1993
Britannica
Book of the Year

Encyclopædia Britannica, Inc.

Chicago

Auckland/Geneva/London/Madrid/Manila/Paris
Rome/Seoul/Sydney/Tokyo/Toronto

CONTENTS

The Not-So-New World Order

BY HEDRICK SMITH

In the long sweep of time, scholars can point to certain decisive, watershed years when human history is suddenly thrust across an irrevocable divide—when with stunning swiftness a new leader or a political movement seizes control in a powerful nation or when revolution shakes the foundations of an empire, and the aftershocks of this one earthquake radiate outward, altering the destiny of the entire world.

In the 20th century, humankind has witnessed several such defining moments: the Bolshevik Revolution of 1917; the ascent of Adolf Hitler in 1933; the defeat of Nazi Germany and the onset of the cold war in 1945; Mikhail S. Gorbachev's rise to power in 1985 and his launching of *perestroika* to transform the Soviet Union and curb the nuclear arms race; and, finally, the breach of the Berlin Wall in 1989. Each of these developments had shock impact. Each bent the path of human history in a new direction.

A similar bolt of lightning struck Moscow in August 1991 at the climax of the Second Russian Revolution, when unarmed citizens at the barricades stopped the tanks sent by hard-line factions of the military, KGB, and Communist Party to halt *perestroika* and reverse Russia's momentum toward greater openness and democracy. That one brief week in 1991—when the icons of communism were toppled and the Soviet state was shattered—electrified the world and kindled the hope that the death knell of Leninist totalitarianism also sounded the dawning of a new, more peaceful and more promising era. So in 1991, it seemed, the trend lines of history were pointing upward.

Then came 1992, and the trend lines suddenly slanted downward. Dreams of global harmony and exaggerated expectations of democracy and prosperity generated by the collapse of communism and the end of the cold war were harshly jolted, if not exploded. U.S. Pres. George Bush might utter that hopeful, vague phrase about a "new world order," but suddenly the world seemed more chaotic. And meaner, too, whether in the murderous clashes of Hindu and Muslim in India or the epidemic-scale famine fanned by corrupt warlords in Somalia. Even amid the promise of new democracies in the Philippines, Nicaragua, or South Africa, the path seemed more vulnerable.

In eastern Europe, lifting the dead hand of tyranny from long-captive peoples brought not just the anticipated burst of democracy and self-determination but a violent explosion of long-suppressed ethnic hatreds. The world watched in horror as proud assertions of independence in what used to be Yugoslavia turned into a barbarous civil war among Serbs, Croats, and Bosnians, conducted under the banner of "ethnic cleansing" with its echoes of Nazi racism. Czechoslovakia broke in two, its "velvet revolution" unable to sustain the unity of Czechs and Slovaks. In the Caucasus, civil conflict brought new bloodshed between Christian Armenians and their Islamic neighbours in Azerbaijan. The old Soviet state of Georgia was torn by warfare among Georgians, Ossetians, and Abkhazians.

Elsewhere, liberation brought suffering along with new freedoms. Amid progress in privatizing their economies, Poland and Hungary suffered from mass unemployment and other painful symptoms of readjustment. Russia's fragile experiment in democracy and market reforms was threatened by industrial collapse, political deadlock, and a rampant, malignant inflation that ate away the savings, living standards, and stoic hopes of the nation's 150 million people. Dramatic arms-control agreements announced at year's end by President Bush and Russian Pres. Boris Yeltsin, to reduce their arsenals by two-thirds in 10 years, seemed in danger from the rising assertiveness of Russian nationalists and from the reluctance of the new nuclear states of Ukraine, Belarus, and Kazakhstan to conform even with earlier treaties signed when these states were part of the old Soviet Union.

The flood of refugees from eastern Europe into Germany ignited waves of neo-Nazi violence against foreigners, shaking the confidence of bourgeois Germans in their own postwar democracy. The pace of German reunification was set back by the harsh realities of transition. By 1992 many western Germans were balking at the high price of implementing Chancellor Helmut Kohl's ambitious plan to reintegrate the once-communist regions of former East Germany with the prosperous West. More broadly, the German and Japanese economies, so long engines of global economic growth, both reeled into recession in 1992, and the U.S. economy laboured wearily to climb out of an economic trough. Britain suffered its worst downturn since the 1930s. People the world over felt the pain of economic contraction. In the U.S. the protracted economic downturn cost President Bush his reelection. This harsh economic climate contributed, moreover, to the undermining of the much-anticipated "year of European unity" in 1992. Expectations of swift movement toward unity had been high as 1991 ended. Yet 1992 became not a time of crowning achievement but a test of the very idea of European cohesion.

Of course, there were events that countered the dominant trends: the holding of the global environmental summit in Rio de Janeiro; the election of a new Israeli prime minister, Yitzhak Rabin, who began at once to revive serious peace negotiations with Israel's Arab neighbours; new bursts of democratic activism in Thailand and the election of a former dissident to the presidency of South Korea; the relentless

---

Hedrick Smith is a writer, author, lecturer, TV commentator, and documentarian. His books include The Russians, The Power Game, How Washington Works, *and* The New Russians.

efforts of Secretary-General Boutros Boutros-Ghali to push the United Nations into a more forceful peacemaking role; the belated intervention of American-led forces to distribute famine relief in Somalia; and the election of a new U.S. president, Gov. Bill Clinton of Arkansas, a spokesman for a new generation. But by and large, the first full year of the new post-cold war era offered less triumph than tragedy, less economic and political liberation than economic dislocation and political disintegration, less renaissance and reassurance than disenchantment and despair.

Whither European Unity. Amid the ashes of a war that had bitterly divided Europe in the 1940s was born the vision of European unity, a unity that not only would underpin peace but would give the old continent greater strength and prosperity by forming the world's largest common market. By surrendering some sovereignty to a supranational entity, Europhiles foresaw not only economic but security dividends: Germany's inclusion in a united Europe would remove the danger of a powerful, independent, and re-united Germany menacing Europe in war, as had happened three times in the previous century. In 1957, six countries had signed the Treaty of Rome establishing the European Common Market, a symbol of postwar reconciliation be-tween Germany and France. In 1985, the British and five more countries endorsed the concept of "Europe '92," an expanded, 12-nation regional market.

So there were great expectations when the leaders of the 12 members of the European Communities gathered in the medieval Dutch city of Maastricht in December 1991. "The train to European union is standing at the platform" was the hopeful prognosis of Hans-Dietrich Genscher, the German foreign minister. Three days later, on December 10, the train was moving: the 12 countries had agreed to form a single central bank and, with some loopholes, to adopt a single currency by 1999, to converge their economic policies in the mid-1990s, to adopt the concept of European citizenship and parallel welfare and social benefits, and to move toward a common European foreign policy with the goal of "the eventual framing of a common defense policy." The Maastricht Treaty laid the foundation for the most powerful economic market of the 21st century, 340 million people strong. French Pres. François Mitterrand summed it up: "A great power is being born, one at least as strong commer-cially, industrially, and financially as the United States and Japan."

Euroskeptics quickly noted, however, that obstacles marred the blueprint, including the requirement that Maas-tricht be ratified by all 12 countries and Britain's open reluctance to accept a common currency. Some Europeans were uneasy about the sweeping provisions for unified poli-cies and suspicious of giving too much power to the union's executive commission, the central bureaucracy in Brussels. Some bankers feared domination by the German Deutsche Mark and the Bundesbank, the most powerful financial in-stitutions in Europe. A real jolt came in June 1992, when Danish voters rejected the Maastricht Treaty, fearing that Danish sovereignty would be swallowed up by larger neigh-bours. With unity suddenly in jeopardy, France voted nar-rowly in September for Maastricht, saving the concept from extinction, but the slim 51% French majority left serious doubts. Britain put off its consideration of union.

As the debate mounted, the pull of nationalist feelings became an increasing force in one country after another. In each referendum, opposition leaders objected to giving up national currencies, national symbols, national sovereignty. Ironically, the end of the cold war and the disappearance of the Soviet threat seemed to have diminished rather than reinforced the Western sense of urgency for union and forging common policies. Deprived of the unifying mission of opposing communism, European governments fell to squabbling about each other's economies. Germany's high interest rates cast a pall over other countries seeking lower rates to rekindle growth. Unable to match the strength of the D-mark, England and Italy temporarily pulled out of the European monetary system. The richer countries of northern Europe were reluctant to increase their support of poorer partners such as Spain, Portugal, Ireland, and Greece.

To revive the flagging unity drive, Chancellor Kohl pushed the Maastricht Treaty through the German Bundestag in December, making Germany the ninth nation to give formal ratification. Nonetheless, western European governments backed away from the continent-wide unification of pass-port controls that had once been considered routine. At a gloomy gathering in Edinburgh in December, a year after the triumphant session at Maastricht, the 12 western Eu-ropean leaders approved new loopholes and qualifications to the Maastricht formula in hopes of luring British and Danish assent. The British were promised less "meddling" by the Brussels bureaucrats. The Danes were even told they could renege on the common pledge to adopt a single cur-rency, a single citizenship, and a common defense. In short, for the facade of unity, advocates were prepared to water down the principles of union.

Balkanization. For all its menace, the cold war had pro-vided stability in the heart of Europe. The Soviet Union and the United States might engage in proxy wars in Indochina, Afghanistan, or Central America, but they were careful not to tread heavily on each other's interests in Europe, for fear of touching off a military conflict that could escalate into nuclear cataclysm. But with the end of the cold war, with nuclear holocaust no longer a deterrent and without nuclear "policemen" on both sides ready to intervene at once against any real or perceived threat to their interests, smaller nations and peoples were suddenly freer to fight petty wars. Not surprisingly, perhaps, what first emerged from the collapse of the Soviet empire was not a new order but old disorder—old passions, old feuds, old hatreds, old conflicts, in the same old places. The dateline of Sarajevo came to symbolize war in 1992, just as it had in 1914.

Indeed, the world's worst conflicts in the immediate after-math of the cold war have so far been not those between states but those within states, among rival peoples moved to action by the promise of freedom and self-determination. Once the cold war order had been overthrown, historic peoples, long suppressed, moved to fill the vacuum. In the newly independent Baltic states of Estonia, Latvia, and Lithuania, passionate nationalists wanted the Russians out. In the Caucasus and Central Asia, where Moscow's mili-tary writ no longer ran, violence exploded. But nowhere in the world did it approach the scale, the ferocity, and the brutality of the cauldron of animosities in what used to be Yugoslavia. Even before the Soviet Union broke up in late 1991, Yugoslavia had disintegrated. In defiance of the Serb-dominated Yugoslav federation based in Belgrade, Croatia and Slovenia declared independence, followed by the re-public of Bosnia and Hercegovina, which contained a large Muslim population. All were recognized abroad and made members of the United Nations. But Serbian-led federal military forces under Pres. Slobodan Milosevic, a former Communist leader, moved to reimpose central rule and to form "Greater Serbia." Once again, the Balkans became synonymous with fragmentation and fratricide.

The savagery of the Balkan bloodshed horrified the world. This "cancer in the heart of Europe" left more than 50,000 people dead, mostly civilians, and more than two million people homeless refugees, according to some estimates. The siege of Sarajevo, a city of Muslims and the capital of Bosnia, epitomized the carnage. Ringed by Serbian artillery in the surrounding mountains, Sarajevo was pounded mercilessly for more than six months. A bus attempting to evacuate 50 children under four years of age was riddled by gunfire, and the next day, during the burial of one of the dead children, Serbian mortars bombarded the cemetery, wounding the child's grandmother. Not far from Sarajevo, in the town of Kozarac, Muslim refugees told of the Serbian policy of "ethnic cleansing"; Serbian commanders had forced the evacuation of 25,000 inhabitants to clear the way for an ethnically pure Serbian state. Croatian troops also moved into Bosnia. People fled by the tens of thousands. Prisoners emerged from Serbian camps to describe a Serbian Gulag: torture and the gunning down of unarmed civilians in cold blood. Other stories of mass killings, allegedly by Serbian forces, surfaced in Croatia. After the U.S. State Department reported that as many as 3,000 people might have been killed in Serb-run camps, the UN Security Council set up a war-crimes commission to investigate alleged atrocities, the first such commission since World War II.

For Europe, for NATO, for the West as a whole, the Balkan war was a test of President Bush's "new world order." Both the Europeans in NATO and the United States shied away from military involvement, initially on grounds that this was an internal conflict, later arguing that intervention would be a quagmire. Western generals said the mountainous Balkan terrain and the guerrilla-warfare traditions of the inhabitants would make it impossible to take full control. Even the Nazi occupiers, they said, could not quell the Yugoslav partisans during World War II. So throughout the year, both the UN Security Council and the NATO governments passed resolutions—condemning the violence, offering humanitarian aid to Sarajevo and other besieged Bosnian regions, imposing economic sanctions against the Serbian government, sending 14,000 military and civilian staff members to supervise a cease-fire between Serbia and Croatia, and eventually sending 6,000 more to try to protect the Sarajevo airport and open up a land corridor for transports carrying relief supplies to Bosnia. To block Serbian air force planes from aiding Serbian ground gunners, the UN declared a "no-fly zone" over Bosnia, but the ban went unenforced. After repeated futile denunciations of Serbia, the UN General Assembly on September 22 took the unprecedented step of expelling Yugoslavia (now consisting only of Serbia and Montenegro). In defiance of the world, Serbs reelected Milosevic, their hard-line leader, amid the rising danger that the carnage would be escalated by Islamic nations. Islamic militants adopted the cause of Bosnia's Muslims as a holy war. Several hundred men, many of them veterans of the war in Afghanistan, volunteered for the Bosnian forces.

Economic Reform in Russia; Reunification of Germany. For many in the West, the real test of the future in eastern Europe would come not in Yugoslavia—nor in Hungary, Poland, or Czechoslovakia, where economic reforms were being pushed—but in Russia. Over six years, Gorbachev had introduced elections, parliaments, popular movements, and a freer press, albeit in imperfect form, to challenge the Communist *nomenklatura*. But by late 1991, he had done little to alter the centralized Soviet economic system. Yeltsin, his successor as leader of Russia, set out to introduce a market economy, with Yegor Gaidar, a 36-year-old Western-minded economist, as acting prime minister and architect of the transition from Soviet socialism to a mixed market economy. Under Gorbachev, the old state distribution system had largely collapsed, and production had

fallen. To placate the masses, workers had been given more pay, without more output. The Yeltsin-Gaidar strategy was "shock therapy": cutting off massive state subsidies to the old Soviet complex of military and heavy industries, phasing out subsidies on consumer goods, driving to balance the state budget to halt the inflation that had mounted ominously under Gorbachev, and privatizing farms, small retail trade, and eventually larger enterprises.

The first blow of "price liberalization" (freeing up fixed state prices) fell hard on consumers on Jan. 2, 1992. Bread prices tripled. Energy prices rose 10-fold. Milk prices shot up eight times overnight. Pensioners and workers screamed that their life savings were eaten up. Yeltsin's strategy of using higher prices to lure more goods into the market and gradually end Russia's chronic shortages was undercut by the old state monopolies and distribution cartels, which sat on their stocks, choked the flow of goods to stores, and made big profits by jacking up their prices to the maximum allowed. As a matter of survival, barter and gray-market deals became a national way of life.

Several hundred commodity exchanges were launched by private entrepreneurs, the first step toward a wholesale market for industry. But supplies were drastically inadequate, and prices soared. Middlemen dealing in commodities, often obtained through bribery of local officials, reaped enormous profits, giving capitalism and market economics a bad name. Deprived of state subsidies by Yeltsin, industrial plant managers demanded massive loans from state banks to pay their workers, while production fell because the wholesale trade on the commodity markets was far too small to replace the Soviet state-run distribution system. Encouraged by conservatives in Parliament opposed to Yeltsin's reforms, the central bank authorized hundreds of billions in unfunded credits to industry, undermining Yeltsin's reforms and fueling inflation. The ruble plummeted from 60 to more than 400 to the U.S. dollar. By some estimates, national output fell by 25% while inflation raced to 25% a month. To stem the hemorrhaging, Yeltsin needed outside funds to stabilize the ruble. The West promised $24 billion in loans, but the package was not delivered. Catch-22: Yeltsin, who needed the loans to slow inflation, had to check inflation in order to qualify for the loans.

The mounting economic strains were compounded by political deadlock and the breakup of the Soviet Union. In the new spirit of nationalism, Ukraine, Belarus, the Baltics, Caucasian Republics, and Central Asian Republics all declared their independence. Yeltsin and Ukrainian Pres. Leonid Kravchuk avoided the precipice of open warfare, à la Yugoslavia. But they clashed over who should control the Soviet Black Sea Fleet and various disputed territories, and Kravchuk imposed embargoes on Ukrainian industrial exports to Russia after Yeltsin tried to put the squeeze on Ukraine by restricting its imports of Russian oil. Industries on both sides were hobbled by lack of components from the other side, and this problem was multiplied in every former Soviet republic.

In Moscow, the old guard of the Soviet bureaucracy still had a stronghold in the Russian Parliament, where nearly one-third of those elected in 1990 had been Communist leaders opposed to Yeltsin. Moreover, the shock impact of the Yeltsin-Gaidar economic strategy became so unpopular with ordinary Russians that a middle bloc of deputies, rallying around former Gorbachev aide Arkady Volsky, demanded a slower pace of reform and support for the old Soviet industries. In a confrontation at year's end that symbolized the deadlock crippling Russia, the Congress of People's Deputies rejected Yeltsin's bid to reappoint his reformist prime minister. To salvage his own political neck,

Yeltsin had to make concessions, and his new prime minister backed away from market reforms, reimposing some price controls.

If one region of eastern Europe seemed likely to ride out the wrenching change from socialism to capitalism, it was East Germany. West Germany was to fill the gap. But even Germany felt the strains of the post-cold war era. Chancellor Kohl had committed the prosperous West German economy to pumping $100 billion a year into the east for several years—on a per capita basis, nearly 40 times as much each year as the West had promised, but not delivered, to Russia in one year. Moreover, a common cultural heritage supposedly offered avenues for lifting east Germans to the west German level. In the first blush of enthusiasm, big corporations like Krupp and Daimler-Benz announced plans to set up new factories in the eastern region. But Kohl had underestimated the problems and had failed to spell out the high cost of reunification. By 1992, west Germans were protesting over increased taxes and other costs. Public employee unions went on strike to protest, and as Germany sank into recession under the weight of reunification, Krupp and Daimler-Benz, among others, canceled their plans for new investments in the east. Chancellor Kohl was forced to scramble in late 1992 to patch together a national solidarity pact to save his reunification policy.

Germany's problems were magnified by the unprecedented inflow of some 450,000 refugees from eastern Europe, fleeing both the Balkan war and the eastern European economic collapse. Frictions with this new mass of foreigners, especially in former East Germany, where unemployment was high, produced outbursts of neo-Nazi violence. Foreigners became scapegoats for the powerful frustrations of young German skinheads, angered by the lack of jobs and the bleak prospects of only a slow rise to Western living standards. Sitting on a powder keg, the German government moved simultaneously to crack down on neo-Nazi groups and to alter the extremely liberal political asylum provisions of Germany's Basic Law. Germany's action was bitter testimony to the imperatives of nationalism in the new post-cold war Europe: each nation would have to protect its own citizens, even if doing so meant friction with the rest of Europe.

Globalism. If the end of the cold war was to open the way toward common global efforts to combat problems of poverty, hunger, crime, human rights, and environmental protection, the most visible symbol of that impulse in 1992 was the 12-day "Earth Summit" in Rio de Janeiro in June. The gathering attracted 10,000 environmentalists, 8,000 journalists, and 116 heads of state. It adopted a global-warming convention that recommends curbing emissions of carbon dioxide, methane, and other "greenhouse" gases thought to warm the Earth's climate by trapping the Sun's heat in the atmosphere close to Earth; a biodiversity convention that requires inventories of plants and wildlife and offers plans to protect endangered species; a nonbinding Rio Declaration of 27 broad principles for guiding national environmental policies; and "Agenda 21," an 800-page blueprint for cleaning up the environment and ensuring that economic development is carried out in an environmentally sound manner. Activists were frustrated by the vague statement of principles and the lack of clear targets and binding legal requirements for compliance. Several times, the Bush administration watered down tough language. Norwegian Prime Minister Gro Harlem Brundtland voiced disappointment that the need for consensus meant that progress was dictated by "the pace of the most reluctant mover in each field." Secretary-General Boutros-Ghali echoed, "The current level of commitment is not comparable to the size and gravity of the problems."

But others hailed the Rio conference as the first global summit devoted to the environment, rather than to military security or world trade issues.

Like the global environment, global economics has become a byword of the new era. With economics rather than the nuclear arms race now driving world diplomacy, trade is a top priority for every government. One global target pursued by multinational negotiators over six torturous years has been a new world trade accord under GATT, the General Agreement on Tariffs and Trade. Late in 1992, the Bush administration, wielding the threat of heavy tariffs on European white wines and other items, broke a long deadlock over the U.S. demand for a reduction in farm subsidies. The French government, politically weak and worried about the anger of French farmers, threatened a veto. But Europe and America proceeded, doubtful that the French would dare to topple the edifice of free trade over that one issue.

Another globalist trend in 1992 was the increasing use of United Nations peacekeeping forces—more than 50,000 on duty around the world by year's end. But even with 22,000 UN troops in the Balkans, 17,000 in Cambodia to promote and oversee free elections, and 12,000 scattered from Cyprus to India and Pakistan, Secretary-General Boutros-Ghali was not satisfied. He pushed member states to send a military force to stop the widespread looting of humanitarian relief supplies in Somalia (a role taken over in December by 26,000 U.S. troops) and another 7,500 troops to supervise elections in Mozambique. The growing use of military escorts to protect relief efforts, Boutros-Ghali acknowledged, comprised "a new dimension of peacekeeping" for UN forces. Another departure was the use of UN teams, including Russians and Americans, for highly visible inspections of Iraq's mass-destruction weapons programs, a potential harbinger of greater UN activity against the worrisome concern of nuclear proliferation.

If President Bush was reluctant to engage deeply in several of the UN initiatives, President-elect Bill Clinton foreshadowed a more forward American policy in Somalia and Bosnia and perhaps elsewhere. Rather than insisting, as Bush had, on the withdrawal of U.S. forces from Somalia by Jan. 20, 1993, the new American leader suggested even before taking office that he would be ready to keep U.S. troops in Somalia longer, to ensure the rebuilding of national stability. On Bosnia, too, he took a more assertive stand, hinting at his readiness to use American air power to enforce the ban on Serbian flights over Bosnia and Hercegovina. Policymakers spoke of the need for a common strategy to aid "failed nations."

But the main promise of the Clinton administration, on an issue of both domestic and global importance, was greater activism to stimulate the rebound of the U.S. economy and, indirectly, the world economy beyond. For the U.S. elections of 1992 carried two messages of global significance. First, that publics everywhere, in Russia, America, and perhaps Britain, France, and Germany as well, will turn away from leaders like Gorbachev, Bush, and maybe Yeltsin who fail to deliver a better economic life. And, second, that a new generation of Americans, geared for greater governmental activism and for expanded social policies at home and abroad, are ready to move away from the laissez-faire economics of the Reagan-Bush period and adopt deliberate policies to make America a more dynamic and competitive player in the global economy. Thus, though the world might be mired in difficulties as it tried to move beyond the cold war, America in 1992 summoned new leadership for that purpose.

Chronology of 1992

JANUARY

1 **United Nations gets new leader.** Boutros Boutros-Ghali, who had been deputy prime minister of Egypt, assumed office as the sixth secretary-general of the United Nations. Boutros-Ghali, the first Arab and the first person from Africa to head the international organization, replaced Javier Pérez de Cuéllar of Peru, who had completed two successive five-year terms.

4 **Tunisia opposes fundamentalists.** During a meeting in Tunis with the interior ministers of 16 Arab nations, Tunisian Pres. Zine al-Abidine Ben Ali called for a concerted effort to suppress militant Islamic fundamentalists, who, he said, were using religion as a guise to gain political power. The Tunisian government had rounded up hundreds of supporters of al-Nahda, a banned political party bent on turning the country into an Islamic state. Both inside and outside the country, fears were expressed that Tunisia might be having second thoughts about the steps it had taken to evolve into a true multiparty democracy.

6 **Gamsakhurdia yields to pressure.** Zviad Gamsakhurdia, president of the former Soviet republic of Georgia, fled the capital city of Tbilisi with about 100 of his supporters. The convoy that carried them to safety in Armenia included buses and armoured vehicles. Gamsakhurdia, who informed reporters that he had no intention of resigning the presidency, had become the first freely elected president of the republic in May 1991. Charges that he was attempting to amass dictatorial powers finally led to a military assault on the parliament building and to Gamsakhurdia's departure. The military council that took over the government announced that it would hand over power to civilians as soon as possible.

7 **China expels Canadian legislators.** Three Canadian members of Parliament, who had openly declared that they intended to visit Tiananmen (T'ien-an-men) Square in Beijing (Peking) to honour the pro-democracy demonstrators who had been killed by the military in June 1989, were summarily deported by the Chinese government. The legislators had also planned to visit a Beijing prison and speak with dissidents who were known to be held there. Chinese officials had always contended that the Tiananmen incident and the government's treatment of dissidents was an internal affair. Government policy in this regard could not, they insisted, be a legitimate concern to outsiders.

10 **Bush winds up Asian trade talks.** After hearing criticism that his administration was harming Australian farm exports by subsidizing farmers in the U.S., Pres. George Bush departed Australia for Singapore on January 3. The following day he announced a tentative agreement to relocate the headquarters of the U.S. Navy's 7th Fleet from the Philippines to Singapore. During Bush's visit to South Korea, talks focused on open trade, trade deficits, and efforts to reunite North and South Korea. Bush's visit to Japan was, as expected, the most important stop on his itinerary and proved to be the most controversial. Among those who accompanied him were leading U.S. industrialists, including the heads of the three largest U.S. automobile companies. They openly declared their determination to improve their competitiveness by exacting concessions from their Japanese counterparts. The latter agreed, among other things, to nearly double their purchases of U.S.-made auto parts and to supply Japanese distributors with more U.S. cars. They also agreed to open up their computer, paper, and glass markets. Bush, however, was criticized at home for going to Japan "to beg" and for assuming the role of "a car salesman." The *New York Times* called the visit a fiasco.

11 **President of Algeria resigns.** Chadli Bendjedid, president of Algeria since 1979, announced his resignation in the face of potential political chaos. Top military officers had reportedly insisted on the resignation as a necessary step in preventing the fundamentalist Islamic Salvation Front (FIS) from gaining control of the National People's Assembly and establishing an Islamic state. In the December 1991 legislative elections, the FIS had captured a stunning 188 of 231 seats. There was little doubt that, in the runoff election scheduled for January 16, the FIS would capture more than 28 of the 199 contested seats needed to constitute a majority. On January 12 the High Security Council, which included Prime Minister Sid Ahmed Ghozali and senior military officers, invalidated the results of the December elections and announced that no further elections would be held until "conditions are achieved for the normal functioning of institutions" of government. On January 22, Abdelkader Hachani, the leader of the FIS, was taken into custody. On February 9 Algeria's new High State Council closed the headquarters of the FIS in Algiers and proclaimed a severe yearlong state of emergency.

15 **Yugoslav federation crumbles.** The demise of the federal republic of Yugoslavia was assured when 11 members of the European Communities (EC) followed Germany's lead and formally recognized Croatia and Slovenia as independent states. Austria, Switzerland, and the Vatican also recognized the sovereignty of the two republics. There was little international concern about the future of Slovenia, but the fate of Croatia remained very much in doubt. About one-third of

The parliament building in Tbilisi stands in ruins after attack by Georgian opposition forces. Zviad Gamsakhurdia, president of Georgia for less than eight months, was toppled from power.

its territory was occupied by the Yugoslav People's Army and Serbian irregulars, and the Serbian-dominated central government in Belgrade had vowed to use whatever military force was necessary to prevent some 600,000 ethnic Serbs from ever becoming part of an independent Croatia. According to EC estimates, about 6,000 Croats and 4,000 Serbs had already died in the fighting. The suffering was expected to increase as the civil war intensified.

16 **Peace comes to El Salvador.** The bitter 12-year civil war that had claimed some 75,000 lives in El Salvador formally ended with the signing of a treaty in Mexico City. Most of the worries of the government and of the guerrillas had been put to rest during discussions with Javier Pérez de Cuéllar, who successfully mediated the settlement during his final hours as secretary-general of the United Nations. The ceremonial signing of the treaty was unusually emotional. Six government negotiators, five guerrilla commanders, and five rebel negotiators signed the pact one after the other. The treaty was then placed in front of Salvadoran Pres. Alfredo Cristiani, who had earlier declared that he would not be among the signatories. Instead, in the presence of nine other heads of state, Cristiani affixed his name to the document. He then left the podium to shake hands for the first time with his longtime military foes.

17 **Court exonerates Papandreou.** A special court made up of 13 high-ranking judges voted 7–6 in Athens to acquit Greece's former prime minister Andreas Papandreou of complicity in a bank scandal. The accusations had helped bring down Papandreou's socialist government in 1989. The same court found two members of Papandreou's former Cabinet guilty as charged. The principal accusations against Papandreou were that as prime minister he had ordered state companies to deposit funds in the Bank of Crete and had accepted bribes from George Koskotas, who, while head of the bank, allegedly embezzled some $210 million. Koskotas, who was due to be tried separately at a later date, had been the prosecution's chief witness against Papandreou.

18 **Kenyans hold legal protest rally.** More than 100,000 Kenyans attended a daylong rally in Nairobi, the first antigovernment gathering since Pres. Daniel arap Moi's administration sanctioned opposition political parties in December 1991. The rally was sponsored by the Forum for the Restoration of Democracy, the only opposition political party thus far officially registered with the government. Its leader was 75-year-old Oginga Odinga, who had spearheaded the campaign for multiparty democracy. He now urged his compatriots to oust Moi when presidential elections were held sometime later in the year.

19 **Zhelev wins Bulgarian election.** Zhelyu Zhelev, president of Bulgaria, won a relatively close runoff election against Velko Valkanov, the candidate of the Socialist (former Communist) Party. It was the nation's first presidential election decided by popular vote. Zhelev's

On January 16, Boutros Boutros-Ghali, UN secretary-general, signs a treaty aimed at ending El Salvador's civil war. The country's president and guerrillas also signed the agreement.
KEITH DANNEMILLER—SABA

election to a five-year term consolidated power in the hands of the Union of Democratic Forces party, which had already gained control of the government by winning a plurality of seats in the October 1991 parliamentary elections.

Saudi Arabia welcomes Jews from U.S. Seven leaders of the American Jewish Congress arrived in Saudi Arabia, where on January 21 the pro-Israeli group held discussions with Saudi Foreign Minister Prince Sa'ud al-Faisal as-Sa'ud. It was a historic event because Jews were normally not permitted to enter the Saudi kingdom. The delegates later reported that the Saudi government recognized Israel's right to exist and appeared ready to assume a more active role in the current negotiations to end the Arab-Israeli conflict. The Saudis were said to believe that the animosity that characterized the relationship between Jews and Arabs was more political than religious in nature and could, therefore, be mitigated if both sides agreed to compromise.

22 **Japanese lose railcar contract.** The Los Angeles County Transportation Commission voted unanimously to rescind a $122 million contract that it had recently awarded to the Japanese-owned Sumitomo Corp. to build 41 railcars for a proposed 650-km (400-mi) transportation system. The total cost of the project was estimated to be $150 billion. Although Sumitomo had submitted a bid that was about $5 million higher than the one made by Morrison Knudsen Co., the U.S. bidder, Sumitomo was judged better qualified. County officials reversed their decision after local workers complained that many of them had lost their jobs in the defense and auto industries and were now being denied jobs that they desperately needed.

24 **Mauritania holds free election.** In Mauritania's first multiparty election, the nation's military leader, Col. Maaouya Ould Sidi Ahmed Taya, was elected president with 62.8% of the vote. The main opposition candidate later

claimed that the balloting had been fraudulent and that at least five antigovernment protesters were killed by police on January 26. To control the unrest, the government imposed a night curfew in the capital and in the country's main port city. The election was made possible in April 1991 when Colonel Taya unexpectedly announced that he was terminating military rule. Opposition parties were legalized, and in July a new constitution was overwhelmingly approved by the voters. Several weeks later Taya proclaimed a general amnesty.

30 **Prime Minister Haughey to quit.** Charles J. Haughey, prime minister of Ireland, announced his decision to resign on February 10. Haughey, the leader of Fianna Fail and one of the nation's most influential politicians, said that he felt compelled to step aside "to end the political uncertainty." The prime minister had been under attack for alleged corruption on the part of friends and acquaintances. He had also been hurt politically by new accusations that he had known about the government's tapping of journalists' phones in 1982. On February 6 Albert Reynolds, whom Haughey had dismissed as his finance minister in November 1991, was elected leader of Fianna Fail. He assumed the prime ministership on February 11.

31 **Security Council holds summit.** For the first time in history, the leaders of the nations that hold seats on the 15-member Security Council met at the UN headquarters in New York City to discuss ways of enhancing the role of the UN in world affairs. The leaders issued a joint communiqué that, among other things, recognized "the responsibility of the Security Council in the maintenance of international peace and security." The document cited the UN's role "in enabling Kuwait to regain its sovereignty and territorial integrity, which it had lost as a result of Iraqi aggression." It also applauded "the valuable contributions being made by United Nations peacekeeping forces now operating in Asia, Africa, Latin America and Europe."

FEBRUARY

1 **Cold war relegated to history.** Pres. George Bush and Russian Pres. Boris Yeltsin signed a statement of general principles that brought an end to decades of intense East-West rivalry and ushered in a new era of friendship and cooperation. The first section of their joint declaration read: "Russia and the United States do not regard each other as potential adversaries. From now on, the relationship will be characterized by friendship and partnership founded on mutual trust and respect and a common commitment to democracy and economic freedom." The two leaders also agreed to "work to remove any remnants of cold war hostility, including taking steps to reduce our strategic arsenals."

U.S. begins repatriating Haitians. The U.S. government began the involuntary repatriation of thousands of Haitians who had been picked up at sea while trying to escape the hardships of their homeland. On January 31 the U.S. Supreme Court had ruled 6–3 to void a district court injunction that prohibited repatriation. On February 3 the first group of 381 refugees arrived in Haiti aboard U.S. Coast Guard cutters. The U.S. Immigration and Naturalization Service, after interviewing thousands of refugees, had decided that some 3,400 had credible claims to political asylum in the U.S. In time, all those judged to be victims of political repression would be transported to Florida for further processing. Most of the refugees were currently being housed at the U.S. military base at Guantánamo Bay, Cuba; others were temporarily living on U.S. Navy ships.

Fumio Abe charged with bribery. Fumio Abe, who had been arrested on January 13, was formally indicted in Tokyo on charges of having accepted $640,000 in bribes from a top executive of the Kyowa Corp. In exchange for money, Abe reportedly passed on information about future government development projects that he learned about as a Cabinet minister. Abe strongly denied that he had violated the law by doing favours in return for gifts. His indictment further damaged the reputation of the ruling Liberal-Democratic Party (LDP), which was still under a cloud of mistrust because of other recent financial scandals involving LDP politicians.

3 **Ershad sentenced in Bangladesh.** A special court sitting in Dhaka, Bangladesh, sentenced Hossain Mohammad Ershad to three years in prison for possessing wealth inconsistent with his income. The former president, who had been forced to resign in December 1990 after eight years in office, was already serving a 10-year sentence for illegal possession of firearms. Ershad, moreover, still had to answer charges of corruption and abuse of power while in office. Meanwhile, the country, one of the poorest in the world, was being deluged with tens of thousands of Muslim refugees who were fleeing predominantly Buddhist Myanmar (Burma) to escape the savage onslaughts of government troops.

4 **Army coup in Venezuela fails.** Troops loyal to Venezuelan Pres. Carlos Andrés Pérez successfully repulsed an early-morning tank attack against the presidential palace in Caracas. A rebel colonel later explained that the insurgents wanted to "rescue the Venezuelan people from politicians, from demagoguery, and bureaucracy." The violent protests and labour unrest that had preceded the failed coup were widely interpreted as expressions of despair on the part of ordinary citizens. The government admitted that nearly half of the population could afford only one meal a day, and soldiers complained that their salaries were being gobbled up by runaway inflation. The European Communities, the Organization of American States, and the U.S. were among those who condemned the coup, in part because Venezuela ranked second behind Colombia as the oldest democracies in South America.

6 **Ethiopia promised financial aid.** The World Bank, the International Monetary Fund, and other organizations expressed cautious optimism that Ethiopia would begin recovering from years of civil war and disastrous economic policies if given financial assistance. Together they pledged a total of $672 million, the first $7 million of which was designated for emergency medical needs. The remaining funds, to be dispensed over a 30-month period, would be used to build roads, bridges, and schools and help satisfy other basic needs. Ethiopia's minister for foreign economic relations summed up the situation in these words: "Our poverty is devastating. We have 1.2 million demobilized soldiers in need of jobs and 100,000 children living on the streets. We have an urgent need for fertilizer and seeds. Industries are idle for lack of raw materials and spare parts."

14 **Somalians accept a cease-fire.** Leaders of the two warring factions within the United Somali Congress accepted an immediate cease-fire that had been mediated by UN Under Secretary-General James Jonah. Three months of fierce fighting in and around the capital city of Mogadishu had left more than 20,000 dead or wounded and caused more than 50,000 refugees to flee across the border into Kenya. The situation became chaotic soon after the ouster of Pres. Muhammad Siyad Barrah in January 1991 because Ali Mahdi Muhammad and Gen. Muhammad Farah Aydid both claimed the presidency. The two men represented different clans within the same Hiwiye tribe. Their acceptance of a cease-fire was tied to an agreement to work out details of a comprehensive settlement in the near future. The country's most urgent needs, however, continued to be food and medicines.

CIS at odds over unified military. Leaders of 11 former Soviet republics, now loosely joined in a union called the Commonwealth of Independent States (CIS), met in Minsk, Belarus, to discuss the feasibility of a unified defense force that would replace the former Soviet Union's Red Army. Ukraine adamantly opposed the plan because it would give Russia, the largest and wealthiest member of the CIS, virtual control of all conventional forces. Ukraine was especially concerned about the Black Sea Fleet, part of which it laid claim to. Ukrainian Pres. Leonid Kravchuk, flanked by representatives of Belarus and Armenia, told reporters that the Commonwealth meeting had merely underscored the differences that separated the republics into two distinct groups, one supporting him and the other supporting Boris Yeltsin.

16 **Shi'ite leader killed in Lebanon.** Sheikh 'Abbas al-Mussawi, the 39-year-old leader of the militant wing of Hezbollah ("Party of God"), was killed along with his wife, small son, and several bodyguards when two Israeli helicopter gunships attacked his seven-vehicle motorcade near the town of Jibchit in southern Lebanon. The Israeli air raid was part of a wave of violence that occurred after the February 14 murders of three Israeli soldiers by four guerrilla assassins who had slipped into an Israeli army camp under cover of darkness. On February 18 the leadership council of Hezbollah elected Sheikh Hassan Nasrallah as Mussawi's successor.

19 **Seoul and Pyongyang sign pacts.** The prime ministers of North and South Korea, during the sixth round of high-level talks between the two countries, formally exchanged three signed pacts in Pyongyang that were designed to lessen tensions and lead to the eventual reunification of the divided peninsula. The three documents were entitled "Agreement on Reconciliation, Nonaggression, and Exchanges and Cooperation," "Agreement on

STEVE BENT/KATZ—SABA

Lebanese villagers carry the coffin and a photograph of Sheikh 'Abbas al-Mussawi. Israelis killed the Shi'ite leader and his family in retaliation for attacks on Israeli troops.

Formation and Operation of Intra-Korean Subcommittees," and "Joint Declaration for a Non-Nuclear Korea." North Korea's nuclear weapons program remained a matter of serious concern even though the government had signed the Nuclear Non-proliferation Treaty in 1985. This was so because Pyongyang continued to resist international inspection of its nuclear facilities.

21 **Yugoslavia to get UN forces.** The UN Security Council voted unanimously to begin sending a 14,000-member peacekeeping force to Yugoslavia to oversee the cease-fire accepted by Croatia, which had recently seceded from the Yugoslav federation, and by Serbia. Some 16,000 UN personnel were currently involved in 10 peacekeeping missions in Africa, Asia, the Middle East, and South America. Since 1948, at a cost of $5.8 billion, more than half a million United Nations troops had participated in 23 peacekeeping missions in various parts of the world.

The 1992 Winter Olympics open on February 8 in Albertville, France. Among the 64 nations participating were several republics of the former Soviet Union, under the name Unified Team.
GAMMA LIAISON

The Sudan drives 400,000 into desert. Andrew Natsios, director of foreign disaster assistance for the U.S. Agency for International Development, reported that the military government of The Sudan had driven more than 400,000 squatters out of Khartoum, the capital, and into the desert. He called the expulsion at gunpoint a death sentence because the areas to which the people were being driven had "minimal to nonexistent" food, water, or shelter. Many victims of the forced migration were Christians or followers of traditional beliefs who had trekked to the capital to escape drought and the ravages of civil war. Natsios also reported that the government refused to allow UN personnel to assist the newly displaced. Several local groups, however, were said to have offered help to the refugees, but only if they first converted to Islam.

23 **Winter Olympics end in France.** After two weeks of competition, the 16th Winter Olympic Games came to an end in Albertville, France. A record 2,289 athletes representing a record 64 countries competed at 13 sites

spread over some 1,600 sq km (640 sq mi). The great distances that separated the venues somewhat diminished the camaraderie that usually characterized the international sports extravaganza. For the first time since 1964, Germany competed as a single team; it won 26 medals, the most by any nation. Athletes from five former Soviet republics formed what was officially called the Unified Team and finished with 23 medals. When members of the team received their gold medals, the Olympic hymn was played because no national anthem would have reflected the status of the newly independent republics represented on the Unified Team.

24 **U.S. will not back Israel loans.** U.S. Secretary of State James Baker told members of the House Foreign Operations Subcommittee that the Bush administration would not guarantee $10 billion in loans to Israel as long as it refused to halt all activity related to the building of Jewish settlements in the West Bank and Gaza. The request for such guarantees had come from Prime Minister Yitzhak Shamir, who promised

that the money would be used exclusively to facilitate the absorption of former Soviet Jews. Such an assurance meant nothing, Baker noted, because Israel could continue to finance new settlements in the occupied territories by simply using funds currently allocated for other purposes and then replacing them with funds that became available through new loans. The U.S. and Israel thus appeared to be at an impasse because Shamir had vowed that he would never halt the construction of Jewish settlements "even for a day."

28 **More UN help for Cambodia.** All 15 members of the United Nations Security Council approved a resolution calling for an additional 22,000 soldiers, police, and administrators to go to Cambodia to bolster UN efforts to conduct a free and fair election. In October 1991 the Khmer Rouge and its three allied opponents had authorized a pivotal role for the UN in an effort to terminate the fighting and give the nation a stable government. One of the UN's most difficult tasks was to persuade the various factions to disarm.

MARCH

1 **Saudi government to be revamped.** King Fahd of Saudi Arabia proclaimed a new constitution that provided for a 60-member Consultative Council selected by the king. Its responsibilities would include conferring with and advising the Cabinet and evaluating the appropriateness of various laws. The king and the royal family would still retain near absolute power, but for the first time dissenting voices would be heard. This fact alone was a major change in Saudi Arabia's traditional governmental structure. During an interview published on March 29, King Fahd ruled out free elections in Saudi Arabia on the grounds that Western democratic institutions were not suitable for Arab states in the Persian Gulf. He also called Islam the only acceptable ideology

for his country, but he strongly rejected Islamic fundamentalism.

5 **Fighting halts UN aid to Somalia.** A ship carrying relief food for the starving people in Mogadishu, the capital of Somalia, was unable to reach port because of heavy shelling. James Jonah, the under secretary-general of the UN in charge of the relief effort, resoundingly condemned both rebel groups fighting to take over the government since the overthrow of the previous president. In a message to the two rival leaders, Jonah acknowledged that he was deeply depressed by their reckless disregard for others and warned them that "it should not be taken for granted that the international community, in the face of such behaviour,

will continue to exert all efforts to bring food to Mogadishu when there are equally competing demands in other parts of the world."

6 **President of Azerbaijan quits.** Ayaz Mutalibov resigned the presidency of Azerbaijan just six months after assuming office. The collapse of his government was directly related to unsuccessful attempts to control the ethnic violence in Nagorno-Karabakh, an enclave within Azerbaijan that was heavily populated by ethnic Armenians. The four-year-old war for control of the region was also the product of religious differences; most Azerbaijanis were Muslims, whereas the majority of Armenians were Christians. Children and women were among the thousands of victims either killed or maimed in the ferocious fighting. On March 15, during a meeting in Iran, the deputy foreign ministers of Armenia and Azerbaijan accepted a cease-fire. It was quickly ignored, like others before it.

17 **South Africans cast historic vote.** In what many considered to be one of the most important events in South African history, white voters, who constituted only 18% of the nation's population, approved a referendum supporting Pres. F.W. de Klerk's efforts to negotiate an end to white-majority rule. More than two-thirds of the 2.8 million whites who cast ballots favoured an end to apartheid, the policy of racial separation that also denied suffrage to blacks. De Klerk had already taken dramatic steps to remove some of the burdensome restrictions on blacks despite angry denunciations by white extremists. After the election results were announced, de Klerk remarked that the massive yes vote was "a powerful message to all South Africans" that the vast majority of whites really wanted to share power with the blacks.

Sudanese military drives south. Armed with newly acquired Libyan, Iranian, and Chinese heavy weapons, an enlarged Sudanese military force pressed its offensive into the south. A week earlier it had captured Pochala, and on March 13 it had bombed Kapoeta, the most important centre held by the Sudan People's Liberation Army. A UN official reported that the escalating war was impeding UN efforts to transport food from northern Kenya to southern Sudan, where some 200,000 displaced persons were in dire need of sustenance. The war pitted the Arab Muslim fundamentalists in the north against southern rebels who were Christians and animists. Some political analysts believed that Iran's support of the Sudanese government was part of a larger plan to extend the influence of Islamic fundamentalism to other parts of Africa.

19 **White farms seized in Zimbabwe.** Zimbabwe's Parliament passed new legislation giving the government

Sali Berisha, head of Albania's Democratic Party, campaigns in Tirane. In elections held on March 22, his party gained control of Parliament from the Socialist (former Communist) Party.
REUTERS/BETTMANN

the right to confiscate white-owned farms with little compensation and no right of appeal. The intent of Parliament was to provide homelands for some one million blacks. Critics of the law contended that in time agricultural lands would be transformed into subsistence farms and Zimbabwe would cease to be an exporter of food. The 4,500 white farmers, who owned one-third of the land, accounted for most of the nation's export earnings and employed the largest work force in the country. Under Pres. Robert Mugabe, the government had already settled some 160,000 blacks on farms that white owners had sold voluntarily.

20 **Kenya bans political meetings.** Kenyan Pres. Daniel arap Moi banned all political meetings in the wake of the nation's worst ethnic violence since independence in 1963. According to observers, members of the Kalenjin tribe, to which Moi belonged, had initiated the fighting by attacking Luo settlements. An intense tribal and political rivalry existed between the two groups because the Luo, unlike the Kalenjin, had long been prominent in politics and was second in size only to the Kikuyu. Some surmised that Moi himself was slow to intervene because the unrest provided an opportunity

to slow the democratic process and curb the power of the opposition Forum for the Restoration of Democracy, which was led by Oginga Odinga, a Luo.

22 **Socialists defeated in Albania.** The Socialist (former Communist) Party of Albania (SPA) lost control of the government when candidates of the opposition Democratic Party emerged from the national election with an impressive majority in the People's Assembly. The Democrats' victory, spearheaded by 47-year-old cardiologist Sali Berisha, was especially significant because the SPA had gained power just a year earlier in a free election. Berisha attributed his party's success to a dramatic change of attitude among rural voters.

Military profits from Thai election. In the first national election since the February 1991 military coup that toppled the democratically elected government of Thailand, candidates of four political parties supporting the junta won 191 of the 360 seats in the lower house of the National Assembly. That same day the junta, which called itself the National Peacekeeping Council, filled all 270 seats in the upper house of parliament with its appointees. More than half of that number were military or police officers. Thailand's deeply rooted practice of vote buying received a jolt in Bangkok, the capital, when the Palang Dharma (Righteous Force), led by "Mr. Clean" Chamlong Srimuang, won 41 seats in the lower house after campaigning on a platform of honest government.

24 **Koreans elect National Assembly.** South Korea's ruling Democratic Liberal Party (DLP) suffered a significant setback in elections to the National Assembly when it captured only 149 seats in the 299-seat assembly. With the support of some of the 21 newly elected independents, however, the DLP expected to have a functioning majority. The opposition Democratic Party made impressive gains by winning 97 seats. The Unification National Party won 31. Emphasizing the more positive aspects of the election, the government noted that its 38.5% share of the popular vote was 4.6% greater than in 1988. It also cited the election results as evidence that South Korea had discarded its authoritarian past in favour of genuine democracy. With Roh Tae Woo ineligible

DEREK HUDSON—SYGMA

Whites in Cape Town go the polls on March 17 to vote on Pres. F.W. de Klerk's proposal to negotiate an end to white-majority rule in South Africa. The referendum passed overwhelmingly.

to run for reelection, politicians and the voting public were looking forward to the presidential election later in the year.

25 **Turkish Kurds battle government.** In five days of violent clashes between Kurdish separatists and Turkish security forces, at least 70 persons were killed in the southeastern region of the country. The Kurds, who by and large were adherents of Islam, had long inhabited an area in the Middle East called Kurdistan, which basically included contiguous parts of Iran, Iraq, and Turkey. The Kurds had never achieved political autonomy. Their latest military challenge to Turkish authority resulted in retaliatory air strikes against two of their guerrilla bases inside Iraq. A year earlier, the Kurds had made an even more disastrous attempt to gain autonomy. After Iran's ignominious defeat in the Gulf war, rebellious Iraqi Kurds renewed their fight for independence. In short order they discovered that they were no match for the better trained and better equipped Iraqi troops. Frantically seeking safety, they fled toward Turkey and Iran into snow-covered mountains, where they endured unspeakable hardships until UN forces came to their assistance.

31 **Security Council pressures Libya.** The United Nations Security Council voted 10–0 with 5 abstentions to ban air flights and arms sales to Libya if it did not surrender suspected international terrorists by April 15. For the present at least, Libya's exportation of oil would not be affected. Strong evidence indicated that two of the suspects had been deeply involved in the bombing of Pan Am Flight 103 over Scotland in December 1988 and four others in the destruction of a French UTA flight over the Sahara in September 1989. The two bombings killed 441 people from some 30 countries. The Security Council resolution obliged all members of the UN to observe the ban if Libya did not comply by the stated deadline. Once the ban took effect, those who wished to depart Libya would have to arrange transportation by ship.

IMF approves Russia's plan for reform. The International Monetary Fund (IMF) announced that it had approved Russia's plan for economic reforms and that as a consequence the republic was qualified to receive up to $4 billion in IMF assistance during the next year. In return, Russia would have to meet certain conditions laid down by the IMF, including exercising tight control over inflation and the national budget. Neither Russia nor any of the other republics that constituted the former Soviet Union had yet been admitted to membership in the IMF. To date, those republics had received about $35 billion from Germany, which stipulated that most of the money was to be used to cover the cost of removing former Soviet troops from what had been East Germany.

APRIL

2 **Mitterrand appoints Bérégovoy.** Pres. François Mitterrand announced that Finance Minister Pierre Bérégovoy would replace Edith Cresson as prime minister of France. Mitterrand apparently felt compelled to make the change because Cresson's popularity had plummeted during her less than 11 months in office. During that time she had made widely publicized derogatory remarks about people of other countries that many French found embarrassing. Mitterrand's Socialist Party, moreover, had won only 18.3% of the popular vote in regional elections on March 22. The government was also plagued by financial scandals, an intense controversy over immigration, a faltering economy, and an unemployment rate near 10%. Bérégovoy's success in attacking France's festering problems before the parliamentary elections in 1993 could well determine the political future of the minority Socialist government.

3 **Serbs attack Bosnia-Hercegovina.** Serbian irregulars and units of the Serbian-dominated Yugoslav army intensified their attacks against Muslim Slavs and Roman Catholic Croats in Bosnia and Hercegovina, which had voted in late February to secede from the Yugoslav federation. The Serbs, who were predominantly Orthodox Christians, warned the European Communities (EC) that diplomatic recognition of Bosnia and Hercegovina would have dire consequences. Undeterred, the EC voted on April 7 to grant such recognition. It did not, however, extend recognition to Macedonia, another former Yugoslav republic, because Greece vigorously opposed having a new neighbouring country bearing the same name as its northern province; among other things, identical names would tend to emphasize the historical affinity between the two regions and perhaps perpetuate old territorial disputes. It became clear in the days that followed that the Serbs were determined to dominate all of Bosnia and Hercegovina, if possible. Tens of thousands of refugees had already fled or been driven from their homes, but greater suffering appeared to lie ahead, especially for Muslims and Croats living in Sarajevo, the capital.

6 **Nepalese killed during protest.** At least 7 Nepalese were killed and some 50 injured in Kathmandu, the capital of Nepal, when police fired on striking protesters demonstrating against price increases and alleged government corruption. The strike, organized by the United Nepal Communist Party and backed by other leftist groups, turned violent when the mob began attacking government buildings and vandalizing shops. The ruling Nepali Congress party had assumed leadership of the country in May 1991 following the first democratic election in 32 years. The move toward democracy came after a popular uprising in 1990 that forced King Birendra to relinquish his rights as absolute ruler.

8 **PLO leader survives plane crash.** Yasir Arafat, the 62-year-old leader of the Palestine Liberation Organization (PLO), was found alive in the Libyan desert some 12 hours after his plane had crash-landed during a violent dust storm. Three of the 13 persons aboard the plane were killed. There had been no contact with the plane after the pilot radioed that he was in trouble. Until a search party located the aircraft and reported that Arafat had not been seriously injured, deep anxiety gripped the Palestinian communities in the Middle East because there was no obvious choice to succeed him as leader of the PLO.

9 **Conservatives win U.K. election.** Britain's Conservative Party, under the leadership of Prime Minister John Major, retained control of the government by winning 336 of the 651 seats in Parliament, a net loss of 31. The Labour Party, which many political pundits had predicted would win control of Parliament, gained 44 seats for a new total of 271. The Liberal Democrats finished far behind in third place with 20 seats; the remaining 24 seats were shared by 6 other minor parties. On April 13, Neil Kinnock announced that he would resign as leader of the Labourites when a successor was chosen during a special party convention in July.

Noriega convicted of trafficking in drugs. Gen. Manuel Noriega, the 58-year-old former strongman leader of Panama, was convicted by a U.S. federal jury in Miami, Fla., on 8 of 10 counts involving drug trafficking, racketeering, and money laundering. Sentencing was scheduled for July 10. The seven-month trial was unusual because it was the first in U.S. history that led to the conviction of a foreign former head of state. It also featured a major drug dealer whose friendship the U.S. government had cultivated even when it had abundant evidence that he was criminally involved in drugs. After the U.S. invaded Panama in December 1989, Noriega sought and received sanctuary in the Vatican nunciature in Panama City. On Jan. 3, 1990, he surrendered to U.S. authorities.

Nigeria welcomes Pres. F.W. de Klerk. South African Pres. F.W. de Klerk, who had taken dramatic steps to end white-minority rule in South Africa, was warmly welcomed in Abuja, Nigeria's new capital. The visit was especially significant because Nigerian Pres. Ibrahim Babangida, who had invited de Klerk to visit his country, was a militant leader of black Africa's campaign against apartheid. Before departing, de Klerk told reporters that the visit had been "extremely constructive" even though Babangida had not suggested that he was prepared to grant diplomatic recognition to South Africa.

10 **UN pushes for Cyprus settlement.** The UN Security Council unanimously approved a resolution calling on Greek and Turkish leaders to begin serious discussions to end the dispute that had split Cyprus into separate Turkish and Greek regions. The Security Council drafted the resolution after both Canada and Denmark warned that they might withdraw their peacekeeping forces from Cyprus if no serious effort was made to reunify the island nation. Austria and Great Britain had also committed troops to the peacekeeping mission. The Security Council hoped that the threat of withdrawing UN forces would spur Turkey and Greece to reach a compromise. In 1974 Turkey had occupied the northern third of Cyprus after Greek Cypriots ousted Archbishop Makarios III, the president. Key elements in the long dispute involved the right of the minority Turkish community to govern itself and the determination of Greek extremists to make Cyprus an integral part of Greece. In November 1983 Turkey announced the establishment of the Turkish Republic of Northern Cyprus, which no other country had ever recognized.

Judge gives Keating 10 years for fraud. A judge of the California Superior Court in Los Angeles sentenced 68-year-old Charles Keating, Jr., to 10 years in prison, the maximum allowed by law, and fined him the maximum $250,000 for having duped thousands of clients, many of them elderly, into purchasing worthless junk bonds issued by the American Continental Corp. (ACC), the parent company of the Lincoln Savings and Loan Association, which collapsed financially. Keating was both chairman and chief executive officer of the ACC. The judge also refused to allow Keating to remain free on bail during his planned appeal. For many, Keating had come to symbolize the kind of conduct that had wreaked havoc with the savings and loan industry. The total cost of the federal bailout of the Lincoln S & L was estimated at $2.6 billion.

14 **War interrupts aid to Sudanese.** Dangers posed by a new government offensive in the south-

Afghan refugees living in Pakistan prepare to return to their homeland after the collapse in April of the Soviet-backed regime of Mohammad Najibullah. Many refugees chose to go home even before a stable government could be formed.
REUTERS/BETTMANN

ern region of The Sudan forced several international humanitarian organizations, including two UN agencies, the World Food Program and UNICEF, to withdraw from the area and suspend their efforts to feed several million starving people. All told, the relief operations were taking care of more than seven million Sudanese facing starvation. The Sudan, Djibouti, Ethiopia, and Kenya had pledged during a meeting in Addis Ababa, Eth., not to use food and medicine as weapons of war against those living in areas occupied by groups opposing their governments. The leaders of those nations approved a declaration asserting that they would always "be guided by the objectives of saving lives, of delivering timely assistance to people in distress and of alleviating human suffering." Nonetheless, Lieut. Gen. Omar Hassan Ahmad al-Bashir, the Muslim leader of The Sudan, appeared to consider suppression of the predominantly Christian rebels in the south to be of greater importance.

15 **United Nations isolates Libya.** United Nations sanctions against Libya went into effect when Libyan

leader Muʿammar al-Qadhdhafi disregarded a Security Council deadline to turn over suspected international terrorists for trial. As a consequence, all members of the UN were obliged immediately to sever air links with Libya, suspend arms sales, restrict the movement of Libyan diplomats within their respective countries, and reduce the size of their staffs at diplomatic missions in Libya. Libya was thus punitively isolated from the rest of the world for refusing to comply with a resolution passed by the UN Security Council. The Arab League had attempted to arrange a compromise solution to the dispute, but after a meeting with Qadhdhafi on April 21, Egyptian Pres. Hosni Mubarak acknowledged that further efforts were needed to resolve the impasse.

16 **Scandals besmirch U.S. Congress.** Reacting to intense public anger, the Committee on Standards of Official Conduct of the U.S. House of Representatives released information on 303 current and relatively recent members of Congress who had overdrawn their accounts at the House's private bank. Although the facility was not a bank in the usual sense and the overdrafts cost taxpayers nothing, the use of money that belonged to other congressmen was widely viewed as unethical because it was, in effect, borrowing money interest free. One of the worst abusers of banking privileges had reportedly written 996 overdrafts during the 39-month period under review (up to Oct. 3, 1991). On April 9, while a heated debate was still raging in the House over which details of the bank scandal should be made public, a federal grand jury charged Wendell Magruder, a former clerk in the House post office, with selling illegal drugs, including cocaine, and conspiring with other employees to conceal thefts of postal funds. Three post office employees had already pleaded guilty in February to charges of embezzlement. Frightened by a rising tide of voter outrage over the scandals, the House closed its bank, which had been operating for more than 150 years, and severely restricted other perks ranging from the use of government aircraft and limousines to free use of a private gymnasium.

SCOTT DANIEL PETERSON—GAMMA LIAISON

Christian rebels march in The Sudan. The country's Islamic government continued its military campaign against non-Muslims in the south, impeding international efforts to alleviate famine.

President of Afghanistan resigns. Mohammad Najibullah, whom the Soviet Union had installed as head of the Afghan government in 1986, before it began withdrawing its troops from the war zone, was reported to have resigned the presidency and gone into hiding as Islamic guerrillas and disaffected government soldiers advanced rapidly toward the capital. By April 24 most areas in Kabul were in the control of various heavily armed rebel armies. Despite the collapse of Najibullah's Communist regime, the end of 14 years of civil war, and termination of the Soviet military intervention that began in December 1979, there were serious doubts that the fighting had ended. The leaders of two of the most powerful military factions both wanted to rule the country. One was Ahmad Shah Masood, the military commander of the Islamic Party, and the other was Gulbuddin Hekmatyar, who commanded the Islamic Society. On April 28, Sibgatullah Mojadedi arrived in Kabul. During a meeting in Pakistan he had been elected interim president because he had few political supporters and was highly regarded as a religious leader. The 51 members of his temporary government, moreover, had been drawn from most segments of Afghanistan's highly diverse society.

29 **Los Angeles trial ignites riots.** After deliberating for seven days, a Superior Court jury in Simi Valley, Calif., acquitted four Los Angeles policemen on 10 of 11 charges connected with the severe beating of Rodney King, a black motorist they had sought to arrest after a car chase. Other officers at the scene had made no attempt to intervene. The jury was deadlocked on only one count against a single defendant. Millions of people across the nation were stunned by the verdict because they had repeatedly watched an 81-second videotape of the incident, shot by an amateur, on local and network television newscasts. Within hours of the verdict, rioting in the predominantly black and Hispanic area of south-central Los Angeles was out of control. By the time the National Guard restored order, 51 persons had been killed, a thousand businesses destroyed, and perhaps as much as $1 billion in physical damage inflicted on an area that was already struggling just to survive. In retrospect the jury's verdict did not seem to be so much the cause of the rioting as an incident that provided an opportunity for the community to release its profound frustration over

miserable housing, unemployment, lack of opportunities, and what appeared to be government indifference to the desperate plight of many living in the area.

30 **Troops take over Sierra Leone.** Rebellious soldiers informed the people of Sierra Leone that "patriotic officers" and other members of the armed forces had ousted Pres. Joseph Saidu Momoh and had set up a provisional government. A dusk-to-dawn curfew was imposed, and the people were warned that violators would be shot. Momoh's fate was reportedly linked to developments in Liberia, where a West African peacekeeping force had prevented Charles Taylor, one of two rival rebel leaders, from seizing power. The fighting in Liberia had then spilled across the border when Taylor's troops invaded Sierra Leone to punish Momoh for supporting the peace force. Soldiers sent to retake towns that Taylor had captured were said to resent their involvement in the conflict and to have complained that they had not been paid and had not received sufficient food or ammunition to enable them to carry out their orders.

MAY

4 **Religious groups clash in Egypt.** Fourteen Coptic Christians were reported killed and five others wounded in the Egyptian village of Manshiet Nasser when militant Muslims opened fire on farmers and schoolchildren. The deadly attack was apparently an act of revenge for the killing of a Muslim fundamentalist leader two months earlier. In another incident in late April, a policeman shot and killed a Muslim while a mob was stoning a Coptic church. The policeman said that the man had tried to grab his weapon. Two days later another person was killed by Muslims seeking to avenge the death of their coreligionist. The victim was a 13-year-old girl.

6 **Lebanese government collapses.** Unable to control public anger over the chaotic state of Lebanon's economy, Prime Minister Omar Karami and his government resigned. The announcement came amid mounting chaos in Beirut, where demonstrators were ransacking banks, burning tires, and blocking roads. The previous day labour unions had proclaimed a general strike to protest soaring prices and the plummeting value of the local currency. Schools, banks, and businesses closed down, and the home of the finance minister was set ablaze. On May 13, Pres. Elias Hrawi, whose son had been beaten during the turmoil, asked 66-year-old Rashid as-Solh, a member of the National Assembly, to form a new government. As-Solh had held the post of prime minister in 1975 when Lebanon became engulfed in a devastating civil war.

7 **Germans end nationwide strike.** An 11-day nationwide strike ended in Germany when government officials and labour leaders agreed to an average pay increase of about 5.4% for

some 2.3 million public-sector workers. Those at the lower end of the wage scale would receive larger increases than those above them. The government had originally offered a 4.8% raise, but the unions demanded 9.5%. An arbitrator suggested that they settle for 5.4%. The rank and file of one union rejected the pact, but its leaders, who had authority to disregard the vote, said that a renewal of the strike was unlikely. The job action, which had affected most cities in western Germany, disrupted land and air transportation, postal service, and the collection of garbage. The strikers had flexed their muscles on May 5 by temporarily closing down the Frankfurt airport, the biggest in continental Europe. Meanwhile, labour trouble was also brewing in the private sector, where the leadership of IG Metall, the country's largest union, threatened a full-scale strike unless new wage demands were met. The union represented some 3.5 million workers in the automobile, steel, electronics, and other manufacturing industries. German Chancellor Helmut Kohl warned that any wage increase would have to be "bearable in relation both to the challenges of German unity and growing international competition." Kohl was referring to the huge amount of money the government was committed to spend to revitalize what had been East Germany.

Amendment added to U.S. Constitution. In one of the most unusual developments in U.S. constitutional history, an amendment proposed 203 years earlier by James Madison and sent by the first U.S. Congress to the states for ratification in 1789 automatically became law when Michigan became the necessary 38th state to ratify the legislation. The amendment read in its totality: "No law varying the compensation for the services of the

Senators and Representatives shall take effect, until an election of Representatives shall have intervened." On May 19 the new amendment was published in the Federal Register and formally recognized as part of the U.S. Constitution. Initially there was some uncertainty about the validity of the ratification procedure because the nation had changed dramatically during the past two centuries. No one, however, seriously challenged the law, least of all any member of Congress. On May 20, in fact, both houses of Congress, well aware that voters were deeply dissatisfied with their performance in office, warmly endorsed the new restriction placed on their pay increases.

11 **Ramos wins Philippine election.** Fidel Ramos, a retired army general and former defense secretary, was elected president of the Philippines with 24% of the popular vote. He had been endorsed by Philippine Pres. Corazon Aquino, who during her term in office survived six coups, in part because Ramos came to her defense. Ramos had also had a key role in the pro-democracy movement that forced Ferdinand Marcos out of office in 1986. Miriam Defensor Santiago, a colourful former judge who made government corruption a major theme of her campaign, finished second in the field of seven. Eduardo Cojuangco, a wealthy businessman who had accompanied Marcos when he was flown out of the Philippines, finished third. Imelda Marcos, widow of the former president, and the three other candidates trailed far behind. Although the counting of ballots was agonizingly slow, there was general agreement that the election had been unusually free of fraud. Voters had also been asked to elect a national legislature and to fill numerous local offices.

Tajik president accepts coalition. Four days after Islamic and pro-democracy opposition groups announced that they had taken over control of the republic of Tajikistan, Pres. Rakhman Nabiyev, an old-style Communist leader, declared his willingness to form a coalition government that would give his political rivals control of 8 of the 24 Cabinet ministries. These included the key Defense, Foreign, and Interior ministries; the Agriculture, Economy, and Trade ministries; the Radio and Television Ministry; and the Committee for National Security, the Tajik equivalent of the Soviet KGB. The new government would also have a restructured parliament with equal representation given to members of the opposition and to former parliamentarians, most of whom belonged to the Communist Party. All were aware that great care had to be taken to preserve a sense of unity in a republic that had been artificially created as part of the former Soviet Union.

12 **Australia to curtail immigration.** With citizens clamouring that something be done to alleviate Australia's 10% unemployment rate, the government announced a plan to reduce by about 27% the number of new immigrants allowed into the country each year. Roughly speaking, the total would drop to about 80,000 from 111,000. After quotas were readjusted, the total number of refugees would diminish slightly and the number of new immigrants with ties to families already settled in Australia would increase slightly, but the number of independent skilled workers admitted would be cut by more than 50%.

13 **West suspends aid to Malawi.** Western donor nations and the World Bank suspended development aid to Malawi for 1992 and 1993 in an effort to force Pres. Kamuzu Banda to improve his human rights record in the one-party African republic. The cutoff of funds, however, would not affect drought relief programs or humanitarian aid to some 900,000 refugees who had fled the civil war in neighbouring Mozambique. A decision to suspend aid was virtually assured a week earlier when dozens of demonstrators were killed in Lilongwe, the capital, and in Blantyre. The deaths occurred when angry mobs turned to arson and looting to reinforce demands that Banda resign. Banda was the only ruler Malawi had had since it gained independence in 1964.

U.S. astronauts rescue errant satellite. In an unprecedented and highly dangerous maneuver, three U.S. astronauts left the space shuttle *Endeavour* to retrieve a 4.5-ton communications satellite by using only their hands. Exercising extreme caution not to tear their gloves, they first succeeded in stopping the rotation of the satellite, then worked it slowly into the shuttle's payload bay. The next day the errant satellite was successfully launched toward its proper orbit. For two years the $150 million satellite had remained in a uselessly low orbit while the National Aeronautics and Space Administration devised a plan to rescue it with a metal bar. After two failed attempts, the three astronauts were given permission to make one last effort, this time using only their hands.

Debris litters a Bangkok street damaged by demonstrations in May against the prime minister, a former Thai military commander. The protests were led by a pro-democracy movement.
SERGE CORRIERAS—GAMMA LIAISON

17 **Troops kill Bangkok protesters.** With thousands upon thousands of demonstrators shouting in the streets of Bangkok, Thailand, for an end to military involvement in politics, the government declared a national emergency. The protesters were especially angry over the April 7 appointment of Suchinda Kraprayoon, the nation's top military commander, as prime minister. Opponents claimed that the appointment was illegal because Suchinda had failed to win a seat in the parliament in the March 22 election. During the next three days, tensions reached new heights when government troops fired on the rioters. By some estimates as many as a thousand were killed. The violence appeared to increase after the May 18 arrest of Chamlong Srimuang, a former governor of Bangkok nicknamed "Mr. Clean," whose pro-democracy hunger strike had originally ignited the protest movement. With emotions at fever pitch, the crowd set fire to hundreds of buildings and thousands of cars. The immediate crisis ended on May 20 when King Bhumibol Adulyadej, a man of extraordinary prestige, called Suchinda and Chamlong to the royal palace. The monarch ordered the two men kneeling before him to end their confrontation.

18 **Swiss moving to end isolation.** One day after Swiss voters approved a plan to join the World Bank and the International Monetary Fund, Switzerland announced that it would immediately apply for membership in the European Communities (EC). The decision appeared to end Switzerland's proud tradition of neutrality and self-imposed isolation, but there was no certainty that the notoriously independent electorate would sanction membership in the EC when it was presented with the question in a national referendum. Switzerland remained one of the few countries in the world that was still outside the United Nations. In 1986 voters had rejected UN membership by a 3–1 margin.

19 **Troops suppress Nigerian riots.** Government troops, some in helicopters, others in armoured vehicles or on foot, ended a three-day battle between Christians and Muslims in Nigeria's northern state of Kaduna. A curfew was then imposed to maintain the peace. During the fighting more than 200 had been killed and hundreds injured. A businessman, eyewitness to the rioting, remarked, "People were killed as if they were dogs." Tribal and religious differences as well as land disputes repeatedly caused smoldering animosities to burst into flames. In the latest incident, in addition to the human toll, five churches were destroyed and numerous other buildings consumed by fire. On May 25, Gen. Ibrahim Babangida, Nigeria's president, announced the formation of a national guard, which would have full responsibility for controlling future riots. He was said to share with others the fear that Nigeria could slip into anarchy unless strong measures were taken.

21 **China tests large nuclear device.** Richard Boucher, a spokesman for the U.S. State Department, reported that China had detonated a nuclear device thought to have a yield of about one megaton. A device of that magnitude would be about 70 times more powerful than the atomic bomb dropped on Hiroshima during World War II. The test was the most powerful China had ever undertaken and was nearly seven times larger than the limit agreed to in the U.S.-U.S.S.R. treaty signed in 1974, but it was only one-fifth as powerful as the one the U.S. had conducted underground in 1971. Arms-control experts chided China for its lack of restraint and criticized the U.S. again for opposing a comprehensive international treaty that would ban all testing of large nuclear devices. In the U.S. Congress there was harsh criticism of China because it was reportedly selling missile technology to countries of the Middle East and was still violating the basic human rights of its citizens. The Bush administration had come under attack from those who felt it was following a much too conciliatory policy toward China.

24 **Austrians elect Thomas Klestil.** Early election returns indicated that 59-year-old Thomas Klestil, candidate of the conservative People's Party, had been elected president of Austria with about 56% of the popular vote, the largest margin of victory in any presidential election since World War II. His opponent in the runoff election was Rudolf Streicher, a Social Democrat. Klestil, a relatively unknown career diplomat before his nomination, appeared to have won a vast majority of the votes that had gone to Heide Schmidt, candidate of the far-right Freedom Party, in the inconclusive election on April 26. When Klestil assumed office on July 8, a veil of embarrassment shrouding the presidency would be lifted. His predecessor, Kurt Waldheim, who had been secretary-general (1972–81) of the UN, had been ostracized by a large part of the world after it became known in 1986 that he had been an intelligence officer in a German army unit that subjected Yugoslavs to brutal reprisals during World War II. His commanding officer was later executed for war crimes.

30 **UN approves Belgrade sanctions.** The UN Security Council voted 13–0 with two abstentions (China and Zimbabwe) to impose economic sanctions on Yugoslavia because its Serb-

A convoy carries ethnic Serbs from their homes in Bosnia and Hercegovina to Serbia. It was estimated that the fighting in the Balkans had created well over two million refugees.

JON JONES—SYGMA

dominated government refused to halt military operations designed to carve up the republic of Bosnia and Hercegovina along ethnic lines. The UN resolution called on all nations to sever trade links with Yugoslavia, to freeze its foreign assets, to terminate financial deals that were not humanitarian in nature, to cancel airline schedules, to suspend scientific and technological cooperation, and to ostracize

Yugoslavia from all international sports and cultural events. The UN urged all parties to the conflict to do their part to stop the slaughter, especially in Sarajevo, so that humanitarian aid could reach those most in need of help. The following day tens of thousands of protesters marched in downtown Belgrade to demand the resignation of Serbian Pres. Slobodan Milosevic, a hard-line Serbian nationalist.

JUNE

2 **Denmark rejects European unity.** Danish voters, by a tiny majority, rejected the Treaty on European Union that the European Communities (EC) had worked out during a 1991 summit meeting in Maastricht, Neth. The failure of the referendum dealt a serious blow to the pact because it could not take effect in 1993 as planned unless all 12 EC member nations had ratified it. A suggestion by Denmark's prime minister that sections of the treaty be reworked to satisfy his countrymen was flatly rejected by the prime minister of Portugal, who held the EC's rotating presidency.

14 **World leaders discuss ecology.** Some 35,000 delegates from 178 countries concluded a 12-day United Nations Conference on Environment and Development in Rio de Janeiro after signing several historic agreements. One delegate predicted that in five years "we will look back on Rio and see it

was a point of transition on how we deal with global environmental issues." Brazilian Pres. Fernando Collor de Mello remarked: "Much more than 12 days ago, the world today is aware that the questions of environment and development cannot be treated separately." UN Secretary-General Boutros Boutros-Ghali, reminding the delegates of the task ahead, said: "Today we have agreed to hold to present levels the pollution we are guilty of. One day we will have to do better—clean up the planet."

15 **Japan to join UN peacekeepers.** After months of animated debate, the lower house of Japan's Diet (parliament) approved a bill sanctioning the participation of up to 2,000 military personnel in United Nations peacekeeping missions in various parts of the world. The bill had already passed the upper house on June 9. To appease local critics the bill included restrictions that limited the

force's weapons to small side arms and ruled out deployment in any trouble spot where a cease-fire had not been accepted by opposing groups or where a declared cease-fire had broken down.

U.S. high court permits kidnappings. The U.S. Supreme Court ruled 6–3 that the U.S. government could legally abduct a criminal suspect in a foreign country and transport that person to the U.S. to stand trial in a federal court even over the objections of the country involved and regardless of the conditions set down in an extradition treaty with that country. The court's decision invalidated the rulings of two lower federal courts, which had declared that the seizure of a Mexican doctor in Mexico had been illegal. The man was accused of having taken part in the torture and murder of a U.S. narcotics agent in Guadalajara in 1985. Associate Justices John Paul Stevens, Harry Blackmun, and Sandra Day O'Connor dissented. The court's ruling stunned many Americans, who wondered how the U.S. would react if a foreign power abducted a U.S. citizen on U.S. soil in similar circumstances. The case of Gen. Manuel Noriega would not have been affected one way or another by the court's ruling because Panamanians were overwhelmingly relieved when the former dictator was ousted from power and flown to Miami, Fla., after U.S. troops invaded the country.

17 **De Klerk blamed for massacre.** About 200 Zulu tribesmen, believed to be associated with the Inkatha Freedom Party, slaughtered at least 40 people in the township of Boipatong and in a neighbouring slum some 60 km (40 mi) from Johannesburg, South Africa. The victims of what was called the worst

REUTERS/BETTMANN

Yitzhak Rabin speaks to supporters after Labour had defeated the ruling Likud in elections on June 23. As head of his party, Rabin became prime minister in a coalition government.

single incident of wanton killing in many years were mostly women, children, and the elderly. When Pres. F.W. de Klerk tried to visit the scene, he was besieged by angry demonstrators. During the confrontation that followed, the police fired into the crowd, killing three more persons. The grief-stricken townspeople accused the government of doing virtually nothing to halt violence in the black townships, which had claimed more than 1,500 lives since the beginning of the year.

German hostages released in Lebanon. After more than three years in captivity, Heinrich Strübig and Thomas Kemptner, two German relief workers, were set free in Lebanon by their Shi'ite guerrilla kidnappers. The Germans were believed to be the last Western hostages held in Lebanon. The person responsible for their abduction was said to be the brother of two international terrorists imprisoned in Germany. Rumours that Germany had bargained for the release of the two men were vehemently denied by Klaus Kinkel, the foreign minister. Analysts were more inclined to believe that Syria and Iran, which had the greatest influence over groups known to take hostages, had engineered the release in order to improve relations with Western nations.

20 **Czechoslovakia faces breakup.** Vaclav Klaus, the premier designate of Czechoslovakia, and Vladimir Meciar, a leader of Slovak nationalism, agreed to the formation of a national caretaker government and on steps leading to the division of Czechoslovakia into two separate nations, one Czech, the other Slovak. Whatever agreements were reached by the Czech and Slovak National Councils regarding such things as the division of federal assets, the repayment of Czechoslovakia's debts, and the realignment of the nation's armed forces would have to be approved by the national parliament. Vaclav Havel, president of Czechoslovakia, continued to urge the nation to remain united and said that a national referendum on the issue was the only constitutional and moral way to decide the momentous issue.

23 **Yitzhak Shamir loses election.** In one of the most important elections in Israeli history, Prime Minister Yitzhak Shamir's ruling Likud bloc was soundly defeated by the Labour Party in elections for the 120 seats in the national Knesset (parliament). With 25 parties competing for representation, the Labour Party appeared to have won 44 seats (+5) and Likud 32 (−9). Yitzhak Rabin, who had replaced Shimon Peres as leader of the Labour Party on February 19, provided Israelis with a clear alternative to the Shamir government. He supported

Ships of the Black Sea Fleet lie at anchor in the Crimean port of Sevastopol. Russia and Ukraine agreed in June to divide the fleet but to share bases.
BILL SWERSEY—GAMMA LIAISON

the Middle East peace talks, favoured Palestinian self-rule and the suspension of new Jewish settlements in occupied lands, and expressed a willingness to exchange some occupied lands for peace with the Arabs. At the same time, Rabin made it clear that his top priority remained the national security of Israel.

Russia and Ukraine resolve problems. Russian Pres. Boris Yeltsin and Ukrainian Pres. Leonid Kravchuk signed an 18-point agreement that resolved in principle major disagreements that had soured relations between the two former Soviet republics. One of the most contentious issues, disposition of the Black Sea Fleet, was resolved by an agreement to divide the fleet and share the cost of maintaining its naval bases.

26 **U.S. Navy rocked by sex scandal.** H. Lawrence Garrett resigned as U.S. secretary of the navy amid a growing controversy over the handling of accusations that 26 women, including 14 officers, had been sexually abused at a 1991 convention of some 5,000 current and former navy and Marine Corps fliers. The incident, which occurred at the Hilton Hotel in Las Vegas, Nev., was widely reported by the news media after Lieut. Paula Coughlin, a 30-year-old helicopter pilot, went public. She decided to speak out after navy officers had either failed to take her accusations seriously or temporized in the apparent hope that the matter would die without the need to take serious disciplinary action against those found guilty of misconduct. When investigators encountered a conspiracy of silence, the Senate Armed Services Committee intensified the pressure by holding up the promotions and transfers of some 4,500 navy and marine personnel.

28 **Mongolian ex-Communists triumph.** Unofficial tallies indicated that the Mongolian People's Rev-

olutionary Party had won 70 of the 76 seats in the nation's new parliament. Opposition parties acknowledged that they had been overwhelmed because they were in no position to match the financial and organizational resources of the ruling party. Two years earlier the Revolutionary Party had renounced communism and moved toward greater democracy by initiating free elections, permitting greater freedom of the press, and introducing more liberal economic and political policies. The country, however, still faced serious problems, including chronic shortages of basic necessities.

29 **President of Algeria murdered.** Mohammad Boudiaf, who had been president of Algeria's High State Council since January 11, was shot and killed during an address in Annaba. The assassin was said to have been a uniformed member of Boudiaf's security guard and to have fired an automatic weapon. There were also reports of two explosions, but conflicting reports made it nearly impossible to reconstruct what actually happened or who was ultimately responsible for the assassination. On July 2, with the joint approval of the State and Security Councils, Ali Kafi was named Boudiaf's successor.

Norway soon to ignore whaling ban. Norway announced that starting in 1993 it would no longer observe the international moratorium on commercial whaling because certain species, including minke whales, were no longer in danger of extinction. Echoing that same argument, Iceland resigned from the International Whaling Commission because it had been taken over, Iceland said, by a rabid minority opposed to whaling even though scientific data could no longer be cited to support a continuation of the ban. Japan, which had never viewed the ban as legitimate, was also reported considering a resumption of minke whaling.

JULY

4 **Nigerians vote for legislators.** Nigerians went to the polls for the first time in 12 years to elect members to both houses of the nation's new National Assembly. The military

government of Pres. Ibrahim Babangida permitted only two parties to participate to lessen the possibility, he said, that parties would be formed along religious and tribal lines. Critics complained that although the

election moved the country closer to a restoration of civilian rule, it fell short of true democracy because 32 candidates had been disqualified without explanation just days before the election. Voters, moreover, had to cast their ballots publicly by lining up behind pictures of the candidates of their choice. Preliminary vote tallies indicated that the left-of-centre Social Democratic Party had won a majority in both the Senate and the House of Representatives. What role the assembly would play before the presidential election in January 1993 was still unclear.

5 **Durán wins election in Ecuador.** Sixto Durán, candidate of the United Republican Party, handily defeated Jaime Nebot, head of the Social Christian Party, in a runoff election for the presidency of Ecuador. The constitution did not permit Pres. Rodrigo Borja to enter the race. Both presidential candidates had promised to move Ecuador, South America's second largest oil-producer (after Venezuela), toward a free-market economy. They also pledged to take steps to lower the country's more than $12 billion foreign debt, its 50% inflation rate, and its 15% unemployment rate.

6 **World leaders meet in Munich.** The leaders of the seven major industrialized democracies (Britain, Canada, France, Germany, Italy, Japan, the U.S.) convened in Munich, Germany, for their 18th annual economic summit. Before adjourning on July 8, they held extensive discussions on international trade and on ways to stimulate the world's faltering economies, but they did not reach any specific agreement on what should be done to improve the situation. The final communiqué, however, stated that a successful completion of the Uruguay round of international trade talks under the auspices of the General Agreement on Tariffs and Trade would be a "significant contribution to the future of the world economy."

9 **Patten posted to Hong Kong.** Chris Patten, former chairman of Britain's Conservative Party, was sworn into office as governor of Britain's Crown Colony of Hong Kong. Patten faced the difficult and delicate task of guiding Hong Kong during the years preceding 1997, when the territory would revert to China. In his inaugural speech, Patten pledged to support Hong Kong's free-market economy and to improve relations with China, whose leaders were patently unhappy over mounting demands by Hong Kong residents for genuine democracy. Talks with China on a new Hong Kong airport, approved in principle by both parties, had stalled a week earlier because China feared that escalating costs would bankrupt the colony before it reclaimed the territory. Both sides had rejected the other's plan for financing the project.

10 **Noriega gets 40-year sentence.** U.S. District Court Judge William Hoeveler sentenced Gen. Manuel Noriega, the former strongman leader of Panama, to 40 years in prison. On April 9 he had been convicted by a federal jury in Miami, Fla., on 8 of 10 counts involving drug trafficking, racketeering, and money laundering. Although Noriega would be eligible for parole in 10 years, he still faced charges in Tampa, Fla., of smuggling marijuana.

18 **Smith to lead U.K. Labour Party.** John Smith, a 53-year-old Scottish lawyer, was elected leader of Britain's Labour Party by 91% of its electoral college. He replaced Neil Kinnock, who had announced his resignation after Labour failed to defeat the ruling Conservatives in the April national election. Many had predicted a Labour victory. In his acceptance speech, Smith declared that Labour would try to win back popular support before the next election by "embarking on a great journey, a journey to eliminate poverty, injustice, and homelessness."

19 **Mafia defies Italian government.** Paolo Borsellino, the 54-year-old chief prosecutor in Palermo, Sicily, was killed along with five of his bodyguards when a massive remote-controlled car bomb was detonated near his mother's home. Eighteen others were injured by the explosion. Borsellino had been a key figure in the prosecution and conviction of more than 300 mafiosi in 1987 and had been expected to head a new anti-Mafia super magistrate task force being set up in Rome. The person originally slated for that job had been assassinated in Palermo on May 23. Four days after being excoriated by angry citizens at a state funeral for the victims of the bombing, government officials authorized the deployment of 7,000 anti-Mafia troops to Sicily with orders to hunt down mafiosi and guard important installations.

22 **Colombian drug lord escapes.** Pablo Escobar, the notorious head of the Medellín cocaine cartel in Colombia, escaped from his luxurious prison quarters when government troops attempted to transfer him temporarily to a military installation. Prison guards held the warden and two high-ranking government officials hostage while Escobar and 10 associates made their way to freedom past a security fence. They were well armed and believed to be wearing army uniforms. Six persons were killed before troops were able to rescue the hostages. The escape led to the dismissal or resignation of a handful of top military and government officials.

24 **AIDS discussed in Amsterdam.** The eighth international conference on AIDS, attended by more than 9,000 health experts and others from around the world, concluded in Amsterdam after lengthy discussions about the medical, social, ethical, and economic aspects of the disease. For the first time, AIDS activists were allowed to address the gathering as official participants. The original site of the conference was to have been Boston, but the location was changed because the U.S. denied visas to anyone with AIDS or infected with HIV, the virus that causes AIDS. The director of the World Health Organization's AIDS program told his audience that the number of AIDS patients would total about 40 million by the year 2000.

26 **Japan's ruling LDP triumphs.** Japan's ruling Liberal-Democratic Party (LDP) regained effective control of the upper house of the Diet (parliament) when it won 69 of the 127 contested seats in national elections. Voter turnout was the lowest since democratic elections were instituted in 1947. The LDP's new total of 108 of the 252 seats in the House of Councillors would allow the LDP to form a working coalition with its allies. It already held a satisfactory majority in the lower house, which controlled the prime ministership. The Social Democratic Party (SDP), formerly called the Socialist Party, won only 22 of the contested seats. The SDP had portrayed the election as a referendum on Japan's participation in UN peacekeeping missions, which the SDP vigorously opposed. The peacekeeping operations bill had already been approved by the Diet on June 15. The current low popular appeal of the SDP contrasted sharply with the support it had received in 1989 when it won a stunning victory over the LDP and formed the largest bloc in the upper house with the support of its leftist allies. The latest election was something of an anomaly. Japan's highest judicial authority, the Grand Bench of the Supreme

ALBERTO PIZZOLI—SYGMA

Flowers mark the site in Palermo, Sicily, where a public prosecutor was killed on July 19. The assassination, carried out by the Mafia, occurred as the man visited his mother.

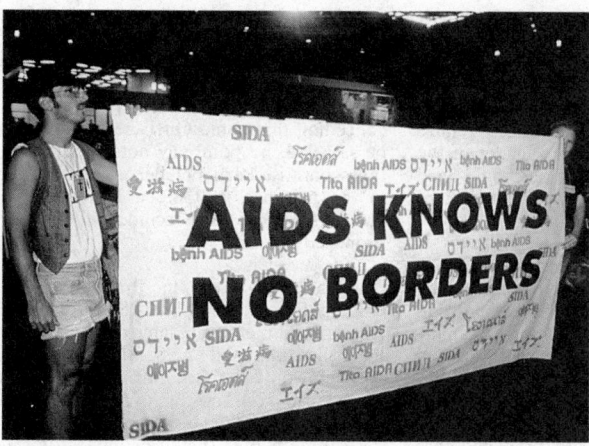

Protesters carry a banner at the July AIDS conference in The Netherlands. It was the eighth international conference held to discuss the disease.
DANIEL GEERAERTS—GAMMA LIAISON

Court, had ruled on several occasions that national elections, which gave rural areas vastly more representation than their numbers warranted, violated constitutional law. Nonetheless, the justices declared the election valid because voiding the results would create political chaos.

U.S. disabilities act takes effect. The employment rights provision of the 1990 Americans with Disabilities Act went into effect throughout the country. It required all companies with 25 or more employees to abandon any hiring practices that discriminated against the physically or mentally impaired provided such people were otherwise capable of performing the job. Employers would be required to make "reasonable accommodations" to assist such persons unless compliance would cause undue hardships. Flexible work schedules, special tools or equipment, and wheelchair

access were cited as examples of "reasonable accommodations." The government estimated that 14 million Americans and some 500,000 businesses would be affected by the new legislation. In two years the law would extend to businesses with 15 or more employees.

29 Honecker extradited to Germany. Erich Honecker was extradited to Germany to face charges of corruption and manslaughter during his years (1971–89) as ruler of East Germany. Because he had ordered border guards to use whatever means were necessary to stop anyone trying to escape to the West, Honecker was being held responsible for the deaths of 49 persons who were killed trying to flee East Germany. The actual number of those who had died was believed to range between 350 and 400. Honecker, now 79 years old, had been living in the

Chilean embassy in Moscow for six months when he was asked to leave. Russian security officers then put him on a military flight to Berlin, where he was taken into custody.

Clark Clifford and partner indicted. Clark Clifford and Robert Altman, two prominent lawyers in Washington, D.C., were indicted by the federal government and by New York state for alleged complicity in the scandal involving the Arab-owned Bank of Credit and Commerce International (BCCI), which had its headquarters in Luxembourg. The two men had been the top executives of First American Bankshares Inc., the largest bank in the nation's capital. A district attorney for New York charged the men with conspiracy, bribe taking, falsifying bank records, and conspiring to commit fraud. He also charged that both men were aware that BCCI had acquired control of First American in 1982 and had accepted bribes to alter records. The federal charges focused mainly on allegations that the men had misled federal banking regulators about the degree of control BCCI exercised over the bank in Washington. Clifford and Altman claimed that they had been duped by BCCI officials.

30 Iran expropriates Iraqi planes. Saudi and Kuwaiti officials confirmed a published report that Iran had decided to expropriate scores of Iraqi planes that had been flown to Iran during the Gulf war to prevent their destruction by UN forces. The total value of the military and civilian aircraft was estimated at $1.2 billion. Iran reportedly confiscated the planes as partial payment for the damages it said it had incurred during its 1980–88 war with Iraq.

AUGUST

6 Israel makes gestures for peace. The Israeli government of Prime Minister Yitzhak Rabin announced further restrictions on new Jewish settlements in the occupied territories by suspending land grants to settlers wishing to build their own homes. On August 24 Rabin took another step to advance the Middle East peace process by canceling the deportation of 11 Palestinians accused of fostering terrorism. The next day, Israeli negotiators presented their Palestinian counterparts with detailed proposals for Palestinian self-rule in the West Bank and Gaza. Although no one expected a sudden breakthrough in the complicated negotiations, a new spirit of goodwill appeared to permeate the arduous search for lasting peace.

7 Truce declared in Mozambique. After 16 years of civil war that claimed an estimated 600,000 lives and forced some four million people to flee to neighbouring countries, the warring factions in Mozambique finally terminated hostilities. The political atmosphere had begun to change significantly in 1991 when the Marxist government of Pres. Joaquim Chissanó acceded to demands from the Mozambican National Resistance

(Renamo) guerrillas that the country become a multiparty democracy. Chissanó and Afonso Dhlakama, head of Renamo, had never met face-to-face before their three-day meeting in Rome. A variety of disparate factors finally brought them together to discuss and then sign a truce.

8 Sri Lankan commanders killed. Maj. Gen. Denzil Kobbekaduwa, commander of the Sri Lankan task force fighting the Liberation Tigers of Tamil Eelam, was killed along with nine other top military officers when their vehicle hit a land mine on Kayts Island. The Tigers, who took credit for the killings, had been waging guerrilla warfare against the government for more than 10 years. Their goal was to gain a homeland for ethnic Tamils, who comprised about 18% of the island nation's 17 million inhabitants. Most Tamils resided in the northern section of the country, where the officers were killed.

9 Summer Olympics come to an end. The Games of the XXV Olympiad concluded in Barcelona, Spain, after two weeks of competition involving some 10,600 athletes from 172 nations and territories. It was the first Summer Games since 1972 unaffected by a political

boycott and the first time in 32 years that South African athletes were allowed to participate. South Africa had been ostracized by the International Olympic Committee because the nation's leaders had, until recently, shown no willingness to abandon apartheid, the policy of racial separation. Seven athletes were expelled from the Games (Britain 3, U.S. 2, Unified Team 1, China 1) after testing positive for banned drugs. The most stunning upset of the games was Sergey Bubka's failure to clear any height in the pole vault. With 30 world records to his credit in that event, he had been considered unbeatable.

12 NAFTA trade pact takes shape. After 14 months of negotiations, Canada, Mexico, and the U.S. completed the draft of an economic pact called the North American Free Trade Agreement (NAFTA). Some modifications were likely before the agreement attained its final form, but when it was ratified by each of the three nations, tariffs and other barriers to free trade and investments were expected to disappear over a period of 15 years. Canada and the U.S. had already been operating under a bilateral free-trade agreement since January 1989. NAFTA's huge internal market of 370 million people

Chinese Pres. Yang Shangkun welcomes South Korean Pres. Roh Tae Woo (right) to Beijing in September. On August 24 the two countries had established relations.

FORREST ANDERSON—GAMMA LIAISON

would represent a combined domestic product in excess of $6 trillion. Most Americans who opposed the agreement predicted that whole U.S. industries would be exported to Mexico, where manufacturing costs were well below those in the U.S. Those who supported NAFTA expressed confidence that in time free trade would create jobs in the U.S., not destroy them.

13 **Belgrade faces new pressures.** The UN Security Council voted 12–0 with 3 abstentions (China, India, Zimbabwe) in favour of a resolution authorizing the use of whatever means were deemed necessary to deliver humanitarian aid to the beleaguered people of Bosnia and Hercegovina, a former constituent republic of Yugoslavia. Evidence continued to mount that Yugoslavia's Serbian-dominated army was decimating and brutalizing the Bosnians, especially Muslims, in a relentless drive to gain mastery of the region through "ethnic cleansing." Bosnia's ambassador to the United Nations, clearly disappointed that the Security Council had no desire to involve the UN as such in any military operation, accused the Security Council of doing only what it thought was absolutely required in order to appease public outrage over what was taking place in his homeland. He had earlier pleaded in vain for an end to an arms embargo that, he said, stripped Bosnians of the "basic right" to defend themselves, especially against a vastly superior military force.

19 **Bahamian voters oust Pindling.** Bahamian Prime Minister Lynden Pindling was swept from power when his Progressive Liberal Party (PLP) was soundly defeated by the Free National Movement (FNM) under the leadership of Hubert Ingraham, Pindling's former protégé. The FNM, which had held 17 of

the 49 seats in the House of Assembly before the election, upped its total to 31. The PLP lost 14 of the 32 seats it had controlled, giving it a new total of 18. Pindling, whose 25 years as head of government constituted the longest tenure of any democratically elected leader in the Western Hemisphere, said he would lead the opposition as a reelected member of the House.

24 **South Korea recognizes China.** South Korean Pres. Roh Tae Woo announced that an agreement had been signed in Beijing (Peking) formally establishing diplomatic relations between South Korea and China. The decision meant that existing diplomatic ties with the Republic of China in Taiwan were automatically severed. Roh predicted that "Korea and China together will forge a new order in East Asia." Observers noted that, perhaps significantly, no mention was made of Japan except to recall that it had invaded Korea and occupied it from 1910 to 1945. During three months of negotiations, China and South Korea discussed the situation in North Korea at great length. China reportedly promised to use its influence with its longtime ally to promote a peaceful reunification of the Korean peninsula.

Brazilian president in deep trouble. The political future of Brazilian Pres. Fernando Collor de Mello was dealt a severe blow when a special congressional commission of inquiry approved (16–5) a 200-page report charging the chief executive with using his position for "improper economic benefits." The findings were judged sufficiently serious for impeachment proceedings to be initiated. A two-thirds majority in the 503-seat lower house of Congress was needed to initiate the process. Collor's campaign treasurer was named as the go-between in an alleged series of illegal dealings.

27 **Canada moves to preserve unity.** Leaders of Canada's diverse political groups met in Charlottetown, Prince Edward Island, to resolve details of certain proposed constitutional changes that, they hoped, would preserve the nation's unity. They also discussed the desirability of holding a national referen-

dum on the changes to hasten ratification. Two days later Robert Bourassa, head of Quebec's ruling Liberal Party, vigorously lobbied some 3,500 party delegates in Quebec City to back the reforms. While conceding that some Quebecers would not be satisfied, he pointedly noted that when the separatist Parti Québécois held power in the province in 1982, it had failed to gain concessions now included among the proposed reforms.

Iraq warned to avoid "no-fly zone." Great Britain, France, and the U.S. warned the Iraqi government that any of its military or civilian planes flying south of the 32nd parallel would be instantly attacked and shot down. The "no-fly" order was issued to protect some 200,000 Shi'ite Muslims in the southern part of the country from air attacks. Iraqi ground troops in the zone were estimated to number between 60,000 and 100,000. A similar "no-fly" prohibition had been in effect north of the 36th parallel since April 1991 to protect Kurds from Iraqi aerial bombardments.

Japanese politician forced to quit. Shin Kanemaru, one of Japan's most powerful politicians, resigned as vice-chairman of the ruling Liberal-Democratic Party (LDP) and as head of a formidable faction within the LDP after admitting that he had improperly accepted a large sum of money from Japan's second largest trucking company. Kanemaru retained his seat in the lower house of the Diet (parliament), but he had probably lost much of his political influence as a staunch supporter of Prime Minister Kiichi Miyazawa, whose election he had promoted.

28 **U.S. begins airlift to Somalia.** A fleet of U.S. C-130 Hercules aircraft began delivering relief supplies to 1.5 million Somalis facing starvation in their northeastern African country, devastated by war between opposing factions. The Red Cross and other private agencies accepted responsibility for distributing the food because the U.S. had agreed that no U.S. military personnel would be involved in the operation after the planes had landed. A week earlier, U.S. planes had begun stockpiling the supplies in Kenya, near its border with Somalia.

REUTERS/BETTMANN

Somali refugees wait at a food distribution point. In August the U.S. military began flying food into the famine-stricken country.

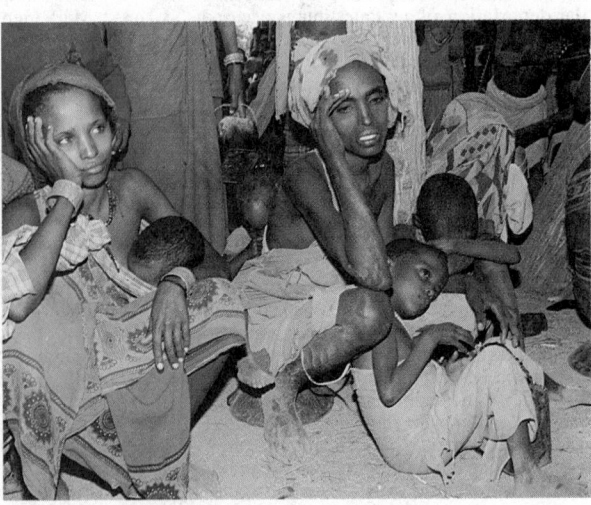

SEPTEMBER

1 **Nonaligned weigh future role.** Indonesian President Suharto welcomed delegates from 108 nations who had gathered in Jakarta to discuss the future of the Non-Aligned Movement (NAM), to which they all belonged. When NAM was formally established in Belgrade, Yugos., in 1961, its fundamental premise was that Third World nations should not align themselves with either of the two superpowers, the U.S.S.R. and the U.S. The current delegates to the Jakarta summit concluded that, despite the collapse of the Soviet Union, their organization still had important roles to play. One of its major responsibilities would be representing the interests of small, impoverished, and less developed countries, which individually had no voice in world affairs.

4 **Moroccans approve constitution.** The citizens of Morocco voted overwhelmingly in favour of a new constitution that had been drawn up by King Hassan II as part of an overall plan to institutionalize greater democracy in his country. As a result, the next parliament would have much broader authority, including the right to enact laws. The prime minister would be nominated by the king, but his choice would have to be satisfactory to the majority of parliamentarians. Among its many other provisions, the constitution gave the prime minister the right to select his own Cabinet. Moroccans who had urged voters to boycott the election included antimonarchists who wanted the king to become a mere figurehead, not unlike monarchs in Britain, Scandinavia, and other parts of the world.

Zhivkov given seven-year term. Todor Zhivkov, who had ruled Bulgaria from 1954 to 1989, was convicted by a seven-judge panel in Sophia of embezzling $1 million and using state funds to provide lavish living for himself, his family, and his political friends. The 18-month open trial ended when Zhivkov was sentenced to seven years in prison. Other former Bulgarian leaders were also expected to stand trial, including three former premiers: Grisha Filipov, arrested in July, who had served from 1981 to 1986; his successor, Georgy Atanasov, arrested in April, who had held office from 1986 to 1990; and Andrey Lukanov, also arrested in July, who had been premier during most of 1990.

6 **German racism alarms nation.** Groups of German racists resumed their wanton attacks on refugees who had taken advantage of the government's generous immigration policy and moved to Germany. Even ethnic Germans who had emigrated from Eastern Europe had become victims of firebombings and other acts of terrorism. A Jewish cemetery was also vandalized. The fierceness and ugliness of the attacks alarmed government officials and the general public alike because all knew what Nazi racism had wrought in Europe during World War II. It appeared likely that Germany would soon have to reevaluate its immigration policy. It was also clear that the reunification

of Germany had been more costly than expected and that such other problems as unemployment were partly responsible for the racist attacks on recent immigrants.

Italy captures top Sicilian mafioso. Italian police arrested Giuseppe Madonia, one of the five most powerful crime figures in Sicily. Madonia, who had been on the police's most-wanted list, complimented the police on doing a very professional job. The men who controlled organized crime in Sicily were believed to have ordered the assassinations of two dedicated crime fighters earlier in the year. In a related development, law-enforcement officers in Italy, Colombia, and the U.S. reported on September 28 that more than 165 persons suspected of drug trafficking had been arrested in the U.S., Italy, Canada, England, Spain, and Costa Rica. All were believed to be connected to a money-laundering scheme that involved the Italian Mafia and Colombian drug rings. The international undercover operation, the first of its kind, had also netted $42 million.

11 **Ancient border dispute settled.** The International Court of Justice (World Court), from its headquarters at The Hague, resolved a 130-year-old border dispute between Honduras and El Salvador. The head of the five-judge panel that decided the case remarked that defining the borders had been one of the most complicated cases the court had ever handled. In 1986 the two countries agreed to turn the matter over to the World Court, the judicial arm of the United Nations. After meticulously studying reams of old documents, the judges determined the political status of six zones along the 250-km (160-mi) border that separated the two nations.

14 **UN troops arrive in Somalia.** A small United Nations contingent of Pakistani troops arrived in Mogadishu, Somalia. They were the advance contingent of 500 Pakistani soldiers

whose mission it would be to protect supplies destined for starving Somalis. More than 1,000 persons, mostly children, were reported to be dying every day from lack of food or from disease. Much of the food that had already been delivered had been looted or stolen by armed bands who roamed the country with impunity. One of two powerful warlords, during discussions with UN officials, refused to allow the deployment of 3,000 additional UN troops, saying his own men, who had reportedly done much of the looting, could handle the distribution of the desperately needed supplies.

20 **French wary of European unity.** French voters, by the smallest of margins, approved the so-called Maastricht Treaty, which was designed to bind the European Communities (EC) closer together. Besides adopting a common currency, the EC would, under terms of the treaty, also work more closely to coordinate foreign and defense policies. Because so many French voters opposed the treaty, the future of the pact, at least in its current form, remained in doubt. The fate of the treaty also depended on Denmark, which had rejected ratification earlier in the year. There was a real possibility, therefore, that the document would have to be revised to some degree because ratification by all 12 members was needed before the treaty could take effect.

21 **Vatican and Mexico restore ties.** The Vatican and Mexico formally resumed diplomatic relations after 130 years of mutual antagonism. The path of reconciliation was paved in July 1992 when Mexico's Chamber of Deputies voted to revise anticlerical sections of the 1917 constitution that had denied legal status to the Roman Catholic Church and other religious groups. As legal nonentities, the churches had no right to own property or provide religious education. The clergy, moreover, could not wear distinctive garb in public and could not vote. With the

N. QUIDU/A. REID—GAMMA LIAISON

Demonstrating German youths give the neo-Nazi salute. Attacks on immigrants, mostly attributed to right-wing groups, occurred in several parts of Germany during 1992.

French citizens attend a rally in support of the Maastricht Treaty on European economic and political union. On September 20, voters in France approved the treaty by a narrow margin.

PASCAL PARROT—SYGMA

passage of time, however, many of the legal restrictions on church activities were not enforced. Before the reconciliation with Rome, Mexico, with a population that was more than 90% Roman Catholic, had been the only major country in Latin America that did not have diplomatic relations with the Vatican. The church expressed the hope that in the future it would win other concessions from the Mexican government, including the right to operate radio and television stations.

22 **United Nations expels Yugoslavia.** The United Nations General Assembly, responding to heavy pressure from members of the European Communities, voted 127–6 with 26 abstentions to declare Yugoslavia's seat at the UN vacant. Three days earlier the UN Security Council had voted 12–0 with 3 abstentions (China, India, Zimbabwe) to recommend the de facto ouster of Yugoslavia, whose Serb-dominated government was considered largely responsible for the atrocities being perpetrated against Muslims and Roman Catholic Croats in Bosnia and Hercegovina. Yugoslav Prime Minister Milan Panic, a moderate, was unable to persuade the foreign ministers of the Security Council member nations to cancel the planned vote. Later, in his address to the General Assembly, Panic condemned the "ethnic cleansing" taking place in Bosnia and warned that expelling Yugoslavia from the UN would only strengthen the "militant nationalists" who opposed him. His plea fell on deaf ears, and the voting took place as scheduled.

23 **Thailand gets new government.** Chuan Leekpai was officially named prime minister of Thailand after he succeeded in bringing various factions together in a coalition government. Chuan's appointment as head of government was a milestone in the world of Thai politics because, for the first time in modern history, the country had a prime minister with no ties to the military or to the aristocracy. Chuan was generally considered to be honest, cautious, and perhaps conciliatory to a fault. Only time would tell if he would be assertive enough to stand up to the military, which had long played a major role in the government, and to resist the pressure of politicians who hoped to continue profiting from their ties to the military. Chuan had already demonstrated his inclination to compromise by including a pro-military party in his coalition government.

29 **Angolans vote in free election.** Angolans began two days of balloting in the first free election in the nation's history. Only 2 of the 11 presidential candidates received substantial support from the electorate. Pres. José Eduardo dos Santos, leader of the Popular Movement for the Liberation of Angola (MPLA), failed to avoid a runoff presidential election because his 49.6% of the popular vote fell short of the 50% required for outright victory. Jonas Savimbi, a former guerrilla leader who headed the National Union for the Total Independence of Angola (UNITA), received 40.1% of the vote. During the 16-year civil war that preceded the current cease-fire, Soviet advisers and Cuban troops had supported dos Santos, while the U.S. and South Africa had backed Savimbi in his struggle against dos Santos' Marxist regime. Voters also favoured MPLA candidates in parliamentary elections, giving them control of the new 223-seat legislature. According to UN and other outside observers who monitored the election, there was no evidence of significant irregularities in the balloting, despite charges of fraud brought by Savimbi. A renewal of sporadic violence delayed the fixing of a date for the runoff presidential election.

President of Brazil impeached. By a vote of 441–38, Brazil's Chamber of Deputies impeached Pres. Fernando Collor de Mello on charges of bribery. As a consequence, his powers were suspended for 180 days, during which time he would be tried by the Senate. Vice Pres. Itamar Franco became acting president on October 2. In 1989 Collor, who had campaigned on a promise of clean government, won the nation's first presidential election in 30 years. Before that, the country had been under a military dictatorship.

OCTOBER

2 **Hundreds die in prison riot.** As many as 400 inmates of the House of Detention in São Paulo, Brazil, were killed during a riot that began with a fight between two convicts. The prison, built to hold 3,500 criminals, had more than twice that number. Once it became apparent that the 15 guards could not control the disturbance, 340 military police were ordered to restore order. When word spread that troops were on their way, the prisoners went on a rampage, burning everything combustible within their reach. On October 6 a spokesman for the Ministry of Justice acknowledged 200 prisoner deaths, contradicting an earlier official count of 111, but other estimates ran as high as 400. Government officials announced that they would investigate charges that the troops had shot prisoners indiscriminately and had committed other atrocities.

4 **Mozambique moves toward peace.** Joaquim Chissanó, president of Mozambique, and Afonso Dhlakama, leader of the Mozambican National Resistance rebels (Renamo), signed a peace treaty in Rome that, after ratification by the parliament, would end 16 years of civil war. The signing was witnessed by Robert Mugabe, the president of Zimbabwe and a strong supporter of Mozambique's government, and by Roelof Botha, the foreign minister of South Africa, which had backed Renamo. Under terms of the agreement, both sides would surrender their arms to UN personnel, then contribute about 15,000 soldiers each to constitute a new army. There was cautious optimism that the plan would work, even though neither side had total control over troops fighting in its name. Relief workers in the area urged that the distribution of food and water be given top priority.

5 **Cheddi Jagan to lead Guyana.** Cheddi Jagan, who headed the People's Progressive Party's (PPP) parliamentary list, replaced Desmond Hoyte as president of Guyana when the PPP won a plurality of 32 seats in the 65-seat unicameral legislature. Hoyt's People's National Congress (PNC) party captured 31 seats. Two of nine other parties that had fielded candidates won one seat each. With virtually all votes tallied, the nonpartisan Election Commission reported that the PPP had garnered 54% of the popular vote and the PNC 41%. Former U.S. president Jimmy Carter and other foreigners who had traveled to South America to monitor the electoral process reported that the voting was a model of democratic reform despite very formidable problems in getting the ballots from jungle areas to Georgetown, the capital.

Kuwaitis elect new National Council. Kuwait made a token gesture in the direction of genuine democracy by allowing a small segment of its population to select members of the National Council. Women, however, were not permitted to vote, and only men 21 years of age or older whose families had been in Kuwait since before 1921 had the right to cast ballots for any of the 278 candidates. When the power of the Sabah family was challenged in the 1985 election, the emir, Sheikh Jabir al-Ahmad al-Jabir as-Sabah, responded by disbanding parliament and suspending the constitution the following year. Kuwait had agreed to restore the council under pressure from the U.S. and its allies, whose troops had driven Iraq out of Kuwait during the Persian Gulf war in 1991. Current dissatisfaction with the government became evident when the opposition won 31 of the 50 seats in the National Council. On October 13 the opposition expressed outrage when the emir reappointed Crown Prince Sheikh Saad al-Abdullah as-Salim as-Sabah to the post of prime minister rather than someone representing the majority in parliament.

11 **Shevardnadze wins in Georgia.** Eduard Shevardnadze, who had gained great respect in the West as the foreign minister of the Soviet Union, was elected unopposed as speaker of a new independent parliament in the former Soviet republic of Georgia. The post was equivalent to that of president. Shevardnadze, who had been serving as chairman of the provisional State Council, was viewed as the best hope for stabilizing the government and reestablishing control over the province of Abkhazia. Secessionist guerrillas had reclaimed about half of the province during a surprise offensive earlier in the month. Under terms of a September 3 cease-fire brokered by Russian Pres. Boris Yeltsin, the government had withdrawn most of its troops from the region.

13 **Khmer Rouge ordered to disarm.** The UN Security Council unanimously approved a resolution reaffirming its commitment to the 1991 Paris Peace Agreements, which called for free elections in Cambodia in May 1993. The Security Council resolution included a demand that the Khmer Rouge rebels lay down their arms, as stipulated in the painstakingly negotiated Paris accords, and permit UN representatives to enter areas under their control so that voters could be registered and preparations made for the national election. Alexander Watson, a spokesman for the U.S., reflected the views of the Security Council when he remarked that he hoped the Khmer Rouge realized it had "nothing to gain and much to lose by continuing to obstruct the peace process." He further remarked that "we must all be prepared to consider and adopt the measures necessary to insure a stable new government and the peace that the Cambodian people deserve, with or without the participation of the Khmer Rouge."

18 **China ends a historic congress.** The Communist Party of China (CPC) concluded its historic 14th congress in Beijing (Peking) after endorsing the liberal economic policies endorsed by Deng Xiaoping (Teng Hsiao-p'ing), China's 88-year-old paramount leader, who held no official post in the government. While embracing, in effect, a free-market capitalist economy, the government reaffirmed its determination to maintain tight political control over the nation. In line with this principle, the party's Central Committee took no steps to rehabilitate Zhao Ziyang (Chao Tzu-yang), the former general secretary of the CPC, who had been purged for showing sympathy to the pro-democracy activists gathered in and around Tiananmen (T'ien-an-men) Square. The 1989 movement was brutally suppressed by the military. The congress also approved an expanded Central Committee, about half of whose full members were new. On October 19 the newly formed Central Committee drastically revamped the Political Bureau and expanded its membership from 14 to 20 full members with two alternates rather than one. One of the most significant accomplishments of the congress was giving the nation new leaders who generally were younger and better educated than those they replaced.

20 **Hong Kong governor visits China.** Chris Patten, who became governor of the British Crown Colony of Hong Kong in July, arrived in Beijing (Peking), where he was given a cool welcome. On October 7 Patten had infuriated the Chinese government by unveiling his plan for greater democracy in Hong Kong during the five remaining years before Britain's lease expired and China reclaimed the territory. Standing firm in the face of withering criticism, Patten insisted that he was not violating the Basic Law when he broadened the electoral basis for choosing members of Hong Kong's Legislative Council. China responded that Patten had most certainly violated at least the spirit and intent of the Basic Law, which Britain and China had both signed. China's foreign minister accused Patten of deliberately challenging the Chinese government rather than cooperating with it and of introducing universal suffrage rather than "corporate voting" in selecting members of the Legislative Council. Patten gave no indication that he would yield to pressure and modify his plans, even though China threatened to undo all his "democratic reforms" when it absorbed the territory in 1997.

23 **Japanese emperor visits China.** Japanese Emperor Akihito and Empress Michiko arrived in Beijing (Peking) for an official state visit. It was the first time in history that a Japanese emperor had set foot in China. The historic event occurred 20 years after Japan and China had ended four decades of hostility and animosity by reestablishing diplomatic relations. At that time China also relinquished its right to war reparations. Many Japanese who opposed the emperor's visit were especially concerned that the monarch, who had no political role in Japan, would in effect assume that role by apologizing for atrocities committed by Japanese soldiers during the war. During the state dinner on the day of his arrival, the emperor handled the delicate matter by saying: "In the long history of relations between our two countries, there was an unfortunate period when our country inflicted profound suffering on the Chinese people. About this I feel deep sadness." Chinese officials appeared satisfied with the statement. In 1972 Kakuei Tanaka, the first Japanese prime minister to visit China after the war, expressed similar sentiments: "The Japanese side is keenly aware of Japan's responsibility for causing enormous damage in the past to the Chinese people through war and deeply reproaches itself."

Vietnam releases new data on U.S. MIAs. President Bush, during a brief news conference at the White House, announced that the Vietnamese government had agreed to turn over all the information and material evidence it possessed on U.S. personnel still unaccounted for in the Vietnam conflict. The U.S. Defense Department listed 1,166 as missing in action (MIA) and an additional 1,100 as killed in action. On October 20 the U.S. acknowledged that it had already received from the Vietnamese some 5,000 photographs of dead Americans, which the U.S. hoped would help resolve some of the MIA cases still pending. U.S. officials believed that the material could not have been removed from Vietnam's military archives

STEVENS—SIPA

Emperor Akihito (left) and Empress Michiko of Japan tour Beijing (Peking). It was the first time a Japanese emperor had visited China.

without the knowledge and consent of high-ranking officials. In other ways, also, it appeared that Vietnam was trying to improve relations with the U.S. One of the most fundamental obstacles standing in the way of U.S. diplomatic recognition, trade, and investment continued to be the unresolved issue of the MIAs.

25 **Lithuanians back ex-Communists.** Lithuanian voters, apparently disgruntled over the country's faltering economy and disenchanted with political bickering that was paralyzing the government, gave the Democratic Labour Party (DLP), led by former Communist Algirdas Brazauskas, a plurality of the 141 seats in the Supreme Council (parliament). Brazauskas, who had exhorted his fellow Communists to push for Lithuanian independence from the Soviet Union, was expected to form a coalition government with other left-wing partners. The election was a bitter disappointment for the leader of the Sajudis Movement, Vytautas Landsbergis, because he had declared Lithuanian independence on March 11, 1990. Running the government and solving the nation's economic problems, however, had proved more difficult than Landsbergis had expected. Voters also approved a new constitution that, among other things, provided for the direct election of the

president. On November 15, in the second round of national elections, the DLP secured a solid majority in parliament.

26 **Canadians divided over reforms.** Canadian voters in 7 of the nation's 12 provinces and territories rejected a nonbinding referendum that, the government hoped, would foster greater harmony among the various segments of Canada's diverse society. The final election returns showed that voters in Alberta, British Columbia, Manitoba, Nova Scotia, Quebec, Saskatchewan, and the Yukon Territory rejected the accord that had been worked out in Charlottetown, Prince Edward Island, in late August. The majority of voters in the provinces of New Brunswick, Newfoundland, Ontario, and Prince Edward Island and in the Northwest Territories backed the referendum. Because the approval of all 12 regional assemblies was needed for the constitutional changes to take effect, the matter was for the time being a dead issue. The proposed changes included self-government for the country's native population and special rights for the French-speaking people of Quebec. Joe Clark, the constitutional affairs minister, summed up the situation by saying: "We thought after two decades of failure, the failure of six rounds of constitutional discussions, we had found

Separatists in Montreal rally against the Charlottetown accord. It was defeated in a national referendum on October 26.
CHRISTOPHER MORRIS—SABA

in the Charlottetown accord a way to resolve these deep and dividing problems in Canada, or begin their resolution." He then added: "What's not clear tonight is what solution might be available to us."

NOVEMBER

3 **Bill Clinton wins U.S. presidency.** Bill Clinton, the Democratic governor of Arkansas, easily defeated Republican Pres. George Bush in a race for the U.S. presidency. Although Clinton emerged with a substantial margin of victory in the electoral college (370–168) by winning 32 states and the District of Columbia (D.C.), he received a majority of the popular vote only in his home state and in D.C. Independent candidate Ross Perot, a maverick Texas billionaire, ran an unorthodox, self-financed, anti-status quo campaign and won 19% of the popular vote with support from all parts of the country. He won no state, however, and thus no electoral votes. Clinton's vice presidential running mate was Sen. Al Gore of Tennessee, who had sought the Democratic Party's presidential nomination in 1988.

The final totals showed that Clinton had won 43% of the popular vote, Bush 38%, and Perot 19%. Clinton, who was born in 1946, was scheduled to assume office as the 42nd president of the United States on Jan. 20, 1993. In races for the U.S. Senate, the final totals showed no net change: Democrats 57 seats, Republicans 43. There were, however, significant changes in personnel. Four new women were elected, bringing the total of female senators to six. Changes in the House of Representatives were far more extensive, mostly because scores of congressmen, for a variety of reasons, chose not to run for reelection. To nearly everyone's surprise, only 24 incumbent congressmen were defeated in the general election. Despite the overall loss of six seats, Democrats retained firm control of the House by a 258–176 margin.

One seat went to an independent. Women gained 19 additional seats, blacks 13, and Hispanics 7. The Democrats picked up 2 additional governorships, raising their total to 30. In states where voters were asked their opinions, there was wide support for limiting the terms of U.S. senators and congressmen. The constitutionality of such local laws, however, would have to be decided in court.

8 **Colombia faces up to drug lords.** Colombian Pres. César Gaviria, after an urgent meeting with his Cabinet, declared a 90-day state of emergency to facilitate an all-out attack on the leftist Revolutionary Armed Forces of Colombia (FARC) and on drug-trafficking terrorists in Medellín. Gaviria took action because the country was in a state of shock over the murders of 26 policemen the previous day and the bombing of dozens of public buildings. About a month earlier FARC had begun to escalate the violence by murdering more than a hundred people, blockading highways, invading villages, and repeatedly blowing up the country's two main pipelines. The president's emergency powers, which were provided for in the constitution, would allow him to take counterterrorism measures without first having to seek approval of Congress or the courts.

9 **Thai officers granted amnesty.** A special panel in Thailand, headed by the president of the parliament, concluded that the government of Prime Minister Chuan Leekpai did not have authority to put on trial top military officers who allegedly had been involved in the

CYNTHIA JOHNSON—TIME MAGAZINE

President-elect Bill Clinton (left) and running mate Al Gore celebrate their victory on election night. Democrats would control the U.S. presidency for the first time in 12 years.

massacre of hundreds of pro-democracy demonstrators in May. The military officers had earlier been granted an amnesty by Gen. Suchinda Kraprayoon while he held the post of prime minister. The fact that he had been named prime minister after failing to win a seat in the parliament so infuriated the citizenry that they took to the streets in rage and forced Suchinda to resign.

11 Female priesthood gets support. Each of the three bodies constituting the General Synod of the Church of England approved, by the necessary two-thirds majority, the ordination of women priests. The vote in the House of Bishops was 39–13, in the House of Clergy 176–74, and in the House of Laity 169–82. If the laity had voted 167–84, the measure would have gone down to defeat because 168 votes were the minimum needed for a two-thirds majority. The decision of the Synod was expected to be confirmed by Parliament and by Queen Elizabeth II. As the reigning monarch, the queen was head of the Church of England, one of 28 national bodies within the Anglican Communion. Of the 1,500 Anglican women already ordained, some 1,000 belonged to the U.S. Episcopal Church. In England the ordination of women was considered so important and fundamental an issue that some clergy and lay people warned that they would leave the church if the measure won approval.

15 Endara proposals unacceptable. The majority of Panamanians who exercised their right to vote decisively rejected a package of 58 constitutional amendments proposed by Pres. Guillermo Endara. One amendment called for the abolition of a standing army. Others called for raising educational standards and improving social welfare benefits. The executive and legislative branches of government would also have been reformed. Endara had been elected president in May 1989, but Gen. Manuel Noriega prevented him from assuming office. Endara finally took the oath of office at a U.S. military installation after U.S. troops invaded the country. Once Noriega had been captured and taken to Miami to stand trial, the armed forces ceased to exist as an organization, but policemen continued to maintain order. In time, Endara was seen as ineffective, indecisive, tolerant of corruption, and indifferent to or incapable of solving such important social problems as unemployment. Some observers believed that Endara sought to bolster his sagging popularity by winning support for his package of constitutional reforms, but most voters viewed them as insignificant or inadequate. There were calls for a totally new constitution that would replace the one written under a military dictatorship.

16 UN votes to blockade Yugoslavia. The UN Security Council authorized a naval blockade of Yugoslavia, which was engaged in a ferocious civil conflict in Bosnia and Hercegovina. The vote was 13–0; China and Zimbabwe abstained. The blockade empowered ships of all nations to halt and inspect all vessels entering or leaving Yugoslav waters. The areas affected included the Adriatic Sea

Smoke rises from the burning Windsor Castle, a residence of British monarchs for nearly 900 years. The fire caused extensive structural damage to some parts of the castle.
MARTYN HAYHOW—SIPA

and the Danube River, an international waterway that flowed through Yugoslavia to the Black Sea. It was difficult to predict how effectively the embargo could or would be enforced. There was already a UN ban on military flights over Bosnia, but no punitive action against violators had been authorized. The U.S. continued to press the Security Council to sanction the shooting down of Yugoslav military aircraft that continued to defy the UN ban.

18 Bishops discuss role of women. The majority of U.S. Roman Catholic bishops, during a meeting in the nation's capital, approved a proposed pastoral letter that reaffirmed the traditional roles of women in the church. The 137–110 vote, however, fell far short of the two-thirds majority needed for passage. The bishops then voted to return the document to the bishops' standing committee for further study. Among other things, the bishops' letter, which was considered more conservative than any of the three previous drafts, condemned violence against women, gender discrimination, family abuse, premarital sex, birth control, and abortion. The letter also severely condemned sexual abuse of minors by clergymen and urged that offenders be immediately removed from their posts; the bishops also recognized the need to provide emotional and spiritual support to the victims and their families. During their meeting the bishops discussed at length the question of ordaining women to the priesthood, even though the Vatican had repeatedly insisted that the issue was not open to debate.

20 Fire devastates Windsor Castle. Windsor Castle, a centuries-old residence for British monarchs, was severely damaged by a fire that took hundreds of fire fighters hours to extinguish. Structural damage in some areas was so severe that restoration of the historic castle would take years to complete. A controversy immediately arose over who would bear the cost of rebuilding. Some Britons expressed a willingness to help

restore one of the nation's most prized treasures. Others, perhaps resentful of royal privilege and weary of hard economic times, said it was the responsibility of the royal family itself to bear the cost. On November 26 Prime Minister John Major told the House of Commons that Queen Elizabeth II had volunteered to begin paying taxes on her private income and to contribute $1.3 million annually toward the support of the royal family, which by law and tradition had always been supported by public funds.

24 UN wants end to Cuban embargo. The UN General Assembly passed a nonbinding resolution calling for an end to the United States' 30-year embargo against Cuba. The vote was 59 in favour, 3 against (the U.S., Israel, Romania), and 79 abstentions. The latter group included Russia and the European Communities. The UN resolution, sponsored by Cuba, followed the signing of a new U.S. law called the Cuban Democracy Act of 1992. It extended the U.S. embargo to foreign subsidiaries of American firms. Although the UN resolution did not mention the U.S. specifically, everyone understood that the U.S. was being rebuked for "the promulgation and application . . . of laws and regulations whose extraterritorial effects affect the sovereignty of other States and the legitimate interests of entities or persons under their jurisdiction."

25 Czechoslovakia to be divided. Czechoslovakia's Federal Assembly, taking its third vote in less than two months, approved a constitutional amendment that would dissolve the federation without a national referendum. As a consequence, independent Czech and Slovak republics would become realities on Jan. 1, 1993. On November 17 the two regional parliaments had paved the way for separation by passing a joint resolution approving dissolution of the federation. The vote in the Czech National Council was 106–67; in the Slovak National Council it was 73–16. The peaceful breakup of the federation stood in marked contrast to the vicious fighting that characterized the dissolution of Yugoslavia.

27 **Germany reins in neo-Nazis.** Rudolf Seiters, Germany's interior minister, announced that he was outlawing the explicitly neo-Nazi and anti-Semitic National Front, which he described as an "active fighting group whose goal is to destroy the democratic order." Seiters called the ban "a clear and unmistakable warning signal against right-wing extremism, agitation, and violence" and pointedly added that other organizations were under investigation. The government also announced the formation of a new police unit whose task would be to monitor and repress the activities of extreme rightists. An estimated 350,000 Germans had gathered in Berlin on November 8 to vent their anger over the nearly 2,000 attacks that had been made against foreigners during the year and to demand that the government take decisive action to end the racial violence. A few hundred rioters, later identified as leftists, managed to disrupt the rally by cutting off the electricity to Pres. Richard von Weizsäcker's microphone and by pelting him with eggs, tomatoes, and paint bombs. On November 29 the National Front said it would go to court to defend its right to exist.

30 **Court backs Boris Yeltsin's ban.** Russia's 13-member Constitutional Court, after listening to months of heated arguments, ruled that Pres. Boris Yeltsin had acted within his powers when he banned the official Soviet and Russian Communist parties in 1991 after a failed coup against Mikhail Gorbachev, who at the time was president of the Soviet Union. The court, however, made no ruling on the disposition of party property, saying that the matter fell within the jurisdiction of the civil courts. At least eight new die-hard Communist parties had been formed in Russia, but none was large or strong enough to make a credible claim to be the logical or legal successor of either the old Russian or Soviet Communist Party. The Constitutional Court did provide some comfort to the Communists by ruling that Communist cells were legal and could continue to operate freely. Anti-Communists had hoped that the court would outlaw all organized Communist activities.

DECEMBER

6 **Hindus level mosque in Ayodhya.** Several thousand militant Hindus, defying an order of India's Supreme Court, totally destroyed the 16th-century Babri Mosque in Ayodhya, Uttar Pradesh state. During the sectarian rioting that followed, more than 1,000 Muslims and Hindus were killed and scores of temples and mosques damaged or destroyed, including some in neighbouring Pakistan and Bangladesh. Prime Minister P.V. Narasimha Rao deplored the mob action, calling it "a betrayal of the nation and a confrontation with all that is sacred to all Indians as a legacy which we have inherited as part of our national ethos." Hindu revivalists from several political and religious groups had called for volunteers to travel to Ayodhya to build a temple to Lord Rama, a widely worshiped Hindu deity. The chosen site, said to be the birthplace of Lord Rama, was partially occupied by the Babri Mosque. In 1990 an attack on the same mosque had brought down the central government. On December 27 the government announced that it would acquire the disputed land and build both a mosque and a temple on the site "to ensure that the balance of both communities is maintained."

9 **U.S. troops land in Somalia.** The first contingent of U.S. Marines, acting in the name of the United Nations, landed on the east coast of Somalia to begin Operation Restore Hope. Their immediate mission was to secure the area, then move into the capital city of Mogadishu so that emergency relief teams could begin distributing food to the starving population. With no functioning government to maintain order, rival bands of heavily armed marauders had hijacked or stolen supplies that relief agencies were trying to deliver to the helpless people. Ships carrying food had also been heavily shelled in the port of Mogadishu and were forced to withdraw. Because hundreds of people, especially young children, were dying from hunger and disease every day, the United Nations urged the U.S. to intervene with troops. Unless roads were secured, supplies could not be delivered to the interior. Some 10 other nations also dispatched troops to Somalia, but far fewer than the 28,000 the U.S. was to deploy. Even after the UN-sponsored troops had set up operations in Mogadishu, the city remained a very dangerous place because rival gangs controlled separate parts. After evaluating the situation, UN Secretary-General Boutros Boutros-Ghali urged the U.S. to expand its mission by disarming the gangs, but U.S. commanders insisted that it was a practical impossibility. On December 16 large quantities of food reached Baidoa, where relief workers had been begging for protection and supplies. Soon after that, other feeding centres in the interior were dispensing food and medicine, but for many the help had come too late. Given the overall condition of the country, no one could offer a long-term solution to the severe problems Somalia faced, but virtually everyone agreed that humanitarian aid could not in conscience have been denied or delayed any longer.

Charles and Diana agree to separate. British Prime Minister John Major, speaking to a national television audience from the House of Commons, announced that Charles and Diana, the 44-year-old Prince and the 31-year-old Princess of Wales, had agreed to separate. Major said that the couple had no plans to divorce and that their "constitutional positions were unaffected." The couple would share the responsibility of raising their two sons and would carry out their royal duties as the future king and queen of England. The formal announcement came after months of media reports that the 1981 storybook wedding had turned into a loveless and sometimes bitter relationship. The prince and princess no longer appeared together except on special occasions, and when they did, neither seemed interested in the other. With the separation official, many Britons doubted that Charles would ever become king. Some said they believed that he would renounce the throne in favour of his eldest son, 10-year-old William. There was even talk that the breakup of the marriage might have dealt a fatal blow to the monarchy itself, which was under great stress. Earlier in the year Andrew, the

PETER TURNLEY—BLACK STAR

Somali citizens greet a U.S. Marine, part of the force sent in December to restore order. Within a few days of the troops' arrival, food was again being distributed to starving Somalis.

Duke of York, had separated from his wife, Sarah. The tabloids had created a sensation by publishing photos of the topless duchess in the company of a Texas millionaire beside a swimming pool. Princess Anne had divorced in the summer and remarried in December. Prince Edward, the fourth child of Queen Elizabeth II and Prince Philip, was not married. At year's end, the queen summed up 1992 as an "annus horribilis" ("horrible year") for the royal family.

14 **Congress vetoes Yeltsin's choice.** Russian Pres. Boris Yeltsin, yielding to the demands of a hostile Congress of People's Deputies, withdrew his nomination of Yegor Gaidar to be prime minister. Gaidar had been a central figure in planning Yeltsin's economic reforms and symbolized the new order Yeltsin was attempting to establish in Russia following the dissolution of the Soviet Union. By abandoning Gaidar, Yeltsin in effect enhanced the prestige of his hard-line political opponents and lost favour among his most ardent supporters, some of whom accused him of lacking courage.

17 **Canada to restrict immigration.** Canada, long known for its generous acceptance of refugees and immigrants, passed a new law that was expected to slow the rate of immigration without, however, resorting to policies as restrictive as those followed by the United States. Applicants would still be judged, albeit more strictly, on the basis of their education, professional qualifications, and financial independence. The new legislation was partly a response to Canada's current economic problems, which included an unemployment rate exceeding 10%. This in turn generated resentment against foreigners, who were perceived by some as outsiders who had taken away jobs that rightfully belonged to Canadian citizens.

18 **Kim Young Sam wins presidency.** Kim Young Sam, the 65-year-old candidate of the ruling Democratic Liberal Party (DLP), was elected 14th president of the Republic of Korea with 42% of the popular vote. Runner-up Kim Dae Jung, head of the Democratic Party, finished with 34%. He then resigned from politics. Chung Ju Yung, the 77-year-old billionaire who led the United People's Party, was backed by 16% of the voters. Four other candidates finished far behind. Kim Young Sam's victory was a turning point in South Korea's turbulent history because it gave the country a president who, for the first time in three decades, had no ties to the military. The election also indicated that the people preferred political stability, continuity, and moderate change rather than the drastic reforms proposed by some other politicians. Unlike 1987, when the opposition candidates campaigned for "an end to military dictatorship," the 1992 campaign focused on proposed solutions to the nation's economic problems. Roh Tae Woo had won the 1987 election in great part because neither of his two major opponents, Kim Young Sam and Kim Dae Jung, was willing to step aside to allow the antigovernment forces to unite behind a single candidate. The vote split when each candidate got overwhelming support from

Palestinians deported by Israel wait in camps in southern Lebanon. Israel charged that the deportees were security risks, but the government's action was internationally condemned.
LAMIA MOUBAYED—SYGMA

voters in his home province. The 1992 election results showed that regionalism was still a very major factor in South Korean politics. But the political landscape had changed dramatically in 1990 when President Roh and Kim Young Sam agreed to join forces and create a new party. Kim was then in a favourable position to seek the presidency in 1992 because the constitution did not permit Roh to run for a second term.

UN rebukes Israel for deportations. The UN Security Council passed a resolution strongly condemning Israel for deporting 415 Palestinians from the occupied West Bank and Gaza Strip. Israel contended that the Palestinians were trying "to kill Israelis and others and to kill the peace process." Lebanon's claim that Israel had violated international law by depositing the Palestinians in a buffer zone that Israel had created north of its border was strongly supported by the Security Council. The resolution that it passed specifically reaffirmed the independence, sovereignty, and territorial integrity of Lebanon. On December 28 Israel announced that 10 Palestinians, deported without a proper "legal decision," would be allowed to return. While both Israel and Lebanon remained deadlocked over the issue, various relief agencies attempted to reach the Palestinians, who were trapped in a barren and frigid environment with no means to sustain themselves.

19 **Taiwan elects new legislature.** For the first time since the government of the Republic of China moved to Taiwan in 1949, voters were allowed to vote for an entirely new 161-seat Legislative Yuan. No interim election had been held because the Chinese constitution stipulated that representatives be chosen from all the provinces of China. Under new laws the people in Taiwan cast ballots for 125 regional legislators, 30 chosen nationwide, and 6 representing overseas Chinese. The final vote tallies gave the ruling Kuomintang a total of 102 seats, the chief opposition Democratic Progressive Party (DPP) 50, the Chinese Social Democratic Party 1, and independents 8. The solid support given to

DPP candidates moved the country much closer to a strong two-party legislature than ever before.

29 **Kenya holds multiparty election.** Kenyan voters, casting ballots in the country's first multiparty election in more than 25 years, reelected Daniel arap Moi president, but they gave the opposition some 80 of the 200 seats in the unicameral legislature. Western diplomats were inclined to encourage the opposition to be satisfied with the results rather than demand a new election on the grounds that the first one had been rigged. Antigovernment groups had, in fact, scored an impressive victory. They not only constituted a strong opposition bloc in the parliament but had the satisfaction of knowing that more than a dozen members of Moi's Cabinet had failed to win reelection to the parliament. Moi, who had been elected president in 1978, presided over a country that continued to be plagued by tribal rivalries and corruption. Nonetheless, Kenya was considered to be relatively prosperous, and there was no sign that the civilian government was threatened by the possibility of a military coup.

Serbs vote no confidence in Panic. Ultranationalist Serbs and Communists in both houses of the Yugoslav parliament voted no confidence in the government of Prime Minister Milan Panic, thereby increasing pressure on the moderate leader to resign. He had already suffered a severe political setback on December 20 when he challenged Pres. Slobodan Milosevic for the presidency and was soundly defeated. Panic, a Serbian-American millionaire from California, had gone to Yugoslavia in the hope that he could somehow inject a measure of common sense into a situation that had gotten completely out of control after the nation began breaking apart in 1991. The Serb-dominated government of Yugoslavia was now engaged in a merciless campaign of "ethnic cleansing" directed against Croats and Muslims. Milosevic's name appeared on a U.S. list of persons who would perhaps one day be tried as war criminals. The list included the names of Croats as well as Serbs.

People of 1992

NOBEL PRIZES

Prize for Peace

Rigoberta Menchú, a 33-year-old Guatemalan Indian-rights activist, won the 1992 Nobel Peace Prize. Perhaps one of the Norwegian Nobel Committee's most controversial honorees, Menchú, who lacked a formal education and who did not learn to speak Spanish until she was 20, became an eloquent spokeswoman for indigenous peoples and the victims of oppression. In its announcement, the committee said, "Rigoberta Menchú grew up in poverty, in a family that has undergone the most brutal suppression and persecution. In her social and political work, she has always borne in mind that the long-term objective of the struggle is peace. Today [she] stands out as a vivid symbol of peace and reconciliation across ethnic, cultural and social dividing lines, in her own country, on the American continent, and in the world." Guatemalan government officials were stunned by the award, having considered Menchú and her followers leftist guerrillas. While she had neither backed nor denounced rebels in her country, the committee concluded, after an investigation of her career, that peace was indeed her goal.

Menchú, a Mayan of the Quiché group from northwestern Guatemala, fled to Mexico in 1981 after her parents and a brother were killed in separate incidents. She had been in Guatemala very few times since, although she awaited news of the prize in San Marcos, a town near her native village. She gained international prominence in 1983 through her book, *I, Rigoberta Menchú* (published in 11 languages), which told the story of her impoverished youth as a farm labourer and also her years as a domestic servant in the household of a wealthy white family. In the book she described in horrifying and graphic detail the torture and murder of members of her immediate family.

AP/WIDE WORLD

Rigoberta Menchú, awarded the Peace Prize for her work on behalf of Indian rights in Guatemala, greets well-wishers.

She was cared for in Mexico by the liberal Roman Catholic Guatemalan Church in Exile and resumed her activities on behalf of human rights in a group called the Committee of Peasant Unity, which at one time had been led by her father. As Menchú became increasingly involved in putting pressure on her government, she was invited to lecture in the U.S. and Europe by others critical of the situation in Guatemala. However, this was not enough to bring the country's plight to the world stage. Menchú said of Guatemala's problems: "[They seem] insignificant in the lives of other people. I mean, they are amazed when they hear that 46,000 people have disappeared in Guatemala. They say, 'How horrible,' and they are very impressed. But it does not go beyond that."

Menchú campaigned successfully for designating 1993 as the International Year for Indigenous Populations. She planned to use her $1.2 million Nobel Prize money to campaign for peace in her country and for Indian rights throughout the hemisphere, by establishing a foundation in her father's name to defend the rights of indigenous peoples. "The only thing I wish for is freedom for Indians wherever they are. As the end of the 20th century approaches, we hope that our continent will be pluralistic." (BONNIE OBERMAN)

Prize for Economics

The 1992 Nobel Memorial Prize in Economic Science was awarded to University of Chicago professor Gary S. Becker. This was the third time in as many years that the university had been the home of the economics prizewinner. Becker, known for applying traditional economic theories to unorthodox subjects, was honoured by the Royal Swedish Academy of Sciences for "having extended the domain of economic theory to aspects of human behavior which had previously been dealt with—if at all—by other social science disciplines such as sociology, demography and criminology." Indeed, one of Becker's proudest accomplishments was his 1955 dissertation about the economics of discrimination—having to do not with price inequities but rather with how racial and ethnic discrimination affects labour markets. He argued forcefully that discrimination costs not only the victims but the perpetrators as well. While this way of thinking was not uncommon in the 1990s, in the '50s it was revolutionary. So were Becker's ideas about how economics affects marriage, childbearing, crime, prejudice, and other typically noneconomic areas.

Becker was born in Pottsville, Pa., Dec. 2, 1930. He graduated from Princeton University in 1951. He received his master's degree and doctorate from the University of Chicago in 1953 and 1955, respectively, and was invited to remain as an assistant professor—a considerable honour at what was already an elite graduate department. He moved to Columbia University in New York City in 1957 and returned to Chicago in 1970.

In 1964, in his book *Human Capital,* Becker made the case for thinking about education as an economic decision; this, in turn, led to new theories regarding labour economics, and how capitalist economies determine wages and incomes. Four years later, in an article entitled "Crime and Punishment," Becker debated whether either the threat of arrest or an increase in the severity or certainty of punishment would deter rational decisions to commit certain types of crimes.

The academy said Becker applied economics to "areas where researchers formerly assumed that behaviour is habitual and often downright irrational." While highly controversial, Becker's ideas led to the testing of various policies ranging from capital punishment to beat policing.

Even more hotly debated were Becker's theories pertaining to the economics of the family, which he saw as a productive unit whose decisions could be analyzed and dissected in the same way as those of a business. Economic incentives, according to Becker, determine how much and what kind of work is undertaken by partners in a marriage, as well as how many children they have and how they make materialistic decisions regarding their welfare. As one of Becker's colleagues noted, "Economics has a tendency to steer away from the real world. Becker brings them back." His theories transformed the understanding of why people marry, why wealthy couples have fewer children than poor ones, why criminals commit crimes; answers to these questions have affected family-planning policy, employee training, and welfare programs.

Known throughout the world for integrating economics with the other social sciences, Becker was credited with an enormous expansion of the boundaries of economics. Probably best known as a conservative columnist for *Business Week* magazine, in which he advocated legalization of certain drugs, he was currently studying the economic bases of all addictions, including alcohol and cigarettes. (BONNIE OBERMAN)

Prize for Literature

An advocate of multiculturalism long before it became fashionable, West Indian poet, playwright, journalist, and painter Derek Walcott was awarded the 1992 Nobel Prize for Literature for his "historical vision." The Swedish Academy of Letters, in announcing the $1.2 million prize, noted, "In his literary works Walcott has laid a course for his own cultural environment, but through them he speaks to each and every one of us. In him, West Indian culture has found its great poet." Walcott's readers had been predicting for years that the prize would one day belong to this professor of literature and creative writing whose poetic and dramatic themes are timeless and whose verse derives from the cadences and traditions of the tiny Caribbean island of his birth. Walcott was currently teaching at Boston University and divided his time between the U.S. and Trinidad.

He was born Jan. 23, 1930, in the town of Castries in St. Lucia, an isolated volcanic island in the Lesser Antilles, which was then a British colony. His birthplace, his African origin, and his command of the English language combined to give Walcott his complex inspirations. Both his parents were schoolteachers who filled their home with books. Walcott's father died when Derek and his twin brother, Roderick, were a year old. Derek's earliest work, a privately printed collection of poetry, was published when he was a teenager. Although a poor math student, he managed to win a scholarship to the University of the West Indies, where he majored in three languages—French, Spanish, and Latin. Living on a Rockefeller Foundation grant in New York City when he was 27, he attended directing classes and rehearsals at the Phoenix Theater's repertory company. By the time he was 30 he had published two more volumes of poetry, established the Trinidad Theatre Workshop, and achieved recognition for his plays, which were being performed throughout the Caribbean islands and in England.

Walcott's love of the classics, folklore, and history are expressed through universal themes. He has written eloquently on subjects ranging from the struggles of Caribbean natives who confront their colonial past to reactions to his own mixed-race African, Dutch, and English ancestry to the bitter legacy of slavery and the effect of the natural landscape of one's birthplace. In citing the "great luminosity" of Walcott's work and his "melodious and sensitive" style, the academy noted especially his 1990 "majestic" epic poem "Omeros," a 64-chapter modern Odyssey composed in terza rima; while it explores several cultures, it is intended to capture the experience of the Caribbean people. Walcott regularly published plays and poetry from the early '50s. His latest play was The Odyssey (1992); The Last Carnival (1986) was being performed at Stockholm's Royal Dramatic Theatre at the time the prize was awarded.

Although he was stunned by his award, what immediately came to Walcott's mind was how "all the races of the world" live in the Caribbean, which of course provides a terrific illustration of the "tremendous possibility of an example of unity." (BONNIE OBERMAN)

Prize for Chemistry

The winner of the 1992 Nobel Prize for Chemistry, Rudolph A. Marcus of the California Institute of Technology (Caltech), was cited for his contributions to the theory of electron-transfer reactions in chemical systems. The processes that Marcus studied, the transfer of electrons between molecules in solution, underlie a number of important chemical phenomena in the living and nonliving worlds, and the practical consequences of his theory extend to all areas of chemistry. The Marcus theory, which by the 1990s was standard fare for modern undergraduate science textbooks, helped scientists better understand such widely differing phenomena as photosynthesis in green plants, chemiluminescence ("cold light") in fireflies, metabolism in living cells, the conductivity of electrically conducting polymers, the emission of light by diodes, and simple corrosion.

Intrigued by a graduate student's question, Marcus began formulating his theory in 1952. He published his first paper on the subject in 1956 and continued to develop and refine his ideas in a series of papers for the next nine years while at the Polytechnic Institute of Brooklyn, N.Y. (later Polytechnic Institute of New York and Polytechnic University), and later at the University of Illinois. Marcus described what is perhaps the simplest of all chemical reactions—the transfer of an electron between two molecules. Although no chemical bonds are broken in such a reaction, changes do take place in the molecular structure of the reacting molecules and their nearest neighbours in solution. These molecular changes influence the ability of electrons to jump between the molecules. Marcus found simple mathematical expressions for the way in which the energy of the molecular system is affected by the structural changes. Using those expressions, he was able to calculate and explain the great differences in the rates that are observed for various electron-transfer reactions.

Because certain of Marcus' predictions were counterintuitive, his theory initially caused considerable controversy. Most notably, the theory predicts that, for a sufficiently large driving force, the larger the driving force becomes, the slower the chemical reaction proceeds. Chemists long found this prediction difficult to accept and confirm, and it was not until 1985 that they succeeded in verifying it experimentally.

The Marcus theory has since proved useful in interpreting many chemical processes. Scientists use it to predict whether an electron-transfer reaction will proceed and how fast it will go. According to the Nobel citation, "In the mathematical connection the Marcus theory makes between theoretical and experimental quantities, experimental chemists gained a valuable tool."

Marcus was born in Montreal on July 21, 1923. He received a Ph.D. in physical chemistry from McGill University, Montreal, in 1946. After graduation, Marcus worked at the National Research Council of Canada as postdoctoral research associate until 1949. Because Canada was not then conducting theoretical research in his area of interest, he moved to the U.S. to investigate theories of electron-transfer reactions in chemical systems. He continued his postdoctoral work at the University of North Carolina until 1951. Marcus then joined the faculty of the Polytechnic Institute of Brooklyn, where he became a full professor in 1958. That same year he became an American citizen. (When he later investigated the idea of obtaining dual citizenship, he found that it was not possible under the Canadian law of the time.) In 1964 Marcus became a professor of physical chemistry at Illinois, and in 1978 he accepted the Arthur Amos Noyes chair of chemistry at Caltech.

Marcus held numerous professional positions during his career. In 1968–69 he served as chairman of the board of trustees of the Gordon Research Conferences. In 1970 he was elected to the U.S. National Academy of Sciences. He was a member of the chemistry department advisory councils of Princeton University (1972–78), Caltech (1977–78), and the Polytechnic Institute of New York (1977–80). He also served on the Panel on Atmospheric Chemistry of the National Research Council-National Academy of Sciences (NRC-NAS) Climatic Impact Committee (1975–78) and its Committee on the Chemical Sciences (1977–79) and as chairman of the NRC-NAS Committee on the Kinetics of Chemical Reactions (1975–77).

Marcus received many scientific distinctions, including the Alexander von Humboldt Foundation's senior U.S. scientist award (1976), the Langmuir and Pauling awards of the American Chemical Society (1978 and 1991, respectively), the Robinson and Centenary medals of the Royal Society of Chemistry (1982 and 1988, respectively), the prestigious Wolf Prize for Chemistry (1985), and the National Medal of Science (1989). He also received honorary D.Sc.'s from the University of Chicago (1983), Polytechnic University (1986), the University of Göteborg, Sweden (1987), and McGill University (1988). In 1986 the Journal of Physical Chemistry devoted a special issue to the 30th anniversary of the Marcus theory. (CAROLYN D. NEWTON)

Prize for Physics

The 1992 Nobel Prize for Physics was awarded to Georges Charpak of CERN (European Laboratory for Particle Physics), Geneva, for his invention of a particle detector known as the multiwire proportional chamber. Largely as a result of his pioneering work, which was carried out in 1968, particle physicists have been able to study very rare particle interactions—as rare as one interaction in a billion.

Particle physics has long relied on recording the trail of ionizations (the creation of electrically charged atoms or molecules) left by a high-energy particle as it passes through matter. The photographic methods that traditionally had been used, although adequate to track comparatively common particles, were not precise or fast enough to allow detection of more exotic particles. Such methods could not discern the few relevant interactions from the multitude of irrelevant ones that occurred in particle-beam collision experiments, and their recording speeds were not high enough to match increasingly intense accelerator beams. Charpak's chamber used electronics to increase the speed of data collection by a factor of a thousand and to improve the spatial resolution. According to the Nobel committee, "His fundamental idea has since been developed and for more than two decades Charpak has been at the forefront of this development."

A single interaction, or collision, between two high-energy particles can create as many as several hundred particles that spray out in all directions. To interpret such an event, scientists often must record the trajectory of every emerging particle. In the years before Charpak's contribution, the event was usually recorded photographically in a bubble chamber, a tank of superheated liquid hydrogen that revealed the passage of particles as trails of gas bubbles. The photographs were then analyzed with the help of special measuring devices in a slow and laborious process.

Charpak's invention used an earlier development, the proportional counter, in an unconventional way. The classic proportional counter consists of a thin wire running down the long axis of a gas-filled tube about a centimetre (0.4 in) in diameter. When a high voltage is applied between the wire and the tube wall and an electric field established between them, a charged particle passing through the tube will ionize the gas. In this process negatively charged electrons are liberated from the neutral gas atoms, which then become positively charged ions. In the electric field the electrons move toward the central wire, the anode, which is positively charged, while the ions move toward the glass wall, the cathode, which is negatively charged. As the electrons approach the wire, they are accelerated by the increasingly strong electric field. They gain enough energy to ionize gas atoms with which they collide, liberating more electrons and ions, and the process continues. The cumulative result is an avalanche of electrons and positive ions moving in opposite directions in the tube. It is this movement that gives rise to a detectable electric signal in the circuit connecting the elements of the counter.

By the use of a classic proportional counter, the position of the charged particle that started the ionization in the gas can be determined with a precision of only about a centimetre—the diameter of the tube. To cover larger surfaces with layers of proportional tubes is impractical and does not allow for the spatial precision necessary in particle-collision experiments. Charpak's invention of the multiwire proportional chamber provided the breakthrough. It consists of a large number of thin parallel wires, about a tenth of a millimetre (0.004 in) in diameter, arranged at intervals of a few millimetres in a plane passing between two cathode plates that are a few centimetres apart. Charpak realized, contrary to the general belief of the time, that each wire in the chamber would behave as a proportional counter and result in a spatial precision of about a millimetre or less. In addition, each wire could handle several hundred thousand particle encounters per second, at that time an exceptionally high rate. Each wire is equipped with an electronic amplifier, and the signals are analyzed with computers, speeding the process enormously.

Charpak also suggested possible refinements of the multiwire proportional chamber. Most significantly he pointed out that it was possible to make use of the time it takes between the initial ionization of the gas and the arrival of the electron pulse at the anode wire, an interval called the drift time. A measurement of the drift time results in an improved spatial precision—better than a tenth of a millimetre in some cases.

Charpak's invention launched a massive development of different types of wire chambers. By the early 1990s practically every experiment in particle physics used some type of detector derived from Charpak's original concept. Charpak was at the centre of this development, from which thousands of scientists, both at CERN and elsewhere, subsequently profited. When the J/psi particle (and support for the existence of charmed quarks) was found in 1974, resulting in the award of the 1976 Nobel physics prize to Burton Richter and Samuel C.C. Ting, several multiwire proportional chambers were used. The wire chamber was also used in the discoveries of the W and Z intermediate vector bosons at CERN in 1983; for that achievement the 1984 Nobel physics prize was awarded to Carlo Rubbia and Simon van der Meer. In the 1990s detectors developed by Charpak were being used increasingly in applications outside physics—for example, in medicine to detect X-rays and in the autoradiography of biological samples.

Charpak, a French citizen, was born on Aug. 1, 1924, in Poland. He moved to Paris with his Polish parents in 1932 at the age of seven. During World War II he served in the resistance and was jailed

The 1992 Nobel laureates (left) and officials attend the awards ceremony in Stockholm. Following custom, the Peace Prize was presented separately in Oslo, Norway, on December 10, the anniversary of Alfred Nobel's death.

TORBJORN F. GUSTAFSSON—REPORTAGEBILD/ PHOTOREPORTERS

by the Nazis for a year at the infamous Dachau concentration camp. In 1955 Charpak received a Ph.D. from the Collège de France, Paris. He began working at CERN in 1959 and also became Joliot-Curie professor at the School of Advanced Studies in Physics and Chemistry, Paris, in 1984. He held an honorary doctorate from the University of Geneva and in 1985 was made a member of the French Academy of Sciences. In 1989 he received the High Energy and Particle Physics Prize from the European Physical Society.

Charpak was a member of an international coalition of scientists who offered in 1984 to trade places with Yelena Bonner, wife of physicist and dissident Andrey Sakharov, if Soviet officials would let her go abroad for medical treatment.

(CAROLYN D. NEWTON)

Prize for Physiology or Medicine
The 1992 Nobel Prize for Physiology or Medicine was awarded jointly to University of Washington emeritus professors Edmond H. Fischer and Edwin G. Krebs for their discoveries concerning a biochemical mechanism that governs the activity of cell proteins—a process called reversible phosphorylation.

A large number of proteins in a living cell participate in regulating the cell's reactions and activities. Their functions in turn are governed by complex, delicately balanced interactions with other proteins. For example, various proteins maintain the cell's metabolic flux, dictate growth and cellular division, release hormones, and mediate muscular work. One of the more important means of controlling those proteins is reversible phosphorylation—the attachment or detachment of phosphate groups to the protein—a mechanism regulated by enzymes. (Enzymes are themselves proteins with the specific role of catalyzing biochemical reactions.) Fischer and Krebs were the first scientists to purify and characterize one of the enzymes involved in these processes. According to the Nobel citation, "Their fundamental finding initiated a research area that today is one of the most active and wide-ranging."

The three-dimensional structure of a protein molecule, which is made up of a folded chain of amino acid building blocks, determines its function. Phosphorylation, the attachment of phosphate groups to the protein, and dephosphorylation, the reverse process, change the structure and charge of the protein and thereby its function. In this manner the biological function of a protein is regulated.

Fischer and Krebs made their basic discoveries in the mid-1950s while studying muscle systems. Muscles are composed of a large number of cells

capable of contraction and relaxation. For a resting muscle to contract, it must get energy in the form of the simple sugar glucose. That glucose is released from glycogen, the form in which the body stores sugar in the liver and in muscle cells. When muscles begin to contract, they quickly mobilize their glycogen deposits, converting them to glucose. To accomplish the conversion the body uses a specific protein, an enzyme called phosphorylase. (The discovery of that enzyme won biochemists Carl and Gerti Cori the 1947 Nobel Prize for Physiology or Medicine.)

Fischer and Krebs wanted to find out exactly how phosphorylase worked and how the activity of the enzyme could switch on and off on demand. They discovered that phosphorylase is converted from an inactive to an active form by the attachment of a phosphate group and that the removal of the phosphate group inactivates the phosphorylase again. The scientists demonstrated that it is the phosphorylation-dephosphorylation mechanism that turns muscle contraction on and off. Their discovery was first reported in a scientific journal in 1956.

The enzymes that catalyze the attachment of phosphate groups to proteins are called protein kinases. The enzymes that catalyze phosphate detachment are known as phosphatases. After the laureates' initial work, scientists discovered scores of additional kinases and phosphatases that regulate specific processes in cells. The innumerable cellular processes governed by reversible protein phosphorylation affect almost all processes necessary for life. Imbalance between kinases and phosphatases can cause disease. According to the Nobel committee, "We therefore expect the development of drugs that make it possible to influence imbalances by supplying inhibitors and activators directed against the phosphorylation/dephosphorylation components."

The laureates' work led to a greater understanding of the immune response, in which certain kinases add phosphates to other kinases in a biochemical cascade that amplifies the initial immune reaction. Cyclosporine, a drug used to suppress graft rejection, was shown to work by inhibiting a phosphorylation reaction and inactivating a phosphatase. Protein phosphorylation also plays a role in the development of cancer. In several cases, chronic myelogenous leukemia, for example, poorly regulated kinase activity is responsible for the abnormal cellular growth characteristic of cancer.

Fischer was born of Swiss parents in Shanghai on April 6, 1920. He received a Ph.D. in chemistry from the University of Geneva in 1947 and then conducted research there until 1953, when

he went to the U.S to work as a research associate in biology at the California Institute of Technology. That same year he joined the faculty of the University of Washington as an assistant professor of biochemistry. He became a full professor at the university in 1961. In 1992 he was engaged in research on the cell transformation involved in the development of cancer.

Fischer served in an advisory capacity for numerous associations, including the U.S. National Institutes of Health (1959–64), the Friedrich Miescher Institute, Ciba-Geigy, Basel, Switz. (1976–84), the American Heart Association (1977–80), the Muscular Dystrophy Association (1980–88), and the Biozentrum of the University of Basel (1982–86). Among his professional honours were the Warner Medal of the Swiss Chemical Society (1952), the Guggenheim Foundation Award (1963–64), the Jaubert Prize of the University of Geneva (1968), and the Laureate Passano Foundation Award (1988). He held honorary degrees from the University of Montpellier, France (1985), and the University of Basel (1988). He was a dual citizen of the U.S. and Switzerland.

Krebs was born on June 6, 1918, in Lansing, Iowa. He attended the University of Illinois, where he earned a B.A. in chemistry in 1940. He received a medical degree from Washington University, St. Louis, Mo., in 1943. After a residency in internal medicine, he took up research at the University of Washington in 1948, becoming a full professor of biochemistry in 1957. He left that university in 1968 to work for several years at the University of California at Davis but returned in 1977. In 1992, as a professor of pharmacology and biochemistry at the University of Washington and a senior investigator emeritus for the Howard Hughes Medical Institute, he was focusing on the processes of hormonal regulation and their role in such diseases as diabetes.

Krebs served as an adviser for the National Institutes of Health, the Biochemistry Test Commission of the National Board of Medical Examiners (1968–71), the American Heart Association (1970–74), the International Board of Review of the Alberta Heritage Foundation for Medical Research (1986), and the External Advisory Commission of the Weis Center for Research (1987–91). His numerous professional honours include Canada's Gairdner Foundation Award (1978), the George W. Thorn Award for scientific excellence (1983), the Research Achievement Award of the American Heart Association (1987), the 3M Life Sciences Award, FASEB (1989), the Albert Lasker Basic Medical Research Award (1989), and the CIBA-Geigy-Drew Award in chemistry (1991).

(CAROLYN D. NEWTON)

BIOGRAPHIES

Adams, Bryan

The son of a career military officer and diplomat, Bryan Adams wanted to prove that he could be the first in his family to survive outside the military. He did it by becoming a successful songwriter and rock singer. He was named best male vocalist at the Canadian Juno Awards for 1982, 1983, and 1986. His albums *Reckless* (1984) and *Waking Up the Neighbours* (1991) both earned diamond records in Canada, and *Reckless* won the Juno Album of the Year Award for 1985. "(Everything I Do) I Do It for You," written for the feature film *Robin Hood: Prince of Thieves* (1991), won a Grammy award for Adams and was nominated for an Oscar. The song became an international hit and was the best-selling single ever in the U.S. At the 1991 Australian Music Awards, Adams was

CANAPRESS

named International Male Singer of the Year. In 1992 he was named Canadian Entertainer of the Year at the Juno Awards.

Born Nov. 5, 1959, in Kingston, Ont., Adams attended school on military bases in Europe and the Middle East before settling in Vancouver, B.C. He believed that the discipline of the military schools taught him to focus on things, and once he decided to become a musician, he pursued his goal with single-minded fervour. At age 16, Adams quit school and joined a rock band as a vocalist. Two years later he met Jim Vallance, with whom he collaborated in songwriting. Their first hit was "Let Me Take You Dancin'" (1979). Adams' first solo album, *Bryan Adams* (1980), was unsuccessful, but his third album, *Cuts like a Knife* (1983), with its companion music video catapulted him to stardom.

Adams gained his early reputation as a songwriter for such rock groups as Kiss and Prism. Even after he had attained fame as a singer, he stated that he would rather be a songwriter. His early albums were considered mainstream rock and roll. However, he believed it was necessary to continue learning, and he used music as a means of making people think. He co-wrote and performed "Tears Are Not Enough" for the Ethiopian relief effort's Live Aid concert. His 1987 album *Into the Fire* explored such themes as personal freedom and native rights. He was displeased when the Canadian Radio-Television and Telecommunications Commission declared that his album *Waking Up the Neighbours* was not Canadian because he wrote the songs in collaboration with British producer Robert Lange. The Canadian public was impressed with the album, and it sold over one million copies in Canada. For his contributions to music in Canada, Adams received the Order of Canada and the Order of British Columbia.   (DIANE LOIS WAY)

Akashi, Yasushi

When Yasushi Akashi arrived in Phnom Penh in mid-March to set up the United Nations Transitional Authority in Cambodia (UNTAC), he said his mission was a historic, complicated, and ambitious challenge and undoubtedly the most expensive such operation in the 47-year history of the UN. The UNTAC mission, at a cost of some $2 billion, was to disarm more than 200,000 soldiers, clean up land mines, repair roads and bridges, repatriate more than 350,000 refugees, and prepare for nationwide free elections in May 1993. The ultimate goal was to bring peace and stability to a country devastated by two decades of relentless war.

The UN dispatched Akashi and some 16,000 multinational "Blue Berets" to work out solutions with the four warring Cambodian factions, including the Phnom Penh government set up by Vietnam after the ouster of Pol Pot's bloody Khmer Rouge regime, which was responsible for the deaths of more than a million Cambodians. When Akashi, a veteran Japanese diplomat, met with Prince Norodom Sihanouk, head of the reconciliation council, the two men pledged to work together to implement the peace accord signed in Paris in October 1991. During the early phase of the peacekeeping operation, the Khmer Rouge was cooperative, but gradually it stiffened its stance and accused the Vietnam-created government of violating the Paris agreement. The Khmer Rouge claimed that Vietnamese troops disguised as civilians were still in Cambodia. This was denied, but the Khmer Rouge used the issue to sporadically disrupt UNTAC's operations. In November the Japanese government said its peacekeeping team was suspending repair work in four sectors of war-torn Cambodia because of terrorist acts by the Khmer Rouge.

Akashi was born in 1931 in Akita, northern Japan. After graduating from the University of Tokyo in 1954, he continued his studies at Columbia University, New York City, hoping to return as a teacher. Instead, he became the UN's first Japanese official. Akashi spent most of his UN career in New York City. Before his appointment to Cambodia, he served as under secretary for disarmament. His life-style changed so much during his years in the U.S. that Akashi seemed un-Japanese to members of the Japanese Foreign Ministry. Akashi saw himself as very international and felt very comfortable in an international environment. The Khmer Rouge, however, resented his blunt talk and wanted to see him replaced. But Akashi sympathized with Cambodia, which he felt had had so much war that it was sick and tired of fighting. The problem was that, after 20 years of war, mutual distrust was difficult to dispel.

Meanwhile, the situation in Cambodia remained shaky. In mid-November UN Secretary-General Boutros Boutros-Ghali reported that UNTAC had found no evidence of foreign units in Cambodia after checking all areas except the 15% of the country controlled by the Khmer Rouge. Nevertheless, the Khmer Rouge, with a military force of 15,000 to 25,000, continued to refuse to cooperate, and in late November the UN announced that it would impose trade sanctions on areas under its control.   (KAY K. TATEISHI)

Amato, Giuliano

Facing the triple demons of budget deficit, government corruption, and organized crime, Giuliano Amato of the Socialist Unity Party (formerly Italian Socialist Party and still popularly called PSI) assumed office as prime minister of Italy on June 28, 1992. A comparative outsider, deputy Socialist leader Amato had received his appointment by Pres. Oscar Scalfaro on June 18, one day following the withdrawal of PSI front-man Bettino Craxi from consideration. Amato's government, constituting a weakened version of the four-party coalition headed by his predecessor, Christian Democrat Giulio Andreotti, was Italy's 51st government of the post-World War II era.

Amato was born in Turin on May 13, 1938. He received a bachelor of laws degree from the University of Pisa in 1960 and a master's degree in comparative constitutional law from Columbia University, New York City, three years later. From 1964 to 1969 he served as assistant professor of Italian and comparative constitutional law at the University of Rome, returning there as a full professor in 1975 after interim tenures at the Universities of Perugia and Florence. In 1967–68 and again in 1973–74, he directed the legislative office of the Ministry of the Budget and of Economic Planning in Rome.

Amato became a member of Parliament in 1983, serving as under secretary of state in the administration of Bettino Craxi, with whom he had reconciled after earlier differences over style of government. Under subsequent Christian Democrat Prime Ministers Giovanni Goria and Ciriaco De Mita, Amato was minister of the treasury from 1987 to 1989. In May 1992, following disclosures of payoffs to government officials by contractors in Milan in exchange for lucrative public works contracts, Amato succeeded Bobo Craxi, son of the PSI leader, as secretary of the city's party organization. Investigation of the Milan scandal subsequently expanded to address similar corruption nationwide.

Voting in the April general election was dissentious, with 16 parties winning parliamentary representation. The Amato coalition, which comprised the PSI and the Christian Democrats along with the Liberal and Social Democratic parties, held a majority of only 16 seats in the 630-member Chamber of Deputies. In order to bolster this precarious alliance, Amato sought support from the Democratic Party of the Left, formerly the Italian Communist Party. In addition to his campaigns against corruption and organized crime, the new prime minister's major agenda included reduction of the nation's budget deficit and implementation of electoral reform. The former effort was regarded as crucial to Italy's continued role as a leading member of the European Communities. Prime Minister Amato's first step in governmental restructuring was to reduce the number of Cabinet ministries from 32 to 25.   (JIM CARNES)

Ando, Tadao

Tadao Ando, one of Japan's most admired and iconoclastic architects, moved centre stage in 1992 when he traveled to Copenhagen in May to receive the first Carlsberg Architectural Prize, at $235,000 the largest award in the field. In addition, his design for the 27.5-m (90-ft)-high Japanese pavilion at the world's fair in Seville, Spain, won international acclaim. The taut, dramatic lines of the open wooden structure embodied the high energy and tension that characterized Ando's works.

Ando viewed architecture as something more than a mere tool to satisfy man's needs and wanted his works to "confront people with nature's vital energy" and through those encounters to "awaken the spiritual sensibilities, still covetous of sleep, in contemporary humanity." Critical of present-day culture, Ando sought to revive inquiry into the relationships that bind architecture and people and nature together.

The stoicism underlying Ando's philosophy was evident in the small Azuma House in Osaka that brought him initial fame in 1976. Born in an old-style Osaka row house himself on Sept. 13, 1941, he later re-created the spatial effect of such houses in an abstract manner in his residential design. The minimalist structure in exposed concrete was divided into two bridged-together sections with a courtyard in the centre open to rain, wind, light, and sound. His genius was expressed in the ways he used voids, natural light, and passages. Ceiling skylights, slits, and curved walls were employed to transform light itself into architecture, as a "mediator between space and form."

More a builder than an architect, Ando was self-taught except for a brief apprenticeship with a Japanese carpenter. He admitted to only two influences, the depth of Japan's building culture and the study tours he made abroad in the late 1960s, which gave him a self-consciously cross-cultural perspective. Working to achieve a contemporary synthesis, Ando viewed Western form-making as irreducibly geometric, volumetric, and vertical and the Japanese tradition as natural, horizontal, and spaceless. In 1969 he established Tadao Ando Architect and Associates, and he subsequently executed some 50 private houses and public buildings. Examples in Japan were Rokko Housing in Kobe (1983), the Church of Light in Osaka (1989), and Water Temple in Hyogo (1991). Works commissioned abroad included the Japanese Gallery at the Art Institute of Chicago. Besides numerous Japanese awards, Ando received the Finnish Alvar Aalto Medal (1985) and the French Gold Medal of Architecture (1989). He also exhibited widely abroad and held a one-man show at the New York Museum of Modern Art in 1991.   (GERD LARSSON)

Ashrawi, Hanan

Dubbed by journalists the "First Lady of the Palestinians," Hanan Ashrawi served as spokeswoman for the Palestinian delegation to the U.S.-initiated Middle East peace talks from the time they

CAMERA PRESS/GLOBE PHOTOS

began in the fall of 1991. Although an outspoken supporter of the *intifada* (Palestinian uprising) and the Palestine Liberation Organization (PLO), Ashrawi disarmed critics of Palestinian radicalism during her frequent appearances on American television. Her command of English, dignified demeanour, and insightful analysis of her people's plight permitted her to press the case for Palestinian self-determination in a way that captured world attention.

Born in 1946 in the town of Ramallah—then in Palestine, now in the Israeli-occupied West Bank—Ashrawi grew up in a Christian family. Inspired by her physician father, who became a Palestinian political leader, Ashrawi joined the General Union of Palestinian Students while attending the American University in Beirut, Lebanon. Her primary focus at that point in her life, however, was academic, and she went on to earn an M.A. in literature from American University and a Ph.D in English literature from the University of Virginia. When she returned to Ramallah, she joined the faculty of Bir Zeit University as professor of medieval and comparative literature. Until the Israeli army forced Bir Zeit to close its doors, she also served as dean of the university's School of the Arts.

It was the brutal raids on refugee camps by Israeli-backed Lebanese Christians during Israel's 1982 invasion of Lebanon that prompted the

scholar to turn spokeswoman for the Palestinian cause, but she did not attract more than local attention until the *intifada* broke out in December 1987. Frequent appearances on ABC's "Nightline" and PBS's "MacNeil/Lehrer NewsHour," however, allowed viewers to see a Palestinian who contrasted sharply with the rock-throwing youths who had come to personify the uprising. The well-dressed, articulate professor, mother of two, appealed to the world to recognize the legitimacy of Palestinian rights on humanitarian grounds, rejecting (at least implicitly) terrorism and the ultimate destruction of the State of Israel.

After U.S. Pres. George Bush announced his peace initiative in 1991, she met with Secretary of State James Baker to protest Israeli insistence that the Palestinian delegation include no one—like Ashrawi—who was a resident of Jerusalem or who had overt ties to the PLO. Her protest failed, but the U.S. eventually persuaded Israel to allow Ashrawi to serve as a member of the advisory committee to the Palestinian delegation and as its official spokeswoman. By late 1992 she was acknowledging that "skepticism is mounting" regarding the lack of progress in the peace talks. She was particularly distressed at Bush's agreement to provide up to $10 billion in loan guarantees for Israel while allowing Israel to complete nearly 10,000 new housing units in the occupied territories. "Many Palestinians," she charged, "see this and say, 'Only the voice of power works.' "
                              (JEROLD L. KELLMAN)

Bérégovoy, Pierre

In April 1992 Pierre Bérégovoy, a self-taught economist, was appointed prime minister of France. His humble upbringing and reputation for pragmatism made the longtime Socialist leader initially a popular choice among the French electorate. For the ruling Socialist Party, 1992 was not a good year. In fact, by gaining only 18.3% of the vote in the March regional elections, it appeared to be heading for political disaster. The nation's unemployment rate hovered near 10%, and allegations of corruption—especially reports that government officials knowingly allowed HIV-infected blood to be used for transfusions—caused the party to plummet in the polls. Many also blamed the party's decline on the seemingly unfocused program and intemperate remarks of Bérégovoy's predecessor, Edith Cresson.

Bérégovoy's appointment by Pres. François Mitterrand was seen as a cautious move. Until April Bérégovoy had been head of the government's Finance Ministry, where he gained wide respect for his policies to lower inflation and the budget deficit. While his appointment thus appeared to provide reassurance to the financial community, it did little to assuage the increasingly angry and alienated working class—the core voting constituency of the Socialist Party—which was more concerned with the bleak employment situation. It was Bérégovoy's rigorous economic policies as finance minister that some blamed for the high unemployment rate, and it appeared that his political future, as well as that of his party, would be at least partially tied to his ability to promote job growth before the 1993 parliamentary elections. Bérégovoy announced soon after his appointment that fighting unemployment would be his first priority.

Bérégovoy was born on Dec. 23, 1925, in Déville-les-Rouen, a town in northern France. His father was a miner, and his mother was a grocery store clerk. At age 15 he left school to become an apprentice lathe operator, and he was later employed by the government-run railroad. In 1950 he took a job at Gaz de France, the national gas utility. It was at Gaz de France that Bérégovoy was able to move up in the ranks, and in 1978 he became a director.

After working as the campaign manager of Mitterrand's successful 1981 presidential bid, Bérégovoy became the president's chief of staff. The following year he was appointed the minister of social affairs. Bérégovoy was finance minister from 1984 until the 1986 election of a conservative government but regained the post after the Socialists again took power in 1988.
                              (THOMAS RIGGS)

Bergen, Candice

Although accustomed to the attention that surrounds celebrity, American actress, photojournalist, and writer Candice Bergen was caught by surprise in 1992 when her television character, Murphy Brown, became the centre of an election year political controversy. In a speech before the Commonwealth Club of California on May 19, in which he criticized Hollywood for "glamorizing" illegitimacy, Vice Pres. Dan Quayle (*q.v.*) targeted, in particular, the character of Murphy Brown for choosing to have a child outside of marriage. The fire storm that followed the speech focused on the Republican Party's upholding of the traditional family (mother, father, and children) to the exclusion of many nontraditional ones. Unlike her character, who is known for her quick, sharp-tongued, and sometimes ill-considered responses, Bergen chose not to participate in the controversy until after the August 30 Emmy telecast, when she (with humour) thanked Quayle for helping her win the award.

After spending the summer in France with her husband, French director Louis Malle, and their daughter, Bergen entered the fray in September. She defended her character's decision to become a single mother, declaring that poverty had contributed more to the erosion of family values in the United States than the media. Finally, Murphy herself (created by Diane English) answered Quayle in the first show of the season. She acknowledged that it had been an agonizing decision to have the baby and pointed out how many nontraditional families are in the truest sense real families.

Born in Beverly Hills, Calif., on May 9, 1946, Bergen began life in the limelight—her very high-profile parents were ventriloquist Edgar Bergen and model Frances Westerman. While she grew up surrounded by Hollywood's glitterati, Bergen's life was not entirely a fairy tale. From birth she was engaged in a fierce competition with her "brother"—the wooden dummy Charlie McCarthy—for her father's affection. Despite her father's aloofness, detailed in her autobiography, *Knock Wood* (1984), Bergen recognized that she was blessed, and it was at her father's urging that she turned to comedy.

While enrolled at the University of Pennsylvania, Bergen began a highly successful modeling career. Her first motion picture, at age 19, was *The Group*, in which she played Lakey, one of the members of a Vassar clique. Other motion pictures of note in which Bergen appeared were *The Sand Pebbles, Soldier Blue, Getting Straight, Carnal Knowledge, The Wind and the Lion, Starting Over,* and *Rich and Famous*. In 1988, after several other appearances on television, Bergen captured the role of Murphy Brown; she received the Emmy award for lead actress in a comedy series in 1989, 1990, and 1992.
                              (SUSAN MARTS MYERS)

Bhumibol Adulyadej

Thailand's soft-spoken constitutional monarch served as a unifying force and a symbol of peace during the country's 1992 political turmoil. Although without legal control over political matters, the king was able to use his moral authority—as well as the devotion of the Thai people—to force the military-led government and the growing civilian opposition movement to work out a compromise. "It's useless," he said, "to live on burned ruins."

Much of Thailand's political opposition was focused on Gen. Suchinda Kraprayoon, who in 1991 led a successful coup against the country's nominally civilian government. In April 1992, despite promises to the contrary, Suchinda made himself prime minister. Demands for Suchinda's resignation began immediately, not only from angry students and workers but also from businessmen in the country's newly emerging middle class. Demonstrations followed, but on May 17 Suchinda ordered a violent crackdown. For days King Bhumibol watched quietly as government forces left scores of protesters dead and the capital city of Bangkok at a near standstill. The normally bustling and congested city began to look like a war zone.

The king finally acted on May 21, ordering a meeting with Suchinda and opposition leader Chamlong Srimuang, who had been jailed by Suchinda's forces. As is custom, when the two men came to the king's ornate hall, they approached the monarch on their knees and sat humbly at his feet. "I would like both of you to talk face-to-face, not to confront each other," King Bhumibol said in the 15-minute televised meeting. Remarkably, with the mediation of Gen. Prem Tinsulanond, a former prime minister, the two opposing leaders announced a political compromise within hours. On May 24, Suchinda resigned.

Bhumibol was born on Dec. 5, 1927, in Cambridge, Mass., where his father, a royal prince not directly in line to the throne, was attending Harvard University. His mother was training to be a nurse. After his father's death in 1929, Bhumibol was taken to Switzerland for his education. Prince Anand, Bhumibol's brother, became king in 1935 when his uncle, Prajadhipok, abdicated the throne, but in 1946 Anand died mysteriously. He was found in the palace with a bullet in his head. Bhumibol, next in line, was officially crowned in 1950 and became the ninth king of the Chakkri dynasty.

During Bhumibol's reign, Thailand had undergone a turbulent period of military domination and 10 successful coups, but it also experienced high growth rates and industrialization. King Bhumibol's initiation of development projects, as well as his moral presence in times of crisis, provided a moderating and stabilizing force for the country. (THOMAS RIGGS)

Boulez, Pierre
Widely acclaimed as one of the most important contemporary composers, Pierre Boulez nonetheless probably became better known as an interpreter of other composers' works. His own music was atonal and thought to be complex and difficult, yet he was noted for the clarity of his interpretations of others' works. An incisive, and sometimes polemical, critic, he championed modern music throughout his career. In 1992 he released the first compact discs in his project to rerecord with the Cleveland (Ohio) and Chicago Symphony orchestras several of the masterworks of the 20th century.

Boulez was born on March 26, 1925, in Montbrison, a small town in central France. He began piano lessons as a young child. At the urging of his father, he went to Lyon in 1941 to study mathematics, but after an unhappy year he left to study music. In 1942 Boulez entered the Paris Conservatory, where his teachers included the organist and composer Olivier Messiaen.

He was influenced by the 12-tone method (a form of serialism) of Arnold Schoenberg, as well as by works of Schoenberg's pupil Anton Webern and of his own teacher Messiaen. Boulez extended serialism beyond melody to include rhythm, timbre, dynamics, and other elements. He also used aleatory (chance) techniques, in which the performer had the discretion, for example, of reordering the movements of a work or of playing or omitting passages. Among the best known of his compositions were *Le Marteau sans maître* (1954) and *Pli selon pli* (1962).

In 1954 Boulez founded a concert series (originally Concerts du Petit Marigny; later Domaine Musical) to introduce 20th-century music to the French public. In the late 1950s he began an association with the Southwest Radio Symphony Orchestra, in Baden-Baden, West Germany, which had a tradition of performing new music. At about this time he became alienated from the French cultural establishment, which he found regressive.

Boulez began conducting in the United States in the mid-1960s, and from 1967 to 1972 he was principal guest conductor of the Cleveland Orchestra. He became chief conductor of the BBC Symphony Orchestra (London) in 1971 and music director of the New York Philharmonic that same year. With these and other orchestras Boulez made highly acclaimed recordings of works of Debussy, Ravel, Schoenberg, Webern, Berg, Bartok, Stravinsky, Messiaen, and others. During the 1960s and '70s he also conducted Wagner at Bayreuth, and in 1974 he was appointed head of the Institut de Recherche et de Coordination Acoustique/Musicale in Paris. With the Ensemble InterContemporain, he continued to present his and others' works. In the early 1990s he returned to Cleveland and Chicago as a regular guest conductor, and on Dec. 7, 1992, he participated in the 150th anniversary concert of the New York Philharmonic. (THOMAS RIGGS)

Boutros-Ghali, Boutros
A scholar and former Egyptian diplomat became, in 1992, the first Arab and first African secretary-general of the United Nations. The selection process was dominated by demands from the Organization of African Unity (OAU) that a leader from their continent be chosen for the UN's top post. From the creation of the UN in 1945 until the selection of Boutros Boutros-Ghali, there had been five secretaries-general—three from Europe, one from Asia, and one from Latin America.

Although he campaigned hard for the position, Boutros-Ghali's selection as secretary-general was generally unexpected. He was only one of six candidates the OAU had recommended, and his inclusion on the list was apparently an afterthought, brought about by pressure from France on the OAU to recommend at least one fluent French speaker. Boutros-Ghali's credentials as an African and an Arab were also in question. The OAU reportedly wanted a sub-Saharan black, and Boutros-Ghali's membership in the Coptic Christian church had put him in disfavour with Arab Muslims. Even his claim to be a representative of the Third World—a quality that helped gain the important vote of China—stood in sharp contrast to his Westernized habits. It was his Western outlook, however, that may have won him the eventual approval of Britain and the U.S. in the Security Council. Replacing Javier Pérez de Cuéllar of Peru on Jan. 1, 1992, Boutros-Ghali hoped to become a champion of Third World causes and reform the bloated UN bureaucracy. Before long, however, he was facing major crises in—most notably—Somalia and the newly independent republics of former Yugoslavia.

Scion of a distinguished Egyptian family, Boutros-Ghali was born on Nov. 14, 1922, in Cairo. His father served as finance minister for the Egyptian government, and his grandfather was prime minister from 1910 until 1920, when he was assassinated by a radical Muslim student. In 1949, after receiving a doctorate in international law from the University of Paris, Boutros-Ghali became a professor of international law and international relations at Cairo University. His academic career was marked by more than 100 publications, mostly in French but also in English and Arabic.

Boutros-Ghali's political life began in 1977 when, in an effort to bring more Egyptian Christians into the government, Pres. Anwar as-Sadat

AP/WIDE WORLD

appointed Boutros-Ghali to his Cabinet, first as acting foreign minister and then as deputy foreign minister. Boutros-Ghali gained international attention for his work on the 1979 Egyptian-Israeli peace treaty. In 1991, following his appointment as foreign minister by Pres. Hosni Mubarak, he played a major role in securing Arab support for the Gulf war. (THOMAS RIGGS)

Brittan, Sir Leon
More than with most U.K. politicians, Sir Leon Brittan's public life was shaped by the continuing controversy over the country's relationship with the rest of Europe. It destroyed his career as a Westminster politician but provided his opportunity for a new career—as a vice president of the European Commission in Brussels.

Brittan was born in London on Sept. 25, 1939. An active member of the Conservative Party at the University of Cambridge, he finally achieved his ambition of becoming a member of Parliament in 1974, when he was elected for the Yorkshire constituency of Cleveland and Whitby. A libel lawyer by profession, he was appointed minister of state at the Home Office when the Conservatives won power in 1979. Two years later he joined the Cabinet as chief secretary to the treasury. After a period as home secretary (1983–85), he was appointed secretary of state for trade and industry.

After four months, however, Brittan was forced to resign. He was engaged in a battle with Michael Heseltine, the defense secretary, over a small, ailing helicopter company, Westland PLC. The issue itself was trivial: should the government allow Westland to be sold to an American bidder (as Brittan and the company management wanted), or should it be incorporated into a European consortium (Heseltine's preference).

The issue, however, was inflated into a row that at one point threatened Prime Minister Margaret Thatcher's government. Heseltine was forced to resign in January 1986—followed later that month by Brittan's resignation, when he was accused of authorizing the leaking of a confidential letter by one of the government's law officers.

Brittan hoped to resume his ministerial career in due course. Instead, in 1988 Thatcher nominated him for a knighthood and appointed him to represent the U.K. as vice president of the European Commission. He was given the specific post of commissioner for competition and financial services. This ensured him a leading role in the negotiations over the completion of the European Communities' single market. He became a leading exponent of the view that a free and open market required a battery of Europe-wide regulations—concerning everything from corporate takeover rules to the amount of asbestos allowed in the tips of billiard cues—in order to ensure genuine free competition on a level economic playing field. (PETER KELLNER)

Brooks, Garth
Dubbed the first entertainment phenomenon of the 1990s, Garth Brooks, a humble country boy with a dash of rock-star charisma, burst into the country music spotlight in 1989. When his third album, *Ropin' the Wind,* was released in 1991, it immediately made music history by becoming the first album to enter *Billboard*'s country and pop charts at number one in both categories. In January his appearance on NBC's "This Is Garth Brooks" pushed the network to its highest Friday night ratings in over two years. His shows sold out within 20 minutes after the ticket windows opened. Brooks sold more albums, faster, than anyone else in the history of country music. He captivated audiences with his unlikely pairing of flamboyant showmanship and sensitive lyrics. His down-home smile and trademark black Stetson graced the covers of *Life, Time,* and *Forbes* magazines. Nonetheless, the king of the country charts was talking about retiring at the zenith of his musical career, claiming that the birth in 1992 of his first child meant more to him than money and fame. Brooks was starting to have second thoughts about making so many commitments that would keep him away from his family, now his first priority.

PAUL NATKIN—PHOTO RESERVE

Troyal Garth Brooks was born Feb. 2, 1962, in Tulsa, Okla., but he grew up in the small town of Yukon. The youngest of six children, Brooks learned how to strum and sing from his mother, who had a brief career as a country singer in the 1950s. In high school Brooks not only participated in football, basketball, baseball, and track and field but also played in a band. Music took a backseat to sports when he was awarded a track scholarship to Oklahoma State University, where he majored in marketing and advertising and competed in the javelin throw. Brooks's failure to make the Big Eight Conference finals his senior year turned his attention back to country music.

Hoping for instant stardom, Brooks headed for Nashville, Tenn., in 1985 but left, daunted, after less than a day. Two years later, accompanied by his bride, Sandy Mahl, he returned to Nashville, this time determined to succeed. Brooks was noticed six months later by a Capitol Records talent scout. *Garth Brooks*, his first album, was released in 1989 and generated four number one country singles, catapulting him to almost overnight success. Brooks—whose musical idols during the 1970s included Queen, Kiss, and James Taylor—represented a new breed of country music entertainer. His songs appealed to a mainstream audience, with their mix of rock and country elements and their sometimes pithy messages based on Brooks's homespun philosophy. His many awards included the Country Music Association Entertainer of the Year and Album of the Year, 1991 and 1992, and *Billboard* magazine's number one pop artist and number one country artist, 1992.

(VIRGINIA M. LA FLEUR)

Brown, Tina

As much a celebrity as those who populated the pages of her magazines, Tina Brown found herself in a whirl of publicity in 1992 upon being named editor of *The New Yorker*. Brown, only the fourth editor in the magazine's 67-year history, had a record of resuscitating moribund publications. The staid *New Yorker* was apparently in for the same treatment, whether its devotees wanted it or not.

Brown was born in Maidenhead, England, on Nov. 21, 1953. Her father was a film producer and her mother a press agent. A precocious and spirited child, Brown was expelled from several boarding schools, but at 20 she graduated from the University of Oxford with a degree in English. While at Oxford she wrote for the literary magazine *Isis*. For that work, *The Sunday Times* voted her Most Promising Female Journalist. After graduation Brown was assigned by Harold Evans, a *Sunday Times* editor, to write profiles on leaders of the U.S. women's movement. Her humorous pieces about her own experiences there

were collected in *Loose Talk: Adventures on the Street of Shame* (1979). Brown joined the British humour magazine *Punch* as a columnist in 1976 and won the 1978 Britain's Young Journalist of the Year Award. That year she was made editor of the *Tatler*. Published since the 1700s, the aristocratic, stodgy magazine had seen its circulation drop dangerously low. Brown, with no editorial experience, broadened its appeal, infusing it with exciting visuals, celebrity reports, and a satirical edge. By 1983 the *Tatler* was voted England's Magazine of the Year.

Meanwhile, in the U.S., Condé Nast's legendary *Vanity Fair*, defunct since 1936, was revived. Expectations were high, but the magazine's elitism and lack of editorial focus soon became apparent. The new *Vanity Fair* was verging on extinction in 1983 when Brown was called in as a consultant. She pronounced it verbose, pretentious, and visually confusing and prescribed a strong look, top-notch writing, and more "crackle and excitement." Invited to become editor in chief, she moved to the U.S. with Evans, whom she had married in 1981.

It was thought that, in her own words, "a great intellectual endeavour had failed and that Condé Nast . . . had brought in Little Miss Celebrity . . . to trash it up." Trash or not, she made *Vanity Fair* the hottest magazine of the 1980s. Her editorial creed encompassed not only the best (and most expensive) writers and provocative as well as intellectual material but also occasional lapses of taste, which she said kept readers on their toes.

Brown expected to stay at *Vanity Fair* through her 10th year, but in mid-1992 she got the call from S.I. ("Si") Newhouse, owner of both *The New Yorker* and Condé Nast, to replace Robert

MARIO RUIZ—TIME MAGAZINE

Gottlieb as *The New Yorker* editor. Gottlieb had himself been a controversial choice for the job in 1987, but he had honoured the status quo at the admittedly idiosyncratic magazine. Longtime staffers and writers panicked, but Brown said *The New Yorker* needed little change to become relevant again. She seemed set on pulling *The New Yorker* into the 1990s, but gently and one step at a time.

(LORRAINE MURRAY)

Bush, George Herbert Walker

On Nov. 3, 1992, while casting his ballot in the U.S. presidential election in Houston, Texas, Pres. George Bush called 1992 "the most unpleasant year of my life." Not only did he lose his presidential bid for a second term in office to Arkansas Gov. Bill Clinton (*q.v.*), but he spent most of the year trying to spark life into a lack-

lustre campaign, cope with a weak economy, and persuade the U.S. electorate that he was sensitive to their domestic policy concerns. His travails continued even after the election—he buried his mother, Dorothy Walker Bush, the Monday before Thanksgiving.

In the wake of the U.S. victory in the Gulf war in 1991, many believed Bush would be unbeatable in the 1992 presidential race. He secured the nomination at the Republican national convention in Houston on August 20 after fending off a stronger-than-expected challenge by right-wing commentator Patrick Buchanan. As it became increasingly clear that voters were not as concerned with foreign policy as with reviving the sagging U.S. economy, Bush crisscrossed the nation, promising changes in health care, expressing regret at having agreed to raise taxes in 1990, and inviting comparisons between his "character" and Clinton's. When the polls showed that Clinton was in the lead and independent H. Ross Perot (*q.v.*) was making a respectable showing, Bush asked Secretary of State James Baker to resign his Cabinet post and work to revitalize the campaign, as he had done so well in 1988. The campaign still foundered; Bush received 38% of the vote, Clinton 43%, and Perot 19%.

Earlier in 1992 Bush traveled to Australia, Japan, Singapore, and South Korea to forge the way for better trade. He was criticized, however, for "begging" those host nations to buy more U.S. products, while the media dwelt on his illness at a state banquet in Japan. In June he reluctantly attended the UN Conference on Environment and Development in Rio de Janeiro, and he was taken to task for not agreeing to deadlines on specific environmental goals. While in Munich, Germany (July 6–8), for a meeting of the heads of government of the Group of Seven, he and Russian Pres. Boris Yeltsin worked out plans to aid Russia, though former president Richard Nixon castigated him for not doing enough. During the year Bush also met with the presidents of Mexico and Canada to initial a North American Free Trade Agreement.

After the election Bush vowed to "finish this job with style." In December he approved plans to send 28,000 forces to Somalia as part of a UN effort to aid the famine-stricken country, and he paid a New Year's Eve visit to the troops. He and Yeltsin were scheduled to sign a second Strategic Arms Reduction Treaty early in January. More controversially, he granted Christmas Eve pardons to six government officials involved in the Iran-*contra* scandal; independent counsel Lawrence Walsh hinted that Bush might yet be implicated in the affair.

Born in Milton, Mass., on June 12, 1924, and raised in Greenwich, Conn., Bush served in the U.S. Navy during World War II, graduated from Yale University in 1948, and worked in the oil industry, mostly in Texas. He entered politics in 1959 and served eight years as U.S. vice president before becoming president on Jan. 20, 1989.

(CHARLES JOHNSON TAGGART)

Buttrose, Ita Clare

In 1992 Ita Buttrose found time to take a tour of Alaska while continuing to expand her horizons as a role model for Australian businesswomen by publishing her views in *Ita*, a magazine she founded (1988) and named after herself. She combined a general concern for the underprivileged and suffering members of the Australian community with a commitment to expanding the rights of women. Buttrose, who possessed an engaging lisp, hypnotic smile, and robust self-confidence, was a pathfinder. She branched out from her major task as chairwoman of the National Advisory Committee on AIDS to launch a vital new government program aimed at raising awareness of the importance of training employees for the work force. Buttrose was appointed to this post by Kim Beazley, the minister for employment, education, and training. She was convinced that Australia had a responsibility to train its staff to the highest level. "The main assumption made by many companies," she said, "is that it's a waste of time training women because women leave to have babies. This excuse was pulled out whenever companies wanted to avoid the real issue—their responsibility to provide the best training for all their staff, including women."

Buttrose, who was born on Jan. 17, 1942, was educated at Dover Heights Domestic Science School in Sydney. Her career in publishing began as an editor of the English *Woman's Own.* Thereafter she overshadowed all other women involved in magazine publishing in Australia. She was founding editor of *Cleo,* edited *The Australian Women's Weekly,* and controlled Australian Consolidated Press Ltd. women's magazines, including *The Australian Women's Weekly, Cleo, Belle, Bride,* and *Mode.* She reigned as one of Australia's most successful women company directors, serving on the boards of Australian Consolidated Press Ltd. (1974–80) and News Ltd. (1981–84). She was editor in chief of both the *Daily Telegraph* and the *Sunday Telegraph.* Besides her hectic life as a publisher and board member, she was a radio and television broadcaster, a columnist, and a member of a large number of philanthropic, charitable, and cultural organizations, including the Royal New South Wales Institute for Deaf and Blind Children and the Australian Ballet Foundation. She was also a patron of the Australian Opera, worked to help youth through drug education, and assisted children with anorexia and bulimia problems.   (A.R.G. GRIFFITHS)

Carey, Ronald Robert
In the first secret ballot election for international leaders in the 88-year history of the International Brotherhood of Teamsters, Ron Carey, a former United Parcel Service driver, was elected to a five-year term as president of the 1.5 million-member union. Observers of organized labour saw Carey's election as a victory for the union's rank and file over a bureaucracy bloated by years of greed and corruption.

Carey was born in New York City on March 22, 1936. Following service in the Marine Corps, he went to work as a driver for United Parcel Service in 1956, becoming union shop steward in 1958. In 1967 Carey ran for president of Teamster's Local 804. He won, despite efforts by company management to force his resignation from his delivery position, thereby making him ineligible for union office. Carey gained a reputation as an honest and dedicated unionist as well as a skilled negotiator and organizer. He kept Local 804 relatively independent, protecting it from the corruption and organized-crime influence then endemic among the Teamsters' leadership while still remaining supportive of the strikes and work stoppages of other locals. He was reelected to the presidency of Local 804 eight times.

Carey's rise to national prominence was aided by federal investigations of corruption in the international union. Prior to his election, three of the Teamsters' last five presidents—Jimmy Hoffa, Dave Beck, and Roy Williams—had served prison sentences, and a fourth, Jackie Presser, had been indicted on embezzlement charges but died before trial. A 1988 antiracketeering lawsuit filed by the U.S. Justice Department led to the appointment of a federal administrative panel authorized to oversee the union's affairs. In 1989 the union settled the lawsuit by granting the government authority to expel corrupt leaders. Following the removal of 138 international officers, the union agreed to a new election by secret ballot; previous leaders had been elected by delegates chosen by union officials.

Carey promised to streamline the bloated union bureaucracy, cut the exorbitant salaries and expense accounts of union officials, and return the control of the union to its membership. He received the backing of Teamsters for a Democratic Union, an organization formed by the union's rank and file to fight corrupt leadership, and was supported by small contributions from union members throughout the country. In a three-way race Carey received 188,883 votes against 129,538 for R.V. Durham and 71,227 for Walter Shea, both of whom had close ties to the union bureaucracy. Promising a new union for members and their families, Carey stated, "It's their union. They want it to work for them. We're only caretakers."   (JOHN H. MATHEWS)

Carreras, José
In July 1992, five years after undergoing radiation and chemotherapy treatment for leukemia, tenor José Carreras had the double distinction of both singing at the summer Olympic Games in Barcelona, Spain—alongside fellow Spanish opera stars Placido Domingo, Montserrat Cabellé, Giacomo Aragall, Juan Pons, and Teresa Berganza—and serving as music director of both the opening and closing Olympic ceremonies. Except for a bit of controversy—Alfredo Kraus, another well-known Spanish tenor, was not invited—the events went smoothly. In 1990 Carreras, Domingo, and Italian tenor Luciano Pavarotti had performed in Rome's open-air Caracalla Theatre before a television audience of several hundred million people. The event was called "the concert of the century," but when Kraus disagreed and publicly made negative remarks, Carreras and Kraus became estranged.

José Carreras Coll was born in Barcelona on Dec. 5, 1946. The youngest of three children, he was the only member of his family who displayed any particular interest in music. After seeing Mario Lanza perform in the film *The Great Caruso,* young Carreras returned home and sang and staged everything he had seen and heard on the screen. He often organized make-believe recitals and operas in his room, singing arias he had heard on records and on the radio. When he was seven, his parents enrolled him in the Barcelona Conservatory to study music. Carreras entered the University of Barcelona in his late teens to study chemistry—both his brother and sister were chemists. While at the university he began vocal training with Jaime Francisco Puig, the voice teacher of his friend Aragall.

In January 1970 Carreras sang the minor part of Flavio in the Bellini opera *Norma* and met Cabellé, who sang the title role. She and her brother, Carlos, took Carreras under their wings, and the two helped him embark on an international career. Carreras made his Italian debut as Rodolfo in *La Bohème* in Parma and then his American debut at the New York City Opera as Pinkerton in Puccini's *Madama Butterfly.* He made his Metropolitan Opera debut as Cavaradossi in *Tosca* in 1974. During the next decade Carreras sang a wide variety of roles all over the world and recorded extensively. *Hollywood Golden Classics,* an album of popular songs, was released in 1991. In May 1992 he returned to New York City and performed before a sold-out audience at Carnegie Hall.   (EDWARD PAUL MORAGNE)

Chiluba, Frederick J.
Frederick J. Chiluba defeated Kenneth Kaunda to become Zambia's president on Nov. 2, 1991, ending the regime of one of the last of post-colonial Africa's founding fathers. Kaunda had been president since the country gained independence in 1964.

Born in 1943, the son of a copper miner, Chiluba spent most of his life as a labour leader. He led the fight for multiparty democracy in Zambia as chairman of the influential Zambia Congress of Trade Unions. A pugnacious five-footer, he earned a reputation as a tough fighter long before he entered the political arena as one of the founders in 1990 of the Movement for Multiparty Democracy (MMD). His popularity on Zambia's Copperbelt was demonstrated by the huge crowds that gathered whenever he spoke. Chiluba's union background and sharp tongue did not appeal to the businessmen and professionals who were prominent in the fight against President Kaunda, but in the ballot for leadership of the MMD he easily defeated his rivals and proved a formidable vote getter in the contest against the veteran Zambian president.

Chiluba, a born-again Christian, had considerable charm, with a winning smile that transformed his pugilist face, skimpily adorned with a wispy moustache and a straggling beard. He was awarded the George Meany Human Rights Award by the AFL-CIO in 1992. In his speech of acceptance he said: "We in Zambia . . . know what works; freedom works. We know what is right; democracy is right."   (COLIN LEGUM)

Clinton, Bill
Emphasizing change and appealing to voters as the candidate from Hope, Arkansas, Gov. Bill Clinton was elected the 42nd president of the United States on Nov. 3, 1992. He and his Democratic running mate, Sen. Albert Gore, Jr. (*q.v.*), symbolized a baby-boomer ticket ushering in a new generation of presidential politics.

Clinton was born William Jefferson Blythe IV on Aug. 19, 1946, in Hope, Ark. His father had died in an automobile accident three months before his birth. His mother went to nursing school in New Orleans, La., when he was two years old; the boy lived for two years with his maternal grandparents. Three years after his mother returned, she married Roger Clinton, who moved the family to Hot Springs. Despite his stepfather's alcoholism and violent tendencies, the young Blythe legally changed his name to Clinton at age 15 in a gesture to hold the family together after his mother and stepfather divorced and soon remarried.

As a high school "senator" to the American Legion Boys Nation, Clinton met his hero, Pres. John F. Kennedy, and began a political career from which he never wavered. He received a B.S. (1968) in international affairs from Georgetown University, Washington, D.C., and won a Rhodes scholarship to the University of Oxford, where he began studies in the autumn of 1968. His opposition to the Vietnam war and efforts to avoid being drafted came under attack during the 1992 campaign.

At Yale Law School, Clinton met Hillary Rodham, whom he married in 1975. After graduation he taught at the University of Arkansas School of Law and practiced law. He ran unsuccessfully for Congress in 1974 but was elected the state's attorney general three years later. In 1978, at age 32, he became the nation's youngest governor. Although he made progress in improving education and economic growth, he was criticized for admitting "outsiders" into his administration, for too hastily proposing a flurry of programs, and for instituting unpopular licenses and fees. Critics were even upset that his wife continued to use her maiden name. Clinton lost a 1980 reelection bid. He won the 1982, 1984, and 1986 races, however, and helped his state attain educational and economic goals. In 1990 he gained a fifth term (in 1986 the state constitution had been changed to mandate four-year terms).

A 1986 poll of governors named him one of the five most effective governors in the nation; by 1991 he was ranked number one. Clinton's national recognition had grown with his chairmanship of the National Governor's Association (1986–87); he was also a cofounder and chairman of the moderate Democratic Leadership Council

(1990). At the 1988 Democratic national convention, he gave the nominating speech for Michael Dukakis, an event most remembered for its excessive length.

On Oct. 3, 1991, Clinton announced his candidacy for president. His campaign was nearly sunk several times by charges of marital infidelity and criticism of his avoidance of the draft, but he clinched the nomination on June 2. His campaign

ROBERT KUSEL

then gained strength, helped by his selection of Gore as his running mate, a unified Democratic convention, and strong debate performances that highlighted his connection to the electorate. Clinton was elected president with 43% of the popular vote; Pres. George Bush (q.v.) received 38% and independent Ross Perot 19%.

(BETSY ROSSEN ELLIOT)

Coughlin, Lieut. Paula
Given the large number of people who refused to believe Anita Hill's accusations of sexual harassment during the Clarence Thomas confirmation hearings in 1991, it would not have been surprising if women thereafter had been reluctant to bring similar charges. Sexual harassment in the military, therefore, might have gone on being tolerated had it not been for Lieut. Paula Coughlin's willingness to speak out, regardless of the risk to her career. Coughlin, a navy helicopter pilot and an aide to Rear Adm. Jack Snyder at the Patuxent River Naval Air Test Center in Maryland, was one of at least 26 women assaulted by members of the Tailhook Association, an organization of navy and Marine pilots, at their 1991 convention at the Las Vegas (Nev.) Hilton. The women were forced to run a gauntlet of male officers who pawed and fondled them and tried to remove their clothes. When Coughlin complained, the incident was treated as the sort of thing to be expected at such a gathering—indeed, navy officials had for several years been aware of such conduct at the conventions but had done nothing about it—and she was either warned to back off or simply ignored. Her complaint was finally examined by the Naval Investigative Service, which failed to uncover much information and was itself accused of foot-dragging and otherwise attempting to protect the officers involved rather than to discover the truth.

In June Coughlin went public in interviews with ABC News and the Washington (D.C.) Post. In the aftermath of her revelations came the resignation of Navy Secretary H. Lawrence Garrett III, who had attended the convention and had been in the vicinity of the assault. A Pentagon investigation led to the forced retirement of two admirals—because of their leadership failure in supervising the original inquiry—and the reassignment of another admiral. Further examples of the extent of sexual harassment in the armed forces, including

numerous accounts of sexual attacks on women serving in the Middle East during Operation Desert Storm, were also elicited during the investigation, and military officials realized that the time had come to institute procedures to combat sexual harassment in the military.

Coughlin, whose father was also a navy pilot, was born on Nov. 15, 1961, in Warwick, R.I. She graduated from Old Dominion University, Norfolk, Va., in 1984 and was commissioned in December of that year.   (BARBARA WHITNEY)

Cunningham, Jack
One of John Smith's first acts following his election as leader of the Labour Party in July 1992 was to appoint John (generally known as Jack) Cunningham as shadow foreign secretary. It was a significant, if predictable, appointment: Cunningham shared Smith's pro-European views, and the two men were equally scornful of the left wing's antinuclear, anti-American rhetoric.

Cunningham was born in Newcastle upon Tyne in northern England on Aug. 4, 1939. He gained a doctorate in chemistry at Durham University and entered Parliament in 1970 as member for Whitehaven (later renamed Copeland, following boundary changes), Cumbria. His constituency contained the Sellafield nuclear power and reprocessing plant. In defending the interests of his constituents, Cunningham defended nuclear power against the antinuclear policies espoused by many left-wingers.

In 1976 Cunningham led the team that successfully campaigned among Labour MPs for the election of James Callaghan as party leader and prime minister. Cunningham's reward was his appointment later that year as a junior minister for energy, a position he held until Labour's defeat in the 1979 general election.

Cunningham coordinated Roy Hattersley's unsuccessful bid to become party leader in 1983, following Michael Foot's resignation, but directly afterward he joined the shadow cabinet of the victor, Neil Kinnock, as shadow environment secretary. In this post Cunningham led Labour's opposition to the legislation that produced the widely disliked poll tax. At the same time, he condemned a minority of local Labour councillors who declared their intention to break the law and not pay the new tax.

In 1989 Cunningham was switched to shadow leader of the House of Commons and party campaigns coordinator. His main task was to prepare the campaign for the general election of April 1992. Labour lost the election, but its campaign was widely regarded as the most professional ever run by a British party. Although Cunningham was not well known among the general public, his reputation among Labour MPs as a backroom fixer was greatly enhanced.   (PETER KELLNER)

Dawkins, John Sydney
John Dawkins consolidated his position as understudy to the prime minister with a strong performance as Australian treasurer throughout much of 1992. However, in November the ruling Australian Labor Party (ALP) came under fire when a Senate inquiry into government borrowing practices was launched at the request of the opposition. It was charged that Dawkins allegedly had concealed a $1.3 billion increase in borrowing by the former Labor government in Victoria to ensure a victory for that party in the November elections. Though Labor was defeated in a landslide, the controversy escalated and contributed to a weakness in the Australian dollar.

Dawkins administered a difficult portfolio in a period of high unemployment and economic recession. Earlier in the year, his high international prestige was underscored by the seriousness with which the British press received his attack on Tory politics in the United Kingdom. Dawkins viewed conditions in London under Prime Minister John Major as a model for life in Australia should the Australian Conservatives ever win office. In a vivid description to the Australian Parliament, Dawkins said, "At about 5 o'clock every evening there is a rush to see who can occupy the doorways of Australia House in London in order to have somewhere to sleep at night." Address-

ing Australia's Conservatives, Dawkins continued, "You can see the results of your policies every day in Britain as people go around looking for a doorway in which to huddle and go into subways to beg for some kind of support that their government will not give them."

Besides having responsibility for the economic recovery on which election victory depended, Dawkins assumed the responsibility of party fireman, hosing down injudicious remarks from Prime Minister Paul Keating and from other members of the party. Dawkins kept a tight rein on economic policy, forcing errant ministers to back down when they stepped out of line and criticized party orthodoxy. When Industry, Technology and Commerce Minister Sen. John Button criticized Dawkins' prediction of a 2% annual growth rate for Australia, Dawkins quickly retorted that the growth estimate was on target.

Dawkins was born on March 2, 1947, and was educated at Scotch College, Western Australia, and Roseworthy Agricultural College, South Australia. In 1977 he was elected member of the House of Representatives for Fremantle, Western Australia. During the 1980s Dawkins served in the Ministries of Trade, Youth Affairs, Finance, and Public Service. He also briefly held the seat of Tangney (1974–75).   (A.R.G. GRIFFITHS)

Dehaene, Jean-Luc
Flemish Christian Democrat Jean-Luc Dehaene, sworn in as Belgium's prime minister on March 7, 1992, was the third Belgian politician in as many months to seek a practicable coalition among the country's disparate political factions. General elections on Nov. 24, 1991, prompted by the collapse of the four-party government headed by Wilfried Martens, also a Flemish Christian Democrat, reduced the representation of the coalition parties without producing a clear alternative. Guy Verhofstadt, whose opposition Flemish Liberal Party showed the only gains in the parliament, failed to establish a government, as did Melchior Wathelet of the Christian Democrats' French-speaking wing. Martens, who had led nine different coalitions since 1979, stayed on as caretaker prime minister until Dehaene took office.

Dehaene was born in Montpellier, France, on Aug. 7, 1940. He was educated at the University of Namur, and he held various governmental advisory positions before serving as minister of social affairs and institutional reforms from 1981 to 1988. In the latter year, he became deputy prime minister after engineering a new coalition that retained Martens at its helm. Concurrently, Dehaene directed the Ministry of Communications and Institutional Reforms until he assumed the prime ministership.

An enthusiast of association football (soccer), Dehaene was an aggressive pragmatist on the political playing field, as attested by his nickname, "the Bulldozer." The entrenched factionalism he faced upon accepting King Baudouin's request to seek a coalition had led some observers to consider Belgium ungovernable. Some 39 parties had fielded candidates in the November elections. Constitutional reforms whereby the French and Flemish linguistic areas, along with Brussels, would acquire regional autonomy had been inaugurated in 1988 but remained controversial. Dehaene's primary goal was to secure a two-thirds majority in the 212-seat Chamber of Representatives in order to ensure that the federalization process continued. While his government represented a trimmer version of the previous four-party array, it fell significantly short of a majority. Dehaene hoped to enlist further support from opposition Liberals, the Green party, and moderate nationalists. During the first month of its installation, the Dehaene government prepared in three days an emergency budget for the remainder of the year, a swift measure necessitated by the long economic lapse following the inconclusive elections.   (JIM CARNES)

Devers, Gail
After she learned to walk again, Gail Devers ran faster than any other woman in the world. She won the Olympic gold medal in a 100-m dash of 10.82 seconds at Barcelona, Spain, on Aug. 1,

1992, less than 17 months after doctors considered amputating her swollen and bleeding feet. Even at the Olympics she felt the lingering effects of her virulent thyroid condition when she could not feel her feet in the starting blocks before her quarterfinal heat. That night she cried in her room. But days later Devers outran four pursuers in the closest group finish in Olympic history.

Devers had hoped to become the first woman to win Olympic gold in both the 100-m dash and the 100-m hurdles, but she finished fifth in the hurdles, historically her better event. Leading at the last hurdle, she clipped it with the heel of her lead leg and stumbled across the finish line. Her time was only 0.27 second slower than the American record of 12.48 seconds that she had set on Sept. 10, 1991, in Berlin.

Yolanda Gail Devers was born Nov. 19, 1966, in Seattle, Wash. As a senior 100-m runner for Sweetwater High School in National City, Calif., she finished second in the 1984 national junior championships and third in the Pan-American juniors. The next year, competing for UCLA, she finished sixth in both the 100- and 200-m dash and also in the 100-m hurdles in her first National Collegiate Athletic Association (NCAA) championships.

She won the NCAA 100-m dash in 1988 but concentrated on the hurdles for the Olympics after setting, on May 10, 1988, an American record of 12.61 seconds in the 100-m hurdles, which she held or shared for three years. Between her second-place finish in the Olympic trials and the Olympic Games that September in Seoul, South Korea, Devers' health began to deteriorate. It was two years before her hyperthyroidic condition was properly diagnosed as Graves' disease.

In the meantime, Devers suffered from migraine headaches, loss of sleep, fainting spells, muscle injuries, uncontrollable shaking, difficulty in breathing, hair loss, psoriasis, weight fluctuations, and brief losses of sight in her left eye. When a doctor finally diagnosed her condition, he said her thyroid had a cyst the size of a child's fist and that the cyst was 2½ weeks from becoming irreversible cancer.

Devers rejected the conventional treatment of beta blockers because they were banned for Olympic competitors. Radiation treatments controlled her thyroid condition but left her skin so sore that just walking made her feet blister, swell, and bleed. In March 1991, when she was just two days away from having both feet amputated, doctors finally determined that her radiation dosage was too high.

Later that month Devers began walking around the UCLA track in stocking feet. Within three months she had won the Athletics Congress championship with a time of 12.83 seconds in the 100-m hurdles. On Aug. 30, 1991, she finished second in the world championships at Tokyo. As 1992 began, Devers said, "There is no hurdle too high I can't conquer."   (KEVIN M. LAMB)

Durán Ballén, Sixto

When Sixto Durán Ballén was elected president of Ecuador on July 5, 1992, carrying 19 of 21 provinces, it represented the culmination of more than 40 years of public service. A strong proponent of free-market reform and foreign investment, Durán called for a "national consensus" and vowed to implement economic liberalization to address the country's rising inflation, burgeoning deficit, escalating external debt, and declining reserves. Such changes would place Ecuador more in the mainstream of Latin-American economic policy.

He had his work cut out for him. Durán's conservative Republican Unity Party (PUD) lacked a majority in Congress, and an expected and natural coalition with the conservative Social Christian Party (PSC) seemed doomed to failure because of the personal rivalry between Durán and Jaime Nebot, the PSC presidential candidate. Durán had been the PSC's candidate in 1988; he founded the PUD in 1991 when the PSC chose Nebot to contest the 1992 election. Although the two agreed on many substantive political issues and shared an ideological affinity, it seemed unlikely that they would come to agreement.

AP/WIDE WORLD

Durán's strength lay in his years of public service; he was the best-known Ecuadoran politician and exuded statesmanship. He was well respected in international financial communities and had close ties to Ecuador's business community. (His Cabinet was dominated by the business sector.) And he and his vice president, Alberto Dahik (leader of the Conservative Party, who did postgraduate work in economics at Princeton University), were expected to improve relations with the U.S.

Durán was born in 1922 in Boston, where his father was engaged in business. The family home was Quito, and the family was considered one of the "120 families" reputed to run Ecuador's economy. Durán attended U.S. schools and received a degree in architecture and urban planning from Columbia University, New York City. In 1951 he began his career as minister of public works, and in the 1960s he worked for the Inter-American Development Bank. Durán was mayor of Quito during the oil-boom years in the 1970s, overseeing its growth from sleepy highland town to prosperous capital city. The interests he developed then in public works projects and low-cost housing were reflected in his creation as president of a Ministry of Urban Development. (He also formed a Ministry of Information and Tourism to promote foreign investment.) In July 1978 Durán made his first bid for the presidency as the candidate of a coalition of rightist parties. He finished second in the initial round of voting; the second round was delayed nine months because of political tensions, and Durán lost that election by a large margin. He ran again in 1988 for the PSC, finishing third in the initial balloting.
(ELLEN FINKELSTEIN)

Eaton, Robert J.

Robert Eaton, a veteran of 29 years with the General Motors Corp. (GM), flew from Hungary to New York City on March 14, 1992, for a conference with the outside directors of the Chrysler Corp. and Lee A. Iacocca, Chrysler's public embodiment. Two days later Chrysler's full board of directors elected Eaton vice-chairman of the board and chief operating officer, and it was announced that he would succeed Iacocca as chairman of the board and chief executive officer on December 31. Many observers thought Eaton's position a delicate one. Chrysler had lost $795 million in 1991. The aging but flamboyant Iacocca, said to be reluctant to renounce any titles, would remain chairman of the executive committee of the board. Chrysler's president, Robert Lutz, acknowledged disappointment at being passed over. Many senior executives had strong loyalties to Lutz, whose skills were similar to Eaton's. Outwardly calm before a possible gathering storm, Eaton toured Chrysler factories, test-drove cars, answered questions, and appointed a team to study new production methods. In August, after

difficult negotiations, Eaton and Iacocca arranged new financing for the company.

Eaton was born in Buena Vista, Colo., on Feb. 13, 1940. In 1963 he received a B.S. in mechanical engineering from the University of Kansas and became a college-graduate-in-training for the Chevrolet Division of GM. He held several engineering jobs before attending the Executive Program at Dartmouth College, Hanover, N.H., in 1981. In 1982 he served briefly as director of quality and reliability for GM's Oldsmobile Division, then became a vice president of GM and head of its advanced engineering staff. In 1988 he became group executive in charge of technical staffs. In 1988, after working mostly in the Detroit area, he became president of GM Europe, a group of subsidiaries with headquarters near Zürich. He supervised the marketing of new lines and improved efficiency. His group performed well, earning a profit of $1,790,000,000 in 1991, while GM as a whole lost $4.5 billion. Eaton established a joint venture in Hungary in 1990 and negotiated an agreement for a joint venture in Poland in February 1992. On March 13, 1992, Eaton went to the Hungarian venture's factory to be present as the first car came off its production line. For political reasons, Hungary had been without a passenger-car industry for more than 25 years.   (CHARLES JOHNSON TAGGART)

Eckersley, Dennis Lee

As the American League's Most Valuable Player and Cy Young Award winner in 1992, Dennis Eckersley was a monument to control. He was a recovering alcoholic who had been sober for six years. He was a fastball specialist who kept his pitches in the strike zone. He was a dominant relief pitcher whose appearance almost invariably took the game out of the other team's reach.

Eckersley set a major-league baseball record by saving 36 games for his Oakland Athletics team in his first 36 opportunities through August 8. He finished the season with 51 saves, the second most in baseball history, in 54 opportunities. The A's won the first 52 games in which he pitched and finished with 65 victories in his 69 appearances and their fourth American League West Division championship in Eckersley's five full years as their closer—their best reliever. He entered games with 31 runners in scoring position and led the league by allowing only two of them (6.45%) to score.

As the team's closer since 1988, Eckersley rarely pitched more than an inning and usually did so with an opportunity for a save. From 1988 to 1992, Eckersley had 220 saves in 246 opportunities, 43 more saves than the runner-up in that period. He was the only pitcher ever with four seasons of more than 40 saves.

Eckersley's 7–1 record and 1.91 earned-run average (ERA) in 1992 gave him five-year totals of 24–9 and 1.90, with 378 strikeouts in 310 games and 359⅔ innings. His most remarkable statistic over that time was 38 walks, 12 of them intentional, or 0.95 walks per nine innings. He pitched 52 consecutive innings, facing 186 batters, without a walk through June 12, 1990. That was the year

AP/WIDE WORLD

his ERA was a career-low 0.61, and it was his fourth of five All-Star seasons, three as a reliever.

Before going to Oakland in 1987, Eckersley was a starter for 12 seasons with a record of 151–128. He was the only pitcher ever with both 100 saves and 100 complete games. He began his career with a shutout for Cleveland in 1975 and set a major league rookie record by not allowing an earned run in his first 28⅔ innings. Two years later his streak of 22⅓ hitless innings was the second longest in major-league history.

In 1986, though, Eckersley's career appeared to be washed up in a sea of alcohol. The Chicago Cubs soon traded him to the A's, who converted him to a relief pitcher. He became the closer after another player's midseason injury in 1987 and finished second the next year in voting for the Cy Young Award.

Eckersley was born Oct. 3, 1954, in Oakland, Calif. He played baseball, basketball, and football at Washington High School in nearby Fremont. During his major league career he had disappointments, blowing save opportunities in memorable A's defeats in the 1988 World Series and the 1992 American League championship series, but A's pitching coach Dave Duncan called him "the game's greatest closer." (KEVIN M. LAMB)

Egerszegi, Krisztina

She appeared almost relaxed as she swam, making barely a ripple in the water but whitecapped splashes in the record books. Krisztina Egerszegi's three gold medals at the 1992 Olympic Games in Barcelona, Spain, were the most by any woman in individual events. She won the 400-m individual medley in 4 min 36.54 sec and set Olympic records in both backstroke events, at 1 min 0.68 sec for the 100 m and 2 min 7.06 sec for the 200 m. She was named Female World Swimmer of the Year for the second straight year.

Egerszegi began dominating women backstrokers at age 16, when she won both events in the January 1991 world championships at Perth, Australia. Seven months later she broke venerable world records for both distances in the European championships at Athens. Her 1-min 0.31-sec time at 100 m on Aug. 22, 1991, cut 0.28 sec off the previous, seven-year-old record. Three days later, in the 200-m backstroke, she broke the five-year-old record of 2 min 8.60 sec by nearly two full seconds, finishing in 2 min 6.62 sec. She also had the fastest 1991 time in the world for the individual medley.

Egerszegi was born Aug. 16, 1974, in Budapest and was a national heroine almost from her first international competition at the 1987 European championships, when she finished fifth in the 200-m backstroke. The next year, at 14, she became the youngest swimming gold medalist in any Olympic Games when she won the 200-m backstroke at Seoul, South Korea, where she also finished second in the 100 m.

Egerszegi's Budapesti Spartacus sports club rewarded her world records in late 1991 by giving her a more generous contract and her family a new apartment after her father, Janos, the manager of a travel agency, said she would change affiliations. Hungarian swimming made a smooth transition from state subsidy to the private sponsorship of wealthy Gyorgy Zemplenyi, who boasted, "Twenty-four hours a day, my children train." Swimmers from that country of 10 million people won five Olympic golds in 1992 and set six world records in 1991, while the rest of the world set eight. But shortly after the Olympics, Zemplenyi disappeared under suspicion of embezzling $7 million. (KEVIN M. LAMB)

Fishburne, Larry

In 1992 Larry Fishburne witnessed two major firsts in his 20-year career as an actor—his first motion picture lead role in the cop-thriller *Deep Cover* and a Tony award for best featured actor in a play for his role in *Two Trains Running*. Although he had been appearing onstage, on television, and in the movies for some time, major success had long eluded him.

Laurence John Fishburne III was born in Augusta, Ga., on July 30, 1961, the only child of parents who later divorced. He was raised in

LISA ROSE—GLOBE PHOTOS

Brooklyn, N.Y., by his mother, who encouraged him with his acting and got him an agent. At the age of 11 he had a role on the soap opera "One Life to Live." From there he landed a role in his first feature film, *Cornbread, Earl and Me*. In 1976 he appeared in the Negro Ensemble Company's production of *Eden*. Then came the Francis Ford Coppola-directed epic *Apocalypse Now*, the film that Fishburne later called the most formative event of his life. He was a teenager when he went off to the Philippines to spend several months filming with Marlon Brando, Robert Duvall, and Martin Sheen. As a result of his experiences there, he returned to the U.S. full of self-confidence and ready to take on Hollywood.

What he found was that he could not get work. "I think a lot of people thought I was crazy, and I probably was," he said later. Coppola was not one of those people, however, and he later directed Fishburne in three other pictures. Between films, Fishburne kept busy with television work. Among his roles was the recurring part of Cowboy Curtis on the children's program "Pee-wee's Playhouse." There he met John Singleton, who was working as a production assistant. Impressed with Fishburne, Singleton had him in mind for the role of Furious Styles when he wrote and directed his first film, *Boyz N the Hood*. Fishburne's portrayal of an inner-city father attempting to steer his son clear of the temptations of the streets helped propel Singleton to an Academy Award nomination for best director of 1991.

As Russell Stevens, Jr., in *Deep Cover*, Fishburne realized his first lead role. "I'm glad it took this long. I probably wouldn't have been able to deal with it when I was frustrated about it," he said. His performance in the Broadway production of *Two Trains Running* was equally rewarding. The sixth installment in playwright August Wilson's anthology of African-American experience during each decade of the 20th century, *Two Trains Running* was nominated for four Tony awards almost immediately after it opened, including the one Fishburne subsequently won. He also garnered an Outer Critic's Circle Award, a Drama Desk Award, and a Theatre World Award for his performance. (ANTHONY L. GREEN)

Foster, Jodie

In 1992 actress Jodie Foster won a second Academy Award for best actress for her portrayal of Clarice Starling, a novice—yet ambitious—FBI agent with a traumatic, hidden past who must catch a serial killer with the aid of another serial killer—Hannibal Lecter, a brilliant psychologist—in Jonathan Demme's dark psychological thriller *The Silence of the Lambs*.

During most of her career Foster chose to portray people who were, in one way or another, outsiders in society—the disinherited and disil-

lusioned. "Part of my agenda . . . is out of some kind of need to save them," she explained in a *Rolling Stone* interview. Her portrayal of a rape victim in *The Accused*, a 1988 sleeper that became one of the year's most talked-about films, was her first Oscar-winning performance.

Alicia Christian ("Jodie") Foster's parents divorced before she was born in Los Angeles, on Nov. 19, 1962, the youngest of four children. A gifted child, Foster began talking at nine months and could read by the age of three. She launched her career in show business as the bare-bottomed Coppertone child seen in television commercials. By age five Foster could understand scripts, and she subsequently appeared in more than 45 commercials. She made her acting debut in May 1969 on television in an episode of "Mayberry, R.F.D." and appeared in more than a dozen television programs during the next five years.

In 1972 Foster was hospitalized after being mauled by a circus lion during the filming of *Napoleon and Samantha*, in which she made her motion-picture debut. Undaunted, she continued acting and appeared in several films, among them *Alice Doesn't Live Here Anymore* (1974). Her portrayal of Iris, a 12-year-old prostitute, in *Taxi Driver* (1976) generated much controversy but nonetheless earned her an Oscar nomination as best supporting actress. After roles in *Bugsy Malone* (1976) and *Candleshoe* (1977), Foster earned favourable reviews when she starred in her first nonjuvenile role, *The Little Girl Who Lives Down the Lane* (1977).

In June 1980 Foster graduated at the head of her class from the Lycée Français in Los Angeles, and she enrolled at Yale University that fall. During her freshman year she became the object of national media attention when on March 30, 1981, John W. Hinckley, Jr.—whom she had never met—tried to kill Pres. Ronald Reagan, apparently in an effort to impress her. She acted in a few films during her tenure at Yale and in 1985 graduated magna cum laude with a B.A. degree in literature. Foster formed her own production company and made her motion-picture directorial debut in 1991 with *Little Man Tate*, a story about a child prodigy. Her latest role was in *Sommersby*, a film set immediately after the U.S. Civil War.
(EDWARD PAUL MORAGNE)

Gore, Albert H., Jr.

On Nov. 3, 1992, Sen. Albert Gore, Jr., of Tennessee was elected vice president of the United States. He thus succeeded where his own father had failed and completed the country's first baby-boomer ticket with his running mate, Bill Clinton (*q.v.*).

Gore was born on March 31, 1948, in Washington, D.C., to Albert Gore, Sr., and Pauline La Fon Gore. The elder Gore was then serving his 10th year in what would be 14 years in the U.S. House of Representatives as a Democrat from Tennessee. He later served three terms as a U.S. senator and was a strong contender for vice president in 1956 but was not selected.

Gore, Jr., received a B.A. degree cum laude in government from Harvard University in 1969. He was drafted for military service in Vietnam, creating a dilemma for him and his family; like his father, he opposed the war, a position that he thought might jeopardize his father's 1970 reelection chances. Gore decided to serve (though his father was narrowly defeated), and when he completed his tour of duty in 1971, he joined the staff of the *Tennessean*, a Nashville newspaper. A devout Baptist, he studied philosophy and phenomenology at Vanderbilt University's Graduate School of Religion, Nashville (1971–72); he also attended Vanderbilt's Law School (1974–76).

When Democratic Rep. Joe L. Evins unexpectedly decided in 1976 not to seek reelection from the state's 4th District, Gore jumped into politics; he won the primary over seven other candidates and was an easy victor in the general election. He coasted to three reelections and in 1984 won a Senate seat when Republican Majority Leader Howard Baker declined to run for another term. Calling himself a "raging moderate," Gore focused much of his attention on health-related and environmental issues; in the House he was

a key player in the development and passage of the 1980 "Superfund" bill to clean up chemical spills, and he sponsored the Organ Procurement and Transplantation Act of 1984. His mastery of defense issues, particularly nuclear disarmament, brought more national attention.

In 1988 Gore ran for president, running a credible campaign in Southern primaries before self-destructing in New York City by aligning himself with Mayor Ed Koch against Jesse Jackson. The following year his six-year-old son, Albert III, was struck by a car and nearly killed. The months of recovery and extensive surgery redefined Gore's priorities and, according to many, helped him mature into a "ready for prime time" political player. Nevertheless, he decided against a 1992 presidential run and, in his son's hospital room, began writing his examination of environmental issues, *Earth in the Balance* (published in early 1992). In 1990 he won reelection and was one of only 10 Senate Democrats who voted to support Pres. George Bush's use of force to expel Iraqi Pres. Saddam Hussein's invasion troops from Kuwait.

By selecting Gore, Clinton shored up his weak areas: military service, foreign policy, and the environment. Gore also gave Clinton an edge in the "family values" war waged by the Republicans, for the campaign of his wife, "Tipper," to get record companies to voluntarily rate and label recordings with sexually explicit lyrics, a detriment for her husband in 1988, was this time seen as a plus.

(BETSY ROSSEN ELLIOT)

Hosokawa, Morihiro

Morihiro Hosokawa, an 18th-generation descendant of a feudal warlord in Kyushu, southern Japan, quit the ruling Liberal Democratic Party (LDP) and formed his own party two months before the July 26, 1992, upper house election. In his view, the current government was incurably corrupt, too centralized, and inefficient. "I've started playing solo," Hosokawa said in announcing formation of Nihon Shinto (Japan New Party; JNP). He then added that he hoped eventually to be part of "a large orchestra." Two days later he published a 12-page manifesto that depicted Japan's political system as moribund and out of touch with reality. He said the central government was so busy interfering with local governments that it was losing its sense of priority. Its success in generating economic expansion, Hosokawa believed, was now stifling progress. He cited the evolution of Japanese educational standards as an example of what needed changing. Because the system, according to Hosokawa, produced uniform academic achievement, it discouraged individual talent and independent thinking. On the basis of his personal experience as a prefectural governor, Hosokawa also complained that local officials had to get approval from central authorities for such trivial matters as moving a bus stop and laying out pigpens.

Hosokawa, tall and soft-spoken, was born in Kumamoto, Japan, on Jan. 14, 1938. His grandfather Prince Fumimaro Konoe was twice chosen prewar prime minister. His failure to check Japanese imperialism in East Asia led to World War II. Konoe committed suicide after the war, shortly before he was to be arrested and charged with war crimes.

Hosokawa graduated from Sophia University in Tokyo, then worked for the influential newspaper *Asahi shimbun.* When he was elected to the first of two six-year terms in the upper house of the Diet (parliament) in 1971, he was the youngest person ever to reach that position. He then won the governorship of Kumamoto prefecture (1983–91), where he pursued an aggressive economic policy and strengthened environmental laws. Beneficiaries of this policy include the Minamata victims of mercury poisoning, who had eaten contaminated fish. Hosokawa also fostered regional activism and became chairman of the "Affluent Life-style" section of the Council to Promote Administrative Reform. Its task was to recommend to the prime minister ways to improve the domestic standard of living. But the recommendations, Hosokawa said, were sabotaged by those who were afraid that such measures would reduce their power to make discretionary decisions. This convinced him that winning control over policy-making would be a Herculean task.

The JNP fielded 16 candidates in the July 26 election, but it won only 4 of the 127 contested seats. Hosokawa nevertheless expressed optimism as the party began preparations for the pending lower house elections; the newly elected JNP parliamentarians were equally upbeat, describing themselves as "proud independent amateurs."

(KAY K. TATEISHI)

Indurain, Miguel

His 1992 victories in the Tour of Italy and the Tour de France made Miguel Indurain only the sixth cyclist to win both races in the same year, and he won them both by enormous margins. He defeated the runner-up in Italy by 5 min 14 sec on June 14 and then outraced the field in France by 4 min 35 sec on July 26. He was unable to become cycling's third triple-crown winner when he finished sixth in the world road-race championship in his native Spain, but he was in the lead pack of 17 racers at the finish. Even so, with the Spanish road-racing championship and victory in Spain's Tour of Catalonia, Indurain was his sport's top-ranked athlete in points and the recipient of *VeloNews* magazine's International Cyclist of the Year award.

In the Tour of Italy, he led from the third stage through the end to become its first Spanish winner. In the Tour de France, his second consecutive victory was the fastest in the race's 79 years, averaging 39.5 km/h (24.5 mph) over 3,983 km (2,475 mi) in 23 days. "It was easier than last year," Indurain said. "Since my first win, I've gained an enormous calm that keeps me cool in handling the stages and warding off the attacks of others."

Indurain was always known for his laid-back, smooth pedaling style. He won his fourth and fifth consecutive Tour de France time-trial stages, always his strength, where cyclists race against the clock with no one benefiting from a competitor's slipstream. His 49.046-km/h (30.48-mph) speed over 65 km (40.4 mi) in the ninth stage beat the field by three minutes and prompted reigning world champion Gianni Bugno of Italy to say, "He must be from another planet." Then his 52.35-km/h (32.53-mph) speed in the later 64-km (39.8-mi) time trial was the race's best ever in a time trial of more than 50 km (31.07 mi).

Indurain was born July 16, 1964, in Villava, Spain, near Pamplona in the province of Navarra, one of five children of Basque farmers. He started racing at age 11, when his cousins persuaded him to compete in a nearby race and he finished second. He won his next race, and cycling displaced running and soccer to become his best sport. After winning several races a year at lower competition levels, he won the Spanish amateur road championship in 1983 and competed in the 1984 Los Angeles Olympics before turning professional

in 1985. In 1989 he won a mountain stage of the Tour de France and finished 17th. The next year he finished 10th and likely would have been in the top three if he had not sacrificed himself as a support rider for Banesto team leader Pedro Delgado.   (KEVIN M. LAMB)

Ingraham, Hubert

Ousting the longest-serving political leader in the Western Hemisphere (except for Cuba's Fidel Castro), Hubert Ingraham became only the second prime minister of The Bahamas since the 700-island nation achieved independence from Great Britain in 1973. Ingraham defeated Sir Lynden Pindling, who had long been accused of enriching himself by allowing Colombian drug dealers to use The Bahamas for drug-trafficking purposes.

A 45-year-old lawyer who had once been Sir Lynden's political protégé, Ingraham had been dismissed from the Cabinet in 1986 for accusing his former mentor and fellow leaders of the ruling Progressive Liberal Party of corruption. In the August 1992 election, Ingraham's rival Free National Movement won 31 of the 49 seats in the House of Assembly. The new prime minister profited from a strategic mistake by Sir Lynden, who scheduled the election during the summer, when many Bahamian young people were home from college. Many first-time voters apparently supported Ingraham as the leader better able to revive the ailing tourist trade and thereby provide more jobs. The tourist trade is, by far, the nation's biggest employer and the most important revenue producer, but hotel workers had been laid off by the hundreds as The Bahamas struggled to compete with other vacation spots.

To many older voters, Sir Lynden was the father of his country, but accusations of bribe taking had begun to surface in the early 1980s. An official commission of inquiry in 1984 said that Sir Lynden and his wife had at least $3.5 million in the bank, a sum that could not be explained by the prime minister's official compensation. For the better part of a decade, officials of the U.S. Drug Enforcement Administration had complained about Bahamian involvement in the international drug trade.

Immediately following his swearing in, Ingraham predicted that his country's relations with the U.S. "can only get warmer" as he proceeded to crack down on drugs and to encourage foreign investment, but he rejected any notion that his government would extradite Sir Lynden or any other member of the defeated Progressive Liberal Party to the U.S. to face drug-trafficking charges. He promised his people a more open government. Citing his own rise from humble beginnings (his father was a stevedore and his mother a maid), he vowed that his government would "assure equality of opportunity" for every citizen. "I will be Prime Minister for all in our Bahamaland."

(JEROLD L. KELLMAN)

Javed Miandad

There are few more glorious sights in the game of cricket than Javed Miandad in full flow. In 1992 the Pakistan right-hander was already the leading Test match run scorer for his country, with 8,465 runs at an average of 54.26, but his quick footwork, strong wrists, and cavalier aggression had made him one of the most attractive batsmen in the world, as well as one of the most prolific. He was one of the fastest runners between the wicket and, because of the quickness of his eye and foot, one of the best players against spin bowling.

A lively character whose provocative manner was not always appreciated by his opponents, he was involved in several on-field incidents, notably when clashing with the Australian fast bowler Dennis Lillee. That love of controversy hindered his career as Pakistan captain, though he began to show genuine skill as a leader in taking his side to victory over England in the 1992 Test series, and there were signs that he was becoming less volatile and more responsible in his middle age.

Javed was born on June 12, 1957. As a batsman he did not take long to show his promise. He made his first-class debut at the age of 16 and marked his first Test, two years later, by hitting 163 against New Zealand. Soon after, at the age

of 19 years 4 months, he became the youngest
player ever to score a Test match double hundred.
With his flashing cover drives and square cuts,
he had made six Test centuries before his 22nd
birthday. His talent was quickly recognized by the
English county Sussex and later by Glamorgan,
for which he played perhaps the innings of his
life, an unbeaten 200 on a turning pitch against
Essex in 1981.

His critics said that too many of his 23 Test
centuries were made inside Pakistan, where the
conditions were advantageous for batting and the
umpires tended to be favourable, but he had
made enough runs in Australia, England, and the
West Indies against the best bowlers to refute
the allegations. Despite his many record-breaking
feats, the stocky and strong Pakistan captain was
still only 35, and he had the ability and the time
to become the highest run scorer in Test history.

(ANDREW LONGMORE)

Jemison, Mae
Ever since she was a small child, Mae Jemison
had looked toward the sky and wondered what
was out there. At 10:23 AM on Sept. 12, 1992, she
got her chance to take a closer look when she became the first African-American woman launched
into space. Although it took only minutes after
liftoff for the seven-member crew of the space
shuttle *Endeavour*—which also included the first
married couple in space—to reach orbit far above
the Earth, Jemison's journey to the launchpad at
the Kennedy Space Center had begun some 33
years earlier.

Mae Carol Jemison was born on Oct. 17, 1956,
in Decatur, Ala., the youngest of three children.
Her parents, who always took care to encourage
and support their children's interests and abilities,
moved the family to Chicago when Jemison was
three to take advantage of educational opportunities. There she nurtured her love for science
and the arts by making great use of the city's museums, libraries, and schools, unknowingly laying
the foundation for a career that would later propel her not only into space but into the history
books as well.

Jemison graduated from high school as an honour student in 1973 and entered Stanford University on a National Achievement Scholarship
at the age of 16. Four years later she entered
Cornell University Medical School, New York
City, having received both a B.S. in chemical
engineering and a B.A. in Afro-American studies from Stanford. After obtaining her M.D. in
1981, she completed a year of internship. From
1983 to mid-1985 Jemison worked as the Area
Peace Corps Medical Officer for Sierra Leone
and Liberia. While in Africa, she developed and
participated in research projects on hepatitis B
vaccine, schistosomiasis, and rabies. In 1985 she
returned to the U.S. and worked as a general

NASA

practitioner in Los Angeles, at the same time
attending graduate engineering classes. During
this time she was accepted into the National
Aeronautics and Space Administration (NASA)
space program. After the *Challenger* accident in
January 1986, NASA temporarily suspended astronaut selection, but once the selection process
was restarted, Jemison renewed her application
and was chosen in June 1987. She was assigned in
1989 to STS-47 Spacelab-J, a joint U.S.-Japanese
mission. As science mission specialist, Jemison
was responsible for conducting research on space
motion sickness and how it could be avoided. She
also served as coinvestigator in bone cell research
and oversaw an experiment that studied the effect
of weightlessness on the development of frogs
from eggs to tadpoles.

After just over 190 hours in space, *Endeavour* returned to Earth, NASA's most successful
mission to date. Jemison put her name back
into the pool of astronauts eligible for upcoming
space flights and said that should there ever be a
manned mission to Mars, she would be ready.

(ANTHONY L. GREEN)

Josephson, Karen and Sarah
When the name of the game is perfectly matched
movements, the ideal partner would be a mirror
image. Karen and Sarah Josephson were as close
to the ideal as possible. When they won the
1992 Olympic gold medal for the synchronized
swimming duet competition, the world was literally seeing double. Karen and Sarah are identical
twins. Their August 7 victory marked the U.S.
dynamic duo's 16th consecutive championship—a
record in the sport's history.

The Js, as the twins were known on the synchronized swimming circuit, received four perfect
marks for technical merit and four more 10s
for artistic impression, earning a total score of
99.600 points for their five-minute Olympic routine. Added to the average of their individual
compulsory figure marks, they tallied a winning
total of 192.175 points, beating Canadian identical twins Penny and Vicky Vilagos by 2.8 points.

Sarah Josephson was born seven minutes after
Karen on Jan. 10, 1964, in Bristol, Conn. The sisters began their 22-year synchronized swimming
partnership with lessons at the Bristol Girls Club,
later joining the Rocky Hill Spindrifts and then
the Hamden Heronettes. At 12 the Josephsons
entered their first senior nationals synchronized
swim meet, and at 16 they joined the U.S. national team.

In 1985, after four years as roommates at Ohio
State University, the twins graduated with almost
identical grade-point averages, Karen earning a
degree in biochemistry and Sarah one in genetics. Both had been named Outstanding Scholar-
Athletes four times, and each had been a three-
time recipient of the U.S. Synchronized Swimming
Athlete of the Year Award. After graduation the
Josephsons moved to Concord, Calif., joining the
Walnut Creek Aquanuts, an Olympian-coached
club specializing in synchronized swimming training. By 1986 the Js had decided to stop competing
as soloists, instead concentrating on their duet
performances.

After winning the silver medal in the 1988
Olympics at Seoul, South Korea, the twins retired for what turned out to be only a year.
At their first international competition after returning from retirement, the 1991 world championships, they recorded the highest overall total
score, 199.762 points, for a duet in international
synchronized swimming history and captured their
first world duet title. Thereafter, they dominated
the sport, remaining undefeated after their return
to competition.

Upon achieving their ultimate goal in the 1992
Olympics, the Josephsons retired from competition. Although they planned to occasionally swim
in exhibitions to promote their sport and for in-
structional clinics, they applied to medical schools,
ready to focus on interests away from the pool.

(BEVERLY E. SORKIN)

Keating, Paul John
Paul Keating became the new Australian Labor
Party (ALP) prime minister in December 1991

following a party room decision, which he largely
engineered, to replace an old leader, Robert
Hawke, before he became—in Keating's words—
as old as Methuselah. In his first months as prime
minister, Keating injected new vitality into the
parliamentary process. Against all predictions but
his own, Keating turned around the tide of disapproval for his government in the early months of
1992. He set forth a bold new vision of Australia's
eventually becoming a republic under its own flag,
and he established links with Asia and the U.S.
while largely ignoring European affairs. He sometimes forgot, however, that the general public was
more concerned with the record unemployment
figures than with his stinging criticisms, which he
delivered during debates with the opposition. In
October Keating made his biggest blunder since
1986, when he described Australia as heading for
"banana republic" status. He claimed in Parliament that the recession was "long over." This
remark was seized upon by newspaper editors,
one of whom commented that, expressed as it
was, it took on the proportions of other notoriously extravagant and insensitive Keating errors.
It was, said the *Advertiser,* "a damaging and revealing mistake. Damaging, because millions of
Australians are still hurting from a recession that
may be technically behind us but which in real
terms is still very much with us. Revealing, because in its very exclusiveness and insensitivity it
serves as an insight into the pressures that Keating must be feeling." Near the end of the year,
Keating's approval rating plummeted.

On a personal level, Keating experienced in
1992 what he said was his most moving day in
public life. At a ceremony on the Kokoda trail
in Papua New Guinea, Keating knelt to kiss the
stone base of a memorial to an Australian soldier
who had died fighting the Japanese at Kokoda.
Keating, standing on the bamboo dais with a garland of boar's teeth and tusks around his neck,
mystically declared that it was on the Kokoda
trail that young Australians decided to confirm
the tradition of heroic resistance that Australian
soldiers exhibited in the World War I battle of
Gallipoli.

Keating was born Jan. 18, 1944, and was educated at De La Salle College, Bankstown. He was
an industrial advocate with the Federated Municipal and Shire Employees Union before launching
a political career. He was elected member of the
House of Representatives for Blaxland in 1969
and served (1979-83) as president of the New
South Wales branch of the ALP. Keating was
minister for Northern Australia (1975-83) and
shadow treasurer (1983) before becoming federal
treasurer in 1983.   (A.R.G. GRIFFITHS)

King, B.B.
It was said that blues musicians fall into two
categories: B.B. King and everyone else. A bit
too pop for traditionalists and too bluesy for pop
radio, King, a self-described "in-betweener," became one of America's—and the world's—most
well-known and respected blues artists. In his 45
years in the music business, the singer-guitarist
and songwriter recorded more than 50 albums,
performed everywhere from the "chitlin circuit"
to Carnegie Hall, won five Grammy awards—including a Lifetime Achievement award—and was
inducted into the Rock and Roll Hall of Fame.
He played with such superstar musicians as Sting
and Stevie Wonder and toured with the Rolling
Stones and, more recently, U2—he recorded the
hit song "When Loves Comes to Town" with the
latter group. These accomplishments and acco-
lades, just a few among many, were remarkable
in that they were earned and received by a man
who came from a very humble beginning.

Riley B. King's musical journey started on Sept.
16, 1925, in Itta Bena, Miss. His parents divorced
when he was four years old, and his mother died
when he was nine. King was left to fend for himself, working on a plantation until his father took
him to Indianola, Miss., five years later. After an
uncle taught him basic chords, King became interested in playing guitar. In 1947 he hitchhiked
north to Memphis, Tenn., where he worked as a
disc jockey at WDIA, a black radio station, and
became known as Riley King, the Blues Boy from

JULIUS DOMONEY—CAMERA PRESS/GLOBE PHOTOS

Beale Street (later shortened to Blues Boy King and then to B.B. King). He started recording on the RPM label in 1949, and by 1950 his recording of "Three O'Clock Blues" had gone to the top of the rhythm and blues charts. After quitting his disc jockey job, he performed with Lucille—his famous musical partner, a guitar—in small clubs and venues around the country; his record of 342 one-nighters in one year still stood in 1992.

King signed with the ABC-Paramount record label in 1961 and in 1964 recorded *Live at the Regal*, considered a classic album. His first big hit single, "The Thrill Is Gone," climbed up the pop charts in 1970. He was named the world's top blues guitarist that same year by *Guitar Player* magazine. His most recent release, *King of the Blues*, a four-compact-disc retrospective collection spanning 40 years of his recorded output, appeared on the MCA label in October 1992. Still, King considered *There Is Always One More Time*, an album he recorded in 1991, his best work. At age 67 he continued to tour throughout the country and performed in more than 250 one-nighters. A confirmed workaholic, King admitted that he might not be the hardest-working man in show business, "but I'm in the top five."

(EDWARD PAUL MORAGNE)

Krzyzewski, Mike

Not only did coach Mike Krzyzewski lead Duke University to consecutive national basketball championships in 1991 and 1992, he did it, as Indiana coach Bob Knight put it, "with college students." His players excelled in the classroom as well as on the court. Krzyzewski insisted on this. He would not allow Duke to hang the banner for its national runner-up finish in 1990 because two of that team's players did not graduate.

With its 71–51 victory over Michigan on April 6, Duke became the first school in 19 years to win two National Collegiate Athletic Association (NCAA) basketball tournaments in a row, and it was only the second defending champion in that period to reach the championship game. "Coach K wouldn't let us lose," guard Bobby Hurley said of Duke's one-point halftime deficit. The Blue Devils ranked number one the entire 1991–92 season and finished with a won-lost record of 34–2 to follow their 32–7 record in 1990–91, when they defeated Kansas 72–65 for the championship.

In the seven seasons beginning with 1985–86, Duke reached the tournament's Final Four six times and finished the 1986 and 1992 regular seasons ranked number one. Krzyzewski had a seven-year record of 212–45 (.825) with various Coach of the Year honours in 1986, 1989, 1991, and 1992; his five consecutive Final Four appearances in 1988–92 ranked him second to former UCLA coach John Wooden. He finished the 1991–92 season with records of 370–169 (.686) for his 17-year head-coaching career and 33–7 for his nine NCAA tournaments.

Michael William Krzyzewski was born in Chicago on Feb. 13, 1947. At Weber High School, he was senior class president and led Chica-

go's Catholic League in basketball scoring for two years. He played guard for Knight's Army team, which he captained as a senior in 1968–69. He coached service teams and the U.S. Military Academy Prep School for five years, then was Knight's assistant at Indiana for one season before Army hired Krzyzewski in 1975. He was a surprising selection in 1980 to coach Duke in the Atlantic Coast Conference—on Knight's advice—and his career there began shakily with no recruits in 1981 and a combined record of 21–34 the next two seasons. But Krzyzewski's fourth Duke team, in 1983–84, went 24–10 and began a streak of nine consecutive seasons with at least 20 victories and NCAA tournament berths. His 1985–86 team went 37–3 and set an NCAA record for victories. He became so successful a national recruiter that the top seven players on his 1991–92 team were from seven states.

The professional Boston Celtics tried to hire Krzyzewski in 1990. But he decided, "I'm not just a basketball coach. . . . I want to be a teacher and work with kids and see them grow up."

(KEVIN M. LAMB)

Leno, Jay

On Monday, May 25, 1992, with a strange succession of opening curtains, with Branford Marsalis as music director, and minus a sidekick, comedian Jay Leno made his premiere bow as the fourth host of television's "Tonight" show. His predecessor, Johnny Carson, had ended his 30-year reign as the king of late-night television talk shows the previous Friday.

James Douglas Muir Leno was born on April 28, 1950, in New Rochelle, N.Y., and was raised in Andover, Mass. Unlike those who derive much of their humour from difficult childhoods, Leno had a happy one with his parents—Catherine Muir, a Scottish immigrant, and Angelo Leno, an insurance salesman and the son of Italian immigrants.

By his sophomore year at Boston's Emerson College, he was performing at night spots in that city and in New York City on weekends. After graduation he toiled in the trenches of comedy life, making the rounds of bar mitzvahs, birthday parties, coffeehouses, strip joints, rock concerts, and Playboy clubs.

Working as a part-time mechanic and automobile delivery man, Leno frequently conveyed cars to clients in New York City, where he performed in such comedy clubs as the Bitter End and Catch a Rising Star. He became friends with other young comedians, including Robert Klein, Freddie Prinze, and David Brenner, who urged him to move to Manhattan. His comedy evolved from telling jokes to telling stories, especially about the funny side of everyday life, in the style of the "observational school" popularized by such comics as Klein, George Carlin, and Richard Pryor. In 1974 he moved to Los Angeles and auditioned at the Comedy Store, where he eventually met another comedian, David Letterman, whose career Leno was able to influence. He introduced Letterman to Jimmie Walker, then the star of the television series "Good Times," who added Letterman to his staff of gag writers. At the Comedy Store he also met Mavis Nicholson, an aspiring writer, whom he married in 1980.

By the mid-1970s Leno had appeared on the "Merv Griffin" and "Mike Douglas" television shows. On March 2, 1977, he made the first of many appearances on the "Tonight" show. But it was the heavy travel schedule to college campuses and comedy clubs in the 1980s, coupled with his frequent guest shots on "Late Night with David Letterman," that sent his popularity skyrocketing. In 1987 Carson named him permanent guest host of "Tonight," appreciating that Leno had an appeal to both the hip and the ordinary. Ironically, Letterman was said to be miffed with NBC for selecting Leno over him as the new host. In December Letterman agreed to move to CBS for $16 million a year to compete directly with Leno in the 11:30 PM EST slot.

Leno's passions included his wife, vintage automobiles, motorcycles, and the Samuel Jared Kushnick Foundation of pediatric AIDS services and research (all royalties from his best-selling *Headlines* books went to that charity). By late

1992 his future on "Tonight" had been further challenged by myriad talk shows; scandal over the firing of his manager, Helen Kushnick, as the show's executive producer; and a reported feud with Arsenio Hall. (BETSY ROSSEN ELLIOT)

Lineker, Gary Winston

Among high-profile professional soccer players Gary Lineker was almost unique. Nothing appeared to have tarnished the reputation of this squeaky-clean "Mr. Nice Guy," the devoted family man. This image mirrored his exemplary conduct on the field; he had never been cautioned or sent off in more than 600 matches. But the fact that he enjoyed a lucrative income was a surprise to the schoolteacher who told him he would never earn his living from the game.

Expert advice had helped to fashion this quiet-spoken young man with a boyish grin into a sports star, but there was sufficient suitable raw material to work on. Lineker was born in Leicester, England, on Nov. 30, 1960. He joined his local club, Leicester City, as an apprentice in July 1977 and turned professional in December 1978 at 18. Yet he was no instant, overnight success. As a schoolboy he had a reputation for scoring goals and having a keen eye for a goal chance, but Leicester had difficulty in finding a role for him except playing wide on the right flank. Indeed, he did not establish himself as a more central striker until the 1981–82 season, when Leicester was still in the Second Division.

During the next season, with Leicester promoted to the First Division, Lineker improved his close control, allowing him to dictate the point of attack. With his scoring knack, pace, and razor-sharp awareness, half chances were turned into gilt-edged ones. After topping the Leicester goal scorers for four seasons, he was traded to Everton for £800,000. His international career took off during the 1986 World Cup finals, when he was top scorer for England with six goals. Barcelona, managed by Terry Venables, then paid £2,750,000 for Lineker, and his game developed further in Spain until differences with new coach Johan Cruyff led to an eventual move to Venables' Tottenham Hotspur in June 1989 for £1.2 million.

In 1992 he was elected Player of the Year by

CAMERA PRESS/GLOBE PHOTOS

the Football Writers Association. It was his second such trophy; in 1986 he had won both that award and one from the Professional Footballers Association. Lineker achieved his crowning glory, however, when he was named an Officer of the Order of the British Empire in the 1992 New Year's Honours list. His financial future was secured by a contract worth £3 million to play in Japan in 1993 for Nagoya Grampus Eight. His international competition in 1992 ended in disappointment, however. While captaining England in the European championship against Sweden, he was withdrawn when, having scored 48 goals in 80 appearances, he still needed one goal to equal Bobby Charlton's record. Nevertheless, his overall tally of 322 goals in 631 games remained a remarkable average. (JACK ROLLIN)

MacKenzie, Kelvin

On the day the Conservatives won the U.K.'s April 1992 general election, the front page of Britain's biggest-selling daily newspaper, *The Sun*, depicted Labour leader Neil Kinnock with his head inside a light bulb and told its readers: "If Kinnock wins today will the last person to leave Britain please turn out the lights?"

That front page—brash, memorable, and vicious—was the brainchild of Kelvin MacKenzie, *The Sun*'s editor. Two days after the election, he claimed that *The Sun* had won the election for Prime Minister John Major. Yet six months later, his tabloid newspaper was attacking Major with the same verve with which it had supported him in April. It accused him of weak leadership and of pursuing policies that were making Britain's recession worse. For the second time in a year, MacKenzie had produced evidence of his power to produce political shock waves, for no politician could ignore a newspaper that was bought by almost 4 million people daily and read by 10 million—one-quarter of the country's electorate.

MacKenzie was born in London on Oct. 22, 1946. Like Major, he was educated at state-funded schools in south London, where he passed few exams and learned to despise Britain's traditional elite groups. He left school at 17 and became a reporter—like both his parents and both his brothers. He joined *The Sun* in 1973 and quickly attracted the attention of its owner, Rupert Murdoch, who shared his antielite sentiments and sent him for a spell in the mid-1970s to the *New York Post* as managing editor.

MacKenzie took over as editor of *The Sun* in 1981 and quickly stamped his mark on the paper. One trademark was jingoism; during the 1982 Falkland Islands/Islas Malvinas war, *The Sun* announced the sinking of the Argentine ship *General Belgrano* under the headline "Gotcha." In 1990 it exclaimed to the president of the European Commission: "Up Yours Delors." MacKenzie was criticized for publishing a series of false stories. The newspaper had to pay £1 million to the rock singer Elton John for publishing untrue stories about his private life, and it shocked doctors by proclaiming, "Straight sex cannot give you AIDS—official." But MacKenzie followed the adage: "Never complain, never explain." As long as *The Sun* remained Britain's most popular daily newspaper, MacKenzie's general response to his critics—who included most other editors—was: "Up yours."   (PETER KELLNER)

Major, John Roy

In 1992 John Major confounded most political observers by leading the U.K.'s Conservative Party to its fourth consecutive election victory—and then confounded many political friends by his faltering judgment in the months that followed.

During the first three months of the year, Major seemed likely to lose power. Parliament was close to its five-year maximum term, and there had been speculation for months on when Major would call a general election. On March 11 he called it for April 9, even though his party lagged behind Labour in the opinion polls. Even when the polls continued to show the Conservatives lagging, he told interviewers that he was "stone-cold certain" that his party would win. In the event, it did, although with a greatly reduced majority.

After his election triumph, Major turned his attention to events in Europe. From July to December 1992, the U.K. enjoyed its turn to hold the presidency of the European Communities. Major wanted to assert his credentials as an international statesman by building on the Maastricht Treaty, agreed to the previous December. But he was unable to ward off ferocious resistance to the treaty from a minority of Conservative members of Parliament, and he was saved from a humiliating defeat in the House of Commons only by the Liberal Democratic Party, which voted with the government in a crucial vote on the treaty on November 4.

Major's handling of the European issue provoked widespread criticism—as did other aspects of his leadership. In particular, he attracted much of the blame for overseeing economic policies that deepened the U.K.'s recession—and then failing

to dismiss Norman Lamont, the chancellor of the Exchequer, when the government had to devalue the pound in September. By late October opinion surveys found that Major was Britain's least popular prime minister in 50 years of polling.

Major was born in south London on March 29, 1943, and entered Parliament in 1979. He joined Prime Minister Margaret Thatcher's Cabinet as chief secretary to the treasury in 1987. He became foreign secretary in July 1989 and was switched to chancellor of the Exchequer three months later. In November 1990, when Thatcher was forced to resign, he defeated Douglas Hurd and Michael Heseltine in the battle to succeed her.

(PETER KELLNER)

Mansell, Nigel

After six years in the shadow of other Grand Prix race car drivers, Nigel Mansell was the most brilliant star in Formula One history in 1992. He went into the season with three second-place rankings since 1986 and 21 victories in his career, the most by anyone who had never been world champion. He began the season with five consecutive victories, breaking Ayrton Senna's 1991 record of four, and then clinched the Formula One championship on August 16, the earliest winner since Jackie Stewart in 1971.

In the clinching race at Budapest, Mansell charged from sixth place to second in the final 16 laps. "When I went across the line, I didn't know where the heck I was," he said. "I can just smile." He finished the season with victories in the Grand Prix races of South Africa, Mexico, Brazil, Spain, San Marino, France, Britain, Germany, and Portugal in addition to his second-place finishes at Monaco and Hungary. His 9 victories and 14 pole positions, awarded for the fastest qualifying time, broke Senna's records of 8 and 13 in 1988.

Nine days before his ninth victory at Estoril, Port., on September 27, Mansell announced his 1993 plans to drive exclusively for the Newman-Haas team in the IndyCar series. He thus became the first reigning Formula One champion on that circuit. He retired from Formula One with 31 poles and 30 victories. Only Alain Prost and Senna had more victories, and Mansell also ranked third in poles. All of Mansell's victories came in the last eight years, and 28 of them were in six seasons with well-equipped Williams teams.

Mansell was born Aug. 8, 1953, in Upton-on-Severn, England. Before he began racing full-time in 1976, he worked as a laboratory technician and production manager at Lucas Aerospace and as a senior sales engineer in the tractor division at Girling.

In 1977 Mansell won 32 of 42 starts and the Formula Ford championship despite frequent misfortune. He lost a wheel off his car five times during the season, and after he broke his neck in a crash, doctors told him he would spend six months in the hospital and might never race again. Mansell ignored them, discharged himself from the hospital, and sold his house the next year to pay for four events on the Formula Three March circuit in 1978. He won the pole in his first race and earned a spot on the Uniport team in 1979, when he won one race and finished second twice. He became a full-time Formula One racer in 1981 for the Lotus team but did not win a race until 1985, his first year with the Williams team, when he ranked sixth on the circuit. Mansell nearly won championships in both 1986 and 1987 but had to settle for close and discouraging second-place finishes in both years.   (KEVIN M. LAMB)

Martini, Cardinal Carlo Maria

Carlo Maria Cardinal Martini, archbishop of Milan since 1980, became in 1992 the leading moral force in Italy and the man judged most likely to succeed Pope John Paul II. The diocese of Milan, founded by St. Ambrose in the 4th century, was Italy's richest, largest, and most prestigious. Two popes had already come from there in the 20th century (Pius XI and Paul VI). Yet Martini's Milan appointment was a surprise, for he was a member of the Society of Jesus, and Jesuits do not usually become bishops except in mission territories. He was, in any case, an unusual Jesuit, having been ordained a priest in 1952 at age 25.

He had been singled out as an especially able biblical scholar with a remarkable grasp of Hebrew, Syriac, and other Middle Eastern languages. He became professor of fundamental theology at the Biblical Institute in Rome in 1958 and its rector in 1969, specializing in textual criticism. Appointed rector of Rome's Gregorian University in 1978, he was also spiritual adviser to many Italian bishops. This may have prompted Pope John Paul to name him to Milan—if he could advise them, he could join them; another theory said it was to prevent him from becoming general of the Jesuits, a position that would give him too much power.

Martini, in any event, showed himself to be a great communicator. Once a week he filled the cathedral with young people learning how to pray. He invited Jews to give lectures on "the silence of God." He declared that he would leave Milan only to go to Jerusalem (the choice might not be his). His pastoral letters, always with a strong biblical content, had become national events, and he was, said the Rome daily *La Repubblica*, "the only truly moral authority left in Italy today." Meanwhile, his international reputation had grown through his presidency, since 1986, of the European Bishops' Council. Present at the great ecumenical meeting in Basel, Switz., in the spring of 1989, he formed friendships with Protestant and, especially, Orthodox leaders like Patriarch Aleksey of Moscow that survived the tensions of postcommunism.

Martini's chances for the papacy would depend entirely on when the next conclave took place. The longer it was delayed, the further he would be in the wrong age bracket. He had enemies, as well, on the right wing who would try to prevent him from becoming the first Jesuit pope.

(PETER HEBBLETHWAITE)

Montagnier, Luc

Since the outset of the controversy over who deserved the glory for first isolating the AIDS virus, or HIV (human immunodeficiency virus), Luc Montagnier was confident that he and his coworkers at the Pasteur Institute would eventually receive the credit. It was not until 1992, however, that the competing claim of Robert Gallo of the U.S. National Cancer Institute was clearly repudiated. By this time Montagnier was enmeshed in other AIDS-related disputes.

Born Aug. 18, 1932, Luc Montagnier reached adolescence during World War II. He was educated at the Universities of Poitiers and Paris, earning degrees in science and medicine. A research scientist since 1955, he had been associated with the Pasteur Institute in Paris since 1972. Montagnier was currently serving as president of the Administrative Council of the European Federation for AIDS Research.

The conflict between Montagnier and Gallo dated back to 1984, when the American announced that his research team had isolated the AIDS virus and developed a test to screen blood for the new pathogen. Montagnier—who

had earlier sent Gallo samples of a virus that French researchers had isolated—challenged the Gallo claim. Although Gallo responded that the French specimens had played only a minor role in the American breakthrough, it was later revealed that the two viruses—French and American—were nearly identical. Since HIV is highly variable depending upon its source, this duplication could be explained only by American use—either by accident or intent—of the French virus.

A bitter dispute over the rival claims was resolved in 1987 when Gallo and Montagnier agreed to share credit and the U.S. government and Pasteur Institute agreed to split the royalties from the blood test. Beneath the surface, however, the conflict continued. In 1989 *Chicago Tribune* reporter John Crewdson wrote a lengthy account of the matter, prompting an investigation that supported Montagnier's primacy and led to charges of misconduct against Gallo.

Meanwhile, Montagnier had plunged into other AIDS-related controversies. In August 1992 he questioned the significance of a report by a scientist at the University of California at Irvine that suggested the existence of a new virus causing an AIDS-like disease.

More controversial was his suggestion that bacteria-like organisms called mycoplasmas might play a crucial part in the progression from HIV infection to symptomatic AIDS. Although by no means the sole proponent of this theory, Montagnier recognized that his was a minority view. "Some people say, 'Let's focus on the virus, let's strike at it, and when we have succeeded, the disease will be cured.' I find this hypothesis too simplistic, given that it is precisely when the virus is least virulent . . . that the unexplained deterioration of the immune system takes place."

(JEROLD L. KELLMAN)

Moseley-Braun, Carol
"Hope has two lovely daughters: anger and courage. Anger at the way things are and courage to change them." That part of Carol Moseley Braun's speech at the Democratic national convention in July described the inspiration behind her entrance into the 1992 Illinois senatorial race. Having been elected, she made history by becoming the first African-American woman and the only single mother in the U.S. Senate. Largely credited with starting the "Year of the Woman," she was an underdog going into the primary race against incumbent Sen. Alan Dixon. Her upset win in that election propelled her into the limelight. (Just before being sworn in the following January, the senator-elect added a hyphen to her name, making it "Moseley-Braun.")

Moseley-Braun was born into a middle-class family in a segregated neighbourhood on Chicago's South Side on Aug. 16, 1947. She attended the University of Illinois at Chicago, later earning a law degree from the University of Chicago. In 1978 she was elected to the Illinois House of Representatives. During her 10 years there, she became known for her advocacy of health care and education issues. Impressed by her abilities, Chicago Mayor Harold Washington encouraged the Cook County Democratic Party to endorse her for the office of recorder of deeds in the 1988 primary. Although Washington died before the election, she won the race, becoming the first woman and first African-American to hold executive office in Cook county government.

The turning point in her career came on Oct. 15, 1991, when Clarence Thomas was confirmed as a justice of the U.S. Supreme Court following Senate hearings in which he was accused by law professor Anita Hill of sexual misconduct. Infuriated by the fact that Dixon was one of the Democrats who voted for the confirmation, Moseley-Braun announced her candidacy. Within a month, however, she was almost forced out of the race because of a lack of money—at one time there was only $300 in the campaign fund. She was outspent by her opponents, Dixon and lawyer Al Hofeld, 10–1 and had virtually no media coverage. Hofeld launched a $5 million smear campaign against Dixon, a two-term incumbent who had not lost an election in 40 years. Moseley-Braun stayed out of the cross fire.

Although little attention was paid to her, thousands of people, including Republicans, were volunteering and donating money for her campaign. Two weeks before the election, she was still 12 points behind Dixon in the polls, but she surprisingly won the primary. Her Republican opponent in the senatorial race was Richard S. Williamson, a little-known former Bush administration aide. After her primary victory, Moseley-Braun began receiving extensive media coverage and large donations. She raised nearly $1.8 million in the three months ended June 30 and earned the nickname "The Smile."

In late September, Moseley-Braun was accused of failing to report a $28,750 inheritance royalty, paid to her mother in 1989, to the Illinois Department of Public Aid. Williamson quickly took advantage of this scandal, closing in on what had been a 30-point lead by Moseley-Braun. However, her existing support overcame negative factors to help her win the race by 54% to Williamson's 46%.

(SANDRA MARIE KIEFFER)

N'Dour, Youssou
When Senegal became independent from France in 1960, local musical instruments and traditions at last began to infiltrate mainstream, urban contemporary music after years of suppression in favour of French styles. Into the mainstream

JACK VARTOOGIAN

flowed *mbalax,* modern Senegalese rock characterized by a 500-year-old tradition of percussion featuring an improvised solo on a native drum. Because singer, drummer, and composer Youssou N'Dour's style of *mbalax* became so wildly popular in the late 1980s, he was often credited with inventing "Afro-pop" or "world beat" music, as it was known in the West.

N'Dour was born into a traditional West African community in Dakar in 1959. Though his garage-mechanic father discouraged him from pursuing a musical career, his mother, a griot (a West African troubadour and oral tribal historian), encouraged and influenced him. In 1979 N'Dour formed the group with which he recorded three albums and had a hit single, "Xalis." After penetrating even the remote regions of West Africa thanks to a thriving bootleg market, the group relocated to Paris in 1984. Renamed and reformed into Le Super Étoile de Dakar, it consisted of a rhythmic dance band with as many as 14 members that included multiple guitarists, saxophonists, and percussionists. Surrounded by European influences, N'Dour's traditional sound absorbed some of the flavour of salsa, soul, and disco to create a distinctive syncopated hybrid, highlighted by N'Dour's trademark wailing tenor.

This distinctive sound brought N'Dour to the attention of American singer Paul Simon, who featured N'Dour as a drummer on his *Graceland* album of 1986. British rock star Peter Gabriel persuaded him to be the opening act for Gabriel's U.S. tour of the same year. N'Dour courted even greater international stardom in the fall of 1988 as

part of Amnesty International's "Human Rights Now!" world tour, which also featured Bruce Springsteen, Sting, Gabriel, and Tracy Chapman.

On his earlier albums *Nelson Mandela* (1986) and *Immigrés* (1988), N'Dour had sung mostly in his native dialect, Wolof. Beginning to cross over to English-speaking audiences with *The Lion* (1989), N'Dour finally had a critical success with *Set* (1990). With *Eyes Open* (1992), N'Dour hoped to further entice Western audiences with songs featuring political and social commentary. However, commercial success was not necessarily his ultimate goal: "For me, the measure of success is more than anything how well I arrive at exposing my music as a representation of not only African music but of African life and the whole image of Africa."

(SUSAN RAPP)

Ondaatje, Michael
For his 1992 novel *The English Patient,* Michael Ondaatje became the first Canadian writer to win the prestigious Booker Prize, an award open to authors in the British Commonwealth. This tale of a young Canadian nurse tending a badly burned British airman in an abandoned Italian villa at the end of World War II also won the 1992 Canadian Governor General's Literary Award for fiction. Ondaatje had earned earlier honours for other writings. *The Collected Works of Billy the Kid* (1970), a collage of photographs, poems, and prose sketches, won the Governor General's award, as did his book of poetry *There's a Trick with a Knife I'm Learning to Do* (1979), a collection from between 1963 and 1978. *Coming Through Slaughter* (1976), a novel based on the life of U.S. jazzman Buddy Bolden, won the Books in Canada First Novel Award. *In the Skin of the Lion* (1987), a novel about the immigrant community of Toronto during the 1920s and '30s, won two Canadian awards.

Ondaatje was born in Colombo, Ceylon (now Sri Lanka), in 1943. In a family memoir, *Running in the Family* (1982), he recounted life there. After settling in Canada in 1962, he considered himself a Canadian author. He assisted his wife, Linda Spalding, in the production of each issue of the Canadian literary magazine *Brick.* In 1990 he edited *From Ink Lake,* an anthology of Canadian fiction. Ondaatje studied at Bishop's University in Lennoxville, Que., the University of Toronto, and Queen's University in Kingston, Ont. He then taught English literature at the University of Western Ontario for four years. In 1971 he began teaching contemporary international literature in Toronto at Glendon College, York University.

Ondaatje first became known as a poet. *The Dainty Monsters,* his first book of poetry, was published in 1967; it was followed by *Rat Jelly* in 1973. Ondaatje preferred writing prose or poetry because he believed that these literary forms allowed him a more subtle approach. He did, however, write stage adaptations of two of his books, *The Collected Works of Billy the Kid* and *Coming Through Slaughter.* He also occasionally ventured into the medium of film. He directed *Sons of Captain Poetry* (1970), a documentary on poet bp Nichol, and *The Clinton Special* (1974), which documented Theatre Passe Muraille's production of *The Farm Show.* While on sabbatical at the Canadian Film Centre, he made *Love Clinic* (1991), which was well received at the Bombay Film Festival.

Ondaatje was also a dog breeder. He made a film entitled *Great Canadian Hounds,* published (1971) *How to Train a Bassett,* and developed and bred a new strain of spaniel called the Sydenham spaniel.

(DIANE LOIS WAY)

Panic, Milan
The already baffling political situation in Yugoslavia took another bizarre twist in July 1992 when an American businessman who had defected from the strife-torn nation nearly 40 years earlier returned to serve as its prime minister. Milan Panic, multimillionaire head of the huge ICN pharmaceuticals company, vowed that he would use his position as Yugoslav head of state to halt the bloodshed in Bosnia and Hercegovina.

Born in Serbia on Dec. 20, 1929, Milan Panic as an adolescent joined the Yugoslav anti-Nazi resistance during World War II and served as a messenger for the communist partisans. After the war he worked as a chemist, but he became better known as a member of Yugoslavia's bicycle-racing team. While touring with the team in 1955, Panic defected to the West. The following year he and his wife arrived in the U.S., and—with just two suitcases and $20—went to California. After studying at the University of Southern California, he launched International Chemical & Nuclear.

ICN, however, had a checkered history. In 1972 the Securities and Exchange Commission accused the company and Panic of making misleading financial forecasts, and while the case was resolved without an ICN admission of guilt, the company faced a host of shareholder suits. In 1991 ICN paid the Food and Drug Administration (FDA) $600,000 to settle charges that it had improperly promoted its antiviral agent ribavirin (brand name Virazole). Panic had positioned ribavirin as a treatment for influenza, hepatitis, measles, herpes, and a number of other viral diseases, but it was ICN's claims that Virazole delayed the onset of AIDS in people infected with HIV (human immunodeficiency virus) that elicited the FDA charges.

On July 2, 1992, after receiving permission from the U.S. government to travel to Yugoslavia, Panic left on what he called a "peace mission" to end the bloodshed in the Balkans. Chosen prime minister by Serb leaders wanting to establish better relations with the U.S., Panic became the head of government in a country that consisted of just two of its original six republics—Serbia and Montenegro. He was sworn in July 14 and immediately criticized Serb-backed attacks on Bosnia and Hercegovina. "We respect the fact that Bosnia-Hercegovina is an independent state. The most important thing for all Serbs is to stop shooting." He also said that "ethnic cleansing is the disgrace of our nation. People are thinking that we are barbarians. I am determined to bring order to Belgrade, Serbia, and Yugoslavia."

Panic began to draw praise from critics who earlier had viewed him as a puppet of Serbian Pres. Slobodan Milosevic. He formed a Cabinet consisting of both pro- and anti-Milosevic elements and removed Serb extremists from positions of power in the Yugoslav government. "We are removing the causes of cancer," he said.

A citizens' group nominated the American millionaire to run for president of Serbia. Although an electoral commission barred Panic from challenging Milosevic, the Serbian Supreme Court overturned that decision. On December 20 Milosevic won a decisive reelection victory, and nine days later Panic lost a unanimous parliamentary vote of no confidence.   (JEROLD L. KELLMAN)

Patten, Christopher Francis
In 1992 Christopher Patten, the architect of the U.K. Conservative Party's April election victory, suffered the humiliation of being the only Cabinet minister to lose his own seat as member of Parliament. He was compensated, however, with his appointment as the last governor of Hong Kong, pending its transfer to China in 1997.

Patten was born in Lancashire, England, on May 12, 1944. After graduating from the University of Oxford, he won a traveling scholarship to the U.S., where he worked on John Lindsay's 1965 campaign to become the liberal Republican mayor of New York City. Back in London, Patten joined the Conservative Party research department in 1966, becoming its director in 1974.

He entered Parliament in 1979 as member for Bath, Somerset. His consensual economic views and liberal outlook on social issues contrasted with the right-wing values espoused by Prime Minister Margaret Thatcher. In the end, however, Thatcher decided that he was less dangerous inside her government than outside. He became a junior minister for Northern Ireland in 1983.

In 1985 Patten was appointed minister of state for education, and a year later he was made minister for overseas development. In 1989 he entered Thatcher's Cabinet as environment secretary, with the thankless task of introducing the widely disliked poll tax for financing local government. Following John Major's election as prime minister in November 1990, Patten was appointed chairman of the Conservative Party—and given the responsibility of rescuing the party from the depths of unpopularity in time for a general election that was due to be held within 18 months.

The Conservatives' victory in April 1992 owed much to Patten's skills—although in the process his necessarily robust campaign tactics lost him much of the cross-party admiration he had won in earlier years for his humane, nonconfrontational approach to politics. His change of style also lost him some support in his own constituency, which he lost to the Liberal Democrats. On April 24, Major offered Patten the challenging consolation prize of the governorship of Hong Kong.

Patten was sworn in on July 9 and immediately set about challenging the status quo. He questioned details of Hong Kong's Basic Law, proposed ambitious democratic reforms to be instituted prior to 1997, and approved preparation of the site for a controversial new airport, despite China's continuing refusal to approve the financing. His actions angered the Chinese government as well as conservatives in Hong Kong and presaged a stormy transition period for the British colony.   (PETER KELLNER)

Perot, H(enry) Ross
Early in 1992 H. Ross Perot, a billionaire from Texas, announced on a television talk show that he would run as an independent for U.S. president if the people wanted him; that is, if they could get his name on the ballot in all 50 states. Perot espoused a populist message that seemed to offer a businesslike approach to solving the country's economic woes. In July, just as many Americans were beginning to view Perot as a viable third candidate, he pulled out of the race. He reentered the race in October, however, and won a surprising 19% of the popular vote in the November election.

Perot was born June 27, 1930, in Texarkana, Texas. He was a mediocre student but an ace Boy Scout—he cited the *Boy Scout Handbook* as one of his favourite books. In 1949 he entered the U.S. Naval Academy, and he served in the Navy until 1957. In 1962 he started his own company, Electronic Data Systems Corp. (EDS), which designed, installed, and operated data processing systems for clients, mainly insurance companies, on a contract basis. Perot ran a tight ship—there was no room for slackers or those whose "morals" were deemed lax. Employees were expected to put the company first. In return Perot let them know they were appreciated. Though his company did fairly well, business really boomed in the mid-1960s when national Medicare legislation dramatically increased the number of insurance claims processed by EDS. When EDS went public in 1968, the stock took off, and Perot became a billionaire.

In the 1970s Perot tried to salvage two foundering Wall Street brokerage firms; he lost a large sum of money and created enormous friction and resentment. One broker commented that Perot's employees' "intention [was] to train people their way, so they won't think for themselves." The venture failed and EDS faced financial trouble. However, in the 1980s Perot received another godsend from the U.S. government in the form of "megacontracts"—long-term contracts involving huge amounts of money, including the overhaul of computer systems at 47 army bases.

Even though EDS's good fortune was ensured for the foreseeable future, in 1984 Perot sold EDS to General Motors for $2.5 billion in GM stock. The deal made him a member of the GM board of directors and the owner of more stock than any other individual. Perot tried to "reform" GM à la EDS by visiting factories and lunching with the line workers. He was seen by GM executives as an intolerable meddler, and he was finally paid $700 million to give up his board seat and his chairmanship of EDS. Almost immediately Perot started a new firm—one that would compete directly with EDS—and went about trying to wrest contracts from his former company.

At various times people had suggested that Perot try politics, but he had always declined because of "the red tape and the inactivity." After his decampment in July, however, Perot continued to fund his supporters, who were still collecting names for his petitions. In October, with his name on all the ballots, Perot relaunched his campaign. He bought a series of 30-minute television advertisements—"infomercials"—and presented viewers with charts detailing economic and other problems and gave his solutions for correcting them. Perot sold himself to the American people remarkably well; in a poll of voters, 86% said his presence as a third candidate was "good," regardless of how they planned to vote.

(ELIZABETH LASKEY)

Pfeiffer, Michelle
To contented fans, she was the cat's meow. But in 1992, fetching actress Michelle Pfeiffer became the cat itself, her "meow" emphasizing the "ow," making it a cry of discontent and pain. Costarring in the hit film *Batman Returns*, Pfeiffer played bland Selina Kyle, a nervous and mousy secretary who is ignored romantically and abused professionally. Shoved out a window by her evil, monstrously sexist boss, she lands in a feline-filled alley and comes to life with strange new powers and a more than slightly altered ego. "I am Catwoman, hear me roar," hisses Selina after she slips into a shimmering, smoldering black-cat outfit that hugs her curves like fresh blacktop on a winding roadway. Her nighttime wanderings bring Catwoman mask-to-mask with an equally conflicted and neurotic Batman, and their battles on the city rooftops suggest a mean, kinky form of courtship. While their provocative adventure sold fewer tickets than the first *Batman*, it appealed to a greater number of critics, in part because of Pfeiffer's performance, which *The New Yorker* called "ferociously sexy" and *Rolling Stone* said possessed "a tough core of intelligence and wit."

Catwoman was a typical role for Pfeiffer. Despite her camera-ready looks—the flowing yellow hair, teary blue eyes, and pouting red lips—Pfeiffer felt most comfortable performing in disguise, revealing just enough tenderness and steel to intrigue viewers. In *Married to the Mob* (1988), the first film to bring her widespread acclaim, a dark-haired Pfeiffer played a gum-chomping housewife running away from her husband's materially rich and morally poor Mob life-style. The same year, in *Dangerous Liaisons*, she earned an Oscar nomination for her wan and brittle, devout and devoted 18th-century wife who gradually succumbs to a notorious womanizer. Then, after her Oscar-nominated performance as a streetwise but glamorous chanteuse—a Grace Kelly with claws—in *The Fabulous Baker Boys* (1989), Pfeiffer went back into hiding to play a thick-accented Russian in *The Russia House* (1990), a bedraggled-looking waitress in *Frankie and Johnny* (1991), and a Southern blond in *Love Field* (1992).

RALPH DOMINGUEZ—GLOBE PHOTOS

Born on April 29, 1958, in Santa Ana, Calif., Pfeiffer led an undistinguished life until, at 20, she attracted Hollywood's eye by winning the Miss Orange County beauty pageant. But if her looks gave her a start, they also almost proved her finish, confining Pfeiffer to blonde bimbo parts in television and movies. She did not get to lose herself in a role—and to find her ability as a character actress—until her coke-snorting moll in *Scarface* (1983). When subsequent films made her into a cover-girl star, however, she refused the part. "When I walk into a room, I try to find a corner where no one's going to notice me," said Pfeiffer, sounding like a cat long before she became a Catwoman. (MICHAEL AMEDEO)

Polgar, Zsuzsa, Sofia, and Judit

Chess had always been the domain of the male gender, and although good women players had appeared from time to time, they had never achieved the ranking of the best men. Male domination of this game might have experienced the first chink in its armour, however, as three young and engaging Hungarian sisters moved into the front line of world class players. The feats of the Polgar sisters at early ages, in fact, matched or surpassed some of those of the great male players. In December 1991, at age 15, the youngest sister, Judit (b. July 23, 1976), achieved the rarefied rank of grandmaster against male competition, replacing Bobby Fischer as the youngest person in chess history to have won this honour. She was, however, only the second female to become a grandmaster in the male field; the honour of being first went to her oldest sister, Zsuzsa (b. April 19, 1969), who managed her accomplishment earlier in 1991. Although Zsuzsa was the eldest, she ranked as the number two woman player in the world behind Judit, now acclaimed number one. The other sister, 17-year-old Sofia (b. Nov. 2, 1974), lagged a bit behind: she was "only" the world's sixth-ranked woman player.

The chess-playing Polgar sisters, according to their father, Laszlo, achieved their uncommon abilities as the result of a carefully planned educational program. A psychologist, Polgar held a theory that "geniuses" are made, not born, and that early training and specialization were the key. He set out to prove his theory and determined that his progeny would focus on chess when Zsuzsa at age four expressed interest in the game. From that time Zsuzsa—and the others, when they came along—were immersed in a chess environment. Each of the girls began learning the game at age four, and eventually their daily regimen included five or more hours a day of playing time. Physical training was also included in the schedule for diversion and in order to build endurance for grueling matches.

The sisters never attended school, having been tutored entirely at home by their parents. Through their mother, who taught several languages, and their international travels, the three learned English, Russian, Spanish, German, and even some Esperanto. It might be expected that this unconventional upbringing would have produced insular and rather quirky individuals. But Zsuzsa, Sofia, and Judit appeared to be normal young women in every respect, displaying a proper interest in pop music, clothes, and males.

By 1992 Judit was regarded by some observers as the first woman who would challenge for the world championship of chess. The most optimistic authorities agreed, however, that even at Judit's rapid rate of progress, she was still 7 to 10 years away from a championship match. (MARVIN MARTIN)

Popcorn, Faith

The woman whom *Fortune* magazine called "the Nostradamus of Marketing," Faith Popcorn, achieved guru status in 1992 after publishing her first book in 1991. Marketing consultant, futurist, and trend analyst, she designed *The Popcorn Report* so that people could plan their own future for the 1990s: where they should live, what their children should study, and how they could make money. Popcorn believed that the number one trend of the 1990s was control and that all trends constituted a form of control. Her book,

which highlighted top trends and her predictions for the '90s, revealed an inventory of "Popcornisms": cocooning (the stay-at-home syndrome), brailling the culture (scanning for signs of the future), cashing out (opting out of corporate life), and trend bending (shaping a product or strategy around an emerging trend).

Popcorn was born Faith Beryl Plotkin on May 11, 1947, in New York City. She changed her name legally in 1969 to Faith Popcorn. The daughter of two lawyers, she grew up in Shanghai and New York City. As a child she wanted to live in the West, and as an adult she collected cowboy and Indian paraphernalia. She enjoyed studying people as they shopped in malls. She liked to listen to people talk and watch them interact. Popcorn capitalized on this interest by launching a career in marketing. She worked in advertising and marketing and became creative director of Smith Greenland Advertising in New York City before forming her own company. BrainReserve Inc., started in 1974 in Manhattan, served as marketing consultant to corporate America.

Popcorn believed that companies sold not only their products but also themselves and that advertisers needed innovative ideas to persuade customers to part with their money. She helped companies with long-range marketing plans to adapt to rapid social change. To improve a company's marketing strategy, Popcorn would work out a problem statement after analyzing marketing and the media and would then call in outside consultants to gain new strategies.

BrainReserve employees, trend analysts for dozens of Fortune 500 companies, kept abreast of the culture by annually reading over 250 magazines, watching top-rated television programs, reading best-sellers, and interviewing thousands of people. Popcorn was considered an extraordinary trend spotter—she was the first to declare the new Coke a disaster. On the basis of her analysis of trends, Popcorn invented the "Bacardi Breezer," a rum-fruit drink that became a success in North America within six months. She boasted a 95% accuracy record and predicted that Bill Clinton would be elected president of the United States in 1992. (DIANE LOIS WAY)

Quayle, James Danforth

From an ongoing feud with television's Murphy Brown to misspelling the word *potato(e)* in a student spelling bee and finally to losing his job, U.S. Vice Pres. Dan Quayle probably would like to forget 1992. Since Quayle's tenure in office rested solely upon the political fortunes of Pres. George Bush (*q.v.*), it ended when the president was defeated in the November elections.

Republican presidential nominee Bush surprised the pundits in 1988 by picking Quayle as his running mate. An instant lightning rod to criticism, Quayle faced numerous questions on his background. His verbal flubs and poor debate performance only added to the ridicule. Yet his tenure as the nation's vice president was arguably the most influential and powerful in the history of the office. He chaired the Council on Competitiveness, exempting businesses from excessive regulations, and headed the National Space Council, playing a key role in reviving the National Aeronautics and Space Administration.

In a May speech Quayle said, "It doesn't help matters when prime-time TV has Murphy Brown . . . mocking the importance of fathers, by bearing a child alone, and calling it just another 'life-style choice.'" That one sentence in a 2,800-word speech sparked a summer-long controversy between "family values" and the Hollywood "cultural elite." In spite of pressure from critics who urged Bush to dump Quayle, the president chose to keep him on the ticket. At the Republican convention Quayle "reintroduced" himself to America by once again stressing family values. Needing to abolish the gaffe-prone, bungling image, Quayle campaigned heavily in smaller towns, rallying the right wing and deflecting criticism with supportive audiences. More at ease, more polished than in 1988, Quayle sometimes resorted to props by having the audience toss waffles to represent Democrat Bill Clinton's "waffling" on issues. In the vice presidential debate, Quayle took the

offensive and was more aggressive and combative. Yet despite an improved campaign style, the Bush-Quayle ticket was defeated by the Clinton-Gore team in a 370–168 electoral landslide.

James Danforth Quayle, born in Indianapolis, Ind., on Feb. 4, 1947, was descended from the Pulliam family, publishers of newspapers in Arizona and Indiana. Quayle, an admitted "C" student at DePauw University, Greencastle, Ind., received a bachelor's degree in 1969. While attending Indiana University Law School (graduated in 1974), he served in the Indiana National Guard (1969–75) and married Marilyn Tucker after a 10-week courtship (1972). In 1976, persuaded to run for Congress by local party officials, he defeated an eight-term incumbent to capture a House seat in northeastern Indiana. Quayle took on three-term U.S. Sen. Birch Bayh in 1980, defeating him in part because Republicans swept the country when Ronald Reagan was elected president.

An avid golfer, Quayle would have plenty of time to work on his game during the next four years—and to decide whether to make a run for the presidency in 1996. (JAMES T. BANNEN)

Rabin, Yitzhak

When the Labour Party was declared the winner of the general election in Israel on June 23, 1992, Israelis knew exactly what they were getting. At the party's helm was Yitzhak Rabin, a man who had been in public life for more than 40 years. When he served his first term as prime minister, from 1974 to 1977, he was the first native-born Israeli ever to hold the post. His matter-of-fact speaking style, low, growling voice, and views on issues such as peace negotiations with Arab neighbours were well known to the Israeli public.

Rabin was born in Jerusalem on March 1, 1922. He studied at the prestigious Kadoorie Agricultural School and was a brigade commander in Israel's War of Independence in 1948. He rose quickly in the ranks and was chief of staff from 1964 to 1968, during which time he presided over Israel's spectacular victory in the Six-Day War. He served as ambassador to the U.S. (1968–73), succeeded Golda Meir as prime minister in 1974, and ordered the daring rescue of 103 Israeli hostages in Entebbe, Uganda, in 1976. Rabin resigned in 1977 amid a scandal involving dollar accounts he kept in the U.S. During a stint as defense minister (1984–90), he was criticized by both the right-wing and left-wing parties for his handling of the Palestinian *intifada* (uprising) that began in December 1987. In February 1992 he faced Labour Party leader Shimon Peres in a hard-fought primary. The party members chose Rabin, believing he had the best chance to defeat Prime Minister Yitzhak Shamir's hard-line Likud-led government and bring progress on domestic issues as well as on peace talks.

In his first few months as prime minister, Rabin had to contend with crises in the fragile coalition that gave him a majority in the Knesset (parliament). The religious parties had less influence over Rabin's government than had sometimes been the case in previous years. Nevertheless, he often needed their support to carry out his policies, including efforts to negotiate autonomy agreements with Palestinians and land deals with Syria over the Golan Heights.

Rabin also put a freeze on new settlements in the occupied territories and canceled building contracts on thousands of new units to be constructed there. In response, U.S. Pres. George Bush said in August that loan guarantees of up to $10 billion that had been denied Rabin's predecessor could be approved. In December, however, after the murder of several Israeli soldiers, Rabin's government expelled 415 Palestinians accused of involvement with the Islamic fundamentalist group held to be responsible. The Israeli public was again looking to Rabin to be tough in his handling of foreign affairs, the economy, election reform, and peace negotiations with the country's Arab neighbours. (FRANCINE SHONFELD SHERMAN)

Radice, Anne-Imelda

From her appointment on May 1, 1992, as acting chair of the U.S. National Endowment for the

Arts, Anne-Imelda Radice strove to bring some degree of "decency" to the arts community. The NEA had been under scrutiny by Congress and right-wing religious organizations because of the controversial content of work funded by federal government grants.

Radice was originally brought to the NEA at the suggestion of former White House chief of staff John Sununu, and she had served as its senior deputy chair since March 1, 1991. She centred her policy in the belief that grants should "promote the widest access of Americans" to the arts. In her attempt to reach this goal, however, she met resistance from many individuals and organizations within the arts world. Protesters criticized her as a "decency czar" and contended that her encouragement of artistic endeavours was grounded in censorship. Radice refused to award federal funding for projects that were considered to be primarily sexually explicit or for art that could offend strongly held religious beliefs.

Radice did not evaluate grant proposals exclusively on artistic excellence and promise. Rather, she felt it was equally important to take public and congressional sensibilities into consideration, and she claimed that potentially "questionable" art containing difficult or mature subject matter was best served by the private sector. Activists in arts circles believed that the premise "art for art's sake" had been abandoned since Radice's appointment, and many refused to accept NEA funding on the grounds that their artistic freedom of expression could be threatened. Others applauded Radice's attempts to institute change and clean up the arts community.

Radice was born in Buffalo, N.Y., on Feb. 29, 1948. She earned a bachelor of arts degree in art history from Wheaton College in Norton, Mass., a master's degree in art history from Villa Schifanois in Florence, an MBA with an emphasis on finance from the American University in Washington, D.C., and a doctorate in architectural and art history from the University of North Carolina at Chapel Hill. Prior to her involvement with the NEA, Radice had spent much of her career in the art world, serving as chief arts adviser directing the Division of Creative Arts at the U.S. Information Agency and as the first director of the National Museum of Women in the Arts, which opened in 1987. She was also curator and architectural historian for the architect of the United States Capitol and an assistant curator and lecturer at the National Gallery of Art.

(DEBORAH A. MARS)

Ramos, Fidel Valdez

The Philippines held an election on May 11, 1992, but because of the care taken in counting the votes, as well as some technical problems, the results were not announced until June 16. Chosen as president was Fidel Ramos, who had campaigned against the country's long tradition of graft and favouritism. Ramos had won a seven-way race with only 24% of the vote. He lacked a strong party organization and had been criticized for having served the Marcos dictatorship. After being inaugurated to a six-year term on June 30, Ramos announced plans to improve the often unreliable electric-power system, tried to make contact with insurgents, and secured an end to controls on foreign exchange.

Ramos was born in Pangasinan province in 1928. After graduating from the United States Military Academy in 1950 and receiving a master's degree in civil engineering from the University of Illinois, he became an officer in the Philippine armed forces and worked his way up through the ranks to become a general. In 1972 Pres. Ferdinand Marcos appointed him commander of the Philippine Constabulary, a paramilitary law-enforcement agency. As such, he was responsible for enforcing Marcos' declaration of martial law. On Marcos' orders, he arrested opponents of the regime, notably Benigno Aquino, who was imprisoned in 1972 and sentenced to death before going into exile in 1980. In 1981 Marcos appointed Ramos deputy to Fabian Ver, the unpopular chief of staff of the armed forces. Ver reportedly insisted on running the Constabulary, Ramos' command.

Tolerance for the Marcos dictatorship declined after Aquino was murdered at the Manila airport as he was returning from exile in 1983, and Ver was accused of complicity. In 1986, after Marcos apparently tried to steal the presidential election from Corazon Aquino, Benigno's widow, Ramos joined Juan Ponce Enrile, the secretary of national defense, in seizing the headquarters of the armed forces. This inspired the People Power movement, in which civilian demonstrators throughout the country forced Marcos into exile. Corazon Aquino, as president, appointed Ramos chief of staff in 1986 and secretary of national defense in 1988. He was responsible for blocking six attempts by the armed forces to overthrow the government. In 1991 he resigned and unsuccessfully sought the nomination of the Democratic Filipino Struggle. On Jan. 2, 1992, he announced that he was the presidential candidate of the new People's Power Party. Aquino, who was barred by the constitution from seeking a second term, endorsed him on January 26.

(CHARLES JOHNSON TAGGART)

Reichmann, Albert, Paul, and Ralph

Reclusive and *private* were words often used to describe the Reichmann brothers, who shunned publicity about their private lives. In November 1987, *Toronto Life* magazine published an article on the family. Paul Reichmann claimed that it defamed his parents and launched a libel suit, which was settled in 1992 in favour of the Reichmanns. These three brothers, who avoided the limelight, were the guiding forces behind a family-held international conglomerate with holdings in real estate, natural resources, and transportation. Born in Vienna, Albert, Paul (b. 1931?), and Ralph (b. 1934?) were sons of Samuel Reichmann, who established a business as a currency trader in Tangier, Morocco, about 1940.

Beginning with a small tile and carpet business in Toronto in 1956, the brothers built Olympia & York Developments Ltd. (O&Y) into one of the richest and most powerful real estate developers in the world. They bought undesirable properties and transformed them into prominent office properties, erecting high-quality buildings at high speed and low cost. In Toronto, First Canadian Place, the world's tallest bank building, was completed in 1978. The Reichmanns' first success in New York City was the building at 55 Water Street, the largest privately owned office tower in the city. In the 1980s, O&Y built the World Financial Center in New York and became the city's largest private landlord. Begun in 1987, Canary Wharf in London's Docklands was the Reichmanns' most ambitious project and, at 28 ha (71 ac), the largest real estate development in Europe.

Soft-spoken Paul Reichmann, a calm and persuasive businessman, crafted the strategies of O&Y. He claimed that he obtained the key to his business success from his study of the Talmud. In the 1970s he made the decision to diversify the company's holdings. In 1985 the company ventured into the oil business with its acquisition of Gulf Canada, and shortly thereafter, O&Y purchased Abitibi-Price, the Canadian forest products company. In an attempted hostile takeover of Hiram Walker Resources, O&Y gained only 49% of the distillery business.

Diversification, however, did not strengthen the empire; oil prices dropped, and by 1990 Abitibi-Price was a losing investment. In 1984 O&Y had begun using short-term debt to finance long-term assets. At first this worked well, but by 1991 a severe recession in the London and New York real estate markets had strained the company's cash flow. In 1992 O&Y, one of the world's most respected real estate investors, was forced to file for bankruptcy protection for its Canadian real estate holdings and place others of its worldwide holdings in receivership.   (DIANE LOIS WAY)

Reynolds, Albert

After less than a year in office, Irish Prime Minister Albert Reynolds provoked a crisis when he used the words "reckless, irresponsible, and dishonest" to describe testimony given by Progressive Democrat leader Desmond O'Malley to

the Tribunal of Inquiry into the Beef Processing Industry. Both Reynolds and O'Malley were state witnesses in an investigation of possible fraud in Irish beef sales to Iraq. Fueled by anger over the suggestion that O'Malley had committed perjury, the Progressive Democrats joined other parties to defeat a motion of confidence in Reynolds and his Fianna Fail party on November 5 and forced new elections. There was speculation that Reynolds had provoked an electoral battle in a bid for majority rule for Fianna Fail in the Dail (parliament), breaking the coalition with the Progressive Democrats.

However, as the election neared, Reynolds saw his approval ratings drop from 60 to 31%. Similar to George Bush's presidential reelection bid in the U.S., Reynolds' efforts were hurt by a stagnant economy and a high unemployment rate. Reynolds and Fianna Fail introduced a Six-Point Plan for National Progress with an emphasis on job creation, but the offer came too late. In the election on November 25, Fianna Fail lost its majority, and the Labour Party doubled its representation in the Dail. At the year's end no workable coalition had been formed in the Dail, but Reynolds remained prime minister.

Reynolds was born Nov. 3, 1933, in the village of Roosky, County Roscommon. He attended Summerhill College in Sligo but did not complete his studies. Before his first election to the Dail (1977), Reynolds operated a chain of big-band dance halls that flourished until the 1960s. From the entertainment world he ventured into the pet-food industry, where he also found success.

Among his Cabinet positions were minister for transport from December 1979 to June 1981, minister for industry and energy from March 1982 to December 1982, and minister for industry and commerce from March 1987 to November 1988. Appointed finance minister in 1988, Reynolds served as a top official under controversial Prime Minister Charles Haughey but was dismissed in 1991 after his attempt to have Haughey removed from office was unsuccessful. In January 1992 Haughey resigned amid increasing charges of corruption after a decade in power.

In his bid to replace Haughey, Reynolds faced two opponents and received 61 of the 77 votes cast in the Dail. Upon his election on Feb. 11, 1992, he sacked many Fianna Fail ministers, vowing to distance the party from accusations of corruption.   (STEPHEN S. SEDDON)

Rimington, Stella

With the collapse of the Soviet Union and the end of the cold war, the intelligence and counterintelligence agencies of the Western democracies faced a reassessment of priorities. Nowhere were these changes more evident than in the U.K., where the Security Service (popularly known as MI-5), the agency responsible for counterintelligence and domestic security, broke with the tradition of secrecy that surrounded its employees and publicly named its new director-general. Even more surprising, the new head of the agency was Stella Rimington, who became the first woman director-general in the 82-year history of the supersecret agency.

Rimington was born in London in 1935. She read English at the University of Edinburgh and worked as an archivist before moving to India with her husband, who was posted to Delhi as a first secretary in the commercial section of the British High Commission. Following her return to England in the late 1960s, she joined MI-5. Rimington gained experience as a political researcher and analyst in MI-5's F branch, which was responsible for monitoring the activities of political subversives.

In the early 1980s Rimington was appointed head of F-2, a section within F Branch that was responsible for countering the activities of suspected political extremists. In the late 1980s she was named director of counterterrorism, responsible for dealing with attacks by the Irish Republican Army (IRA) in the U.K. and Europe and for countering the activities of other terrorist groups within the U.K. Rimington's tenure was marked by the rapid expansion of this section as resources previously earmarked for combating Soviet-backed subversion were freed by the collapse of the Soviet bloc. It was also her duty to deal with the threat of terrorism during the Gulf war, when fear of Iraqi-sponsored terrorist attacks on the U.K. led to the detention of people of Middle Eastern origin, an action for which MI-5 was widely criticized.

Following her appointment as director-general, Rimington proclaimed her intention to direct the combined resources of MI-5 and the Metropolitan Police Special Branch in a cohesive effort to eradicate IRA terrorism. Known as a talented intelligence analyst and a skilled consensus builder in committee, she faced a stiff challenge in a changing world: protecting her nation's security while reconciling the often thorny relationship between MI-5 and other British intelligence agencies.
(JOHN H. MATHEWS)

Sharma, Shankar Dayal
On July 25, 1992, Shankar Dayal Sharma was administered the oath of office that made him the ninth president of India. Sharma succeeded Ramaswamy Venkataraman in the largely ceremonial position, having won 64.8% of the vote in the electoral college, composed of the elected

members of both houses of parliament and of the state legislatures. Moving up from the post of vice president, Sharma began the presidency after five decades in public life, during which he had been a freedom fighter and had held important offices at both the state and national levels. Delivering his emotionally charged inaugural address amid a colourful and joyous ceremony, the new president called for equal respect for all religions as a basis for the achievement of national goals. The difficulty of attaining that ideal was made frighteningly apparent a few months later when Hindu extremists destroyed a mosque built centuries before on the site of a Hindu temple, setting off bloody Muslim-Hindu riots throughout India.

"Freedom has little meaning without equality," Sharma declared, "and equality has little meaning without social and economic justice." He pleaded for a strong and united country capable of finding the strength in ethical and moral values to help overcome the massive problems of terrorism, ethnic frictions, oppression of caste and gender, and persistent poverty, ignorance, and disease.

Sharma was born on Aug. 19, 1918, in Bhopal, later the capital of Madhya Pradesh state. His higher education began at St. Johns College in Agra and was continued at Lucknow University; he took his doctorate of law at the University of Cambridge, and he also attended Lincoln's Inn and Harvard Law School. Sharma taught law at Cambridge. He began his legal practice in Lucknow in 1940 and at about that same time became actively involved in India's freedom struggle. For his role in the independence movement in Bhopal, he was imprisoned for eight months.

After India gained independence (1947), Sharma's political career developed through a long association with the Indian National Congress. He was a member of the All India Congress

Committee for 32 years beginning in 1950, and from 1950 to 1952 he was president of the Bhopal State Congress Committee. He also served the former Bhopal state as its chief minister from 1952 to 1956. Sharma was a member of the Madhya Pradesh legislative assembly from 1956 to 1971, and during that period he held a Cabinet post for some 11 years. He then moved into the national arena, becoming a member of the Lok Sabha (House of the People; the lower house) in 1971 and serving in that body until 1977. From 1972 to 1974 he held the post of president of the Indian National Congress. He was again elected to the Lok Sabha in 1980.

Before becoming vice president in 1987, Sharma held governorship posts in Andhra Pradesh (1984–85), Punjab (1985–86), and Maharashtra (1986–87). The best known of his published works was *Congress Approach to International Affairs*.
(MARVIN MARTIN)

Sherbo, Vitali
From his first gymnastics competition at the age of seven, Vitali Sherbo's ambition was to become an Olympic champion. In 1992 he won more gold medals than anybody else at the Olympic Games in Barcelona, Spain, and became the first gymnast to win six gold medals in one Olympics. He won individual golds in the pommel horse, still rings, vault, parallel bars, and all-around competition (which encompasses all six disciplines) and a team medal as a member of the gold-medal winning Unified Team of athletes from the former Soviet republics.

Sherbo was born Jan. 13, 1972, in Minsk, Belarus. The son of two athletes, he moved quickly up the developmental pyramid of Soviet sports and became a member of the Soviet national team at 15. His first significant success in senior competition came two years later, in 1989, when he placed fourth in the all-around at the Chunichi Cup at Nagoya, Japan.

In 1990 in Minsk Sherbo won his first national championship with an all-around victory in the last tournament to use the U.S.S.R. national championship name. He also burst into the international spotlight with all-around victories in the Goodwill Games at Seattle, Wash., the Blume Memorial at Barcelona, and the Chunichi Cup, where he also won four individual events. Although he finished second in the World Cup all-around at Brussels and fifth in that competition in the European

championships at Lausanne, Switz., Sherbo won individual gold medals at the European championships in the horizontal bar and the floor exercise (his favourite event), and at both meets in the vault. He scored a perfect 10, which was much rarer in men's gymnastics than in women's, in the

vault at the 1990 Goodwill Games, and another 10 in the pommel horse at the 1991 U.S.S.R. Cup, where he won the all-around.

In world championships Sherbo finished second in the all-around, floor exercise, and vault in 1991 at Indianapolis, Ind. In 1992 at Paris he was first in the pommel horse and the rings (his least preferred event) and second in the floor exercise. He placed first or second in four events of the 1992 European championships at Budapest, winning the floor exercise and the vault.

Although still a resident of Minsk and affiliated with the Trudovye Rezervy Club, Sherbo drifted away from his homeland in search of better economic opportunities in the U.S. He said that he and his wife contemplated leaving Minsk because top athletes had become targets of resentment in the economic depression that followed the collapse of the Soviet Union. After the 1992 Olympics he joined a multicity U.S. tour from September 27 through November 4 in conjunction with the U.S. Gymnastics Federation.
(KEVIN LAMB)

Shevardnadze, Eduard Amvrosiyevich
The most famous living native of the Republic of Georgia, Eduard Shevardnadze became chairman of the State Council on March 10, 1992, three days after returning home from six years in Moscow. Internationally known for his role in ending the authority of the Communist Party of the Soviet Union (CPSU), Shevardnadze was remembered in Georgia as a former agent of that authority. His new job was the gift of two military leaders who had seized the government in January after a bloody struggle against Zviad Gamsakhurdia, a popularly elected but increasingly dictatorial president. Georgia had no diplomatic relations, but Shevardnadze quickly established them and, over time, he persuaded most Georgian interest groups to cooperate with the Council. On June 24 he reached an agreement with Russian Pres. Boris Yeltsin to let Russian troops join in the peacekeeping coalition that was to occupy the borders of the homeland of the South Ossetian minority, where fighting between South Ossetians and Georgians was rampant. In October part of the homeland of the Abkhaz minority was seized by an irregular army of Abkhaz and adventurers. Nevertheless, on October 11 elections held throughout the rest of Georgia—including the Ossetian area—for a parliament and a popularly elected chairman attracted 83% of the qualified voters. Shevardnadze, the only candidate for chairman, was endorsed by 90% of those voting.

Shevardnadze was born in Mamati, Georgia, on Jan. 25, 1928. A precocious leader in Komsomol, the CPSU's youth group, he graduated from the Party School of the Communist Party of Georgia in 1951 and from the Kutaisi Pedagogical Institute in 1959. He was a district secretary of the party (1961–64), deputy minister of the Georgian ministry in charge of internal affairs (1964–65) and then minister (1965–72), and first secretary of the Communist Party of Georgia (1972–85).

Shevardnadze was the Soviet Union's minister of foreign affairs from July 1985 to December 1990 and from November to December 1991, chosen because of his acquaintance with Soviet leader Mikhail Gorbachev. Both men eventually accepted non-Communist governments in eastern Europe and favoured the emerging open society in the U.S.S.R. Concerned about some of Gorbachev's personnel choices, Shevardnadze, in December 1990, warned of dictatorship and asked to be replaced. Out of office in 1991, he founded the Soviet Foreign Policy Association, quit the CPSU, and helped stop the hard-line coup against Gorbachev in August. Opposing the increasing disdain of the republics for the Union, Shevardnadze resumed office as minister of foreign affairs in November 1991, but Russia took over his ministry's headquarters in December.
(CHARLES JOHNSON TAGGART)

Singletary, Mike
After Mike Singletary played his last game for the Chicago Bears on Dec. 27, 1992, the National Football League lost a link to its past and a touch of class. In an era of inside linebackers in 3–4

defenses, he was the last great middle linebacker. In an era of specialists, he played every down for more than five seasons.

"My goal has always been to be a complete player," Singletary said. "To do whatever I can the best I can, better than anyone else." His work ethic and performance inspired teammates through a 12-year career that included six division championships, seven play-off berths, and the 1985 NFL championship in a 46–10 Super Bowl victory over New England that was the most lopsided at the time. In his last season, with a disappointing won-lost record of 5–11, the Bears' only victory in their last nine games was a retirement present to Singletary at his last home game.

Singletary led the 1992 Bears with 135 tackles, the seventh time he led them and the fifth in a row. He played in the nine Pro Bowls of 1983–91 and was consensus all-NFL the first seven of those seasons. He was the NFL's Defensive Player of the Year in 1985 and 1988, when he had a career-high 170 tackles. He won the 1990 NFL Man of the Year award for performance and community service. Starting 172 games from the middle of his rookie year, he missed only two because of injury and finished with 1,488 tackles, 885 solo tackles, 14 forced fumbles, and 13 recoveries.

Singletary looked both scholarly in black-rimmed glasses and frenzied with wide, eager eyes. He was indeed both, often shouting an offense's upcoming play before the snap and then dashing to the line to stop the ball carrier. He urged teammates to join him in both Bible study and game-film study. He built specialized video and exercise rooms in his house so that he could work more at night and on days off. Even when the 1985 Bears were winning 18 of 19 games and setting defensive records, he talked repeatedly of the elusive perfect game.

The nickname "Samurai" stuck early in his career, inspired by Singletary's reckless abandon and his excited grunts and growls as he played. He said, "When you hit a guy straight-on, with good form, the helmet right where it should be, the right lift, that's thrilling."

Singletary was born Oct. 9, 1958, the youngest of 10 children in Houston, Texas. Linebacker was the only position he wanted to play. In college at Baylor, he averaged 15 tackles a game and was consensus all-American and Southwest Conference Player of the Year in both 1979 and 1980.

(KEVIN M. LAMB)

Siskel, Gene, and Ebert, Roger

In 1992 the most famous and influential thumbs in America still belonged to Gene Siskel and Roger Ebert, Chicago-based film critics whose imperial judgments could mean life or death at the box office. "Siskel & Ebert," their syndicated television show, attracted a weekly audience of 15 million, among them Hollywood movers and shakers (who hoped to be moved rather than shaken when their work was reviewed). Seated across the aisle from one another in a mock theatre balcony, the discriminating duo took turns introducing clips of new releases, periodically launching into short, sometimes face-flushing, finger-jabbing discussions about the films and finally rendering their verdicts—thumbs heavenward for the sublime, netherward for the ridiculous. To the viewer, the spectacle of two knowledgeable critics going *mano a mano* over the movies was good theatre. But to the Hollywood publicist it was good business, especially when the film got "Two Thumbs Up!," the good-filmgoing seal of approval in 1990s America.

There were some who would not have minded seeing those thumbs broken—figuratively speaking, of course. Expressing a fear shared by others in Hollywood, Eddie Murphy said, "Siskel and Ebert go 'horrible picture,' and, I'm telling you [they] can definitely kill a movie." Meanwhile, some journalists objected that the show, which paid each host a million dollars a year, was devoid of serious film criticism. One called it "a sitcom starring two guys who live in a movie theater and argue all the time." Responding to their critics, Siskel and Ebert often pointed to the seriousness of their occasional issue-oriented shows.

The show's longer, thinner thumb belonged to Siskel, the shiny-domed, shadow-cheeked Yale graduate on the left of the aisle. Born in Chicago on Jan. 26, 1946, he began his career 23 years later as a reporter for the *Chicago Tribune,* moving up to film critic soon thereafter.

Wielding the shorter, stubbier thumb, from the right side of the aisle, was the round-faced, bespectacled Ebert, who looked more like a high school teacher than a show biz celebrity. He was born on June 18, 1942, in Urbana, Ill., close to the University of Illinois, from which he would later graduate. Ebert became film critic for the *Chicago Sun-Times* in 1967 and won a Pulitzer Prize eight years later.

Working for rival dailies, Siskel and Ebert were not even on speaking terms until 1975, when they were paired for a Chicago-area movie-review show, "Opening Soon at a Theatre near You." The program evolved into the PBS series "Sneak Previews" (1978), the syndicated "At the Movies" (1982), and finally "Siskel & Ebert" (1986), picking up more viewers and garnering bigger paychecks for its stars along the way. Siskel and Ebert faced competitors, but viewers—in a role reversal—turned thumbs down on the copycat shows.   (MICHAEL AMEDEO)

Smith, John

On July 18, 1992, John Smith was elected by a massive 91% majority to lead the U.K.'s Labour Party following its fourth consecutive election defeat at the hands of the Conservatives. Opinion polls found him by far Labour's most popular politician—more popular even than the party's previous leader, Neil Kinnock—and his victory was never in doubt. Smith, who was moderate in his politics and strongly pro-European in his outlook, had also established a reputation as one of Parliament's most effective debaters.

Smith was born in Argyll, Scotland, on Sept. 13, 1938. He entered the House of Commons in 1970 as member for Lanarkshire North (subsequently Monklands East) and swiftly brought his training as a barrister to bear in debates. He occupied the right wing of the Labour Party; in 1972 he defied the party's anti-European policy and voted in favour of the Conservative government's proposal that the U.K. join the European Communities (EC).

Smith was appointed minister of state for energy in 1975 following Labour's return to power, and in 1978 Prime Minister James Callaghan elevated him to the Cabinet post of trade secretary. After 1979 Smith became a leading member of Labour's opposition shadow cabinet, although his views were out of sympathy with those of the left-wingers who came close to dominating the party in the early 1980s. Apart from his stand on Europe, Smith differed from the left in advocating multilateral, rather than unilateral, nuclear disarmament. Gradually, however, left-wing influence waned, and Smith's influence grew. In 1987 Kinnock appointed him shadow chancellor of the Exchequer. He used this appointment to help steer Labour toward a pragmatic acceptance of market forces and private ownership.

Smith also used his post to swing Labour behind moves toward European unity. He supported the U.K.'s membership in Europe's exchange rate mechanism and advocated that the U.K. play a full part in the long-term strategy to create a single European currency. After Kinnock's resignation in the wake of Labour's April 1992 election defeat, Smith's pro-European stance contrasted with the anti-EC posture adopted by his rival, Bryan Gould. However, by then the mood among Labour's ordinary members had shifted decisively from the left-wing, anti-EC policies of a decade earlier, and Smith won a 10–1 victory over Gould.

(PETER KELLNER)

Spiegelman, Art

Holocaust literature is an expansive, compelling genre that continues to grow and diversify as it struggles to convey events so horrible they are often difficult to accept. By contrast, comic books are rarely recognized for their literary competence or historical value. In his two volumes *Maus I: A Survivor's Tale: My Father Bleeds History* and *Maus II: A Survivor's Tale: And Here My Troubles Began,* author and artist Art Spiegelman not only established the comic book as a mainstream art form but also produced a work that, in chronicling one man's Holocaust ordeal, deepens the reader's understanding of those events.

Maus II, published five years after its predecessor, concludes the powerful and true story of Spiegelman's parents—Vladek and Anja—both survivors of the Auschwitz death camp. Compelling in its ironic anthropomorphic animal depictions—the Jews are drawn as mice and the Nazis as cats—its historical veracity, and its personal accounts, the story is made more complex by its framework. Spiegelman portrays himself as Artie Spiegelman attempting to understand and reconstruct his parents' past while coping with his mother's suicide, his stingy, manipulative father, and his own sense of guilt.

The commercial and critical success of *Maus* earned Spiegelman a "Special Award" Pulitzer Prize in 1992 and a solo exhibit at New York City's Museum of Modern Art. In addition, *Maus II* became a *New York Times* best-seller. Initially appearing on the fiction list, it was moved to nonfiction after Spiegelman appealed for the transfer on the basis of the book's carefully researched, factual scenes.

Born Feb. 15, 1948, in Stockholm, Spiegelman immigrated to the U.S. with his family. He began selling cartoons and illustrations to the *Long Island* (N.Y.) *Post* at age 14. Spiegelman attended Harpur College (now the State University of New York at Binghamton) from 1965 to 1968 and worked as a designer, writer, and artist for Topps Chewing Gum, where he helped develop the satirical "Garbage Pail Kids" and "Wacky Packages" bubble-gum cards.

In 1980 he cofounded and coedited *Raw,* an underground comic and graphics journal. With his wife, Françoise Mouly, an artist and publisher, he sought to present graphic novels and "comix" (comics written for a mature audience, as distinguished from the mass-produced variety created for children and adolescents) to a wider public. Recognized as the leading avant-garde comix journal, *Raw* featured the work of European artists as well as previewing Spiegelman's own work. The success and acceptance of *Raw* and *Maus* resulted in a wider commercial audience for Spiegelman and work as a *New York Times* illustrator and *Playboy* cartoonist.   (KATHLEEN HARTMAN)

Spinal Tap

Blurring the distinction between fiction and fact, satire and seriousness, the cinematically created Spinal Tap—"the loudest band in Britain"—became a real-life heavy metal band in 1992. The group had been the most popular nonexistent

PETER DARLEY MILLER

band in music history thanks to its 1984 mock documentary *This Is Spiñal Tap,* which satirized the rock music industry in general and bands with more volume than virtuosity in particular. But in taking their reel act to the real world eight years later, a rather long-in-the-tooth, thick-in-the-flesh Christopher Guest, Michael McKean, and Harry Shearer sought to meet the challenge, in Guest's words, "of fictionalizing something on a very deep level, not just doing parody." Even as the three showed their metal in the musical marketplace, however, people differed on whether they were a light comedy act, a heavy metal band, or both. The songs in Tap's "comeback" album, *Break like the Wind,* seemed to blow in two directions: serious but inane and inane but funny. Meanwhile, on a 20-city tour, as they played, postured, and pulsated, the trio punctuated their concerts with hilarious gaucheries—from malfunctioning props to shamelessly clichéd stagings. Reviewing one of their shows, the *New York Times* applauded the group for being able to traverse the border between "accuracy and parody." The question was whether Tap's nebulous approach would attract a significant, long-term following.

Spiñal Tap was born in 1978 on the ABC special "The TV Show." Introduced by television actor and comic Rob Reiner, the then 30-year-old Guest (co-writer and costar of "The Lily Tomlin Special"), 30-year-old McKean (a featured player on the sitcom "Laverne & Shirley"), and 34-year-old Shearer (co-writer of the Albert Brooks comedy "Real Life") performed "Rock and Roll Nightmare" in long-haired wigs and skin-tight pants. Thinking that the parody was funny enough to be the focus of a movie, the four made a demo tape to peddle around Hollywood.

They did not get the chance to make the movie until five years later, however. Shot with handheld cameras by director Reiner and stocked with rock songs co-written with Reiner and performed by Guest, McKean, and Shearer, *This Is Spiñal Tap* followed the adventures of a big-headed, half-witted, over-the-hill British band as it sought to drum up interest in its new album, *Smell the Glove,* through an American concert tour. Guest played perpetually petulant guitarist Nigel Tufnel; Shearer portrayed pompous, pipe-smoking bass player Derek Smalls; and McKean peered—with dope-dead eyes—through reams of blonde hair as vocalist David St. Hubbins, whose willful girlfriend eventually took over the band and turned its decline into a free fall. Seeming to extend the joke into real life, viewers bought 200,000 copies of *Smell the Glove*—approximately 200,000 more than fans in the movie did. (MICHAEL AMEDEO)

Suchocka, Hanna

On July 10, 1992, when the Sejm (parliament) approved Hanna Suchocka, Polish Pres. Lech Walesa's nominee, as prime minister, she became the first woman to hold the post and the fifth prime minister of Poland since the fall of communism in 1989. Her first orders of business were to resolve political disputes and to improve Poland's faltering economy. She favoured the continuation of the austerity program and was committed to economic reform, but she also promised aid to those citizens adversely affected by the Polish transition to a market economy. Her opposition to abortion earned her support among the more conservative church-based parties.

Suchocka, born in 1946 in Pleszew, near Poznan, in western Poland, was the daughter of a pharmacist. She studied law at the University of Poznan and graduated in 1968. Her expertise in constitutional law and human rights led to lecturing positions at the University of Poznan and the Catholic University of Lublin.

In 1980 she joined the Sejm as a member of the Democratic Party, which was then affiliated with the Communist Party. In 1981 she voiced opposition to the imposition of martial law. After she voted against the 1984 law that banned Solidarity, she was expelled from the Democratic Party.

As a member of Solidarity and the centre-left Democratic Union that grew out of Solidarity, Suchocka was elected to the Sejm in 1989 and 1991. The coalition that gave Suchocka a majority in the Sejm—the first for a prime minister since

1989—included several Solidarity-based parties. The three key parties of the ruling coalition were Suchocka's own Democratic Union, the church-based Christian National Union, and the centre-right Liberal Democratic Congress.

Her government faced its first crisis at the end of July, when a wave of industrial strikes erupted. By early September, however, leaders of the biggest strike—at a car parts factory in Tychy—had scaled back their wage demands. A parliamentary victory for Suchocka came on August 4, when the Sejm passed a constitutional amendment allowing her government to bypass parliamentary procedures and implement economic policy by decree. Labour troubles erupted again at year's end with rail and coal strikes.

Suchocka, who was fluent in English, French, and German, also served as vice-chairman of the legislative committee and as head of the Polish delegation to the Council of Europe. Many believed that her organizational and managerial skills would help her secure a compromise between Poland's traditionalists and those who insisted on immediate radical reform.

(FRANCINE SHONFELD SHERMAN)

Terkel, Louis ("Studs")

In 1992 Studs Terkel, perhaps the United States' best known oral historian, published *Race,* a book that dealt with a subject he interpreted as "the American obsession."

JERRY BAUER

Born May 16, 1912, in New York City, Terkel and his family moved to Chicago (the city that he is most frequently identified with) when he was nine. Despite the Great Depression, he managed to finish his schooling at the University of Chicago Law School. Terkel failed his first bar examination and decided not to pursue a career in law. In the 1930s, while holding down a job as a civil servant, he also embarked on a somewhat successful career as a radio actor. His acting jobs led to other radio spots, including news commentator, sportscaster, and disc jockey. In 1945 he began his long association with the Chicago fine arts station WFMT by inaugurating the "Wax Museum," a program that brought out his knack for engaging people in impromptu interviews. His talk show was still a daily feature on WFMT in 1992.

In the late 1960s, Terkel began to use a tape recorder to chronicle his conversations with people. In 1967 he published *Division Street: America,* a book consisting of 70 conversations he had recorded with people in the Chicago area. He said that the tape recorder "can be used to capture the voice of a celebrity. . . . It can be used to capture the thoughts of the non-celebrated—on the steps of a public housing project, in a frame bungalow, in a furnished apartment, in a parked car—and these 'statistics' become persons, each one unique.

I am constantly astonished." *Division Street* was a best-seller and was followed by *Hard Times: An Oral History of the Great Depression* (1970). Two other books expanded the genre: *Working: People Talk About What They Do All Day and How They Feel About What They Do* (1974) and *American Dreams, Lost and Found* (1980). Both poignantly revealed that, at times, many Americans felt demoralized and disillusioned by their lots in life. *Working* was made into a stage musical.

In 1992 Terkel published his most daring book—*Race: How Blacks and Whites Think and Feel About the American Obsession.* Perhaps even more than his earlier books and in light of the fact that the U.S. was feeling the pinch of a recession, this "oral history" exposed a deep sense of disenchantment and even resentment among the interviewees. Despite the less-than-optimistic current that pervades *Race,* Terkel's latest endeavour provided a unique perspective on an emotionally charged issue. (ELIZABETH LASKEY)

Tomba, Alberto

In just over two minutes of sheer brilliance, the career climax for Alberto Tomba was attained at Albertville, France, on Feb. 18, 1992, when the charismatic Italian from Bologna produced a superlative finish in the giant slalom to become the first Alpine ski racer to retain that Olympic title; he had first gained the crown four years earlier in Calgary, Alta. He took the bronze medal in the giant slalom at the world championships in 1987 before winning both the slalom and giant slalom at the 1988 Olympics.

That season he showed off his exceptional talent with top points in each of the slalom and giant slalom World Cup ratings. He finished second in the World Cup slalom in 1989 and 1990, first in the giant slalom in 1991, and first in both slalom and giant slalom in 1992. An outstanding specialist slalom racer who shunned even entering downhill races, Tomba remarkably overcame that handicap against more versatile all-rounders by four times finishing close to the overall cup winner. He was runner-up in 1988, 1991, and 1992 and placed third in 1989 in spite of being sidelined for several weeks after breaking a collarbone in two places. After just seven years on the World Cup circuit, he had gained 28 individual race victories—17 in the slalom and 11 in the giant slalom.

Born the son of a wealthy textile merchant on Dec. 19, 1966, at San Lazzaro di Savena, Italy, "La Bomba," as Tomba is affectionately known by his fans, quickly cultivated a colourful playboy image, and it took time and much self-discipline to control his unhelpful nightlife and excess weight. His excitable temperament often proved a handicap, sometimes causing him to lose concentration.

Most experienced slalom racers tend to exercise more caution in the first of a race's two descents, but Tomba was inclined to go all out each time, an all-or-nothing policy that could either gain him a medal or result in no points at all. Extremely light-footed despite a heavy frame, he had a stylish, almost balletic grace when zigzagging from gate to gate, seldom touching the posts.

Inspired often by the roars of exultant supporters, Tomba once claimed to be "the new messiah of skiing," but his trainer, Gustavo Thoeni, subsequently made him more professional, more serious, and calmer. His extroverted nature hid a steely determination to prove best in deeds as well as words. (HOWARD BASS)

Turabi, Hassan ʿAbdallah at-

By most assessments, in the years following the forcible installation in 1989 of a fundamentalist Islamic military regime in The Sudan, Sunni Muslim jurist and political activist Hassan ʿAbdallah at-Turabi assumed the determining role in Sudanese government. The National Islamic Front (NIF), the political party that at-Turabi founded in 1986, had participated in the coalition government of elected president Sadiq al-Mahdi (at-Turabi's brother-in-law) but was implicated in the coup that replaced al-Mahdi with Gen. Omar al-Bashir. Although al-Bashir banned all political parties, the titular leader relied increasingly on advisers and officials drawn from the NIF elite.

On March 22, 1991, the government instituted in the predominantly Muslim northern states a stringent code of Islamic religious law that at-Turabi had originally drafted in 1983 as attorney general under the dictator Gaafar Nimeiry.

At-Turabi was born in 1930 in the Sudan. He earned a bachelor of laws degree from the Uni-

versity of Khartoum, The Sudan, in 1958, a master of laws degree from the University of London in 1961, and a doctorate in public law from the University of Paris in 1964. He became dean of the faculty at the University of Khartoum, subsequently resigning to serve as secretary-general of the Islamic Charter Front. From 1965 to 1968 he was a member of the Constituent Assembly. Although at-Turabi was originally a prominent opponent of the Nimeiry regime and was often detained for his activities during the 1970s, he later reconciled with the dictator and served in his Cabinet. The original implementation of Shari'ah (Islamic law) under at-Turabi's counsel in 1983 led to his imprisonment two years later following the fall of the Nimeiry regime.

Educated in Europe and fluent in French and English, at-Turabi lent to Islamic fundamentalism a cosmopolitan, intellectual cast. His eloquent writings on legal theory and politics espoused a conservative form of populism, ostensibly somewhat at odds with traditional clerical authority. The state, in his view, represented a fusion of popular will and divine law. In 1992 at-Turabi predicted that Islamic fundamentalists would control the governments of most Muslim countries 10 years hence.

Among the more progressive proposals enumerated in at-Turabi's published works were a call for relaxation of strictures governing Muslim women and a rejection of hostage taking and other coercive measures. In practice, however, in a strife-torn, poverty-stricken country that was one-third non-Muslim, at-Turabi's theories and legal formulations advanced a brutal repression. His unofficial visit to Washington, D.C., in May 1992, which included appearances at the Center for Strategic and International Studies and before a House Foreign Affairs subcommittee, elicited protests from human rights advocates and Sudanese opposition groups.   (JIM CARNES)

Van Duyn, Mona
In October 1992 Mona Van Duyn became the first woman U.S. poet laureate, consultant in poetry to the Library of Congress. Frequently described as a "domestic poet" who celebrated "married love," Van Duyn was much more. Her poetry examined the daily lives of ordinary people, mixing prosaic with unusual, simple with sophisticated. Her clear vision illuminated much of life's "motley and manifold." She used wry humour, insight, irony, and technical skill to find meaning and possibility in a merciless world. Love and art offer

the possibility of redemption—"but against that rage slowly may learn to pit / love and art, which are compassionate."

Van Duyn's work is filled with literary references, as in "Leda Reconsidered," a reference to Yeats's "Leda and the Swan," and in "An Essay on Criticism," which employs the genre and heroic couplets of Alexander Pope. Interspersed with references to philosophy, psychology, and the arts (Freud, Plato, Camus, Norman O. Brown are used in epigraphs and elsewhere) are those to nursery rhymes, the Bible, and Greek myths. She often extended images, a complex metaphor with all its possibilities being developed throughout a poem. Her characteristic use of formal verse set her apart from many of her contemporaries. In "Since You Asked Me . . . ," she explained: "Why rhyme? / To say I love you to language, especially now / that its only viable components seem to be / 'like,' 'y'know?,' and 'Wow'! " and "It's a challenge to chaos *hurled*. / Why use it? Why, simply / to save the world." She defended the use of meter as "not just style but lifestyle."

Van Duyn was born May 9, 1921, in Waterloo, Iowa. She attended Iowa State Teachers College (now the University of Northern Iowa; B.A., 1942) and the University of Iowa (M.A., 1943). During the 1940s she taught at the University of Iowa Writers' Workshop and later at several other universities and writers' workshops. In 1947 with her husband, Jarvis Thurston, she founded *Perspective: A Quarterly of Literature,* which she coedited until 1967. Her first volume of poetry, *Valentines to the Wide World,* was published in 1959. She won well-deserved recognition following the publication of *To See, to Take* (1970), receiving the 1970 Bollingen Prize for achievement in American poetry and the 1971 National

Book Award. She was awarded the 1991 Pulitzer Prize for poetry. Her other works include *A Time of Bees* (1964), *Merciful Disguises* (1973), and *Near Changes* (1990). *Firefall* and *If It Be Not I: Collected Poems 1959–1982* were scheduled for publication in early 1993.   (ELLEN FINKELSTEIN)

Williams, Willie L.
The worst rioting in the history of Los Angeles erupted on April 29, 1992, sparked by the acquittal of four Los Angeles police officers who had been charged with police brutality. The trial garnered wide publicity because the beating of black motorist Rodney King by the white officers had been captured on videotape and shown on nationwide television. Many viewers saw the videotape not as a single incident but as concrete evidence of a chronic problem of police brutality toward racial minorities.

Even before the riots, it had been clear that a major change would have to be made in the Los Angeles Police Department to restore its credibility. The change took place when the city's controversial chief of police, Daryl F. Gates, nearing retirement, was encouraged to step down in favour of an outsider from Philadelphia, Willie L. Williams. By the time Williams actually assumed control of the department, the riots had broken out, the definition of his position had been changed by voter referendum, and budget cuts loomed on the horizon.

Williams was born in West Philadelphia on Oct. 1, 1943, the son of a meatcutter and carpenter. He began his law-enforcement career in 1964 as an officer in the Fairmount Park Guards and rose to become a police captain in 1984. Four years later he was appointed police commissioner of the city of Philadelphia. In that post he gained a reputation as a capable administrator who effectively reduced police brutality. His successful career in police work in a major urban centre and his willingness to address and resolve racial division matched the needs of Los Angeles as it sought to replace Gates.

The appointment of Williams marked a new direction for the LAPD in two important ways: he was black and he was an outsider. These two points, in addition to his excellent qualifications and leadership in community-based policing, were highly visible signals to the people of Los Angeles that the department was serious about improvement. As Chief Williams assumed the helm of the LAPD, the city was still reeling from the riots, antipolice sentiment was running high, and the force itself was split by inner tensions and strained by budget cuts. In 1992 its budget was trimmed by almost $28 million, and its personnel numbered just over 7,800, a decline of 600 employees since 1991. In addition, Proposition F, passed in the June 1992 election, limited the police commissioner to two terms of five years each. Tackling the problems of a riot-torn city with a fractured force and a tight budget was an enormous task, but even in his first months in office Chief Williams was demonstrating his commitment to reform.   (AMANDA McCLURE)

Xuxa
Every morning from Monday to Saturday, nearly four million Brazilian children sat glued to their television screens avidly watching the antics of their hero, the actress-singer-model Xuxa (pronounced SHOO-sha). By 1992 the four-and-a-half-hour "Xuxa Show" was the highest rated daytime television program in Brazil and drew a large children's audience from 16 other countries worldwide, including the U.S., Puerto Rico, and Spain. Her show was a mixture of fantasy and reality, combining fairy tales and games with serious matters, such as ecological themes. By way of explaining her success, Xuxa said, "I try to create fantasies and help people to dream." Xuxa was more than a fad; she became an indelible part of the childhood of an entire generation of Brazilians.

The tall, blond, blue-eyed Xuxa was born Maria da Graça Xuxa Meneghel on March 27, 1963, in Santa Rosa, Brazil. Not exactly a conventional role model for Brazilian youth, she was the descendant of Austrian-Italian immigrant grandparents and a military-officer father. At 16 she became a Ford Agency model and shortly thereafter made her debut in soft-core pornography films. Cleaning up her act and capitalizing on the sort of "glamorous mother image" she presented to children, Xuxa skyrocketed to fame with a series of children's films, including *A Blunderer in Noah's Ark, The Blunderers in the Kingdom of Fantasy,* and *The Blunderers and the Wizard of Oz;* television appearances; and record album releases. After the debut of the Spanish-language version of her megahit "Xuxa Show" in 1991, Xuxa became the first Latin American to make the *Forbes* list of top entertainers by earning a total of $10 million in 1991 alone and by having a reported net worth of $100 million.

Although Xuxa was once known only as soccer star Pelé's girlfriend and was later referred to as the Brazilian version of pop singer Madonna, her contributions to society were not as shallow as these descriptions would imply. Herself a drug-free, alcohol-free vegetarian, Xuxa took part in antidrug campaigns, public information programs

BILL CRESPINEL—CAMERA PRESS/GLOBE PHOTOS

on AIDS, and polio vaccination campaigns. To demonstrate her concern for the plight of those in need, Xuxa used a large portion of the revenues she earned from the sale of some 50 licensed products bearing her name (toys, children's clothing, a children's dictionary, yogurt, shampoo, and comic books, to name a few) to shelter, feed, and educate 250 needy children via the Xuxa Meneghel Foundation. She also donated time and money to several philanthropic causes worldwide.

(SUSAN RAPP)

Yamaguchi, Kristi

A recent upsurge in technique in women's figure skating was epitomized by a petite fourth-generation American of Japanese ancestry, Kristi Yamaguchi. In the space of three months during 1992, she achieved a significant triple crown: the U.S. national title at Orlando, Fla., the Olympic gold medal at Albertville, France, and the world championship on home ice at Oakland, Calif.

Although it had been obvious to discerning observers several years earlier that Yamaguchi had championship potential, it was not until the 1989 U.S. figure skating championships that she gained worldwide attention by finishing second. The tiny powerhouse from Fremont, Calif., then 17, also won the pairs and thus became the first American to win medals in two events at the national championships since Margaret Graham 35 years earlier. At the 1989 world championships in Paris, Yamaguchi placed fifth in pairs with partner Rudi Galindo and sixth in the singles.

Yamaguchi was born July 12, 1971, in Hayward, Calif. She began taking skating lessons at the age of five and took part in her first competition three years later. From 1983 to 1990 she competed in the pairs event with Galindo. In 1988 she became the first girl to win gold medals in two events, singles and pairs, at the world junior championships.

Success did not come easily, however. Born with severely clubbed feet, Yamaguchi was fitted with casts when only two weeks old. "Her feet were turned in all the way," her mother recalls. "Because she was growing so fast, the casts had to be changed every seven weeks. This went on for several months and then she had to wear special shoes."

Jim Hulick, her pairs coach, said that "she may be small and look frail, but don't be deceived. I sometimes wonder where she gets the strength, but it is almost endless. She is an extraordinary athlete." Her Canada-based singles coach, Christy Kjarsgaard Ness, said, "My task has been made

easier because Kristi is a very attentive listener with a retentive memory and has the ability to give undivided concentration." An outstanding jumper, Yamaguchi completed five triples in her free-skating routine at the Olympics. (See SPORTS AND GAMES: Ice Skating.)   (HOWARD BASS)

Yamauchi, Hiroshi

When Hiroshi Yamauchi, president of Nintendo Corp., put up 60% of the $125 million purchase price for the Seattle (Wash.) Mariners professional baseball team, he dismissed his investment as "no big deal." Many die-hard U.S. sports fans disagreed. But the Mariners were in deep financial trouble, so in June all but one of the 26 U.S. owners of major league clubs voted to accept Yamauchi's offer. The deal gave the Japanese businessman less than 50% of the voting stock and included a promise to the fans that the Mariners would remain in Seattle.

Yamauchi was born on Nov. 7, 1927, in the old cultural city of Kyoto. He took over Nintendo in 1949 after the death of his grandfather, whose small shop, set up in 1889, was hand producing Japanese playing cards. When Yamauchi became president of the company, he was a 22-year-old sophomore at Waseda University in Tokyo. In 1959 he scored a coup when the Disney characters he was licensed to produce on the back of his playing cards caught the public's fancy. He then began concentrating on portable video games. His biggest hit, Game Boy, was followed by Donkey Kong, and they became sensations in arcades. In 1983 Yamauchi introduced Famicom, a computer game system renamed Nintendo Entertainment System when it was introduced into the U.S. market in 1985. Nearly 190 million units were sold in Japan and 77 million overseas. His latest hits were the Super Mario games, which featured big-eyed, bushy-haired, black-mustachioed Mario, his twin, Luigi, and a host of friends.

Yamauchi remarked that the headquarters of his global company could be anywhere. In fact, two-thirds of his 3,000 employees were based in the U.S., where his son-in-law Minoru Arakawa ran operations from Redmond, a Seattle suburb. Nintendo's earnings came from sales of machines and from license fees paid by some 120 firms producing Nintendo games. With about an 80% share of the U.S. market, Nintendo was in a class by itself. Its sales in 1991 exceeded $4 billion, and profits reached a record $699 million. Its pretax figures surpassed those of such major Japanese industrial giants as Nippon Steel Corp. and Hitachi Ltd.

Yamauchi lived in a huge tiled-roof house with his wife and daughter, one of three children. He was fond of Go, a deceptively simple Japanese board game, and held the rank of 6-dan (degree). He was stubbornly aloof, shunned publicity, and shied away from foreign travel. Except for the rare occasions when he dressed casually to play a few pocket Game Boy games displayed in shops at the Kyoto train station, little was seen of Kyoto's largest taxpayer.   (KAY K. TATEISHI)

Zhang Yimou

That Zhang Yimou (Chang Yi-mou), China's best known and most respected modern director, would draw government censure was not surprising. The country's cultural policies favoured upbeat socialist realism, while Zhang's films were visually arresting, sensual, and often tragic. Yet, despite frequent bans on his work, the director intended to remain in the country.

Zhang was born in Xi'an (Sian), Shaanxi (Shensi) province, in 1951. His father, a former major in the Kuomintang army, was blacklisted by the Communists. During the Cultural Revolution, Zhang spent years in enforced farm labour; afterward he worked in a factory. It was only in 1974, when he tried photography, that he found relief from boredom and pessimism. In 1978 Zhang persuaded the minister of culture to allow him to attend the Beijing (Peking) Film Academy, though at age 27 he had been deemed too old.

At the academy the strongest influence on Zhang and his classmates was negative. After comparing the brilliant pre-Communist-era Chinese films to poor, unimaginative modern works,

they vowed never to make such "backwards trash." After graduation in 1982 Zhang worked in cinematography. He bartered with Wu Tianming (Wu Tien-ming), the head of Xi'an Film Studio, agreeing to photograph Wu's 1987 film The Old Well if Wu would sponsor his directorial debut. Zhang starred in Wu's film as well and won the best actor award at the Tokyo International Film Festival.

With Wu's help Zhang then made Red Sorghum (1987), about a young woman's illicit love affair. Popular in China, it found critical acclaim abroad and won the Berlin Film Festival's Golden Bear award. His next film, Operation Cougar (1989), was also successful but was to be Zhang's last film seen in China for some time. His fame grew with Ju Dou (1990), a fatalistic love story, and Raise the Red Lantern (1991), both nominated for Academy Awards. But after the Tiananmen (Tien-an-men) Square massacre in 1989, the country's leaders initiated strict artistic controls. They banned Ju Dou in China, attempted to withdraw the film from Oscar competition, and refused to allow Zhang to travel to the awards ceremony. (He was finally allowed to attend the 1992 ceremony.) Raise the Red Lantern was also censored because of its tragic story line—the tense and ultimately fatal competition between four wives for the favour of their elderly husband. The ban was finally lifted in September 1992.

Zhang meanwhile continued to work. Qiuju Goes to Court (1992) told the story of a young pregnant woman who brought suit to force the village chief to apologize to her husband. It won the Changchun (Ch'ang-ch'un) Film Festival Gold Cup. With or without government approval, however, Zhang seemed determined to remain in China. He insisted, "I wouldn't be able to make movies in another place. I can only make films in China, because it is my place, my land, my people."   (LORRAINE MURRAY)

Zhu Rongji

The elevation of Zhu Rongji (Chu Jung-chi) to the Political Bureau Standing Committee of China's Communist Party in October 1992 was widely interpreted as a harbinger of accelerated economic reform. Many observers considered Zhu the most likely successor to Prime Minister Li Peng (Li P'eng), who faced possible replacement at the expiration of his term in the spring of 1993. Zhu was one of three new members appointed to the seven-member Standing Committee, which was to steer China's government for the next five years. The prominence of free-market advocates in the new lineup reflected the influence of Deng Xiaoping (Teng Hsiao-p'ing), the nation's 88-year-old "paramount leader," who no longer held an official title.

Zhu was born on Oct. 20, 1928, in Changsha (Ch'ang-sha), Hunan province. He joined the Communist Party in 1949 and earned a degree in electrical engineering from Qinghua (Ch'ing-hua) University in Beijing (Peking) two years later. He worked for a time in the Northeast China Industrial Ministry as deputy head of the Production Planning Office. Comments by Zhu mildly criticizing the Communist Party resulted in his being denounced as a "rightist" in 1957. Following his rehabilitation in 1978, he joined the State Planning Commission and the State Economic Commission, serving the latter as director of the Technical Transformation Bureau in 1982–83 and as vice-minister from 1983 to 1988. During this period he headed economic delegations to Western Europe and the Soviet bloc countries.

Zhu became deputy secretary of the Shanghai Municipal Committee, advancing to secretary in 1989. Concurrently, from 1988 to 1991, he was mayor of the city, where he established a reputation for fiscal accomplishment. In the tumultuous month of June 1989, Zhu declined to call in troops to quell student protests that disrupted transportation and other municipal functions in response to the central government's crackdown on pro-democracy demonstrators in Beijing. Named China's deputy premier in April 1991, Zhu earned the sobriquet "China's Gorbachev" for his assertive approach to economic reform.   (JIM CARNES)

OBITUARIES

Acuff, Roy Claxton, U.S. singer, fiddler, and songwriter (b. Sept. 15, 1903, Maynardsville, Tenn.—d. Nov. 23, 1992, Nashville, Tenn.), reigned as the "King of Country Music" at Nashville's Grand Ole Opry (1938–92) with his booming country tenor voice, which regaled listeners with such all-time favourite songs as "The Great Speckled Bird," his first and one of his biggest hits, and "Wabash Cannonball," featuring his train-whistle imitation. Acuff, a gifted athlete, played semiprofessional baseball before a series of sunstrokes ended that career and prompted him to practice and master the fiddle, given to him by his mother, during his nearly two-year recuperation. He performed in a medicine show before forming his own string band, the Tennessee Crackerjacks, who were renamed the Crazy Tennesseans and finally the Smoky Mountain Boys when Opry management urged the band to adopt a more dignified name. Acuff's emotive, white-gospel singing style helped brand him a "hillbilly music" traditionalist. The Smoky Mountain Boys served as his acoustic backup and as a comedy troupe, which enhanced his trademark antics. Acuff was a yo-yo virtuoso, sported a collection of hand-painted ties, and often balanced a fiddle bow on his nose. Besides his standard Grand Ole Opry radio broadcasts on Saturday nights from the 1940s onward, Acuff was a cofounder in 1942 with Fred Rose of the Acuff-Rose Publishing Co., the world's leading country-music publisher. Acuff recorded extensively and scored such 1940s hits as "Wreck on the Highway," "Night Train to Memphis," "Fireball Mail," and "Pins and Needles." Other hits included "The Precious Jewel," "Steamboat Whistle Blues," "The Great Shining Light," "The Broken Heart," and "It's Too Late to Worry Anymore." Acuff and his band traveled extensively to entertain troops during and after World War II, and he and his band also enjoyed engagements in Europe. Though he ran for governor of Tennessee in the 1940s, he was defeated. In 1962 Acuff, who had sold more than 25 million records, was elected as the first living member of the Country Music Hall of Fame. He was also the recipient of a Lifetime Achievement Award in 1987 from the National Academy of Recording Arts and Sciences and of a National Medal of Art in 1991.

Adler, Stella, U.S. actress and teacher (b. Feb. 10, 1901, New York, N.Y.—d. Dec. 21, 1992, Los Angeles, Calif.), was an accomplished stage actress and founder (1949) of the Stella Adler Conservatory of Acting in New York City, where she tutored a generation of sterling performers, including Marlon Brando, Warren Beatty, and Robert De Niro, in the Method technique of acting developed by Konstantin Stanislavsky. Adler was the daughter of Jacob and Sara Adler, the leading U.S. classical Yiddish stage tragedians. She made her stage debut in her father's production of *Broken Hearts* at the age of four, but she gained her reputation appearing with the experimental Group Theatre in such productions as *The House of Connelly, Big Night, Paradise Lost,* and *Awake and Sing!* In 1934 she studied with Stanislavsky; her interpretation of Method acting stressed that an actor should create by using imagination and differed from the Method approach taught by Lee Strasberg, who headed the Actors Studio and instructed actors to draw from their experiences. Adler also believed that the art, architecture, and clothes of an era were an integral part of role development. She taught her students that self-awareness coupled with creative imagination was vital to forming characterizations. Besides teaching, Adler directed several New York stage productions; appeared in such films as *Love on Toast* (1938), *Shadow of the Thin Man* (1941), and *My Girl Tisa* (1948); and starred onstage in *He Who Gets Slapped* (1946) and *Oh Dad, Poor Dad, Mama's Hung You in the Closet and I'm Feelin' So Sad* (1961). In 1988 she published *Stella Adler on Acting.*

Almendros, Nestor, Spanish cinematographer (b. Oct. 30, 1930, Barcelona, Spain—d. March 4, 1992, New York, N.Y.), turned the essentially technical craft of cinematic photography into a creative art form in a series of strikingly beautiful French and American films, most notably *Days of Heaven* (1978), for which he won an Academy

AP/WIDE WORLD

Award. Almendros moved to Havana in 1948 to join his exiled father, who had fought with the defeated loyalist forces during the Spanish Civil War. In the early 1950s he studied in Cuba and in Rome and then taught in the United States. He returned to Cuba in 1959 to make documentaries, but in 1961 he came into conflict with the Communist government and moved to Paris. Almendros' use of camera angles, visual imagery, colour, and luminous lighting effects enhanced some of the most critically acclaimed French motion pictures of the 1960s and '70s. He worked with director Eric Rohmer on such films as *Ma Nuit chez Maud* (1968; *My Night at Maud's*), *Le Genou de Claire* (1970; *Claire's Knee*), *L'Amour l'après-midi* (1972; *Chloe in the Afternoon*), and *Pauline à la plage* (1982; *Pauline at the Beach*). He also collaborated with François Truffaut on *L'Enfant sauvage* (1970; *The Wild Child*), *L'Histoire d'Adèle H.* (1975; *The Story of Adele H.*), and *Le Dernier Métro* (1980; *The Last Metro*). In addition to *Days of Heaven,* Almendros' English-language films include *Kramer vs. Kramer* (1979), *The Blue Lagoon* (1980), *Sophie's Choice* (1982), *Places in the Heart* (1984), and *Billy Bathgate* (1991). His autobiography, *A Man with a Camera,* was published in 1985.

Alzado, Lyle, U.S. football player (b. April 3, 1949, New York, N.Y.—d. May 14, 1992, Portland, Ore.), as a ferocious defensive lineman for the Denver Broncos (1971–79), Cleveland Browns (1979–82), and Los Angeles Raiders (1982–85) professional football teams, was admired by fans for his bone-jarring, aggressive playing style but was feared by opponents who faced his 1.91-m (6-ft 3-in), 118-kg (260-lb) hulking frame. Alzado maintained his formidable physique by taking massive doses of anabolic steroids, drugs that he claimed (although it could not be proved) served as a catalyst for the rare type of brain cancer that claimed his life. After his disease was diagnosed in April 1991, he became a self-anointed symbol of the dangers of steroid use as his massive muscles were reduced to a frail form. Alzado was named Little All-American for his playing with Yankton College, Yankton, S.D. He confessed that it was then that he began taking steroids. Alzado continued to take body-enhancing drugs throughout his professional career, and he revealed that he was so addicted to them that he took them even after his retirement. A maverick on the gridiron,

Alzado was also noted for his temper; he once ripped a helmet off an opponent in retaliation for what he thought was a personal foul against him. Alzado was named the NFL's defensive player of the year in 1977, when he was with the Broncos, but many felt that he reached the pinnacle of his career with the Raiders. He played on the Raider team that routed the Washington Redskins 38–9 in the 1984 Super Bowl. After retiring in 1986, Alzado embarked on an acting career; he attempted a comeback with the Raiders in 1990 but was unsuccessful.

Anderson, Dame Judith (FRANCES MARGARET ANDERSON), Australian-born actress (b. Feb. 10, 1898, Adelaide, Australia—d. Jan. 3, 1992, Santa Barbara, Calif.), had a distinguished stage and screen career for more than 70 years, but she was best known for her Oscar-nominated performance as the malevolent housekeeper, Mrs. Danvers, in the 1940 motion picture *Rebecca* and for her Tony award-winning portrayal of the title character in Robinson Jeffers' play *Medea* (1947–49; staged for television 1959). Anderson made her stage debut in Sydney, Australia, in 1915 and in 1918 moved to the United States, where she scored her first major success in *Cobra* (1924) in New York City. Her striking appearance and intense dramatic style were perfectly suited to complex villainous characters, notably Nina in Eugene O'Neill's *Strange Interlude,* Lavinia in O'Neill's *Mourning Becomes Electra,* Gertrude in *Hamlet,* and a chillingly effective Lady Macbeth, a

AP/WIDE WORLD

role that garnered her television's Emmy awards in 1954 and 1961. After *Rebecca,* Anderson's film roles often exploited her theatrical intensity and her ability to invoke a sinister mood from the smallest vocal inflection or gesture, as in *King's Row* (1941), *All Through the Night* (1942), *Laura* (1944), and *The Furies* (1950). She could be equally effective, however, when cast against type, as in her portrayal of the long-suffering Big Mama in Tennessee Williams' *Cat on a Hot Tin Roof* (1958) and the austere priestess in *Star Trek III: The Search for Spock* (1984). In the 1980s she appeared as a domineering matriarch on the popular U.S. daytime soap opera "Santa Barbara." Anderson was made Dame Commander of the Order of the British Empire in 1960.

Andrews, (Carver) Dana, U.S. actor (b. Jan. 1, 1909, Collins, Miss.—d. Dec. 17, 1992, Los Angeles, Calif.), was a handsome and durable leading man who turned in sensitive performances in such 1940s films as *Laura,* as a cynical detective obsessed by a portrait of a woman whose apparent murder he is investigating; *The Ox-Bow Incident,* as an innocent victim of a lynch mob; *A Walk in the Sun,* as a tough sergeant leading a platoon; and *The Best Years of Our Lives,* as a heroic World

War II veteran returning to an uncertain future. Andrews, a onetime accountant, hitchhiked to Los Angeles in 1931 to try to break into show business. He worked in a gas station and attended the Pasadena Playhouse before making his motion-picture debut in *The Westerner* (1940). Some of his other notable films include *Beyond a Reasonable Doubt, Boomerang, My Foolish Heart,* and *While the City Sleeps.* After his career began to wane in the 1960s, he briefly performed onstage and from 1969 to 1972 appeared in the television soap opera "Bright Promise" before returning to the screen in *Airport 1975* (1974) and *The Last Tycoon* (1976). During the 1950s he was arrested twice for drunken driving, and though he did not believe in making commercials, he appeared on television in 1972 as a spokesperson for sobriety for the Federal Department of Transportation.

Arletty (ARLETTE-LÉONIE BATHIAT), French actress (b. May 15, 1898, Courbevoie, France—d. July 24, 1992, Paris, France), was a legendary star of the French cinema in the 1930s and '40s; she was best known for her stunning portrayal of the courtesan Garance in director Marcel Carné's classic film *Les Enfants du Paradis* (1945; *Children of Paradise*). Arletty grew up in a working-class suburb of Paris and worked in a factory and as a secretary before turning her sensual good looks to her advantage as an artists' model and music-hall chorus girl. She made her motion-picture debut in *Un Chien qui rapporte* (1930) and had minor roles in numerous films, but she achieved star status with *Hôtel du Nord* (1938), the first of her five collaborations with Carné. The others were *Le Jour se lève* (1939), *Les Visiteurs du soir* (1942), and *L'Air de Paris* (1954). Arletty was briefly jailed as a collaborator in 1944 because of a wartime liaison with a German officer. She did not make another movie until 1949 (*Portrait d'un assassin*), the same year she triumphed as Blanche in Jean Cocteau's stage production of Tennessee Williams' *A Streetcar Named Desire.* Arletty's later work included the film version of Jean-Paul Sartre's *Huis-clos* (1954; *No Exit*) and *The Longest Day* (1962), her only English-language film. She also appeared on stage in Brendan Behan's *The Hostage* (1962) and Cocteau's *Les Monstres sacrés* (1966). She lost most of her eyesight in the mid-1960s. Arletty published two volumes of memoirs, *La Défense* (1971) and *Je suis comme je suis* (1987).

Asimov, Isaac, U.S. science-fiction writer, science popularizer, and biochemist (b. Jan. 2, 1920, Petrovichi, Russia—d. April 6, 1992, New York, N.Y.), explored extraterrestrial horizons and the role of robotics in a futuristic society as the enormously popular and prolific author of more than 400 books, notably *Foundation* (1951), *Foundation and Empire* (1952), and *Second Foundation* (1953), a panoramic trilogy detailing the impending collapse of a far-flung galactic empire and the work of an organization of psychologists and social scientists to sow the conditions for a better empire to follow. Asimov, a self-styled compulsive writer, was renowned for the clarity of his writing and for his superb storytelling. He was credited both with popularizing science-fiction writing and with elevating the genre from pulp-adventure stories to a higher intellectual plane, encompassing sociology, history, mathematics, and science. He also published nonfiction books on such wide-ranging subjects as the Bible, Shakespeare, Gilbert and Sullivan, humour, limericks, history, and a variety of scientific topics. A precocious child who immigrated to the U.S. with his family when he was three, Asimov sold his first story, "Marooned off Vesta," to the magazine *Amazing Stories* in 1938. Three years later *Astounding Science Fiction* magazine published "Nightfall," which describes the shattering events that take place on the planet Lagash, a world with six suns, when, during an eclipse, the stars make their once-in-2,000-year appearance. The story was hailed as a masterpiece and 30 years later was voted by the Science Fiction Writers of America as the best science-fiction short story ever written. A year after earning (1948) a Ph.D. in chemistry from Columbia University, New York City, Asi-

THE NEW YORK TIMES

mov joined the faculty of Boston University; after 1958 he did not teach or receive a salary, but he remained professionally associated with the university. Asimov published his first book, *Pebble in the Sky,* in 1950 and followed it with the short-story collection *I, Robot,* which included his famous "Three Laws of Robotics" that helped establish the popular conception of robots, both fictional and real, as benign creations rather than monsters bent on destroying humanity. Asimov was awarded numerous prizes and awards for his works, including five Hugos (given by fans) and three Nebula Awards (given by fellow science-fiction writers). Among his remarkable output are *The Stars, like Dust* (1951), *The Chemicals of Life* (1954), *The Caves of Steel* (1954), *Inside the Atom* (1956), *The Naked Sun* (1957), *The Human Brain* (1964), *ABC's of Ecology* (1972), *Asimov's Guide to Science* (1972), *The Gods Themselves* (1972), *Our World in Space* (1974), *Views of the Universe* (1981), *The Robots of Dawn* (1983), *Foundation's Edge* (1982), *Foundation and Earth* (1986), *Prelude to Foundation* (1988), *Nemesis* (1989), *Asimov Laughs Again* (1992), and *Forward the Foundation,* scheduled to be published posthumously. Besides two volumes of autobiography, *In Memory Yet Green: The Autobiography of Isaac Asimov, 1920–1954* (1979) and *In Joy Still Felt: The Autobiography of Isaac Asimov, 1954–1978* (1980), he regularly contributed to several magazines, including *Fantasy and Science Fiction, Isaac Asimov's Science Fiction,* and *American Humanist.*

Atassi, Nureddin al-, Syrian politician (b. Homs, Syria, 1929—d. Dec. 3, 1992, Paris, France), was swept into power and named president in 1966 after Syria's 10th coup in 20 years. His turbulent reign set the stage for the eventual takeover by strongman Hafez al-Assad. Atassi trained as a doctor, receiving his M.D. from Damascus University in 1955. He entered politics during the 1960s, becoming embroiled in the internal intrigues of the Ba'th Party, at that time divided between two factions. Atassi became a leader of the "progressive" wing, which advocated Marxist-inspired economic policies and a strong relationship with the U.S.S.R. After the party seized power in 1963, he was named minister of the interior. In 1964 he served as deputy prime minister, and in 1965 he was made a member of a five-man Presidential Council. After a military junta orchestrated by members of the progressive faction took power in 1966, Atassi was named president; he served as secretary-general of the party as well. Atassi managed to stay in power for four years (through the Six-Day War in 1967) and became prime minister in 1968, yet his position was always tenuous at best. In 1969 an attempted coup led by Assad, who headed the competing "nationalist" wing of the party, was thwarted only by Moscow's threatened withdrawal of all military and economic aid. The next year Atassi sought

to support Palestinian guerrillas (who were based in Jordan and fighting King Hussein's army) by sending Syrian army troops; Assad, as minister of defense, refused to send air cover, and they were defeated. Atassi, who was placed under house arrest in 1970 after Assad assumed power, was later reportedly moved to al-Mezze military prison in Damascus. In November 1992 Atassi was sent to Paris because of ill health.

Babbitt, Arthur, U.S. animator (b. Oct. 8, 1907, Omaha, Neb.—d. March 4, 1992, Los Angeles, Calif.), as a master artist during the golden era of animation, created such classic Disney cartoon characters as Geppetto the wood-carver in *Pinocchio* (1940), the evil queen in *Snow White and the Seven Dwarfs* (1937), and the drunken mouse in *Country Cousin* (1936), which won an Academy Award for his employer, Walt Disney. Babbitt worked (1929–32) for Terrytoons before joining Walt Disney Studios in Los Angeles, where he also gave life to the dancing mushrooms in *Fantasia* and the stork in *Dumbo.* His special fascination was with movement and the personality development of characters, and he was dubbed "the father of Goofy" for shaping that simpleminded dog into a major star. In 1941 Babbitt was fired from Disney for his union activities, but he was reinstated after the U.S. Supreme Court ruled that he had been illegally dismissed. Despite his poor vision, he served in a combat unit with the marines during World War II. Babbitt then returned to Disney until 1947, when he became a free-lance animator. For United Productions of America he created *The Family Circus* cartoons in 1951, and as director of the commercial department at Hanna-Barbera Studios he garnered more than 80 awards for his television advertisements, notably those for (Fred) Flintstone vitamins. Babbitt also taught classes at Richard Williams Animation in London, the studio that won Academy Awards for the animated *Christmas Carol* (1971) and the 1988 *Who Framed Roger Rabbit* (1988). His last animation was in Williams' *The Thief and the Cobbler,* which appeared posthumously.

Bacon, Francis, British painter (b. Oct. 28, 1909, Dublin, Ireland—d. April 28, 1992, Madrid, Spain), as the "master of the macabre," was simultaneously lauded as one of the towering figures of contemporary British art and derided as a morbid sensationalist. Using photographs, films, or paintings by other artists as inspiration for his visually disturbing portraits, Bacon twisted, distorted, and smeared figural images to express anger, isolation, and horror. His most powerful works included the 1944 triptych "Three Studies for Figures at the Base of a Crucifixion," which he reworked in 1988 as "Second Version of Triptych 1944"; the "screaming popes," a series based on Diego Velázquez' "Portrait of Pope Innocent X"; and numerous paintings of the human body taken from motion studies by the 19th-century photographer Eadweard Muybridge. Bacon, the son of a British horse trainer in Ireland, was educated at home. At the age of 16 he was banished by his parents for his homosexual activities, and despite his lack of formal training, he was drawn to the London art scene. For several years he moved between London, Paris, and Berlin, painting and selling furniture and rugs of his own design. He destroyed most of these early paintings, however, and did not exhibit again until the end of World War II. After the war Bacon settled in London and devoted his life to painting, gambling, and swilling champagne at the Colony Room, a Soho drinking club. Although he refused to accept a knighthood, he received many artistic honours and was the subject of important retrospectives in New York City, Tokyo, Paris, Moscow, and Washington and twice at the Tate Gallery in London. In May 1990 a triptych by Bacon sold for the record price of $6,270,000.

Bacon, Francis Thomas, British engineer (b. Dec. 21, 1904—d. May 24, 1992), developed the first practical hydrogen-oxygen fuel cells, which convert air and fuel directly into electricity through electrochemical processes. This high-efficiency, pollution-free technology gained its first practical application in the U.S. space program, which used Bacon's alkaline fuel cells to provide in-flight power, heat, and clean drinking water (a by-product of the electrochemical reaction) in Apollo space vehicles. A graduate of Eton College and Trinity College, Cambridge (B.A., 1925; M.A., 1946), Bacon became intrigued with fuel cells while working (1925–40) for the electrical company C.A. Parsons Co. Ltd. in Newcastle-on-Tyne. Although Sir William Grove had discovered the principle of fuel cells in 1842, they were considered a scientific curiosity until the early 1940s when Bacon, then working at King's College, London, proposed their use in submarines. He continued his research with the Anti-submarine Experimental Establishment, then returned (1946) to Cambridge, where he demonstrated a successful six-kilowatt fuel cell in 1959. As principal consultant to National Research Development Corp. (1956–62), Energy Conservation Ltd. (1962–71), and the U.K. Atomic Energy Authority (1971–73), Bacon sought new applications for fuel cells. By the 1990s there were fuel-cell power plants in operation in Japan, and the technology was being developed in many other countries. Bacon was made an Officer of the Order of the British Empire (1967), elected a fellow of the Royal Society (1973), and awarded the first Grove Medal (1991).

Barber, Walter Lanier ("Red"), U.S. baseball broadcaster (b. Feb. 17, 1908, Columbus, Miss.—d. Oct. 22, 1992, Tallahassee, Fla.), as the home-spun announcer, notably on radio, for the Cincinnati Reds (1934–39), Brooklyn Dodgers (1939–53), and New York Yankees (1954–66) professional baseball teams, enthralled audiences with his colourful play-by-play images of the game. The much-beloved announcer "sittin' in the catbird seat" delighted listeners with his folksy expressions, including such famous analogies as depicting the baseball diamond as "the pea patch" and a sewn-up game as "tied up in a crocus sack." Barber, who was revered as the greatest baseball broadcaster of his era, combined technical expertise with intriguing between-play asides, and punctuated spectacular plays with his signature, "Oh-ho Doctor!" Known for his integrity, Barber left the Dodgers after he was urged to make his

AP/WIDE WORLD

commentary more supportive of the team, and he was fired by the Yankees after he reported that the last-place team had attracted a mere 413 fans for a September game. Though he also appeared on television, radio remained his favourite medium. The first baseball radio announcer for New York blew a kiss to Brooklyn when he was dismissed by the Yankees. He became, however, a mainstay on National Public Radio from 1981 with his Friday-morning commentary, and in 1978 he was inducted into the Baseball Hall of Fame. Barber was also the author of several books, including *The Rhubarb Patch: The Story of the Modern Brooklyn Dodgers* (1954), *1947, When All Hell Broke Loose in Baseball* (1982), and an autobiography, *Rhubarb in the Catbird Seat* (1968).

Barnett, Marguerite Ross, U.S. educational administrator (b. May 21, 1942, Charlottesville, Va.—d. Feb. 26, 1992, Wailuku, Hawaii), became the first black woman to head a major university when she was named (1990) president of the University of Houston, Texas. Barnett earned an undergraduate degree (1964) from Antioch College, Yellow Springs, Ohio, before receiving an M.A. (1966) and a Ph.D. (1972) in political science from the University of Chicago, where she was a lecturer. She was on the faculty at Princeton University (1970–76), Howard University, Washington, D.C. (1976–80), and Columbia University, New York City (1980–83), before serving as vice-chancellor (1983–86) of the City University of New York and chancellor (1986–90) of the University of Missouri at St. Louis. An able administrator, she implemented programs to assist poor high school students in making the transition to college and in finding good jobs. Barnett was a skilled fund-raiser and helped secure substantial donations for urban universities by stressing their important role in fostering economic growth. She routinely downplayed the racial element of her appointment, especially when asked by interviewers how it felt to be the first black woman to head a large university. Her skin colour, she felt, was as insignificant as her redheaded assistant's hair colour. During her short tenure at the University of Houston, Barnett raised more than $150 million.

Bartholomew, Freddie (Frederick Llewellyn Bartholomew), British-born child actor (b. March 28, 1924, London, England—d. Jan. 23, 1992, Sarasota, Fla.), epitomized Hollywood's vision of a proper little English boy in such Depression-era motion pictures as *Little Lord Fauntleroy* (1936) and *Captains Courageous* (1937). At the peak of his short film career, the angelic-faced, tousled-headed Bartholomew was the second highest paid child star, after Shirley Temple. He was born into a modest family and was reared by his aunt, Millicent Bartholomew. She found small stage and screen roles for him in Britain before taking him to Hollywood, where his first major role, as the title character in *David Copperfield* (1935), made him an overnight star. Bartholomew's popularity soared with his later films, which included *Anna Karenina* (1935), *Kidnapped* (1938), *Swiss Family Robinson* (1940), and *Tom Brown's School Days* (1940). However, his fame and rising income soon brought out his long-absent parents, who filed an unsuccessful but enormously expensive lawsuit to wrest custody from his aunt. After serving in World War II, Bartholomew returned to acting, but his fortune and his wistful cinematic appeal were both gone. In the early 1950s he moved to New York City, where he became a successful advertising executive.

Bath, Henry Frederick Thynne, 6th Marquess of, British nobleman (b. Jan. 26, 1905, Longleat House, Wiltshire, England—d. June 30, 1992, Longleat House), shocked the British aristocracy in 1949 when he turned his financially distressed family's 16th-century home into a tourist attraction and again in the 1960s when he introduced lions and other African wildlife in a safari park on the estate's grounds. Other peers soon followed suit, however, and the master of Longleat was recognized as the forerunner of the booming "stately home business." After failing his entrance exams at Eton College, he attended Harrow and Christ Church, Oxford, but he was unable to settle on a suitable career. When his father died in 1946, the new Lord Bath inherited a stunning 100-room Elizabethan house that was badly in need of repair, a superb art collection, one of the world's finest private libraries, and crippling death duties that topped £600,000. In order to avoid selling the family valuables, he determined to make the estate support itself, and within three years the renovated house was opened to the paying public. Lord Bath, who cultivated his public image as an eccentric, often worked in the garden, while his sons parked cars and his wife served tea to the visitors. The estate drew tens of thousands of tourists per year, especially after the arrival of the

lions of Longleat in 1966, and it was frequently used as a movie set.

Begin, Menachem Wolfovitch, Polish-born Israeli politician (b. Aug. 16, 1913, Brest-Litovsk, Russia—d. March 9, 1992, Tel Aviv, Israel), was the leader of Irgun Zvai Leumi (an underground

AP/WIDE WORLD

guerrilla group within the Zionist movement to establish a Jewish state on both sides of the Jordan) who eventually became Israeli prime minister (1977–83) and corecipient with Egyptian Pres. Anwar as-Sadat of the 1978 Nobel Prize for Peace. As a teenager Begin joined Betar, a militant Zionist youth movement, and in 1937 he was briefly imprisoned for leading an anti-British demonstration. He received a law degree (1935) from the University of Warsaw, but he never practiced law. In 1940 he was arrested as a dissident and was sentenced to eight years in a Soviet labour camp, but he was released in 1941 to join the Polish army in exile, with which he went to British-administered Palestine. As Irgun commander (1943–48), Begin was held responsible for the group's terrorist activities, including the July 1946 attack on the King David Hotel in which 91 civilians were killed, the 1947 execution of two British soldiers, and the massacre on April 9, 1948, of some 250 Arabs in the village of Dayr Yasin. After the establishment of Israel in May 1948, he emerged from hiding and founded the Herut political party. Begin, a formidable speaker and strategist, courted the votes of Sephardic Jews from North Africa and gradually gained influence and power. In May 1977 the right-wing Likud coalition, of which Herut was a part, won a majority in the Knesset (parliament), and Begin was named prime minister. Although he encouraged the settlement of territories occupied in the 1967 Arab-Israeli war, in late 1977 he unexpectedly accepted Sadat's offer to open a peaceful dialogue. These negotiations eventually led to the awarding of the Nobel Prize and to the return of the occupied Sinai Peninsula to Egypt in 1979. Begin sacrificed much of the world's goodwill, however, when he authorized the 1982 invasion of Lebanon by Israeli forces. He came under increasing foreign and domestic criticism after an official inquiry held Israel indirectly responsible for the massacre of hundreds of Palestinians at the Sabra and Shatila refugee camps in West Beirut. He resigned from office in August 1983.

Black, Eugene Robert, U.S. financier (b. May 1, 1898, Atlanta, Ga.—d. Feb. 20, 1992, Southhampton, N.Y.), as the prudent president (1949–62) of the International Bank for Reconstruction and Development (World Bank), expanded the membership from 48 nations with a capital of $8.3 billion to 80 members with a capital of $20.5 billion and formed two affiliates—the International Development Association, charged with making concessional loans to the poorest countries, and the International Finance Corp., the arm of the bank promoting the private sector. Black, the son of a governor of the Federal Reserve Bank of Atlanta, was a graduate of the University of Georgia and served in the navy during World War I before becoming a successful investment banker on Wall Street, specializing in the bond market. He was propelled into the world of international finance after joining (1947) the World Bank as U.S. executive director under its president, John J. McCloy. During his tenure as president of the bank, he established that institution's credibility with financial markets in the developed world and secured a reputation as a troubleshooter after forging an accord (still existing) between India and Pakistan for distributing the waters of the Indus River. A skilled and hard-boiled negotiator, Black played a vital role in securing loans for Third World countries, although the bank was originally formed (1946) for post-World War II reconstruction in Europe. While Black was at its helm, the bank shifted its emphasis to providing loans for economic development, and it lent more than $6 billion of its own capital in addition to funds from private sources without a default. Upon his resignation in 1962, Black served as Pres. Lyndon Johnson's emissary to Southeast Asia; helped lay the foundation for the creation of the Asian Development Bank; served as chairman of the Brookings Institution, a liberal Washington think tank; and was on the board of directors of numerous companies and financial institutions.

Blackwell, Ed(ward) Joseph, U.S. jazz drummer (b. Oct. 10, 1929, New Orleans, La.—d. Oct. 7, 1992, Hartford, Conn.), was known for his role in the development of free jazz beginning in the

JACK VARTOOGIAN

1960s. Although the snare drum was prominent in his playing, he was often praised as one of the most melodic of drummers. Blackwell grew up in New Orleans, where he was influenced by the city's musical tradition and by such early drummers as Paul Barbarin. After playing with rhythm and blues groups, in 1951 he went to Los Angeles and first performed with saxophonist Ornette Coleman, who was later at the forefront of the free jazz movement. Blackwell moved to New York City in 1960, where he gained recognition as the regular drummer in Coleman's quartet. He also performed with a number of other avant-garde musicians, including trumpeter Don Cherry and the group headed by trumpeter Booker Little and saxophonist Eric Dolphy. In 1975 he became

artist in residence at Wesleyan University, Middletown, Conn. Beginning in 1976 he performed and recorded with other former Coleman associates under the name Old and New Dreams.

Bloom, Allan David, U.S. philosopher and author (b. Sept. 14, 1930, Indianapolis, Ind.—d. Oct. 7, 1992, Chicago, Ill.), was best remembered as the author of the controversial thought-provoking best-seller *The Closing of the American Mind: How Higher Education Has Failed Democracy and Impoverished the Souls of Today's Students* (1987); he was also known in academic circles for his scholarly volumes of interpretive essays and translations of works by Rousseau and Plato. Bloom earned a B.A. (1949), an M.A. (1953), and a Ph.D. (1955) from the University of Chicago, where, under the tutelage of the German-born political philosopher Leo Strauss, he became a devotee of the Western classics and a proponent of the philosophical tenet of "transcultural truth." Bloom taught at the University of Chicago (1955–60) before teaching at Yale University (1962–63) and Cornell University, Ithaca, N.Y. (1963–70). He was also a member of the faculties of the Universities of Tel Aviv, Israel (1969–70), Paris (1970), and Toronto (1970–79). At Cornell he published such well-received works as *Shakespeare's Politics* (1964), a collection of essays, and a translation of Plato's *Republic* in 1968. The following year, when an armed group of students took control of Cornell's administration building and demanded that certain mandatory classes be dropped in favour of those deemed more relevant to them, Bloom tendered (1970) his resignation after the university yielded to their demands. He returned to the University of Chicago in 1979 as a professor with the Committee on Social Thought; he became codirector in 1984 of the university's John M. Olin Center for Inquiry into the Theory and Practice of Democracy. In *The Closing of the American Mind,* Bloom argued that universities no longer taught students how to think; that students, especially those attending the top schools, were unconcerned about the lessons of the past or about examining ideas in a historical context; and that students seeking a liberal education would not be able to get one. His blistering critique, which offered no solutions to the crisis in education, blamed misguided curriculum, rock music, television, and academic elitism for the spiritual impoverishment of students.

Booth, Shirley (THELMA BOOTH FORD), U.S. actress (b. Aug. 30, 1898, New York, N.Y.—d. Oct. 16, 1992, North Chatham, Mass.), gave an unforgettable dramatic performance as the shabby housewife Lola Delaney in *Come Back Little Sheba*; she won a Tony award for her stage role in 1950 and an Academy Award for best actress in 1952. Booth, however, was probably best remembered for her Emmy-winning title-role portrayal

AP/WIDE WORLD

of the irrepressible maid on the television series "Hazel" (1961–66). An amateur actress from the age of 12, Booth made her Broadway debut in 1925 in a supporting role in *Hells Bells.* On radio she was the voice of cashier Miss Duffy on the popular program "Duffy's Tavern," which featured Ed Gardner, her first husband, as Archie. During Booth's Broadway career she often portrayed quick-witted women adept at wisecracking. She appeared in some 40 plays, notably *Three Men on a Horse, The Philadelphia Story, My Sister Eileen, The Time of the Cuckoo,* and the musical version of *A Tree Grows in Brooklyn.* Her film credits include *Main Street to Broadway* (1953), *About Mrs. Leslie* (1954), *The Matchmaker* (1958), and *Hot Spell* (1958).

Boudiaf, Muhammad, Algerian political leader (b. June 23, 1919, M'Sila, Alg.—d. June 29, 1992, Annaba, Alg.), was a founder of the revolutionary National Liberation Front (FLN) and a hero of the Algerian war of independence (1954–62). He broke with his former comrades-in-arms in the early 1960s, but he was unexpectedly recalled in 1992 after more than 27 years in exile to become the nation's president. Boudiaf fought in the French army in World War II, but by 1950 he was a central figure in the nationalist movement against France, and in 1954 he joined Ahmad Ben Bella on the FLN leadership council. In 1956 he and Ben Bella were captured and imprisoned by the French. They were released in 1962 and formed a provisional government in newly independent Algeria, with Boudiaf as deputy premier. He opposed President Ben Bella's autocratic rule, however, and after being interned for several months by his old partner, he went into exile (1964). Boudiaf settled in Morocco, where he managed a brick factory and denounced the increasingly corrupt FLN. In January 1992, with the Islamic fundamentalists on the verge of winning parliamentary elections, he was invited to return as the head of a military-backed council of state. Although he appeared to have gained public support for his announced reforms, Boudiaf was shot and killed while giving a speech at the opening of a new cultural centre; one of his bodyguards was suspected of the shooting.

Bovet, Daniel, Swiss-born Italian physiologist (b. March 23, 1907, Neuchâtel, Switz.—d. April 8, 1992, Rome, Italy), won the 1957 Nobel Prize for Physiology or Medicine for his discoveries of certain synthetic chemotherapeutic substances, notably curare-like muscle relaxants, which are used in conjunction with anesthetics to facilitate surgery, and the first antihistamines, which are effective in the treatment of allergic reactions. Bovet was educated at the University of Geneva (D.Sc., 1929) and took a research position at the Pasteur Institute in Paris. There he found that the dye Prontosil, which had been shown to cure bacterial infections, actually contained a simpler active compound, sulfanilamide. This discovery led to the development of hundreds of antibacterial sulfa "wonder drugs." Bovet was named director of the Pasteur Institute in 1936, and in 1944 he discovered pyrilamine (mepyramine), the first antihistamine. In 1947 he was invited to establish a laboratory of chemotherapeutics at the government-sponsored Superior Institute of Health in Rome. Although he synthesized some 400 compounds that produced curare's paralyzing effects in differing degrees, Bovet filed no patents and received no income from any of his discoveries. Later he moved away from pure research, becoming professor of pharmacology at the University of Sassari (1964–71), director of the psychobiology and psychopharmacology laboratory at the Italian National Research Council (1969–75), and professor of psychobiology at the University of Rome (1971–82).

Boyle, Kay, U.S. author (b. Feb. 19, 1902, St. Paul, Minn.—d. Dec. 27, 1992, Mill Valley, Calif.), gained critical acclaim for her poetry and novels and especially for her short stories, notably "The White Horses of Vienna" (1936) and "Defeat" (1941), for which she won O. Henry Awards. Boyle spent much of her childhood and the early years of her first marriage in Europe and, after briefly returning to the U.S. with her second husband in 1941, she returned to Europe during World War II. After the war she served in France and West Germany as a correspondent (1946–53) for *The New Yorker* magazine. Boyle's thematic works, which stressed the moral responsibility of the individual in desperate situations, showcased her mastery of style. She employed such literary techniques as grammatical simplification, rhythmic repetition, stream of consciousness, radical imagery, and experiments with Surrealism. Her first offerings were romances, but in later works she documented the spirit of the times with fictional works of social realism. When she and her third husband, Joseph von Franckenstein, were blacklisted as Communists during the 1950s witch-hunts conducted by U.S. Sen. Joseph McCarthy, she spoke out against that injustice; she later openly opposed the Vietnam war and the U.S. bombing of Libya in the 1980s. Among her novels were *Plagued by the Nightingale* (1931), *Monday Night* (1938), and *Death of a Man* (1963). Her collections of short stories include *The First Lover and Other Stories* (1933), *The Smoking Mountain: Stories of Post-War Germany* (1951), and *Fifty Stories* (1980).

Brandt, Willy (HERBERT ERNST KARL FRAHM), German statesman (b. Dec. 18, 1913, Lübeck, Germany—d. Oct. 9, 1992, Unkel, Germany), was seen as the moral voice for peace and, while serving as German chancellor, won the 1971 Nobel Prize for Peace for promoting *Ostpolitik*, which set the stage for the eventual reunification of Germany. Born Herbert Ernst Karl Frahm, he was the illegitimate son of a 19-year-old salesclerk. Frahm was strongly influenced by his passionately socialist grandfather and began contributing articles to the local party newspaper at age 14. He had joined the Social Democratic Party (SPD) by age 17. In 1931, however, he felt uncomfortable with what he saw as the party's dangerously moderate views, especially toward the Nazis, and he left the SPD and joined a Marxist splinter group called the Socialist Workers Party. Soon after Hitler came to power in 1933, Frahm fled to Norway, where he became a journalist. By this time he was working under the name Willy Brandt and was keeping in contact with the resistance both inside and outside Germany. After the war he returned to Berlin as the Norwegian press attaché; in 1947 he applied to renew his German citizenship and rejoined the SPD. Brandt was elected mayor of West Berlin in 1957, a post he held until 1966; he became chairman of the SPD in 1964. It was during his tenure as mayor, and especially after the building of the Berlin Wall in 1961, that he began to see the policies of the West as unrealistic and ineffective. Brandt saw that the acceptance of the status quo and thus the normalization of relations between East and West was necessary for any future change. Brandt became chancellor of West Germany when the SPD gained power in 1969. He immediately set about normalizing relations with East Germany (by accepting that "two states exist in Germany"), Poland (by acknowledging the Oder-Neisse line as the border of that country), and the Soviet Union (by signing a treaty in which both sides agreed to "refrain from the threat of force or the use of force in any matters affecting security in Europe and international security"). In 1974 Brandt was forced to resign as chancellor after it was discovered that one of his closest aides was an East German spy. He continued on as party chairman until his resignation in 1987. With tears of joy he watched the Berlin Wall fall in 1989.

Bratby, John Randall, British painter (b. July 19, 1928, Wimbledon, Surrey, England—d. July 20, 1992, Hastings, East Sussex, England), rose to prominence in the 1950s as a member of the Kitchen Sink School, a group of British social-realist artists who paralleled the literary Angry Young Men of the decade. He was particularly known for the feverish speed at which he worked and for the extremely thick texture of his vividly coloured, Expressionistic paintings, into which he often incorporated beer bottles and other every-day items. Bratby was accepted at the Slade School of Fine Art, but he abruptly switched to the Royal College of Art (1951–54). He mounted his first solo exhibition at the Beaux Arts Gallery in London in 1954 and captured the public's fancy almost overnight. In 1957 he was commissioned to provide paintings for the motion picture *The Horse's Mouth,* and for many years thereafter he was identified in the popular imagination with the Bohemian artist at the centre of the film. Although he fell out of critical favour in the 1960s, Bratby continued to work, producing thousands of sketches and paintings, including hundreds of portraits. He also wrote several autobiographical novels, notably *Breakdown* (1960), and served as editor in chief of *Art Quarterly* from 1987.

Brooks, Richard, U.S. screenwriter and motion-picture director and producer (b. May 18, 1912, Philadelphia, Pa.—d. March 11, 1992, Beverly Hills, Calif.), was known for producing films characterized by gritty social realism, especially *The Blackboard Jungle* (1955), and also specialized in adapting literary works to the screen, notably the superb *Elmer Gantry* (1960), for which he won an Academy Award for screenwriting. After attending Temple University in Philadelphia, Brooks began his writing career as a sports journalist. He helped Orson Welles on radio scripts before collaborating on screenplays for such forgettable films as *White Savage* (1943) and *Cobra Woman* (1944). During World War II he served (1943–45) in the marines and wrote a novel about the persecution of a homosexual in *The Brick Foxhole* (1945), which was later adapted to the screen as a film about anti-Semitism and renamed *Cross-fire* (1947). His screen adaptation for *Key Largo* (1948) was critically acclaimed for its taut, tension-building structure, and he made his directing bow with another thriller, *Crisis* (1950). Following the success of *Deadline USA* (1952), Brooks adapted Evan Hunter's novel *The Blackboard Jungle* and directed Glenn Ford in the compelling film about a teacher grappling to earn the respect of ghetto teenagers. Some of his later efforts at literary adaptation were considered somewhat long, including *The Brothers Karamazov* (1958), *Lord Jim* (1965), and *Elmer Gantry,* yet the latter, with strong performances by Burt Lancaster and Shirley Jones, became a classic and was perhaps Brooks's best film. He evoked strong performances from Elizabeth Taylor and Paul Newman in Tennessee Williams' *Cat on a Hot Tin Roof* and again from Newman in another Williams adaptation, *Sweet Bird of Youth.* Brooks's script for Truman Capote's *In Cold Blood* (1967) created a sensation for its brutality, but he did not score another success until 1977, when he adapted Judith Rossner's *Looking for Mr. Goodbar,* which starred Diane Keaton. A tough, intractable director who often delivered scripts at the last moment, he analyzed Hollywood in his unflinching, probing novel *The Producer* (1951). Brooks, who directed the classic Western *The Professionals* in 1966, the year after he became an independent producer, returned to the studios for two films in the 1980s.

Brown, Georgia (LILLIAN KLOT), British actress (b. Oct. 21, 1933, London, England—d. July 5, 1992, London), was an earthy, husky-voiced singer best known for her portrayal of the ill-fated prostitute Nancy in Lionel Bart's musical *Oliver!* Brown began singing jazz and bluesy ballads in nightclubs as a teenager and took her stage name from a popular song. She made her London stage debut in 1956 as Lucy in Kurt Weill's *The Threepenny Opera,* and the next year she repeated the role off-Broadway. After her triumph as Nancy in London (1960–62), on a U.S. tour (1962), and on Broadway (1963–64), she joined the cast of *Maggie May,* which Bart had written for her. She later starred in *Carmelina, Greek, Roza, Man Is Man, 42nd Street, Side by Side by Sondheim, 3 Penny Opera* (a 1989 revival on Broadway), and a one-woman show, *Georgia Brown and Friends.* She also recorded acclaimed solo albums. However, she failed to win the part of Nancy in the 1968 movie of *Oliver!* and had limited success on screen. Brown appeared on television, most notably in a production of Bertolt Brecht's *Mother Courage* and in "Shoulder to Shoulder," a miniseries she produced for the BBC.

Bryceland, Yvonne, South African actress (b. Nov. 18, 1925, Cape Town, South Africa—d. Jan. 13, 1992, London, England), brought passion and political conviction to the theatre through her inspired interpretations of the antiapartheid works of South African playwright Athol Fugard. Bryceland and her second husband, Brian Astbury, also defied South Africa's racially segregated system and founded (1972) the country's first nonracial theatre, the Space Theatre, in Cape Town. She was born Yvonne Heilbuth and worked as a newspaper librarian and amateur actress until after her divorce from her first husband. She made her professional acting debut in *Stage Door* in 1947 but had only moderate success until she joined the Cape Performing Arts Board in 1964. In 1969 Bryceland triumphed in Fugard's *People Are Living There* and *Boesman and Lena* (in which she made her London debut and then toured Europe). Their inspired collaboration blossomed with several more plays, most notably *Orestes, Statements After an Arrest Under the Immorality Act, Hello and Goodbye,* and *The Road to Mecca* (in which she made her U.S. debut). Bryceland's repertoire also included Dario Fo's *One Woman Plays,* Eugene O'Neill's *Long Day's Journey into Night,* Tennessee Williams' *The Glass Menagerie,* Bertolt Brecht's *Mother Courage and Her Children,* Henrik Ibsen's *The Wild Duck,* and Euripides' *Medea.* In 1978 she moved to London, where she joined the National Theatre.

Buchanan, Junious ("BUCK"), U.S. football player (b. Sept. 10, 1940, Gainesville, Ala.—d. July 16, 1992, Kansas City, Mo.), as a towering (2-m [6-ft 7-in]) defensive tackle for the Kansas City Chiefs professional football team (1963–75), combined his size, strength, and agility to set a new standard for defensive lineman during the era of the passing game by consistently knocking down balls thrown by opposing quarterbacks. Buchanan, a basketball and football star at Birmingham (Ala.) Parker High School, attended the small, predominately black Grambling (La.) State University and in 1962 was unanimously named to the National Association of Intercollegiate Athletes (NAIA) All-American team. Buchanan also played on the 1963 College All-Star team that defeated the world champion Green Bay Packers (NFL) in an exhibition game in Chicago. That same year he was the number one draft pick of the AFL Dallas Texans (later Kansas City Chiefs; AFL, 1963–69, and AFC of NFL from 1970). He powered his team during Super Bowl I against the Green Bay Packers and in Super Bowl IV, when the Chiefs beat the Minnesota Vikings 23–7. After retiring as a player in 1975, Buchanan coached for the New Orleans Saints (1975 and 1977) and Cleveland Browns (1978) and became a much-admired civic and business leader in Kansas City. He was named to the NAIA Hall of Fame in 1968 and was inducted into the Professional Football Hall of Fame in 1990, just days after being diagnosed with cancer.

Cage, John, U.S. composer, writer, and philosopher (b. Sept. 5, 1912, Los Angeles, Calif.—d. Aug. 12, 1992, New York, N.Y.), moved beyond established musical language to create works that expanded the idea of what music might be; he was thought by many to have been the greatest single influence in music and the arts after World War II. His education in the arts began early, and he continued formal instruction into his 20s, including study with such composers as Henry Cowell and Arnold Schoenberg. During that time Cage became interested in percussion ensembles, and in 1938 he invented the prepared piano, in which objects of various kinds (nuts, bolts, paper) were attached to the strings so as to emphasize the instrument's percussive qualities. In 1943 one of Cage's percussion groups gave a concert at the Museum of Modern Art in New York City, the beginning of his public reputation. At about this time he began collaborating with the dancer and choreographer Merce Cunningham, an association that lasted until Cage's death. His interest in the thought and culture of the East, including the *I Ching* ("Book of Changes"), led him to introduce chance as an element in composition. *Music of Changes* (1951), a piano piece derived from tosses of coins, and *Imaginary Landscape No. 4* (1951), in which the performers adjusted the volume and tuning of 12 radios, were among such works. Cage later also applied chance operations to performance, so that a work varied from one performance to the next. In addition to compositions using electronically produced sounds, he created a number of works using magnetic tape, as in *Imaginary Landscape No. 5* (1952), in which he cut tapes into pieces and then recombined them according to chance operations. *HPSCHD* (1967–69), with Lejaren Hiller, for harpsichords, tapes, films, slides, and coloured lights, was one of his multimedia works. In *4′ 33″* (1952) the performer remained silent for four minutes and 33 seconds so that the attention of the audience was drawn to whatever sounds happened to be audible. This and other works were examples of Cage's attempts to break down the distinction between musical and nonmusical sounds, and they illustrated his belief that the artist should not so much impose order as draw attention to whatever occurred. Throughout his career Cage taught at schools in the U.S. and other countries, and he was the recipient of numerous honours and awards. Among his many writings were *Silence* (1961) and *A Year from Monday* (1967), both collections of essays and lectures.

Camarón de la Isla (JOSÉ MONGE CRUZ), Spanish Gypsy singer (b. Dec. 5, 1950, San Fernando, Spain—d. July 2, 1992, Barcelona, Spain), revolutionized flamenco music by linking classic *cante hondo* ("profound song") with elements of progressive rock, thus introducing the traditional Andalusian folk music to a new generation of young fans. Despite his shy onstage demeanour, a long history of drug abuse, and occasional outbursts of "artistic temperament," Camarón was adored by rock fans and traditionalists alike. He thrilled audiences with his remarkably expressive voice and his unmistakable *duende*, the elusive spark of genius considered essential to truly great flamenco. He became a professional singer in his teens and took the stage name Camarón de la Isla ("shrimp of the island"), a childhood nickname he had acquired because of his pale skin and slender build. He began singing in nightclubs, but he later concentrated on concerts, usually accompanied by a solo guitarist, and on recording. Camarón's final bout with lung cancer drew intensive media coverage, and his death was followed by three days of public mourning.

Carnovsky, Morris, U.S. actor (b. Sept. 5, 1897, St. Louis, Mo.—d. Sept. 1, 1992, Easton, Conn.), was superb in dialectal character roles and gained renown on both stage and screen with his portrayals of thoughtful, troubled men. After making his New York City stage debut in *The God of Vengeance* (1922), Carnovsky joined (1924) the Theatre Guild's acting company; he had important supporting roles in such plays as *Saint Joan, The Brothers Karamazov,* and *The Doctor's Dilemma* and played the title role in *Uncle Vanya.* He then helped found (1931) the Group Theatre, which specialized in dramas, and he gave an unforgettable performance as Mr. Bonaparte, the father whose son refuses to become a violinist and becomes a prizefighter, in *Golden Boy* (1937). After the Group Theatre disbanded, Carnovsky went to Hollywood and made his motion-picture debut as Anatole France in *The Life of Emile Zola* (1937). In some of his other notable supporting roles, he appeared as a priest in *Edge of Darkness* (1943), as the kindly Gershwin father in *Rhapsody in Blue* (1945), and as an evil nightclub owner in *Dead Reckoning* (1947). His screen career abruptly ended during the 1950s when he was blacklisted by the House Un-American Activities Committee for refusing to testify. He was, however, invited by actor John Houseman to join the American Shakespeare Festival in Stratford, Conn., where he gained renown in such parts as Shylock in *The Merchant of Venice* and the title role in *King Lear.* Carnovsky later made two more motion pictures,

A View from the Bridge (1962) and *The Gambler* (1974). He was inducted into the Theatre Hall of Fame in 1979.

Carstens, Karl, German politician (b. Dec. 14, 1914, Bremen, Germany—d. May 30, 1992, Meckenheim, Germany), overcame harsh criticism for his youthful membership in the Nazi Party to play an instrumental role in forming West Germany's place in postwar Europe and to serve as the republic's president (1979–84). Carstens studied law and political science at the Universities of Frankfurt, Munich, Königsberg, and Hamburg (doctor of law, 1937). In 1937 he joined the Nazi Party in order to obtain a scholarship and to further his future legal career, but he never was an active member of the party. He served in an army antiaircraft unit in World War II, and after the war he was cleared by an Allied denazification court. Carstens continued his studies in Dijon, France, and at Yale University (LL.M., 1949) and returned home to practice law. He represented Bremen (1949–54) in the new central government, and in 1954 he was chosen to represent West Germany in the Council of Europe. Three years later he was one of the architects of the Treaty of Rome, which established the European Economic Community. As a member of Chancellor Konrad Adenauer's Christian Democratic Union (CDU), Carstens served as state secretary of foreign affairs (1960–66), deputy defense minister (1966–67), and head of the chancellor's office (1968–69). In 1972 he was elected to the Bundestag (parliament), where he was subsequently CDU party leader (1973–76) and parliamentary president (1976–79). Despite the controversy over his nomination as West German president, Carstens was an effective and popular head of state. He retired from public office in 1984 at the end of his term.

Carter, Angela, British writer (b. May 7, 1940, Eastbourne, Sussex, England—d. Feb. 16, 1992, London, England), took motifs from mythology, legends, and fairy tales and reshaped them with macabre humour and eroticism in a series of novels and short stories that owed more to the so-called magical realism of Gabriel García Márquez and other Latin-American writers than to more traditional British realism. Carter, who was born Angela Olive Stalker, rejected an Oxford education in favour of a job as a journalist with the *Croydon Advertiser.* In 1961 she moved with her first husband to Bristol, where she studied medieval literature at the University of Bristol (B.A., 1965). She had moderate success with her novels *Shadow Dance* (1966; U.S. title *Honeybuzzard,* 1967) and *The Magic Toyshop* (1967; filmed 1986). After her third book, *Several Perceptions* (1968), won the Somerset Maugham Award in 1969, she used the prize money to leave her unhappy marriage, move to Japan for two years,

and write. Carter's later novels included *The Infernal Desire Machines of Doctor Hoffman* (1972), *The Passion of New Eve* (1977), and *Wise Children* (1991). Her fiction gained new popularity in the 1980s, notably after the release of *The Company of Wolves* (1984), the motion picture she cowrote that was based on a story from *The Bloody Chamber* (1979), a collection of adult adaptations of fairy tales. Carter's interest in the macabre and the sensual was reflected in her chief nonfiction work, *The Sadeian Woman: An Exercise in Cultural History* (1979), a polemical study of the Marquis de Sade's female characters. She also wrote radio plays, children's books, and essays.

Casson, A(lfred) J(oseph), Canadian painter (b. May 17, 1898, Toronto, Ont.—d. Feb. 19, 1992, Toronto), produced watercolours featuring landscapes of sun-drenched Ontario towns and was the last surviving member of the Group of Seven painters (1920–32), who forged a national identity through the visual arts with canvases reflecting the Canadian landscape. Casson studied at Hamilton (1913–15) and Toronto (1915–17) before joining a commercial art firm. In 1926 he was invited to join the Group of Seven, replacing Frank Johnston. By then the painters had turned from exclusively depicting harsh landscapes to including urban scenes. Casson helped revive the watercolour medium, and in later years he was instrumental in helping the Ontario Provincial Police identify forgeries, especially of Group of Seven works. A commercial artist for 32 years, Casson could not afford to paint full time until he retired at 61. An especially harsh critic of his own works, Casson destroyed, to his later regret, many of his first paintings. In his later years he saw some of his early canvases fetch as much as $200,000. His most famous work was "Anglican Church at Magnetawan."

Coles, Charles ("HONI"), U.S. dancer (b. April 2, 1911, Philadelphia, Pa.—d. Nov. 12, 1992, New York, N.Y.), was a self-taught tap-dancing virtuoso whose feathery light footwork reputedly made "butterflies look clumsy." Coles performed in vaudeville during the 1920s, and for many years he showcased his soft-shoe elegance with partner Cholly Atkins. The duo performed with many of the top jazz bands of the 1940s, fronted by Cab Calloway, Count Basie, Duke Ellington, and Fats Waller. Coles's artistry was honed during long hours of practice as he devised intricate footwork patterns by extending the duration of his steps and worked to become the fastest dancer in show business. His dancing gained recognition in 1949 when he and Atkins made their Broadway debut in *Gentlemen Prefer Blondes.* Coles also appeared on Broadway in *Hello, Dolly!* and in a production of *Bubbling Brown Sugar.* During the 1960s and '70s, when the popularity of tap dancing waned, he served as production manager of the Apollo Theater in New York City. At the age of 73, he won a Tony award for his show-stopping performance in Broadway's *My One and Only,* and in 1991 he was awarded a National Medal of the Arts.

D'Aubuisson, Roberto, El Salvadoran political figure (b. Aug. 23, 1943, San Salvador, El Salvador—d. Feb. 20, 1992, San Salvador), was the founder, in 1981, of the extreme right-wing political party Nationalist Republican Alliance (Arena) and was widely characterized as the brains behind the Union of White Warriors, which allegedly conducted assassinations by "death squad" during El Salvador's civil war (1979–92), which claimed some 75,000 lives. D'Aubuisson, born of French immigrant stock, was not among the ruling oligarchy of 14 wealthy families that held power during his youth. After being educated by the Jesuits, he attended military school and joined the National Guard, which had a reputation for brutality. He attended the International Police Academy in Washington, D.C., and the Political Warfare Cadres Academy in Taiwan before serving as an intelligence officer with the National Guard and then as deputy director of Ansesal, the presidential security agency. When reformists in the military overthrew the de facto government

AP/WIDE WORLD

of Gen. Carlos Humberto Romero, D'Aubuisson was given backing by the coffee oligarchs, who resisted demands for land redistribution and political reforms, to organize new political parties. D'Aubuisson was thrown out of the army in 1979 after gaining a reputation for right-wing terrorist activity and coup attempts. He was implicated in the 1980 abortive coup to unseat Majano Ramos and in the murder of Roman Catholic Archbishop Oscar Romero that same year. He took refuge in Guatemala before returning to El Salvador to form Arena and served as president (1982–83) of the Constituent Assembly. In 1984 he lost the presidential election to José Napoleón Duarte of the Christian Democratic Party. D'Aubuisson, who was characterized by a U.S. ambassador to El Salvador as a "pathological killer," denied any link to those killings he was accused of masterminding, including the 1980 murder of Mario Zamora Rivas, El Salvador's attorney general, and the 1989 slayings of six Jesuit priests. In 1989 Arena's candidate, Alfredo Cristiani, became president. D'Aubuisson tried to uphold the party hard line amid Cristiani's attempts to negotiate an end to the civil war with the left-wing guerrillas. Just five weeks before d'Aubuisson's death from throat cancer, a formal cease-fire was signed.

David, Elizabeth, British food writer (b. Dec. 26, 1913—d. May 22, 1992, London, England), celebrated the joys of cooking in a series of magazine columns and books that revolutionized the everyday kitchens, shops, and restaurants of Britain in the years following World War II. Although the recipes in her books were sometimes sketchy, David conveyed an enthusiasm for good food and for European culture that even non-cooks found enticing. While studying literature and history at the Sorbonne in Paris, she was captivated by the local cuisine, and after a brief stint as an actress and an unsuccessful marriage, she resolved to share her culinary passion. In *A Book of Mediterranean Food* (1950), David conjured up both the romance of sunnier climes and the succulence of bouillabaisse, ratatouille, and other dishes filled with such authentic ingredients as fresh garlic, olive oil, Parmesan cheese, and butter—items that were unknown or unobtainable in ration-weary postwar England. She continued with *French Country Cooking* (1951), *Italian Food* (1954), *Summer Cooking* (1955), *French Provincial Cooking* (1960), *Spices, Salt and Aromatics in the English Kitchen* (1970), and *English Bread and Yeast Cookery* (1977). In 1965 she opened the first kitchen shop in London, but she quit the business in 1973 after a falling out with her partners. A collection of early essays, *An Omelette and a Glass of Wine,* appeared in 1984. David was made Chevalier du Mérite Agricole of France in 1977 and Commander of the Order of the British Empire in 1986.

Deng Yingchao (Teng Ying-ch'ao), Chinese political figure (b. Feb. 4, 1904, Guangshan [Kuangshan] county, Henan [Honan], China—d. July 11, 1992, Beijing [Peking], China), was a revolutionary hard-liner who with Premier Zhou Enlai (Chou En-lai), her husband, weathered the chaotic factionalist fighting during the Cultural Revolution (1966–76). After her husband's death (1976) and the rise of Deng Xiaoping (Teng Hsiao-p'ing), she became a high-ranking official and emerged, like her husband, as a much beloved figure. Deng was given (1978) a seat on the Communist Party's Political Bureau, and she served (1983–88) as head of the Chinese People's Political Consultative Conference. Her commitment to expanding women's rights was manifested early in life when she joined the movement to abolish the custom of binding women's feet. She took part in the May Fourth Movement (1917–21), a revolution by young intellectuals aimed at preserving Chinese society and culture in the wake of Japanese encroachment. When she was 15, Deng joined the Awakening Society, a liberal student movement headed by Zhou, and was arrested for her radical activities. She joined the Communist Party in 1924. After Deng and Zhou married in 1925, the newlyweds were forced underground after the Kuomintang massacred their Communist comrades in Shanghai in 1927. Deng reportedly underwent an abortion late in her pregnancy in order to flee the Nationalist police, and she was never again able to conceive. She and Zhou fled to Moscow before returning (1930) to Shanghai, where they joined Mao Zedong's (Mao Tse-tung's) followers on the epochal Long March (1934–35). Deng was one of only 50 women on the 10,000-km (6,000-mi) trek and was carried on a stretcher for hundreds of kilometres after contracting tuberculosis. While seeking medical attention in Beijing in 1936, she eluded detection by posing as American journalist Edgar Snow's servant. After the Communist victory in 1949, Deng was revered as the nation's "elder sister." She was instrumental in promoting women's rights, and in 1956 she became a member of the Communist Party Central Committee. A party loyalist, she advocated the use of military force against the student-led 1989 pro-democracy movement.

Dennis, Sandy (SANDRA DALE DENNIS), U.S. actress (b. April 27, 1937, Hastings, Neb.—d. March 2, 1992, Westport, Conn.), was alternately praised and criticized for her quirky mannerisms, which became a hallmark of her career, and turned in an Academy Award-winning performance as best supporting actress as the mousy and nervous faculty wife in *Who's Afraid of Virginia Woolf?* (1966). Dennis hit her stride during the 1960s, making her film debut in *Splendor in the Grass* (1961) and then winning Tony awards for her Broadway roles as a social worker in *A Thousand Clowns* (1962) and as the unconventional mistress of a tycoon in *Any Wednesday* (1964). She also gained critical acclaim for her convincing performance as an idealistic schoolteacher recruited to a tough New York City school in *Up the Down Staircase* (1967). Her screen roles were mostly solemn ones, including the unstable women she portrayed in two Robert Altman films: *That Cold Day in the Park* (1969) and *Come Back to the Five and Dime, Jimmy Dean, Jimmy Dean* (1982). In *Sweet November* (1968) Dennis starred as a woman dying from an incurable disease; in *The Out-of-Towners* (1970) she was a hapless victim of crime and circumstance; and in *The Four Seasons* (1981) her husband betrayed her for a younger woman. In one of her last roles, a cameo, she appeared in *Another Woman* (1988) as a bitter actress coming to terms with her past. Dennis succumbed to ovarian cancer.

DeRoburt, Hammer, Nauruan politician (b. Sept. 25, 1922, Nauru—d. July 15, 1992, Melbourne, Australia), as Nauru's head chief and longtime president, was at the centre of political life on the central Pacific island for more than 30 years. DeRoburt was educated at Geelong Technical College in Australia and returned to his native island to teach in 1940. After Japanese forces invaded Nauru in 1942, he was deported (along with

most of the population) to Truk (now Chuuk) in Micronesia until 1946. As a member of the local government council (from 1955) and head chief (from 1965), DeRoburt led the negotiations for local control over Nauru's immensely rich phosphate industry and for political independence from Australia, which administered the island as a UN-mandated trust territory. In 1968 he was elected the first president of independent Nauru, and he remained in power until 1989, except for a two-year span (1976–78) when he was voted out of office and a brief period in late 1986 when he was temporarily ousted by government opponents. In 1982 he was awarded an honorary knighthood by Britain's Queen Elizabeth II. DeRoburt was finally replaced as president in August 1989.

Deutsch, Helen, U.S. screenwriter (b. 1907?, New York, N.Y.—d. March 15, 1992, New York), was the prolific and critically acclaimed author of such diverse screenplays as *Lili* (1953), a heartwarming story starring Leslie Caron as an orphan; *I'll Cry Tomorrow* (1955), a drama featuring Susan Hayward in the role of alcoholic singer-actress Lillian Roth; and the brassy musical *The Unsinkable Molly Brown* (1964), with Debbie Reynolds as the indomitable *Titanic* survivor. Deutsch scored her first success as co-writer of the blockbuster film *National Velvet* (1944), featuring Elizabeth Taylor as a young girl training her horse for the Grand National Steeplechase. Earlier Deutsch ran a theatre company, covered theatre for the *New York Herald-Tribune* and the *New York Times,* and established the New York Drama Critics Circle in protest against the Pulitzer Prize-winning selections. She wrote scores of newspaper articles, short stories for magazines, and several plays and television scripts. A sometime lyricist, she created the words for "Hi Lili Hi Lo," which she described as "dreadful." Among her other scriptwriting credits were *The Seventh Cross* (1944), *King Solomon's Mines* (1950), *It's a Big Country* (1952), *Forever Darling* (1956), and the popular success but critically reviled *Valley of the Dolls* (1967), her last effort. Deutsch then returned to New York City, where she became a recluse.

Devi, Kanan(bala), Indian motion-picture actress (b. 1916?, Bengal, India—d. July 17, 1992, Calcutta, India), brought glamour, technical skill, and a mellifluous singing voice to Bengali cinema for more than three decades, but she retired in the 1960s when she became disillusioned with the increasingly raucous style of Indian films. Devi, who came from a poor family, began acting in silent movies in 1926 and made a smooth transition when talkies arrived in 1931. By 1936 she was an established star, and she joined the innovative New Theatres studio. Although she appeared in several popular Hindi-language films, including *Vidyapati, Abhinetri,* and *Lagan,* she refused to leave Calcutta and move to the industry capital, Bombay. Devi eventually launched her own production company to produce and direct her films. In 1968 she was honoured by the Indian government with the Padma Shri, one of the nation's highest civilian awards, and in 1976 she received the Dada Saheb Phalke prize for her lifetime contribution to Indian cinema.

Devlin, Patrick Arthur Devlin, BARON, British jurist (b. Nov. 25, 1905, Chislehurst, Kent, England—d. Aug. 9, 1992, Pewsey, Wiltshire, England), capped a distinguished legal career as a barrister (1929–48), a High Court judge (1948–60), a lord justice in the Court of Appeal (1960–61), and a law lord in the House of Lords (1961–64) by abruptly resigning at the age of 58 to lecture and campaign for reforms in the British legal system. Devlin was educated at Stonyhurst College and Christ's College, Cambridge, and was called to the bar in 1929. He established a thriving practice in commercial law and worked for the Ministry of Supply during World War II before taking silk in 1945. Two years later he was named attorney general of the duchy of Cornwall, and the next year he became, at age 42, the youngest High Court judge of the century. In 1961 he was made a life peer and elevated to the nation's highest appeals court, but after three years he resigned, declaring he found his work in the House of Lords "so utterly boring." Lord Devlin remained active, however, as chairman of the press council (1964–69) and high steward of the University of Cambridge (1966–91). He also sought reforms that would create a U.S.-style supreme court in Britain, campaigned for the release of the Guildford Four (wrongly convicted of engineering two IRA bombings in 1974), and wrote numerous books, notably *The Enforcement of Morals* (1959) and *Too Proud to Fight: Woodrow Wilson's Neutrality* (1974).

di Donato, Pietro, U.S. writer (b. April 3, 1911, West Hoboken, N.J.—d. Jan. 19, 1992, Stony Brook, N.Y.), captured the gritty realism of the lives of immigrant Italian labourers in the largely autobiographical best-seller *Christ in Concrete,* which was hailed as a masterpiece when it was published in 1939. The novel provided a richly detailed portrait of the life of di Donato's father, Geremio, a bricklayer who was buried in concrete when a building collapsed and killed him. The book, which blended religious and philosophical themes, was a powerful testimony to di Donato's riveting storytelling. He was only 12 when his father died. When his mother died shortly thereafter, he became a bricklayer. He learned to write by frequenting libraries, where he gained inspiration reading the works of French and Russian writers. His other literary offerings were modest in both number and popularity. They included *Immigrant Saint: The Life of Mother Cabrini* (1960), a biography; *Three Circles of Life* (1960), the sequel to *Christ in Concrete; The Penitent* (1962), a biography; and *Naked Author* (1970), a collection of short stories. Di Donato also wrote a few plays and regularly contributed short stories to magazines.

Dietrich, Marlene (MARIE MAGDALENE VON LOSCH), German-born actress (b. Dec. 27, 1901, Berlin, Germany—d. May 6, 1992, Paris, France), exuded a seductive charm and smoldering sensuality that, coupled with her sinuous figure and sultry voice, made her one of the most glamorous stars in Hollywood during the 1930s and '40s. In Germany she studied to be a violinist before a wrist injury ended her ambitions for a professional career. She then studied acting under theatrical director Max Reinhardt, and she made her film debut in *Der kleine Napoleon* (1923) and appeared in other bit roles before being discovered by Austrian director Josef von Sternberg. He cast her in *Der blaue Engel* (1930; *The Blue Angel*) as cabaret singer Lola-Lola, a heartless femme fatale who enticed and destroyed a schoolteacher; her remarkable performance and her rendition of the song "Falling in Love Again" in her trademark white tie, tails, and top hat made her an international star. After the premiere of *The Blue*

Angel, Dietrich went to the U.S. with Sternberg, who cultivated her screen persona and starred her in such masterpieces as *Morocco* (1930), as the smitten cabaret singer who followed foreign legionnaire Gary Cooper into the desert in her evening gown; *Dishonored* (1931), as the notorious spy who applied lipstick and adjusted her stockings before being executed by a firing squad; *Blonde Venus* (1932), as a devoted mother and café singer who donned a gorilla suit for a routine; *Shanghai Express* (1932), as a woman of easy virtue who proclaimed, "It took more than one man to change my name to Shanghai Lily"; and *The Scarlet Empress* (1934), as a resplendent Catherine the Great. However, her last film with Sternberg, *The Devil Is a Woman* (1935), was a flop. Dietrich's career faded and she was dubbed "box-office poison," but she made a comeback in *Destry Rides Again* (1939), which showcased her gift as a comedienne as the barroom-brawling Frenchie. She then appeared in a string of forgettable films before using her considerable talents and million-dollar-insured legs to entertain Allied troops in Italy, France, and the U.S. during World War II. Earlier she reportedly had rebuffed Adolf Hitler's request to be his mistress, and she became a U.S. citizen in 1939. For her war efforts, which included making anti-Nazi broadcasts in German and entertaining troops under battle conditions, she was awarded the U.S. Medal of Freedom. After returning to the screen, she shone in *Stage Fright* (1950), *Rancho Notorious* (1952), *Witness for the Prosecution* (1957), *Touch of Evil* (1958), and *Judgment at Nuremberg* (1961) before making her final bow in *Just a Gigolo* (1979). During the 1950s she starred in a series of successful appearances in cabarets and one-woman Broadway shows, and during '60s and '70s tours she vaunted her still-delectable form in skintight gowns, which reportedly covered an ironlike body stocking. She left the stage in 1975 when she broke a leg, but the image she projected remained incomparable. Though she loved to wear trousers, she glimmered in gowns; though she was married and never divorced her husband, she had numerous liaisons; though she was an accomplished seductress, she remained aloof. In 1986 her offscreen voice gave life to the documentary *Marlene.* Even as Dietrich lived the last years of her life in reclusion in Paris, her enigmatic personality continued to entrance admirers intent on unraveling her mystique.

Dixon, Willie (WILLIAM JAMES DIXON), U.S. blues musician (b. July 1, 1915, Vicksburg, Miss.—d. Jan. 29, 1992, Burbank, Calif.), exerted an extraordinary influence on modern blues and the emergence of rock and roll as the behind-the-scenes creator of blues classics, notably "I'm Your Hoochie Coochie Man," which was interpreted by such recording stars as Jimi Hendrix, the Allman Brothers, and Muddy Waters. In 1936 Dixon moved to Chicago, where he began selling some of his songs. That same year he captured the Illinois Golden Gloves amateur heavyweight boxing title as James Dixon, but he soon returned to music and played the double bass with such groups as the Five Breezes and the Four Jumps of Jive. His next band, the Big Three Trio, played blues and harmony at Chicago clubs (1946–52), but when that group dissolved, he began working full time for Chess Records, expertly serving as artists and recording manager, producer, composer, musician, talent scout, and middleman between the artists and the company, which was headed by Polish-born brothers. As blues clubs were established in black Chicago neighbourhoods, they became a virtual mecca for bluesmen. Dixon's upbeat blues compositions, which he sold for as little as $30, helped usher in the Chicago blues sound during the 1950s and were standard numbers for any young white rock group trying to make the record charts during the 1960s. His original songs included "Little Red Rooster" (Howlin' Wolf, the Rolling Stones), "You Shook Me" (Led Zeppelin), "Back Door Man" (Howlin' Wolf, the Doors), "I Ain't Superstitious" (Howlin' Wolf, Jeff Beck, Savoy Brown), and "I Just Want to Make Love to You" (Muddy Waters, the Rolling Stones, Foghat). Dixon's songs were also adopted

by Elvis Presley, the Everly Brothers, the Yardbirds, Cream, and Aerosmith. Dixon later led a band called the Chicago All-Stars and traveled widely throughout the U.S. as well as in Europe, where he was revered. The magnitude of his influence was summed up by Big Willie himself with his release of the album called "I Am the Blues" and a 1989 autobiography with the same title. He was the founder of the Blues Heaven Foundation, a nonprofit organization to benefit older blues performers and provide scholarships to young musicians.

Douglas-Home, William, British playwright (b. June 3, 1912, Edinburgh, Scotland—d. Sept. 28, 1992, Kilmeston, Hampshire, England), was the prolific creator of more than 40 plays in four decades. His most successful works were light drawing-room comedies that featured the top stars of the British theatre. At one time he had four plays running simultaneously in London's West End. Many of his plays were produced on Broadway and made into motion pictures. Douglas-Home was educated at Eton and New College, Oxford. It was at Eton that he wrote his first play—a 10-minute piece. He went on to study at the Royal Academy of Dramatic Art and appeared onstage in London before making writing his career. Douglas-Home drew on his own experiences for many of his plays. During World War II, for example, he was court-martialed for refusing to take part in an attack that killed more than 2,000 civilians in the French port of Le Havre. His prison experiences formed the basis for *Now Barabbas* (1947), his first West End play. His three unsuccessful candidacies for Parliament and the political career of his brother, former prime minister Sir Alec Douglas-Home (later Lord Home), also became sources for such plays as *The Chiltern Hundreds* (1947) and *The Reluctant Peer* (1964). Other successes included *The Reluctant Debutante* (1955), *The Secretary Bird* (1968), *The Jockey Club Stakes* (1970), *Lloyd George Knew My Father* (1972), *The Kingfisher* (1977), and *Portraits* (1987). Among his books were three volumes of autobiography: *Half Term Report* (1954), *Mr. Home Pronounced Hume* (1979), and *Old Men Remember* (1991).

Drake, Alfred (ALFRED CAPURRO), U.S. actor (b. Oct. 7, 1914, New York, N.Y.—d. July 25, 1992, New York), breathed new life into musical theatre as the star of Broadway's *Oklahoma!* (1943), which featured his rich baritone voice in exuberant renditions of such enduring songs as "Oh, What a Beautiful Morning," "People Will Say We're in Love," and "The Surrey with the Fringe on Top." Drake was a chorus singer before being discovered while performing in the Broadway musical *Babes in Arms* (1937). That role helped him land the romantic lead, the part of Curly, in

Oklahoma! He appeared in *Sing Out, Sweet Land* (1944), *Beggar's Holiday* (1946), and *The Cradle Will Rock* (1947) before scoring critical acclaim as shrew-taming Fred Graham in *Kiss Me, Kate* (1948), as the wily Hajj in *Kismet* (1953), and as suave Honoré Lachalles in *Gigi* (1973). His talents also extended to drama. He had serious roles in *Much Ado About Nothing* (1957) and *Hamlet* (1964). Drake won Drama Critics Awards for his roles in *Oklahoma!* and *Kismet* and a Tony award for *Kismet*, and in 1990 he received the Tony Honor of Excellence award. Drake was inducted into the Theatre Hall of Fame in 1981.

Dubcek, Alexander, Czechoslovak politician (b. Nov. 27, 1921, Uhrovec, Czech.—d. Nov. 7, 1992, Prague, Czech.), was the Communist Party leader whose attempt in 1968 to give his country "social-

REUTERS/BETTMANN

ism with a human face"—known as the "Prague Spring"—ended in invasion by Soviet-led Warsaw Pact troops. Dubcek attended school in the Soviet Union, where his father, one of the first members of the Czechoslovak Communist Party, was helping to build the new Communist nation. The family returned to Czechoslovakia in 1938, and Dubcek became a member of the outlawed Communist Party of Slovakia. During the World War II Nazi occupation, he took part in the underground resistance. After the war Dubcek began to rise through the party ranks, and by 1962 he had become a full member of the Presidium of the Central Committee. The next year he became a full member of the party, and in January 1968 he became first secretary. He almost immediately began to allow greater freedom: control of the news media was relaxed; travel abroad was allowed; and plans were made for economic reform and the reinstatement of human rights. Leaders of the other Warsaw Pact nations denounced Dubcek's action, however, and relations rapidly deteriorated. Soviet pressure increased and, though compromises were made, Warsaw Pact troops invaded Czechoslovakia on the night of Aug. 20–21, 1968. Dubcek was arrested, taken to Moscow, and forced to grant major concessions and legitimize the invasion before being returned to Prague. He remained in office until he was demoted (April 1969) and then served as ambassador to Turkey (1970) and as a forestry official (1970–88). With the democratization of the government in 1989, however, Dubcek reemerged, and until June 1992 he held the largely symbolic post of chairman of the Federal Assembly.

Dupain, Maxwell Spencer, Australian photographer (b. April 22, 1911, Sydney, Australia—d. July 27, 1992), captured visually the powerful geometric forms inherent in architectural and industrial subjects, thus developing an influential style of Australian nonpictorial commercial photography. Dupain exhibited his first landscape photographs while attending grammar school. He studied at the East Sydney Technical College and the Jul-

ian Ashton art school (1933–35) and apprenticed (1930–34) with Cecil Bostock. During World War II Dupain, by then a successful fashion and portrait photographer, left his studio to work for the army camouflage unit; he then worked for the Department of Information (1945–47). On his return he de-emphasized picturesque landscapes and portraiture in favour of the more abstract architectural and industrial imagery that established him as one of Australia's most significant Modernist photographers. Dupain was the subject of numerous exhibitions and retrospectives, notably an 80th-birthday-celebration exhibit at the Photographers' Gallery in London, and was made an Officer of the Order of the British Empire.

Elliott, Denholm, British actor (b. May 31, 1922, London, England—d. Oct. 6, 1992, Ibiza, Spain), enjoyed a 47-year career in theatre, in motion pictures, and on television—usually in supporting character roles—and gained a reputation for stealing any scene he was in. Elliott was educated at Malvern College and briefly studied at the Royal Academy of Dramatic Art. During World War II he was a radio operator and gunner in the Royal Air Force. While spending three years in a German prisoner-of-war camp, he organized the No Name Players and developed an interest in acting. After the war Elliott appeared in London's West End in *The Guinea Pig* (1946). He soon caught the attention of Laurence Olivier and appeared as his son in *Venus Observed* (1949). Elliott made his Broadway debut the next year in *Ring Round the Moon* and began appearing in films, making his debut in *Dear Mr. Prohack* (1949). He followed that with notable roles in *The Sound Barrier* (1949) and *The Cruel Sea* (1953). As Elliott matured, his roles and performances became increasingly more interesting. A breakthrough occurred after he portrayed the black sheep of the family in *Nothing but the Best* (1964) and the back-street abortionist in *Alfie* (1966). In his most successful roles Elliott depicted somewhat rumpled men with a few guilty secrets: a drunken has-been director in *The Apprenticeship of Duddy Kravitz* (1974), a corrupt, greedy doctor

THE NEW YORK TIMES

in *A Private Function* (1984), the emotive father in *A Room with a View* (1986), and an aging drunken actor in *Noises Off*, his last motion picture. Other successes included *Trading Places* (1982) and two Indiana Jones movies, *Raiders of the Lost Ark* (1981) and *Indiana Jones and the Last Crusade* (1988). His last stage appearance was in David Mamet's *A Life in the Theatre* (1989) in London. Elliott was made Commander of the Order of the British Empire in 1988.

Evans, Sir Geraint, Welsh opera singer (b. Feb. 16, 1922, Cilfynydd, Wales—d. Sept. 19, 1992, Aberystwyth, Wales), was one of Britain's leading operatic baritones and had an international reputation as one of the finest interpreters of such

roles as the title characters in *Falstaff* and *The Marriage of Figaro*, Leporello in *Don Giovanni*, and Beckmesser in *Die Meistersinger*. Although many of his most successful roles drew on his genius for comedy, his acting ability and his careful attention to character also resulted in powerful portrayals in many tragic roles. Evans, the son of a coal miner, won a gold medal in a singing competition at the age of four and as a teenager won a solo spot on the "Welsh Rarebit" radio program. After service in the Royal Air Force in World War II, he was stationed in Hamburg, West Germany, and worked for the British Forces Radio Network, occasionally performing. In 1948 he joined the opera company at London's Covent Garden, making his debut in the small role of the Nightwatchman in *Die Meistersinger*. His potential was noticed, and the next season he sang his first Figaro, a role he would go on to sing all over the world—notably in his debuts at La Scala, Milan (1960), and the Salzburg (Austria) Festival (1961)—until he thought he looked too old. Evans sang his first Falstaff, which became his signature role, at the Glyndebourne (England) Festival in 1957 and made his debut at New York City's Metropolitan Opera in that role in 1964. Other major roles were Bottom in *A Midsummer Night's Dream*, Balstrode in *Peter Grimes*, Papageno in *The Magic Flute*, and Dulcamara in *L'Elisir d'amore*, which he sang at his farewell performance at Covent Garden in 1984. Evans was made Commander of the Order of the British Empire in 1959 and was knighted in 1969. His autobiography, *A Knight at the Opera*, was published in 1984.

Falcone, Giovanni, Italian judge (b. May 18, 1939, Palermo, Sicily, Italy—d. May 23, 1992, near Palermo), as the most prominent member of a special "pool" of anti-Mafia magistrates, orchestrated Italy's crusade against that secret criminal organization. Falcone grew up in a tough working-class area of Palermo, the centre of Mafia activity. He began his legal career as a prosecutor and then became a bankruptcy judge. In 1978 he was assigned to Palermo and prosecuted cases against the Mafia, and in the early 1980s he and several other magistrates were pooled into a legal team to share the responsibilities and the risk of assassination. In 1987 Falcone's efforts led to the conviction and sentencing of 338 top mafiosi. He was appointed Palermo's deputy attorney, and later he was named director-general of the Justice Ministry's criminal affairs division in Rome. Falcone's campaign against the Mafia in Italy, the U.S., and South America and the unsuccessful attempts on his life made him an international figure and the subject of a profile on the U.S. TV show "60 Minutes." He was killed, along with his wife and three bodyguards, when a one-ton bomb exploded under his car. On July 19, Judge Paolo Borsellino, another member of the pool, who was expected to be Falcone's successor, died in a similar car bombing.

Ferrer, José (JOSÉ VINCENTE FERRER OTERO Y CINTRON), U.S. actor and director (b. Jan. 8, 1912, Santurce, P.R.—d. Jan. 26, 1992, Coral Gables, Fla.), movingly portrayed the lovelorn, long-nosed swordsman with the soul of a romantic poet in the film *Cyrano de Bergerac* (1950), for which he won an Academy Award as best actor; he was nominated again as best actor in 1953 for his sterling performance as the diminutive artist Toulouse-Lautrec in the 1952 film *Moulin Rouge*. For the latter role he strapped up his legs and performed on his knees to emulate the crippled Lautrec. Ferrer, a 1934 graduate of Princeton University, was a gifted pianist and had intended on becoming an architect before being stagestruck. He had various theatrical roles from 1935 until he gained a reputation in the comic title role in the Broadway hit *Charley's Aunt* (1940). Ferrer demonstrated his versatility as an actor in the dramatic role of Iago to Paul Robeson's Othello (1943). He earned his first Tony award in 1947 for his stage performance in *Cyrano de Bergerac* and won two more in 1952, the first for directing the plays *Stalag 17*, *The Fourposter*, and *The Shrike* and the second for acting in *The Shrike*.

AP/WIDE WORLD

He made his motion-picture debut as the dauphin in *Joan of Arc* (1948) and earned an Academy Award nomination as best supporting actor for that role. His unmistakable voice, marked by precise diction, was one of his trademarks. Some of his most memorable film roles were a murdering hypnotist in *Whirlpool* (1949), a South American dictator in *Crisis* (1950), the defense lawyer in *The Caine Mutiny* (1954), a henpecked husband in *The Shrike* (1955), a Turkish bey in *Lawrence of Arabia* (1962), and Herod in *The Greatest Story Ever Told* (1965). As a director he cast himself in starring roles in *The Great Man* (1956), *I Accuse* (1958), and *The High Cost of Loving* (1958). The last films he directed were *Return to Peyton Place* (1961) and *State Fair* (1962). During the 1970s and '80s, the durable Ferrer was cast mainly in villainous roles, mostly for television. He was married four times, and among his wives were actress Uta Hagen (1938–48) and singer Rosemary Clooney (1953–67). In 1985 Ferrer was the first actor to receive the National Medal of Arts. He made his final stage appearances in 1990.

Ffrangcon-Davies, Dame Gwen, British actress (b. Jan. 25, 1891, London, England—d. Jan. 27, 1992, Halstead, Essex, England), was a legendary figure of the classical British stage; she made her debut in 1911 in a walk-on part in *A Midsummer Night's Dream* and taped her last television appearance 80 years later, at the age of 100. At first Ffrangcon-Davies played bit parts and sang in the chorus, but by 1921 she was taking leading roles with the Birmingham Repertory Company, and in 1922 she originated the role of Eve in George Bernard Shaw's *Back to Methuselah.* Her long association with Shakespeare's heroines began in 1924 with Cordelia in *King Lear* and with Juliet (which was to become her signature role). Eventually her credits included Cleopatra, Portia, Titania, Ophelia, Regan, Beatrice, Henry VIII's Queen Katharine, and Lady Macbeth. She displayed equal variety in her other roles, most notably Elizabeth Barrett in *The Barretts of Wimpole Street* (1930, revived in 1935), Gwendolen in Oscar Wilde's *The Importance of Being Earnest* (1940), Mary Tyrone in Eugene O'Neill's *Long Day's Journey into Night* (1958), and Amanda Wingfield in Tennessee Williams' *The Glass Menagerie* (1965). She last appeared on stage in Anton Chekhov's *Uncle Vanya* in 1970, but she continued to act for television and radio. Ffrangcon-Davies was honoured in a 1988 television documentary, "Gwen: A Juliet Remembered," and in 1991 she was finally made a Dame Commander of the Order of the British Empire.

Fieldhouse of Gosport in the County of Hampshire, John David Elliott Fieldhouse, BARON, admiral (ret.) British Royal Navy (b. Feb. 12, 1928—d. Feb. 17, 1992, Southampton, Hampshire, England), rose through the naval ranks from cadet (1944) to chief of the defense staff (1985–88); he was particularly esteemed for his role as commander in chief of the British naval task force that expelled Argentine forces from the Falk-

land Islands/Islas Malvinas in 1982. Fieldhouse attended the Royal Navy College at Dartmouth, served in the East Indies fleet as a midshipman (1945–46), and joined the submarine service in 1948. He became a commanding officer in 1955 and was made commander of the first British nuclear-powered submarine, HMS *Dreadnought,* in 1964. Three years later he was promoted to captain and made the first commander of the Polaris submarine squadron. In 1975 he was elevated to commander of the submarine forces in the eastern Atlantic Ocean. As a member of the Admiralty Board and controller of the navy (1979–81), he was a strong advocate for the advanced Trident submarine that replaced the Polaris. In 1981 he was promoted to admiral and made Knight Commander of the Order of the British Empire. As allied commander in chief of the eastern Atlantic (1981–82), Fieldhouse was put in command of the Falklands naval campaign, which he directed from his headquarters at Northwood. The successful completion of the campaign brought him advancement to first sea lord and chief of the naval staff (1982–85) and then chief of the defense staff. Fieldhouse retired in 1989 and was made a life peer in 1990.

Fisher, Mary Frances Kennedy, U.S. writer (b. July 3, 1908, Albion, Mich.—d. June 22, 1992, Glen Ellen, Calif.), embraced the notion that "our three basic needs, for food and security and love, are so mixed and mingled and entwined that we cannot straightly think of one without the others" in more than a dozen books that extolled the pleasures of preparing and partaking of food. Her eloquent essays conjured sensuous images of gastronomic delights, and poet W.H. Auden was so enamoured of her writing style that in 1963 he christened her "America's greatest prose writer." Fisher's first three books, *Serve It Forth* (1937), *Consider the Oyster* (1941), and *How to Cook a Wolf* (1942), were all published under the name Mary Frances Parrish. She was later better known to readers of her books and *The New Yorker* magazine as M.F.K. Fisher. Her essays were collected in such best-selling books as *The Gastronomical Me* (1943), *Here Let Us Feast* (1946), *An Alphabet for Gourmets* (1949), and *With Bold Knife and Fork* (1968). She was proudest, though, of her translation into English of French epicurean Jean Anthelme Brillat-Savarin's 1825 treatise *The Physiology of Taste* (1949). Besides her gastronomic offerings, Fisher published books on aging, and a children's book, *The Boss Dog,* appeared in 1991. Her life story was recounted in the documentary *M.F.K.,* which was released in March 1992.

Franjieh, Suleiman Kabalan, Lebanese politician (b. June 14, 1910, Zgharta, northern Lebanon, Ottoman Empire—d. July 23, 1992, Beirut, Lebanon), was a ruthless warlord at the head of one of Lebanon's powerful Maronite Christian clans and president (1970–76) of Lebanon; he was considered by many to be in large part responsible for the country's descent into civil war in the mid-1970s. Franjieh was educated in Tripoli and Beirut and operated an import-export firm in Beirut. In 1957 he was implicated in the murder of several members of a rival clan and fled to Syria, where he became friends with a young air force officer, Hafez al-Assad. He soon returned to Lebanon, however, to succeed his popular elder brother, Hamid, as clan leader. After being elected (1960) to his brother's former seat in parliament, Franjieh held a succession of ministerial posts. On Aug. 17, 1970, the Lebanese parliament elected him president by one vote on the third ballot, but he soon alienated Muslims and Christians alike by his autocratic rule and his promotion of incompetent and often corrupt clansmen, notably his son Tony. In June 1976, shortly before he left office, Franjieh reportedly invited his old friend Assad, by then president of Syria, to send troops into Lebanon to assist the Maronite Christians in their growing war against left-wing Muslim and Palestinian forces. Rival clans who opposed Syrian intervention allied themselves with Israel. In June 1978 members of the Phalange, a rival Christian militia, murdered Franjieh's son Tony, along with Tony's wife and daughter, thus cementing the rift

between the clans and precluding a quick end to the war.

Franks of Headington, Oliver Shewell Franks, BARON, British civil servant and diplomat (b. Feb. 16, 1905, Bristol, England—d. Oct. 15, 1992, Oxford, England), had a long career in public service that began during World War II and extended into the 1980s. Franks was educated at Queen's College, Oxford, and then taught there until 1937. After leaving Oxford, he taught at the University of Glasgow, Scotland (1937–45). During World War II Frank was also a civil servant (1939–45) in the Ministry of Supply, and his analytic and managerial talents earned him a promotion to permanent secretary of supply and aircraft production (1945–46). He was provost of Queen's College from 1946 to 1948, and in 1947 he was also head of the British delegation to the conference that negotiated Marshall Plan aid. As the British ambassador to the U.S. (1948–52), Franks was instrumental in creating the close friendship and understanding that developed between the U.S. and Britain. From 1953 to 1975 Franks was a director of Lloyd's Bank, and for eight of those years (1954–62) he was chairman. In addition, from 1962 to 1976 he was provost of Worcester College, Oxford. His last high-level appointment was the chairmanship (1982) of the committee investigating the Argentine invasion of the Falkland Islands/Islas Malvinas. It was that position that brought him his greatest public prominence. Franks was made Commander of the Order of the British Empire in 1942, was knighted in 1945, and was made a life peer in 1962.

Frum, Barbara, U.S.-born Canadian broadcast journalist (b. Sept. 8, 1937, Niagara Falls, N.Y.—d. March 26, 1992, Toronto, Ont.), earned a reputation for integrity as a hard-driving, curious, and well-informed interviewer. She was a thoughtful yet sometimes acerbic inquisitor of international celebrities on radio's popular phone-out show "As It Happens" (1971–81) and then starred on television's nightly current-affairs program "The Journal" (1982–92). Frum, one of the country's best-known moderators, won numerous awards and set new journalistic standards with her flair for flushing out the facts in an incisive manner during interviews. She became a fixture on television, reaching 1.3 million homes with "The Journal." Though diagnosed with leukemia in 1974, Frum endured until complications from the disease claimed her life.

Gaines, William Maxwell, U.S. publisher (b. March 1, 1922, New York, N.Y.—d. June 3, 1992, New York), was the creative genius who launched (1952) and published *Mad* magazine, an irreverent monthly that featured the goofy-faced, gap-toothed cover boy Alfred E. Neuman, whose motto "What, me worry?" became the punch line for numerous jokes and the catch-

MICHAEL FERGUSON—GLOBE PHOTOS

phrase of teenage readers. Gaines's magazine, which carried no advertising, satirized advertisers, politicians, celebrities, and comic books with brilliant drawings and illustrations accompanied by punchy writing "in a jugular vein." Gaines, who inherited EC (Educational Comics) after his father died in 1947, had a weight problem, suffered from insomnia, and had an obsession for neatness (he measured the position of all objects on his desk). The stringy-haired, bespectacled, bearded eccentric cultivated the zany environment at his publishing headquarters. He changed Educational Comics to Entertaining Comics and pioneered the horror comic genre. After a 1954 Senate inquiry on the influence of violent comic books on youth, a standards code was adopted and distributors refused to stock his publications. That was when *Mad* was born, and its "gang of idiots" lampooned scores of sacred institutions, including family values, television, and films. From 1956 the demented-looking, freckle-faced Neuman was nominated as a write-in candidate in every presidential election, and Gaines once hung a Neuman campaign poster atop the Leaning Tower of Pisa in Italy. His wacky brand of humour was essential to the baby-boom generation, and at the peak of its popularity, *Mad*'s yearly circulation was 2.4 million. Even after *Mad* was acquired in 1968 by Kinney (later Warner Communications), Gaines continued to occupy his office.

Gleason, Thomas William ("TEDDY"), U.S. labour leader (b. Nov. 8, 1900, New York, N.Y.—d. Dec. 24, 1992, New York), presided for 24 years (1963–87) as the iron-fisted president of the International Longshoremen's Association (ILA) and negotiated a guaranteed annual income (effective in 1964) for union members (as much as $32,000 a year whether they worked or not) when containerized shipping threatened their livelihood. Gleason left school after the seventh grade to become a dockworker, and he joined the ILA in 1919, at a time when its members were branded as rebels. Gleason, who worked as a checker, billing clerk, longshoreman, winch driver, truck loader, and timekeeper, developed his political and organizational skills during the bitter union battles of the 1920s and '30s. He had risen to dock superintendent when he was fired for honouring a picket line in 1932. He worked in a sugar factory and sold hot dogs until New Deal policies and union legalization allowed him to return to the ILA. Gleason served as president of various locals before his friend William V. Bradley became ILA president in 1953 (after the ILA was expelled that year from the American Federation of Labor over corruption) and appointed him to the newly created office of general organizer. Gleason became executive vice president in 1961 and president of the ILA in 1963. A powerful and influential leader, he could be as tough as nails or as smooth as silk—whichever the occasion demanded. Gleason led a successful 1965 strike of longshoremen and served on Pres. Lyndon Johnson's Maritime Advisory Committee. At the time of Gleason's retirement, union membership had shrunk to 110,000 members from 250,000.

Godfree, Kathleen McKane ("KITTY"), British tennis player (b. May 7, 1896, London, England—d. June 19, 1992, London), was one of the dominant figures in women's tennis in the 1920s, racking up two singles titles at the All-England Championships at Wimbledon, five doubles titles in Grand Slam events, and five Olympic medals, including a gold in women's doubles in 1920. Under her maiden name, Kitty McKane, she lost the 1923 All-England final to Suzanne Lenglen of France, but she returned the next year to become the only woman ever to beat American Helen Wills at Wimbledon. She won the mixed doubles championship at the same tournament with her partner, Jack Gilbert. In 1926 she repeated that feat, again winning both the singles and the mixed doubles (now paired with her new husband, Leslie Godfree). She won the U.S. championships in women's doubles (1923 and 1927) and in mixed doubles (1925), and she represented England in the Wightman Cup series every year until 1934, when she retired with a 17-year-career total of 46

BETTMANN

singles and 107 doubles titles. Godfree was also All-England badminton champion four times in the early 1920s and was a member of the national lacrosse team in 1918. She was made a vice president of the All-England Club in 1989.

Goodson, Mark, U.S. radio and television producer (b. Jan. 24, 1915, Sacramento, Calif.—d. Dec. 18, 1992, New York, N.Y.), was the creative force behind the development of the first television game show—"What's My Line?"—which aired for 17 years, and he conceived such other popular shows as "The Price Is Right," "To Tell the Truth," "I've Got a Secret," "Password," "Concentration," and "The Match Game." Earlier he produced such radio game shows as "Stop the Music" and "Hit the Jackpot." Goodson's name was identified for many years in conjunction with Bill Todman, who sold Goodson's game shows to the networks. Goodson, a radio announcer, met Todman in 1941 while they were in New York City working on the radio quiz program "Battle of the Boroughs." They sold "Winner Take All" to a radio station in 1946 and launched what would become a game show empire. Their shows always ended with the tag line "This has been a Mark Goodson-Bill Todman production." After Todman died in 1979, Goodson continued to produce some of the longest-running and best-known game shows in television history. He was honoured in 1990 with an Emmy award for lifetime achievement, and in December 1992 he was selected for 1993 induction into the Hall of Fame of the Academy of Television Arts and Sciences.

Guattari, (Pierre-)Félix, French psychiatrist (b. April 30, 1930, Colombe, France—d. Aug. 29?, 1992, near Blois, France), as a leader in the "antipsychiatry" movement, publicly challenged established thought in psychoanalysis, philosophy, and social politics. Guattari, who studied philosophy, joined the psychoanalyst Jean Oury at La Borde, an innovative psychiatric clinic where unrestrained patients actively participated in running the facility. Beginning in 1964, Guattari worked with the noted psychoanalyst Jacques Lacan in Paris and, despite his increasing skepticism about Lacan's theories, he divided his time between La Borde, his private psychoanalytic practice, and Lacan's Freudian School of Paris until Lacan dissolved the institution in 1980. Although he was expelled from the Communist Party for opposing the 1956 Soviet invasion of Hungary, Guattari remained a left-wing activist. He supported the 1968 student rebellion in France while criticizing the rebels for their own failings, and he was close friends with known terrorists despite his avowed rejection of terrorism. In 1969 he became associated with Gilles Deleuze, an "antiphilosopher" with whom he wrote a series of influential books, notably *L'Anti-œdipe* (1972), *Mille plateaux* (1980), and *Qu'est-ce que la philosophie?* (1991). Guattari ran

unsuccessfully as a Green Party candidate in regional elections in March 1992.

Guimarães, Ulysses, Brazilian politician (b. Oct. 6, 1916, Rio Claro, São Paulo, Brazil—d. Oct. 12, 1992, near Angra dos Reis, Brazil), as the "grand old man of Brazilian politics," spent 44 years in Congress, many of them opposing the military government that ruled from 1964 to 1985. Guimarães, a constitutional lawyer by profession, presided over the 1987 convention that wrote a new constitution to replace the one written by the military. He possessed a sterling political reputation and was respected for his vigorous fight against political and economic corruption. When the military was obliged to call for democratic elections in 1989, Guimarães ran for president as the candidate of the Party of the Brazilian Democratic Movement (PMDB), which he led from 1970 to 1990. Though he finished a distant fifth in the election, he initially supported the winning candidate, Fernando Collor de Mello, until it became evident in 1992 that Collor had apparently participated in such practices as influence peddling and embezzlement. Guimarães then led a campaign to impeach Collor. Guimarães and his wife were killed when the helicopter in which they were flying crashed into the Atlantic Ocean during a violent thunderstorm.

Habib, Philip Charles, U.S. diplomat (b. Feb. 25, 1920, New York, N.Y.—d. May 25, 1992, Puligny-Montrachet, France), had a distinguished 30-year career as a U.S. foreign service officer who served as a skilled troubleshooter and negotiator, notably when Israel invaded Lebanon in 1982; he brokered a tenuous peace agreement (which later collapsed) following the evacuation of the Palestine Liberation Organization (PLO) forces from Beirut under the supervision of the U.S. Marines. Habib, the son of a Lebanese grocer, was raised in a Jewish section of Brooklyn. He graduated (1942) from the University of Idaho with the intent of becoming a forest ranger and was studying for his Ph.D. in agricultural economics at the University of California at Berkeley when he decided to take a test to enter the State Department. His passing grade launched his diplomatic career, and he was posted to Canada, New Zealand, Trinidad, and South Korea before going to Vietnam as chief political adviser to Ambassador Henry Cabot Lodge. It was there, in Saigon, that he became a recognized expert on Asian affairs. Several U.S. presidents sought his counsel, and as head of a task force studying the situation in war-torn Vietnam, he persuaded Pres. Lyndon Johnson to restrict the bombing of North Vietnam. He led the U.S. delegation to the 1968 Paris peace talks but was recalled in 1970 by Pres. Richard Nixon when no agreement was forthcoming. Habib then served as U.S. ambassador to South Korea (1971–74) and as assistant secretary of state for East Asian and Pacific affairs (1974–76). In the latter position he was openly critical of the regimes of Ferdinand Marcos in the Philippines and Park Chung Hee in South Korea. After being named under secretary of state for political affairs by Pres. Gerald Ford, Habib concentrated on the Middle East. He was credited with persuading Egyptian Pres. Anwar as-Sadat and Israeli Prime Minister Menachem Begin to meet together with U.S. Pres. Jimmy Carter at Camp David, Md., for a 1978 Middle East peace summit. Habib traveled extensively, shuttling between Washington and the Middle East, and in 1978, after suffering a massive heart attack (his second), he retired from the foreign service. He was called out of retirement in 1981 by Pres. Ronald Reagan, who needed the skills of a veteran diplomat to defuse the situation in Lebanon. For those efforts Habib was awarded the Presidential Medal of Freedom in 1982. He later served as special envoy to the Philippines and Central America and helped persuade Marcos to go into exile. He retired for a second time in 1987. Habib was decorated commander of France's Legion of Honour in 1988.

Hale, Clara M., U.S. social activist (b. April 1, 1905, Philadelphia, Pa.—d. Dec. 18, 1992, New

York, N.Y.), was the founder of Harlem's Hale House, where she sheltered and nurtured hundreds of abandoned and orphaned children of drug addicts in New York City. She was in her 60s and retired when in 1969 her daughter, Lorraine, persuaded a drug-addicted mother (whom she saw dozing off on the street while holding a two-month-old infant) to temporarily entrust her child to Hale while she sought treatment for her addiction. Hale's benevolence was made known to other addicts, and within two months she was caring for 22 babies, themselves suffering the withdrawal pangs of maternal drug abuse. During the early 1970s her project was granted funding by New York City, and in 1975 a five-story brownstone was refurbished and christened Hale House. Hale's newly appointed and cheerfully decorated haven boasted a kitchen, mirrored dining room, playroom, and second-floor nursery. New arrivals would spend their first days with Mother Hale, as she became known, in her third-floor bedroom, where she would gently rock and care for them around the clock. Hale's daughter, who held Ph.D.'s in developmental psychology and child development, became executive director of Hale House in the mid-1980s. In 1989, however, government funding for the home was curtailed, yet the flow of children remained steady. Hale House relied on private financing and continued to expand its programs to include housing and education for mothers after their detoxification, apprentice training for youths, and a home for mothers and infants with AIDS. Hale was saluted in 1985 by Pres. Ronald Reagan as an "American hero." She earned her high school equivalency diploma shortly before her death.

Haley, Alex Palmer, U.S. writer (b. Aug. 11, 1921, Ithaca, N.Y.—d. Feb. 10, 1992, Seattle, Wash.), scrupulously traced his maternal African ancestry to West Africa by conducting research on three continents and combined factual data with fictional drama to create the blockbuster and Pulitzer Prize-winning book *Roots: The Saga of an American Family* (1976), which sold more than 5.5 million copies, was translated into 37 languages,

and was the basis for one of the most-watched miniseries in the history of television. Haley, who completed only two years of college, spent 20 years (1939–59) in the U.S. Coast Guard and began writing during long sea voyages. His first best-seller was *The Autobiography of Malcolm X* (1965), for which he interviewed the black Muslim leader, who was assassinated just two weeks after Haley's manuscript was completed. That book, which was deemed a classic of African-American autobiography, sold six million copies in eight languages and, like *Roots,* helped etch an identity

for African-Americans who had no recorded history. Haley's obsession with documenting the oral history of the heritage provided by his maternal grandmother was the grist that propelled him to travel over three-quarters of a million kilometres to find his origins in the present nation of The Gambia. There he found a *griot,* a tribal oral historian, who chanted for Haley the history of the Kinte tribe and the fate of Kunta Kinte, who was enslaved and taken to Maryland. Haley came to believe that this man, "Kin-tay," was his ancestor. His 12-year odyssey culminated in *Roots,* which chronicled seven American generations beginning with Kinte and ending with Haley's own quest. The story, published during the U.S. bicentennial, sparked interest in their genealogy not only among African-Americans but also among Americans of many other ethnic heritages. The sequel, "Roots: The Next Generation," was broadcast in 1979 and was also a popular success. Haley spent much of his subsequent time lecturing but did complete a novella, *A Different Kind of Christmas* (1988), the story of a plantation owner who rejects slavery. At the time of his death, Haley was researching the paternal side of his family, and he had completed research on Henning, Tenn., the town in which he was raised.

Hamburger, Jean, French physician (b. July 15, 1909, Paris, France—d. Feb. 1, 1992, Paris), was a pioneer in the field of nephrology and founding president (1960–63) of the International Society of Nephrology. On Feb. 12, 1962, Hamburger and his medical team at Necker Hospital in Paris performed the first successful kidney transplant between nonidentical twins (the first successful organ transplant of any kind in France), and the next year they performed one of the first successful cadaver transplants using immunosuppressive therapy. Hamburger was born in Paris and graduated (1928) from the Sorbonne with a degree in the natural sciences before his growing interest in the physiology of fluid and electrolyte balance induced him to switch to medicine. During the 1930s and '40s he did clinical research at the Paris Hospitals, where he developed improved methods of intensive care treatment, studied the connections between electrolyte disturbances and renal failure, and supervised the creation of an early artificial kidney. In 1952 Hamburger's team transplanted a woman's kidney to her healthy son, whose only kidney had been damaged in an accident. The recipient's temporary survival was a turning point in the study of histocompatibility, and Hamburger championed the research that led to the human leukocyte antigen (HLA) system of genetic markers used in establishing donor compatibility. He later did extensive research into renal histology and immunology and wrote many papers and books, including *Néphrologie* (1966) and *La Transplantation rénale* (1971). Hamburger was awarded the Legion of Honour and the National Order of Merit. He was president (1968–70) of the International Society of Transplantation, a member of the National Academy of Medicine, and a fellow of the American College of Physicians and the Royal College of Physicians. In 1991 he was named president of the French Academy of Sciences.

Hancock, Langley George, Australian mining industrialist (b. June 10, 1909, Perth, Australia—d. March 27, 1992, Perth), was an outspoken and controversial prospector who unearthed some of the largest iron-ore reserves in the world; the royalties from these deposits made him one of Australia's richest men and financed his campaign to form a right-wing political party and to fight for Western Australian independence. Hancock began prospecting while managing his family's sheep station in the Hamersley Range. In the 1930s he and his business partner, Peter Wright, established an asbestos-treatment plant and a mining company to process the asbestos deposits he had discovered. In 1952 when he was forced to land his private aircraft in bad weather, Hancock stumbled across vast iron-ore deposits in the Pilbara region of northwestern Western Australia. It was several years before he could convince the authorities of his find, but eventu-

ally he and Wright founded Hamersley Iron and signed a royalty agreement with a major mining company. By the late 1960s Hancock had discovered hundreds of deposits that totaled millions of tons of iron ore and generated millions of dollars in annual royalties. In 1974 he founded the Western Secession Movement and the newspaper *National Miner* to advance his controversial ideas, which included the use of nuclear explosions to excavate mines and harbours and the addition of sterilizing drugs to the water of half-caste Aborigines. In the 1980s he arranged a controversial trade agreement with Romanian strongman Nicolae Ceausescu.

Harris, Reginald Hargreaves ("REG"), British cyclist (b. March 1, 1920, Bury, Greater Manchester, England—d. June 22, 1992, Macclesfield, Cheshire, England), won five world sprint titles (one as an amateur; four as a professional) between 1947 and 1954; 20 years later he came out of retirement to win the British sprint championship at age 54. Harris was known for his raw physical power and for his wily racing strategy. He was named to his first national cycling team in 1939, but the world championships were canceled when World War II broke out. He was wounded in action in North Africa, and after a year in a hospital he was invalided out of the army. By 1944 he had returned to form as British amateur sprint champion, and he won the world sprint title in 1947. The next year he fractured his spine in an auto accident, broke his wrist in a cycling spill, and was almost dropped from the national team in a dispute over training procedures, but he held on to win two silver medals at the 1948 Olympic Games. He turned pro later that year and captured the professional sprint title in 1949, 1950, 1951, and 1954. Harris retired from competition in 1957, but he staged a spectacular comeback in 1974–75. He died after suffering a stroke while cycling.

Hassuna, (Muhammad) 'Abd al-Khaliq, Egyptian diplomat (b. Oct. 28, 1898, Cairo, Egypt—d. Jan. 20, 1992, Cairo), was secretary-general of the League of Arab States for 20 years (1952–72) and a skillful mediator, particularly during the international crisis that ensued after Egyptian Pres. Gamal Abdel Nasser nationalized the Suez Canal in 1956 and in the difficulties surrounding the independence of Kuwait in 1961. Hassuna graduated in law (1921) from the University of Cairo and in economics and political science (1925) from the University of Cambridge. He spent most of his early career with the Egyptian Foreign Ministry and served in a variety of posts, including under secretary of state (1939), governor of the city of Alexandria (1942), minister of social affairs (1949), and foreign minister (1952). He was named to head the Arab League shortly after King Farouk I of Egypt was overthrown in 1952. Hassuna proved to be a persuasive and respected negotiator, mediating between Arab nations and between the league and countries outside the region. In 1961 he coordinated the creation of a league force to protect newly independent Kuwait from Iraqi invasion. When he retired in 1972, he was succeeded by another Egyptian, Mahmoud Riad (*q.v.*). Hassuna's numerous awards included the French Legion of Honour.

Haury, Emil Walter, U.S. anthropologist and archaeologist (b. May 2, 1904, Newton, Kan.—d. Dec. 5, 1992, Tucson, Ariz.), was for more than 50 years considered one of the preeminent scholars of southwestern U.S. prehistory. Haury credited a chance introduction to archaeology at a National Geographic Society project site with inspiring him to explore the cultures of the ancient Americas. He received both a B.A. (1927) and an M.A. (1928) from the University of Arizona and a Ph.D. (1934) from Harvard University. Returning to the University of Arizona, he served as head of the department of anthropology (1937–64) and was a full professor (1938–80). During his tenure his department was widely recognized for the excellence of its research and education programs. Haury's own scholarship was exceptionally wide ranging, covering the three major prehistoric cultures—the Hohokam, Mogollon, and Anasazi Indians. His fieldwork and analyses were considered of the highest order. Haury also served as director (1938–64) of the university's Arizona State Museum. He was a member of many boards and committees, was chairman of anthropology at the National Academy of Sciences, and served as an adviser to the National Park Service. His last book was *The Hohokam, Desert Farmers and Craftsmen: Excavations at Snaketown, 1964–1965* (1976).

Hayakawa, S(amuel) I(chiye), Canadian-born semanticist, educator, and politician (b. July 18, 1906, Vancouver, B.C.—d. Feb. 27, 1992, Greenbrae, Calif.), captured national newspaper headlines on his first day (Dec. 2, 1968) as the authoritarian acting president of San Francisco State College when he confronted striking students who had presented the administration with a list of "nonnegotiable demands," including the admission of all black applicants and the institution of an autonomous department devoted to minority studies, by climbing aboard their sound truck and ripping out the wiring inside the loudspeaker. His dramatic action, which was applauded by conservatives and critics of the nationwide anti-Vietnam war protests on college campuses, helped him win election to the U.S. Senate in 1976. Hayakawa immigrated to the U.S. in 1929 and earned a Ph.D. from the University of Wisconsin in 1935. His early claim to fame was as a linguist, and his book *Language in Action* (1941; rev. ed., *Language in Thought and Action,* 1949), written for the general public, became a popular high school semantics text. His theory, that words are not the same as reality and at best can only lead to an understanding of real meaning and at worst can actually obscure it, was later identified by scholars as a popularization of the work done by Polish scholar Alfred Korzybski. Hayakawa denied the charge, but his contribution to the field of theoretical research was regarded by scholars as interpretive rather than original. During and after World War II, Hayakawa and his wife lived in Chicago, where from 1950 to 1955 he lectured at the University of Chicago. His Canadian citizenship spared him from being interned in a camp as other Japanese-Americans had been, and he angered many when he supported the practice. He became a U.S. citizen in 1954 and the following year joined San Francisco State College as a lecturer. He was a professor of English there when the governor of California, Ronald Reagan, appointed him president of the college after two others had resigned and the school had been closed by student strikes. A colourful administrator who sported a trademark tam-o'-shanter, the diminutive Hayakawa established himself as an authority figure and reopened the college. He served as president (1969–73) of the college before running as the Republican candidate for the U.S. senate in 1976 at the age of 70. During his term in office (1977–83), he introduced a constitutional amendment making English the nation's official language, supported a lower entry-level minimum wage for teenagers, and earned the moniker "Sleepin' Sam" for frequently dozing during briefings.

Hayek, Friedrich August von, Austrian-born British economist (b. May 8, 1899, Vienna, Austria—d. March 23, 1992, Freiburg im Breisgau, Germany), shared the 1974 Nobel Prize for Economics with Gunnar Myrdal of Sweden. Hayek, who was often referred to as the "father of monetarism," argued that government intervention in a free-market economy is counterproductive and potentially damaging to society. In his most successful book, *The Road to Serfdom* (1944), he predicted the inevitable failure of the centrally planned Communist states and warned against government involvement in capitalist economies. Although his theories fell out of favour after World War II, in the 1970s and '80s Hayek's works gained new attention and influenced the conservative monetarist policies of U.S. Pres. Ronald Reagan and British Prime Minister Margaret Thatcher. Hayek received advanced degrees in law, political science, and economics from the

University of Vienna, and after a brief stint in the civil service he returned there as a lecturer and director of the Austrian Institute for Economic Research (1927–31). In 1931 he accepted a post at the London School of Economics (LSE), where he led an intense but amicable debate against his Cambridge-based rival John Maynard Keynes. Hayek left the LSE in 1950 and pursued his academic career as a professor of social and moral science at the University of Chicago (1950–62), professor of economics at the University of Freiburg (1962–69), and visiting professor at the University of Salzburg. Hayek's other books include *The Pure Theory of Capital* (1941), *The Constitution of Liberty* (1960), and *The Fatal Conceit* (1988). He became a British citizen in 1938 and was awarded the highest civilian honours in Britain (Companion of Honour in 1984) and the U.S. (Medal of Freedom in 1991).

Henreid, Paul (PAUL GEORGE JULIUS VON HERNREID), Austrian-born actor (b. Jan. 10, 1908, Trieste, Austria-Hungary—d. March 29, 1992, Santa Monica, Calif.), charmed movie audiences with good looks, elegant sophistication, and a smooth, middle-European accent that made him ideal for romantic character roles. Henreid was best known for his work in two classic 1942 films—*Casablanca,* in which he portrayed the gallant Resistance leader Victor Laszlo, and *Now, Voyager,* in which he created one of Hollywood's most enduring romantic images by simultaneously lighting two cigarettes and then passing one to his costar, Bette Davis. This gesture was copied by countless

parodists and would-be continental lovers around the world. Henreid, the son of an aristocratic Viennese banker, trained for the theatre in Vienna and made his stage debut under the distinguished director Max Reinhardt. He left Austria in 1935 and appeared in such British films as *Goodbye, Mr. Chips* (1939) and *Night Train to Munich* (1940) before moving to the U.S. Henreid's other films included *The Spanish Main* (1945), *Of Human Bondage* (1946), *Song of Love* (1947), *Siren of Bagdad* (1953), and *The Four Horsemen of the Apocalypse* (1961). In the 1950s he began a second career as a director, particularly for television. In his 1984 autobiography, *Ladies Man,* he claimed that his acting career suffered from Hollywood blacklisting when he protested against the House Committee on Un-American Activities. Henreid died just days before *Casablanca* was rereleased in honour of its 50th anniversary.

Herman, Billy (WILLIAM JENNINGS BRYAN HERMAN), U.S. baseball player (b. July 7, 1909, New Albany, Ind.—d. Sept. 5, 1992, Palm Beach county, Fla.), was a phenomenal second baseman for the Chicago Cubs (1931–41), Brooklyn Dodgers (1941–46), and Pittsburgh Pirates (1946–47) professional baseball teams. He was named to 10 All-Star teams during his 15-year career

and held the National League batting average record (.433) for All-Star Games. Herman, who was touted as one of the smartest players in the National League during the 1930s and '40s, was especially adroit at stealing opponents' signals. He helped the Cubs capture pennants in 1932, 1935, and 1938, and he led the Dodgers to a pennant in 1941. A hard-nosed player, he was once fined $200 (at that time the heaviest fine ever imposed on a player during a World Series) for using "vile and unprintable language" during a game against Detroit. When asked which words he used, he replied, "All of them." During World War II, Herman left the Dodgers to serve in the navy. In 1946 he was traded to the Pirates, and he retired the following year with a .304 lifetime batting average, 1,163 runs scored, 839 runs batted in, 2,345 hits, 486 doubles, 82 triples, 47 home runs, and 67 stolen bases. He served as a manager for several professional teams from 1947 to 1966 and was inducted into the Baseball Hall of Fame in 1975.

Hill, Benny (ALFRED HAWTHORNE HILL), British comedian (b. Jan. 21, 1925, Southampton, Hampshire, England—d. April 18?, 1992, Teddington, Middlesex, England), created, wrote, and starred in "The Benny Hill Show" (1955–88), a fast-paced television program filled with risqué jokes, satiric impersonations, sight gags, and saucy music-hall-style songs. He was sometimes accused of being lewd and sexist, but his good-natured jests more often skirted the edges of vulgarity, and his cherubic face and mischievous grin were adored by millions in more than 80 countries around the world. Hill showed an early interest in show business and entertained fellow soldiers during World War II. By 1950 he was well established on television, and in 1954 he was voted TV personality of the year. The next year he got his own program, which was syndicated in the U.S. in 1979. Hill frequently played multiple characters in a comedy skit, but he also surrounded himself with a regular supporting cast and a bevy of scantily clad women known as "Hill's Angels." Prevailing fashions in comedy turned against him, however, and despite an international popularity that approached cult status, Hill's program was abruptly canceled in 1988. His other work included the films *Those Magnificent Men in Their Flying Machines* (1965) and *Chitty Chitty Bang Bang* (1968) and a TV version of *A Midsummer Night's Dream* (1964). Hill was found dead of an apparent heart attack in his home.

Hobson, Sir Harold, British theatre critic (b. Aug. 4, 1904, Thorpe Hesley, Yorkshire, England—d. March 12, 1992, Chichester, West Sussex, England), as drama critic for *The Sunday Times* for nearly three decades (1947–76), used his position and influence to champion such controversial new playwrights as Samuel Beckett, Eugene Ionesco,

Harold Pinter, John Osborne, Marguerite Duras, and Tom Stoppard. Hobson was partially paralyzed by polio as a child and studied at home before winning a scholarship to Oriel College, Oxford. He became drama critic for the *Christian Science Monitor* in the early 1930s and a decade later joined *The Sunday Times* as assistant literary critic. He was soon made assistant drama critic under James Agate, whom he succeeded in 1947. Hobson was a tireless campaigner for actors, playwrights, and plays he considered deserving and was often credited with saving Beckett's *Waiting for Godot* and Pinter's *The Birthday Party* from oblivion. Although his strong religious beliefs and occasionally idiosyncratic viewpoints drew criticism, Hobson's passion for the theatre and the sharp contrast he provided to Kenneth Tynan, his counterpart at *The Observer*, delighted even his critics. Hobson was forced into retirement in 1976, but he continued to write special features for *The Sunday Times* and published an autobiography, *Indirect Journey* (1978). He was knighted in 1977.

Holm, Hanya (JOHANNA ECKERT KUNTZE), German-born U.S. choreographer (b. March 3, 1893?, Worms, Germany—d. Nov. 3, 1992, New York, N.Y.), was a pioneer of modern dance and a major Broadway choreographer. Her emphasis on individual, creative thinking inspired the choreography of many of her students, notably Alwin Nikolais, Murray Louis, Glen Tetley, and Lucinda Childs. Holm studied in Germany under Émile Jaques-Dalcroze and then joined (1921) Mary Wigman's company and taught at her school. Wigman sent her to New York (1931) to found a school there, but after five years she abandoned Wigman's approach, renamed the school after herself, and started a dance company. The school closed in 1967. She also taught at the Bennington (Vt.) College Summer School of Dance (1934–39)—where she choreographed one of her most famous works, *Trend* (1937)—and at the summer school she established at Colorado College (1941–83). Her *Metropolitan Daily* (1938) was reported to have been the first modern dance to be televised. Her successful choreography of a section of *Broadway Ballads* (1948) led to an invitation to choreograph *Kiss Me, Kate* the same year. The latter won her the New York Drama Critics Award for choreography. In 1952 she copyrighted the dances from that show (recorded in Labanotation), becoming the first choreographer to do so. Her ability to adapt her style to the needs of a particular show resulted in such successes as *Out of This World* (1950), *My Fair Lady* (1956), and *Camelot* (1960). She also choreographed for opera, television, and motion pictures.

Hopper, Grace Murray (GRACE BREWSTER MURRAY), mathematician and rear admiral (ret.), U.S. Navy (b. Dec. 9, 1906, New York, N.Y.—d. Jan. 1, 1992, Arlington, Va.), as a pioneer in developing computer technology, helped devise Univac I, the first commercial electronic computer, and used her expertise to develop naval applications for COBOL (computer business oriented language). After earning (1928) a degree in mathematics and physics from Vassar College, Poughkeepsie, N.Y., she received an M.A. (1930) and a Ph.D. (1934) from Yale University. Hopper taught mathematics at Vassar before joining the Naval Reserve in 1943. She became a lieutenant and was assigned (1944) to the Bureau of Ordnance's Computation Project at Harvard University, where she worked on Mark I, the first large-scale automatic calculator and a precursor of electronic computers. Hopper remained at Harvard as a civilian research fellow while maintaining her naval career as a reservist. It was at Harvard that she coined the term *bug* to refer to unexplained computer failures. The first such mysterious occurrence was actually caused by an insect, a moth that had infiltrated the circuits of the Mark I. In 1949 Hopper joined the Eckert-Mauchly Computer Corp., where she designed an improved compiler (a program for translating a programmer's instructions into codes that a computer can read). She remained with the firm when it was taken over by Remington Rand in 1951 and by the Sperry Corp. in 1955. In 1957 her division developed the first English-language

data processing compiler, which was known as Flow-Matic. By 1961 Hopper had risen to the position of staff scientist, and in the following year she was elected a fellow of the Institute of Electrical and Electronic Engineers. In 1966 she retired from the navy as a commander, but she was recalled to active duty the following year to help standardize the navy's computer languages. She was the oldest officer on active U.S. naval duty when she retired in 1986, just months short of her 80th birthday. In 1969 Hopper was named the first computer science Man of the Year by the Data Processing Management Association, and in 1991 she was awarded the National Medal of Technology by Pres. George Bush.

Howerd, Frankie (FRANCIS ALEX HOWARD), British comedian (b. March 6, 1922?, York, England—d. April 19, 1992, London, England), a rubber-faced master of the "nudge-nudge, wink-wink" style of ribald humour, was best known for his stammering narrative style, his expressive gestures, and such mocking catchphrases as "titter ye not" and "Well, please yourselves." Howerd began as a stand-up comedian in music halls and on the radio, notably on the BBC program "Variety Bandbox." He quickly gained stardom on the variety theatre circuit and performed at Buckingham Palace in 1949. After appearances onstage in the revue *Pardon My French* and the plays *Charley's Aunt, Hotel Paradiso,* and *A Midsummer Night's Dream,* Howerd fell into a career slump. His triumphant return on the satiric television program "That Was the Week That Was" (1963) was followed by his award-winning portrayal of Prologus and Pseudolus in *A Funny Thing Happened on the Way to the Forum* (1963; revived in 1986) and his Broadway debut in *Rockefeller and the Red Indians* (1968). His role as the slave Lurcio in the bawdy television show "Up Pompeii" (1970–71) triggered another revival in his career. In the 1990s he returned to doing stand-up routines in front of a new generation of appreciative college students. Howerd's films include *The Ladykillers* (1956), *The Runaway Bus* (1954), *The Mouse on the Moon* (1963), *Carry On Doctor* (1968), and *Up Pompeii* (1971). He was made an Officer of the Order of the British Empire in 1977.

Hutchison, (William) Bruce, Canadian journalist and novelist (b. June 5, 1901, Prescott, Ont.—d. Sept. 14, 1992, Victoria, B.C.), chronicled the history of Canada and the spirit of its people in two widely read books: *The Unknown Country* (1942; rev., 1948) and *Canada: Tomorrow's Giant* (1957). He was revered for his insightful novels and journalistic writings as associate editor of the *Winnipeg* (Man.) *Free Press* (1944–50), editor of the *Victoria Times* (1950–63), and editorial director of the *Vancouver* (B.C.) *Sun* (1963–74). Hutchison's books, which helped define the national identity, were witty and filled with colourful descriptions of the country and its politicians. In 1952 he published *The Incredible Canadian*, a mostly unflattering yet highly regarded biography of politician MacKenzie King. Some of his other works include *The Hollow Men* (1944), *Canada's Lonely Neighbour* (1954), *Mr. Prime Minister, 1867–1964* (1964), and *The Unfinished Country* (1985). Hutchison published his autobiography, *The Far Side of the Street*, in 1976.

Ireland, John Benjamin, Canadian-born actor (b. Jan. 30, 1914, Vancouver, B.C.—d. March 21, 1992, Santa Barbara, Calif.), reached the pinnacle of his career portraying the ruthless intellectual Jack Burden, who became corrupt Willie Stark's crony in *All the King's Men* (1949). For his performance Ireland was nominated for an Academy Award as best supporting actor. He launched a career in show business by staging underwater stunts at a carnival. After taking acting lessons, he made his Broadway debut in *MacBeth* (1941). His resonant and distinctive voice was especially well suited to Shakespearean roles, and he later narrated a number of films. Ireland was featured in *A Walk in the Sun* (1946), his motion-picture debut, and in the classic western *My Darling Clementine* (1946). He was soon cast in cynical tough-guy roles and appeared in *Red River* (1948),

I Shot Jesse James (1949), *Gunfight at the OK Corral* (1957), and *Spartacus* (1960). His career took an unaccountable nosedive during the mid-1960s, and he was soon accepting bit parts. On television Ireland appeared in "Rawhide" and made guest appearances on "Bonanza" and other programs.

Irving, K(enneth) C(olin), Canadian industrialist (b. March 14, 1899, Buctouche, N.B.—d. Dec. 13, 1992, St. John, N.B.), methodically expanded his business holdings for over 50 years into a vast empire that dominated the lives of many in the province of New Brunswick, where he employed one of every 12 workers; he was a hardworking and austere man who became one of Canada's richest persons. Irving was born in a small fishing village in New Brunswick and, after attending college for several years (but not graduating) and serving in the Royal Flying Corps, he returned there to sell Model T Fords and gasoline (petrol). After his gasoline station franchise was revoked—reportedly under pressure from competitors—Irving borrowed several thousand dollars in the mid-1920s and opened his own oil business, starting with a used tank and a few trucks. The Irving Oil Co. proved to be the cornerstone of his holdings. He bought bus lines (to use the oil), then tankers (to transport it), and finally a shipyard (to build the tankers). Further diversification took him into the pulp and paper business, and his holdings included 1.4 ha (3.4 million ac) of New Brunswick timberland, more than 25% of the province's timber. He owned the province's four English-language newspapers and two of its three English-language television stations. In 1990 *Forbes* magazine estimated his worth at $5 billion, although the complexities of the structure of a series of offshore holding companies made the exact worth of his some 300 companies unknown. After a lifetime of 12-hour days, Irving technically retired to Bermuda in 1972 after handing over the conglomerate's day-to-day control to his three sons, but he still held ultimate authority. He had few outside interests and when asked what he did for entertainment, replied, "I work."

Jacobs, Lou (JACOB LUDWIG), U.S. performer (b. 1903, Bremerhaven, Germany—d. Sept. 13, 1992, Sarasota, Fla.), entertained audiences for more than 60 years as the master clown of the Ringling Brothers and Barnum & Bailey Circus. He was easily recognized by his bulbous red nose, arching eyebrows, goofy grin, and minuscule hat perched atop a pointy head, an image that was emblazoned on a U.S. postage stamp in 1966 and served as an emblem for the Ringling circus. Although he was 1.86 m (6 ft 1 in) tall, he regularly opened the show by squeezing his frame into a 61 × 91-cm (2 × 3-ft) fully operational minicar and then entering the ring with one giant clown shoe dangling in the air. This vehicle and his feisty Chihuahua, Knucklehead, were his trademarks. Two of his most famous routines were sliding around the hippodrome track on water skis and gliding past spectators in a motorized bathtub. In 1952 he had a cameo role in the film *The Greatest Show on Earth*, teaching his craft to apprentice

James Stewart. Jacobs, a professional clown from 1925 to 1985, was a founding professor (1968) at the Clown College of the Ringling Circus in Venice, Fla. He was inducted into the Circus Hall of Fame and the Clown Hall of Fame in 1989.

Jaroszewicz, Piotr, Polish politician (b. Oct. 8, 1909, Nieswiez, Warsaw province, Russian Empire [now Belarus]—d. Sept. 2, 1992, Anin, Poland), as premier of Poland (1970–80) implemented the policies of Edward Gierek, first secretary of the Polish United Workers' (Communist) Party; their government policies led to a crippled economy, huge price increases, and long lines for goods. The strikes and unrest that followed gave rise to the Solidarity trade union movement. Jaroszewicz was a teacher until he joined the Soviet-backed Polish army (1943). He progressed rapidly, rising to the rank of brigadier general by 1950. In 1944 he joined what effectively was the Communist Party, and he rose through a number of posts to become deputy premier, remaining in that office until he became premier. He joined the party's Politburo in 1964 and became a full member three days before his appointment as premier. During the unrest caused by the government's economic failures, Jaroszewicz was made a scapegoat, and he was dropped from the Politburo and forced to resign from office. He and Gierek were expelled from the party the following year. Jaroszewicz and his wife were found murdered in their home; he had been tortured and strangled, and she had been shot.

Jenkins, Peter, British journalist (b. May 11, 1934, Beaconsfield, Buckinghamshire, England—d. May 27, 1992, London, England), chronicled the political and social changes in Britain and the world for more than 30 years as a newspaper correspondent and political columnist for *The Guardian* (1960–85), *The Sunday Times* (1985–87), and *The Independent* (1987–92). Jenkins grew up in Suffolk, received a master's degree in history from Trinity Hall, Cambridge, and did national service in the British navy. After two years as a reporter for the *Financial Times* (1958–60), he joined the staff of *The Guardian* as a reporter (1960–63), later becoming labour correspondent (1963–67), Washington correspondent (1972–74), and political commentator and policy editor (1974–85); he contributed three or more political commentaries per week to the paper, and his breadth of knowledge and shrewd judgment soon brought him national attention. Jenkins, whose personal beliefs were essentially socialist and pro-European, went to work for the conservative *Sunday Times* in 1985, but he quit two years later to sign on with the newly founded *Independent* as associate editor and chief political commentator. In the 1970s and '80s he made frequent radio and TV appearances. He also wrote a play, *Illuminations* (performed in 1980), as well as theatre reviews for *The Spectator* (1978–81), in-depth articles and interviews for the magazine *Modern Painters,* and two books, *The Battle of Downing Street* (1970) and *Mrs. Thatcher's Revolution: The Ending of the Socialist Era* (1987).

Joseph, Helen Beatrice May, British-born South African political activist (b. April 8, 1905, Midhurst, England—d. Dec. 25, 1992, Johannesburg, South Africa), was one of the first whites in South Africa to struggle for change; she fought the inequities of the white minority government for 40 years despite government harassment, ill health, and advancing age. Educated at the University of London (1927), Joseph settled in South Africa in 1931. She married and lived as a homemaker until World War II, when, as an information officer in the women's auxiliary air force, she gave lectures on the conditions in South Africa to British troops. After the war she returned to college, got a divorce, and became a social worker in a Coloured (mixed race) area in Cape Town, where she discovered the daily realities of government-sanctioned injustice, especially as racial separation evolved into official policy. In 1955 Joseph was a founding member of the Congress of Democrats, the white wing of the then outlawed African National Congress (ANC). In 1957 she was arrested

for treason and banned (not allowed to attend meetings); she was acquitted in 1961, put in detention for five months, and then (1962) placed under house arrest. She continued to speak out, and in 1964 she was listed as a communist, which barred her from being quoted in the press. When she was hospitalized with cancer in 1971, her house arrest was lifted. Joseph was arrested again in 1980 and banned until 1982. In 1983 she was elected one of the patrons of the United Democratic Front (UDF), which waged a battle nationally and internationally on behalf of the ANC and whose work eventually led to the dismantling of apartheid. The UDF hailed Joseph, who wanted to be remembered as a "tough old bag," as the "mother of the struggle." Her books include *If This Be Treason* (1963), *Tomorrow's Sun* (1966), and *Side by Side* (1986).

Kaufman, Irving Robert, U.S. judge (b. June 24, 1910, New York, N.Y.—d. Feb. 1, 1992, New York), was the presiding federal judge during the 1951 Julius and Ethel Rosenberg cause célèbre and sentenced the two to death in the electric chair after finding them guilty of having conspired to deliver atomic-bomb secrets to the Soviet Union. It was the only death sentence for espionage by American civilians ever carried out in the U.S. (the Rosenbergs were electrocuted in 1953), and the order haunted Kaufman throughout his career, which was otherwise marked by liberal rulings. After graduating (1931) from Fordham Law School, New York City, Kaufman practiced law before serving as an assistant U.S. attorney. He was appointed (1949) to the federal bench by Pres. Harry S. Truman and in 1961 was elevated to the U.S. Court of Appeals for the 2nd Circuit in New York, serving as chief judge from 1973 until mandatory retirement in 1980. He remained as a regular judge until 1987, when he retired to a senior judgeship. During his years on the bench, Kaufman specialized in First Amendment cases and consistently championed the freedom of the press. He cast the lone dissenting vote in 1971 when the court ruled not to allow the *New York Times* to publish the sensitive Pentagon Papers about the Vietnam war. The Supreme Court agreed with Kaufman and overturned the ruling. In 1961 Kaufman ordered the first desegregation of a predominantly black public school in the North, saying that "compliance with the Supreme Court's (1954) edict was not to be less forthright in the North than in the South." He also wrote a number of landmark decisions involving antitrust suits and race relations. Kaufman was excluded from a seat on the Supreme Court because of his controversial role in the Rosenberg spy case; he was taken to task by liberals for invoking divine guidance in determining the Rosenbergs' sentencing and for imposing the harshest sentence on them, and some accused him of being influenced by Sen. Joseph McCarthy's anti-Communist witch-hunting.

Kaysone Phomvihan, Laotian political leader and revolutionary (b. Dec. 13, 1920, Na Seng, Laos—d. Nov. 21, 1992, Vientiane, Laos), was a Communist leader from 1955 and ruler from 1975 of Laos, one of the poorest and least developed nations in the world; earlier he had fought in the struggle for a liberated Laos against Japanese occupiers, the French colonial government, and finally the U.S. military. Kaysone was best remembered, though, as one of the revolutionary leaders responsible for the 1975 overthrow of the 600-year-old monarchy and for allowing the last king, Savang Vatthana, and his wife, Queen Khamphouis, to perish (reportedly in 1981) in a detention camp. He was born in southern Laos of a Lao mother and a Vietnamese father, a civil servant in the French colonial government. Kaysone protested against Japanese occupation of his country during World War II and, while studying law at the University of Hanoi, he became involved with the nascent Indochinese Communist Party. Soon Kaysone was sent back to Laos by his Vietnamese friend Ho Chi Minh to join the anti-French revolutionary movement that came to be known as the Pathet Lao. In 1955 he cofounded and became general secretary of what would later be called the Lao

People's Revolutionary Party (a post he would hold until his death). In 1958 Kaysone unsuccessfully ran for a seat in the Supreme People's Assembly. After the resumption of hostilities in 1964, he moved the Pathet Lao into caves in the northern mountains, withstanding U.S. carpet bombing of the area. After the disintegration of a short-lived, U.S.-backed postwar government in 1975, Kaysone became prime minister of the newly created Lao People's Democratic Republic.

Kaysone kept the country closely allied with Vietnam and isolated from Western influence. With the end of the cold war, however, he sought new donors, visiting France and Japan in 1989. After a new constitution was adopted in 1991, Kaysone became president. In 1992 he relaxed some government controls and scheduled December elections for the Supreme People's Assembly. He also released most political prisoners, including those army officers from the pro-Western regime held in detention camps since 1975, and he also distanced Laos from Vietnam by improving relations with China.

Kelly, Petra, German political activist (b. Nov. 29, 1947, Günzburg, West Germany—found dead Oct. 19, 1992, Bonn, Germany), as a cofounder of the Green Party, tirelessly advocated and fought for world peace and nuclear disarmament. Born Petra Lehmann, she moved to the U.S. at age 13 after her mother married an Irish-American army officer. Kelly became involved in the protest culture that swept the U.S. during the 1960s, taking part in antiwar and civil rights demonstrations before graduating from American University, Washington, D.C., with a degree in international studies in 1970. That year her younger sister died of cancer after years of radiation therapy; soon thereafter Kelly made an "emotional connection" between cancer and nuclear power. After returning to Europe, she worked for the European Communities and joined the Social Democratic Party, but she eventually became disillusioned with its defense and energy policies; in 1979 she and a few others founded the Green Party. In 1983 the Greens received enough votes to send Kelly and 26 others to the Bundestag. Over time, the party split into various competing factions, and Kelly found herself an internationally acclaimed figure within a party that distrusted individual power and the cult of personality. The Greens lost representation in the "unification election" of 1990, but Kelly continued to work ceaselessly for international causes. Since the early 1980s, Kelly had been involved with Gert Bastian, an army general who had resigned his commission and had become active in Green politics; their bodies were found about three weeks after Bastian, without explanation, apparently shot Kelly and then himself in the house that they shared.

Kendricks, Eddie, U.S. singer (b. Dec. 17, 1939, Union Springs, Ala.—d. Oct. 5, 1992, Birmingham, Ala.), as lead tenor of the Temptations, propelled them to electrifying heights with his spine-tingling falsetto, which was featured in a string of hits, including "Girl (Why You Wanna Make Me Blue)," "Just My Imagination," and "The Way You Do the Things You Do." In Detroit, Mich., Kendricks and baritone Paul Williams formed the Primes quintet with baritone Otis Williams, high tenor Eldridge Bryant, and bass Melvin Franklin. After they were signed by Motown Records in the early 1960s, Bryant left the group and was replaced by David Ruffin, who often shared the lead with Kendricks. The group was then renamed the Temptations. Their first number one hit was "My Girl" (1965), and they became one of the top black male vocal groups of the 1960s with their soulful five-part harmonies. In 1971 Kendricks struck out on a successful solo career, and he scored hits with such singles as "It's So Hard to Say Good-bye," "Can I," "If You Let Me," and "Keep on Truckin'." Some of his finest albums included *Goin' Up in Smoke* and *Eddie Kendricks at His Best.* His career began to falter, however, during the late 1970s. He rejoined the Temptations in 1982 for a reunion tour and again in 1989. In that same year, Kendricks and the other members of the Temptations were inducted into the Rock and Roll Hall of Fame.

Khoei, Abolqassem al-, Iranian-born cleric (b. Nov. 19, 1899, Khvoy, Iran—d. Aug. 8, 1992, al-Kufah, Iraq), as the grand ayatollah based in an-Najaf, Iraq, was spiritual leader of the millions of Iraqi Shi'ite Muslims. The scholarly Khoei was revered by most Shi'ites, particularly those living outside of Iran, and he was widely regarded as the chief spokesman for the "quietists," Muslims who believe that Shi'ite jurists should avoid political activism. As such, he was a leading opponent of Ayatollah Ruhollah Khomeini's 1979 Islamic revolution in Iran. Khoei studied Persian poetry and religion as a child and at the age of 13 was sent to study traditional law in the Islamic holy city of an-Najaf, where he remained. He established an international charitable foundation and wrote more than 90 books on Shi'ite theology. Although he openly criticized Mohammad Reza Shah Pahlavi of Iran, Khoei refused to endorse Khomeini and he staunchly refused to take sides during the Iran-Iraq war (1980–90). After the unsuccessful 1991 Shi'ite uprising in Iraq, he was placed under house arrest. The Iraqi government refused to allow a large public funeral for Khoei, but both Iran and Iraq declared an official three-day mourning period.

King, Albert (ALBERT NELSON), U.S. blues musician (b. April 25, 1923, Indianola, Miss.—d. Dec. 21, 1992, Memphis, Tenn.), created a unique string-bending guitar style that influenced three generations of musicians and earned him the nickname "godfather of the blues." King, who was left-handed, taught himself to play a right-handed guitar upside down by pulling the strings down, coaxing distinctive wailing sounds out of his trademark Gibson Flying V, "Lucy," that were widely imitated by such contemporary blues rock performers as Jimi Hendrix, Joe Walsh, Stevie Ray Vaughan, and Eric Clapton. King was one of 13 children born to an itinerant Mississippi preacher and his wife. When he was eight years old, his widowed mother moved the family to eastern Arkansas, where he worked as a farmhand on a cotton plantation and later as a bulldozer operator. In the early 1950s he moved to Gary, Ind., joined the Chicago-based music scene, and made (1953) his first record, "Bad Luck Blues," for the Parrot label. He moved to St. Louis, Mo., in 1956 and continued performing his blend of simple, declamatory vocals and soaring guitar licks in clubs and roadhouses. His career took off in the 1960s after he joined Stax Records in Memphis and released such acclaimed albums as *Born Under a Bad Sign* (1967) and *Live Wire/Blues Power* (1968). King toured extensively and made an acclaimed appearance at the Montreux (Switz.) Rock/Blues Festival in 1975. He reemerged in the 1980s, capturing a new generation of fans with the albums *San Francisco '83* (1983), *Laundromat Blues* (1984), and *I'm in a Phone Booth, Baby* (1984).

Kirsten, Dorothy, U.S. opera singer (b. July 6, 1910, Montclair, N.J.—d. Nov. 18, 1992, Los Angeles, Calif.), as a lyric soprano with the Metropolitan Opera for 30 years, specialized in title role interpretations of such Puccini works as *Manon Lescaut, Tosca,* and *Madama Butterfly.* Kirsten was a popular singer on radio and a student at Juilliard in New York City before becoming the protégé of soprano Grace Moore, who sponsored her trip to Rome for studies with Astolfo Pescia. When Kirsten returned to the U.S. at the outbreak of World War II, she made her professional concert debut in a stage show at the New York World's Fair. Moore helped her secure an engagement with the Chicago opera, where in 1940 she made her operatic debut as Poussette in *Manon.* She later debuted with the San Carlo

Opera (1942), the New York City Opera (1944), and the San Francisco Opera (1947). Kirsten made her bow with the Metropolitan as Mimi in *La Bohème* on Dec. 1, 1945. At the Metropolitan she prided herself on accepting only roles that showcased her clear voice to its best advantage. Besides Puccini portrayals, Kirsten also performed the leads in Gounod's *Roméo et Juliette* and *Faust,* Leoncavallo's *Pagliacci,* and Verdi's *La Traviata.* She also appeared on television and in such motion pictures as *Mr. Music* and *The Great Caruso.* Though Kirsten formally retired from the Metropolitan in 1975, she continued to return there for special engagements.

Kitagawa, Joseph Mitsuo, Japanese-born U.S. theologian and educator (b. March 8, 1915, Osaka, Japan—d. Oct. 7, 1992, Chicago, Ill.), was a scholar in the vanguard of establishing religion as an independent academic discipline on U.S. university campuses and was instrumental in introducing the religions of Japan to the West. After graduating (1938) from Rikkyo (St. Paul's) University, Tokyo, Kitagawa went to the U.S. in 1941 to continue his theological studies, but he was interned for four years, like others of Japanese ancestry, in detention camps during World War II. During that time he was ordained an Episcopal priest and, while incarcerated in Idaho, he served as an Episcopal minister. After earning a Ph.D. (1951) from the University of Chicago, Kitagawa joined the faculty there as an assistant professor. He became professor of the history of religion in 1964 and, from 1970 to 1980, served as dean of the university's Divinity School. Kitagawa wrote a number of highly regarded books, including *Religions of the East* (1960; rev. ed., 1968), *Religion in Japanese History* (1965), *The Great Religions: An Anthology* (1969), *Spiritual Liberation and Human Freedom in Contemporary Asia* (1990), and *The Christian Tradition: Beyond Its European Captivity* (1992). He was a founding member and editor of the international journal *History of Religions.* Kitagawa was also for many years a valued adviser and contributor to *Encyclopædia Britannica.*

Klineberg, Otto, Canadian-born social psychologist (b. Nov. 2, 1899, Quebec, Que.—d. March 6, 1992, Bethesda, Md.), conducted ground-breaking studies on intelligence scores of black students, and his pioneering findings helped influence the U.S. Supreme Court's landmark 1954 school desegregation case *Brown* v. *Board of Education.* By comparing intelligence scores of students attending underfunded Southern black schools with those of Southern whites and Northern blacks and whites, Klineberg discovered that the Southern black students' scores were lower but that when Southern blacks moved to integrated schools in the North, their intelligence scores eventually equaled those of Northern-born blacks. His studies showed that segregated schools were inferior and provided unequal education. Klineberg earned a B.A. (1919) from McGill University in Montreal, an M.A. (1920) in philosophy from Harvard University, an M.D. (1925) from McGill, and a Ph.D. (1927) from Columbia University, New York City, where he began studying Native Americans and chaired the social psychology department. From 1961 to 1982 he directed the International Center for Intergroup Relations at the University of Paris. He then returned to New York City, where he taught part-time at City University until he was 90.

Lerner, Max(well Alan), U.S. educator and author (b. Dec. 20, 1902, Minsk, Russia—d. June 5, 1992, New York, N.Y.), was an influential spokesman for liberal political and economic views. Beginning in 1949, he was for many years a widely read, often controversial syndicated columnist for the *New York Post,* and many of his books, some of them collections of his columns and articles, had great impact when they appeared. Lerner, originally named Mikhail, immigrated to the U.S. with his parents in 1907. He received a B.A. degree from Yale University in 1923 and then studied law there the following year. He received an M.A. degree from Washington University, St. Louis, Mo., in 1925 and a Ph.D. from the Robert Brookings Graduate School of Economics and Government, Washington, D.C., in 1927. From 1927 to 1932 he edited the *Encyclopaedia of the Social Sciences,* and he later edited the magazine *The Nation* (1936–38) and *PM,* a New York newspaper with no advertising (1943–48). He contributed to many magazines, including *The Atlantic, The New Republic,* and *Saturday Review.* Lerner's long teaching career, largely in government and political science, included appointments at Sarah Lawrence College, Bronxville, N.Y.; Harvard University; Williams College, Williamstown, Mass.; and Brandeis University, Waltham, Mass. Throughout his life he advocated the right of Soviet and Eastern European Jews to emigrate to Israel. Lerner's last book, *Wrestling with the Angel* (1990), described his encounters with the doctors who treated him during a long series of illnesses.

Li Xiannian (Li Hsien-nien), Chinese politician (b. June 23, 1909, Hongan [Hung-an] county, Hubei [Hupeh] province, China—d. June 21, 1992, Beijing [Peking], China), exerted enormous influence as one of the eight "revolutionary elders" and as a leftist hard-liner who opposed economic reform. He supported Deng Xiaoping (Teng Hsiao-p'ing) in the military suppression of the student-led 1989 Tiananmen (T'ien-an-men) Square pro-democracy movement. Li, a member of the Communist Party by 1927, was a veteran of the Long March (1934–35), having served as army captain and political commissar. After the 1949 Communist victory and Mao Zedong's (Mao Tse-tung's) rise to power, Li became governor in his native province. Later in Beijing he served as finance minister (1954–78) and became a self-taught economist who favoured the Soviet economic model of central planning. He was instrumental in helping to rebuild the economy after the 1960–62 famine that resulted from Mao's Great Leap Forward in collectivization. After Mao died in 1976, Li, who survived numerous purges, initially urged party leaders to "deepen the struggle against Deng Xiaoping," but when the latter emerged as China's premier leader, Li recanted and blamed himself for the deficit-plagued economy. Li served in the largely ceremonial post of president of the country from 1983 to 1988. He exercised his political power as one of five members of the Communist Party Political Bureau Standing Committee (1982–87); as a member of the party's Central Advisory Commission, an influential body of party veterans; and as chairman of the People's Political Consultative Conference, a post he held at the time of his death.

Lorentz, Pare, U.S. filmmaker (b. Dec. 11, 1905, Clarksburg, W.Va.—d. March 4, 1992, Armonk, N.Y.), dramatically recorded the images of the Great Depression in two classic government-sponsored documentaries that used lyrical images, the powerful narrative of Thomas Chalmers, and compelling scores by Virgil Thomson to capture the social consciousness of the American public. The first, *The Plow That Broke the Plains* (1936), chronicled the misuse of the Great Plains and the subsequent plight of the farmers in the resulting Oklahoma Dust Bowl. The second documentary, *The River* (1937), was a history of the Mississippi River Basin and the effect of the Tennessee Valley Authority on the area. As a film critic for *Judge* magazine (1926–34) and the *New York Evening Journal* (1931–32), Lorentz gained a national reputation by criticizing filmmakers for not making more realistic films. He was given a budget of $6,000 by the Resettlement Administration (later part of the Department of Agriculture) under Pres. Franklin D. Roosevelt to direct a film about the Oklahoma Dust Bowl. His effort met resistance by filmmakers and, until King Vidor intervened, they refused to lend stock footage to what they considered a propaganda effort. Following the resounding critical and artistic success of *The Plow That Broke the Plains* and *The River*, Roosevelt appointed Lorentz chief of the U.S. Film Service in 1938. He then directed *The Fight for Life* (1940), a docudrama about the hazards of childbirth among the poor. After the Film Service was disbanded in 1940, Lorentz made only one more documentary, *The Nuremberg Trials* (1946). During World War II he served in the Army Air Forces, making more than 200 briefing films to be shown to pilots. Lorentz formed his own film-production company in 1948, but his plan to produce a documentary about atomic-bomb testing was never realized. Besides serving as a film consultant and lecturer, he also published *Censored: The Private Life of the Movies* (1930; with Morris Ernst), *The Roosevelt Year: 1933* (1934), and an autobiography, *FDR's Moviemaker,* which appeared posthumously.

Loutit, John Freeman, Australian-born hematologist and radiobiologist (b. Feb. 19, 1910, Perth, Australia—d. June 11, 1992, Oxfordshire, England), was a pioneer in the study of the biological effects of radiation. As the founding director (1947–69) of the Radiobiology Unit of the British Medical Research Council (MRC), he assembled and led interdisciplinary teams that explored the possibility of biological hazards from the peaceful use of atomic energy and indicated that radiation could be effective in the treatment of leukemia and certain other forms of cancer. He also developed a storage medium of acidified citrate and dextrose that extended the shelf life of red blood cells. Loutit began his studies in Australia and accepted (1930) a Rhodes scholarship to the University of Oxford, where he eventually completed his medical education (M.S., 1938; D.M., 1946). He held several clinical appointments (1935–39) and served as director of the South London Blood Transfusion Service (1940–47) before heading the MRC Radiobiology Unit. Loutit resigned as director in 1969, but he continued to work in the unit laboratory until 1988. His best-known book, *Irradiation of Mice and Men,* was published in 1962. Loutit was made Commander of the Order of the British Empire in 1957 and elected a fellow of the Royal Society in 1963.

Ludwig, Daniel Keith, U.S. shipping tycoon (b. June 24, 1897, South Haven, Mich.—d. Aug. 27, 1992, New York, N.Y.), was a savvy entrepreneur who amassed a fortune and parlayed a $5,000 loan from his father into a global shipping and real

estate empire. Ludwig left school after the eighth grade and worked for a marine engine company before going into business for himself at the age of 19. He purchased an old steamer, converted it into a barge, and started hauling molasses in the Great Lakes region. During the 1920s he turned to transporting oil and formed the American Tankers Corp. in 1925. The following year Ludwig was aboard an oil freighter when it exploded. The accident fused three vertebrae in his spine, and he suffered constant pain until an operation 28 years later helped alleviate some of his discomfort. The foundation of his shipping concern was the New York-based National Bulk Carriers Inc., which he owned outright and turned into a colossal private multinational corporation. Ludwig was also well known for his innovations and creative financing. During the 1940s one of his shipyards pioneered a timesaving process of welding rather than riveting the hulls of ships, and by the end of World War II, he owned the nation's fifth largest tanker fleet, with scores of supertankers. Ludwig acquired his fleet by borrowing against the future lease income that they would generate. He secured loans by using these contracts as collateral and then used the money he borrowed to buy more ships. He also made millions in stock investments. Ludwig earned a reputation as a crusty taskmaster, a visionary investor, and a reclusive personality who shunned the press. It was his foresight that prompted him to correctly predict a shortage of wood products and to begin in the 1960s the billion-dollar large-scale development of the Jari River valley in Brazil to tap its lumber potential. In 1982, however, he was forced to abandon the costly project, which had led to the destruction of large tracts of tropical rain forest. It was reported that the project had eroded billions of dollars from his fortune, yet in 1991 his worth was estimated at $1.2 billion. Some of his other ventures included citrus farms in Panama, coal mines in Australia, and hotels in the Caribbean, and in the early 1970s he established the Ludwig Institute for Cancer Research, which commanded much of his attention during his later years. In 1986 a biography, *The Invisible Billionaire,* appeared.

MacBeth, George Mann, British poet (b. Jan. 19, 1932, Shotts, Lanarkshire, Scotland—d. Feb. 16, 1992, Tuam, County Galway, Ireland), was a prolific and versatile writer whose verse encom-

JERRY BAUER

passed moving personal elegies, highly contrived poetic jokes, loosely structured dream fantasies, and macabre satires. MacBeth published his first collection of poetry, *A Form of Words* (1954), while still an undergraduate at New College, Oxford. After graduating (1955) he joined the BBC, and by the end of the decade he was one of the BBC's top talk-radio producers. On such programs as "The Poet's Voice" (1958–65; renamed "Poetry Now," 1965–76) and "New Comment" (1959–64), he induced a wide variety of major and minor poets to read their own work. He quit

the BBC in 1976, shortly after the publication of his first two novels, *The Transformation* and *The Samurai* (both 1975). Although his second verse collection, *The Broken Places,* did not appear until 1963, from 1965 MacBeth published at least one volume of poetry almost every year, including *The Colour of Blood* (1967), *Shrapnel* (1973), *Poems of Love and Death* (1980), *Anatomy of a Divorce* (1988), *Trespassing* (1991), and two volumes of collected poems. He also penned children's verse, edited poetry anthologies, and wrote several more novels, notably *Anna's Book* (1983) and *Another Love Story* (1991). His last novel, *The Testament of Spencer,* was published posthumously.

McClintock, Barbara, U.S. geneticist (b. June 16, 1902, Hartford, Conn.—d. Sept. 2, 1992, Huntington, N.Y.), during the 1940s and '50s uncovered complex and profound discoveries about the na-

AP/WIDE WORLD

ture of mobile genetic elements; the findings were so revolutionary at the time she presented (1951) them that scientists were unable to verify or comprehend the immensity of her early discovery, which won her the Nobel Prize for Physiology or Medicine in 1983. McClintock, the daughter of a doctor, earned a Ph.D. in botany (1927) from Cornell University, Ithaca, N.Y. She taught there and helped show through her laboratory experiments that trait-determining (genetic) information was transferred between chromosomes—a process called crossing over—during cell division. McClintock joined the Carnegie Institution of Washington (D.C.) and conducted research on the Indian corn plant (maize) for Carnegie's Cold Spring Harbor (N.Y.) Laboratory, which later became a self-governing organization. There, from 1941 until her death, the maverick researcher worked alone by choice and earned the reputation of a loner; she preferred receiving letters to telephone calls and only reluctantly installed a telephone in 1986. She possessed an uncanny ability to decipher the nature of genes and was a scrupulous investigator. Using pigmentation changes in the kernels of corn as her model and microscopically examining their chromosomes, she traced how mobile genetic elements (nicknamed "jumping genes" by a later generation of geneticists) cause mutations and control growth and development in cells. Her work was not validated until James D. Watson and Francis Crick discovered the molecular structure of DNA, which led to a rediscovery of mobile elements in the chromosomes of many plants and animals. McClintock won belated acclaim for her work and was revered as a giant in the field of genetics. Besides her Nobel Prize, she was the recipient of the National Medal of Science (1970) and the first MacArthur Laureate Award (1981), a lifetime annual prize of $60,000. A biography that detailed her pioneering work, *A Feeling for the Organism,* appeared in 1983.

MacMillan, Sir Kenneth, British choreographer (b. Dec. 11, 1929, Dunfermline, Scotland—d. Oct. 29, 1992, London, England), created more than 40 ballets during his career and was said to have revived the tradition of full-length ballet in Britain. His family was impoverished, but MacMillan—inspired by films starring the dancer Fred Astaire—found a ballet teacher who would give him free lessons. He was awarded a scholarship to the Sadler's Wells Ballet School and a year later (1946) became one of the original members of the Sadler's Wells Theatre Ballet (the second company of the Sadler's Wells Ballet, which later became the Royal Ballet), making his debut in *The Sleeping Beauty.* He began choreographing for workshop performances in the early 1950s and created his first professional work, *Danses Concertantes,* in 1955. *Romeo and Juliet* (1965), his first full-length ballet, made an international impact and became a mainstay of both the Royal Ballet and American Ballet Theatre (ABT). It was danced at its premiere by Margot Fonteyn and Rudolf Nureyev and later by Christopher Gable and Lynn Seymour, one of MacMillan's favourite muses, on whom it had been choreographed. Also in 1965 he created another of his most acclaimed works, *Song of the Earth,* for the Stuttgart (Germany) Ballet. The next year he became director of the Deutsche Oper Ballet in West Berlin, but in 1970 he returned to London to succeed Sir Frederick Ashton as a codirector, with John Field, of the Royal Ballet. Three months later he became sole director, and he remained in that post until 1977, when he resigned so he could concentrate on choreography. For the rest of his life, he was the Royal Ballet's principal choreographer. He also became an artistic associate of ABT (1984) and the Houston (Texas) Ballet (1988). Among MacMillan's other successes were *Anastasia* (1971), *Manon* (1974), *Mayerling* (1978), and *Isadora* (1981). At the time of his death he had nearly completed the choreography for a new production of the musical *Carousel.* He died backstage at the Royal Opera House at Covent Garden during a revival of *Mayerling.* MacMillan was knighted in 1983.

McWilliam, F(rederick) E(dward), Irish sculptor (b. April 30, 1909, Banbridge, County Down, Northern Ireland—d. May 13, 1992, London, England), worked in wood, stone, and bronze to create surreal, abstract, and semiabstract sculptures that defied easy categorization. In his best-known pieces he "reinvented anatomy," placing distorted human figures or body parts in juxtaposition to achieve a dramatic or whimsical effect. McWilliam studied at the Belfast College of Art and the Slade School of Fine Art in London (1928–31) before moving to Paris. The 1932–33 collapse of sterling forced him to return to England, where he began carving in the local Buckinghamshire cherrywood. After serving in the Royal Air Force in India during World War II, McWilliam taught drawing and sculpture in Bengal (1944–46), at the Chelsea School of Art (1946–47), and at the Slade (1947–66). Although his work was seldom overtly political, in 1972–73 he made a series of powerful bronzes, "Women of Belfast," in response to the bombing of the Abercorn Tea Rooms in Belfast. McWilliam was made Commander of the Order of the British Empire (1966) and was elected to the Royal Academy (1989). He was the subject of a major retrospective at the prestigious Tate Gallery in London in 1989.

Maglie, Sal(vatore) Anthony ("THE BARBER"), U.S. baseball player (b. April 26, 1917, Niagara Falls, N.Y.—d. Dec. 28, 1992, Niagara Falls), sported a five-o'clock shadow and adopted a fierce scowling grimace when he pitched his specialty fastball, which was so high and close to (shaving) the face of batters that he earned the nickname "Sal the Barber." During his heyday in the 1950s, Maglie played for all three New York professional baseball teams: the New York Giants, the Brooklyn Dodgers, and the New York Yankees. His phenomenal pitching also included a curveball that helped the Giants capture a National League pennant in 1951. In 1950 he led the league with 18 wins and 4 losses, and the following year he had a 23–6 record. He pitched for the Cleveland Indians in 1955 before moving to the Dodgers in 1956. His 13–5 record helped propel that team to a National League pennant. Though Maglie won in the 1956 World Series opener against the Yankees, he lost the fifth game 2–0 when Don Larsen pitched a perfect game. Maglie ended his pitching career with the Yankees in 1957 and became a coach the following year. His career record included 119 wins, 62 losses, a 3.15 earned-run average, and 25 shutouts.

Martin, Paul Joseph James, Canadian politician and diplomat (b. June 23, 1903, Ottawa, Ont.—d. Sept. 14, 1992, Windsor, Ont.), served with distinction in the Cabinets of four Liberal Party prime ministers (from Mackenzie King to Pierre Trudeau) and, as minister of national health and welfare from 1946 to 1957, was instrumental in writing most of the country's social legislation. Martin, who was stricken with polio at the age of four, experienced a miraculous recovery, but his affliction left a lasting impression on his life-style and the legislation he supported. He studied at the University of Toronto, Harvard Law School, Trinity College, Cambridge, and the School of International Studies in Geneva. Martin was elected to the House of Commons in 1935 and represented the Windsor riding of Essex East (now Windsor-Walkerville) until 1968. He was appointed parliamentary assistant to the minister of labour in 1943, and in 1945 he joined the Cabinet as secretary of state. As minister of national health and welfare, he guided important legislation through Parliament, including the National Health Program (1948), the federal Old Age Security Act (1951), and the Hospital Insurance and Diagnostic Services Act (1957). He was also responsible for ordering the manufacture of vast quantities of the polio vaccine developed by Jonas Salk so that, when it was approved safe for distribution, Canadians could be quickly vaccinated. A skilled diplomat, Martin was a delegate to the League of Nations in the 1930s, the principal architect of an expanded UN membership plan (1955), minister of external affairs (1963–68), and high commissioner to Britain (1974–79). His memoirs, *A Very Public Life,* were published in two volumes (1983 and 1985).

Messiaen, Olivier-Eugène-Prosper-Charles, French composer and musician (b. Dec. 10, 1908, Avignon, France—d. April 28, 1992, Paris, France), was the last in a long line of distinguished French organist-composers; he was also one of the 20th century's most influential teachers, and his students included Iannis Xenakis, Pierre Boulez, and Karlheinz Stockhausen. Messiaen began composing as a child, and at age 11 he entered the Paris Conservatory, where his teachers included organist Marcel Dupré and composer Paul Dukas. In 1931 he became resident organist at the church of the Trinity in Paris. He began teaching in 1936 but left to enter the French Army in World War II. It was while he was interned by the Germans that Messiaen wrote *Quatuor pour la fin du temps* (1940; *Quartet for the End of Time*) to be performed by fellow prisoners. In 1942, after he was released, Messiaen began teaching at the Paris Conservatory, where he remained until 1978, and in 1942 he resumed his position at Trinity Church, which he held until his death. Among his principal compositions were the orchestral works *L'Ascension* (1933; arranged for organ, 1934) and *Turangalîla-Symphonie* (1946–48), the organ cycle *La Nativité du Seigneur* (1935), and the piano works *Vingt Regards sur l'Enfant Jésus* (1944) and *Catalogue d'oiseaux* (1956–58). His only opera was *Saint François d'Assise* (1975–83). *Éclairs sur l'au-delà,* commissioned by the New York Philharmonic Orchestra in celebration of its 150th anniversary, received its premiere posthumously. Messiaen developed a highly personal style noted for its rhythmic complexity, rich tonal colour, and unique harmonic language. He was particularly fascinated with birdsong, which he transcribed in many of his compositions. The principal extramusical influence on his work, besides his interest in nature, was his deep religious devotion. Messiaen was elected a member of the French Institute in 1967 and received many other honours, including the Grand Cross of the Legion of Honour.

Meyendorff, John, U.S. theologian (b. Feb. 17, 1926, Neuilly-sur-Seine, France—d. July 22, 1992, Montreal, Que.), as a prominent U.S. leader in the Eastern Orthodox Church, helped forge unity among members of the ethnically diverse Orthodox churches and promoted ecumenism among other Christian denominations. Meyendorff was the son of Russian émigrés who fled their homeland during the Russian Revolution of 1917. After graduating (1949) from the Orthodox Theological Seminary of St. Serge in Paris, he earned a doctorate from the Sorbonne in 1958. The following year he joined the faculty of St. Vladimir's Orthodox Theological Seminary in Crestwood, N.Y., and from 1984 he served as its dean. Meyendorff played a vital role in modernizing the church's liturgy from Old Slavonic to English, and he became an esteemed figure within the church. In the Orthodox Church in the U.S., he served as adviser to the Holy Synod and was editor of its monthly newsletter. In a wider capacity, he was cofounder and the first general secretary of Syndesmos, an international coalition of Orthodox youth organizations. Meyendorff's scholarship was evidenced in his many writings; he wrote in English, Russian, and French. His religious and historical books were published in eight languages, and for many years he was a valued contributor to *Encyclopædia Britannica.* He was also a lecturer at Harvard University; Fordham University, Bronx, N.Y.; and Columbia University, New York City. Meyendorff represented the Orthodox Church in America on the Central Committee of the World Council of Churches and was a past president of the Orthodox Theological Society of America and of the American Patristics Association. An expert on Byzantine history, he was a member of the executive committee of the U.S. Committee of Byzantine Studies and was senior fellow and acting director of Harvard's Byzantine Research Centre in Washington. As the Soviet Union disintegrated, Meyendorff made numerous trips to Russia, where he visited Patriarch Aleksy II of the Russian Orthodox Church during the time of the attempted coup against Pres. Mikhail Gorbachev in 1991. Meyendorff died of pancreatic cancer while on vacation in Canada.

Miller, Roger, U.S. singer and songwriter (b. Jan. 2, 1936, Fort Worth, Texas—d. Oct. 25, 1992, Los Angeles, Calif.), composed witty and lyrical songs that relied on his clever use of puns, wordplay, wisecracking, and wry country humour, including such all-time favourites as "Dang Me," " England Swings," and "King of the Road," which became an anthem for hobos. A versatile and self-taught musician, Miller played the drums, fiddle, banjo, piano, and guitar and composed his first song at the age of five. He left school after the eighth grade and served in the U.S. Army in Korea before moving to Nashville, Tenn., where he launched his songwriting career, turning out hits for Jimmy Dean, George Jones, Ray Price, and Ernest Tubb. After signing with RCA Records in 1960, he scored his first top-10 country hit the following year with "When Two Worlds Collide." Soon after, he made a successful crossover to pop music, and he enjoyed a string of hits with such novelty and folksy songs as "Chug-a-Lug," "Do Wacka Do," "Can't Roller Skate in a Buffalo Herd," "Walkin' in the Sunshine," and "Little Green Apples." Between 1964 and 1966 Miller garnered a record 11 Grammy awards. His popularity began to wane in the '70s before he climaxed his career in 1985 as the songwriter for the smash Broadway hit *Big River,* which ran for two and a half years, captured seven Tony awards, and earned Miller his own Tony for best score for a musical.

Mills, Wilbur Daigh, U.S. lawyer and politician (b. May 24, 1909, Kensett, Ark.—d. May 2, 1992, Kensett), exerted extraordinary influence in the political arena as the longtime Democratic representative from Arkansas's Second District (1939–77) and as the chairman of the powerful House Ways and Means Committee (1957–74) before he was toppled from his lofty position on Oct. 7, 1974. On that day the driver of his limousine was pulled over, and Mills was discovered to be intoxicated and in the company of a stripper known as Fanne Foxe, who then bolted from the vehicle and dived into the Tidal Basin formal pond. Mills graduated (1933) from Harvard University with a law degree but entered local politics because the Great Depression limited his legal opportunities. At the age of 29 he was elected to the House of Representatives, and in his first 15 years in office he voted against civil rights, the construction of the St. Lawrence Seaway, statehood for Hawaii, and the admission of refugees from Communist countries; Mills also voted for making membership in the Communist Party a crime. During the 1960s he shifted his ultraconservative stance and supported the national health insurance program known as Medicare, an upgrading of welfare laws, a major tax revision, and several foreign-trade tariff laws. As chairman of the House Ways and Means Committee, Mills wrote most of the federal tax code, exercised control over nearly all legislation involving federal spending, and held large sway in the selection of chairmen for other major House committees, including Agriculture, Foreign Affairs, and Armed Services. His skills as an intelligent administrator coupled with his influence prompted some to mention him as a possible nominee to the U.S. Supreme Court or even the presidency. After the scandalous incident, Mills was forced to resign his chairmanship of Ways and Means, though he was reelected to one more term in the House. In 1982 he spoke before a Senate subcommittee on health, recounting his own experience as a recovered alcoholic. He said, "I thought it was a failure on my part. It's a disease from which you can recover and gain back your position in life."

Milstein, Nathan, Ukrainian-born violinist (b. Dec. 31, 1904, Odessa, Ukraine, Russian Empire—d. Dec. 16, 1992, London, England), was hailed as one of the finest interpreters of Bach's unaccompanied violin sonatas and of works in the Romantic style and for his superb mastery of the instrument in a distinguished career of more than 60 years. Milstein, raised in the Jewish ghetto in Odessa, started playing at age five "because my mother made me," he said. When Milstein was 11, the renowned violinist Leopold Auer heard him play and invited him to study under him at the St. Petersburg Conservatory of Music. Milstein's first public recital was in 1919—with his sister as piano accompanist—and they continued to play together, especially as his family was suffering financially in the aftermath of the Russian Revolution. He met and grew close to pianist Vladimir Horowitz, and they sometimes performed together, occasionally touring Russia. In 1926 Milstein left for Paris—without money or a violin—and decided to stay. He studied under the famed Belgian violinist Eugène Ysaye and eventually secured a patron; he went on to become one of the continent's most highly regarded violinists, touring regularly. Milstein made his U.S. debut in 1929 and then returned to play annually, eventually becoming a citizen in 1942. Milstein earned an international reputation as an exceptional musician; he continued touring annually into his 80s. He received the Kennedy Center Award for Lifetime Achievement in 1987 and published a memoir, *From Russia to the West,* in 1990.

Mitchell, Joan, U.S. expatriate painter (b. Feb. 12, 1926, Chicago, Ill.—d. Oct. 30, 1992, Paris, France), was an important figure in the second generation of Abstract Expressionists and drew inspiration from landscapes in Saugatuck, Mich., New York City, and her adopted home in Vétheuil, France. Her colourful and enormous canvases, which were filled with heroic-sized slashes of lines, clusters or blocks of colours, and sequential panels, were painted in a controlled manner yet suggested a spontaneous freedom of movement. After attending (1942–44) Smith College, Northampton, Mass., Mitchell studied at the Art Institute of Chicago before traveling (1948–49) to France on a $2,000 fellowship. When she

returned to the U.S., she settled in New York City and became one of the few women members of the influential Eighth Street Club (The Club), which included such luminaries as Willem de Kooning, Franz Kline, and other exponents of the New York school of Abstract Expressionists. In 1951 her works were exhibited in the seminal Ninth Street Show, and she had her first solo exhibit the following year. Critical acclaim and a move to Paris followed in 1955. From that date until 1979, she was companion to the French-Canadian painter Jean-Paul Riopelle. In 1968 Mitchell settled on a small country estate in the village of Vétheuil, where she remained for the rest of her life. Her enormous paintings, some as wide as 8 m (20 ft), were featured in a major retrospective at the Whitney Museum of American Art (1974), in the Musée d'Art Moderne de la Ville de Paris (1982), and in a 1988 U.S. touring exhibit. In 1991 Mitchell was the recipient of the Grand Prix des Arts given by the City of Paris.

Mitchell, Peter Dennis, British biochemist (b. Sept. 29, 1920, Mitcham, Surrey, England—d. April 10, 1992, Glynn, Cornwall, England), received the 1978 Nobel Prize for Chemistry in recognition of his chemiosmotic theory explaining the mechanisms by which energy is converted for use within the cells of living creatures. In 1961 Mitchell and his longtime research associate, Jennifer Moyle, published his theory that the enzyme-studded interior membranes of mitochondria (in animal cells) and chloroplasts (in plant cells) are actively involved in the transfer of energy in food, sunlight, and oxygen to adenosine triphosphate (ATP), the molecule that serves as the "currency" of exchange in cell processes. This breakthrough theory, for which Mitchell had no experimental proof, contradicted all conventional wisdom up to that time and was vehemently opposed by most of the scientific community. He persisted in the development of this hypothesis, however, and experimental evidence eventually proved him correct. In 1974 he was made a fellow of the Royal Society, which awarded him its highest honour, the Copley Medal, in 1981. Mitchell studied biochemistry at Jesus College, Cambridge (Ph.D., 1950), and taught there until 1955, when he was named director of the chemical biology unit at the University of Edinburgh. In 1963 he moved to Cornwall, where he founded the Glynn Research Laboratories (from 1987 Glynn Research Institute).

Morley, Robert, British actor and playwright (b. May 26, 1908, Semley, Wiltshire, England—d. June 3, 1992, Reading, Berkshire, England), was a jowly character actor whose imposing girth, bushy eyebrows, and irreverent wit made him an audience favourite in stage and screen comedies and comedy-dramas. Morley studied at the Royal Academy of Dramatic Art and made his stage debut in Margate in 1928. He made his London debut the next year, but his breakthrough came as the title character in *Oscar Wilde* (1936), which he played on Broadway to equal critical acclaim in 1938. Morley starred mainly in comedies, such as *Pygmalion* (1937), *The Man Who Came to Dinner* (1941), *The First Gentleman* (1945), *The Little Hut* (1950), *A Majority of One* (1960), and *How the Other Half Loves* (1970). His most memorable role, however, was probably the ruthless Arnold Holt in *Edward, My Son* (1947), which he cowrote with Noel Langley and which he took on tour to the United States (1948) and to Australia and New Zealand (1949–50). Morley also made more than 60 motion pictures, including *Major Barbara* (1941), *The African Queen* (1951), *Beat the Devil* (1953), *Take Her, She's Mine* (1963), *Topkapi* (1964), *The Blue Bird* (1976), *High Road to China* (1983), and the 1960 adaptation of *Oscar Wilde.* He received an Academy Award nomination for his first film appearance, *Marie Antoinette* (1938), and was named best supporting actor by two major film critics societies for *Who Is Killing the Great Chefs of Europe?* (1978; U.K. title, *Too Many Chefs*). Morley's frequent appearances on U.S. television began with a live production of *Edward, My Son* in 1955, and by the 1980s he was a much-sought-after talk-show guest and the droll

TV spokesperson for British Airways. In addition to writing or co-writing eight plays, Morley wrote five books of reminiscences and an autobiography, and he was a prolific contributor to *Punch* and *Playboy* magazines. He was made Commander of the Order of the British Empire in 1957, but he refused to accept a knighthood.

Muldoon, Sir Robert David, New Zealand politician (b. Sept. 25, 1921, Auckland, N.Z.—d. Aug. 5, 1992, Auckland), was at the eye of every political storm throughout his long career, particularly during his turbulent years as prime minister of New Zealand (1975–84). Muldoon identified with the average New Zealanders he called "Rob's Mob," and he retained his leader-of-the-mob image even after he was knighted (1984). His father returned from World War I an invalid, leaving his mother to support the family. Muldoon won a scholarship to a suburban grammar school, but he left to take a pound-a-week job as a junior clerk. He studied accountancy while in the army

territorials at the start of World War II, served as a corporal in the Middle East and Italy, and continued his studies on an army grant in England after the war. He joined the youth section of the conservative National Party (NP), and after two unsuccessful bids for Parliament, he won a seat in 1960, the same year Sir Keith Holyoake led the NP to power. As under secretary of finance (1963–66), Muldoon supervised the country's conversion to a decimal currency. He rose to minister of finance in 1967 and developed into an interventionist who referred to his budget tinkering as "fine-tuning." When Holyoake retired in 1972, the NP elected Muldoon deputy to the new leader, Sir John Marshall, but a general election defeat two years later left Marshall defenseless against a challenge from his deputy. As prime minister, Muldoon retained his finance portfolio, froze wages and prices, increased subsidies, and borrowed to balance the budget. He distracted attention from negative policies through a barrage of invective against critics and the disablement of those who crossed him. He was defeated in an ill-advised snap election he called in July 1984 and lost the party leadership soon afterward, but he retained his seat in Parliament until 1991. Muldoon wrote several volumes of memoirs and kept his unpretentious style as the host of a radio call-in program.

Muliro, Masinde, Kenyan politician (b. June 30, 1922?, Matili, Kenya—d. Aug. 14, 1992, Nairobi, Kenya), as a longtime leader of the opposition in Kenya, was instrumental in the rebirth of multiparty politics in that country at the end of 1991. Muliro, a member of the Luhya, Kenya's third largest ethnic group, was educated at Roman Catholic mission schools, St. Peter's College in Tororo, Uganda, and the University of Cape

Town (B.A., 1954). He taught school in Kenya until 1957, when he was elected to the colonial legislative council. He was the founding vice president of the Kenya African Democratic Union (KADU; 1960–64), but after Kenya gained its independence (1963) KADU was dissolved and Muliro reluctantly joined the governing Kenya African National Union (KANU). Despite his frank opposition to KANU's single-party rule, Muliro held on to his seat in parliament (1963–79, 1983–88) and served as minister of cooperatives and social services (1969–75). In 1991 he and other opposition leaders formed the coalition Forum for the Restoration of Democracy, which led a successful international effort to pressure Pres. Daniel arap Moi to restore multiparty democracy. Shortly before his death Muliro announced his intention to run for president.

Murphy, George Lloyd, U.S. actor and politician (b. July 4, 1902, New Haven, Conn.—d. May 3, 1992, Palm Beach, Fla.), was best remembered as an amiable song-and-dance man in a succession of Hollywood musicals but also gained attention for some dramatic roles and finally for his term as a Republican senator representing California (1965–71). Murphy attended Yale University but dropped out in his junior year and held jobs as a Wall Street messenger, a miner, and a toolmaker before teaming up with Juliette Henkel (stage name, Julie Johnson) to form a dancing team and perform in cabarets and nightclubs. The two married in 1926, and the following year Murphy made his Broadway debut as a member of the chorus in *Good News*. He appeared in three other Broadway shows—*Hold Everything!, Of Thee I Sing,* and *Roberta*—before heeding the call from Hollywood and making his bow in *Kid Millions* (1934). Murphy's agility and grace were evident as he danced with Shirley Temple in *Little Miss Broadway* (1938), played opposite Judy Garland in *Little Nellie Kelly* (1940), and partnered Fred Astaire in a top-hat-and-walking-stick routine in *Broadway Melody of 1940*. A year earlier he had switched from the Democratic to the Republican Party, and he became a close political ally of Ronald Reagan, with whom he appeared in *This Is the Army* (1943). During World War II, Murphy's patriotic dramatic roles in *The Navy Comes Through* (1942) and *Bataan* (1943) were critically hailed. Among his other 45 films were *Broadway Melody of 1938, Hold That Co-ed* (1938), and *Walk East on Beacon* (1952), his final film. Murphy served on the board of directors of the Screen Actors Guild (1937–53) and was its president (1944–46); in 1950 he was honoured with a special Academy Award for career achievement. After retiring from films, he worked as a motion-picture business executive until he won election to the U.S. Senate, defeating Pierre Salinger. His 1970 reelection bid failed after it was revealed that he had continued to accept a salary from a film company while serving in the Senate, and he was hampered by a raspy voice, the result of surgery needed to remove a cancerous growth from his vocal chords. His autobiography was titled *Say . . . Didn't You Used to Be George Murphy?* (1970).

Mussawi, 'Abbas al-, Lebanese Shi'ite Muslim cleric (b. 1952?, an-Nabi Sheet, Lebanon—d. Feb. 16, 1992, southern Lebanon), was a relatively moderate member of the radical Hezbollah ("Party of God") movement; he was named the group's secretary-general in May 1991. Mussawi studied Shi'ite theology in an-Najaf, Iraq, where he fell under the influence of the fundamentalist Iranian cleric Ayatollah Ruhollah Khomeini. Mussawi returned to Lebanon in 1978, and four years later he helped to form Hezbollah in response to the Khomeini-led Islamic revolution in Iran (1980) and the Israeli occupation of southern Lebanon (1982). Although he denied any direct involvement in terrorist activities or in the kidnapping of Western hostages, Mussawi was believed by many Western observers to be responsible for numerous terrorist acts, including the 1983 bombing attacks in which some 300 U.S. and French peacekeeping troops were killed. After he was named Hezbollah's secretary-general in 1991, Mussawi publicly

AP/WIDE WORLD

denounced such attacks and endorsed a shift to more moderate policies. He was killed, along with his wife, their son, and several bodyguards, when the motorcade in which they were traveling came under rocket attack by Israeli helicopters.

Naughton, Bill (WILLIAM JOHN FRANCIS NAUGHTON), Irish-born British playwright (b. June 12, 1910, Ballyhaunis, County Mayo, Ireland—d. Jan. 9, 1992, Ballasalla, Isle of Man, England), delighted playgoing audiences in the 1960s with a series of working-class comedies, most notably *Alfie* (1963; filmed 1966), an episodic, unsentimental tale of an egocentric Cockney womanizer. When Naughton was a child, his family moved from Ireland to Bolton, Lancashire, where he later worked as a weaver, truck driver, and coal bagger. *A Roof over Your Head* (1945), a semiautobiographical study of life in northern England in the 1920s, was followed by several moderately successful novels and short-story collections. Naughton moved to London in the 1950s to write for the humour magazine *Lilliput* and for radio and television. He drew critical and popular acclaim for his first three plays—*All in Good Time* (1963; film title, *The Family Way,* 1967), *Alfie,* which was based on Naughton's 1962 radio play *Alfie Elkins and His Little Life,* and *Spring and Port Wine* (1964; U.S. title, *Keep It in the Family,* 1967; filmed 1969). Naughton had less success with his later plays and novels, including *June Evening* (1966), *Annie and Fanny* (1967), and *Alfie Darling* (1970).

Newman, Joe (JOSEPH DWIGHT NEWMAN), U.S. jazz trumpeter (b. Sept. 7, 1922, New Orleans, La.—d. July 4, 1992, New York, N.Y.), who played in both the swing and bop styles, was perhaps best known for his long association with the Count Basie orchestra. He was the son of pianist Dwight Newman and briefly attended college in Alabama before joining Lionel Hampton's big band in 1941. From 1943 to 1946 he played with Basie's orchestra, and he rejoined the group in 1952, when he replaced longtime Basie trumpeter Harry ("Sweets") Edison. Newman left the orchestra in 1961, and in 1962 he toured in the Soviet Union, the first of two visits there, with Benny Goodman. In the early 1960s he became active in Jazz Interactions, working to promote jazz. During later years Newman taught and performed with his own and other jazz groups, as well as on television and the Broadway stage. He made many recordings, both under his own name and with other leaders and as an accompanist for pop singers.

Nolan, Sir Sidney Robert, Australian painter (b. April 22, 1917, Melbourne, Australia—d. Nov. 27, 1992, London, England), was one of the best-known and most influential Australian artists. He was most famous for two series of paintings depicting the 19th-century outlaw Ned Kelly, but

he was also noted for having invigorated modern Australian painting, bringing it to a wider audience around the world. Nolan began studying design at a technical college when he was 14 and was first employed by a hat company to paint posters. At the time of his first one-man show (1940), which he held in his studio in Melbourne, his paintings were abstract. He developed a more representational style over the years, however, and began basing his paintings on Australian folklore. The historian Kenneth Clark, having seen Nolan's work in a group exhibition in the late 1940s, encouraged him to exhibit in London, which he did in 1951. He moved to England in 1955 and thereafter lived there or traveled throughout the world. Besides painting, Nolan also designed for such productions as Serge Lifar's ballet *Icarus* (1941), Kenneth MacMillan's (*q.v.*) version of the ballet *The Rite of Spring* (1962) at London's Covent Garden, and the opera *Samson and Delilah* (1981) at Covent Garden. Nolan was knighted in 1981 and became a member of the Order of Merit in 1983.

Norton, Mary, British children's writer (b. Dec. 10, 1903, London, England—d. Aug. 29, 1992, Hartland, Devonshire, England), created the Borrowers, a resourceful race of beings only 15 cm (6 in) high, who secretly live under the floorboards and "borrow" what they need from the humans among whom they reside. Norton introduced the Clock family—Pod, Homily, and their daughter, Arrietty—and their friends in *The Borrowers* (1952), which won the Carnegie Medal. She chronicled their further adventures in *The Borrowers Afield* (1955), *The Borrowers Afloat* (1959), *The Borrowers Aloft* (1961), *Poor Stainless* (1971), and *The Borrowers Avenged* (1982). Norton was born Mary Pearson and trained as an actress with the Old Vic Theatre Company in London. In 1927 she accompanied her husband to Portugal, where they lived until the outbreak of World War II. While working for the British Purchasing Commission in the U.S. (1940–43), she published *The Magic Bed-Knob* (1943), concerning the adventures of three children and an amateur witch. After returning to England, Norton penned a sequel, *Bonfires and Broomsticks* (1947). She later combined the two into a single volume, *Bed-Knob and Broomstick* (1957; filmed as *Bedknobs and Broomsticks,* 1971). Norton also wrote *Are All the Giants Dead?* (1975), a humorous story of aging fairy-tale characters. The Borrowers tales were adapted for television in the early 1970s and again in 1992.

Obraztsov, Sergey Vladimirovich, Russian puppeteer (b. July 5 [June 22, old style], 1901, Moscow, Russia—d. May 8, 1992, Moscow), established puppetry as an art form in the Soviet Union and enchanted audiences with spectacular musical productions in Moscow and on a series of world tours. He was equally adept at controlling complex rod puppets and at demonstrating his virtuoso finger-puppet technique with bare hands. Obraztsov studied painting at the Moscow Higher Art and Technical Studios (1918–26) and tried acting at the Nemirovich-Danchenko Music Theatre (1922–30) and the Moscow Art Theatre (1930–31). His real love, however, was the vaudeville act he developed using hand puppets, and in 1931 he was named artistic director of the new State Central Puppet Theatre in Moscow. Despite the satiric content of many of his elaborate productions, he was a great favourite of Joseph Stalin and was permitted to travel extensively outside the country. Obraztsov published several books, notably *Akter s kukloi* (1938; "Actor with a Puppet"), *Moya professiya* (1950; "My Profession"), and *Teatr kitayskogo naroda* (1957; *Chinese Puppet Theatre,* 1961). He was elected vice president of the International Union of Puppeteers in 1957 and president in 1976.

Olson, Elder James, U.S. poet, playwright, and critic (b. March 9, 1909, Chicago, Ill—d. July 25, 1992, Albuquerque, N.M.), was a leading member of the Neo-Aristotelian (also called the critical pluralist, or Chicago) school of literary criticism that developed at the University of Chicago during the 1940s. He received B.A., M.A., and

Ph.D. degrees from the University of Chicago and taught at the Armour (later Illinois) Institute of Technology from 1935 to 1942. In 1942 he returned to the University of Chicago to teach, and he remained a member of the faculty there until his retirement in 1977; during this time he also held visiting appointments at several universities in the U.S. and other countries. At Chicago he was a member of the group advocating a critical approach based on principles of Aristotle's *Poetics,* a movement that was in part a reaction against the linguistic emphasis of the New Criticism, which was then in vogue. Olson was a contributor to *Critics and Criticism* (1952), edited by his colleague R.S. Crane, considered the manifesto of the Neo-Aristotelian movement. His own best known work of criticism was probably *The Poetry of Dylan Thomas* (1954). Olson's works of poetry include *The Scarecrow Christ and Other Poems* (1954) and *Olson's Penny Arcade* (1975), the latter also containing one of his verse dramas. He received many honours for his work, including the Poetry Society of America Chap-book Award in 1955 for his book on Thomas.

O'Neill, Gerard Kitchen, U.S. physicist (b. Feb. 6, 1927, New York, N.Y.—d. April 27, 1992, Redwood, Calif.), formulated in 1956 the colliding-beam storage-ring principle—that the collision of beams of subatomic particles traveling in opposite directions in storage rings would increase the energy output from particle accelerators—and was an early proponent of establishing permanent, self-sustaining colonies in space as a solution to such terrestrial problems as pollution, overpopulation, and energy shortages. After earning a Ph.D. in physics from Cornell University, Ithaca, N.Y., in 1954, O'Neill joined the faculty at Princeton University, where he taught until his retirement in 1985. Besides his storage-ring principle, which provided the basis for much of the research in particle physics in recent decades, O'Neill designed and publicized during the late 1960s a blueprint for establishing self-supporting habitats in space that would be positioned equidistant from the Earth and the Moon and powered by solar energy. In his book *The High Frontier* (1976), O'Neill maintained that a "breakout" of human beings from Earth was unavoidable. He was also the author of the graduate-level textbook *Elementary Particle Physics: An Introduction* (1979; with David Cheng), *2081: A Hopeful View of the Human Future* (1981), and *The Technology Edge: Opportunities for America in World Competition* (1983). He formed various private nonprofit organizations devoted to technological development, including the Space Studies Institute and the Geostar Corp., the latter of which supplied the first private satellite navigational system used to guide travel on Earth. At the time of his death, O'Neill was working on a high-speed ground-based form of transportation called a magnetic flight system, comprising a small-diameter car that would "float" on a magnetic field in a vacuum tube on land or underground, enabling it to traverse the distance from Boston to Los Angeles in about an hour.

JIM WILSON—THE NEW YORK TIMES

Oort, Jan Hendrik, Dutch astronomer (b. April 28, 1900, Franeker, Neth.—d. Nov. 12, 1992, Leiden, Neth.), dominated the quest to understand the nature of the Milky Way Galaxy and was respected as one of the world's preeminent astronomers; he was considered by many to be the father of Dutch astronomy. Oort first studied at the University of Groningen under Jacobus Kapteyn, a pioneer devoted to mapping the galaxy from photographic plates. Building from

THE NEW YORK TIMES

this work, Oort focused his attention on stars of high velocity after joining the Leiden Observatory in 1924. By calculating the speeds of various stars, he confirmed in a series of papers published in 1927 that the galaxy rotates in its own plane around its distant centre, a hypothesis first put forth by Bertil Lindblad and now generally accepted. Soon after having been named a professor at Leiden (1935), Oort used the newly emergent science of radio astronomy to determine that the Sun is 30,000 light-years from the centre of the galaxy and takes 225 million years to complete an orbit around it. In 1950 he proposed that a vast cloud containing billions of Sun-orbiting comets existed beyond the solar system and that when other stars approach it some comets' orbits are altered and can then pass close to the Sun; the existence of the "Oort cloud" became generally accepted by astronomers. Oort lobbied for the construction of what was then the world's largest steerable radio telescope at Dwingeloo; upon its dedication he noted that "the heavens are now wide open." Oort also served as general secretary (1935–48) and president (1958–61) of the International Astronomical Union.

O'Reilly, William Joseph ("TIGER"), Australian cricketer (b. Dec. 20, 1905, Wingello, New South Wales, Australia—d. Oct. 6, 1992, Sydney, Australia), was one of the finest leg-spin bowlers of the 20th century. In a first-class career that lasted from 1927 to 1946, he took 774 wickets (average 16.60), with 144 (average 22.59) in 27 Test matches. Sir Donald Bradman, who batted against O'Reilly in up-country and first-class cricket, declared in a tribute that his old friend and rival was "the greatest bowler that I ever faced or saw, and in my opinion certainly the best bowler Australia ever produced." As a young schoolteacher, O'Reilly was posted to isolated rural areas, and he was unable to play regularly for New South Wales until the 1930s. A tall, powerful man with a formidable googly, he burst onto the international scene in 1931–32 when he was called up to bowl in his first Test against South Africa. Thereafter he was never dropped from the side, and in 19 Test matches against England he captured 102 wickets. After World War II O'Reilly appeared in his last Test, taking 8 for 33 against New Zealand. He retired to become a cricket columnist for the *Sydney Morning Herald,* a post that gave him ample opportunity to express his passionate views on society, politics, "pyjama cricket," and the unfortunate decline in

spin bowling. O'Reilly was made Officer of the Order of the British Empire in 1971.

Page, Robert Morris, U.S. physicist (b. June 2, 1903, St. Paul, Minn.—d. May 15, 1992, Edina, Minn.), during the 1930s invented the technology for pulse radar, a system that detects and locates distant objects by sending out short bursts of electromagnetic radiation and then using the intervals between bursts to receive and display the echoes that return from the objects. His invention was vital to the Allies during World War II for detecting enemy planes and other targets. Page initially studied theology while attending Hamline University in St. Paul, but he changed his major to physics in his senior year. After graduating in 1927, he joined the U.S. Naval Research Laboratory (NRL) in Washington, D.C., and he earned an M.A. (1932) from George Washington University, Washington, D.C. Page conducted pioneering experiments in radar with A. Hoyt Taylor, Lawrence A. Hyland, and Leo C. Young at the same time that the British scientist Sir Alexander Watson Watt was doing similar studies. In the 1940s the U.S. and British scientists pooled their work at the Radiation Laboratory of the Massachusetts Institute of Technology. Page, who held 75 patents on inventions in precision electronics, developed the first radar duplexer capable of using a single antenna for transmitting and receiving; the planned position indicator, the first radar technology to identify the direction and range of a target simultaneously; and Project Madre, a radar system that could bend its beam to the curve of the Earth and thus "see" over the horizon. Page successively served at the NRL as a physicist and head of the Radar Research Section (1938–45), superintendent of Radio Division III (1945–52), associate director of research in electronics (1952–57), and director of research (1957–66). He was the recipient of the Distinguished Civilian Service Award (1945), the Presidential Certificate of Merit (1946), and the President's Award for Distinguished Federal Civilian Service (1960). Page was the author of *The Origin of Radar* (1962).

Parks, Bert (BERT JACOBSON), U.S. entertainer (b. Dec. 30, 1914, Atlanta, Ga.—d. Feb. 2, 1992, La Jolla, Calif.), was a fixture on television for

MICHAEL OCHS ARCHIVES

25 years as the engaging master of ceremonies of the "Miss America Pageant" who serenaded the newly crowned beauty queen as she took her traditional walk down the runway with his signature song, "There She Is." Parks, the gap-toothed emcee of such radio quiz shows as "Break the Bank" and "Stop the Music," also starred as the host of those programs when they moved to television and of the popular game show "Double or Nothing." He had worked as an announcer for CBS from 1933 to 1939. Parks was best remembered, however, for his annual stint (1955–79) on the "Miss America Pageant." When officials dropped him as host in 1980 because of his age, Johnny Carson launched a major though

unsuccessful nationwide letter-writing campaign. Parks made one last special appearance as host of the beauty pageant in 1990, and in the same year he made a cameo appearance in a comic send-up of his own beauty pageant performances by crooning a satirical version of "There She Is" to a lizard in the film *The Freshman*. Parks was also lauded for his starring role on Broadway in *The Music Man* (1960–61), and he continued to maintain a presence on television, appearing as ringmaster of the "Circus" series and in guest appearances on "Burke's Law," "Ellery Queen," and "The Bionic Woman."

Parnis, Mollie, U.S. fashion designer (b. March 18, *c.* 1900, New York, N.Y.—d. July 18, 1992, New York), created a tasteful and fashionable line of comfortable dresses made of fine fabrics and attracted a conservative clientele, notably such first ladies as Mamie Eisenhower, Betty Ford, and Lady Bird Johnson. Parnis, who could neither sketch nor sew, briefly served as an assistant salesclerk with a blouse manufacturer before marrying textile salesman Leon Livingston and forming Parnis-Livingston in 1933. Their enterprise was an instant success, and she earned a reputation for eschewing faddish designs in favour of smart ones. Parnis was a fixture in New York City with her Seventh Avenue dress showroom and her Park Avenue duplex apartment, which she turned into a salon for journalists, actors, and Democratic politicians. One of her greatest disappointments, however, was her lack of a formal college education, so she became an avid reader with a dictionary close at hand. After her husband's death in 1962, she retired for three months but soon returned to retailing. She closed her Seventh Avenue store in 1984 only to return to work for her nephew, designing Mollie Parnis At-Home fashions. Parnis never disclosed the year of her birth, but it was believed that she was in her 90s when she died.

Perkins, Anthony, U.S. actor (b. April 4, 1932, New York, N.Y.—d. Sept. 12, 1992, Hollywood, Calif.), was forever identified with his portrayal of the murderous motel owner Norman Bates in the chilling Alfred Hitchcock thriller *Psycho* (1960), and he reprised this role in three sequels (1983, 1986, and 1990). Perkins made his film debut in *The Actress* (1953) while still studying at Columbia University, New York City. The following year he starred on Broadway as the sensitive adolescent, Tom Lee, in *Tea and Sympathy*. In the film *Friendly Persuasion* (1956), he portrayed a young Quaker worried about protecting his family's homestead while being true to his religious beliefs. That performance earned him an Academy Award nomination for best supporting actor. He then specialized in playing awkward, anxious, and gawky young men, notably in *Fear Strikes Out* (1957), *The Tin Star* (1957), and *Desire Under the Elms* (1958), before achieving international stardom in *Psycho* as the maniac

ARCHIVE PHOTOS

who stabbed Janet Leigh in the shower. Perkins then appeared in several films in Europe, including *The Trial, The Champagne Murders,* and *Ten Days Wonder,* before playing an assortment of roles in U.S. motion pictures. He was a psychotic arsonist in *Pretty Poison* (1968), the chaplain in *Catch-22* (1970), and a political assassin in *WUSA* (1970), but he never recaptured the success of the original *Psycho*. Some of his other screen credits include *The Life and Times of Judge Roy Bean* (1972), *Murder on the Orient Express* (1974), and *Edge of Sanity* (1989). Perkins also appeared in such plays as *Look Homeward, Angel, Harold, Steambath,* and *Romantic Comedy*. In one of his last roles Perkins starred as a police detective in the television movie *In the Deep Woods,* which appeared posthumously. His death was attributed to complications from AIDS.

Piazzolla, Astor, Argentine musician (b. March 11, 1921, Mar del Plata, Arg.—d. July 5, 1992, Buenos Aires, Arg.), was a bandoneon (a square-built button accordion) virtuoso who performed until 1955 with traditional Latin-American tango bands but then dramatically departed from the stylized music associated with traditional tango and composed some 750 compositions that blended elements of jazz and classical music into what he christened the "new" tango. Piazzolla's innovations, including counterpoint and new rhythms and harmonies, were not well received in his country. His music was greatly admired in the U.S. and Europe, however, and from 1974 to 1985 he lived in Paris. Earlier, during the 1950s, Piazzolla had studied in that city under Nadia Boulanger, who had urged him to experiment with the tango. After returning to Argentina, he formed (1960) the influential Quinteto Nuevo Tango, featuring violin, guitar, piano, bass, and bandoneon. Though most of his compositions were written for that quintet, he also composed pieces for orchestra, big band, bandoneon, and cello. In Argentina his new tango gradually gained acceptance, and his music influenced a new generation of tango composers and was featured during the 1970s and '80s in film scores, television programs, and commercials.

Picon, Molly, U.S. actress and singer (b. June 1, 1898, New York, N.Y.—d. April 5, 1992, Lancaster, Pa.), reigned as the Yiddish theatre's "Sweetheart of Second Avenue" during the 1920s and '30s and captivated New York City audiences with her impish charm and comedic talents, which were showcased by her gift for mimicry and superb sense of timing, notably in such unforgettable productions as *Yankele, Raizele, Oy, iz dos a meydl!* ("Oy, what a girl!"), and *Hello Molly*. A child star, she first appeared (1904) in vaudeville before being persuaded (1919) by playwright Jacob Kalich to join the Yiddish theatre he managed. Picon and Kalich married the same year, and they toured Europe in 1921 so that Picon could perfect her Yiddish. After returning to the U.S., she beguiled audiences as the diminutive and effervescent star of more than 200 Yiddish productions, evoking laughter with her comical renditions of "The Woiking Goil" and "The Story of Grandma's Shawl." In 1940 Picon made her Broadway bow in *Morning Star,* her first English-speaking starring role. During World War II she toured worldwide, and after the war she turned the tears of concentration camp survivors to laughter as she serenaded them with Jewish songs. Her starring role in London opposite Robert Morley in the comedy *A Majority of One* (1960) earned her critical acclaim. As Yiddish theatre receded from the limelight, Picon turned to stage and film. She was a huge success playing an American widow searching for a husband in Israel in the Broadway musical *Milk and Honey* (1961), and she was memorable in such films as *Yiddle with His Fiddle* (1937), *Mamele* ("Little Mother"; 1938), *Come Blow Your Horn* (1963), and *Fiddler on the Roof* (1972). Picon had a Jewish theatre named for her in 1931, and she continued to perform well into her 80s.

Piper, John Egerton Christmas, British artist (b. Dec. 13, 1903, Epsom, Surrey, England—d. June

28, 1992, near Henley-on-Thames, Oxfordshire, England), despite a widely varied career, was best known for his architectural and topographic paintings. Piper attended Epsom College, Richmond School of Art (1926–27), and the Royal College of Art (1927–29). In the early 1930s he painted visually powerful cubist works and was elected to the "7 & 5 Society" of nonrepresentational artists. He found abstract art limiting, however, and in 1937 he returned to an early love of architectural form. As an official war artist during World War II, he depicted the poignancy of bombed-out buildings, notably the devastation of Coventry Cathedral. He was also commissioned by the queen to paint 26 watercolours of Windsor Castle in case it was destroyed. After the war Piper continued to paint neoromantic portraits of historic country houses and landscapes while he branched out into nearly every related field. He contributed articles to *Architectural Review,* wrote and provided sketches and photographs for Shell county guides, designed sets and costumes for most of Benjamin Britten's operas, worked on a tapestry for the high altar at Chichester Cathedral, created public fireworks displays, produced a series of art prints, and illustrated several books. He was particularly admired for his later work in stained glass, notably windows for Liverpool Cathedral, Eton College Chapel, and the baptistery wall at the rebuilt Coventry Cathedral. Piper was made a Companion of Honour in 1972.

Poiret, Jean (JEAN-GUSTAVE POIRÉ), French actor and playwright (b. Aug. 17, 1926, Paris, France—d. March 14, 1992, Paris), wrote and starred in the original 1973 Paris production of *La Cage aux folles,* a contemporary farce revolving around a homosexual couple. The play, which ran for more than 2,000 performances, was made into an internationally popular film (co-written by Poiret), inspired an almost equally successful movie sequel, and was adapted into a Tony award-winning Broadway musical. Poiret's career took off in the early 1950s when he formed a cabaret act (and an enduring professional partnership) with comic actor Michel Serrault. Poiret wrote or adapted and starred in numerous successful comedies, including *Douce Amère* (1970), *Joyeuses Pâques* (1980), and a French production of Neil Simon's *Rumors* (1991). However, none of these matched the cult status of *La Cage aux folles,* which provided the perfect vehicle for Poiret's suave charm and Serrault's flamboyance. Although he did not appear with Serrault in the two films based on *La Cage,* Poiret made some 40 motion pictures, notably *Le Dernier Métro* (1980; *The Last Metro*), *Poulet au vinaigre* (1985; *Cop au Vin*) and its sequel, *Inspecteur Lavardin* (1986), and *Le Miraculé* (1986). At the time of his death, Poiret had just completed directing the film *Le Zèbre* and had been nominated for Molière awards for his stage adaptations of two different English comedies.

Price, Sammy (SAMUEL BLYTHE PRICE), U.S. pianist and bandleader (b. Oct. 6, 1908, Honey Grove, Texas—d. April 14, 1992, New York, N.Y.), was one of the last jazz musicians to have grown up in the old rhythm and blues and boogie-woogie traditions, and he was at home in these and other styles, including ragtime and stride. He had a long career as a soloist and accompanist and was also known as a bandleader, organizer, and educator. Price first toured as a dancer before working in bands in the Southwest and Midwest during the 1920s and '30s. He moved to New York City in 1937, where he became a staff musician and a musical director for Decca Records. There he organized and supervised recording sessions, and he himself frequently accompanied such singers as Trixie Smith, Sister Rosetta Tharpe, and Ella Fitzgerald. Later he formed his own band, the Texas Blusicians, which for a time included the saxophonists Ike Quebec and Lester Young. During the 1940s and '50s, Price recorded as a soloist and with other musicians, including saxophonist Sidney Bechet, clarinetist Mezz Mezzrow, and trumpeter Doc Cheatham; operated nightclubs in Dallas, Texas; and toured in Europe. He organized jazz festivals in Philadelphia, and in New

York City he was involved in Harlem politics and worked as a probation officer. Price was artist in residence at Harvard University in 1985, and his autobiography, *What Do They Want?*, was published in 1989.

Pucci, Emilio (MARCHESE DI BARSENTO), Italian fashion designer (b. Nov. 20, 1914, Naples, Italy—d. Nov. 29, 1992, Florence, Italy), created the brightly coloured prints—incorporating both geometric and Art Nouveau designs—that became emblematic of fashion in the 1950s and early '60s. He revolutionized sportswear and added casual fashions and sports clothes to the wardrobes of rich women more accustomed to city clothes.

Pucci was born into an aristocratic family whose history in the silk industry extended back to the 14th century. He was a member of Italy's 1932 Olympic ski team before studying at the University of Milan, the University of Georgia, and Reed College, Portland, Ore., from which he received a master's degree in 1939. He went on to earn a Ph.D. in political science from the University of Florence in 1941. He had joined the Italian air force in 1938, and during World War II he was a bomber pilot. On a skiing holiday while on leave in 1947, he was noticed by a fashion photographer because of his snug-fitting ski clothes, which he had designed himself. Photographs appeared in *Harper's Bazaar*, and his career was launched. By 1950 he had established a boutique, Emilio of Capri, and he set the standard for resort elegance and became an international success. His bold prints began appearing on such varied products as towels, jewelry, wall coverings, underwear, and airline uniforms, and his signed shifts became collectors' items. Besides his fashion work, Pucci was also active in politics. He held a seat in the Chamber of Deputies (1963–72) and continued to serve as a Florence city counsellor. By the late 1980s his designs were enjoying a revival, and Pucci became one of the few designers to peak twice in fashion popularity.

Pyke, Magnus, British food scientist and media personality (b. Dec. 29, 1908, London, England—d. Oct. 19, 1992, London), had a gift for presentation and lively expression that enabled him to vividly communicate scientific knowledge—especially little-known facts about food science—to nonscientists. In 1975 readers of *New Scientist* named him the best-known living scientist, and only Newton and Einstein topped him on the all-time best-known list. Pyke received (1933) a B.Sc. in agriculture from McGill University, Montreal, and became a research chemist in London while also doing research on vitamins and earning (1936) a Ph.D. in biochemistry at University College, London. At the Ministry of Food (1941–45 and 1946–48), he conducted research related to nutrition under wartime restrictions. His lectures on nutrition were published (1945) as the ministry's *Manual of Nutrition*, which became a bestseller. From 1949 to 1973 Pyke worked for the Distillers Co. in Scotland, and from 1973 to 1977 he was secretary and chairman of the council of the British Association for the Advancement of Science. His success in a Yorkshire Television documentary led to his being (1974–80) one of the hosts of "Don't Ask Me"—which became the most popular science series in British television history—and its successor, "Don't Just Sit There." He participated in a number of other programs, lectured throughout the world, and wrote more than 25 books. Pyke was made Officer of the Order of the British Empire in 1978.

Quadros, Jânio da Silva, Brazilian politician (b. Jan. 25, 1917, Campo Grande, Mato Grosso, Brazil—d. Feb. 16, 1992, São Paulo, Brazil), touched off a constitutional crisis when he unexpectedly resigned as president after having served only seven months in office (Jan. 31–Aug. 25, 1961) as a colourful and sometimes eccentric populist who had attracted a widespread following by campaigning with a broom as a symbol of his pledge to "sweep out corruption." Quadros entered the political arena when he was elected to the São Paulo city council in 1947. He adopted the broom for his successful 1951 campaign for state deputy of São Paulo, and two years later he became mayor of São Paulo. He balanced that city's budget in less than a year, and as governor of the state (1954–58), he used his financial wizardry to make it into one of the most prosperous states in the country. A charismatic master-manipulator, he affected the image of a commoner and attracted the votes of the poor with his rumpled appearance. A favourite ploy was to pull a sandwich from his pocket while delivering a speech and then apologize, explaining he had not had lunch. As president Quadros banned bikinis, cockfights, and advertising in movie theatres, and he created a stir in foreign affairs when he reestablished diplomatic relations with the Soviet Union, refused to back U.S. Pres. John F. Kennedy's Bay of Pigs invasion of Cuba, and decorated the Latin-American guerrilla leader Che Guevara. Quadros stunned the country when he suddenly resigned, enigmatically citing the "terrible forces" conspiring against him. It was believed that he had intended to return to office as a dictator after being coaxed back into office by Congress, but his resignation was accepted, and the vice president, João Goulart, came to power. Four years later the military ousted the latter in a coup, and in 1968 Quadros was stripped of his rights and sent into exile. After a 1980 amnesty he returned to São Paulo and unsuccessfully ran for governor of that state. He later served two terms (1985–88) as mayor of São Paulo before ill health forced him to retire from the limelight.

Rauh, Joseph Louis, Jr., U.S. lawyer (b. Jan. 3, 1911, Cincinnati, Ohio—d. Sept. 3, 1992, Washington, D.C.), championed liberal causes and as a prominent defender of civil and individual rights helped establish (1947) Americans for Democratic Action, a liberal bastion. After graduating magna cum laude from Harvard University in 1932, Rauh entered Harvard's Law School and graduated first in his class in 1935. He then served as a law clerk to two Supreme Court justices, Benjamin N. Cardozo and Felix Frankfurter. After serving in the army during World War II, he went into private practice in 1947. The following year, at the Democratic national convention, he had a leading part in writing the strong civil rights language that was adopted into the party's platform. He played a leading role as an ardent lobbyist for passage of the Civil Rights Act of 1964, the Voting Rights Act of 1965, and the Fair Housing Act of 1968. During the 1950s he defended writers Lillian Hellman and Arthur Miller, who were called before the House Un-American Activities Committee to identify contemporaries with leftist sympathies. Some of his other clients included the United Automobile Workers led by Walter Reuther, the Mississippi Freedom Democratic Party, and the Leadership Conference on Civil Rights. Rauh was also a member of the executive board of the National Association for the Advancement of Colored People. In recent years he had given up his law practice, but he continued to lobby against the nominations of conservatives to the Supreme Court.

Ray, Satyajit, Indian filmmaker (b. May 2, 1921, Calcutta, India—d. April 23, 1992, Calcutta), gained international critical acclaim for a series of poetic Bengali-language motion pictures over which he had complete control as writer, director, and film editor and often as cameraman, composer, and costume and set designer. To achieve a sense of spontaneity and realism, Ray frequently used nonprofessional actors and a loose, unfinished script. His father was a popular writer and illustrator of nonsense verse, while his grandfather, a painter and writer, founded a well-known children's magazine. Ray graduated in economics from the University of Calcutta and then turned to artistic studies at Visva-Bharati University, Santiniketan, under the Nobel Prize-winning poet Rabindranath Tagore, a close family friend. In 1943 he joined an advertising agency in Calcutta as a layout artist, and in 1949 he was named art director. The next year, while working for the agency in London, he saw Vittorio de Sica's neorealist film *The Bicycle Thief,* and he began to write a screenplay based on a novel by Bibhuti Bhusan Banerjee. Unable to find financial backing, Ray borrowed money, pawned his wife's jewelry, and filmed part-time for three years with amateur actors and largely unpaid help. The Bengali government finally agreed to provide financing, and the resulting feature, *Patha Panchali* (1955; *The Song of the Road*), won a special prize at the 1956 Cannes Film Festival. *Patha Panchali,* the first in the so-called Apu Trilogy, was followed by *Aparajito* (1956; *The Unvanquished*) and *Apu Sansar* (1959; *The World of Apu*) and established Ray as a world-class moviemaker. However, his low-budget black-and-white films, which deviated from the musical extravaganzas that dominated Indian cinema, had limited release in his home country. He did not make his first Hindi film, *Shatranj Ke Khilari* (*The Chess Players*), until 1977. Other notable films include a 1961 documentary biography of Tagore; family dramas such as *Devi* (1960; *The Goddess*) and *Charulata* (1964; *The Lonely Wife*); the children's fantasy *Goopy Gyne Bagha Byne* (1969; *The Adventures of Goopy and Bagha*); *Ashani Sanket* (1973; *Distant Thunder*), an epic treatment of the 1943 Bengali famine; and *Ganashatru* (1989), based on Henrik Ibsen's *An Enemy of the People.* Shortly before his death Ray received a special Academy Award for lifetime achievement in film. He also received the Bharat Ratna, India's highest civilian honour, and his last work, *Agantuk* (1991; *The Stranger*), won top Indian awards for best picture and best director.

Reshevsky, Samuel Herman, Polish-born chess grand master (b. Nov. 26, 1911, Ozorkow, Poland—d. April 4, 1992, Suffern, N.Y.), was recognized as a tenacious player and brilliant tactician during a longtime career in which he reigned as U.S. champion (1936, 1938, 1940, 1942, 1946, 1969, and 1971) and beat formidable opponents and world champions in prestigious tournaments but was unable to capture the world championship title. Reshevsky, who was taught to play the game by his father when he was about four, was a child prodigy who toured Europe at the age of six and had gained master status by the time he was nine. His stunning victories, in which he took on as many as 75 opponents at a time, astounded players, and he was dubbed the "boy wonder of chess." In 1920 Reshevsky immigrated to the U.S. with his parents. He became famous that same year after he beat 19 top faculty chess players at the United States Military Academy, West Point, N.Y. A few days later he solved three complex chess problems in a record 3 minutes 25 seconds and was awarded a gold medal by then U.S. champion Frank J. Marshall, who had presented him with the challenge. Reshevsky's playing as a professional prodigy was ended when child-welfare officials intervened after sighting him at a late-night exhibition. His formal education was sponsored by wealthy patrons under the condition that he suspend his chess playing. After graduating (1933) from the University of Chicago with a degree in accounting, he returned to the chessboard, and though he was able to score spectacular victories, including ones against José Raúl Capablanca in 1935 and Mikhail Botvinnik in 1955, some felt that his interrupted career, stereotyped opening, and addiction to time pressure may have cost him the coveted world title. His 1961 16-game match with another prodigy, Bobby Fischer, was terminated after 11 games when Fischer walked out over a scheduling dispute. Though the score was tied (5½ to 5½), Reshevsky was given the victory by default, but his career at the world level declined. He continued to delight fans with his persistence, and in 1984 he won first place at the Reykjavik (Iceland) International Tournament at the age of 72. He was the author of *Reshevsky on Chess* (1948) and *How Chess Games Are Won* (1962).

Riad, Mahmoud, Egyptian diplomat (b. Jan. 8, 1917, Qalubiyah, Egypt—d. Jan. 25, 1992, Cairo, Egypt), reached the culmination of a distinguished career when he was named secretary-general of

the League of Arab States in 1972, but he was unable to prevent Egypt's expulsion from the league in 1979 after his country signed a separate peace treaty with Israel. Riad studied at the Egyptian military academy and received a doctorate in engineering. After fighting in the first Arab-Israeli war (1948–49), he was a member of the mixed armistice committee. Following the 1952 coup that deposed King Farouk I, Riad joined the Foreign Ministry, where he served as head of the Palestine desk (1952–53), director of Arab affairs (1953–55), ambassador to Syria (1955–58), special adviser to Pres. Gamal Abdel Nasser (1958–62), and permanent ambassador to the UN (1962–64). As Egyptian foreign minister (1964–72) and deputy premier (1971–72), he urged a peaceful settlement of the Arab-Israeli conflict and persuaded many nations to join in an international boycott of Israel to force concessions. In 1972 he was named to succeed Muhammad 'Abd al-Khaliq Hassuna (*q.v.*) as secretary-general of the Arab League. Although he disagreed with Pres. Anwar as-Sadat's peace negotiations, Riad struggled to hold the league together. In 1979, after the other Arab states voted to expel Egypt from the league and move its headquarters from Cairo to Tunis, Tunisia, Riad resigned from public office, but he remained a respected government adviser.

Roach, Harold Eugene ("HAL"), U.S. motion-picture producer and director (b. Jan. 14, 1892, Elmira, N.Y.—d. Nov. 2, 1992, Bel Air, Calif.), as the pioneering executive (1915–55) of his own studio, produced some 1,000 motion pic-

tures and more than 2,000 two-reel comedies that showcased the talents of such long-ago stars as Harold Lloyd, Will Rogers, Harry Langdon, Charlie Chase, and especially the renowned team of Laurel and Hardy. Together with rival Mack Sennett, Roach created some of the classic early Hollywood comedies. His trademark style relied less on sight gags and more on strong scripts and characterization. After striking out on his own at the age of 17, Roach held various jobs before settling in Los Angeles, where he began working as a film extra. When he came into an inheritance, he founded his own studio and made Lloyd a star in the "Willie Work" comedies, in the "Lonesome Luke" series, and in such films as *Just Nuts* (1915) and the unforgettable stunt classic *Safety Last* (1923), featuring Lloyd dangling from the face of an enormous clock. During the 1920s Roach originated the "Our Gang" (later known as "The Little Rascals") films, one of the most popular juvenile series ever made. Though Roach parted with Lloyd in 1923, he had an impressive roster of comics in his all-star performing stock of players. He was credited with rediscovering Stan Laurel and Oliver Hardy, who had appeared together in a forgotten 1917 short, and with developing their unique mannerisms, notably Laurel's head scratching and Hardy's twittering and tie-twiddling. Roach starred them in *The Battle of the Century* (1927), *Leave 'em Laughing* (1928), and *The Music Box* (1932), in which they moved a player piano up a long flight of stairs. For the latter he won an Academy Award, and he won a second for the Our Gang short *Bored of Education* (1936). When the popularity of the comedy shorts began to wane during the Great Depression, Roach began producing feature films, including *One Million B.C.* (1940), a special-effects masterpiece; *Topper* (1937) and *Topper Returns* (1941), fantasies about a befuddled mortal helped by amiable ghosts; and *Of Mice and Men* (1939), a poignant drama. During World War II his production company made training and propaganda films for the government; after the war it produced television programs. Roach sold the studios to his son in 1955, but by 1959 the son had been ousted, and the company soon went bankrupt. The studios were demolished in 1963. Roach garnered a third Oscar in 1984 for "life achievement," and even at the age of 100 he continued to campaign for the return of the two-reel comedy.

Rocard, Yves-André, French mathematician and physicist (b. May 22, 1903, Vannes, France—d. March 16, 1992, Paris, France), contributed to the development of the French atomic bomb and to the understanding of such diverse fields of research as semiconductors, seismology, and radio astronomy. Rocard received doctorates in mathematics (1927) and physical science (1928) from the École Normale Supérieure (ENS) in Paris and took a job in the electronics industry. During World War II he worked with the Resistance and supplied British scientific intelligence with vital information, including details on a new radio navigational beam station. For this assistance he was made Commander of the Order of the British Empire (1946). He was later awarded the French Legion of Honour and the Order of Merit. After the war Rocard returned to the ENS as head of the physics department, and in 1951 he was named to the French Atomic Energy Commission. His professional reputation suffered somewhat in later years when he concentrated on the scientific study of biomagnetism and dowsing. Rocard's son, Michel, served as French prime minister from 1988 to 1991.

Romanov, Prince Vladimir Kirillovich, Russian pretender to the throne (b. Aug. 30, 1917, Borgo, Fin.—d. April 21, 1992, Miami, Fla.), declared himself grand duke, head of the Romanov family, and heir to the Russian throne in 1938 on the death of his father, Grand Duke Kirill Vladimirovich, first cousin to Tsar Nicholas II. Some Russian monarchists and members of the Romanov family, however, disputed his claim to the title grand duke and to the throne. Vladimir Kirillovich was born in exile during the Russian

Revolution and was reared and educated mainly in France. He spent most of World War II living in Nazi-occupied France, moved to Spain in 1945 to avoid possible repatriation as a collaborator, and returned to the family estate in Brittany in the early 1950s. Although he continued to work for the restoration of the monarchy, he did not make his first visit to Russia until November 1991. His body was returned to St. Petersburg for eventual burial in the family tomb at the Peter-Paul Fortress, and he was accorded a Russian Orthodox funeral with full imperial regalia.

Ross, Steven Jay (STEVEN JAY RECHNITZ), U.S. business executive (b. Sept. 17, 1927, New York, N.Y.—d. Dec. 20, 1992, Los Angeles, Calif.), was a passionate risk taker who parlayed a funeral parlour business into Time Warner Inc., the world's largest media and entertainment empire. Ross transformed his in-laws' funeral business into Kinney Services Inc., whose businesses included parking garages, cleaning services, limousine rentals, and magazine distribution. That catchall conglomerate was merged with Warner Bros.-Seven Arts in 1969, and Ross soon sold Kinney's holdings to concentrate on films, pop music, and television. That company was renamed Warner Communications Inc. in 1972 and then became Time Warner Inc. after a 1990 megamerger with publishing and cable television giant Time Inc. Ross, a hands-off manager and self-proclaimed dreamer, encouraged his employees to take risks, and he handsomely rewarded them for their successes. He loved to associate with celebrities and indulged in a lavish life-style. The visionary Ross was one of the first to promote pay-per-view television and to back such specialized channels as weather, MTV (Music Television), and sports. He also envisioned a global expansion through alliances with foreign countries. In 1982, however, Warner's Atari video-games division collapsed, and the parent company lost $1 billion. His freewheeling style was the subject of controversy when he presided over the Warner merger with Time, which plunged the new company into a debt of more than $11 billion. At the same time, his salary, bonuses, and stock sales totaled $78.2 million in 1990 and highlighted the national outrage over executive pay. As Time Warner's chairman and co-chief executive (with Gerald M. Levin, who would succeed Ross as sole chief executive), he increased that company's revenue to more than $12.1 billion by 1991.

Rothenstein, Sir John Knewstub Maurice, British art historian and curator (b. July 11, 1901, London, England—d. Feb. 27, 1992, Dorchester-on-Thames, Oxfordshire, England), as director (1938–64) of the prestigious Tate Gallery in London, supervised the evacuation of the artwork from the museum at the beginning of World War II, oversaw the gallery's postwar reconstruction, and expanded the collection's holdings of modern English painters. He was the son of Sir William Rothenstein, the painter and principal of the Royal College of Art, London, and spent his childhood among some of the most important British artists of the early 20th century. After attending Worcester College, Oxford, he taught in the U.S. for two years. In 1932 he was named director of the Leeds City Art Gallery, and two years later he moved to the gallery in Sheffield. When Rothenstein took charge of the Tate, the facilities were in disarray, the collection was short of contemporary British art, and the war was looming. He quickly moved the collection to safety in Wales, and after the war he devoted his energies to rebuilding the museum and its reference library and to raising public awareness of English artists. In the 1950s his tenure at the Tate was rocked by his dislike of the emerging forms of modernist art and by a personal rivalry with the gallery's deputy director. Rothenstein's many books include *Modern English Painters: Sickert to Hockney* (published in three volumes, 1952–74) and a three-volume autobiography. He was knighted in 1952.

Salk, Lee, U.S. child psychologist (b. Dec. 27, 1926, New York, N.Y.—d. May 2, 1992, New York), as an expert on family relationships, stressed the crucial role played by the family in fostering the development of children; he popularized his views about the emergence of changing American values on the upbringing of children as the author of eight books, as a columnist for *McCall's* magazine, and as a frequent guest on such television shows as "Today," "Good Morning America," and "Nightline." Salk earned his A.B., M.A., and Ph.D. from the University of Michigan and first gained public acclaim when he published (1960) a study demonstrating that newborn babies exposed to the sound of a mother's heartbeat were more tranquil than those who were placed in a quiet environment. He advised parents to pick up their crying babies without worrying about spoiling them and stirred controversy when he cautioned against abandoning full-time motherhood in his 1973 book, *What Every Child Would Like His Parents to Know*. His popularity was attributed to his reliance on common sense, and he urged parents to tell their children the truth and to discipline them in a consistent manner. He pioneered research in sudden infant death syndrome and on the effects of early experiences on later behaviour and at the time of his death was studying the relationship between adolescent suicide and conditions at the time of a child's birth. Some of his books include *How to Raise a Human Being* (1969), *Preparing for Parenthood: Understanding Your Feelings About Pregnancy, Childbirth, and Your Baby* (1975), *Fathers and Sons, an Intimate Relationship* (1982), and *Familyhood, Nurturing the Values That Matter,* which was published posthumously. At the time of his death, Salk was a professor of psychology in pediatrics and psychiatry at Cornell University Medical Center, Ithaca, N.Y., attending psychologist at two New York City medical centres, and adjunct professor at Brown University, Providence, R.I. His older brother, Jonas, developed a vaccine for poliomyelitis, and his other brother, Herman, was a renowned veterinarian.

Schuman, William Howard, U.S. composer, educator, and administrator (b. Aug. 4, 1910, New York, N.Y.—d. Feb. 15, 1992, New York), was known for music that combined traditional forms with American themes and for his contributions to teaching and the development of arts institutions. Although he had music lessons in his youth, Schuman entered college to study business. At the age of 19, however, after attending a performance by the New York Philharmonic conducted by Arturo Toscanini, he turned to the study of music. In New York City he enrolled at Malkin Conservatory and then at Teachers College, Columbia University, where he received B.S. (1935) and M.A. (1937) degrees. He also studied with the composer Roy Harris at the Juilliard Graduate School. In 1935 Schuman began teaching at Sarah Lawrence College, Bronxville, N.Y., and in 1945 he began an association with the music publisher G. Schirmer, Inc. Later in that same year he was appointed president of Juilliard, where his many innovations included changes in the curriculum, establishment of divisions for opera and dance, and development of the Juilliard String Quartet, which became a model for chamber groups in residence. After participating in the planning for the Lincoln Center for the Performing Arts, of which Juilliard became a part, he served as its president from 1962 to 1969. Early in his career as a composer, Schuman wrote songs and short pieces influenced by popular music. He soon turned, however, to longer, more formal works, and his output included symphonies, concerti, ballets, and choral and chamber works. Several of his best-known compositions—*American Festival Overture* (1939); *Third Symphony* (1941); *A Free Song* (1943), a cantata based on poetry of Walt Whitman; and *Symphony for Strings* (1943)—received their premieres under Serge Koussevitzky, a champion of new music. Other works include the opera *The Mighty Casey* (1953), later revised as the cantata *Casey at the Bat* (1976); *New England Triptych* (1956); and an orchestration of Charles Ives's *Variations on America* (1963). Among Schuman's many honours were the first Pulitzer Prize ever awarded in music, in 1943 for *A Free Song*, and a second Pulitzer, in 1985, for

his achievements both as a composer and as an educator and administrator.

Sergeyev, Konstantin Mikhailovich, Russian ballet dancer and director (b. March 5 [Feb. 20, old style], 1910, St. Petersburg, Russia—d. April 1, 1992, St. Petersburg), was a premier danseur with the renowned Kirov Ballet for three decades (1930–61) and twice served as the company's artistic director and chief choreographer (1951–55; 1960–70). As a performer Sergeyev was much admired for his lyrical interpretations of romantic leading roles and for his partnering skills; as a director he introduced the world to the Kirov's exquisite artistry in a series of international tours. In 1930 he completed his studies with the State Academic Theatre of Opera and Ballet (renamed the Kirov in 1935) and joined the company. He quickly rose to leading roles in the standard repertory and in new ballets, notably *Fountain of Bakhchisaray, Lost Illusions,* and *The Bronze Horseman*. After his acclaimed partner Galina Ulanova transferred to the Bolshoi Ballet in 1944, he danced with Natalya Dudinskaya (whom he married). As a choreographer and as artistic director, Sergeyev focused mainly on classical ballet techniques in the standards and in such new productions as *Hamlet* (1970). He was dismissed from the company in 1970 after Natalya Makarova defected while on tour in the U.K., but he was reinstated as director of the choreographic school in 1973. Sergeyev was awarded numerous state honours, including the Lenin Prize (1970).

Sevareid, (Arnold) Eric, U.S. broadcast journalist (b. Nov. 26, 1912, Velva, N.D.—d. July 9, 1992, Washington, D.C.), was an eloquent commentator and scholarly writer whose finely crafted essays

became a hallmark of his career with CBS News (1939–77) and who pioneered a new journalism by introducing opinion and analysis in news reports. Sevareid, a stately Norwegian, felt that he was "cursed with a somewhat forbidding Scandinavian manner, with a restraint that spells stuffiness to a lot of people." His newscasts were delivered in sonorous if not grave tones, but his forthright manner projected a sense of trust to his peers and audiences. After graduating (1935) from the University of Minnesota, Sevareid worked as a reporter (1936–37) for the *Minneapolis Journal,* which had hired him as a cub reporter in 1930. He then secured a job with the *New York Herald Tribune* in Paris. In 1939 Edward R. Murrow, who was based in London, recruited Sevareid to join CBS as a news correspondent to cover the outbreak of World War II in Europe. As one of "Murrow's Boys" he was the last American to broadcast from Paris, and in 1940 at Bordeaux he scored a journalistic scoop by being the first to announce that France was poised to surrender to the Germans. After fleeing Paris with his wife and

newborn twin sons, Sevareid joined Murrow in London for broadcasts during the Battle of Britain bombing raids. When he returned to the U.S. in late 1940, he covered Pres. Franklin D. Roosevelt and the war effort, but he became restless and was assigned to the China-Burma-India theatre in 1943. While flying into China, the aircraft he was aboard experienced engine failure, and the crew and passengers were forced to parachute out into Japanese-controlled jungles. With help from a supply plane, which dropped provisions, he was instrumental in leading the group out of the jungle on foot. He recounted many of his adventures in his books, notably *Not So Wild a Dream* (1946), which was reprinted twice. Sevareid's postwar assignments were in France, Germany, Britain, and Washington, where he became a formidable and vocal foe of Sen. Joseph McCarthy's Communist witch-hunts. Sevareid became a celebrity in the U.S. during the 1960s, when his commentaries were featured on the "CBS Evening News with Walter Cronkite." Besides his two-minute television editorials, which aired until his retirement in 1977, Sevareid wrote a weekly syndicated column and published such books as *In One Ear* (1952), *Small Sounds in the Night* (1956), and *This Is Eric Sevareid* (1964).

Shawn, William, U.S. editor (b. Aug. 31, 1907, Chicago, Ill.—d. Dec. 8, 1992, New York, N.Y.), headed *The New Yorker* for 35 years, from 1952 to 1987, during which time it was one of the most avidly read and influential of U.S. publications. He left college after two years and briefly worked in journalism and as a composer and pianist. In 1933 he began working for *The New Yorker,* at first as a free-lancer, and in 1939 he became a managing editor. In 1952, after the death of founding editor Harold Ross, Shawn became editor. Under him the magazine gave up much of its lighthearted irreverence—but never its sense of humour or its famous cartoons—and became known for serious reporting of major social and political issues. Among others, Shawn published writing by Hannah Arendt, on the trial of Adolf Eichmann; James Baldwin, on race; and Rachel Carson, on the environment. Truman Capote's *In Cold Blood* was first serialized in the magazine. *The New Yorker's* distinguished writers of fiction included John Cheever and John Updike, and Pauline Kael, on film, and Roger Angell, on baseball, were among its longtime critics and reporters. Shawn was esteemed as an editor who knew when to leave prose alone but who also demanded accuracy and sought perfection—the magazine's fact-checking department being legendary—and as a person who nurtured writers and other editors. When new owners forced him to retire in 1987, more than 150 of his colleagues protested by asking his replacement to decline the position.

Sirica, John Joseph, U.S. lawyer and judge (b. March 19, 1904, Waterbury, Conn.—d. Aug. 14, 1992, Washington, D.C.), presided over the historic Watergate scandal proceedings, doggedly searching for the truth and the identity of those responsible for the burglary (June 17, 1972) of the Democratic National Committee headquarters at the Watergate hotel-office-apartment complex in Washington, D.C.; he became an American folk hero after unraveling the cover-up, which prompted the resignation (Aug. 9, 1974) of Pres. Richard Nixon and the convictions of many of Nixon's top White House aides. After graduating (1926) from Georgetown University in Washington, D.C., Sirica boxed in several bouts in Miami, Fla., before opening a law practice in the nation's capital. He served as U.S. attorney (1930–34) before returning to private practice. During World War II, he enlisted in the navy but was deferred after failing the physical. Instead, he and boxer Jack Dempsey toured the U.S. selling war bonds. In 1957 Sirica was appointed to the federal bench. As chief judge of the U.S. District Court for the District of Columbia, Sirica assigned himself the case (January 1973) of the seven men charged with the Watergate burglary. During their sentencing (five pleaded guilty and two were convicted by a jury), Sirica read a letter from one of the defendants, James W. McCord, Jr., stating that there had been a White House "cover-up" and that several witnesses had perjured themselves. After Nixon refused to respond to a subpoena requiring him to release tape recordings of conversations that could implicate the White House, Sirica ruled that he had to comply. The U.S. Court of Appeals upheld his order, and the epic tape battles ensued. Under public pressure, Nixon released the tapes after the Supreme Court upheld another of Sirica's rulings. Nixon was ultimately forced to resign. Sirica felt that Nixon "should have stood trial," but he was pardoned by Pres. Gerald Ford on Sept. 8, 1974. In 1977 Sirica went into semiretirement as a senior judge, and in 1986 he retired. He was named *Time* magazine's Man of the Year in 1973.

Smith, Cyril Stanley, British-born U.S. metallurgist (b. Oct. 4, 1903, Birmingham, England—d. Aug. 25, 1992, Cambridge, Mass.), made important contributions to several different scientific disciplines during his longtime career; he was first noted for determining (1943–44) the properties and technology of plutonium and uranium—needed for the construction of the atomic bombs that were first exploded in 1945—and he later advanced the use of metallography in the examination of archaeological artifacts. After graduating (1924) from the University of Birmingham, Smith pursued his studies in the U.S. at the Massachusetts Institute of Technology (MIT), where he earned a Ph.D. in 1926. He then spent 15 years with the American Brass Co. at Waterbury, Conn., conducting research on copper alloys. From 1936 to 1942 he helped Martha Teach Gnudi translate Vannoccio Biringuccio's *Pirotechnia,* which appeared in 1540 in Italian and was the first printed work on metallurgy. Smith, who was recognized as an expert on metals through his various writings, was recruited to join the Manhattan Project at Los Alamos, N.M., where he directed (1943–46) the preparation of the active metals for the first three atomic bombs and did research on tungsten carbide and boron. He then served as founding director (1946–56) of the Institute for the Study of Metals at the University of Chicago before moving to MIT in 1960 to hold dual posts in the departments of metallurgy and humanities. There he established the laboratory for research in archaeological materials and examined the structure of inorganic matter by analyzing the shape of metal grains. Some of his writings include *A Search for Structure* (1981), *From Art to Science* (1980), and *A History of Metallography: The Development of Ideas on the Structure of Metals to 1890* (1988). Smith was awarded the Presidential Medal for Merit (1946), the Platinum Medal of the Institute of Metals, London (1970), and the Dexter Award of the American Chemical Society (1981).

Smogorzewski, Kazimierz Maciej, Polish journalist (b. Feb. 24, 1896, Sosnowiec, Poland—d. Nov. 4, 1992, Shepperton, Middlesex, England), chronicled European events as a newspaper correspondent in Paris (1919–25), Berlin (1933–39), and London (1957–81) and as editor of the Paris-based monthly *La Pologne* (1929–33) and the London-based bimonthly *Free Europe* (1939–45). Smogorzewski was educated at the School of Political Science in Paris. He fought with the French Foreign Legion during World War I, but he was seriously wounded in 1915, received the Croix de Guerre, and was invalided out (1917). In 1919 he became the Paris correspondent for the conservative *Gazeta Warszawska,* and he remained in Paris throughout the 1920s. As Berlin correspondent for the semiofficial Polish daily *Gazeta Polska* from 1933, Smogorzewski interviewed Hitler and recorded the events leading up to the German invasion of Poland. In August 1939 he fled to London, where he became a central figure in the expatriate Polish community. It was later discovered that his name appeared on the Nazi arrest list in the event of a German invasion of England. His books included *La Pologne restaurée* (1927) and *Poland's Access to the Sea* (1934). Smogorzewski was associated with *Encyclopædia Britannica* from 1942 until shortly before his death.

Stirling, Sir James Frazer, British architect (b. April 22, 1926, Glasgow, Scotland—d. June 25, 1992, London, England), designed public buildings and multiunit housing that, while often criticized or misunderstood by the general public, were regarded as classics of Postmodernism. Stirling trained at the University of Liverpool's School of Architecture (1945–50) and worked for the firm of Lyons, Israel and Ellis in London until 1956, when he formed a partnership with James Gowan. Stirling and Gowan's projects were commonly identified as New Brutalist (an English reaction against the International Style), which emphasized functional principles and materials, including exposed concrete and brick masonry.

Their commissions included low-rise housing units in London's Ham Common (built in 1957) and the award-winning engineering building at Leicester University (1959–63). After Stirling's breakup with Gowan in 1963, his style evolved into a more avant-garde High Tech Postmodernism. One building, the University of Cambridge history faculty library (1964–67), proved to be so unpopular that British anti-Modernists used it as a rallying point, while a concrete housing project at Runcorn New Town (1967–76) was later demolished. The Neue Staatsgalerie (1977–84) in Stuttgart, Germany, a combination of classicism and colourful geometric abstraction designed by Stirling and his partner (from 1971) Michael Wilford, was heralded as an icon of Postmodernism. Stirling won the Royal Institute of British Architects' Gold Medal in 1980 and the Pritzker Prize in 1981. In 1991, after a long and bitter fight, planning permission was granted for his controversial No. 1 Poultry, to be built in the heart of London's conservation area. He was knighted only 18 days before his death from complications after surgery.

Stommel, Henry Melson, U.S. oceanographer and meteorologist (b. Sept. 27, 1920, Wilmington, Del.—d. Jan. 17, 1992, Boston, Mass.), conducted important field studies on the dynamics of ocean currents and became a respected theoretician in that field of research. In 1977 Stommel and Friedrich Schott developed a method of determining, in principle, the absolute velocity of mean ocean currents from observations of the density alone. After earning a B.S. from Yale University in 1942, he taught mathematics and astronomy (1942–44) there before moving to the Woods Hole (Mass.) Oceanographic Institution, where he was research associate (1944–59) and, from 1978, oceanographer. Stommel was professor of oceanography at the Massachusetts Institute of Technology (1959–60 and 1963–78) and at Harvard University (1960–63). In 1947 he published *The Gulf Stream,* one of the first books to explore that ocean current and other currents in general. He set forth the idea that the Earth's rotation was responsible for pushing the Gulf Stream westward along the coast of North America, and he also theorized that its northward flow must be balanced by a deep, southward flow beneath it. Many of his theories were later proved. Stommel set up observational stations to monitor ocean current, including the PANULIRUS (begun in 1954) in Bermuda and the MEDOC study of deep-water formation in the Mediterranean (1969–72). He was credited with having helped to formulate a physical-mathematical treatment of the entrainment of surrounding air into the ascending current of a cumulus cloud. Stommel, who earned honorary Ph.D.'s from Göteborg (Sweden) University in 1964 and Yale University and the University of Chicago in 1970, was elected to the National Academy of Sciences in 1962 and was awarded the National Medal of Science in 1989.

Stotz, Carl E., U.S. sports figure (b. 1910?, Williamsport, Pa.—d. June 4, 1992, Williamsport), was the enthusiastic founder, in 1939, of Little League baseball, which he established after brainstorming the idea while nursing a leg injury caused when he stumbled over a lilac bush while playing a backyard game of catch with his two nephews. Stotz, a lumberyard clerk, gained sponsorship for the league from local businesses and devised his own field with youth-size dimensions. The birth of Little League was written into history when Lundy Lumber beat Lycoming Dairy 23–8 on June 6, 1939. Stotz modified the playing diamond for little leaguers by spacing their bases 60 ft apart (compared with 90 ft for major leaguers), by making the pitcher's mound 40 ft from home plate, and by introducing lighter bats and balls. Stotz, who together with George and Bert Bebble managed the first three Little League teams, organized the game for boys too small or too young to get into their big brothers' games. They sported regulation uniforms and had adult managers and coaches. By 1942 a permanent field had been completed, and in 1947 there were 48 teams in 12 leagues. The first national tournament was held in 1949 in Williamsport, which became the permanent home of the Little League World Series. As commissioner of Little League baseball, Stotz became embroiled in a controversy with the organization in 1955 when he filed suit because he felt that the league had grown too large and that increasing team rosters to 15 players from 12 was detrimental to less talented players, who would have their playing time reduced. The suit was settled out of court, but in early 1956 Stotz was barred by a federal court from forming a rival group. It was never clear whether Stotz was fired or quit as Little League commissioner. He later served as a tax collector in his hometown.

Strang, Gunnar Georg Emanuel, Swedish politician (b. Dec. 23, 1906, Jarfalla, near Stockholm, Sweden—d. March 6, 1992, Stockholm), as finance minister (1955–76) in a succession of Social Democratic Cabinets, was the chief architect of the renowned Swedish social welfare system. Strang was a self-educated agricultural labourer and trade union organizer who rose to become president of the Swedish Agricultural Workers' Union in 1938. After World War II he was elected to the Riksdag (parliament), joined the government as a consulting minister (1945–47), and later was head of the Ministries of Supply (1947–48), Agriculture (1948–51), and Social Affairs (1951–55). As minister of finance, Strang sought the redistribution of wealth through a highly progressive system of taxes on personal income, capital, and private employers. He supported the extensive welfare system that included generous health care benefits, pensions, and unemployment coverage. He also put considerable emphasis on job creation and the need for a balanced budget. In 1969 Strang introduced Sweden's first value-added tax, which took on even greater significance in the late 1980s when the government introduced a series of cuts in other forms of taxation. Strang left office after the Social Democrats lost the 1976 elections, but he remained in the Riksdag until 1985.

Summerson, Sir John Newenham, British architectural historian (b. Nov. 25, 1904, Darlington, England—d. Nov. 10, 1992, London, England), was an important influence on architectural preservation in Britain and helped record that country's architectural history. Several of his books became popular classics and set a professional standard for works on that subject. Summerson was educated at Harrow and at University College, London. After he received his architect's license, he worked in a number of architects' offices but then decided that he preferred teaching and writing. He was assistant editor of *The Architect and Building News* (1934–41) and deputy director of the National Building Record (1941–45) before becoming (1945) curator of Sir John Soane's Museum, where he remained until 1984. During these years with the museum, Summerson also held professorships and lectureships at a number of colleges and universities—among them Oxford (1958–59), Cambridge (1966–67), and Columbia, New York City (1968)—and wrote many books, some of them based on his lectures. *Architecture in Britain 1530–1830* (1953) surveyed almost all of his most important work and became a classic, and *The Classical Language of Architecture* (1964; rev. 1980) was considered a masterpiece. In addition, he served on numerous committees. Summerson was made a Commander of the Order of the British Empire in 1952, knighted in 1958, awarded the Royal Gold Medal for Architecture of the Royal Institute of British Architects in 1976, and appointed Companion of Honour in 1987.

Sutcliff, Rosemary, British children's writer (b. Dec. 14, 1920, West Clandon, Surrey, England—d. July 23, 1992), produced some 50 volumes of richly detailed historical fiction that entertained children while teaching them about British history from the pre-Roman era to the 17th-century English Civil Wars and beyond. Sutcliff, who was never overly sentimental or condescending to her readers, introduced a vast amount of carefully researched detail into her novels and did not shy away from such complex, emotion-charged issues as war, loneliness, and death. Stricken by a crippling form of arthritis as a child, she had little formal education until she entered the Bideford School of Art at age 14. She became an accomplished miniature painter and did not publish her first book, *The Chronicles of Robin Hood,* until 1950. *The Eagle of the Ninth* (1954), which brought her nationwide fame, was the first of several artfully linked novels set mainly in Roman Britain, including *The Shield Ring* (1956), *The Silver Branch* (1957), *The Lantern Bearers* (1959), *Dawn Wind* (1961), and *Frontier Wolf* (1980). Among her other novels were *Warrior Scarlet* (1958), *The Mark of the Horse Lord* (1965), *Blood Feud* (1976), *Flame-Coloured Taffeta* (1986), and an Arthurian trilogy. She also wrote several books based on ancient legends and tales, as well as historical fiction for adults and an autobiography, *Blue Remembered Hills* (1983). Sutcliff won the Carnegie Medal in 1960 and was made Commander of the Order of the British Empire shortly before her death.

Takano, Shizuo, Japanese electronics engineer (b. 1923, Yokohama, Japan—d. Jan. 19, 1992, Tokyo, Japan), as chief of the video products division of the Victor Co. of Japan (JVC) from 1970 to 1976, spearheaded the successful market development of the VHS (video home system) videocassette recorder, which debuted in 1976. His company became engaged in a fierce competition with the Sony Corp., which had introduced the Betamax video system in 1974. Takano insisted that engineers design the VHS system so that two hours of normal recording (versus one hour for Betamax) were possible, and he licensed the secret VHS technology to other manufacturers. Consequently, more video rental tapes had a VHS format, and because VHS and Betamax tapes had to be played on recorders suited to their own respective formats, VHS tapes became standard. Soon video rental stores ceased stocking Betamax videotapes (even though it was generally agreed that they had greater clarity), and by 1988 Sony had been forced to begin manufacturing VHS recorders. Takano, a graduate of Hamamatsu Technical College, served two years

in the navy before joining JVC in 1946. Some of his other executive posts were director (1976–80) of the video products division, managing director (1980–83), senior managing director (1983–86) of video research and development laboratories, vice president (1986–90), and auditor (1990–92).

Tal, Mikhail Nekhemyevich, Latvian chess grand master (b. Nov. 9, 1936, Riga, Latvia—d. June 28, 1992, Moscow, Russia), became at 23 the youngest man to have won the world chess championship when he defeated the defending champion, Mikhail M. Botvinnik, in a stunning upset (12½–8½) in 1960. Tal, who learned to play chess at the age of six, was known for his unbelievably complex and audacious moves. He became a national master and Latvian champion in 1953, at age 16. In 1957, the year he graduated from Riga University, Tal became an international grand master and won the first of his six titles as champion of the U.S.S.R. He established his right to challenge Botvinnik with impressive victories in the 1958 interzonal and 1959 candidates' tournaments, both held in Yugoslavia. Tal was taken seriously ill with kidney disease shortly before he lost to Botvinnik in a 1961 rematch, and he never again challenged for the world championship. Despite continuing bouts with liver and kidney ailments, however, he won five more U.S.S.R. titles (1958, 1967, 1972, 1974, and 1978) and numerous other international competitions, notably the high-speed world blitz championship in Canada in 1988.

Tanada, Lorenzo, Philippine politician (b. Aug. 10, 1898, Gumaca, Phil.—d. May 28, 1992, Manila, Phil.), devoted his life to ending foreign domination of the Philippines and particularly to the expulsion of U.S. troops from his country. Tanada, who was born into a wealthy landowning family, studied law at the University of the Philippines and at Harvard University. As a young prosecutor in Manila, he protested against the U.S. presence in the Philippines. He was an anti-Japanese guerrilla during World War II, and after the war he served on the legal team that prosecuted Filipino collaborators. In 1947 Tanada was elected to the newly created Senate, where he promoted Philippine nationalism. After Pres. Ferdinand Marcos abolished the legislature under martial law (1972), Tanada took to the streets in protest, and when the opposition leader, Benigno Aquino, was charged with subversion, he joined the legal defense team. Later he was a member of the so-called convenors group that endorsed Aquino's widow, Corazon, for president. Despite his failing health, Tanada attended the crucial 1991 Senate vote that narrowly rejected the treaty that would have allowed the U.S. to retain its naval base at Subic Bay.

Tanenbaum, Marc Herman, U.S. rabbi (b. Oct. 13, 1925, Baltimore, Md.—d. July 3, 1992, New York, N.Y.), as a prominent interfaith leader in the U.S., helped forge better relations between Jews and Christians, especially Jews and Catholics, and was the only rabbi present when the Second Vatican Council was convened by Pope John XXIII during the early 1960s. After graduating (1945) from Yeshiva University in New York City, Tanenbaum entered the Jewish Theological Seminary of America there to begin his rabbinical studies. He was ordained a rabbi in 1950 and devoted the remainder of his career to establishing a dialogue between Jews and Christians and to dispelling anti-Semitism. In New York City he became host in 1965 of a local radio broadcast of religious commentary. He was proudest, though, of his roles as founder and chairman of the National Interreligious Task Force on Soviet Jewry, which interceded for both Jews and Christians who were persecuted because of their religious beliefs before the collapse of the Soviet Union, and as a member of the International Rescue Committee, which helped save thousands of Vietnamese boat people during the early 1980s. A respected figure whose leadership and scholarship were greatly valued, Tanenbaum served as consultant to motion-picture and television producers on Jewish matters, including the

television series "Holocaust." He also was a panelist on White House commissions that discussed children, the elderly, and the Holocaust.

Tippet, Clark, U.S. ballet dancer and choreographer (b. Oct. 5, 1954, Parsons, Kan.—d. Jan. 27, 1992, Parsons), with his powerful build and imposing height possessed a commanding stage presence as a dancer (1972–78 and 1982–86) with American Ballet Theatre (ABT); he later showed promise as a ballet choreographer. Tippet, who began dancing at age 5, was 11 when he followed his teacher, Joyce Gandy, to New York City, where he enrolled at Thalia Mara's National Academy of Ballet. In 1972 he became a member of ABT's corps de ballet, and he was promoted to soloist in 1975 and principal dancer the following year. His height gained him advantage in earning roles in which he partnered tall ballerinas. He was particularly praised for creating roles in Antony Tudor's *The Leaves Are Fading* (1975) and Twyla Tharp's *Push Comes to Shove* (1976). Tippet had featured roles in Glen Tetley's *Sphinx, Gemini,* and *Sacre du Printemps;* Dennis Nahat's *Brahms Quintet* and *Some Times;* and ABT's productions of *Coppélia* and *The Nutcracker.* Shortly after appearing in the motion picture *The Turning Point* (1977), he left ABT owing to intense psychological pressure and because he needed knee surgery. He was persuaded to return to dancing in 1979 with the Cleveland (Ohio) Ballet, and he performed with several other companies before returning to ABT in 1982. Instead of dancing in big classical roles as he had earlier, Tippet began experimenting in works by modernist choreographers, including David Gordon and David Parsons. He turned to choreography in 1986 and earned raves with his first ballet offering, *Enough Said.* He was especially known for tailoring his choreography to each performer's best dancing skills and for incorporating inventive movements that reflected contemporary life. Some of his other choreographic credits include *Bruch Violin Concerto No. 1* (1988) and *Some Assembly Required* (1989). Tippet died of AIDS.

Tomasek, Frantisek Cardinal, prelate of the Roman Catholic Church in Czechoslovakia (b. June 30, 1899, Studenka, Moravia, Austrian Empire—

d. Aug. 4, 1992, Prague, Czech.), was the archbishop of Prague (1977–91) who maintained a cautious but resolute opposition to the Czechoslovak Communist authorities and helped to free his country in the 1989 "velvet" revolution. Tomasek was ordained in 1922 and taught (1934–40) in Olomouc at the Saints Cyril and Methodius Theological Faculty, where he also received a doctorate (1938). The school was closed under the Nazi occupation during World War II. Tomasek reclaimed his teaching post in 1945 and completed his second doctorate, but all Roman Catholic schools were again closed after the 1948 Communist takeover. In 1949 Tomasek was consecrated auxiliary bishop of Olomouc; within months he was arrested and interned in a labour camp. After his release in 1954, he served as a parish priest until he was unexpectedly sent as a representative to the Second Vatican Council (1962–65). When the archbishop of Prague, Josef Cardinal Beran, was forbidden to return from Rome, Tomasek was appointed apostolic administrator of Prague. He was secretly elevated to cardinal in 1976 and was publicly proclaimed archbishop of Prague in December 1977. Although Tomasek had supported the brief period of liberalization (the "Prague Spring") in 1968, he remained conciliatory to the government until Pope John Paul II encouraged his old friend in 1978 to take a more active role in the dissident human rights movement. In 1989 Tomasek openly endorsed the peaceful overthrow of the Communist regime.

Trace, Christopher, British television personality (b. March 21, 1933, Cranleigh, Surrey, England—d. Sept. 5, 1992, London, England), was the original male host of the BBC television program "Blue Peter," a show developed for five- to eight-year-olds to fill a gap in children's programming. For nearly nine years (1958–67) and more than 500 shows, he was a reliable and adventurous surrogate older brother to a generation of youngsters. Trace was especially effective when he demonstrated do-it-yourself projects, and he originated the much-parodied phrase "Here's one I made earlier." After service in the army, Trace decided to become an actor; until "Blue Peter," however, being Charlton Heston's double in *Ben Hur* was the closest he came to fame. After leaving "Blue Peter," he joined the Spectator feature film company. It failed after two years, though, and Trace's life savings were depleted. He went on to work for the BBC's "Nationwide" program but then left show business and worked at a number of odd jobs before returning to broadcasting as a regular guest on the radio program "Are You Sitting Comfortably?"

Vafiades, Markos, Greek insurgent (b. Jan. 28, 1906, Asia Minor [now in Turkey]—d. Feb. 22, 1992, Athens, Greece), as a founding member of the Greek Communist Party and commander of the Communist-led Democratic Army, directed the civil war (1946–49) against the Greek government. Vafiades worked as a labourer in Istanbul and fled to Greece as a refugee in 1923. He became a Communist in his teens and fought with the partisans against the Germans during World War II. After the war he remained with the Communist guerrilla forces, rising to commander under the title General Markos. In December 1947 he proclaimed a provisional Greek government in the north with himself as prime minister, but it was never internationally recognized, and when nationalist troops crushed the civil war (1949), he was forced into exile. Vafiades settled in the Soviet Union, where he clashed with party leadership and was alternately purged (1950), rehabilitated (1956), purged (1964), and restored (1969) to party membership. He returned (1983) to Greece after a general amnesty was declared, and in 1989 he was elected to parliament as a supporter of the Panhellenic Socialist Movement.

Van Fleet, James Alward, general (ret.), U.S. Army (b. March 19, 1892, Coytesville, N.J.—d. Sept. 23, 1992, Polk City, Fla.), was an expert strategist who commanded troops during crucial World War II battles, notably on D-Day at Utah Beach, Normandy, and at the Battle of the Bulge. He was also field commander of the 8th Army in Korea and was credited with scoring a major tactical victory after his troops chased the Chinese Communists from South Korea back to the 38th parallel during that conflict. After graduating from the United States Military Academy at West Point, N.Y. (1915), Van Fleet was commissioned in the infantry. He spent much of World War I in France as a captain in charge of an infantry division and also with occupation forces. He spent several years as a reserve training instructor at Kansas State College, South Dakota State College, and the University of Florida before rising to colonel and taking command of the 8th Army in 1941. After his distinguished World War II service, he served (1947–48) as deputy chief of staff of the army's European Command in

AP/WIDE WORLD

Frankfurt, West Germany. In 1948 Van Fleet was appointed by Pres. Harry S. Truman to direct the military adviser missions to Greece and Turkey, and he played a vital role in the defeat of armed Communist partisans in those countries. In Korea Van Fleet's troops repulsed two major offensives by the Communists in 1951 but were forced to retreat from their June counteroffensive when the Communists called for peace talks, which lasted two years before an armistice was finally negotiated. Van Fleet was promoted to general in 1951 and retired as a four-star general in 1953. He was the recipient of the Purple Heart, Distinguished Service Cross, Silver Star, Bronze Star, and his most prized commendation, the Combat Infantryman's Badge. He devoted the rest of his life to business pursuits.

Vieira da Silva, Maria Helena, Portuguese-born painter (b. June 13, 1908, Lisbon, Port.—d. March 6, 1992, Paris, France), used strong linear and geometric forms to create labyrinthine abstract paintings with a powerful (if sometimes warped) sense of perspective and mosaic-like patterns that were often reminiscent of traditional Portuguese tilework. Vieira da Silva studied painting and drawing in Lisbon, then went (1928) to Paris to study sculpture, painting, and printmaking. In 1930 she married the Hungarian painter Arpad Szenes, and at the beginning of World War II they fled from Nazi-occupied Europe to Brazil. During their years of exile, Vieira da Silva had major solo exhibitions in Rio de Janeiro (1942) and New York City (1946). In 1947 they returned to Paris, where they took French citizenship (1956), and Vieira da Silva became a key figure in the informal group of abstract artists known as the École de Paris (School of Paris). Her many awards included the grand prize at the 1961 São Paulo Biennial, the National Grand Prize of the Arts of France (1966), the Legion of Honour, and honorary membership in the British Royal Academy. In 1988 official retrospective exhibitions of her work were mounted in Lisbon and Paris.

Walker, Nancy (ANNA MYRTLE SWOYER BARTO), U.S. actress (b. May 10, 1922, Philadelphia, Pa.—d. March 25, 1992, Los Angeles, Calif.), was a feisty, diminutive redhead who used her gift for wisecracking to create such unforgettable television characters as manipulative mom Ida Morgenstern on "Rhoda," Mildred the sardonic housekeeper on "McMillan and Wife," and Rosie the brassy waitress who advocated the "quicker picker-upper" in a series of paper towel advertisements from 1970 to 1990. Walker, the daughter of vaudevillians, initially launched a career as a serious singer before producer George Abbott guided her at the age of 19 to the stage in comedy roles. She appeared in three MGM musicals of

the 1940s—*Best Foot Forward* (1941), *Girl Crazy* (1943), and *Broadway Rhythm* (1944), introducing the hit songs "Alive and Kicking" and "Milkman Keep Those Bottles Quiet"—but her unique slapstick style was better suited to the stage, where she scored a huge success as taxicab driver Brunhilde Esterhazy in *On the Town* (1944), stopping the show with her rendition of "I Can Cook Too." Some of her other stage credits were *Barefoot Boy with Cheek* (1947), *Look Ma, I'm Dancin'* (1948), *Copper and Brass* (1957), *Along Fifth Avenue* (1949), *Do Re Mi* (1960), and *A Funny Thing Happened on the Way to the Forum* (1971). Later films included *Stand Up and Be Counted* (1972), *Forty Carats* (1973), and *Murder by Death* (1976). Two 1976 television programs, "The Nancy Walker Show" and "Blansky's Beauties," were flops, but she returned to form in 1990 in "True Colors," in which she portrayed a Jewish mother whose daughter had married a black man. Walker was

MICHAEL OCHS ARCHIVES

one of the few women to have the distinction of both directing and acting on Broadway and in television, having directed, for example, *UTBU* on Broadway (1956) and episodes of the "Mary Tyler Moore Show," "Rhoda," and "Alice." She also directed the movie *Can't Stop the Music* featuring the Village People (1980).

Walton, Samuel Moore, U.S. retail magnate (b. March 29, 1918, Kingfisher, Okla.—d. April 5, 1992, Little Rock, Ark.), was a shrewd merchandising maverick who as founder in 1962 of Wal-Mart Stores Inc. wrought a revolution with a retailing strategy that included offering name-brand merchandise, everyday low prices, and homespun personal service to attract customers to his discount-store chain; in 1991 Wal-Mart surpassed Sears, Roebuck & Co. to become the largest retailer in the U.S., with sales in excess of $43 billion. After graduating from the University of Missouri in 1940 with a degree in economics, Walton entered a J.C. Penney management-training program in Iowa and, shortly after, opened his first five-and-dime store in Newport, Ark. He relocated to Bentonville, Ark., some five years later, and by the 1960s he and his brother, James, were operating a regional chain of Ben Franklin dime stores. When Franklin executives rejected Walton's concept for a new discount-store chain, Walton independently opened (1962) the first Wal-Mart store in Rogers, Ark. The enterprising Walton developed centralized distribution centres that made it economically possible to open stores in towns with as few as 5,000 residents; some local businesses, unable to compete, were shut down. A colourful character with a folksy style, he routinely wore blue jeans and an open-collared shirt and insisted that his "associates" (employees) call him "Mr. Sam." He visited as many as six stores each day, either dropping by in his beat-up pickup truck or piloting his own plane, to conduct impromptu pep rallies. In 1983 he donned a grass skirt and danced the hula on Wall Street when his profits exceeded all expectations. Two years later, with a net worth of $2.8 billion, he was identified by *Forbes* magazine as the "richest man in America." Walton continued to slash costs and keep salaries low, but he inspired company loyalty in employees, who retired with lucrative pensions as a result of the profit-sharing plan. In 1988 Walton stepped down as chief executive officer, and in 1990, after being diagnosed with multiple myeloma (a form of bone cancer), he divided his fortune among his four children; each received $4.4 billion. At the time of his death, Walton had expanded into 43 states; had established 1,735 Wal-Marts, 212 Sam's Clubs (a wholesale subsidiary), and 13 SuperCenters and Hypermarts; and employed 380,000 people. When Walton was awarded the Presidential Medal of Freedom a month before his death, he was cited as "an American original, embodying the entrepreneurial spirit and epitomizing the American dream." He remained chairman of the company until his death.

Wang Hongwen (Wang Hung-wen), Chinese political figure (b. 1935?, Jilin [Chi-lin] province, China—d. Aug. 3, 1992, Beijing [Peking], China), was a member of the notorious Gang of Four, who gained great political power during the Cultural Revolution (1966–76), which was launched by Chairman Mao Zedong (Mao Tse-tung) to purge thousands of moderate party officials and intellectuals. Wang was reportedly born in either 1934 or 1935 and was a textile worker before becoming the henchman of Jiang Qing (Chiang Ch'ing), the ringleader of the Gang of Four and Mao's wife. Wang was apparently recruited because Jiang and Mao recognized that his youth would attract the younger generation. By 1973 he was vice-chairman of the Communist Party of China (CPC) and was angling to first replace Premier Zhou Enlai (Chou En-lai) and to then succeed Mao. After the latter's death in 1976, Wang and the other members of the Gang of Four were arrested and expelled from the CPC. During his 1981 trial he expressed remorse and pleaded guilty to charges that, among other allegations, he had incited armed riots in Shanghai. Wang was sentenced to life imprisonment, but in 1986 he was hospitalized because of a liver ailment that ultimately claimed his life.

Welk, Lawrence, U.S. bandleader and accordion player (b. March 11, 1903, Strasburg, N.D.—d. May 17, 1992, Santa Monica, Calif.), as perhaps television's most popular musical maestro, entertained middle-aged audiences for more than 30 years with his effervescent brand of "champagne music" that was a featured ingredient on his successful show, the longest running on television. Welk, who was raised in a German-speaking hamlet in North Dakota, did not learn English until he was 21. Part of his enduring charm was his accent, which flavoured many of his trademark phrases, including "wunnerful, wunnerful." From the age of 13, Welk earned money playing the accordion, and he later formed two groups, the Biggest Little Band in America and the Hotsy-Totsy Boys, before leading larger bands and orchestras, mainly in the Midwest. He then moved to Los Angeles, where "The Lawrence Welk Show" was first telecast in 1955. His "squarest music this side of Euclid" made him the second-wealthiest performer in show business, behind Bob Hope. Welk was a demanding taskmaster dedicated to producing a wholesome show. He reportedly fired a performer for wearing a dress with a too-short hemline, and he kept his musical regulars, including the Champagne Lady and the Lennon Sisters, on the show for years, sometimes even arbitrating marital disputes in order to do so. Welk's folksy appeal (he introduced band selections with the trademark phrase "ah-one an' ah-two") and the orchestra's bubbly sound kept him on the airwaves from 1955 to 1971. When the network dropped the program, he signed up more than 250 independent television stations in the U.S. and Canada, and "Memories with Lawrence Welk" stayed on the air until 1982. From 1987 the program appeared

on public television. The multimillionaire had a vast real-estate empire, owned royalty rights to 20,000 songs, including the entire body of Jerome Kern's work, and chronicled his rags-to-riches tale in two books, *Wunnerful, Wunnerful!* (1971) and *Ah-One, Ah-Two!* (1974).

Whiteley, Brett, Australian painter (b. April 7, 1939, Sydney, Australia—d. June 15?, 1992, near Wollongong, New South Wales, Australia), was admired for the exuberance and sensuous power of his painting and his superb draftsmanship. Whiteley studied at the Julian Ashton art school in Sydney and spent several months in Italy on a traveling art scholarship. He arrived in London just in time to be included in the Whitechapel Gallery's "Recent Australian Painting" exhibition (1961), in which he was an instant success. The Tate Gallery purchased his "Red Painting" from that exhibit, making him the youngest artist ever bought by the Tate. Under the influence of such artists as his friend and mentor Francis Bacon (*q.v.*), whose portrait he painted in 1972, Whiteley abandoned his early abstract style in favour of a more figurative Expressionism. His best-known work of the 1960s included a series of paintings inspired by the British mass murderer John Christie. In the mid-1960s Whiteley traveled to the U.S. and Fiji before returning to Australia, where he portrayed his homeland in a series of Expressionist landscapes. In 1991 he was made an Officer of the Order of Australia. Whiteley, whose use of heroin and other drugs had been well publicized, was found dead in a beachside motel, and it was thought that he was the victim of a drug overdose.

Whitney, Cornelius Vanderbilt, U.S. businessman, horseman, aviation pioneer, and film producer (b. Feb. 20, 1899, Roslyn, N.Y.—d. Dec. 13, 1992, Saratoga Springs, N.Y.), despite the fact that vast inherited wealth made achievement on his part unnecessary, turned a variety of interests into several fortunes. Whitney was born into two of America's most prominent and wealthy families (his mother was Gertrude Vanderbilt Whitney, sculptor and founder of the Whitney Museum of American Art and heiress to a railroad and steamship fortune; his father, Henry Payne Whitney, was heir to fortunes in oil and tobacco). Whitney's early years were spent at the exclusive Groton prep school. With the onset of World War I, he enlisted in the Aviation Section of the U.S. Army and became a flying instructor. After he graduated from Yale in 1922, he headed west to make his fortune. He worked in a series of mining camps until he became involved with a salvage operation that extracted ore from mining scraps; this grew into the Hudson Bay Mining and

Smelting Co., which he founded in 1927. With another Yale graduate he founded Pan American Airways that same year, serving as chairman of the board until 1941. Whitney next turned to the motion-picture business; he coproduced such films as *Gone with the Wind* and *A Star Is Born*. In 1937 Whitney founded what became known as Marineland in St. Augustine, Fla. With the purchase of his father's horse farm and racing stable, he embarked on a lifelong involvement with horses and horse racing. During World War II he served as staff officer in the U.S. Army Air Force, rising to the rank of colonel. Whitney served in Pres. Harry S. Truman's administration as the first assistant secretary of the newly independent U.S. Air Force (1947–49) and then as under secretary of commerce (1949–50). His fourth marriage, in 1958, turned his interests to many philanthropies, especially in the arts, and much social activity. In 1985 he was given the Eclipse Award in recognition of lifetime achievements in the sport of Thoroughbred horse racing. An autobiography, *High Peaks*, was published in 1977.

Williams, Tony, U.S. singer (b. April 5, 1928, Elizabeth, N.J.—d. Aug. 14, 1992, New York, N.Y.), was the lead vocalist of the rhythm-and-blues group the Platters, which became the most successful black group of the 1950s, recording such smash hits as "Only You," "The Magic Touch," and "Smoke Gets in Your Eyes." It was Williams's unearthly tenor voice that propelled the harmonizing quintet to 16 gold records, notably for "My Prayer," "Harbor Lights," and their top seller, "The Great Pretender." Williams was a parking-lot attendant before being chosen in 1953 by songwriter Buck Ram to front the group. In 1960 Williams left the group that had been billed as "the Platters featuring Tony Williams" to pursue a solo career, but neither he nor the group, which underwent numerous personnel changes, ever recaptured the group's original success. In 1990 the Platters were inducted into the Rock and Roll Hall of Fame.

Zygmund, Antoni, Polish-born mathematician (b. Dec. 26, 1900, Warsaw, Poland—d. May 30, 1992, Chicago, Ill.), as a university professor in Europe and after 1947 at the University of Chicago, exerted a major influence on 20th-century mathematics through his work, teaching, and students. Zygmund's interest lay in the broad division of mathematics known as analysis, and he was particularly well known for his contributions to harmonic analysis, a field relied on in science and technology for the formulation of descriptions of periodic phenomena such as waves, vibrations, and regularly repeating structures. In 1986 he received the U.S. National Medal of Science for creating the so-called Chicago School of Analysis, the "strongest school of analytical research [particularly Fourier analysis and its applications to partial differential equations] in the contemporary mathematical world." Zygmund's legacy from nearly six decades of teaching included more than 80 Ph.D. students and hundreds of second-generation mathematical descendants. His book *Trigonometric Series* (1935 and later editions) remained the definitive treatment of the subject. Zygmund obtained his Ph.D. from the University of Warsaw in 1923. Between 1922 and 1929 he taught at the Polytechnical School in Warsaw, and between 1926 and 1929 he was also at the University of Warsaw. After a year in England on a Rockefeller fellowship, he became professor of mathematics at the University of Wilno (later Vilnius, Lithuania). In 1940, following a period of service in the Polish army, Zygmund escaped with his wife and son from his German-overrun homeland to the U.S. Successive posts at Mount Holyoke College, South Hadley, Mass., and the University of Pennsylvania led to an invitation in 1947 to join the faculty of the University of Chicago, where Zygmund remained until his retirement in 1980. His other books include *Analytic Functions* (1938, with Stanislaw Saks) and *Measure and Integral* (1977, with R.L. Wheeden). Zygmund held membership in the national academies of science of four countries: the U.S., Poland, Argentina, and Spain.

Events of 1992

Agriculture and Food Supplies

World agricultural and food production did not increase in 1992, according to preliminary estimates of the United Nations Food and Agriculture Organization (FAO). Disruptions in both the overall economy and agricultural sectors of the former Soviet Union and drought in western Europe restrained the expansion. Famine in Somalia resulting from the complete breakdown of law and order led to the intervention of U.S. troops to alleviate widespread starvation and suffering. The tragedy there tended to obscure the continuation of acute food shortages elsewhere in Africa; these were caused largely by civil strife but also by the worst drought in southern Africa in a century.

Food issues were the focus of an international nutrition conference. Environmental issues in agriculture also received more attention at the global level, as evidenced by a major UN-sponsored study assessing soil degradation.

The European Communities (EC) initiated major changes in the common agricultural policy (CAP), which provided some hope of concluding the long-running multilateral trade negotiations (MTN) carried out under the General Agreement on Tariffs and Trade (GATT). Before resolving the issue, the U.S. and the EC moved to the brink of a major trade war over EC import rules that restricted oilseed imports from the U.S. Their agreement went beyond oilseeds to deal with broader agricultural issues that had been blocking completion of the MTN. France, however, challenged the validity of the agreement, adding to the uncertainty about the MTN's fate in 1993. The U.S. complemented its Free Trade Agreement (FTA) with Canada with the North American Free Trade Agreement (NAFTA) it signed with Canada and Mexico.

Food Emergencies. Following the outbreak of civil war in 1988 and the overthrow of Pres. Muhammad Siyad Barrah in January 1991, warfare between the factions and clans in Somalia killed thousands of people, uprooted hundreds of thousands more, destroyed the country's infrastructure, crippled its economy, and resulted in the dissolution of the Somali government and a complete breakdown of law and order. By November 1991 relief officials were predicting imminent famine. The country was also gripped by a devastating drought that cut grain production by 50% in 1992 and decimated the livestock sector, upon which three-fourths of the population depended for its livelihood. Food

Table I. Selected Indexes of World Agricultural and Food Production
(1979–81 = 100)

Region or country	Total agricultural production						Total food production						Per capita food production					
	1987	1988	1989	1990	1991	1992[1]	1987	1988	1989	1990	1991	1992[1]	1987	1988	1989	1990	1991	1992[1]
Developed countries	108	105	109	110	107	106	108	105	110	111	107	107	103	100	104	104	100	99
United States	99	93	102	106	105	112	99	92	103	106	104	112	93	86	94	97	94	101
Canada	118	105	116	131	130	119	120	106	117	132	131	121	112	99	107	119	118	108
Europe	109	109	110	109	108	104	109	108	110	109	108	104	106	106	107	106	105	100
Japan	106	103	104	103	100	99	108	105	106	105	103	102	104	100	100	99	97	95
Oceania	109	114	110	111	112	115	106	111	109	110	110	114	97	100	96	96	94	97
South Africa	101	104	110	103	106	88	102	105	111	104	106	88	88	88	91	83	84	67
Former U.S.S.R.	117	116	120	119	104	100	119	118	122	122	105	102	112	109	113	112	96	92
Less developed countries	125	131	135	140	143	145	125	131	135	140	143	146	108	111	112	114	113	113
South and East Asia[2]	129	136	142	148	150	155	129	136	142	148	150	155	113	117	120	123	123	124
Bangladesh	112	113	122	123	124	125	112	114	124	125	125	128	92	92	97	96	93	92
China	141	145	148	160	166	169	139	142	146	158	162	167	127	128	130	139	139	142
India	121	135	143	145	148	151	123	137	144	147	149	153	106	116	119	119	118	118
Indonesia	132	139	149	149	151	156	133	140	146	152	154	159	116	120	122	124	124	125
Korea, South	107	111	111	109	108	110	109	113	113	111	110	112	97	102	92	100	99	98
Malaysia	139	149	160	161	159	167	155	168	191	196	196	207	129	136	151	151	146	152
Myanmar (Burma)	119	114	110	112	110	116	119	115	111	114	111	117	103	97	92	92	89	91
Pakistan	132	139	148	154	165	168	125	134	144	147	152	155	96	100	104	103	103	102
Philippines	100	102	107	109	109	112	99	101	106	108	108	111	82	82	84	84	82	82
Thailand	115	127	133	122	133	140	113	126	132	119	131	136	99	109	112	100	108	111
Vietnam	137	150	160	167	178	171	134	146	157	161	170	166	115	123	129	130	134	128
Western Asia	120	126	119	133	133	137	120	126	119	133	133	138	99	101	93	101	99	99
Iran	152	140	140	170	166	176	154	142	141	173	168	180	118	106	104	124	118	123
Turkey	114	124	115	126	125	128	115	124	114	125	126	128	97	102	92	100	99	98
Africa[3]	115	122	125	126	130	126	118	126	130	131	135	132	95	99	99	97	96	92
Egypt	120	121	124	134	137	138	128	130	135	146	149	150	107	106	107	114	114	112
Ethiopia	101	104	107	112	111	108	102	105	108	113	114	110	87	87	87	88	87	82
Morocco	132	156	160	156	174	141	130	155	159	154	174	139	109	126	126	119	131	102
Nigeria	123	144	151	162	170	184	123	144	151	163	170	184	98	112	113	118	119	125
Sudan, The	96	111	93	88	104	112	93	110	91	88	105	114	76	87	70	66	76	80
Zaire	121	124	127	129	131	132	121	125	128	129	132	133	98	98	97	95	94	92
Latin America	118	122	125	126	127	128	119	124	127	128	130	131	103	105	105	104	103	102
Argentina	102	108	100	109	114	109	103	107	99	108	113	110	94	96	88	95	98	93
Brazil	138	140	145	141	142	150	139	144	150	145	147	156	119	121	123	117	116	121
Colombia	106	112	120	127	129	129	109	117	127	131	132	131	94	99	105	107	105	103
Mexico	115	120	124	127	125	121	116	121	127	129	128	127	98	100	103	102	100	97
Peru	114	123	120	112	114	111	116	125	120	115	118	114	99	104	98	92	93	89
Venezuela	120	125	128	131	132	134	116	125	120	115	118	116	99	104	98	92	93	89
World	116	119	123	125	126	126	117	119	123	126	125	127	103	103	105	106	104	103

[1]Preliminary. [2]Excludes Japan. [3]Excludes South Africa.
Source: Food and Agriculture Organization of the United Nations, *FAO Quarterly Bulletin of Statistics.*

distribution was hindered by the collapse of the distribution network and by widespread looting and hoarding of relief supplies. By December 1992 more than 300,000 Somalis were estimated to have died of starvation. The International Committee of the Red Cross (ICRC) estimated that, of Somalia's population of 6.7 million, some 1.5 million, beyond the reach of international relief efforts largely because of the poor security situation, were in dire need of immediate assistance. As many as another 4.5 million people were in desperate need of food and other forms of assistance. It was estimated that at least 52,000 tons of food per month were needed to feed the hungry.

At U.S. urging, the UN Security Council on December 3, by Resolution 794, authorized member nations to use all necessary means to establish a secure environment for humanitarian relief operations in Somalia. On December 8, U.S. troops under U.S. command landed unopposed in Somalia under orders to support the resolution.

The Somali tragedy tended to obscure the continuation of acute food shortages elsewhere in Africa. Although the 1992 grain harvest in The Sudan was much larger than expected, food shortages remained acute in many areas of that nation because of the continuing civil war. Some areas, such as Juba, had been inaccessible by surface transport for four years and remained totally dependent on airlifts for food supplies. In Ethiopia food supplies remained tight because of disruptions caused by its recently ended civil war, continuing drought in pastoral areas, and large numbers of returnees and displaced persons, including increasing numbers of refugees from The Sudan and Somalia. Parts of the south and east were still experiencing ethnic conflicts that were disrupting relief operations. Kenya, experiencing its third consecutive year of drought, had a large number of internally displaced persons, and the number of refugees from Somalia, The Sudan, and Ethiopia was growing.

Southern Africa was devastated in 1992 by the worst drought of the century. In Malawi grain production fell 60%, with nearly total crop failures in parts of the south and central regions; perhaps one-third of the nation's population was left with little or no food, including some one million

refugees from Mozambique. In the latter country, beset by protracted civil war, an October cease-fire gave hope of relieving shortages in previously inaccessible regions. More than three million people were at risk from hunger and disease in government-controlled areas. Zambia, whose grain crop declined 50%, acted quickly to increase food imports, but the country faced major transportation obstacles in distributing food to the needy. Zimbabwe, normally a grain exporter, saw its grain output cut by two-thirds, and more than 60% of the country's communal cattle herd died.

Crops were generally better in the Sahel and West Africa in 1992, but farming and relief operations in parts of Liberia and Sierra Leone were disrupted by civil strife. Conditions were improved around Monrovia following deployment of a peacekeeping force of the Economic Community of West African States in midyear. Madagascar, Rwanda, and Zaire also remained on the FAO's list of countries requiring exceptional or emergency assistance.

In Asia the food-supply situation deteriorated in Afghanistan as the result of a below-average grain harvest and the return of hundreds of thousands of refugees in need of assistance. Food shortages requiring exceptional or emergency assistance continued to be reported also in Cambodia, Laos, and Lebanon. In the Western Hemisphere grain supplies were short in Haiti, and grain and potato crops in Peru were seriously damaged by drought or floods.

In Europe the food-supply situation was grave in Bosnia and Hercegovina and serious in neighbouring newly independent republics, a situation made worse by the presence of some 2.7 million refugees and displaced persons. Exceptional or emergency assistance was also required in Albania. The tight food situation in the former Soviet republics eased in 1992. The problem became more a matter of re-

Table II. World Cereal Supply and Distribution
In 000,000 metric tons

	1989–90	1990–91	1991–92	1992–93[1]
Production				
Wheat	533	588	542	555
Coarse grains	793	820	801	838
Rice, milled	343	351	348	351
Total	1,668	1,759	1,691	1,745
Utilization				
Wheat	530	565	555	550
Coarse grains	817	807	806	821
Rice, milled	336	346	352	354
Total	1,683	1,718	1,712	1,725
Exports				
Wheat	97	95	108	103
Coarse grains	102	88	94	91
Rice, milled	12	13	15	14
Total	211	195	216	208
Ending stocks[2]				
Wheat	121	144	131	136
Coarse grains	125	138	134	151
Rice, milled	55	60	57	54
Total	301	342	322	341
Stocks as % of utilization				
Wheat	22.8%	25.4%	23.7%	24.8%
Coarse grains	15.3%	17.1%	16.6%	18.4%
Rice, milled	16.4%	17.5%	16.1%	15.1%
Total	17.9%	19.9%	18.8%	19.8%
Stocks held by U.S. in %				
Wheat	12.1%	16.4%	9.4%	9.9%
Coarse grains	36.6%	34.6%	25.5%	40.1%
Rice	1.6%	1.3%	1.6%	2.1%
Total	20.3%	21.1%	14.7%	22.0%

[1] Forecast.
[2] Series includes estimates of Chinese and Soviet stocks. Data not available for all countries, including parts of eastern Europe and Asia.
Source: USDA, Foreign Agricultural Service, December 1992.

Table III. World Production of Oilseeds and Products
In 000,000 metric tons

	1990–91	1991–92[1]	1992–93[2]
Production of oilseeds	215.9	223.1	224.2
Soybeans	104.0	106.1	112.4
U.S.	52.4	54.1	59.0
China	11.0	9.7	9.7
Argentina	11.5	10.8	10.8
Brazil	15.8	19.1	20.0
Cottonseed	33.5	37.0	32.9
U.S.	5.4	6.3	5.7
Former Soviet republics	4.9	4.4	3.7
China	7.7	9.7	7.8
Peanuts	22.3	22.4	22.3
U.S.	1.6	2.2	2.0
China	6.4	6.3	5.3
India	7.6	7.3	8.3
Sunflower seed	22.9	21.1	22.2
U.S.	1.0	1.6	1.3
Former Soviet republics	6.6	5.6	6.1
Argentina	3.9	3.6	3.6
EC[3]	4.3	4.0	4.1
Rapeseed	25.1	28.5	26.4
Canada	3.3	4.2	3.7
China	7.0	7.4	7.1
EC[3]	6.2	7.3	6.2
India	5.2	6.0	6.5
Copra	4.8	4.6	4.5
Palm kernel	3.3	3.4	3.6
Crushings of oilseeds	177.4	184.8	184.7
Soybeans	87.6	91.9	93.7
Ending stocks of oilseeds	22.8	21.2	22.1
Soybeans	20.1	18.1	19.5
World production[4]			
Total fats and oils	71.4	...	...
Edible vegetable oils	56.9	58.4	59.4
Soybean oil	15.9	16.7	16.8
Palm oil	11.1	11.5	12.3
Animal fats	12.4	...	...
Marine oils	1.4	1.4	1.4
High-protein meals[5]	114.1	118.7	119.3
Soybean meal	69.5	72.8	74.2

[1] Preliminary.
[2] Forecast.
[3] Includes former East Germany.
[4] Processing potential from crops in year indicated.
[5] Converted, based on product's protein content, to weight equivalent to soybeans of 44% protein content.
Source: USDA, Foreign Agricultural Service, June and December 1992.

A Japanese rice farmer harvests the crop. Japan's farmers opposed a proposal before the General Agreement on Tariffs and Trade (GATT) to replace the ban on rice imports with high tariffs.
KAREN KASMAUSKI—MATRIX

duced purchasing power restricting consumption by poorer elements of the population rather than of acute, life-threatening food shortages.

Nutrition Conference. The International Conference on Nutrition (ICN), convened in December by the FAO and the World Health Organization (WHO) and attended by representatives from 160 nations, dealt with a broad range of nutrition issues. The conference noted that more than 700 million people—mostly in Africa, southern Asia, and Latin America—did not receive enough food to meet basic needs. Reflecting a new emphasis on micronutrients, it pointed out that two billion people subsisted on diets that lacked the essential vitamins and minerals required for normal growth and development. It also concluded that on a worldwide basis there was enough food, but that "inequitable access is the main problem."

To deal with these problems, the conference took two main steps. The first was a Global Declaration on Nutrition that recognized access to nutritionally adequate food as a right of every individual and pledged the participating countries to make all efforts to eliminate famine and famine-related deaths before the end of the 1990s. It also pledged to "reduce substantially within this decade" starvation and widespread chronic hunger, undernutrition, micronutrient deficiencies, diet-related diseases, impediments to breast-feeding, and inadequate sanitation and poor hygiene.

By itself the declaration no more guaranteed an end to hunger than had the resolution adopted by the World Food Council of 1974, which pledged that "no child would go to bed hungry" by the end of that decade. Probably more important was the ICN's call for each nation to develop by the end of 1994 a nutrition plan of action to meet the declaration's goals. Such plans were to include measurable nutrition targets. The FAO, WHO, and other international organizations were also asked to increase their capacity for implementing the declaration and plans of action.

Soil Degradation. A study financed by the UN Environment Program found that more than 1.2 billion ha (3 billion ac) of land, about 10.5% of the world's vegetated surface, had been seriously damaged by human activity since 1945. The study, carried out by the nonprofit World Resources Institute in the U.S. with coordination by the International Soil Reference and Information Centre in The Netherlands, took three years and surveyed the work of more than 250

soil scientists throughout the world. It found that much of the damage had been masked by a general rise in global agricultural productivity resulting from expanded irrigation, better plant varieties, and greater use of production inputs such as fertilizers and pesticides.

More than a third of the damaged land was in Asia, almost a third in Africa, and a quarter in Central America. Some 9 million ha (22 million ac) were considered damaged beyond restoration. The study considered the measures needed to restore the productivity of the remainder to be beyond the means of most farmers in the less developed countries. The greatest sources of soil degradation were overgrazing, unsuitable agricultural practices, and deforestation.

Commodities. *Grains.* World grain output was expected (in December) to increase in 1992–93, thanks largely to a recovery of grain production in the U.S. and the former Soviet republics. A moderate increase in world grain stocks was in prospect despite a continuing rise in global grain use. Drought reduced grain output, however, throughout much of Europe, especially in eastern Europe. Smaller grain supplies in eastern Europe, together with inadequate foreign exchange to finance imports and the effects of market reforms, were further cutting grain consumption there. Drought during the spring and summer in southern Africa resulted in large grain imports by a region that was normally a net exporter.

Global grain trade was likely to be smaller in 1992–93, largely because bigger grain harvests in the former Soviet republics and wheat harvests in China reduced the import requirements of those countries. Grain imports by the former Soviets were also being limited by the region's increasing dependence on the availability of export credit and credit guarantees. Overdue payments to U.S. suppliers resulted in the suspension in November of new U.S. grain sales on credit to Russia, followed by reinstatement shortly thereafter following some payments, and then a suspension that remained in effect through year's end.

The EC policies that were the subjects of CAP reform had helped make the EC the world's second largest grain exporter after the U.S. The intervention prices paid its grain farmers were set well above world grain prices and generated excess production that was exported with the help of extensive export subsidies. The CAP reform would reduce the average EC intervention price for grains by 55 European

Currency Units (ECU; about $52) to ECU 100 (about $146) per ton by 1995–96. New direct income supports of ECU 45 (about $42) per ton of grain were to substitute for part of the support lost through the reduction of intervention prices. Larger, so-called professional farms had to set aside (idle) part of their land to be eligible for payments. Such farms—those that produced more than 92 tons of grain annually and were ordinarily 20 ha (about 50 ac) or larger—represented some 35% of all farms and 65% of the total area planted to the crops covered.

The 1992–93 world wheat crop was the second largest on record although well below the 1990–91 record. Crops in both the U.S. and the former Soviet republics were more than 20% larger than a year earlier. Eastern Europe's wheat production, however, was 30% smaller. Wheat imports by eastern European countries were expected to be heavily dependent on the availability of credit and donation programs by exporters. Stocks of EC wheat from the 1991–92 harvest were sufficient to increase exports in 1992–93, despite the drought-reduced EC wheat crop.

A relaxation of government planting restrictions and favourable weather conditions resulted in the largest U.S. coarse grain crop since 1985–86—up one-fourth from 1991–92 to 274 million tons. That, together with a substantial recovery in production in the former Soviet republics, more than offset the much smaller crops in eastern Europe and the EC.

Oilseeds. A modest increase in 1992–93 global oilseed production was expected (in December), largely the result of a U.S. soybean crop favoured by unusually good weather. The strong expansion of 1991–92 oilseed output—led by cottonseed, rapeseed, and soybeans—together with the availability of substantial carryover soybean stocks, fueled strong increases in production of both high-protein meals and edible vegetable oils. The ample oilseed supplies were reflected in soybean prices (c.i.f., Rotterdam, U.S. No. 2 yellow), which were trending slowly downward, averaging $237 per ton from October 1991 through September 1992, compared with $241 in 1990–91 and $247 in 1989–90.

The demand for protein meal strengthened a little in 1991–92, stimulated by the expansion of the hog and poultry sectors of the U.S., EC, and those Latin-American and Asian countries that were experiencing rapid economic growth. The price of soybean meal increased from an average of $198 per ton (c.i.f., Rotterdam) in 1990–91 to $203 in 1991–92. Although soybean oil prices (f.o.b., Rotterdam) fell from an average of $454 per ton in 1990–91 to $437 in 1991–92, about the same as in 1989–90, strong price increases were recorded for coconut and palm oil in 1991–92.

In response to an earlier GATT finding that the EC's oilseed policy denied the U.S. and other oilseed exporters the benefits of a 30-year-old tariff concession that reduced EC tariffs on oilseeds and oilseed meals, the EC adopted a new set of oilseed policies in December 1991. The U.S. was not satisfied and requested another panel, which ruled in March 1992 that the new policies continued to deny U.S. oilseed exporters—mainly of soybeans—the benefits of the concession. The EC rejected the ruling, and the U.S. threatened to restrict imports worth $1 billion from the EC—the

Table IV. Livestock Numbers and Meat Production in Major Producing Countries
In 000,000 head and 000,000 metric tons (carcass weight)

Region and country	1991[1]	1992[2]	1991	1992[2]
	Cattle and buffalo		Beef and veal	
World total	1,055.9	1,047.9	48.92	47.98
Canada	11.4	11.6	0.89	0.93
United States	100.1	102.3	10.53	10.65
Mexico	30.2	30.7	1.58	1.66
Argentina	56.5	56.7	2.65	2.60
Brazil	130.1	129.4	3.70	3.80
Uruguay	9.9	10.4	0.32	0.32
Western Europe	87.7	85.9	9.34	8.94
EC[3]	80.4	78.7	8.68	8.29
Eastern Europe	24.6	23.7	2.08	1.83
FSU[4]	106.0	97.0	7.81	6.97
Baltic states	4.3	3.9	0.41	0.36
Australia	24.7	24.4	1.72	1.74
India	271.2	271.3	2.03	2.04
China	104.6	105.7	1.54	1.76
	Hogs		Pork	
World total	762.6	761.1	65.91	67.06
Canada	10.6	10.4	1.13	1.18
United States	57.7	58.9	7.26	7.83
Mexico	9.9	11.2	0.82	0.83
Western Europe	115.0	118.0	14.86	14.88
EC[3]	106.2	109.2	13.75	13.78
Eastern Europe	55.2	52.9	5.49	5.31
FSU[4]	64.6	56.9	5.64	4.80
Baltic states	4.4	3.7	0.45	0.38
Japan	11.0	10.8	1.48	1.44
China	369.7	371.7	24.52	26.00
	Poultry		Poultry meat[5]	
World total	...	...	37.78	39.33
United States	...	...	11.20	11.75
Brazil	...	...	2.69	2.96
EC[3]	...	...	6.85	6.96
Eastern Europe	...	...	1.69	1.62
FSU[4]	...	...		
Baltic states			0.12	0.10
Japan	...	...	1.42	1.37
China	...	...	3.95	4.50
	Sheep[3]		Sheep, goat meat	
World total[6]	845.1	818.5	6.49	6.34
			All meat	
Total			159.10	160.70

[1] Preliminary livestock numbers at year's end. Consists of 51 countries for beef and veal, 38 for pork, 51 for poultry meat, 30 for sheep and goat meat, and roughly the same coverage for animal numbers. Includes nearly all European producers, the most significant in the Western Hemisphere, and scattered coverage elsewhere.
[2] Forecast.
[3] Includes united Germany.
[4] Former Soviet Union, comprising 12 nations, excluding its Baltic states.
[5] Ready-to-eat equivalent.
[6] Coverage includes China.
Source: USDA, Foreign Agricultural Service, August and October 1992.

Table V. World Production of Dairy Products[1]
Production of cow's milk
In 000,000 metric tons

Region and country	1990	1991	1992[2]
North America	84.6	85.4	87.3
United States	67.3	67.4	68.8
South America	24.5	24.2	25.2
Brazil	14.5	14.2	14.8
Western Europe	133.4	128.7	126.2
EC	118.0	113.9	111.5
France	26.4	25.7	25.5
Germany (united)	31.2	28.9	27.8
Italy	11.5	11.4	11.1
Netherlands, The	11.3	11.0	10.7
United Kingdom	15.0	14.5	14.5
Other western Europe	15.3	14.9	14.7
Eastern Europe	34.7	31.5	28.3
Poland	15.8	14.5	12.8
Former Soviet republics	102.0	95.4	82.2
Baltic states	5.8	5.1	4.9
China	4.2	4.6	5.2
India	27.5	28.2	29.4
Australia/New Zealand[3]	14.2	14.7	15.4
Japan/South Africa	10.7	10.7	10.8
Total	442.0	429.4	415.0

	Production		Year-end stocks	
Product/Region	1991	1992[2]	1991	1992[2]
	In 000 metric tons			
Butter	6,307	6,056	1,006	924
EC	1,801	1,619	538	458
U.S.	606	615	249	225
Cheese	10,169	11,127	1,629	1,627
EC	4,892	4,982	1,088	1,120
U.S.	2,763	2,920	189	175
Nonfat dry milk	3,474	3,177	769	354
EC	1,499	1,208	482	130
U.S.	398	390	98	45

[1] Based on 37 major producing countries. Those not shown individually include (North America) Canada and Mexico; (South America) Argentina, Chile, Peru, and Venezuela; (EC) Belgium-Luxembourg, Denmark, Greece, Ireland, Portugal, and Spain; (other western Europe) Austria, Finland, Norway, Sweden, and Switzerland; and (eastern Europe) Czechoslovakia and Yugoslavia. Coverage of production and stocks of other dairy products is not as comprehensive or uniform for the countries not shown above individually.
[2] Preliminary.
[3] Year ended June 30 for Australia and May 31 for New Zealand.
Source: USDA, Foreign Agricultural Service, November 1992.

U.S. estimate of the damage to U.S. export sales. Following unsuccessful EC attempts to renegotiate its tariff bindings on oilseeds and oilseed meal, the U.S. in September asked for binding GATT arbitration to rule how much compensation the EC owed the U.S. and oilseed exporters for the damage caused them by the EC policies. More negotiations ensued after the EC unilaterally blocked the proposal for arbitration.

On November 2 the U.S. announced the first installment of its retaliation should the dispute not be resolved to its satisfaction by December 5. It withdrew U.S. tariff reductions negotiated in earlier years on $300 million worth of EC exports to the U.S. Prohibitive duties were announced on a list of EC exports that included white wine, rapeseed oil, and wheat gluten. U.S. imports of agricultural products from the EC (excluding distilled spirits) amounted to $4.4 billion in 1991.

The EC and the U.S. announced on November 20 that they had resolved the oilseed dispute and several other differences between them that were delaying the GATT multilateral trade negotiations. The agreement on oilseeds was based on an EC commitment to limit its oilseed production by setting aside in the first year of the agreement 15% of the area now planted to oilseeds and 10% in subsequent years. The outcome of the issue, however, remained in doubt because of a bitter French claim that the agreement was invalid.

Meat and Livestock. Another decline in the world cattle herd, by about 1%, was expected in 1992 (in October) because increases in the U.S. and China were overwhelmed by large reductions in the former Soviet republics and eastern Europe and smaller declines in the EC. The formerly Communist countries were also the source of the largest reductions in beef production in 1992, resulting in an estimated 2% reduction globally.

World pork production continued to expand at almost 2% annually, led by strong growth in Chinese output that more than offset substantially smaller production in the former Soviet republics. World poultry output continued to grow briskly, but not quite as rapidly as the 5% rate achieved in 1991. The growth in Chinese poultry production also slowed a little from the 7.5% expansion recorded in 1991.

CAP meat-industry reforms created a new support mechanism that made direct payments to beef and sheep farmers based on the number of animals owned up to a designated maximum, with premiums for a certain number of animals per hectare of land used. The intervention price (government purchase guarantee) for beef was cut 15% to maintain the competitiveness of beef with other meats, but this was offset to some extent by reductions in feed costs resulting from CAP reforms that lowered intervention prices for grains. Much less EC pork and poultry than beef was purchased under EC support programs, but they would also benefit from the lower grain prices.

Dairy Products. The production of cow's milk by 37 major producing countries in 1992 was expected (in November) to decline for the second straight year, again falling about 3%. Economic upheaval in the former Soviet republics was primarily responsible, but drought also compounded the problems of reorganizing the dairy industries of eastern Europe. EC milk production again fell as the buyout of production quotas held by EC milk producers continued. Many small producers were leaving the industry, contributing to an increased slaughter of dairy cows and smaller dairy surpluses.

Cheese production increased in most areas outside the former Soviet republics and eastern Europe in 1992 as a greater proportion of fluid milk was converted into cheese in response to strong consumer demand. International dairy

prices (f.o.b., North European and selected world ports) strengthened a little in 1992 from spring onward, peaking in October at $1,400–$1,750 per ton for butter, $1,750–$2,150 for butter oil, $2,050–$2,450 for cheese, and $1,650–$2,060 for nonfat dry milk (NFDM). The increases were greater for cheese and NFDM than for butter, partly reflecting a long-term trend in many countries toward lower per capita consumption of butter because of dietary concerns and competition from vegetable margarine. Butterfats were also tending to receive lower levels of support, particularly in EC and U.S. dairy programs, relative to NFDM.

The EC in May 1992 adopted important changes in its dairy policy, which cost it some $7 billion annually, as part of overall CAP agricultural reforms. The reforms were less drastic than were those for the grains and oilseed sectors; a 2% cut in milk quotas for 1991–92 resulted in a reduction in EC dairy surpluses and reduced pressures for further production cuts. The reforms provided for only small reductions in support prices, leaving most adjustments to future years. A 5% cut in the support (intervention) price for butter was approved.

Sugar. World sugar production in 1992–93 was expected (in November) to about match output in 1991–92, when unexpectedly large increases in output in Asia, especially by China and India, disproved early forecasts of a smaller harvest. Global sugar output was expected to exceed consumption for the fourth straight year. The prospects of continuing growth in world sugar stocks helped keep the average monthly spot prices of freely traded raw sugar mostly in the 8–10-cent-per-pound range. World prices of refined sugar moved mostly in the 12–13-cent range.

The dissolution of the Soviet Union and the economic crisis faced by its successor states resulted in a breakdown of the barterlike arrangements under which Cuba had traded

Table VI. World Production of Centrifugal (Freed from Liquid) Sugar

In 000,000 metric tons raw value

Region and country	1990–91	1991–92	1992–93[1]
North America	10.3	10.2	10.7
United States	6.3	6.6	6.8
Mexico	3.9	3.5	3.8
Caribbean	8.8	8.1	7.2
Cuba	7.6	7.0	6.0
Central America	2.2	2.4	2.5
Guatemala	1.0	1.1	1.2
South America	13.2	14.7	14.9
Argentina	1.3	1.6	1.4
Brazil	7.9	8.9	9.2
Colombia	1.6	1.8	1.8
Europe	23.0	21.3	22.1
Western Europe	18.2	16.9	18.1
EC	17.0	15.8	17.0
France	4.7	4.4	4.7
Germany (united)	4.7	4.2	4.5
Eastern Europe	4.8	4.5	4.0
Poland	2.2	1.6	1.6
Former Soviet republics	9.2	6.9	7.5
Baltic states	0.1	0.1	0.1
Africa and Middle East	10.6	10.9	9.6
South Africa	2.2	2.4	1.6
Turkey	2.0	2.1	1.8
Asia	32.7	38.3	37.4
China	6.8	8.5	8.6
India	13.7	15.5	14.6
Indonesia	2.1	2.3	2.1
Pakistan	2.1	2.5	2.4
Philippines	1.7	2.0	1.9
Thailand	4.0	5.1	5.5
Oceania	4.1	3.4	4.3
Australia	3.6	3.0	3.4
Totals			
Beginning stocks	19.5	22.0	24.6
As % of consumption	17.7%	19.5%	21.5%
Production	114.0	116.3	116.2
Imports[2]	27.3	27.2	27.1
Consumption	110.3	112.9	114.6
Exports[2]	28.6	28.0	28.3

[1] Preliminary.
[2] Exports do not equal imports because "Totals" are a composite of slightly differing marketing years, not all beginning in the same months.
Source: USDA, Foreign Agricultural Service, November 1992.

its sugar on very favourable terms for petroleum and other raw materials produced by the U.S.S.R. and the European countries under its influence. These new states of the former Soviet Union at first sought to eliminate the subsidies to Cuba by exporting for hard currency to the highest bidder. However, many eventually found it convenient to establish their own barter arrangements with Cuba because of severe foreign exchange shortages and a continuing need for large quantities of imported sugar. Cuba's exports declined from about seven million tons to a forecast five million tons in 1992–93. A shortage of fuel and spare parts and antiquated machinery were contributing to further declines in Cuban sugar output.

In China large stocks of sugar and a desire to earn foreign exchange continued to support growth in both consumption and exports—which now exceeded imports—despite a smaller sugar crop in 1992–93. In October Brazil ordered an increase in the required alcohol content of gasoline from 14 to 22% as part of a plan to cut carbon emissions in half by 2000. About 4 million of Brazil's estimated 12 million motor vehicles used fuel alcohol derived from domestic sugar or imported methanol exclusively.

Coffee. The 1992–93 world coffee harvest was expected (in December) to be the smallest since 1988–89, primarily because of a sharp drop in Brazilian output. Weak market prices, the high cost of credit, and the Brazilian government's suspension of guarantees to buy surplus coffee

production influenced the replacement of some 650 million lower-yielding coffee trees with other crops and the adoption of less intensive cultivation there.

International prices for raw coffee had moved steadily downward since the July 1989 suspension of export quotas under the International Coffee Agreement (ICA). The ICA composite indicator price (15-day moving average, New York), which had averaged better than $1.16 per pound in the year prior to suspension, declined steadily to an average of about 67 cents per pound in 1991, falling to a 10-year low of about 46 cents in August 1992 before strengthening a little on prospects of a much smaller 1992–93 coffee harvest. The low prices reflected the large stocks held in both exporting and importing countries.

Negotiators extended the deadline for completing a new ICA to March 31, 1993, after failing to meet their year-end goal. They agreed to the principle of a "universal quota" to govern exports to both ICA members and nonmembers and were close to agreeing on how to achieve "selectivity," which seemed to imply separate export quotas and indicator prices for different classes of coffee—both questions of critical concern to importing countries. Among the many issues remaining to be resolved were the allocation of quotas among exporting countries and how the arrangement would respond to market forces.

Cocoa. African cocoa bean production, along with global cocoa production, was expected (in October) to recover in 1992–93. Producers in many countries cut back on new plantings because low world cocoa bean prices caused them to produce at a loss or barely recover production costs. Prices for cocoa beans (nearest three-month average, New York futures) fell steadily from an average of $1.06 per pound in 1984 before holding at about 55 cents per pound in 1989 and 1990, slipping to 52 cents in 1991, and drifting even lower through October 1992. In Indonesia, however, low production costs made cocoa profitable, and output continued to expand rapidly.

Cocoa bean grindings declined in 1991–92 largely because grindings and cocoa imports in the former Soviet republics were sharply reduced; however, they still exceeded production, resulting in a small drawdown in stocks. Cocoa grindings and consumption declined sharply in the former Soviet Union—once the world's second largest consumer—because of depressed economic conditions and a shortage of foreign exchange. Nigeria's capacity to produce cocoa products such as cocoa butter, cocoa cake, and chocolate liquor for export exceeded domestic cocoa bean production in 1992 and could lead to a ban on bean exports.

Table VII. World Green Coffee Production
In 000 60-kg bags

Region and country	1990–91	1991–92[1]	1992–93[2]
North America	17,350	18,121	16,990
Costa Rica	2,565	2,530	2,375
El Salvador	2,603	2,357	2,500
Guatemala	3,282	3,444	3,150
Honduras	1,685	2,200	2,000
Mexico	4,550	4,620	4,200
South America	50,010	51,197	45,955
Brazil	31,000	28,500	24,000
Colombia	14,500	17,980	17,000
Ecuador	1,830	1,800	1,900
Africa	18,516	18,971	18,565
Cameroon	1,450	1,485	1,470
Côte d'Ivoire	3,300	3,967	4,000
Ethiopia	3,500	3,000	3,000
Kenya	1,455	1,572	1,550
Uganda	2,700	3,000	3,000
Zaire	1,695	1,500	1,300
Asia and Oceania	14,589	14,604	14,370
India	2,970	3,200	2,500
Indonesia	7,480	7,100	7,350
Total production	100,465	102,893	95,880
Exportable[3]	76,564	81,103	73,786
Beginning stocks[4]	39,218	39,301	39,489
Exports	76,903	81,128	76,412

[1] Preliminary.
[2] Forecast.
[3] Production minus domestic use.
[4] In exporting countries.
Source: USDA, Foreign Agricultural Service, December 1992.

Table VIII. World Cocoa Bean Production
In 000 metric tons

Region and country	1990–91	1991–92	1992–93[1]
North and Central America	102	107	107
South America	568	469	466
Brazil	375	295	290
Ecuador	104	83	85
Africa	1,398	1,236	1,319
Cameroon	100	95	95
Côte d'Ivoire[2]	804	750	780
Ghana	293	242	270
Nigeria[3]	160	110	135
Asia and Oceania	458	448	459
Indonesia	165	180	200
Malaysia	235	210	200
Total production	2,526	2,259	2,351
Net production	2,500	2,236	2,327
Cocoa grindings	2,355	2,330	2,350
Change in stocks	145	−94	−23

[1] Forecast.
[2] Includes some cocoa marketed from Ghana.
[3] Includes cocoa marketed through Benin.
Source: USDA, Foreign Agricultural Service, October 1992.

Table IX. World Cotton Production
In 000,000 480-lb bales

Region and country	1990–91	1991–92	1992–93[1]
Western Hemisphere	23.5	25.2	22.1
United States	15.5	17.6	16.3
Mexico	0.8	0.8	0.2
Argentina	1.4	1.1	0.9
Brazil	3.2	3.4	3.0
Paraguay	1.2	0.7	0.9
Europe	1.4	1.5	1.7
Former Soviet republics	11.9	11.3	9.4
Africa	5.7	5.5	6.0
Egypt	1.4	1.3	1.5
Sudan, The	0.4	0.4	0.4
Asia and Oceania[2]	44.4	52.5	46.7
China	20.7	26.1	21.0
India	9.1	9.4	10.0
Pakistan	7.5	10.0	9.0
Turkey	3.0	2.6	2.8
Australia	2.0	2.3	1.6
Total	86.9	96.0	85.9

[1] Estimate.
[2] Includes Middle East.
Source: USDA, Foreign Agricultural Service, June and December 1992.

A new corn plant sprouts in the previous year's stubble. No-till farming, in which seeds are planted among the remains of the previous crop, was being adopted by farmers to conserve soil and moisture.

STEVE LISS—TIME MAGAZINE

A negotiating conference convened in April under the auspices of the UN Conference on Trade and Development (UNCTAD) made little progress in developing a new International Cocoa Agreement (ICCA). The conference demonstrated that producing countries wanted an export-quota system to control supply, while consuming countries wanted producing countries individually to withhold cocoa in conjunction with the existing ICCA buffer stock. Another meeting in July saw the negotiators still divided over key issues, such as how to deal with the structural oversupply of raw cocoa, the nature and financing of a withholding scheme, and what price level to defend. A November conference brought some narrowing of positions, and negotiators planned to meet again in February 1993.

Cotton. The sharp downturn in world cotton production in 1992–93 (estimated in December) was expected to result in output approximately matching cotton use and would end a two-year buildup in global cotton stocks. The largest reduction was in China, which was affected by drought and insect damage. Depressed cotton prices resulting from the record crop of 1991–92 also led to smaller cotton plantings elsewhere, especially in the U.S. Output was also reduced by unseasonably cool, wet weather in the former Soviet republics and by flooding in Pakistan.

The Chinese harvest, nevertheless, remained large enough to permit a substantial increase in cotton use without drawing down stocks, which represented about 35% of world cotton stocks at the beginning of the 1992–93 season. Low world prices prevented China from moving much surplus cotton onto world markets without large subsidies that would greatly increase its already dangerously high budget deficit and make it more difficult to gain admission into the GATT.

Cotton use continued to grow worldwide about 2% annually. Increases tended to be largest in countries that were large exporters of cotton—such as China, India, and Pakistan—but that also were producing more textiles to meet increased domestic demand caused by rapidly growing populations. International prices of cotton (Northern European Cotlook Index "A"), which averaged a little under 83 cents per pound in 1990–91 (August–July), fell to an average of 63 cents in 1991–92, and slid to about 52–53 cents in late 1992.

The international Multi-Fiber Agreement (MFA), which was to expire Dec. 31, 1992, was extended one year in December when it became clear that the GATT multilateral trade negotiations would not be completed in time to replace MFA rules governing the importation of textile products. The agreement, which sanctions restrictions on such imports by its members, falls outside the GATT. Less developed countries that were members of the MFA sought liberalization of such restrictions by the developed countries and were said to demand increased market access as a condition of the MFA's extension.

Agricultural and Trade Policies. *EC CAP Reforms.* After long and difficult debate, the EC's agricultural ministers on May 21 adopted a package of measures aimed at reducing the large budgetary expenditures and agricultural surpluses generated by its CAP. About one-half of EC agricultural output, in terms of value, was affected. These major reforms were to be carried out over three years beginning in 1993–94. They focused on the grains, livestock, and dairy sectors and extended the reform process initiated with the oilseed-sector reforms of 1991.

Previously, the EC had provided both price and income support to EC farmers primarily through government guarantees to intervene in markets in a manner similar to the U.S. loan-rate system; the EC purchased products at a minimum "intervention price" that was usually set well above world prices. The CAP reforms relied more on supply controls, in the form of land "set-asides" for crops, to support prices and to reduce government acquisition of stocks. Intervention prices were retained but at substantially reduced levels. Income support was provided largely by direct compensation payments similar to U.S. deficiency payments.

The reforms created some practical obstacles to how far the EC could go in reducing its trade restrictions in a GATT agreement. The need for import barriers and export subsidies, the focus of the concerns of the EC's negotiating partners, depended on the level of support provided by the EC countries. When domestic supports are reduced, as in the CAP reforms, individual countries have less need to enact trade-distorting measures to protect their domestic markets. A country may reduce such barriers even further, but the cost could be prohibitive without costly expenditures or further reductions in domestic support, both of which are likely to be controversial. This explains the mandate given by the EC countries to its negotiators on the EC Commission that any agreement it reached with the U.S. or in the MTN had to be compatible with CAP reform.

The MTN and the Oilseeds Agreement. The EC-U.S. oilseeds agreement also dealt with the much broader agricul-

Table X. Shipment of Food Aid in Cereals
In 000 metric ton grain equivalent

Region and country	Average 1987–88, 1989–90	1990–91	1991–92	1992–93[1]
Australia	338	349	415	300
Canada	1,064	1,149	1,005	1,000
EC	2,687	2,609	3,487	3,500
By members	1,018	944	991	N/A
By organization	1,669	1,665	2,496	N/A
Japan	477	512	363	350
Norway	38	47	75	40
Sweden	110	96	128	90
Switzerland	56	103	44	50
United States	6,417	7,260	7,533	7,200
Others[2]	502	231	472	270
Total	11,689	12,356	13,522	12,800
To less developed countries	11,160	11,012	11,895	11,300

[1] Estimated.
[2] Includes Argentina, Austria, China, Finland, India, OPEC Special Fund, Saudi Arabia, Turkey, and World Food Program, but not necessarily for all years.
Source: FAO, *Food Outlook*, December 1992.

tural issues dividing them that had blocked conclusion of the MTN in 1991. The starting point for the agreement was the so-called "Dunkel Proposal," which GATT's director general, Arthur Dunkel, put forward to revive the MTN after it collapsed in December 1991 because of EC-U.S. differences over agriculture. Initially rejected by both the EC and Japan, the Dunkel paper eventually was accepted by all GATT members as a basis for negotiations. Various attempts were made to move the agricultural negotiations forward during the year, but all failed because of the EC-U.S. deadlock. If an overall MTN agreement was reached in 1993, it would likely substantially incorporate the EC-U.S. oilseeds accord. These were among its major features:

1. The average level of internal farm supports across commodities would have to be reduced 20% from a 1986–88 base. Reducing average support—as opposed to Dunkel's proposal to cut support of each commodity—and allowing credit for reductions already made would mean that neither party would have to reduce domestic support for any specific commodity from current levels. The reason was that prices that depressed the market pushed supports to unusually high levels in the 1986–88 base period, while changes in policies and stronger market prices thereafter brought reductions in support greater than 20% for many commodities. The reductions of more than 20% for some commodities would allow retention of support on others—such as dairy products and sugar—for which support had fallen less than 20%.

2. Internal support in the form of direct payments—such as the U.S. deficiency and the EC's new compensation payments—would not have to be limited for crops if they were based on a fixed acreage base and fixed yields or were paid on less than 85% of base-level production; for livestock, payments would have to be based on a fixed number of animals. The intent was to eliminate the incentive to gain larger government payments by increasing production.

3. For each agricultural commodity, the volume of exports receiving export subsidies would have to be reduced by 21% and the amount of such subsidies would have to be cut by 36% from a 1986–90 base. These provisions corresponded to the Dunkel proposal, except that the latter limited the volume of commodities subsidized to 24%. The provision

of food aid would not be restricted because it would not be counted as a subsidy under this agreement.

4. The agreement accepted the conversion of nontariff import barriers such as import quotas, licenses, and variable levies into tariffs. The new and existing tariffs on imported commodities would be cut an average of 36% from those in a 1986–90 base period over six years, with those on individual commodities reduced at least 15%. EC concerns about "rebalancing" its grain- and oilseed-import restrictions were dealt with by a commitment to consultations seeking a mutually acceptable solution if future EC imports of nongrain feed ingredients, in comparison with those in 1986–90, undermined the implementation of CAP reform. The agreement also included special safeguards to deal with disruptions caused by imports and adopted a "peace clause" sought by the EC: Internal support measures and export subsidies during the six-year implementation period that fully conformed to the agreement would not be subject to challenge under GATT rules on subsidies.

The French, however, immediately denied the validity of the agreement, claiming that the EC negotiators had exceeded their mandate by accepting provisions that were not compatible with the CAP reforms approved by the EC's members. They stated that they would wait to see what the final GATT agreement looked like and would then use all means to defeat it if it involved concessions by the EC that went beyond CAP reform. Adding to the uncertainty was how the changeover in the administration and the Congress in the U.S. would affect prospects for ratification of a GATT agreement.

Agriculture and the NAFTA. U.S. Pres. George Bush signed the NAFTA on behalf of the U.S. with Mexico and Canada on December 17, but he appeared to intend leaving submission of the agreement to Congress to the incoming administration of Bill Clinton. The NAFTA, with a target date for enactment of Jan. 1, 1994, would apply to a market with more than 360 million consumers and more than $6.4 trillion in annual output.

The NAFTA contained separate bilateral undertakings between Mexico and its U.S. and Canadian trading partners. It also incorporated the Canada-U.S. Free Trade Agreement, leaving intact its rules on agricultural tariff and

Bicentennial of Old Farmer's Almanac

For millions of Americans today, their closest brush with farm living is reruns of the television series "Green Acres." Yet (and that zany TV chestnut only proves it), the idea of the small farm remains firmly rooted in the American national consciousness. How else to explain the perennial vigour of *The Old Farmer's Almanac*, at 200 the oldest continually published periodical in the United States?

The *Almanac*'s abundant yield of horse sense and homespun humour has weathered the transition from a predominantly rural to a predominantly urban America. Its trusty nature lore, household hints, and meteorological forecasts have served generations of farm families, as well as transformed countless couch potatoes into armchair agriculturalists.

When Robert B. Thomas introduced his publication in Boston in 1792, the field of almanacs was a crowded one. Only Thomas', however, survived the next 50 years. According to the 1992 bicentennial issue, this success is attributable at least in part to a printer's joke or error

that correctly predicted a freak summer snowfall in 1816. Another windfall of publicity came in 1858, when prominent trial lawyer Abraham Lincoln used the *Almanac*'s lunar table to persuade a jury that on the midnight in question there was insufficient moonlight for his client to have murdered a man with a "slungshot." In the words of the 12th and current editor, Judson D. Hale, Sr., of Dublin, N.H., the *Almanac*'s "calendar pages and astronomical charts reflect the perfection of our Universe and its Creator, but we humans can only strive mightily to minimize our imperfections."

In true *Almanac* fashion, the commemorative edition devotes two pages to the question "What Else Is 200 Years Old This Year?" Answers include the French Republic, tomato ketchup, the presidential veto, and the formal practice of cremation in the United States. This compendium of fellow bicentenarians exemplifies the conciseness, eclecticism, and leavening wit that have kept *The Old Farmer's Almanac* in flower for two centuries.   (JIM CARNES)

nontariff barriers and transitional safeguards that went into effect in 1989. Some trilateral provisions dealt with domestic support and export subsidies. Mexico and the U.S. agreed to convert all nontariff barriers to their agricultural trade either to tariff-rate quotas or to ordinary tariffs.

Food Aid. Food aid commitments for 1992–93 were estimated by the FAO (as of December) to be smaller than the 13.5 million tons of cereal grains shipped in 1991–92. Some 6.3 million tons were moved to Africa (4.3 million to nations south of the Sahara) in 1991–92 and about 1.6 million to the former Soviet republics and eastern Europe.

Pledges by 63 donors to the regular resources of the World Food Program (WFP) for the 1991–92 biennium by the end of September totaled $1,169,000,000 (70% commodities and 30% cash), against a pledging target of $1.5 billion. Pledges through November for the 1993–94 biennium were the equivalent of $594 million. In 1992 pledges to the WFP's International Emergency Food Reserve totaled 1.2 million tons of food commodities (90% cereals) plus an additional 948,448 tons (88% cereals) devoted to protracted refugee operations of the WFP's regular resources.

The Food Aid Committee of the International Wheat Agreement approved extension to June 1995 of the Food Aid Convention, which was due to expire in June 1993. Members of the convention pledged to supply a minimum of 7,517,000 tons of grain (wheat equivalent) annually.

(RICHARD M. KENNEDY)

See also Gardening.
This article updates the *Macropædia* article The History of AGRICULTURE.

FISHERIES

According to the latest statistics compiled by the Food and Agriculture Organization (FAO) of the United Nations, total world fish catches declined in 1990, for the first time in 20 years. The 1990 total world catch was confirmed at 97,245,600 metric tons, some three million tons below the 100 million-ton record catch achieved in 1989.

The reduction in total catches was attributed largely to sharp drops in catches of Peruvian anchovy (anchoveta), which fell from 5,407,527 tons in 1989 to 3,771,477 tons in 1990, and of Alaska pollock, which fell from 6,320,902 tons to 5,792,813 tons in the same period. Declining catches were noted, however, for most of the world's top 10 commercially harvested species. The top 10 species landed in 1990 were (in order of tonnage) Alaska pollock, Japanese pilchard, South American pilchard, Chilean jack mackerel, anchoveta, European pilchard, Atlantic herring, Atlantic cod, silver carp, and chub mackerel. These species produced a combined total world catch of 29,773,392 tons against 33,066,730 tons in 1989, a reduction of 3,293,338 tons. Catches of other major species such as skipjack tuna, common carp, grass carp, yellowfin tuna, capelin, large hairtail, bighead carp, and Atlantic mackerel rose slightly, while notable increases were recorded for blue grenadier, Atlantic horse mackerel, Japanese anchovy, and European anchovy. However, none of these was sufficient to offset the deficit.

China emerged as the world's top catching nation in 1990, increasing its total catch from 11,219,992 tons in 1989 to 12,093,363 tons. The U.S.S.R. fell into second position, with total landings of 10,389,030 tons in 1990 against 11,310,091 tons the previous year. The top 10 catching nations in 1990 were China, the U.S.S.R., Japan, Peru, the U.S., Chile, India, Indonesia, South Korea, and Thailand. Together, they accounted for landings totaling 63,033,489 tons in 1990 against 64,710,344 tons in 1989. Thus the world's 10 major fishing nations were responsible for more than half the 3,090,000-ton shortfall in 1990 total world catches.

Worldwide, the matter of overfishing remained of great concern. Despite the continuing imposition of stringent quotas and other restrictions on fishing, major fish stocks remained under pressure. The consequently reduced catches contributed greatly to the economic hardship faced by fishing communities in several coastal fishing nations. Notable among these were Iceland, with an economy based largely on fishing, and Canada's provinces of Newfoundland and Nova Scotia, where layoffs and bankruptcies became the order of the day.

In recent years Canada had campaigned vigorously to reduce what it described as illegal fishing by European Communities (EC) fishermen operating on the boundary of Canada's 200-mi exclusive economic zone on the Grand Banks. In this area valuable northern cod and flatfish stocks straddle the 200-mi demarcation line between Canadian and international waters. The Canadian government claimed that overfishing of straddling stocks by EC fleets in the Northwest Atlantic since 1986 had totaled more than 400,000 tons above internationally established quotas, and depletion of these stocks in the past five years had caused quota reductions of 50% in some stocks, with the loss of 300,000 tons of fish by Canada. This, Canada claimed, had contributed to a one-third reduction in its offshore fleet and caused considerable hardship in traditional fishing communities. The issue became one of significant political and economic importance, with Canada—supported by the World Wildlife Fund—and the EC at loggerheads. In a move to protect fish stocks, Canada imposed a two-year ban on domestic fishing for northern cod along the northeastern coast of Newfoundland and Labrador and called on the EC to withdraw its fleets. The EC subsequently imposed a temporary ban on fishing for cod in the area, but not in recognition of Canada's claims; rather, it moved on the basis that the EC quota had been fulfilled. The EC denied Canada's claims and said that the presence of the EC fleets on the Grand Banks was minor compared with that of others.

Europe was not without its share of problems at home, and there was concern that reduced EC catches of fish for human consumption rendered the EC less self-sufficient and more dependent on imports of fish to satisfy growing consumption. Until 1988 the EC had been able to meet its own demand for fish, but it was predicted that, despite increased aquaculture production, the early 1990s would find the EC becoming more and more dependent on imports of popular fish and shellfish species such as cod, herring, and shrimp.

The poor situation prevailing in most of the world's fisheries showed little prospect of recovery and indeed seemed unlikely to improve until the mid-1990s. High costs and limited access to fishing grounds led to bankruptcies among fishing companies and fish processors and did nothing to aid the plight of the shore-based infrastructure; shipyards continued to report lack of orders for new buildings, especially for larger, oceangoing vessels, and banks remained reluctant to lend. The economic impact was severe among smaller- and larger-sized suppliers and manufacturers alike and led to a spate of acquisitions, mergers, bankruptcies, and insolvencies.

The growing trend toward healthy eating continued to stimulate demand for fish and shellfish products. In Europe, for example, consumption of finfish products was predicted to reach 5,320,000 tons by the mid-1990s, while shellfish consumption would rise to 2,350,000 tons. Spain, Germany, and France would remain the most important European markets for these products. In response to anticipated continuing growth in demand for fish and fish products, fishermen and producers sought new grounds and more efficient processing techniques to increase yield. Deepwater trials had already proved successful in several countries, including New Zealand and Australia, where the discovery and commercial exploitation of such species as hoki and orange roughy proved to be an outstanding success. Newly discovered stocks of deepwater redfish and grenadier also seemed poised for success, with the latter already commanding high prices on the market in Spain, France, Italy, and Germany.

Similarly, the fish meal and fish oil industries were forced to seek new or underutilized stocks and to improve production efficiency. For decades, fish meal had been sold on the world market as a commodity for the animal feed industry, in competition with such products as soybeans and with prices based on protein content as the major quality criterion. It was only about 10 years since serious development of specialized fish meal products had started in Norway with the mink feed and expanding fish feed industries in mind. The high costs of fresh raw material and of the energy-intensive production process, coupled with a more discerning demand by fish farmers, paved the way for the introduction of newer, more specific product types and less energy-intensive production methods. For the past five years world fish meal production had been steady at about 6.5 million tons, with fish oil at about 1.5 million tons. This represented some 32 million tons of fish, or approximately one-third of the world's catch. The major producing countries were Chile, Peru, Japan, the U.S., the U.S.S.R., Norway, Denmark, and Iceland.   (VIVIANNE L. AERS)

This article updates the *Macropædia* article Commercial FISHING.

Table XI. World Fisheries, 1990[1]

Country	Catch in 000 metric tons		Trade in $000,000	
	Total	Inland	Imports	Exports
China	12,095.4	5,237.4	183.9	1,622.1
U.S.S.R.	10,389.0	974.9	162.9	933.4
Japan	10,353.6	208.1	10,668.3	807.5
Peru	6,875.1	31.3	1.4	506.8
U.S.	5,865.0	255.8	5,873.2	3,019.9
Chile	5,195.4	1.2	4.1	866.4
India	3,790.6	1,484.8	—	504.9
Indonesia	3,080.4	795.0	42.8	978.6
South Korea	2,750.0	33.0	364.7	1,363.3
Thailand	2,650.0	200.0	794.4	2,264.9
Philippines	2,208.8	585.8	84.8	396.0
North Korea	1,750.1	110.0	—	52.0
Norway	1,747.1	483.0	237.4	2,059.8
Canada	1,624.3	50.3	620.3	2,269.8
Denmark	1,517.2	35.8	1,116.1	2,165.5
Iceland	1,507.6	0.7	17.1	1,240.3
Spain	1,458.1	29.1	2,360.8	743.4
Mexico	1,401.0	194.6	42.2	361.4
France	896.8	48.0	2,809.0	931.2
Vietnam	850.0	240.0	—	229.2
Bangladesh	847.8	594.4	—	174.8
United Kingdom	803.5	15.9	1,811.2	961.9
Brazil	800.0	209.7	88.3	153.0
Myanmar (Burma)	743.8	114.6	—	13.0
Malaysia	602.5	14.7	145.8	228.5
Morocco	565.5	1.4	2.5	522.2
New Zealand	565.4	0.1	36.2	439.2
Argentina	555.6	10.6	6.2	318.8
South Africa	536.4	2.3	115.2	107.5
Italy	525.2	57.2	2,458.1	238.5
Pakistan	479.0	113.2	0.3	83.5
Poland	473.0	45.0	48.3	192.2
The Netherlands	438.3	5.4	843.6	1,332.8
Ghana	391.8	58.0	30.3	22.6
Ecuador	391.1	1.9	—	488.6
Germany	390.7	54.3	1,716.8	673.2
Turkey	382.2	41.7	27.8	69.5
Tanzania	337.0	330.0	0.3	6.6
Venezuela	332.3	18.8	1.3	65.6
Portugal	321.9	2.6	606.0	279.9
Nigeria	316.3	98.7	155.8	14.6
Egypt	313.0	237.7	69.0	11.4
Senegal	299.6	17.0	37.4	339.2
Namibia	289.8	0.1	...	...
Other	7,498.6	1,370.1	5,827.0	6,374.7
World	97,245.7	14,444.4	36,410.8	36,428.2

[1]Excludes aquatic mammals, crocodiles and alligators, pearls, corals, sponges, and aquatic plants.
Source: United Nations Food and Agriculture Organization, *Yearbook of Fishery Statistics*, vols. 70 and 71.

FOOD PROCESSING

While economic pressure forced many families to restrict spending on food, the trend away from traditional meals continued as more consumers combined healthy eating with convenience products. Consumption of dietary foods and fresh produce increased. In the U.K. sales of vegetarian products rose 49% over the previous year, a phenomenon not matched anywhere else in the world. The U.S. government announced new food-labeling regulations. However, ingredient and nutritional information on product labels was largely ignored by the majority of purchasers in Europe and the U.S. Fear of additives declined, and processed foods gained wider acceptance. Food-poisoning incidents continued to rise, showing that many caterers, in particular, were still not giving proper attention to hygiene.

Business Trends. The effect of recession on the food industry was hard to assess, and opinions ranged from "none" to "severe." Acquisitions and mergers worldwide were down by nearly half during the year. Many companies tried to save money by cutting their marketing budgets but were left with a reduced share of the market as a result.

German reunification and liberalization in eastern Europe provided growth opportunities that were seized by many major food companies. Salesmen were pleasantly surprised by the high brand awareness of east Germans, who for years had watched West German TV advertising. Of the 103 large food companies in eastern Germany, 52 had been privatized by March 1992. The food industry in the former Soviet Union was in a horrendous condition, with obsolete equipment and a distribution system in which half the food was wasted or stolen between producer and consumer. The U.S. Department of Agriculture (USDA) accepted an offer from U.S. food manufacturers to provide the former U.S.S.R. with technical assistance.

Campden Food Research Association in the U.K. set up a National Consumer Complaint Database to pool information provided by companies' own computer-based systems for handling customers' complaints. This could produce detailed analyses of complaints and help to identify their nature and cause. The U.K. food workplace became disproportionately perilous, with an accident rate second only to the construction industry. The Health and Safety Executive launched a campaign to cut the number of serious accidents. Major retailers, especially in the U.S., moved closer to a "no-stock" policy by imposing "just-in-time" deliveries on manufacturers to eliminate warehousing, a trend seen also in Europe. The additives market in the European Communities (EC) continued to grow, with flavours, phosphates, and intense sweeteners increasing the fastest in line with the rise of convenience products. Germany was the largest national market.

Technology. Despite fierce opposition from consumer groups, a new company, Vindicator Inc., started up the first U.S. irradiation plant for treating fresh foods; the $7 million plant at Mulberry, Fla., was irradiating citrus fruit, strawberries, tomatoes, and other local produce. British Technology Group USA of Philadelphia developed a process for removing from cocoa powder the protein allergens that cause rashes and migraine in some people. The proteins are denatured rather than extracted, so the taste of the finished chocolate is unaltered. ABC Research of Gainesville, Fla., perfected a method of defatting and restructuring beef to give it the fat content of turkey meat. SKW Chemicals of Trostberg, Germany, developed a process for extracting concentrated citrus oils with supercritical carbon dioxide instead of solvents; the process could be extended to the decaffeination of coffee and tea and to other food extraction processes in which organic solvents, now thought to carry a possible cancer risk, had hitherto been used. Freshtainer GmbH of Austria teamed up with the BOC Group of the U.K. to launch a system for preserving fruits and vegetables during transportation over long distances. The system controls the composition and humidity of an artificial atmosphere in the container comprising oxygen, carbon dioxide, and ethylene. It would be used by a joint venture company set up to distribute food in the former U.S.S.R. and eastern Europe.

New Products and Ingredients. While the number of new food products fell as a result of the recession, new beverages did not. Worldwide, dairy product launches plunged by half compared with the year before. Lymeswold, introduced in the U.K. in 1982 as the first new English cheese in 200 years, was withdrawn in the face of falling sales. In the U.S. new products featured less fat, cholesterol, salt, calories, and sugar, with the greatest increase in products claiming low or no fat. Another noteworthy trend was the growth of "green" marketing; the number of new products making environmental claims rose to a record level. The U.K. snack-food market was growing faster than the overall food market, and this was reflected in the number of new product launches in that sector, with savory snacks accounting for about half. Scientists at the University of Melbourne, Australia, discovered a protein that combats tooth decay and can be used in chocolate and other high-sugar products. It was patented in the U.S. and was expected to be cleared for commercial production within seven years.

Ault Foods Ltd. of Ontario developed Dairylite, a milk-based fat replacer containing no chemicals or additives. The result of a $5 million research investment, the product could be used in low-fat and fat-free products; the technology was to be licensed around the world. Hercules in the U.S. introduced Slendid, a fat replacer made from natural fruit pectin. Japan led the world in new product launches with around 4,000 and also led in failure rate—about 99%, compared with 80–85% in other countries. New Japanese products included a breakfast cereal made from green peas, an alcoholic milk drink, a cosmetic drink said to beautify the skin, a mineral water claimed to prevent hangovers when taken at bedtime after heavy drinking, and "healthy" fruit drinks formulated to match consumers' blood groups.

Packaging. In the U.S., where renewed interest was being shown in edible films and coatings, some eight universities

and the USDA were researching the technology. A major focus was on preserving and packing fruits and vegetables; edible wax for apples and pears was already being used. In Australia gelatin-based edible films were in use, as was an edible wrap made from rice paper in Japan. The Potato Cup Co. of Queensland, Australia, produced an edible food container for potato chips and french fries. Japanese companies were taking the lead in the emerging technology of "intelligent" packaging. Examples included a bar code printed in special ink so a bar code reader could tell instantly whether a product was past its "use by" date, and "microwave doneness" indicators. The Coca-Cola Co. introduced the first plastic soft drink bottles made with recycled plastic, with U.S. Food and Drug Administration (FDA) approval. The bottles, currently under trial, contained 25% recycled material.

Company Developments. The Swedish food machinery and packaging companies Tetra Pak and Alfa-Laval, which merged in 1991, announced that the merged group would become Tetra Laval on Jan. 1, 1993. With 35,000 employees worldwide and a turnover in 1992 of $8.5 billion, the group was one of the biggest privately owned companies in the world. Tetra Pak signed a joint venture agreement with the Kuban cooperative in Russia to manufacture, pack, and distribute a wide range of fresh and frozen food and drink products and also to make aseptic packaging materials and equipment. Nestlé of Switzerland and BSN of France formed a joint venture to purchase Cokoldovny, a large Czech food manufacturer, for $96 million. Nestlé acquired the French Perrier business for $2,760,000,000, but it was warned that the deal might contravene EC laws on competition. Nestlé also bought control of the Hong Kong and southern China business of Dairy Farm International. Taking advantage of the expiration of NutraSweet's U.S. patents on the intense sweetener aspartame, Holland Sweetener Co. invested over $30 million to quadruple its aspartame-manufacturing capacity and challenge NutraSweet's market dominance. NutraSweet responded by beginning construction of its first factory in Europe, a $45 million plant at Dunkirk, France. In the U.S. Philip Morris Companies announced plans to buy RJR Nabisco's cold cereal business.

Government Action. On December 2 the U.S. government announced new labeling rules for processed foods that would standardize such terms as *low fat, less* and *reduced* (which would now be synonymous), and *healthy* and

A protester demonstrates against the sale of irradiated strawberries. Although consumer groups opposed the practice on the grounds of safety, a company in Florida began irradiating several types of produce in 1992.

would allow consumers to determine the nutritional content of food products. The rules did not apply to fresh meat, poultry, fish, and produce. Manufacturers had until May 1994 to comply. The number of U.S. states with labeling laws regulating "green" claims reached 14. An EC directive on nutrition labeling for foods came into force on April 1, 1992. A regulation controlling the production of organically grown foods and the labeling of products containing them also appeared in the EC, as did the final draft of a packaging waste directive setting recycling and recovery targets. The U.K. government introduced regulations setting a maximum limit of 125 mg of caffeine per litre of beverage and abolishing the minimum sugar level requirement in soft drinks.   (ANTHONY WOOLLEN)

See also Environment; Health and Disease; Industrial Review: *Beverages; Textiles; Tobacco.*

This article updates the *Macropædia* article FOOD PROCESSING.

Anthropology

The ancestors of the modern prosimians (lemurs, lorises, and tarsiers), the "prosimian primates of modern aspect," were well established by the mid-Eocene, about 45 million years ago. They must have originated in the previous epoch, the Paleocene, but all that has been found so far are the "archaic primates" or Plesiadapiformes, which probably were not really primates at all. Two new fossils from that group, *Ignacius* and *Phenacolemur,* from the earliest Eocene of Wyoming, do have some anatomic similarities to the primates, but what they most resemble are the Dermoptera, represented today by the "flying lemur"—an animal that does not fly (it glides) and certainly is not a lemur. Thus the "archaic primates" from the Paleocene of North America and Europe are not the ancestral primates they were once thought to be. Where, then, did the primates originate? A new find from the Paleocene of Morocco, *Altiatlasius,* may be a primate. If so, it provides additional support for an African origin of the Primate order. Another new fossil, *Algeripithecus,* from the Late Eocene and Early Oligocene of Africa, is an early anthropoid. This is part of the growing evidence that the ancestors of the monkeys diverged from those of the prosimians far earlier than had previously been believed.

In 1992 Meave Leakey reported the discovery of a hominoid fossil from the Oligocene of Kenya, 27 million to 24 million years ago. Since it is estimated that the ape/human line split from the monkey line somewhere between 32 million and 22 million years ago, this is not only the oldest hominoid found to date but one very near that important divergence. In the Miocene there was an extensive radiation of these hominoids in Africa, Asia, and Europe. These were diverse groups, but after the Middle Miocene, during the period 14 million to 4 million years ago, there is a great gap in the fossil record. A new find in that gap was a relatively complete fossil skull from Greece. It was dated at 9 million–10 million years ago and assigned to the genus *Ouranopithecus.* Some considered it to be a hominid—a member of the Hominidae.

An interesting new *Australopithecus* fossil was found in an area that is geographically between eastern and southern Africa, the areas where all previous finds have been made. It was described as being morphologically gracile—somewhat intermediate between the less rugged australopithecines and *Homo habilis.* With Ethiopia once again open to paleontologists, a number of new finds were reported. At Hadar, *A. afarensis* bones were discovered that date 500,000 years prior to the well-known *A. afarensis* fossil Lucy. They had

not yet been fully described, but it appeared that there was a great diversity of shapes and sizes and that in general these hominids were more powerful in their arms and shoulders than Lucy. At a different site in the area called Fejej, hominid teeth were found that date between 3.7 million and 4.4 million years ago.

In the "taxonomic space" between the australopithecines and *H. erectus,* during a period of about 2.4 million–1.6 million years, is *H. habilis.* In 1991 Andrew Hill was able to use an argon-dating technique on a *Homo* temporal bone originally found in Kenya in 1965. The date of 2.4 million years ago made this the earliest date for the genus. This coincides with a time when that part of Africa shifted to a dryer climate, and it is close in time to the date of the first stone tools. *H. habilis,* first identified at Olduvai Gorge in 1959, was now represented by a number of specimens from the Rift Valley and even one from South Africa. But are they all one species? Bernard Wood believed not. He saw evidence for a substantial radiation of these early members of the genus *Homo.* At the Kenyan site of Koobi Fora he could identify three species, all representing adaptive shifts away from the australopithecine ancestral forms.

The year 1990 marked the hundredth anniversary of the discovery of Java Man, and two monographs on *H. erectus* were published, one by G.P. Rightmire, the other by Jia Laupo and Huang Weiwen. A number of African fossils were getting a second look, as it were, to determine whether they indeed warranted designation as *H. erectus.* Among them were the fossils at Ternifine in North Africa and Swartkrans in South Africa and a number of specimens from Olduvai Gorge, Lake Turkana, and Koobi Fora. The early European hominids, on the other hand, were still not considered *H. erectus* by most investigators. One recent find, a mandible with 16 teeth from Georgia in Transcaucasia, was of great interest since it was dated at between 900,000 and 1.6 million years ago. That was older than any western European hominid, although million-year-old stone tools had been found in France.

Neanderthal research included the redating of the St. Césaire fossil by thermoluminescence at 36,000 (±3,000) years ago. The previous dates were 31,000 to 34,000 years ago. This was still the last of the known Neanderthals who used an Upper Paleolithic stone industry, and it may have coexisted with anatomically modern humans. It is a problem that this interesting period of 50,000 to 30,000 years ago is beyond the reach of radiocarbon dating, but the thermoluminescence, uranium series, and electron-spin resonance techniques should yield some interesting information for the time period when Neanderthals and moderns may have lived side by side in parts of Europe, Asia, and the Middle East. The Israeli Neanderthal cave sites of Tabun and Kebara are dated at 120,000 and 60,000 years ago, respectively, while the caves occupied by modern humans are dated at 100,000 years ago. Recent fossil finds in China also indicate the possible coexistence, about 350,000 years ago, of modern humans with anatomically less modern forms, in this case presumably *H. erectus.*

The "Eve hypothesis" of a common African ancestor of anatomically modern humans, as first published in 1987, was criticized for methodological shortcomings: the mitochondrial DNA (mtDNA) analysis could have been better done, African-Americans should not have been used to represent Africans, and the computer program used to build the tree of relationship had its shortcomings. In 1991 Allan Wilson and colleagues corrected these flaws and, if anything, their original findings were reinforced. Then it was found that the conclusions of the study were a product of how the data

(continued on page 96)

The Changing Status of Women in Muslim Societies

BY KHAWAR MUMTAZ

Since the turn of the century, the condition of women in Muslim societies has been undergoing change—slow in some instances, cataclysmic in others, but complex everywhere. To comprehend this one must bear the following factors in mind:

- While Islam remains a major reference point, a strong determinant of the role and status of women has been the social, political, and economic development of each society. The Muslim world is not a single homogeneous entity; it comprises diverse societies and peoples with diverse histories of state and class formation. The situation of Muslim women is differentiated by country and also, within each society, by class, ethnicity, rural or urban location, and level of development.

- Though significant variations exist among Muslim societies, there are also persistent similarities, specifically in the condition of women. These emanate in large part from Islam. Culture, class, kinship, and political system interact with Islamic tenets to determine women's position or the extent of their subordination. Thus the desire to control women seems to pervade all Muslim societies.

- The ferment of change accompanying the collapse of colonialism and the concomitant global rearrangements left Muslim societies caught between the economic compulsion to integrate with world capitalism and the psychological need to assert their identity. In the absence of appropriate social structures to cope with transition, Muslim states have looked toward Islam to provide legitimizing ideologies. In the process women have been used as both instruments of change—inducted into nationalist struggles (Algeria, Iran) and subsequently into the industrial sector—and repositories of identity, pushed behind the veil and denied autonomy.

- Islam as a religion operates at many levels—as personal faith, symbol of identity, political motivator/mobilizer, instrument to be used in the pursuit of legitimacy and power. Sometimes one aspect dominates, sometimes another.

- With the rise of the "fundamentalists," drawn largely from the alienated, newly urbanized, and upwardly mobile classes, the struggle for power between various forces—secularists, reformists, and obscurantists/traditionalists—has sharpened. From this perspective, recent "Islamic" movements are more a political phenomenon than a religious revival. Against this background, the woman question has emerged as central in defining the nature of the Muslim society. Proper dress, modest behaviour, visibility in public spaces, women's roles—all have become major issues of debate.

Religious Sources. The two main sources of Islam are the Qur'an, embodying the texts revealed to the Prophet

Khawar Mumtaz is coordinator of the Shirkatgah women's resource centre in Lahore, Pak. She is the coauthor of Women of Pakistan: Two Steps Forward, One Step Back? (London, Zed Books, 1987).

Muhammad at Mecca and Medina in AD 607–632, and sunna, his practice. Hadith documents the sunna and is the form in which the sayings and actions of the Prophet are transmitted. Qur'an, sunna, and Hadith are considered the keys to understanding Islam as a doctrine and as a code of conduct for Muslims. Shari'ah is Islamic law based on these sources. The authenticity of the overwhelming volume of Hadith literature, collected and compiled from oral transmissions traced to the Prophet's time, has been the subject of controversy. The authenticity of each Hadith is determined by the integrity of the chain of transmitters. A substantial number of Hadith relating to women have been faulted on this count, but they have remained in circulation. Their status (authenticity) has blurred over time, but their emotive aspect is ingrained in the Muslim psyche.

Muslims are divided into Sunnites, the followers of the Prophet's tradition, and Shi'ites, those who accept only the traditions of the Prophet's family. The split occurred in AD 658 over the selection of the fourth caliph. Each group follows its specific texts of fiqh (religious knowledge) as sources of the Shari'ah. Sunni Islam has four major schools of law, developed on the basis of interpretation of theology and law during the first century of the introduction of Islam: Hanafi, Maliki, Shafi'i, and Hanbali. The Hanafis are spread across Turkey, The Sudan, Egypt, Syria, and Central and South Asia; the Maliki school is dominant in North and West Africa; the Shafi'i school in Indonesia, Malaysia, Lower Egypt, and parts of the Arabian Peninsula, Central Asia, and East Africa; and the Hanbali in Saudi Arabia. On the question of women's rights, status, and role, the four schools agree in principle. The differences between them relate to details of legal procedures.

Women in Muslim Societies. Given the complexity of the Muslim world—diverse on the one hand, unified through Islam on the other—women's situation has improved not in a linear fashion but with a forward-and-backward movement. Two processes of change were discernible as Muslim countries came into their own. One, initiated by reformist leadership (sometimes within the Islamic framework, sometimes not), was committed to modernization and women's emancipation (e.g., Tunisia, Pakistan, Egypt, Turkey). Educational institutions for women were opened; women got the vote and representation in legislatures; new employment opportunities became available. Initially, privileged women benefited, but the overall impact was greater than their numbers warranted. At the same time, pressures of economic development and sheer survival drew women into the modern industrial and services sectors. The other process of change arose from resistance to this modernizing trend by indigenous emerging elites galvanized by traditional Islam. As these forces grew, their ability to manipulate gains for themselves within existing systems also increased. Women, weak and unorganized in most countries, found their rights falling victim to political bargaining.

In Algeria following the liberation struggle, the constitution of 1963 guaranteed women the same rights and duties as men. These, however, were contravened in 1984 by passage of the Family Code. Women's status was thus frozen in line with the existing patriarchal traditions. A woman is given in marriage by the (male) guardian; she does not have the right of divorce; polygamy is not curtailed; and her subordination continues. The rise of the Islamic Salvation Front (FIS) in Algeria, the forced and unforced spread of the veil, the debates over what women can or cannot do (e.g., the woman runner who won a gold medal in the Barcelona Olympics was bitterly opposed by the FIS for her participation) exemplify the tensions in society.

In Iran, a predominantly Shi'ite state, new political forces—merchant class, clerics, urbanized petit bourgeoisie—succeeded in overthrowing a monarchical system. Women, who under the shah had gotten the vote, the right to enter paramilitary forces and universities, and some measure of protection under progressive family laws, mobilized in the thousands against his oppressive political system, donning the black chador (veil) as a dual symbol of resistance and identity. However, the subsequent introduction of orthodox religious laws was a step back for women. The minimum age of marriage was reduced to 13; polygamy was permitted and *mut'a* (temporary marriage) was restored; a woman's right to travel abroad and hold a passport was made conditional on the husband's permission; a dress code requiring the use of the veil was introduced; women were excluded from certain services like the judiciary. Women's education in segregated schools continues, however, as does women's entry into universities. They have the vote, have been elected to assemblies, and in recent years have vocally advocated their rights as "prescribed by Islam."

In Pakistan women experienced a setback after the 1977 military coup of Gen. Mohammad Zia-ul-Haq, who opted to use Islam as propagated by the obscurantists to legitimize his hold on power (unlike Pakistan's previous military dictator, Gen. Mohammad Ayub Khan, who had used progressive interpretations of Islam to provide relief to women). Women became the worst victims of Zia's discriminatory so-called Islamic legislation. Paradoxically, the leader of the main opposition party is a woman, Benazir Bhutto, who triumphed in the general elections of 1988 and was the first woman to head the government in a Muslim state in contemporary times.

In Saudi Arabia, a monarchy where conservative Islam prevails and no codified system of law exists, women's mobility is strongly curtailed. Women are not allowed to move out of the house without a *mehram* male (father, brother, husband, son), and their spheres of activity are determined by the state. Female education is encouraged (in segregated institutions), and women may run small, all-female businesses, such as boutiques. But in 1991, when women staged an unprecedented demonstration to demand the right to drive automobiles, they were categorically told that this was un-Islamic.

In Indonesia indicators of women's development are better than in other parts of the Muslim world (49% literacy, 53.7% female labour force participation, suffrage in 1941). There, as in parts of Malaysia, a number of Islamic legal concepts have been absorbed into customary laws that favour women. Women's mobility and entry into professions are not curtailed (women can be judges and can sit on Islamic religious courts), nor is veiling compulsory. The Islamic marriage code is applicable, however; polygamy is not banned, but monogamy may be ensured through a clause in the marriage contract, and the woman also has the right of divorce. Frenetic religious conflict is not characteristic of Indonesia, certainly as compared with other Muslim societies.

Women who benefited from past reforms have resisted the upsurge of "fundamentalist" Islam in their countries. Algerian women first demonstrated in a major way (20,000 strong) in 1982 against the Family Code. In Pakistan the Women's Action Forum was a direct response to Zia's so-called Islamization. The women's demonstration in Riyadh reflects the debate regarding expansion of women's space. At the same time, new groups of women have emerged, vocal and veiled, asserting "Islamic" rights—in Pakistan, Malaysia, Iran. The ferment and tension, debate and conflict, over definition and redefinition of women's roles is likely to continue in Muslim societies and to shape women's condition.

(continued from page 94)

were entered into the computer program and that many, many other conclusions could be equally valid. Nevertheless, what remained was a consensus that African populations of modern humans are in fact more variable in their mtDNA than peoples elsewhere and are therefore older. Beyond that, the proponents of the "out of Africa," single-point origin continued to challenge those who interpreted the data as evidence of regional continuity in all areas of the Old World. Their competing analyses remained one of the most interesting areas of research in anthropology.

Human population geneticists joined linguists and archaeologists in research on the origins of the Indo-Europeans. Are they descendants of horse-riding Kurgan invaders from the Pontic steppes or of early farmers migrating from Turkey and Asia Minor? Did agriculture spread as an idea or with the migrants? The hope was that the genetics of current populations might shed some light on these questions. In most cases, gene frequency and linguistic boundaries coincide, although there is considerable local genetic diffusion because people mate with their geographic neighbours, regardless of linguistic differences. Mass movements of populations over generations are thus difficult to measure. Also, languages, like anything that is learned, including farming, can spread horizontally. Robert Sokal found that in Europe genetic differences do associate closely with linguistic differences, even when geography is controlled for. He suggested that this may indicate that there were numerous invasions and movements of Indo-Europeans at different times, an interpretation that does not support either the Kurgan or the eastern farmer hypothesis. Luigi Luca Cavalli-Sforza, on the other hand, believed Sokal's analysis might really indicate that the Kurgans were themselves somewhat later descendants of the Indo-European-speaking farmers. Their research continued. (HERMANN K. BLEIBTREU)

See also Archaeology.
This article updates the *Macropædia* article Human EVOLUTION.

Archaeology

Eastern Hemisphere. There were two remarkable discoveries in 1992, one in France and the other in Oman on the Persian Gulf. Also, much more was learned from the frozen body of a man that melted out of an Alpine glacier in 1991. The find in France, in a cave with a deep underwater entrance on the Mediterranean coast near Marseille, was of late Pleistocene engravings and paintings. In Oman the "lost city of Ubar," on the frankincense road, was discovered with the aid of satellite photos, and preliminary excavations were begun. The previous year's remarkable find (about 5,000 years old), the body of a fully clothed man and his possessions, gave valuable information on what life was like in the late Neolithic in central Europe.

The use of special cameras carried on satellites was becoming more widespread and useful. The traces of very old sites and of roads, fields, and other remains of ancient use—not easily visible on the ground—could be located in this way. There was also increasing use of computers for handling great quantities of descriptive data in the records of finds from large excavations. At Pompeii, for example, a new data base was set up to help untangle records reaching back almost 200 years.

There were many archaeologically important regions of the Old World where, because of political turmoil, no fieldwork could be done. Field excavations in Iraq, for example, were terminated by the Gulf war, and few foreign archaeologists had even been allowed to visit the country. It was

In April archaeologists announced the discovery of remains of the ancient fortified city known as Saffara Metropolis, in what is now southern Oman. The city, a centre in the trade in frankincense, was located with the aid of satellite photography.

JURIS ZARINS

known that art markets in the West were selling artifacts from Iraqi museums.

Pleistocene Prehistory. The European cave art (about 20,000 years old) in the cave near Marseille was of great importance. The late Pleistocene sea level was 37 m (121 ft) below the present surface of the Mediterranean. From a rocky bluff, now underwater, a cave gallery sloped up from the beach to a large chamber. This chamber itself is mostly above the present water-fill of the gallery. A French deep-sea diver, searching for evidence of Paleolithic art, entered the gallery and made his way up to the open chamber. Many engravings of human hands, usually with incomplete fingers, were present, as well as engravings and paintings of bison, ibex, stag, chamois, horse, felines, seals, and penguins. A real problem was whether the public could ever visit the gallery. Two other end-Pleistocene sites were of interest. In southern Egypt, some 95 km (about 60 mi) west of Abu Simbel in the desert, the remains of seeds of sorghum and millet were recovered. It was not clear that actual domestication of these food plants was involved, but they were apparently being harvested. On Cyprus a collapsed and eroded rock shelter yielded many animal bones, mostly of the now extinct pygmy hippopotamus. It was suggested that early human settlers on Cyprus were the cause of the hippo's extinction.

Middle East. In Egypt considerable activity took place around Giza, as well as in the Luxor region. At the yearly meeting of the American Association for the Advancement of Science, a sharp debate focused on the date for the Sphinx; a geologist claimed that it was several thousand years older than the 2500 BC date supported by archaeologists. Mark Lehner of the University of Chicago urged the later date on archaeological grounds. He had also undertaken a computer "re-creation" of the Sphinx's original appearance. At Abydos, 12 3rd-millennium boats, encased in mud bricks (as burials), were exposed. The restoration of the magnificent tomb of Queen Nefertari was completed.

In Israel a geologist, after carefully examining Jerusalem's ancient subterranean waterworks, showed that they were adapted from a natural karst system and not dug out by hand. A Harvard University excavation at Ashkelon, on the coast in southern Israel, suggested that the Philistines were linked to the early Greeks. The family tomb of Caiaphas, the Jewish high priest who presided at the trial of Jesus, was discovered in a desert cave near Jerusalem. Israeli archaeologists continued their work at the port town of Caesarea, near Haifa, and at the Roman-Byzantine portion of the site of Bet She'an.

In Jordan the work of German excavators at the early pre-ceramic village of Basta was of particular interest. In the port area clearances at Aqaba, an Oriental Institute (Chicago) exposure encountered a horde of gold coins; probably they had belonged to a pilgrim coming from southern Morocco en route to Mecca around AD 1000. A report on the work at Tell Sabi Abyad, a large Halafian site in northern Syria, appeared in the *American Journal of Archaeology.* The yield showed the settlement's transition from a pre-Halafian early village to a fully developed, large Halafian town.

There was a fair amount of archaeological activity in Turkey, covered in Machteld Mellinck's yearly survey in the *American Journal of Archaeology.* Increased attention was being paid to the regions of Anatolia south of the Tauros, where the beginnings of the region's settled village life developed, with linkages toward Mesopotamia. New evidence of a somewhat different early village development, more to the north and west, was also being recovered. Nevali Cori and the even earlier Hallan Cemi were important very early village sites in the south and east; Asikli was a promising example of further developments toward the northwest. In west coastal Thrace, Hoca Cesme was a site with important linkages to eastern Europe.

The Greco-Roman World. Satellite remote-sensing techniques used in Greece near Preveza, at the site of Nikopolis, showed changing relationships in the area, from earlier prehistoric to medieval times. At the site of Midea, in the Argolid, an important yield of Mycenaean material was recovered. Elizabeth Gebhard of the University of Illinois at Chicago made new clearances in the temple of Poseidon at Isthmia. In the central Mediterranean, Sardinia and Sicily received attention, especially for their occupations during pre-Classical times. On Sardinia some paleolithic remains had been recovered, as well as evidence of a long sequence of developments from 5000 BC onward. A report on the examination of the gardens of Hadrian's Villa in Rome yielded interesting evidence of how Roman gardens were managed. On the Adriatic coast, near Brindisi, a diver discovered over 1,000 pieces of Roman bronze statue fragments and tools at a depth of about 15 m (50 ft).

On the extreme eastern end of the Greco-Roman world, and perhaps reaching much further back in time, was the site taken to be the so-called lost city of Ubar, located in the desert of Oman by satellite photos. The effort was instigated by a pair of amateurs, whose interest focused on the location of the ancient frankincense route and the possibility that satellite photos might be used to locate it. Once the surface indications had been found, Juris Zarins of Southwest Missouri State University, an expert on the Arabian area, was appointed field director, and preliminary investigations were begun.

Pre-Classical Europe. Further investigations of the Alpine "mummy" confirmed that the man had been high in the mountains, probably hunting, when a freezing fog caused his death. Details of his clothing and the tools and weapons he carried give a very personal picture of what life must have been like for a late prehistoric European of about 5,000 years ago. The fact that he had a copper ax was of added interest.

New radiocarbon dates placed Great Orme Head in Wales, long taken to be the remains of a Roman copper mine, at between 1800 and 600 BC. In England, Flag Fen, adjacent to Peterborough, Cambridgeshire, had an alignment of wooden posts and a wooden platform about 1.4 ha (3.5 ac) in area. The late Bronze Age site was being recovered from a region where the wetlands were drying out. At Svenloji, Lithuania, the remains of huts around an extinct lake yielded evidence of the lives of hunter-gatherers and fishers of about 3500–2000 BC near the Baltic Sea.

Africa, Asia, and the Pacific. Political turmoil in Africa probably had much to do with the lack of archaeological news from that region. New work on the impressive remains of stone buildings in Kenya indicated that they were probably built by the indigenous inhabitants. In the Deccan, in India, excavation on two early 2nd-millennium BC sites yielded evidence of craft specialization. Liangzhu (Liang-chu), China, showed evidence of late Neolithic development, with much attention to the working of jade ornaments. Interest in the problem of when Pacific voyagers first reached New Zealand was being stimulated by an impressive series of radiocarbon age assays. The samples began their cluster around AD 1200.   (ROBERT J. BRAIDWOOD)

Western Hemisphere. Archaeological research and a series of new discoveries in North and Latin America focused attention in 1992 on the insights that can be derived from

Stencils of hands are among prehistoric drawings, said to rival those at Lascaux, found in a cave on the coast of France near Marseille. Because of a rise in sea level, the entrance to the cave was submerged although the chamber itself remained mostly dry.

the proper documentation of human remains. In addition to the announcement of extensive new discoveries of both precontact and historic-period burials of the Maya and Aztecs in Mexico, there was confirmation of the earliest dated human remains in North America. At Jamestown, Va., archaeologists exposed the remains of the first Indian village destroyed by the English colonists. While archaeologists have often been noted for their use of modern scientific techniques to study the past, the year saw the vivid application of traditional archaeological procedures toward the documentation of recent mass burials, in this instance the mass graves of villagers in El Salvador who fell victim to right-wing death squads.

In October the *New York Times* featured a front-page article coupled with a large photograph of forensic archaeologists exposing the mass grave of 38 children, reported to have been among 792 victims massacred by U.S.-trained Salvadoran soldiers over a decade earlier. Local Indian farmers had claimed that counterinsurgency units "rampaged" through El Mozote province in eastern El Salvador, and the stark archaeological evidence verified their claims. The team of forensic archaeologists from Argentina was exposing the remains to provide evidence to present to the Truth Commission, set up under the El Salvador peace agreements to investigate human rights abuses. Once documented and exhumed, the remains would be sent to the University of California at Berkeley for genetic analysis aimed at matching the archaeological traces of DNA with that of survivors.

Improvements in the techniques of radiocarbon dating permitted the evaluation of increasingly smaller samples. In 1992, 0.5 g of ancient skull material provided fresh evidence that the skeletal remains of a woman, found by amateur archaeologists in 1953 near Midland, Texas, date back to at least 11,600 years before the present, with a standard deviation of plus or minus 800 years. Announced by Curtis McKinney of Southern Methodist University, Dallas, Texas, the new chronometric results established the earliest known human remains in North America and the only known example of an individual of the Clovis culture, which was distinguished by the manufacture of distinctive chipped-stone spear points.

Archaeologists conducting a salvage excavation at a construction site eight kilometres (five miles) west of Akron, Ohio, under the direction of David Brose, chief curator of archaeology at the Cleveland (Ohio) Museum of Natural History, announced the discovery of traces of the oldest known structural remains in North America, dating to 10200 BC. The find, consisting of three postholes and two pits covering a 14-sq m (150-sq ft) area, was described by John Blank of Cleveland State University as among the most important in the eastern U.S. in 20 years. The antiquity of the ancient structural remains was supported by the discovery of associated Clovis fluted points, which have been dated elsewhere to 12,000 years before the present.

Salvage excavations at a site being developed into a golf course near Jamestown yielded Native American human and structural remains from the village of Paspahegh, the Indian village closest to Jamestown, the first English colony to survive in North America. The project field supervisor, Mary Ellen Hodges, working under the direction of Nick Luccketti, director of the James River Institute of Archaeology, reported to the Associated Press that the work to date had exposed seven whole skeletons and partial remains of five other individuals. The village site included at least 40 structures, apparently dating to between 1500 and 1610. The village was attacked by the British settlers under Lord Thomas De La Warr; 60 people were murdered, and the village was burned to the ground. According to Hel-

Archaeologists digging at the Mayan city of Copán, in western Honduras, found what they believed was the tomb of a 6th-century king who had died before age 30. Of the contents, ceramic vessels were especially well preserved.
WENDY MURRAY ZOBA

en Rountree, professor of anthropology at Old Dominion University, Norfolk, Va., the event marked the first attempt by the English to take over native territory and the first recorded instance in which Native American women and children were killed.

The issue of national rights and responsibilities with regard to marine archaeological resources was brought to the fore by the discovery and salvage of a Spanish cargo ship found untouched in the estuary of the Río de la Plata offshore from Montevideo, Uruguay. A team headed by a private investment and salvor group under the direction of Rubin Collado, an Argentine treasure hunter and investor, announced the recovery to date of 1,600 gold coins, 3.3 kg (7.3 lb) of gold bullion bars, and three additional "masses" of consolidated gold coin hoards weighing 2.3 kg (5 lb) apiece. While estimates varied wildly, some government functionaries projected that the government's 50% share would be sufficient to cover the national debt. At least one scientist, marine archaeologist James Parrent, cautioned to the *New York Times,* however, that by the 18th century few Spanish ships were carrying large stocks of gold since the sources in Peru had been largely exhausted by that time.

Caribbean archaeology was advanced by the discovery by Robert Carr, while working for the Spanish Wells Museum, of the remains of the first British settlers in the Bahamas. In May archaeologists and government officials announced the discovery in Preacher's Cave on North Eleuthera, some 320 km (200 mi) east of Miami, Fla., of the domestic remains of a small sect, remembered as the "Eleutherian Adventurers." Their ship was breached on a reef in 1648, and they used the cave until the 1660s. In addition to the bodies of three children found in a small cemetery within the cave, the archaeological team documented the recovery of a range of datable 17th-century historic artifacts. The findings represented the earliest evidence of British settlement on the island.

Working just ahead of the bulldozers constructing Mexico City's new subway system, teams of Mexican archaeologists under the direction of Salvador Pulido discovered the colonial-era graves of hundreds of Aztecs, possibly the first victims of European diseases taken to the capital by the conquistadors. After the initial discovery of 50 graves in March, extensive interments were found adjacent to one of the New World's first hospitals, which operated until the 20th century. In a press account, Pulido indicated that the majority of the dead, many of them children, were found

clasping rosaries and crucifixes. Imported diseases reduced the Aztec population of Mexico City from 60,000 to 18,000 within two years of the arrival of Cortés.

In Honduras the year was marked by the discovery of what appeared to be an almost undisturbed royal tomb at the ancient Mayan capital of Copán. The tomb dated to the 6th century AD, the peak of the Classic period, nearly three centuries before the city collapsed. In April, José María Casco of the Honduran Institute of Anthropology and History announced the discovery of a 3.7 × 1.5-m (12 × 5-ft) stone-lined tomb with a 1.5-m-high roof of stone arches. The find was made by a joint Honduran–U.S. team under the overall direction of William L. Fash of Northern Illinois University. The actual discovery was made by an anthropology graduate student from the University of Pennsylvania, excavating under the direction of Robert J. Sharer of the University Museum.

The moment of discovery matched the romantic images of an Indiana Jones movie. The student came upon the tomb while excavating to clear a stone stairway. Under the staircase she recognized a line of eight stone beams, one of which had partially collapsed. In the gap between the beams, the archaeologist saw the chipped interior of a red plaster-lined stone chamber containing a royal body, raised on a stone slab covered with jade beads, carved shells, and other jewelry. Around it on the floor were over two dozen decorated ceramic pots filled with shells, beads, and animal bones. Initial photographs taken by remote cameras showed the teeth to be in good condition, possibly implying a relatively young man. The stylistic details of the well-preserved pottery offerings suggested the 6th-century date for the find.

The tomb, with its apparently unlooted burial offerings, provided for the first time an undisturbed, scientifically documented sample from this least known period of Copán Mayan history. Sharer speculated that, on the basis of the age and wealth of the tomb's contents, the chamber could be that of one of the four rulers who dominated Mayan politics from Copán during the 6th through 9th centuries. Archaeologists had identified the first of these rulers as Water Lily Jaguar, who was followed by two successors known only as Rulers 8 and 9 and finally by Moon Jaguar, who ruled until the apparently sudden collapse of Copán as a key Mayan urban centre.   (JOEL W. GROSSMAN)

See also Anthropology.

This article updates the *Macropaedia* article The Study of History: *Archaeology.*

The Chiat/Day/Mojo Building, designed by Frank Gehry, includes a section in the form of giant binoculars by sculptor Claes Oldenburg. Built as headquarters for an advertising agency in Venice, Calif., the structure won a design award in 1992.
GRANT MUDFORD

Architecture

France and Spain were among the busiest sites for new architecture in 1992. Euro Disney, the vast entertainment complex in the Paris suburb of Marne-la-Vallée, opened in April. Also opening during that month was Expo 92, a world's fair in Seville, Spain. And the Olympic Games were held in Barcelona, Spain, in July and August.

Euro Disneyland comprised six hotels, an entertainment centre, a campground, and the usual theme park, at a cost of $4.4 billion on 2,000 ha (4,800 ac). The architecture—much of it designed by famous architects—received mixed reviews. The Disney Corp. was known for "theming" its architecture, which means echoing familiar buildings from history or literature. A hotel by Robert A.M. Stern, the Newport Bay Club, was modeled after American Victorian seaside resorts, and another Stern design, Hotel Cheyenne, was intended to resemble the movie set for a western. Hotel New York, by Michael Graves, embodied a jazzy Manhattan theme, and Hotel Santa Fe, by Antoine Predock, used motifs from the American Southwest. The only French architect asked to design for Euro Disneyland, Antoine Grumbach, produced an imitation Montana hunting lodge. Most observers found the themes banal. The most-praised architecture at Euro Disneyland proved to be the nonthematic entertainment complex, Festival Disney, designed by U.S. architect Frank O. Gehry, a street of shops and restaurants and shows— "Electric Avenue"—lined with 20-m (66-ft)-high ruby-and-silver-striped stainless-steel towers.

In Barcelona the architecture fared better. Barcelona in recent years had been regarded architecturally as one of the most progressive cities in the world. Designers, led by Oriel Bohigas, deliberately used the Olympics to reshape the city, placing Olympic facilities in locations where they could stimulate urban renewal. Among prominent individual buildings were the Olympic stadium by Arata Isozaki of Japan, a sports palace by Bonell & Gil, and archery pavilions by Miralles & Pinos. The city of Atlanta, Ga., meanwhile, began work on its 1996 Games, embarking on a master plan for 26 sports facilities.

In Seville, Expo 92 similarly stimulated $10 billion in civic improvements, including the stunning new Alamillo Bridge by architect/engineer Santiago Calatrava and a new airport by Rafael Moneo. Among the national pavilions were a high-tech British design by Nicholas Grimshaw and a more traditional wood-framed Japanese effort by Tadao Ando (see BIOGRAPHIES).

Awards. Ando was also the winner of the first Carlsberg Prize, a $225,000 honour sponsored by the well-known brewery and intended to be the architectural equivalent of the Nobel Prize. Ando was chosen by a multicultural jury that included filmmaker Wim Wenders and composer Andrew Lloyd Webber. Known for severe sculptural buildings, built usually of plain concrete, Ando was praised for "his fear of impending chaos, his will to create a haven of calm, an artistic moment amidst the overstimulation of the senses and the hysterical search for the new that is the mark of late modernity." Ando donated his prize to help young European architects travel to Japan for study.

The rival $100,000 Pritzker Prize, also promoted as a Nobel equivalent, went to Alvaro Siza of Portugal. The $115,000 Japanese Praemium Imperiale award was given to Gehry for lifetime achievement in the arts. Gehry also shared the 1992 Wolf Prize in the Arts with architects Jørn Utzon of Denmark and Sir Denys Lasdun of Britain, all sharing $100,000. In September, at ceremonies in Samarkand, Uzbekistan, the triennial Aga Khan Awards for architecture were presented to nine projects from the Islamic world, including not only buildings but also programs for restoration or construction. This was the fifth round of the Aga Khan Awards since 1980, their purpose being to nurture architecture that sustains Muslim culture while still responding to a changing world.

Massachusetts architect Benjamin Thompson received the 1992 Gold Medal of the American Institute of Architects (AIA), the highest U.S. honour. Thompson was best known for his "festival marketplaces" such as Faneuil Hall Marketplace in Boston, South Street Seaport in New York City, and Harborplace in Baltimore, Md. In December it was announced that in 1993, for the first time, there would be two Gold Medals: one posthumously to Thomas Jefferson, architect of Monticello and the University of Virginia; and the other to Kevin Roche, Irish-born, Connecticut-based architect of the Oakland Museum in California and of corporate headquarters such as the Ford Foundation in New York City and General Foods in Rye, N.Y.

The AIA also picked 10 new buildings for its annual Honor Awards. Among the better known were the Paramount Hotel renovation in New York City by Philippe Starck; Team Disney Building in Lake Buena Vista, Fla., by Isozaki; the Sainsbury Wing of the National Gallery in London by Venturi, Scott Brown; and the Canadian Centre for Architecture in Montreal by Peter Rose. The AIA's 25-Year Award for a building of lasting merit was presented to the Salk Institute in La Jolla, Calif., designed by Louis I. Kahn. The Salk was the subject of intense controversy during 1992 over a proposed addition, which by the end of the year seemed certain to be built. The New York City firm of James Stewart Polshek & Partners won the AIA's Firm Award. The Gold Medal of the Royal Institute of British Architects went to a structural engineer, Peter Rice, who collaborated with architects on such notable buildings as the Sydney (Australia) Opera House and the Pompidou Centre in Paris.

Cultural Buildings. Perhaps the biggest event in U.S. architecture in 1992 was the reopening in June of the Guggenheim Museum in New York City, a 1960 masterpiece designed by Frank Lloyd Wright. It was completely refurbished by the firm of Gwathmey Siegel, which also added a new 10-story wing of galleries and offices. Long controversial, the Gwathmey Siegel redesign restored the great spiral rotunda interior to a condition that was closer than ever before to Wright's intentions. But the new wing was widely criticized for crowding and taming the spiral as seen from outside. The Guggenheim also opened a branch in a loft building in lower Manhattan, with interiors by Isozaki, and announced an ambitious plan for other satellites in Bilbao, Spain (by Gehry), and Salzburg, Austria (by Hans Hollein).

A new Seattle (Wash.) Art Museum by Robert Venturi and Denise Scott Brown was a big curved box of grooved limestone, exhibiting a mix of pop and esoteric motifs typical of that firm. Jaipur, India, was the site of a new crafts museum by the noted Indian architect Charles Correa. Among smaller works much attention was paid to a museum for a private collector in Los Angeles by Franklin Israel. Perhaps the most eagerly anticipated U. S. building, the Disney Concert Hall for Los Angeles by Gehry, went into construction and was scheduled to open in 1996.

Commercial Buildings. Probably the most noteworthy office tower of the year was Century Tower in Tokyo by British architect Norman Foster. Overlooking the Imperial Palace at the heart of the city, Century Tower consisted of two towers of 19 and 21 stories with a full-height glass atrium between. The building responded to the earthquake threat in Tokyo with an exterior of bold, bridgelike trusses.

Chiat/Day/Mojo, an advertising agency, moved into a new three-story headquarters in Venice, Calif., designed by Gehry in collaboration with sculptors Claes Oldenburg and Coosje van Bruggen, who created an entrance lobby in the shape of a 9-m (30-ft)-high pair of binoculars. Visitors entered between the lenses. Gehry—surely the architect of the year for 1992—won further notice for his design of a remarkable line of laminated bentwood chairs and tables, unveiled in January at the Museum of Modern Art in New York City.

In Bloomington, Minn., appeared the vast Mall of America, a $625 million "megamall" designed by the Jerde Partnership of Los Angeles, with 13,000 parking spaces, 281 retail stores, 48 food stores, 21 restaurants, and 9 nightclubs, all wrapped around an amusement park. In Orlando, Fla., the ever busy Disney Corp. opened an elegant small convention centre and a golf club by Gwathmey Siegel.

Civic Buildings. A popular and critical home run was hit by the new Oriole Park at Camden Yards, a ballpark in Baltimore designed by Hellmuth, Obata & Kassabaum of St. Louis, Mo. Fans and architects alike praised its heart-of-the-city downtown location; its asymmetrical playing field, which was thought to make for a more interesting game than a more standardized layout; the intimacy with which spectator seats were placed close to the action; and the decision to integrate an 1898 freight warehouse and 1857 rail terminal into the new complex.

Cities continued to build aquariums at a record pace, including a new Tennessee Aquarium in Chattanooga by Cambridge Seven Associates and a New Jersey State Aquarium in Camden by Hillier Group. Genoa, Italy, acquired a new soccer stadium by Vittorio Gregotti, in which a piece of a demolished older stadium was preserved and applied to the facade of the new one to reduce its apparent size. The stadium's roofs were hung by cables from towers, as in a suspension bridge, for column-free viewing.

Competitions, New Commissions, and Exhibitions. Canadian/Israeli architect Moshe Safdie won a competition for a new central library in Vancouver, B.C., with a design that echoed the ancient Roman Colosseum with a curved

FREDERICK CHARLES

Although many people expressed outrage at the addition (at left of photo) to Frank Lloyd Wright's Guggenheim Museum in New York City, it was pointed out that the architect himself had proposed a similar structure. The addition, designed by Charles Gwathmey and Robert Siegel and opened in 1992, provided much-needed space for exhibitions and office functions and also allowed the interior of the original building to be restored.

The departure concourse of the new airport terminal in Seville, Spain, features arches that span the width of the broad hall. Designed by Rafael Moneo, the complex opened in time for the city's Expo 92.
DIDA BIGGI

four-story wall of reading rooms. Isozaki was winner of an international design competition for a convention centre in Nara, Japan. (An exhibition of the 10 finalist designs for Nara opened at the Museum of Modern Art in New York City in November.)

Venturi, Scott Brown bested five other finalists with a design for the Whitehall Ferry Terminal on the Battery at the tip of Manhattan Island, intended to replace a Staten Island Ferry terminal destroyed by fire. The Venturi design featured a 12-m (40-ft)-tall illuminated clock facing the harbour and a vaulted waiting room for passengers. Robert A.M. Stern was commissioned to revitalize existing theatres and other buildings along 42nd Street in New York City's Times Square after a long-controversial proposal for a group of four giant towers, by John Burgee and Philip Johnson, was quietly scrapped.

"Czech Cubism: Architecture and Design," an exhibit organized by the Vitra Design Museum of Germany and the Museum of Decorative Arts of Prague, traveled in Europe, Canada, and the U.S., displaying the work of avant-garde architects who worked in Prague in the years 1911–18. The Canadian Centre for Architecture produced an exhibit, cocurated by the centre's founder, Phyllis Lambert, entitled "Opening the Gates of Eighteenth-Century Montreal." Some 400 objects—letters, maps, portraits, drawings, deeds, and computer simulations—were deployed to explore the sources of the architecture and urban form of the city.

Preservation Issues. The Piazza d'Italia in New Orleans, La., designed by Charles Moore and regarded as an early (1975) icon of the Postmodern movement, was falling apart, and its site was threatened by redevelopment. At Ellis Island in New York Harbor, the U.S. National Park Service withdrew, under fire from preservationists, a proposal to demolish 12 historic buildings for a new hotel and conference centre. Boston's most historic structure, the Old State House, was restored by architects Goody, Clancy in a manner that preserved remnants of each period of its history.

The Art-Deco Union Terminal in Cincinnati, Ohio, perhaps the most architecturally distinguished of surviving U.S. railroad structures, reopened as home to a group of museums, as well as—for the first time in 20 years—an active rail station, used by Amtrak. At Taliesin East, the onetime

home of Frank Lloyd Wright in Wisconsin, work began on a massive renovation effort expected eventually to cost tens of millions of dollars. Wright's "Romeo and Juliet" windmill of 1897 was restored and, for the first time, members of the public were permitted to tour the house itself in small, advance-reservation groups.

Controversies. Perhaps the most controversial building design in the world in 1992 was the proposed new Bibliothèque de France in Paris by Dominique Perrault, an arrangement of four glass book towers around a podium. The towers were reduced in height by 7 m (23 ft), but that still left them at 79 m (259 ft). It was also announced that books in the towers would be protected from the sun by movable wood panels, raising the question of why the towers were glass in the first place. Construction on a modified design began in March.

The always-controversial Prince Charles of Great Britain launched a new school, the Prince of Wales Institute of Architecture, in London, with an illustrious faculty of architects of conservative tastes, including Leon Krier, Demetri Porphyrios, and Christopher Alexander, as well as the U.S. team of Andres Duany and Elizabeth Plater-Zyberk, creators of the model community of Seaside in Florida. In his inaugural speech the prince, a noted anti-Modernist, said he hoped to restore "an architecture of the heart." He was also involved in sponsoring three urban redevelopments: Paternoster Square in London, a project to erase modern buildings and restore portions of the medieval street plan near St. Paul's Cathedral; the South Bank Arts Centre, where raw concrete buildings of the late 1960s in the so-called Brutalist style of architecture were to be partially demolished and replaced with new shops, cafes, and galleries; and, largest of all, a new town called Poundbury near the city of Dorchester, to be designed by Krier.

Urban Design and Planning. Two huge waterfront developments continued in 1992. Phase one of Canary Wharf, part of the vast Docklands redevelopment on the River Thames in London, reached completion, comprising a total of 600,000 sq m (6,450,000 sq ft) of floor area, including the tallest building in Europe, a 245-m (800-ft) office tower by U.S. architect Cesar Pelli. By the year's end, however, the developer, the Canadian firm of Olympia & York, was in financial collapse, leaving the future of Canary Wharf uncertain.

In Genoa, the birthplace of Christopher Columbus, a complete renovation of the harbour was undertaken under the leadership of architect Renzo Piano. Piano had been known for such new buildings as the Pompidou Centre in Paris (with Richard Rogers) and the De Menil Collection in Houston, Texas, but in Genoa he meticulously restored historic structures, as well as collaborating on such new works as an aquarium with Cambridge Seven Associates.

Business and Practice. Times continued to be difficult for the architectural profession, mired in a worldwide recession. Seminars and conferences on finding new ways to practice were common. The so-called Earth Summit in Rio de Janeiro in June stimulated many to think about the relation between architecture and the environment, and the term *sustainable architecture* gained currency. Flooding in Chicago and rioting in Los Angeles were seen as symptoms of both physical and social decline in U.S. cities, and many architects, including the AIA, called for a new urban political agenda. Architects in Miami, Fla., established an Architecture Recovery Center to assist the rebuilding effort after Hurricane Andrew. Nine thousand people attended the annual convention of the AIA, held in Boston in June, where L. William Chapin II of Rochester, N.Y., was elected first vice president/president-elect.

James Stirling, one of the world's leading architects, died in June, at the age of 66, 12 days after being knighted by Queen Elizabeth. Stirling was noted for having changed his style radically several times during his career. His best-known work, regarded as a masterpiece of 20th-century design, was the Staatsgallerie museum of art (1983) in Stuttgart, Germany (*see* OBITUARIES). Other deaths included those of historian Spiro Kostof, 55, who was posthumously awarded the AIA Topaz Medallion for Excellence in Architectural Education; Craig Ellwood, 70, noted architect of modern houses in California; and Paul Gapp, 64, Pulitzer Prize-winning architecture critic of the *Chicago Tribune*.

(ROBERT CAMPBELL)

See also Engineering Projects; Industrial Review: *Building and Construction.*

This article updates the *Macropædia* article The History of Western ARCHITECTURE.

Art Exhibitions and Art Sales

The 500th anniversary of Columbus' voyage to America in 1492 was the occasion for a number of exhibitions in 1992. Genoa, birthplace of the explorer, was a natural venue, and one of the largest shows was mounted at the Palazzo Ducale in that city. Entitled "Due Mondi a Confronto," it comprised a multimedia presentation covering the period 1492–1728 and focusing on exploration of Europe and America. Two Columbus-year exhibitions were shown at the New York Public Library, "Mapping the New World," devoted to American mapmaking from the 16th to the 19th century, and "Native Americans in Prints and Photography." At the American Museum in Bath, England, "Columbus and His World 1451–1506" consisted of engraved maps, mostly by the cartographer Theodor de Bry, that illustrated the explorer's voyages. Two important exhibitions formed part of Expo 92, the world's fair held in Seville, Spain, in the summer. "Art and Culture in the World of 1492" drew together late 15th-century objects from many different cultures, while "Treasures of Spanish Art" included important works by major Spanish painters, among them Goya, Picasso, and Dali.

The year 1492 was also the year of the death of Lorenzo de' Medici, the great Florentine patron of art. A number of exhibitions were mounted in Italy commemorating the anniversary, including one devoted to the drawing of his time at the Uffizi. Others concentrated on manuscripts, books, and documents relating to Lorenzo and aspects of his many and varied intellectual interests.

Exploration was also the theme of a fascinating exhibition held in London at the Accademia Italiana and entitled "Rediscovering Pompeii." Unlike the last major exhibition on Pompeii in London, at the Royal Academy in 1976–77, this show concentrated not on the more famous findings and well-known aspects of Pompeiian life but rather on unknown finds, many recently discovered. It comprised only 193 exhibits, making it quite selective. Included were sculptures, frescoes, and decorative objects such as jewelry. Highlights were a fine statue of Bacchus and a complete

"Adoration of the Magi" was included in a 1992 exhibition devoted to the Italian Renaissance painter Andrea Mantegna. Organized by the Royal Academy of Arts in London and the Metropolitan Museum of Art in New York City, the large exhibition included some 130 works.

painted room with frescoes. Computer terminals offered varied experiences, among them re-creations of the eruption of Vesuvius and the experience of a Roman bath. One of the programs enabled visitors to "walk around" a Pompeiian house, examining the decorations room by room and wall by wall.

The art year was notable for the number of fine shows about sculpture and sculptors. A large exhibition at the Museo Correr in Venice devoted to the work of the neoclassical sculptor Antonio Canova was on view throughout the summer months. Paintings and drawings as well as sculpture were included. This provided the first opportunity in about 20 years for visitors to enjoy a significant number of works by this sometimes underrated artist. The show comprised 152 works, including 35 of the marbles for which he is probably best remembered. The centrepiece of the show was the collection of 11 marbles lent by the Hermitage in St. Petersburg, but works were also lent by collections in Florence, Munich, Paris, Vienna, and elsewhere, and these were added to the important holdings of the Museo Correr and other Venetian collections. There were also a number of portraits of Canova himself, together with a selection of drawings and models illustrating major sculptures and showing his expertise as a draftsman. The most important marbles were those dedicated to mythological subjects and dating from the final two decades of the 18th century. The complexity of composition was clear, as was the exquisite surface of his works. The French sculptor Clodion, a contemporary of Canova, was represented by a major summer exhibition at the Louvre in Paris, allowing a reassessment of the works of one of the greatest French sculptors of the 18th-century rococo. His subjects ranged from mythology to portraiture. Terra-cotta was his preferred medium.

Modern sculptors were not neglected. An important retrospective of the work of the 20th-century Italian sculptor

The painting "Woman in a Purple Robe" was on view in the Henri Matisse retrospective that opened in September 1992 at the Museum of Modern Art in New York City. Part of the popular exhibition was to appear in 1993 at the Pompidou Centre in Paris.

Alberto Giacometti was shown at the Musée d'Art Moderne de la Ville de Paris in the spring, one of a series of shows at that museum focusing on important artists who influenced Parisian modern art. On view were well over 100 sculptures, more than 60 paintings, and about 150 works on paper, as well as books, catalogs, special editions illustrated by the artist, and even sections of a grafittoed studio wall. In the 1920s Giacometti worked with Antoine Bourdelle, and his working life was closely connected with major French artists of the time. A major retrospective of the work of the English sculptor Henry Moore was on view at the Art Gallery of New South Wales in Sydney, Australia. It comprised nearly 200 sculptures, prints, and drawings and was the first large-scale showing of the artist's work in Australia in nearly half a century.

The Australian National Gallery in Canberra held an important exhibition entitled "Rubens and the Italian Renaissance" illustrating the influence of Italian Renaissance art and scholarship on the Flemish artist and demonstrating Rubens' vital role in disseminating Italian influence in northern Europe. A major Renaissance show devoted to the works of the Italian painter Andrea Mantegna was seen at the Royal Academy in London in the spring and from May to July at the Metropolitan Museum of Art in New York City. It was the first such exhibition in 30 years and gave a good overview of the artist's personal style and varied talent. Paintings, drawings, and prints were shown together at the Royal Academy, and the selection of prints and drawings was very large indeed, with loans from most of the major European and Italian collections.

Western art remained highly regarded in Japan, and Japanese art enthusiasts enjoyed a number of exhibitions comprising loans from European collections. Notable among them was a show at the National Museum of Western Art in Tokyo in the summer that included exquisite items of jewelry and glass by the French artist René Lalique. Opera sets and costumes designed by David Hockney were shown in Tokyo at the Bunkamura Museum of Art, and the National Museum of Modern Art at Kyoto held a large retrospective of sculpture by Isamu Noguchi, an artist as well known in the West as in Japan. In Yokohama the Sogo Museum exhibited a selection of 69 German works from the 17th to the 19th century lent by the Wallraf-Richartz Museum in Cologne. The Isetan Museum of Art in Tokyo showed "British Landscape Paintings," a survey of work by the major British artists of the 18th to 20th century, including Gainsborough, Constable, and Turner.

As usual, Paris was home to an important selection of internationally praised art exhibitions. A retrospective of the work of Toulouse-Lautrec, which had been at the Hayward Gallery, London, in the winter, moved to the Grand Palais in Paris in the spring. The selection of works on show covered 20 years of the artist's working life and included posters and lithographs as well as paintings. The integration of printed images with painterly effects was best seen in the famous posters. The show was arranged by theme, making it easy to appreciate Lautrec's variety and continuity. Almost all of Lautrec's most famous paintings were on view, but two important works, "Au Cirque Fernando" and "Bal au Moulin de la Galette" from the Art Institute of Chicago, were seen only in Paris.

"The Loves of the Gods," also at the Grand Palais in the winter, traveled to the Philadelphia Museum of Art in the spring and to the Kimbell Art Museum in Fort Worth, Texas, in the summer. This was a traveling exhibition of Old Master paintings, with works drawn from international sources—the type of exhibition that was becoming more and more difficult to mount. Sixty-eight important works were brought together, concentrating on French mythological subjects. The subtitle, "Mythological Painting from Watteau to David," demonstrated the intelligence and seriousness of the subject matter, often wrongly assessed on its purely decorative qualities. Works were lent by such diverse collections as the Philadelphia Museum of Art, the Trianon at Versailles, France, and museums in Geneva and Stockholm.

An exhibition at the Grand Palais in the autumn focused on Picasso's still-life paintings over a period of 50 years. Entitled "Picasso & les Choses," it illustrated the artist's amazing inventiveness and variety, which could infuse even the most ordinary items with artistic quality. The earliest painting, dating from 1901, was executed when Picasso was only 20. A thrilling image of the skull of a bull, painted in 1958 when the artist was nearly 80, completed the time span. The German Expressionist painter Otto Dix was another 20th-century artist honoured with a retrospective, this time at the Neue Nationalgalerie in Berlin on the occasion of the centenary of the artist's birth. A slightly revised version was also shown in London at the Tate Gallery. Little-known works from the period 1946–69 were shown with more familiar works dating from the prewar years. Many of the canvases were extremely fragile and unlikely ever to be brought together again in such a large retrospective. Part of the fragility was due to the artist's unusual technique, developed in about 1925, of painting in oil over tempera, as well as his method of using pigments, intended to re-create effects achieved by German Old Masters.

"Allegories of Modernism" at the Museum of Modern Art in New York City in the spring was a major international show devoted to drawings, an unusual subject for such an important event. The overwhelming majority of artists represented were from the U.S. or Germany, and the exhibition illustrated the varied purposes of drawing, with examples ranging from traditional studio drawings to those intended as "stand alone" works of art. Many thought-provoking examples of Postmodernism were included, providing evidence of how far drawing as an art in itself had moved in the 20th century. "Helter Skelter: L.A. Art in the 1990s," organized by the Los Angeles Museum of Contemporary Art, wanted to be provocative and succeeded. Violence, tawdriness, and cult religion were common images in the works by 16 artists, including Chris Burden, Manuel Ocampo, and Llyn Foulkes. Burden's "Medusa's Head," an enormous meteorite covered by miniature railroad tracks, was a vision of ecological disaster and one of the show's potent images.

Twentieth-century art was also the focus of the exhibition at the Guggenheim Museum in New York City celebrating that museum's reopening after two years of renovation. "The Guggenheim Museum and the Art of this Century" was a two-part show comprising "Masterpieces" and "From Brancusi to Bourgeois." The first included works selected from the collection, and the second emphasized recent art. The museum's first major loan exhibition was a show of Russian avant-garde art seen earlier at the Stedelijk Museum in Amsterdam. A major retrospective at the Museum of Modern Art in New York was devoted to the works of Henri Matisse and included some 300 paintings and more than 100 works in other mediums. The works lent included some from important Russian collections in Moscow and St. Petersburg and from the Musée National d'Art Moderne in Paris. As with many popular shows, timed admission and prebooking were employed to prevent overcrowding.

A major exhibition of the work of the Belgian Surrealist René Magritte was held at the Hayward Gallery and traveled to the Metropolitan Museum of Art. The last major exhibition devoted to Magritte had been at the Tate Gallery

"The Treachery of Images," a painting of a pipe above the text "This is not a pipe," was part of the René Magritte retrospective organized in 1992 by the Hayward Gallery in London. From there the exhibition was to travel to three U.S. cities—New York; Houston, Texas; and Chicago.
LOS ANGELES COUNTY MUSEUM OF ART, THE MR. AND MRS. WILLIAM PRESTON HARRISON COLLECTION

in 1969. The Galleria d'Arte Moderna in Verona, Italy, was the venue for the largest retrospective devoted to the work of the Swiss artist Paul Klee ever seen in Italy. The show, on view during the summer, included more than 350 paintings, watercolours, and drawings, many selected from the Klee Foundation. At the Royal Academy a retrospective devoted to the work of Alfred Sisley, one of the less famous French Impressionists, included 72 canvases illustrating the artist's work at its best. The exhibition moved from his early works in the style of Corot to his splendid, fully Impressionist landscapes of the 1870s.

The American artist Stuart Davis was the subject of a major exhibition mounted by the Metropolitan Museum of Art and also shown at the Museum of Modern Art in San Francisco. The exhibition catalog included 175 works, providing a representative overview of the artist's output during his 50 years of activity. The show included portraits and landscapes along with his well-known still-lifes. Though influenced by such movements as Cubism, Davis remained quintessentially American. An important traveling exhibition, "Master European Paintings from the National Gallery of Ireland," was shown at the Art Institute of Chicago. It comprised 44 of that museum's most important paintings, including works by Hogarth, Reynolds, Chardin, and Velázquez. The show traveled on to San Francisco, Boston, and New York.

At Dulwich College Picture Gallery in London, "Treasures of a Polish King" comprised a selection of works collected by Stanislaus Augustus, the last king of Poland. The show included works by Rembrandt, Fragonard, and Boucher lent by various public collections. An exchange exhibition in Warsaw, entitled "Collection for a King," included works by Rembrandt, Tiepolo, and Poussin, purchased for Stanislaus Augustus but undelivered at the time of his abdication and eventually given to Dulwich. "The Making of England" was the title of an exhibition at the British Museum in the late winter that concentrated on Anglo-Saxon art of AD 600–900. Included were the sole surviving copy of the epic poem *Beowulf,* the Rome Gospel, and the Stockholm Codex Aureus. A section devoted to the Northumbrian church included relics of St. Cuthbert, such as a leather-bound copy of St. John's Gospel closely connected with the saint's cult and his own altar and cross. Artifacts, manuscripts, carving, and jewelry were featured prominently. The exhibition provided a unique chance for visitors to reconsider many of the finest surviving art works from early medieval England.

(SANDRA MILLIKIN)

ART SALES

The 1991–92 auction season recorded the worst results in five years. Turnover for the year fell by 14% at Sotheby's and 10% at Christie's. This compounded the adverse effects of the previous season, when the turnover of both houses fell by around 50% from the all-time high in 1989–90, the peak of the '80s speculative boom. The decline was a direct reflection of world recession. The year also saw a steady succession of gallery closings in London, Paris, and New York, including Ackerman's, the London dealers in sporting pictures established in the 18th century, and Kasmin, David Hockney's dealer and one of the stars of the 1960s contemporary art scene. The question of central importance to the future of the art market, however, was whether A. Alfred Taubman, the U.S. tycoon, would manage to hold on to Sotheby's. *Forbes* magazine estimated that his personal fortune had fallen from $2 billion to $600 million. He sold 8 million Sotheby's shares in July for $100 million, retaining 14 million special "B" shares that carried 10 votes each and left him control of the company.

Much less material came up at auction than in previous years. The most expensive paintings came from British aristocratic collections—largely as a result of the threat that they might be banned from export by a heritage "list," a scheme subsequently rejected by the government. It appeared that Holbein's "Portrait of a Lady with a Squirrel" would make the year's top auction price when Christie's announced its forthcoming sale on behalf of the Marquess of Cholmondeley in February, but the National Gallery managed to negotiate its purchase before the auction at a tax-exempt figure of £10 million. This might have been equivalent to anything from £15 million to £25 million at auction, depending on how the Treasury decided to calculate Cholmondeley's tax bill.

That left the two highest auction prices of the year as the £10,120,000 paid by the composer Andrew Lloyd Webber for Lord Malmesbury's large Canaletto view of "The Old Horse Guards, London, from St. James's Park" and the surprise £7,480,000 for Lord Normanton's "Venus and Adonis" by Titian. The latter came up at Christie's in December cataloged as by "Titian and workshop" and estimated at £1 million. However, everyone decided it was a real Titian, especially the J. Paul Getty Museum of Malibu, Calif. The Getty paintings curator, George Goldner, did not have time to convince his trustees before the sale; Hazlitt, Gooden and Fox in London and Hermann Schickman in New York bought it together, in the hope that the Getty might take it later. It was duly bought by Malibu. Goldner remained the dominant buyer in the market. He rescued Agnew's, the Bond Street dealers, from severe financial difficulties in late 1991 by paying around £7 million for Sebastiano del Piombo's portrait of "Pope Clement VII," and he rescued a consortium of dealers by taking a large Canaletto "View of the Grand Canal" off their hands for roughly the same price.

Old Master sales remained the strongest sector of the picture market, but with few buyers around, prices were erratic. In April Christie's could not find a buyer prepared to pay the £6 million they were asking for a ravishing tiny Rembrandt, "Daniel and Cyrus Before the Idol of Bel," but Sotheby's persuaded Milwaukee (Wis.) collector Alfred Bader to give Rembrandt's portrait of Johannes Uyttenbogaert a home at £4,180,000 in July. In the Impressionist and contemporary markets, where prices collapsed in 1990, something called "bottom fishing"—seeing how low one could buy a picture—became fashionable. Christie's had the two best sales of the year, the Tremaine and McCarty-Cooper collections, and scored $7.7 million for both Tremaine's Léger, "Le Petit Dejeuner," and Cooper's Braque, "Atelier VIII." In the

---

Reattribution, or Where Have All the Rembrandts Gone?

"A thing of beauty is a joy forever." Or so observed John Keats on the immortality of great works of art. To a growing number of collectors and curators, however, the poet's words offer scant consolation. What is one to make of a Rembrandt that suddenly isn't?

In 1968 the Rembrandt Research Project (RRP), an international committee of art historians and connoisseurs based in Amsterdam, began a systematic, high-tech reassessment of the entire body of oil paintings conventionally attributed to the 17th-century Dutch master. This corpus at its most generous reach—in the flush of a 19th-century Rembrandt "revival"—exceeded 1,000 works. Subsequent inventories based on examination of technique and subject matter trimmed the number by nearly half. The esoteric pursuit of art authentication became public drama in 1992 when the RRP committee "deattributed" a number of paintings—including "The Polish Rider" (Frick Museum) and "The Girl at the Door" (Art Institute of Chicago)—formerly esteemed as unassailable masterworks.

This uncertainty in the Rembrandt canon owes more to Dutch socioeconomic history than to any grand deception. The medieval craft guild system, in which learners of all trades, including painting, served formal apprenticeships with exacting masters, still flourished in 17th-century Amsterdam. Rembrandt supervised a large studio of paying novices who diligently imitated his style. The most talented students often collaborated with the mentor himself, and several went on to achieve their own measure of fame. Rembrandt's enormous popularity encouraged anyone who owned a "Rembrandtesque" painting to consider it the real thing. It should also be noted that some painters, such as Rembrandt's Flemish contemporary Peter Paul Rubens, were more fastidious in distinguishing their own work from that of their disciples.

In its monumental effort to clarify this muddle, the RRP is employing an unprecedented combination of informed judgment and scientific objectivity. Traditional scholarly appraisal, newly focused, has accounted for most of the "demotions" thus far. But, interestingly, it is the cooler eye of technology—the X-ray and so-called dendrochronological analysis (dating of the paintings' wooden panels)—that has shown even the deattributed works to date from Rembrandt's time.

The first three volumes of a projected five-volume Corpus of Rembrandt Paintings have received a largely favourable response. A major exhibition reflecting the committee's findings thus far attracted large crowds in Amsterdam, Berlin, and London. While some owners of "former" masterpieces remained predictably unconvinced, others looked for a silver lining, such as a new interest in the often brilliantly gifted figures who laboured in Rembrandt's shadow.   (JIM CARNES)

contemporary field, 1980s art was selling much better than '60s or '70s; Charles Saatchi, the British advertising mogul, and the bankrupt estate of Swedish collector Fredrik Roos put a lot of good 1980s material on the market. There were many new price records for Latin-American artists. Diego Rivera's "The Flower Seller" set an all-time high at $2,970,-000—matching the new record for a Victorian painting, Richard Dadd's "Contradiction," paid, again, by Andrew Lloyd Webber.

In virtually every field, auctions were dominated by private buyers rather than dealers. This was notably true of the sales of important French and Continental furnishings. Some of the extraordinary prices included F 23 million for an exquisite jewel cabinet made for Queen Marie-Antoinette, $1,980,000 for a Louis XVI commode painted with roses from the Ortiz-Patino collection, $1.8 million for a pair of silver ice buckets made in Paris for Horace Walpole, £770,000 for a rococo bureau by Pietro Piffetti of Turin, and $1,210,000 for a Savonnerie carpet, the highest auction price for a carpet on record. Prices for English furniture were more hit or miss. Christie's had two hits—the sale of the Samuel Messer collection in December and Chippendale furnishings from Harewood House in July. Messer's Chippendale commode made £935,000, while a pair of Harewood silvered mirrors made £319,000.

It was generally a quiet year for the Oriental market. Chinese sales were not doing well, and Japanese buyers were suffering from recession and art market scandals back home. Korea proved to be the new wild card in the pack; a 14th-century Korean painting made 10 times estimate at $1,760,000 in October, and an 18th-century blue and white vase made seven times estimate at £418,000 in December.

Book Sales. The impact of the recession on the book market was much less marked. Heavily publicized auctions no longer made prices out of line with the market, but competition for real rarities was as strong as ever. Average prices had probably dropped some 10–15% from their peak.

It was notable that a high proportion of the year's star turns were handled by Christie's, which traditionally had done much less book business than Sotheby's. On Oct. 30, 1991, Christie's sold a pair of terrestrial and celestial globes dated 1579 and attributed to the workshop of Gerard Mercator for £1,023,000. They followed up with a 36-line Bible at £1.1 million on November 27; dating from before 1460, it was set from matrices struck in the Mainz workshop of Gutenberg. Only 14 copies were known to have survived, and this one was sold, via New York dealer H.P. Kraus, to the Scheide Library in Princeton. Christie's also set a new price record for an American letter in New York on December 5 with Abraham Lincoln's 2¼-page defense of his Emancipation Proclamation written to Major General McClernand; it sold for $748,000 to Profiles in History of Los Angeles. Sotheby's scored the other big price of the autumn, £1.1 million for one of the last complete autograph manuscripts of a major work by Beethoven in private hands, his *Piano Sonata in E Minor,* Opus 90, written in 1814. It was the highest price ever recorded for a music manuscript.

Christie's handled the top-priced books of 1992. Audubon's *The Birds of America,* with its sensational elephant folio illustrations, is always among the most expensive books in the world. A new high of $4,070,000 was set on April 24 for a copy conserved since its publication by the University of Edinburgh. Back in London on May 20, one of the first pictorial records of garden flowers, a manuscript containing 473 drawings of ornamental plants from the garden of the Nürnberg botanist and physician Joachim Camerarius (1534–98), was sold at Christie's for £638,000 to the University Library of Erlangen.

Other notable sales included the autograph manuscript of Charles Dickens' "The Haunted Man and the Ghost's Bargain," $308,000 at Sotheby's on October 11; a magnificent high Renaissance binding made in Paris for Peter Ernst von Mansfeld in 1556, £308,000 at Sotheby's on December 5; the first German edition of the Nuremberg Chronicle, $264,000 at Sotheby's on June 18; and a 1455 manuscript of Basinio da Parma's astrological poem "Astronomicon," £115,000 at Sotheby's on June 16. The most unexpected high of the year was the £253,770 realized at Phillips, London, on June 11 for the papers of the 18th-century bluestocking Catharine Macaulay (1731–91)—against a presale estimate of £20,000 to £30,000.   (GERALDINE NORMAN)

This article updates the *Macropædia* articles The History of Western PAINTING; The History of Western SCULPTURE.

Astronomy

For astronomy, 1992 was the year of Galileo, Hubble, and Compton. More than three and a half centuries ago the great astronomer and physicist Galileo Galilei was sentenced to house arrest by the Roman Catholic Church and forced to recant his view that the Earth moves around the Sun. After deliberating for 13 years, a commission appointed by the church finally announced intentions to find Galileo "not guilty." Though operating with defective optics, the orbiting Hubble Space Telescope (HST) achieved many firsts in providing exciting new images of the universe. And the Compton Gamma Ray Observatory (GRO), the first true gamma-ray telescope launched into orbit, made a host of findings about sources of these very high-energy photons coming from the Milky Way Galaxy and beyond.

Solar System. Within the solar system lie the Sun, the nine major planets and their moons, and the asteroids, comets, and other debris. New discoveries were made about each of these during the year. Earth's nearest cosmic neighbour, the Moon, always keeps one side facing Earth. Despite manned landings on the near side of the Moon, the far side still held deep mysteries. In 1992 the spacecraft Galileo, launched in 1989, returned to the Earth-Moon region as part of the complicated trajectory it was following to reach its ultimate destination in 1995, Jupiter. Galileo obtained spectacular new images of the far side of the Moon at many wavelengths, allowing scientists to assess the composition of various lunar craters. Analysis revealed that ejecta from the Orientale Basin, an impact-created feature some 1,000 km across, were excavated from the Moon's crust and not from its mantle, as had been previously thought. (One kilometre is about 0.62 mi.) On the other hand, another crater in the South Pole-Aitken Basin, which is some 2,000 km in diameter, indicated the presence of iron-rich materials, suggesting that the impact making that crater may well have penetrated into the lunar mantle.

As reported widely in 1991, Galileo was the first spacecraft to have made a close encounter with an asteroid. Although early images of the asteroid Gaspra were released that year, because of a defect in the telemetry system of the spacecraft, scientists had to wait until 1992 to get a full-colour look at the object. The newer view, which was three times sharper than before, revealed more than 600 meteorite impact craters on the 20-km-long rock. Because of the calculated high impact rate, however, scientists concluded that the asteroid must be very young, perhaps less than 200 million years old, compared with the 4.2 billion-year age of the solar system. Gaspra probably formed as a splinter of a larger asteroid following a cataclysmic interplanetary collision with another solar system body.

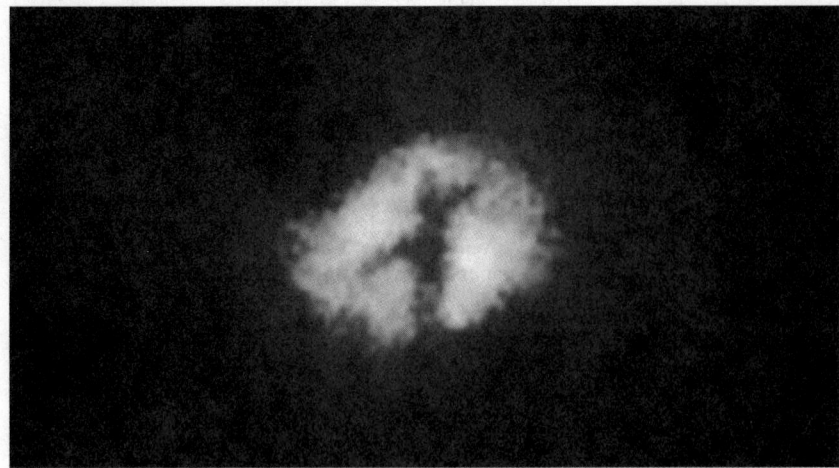

Image of the nucleus of the Whirlpool Galaxy (M51) taken with the Hubble Space Telescope reveals what astronomers believed was the first view of the dust ring surrounding a massive black hole at the galaxy's core. Forming the thicker bar of the X, the light-absorbing, doughnut-shaped ring lies almost perpendicular to the disk of the galaxy, which is oriented nearly face-on to the Earth. Hidden within the intersection of the X may be a black hole with as much mass as a million Suns.
NASA

David Jewitt of the University of Hawaii and Jane Luu of the University of California at Berkeley discovered what may be the first of a new class of objects at the edge of the solar system, beyond the orbits of Pluto and Neptune. The "planetesimal" is about 200 km in diameter. It lies 1.6 billion km beyond Neptune, or about 42 astronomical units from the Sun. (An astronomical unit, or AU, is the Earth–Sun distance.) The object, currently dubbed 1992 QB1, may well belong to a belt of icy objects whose existence the astronomer Gerard Kuiper predicted in the early 1950s. He had suggested such a belt as the source of short-period comets, such as Halley's Comet, which orbit the inner solar system with periods of less than about 200 years.

Observations of the Sun revealed for the first time the presence of fast neutrons produced in solar flares. In June 1991 GRO recorded high-energy gamma-ray emission from the Sun at the time of some very large flares. Following the optical emission from the flares, GRO found an "afterglow" of gamma rays and neutrons lasting several hours. Analysis of the data, reported in 1992, supported the notion that energetic protons are accelerated in a flare and then get trapped in loops of solar magnetic fields, subsequently striking the gas present and producing neutrons and gamma rays. Neutron images of the Sun derived from GRO data were the first-ever such images of any extraterrestrial object.

Stars. The solar system is not the only place to look for planets. In seeking possible places for life beyond Earth, scientists have usually searched for signs of planets around stars like the Sun. In 1991 scientists announced what they believed to be the discovery of a planet circling a pulsar, a highly magnetized rotating neutron star. Since a pulsar represents the last stage in the evolution of a star and is usually formed in a supernova explosion, it seemed a most unlikely place for an orbiting planet. "Detection" of the planet was based on reported slight variations in the clock-like radio pulses coming from the pulsar PSR 1829–10. In 1992, however, the discovery was withdrawn, owing to an error in the analysis of the arrival time of the pulses. Meanwhile, another detection of at least two planets around a different pulsar was reported by Alexander Wolszczan of Cornell University, Ithaca, N.Y. This object, named PSR 1257+12, appeared to have planets roughly three times the mass of the Earth that circle the pulsar in orbits similar to that of the planet Mercury about the Sun. If confirmed by further observations, the discovery would raise many questions about the late stages of stellar evolution, not to mention the origin of planets around old pulsars.

Before GRO began systematically mapping the sky in gamma rays, there had been limited satellite studies of the

gamma-ray sky. Perhaps the most perplexing discovery in the preceding two decades of gamma-ray astronomy was the object dubbed by its discoverers Geminga, which is derived from an Italian expression meaning "It's not there." Although it is the second brightest source of gamma rays in the sky, it was initially undetectable at any other wavelength. Later, weak optical and X-ray emission was detected from Geminga, but its true nature remained a mystery. Finally in 1992, observations by GRO as well as by the X-ray–detecting Röntgensatellit (ROSAT) settled part of the puzzle. Both satellites detected pulsations from the object with a period of 237 milliseconds (thousandths of a second), from which astronomers concluded that the object is a pulsar. Why its radiation properties are so different from all other pulsars, however, was still unclear.

Extragalactic Astronomy. Black holes remain an elusive quarry for detection. Though a black hole cannot be seen directly, every year astronomers report new indirect means of demonstrating the presence of these invisible, alleged denizens of the universe. In particular, black-hole mania swept over HST users in 1992. The active galaxy M87 (Virgo A), well known for the luminous jet emanating from its nucleus, was studied by Tod R. Lauer of the National Optical Astronomy Observatories in Arizona and collaborators using the HST. The galaxy lies some 50 million light-years from Earth in a comparatively nearby cluster of galaxies in the constellation Virgo. They found that the light coming from its centre is some 300 times brighter than would be expected if there were only stars at the centre. The observation, combined with the existence of a jet extending some 4,000 light-years from its core, suggests that M87 may contain a black hole having a mass two billion to three billion times that of the Sun.

Holland Ford of Johns Hopkins University, Baltimore, Md., and co-workers used the HST to make a dramatic image of what was interpreted to be a massive black hole at the centre of the spiral galaxy M51, the Whirlpool Galaxy, lying some 20 million light-years from Earth. The object's presence is marked by a dark X across the centre of the nucleus of the galaxy. The thicker of the two bars of the X was suggested to be a doughnut, or torus, of cold gas and dust about 100 light-years across that is rotating around the otherwise unseen million-solar-mass central black hole.

And closer to home in the elliptical galaxy M32, which lies only about two million light-years from Earth, Lauer and collaborator Sandra M. Faber of the University of California at Santa Cruz, using the HST, found that the density of stars increases to form a sharp "cusp" as one gets closer to the centre of the galaxy. They concluded that at its very

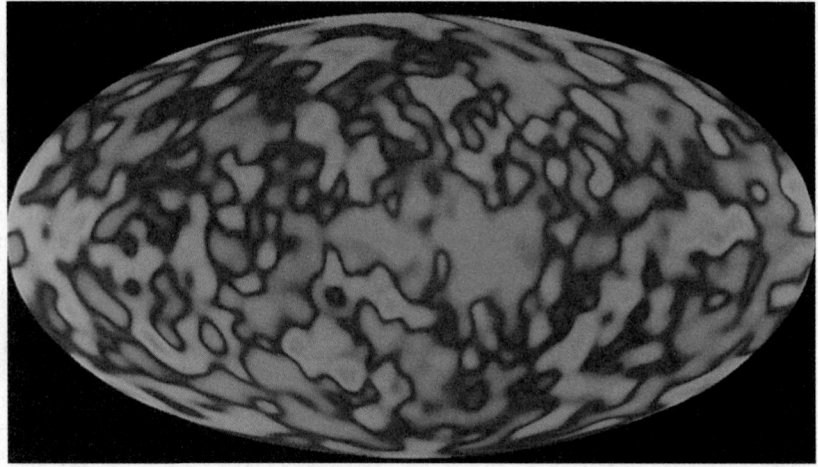

Tiny temperature fluctuations in the cosmic background radiation lurk among pink and blue patches of signal noise in this computer-enhanced map of the sky made from data collected by the Cosmic Background Explorer (COBE) satellite. The long-awaited discovery of the fluctuations, announced in April, offered critical input to theories attempting to account for the present lumpiness of matter in the universe in the form of galaxies and larger-scale structures.

NASA

core lies a black hole of perhaps three million solar masses. To some astronomers, however, the lack of jets or other sign of activity at the centre of this galaxy made the claim for a black hole less viable.

Cosmology. Hubble's name appeared in another guise throughout 1992. Edwin Hubble, for whom the HST is named, is credited with having discovered the expansion of the universe by producing the first detailed correlation between the distances to galaxies and the rate at which they appear to recede from the Milky Way and from one another (now called the Hubble law). During the past half century, astronomers have sought to establish an accurate distance to nearby galaxies, thus allowing an accurate calibration of the current expansion rate of the universe, a number called Hubble's constant. From this, one can deduce the approximate age of the universe, the time since the original big bang. Using the HST, Allan Sandage of the Observatories of the Carnegie Institution of Washington and co-workers measured the luminosity of 27 Cepheid variable stars (a class of stars whose periods of variation are proportional

to their true brightness) in the small galaxy IC 4182. This galaxy contains even brighter yardsticks called type Ia supernovas, which can also be used to calibrate Hubble's constant since these stellar explosions peak at the same brightness. Combining these observations with the best estimates for the average mass density of the universe, Sandage found that the universe is at least 15 billion years old, in good agreement with independent estimates of the ages of the oldest stars in the Milky Way. Nonetheless, at year's end many observational cosmologists—perhaps the majority—remained skeptical, arguing that the universe is younger, perhaps only half this age.

Though 1992 was an active year in astronomy, the discovery that received the greatest attention, at least in the popular press, was the detection by the Cosmic Background Explorer (COBE) satellite of small fluctuations in the microwave background radiation. The big bang model rests on four crucial observational pillars: the already mentioned Hubble law; the age of the oldest known stars; the measured abundance of the various chemical elements; and the existence of background radiation pervading the sky with a temperature of about 2.7° above absolute zero (2.7 K; $-455°$ F, or $-270°$ C). The big bang model predicts that if the universe began with an initial hot, high-density explosion, some of the lightest elements would be synthesized and radiation would be produced, initially as gamma rays, that would subsequently cool as the universe expanded. COBE had already confirmed that the cooled radiation has the predicted temperature and spectrum. And it had already found that the radiation comes from all over the sky. But the model also requires that, at some level of strength, fluctuations be seen in the radiation corresponding to places where there is structure in the universe, such as in the directions of superclusters of galaxies.

In a dramatic announcement in April, George Smoot of the University of California at Berkeley, speaking for the COBE instrument team that made the measurements, said that COBE had seen what one scientist called "the handwriting of God." What COBE found were small fluctuations, only a few parts in a million, in the temperature of the radiation observed coming from different directions in the sky. Though the significance of the discovery was still being assessed at year's end, 1992 was definitely a year for astronomy that, to rephrase T.S. Eliot, ended with a bang, not a whimper. (*See* PHYSICS.)　(KENNETH BRECHER)

See also Space Exploration.

This article updates the *Macropædia* articles THE COSMOS; GALAXIES; THE PHYSICAL SCIENCES: *Astronomy;* THE SOLAR SYSTEM; STARS AND STAR CLUSTERS.

Earth Perihelion and Aphelion, 1993

Jan. 4	Perihelion, 147,097,000 km (91,402,000 mi) from the Sun
July 5	Aphelion, 152,091,000 km (94,505,000 mi) from the Sun

Equinoxes and Solstices, 1993

March 20	Vernal equinox, 14:41[1]
June 21	Summer solstice, 09:00[1]
Sept. 23	Autumnal equinox, 00:22[1]
Dec. 21	Winter solstice, 20:26[1]

Eclipses, 1993

May 21	Sun, partial (begins 12:18[1]), visible in the central and western coterminous United States, most of Canada and Alaska, the entire Arctic region (including Greenland, northern Russia, Scandinavia, and the Baltics), and eastern Europe (including Belarus and Ukraine).
June 4	Moon, total (begins 10:10[1]), the beginning visible along the east coast of Asia, Australia, Antarctica, southern Alaska, extreme western Canada, western United States, most of Mexico, the coastal regions of Peru and Ecuador, southwestern South America, the Pacific Ocean, and the southeastern Indian Ocean; the end visible in most of eastern and south central Asia, Madagascar, Australia, Antarctica, the Hawaiian and the Aleutian islands, the Indian Ocean, and the western Pacific Ocean.
Nov. 13	Sun, partial (begins 19:46[1]), visible in Antarctica, the southern tip of South America (including the Falkland Islands), New Zealand, Tasmania, and the south central and southwestern regions of Australia.
Nov. 29	Moon, total (begins 03:27[1]), the beginning visible in extreme eastern and northern Asia, the Hawaiian Islands, North America, Central America, South America, the Arctic, Greenland, Europe, western Africa, extreme western Russia, the eastern Pacific Ocean, and the Atlantic Ocean; the end visible in northeastern Asia, most of New Zealand, the Hawaiian Islands, North America, Central America, South America except the extreme east, the Arctic regions, Greenland, the Pacific Ocean, and most of the North Atlantic Ocean.

[1]Universal time.

Source: *The Astronomical Almanac for the Year 1993* (1992).

Botanical Gardens and Zoos

Botanical Gardens. The contemporary botanical garden has many urgent tasks, the conservation of plant resources being paramount. A number of botanical gardens were showing great flair and imagination in taking their conservation messages to the public. The Royal Botanic Garden, Edinburgh, built a Bornean longhouse within a tropical greenhouse, while the New York Botanical Garden built a traditional South American healers' house. The Botanic Garden of the National Autonomous University of Mexico, Mexico City, used the celebrations for the Day of the Dead to promote the role of the festival's plant components.

The topics of major international meetings reflected the historical legacies and contemporary challenges of botanical gardens. In March 1992 the botanical gardens of the Southwest Pacific region were discussed at the Wellington (N.Z.) Botanic Garden. The Etnobotanica-92, meeting in Córdoba, Spain, examined the effects of plant transfer between the Old and New Worlds. The third International Botanic Gardens Conservation Congress, held in October 1992 in Rio de Janeiro, examined the theme "Botanic Gardens in a Changing World." The last few years had seen a spectacular and welcome surge in botanical garden activity in the Spanish-speaking world. The botanical gardens of Colombia, Cuba, Mexico, and Venezuela were expanding in influence and importance. In some respects the new botanical gardens and plant germ-plasm centres of South America were showing the way in the evolution of the contemporary tropical botanical garden. Botanic Gardens Conservation International started issuing a special bulletin for Latin America, *Boletin de los Jardines Botanicos de America Latina*. In January 1991 the Brazilian botanical gardens had formed a collaborative network, Rede Brasileira de Jardins Botanicos, and the Venezuelan botanic gardens met to form a national network in August 1992.

Many of the old colonial botanical gardens of the tropics had suffered from political and financial neglect. The Limbe Botanic Garden in Cameroon, established by the German colonial authorities in 1892 as a centre for the development of plantation crops, had been in decline since the 1960s. In 1988, however, a renovation program for the garden and its associated rain forest reserves was initiated as a collaborative project between the Cameroonian government, the Overseas Development Agency of the British government, and the Royal Botanic Gardens, Kew. As a result, the garden was able to celebrate its centenary in 1992 as a centre for plant conservation and environmental education.

Botanical gardens were increasingly having to adopt new skills for the management of rare plants in cultivation. The cultivation of a single specimen of a rare species does not constitute conservation of that species. Genetic variability must be retained to ensure long-term survival. One of the most eagerly awaited publications for botanical garden conservationists was *Genetics and Conservation of Rare Plants*, edited by Donald Falk and Kent Holsinger. The book reviews the available literature on the genetic management of rare plant species, both in cultivation and in the wild. A growing number of botanical gardens were undertaking collaborative projects with endangered species. The university botanical garden of Bonn, Germany, was working with the Göteborg (Sweden) Botanic Garden on the conservation of *Sophora toromiro*, a tree extinct in its native Easter Island. All known plants in cultivation in Europe appeared to be descended from a single seed collection. In 1992, in common with many other gardens, the Berlin-Dahlem Botanic Garden started a reintroduction program for rare

native species. In late summer two major tropical botanical gardens renowned for conservation work, the Fairchild Tropical Garden in Florida and the Waimea Botanical Garden in Hawaii, were devastated by hurricanes.

(MICHAEL MAUNDER)

Zoos. The most important international conference of 1992, the sixth World Conference on Breeding Endangered Species, held in May in Jersey, was attended by over 250 delegates from 40 countries. The main emphasis of the papers and discussions was on the increasing importance of the conservation role of zoos, especially the interlinking of work on animals in captivity and in the wild. This theme was also stressed at the annual meetings in Vancouver, B.C., of the Captive Breeding Specialist Group (Species Survival Commission of the International Union for the Conservation of Nature and Natural Resources), September 4–6, and the International Union of Directors of Zoological Gardens, September 7–10.

That zoos are an integral part of the conservation movement was accepted and endorsed by the major international conservation organizations in their *Global Biodiversity Strategy*, published in 1992. The document stated that the conservation role of zoos should be strengthened, especially in conservation/education, research, and cooperative animal-management programs and by support of the global, regional, and national network of zoos. The loss of London Zoo, one component in this coordinated network of over 1,000 zoos, would be tragic. The soap-opera drama of London Zoo and its proposed closure continued throughout the year, and though a reprieve was announced in September by the parent-body council of the Zoological Society of London, further cliff-hanging developments were likely. In war-torn Sarajevo, Bosnia and Hercegovina, the last surviving animal in the city's zoo, a bear, died in November. On a happier note, the Miami (Fla.) Metrozoo reopened in December, four months after suffering extensive damage in Hurricane Andrew.

The taxonomically unique aye-aye (*Daubentonia madagascariensis*), endemic to Madagascar and listed as critically endangered, had high conservation priority. The population in the wild had certainly declined, and there were only 16 in captivity, in three institutions. Encouragingly, the first captive births outside Madagascar were recorded in 1992: one, conceived in the wild, at Duke University Primate Center, Durham, N.C., and one, conceived in captivity, at Jersey Wildlife Preservation Trust.

Other births and hatchings of particular interest included: Poor Knight's Island giant weta (*Deinacrida fallai*) at Wellington (N.Z.) Zoo; frilled lizard (*Chlamydosaurus kingii*) at Melbourne (Australia) Zoo; Attwater's prairie chicken (*Tympanuchus cupido attwateri*) at Fossil Rim Wildlife Center, Texas; a number of rare parrots including Spix's macaw (*Cyanopsitta spixii*) at Loro Parque, Tenerife; San Clemente Island loggerhead shrike (*Lanius ludovicianus mearnsi*) at San Diego (Calif.) Zoo; streak-bellied woodpecker (*Picoides macei*) at Carl Hagenbeck Tierpark, Hamburg, Germany; purple-crowned fairy wren (*Malurus coronatus*) and Calaby's mouse (*Pseudomys laborifex calabyi*) at Territory Wildlife Park, Australia; Verreaux's sifaka (*Propithecus verreauxi*) at Los Angeles Zoo; and Malagasy giant jumping rat (*Hypogeomys antimena*) at Jersey Wildlife Preservation Trust.

There were a number of important advances in the use of artificial insemination techniques. Collaborative work of the National Zoo, Washington, D.C., and Salisbury (Md.) Zoo, using semen preserved at low temperatures, resulted in the birth of seven Eld's deer (*Cervus eldi*) in December 1991 and January 1992; collaborative work between New

The Lied Jungle, opened in 1992 at the Henry Doorly Zoo in Omaha, Neb., includes 0.6 ha (1.5 ac) of rain forest along with several hundred rare animals. Much of what appeared to be natural vegetation was actually man-made, but the simulated material would eventually disappear from sight as the living plants grew.
NEBRASKALAND MAGAZINE/NEBRASKA GAME AND PARKS COMMISSION

York Zoological Park and the National Zoo, using frozen/thawed semen, resulted in the birth of two leopard cats (*Felis bengalensis*) in February; collaborative work of Point Defiance Zoo and Aquarium, Tacoma, Wash., and the U.S. Fish and Wildlife Service, using fresh semen, resulted in the birth of three red wolves (*Canis rufus*) in May.

The California condor (*Gymnogyps californianus*) captive-breeding and reintroduction program continued. In January two eight-month-old birds, together with two captive-bred Andean condors, were released in the Sespe Condor Sanctuary in California, but the male died in October after drinking from a puddle of antifreeze. It was just under five years since the last bird in the wild had been taken into captivity. A census of the only population of Bali starling (*Leucopsar rothschildi*) left in the wild showed an increase from fewer than 20 in 1990 to an estimated 52–56 birds in 1992, due mainly to the introduction of captive-bred birds, a decrease in poaching, and a series of relatively good breeding seasons. Ling-ling, the 23-year-old female giant panda at the National Zoo, died in December.   (P.J.S. OLNEY)

See also Environment; Gardening.

Chemistry

Molecular Cluster Chemistry. The scope of molecular cluster chemistry expanded beyond the fullerenes in 1992 with the synthesis of several members of what appeared to be a new class of molecules composed of atoms arrayed in a highly symmetrical and stable cagelike structure. Although structurally similar to the ball-shaped carbon molecules that make up the fullerene family, the new molecules have different chemical and physical properties.

Chemists at Pennsylvania State University led by A. Welford Castleman, Jr., initially made the cluster Ti_8C_{12}, which contains 8 titanium atoms and 12 carbon atoms. Ti_8C_{12} has a dodecahedral structure, with its 12 faces made up of pentagonal rings. A ring contains two titanium atoms, each bonded to three carbon atoms. The chemists synthesized Ti_8C_{12} through laser vaporization of titanium, with the metal reacting with carbon atoms supplied by hydrocarbons like methane, ethylene, and benzene. Castleman named the molecule a metallo-carbohedrene, or met-car, and predicted that it may be the first of a broad class of molecular clusters with unique properties and practical applications, including catalysts. Soon thereafter, Castleman's team reported mak-

ing other versions of the 20-atom cage in which titanium is replaced by vanadium, zirconium, or hafnium. They also presented evidence for their synthesis of larger clusters comprising two or more of the small cages linked together by shared faces.

Intense interest in the fullerenes continued as researchers learned more about fullerene properties while isolating and characterizing new varieties of the molecules. Typified by the 60-carbon-atom, soccer-ball-shaped buckminsterfullerene (C_{60}), fullerenes are all-carbon molecules with an even number of atoms arranged in a framework resembling a cage. Each fullerene cage comprises 12 pentagons and 2 or more hexagons.

American and Swiss chemists demonstrated conclusively that fullerene coalescence reactions occur, with smaller fullerene molecules fusing to produce giant fullerenes. Robert L. Whetten and his associates of the University of California at Los Angeles and François Diederich of the Federal Technical Institute, Zürich, Switz., used a laser to vaporize C_{60}, C_{70}, or mixtures of both under conditions that yielded multiples and near multiples of the original molecules—for example, C_{118} and C_{120} from C_{60} starting material. By controlling the density and temperature of the vapour, Whetten and Diederich were able to obtain different distributions of giant fullerenes. They suggested that controlled coalescence could be used selectively to produce large quantities of specific giant fullerenes including large endohedral complexes, in which one or more atoms are trapped inside the fullerene cage.

Richard E. Smalley of Rice University, Houston, Texas, reported making a family of small fullerene-uranium endohedral complexes. Previous efforts at encapsulating metal atoms inside fullerenes had resulted only in large complexes having 60 or more carbon atoms in the cage structure. Smalley's group laser-vaporized graphite impregnated with uranium dioxide to obtain a series of fullerene-uranium complexes ranging from C_{28} to C_{60}, or U@C_{28} to U@C_{60}. (Proposed nomenclature for endohedral fullerenes uses the symbol @ to indicate an atom encapsulated by a fullerene.) Smalley believed that C_{28}, like C_{60}, may have an extraordinarily stable geometric structure. C_{28} is extremely small yet is able to encapsulate uranium, one of the largest atoms, without bursting, whereas larger fullerenes proved unable to encapsulate smaller atoms. Smalley's group also prepared complexes of C_{28} encapsulating single atoms of hafnium, titanium, and zirconium.

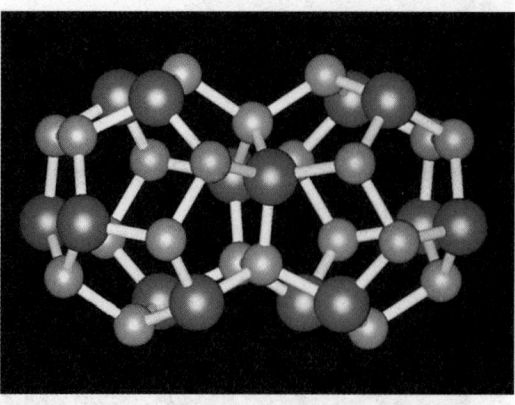

The symmetrical, cagelike molecule Ti_8C_{12} (far left), made of 8 titanium atoms (purple spheres) and 12 carbon atoms (green spheres), is the first member of a newly discovered class of metal-carbon cluster molecules, dubbed met-cars, to be synthesized. Chemists also reported making larger met-cars comprising two or more of the small cages, including the double-cage structure at left.

PHOTOGRAPHS, A. WELFORD CASTLEMAN, JR., PENNSYLVANIA STATE UNIVERSITY

At Sandia National Laboratories in New Mexico, Douglas Loy and Roger Assink reported making a fullerene polymeric material, a copolymer containing C_{60} as one of the monomers. Their process used simple free-radical chemistry in which paracyclophane was sublimed at 650° C (1,200° F) to obtain xylylene, which then was reacted with a solution of pure C_{60} dissolved in toluene (*see* 1). The result was an insoluble brown precipitate consisting of the copolymer C_{60}-*p*-xylylene. The results indicated that fullerene polymers can be produced with straightforward free-radical reactions. Fullerene-based plastics with practical industrial and commercial applications could result.

Inorganic Chemistry. Researchers at the Carnegie Institution of Washington (D.C.) and the University of Amsterdam reported producing the first solid compound of the noble gas helium. The material, $He(N_2)_{11}$, formed when helium and nitrogen were mixed together and subjected to a pressure of 7.7 gigapascals, about 77,000 times normal atmospheric pressure. Carnegie's Willem L. Vos conjectured that it may be the first of a new family of chemical compounds that are formed at high pressure and held together by weak interactions known as van der Waals forces. He felt that studies of such compounds may be important in understanding the structure and properties of matter in the interiors of the gas-giant planets of the outer solar system.

Names for the three heaviest known chemical elements were formally proposed in September by researchers at GSI (Laboratory for Heavy Ion Research), Darmstadt, Germany. The elements, which bear the atomic numbers 107, 108, and 109, were synthesized at GSI between 1981 and 1984 by a group headed by Peter Armbruster and Gottfried Münzenberg. Discoverers of new elements traditionally select the names. The GSI group named element 107 nielsbohrium

(Ns) after Niels Bohr, the Danish scientist who pioneered the modern theory of atomic structure; element 108 hassium (Hs) after the German state of Hesse, site of Darmstadt; and 109 meitnerium (Mt) after Lise Meitner, the Austrian physicist and pioneer in nuclear fission. All three elements are radioactive and extremely short-lived. Once accepted by the International Union for Pure and Applied Chemistry (IUPAC), the new names would replace interim names previously suggested by IUPAC.

Next to oxygen, silicon is the most abundant element in the Earth's crust. Silicon occurs with oxygen in compounds called silicates that form sand, clays, and other minerals representing fully 75% of the crust. Silicates exist in a particular molecular structure, with each silicon atom bonded to four oxygen atoms in a tetrahedron. The exceptional stability of that structure poses difficulties for chemists who want to exploit silicon's properties in new forms of glass, electrically conducting polymers, and other materials. In order to exploit silicon at present, they must strip the oxygen atoms out of the tetrahedron in a tedious, costly process. During the year a group led by Richard Laine of the University of Michigan reported a simpler technique for making silicates possessing greater chemical reactivity. The process involves dissolving silica gel or fused silica in ethylene glycol, under the influence of a strong alkali, to produce silicates in which the silicon is bonded to five or six oxygen atoms (*see* 2). Such bonding states provide enough reactivity for conversion to silicate polymers, glasses, and other materials.

Organic Chemistry. Dutch chemists took an important step toward developing metal-like organic compounds that could complement or replace the inorganic semiconductors now used in transistors and other electronic devices. Such organic compounds would have a number of advantages,

650° C

xylylene

xylylene diradical

paracyclophane

toluene, C_{60}
−78° C

$(C_{60})_n$ $\left[\left[\right]_m\right]_x$

1

C_{60}-*p*-xylylene copolymer

including lower cost and greater ease of fabrication. Hans Wynberg and Wolter ten Hoeve of the firm Syncom in Groningen and Edsko E. Havinga of Philips Research Laboratories in Eindhoven reported new organic polymers that have electrical properties more like metals than previously identified polymers. The materials, polysquaraines and polycroconaines, were synthesized via a simple condensation reaction from croconic acid or squaric acid, both of which are used industrially to make certain dyes. Polysquaraines and polycroconaines appeared to be stable at room temperature, and some of them remained so at 300° C (570° F). The polymers have potential for electronic components because their band gaps are small, the smallest ever observed in organic compounds. The band gap, which is expressed in electron volts, determines the electronic properties of a material. It is a measure of the amount of energy needed to move an electron in the material's molecular structure to the next highest valence band or energy level. Metals are such good conductors because they have a zero band gap, and their electrons can move easily. The band gap is larger in insulators, whose electrons move with difficulty.

A new synthetic process for making ethylene glycol and dimethylcarbonate simultaneously was reported by Roger G. Duranleau and co-workers of Texaco Chemical Corp., Houston. Ethylene glycol is a key chemical feedstock used to make solvents, inks, and other products. Dimethylcarbonate is an intermediary in the production of tough polycarbonate plastics and also serves as a methylating agent in other chemical processes. The two chemicals traditionally have been synthesized in separate processes, with ethylene glycol made by hydration of ethylene oxide and dimethylcarbonate made with a condensation reaction that uses methanol and carbon monoxide. Duranleau's process for cosynthesis of the compounds involves transesterification of ethylene carbonate with methanol.

Metal phosphonates and metal phosphates have been used to make microporous solids having an internal structure riddled with microscopic chambers much like that of zeolites, which are widely used as catalysts in various processes. Like zeolites, microporous solids also have catalytic properties and thus have been under study as zeolite analogues. During the year groups led by Guang Cao of Exxon Research & Engineering Co., Annandale, N.J., and Thomas Mallouk of the University of Texas at Austin produced microporous solids capable of chiral recognition; that is, of distinguishing between mirror-image, or left- and right-handed, forms of the same molecule. Cao and Mallouk produced the microporous solids by incorporating a quaternary ammonium derivative of N-(3,5-dinitrobenzoyl)-L-leucine into the interlayer region of a layered zirconium phosphate material. They speculated that microporous solids having chiral selectivity could be used as process catalysts to make specific left- or right-handed forms of a compound.

Electrochemistry. A process that combines electrochemistry with enzymatic reactions could permit development of new bioreactors that remove nitrates and other contaminants from groundwater, which is used as drinking water in many parts of the world. Stephan Diekmann of Mobitec GmbH, Göttingen, Germany, headed the group that developed the process, which uses a series of enzymes isolated from denitrifying bacteria (microorganisms that naturally convert nitrates in soil into free nitrogen). The enzymes are immobilized on a plastic matrix that is incorporated into an electrochemical cell. Nitrates in water that is passed through the cell are completely converted into gaseous nitrogen. Diekmann noted that no practical methods currently exist for removing nitrates from contaminated groundwater. Through the incorporation of different enzymes, the process

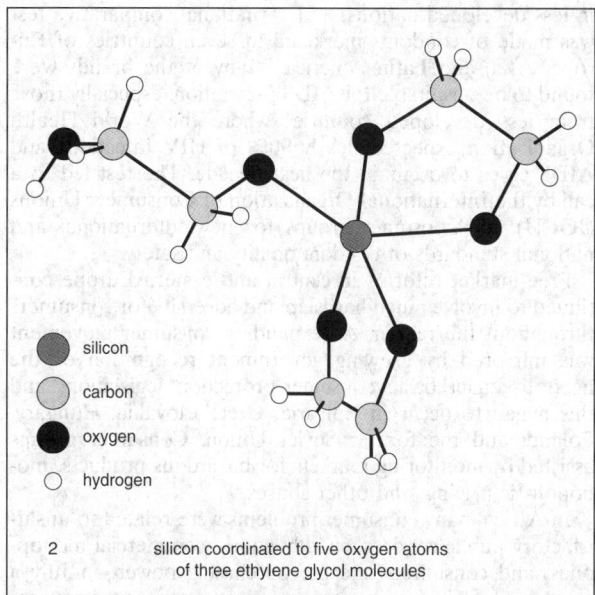

2   silicon coordinated to five oxygen atoms of three ethylene glycol molecules

silicon
carbon
oxygen
hydrogen

also could be modified for use in removing pesticides and other pollutants.   (MICHAEL WOODS)

This article updates the *Macropædia* articles CHEMICAL COMPOUNDS; CHEMICAL ELEMENTS; CHEMICAL REACTIONS; The PHYSICAL SCIENCES: *Chemistry*.

Consumer Affairs

A huge gap separated people occupying the upper and lower rungs of the global consumption ladder. Many if not most of the problems and needs of consumers in 1992 were directly related to their purchasing power and the availability of basic, affordable goods and services in the marketplace. Even in affluent countries, between 10 and 20% of the population was estimated to be living below national poverty lines, in situations varying from high debt to inadequate food, shelter, and education to homelessness. Many public and private consumer bodies were addressing this fundamental issue of consumer access to essential goods and services as part of their overall effort to protect and promote consumers' rights. Also of concern was the fact that many consumers lacked sufficient information and awareness to protect themselves in the marketplace and to make knowledgeable buying choices.

In Latin America democratization and gradual recovery from a decade-long economic crisis led to modest economic growth, renewed foreign direct investment, and increased social spending in 1992. However, lack of effective consumer-protection legislation in the region still left people vulnerable to disreputable services, faulty products, fraudulent sales practices, and other pitfalls. Similar problems were faced by millions in Asia and the Pacific, where the gap between rich and poor had broadened even as explosive economic growth rates were achieved by the region's newly industrializing countries. National consumer movements appeared to be growing most rapidly in China, India, Nepal, Vietnam, and Sri Lanka. In the South Pacific, consumer representatives from 12 island nations cooperated in drafting a "model law" to be used in the development of future consumer-protection legislation. A comprehensive national consumer-protection law was enacted in the Philippines.

In an example of cooperation between large consumer organizations in developed countries and their counterparts in less developed nations, an international comparative test was made of condoms marketed in seven countries of Europe, Asia, and Latin America. Many of the brands were found to be unsuitable for AIDS prevention, especially those from less developed countries where the World Health Organization expected nearly 90% of HIV infections and AIDS cases to occur in the next decade. The test led to a call by the International Organization of Consumers Unions (IOCU) and consumer groups for new international and national standards of condom quality and safety.

Free-market reforms in central and eastern Europe continued to involve much hardship and adversity for consumers throughout the region. An expanding consumer movement was mirrored by growing government recognition of the need to enact basic consumer-protection legislation, and this began to occur in Bulgaria, Czechoslovakia, Hungary, Poland, and the former Soviet Union. Consumer groups assisted by monitoring markets for hazardous products, monopolistic pricing, and other abuses.

In Africa many consumer problems were related to unsatisfactory public services, shoddy goods, commercial monopolies, and consumers' meagre purchasing power. In July a number of African consumer organizations met with government consumer-protection representatives and advisers in Dakar, Senegal, and Harare, Zimbabwe, to discuss progress made by African nations in implementing the UN Guidelines on Consumer Protection. Adopted by the UN General Assembly in 1985, the Guidelines provided a framework for less developed countries to use in elaborating and strengthening policies to protect consumers' health and security.

A global report on consumer protection was presented to the UN Economic and Social Council in June by UN Secretary-General Boutros Boutros-Ghali. He pointed to the need for international cooperation to promote consumer protection, especially in less developed countries and those with emerging market economies. He also called on all UN member states to provide a legal basis for enforcing basic consumer rights, through consumer-protection legislation covering physical safety, promotion and protection of consumers' economic interests, standards for the safety and quality of goods and services, and education and information programs for consumers.

World investment trends and the rising dominance of transnational corporations (TNCs) in the global economy drew the close attention of consumer organizations. After nearly two decades of stalled negotiations on a proposed UN Code of Conduct on Transnational Corporations, it appeared that the chances of adopting such a code had all but vanished, owing to the changing climate of international economic and business relations. In these circumstances, the world consumer movement, spearheaded by the IOCU, turned its energies toward a search for viable alternatives. Consumer organizations urged that important provisions of the code be taken up in a new, more relevant UN initiative that could provide far-reaching and universally accepted principles to guide the relationship of TNCs with their host governments while also safeguarding consumers.

Two international events provided opportunities to emphasize the destructive effects of overconsumption on the global environment. Through World Consumer Rights Day, commemorated annually on March 15, many consumer organizations stressed the importance of consuming less and conserving more. The June "Earth Summit" in Rio de Janeiro also provided a platform for organizations to inform consumers about the environmental consequences of overconsumption. Throughout the year consumer organizations called on local and national governments to do their part by providing more waste-collection and recycling facilities, establishing "eco-labeling" schemes for products, and developing or supporting programs to educate consumers about environmental problems and their causes.

Issues of health, food, and nutrition were of leading concern to consumers and consumer organizations. The International Conference on Nutrition was convened by the UN in Rome in December for the purpose of drawing up a global agenda for nutrition policy. Attended by government officials from over 150 countries, the conference also attracted the participation of consumer organizations and

EC Duty-free Trade: Stay of Execution

Duty-free privileges for travelers moving by air or ferry between European Communities (EC) countries were reprieved in 1992. The concessions were obviously economic nonsense once the EC became a single market from Jan. 1, 1993, so the logical bureaucrats of Brussels planned to kill off this $2,330,000,000-a-year trade from that date. But the politically sensitive EC Council of Ministers vetoed the plan, deciding instead that the trade could survive until mid-1999.

In allowing a dynamic field of EC commerce a 6½-year stay of execution, the Council had in mind, particularly, the huge subsidies that duty-free trade reluctantly gives to intra-EC travel. The heavy concession fees taken by the airport authorities and shipping lines from the profits of duty-free traders with shops at international airports or aboard ferryboats are used to subsidize travel by, for example, cutting airport landing fees and the fares that ferry passengers pay. Similarly, scheduled and charter airlines (the latter are big business in the EC) use profits from duty-free sales on board to subsidize fares.

Denial of duty-free purchase opportunities to travelers moving by air and sea among the 12 countries of the new single market would eliminate about half the EC's duty-free trade (the other half, involving travelers heading for more distant destinations, was not threatened). The trade had always had its inequities. It was mainly buyers of duty-free wines, spirits, and tobacco (the only merchandise on which heavy excise duties are common) who financed the travel subsidies that all enjoyed, and travelers crossing internal EC frontiers by car or train had no opportunity to buy duty free en route.

Before the new extinction date, June 30, 1999, multi-million-dollar questions about duty-free trade would arise if, as expected, the European Free Trade Association countries (Sweden, Finland, Norway, Iceland, Switzerland, Austria, and Liechtenstein) became full members of the EC. The Nordic countries, which tax liquor and tobacco heavily, had a vigorous duty-free trade on Baltic ferries.

Europe, where modern-era duty-free trade began in 1951 at Shannon Airport in Ireland, still dominated world duty-free trade, with about 52% of annual worldwide sales, which now exceeded $15 billion.

(MICHAEL F. BARFORD)

other public interest groups working to ensure that future UN policy would provide adequate safety, quality, and security for consumers throughout the world.

(KEVIN G. COOK)

In the U.S. state regulators approved a new plan to change the way life insurance companies are evaluated. The move was prompted by the failure in 1991 of Mutual Benefit Insurance Co. and First Executive Corp. The previous system of evaluation had been based solely on reviews by state examiners. The new plan created a national standard to measure the financial strength of life insurance companies by putting more emphasis on capital requirements. Companies with 100% or more of the required capital level would be considered financially healthy, while those not meeting this standard would be subject to specific actions by state regulators. Enforcement would still be under state jurisdiction. The financial strength of each company would be assessed according to the riskiness of its assets and operations. Thus companies with major investments in real estate and common stocks would be looked at more closely than those investing mainly in government bonds. The new system, designed by the National Association of Insurance Commissioners, went into effect in late 1992. A similar system for property and casualty insurance companies was to be implemented in late 1993.

A law signed by Gov. Jim Edgar of Illinois in September restricted lawsuits by fans injured by batted balls at baseball games. Owners and operators of baseball teams, including schools and municipal leagues, were exempted from lawsuits unless an injury resulted from defective equipment or reckless behaviour. The legislation was passed after a state appeals court ruled that juries could decide whether screening between spectators and players at a ballpark provided adequate protection. The ruling went against earlier decisions that fans assumed the risk of being hit by a ball when they attended a game.

After completing an investigation into claims made by more than a dozen weight-loss chains, the Federal Trade Commission issued new advertising guidelines requiring that before-and-after testimonials show typical clients, not just successful ones. A report by the National Institutes of Health found that within a year virtually all dieters have regained two-thirds of the weight lost, and within five years they have regained all of it. As a result of increased government interest in the weight-loss industry, diet companies revised their marketing strategies. Weight Watchers moved its meetings out of church basements and schools to storefront locations and introduced a new line of prepared foods, while Jenny Craig was testing a program to supply its food and services to rehabilitation companies in order to get diet programs covered by insurance. The sale of products and services to dieters was a $33 billion-a-year industry if health club fees, artificial sweeteners, and diet soft drinks were included.

The U.S. Supreme Court overturned an appeals court ruling that tobacco companies could not be sued by people who smoked after warnings were placed on cigarette packages in 1966. The Supreme Court ruling would allow plaintiffs to sue tobacco companies for fraud if they could prove the company had covered up information that smoking is harmful. Tobacco companies claimed the ruling was a victory for the industry, while personal injury attorneys said it opened up new possibilities for state and local regulations favouring their clients. Advertising and labeling of tobacco products were still under federal regulation, but states could require tobacco companies to disclose warning information in other ways, such as by an 800 telephone number. Meanwhile, consumers were beginning to sue tobacco companies over the issue of passive smoking. Seven nonsmoking flight

The Mall of America, the largest in the U.S., included the world's largest indoor amusement park, Camp Snoopy. Opened in Bloomington, Minn., in 1992, the megamall covered 31.5 ha (78 ac), although a little less than half of the total area was given to retail stores.
STEVE WOIT

attendants sued a tobacco company for concealing the dangers posed to nonsmokers by smokers.

The Federal Communications Commission adopted rules regulating the use of automatic dialers, prerecorded messages, and fax machines by direct marketing companies. Under the new rules, telemarketers would be required to maintain an in-house list of residential telephone subscribers who do not want to be called. Telemarketing calls to homes before 8 AM and after 9 PM were banned, as were calls to emergency phones, health care facilities, and numbers for which the recipient may be charged. The new rulings did not apply to nonprofit and public organizations or political fund-raising activities.

(EDWARD MARK MAZZE)

See also Economic Affairs: *World Economy;* Environment; Industrial Review: *Advertising.*

Crime, Law Enforcement, and Penology

Violent Crime. *Terrorism.* A welcome reduction in the number of major international terrorist attacks appeared to be continuing in 1992. According to a U.S. State Department report released in April, 87 people died in 557 terrorist attacks in 1991, compared with 200 deaths in 456 attacks in 1990. Half of the attacks in 1991 occurred during January and February, while Operation Desert Storm was in progress, and most were low-level incidents causing few deaths and injuries. With the end of the Gulf war, the number of terrorist attacks fell sharply to levels below those of 1990. This decline was especially marked in Asia, where attacks dropped from 92 in 1990 to 43 in 1991, and in Africa, where 3 incidents were recorded, compared with 53 the previous year.

Spanish authorities were fearful that the Basque separatist guerrilla movement ETA would seek to stage a spectacular terrorist attack during the Olympic Games in Barcelona in

John Gotti, found guilty in a U.S. federal court in April 1992 of charges that included murder and racketeering, listens to testimony in an earlier (1990) trial. The boss of the Gambino crime family, Gotti had avoided conviction in three previous trials.

AP/WIDE WORLD

August. In March, French and Spanish authorities captured a number of leading ETA members in a raid on a safe house in Bayonne, France, and that decapitation of the ETA leadership, coupled with a massive security operation throughout Spain, avoided any repetition of the 1972 Munich Games massacre. On September 12 Peruvian authorities scored a spectacular success against the Maoist guerrilla group Sendero Luminoso (Shining Path) with the capture in Lima of its shadowy leader, Abimael Guzman, and other high-ranking Shining Path officials. Peruvian police claimed that Guzman, a former philosophy professor who had been in hiding since 1979, was caught after detectives watching a guerrilla hideout discovered notes in his handwriting in a rubbish bin. Guzman and two other rebel leaders were convicted of treason, sentenced to life imprisonment, and ordered to pay $25 billion in damages.

In the Middle East a decade-long hostage drama came to an end in June with the release, after months of negotiations, of the only two remaining Western prisoners held in Lebanon, German aid workers Heinrich Strübig and Thomas Kemptner, after 1,127 days in captivity. U.S.-sponsored peace talks between the Israelis and Arabs continued during the year, but the bitter conflict between them still exacted a heavy toll of deaths and injuries. On February 16 Israeli helicopter gunships ambushed a convoy of seven vehicles in southern Lebanon, killing the head of the pro-Iranian Hezbollah movement, Sheikh 'Abbas al-Mussawi (*see* OBITUARIES), his wife and six-year-old son, and five bodyguards. The action was thought to be in retaliation for Hezbollah raids on Israeli soldiers, including an attack by three Arabs on a military camp near Tel Aviv in which three Israeli soldiers were hacked to death. On March 17 a massive car bomb explosion ripped apart the Israeli embassy in Buenos Aires, Arg., killing 29 people and injuring some 252. The pro-Iranian Islamic Jihad claimed responsibility.

Algeria's head of state, Muhammad Boudiaf (*see* OBITUARIES), was assassinated on June 29 as he addressed a crowd in the eastern Algerian coastal town of Annaba. His assassin wore a police uniform. No one claimed responsibility, but Algerian authorities who captured the assassin said he was a member of the security service who acted out of "religious conviction." Muslim fundamentalists were thought to be behind the slaying. On January 21 the UN Security Council unanimously approved a resolution ordering Libya to cooperate with British, French, and U.S. investigations into the terrorist bombings of Pan Am Flight 103 over Lockerbie, Scotland, in 1988, which killed 270 people, and of UTA Flight 772 over Niger in 1989, which resulted in 171 deaths. The resolution required Libya to hand over for trial in either the U.S. or Britain two indicted intelligence agents alleged to be involved in the Lockerbie bombing. This was the first time the Security Council had demanded the extradition of citizens of one country to stand trial in another. On April 15 the Security Council imposed an air and arms embargo on Libya because the suspects had not been surrendered.

The Irish Republican Army (IRA) continued its bloody struggle over the future of Northern Ireland. In January eight Protestant workers, returning home from a construction site at a British army base in County Tyrone, were killed by a remotely detonated IRA bomb. On February 4 a policeman, distraught over a colleague's death, killed three people and wounded two at the offices of the IRA political party in Belfast before taking his own life. The IRA's offensive extended to the British mainland, where bomb alerts and explosions caused widespread disruption in a number of cities prior to the British national election on April 9 and again in the fall. On April 10 a huge IRA car bomb planted in the heart of London's financial district killed 3 people, injured 91, and caused hundreds of millions of dollars of property damage. In June the British Court of Appeals quashed the 1974 conviction and jailing for life of Judith Ward for the murder of 12 people in the IRA bombing of an army coach in northern England. Ward was among 17 people jailed in the 1970s for IRA crimes but subsequently released on appeal on the grounds that their convictions were miscarriages of justice. A royal commission established to review the criminal justice system in the wake of these releases continued its deliberations.

Drug Trafficking. In a ruling widely criticized by jurists in the U.S. and abroad, the U.S. Supreme Court refused in June to block the exceptional powers given to U.S. government agents to kidnap and forcibly abduct foreign nationals from their own countries to stand trial in U.S. courts. The ruling arose in a case involving a Mexican physician, Humberto Alvarez Machain, who was smuggled across the border to be tried for his alleged role in the 1985 torture and murder of a U.S. Drug Enforcement Agency agent, Enrique Camarena. Following the ruling Mexico suspended all cooperation with the U.S. against drug trafficking. Machain was later freed for lack of evidence. (*See* LAW.) After a seven-month trial that ended in April, the deposed Panamanian leader Gen. Manuel Noriega was found guilty by a Miami (Fla.) jury of 8 out of 10 drug trafficking, money laundering, and racketeering charges. He was sentenced in July to 40 years in prison.

On July 10 Colombia's Pres. César Gaviria Trujillo invoked emergency powers to block the release of more than 1,300 prisoners suspected of drug trafficking, murder, and other violence. Under a new law that went into effect on July 1, any person detained for more than 180 days without charges had to be released immediately. Without the presidential decree, Colombian authorities asserted that the top leaders of the Medellín drug cartel would have been eligible for release, including cocaine baron Pablo Escobar. Following the July 10 decree, Colombian authorities sought to move Escobar from a luxurious ranchlike prison to a higher security military jail. During the transfer Escobar and nine fellow detainees escaped through a tunnel. Escobar offered a conditional surrender, but an embarrassed Colombian government refused.

Murder and Other Violence. Violent crime in the U.S. reached a record high in 1991. The rate of violent crime, which included murder, robbery, rape, and assault, rose by 3.6% although, overall, crime increased at a rate of only 1% for the year. There were 24,703 murders in 1991, up 5.4% from 1990, and the murder rate was almost 10 per 100,000 people. Washington, D.C., with a murder rate of 80.6 per 100,000, again topped the list of cities with populations exceeding 100,000. Firearms were used to commit about 6 in every 10 murders, and the number of homicides committed with handguns increased by 13%. Youths aged 15–19 were responsible for nearly one-sixth of all murders. A report released in July by the American Medical Association said violent deaths in the U.S. from handguns had now become a "public health emergency." The U.S. now had the highest murder rate of any industrialized country, with murder the leading cause of death among 15–34-year-old black males and the third leading cause of death among 15–24-year-old white males. During 1992 a rash of armed automobile robberies or "carjackings," in some cases involving violence, received wide publicity.

In February, following a sensational nationally televised trial, a Milwaukee, Wis., jury convicted Jeffrey Dahmer, 31, of 15 counts of murder. Dahmer, who pleaded guilty but insane, was involved in a gruesome decade-long series of killings of young men and boys. In the absence of the death penalty in Wisconsin, the trial judge sentenced him to 15 consecutive life sentences. An even grimmer case of serial killing surfaced in Rostov-na-Donu, Russia, where Andrey Chikatilo, a 56-year-old former schoolteacher, was accused of murder, mutilation, and cannibalism in connection with the deaths of more than 50 young women, girls, and boys over a period of 12 years. Chikatilo, who was arrested in November 1991, confessed to most of the killings, but Russian law required that every case be reviewed. After a trial lasting several months, he was found guilty of 52 counts of murder and sentenced to death by one bullet in the back of the head.

In what was called the most dramatic kidnapping since the abduction of the Lindbergh baby in 1932, Sidney Reso, the international president of the Exxon Corp., vanished on his way to work on April 29 in New Jersey. His kidnappers later attempted to extort $18 million from Exxon. In June the FBI arrested Arthur Seale, a former Exxon security officer, and his wife, Irene, after tracing their ransom requests through cellular phone calls made by the couple. Reso's body was subsequently found buried in a southern New Jersey pine forest. In September, faced with the possibility that his wife would testify on behalf of the prosecution, Seale pleaded guilty to extortion charges and revealed that Reso had been accidentally shot at the time of his capture and lived for four days imprisoned in a crate. Seale was sentenced to 95 years in prison without parole.

In April the National Victim Center, a nonprofit group dedicated to promoting crime victims' rights, released a study showing that at least 12.1 million American women, or one out of every eight adult women, had been raped, but only 16% had reported the offense to the police. In February, following a highly publicized 13-day trial, former world heavyweight boxing champion Mike Tyson was found guilty of having raped an 18-year-old contestant in the Miss Black America pageant. He was sentenced to six years in prison with eligibility for parole in 1995, but his lawyers appealed both the verdict and the sentence.

Nonviolent Crime. *Political Crime and Espionage.* Investigations continued throughout the year in many parts of the world into the labyrinthine operations of the Bank of Credit and Commerce International (BCCI). The bank, with 417 branches in about 70 countries, was shut down in 1991 after evidence emerged that it had defrauded depositors of up to $12 billion and was involved in global bribery and corruption, terrorist networks, drug running, and political influence peddling. On July 29 New York state and federal officials charged Clark Clifford, 85, a longtime Democratic presidential adviser, and his law partner, Robert Altman, on counts of fraud, conspiracy, and receiving millions in bribes relating to BCCI activities. U.S. prosecutors disclosed that one of BCCI's directors, Sheikh Kamal Adham, the head of Saudi Arabian Intelligence, had pleaded guilty to conspiracy charges and had agreed to pay a fine of $105 million and to reveal all he knew about BCCI's operations in return for a reduced sentence.

In September Brazil's Chamber of Deputies voted 441 to 38 to impeach Pres. Fernando Collor de Mello on charges of illicit enrichment and perjury. Collor faced trial before the Brazilian Senate but resigned before the proceedings began. (*See* WORLD AFFAIRS [Latin America and the Caribbean]: *Brazil.*) Deposed Bulgarian Communist leader Todor Zhivkov, 81, was sentenced by a court in Sofia in August to seven years in prison for abuse of power and

Kevin Maxwell, son of the late publisher Robert Maxwell, is escorted by policemen after his arrest in London on June 18. Maxwell and his brother, Ian, were charged with crimes involving pension funds and other assets of the family empire.

embezzlement of $1 million. Zhivkov, who ruled Bulgaria for 35 years, was the first former Eastern European Communist head of state to be convicted in a criminal trial. Erich Honecker, 80, who ruled East Germany for 18 years, was charged in a Berlin court in August with 49 counts of manslaughter, 25 counts of attempted manslaughter, and several counts of embezzlement. The manslaughter charges related to the "shoot to kill" policy adopted by Honecker's regime against those seeking to flee to the West. The trial continued at year's end, although Honecker was suffering from cancer and was not expected to live more than a few months.

White Collar Crime and Theft. The fallout from the collapse of the late Robert Maxwell's fraud-ridden multinational empire reached his sons Ian and Kevin in June. Together with Maxwell's former financial adviser, Larry Trachtenberg, they were arrested by British authorities and charged with counts of theft and conspiracy to defraud involving $260 million, some of which came from Maxwell staff pension funds.

In April a three-judge court in Milan convicted and sentenced Carlo De Benedetti, the Italian financier who built up the Olivetti business empire, to six years in prison for his role in the fraudulent bankruptcy of Banco Ambrosiano. The so-called Vatican bank collapsed in 1982 with debts of $1 billion. De Benedetti, who immediately lodged an appeal, was one of 33 people sentenced in the Ambrosiano affair. Legal experts said the appeal process could stretch out for years, and it was unlikely that De Benedetti would ever have to serve a jail sentence.

India's biggest-ever financial scandal shook the Bombay Stock Exchange in April as a long bull market on the exchange ended amid allegations of insider trading, stock manipulation, and illegal diversion of bank depositors' funds. In June Harshad Mehta, a flamboyant Bombay stockbroker, and nine others were arrested on an array of forgery, conspiracy, bribery, and cheating charges. Alan Bond, the Australian tycoon who became a national hero in 1983 when he mounted a successful challenge for the America's Cup yachting trophy, was convicted of a securities offense and sentenced to two and a half years in prison. An appeals court ordered a new trial, however, and in November he was found not guilty. In July the Alaskan Appeals Court reversed the conviction of the captain of the supertanker *Exxon Valdez* for negligently discharging oil into Alaska's Prince William Sound when his ship grounded there in 1989. The court said that Capt. Joseph Hazelwood was entitled to the immunity granted by a federal law to those who promptly report any spill to the appropriate authority. Alaskan officials said they would appeal.

Law Enforcement. On April 29 a jury in Simi Valley, Calif., an overwhelmingly white middle-class community northwest of Los Angeles, acquitted four white Los Angeles Police Department (LAPD) officers on all but one count of beating a black motorist, Rodney King, while arresting him on March 3, 1991. The beating, captured on videotape by an amateur photographer, had provoked a nationwide debate in the U.S. about the misuse of force by police. Within hours, the acquittal sparked the worst urban violence experienced in the U.S. since the Watts riots in Los Angeles in 1965. By the time the situation was brought under control, with the assistance of National Guard and federal forces, at least 53 persons were dead and 2,400 injured. Property damage, much of it in the inner city, was estimated to exceed $1 billion. In a move intended to dampen tensions, the U.S. government handed down indictments in August against the LAPD officers involved, alleging they had violated King's civil rights. In June Willie L. Williams (*see* BIOGRAPHIES),

a former chief of police in Philadelphia, replaced the much-criticized and controversial Daryl Gates as chief of the LAPD.

The campaign by Italian law-enforcement authorities to curb the Mafia suffered a number of major setbacks during the year. On May 23 one of Italy's leading anti-Mafia fighters, Judge Giovanni Falcone (*see* OBITUARIES), his wife, and three bodyguards were killed when a massive bomb detonated on an expressway where he and his family were driving. In July Paolo Borsellino, an anti-Mafia prosecutor since 1985, was blown to pieces, along with five bodyguards, when a powerful bomb exploded under a parked car as they passed by. Borsellino had just visited his mother in Palermo, an appointment known only to his most trusted aides. More than 8,000 people attended Borsellino's funeral to show solidarity with his struggle against the Mafia. It was believed that the Sicilian Mafia controlled up to 30% of heroin traffic to the U.S.

In the U.S. the passage of effective federal and state laws in recent years, notably the Racketeer Influenced and Corrupt Organizations (RICO) acts, was said to be responsible for an ongoing series of successful prosecutions of major Mafia figures. Since 1981 U.S. authorities had convicted 24 leading Mafia bosses and dozens of underbosses of organized crime groups. In April a jury in Brooklyn found John Gotti, the head of the Gambino crime family, guilty of 13 racketeering crimes including five murders, murder conspiracy, gambling, loan sharking, and obstruction of justice. The verdict was the culmination of a five-year investigation. On three previous occasions Gotti had eluded federal prosecutors, earning for himself the nickname of the Teflon Don. In June he was sentenced to life imprisonment.

As South Africa stumbled toward a multiracial society, a number of scandals involving that nation's police and security forces rocked the government of Pres. F.W. de Klerk. In July Jonathan Gluckman, South Africa's leading pathologist, gave graphic details of deaths occurring in police custody. Gluckman revealed that his office had more than 200 files of postmortems he had performed on blacks who had died in detention; he was convinced that 90% of the detainees had been killed by the police. Gluckman's revelations came at a time when the South African police were already under harsh criticism from a report condemning their actions at a massacre on June 17 in which more than 40 people were killed in the township of Biopatong. In July an international panel recommended that the police stop using a newly formed national antiriot unit to deal with demonstrations and refrain from resorting hastily to lethal force. (*See* WORLD AFFAIRS [Africa South of the Sahara]: *South Africa.*)   (DUNCAN CHAPPELL)

Prisons and Penology. Prison populations continued to rise in many parts of the world in 1992. According to the Sentencing Project, the United States continued to have the highest incarceration rate, 455 prisoners per 100,000 inhabitants. With the total cost of imprisonment in the U.S. estimated at $20.3 billion, however, there were some indications that the rate of growth might be slowing down. Second was South Africa with a rate of 311, although this represented a 7% decline from the previous year. Rates rose in a number of European countries, including the United Kingdom, France, and Spain. Poland had reduced its prison population by about two-thirds in 1989, but numbers in 1991–92 increased sharply.

Several countries lowered their prison population through amnesties. In Tanzania a presidential decree ordered 23,-000 prisoners released, and in Russia 20,000 prisoners were granted release by this means. An even more substantial amnesty involving 25,000 persons took place in Thailand.

Inmates of a prison in São Paulo, Brazil, where on October 2 some 200 were killed, hang a banner reading "We are mourning justice." Reports were that police initially moved in to suppress a riot, but survivors later accused security forces of atrocities against prisoners.

ANGULAR—SIPA

Other countries announcing amnesties included Tunisia, Nicaragua, and South Africa.

Prison Conditions. Many prisoners continued to be held under conditions that varied from poor to atrocious. A study of 56 prisons in Nigeria found that in some institutions prisoners had to take turns sleeping, one group standing around the walls of the cell while the remainder slept on the floor. There were also a large number of "extrajudicial deaths," with some prisons experiencing two or more deaths per week. It was not uncommon for prisoners to spend up to 10 years awaiting trial. In Tunisia cells designed for two persons sometimes held in excess of 10 prisoners. High levels of prison overcrowding were also reported in many other countries, including Venezuela, Spain, Guyana, Barbados, and in many systems across the U.S. Three prisons in Britain were strongly criticized by the Council of Europe Committee for the Prevention of Torture and Inhuman or Degrading Treatment or Punishment, which found a "pernicious combination" of overcrowding, inadequate activities, and poor sanitation and hygiene. In Australia reports of untreated illnesses and suicides among Aboriginal people held in jails continued to cause concern, despite the report of a royal commission in May 1992.

There were fewer reported prison disturbances than in recent years. In Spain five prisoners had been killed in a series of riots during the summer of 1991. The authorities blamed the disturbances on heat, overcrowding, drugs, and AIDS. Prisoners had demanded improvements in medical treatment, work opportunities, and food. Serious incidents took place at two French prisons in September 1992. A 15-hour rebellion was put down at Moulins-Iseure prison, and at Clairvaux prison a prison officer and a prisoner were killed during a shoot-out that led to the escape of eight prisoners. At the Miguel Castro Castro prison in Lima, Peru, 500 prisoners seized part of the prison in May 1992. After the authorities retook the prison, they reported that 35 prisoners and 2 police officers had been killed. However, sources close to the guerrilla group Sendero Luminoso claimed that 80 of its members had died and that many others remained unaccounted for. The year's most serious disturbance took place in the House of Detention in São Paulo, Brazil, in early October, when, according to official accounts, police moved in to stop a fight between inmates. Estimates of the death toll ranged from the official report

of 111 to between 200 and 400, and there were accusations of police brutality and human rights violations.

Death Penalty. According to Amnesty International, death sentences were judicially imposed or carried out in 90 countries. These included every country in the Middle East, with over 700 death sentences estimated to have been imposed in Iran. In October 1991, 65 persons (including 4 women) were hanged in Mashad after being convicted of offenses that included drug trafficking. In June 1992 nine persons were sentenced to death (four were promptly executed) after disturbances in Shiraz during which security forces acted against disabled war veterans holding a rally.

In the U.S. some 2,590 persons were being held on death rows in most of the 36 states where the death penalty had been restored. This number included 31 juveniles, and Amnesty International accused the U.S. of flouting international standards by sentencing juveniles to death. According to Human Rights Watch, some death row prisoners in Florida had been held in solitary confinement within windowless cells for up to 17 years. In December 1992 a Texas prisoner became the 187th person to be executed since 1976, when the Supreme Court permitted new death penalty statutes. Delaware and Arizona carried out their first executions in 46 and 29 years, respectively. In California the execution of Robert Harris in April 1992, the first in that state in 25 years, received international attention; his execution date had been set and then postponed four times. Considerable publicity also attended the electrocution of Roger Coleman in Virginia, which went ahead despite doubts as to his guilt. The rate of executions was expected to increase as a result of the drastic curtailment of the appeal process for condemned persons by the Supreme Court.

A number of countries extended the applicability of the death penalty. In Vietnam the penal code was amended to permit the death penalty for bribe taking and "defrauding the socialist party." Use of the death penalty in Iraq was widened to cover crimes ranging from looting to car theft. By contrast, Switzerland abolished the death penalty for wartime offenses, 50 years after it had taken similar action with respect to offenses committed in peacetime.

(ANDREW RUTHERFORD)

See also Law.

This article updates the *Macropædia* articles CRIME AND PUNISHMENT; POLICE.

Dance

North America. New York no longer held the position of leadership it once did in North American dance. With companies such as the New York City Ballet (NYCB), American Ballet Theatre (ABT), and the Martha Graham Dance Company now functioning as inherited institutions rather than vanguard forces, the city had lost some of its influence. No other single location, however, had replaced it. Companies still sought both public and journalistic New York responses, but more and more these visiting groups showed strengths comparable to those of once superior resident New York troupes. Anna Kisselgoff of the *New York Times* painted a dollars-and-cents picture of ballet around the U.S. for her analysis of the dramatic changeover at ABT after the May resignation of artistic director Jane Hermann. Looking at the task ahead for Kevin McKenzie, ABT's new director, she reported that annual budgets for companies outside New York were no longer far below those in the "dance capital." Companies once considered regional were reaching parity with groups once thought of as national trendsetters.

ABT had what could best be called a conservative year. The repertory was significantly enriched by only one work, a revival of Frederick Ashton's cool but voluptuous 1946 *Symphonic Variations.* New ABT works ranged from the appallingly chic to the blandly predictable. Essentially the dancers, most of whom had been developed during the decade Mikhail Baryshnikov directed the company, gave the repertory its real interest. In particular, Julie Kent, Amanda McKerrow, and Wes Chapman shone. The company's sometime fixation on stars was largely concentrated in one performance of *Romeo and Juliet,* danced by Paris Opéra guests Laurent Hilaire and Sylvie Guillem and conducted by Rudolf Nureyev, whose rumoured ill health was evident in his frail curtain calls.

NYCB enlivened its annual spring season with a kind of festival. Called the "Diamond Project" (after a principal funder), the week-long series offered 11 premieres by as many choreographers, some familiar to the company, some new. At best, the event showcased the company's current dancers and produced a few works worth keeping, such as Miriam Mahdaviani's *Images* and Richard Tanner's *Ancient Airs and Dances.* Getting the much-sought-after William Forsythe to create a new work proved more newsworthy than artistic. Though the star of the American-born Forsythe, who worked mostly with his company in Frankfurt, Germany, was starting to wane, he still captured the interest of a good many individuals who practiced, directed, and watched dancing. His *Herman Schmerman* looked like the same one-note, attitudinizing dance he usually did. The influence of Forsythe's relentless, assertive aesthetic, however, pervaded more than one of the "Diamond Project" works.

The proudly eclectic Joffrey Ballet had the roughest year of the country's Big Three. After some engagement cancellations due to uncertain finances, the company had to forgo its important Los Angeles season in the wake of the riots there. It finally got to perform its major revival of Leonide Massine's 1933 *Les Présages* in July in San Francisco, but the loss of its great ballerina Tina LeBlanc to the San Francisco Ballet (SFB) mostly presaged good fortune for the California troupe. SFB continued to showcase its interesting

Twyla Tharp and Kevin O'Day perform *Men's Piece,* a mostly humorous look at relationships between the sexes. The work was one of several premiered in 1992 by Tharp's newly formed group.

dancers and to add both Balanchine classics and contemporary premieres to its repertory. With Elizabeth Loscavio and LeBlanc in his troupe, artistic director Helgi Tomasson had to be the envy of many ballet directors. Tomasson's pervasively strong male contingent also deserved remarking on. A genuinely sterling roster of women produced by Kent Stowell and Francia Russell at Pacific Northwest Ballet also warranted mention. Barely five years old, Ballet Chicago, directed by Daniel Duell, made an especially vivid impression in New York, due to the radiance and expertise of its dancers and the inspired dances of resident choreographer Gordon Peirce Schmidt.

Houston (Texas) Ballet had to cancel its scheduled New York season owing to financial losses incurred in the same Los Angeles unrest that affected the Joffrey. Boston Ballet, whose enthusiastic director Bruce Marks was reportedly sought after by ABT, produced a special "On the Edge" series that included works by such expert dancemakers as Twyla Tharp and Mark Morris. Dance Theatre of Harlem, back in circulation after a hiatus for financial restructuring, gave strong and appealing performances and initiated a special expansion project for its school. Eliot Feld continued to fuel his youthful company, Feld Ballets/NY, with feisty and eccentric explorations of classical dancing, while his school, the New Ballet School, was awarded a $250,000 grant by the Andrew W. Mellon Foundation.

Almost concurrent with the annual performances of the School of American Ballet, NYCB's affiliate, the school of the Paris Opéra Ballet visited New York with a lecture-demonstration and repertory program. Both institutions were doing front-rank work in training dancers. Their respective appearances indicated that the Americans were more mature performers, the Parisians more careful. Visiting companies included the Kirov (also known as the Mariinsky) Ballet, the Royal Danish Ballet, and the Stuttgart (Germany) Ballet. The Russian company looked less firmly focused than when it was under Soviet auspices. NYCB ended the year with Kirov firebrand Igor Zelensky and stellar Dane Nikolaj Hübbe on its roster, but it lost, for at least a year, the prodigious Ethan Stiefel, who was working in Europe.

The financially pressed Graham company performed a mere one-week New York season and, except for its opening gala performance, was forced to use taped music. The highlight was a handsomely restaged fragment of *Panorama,* an early, large-group piece of Graham's from 1935. Merce Cunningham showed three premieres during his company's two-week season. Each was compelling, with *Loosestrife* showcasing the company's expert dancers both as fine soloists and as a fine-tuned ensemble. Paul Taylor, also in a two-week season, offered only one new dance—*Oz,* a prettily produced suite-form reverie on the characters in the books of L. Frank Baum. Judith Jamison's direction continued to give fresh life to the personal legacy Alvin Ailey left to the company he founded. Morris and his dance group resettled in the states after three years in Belgium. In the spring the troupe showed two weeks of two strong, mixed programs. It closed the year with two weeks of *The Hard Nut,* Morris' personal take on *The Nutcracker,* which was 100 in 1992.

Pilobolus, at least three generations away from its founding, showed that it could still be popular and innovative. Demetrius Klein brought to New York another impressive sampling of the dances he created out of his own school and ensemble in Florida. Tharp, who published her autobiography in November, showed some of her most fluent crossover ballet work in a "project" of temporary dancers and dances in January. She finished the year touring alongside Baryshnikov in "Cutting Up," a specially arranged showcase for

Aria, by choreographer Bill T. Jones, develops contrasts between ballet and modern dance. The work received its premiere in New York City in 1992.
JACK VARTOOGIAN

herself and the Russian superstar plus nine other dancers. For a second year running, the Judson Memorial Church was the site of free showings of experimentalist work, happily reclaiming its 1960s legacy as a laboratory for iconoclasm and new directions in dance theatre.

Les Grands Ballets Canadiens offered *Paukenshlag,* a new Morris ballet. Montreal's annual international festival of "new" dance offered works from six countries, including Canada. Toronto's National Ballet of Canada lost the Barbados-born John Alleyne, one of its young balletmasters, to Ballet British Columbia, where he would become director, but it gained back James Kudelka, a dancemaker almost as well known in the U.S. as in his native Canada. The Royal Winnipeg Ballet, which gave a couple of admirable performances in New York, acquired Ashton's *The Dream.*

Deaths included ABT dancer and choreographer Clark Tippet, choreographer Hanya Holm, tap dancer Charles ("Honi") Coles (*see* OBITUARIES), ex-Graham dancer Gertrude Schurr, dance writers Lydia Joel and Burt Supree, dance photographer Barbara Morgan, and designer Rouben Ter-Arutunian, who collaborated on Balanchine's landmark production of *The Nutcracker.*   (ROBERT J. GRESKOVIC)

Europe. Two leading European dance companies long absent from Britain were scheduled to return as part of a six-month multimedia arts festival organized with special government funds to mark Britain's presidency of the European Communities (EC), July to December. From Germany, Pina Bausch's Tanztheater Wuppertal had notable success in the Edinburgh Festival, and Netherlands Dance Theatre, directed by Czech-born Jiri Kylian, was announced for a December season at Bradford, Yorkshire.

What used to be a matter of cultural prestige in the international exchange of dance companies, particularly between East and West, had become an increasingly commercial matter. More and more tours from the former U.S.S.R. were made in search of hard currency, ranging from seasons of regular repertory by major companies to a confusion of identity between St. Petersburg Dance Theatre in its U.K. debut and a hitherto unknown National Ballet of St. Petersburg touring one- and two-night stands of *Swan Lake.* Visits also featured "Stars of the Bolshoi Ballet" in assorted showpieces of moderate quality, Moscow City Ballet in a

better-produced and danced *Swan Lake,* and a mixed ballet and opera gala at Covent Garden entitled "Welcome Back St. Petersburg."

Whatever the EC's future, rampant internationalism was greatly benefiting the art of dance, even Britain's Royal Ballet, whose founder-director, Dame Ninette de Valois, at age 94 received "lifetime achievement" awards from Britain (a Laurence Olivier Special Award) and Italy (the Porselli Prize). The company toured to Japan for four weeks in Tokyo and 11 other cities, and at home it received another Olivier Award for the year's best dance: *In the middle, somewhat elevated* by Frankfurt Ballet's Forsythe, a plotless work of modern classicism starring Guillem, the company's resident French ballerina. Principal choreographer Sir Kenneth MacMillan premiered *The Judas Tree,* a dance-drama on the theme of betrayal, establishing a vivid new partnership between Italian-born Viviana Durante and Russian-born Irek Mukhamedov and with powerful new music by Brian Elias, a newcomer to dance born in India to emigrants from Iraq. Sir Kenneth, one of the giants of 20th-century ballet, died in October (*see* OBITUARIES).

Myriad small groups performing the work of one man or woman made up the modern-dance scene. A variety of visitors supplemented British groups for concentrated spring and fall seasons. Among them were two notable Belgian choreographers, Anne Teresa de Keersmaeker and Wim Vanderkeybus, working separately in a "postmodern" dance idiom more closely related to acrobatics. London Contemporary Dance Theatre lost its American-born director, Nancy Duncan, after less than a year, highlighting problems of finance and artistic policy affecting companies dependent on mixed repertory. LCDT continued to perform new work pending the search for a successor and received government funds to set up an exchange project of teaching and performance with Czechoslovakia. A new Prague Festival Ballet gained commendation on its British debut. From South Africa, Cape Town's PACE Dance Company went to Europe for the first time, touring centres in France and Britain with a program emphasizing mixed-race performance and an exhilarating integration of tribal and modern-dance styles. Britain's first national South Asian dance company, Yuva, was founded by Calcutta-born Ranjabati Sircar.

Dancers perform in the Kirov Ballet's revival of a 1940 production of *Romeo and Juliet.* The production, originally a product of Soviet Socialist Realism, emphasized dramatic elements in dancing and staging.
JACK VARTOOGIAN

Increasing attention was focused on dance especially made for video, not theatre, performance. Vienna's International Dance Weeks showed 64 video productions from 16 countries; Frankfurt's Dance Screen Award chose de Keersmaeker's *Rosa* from 177 entries representing 25 countries. Britain's BBC Television and the Arts Council combined to invest over £500,000 in a two-year "Dance for the Camera" project.

A boom in French contemporary dance in the last decade, "unparalleled anywhere else in the world" according to one (British) report, was credited to the innovative policies of the Ministry of Culture headed by Jack Lang. Even the conservatively classical Paris Opéra Ballet, directed by Patrick Dupond, commissioned new works from two prominent modern-dance choreographers, Odile Duboc and Daniel Larrieu, to diversify its repertory, incidentally highlighting a current dearth of classical ballet choreographers. The national Paris company paid tribute to Picasso in a triple bill of works he first designed (*Le Tricorne, Le Train bleu, Le Rendez-vous*) and to the American choreographer Jerome Robbins, who himself directed his triple bill of *Dances at a Gathering, En Sol,* and *Glass Pieces.* Another American, John Butler, was celebrated for 50 years as a choreographer with a double bill of his *Carmina Burana* and *Catulli Carmina* at Italy's Verona Festival.

Swedish-born Ivo Cramér had won special respect for his stylish reconstructions of forgotten historical ballets. France's Ballet du Rhin (Strasbourg) brought his version of Jean Dauberval's original *La Fille mal gardée* (1786) to London; he staged Jean-Georges Noverre's *Jason et Médée* (1763) with the same company at Strasbourg, and for the Royal Swedish Ballet he produced a new version of Louis Duport's *Figaro, or Love and Almaviva* (1806). The Royal Danish Ballet with a continuous tradition of August Bournonville's 19th-century ballets, celebrated the 150th anniversary of his *Napoli* with a new staging by Dinna Bjørn, Henning Kronstam, and Frank Andersen. For the 25th wedding anniversary of Denmark's Queen Margrethe, choreographer Flemming Flindt created *Lucifer's Daughter,* a ballet on the life of Danish author Karen Blixen (who wrote under the name Isak Dinesen).

New biographical ballets elsewhere included Eugene Polyakov's *Lorenzo il magnifico* for MaggioDanza at Florence, two versions of *Elvira Madigan* in Sweden, by Regina Beck-Friis in Stockholm and Robert North in Göteborg, and at least three on Christopher Columbus in the quincentenary year—by Alberto Mendez at Milan's Teatro Lirico, by Gabor Kevehazi for the Budapest Opera Ballet with Nureyev as the explorer's guardian angel, and by Jean-Paul Comelin for France's Ballet du Nord (Roubaix). Spain's 12th International Dance Festival at Seville drew 15 visiting companies, while still others toured to Madrid and Barcelona to fly cultural flags at Expo 92. The locally based Ballet Lirico Nacional and Ballet Victor Ullate, both nationally funded, produced Nacho Duato's *Valencia* and Ullate's *De Madrid al cielo,* respectively, both celebrating Spain's indigenous heritage of dance and music.

Shakespeare remained unshakably relevant to narrative ballets. Besides the now-universal *Romeo and Juliet,* which Prokofiev's music had made the most popular three-act ballet since Tchaikovsky, the Norwegian National Ballet toured Glen Tetley's *The Tempest* in a double bill with Antonio Bibalo's opera *Macbeth;* André Prokovsky staged his greatly condensed version of *Macbeth* for Scottish Ballet, and a *Hamlet* by Jonathan Taylor was scheduled for a late-November British debut by the Royal New Zealand Ballet. The New Zealand company was now directed by former Royal Ballet and Stuttgart Ballet principal Ashley Killar, in succession to Harry Haythorne. Other directorial changes included Jorma Uotinen at the Finnish National Ballet following Doris Laine's move to the Berlin Komische Oper; Carlo Maier was reportedly newly incumbent at Turin, Italy; and the Greek National Opera Ballet at Athens was reorganized under former U.K. Ballet Rambert dancer Yannis Metsis.

Deaths during the year included, besides MacMillan, Joan-Denise Moriarty, founder-director of the short-lived Irish National Ballet; Alexis Rassine, Lithuanian-British principal of Sadler's Wells Ballet (now the Royal Ballet); Brian Shaw, Royal Ballet teacher and former principal; and three leading figures in post-Revolution dance in Russia: Vakhtang Chabukiani, dancer; Asaf Messerer, dancer, teacher, sometime director of the Bolshoi Ballet; and Konstantin Sergeyev (*see* OBITUARIES), dancer, choreographer, and longtime director of the Kirov Ballet. (NOËL GOODWIN)

See also Music; Theatre.

This article updates the *Macropædia* article The History of Western DANCE.

Disasters

The loss of life and property from disasters in 1992 included the following:

Aviation

January 20, Near Mont Sainte-Odile, France. A French Airbus A-320 traveling from Lyon to Strasbourg sliced through treetops before crashing in snow and fog on a wooded ridge; only 11 of the 96 persons aboard survived the crash.

Early February, Brazil. A Brazilian-made Bandeirante airliner slammed into a mountain; all 12 persons aboard perished.

February 6, Evansville, Ind. A C-130 Hercules transport plane, which was practicing takeoffs and landings, exploded after crashing into a crowded motel and adjacent restaurant; all five crewmen were killed, nine persons in the motel died, and two others in the restaurant lost their lives in the burning wreckage.

February 9, Diouloulou, Senegal. A plane chartered by Club Méditerranée to ferry tourists from Dakar to its coastal resort at Cap Skirring crashed some 48 km (30 mi) short of its destination when the pilot apparently mistook lights in a hotel garden for those marking his intended landing strip; the governor of the region reported that there had been 59 persons aboard the craft and that 31 of them lost their lives.

March 14, North Sea. A helicopter shuttling workers from an oil platform to a nearby accommodation vessel suddenly fell from the sky into the icy sea during a snowstorm; of the 17 persons aboard the craft, only 6 were rescued.

March 22, New York City. A USAir plane en route to Cleveland, Ohio, was twice briefly airborne during takeoff but fell off the runway and crashed into an embankment before landing upside down in Flushing Bay near La Guardia Airport; of the 51 persons aboard, 24 miraculously survived in the tangled wreckage. Though the plane had been deiced twice, some speculated that the pilot should have requested a third treatment prior to the aircraft's departure in a snowstorm some 30 minutes after the last application had been made.

March 25, Oaxaca state, Mexico. A helicopter carrying 10 government officials who were mapping out preparations for a presidential visit to that state the following week slammed into a fog-shrouded mountain; there were no survivors.

April 16, Nairobi, Kenya. A Kenyan air force plane lost power in its left engine and plowed into a block of flats, where it exploded in a fireball; all 45 persons aboard the craft were killed, and 5 persons on the ground lost their lives.

April 22, Perris, Calif. A twin-engine plane carrying sky divers crashed during takeoff; 16 of the 22 persons aboard were killed, and the others were seriously injured in the crash, which was attributed to tainted fuel that caused the right engine to stall.

April 26, Iran. A chartered plane carrying 39 persons crashed while making a routine domestic flight from Tehran to Mah Shahr.

Mid-May, Near Dargachi, Russia. Two Russian military planes collided; 12 of the 14 crewmen aboard the crafts were killed.

June 6, Near La Palma, Panama. A Panamanian airliner carrying 47 persons crashed in the jungle during stormy weather; there were no survivors.

Mid-June, Jauja, Peru. A military helicopter slammed into an army barracks; 11 soldiers were killed, and 25 others were injured.

June 19, Near Kingman, Ariz. A small sightseeing plane crashed near Lake Mead; all 10 persons aboard died.

July 14, Near Aden, Yemen. A military aircraft carrying both military personnel and civilians crashed during a sandstorm after being unable to land because of the swirling winds; 58 persons lost their lives in the desert crash.

July 14, Nakhichevan, Azerbaijan. An aircraft shuttling families of Russian soldiers to Rostovna-Donu crashed during takeoff; 29 persons were killed.

July 24, Near Pattimura, Indon. A passenger plane carrying 71 persons slammed into a fog-shrouded hill and was completely destroyed; none of those aboard the plane survived.

July 31, Near Kathmandu, Nepal. A Thai Airways jetliner carrying 113 persons, many of them tourists, crashed into a mountainside during heavy monsoon rains; soldiers assisting in the rescue effort climbed the rain-drenched Himalayan mountain on their hands and knees but found no survivors.

July 31, Nanjing (Nanking), China. A Chinese airliner burst into flames during takeoff; of the 126 persons aboard, only 17 survived.

August 11, Near Beijing (Peking), China. A helicopter carrying Japanese tourists crashed near the Great Wall; 15 persons lost their lives.

August 27, Ivanovo, Russia. An Aeroflot jet crashed some three kilometres (two miles) short of the runway while attempting to land in heavy fog; 82 persons perished.

September 7, Near Hinckley, Ill. A small plane carrying members of a skydiving club crashed and burst into flames shortly after takeoff when it apparently experienced engine problems; all 12 persons aboard perished.

September 19, Bogotá, Colombia. A cargo plane crashed during takeoff; 11 persons were killed in the fiery wreckage.

September 26, Near Lagos, Nigeria. A Nigerian military transport plane carrying 163 army, navy, and air force officers nosedived minutes after takeoff into a swampy area; there were no survivors.

September 28, Near Kathmandu. A Pakistani Airbus with 167 persons aboard, including mountain climbers and missionaries, slammed into a pine-covered hillside while making its landing approach; all aboard perished in the crash, which was attributed to pilot error. The pilot had flown below the required flight path in his descent over the Himalayas.

October 4, Amsterdam. An El Al Boeing 747 jumbo jet with four persons aboard crashed into an apartment complex in a rundown section of the city known as Bijlmermeer after the pilot reported that two of the airliner's engines were ablaze; all aboard the craft were instantly killed when the jet plowed into two connected 10-story apartment buildings, and at least 70 others, some of them unregistered immigrants, were believed to have died in 80 incinerated apartments.

October 9, Northwestern China. A charter plane carrying French tourists crashed in a remote village; nine tourists and a crew of five were killed.

October 18, Western Java, Indon. A domestic airliner with 31 persons aboard slammed into a mountain; all aboard perished.

October 29, Great Salt Lake, Utah. A military helicopter carrying 13 persons on a training mission crashed during a violent storm; only one soldier survived.

November 5, Henan (Ho-nan) province, China. A helicopter hired to drop leaflets for a cosmetics sales promotion crashed into a building and exploded; 33 persons were killed.

November 5, Near Anapa, Russia. A military helicopter crashed after apparently hitting the side of a cliff; at least 30 persons lost their lives.

November 15, Near Puerto Plata, Dominican Republic. A Cuban airliner en route to Havana crashed after experiencing engine failure in a storm; 34 persons died, including 6 Dominican chess players.

Mid-November, Southern Vietnam. A plane carrying 30 persons crashed in a jungle during bad weather; only one woman, who was found more than a week after the crash, was rescued.

November 24, Near Guilin (Kuei-lin), China. A Boeing 737 jetliner rammed into a mountain moments after it reportedly had belched smoke; 141 persons were killed in the country's worst air disaster to date.

November 30, Montana. Two U.S. Air Force cargo planes collided in midair during a training exercise; 13 crewmen were feared dead.

December 10, Quito, Ecuador. A small plane carrying Ecuador's army chief, his son, and at

AP/WIDE WORLD

Workers search the ruins of an apartment complex in the Bijlmermeer area of Amsterdam after a cargo plane slammed into it on October 4 and burst into flames. The accident, which claimed at least 70 lives, was called the worst air disaster in Dutch history.

Residents of Guadalajara, Mexico, watch as rescue workers search the rubble produced by a series of explosions on April 22. The blasts, which killed more than 200 people, were blamed on gasoline that had leaked into the city's sewer system.

JOHN DAVENPORT—GAMMA LIAISON

least eight other military personnel slammed into a 10-story building; all were killed.

Mid-December, Eastern Zaire. A passenger plane carrying 37 persons crashed in a mountainous area near the Rwandan border; all aboard perished.

December 22, Near Souq as-Sabt, Libya. A domestic airliner with at least 157 persons aboard went down apparently after colliding in midair with a military aircraft; there were unconfirmed reports that the military crew parachuted to safety, but there were no survivors on the passenger plane.

December 22, Faro, Port. A chartered DC-10 Dutch jumbo jet slammed into the runway while attempting to land in a rainstorm, broke apart, and then burst into flames; a sudden wind gust was blamed for the crash, which claimed the lives of 54 of the 340 persons aboard the jetliner.

Fires and Explosions

March 24, Dakar. A tanker truck filled with liquid ammonia inexplicably exploded at a peanut-processing factory; at least 60 persons were killed, some of them by toxic fumes.

April 22, Guadalajara, Mexico. A series of explosions in the city's sewer system, precipitated by a buildup of gasoline fumes caused by a leak in a pipeline belonging to Pemex, the state-owned oil company, rocked more than 20 blocks of the downtown area; at least 206 persons were killed in the blasts, which caused some $300 million in damages.

April 23, Nagorno-Karabakh, Azerbaijan. A passenger bus exploded after driving over a land mine; at least 14 persons, some of them children, were killed in the blast.

May 15, Northern Taiwan. A bus carrying kindergarten students and teachers to a zoo burst into flames after experiencing mechanical problems; 20 children and 4 adults were killed when several bottles of butane stored behind the driver's seat ignited and they were unable to open the emergency exit doors.

Late May, Ukraine. A bus carrying 40 persons burst into flames after containers filled with petroleum ignited; 10 persons were incinerated.

June 2, Detroit, Mich. A fast-burning fire in a three-story brick-and-wood boarding house apparently started on the ground floor; 10 persons on the second and third floors lost their lives in the blaze, which may have been started by a cigarette.

June 21, Off the coast of Port Klang, Malaysia. A chemical tanker sank after being

rocked by oil explosions; 13 persons lost their lives in the roaring blaze.

July 7, Mostoles, Spain. A fire swept through an apartment building, claiming the lives of 12 persons and injuring at least 7 others, who suffered from smoke inhalation and injuries sustained after they jumped from the blazing inferno.

August 8, Tekirdag province, Turkey. A huge explosion in a textile factory in Corlu annihilated the cafeteria, which plunged into a lower-level water-storage area during the crowded lunch hour and destroyed walls and windows; at least 32 workers lost their lives by being either charred by the blast or drowned in the water-storage unit, and 27 others were seriously injured.

Mid-September, The Hague. A fiery blaze in a hostel for the mentally ill and homeless claimed the lives of at least 11 persons.

September 18, Port-au-Prince, Haiti. A chemical explosion in a pharmaceutical laboratory,

which was located in a three-story building, toppled the structure, claimed the lives of at least 15 persons, and injured hundreds of others on a busy downtown street.

Late October, Jaria, India. An explosion in a fireworks store killed at least 25 persons and injured more than 100.

Marine

January 16, Punjab province, Pak. An overloaded ferry carrying religious pilgrims capsized in the icy Jhelum River; more than 200 persons were feared drowned, but 50 others swam to shore.

Mid-January, Uganda. A cargo ship capsized in Lake Victoria during a brutal storm; 50 persons perished, and 18 were rescued.

February 6, Off the coast of Puerto Rico. Two boats filled with refugees from the Dominican Republic capsized in rough seas; only a dozen of the estimated 80 persons aboard the vessels reached shore.

March 8, Off the coast of Thailand. A ferryboat carrying Buddhist pilgrims was rammed by an oil tanker after trying to cut across its path and broke in two; 112 persons aboard the ferry were killed.

April 15, Gulf of Guinea. Two ferryboats collided in high seas between Nigeria and Cameroon; of the estimated 500 persons aboard the two vessels, at least 356 were missing and feared drowned.

Early May, Dubrovnik, Croatia. Two ferryboats collided in Dubrovnik Harbour; 10 persons were killed, and 51 were missing and feared drowned.

Mid-May, Off the coast of Maisi, Cuba. A boat carrying Haitian refugees back to their homeland sank; 18 persons were known dead, and 2 were missing.

June 27, Near Bali, Indon. An overloaded ship sank; 69 persons were missing and feared drowned, but 137 were rescued.

July, Off the coast of Yemen. A ship harbouring Somali refugees was forced aground; 70 persons lost their lives.

July 19, Off the coast of Source Matelas, Haiti. An overcrowded boat carrying some 100 Haitian refugees sank shortly after it was launched; at least 90 were feared drowned.

Late July, Off the coast of Djibouti. A dhow carrying Somali refugees sank in rough seas; at least 45 persons were killed, and only 5 were rescued.

September 20, Off the coast of Indonesia. An oil tanker burst into flames after colliding with a cargo ship in the Strait of Malacca; more than 20 crewmen were missing.

SAKHAI WONG—GAMMA LIAISON

Rescue workers recover the body of a victim of a predawn ferry accident on March 8 in the Gulf of Thailand. The ferryboat sank almost immediately after being struck by an oil tanker.

Men clear away debris produced by an earthquake that killed more than 550 persons in Cairo on October 12. The centre of the quake, the strongest in Egypt in recent history, was located just southwest of the capital.

October 26, Off the coast of Abkhazia, Georgia. A fishing boat carrying more than 200 passengers, many of them women and children fleeing from the two-month civil war in the strife-ridden region of Abkhazia, sank during a storm; only 36 persons were rescued.

Mining

Early February, Near Johannesburg, South Africa. Rockfalls claimed the lives of at least 10 miners at Western Deep Levels gold mine.

March 3, Kozlu, Turkey. A methane gas explosion in a government-run coal mine filled shafts with toxic gas and buried more than 200 miners; 122 bodies were recovered, but as many as 150 more miners were missing and presumed dead. Rescue workers were unable to reach victims because of new blasts and underground fires in the country's worst mining accident to date.

April 17, Heilongjiang (Hei-lung-chiang) province, China. A gas explosion at a colliery in Jixi (Chi-hsi) killed 28 miners.

May 5, Nyeye, Sierra Leone. A tunnel dug in a diamond mine by unlicensed miners caved in and claimed the lives of more than 100 persons.

May 9, Plymouth, Nova Scotia. An explosion in a coal mine, apparently caused by methane gas, crippled the mine's ventilation system, knocked out its power, and claimed the lives of 26 miners.

June 9, Near Krasnodon, Ukraine. A methane gas explosion in a coal mine killed 8 miners instantly and caused a release of lethal carbon monoxide into the mine's ventilation system that suffocated at least 38 others.

August 21, Near Donetsk, Ukraine. A series of explosions caused by a buildup of gas ripped through a coal mine and claimed the lives of at least 17 persons.

November 25, Stavropol, Russia. A methane gas explosion in a coal mine entombed at least 13 miners.

Miscellaneous

January 1, Bombay. Toxic liquor that was laced with methyl alcohol by the owners of a bar dispensing drinks to impoverished New Year's Eve revelers killed at least 91 persons and caused countless others to suffer permanent kidney and vision damage.

February 7, Bangkok, Thailand. Scaffolding supporting workers who were constructing a 30-story apartment building collapsed; at least 20 workers died.

February 18, Kumbakonam, India. A stampede occurred during a Hindu bathing festival when a wall collapsed, killing several persons standing on it and causing the crowd to surge toward the sacred lake of Kumbakonam; as many as 47 persons were feared dead in the melee.

February 29, Jerusalem. The roof of an Arab café caved in after being hit by the collapsing rain-weakened retaining wall of an adjacent cemetery; 23 persons were killed and about 20 injured.

Early May, Orissa state, India. Poisonous liquor claimed the lives of more than 200 persons who drank the illegally brewed beverage, which contained a lethal percentage of methyl alcohol; more than 600 persons suffering from convulsions and stomach pains sought treatment at hospitals.

May 4, Srinagar, India. A three-story house packed with about 200 funeral mourners collapsed when the wooden floorboards on the top floor gave way; 81 persons were killed, and 100 were injured.

May 5, Bastia, Corsica. A temporary soccer stand that was erected to expand capacity at a French Cup semifinal match between Bastia and Marseille collapsed moments before the kickoff; 14 persons were killed, and more than 700 were injured.

Late July–Early August, Russia and Ukraine. Widespread poisonings were reported across the two countries among those who had eaten wild mushrooms contaminated with deadly toadstool toxins; at least 24 deaths were attributed to mushroom poisoning, and more than 150 persons were hospitalized.

August 3, Anhui (An-hui) province, China. Food poisoning claimed the lives of 11 restaurant patrons who ate breakfast buns made from flour that had been contaminated with farm chemicals; the exposure occurred when a truck driver loaded his truck with flour after having spilled chemicals in his vehicle.

Mid-November, Bangladesh. Food poisoning claimed the lives of at least 11 persons who had unknowingly eaten a poisonous variety of patka fish.

Late December, Vijayawada, India. An overhead water tank that was filled to capacity collapsed and unleashed a torrent of water that swept away a row of thatched huts; at least 15 persons were killed.

Natural

January 5, Rio de Janeiro. A brutal storm accompanied by heavy rains and high winds caused massive flooding and mud slides; at least 25 persons were killed, most of them buried in their hillside homes by mudflows, and hundreds were left homeless.

Early February, Eastern Mediterranean. The harshest winter in 40 years claimed at least 15 lives when blizzards blanketed Israel, Lebanon, Syria, Jordan, and Turkey.

February 1–7, Southeastern Turkey. A weeklong onslaught of blizzards accompanied by bitter cold caused widespread avalanches, which buried the Kurdish mountain hamlet of Gormec and the village of Akcayul in Sirnak province; the devastating snowslides claimed at least 201 lives.

Mid-February, California. Relentless rainstorms for nearly a week precipitated widespread flooding in Los Angeles and Ventura counties and caused $23 million in damage and at least eight deaths.

Mid-March, Jiangxi (Chiang-hsi) province, China. Several days of torrential rains caused severe flooding; 29 persons were killed, 70 were injured, and more than a million were affected by the floodwaters.

March 13, Erzincan, Turkey. A powerful earthquake measuring 6.8 on the Richter scale decimated nearly one-quarter of the city, left more than 500 persons dead and more than 1,000 injured, and unleashed avalanches and landslides, which blocked roads, railways, and bridges; strong aftershocks followed for two days, and frightened survivors remained outdoors despite freezing temperatures.

March 18, Near Belo Horizonte, Brazil. A thundering landslide buried a hillside shantytown and killed more than 30 persons who were buried in their shacks in the Barraginha slum. The slide, which possibly entombed 100 to 150 residents, was variously attributed to rain and to a waste deposit piled atop the hill by construction workers in the area.

May 13–15, Tajikistan. Torrential rains caused heavy flooding and mud slides that killed at least 200 persons.

May 20, North-West Frontier province, Pak. A strong earthquake measuring 5.5 on the Richter scale shook the area and destroyed mud and stone houses; at least 36 persons were killed and 100 injured in the temblor.

Late May–Early June, Argentina, Brazil, Paraguay. Two weeks of heavy rains caused the Paraguay, Paraná, and Iguaçu rivers to overflow their banks and inundate hundreds of towns and villages; at least 28 persons were killed, and more than 220,000 others were evacuated from their homes.

June 7, Dushanbe, Tajikistan. Torrential rains unleashed mud slides that entombed homes in low-lying areas; at least 10 persons lost their lives.

Early–Mid July, China. Torrential rains caused massive flooding in Fujian (Fu-chien) and Zhejiang (Che-chiang) provinces; more than 1,000 were killed in the floods, thousands of homes collapsed or were destroyed, and vast areas of farmlands were inundated.

July 23–24, Cao Bang province, Vietnam. A mud slide reportedly buried hundreds of persons according to the official Voice of Vietnam radio, but a casualty figure of only 23 was reported in the country's Communist Party newspaper.

A camel from Miami's zoo stands amid the wreckage of Hurricane Andrew, which struck Florida on August 24. The hurricane was one of a number of major U.S. disasters in 1992.

JOHN BERRY—GAMMA LIAISON

Late July–Mid-August, Southern Pakistan. Three days of relentless monsoon rains precipitated heavy flooding, which claimed the lives of at least 56 persons and left thousands of others homeless as their mud-and-brick homes collapsed.

August 9, Mizoram, India. A thundering landslide caused by monsoon rains buried makeshift homes; at least 60 persons were feared dead.

August 19, Kyrgyzstan. A powerful earthquake shook the region, causing rockfalls to devastate remote mountain villages located near the border with China; at least 50 persons perished in the temblor.

August 23–26, The Bahamas, Florida, Louisiana. Hurricane Andrew, the costliest natural disaster in U.S. history, struck The Bahamas before rampaging across southern Florida, where it virtually annihilated the towns of Homestead and Florida City with wind gusts up to 264 km/h (164 mph), and unleashing its fury on Louisiana's Cajun country, notably Morgan City and Lafayette; 38 persons were killed in Florida alone, where 63,000 homes were destroyed, $20 billion in damages were assessed, and 3 million homes and businesses were without power. Louisiana, which sustained damages of at least $300 million and where some 44,000 persons were left homeless, was faced with the probable loss of at least half of its sugarcane crop.

August 30–31, China. Tropical Storm Polly lashed the country with waves as high as 6 m (20 ft) in the northern port of Tianjin (Tientsin), but most of the fatalities occurred along the southeast coast, where 165 persons were killed and more than 5 million were left homeless.

September 1, Western coast of Nicaragua. A major earthquake at sea spawned huge tidal waves that swallowed coastal communities from Corinto to San Juan del Sur; at least 105 persons were killed, 489 were injured, and some 27 communities sustained serious damage.

September 2, Near Gulbahar, Afghanistan. Heavy rains precipitated devastating flash floods that wiped out numerous villages as they roared through three valleys in the southern foothills of the Hindu Kush Mountains; as many as 3,000 persons were feared dead.

September 11–16, Pakistan and India. Torrential monsoon rains that began on September 8 caused the swollen Indus River to overflow its banks; the massive flooding in Pakistan claimed more than 2,000 lives, and at least 500 persons died in India as a result of the advancing waters.

September 15, Manila. A rush-hour rainstorm caused flash flooding that unleashed mud slides onto the capital; at least 10 persons were killed.

September 22, Southeastern France. Torrential rains caused deadly flash floods that rampaged through the Ardèche, Vaucluse, and Drôme regions; at least 80 persons were feared dead, and 30 others were missing.

Early October, Kerala, India. Floods and landslides in the southern state claimed the lives of at least 60 persons and left thousands homeless.

October 12, Cairo. A devastating earthquake, 5.9 on the Richter scale, rumbled through the capital; the temblor toppled many old buildings, destroyed more than 5,000 homes, killed more than 550 persons, injured nearly 10,000, and left some 3,000 families homeless.

October 18, Near San Pedro de Uraba, Colombia. A severe earthquake, the second in two days, touched off an eruption of mud and steam at thermal baths; 10 persons were known dead, 25 were missing, and 16 victims suffered severe burns.

Mid-November, Southern India. Four days of torrential rains precipitated floods and mud slides; more than 230 persons were killed, and thousands were left homeless.

Mid-November, Ukraine. Severe floods took the lives of at least 17 persons and caused extensive damage to homes and roads.

Mid-November, Albania. Widespread flooding occurred when the Mati River overflowed its banks; at least 11 persons died as a result of the deluge.

November 21–23, Southern and midwestern U.S. As many as 45 freak tornadoes zigzagged across 11 states from Texas to as far north as Ohio, creating massive destruction, especially in trailer parks, killing at least 25 persons, and injuring hundreds; hardest hit was Mississippi, where at least 15 persons lost their lives.

December 7, Caranavi, Bolivia. Torrential rains triggered a massive mud slide that buried a goldmining town and pushed some shacks into the swollen Tipuani River; 153 persons were known dead, some 130 were injured, and an uncertain number (100–200) were presumed dead.

December 10–11, Northeastern U.S. A brutal and deadly winter storm that was designated an extratropical cyclone by the U.S. National Weather Service alternately dumped rain and snow (as much as 1.2 m [4 ft] of snow in parts of Massachusetts), packed strong winds that inflicted some $10 million in damages on New Jersey's Atlantic City and sucked out skyscraper windows in New York City, and claimed the lives of at least 17 persons.

December 12, Flores, Indon. A powerful earthquake rocked the island, destroyed 80% of the buildings in the coastal city of Maumere, and killed more than 1,200 persons living there; a total of 2,500 persons lost their lives in the quake.

Railroad

March 3, Near Nelidovo, Russia. An express train and a freight train collided, apparently when one of the engineers failed to observe railroad signals; at least 27 persons died in the crash.

April 5, Andhra Pradesh, India. A passenger train slammed into the rear of a stationary freight train awaiting clearance to enter Tsundur railway station; at least 21 persons were killed in the high-impact crash, and 15 were injured.

August 7, Near Lazaro Cardenas, Mexico. A passenger train and freight train collided; 10 persons were killed, and more than 220 passengers were injured.

November 1, Reti, Pak. A passenger train filled with sleeping passengers slammed into the rear of a parked freight train after a signal apparently diverted the express train to the same track as the freight train; at least 14 persons were killed, and as many as 150 were injured.

November 15, Northeim, Germany. A passenger train crashed into a derailed freight train; 11 persons died, and at least 51 were injured.

Traffic

Mid-February, Near Belbeis, Egypt. A bus hit a tree and cracked in two; 14 persons were killed, and 42 were injured in the crash.

Early March, Near Nilphamari, Bangladesh. A bus skidded off a bridge into a river; 35 persons were killed, and 42 were missing and feared drowned.

March 12, Göteborg, Sweden. A runaway tram rolled backward down a hill, slammed into a car, collided with a taxicab, jumped the rails, and plowed into a queue of passengers standing at a tram stop before it jackknifed and came to a halt; the two-carriage tram had been emptied of passengers because a fallen electrical cable blocked its path. Of the 13 fatalities, 4 were from the car, which had burst into flames.

March 14, Russia. A prison van overturned during a gust of high wind and then burst into flames; 16 prisoners and one guard were incinerated in the blaze.

Mid-March, Bursa, Turkey. A 10-vehicle pileup occurred when a truck skidded into a bus and collided with other oncoming traffic during a rainstorm; 14 persons were killed, and 11 were injured.

April 11, Near Dundee, South Africa. A school bus transporting teenagers and teachers crashed into a steel railing while crossing a single-lane bridge after swerving to avoid an oncoming car; 30 students and 3 teachers were killed, and at least 36 others were injured.

Mid-April, Near Buenos Aires, Arg. A passenger bus carrying Easter holiday tourists exploded after slamming into three cars; at least 41 persons were killed, and 20 were injured.

May 9, Near Vitoria, Spain. A bus overturned while rounding a bend in the road; 17 persons were killed in the crash.

June 17, Near Mersa Matruh, Egypt. A military bus and an oil tanker collided; 48 persons were killed in the fiery wreckage.

August 8, Mailänd, Germany. A tour bus collided with a car; 11 persons perished in the crash.

Mid-August, Madhya Pradesh, India. A bus loaded with passengers fell into a flooded river; 19 persons were killed and 25 were missing and presumed drowned.

August 19, Torreblanca, Spain. A speeding bus carrying tourists from Barcelona to Seville somersaulted off a coastal highway and landed on its roof after swerving off a tight curve at twice the appropriate speed; 45 persons were killed, and 11 were injured.

September 6, Near Donau-Eschingen, Germany. A tour bus was struck by a car on a highway near the Black Forest; 21 persons were killed, and 37 were injured.

September 6 and 7, Nepal. Two bus accidents on successive days occurred when the vehicles rolled off a mountain cliff at the same spot and plunged into the Thopla River; 10 persons were killed in the first accident, and 12 passengers died in the second disaster.

September 16, Kaliningrad, Russia. A bus and train collided; 17 persons from the bus died in the crash.

Late September, Central Spain. A bus and truck collided head-on; 10 persons lost their lives, and 9 were injured.

Early November, Near Safaga, Egypt. A school bus collided with a truck; 18 children and 8 teachers were killed, and 17 other passengers were injured.

November 12, The Gambia. A bus carrying more than 100 persons to a dock experienced brake failure and plunged into a river; there were only three survivors.

Early December, Kenya. A bus carrying 112 persons skidded out of control, slammed into a bridge, and plunged into a river; nearly 100 persons were killed in the country's worst road accident to date.

December 11, South Africa. The driver of an overloaded pickup truck lost control of the vehicle, which slid under an oncoming truck; 20 children and 3 adults were killed.

December 21, Pakistan. A bus left the road and plunged into a 763-m (2,500-ft)-deep gorge in Malakand region; at least 22 persons lost their lives, and 8 were injured.

December 24, Southeastern Turkey. Two buses collided head-on during a blinding snowstorm; 13 persons were killed, and 21 were injured.

Earth Sciences

GEOLOGY AND GEOCHEMISTRY

In 1992 the U.S. Congress passed and Pres. George Bush signed the National Geologic Mapping Act, which was expected to reverse the drastic curtailment in geologic-map production that had taken place since the 1970s. The act would expedite production of a geologic-map data base for the U.S. that could be applied to land-use-management assessment, conservation of natural resources, groundwater management, and environmental protection. The growing importance of those areas of the geologic sciences was evident from the program of the 29th International Geological Congress (quadrennial) held in Kyoto, Japan, during the year. The growth of world population, and especially of urban populations, increased the need for improved public awareness of the relevance of geologic-map information to issues of land-use management.

Development of a global standard of geologic time has been based largely on correlation of the relative order and fossil content of rock strata found around the world (chronostratigraphy and biostratigraphy). Since the late 1970s an alternate approach, developed by Peter Vail and colleagues of Exxon Production Research Co., Houston, Texas, has been that of sequence stratigraphy, based initially on data obtained from seismic reflection profiling, an acoustic technique for imaging buried sediment layers. The approach assumes that rock successions of precisely similar age exist in tectonically independent basins worldwide, implying that there are records of sea-level fluctuation cycles that can be correlated globally and that all sediments in the geologic record for the past 250 million years can be identified and dated with reference to those cycles.

A.D. Miall of the University of Toronto challenged the validity of the approach, which was embodied in a sea-level cycle chart published by Exxon, as an independent standard of geologic time on the grounds that the basic premise remained unproven. The critical test is to demonstrate that successions of cycles of precisely the same age do indeed exist in many tectonically independent basins around the world. According to Miall, none of the events in the Exxon chart received independent global confirmation by careful chronostratigraphic work and that most of the careful local studies indicated significant departures from the Exxon chart. Stratigraphic correlation with the Exxon chart will almost always succeed because there are so many Exxon sequence-boundary events from which to choose, but it is questionable what this proves. Miall emphasized the dangers of circular reasoning when the Exxon chart was used as a template for stratigraphic correlations.

The identification in the early 1980s of relict coesite, a form of silicon dioxide that can be made only under high pressure, in mineral samples from the Dora Maira massif in the Italian Alps provided the first evidence that large masses of continental rocks (in contrast to thin slabs of oceanic crust in subduction zones) had been carried to depths in the Earth of at least 100 km (60 mi). That startling conclusion was confirmed by the discovery of similar high-pressure continental rocks in several other collision belts. What still was lacking, however, was an explanation of how these rocks returned to the surface without the mineralogical signature of high pressure being erased by recrystallization.

D. Avigad of the École Normale Supérieure, Paris, studied the internal structure of the Dora Maira massif and concluded that its structural units were juxtaposed in the mountain-building process after the high-pressure metamorphism had been completed and, thus, that the structure of the massif was shaped during an overall decompression of the rocks as they rose through the crust. The mountain range was built within a setting in which the European and Adrian tectonic plates were converging. Before the plates sutured, a period of extensional tectonics, or stretching, occurred. This was associated with shallow-dipping shear zones that aided movement of the upper parts of the growing mountain range and dispersal of the rocks laterally away from the mountains. The relatively rapid removal of the rocks from the mountain heights permitted concomitant uplift of the deep-seated rocks, and this process helped unroof the high-pressure coesite-bearing rocks. Although the deep burial of these rocks was caused by compression between tectonic plates, their exhumation was caused by extensional tectonics within the overall plate-convergent setting.

Recent advances in isotope geochemistry have made it possible to decipher the rates of uplift and erosion of mountain ranges. Techniques for precise determination of argon isotopes in minerals have been greatly improved, as has an understanding of how isotope "ages" can be interpreted in terms of the times at which certain events occurred; *e.g.,* the time at which a granite cooled through a particular temperature. Mark Harrison of the University of California at Los Angeles used argon-argon isotope dating, combined with tectonic studies, to develop an intriguing story about the uplift of Tibet and the exhumation of the Himalayas. As

Mineral veins at Nevada's Yucca Mountain figured in a debate over the proposed use of the site as a nuclear waste repository. Some thought that the veins had been formed by upwellings of groundwater and that the stored waste could be threatened by future rises in the water table.

Dante, an aptly named eight-legged robot, undergoes tests before being sent on its mission into the smoldering mouth of Mt. Erebus, an Antarctic volcano located on Ross Island. Designed and built at Carnegie Mellon University, Pittsburgh, Pa., Dante was to rappel down the crater wall of the active volcano, which was inaccessible to humans. On the way to the lava lake on the crater floor, it would make television observations, take gas samples, retrieve minerals, and conduct a variety of other experiments. In the process the robot would help validate robotic exploration concepts being envisioned for the Moon and Mars.

ROBOTICS INSTITUTE, CARNEGIE MELLON UNIVERSITY

the Indian continental mass indented the Asian continent, India was accommodated to a significant extent by eastward displacement of a large mass of China along a major fault system. About 20 million years ago this lateral displacement terminated, and extremely fast uplift of the Himalayas occurred within a couple of million years. The enhanced erosion associated with the exhumation of the towering mountain range is also recorded in the stratigraphy of the immense sedimentary fan beneath the Bay of Bengal. Rift valleys that opened transverse to the mountain ranges during the past seven million years indicate that the Himalayas may be in the process of collapse. The history of the uplift and erosion of this large mountain massif provides critical information for paleoceanographers and paleoclimatologists working on the history of monsoon conditions in the region.

The Earth's climate also may be affected by volcanic eruptions, with such gases as sulfur dioxide (SO_2) and carbon dioxide (CO_2) being particularly influential. Attempts to estimate the amounts of these gases emitted from ancient volcanoes have relied largely on petrologic studies based on the concentrations of sulfur and CO_2 trapped in glass inclusions within minerals and in pumices produced by the volcanoes. H.R. Westrich of Sandia National Laboratories, Albuquerque, N.M., and T.M. Gerlach of the U.S. Geological Survey, Vancouver, Wash., tested the validity of the technique by studying the minerals and glasses associated with the June 15, 1991, eruption of Mount Pinatubo in the Philippines and by comparing the results with the amount of SO_2 measured in the stratosphere on the basis of TOMS (total ozone mapping spectrometer) satellite data. The petrologic method predicted a stratospheric injection of about 110,000 tons of sulfur (220,0000 tons of SO_2), which was almost two orders of magnitude less than the amount determined from TOMS data. The difference suggested a source of sulfur in excess of that dissolved in silicate melt (lava). The authors concluded that the glass inclusions formed after most of the sulfur was already separated from the melt in the form of a water-rich, free gas phase given off from the magma at depth. The gases released during the eruption, therefore, were underrepresented in the composition of the inclusions. The standard petrologic method for estimating sulfur degassing thus appeared prone to substantial underestimations of sulfur releases by past eruptions and of the potential effects of those releases on climate.

The proposed nuclear waste repository site at Yucca Mountain, about 160 km (100 mi) northwest of Las Vegas,

Nev., has been the subject of debate for several years. The present groundwater level is about 300 m (1,000 ft) below the site, but Jerry Szymanski of the U.S. Department of Energy reported in 1987 that groundwater had risen to much higher levels in the past and that radioactive wastes stored at the site would potentially threaten the environment if groundwater rose as high in the future. A 1992 panel report from the National Research Council found Szymanski's evidence and proposed mechanism to be inadequate and concluded that no known mechanism could raise the water-table level high enough to reach the repository site. Continued site characterization was recommended for more detailed assessment of the future geologic processes at Yucca Mountain.

That fossil bones contain preserved proteins had been revealed in a general way by bulk amino acid assays, but recently the preservation of a specific protein, osteocalcin, was documented in dinosaur bones at least 75 million years old by Gerard Muyzer of the University of Leiden, Neth., and Philip Sandberg of the University of Illinois. The discovery constituted the oldest record of specific protein preservation and held real potential for addressing the question of dinosaur evolutionary relationships and the genetic relationship of dinosaurs to birds and to other reptiles.

(PETER JOHN WYLLIE)

GEOPHYSICS

Although seismic activity worldwide was moderate during the year, California was subjected to more than its usual share of strong earthquakes in several series going back to mid-1991. On July 12, 1991, a shock of magnitude 6.9 on the Richter scale occurred off the coast near the Oregon border. It was followed on August 16 by a magnitude 6.2 quake and on August 17 by two shocks of magnitudes 6.0 and 7.1, all south of the first, near Cape Mendocino. This series was widely felt throughout northern California and southern Oregon but caused negligible damage. Then on April 25, 1992, another series began off Cape Mendocino with a shock of magnitude 6.9, followed the next day by two of magnitudes 6.5 and 6.6. The April 25 quake, which caused considerable damage to towns in Humboldt county, produced an acceleration more than twice that of the Earth's gravity, the largest ever recorded.

Almost coincident with this activity, another series began in south-central California on April 22, 1992, with a shock of magnitude 6.1. It was followed on June 28 by a quake of magnitude 7.4 in Yucca Valley about 150 km east of Los Angeles, and among the many aftershocks was one of magnitude 6.6 just over three hours later. (One kilometre is about 0.62 mi.) The main shock reached as far north as Boise, Idaho, and as far east as Santa Fe, N.M., and Denver, Colo. One person died, 350 were injured, and damage totaled $92 million. Had any of these earthquakes been located in an urban area, the smallest would have been very destructive, and those with magnitude of 7.0 or greater would have been devastating.

Much of Erzincan, Turkey, was destroyed March 13 by a magnitude-6.8 shock, which left more than 500 persons dead and unleashed landslides that blocked transportation arteries. On August 19 a magnitude-7.5 earthquake, one of three major shocks to hit Kyrgyzstan in 1992, devastated a number of mountain villages near the border with China and killed at least 50 people. Another severe quake on September 1, of magnitude 7.0, near the coast of Nicaragua killed at least 105 and left thousands homeless; most of the casualties and damage resulted from tsunamis (seismic sea waves) triggered by the quake. Two destructive shocks, one of magnitude 6.6 on October 17 and the other of magnitude 7.2 a day later, occurred in Colombia about 300 km northwest of Bogotá. On December 12 a magnitude-7.5 quake rocked the eastern part of the Indonesian island of Flores, virtually destroying the town of Maumere and inundating entire coastal villages with tsunamis.

Several lesser tremors were notable for being located in areas of comparatively infrequent activity, among them a magnitude-5.8 shock April 13 near Roermond, Neth., near the Belgian and German borders, the strongest to hit the region since 1756. On October 12 a magnitude-5.9 quake, the most powerful recorded for Egypt, struck about 30 km southwest of Cairo. More than 550 people were killed and nearly 10,000 injured, many of them residents of crowded, substandard buildings in the city's slums. Egypt's famed Sphinx and pyramids were spared.

The international Ocean Drilling Program (ODP) completed and reported on Legs 137 through 141. Legs 137 and 140 revisited Hole 504B, the world's deepest sub-seafloor hole, which was located in the Pacific Ocean at about 1° N latitude, 84° W longitude, off the coast of Ecuador. It was first drilled in 1979 and was revisited in the early 1980s and then again in 1986, at which time the scientific drilling ship *JOIDES Resolution* had to leave some down-hole gear owing to time constraints and the lack of adequate retrieval equipment. The main objective of Leg 137 was to clear the hole and prepare it for further drilling. Found to be in good condition, the hole was drilled 59.2 m deeper to a depth of 1,621.5 m below the seafloor. (One metre is about 3.3 ft.) Leg 140 extended the hole to 2,000.4 m, nearly three times deeper than the second-deepest hole. Over its total depth the hole penetrated in succession 274.5 m of sediment, 571.5 m of pillow lavas, a 209-m transition zone, and 945.5 m into competent rock. Throughout the years the down-hole temperatures had been logged, from which a gradient of 61° C (109.8° F) per 1,000 m was established, indicating a temperature of 195° C (383° F) at the 2,000-m level.

To examine the sedimentary history of the eastern equatorial Pacific, two transects comprising 11 holes were drilled across the equator on Leg 138. Seven holes were in a north-south line at about the 100° W meridian, and four were drilled farther east off Central America and Ecuador. A large amount of digitized data was collected for colour analysis by means of a new automated colour-scanning instrument developed at Oregon State University. A continuous record of sediments for the past 7 million years were gathered at all sites and for the past 18 million years at

three sites. The analysis provided a continuous history of deposition and valuable information concerning long-term changes in the climate of the eastern Pacific.

The Middle Valley region of the northern Juan de Fuca Ridge in the eastern North Pacific is unique in that, even though it is an area of seafloor spreading, the upwelling material is not cooled or scoured away by seawater but is contained by an overlying cap of thick sediments. The sediments form a seal over the volcanic rocks, trapping extremely hot water beneath the sea bottom. On Leg 139 22 holes were drilled into this overburden at critical points. Scientists were able to measure the temperature regime, rates of fluid flow, and the chemical composition of the various elements of the newly forming crust.

Off the Taitao Peninsula in southern Chile, the Chile Ridge, the Chile Trench, and the spreading boundary between the Nazca and Antarctic plates all converge. Leg 141 was planned to explore this singular juncture where a mid-oceanic ridge is being subducted and the overriding plate is the continental lithosphere. Three holes were drilled across the accretionary complex about 35 km north of the triple junction. Unexpectedly, no evidence of extensional deformation or subsidence was found, which seemed to indicate that subduction erosion has not yet begun. A fourth hole was drilled on the seaward extensions of the Taitao Ridge, where, rather than the expected uniform basalt, interlayers of lava were found, apparently the result of the migration of arc magmas into the oceanic plate through the Taitao Fracture Zone. A fifth hole was located on the prism directly above the subducted spreading axis. Normal faulting was encountered, indicating that subduction erosion and subsidence has begun at that point.   (RUTLAGE J. BRAZEE)

HYDROLOGY

Extensive irrigation projects beginning about 1960 were depleting river inflow to the Aral Sea in the former Soviet Union, resulting in the shrinking of what was once the world's fourth largest lake. By 1992 the lake's volume was less than a third of its 1960 figure, while its surface was diminished by almost a half. The Middle East continued to suffer water shortages. Jordan, already water short, experienced increased water demands because of an influx of refugees. Water supplies in Israel were being taxed by a million immigrants from former Soviet countries.

Libya completed the first phase of an enormous water-supply project that was to deliver water from wells in the central and southern desert areas to reservoirs along the Mediterranean coast for irrigation and urban use. Part of the project, a pipeline 4 m (13 ft) in diameter and nearly as long as the Rhine, was capable of delivering more than 1,900 cu m (500,000 gal) of water per day.

As the 1992 water year began (Oct. 1, 1991), nearly 15% of the U.S. experienced long-term drought conditions. In the Missouri River Basin the drought was the third worst of the 20th century. Soil moisture conditions and reservoir storage in the western states were below average at the start of the water year. By contrast, streamflow was in the normal to above-normal range at 77% of the index-stream-gauging stations in the conterminous U.S. Streamflow and reservoir contents were well below average in the Pacific Northwest by early spring of 1992. Both the East Coast and West Coast continued in a drought situation throughout the year. The June flow of the Snake River reached the lowest level in 81 years, an indication of the severity of drought in the northwestern U.S. By midsummer below-normal streamflow occurred in 36% of the conterminous U.S.

The combined flow of the Columbia, Mississippi, and St. Lawrence rivers was 18% below normal at the beginning of the 1992 water year, remained in the normal range throughout the winter and spring, and dropped into the below-normal range by midsummer. Mean water levels in the Great Lakes were slightly below the median going into the winter but remained in the normal range throughout the remainder of the year.

In 1992 groundwater consumption in the U.S. exceeded 300 million cu m (80 billion gal) per day, a figure more than double the consumption in 1950. Two-thirds of the water was used for irrigation of crops, 17% for domestic water supply, 14% for industry, and 2% for livestock watering. Forty-four states had adopted or were in the process of adopting groundwater-protection strategies to encourage the conservation and wise use of groundwater resources. Artificial recharge of aquifers offered one solution for the problem of dwindling groundwater supplies. The U.S. Bureau of Reclamation was conducting a groundwater-recharge demonstration program under the authority of the High Plains States Groundwater Demonstration Program Act of 1982. Projects located in Montana, South Dakota, Colorado, Nebraska, Oklahoma, Idaho, Arizona, and Texas were operational; several additional projects were in the construction stage.

The conservation group American Rivers named the Columbia and Snake rivers in Oregon and Washington the most endangered river systems in the U.S. for 1992. Dam and reservoir operations had dramatically reduced the populations of wild salmon in those river systems.

K.B. Crandall and colleagues, writing in the April 1992 issue of *Rivers,* compared the economic benefits of perennial and intermittent flows in Arizona's Hassayampa River Riparian Preserve. The study revealed a large potential loss of benefits to the local economy if streamflows were to diminish from steady perennial flows to intermittent, seasonal flows. The study confirmed that streamflows and aquatic ecosystems generate economic benefits. Instream flows, or streamflow levels that support such resources as riparian (riverbank) habitats, had been neglected in the competition for water because the benefits they provided tended to be public goods and amenities not previously recognized as beneficial uses of water. Current trends in water resources management, water law, and natural resource economics indicated that nonconsumptive uses of water needed to be included in future water budgets.　(BRUCE P. VAN HAVEREN)

METEOROLOGY

In sharp contrast to the widespread, persistent warmth observed over much of the world in the 1980s and early 1990s, several large areas of the globe experienced abnormally low temperatures during 1992. The oceanic and atmospheric anomaly patterns of the moderate El Niño (a periodic appearance of abnormally warm surface water in the eastern equatorial Pacific) that commenced in 1991 rapidly faded as conditions returned nearly to normal by mid-1992. In addition, parts of the U.S. were devastated by hurricanes, while the island of Guam was hit by five different typhoons.

Hurricane Andrew, the costliest natural disaster ever to strike the U.S., was one of the more newsworthy meteorologic events of the year. Andrew raced through the northern Bahamas and southern Florida in late August with sustained winds as high as 225 km/h (140 mph). Although the eye of the storm was inland less than four hours, Andrew inflicted an estimated $30 billion in damages and caused 38 fatalities, directly and indirectly, in Florida alone. Millions of homes and businesses lost power, and an estimated 250,000 people were left homeless. Once in the Gulf of Mexico, Andrew took aim at south-central Louisiana, making its second landfall near Morgan City. Fortunately, the brunt

of the storm affected sparsely populated agricultural and wetland regions. All told, Andrew took a total of 60 lives in Louisiana, Florida, and The Bahamas.

Despite Andrew's effects, 1992 was the second consecutive year having a subnormal Atlantic hurricane season, with only 6 named storms (versus a long-term average of 10). In the Pacific Ocean, Hurricane Iniki became the strongest storm in at least 90 years to affect Hawaii. Iniki's sustained winds reached 225 km/h just before it struck the island of Kauai in early September. Civil defense authorities estimated that major damage covered 75–80% of the island, with half of its 21,000 homes and most of its 70 hotels badly damaged. Damage estimates rose to nearly $2 billion by the end of the year, making Iniki the most destructive storm to strike the Hawaiian islands. Farther west, Typhoon Omar slammed into Guam in late August with winds gusting to 250 km/h (155 mph), causing $700 million in damage and destroying or badly damaging more than 2,100 homes. Later the island was clipped by typhoons Brian, Elsie, Gay, and Hunt, which caused only minor damage.

In the contiguous U.S. numerous storm systems and ample moisture spread across the southern tier of states during the first half of the year. The 1991–92 wet season in the western U.S. brought enough precipitation across some southern sections to nearly alleviate the effects of the six-year drought, prompting several municipalities to ease or eliminate water-use restrictions. Farther north, however, subnormal winter precipitation allowed the drought to continue. Along with unusually high temperatures and ample fuel, the drought abetted several outbreaks of wildfires during the summer and fall months, particularly in Idaho, California, Nevada, and Oregon. By contrast, June–August

Residents of Jerusalem enjoy the half metre of snow that fell on January 2 in the city's heaviest snowstorm in more than 40 years. Several areas of the Middle East had periods of unusually cold weather during the first half of 1992.

temperatures averaged much below normal east of the Rockies, making 1992 the third coolest summer nationally.

For the Middle Eastern countries the winter months were characterized by repeated invasions of cold air and heavy precipitation, frequently as snow. Abnormally low temperatures persisted across the region into midsummer. Even northern Africa was not immune to the invading cold-air masses. A frigid mid-January outbreak claimed 17 lives in Nigeria's northern city of Kaduna, and repeated intrusions of cold air enveloped much of north-central Africa into May. In the western Sahel the 1992 rainy season started slowly, but surplus July and August rains brought seasonal totals near average. The most notable exceptions included northern Senegal and Mauritania. Farther south an extreme drought, described as the worst in 100 years, afflicted much of southern Africa during the 1991–92 rainy season, profoundly cutting agricultural production.

Unusually dry conditions affected much of continental Europe during mid-1992. Late-summer rains finally ended the dry spell in northern Europe, but a series of September and October storms dumped heavy rains on northern Spain, southern France, and northern Italy, producing localized flooding that claimed over a dozen lives.

In early September torrential downpours in extreme northern Pakistan and India melted mountain snowpack, producing landslides and catastrophic downstream flooding. An estimated 4,000 lives were lost, millions were displaced, and agricultural and property damage was immense in Pakistan's worst flooding since the country was founded in 1947. Surplus March precipitation across much of eastern China, Taiwan, the Ryukyu Islands, South Korea, and western Japan produced effects ranging from severe flooding to welcome relief from the previous year's dryness. However, the wet spell abruptly ended in interior southeastern China in midsummer, damaging crops. In mid-July a series of tropical systems dumped inundating rains on the central and northern Philippines, while in late August and early September more rain generated deadly flows of lahar (a mixture of volcanic ash and water) near Mt. Pinatubo that destroyed dwellings in nearby villages and took numerous lives.

The rainy season in northern Australia, typically November to March, was slow to start until heavy mid-January rains fell on the east-central and northeastern sections of the country. Then, in late February, cyclones Daman and 18P dumped excessive rains on parts of southeastern Queensland. The rain benefited many previously stressed crops in central and northern Queensland, but in southeastern Queensland it generated some of the region's worst flooding of the century.

Much of central South America experienced very wet weather in the first months of 1992. In May, though, a month when totals normally decline, rainfall dramatically increased. The Brazilian states of Rio Grande do Sul and Santa Catarina were drenched, and downstream river flooding became a chronic problem along the Iguassu, Paraguay, and Paraná rivers in northern Argentina. Unusual warmth dominated large areas of South America between March and June; during midyear, however, unseasonably cool air covered most of the continent.   (ELBERT W. FRIDAY, JR.)

This article updates the *Macropædia* article CLIMATE AND WEATHER.

OCEANOGRAPHY

The Earth's climate depends on the global distribution of the Sun's radiation and on the way atmospheric winds and ocean currents carry heat over the globe. Paleoceanographers and geochemists have learned in the past few decades that the intensity and duration of the most severe climate fluctuations, i.e., the ice ages, are recorded in polar ice and in seafloor sediments as changes in their content of oxygen-18 (^{18}O), a heavy isotope of oxygen, relative to the content of the far more abundant and lighter isotope oxygen-16 (^{16}O). Water whose molecules contain ^{18}O vaporizes at a slightly higher temperature than water whose molecules contain ^{16}O; thus the $^{18}O/^{16}O$ ratio in, for example, an ice core sample serves as a record of the air temperature when the water making up the ice last evaporated.

From such records researchers have generally concluded that variations over tens of thousands to hundreds of thousands of years in the amount of solar heat reaching the Northern Hemisphere—variations thought due to cyclic changes in the Earth's orbit and in the inclination of its axis—were responsible for the coming and going of the major ice ages. A surprising and controversial development in 1992 was the result from an analysis of the $^{18}O/^{16}O$ record preserved at the Devil's Hole aquifer in Nevada in calcite that had been deposited continually from mineral-rich water over the past few hundred thousand years. That record showed the familiar sequence of ice ages but at revised times of occurrence, some of which conflicted with the previously accepted correlation between ice age occurrence and Earth orbit-inclination changes.

The great ice ages developed gradually and terminated suddenly. During the year reports suggested that profound changes in the circulation of the North Atlantic Ocean accompanied the most recent deglaciation. Today fully a quarter of all the heat that goes into the atmosphere over the North Atlantic is taken there by ocean currents. Warm surface water enters the far North Atlantic and cools, giving up its heat to the atmosphere. The cooled water sinks deeply in isolated locations and then returns southward; the deepest such water is called North Atlantic Deep Water (NADW). Eventually NADW reaches the South Atlantic, whence it goes around Antarctica via the Circumpolar Current and, in diluted form, fills the deep Pacific and Indian oceans. There it gradually rises to the surface, finally to return to the North Atlantic by pathways that were only beginning to be elucidated.

By contrast, near the end of the last glacial period, about 18,000 years ago, warm surface water did not flow into the far North Atlantic. The far North Atlantic was much colder than it is now, and no NADW was produced. Because NADW is poor in nutrients relative to other waters of the global ocean, the nutrient content of deep water as recorded in the carbon-13 content of deep ocean sediments may be used to map the extent of NADW in past times. Work published in 1992 showed that there was no NADW in the South Atlantic until about 13,000 years ago. At that time, according to available evidence, the surface temperature of the Norwegian Sea suddenly increased, and the sea surface became ice free, all this apparently indicating that the circulation resulting in the production of NADW had suddenly turned on.

Of particular interest to students of the Earth's climate is the fact that the production of NADW, with its associated strong heating of the atmosphere over the North Atlantic, started up about 13,000 years ago but then temporarily ceased about 1,500 years later when Norwegian Sea surface temperature and North Atlantic air temperature again fell to glacial values. The return once more to almost present-day conditions occurred very suddenly less than 1,000 years later; both sea-surface and air temperatures rose by 5°–7° C (9°–13° F) in less than 40 years. Not surprisingly, extended melting of glacial ice sheets was happening about this time; sea-level records preserved in fossil coral reefs around Barbados show two pulses of rapid melting, one just before the temporary shutdown of NADW production and one just after its resumption. The interaction between the melting events and NADW production needed further study.

Regions where ocean waters change depth by thousands of metres, as occurs in the production of NADW, are rare. But for most of the ocean scientists know little about, and cannot predict, the vertical transfer or dispersion of heat, nutrients, or pollutants. During the year an experiment designed to observe such vertical activity directly was begun in the mid-latitude North Atlantic. During a week in May scientists injected streaks of a tracer compound, sulfur hexafluoride, into a patch of ocean water located vertically at about 300 m (980 ft) depth and extending horizontally about 16 km (10 mi). The patch was also seeded with acoustically trackable floats ballasted to float freely at the same depth; their purpose was both to outline the horizontal motion of the patch, so that it could be easily followed and found at later times, and to carry instruments to measure gradients of temperature, salinity, and velocity within the patch. The marked patch was followed from shipboard for two weeks, and tracer concentration was measured directly by a vertical rake of 20 tracer sensors repeatedly towed through it.

During the two-week sampling period, the tracer appeared to spread vertically by a few metres, but this amount was so small that it could not be told reliably from vertical variations in the injection depth or from uneven mixing with seawater occurring at the time of injection. The patch, tracked by the floats, was to be revisited periodically; on those visits researchers would make measurements needed to test theoretical predictions of vertical dispersal. The predicted vertical dispersal intervals are on the order of several tens of metres over one year.   (MYRL C. HENDERSHOTT)

See also Astronomy; Disasters; Energy; Environment; Life Sciences; Mining; Space Exploration.

This article updates the *Macropædia* articles ATMOSPHERE; The EARTH; The EARTH SCIENCES; EARTHQUAKES; GEOCHRONOLOGY; The HYDROSPHERE; OCEANS; PLATE TECTONICS; RIVERS.

Economic Affairs

Partial statistics available in late December pointed to a growth of around 1% for the world economy in 1992. Although this was an improvement on the virtual stagnation seen in the preceding year, it was regarded as a somewhat disappointing performance for a number of reasons. Excluding 1991, it was the lowest growth rate recorded since 1982. Furthermore, in terms of a recovery from the previous year's recession, it was fairly unimpressive by historical standards. In the last world recession, seen in 1982, world output fell by 0.4%, but it was followed in 1983 by a growth rate of 2.6%. Nor was 1992's growth very much to show for the reasonably growth-oriented monetary and fiscal policies pursued by countries such as the U.S., Japan, and, to a lesser extent, the U.K. This, in turn, raised some doubts about the continued efficacy of these previously tried and true policies. In particular, it was being suggested that, mainly in reaction to the conspicuous consumption of the 1980s and the sharp fall in property values in a number of countries, there may have been some weakening in the consumers' underlying propensity to spend. There was, in late 1992, considerable uncertainty about the underlying strength of, and the outlook for, the world economy.

Unlike the situation in previous years, most of the doubts concerned performance in the developed countries. Collectively these were estimated to have boosted their combined gross domestic product (GDP) by 1.7%, compared with a gain of 0.6% in 1991. However, the bulk of this improvement came from North America, which pursued a low-interest-rate policy for well over a year. Partly as a result of this, the U.S. economy turned a GDP decline of 1.2% in 1991 into a gain of 1.9% in the subsequent year, while Canada achieved an advance of around 2%, compared with a drop of 1.7% a year earlier. In Europe the U.K. saw a relative improvement in performance, but—following a GDP fall of 2.2% in 1991—it was still expected to register a decline of around 1% in 1992. Although British policy was modestly expansionary for most of the year, it was only when sterling and interest-rate constraints were eased on Britain's departure from the European exchange-rate mechanism (ERM) in September that the authorities were able to institute a significant cut in the cost of borrowing. Japan, by contrast, maintained an increasingly relaxed monetary policy but still faced a slowdown in its growth rate from 4.4 to 2%. The western part of Germany saw a spectacular cutback in growth from 3.7 to 1%, largely because the Bundesbank maintained interest rates at a relatively high level in an attempt to counter the inflationary effects of financing unification with former East Germany, where there was some recovery, with the result that the nation's combined growth rate was around 1.8%. The Bundesbank's high-interest-rate policy had a strongly undesirable effect on economic growth in other European countries. Because currency parities within the ERM were anchored to the Deutsche Mark, Germany's high cost of borrowing and the obligation to maintain the agreed parities within relatively narrow bands greatly reduced the ability of other European Communities (EC) members to cut interest rates to stimulate domestic economic activity.

Rather more encouragingly, in the less developed world, growth exceeded that seen in industrially advanced countries for the fourth successive year. Estimates by the International Monetary Fund (IMF) put the overall gain for 1992 in excess of 6%, nearly twice as large as in the previous year and some 56% above the average advance achieved during the 1984–91 period. However, although most countries did better than in 1991, a significant part of the improvement in the overall growth rate was the result of the sharp pickup in activity in the Middle East in the wake of the earlier disruption caused by the Gulf war. The available information suggested that GDP in this area might have grown by around 10%, compared with a largely static performance 12 months earlier. The second fastest growth among less developed countries (LDCs) was achieved in Asia, with an estimated advance of nearly 7%, as against 5.7% in 1991. This seemed to be fairly well spread, although a significant boost to the figure came from the strong performance put in by China as well as the four newly industrializing Asian economies (Taiwan, Hong Kong, Singapore, and South Korea). LDCs in the Western Hemisphere grew at around the same rate as in the previous year (2.8%), but in Africa there was a modest acceleration from 1.5 to 1.9%. The former centrally planned economies faced a decrease in output of some 17%—significantly more than the loss of 10% seen in 1991. Eastern Europe managed to slow down the rate of decline, but in the former Soviet Union the fall in output was thought to have doubled to 18%.

There was some improvement in most principal components of demand. The sharpest turnaround appeared to have been in fixed-investment expenditures, which rose by some 2%, as against a fall of 2.7% in 1991. However, performance was very uneven from country to country. Business confidence remained at low levels in Japan, Germany, and the U.K., with the result that spending on plant and equipment recorded a slowdown in growth or a decrease from the preceding year's level. In contrast, the low-interest-rate policy pursued in the U.S. resulted in a 4.5% rise in investment activities in the wake of an unprecedented fall of 8.5%. Consumer expenditure also strengthened in the developed world, but the extent of the improvement—from 1 to 2%—was far from spectacular. This reflected almost universal caution and uncertainty by consumers, which seemed to signify a fundamental change in attitude. It appeared that the previous balance between consumption and reducing debt/increasing savings had shifted in favour of the latter, possibly because of the rising danger of unemployment and the fall in property and equity prices. This made it difficult to get the recovery going by the established demand-boosting measures. Accordingly, consumer expenditure remained relatively sluggish in most countries. In Japan it rose by just over 2%, compared with a gain of 2.7% 12 months earlier, and in the EC the growth rate was largely unchanged at 1.7%. Even in the U.S., where there was a strong rebound in consumer spending from the decline of 0.6% recorded in 1991 to a gain of 1.7%, the 1992 figure was low by historical standards.

Interestingly, this apparent reduction in the propensity to consume came about despite a significant fall in inflation. Taken together, industrially developed countries saw a rise in prices of only 3.3%—lower than at any other time since 1988—compared with 4.1% in the previous year. The rate of increase slackened in every major country, with the most spectacular change seen in Canada (1.6%, as against 5.6% a year earlier) and the U.K. (3.8%, compared with 5.8%). In the less developed world, however, the rate of inflation appeared to have matched that of the preceding year after the significant slowdown secured in 1990. Thus, largely because of structural reforms and stabilization programs, the rise in consumer prices was cut from a weighted average of 80% in 1990 to 42% in 1991, and the available evidence indicated that for 1992 the final figure would be at around the 40% mark. The position could not have been more different in the former centrally planned economies. Because of the structural free-market-oriented reforms, the ending of the previously tightly controlled and artificial price structure resulted in spectacular price increases. Thus in eastern Europe consumer prices were thought to have risen eightfold, compared with a mere doubling in 1991, while in the former U.S.S.R. the increase was said to be 13-fold.

Unemployment is usually defined as a lagging indicator, which means that it tends to rise fairly late in the course of a recession but does not fall until the subsequent recovery is well under way. Therefore, it was not surprising that, despite the modest pickup in the tempo of activity in 1992, there was a further increase in joblessness in the developed world. The number of people out of work expressed as a percentage of the labour force rose from 7 to 7.7%, with the situation deteriorating in most countries. The highest figures—in excess of 11%—were seen in Italy and Canada, and even in the U.S., where the economic recovery was relatively strong, the rate of joblessness rose from 6.8 to 7.5%. If, as expected, the fragile world economic recovery continued, unemployment would begin to fall toward the end of 1993. Looking at some longer term trends, however, there was room for both concern and qualified optimism. The unemployment rate was unlikely to hit the peak of 8.7% seen in 1983, but it was not likely to return to the 4% mark seen in the 1970s. The lowest rate reached at the height of the previous economic boom was 6.3%, and it was widely felt that, mainly because of structural changes, this figure would become the norm in times of relative economic buoyancy.

There was something of a schism in monetary policy between Europe and the other developed countries in 1992. In Canada, the U.S., and Japan, short-term interest rates were

Table I. Real Gross National Products of Selected OECD Countries
% annual change

Country	1988	1989	1990	1991	1992*
United States	3.9	2.5	0.8	−1.2	1.9
Japan	6.2	4.7	5.2	4.4	2.0
Germany†	3.7	3.8	4.5	0.9	1.8
France	4.5	4.1	2.2	1.2	2.2
United Kingdom	4.3	2.3	1.0	−2.2	−0.8
Canada	5.0	2.3	−0.5	−1.7	2.1
Italy	4.1	2.9	2.2	1.4	1.3
All developed countries	4.3	3.3	2.4	0.6	1.7
Seven major countries above	4.5	3.3	2.4	0.6	1.7
European Communities	4.0	3.5	2.8	0.8	1.4

*Estimated.
†From 1991 figures include former East Germany.
Source: International Monetary Fund, *World Economic Outlook*, October 1992.

on a downward trend for well over a year, with the U.S. discount rate reaching 3% in July—its lowest level since 1963. In Europe, on the other hand, rates moved up slightly because Germany's high-interest-rate policy forced its ERM partners to follow suit in order to protect their agreed parities under ERM rules. Thus France, Italy, and other, smaller countries all saw a largely undesirable hardening in their short-term interest rates. The only exception was the U.K., which recorded a very gentle reduction while still in the ERM, followed by a sharp drop in the few months after the government's decision to float sterling.

Unfortunately, while the policy of keeping interest rates high succeeded in prejudicing economic recovery, it failed to stabilize exchange rates and defend unsupportable parities. In consequence, the last three months of the year saw considerable turmoil in European foreign-exchange markets. Sterling left the ERM and was devalued from DM 2.95 to around DM 2.40; Italy devalued and was forced to allow the lira to float; the Spanish peseta was devalued twice; Portugal cut its parity once; and Sweden, Finland, and Norway were forced to abandon their formal links with the European currency unit (ECU). The French franc was also under pressure, spending much of its time near the floor of its permitted parity band, kept inside the band only by strong (but increasingly less enthusiastic) German support. The U.S. currency was not significantly affected by Europe's turbulence, but for the greater part of the year the dollar was losing against the Deutsche Mark and the Japanese yen because of the U.S.'s low-interest-rate policy.

NATIONAL ECONOMIC POLICIES

Developed Market Economies. *United States.* The U.S. economy performed more strongly during 1992 following a short-lasting recession in 1991. However, the pace of recovery was not as quick as it had been from the previous recessions—despite rock-bottom interest rates and a large budget deficit. Public perception of the economy remained pessimistic through most of the year, and this lack of consumer confidence was widely seen as a factor in Pres. George Bush's losing the election in November. Real GDP advanced by an estimated 1.9% during 1992, compared with a 1.2% decline in 1991. The pace of economic growth during the year was surprisingly uneven. Having started 1992 strongly with an annualized increase of 2.9%, growth slowed to a disappointing 1.5% in the second quarter. However, faster growth resumed during the summer, with a robust GDP growth of 3.9% in the third quarter. The confirmation of the summer rebound came after the presidential elections. Economic indicators available in December 1992 suggested that the economy continued to gather momentum and was heading toward a sustained recovery.

There were several reasons why the upswing was relatively sluggish, in the first half at any rate. Perhaps the main reason was that private consumption was subdued for most of the year. As in other developed countries, private consumers in the U.S. were holding back from major purchases, as they were concerned with reducing the high level of debts they had built up in the 1980s and/or were worried about the possibility of losing their jobs. Another factor was economic slowdown in Europe and Japan, which reduced export opportunities. Finally, business faced uncertainty in a presidential election year, with the incumbent looking vulnerable and fears that the Democratic candidate's economic-recovery program would comprise an unexciting cocktail of more spending and higher taxation.

In the main elements of domestic demand, total consumer expenditure rose by about 1.7% in real terms, while the volume of retail sales expanded relatively faster, with an estimated 2.8% increase. Furniture and appliance sales lagged behind the sector average, as did spending on food and automobiles. However, figures available in the closing months of the year pointed to a stronger retail sales trend. The earlier weak trend in retail sales was reflected in consumer credit. Consumer credit outstanding increased $1.6 billion in September for the first time since January 1992, but it was still more than $6 billion below the figure at the start of the year. Preliminary figures indicated that retail sales during the Christmas season were markedly better than in 1991.

Government expenditure in real terms followed a similar path and rose at an annual rate of 3.3% in the third quarter, reversing the previous quarter's 1.2% fall. For the year as a whole, it was estimated to have dropped by over 0.7%. Federal defense spending fell more than nondefense expenditure, while state and local expenditure remained largely unchanged.

Overall, investment spending in real prices was relatively stronger, with an estimated 4.5% increase for the year. However, it was highly volatile, with violent swings from one quarter to the next reflecting the changes in business inventories and residential-housing investment. The latter declined for five quarters before picking up in the autumn.

Against a background of hesitant domestic demand, it was not surprising that recovery in industrial production was patchy. A month-to-month increase of 0.4–0.6% in the first half of the year gave way to a decline of similar magnitude in the summer. Manufacturing industry was less severely affected by the downturn than mining and food industries. Despite this seesaw, industrial output rose by 1.4% during the first 10 months of 1992, compared with a 1.9% decline for the whole of 1991. Capacity utilization mirrored industrial output and fell to 78.5% in October from the year's peak of 79.1% in July. It had risen from the low point of 78% in January. Corporate after-tax profits rose by 1.3% in the second quarter after a 10.8% increase in the opening quarter. The first-quarter increase was the largest in four years and followed a 3.7% fall in 1992.

Reducing unemployment turned out to be particularly tough in a sluggish economy, as the labour force continued to grow. Unemployment continued to rise in the first half of the year and exceeded 10 million, giving an unemployment rate of 7.8% (the highest since 1984). June marked a turning point, and the unemployment rate declined steadily in the summer to reach 7.4% in October. While all sections of the labour force found it difficult to find a job, the hardest hit were teenagers entering the job market for the first time and those who had been laid off and were waiting to be called back to employment.

The slack labour market kept wage increases down, squeezing the spending power of many workers. Although in October average weekly earnings rose 0.8% (in nominal

terms), this was from a slight decline in September. During the first 10 months of the year, they had risen by 2.75% over the same period in 1991. Adjusted for cost of living, this represented a 0.3% decline in real terms during the same period. Moreover, the rise in hourly earnings was nearly one percentage point lower in real prices. One beneficial effect of the slack labour market and low wage increases was an improvement in business productivity and a reduction in unit labour costs in manufacturing. The overall inflation rate, having declined from 5.4% in 1990 to 4.25% in 1991, continued its downward trend in 1992. In October it stood at just over 3%. The absence of inflationary pressures was also reflected in producer prices, which were running at around 1.8% in the final quarter. Given higher import prices, caused by the dollar's decline in the summer, this was an impressive outcome.

After several years of reduction, the merchandise trade deficit was likely to have slightly widened in 1992 to $74 billion from the previous year's $65 billion. The steady improvement in recent years was due partly to the lower value of the dollar but also to the added attention U.S. exporters were paying to the requirements of their foreign customers. As the invisibles surplus and investment-income surplus also declined during 1992, the current account was heading for a wider deficit. A current account deficit of around $35 billion appeared to be in the cards in December 1992. As the previous year's exceptionally low deficit was due to large cash contributions from the U.S. allies in the Gulf war, a bounce back in 1992 was not a serious setback. The signing on December 17 of the North American Free Trade Agreement (NAFTA) with Mexico and Canada to create a common market with 365 million consumers (the EC had 345 million) was potentially of significant long-term importance to U.S. trade.

The lax monetary policy, which dated back to mid-1989, remained at the forefront of policy to revive the economy. Concerned that money-supply growth remained well below its target range, the Federal Reserve cut its discount rate in July by 0.25% to 3% (the lowest level since 1963) after unexpectedly weak unemployment data. The commercial banks responded by a 0.5% cut in the prime rate to 6%. Further technical moves in September and turmoil in the European currency markets raised hopes that there might be room for another cut, but rates remained unchanged at year's end. Although fiscal policy was constrained by the Omnibus Budget Reconciliation Act, the federal deficit continued to widen. For fiscal 1992 (ended September) it rose to a record $290.2 billion, compared with the previous record of $269.5 billion in fiscal 1991. President Bush's budget proposals for fiscal 1993 envisaged the deficit rising to $333.5 billion. Despite his campaign pledges to reduce the deficit, President-elect Bill Clinton was unlikely to rein in the deficit for several years. Thus the economy would continue to benefit from a budgetary stimulus when the interest rates began to rise again.

United Kingdom. During 1992 the British economy performed extremely poorly, partly because of the weakness of the world economy but primarily because of the government's failure to develop a consistent and credible economic strategy. The result was a decline in GDP for the second year in succession, a massive rise in unemployment, a collapse in property values, a fall in manufacturing output, a spate of company failures, a large drop in the external value of sterling, and a doubling in the country's current account deficit. Set against these developments, the one modestly encouraging feature of the year—a slowdown in inflation in the U.K. from 5.9 to around 4%—faded into utter insignificance.

Given the weakness of the world economy, the year would have been difficult for the U.K. even if the government had adopted a less disastrous economic strategy. Unfortunately, instead of taking action to boost the economy, which was already in the throes of recession in late 1991, the government remained rigidly focused on fighting the steadily receding danger of inflation and maintaining an unrealistic sterling/ Deutsche Mark parity of DM 2.95 within the ERM. The preoccupation with parity, coupled with Germany's high-interest policy designed to counter the inflationary effects of reunification, ruled out any major confidence-boosting measures to stimulate business activity. Despite consistently falling output and rising unemployment, the government refused to cut interest rates until May, when it instituted a cut of 0.5%, to 10%. This and one or two other measures of marginal importance did nothing for the economy, but the chancellor of the Exchequer, Norman Lamont, remained firmly wedded to fighting an inflationary danger that was becoming nonexistent and supporting a parity that was becoming less supportable by the day. As a result of the European currency uncertainties following the rejection of the Maastricht Treaty by Denmark in June, Britain's position was becoming increasingly vulnerable until finally on September 16 market pressures became irresistible and sterling was forced out of the ERM and left to float.

Having seen the central plank of his strategy destroyed in the course of a few hours, Lamont let the base rate fall by 1% (to 9%), reiterated his intention to fight inflation, and did, and said, little more. This suggested that, despite its high-risk policy of attempting to buck currency markets, the government had no idea of what to do in the new situation. This dealt another blow to the already weak business confidence, which even another 1% cut in the base rate in October failed to revive. Nearly two months later, on November 12, the chancellor announced a package of measures—including a further cut in the base rate to 7%, assistance to exporters, a reduction in the car tax, modest help for the depressed housing sector, and some large capital expenditure projects—to stimulate the economy. So, as one of the most difficult years in the U.K.'s recent economic history drew to a close, there was at least some hope of a modest recovery, although there remained widespread fears

that, once again, the government acted too late and did too little to lift the economy out of recession.

On the basis of partial statistics available in late 1992, GDP for the year as a whole was heading for a fall of around 1% in the wake of a 2.2% decrease in 1991— the first time in over 10 years that the government had seen two consecutive years of decline. Virtually all areas of demand were weak. Thus consumer expenditure, which in past recessions had often acted as the engine of recovery, fell by an estimated 0.5% after having recorded a drop of just below 2% in 1992. The principal reason for this was not so much a slowdown in the rise of earnings— moving to 6.2% in 1992 from 8.4% in the previous year— but the relentless rise in unemployment and the attendant uncertainty among consumers. Unemployment rose from a total of 2.5 million in December 1991 (accounting for 9% of the labour force) to 2.9 million, or 10.1% of the labour force, in November 1992—its highest level since 1987. With the attendant concerns about job security, consumers were reluctant to spend despite heavy discounting by retailers, preferring instead to build up their savings. As a result, the savings ratio—the ratio of savings to disposable income— continued to rise, reaching near-record levels of 10.5% for the first half of 1992.

Investment expenditure was also extremely sluggish. Investment activity in manufacturing was adversely affected by a decline in output (by around 1% in the wake of a 5.3% fall in 1991), uncertainty, and a growing number of corporate bankruptcies. At the same time, housing investments were decimated by the slump in the residential property market. High real interest rates and unemployment resulted in large-scale failures to service housing loans, with lenders repossessing a substantial number of properties. Furthermore, because of the lack of confidence in the future, new buyers were few and far between, leading to a glut of unsalable houses. Fixed investment of all kinds was expected to drop 3.5%, following a decrease of some 10% in 1991.

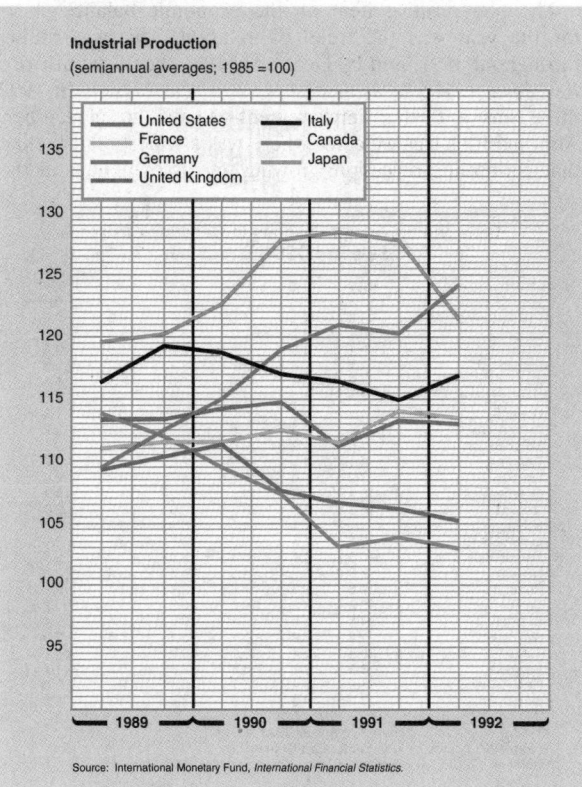

Inflation Rate
(Percentage change from December to December)

United States
France
Germany
United Kingdom
Italy
Canada
Japan

1989   1990   1991   1992   *

*Percentage change from October 1991 to October 1992.

Source: *The Economist*, Economic and Financial Indicators.

Industrial Production
(semiannual averages; 1985 =100)

United States   Italy
France   Canada
Germany   Japan
United Kingdom

1989   1990   1991   1992

Source: International Monetary Fund, *International Financial Statistics*.

In the past when domestic demand was sluggish, U.K. imports tended to become weaker while exports strengthened as domestic producers attempted to make up for the shortfall of local orders by selling abroad. The overall effect was usually an improvement in the balance of payments. However, although this was the scenario realized in 1991 with the current account deficit falling from £17 billion in 1990 to £6.3 billion, 1992 saw a significant rise in the external deficit in spite of the domestic recession. Thus, largely because of the erosion of the domestic manufacturing base, the availability of locally made products was reduced while—because of the artificially high sterling/Deutsch Mark exchange rate until September—imported goods had a strong competitive advantage. The effect of these factors was to boost the volume of imports by an estimated 6%. At the same time, exports were adversely affected by the high sterling exchange rate and the sluggishness of the world economy and were heading for a volume increase of only some 2%. The net result was a massive increase in the external payments deficit from £6.3 billion to over £12 billion. This appeared to be an unequaled "achievement" since in the course of the previous 20 years there had been no occasion when a slump in GDP was accompanied by an increase in the balance of payments deficit.

During the first half of the year, exchange rates were relatively stable, with the rate against the Deutsche Mark fluctuating within the DM 2.80–DM 2.90 band and that against the U.S. dollar moving between $1.75 and $1.95. This was largely the result of the government's commitment to the central ERM parity of DM 2.95—a commitment that was the cornerstone of economic policy and that made it impossible for the government to stimulate the economy. In late November, after sterling had been forced out of the ERM and left to float, the rate was around DM 2.40, while against the dollar it was around $1.50. Subsequently, however, worries about the deepening German recession reversed the trend, and the rate hit DM 2.49 before ending the year at DM 2.45.

The one positive item on the economic balance sheet for the year was the trend of inflation. This was falling throughout 1991, and by December 1991 the 12-month rise was down to 4.5%, as against 9.3% a year earlier. In 1992 there was a further improvement—to 3% in November. Although this was welcome, there was a widespread feeling that continuing recession, growing unemployment, and ris-

ing corporate bankruptcies constituted too high a price for a reduction of a little more than one percentage point in an already low inflation rate.

Japan. It was a disappointing year for the Japanese economy. Although the government pursued reasonably growth-oriented policies, there was a severe slowdown in most areas of business activity compared with the preceding year. One of the main reasons for this was a significant loss of confidence among both consumers and corporations arising out of a structural readjustment of real-estate and equity values. Stock prices rose rapidly in the four years to 1990, greatly outperforming other major stock markets and giving rise to unsustainable price-to-earnings ratios. This gave rise to a strong downward correction in 1990, but instead of the widely expected sharp but short adjustment, prices continued to plummet throughout 1991 and most of 1992. Apart from damaging people's perception of their personal wealth, this also reduced asset values throughout the financial system and made it extremely difficult for business to raise investment capital by issuing equity. Real-estate prices, which rocketed in the mid-1980s, also fell back rapidly and, since property companies and developers relied extremely heavily on bank finance, the slump in the market resulted in a massive rise in bad debts, forcing banks to adopt a much more restrictive approach to lending.

The combined effect of these developments was to engender a pervasive feeling of insecurity and lack of confidence that could not be overcome by government attempts to boost growth. The Bank of Japan reduced its discount rate from 4.5 to 3.75% in April and to 3.25% in July. Also in April, it was decided to front-load 75% of the public works budget for the 1993 fiscal year. These measures failed to boost economic activity to a significant extent. The two main sources of domestic demand—private consumption and investment—remained sluggish, with the result that, after a GDP gain of 1.1% in the first quarter of 1992, the following three months recorded an advance of only 0.3%. Consumers' expenditure was also affected by the virtual saturation of the market for certain products, such as automobiles and consumer electronics; the weakness of the residential housing sector, which cut back home-related spending; and relatively low bonus payments (approximately one-quarter of employees' remuneration packages was normally accounted for by bonuses), reflecting the deterioration in corporate profitability. This, together with the greater difficulty of obtaining bank finance and the absence of any clear signs of an upturn in demand in the near future, also had an adverse effect on expenditures for private plants and equipment.

Inevitably, the weakness of domestic demand was reflected in the trend of industrial production. Although export volumes held up reasonably well, shipments for domestic markets fell in most sectors, leading to a rise in producers'

Table II. Percentage Changes in Consumer Prices in Selected OECD Countries

Country	1987	1988	1989	1990	1991	1992*
United States	3.6	4.1	4.8	5.6	4.3	3.0
Japan	0.1	0.7	2.3	3.1	3.3	2.0
Germany†	0.2	1.3	2.8	2.7	3.5	3.6
France	3.1	2.6	3.7	3.4	3.2	2.6
Italy	4.6	5.0	6.6	6.0	6.5	5.1
United Kingdom	4.1	4.9	7.8	9.6	5.8	3.6
Canada	4.4	4.0	5.0	4.8	5.6	1.3
Austria	1.4	2.0	2.5	3.3	3.4	3.9
Belgium	1.6	1.2	3.0	3.5	3.2	2.3
Denmark	4.1	4.5	4.8	2.6	2.4	2.0
Finland	3.9	5.0	6.6	6.1	4.2	2.0
Greece	16.4	13.5	13.8	20.5	19.5	15.3
Iceland	18.8	25.5	20.3	14.6	6.8	2.0
Ireland	3.1	2.1	4.0	3.3	3.2	2.8
Luxembourg	−0.1	1.5	3.3	3.7	3.1	3.0
Netherlands, The	−0.6	0.7	1.1	2.5	3.9	3.4
Norway	9.3	6.7	4.6	4.2	3.4	2.0
Portugal	9.3	9.7	12.6	13.3	11.4	9.1
Spain	5.2	4.8	6.8	6.8	5.9	5.8
Sweden	4.1	5.8	6.4	10.5	9.4	2.4
Switzerland	1.5	1.9	3.2	5.4	5.8	3.5
Turkey	38.5	75.4	63.1	60.3	65.6	67.7
Australia	8.5	7.3	7.6	7.3	3.2	1.2
New Zealand	15.8	6.4	5.7	6.1	2.7	1.0
OECD Total	3.2	4.9	5.9	5.8	5.2	4.3

*Twelve-month rate of change in August 1992.
†From 1991 figures include former East Germany.
Sources: OECD, *Main Economic Indicators,* November 1992.

Table III. Unemployment Rates in Selected Developed Countries
% total labour force

Country	1987	1988	1989	1990	1991	1992*
Canada	8.9	7.8	7.5	8.1	10.3	11.1
United States	6.2	5.5	5.3	5.5	6.8	7.5
Japan	2.8	2.5	2.3	2.1	2.1	2.1
France	10.5	10.0	9.4	8.9	9.3	10.0
Germany†	7.6	7.6	6.8	6.2	6.7	7.8
Italy	12.0	12.0	12.0	11.0	10.9	11.1
United Kingdom	10.0	8.1	6.3	5.9	8.0	9.8
Other developed countries	10.0	9.5	8.7	8.4	9.3	10.0
All developed countries	7.5	6.9	6.3	6.2	7.0	7.7

*Estimated.
†From 1991 figures include former East Germany.
Source: International Monetary Fund, *World Economic Outlook,* October 1992.

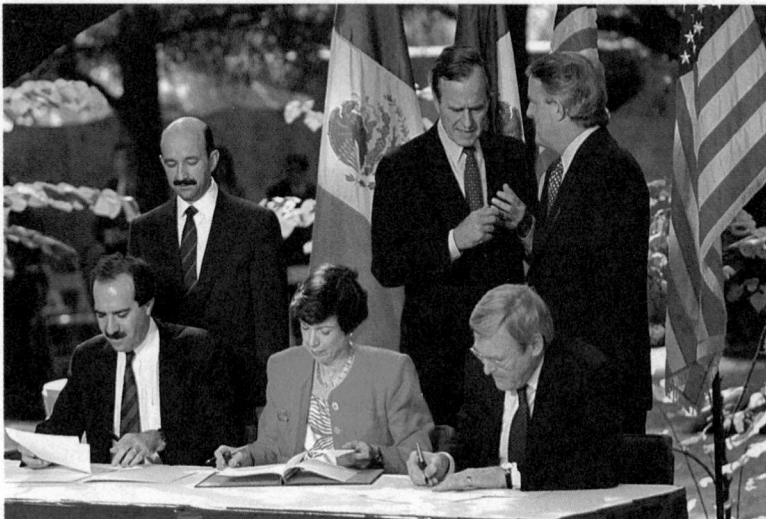

Mexican Pres. Carlos Salinas de Gortari (standing from left), U.S. Pres. George Bush, and Canadian Prime Minister Brian Mulroney watch as trade officials of the three countries initial the North American Free Trade Agreement in San Antonio, Texas, on October 7. The treaty, which required ratification by the respective legislatures, faced considerable opposition in the U.S. and Canada.

DIRCK HALSTEAD—GAMMA LIAISON

inventories of finished products. This, in turn, resulted in cutbacks in output, putting the index of mining and manufacturing output on a steady downward trend for the first three quarters of the year. Not unexpectedly, this reduced the demand for labour, with the result that the job offer-to-seeker ratio—a key indicator for labour—saw a marked decline for most of the year. The rate of unemployment, however, remained very low and moved little—it stood at 2.1% in 1992. This was because the Japanese tradition of companies providing lifetime employment ruled out large-scale redundancies and layoffs as a means of coping with the financial consequences of a downturn in business. As the year progressed, there were indications that employers were beginning to look closely at staffing levels, and a number of corporations admitted the need for a long-term cut in employee numbers. These and other developments raised fears about long-term job security, which, in turn, contributed to the strong underlying feeling of uncertainty and pessimism.

By the time the year entered the second half, there were widespread fears of a recession, with growth slowing to around 2% for the year, compared with a gain of 4.4% in gross national product (GNP) during 1991. Faced with this prospect, the government announced an unexpectedly large $85 billion demand-boosting package in August. According to established practice, approximately 60% of the $85 billion boost was for additional public works projects. A further 20% was earmarked for housing loans and land purchases in an attempt to stimulate the real-estate market, while the remaining 20% went to financial institutions for nonhousing lending purposes. The authorities also announced the allocation of an extra $8.5 billion to be devoted to equity purchases by public bodies in the hope that this would underpin stock market prices. Further measures included changes to tax and other regulations with a view to making it easier for banks to write off bad debts arising out of the collapse of property values.

The size of the package was the largest in recent history and illustrated the extent of the problems faced by the Japanese economy. Government officials estimated that it would add 2.4% to economic growth, but—although it was widely welcomed—there were fears that it would do little for economic activity in 1992 and that, even in the longer term, it would not be sufficient to bring growth to the desired 3.5% per annum. There was, therefore, growing pressure for a cut in income tax to underpin consumption, although, given the need for large-scale deficit financing already, the government was resisting such suggestions.

All in all, the evidence available at the end of 1992 pointed to a GDP gain for the year of around 2%, less than half of the advance secured for 1991. Consumption was heading for an annual growth of 1.5%, as against 2.6% in the preceding year, while private plant and equipment investments were expected to show virtually no growth, a considerable deterioration from the 6% increase achieved in 1991. The one area of the economy that continued to perform well was exports. Despite the strong appreciation of the yen in 1991, the volume of Japanese sales abroad was estimated to have risen very much faster (one estimate suggested a gain of 10%) than the 2.5% advance recorded in 1991. This was partly due to a very strong performance in the U.S. and Asia, where economic growth was very much more buoyant than in European countries. Although this provided much-needed support for industry, combined with a relatively weak uplift in imports, it resulted in an embarrassingly large increase in the external payments surplus. During the first half of fiscal 1992, the current account surplus reached $58 billion, up by 50% over a year earlier. All the indications suggested that exports would continue to outperform im-

Table IV. Changes in Output in the Less Developed Countries
% annual change in real gross domestic product

Area	1987	1988	1989	1990	1991	1992*
All less developed countries	4.5	3.8	3.7	3.5	3.2	6.2
Oil-exporting countries	0.9	0.3	3.7	4.7	1.5	8.7
Non-oil-exporting countries	6.4	5.8	3.6	3.2	4.0	5.0
Africa	0.3	3.6	3.2	1.0	1.5	1.9
Asia	8.1	8.9	5.3	5.5	5.7	6.9
Middle East	3.3	−1.0	3.8	5.4	0.3	9.7
Western Hemisphere	2.2	0.4	1.0	−0.1	2.9	2.8

*Estimated.
Source: International Monetary Fund, *World Economic Outlook,* October 1992.

Table V. Changes in Consumer Prices in Less Developed Countries
% annual change

Area	1987	1988	1989	1990	1991	1992*
All less developed countries	36.4	57.3	70.2	80.2	42.5	42.4
Oil-exporting countries	32.0	32.2	18.1	15.4	18.1	12.1
Non-oil-exporting countries	38.8	71.1	100.0	117.4	54.7	59.4
Africa	14.4	19.3	18.7	16.2	27.1	28.6
Asia	12.6	18.6	13.1	8.7	9.0	8.4
Middle East and Europe	20.1	22.3	17.8	16.6	22.1	16.4
Western Hemisphere	117.8	243.2	434.3	649.7	163.2	178.9

*Estimated.
Source: International Monetary Fund, *World Economic Outlook,* October 1992.

ports, and the expectations were that—despite the various domestic demand-boosting measures announced during the year—the current account surplus would reach $110 billion for the full year, as against $72 billion in 1991.

Given the sluggish undertone of the economy and the relatively low rise in average earnings, it was not surprising that price inflation, which in 1991 was judged to be a potential problem, was all but squeezed out of the system. The available figures to September 1992 showed that wholesale prices were running well below those of the previous year, with the 12-month average promising an overall drop of around 2.2%. Retail prices, however, were still showing some increase over 1991, with the average for the year heading for just under 2%, compared with a gain of 2.6% in the preceding 12-month period.

Germany. While it remained among the strongest economies in Europe, during 1992 Germany found it increasingly difficult to avoid drifting toward a recession. After a strong start to the year, with real GNP growing by 1.9% in western Germany, the pace of activity slowed, and GDP declined by 0.2% in the second quarter. This was followed by a larger fall of 0.5% in the third quarter. The economy remained weak in the closing months of the year and, on the basis of economic indicators available in December, real GNP for the year was likely to have expanded by 1.2%, compared with the previous year's 3.7%. GNP in eastern Germany rose by an estimated 5–8%, reversing the steep decline (30%) of the previous two years. This was likely to produce overall growth of around 1.5% in 1992. Despite this improvement in the east, a large gap remained between the two regions, and at this rate it was estimated that it would take eastern Germany nearly 30 years to catch up with the western sector instead of the 15 years initially thought.

The sharp slowdown in former West Germany was due to a combination of high interest rates and continuing sluggish economic activity among its trading partners, including the U.S. The reason for the high interest rates—the highest in 60 years—was to curb the rise in inflationary pressures caused by the higher-than-expected cost of unification and relatively high wage settlements. In the event, while the headline inflation rate eased, largely owing to technical reasons, the rapid increase in monetary growth and the large budget deficit both remained stubbornly high.

The inflation rate continued to rise during the spring while the wage round was under way, fueling demands for

higher wages. This was seen most clearly in public-sector strikes—the most widespread in 18 years. Once 1991's higher oil prices dropped out of the calculation, together with some of the temporary tax increases imposed to help fund unification, the inflation rate fell sharply. From a nine-year peak of 4.8% in March, it dropped to around 3.5% by the late summer, and it was lower still in December. The inflation rate was expected to average close to 4% for the year, compared with 3.5% in 1991. In eastern Germany inflation moderated, too, and was expected to fall to 11% by year's end from 16% in January.

With export earnings contributing to a much higher proportion of GDP than in other European countries, it was not surprising that high German labour costs and the Deutsche Mark's rise against the dollar and other European currencies had a disproportionate effect on the economy and business confidence. In the second quarter the seasonally adjusted value of exports fell by 7.5% compared with the previous quarter. Although there was a small recovery in the third quarter, a minimal growth in export volume was expected, compared with a 12% growth in 1991. Economic slowdown also reduced the demand for imports, enabling the trade surplus to register a modest improvement over the previous year's DM 21 billion.

The economic slowdown during 1992 was much in evidence in most areas of domestic demand. Retail sales volume fell by an average of 3.5% in the first eight months of the year compared with the same period in 1992. A slight improvement, however, was evident in the summer after the one-year unification taxes imposed in July 1991 were removed. Likewise, automobile sales followed a declining trend; in the three months to August 1992, they were 4% lower than they had been in the previous three months. As a result of the continuing high cost of money and weak external demand, investment in manufacturing weakened during the year. Construction investment fell, too, but this was to be expected, as the unification-related boost could not be maintained. In 1992 as a whole, total investment was expected to rise by around 2%, compared with 6.2% the previous year.

Given the weaknesses in domestic and external demand, a slowdown in industrial output was unavoidable. In the opening months of 1992, industrial production was comfortably ahead of the previous year's level, but output progressively declined and by October it had sunk 3.3% below the Oc-

AFP

In Strasbourg, France, seat of the European Parliament, farmers protest a U.S.-European trade accord reached in November. The agreement would reduce European production of oilseeds, including soybeans, as well as subsidies for all exported grains.

tober 1991 level. Particularly hard hit was the automotive sector. Construction activity fared relatively better and was still ahead of 1991 despite a significant slowdown. In former East Germany the year-to-year decline in the volume of industrial production improved to 2% from 4% in the first quarter and about 30% in the second half of 1991.

The trends in industrial production were mirrored in capacity utilization in manufacturing. In the third quarter it fell to 83.1% from 85.1% in the second quarter of 1992. Thus, having reached a peak of 90% in the third quarter of 1990, capacity utilization fell to the lowest level in seven years. As 1992 drew to a close, capacity utilization was lowest in the capital goods sector and highest in consumer durables.

As a consequence of the deteriorating economic situation, unemployment rose rapidly, reaching 7.8% in October, compared with 6.3% a year before. The number of unemployed stood at 1.9 million and those working part time at 327,000. In eastern Germany unemployment fell slightly to 13.9%, compared with 17% at the beginning of the year, largely as a result of government work schemes and early retirement. The jobless total in eastern Germany at over one million disguised the full extent of the problem, as another 900,000 were working part time or in special training schemes.

In these circumstances it was not surprising that the Bundesbank came under increasing pressure at home and from EC partners to relax its monetary policy somewhat and cut interest rates. However, these calls were largely ignored, and the monetary policy remained tight. Concerned with money supply growing well above target and a rising budget deficit, the Bundesbank raised the discount rate by 0.75 to 8.75% in the summer—the highest rate in 60 years. The Lombard rate, which traditionally had a greater impact on money-market rates, was left unchanged. A surprise 0.5% cut in the discount rate, together with a smaller 0.25% cut in the Lombard rate, on September 13 did not signal a change in the tough monetary policy. It was a failed political move to stave off a crisis in the ERM. The strength of the Deutsche Mark had pushed sterling and the lira to their ERM floors, causing tension within the system and providing the currency speculators with ammunition. In the event, despite the devaluation of the lira within the system, a currency turmoil could not be avoided, and it resulted in both the lira and the pound withdrawing from the ERM. The following month both the Spanish peseta and the Portuguese escudo were devalued within the ERM. As the year drew to a close, with the currency markets still unsettled and the German money-supply growth strong, there was no perceptible change in the Bundesbank's policy to allow the much-needed cut in interest rates to get the economy moving again.

France. Despite an economic recovery from 1991, the lowest inflation rate in Europe, and a stable currency, the French public was still dissatisfied with its country's economic performance. This was mainly because of rising unemployment and political instability. As the pace of economic growth was relatively faster in the latter part of the year, GDP was likely to have expanded by just over 2%, compared with 1.2% in 1991.

Economic recovery in 1992 was based principally on a recovery in exports and to a lesser extent on consumer spending. Household consumption was stimulated by a reduction in the top rate of the value-added tax (VAT) and would probably have grown faster had it not been for high unemployment and a slow growth in real income. Household consumption was projected by the government to have grown by 1.8% in 1992, up from 1.3% in 1991.

Exports surged by nearly 8% in the first six months of 1992, stimulated by relatively strong demand from Germany

Table VI. Balance of Payments on Current Account						
In $000,000,000						
Area	1987	1988	1989	1990	1991	1992*
All developed countries	−61.7	−55.4	−78.5	−104.4	−23.5	−22.9
All less developed countries	−5.5	−23.9	−16.0	−14.2	−78.2	−51.8
Oil-exporting countries	−11.8	−28.9	−10.9	−2.5	−66.5	−29.2
Non-oil-exporting countries	6.3	5.0	−5.2	−11.7	−11.7	−22.5
Africa	−5.1	−10.2	−6.5	−1.9	−3.6	−9.0
Asia	22.1	10.6	1.6	−1.4	−4.3	−10.7
Middle East and Europe	−12.0	−13.8	−2.5	−3.7	−50.5	−6.1
Western Hemisphere	−10.3	−10.5	−8.6	−7.2	−19.9	−26.0

*Estimated.
Source: International Monetary Fund, *World Economic Outlook,* October 1992.

and aided by the competitiveness of French products as a result of the low inflation rate. Export growth slowed in the autumn as external demand weakened and the franc strengthened. Nevertheless, France was able to record a trade surplus of F 23.9 billion in the first 10 months of 1992, compared with a deficit of F 27.4 billion a year earlier.

Industrial production mirrored the trends in household consumption and exports and weakened in the second half of the year. Given a sluggish economy, total investment remained on a downward trend and was officially expected to have declined by 1% in 1992—a smaller fall than the previous year's 1.3%. This was despite measures announced in the spring to boost the construction industry and boost investment in roads and public transport. Not surprisingly, capacity utilization in industry fell during 1992 to its lowest level since early 1984.

Unemployment remained the black spot in the economy, and it upset the voters so much that it seemed likely to lose the ruling Socialist Party the parliamentary elections in March 1993. The number of unemployed had risen to 2,930,000 (a rate of 10.4%) in October and was expected to go on rising. In protest against rising unemployment, low wage rises, and the government's tough anti-inflation policies, several groups of workers went on strike. One of the bright features of the French economy in 1992 was its success in maintaining an inflation rate well below that of Germany and most other EC countries. The year-to-year inflation rate in October was 2.4%, and in the preceding three months it had grown at an astonishingly low annual rate of 1.4%.

Given its commitment to maintaining the value of the franc against the Deutsche Mark, the government was forced to follow a tight monetary policy and keep interest rates relatively high. Nevertheless, the banks were able to trim the prime lending rate twice during the year. The first cut came in May after the Bank of France had reduced the interest-free deposits that it required the commercial banks to maintain with it. This lowered the banks' costs and enabled a 0.5% cut in the prime rate. The second opportunity came in November after the Bank of France cut two key interest rates by 0.25%. Following the November reduction of 0.25%, the prime rate stood at 9.65%, implying a real interest rate of 7%—far too high for an economy losing momentum. Not surprisingly, in the closing months of the year, the government came under increasing pressure to relax its tough monetary policy and budgetary discipline in order to stimulate the flagging economy. However, having narrowly survived frenzied speculation against the franc in September, the government felt that it had little room to maneuver until the Bundesbank had cut the German interest rates.

Although the 1992 budget deficit was heading to F 180 billion, well above the revised target of F 135 billion (originally F 90 billion), it was not stimulatory, as the wider gap was largely due to lower tax revenue following slower-than-expected economic growth. The cut in VAT rates also played a role in reducing government revenues. To avoid increasing the tax burden, the government selectively restricted its expenditure, maintaining a relatively tight fiscal stance.

Less Developed Countries. In contrast to the relatively sluggish economic growth in the industrialized countries, the pace of economic activity quickened among the LDCs. According to IMF estimates, GDP growth in the LDCs in 1992 was around 6%, compared with 3.25% the year before, and double the medium-term trend rate. However, as the population growth rate was comparatively high, the growth rate in GDP per capita was halved to an estimated 3.3%. This improvement in economic performance was attributable to a number of factors, including a rebound in economic activity in the Middle East, lower interest rates in the U.S., and measures introduced by many governments to stabilize their economies. The structural reforms introduced to encourage competition and international trade also helped to offset the negative influences of the weak oil and nonfuel commodity prices.

While an upswing in economic activity was seen in many regions of the world, the fastest growth in output occurred in the Middle East. This was to be expected following the normalization of oil production and exports from Kuwait. Although oil production restarted in Iraq, it was for domestic consumption only, as its export was still embargoed by the UN. Regional growth in the Middle East was augmented by the continuation of the strong economic growth in Iran that got under way in 1991.

Output in Asia also gathered momentum and was estimated to have increased by nearly 7% in 1992, compared with around 5% the year before. Strong domestic demand and increased intraregional trade were the main stimuli for growth. This rapid growth rate for the region as a whole, however, masked significant variations in individual country performances. Continued rapid growth in China, Hong Kong, Indonesia, South Korea, Malaysia, Singapore, Taiwan, and Thailand contrasted with the comparatively sluggish growth in other countries, such as India, Pakistan, Sri Lanka, and the Philippines. Some of these countries were still recovering from the adverse effects of the Gulf war and the breakup of the former U.S.S.R.

Thanks to a number of reforms introduced by the LDCs in the Western Hemisphere, the growth momentum established in 1991 was maintained during 1992. The main beneficiaries of economic deregulation, trade liberalization in the region, and privatization of public companies were the larger countries, notably Argentina, Chile, Colombia, and Mexico. The economies of some smaller countries also picked up during the year. The economic growth rate in Brazil was once again constrained by the restrictive policies in force aimed at combating high inflation.

While GDP growth in Africa was estimated to have increased slightly more than the previous year's 1.5%, it was still adversely affected by declining terms of trade, drought, and political unrest. Another negative development was the likely slippage in economic stabilization and structural reform programs previously introduced. Food shortages also continued in a number of countries, including The Sudan, Ethiopia, Mozambique, and Somalia. In an attempt to end mass starvation in Somalia, President Bush sent U.S. troops to undertake a mercy mission of food distribution at year's end.

After the sharp deterioration in the external accounts of the LDCs during 1991, caused largely by the recession in the industrialized countries and the Gulf crisis, there was a welcome improvement during 1992. Continuing low inflation and relatively stable interest rates in the developed world contributed to this improvement. As a result of higher borrowings to finance development projects and maintain economic activity levels, the external deficits increased in some non-Middle Eastern countries. However, the overall debt-servicing burden in these countries remained comparatively easy during the year, slightly improving their import capacity.

According to IMF projections, the aggregate current account deficit of the LDCs decreased to $52 billion in 1992 from $78 billion in 1991. Despite a slight deterioration in the terms of trade, exports rose faster than imports both in value (measured in U.S. dollars) and in volume terms. While most of the higher exports were from the fuel-exporting countries, there was a slight improvement in the trade balances of some of the least developed countries. As this was offset by a decline in official transfer payments (grants) and private flows, it resulted in larger current account deficits by the non-fuel-exporting LDCs. Thus, excluding the Middle East, the aggregate deficit of the other regions increased by an estimated $18 billion in 1992.

The financing of the current account deficit once again remained relatively easy, as net financial flows rose from $101 billion in 1991 to an estimated $133 billion in 1992. The IMF attributed some of the increase in capital inflows to improvements in the economic performance of the LDCs, as well as to economic reforms they introduced. These reforms were thought to have reduced the risks perceived by the lenders, who improved their assessment of the economic prospects of the LDCs concerned. As the conditions in Africa remained relatively less attractive, there was no increase in the net flow of funds into that region. The main beneficiary region was the Western Hemisphere, followed by Asia.

In 1991 the total external debt of the LDCs rose by 6.5% (more slowly than expected) and reached $1,360,000,000,000. This trend continued into 1992, and the total external debt was projected by the IMF to have increased by around 4%. Another favourable related development was a reduction in the aggregate debt-export ratio of the LDCs. In addition to lower world interest rates and debt-reduction operations, export-promoting reforms played a role in this. During 1992 debt-restructuring arrangements were concluded in Argentina and the Philippines, for example. Nigeria, Mexico, and Brazil also benefited from programs concluded in 1991 or 1992.

Inflation, after being halved to around 40% in 1991, was broadly unchanged during 1992. Inflation declined fastest in the Middle East, reflecting the return to normalcy after the Gulf crisis. Assessed over a longer term, the most dramatic decline occurred in the Western Hemisphere, where inflation, having reached 650% in 1990, dropped to 160% in 1991. It was estimated to have upturned slightly during 1992, but further progress was expected during 1993. The underlying improvement was largely due to economic stabilization and structural reforms being introduced. In China and other Asian countries capacity constraints and rapid credit expansion contributed to an upward pressure on prices. Thus inflation in the Asian region as a whole had not improved since 1990. In Africa the inflation rate was expected to rise further in 1991, as a result of wage increases, the lifting of price restrictions in Algeria, the large public-sector deficit in Nigeria, and the adverse impact of the drought in southern Africa.

Reflecting the trends in the industrialized countries, unemployment increased in the LDCs during 1992, but it was partly offset by a decline in unemployment in the Middle

East and in some Asian countries closely linked with the Middle Eastern labour market. There was also an increase in unemployment in some Latin-American countries where counterinflationary measures were still in operation. By contrast, unemployment levels remained very low in the newly industrializing countries in South Asia.

The Formerly Centrally Planned Economies. Economic output in the formerly centrally planned economies continued to decline in 1992. This reflected the restructuring that was taking place in the wake of political and economic reforms. In eastern Europe output was estimated to have fallen by nearly 10% following a 14% decline in 1991. In the 15 former Soviet republics, the economic chaos that accompanied the breakup of the U.S.S.R. contributed to an estimated 18% decline on top of the 9% fall in 1991. These countries had had less exposure to free markets than had most of eastern Europe and were less able to respond to the new market conditions. (*See* Special Report.) The entire region suffered from distortions caused by macroeconomic imbalances and the liberalization of prices without accompanying stabilization measures. Necessary reforms were far from complete, and many were still at the planning stage. In Russia measures to create a market economy were having limited success, and output, investment, and private consumption were declining rapidly. In Armenia, Georgia, and the former Yugoslavia, in particular, drops in output were made more severe by natural disasters or social unrest that culminated in civil war. Government economic policies were under pressure because of the high unemployment and severe hardships that were inevitable parts of the transition process. Tax revenues fell sharply, making budget deficits hard to control.

Economic performances were mixed, however, and the official statistics were misleading. In previous years, output had often been overstated for political reasons. In eastern Europe statistics were being collected mainly from large companies, which meant that much of the economic activity from the new, small entrepreneurial enterprises was not recorded. New businesses were being established—in Hungary alone, more than 60,000 had emerged by late 1992.

The economies of Czechoslovakia, Hungary, and Poland had opened up more than elsewhere in eastern Europe. Exchange-rate controls virtually disappeared and, although economic output had declined in 1992, the downward trend was expected to be reversed in 1993. In Bulgaria and Romania falls of about 8% in 1992 were expected to moderate to about 2% in 1993. In the newly independent states of the former Soviet Union, the declines in output, which ranged from 2% in Kyrgyzstan to 23% in Kazakhstan in 1991, persisted. Clear reform strategies had not been formulated in many of the republics.

A major factor in the poor economic performance was the falloff in intraregional trade that followed the dissolution of the Council for Mutual Economic Assistance (CMEA, or Comecon) in June 1991. The region's trade position was helped by improved access to markets in the developed countries. Poland, Hungary, and Czechoslovakia increased their exports to EC markets when their association agreements with the EC came into effect on March 1, 1992, but many enterprises were unable to switch sales to the West. Without subsidies, products were no longer price-competitive, and the quality was often poor. As a result, current account balances deteriorated further in 1992, and for the region as a whole they were expected to exceed $8 billion in 1992, compared with an estimated $1 billion in 1991.

Privatization—the key to the transformation from a centrally planned to a free-market economy—made slow progress. In free-market economies the shift of assets from the state to the private sector was relatively simple because state enterprises were under the control of strong central authorities. In eastern and central Europe, however, these authorities had been discredited, leaving a vacuum during and after the transfer. Governments often faced strong employee resistance because of the high proportion of layoffs that were accompanying privatization. Whereas legal systems and financial sectors in the West were competent to handle

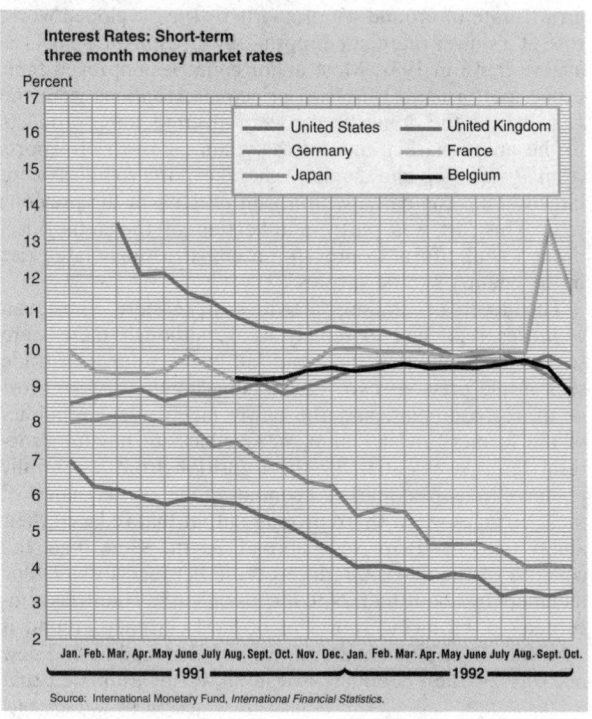

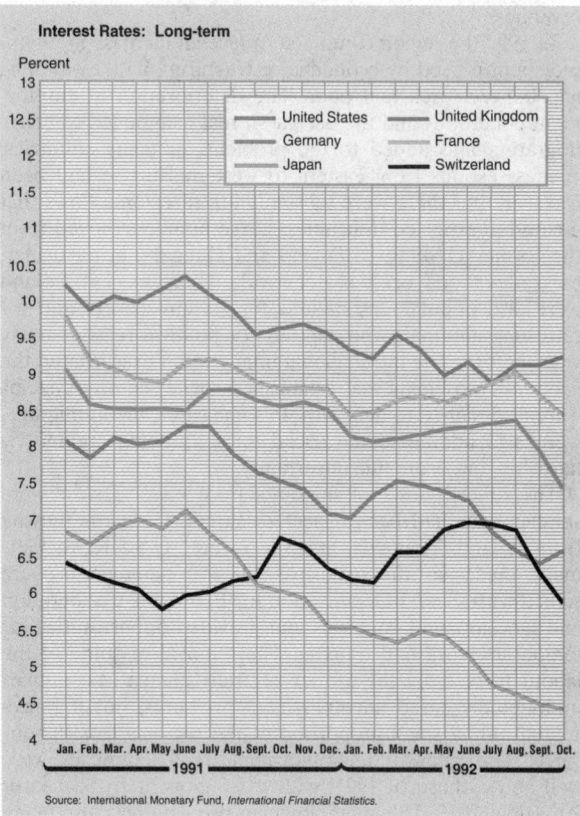

the transfer of public assets, the former centrally planned economies still needed to create the necessary infrastructure. Legally binding private-property rights, bankruptcy laws, the means to allocate capital efficiently, and well-developed financial markets were almost nonexistent.

Many small enterprises had been successfully privatized prior to 1992. In 1992 the emphasis was shifting to medium and large companies in Hungary, Romania, and Bulgaria. In Czechoslovakia, under the auspices of the Czech and Slovak Ministries of Privatization, the majority of the country's 5,500 large enterprises were scheduled for the rapid privatization of both their assets and their liabilities. Over half the book value of enterprises was being sold through an ingenious voucher scheme. This enabled those citizens who wished to—either individually or through a private intermediary—to purchase "shares" in the new enterprises. The voucher scheme proved extremely popular and overcame many of the practical problems associated with the sale of state holdings. A stock market using similar technology was also being set up. The rapid changes caused considerable upheaval in Slovakia, however, and in November it negotiated a peaceful separation from the Czech lands, to take effect on Jan. 1, 1993. The new Slovak Republic was expected to slow the pace of privatization.

In most of the former U.S.S.R. republics, a common problem hampering privatization was the sheer size of state enterprises. Their physical coverage was extensive, as was their sphere of economic activities. In Russia, although ambitious plans for privatization had been announced in March 1992, they made little progress. In Romania, however, most of the agricultural lands were expected to be privately owned by the end of 1992.

Despite privatization, state enterprises remained important. Even in Poland, Hungary, and Czechoslovakia, over half the assets were expected to remain in the control of the government for the foreseeable future. The financing of these operations was a problem in the face of falling tax revenues.

In 1992 the region continued to face an increase in unemployment caused by economic restructuring and a widening gap between rich and poor. The deterioration in employment conditions and the decline in real income led to heavy migration and added to the problems in many countries. A mass exodus from eastern to western Europe had been foreseen, but there were substantial intraregional flows that created unexpected difficulties. Large numbers moved from the former U.S.S.R. to Poland and Hungary, in particular, to trade goods or look for work. Hungary and Poland were also popular destinations for asylum-seekers and for returning nationals who had left for political reasons many years before. The intraregional immigration exacerbated the economic problems that established social security systems were ill-designed to deal with. In some cases, the immigrants were also adding to the social tensions being created by hardship and economic uncertainty.

The official flows of migrants from east to west were smaller than had been expected. Ethnic Germans moving from Poland, Romania, and the former U.S.S.R. to Germany made up the majority. Bilateral agreements were signed with several Organization for Economic Cooperation and Development countries and provided opportunities for temporary work and training. The removal of some of the labour force from the former centrally planned economies undoubtedly eased unemployment pressures, but it represented only a small proportion of the region's total labour force. The rates of unemployment in all countries were well above those of 1991, with most thought to be nearer 20% than 10%. The unemployment problem was also being blamed for the rising crime rates. There were wide and growing disparities, with, for example, unemployment levels in Slovenia being three times higher than in the Czech regions. The resolve of governments to maintain their stabilization policies was being challenged, and labour-market policies were being urgently reviewed.

The tighter financial policies that were being adopted brought a decline in inflation in eastern Europe except in Romania and former Yugoslavia, where civil war resulted in hyperinflation. Throughout the former Soviet Union, however, prices escalated in 1992, and in Russia inflation was expected to reach 2,000%. The greater supply of consumer goods, together with the increase in prices, brought a sharp decline in savings following many years during which the savings ratio remained stable.

INTERNATIONAL TRADE

After a fairly indifferent performance in 1991, the growth of world trade was thought to have staged a modest recovery in 1992. Final figures would not be available until the second half of 1993, but partial statistics and other indicators suggested volume growth of around 4%. Although this compared favourably with the growth rates of 3.9 and 3% achieved in the two preceding years, it was well below the average of 6% seen in the five-year period to 1989.

Improvement was largely the result of the modest upturn in world economic growth. Most of the boost came from the industrialized world; the trade of LDCs rose broadly at the same rate as in the previous year. Even among developed economies, performance was fairly uneven. Overall, their imports were estimated to have risen by 4.1%, as against 2.4% in 1991. However, this was almost entirely accounted for by rapidly rising import volumes in the U.S. and Canada, as well as an estimated growth of 6% in the U.K., which staged a recovery from the 2.8% decline of the preceding year. Most other major industrialized countries recorded a slowdown. Japan, facing a significant fall in GDP growth, saw imports rise by only 2.8%, as against 6% in 1991, while Germany—which boosted the volume of its overseas purchases by over 14% in 1991 to satisfy pent-up demand from the former East Germany—returned to a more normal growth rate of around 4%. Exports by the developed world rose at a slower rate than imports—by an estimated 3.8%, as against 2.9% in 1991. Most major countries improved their export performance; the two principal exceptions were the U.S., where the domestic recovery diverted some products to the home market and cut the volume growth of exports from 7 to 6%, and Japan, where export volumes were largely static compared with a gain of 2.5% in the previous year. This last was partly a reflection of the authorities' unsuccessful efforts to prevent an embarrassingly large rise in the country's trade surplus.

The level of trading activities in eastern European countries remained extremely weak, although there were some indications that the rapid fall in the volume of trade seen in the previous two years was beginning to slow. Most of these economies, and the newly independent republics of the former Soviet Union, were subject to painful structural reforms essential for the transition from a centrally planned to a free-market economy. One consequence of these changes was a sharp drop in output that reduced their ability (and need) to trade abroad. At the same time, the collapse of the CMEA reduced trade between former bloc members by about half. Not surprisingly, the countries concerned—often facing shortages of hard currency—found it very difficult to shift to alternative suppliers and to find new markets for their products. All in all, it was estimated that

(continued on page 144)

Eastern Europe's Problems of Transition

BY KENNETH L. ADELMAN

Since the revolutions of 1989, the nations of central and eastern Europe—Albania, Bulgaria, Czechoslovakia, Hungary, Poland, Romania, and Yugoslavia—have faced the most exacting of problems: managing a first-ever transformation from a central economy to a market-driven economy. Most started with bankrupt political and financial structures, and they seek to end the process soon enough to forestall unmanageable social unrest. They have faced this predicament with little historical or intellectual guidance. While libraries are full of books on the transition from capitalism to communism, few have been written on its opposite. Thus there is little to guide the new leaders of these nations, worried that their plans for radical change will be overtaken by economic collapse, civil war, authoritarianism, or all of the above.

The Rocky Road to Capitalism. If the new leaders lack specific guidance on how to manage the transition, they have agreed on the final destination. That a centrally controlled economy does not and cannot work has become universally accepted. The old argument between capitalism and communism, central control and free enterprise, was ended by the stark contrast between the economies of East and West Germany, China and Taiwan, Cuba and Puerto Rico, and North and South Korea. Also in their favour, few of the central or eastern European countries were as thoroughly militarized, economically failing, politically splintered, ethnically clashing (except for Yugoslavia), or bureaucratically stifling as the former Soviet Union. Being smaller, mostly more homogenous, and certainly more manageable, these countries provided greater opportunities for outside aid to make a genuine contribution. Finally, in most of eastern Europe—excepting Albania and possibly Romania—the standard of living was higher and the work ethic stronger than in the former Soviet republics. Forty-five years of communism in eastern Europe had proved less corrosive than 75 years in the Soviet Union.

Clearly, these countries are heading in the right direction, toward privatization and free-market economies less reliant on defense business. Over half the defense plants in Czechoslovakia, Poland, and Hungary have been slated for conversion or closure. Often governments have simply flung defense concerns into the commercial marketplace—the "sink-or-swim school" of conversion. Unfortunately, these were not real "companies" at all but merely factories. Their managers were told what to build, their workers when and how to build it. Much to their current disadvantage, most used production specifications prepared in the Soviet Union.

Yet the demands on industrial managers suddenly thrown into a competitive world pale compared with those placed on the policymakers directing the transformation. Many of the new leaders were former dissidents—intellectuals, poets, or unionists but not managers or politicians experienced in parliamentary ways.

Problems Abroad. The biggest external problem facing the new governments was the collapse of trade with their biggest trading partner, the Soviet Union. In the first year after the 1989 revolutions, eastern European imports to and exports from the U.S.S.R. dropped by more than 40%. This cost Czechoslovakia, for one, more than $2 billion. Then Moscow ended its subsidies of oil just before the Gulf crisis sent world oil prices skyrocketing.

Foreign assistance was prompt but somewhat disappointing. The European Bank for Reconstruction and Development was begun to stimulate private-sector investment and lending in the region, while the European Communities' "Group of 24" was given the task of donor coordination. The International Monetary Fund made standby arrangements in most eastern European countries. Western donors increased their efforts, with the U.S. government spending some $450 million yearly on aid to the region.

Nonetheless, the biggest generator of growth, foreign investment, initially proved scant. Many outsiders remained uncertain about the viability and sustainability of the reforms. Legal worries—who owns what, how contracts are made and enforced, what the limits to environmental liability are—were a deterrent. So were overvalued exchange rates. Furthermore, there proved to be fewer concrete investment opportunities in these countries than had been expected. Most firms turned out to be huge, overstaffed factories that were full of pathetically outdated technology. Governments might be headed by ex-dissidents, but they had to rely heavily on apparatchiks from the old regime. Even those not so tainted were ill informed about the workings of a free economy.

Country by Country. *Poland* adopted radical and quick reform, dubbed "shock therapy," which set the pace for the region. The new government rapidly freed prices, eliminated trade barriers, tied some local currency to convertible currency, cut or ended many subsidies to state industries, beat down inflation, and reduced its budget deficit. The result was a rapid expansion of the private sector, but problems arose. Many bureaucratic and tax obstacles remain for businesses, and foreign investment has not rushed in. While all retail trade has been privatized, the state still owns most industrial production. Sale of these state-owned companies has been slower than anticipated.

In contrast, *Czechoslovakia* waited until January 1991 before undertaking a "big bang" approach that included an innovative and extensive privatization program. It began its postcommunist phase with one of the strongest economies in the region. Citizens enjoyed a fairly high standard of living, and the country had little foreign debt. The new government held down inflation and the budget deficit while implementing its program of "coupon privatization." Sold inexpensively to citizens, these vouchers allowed people to purchase shares in individual companies or in investment funds that in turn purchased state firms with the best prospects for growth. More than 80% of the citizens participated in the program, which led to the sale of some 500 state firms with a total valuation of more than $10 billion. However, business taxes remain high, and government regulation is still heavy. Though foreign investors began to flock into Czechoslovakia in 1992, the agreement between the country's two parts to separate adds political uncertainty to the economic promise.

Hungary had a head start on reform. Since the late 1960s it had undertaken economic liberalization at home while toeing the communist line on policies abroad. Though saddled with considerable debt, the government initially attracted nearly two-thirds of the foreign investment going into the region, held inflation down, and removed trade barriers. Its government, though relatively weak, is on its way to privatizing half the economy by 1995. Taxes remain relatively high.

Bulgaria took dramatic action only after sorting out its new domestic politics. Its 1990 election returned many ex-Communists, and change had to wait until the October 1991 elections empowered genuine reformers. Then the government quickly freed most prices, brought inflation down, liberalized trade, and cut taxes. Little privatization was implemented, however, until quite recently.

The Ceaucescu dictatorship left *Romania* impoverished economically as well as politically and spiritually. Its per capita income is among the lowest in the region, and the harshness of the leadership left few if any reformist political leaders available to take over. Strikes and political instability have added to the climate of uncertainty. Taxes remain high, legal rights to private property are hazy, and few real reforms have been implemented. Government leaders and citizens mostly try just to stay afloat.

Albania was a wasteland before 1989, with few roads and no base for progress. Strikes in 1991 caused already-low industrial and agricultural production to fall by half. The new government of Albania, like that of Romania, has decided on a radical reform package but spends most of its energy coping with daily crises—including the need to import enough food to keep its people going.

The former *Yugoslavia* is tearing itself apart politically, economically, culturally, and socially. The first requirements for real reform, political stability and participation, are lacking.

A Long Haul. The countries of central and eastern Europe differ considerably, but in all cases their transitions will prove longer and tougher than most people expected in the euphoria of 1989. After all, it took the already-developed nations of Japan and West Germany a quarter century after World War II—aided by benevolent foreign occupation and massive infusions of foreign assistance—to become prosperous, free-market democracies. It took South Korea about the same time after its war in the early 1950s, again with massive aid.

While the main burden of creating the conditions for prosperity lies with the eastern European governments, outsiders can help. Foreign assistance can prove beneficial, as it has. Foreign investment is more important, but it depends on local conditions. Money is a coward, and few businesses are willing to risk vast sums in periods of great uncertainty—especially when the world from Malaysia to Mexico and Chile to Canada is rich with opportunities for risk capital.

Enabling trade to flourish is also essential. Lowering or even scrapping the European Communities' protectionist wall against commerce with countries to the east remains the most critical contribution outside governments can make. It is ironic that the most formidable wall harming the peoples of eastern Europe may be that erected and maintained by the western Europeans.

Above all, time and determination will prove critical. While the newly liberated people of the eastern European nations fixate on near-term problems, including defense conversion, they are embarked on a much grander and nobler conversion, into a system of freedom and free markets. Theirs is an effort worthy of strong support.

Kenneth L. Adelman, a former U.S. ambassador to the United Nations (1981–83) and director of the U.S. Arms Control and Disarmament Agency (1983–87), is vice president of the Institute for Contemporary Studies and a nationally syndicated columnist.

(continued from page 142)

the foreign trade of formerly communist countries fell by around 20%, compared with a drop of some 35% in 1991.

Although LDCs saw little or no acceleration in the growth of their trade, in absolute terms they did considerably better than the developed world. Partly boosted by China's rapidly growing economy and overseas sales, developed country export volumes were estimated to have risen by 8%, perhaps 1% faster than in the previous year. However, fuel-exporting countries—benefiting from the weak recovery in the industrialized world and modest weakening in oil prices—saw a marked acceleration in export volume growth, from 2.7 to 4.7%. Asian economies secured a gain of around 10%, but Africa produced an advance of only some 2–3%. As far as imports were concerned, overall volumes for the less developed world were down by one percentage point to approximately 9%. Most major groupings saw a slowdown in 1992; an exception was Africa, where—in reaction to a drop of 3% in imports during 1991—partial figures pointed to an overall gain of 5–6%.

During 1992 the trend of world trade prices was modestly unfavourable to the LDCs. Food prices, in particular, were fairly weak; according to UN estimates, prices for LDCs' food products saw no improvement at all, despite three successive years of decrease that had pushed them to a very low level. At the same time, the price of agricultural nonfood products was estimated to have fallen by 3% after a cut of over 6% in the preceding year. There was, however, a modest improvement of 1.3% in mineral and metal prices; this was largely due to the recovery in output in some industrialized countries, but it made up for only a fraction of the 9.4% slump recorded for 1991.

Oil prices showed little change. Depending on the measure used, they were static or slightly weaker than in the previous year. All in all, exporters of primary products earned less per unit of exports than in 1991. At the same time, partly because of currency movements, they faced an increase of some 6% in prices of manufactured products. The result was a further deterioration in terms of trade. The adverse movement for LDCs as a whole was estimated by the IMF at 1.8% in the wake of a 3.6% fall in 1991. The adverse movement for Asian economies was only some 0.7%, whereas for the more vulnerable Western Hemisphere and African LDCs, the terms of trade fell by 4–6%. The terms of trade for the industrialized world improved by just over 1% (on top of a gain of 1.6% in 1991), ranging from 7% for Japan to 2% for the U.K. and less than 1% for most other major countries.

The General Agreement on Tariffs and Trade (GATT) negotiations launched in Uruguay in 1986 continued at a somewhat leisurely pace for most of 1992 but reached a dramatic climax toward the end of the year. In late October the U.S. and the EC were still in disagreement over the level of subsidized European oilseed production, and the U.S., accusing Europe of not negotiating seriously, pulled out of the talks and threatened to impose punitive tariffs on a range of agricultural imports from EC countries. This caused a flurry of activity in Brussels, and in early November further talks were held in Chicago. These were said to have been on the verge of success when Ray MacSharry, the EC's chief negotiator, resigned and accused Jacques Delors, the president of the EC Commission, of undue interference and an attempt to sabotage the negotiations. Delors, who was widely tipped as a likely candidate in the next French presidential election and who could not afford to lose farming support at home, denied the charge. A few days later MacSharry was reinstated as the EC negotiator. In the meantime, the U.S. published details of its proposed retal-

Viktor Chernomyrdin (standing right), on December 14 elected prime minister of Russia by the Congress of People's Deputies, walks ahead of the man he replaced, Yegor Gaidar (centre). A former deputy prime minister for fuel and energy, Chernomyrdin was expected to modify Gaidar's free-market economic reforms.
AP/WIDE WORLD

iatory measures, which affected some $300 million worth of EC exports and were concentrated on white wine (mainly French). Following MacSharry's reinstatement, talks were resumed, and they resulted in an agreement announced on November 20.

Most EC member countries welcomed the agreement, which was seen as a last-minute opportunity to avert a potentially disastrous trade war with the U.S. The principal exception was France; in deference to the country's relatively inefficient and extremely militant farmers, the French government took a strongly negative line throughout the negotiations and, despite the approval of the EC Commission and most other members of the Community, pronounced the agreement unacceptable. It also threatened to use its right to veto the deal, although it was not clear if such a right actually existed. In any event, France succeeded in transforming the widespread relief that greeted the EC-U.S. accord into a feeling of apprehension.

Although the farm deal removed a major stumbling block, the global GATT agreement remained dependent on the successful conclusion of other fairly complex multilateral negotiations on a wide range of issues. These included the agreement of the Cairns Group (agricultural exporters, including New Zealand, Australia, and Canada), which had walked out earlier and was not a party to the U.S.-EC agreement; compromises by Japan with regard to its policy of protecting its rice growers; a reconciliation of the disagreement on quotas and tariffs for trade in bananas; and a range of potentially difficult differences of opinion between the developed and less developed worlds on the liberalization of trade in services. Given the number and complexity of issues that were still outstanding, it was feared that France and other aggrieved parties would have a number of opportunities to reopen the farm dispute and endanger or delay agreement on the most ambitious package of multilateral trade-boosting measures ever put forward. The package included freer trade in financial, telecommunication, audiovisual, and maritime services; a 30% cut in tariffs across the world; new rules for protecting patents and copyrights; and better rules for settling international disputes. There was additional concern over France's strategy of using other controversial issues within the EC as a means of gaining support for its anti-GATT stance from other members; this appeared to be partially successful in modifying the original Belgian, Spanish, and Italian positions. The general gloom and dismay was reinforced by the vivid pictures of French farmers protesting on the streets of Paris, Strasbourg, and

other cities, damaging cars and other property, and burning farm produce.

Nevertheless, as the year drew to a close, most negotiating partners pressed ahead with the discussions in an attempt to conclude a global deal by March 1993, before the expiry of the special negotiating authority granted by the U.S. Congress. It was feared that President-elect Clinton would adopt a tougher approach in future negotiations.

INTERNATIONAL EXCHANGE AND PAYMENTS

The most notable feature of the international monetary scene during 1992 was widespread and prolonged exchange-rate instability. This was centred principally on the ERM. In previous years the ERM had been a strong stabilizing force, limiting fluctuations in member currencies within relatively narrow bands by central bank support operations and by the flexible use of interest rates. In 1992 this carefully constructed edifice came under considerable strain, partly because of the emergence of serious structural divergences among member countries and partly because of the inappropriate policies pursued by the principal participants. The central parity for currencies within the ERM was expressed in Deutsche Marks, which, on the basis of a record of relatively rapid, consistent, and noninflationary growth in the German economy, was considered the strongest and most stable European currency. However, during 1992 the method of financing German unification gave rise to strong inflationary pressures that caused the Bundesbank to adopt a high-interest-rate policy. This, in turn, put considerable pressure on the weaker currencies. The sluggish economic conditions made it impossible for interest rates to be raised sufficiently to provide protection, while, at the same time, periodic statements by Bundesbank officials encouraged currency speculation by raising doubts about Germany's willingness to continue support for the currencies under pressure.

In early September EC finance ministers conferred and announced that German interest rates would not be lowered and the ERM currencies would not be realigned. A week later Germany was prevailed upon to institute a minor interest-rate change, and the Italian lira was devalued by 7%, making it clear to currency speculators that statements by EC finance ministers should not be taken unduly seriously. Less than a week and several ambiguous Bundesbank statements later, sterling and the lira came under attack and were forced out of the ERM to find their own level. At the same time, the Spanish peseta was devalued by 5%.

This was followed by very strong pressure on the French franc, which was eased by heavy German support. Throughout October currencies such as the peseta, the Portuguese escudo, the Danish krone, and the Irish punt came under pressure, and finally, at the end of November, the peseta—this time accompanied by the escudo—was devalued by a further 6%. Not surprisingly, the turmoil within the ERM had a wider effect; the Swedish and Finnish currencies, which were pegged to the ECU, also suffered and—after some desperate countermeasures, including overnight rates in excess of 100%—were forced to float and find their own level. Norway resisted a little longer but had to follow suit in early December. At the end of the year, currencies such as the franc, the krone, and the punt faced repeated bouts of pressure, giving rise to widespread skepticism about the future of the ERM as well as the EC's ambitious plans for monetary integration.

Away from Europe currency movements were less spectacular. Between January and March the U.S. dollar moved upward against most other currencies. However, largely because of a fall in relative interest rates, the trend was reversed in subsequent months, and by October 1992 the dollar's effective rate was 79.5, compared with 83.9 during the second quarter of the year. Generally, the dollar grew weaker against most other currencies, including the Deutsche Mark, the franc, and the yen, although—as a result of the turmoil in the ERM from September—it gained considerable ground against sterling and the lira.

Balance of payments positions across the world did not change dramatically during 1992. Following a massive reduction in the industrialized world's current account deficit between 1990 and 1991, 1992 saw little change, with the overall shortfall expected at around $23 billion. This figure concealed significant variations in the performance of the main members of this bloc. In fact, despite the relatively sluggish growth in their economies, most developed countries faced a growing deficit. This was particularly true of the U.S., where the stronger-than-average growth in the economy sucked in imports at a rapid rate and resulted in an estimated negative balance on the current account of approximately $35 billion, compared with a deficit of only $3.7 billion in the preceding year. Large as the 1992 figure was, set against the recent external payment record of the U.S., it seemed somewhat less spectacular; between 1984 and 1991 the average annual current account deficit in the U.S. totaled $107 billion.

The EC also saw a modest widening in its negative balance. The principal culprits were the U.K., where—despite a fall in GDP—the current account shortfall was estimated to have nearly doubled to just under $20 billion, as well as Italy—up from $21 billion to $25 billion—and Germany, which faced an estimated deficit of $22 billion. Although this represented only a 10% increase over the previous year in Germany, it was a very dramatic change from the recent record. Attributable almost entirely to the economic problem of unification, it was only the second negative figure in recent history and compared with an average annual surplus of $31 billion in the period 1984–91. In sharp contrast, however, it would seem that nothing could stop the steady rise in Japan's current account surplus. Mainly as a result of a significant slowdown in the rise of imports consequent on the sluggishness of the domestic economy, the 1992 surplus was thought to have grown to about $110 billion, an increase of some 50% over 1991 and the highest level in at least the preceding 10 years.

The LDCs saw a significant cut in their payments deficit, from $78 billion in 1991 to an estimated $52 billion in 1992. However, all of this improvement was attributable to the normalization of oil production after the Gulf war, the effect of which was to cut the deficit of oil-producing countries from $67 billion to $29 billion. Most other LDCs faced higher current account deficits than in 1991. In African countries, which saw a strong growth in imports, weak overseas demand, and a deterioration in their terms of trade, the deficit was thought to have trebled to $9 billion. A significant increase of 100% to $11 billion was also estimated for Asian LDCs. By contrast, the former communist countries of eastern Europe were expected to do significantly better than in 1991. The main factors were a substantial inflow of foreign capital, the gradual reorientation of local industry to serve Western markets, sluggish import growth resulting from official efforts to protect the balance of payments, and a lack of purchasing power consequent on a low level of disposable income. In October the IMF estimated eastern Europe's 1992 current account deficit at $2.9 billion, compared with $6.4 billion in the preceding year. These figures excluded those for the republics of the former Soviet Union, for which the sketchy information available pointed to a significant worsening in their external payments position in 1992.

Contrary to some fears expressed in 1991, the debt problem of the less developed world did not become more acute. Although IMF estimates suggested that total debt rose by about 6% to $1,360,000,000,000, expressed as a ratio to the value of exports of goods and services, it actually fell from just over 126 to 123. While the improvement was far from spectacular, it came in the wake of a modest deterioration in 1991 and reestablished the downward trend seen since 1986, when the figure stood at a peak of 176. The level of indebtedness also showed a decline as a proportion of GDP. For 1992 this ratio was estimated at just over 29%, below the 30% mark for the first time in over 10 years and some 25% lower than the peak reached in 1986. Thus, although debt among the LDCs remained at an uncomfortably high level, in the latest six years, except for 1991, there was a sharp fall in its relative importance.

The 1992 good performance was attributable to further efforts by official lenders to restructure debt, as well as to the trend of interest rates. Interest rates in the U.S., Japan, and the U.K. were on a downward curve, which had a beneficial effect on LDCs' debt-servicing burden. In fact, estimates suggested that, expressed as a percentage of exports, these remained broadly unchanged in 1992. There were also a number of official debt-restructuring and buy-back arrangements, including a deal covering the $44 billion Brazilian commercial debt, a scheme to reduce Argentina's medium- and long-term debts to foreign banks, a scheme to cut Nigeria's indebtedness by $3.5 billion, and an agreement with commercial lenders about existing debt restructuring, debt buybacks, and the provision of new finance for the Philippines.

However, although the overall picture was largely satisfactory, the performance of individual countries varied considerably. Asia and the Middle East were in the most favourable position; the former's debt-to-export ratio declined from 68 to 66, while that of the latter remained largely unchanged at around 133. By contrast, African economies—which saw a strong improvement in their relative indebtedness toward the end of the 1980s—faced a rise (for the second year in succession) in the size of their debt burden to 230% of their exports, while in the case of the LDCs of the Western Hemisphere the comparable figure was put at 267%, broadly the same as in the preceding year but 6% above 1990. Nevertheless, for most LDCs, including those in Africa, the long-term trend was one of improvement. The same could not be said of the formerly centrally planned countries. Although eastern Europe's debt-to-export ratio fell from 167 to 163, because of the financing needs of the economic restructuring program, this was well above the 130 mark seen in the mid-1980s and the average figure of 70 common at the start of that decade. Projections indicated that in 1991 Soviet external debt had risen to $66 billion, but because of a massive fall in overseas sales, the debt-to-export ratio jumped from 53 to 88%. Partial indications for 1992 suggested that there had been a further deterioration in the position.   (IEIS)

This article updates the *Macropædia* articles BANKS AND BANKING; ECONOMIC GROWTH AND PLANNING; GOVERNMENT FINANCE; INTERNATIONAL TRADE.

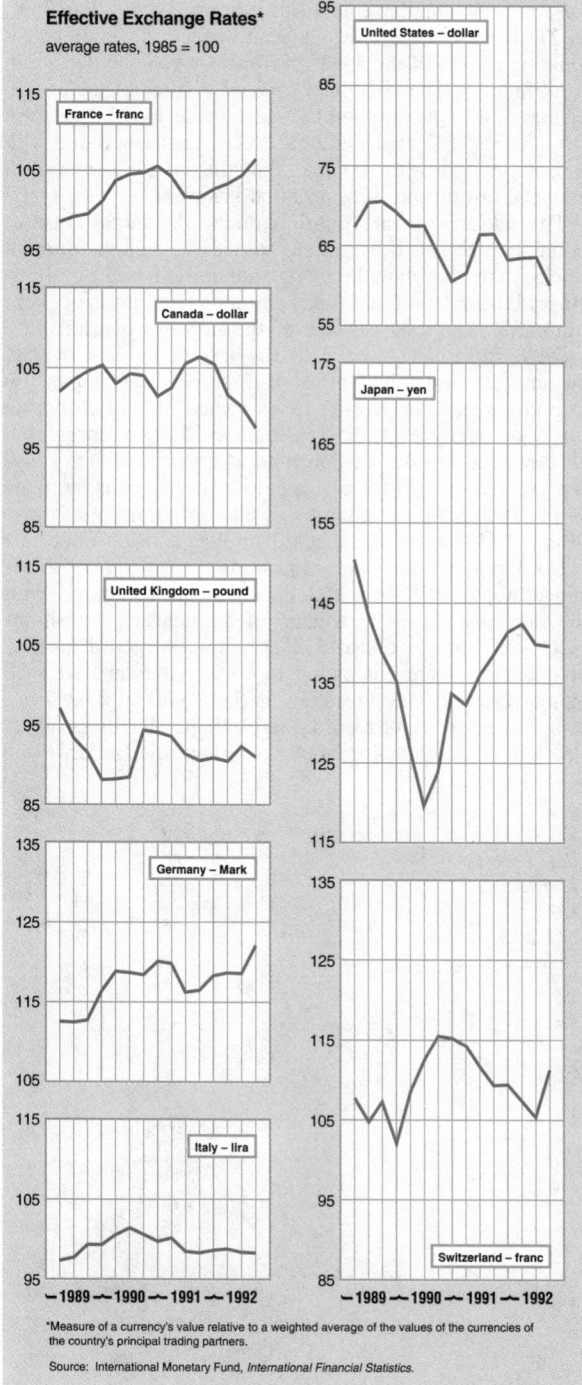

STOCK EXCHANGES

Many of the world's leading stock exchanges declined during 1992 in response to sluggish global economic growth, static or declining corporate profitability, and reduced dividend payout. In the absence of major international factors, investor demand was influenced by domestic and regional concerns. Thus the modest gains seen in the U.S., the U.K., and Hong Kong were offset by declines in Japan, Australia, Taiwan, and most of continental Europe. Overall, world stock markets in 1992 registered about a 5% fall, as measured by the *Financial Times* World Markets Price (FTA World) Index.

Yields from fixed-income securities declined during 1992, allowing prices to appreciate, but not as much as in the previous year. The attractions of fixed-income securities were boosted by stable inflation rates and gently declining interest rates. The main exception to this trend was among countries that were members of the European exchange-rate mechanism (ERM). The continuing high interest rates in Germany, reflecting the tight anti-inflationary policy of the Bundesbank, prevented members of the ERM from reducing their interest rates significantly without risking currency instability. This maintained a relatively high yield on their government bonds and other fixed-income securities. (IEIS)

United States. Stock market prices were relatively flat during 1992, with the narrowest margins in history between highs and lows. For the first time since 1986, the Dow Jones

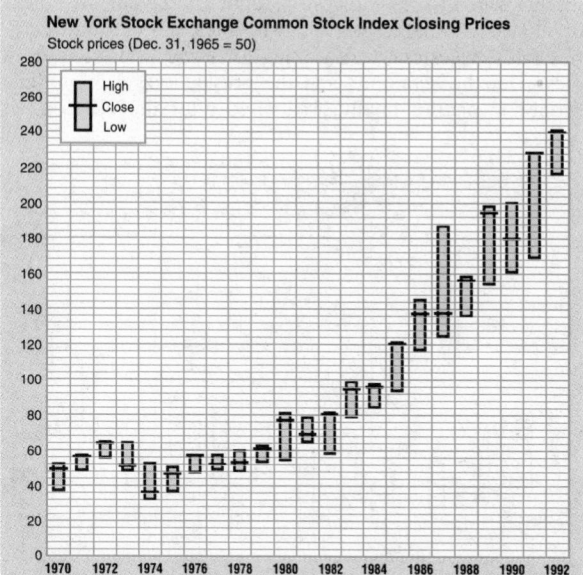

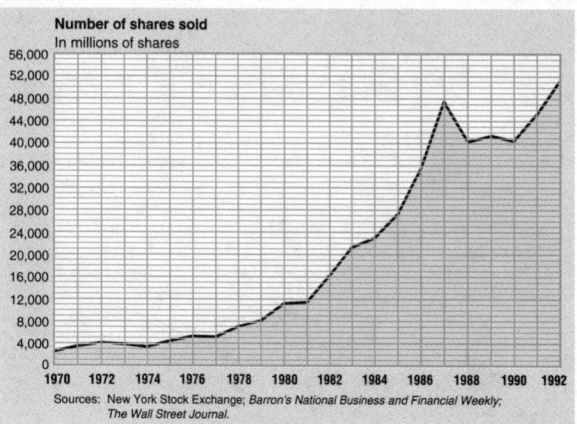

industrial average (DJIA) had no major fluctuations. There were no 100-point intraday changes. The DJIA traded in a range of 8.8%, the narrowest ever. The Standard & Poor's (S&P) 500 stock index traded in a range of just 11.9% between its annual high and low, also the narrowest range ever.

The DJIA started the year at 3168.83 and hit new highs throughout January in response to the Federal Reserve's (Fed's) attempt to jump start the economy by aggressively cutting interest rates. The DJIA first crossed the 3300 mark on April 14 and the 3400 mark on June 1. It peaked at 3413.21 on June 1, but the broader averages continued hitting new all-time highs into December. The DJIA closed the year at 3301.11, up 132.28 points, or 4.2% for the year. In 1991 the DJIA rose 535.17 points, or 20.3%. Stock prices climbed after the November 1992 presidential election on evidence of the economy's growing strength. The S&P 500 gained 4.5%, not including dividends, and about 7.6% with dividends reinvested. On the over-the-counter (OTC) market, the National Association of Securities Dealers automated quotation (Nasdaq) composite index ended the year at a record high, up 15.5% from a year earlier.

The business and economic news was mostly gloomy in 1992, as weakness in the economy forced dozens of companies to retrench—laying off thousands of employees, closing plants, and, in many cases, filing for bankruptcy. The market was depressed by deeply troubled blue-chip stocks, such as IBM and General Motors. On July 2 the Fed cut interest rates to the lowest level in almost 30 years, but the stock market failed to rally. Investors tended to favour the stocks of smaller companies and built up their mutual fund equities. Most investors were waiting for lower interest rates, a pickup in the economy, and the presidential election. The economic picture finally brightened after the election, as

retail sales began to inch up and the consumer confidence index soared. By year's end investors were bullish. The index of leading economic indicators was rising during the last quarter of the year. The most favoured industry groups included semiconductors, autos, manufactured housing, and banks; least popular were drug stocks and other health care issues.

While unemployment remained high, averaging 7.5%, up from the prior year, gross domestic product (GDP) rose about 2% to $5,943,400,000,000. The Consumer Price Index rose by only about 3%. More companies reinstated dividends, announced higher dividends, or gave extra dividends in 1992 than in either of the previous two years. Favourable dividend announcements totaled 1,703, a 16.8% jump over the results of 1991, the worst year on record. The number of unfavourable announcements also dropped more than 36%, to 277 from 437 the previous year. Among the confidence-building factors of the 1992 stock market was the decline in bank failures. The combined total of failures of banks and savings and loans dropped to a seven-year low. There were 181 failures: 122 banks and 59 S&Ls. That compared with 295 in 1991 and was less than half that of 1989, when 535 financial institutions were declared insolvent.

The nation's private pension funds, the largest institutional holders of U.S. stocks, sold $16.6 billion more in stocks than they bought on an annualized basis in 1992. Heavy buying by mutual funds and individual investors kept stock prices high in the face of the negative pension fund activity. Individuals were still the largest holders overall, owning just under half of all U.S. stocks outstanding. As of midyear, private pension funds owned 21% of corporate stock, or nearly $1 trillion in equities. Stocks represented 59% of total private pension fund assets in 1992. They also represented 46% of the assets held by public pension funds (some $400 billion in equities), while corporate bonds represented 21% of all assets held by public pension funds.

Corporate merger and acquisition activity in 1992 declined about 9.7% on a dollar basis as compared with the previous year. The volume of announced acquisitions of U.S. companies fell to $123.9 billion. A record number of financings were completed in 1992. An estimated $838 billion raised in U.S. financing markets marked a 42% rise over the prior year's record $590 billion. Merrill Lynch & Co. led in every major branch of domestic underwriting

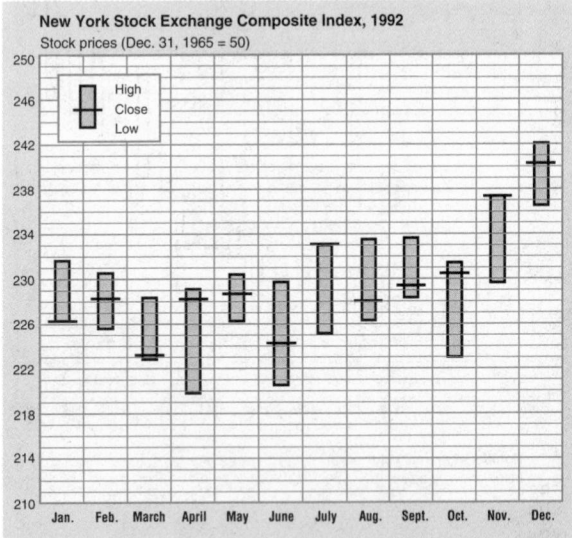

New York Stock Exchange Composite Index, 1992
Stock prices (Dec. 31, 1965 = 50)

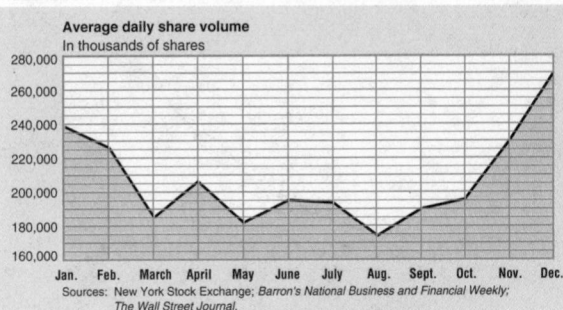

Average daily share volume
In thousands of shares

Sources: New York Stock Exchange; *Barron's National Business and Financial Weekly*; *The Wall Street Journal.*

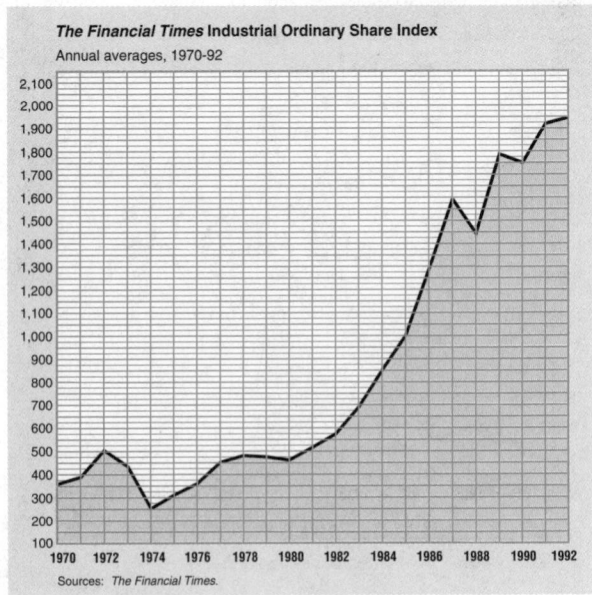

***The Financial Times* Industrial Ordinary Share Index**
Annual averages, 1970-92

Sources: *The Financial Times.*

except mortgage and asset-backed markets. Goldman, Sachs & Co. remained second, and the Lehman Brothers division of Shearson Lehman Brothers Inc. was third. Merrill Lynch earned more than 21% of the $6.7 billion in Wall Street underwriting revenues, or approximately $1.4 billion. A total of $72.4 billion in new common stock was sold in 1992. More than $301 billion was raised in the debt markets, excluding the mortgage and asset-based sectors. This was equal to the cumulative amount raised in the two prior years. Lower rates made it attractive for bond issuers to refinance long-term debt. Junk bonds (high-risk, high-yield debt) made a remarkable comeback, with an all-time record $38 billion in new issues in 1992, up almost 300% from the $10 billion in 1991. The previous record was $31 billion in 1986, during the heyday of the junk-bond market.

Interest rates were down across the board in 1992. The bank prime rate ended the year at 6%, compared with the prior year's 6.5%. The yield on the U.S. Treasury's main 30-year bond closed at 7.37%, down from 7.46% in 1991; the discount rate was 3% compared with 3.5%; and the Fed funds rate was 2.5%, contrasted with 4.6% the prior year. Three-month Treasury bills ended the year yielding 3.05%, contrasted with 3.86% the previous year, while six-month bills closed at 3.23%, down from 3.87%. Municipal bond average yields fell from 6.7% in 1991 to 6.39% in 1992.

Turnover of shares on the New York Stock Exchange (NYSE) rose 13.1% in 1992 to 51,375,671,500 shares, as compared with the prior year's 45,424,500,000. A total of 1,811 issues advanced, 831 declined, and 53 were unchanged. The total number of issues traded was 2,695, up from 2,464 in 1991. Most of the best gainers for the year were small, little-known stocks, while the best industries were semiconductors (up 65.7%) and communications (56.5%). The most active issues on the Big Board were: Glaxo Holding, with a volume of 569,397,600 shares traded; RJR Nabisco, 543,-237,800; General Motors, 537,620,700; IBM, 512,988,300; Philip Morris, 472,418,900; Teléfonos de México, 464,883,-400; Citicorp, 453,483,600; AT&T, 428,898,700; Chrysler, 427,798,300; Merck, 406,015,700; and Ford Motor, 395,743,-500. Short sales, in which traders sell borrowed stock in the expectation that the stock's price will fall and that they can profit by buying the shares back later at a lower price to replace the borrowed stock, passed the billion-share mark for the first time in mid-December 1992, with 1,010,000,-000 shares sold short. Bond sales were down by 9%, from $12,693,690,000 in 1991 to $11,629,012,000 in 1992. The number of traded issues declined from 2,087 in 1991 to 1,382 in 1992.

On the American Stock Exchange (Amex), annual sales of shares increased 6.75%, from 3,368,380,000 in 1991 to 3,595,779,000 in 1992. There were 579 advances, 345 declines, and 24 issues unchanged for a total of 948 issues traded, down from 1,049 the prior year. Held back by the poor performance of many small energy and mineral stocks that traded on the Amex, the market-value index rose by just 1.1% for the year. Bond sales declined 6.8%, from $952,360,000 in 1991 to $891,913,000 in 1992. The number of issues traded fell from 262 to 158. The "Emerging Issues Market" on the Amex, designed to facilitate the entry of smaller companies into the market, continued to expand with the addition of many new entrants. Trading volume on the Pacific Stock Exchange (PSE) was 1,990,389,794 shares, virtually unchanged from the prior year. The value of shares traded on the PSE was up 5.7% from 1991—$54.9 billion, compared with $51.9 billion. The Philadelphia Stock Exchange set a record for volume in its stock and currency markets in 1992. Equity volume was 1.1 billion shares, up 24% from 1991.

On the OTC market, average prices reflected a more bullish attitude than was reflected on the major exchanges. The Nasdaq composite index of 4,000 mostly small stocks achieved a high of 676.95 at year's end, a rise of 15.5%, compared with 56.8% in 1991. The number of shares traded on the Nasdaq exchange, 48,396,600,000, rose 17.2% in 1992, from a level of 41,310,043,000 in 1991, and surpassed the volume on the NYSE on 83 of the 252 trading days. Of a total 4,667 issues traded, 3,119 advanced, 1,463 declined, and 85 were unchanged. Nasdaq's most active issues, which

Table VII. Selected Major World Stock Market Indexes*

Country and index	1992 range† High	Low	Year-end close	Percent change from 12/31/91
Australia, Sydney All Ordinaries	1685	1357	1550	−6
Austria, Credit Aktien	578	291	313	−17
Belgium, Brussels BEL20	1235	1046	1127	+3
Canada, Toronto Composite	3666	3195	3350	−5
Denmark, Copenhagen Stock Exchange	365	250	262	−26
Finland, HEX General	936	541	829	+6
France, Paris CAC General	556	442	484	+1
Germany, Frankfurt FAZ Aktien	725	566	603	−6
Hong Kong, Hang Seng	6447	4302	5512	+28
Italy, Milan Banca Comm. Ital.	552	355	446	−12
Japan, Nikkei Average	23,801	14,309	16,925	−26
Netherlands, The, CBS All Share	216	190	198	+4
Norway, Oslo Stock Exchange	773	532	667	...
Singapore, SES All-Singapore	417	351	395	−2
South Africa, Johannesburg Industrials	4689	3936	4363	+5
Spain, Madrid Stock Exchange	267	179	214	−13
Sweden, Affarsvarlden General	1015	639	913	−1
Switzerland, SBC General	682	596	688	+16
Taiwan, Weighted	5392	3352	3377	−27
Thailand, Bangkok SET	963	668	893	+26
United Kingdom, FT-SE 100	2792	2281	2847	+14
United States, Dow Jones Industrials	3413	3137	3301	+4

*Index numbers are rounded.
†Based on daily closing price.
Source: *Financial Times.*

Table VIII. U.S. Stock Market Prices

Month	Transportation (20 stocks) 1992	1991	Public utilities (40 stocks) 1992	1991	Industrials (400 stocks) 1992	1991	Composite (500 stocks) 1992	1991
January	340.35	241.37	149.70	138.38	493.37	382.78	416.08	325.49
February	348.31	279.36	143.06	143.19	490.89	427.94	412.56	362.26
March	346.73	267.91	139.45	142.84	484.86	441.87	407.36	372.28
April	344.98	273.89	141.61	143.13	484.53	450.17	407.41	379.68
May	356.62	284.72	147.25	138.66	470.72	450.05	414.81	377.99
June	342.07	296.23	146.79	135.73	481.96	450.87	408.27	378.29
July	334.44	294.32	153.70	137.75	487.16	453.38	415.05	380.23
August	321.77	295.57	149.97	140.88	490.88	463.26	417.93	389.40
September	323.19	295.12	155.36	142.84	493.56	459.11	418.48	387.20
October	327.46	314.42	154.28	144.54	483.33	457.39	412.50	386.88
November	...	315.86	...	146.66	...	454.97	...	385.92
December	...	312.73	...	148.81	...	458.00	...	388.51

Source: U.S. Department of Commerce, *Survey of Current Business.* Prices are Standard & Poor's monthly averages of daily closing prices, with 1941–43 = 10, except Transportation, 1982 = 100.

Table IX. U.S. Government Long-Term Bond Yields

Month	Yield (%) 1992	1991	Month	Yield (%) 1992	1991
January	7.48	8.33	July	7.40	8.50
February	7.78	8.12	August	7.19	8.17
March	7.93	8.38	September	7.08	7.96
April	7.88	8.29	October	7.26	7.88
May	7.80	8.33	November	...	7.83
June	7.72	8.54	December	...	7.58

Source: U.S. Department of Commerce, *Survey of Current Business.* Yields are for U.S. Treasury bonds that are taxable and due or callable in 10 years or more.

Table X. U.S. Corporate Bond Yields

Month	Yield (%) 1992	1991	Month	Yield (%) 1992	1991
January	8.20	9.04	July	8.07	9.00
February	8.29	8.83	August	7.95	8.75
March	8.35	8.93	September	7.92	8.61
April	8.33	8.86	October	7.99	8.55
May	8.28	8.86	November	...	8.48
June	8.22	9.01	December	...	8.31

Source: U.S. Department of Commerce, *Survey of Current Business.* Yields are based on Moody's Aaa domestic corporate bond index.

had turnovers comparable to or better than those of the NYSE, were primarily computer-related stocks, including Intel Corp., with 553,729,200 shares traded; Novell Inc., 434,325,000; and Microsoft Corp., 402,467,700.

Mutual fund managers had a mediocre 1992 in terms of investment performance. The average equity mutual fund recorded just an 8.88% gain for the year. The results were far below the 35.61% gain in 1991 or the 11.1% average gain over the previous 30 years. Small-company stock funds were the performance leaders, surging 9.77%. Mutual funds bought $68.6 billion in 1992. In 1991 net stock purchases were 44.6 billion, up from 14.4 billion in 1990 and just 1.2 billion in 1989. Mutual funds had become the second largest institutional holders of equities, owning 9% of all U.S. stocks. The bulk of mutual fund assets still were held in government and corporate bonds. In the 1950s and 1960s nearly 90% of all mutual funds' assets were invested in stocks.

The S&P 500 composite index (Table VIII) averaged 416.08 in January, 27.8% above the corresponding 325.49 figure of the previous year. The index declined to 407.36 in March, rose modestly to 414.81 in May, and moved within a narrow range until year's end. The high for the index was 441.28, the low was 394.50, and the closing figure was 435.71. The S&P industrials index registered a 1992 high of 515.75, with 470.91 as the low and 507.46 at the close. After the January average of 493.37, it dipped to 470.72 in May before beginning a climb in June and breaking through the 500 mark in December. Public utilities stock prices paralleled the movements of the broader indexes with a high of 161.98, a low of 135.59, and a close of 158.46. Transportation stocks were above the previous year's levels throughout 1992, but the year-to-year comparative differences narrowed from 99 points in January to 13 points in October. The high for the year was 369.97, the low was 307.94, and the close was 363.75.

U.S. government long-term bond yields were lower in 1992 than in the previous year. The January average (Table IX) was 7.48%, compared with 8.33% in 1991. After a modest gain to 7.93% in March, the average yield slid slowly through September at a level of 7.08% and then climbed to close the year at 7.39%.

Corporate bond yields (Table X) declined during 1992 from an average level of 8.2% in January to 7.92% in September before a modest year-end gain. The junk-bond market was strengthened, as the default rate fell to 3.9%, down sharply from 9.7% in 1991 and below the average of 4.65% for the previous 21 years.

Traders in the futures pits had a discouraging year, as the lagging economy lessened demand for basic industrial commodities such as copper and silver. The Commodity Research Bureau's widely watched index of 21 futures contracts ended the year at 202.76, down 2.6%. The CRB Futures Index (1967 = 100) began the year at 208, traded irregularly to reach a high of 211 in June, declined to 200 by August, and climbed back slowly to year's end.

The securities industry enjoyed record profits in 1992. Member firms of the NYSE that dealt with the public achieved record pretax profits, with estimates ranging to as much as a total of $7 billion. Underwritings rose sharply in 1992. Total U.S. corporate financing was $846 billion, up 45% from 1991. Initial public offerings of stock raised a record $39.4 billion from investors in 1992, up 57% from 1991, fueled by a bull market in OTC stocks. Once issued, new stocks did well in 1992 but not as spectacularly as 1991's new issues. Secondary offerings raised $33 billion, up 7% over 1991, compared with preferred stock ($29 billion, up 47%), mortgage debt ($377 billion, up 51%), investment grade debt ($271 billion, up 42%), asset-backed debt ($51 billion, up 2%), junk bonds ($38 billion, up 280%), and convertible debt ($7 billion, down 7%), according to the Securities Data Co. The five largest common-stock offerings in 1992 were: General Motors, 1.5 billion shares; Blackrock 2001 Term Trust, 1.3 billion; Chemical Banking, 1,226,000,-000; Wellcome Group (ADRs), 1,068,000,000; and GTE, 789 million. The largest debt issuers were Federal Home Loan Mortgage and Federal National Mortgage. More than a third of corporate debt issued was refinancing at lower interest rates.

The Securities and Exchange Commission took a number of important initiatives during the year, including a program to facilitate capital raising by small businesses by reducing the compliance burdens placed on them by federal securities laws; implementation of new disclosure requirements for broker dealers in penny-stock transactions; increased net capital requirements for broker dealers who served as market makers; and increased investment adviser oversight.

Canada. Canadian stock prices lost ground in 1992 as investors worried about a depressed economy, a weak dollar, concerns about constitutional reform, and the financial health of several of Canada's largest corporate empires, including Olympia & York Developments, Ltd., and Bramalea, Ltd. The unemployment rate rose to a cyclical high of 11.8% in November, up from 11.3% in October. The Canadian dollar traded at new lows in November amid slim evidence of a recovery. Domestic demand was weak, and employment growth and income gains remained sluggish. Interest rates were subject to major fluctuations during the year. The prime rate, which hit a low in September at 6.25%, the lowest level since 1971, was raised, in response to wild gyrations in the currency market, to shore up the dollar's sagging fortunes. During July the dollar tumbled against major currencies, brushing close to all-time lows. The rate rose to 9.95% in late November, the highest level in two years. After the market's initial sigh of relief over the failure of the October 26 referendum on constitutional reform, the Canadian market sold off sharply in November. Downward pressure on the currency was met with higher short-term interest rates, with the prime rate rising from 7.75 to 9.75% over the month. During December the banks dropped the rate six times in seven days to 7.25%. Canadian fixed-income markets experienced attractive gains during the last quarter. Investors earned an average 7.69% on Canadian bonds in the 11 months to November 30, measured by the Scotia-McLeod Universe Index, well below the 19.47% in the corresponding period of 1991.

The Toronto Stock Exchange composite index, which was above 3600 in January 1992, dipped to 3325 by April, fell to 3200 in October, jumped to 3350 in November, and closed the year at 3350.44. The index, including dividends, was down 1.4% for the year. The 90- and 200-day averages both trended downward throughout the year. Advancing groups included industrial products, transportation, and gold stocks. Oil and metal prices were down. The Vancouver Stock Exchange's share of volume on all Canadian exchanges was 29%, while its share of total value remained at 3%. At the end of November there were 1,903 issues listed on the VSE. Mining companies continued to account for the largest share of capital raised by VSE companies, at 43% of money raised. High-tech companies maintained a 14% share.

Investors turned bullish toward the end of the year in anticipation of a U.S. recovery spurring demand for Canada's mining and forestry products. U.S.-Canadian trade reached another record in 1992. For the first 10 months of the year, U.S. imports from Canada totaled U.S. $78,060,000,000, an 11.2% increase from 1991. U.S. exports to Canada showed a 9.3% increase. The U.S. took more than 77% of Canada's exports and supplied more than 70% of Canada's imports.

(IRVING PFEFFER)

Western Europe. With few exceptions, stock markets in Europe underperformed their North American counterparts; they declined more than Wall Street early in the year and failed to recover in the autumn. An overall gain of 3%, as measured by the *Financial Times* European index, disguised losses investors suffered in many European bourses in 1992. The star performers in Europe were Switzerland and the U.K., with around 16% and 14% rises, respectively, from the beginning of the year. By contrast, the worst performers in 1992 were Denmark, Austria, and Spain. Investors in Germany, France, Italy, and Sweden also saw their investments valued on Dec. 31, 1992, at a lower level than at the beginning of the year.

The London Stock Exchange (LSE) took off only after the government's spectacular U-turn in September following the European currency crisis that forced the pound to withdraw from the ERM. No longer constrained with maintaining the value of the pound against the Deutsche Mark, British economic strategy shifted from low inflation to high growth, and interest rates were cut by three points in successive stages between mid-September and mid-November. Growth-stimulating and job-generating capital-investment projects were given greater priority at the expense of current spending.

This was the second powerful rally in London. The year had opened with moderate gains correcting the previous autumn's weakness. As the general election campaign got under way and the opposition Labour Party, despite a commitment to raise income taxes, remained ahead in the opinion polls, the market took fright. The *Financial Times* Stock Exchange (FT-SE 100) Index dropped by around 100 points to 2400. It soared to 2740 when Prime Minister John Major was unexpectedly returned with a working majority. However, the postelection euphoria did not last long, as it became evident that the recession was worsening instead of ending. During the summer, as corporate results disappointed, some large corporations cut their dividends, unemployment climbed, and company failures reached record levels, the FT-SE 100 Index dropped to 2300. Then came the U-turn, with lower interest rates, and the LSE established a new all-time high. At year's end the market was firmly above 2800, as it was encouraged by expectations of recovery at home and in the U.S.

Given the speed with which the German economy approached a recession, it was not surprising that the Frankfurt Stock Exchange reacted adversely. Encouraged by better-than-expected economic growth, the FAZ Aktien Index rose steadily during the spring to 720—a gain of 13%. The market consolidated during the summer and occasionally tested higher levels on hopes of lower interest rates as the inflationary pressures eased somewhat. The bubble burst in July when the Bundesbank raised its discount rate at a time when the rapid appreciation of the Deutsche Mark was hurting exporters, domestic demand was weakening, and it was painfully clear that unification was costing much more than previously expected. As international investors bailed out, the market fell, dragging the FAZ Aktien Index close to 580 by the beginning of September. As the economic downturn deepened in the autumn, with forecasts of minimum growth in western Germany in 1993, the markets remained depressed. In September Germany came under pressure from other European countries to cut its interest rates to relieve the currency tensions within the ERM. In the event, a 0.25% cut was less than expected. Afterward the Bundesbank reaffirmed its concern with the strong growth

in money supply rather than the looming recession. As the year drew to a close, investors remained cautious and the market drifted sideways, nursing capital losses close to 6%.

Given the French economy's close ties with Germany and the fact that it was hampered by sluggish global economic activity and political uncertainty, it was not surprising that the Paris Bourse underperformed in 1992. As with other major stock markets, it rose strongly in the opening months of the year, taking the CAC 40 Index to 2078 in May, up from the January 2 level of 1750. However, as the prospects of lower interest rates receded and economic growth lost momentum, the Paris Bourse looked expensive and declined steadily in the summer. Following the Danish rejection of the Maastricht Treaty, uncertainty surrounded the outcome of the French referendum and was heightened by the news that Pres. François Mitterrand was suffering from cancer. The narrow "yes" vote was initially well received, but soon the Paris Bourse went into a steep decline as the crisis in the ERM hit the franc, forcing it to its ERM floor. A hike in interest rates to protect the franc and considerable support from the Bundesbank forestalled a devaluation that could have wrecked the whole system. The stock market remained unimpressed by two small cuts in prime interest rates in November, as the real interest rates, at around 7%, were inimical to corporate profits, and economic outlook remained uncertain.

Switzerland benefited from the rest of Europe's uncertainties. It was a market dominated by big banks and multinational drug and industrial companies. This provided better defensive qualities, and the market was up some 16% overall during 1992. Having moved up swiftly in the spring, it was nearly 17% higher in May, but it gave up some of the gains as the corporate earnings for 1993 were revised downward in the summer. However, an autumn rally developed as the investors shrugged off a "no" vote on a referendum on closer economic integration with the European Communities.

The Benelux countries, which were heavily dependent on international trade, were caught up in the higher Deutsche Mark valuation and suffered depressed exports. The stock markets broadly reflected the trends in Germany and France and gave up their earlier gains to end the year with very small gains.

The Scandinavian stock exchanges were also disappointing for the investors. Denmark's rejection of the Maastricht Treaty in June marked a turning point, and the Copenhagen Stock Exchange lost over 100 points, or 25% of its value, in the second half of the year. Sweden's fundamental economic weakness and high interest rates drove the Affarsvarlden General Index nearly 15% below its level at the beginning of the year, but it staged a strong recovery in late November, following the devaluation of the krona, and recouped most of the earlier losses. Finland, a comparatively smaller market, picked up in 1992, ending a long period of sustained underperformance in the wake of the collapse of the former Soviet Union.

The southern European bourses were among the worst performers in 1992. The Milan Bourse fell steadily until October and was more than 12% down year to year, despite a sustained rally in the closing months. Investors reacted adversely to Italy's growing economic crisis, which was accentuated by financial and political scandals. While Prime Minister Giuliano Amato's tough austerity measures were welcomed as long overdue to address the country's structural economic problems, investors were jolted when the September ERM crisis initially led to 21% short-term interest rates. This was followed by a small devaluation and the withdrawal of the lira from the system. Once a favourite

Dealers on the Tokyo exchange watch on March 16 as the Nikkei Price Index drops 3% to below 20,000, the lowest level in five years. The Japanese stock market later fell another 6,000 points, to a six-year low, increasing concern for the stability of the country's financial institutions.
AP/WIDE WORLD

of international investors and a star performer, the Madrid Stock Exchange found it heavy going in 1992 and fell by around 13%. While many European stock exchanges rose in the spring, Madrid was shunned as the economic prospects and the inflationary outlook in Spain seemed relatively less attractive. The steady decline through the summer, however, turned into a slump in September as Spain, like Italy, was caught up in the currency crisis and had to raise interest rates and devalue. What discouraged investors most was an unexpected temporary reintroduction of capital controls.

Other Countries. With the exception of Hong Kong and the Southeast Asian "tiger countries," stock exchanges in Southern Hemisphere countries fell in 1992. A delayed economic recovery in Australia, coupled with poor corporate profitability, meant that the stock exchange could not hold on to earlier gains and ended the year down 6%. Likewise, political deadlock, tribal clashes, and declining gold and diamond prices meant that South Africa experienced a volatile year with a small gain on the Johannesburg Stock Exchange. Hong Kong, with an overall gain of more than 28%, was the best performing stock exchange in 1992, despite a severe setback in the autumn. Encouraged by rapid economic growth in the colony, international investors looking for an alternative to Japan in East Asia and for exposure to China's rapid economic growth piled into Hong Kong, doubling the Hang Seng Index in less than two years. The growing economic link between Hong Kong's industrialists, who employed more than two million workers in China's southern region, and Beijing (Peking) was perceived to outweigh the political tension between Gov. Chris Patten and China's rulers over attempts by the former to introduce certain democratic changes into the colony before the 1997 handover. In late November, however, investors took fright from renewed Chinese sabre rattling, and the market went into a headlong dive. In a week it fell 17% before stabilizing. At year's end the Hang Seng Index was nearly 15% off its early November high.

Japan, the world's second largest stock market, defied expectations of a recovery and fell by another 26% during 1992. From the December 1989 peak, the Nikkei Price Index had fallen 56.5%. The fundamental problem with Japan remained one of economic weakness. Consumption and capital spending, which between them accounted for nearly 80% of GDP, fell during 1992. Corporate earnings suffered, too, as the imbalance between revenues and fixed costs sharply eroded profits. The Nikkei Price Index staged a halfhearted rally in the spring as short-term interest rates were cut, but it continued to lose ground. Another rally in September fizzled out. The year ended as it started, with the Nikkei Price Index back in sick bay. In sharp contrast to Japan, many of the smaller stock exchanges in the region registered good increases. Indonesia and Malaysia outperformed South Korea and the Philippines, where the gains were smaller. Singapore went against the trend and fell slightly.

Commodity Markets. The continuing global recession held down the prices of many commodities. The *Economist* Commodity Price Index, which measured spot prices in U.S. dollars and sterling for 28 internationally traded foodstuffs, nonfood agricultural products, and metals, was largely unchanged in dollar terms from the beginning of the year. As the dollar depreciated against other currencies, especially in the summer, there was a 13% gain in sterling terms (despite the September devaluation of sterling).

The price of crude oil, which was not included in the *Economist* Index, fell by around 7% in 1992. North Sea (Brent) crude oil fluctuated between $17 and $21 per barrel during the year, and in mid-December it was selling at $17.70 per barrel for January delivery. This price weakness was largely a result of sluggish demand from the recession-hit industrial countries, as well as a mild winter. An agreement in November by OPEC countries to cut production did not stabilize prices, as the level of production was still thought to be above the likely global demand. Furthermore, the revised ceiling did not include Ecuador, which had left OPEC.

The two major sectors of the *Economist* Index performed slightly differently. The food index declined 2%, while the industrials index was up by a similar magnitude. Nonfood agricultural products such as wool, cotton, and rubber were held back either by slack demand or by overproduction. An exception was New Zealand wool prices, which climbed 30% thanks to Chinese and Russian buying. The *Economist* metal index, which was largely unchanged in dollar terms, was the weakest of the subindexes. Although investment buying boosted metal prices in the summer, this was short-lived. With the economic recovery proving elusive, industrial demand was weak, and prices drifted. There were large surpluses, particularly in aluminum and nickel, owing to large Russian exports.

Gold, while cheap by historical standards, traded in a narrow price range and ended 1992 with a 9% fall. As an ultimate safe haven, it had lost its appeal in the post-cold war, low-inflation era. While rock-bottom interest rates in the U.S. also reduced the demand from gold fund managers, industrial demand for the metal was stronger, as the electronics industry and jewelers purchased more. Supply, however, was also higher as sales by central banks in Japan, Brazil, and Canada supplemented newly mined gold. The price, having started the year at around $360 per troy ounce, drifted to $330 in December, raising hopes that at this lower level it would begin to attract buyers. However, as the year drew to a close, there was still no life in gold prices.

(IEIS)

This article updates the *Macropædia* article MARKETS.

Education

Noteworthy topics in 1992 included academic-achievement testing, ways to expand educational opportunities, the rebuilding of war-damaged educational systems, and students' political activism.

Comparisons of academic performance across nations were highlighted in two reports of educational achievement that compared the success of pupils from a number of countries in reading, mathematics, and science. The study of reading literacy, sponsored by the International Association for the Evaluation of Educational Achievement (IEA), tested 210,000 students, ages 9 and 14, from 9,000 schools in 52 countries. The tests measured skill in reading expository and narrative matter and in comprehending documents containing graphs, maps, and charts. Pupils in Finland earned the highest scores. Relatively strong scores were also achieved by participants in Sweden, France, the U.S., and New Zealand. Factors that consistently distinguished high-scoring from low-scoring countries were large school libraries, large classroom libraries, regular book borrowing, frequent silent reading in class, frequent story reading aloud by teachers, and more class hours spent in language instruction. Although in most school systems urban children achieved at higher levels than their nonurban age-mates, in a few highly developed nations rural pupils scored as high as, or higher than, those in city schools.

The Educational Testing Service (ETS) measured the mathematics and science achievement of 9-year-olds in 10 countries and of 13-year-olds in 15 countries. Among the nine-year-olds, South Korea placed first in mathematics, followed by Hungary, Taiwan, the former Soviet Union, and Israel. The U.S. ranked ninth. In science, South Korean nine-year-olds were again first, followed by Taiwan, the U.S., Canada, and Hungary. Among 13-year-olds, South Korea and Taiwan tied for first place in mathematics, followed by Switzerland, the former Soviet Union, and Hungary. In the science test for 13-year-olds, South Korea was first, followed by Taiwan, Switzerland, Hungary, and the former Soviet Union. U.S. 13-year-olds were 14th in math and 13th in science. A total of 174,000 pupils participated in the survey. Analysts of the ETS results concluded that success on the test could not be accounted for by such variables as class size, length of the school year, or the amount of money spent on education. Factors that appeared more significant were curriculum, parental expectations, and the amount of time pupils spent on homework or on reading as opposed to watching television.

Educational opportunity in the European Communities (EC) took a step forward with the implementation of a policy permitting children from the Community to attend school in any EC country, with the host nation paying the cost. In Britain, where the enrollment of boarding students had declined, 43 state boarding schools enthusiastically welcomed the program as a way to fill empty beds.

The Council of Europe, formed by 10 countries in 1949 as a forum for political discussion, had 27 member nations by 1992 and an agenda featuring cultural and educational cooperation. Major projects in 1992 included establishing a common framework for language learning in member countries and a secondary-school curriculum focusing heavily on European affairs.

Primary and Secondary. School attendance continued to be a topic of general concern. According to the French Ministry of Education, 62% of young people aged 2–29 in France were in education programs, higher than the 50–57% reported for other developed countries. Enrollment at the bottom of the schooling ladder was considerably more stable than at the top; over 80% of French children aged two to five were regularly in nursery schools, while half the students attending universities dropped out during the first two years. After four years as France's minister of education, Lionel Jospin was replaced by Jack Lang, who added education to his existing responsibilities as minister of culture. Jospin's record in office included increased salaries for educators, more flexible teaching methods in primary schools, a unified teacher-education system, a major expansion of higher education, and a new training partnership between industry and the schools.

In eastern Europe there was increasing change in the schools of former socialist countries. In Czechoslovakia, for example, world history books over four decades had focused chiefly on the Soviet Union and the triumph of communism, but newly revised textbooks emphasized Czechoslovakia's place in European history and the influence of the nation among world powers. The annual conference of the U.S.-based Comparative and International Education Society in March was attended by the ministers of education from 14 of the 15 countries that formerly made up the Soviet Union. The occasion provided the ministers with their first opportunity to meet each other and discuss education issues. The visit to the U.S. was financed by donations solicited from U.S. industries.

Civil war in Yugoslavia forced the closing of most schools in the regions under siege. In Croatia, 65,000 pupils and 6,000 teachers had to leave their homes. A total of 81 preschools, 204 primary schools, 61 secondary schools, and 17 colleges were damaged or totally destroyed. During the shelling of the town of Karlovac, educators attempted to teach textbook-based lessons over the local radio stations but were constrained by limitations on air time that permitted only five minutes per subject per class each week. Another area where schooling fell victim to unrest was Iraqi Kurdistan. In the town of Said Sadiq, volunteer Kurdish teachers set up school in seven tents and operated three shifts of classes each day in an effort to serve nearly 15,000 children.

Following the breakup of the Soviet Union, officials in control of China's schools reemphasized the teaching of Marxist-Leninist-Mao Thought, often accompanying study sessions with military drills intended to maintain political discipline among the young. As a further means of preventing students from straying off the communist path, the government endeavoured to suppress news of events in the former U.S.S.R.

With the unification of Germany, schools in the eastern sector, which had followed state atheism for 40 years, were now obliged to reintroduce religion as a regular part of the curriculum. Under the German constitution, students are to be taught "in accordance with the tenets of the religious communities," which in most west German schools meant Catholic or Protestant instruction. Four new federal states in the east adopted this pattern, but Brandenberg intended to integrate religion into a life orientation and ethics course being introduced in 44 schools on a trial basis. Church leaders objected to the Brandenberg plan on the grounds that teachers trained under the former regime were unqualified to teach religion and that religion was in danger of receiving short shrift in a course that also focused on such topics as unemployment, tolerance of minorities, ethics, and sexuality.

In the latest chapter of the effort to define the constitutional ban on the establishment of religion in the U.S., the Supreme Court barred public prayer at high school graduation ceremonies. The ruling was more specific than the

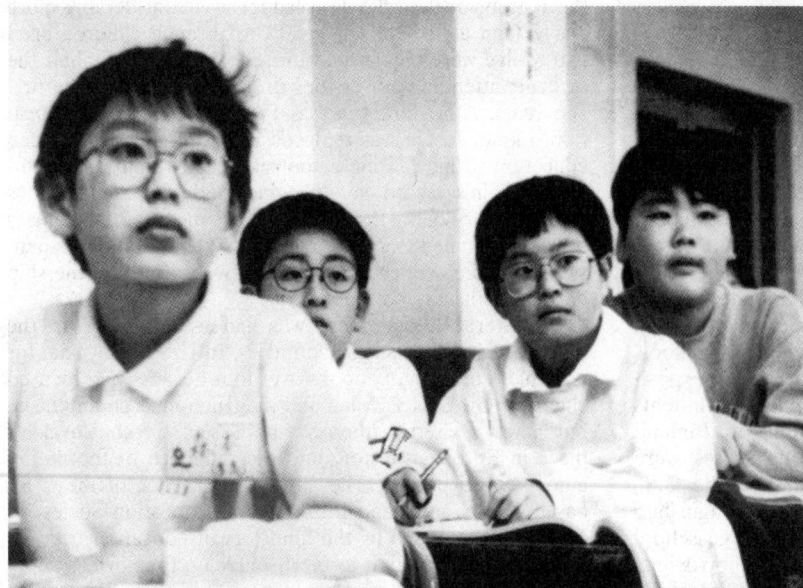

Japanese students attend a science class at a *juku*, or cram school. As a supplement to regular schools, *juku*s have become increasingly common in Japan.
KAKU KURITA—THE NEW YORK TIMES

court's 20-year-old, three-part test for maintaining the wall of separation between church and state. Since graduation is an official ceremony, prayer during it was viewed as a state-sanctioned religious activity. Some experts conjectured that a moment of silence might be permissible.

Sex education in the era of AIDS continued to be a contentious subject. Britain's Basil Cardinal Hume urged participants at a Catholic education conference to include sexuality and AIDS as topics in religious education classes so pupils might achieve a moral awareness extending beyond the physiological knowledge taught in science classes. In the U.S. the distribution of condoms in schools as a means of stemming the spread of AIDS was a source of conflict in a number of districts, although 68% of respondents in a Gallup Poll favoured it. One-fourth supported distribution only if parents consented.

Spending on education at all levels in the U.S. during the 1992–93 school year was estimated at some $445 billion, an increase of 5% over the preceding year. Education spending had risen by 40% in 10 years (adjusted for inflation), according to the U.S. Department of Education. More than seven million Americans were employed in education at all levels, and some 70 million persons, one-fourth of the population, were involved as students, administrators, or support staff.

Reform of the nation's schools was a major topic in the U.S. presidential election campaign, despite the fact that control of the schools rested largely with state and local governments. The major candidates all claimed to support education as a national priority. Pres. George Bush pointed to his America 2000 initiatives to reform education, Bill Clinton to improvements made in Arkansas schools during his governorship, H. Ross Perot to his leadership role in citizen-led reforms in Texas education. All pictured education as essential to improvement of the nation's lagging economy. Both national teachers' unions, the National Education Association (NEA) and the American Federation of Teachers (AFT), endorsed Clinton. The NEA was the single largest group represented at the Democratic convention.

In July U.K. Education Secretary John Patten published a White Paper, *Choice and Diversity,* setting out proposals for a rapid increase in the opting-out process, whereby schools in England and Wales could switch from the control of local education authorities to grant-maintained status—in effect, control by the central government. A new centralized fund-

ing agency would take over many of the local authorities' responsibilities in areas where more than 10% of pupils had opted out. The White Paper also outlined strong measures for schools deemed to be badly run, encouragement for schools that had opted out to specialize, a crackdown on truancy, a review of religious education, and an emphasis on the teaching of moral standards. So far fewer than 300 schools had chosen to opt out, but it was expected that the process would speed up significantly when the proposals outlined in the White Paper became law.

It was reported that half a million pupils in Japan were staying away from their classrooms more than 50 days a year because they found school life oppressive. Analysts charged that the rapidly rising number of absentees (*tokokiyohi*) was caused by the schools' rigid regimentation and strict discipline, the breakdown of family control over the young, and a demanding national curriculum that discouraged slow learners.

Attempts in Australia to provide suitable education for the country's 340,000 Aboriginal people featured curricula adjusted to the students' backgrounds, teacher training for Aborigines via radio and correspondence, bilingual programs, and newsletters produced in remote communities by means of desktop publishing. The Israeli Ministry of Education instituted a special program to train Ethiopian immigrants to teach in schools enrolling Ethiopian Jews, who had been airlifted to Israel in 1991. More than half the newcomers were under age 18. The training program included such subjects as the study of Israeli society, democracy, and civics.

Unequal educational opportunities for women in the U.S. were highlighted in a report titled *How Schools Shortchange Women,* published by the American Association of University Women. A summary study of hundreds of research reports, the AAUW report traced how girls end their high school careers trailing boys. Girls start school on an equal footing and fall behind as a result of discrimination by teachers, stereotypes in textbooks, biased tests, and male peer harassment. A study of 40,000 schools by Gary Orfield of Harvard University revealed a dramatic increase in the segregation of Hispanic students in the U.S. The rate had doubled during the past two decades, and dropout rates for Hispanics were nearly triple the national average. Among other findings in the report, school desegregation progress had been greatest in the Deep South, while central cities had been largely vacated by whites and were increasingly being abandoned by middle-class African-Americans.

A study published by the NEA found that 13.3% of teachers belonged to minority groups, a small drop from previous years. Of the approximately 2.4 million teachers in the U.S., 53.1% had earned advanced degrees. The average workweek for a teacher was 46.5 hours. Teacher salaries averaged $34,213 during the 1991–92 school year, according to the AFT. This represented a 3.6% increase from the preceding year, but the union noted that the outlook was clouded by economic difficulties. More than 20 strikes were reported as the 1992–93 school year started. Detroit, Mich., the nation's seventh largest school district, experienced a 27-day strike over a demand for an 8% pay raise. Some 168,000 students were affected. In another large district, Philadelphia, a strike was averted by a last-minute settlement.

A stalemate in salary negotiations between the Italian government and the teachers' unions motivated teachers to adopt a novel mode of industrial action. To display their dissatisfaction, while still honouring a no-strike agreement, the teachers refused to order textbooks for the coming year. The teachers contended that they were among the lowest paid in Europe. However, the government noted that Italian teachers enjoyed the lowest teacher-pupil ratio on the continent (1 to 9) and that salaries accounted for 98% of the nation's education budget. Over 98% of New Zealand's secondary school teachers staged a one-day walkout, followed by a series of regional strikes, to protest the government's move to eliminate traditional collective pay agreements and require each teacher to negotiate an individual contract. Opinion polls showed that 80% of the public supported the teachers.

In the U.S. Channel 1, a private, for-profit news program beamed to high schools, entered its second year with an audience estimated at 8.1 million students. The program continued to be controversial because it included commercials. Meanwhile, Whittle Communications, the developers of Channel 1, began plans for a network of private schools. Benno Schmidt resigned as president of Yale University to head the program.

Higher Education. In an effort to improve instruction in German universities, students launched a nationwide "test the teacher" (Prüf-den-Prof) project that involved collecting student assessments of instructors by means of questionnaires, with the results leading to awards for faculty members identified as the best teachers. The program was intended to encourage instructors to place at least as much emphasis on teaching as on research. The German university system, designed for 900,000 students, currently struggled to accommodate twice that many.

From 1963 through 1992, the number of British youth enrolled in higher education rose from 7.2 to 21% of the age group, with the greatest increase occurring among women, particularly those attending part-time. Although the British population was 40% working class and 60% middle class, only 20% of degrees in higher education were earned by working-class students, a proportion that had not changed over the past two decades. During that 20-year period, the percentage of university applicants entering with high test scores had risen.

To enhance the quality of faculty members at Brazil's leading university, officials of the University of São Paulo successfully challenged the clause in the nation's constitution that prohibited the permanent appointment of professors from abroad. At the same time, Brazil's Ministry of Education planned to expand its program of bringing researchers from the former Soviet Union and eastern Europe to the

nation's institutions of higher education. The Australian government, in a similar move, established a loan fund to help finance the immigration of highly qualified scientists from the former Soviet republics to take research positions in Australian universities. Meanwhile, institutions in the U.S. were appointing substantial numbers of former Soviet scientists, particularly those with international reputations in theoretical physics and fundamental mathematics. Over 2,000 academics who had immigrated to Israel from the Soviet Union were still unable to find teaching or research posts in Israeli institutions, partly because of the newcomers' lack of fluency in Hebrew. During the previous two years, an estimated one-third of such new arrivals had been placed in suitable positions.

In the aftermath of social upheaval, higher-education institutions in many countries struggled to reestablish normal operations. Two years after the end of Sandinista rule in Nicaragua, the country's four universities faced the prospect of a 22% cut in government funding as a result of the nation's dire economic state. With government allocations barely covering modest faculty salaries, few funds were available for research, equipment, or supplies. Kuwait University was gradually recovering from the destruction of its seven campuses during the 1990–91 Iraqi occupation. Officials were seeking to replace books and valuable equipment taken to Iraq, and damaged buildings were being repaired. Enrollment totaled around 9,000 students, 15% below the number prior to the invasion.

Following the October 1991 peace agreement that ended 13 years of civil war in Cambodia, universities and institutes in the capital of Phnom Penh were endeavouring to rebuild campuses abandoned during the hostilities. Students who had been refugees in Thailand were returning to attend classes alongside members of the Khmer Rouge, whom they still viewed as enemies. Thus university officials faced problems not only of providing learning resources and qualified instructors but also of subduing the conflicting political philosophies that many students and faculty members were seeking to propagate.

In Finland the loss of the nation's profitable trade arrangement with the former Soviet Union seriously weakened the economy, causing the government to cut funds for the country's 20 higher-education institutions by 4%. The revenue reduction forced a deferment of building and maintenance programs and the elimination of 150 faculty positions.

Student demonstrations were launched in several nations to effect political change. The pro-democracy uprising in Bangkok, Thailand, led by students from Ramkhamhaeng University, led to the resignation of the military-controlled government. Nigerian students periodically clashed with police on campuses across the nation during protests against ineffective university administration, human rights violations, and economic austerity programs that resulted in the deterioration of campus facilities. During July more than 15,000 Yugoslav students seized 12 university buildings in Belgrade in a demonstration against the government of Serbian Pres. Slobodan Milosevic. The takeover followed antiwar protests in which Milosevic's regime was blamed for the nation's civil war and deteriorating economic condition. In retaliation, the government passed legislation drastically limiting the university's traditional autonomy.

Shortly after Peru's Government of Emergency and National Reconstruction took control of the country in April, Pres. Alberto Fujimori moved to cleanse the universities of left-wing activists. Hundreds of students were detained by police for several days to prevent them from organizing protests against the government's action. As in other

Thomas A. Fleming, 1992 Teacher of the Year, works with his class at a juvenile detention centre in Ann Arbor, Mich. Sponsored by Encyclopædia Britannica, Inc., and the Council of Chief State School Officers, the award is given in recognition of excellence in teaching.
MICHELLE ANDONIAN

Latin-American countries, student governments in Peru's state universities over recent decades had favoured such leftist doctrines as those advocated by the Maoist guerrilla movement Sendero Luminoso (Shining Path). Right-wing military forces that opposed Shining Path had also been using the universities as an ideological battleground. In the midst of this struggle, the politically moderate rector of San Cristóbal de Huamanga National University, Pedro Villena Hidalgo, was the target of frequent death threats.

Youths in several countries demonstrated against proposed increases in tuition. The University of Zambia expelled all 10,000 of its students after weeks of mass protests against a 25% fee increase ordered by the government. In Chile students boycotted classes and took over university buildings in response to financial-aid procedures they claimed were slow and required an unreasonable rate of repayment, particularly for graduates who entered teaching posts that, in Chile, were notoriously underpaid.

The National Autonomous University of Mexico (UNAM), with an enrollment of 270,000, faced the threat of a student strike if authorities raised the tuition rate, which had not changed in 44 years. The established fee of 250 pesos, the equivalent of about U.S. $170 in 1948, barely equaled 8 cents in 1992. Current rates at other public universities ranged from $46 to $240, while fees at leading private institutions went from $4,500 to over $5,000. Authorities at UNAM planned to raise their annual fee to about $670. One objection to the tuition increase was that it appeared to conflict with the nation's constitutional commitment to free education for all citizens, a provision that some observers interpreted as extending to university studies.

Renewal of the international boycott of South Africa's institutions of higher education was averted in mid-1992 when representatives of the African National Congress and the Union of Democratic University Staff Associations counseled against it on grounds that it would be counterproductive, hastening the exodus of talented academics from the country without advancing political negotiations. The boycott had officially ended in October 1991 when the Commonwealth nations agreed to lift person-to-person sanctions against South Africa. When it was in force, it had prevented many South African academics from attending international conferences or publishing their works abroad. The possibility that it would be renewed in 1992 was occasioned by the breakdown in political negotiations between the ANC and the South African government.

Colleges and universities in the U.S. began the 1992–93 academic year prepared to receive 14.3 million students; more than 60% of U.S. high school graduates attended college. Institutions of higher education planned to spend more than $172 billion in the 1992–93 school year, a 36% increase since 1982–83. The total dollar outlay per college student was more than $16,000, a 25% increase over the past 10 years. Degree completions for 1992–93 were projected at 470,000 associate degrees, 345,000 master's degrees, and 41,000 doctorates.

The expected increase in job recruiters on campus did not occur. Job opportunities for the current crop of graduates were curtailed by competition with the previous year's graduates, who were still job hunting. Engineers were still in demand, and their salaries were in the mid- to high $30,000s—about $10,000 higher than the offers being received by accounting and business majors. Many employers were adopting a wait-and-see attitude about the possibility of economic recovery, and this was reflected in conservative hiring.

Many colleges experienced increases in freshman applications, especially from minorities and transfer students. Of 627 colleges responding to a survey, 70% reported increases in applications. Financial aid to students rose 7.5%, to $30.8 billion, according to the College Board. This included grants ($15.1 billion), loans ($14.9 billion), and work-study earnings ($791 million). The fastest-growing source of aid was the colleges and universities themselves.

The College Board reported that for the fourth year average scores on the ACT (American College Testing Program) had not changed. Scores of college-bound high school seniors taking the Scholastic Aptitude Test (SAT) improved slightly in 1992, the first time since 1985 that the combined verbal and math scores had risen. However, urban and rural seniors continued to score significantly below their counterparts in suburbs and medium-sized and small cities and towns.

The Massachusetts Institute of Technology was found guilty in federal district court of violating antitrust laws by engaging in a conspiracy with eight Ivy League schools to limit financial-aid packages for students. The other universities involved—Brown, Columbia, Cornell, Dartmouth, Harvard, Princeton, Yale, and the University of Pennsylvania—had avoided a trial by pleading no contest and agreeing to cease sharing information. The Overlap Group of nine institutions, as it was called, began meeting in the early 1960s with the aim of preventing bidding wars for outstanding students. MIT argued that without such agreements, the universities would have been forced to compete for the best students and other needy students would have suffered. However, the judge ruled that "no reasonable person could conclude that the Ivy Overlap agreements did not suppress competition." Some observers believed the decision would open MIT to damage suits by students claiming they had been denied financial aid because of the conspiracy, although proving that an individual student had been injured would be difficult.

Many state-supported institutions were facing cutbacks as state governments, forced to tighten their budgets, were reducing support. In California, where the economy had been especially hard hit by recession, the state university system, long considered one of the nation's finest, was facing the possibility of limiting enrollments, cutting back on programs, seeking early retirement for faculty members, and raising student fees.   (JOEL L. BURDIN; ROBERT MURRAY THOMAS)

See also Libraries; Motion Pictures.

This article updates the *Macropædia* articles History of EDUCATION; TEACHING.

Energy

Some major changes in U.S. energy policy took place during 1992. As one of its last actions before adjournment in October, Congress passed the first comprehensive energy policy bill in 10 years. One of the most sweeping provisions concerned automotive vehicles, setting goals for the introduction of vehicles capable of using fuels other than standard gasoline. The goal set for federal government fleets was 75% of vehicle purchases by 1999; for state fleets the goal was 10% in 1995; and for municipal and private vehicles the goal was 20% around the turn of the century and 70% by 2005. The bill also raised energy efficiency standards in building codes and for lighting, motors, and heating and cooling equipment in homes and commercial buildings. Another important provision changed the Public Utility Holding Company Act of 1935, restructuring the electric utility industry by creating a new class of independent power producers and giving them access to the transmission lines of the integrated electric utilities. Among proposals deleted from the bill as passed were higher mileage standards for new cars and permission for the oil industry to drill in Alaska's Arctic National Wildlife Refuge.

A policy event of smaller but still significant scope was the establishment by the U.S. Federal Energy Regulatory Commission of broad new rules designed to complete the process of deregulation of the natural gas pipeline industry begun in the mid-1980s. The rules laid the foundation for a major restructuring in gas pipeline operations by requiring pipelines to charge separately for each of their services (chiefly transportation and storage) and by making them available on an equal basis to anyone desiring to use them. The ultimate effects of this action were expected to be felt by all segments of the gas industry—producers, pipelines, and distributors—as well as consumers.

Petroleum. In contrast to the preceding two years of large swings in oil prices as a consequence of the Persian Gulf war, oil markets were relatively quiet in 1992. The year opened with the market on the weak side, with prices of world benchmark crude oils below $17 per barrel. Production cuts by members of the Organization of Petroleum Exporting Countries (OPEC) in January strengthened the market somewhat, but additional cuts agreed on at an OPEC meeting in February initially failed to strengthen the market further, as production actually increased. Prices in the second quarter were firmer as a result of a decision by Saudi Arabia to shift from a moderate price policy to one of higher prices. The result was a rise above the OPEC target price of $21 per barrel. Prices were weaker during the summer (traditionally the period of peak demand) but in September rose briefly in the U.S. as a result of the reduced output in Louisiana caused by Hurricane Andrew. Market weakness returned in October, and in December there was a sharp drop below $20. Once again, the failure of OPEC members to limit production was responsible.

In April the streets of Guadalajara, Mexico, erupted in a series of explosions that killed at least 190 and damaged over 2,000 buildings. The disaster was caused by leakage of gasoline from a corroded underground pipeline into the sewer system. It was blamed on authorities who were aware of the leak but failed to notify the population or evacuate the areas in danger.

In May U.S. dependence on imported oil exceeded domestic production as the nation's output fell to the lowest level in 31 years. The government resumed purchases for the Strategic Petroleum Reserve for the first time in 20 months.

Ecuador, dissatisfied with its treatment by OPEC, stunned that organization by announcing in September its intention to renounce its membership—the first such action in OPEC's history. The discovery of a giant oil field in Colombia was announced in October. At 1.5 billion bbl, it was the world's largest discovery since the 1970s.

MALCOLM W. BROWNE—THE NEW YORK TIMES

Operators work at the Soviet-built Ignalina nuclear power plant in Lithuania. Some authorities expressed concern about poor maintenance at Ignalina, which, like the plant at Chernobyl (in what is now Ukraine), was designed with a graphite core reactor.

Natural Gas and Coal. Events in the natural gas industry were dominated by the behaviour of gas prices. The year opened with a sharp price decline, with futures prices reaching a low of $1.04 per thousand cubic feet (28.3 cu m). The weakness continued into February as spot prices declined to $1. In response, producers shut down about 6% of total capacity, and Louisiana, Oklahoma, and Texas, which together supplied about three-quarters of total U.S. output, exercised tighter control of their gas production. This strengthened the market, and by April gas futures had reached $1.60. The minor supply interruption caused by Hurricane Andrew triggered a rush by gas suppliers to line up commitments for the coming winter, and by late September prices had reached $2.75. This in turn caused considerable scrambling by industrial consumers to arrange for supplies of alternative fuels, and prices remained well above $2 during the fourth quarter.

Available gas supply in the northeastern states received a boost in January when a new international pipeline began operation. The 595-km (370-mi) line through New York and Connecticut connected producers in western Canada with regional and local distribution systems in New York and New England. This added supply offered the northeastern states a chance for relief from their traditional high dependence on oil for heating and power generation. In April two gas discoveries in Canada offered the promise of a significant boost in that country's reserves and productivity capacity. A potentially giant field, 28 billion cu m (1 trillion cu ft) or more of reserves, was discovered on the south shore of the St. Lawrence River, and a claimed "world-class" discovery in northeastern British Columbia hinted at a major new gas province in western Canada.

The only development of note in coal was the announcement by the British government in October that the national coal company, in the face of large unsold stockpiles (equivalent to an 18-month supply) and declining demand, would close 31 mines and eliminate 30,000 jobs. This would reduce the mine force by 75% and leave only 19 working mines. Within a week public uproar over such drastic action in the face of a prolonged recession and high general unemployment forced the government to retreat. Ten mines were to be closed only after "statutory consultation" with interested parties; closing of the other 21 was deferred pending further study, giving temporary job security to 22,000 miners. In December the High Court declared even this action unlawful, ruling that the situation at all 31 mines had to be reviewed before any action could be taken. The court did not order any government action, however, and the 10 closed mines remained closed.

Nuclear Energy. There were several events of note in the field of nuclear energy. In February the utility operating the Yankee Rowe plant at Rowe, Mass., decided to close it down rather than incur the more-than-$23 million expense of demonstrating to the Nuclear Regulatory Commission that the reactor vessel could continue to meet safety standards after 32 years of operation. It was the oldest operating nuclear plant in the U.S. The decision followed by a month a similar move to shut down the 24-year-old San Onofre I reactor in California. Demolition began during the year at the Shoreham nuclear plant on Long Island, New York. After completion at a cost of $5.5 billion, it had generated electricity for only 30 hours. The utility owning the plant had never been able to obtain an operating license in the face of local opposition and the failure to obtain approval of emergency evacuation plans.

In Russia two reactors were closed at a power station at Krasnoyarsk in Siberia. In September the U.S. announced that it would buy bomb-grade uranium from dismantled

Russian nuclear warheads for conversion into fuel for commercial nuclear power plants. The U.S. agreed to buy at least 10 tons of highly enriched uranium for five years and at least 30 tons a year thereafter. One ton of such uranium can yield about 272,000 kg (600,000 lb) of low-enriched uranium oxide for use in nuclear reactors. In a similar scheme, Japan proposed to buy weapons-grade plutonium from scrapped Russian nuclear weapons.

In July representatives of the European Communities, Japan, Russia, and the U.S. signed an agreement to cooperate in the design of an International Thermonuclear Experimental Reactor. The goal of the six-year project was to produce a design for a working thermonuclear reactor.

Other Developments. A radical new light bulb was introduced in June. The bulb is essentially a fluorescent lamp but uses a tiny radio-frequency generator to excite atoms of mercury. The mercury atoms then emit ultraviolet light, which in turn causes a phosphor coating on the inside of the bulb to emit visible light, as in a conventional fluorescent lamp. The principle was not new; the innovation was in the prevention of interference with the radio waves with other electronic devices such as television and radio receivers. The new bulb also had the advantages of being about the size and shape of incandescent light bulbs and fitting into standard sockets.

In July power generation began at the Ataturk Dam, the ninth largest in the world, in southwestern Turkey near the Syrian border. In addition to generating power, the dam would use the waters of the Euphrates River to irrigate a large area between the Tigris River and the Euphrates.

Andrew, the devastating hurricane that struck Florida and Louisiana at the end of August, effectively wiped out the transmission and distribution system of the local electric utility in the part of Dade county lying south of Miami. The storm knocked down more than 20,000 km (12,600 mi) of power lines and more than 1,000 km (620 mi) of feeder lines as well as destroying more than a dozen substations and thousands of transformers and power poles. In Louisiana the oil and gas industry suffered an estimated $200 million worth of damage to offshore production platforms and pipelines in the Gulf of Mexico and experienced operating difficulties at oil refineries. Of the 3,800 operating platforms in the Gulf, 13 were totally destroyed and 243 facilities damaged. With round-the-clock work, power was restored in Florida to all residences and businesses capable of receiving it by early October, but essentially full restoration of oil and gas production in the Gulf was not achieved until late in the year. Hurricane Iniki, an equally severe storm that struck Kauai in the Hawaiian Islands two weeks later, damaged all 2,800 of the power poles on the island. Full restoration of service took about a month.

In the field of unconventional energy, Japan launched the world's first ship that used a radically new propulsion technology. The ship is powered by electromagnetic propulsion, combining the technology of magnetohydrodynamics with superconductivity. By passing an electric current through a strong magnetic field (created by a superconducting coil), water taken into ducts at the bow of the ship is ejected at high speed at the stern, propelling the ship forward with no moving parts. The 30-m (98-ft), 280-ton experimental ship was limited to a speed of a modest 8 knots, but in principle 100 knots could be attained. Another Japanese company announced the development of the first portable fuel cell for commercial use.　　　　(BRUCE C. NETSCHERT)

See also Engineering Projects; Industrial Review; Mining; Transportation.

This article updates the *Macropædia* articles ENERGY CONVERSION; Fossil FUELS.

Explosive charges send a section of the Central Bridge, which had connected Cincinnati, Ohio, to northern Kentucky since 1891, crashing into the Ohio River. The pieces of the bridge were later removed from the river.
BRUCE CRIPPEN—THE CINCINNATI POST

Engineering Projects

Bridges. Bridges in the 1990s were becoming much longer, much taller, and, in regard to their foundations, much deeper. Engineering advances with new materials, new uses of conventional materials, and computer-enhanced analyses were notable features of the year.

The largest bridge under construction was Japan's Akashi, which was well out of the ground with its towers beginning to push skyward. By the year's end they reached 100 m and were aiming for 297 m, just short of the height of the Eiffel Tower (1 m = 3.3 ft). The bridge was to carry six lanes of traffic between Japan's main island of Honshu and the smaller Shikoku, completing the second of three massive multibridge links.

Akashi would easily be the world's longest bridge on its scheduled completion in 1998, when its 1,990-m central span across the Akashi Strait would exceed Britain's Humber Bridge by more than 500 m. Akashi would also outstrip the bridge that by then would be the world's longest, the 1,624-m-long Store Bælt (Great Belt) in Denmark, which in 1992 was in the early stages of foundation construction. Third longest of these new structures was the Tsing Ma Bridge from Kowloon, Hong Kong, to the new airport on Lantau Island. It was to have a 1,377-m double-deck span for road and rapid transit.

But even before the superstructures were begun for most of these awesome spans, two other remarkable bridges were attracting serious attention. Italy's much-debated Messina crossing, a single span that would stretch 3,300 m across the strait between Italy and Sicily, was due for approval by the government. During 1992 it was the subject of intensive engineering investigation; work could begin in a couple of years if the recession eased. If built, it would have towers 376 m high that would carry main cables almost five kilometres (three miles) long for the suspenders to the bridge deck. Huge earthquake-resistant foundations would be required because the bridge would be located in an area at least as prone to earthquakes as California. Even more symbolic of the next millennium would be a 28-km (17 mi) multiple-bridge crossing of the Strait of Gibraltar; this gateway to the Atlantic Ocean was once the limit of the known world. The project was only in an early design stage, but it could include spans as long as 5,000 m.

All these structures employed the well-established suspension principle also used in such earlier record breakers

as the Verrazano-Narrows—at 1,298 m a mere one-third of the proposed Messina—and the Golden Gate. In such bridges loads are taken by cables hung onto cables that tug at giant anchorages ashore, and so far nothing else could produce the largest spans.

In recent years, however, the cable-stay bridge had gained much ground. In this type the cables do not "hang" from larger slung cables but tie straight back onto the towers in a fan shape; the advantage was that no shoreside anchorages were needed and most of the load went straight down into the tower foundations. The disadvantage was that towers had to be higher and, so far, spans could approach only half the size of suspension bridges.

But the limits were being tested, and in 1992 progress on the biggest cable-stay bridge was well advanced. This was the Pont de Normandie, crossing the Seine estuary on the north coast of France near Le Havre. Towers had already reached 150 m and were designed to top out at 214 m. Engineering for this bridge also took technology to the limit; the deck, for example, would require a cantilever in high-strength concrete and then steel, extended from each side for more than 400 m before the 856-m central span was joined to produce a bridge nearly twice the length of the current longest cable stay, Norway's 530-m Skarnsundet, which opened in December 1991. Canada's Alex Fraser Bridge in Vancouver, B.C., once the longest cable stay at 465 m, would also be dwarfed by the 890-m Tatara in Japan, though this was not due for completion until 1999; by a 602-m bridge across the Huang Pu (Huang-p'u) in Shanghai; and by the 590-m Meiko Chuo in Tokyo Bay, also scheduled for completion later in the decade.

The cable-stay bridge most noticed in 1992, though, was the beautiful harp-shaped Alamillo Bridge in Seville, Spain, built for the Expo 92 exhibition. Designer Santiago Calatrava aroused controversy by using a single, expensive, backward-leaning tower for the 220-m span, but the result was delightful.

All was not rosy during the year, however. The New Haengju concrete cable-stay bridge in South Korea collapsed when failure of elements led to total disintegration of about half the bridge. The causes were under investigation, though weak concrete might be to blame. More embarrassing but less disastrous was a stuck bridge in Chicago, where a 3,750-ton steel bascule section for a lifting bridge across the Chicago River became stuck in the upright position for two months after it was unseated from its hinges.

(ADRIAN LEE GREEMAN)

Buildings. Hong Kong's Central Plaza building, its 306.5-m-high superstructure making it the world's tallest reinforced-concrete building, was topped out in April 1992. A steel mast would bring the total height to 374 m. The building was an equilateral triangle in shape with each side approximately 50 m in length. The floors extended from closely spaced perimeter columns and around a central core area of elevators and service ducts. The use of concrete for such a tall building was made possible by the employment of high-strength concrete. There were three stories below ground, and under those the building rested on deep caissons up to 7.4 m in diameter.

In an advanced stage of planning was the Tour Sans Fins in Paris. This was to be 426 m in height with a circular plan form 43 m in diameter. This caused it to be very slender in terms of building structures and, while the circular plan shape was efficient from the point of view of wind drag, it introduced the problem of wind vortex excitation. This phenomenon arises with rounded shapes and is caused by the periodic shedding of the vortices from alternate sides of the cylinder. At a certain wind speed this shedding can be at the same frequency as that of the building, causing the system to reach a high level of oscillation.

Concrete was being chosen for the structure on account of its efficient stiffness and damping properties (properties that diminish the amplitude of an oscillation) compared with those of steel. Even so, accelerations would likely exceed acceptable limits, and a damper at the top of the building was being considered. This would comprise a pendulum with a mass of only a fraction of that of the building and with a predetermined damping factor introduced between it and the structure. The Tour Sans Fins was to be a peripheral pierced and framed tube with no central core, thereby concentrating the load-carrying members in the area where they would contribute most to the strength and stiffness of the structure.

Another building of significant engineering interest was the Hotel de las Artes Tower in Barcelona, Spain, completed during 1992. The main structure was a 45-story, 135-m-high hotel-apartment tower with an externally expressed structural-steel frame. One of the main design features in a steel-framed building, after strength and stability, is fire resistance. Normally this is achieved by sprayed-on fire protection and/or cladding and encasement. In this case, however, the designers predicted that by having the structural members at least 1.5 m from the window wall, the steel, in the event of fire breaking through the facade, would not overheat. This feature was in addition to careful fire compartmenting within the building to reduce the risk of fire spread. The structural concept was bold. The tower was 30 m square in plan, and each elevation was divided into three bays, the outer ones being cross braced for the full height of the tower; at three levels the central bay was also cross braced, which significantly increased the stiffness of the building and reduced wind movement. Vertical loads were transferred from the floors to the external frame by fire-protected steel beams, four on each elevation. Detailed studies had to be made to predict the likely temperatures that the steel would reach in the event of a fire and to check that the stresses and deflections arising from those temperatures would be acceptable.

Under construction during 1992 were Norway's sports stadiums for the 1994 winter Olympic Games. Because Norway is heavily forested, it was not surprising that timber was being used extensively for the roofs of the stadiums. The largest of them was 260 m long and 96 m wide, believed to be the largest roof of its type. In order to span the 96 m, the designers chose trussed beam arches, which allowed prefabrication and trial assembly at the factory before being transported to the construction site in 25-m-long sections. The main design problem to overcome in this type of timber structure is that of the joints, from both the structural and appearance points of view. To address this, the designers added new developments to an existing jointing system, using concealed slotted-in plates that were secured on either side by steel dowels. Tests showed that joints of this type had both greater strength and better fire resistance than conventional bolted connections and also had a cleaner appearance. Some of the joints used as many as six steel plates and 30 dowels, both of which served to distribute the load transfer through a large volume of the timber and to minimize high stress concentrations. Several smaller stadiums also had timber roofs of various forms.

(GEOFFREY M. PINFOLD)

Dams. A study by the International Commission on Large Dams revealed that 1,190 dams were under construction at the beginning of 1991, of which 368 were completed during the year; 294 new dams were placed under construction, and so, as of Jan. 1, 1992, there were 1,116 dams under construction. Of the total, two-thirds of the dams were of the embankment type, while one-third used concrete to make gravity, arch, and buttress dams. Approximately 95%

Work goes forward on a dam at Gabcikovo, in the Slovak Republic of Czechoslovakia. Although Hungary and other countries charged that the dam would harm both the environment and Danube River shipping, the Slovak government finished the project, designed as a source of electric power, in November.

Major World Dams Under Construction in 1992[1]

Name of dam	River	Country	Type[2]	Height (m)	Length of crest (m)	Volume content (000 cu m)	Gross reservoir capacity (000 cu m)
Aguamilpa	Santiago	Mexico	E,R	187	642	13,000	6,950,000
Al-Wehda	Yarmuk	Jordan/Syria	E,R	164	700	21,000	486,000
Arakhthos/Kalaritiko	Arakhthos	Greece	E	185	238	1,500	1,840,000
Bakun	Rajana	Malaysia	R	204	900	29,400	43,800,000
Banje	Devoll	Albania	E,R	100	1,350	15,000	700,000
Bekme	Greater Zab	Iraq	E,R	204	600	34,000	17,000,000
Berke	Ceyhan	Turkey	A	201	270	745	427,000
Bureya	Bureya	Russia	G	139	810	3,561	20,900,000
Chapeton	Paraná	Argentina	E,G	35	224,000	296,000	60,600,000
Chisapani	Karali	Nepal	E,R	210	850	35,000	15,000,000
Cipasang	Cimanuk	Indonesia	E,R	200	640	90,000	860,000
Corpus Pasadas	Paraná	Argentina/Paraguay	E,R	65	8,474	18,200	13,000,000
Dongfeng	Wujiang	China	A	168	265	622	915,000
Ertan	Yalongjiang	China	A	245	779	4,742	5,800,000
Geheyan	Qingjiang	China	A	151	674	3,060	3,400,000
Guayillabamba	Guayillabamba	Ecuador	A	165	413	704	105,000
Hrusov-Dunakiliti-Gabcikovo	Dunaj	Czechoslovakia/Hungary	E,G	29	31,500	18,340	199,000
Ingapata	Paute	Ecuador	G	166	430	1,600	413,000
Kambaratinsk	Naryn	Uzbekistan	E,R	255	560	112,000	4,650,000
Kanev	Dnieper	Ukraine	E,G	40	16,479	33,000	2,620,000
Karun No. 3	Karun	Iran	A	200	831	7,600	623,000
Katse	Malibamatso	Lesotho	A	180	710	2,200	2,000,000
Katun	Katun	Russia	E,R	185	760	32,700	5,800,000
Kishau	Tons	India	E,G	236	680	9,500	1,810,000
Kumgang	North Itan	North Korea	E	215	1,120	8,760	9,250,000
La Vueltosa	Caparo	Venezuela	E	118	1,200	15,000	5,300,000
Lijiaxia	Huang He	China	A	165	402	3,030	1,720,000
Longtan	Hongshui He	China	RCC	285	790	7,610	27,280,000
Maroun	Maroun	Iran	E,R	168	350	7,490	1,200,000
Mashai	Malibamatso	Lesotho	E	155	680	14,400	3,306,000
Messochora	Acheloos	Greece	R	150	300	4,200	625,000
Miyagase	Nakatsu	Japan	G	155	400	2,000	193,000
M'Jara (Wahada)	Ouegha	Morocco	E	87	1,600	25,000	4,000,000
Namakhvani I	Rioni	Georgia	A	161	460	1,200	560,000
Nukui	Takiyama	Japan	A	155	382	800	82,000
Pati	Paraná	Argentina	E,G	36	174,900	238,180	38,000,000
Piedra del Aguila	Limay	Argentina	E,G,R	163	820	2,520	11,300,000
Potrerillos	Mendoza	Argentina	E	146	550	17,120	860,000
Roncador	Uruguay	Brazil/Argentina	E,R	78	1,598	9,940	33,580,000
San Roque	Agno	Philippines	E	210	1,130	43,150	990,000
Sardar Sarovar	Narmada	India	G	163	1,202	7,472	9,500,000
Serra da Mesa	Tocantins	Brazil	E,R	150	1,510	12,619	54,400,000
Songwon	Chungmangang	North Korea	R	160	630	1,100	3,200,000
Tehri	Bhagirathi	India	E,R	261	575	25,645	3,540,000
Thissavros	Nestos	Greece	E,R	172	480	10,000	700,000
Tianshengqiao	Hongshui	China	E,R	180	1,137	18,000	8,400,000
Urayama	Takiyama	Japan	G	155	400	1,730	58,000
Valea Sadului	Jiu	Romania	E,R	56	7,150	18,250	306,000
Xiaolangdi	Yellow	China	E,R	152	1,200	12,650	N/A
Yacyreta-Apipe	Paraná	Paraguay/Argentina	E,R	43	69,600	67,700	21,000,000
Zimapan	Moctezuma	Mexico	A	200	80	280	1,426,000

Major World Dams Completed in 1991 and 1992[1]

Name of dam	River	Country	Type[2]	Height (m)	Length of crest (m)	Volume content (000 cu m)	Gross reservoir capacity (000 cu m)
Kabalebo	Kabalebo	Suriname	E,R	45	1,650	3,790	19,000,000
Kayraktepe	Gaksu	Turkey	E,R	199	580	17,000	4,800,000
Kouilou	Kouilou	Congo	A	137	345	390	35,000,000
La Grande 2A	La Grande	Canada	R	168	2,826	23,192	61,715,000
Lhakwar	Yamuna	India	G	204	454	2,871	580,000
Naramata	Naramata	Japan	E,R	158	520	13,100	90,000
Porto Primavera	Paraná	Brazil	E,R	38	11,300	37,644	20,000,000
Thein (Rajit)	Ravi	India	E,R	160	565	14,213	3,280,000
Turkwell Gorge	Turkwell	Kenya	A	153	150	170	1,641,000
Warma	Warma	India	E,G	91	1,580	15,310	964,000

[1] Having a height exceeding 150 m (492 ft); or having a volume content exceeding 15 million cu m (196 million cu yd); or forming a reservoir exceeding 14,800 × 10^6 cu m of capacity (12 million ac-ft).
[2] Type of dam: E = earth; R = rockfill; A = arch; G = gravity; RCC = roller-compacted-concrete.

(T.W. MERMEL)

of the dams were less than 150 m in height, and thus only 5% were in the major dam category. Worldwide hydroelectric potential was estimated at 35 million GWh (gigawatt-hour) per year, of which one-half was technically feasible and only one-third of which was developed. Each year only about 18% of the electrical energy generated throughout the world is by water power.

As of Jan. 1, 1992, there were 154 dams under construction in Japan, of which 16 were higher than 100 m. Turkey had 157 dams under construction, with 9 higher than 100 m. In Iran 20 dams were under construction, with one higher than 100 m. Spain had 58 dams under construction, with 3 higher than 100 m; 23 were completed in 1991. In the United States there were 49 dams under construction, with only one over 100 m high. In China 250 dams were in various stages of construction, compared with 500 a decade earlier. Ten of the dams under construction were more than 100 m high.

A strong movement developed to rehabilitate and modernize old dams and hydroelectric plants, especially where the dams required little or no reconstruction expenditures. In the U.S. the Roosevelt Dam, built between 1903 and 1911, was to be raised 24 m to increase the reservoir capacity by 20%. In Austria the Albbruck-Dogern plant built 60 years earlier was being refurbished to increase its output by 15%. In China the Sanmenxia (San-men-hsia) project, built in 1957, had not anticipated siltation of the reservoir, and the turbines became badly eroded. With a change in the method of operation of reservoir releases and installation of a different type of turbine, the output of the plant could be increased by 17%.

Chile approved the construction of a 113-m-high roller-compacted concrete (RCC) dam that would have a volume content of 700,000 cu m (1 cu m = 35.3 cu ft), a crest length of 450 m, and a reservoir capacity of 175 million cu m. Construction was to start in 1993.

Greenland began construction of its first hydroelectric plant, which was designed to produce 30 MW. The dam was to be 15 m high and have a reservoir capacity of 1.9 billion cu m of storage. It would supply the power to the capital city of Nuuk, which had a population of some 13,000 people. The dam was to be a slab concrete structure.

In California a major earthquake registering 7.4 on the Richter scale caused minor transverse cracking of the 17-m-high Glen Martin Dam and the 26-m-high Wide Canyon Dam. Both embankment dams, they were located about 29 km (18 mi) from the earthquake's epicentre.

Iraq completed the reconstruction of the Mosul Dam (now Saddam Dam) on the Tigris River; it had been damaged during the Gulf war. It was now providing 880 MW. Construction resumed at the Badush Dam on the Tigris River and at the year's end was about 50% completed.

In Lesotho progress was being made to complete a series of dams, tunnels, and canals to transfer water from Lesotho to South Africa. Five major dams were involved, ranging in height from 126 to 180 m, and there were to be 225 km of tunnels and three pumping stations. The power generated by the dams would be used by Lesotho.

China approved the study of the Xiaowang (Hsiao-wang) Dam to be built on the Lancanjiang (Lan-ts'an River). It was to be 296 m high with a total storage capacity of 15 billion cu m. Construction started on the Longtan (Lung-t'an) Dam on the Hongshui He (Hung-shui River). It was to be the largest RCC dam in the world and would produce 5,400 MW of power. (T.W. MERMEL)

Roads. Economic and environmental pressures continued to affect the road-building industry worldwide. In a bid to stimulate the nation's economy, the government of Japan announced a 500 billion yen road-construction program. The Australian government announced a similar set of measures, valued at $A 600 million.

In Germany the enormous cost of improving the road network in the former East Germany was to be financed in part by the introduction of tolls on the autobahns (expressways). Scheduled for introduction in 1993, the tolls were to be supplemented by a new fuel tax. Tolls had never before been collected on German autobahns. Several road-construction projects, including a new tunnel under the Elbe River at Hamburg, were to be built and operated by private companies.

Many other countries joined the movement toward using tolls to finance road projects. In the United States legislation was passed to increase the application of tolls on highways, bridges, and tunnels. The Intermodal Surface Transportation Efficiency Act allows federal and private funding to be combined on new road-construction projects and conversion of existing toll-free roads to toll roads.

Changes to Mexico's General Highways Law would allow privatization of 3,400 km (2,000 mi) of existing highways, with the revenue generated used to finance the construction of new roads. The first new project to be financed this way was to be a highway connecting Mexico City and Cuernavaca; cost was estimated at $330 million.

Argentina, Uruguay, and Brazil announced plans for a 2,500-km (1,500-mi) superhighway to link Buenos Aires with São Paulo at an estimated cost of $2.5 billion. The road was to be privately financed and tolled and would include a 55-km (34-mi) bridge across the Río de la Plata estuary.

Much activity was focused on the Asia Pacific region. When completed in 1995, the Malaysian North-South Expressway was to be a four-lane dual expressway running 800 km (500 mi) from the border with Thailand to that with Singapore. Construction of this project began in 1988. Indonesia was expanding its highway network throughout the country, with most activity concentrated on the island of Java. The two main cities, Jakarta and Bandung, were to be connected by a high-speed road that in 1992 was two-thirds complete. In Jakarta itself new arterial roads were

being built to ease the urban congestion that resulted from the high rate of growth of car ownership—15% per year. Singapore announced plans to build a new arterial road in a 14-km (9-mi) ring tunnel under the city centre. The system was intended to increase the total road capacity by 40%. Other cities in the region that were building new roads to relieve traffic congestion included Bangkok, Thailand, and Seoul, South Korea.

Taiwan announced a vast six-year infrastructure-development program in 1991, including more than 700 projects valued at $300 billion. In its first year, however, the program got off to a bumpy start, and it was now accepted that many of the projects, including road, rail, and airport construction, might not be completed for 15 years.

Increasing environmental sensitivity caused some projects to be delayed or even shelved. The European Commission began legal action against the United Kingdom, Portugal, Spain, and Germany for beginning construction work on new projects without first completing environmental-impact assessments. Despite this, the most environmentally sensitive project in Britain, the extension of the M3 motorway through Twyford Down, Hampshire, was begun.

Concerns over the noise generated by highways led the local government of Kent, England, to ban concrete roads in favour of quieter asphalt surfaces. In Spain terrorists seeking an independent Basque homeland disrupted construction of a new highway between San Sebastián and Pamplona, joining with environmental protesters to attempt to have work halted. The year was also marked by the approaching completion of some of the most ambitious projects ever conceived. The Limehouse Link road in the rejuvenating Docklands area of London was structurally completed. Costing almost £350 million, the 1.8-km (1.1-mi) road was almost entirely underground.

Even that fantastic cost was exceeded by the final section of the U.S. interstate highway network in Seattle, Wash. The 11-km (7-mi)-long stretch of Interstate 90 formed the western terminus of the 72,000-km (45,000-mi) network begun in 1956. Under construction for almost 30 years, the final section of the I-90 cost $1,550,000,000 to complete—$137 million per kilometre ($221 million per mile)—as a result of the extensive tunneling, bridge, and environmental-protection measures it required. (RUSS SWAN)

Tunnels. Apart from a few bright spots, tunneling throughout the world was seriously depressed in 1992. The widespread recession cut public investment; private investment in public projects, a concept that initiated the Channel Tunnel in the mid-1980s, was in disrepute; and joint private- and public-sector developments stalled as one party or another reneged on financial commitments.

In London British Rail failed to meet the private owner of Heathrow Airport with its 20% public capital share of the £250 million Heathrow–Paddington high-speed rail link, involving nine kilometres of tunnels and two underground stations at the airport. The financial collapse of private developer Olympia & York placed the Jubilee Line Extension of the London Underground in jeopardy. Government support of these projects was seen as an immediate move to help Britain out of its recession. Most detailed design work was complete, and letters of intent for several construction contracts had been issued.

In southern Africa the Lesotho Highlands Water Project took over from the Channel Tunnel as the largest tunneling project in the world. Five full-face tunnel-boring machines (TBMs) mobilized to excavate the 82 km of 5-m-diameter tunnel for the first phase. The scheme was designed to divert up to 70 cu m of water per second from the rivers rising in the mountains of Lesotho and export it north to the Vaal Dam some 70 km south of Johannesburg to secure future supplies to the industrial heart of South Africa.

Despite recession in North America, tunneling started in Dallas, Texas, on the Cityplace underground station for the Light Rail Transit. With its 5.5 km of twin-tube tunnels, it was the only underground portion remaining of an original 11-km underground section on the 32-km starter system. In Boston two full-face TBMs were launched on the $6.1 billion Boston Harbor cleanup project. One was excavating the 3.5-m-diameter, 8-km-long interisland connecting tunnel to take sewage from the city to the new treatment works on Deer Island. The second started the 7.5-m-diameter, 15-km-long undersea outfall tunnel through which treated wastewater would be discharged far out in the ocean. Also in Boston, work started on the 1.2-km-long, four-lane Third Harbour road tunnel providing a new link to Logan Airport. Design work continued on the new 27-km-long, 4.2-m-diameter Sudbury Aqueduct water-supply tunnel as well as on the Central Artery North Project, a major undertaking to replace underground a two-kilometre section of the six-lane expressway that passes through the heart of Boston on an aging and congested elevated structure.

The Great Chicago Flood

On the morning of Monday, April 13, 1992, the Chicago River started flooding downtown Chicago, commonly called the Loop. It was unlike most floods, however, for it could not be seen from the streets; a section of an old tunnel system unfamiliar to most Chicagoans had sprung a leak, affecting everything from income-tax filing to the survival of downtown retailers.

The first signs came when basements and subbasements started filling with murky water. By the time a whirlpool was found near the Kinzie Street bridge and city workers had lowered a sonar measuring device, the breach had grown to the size of an automobile. Before it could be plugged, more than about 950 million litres (250 million gal) of river water had coursed through the approximately 95 km (60 mi) of freight tunnels. Built at the turn of the century to take coal to buildings and cart away goods and refuse, the tunnels had been all but abandoned by the 1940s. In recent decades they had been used by utility companies to house fibre-optic and other cables.

The hole was believed to have been caused when two clusters of new pilings, installed in the river the previous September by Great Lakes Dredge & Dock Co. to protect the bridge from passing boats and barges, cracked a tunnel wall. A city contract warned that "even slight position changes may cause serious damage to various underground cables and structures," but the pilings were placed a few metres away from the old ones instead of replacing them. The river bed is 6 m (20 ft) below street level; the tunnel, 4.5–5.8 m (15–19 ft) below that. Tunnel walls there are constructed of concrete that is 25 cm (10 in) thick but is not reinforced by steel, as would be required today. The leak was discovered in January by a cable television company filming a documentary. Although at least two city departments were notified of the need for fast action, what would have been a $10,000 repair job was delayed by City Hall bureaucracy and underestimation of the severity of the damage.

Immediate efforts to plug the hole included the use of gravel, sandbags, concrete blocks, and even mattresses. Rapid-set hydraulic concrete was poured by a hose into the breach, hardening to structural strength within two hours (compared with the normal 28 days). Permanent repair, however, proved more difficult than first estimated; steel shafts were driven to isolate the affected area, and then a rubber bladder sealed the area in preparation for a permanent concrete plug. The city's initial plan to drain the tunnels by digging through to the high-capacity Deep Tunnel storm-water sewer system 67 m (220 ft) below ground level was vetoed by the U.S. Army Corps of Engineers. Rather than risk soil and foundation shifting by this more rapid method, they chose to pump the water from many locations to the river and to the Deep Tunnel in a process that took up to two weeks.

Despite concern over older buildings with brick foundations, no structural damage was caused. Flood damages totaled an estimated $300 million in business losses and building repairs and another $37 million in costs to the city. Fifteen buildings were closed for at least a week and some for as long as three weeks. The emergency was viewed by many as emblematic of the infrastructure problems of older cities.

(BETSY ROSSEN ELLIOT)

AP/WIDE WORLD

Water is pumped from Marshall Field's department store, one of several Chicago Loop businesses that suffered losses in April from the flooding of a tunnel system. The disaster called attention to the problems of aging infrastructure in the U.S.

Federal funding for the 87 km of tunneling for the Superconducting Super Collider project in Waxahachie, Texas, was jeopardized, but it was secured for continued tunneling on the Los Angeles subway system. Design work began on the new 2.2-km-long, 8.7-m-diameter railway tunnel under the St. Clair River between Sarnia, Ont., and Port Huron, Mich., and on the 32-km-long, 12.2-m-diameter Passaic River flood-relief tunnel in New Jersey.

There were better times for the Store Bælt railway tunnel project in Denmark. After a catalog of troubles, including the inundation of two headings, three of the four TBMs were under way again by the end of the year. Only 2.6 km of the required 14.8 km of twin-tube rail tunnel was complete at the end of October, and the project was about 18 months behind schedule. Troubles continued for the Channel Tunnel. Delays in the manufacture of the rolling stock and installation of operating services pushed inauguration of the project from an original May 1993 deadline to as late as December 1993.   (SHANI WALLIS)

This article updates the *Macropædia* articles BUILDING CONSTRUCTION; PUBLIC WORKS.

Environment

The UN Conference on Environment and Development (UNCED), nicknamed the "Earth Summit," was held in June 1992 in Rio de Janeiro and was generally thought to have been a success. Much of the debate at the conference centred on the risk of global climatic warming and appropriate responses to it. Scientifically, many doubts remained. Although most climatologists believed a risk of climate change existed, reports published during the year demonstrated no agreement on its extent, timing, or regional effects.

The eruptions in 1991 of Mt. Pinatubo in the Philippines and Mt. Hudson in Chile were believed to have aggravated the seasonal depletion of the ozone layer over both Antarctica and the Northern Hemisphere. Several countries announced that they would phase out production and use of ozone-depleting compounds ahead of the deadlines set in the Montreal Protocol, and those deadlines were also moved up. A study showed pollution caused by the release of oil into the Persian Gulf during the Gulf war was less se-

vere than had been feared. A 50-year moratorium on mining was among measures to protect the Antarctic environment that formed the basis of a protocol to the Antarctic Treaty initialed in October 1991 by 23 of the 26 treaty signatories.

INTERNATIONAL COOPERATION

UN Conference on Environment and Development. The 12-day Earth Summit was opened on June 3 by UN Secretary-General Boutros Boutros-Ghali, who linked economic problems in less developed countries with environmental degradation. Leaders from 178 countries attended, making UNCED the largest summit meeting ever held. By the end, a range of agreements had been signed. The Convention on Protecting Species and Habitats (the so-called biodiversity convention) was signed on behalf of more than 150 countries. Controversy and confusion—arising from diverging statements from U.S. Pres. George Bush and William Reilly, head of the Environmental Protection Agency and leader of the U.S. delegation—surrounded Bush's decision not to sign the convention, a decision that was made in order to protect U.S. patents on products developed from materials obtained overseas. It was believed, however, that the U.S. would observe most of the conditions of the convention and might sign it at some time in the future. The Rio Declaration on Sustainable Development was also signed. There was agreement that it, together with Agenda 21, the outline action program, would be passed to the UN Sustainable Development Commission, a body to be established later by the General Assembly.

The legally binding treaty on climate change was signed on behalf of more than 150 countries. There were also plans to develop a convention on desertification, and a consensus was reached on principles for the management of forests, although there would be no convention on the subject because of resistance from less industrialized countries, led by India and Malaysia. The state of global fish stocks was to be the subject of a future conference.

It was agreed that the World Bank, the UN Development Program (UNDP), and the UN Environment Program would manage the Global Environment Facility (GEF), established in 1990, and would control two-thirds of its funds, with the remainder to be handled by the UNDP. The International Development Association, affiliated to the World

ALLAN TANNENBAUM—SYGMA

UN Secretary-General Boutros Boutros-Ghali (right) applauds as Fernando Collor de Mello, president of Brazil, signs the convention on climate at the "Earth Summit" held in Rio de Janeiro in June. The UN-sponsored conference was the largest such meeting on the environment ever held.

Bank, would take a larger environmental role, with a 15% increase in its funds as well as a separate "Earth Increment" fund of $3 billion to $5 billion a year that would be used to implement Agenda 21 proposals.

It was also agreed that official development assistance should be increased to 0.7% of the gross domestic product of wealthy industrialized nations. There was no deadline proposed for achieving this, although Japan pledged $7.7 billion over five years for environmental assistance. By the end of the year, however, the deteriorating economic situation in many industrialized countries had led to doubts about the attainment of the aid target.

Other Developments. On February 27 the Royal Society of London and the U.S. National Academy of Sciences issued a joint statement warning that poverty in the less industrialized countries would continue and that the global environment might be damaged irreparably unless remedial action was taken within the next 30 years. The paper, the first statement ever to be issued jointly by the two institutions, warned that species were being lost at a rate greater than at any time since the Cretaceous–Tertiary extinction and drew attention to human health, soil erosion, desert expansion, potential climate change, and the rate and pattern of resource consumption. The two groups urged action to accelerate development and thus a demographic transition to stabilize population growth and emphasized the need to introduce conservation measures and less wasteful use of fuels and other resources.

Dissatisfaction with the economic relationships between industrialized and less industrialized countries led to proposals for environmental trade-offs. In February the presidents of Brazil, Ecuador, Colombia, Guyana, Suriname, and Bolivia signed a declaration calling for financial and technological assistance in return for agreeing on measures to reduce emissions of greenhouse gases, establish sustainable forestry regimes, and protect biodiversity. The declaration reaffirmed the sovereignty of nations over the natural resources within their territories, blamed industrialized nations for global warming, and demanded that an environmental treaty not have an adverse effect on the economies of less industrialized countries. On April 28, at the end of a two-day meeting in Kuala Lumpur, Malaysia, representatives from more than 50 less developed countries called for the establishment of a fund, separate from existing aid, to finance environmental programs.

There was no firm commitment at the Earth Summit to set limits for emissions of carbon dioxide. The U.S. refused to allow mention of "climate change" in the draft convention and was reportedly prepared to veto proposals imposing limits on carbon dioxide emissions. In May, however, at a New York City meeting to prepare a climate convention, the U.S. agreed to take measures that would stabilize emissions at their 1990 level by 2000, provided the treaty was worded in such a way as to make it nonenforceable, thus protecting it from challenge in U.S. courts. The accepted version committed countries to prepare and report on those national programs that "recognize that the return to earlier levels of anthropogenic emissions of carbon dioxide by the end of the decade would be an appropriate signal by developed countries that longer-term emission trends have been modified." The U.S. agreement to the document, which was accepted by more than 150 nations, meant that all the members of the Organization for Economic Cooperation and Development had accepted the 1990-level-by-2000 target. The European Communities (EC) Environment Commission had earlier approved a tax on greenhouse gas emissions, agreeing that it would come into force on Jan. 1, 1993, provided the U.S. and Japan took similar action.

The meeting of environment ministers on May 26 failed to approve the tax, however, and the EC members signed the nonenforceable climate convention.

It was reported in February that the first project to be financed by the $1.4 billion GEF would aim to rescue and upgrade forests damaged by pollution in eastern Europe, including those in the "Black Triangle" covering parts of Poland, Czechoslovakia, and former East Germany. In early May representatives from 32 governments agreed at a meeting in Washington, D.C., to enlarge and restructure the GEF, establishing a permanent fund and making the GEF accountable to contributors and beneficiaries.

As part of the Uruguay round of trade negotiations, an agreement was reached between industrialized and less industrialized countries in October 1991 to take account of the environmental effects of trade accords reached through the General Agreement on Tariffs and Trade.

In November 1991, 19 European countries, Canada, and the U.S. agreed in Geneva to a 30% reduction in emissions of volatile organic compounds (small, carbon-based molecules that cause photochemical pollution) by 1999, although most eastern European countries said they would be unable to comply. Most EC countries, Bulgaria, Ukraine, and the U.S. agreed to cut emissions over their whole territories, while Canada and Norway consented to cut them in their industrialized regions.

Greenpeace. It was reported in June 1992 that declining public donations had compelled Greenpeace International to reduce its 1993 budget by $9 million from the 1992 figure of $36 million. It also planned to sell the *Gondwana,* the largest of its seven ships, and lay off 25% of its 500 employees. In November Greenpeace reported that its ship *Solo* had been rammed by a Japanese warship off the coast of France. The *Solo* had been following the Japanese freighter *Akatsuki Maru,* which was carrying a cargo of radioactive plutonium. Greenpeace's position as a radical campaigning body was being taken by Earth First!, a U.S.-based group that operated through cells of members who took direct action. Earth First!'s rise was said to be worrying security authorities in Britain, where there were believed to be 10 groups and 4,000 members.

NATIONAL DEVELOPMENTS

European Communities. On June 29, Carlo Ripa de Meana left his post as environment commissioner to become an environment minister in the new Italian government. The EC transport commissioner, Karel van Miert, became acting environment commissioner.

On January 27, at the UN Conference on Water and the Environment held in Dublin, André Piavaux, deputy head of the division responsible for water protection, revealed that a draft EC ecological water quality directive broke new ground by establishing a philosophical, rather than practical, goal for water quality. It called for the quality of all stream, river, and lake waters to be restored to the condition they would have were they completely uninfluenced by human activities.

Environment ministers met in Portugal on February 22 amid concern over an EC report that the Community had paid £143 million to subsidize an iron-ore mine in the Carajas region of Amazonia. This, the world's largest iron-ore mine, with reserves estimated at 18 billion tons, had caused large-scale clearance of rain forest and the removal of many indigenous people from their land. The mining company, Companhia Vale do Rio Doce, defended its record by stating that local people had long been Westernized and urbanized, the company subsidized local education and health projects, and it had directly created 1,700 jobs.

The adverse environmental effects of construction projects in poorer regions led to the condemnation of the use of EC structural funds for this purpose in a joint statement made in February by 66 environmental organizations. They called for the environmental effects of development to be given greater prominence, for a budget to be established for training local managers in environmental protection, for all proposals to be open for public comment, and for projects that breach EC environmental law to be canceled. European Commission officials described the objections as "ironic" since the structural funds provided the only EC financing for environmental projects such as sewage treatment.

On March 23, environment ministers agreed in Brussels to limit cross-border shipments of hazardous industrial wastes, even within the EC. Such movements would not be banned, but the aim would be for each country to dispose of its wastes within its own territory. This, it was believed, would eventually end shipments of waste to less developed countries. It was reported in July that the Court of Justice of the EC had ruled that the Wallonia region of Belgium had violated EC laws on free trade by banning the import of wastes. Dutch and German haulers had been using Wallonian dumps because the regulations controlling them were laxer than those in their own countries and enforcement was weak. The court allowed that countries were entitled to ban the import of materials dangerous to the environment or human health and that Wallonia could reintroduce its ban if it could prove such a threat. EC commitment to more satisfactory methods of waste disposal was emphasized when, on July 15, the Commission said that within 10 years EC members should be recycling 90% of their waste or using it for power generation.

British plans for seven major building projects for which environmental-impact assessments had not been obtained led, on Oct. 17, 1991, to the start of legal proceedings under Article 169 of the Treaty of Rome for alleged breach of an EC planning directive and to a well-publicized controversy. Work on one of the developments, an extension of the M3 expressway through an environmentally sensitive area of Twyford Down, Hampshire, commenced in February despite protest marches involving up to 700 people. Similar legal action was initiated against Ireland, France, The Netherlands, Italy, and Portugal, in each case in response to pressure from environmental groups. In July the EC dropped five of the seven British cases; the two remaining involved a river crossing in London and a British Petroleum terminal at Kinneil, Scotland.

Brazil. In March the environment minister, José Lutzenberger, was dismissed and replaced by José Goldemberg, who was already minister of education. At meetings in New York City to prepare for UNCED, Lutzenberger had praised the Group of Seven countries for reducing by one-sixth their scientific and environmental aid to Amazonia because, he said, the corrupt government would squander the $1.5 billion originally pledged. He questioned the integrity of the Institute of the Environment and Natural Resources, which formed part of his own ministry. The director of the institute, Eduardo Martins, was also dismissed.

It was reported in November 1991 that mercury released into rivers in the Amazon Basin by miners panning for gold was poisoning people downstream, probably through the fish that formed their staple food. Fernando Branches, a doctor in Santarém, analyzed hair from 20 people and found that all of them had mercury levels above the World Health Organization (WHO) limit of two micrograms per gram of hair and that some had more than three times the limit. Branches said he first treated a victim of mercury poisoning in 1986. In July 1989 he treated 20 cases; by November 1990 he had 84 cases a month; and by July 1991 there were 132 cases a month. One patient had 1,158 micrograms of mercury per litre of urine, well above the WHO limit of 50. Another study found serious contamination in Tucuruí, on the Tocantins River, and in Crepori one patient had 843 micrograms of mercury per litre of urine.

Britain. The structure of the proposed Environmental Agency for England and Wales was announced on July 15. Under the system of integrated pollution control introduced in 1991, a single body would assume the functions of the

---

Biosphere 2: Hard Science or Soft Sell?

On Sept. 26, 1991, four women and four men were sealed into Biosphere 2 in Oracle, Ariz. They joined monkeys, birds, and 3,800 other species of animals and plants in a two-year experiment designed to replicate Biosphere 1 (the Earth) in miniature. Biosphere 2 comprised seven biomes, or habitats: rain forest, savanna, miniocean with coral reef, desert, marsh, farm, and human living quarters. The project was financed by Texas multimillionaire Edward P. Bass, who contributed $150 million to build the steel-and-glass-enclosed, 1.2-ha (3-ac) environment. The head of the project and of Space Biospheres Ventures (SBV)—its parent organization—was John Allen, who once went by the name Johnny Dolphin and ran a commune in New Mexico called the Synergia Ranch. Allen, a poet, playwright, and engineer with an MBA from Harvard, had many critics. In February 1992, amid allegations of fraud and accusations that the team had secretly pumped in fresh air, a panel of eight scientists was appointed without pay by SBV to examine Biosphere 2's scientific credibility. The scientists would report to Bass.

Planning for Biosphere 2 began in 1984. It was originally conceived as a 100-year project, with groups of "biospherians" entering and exiting every two years. The object was to create a model for stations on the Moon or Mars and to experiment in cleaning up polluted environments and helping Earth's ecology. The complex was designed to be isolated, except for inputs of energy, such as generators for electrical power and computers. However, a device to remove carbon dioxide from the air was installed even after SBV insisted it would be an experiment in closed recycling. The project also came under fire from those who suspected that it was too vast to be well monitored. Biosphere 2 was a for-profit venture and quickly became a major tourist attraction.

Of the eight biospherians, Roy Walford of the University of California at Los Angeles was the only scientist of distinction. Some of the others boasted degrees from the Institute of Ecotechnics in London, an unaccredited institution that was set up by Bass to be a consultant to the project. In December 1992 Walford published a scientific paper on the physiological effects of the crew's low-calorie, low-fat diet, but outside researchers said the paper merely confirmed earlier studies.   (FRANCINE SHONFELD SHERMAN)

National Rivers Authority (NRA), the inspectorate of pollution, and the waste-regulation tasks of local government. Some NRA functions relating to land drainage and coastal protection would be privatized. A leaked memo from NRA staff, reported on August 24, warned that this could allow pollution-control standards in rivers to deteriorate to those of the 1950s. Instead of the NRA testing emissions from 5,000 major factories, companies would test their own emissions and report breaches of the law to the new body, which lacked the staff to conduct effective monitoring.

The Environmental Law Foundation was launched in London on January 7. Backed by leaders of the legal profession and with a network of about 100 lawyers, economists, and environmental experts throughout the country, it aimed to support ordinary citizens who were objecting to pollution and planning developments by large, wealthy organizations.

The Green Party held its annual conference in Wolverhampton in September. Membership had fallen to fewer than 8,000 from a 1990 peak of nearly 20,000, and in the 1992 general election its poll share was just over 1%. Factional divisions in the party led to the resignation of its best known figures, Sara Parkin and Jonathon Porritt, from active involvement.

Draft regulations issued by the Department of the Environment in August revealed that initially the proposed register of contaminated land in England and Wales would include only 10–15% of industrial sites and eight industrial processes. In October the Royal Commission on Environmental Pollution said the limited scope of the register would increase the difficulty of protecting water resources from contamination and that a firm timetable should be set for its expansion.

Canada. In April an official report describing the country's environmental decline said the old-growth forests of British Columbia would disappear within 16 years, intensive farming had depleted the organic-matter content of soils in the western prairies by up to 50% (rendering them vulnerable to erosion already costing $500 million to $900 million a year in lost production), and deterioration in freshwater supplies was a major health concern. More than 300 chemical contaminants had been detected in the Great Lakes, and more than 14,000 lakes suffered acid rain damage. The environment minister, Jean Charest, said the government's $6 billion Green Plan to tackle environmental problems addressed most of the items in the report, although some environmentalists disagreed.

China. It was reported in April that the Three Gorges Dam project had aroused strong opposition. Proponents said the 185-m (607-ft)-high dam on the Chang Jiang (Yangtze River) would prevent frequent catastrophic flooding, improve navigation, and generate 84 billion kw-hr of electrical power a year. The dam would take 18 years to complete at a cost of 57 billion yuan. Opponents objected to the extensive flooding of the reservoir area, which would force farmers to move to less productive land, and to the destruction of the gorges, which were a major tourism asset.

France. In regional elections held on March 22, the two green parties, the Greens and Generation Ecology, won 7.1 and 6.8% of the national vote, respectively. Their total of 13.9% placed them in joint third position with the National Front and gave them the balance of power in some regions.

In July two prototype pumps were installed to oxygenate the Seine near Paris—one at Colombes, the other at Rueil-Malmaison. The larger pump, Air Liquide, delivered oxygenated water, while the smaller one, Linde Gaz, delivered oxygen bubbles. Between them the two pumps delivered 15 tons of oxygen a day.

Emissions from the many factories in Benxi (Pen-hsi), a major Chinese centre of heavy industry that was sometimes called the most polluted city in the world, produce intense smog. China declared that it would choose development over protection of the environment.
ADRIAN BRADSHAW—SABA

Mexico. Urban air pollution remained a serious problem. In November 1991 up to 26,000 taxis and minibuses were banned from the streets of Mexico City for one day each week in an attempt to reduce air pollution. A similar ban on private cars, based on a system of coloured disks and affecting about 500,000 cars a day, had been introduced in November 1989, but many people bought second cars to circumvent it. On March 16, ozone levels in the southwest of the city reached 460 parts per billion by 2 PM, falling again later. This was four times the international safety level, and people complained of sore eyes and breathing difficulties. A one-week driving ban was already in place, but factories were ordered to reduce output by up to 75%, schools were closed, and the use of official vehicles was restricted.

The Netherlands. In 1991, emissions of nitrogen oxides and sulfur dioxide decreased for the first time. Nitrogen oxides fell by 4,000 tons to 549,000 tons, and sulfur dioxide dropped by 7,000 tons to 201,000 tons. Emissions of volatile organic substances fell by 18,000 tons, to 446,000 tons. The improvement was attributed to the increasing use of catalytic converters on cars.

Russia. It was reported in August that members of the Russian parliament had asked for the release of data concerning the alleged dumping of large quantities of radioactive waste in the shallow Karas and Barents seas. The dumping was said to have begun in the 1960s and ended in 1991. Scientists from the U.S., Canada, and Russia met at Woods Hole, Mass., in July to devise strategies for dealing with the situation.

Thailand. Under an updated environmental protection act, which came into force in June, the tourist resorts of

Plastic bottles overflow a container at a recycling centre. Enthusiasm for recycling some materials exceeded facilities and demand.

CHRISTOPHER FITZGERALD—PICTURE GROUP

Phuket and Pattaya were declared the first pollution-control zones. A £100 million environment fund was established to pay for rehabilitation, nearly 80% of it being devoted to the two resorts, mainly to build sewage-treatment works. During the year the government also introduced acts concerned with hazardous substances, promotion of energy conservation, public health, and factories.

U.S. It was reported in November 1991 that Department of Energy officials had assembled experts to develop a coordinated federal program to examine possible links between exposure to low-frequency electromagnetic fields and health, including cancer incidence. The 1992 appropriations bill did not include an increase in funding for this study, however, and it remained at $5 million.

It was reported in February that the Bush administration was planning to downgrade the research program on global climate change. Presidential science adviser D. Allan Bromley told members of the President's Council of Advisers on Science and Technology that the research had matured and emphasis should switch to assessing the results obtained.

American enthusiasm for recycling wastes was reported to have resulted in a supply of recycled material overwhelming the demand, with a consequent fall in prices. Aluminum remained profitable at about $600 a metric ton, but clear glass was selling for only $20 a ton and sorted plastic for $6 a ton. Green glass, mainly from imported bottles, was a particular problem. Wisconsin Power and Light became the first U.S. company to trade a "right to pollute" when, on May 12, it sold permission to emit 10,000 tons of sulfur dioxide to the Tennessee Valley Authority, for a sum believed to be close to $3 million ($300 per ton).

MAJOR CONCERNS

Climate Change. Calculations by the Intergovernmental Panel on Climate Change (IPCC), reported in October 1991, suggested that the loss of stratospheric ozone significantly reduced global greenhouse warming by allowing heat to escape from the upper atmosphere. This was confirmed by several other studies, as was the IPCC finding that, by reflecting incoming solar radiation, sulfate particles shielded the surface and also reduced warming in the Northern Hemisphere, where the particles form as a result of pollution by sulfur dioxide. When increased photosynthesis by plants was taken into account, the overall result was a downward revision in estimates of the warming and sea-level rise to be expected from a doubling of atmospheric carbon dioxide.

Ozone Layer. The Antarctic ozone level on Oct. 6, 1991, was the lowest ever recorded, although the area of the "hole" was unchanged from previous years. The situation appeared to be even worse in October 1992. Particles from the 1991 eruptions of Mounts Pinatubo and Hudson were believed to have increased ozone depletion.

On April 7, 1992, scientists from the European Arctic Stratospheric Ozone Experiment reported that in the previous December and January the ozone layer over northern Europe was depleted by 10 to 20% and in February by 10 to 15% owing to accumulations of chlorine compounds up to 70 times higher than natural levels, particles from the Mt. Pinatubo eruption, and the formation of the largest high-pressure system in a century over Europe and the North Atlantic. This caused tropospheric air to swell upward, mixing with and diluting stratospheric air containing ozone. On May 1, NASA scientists reported that ozone levels over the Arctic fell to their lowest level ever.

On February 12 the British firm ICI announced that its Runcorn, Cheshire, chlorofluorocarbon (CFC) plant would close in 1995, two years ahead of the EC's compulsory deadline for phasing out CFCs. Germany, France, and The Netherlands planned to phase out CFCs by Jan. 1, 1995. In early February, Germany prohibited the sale of products containing CFC propellants, and President Bush announced that the U.S. would also phase out CFCs by 1995. On March 4 the European Commission announced that methyl chloroform, carbon tetrachloride, and halons used in fire extinguishers would be banned from the end of 1995. In November the parties to the Montreal Protocol, meeting in Copenhagen, agreed to move the deadline for CFCs to Jan. 1, 1996, and for halons to Jan. 1, 1994. A timetable was set for eliminating hydrochlorofluorocarbons, used by industry as an interim substitute for stronger ozone-depleting chemicals, but no action was taken on the pesticide methyl bromide, which some scientists believed would account for 15% of ozone depletion by 2000.

Lead. In September WHO introduced new recommended limits of 10 micrograms per litre for lead in drinking water, compared with the previous limit of 50. Studies of children in Edinburgh in 1987, which confirmed earlier studies, and a follow-up in Boston had suggested a small but significant adverse effect on children from elevated blood-lead levels. A study of children living near a lead smelter at Port Pirie, South Australia, reported in February 1992, linked exposure to lead to a permanent reduction in intelligence.

Marine Pollution. On April 9, delegates from Denmark, Estonia, Finland, Germany, Latvia, Lithuania, Poland, Russia, and Sweden signed a convention on the protection of the marine environment of the Baltic Sea and agreed on an action plan to reduce pollution in areas around the sea.

A newspaper report on September 2 warned of pollution from an underwater uranium dump in Estonia. It said four million tons of uranium ore waste had been dumped in an artificial lake near Sillamae, on the Gulf of Finland. Although radiation levels were raised in the sea near the dump, levels were normal several kilometres offshore. The plant attracted attention in 1990 with reports of inexplicable hair loss and allergies among the 25,000 population of Sillamae.

A study of the pollution caused by the Gulf war, reported in August, found it did not extend beyond about 400 km (250 mi) from the spillages and mainly affected the Saudi Arabian coast. During the four months following the war, much of the oil degraded, and concentrations of hydrocarbons in sediments and bivalve mollusks from Bahrain were found to be lower in June 1991 than levels recorded in 1983–86, probably because of reduced tanker traffic.

On December 3 the Greek tanker *Aegean Sea* ran aground off the northwestern coast of Spain, broke apart, and caught fire. By December 13 it was estimated that the ship had lost 500,000 bbl of crude oil, but an unknown amount of this had burned off. Greenpeace reported that some 200 km (125 mi) of coastline had been damaged by the spill.

After 18 months of negotiations, the North Sea states agreed on September 22 to revisions to the 1974 Paris Convention. Britain and France accepted a 15-year ban on dumping nuclear wastes. (MICHAEL ALLABY)

WILDLIFE CONSERVATION

As pressures on wild plants and animals continued to increase, some countries introduced new controls to help threatened species. Toward the end of 1991 India had amended its Wildlife (Protection) Act of 1972 to ban or severely restrict hunting, exploitation, and trade in wildlife and to give stronger protection to wildlife sanctuaries. Thailand published a Wildlife Preservation and Protection Act of 1992, which prohibited hunting and trade in certain species and required owners of captive "preserved and protected species" to register them with the wildlife authorities. Malawi's new National Parks and Wildlife Act introduced tough penalties for offenders. On July 22 the European Commission published the Habitats Directive. Its main objective was the creation of the Natura 2000 network of sites considered essential to the survival of 42 priority habitat types and 184 priority species.

Conservation efforts continued for many species that survived only in very low numbers. Six Livingstone's fruit bats were captured on Anjouan Island in the Comoros for a breeding program. There were only about 120 left in the wild, and future relocation would depend on whether their forest habitat could be restored and protected. California condor numbers in captivity stood at 63. On January 14, as part of the effort to reintroduce the species to the wild, two captive-bred California condors were released about 80 km (50 mi) from Los Angeles, but one died on October 8. On April 11, 11 Hawaiian crows were found by U.S. federal biologists on McCandless Ranch in Kona, the only place where the bird occurred in the wild. The ranch owners had previously denied access to officials, but a lawsuit brought and won by the Audubon Society against the ranch and the U.S. Fish and Wildlife Service compelled the service to carry out a recovery plan for the endangered bird. In July six young black-footed ferrets were seen in the wild in the Shirley Basin in southeastern Wyoming, proof that the captive-bred individuals released in 1991 in the first reintroduction effort for this species were thriving and breeding. It was reported that efforts to prevent poaching in Indonesia's Bali Barat National Park had been successful and that after the 1992 breeding season there were 55 Bali starlings, an encouraging increase from the all-time low of 13–18 in 1990.

The biennial meetings of the Convention on International Trade in Endangered Species of Wild Fauna and Flora were important markers in the progress of wildlife conservation. At the eighth meeting held March 2–13 in Japan, which was attended by representatives of the 112 parties to the convention, Brazilian rosewood, several genera of cacti, and Geoffroy's cat were among species added to Appendix I, which banned international trade. Other species were added to Appendix II so that trade could be monitored and controlled. Proposals to remove international trade bans on ivory from African elephants and on rhino horn were rejected. The ban on ivory was clearly helping populations of elephants to recover from years of poaching. However, the ban on rhino horn had not resulted in conservation gains. From 1970 the number of rhinos worldwide had fallen by 85% owing to poaching for their horn. In June Zimbabwe followed Namibia's lead and set out to dehorn its black rhinos to make them valueless to poachers. The dehorning teams were shocked to find only about 500 black rhinos left in the country rather than 2,000, the official figure. Late in the year it was reported that Zimbabwe, South Africa, and Namibia had decided to combat poaching by entering the rhino horn trade on a regulated basis and using the profits for management of the animals.

June was the deadline for the UN ban on drift nets in the world's oceans. These nets had been called "walls of death" because of the huge numbers of marine mammals, birds, and turtles that became ensnared in them.

At the 44th annual meeting of the International Whaling Commission (IWC) held in Glasgow, Scotland, from June 29 to July 3, Iceland announced that it was leaving the commission, and Norway said that it would resume commercial harvesting of minke whales, whether or not the IWC agreed on a quota. A French proposal to declare a whale sanctuary in the Antarctic was referred to the 1993 meeting. Requests

RON SANFORD—BLACK STAR

Wolves flourished in Alaska, and officials there were considering killing them to increase the populations of moose, caribou, and other of their prey. At the same time, Montana was trying to reintroduce wolves 50 years after they had been hunted to extinction in the U.S. West.

from Japan for a continued kill of minke whales in Antarctica for scientific research were granted. The meeting agreed on the procedure to be used to calculate catch quotas if commercial whaling was resumed but said that many more features needed to be in place before it could be used as part of a revised management system. Meanwhile, the existing moratorium on commercial whaling was extended for a further year, and the Indian Ocean Whale Sanctuary was extended for another 10 years. In September four whaling countries—Norway, Iceland, Greenland, and the Faeroe Islands—which argued that the IWC had become dedicated to protecting rather than managing whales, agreed to set up the North Atlantic Marine Mammals Commission, aiming to assume management of certain whale and seal stocks in the North Atlantic.

The drought in southern Africa caused problems for wildlife. In southern Zimbabwe officials dealt with the drought by culling some animals, feeding others, and translocating some to private ranches farther north. In July South Africa and Botswana agreed to feed the hippos along the Limpopo River—the border between the two countries—because there was no grazing left. (JACQUI M. MORRIS)

See also Agriculture and Food Supplies; Botanical Gardens and Zoos; Energy; Life Sciences; Transportation.

This article updates the *Macropædia* article CONSERVATION OF NATURAL RESOURCES.

Fashion and Dress

Fashion designers, bogged down by sluggish sales during the lingering recession, tried to entice women to shop by blitzing them with options in 1992. They brought back 1940s, '50s, and '70s styles, including short skirts, long skirts, and trousers. Some designers offered seemingly contradictory styles, such as menswear looks and bouffant cocktail dresses, within the same collection. Western styles, leopard prints, and gingham checks were some of the passing fads.

Responding to price resistance by consumers, several U.S. manufacturers announced early in the year that they were lowering wholesale prices between 10 and 25%. Even upscale specialty stores put a stronger emphasis on lower priced merchandise and devoted more space to bridge clothes, which were priced a notch below designer fashions.

Unlikely juxtapositions of casual and dressy items marked some of the most memorable showings. Both Gianni Versace in Italy and Marc Jacobs for Perry Ellis in New York showed denim shirts tied at the waist over ball gown skirts for spring. At Chanel designer Karl Lagerfeld paired a man's ribbed undershirt with spring suits. Just as it was chic to mix high and low culture in the media and the arts, it was hip to combine high and low fashion in the same outfit. Women were able to turn their designer suits into weekend wear by pairing their Chanel jacket (or look-alike) with jeans.

Seemingly innocuous fashion basics were touted as essentials. Retailers declared white cotton shirts the must-have item for spring, while twin sweater sets became a fall necessity. Personal style became the catchphrase for the '90s, and retailers offered women all of the elements for creating their own.

Hemlines threatened to become an issue after designers began showing longer lengths for spring, but retailers played down the controversy by treating long skirts as an option. Short remained the predominant length for the year, although women in ultra-fashion-conscious cities like New York and Paris began sporting long, skinny skirts for fall. Short skirts became longer as the year wore on, ending slightly above the knee.

A necktie, bowler, and walking stick complete Ralph Lauren's version of an Edwardian suit. Several designers showed adaptations of men's clothing for women in 1992.
DAN LECCA

Perennial fashion themes, such as the Western look, were treated with a sense of humour. Tiered miniskirts, gingham *bustiers,* denim shirts, bandanna prints, fringe, and cowboy boots were all part of the spaghetti western equation. Cowboys, Indians, and Holstein cows turned up as print motifs. Gingham checks became the ubiquitous pattern for spring. Although casual ginghams were tied in with Western looks, the more-tailored versions went to the office.

Madras was another strong pattern, turning up on casual sarong skirts and beaded evening wear. Scarf prints, which took their name from their resemblance to Hermès scarves, were popularized by Versace and became the preferred pattern for dressy blouses.

Sheer fabrics continued to gain in popularity. A transparent black bodysuit worn over a black bra in Isaac Mizrahi's fall '91 collection spawned a legion of look-alikes. Sheer insets and fishnet fabrics trimmed everything from cocktail dresses to swimsuits and exercise clothes.

Shirts became a basis for dressing. Crisp cotton shirts teamed up with trouser suits or long, slim skirts. Shirtwaist dresses from the '50s in both long and short versions appeared in cotton or linen for day and in organza for evening. U.S. designer Byron Lars continued to evolve shirt dressing by wrapping and draping striped cotton fabric into sensuous shapes.

Designers offered long skirts as an option for warm weather, but they used sheer fabric, button fronts, or slits to reveal legs. Some of the long, full skirts were designed to be worn unbuttoned to show shorts underneath. Women in both the U.S. and Europe took to wearing long, fluid dresses and skirts in tiny prints reminiscent of '40s housedresses. Women throughout France opted for either short or long versions of the lightly fitted princess dress in burgundy or blue prints. "French country" prints, particularly in blue-and-white patterns, were widely worn in either short- or long-tiered skirts in trend-setting southern France.

By fall, the '40s had become a full-fledged inspiration. Long, slim skirts with side or back slits, dressmaker suits, and softly waved hair showed a return to more elegant clothing. A long, lean line became the most dominant silhouette, prompting coat manufacturers to revive longer lengths. Platform shoes were a favourite for several seasons among the avant-garde. The most popular versions sported platforms less than 1.25 cm (0.5 in) thick.

Since the '70s took its inspiration from the '40s, it was often hard to separate the two influences for fall. Long, dandyish jackets over jeans, ruffled pirate shirts, and clogs were among the indicators that the '70s were about to become the next font of inspiration for designers in the '90s. Leopard patterns went from classic to fad status for fall, much like plaid in 1991. Other jungle prints, like zebra, joined leopard as patterns on jeans, jackets, blouses, fake furs, lamé evening gowns, platform shoes, handbags, and belts.

Menswear styles began to return for spring, and by fall, pinstripes were patterning suits, vests, and underwear. Trouser suits proliferated, but they usually featured jackets with fitted waists to give them a feminine silhouette. Vests in either menswear patterns, whimsical prints, or leather were an important element. They were often worn in place of a jacket and were sometimes elongated into short dresses. Tailored shorts in wool, corduroy, or leather provided an option for women who were tired of miniskirts but still wanted to show their legs. Knits began to stage a comeback as women once again embraced their practicality. The spring mall uniform for teens and young women in the U.S. consisted of a loose, cotton knit ribbed tunic over a matching miniskirt or patterned leggings. For fall, knits showed their versatility as tailored suits, twin sweater sets, ribbed dresses, and slinky evening gowns.

Comfort was also an important factor in footwear, especially among teens and young adults. Birkenstock sandals and Doc Martens were commonplace on college campuses across the U.S., as were Teva sandals (sports sandals constructed of strips of nylon webbing attached to rubber bottoms). Many college students returned to campus in rugged, outdoorsy clothes similar to the ones worn on the television series "Northern Exposure." Jeans dyed to dull shades of brown, green, and red became widely accepted. Leather also regained its status for fall, allowing women to present a slick, tough exterior. Elongated motorcycle jackets, trench coats, jeans, long skirts, and shorts were some of the key looks in leather.

The warm months were full of soft pastels and upbeat hues like marigold, coral, and rose. Fall colours revolved around black, gray, brown, and camel punctuated by doses of red. Earthy colours in touch with ecology were also popular.

Colours associated with Africa, such as black, gold, green, and red, continued to gain fans among blacks. Cross Colours, a Los Angeles sportswear manufacturer that used African colours and symbols, became a status brand among inner-city youths and was widely praised for its antigang stance.

Several outsider trends worked their way toward the mainstream. Tattoos proliferated among college students and young adults, while the application of temporary tattoos became a form of entertainment at nightclubs and bars. Lapel pins became a craze in France following the winter Olympic Games in Albertville. Small enamel pins traded among the athletes and spectators gave birth to a host of pins that promoted products. Fashion intellectuals,

primarily a small group of Paris-based designers, promoted "deconstructivism." Exposed linings, unraveled seams, and uneven hems were part of the message. The only apparent mass-market trend to result from the movement was skirts slashed into ribbons, offering a dozen revealing slits. A similarly disheveled style originating among the U.S. young was the "grunge" look, which relied on ragged, thrift-shop-type apparel.

Italian fashion designer Emilio Pucci, who was renowned for his bold, brightly coloured prints, died in November (*see* OBITUARIES). (LISBETH LEVINE)

Men's Fashions. In 1992 men's fashions suffered from the continuing worldwide economic recession. Sales of men's suits, for example, remained static in most countries, with the exception of Japan, where some 12.5 million suits were sold; some retail chains reported increases of up to 30%. In the U.S. and in most European countries, there was a standstill in the sales of men's outer clothing. In contrast, men bought more shirts and ties, which were multicoloured and in bold floral and geometric patterns.

During the beginning of the year the fashion pendulum swung from single-breasted to double-breasted suit styles, but by the end of the year men in most age groups were sporting single-breasted styles. The best-selling colour in suits was gray—way ahead of blue and brown.

The emphasis in most forms of clothing was on comfort in lighter and brighter jackets and slacks. In casual clothes the most ubiquitous garments, not surprisingly, were jeans and T-shirts, mostly in woven cottons. Even before the summer Olympic Games in Barcelona, Spain, many more men were wearing stretch garments in elastomeric fibres such as Lycra, which molded their figures both on and off the track. The shell suit ensembles, on the other hand, were not as popular as they had been previously among either the athletic or nonathletic members of the community.

The double-breasted blazer established itself as a year-round garment, usually worn with lightweight cotton or linen slacks in soft colours for the spring and summer and with heavier Cavalry twill or Bedford cord cloth for the autumn and winter. The top hat story in Europe for the summer of 1992 was the Panama hat. The Panama Montecriste, supplied by the French company of the same name, was shown in Paris.

The footnote to men's fashions in 1992 was supplied by Reebok and other brand-name athletic shoes. Another footwear trend that emerged in European cities was men wearing plimsolls (a canvas shoe with rubber sole). Men often wore them with no socks and in colours such as blue, red, or green to match the colour of their garments.

(STANLEY H. COSTIN)

See also Industrial Review: *Furs.*

This article updates the *Macropædia* article DRESS AND ADORNMENT.

Gardening

In 1992 gardening continued to gain popularity in the U.S., moving from the nation's most popular outdoor activity to the number one leisure pursuit. An estimated 60 million gardeners in the U.S. spent nearly $9 billion annually on gardening products, supplies, and equipment. British gardeners were bedeviled by both drought in the early part of the season and flooding in the summer months. Because of bans on water hoses in parts of Kent, East Surrey, and Yorkshire, many gardeners conserved water by installing devices that automatically diverted rainwater from the downspouts of their homes and garages into holding tanks.

Environmental concerns continued to be important to both U.S. and European gardeners. In the U.S., gardeners who regularly used organic fertilizers instead of chemical types outnumbered those who exclusively used chemicals. However, the vast majority of gardeners relied on integrated pest management, which combined both chemical and organic methods. In Britain organic gardening techniques continued to gain popularity, and there was an increased interest in the use of biological pest control. With this technique, natural predators instead of chemical pesticides were employed to control pests. Some of the most effective agents included a parasitic wasp, *Encarsia formosa,* to control whitefly, a predatory mite; *Phytoseiulus persimilis* for the control of red spider mite; and a bacterial spray based on *Bacillus thuringiensis* to kill caterpillars.

One destructive pest that had caused considerable damage in gardens and nurseries during recent years was the vine weevil, with grubs devouring roots and underground parts of plants and adults eating the foliage. Few chemical controls existed, but growers resorted to a microscopic parasitic nematode that had an insatiable appetite for vine weevil larvae. An exciting new organic weed killer, which was introduced at a British gardening trade show in September, used a safe but unusual active ingredient—soap. This unique product used fatty acids to break down the leaf cuticle, causing leaves to dehydrate in the sun and die in just 24 hours. In August the first Organic Gardening Weekend was held in Britain.

The use of powered lawn and garden tools also came under the scrutiny of environmentalists. Several communities in California outlawed the use of power blowers because of excessive noise pollution. The Environmental Protection Agency (EPA) released information on harmful emissions from lawn mowers, revealing that in one hour one unit could spew as much smog-producing hydrocarbon into the air as a modern automobile, even though the car had 30 times the horsepower. As a result, the EPA launched a program to purify lawn mower emissions and announced it would investigate other gas-powered machines, including weed cutters, leaf blowers, and chain saws. Two new lawn mowers unveiled at the National Hardware Show operated on rechargeable batteries.

Another issue of concern was the collection of wild bulbs. Plantlife, an environmental group, strengthened its campaign to stamp out the trade in the commercial, worldwide collection of bulbs, including bluebells from the British countryside. Many bulbs extracted from the wild were sold through the Dutch horticultural trade, and it was impossible to tell whether a packet sold as a "product of Holland" had originated in the wild. In the U.S. dedicated propagators of old roses roamed old churchyards and vacant lots looking for remnants of roses that thrived in the 19th century or earlier. These "rose rustlers" took cuttings and sought to protect antique specimens that might otherwise be lost.

The first international floral and garden exhibition ever held in the U.S.—Ameriflora 92—ran for five months in the 100-year-old Franklin Park in Columbus, Ohio. Ameriflora, with 36 ha (88 ac) of exhibits, was an important part of the nation's celebration of the quincentenary of Christopher Columbus' voyage to America. Some of the attractions included the Franklin Park Conservatory, which showcased nine different climate areas and featured the plants and flowers indigenous to them; a two-week-long internationally sanctioned Grand International Indoor Horticultural Exhibition and Competition; a 930-sq m (10,000-sq ft) Midwestern Victory Garden; and the Community of Nations display, featuring garden design and horticulture.

The biggest floral event in Europe, the Dutch Floriade, ran from April to October and covered 69 ha (170 ac) of landscaped parkland near The Hague. Floriade, staged once every decade, incorporated a host of horticultural and educational exhibits. In Britain, Garden Festival Wales was open from May to October in the Welsh mining valley of Ebbw Vale. It was the last of five National Garden Festivals designed to revitalize derelict and inner-city areas.

Fleuroselect, the European seed-testing organization, awarded gold medals for outstanding garden performance to pansy Imperial Frosty Rose, violet-blue *Verbena* Imagination, *Nierembergia* Mont Blanc, and statice Forever Gold. Seven plants were chosen as All-America Selections for 1992, including *Verbena* Peaches and Cream, carrot Thumbelina, cana Tropical Rose, *Dianthus* Ideal Violet, *Vinca* Pretty in White, dill Fernleaf, and *Salvia* Lady in Red. The 1992 Rose of the Year, Top Marks, was a low-growing patio rose covered with vibrant orange-red flowers. A new world record was set for the heaviest onion; it weighed 5.05 kg (11 lb 2 oz).

(KAY MELCHISEDECH OLSON; ADAM GERHOLD PASCO)

See also Agriculture and Food Supplies; Botanical Gardens and Zoos; Life Sciences.

This article updates the *Macropædia* article GARDENING AND HORTICULTURE.

Health and Disease

Recognition of the astonishing reemergence of pulmonary tuberculosis (TB) in the big cities of the U.S. and Europe was a major development in 1992. The resurgence followed a century during which the disease had been repelled, initially as a result of improved nutrition and hygiene, then by immunization, and, most spectacularly in the 1940s and '50s, by antibiotic drugs such as streptomycin.

In the U.S. the number of new cases of TB reported annually had grown by 16% over the past six years, reversing the trend of the previous three decades, which saw an average annual decline of 6%. Several factors contributed to the growing American epidemic: homelessness, drug abuse, increased immigration from countries with a high prevalence of TB, and overcrowding in prisons, shelters, and the homes of the poor were each partly to blame. The mechanisms linking these social determinants with the actual disease included malnutrition, impaired immunity, and enhanced dissemination of the tubercle bacillus, the disease-causing organism.

On a worldwide scale, the resurgence of TB could be attributed in large part to the spread of the human immunodeficiency virus (HIV), the virus that causes AIDS. Although not everyone infected by the tubercle bacillus would go on to develop tuberculosis, the chances of doing so were much higher if the individual's immune system was compromised by HIV. Thus, while only about 30% of people with normal immune systems who were exposed to the bacillus became infected—and only about 10% of those became ill—up to 40% of people with AIDS had active TB. In the U.S. outbreaks of TB among HIV-infected individuals reported during 1992 were characterized by their rapid spread and by the speed with which the TB progressed. The inexorable, concurrent spread of those two microbes could pose an even greater public health threat in many parts of the Third World, particularly Africa.

The picture was complicated further by a pronounced increase in the resistance of the tubercle bacillus to the drugs normally given to treat the disease. In many less developed countries this occurred because antituberculosis drugs had been freely distributed without controls over the way they were used. Elsewhere, especially in the U.S., the cause seemed to be that many patients discontinued treatment before the bacillus was completely eradicated from the body, a process that might take up to 18 months. In each of these situations not only did the infection continue to spread, but the emergence of resistant strains of disease-causing organisms was encouraged, too.

Another feature of the resurgence of TB was that, having ostensibly been defeated as the great social scourge of past centuries, the disease had been marginalized both as a challenge to medical science and as a target of public health efforts. With TB under control, there had been no reason for pharmaceutical companies to develop new drugs that could be used against resistant strains. In the U.S. production of streptomycin had declined to the point where it was virtually unobtainable. Moreover, with the decline in the number of cases of TB in the U.S. since the 1950s, the medical community had become increasingly unfamiliar with the subtleties of diagnosis and treatment of the disease.

AIDS. Although they disagreed on the exact numbers, two international organizations were in concert in issuing bleak predictions of the worldwide spread of AIDS during the year. The World Health Organization (WHO) estimated that approximately 10 million people were already infected with HIV, while the Harvard University-based Global AIDS Policy Coalition said the figure was more like 13 million. According to WHO, by the year 2000, 30 million to 40 million would be infected; the Harvard group believed that the number could be as high as 110 million. Major epidemics were emerging in Asia and Latin America.

In the U.S. concern grew over the increasing spread of HIV infection among teenagers; AIDS was reported to be the sixth leading cause of death among 15- to 24-year-olds. A continuing concern was the infection of newborn infants by their HIV-positive mothers. However, one small study showed that zidovudine (also called azidothymidine, or AZT) given during pregnancy was well tolerated by mothers and fetuses and could apparently interrupt perinatal HIV transmission; a larger national study was under way. Another proposed study, sponsored by the National Institutes of Health, was to assess whether giving HIV immune globulin (a blood product containing antibodies to HIV) to infected pregnant women and to infants after birth would prevent transmission. Other research was aimed at developing better methods of detecting infection in newborns so that treatment with potentially toxic anti-AIDS drugs could be given only when truly needed.

A report in the *New England Journal of Medicine* showed that early treatment of HIV-infected people with zidovudine could, as hoped, delay the onset of AIDS and prolong survival. Zalcitabine (also called dideoxycytidine, or ddC) received the approval of the U.S. Food and Drug Administration (FDA) for use in conjunction with zidovudine and, under the FDA's expanded access program, a still-experimental drug, stavudine (also called D4T) was being made available to patients who were unable to tolerate approved anti-HIV drugs.

MAX AGUILERA-HELLWEG

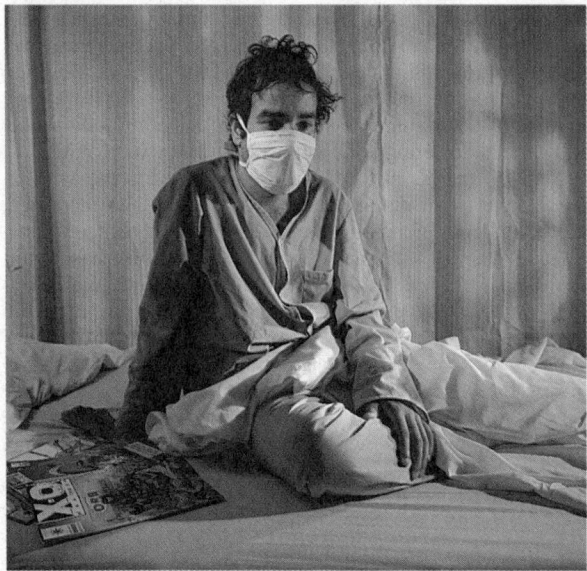

A homeless man with tuberculosis is hospitalized in New York City. The disease, now often resistant to the drugs normally used to treat it, continued to increase among certain groups, including persons with AIDS, drug users, prisoners, and the homeless.

Demonstrators charge complicity at the highest levels of the French government as they march outside the courtroom where four former health officials were on trial for authorizing the distribution of blood products known to be contaminated with the virus that causes AIDS. In October three of the officials were found guilty.
CHRISTIAN VIOUJARD—GAMMA LIAISON

The Centers for Disease Control and Prevention (CDC) finally expanded the official case definition of AIDS, a measure that was expected to double the number of reported cases. The revised definition included HIV-positive persons who had fewer than a certain number of immune cells (called CD4 lymphocytes) and added three more maladies often found among HIV-infected women and drug abusers to the list of complicating conditions: invasive cervical cancer, pulmonary TB, and recurrent bacterial pneumonia.

The public reacted with alarm to reports of a mysterious new AIDS-like illness whose victims showed no evidence of HIV. Whether some other microorganism was causing the disease was not clear. A meeting convened by WHO revealed that the incidence of the disorder was very low—some 100 cases worldwide—but research was scheduled to continue. There were also reassurances that the blood supply was safe.

Heart Disease. Several issues in 1992 stood in sharp contrast to previous years. Perhaps chief among them was the worry about the possible ramifications of low cholesterol levels (below 160 milligrams per decilitre [mg/dL]) and whether the efforts at decreasing total cholesterol by means of drugs may have been somewhat misguided. Several studies had shown that lowering total cholesterol (with diet or drugs) below 160 mg/dL not only failed to decrease the rate of death from heart disease but was associated with increased mortality from noncardiac causes, including cancer, lung disease, suicide, and alcoholism. One possible reason for the slight—or absent—improvement in cardiovascular mortality was that lowering total cholesterol also lowers levels of the "good" cholesterol, high-density lipoprotein (HDL) cholesterol. One study published in the journal *Circulation* during the year showed that even in heart disease patients with a total cholesterol level of 175 mg/dL or under—a desirable level—those with low HDL levels (under 35 mg/dL) had twice the risk of suffering a subsequent heart attack or possibly dying from heart disease as those with higher levels.

If there was less interest in the drastic lowering of total cholesterol, this change in attitude might have been partly attributed to the discovery of rival risk factors for coronary heart disease. High levels of stored iron were one such factor according to a Finnish report published during the year. A five-year study of nearly 2,000 healthy men showed that every 1% increase in stored iron was associated with a greater than 4% increase in heart attack risk. The report seemed to confirm a theory advanced 11 years before by Jerome L. Sullivan of the Veterans Affairs Medical Center, Charleston, S.C., which suggested that the relatively low level of iron in the bodies of menstruating women accounts for that group's lower risk of heart attack compared with men or postmenopausal women.

Another heretofore overlooked risk factor for cardiovascular disease might be fibrinogen, a protein that participates in blood clotting. Investigators in London reported in 1992 that for patients with symptoms of angina, high fibrinogen levels may be a more important risk factor than cholesterol level.

In other research, studies published during the year indicated that intravenous injection of magnesium might be helpful to victims of heart attack. According to these data, treatment begun as soon as possible after a heart attack might reduce mortality by about 25%. An attractive feature of magnesium was that it was inexpensive.

Prospects improved substantially for those heart attack victims in danger of a subsequent attack due to malfunction of the left ventricle, the heart's main pumping chamber. A study involving over 2,000 such patients, based at Harvard Medical School and other centres in the U.S. and Canada, showed that captopril, a member of the group of drugs known as angiotensin converting enzyme (ACE) inhibitors, greatly improved their chances of surviving and reduced the likelihood of death or further illness due to the heart condition. This conclusion was supported by the results of an even larger study with another ACE inhibitor, enalapril, carried out at the U.S. National Heart, Lung, and Blood Institute, Bethesda, Md.

Finally, two possibly improved methods of cardiopulmonary resuscitation (CPR) were reported during the year. One called for the application of rhythmic abdominal pressure along with the standard method of chest compression (at least two people would be needed to do CPR); the other involved substitution of a device similar to a toilet plunger that would compress and decompress the chest.

Genetics. Several major advances occurred in the location of genes responsible for particular diseases—advances that should help in screening for these conditions, prevention, and possibly treatment, too. Researchers in London and Cardiff, Wales, announced that they had identified, on human chromosome 19, the genetic defect that causes myotonic dystrophy, the most common form of adult muscular dystrophy. Research in Britain also indicated that deletions of genetic material in chromosome 22 are an important cause of familial congenital heart defects, while a U.S. study showed that DNA markers could be used to make a diagnosis in some families affected by the type of potentially fatal heart arrhythmia known as long QT syndrome. Additional genetic defects that seemed to predispose people to heart attack, hypertrophic cardiomyopathy, and a rare, severe form of hypertension were reported during the year.

A collaborative investigation in the U.S. and the U.K. suggested that Marfan's syndrome is attributable to mutations in a particular gene on chromosome 15. As a result, this common hereditary disease, characterized by skeletal anomalies, vision problems, and life-threatening circulatory complications, could now be diagnosed in many affected families. Another U.S.-U.K. collaboration, supported by work in France, pinpointed defects in a particular gene in the causation of the variety of diabetes known as maturity-onset diabetes of the young. The gene is one that normally produces an enzyme responsible for regulating sugar metabolism in the pancreas and liver.

Studies in Oxford and Paris threw light on the genetic basis of atopy, an inherited state of hypersensitivity that underlies allergic asthma and rhinitis. Although the condition had been traced to a gene on chromosome 11, the trait was detectable only when transmitted through the mother. This appeared to be an example of the recently recognized phenomenon of genomic imprinting, in which a particular gene behaves differently when passed down through the maternal or paternal line.

Further complicating the ongoing research into Alzheimer's disease, a progressive, irreversible dementia, researchers at the University of Washington announced the finding of a gene defect on chromosome 14 that is associated with an early-onset form of the disease in a few families. Earlier studies had implicated sites on chromosomes 21 and 19 in families with a history of Alzheimer's.

Previously, once researchers had located genes responsible for particular diseases (or marker genes very close to them on the same chromosome), tests for those genes were used principally as a basis for selective abortion of affected fetuses. In 1992, however, there was the first detailed report of the birth of a normal, healthy baby following a more positive type of screening to eliminate the possibility of a genetic defect. Collaborators at the Hammersmith Hospital, London, and Baylor College of Medicine, Houston, Texas, used the new approach, termed preimplantation diagnosis, to screen embryos fertilized in the laboratory prior to implantation in the mother's uterus. In this case, both the

Breast Implants

In April 1992 the U.S. Food and Drug Administration (FDA) severely restricted the use of silicone-gel-filled breast implants, limiting them initially to women aged 18 and older who had a medical need for the devices (such as breast reconstruction after mastectomy) and for whom saline-filled implants were medically unsatisfactory. All implant recipients were to be enrolled in FDA-approved clinical trials and would have to be followed medically for five years by a surgeon participating in the trial. Later on, the devices would be available under similar controlled study conditions to perhaps a few thousand women who wanted them for cosmetic breast enlargement. At the same time, the agency recommended that women who were not experiencing problems with their silicone-gel implants should not consider having them removed.

In January it became known that the major manufacturer of the implants, the Dow Corning Corp., had concealed some information on implant difficulties. The main problems—which seemed to have occurred in about 5% of patients—included implant rupture, leakage of silicone, infection, loss of sensation, inflammation, and hardening of surrounding breast tissue due to calcium deposits or capsular contracture (shrinking of the capsule of scar tissue that forms around the implant). However, more serious ailments—autoimmune disorders and neurological problems—were also associated with implants in some women, although a cause-and-effect relationship could not be demonstrated. Two studies, one published before and one after the decision, discounted any increased risk of breast cancer in implant recipients.

Ultimately, Dow Corning decided to withdraw from the breast implant market. The company set up a $10 million breast implant research fund and offered $1,200 to any woman who wanted to have an implant removed but could not afford it. In the meantime, research moved forward on other materials to fill breast implants. Peanut oil and umbilical cord jelly were two possibilities. The FDA was also reviewing saline implants.   (GAIL W. MCBRIDE)

A U.S. Food and Drug Administration (FDA) panel votes on recommendations for the use of silicone-gel breast implants. In April the FDA followed the panel's suggestions and adopted regulations largely restricting their use to reconstructive surgery.

husband and wife were carrying a genetic defect known to be associated with cystic fibrosis. Cells removed from the embryos three days after fertilization were screened for the genetic abnormality. Some were affected and some unaffected. Following reimplantation of an unaffected embryo, the woman gave birth to a girl free of both cystic fibrosis and the aberrant gene.

Other Developments. The era of animal-to-human transplants may have begun in 1992 with the transplantation of a baboon's liver into a man whose liver had been almost destroyed by hepatitis B. The patient died of a brain aneurysm 71 days after surgery, but the surgeons said more such transplants were planned. Shortly after this, doctors at Cedars-Sinai Medical Center in Los Angeles transplanted a pig liver into a woman dying of liver failure as a temporary measure until a human liver could be found. Unfortunately, the woman died of complications of liver failure right before a newly obtained human liver could replace the pig liver.

A number of pediatric issues were in the news in 1992. Confirming what many parents had long suspected, U.S. researchers reported in the journal *Science* that babies grow in spurts—sometimes as much as 2.5 cm (one inch) in 24 hours—rather than steadily and continuously. Following upon a reduction in the CDC's official threshold for potentially dangerous levels of lead in the blood—from 25 micrograms per decilitre to 10 micrograms per decilitre—it was announced in 1992 that virtually all children on Medicaid would undergo blood screening for lead poisoning. It was estimated that more than six million children under age six would be eligible for the screening. That intellectual development can be significantly impaired by lead exposure—independent of any detrimental influences exerted by socioeconomic factors—was confirmed by an Australian study that documented the adverse effects on cognitive abilities of low levels of lead in school-age children in a middle-class community. It was the largest long-range investigation of the effects of lead exposure ever conducted.

A recently introduced vaccine against the bacterial infection haemophilus influenzae type B, the leading cause of meningitis in children, was shown to be exceedingly effective, reducing the number of cases of meningitis in children by 90%. And an as-yet-unlicensed vaccine against hepatitis A, a severe and sometimes deadly liver infection, was 100% effective in a population of children at risk for the disease.

A study conducted on the Isle of Wight in the U.K. threw new light on the occurrence of disorders such as allergic asthma and eczema in the early years of life. Although a family history of conditions of this sort had long been known to indicate an increased risk, the possible triggering role of certain foods and other substances was uncertain. The study clearly showed that among infants at risk for allergic disorders, exposure to allergens in food and house dust in the first years of life contributes to the development of allergy and eczema, with passive smoking a particularly important factor.

The outcome of another study from the U.K., based at Cambridge, strongly suggested that breast feeding has a beneficial effect on brain development in preterm infants. When children's IQs were assessed at ages 7½ to 8, they were found to be significantly higher in those who had received maternal milk than in those who had been bottle-fed. This extended a previous report from the same investigators showing high development scores at 18 months in the breast-fed children.

A major drug trial, carried out at a number of centres in the U.S. and Russia, showed that low doses of methotrexate, given once weekly for a six-month period, are an effective treatment for juvenile rheumatoid arthritis, the most com-

mon rheumatic condition of childhood. Whether the drug would prove effective—and nontoxic—in the long term remained to be seen.

Concern was expressed during the year about the dangers of excessive vitamin D intake, caused by drinking milk overfortified with the vitamin. Although supplementation of milk with vitamin D (first begun in the 1930s) has since greatly reduced the incidence of rickets, U.S. investigators identified several cases of hypervitaminosis D in the U.S. during 1992, in patients ranging in age from 15 months to 81 years. Subsequent analysis of milk and infant-formula preparations showed that they often contained too much—or too little—vitamin D. This finding led to calls for better monitoring of the fortification process.

There was a call for greater care in the use of bronchodilator sprays containing beta-agonist drugs for the relief of asthma. This followed the publication of a study from New Zealand, confirmed by findings in Canada, that brought to light a heightened risk of death or near death in patients using these sprays regularly—and particularly in those using more than the prescribed amount. It was unclear whether beta-agonists were themselves responsible for the adverse effects or whether the fatalities and near fatalities indicated the emergence of a more severe form of asthma. Nevertheless, physicians were warned to reevaluate the condition of patients using such sprays heavily.

(BERNARD DIXON; GAIL W. MCBRIDE)

MENTAL HEALTH

The year 1992 saw three important steps toward a deeper understanding of schizophrenia. The advances came from different types of investigation and seemed to confirm that it was unlikely that the condition had any one specific cause.

In the first of these studies, psychiatrists at Harvard Medical School and other centres in Massachusetts investigated 15 male schizophrenics by means of the innovative technique of magnetic resonance imaging (MRI). Although comparable to conventional radiography, MRI provided much more detailed information about the inside of the body. It also enabled three-dimensional structures to be reconstructed, facilitating accurate measurements of their size. Previous work had suggested that schizophrenics might have abnormalities in one particular part of the brain, the left temporal lobe. The Harvard researchers showed that, compared with 15 normal control subjects, their 15 patients had significant reductions (13–19%) in the volume of gray matter in three specific regions of the left temporal lobe. There were no such differences in any other parts of the brain. The researchers also were able to show that the severity of the patients' thought disorders was paralleled by the reduction in volume of a part of the brain associated with language.

Psychiatrists had known for many years that schizophrenia was more common in modern industrialized city centres and occurred more frequently in urban than in rural areas. This pattern was thought to reflect the drifting of schizophrenics into cities. This hitherto unverified hypothesis was tested by scientists at Huddinge (Sweden) University Hospital and the Institute of Psychiatry in London. Data about the childhood locations of a group of some 50,000 young men, drawn from the Swedish Conscript Survey, revealed that schizophrenia was 1.65 times more common among individuals brought up in cities than among those who spent their youth in a rural area. Even when the investigators adjusted their figures to compensate for potentially relevant factors such as parental divorce, use of marijuana, and family history of psychiatric disorder, the clear association remained. They concluded that as-yet-unidentified environmental factors found in cities increased the risk of schizophrenia.

Still a third study supported the notion that malfunctioning of the body's immune defenses was responsible for some cases of schizophrenia. There had been previous suggestions that the disease was initiated in one subgroup of individuals when the immune system began to attack nerve cells in the brain. Researchers in New York City confirmed this theory. They analyzed blood samples from 32 otherwise healthy institutionalized schizophrenics. Fourteen of them (44%) were found to have antibodies against a particular protein that occurs in a human nerve cell malignancy. Although the patients were not suffering from this or any other type of tumour, the discovery indicated that schizophrenia was related to abnormal antibody production in a substantial minority of patients.

The British policy of transferring psychiatric care out of hospitals and into the community was vindicated by the results of a study conducted at St. Mary's Hospital, London. Researchers randomly assigned 100 psychiatric emergency patients, aged 16–65, to either conventional hospital outpatient services or multidisciplinary care in the community. There were no restrictions on the treatment given in either setting, and all patients received inpatient treatment when required. Rated by an independent assessor 2, 4, and 12 months later, the individuals referred for community care showed a significantly greater improvement in their symptoms and were more satisfied with their treatment, as compared with the hospital outpatients. Moreover, the latter had spent eight times as many days as hospital inpatients as those treated in the community.

There was a major extension in the understanding of dyslexia, a learning disorder whose victims have great difficulty in learning to read. Hitherto, dyslexia was thought to be a distinct, all-or-nothing condition, caused by a discrete abnormality in the brain. Careful monitoring of over 400 Connecticut children from school grades one to six showed this to be untrue. The real pattern of differences in reading ability was much more like that of variations in height or blood pressure—a continuum on which no particular group was sharply demarcated from the rest of the population. The researchers concluded that there were actually different degrees of dyslexia, which formed a continuum with normal reading ability. (BERNARD DIXON)

This article updates the *Macropædia* article MENTAL DISORDERS and Their Treatment.

DENTISTRY

Economists at the National Institute of Dental Research (NIDR) in Bethesda, Md., and the University of Connecticut School of Dental Medicine reported during 1992 that Americans saved nearly $100 billion in dental bills during the 1980s. L. Jackson Brown, an economist and NIDR's chief epidemiologist, observed that this decline of dental expenditures—despite less favourable economic conditions—could be attributed to the fact that more Americans had dental insurance and were seeking dental care on a regular basis. Geraldine Morrow of Anchorage, Alaska, president of the American Dental Association (ADA), noted, however, that certain segments of the population still lacked proper dental care, particularly the indigent elderly and disabled and institutionalized and uncared-for children.

Researchers successfully immunized rats against a form of periodontal (gum) disease in tests that could eventually lead to a vaccine for humans. Led by Richard Todd Evans, associate professor of oral biology and microbiology at the State University of New York at Buffalo, a team that included scientists from the University of Copenhagen and the State University of New York at Stony Brook immunized the animals by using a small synthetic peptide that is based on known gingival (gum tissue) bacteria. Combined with a "carrier" molecule, the peptide was injected into germ-free rats, where it produced adequate levels of immunity to dramatically halt and prevent loss of bone supporting the teeth. The researchers acknowledged that vaccines for human use would have to contain antigenic components against a handful of other bacteria found in the oral cavity to provide the broadest protection against periodontal disease.

Only nature can heal canker sores, but new research showed that topical remedies, pain relievers, and proper nutrition would help alleviate discomfort. In a University of Florida study of 300 patients, pediatric dentist Daniel Barnes found that immune and nutritional deficiencies may play a role in causing this common condition. Barnes suggested the use of over-the-counter preparations such as anesthetics, antiseptics, and anti-inflammatory agents. For some individuals, vitamin supplements such as folic acid might be useful.

People using nicotine gum to help them quit smoking should not drink coffee while chewing the gum, according to a study by the Addiction Research Center of the National Institute on Drug Abuse in Baltimore, Md. Coffee inhibits the body's ability to absorb the nicotine, which quitters need to minimize their withdrawal symptoms. Cigarette smokers are generally heavy coffee and tea drinkers, according to Jack E. Henningfield, who conducted the study. Henningfield's research showed that drinking coffee—or other acidic beverages such as tea, fruit juices, and cola—while chewing nicotine gum completely eliminated any measurable levels of nicotine absorption. Withdrawal regimens using nicotine skin patches were not affected by coffee drinking because the nicotine was transmitted into the body through the skin rather than via the oral tissues. (LOU JOSEPH)

VETERINARY MEDICINE

The collection of data on the geographic pattern of rabies, as well as efforts to contain or eradicate it, continued during 1992. In the U.S. the CDC reported that the number of cases of animal rabies had risen only slightly (by 1.5%); 30 states had experienced a decrease. In some areas, however, notably New Jersey and New York states, the numbers had increased markedly. Over the two years 1989 and 1990 (the most recent data quoted by the 1992 report), reported cases of animal rabies rose from 50 to 460 in New Jersey and from 54 to 242 in New York. A large rise in the incidence of rabies in wild raccoons was the major factor in this increase.

In the past, efforts to prevent the spread of rabies usually have relied on the quarantine of imported animals where this strategy was possible. Obviously it was practical mainly in such places as the U.K.—islands that had effective customs regulations. The soon-to-be-completed Channel Tunnel from France to England would incorporate sophisticated traps to prevent animals from entering Britain from the Continent.

Whereas raccoons were the main vector of rabies in the U.S., foxes were largely responsible for the spread of the disease in continental Europe. Success had been claimed for control efforts in which bait—chicken heads that contained an oral rabies vaccine—had been placed in known fox runs. Trials of similar methods had been carried out with varying results in other parts of the world. In Zimbabwe, for example, where the target animal was the jackal, meat dosed with rabies vaccine proved attractive to baboons, which ate the bait. Unfortunately, the vaccine strain used, although harmless in jackals, caused the baboons to become infected with rabies.

Concern over the health implications of ozone depletion in the atmosphere—the so-called greenhouse effect—was

A veterinarian releases a raccoon that has been inoculated with a rabies vaccine. In some countries an oral vaccine given in bait was being tried.
MICHAEL J. OKONIEWSKI—THE NEW YORK TIMES

extended during the year to animals. S.J. Mayer, a veterinary scientist with the environmental organization Greenpeace, pointed out that any increase in ultraviolet B radiation resulting from significant losses of ozone might be expected to cause an increase in disease in animals with exposed nonpigmented areas of skin such as the nose and eyes. Skin cancers in dogs and cats and eye tumours in cattle were cited as the most likely potential problems. Farmed fish might also be at risk, Mayer suggested.

A study conducted by a group of veterinarians centred at the University of California at Davis appeared to confirm the long-held belief that pups bought from pet stores tended to have more health problems than those bought privately. The researchers, who surveyed the health records of pups over a two-year period and checked those records against the source of purchase, found a significantly higher rate of sickness in the store-bought pups due to conditions such as kennel cough, diarrhea, and intestinal parasites.

(EDWARD BODEN)

See also Life Sciences: Molecular Biology.

This article updates the *Macropædia* articles Diagnosis and Therapeutics; Disease; Infectious Diseases; Medicine.

Industrial Review

The years 1991 and 1992 were marked by a diversity of experience across the major economic regions. The industrialized economies struggled to escape from what proved in many countries to be an unexpectedly protracted recession. In eastern Europe and the republics of the former Soviet Union, the move away from central planning to a market-based economic system proved to be fraught with difficulties, and industrial production plummeted. In complete contrast, parts of the less developed world expanded rapidly, most notably the economies of Latin America and the Pacific Rim, including China.

The recession that began in North America and other English-speaking countries spread in 1992 across the whole industrialized world. By the second half of 1991, it had appeared that the downturn might be drawing to a close and that the recession would be limited both in its duration and in its incidence. A year later, however, such confidence

appeared to have been premature. Output was rising in the U.S., though at a rate uncharacteristically slow by the standards of earlier recoveries, but in Japan and Germany it was on the slide.

As recently as the start of 1992, it appeared that the economies of continental Europe and Japan might be able to avoid recession. Despite a severe monetary tightening on the part of the Bundesbank, the rise in demand stemming from German unification had not run its course. In Japan it remained possible that the tight monetary policies put in place by the Bank of Japan in an effort to burst the bubble of asset market inflation might not spill over into the real economy.

Neither of these hopes was fulfilled. Tight money in Germany brought not only Germany but also the bulk of its partners across western Europe to recession—with the added effect of all but wrecking the exchange-rate mechanism of the European Monetary System. In Japan the downturn in business confidence produced a 7% decline in industrial production in 12 months.

Table I. Annual Average Rates of Growth of Manufacturing Output, 1981–91
Percent

Area	1981–84	1985–88	1989	1990	1991
World[1]	4.1	1.7	4.3	0.9	0.8
Industrial countries	1.4	3.5	4.0	−0.4	−1.1
Less industrialized countries	3.4	6.9	6.3	7.0	8.7
Eastern Europe and former Soviet Union	3.3	4.0	1.4	−5.0	−2.0

[1] For definition, see Table IV.
Source: UN, *Monthly Bulletin of Statistics.*

Table II. Manufacturing Production in Eastern Europe and the Former Soviet Union[1]
1980 = 100

Country	1987	1988	1989	1990	1991	%[2]
Bulgaria[3]	134	141	139	...	102	...
Czechoslovakia	122	124	125	121	89	−26
East Germany[3]	126	130	133			
Hungary	117	117	111	101	76	−25
Poland	105	111	109	80	68	−15
Former Soviet Union	131	136	139	139	126	−9

[1] Romania not available.
[2] % change 1990–91.
[3] All industries.
Source: UN, *Monthly Bulletin of Statistics.*

Manufacturing industry was bearing the brunt of the slow-down, and measures of business confidence were uniformly weak. Particularly badly affected were the investment goods sectors; the boom of the late 1980s had produced a surge in industrial investment, which in the recession of the early 1990s resulted in excess capacity in many sectors. This led to large cutbacks in investment spending as companies adjusted to the weaker outlook.

One of the factors contributing to the weakness of the industrial economies was the rapid progress of many less developed economies, which had been gaining market share at the expense of higher-cost competitors. This was particularly true in the Pacific Rim, where the well-documented success of the "four dragons" (Hong Kong, Singapore, South Korea, and Taiwan) was being emulated across the region, nowhere more obviously than in China, where industrial production was increasing at a 20% rate. Japanese capital, in search of low-cost production sources, was the catalyst for much of this development and produced a one-third increase in bilateral trade with China during the year. In Latin America the sharp drop in U.S. interest rates also helped because fewer resources had to be devoted to debt service. The signing on December 17 of the North American Free Trade Agreement between the United States, Canada, and Mexico was spurring industrial development in the latter country. These trends were also apparent over the longer term. Since 1980 there had been a 25% increase in manufac-turing output in the industrial nations; the equivalent figure for the less developed nations as a whole was 85%, with Asian output (outside Japan) 150% higher. In the former centrally planned economies, by contrast, industrial output fell by as much as one-half in two years. In Czechoslovakia, Hungary, and Poland (as well as the former East Germany), the drop may have run its course by the end of 1992; in the republics of the former U.S.S.R. the decline in output was still accelerating.

There was also a marked shift in the composition of world industrial output over the past decade. In some sectors, notably textiles, clothing, and footwear, output rose only slightly; however, in chemicals, paper, printing and publishing, and metal products, the rise was in excess of 40%. In the less developed economies, output in the latter categories had doubled in 10 years. While this, to a considerable extent, reflected industrialization from a low base, it served to increase the share of the less developed economies from 14% of world industrial production in 1980 to about 20% in 1992.

The recession in the industrial economies took a severe toll of employment in the manufacturing sector, notably in Scandinavia and the U.K. In contrast with earlier downturns, therefore, the decline in employment for the most part kept pace with or even exceeded the drop in output, with the result that productivity growth was maintained.

(GEOFFREY R. DICKS)

Table III. Pattern of Output, 1988–91
Percent change from previous year

	World[1]				Developed countries				Less developed countries				Eastern Europe and former Soviet Union[2]			
	1988	1989	1990	1991	1988	1989	1990	1991	1988	1989	1990	1991	1988	1989	1990	1991
All manufacturing	6	4	0	0	6	4	0	−1	6	6	7	9	5	1	−5	−2
Heavy industries	7	4	0	0	8	5	0	−1	7	7	8	10	5	1	−5	−3
Base metals	7	2	−1	−1	9	2	−2	−3	5	9	9	9	3	−1	−8	−5
Metal products	8	5	0	−1	8	6	0	−1	7	6	6	7	5	1	−4	−3
Building materials, etc.	5	4	−1	−1	6	3	−1	−4	4	8	4	7	4	2	−5	−2
Chemicals	6	4	0	3	6	4	−2	0	9	6	9	12	4	1	−5	−2
Light industries	4	3	0	1	3	2	−1	−1	5	6	6	7	4	3	−5	−1
Food, drink, tobacco	3	4	2	4	3	2	1	1	5	9	9	11	3	2	−2	1
Textiles	1	2	−4	−2	0	1	−5	−2	0	2	2	2	4	3	−7	−3
Clothing, footwear	1	1	−3	−2	−2	−1	−6	−5	4	6	0	2	4	3	−1	1
Wood products	5	2	−1	−2	4	2	−2	−4	6	2	5	3	5	2	−5	3
Paper, printing	5	4	2	1	5	3	2	0	7	9	11	11	4	1	−4	−4

[1] Excluding Albania, China, North Korea, and Vietnam.   [2] Excluding former East Germany.   Source: UN, *Monthly Bulletin of Statistics.*

Table IV. Index Numbers of Production, Employment, and Productivity in Manufacturing Industries
1980 = 100

Area	Relative importance[1] 1980	1991	Production 1990	1991	Employment 1990	1991	Productivity[2] 1990	1991
World[3]	1,000	1,000	132	133	...	...	...	...
Industrial countries	861	805	126	124	...	...	...	...
Less industrialized countries	139	195	171	185	...	...	...	...
North America[4]	282	271	132	128	...	...	...	...
Canada	22	18	118	110	...	...	...	...
United States	260	253	139	136	95	92	146	148
Latin America[5]	79	84	143	163	...	...	...	...
Brazil	26	19	98	97	...	...	...	...
Mexico	18	17	125	129	...	...	...	...
Asia[6]	183	246	171	179	...	...	...	...
India	11	...	205		...	...	...	...
Japan	131	149	149	152	115	120	130	127
South Korea	6	15	312	338	...	...	...	...
Europe[7]	422	359	115	113	...	...	...	...
Austria	9	9	133	137	87	86	156	159
Belgium	13	12	125	123	...	...	...	...
Denmark	5	5	133	135	102	99	129	136
Finland	6	5	130	118	88	79	148	149
France	75	61	110	108	...	...	...	...
West Germany	114	110	124	128	...	...	...	...
Greece	4	3	103	102	...	...	...	...
Ireland	2	3	196	202	85	85	231	238
Netherlands, The	14	14	128	130	...	...	...	...
Norway	5	4	111	109	...	...	...	...
Portugal	3	...	150		...	...	...	...
Spain	23	20	119	117	...	...	...	...
Sweden	13	10	117	107	90	80	127	134
Switzerland	13	...	123		...	...	...	...
United Kingdom	58	51	123	116	...	...	...	...
Rest of the world[8]	34	30	...	...	...	...	...	...
Oceania	15	12	110	108	...	...	...	...
South Africa	8	6	107	104	104	...	100	...
Former centrally planned economies[9]	...	...	128	126	...	...	...	...

[1] The 1980 weights are those applied by the UN Statistical Office.
[2] This is 100 times the production index divided by the employment index, giving a rough indication of changes in output per person employed.
[3] Excluding Albania, Bulgaria, China, Czechoslovakia, East Germany, Hungary, Mongolia, North Korea, Poland, Romania, the Soviet Union, and Vietnam.
[4] Canada and the United States.
[5] South and Central America (including Mexico) and the Caribbean islands.
[6] Asian Middle East and East and Southeast Asia, including Japan, Israel, and Turkey.
[7] Excluding Albania, Bulgaria, Czechoslovakia, East Germany, Hungary, Poland, Romania, the Soviet Union, and former Yugoslavia.
[8] Africa and Oceania.
[9] Bulgaria, Czechoslovakia, Hungary, Poland, Romania, and the former Soviet Union.
Source: UN, *Monthly Bulletin of Statistics.*

ADVERTISING

Bill Cosby and Jimmy Stewart were the nation's top entertainment personalities in 1992 according to Marketing/Evaluations/ TVQ's 1992 Performer Q survey. The survey was used by marketing firms and advertising agencies to choose celebrity endorsers as well as by television networks and movie producers to cast their shows and movies. Other personalities with high Q scores were Clint Eastwood, Steven Spielberg, Robin Williams, Whoopi Goldberg, Billy Crystal, Mel Gibson, and Damon Wayans. Michael Jordan, who placed fourth in the 1991 ratings, was number 31 in the 1992 survey but still the top athlete. The decline of the sports personalities in the Q survey, according to members of the advertising community, reflected a growing backlash against athletes perceived as too egotistical or mercenary. However, teenagers still ranked Jordan number 1; his Chicago Bulls teammate Scottie Pippen was number 9, and Texas Rangers pitcher Nolan Ryan was rated number 10. Among children aged 6 to 11, Jordan was ranked number 2 and Ryan number 6. The number 1 personality in 1991, television actor Jaleel White, who played Steve Urkel on ABC's "Family Matters," fell to 13th in 1992.

The cost of advertising on television increased in 1992, with CBS charging advertisers $850,000 for a 30-second commercial for the Super Bowl, compared with $800,000 in 1991. "Murphy Brown" (CBS) charged $310,000 for a 30-second commercial, making it the most expensive regularly scheduled series on television. "Cheers" (NBC) charged $300,000; "Roseanne" (ABC), $290,000; "Coach" (ABC), $280,000, and "Monday Night Football" (ABC), $265,000.

U.S. advertising agencies were opening in China, responding to increases in per capita income there and a growing demand for luxury products. DDB Needham Worldwide and Grey Advertising opened offices in Beijing (Peking) and Guangzhou (Canton). DDB Needham's operations were a joint venture with Beijing Advertising Corporation, a government-owned unit. Clients included McDonald's Corp., Fuji Photo Film Co., Mobil Oil Corp., and the Hong Kong Trade Development Council. Dentsu, Young and Rubicam, which had been in China for six years, billed $12 million in 1992, compared with $8 million in 1991. Its clients included Colgate-Palmolive Co., Xerox, Johnson & Johnson, Kentucky Fried Chicken, and Philips Electronics N.V. A locally produced Colgate toothpaste was the first product made in China to be launched by a U.S. advertising agency.

Chinese government statistics indicated that the average monthly income of most Chinese workers was $30, with a higher figure estimated for Beijing and the southern coastal provinces. However, a survey by the J. Walter Thompson China agency indicated that the average annual household income in Guangzhou was about $2,500, in neighbouring Shenzhen (Shen-chen) it reached around $3,300, and in Beijing and Shanghai workers earned some $1,300. The improving economy and the influx of multinational companies in China made the market attractive to U.S. advertising agencies. Most agencies estimated that it would take two or three years before they showed a profit there, but they expected China to develop into a major market.

Pharmaceutical companies spent $350 million a year advertising in medical journals, but a study conducted by researchers at the University of California at Los Angeles found that such ads are often unreliable. Experts from appropriate fields were asked to rate 109 advertisements in 10 leading medical journals in terms of educational value, scientific rigour, and compliance with U.S. Food and Drug Administration (FDA) standards. Of the 109 ads, 100 contained deficiencies in areas for which the FDA had established explicit standards: 40% failed the fair balance test by exaggerating a drug's benefits or downplaying its known hazards; 30% cited statistics from inconclusive, dissimilar, or poorly designed studies; and 30% included misleading graphs or tables. As a result of the UCLA study and its own investigations, the FDA started to tighten its scrutiny of journal advertisements and other prescription drug promotions. Past studies had found that many physicians keep abreast of new treatments by reading advertisements rather than by looking at data from clinical trials.

Leading the 100 top national advertisers in the U.S. in 1991, as listed in the Sept. 23, 1992, issue of *Advertising Age,* was Procter & Gamble, with expenditures of $2.1 billion. It was followed by Philip Morris, General Motors, Sears, Roebuck, and PepsiCo, all of which except PepsiCo spent over $1 billion. Monsanto remained number 100 on the list, spending $100.8 million in 1991 as compared with $114.9 million in 1990.

The top 100 spent a total of $33.7 billion on advertising in 1991, a 3.9% drop from 1990. The decline was attributed to the recession and the Gulf war. Spending for advertising in newspapers, magazines, and television all declined. On the other hand, unmeasured forms of advertising such as sales promotions and direct marketing were not affected by the recession since companies tend to use them more when consumers become price conscious and move away from premium-priced brands. The five industries spending the greatest amount of money for advertising in 1991 were automotive, retail, business and consumer services, food, and entertainment. Sears was the largest user of network radio in 1991, spending $66.5 million, while Philip Morris was the largest user of spot radio advertising with $33.5 million. Retailers were the leading advertisers in newspapers; the May Department Stores, ranked number one, spent $155.2 million. GM led network television advertisers with $527.8 million, while Procter & Gamble was the top spot television advertiser with $283.7 million.

(EDWARD MARK MAZZE)

AEROSPACE

The authoritative journal *Aviation Week & Space Technology* put the international aerospace situation in a nutshell when, in a report on Britain's Farnborough Air Show, it commented:

"The worldwide aerospace/defense industry faces continuing uncertainty and challenges as the expected recovery from global recession remains elusive, effects of the gulf war on civil aviation linger and the thaw in the Cold War progresses unabated."

Taken as a whole, these "new realities," as they were termed, comprised falling defense budgets, declining markets, sharper and even destructive competition, corporate restructuring, uncertainty in the defense sector as to aims and goals following the new geopolitical alignments, and an increasing shift to nonwestern partners.

The airlines continued to suffer financial loss, and the three principal airframe companies also had to scale back on deliveries. Boeing continued to hold about 60% of the world market for civil transports, the balance being shared almost equally by McDonnell Douglas and Europe's multinational Airbus Industrie. The desert storage parks in the southwestern U.S. displayed row upon row of airliners—many of them new—put into storage until better times arrived. The failure of a top aircraft leasing company, Guinness Peat Aviation, to float itself on the world's equity markets was another, and delayed, recognition of the trou-

UNITED COLORS OF BENETTON; CONCEPT, O. TOSCANI; PHOTOGRAPH, T. FRARE

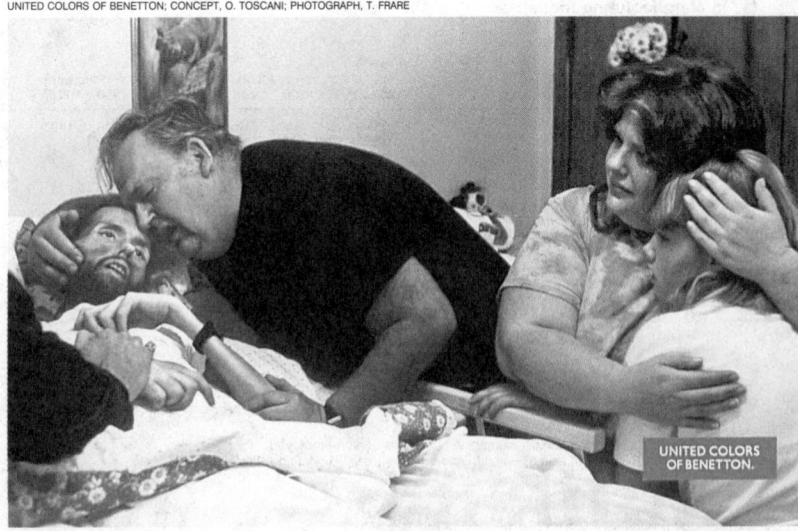

"Family," an advertisement by the clothing retailer Benetton, shows a young man dying of AIDS. The company's controversial ad campaign, which used documentary-like photographs without captions, was aimed at encouraging thought and discussion on important social issues such as AIDS, violence, racism, and terrorism.

With engines sealed, planes from various airlines are lined up in rows on a giant desert "parking lot" in the southwestern U.S. As hard times for airlines continued in 1992, many carriers found themselves with too much capacity and resorted to temporary storage for excess craft.
DOUGLAS BURROWS—GAMMA LIAISON

bled state of the airline industry. It was a sign that the time of speculative acquisition by middlemen of expensive aircraft in the expectation of selling them at a premium had ended. Some observers were predicting that the airline industry would continue to shrink as weaker operators collapsed.

The uncertainty of the situation was highlighted by the announcement in September that Britain's Hatfield factory, famous since 1930 as the home of de Havilland, was to close. Half of its BAe 146 regional airliner production was to be transferred to Scotland, and the rest was to be shared with Taiwan on a 50-50 joint-venture basis. As a partial measure to retain capital, a number of airlines asked that the deliveries of new aircraft be postponed. In total, delivery extensions covering some $20 billion of new aircraft were agreed on for the U.S. airline industry. Thus the airlines themselves prepared to meet their third successive unprofitable year. The problem was not so much a decline in traffic as the effect of overcompetition and fare wars. Many operators actually recorded substantial traffic increases during the summer, but heavily discounted fares, which had become commonplace, bit deeply into their revenues. The challenge was to increase fares to a viable level without causing the fragile market to collapse again. Despite falling revenues, overcapacity, and rollbacks in deliveries, however, U.S. airlines still expected to increase their capacity by about 4–5% during 1993.

In the airframe business, after its worst-ever recession and despite the stretch-out in deliveries, some recovery appeared to be under way, though it was likely to be four or five years before, as one observer put it, "the bunting comes out in the streets of Seattle, Long Beach, Toulouse, Hatfield, and Amsterdam." In March came the first indications of an improvement when during successive days three airlines ordered 30 Boeing 737s, 4 747-400s, and 2 Boeing 777s. Then, during July, United Airlines announced that it would lease 50 Airbus A320s from the manufacturer and then option 50 more leased A320s.

Airbus flew its first A340 four-engined transport in October 1991 and was planning to certify it for service in early 1993. The virtually identical but twin-engined A330 made its first flight on November 2. Meanwhile, Douglas froze the design of its 511-seat MD-12 long-range transport, a direct challenger to the Boeing 747 as the world's number one large airliner. The program was to have been launched during the year but was postponed owing to the predicted poor financial returns for 1992. Farther into the future perhaps was Airbus's proposed 600-seat UHCA (ultra-high capacity aircraft), for possible launch in 1997.

The military sector suffered at least as badly as the airlines and commercial aircraft industry. The collapse of the Soviet Union and its new reliance on the West had two effects. First, the disappearance of the perceived threat from the former Soviet Union resulted in pressure to cut Western defense budgets in favour of increased social expenditure, and second, competition in export markets from relatively cheap aircraft from Russia, now equally eager to become part of the capitalist system, was expected to increase.

Russia's desire and ability to enter world markets, and to show itself a technological equal of the West, was evidenced at the Farnborough Air Show in September when it brought along a large number of notable new types of aircraft. Advanced versions of the MiG-29 Fulcrum and Su-27 Flanker fighters flew impressive flight schedules, and visitors could inspect the Tupolev Tu-22M3 Backfire swing-wing bomber, equivalent to the U.S. Rockwell B-1B, and the unique Yakovlev Yak-141 supersonic V/STOL (vertical/short takeoff and landing) experimental fighter.

The fear among U.S., U.K., and French observers at Farnborough was that the unregulated selling of advanced Russian aircraft and missiles to North Korea, China, and volatile countries in the Middle East would change the balance of power in strategic areas of the world. Military budgets in the former Soviet republics had virtually collapsed, and so top-class companies such as Mikoyan and Sukhoi had no alternative but to sell abroad if they were to survive.

Added to the potential competition from those companies was the steady rise to prominence of competitive Third World products such as Taiwan's IDF defensive fighter; this plane could be politically attractive to countries that did not wish to be associated with the U.S. or Europe, and it was also less expensive.

The "new world order" aspect of the industry was emphasized by Germany's announcement that it would pull out of the multinational European Fighter Aircraft (EFA) project on the basis that such a costly aircraft could not be justified with the disappearance of the Soviet threat. EFA supporters countered that top-class Russian fighters would be operated by increasingly volatile Third World nations and perhaps by former Soviet republics. In the U.S., companies were preparing to bid for a new U.S. Air Force/U.S. Navy AX multimission strike fighter.

But some things do not change. At Farnborough two companies were offering Douglas DC-3s, with turbine engines and "as new" airframes, and were recording brisk sales. The DC-3 first flew in 1936, and salesmen predicted that several hundred would be flying well into the next century.

(MICHAEL WILSON)

AUTOMOBILES

The production of automobiles throughout the world fell 5% in 1991 compared with 1990. The total of 33,518,000 cars produced was the lowest since 1987. Production of trucks and buses (commercial vehicles) was 4.7% lower in 1991, at 10,998,000 vehicles. This was nearly 15% below the record production of 12,903,000 units in 1988.

Among major car-manufacturing nations the only gains in 1991 over 1990 were by South Korea, up from 987,000 to 1,158,000 cars, and Spain, up from 1,679,000 to 1,774,000. Smaller manufacturing countries with increased output in 1991 included Argentina to 120,755, Brazil to 705,633, and Turkey to 195,574. Small gains in the production of commercial vehicles were recorded in 1991 by Argentina, Austria, Belgium, Brazil, Germany, Korea, Turkey, and the Soviet Union.

New car sales in 1991 in the countries of the European Communities (EC), at 11,805,000, were 3% lower than in 1990; the greatest decline took place in the U.K., where sales slumped from 1,930,000 to 1,530,000. EC commercial vehicle sales fell 8% to 1,512,000, the biggest drop again being recorded in the U.K. In the European Free Trade Area (EFTA) nations—Austria, Finland, Iceland, Norway, Sweden, and Switzerland—car sales declined 4% to 957,000, but commercial vehicle sales were 19% lower at 112,000. For all of Asia car sales fell 3.4% to 6,850,000, and commercial vehicles were down 7.8% to 3,580,000. Declines in Japan, Taiwan, and the Philippines more than offset gains in South Korea, Malaysia, Hong Kong, and Thailand. Commercial vehicle sales were also lower in Hong Kong and Thailand in 1991.

The initial enthusiasm for rapid growth in demand for new cars and production facilities in the former communist nations of eastern Europe was tempered by a growing realization of the scale of the economic malaise in most of those countries. While Western automakers, including Opel-GM, Volkswagen, and Mercedes-Benz of Germany and Italy's Fiat group, entered manufacturing agreements in many of those countries, their rewards were expected to be small for several years.

In late 1992 Honda and Toyota joined Nissan as Japanese carmakers starting production at new factories in Britain. Nissan had begun manufacturing in volume in the

U.K. in 1986. In 1991 British production of the Nissan Primera rose 64% to 124,666, and for 1992 it was scheduled to increase again to 175,000. The introduction of a second car, the smaller Micra, in late 1992 was expected to boost Nissan production to 270,000 units in 1993.

Honda began manufacturing automobiles in the U.K. at Swindon, Wiltshire, in October 1992. Toyota's more ambitious plant at Burnaston, near Derby, began production in December. For established British and mainland European manufacturers, those new factories represented important competition and provided a preview of the free access of Japanese cars from Japan due at the end of the century.

Britain was not Japan's only springboard into Europe, and Japanese vehicle production capacity in Europe was expected to top 1.2 million by the year 2000. (In 1991 EC car production totaled 12.7 million; Volkswagen Group led the field for the seventh year with 2,440,000.) Suzuki produced its first Swift models in Hungary in 1992, and Daihatsu began making small vans and pickup trucks in a joint venture with Piaggio in northern Italy. Volkswagen was expected to link with Suzuki to produce small cars in Spain beginning in 1995. Nissan was investing heavily in new models at its Spanish commercial vehicle maker, Nissan Motor Iberica. Ford Motor Co. planned to take some Spanish-built Nissan four-wheel-drive models and rebadge them for sale as Fords in Europe. (JOHN R. WEINTHAL)

United States. Robert Stempel in 1992 became only the second chairman in the history of the General Motors Corp. to be ousted from office when a group of outside directors led by former Procter & Gamble chairman John Smale forced him to resign from office 27 months after he had succeeded Roger Smith in the job. Stempel's departure was expected since the directors earlier had demoted GM president Lloyd Reuss and made him an executive vice president while promoting John F. ("Jack") Smith to the office of president.

The purge was viewed by many with bitter irony since most of the directors who were responsible for Stempel's ouster had been on the board for at least 10 years. Thus they had been on the board during GM's loss of market share from 45 to 35% and had been in office as GM posted staggering losses, culminating in a $4.5 billion deficit in 1991. The same board members also had been in control when Stempel announced major plant closings and employee layoffs. Smale was named chairman to succeed Stempel, and John Smith was named chief executive officer to run the company's day-to-day operations.

The only other time a GM chairman had been driven from office was when company founder William Durant was forced to resign in the 1920s.

On the same day the board of directors forced Stempel to resign (November 2), a trio of his allies and men who had been loyal to former chairman Roger Smith resigned as well. Reuss, vice-chairman Robert Schultz, who headed the automaker's nonautomotive units, and F. Alan Smith, who was in charge of overseeing marketing operations, also quit.

At the same time that GM was embroiled in executive turmoil, the Chrysler Corp. quietly elected Robert Eaton, the former head of GM's overseas operations, to take over as chairman from Lee Iacocca, who was retiring after 14 years with that automaker. At Ford Motor Co. Harold ("Red") Poling was also planning to step down. Alex Trotman, head of Ford's North American Automotive Operations, and Allan Gilmour, president of the North American Automotive Group, were in line to succeed him. Neither Trotman nor Gilmour waged a power struggle for the post.

U.S. automakers ended the 1992 model year by selling 8,160,000 new cars, down from 8.3 million in 1991. Truck sales, however, rose to 4.7 million units from 4.2 million the prior year. It was the second year in a row that the industry had failed to reach the 13 million sales level.

General Motors sold 2.9 million cars, even with a year earlier; Ford sold 1.7 million cars, up from 1.6 million in 1991. Both Honda, with sales of 771,321 cars, and Toyota, with sales of 764,480 cars, topped Chrysler, whose sales reached 671,936. However, when car and truck sales were combined, Chrysler was still able to retain the rank of third in the industry with combined sales of 1.5 million units versus 1.1 million at Toyota, which sold 263,171 trucks. Honda sold no trucks in the U.S.

Ford topped Chevrolet in sales with 1,158,591 cars and 1,399,639 trucks to Chevrolet's 1,039,522 cars and 1,120,148 trucks. The full-size Ford F-Series pickup truck was the industry's top-selling vehicle at 488,146 units. The Chevrolet full-size C-K series pickup truck finished second with sales of 424,933 units. The best-selling car was the Honda Accord at 387,883 units, followed by the Ford Taurus at 347,534 units, which made those two cars the third and fourth best-selling vehicles in the industry, respectively.

Rounding out the top 10 sales leaders were the Ford Explorer utility vehicle (292,069), the Toyota Camry (277,789), the Ford Ranger compact truck (244,661), the Ford Escort (244,231), the Dodge Caravan (234,792), and the Chevrolet Lumina (219,120). The top 10 cars were the Accord, Taurus, Camry, Escort, Lumina, Ford Tempo (213,352), Chevrolet Cavalier (212,675), Toyota Corolla (206,560), Honda Civic (204,839), and Pontiac Grand Am (198,596). Four of the top 10 cars were Japanese nameplates—Accord, Camry, Corolla, and Civic, all of which were built in the U.S. Japanese nameplates accounted for a 30.1% share of the U.S. market, up from 29.7% a year earlier.

In an attempt to soothe consumer unrest over high new-car prices, the domestic automakers surprised observers by holding the line on price increases on the 1993 models when they appeared in the fall. Ford increased prices by 0.3%, General Motors by 1.6%, and Chrysler by 1.9%. That translated into an average $63 increase at Ford, $290 at GM, and $400 at Chrysler.

The pricing action by U.S. automakers magnified the increases imposed by the Japanese, who were forced to boost prices to account for the lower value of the U.S. dollar against the Japanese yen and a weak economy in the home country. Toyota, for example, raised the price on its compact Corolla by $1,046–$1,521, making it $2,000–$3,700 more expensive than the compact Saturn from GM.

The Europeans in some cases also lowered prices. Jaguar, for example, dropped sticker prices by $10,750 on its XJ-S coupe line because it replaced the car's V-12 engine with a six-cylinder model. Mercedes-Benz raised prices, but modifications to its engines to increase mileage and therefore reduce federal gas-guzzler taxes canceled out much of the increase. On a 300SE, for example, the sticker price went up by $500, but the gas-guzzler tax was trimmed by $400 down to $1,700. The net price increase, therefore, was only $100.

A host of new domestic and imported vehicles were introduced in the fall for the 1993 model year. At GM, Chevrolet brought out a new version of the GEO Prizm, a version of the Toyota Corolla that was built in conjunction with the Japanese automaker at Fremont, Calif. Chevrolet dropped the hatchback version of the GEO Storm only one year after it was introduced. The Corvette ZR-1 gained engine modifications to boost horsepower to 405 from 375, but at the same time, Chevrolet said that, starting with the 1993 model year and extending through 1995, it would build and sell only 380 ZR-1s annually, a hint that the car would then be discontinued.

ROGER MASTROIANNI

A worker operates machinery at the General Motors assembly plant in Lordstown, Ohio. The factory instituted a number of changes—including round-the-clock production and retraining of workers to handle a greater number of tasks—designed to make operations more efficient.

At Cadillac the full-size, rear-wheel-drive Brougham, Cadillac's biggest car, was redesigned and renamed Fleetwood, a name that previously had been used to denote the top-of-the-line Deville sedan. The Deville was renamed the Sixty Special. Cadillac also added a new 4.6-litre, 32-valve, 295-hp V-8 engine, dubbed Northstar, to its Allanté, Seville STS, and Eldorado Touring Coupe. In November it announced plans to drop the Allanté luxury roadster.

Saturn added a pair of station wagons as well as a new low-priced base model in its coupe lineup. Saturn also made driver-side air bags standard in all of its cars and for the first time offered traction control as a $50 option for buyers who also purchased automatic transmission and antilock brakes.

Ford introduced a restyled version of the compact Probe and a front-wheel-drive minivan, called Villager, in the Mercury line. The Taurus SHO high-performance sedan offered automatic transmission for the first time, while the subcompact Mustang unveiled a limited-edition, high-performance model called Cobra, as well as a high-performance full-size F-Series pickup truck called Lightning. Ford's Lincoln-Mercury division brought out the next generation of the Mark, called the Lincoln Mark VIII, with a 4.6-litre, 32-valve, 280-hp engine.

Chrysler's long-awaited LH sedans were introduced, the first all new car platform from the automaker since the K-car in 1981. The LH cars were the Chrysler Concorde, Eagle Vision, and Dodge Intrepid. There was no Plymouth version, which fueled even more the speculation that Chrysler was eventually going to drop that nameplate.

The LH cars were billed as family-size models built on 287-cm (113-in) wheelbases and 508–514 cm (200–202 in) long. Early in 1993 Chrysler prepared to bring out two additions to the LH lineup, the Chrysler New Yorker and Chrysler LHS, built on the same wheelbase but longer at 526 cm (207 in). All LH cars offered a choice of two engines, a 3.3-litre V-6, the same as that offered in the Chrysler minivans, and a new 3.5-litre, 24-valve V-6. All LH cars also boasted as standard features four-wheel antilock brakes and air bags on both the driver and passenger sides. In the Jeep utility vehicle line, Chrysler added a Grand Wagoneer companion to its Grand Cherokee version. It had a 5.2-litre V-8 engine as a standard feature; that engine was made optional in the Grand Cherokee.

There was also a flurry of activity among the imports. Toyota redesigned the subcompact Corolla and in doing so stretched it in size to a compact. Nissan replaced the compact Stanza with a new car called Altima. In a move to preserve the low insurance-premium ratings won by the Stanza, Nissan put Stanza decals on the Altima even though formally refusing to use that name. Nissan also brought out a new front-wheel-drive minivan called Quest, a companion version of the Villager at Mercury.

Honda took the wraps off a new convertible hardtop, the Civic del Sol. The metal roof of the two-seater del Sol was removable for open-air driving. The del Sol replaced the CRX line. The Civic series also added a new coupe, while Accord added a luxury SE sedan version with both driver- and passenger-side air bags.

Mazda rolled out restyled 929, MX-6, and RX-7 models but made the most im-

The Ford Explorer, an off-road utility vehicle, was among the top 10 in sales in the U.S. in 1992. The Explorer was one of 10 current models produced as a joint venture between Ford and Mazda, which had been working together for 13 years in development, production, and marketing.
FORD MOTOR COMPANY

pact by announcing that it was dropping plans to unveil in 1995 a new luxury line called Amati that was designed to compete against the Toyota Lexus, Honda Acura, and Nissan Infiniti. Mazda said that uncertainty in the luxury-car market was the primary reason, though admitting that a decline in profits was also responsible for the decision. Mitsubishi redesigned the Mirage, while Subaru brought out an all-wheel-drive, turbocharged Legacy station wagon and a new Impreza sedan and wagon that it said would eventually replace the Loyale.

Among the European imports BMW replaced the 735 series with a new 740i and 740iL sedan powered by a 32-valve, 4-litre, V-12 engine. In addition to replacing the V-12 with a six-cylinder engine in its XJ-S coupes, Jaguar added an XJR-S coupe powered by a 6-litre V-12 engine and for the first time in two decades made a five-speed manual transmission available in the XJ-S coupe.

Mercedes-Benz added a 300CE Cabriolet, its first four-passenger convertible since the 1971 model 280SE 3.5, while preparing to add a V-12-powered 600SL, a V-8-powered 500SEC, and a V-12-powered 600SEC later in the model year. The 400SE sedan was dropped in favour of a longer 400SEL version. Porsche expanded the 911 lineup with both America Roadster and RS America models, while Rolls-Royce brought out a new Bentley Brooklands model with a $138,500 price tag and such options as a picnic table and cocktail cabinet.

Saab introduced a four-door 9000CS hatchback and Volvo an 850GLT front-wheel-drive sedan. Volkswagen dropped the Vanagon and replaced it with a new model called the Eurovan with front-wheel drive.

The two most significant new models, however, were the Dodge Viper, a two-seater roadster that listed at $55,000, including a $5,000 gas-guzzler tax, and a Toyota pickup truck. Only 200 1992 Vipers were built, and they came only in red. The pickup truck, a new full-size model, was seen as the first import that threatened to wrest the title of top-selling truck from Ford's F-Series. Ford and Chevrolet had always dominated the full-size truck market, and no full-size import trucks had ever before been offered in the U.S.

BMW announced during the year that it would set up assembly in South Carolina, its first U.S. production plant and only the second attempt at U.S. assembly by a European car company. (Volkswagen built subcompact Rabbit cars at a plant in Westmoreland, Pa., before closing that operation and focusing on European assembly only.) Three other European automakers decided to give up on the U.S. market. Yugo, the Yugoslav-built mini that captured attention at $3,990 before attracting criticism for quality problems, left the U.S. market, as did Peugeot of France and Sterling of Great Britain.   (JAMES L. MATEJA)

Japan. Sales of new cars in Japan for 1992 were expected to fall below those of the previous year for the second year in a row. For the three quarters of the year ended in September, sales totaled 5,332,191 units, 6.4% lower than during the same period of 1991.

Because of the sales decline, automakers were becoming increasingly reluctant to launch new models into the market, and Isuzu announced that it would stop making passenger cars entirely. This hurt related industries, especially manufacturers of metal molds. Car production was sluggish, totaling 6,334,774 units in the first half of 1992, 3.5% below the same period of the previous year. The bright side was the number of exports, 2,896,552 units, up 1.7% and the first upward turn since 1986.

The used-car market, by contrast, was booming. Used-car sales in the first half of 1992 rose 17% to about 2.8 million units, slightly over that of the new cars. The price tags, particularly of the luxury cars, were soaring, and used-car dealers even claimed shortages of supply.   (RINZO SAKAUCHI)

BEVERAGES

Beer. In contrast to the onslaught of new labels and varieties released in the past few years by major U.S. brewers, the only debut product of note from one of these firms in 1992 hardly qualified as a beer. Zima, a clear, alcoholic malt beverage from Coors, was intended to appeal to drinkers seeking a "lighter" taste. Crazy Horse malt liquor, marketed by the small Hornell Brewing, was immersed in controversy because of its name, taken from a famous Sioux tribal

Table V. Estimated Consumption of Beer in Selected Countries In litres[1] per capita			
Country	1988	1989	1990
West Germany	143.0	142.9	143.1
East Germany	143.0	145.7	141.3
Czechoslovakia	131.7	131.8	135.0
Denmark	119.9	123.4	126.2
Luxembourg	115.8	119.3	121.4
Austria	117.8	119.3	121.3
Belguim	118.6	114.9	120.7
Ireland	109.0	115.6	117.0
New Zealand	115.2	116.8	110.6
United Kingdom	110.9	110.4	110.2
Australia[2]	113.1	111.6	108.2
Hungary	101.5	103.0	107.0
United States	89.3	88.6	90.8
Netherlands, The	83.3	87.5	90.0
Finland	74.1	79.4	83.5
Canada[3]	81.8	80.6	...
Spain	68.7	71.7	71.8
Switzerland	68.7	69.3	69.8
Bulgaria	67.4	70.3	66.8
Portugal	53.1	63.8	65.1
Venezuela	82.3	61.8	63.5
Colombia	59.5	57.7	60.7
Sweden	54.8	57.6	59.8
Cyprus	50.5	54.1	57.1
South Africa	50.9	52.0	c. 52.5

[1] One litre = 1.0567 U.S. quart = 0.8799 imperial quart.
[2] Years ending June 30.
[3] Years ending March 31.

Table VI. Estimated Consumption of Distilled Spirits in Selected Countries In litres[1] of pure alcohol per capita			
Country	1988	1989	1990
East Germany	5.2	c. 5.2	c. 5.2
Hungary	c. 4.6	c. 4.8	c. 4.3
Poland	4.6	4.5	3.8
Czechoslovakia	3.3	3.4	3.3
Bulgaria	2.9	3.2	3.2
Cyprus	3.0	3.0	3.2
Finland	3.1	3.2	3.0
Spain	2.8	2.8	2.7
France	2.5	2.6	2.5
United States	2.4	2.4	2.4
Canada[2]	2.4	2.3	...
West Germany	2.1	2.0	2.2
Japan	2.5	2.1	2.2
Iceland	c. 2.4	2.2	2.1
Soviet Union	1.8	2.0	2.0
Romania	c. 2.0	c. 2.0	c.2.0
Netherlands, The	2.1	1.9	2.0
Cuba	1.9	1.9	...
Switzerland	2.0	1.9	1.8
Sweden	1.9	1.8	1.7
United Kingdom	1.8	1.7	1.7
Ireland	1.7	1.7	c. 1.7
Yugoslavia	1.5	1.6	1.6
Uruguay	1.6	1.6	1.6
New Zealand	1.3	1.4	1.6

[1] One litre = 1.0567 U.S. quart = 0.8799 imperial quart.
[2] Years ending March 31.

Table VII. Estimated Consumption of Wine in Selected Countries In litres[1] per capita			
Country	1988	1989	1990
France	74.3	74.1	73.1
Italy	70.0	69.7	61.4
Luxembourg	58.3	61.4	58.2
Argentina	56.5	54.7	54.2
Switzerland	49.9	49.5	49.4
Portugal	54.0	53.0	47.5
Spain	40.6	36.9	37.4
Austria	34.2	35.2	35.0
Greece	29.9	29.9	32.6
Uruguay	26.0	27.5	30.4
Chile	35.0	35.0	30.0
West Germany	25.9	26.3	26.1
Romania	c. 26.0	16.9	26.0
Belgium	23.2	23.0	24.9
Hungary	20.5	20.0	24.0
Bulgaria	23.2	21.8	23.4
Denmark	21.6	19.2	21.3
East Germany	12.1	12.0	20.0
Yugoslavia	21.1	21.1	18.6
Australia[2]	19.1	18.3	17.6
New Zealand	14.8	14.3	14.7
Netherlands, The	14.8	14.9	14.5
Czechoslovakia	13.0	13.8	13.9
Cyprus	13.7	13.6	13.5
Sweden	12.1	12.5	12.2

[1] One litre = 1.0567 U.S. quart = 0.8799 imperial quart.
[2] Years ending June 30.

Source: *World Drink Trends*, in association with Produktschap voor Gedistilleerde Dranken, Schiedam, The Netherlands.

leader; Native Americans suffer from alcoholism at highly disproportionate rates.

In February, Anheuser-Busch undertook its first major campaign for Michelob in four years, running a series of ads wooing women as well as men—something of a rarity in the U.S. In August the top brewer began a series of ads disparaging Coors, the third-leading U.S. brewer, for touting Coors Light for its "Rocky Mountain water" because some Coors Light contains water from Virginia. After losing a court suit to stop the negative assault, Coors responded with TV commercials featuring its president, Peter Coors, wandering through the Shenandoah Valley declaring that water there is just as pure as that from the Rockies. Such negative advertising was unusual for beer, but it was fitting in a way. U.S. beer volume growth was negative in 1991, falling from 90.8 litres per capita in 1990 to 87.8 litres (1 litre = 1.057 quarts). Poor weather, continued antialcohol pressure, and increased tariffs on Canadian imports contributed to lagging sales in 1992, and brewers resorted to discounting.

Coors began distributing its Extra Gold in parts of the U.K., with the help of Scottish & Newcastle Breweries. Miller High Life became the first foreign beer to be made in Beijing (Peking) after Miller Brewing signed an agreement with Shuang He Sheng Five Star Brewery. Pittsburgh Brewing took its aptly named American Beer to Russia, while Heineken finally began selling its Dutch beer in Germany.

(GREG W. PRINCE)

Spirits. The ability to increase share in a mature industry remained a problem for the spirits industry in 1992. Marketers had discovered that, just as low alcohol content and single-serve portions had been keys to increasing sales in the 1980s, so convenience had now become an important consumer preference. Drinking habits of many consumers in the U.S. changed because of the recession of the early 1990s. They not only drank less but paid less for what they did drink.

Consumers increasingly wanted more taste choices. Flavoured spirits, such as a Puerto Rican coconut-based rum introduced in 1992, were designed to meet this new demand. Sales of white spirits (gin, vodka, rum, and tequila) in the U.S. remained stronger than those of brown spirits (whiskeys). Sales of tequila products in particular continued to grow. A single-serve premium tequila margarita product introduced in April 1992 was thought to be promising. A margarita-flavoured schnapps was the fastest growing line of a major U.S. producer of cordials. A new premium rum from Trinidad and Tobago was said to be based on a recipe unchanged since the 17th century, and new ultrapremium, small-batch bourbons from Jim Beam Brands Co. were said to be based on recipes predating the 20th century.

In a major deal between distilled spirits companies in late 1991, Seagram Co. Ltd. sold trademark rights to seven of its mid-priced brown and white brands to Jim Beam. Paddington Corp. of Ireland attempted to increase U.S. sales of cordials by introducing Baileys Light, a low-fat, low-calorie version of Baileys Original Irish Cream. The Louisville, Ky.-based distiller Brown-Forman Corp. recorded a 0.8% increase in sales over fiscal year 1990–91, attributed to the strong performance of Jack Daniels overseas.   (STEPHEN NEHER)

Wine. After an exceptionally poor harvest in 1991 (251.6 million hl worldwide, including 175.6 million hl in the European Communities [EC]; 1 hl = 26.4 U.S. gallons), the first estimates for 1992 were encouraging. World production was set at close to 300 million hl and EC production at about

AGRITROPE

A laboratory worker examines cultures of grapevine rootstock resistant to phylloxera. As infestations of the microscopic insects continued to destroy vineyards in California, cloning techniques for producing large quantities of new plants quickly were being tried.

190 million hl. Italy, which had just passed a law mandating the labeling of wine by region of origin, was the world's leading wine producer, with 68 million hl. France, with 63.5 million hl, had an excellent harvest. Other major producers included Spain (36.1 million hl), the U.S. (17 million), Argentina (16.5 million), Germany (13.4 million), the former U.S.S.R. (13 million), Portugal (10 million), and South Africa (9.7 million).

The worldwide decline in wine consumption continued. Sharp falls in the great wine-producing countries (France, Italy, Spain, Portugal, Argentina) were not compensated by the increases in countries that were currently self-sufficient (Australia, South Africa), net importers (Belgium, Luxembourg, the U.S., Canada, Japan), or non-producers (the U.K., The Netherlands, the Scandinavian countries). The downward trend in demand aggravated the instability of the market. Trade was stagnant overall, and the Western Hemisphere nations were expanding their exports at the expense of the major EC producers. It seemed likely that chronically excessive supply at the international level would continue until the year 2000, since the European regulatory mechanisms had proved to be largely ineffective. Offering some hope of improvement was the spectacular effect on U.S. consumption of red wines generated by a television broadcast announcing that vascular diseases were less frequent among consumers of French wines than among nonconsuming Americans.

It was reported that the grape phylloxera, which devastated European vineyards in the last century, had infested 20% of California grapevines. The Wine Institute estimated that 75% of the infested vines would have to be uprooted within 10 years.

(MARIE-JOSÉ DESHAYES)

Soft Drinks. Both Coca-Cola and Pepsi-Cola moved into categories they had previously ignored, after seeing their potential cultivated by others. Bottled and canned tea experienced a renaissance. Coca-Cola and Nestlé consummated their previously announced relationship by releasing a line of packaged Nestea products in the U.S., while Pepsi-Cola and Lipton formed the Pepsi Lipton Tea Partnership. Also getting together were A&W and Tetley and Cadbury and All Seasons. This activity was, in part, a reaction to the success of Snapple, a New York-based firm whose real-brewed bottled teas had given it a leadership position in this burgeoning category. U.S. sales of canned and bottled tea were reportedly growing by 20% in 1992.

The other segment catching Coke and Pepsi's attention was that of "New Age" clear beverages. The motivating factor was the advent of Clearly Canadian, an amalgamation of sparkling Canadian water, natural flavourings, and high fructose corn syrup in stylish glass bottles. Coke responded with a new "sparkling water beverage" called Nordic Mist, and Pepsi unveiled Crystal Pepsi, a differently flavoured version of its flagship cola. A number of smaller North American companies were also taking their shots at Clearly Canadian with like products.

The reason for the "innovations" was the basic flatness of the primary soft drink category. U.S. volume was up a scant 1.7% to 46 billion litres in 1991 (183 litres per capita). Even slighter growth was noted through 1992, attributable to an unseasonably cool summer. Volume was also sluggish through most of Western Europe, with slight gains in France (up to 23.4 litres per capita in 1991) and Italy (20.1 litres) offset by losses in Spain (down to 15.7 litres) and the U.K. (8.8 litres). Germany got a boost from Coke's activity in the eastern half of the country. Both Coke and Pepsi took steps to expand their product lines in the Far East. Coke brought Sprite to Korea, and Pepsi signed an agreement with A&W to distribute that company's root beers across the region.

(GREG W. PRINCE)

BUILDING AND CONSTRUCTION

The U.S. Department of Commerce reported in September that expenditures for building and construction in the U.S. during the first eight months of 1992, on a seasonally adjusted annual-rate basis, were higher in each month of 1992 than in the comparable month of 1991. On this basis, total outlays were $424 billion in August 1992, compared with $405 billion a year earlier. The Commerce Department also reported that the number of employees in construction was higher in the third quarter of 1992 than in the same quarter of 1991. In September 4.8 million employees were reported to be on construction payrolls. While the increases over 1991 were good news, the bad news was that both total expenditures and employment in construction were lower than they had been in 1988, 1989, or 1990.

The number of housing units started in the U.S. in the first nine months of 1992 was also reported to be higher than in the comparable months of 1991 but still lower than in the comparable months of 1986 through 1989. The monthly average prices of new homes sold were down in 1992 compared with prices in the three preceding years. The average price in August 1992 was $140,200. The Composite Cost Index of the U.S. Bureau of the Census showed little increase in the cost of construction materials in 1992; in August it stood at 112.4 (1987 = 100). Mortgage interest rates in 1992 were at the lowest levels in 20 years. In several months of the year the rate fell below 8% on a 30-year fixed-rate mortgage. The lower prices and mortgage rates contributed to monthly increases in the sales of new houses during the second and third quarters.

In Canada investment in housing and business had declined greatly in 1990 and 1991. In 1992 there was recovery over those two very depressed years, but the increase in construction was slow even though interest rates on mortgages were very low.

The *National Economics Review* provided information on economic developments in Great Britain, selected European countries, and Japan. The August 1992 issue showed that in Great Britain depressed economic conditions had brought investment in housing and business to very low levels in 1990, in 1991, and into the first half of 1992. It was projected that investment in housing and business would be conditioned by the level of consumer confidence.

Germany's economy was reportedly still experiencing problems resulting from the reunification of the eastern and western parts of the country. This had proved very expensive for the government and delayed plans for additional governmental expenditures in 1992 to stimulate investment. If the government went forward with its spending plans, the added stimulus should increase investments in housing and business in 1993. In France the economy grew at about 1.2% in 1991, compared with 2.2% in 1990. Production figures for the first half of 1992 indicated that growth for the year would be slow. Housing investment was expected to rise very little, and business investment was forecast to decline.

In Japan the substantial decline on the stock market that began in 1990 and continued into 1992 had extensive repercussions throughout the economy. The decline in equity prices influenced investment in business and housing. Business investment rose only 6.2% in 1991, compared with 16.5% in 1989 and 12.4% in 1990. It appeared that there would be little gain in 1992. Housing investment was down 7.7% in 1991 and appeared headed for a further decline in 1992.

(CARTER C. OSTERBIND)

CERAMICS

Worldwide sales of ceramic materials and components in 1991 totaled approximately $82 billion, according to a survey by *Ceramic Industry*. Captive production—that for a specific consumer and not intended for the open market—was not included in this number since those data were not reported to the U.S. Department of Commerce or similar government agencies in other countries. Captive manufacture of advanced ceramic materials and components for use in high-tech industries was estimated as approximately equal to the total for the open market. This would increase production to more than $150 billion. The captive production of ceramic materials and components continued to grow as advanced ceramics were being used at an increasing rate to develop market advantages in the electronics, machine-tool, automobile, aerospace, and other industries.

The advanced ceramics market was much more international than were the markets for traditional ceramics, because of the higher value per kilogram of the advanced materials. According to a *Ceramic Industry* survey, the worldwide market for advanced ceramics in 1990 was approximately $15.3 billion, and the U.S. market was approximately $5 billion. If the value of captive production was included, the value for worldwide advanced ceramics production could be as high as $30 billion. Electronic ceramics continued to dominate the market for advanced ceramics with about two-thirds of total sales. This market included electronic substrates, electronic packages, capacitors, ferrites, piezoelectrics, and sensors. Sales of engineering ceramics grew significantly to approximately $1.7 million.

Optical fibre production in the U.S. was growing at a rate of approximately 20% per year, and the worldwide thrust to install local area networks of optical fibre was projected to cause this market to continue to grow at a 20% rate through at least 1996. Sales in 1991 were approximately $1 billion, and a $2.5 billion market was projected for 1992. Ceramic ferrules for use as fibre-optic connectors accounted for $71 million in sales in 1991, and sales of $172 million were projected for 1996.

The introduction by General Electric Co. of ceramic scintillators for advanced medical X-ray detectors clearly illustrated the value-added potential of advanced ceramics at the systems level. These scintillators were being used in X-ray computed tomography (CT) scanners, where they provided greater sensitivity and higher resolution than previous scanners. This performance enhancement allowed cancer to be detected at an earlier stage than was possible with previous scanners. As a result, the presence of this advanced ceramic scintillator in a $1 million CT scanner gave that machine a significant edge in the multibillion-dollar market for scanners. That market potential created the major incentive needed for GE to develop the special advanced ceramic.

Worldwide whiteware sales totaled $8 billion–$8.5 billion in 1991. This included tile, sanitaryware, dinnerware, and electrical porcelain. Tile sales continued at 1989 levels because of a weak housing market; Italy was the leading producer. Sanitaryware sales were approximately $2.5 billion on a worldwide basis.

U.S. shipments of refractory materials decreased 5.6% to $1.9 billion in 1991 owing to decreased steel production caused by weakness in construction and the production of automobiles and appliances. Worldwide sales were approximately $6 billion. The market for refractories continued to demand materials with improved higher performance and longer life in order to reduce downtime and increase productivity. The shift in steel-production technology to continuous casting was also affecting the mix of refractories sold. The outlook for 1992 was for slowly improving sales due to an increase in steel consumption.

Porcelain enamel sales dropped approximately 9% in 1991 owing to the weak market for appliances. Worldwide sales totaled more than $7.5 million.   (DALE E. NIESZ)

CHEMICALS

"They're hanging crepe all over the world," remarked Robert Kennedy, chief executive officer of Union Carbide Corp. in October 1991, and his words well characterized the chemical industry in 1992. Following a dismal 1991, there were gusts of hope that 1992 was going to be a recovery year. Instead, virtually everywhere in the world, difficulties continued, and the hints in 1991 that recession would affect the important chemical industries of Germany, France, and Italy turned into grim reality. Japan's chemical industry also began to sag. Suffering worst of all was the chemical industry of the former communist countries of eastern Europe. Nowhere did there seem to be clear indications that the industry, so closely tied to the construction and automobile industries, had a way out of its troubles.

Compared with many of their customer industries, however, chemical makers were fortunate. While the 2–3% growth for the chemical industries of the industrialized countries was disappointing, it was generally better than the growth experienced by other manufacturing industries.

There were some bright spots, but they were few and decidedly small. For the U.S. petrochemical companies there were "oxygenates" for motor fuel. These compounds, of which methyl tertiary butyl ether (MTBE) had become most prominent, were important mainly because of recent U.S. laws designed to reduce the smog problems attributed to automobile exhaust gases. The laws were put into effect in many smog-

troubled cities as the winter of 1992–93 began. Because the U.S. used 10 times the motor fuel burned in any other nation in the world, it had a singularly serious problem that oxygenates could help solve. Within decades, though, a large market for oxygenates would probably develop in most of the industrial countries. The recession made U.S. companies skittish about building huge additional MTBE units, however. Plants in the planning stages now were being nursed along slowly, in hopes that they would be ready about the time that the U.S. demand maximized—estimated to be about 1995.

The use of industrial gases also grew substantially in 1992. Oxygen and nitrogen continued to sell in the highest volumes, but a variety of other expensive, ultrahigh-purity gaseous compounds were important for electronic chip making and thus had excellent growth prospects. Oxygen and nitrogen, derived from the air, carried no burden of hazardous waste products or worrisome by-products. Their only obvious negative was that separating them consumed considerable amounts of energy. Even in the recession, their growth exceeded that of most chemicals.

Worldwide, and in virtually all branches of the chemical industry (organics/petrochemicals and inorganics), 1992 held little prospect of being much better than 1991. Although the 1991 statistics showed East Asia to have the most encouraging record, the fact that it rose from a comparatively small base had to be considered.

In 1991 half of the world's 21 leading industrial nations reported production down, and only one could boast of an output volume increase of more than 3%—Ireland, up 21.8%. Ireland's $5,140,000,000 1991 chemical industry, however, was only 1.4% of the European Communities' (EC's) total of $373 billion.

Combined, western Europe's 15 nations achieved a 1% production growth in 1991. The 12 nations in the EC hiked production 1.6%. The U.K. managed a 3% production gain (value up to $50.9 billion despite its third successive year of recession). France, which had been making a government-aided effort to strengthen its chemical position worldwide and had become Europe's second largest chemical producer (with a 1991 sales volume of $66.1 billion), also increased production 3%. Germany (excluding contributions by the former East Germany) remained the leader in Europe with a sales volume of $99,780,000,000 and a 2.2% production gain in 1991. Italy's $50.3 billion chemical industry slumped 1.4% in output. Spain, which had an excellent 1990, dipped in volume in 1991 roughly 1.2% and dropped about the same in sales volume.

Detailed data from the former Soviet Union were almost entirely lacking, as were believable statistics on the chemical industry of the eastern European nations. *Chemical and Engineering News* magazine, using a combination of U.S. Central Intelligence Agency reports, data from the private concern PlanEcon Inc. (London), and sparse national data along with its own projections, estimated that the former Soviet Union chemical output dropped 10%, Poland 14%, Bulgaria 34%, Czechoslovakia 20%, Hungary 16%, and Yugoslavia 16%. Nowhere were there any indications that the downslide in eastern Europe would

be stopped; in fact, further losses seemed likely in 1992.

U.S. chemical makers in 1991 managed a 0.6% output increase to a $287.5 billion level, aided by slight growth in plastics (3%) and fibres (1%), and a rise in MTBE output of 8%. Also contributing gains were nitrogen (output up 5%), oxygen (up 2%), and two paper-bleaching chemicals, hydrogen peroxide (up 11%) and sodium chlorate (up 44%).

The hopes for a substantially better 1992 for the U.S. chemical industry had largely evaporated by the end of September. "We fell off a cliff," lamented one industry executive who had been encouraged by growth through the first half.

East Asia continued to thrive in comparison with the rest of the world, but downturns were evident. Japan's growth was halved (compared with the 1990 gain over 1989) to 2.2%, but its $183 billion industry (second in size in the world only to the U.S.) was the Pacific Rim leader. South Korea continued its rapid growth—estimated at 10% over 1990, although sales volume data were unavailable. China posted gains of 3 to 11% on products such as ammonia, sulfuric acid, and ethylene, with plastics production up 17% (sales volumes not available). Taiwan's economic planning and development group announced a 15% increase in chemical output, with fibres output up 21% (polyester up 13%) and growth in acrylonitrile-butadiene-styrene plastic up 23%. Australia, on the other hand, saw its overall chemical industry production slide 2.5%, with sales of $9 billion.

(J. ROBERT WARREN)

ELECTRICAL

New markets in eastern Germany and continuing development in Asian countries relieved some of the gloom of the recession in the electrical equipment market in 1991. The Asea Brown Boveri (ABB) multinational reported that the markets worst hit by the depression were those in North America and other English-speaking countries, plus Scandinavia and southern Europe.

However, manufacturers that had taken advantage of the prosperous 1980s to invest, restructure their management, and consolidate, such as General Electric (GE) in the U.S., were largely insulated from the worst effects of the downturn in trade. John Welch, chairman of GE, said in the company's annual report that 1991 was the "first real test when much of the global economy settled into a full year of steady decline." But at GE both revenues and earnings increased by 3% in 1991, mainly as a result of increases in "total cost productivity," which stood at a remarkable 4%. Welch's formula for increasing productivity was to clear away impediments to growth, such as management layers, functional boundaries, and "all the other trappings of bureaucracy."

Another company that seemed satisfied that it could overcome the negative effects of weak markets was ABB. According to the president, Percy Barnevik, "Our decentralized organization has adapted capacity and cost early enough to limit the impact of the recession." At ABB earnings rose by 2% in 1991 to $1,153,000,000 on a global income of $28,883,000,000, up 8%.

GE's worldwide revenue in 1991 was $58,414,000,000, but the company had many activities outside the electrical industry, such as the Aerospace and Aircraft Engines divisions with a combined revenue of $13,225,000,000. Siemens in Germany, a multinational similar in size to GE, had global net sales to Sept. 30, 1990, of about $48,672,000,000, but most of its operations were in the electrical industry.

For comparison, the combined revenue of Siemens' Power Generation and Power Transmission and Distribution businesses was DM 10,262,000,000 (about $6,841,000,000), while the revenue of the equivalent GE business, Power Systems, was $6,185,000,000. (The operating profit at GE's Power Systems was up a stupendous 26% from 1990 following massive productivity gains.) Like most other multinationals in this consumer-driven depression, GE's industrial and appliance businesses saw revenues fall in 1991, down to $6,928,000,000 (−1.6%) and $5,451,000,000 (−4.5%), respectively, with profits down by 5 and 7%. In late 1992, in the face of military spending cuts, GE announced that it would sell its Aerospace Division to Martin Marietta.

Each of the three giants in the industry, ABB, GE, and Siemens, was tempted by the new markets in eastern Europe, with Siemens having the advantage following German unification in October 1990. Siemens' investments in eastern Germany included the acquisition of 11 plants as well as establishment of a distribution and service network covering the entire region.

For many years Siemens had been seen as the "sleeping giant" of the electrical industry, but this had changed dramatically during the past two years. Apart from its enormous potential expansion into what was communist East Germany, Siemens in October 1990 merged its information systems business with the ailing German computer manufacturer Nixdorf; this resulted in larger losses than expected (about DM 700 million). Then, in August 1992, Siemens purchased the U.S. Sylvania lighting interests from GTE, giving Siemens' Osram subsidiary a leading position in the world lighting and light bulb market. GE spent 3.8% of its revenue on new plant and equipment in 1991 and 6.7% on research and development; the equivalent figures for Siemens were 12 and 9.2%, and for ABB, 3.6 and 8.1%.

Sales at Britain's General Electric Co. (GEC) totaled £9,435,000,000 (about $15,379,000,000) in the year ended March 31, 1992, a decline of 0.5% from the previous year, with operating profits at £702 million (about $1,144,000,000), up 2%. These figures include the activities of GEC Alsthom, the Anglo-French heavy electrical group. Sales there were about $9,782,000,000 in the year ended March 31, 1992, a rise of 8.4% from the previous year, with net income of about $366 million, up 14%.

Toward the end of 1992, sales figures showed that the electrical equipment market remained weak. For the first six months of 1992, revenue at ABB was $13,838,000,000, up 2% from the first half of 1991, but earnings, at $518 million, fell by 0.4%. The outlook was for continuing stagnation in all but the Asian markets. At Siemens, orders for transportation equipment for eastern Germany resulted in an 8% rise in profits to DM 292 million in the six months to March 31, 1992, compared with the same period a year earlier.　　　(T.C.J. COGLE)

FURNITURE

Change was in the air in the U.S. in 1992, and the previously status-quo-oriented furniture industry was no exception. One indication was its expanding global mind-set as North America took steps toward becoming a single megamarket under the North American Free Trade Agreement. Thus, for the first time, *Furniture/Today*'s annual ratings of manufacturers and retailers included some from outside the U.S. Also, exports were up; U.S. furniture exports had risen by 300% between 1987 and 1991, and they continued to increase in 1992. The industry was involved in aspects of the trade negotiations under the General Agreement on Tariffs and Trade and in Europe's efforts to establish closer union. Another change was marketing creativity. In hard times, the industry was putting a new twist on an old expression: Anxiety is the mother of invention. Thomasville Furniture, for example, began participation in Air Miles, a free air travel program, as a method of boosting sales.

The spur for these changes was the dismal economic situation of the previous three years, and apparently the changes made a difference. According to the American Furniture Manufacturers Association (AFMA), projected shipments for 1992 would be $16,195,000,000—a 6% increase over 1991, which had finished higher than anticipated at $15,273,000,000. At the top of the 100 leading North American retailers listed by *Furniture/Today* was Levitz with $885 million in sales. Second was Ethan Allen Home Interiors, which sported a new name and a non-Colonial logo. The fact that the stores in third and fourth place

TED MORRISON

An office worker stands at an award-winning desk. Because the height was adjustable, the desk could also be used by a worker who preferred to sit down, and the hinged top was designed to support books or papers.

were IKEA, a Swedish-based firm, and Pier 1, which specialized in imported furnishings, reflected the international influence. Heilig-Meyers, in fifth place, spent the year expanding. New to the list were several firms from Canada, led by Leon's Furniture in 11th place. The single entry from Mexico was Muebles Dico, which ranked 62nd. A major change in retailing was market composition. Specialty stores outpaced conventional furniture stores in units sold, even though furniture stores comprised 45% of the market and specialty stores accounted for only 38%.

Masco Home Furnishings, reporting $1,430,000 in sales, was number one in *F/T*'s survey of the top 25 North American furniture manufacturers. Broyhill/Lane was runner-up, with La-Z-Boy, Ladd, and Thomasville in the next three positions. All had the same rankings as in 1991. Two Canadian firms made their first appearance: Dorel (14th) and Palliser (15th). Buyouts of manufacturers seemed to have stopped as the existing companies regrouped.

The use of computers in the industry continued to expand. For example, AFMA provided its members with an electronic bulletin board. Advances in video catalogs included electronic ordering, updated pricing, and direct-response television. Catelist, a joint development of AT&T, McGraw-Hill, and Image Technology, offered an online data base network for international marketing.

With the exception of the "Lodge Look" and "Western Motif" influences, design inspiration sprang from sociological and technological changes rather than decorative or style categories. The three major innovations were the home office, the home theatre, and the new feature-filled recliner. Furniture for electronics alone was expected to reach $1 billion in sales.

(ABBY CHAPPEL)

FURS

Demand for fur apparel improved somewhat in 1992 following two years of decline, attributed to a combination of poor economic conditions and abnormally mild winters. Although many countries were still struggling through a continuing recession, retail sales of big-ticket items in the U.S., including furs, were showing signs of improvement. One reason was early forecasts of a cold winter, which gained credibility as a result of a cooler-than-normal summer and fall. Another was pent-up demand among upper-income consumers, who may not have been affected by the recession but had shied away from conspicuous consumption. By year's end it was estimated that retail fur sales in the U.S. totaled just under $1 billion, or about half what they were in the peak year of 1986.

While sales of conventional furs were showing modest improvement, retailers found healthy growth in the demand for outerwear combining fur with leather or fabric. The popularity of these items was linked to the trend to a more casual lifestyle, as well as their greater versatility and substantially lower price.

The industry shrank in virtually all sectors, from primary markets through the retail level. In part this reflected normal attrition, but much of it was due to severe losses resulting from declining sales and depressed prices. The overexpansion of the early to mid-1980s contributed to unjustifiably high overhead costs. Trade sources estimated that the number of stores carrying furs diminished by 20%, and with fewer stores to serve, the manufacturing sector also shrank. Imports of fur apparel into the U.S., which had reached a high of $477 million in 1987, were expected to be little more than $100 million by the end of 1992.

Although pelt prices recovered somewhat, most farmed types remained well below production costs. This resulted in a further cutback, both in the number of farms in operation and in the crop itself. On the basis of U.S. Department of Agriculture and trade data, there were only about 600 mink ranches still operating by the end of 1992, and the year's crop was estimated at under three million pelts. Harvesting of wild furs was also down, reflecting the fashion swing away from long-haired furs except as trimming.

A new U.S. law was enacted making it a federal crime to release animals or damage farm and research facilities. Similar laws were already in effect in 30 states. In general, however, activities by animal protection groups appeared to be on the wane.

(SANDY PARKER)

GAMES AND TOYS

The international toy business moved at a pace in 1992 that kept even industry experts on their toes. Acquisitions, mergers, massive overseas growth, and radical product development all were notable during the year. And all this took place at a time when video games were becoming even more popular. Predictions that the video games boom would sink the traditional toy industry proved to be unfounded. "We have learned to live with video games," was the comment most often heard, and the top four U.S. public toy companies provided the best evidence. Hasbro, Mattel, Tyco Toys, and Fisher-Price—the top four in terms of size—all increased their business dramatically, with core brands becoming stronger and new lines taking them into fresh categories. Stable core businesses backed by innovative new product departures seemed to have been the key.

The year began with Mattel acquiring International Games and thus gaining ownership of the world's best-selling boxed game, UNO. Tyco then began to flex its muscles internationally, with subsidiaries being opened in Spain and Belgium and then later in Germany, Italy, Australia, Switzerland, and Austria. And all this came on top of the year's largest acquisition when Tyco launched its bid for Universal Matchbox Group, the Hong Kong-based maker of Matchbox miniature cars. That purchase, coupled with Tyco's natural growth, should make the company worth more than $1 billion within the next 18 months.

The world's favourite toy retailer, Toys "Я" Us, kept getting bigger and marked the start of the year with the opening of its second store in Japan, officially opened by U.S. Pres. George Bush. While the company continued to expand internationally, its domestic market was boosted by the news that rival toy superstore operator Child World had filed for bankruptcy before eventually going out of business.

In Europe, the Ideal Group provided the best success story with offices now open in most countries. Their strength did not

go unnoticed, as Playmates International Holdings, makers of the Teenage Mutant Ninja Turtles, then swooped to buy 37.5% of the company. The short-term result was that, in Europe, Ideal gained the exclusive distribution rights to the Turtles, which remained among the world's most popular toys.

Elsewhere in Europe the prospect for full European harmonization—as signaled by the Maastricht Treaty—was looking bleak, and when the Danish people voted no in a midyear referendum, Lego Systems, Denmark's best-known toy company, announced the postponement of many planned European investments.

In the U.S. toys that had been popular in previous years enjoyed renewed success. Trolls moved up to the top of the charts, and the 30-cm (12-in) version of Hasbro's GI Joe returned at Christmas after a more than 10-year absence. Mattel's Barbie in her many versions earned $1 billion in a record-breaking year. The new longhaired Totally Hair Barbie earned $100 million by itself.

Other intriguing products included Buddy L's Voice Command, vehicles that started their engines roaring and moved away when commanded by a young child; Hasbro's Starla doll, which moved her mouth in sync when her microphone was sung into by a child; Teen Talk Barbie, who was the centre of some controversy when some of the dolls dared include among their utterances the politically incorrect words: "Math class is tough!"; and Danish toymaker Villy Nielsen's the Mommy-to-Be Doll, whose swollen abdomen could be removed to reveal a baby girl or boy. A legal battle in Britain between Hasbro and Mattel ended when Hasbro agreed to change its popular Sindy doll to look less like Barbie.

Among the year's other leading toys were Tyco's Incredible Crash Dummies; Rollerblade dolls; the innovative Nerf Bow and Arrow from Kenner; the purple dinosaur Barney, based on a children's television show; and Mattel's Gak, a combination of Play-Doh and Silly Putty. And all

the while, video games remained hot news. Nintendo clawed back into the lead it had lost to Sega's Genesis, but two factors had to be worrying Nintendo: the pre-Christmas launch of the Sonic 2 cartridge for Genesis featuring Sonic the Hedgehog (its launch date was dubbed Sonic 2sday) and the arrival in November of the Sega CD, the first mass-market CD-ROM peripheral that could signal a new era for video games.

(JONATHAN M. SALISBURY)

GEMSTONES

Though an end to recession in the Western world was confidently forecast in the closing months of 1991, by mid-1992 signs of recovery were patchy. Despite this, the jewelry and gemstone sectors managed to survive reasonably well, with the top end of the market giving, as always, the greatest cause for optimism. Salesroom reports indicated that the number of jewelry sales had declined slightly, with at least one firm going out of business at the expensive end of the market. A number of lots remained unsold at major auctions, and customers appeared to prefer items of tried and trusted resale value. Nevertheless, the best modern items continued to move, and this was reflected in the retail market. Small jewelry manufacturers were hard hit by recession, and newer firms went out of business in large numbers.

Ruby from Vietnam was well established in the gemstone market; the colour at best was almost equal to the best Burmese stones, traditionally considered the world's finest. Colour remained attractive down to small sizes. Fine colour-change Brazilian alexandrite had not reappeared in any quantity. At the 1992 Basel (Switz.) Fair, a good indicator of the strength of the European gemstone market, the quality of the merchandise was described as uneven, with no single species attracting excited attention. Some emerald and other species were reappearing from the former Soviet Union, though the quality did not yet equal that seen in earlier years. Some demantoid gar-

Barney the purple dinosaur receives the attentions of an adoring fan. The PBS television show "Barney & Friends," which enchanted the toddler set (if not always their somewhat bored parents), spawned a brisk business in Barney books, dolls, clothing, and other merchandise.

Wildcat miners search for diamonds in Angola. It was estimated that in 1992 as many as 50,000 prospectors were digging in Angola, and the resulting flood of diamonds threatened the stability of world markets, which were normally tightly controlled.

REUTERS/BETTMANN

net from the same source was reportedly back on the market. Fine and varied colours of diamond continued to come from the Western Australian mines, where a significant proportion of total production was of gem quality. Some gem minerals were once more appearing from Nigeria (emerald of reasonable quality); supplies from Madagascar were still uneven.

The main question still occupying the attention of gemstone dealers was alteration/improvement of colour. Some merchants suggested that at least 90% of sapphire was routinely heat-treated, and the question of whether treatment should be disclosed to customers continued to be a vexed and unresolved issue. There was no likelihood that earlier conditions, where stones were not interfered with, would return, so the disclosure problem passed to the gem and jewelry regulatory bodies. Most treatment was carried out in Bangkok, Thailand.

(MICHAEL O'DONOGHUE)

GLASS

Competitive pressures and a sluggish world economy in industrialized countries combined to make profitability and long-term viability in the glass industry much more of a challenge than ever before. In expanding markets, such as Southeast Asia and South and Central America, investment in capacity and production technology was occurring to meet demands that were expected to double or even triple in the next decade. In eastern Europe, however, there was considerable economic distortion since production and labour costs were cheaper than in the West and the ecological constraints that were becoming increasingly stringent in the West were virtually nonexistent. Exports to the West rose to compensate for the collapse in the domestic market and the dramatic drop in trade volume in eastern markets. A number of large enterprises were considering the possibilities of investing in eastern European companies.

In Czechoslovakia two recent partnerships developed, and a major flat glass producer invested in Poland and intended to build the country's first full-size float line for making plate glass.

Shipments of glass containers in the U.S. declined by 2.6% in 1991 to 277,760,000 gross units. However, in the first quarter of 1992 market demand strengthened appreciably as shipments rose 6.4% above those for the first three months of 1991.

Production of glass containers in the European Communities (EC) grew by slightly less than 5% in 1991, with production at 95% of capacity. Market penetration by imports, although still relatively low (6.5%), was growing. The trend was expected to continue for some time as imports originating from the EC's main competitors, the countries of eastern Europe, were encouraged by the liberal import policy and tariff concessions that the EC had granted them.

Weakness in the construction and automotive industries caused flat glass shipments in the U.S. to dwindle by 3.3% in 1991 to 297,280,000 sq m (3.2 billion sq ft). This was the third consecutive annual decline in shipment volume, although the downward trend was expected to reverse in 1992. Flat glass demand in the EC moved from a position of very strong growth in 1987 and 1988 to a drop in sales of 1% in 1991. Capacity utilization dropped from 91% in 1987–88 to a situation of increasing surplus capacity in 1992 and 1993. This was exacerbated by increasing imports from outside Europe, notably the U.S. The value of flat glass also declined. Glass prices in 1991 were 25% lower than two years before in Europe and the U.S. and 38% lower than they had been in Australia.

Demand for glass fibre, which grew 8–10% per annum in the latter half of the 1980s, continued to slow down following a downturn in activity for its more traditional applications in the construction, automotive, and defense industries. Sales fell by

3% during both 1990 and 1991. Worldwide sales of fibre-reinforced composites were expected to rise between 4 and 5% in 1992.

(HEIDI C.D. BROWN)

INSURANCE

The insurance world would remember 1992 as the year of disasters. Even before midyear, there had been two earthquakes and the billion-dollar Los Angeles riot in California, a flood in Chicago, and two freak hailstorms in central Florida. Then, in August, Hurricane Andrew swept across southern Florida and Louisiana causing an estimated $15 billion–$16.5 billion of insured losses, the highest in history. Almost three weeks later Hurricane Iniki battered Hawaii for some $2 billion more in losses. Outside the U.S., the worst windstorm in three decades in France resulted in 50 deaths, an earthquake in Cairo killed 400, and a jumbo jet crashed into an Amsterdam apartment complex, with expected claims of $100 million–$300 million.

British insurers faced these disasters following a year in which net losses, after considering £3.5 billion investment earnings, were 12% of nearly £30 billion premium income. Household insurance crime losses rose 75%, while subsidence damage claims were four times as severe as in an average year. Life insurance was a bright spot, with premiums growing by 17% to £47 billion. Many employees exercised their recently gained freedom to opt out of employers' pension plans in favour of personal insurance pensions.

Lloyd's of London had a traumatic year. The latest year (1989) under its three-year accounting system showed a record loss of £2 billion. Particularly hard hit were about 4,500 of some 30,000 members of syndicates writing catastrophe reinsurance. Although few calls for claims were made on Lloyd's Central Fund, a levy was increasing the fund by £500 million. The number of syndicates fell from 384 to 279 as legal actions against them rose sharply. Lloyd's weathered the short-term capacity crisis with £6.5 billion of net resources, nearly the same as two years earlier.

The European Communities adopted directives to ensure a common market in both general and life insurance by 1994, but a few countries, such as Greece and Portugal, might postpone the changes. In eastern Europe new insurers were replacing state insurance monopolies that existed under communism. European brokers were opening offices there, with the most progress reported in Hungary and Poland. Banks were increasing their involvement in insurance, particularly life insurance.

With policyholder surplus of approximately $160 billion and premiums of $223 billion for the first half year, U.S. property-liability insurers were challenged by the disasters but not seriously threatened. Individual company results varied considerably, however. Additional capital was pumped into several large insurers, notably the ITT Hartford Insurance Group ($680 million) and Prudential ($900 million). Mergers and reorganizations proliferated with the large losses. Aetna and Continental Corp. decided to sell their reinsurance units, and Sears put 20% of Allstate up for sale. Other insurers stopped or reduced business in troubled states, particularly California, Florida, Texas, and New Jersey.

Buildings and vegetation in south Florida lie devastated by Hurricane Andrew, which struck the area in August. For insurance companies the storm was the single most costly disaster in history, and as a result, several had their credit ratings lowered later in the year.

ALLAN TANNENBAUM—SYGMA

Pressure grew on insurers to raise prices. In liability insurance, for example, tort costs had grown four times faster than the U.S. economy during the past half century. Of total annual tort costs of $132 billion in 1991 (including $9 billion for rising malpractice costs), 43% went for legal costs. Pollution liability costs were notoriously uncertain, with four recent court decisions denying coverage for gradual pollution and four granting such protection. Continued worker's compensation losses prompted cost-cutting reform bills in Maine and other states, and 24-hour health insurance as an alternative to reduce claim abuses was advocated.

Assets of U.S. life-health insurers reached a record $1.5 trillion, but declining interest rates and depressed real estate values were major problems. Corporate readjustments included demutualization of several insurers, the largest by far being that of the Equitable Life Assurance, which included a $450 million stock sale. The number of mutual life insurance companies had fallen 32% during the past 50 years. One of the largest of numerous mergers combined Phoenix Mutual and Home Life. Mutual Benefit of New Jersey went into conservatorship. The capital and surplus of many life insurers was lowered at the end of 1992 by new interest maintenance reserve regulations of the National Association of Insurance Commissioners. (See CONSUMER AFFAIRS.)

The sale of variable annuities rebounded during the first six months of 1992, up 75% compared with the previous year. Variable universal life insurance policies were also popular, but overall their one-fourth share of new premiums dropped as interest earnings diminished. Sales of "first-to-die" life contracts, insuring two or more persons but paying off only at the first death, were growing because they could reduce costs for dual-income married couples and for business partners.

Although AIDS-related life and health claims rose only 11% in 1991, the smallest

jump in five years, the $1.3 billion paid was significant. A federal court ruling permitted employers to reduce health coverage for victims of AIDS and other costly illnesses. Health insurance was likely to be the number one issue for insurers for some time to come. With annual health care costs skyrocketing to more than $800 billion, major changes seemed likely.

(DAVID L. BICKELHAUPT)

IRON AND STEEL

As a result of the increasingly sluggish economies in the major countries, the market for steel products in 1992 was very weak. In most of the industrialized nations, estimates of the year's apparent steel consumption were for a decrease, with a very strong decline from 1991 (13%) expected for Japan and a slighter reduction (1.7%) in the countries of the European Communities (EC). Altogether, steel demand in the industrialized countries was expected to reach only 309 million metric tons of finished steel products, the lowest level since 1988.

Steel demand in the less developed countries, although still anticipated to rise marginally in 1992, lost some of its earlier vigour; it was expected, however, to amount to 124 million metric tons of finished steel products, with most of the 4.8% increase coming from the newly industrializing countries in Asia. Steel consumption in the West would remain at the 1991 level of 432 million metric tons.

Estimates of steel consumption in the former planned economies of eastern Europe and the Commonwealth of Independent States (CIS; republics of the former Soviet Union) were fraught with considerable uncertainty; the economic turmoil and the virtual collapse of investment activity and of international trade in the region were expected to result in a substantial fall in steel requirements in 1992; at best, finished steel consumption could reach 120 million metric tons, compared with about 170 million metric tons in the peak years

before the drastic changes in the political and economic system occurred. Taking account of some further expansion of steel needs in China, the International Iron and Steel Institute (IISI) estimated that world finished-steel consumption in 1992 would remain at about the previous year's level of 623 million metric tons.

Given the slack in steel demand, steel production in 1992 was also at a low level; during the first nine months of the year, crude steel output in the 65 countries covered by the IISI monthly statistical reports was down by 2.8%, to 523 million metric tons, 15 million metric tons less than in the corresponding period of 1991. The bulk of this decline occurred in the industrialized countries, which, taken together, produced 7 million fewer tons; crude steel output in Japan was nearly 11 million tons below that of the first nine months of 1991. The countries of eastern Europe and the CIS reduced crude steel production by as much as 20 million metric tons (15.6%). For all of 1992 world crude steel production was estimated to amount to 715 million metric tons, compared with 734 million metric tons in 1991. The geographic breakdown was expected to be as follows: industrialized countries, 370 million metric tons (−2.6%); less developed countries, 115 million (+4.5%); total Western world, 485 million (−1%); eastern Europe and CIS, 144 million (−13.3%); and China and other eastern Asian countries, 86 million (+12.2%).

As a consequence of weakening demand, steel prices were under pressure worldwide. The f.o.b. Antwerp export prices—relatively reliable general indicators of overall world price developments—in October 1992 were, for certain products, at levels below those in 1981, when the authorities of the EC had declared the industry in a state of "manifest crisis." Apart from the general economic slowdown, the price fall was ascribed to increased low-priced imports from the eastern European countries and to excess capacity in a number of western European economies.

The rather bleak market situation gave rise to a number of trade conflicts and defensive measures, including the filing of 84 lawsuits by many major steelmakers in the U.S. against producers in Japan, western Europe, Brazil, and South Korea. Steelmakers in the EC reintroduced import quotas for certain products originating from eastern Europe. The so-called Multilateral Steel Agreement negotiations, held parallel to the stalled General Agreement on Tariffs and Trade Uruguay round proceedings, had come to a virtual standstill.

It was not likely that the next year would bring any substantial improvement in the demand for steel products. In the U.S. the weak and hesitant economic recovery was expected to generate only a marginal rise in steel consumption, and similarly slow growth was expected for the countries of the EC and for Japan. The principal driving force for steel demand—investment spending—remained hesitant; apart from the uncertain economic outlook, the main reasons for this were the disturbances that had occurred in the international financial markets and the rather violent and erratic fluctuations of exchange rates.

For the West as a whole, steel consumption was expected to attain at best about

Table VIII. World Production of Crude Steel
In 000 metric tons

Country	1987	1988	1989	1990	1991	1992 First 9 months	Percent change 1992/91
World	736,414	780,062	786,182	769,991	733,734	¹	¹
Soviet Union/CIS	161,874	163,037	160,096	154,414	132,666	86,400	−15.6
Japan	98,513	105,681	107,908	110,339	109,649	72,832	−12.9
U.S.	80,877	90,650	88,834	89,723	79,203	62,457	+6.2
China	56,280	59,430	61,590	66,349	70,436	58,810	+14.2
Germany²	36,248	41,023	41,073	38,434	42,169	31,225	−2.2
Italy	22,859	23,760	25,213	25,510	25,007	18,931	+2.9
Brazil	22,228	24,657	25,055	20,567	22,617	17,829	+6.1
France	17,693	19,122	19,335	19,015	18,434	13,921	+0.6
Poland	17,147	16,873	15,094	13,625	10,439	7,508	−9.4
Czechoslovakia	15,416	15,379	15,465	14,775	12,071	8,424	−11.8
U.K.	17,414	18,950	18,740	17,841	16,474	12,338	+0.3
South Korea	16,782	19,118	21,873	23,125	26,001	20,195	+5.0
Romania	14,962	14,314	14,415	9,754	7,092	4,135	−27.2
Canada	14,737	14,866	15,458	12,281	12,987	10,318	+7.3
India	13,121	14,309	14,608	14,963	16,394	12,841	+5.6
Spain	11,691	11,886	12,765	12,935	12,867	9,547	−0.6
Belgium	9,783	11,217	10,948	11,414	11,331	7,929	−6.6
South Africa	8,991	8,837	9,337	8,619	9,358	6,808	−4.9
Mexico	7,642	7,779	7,851	8,726	7,883	6,253	+5.1
Australia	6,100	6,387	6,735	6,676	6,141	5,122	+12.8
North Korea	6,730	6,830	6,930	7,000	7,000³	—	—
Turkey	7,044	7,982	7,799	9,322	9,336	7,411	+6.3
Taiwan	5,771	8,288	9,047	9,747	10,957	8,184	+2.7
Netherlands, The	5,082	5,518	5,681	5,412	5,171	4,067	+7.3
Yugoslavia	4,367	4,485	4,500	3,608	2,497	1,129	−37.1
Austria	4,301	4,560	4,717	4,291	4,186	3,073	−5.0
Sweden	4,595	4,779	4,692	4,454	4,248	3,161	+3.1
Hungary	3,622	3,582	3,315	2,866	1,862	1,133	−25.0
Luxembourg	3,302	3,661	3,721	3,560	3,379	2,250	−11.6
Venezuela	3,699	3,646	3,196	2,998	3,119	2,713	+18.1
Argentina	3,633	3,652	3,908	3,657	2,992	1,977	−14.6
Bulgaria	3,044	2,880	2,899	2,180	1,703	—	—
Finland	2,669	2,798	2,921	2,860	2,890	2,287	+7.2
Indonesia	2,059	2,054	2,383	2,892	3,000³	—	—
Egypt	1,433	2,025	2,114	2,235	2,541	1,854	−4.2

¹1992 figures not yet available. ²Includes the former East Germany from 1991. ³Estimate.
Source: International Iron and Steel Institute.

Table IX. World Production of Pig Iron
In 000 metric tons

Country	1987	1988	1989	1990	1991
World	508,811	538,164	544,826	531,835	507,876
Soviet Union/CIS	113,900	114,559	113,928	110,167	90,953
Japan	73,418	79,295	80,197	80,229	79,985
China	55,030	57,040	58,200	62,606	67,164
U.S.	43,917	50,572	50,677	49,666	43,999
Germany	28,517	32,453	32,777	30,097	30,969
Brazil	20,944	23,454	24,363	21,141	22,695
France	13,449	14,786	15,071	14,415	13,646
Italy	11,335	11,375	11,795	11,882	10,862
India	10,923	11,714	12,074	12,645	14,176
Poland	10,023	9,929	9,167	8,423	6,355
U.K.	12,017	13,056	12,638	12,319	11,883
Czechoslovakia	9,788	9,706	9,911	9,667	8,479
Romania	9,500	8,941	9,051	6,355	4,700²
Canada	9,719	9,498	10,139	7,346	8,268
South Korea	11,057	12,578	14,846	15,339	18,510
Belgium	8,239	9,184	8,923	9,416	9,353
Australia	5,581	5,723	6,084	6,127	5,633
South Africa	6,317	6,171	6,543	6,257	6,968
North Korea	5,900	5,900	5,900	5,900	6,000²
Spain	4,804	4,691	5,535	5,482	5,588
Netherlands, The	4,575	4,994	5,163	4,960	4,696
Taiwan	3,732	5,487	5,780	5,491	5,561
Mexico	3,712	3,639	3,230	3,645	3,039
Turkey	4,068	4,462	3,508	4,827	4,594
Austria	3,451	3,665	3,823	3,452	3,439
Yugoslavia	2,867	2,916	2,898	2,313	1,266
East Germany	2,743	2,786	2,732	2,159	—
Luxembourg	2,305	2,519	2,684	2,645	2,463
Sweden	2,314	2,492	2,638	2,736	2,812
Hungary	2,109	2,093	1,954	1,708	1,311
Finland	2,063	2,173	2,284	2,283	2,331
Argentina	1,752	1,596	2,248	2,003	1,437

¹Includes the former East Germany from 1991. ²Estimate.
Source: International Iron and Steel Institute.

445 million metric tons; for the CIS and eastern Europe, there was expected to be a further decrease in steel demand, to 115 million metric tons. With some expansion of steel use in China, world steel demand in 1993 could reach a maximum of 633 million metric tons, which would require crude steel production of roughly 725 million metric tons.   (D.F. ANDERSON)

MACHINERY AND MACHINE TOOLS

Data collected for the year 1991 revealed that, for the United States, exports of machine tools reached a record total of $1,070,000,000. Total U.S. export sales had climbed each year since 1983. As a percentage of total production, exports continued their rise and approximated 27% in 1991. The principal foreign markets for U.S.-built machine tools included Canada, Mexico, Germany, Japan, and South Korea, in that order. Sales to Mexico, Germany, Japan, South Korea, and China all posted significant gains over the levels registered in the preceding year.

Imports of machine tools to the U.S. fell for the third straight year in 1991 to a total of $2.1 billion, the lowest level since 1988. The drop in imports plus the previously noted rise in exports combined to improve the U.S. machine tool trade deficit by 15% in 1991 compared with 1990.

Machine tool consumption (the measure of new machine tools installed) fell in the U.S. by 7% from 1990 to 1991. This was a result of the economic slowdown that affected most sectors of the U.S. economy and the economies of other countries as well. In 1991 U.S. machine tool consumption totaled $4.3 billion, the lowest level since 1988. Imports as a share of total U.S consumption fell to 45.4% in 1991, down from 46.2% in 1990.

Net new orders for U.S.-built machine tools fell in 1991 to $2.6 billion, down 12% from order levels in 1990. However, the export portion of those orders jumped 26%—to their second highest level ever.

Figures for 1991 indicated that Japan continued to lead the world in machine tool production with machines worth $11.6 billion. Following in order were Germany, $8.8 billion; Italy, $3.5 billion; the U.S., $3.3 billion; the Soviet Union and its successor, the Commonwealth of Independent States (CIS), $2.5 billion; Switzerland, $2 billion; China, $1.4 billion; and the U.K., $1.3 billion. The corresponding order of countries for 1990 was Japan, Germany, the U.S.S.R., Italy, the U.S., Switzerland, the U.K., and China.

Regarding consumption, figures for 1991 indicated that Japan installed $8.3 billion worth of new machine tools, more than any other country. The countries that followed were, in order, Germany, $6 billion; the U.S., $4.3 billion; the Soviet Union and CIS, $3.4 billion; Italy, $2.7 billion; France, $1.8 billion; China, $1.8 billion; South Korea, $1.6 billion; and the U.K., $1.4 billion. The order in 1990 was: Japan, Germany, the Soviet Union, Italy, France, the U.K., South Korea, China, and Spain.

(JOHN B. DEAM)

MICROELECTRONICS

Projected worldwide sales of semiconductors rose again in 1992 by 7.8% to $58.9 billion, according to the Semiconductor Industry Association (SIA). Although falling 7% from a year earlier, Japan retained its lead with $19.5 billion, with the U.S. a close second at an estimated $17.9 billion. The largest gain in consumption, 25.3%, was achieved by the Asia Pacific market, which in 1992 claimed 17.4% of the worldwide market to Western Europe's 19.1%.

The Intel Corp., the largest chip producer in the U.S. and supplier of the 386 and 486 microprocessors used in IBM and IBM-compatible personal computers that run the DOS Operating System and Windows, announced that its new chip, code-named P5, would break from tradition and be called Pentium instead of the 586 processor. During the year Intel introduced its second-generation 486 chip, the 486DX2 processor, operating at 50 MHz. This was later improved to operate at 66 MHz. In addition, Intel introduced its low-voltage 386SL and 486SL microprocessors for use in portable and notebook computers. It also announced a $50 million joint venture with VLSI Technology, Inc., to design the chip sets that would be used in the next generation of portable computers—the hand-held or personal digital assistant.

In the race to make portable computers smaller, lighter, more efficient, and less power hungry, new plug-in devices the size of credit cards were introduced; they were being used to attach modems, networking interfaces, and solid-state mass-storage devices to small, notebook-size computers. Conforming to the Personal Computer Memory Card International Association (PCMCIA) standard and Intel's new Exchangeable Card Architecture (ExCA) specification, these cards could be exchanged between different vendors' products that conformed to the standards.

The PCMCIA cards were using the newest development in nonvolatile memory (memory that retains its information even without power). Called resident flash memory, it was already replacing some of the components in portable computers. Using the PCMCIA and ExCA specifications, the floppy disk drive on portable computers would be replaced by flash cards that ranged in size from 2.5 to 20 megabytes.

All the major U.S. chip manufacturers entered into strategic partnerships to develop "fuzzy logic" applications for their microcontroller chips. Fuzzy logic and neural networks were being used to solve complex problems by approximating the human thought process and "learning" from past experiences. Applications included object, speech, and handwriting recognition; engine diagnostics; medical diagnostics; and imaging and vision systems. Neural microchips, such as those manufactured by HNC Inc., could perform up to 1,280,000,000 "connections" per second.

Digital Equipment Corp. announced its new Alpha microchip, a reduced instruction set computing (RISC) chip. The 64-bit chip was designed to process up to 400 million instructions per second (MIPS).

(THOMAS E. KROLL)

NUCLEAR INDUSTRY

Data for 1991, released by the International Atomic Energy Agency (IAEA) in 1992, showed that construction began on two units, Wolsong 2 in South Korea and Kashiwazaki-Kariwa 6 in Japan. One unit each in Bulgaria, China, France, and Japan was connected to the grid for the first time, and one project in Bulgaria and three in Germany were suspended or canceled. Nine units were closed permanently. For the first time since 1967, no new unit was brought on-line in the U.S. At the end of 1991 there were 420 units in operation throughout the world, with a total capacity of 326,611 MW (a net fall of three units but a slight rise in total capacity compared with 1990). Nuclear plants produced 2,009.1 TW hr (terawatt hours; one terawatt equals one trillion watts) of electricity in 1991.

Atomic Energy of Canada Ltd. concluded a deal with the Korean Electric Power Co. for two pressurized heavy water reactors (PWRs), units 3 and 4 at Wolsong. The Wolsong site was expected to produce more than 2,500 MW when completed. South Korea planned to add 18 new nuclear power units before 2006; seven units were under construction in 1992, and 11 were planned.

The new nuclear station site at Higashidori would allow Japan to reach its target of 35% nuclear electricity production by 2000. The site, where four boiling-water reactor (BWR) units were planned, was the first to become available in Japan in more than six years. The Japanese Tokai 2 unit became the first BWR in the world to generate 100 million MW hr.

In the U.K. Bradwell 2, one of the two 123-MW Magnox-type nuclear units at the station, won a new lease on life from the U.K. Nuclear Installations Inspectorate, which allowed it to continue operation beyond its already extended 30-year lifetime. The unit began operation in 1962 with a design life of 20 years. It might now continue in operation until 1998.

The U.S. Nuclear Power Oversight Committee, the nuclear power industry's policy-making body, issued formal requests for "advanced nuclear power plant designs" from three groups led by Westinghouse Corp., General Electric Co., and ABB/Combustion Engineering. The winning proposals were expected to obtain U.S. Department of Energy (DOE) funding. The DOE committed more than $100 million over five years for support of the development. The Advanced Reactor Corp., an

Operators work at a Russian nuclear power plant west of St. Petersburg, where a problem with one of the reactors caused radioactive gases to be released into the atmosphere on March 24. There was no reported danger either to workers or to people outside the facility.
ALEXEI ROGOV—SYGMA

industry agglomerate, also pledged $50 million. Westinghouse was proposing a 600-MW "passive" design; General Electric was working on designs for both 600 and 1,300 MW; and the ABB/Combustion group was preparing a 1,300-MW design.

A study of advanced reactor designs by the U.S. Council for Energy Awareness showed that the 30-year average costs of electricity generated by both the medium-sized and large units would be competitive with the output from fossil-fired stations of similar sizes. Costs for various types of plants operating at the end of the decade were (in 1992 U.S. dollars) 3.8 cents per kilowatt hour for one 1,200-MW nuclear unit and 4.5 cents per kilowatt hour for one 600-MW reactor, compared with 4.8 cents per kilowatt hour for a low-emission coal-fired plant or 4.3 cents per kilowatt hour for a combined cycle gas-fired station. The estimates included decommissioning and fuel-cycle costs.

The nuclear power legacy of the Soviet Union to its successor republics resulted in a good deal of "fire-fighting" operations. The Ukraine government, for example, decided to rebuild the sarcophagus enclosing the destroyed reactor at Chernobyl so that it would last for at least 100 years. Cash prizes were offered for the best solution to the problem. Principal requirements were that the new enclosure be completed in five years at the most, normal personnel exposure safety regulations be met, and the processing and disposal of radioactive waste from the site also be included in the proposals.

Early in the year the leaders of Russia affirmed their continuing support for the IAEA in all important nuclear-related areas, including safety and the exchange of information. At a March meeting in Vienna, national regulators and utility managers from Czechoslovakia, Bulgaria, and Russia discussed measures taken or contemplated to improve the safety of the VVER-type pressurized water reactors.

Another joint agreement between the Czechoslovak manufacturer Skoda and a Western company was announced as part of the process of privatization from a single state enterprise into two companies, Skoda Energo and Skoda Transport. Both companies were to have Siemens as a foreign partner to provide a positive link with Western technology. Siemens was to contribute finance, technology, and work orders to the joint-venture companies, while Skoda would provide assets, production capacity, and skilled workers. Skoda Energo would be active in all forms of energy production, with emphasis on ecologically benign sources, encompassing the four original power engineering plants in Plzen and Prague for turbines, nuclear machinery, electrotechnology, and automation engineering.

The French nuclear program, which had been the most intensive in the world (France produced 72.7% of its total output of electricity by nuclear power in 1991), continued the slowdown that had begun in recent years. At the start of 1992 there were 56 units in operation, 5 units being built, and only 6 in the planning stages. The state-owned utility, Electricité de France, approached the government for approval for at least two new units of 1,455 MW.

A report from the French safety authority on the problems with the commercial-scale fast-breeder reactor at Creys-Malville (called Superphénix) pointed to "inherent weaknesses" in the technology, particularly the liquid-sodium cooling system, which had bedeviled the early operating experience with the plant. Even if the government decided to allow the project to continue, the report indicated that it should be for only a limited time to gain as much information as possible from this prototype project. The report called for studies to be made on using the reactor to "burn" actinides in a nonbreeding mode in order to reduce the large stockpile of plutonium accumulating at the La Hague reprocessing plant.

A report by the U.S. National Research Council endorsed advanced versions of the liquid-metal reactor together with the "passive" advanced light water reactors. The council said that they offered the best prospects for long- and near-term development in the U.S.

The new collaboration between old rivals Framatome in France and Siemens in Germany, joining in a search for contracts in a lean market for new and replacement nuclear steam generators, was rewarded with contracts for 12 units in Spain and 3 in Sweden. Mitsubishi, in its first successful foray for nuclear business outside Japan, won an order for three steam-generator replacements at Tihange in Belgium.

Work on the second unit at Angra in Brazil had come to a stop in 1988 after 11 years following the transfer of the nuclear project to Furnas, a concessionary of the state-owned electricity company Electrobras. The World Bank, which does not finance nuclear projects, promptly ceased Brazil's energy financing. A new agreement between the Brazilian government and the German financing agency KFW, together with the Dresdner Bank, was designed to allow the project to be completed by 1997. The negotiations between the governments succeeded after a $130 million reduction was achieved in the projected costs.

The new heavy water plant at Arroyito in Argentina was due to have completed its commissioning by the end of 1992, when it would begin production of heavy water for Atucha 2, the German-built PWR. Argentina might have to sell its two other nuclear plants (Embalse and Atucha 1) to private investors to finance the completion of Atucha 2.   (RICHARD A. KNOX)

PAINTS AND VARNISHES

The economy and the environment continued to weigh heavily on paint makers in the West; expansion was a more typical experience for their counterparts in East Asia. While recession was biting deeply into paint output and profits—in the U.K. and the U.S. in particular—environmental legislation in Europe and North America was making additional demands on the industry. At the same time, Southeast Asia's buoyant paint markets were offering attractive opportunities for joint ventures, technology licensing, and trade. Specialties, such as coil and powder coatings, enjoyed good growth prospects. The Chinese mainland, with its vast, as-yet-untapped market, was beginning to exert an increasing pull. Its paint output rose by 9.3% in 1991 to 928,000 metric tons.

Another market with an as-yet-unrealized potential was eastern Europe. In the wake of the privatization wave, paint production there had fallen drastically. Nonetheless, Western expansion into the area was proceeding. Restoration work in eastern Germany brought a brisk demand for building paint, as shown in the expansion of paint production from only 17,500 tons in the first half of 1991 to 42,000 tons during the same period in 1992. In general, the globalization of marketing strategies was finding expression in worldwide takeovers and joint ventures. The consolidation of the powder coatings market took a step backward, however, when the announced merger between the powder coatings interests of the Ferro Corp. and ICI failed to take place.

In the U.K. the stepwise compliance schedule of the 1990 Environmental Protection Act began with authorization applications for paint makers and industrial users during 1992, but the upgrading deadline for paint manufacture was postponed to April 1999. In the European Communities at large, the seventh amendment to the 1967 Dangerous Substance Directive—with its new "dangerous for the environment" symbol—was adopted. Also adopted during the year was the voluntary EC-wide Eco-Label Regulation. Although its administrative provisions were in place, the individual criteria for paints were still under development. Meanwhile, France produced its own national Eco-Label for paints. In the U.S., air emissions and waste controls continued to dominate the regulatory landscape, but lead abatement in old paintwork was emerging as a major problem. Much of the industry's research and development agenda was now dictated by environmental considerations with the replacement of conventional solvent-based paint the prime goal. Waterborne coatings currently appeared as a viable alternative.

(HELMA JOTISCHKY)

PHARMACEUTICALS

When originally proposed in the mid-1980s, so-called user fees for U.S. Food and Drug Administration (FDA)-regulated industries encountered considerable opposition. The primary objection hinged on the fact that the fees to be paid by manufacturers applying for new drug application (NDA) approvals, certification of food or cosmetic colours or additives, or agency approval of new medical devices were earmarked for general revenues, meaning they could be used for any purpose, not just for improving FDA efficiency or staffing. Small generic drug companies saw the scheme as an unfair burden, since the drugs they were selling were essentially copies of truly innovative drugs and thus needed less reviewer time and effort. The food and cosmetic industries had similar objections.

After several years of stalemate, a compromise was reached in the fall of 1992 involving reconfiguration of the scheme so that user fees could go directly to improving and streamlining the FDA approval process, and limitation of the notion to prescription drugs. The result was passage of the Prescription Drug User Fee Act of 1992. During its five years of life, the measure was expected to bring in about $330 million, allowing the FDA to hire 600 new examiners. The cost to firms submitting NDAs would rise from $100,000 to $233,000 per application over five years, and other fees would also increase.

In the fall a U.S. General Accounting Office study of prescription drug prices over a six-year period found that the price increase of 29 widely used drugs "generally exceeded 100 percent," with some prices rising by 200 to 300%. During this period, the Consumer Price Index (CPI) rose 26.2%, while the CPI for prescription drugs rose by 67%. Findings like these prompted criticism of drug manufacturers during the election campaign. The Pharmaceutical Manufacturers Association asserted that price increases had "moderated" since 1989, but this did not reassure Wall Street analysts, who saw pressure building for government controls on prices and profits.

There were further repercussions of the generic drug scandal, with heavy sentences and fines handed down to generic company officers found guilty of fabricating phony bioequivalence or quality-control records, mislabeling drugs, or attempting to foil FDA investigators. The business of at least a dozen companies was curtailed by FDA

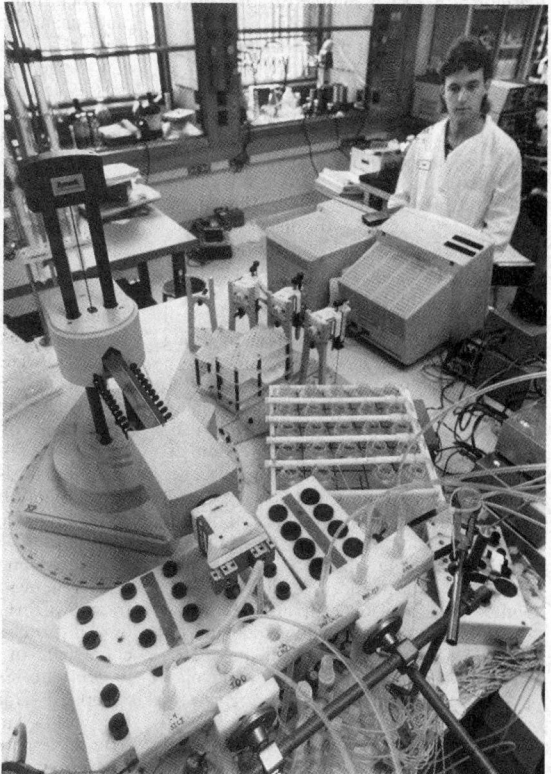

TERRENCE MCCARTHY—
THE NEW YORK TIMES

A lab technician helping in the search for new drugs works with equipment that combines traditional screening methods with modern biotechnology. Rather than testing entire protein molecules for their activity against disease-causing organisms, the new approach tested millions of different, synthesized protein fragments, or peptides, for their molecular interactions with the organisms; once such masses of information were processed by computer, researchers hoped to find clues for building more effective therapeutic proteins.

orders. The generic drug business remained strong, however, in part because of rising prices for innovator drugs and tough cost-containment policies in hospitals and other institutions.

There were clear signals from a few major drug firms that they were preparing to enter the generic drug business with cheaper versions of their original innovative drugs, some before outside competitors could move into the market. Eighty or more very profitable drugs would come off patent by 1995, and one way to freeze generic competition was to switch a profitable prescription drug to over-the-counter (OTC) status. However, the possibility of side effects could make such a switch nonproductive, and a condition requiring physician monitoring was unlikely to yield a drug that could achieve OTC status. Furthermore, the new user fee law prescribed a $100,000 application fee for manufacturers that opted for the switch procedure.

(DONALD A. DAVIS)

PLASTICS

At the start of 1992, the U.S. and the U.K. were experiencing a recession that spread during the year to the rest of Europe and Japan. This severely affected the main plastics users, namely the automotive, appliance, construction, and packaging industries. The depression was still deepening at year's end. However, demand for plastics materials held up better than in the downturn of the early 1980s. Reduced car production, for instance, was to some extent balanced by the still-rising weight of plastics used per unit, while plastics continued to make inroads into packaging because their superior protective properties permitted longer shelf-lives for perishable food products in a time of slower sales.

The industry's problems arose from slack prices and small or negative profit margins rather than volume turnover. Most chemical manufacturers identified the large-tonnage basic thermoplastics as the principal factor in their drastically reduced earnings, and as ever the cause was excess production capacity. This was, and would continue to be, most severe in Europe, where the lessons of the 1980s were clearly unlearned. In addition, European industry leaders expressed worry over the future threat of imports from the many new low-cost plants being erected in less developed countries, especially in the Asia-Pacific region. Plastics imports into western Europe, notably of polyvinyl chloride from eastern Europe and the U.S., were already rising sharply.

It was, therefore, not surprising that the year saw a spate of planned mergers or exchanges (all subject to ratification by the European Communities on competitive grounds). The most important was the proposed joint venture between the Royal Dutch/Shell Group and Montecatini of Italy covering all their interests in polyethylene and polypropylene. Himont, a Montecatini subsidiary, and its licensees together accounted for some 60% of installed world polypropylene capacity. Global demand for polypropylene exceeded 10 million metric tons per year, around 12% of world plastics consumption, and was expected to go on rising.

Engineering plastics were less immune to the general troubles of the industry than in

earlier years. Nevertheless, manufacturers continued to put major effort into developing improved grades of established materials, such as polyamides, polycarbonate, and urethanes. There was some withdrawal from specialties whose prospects no longer seemed promising, given the cutbacks in high-technology industries such as defense. Thus Bayer disposed of its polyphenylene sulfide business, and both ICI and Hoechst ceased polyetherether ketone production. Composite and hybrid materials also experienced a year of mixed fortunes. The most noteworthy effort in this sector was the construction by Montecatini, using extremely advanced technology, of a series of five yachts in the *Il Moro di Venezia* series in a bid to win the 1992 America's Cup race. The boat entered came in second, but much experience in the composites field was gained.

Questions of plastics waste management continued to loom large. There was growing realization—by the industry if not by legislators—that mechanical recycling of all mixed municipal plastics refuse was impractical. Economic end uses for such vast tonnages of material were simply not available. Alternative approaches of clean combustion with energy recovery or chemical recycling (converting plastics back to their original feedstocks) therefore received increasing attention.   (ROBIN C. PENFOLD)

PRINTING

Economic woes cast a shadow over the printing and graphic communications industries, especially in the English-speaking world. In Britain hundreds of printing companies closed down. The world's two largest printing-press manufacturers reported serious declines in sales of machines to Britain and the U.S.

Innovation proceeded apace, however. German offset machine makers, after at first belittling the advances in automatic plate change pioneered by Japanese manufacturers, climbed on the bandwagon. A new range of compact web offset colour presses designed to meet the needs of both newspapers and the medium-quality colour market was launched by Heidelberg Harris, MAN Roland, and Rockwell Graphic Systems. At the lower end of the web offset press market, Indian manufacturers Bandhu and Manugraph made sales to the U.S. and European countries, as well as Southeast Asia. Heidelberg Harris introduced an extra-wide "Sunday Press" for web offset, aimed at competing with rotogravure in magazine and catalog production, primarily in the U.S. The *Daily Mail*, in London, successfully used Koenig & Bauer–Albert flexo presses to print colour on coated paper.

European printers and converters became enthusiastic about ISO 9000 quality assurance standards, but U.S. printers working for multinationals that demanded ISO 9000 certification complained about the added cost burden. However, total production-control systems and management-information systems, such as Bobst Base 2000 from Switzerland, MAN Roland's Pecom, or Ahlstrom Automation, which had become part of Honeywell, were geared to incorporate ISO 9000 steps.

Japan's Dainippon Ink & Chemicals, the world's largest maker of printing inks, opened a new Sun Chemical ink factory in Germany. The Sun Chemical divisions

in the U.S. and Europe introduced environmentally friendly soybean-based inks. America's largest printing group, R.R. Donnelley & Sons, expanded into Mexico, Singapore, and Spain. The latter country also attracted Watmoughs of Britain and Hachette of France.

Security printers found new and rapidly growing markets printing bank notes for the newly independent republics of the former Soviet Union. Britain's De La Rue and Germany's Giesecke & Devrient were the main beneficiaries, but François-Oberthur in France, U.S. Banknote, and Canadian Bank Note also benefited substantially.

(W. PINCUS JASPERT)

RUBBER

After a period of restructuring and rationalization, the rubber industry returned to problems of cost, supply, and recycling in 1992. Higher prices for basic feedstocks such as styrene and butadiene forced most tire manufacturers to raise prices and, for the most part, the increases held. Prices for natural rubber continued to be depressed, however, causing many producing nations to call for a change in the basic pricing mechanism, the International Natural Rubber Agreement (INRA), which would come up for renewal in 1993. Even the purchase of 40,000 tons of natural rubber during the summer by the INRA organization failed to influence the price. Malaysia, Indonesia, and Thailand, the three largest natural-rubber-producing countries, were debating forming an OPEC-like cartel. Meanwhile, increased production from Indonesia, Thailand, and other Southeast Asian countries, coupled with the reopening of Liberia's natural rubber trade, kept prices low. The Liberian plantation, owned by Bridgestone, was shut down again at the end of 1992, a victim of the nation's internal strife. In all, natural rubber production was expected to increase slightly in 1992, to 5.4 million metric tons from 5.3 million tons in 1991.

Usage of synthetic rubber was expected to be 160,000 metric tons lower than in 1991, mainly because of a drop-off in buying by central Europe and the countries of the former Soviet Union. A 2.8% increase in synthetic rubber consumption was predicted for the rest of the world. Worldwide usage was expected to be 9,210,000 tons, making this the second straight year of decline. There was much interest in central Europe and the former U.S.S.R. as these countries began switching to market-driven economies, but outdated equipment and the scarcity of working capital made potential investors cautious. In one significant move, Kautschuk-Gesellschaft, the largest rubber trader in Europe, entered a joint venture with Russia's Efremov to market Efremov's polybutadiene and related products. Earlier in the year, Kautschuk-Gesellschaft had completed its merger with France's Safic-Alcan & Cie.

Elsewhere in Europe, Pirelli planned to lay off more than 1,000 workers and close its Sicilian motorcycle-tire plant; the company also planned to consolidate its European truck-tire-manufacturing operations in one plant. Pirelli sold its antivibration components business in Germany, Spain, and the U.K. to BTR p.l.c. Netherlands-based DSM bought Novacor Chemicals' thermoplastic elastomer business, gaining entry into the North American market.

The centre groove and unique tread design of the Aquatred gives the tire better traction on wet pavements. A product of Goodyear, the award-winning tire was highly successful commercially.

GOODYEAR TIRE & RUBBER COMPANY

Most increases in capacity occurred in Asia and the Pacific Rim. A \$285 million investment for 60 technical rubber projects in Shanghai's "Tyre City" would enable the area to produce six million tires annually when completed. Michelin created a second joint manufacturing venture in Thailand and acquired a minority interest in MRF Ltd., India's largest tire manufacturer. Pirelli started a number of projects, including a light-truck tire plant and a one million-unit radial passenger-car tire plant in China and a passenger-car tire plant in Indonesia.

Elsewhere in the area, the Indonesian tire maker Gadjah Tunggal increased capacity fivefold; Asiatic Development of Malaysia was constructing a 1,200-ton-per-year deproteinized natural rubber facility; and Taiwan Synthetic Rubber increased production by 10%.

In North America much of the news in 1992 concerned marketing strategies. Goodyear, which had sold its tires exclusively through company-owned stores and independent tire dealers, announced it would start selling tires at other outlets when it signed a deal with Sears Roebuck. Firestone announced that it would sell Michelin tires in its stores. Recycling of tires got a boost when Congress passed a bill requiring at least 5% rubber content for asphalt used in federal highway projects. The Rubber Manufacturers Association predicted that this would consume 80 million used tires annually by 1997.

Many rubber-product manufacturers returned to profitability during the year. The top three, Japan's Bridgestone Corp., France's Michelin, and Goodyear of the U.S., all reported earnings reversals in 1992 after a period of record losses. Goodyear reported record earnings of \$279.3 million for the first nine months after posting an \$8.5 million loss for the same period in 1991. Bridgestone reported that its Bridgestone/Firestone subsidiary showed monthly profits in August and September for the first time in "some time," according to a company spokesman, and it expected to finish the year with positive results after losing \$400 million in 1991. Michelin reported more than doubling its operating profits for the first half of 1992, the first time since the second half of 1989 that the firm had been in the black on a net basis.

(DONALD SMITH)

SHIPBUILDING

The world order book, comprising ships under construction and ships on order on which construction has not begun, increased slightly compared with the previous year. The second-quarter figures issued by Lloyd's Register showed the total volume of tonnage in the world order book to be 41,408,594 gross tonnage (gt), an increase of 1,837,812 gt over the same quarter of 1991.

The total order book was made up of 17,726,092 gt of ships under construction and 23,682,502 gt of ships on order. The increased figure for the world order book was in fact due to a large increase of 3,534,844 gt of ships under construction. However, this was offset by a downward trend of ships on order, which showed a decline of 1,697,032 gt.

There were some significant changes in the types of ship being built and on order. The second-quarter figures from Lloyd's Register revealed a reversal of the downward trend for bulk carriers. The total world order book for this type of ship was 9,023,495 gt, a startling increase of 3,510,653 gt. Significantly, much of this was due to an increase of orders on which construction had not begun, totaling 2,754,217 gt. The world order book for oil tankers, on the other hand, decreased by 627,406 gt and for general cargo ships, at 6,091,628, declined by 1,212,081 gt.

There was continuing concern about the vulnerability of bulk carriers to side structural failures that result in total loss of the ship. The figures for 1991 revealed that more than 1,200 seamen died in shipping accidents that resulted in total losses—more than three times as many as in 1990. The cause of many of these sinkings was cracked shell plating, almost certainly resulting from corroded and/or damaged frames.

This continuing concern about bulk carrier safety led to the introduction of on-line stress monitoring of ships' hulls to provide an early warning of any structural weakness. Apart from the appalling loss of life, the financial drain was considerable. Mounting bulk carrier losses brought insurance brokers' discontent with the performance of the ship-classification societies to a head. Insurers in London took matters into their own hands and announced that underwriters would henceforth ask the Salvage As-

sociation to carry out structural condition surveys where there was doubt about the seaworthiness of a vessel. Four leading ship-classification societies responded to this action by saying that underwriters should support the classification system and called for the general application by underwriters of a strengthened Classification Warranty clause.

Specialized ship types of interest included small waterplane area twin hull (SWATH) vessels. During the year the SWATH-design 20,295-gt cruise ship *Radisson Diamond* was delivered to its Finnish owners by Finnyards Oy in Rauma, Fin. The largest ship delivered the second quarter of 1992 was the 322,132-dwt (deadweight ton) ore carrier *Bergeland,* built by Hyundai Heavy Industries at Ulsan, South Korea.

The vexing question of phasing out government subsidies for shipbuilding appeared to be making more headway in Japan than in Europe. The Japanese advisory committee to the minister of transport recommended the termination of all the protectionist measures adopted by Japan for its shipbuilding industry during the last 20 years. However, national differences within the European Communities on the issue of shipyard support were making it more difficult to achieve an international consensus on the phasing out of subsidies.

The second-quarter figures again emphasized the supremacy of Japan as the leading shipbuilding country in the world, even though its share of the world order book, at 35.5%, was about three percentage points lower than in the previous year. Nevertheless, Japan's order book of 14,692,702 gt was 6,605,329 gt more than the next shipbuilding giant, South Korea, which captured 8,087,373 gt of the world order book.

(EDWARD CROWLEY)

TELECOMMUNICATIONS

AT&T announced new long-distance calling records in the United States during 1992. On Mother's Day a holiday record was set when 101 million calls were placed, more than 1½ times the normal volume. During a period when airlines were competing against one another by offering reduced fares, calling volume over an 11-day period reached 1.6 billion, including a one-day record 177.4 million calls on June 1. This volume was 20 million more than the previous record set in 1991 on the traditionally heaviest traffic day, the Monday after Thanksgiving. Another record was set on the four days after the Hurricane Andrew disaster, during which an average 125 million calls per day were placed over a four-day period.

In fact, the telephone network survived a number of disasters during the year. Although localized outages occurred, the overall network was never compromised. Included in those disasters were two major hurricanes, Andrew and Iniki; a major riot in the Los Angeles area; and the flooding of the tunnel system that runs under Chicago's business district. During cleanup efforts after the flood, three Illinois Bell fibre-optic cables were damaged, but a major catastrophe was averted when alternate routes, installed after a disastrous 1988 central office fire, were brought into service.

The U.S. Federal Communications Commission (FCC) ended the monopoly of the local exchange carriers (LECs) by opening

AT&T's VideoPhone 2500 used compression technology to eliminate nonessential features of the colour picture so that it could be transmitted over existing copper wiring. Intended for the mass market, the videophone plugged into a regular wall telephone jack.

AT&T

the local telephone network to competition. The FCC ordered the LECs to permit interconnection in the local exchange, allowing other service providers to locate equipment in the LEC's central offices in order to connect to the public network. The two major providers of alternate access were Teleport Communications Group, Inc., of New York City and Metropolitan Fiber Systems, Inc., in Illinois.

In January United Telecommunications Inc. acquired the final 20% of GTE's interest in U.S. Sprint, which had been formed in 1986 as a joint venture between the two, and in February UTI changed its name to Sprint Corp. At the end of May Sprint announced that it would acquire the Centel Corp., paying about $2,850,000,000 for 85 million shares of Centel stock. Sprint, the third largest long-distance company in the U.S., behind AT&T and MCI, thus became the first telecommunications company to offer local, cellular, and long-distance services.

In November AT&T announced plans to buy a 33% interest in McCaw Cellular Communications, Inc., the largest cellular service provider in the U.S., at a cost of $3.8 billion. This would position AT&T for its return to providing customers with direct service into its telephone network, bypassing the LEC's land-based lines with cellular technology. In 1991 AT&T had paid more than $18 billion to the LECs to connect customers to its network.

The wireless industry was further influenced by the FCC's decision to push ahead with plans for personal communications service (PCS), which would eventually merge the cordless telephone, pager, cellular and personal telephone, and portable computer into the telecommunications network. This concept envisioned a person's having one telephone and one telephone number that would follow him or her from home to car to office to city throughout the world. To facilitate U.S. dominance in this new industry, the FCC assigned high-frequency radio bandwidth in the two-gigaHertz range to PCS. AT&T provided the first personal, portable telephone number when it announced the EasyReach 700 Service, in which a 700 prefix is used to assign

lifetime long-distance telephone numbers to subscribers.

In the latest race to build the world's smallest and lightest cellular telephone, the $995–$1,195, 175.5-g (6.2-oz.) Minivox Lite was announced by Audiovox of Hauppauge, N.Y., in late August. Within a month, Motorola Inc. announced its MicroTAC Ultra Lite at 167 g (5.9 oz.) and $945.

Another innovative product introduced in 1992 was the videophone. In January AT&T announced its VideoPhone 2500. Selling at $1,499, it became the world's first colour videophone that worked over standard telephone lines. In September MCI countered with its own videophone selling at $750.

The $450 million TAT-9 undersea fibre-optic cable was completed during the year. Linking the North American continent with Europe, the 8,993-km (5,586-mi) cable could process the equivalent of 80,000 simultaneous calls, moving voice, data, and video signals.   (THOMAS E. KROLL)

TEXTILES

Depression throughout the world textile industry was expected to last for some time to come and to be followed by only a modest recovery. In the U.S. and throughout Europe the textile industry was again undergoing a major transition, with many small, uncompetitive companies being forced into liquidation.

This implied that larger groups were getting larger. By their very size, large companies are more vulnerable, particularly in the specialist areas where small and more versatile companies can react more quickly. However, electronic communications being developed by the retail trades was linked, increasingly, to textile manufacturing, so even big companies could be alerted almost instantly to changes in fashion trends. "Quick response" was a byword throughout the industry. Parallel with it was "just in time," meaning that production was being scheduled in such a way that stocks of a required product were shipped and arrived just when they were required.

There was a growing feeling that the technologically advanced nations should open their markets to textiles and textile prod-

ucts from the less developed countries. One argument was that it is more economical to convert fabrics into finished products in areas where wages are low. An interesting—but probably only temporary—development involved German companies obtaining textiles made under contract in formerly communist countries.

Another developing trade was the shipment of container loads of suitings into eastern Europe, where the fabrics were converted into garments and returned in the same containers.

(PETER LENNOX-KERR)

Wool. The resumption of a free auction system in Australia and abandonment of the failed reserve price scheme led to a stronger market. After falling back from a June 1991 peak of 597 cents per kilogram (1 kg = 2.2 lb), prices, as measured by the Australian Wool Corporation's market indicator, showed exceptional volatility. A new peak of 648 cents in March 1992 was followed by a gradual softening, with the indicator falling below the 500-cent mark in October.

The prolonged recession in world trade, along with the problems created by the collapse of communism in Russia and eastern Europe, kept wool prices low. A noteworthy exception was China, where the economy expanded, leading to a very welcome improvement in demand for wool in Australia, New Zealand, and South America. Low wool prices and the return to free-market conditions also helped raise wool's competitive position in the fibre market. By March 1992 wool accounted for 34.4% of overall fibre consumption in the wool textile industry, 1.5 percentage points better than a year earlier.

Low wool prices continued to cause reduced production of wool. Total world production figures (in thousand metric tons clean) were: 1990–91 season, 1,934; 1991–92, 1,735; 1992–93, 1,667. The Australian stockpile of 4.5 million bales (1 bale = 348 lb or 158 kg), equal to a full season's production, was reduced by about half a million bales in 1991–92. Sales in the opening months of 1992–93 were low as the Australian Wool Realisation Commission sought to avoid market disruption.

(H.M.F. MALLETT)

Cotton. During 1992 Pakistan, which depends on cotton products for the bulk of its export trade, suffered massive flooding in the Punjab and Sindh provinces. Initial official estimates suggested that 10% of the crop had been destroyed, but others placed the loss at nearer 20%. In Sindh nearly 60% of the crop was destroyed.

In the U.S. there was currently a major move by cotton growers to concentrate increasingly on extra long staple (ELS) cottons. This was taking place at a time when, despite world depression, consumption of cotton was rising.

Textile specialists had stressed the need to develop finer and longer cotton fibres, better suited to the newer spinning processes. That this was being taken seriously by growers could be seen from the expanding ELS program in the U.S. Meanwhile, there was a report from Japan of the development of a "microfibre" cotton, reported to be an ideal raw material for conversion into very-fine-count yarns for ultrahigh-quality shirtings and similar upmarket products.

In Israel, where water availability was a growing problem, a somewhat different line of development was being followed. Sivon and Eldad were two new varieties of medium-staple cotton that offered a 15% greater yield than previous varieties and could be grown with very much less water. It was claimed that water requirements might be reduced by up to 30%. If this proved to be so, there was an exciting prospect for Israeli export of cottonseed to arid countries. (PETER LENNOX-KERR)

Silk. The international silk community continued to undergo a painful process of readjustment following the boom of 1988–89. With the exception of the Chinese domestic market, demand declined everywhere. China suffered severe floods in July 1991, which caused considerable damage to silk-growing areas. Nevertheless, stocks of raw material grew uncomfortably large. The Chinese cut prices by 12–20% in the winter of 1991–92. European manufacturers lost money on their inventories, and confidence was undermined further. A growing number of low-priced silk garments pouring into Europe and the U.S. from East Asia made sales even more difficult for Western manufacturers.

In Japan, where raw silk continued to be protected, demand also declined, and the average price was 12,549 yen per kilogram in 1991, 4% lower than in 1990 and the lowest in several years. The decrease in the world price for silk hit newly developing silk countries, but encouraging news came from southern Africa, where projects aimed at the domestic market began to take off. Frequent offerings of cocoons were made by the former Soviet republics anxious to secure foreign currency.

Production figures in the three most important silk-producing countries in 1991 were as follows: China 48,486 metric tons, India 11,600 tons, Japan 5,526 tons. Because of silk garment importation, consumption of silk products did not decline as much as the gloomy market might imply. Total world silk production was estimated at 71,811 tons in 1990 and 76,526 tons in 1991. (ANTHONY H. GADDUM)

Man-Made Fibres. It was expected that by the turn of the century the largest producer of man-made fibre in the world would be China. Throughout the country massive new plants were being built, most of them for polyester, the leading man-made commodity fibre. Polyester fibres, a British invention now celebrating its first half century, had proved to be the most versatile of all the new polymers introduced to the textile trade.

When polypropylene was "discovered" as a basic polymer for making fibres, it was thought that because the raw material was a gas (propylene) that previously had been burned off in the oil-refining process, it would be the cheapest raw material for the fibre trade.

However, the fibre proved to be almost inert and undyeable in its normal form. Over the years various oil companies became involved in making fibre from polypropylene, but most had little success. Recently, a small U.S. company discovered that the metallurgy of the equipment that had been used—the same as that used to produce nylon or polyester fibres—made it unsuitable for extruding polypropylene. Now a new generation of what were de-

scribed as "enhanced polyolefin fibres" was being introduced. They were produced with the use of a modifying component and extruded on equipment made of metals that would not be affected by the molten polymer flowing through it. It was hard to predict where this development would lead, but already the virtually nonabsorbent fibre had been made into undergarments that could be worn to provide comfort under bulletproof vests and into tennis shirts that would not stick under the arms.
(PETER LENNOX-KERR)

TOBACCO

An all-time record harvest marked the quincentenary of Columbus' transplanting tobacco and the smoking habit from the Caribbean to Europe. More than 117 countries cultivated tobacco in 1992, reaping some 6,866,000,000 kg (15,137,000,000 lb) and generating at least $140 billion per year in taxes.

World consumption in 1992, estimated at 6,549,000,000 kg (14,438,100,000 lb), was fractionally below the previous year's record. Smoking, predominantly of cigarettes, fell only in the 28% of the world where vigorous antitobacco campaigning was allied with high tobacco taxes—the U.S., Canada, most of Western Europe, and Australasia. Other countries, while aware of the health argument, responded sluggishly. Bans on smoking in public places were common, but enforcement was lax. In most of the world, population increase and smoking by newly emancipated women held consumption level or carried it upward.

Tobacco growing was increasingly concentrated in the Third World, which remained indifferent to the implications of the smoking and health debate. For most less developed nations, no other crop could match the cash returns that farmers could earn from tobacco, the price stability of its market, or its huge capacity to generate rural employment.

Tax differentials between adjacent countries and shortages in eastern Europe created a 1992 boom in cigarette smuggling—into Canada from the U.S. and into, around, and westward from the postcommunist states of Europe. Famous-name American-blend brands were the most popular in trade along the line of the former iron curtain. It was expected that the contraband trade would make fresh gains in 1993 as the European Communities abolished internal barriers without harmonizing widely divergent tobacco-tax levels. Soaring taxes also explained unprecedented sales of economy cigarettes and, in Germany, sales of tobacco rolls (cylinders of cut tobacco that could be smoked only when slid into hulls of cigarette paper) big enough to eat into the conventional cigarette trade. A tax loophole allowed rolls to sell at around half the price of factory-made cigarettes.
(MICHAEL F. BARFORD)

TOURISM

The travel industry faced 1992 in an optimistic frame of mind. Package tour bookings were ahead of 1990, previously the best year, and the 500th anniversary of Columbus' voyage to the Americas was to be marked by a number of special events. With the 1991 Gulf war now history, prospects looked good. By midyear, however, with economic recession deepening, the realiza-

tion dawned that 1992 results, while not exceptional, were very satisfactory in the circumstances.

Worldwide international arrivals, which had reached 449 million in 1991, were expected to grow by 4% in 1992 (compared with a 1.4% decline in 1991) to 467 million. Worldwide international tourism receipts rose by 6–7% in 1992 to $278 billion (compared with 2.3% growth and $260,763,000,000 in the previous year). Europe earned 52% of world tourism receipts in 1991, followed by the Americas (29%) and the Asia-Pacific area (15%). Average receipts earned per arrival in 1991 amounted to $581.

U.S. outbound travel moved ahead of the Gulf war-affected totals of 1991 but failed to improve beyond 1990 (though some Asia-Pacific countries like Hong Kong and Singapore were exceptions). One major problem, high U.S. dollar prices, was resolved only in August when the Italian, Spanish, and U.K. currencies were devalued. Meanwhile, hoteliers competed fiercely to maintain their share of the U.S. business market. German travel spending abroad was second only to that of the U.S. in 1991 ($31,650,000,000 as against $39,418,000,000), and the strong currency encouraged outbound travel in 1992. In third place came Japan ($23,983,000,000). Despite the recession, Japanese outbound travel in 1992 was reportedly up 20% in volume terms, and spending soared 30% in dollar terms.

Airline overcapacity, a price war to secure passengers on North Atlantic routes, and relatively attractive dollar prices for meals and accommodations helped boost incoming tourism to the U.S. in 1992 by 14%. U.S. resort tourism was hard hit in the fall by hurricanes that caused millions

Table X. Major Tourism Earners and Spenders
In $000,000

Major earners	Receipts	
	1981	1991
United States	12,168	45,551
France	7,193	21,300
Italy	7,554	19,668
Spain	6,716	19,004
Austria	5,690	13,956
United Kingdom	5,938	12,588
Germany	6,278	10,947
Switzerland	3,981	7,064
Canada	2,552	5,537
Hong Kong	1,449	5,078
Singapore	1,090	5,020
Mexico	1,760	4,355
Thailand	983	4,295
Australia	1,251	4,183
Netherlands, The	1,577	4,074
Portugal	1,023	3,700
Denmark	1,239	3,475
Belgium	1,585	3,468
South Korea	448	3,446
Japan	735	3,435
Major spenders	Expenditure	
United States	11,460	39,418
Germany	17,853	31,650
Japan	4,616	23,983
United Kingdom	6,478	16,793
Italy	1,664	13,300
France	5,752	12,338
Canada	3,200	10,526
Netherlands, The	3,648	7,886
Austria	2,788	7,449
Sweden	2,239	6,104
Switzerland	2,152	5,682
Belgium	2,644	5,543
Spain	1,008	4,530
Australia	1,847	3,940
South Korea	439	3,785
Denmark	1,269	3,377
Norway	1,433	3,207
Finland	536	2,634
Mexico	1,547	2,146
Singapore	438	2,019

Source: World Tourism Organization, Madrid

Visitors to Euro Disneyland crowd Main Street, U.S.A., with Sleeping Beauty's Castle in the background. Located 32 km (20 mi) east of Paris, the park offered the usual complement of Disney attractions and drew tourists from other European countries as well as French visitors.
PASCAL DELLA ZUANA—SYGMA

of dollars of damage in Hawaii and Florida. Caribbean destinations had mixed results, as did mainland South America, though the "Earth Summit" in Rio de Janeiro in June attracted a record number of visitors. The Maghreb countries reported a big improvement in 1992. South Africa showed continued strong growth, and Israel, Jordan, and Egypt recovered strongly from Gulf war reverses.

France targeted a record visitor total of 56 million for 1992. The spring opening of Euro Disneyland east of Paris augured well for the season, and six million visitors were welcomed in the first five months of operation. Nevertheless, slack domestic demand at the new theme park, combined with poor weather and difficulties in handling group visits, suggested scope for improvement. When truck drivers blockaded main highways in France during July to protest new driving penalties, the French National Hotel Federation claimed a 60% "no show" rate for July hotel reservations. In 1991 the French tourism industry had recorded a F 51.3 million trade surplus.

Spain was confident of ending 1992 with at least a 7% increase in tourist arrivals and was on target at midyear. Expo 92, held at Seville from April to October, recorded 42 million visits. World Tourism Day, September 27, was observed at the Expo site. The new Madrid–Seville 300-km/h (186-mph) high-speed train, inaugurated in the spring, operated at over 90% capacity throughout the Expo. The Olympic Games in Barcelona also attracted record crowds. Meanwhile, hoteliers on Spain's Costa del Sol and Costa Blanca expressed concern about low occupancies. In the view of regional hotel associations, there was a need to shut down older properties, accentuate training, and participate actively in environmental programs.

Early figures for Italy showed a continuing decline in tourism, attributed to rising prices and the need to rethink and restructure tourist facilities. London hotels began 1992 with a 10-year trading low, but by the time London's World Travel Market opened in November, the devaluation of

sterling had improved prospects. Tourism in former Yugoslavia, once a popular destination, was virtually nonexistent as the area was torn by civil war.

In the Asia-Pacific region, Australia experienced a 16% increase, and tourism in New Zealand rose 13%. Rules for tourist visits to the Antarctic continent were submitted to the November session of signatories to the Antarctic Treaty. Each year, an estimated 6,500 tourists visited Antarctica aboard specially equipped cruise ships. China continued to make rapid progress in its tourism development, with a 49% increase in arrivals during 1992. Russia estimated foreign tourism at 6.9 million arrivals in 1991, 1.5% of the world total. With the creation in 1992 of a Ministry of Culture and Tourism, it hoped to increase foreign tourism 50% by 1995.

(PETER SHACKLEFORD)

WOOD PRODUCTS

The severe and protracted recession that afflicted most world economies in 1991 persisted into 1992. However, at least in Europe, softwood imports regained lost ground and were expected to grow by around 3% to 25.5 million cu m (1 cu m = 35.3 cu ft), with consumption growing marginally to just under 74 million cu m. The outlook in North America also brightened toward the end of the year. Softwood production had fallen by almost 5% in Canada in 1991 and by more than 6% in the U.S., but an increase in housing starts in both countries sparked a rise in lumber consumption to a potential 19 million cu m.

Environmental concerns continued to dominate forestry thinking worldwide. In March seven Canadian forestry ministers signed an accord designed to ensure sustainability in relation not only to wood products but also to fish and wildlife management, aboriginal concerns, and recreational values. Sweden, which could point back to its first forestry act in 1903, developed a new forestry policy emphasizing the concept of biodiversity.

It was in the tropical forests that the environmental debate raged most fiercely,

however. The International Tropical Timber Organization planned to set up a tropical rain-forest protection fund. Japan, the world's largest tropical hardwood importer, was expected to contribute about 30% of the resources. The World Wide Fund for Nature reiterated its stand that total sustainability in forest management should be reached by 1995. Steps toward this end were taken by some key exporters. Malaysia, which produced about 10 million cu m of sawn hardwood lumber a year, was investing in management and harvesting techniques and instituted severe crackdowns on illegal logging. Ghana also launched a tree-planting project to minimize deforestation caused by small-scale subsistence farming. The scheme, funded by a 1% levy on timber exports, would encourage farmers to replant cleared land with species that would provide fuelwood, fodder, soil enrichment, and timber crops.

Brazil, long castigated as a prime culprit of deforestation, issued decrees weighted to long-term resource management, although their efficacy would vary from state to state. Any forest operation consuming more than 12,000 cu m a year was now required to issue a management plan, and by 1995 it would have to obtain all its timber from sustainable sources. The clock could not be turned back, and the forests burned—predominantly for agriculture in the early '90s—were gone forever. However, the whole Amazonia region still comprised 449 million ha (1,109,000,000 ac) of forest, about 92% of the land area. In the Philippines, where in some areas irreversible damage had been done, the new government cut back the number of timber license agreements issued to private entrepreneurs from 63 to 27. The result would be a drop in the total allowable hardwood cut from 2 million cu m at the start of the year to barely 500,000 cu m.

Technological advances in timber utilization continued. A striking example was laminated veneer lumber, which had gained popularity in North America over the past few years and was edging into the European market. Characteristically manufactured from thin strips of timber edge-glued together, the material is considerably lighter than steel or concrete per unit of volume and gives highly predictable structural and fire performance. Medium-density fibreboard continued to gain market share. More than two million cubic metres were consumed in Europe in 1991, and available supplies were expected to reach four million cubic metres by 1993.

(JEAN CLARK CAMERON KLOOS)

See also Agriculture and Food Supplies; Consumer Affairs; Economic Affairs; Energy; Information Processing and Information Systems; Labour-Management Relations; Mining; Photography; Television and Radio; Transportation.

This article updates the *Macropædia* articles BEVERAGE PRODUCTION; BUILDING CONSTRUCTION; DRESS AND ADORNMENT; ELECTRONICS; ENERGY CONVERSION; FORESTRY AND WOOD PRODUCTION; INDUSTRIAL GLASS AND CERAMICS; Chemical Process INDUSTRIES; Extraction and Processing INDUSTRIES; Manufacturing INDUSTRIES; Textile INDUSTRIES; INSURANCE; MARKETING AND MERCHANDISING; PRINTING, TYPOGRAPHY, AND PHOTOENGRAVING; TELECOMMUNICATIONS SYSTEMS; TOOLS.

Information Processing and Information Systems

During 1992 in the U.S. computer industry, big companies bled red ink, computers became faster and cheaper, virus programs continued to cause more fear than actual damage, and corporate data processing managers continued to demand "open systems," computers that could run any company's software. In other words, the period was much like those that had gone before.

But there were also some twists. For one, there was an increasing public concern about whether computers and networks were protected from electronic eavesdropping by hackers or even by legitimate "tappers." The FBI at one time during this period encountered stiff opposition when it proposed legislation that would require all digital computer networks to make available a means for FBI tapping.

Another new twist was the arrival on the home computing scene of the telephone company. When AT&T's Bell system was broken up into seven regional operating companies in 1984, those "Baby Bells" were banned from entering the information services market, a $10 billion industry that provides on-line information such as stock quotes. In late 1991, however, a court decision lifted the ban, and the Bells were expected to begin offering home computer users electronic Yellow Pages in the short run and on-line interactive video in the long term.

On the cheaper-and-lighter computing front, Apple Computer introduced its first portable computers, including the pocket-size Newton, and released a new line of Macintosh computers that were to sell for far less than any previous Macs. The Powerbook laptop computer was expensive at $2,299–$4,599, but it could run both Mac and IBM personal computer (PC) software, while the Newton, a computerized executive organizer, was equipped with built-in wireless

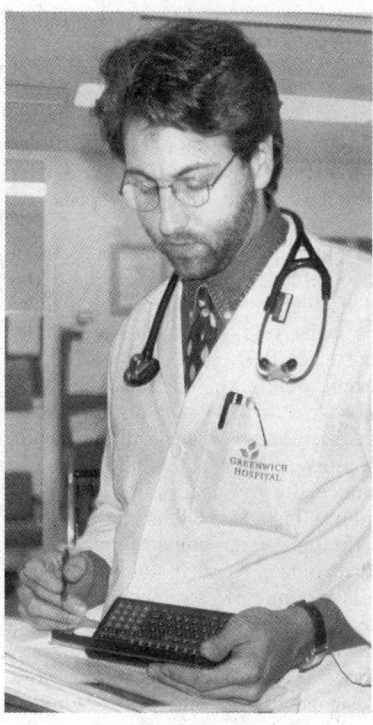

A hospital physician uses a palmtop computer rather than a clipboard to record patient information. The computer could also be used to assist in other tasks, such as checking references for appropriate treatments and obtaining information on drugs and dosages.
MICHELLE BROWN/GREENWICH HOSPITAL

communications ability. Newton was expected to carry a street price of $700 when it went on sale in early 1993.

Another relatively new breed of light computer was the notebook, in which a pen replaces the keyboard as the means to issue commands or enter information. During the year pen computers continued to garner the support of the key PC industry software companies. These included Microsoft, which introduced a version of its Windows operating environment for such machines, and Lotus, the maker

---

Building a Superhighway for Data

With little fanfare the U.S. government in recent months launched a research effort to create nationwide "superhighways for data." This five-year High-Performance Computing and Communications (HPCC) program, the outgrowth of legislation proposed by Sen. Al Gore, Jr. (Dem., Tenn.), would upgrade an existing national computer network to run so fast that the entire *Encyclopædia Britannica* could pass over it in one second.

Speeds of up to one billion bits of data per second were necessary in order to link the nation's supercomputers, making their computing power accessible to smaller universities, libraries, and government research centres that could not afford those multimillion-dollar machines. With supercomputing widely accessible, computer simulation of natural events or new designs would become widespread, said HPCC coordinator Don Lindberg. Using simulation, supercomputers were used to predict accurately the destructive path of Hurricane Andrew in 1992, for instance.

HPCC was not just a network-improvement project, however; most of the $2 billion being spent in the five-year project was to be used to research new "massively parallel" supercomputers and to develop the software that would allow them to communicate over long dis-

tances. Only about 20% of the project's spending was to go toward creating the National Research and Education Network from what was now Internet, a chain of 3,000 computer networks linking researchers worldwide. While Internet had been used mostly for academic research, it was also being increasingly employed for high-speed data communication by businesses.

Of HPCC's three facets, the high-speed network aspect most captured the public imagination. One reason was that high-speed computing and widespread data access were essential to retaining the U.S.'s technological edge. Japan, for instance, planned to have a nationwide high-speed network reaching homes and businesses by 2015. In the long run, HPCC was seen as the proving ground for a national high-speed network that would reach schools and homes, allowing students to browse electronically through rare books at the Library of Congress while their parents watched television programs with which they could interact. To make that a reality, Gore and others wanted to lift the ban that kept telephone companies from providing cable TV service. This would give phone companies the incentive to link each home with fibreoptic cable, the tarmac of the 21st-century data freeway.

(EDWARD S. WARNER)

of 1-2-3, which said that it would produce versions of its top programs for pen computers.

There were, however, still a few hitches to pen computing. The screens on which users wrote were temperature-sensitive, and a pen computer left in a hot car would have a black screen until it cooled down. These computers were supposed to translate their user's writing into typed characters, but many made mistakes in conversion, especially if the user had poor penmanship.

The cheap computer phenomenon caused serious financial problems for several hardware makers, including Compaq, IBM, and Digital Equipment Corp. (DEC). Of these, DEC arguably had the worst year, posting a $138 million loss for the second quarter of 1991, compared with a $111 million profit in the same quarter of the preceding year. One quarter later a new loss of $294 million was posted, down 9% from a year earlier, and by the fourth quarter the red ink remained, with a loss totaling $188 million.

In response DEC launched a reorganization designed to trim 10,000 workers and result in a $1.5 billion charge against earnings. Symbolic of the upheaval, company founder and long-time chief executive officer Kenneth Olsen resigned. DEC's new strategy was to emphasize connecting its mini-computers to networked PCs. The company had an alliance with Microsoft and thus planned to make its products work with Microsoft's Windows. For instance, its Alpha work-stations were being designed to run Microsoft's Windows New Technology software.

IBM, meanwhile, began the period by posting a $1.4 billion loss for the fourth quarter of 1991 and a 4.2% decline in annual revenue for the year. In 1992 the firm lost a record $4,750,000,000 and announced in December that it would cut its work force by 25,000 and reduce its manufacturing capacity in 1993.

At Compaq a 1991 third-quarter loss totaled $70 million, forcing the company to eliminate 1,400 workers, including founder and president Joseph ("Rod") Canion. The company had taken a beating from makers of IBM PC clones that could offer a computer with almost as much reliability as Compaq but for a far lower cost. It ended fiscal 1991, however, with a net income of $130 million.

The biggest financial horror story of all, however, was that of Wang Laboratories, which entered Chapter 11 of bankruptcy after declaring a $45 million loss on sales of $1.2 billion in fiscal year 1992. Wang had helped spark the small-computer revolution with the launch of a dedicated word-processing system but later saw its market eroded by cheap PCs that could run any word processor.

Reflecting the demand for open systems was the formation of an industry consortium organized to develop the Advanced Computing Environment (ACE). The 250 consortium members, which included competitors such as Microsoft and DEC, said that they would make sure that all their workstation computers could run the same open operating system, leaving customers free to buy software from any supplier. Corporate data system managers, however, found that they could already run any software on any computer as long as there was a "middleman" program between the software and the operating system. Therefore, the pursuit of open systems seemed ready to move away from focusing on open operating systems to the development of more intermediary software.

As in years past, workstations powered by reduced instruction set computing (RISC) chips were big news in 1992. DEC introduced a line of non-RISC workstations that carried surprisingly low price tags—one sold for less than $4,000—but customers kept waiting for DEC's Alpha RISC workstations, which could run an open operating system and a DEC operating system simultaneously. Sun Microsystems responded to DEC's thrust with the introduction of a colour RISC system priced at about $5,000.

More importantly, Sun announced a new line in which each workstation would use several RISC processors, resulting in a "parallel" computer that could break each task into parts, with each processor running its part at the same time as the others. Such machines could outrun some super-computers. One Sun workstation was designed to have 20 RISC brains and was to be available in 1993.

IBM's new RISC System/6000 workstations, also parallel processors, could be linked on a high-speed network to operate as a cluster. A cluster of 15 would cost only about $1 million, far less than a supercomputer. The first machines were expected to be delivered in 1993. As of 1992, the cheapest of IBM's "RISC stations" was priced at $6,345.

As for computer viruses, those small "chameleon" programs hackers use to crash other people's computers, only one made a big splash during the year, and it proved a dud. The virus was named Michelangelo and was set to begin its dirty work on the artist's March 6 birthday. Many warnings were issued but, when the day arrived, little damage occurred, largely because users had run antivirus software in time and made copies of the data on their hard disks. Later, however, a $15 manual for making computer viruses was published, making it clear that the virus menace would not go away.

Other types of computer crime also made headlines. In one case the FBI arrested five hackers, aged 18–22, who allegedly broke into computer systems at several *Fortune* 500 firms, including TRW, which had 176 consumer credit records stolen. In another case an FBI raid closed down Davey Jones Locker, a Boston-area computer bulletin board, to which anyone who paid $99 could connect his computer and illegally copy dozens of commercial software packages.

Perhaps the most disturbing hacker news, however, came from the movie *Sneakers,* in which a mathematician has built a black box that would let users decrypt any encoded information and gain access to any computer system. Coincidentally, the national standard for data encryption was up for reconsideration in 1993.   (EDWARD S. WARNER)

Apple's Macintosh computers are displayed in a consumer electronics store in Japan. During the past few years Apple had dramatically increased its share of the Japanese market, partly by encouraging the development of Japanese-language software.

One of the important trends in the information industry in Japan was the formation of new alliances between computer manufacturers. With the development of open operating systems, alliances were being formed that would have been unthinkable in the past. Makers who competed intensively against one another in one submarket were co-operating in another. For example, Hitachi and IBM Japan Ltd. reached an agreement in the PC area. Also, IBM Japan Ltd. concluded a marketing agreement with NEC. Under this agreement NEC was to sell IBM magnetic disk units, while IBM Japan would sell NEC supercomputers.

According to statistics based on the Ministry of International Trade and Industry's *New Survey on Computer Deliveries,* 2,720,000 computers were delivered in Japan in 1991. The value of the deliveries was 4,214,800,000 yen. In this new survey all types of computers were included, such as general-purpose computers, minicomputers, office computers and distributed processing processors, workstations, and personal computers. In terms of value, general-purpose computers ranked first with a share of 51%, followed by personal computers (21.8%), office computers/distributed processing processors (14.8%), workstations (8.7%), minicomputers (3.1%), and others (0.6%).   (YUJI YAMADORI)

This article updates the *Macropædia* articles COMPUTERS; INFORMATION PROCESSING AND INFORMATION SYSTEMS.

Labour-Management Relations

The background to labour-management relations in 1992 was the widespread recession in most countries of the Organization for Economic Cooperation and Development and government efforts to adapt to economic rigour and to stem high levels of unemployment.

The European Communities. Straitened economies did not prevent the EC Commission from pressing on with its efforts to extend Community-wide regulation of labour matters. Progress was slow for several reasons, including problems of ratification of the Maastricht Treaty on closer European union and the new situation opened up by the provision agreed to at Maastricht (the U.K. excepted) envisaging the possibility of management and labour arriving at agreements on some subjects on a European level. The most controversial proposals considered during the year, concerning the establishment of European works councils and the regulation of working time, were substantially diluted in the course of discussion, but no final agreement had been reached at year's end.

Britain and Ireland. On October 13 Britain was shocked by the announcement that 31 of British Coal's pits were to be closed with the loss of 30,000 jobs, leaving only 19 pits in operation. At the same time, the government announced an aid package for the displaced workers and affected areas. The main reason for the decision was the changeover by much of the electricity-generating industry from coal to other sources of energy, particularly natural gas. Faced with strong protests, the government quickly announced a reprieve for all but 10 of the pits. On December 21 the High Court ruled that plans to close all 31 pits were illegal because the government had not followed prescribed procedures. However, Trade and Industry Secretary Michael Heseltine announced that production at the 10 pits would not be resumed.

A government White Paper, "People, Jobs and Opportunity," proposed amending the law to give greater freedom to individuals to belong to the union of their choice, to tighten arrangements for the checkoff of union dues, to extend union members' rights to information about their union's financial affairs, and to give the users of a public service a right to restrain unlawful industrial action affecting that service. A bill introduced in November included provisions for seven days' notice of industrial action. It was reported on March 5 that members of two of Britain's major unions—the Amalgamated Engineering Union and the Electrical, Electronic, Telecommunications, and Plumbing Union—voted to merge to form the Amalgamated Engineering and Electrical Union with over a million members. An even larger merger discussed during the year would bring together the National and Local Government Officers Association, the National Union of Public Employees, and the Confederation of Health Service Employees to form a public service employees union with a potential membership approaching 1.5 million.

In Ireland a Code of Practice on Disputes Procedures was given ministerial authorization. It contained special provisions for essential services, including health services, energy supplies, water and sewage services, fire, ambulance, and rescue services, and certain elements of public transport. There were two notable disputes during the year. One, in the banking industry, was settled after 14 weeks on the basis of a Labour Court recommendation, which provided modest pay increases and more flexible operating hours. The second, in the postal service, concerned resistance to the employer's efforts to implement a cost-reduction program that included the introduction of part-time temporary staff. This dispute was settled after six weeks on the basis of terms, proposed by the Labour Relations Commission, under which the employer undertook to create new permanent jobs and both parties were committed to reorganization.

North America. The most notable event in the U.S. was the dispute about the terms of a new contract between the United Auto Workers and the Caterpillar Co., the world's largest maker of construction equipment. At the root of the conflict was the company's refusal to accept terms similar to those the union had achieved with Deere & Co., reflecting a desire on the company's part to avoid pattern bargaining. On April 14, after five months of dispute, the company announced that it would stop recruiting replacements for strikers who did not return to work. The union then instructed its members to go back, but it later mounted a go-slow campaign. The biggest automobile manufacturer, General Motors, announced that by 1995 it would have to close 21 plants, with an estimated loss of 74,000 jobs. The company was forced to embark on cost cutting, and there were strikes in plants at Lordstown, Ohio, and Lansing, Mich. In Canada the Paperworkers, Communications and Electrical Workers, and Energy and Chemical Workers unions merged to form the Communications, Energy and Paperworkers Union of Canada with 133,000 members.

Continental Europe. In Germany the major labour problems sprang from the heavy costs of unification and the poor economic performance of the eastern (formerly communist) part of the country. Many workers in the west felt they were being expected to pay an unfair proportion of these costs, while workers in the east worried about paying western German prices with eastern German wages. With economic growth low, the government was particularly anxious that any increase in labour costs be modest. The unions sought wage increases in the neighbourhood of 10%, but successive wage settlements in the west, including that in the important metalworking industry, were kept broadly under 6%, just about tolerable for employers and the national economy.

In France the Renault automobile company's historic factory at Billancourt, long known for the militancy of its

Members of the United Auto Workers on strike at a Caterpillar plant in Aurora, Ill., shout at workers entering the factory. After the company began advertising for replacements, union members returned to work without settlement of their demands.
AP/WIDE WORLD

workers, closed at the end of March. The Euro Disneyland theme park to the east of Paris became involved in a dispute even before it opened as unions protested the employer's imposition of a dress code banning, among other things, beards for men and heavy makeup for women. At the end of June there was a rash of strikes and demonstrations across France, including action by farmers, dockers, and airline pilots. The largest action, however, was by truck drivers protesting changes in penalties for road offenses that could result in loss of their licenses for a relatively small number of infractions. The drivers' blockade of key sections of the road network left thousands of motorists and foreign truck drivers stranded. The agreement that ended the action, while retaining the basis of the new regulations, afforded the drivers a measure of protection.

For years the Italian system for relating wage rates to prices, the *scala mobile,* had been the subject of a tug-of-war between governments and employers, concerned about its effects on inflation, and unions, which viewed it as an essential protection for workers' living standards. Italy's new government achieved a major success on July 31 with a central government-union-employer agreement that finally abolished the *scala mobile* while conceding limited flat sum payments over 13 months from January 1993 and undertaking to freeze the prices of public services. The government also committed itself to keeping a more careful watch on the taxes paid by small businesses and the self-employed, with a view to ensuring that the economic burden was equitably shared. The deal did not go down well with union rank-and-file members or with some union officials. Worker dissatisfaction was increased by belt-tightening measures announced by the government on October 1, and a one-day general strike was held on October 13.

The Spanish government, with its eyes on eventual participation in the European Monetary System, was pursuing policies for countering inflation while reducing the high level of unemployment. The unions strongly disagreed with some of its policies, notably proposals to reduce the amount and duration of unemployment benefits and to enact a strict new law on strikes (in the first half of the year strikes cost the country 7,750,000 working days). A half-day general strike was called on May 28. In October the government decided to freeze public-sector pay in the coming year.

The once hugely successful Swedish labour-relations model continued to weaken, with joint administrative boards being replaced by advisory bodies and moves to change long-established bargaining cartels. Unemployment, though

still low by the standards of many countries, rose steadily. In Norway the central trade union and employer bodies reached a two-year agreement on pay and working conditions in the private sector on April 27. A strike by municipal workers disrupted schools, hospitals, and refuse collection outside Oslo; the government ordered compulsory arbitration. Greece experienced another difficult year as the government sought to improve the economy by privatization, reform of state pensions, and a freeze on public-sector pay. In response to a strike by the Athens bus service, the government announced its intention to privatize it.

Former Communist Countries. While labour-relations experience in the ex-Soviet Union and the formerly communist countries of central and eastern Europe was varied, economic difficulties, inflation, uncertain industrial development, and high unemployment were all widespread. In Russia, a Tripartite Commission on Social and Labour Relations was set up in January, and a central agreement, arrived at in March, envisaged legislative and other measures to promote employment and improve living standards and provided changes in social security, working conditions, occupational safety, and the legal basis of labour relations.

East Asia. Japan's working hours were the longest among advanced industrial countries, and for some time the government has urged their reduction. In 1992 the government implemented a 40-hour, five-day week for its own employees, as from May 2, and on June 19 a law was passed encouraging a more general reduction of working hours. In January the extensive plants of the Hyundai Motor Co. at Ulsan, South Korea, were occupied by workers striking for a higher year-end bonus, the dropping of charges against union members who had been arrested, and the reinstatement of members dismissed for allegedly illegal labour activities. The occupation was called off after a week when police threatened to storm the country's largest car plant, using helicopters and armoured vehicles.

South Africa. In South Africa discussion continued about reform of the Labour Relations Act and restructuring of the National Manpower Commission. There were a number of strikes, apart from the 48-hour general strike called in August in support of majority rule. Major strikes included one by 6,000 Toyota workers in Durban that lasted two months and one by 7,400 state health service workers in the Transvaal.   (R.O. CLARKE)

See also Economic Affairs: *World Economy;* Industrial Review.

This article updates the *Macropædia* article WORK AND EMPLOYMENT.

Law

Court Decisions. Sensational cases seldom make enduring law, but some of them dominated the headlines of Europe and the U.S. during 1992, with commensurate political implications. The more important decisions from the viewpoint of the courts and the legal profession—on matters of extradition, abortion, racial harmony, and criminal law—were usually relegated to the back pages by the information media. Thus the rape trial of William Kennedy Smith, a nephew of U.S. Sen. Ted Kennedy, which ended in acquittal on Dec. 11, 1991, attracted a huge television audience. Heavyweight boxing champion Mike Tyson fared less well against charges that he had raped a young beauty contestant. His conviction, also attended by enormous publicity, caused some to assert—in the context of the Smith acquittal—that the U.S. criminal justice system was weighted heavily in favour of rich, politically prominent individuals and against those who were less well situated. Tyson, however, was represented by a criminal lawyer considered by some to be one of the best in the country, and his defense had strong financial and popular backing.

In Europe public attention, particularly in Germany, was directed toward the trial of the "Berlin Wall" guards, who were convicted of manslaughter for shooting a person attempting to cross from East to West Germany. The accused guards relied as a defense on the "shoot-to-kill" policy adopted by the East German government with respect to people trying to flee the country, but the court found that the guards should have disobeyed that order since its execution would be a violation of human rights. The trial of former East German leader Erich Honecker on charges stemming from killings at the Wall continued at year's end. In Greece, Muhammad Rashid, a Palestinian, was convicted of premeditated murder for causing a midair bomb blast that destroyed a Pan American airliner over Hawaii in 1982. The U.S. had attempted to extradite Rashid, but the Greek authorities rejected the request.

Extradition. Some sensational cases, of course, also have jurisprudential significance. *United States* v. *Alvarez-Machain,* decided by the U.S. Supreme Court, involved the question of whether a state or country has jurisdiction to try an individual who has been brought into the state or country by official force and not through extradition. Most countries subscribe to the legal rule that jurisdiction is based on power—that a state has power over, and therefore jurisdiction to adjudicate the legal rights of, all persons and things within its geographic sphere. Under this doctrine courts throughout the world have asserted jurisdiction over individuals who are brought by force into their sovereign territories by bounty hunters and private kidnappers. For the first time, however, the Supreme Court had to determine whether this "law of nations" applied where a country itself abducted another country's citizen. In this case, a Mexican citizen was kidnapped in Mexico by U.S. agents and taken to the United States, where he was charged with a crime committed in Mexico that allegedly violated both Mexican and U.S. law. The case was further complicated by the fact that Mexico and the United States are parties to an extradition treaty that could be read to mean that forcible governmental kidnapping is prohibited. The majority of the court held that the United States had jurisdiction to try the accused for violations of U.S. criminal law. After the decision was rendered, Pres. George Bush announced that the United States, as a matter of policy, would no longer permit its agents to kidnap foreign nationals. The accused was subsequently acquitted and returned to Mexico.

In *R.* v. *Secretary of State ex Sinclair,* the English Divisional Court upheld the decision of the home secretary refusing the request of the U.S. government to extradite an individual who had been convicted in the United States 10 years earlier and who, without serving his sentence, had fled to Trinidad and then to England. The home secretary found that the individual had tried to return to the United States to serve his sentence but was refused permission to enter. This circumstance, plus the fact that the U.S. had waited so long to request extradition, constituted sufficient grounds for the home secretary to deny the request.

Abortion. The U.S. Supreme Court had another opportunity in 1992 to review its position respecting abortion. *Planned Parenthood* v. *Casey* involved a constitutional attack on a new Pennsylvania abortion statute. Under this statute (1) a woman seeking an abortion is required to give her informed consent to the abortion at least 24 hours before it is performed; (2) a minor seeking an abortion is required to obtain the informed consent of one of her parents but has available a judicial bypass option if she does not wish to or cannot obtain such consent; (3) with certain exceptions, a married woman seeking an abortion must notify her husband of her intentions in this regard, but she does not need to obtain his consent; and (4) exemption from compliance with these requirements is given in case of medical emergency.

The Supreme Court held this legislation valid, except for the spousal notice provision, which it found violated the 14th Amendment to the Constitution. The decision pleased neither pro-life nor pro-choice activists. The former had hoped that the case would result in the overturning of *Roe* v. *Wade* and thus allow states to prohibit abortions altogether, but this did not happen. The latter hoped in vain that the court would fortify *Roe* v. *Wade* by declaring unconstitutional any limitations on a woman's right to an abortion.

Adoption was urged by pro-life groups as a good alternative to abortion, but two French cases during the year showed that adoption has its own legal problems. Both cases were decided by the Council of State. The first, *Dept. du Loiret* v. *T.,* held that a male bachelor was eligible to adopt a ward. The second, *Dept. du Doubs* v. *M et Mme F.,* denied the right to adopt to a couple who stated that, on religious grounds, they would oppose a blood transfusion as a medical treatment for their adopted child.

Freedom of Expression. Notorious criminals, such as serial killers, sometimes write books about their crimes after they are incarcerated. In some cases these books become bestsellers, generating substantial royalties for their authors. In an effort to divert these royalties from the criminal to his or her victims, some states enacted "Son of Sam" laws (named after an infamous New York serial murderer) to effectuate such a diversion. The U.S. Supreme Court, in *Simon & Schuster* v. *Crime Victims Board,* held that these laws violate the First Amendment to the Constitution, which guarantees freedom of speech.

Great Britain largely restricts the right of the press to comment on cases being tried by its courts, ostensibly on the grounds that this restraint better assures a fair trial. It has enforced its rule by holding in contempt of court anyone who violates it. In many other countries "the right to know" is accorded a higher value than "fair trial," and in these places the press is largely free to comment on ongoing litigation. Ireland had followed the English rule on this matter, but in 1992 its Supreme Court changed that position. In *Desmond & Dedier* v. *Glackin, Minister for Industry and Commerce and Attorney General,* the court held that comment could be given on cases being tried, particularly when the cases are of great public interest. The decision was

In a courtroom in Orlando, Fla., 12-year-old Gregory Kingsley testifies in his trial to "divorce" his natural mother and be adopted by foster parents. The judge granted the boy's petition, thought to be the first time such action had been taken at the request of a minor.
COURTROOM TELEVISION NETWORK

influenced, to some extent, by Article 10 of the European Convention on Human Rights.

Sex and Sex Discrimination. In 1984 the U.S. Congress passed the Child Protection Act, which criminalized the receipt through the mails of sexually explicit depictions of children. Having determined that one Keith Jacobson may have been predisposed to receiving such materials, the U.S. Postal Service subtly encouraged him to do so and then caused him to be arrested when the materials had been received. In *Jacobson* v. *United States,* the U.S. Supreme Court reversed lower court holdings that Jacobson had not been illegally entrapped and ordered him released. The court did not hold, however, that the Child Protection Act was unconstitutional.

In *State of Israel* v. *Gestetner,* the Israeli National Labour Court found that Gestetner Ltd. had violated the Equality of Labour Opportunity Law, which provides that advertisements for employees must be framed in such a way as to include both men and women, except in those cases where sexual discrimination is "imperative." In handing down its decision, the court reviewed, and found persuasive, similar cases from many countries, including Britain, the United States, Germany, Sweden, Canada, The Netherlands, and Belgium.

School Desegregation. For many years the U.S. federal courts had been supervising the desegregation of the country's public schools. In a few instances, that supervision was terminated when the school districts involved showed that segregation had been eliminated. More frequently, desegregation efforts had been partially but not completely effective, and in 1992 the Supreme Court addressed the question of whether partial withdrawal of supervision would be permitted in these cases. In *Freeman* v. *Pitts* it answered this question affirmatively. The case involved a school district in Georgia that had achieved desegregation with respect to student assignments, transportation, physical facilities, and extracurricular activities but not with respect to teacher and principal assignments, resource allocation, and overall quality of education. The court said that incremental withdrawal of supervision was within the discretion of the responsible federal court.

Cruel and Unusual Punishment. The Eighth Amendment to the U.S. Constitution prohibits the states and the federal government from inflicting "cruel and unusual" punishment on prisoners. The exact meaning of this wording was the subject of controversy among lawyers, prison administrators, and civil libertarians. Some Supreme Court justices, for example, had held that the amendment precludes capital punishment, but this view had not prevailed in actual decisions. In 1992 some light may have been shed as to the scope and range of the amendment in the Supreme Court case of *Hudson* v. *McMillian.* In this case, Keith Hudson, an inmate of the Louisiana state penitentiary, was being taken from his cell to an administrative lockup facility when he engaged in an altercation with the two guards who were removing him. At the time, Hudson was in handcuffs and shackles. As a result of the altercation, Hudson suffered minor bruises and swelling of his face, mouth, and lip. In addition, his teeth were loosened. Hudson brought an action against the guards under a federal statute designed to implement, among other things, the rights provided by the Eighth Amendment. The lower federal court dismissed the action on the grounds that one alleging the use of excessive force in violation of the Eighth Amendment must prove that a significant injury resulted. The Supreme Court reversed this holding, deciding that the prisoner could maintain the claim by showing that the guards had used excessive force under the circumstances, even though that force had caused only minor injuries. (WILLIAM D. HAWKLAND)

International Law. The year 1992 was one of disintegration, and the steady movement toward a new world legal order evident in the previous year was put in question on many fronts. Yet there were signs that this was in fact not a setback but rather a difficult—and dangerous—period of passage.

Disintegration. The dissolution of the Soviet Union at the end of 1991 introduced a series of disintegrative changes in eastern Europe and southwestern Asia. The Commonwealth of Independent States (CIS), which replaced the old U.S.S.R., did not acquire any personality of its own. So much was this so that during the 1992 Olympic Games the ex-Soviet athletes (who still formed a single team) did not appear under the banner of the CIS but were given the embarrassed and meaningless title of the Unified Team. The question of state succession to the U.S.S.R. was also fudged. In particular, the U.S.S.R.'s permanent seat in the UN Security Council was given to Russia by political decision and without any discussion of its entitlement in law to succeed under Article 23 of the UN Charter. Belarus and Ukraine had been founding members of the UN. The other CIS states were admitted to the international organization as ordinary members.

Yugoslavia, although not within the U.S.S.R.'s sphere of influence, was also affected by its dissolution. Almost immediately two of its constituent republics (Slovenia and Croatia) broke away from the federation. The recognition of Croatia by the European Communities (EC) triggered a violent irredentist reaction from the Serbian republic, which used the Yugoslav army to invade the secessionary states. In midyear, when that adventure had reached a military stalemate, Bosnia and Hercegovina made its claim to secede and was in turn invaded by what were now in effect Serbian troops. That led to a vicious civil war with strong religious overtones between Bosnians of, respectively, Serbian, Croatian, and Muslim extraction. By the end of the year the territory had been almost entirely partitioned between the two former groups and their sponsor republics/states. In December Yugoslavia, which had been occupying the Yugoslav seat at the UN though it now consisted only of Serbia and Montenegro, was expelled from the international organization.

The third country to subdivide following the lifting of pressure in eastern Europe was Czechoslovakia, which split by peaceful and formal means into Slovakia and the Czech Republic. (The ancient name of Bohemia was inappropriate because the new Czech Republic also included Moravia.) The new arrangement was to enter into force on Jan. 1, 1993.

Integration. Set against these splits was the continuing worldwide trend toward greater politico-economic union. The North American Free Trade Agreement (NAFTA) between the U.S., Canada, and Mexico, finally concluded on August 12, was scheduled to come into force on Jan. 1, 1994. The U.S.-Canada Free Trade Agreement, which it would supersede, established a dispute-settlement panel in January to resolve a dispute over local content of Japanese cars assembled in North America, a procedure almost identical to that included in the NAFTA system. The Southern Cone Common Market (Mercosur) treaty between Argentina, Brazil, Paraguay, and Uruguay, which was to come into force on Jan. 1, 1995, was ratified by Brazil in late 1991. Guatemala, Honduras, and El Salvador agreed in May to create a free-trade area. The free-trade agreement between Bolivia and Peru came into force in October. Also in October, Venezuela agreed to give duty-free entry to goods from the 13 Caribbean Community and Common Market (Caricom) countries in exchange for most-favoured-nation treatment. Caricom itself agreed on a timetable for reducing the top level of its common external tariff by successive steps in 1993, 1995, and 1997.

Outside the Americas, the Asia-Pacific Economic Cooperation Group (APEC), comprising Australia, New Zealand, the U.S., Canada, Japan, South Korea, Taiwan, Hong Kong, China, the Philippines, Singapore, Malaysia, Indonesia, Brunei, and Thailand, agreed to establish a permanent secretariat to devise and coordinate cooperation programs. In January the fourth Association of Southeast Asian Nations (ASEAN) summit, in furtherance of the Asian free-trade agreement signed the previous autumn, signed a Framework Agreement on Enhancing ASEAN Economic Cooperation and a tariff-reduction agreement. The Southern African Development Community Treaty to establish mechanisms for cooperation and integration was signed in August by Angola, Botswana, Lesotho, Malawi, Mozambique, Namibia, Swaziland, Tanzania, Zambia, and Zimbabwe, with the hope that it would develop into a common market. It was partly inspired by the need to provide a counterweight to a postapartheid South Africa. The Economic Community of West African States (ECOWAS) transformed its West African Clearing House into a West African Monetary Agency and agreed to establish an ECOWAS exchange rate system, inspired by the EC.

In Europe events were more ambivalent. The Maastricht Treaty on European union, agreed to the previous December, was finally signed in February—as a single treaty and not as two separate but interlinked treaties as had been expected. It was intended to enter into force on Jan. 1, 1993, but the first member state to take up ratification, Denmark, put it to referendum, and the popular vote, in June, gave a narrow margin against ratification. The U.K., which was in the process of debating the ratification bill in Parliament, immediately withdrew it. By autumn, when it was taken up again, political opposition within the government party had hardened, and a very ambivalent ratification procedure was begun; the bill was still in committee at year's end. By then, all the other 10 member states had ratified the treaty, and arrangements had been made to satisfy the Danes, who, it was hoped, would hold a second referendum, probably in the spring of 1993.

The other great Community initiative, the creation of a larger common market by partially merging the EC and the European Free Trade Association (EFTA) into a joint European Economic Area (EEA), also suffered shocks. After the negative opinion of the European Court of Justice (ECJ) the previous December, the objectionable passages in the treaty were redrafted to remove the joint EEA court and replace it with a "two-pillar" system of separate EFTA institutions. At the insistence of the European Parliament, the redraft was resubmitted to the ECJ, which gave its approval in April. The treaty was then signed in May by all 12 EC countries, by all 7 EFTA countries, by the EC itself, and also by the European Coal and Steel Community. On the same day, the EFTA states signed a series of related treaties setting up the machinery to enforce the treaty within EFTA under the two-pillar system, particularly an EFTA court and a Surveillance Authority to enforce antitrust provisions.

These treaties, and the EEA treaty, were intended to enter into force on Jan. 1, 1993, at the same time as the Maastricht Treaty and completion of the EC internal market. However, a Swiss referendum in December voted against ratification by an even narrower majority than the Danish rejection of Maastricht. At year's end a joint EC-EFTA committee was exploring ways of ensuring the EEA's survival. Meanwhile, the EC's 1992 program was duly completed just before Christmas, so the full internal market, with its abolition of internal frontiers and remaining technical barriers to movement, would come into force on Jan. 1, 1993, as planned.

In eastern Europe, apart from the association agreements of Poland and Hungary with the EC (the Czech agreement was not ratified because of uncertainty over the country's status), free-trade agreements were concluded between Russia and Estonia in September and between Poland and Hungary in October. In the same month, Moldova and Romania agreed to establish a committee to coordinate their parliaments with a view to greater economic integration.

Violence. The international violence of former years was replaced in 1992 by a series of vicious civil wars in Yugoslavia, Somalia, Liberia, and elsewhere. This led to a new role for the UN of somewhat uncertain legal status. Hitherto, Article 2(7) of the Charter, excluding the UN from intervening in matters within the domestic jurisdiction of a state, had been interpreted to exclude civil wars from UN enforcement action, despite the express reservation in Article 2(7) allowing Chapter VII enforcement in cases of actual or threatened breaches of international peace. Now, however, a change took place. Powerful press reports of the savage fighting in Bosnia and the anarchy in Somalia, in both cases causing terrible suffering among the civilian population, roused international public opinion.

The UN responded traditionally by sending in peacekeeping troops to support the giving of humanitarian aid by international relief agencies—*i.e.,* to convoy food to besieged civilians. Such weapons as were carried were, as usual, not to be used in anger. As news of mass deaths from starvation in Somalia continued, however, the Security Council finally authorized Chapter VII action, and toward the end of the year a largely U.S. force, wearing their own uniforms and without the blue UN headgear, landed in Somalia to protect food distribution directly against armed attack. There was more reluctance to commit combat troops in Bosnia because of the greater possibility of loss of life, and as of year's end no direct UN military action had been authorized. Measures short of counterviolence were nevertheless imposed on Yugoslavia, including economic sanctions (which failed because of an inability to blockade the Danube River along the Serbian border).

Less violent but nonetheless disturbing was the decision of the U.S. Supreme Court in June that the kidnapping of a foreigner in his own country by U.S. agents and his forcible removal to the U.S. to stand trial for violation of U.S. criminal law was not open to review by the U.S. courts. (See *Court Decisions,* above.) The U.S. also continued its extensive exercise of nonviolent extraterritorial jurisdiction, extending its existing embargo through the Cuban Democracy Act, which prohibited foreign subsidiaries of U.S. firms from trading with Cuba, even if it was lawful to do so in the state where the subsidiary was established. The U.K. government insisted that its laws would determine trade practices. In April the U.S. Justice Department extended its claim to control foreign nonresident traders under U.S. antitrust law to include conduct that harmed U.S. exports, and in May the California Supreme Court upheld the right of that state to include foreign earnings in the calculations for assessing the California tax due from foreign multinational companies doing business in the state (*Barclays Bank International Inc.* v. *Franchise Tax Board*).

International Adjudication. In April the International Court of Justice (ICJ) rejected Libya's request for provisional measures against the U.S. and the U.K. in connection with the claimed extradition of two Libyans suspected of complicity in the destruction of an airliner over Lockerbie, Scotland, in 1988. In June it rejected one of Australia's objections to its jurisdiction in *Nauru* v. *Australia* but upheld another. In September it struck off the "Great Belt case," *Finland* v. *Denmark,* on being told that it had been settled. Also in September, it gave judgment on the complex frontier dispute in *El Salvador* v. *Honduras.* In November a new action was filed, *Iran* v. *U.S.A.,* in respect of the destruction of Iranian oil platforms in the Persian Gulf during the Iran-Iraq war.

Nigeria and Cameroon appointed a panel of experts to recommend solutions to their border dispute. The U.K. and Albania reached an agreement to settle their long-standing dispute over deaths arising from the placing of mines in the Corfu Channel in 1946, leading to an ICJ judgment in 1948 ordering Albania to pay damages. An international arbitral tribunal settled the dispute between France and Canada over fishing rights off the French islands of Saint Pierre and Miquelon.   (NEVILLE MARCH HUNNINGS)

See also Crime, Law Enforcement, and Penology; World Affairs: *United Nations.*

This article updates the *Macropædia* articles CONSTITUTIONAL LAW; INTERNATIONAL LAW.

Libraries

Libraries throughout the world were in trouble in 1992. In the less developed countries, as they gained independence after World War II, there had been a real belief in the benefits of education and of libraries. Good collections were built up, and librarians, sent to the U.S. and Europe to learn their profession, returned eager to establish library services that would help their nations on the path to successful development. Unfortunately, education and libraries did not altogether live up to expectations. Much of the world's population had been raised in a bookless culture that depended on the spoken word and memory. Libraries—particularly in Africa but also in many countries of Asia, South America, and Oceania—were not well used, frequently attracting less than 5% of the population. After the euphoria of the '60s, the resources allocated to them were reduced bit by bit. The more urgent problems of development overshadowed concern with libraries. Even education, though still hon-

Books in the Library of Congress in Washington, D.C., carry markers indicating they have been mutilated. The problem, thought to be extensive and affecting a number of irreplaceable works, led the library in 1992 to close its stacks to the general public.
STEPHEN CROWLEY—THE NEW YORK TIMES

oured by many in the less developed world, could not meet expectations because not enough resources were devoted to it. This was particularly true after the oil crisis of the 1970s, when less developed countries began to incur huge debts. Model libraries, set up by Unesco in India and in northern Nigeria, found few if any imitators.

The conservative culture of the library profession did not help. A library in West Africa in 1992, for instance, was likely to look much like a rundown English suburban library of the 1960s. Libraries in the less developed world had not adapted to their societies. Oral societies are no less sophisticated or intelligent than literate ones, but their modes of communication are different. They do not in the first instance depend on Western-style libraries or librarians. Libraries are really in the business of disseminating information, but few librarians in Africa, Asia, South America, or the less developed countries of Oceania gave serious thought to how this could best be accomplished. It was significant that while in Third World libraries new books were often scarce and periodicals even scarcer, video shops managed to import sufficient supplies of videotapes to satisfy their customers and to send equipment overseas for repairs without difficulty.

In the 1990s it was clear that librarians could no longer afford to be merely librarians. Access to information had become more important than an exclusive diet of books. In the less developed world, professional education needed to go further, including the capacity to deal both with illiterates and with university and specialist libraries. Librarians even needed to know the basic technology of desktop publishing and how to design and write simple books in the local language—a genre usually ignored by major publishers. Less developed countries could no longer afford to send their trainees to the industrialized world, only to have them return with inflated ideas but without the ability to apply their knowledge within the constraints of their own cultures.

Libraries in the industrialized world were not without their troubles. In Britain the fine collections built up in the

London boroughs, Birmingham, Liverpool, Manchester, and other cities in the 1960s and 1970s had become a burden to their governing authorities. In London during the year, attention was drawn to the fact that a number of public libraries had sold off their stocks to secondhand booksellers, street traders, or even the general public, sometimes at a fraction of their real value. In Germany libraries of east and west were seeking to harmonize policies, while in Russia libraries were fighting for their existence.

Construction began in March on the Bibliothèque de France, the new French national library. Earlier, French Pres. François Mitterrand agreed to minor modifications of Dominique Perrault's controversial design but did not change the basic plan of four glass towers around a sunken cloister. In Moscow the Lenin Library, one of the last major Russian institutions to retain the name of Bolshevism's founder, was renamed the Russian State Library. The Russian government agreed to fund repairs to the library, which contained some 30 million volumes. The opening of the new British Library was delayed at least until the end of 1994 when it was discovered that 95 km (60 mi) of shelving had begun to rust and would have to be replaced. The library had been under construction since 1982, and in that time the cost had nearly trebled to £450 million.

(P. HAVARD-WILLIAMS)

Libraries on both coasts of the U.S. were hard hit by disasters in 1992. Two branches of the Los Angeles Public Library were destroyed by fire in the April 29 rioting, and a third was looted of equipment. In late August Hurricane Andrew caused some $20.4 million in damage to the Miami-Dade public library system; four branches remained closed two months after the storm.

Northern Illinois University announced that it would phase out its library school by 1994. However, threats to library schools were averted at the University of Maryland, the University of Southern Mississippi, and the University of Iowa. In a suit brought by a homeless man, the U.S. Circuit Court of Appeals in Philadelphia overturned a 1991 ruling that the Morristown, N.J., public library's restrictions on the behaviour and hygiene of patrons were unconstitutional. Following major losses to theft and vandalism, the Library of Congress implemented extensive new security measures that limited access to the stacks.

Public library circulation in the U.S. increased by 15% in 1991, while expenditures rose just 5%, according to the University of Illinois annual survey. In a "Call for America's Libraries Campaign," sponsored by the American Library Association (ALA), 75,743 people called a toll-free telephone number in March and April to register their support for libraries and librarians in the face of budget cuts resulting from the recession; the callers' names were presented to key congressional leaders, along with petitions containing 230,722 signatures.

Gloria Steinem and U.S. Rep. Patricia Schroeder (Dem., Colo.) addressed the ALA's 111th annual conference, which drew 19,261 registrants to San Francisco in June. Linda Crismond abruptly resigned as ALA executive director in May following conflicts with the association's executive board. Commissioner John Duff left the Chicago Public Library in June to become president of Columbia College in that city. Dallas (Texas) Public Library director Patrick O'Brien resigned in October to become director of the Alexandria (Va.) Public Library. The Rev. Timothy Healy, president of the New York Public Library, died December 30. In July Sacramento, Calif., opened a new six-story, $31.9 million central library. (GORDON FLAGG)

This article updates the Macropædia article LIBRARIES AND LIBRARY SCIENCE.

Life Sciences
ZOOLOGY

In 1992 the use of molecular techniques and the finding of new fossils led to advances in the understanding of the evolutionary relationships of several vertebrate groups and in some instances challenged conventional classification systems. Behavioral experiments revealed previously undiscovered abilities of fish and octopuses and called into question the capability of dogs to discriminate among human odours.

Some aquatic animals use electricity generated by modified tail muscles as a sensory technique. For certain nocturnal fish, for example, electrolocation is critical for detecting objects in their habitat. Electric fish are known to be able to tell their own species from others and to determine the sex of another individual by the waveform of that individual's electric discharge. A British study by Peter K. McGregor of the University of Nottingham and G.W. Max Westby of the University of Sheffield added a layer of complexity to the electrosensory abilities of fish by revealing that the South American knifefish *Gymnotus carapo* uses its electrosensory system to discriminate among individuals of its own species. Its discharge is too weak to be used as a weapon, but it will vigorously defend its territory from other knifefish by biting intruders. The researchers used plastic mesh screens to separate electric fish in a large aquarium for a three-month period. Each knifefish was allowed to set up a territory and assume dominance of its compartment. At first the fish in adjacent compartments defended the borders of their respective territories. But eventually they accepted the presence of the neighbouring fish. The investigators then recorded the electric pulse of each individual so that individually characteristic waveforms could be "played back" through an electrode placed in the aquarium. When the scientists exposed fish to recordings of the electric discharges of familiar neighbours at the correct boundary, the fish showed little response. But when the waveform of a stranger, or that of a familiar fish at the incorrect boundary, was used, the knifefish directed attacks and bites toward the electrode, demonstrating their ability to tell one individual from another on the basis of waveform characteristics alone.

Experiments with the octopus *Octopus vulgaris* showed that invertebrates can learn by observation. Graziano Fiorito of the Zoological Station of Naples, Italy, and Pietro Scotto of the Università di Reggio Calabria, Catanzaro, Italy, conditioned octopuses by a reward-punishment system to select one of two simultaneously presented objects, a red ball and a white ball, that differed only in colour. After the octopuses had been trained to select either a red ball or a white ball, another octopus was placed in an adjacent tank as an observer. The observer octopus was allowed to watch a conditioned octopus during four trials in which no errors were made. The observers were then tested in isolation, where they consistently selected the same-coloured ball as the observed octopus. Observational learning, known for humans and some other vertebrates, is considered to be an early step in conceptual thought and related to the cognitive learning abilities of animals. The findings were especially intriguing because octopuses have highly developed invertebrate brains with neural organizations analogous to vertebrate brains.

I. Lehr Brisbin of the Savannah River Ecology Laboratory, Aiken, N.C., and Steven N. Austad of Harvard University performed experiments on dogs trained to discriminate between scents of individual humans in order to evaluate whether they could distinguish scents from particular body parts. In a series of trials the dogs were highly successful in

This aye-aye, a representative of a critically endangered species of lemur from Madagascar, was born in captivity at the Duke University Primate Center in Durham, N.C. The primate uses its long middle finger to detect insect grubs in tree hollows and to poke holes in eggs and coconuts. The new aye-aye was a promising start for researchers attempting to develop a captively bred stock of the animals for repopulating Madagascar.
DUANE HALL—THE NEW YORK TIMES

discriminating between objects touched by the hand of the trainer and those touched by a stranger. But if the scent on an object came from the crook of the trainer's arm, the dogs perceived it as different from an object touched by the trainer's hand. One explanation is that dogs have evolved highly sensitive powers of scent discrimination that are important in the complex details of kin selection and recognition of subtle environmental cues. However, if dogs also make a distinction among such articles as clothing, gloves, or shoes that have acquired scents from different body parts of the same person, law-enforcement officials may need to reevaluate the techniques by which dogs are trained and used to identify suspects.

Determining phylogenetic relationships and origins among major taxonomic groups is fundamental to the understanding of various stages of evolution. To clarify early vertebrate evolution, scientists find it important to establish the relationships among the hagfish and lampreys, which are jawless, and the jawed fish. Formerly, the primitive characteristics shared by hagfish and lampreys had been thought to be due to a closer evolutionary relationship of the two groups to each other than to the jawed fish. In recent years, however, analyses of the physical form and structure (morphology) of all three groups led to a widely accepted revised view that lampreys are more closely related to jawed fish than to hagfish. Conclusions can be equivocal, however, when uncertainty exists about whether particular morphological features are ancestral or derived; i.e., in this case whether they are primitive or a result of degenerative evolution. To avoid such uncertainty David W. Stock and Gregory S. Whitt of the University of Illinois used sequence information in a specific RNA molecule taken from all three groups in order to construct an evolutionary tree of the molecule itself. By comparing similarities and divergences in molecules of ribosomal RNA from lampreys and hagfish with those from jawed fish, urochordates (such as sea squirts), and cephalochordates (lancelets), the investigators obtained results supporting the older hypothesis that lampreys and hagfish are more closely related to each other than either is to the jawed fish.

New information on the early evolution of avian flight and perching abilities was provided by Paul C. Sereno of the University of Chicago and Rao Chenggang of the Beijing (Peking) Natural History Museum on the basis of fossil bird skeletons from the Early Cretaceous (about 135 million years ago) in China. The newly described species, *Sinornis santensis,* was a sparrow-sized bird that retained some of the primitive traits of the 150 million-year-old *Archaeopteryx,* the oldest known bird, but had many characteristics of modern birds. The discovery represented one of the few bird fossils, and the only one with a complete skeleton, from the 50 million-year span following the existence of *Archaeopteryx.*

Conodont elements, minute toothlike fossils having a 300 million-year record ranging from the Late Cambrian to the Late Triassic, are well known to paleontologists because their colour and condition disclose the thermal history of their associated sediments and the chemistry of the ocean that supported the marine organism from which the fossils came. The classification of the conodont organism, however, had been debated for more than a century, being variously assigned to algae, vascular plants, invertebrates, and vertebrates, and it was only in the 1980s that the finding of fossils of the organism's soft tissues allowed it to be identified as a small, vaguely eel-like animal. During the year I.J. Sansom of the University of Birmingham, England, and colleagues reported that their investigation of the microstructure of conodont elements identified cellular bone and other tissue types characteristic of vertebrate skeletons. The confirmation of the vertebrate affinity of the conodont animal extended the known occurrence of vertebrate hard tissues from the Middle Ordovician (about 475 million years ago) to the Late Cambrian (about 515 million years ago).

A finding applicable to the origins of primates, and one that appeared to resolve a recent controversy, relates to whether all modern bats share a single evolutionary origin, as conventionally acknowledged by their classification into one order, Chiroptera. The alternative is that the two recognized groups of bats, megabats and microbats (Megachiroptera and Microchiroptera), evolved independently of each other and that megabats are more closely related to primates than to microbats. Wendy J. Bailey, Jerry L. Slightom, and Morris Goodman of Wayne State University School of Medicine, Detroit, Mich., compared gene sequences from bats, primates, and flying lemurs to establish their relationships. Megabats shared 39 derived gene-sequence changes with microbats but 3 or fewer changes with primates, flying lemurs, or both. Coupled with other recent molecular studies, the findings provided strong support that bats evolved only once and have only a distant phylogenetic relationship to primates.

In a recovery effort for an endangered species, the first two captive-bred California condors were released early in the year in a mountain habitat north of Los Angeles, five years after the last free-ranging birds had been removed from the wild. One of the birds, however, died in October from drinking antifreeze, probably from a puddle left by a motor vehicle. Plans continued for the release of six more condors in December. (J. WHITFIELD GIBBONS)

Entomology. Ashok K. Raina, Timothy G. Kingan, and Autar K. Mattoo of the U.S. Department of Agriculture's Beltsville (Md.) Agricultural Research Center provided evidence of the intricate mechanisms that insects have evolved to enable them to coordinate the timing of reproductive behaviour and offspring production with the availability of food. Females of the corn earworm moth (*Heliothis zea*) mate and deposit their eggs on corn and other host plants; after hatching, the caterpillars feed on the fruiting parts of these plants. The investigators conducted experiments showing that the female moths can detect volatile chemicals released by corn silk in association with the ripening of corn. The chemicals evoke a response in the female to release a sex pheromone that attracts males. Egg laying follows within a few hours. Females thus delay production of their sex pheromone and other reproductive behaviour until the chemical cue from a host plant is perceived, assuring the availability of food for the young.

R. Wehner and S. Wehner of the University of Zürich, Switz., and A.C. Marsh of the University of Namibia investigated factors that restrict the foraging activities of the Saharan silver ant (*Cataglyphis bombycina*), the only arthropod that forages at midday in the Sahara Desert. Silver ants scavenge on invertebrates but limit their foraging to a few minutes during the hottest part of the day, when temperatures that an ant experiences a few millimetres above the surface are above 46° C. (To convert Celsius to Fahrenheit, multiply by 1.8 and add 32; thus 46° C = 115° F.) Surface temperatures at that time are 60°–70° C. Ants discontinue foraging when their body temperature approaches about 53° C, the highest critical thermal maximum recorded for any terrestrial animal. The investigators determined that silver ants forage at such high temperatures to avoid predation by a desert lizard, which retreats from the surface at temperatures close to the threshold at which ants become active. The behaviour of the ant-eating lizard has apparently shaped the ant's behaviour by defining the "thermal window" within which the ant can safely forage, the upper limits being set by heat stress and the lower limits by predation pressure.

Evidence of the aggressive nature of imported fire ants (*Solenopsis invicta*), which have spread throughout much of the southeastern U.S. since their introduction from South America in the early 1900s, was gathered by R.H. Cherry and G.S. Nuessly of the University of Florida's Everglades Research and Education Center. The researchers used a variety of techniques to measure relative abundance of ant species in Florida sugarcane fields. Although imported fire ants had not been reported from the observed habitat in Florida before 1970, the study showed them now to be the dominant ant species, resulting in a lower relative abundance of native ant species.

Recalling the devastation wreaked on eastern U.S. forests by caterpillars of the gypsy moth (*Lymantria dispar*) since its introduction from Europe in the mid-1800s, American and Canadian entomologists expressed concern over the possibility of a similar threat to forests in the Pacific Northwest from an Asian strain, which was detected in Vancouver, B.C., in 1991, apparently carried in on grain ships from the Asian part of Russia. The Asian moth, which also was discovered in Portland, Ore., and Seattle, Wash., was believed to subsist on a broader range of trees than its European counterpart. Asian females were also stronger fliers, suggesting that spread of the moth could be faster and its control more difficult. (ANNE R. GIBBONS)

This article updates the *Macropædia* article INSECTS.

Ornithology. DNA fingerprinting, a technique in which unique patterns present in an individual organism's genetic material can be used to establish identity and determine relatedness among a group of individuals, was being used to study the sexual physiology and behaviour of birds. In *Sperm Competition in Birds: Evolutionary Causes and Consequences* (1992), Tim Birkhead and Anders Moeller collated and synthesized much recent data, some of it derived from DNA fingerprinting, on the topic of avian promiscuity. It long had been held that the large majority of bird species were monogamous, but in recent years "extra-pair" copulations and resulting broods of mixed parentage were shown to be widespread. The proportion of extra-pair matings observed in the field was found to correlate with the proportion of nestlings revealed by DNA fingerprinting to have been sired by promiscuous males. The percentage can be as high as 65% in the splendid fairy wren of Australia and nearly 50% in the indigo bunting of North America. The advantage to male birds who seek out and mate with more than one female is that they hand down more of their genes than if they were strictly monogamous. But females, far from being merely resigned to male promiscuity, appear to be energetic and ready participants. One advantage to females of mating with more than one male could be the improved chance of finding a male of higher quality subsequent to pairing with one of lesser quality.

A new one-volume checklist of the world's birds, *Distribution and Taxonomy of Birds of the World* by C.G. Sibley and B.L. Monroe, was noteworthy for its level of detail and completeness. Covering more than 9,000 species, the list was based on a classification system developed by Sibley and J.E. Ahlquist, and it arranged birds in a revised hierarchy and sequence. Hitherto, classifications had been based on morphology (form and structure) and had involved a degree of subjectivity of assessment. The new system was genetic, based on comparisons of the birds' DNA, and therefore more objective. A major surprise emerging from the new classification was that most Australian true songbirds (oscines) are related to one another, having gone through an adaptive radiation similar to that of the region's marsupial mammals. That fact had been hidden because the birds concerned have no shared morphological character comparable to the mammalian marsupial pouch. Other unexpected relations were the evolutionary closeness of the starlings to the mockingbirds, of the vultures of the New World to the storks (rather than to the Old World vultures), and of the pelicans to the shoebill (an African water bird superficially resembling a stork).

The world's total of just over 9,000 bird species is increased by one or two new species a year. Usually a specimen is killed and the skin preserved, but because a suspected new bush shrike spotted in Somalia could have belonged to a rare or endangered species, it was instead captured alive and later released. That it was indeed new to science was determined by DNA extracted from feather quills and then compared with DNA taken from live bush shrikes of other forms. It was named the Bulo Burti boubou and given the scientific designation *Laniarius liberatus*. The second word, *liberatus,* honoured the fact that for the first time the "type specimen" of a new species was not killed but set free.

The hooded pitohui (*Pitohui dichrous*), an orange-and-black passerine songbird from New Guinea, became the first bird known to be poisonous. John P. Dumbacher of the University of Chicago and colleagues discovered that the feathers and skin of the bird, and subsequently those of two related species of pitohui, contain the alkaloid homobatrachotoxin, the same potent nerve toxin found in the skin of poison-dart frogs of Colombia. The investigators proposed that the compound functioned as a chemical defense against predators. They had yet to learn how the pitohui tolerated the toxin in its own body and whether it synthesized the compound entirely on its own or obtained precursor molecules from insects or plants in its diet.   (JEFFREY BOSWALL)

This article updates the *Macropædia* article BIRDS.

MARINE BIOLOGY

Scientists aboard the U.S. submersible *Alvin* discovered persistent dense swarms (more than 1,000 individuals per litre) of amphipod crustaceans near hot-water vents at a depth of 2,520 m along the East Pacific Rise. (A metre is about 3.3 ft.) The amphipods were new to science, and they exhibited sustained, rapid swimming, highly unusual in deep-sea invertebrates. Researchers aboard *Cyana*, a French submersible, found a remarkably deep (400-m) layer of salps (*Salpa fusiformis;* animals belonging to the urochordate, or tunicate, subphylum) and a new species of appendicularian (a species of *Oikopleura;* also a urochordate), apparently sustained by downward transport of phytoplankton (the plantlike component of plankton) at the Ligurian convergence in the northwestern Mediterranean. Methane seeps in shallow waters of the northern Kattegat Strait off Denmark were shown to form spectacular submarine landscapes ("bubbling reefs") of carbonate-cemented limestone structures colonized by brightly coloured plants and animals.

The spawning location of Japanese eels (*Anguilla japonica*) in the Pacific, elusive for 60 years, was located by a Japanese scientist west of the Mariana Islands (15° N, 140° E). Dispersal of leptocephalan larvae (the leaflike larval young) of these eels was similar to that of the Atlantic eels spawned in the Sargasso Sea. Aggregated settlement of bivalve mollusk larvae has often been attributed to substrate selection behaviour, but Swedish studies on cockle larvae (*Cerastoderma edule*) questioned this since most previous laboratory experiments had been carried out in still, not flowing, water. In moving water cockle larvae were observed to remain undispersed in the viscous layer less than a millimetre (a few hundredths of an inch) above the sediment surface, suggesting that water-flow effects may also induce patchy settlement. The scyphomedusan *Linuche unguiculata* (a jellyfish) was observed to form clusters up to a square kilometre (about 0.4 sq mi) in area along the Belize barrier reef, probably enhancing breeding success. During windy periods clusters were determined by surface circulation, but in calm conditions aggregations persisted by the novel mechanism of swimming in circles.

The nautilus is a zoological oddity, often described as a "living fossil," a rare survivor of an abundance of shelled cephalopods dating back to the Paleozoic Era (570 million to 245 million years ago). A study in Papua New Guinea suggested how mass extinction of shelled cephalopods may have occurred, finding that modern *Nautilus pompilius* is astonishingly well adapted for conditions of low oxygen concentration. If fossil forms such as the ammonites were similarly adapted, then they may have been outcompeted by new species of fish and cephalopods that evolved when concentrations of oxygen in seawater increased following acknowledged increases in atmospheric oxygen during the Mesozoic Era (245 million to 66.4 million years ago).

Canadian studies reported remarkable opportunism by normally scarce shallow-water, near-bottom-dwelling copepods *Tisbe furcata* and *Cyclopina schneideri* in Arctic waters. In midwinter the crustaceans ascended to exploit rich feeding space immediately below the ice cover. There the "ice copepods" flourished very abundantly until the ice melted and survivors returned to the near bottom. Australian studies showed grapsid crabs to be so-called keystone species in mangrove forest ecology; burrowing of the crabs enhanced soil aeration and hence the productivity and reproductive success of mangroves.

Thraustochytriales, generally considered to be fungi, were isolated from Indian mangroves and shown to produce amoebas, which fed by ingesting bacteria. The combined functions of funguslike breakdown of complex organic molecules and ingestion of bacteria suggested a unique position for these organisms within the kingdom Protista. Since the discovery of the ozone hole over Antarctica in the mid-1980s, there had been concern regarding the potential effects of increased ultraviolet (UV) radiation on the Antarctic marine ecosystem. Joint U.S.-Argentine studies showed markedly less resistance to UV in Antarctic phytoplankton compared with tropical forms.   (ERNEST NAYLOR)

This article updates the *Macropædia* articles CRUSTACEANS; FISHES; MOLLUSKS; etc.

BOTANY

Plant physiologists have long wondered how plants respond to gravity with nearly perfect fidelity. Roots always grow down, whereas stems grow up. The response derives from a gravity-sensing (gravisensing) mechanism rather than a light-sensing one, since it is evident in plants grown in either light or darkness. The growth movements that result from the stimulus have been named gravitropisms. The most widely accepted textbook explanation of gravisensing in plants involves the movement of starch grains within certain cells of the root; the grains act as statoliths and fall to the lower side of the cell owing to gravity. The movement of the grains triggers other cellular events, which then result in directed growth of stems and roots. However, the fact that some plants that lack starch grains remain sensitive to gravity leaves unanswered questions about the mechanism involved.

Scientists at Cornell University, Ithaca, N.Y., published papers in 1991 and 1992 that proposed a different mechanism for gravisensing in certain large-celled algae, one that may be applicable to other plants as well. In the alga *Chara corallina*, which has cells that are 2.5–5 cm (1–2 in) in length and that lack starch grains, one can easily observe the movement of structures within the cells, a phenomenon called cytoplasmic streaming. When *Chara* cells are oriented vertically, the cytoplasm streams downward about 10% faster than it streams upward. Because the upward stream becomes thicker than the downward stream, the volume moving in either direction is the same. Reversing the orientation of the cell reverses the streaming rates; what was the slower upward rate becomes the faster downward rate and vice versa. Experiments with both chemical reagents and physical manipulations showed that both ends of the *Chara* cell are involved in its perception of gravity and that the entire cell contents act as ballast. The falling of the cell contents causes compression of the plasma membrane of the lower part of the cell and a tension on the plasma membrane of the upper part of the cell. The compression and tension may cause specific ion channels, such as those that permit the flow of calcium, to respond by opening or closing. The resulting change in intracellular calcium may then regulate the upward and downward cytoplasmic flow.

The universality of the genetic code combined with the techniques of genetic engineering make it possible, at least in theory, to transfer any gene from one organism to another. The result of such a transfer is a transgenic organism that, if the instructions carried by the transferred gene are expressed, can carry out new tasks that were previously restricted to the donor organism. In plant biology, transgenic plants have been under intensive study because the results of such experiments hold great promise for agriculture. In one study a gene that affects the production of the plant hormone cytokinin was inserted into tobacco plants. The

The cotton boll on the left has matured free of damage from caterpillar crop pests, in contrast to the fate of the two other specimens. The difference is that the protected boll is from a plant carrying an inserted gene (from the *Bacillus thuringiensis* bacterium) that allows the plant's tissues to make a natural insecticidal toxin. Agricultural researchers have succeeded in growing successive harvests of the genetically engineered cotton and foresee commercial lines on the market in a few years that require much less pesticide spraying for high yield.

AGRICULTURAL RESEARCH SERVICE, USDA

result was a tobacco plant with viviparous leaves; that is, leaves that could produce plantlets in a way similar to the process that occurs normally in the common houseplant kalenchoe. Another, somewhat similar study using tomato plants demonstrated that expression of a gene that regulates the production of ethylene, another plant hormone, inhibited the ripening process of the tomato fruit. Both studies represented the rapidly expanding use of biotechnology in plant science research.

The accumulation of so-called greenhouse gases, including carbon dioxide (CO_2), in the atmosphere has created great concern and much speculation regarding the potential effect on global temperature and thus on possible changes in vegetation patterns. Since carbon dioxide is the form of carbon used in photosynthesis, some scientists have argued that increasing the forested areas of the planet would help dampen global warming since the increased tree growth, stimulated by initially higher CO_2 concentrations, would eventually decrease atmospheric CO_2. One recent study using yellow poplars, however, suggested that in a natural ecosystem the dampening effect due to increased tree growth may be quite small. Citing climate model simulations, another report argued that the temperature and rainfall changes associated with predicted global warming could shift the equilibrium distribution of natural vegetation over eastern North America as much as 500–1,000 km (300–600 mi) over the next 200–500 years. Such a change would be larger than the overall change that took place over the previous 7,000–10,000 years, after the retreat of glaciers.

(PHILIP D. REID)

MOLECULAR BIOLOGY

A Cancer-Fighting Compound in Broccoli. One of the most effective defenses of animals against physical attack, namely, running away, is denied to plants. Yet plants are constantly subject to attack by insects and grazing animals. Plants have adapted by evolving chemical defenses. They produce and accumulate compounds that are distasteful, or even toxic, to potential predators.

As plants developed chemical defenses, insects evolved countermeasures, such as immunity to the plant toxins or systems of enzymes that modify and so neutralize the toxins. Some insects even developed a liking for specific plant toxins as well as the ability to use them for their own purposes; *e.g.*, to attract mates or to deter attackers.

As a consequence of eons of evolution of chemical defenses by plants and of countermeasures by herbivores, many plants devote a substantial fraction of their metabolism to the synthesis of such defensive toxins. All herbivores, including humans, therefore encounter in their food a variety of

chemicals that are potentially deleterious. Herbivores must possess means of detoxifying those food-derived chemicals or at least of modifying them to increase their solubility in water and so facilitate their excretion in urine.

The first phase of that detoxication entails addition of one atom of oxygen (O) under the catalytic influence of enzymes called mono-oxygenases. Since the atom of oxygen derives from molecular oxygen, which contains two atoms of oxygen, some means of disposing of the second atom must be provided. Disposal is achieved by reducing it to water. The pair of electrons needed for the reduction comes from a coenzyme, derived from the vitamin niacin and designated NADPH. The mono-oxygenation reaction may be written as $NADPH + H^+ + O_2 + R-H \rightarrow NADP^+ + H_2O + R-OH$, in which H^+ is a hydrogen ion and $R-H$ represents the target toxin. It occurs in the membranes of the cellular endoplasmic reticulum and requires the cooperation of two enzymes. One of them is NADPH:cytochrome P_{450} reductase, which catalyzes the transfer of two electrons from NADPH to the second enzyme, cytochrome P_{450}. The reduced P_{450} then interacts with molecular oxygen and with the toxin and catalyzes the actual mono-oxygenation.

There is only one type of NADPH:cytochrome P_{450} reductase, but there are dozens of different P_{450} cytochromes, each of which can accommodate a different set of structurally related toxins. In toto the P_{450} family enables human beings to detoxify not only a wide array of natural toxins but also many of the synthetic organic compounds used in industrial societies as solvents, fuels, dyes, drugs, plasticizers, preservatives, and insecticides.

Simple addition of the hydroxyl (OH) group to the toxin, a process called hydroxylation, does somewhat increase its water solubility. Much greater water solubility can then be achieved by coupling the hydroxylated toxin with very water-soluble compounds like sulfate, glucuronate, or glutathione. That coupling is the second phase of the detoxication process, and it is applied to some compounds that are generated endogenously (within the body) as well as to food or environmental toxins.

Obviously, how much of a given detoxication enzyme is needed at any one time depends on the levels of exposure to the toxins that the enzyme is competent to modify. The level of exposure to specific plant toxins, for example, varies with the diet, which in the natural world varies with geographic location, season, amount of rainfall, and other factors. There is no point in maintaining a high level of a detoxication enzyme for a toxin that is not being ingested.

Economical adaptation to this variability demands that individual detoxication enzymes be produced in proportion to the need for their services. Therefore, specific detoxication enzymes should be, and indeed are, inducible by exposure to the toxins they act on or to compounds that resemble those toxins. The induction of detoxifying enzymes explains the development of tolerance during chronic exposure to given toxins.

A fraction of the toxins to which humans are exposed are capable of reacting with and modifying the DNA that encodes genetic information. Such compounds can cause mutations. Since certain mutations can lead to uncontrolled growth, these mutagenic toxins are sometimes also carcinogens, or cancer-causing agents. And, if there are compounds that can cause cancer, might there not also be compounds that somehow oppose the action of carcinogens and that therefore act as anticarcinogens?

The existence of anticarcinogens was suggested by the observation that diets rich in green and yellow vegetables are associated with a decreased incidence of cancer. Such a correlation was seen in laboratory rats and also in large populations of humans. Since vegetables are rich in the toxins that were evolved to thwart insect herbivores, a vegetable-rich diet should cause the body to produce enzymes devoted to detoxication. It appeared possible that the anticarcinogenic properties of the vegetables were a consequence of the induction of detoxifying enzymes.

This line of thought led a group of scientists at Johns Hopkins Medical School, Baltimore, Md., to look for inductions of detoxifying enzymes by vegetable-rich diets. They found two such enzyme inductions, one being that of glutathione-S-transferase, which couples glutathione to hydroxylated toxins, and the second being that of a quinone reductase, which reduces quinones to hydroquinones. They chose to concentrate on the quinone reductase since its activity is particularly easy to measure, and they found that exposing cultured hepatoma (liver tumour) cells to extracts of broccoli caused induction of quinone reductase in the cells.

In 1992 the Johns Hopkins group reported isolating and identifying the component of the broccoli extracts that is responsible for inducing quinone reductase. That compound is sulforaphane:

$$\begin{array}{c}
\text{H} \quad \text{O} \; \text{H} \; \text{H} \; \text{H} \; \text{H} \\
| \quad \| \quad | \quad | \quad | \quad | \\
\text{H}-\text{C}-\text{S}-\text{C}-\text{C}-\text{C}-\text{C}-\text{N}=\text{C}=\text{S} \\
| \quad\quad | \quad | \quad | \quad | \\
\text{H} \quad\quad \text{H} \; \text{H} \; \text{H} \; \text{H}
\end{array}$$

When added to the culture medium in only minute concentrations, sulforaphane caused a large increase in quinone reductase activity in hepatoma cells in culture. It also increased the activity of glutathione-S-transferase and, when fed to mice, was effective in inducing these enzymes in the liver and other tissues.

Induction of detoxication enzymes by a compound that is not itself a carcinogen would have the effect of decreasing the net body burden of carcinogens. This is a reasonable explanation for the anticarcinogenic effect of green and yellow vegetables. Sulforaphane is an isothiocyanate, and isothiocyanates are found in all cruciferous vegetables, including cabbage, brussels sprouts, broccoli, cauliflower, and mustard. Isothiocyanates other than sulforaphane also probably are able to induce detoxication enzymes. Indeed, several purely synthetic isothiocyanates showed such activity. The next stage of research would be to feed sulforaphane to rats or mice throughout their life spans in order to assess the magnitude of its anticarcinogenic effect.

It thus appears that, while some plant compounds are carcinogenic, others are anticarcinogens in that they elicit an increase in the levels of those enzymes dedicated to detoxication. If anticarcinogens can be found that are tasteless and free of unwanted side effects, they could be added to foods to achieve a decrease in the incidence of cancer.

(IRWIN FRIDOVICH)

The Human Genome Project—Controversy Abounds

Since its inception in the 1980s, the Human Genome Project has been torn by disagreements. One of them, the debate over the patenting of genes, was reportedly instrumental in the resignation in April 1992 of the project's noted leader, James D. Watson, co-winner of a Nobel Prize for determining the double helix structure of DNA. The lofty purpose of the project is to map the human genome—that is, to locate all the genes that the DNA comprises within a human cell's 46 chromosomes—and to determine the precise order of the three billion gene subparts, the nucleotides, that form the genetic code.

Heralded by some as the key to finding the cause and cure for many of humankind's most stubborn diseases, the project from the outset was, nevertheless, criticized by numerous scientists and officials who felt that the rewards would be insufficient justification for the huge amount of projected work, time, and funding. At the time of its endorsement by the U.S. National Academy of Sciences in 1988, the project was expected to cost $3 billion and take 15 years. Less than 10% of the genome is expected to yield useful information, most of it being made of "junk" DNA that does not carry coded instructions for functional proteins.

Other critics have expressed their concerns over moral and ethical issues involving the possible misuse of genetic information. For instance, applicants could be refused insurance or employment on the basis of tests that reveal a genetic predisposition to certain diseases or alcoholism. Such cases of "genetic discrimination" have already been documented. Anticipating this type of conflict, Watson insisted that 3% of the project's budget be set aside for the study of related political, social, and ethical problems.

Watson's opposition to the patenting of genes brought him into direct conflict with Bernadine Healy, director of the National Institutes of Health (NIH), which controls the genome project. Healy has approved gene patenting by the NIH, while Watson has referred to the patenting of thousands of gene fragments whose functions are largely unknown as "lunacy." Watson's resignation was also said to have been precipitated by an investigation of his interests in biotechnology companies, implying a possible conflict of interest. Most sources, however, suggested that the flap over patenting and the control of policy in general underlay the resignation. Watson and other critics of gene patenting felt that international scientific cooperation would be stifled by the process, belying the original "open" policy of the project. Hanging in the balance were the billions of dollars that could be made by biotechnological researchers as the genetic bases of diseases and various human physical and mental traits were discovered.

(MARVIN MARTIN)

Human Gene Therapy. In the simplest of terms human gene therapy is not a new idea but, rather, a very old idea that has recently taken on new form. Its basic premise—that replacing missing or nonfunctional body components with functional substitutes may treat or even cure at least some diseases—underlies much of common medical practice. The treatments of diabetes with insulin and of hemophilia with factor VIII are common examples. In each disorder untreated patients suffer complications resulting from their inability to produce enough of otherwise naturally occurring proteins. And in each case giving the patient regular injections of the appropriate substance relieves the symptoms.

Because both insulin and factor VIII are the products of genes (which happen to be missing or inactive in people with these disorders), such treatments could be called gene-product therapy. By replacing the missing natural gene products, both treatments are quite effective. Nonetheless, because they replace only the gene products, which are broken down quickly within the body, and not the genes themselves, which normally direct the continued production of those proteins, the treatments fall short of being cures; the patients remain absolutely dependent on receiving regular injections. Such diseases are somewhat analogous to a car that, because it has bad gaskets, persistently leaks oil. The car's owner could keep adding oil as needed, but the problem would remain. Alternately, the owner could replace the gaskets and cure the problem. Gene therapy provides the molecular equivalent of such a cure.

Children afflicted with a rare disorder called ADA-deficient severe combined immunodeficiency (SCID) were the first to be offered gene therapy. For years patients with ADA-deficient SCID were treated with regular injections of the natural protein they lacked, adenosine deaminase (ADA). In the absence of ADA, the body accumulates a toxic compound in its immune cells, leading to premature destruction of those cells and consequently to severely impaired immune function. Like the traditional treatments for diabetes and hemophilia, regular injections of ADA can be painful and costly. More importantly, despite such therapy, children with ADA-deficient SCID often continue to suffer the principal symptom of their disease—increased susceptibility to potentially fatal infections. The persistence of symptoms even in treated children probably reflects the fact that unlike insulin and factor VIII, which normally function free in solution within the blood, ADA normally functions within cells. Therefore, ADA injections provide the right protein in the wrong place—better than no protein at all but not fully effective.

In 1990 a four-year-old girl suffering from ADA deficiency became the first patient to receive gene therapy. Although she had taken ADA injections for two years hitherto, she continued to suffer repeated infections and was gradually losing her battle with the disease. Starting in late 1990 she received a series of intravenous infusions of her own immune cells that had been "gene-corrected" by the introduction of normal genes encoding functional human ADA. In response the child's immune function and clinical condition improved. In addition, analyses of the immune cells in her blood indicated that a significant fraction were indeed gene-corrected. After less than a year, therapy was stepped down to a maintenance level, and the child's condition continued to be monitored closely. In addition, a second patient, a nine-year-old girl, began treatment in 1991. As of mid-1992 both children continued to improve and were healthy enough to attend regular schools, suffering no more than the average number of infections.

The landmark protocol initiated in 1990 represented a beginning for gene therapy. By May 1992 there were 11 active clinical gene therapy protocols and almost double that number either approved and awaiting initiation or in various stages of development. Gene therapy was proposed to aid in the treatment of diseases ranging from hemophilia and familial hypercholesterolemia (inherited high cholesterol levels) to cancer and AIDS. In addition, successful experiments in laboratory animals indicated that gene therapy could help in the battle against cystic fibrosis (CF), a serious inherited disorder caused by mutations in a gene, the CF transmembrane conductance regulator (CFTR) gene, that encodes a protein needed for normal passage of chloride ions across the membranes of cells lining the airways, pancreas, and sweat glands, among other tissues.

The CF experiments are particularly novel because they require a new class of gene-delivery vectors, or carriers, distinct from those used in most other gene therapy protocols. Most protocols rely on delivery systems based on retroviral vectors. These vectors carry human genetic material packaged in the form of modified viral particles, capable of infecting human cells and thereby delivering their contents of human genetic material. The problem with such vectors is that they infect only proliferating cells. While the immune cells requiring gene correction in ADA-deficient patients are proliferating, the cells lining the airways of CF patients are not. Researchers thus turned to an alternative vector system based on a virus capable of infecting even nonproliferating cells; namely, adenovirus. Using adenoviral particles engineered to carry the human CFTR sequence, the researchers achieved the introduction and expression of this human DNA in cells of the airway lining of living rats. Although many hurdles remained to be overcome before such newer procedures would be ready for human trials, the implications for treating patients with CF and perhaps related respiratory disorders were clear and enormous.

Technical progress achieved in recent years has moved gene therapy from dream to reality. That reality carries with it not only immense promise for good but also a broad range of social, ethical, and technical questions. Perhaps the most obvious issue deals with boundaries. When is gene therapy ethically justified and when is it not? For example, is any form of gene therapy that involves somatic cells (cells other than eggs or sperm) acceptable but any form of germline therapy (one involving eggs or sperm) unacceptable? At the crux of the question is a deeper one: is it proper to treat patients alive today but improper to alter the genetic makeup of future generations? Furthermore, who is to define the boundary between genetic treatment and genetic enhancement? Because many nongenetic forms of medical "treatment," including plastic surgery and the use of steroid hormones, have certainly crossed this fine line, can genetic forms of therapy realistically be held to a higher standard?

Technical issues regarding safety, efficacy, cost, and ease of use also abound. For example, while significant short-term safety precautions are rigorously enforced prior to approval of any gene therapy protocol, an assessment of long-term safety will become apparent only with the passage of time. As with the basic concept behind gene therapy, none of the issues is new. The challenge remains one of balancing risks and benefits to secure the safest and greatest good for those now living and those yet to be born.

(JUDITH L. FRIDOVICH-KEIL)

See also Botanical Gardens and Zoos; Earth Sciences; Environment.

This article updates the *Macropædia* articles AGRICULTURE; Animal BEHAVIOUR; BIOCHEMICAL COMPONENTS OF ORGANISMS; The BIOLOGICAL SCIENCES; BIOSPHERE; CANCER; CONSERVATION OF NATURAL RESOURCES; DISEASE; The Principles of GENETICS AND HEREDITY; MAMMALS; REPRODUCTION AND REPRODUCTIVE SYSTEMS; SENSORY RECEPTION.

Literature

The 1992 Nobel Prize for Literature was awarded to Derek Walcott (*see* NOBEL PRIZES), the West Indian poet and playwright. The judges remarked that his most fruitful sources and central loyalties were to "the Caribbean where he lives, the English language and his African origins." Walcott's victory was welcomed in Britain, where his play, *The Odyssey,* had recently been well received at Stratford-upon-Avon; it resembled his epic narrative *Omeros,* a novel in verse, which relocated stories from Homer's two epics within a fishing village on Saint Lucia. "Standing astride the chasm between two cultures," declared the London *Independent,* "he has found a toehold in the best of both worlds." Walcott's triumph was similarly welcomed in the U.S.; though born in Saint Lucia and resident in Trinidad, he was currently teaching at Boston University.

In France, too, a writer from the Caribbean won the principal literary award. Patrick Chamoiseau from Martinique was awarded the Prix Goncourt for his novel *Texaco*—Texaco being a district of Martinique threatened by redevelopment. The novel, written partly in the Creole version of French, dealt with the history of the French colony from the days of slavery to the present as recorded by a dominating old woman, a strong opponent of the Texaco redevelopment.

An attempt was made to set up an independent, Western-style literary prize for Russian novels, in Moscow. It was sponsored by Booker plc, the firm that sponsors the main prize for novels in Britain. The judges were an international group, including John Bayley, the British scholar, and Andrey Sinyavsky, the celebrated "dissident" writer of the 1960s. The sorry condition of the Russian publishing industry and the literary journals made the Booker Russian Novel Prize difficult to organize. However, a shortlist of six novels was assembled, and in December the prize of £10,000 (6 million rubles) was awarded to Mark Kharitonov for "Lines of Fate," published as yet only in a literary journal.

Derek Walcott

ENGLISH

United Kingdom. Despite the recession, a great many books were published in the U.K.—more than in any other European country, according to a survey by Datamonitor, presented in November; the U.K.'s output had risen to 70,000 titles from 50,000 in 1986. The survey suggested that foreign publishers would continue to buy into the British market since the English-language market was recognized as potentially the largest in the world.

Nonfiction works, dealing with large themes, were presented by successful novelists. One of these, respectfully received, was a discourse on the English language by the versatile Anthony Burgess, displaying his technical knowledge of linguistics. Another was a "biography" of Jesus Christ, written by the satirical A.N. Wilson. It had long been felt that Wilson's rather sour and generally repellent novels were redeemed by his Christian faith and his stalwart adherence to the Church of England. Having lost his faith, he produced this book as an antireligious thesis, striving "to rescue Jesus from the encrustations of the Christian myth." The book's arguments were found to be familiar and did not stimulate a very lively or lasting controversy.

More serious attention was accorded to *Metaphysics as a Guide to Morals* by Iris Murdoch, an academic philosopher as well as an admired novelist. Reviewing it in the *Times Literary Supplement,* Simon Blackburn described it as a "huge, intelligent, rambling exploration of religion, art, metaphysics and morals." He admired the "incisive things" she had written about the work of celebrated philosophers and artists, while always returning to "the responsible moral spiritual individual" and "the transcendental ideas that it takes to sustain him." But he could not accept her view that "the relation of religion, morality and philosophy is perhaps the great intellectual problem of the age."

The Intellectuals and the Masses by John Carey was a forceful attack on some of the most admired modern (or "Modernist") writers of the century; it was subtitled *Pride and Prejudice Among the Literary Intelligentsia 1880–1939,* with reference to the snobbish disdain for "normal people," or the Common People, expressed by such elitists as James Joyce and Virginia Woolf. Auberon Waugh, the editor of the *Literary Review,* cheerfully admitted his sympathy with the snobbery that Carey opposed; he identified mass culture with "the Mickey Mouse culture of America."

John Gross, a versatile scholar and journalist, was much applauded for *Shylock: Four Hundred Years in the Life of a Legend.* "It broadens out," said Julian Symons, "from consideration of the Elizabethan Shylock into suggestions of shifting attitudes towards Jews" in the centuries during which Shakespeare's play had been performed and interpreted. The words of *The Merchant of Venice,* said Frank Kermode, frequently "subvert the manifest message they are promoting"; the subtexts become clearer with time, "especially when powerful actors and directors dig for them."

Fiction. Novelists in the ambitious, prizewinning category seemed obsessed with past history—particularly the wartime of 50 years earlier. It came as almost a surprise

Barry Unsworth

when Julian Barnes published *The Porcupine,* an up-to-date story about a deposed Communist leader facing a dubious prosecution in a country resembling modern Bulgaria. In fact, the novel was first published there, in Bulgarian.

The novelists on the shortlist for the Booker Prize were less attached to current events. Ian McEwan's *Black Dogs* concerned the physical manifestation of evil to a young British couple in 1946. Keen young Communists, on their honeymoon in France, they are confronted by feral hounds, former Nazi guard dogs, creating an atmosphere of menace strong enough to split the couple apart and drive the woman into a spiritual quest. *Daughters of the House* by Michèle Roberts told of two French girls in the 1950s, trying to interpret the misdeeds of their seniors in World War II. *Serenity House,* by the South African novelist Christopher Hope, dealt with an "eventide home" for retired gentlefolk, including a fine old English gentleman—suddenly exposed as a Nazi war criminal. *The English Patient* was written by Michael Ondaatje (*see* BIOGRAPHIES), a Canadian of mixed Dutch and Asian blood, born in Sri Lanka. His poetic novel was set in a battered Italian villa in 1945—just after the war. It had become a war hospital, where one English patient survived, a badly burned aviator, tended by a Canadian nurse, herself mentally scarred by wartime events.

Ondaatje shared the Booker Prize with Barry Unsworth, whose novel *Sacred Hunger,* concerned with the 18th-century slave trade, was described by a judge as a "rattling historical narrative," as against "the dense poetic meditation" of Ondaatje. Of the six prime competitors, only one was set in our contemporary world: *The Butcher Boy* by Patrick McCabe, the bizarre monologue of a gruesomely deranged Irish youth—"the sort of book you feel guilty enjoying," according to one critic. It was asserted in *The Guardian* that "the workmanlike novels on the Booker shortlist merely confirm the decline of British fiction."

In contrast with these were ambitiously satirical books, described (in the *Indepen-*

dent) as "two new novels that take on slippery modern literary theories." One was *The Death of the Author* by Gilbert Adair, a learned joke about a "deconstructionist" scholar with a Nazi past—evidently modeled on the late Paul de Man of Harvard; his aim was to eliminate the Author from the Text in a manner more literal than was usually recommended by deconstructionists. The other was *Dr Criminale* by Malcolm Bradbury, himself a literary academician. His principal character was another literary philosopher with a high reputation and a nasty past—he had worked for the East German Stasi and had since become attached to the Eurocrats of Brussels. The narrator pursues Dr. Criminale all over Europe, from conference to conference, in a deconstructionist spirit, feeling that "Criminale was the Text and I was the Decoder." Like Adair's satire, *Dr Criminale* was admired by those readers who took his references.

Returning to the past, Hilary Mantel produced *A Place of Greater Safety,* a long novel *about* (rather than set within) the French Revolution—with Camille Desmoulins as the hero, Danton and Robespierre taking leading parts. In the *London Review of Books,* P.N. Furbank marveled at the author's "creative energy and planning power" while doubting that it was possible to write a novel *about* such an extraordinary event. Another widely admired study of the past was *Ulverton* by Adam Thorpe, telling stories from four centuries in what one of the Booker judges, Mark Lawson, described as "both a chronicle of English history and a commentary on the evolution of the English language."

Biography. Revealing and inquisitive books about the lives of modern writers continued to attract attention and dismay. Hugh David's biography of a poet, *Stephen Spender: A Portrait with Background,* was not much admired. It was attacked by Sir Stephen's wife, in the columns of the *Times Literary Supplement,* even before publication. Ian Hamilton offered a lively study, *Keepers of the Flame: Literary Estates and the Rise of Biography,* which demonstrated that the quarrel between writers' kin and biographers was not a new phenomenon. He presented 22 case studies, from John Donne in the 17th century to the contemporary poet Philip Larkin. A somewhat similar historical survey of biographers and their opponents, by Michael Millgate, was entitled *Testamentary Acts: Browning, Tennyson, James, Hardy.*

John Sutherland remarked, in the *London Review of Books,* that Hamilton's study was "that rarest of modern things, lit crit with laughs." However, he found it surprising—in "a study whose main concern is the suppression or revelation of intimate materials"—that there was no discussion of the connections and collisions between James Joyce's family and his biographers; he listed many other recent controversies concerning biographies (authorized or unauthorized) of Nabokov, Laurence Durrell, Sylvia Plath, Anne Sexton, T.S. Eliot, Philip Larkin, and, of course, Stephen Spender. Sutherland noted that Hamilton himself had written a successful biography of the dead American poet Robert Lowell but had been frustrated in his pursuit of the still-living J.D. Salinger.

A compilation of *Selected Letters of Philip Larkin,* edited by Anthony Thwaite, the po-

et's executor, was reviewed by Ian Hamilton in the *London Review of Books;* he remarked that it was unusual for a writer's letters, "all foreground and no background," to come out in advance of the official biography. The quiet, reclusive Larkin was shown to have been very ambitious, "surprisingly alert to questions of literary-world status and to the encroachments of his rivals. No attempt to account for his lifelong unhappiness can now possibly pretend that he was not." But his unhappy life, wrote Mick Imlah in the *TLS,* had produced "hundreds of sharp and sad and funny letters," as well as "dozens of the most generally enjoyed English poems of the century."

Muriel Spark, an admired and formidable novelist, published her autobiography, *Curriculum Vitae.* She was born Muriel Camberg in Edinburgh in 1918, married, bore a child in Africa, suffered a nervous breakdown, and became a Roman Catholic—a surprising decision, perhaps, for a woman of Jewish ancestry, brought up in Scotland. Her autobiography was found to be as chic and rigorous as her novels.

A more vulnerable woman, Lady Ottoline Morell, had been best known as a subject of jokes and parodies in the spiteful writings of her protégés—Lawrence, Strachey, Woolf. Miranda Seymour's appreciative biography of the hostess was reviewed by Sue Gainsford: "At last, you feel, Ottoline has got the treatment she deserved." One of Ottoline's lovers, Bertrand Russell, also received an admired biography, by Caroline Moorehead, who dealt with his troubled and controversial career as political dissenter, academic philosopher, and lover during his 97 years of life.

Keir Hardie, born 16 years earlier than the learned, aristocratic Russell, had long been a hero, semimythical, for the British Labour Party. He began his career as a boy coal miner, became a trade-union activist, a member of Parliament (in 1892), a supporter of women's suffrage, and a campaigner against war. Caroline Benn, the American wife of another Labour Party statesman, worked hard to present a full account and appreciation of his exemplary

Iris Murdoch

life. This was perhaps the most valuable of the year's political biographies, which also included Bernard Wasserstein's study *Herbert Samuel* (about the distinguished Liberal minister and governor of Palestine) and Ben Pimlott's rather cautious biography of a still-living and controversial Labour Party statesman, *Harold Wilson.*

Rupert Murdoch: Ringmaster of the Information Circus was the title of the fifth biography of the famous newspaper magnate; it was written by William Shawcross, who described him as "a lord of the global village." Another expatriate press tycoon, the late Lord Beaverbrook, was candidly presented as a charming rogue in his latest biography—*Beaverbrook: A Life* by Anne Chisholm and Michael Davie.

Poetry. In a year notable for public sneering at the crown and the monarchy, the collection of "Laureate poems" offered by Ted Hughes was found refreshing by many readers and critics. Hughes was "the best Poet Laureate since Tennyson," declared another poet, Andrew Motion. The laureate's book, *Rain-Charm for the Duchy,* was savagely attacked by other critics, and in the *Independent* it was predicted that Hughes would be "the last person in England who will ever try to write meaningful, heartfelt, royalist poetry." From a notable contemporary of Hughes, Thom Gunn, now resident in the U.S., came a very different sort of book, *The Man with Night-Sweats.* These poems, mostly concerned with sufferers from AIDS, were widely admired.

John Burnside was recognized as one of the leading poets with a "numinous urge," declaring themselves for the idea of "God in Nature and for a return to Christian metaphysics" (according to Peter Porter in the *Sunday Telegraph*). Burnside's collection, *Feast Days,* took its name from "missals of feast days in scarlet ink: Laetere, Rogation, Quasimodo"—but he turned his attention to quieter, less formal celebrations. Simon Armitage, with *Kid,* mapped "a degraded Post-Modern landscape" (suggested Nicholas Tredell, in the *LRB*) "where the seedy can tip into the macabre."

In *Red-Haired Android,* Jeremy Reed denounced other poets, thus:

> Their safety-net is Larkin's provincial de-sexualised climacteric; the flat sensibility bred by a library

However, Reed's poems were found to be lacking in the adventurousness and the visionary qualities that he advocated and craved.   (D.A.N. JONES)

United States. In just about every literary genre, marvelous new work was published in the United States in 1992. Some of it also performed quite well at the box office.

Fiction. "He rode on, the two horses following, riding doves up out of pools of standing water and the sun descending out of the dark and discolored overcast to the west where its redness ran down the narrow band of sky over the mountains like blood falling through water and the desert fresh from the rain turning gold in the evening light and deepening to dark, a slow inkening over the bajada and the rising hills and the stark stone length of the cordilleras darkening far to the south in Mexico.... He pointed his horse at the polestar and rode on...."

Nearly 30 years earlier the author of these lines, novelist Cormac McCarthy, had pointed his horse at the polestar and pro-

Robert Stone
MICHAEL A. SMITH

duced one wonderful book after another, none of which sold more than a few thousand copies, yet each of which seemed to a discerning group of serious readers a minor masterwork of contemporary fiction. With the 1992 publication of McCarthy's sixth novel, *All the Pretty Horses* (from which the lines quoted above were taken), McCarthy's public increased 10-fold, and many critics started talking major rather than minor. The story of a pair of troubled Texas ranch boys who in the winter of 1949 hitch up their ponies and cross the border into Mexico in search of their destinies, McCarthy's novel is composed in lapidary prose that burrows deep into the heart at the same time it gestures toward the horizon. This novel alone would have made 1992 an auspicious year for fiction.

Another fine book from one of the country's best fiction writers was Robert Stone's seagoing *Outerbridge Reach.* Like McCarthy's novel, this dark and artful story hit the best-seller list for a respectable number of weeks, and it showed a masterly novelist working at the top of his powers. A middle-aged Vietnam-generation couple undergoing the stress of a troubled marriage, a daring and ultimately hallucinatory oceangoing race in a vessel not built to last, a gifted filmmaker who sees the world as through a lens darkly: Stone's novel possessed all the elements of the brilliance that readers had come to expect of him and told a powerful and resonant story.

A number of other novelists in for the long haul published new work during the year, some with more success than others. On the plus side came *Very Old Bones,* the latest in William Kennedy's "Albany cycle" of novels, a family saga set in the New York state capital from the mid-19th century to the present day. A book of massive proportion and ambition was Richard Marius' third novel, the completely engrossing *After the War.* Thomas McGuane, writing once again from Montana about Montana men in dire social and mental straits, produced *Nothing but Blue Skies,* his finest—and funniest—book in a decade.

Live from Golgotha or, as the subtitle put it, "The Gospel According to Gore Vidal," was either loved or loathed, depending, it

seemed more often than not, on the reviewer's theological orientation. Secular critics claimed to enjoy Vidal's satiric send-up of early Christianity, though the negative reviews, by writers such as Father Andrew Greeley in the *Washington Post*'s *Book World* ("blasphemy") and novelist Wilfrid Sheed in *The New Yorker* ("an ingenious piece of fluff") were more entertaining. Mixed reviews greeted *Brightness Falls,* Jay McInerney's lively challenge to Tom Wolfe's multicharacter serial of contemporary New York City life, *The Bonfire of the Vanities.* Ken Kesey's ecology-minded extravaganza set in an Alaska of the near future—*Sailor Song,* his first novel in decades—also met with a mixed reception.

More solidly praised were a number of fine novels by a miscellaneous group of writers, all of whom deserved wider recognition: *Violence* by Richard Bausch, the story of a murderous robbery at a Midwestern convenience store and its effect on the life of one of the survivors; *Fortunate Lives,* a subtle but piercingly told story of middle-class family life in the wake of personal disaster, by Robb Forman Dew; Gloria Naylor's daring—and successful—allegory *Bailey's Cafe;* Susan Richards Shreve's bold feminist saga *Daughters of the New World;* and Craig Nova's beautifully composed *Trombone,* in which he told the troubling story of an unrepentant California arsonist and his recalcitrant son. Critic Susan Sontag made a hit in intellectual circles with *The Volcano Lover,* a historical workout on the lives of Lord and Lady Hamilton.

Among the writers of short stories there were masters at work and some talented newcomers as well. George Garrett weighed in with *Whistling in the Dark: True Stories and Other Fables,* a brilliant mix of short fiction and lively essays; Robert Olen Butler brought out a collection of fine stories about Vietnamese-Americans living in Louisiana called *A Good Scent from a Strange Mountain;* and *The Stories of John Edgar Wideman* included three previous volumes plus 10 new stories. First-time author Pam Houston briefly hit the best-seller list with her widely noticed collection *Cowboys Are My Weakness,* and South Bronx writer Abraham Rodriguez made an impressive debut with the stories in *The Boy Without a Flag: Tales of the South Bronx.*

Among consistently popular best-selling writers of serious accomplishments, Michael Crichton added his novel *Rising Sun,* a Los Angeles murder mystery set in the context of troubled U.S.-Japanese relations, to his list of triumphs; and Anne Rice delivered the fourth volume of her phenomenally successful gothic series on vampires, a book called *The Tale of the Body Thief. Gerald's Game,* one of Stephen King's less terrifying and thus less interesting novels, hovered near the top of the list for much of the year.

The main flurry of activity among best-sellers that proved truly significant, however, was the success of novels by Toni Morrison—*Jazz*—and Terry McMillan—*Waiting to Exhale*—and Alice Walker—*Possessing the Secret of Joy,* three novels by three African-American woman writers appearing on the list at the same time. The McMillan book became in fact the object of a new indicator of commercial success: urban bookstores throughout the U.S. reported that her novel was being stolen from shops faster than managers could restock it.

Nonfiction. As rich a year as 1992 was in fiction, the quality of the nonfiction was at least equal with the novels and story collections. A number of first-rate, idiosyncratic volumes set the standard.

"The grain . . . It is a trickle at first. Almost single kernels and then half cups as the auger spurts them up and out of the augur chute and tumbling down into the empty wooden grain wagon where a child, always a child for this and for the tops of the haystacks, where a child waits with a shovel almost as big as he is, a huge grain scoop . . . And it comes . . . That little bit comes and then the shocks begin feeding into the threshing machine faster, one on top of another and another, tumbling off the hayracks and into the feed chute and past the twine cutter and down into the guts of the machine and the grain becomes a small stream, then a river, a river of gold pouring from the top of the augur tube into the wagon." In *Clabbered Dirt, Sweet Grass* Gary Paulsen made this elegiac rendering of farm life through the course of the four seasons. As much a memoir of his troubled past as an investigation of the values of western ranching, *Hole in the Sky* by novelist William Kittredge also used elegy to good effect. In the posthumously published *Young Men and Fire,* Norman Maclean meditated on a long-forgotten incident in the history of the U.S. Forest Service, creating an impressive fusion of personal history and social detail.

Beverly Lowry, in *Crossed Over,* offered a powerful picture of family tragedy intersecting with a crime story by telling the story of a young Texas woman on death row and her own coming to terms with the highway death of her younger son. Essayist Richard Rodriguez looked in the mirror—"The wide nostrils, the thick lips . . . such a long face—such a long nose—sculpted by indifferent, blunt thumbs, and of such common clay."—in his impressive collection *Days of Obligation: An Argument with My Mexican Father,* a stimulating series of essays on Mexican-American cultural interplay. The superb essays in Edward Hoagland's *Balancing Acts* took the reader from Yemen to Wyoming and from Thoreau to contemporary academic politics, all in the cunningly casual voice of one of America's most serious and intelligent prose writers.

GILLES PERESS—MAGNUM

Cormac McCarthy

Susan Sontag
MARIO RUIZ—TIME MAGAZINE

Essays, book reviews, class notes, and lectures were among the 21 pieces in cultural critic Camille Paglia's second book, *Sex, Art, and American Culture,* as lively and provocative a collection of assays of the changing nature of U.S. popular culture as was seen all year. Richard Rhodes's *Making Love: An Erotic Odyssey* was a single-minded autobiographical essay on the Pulitzer Prize winner's life as an erotic American.

Biography. Past presidents came under scrutiny on a grand scale in such highly praised volumes as David McCullough's *Truman,* which lent impetus to the frequent—and probably erroneous—invocation of the example of the life of the 33rd president in the rhetoric of the 1992 presidential campaign. *Theodore Roosevelt* by Nathan Miller also appeared. A study on the grand scale of a man nearly as powerful as a president was *Kissinger* by *Time* magazine correspondent Walter Isaacson.

Among biographies of literary figures, a few stood out, either for the fact of calling attention to a writer who had not heretofore come under serious scrutiny or for the breadth and depth of its investigations. Of the former variety there was *Pilgrim in the Ruins* by Jay Tolson, the first major biographical exploration of the life of the late Louisiana novelist Walker Percy. Of the latter there was *Hemingway: A Life Without Consequences* by James R. Mellow, which rounded out the author's trilogy of biographies of Lost Generation figures that included books on Gertrude Stein and a dual biography of F. Scott and Zelda Fitzgerald.

Mary McCarthy's posthumous *Intellectual Memoirs: New York, 1936–1938* revealed more about the novelist's erotic life than her mind. *The Pill, Pygmy Chimps, and Degas' Horse: The Autobiography of Carl Djerassi* offered a rare glimpse into the life and work of a world-renowned scientist.

Literary Criticism. Veteran critics, journalists, and an outstanding newcomer made their presences felt on the scene, beginning with John W. Aldridge, author of the epoch-setting *After the Lost Generation,* weighing in with *Talents and Technicians,* a reasoned polemic against writing schools and a cool critical estimate of the "Brat Pack" generation. *New York Times* writer and novelist/biographer James Atlas published *Battle of*

the Books, a smart survey of the current struggle for the possession of the literary canon within universities around the nation.

Ignoring, with good results, such academic questions as "canonicity," novelist George Garrett was represented in the critical realm during the year with two volumes of entertaining and intelligent essays on the literary tradition and the contemporary literary marketplace, *The Sorrows of Fat City* and *My Silk Purse and Yours: The Publishing Scene and American Literary Art.* A practical critic of the first order, young reviewer and essayist Sven Birkerts produced *American Energies,* an interesting collection of his recent pieces on contemporary American fiction.

Poetry. "Although I'm apparently alone, with a pleasant but unextraordinary feeling of self sufficiency, / I know I'm actually a part of a group of people who for reasons the dream never makes clear / are unavailable to any of my senses, though I'm always aware of the pressure of their presence." Poet C.K. Williams in "The Solid," one of the many dream poems in his pithy and important collection *A Dream of Mind,* might have been speaking of the large number of his contemporaries who also brought out interesting work during the year, among them Louise Glück with *The Wild Iris,* Gerald Stern with *Bread Without Sugar,* Susan Wood's Lamont Poetry Prize-winning *Campo Santo,* Gary Snyder's *No Nature,* and Stephen Sandy's *Thanksgiving Over the Water.*

William Matthews offered his *Selected Poems and Translations, 1969–1991,* and Hayden Carruth published his *Collected Shorter Poems, 1946–1991. Heaven, Collected Poems, 1956–1990* showed the poetic side of novelist Al Young. Elizabeth Macklin's *A Woman Kneeling in the Big City* revealed urban poetryscapes of some accomplishment, and *A Gilded Lapse of Time* by Gjertrud Schnackenberg was made up of a carefully worked triptych on faith and art. Among first books, Susan Prospere's *Sub Rosa* captured some attention.

Prizes and Awards. Jane Smiley won both the Pulitzer Prize in fiction and the National Book Critics Circle Award for Fiction for her novel *A Thousand Acres.* Lawrence Langer won the NBCC Award for criticism with *Holocaust Testimonies,* and Al-

LARRY BARNS

Alice Walker

bert Goldbarth's *Heaven and Earth* took the prize for poetry. The PEN/Faulkner Award for Fiction went to Don DeLillo for his novel *Mao II.* Among the recipients of the new Lila Wallace-Reader's Digest Fund awards to American writers were Richard Bausch and C.K. Williams. (ALAN CHEUSE)

Canada. The big news in Canada in 1992 was Michael Ondaatje (*see* BIOGRAPHIES) sharing the Booker Prize for his novel *The English Patient,* a brilliant collage of the lives of four desperately disparate people—the mysterious, moribund English patient; his Canadian nurse, Hana; the amiable Caravaggio, thief and spy; and Kirpal ("Kip") Singh, a bomb-disposal expert—thrown together in the maelstrom of the last days of World War II. Ondaatje also won the 1992 Governor General's Literary Award.

The mysteries of evil and innocence were a common theme in the year's releases. Sandra Birdsell mirrors both in *The Chrome Suite,* the story of a young woman, a survivor of a lightning bolt who is then nearly flattened by the brisk tattoo of life's fists, psychological and physical. The brute physicalness of violence is made painfully plain in the pungent language of poet Patrick Lane's first book of fiction, *How Do You Spell Beautiful?* From an acutely different angle, *Brud,* a first novel by Ken J. Harvey, tells the story of a simpleminded man whose trust and credulity are severely tested several times. Diane Fletcher, the hero of Sean Stewart's science-fiction mystery-thriller *Passion Play,* is just the opposite, a hellcat of a woman who believes only in herself and her mission of hunting down criminals, apprehending their bodies by comprehending their minds.

The mystery theme continued in *The Substance of Forgetting* by Kristjana Gunnars, a poet's explorations of the romance of opposites in novel form, and Guy Vanderhaeghe's *Things as They Are?,* a collection of short stories in which nothing is taken for granted. Conventions, both literary and scientific, are cleverly contravened in *The Covenant,* a supernatural whodunit by Pauline Gedge, while *The Last Magician* is Janette Turner Hospital's guide to survival in a time-spiraling tour of the circles of Hell and comedy. Laughter of a more sardonic timbre echoes throughout Robin Skelton's excursions into the dreadfully weird in his most recent collection of short stories, *Higgledy Piggledy.*

There were also those books focused on the enigmas of everyday life, including *The Girl with the Botticelli Face,* W.D. Valgardson's darkly comic verbal fandango set among the academics in a smallish West Coast college, and *Man and His World* by Clark Blaise, short stories reflecting the author's life front, back, and sideways. Linda Svendsen relates the stories in her *Marine Life* through a young woman's reflections of herself from the inside as both child and mother. In its own fashion, Janice Kulyk Keefer's novel *Rest Harrow* also peels off a character's stereotypic trappings to reveal the complicated person beneath, while in *Itsuka,* Joy Kogawa traces the labyrinthine interactions of generations.

New works of poetry included *Inventing the Hawk,* Lorna Crozier's deceivingly simple-seeming evocations of the senses and sensibility, light and language; Irving Layton's *Dance with Desire: Selected Love Poems,* a collection from over 35 years of

Michael Ondaatje
JERRY BAUER

practice; *Mother, Not Mother,* di brandt's musings on the various and surprising relationships of mothers to their worlds; and Henry Beissel's quite different meditations on similar themes regarding his father in *Dying I Was Born.*

Richard Sommer's *The Shadow Sonnets* continues his explorations of the other side of things; *Aqua* (1991) by Anne Marriott dives into the blues, classical and contemporary, which are also David Donnell's medium, done up in downtown style in *China Blues: Poems and Stories.* Miriam Waddington escapes the linear confines of language through *The Last Landscape,* a series of graceful greetings and farewells, while *Letters from the Doll Hospital* are Linda Rogers' humorous, trenchant observations of the child in the adult, the adult in the child. A childhood of war and holocaust informs the themes of Liliane Welch's *Life in Another Language. Inkorrect Thots* is bill bissett's most recent outpouring of exuberant enthusiasms, political and lyrical.

Other books worth noting were *The "Patricia" Album and Other Poems* by Colleen Thibaudeau; Erin Mouré's *Sheepish Beauty/ Civilian Love; The Beloved* by David Helwig; *Memories Have Tongue* by Afua Cooper; *Anonymity Suite* by David McFadden; and *Oedipal Dreams* by Evelyn Lau.

(ELIZABETH WOODS)

FRENCH

Fifty years after the fact, the Vichy regime and the period of the German occupation in World War II continued to give rise to controversy. A number of works on the subject appeared in 1992, with the greatest stir caused by the previously unpublished *Journal* that Pierre Drieu La Rochelle kept from 1939 to 1945. It was known that the author had advised collaboration with the Germans, but what this badly written and repetitive *Journal* reveals are true hatreds: of women, Jews, homosexuals, his fellow writers. It might be that these hatreds hid another: hatred of himself.

Drieu La Rochelle appears again in a fascinating selection of letters by Jean Paulhan,

Traité des jours sombres 1937–1945. These were indeed sombre days for *La Nouvelle Revue Française,* which Paulhan edited. In 1940 the Germans sealed the doors of the publisher Gallimard, and the journal ceased publication. Thanks to Drieu La Rochelle's connections, it resumed under his direction, and for a time Paulhan and Drieu—who needed each other—played a kind of chess game. In the end, Drieu helped Paulhan escape the German police. Other works on the period included Serge Added's *Le Théâtre dans les années Vichy* and *Le Régime de Vichy et les Français* by Jean-Pierre Azéma and François Bédarida. Material on the Vichy regime is included in the monumental *Historie des droites,* edited by Jean-François Sirinelli, which places French rightwing political movements within the context of politics and culture.

The 400th anniversary of Montaigne's death was observed with a new edition of his *Les Essais,* prepared by Claude Pinganaud, with modernized spelling. Pierre Leschenelle offered *Montaigne ou le mal à l'âme* (1991), and Madeleine Lazard published *Michel de Montaigne.* François Rigolot presented Montaigne's *Journal de voyage,* a definitive edition of which had not been published to date. The 150th anniversary of Stéphane Mallarmé's birth was celebrated more quietly. In *Un Fantôme dans le kiosque,* Roger Dragonetti recalls a little-known Mallarmé: the author of a voluminous correspondence and the journalist who created *La Dernière Mode.* Daniel Oster, in *Stéphane* (1991), sketches a subtle, emotion-filled portrait written in a language close to that of Mallarmé himself.

In *Les Règles de l'art,* Pierre Bourdieu focuses on the formation, in the 19th century, of the modern literary landscape, particularly its influence on Flaubert. Jean-Marie Goulemot and Oster devote part of their study on *Gens de lettres* to the same subject. In *L'École du désenchantement,* Paul Bénichou pursues his study of the poetic philosophy of French Romanticism. Pierre-Yves Pétillon's remarkable *Historie de la lit-*

PHILIPPE GIRAUD—SYGMA

Patrick Chamoiseau

térature américaine (1939–1989) would undoubtedly give French readers a better understanding of this literature. Finally, in *Lectures 2,* Paul Ricoeur first discusses the authors who have influenced him and then holds a "dialogue" with the principal representatives of structuralism.

The inclusion in the prestigious Pléiade collection of the popular poet Jacques Prévert was not welcomed by everyone. The Pléiade published a second volume of the *Oeuvres complètes* of André Breton, containing works written between 1931 and 1941. The *Journal* that Michel Leiris kept all his life proved to be one of the most moving books of the year. Another notable event was the publication of Louis Althusser's autobiography, *L'Avenir dure longtemps,* written in 1985, in which the philosopher attempts to explain the psychic factors and events that led him to kill his wife. The first volume of a biography of Althusser by Yann Moulier Boutang was also issued. In *Carnets du grand chemin,* Julien Gracq, while not complying with the strict rules of autobiography, expressed some of its emotions. Marguerite Duras published an entirely autobiographical narrative, *Yann Andréa Steiner,* in which she recalls her companion, Yann Andréa, whom she had included in several of her novels. A good study of Duras was written by Christiane Blot-Labarrère.

In *Étoile errante,* J.-M.-G. Le Clézio crosses the paths of two young women, one a Jew, the other a Palestinian. Jean Echenoz, in *Nous trois,* mocks the clichés of modern reality. With *La Septième Terre,* a big, confused novel, Bernard Puech disappointed admirers of his first book, *Sous l'étoile du chien.* In *Les Très-Bas,* Christian Bobin in his own way recalls the figure of Francis of Assisi. Pierre Bergounioux, in *L'Orphelin,* evokes his father, as does Marc Le Bot in *Les Yeux de mon père.*

The Prix Goncourt was awarded to a writer from Martinique, Patrick Chamoiseau, for his third novel, *Texaco,* which recounts much of Martinique's history through the story of a woman, Marie-Sophie Laborieux, and of a district of Fort-de-France. Michel Rio received the Prix Médicis for *Tlacuilo,* and the Prix Renaudot went to François Weyergans for *La Démence du boxeur,* a lyrical novel on the death of the cinema. Anne-Marie Garat received the Prix Fémina for her deceptive *Aden.*

In the field of poetry, *Nouveau nouveau recueil* reassembles—in three volumes—scattered texts published by Francis Ponge. André du Bouchet published two books, *Axiales* and *Matière de l'interlocuteur.* The *Almanach du cinéma,* published by Encyclopædia Universalis, a beautiful, useful, and pleasant volume conceived by Gilles Quinsat and put together by Philippe d'Hugues, salutes 100 years of cinema.

(FRANÇOIS POIRIÉ)

Canada. Among the many novelists capitalizing on the 500th anniversary of Columbus' "discovery" of the New World, Paul Zumthor published a very complex novel, *La Traversée,* whose intrigue is fed by entries from the celebrated navigator's logbook. Written from an entirely different perspective, Louis Lefebvre's novel *Guanahani* dramatizes the reminiscences of one Atobeian, who had made the same perilous crossing some 20 years before Columbus. The two novels gave a quite vivid impression of the clash of cultures in that distant era.

History was also a source of inspiration for Gabrielle Gourdeau, but in her case it was literary history. Her *Maria Chapdelaine, ou le paradis retrouvé* recounts how that famous fictional character became, in the '70s, an avowed *indépendantiste*. Guylène Saucier published a second novel, *Sarabande,* whose intrigue hinges on the mysterious disappearance of Elise Borgia. The interest inseparable from such an intrigue is mainly due to Saucier's cunningly wrought portraiture of Elise, who becomes more and more substantial as the novel goes on. *L'Enfant chargé de songes* by the accomplished novelist Anne Hébert groups together themes that had inspired her earlier works. She focuses anew on the initiatory passage from adolescence to adulthood that she had dramatized in her 1950 short story "Le Torrent."

Can a book of poems make a best-seller list? Yes, if the poet is Gilles Vigneault. In *Bois de marée,* he collects within an elegant format distinctive productions in verse and prose: "When the gardens have been sown, we no longer bear sole responsibility for everything." Another poet, André Roy, published a book of poems that was tragically topical: *On sait que cela avait été écrit avant et après la grande maladie.* The first of its two parts ("Avant") rhapsodically celebrates the vocabulary of love; the second ("Après") emits a cry of distress in the face of AIDS.

Worth noting was the appearance of the play *Pied de poule,* which Marc Drouin wrote in 1982 but tinkered with anew in 1991. It was remarkable for its corrosive social satire as well as for the way it shatters conventional approaches to the theatre. Also worthy of note was the definitive *L'Histoire des femmes au Québec depuis quatre siècles,* a work of historical research that had been completely revised and brought up to date. Its multiple authorship was indicated by the name Clio.   (PIERRE HÉBERT)

GERMAN

A new novel by Günter Grass was always a literary landmark, and *Unkenrufe,* although critics were divided on its merits, was no exception. In it Grass added to his literary bestiary the toad, harbinger of disaster. The private attempt of an elderly couple, one German, one Polish, to reconcile their respective societies ends with the prospect of a new colonization by Germany of its eastern neighbour. Grass's commitment was beyond doubt; his text in places was an uneasy mixture of literature and journalism. German-Polish relations were also the subject of Walter Kempowski's novel *Mark und Bein.* Whereas Grass's novel was set during the revolution in eastern Europe, Kempowski focused on the year 1988 and a journey to Poland in search of a personal identity. Less transparent than *Unkenrufe,* Kempowski's novel was more disturbing in its presentation of both Polish deficiencies and German recidivism.

There were some substantial attempts to come to terms with German unification on the part of writers from the former German Democratic Republic. A number of significant autobiographical texts appeared: *Abspann,* from the ex-president of the Writers Union, Hermann Kant; *Krieg ohne Schlacht,* dramatist Heiner Müller's account of life in "two dictatorships"; octogenarian economist Jürgen Kuczynski's *Ein linientreuer Dissident;* and Günter de Bruyn's highly acclaimed *Zwischenbilanz.* Frank Werner's novel *Haus mit Gästen* is an impressionistic account of German history that parallels the end of the Third Reich with that of the GDR.

Renate Feyl's dryly ironic *Ausharren im Paradies* relates the vicissitudes of a German academic expelled from Czechoslovakia in 1945, who opts for socialism, loses his post when he protests the invasion of Czechoslovakia in 1968, and is reinstated in 1990—while simultaneously his daughter loses her job, an innocent victim of the latest purges in academia. Underlying the avant-garde structures of Volker Braun's *Iphigenie in Freiheit* was a much fiercer attack on what the author regarded as the colonization of the former East by the West.

For the West German Botho Strauss, by contrast, in his volume of reflections *Beginnlosigkeit,* such preoccupations as political utopias, emancipation, and Marxism itself had become mere fossils. Hans Joachim Schädlich's *Schott* likewise rejected the notion of progress; this novel radically abandons the conventions of traditional fiction, eschewing plot and deconstructing the individual identity. The 25 texts of Brigitte Kronauer's *Schnurrer* imply a similar outlook; in these precisely observed vignettes of an eccentric 40-year-old, the two-dimensionality of postmodernist fiction comes once more to the foreground.

The collapse of yet another version of socialism, that of Nicolae Ceausescu, was the background to Romanian-born Herta Müller's novel *Der Fuchs war damals schon der Jäger.* The terror of arbitrary dictatorship is conveyed in fragmentary details of everyday life; here, too, utopia is not easy to find. Of comparable poetic power is Christina Viragh's *Unstete Leute,* in which an emigration is described from a child's perspective, with everything new taking on threatening dimensions. Told in a more conventional style, Roswitha Quadflieg's novel *Die Braut im Park* evokes similar feelings of disorientation in its account of a Baltic countess' years of wanderings across the world.

In *Der Antiquar,* by the Swiss novelist Hansjörg Schertenlieb, the futility of attempts to "chart" one's life—the principal character's passion is for old maps—becomes apparent when the unforeseen breaks into a pedantically ordered life. This existentialist novel moves from Switzerland to South America and back, ending in the snowy wastes of the Alps. South America is also the setting of extensive parts of Austrian Robert Menasse's picaresque novel *Selige Zeiten, brüchige Welt,* a highly sophisticated and witty mixture of social criticism, philosophy, and aesthetics. Günther Rücker's equally picaresque *Otto Blomow,* set in the immediate postwar years and satirizing the political and economic intrigues of the time, was less demanding reading.

The chaos and uncertainty of personal relationships was one of the themes of Menasse's novel. Two comparable novels on contemporary sexual relationships were Peter Schneider's *Paarungen* and Jurek Becker's *Amanda herzlos.* Schneider, himself a veteran of the 1968 movement in West Germany, shows the erstwhile revolutionaries to have made their peace with

Günter Grass

society; the Berlin setting of his novel, with the Wall still intact, symbolizes the gulf that still exists between men and women on the personal level. Becker's entertaining novel also is set in the Berlin of the 1980s; the eponymous Amanda, a writer, is seen through the perspectives of three male admirers.

The third volume of Erwin Strittmatter's historical novel *Der Laden* was an outstanding success with the public in the former East Germany, indicating that, in spite of unification, the two halves of the country still had different expectations from their literature.

Significant collections of poetry included Sarah Kirsch's *Erlkönigs Tochter,* some of them inspired by a recent visit to the United Kingdom; Durs Grünbein's *Schädelbasislektion;* Barbara Köhler's *Deutsches Roulette;* Volker Braun's *Die Zickzackbrücke;* and Peter Maiwald's *Springinsfeld.*   (J.H. REID)

SCANDINAVIAN

Denmark. Svend Åge Madsen's novel for young people, *Jagten på et menneske* (1991), is a fantasy centred on unemployment: the unemployed are fair game for those licensed to kill. Henrik Bjelke's *Rygternes atlas* shows some indebtedness to James Joyce and reflects Bjelke's own Irish roots. In *Frøken Smillas fornemmelse for sne,* Peter Høeg offered a lengthy thriller with wide human and cultural perspectives. A more decided thriller is Anders Bodelsen's *Rød September* (1991), inspired by an actual Copenhagen event. Leif Davidsen's *Den sidste spion* (1991) confirmed its author as a first-rate thriller writer. With *Sidste sommer* (1991), Tage Skou-Hansen completed his series centred on the World War II Danish resistance. A contrast was Vagn Lundbye's *Palindromos* (1991), about an American kidnapped by a primitive jungle people. Western civilization is subjected to a culture it does not understand.

There are overtones of the thriller in Mette Winge's *Sandflugt* (1991), about two women in love with the same spy. Charlotte Strandgaard, in *Vedrørende Heidi* (1991), sticks to the realistic social novel in a study of a child placed with foster parents because her own alcoholic mother cannot cope. Hanne Marie Svendsen's *Kirstines ting og andre historier* ranges from the everyday and ordinary to the fantastic and visionary.

In *Modspil* (1991), Ole Wivel writes of his work as critic, while in *Den frie vilje* Villy Sørensen discusses free will. In his scholarly *Jesus og Kristus,* Sørensen presents Jesus as historical but not as God. Pure autobiography is to be found in Solvejg Bjerre's *Længe siden,* with portraits of famous people, including her own father, Jeppe Aakjær. Carsten Jensen's *Af en astmatisk kritikers bekendelser* is part autobiography, part reflection on the true role of literature.

Distinguished poetry came from Rolf Gjedsted with *Ni måneders mørke* (1991), Peter Poulsen with *Akustiske digte* (1991), Erik Stinus with *Ubekræftede forlydender,* and the tireless Klaus Rifbjerg with one major collection entitled *Bjerget i himlen* (1991) and a second called *Krigen. En digtcyklus.* The inventive Per Kirkeby produced *Meget senere,* and Sven Kaalø added to his hymnlike production with *Fra Stubmarken.* Peter Laugesen, who presented a volume of poems under the modest title of *29 digte,* was awarded the Danish Academy's major prize.   (W. GLYN JONES)

Norway. Johannes Heggland's novel *Det stutte livet* brought to a triumphant close a magnificent tetralogy centred round Karjana, one of the memorable female characters in 20th-century Norwegian literature. The building referred to in Ketil Bjørnstad's satirical novel *Villa Europa* is an Oslo house linking the fates of eight main characters in a cavalcade spanning a century of men's rotten behaviour toward the women in their lives. For inventiveness nothing could surpass Jon Bing's science-fiction novel *En gammel romfarers beretninger,* which takes its readers into the far distant future in a report from an interstellar space journey lasting a thousand years.

Unusual narrative technique and psychological ambiguity characterized Terje Larsen's minimalist novel *Kastanjetid,* where constant repetition is the essence of its enigmatic charm. The lower depths of the Norwegian capital in the early 20th century form the central backdrop to Karsten Alnæs' *Trollbyen.* Herbjørg Wassmo's powerful 19th-century historical novel *Lykkens sønn* deals with the trauma of witnessing one's mother kill her lover. The 16th-century Spanish Inquisition provides the setting for Bergljot Hobæk Haff's *Renhetens pris.* The painting referred to in the title of Fredrik Skagen's riveting thriller *Landskap med kulehull* is an unknown work by Van Gogh, discovered in Poland and the object of a deceitful, murderous arts dealers' chase through Europe.

Existential problems and the enigmatic nature of love, and especially its aftermath, are central themes in Stein Mehren's collection of poems, *Nattsol.* Autobiography and fellow poets figure prominently in Paal Brekke's *Men barnet i meg spør.* Homosexuality found its Norwegian poet in Øystein S. Ziener in his *Fanga. Fanga i flukta.*

In a class of its own among a number of short-story collections was Lars Saabye Christensen's *Ingens,* with its sharp-focused pinpointing of poignant moments. Unforgettable was Finn Carling's hymn to life in his moving novelistic texts about death, *Antilopens øyne. Folket i Plassgrenda* is a collection of short stories by Alf Prøysen, fastidiously selected by Kjell Askildsen, and Prøysen's own life is dealt with in great

detail in a biography by Ove Røsbak. Liv Kølzow's *Den unge Amalie Skram,* covering the years 1846 to 1884 in the life of Norway's leading naturalist and feminist writer, also provides a comprehensive survey of the Norwegian intellectual climate of the period.   (TORBJØRN STØVERUD)

Sweden. Among senior established writers, Sven Lindqvist, in his horrifying account in *Utrota varenda jävel* ("Exterminate the Brutes") of the slaughter of indigenous populations by 19th-century colonizers, sparked controversy regarding its historical accuracy. P.C. Jersild's chillingly entertaining futuristic scenario with a privatized penal system, *En lysande marknad,* was also disturbing, although he had a gift for sweetening the pill of social criticism. Stig Claesson's bittersweet novel *Män i min ålder* featured a Swedish writer's abiding affection for Hungary and his need to come to terms with approaching old age, while Per Agne Erkelius' *Efterträdaren* presented a man haunted by the childhood death of his brother. (Incidentally, the young postmodernist Stig Larsson published *om en död,* detached, enigmatic, faintly absurdist prose pieces on death.) Three plays by Sweden's internationally known dramatist Lars Norén on the tensions of bourgeois family life—*Tre borgerliga kvartetter*—proved him to be highly readable. Theodor Kallifatides' *Vem var Gabriella Orlova?,* about a Greek-American gumshoe working in Athens, was surprisingly truffled with soft porn. Jan Guillou continued his best-selling series about the secret agent Coq Rouge in *Ingen mans land.*

Ernst Brunner published *Edith,* a novel about the Finnish-Swedish poet Edith Södergran, whose short life of privations, illness, and triumphant creativity ended in 1923. The entertainer-cum-writer Jonas Gardell presented the cruelties of a stand-up comic's suburban childhood in *En komikers uppväxt.* Robert Kangas continued in *Vägen hem* to write dense prose, featuring incestuous passions in a harsh rural setting. By contrast, Björn Ranelid's sprawling novel *Mästaren* allowed for the mystically redemptive power of love. Kjell Johansson's *Sju huvudens historia* treated a sad childhood with magic realism.

Among young women writers, Mare Kandre's *Deliria* was prose-poetry to stir thought and emotions, Anna-Karin Palm's short stories *Utanför bilden* were promising, Sigrid Combüchen's novel *Korta och långa kapitel* featured provincial life in a privatized and postpolitical era, while Inger Alfvén's *Elefantens öga* built a picture of changing values and gender roles in a two-generation family. The first publication of letters from the Nobel Prize winner Selma Lagerlöf (1858–1940) to her friend Sophie Elkan provided excitement.

Noteworthy poetry included Kjell Espmark's *När vägen vänder,* Arne Johnsson's *Dess ande kysst,* and Ann Jäderlund's *Rundkyrka och sjukhuslängor.*

(KARIN PETHERICK)

ITALIAN

The enthusiasm and optimism of the '80s came to a sudden end in 1992. The serious economic and institutional crisis, the worsening problem of political instability, the scandal of widespread corruption affecting governing parties, the outrages of the Mafia, and the national preoccupation with

the influx of immigrants from eastern Europe and Africa—all this, compounded with the recent collapse of traditional left-wing alternatives, made the fictions of literature pale into insignificance. The book market, the last industry to feel the beneficial effects of the booming '80s, was the first to face the consequences of the sharp downturn in the '90s. However, though publishers seemed to favour cheap classics in ever more inviting packages, the outpouring of new writing gave no sign of drying up.

In fiction the favourite themes were grim, as though writers had sensed in advance the mood that was to prevail in the country. A Spanish galleon imprisoned on a becalmed ocean, as in Michele Mari's precious *La stiva e l'abisso;* a roadside restaurant, sole survivor of a catastrophic flood, as in Giorgio Calcagno's *Notizie dal diluvio;* an old hotel perched on a cliff over the Adriatic Sea, guarding crimes that detectives do not seem to want to uncover, as in Giuseppe Bonura's *I custodi del silenzio;* or even a health clinic for monstrously obese and opulent people, as in Aldo Busi's *Le persone normali*—all were offered as topical allegories of a directionless universe, a society where truth and falsity had become indistinguishable, justice impossible, and integrity a luxury that did not pay.

In this oblique denunciation of present evils, southern writers were, as usual, at the forefront. Vincenzo Consolo's *Nottetempo, casa per casa,* perhaps the most successful and certainly one of the most accomplished books of the year, confirmed this Sicilian writer's eminent position among contemporary Italian novelists. Set in the early 1920s in Sicily and written in Consolo's distinctive baroque style, the novel consists of a series of flashes of insanity that anticipate the fascist takeover of the country. Caught between the old lethargy of his region and the appeal of new, impossible ideals, the protagonist in the end escapes the overwhelming chaos by sailing away in search of honesty and reason.

Domenico Campana's *I giardini della Favorita,* though set in the Sicily of a later period—between 1943 and 1946—conveyed a message that was no less bleak. This is the story of a tragic love affair in which a gloomy background of Mafia dealings, rampant lawlessness, and political intrigue has the lion's share. Raffaele Nigro offered perhaps the most direct and bloody picture of the social and moral degradation brought about in the South by the craving for money and power—the trouble with his *Ombre sull'Ofanto* being that it mimics cinema fiction too closely to be convincing as a representation of true reality.

Hardly less harrowing was the picture of life in the Roman suburbs in the novels of two new and very different young writers. *Il sole è innocente* by Claudio Camarca is a nightmarish story of violence, drugs, and social degradation, strongly reminiscent of Pier Paolo Pasolini's early fiction but bereft of the myth of natural innocence that somehow redeemed Pasolini's characters. In *Crampi* by Marco Lodoli a man, tied to a goat, compulsively runs along an expressway in a nighttime marathon "for peace and love"; as he remembers his past, he goes well beyond the finish line, only to collapse exhausted in a pool of mud.

Northern writers did not provide much relief either. Again combining history with invention, Sebastiano Vassalli's *Marco e Mattio* is the story, set in Veneto in the late 18th and early 19th centuries, of another of Vassalli's marginalized characters. This time a shoemaker's son, devastated by pellagra, believes himself to be Christ, attempts to crucify himself in order to redeem humankind, and ends his life in a Venetian asylum. Vassalli's attempt to depict a historical fresco of unspeakable suffering and violence, though compelling in places, was on the whole too ambitious and uncontrolled to be totally effective.

A measure of relief was to be found in such books as Ferdinando Camon's *Il Super-Baby,* an amusing satire of the myth of innate genius and the quest for success, and *La casa a nord-est* by Sergio Maldini, who returned to publishing after 40 years of silence, focusing on a house that his protagonist dreams of, buys, and lovingly restores. Yet even houses were far from solid in the year's fiction. In Giampaolo Rugarli's *Una montagna australiana,* the narrator's house suddenly cracks open, revealing that the cement expected to hold it together was in fact just sand—a swindle not unknown to the building trade. In the general turmoil, only literature seemed to be surviving, though with the certainty, on the part of producers and consumers alike, that it is itself no more than a lie and, as Gesualdo Bufalino's stylized autobiography *Calende greche* makes beautifully clear, something quite inadequate as an alternative to, or consolation for, the intractable hardness of experience. (LINO PERTILE)

SPANISH

Spain. While the quincentennial celebration of the Columbian enterprise spawned an avalanche of publications, largely historiographic, devoted to the momentous American "encounter" of 1492, another anniversary was observed in the setting of Spain's young but well-consolidated democracy; in 1992, the centennial year of Francisco Franco's birth, a preoccupation with the deeds and legacies of his long regime (1939–75) was especially evident. Thus a new biography by the American historian Stanley G. Payne, *Franco: El perfil de la historia,* became an instant best-seller. Literary critics and historians were either enthusiastic about or disconcerted by Manuel Vázquez Montalbán's ambitious pseudo-historical novel, *Autobiografía del general Franco,* in which a fictitious ghostwriter of "Franco's memoirs" sabotages his own manuscript with a vindictive running commentary on the "lies" he has been hired to write. Andrés Trapiello won the Plaza & Janés Prize for *El buque fantasma,* a portrait of clandestine student revolutionaries during the final, least repressive phase of the regime. Two other novels—Fanny Rubio's *La sal del chocolate* and Lourdes Ortiz' *Antes de la batalla*—developed a similar "generational" theme: how the radical idealists of the 1960s were corrupted by the political power and material comforts they came to enjoy in the '80s.

The rich Planeta Prize went to Fernando Sánchez Dragó for his novel *La prueba del laberinto,* whose semiautobiographical protagonist, a troubled middle-aged writer assigned to research the life of Jesus of Nazareth, conducts a spiritual peregrination of his own. In *Nubosidad variable* Carmen Martín Gaite returned to a key theme of her earlier fiction: the writing act as a form of self-recovery and an instrument of personal salvation. Another yearlong bestseller was *Corazón tan blanco,* by Javier Marías, a brilliant meditation on marriage, guilt, self-knowledge, and death. Other satisfying fiction included Eduardo Mendoza's melodramatic story of sacrilegious love, *El año del diluvio,* and Rosa Montero's *El nido de los sueños* (1991), narrated from the perspective of a small girl's magical imagination. Juan Eduardo Zúñiga published an extraordinary collection of 40 stories under the title *Misterios de las noches y los días.*

Three important verse collections appeared: Rosa Chacel's *Poesía (1931–1991*); *Las ruinas del mundo (Poesía, 1974–1991*), by César Antonio Molina; and Leopoldo Panero's *Selección poética (1968–1992*).

A month before her 90th birthday, the reclusive Cuban poet Dulce María Loynaz was notified in Havana that she had received the Premio Miguel de Cervantes, the top award in Hispanic letters.

(ROGER L. UTT)

Latin America. Two of Latin America's most renowned writers, the Mexican Carlos Fuentes and the Colombian Gabriel García Márquez, were at the forefront of the year's literary production. Several younger writers, such as Argentina's Ricardo Piglia and Mempo Giardinelli, also published important books. As might have been expected, many writers were concerned with the historical revisionism associated with the quincentennial of Columbus' arrival in the Americas.

The most notable book from Mexico was Carlos Fuentes' book-length essay on Hispanic cultures, *The Buried Mirror,* which appeared in both English and Spanish. A book that was most appropriate for the quincentennial, *The Buried Mirror* is Fuentes' analysis of the multicultural roots of Hispanic history and culture. He traces these roots from the Iberian Peninsula of the Romans to the triethnic cultures of Latin America today. The other major book to appear in Mexico was Elena Poniatowska's *Tinísima,* a historical novel. Other noteworthy novels were Angelina Muñiz' *Dulcinea encantada,*

JERRY BAUER

José Donoso

Bernardo Ruiz' *Los caminos del hotel,* and Pablo Soler Front's *Legión.* The novelist Héctor Aguilar Camín published a volume of short fiction, *Historias conversadas.*

The literary event of the year in Colombia was the publication of *Doce cuentos peregrinos* by Nobel laureate Gabriel García Márquez, his first new book to appear in seven years. The volume consists of 12 short stories written between 1974 and 1992, some of which had appeared in magazines and newspapers. These fine stories do not bear the magic realist stamp of García Márquez' previous fiction, but this Colombian's gift for storytelling is still intact. Death and power, two of the themes appearing consistently in his novels of the 1970s and 1980s, are also constant themes in these stories. Other recent books to appear in Colombia were *El vuelo de la paloma,* a novel by Roberto Burgos Cantor, and *Fantasio,* a volume of short stories by Fabio Martínez.

The most prominent Chilean writer, José Donoso, did not publish any new books in Chile, but a novel published successfully in 1979, *El jardín de al lado,* appeared for the first time in English under the title *The Garden Next Door.* Chile's major woman writer, Diamela Eltit, had a similar year; she published no new novels, but her third novel, *El cuarto mundo* (1988), appeared in French. Several younger writers in Chile continued publishing, including the poet Arturo Fontaine Talavera, whose first novel appeared under the title *Oír su voz.*

Two important books by younger writers appeared in Argentina. Ricardo Piglia published his third novel, *La ciudad ausente.* In his previous fiction, Piglia was engaged in a self-reflexive analysis of Argentine history and culture. *La ciudad ausente* represents a continuation of Piglia's project, as he reconsiders the role of the avant-garde writers Macedonio Fernández and Roberto Arlit. Mempo Giardinelli, the author of several novels and volumes of short stories, published a voluminous historical novel, *Santo oficio de memoria.* His major novel to date, it deals with an Italian family's immigration to Argentina.

Several Latin-American writers published books in late 1991 that had their impact in 1992. The most notable of these were *Parece que fue ayer* by Denzil Romero, *Toro-Toro* by Humberto Mata, *El vuelo de los avestruces* by Boris Izaguirre (all Venezuelans), *Cuerpos prohibidos* by the Chilean Marco Anonio de la Parra, and *La mano de amo* by the Argentine Tomás Eloy Martínez.

A new voice on the Central American scene was Roberto Quesada from Honduras. His novel *The Ships* describes the occasional triumphs of daily life in a world near poverty. It charts the progress of a young writer named Guillermo in the Honduran coastal town of La Ceiba. One of the numerous positive reactions this book evoked was from the American writer Kurt Vonnegut, who described Quesada as a "lively and gifted writer full of amusing and thought-provoking ideas."

(RAYMOND LESLIE WILLIAMS)

PORTUGUESE

Portugal. The year's winner of the prize for fiction awarded by the Association of Portuguese Authors was José Saramago, the only Portuguese writer currently active whose novels were immediately translated into English. The belated recognition by the judges of his national and international success rested, however, less on his latest novel, *O Evangelho segundo Jesus Cristo,* than on the high quality of his continued literary production. The *Evangelho* tells the life of Jesus as seen through his own eyes. Saramago conveys here an intensely humane message. His Jesus is acutely aware of his own body and the bonds of human solidarity. He wants to avoid the mission imposed on him. In his encounter with God and the Devil—the two are always allied in the making of his destiny—he probes the reasons for his sacrifice and discovers the ugly face of power. The poetic beauty of the narrative blends with a breadth of vision that shakes old truths and poses new questions.

The most innovative novel of recent years was *Partes de África* by Helder Macedo. This amusing and brilliant novel chronicles the old days of Portuguese colonialism in Africa and the moral and psychological effects of national independence, symbolically underlined by the death of the narrator's father. Deeply rooted in the tradition of Western literature, the author skillfully uses well-known narrative conventions to reveal the fictions of memory, exposing the borderline between "fact" and invention. By teasing his readers' imagination, he engages them in the making of his story.

In a charming poetic novel, *Litoral,* Wanda Ramos deals with death and the vagaries of memory, linked with love of the soil and the Portuguese roots in Galicia, the northernmost part of the Iberian Peninsula. Trying to find the reasons for the strange death of a distant cousin, who left her his estate, the narrator visits his old house in Land's End. Her reconstruction of his past, through pictures, paintings, his friends, lovers, and an incomplete diary, is as much the work of a detective as of a novelist. The ending shows an uncanny fusing of individual destinies with the spirit of the land.   (L.S. REBELO)

Brazil. Brazilian theatre was active throughout the year. Miguel Falabella's *No coração do Brasil* is a black comedy about the lives of poor people employed at a suburban movie theatre. The 19th-century Brazilian classic *Macário* by Álvares de Azevedo was staged; in it, a 20-year-old considers making a pact with the devil. Plays by Hamilton Vaz Pereira, Zeno Wilde and Wanderley Bragança, and Domingos de Oliveira appeared, as well as the Bahian Group Bando de Teatro Olodum. Aderbal Freire Filho and Carlos Eduardo Novaes' *O Tiradentes, Inconfidência no Rio,* dealing with the 18th-century Mineiran conspiracy against the Portuguese, required the public to travel to five different staging sites. There were also successes abroad for the Brazilian theatre; in New York City director Cacá Rosset's company presented *A Comedy of Errors* in Central Park, and director Gerald Thomas' *Flash and Crash Days* was presented at Lincoln Center's "Serious Fun" festival.

The cultural event of the year was the August celebration of Jorge Amado's 80th birthday in Salvador. Amado published a new volume of memoirs, *Navegação de cabotagem.* Important new works of fiction included a novel by the eminent 81-year-old Rachel de Queiroz, one of the major figures of Brazilian social realism

of the 1920s and 1930s; Silviano Santiago's *Uma história de família;* and Moacyr Scliar's *Sonhos tropicais,* whose protagonist is Oswaldo Cruz, the Brazilian doctor who "conquered" malaria and yellow fever. Ana Maria Machado published *Canteiros de Saturno;* Pascoal Motta also dealt with the Mineiran conspiracy in his *Eu, Tiradentes,* a fictional biography/confession of the movement's leader. Antônio Olinto's *Sangue na floresta* takes place in the Amazon. Rubem Fonseca published a new collection of short fiction, *Romance negro e outras histórias.*

New biographies of Antônio José da Silva, *O Judeu* by Alberto Dines, of Vinícius de Moraes by José Castello, and of Nelson Rodrigues by Ruy Castro appeared. Paulo Coelho added another volume, *As Valquírias,* to his three earlier works of "inspirational" fiction. A major critical study was Nelson Vieira's *Brasil e Portugal: a imagem recíproca,* which investigates the literary and cultural relationship between the two nations. João Cabral de Melo Neto, Brazil's major poet, was awarded the Neustadt Prize for literature. The critic Fábio Lucas received the Juca Pato Trophy from the Brazilian Writers Union as the "intellectual of the year." Writer Ricardo Ramos and publisher Sérgio Lacerda died during 1992.   (IRWIN STERN)

RUSSIAN

Russian literature remained in a state of disarray and confusion throughout 1992. As political and economic uncertainty prevailed in Russia, its literature and its writers were experiencing the painful process of adjusting to new freedoms and the laws of the market economy.

The crisis among journals and literary magazines widened owing to problems of declining readership, inadequate means of distribution, and new market-driven competition. Honoraria for writers steadily decreased, forcing many to look for other means of support. Book publishing also remained in turmoil. Although censorship was virtually nonexistent, making it much easier for established writers to get published, many were forced to publish at their own expense. At the same time, prices of books rose 100 times. Ideological squabbles began tearing writers' organizations apart. A deep schism in the former Union of Soviet Writers was symbolized by one faction's burning the poet Yevgeny Yevtushenko in effigy. Readers became more interested in literary scandals than in literature.

Economics aside, Russian literature faced tough times during the unstable transitional period. Without its social and political mission, the literature of social protest began losing its appeal. Lyudmila Petrushevskaya's brilliant prose, which describes the dark side of human relations, ceased to be a sensation. The public had become weary of literature that deromanticized everyday Russian life solely as a counterweight to the romanticization of life under the doctrine of socialist realism. Readers waited for something new, yet writers of the so-called postmodern wave were frequently at a loss for subjects. Preoccupied with current events, they often produced one-dimensional works, usually with a single message tied to Russia's current spiritual crisis.

As politics took centre stage in the national debate, the circle of readers contin-

Mark Kharitonov
GRIGOR DUKOR—THE NEW YORK TIMES

ued to narrow. Poetry, traditionally popular among Russians, virtually disappeared from the pages of newspapers and journals, forced out by political commentaries. Literature's central place in Russian life shifted dramatically. Not long before, those who wanted to orient themselves in the country's social and political life turned to belles lettres. Writers and poets enjoyed great popularity and status, which explained why so many had actively participated in politics during the Gorbachev era. In the last two years, however, a new group of professional politicians, economists, and commentators had arisen, replacing the writers. In the era of uncensored information, literature as a source of forbidden knowledge lost its importance.

In many ways, literature in Russia was being relegated to the secondary place it occupied in many other countries. In the past, every noteworthy book that successfully passed or bypassed the censor immediately became a sensation. Now nothing qualified as a literary event. In the flood of published books, starting with Joseph Brodsky and Aleksandr Solzhenitsyn and ending with Agatha Christie, sensation was simply impossible. *Strakh* ("Fear"), Anatoly Rybakov's sequel to his celebrated *Deti Arbata* (*Children of the Arbat*), for example, passed virtually unnoticed. Classical literature was not being published, and the popularity of émigré literature was in decline. Bookstores, on the other hand, were overtaken by a wave of Western literature, hastily and often badly translated into Russian, consisting mainly of detective stories, science fiction, and popular romances.

While no new trends were evident in Russian literature in 1992, several notable writers stood out, such as Fridrikh Gorinshtein, Vladimir Makanin, Oleg Blotsky, and Aleksandr Borodina. In addition, Anatoly Kim's *Posiolok kentavrov* ("The Settlement of Centaurs") and Viktor Astafyev's *Posledny poklon* ("The Last Bow"), both published in *Novy Mir,* and Nikolay Glazkov's tragicomedy *Grigory Rasputin,* published in *Oktyabr,* attracted the critics' attention. Most noteworthy among the new emerging writers were Aleksandr Ivanchenko, Mark Kharitonov (who won the first Russian Booker Novel Prize for "Lines of Fate"), Leonid Latynin, Aleksandr Trekhov, Oleg Ermakov, Andrey Shvedov, and Erik Pustynik. Women writers such as Lyudmila Petrushevskaya, Tatyana Tolstaya, Svetlana Vasilenko, Valeria Narbikova, Marina Polei, and Irina Muraveva maintained their strong creative output of previous years.

Several anniversaries were commemorated during the year. Irma Kudrova's new book, *Versty, Dali... Marina Tsvetaeva 1922–39* ("Versts, Vistas... Marina Tsvetaeva 1922–39"), was published in Moscow. *Serebryanny gost* ("The Silver Guest") was the first Russian-language monograph dedicated to the poet Konstantin Balmont. Written by Viktor Dimitrev, it was published in the U.S. Also in the U.S., the 50th anniversary of the oldest Russian émigré journal, *Novyi Zhurnal* ("The New Review"), was celebrated at the New York Public Library. First to publish Nobel laureates Boris Pasternak, Solzhenitsyn, and Brodsky abroad, *Novyi Zhurnal* preserved the traditions of the so-called thick Russian journals, offering on its pages a half-century of Russian culture and civilization, free from totalitarian ideology and censorship. Reflecting wide-ranging political and cultural viewpoints, the journal had a great impact on intellectuals in Russia and abroad.   (EDWARD J. CZERWINSKI;
AGNIESZKA PERLINSKA)

EASTERN EUROPEAN

It was surprising that books continued to be published under the inhospitable conditions prevailing in eastern Europe in 1992. The most important, however, were published abroad. Poetry seemed to be the most popular genre. The first anthology of Bulgarian poetry was published in the U.S.: *Clay & Star,* translated and edited by Lisa Sapinkopf and Georgi Belev, includes the works of 27 of the best contemporary Bulgarian poets (Bulgaria's vice president, Blaga Dimitrova, was represented by seven poems). Stanislaw Baranczak's anthology (edited and translated with Clare Cavanagh), *Spoiling Cannibals' Fun: Polish Poetry of the Last Two Decades of Communist Rule,* contains the best work of 27 contemporary Polish poets. The anthology edited by Daniel Weissbort is fittingly entitled *The Poetry of Survival: Post-War Poets of Central and Eastern Europe;* 28 of the world's finest poets who survived the Holocaust are included. The Serbian writer Veljko P. Bojic, now living abroad, published two significant works: *17-57: Poema* ("17-57: Poem") and *Orlovska gnijezda* ("Eagle Nests"; in two volumes). Jan Kott continued his original research on Shakespeare and world literature in two collections of essays, *The Memory of the Body* and *The Gender of Rosalind.*

Even with pervasive censorship of the media, quality works appeared in Serbia and Croatia. In Radoslav Bratic's *Strah od zvona* ("Fear of the Bell"), his fourth novel, the juxtaposition of childhood reverie and today's reality gives poignancy to a story with tragic overtones. Milisav Savic's *Hleb i strah* ("Bread and Fear") also recounts childhood experiences, culminating with the student riots in Belgrade in 1968. Its theme is the artist in search of reality. It received the prestigious Nin Award in 1992. Miodrag Pavlovic, considered by many the greatest

living Serbian poet, had published 10 volumes during the past three years. His latest, *Kniga staroslovna* ("An Ancient Book"), is a deeply spiritual odyssey, during which the poet visits several holy places associated with the source of Serbian culture.

The Slovene Writers Association, following the lead of Western publishing houses, issued an anthology, *Contemporary Slovene Short Stories,* edited by Jani Virk, Michael Creegan, *et al.* The stories concentrate on the fragmented lives of undistinguished individuals and rarely enter into the province of politics. Still, they present the subdued psychological struggle of men and women caught up in the turmoil of 20th-century politics. Another anthology, *Najbolje price 1990,* edited by David Albahari and Mihajlo Pantic, might be one of the last attempts to bring together writers from the entire Serbo-Croatian region in one book. The best stories belonged to older writers. Croatia's Dubravka Ugresic continued to astound English-speaking readers, this time with her surrealistic novel *Fording the Stream of Consciousness,* translated by Michael Henry Heim. Anthologies also appeared in Hungary. *Hungary: Plays,* edited and translated by Eugene Brogyanyi, includes five contemporary dramatic works by five playwrights. Perhaps the most challenging is Mihaly Kornis' *Kozma,* delineating the ordeal of Kozma, a Christ figure who is murdered by his three lovers.

Romania's Marin Sorescu was fast becoming known to English-speaking audiences. *Hands Behind My Back: Selected Poems* was the fifth collection of his poetry to be translated into English. The first full-length study devoted to Czeslaw Milosz appeared in the U.S. *The Poet's Work* was written by two American scholars with no knowledge of Polish, Leonard Nathan and Arthur Quinn. Working with translations available in English, the two Berkeley, Calif., professors provided readers, both Polish and English, with an excellent introduction to Milosz' poetry and prose. At the same time, *The Mature Laurel: Essays on Modern Polish Poetry,* edited by Adam Czerniawski, effectively evaluates Milosz' poetry. Few works published in Poland provoked great interest. Among those worth mentioning were Zbigniew Herbert's new poems collected in *Rovigo,* Andrzj Szczypiorski's novel *I omineli Emaus* ("And They Bypassed Emaus"), and Wladyslaw Terlecki's *Zabic cara* ("To Kill the Tsar").

The Czech poet Miroslav Holub was gaining a reputation as an excellent prose stylist. Fifty-five of his "essaylets" or "43 liners" were published in Scotland by Bloodaxe Books as *The Jingle Bell Principle,* translated by James Naughton. Several works by older writers were published in Czechoslovakia and received good reviews: Arnost Lustig's *Colette,* his last novel, a masterful description of a young girl from Antwerp facing life's challenges; Vaclav Pavel Borovicka's *Murderers in the Name of the State,* a reconstruction of various violent attacks on historical personages; Frantisek Pavlicek's *The End of the Patriarchate,* a gentle and sensitive study of people against the landscape of childhood; Victor Fischl's *A Cock's Crow,* a highly personal account of the author's philosophical position; and Jiri Grusa's family saga *Virgin's Master.*
(EDWARD J. CZERWINSKI;
AGNIESZKA PERLINSKA)

JEWISH

Hebrew. The main event in Hebrew literature in 1992 was the publication of *Mikdamot,* S. Yizhar's new novel. Acknowledged as one of the best Israeli novelists after S.Y. Agnon, Yizhar had not published any fictional work for almost 30 years, yet his new novel lacks none of the superb qualities of his early works. Other novels by veteran writers included Yonat and Alexander Sened's *Yoman shel Zug Me'ohav,* Aharon Megged's *Yom haOr shel Anat,* and Yoram Kaniuk's controversial *Post Mortem.* The younger generation was represented by Hanoch Levin's *Ish Omed leYad Isha Yoshevet,* Yitzhak Ben-Ner's *Boker shel Shotim,* Orly Castel-Bloom's intriguing *Dolly City,* and Haim Lapid's detective-like novel *Breznitz.*

First novels were penned by Gabriela Avigur-Rotem (*Mozart Lo Haya Yehudi*), Ariana Melamed (*Beit Sefer leBallet*), and Arieh Eckstein (*Doda Ester*). Clearly reflecting the postmodern vein in Hebrew prose, first collections of short stories were published by Etgar Kerrett (*Tsinorot*), Leah Ayalon (*Mashehu Kiyumi*), and Udi Taub (*Mayo leYudaika*).

Other collections of short stories were Yitzhak Averbuch Orpaz' *Ahavot Ketanot,* Terufim Ketanim, Ronit Matalon's *Zarim baBayit,* Savyon Liebrecht's *Sinit Ani Medaberet Eilekha,* and Yitzhak Bar-Yosef's *Venus.*

David Grossman examined the feelings of Palestinians living in Israel toward the state of Israel in his nonfiction *Nokhehim Nifkadim.* Literary reflections on the Arab-Israeli conflict were collected in two anthologies of short stories edited by Ehud Ben-Ezer and Aharon Amir. Notable books of poetry included Yehudah Amichai's *Nof Gluy Yeinayim,* Daliah Rabikovitz' *Ima Im Yeled,* Oded Sverdlik's *Ad Khlot haDvash,* and Ory Bernstein's *Inyan Prati.* Among works of literary scholarship were Dan Miron's controversial essays on the poetry of the War of Independence (*Mul haAh haShotek*) and Avraham Balaban's discussion of A.B. Yehoshua's latest novels (*Mar Molkho*). Miron also edited the two-volume collected poems of Yehudah Karni. The

RINO CASTELNUOVO—THE NEW YORK TIMES

Emil Habibi

prestigious Israel Prize was awarded to the late poet Avot Yeshurun and to the Israeli-Palestinian writer Emil Habibi.

(AVRAHAM BALABAN)

Yiddish. The year witnessed three consequential journalistic anniversaries. *Afn shvel,* the journal of the League for Yiddish, marked its 50th year; New York's weekly *Forverts* celebrated 95 years of continuous publication; and the magazine of the World Congress for Jewish Culture, *Di Tsukunft,* completed its 100th year.

Writing from Moscow, Khaym Beyder continued to make signal contributions to Yiddish literary scholarship. *The Paths We Discover* is the rewarding result of his patient mining of literary and historical archives and personal collections. Yoysef Kerler's *Selected Prose,* imbued with deep pathos, is dominated by vignettes of colleagues. Meyer Ravitsh's *Essays* ranges over major motifs of pivotal 20th-century writers. Mordkhe Tsanin contributed *Summersnow,* a collection of reflective essays.

In addition to several compelling short stories, much of Shire Gorshman's attention in *Perseverence* is given over to Soviet Yiddish writers of her acquaintance. Yoysef Heyblum's *The Comic in the Tragic* scrutinizes Israeli daily life with a bemused smile. Characteristic of Yisroel Kaplan's *Edgés* are historical and humanistic themes. Sh. Simkhovitsh's lyrical mini-epic, *A Stepchild by the Vistula,* takes the reader back to Poland's pre-World War II Jewish community. Historian-novelist Shloyme Vorzoger offered *Generations,* about a family fleeing from Poland to Israel. The versatile and suggestive medley *Eldra Don and Other Stories* by Hirsh-Dovid Meynkes [Katz] is partly autobiographical, partly a celebration of his late father, poet Meynke Katz.

Some of the Yiddish world's finest poets explored new vistas. Rivke Basman's *The Silence Burns* is an imaginative and richly allusive gathering. Binem Heller's *The Spirit of the Storm* brings together a half-century of creativity. Meyer Kharats' *Reckoning 3* is a distinctly crafted anamnesis. The thematic of Canadian poet Sh. Mitsmakher's *Time and Mood* is the ambience of modern history. Charles Dobzynski introduces Moyshe Shulshteyn's provocative volume of poetry, *Secret and Intent.* In his magisterial *The Heir of the Rain,* Avrom Sutskever returns in memory to Vilne and recalls the arrival of Nazi troops. Dore Taytlboym's spare *Steps to the Heights* reflects her courageous confidence in the future.   (THOMAS E. BIRD)

CHINESE

Politics in China was still a potent influence in literary circles in 1992, although that may not have been immediately evident to those who bought books or attended the movies. In a certain sense, the year belonged to Wang Shuo, a 34-year-old novelist whose literary output was quite astounding, both in quantity and in impact. The author of about a dozen novels and novellas over a short span of time, Wang set about adapting many of his works for the movies. He represented an irreverent, nonideological trend in fiction, everything from "ruffian" literature to burlesque, the latter setting him apart from most of his peers. As urbanites in growing numbers turned to works featuring get-rich-quick schemes and Western "decadence," the popularity of more serious literature decreased. This trend also

Ai Bei
COURTESY OF AI BEI

surfaced in Taiwan, where a "brat pack" of youthful novelists relied more on marketing techniques than on creativity to reap substantial financial rewards.

In 1992 Wang published two new books and a four-volume collection of previously published fiction. Meanwhile, his most renowned contemporaries either were engaged in writing movie scripts or were publishing new works in Taiwan, where the monetary payoffs were far greater than in China. Liu Heng, author of the novella and prize-winning movie *Ju Dou,* continued his screenplay success with *Qiu Ju Goes to Court,* which won the Golden Lion award for best picture at the Venice Film Festival.

Mo Yan (Mo Yen), author of the renowned movie and novel *Red Sorghum,* was also busy with a screenplay; more significant, however, was the publication in Taiwan of his fourth novel, *Wineville,* a stunningly innovative work dealing with cannibalism, fiction writing, the culture of drinking, and more. A collection of his short fiction in English translation, *Explosions,* appeared in Hong Kong. Li Jui, another novelist on the verge of gaining an international reputation, published excerpts from *Old Sites* in the Taiwan magazine *Unitas,* which also brought out a special issue on Hong Kong literature. Su Tong (Su T'ung), whose *All My Wives* was made into the film *Raise the Red Lantern,* published *My Life as Emperor* in Taiwan. Lillian Lee's *The Last Princess of Manchuria* was one of several significant works to appear in English during a relatively quiet year for translations.

In Taiwan the new literary house Rye Fields published a collection of recent stories by Chu T'ien-hsin, one of three literary daughters of novelist Chu Hsi-ning, who had set high literary standards in Taiwan three decades earlier. Rye Fields had firmly established itself as a major promoter of contemporary fiction from Taiwan and the mainland. A milestone was reached in Taiwan with the 20th-anniversary issue of *The Chinese PEN,* a quarterly that for two decades had introduced the public to some of the finest writing from Taiwan and overseas communities.

Writers outside China, many of whom continued to live in self-imposed exile, were active both in print (the magazine *Today* remained the primary vehicle for their works) and as participants in literary gatherings. The Academy of American Poets brought the three dissident poets Bei Dao (Pei Tao), Duo Duo (To To), and Gu Cheng (Ku Ch'eng) together with Shu Ting (Shu T'ing) from China for readings in New York and San Francisco, while the novelist Ai Bei (Ai Pei; *Red Ivy, and Green Earth Mother*) was warmly received at the University of Colorado's spectacular autumn gathering of writers from around the world.

(HOWARD C. GOLDBLATT)

JAPANESE

The major news of the year was not any particular book of fiction or poetry but the deaths of three novelists, Mitsuharu Inoue, Kenji Nakagami, and Seicho Matsumoto. Nakagami's death was especially shocking since he was still in his mid-40s and was regarded by many literary critics as one of Japan's most promising novelists. A member of the *burakumin,* or "outcast" class, he was born and raised in Kumano province, the locale of many of his books, including *Kareki nada* ("The Seas of the Dying Woods") and *Pleasures of One Thousand Years.* His last novel, *Derision,* was published in 1992. Inoue was one of the earliest critics of the Communist Party and was expelled from it in 1953, but he kept his leftist credo, and most of his novels were concerned with social protest. Matsumoto, one of the most popular and prolific novelists of postwar Japan, had remained active in such various fields as mystery, historical romance, and nonfiction.

The Tanizaki Prize was awarded to Jakucho Setouchi, who became a Buddhist nun in her mid-50s. Her novels were remarkable for their frankly amorous descriptions, and some considered her "conversion" too sensational to be convincing. However, *Ask the Flowers,* her prizewinning novel, succeeded in evoking the touching image of Ippen, a "dancing Buddhist saint" of the 13th century, while following the amorous career of a modern female character. Kunie Iwahashi's *Floating Bridge,* the Woman Writer's Prize winner, was a sophisticated chain of short stories, mainly concerned with the delicate balance between loneliness and liberation of a widowed middle-aged writer. It was obviously autobiographical. Masahiko Shimada's *Higan Sensei* was a clever, ambitious, "postmodern" novel by a promising young writer.

Jinichi Konishi's multivolume *History of Japanese Literature* was a stupendous achievement, both scholarly and brightly critical. Gen Ansei's *Responses of the Modern Chinese Intellectuals Toward Japan* was an outstanding study of a neglected topic by a Chinese scholar, and Yoko Makino's *Lafcadio Hearn* was a sensitive portrait of the expatriate American writer. The posthumous *Collected Plays* by the celebrated literary critic Mitsuo Nakamura impressed with its irony and bitter sarcasm, exceptional on the Japanese stage.   (SHOICHI SAEKI)

See also Art Exhibitions and Art Sales: *Art Sales;* Libraries; Publishing.

This article updates the *Macropædia* article The History of Western LITERATURE and articles on the literatures of the various languages.

Mathematics

Among noteworthy mathematical events of 1992 was a major breakthrough in the theory of geodesics—shortest curves joining two points on surfaces—made by Victor Bangert of the University of Freiburg, Germany, and John Franks of Northwestern University, Evanston, Ill. Within the context of general relativity theory, geodesics define the paths along which matter travels in gravitationally curved space-time. Where flight restrictions permit, aircraft follow geodesics over the surface of the Earth to conserve fuel. Closed geodesics, which return to their starting point and traverse the same path over and over again, are especially interesting to mathematicians and scientists and have applications in fields ranging from materials science to nuclear fusion research.

On an ordinary round sphere geodesics are great circles, lying on planes that pass through the centre of the sphere, and all of them are closed. On a bumpy sphere many geodesics wind round the bumps and fail to close up. Not all of them, however, show such "bad" behaviour. In 1917 the American mathematician George Birkhoff proved that every bumpy sphere has at least one closed geodesic, a value that was improved to at least three closed geodesics in 1929.

How many closed geodesics must there be? As was shown during the year, three is a wild underestimate. Using methods from dynamical systems theory, Bangert and Franks proved that every bumpy sphere has infinitely many closed geodesics. The proof starts with one closed geodesic, which is viewed as an "equator," dividing the sphere into two parts. Any other geodesic must either stay entirely inside one half or cross the equator. If a geodesic crosses the equator, it does so at some particular point and some particular angle. Following it to the next crossing then produces a new point and a new angle. The pairs of points and angles form coordinates on a cylindrical band, or annulus, and following a geodesic from one intersection to the next defines a mapping from the annulus to itself. Closed geodesics correspond to periodic points of this mapping—points that return to their initial state if the mapping is applied sufficiently many times in succession. The problem thus reduces to showing that the mapping of the annulus possesses infinitely many periodic points. The key is that the mapping is area preserving; that is, small regions of the annulus are mapped to regions with the same area.

What if the chosen geodesic does not cross the equator at all but gets trapped in one hemisphere? Bangert discovered that in this case the hemisphere in question contains a second equator for which the difficulty does not arise. Franks's contribution was a striking proof that every area-preserving mapping of an annulus has either no periodic points or infinitely many. The complete result emerges when their separate theorems are combined.

The year also saw the long-sought answer to a question posed by Mark Kac of Rockefeller University, New York City, in 1966: can you hear the shape of a drum? More generally, what information about a shape can be inferred from its spectrum, the range of frequencies that it produces when it vibrates? When an earthquake hits, the entire Earth rings like a bell, and seismologists deduce a great deal about the internal structure of the planet from the "sound" that it produces and the way the vibrations echo around, bouncing off different layers of rock. Kac's celebrated question is the simplest and tidiest one that can be asked about such techniques. In 1992 Carolyn Gordon and David Webb of Washington University, St. Louis, Mo., and Scott Wolpert

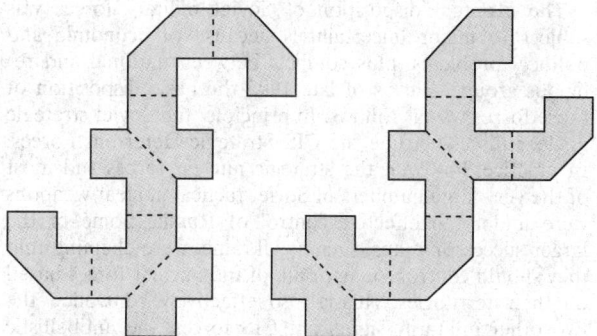

Mathematicians proved in 1992 that these two distinct two-dimensional drumhead shapes produce identical sounds; *i.e.*, they have the same frequency spectrum. Each drumhead is assembled from seven halves of a Greek cross.

of the University of Maryland constructed two distinct mathematical drumheads that produce the identical range of sounds (*see* Figure).

Some features of a drumhead definitely are determinable from its spectrum; for example, its area, as the German mathematician Hermann Weyl proved in 1912, and its perimeter. In 1985 Toshikazu Sunada of Nagoya (Japan) University found a general criterion for two distinct shapes to have the same spectrum. Using it, Peter Buser of the École Polytechnique, Lausanne, Switz., found two distinct curved (three-dimensional) surfaces having the same spectrum. The two-dimensional example found by Gordon, Webb, and Wolpert resulted from squashing one of Buser's examples flat. The two drumheads are each assembled from seven identical pieces. This factor is important in the proof that the spectra are identical because vibrational patterns can be "cut and pasted" from one drum to the other. This technique, based on Sunada's work, was pioneered by Pierre Bérard of the University of Grenoble, France.

(IAN STEWART)

This article updates the *Macropædia* articles GEOMETRY; MECHANICS: *Dynamics*.

Military Affairs

The two most important defense events of 1992 were the final collapse of the massive military machine of the Soviet Union and the worsening civil war in the territories of the former Yugoslavia. The Soviet Union was replaced by a total of 15 nations: the 10 republics of the Commonwealth of Independent States (CIS), Azerbaijan, Georgia, and the three Baltic states (Estonia, Latvia, and Lithuania).

These nations differed significantly in their size, location, and military strength and could be divided into three groups. The first was Russia itself, which was mainly a European power, although it also had an Asian presence because of its territories east of the Ural Mountains, which formed the Siberian, Transbaykal, and Far East military districts. Under Pres. Boris Yeltsin, Russia was sharply cutting its military forces, but it remained the largest military power in Europe and the only European nuclear superpower. The second group of Soviet successor states comprised the nine that formed part of non-NATO Europe. These included the four CIS republics (Armenia, Belarus, Moldova, and Ukraine), Azerbaijan, Georgia, and the three Baltic states (Estonia, Latvia, and Lithuania). The third group of Soviet successor nations was made up of the five Central Asian CIS republics (Kazakhstan, Kyrgyzstan, Tajikistan, Turkmenistan, and Uzbekistan).

The eventual disposition of Soviet military forces was subject to major uncertainties because of economic and political problems, plus conflicts between national and religious groups. But as of late 1992 the basic disposition of those forces was as follows. In principle, the Soviet strategic nuclear forces became the CIS Strategic Deterrent Forces. In practice, however, the strategic nuclear forces and most of the very large numbers of Soviet tactical nuclear weapons were under the effective control of Russia. Some of the larger successor states, such as Ukraine, were claiming that they should control some, or all, of the nuclear forces based on their territories. Russia also effectively controlled the two other militarily significant CIS forces, the antiballistic missile defense system and the Space Forces.

The conventional forces of the former Soviet Union were to be divided. Russia would control all conventional forces on its territory and those in the Groups of Forces (in Germany, Poland, and the Baltic republics), plus the 14th Army (mainly based in Moldova), the forces in Azerbaijan and Armenia, and the former Soviet navy. In principle, the remaining conventional forces were to form the CIS Joint General Purpose Forces (CIS-JGPF) under the joint control of Russia and the republic where they were stationed. Georgia and the three Baltic states would not share in these arrangements and planned to form independent national forces. In practice, Ukraine and Belarus appeared to have assumed control of the conventional forces on their territories. Ukraine and Georgia were negotiating with Russia for control over parts of the Black Sea Fleet of the former Soviet navy. In addition, Ukraine, Belarus, Georgia, and most other successor states were nationalizing conventional forces on their territories by ordering their nationals to serve only in the CIS-JGPF forces.

There was increasing danger of unrest among different nationalities in the successor nations, splitting the armed forces into national components and leading to the possibility of civil wars. Serious clashes had already occurred in Armenia, Azerbaijan, Kyrgyzstan, and Georgia. In Georgia the hard-line former Communist president, Zviad Gamsakhurdia, was forced to resign after his supporters were defeated by a coalition of irregular forces in intensive fighting in the capital, Tbilisi. The Russian military had to establish regional peacekeeping forces to limit two regional conflicts between government and separatist forces. One was between Moldovan forces and the breakaway trans-Dnestr region, mostly inhabited by ethnic Russians and Ukrainians, and the other was between Georgia and the South Ossetia region, which was attempting to leave Georgia and join the Russian autonomous republic of Severnaya Osetiya.

The potential for conflict in the ex-Communist countries was demonstrated by the bitter civil war in former Yugoslavia. By 1992 that country had split into five states, the Federal Republic of Yugoslavia (Serbia and Montenegro), Bosnia and Hercegovina, Croatia, Slovenia, and Macedonia. The Serbian government and the largely Serb former Yugoslav national army, together with Serb irregulars, were trying to establish a Greater Serbia that would include all Serbs living in the neighbouring republics. The governments of Slovenia, Croatia, and Bosnia defended their territories with national militias (though fighting in Slovenia ended in 1991). Military and civilian casualties were heavy, running into the tens of thousands. One particularly chilling feature of the war was what was called ethnic cleansing, the execution or expulsion of members of one ethnic group by another in an effort to create an "ethnically pure" area. It appeared to have been carried out mainly by Serbs against Slav Muslims in Bosnia, though other groups were guilty as well. A UN peacekeeping force deployed to Croatia and

Soldiers from Uzbekistan, stationed in Ukraine as members of the former Soviet army, watch a parade in January. Control of forces and military equipment was one of the difficulties faced in 1992 by the new republics formed from the Soviet Union.
AP/WIDE WORLD

Bosnia was too small to stop the fighting. At year's end the U.S. and the European Communities were debating whether to intervene. (*See* WORLD AFFAIRS [Europe]: *Bosnia and Hercegovina; Croatia; Yugoslavia.*)

UNITED STATES

The U.S. all-volunteer armed forces in 1992 totaled 1,913,-750 personnel (212,600 women). By 1997 proposed force reductions would cut this total to some 1.6 million. The largest cuts would be in the army. Defense spending (budget authority) for fiscal 1992 was $270.9 billion.

The main air force commands were reorganized, and the Strategic Air Command (SAC) was abolished. The new Air Combat Command (ACC) took over SAC's responsibility for U.S. strategic nuclear forces, which were to be greatly reduced. Most modernization programs were to be eliminated. The ACC would retain 95 modern Rockwell B-1B strategic bombers. The elderly B-52 bomber force declined to 81 B-52Gs and 94 B-52Hs (first deployed in 1959 and 1962, respectively). Of the B-52Gs, 40 carried 12 AGM-86B air-launched cruise missiles (ALCM) each, while 41 were equipped with the Harpoon air-to-surface missile and were intended for a nonnuclear antishipping role. Deployment of the first 100 advanced cruise missiles, with low-observable (stealth) technology, began, but production would be capped at 640 instead of 1,000. Only 16–20 new B-2 stealth bombers would be built.

The land-based, fixed-silo intercontinental ballistic missile (ICBM) force was to be reduced, under the July 31, 1991, Strategic Arms Reduction Treaty (START I) and the June 16, 1992, agreement between U.S. Pres. George Bush and Russian Pres. Boris Yeltsin, to 500 silos containing Minuteman III ICBM converted to single warheads. The 50 MX Peacekeepers were large missiles, each weighing 88,-000 kg (195,000 lb) and carrying 10 multiple independently targetable reentry vehicles (MIRV). No more Peacekeepers would be produced. The 500 Minuteman IIIs were modernized missiles, each carrying three MIRV. All 450 Minuteman II ICBM in fixed silos were to be retired and were reduced from alert status, as were strategic bombers. Development of the single-warhead Midgetman ICBM was canceled.

The ballistic missile nuclear submarine (SSBN) force was reduced to 25, carrying 504 submarine-launched ballistic missiles (SLBM). Eight of the 13 modern Ohio-class SSBN each carried 24 Trident I/C-4s, while the other five each carried 24 Trident II/D-5 SLBM; these would eventually replace the Trident I/C-4s on the other eight Ohio-class SSBN. Older SSBN included six Franklin class (96 Trident I/C-4s) and six Madison class (96 Trident I/C-4s). The 10 older SSBN with Poseidon C-3 SLBM were retired. All submarine-launched nuclear cruise missiles (SLCM) were replaced with conventionally armed SLCM on the 18 nuclear attack/cruise missile submarines (SSGN). Plans called for a total of more than 2,300 conventionally armed BGM-109A Tomahawk sea-launched cruise missiles to be deployed.

The U.S. Navy in mid-1992 totaled 188 principal surface combatants, 69 nuclear-powered attack submarines (SSN), and 546,650 personnel. These provided 12 active carrier battle groups, each carrier having an attack wing of some 86 aircraft plus escorting surface vessels and SSN. Of the total of 14 aircraft carriers, 7 were nuclear powered (including one in long refit) and 7 were conventionally powered (including one in a Service Life Extension Program refit). Modern aircraft included 423 F-14A/D Tomcat fighters, 432 A-6 Intruder/Prowler strike planes, 663 F/A-18A/B/C/D.) Hornet fighter/ground attack (FGA) planes, and 92 E-2C Hawkeye electronic warfare/airborne early warning aircraft. All of the four recommissioned World War II Iowa-class battleships had been decommissioned but placed in preservation. The 9 nuclear- and 39 conventionally powered guided-weapons (GW) cruisers included 21 new Ticonderoga-class equipped with the Aegis fleet air defense missile/radar system. Other major surface combatants included 45 destroyers (14 GW) and 83 frigates (51 GW).

The Marine Corps, with 193,000 personnel, was organized in three divisions, each with its own air wing. Modern aircraft included 201 F18-A/D Hornet FGA aircraft, 40 A-6 Intruder strike aircraft, and 165 AV-8A/C Harrier vertical/short takeoff and landing (V/STOL) FGA aircraft.

The 499,300-strong air force had approximately 3,485 combat aircraft plus more than 1,300 in storage. Among modern types were 838 F-15 Eagle fighters, 1,679 F-16 Falcon FGA, and 55 F-117 Stealth FGA, plus 34 E-3 Sentry airborne warning and control systems. Older types included 256 F-4 Phantom FGA/reconnaissance, 275 F-111 A-F medium bombers, and 372 A-10A Thunderbolt ground-support aircraft.

The army, which comprised 674,800 personnel, formed 9 heavy and 1 airborne divisions (about 17,000 men each)— 2 armoured, 5 mechanized, 1 infantry, 1 air assault, and 1 airborne division—plus 4 light infantry divisions (consisting of about 10,200 men each). The light infantry divisions were easier to transport and were intended as part of the Rapid Deployment Force for use outside NATO-Europe. Armour included 7,422 M-1/1A1 Abrams tanks and 5,371 M-2/3 Bradley armoured infantry fighting vehicles (AIFV), plus some 7,311 M-60/60A1 and M60-A3 tanks and 13,102 M-113 armoured personnel carriers (APC). (See *Arms Control and Disarmament,* below.)

By year's end some 18,000 U.S. troops had been sent to Somalia to lead a UN-backed force to safeguard the delivery of supplies in the famine- and war-ravaged country.

NATO

In 1992 the NATO alliance continued to meet, successfully, its greatest challenge since it was founded in 1949; it was assisting the evolution of democratic governments in central Europe and the former Soviet Union while retaining lower levels of defense forces, at lower readiness but with enhanced mobility and flexibility. Some alliance members, notably the U.S., the U.K., and France, were also helping to enforce the terms of the UN cease-fire that followed their defeat of Iraq in the 1991 Gulf war.

NATO was continuing its two-track policy agreed upon in 1989. It would give economic aid to the emerging eastern European democracies and reduce the level of conventional forces through the Conventional Forces in Europe (CFE) Treaty, signed on Nov. 19, 1990. However, subsequent military and political developments, culminating in the collapse of the Soviet Union, enabled NATO, non-NATO Europe, and Russia to use the CFE Treaty framework to codify the much deeper cuts they now planned.

The CFE Treaty established categories of treaty-limited equipment (TLE), such as main battle tanks and combat aircraft, and established four zones of limitation for TLE in the Atlantic-to-the-Urals (ATTU) region. After July 17, 1992, all TLE above the specified limits were to be destroyed (not sold or moved out of the ATTU), and TLE was to be fully limited to CFE Treaty limits by Jan. 17, 1996.

If the CFE Treaty terms were fully complied with, the result would be a new European balance of power. The three most militarily powerful Soviet successor states would be: Russia, with (in the ATTU area) 1,450,000 personnel,

PETER POULIDES

Workers in Texas assemble aircraft at the Fort Worth plant of General Dynamics. In what was widely seen as a move to save jobs, U.S. Pres. George Bush in September approved the sale of 150 F-16 fighters, made at the Fort Worth facility, to Taiwan.

Approximate Strengths of Regular Armed Forces of the World

Country	Military personnel in 000s			Warships[1]			Jet aircraft[3]		Tanks[4]	Defense expenditure as % of 1990 GNP[5]
	Army	Navy	Air Force	Aircraft carriers/ cruisers	Submarines[2]	Destroyers/ frigates	Bombers and fighter- bombers	Fighters/ recon- nais- sance		
I. NATO[6]										
Belgium	54.0	4.4	17.3	—		4 FFG	72 FB	35, 15 R	334	1.5
Canada[7]	22.0	17.0	22.4	—	3	4 DDG, 6 FFH, 8 FF	180 F, 18 MR	—	114	1.9
Denmark	17.3	4.9	7.0	—	5	3 FFG	106 FB	—	499	2.0
France[8]	260.9	64.9	91.7	2 CVS	8, 5 SSN, 4 SSBN	4 DDG, 34 FFG	15 B, 267 FB	240, 53 R, 32 MR	1,343	2.8
Germany	316.0	35.2	95.8		22	3 DDG, 3 DD, 8 FF	567 FB	20 F, 71 R, 19 MR	7,090	1.9
Greece	113.0	19.5	26.8		10	9 DD, 4 FF	162 FB	163, 19 R	1,879	5.9
Italy	230.0	48.0	76.0	1 CVV, 1 CGH	8	1 DDG, 1 DDGH, 8 FFH, 16 FF	177 FB	84 F, 18 R, 18 MR	1,220	1.7
Netherlands, The	60.8	15.5	12.0		5	4 DDG, 12 FF	157 FB	20 R, 14 MR	913	2.7
Norway	15.9	7.3	9.5	—	11	5 FFG	61 FB	20 F, 6 MR	211	3.2
Portugal	32.7	15.3	10.3	—	3	3 FFG, 8 FF	77 FB	6 MR	129	2.4
Spain	146.0	36.9[9]	35.0	1 CVV	8	9 FFG, 6 FF	88 FB	113, 20 R, 7 MR	838	1.6
Turkey	450.0	52.3	58.0	—	12	12 DD, 8 FF	490 FB	20, 26 R	3,928	3.1
United Kingdom	145.4	62.1	86.0	3 CVV	6, 13 SSN, 3 SSBN	12 DDG, 29 FFG	23 B, 356 FB	86, 11 R, 33 MR	1,318	4.2
United States	674.8	739.65[9]	499.3	7 CVN, 7 CV, 9 CGN, 39 CG, 7 LHA, 7 LPH, 12 LPD, 33 LSD/T	69 SSN, 25 SSBN, 18 SSGN,	14 DDG, 31 DD, 51 FFG, 32 FF	270 SB, 275 B, 4,354 FB	2,704, 162 R, 334 MR/ASW	15,629	5.1
II. NON-NATO EUROPE										
Albania	27.0	2.0	11.0	—	2	—	22 FB	70	100	...
Austria	46.0	—	6.0	—	—	—	30 FB	24	159	1.0
Belarus	95.0	—	20.0	—	—	—	130 B, 180 FB	165 F, 92 R	1,850	...
Bosnia-Hercegovina	67.0	—	—	—	—	—	—	—	300	...
Bulgaria	75.0	10.0	22.0	—	3	2 FF	57 FB	141, 40 R	2,100	6.9
Croatia	100.0	5.0	4.2	—	—	—	—	—	200	...
Czechoslovakia	72.0	—	44.8	—	—	—	153 FB	109, 42 R	3,208	2.9
Finland	27.3	2.5	3.0	—	—	—	—	87	123	1.7
Georgia	20.0	—	—	—	—	—	—	—		...
Hungary	63.5	—	17.3	—	—	—	—	59, 11 R	1,357	2.3
Ireland	11.2	1.0	0.8	—	—	—	—	—	—	1.2
Moldova	12.0	—	—	—	—	—	—	30 F		...
Poland	194.2	19.3	83.0	—	3	1 DDG, 1 FF	124 FB	257, 24 R	2,850	2.4
Romania	161.0	19.0	20.0	—	—	1 DDG, 5 FF	140 FB	237, 24 R	2,875	3.1
Slovenia	15.0	—	—	—	—	—	—	—	120	...
Sweden[10]	43.5/700.0	9.5	7.5	—	12	—	97 FB	214, 48 R	785	2.5
Switzerland[10]	20.0/565.0	—	3.0/60.0	—	—	—	87 FB	137, 18 R	812	1.7
Ukraine	150.0	—	50.0	—	—	—	96 B, 290 FB	340 F, 87 R	6,300	...
Federal Republic of Yugoslavia[11]	100.0	6.0	29.0	—	5	4 FF	126 FB	126, 71 R	1,000	18.6
III. RUSSIA										
Russia	1,400.0	320.0	800.0[12]	1 CV, 3 CVV 3 CGN, 1 CGH 29 CG	80, 59 SSN, 55 SSBN, 36 SSGN, 8 SSG	26 DDG, 129 FF	170 SB, 555 B, 2,150 FB	3,735, 365 R, 90 MR	29,000	11.1
IV. MIDDLE EAST AND NORTH AFRICA; SUB-SAHARAN AFRICA; LATIN AMERICA[6]										
Algeria	120.0	7.0	12.0	—	2	3 FF	57 FB	149, 3 R	960	1.4
Egypt	290.0	20.0	30.0	—	4	4 FF	113 FB	205, 20 R	3,090	7.5
Iran[13]	305.0	18.0	35.0	—	—	3 DD, 3 FFG, 2 FF	130 FB	102 F, 8 R	700	7.1
Iraq[14]	350.0	1.6	30.0	—	—	—	6 B, 130 FB	180, 5 R	2,300	...
Israel[10]	134.0/598.0	10.0/10.0	32.0/37.0	—	3	—	600 FB	14 R	3,890	9.9
Jordan	85.0	0.4	14.0	—	—	—	62 FB	32	1,131	14.1
Kuwait	8.0	1.2	2.5	—	—	—	32 FB	15	200	33.0
Lebanon[15]	35.7	0.4	0.8	—	—	—	...		240	3.7
Libya	55.0	8.0	22.0	—	6	3 FF	5 B,133 FB	238, 13 R	2,150	...
Morocco	175.0	7.0	13.5	—	—	1 FFG	32 FB	15	284	4.3
Oman	20.0	3.0	3.5	—	—	—	20 FB	—	78	12.3
Qatar	6.0	0.7	0.8	—	—	—	6 FB	12	24	12.2
Saudi Arabia	73.0	11.0	18.0	—	—	8 FFG	97 FB	102, 10 R	700	33.8
Sudan	75.0	1.5	6.0	—	—	—	28 FB	17	250	...
Syria	300.0	8.0	100.0	—	3	2 FF	170 FB	302, 6 R	4,600	13.0
Tunisia	27.0	4.5	3.5	—	—	1 FF	15 FB	—	84	3.3
United Arab Emirates	50.0	2.0	2.5	—	—	—	32 FB	34	131	14.6
Yemen[16]	60.0	1.5	2.0	—	—	—	48 FB	47	1,275	13.1

6,400 battle tanks, and 3,450 combat aircraft (down from 1,536,000 personnel, 11,000 battle tanks, and 3,950 combat aircraft); Ukraine, with 450,000 personnel (up from the current 230,000), 4,080 battle tanks, and 1,090 combat aircraft (down from 6,300 battle tanks and 1,380 combat aircraft); and Belarus, with 100,000 personnel, 1,800 battle tanks, and 260 combat aircraft (down from 125,000 personnel, 1,850 battle tanks, and 617 combat aircraft). The other major European military powers would be Germany, with 345,000 personnel, 4,166 battle tanks, and 900 combat aircraft (down from 411,800 personnel, 7,090 battle tanks, and 989 combat aircraft); France, with 325,000 personnel, 1,306 battle tanks, and 800 combat aircraft (down from 330,400 personnel, 1,343 battle tanks, and 808 combat aircraft); and the U.K., with 260,000 personnel (up from 222,500), 1,015 battle tanks (down from 1,198), and 900 combat aircraft (up from 721). In addition, Russia, France, and the U.K. would have national nuclear forces.

However, as these figures also show, many countries might cut their forces well below CFE Treaty levels, as did the U.S. Under the CFE Treaty, the U.S. was limited to 250,000 troops, 4,006 battle tanks, and 900 combat aircraft. But U.S. forces had already been cut well below these levels, to 222,500 personnel, and seemed likely to be cut to some 100,000 by 1996.

ARMS CONTROL AND DISARMAMENT

During the year U.S.-Soviet arms control negotiations were replaced by negotiations between the U.S. and Russia, Belarus, Kazakhstan, and Ukraine. At their 1992 meeting in

Country	Military personnel in 000s			Warships[1]			Jet aircraft[3]		Tanks[4]	Defense expenditure as % of 1990 GNP[5]
	Army	Navy	Air Force	Aircraft carriers/ cruisers	Submarines[2]	Destroyers/ frigates	Bombers and fighter-bombers	Fighters/ reconnaissance		
Angola[17]	120.0	1.5	6.0	—	—	—	90 FB	35	230	...
Kenya	20.5	1.2	2.5	—	—	—	11 FB	—	80	...
Madagascar	20.0	0.5	0.5	—	—	—	12 FB	—	—	1.4
Mozambique	45.0	1.2	4.0	—	—	—	43 FB	—	100	15.6
Nigeria	62.0	4.5	9.5	—	—	1 FFG	58 FB	—	157	0.8
South Africa	49.9	4.5	10.0	—	3	—	116 FB	14	250	3.6
Tanzania	45.0	0.8	1.0	—	—	—	—	24	62	...
Zaire	26.0	1.3	1.8	—	—	—	—	8	80	...
Zimbabwe	46.0	—	2.5	—	—	—	17 FB	12	40	7.0
Argentina	35.0	20.0[9]	10.0	—	4	6 DDG, 7 FFG	6 B, 82 FB	—	266	1.7
Brazil	196.0	50.0[9]	50.7	1 CVV	4	6 DH, 12 FFG	68 FB	18	—	0.2
Chile	54.0	25.0[9]	12.8	—	4	2 DDG, 2 DDH, 4 FFG, 2 DD	48 FB	15	171	3.2
Colombia	120.0	12.0[9]	7.0	—	2	4 FFG	28 FB	—	—	3.0
Cuba	175.0	13.5[9]	17.0	—	3	3 FF	20 FB	126	1,700	5.0
El Salvador	40.0	1.3	2.4	—	—	—	—	—	—	2.4
Mexico	130.0	37.0[9]	8.0	—	—	3 DD	—	11	—	0.5
Nicaragua	13.0	.5	1.2	—	—	—	—	—	130	9.1
Peru	75.0	22.0[9]	15.0	2 CA	9	4 DD, 2 DDG, 4 FFG	13 B, 41 FB	24	300	3.8
Venezuela	34.0	11.0[9]	7.0	—	—	6 FFH	76 FB	—	70	3.6

V. SOUTH AND CENTRAL ASIA; EAST ASIA AND OCEANIA[6]

Country	Army	Navy	Air Force	Aircraft carriers/ cruisers	Submarines[2]	Destroyers/ frigates	Bombers and fighter-bombers	Fighters/ reconnaissance	Tanks[4]	Defense expenditure as % of 1990 GNP[5]
Australia	30.3	15.3	22.3	—	5	3 DDG, 5 FFG, 3 FF	18 B, 52 FB	19 MR, 4 RR	103	2.4
Bangladesh	93.0	7.5	6.5	—	—	1 FFG, 3 FF	46 FB	35	50	1.3
China	2,300.0	260.0[9]	470.0	—	38, 1 SSG, 5 SSN, 1 SSBN	19 DDG, 27 FFG, 10 FF	630 B, 600 FB	4,600, 300 R, 20 MR	8,000	3.2
India	1,100.0	55.0	110.0	2 CVV	15, 1 SSGN	5 DDG, 5 FFH, 15 FF	354 FB	298, 18 R, 22 MR	3,800	2.9
Indonesia	215.0	44.0[9]	24.0	—	2	12 FFH, 4 FF	40 FB	14	—	1.3
Japan	156.0	44.0	46.0	—	17	6 DDG, 24 FFH, 34 FF	94 FB	130, 10 R, 104 MR	1,210	1.0
Kazakhstan/C.I.S.	63.0	—	—	—	—	—	140 FB	60 F, 170 R	1,200	...
Korea, North	1,000.0	40.0	92.0	—	22	2 FF, 1 FFG	80 B, 310 FB	376	3,000	26.7
Korea, South	520.0	60.0[9]	53.0	—	—	5 DDG, 4 DD, 7 FFG, 19 FF	190 FB	96, 28 R	1,800	3.8
Laos	33.0	0.5	3.5	—	—	—	29 FB	—	30	...
Malaysia	105.0	10.5	12.0	—	—	2 FFG, 2 FFH	33 FB	17, 4 R	—	3.7
Mongolia	14.0	—	1.5	—	—	—	—	12	650	11.1
Myanmar	265.0	12.0	9.0	—	—	—	12	—	26	4.2
New Zealand	4.8	2.4	3.7	—	—	4 FFH	21 FB	6 MR	—	1.9
Pakistan	515.0	20.0	45.0	—	6	1 DDh, 4 FFG, 6 FF	126 FB	214, 12 R, 4 MR	1,980	7.0
Philippines	68.0	23.0[9]	15.5	—	—	1 FF	—	9	—	2.2
Singapore	45.0	4.5	6.0	—	—	—	90 FB	38, 8 R	—	5.4
Taiwan	260.0	60.0[9]	70.0	—	4	12 DDH, 14 DD, 2FFH 4 FF	420 FB	6 R, 32 MR	459	5.4
Thailand	190.0	50.0[9]	43.0	—	—	3 FFG, 5 FF	30 FB	44	153	2.5
Turkmenistan/C.I.S.	34.0	—	—	—	—	—	60 FB	115 F	750	...
Vietnam	700.0	42.0[9]	115.0	—	—	1 FFG, 6 FF	60 FB	125	1,300	...
Uzbekistan/C.I.S.	15.0	—	—	—	—	—	100 FB	100 F, 35 R	280	...

Note: Data exclude paramilitary, security, and irregular forces. Naval data exclude vessels of less than 100 tons standard displacement. Figures are for June 1991. Because of substantive changes in national forces and reassessments of evidence, data may not be comparable with previous editions.

[1]Aircraft carrier (CV); aircraft carrier, nuclear (CVN); V/STOL and helicopter carrier (CVV); general purpose amphibious assault ship (LHA); amphibious transport dock (LPD); amphibious assault ship (helicopter) (LPH); dock/tank landing ship (LSD/T); battleship (BBG); heavy cruiser (CA); guided missile cruiser (CG); guided missile cruiser, nuclear (CGN); helicopter cruiser (CAH); destroyer (DD); guided missile destroyer (DDG); frigate (FF); guided missile frigate (FFG); helicopter frigate (FFH); N denotes nuclear powered.
[2]Nuclear-powered attack submarine (SSN); ballistic missile submarine (SSB); guided (cruise) missile submarine (SSG); coastal (C); N denotes nuclear powered.
[3]Bombers (B), fighter-bombers (FB), strategic bombers (SB), reconnaissance fighters (R); maritime reconnaissance (MR). Data include jet combat aircraft from all services including naval and air defense. MR also includes propeller drive ASW and ECM aircraft; data exclude light strike/counterinsurgency (COIN) aircraft.
[4]Main battle tanks (MBT), medium and heavy, 31 tons and over.
[5]Figures are for gross national product (GNP).
[6]Only state with significant military forces are listed.
[7]Of Canada's other military personnel, approximately 22,600 are not identified by service.
[8]French forces were withdrawn from NATO command structure in 1966, but France remains a member of NATO.
[9]Includes marines.
[10]Second figure is fully mobilized strength.
[11]Figures refer to force levels for Federal Republic of Yugoslavia composed of Serbia and Montenegro.
[12]Figure includes the Strategic Rocket Forces (144,000) and the Air Defense Force (356,000), both separate services.
[13]Losses in Iran-Iraq war made remaining force estimates uncertain.
[14]Losses in Operation Desert Storm cause remaining force estimates to be uncertain.
[15]Lebanon's civil war and division mean that there are both national forces and militias plus 30,000 Syrian troops in occupation.
[16]The Yemen Arab Republic and the People's Democratic Republic of Yemen formed the Republic of Yemen in 1990.
[17]Opposition UNITA forces total some 28,000 personnel.
Sources: International Institute for Strategic Studies, 23 Tavistock Street, London, The Military Balance 1992–1993, Strategic Survey 1991–92.

Washington, D.C., Bush and Yeltsin signed a Joint Understanding on further cuts in strategic offensive nuclear forces. START II, embodying this agreement, was to be signed early in 1993. However, START I could not be carried out until the other three republics agreed to be nuclear-free.

Under START II, the cuts would be made in two stages. In Stage One, to be completed by 1999, strategic forces would be reduced to an overall total of 3,800–4,250 warheads, of which only 1,200 warheads could be MIRV on ICBM (with a Russian sublimit of 650 heavy SS-18 ICBM); there could be only 2,160 SLBM warheads. In Stage Two, to be completed by the years 2000–2003, strategic forces would be reduced to an overall total of 3,000–3,500 warheads. All MIRV on ICBM would be eliminated, and a maximum of 1,750 SLBM would be allowed.

UNITED KINGDOM

The U.K. defense budget for 1992 totaled £24,240,000,000. Modernization of the U.K.'s national nuclear forces continued, with the ordering of the fourth and final Vanguard-class SSBN to carry U.S. Trident II SLBM with U.K. warheads, to replace the four (now three) SSBN carrying U.S. Polaris A-3 SLBM with U.K. Chevaline warheads. All tactical naval nuclear depth bombs were being withdrawn and destroyed, but a replacement nuclear aircraft bomb was being developed.

The army of 145,400 had 426 new Challenger and 850 Chieftain battle tanks plus 605 Warrior AIFV and 3,501 APC. The Royal Air Force, with 86,000 personnel, had about 466 combat aircraft. Modern aircraft included 198

new Tornado GR-1 and F-2/3 fighter, FGA, and reconnaissance planes; 66 Harrier GR-3/-5/-7/-T-4 V/STOL, 53
Jaguar GR-1 FGA planes; and 3 Nimrod R-1 electronic
countermeasure aircraft and 30 MR-2 maritime reconnaissance aircraft.

The Royal Navy had 62,100 personnel, with 19 attack
submarines (13 nuclear) and 43 principal surface combatants, including 3 small carriers with Sea Harrier FGA, 12
GW destroyers, and 29 frigates (mostly GW). Royal Marine
personnel totaled some 7,600.

FRANCE

The 1992 defense budget for France was F 194,480,000,000.
Modernization of France's national nuclear forces continued, with four SSBN operational, one being refitted, and
two under construction. All carried the M-4 SLBM. Tactical
nuclear forces were reduced.

Military personnel totaled 431,700 (260,900 in the army).
Equipment included 1,343 AMX-30 battle tanks (658 new
AMX-30-B2), 816 AMX-10P/PC Milan AIFV, and about
4,000 APC. These were organized in the equivalent of four
armoured and two mechanized infantry divisions, plus a
Rapid Action Force for overseas intervention consisting of
five light divisions (7,000–8,000 personnel each). The air
force of some 91,700 had 808 combat aircraft, the newer
models including 192 Mirage F-1B/C/CR and 184 Mirage
2000B/C/N, plus 153 Jaguar A/E in fighter, FGA, and reconnaissance roles. The 64,900-strong navy's 41 major surface
combatants included 2 small carriers, 4 GW destroyers, and
34 frigates (mostly GW); the navy also had 13 attack submarines (5 nuclear).

GERMANY

Under the 1992 Final Act of the Conference on Security
and Cooperation in Europe, German forces were no longer
to be subject to special limits but were to be covered by
the overall limits of the CFE Treaty. The German armed
forces would be limited to a total of 345,000 personnel by
1996. No non-German NATO forces would be stationed in
the former East German territory. Russian forces stationed
there, reduced to some 177,000 personnel by the end of
1992, would be withdrawn by 1994, and Germany would pay
their occupation costs.

The German armed forces faced continued problems in
retiring or absorbing former East German military personnel and restructuring the unified force. Despite these difficulties, the unified Germany was emerging as the largest
military power in Europe. Its population of nearly 80 million
gave it the manpower pool needed to maintain its forces at
the CFE Treaty level, with very high-quality personnel and
equipment. In 1992 Germany's defense budget was DM 52,-
130,000,000. Armed forces personnel totaled 447,000. The
316,000-strong army comprised 12 divisions (6 armoured, 4
armoured infantry, 1 mountain, and 1 airborne). Armour
included 2,083 new Leopard 2 (700 to be upgraded) and
2,084 Leopard 1A1 battle tanks (1,258 to be upgraded
to A5), plus 549 T-72M and 1,725 T-54/-55 former East
German tanks. AIFV included 2,100 Marder A1/A2 (to be
upgraded to A3), plus 1,150 former East German BMP-1/
-2. APC, including former East German equipment, totaled
10,955. Large numbers of modern artillery, guided weapons,
and helicopters were also deployed.

The air force had 95,800 personnel (9,300 Eastern Command) with more than 600 combat aircraft. These included
236 new Tornados and 24 new MiG-29, plus 230 older
Phantoms in fighter, FGA, and reconnaissance roles. The
35,200-strong navy (1,900 Eastern Command), designed for
coastal warfare in the Baltic Sea, had 14 major surface

combatants, including 3 GW destroyers and 8 GW frigates,
40 GW fast-attack craft, and 22 coastal submarines. The
naval air arm consisted of 118 combat aircraft, including
102 Tornado attack/reconnaissance aircraft.

NON-NATO EUROPE

In the non-NATO Europe area, the forces in four CIS republics (Belarus, Ukraine, Moldova, and Armenia) were to
form the CIS JGPF. Ukraine deployed the largest military
forces, with personnel totaling 230,000. The ground forces
totaled 150,000 personnel, with 6,300 T-54/-55/-62/-64/-72/
-80 main battle tanks and an air force of 50,000 personnel
and some 1,100 combat aircraft (220 new MiG-29 fighters
and 210 Su-24 FGA aircraft). Belarus deployed the second largest military forces, with personnel totaling 125,000,
mainly ground forces of 95,000 personnel (the total to be
cut to 90,000) with 1,850 main battle tanks (mostly T-72),
and an air force of 20,000 personnel and some 502 combat
aircraft (50 new MiG-29 fighters).

Poland had military forces totaling 296,500, including a
194,200-strong army with 2,850 T-55/-72 main battle tanks
and an 83,000-strong air force with 423 combat aircraft (221
MiG-21U fighters). Czechoslovakia's 145,800-strong forces
comprised an army of 72,000 with 3,208 T-54/-55/-72 tanks
and an air force of 44,800 with 304 combat aircraft. Hungary
had armed forces of 80,800 personnel, including an army of
63,500 with 1,357 T-34/-54/-55/-72 tanks and an air force of
17,300 with 59 MiG-21/-23 fighters.

RUSSIA

The breakup of the former Soviet Union created major
uncertainties about the control of its military forces. These
had been, in 1991, the world's largest, with about 3.4 million personnel plus some 5,239,000 in reserves and 570,000
paramilitary internal security personnel. Provisional transition arrangements called for some forces to be CIS Centrally Controlled Forces (CIS-CCF), including the Strategic
Deterrent Forces, but these were effectively controlled by
Russian Pres. Boris Yeltsin and the Russian military. They
comprised the Strategic Rocket, Naval, and Aviation Forces.
The Strategic Rocket Forces' 144,000 troops and modern
ICBM systems included 36 rail-mobile SS-24 (deployment
capped), more than 340 road-mobile SS-25, and 308 SS-18
heavy ICBM (some 204 deployed in Russia). The Strategic
Naval Forces had 12,000 personnel, manning 55 SSBN carrying 832 SLBM, all based in Russian ports. No new SSBN
had been deployed. Modern SSBN included six Typhoon-
class, each carrying 20 SS-N-20 MIRVed SLBM; 7 Delta IV
(16 SS-N-23); and 14 Delta-III (16 SS-N-18).

Strategic Aviation Forces had 25,000 personnel and included 15 new Blackjack A Tu-160 bombers and 84 Tu-95
Bear-H, each carrying 8 ALCM (plus 66 older Tu-95). Production of both bombers was ended. Medium-range bombers
included 190 modern Tu-26M Backfire B/Cs (which had
strategic capabilities), 80 elderly Tu-22 Blinder A/Bs, and
50 obsolete Tu-16 Badgers.

The CIS-CCF Strategic Deterrent Forces outside Russia
were deployed in Belarus, Kazakhstan, and Ukraine. In
Belarus there were 80 mobile SS-25 ICBM, in Kazakhstan
104 SS-18 ICBM and 40 Tu-95H Bear strategic bombers,
and in Ukraine 176 ICBM (130 SS-19 and 46 SS-24) and 41
strategic bombers (21 Tu-95 and 20 Tu-160).

Russian General Purpose Forces included an army with
about 1.4 million personnel, organized into some 22 tank, 81
motor rifle (mechanized), 16 artillery/missile, and 6 airborne
divisions of 11,100–13,500 men each. Equipment included
approximately 29,000 tanks (modern types comprised 5,300
T-80s and 11,000 T-72s, plus 11,000 older T-54/-55/-62s),

Iranians view a Scud missile on display in Tehran. Iran and other Middle Eastern countries were buying large numbers of weapons from sellers that included China, North Korea, former Soviet-bloc nations, and the U.S.
KAVEH GOLESTAN

28,000 AIFV, and 22,000 artillery pieces, including 6,000 new self-propelled 203-mm, 152-mm, and 122-mm guns. Russian forces and equipment had been withdrawn from Czechoslovakia, Hungary, and Poland, as well as from Mongolia, and were being withdrawn from Germany. The only significant overseas deployment of Russian forces was 4,300 troops in Cuba.

The Russian air force had about 300,000 personnel with some 3,700 combat aircraft. These included 1,800 FGA aircraft (610 new MiG-27 Flogger D) and 1,500 fighters, new types including 430 MiG-29 Fulcrum, 140 Su-27 Flanker, and 110 MiG-25 Foxbat. In addition, Russia controlled some 50–70% of the assets of the former Soviet Air Defense Command, a separate service with about 356,000 personnel, 2,200 fighter aircraft (including new MiG-31 Foxhound), and approximately 7,000 surface-to-air missile (SAM) launchers at some 900 fixed sites.

The Russian navy had 320,000 personnel, 192 principal surface combatants, and 183 tactical submarines, including 59 SSN and 36 SSGN. No new construction was started in 1992, and work on about half of the 130 ships under construction was halted. Naval deployments were ended in the Mediterranean, the Persian Gulf, and the Indian Ocean.

MIDDLE EAST

The military balance in the Middle East was heavily influenced by the defeat of Iraq in the 1991 Gulf war. With much of his military capability destroyed, Saddam Hussein posed less of a threat to neighbouring countries. Iraqi weapons destroyed or captured in the war included some 3,000 tanks, 1,860 armoured vehicles, 2,140 artillery pieces, and 135 combat aircraft, plus 112 aircraft flown to Iran and interned. But Hussein retained sufficient armed forces to ensure his hold on power. Iraqi armed forces totaled some 382,500 personnel, including an army of about 350,000, with 2,300 battle tanks and 900 BMP-1/-2 AIFV. The air force of 30,000, including 15,000 air defense personnel, had some 130 FGA and 180 fighters.

UN economic sanctions against Iraq remained in force. The UN Special Commission succeeded in verifying the destruction of declared stocks of tactical ballistic missiles and the means of manufacturing them and, despite Iraqi obstructions, it located some undeclared manufacturing ca-

pacity. However, it probably had not found any undeclared stocks of weapons of mass destruction, which could include Iraqi-modified Scud missiles and biological-weapons-manufacturing capabilities. Late in the year Iraqi planes breached the no-fly zone set up in southern Iraq to protect the Shi'ite Muslims there, and one Iraqi MiG was shot down by a U.S. F-16. Some observers believed Saddam Hussein hoped to take advantage of the transition period between U.S. administrations.

Israel was still capable of deterring a major attack by Syria, the most aggressive and militarily powerful Arab nation, but it relied increasingly on thinly veiled threats of massive retaliation with its nuclear weapons, estimated to include up to 100 warheads and Jericho 1 and 2 surface-to-surface missiles (ranges of some 500 and 1,500 km [310 and 930 mi], respectively). It remained the region's strongest military power, especially in the quality of its personnel and weapons, but its defense burden, which reached $6,760,000,-000 for 1992, was difficult to support, even with massive aid from the U.S. With a population of only 5,090,000, Israel raised standing armed forces of 175,000, which would increase to approximately 705,000 on mobilization of reserves. The standing army of about 134,000 combined with the reservists to form, on mobilization, 12 armoured and 1 airmobile/mechanized infantry divisions plus 5 mechanized and 10 regional infantry and 7 artillery brigades. These forces had some 3,890 battle tanks and 5,000 APC. The 32,000-strong air force had 662 combat aircraft; modern types included 63 U.S. F-15A/B/C/D Eagles, 209 U.S. F-16A/B/C/D Falcons, 95 Israeli Kfir C2/C7, and 112 U.S. F-4E Phantom fighter/FGA (50 converting to Phantom 2000).

Syria's armed forces personnel totaled 408,000, with an army of approximately 300,000 comprising six armoured divisions, three mechanized divisions, and one Republican Guard division. Equipment included 1,500 new T-72 and 3,100 T-54/-55/-62 battle tanks and 2,250 BMP-1 AIFV. The separate Air Defense Command had 60,000 personnel manning 95 batteries with Soviet Sa-2/-3/-5/-6/-8 SAM. The 40,000-strong air force had some 639 combat aircraft, modern types including 20 MiG-29 and 30 MiG-25 fighters plus 40 Su-20/-24 FGA. Defense spending totaled $1,130,000,000 in 1991.

(continued on page 233)

The Soviet Military Collapse

BY ROBIN RANGER

The most important defense event of 1992 was the collapse of the military machine of the former Union of Soviet Socialist Republics. This collapse finalized the fall of the Soviet empire in Eastern Europe and overseas and also inside the U.S.S.R. itself, which had been the world's last multinational empire. These events represented the most important military and political changes in the world balance of power since World War II ended in 1945 and the cold war started.

In addition, the collapse of the Soviet military machine represented a remarkable success for the long-term U.S. strategy of containment. This strategy had been established by Pres. Harry Truman's 1947 Truman Doctrine and was supported by every subsequent administration, as well as by a bipartisan majority in Congress and by the U.S. electorate. Under the containment strategy the U.S. would contain the expansion of the Soviet empire with nuclear and conventional military forces. The U.S. would also provide military and economic aid to allies who assisted in the containment and would encourage the spread of democratic governments.

Eventually, the crippling economic and social costs of the Soviet empire and its massive military machine would force Soviet leaders to withdraw from much of their realm and radically reform the remainder. This was, indeed, what Mikhail Gorbachev tried to do from 1985 onward, as the last leader of the Soviet Union. However, because the costs had bankrupted the empire, it collapsed both at home and abroad.

Since the death of Soviet dictator Joseph Stalin in 1953, the relationship between the leadership of the Communist Party of the Soviet Union (CPSU) and that of the Soviet military had become one of mutual dependence. The CPSU leadership relied on the Soviet military to keep control of the post-World War II Soviet empire in Eastern Europe (mainly East Germany, Poland, Hungary, and Czechoslovakia) and inside the Soviet Union. The Soviet military leadership, in turn, relied on the CPSU to run the Soviet empire and to give the military first call on Soviet economic resources.

This mutual dependence between the CPSU and the Soviet military increased after the 1962 Cuban missile crisis. The crisis was caused by Soviet leader Nikita Khrushchev's attempt to install nuclear armed medium- and intermediate-range ballistic missiles in Cuba to offset the massive U.S. advantage in strategic nuclear forces (SNF). However, U.S. Pres. John F. Kennedy used this advantage in SNF and in local conventional military forces to force Khrushchev to withdraw the Soviet missiles from Cuba.

In 1964 Khrushchev was overthrown, and a new Soviet leadership took power under Leonid Brezhnev. From 1964 to 1985 the Brezhnev-era leadership based Soviet military policy on three main principles. First, Soviet strategic nuclear forces would be built up until the U.S.S.R. had a level of nuclear superiority over the U.S. comparable to the level of superiority that the U.S. had had over the U.S.S.R. in the Cuban missile crisis. Second, Soviet conventional military forces would be built up until they enjoyed a wide margin of superiority over all possible opposing forces. Third, Soviet nuclear and conventional military superiority would be used to make military, political, and economic gains directly (by occupying territory) and indirectly (by intimidation).

Thus by 1985 the Soviet military machine was the largest and most powerful in the world. Personnel totaled some 5.3 million (including around 1.3 million construction, command, and general support personnel) plus some 5.4 million in reserves. In addition, the Soviet Union had about 675,000 paramilitary internal security personnel. At this time the Soviet Strategic Nuclear Forces Command, a separate service with 300,000 troops, was continuing a major modernization program to further increase its superiority over the U.S. in missile and nuclear warhead numbers and in nuclear warhead yield and accuracy.

Soviet SNF already had a capability to strike first and disable much of the U.S. SNF, a capability the U.S. lacked. Soviet SNF also enjoyed a wide margin of quantitative superiority over those of the U.S. The totals for Soviet versus U.S. forces in 1985 were some 1,400 versus 1,000 intercontinental ballistic missiles and some 1,000 versus 640 submarine-launched ballistic missiles.

The separate Strategic Aviation Force had approximately 380 strategic bombers, as compared with some 300 U.S. strategic bombers. Soviet strategic defensive forces were also large. The Air Defense Command formed a separate service with some 635,000 personnel, 1,200 interceptors, and 9,600 surface-to-air missile launchers at 1,200 fixed sites. The air force had some 570,000 personnel and some 5,900 modern combat aircraft.

The army, totaling approximately two million personnel, was organized into 51 tank, 141 motor rifle (mechanized), 16 artillery, and 7 airborne divisions of 11,100–13,500 men each, plus 424,000 railway and construction troops. Equipment totals were at much higher levels than for the U.S., its NATO allies, and China. Soviet equipment included 52,600 tanks, 70,000 armoured fighting vehicles, and 33,000 artillery pieces. Soviet army force deployments were roughly two-thirds against NATO-Europe and one-third against China.

The Soviet navy had some 480,000 personnel and 289 major surface combatants plus the world's largest submarine force, including 72 nuclear-powered attack submarines and 49 nuclear-powered cruise missile-armed submarines. Soviet naval aviation included approximately 875 combat aircraft. These Soviet naval forces provided a global power capability.

In 1985 these Soviet military forces maintained CPSU control over the Soviet empire, including Eastern Europe and Cuba. Soviet forces had occupied Czechoslovakia since 1968 and Afghanistan since 1979. Large overseas force deployments were in Syria (7,000), Vietnam (7,000), and Cuba (9,000), with smaller ones of 500–2,500 troops each in Algeria, Angola, Ethiopia, Iraq, Laos, Libya, North Yemen, and South Yemen. The Soviet empire was also supported by major overseas deployments of Cuban military forces in Angola (26,000 troops) and Mozambique (750 troops). Cuba also gave significant military assistance to insurgent groups throughout Latin America, notably in El Salvador, and channeled Soviet military aid to the pro-Soviet government of Nicaragua.

Yet only seven years later this massive Soviet military machine had collapsed for four main reasons. First, the Brezhnev-era leadership had grossly underestimated the long-term economic and social costs of achieving military superiority over the U.S. and its allies. The full costs of Soviet defense and empire-related spending remain unclear, but current Western and Russian estimates are that for the 21 years of the Brezhnev era (1964–85) this spending was some 25–35% of the gross national product (GNP) or more. This was comparable to the U.S. level of defense spending in World War II and was also very much higher than the level of U.S. defense spending under Pres. Ronald Reagan, which averaged about 6% of GNP. Thus by 1985 the Soviet Union was a military superpower but bankrupt and, in economic and social terms, a poor Third World country.

Second, the Brezhnev-era leadership overestimated the utility of Soviet nuclear and conventional forces and underestimated the deterrent capabilities of U.S. and allied nuclear and conventional forces. The Soviet leaders found that they had large margins of military superiority but not large enough to launch a major Soviet attack on the U.S. and its allies and win. Any major Soviet attack would risk the large-scale use of nuclear weapons, and Soviet nuclear forces might not be able to knock out U.S. nuclear forces, thus risking potentially fatal damage to the Soviet Union from U.S. retaliatory nuclear strikes. The Brezhnev-era leadership did use Soviet and Cuban conventional forces for limited military interventions in Czechoslovakia (in 1968) and the Third World, but these interventions failed to produce significant lasting political and economic gains. In addition, the 1979 Soviet occupation of Afghanistan proved a costly mistake. Soviet military forces suffered significant casualties, including more than 15,000 killed. Yet the Soviet military was unable to win the war and suffered increasing casualties after Reagan provided effective military aid to the mujahideen resistance fighters from 1983 onward. As a result, many Soviet military officers came to oppose the CPSU leadership.

Third, the Brezhnev-era leadership underestimated the political resolve and the technical military capabilities of the U.S. and its allies, especially in NATO-Europe. The Soviet military buildup and invasion of Afghanistan triggered a U.S. and allied political reaction in favour of increasing defense forces and resisting Soviet political pressures. This reaction helped to bring to power Reagan in the U.S. and his strongest allied supporter, Prime Minister Margaret Thatcher, in the U.K. Under Reagan the U.S. accelerated the development and deployment of a new generation of high-technology weapons whose effectiveness was demonstrated in the Gulf war. The Soviet military leadership then found that the nation's economy could not support the development and deployment of comparable weapons systems, and so Soviet margins of military superiority were being reduced. The Soviet leadership also found that President Reagan, Prime Minister Thatcher, and other allied leaders refused to be intimidated, especially as the U.S. and allied military position improved.

Fourth, from 1985 onward Gorbachev and his allies attempted partial reforms, but these accelerated the collapse of the Soviet military, economic, and social systems. By 1989–90 Gorbachev had been forced to abandon the Soviet empires overseas and in Eastern Europe and to propose major cuts in the Soviet military. But even those radical reforms came too late to save the CPSU and the Soviet Union. The Soviet military played a major role in defeating the August 1991 coup attempt by hard-line CPSU and military leaders and in supporting the democratic leader, Russian Federation Pres. Boris Yeltsin. Subsequently, Yeltsin forced Gorbachev to resign, and in December 1991 the U.S.S.R. was dissolved.

Robin Ranger is vice president of Ranger Associates Inc., Washington, D.C. His books include Arms and Politics 1958–1978: Arms Control in a Changing Political Context.

(continued from page 231)

SOUTH AND CENTRAL ASIA

The breakup of the Soviet Union created a new geostrategic area of South and Central Asia, which consisted of the five Central Asian republics of the former U.S.S.R. (Kazakhstan, Kyrgyzstan, Tajikistan, Turkmenistan, and Uzbekistan), Afghanistan, Pakistan, India, Bangladesh, Sri Lanka, and Myanmar (Burma). Each of the five former Soviet republics had significant former Soviet military forces on its territory. These were, in principle, to form the CIS-JGPF, under the joint control of Russia and the independent republic where the forces were stationed.

Conflict between Pakistan and India remained a danger because of civil unrest in Indian Kashmir and Hindu-Muslim religious clashes in India. Such a conflict could potentially escalate to the use of nuclear weapons. This possibility was underlined by the Pakistani foreign minister's acknowledgement in February that Pakistan had elements that, if put together, would become a nuclear device. Both Pakistan and India increased their military and paramilitary forces.

Pakistan's armed forces had risen to 580,000, mainly an army of 515,000 (an increase of 15,000) with some 2,000 battle tanks (mostly Chinese Type-59/-69). The air force comprised 45,000 personnel and 352 combat aircraft, including 39 F-16A/B Falcon and 58 Mirage 5 fighter-bombers. India continued to be the major regional military power, with armed forces totaling some 1,265,000. The 1.1 million-strong army had some 3,800 battle tanks, 1,300 of which were new T-72s. In addition, paramilitary forces, including a Home Guard of 438,000, totaled over one million personnel. The air force of 110,000 had 674 combat aircraft, including 100 MiG-27 FGA and 54 MiG-29 and 36 Mirage 2000 fighters. Defense spending in 1992 amounted to $6,750,000,000.

EAST AND SOUTHEAST ASIA

Chinese armed forces in 1992 were being reduced from a total personnel strength of about three million but were still the largest in the area. The defense budget for 1992 was $6,760,000,000. China's nuclear stockpile remained small, with limited numbers of comparatively old, vulnerable delivery systems. These included about 8 ICBM (CSS-3/-4), 60 CSS-2 intermediate range ballistic missiles, and 1 Xia-class SSBN with 12 CSS-N-3 (J-1) SLBM (modified DF-3s). The army had 2.3 million personnel but only some 8,000 battle tanks (mostly T-59), while the 470,000-strong air force's 4,970 combat aircraft were mostly modifications of old Soviet models, including 3,000 J-6/MiG-17 fighters. Modern types included 28 Su-27.

Vietnam remained the second largest active military power in the area. However, the collapse of the Soviet Union and the end of most Soviet economic and military aid forced the Vietnamese government to end its military intervention in Cambodia and Laos and cut its armed forces. These were mostly army and were reduced to a total of 857,000. The army had approximately 1,200 T-34/-54/-55/-62/Type 59 battle tanks, and the 15,000-strong air force had approximately 185 combat aircraft.

Japan's 1992 defense budget was $34.3 billion. Armed forces personnel were being reduced from a total of 246,-400, including an army of 156,000 with 1,210 battle tanks. The air force had 46,000 personnel and 440 combat aircraft. The 44,000-strong navy had 6 GW destroyers, 58 frigates (24 helicopter), and 13 tactical submarines.

(ROBIN RANGER)

See also Space Exploration.
This article updates the *Macropædia* article The Technology of WAR.

Mining

Some of the principal influences on the world mining industry during 1992 included: (1) the general world recession, which made development capital scarce; (2) the burgeoning environmental movement, which continued to dictate altered priorities worldwide; (3) the increasing number and influence of regional trading blocs, such as the newly formed Southern Africa Development Council, or the trade area envisioned by the North American Free Trade Agreement (NAFTA); (4) the opening of the mineral deposits of the former U.S.S.R. to investment and active participation by Western and Third World countries; and (5) the political penalties for neglect or undervaluation of the mining sector. The political penalties were particularly apparent in the U.K., following reaction to the October announcement by British Coal of the closing of 31 coal mines and the British government's quick retraction of its earlier acceptance of the closings, and also in Russia, where miners of the Kuznets Basin had disrupted the national economy by a strike in 1991 and in 1992 struck again, this time for back pay. Similar situations developed in Spain during the year when demonstrations in Madrid (by Basque steelworkers) and a 500-km (310-mi) march by coal miners in León brought concessions by the Spanish government.

The United Nations indexes of production (*see* TABLE) indicated continued very strong growth of the coal sector in the less developed market economies, much of it to offset parallel losses in output of petroleum and natural gas; for example, Nigeria was successful in restoring a substantial share of its former coal output. Both the coal and metals sectors of the formerly centrally planned countries declined during 1991 and were sufficiently disorganized in 1992 that data for the year, even for the first quarter, were unavailable at year's end. Very strong long-term growth in the production of metals was recorded in the developed market economies through the end of the second quarter. Overall, however, the mining sector worldwide was producing at levels almost a third below those maintained by manufacturing during the last decade (when compared with the 1980 base year of the UN index).

Latin America—Chile in particular—was the centre of new development activity (*see* below). The signing of the NAFTA document and Mexico's promulgation of a new comprehensive mining law at midyear attracted the interest of a variety of U.S. and Canadian mining companies that were beginning to find the regulatory, tax, and environmental burdens at home too restrictive. At the same time, the need to find bankable large-scale deposits for new development was focusing investors' attention on a still-underexplored Africa. (Beatrice Labonne, chief of the UN's Mineral Resource Branch, drew special attention to Zaire, Angola, Tanzania, Zimbabwe, and Namibia at Price Waterhouse's 1992 Mining Industry Conference.)

Activity in the formerly socialist nations centred on the achievement of more efficient and environmentally sound development and operations at new and existing sites; the participation of Western or Third World companies that had relevant experience was often sought. In the countries of Central Asia, for example, such Western firms as Cyprus, Chilewich, Minproc, and Newmont (U.S.), Candorado Mines (Canada), and Portman Mining (Australia) joined with such Third World investors as Birlesmis Muhendisler Birligi of Turkey. Some of this activity, however, was also directed outward, as the experience of the former Soviet republics in mining was enormous. One such case was the October announcement of a joint venture in Jamaica by Ukraine to revitalize the Lydford mine there in order to ensure future feedstock for Ukraine's Mykolayyiv alumina plant.

In the United States the mining industry continued to display a long-term stability almost unmatched among major industries (*see* below), but it also suffered a fatality rate more than four times higher (32.4 per 100,000 workers) than the average for all other industries (7.2). Although the U.S. had good safety standards overall, meaningful enforcement entailed more than simple voluntary compliance by operators. Dissatisfaction with the existing U.S. General Law Mining Law (1872) did not produce a definitive replacement during the year, but attempts by Congress to achieve a new general law kept the issues before the public. The U.S. Bureau of Mines estimated the value of domestic nonfuel mineral production at $31,713,000,000 in 1992, a modest 3% rise but a rise that had occurred in all but four of the last 32 years. The value of processed minerals was put at $310 billion. The U.S. Postal Service released a new stamp set on September 17 depicting minerals from the Smithsonian Institution's collections, the first such set in 18 years.

Indexes of Production, Mining and Mineral Commodities
(1980 = 100)

	1987	1988	1989	1990	1991	1992 1st quarter	1992 2nd quarter
Mining (total)							
World[1]	91.0	95.7	100.0	99.6	100.8	...	...
Centrally planned economies[2]	112.5	115.3	113.3	105.0	102.6	...	...
Developed market economies[3]	104.3	105.8	106.1	106.4	108.7	111.8	107.4
Less developed market economies[4]	79.2	86.5	94.2	94.4	95.3	93.7	
Coal							
World[1]	107.0	107.6	107.3	99.1	98.8	...	
Centrally planned economies[2]	108.3	110.2	106.4	94.6	92.6	...	...
Developed market economies[3]	103.0	102.7	103.4	95.8	92.6	94.5	90.4
Less developed market economies[4]	149.9	153.5	164.0	170.6	217.0	273.8	
Petroleum and natural gas							
World[1]	83.2	87.9	92.6	92.7	93.2	...	...
Centrally planned economies[2]	114.9	116.5	114.9	109.5	107.5	...	...
Developed market economies[3]	102.6	100.9	98.1	99.3	103.0	109.3	100.5
Less developed market economies[4]	74.4	81.7	89.6	89.5	88.8	86.2	...
Metals							
World[1]	112.6	122.4	129.0	134.7	143.4	...	...
Centrally planned economies[2]	104.9	107.3	107.7	103.0	91.3	...	...
Developed market economies[3]	115.6	128.2	137.6	147.1	157.9	157.9	160.2
Less developed market economies[4]	108.7	114.9	118.0	119.0	127.5	130.1	...
Manufacturing (total)	119.9	126.9	131.7	131.6	131.6	...	...

[1] Excluding Albania, China, North Korea, and Vietnam.
[2] Bulgaria, Czechoslovakia, Hungary, Poland, Romania, and the former U.S.S.R.
[3] North America, Europe (except centrally planned and Yugoslavia), Australia, Israel, Japan, New Zealand, and South Africa.
[4] Caribbean, Central and South America, Africa (except South Africa), Asian Middle East, East and Southeast Asia (except Israel and Japan), and Yugoslavia.
Source: UN, *Monthly Bulletin of Statistics* (November 1992).

What has been called the cleanest coal on Earth is mined on Kalimantan (Indonesian Borneo). Named Envirocoal, it is extraordinarily low in production of sulfur dioxide, nitrogen, and ash.

FREDERICK J. MURRELL

Exploration and Development. Gold dominated the investment profile for the year, especially for smaller properties. An inventory of large projects published by *Mining Magazine* during the year displayed better overall balance among the minerals but noted that selection of listed projects was complicated by the large number that had been scheduled to become operational during 1991 and 1992 but were postponed into the 1993–95 period that was the main focus of the inventory. Of 41 very large projects (processing more than three million tons of ore per year), 11 were in the U.S. Of these 9 were gold only or gold and copper, and 2 of the 11 were copper alone. This pattern held for the rest of the world; the same two metals were the principal product(s) at all the other sites except for the Century (Queensland; lead-zinc-silver) and the Yakabindie and Mount Keith (Western Australia; nickel).

Conferences during the year highlighted the development possibilities available in Latin America, Africa, and Southeast Asia, emphasizing at the same time a growing perception in the U.S., Australia, and other developed countries that regulatory, environmental, safety, tax, and other constraints were making the conduct of business so difficult and even unpredictable that a large-scale flight of jobs in the industry was possible during the 1990s. The NAFTA and Mexico's 1992 mining law made that country a frequently mentioned possibility to attract such investment. Mexico was already in the midst of a five-year program to revitalize and privatize a mining sector that had fully exemplified the inefficiencies and failures of state control during the 1980s.

Markets. In the U.S., mining employment in 1992 declined 24,000, to 629,000, between January and September, paralleling a similar trend in manufacturing. Utilization of capacity, as monitored by the Federal Reserve Board, ranged between 85 and 87%. This was well above the average for all industry, which was about 78% for most of the year. Despite the complaints mentioned above by the mining industry, it was perhaps notable that, of a score of industries monitored by the FRB over the last 20 years, none had had so high a minimum level of utilization.

Gold reserves of central banks fell in June to a 30-year low of 35,344 tons following large sales by Canada and Belgium. This gold represented about one-third of total government financial reserves worldwide. A similar decline in reserve holdings by the Bank for International Settle-

ments (BIS) was thought by some to be connected with the Belgian bank's activities. Holdings at BIS recovered soon afterward.

Aluminum demand, normally about 25 million tons, was boosted during the year by the release of Madonna's new book, *Sex*, which required a reported 340 tons of aluminum to manufacture its covers. The extra demand was probably appreciated, as large aluminum exports from former Soviet republics had reduced prices and demand in Western markets, leading analysts to express opinions ranging from "cautious optimism to qualified pessimism." The chief areas of optimism were recycled aluminum, which continued to raise its market share because it required 5% of the energy needed to produce primary aluminum, and canning, in which steel was steadily losing market share to aluminum.

The James Capel worldwide mining indexes (Jan. 1, 1989 = 100) reached an annual low of 84 in November but recovered to the mid-90s by the end of the year. Significant influences on the year's activity included strong sales of base metals in the West by the countries of eastern Europe and the former Soviet republics, for whom the metals markets were a substantial source of hard currency; strong copper demand by China; and caution induced by the world recession. The end of the cold war rendered much of the U.S. Strategic Reserve (of metals) superfluous or at least of reduced importance. Although Congress authorized substantial dispersals of these stocks, requests were received to postpone dispersals to avoid depressing the prevailing price for the metals any further.

British coal miners achieved their highest rates of output ever just before the announcement in October of the closing of 31 coal pits by British Coal. In the face of public outcry, the number was reduced to 10, and on December 21 Britain's High Court ordered the mines to remain open, ruling that British Coal had failed to submit to independent review procedures mandated by law.

Safety and Environment. China's mining industry was perhaps the world's most dangerous, with more than 10,000 miners (out of a total of some 20 million) having died in 1991. The need for reform was obvious and urgent, and in May China's first mine safety law was promulgated. But even in countries with safety legislation in force, fatalities could occur in illegal, unregulated diggings; on May 5 in Sierra Leone, more than 100 illegal diamond miners were killed, and in an accident in December in Bolivia, a tailings heap collapsed in torrential rains, leaving 153 known dead and another 100–200 presumed dead.

Unfortunately, government regulation provided no guarantee of safety. In the U.S., 13 coal companies pleaded guilty in March to falsification of results of federally mandated coal-dust-monitoring tests. Also in the U.S., in November, mining inspectors who headed regional offices of the Office of Surface Mining, Reclamation, and Enforcement charged the director of their agency, Harry M. Snyder, with having repeatedly obstructed enforcement efforts by terminating investigations, reducing or eliminating fines, and creating a climate that had the effect of chilling enforcement efforts within his agency.

The nations of eastern Europe and the former Soviet republics had allowed industrial development to proceed for so long without meaningful regulation or environmental controls that by 1992 activities involving those facilities consisted of mitigation where the facility continued in operation, remediation where it had closed, or closing where operations could not be made efficient or environmentally responsible enough to operate within modern Western regulations (as was the case in eastern Germany where coal output had fallen by half since reunification). The inventory of environmental problems in the east included unreclaimed strip-mined lands, surface subsidence from underground mining (reportedly damaging as many as one-third of surface structures in one coal basin in Poland), and tailings and other waste that resulted in radioactive, arsenical, or heavy metal damage to soils, vegetation, surface and ground waters, and, especially, the health of persons living in those regions. Though all of those countries were implementing improved environmental controls in 1992, the older practices were so intimately entwined with mining methods, manpower, economic planning, supply of raw materials, and foreign trade that the institution of new practices was slow, painful, and, inevitably, disruptive of every other aspect of the economy and society that they touched. The difficulty of persuading potential investors that these nations' new economic policies would provide enough security and profitability to justify the substantial costs required for refitting mines, buying new equipment, and funding land reclamation resulted in a slow transition and consequent disruption of trade and industrial relations.

Technology. Science, rather than technology, was the principal concern of the industry during the year, especially at the "Earth Summit" in Rio de Janeiro. Though the U.S. delegation pursued U.S. Pres. George Bush's stated goal of balancing development and the environment, it angered many delegates by, in their view, obstructing all efforts to achieve either binding agreements; specific goals, quotas, or timetables; or consensus that existing scientific study demonstrated anything beyond the need for more study. Many observers saw irony as well in the choice of Brazil as the site for this meeting in view of its history, especially its mining industry's history of environmental degradation. However, Brazil could point to responsible mine operations such as the enormous bauxite strip-mining facilities of Trombetas and Alumar, where rehabilitation of soils and vegetation, preservation of aquifers, and reduction of atmospheric emissions provided models for what could be accomplished, even in a less developed country with urgent needs for jobs and export earnings.

(WILLIAM A. CLEVELAND)

See also Earth Sciences; Energy; Industrial Review: *Gemstones; Iron and Steel.*

This article updates the *Macropædia* article Extraction and Processing INDUSTRIES.

Motion Pictures

Domination of the world's screens by Hollywood continued in 1992 to threaten the existence of film production in many other countries. Week by week the U.S. trade magazine *Variety* reported the top 10 films in the major capitals of the world. Only occasionally would a locally produced film take its place alongside the U.S. successes. The single European film of 1992 that maintained a fairly consistent presence in those international listings of audience preferences was James Ivory's *Howards End*—a literary period piece in marked contrast to the violence that characterized 1992's unrivaled audience favourites, *Lethal Weapon 3* and *Basic Instinct.* In many countries—including, for example, Greece and Turkey—production in 1992 was so slight in quantity and quality that they are not mentioned in the brief survey of world production that follows.

English-Speaking Cinema. *United States.* The year brought its predictable run of blockbuster successes. Paul Verhoeven's *Basic Instinct* knowingly mixed horrid violence and wayward sexuality. *Lethal Weapon 3* pursued its predecessors' successful comedy-thriller formula. Among the other big box-office winners of the year, *Batman Returns* gave the comic-strip hero a new collection of weird opponents. Penelope Spheeris enjoyed a major success with her first studio production, *Wayne's World,* an aggressive TV-inspired comedy. Ron Howard's *Far and Away,* starring Nicole Kidman and Tom Cruise as 19th-century Irish immigrants, proved, however, that even big-budget star vehicles were not guaranteed against commercial failure.

An unusual phenomenon of the year was the rivalry of two Columbus quincentennial films. *Christopher Columbus: The Discovery,* directed by John Glen and starring George Corraface (with Marlon Brando as Torquemada), won the race to the screen and surprised critics with more literacy than they had anticipated. Ridley Scott's *1492: Conquest of Paradise,* with Gérard Depardieu in the leading role, proved in the end a two-dimensional and conventional historical epic.

Comedy provided one of the year's major box-office successes. Emile Ardolino's *Sister Act* cast the redoubtable Whoopi Goldberg as a pop singer thrown by accident into a convent run by Maggie Smith. Other notable comedies included John Landis' vampire farce *Innocent Blood* and Charlie Peters' endearing *Passed Away,* about family bereavement. *Sneakers,* an elegant low-key comedy about a misfit espionage group cracking security systems, confirmed the original talent of Phil Alden Robinson's earlier *Field of Dreams. My Cousin Vinny,* a low-budget farce about the triumphs of a shabby New York City lawyer in the benighted South, enjoyed major box-office success.

Hollywood itself was mercilessly lampooned in Robert Altman's well-received comedy about murder, deception, and success in the film business, *The Player.* Of the other Hollywood individualists, Woody Allen countered the much-publicized misfortunes of his private life with one of his best films, *Husbands and Wives.* In a film made earlier in the year, *Shadows and Fog,* Allen attempted a less-than-successful tribute to the German Expressionist cinema of the '20s.

Several actors made debuts as directors in films in which they also starred. The comedian Billy Crystal made a sentimental comedy, *Mr. Saturday Night.* The star of Altman's *The Player,* Tim Robbins, directed *Bob Roberts,* a satire about a fascist folksinger who runs for the U.S. Senate. John Turturro directed and starred in *Mac,* a gentle, touching reminiscence of his builder-father.

A college professor, the Woody Allen character in *Husbands and Wives*, is seduced by a student, played by Juliette Lewis. The film, praised by many critics, was searched by many viewers for parallels with the widely publicized details of Allen's breakup with Mia Farrow and his affair with her adopted daughter.
STEVE SANDS

Outdoor Americana was in evidence. Clint Eastwood made a grandly reflective western, *The Unforgiven,* and Michael Mann a majestic adaptation of James Fenimore Cooper's *The Last of the Mohicans.* Robert Redford directed an adaptation of Norman Maclean's *A River Runs Through It.* Michael Apted's *Thunderheart* was a murder mystery involving racist persecution of an Indian community.

Literary adaptations included Gary Sinise's pedestrian reworking of Steinbeck's *Of Mice and Men.* James Foley adapted David Mamet's stage success *Glengarry Glen Ross;* fine performances by Jack Lemmon and Al Pacino helped offset failure to obscure the work's stage origins.

Notable films that opened late in the year included Rob Reiner's Marine Corps melodrama *A Few Good Men,* with Tom Cruise and Jack Nicholson in strong performances; Danny DeVito's portrait of the Teamsters leader, *Hoffa,* with Nicholson in the title role; Walter Hill's racial drama *Trespass;* Martin Brest's *Scent of a Woman,* about a bitter blinded military man and the prep school student who takes care of him over Thanksgiving vacation; Richard Pearce's *Leap of Faith,* about a phony faith healer who suffers a spiritual crisis; Francis Ford Coppola's remake of the classic *Bram Stoker's Dracula;* Spike Lee's biography of the controversial black leader *Malcolm X;* Mick Jackson's romantic thriller *The Bodyguard;* Barry Levinson's *Toys,* starring Robin Williams; Steve Miner's romantic *Forever Young;* Chris Columbus' sequel to a hit comedy, *Home Alone 2;* and the animated *Aladdin* from Walt Disney Pictures.

Some of the outstanding film work of the year was in low-budget, independent production. Hal Hartley's *Simple Men* was the story of two brothers searching for their wayward errant father. Alexander Rockwell's *In the Soup* was a delightful sketch comedy about an innocent, unsuccessful scriptwriter taken up by a New York con man. Allison Anders' debut film *Gas Food Lodging* showed a working-class woman and her two teenage daughters searching together for emotional security. Anthony Drazan's *Zebrahead* explored the tragic impossibility of a Romeo and Juliet love between a Jewish schoolboy, delighted by African-American culture, and a protected African-American girl.

Homosexuality figured largely in independent production. Tom Kalin's *Swoon* took a new look at the celebrated Leopold and Loeb murder case of 1924, using actual documents of the trial and reviewing it in terms of sexual politics. Gregg Araki's *The Living End* was a road movie involving two gay men, both HIV positive and with a nihilist view of relationships and life.

At the annual awards ceremony of the Academy of Motion Picture Arts and Sciences in Los Angeles in March, Jonathan Demme's *Silence of the Lambs* won Oscars for best film, best direction, best actor (Anthony Hopkins), best actress (Jodie Foster), and best adapted screenplay. Of the nominated films that had seemed most likely winners, Oliver Stone's *JFK* took awards only for best cinematography and best editing and Barry Levinson's *Bugsy* for best costume design and best art direction. The best supporting actor and actress were Jack Palance, in *City Slickers,* and Mercedes Ruehl, in *The Fisher King.* The best original screenplay award went to Callie Khouri for *Thelma and Louise.* The best foreign-language film was the Italian *Mediterraneo.*

Great Britain. British production continued at a low ebb, with only minor financial concessions from the government to alleviate a dire economic situation. Two ambitious productions in 1992, however, were Richard Attenborough's evocation of the life and times of Charlie Chaplin, *Chaplin,* released at the close of the year, and James Ivory's third elegant adaptation from E.M. Forster, *Howards End.*

The ambitions of Roland Joffé's earnest *City of Joy—* a Franco-British coproduction shot in India—were handicapped by predictable plot and characters. Terence Davies' *The Long Day Closes,* a collage of memories of 1950s working-class life and pleasures, confirmed the director's singular talent. Other notable productions of the year were Sally Potter's decorative but vacuous adaptation of Virginia Woolf's *Orlando* and Neil Jordan's *The Crying Game.* This strange picture led from the machinations of Irish Republican Army terrorists to a liaison between a repentant IRA activist and the transsexual "widow" of one of his victims.

Several modestly budgeted films dealt with contemporary issues and characters. Richard Spence's *You, Me and Marley* was a toughly humorous look at the plight of youngsters in Northern Ireland. David Attwood's *Wild West* was a spirited comedy about Pakistani would-be pop stars in the barren soil of Southall. A lively low-budget comedy about a Jewish boy who learns that he was sired by a pig farmer, *Leon the Pig Farmer,* directed by Vadim Jean and Gary Sinyor, enjoyed critical and commercial success.

Australia. The outstanding success of the year, Baz Luhrmann's *Strictly Ballroom,* was a comic contemporary Cinderella story set in the claustrophobic world of ballroom dancers. Gillian Armstrong's *The Last Days of Chez Nous* was a finely crafted and observed study of a group of women. Geoffrey Wright's *Romper Stomper* was a slick story about a gang of neo-Nazi skinheads.

New Zealand. Against a background of economic revival, seven features were released in 1992. Most notable was Ian Mune's tender study of early adolescence, *The End of the Golden Weather.*

Canada. Among the home-produced successes of the year were Bill Robertson's witty low-budget comedy about a dysfunctional family, *The Events Leading up to My Death;* John Pozer's stylish low-budget film noir *The Grocer's Wife,* in which the villain is the killing smog of a British Columbian city; and Jean Beaudin's *Being at Home with Claude,* an original murder mystery, challenging assumptions about sexuality. From French Canada, Patrick Dewolf's debut feature *Memoire tranquée* was an effective drama about a young boy who discovers that his family is living under false identities after being spirited to Canada under the witness-protection program.

Europe. The European Media organization, with its various agencies, was committed to shaping a united European cinema to challenge the U.S. dominance. The result was a growing number of European coproductions, whose dangers were signaled by such a multiaccented film as the British-Italian-German *Utz,* by Dutch director George Sluizer.

Austria. Of the year's 15 productions of feature films, only one attracted attention abroad. Michael Haneke's *Benny's Video* was a chilling Grand Guignol about a child—totally alienated by electronic toys—who coolly experiments with murder.

Belgium. The producer-director-writer-actor trio of Benoît Poelvoorde, Remy Belvaux, and André Benzel made their mark internationally with *C'est arrivé près de chez vous,* a horror comic in which a naive video crew is making a documentary about a crazed hit man.

France. Even though the domestic share of the box office had dropped to below 30% in the face of U.S. competition, the figure was still the highest for Europe, and French production remained buoyant. Among the year's most ambitious productions were Régis Wargnier's sprawling romantic saga *Indochine* and Pierre Schoendoerffer's heavy-handed *Dien Bien Phu.* The year's outstanding commercial success, however, was a frank adaptation of Marguerite Duras's erotic girlhood reminiscence *L'Amant,* produced by Claude Berri and directed by Jean-Jacques Annaud. A major critical success, Alain Corneau's *Tous les matins du monde,* re-created the world of the 17th-century composer Marin Marais—played at varying ages by Gérard Depardieu and his son Guillaume.

Of the established directors, Bertrand Tavernier made two films. The documentary *La Guerre sans nom* collected reminiscences of French soldiers who had fought in the Algerian War. *L.627* was a realistic study of the daily activities of members of a Paris drug squad, struggling against their own prejudices and incapacity. Eric Rohmer continued his "Four Seasons" cycle with *Conte d'hiver,* a charming and absorbing account of a woman torn in the choice of a life partner. Claude Sautet made a strong impression with *Un Coeur en hiver,* a delicately understated study of a triangular relationship. Claude Chabrol returned to form with *Betty,* from a Georges Simenon novel.

Czechoslovakia. Though it was a small, underfinanced production, Jan Sverak's *Elementary School* was outstanding. This attractive study in bittersweet nostalgia was set in 1945–46.

Germany. Production in the united Germany was in the doldrums, the staple fare being cheap farces and thrillers. An exception was *Schtonk,* conceived and directed by Helmut Dietl, which wittily satirized the scandal of the 1980s surrounding the forged Hitler diaries. There was contemporary satire, too, in *Der Brocken,* about predatory businessmen

from the West trying to take advantage of the naiveté of the former East Germans. Essentially designed as a series for television, Edgar Reitz' monumental 26-hour film sequel to *Heimat, die Zweite Heimat,* followed the fortunes of his mythical rural German family to the '60s and migration to the city.

The Netherlands. One of the best productions of a thin year, Digna Sinke's *Above the Mountains* observed the interaction of a group of middle-aged, middle-class people on a hiking holiday.

Hungary. A few Hungarian directors faced the new social problems. Istvan Szabo's *Sweet Emma, Dear Bobe* viewed the tensions of postcommunist Hungary through two young teachers who abandoned the countryside for the lure of Budapest. Janos Rozsa's *Brats* dealt with a group of teenagers turned into a street gang by the sudden new problems of survival.

Italy. The plight of victimized children was explored in several films. Aurelio Grimaldi's *La discesa di Acla a Floristella* movingly described a spirited young boy broken by the feudal working conditions at a quarry in the 1920s. Carlo Carlei's *La Corsa dell'Innocente* related the flight of a child from his southern Italian family after he learns they are kidnappers. Gianni Amelio's *Il ladro di bambini* portrayed social impoverishment through the story of a young policeman escorting two young children in his care. Michele Placido directed, wrote in part, and starred in a serious, delicate drama about an incestuous father, *Le amiche del cuore.*

Romania. After 20 years of exile, Lucian Pintilie returned to head the motion-picture industry and also to make a black horror comedy, *The Oak,* about the last years of the Ceausescu regime, seen from the viewpoint of two eccentric independent spirits.

Russia. Production was already shrinking rapidly from the 1991 boom, during which 400 films were made. In an atmosphere that bred bizarre movements like the "Neonecrophiles," the acknowledged leader of the avant-garde, Aleksandr Sokhurov, made *The Stone,* a bizarre duologue between a young guard at the Chekhov Museum and a stranger who might be the writer himself.

Valery Todorovsky's likable *Love* described two friends who were discovering both love and racism. Vitaly Kanievsky completed the second part of an intended autobiographical trilogy, *An Independent Life,* that portrayed a youngster's odyssey through eastern Russia in the years after World War II.

The former Central Asian republics of the Soviet Union pursued their independent lines of cinema. From Tajikistan came Tolinb Khamidov's *Identification of Desire,* a sinewy comedy about a group of youths who were bent on sexual initiation. Kazakhstan offered Yermek Shinarbeav's mystical *Revenge,* set in China and Korea and spanning several centuries. From Georgia, in the west, came Mikhail Kalatozosischvily's *The Beloved,* loosely based on Prosper Mérimée's "Mateo Falcone" and viewing the Russian Revolution and the Red Army with very different eyes from old Soviet conventions.

Serbia. Goran Paskaljevic's *Tango Argentina* offered an end-of-era portrait of Serbia, interpreted through the eyes of a young boy who finds warmth and understanding only among old people, whom he constantly loses to death.

Scandinavia. In Sweden the British director Colin Nutley made *Angel Farm,* a lovely evocation of a Swedish summer and a village set at odds by the arrival from the city of the heiress to the local manor. Two scripts by Ingmar Bergman were made by other directors. Bille August's *The Best Intentions* treated the early married life of Bergman's parents. *Sunday's Children,* directed by Bergman's son Daniel, caught up with little Ingmar at 8, then flashed forward to his 50th year, the end of his own father's life, and his reassessment of their relationship. A former Bergman actress, Liv Ullman, made her first film as director, *Sofie,* a beautifully acted and staged but excessively long saga about a Jewish family in Copenhagen at the end of the last century.

In Denmark the year's major success was *The Boys from Saint Petri,* a drama about public school boys fighting in the wartime resistance. In Finland, Aki Kaurismaki made a modern-dress version of *La Vie de bohème,* one of his best films, comic yet with a genuine bittersweet sense of tragedy.

Spain. The best and most original Spanish film of the year, Victor Erice's *El sol del membrillo,* observed in loving, lingering—sometimes comic—detail the daily work of the realistic painter Antonio López while painting a quince in his garden. Spanish directors had not lost their fascination with the tragedies of the 1930s and civil war. Jaime Camino's *El largo invierno (The Long Winter)* paid tribute to the Catalan resistance to Franco in 1939. Pilar Miro returned to direction and to the Franco past with *Beltenbros.*

Switzerland. Daniel Schmid's *Hors saison* was a touching, comic memory of the family hotel where he spent much of his boyhood.

Middle East and North Africa. A reinvigorated Iranian production was presented at the Fahr festival in early 1992. Mohsen Makhmalbaf's *Once upon a Time, the Movies . . .* was a somewhat esoteric tribute to Iranian film history. Ebrahim Foruzesh's *The Jar* achieved a fablelike quality in its treatment of poverty, where the breaking of a jar becomes a major social catastrophe. Abbas Kiarostami's unsentimental, moving *Life and Nothing More* related travels through a region devastated by an earthquake in search (unfulfilled) of the children who played in the director's fine earlier film *Where Is My Friend's Home?*

Latin America. A slight revival in production in Argentina in 1992 included Adolfo Aristarain's *Un lugar en el mundo,* a feeling portrait of a couple returning from exile and rediscovering the strengths and flaws of their old country. More ambitious in scale, Luís Puenzo's *The Plague* was a free adaptation that updated Albert Camus's original book and moved the story from Algeria to Buenos Aires, Arg. The ostensible theme was bubonic plague; the real target, political dictatorships.

Generally reckoned the best Chilean film for some years, Riccardo Larrain's *La frontera* related the adventures of a teacher condemned to internal exile by the military government. In Mexico, Dana Rotberg's *Angel of Fire* was a visually exciting, melodramatic allegory set among traveling show people. Gabriel Retes' *1 Bulto (Excess Baggage)* was an intelligent film about a man who was knocked into a coma during student riots in the 1960s and who wakes to react to a very different age.

East Asia. Japanese films evinced a new spirit of self-criticism. Juzo Itami continued his series of social comedies with *The Anti-Extortion Woman*—an attack on *yakusa* (organized crime) methods that led to *yakusa* thugs beating up the director. Mitsuo Kurotsuchi's *Traffic Jam* was a sharp comedy about the Japanese success and work ethic. Hirotaka Tashiro's *Swimming with Tears* investigated the plight of foreign workers in Japan through the misadventures of a runaway mail-order bride from the Philippines. More traditional films included Yoji Yamada's attractive *My Sons,* about the relationship of a widowed father with his independent-minded children.

Perhaps the most remarkable film to come out of China—though its release was obstructed by the authorities—was Zhuang Yuan's *Mama,* about a woman's struggle to bring up her mentally handicapped child in a society with inade-

Vanessa Redgrave (left) and Barbara Hicks appear in a scene from *Howards End,* which won both critical and popular acclaim. The film was another in a series of adaptations of literary classics by producer Ismail Merchant, director James Ivory, and writer Ruth Prawer Jhabvala.
DERRICK SANTINI

quate social services. *The Story of Qiu Ju* confirmed Zhang Yimou (*see* BIOGRAPHIES) as the most accessible of the new Chinese directors. The film told the human, often comic, story of a very pregnant young woman's insistent attempt to bring to justice the village headman who has injured her husband.

The staple diet of violent crime and martial arts films in Hong Kong was offset by Clara Law's *Qiuyue,* an exceptional film about two alienated youngsters—from Japan and Hong Kong—meeting in the island of doubtful future. The year's big production, however, was Stanley Kwan's *Centre Stage,* an ambitious biography of Ruan Lingyu, a star of Hong Kong silent pictures who committed suicide in the early '30s, depressed by malicious gossip.

In his first film, *Searching for Our Class,* South Korean director Hwang Gyu Dok attacked a too demanding and competitive educational system. Kim Yu Din's *Because You Are a Woman* was an equally fierce indictment of the treatment of rape victims. The most ambitious film of the year, Im Kwon Taek's *Fly High, Run Far—Kae Byok,* was a dense epic about a popular 19th-century religious leader.

Unexpectedly lively 1992 production in Taiwan included Ann Hui's *My American Grandson,* a likable culture-clash story about an old man visited by his U.S.-raised grandchild. Amg Lee reversed the situation in *Pushing Hands,* in which the arrival of a Chinese grandfather complicates a Chinese-American marriage. Stan Lai's ingenious comedy *The Peach Blossom Land* relishes the complications when two theatrical companies arrive to rehearse different plays on the same stage at the same time.

India. While production of Bombay-style commercial spectacles continued, a shortage of funds virtually put an end to independent and progressive cinema—significantly in the year of the death of India's greatest film artist, Satyajit Ray (*see* OBITUARIES).

Africa. In South Africa the successful stage musical *Sarafina!* was finally filmed on location in Soweto, where the action is set, with a mixture of Hollywood (Whoopi Goldberg) and African artists.

In Senegal, Djibril Diop Mambrety's *The Hyenas* was a bitter, witty, authentically African transformation of Friedrich Dürrenmatt's *The Visit.* From Cameroon, Jean-Pierre Bekolo's *Quartier Mozart* was a vital picture of contemporary suburban life, with a lively injection of comedy and African magic. (DAVID ROBINSON)

Nontheatrical Films. Winning more recognition than any other nontheatrical U.S. film in 1992 was *The Howie Rubin Story,* produced by Rod Cohen, a student at Loyola Marymount University, Los Angeles. It was honoured at five events, winning the Council on International Nontheatrical Events (CINE) Eagle, the Duisburg (Germany) gold medal, Mons (Belgium) Short Film Festival award for best comedy, Cork (Ireland) Youth International Video and Film Festival Blarney Trophy, and Ebensee (Austria) best of festival as well as a gold medal. The comedy, about a fantasizing, naive 1950s teenage boy growing up in New York City, has the polish of a professional production. It could easily rank as a top-notch Hollywood short feature.

Top winner of the Emily Award at the prestigious American Film and Video Festival was a 52-minute black-and-white documentary, *Indianapolis: Ship Of Doom.* The story was best described by the person for whom the award was named, Emily S. Jones, writing in *Sightlines,* "The haunting and horrifying story of the fate of the cruiser USS *Indianapolis* in the closing days of World War II is told through wartime footage (some from the Japanese), old newsreels and Navy material, contemporary interviews, and some re-created scenes. It was skillfully edited into an engrossing film." (THOMAS W. HOPE)

See also Photography; Television and Radio.

This article updates the *Macropædia* article MOTION PICTURES.

STAN COHEN

The Howie Rubin Story revolves around a teenager's fantasy that he is living in the gangster world in the 1950s. Produced by Rod Cohen, a student at Loyola Marymount University in Los Angeles, the film won the top prize in several competitions both in the U.S. and in Europe.

Museums

There was continuing uncertainty in 1992 about the long-term future of many famous museums and collections in central and eastern Europe as transfers of both buildings and collections continued. A major landmark in this process was the agreement to reverse the 1919 confiscation and conversion into museums of the Kremlin cathedrals in Moscow. The debate in Russia about the legitimacy of the seizure of both church and private collections in the revolutionary period continued. Toward the end of the year it was at last admitted that—as had long been suspected—some priceless western European museum collections missing since World War II had been taken by the former Soviet Union and stored in Russia. This opened up the prospect of return and restitution of these collections to their countries of origin.

Museums and monuments in former Yugoslavia were clearly being viewed as important symbols of cultural and ethnic identity and hence became prime targets in the civil war. There was widespread evidence of large-scale destruction of important museums, archives, and monuments in Croatia and in Bosnia and Hercegovina, and it was alleged that many had been deliberately targeted, despite clear marking with the international symbol set out in the 1954 Hague Convention for the Protection of Cultural Property in the Event of Armed Conflict. On a happier note, the collections of the Kuwait National Museum, removed by Iraq following its invasion of Kuwait, were returned to temporary storage in Kuwait under UN supervision. However, plans for rebuilding the severely damaged museum itself seemed to be in only a very preliminary stage.

Terrorism hit museums in 1992: the Isaac Fernández Blanco Museum of Spanish-American Art in Buenos Aires, Arg., suffered serious structural damage when a car bomb destroyed the nearby Israeli embassy, and the local Regimental Museum in Shrewsbury, England, was severely damaged in a firebomb attack claimed by the Irish Republican Army. Within the space of a week, apparently accidental fires ravaged Windsor Castle in England and the Hofburg in Vienna. Though in each case losses of important items from the respective collections were almost miraculously light, the scale of destruction revived the long-standing concern about the best way to protect such buildings and their contents. In particular, the traditional strong opposition to the installation of water sprinkler systems because of the potential damage to works of art, especially paintings, in the event of accidental discharge was now being questioned.

The deep recession led to a marked slowdown in museum development and provision. In the U.S. this was reflected, for example, in the closing of the Museum of Holography in New York City, even though it had attracted 60,000 visitors annually, and major staff cuts at the Smithsonian Institution in Washington, D.C. A special 18-month tax provision, in effect to mid-1992, had once again permitted the full market value of appreciated property donated to charitable institutions, including museums, to be taken as a tax deduction. As a result, 75 major U.S. museums, which had received 11,582 works of art in 1990, accepted 29,692 gifts in 1991, and during that year New York City's Metropolitan Museum of Art alone received $28.3 million worth of art. An extension of the provision was included in a tax bill passed by Congress, but it was vetoed by Pres. George Bush.

Despite the bleak economic outlook, work continued on new national museums in Australia and New Zealand. In Duisburg, Germany, a fine new museum of the history of the city and the central Rhine/Ruhr inland navigation system opened on the riverfront, almost simultaneously with a

Visitors enjoy reinstalled artwork in the National Gallery of Art in Washington, D.C. Critics praised the results of the two-year remodeling of galleries in the West Building, which included the restoration and reframing of paintings.
KATHLEEN BUCKALEW—NATIONAL GALLERY OF ART

splendid extension that more than quadrupled the size of the Wilhelm Lehmbruch art museum. Completion of the new aviation museum at Frankfurt's Rhein-Main international airport was followed by the opening of the Volkerkund-Museum in a major new building by the New York architect Richard Meier. In Spain the combination of the Seville world's fair, Madrid's designation as Cultural Capital of Europe for 1992, and the Barcelona Olympics (which included the most ambitious "cultural Olympics" festival in more than half a century) put the country's museums to the fore. The innovative Ethnographic Collection within a large, new extension to the National Museum in Copenhagen could be regarded as a major new museum in its own right.

Two important new developments opened in English provincial industrial towns. At Halifax, Yorkshire, the £7 million Eureka! was Britain's first large-scale children's museum, created by a team of staff and consultants who had played leading roles in the La Villette Cité des Sciences et de l'Industrie in Paris and the Boston Children's Museum. The £10 million Snibston Discovery Park and Museum in Coalville, Leicestershire, on the site of a historic coal mine, included a substantial nature reserve and a large-scale outdoor interactive "science play" area. Saroj Ghose, director general of India's National Council of Science Museums, was elected president of the International Council of Museums at the council's triennial conference in Quebec in September.

The Solomon R. Guggenheim Museum in New York City reopened after a two-year, $45 million restoration and expansion that included a new, controversial addition adjacent to the well-known Frank Lloyd Wright structure. The California Palace of the Legion of Honor closed for a two-year renovation that was to cost $25 million, including $11 million for earthquake safety improvements. In Chicago the Museum of Contemporary Art announced the design for its new $55 million structure, and the Art Institute reopened its Asian galleries after a three-year, $5 million renovation. The National Gallery of Art in Washington, D.C., completed a two-year reinstallation of its Old Master, Impressionist, and Postimpressionist paintings. The Musée

d'Art Contemporain de Montréal, entirely funded by the Quebec government, moved to new quarters in Montreal. In London the Tate announced plans to split its British and modern collections, housing the latter in a new museum of modern art. (PATRICK J. BOYLAN; JOSHUA B. KIND)
See also Art Exhibitions and Art Sales.
This article updates the *Macropædia* article MUSEUMS.

Music

Classical. After the "Mozart-mania" of 1991, the bicentenary of the composer's death, 1992 seemed a relatively calm year for classical music. There was no composer's centenary more notable than that of Rossini—Darius Milhaud's was barely noticed—nor were there any dramatically unexpected shifts in music director appointments. Such headlines as appeared in the international press mainly concerned the dramatic accession of Gérard Mortier as artistic director of the Salzburg Festival. After Herbert von Karajan's 34-year dominance of the annual Austrian extravaganza, Mortier, a Belgian who came from La Monnaie in Brussels, made no secret of his intended clean sweep. To an institution known for its guardianship of those Teutonic gods Mozart, Goethe, and Strauss, Mortier brought a revolutionary internationalism—for which he was duly roasted in the Viennese musical press.

The opening concert was conducted by Nikolaus Harnoncourt, the very antithesis of homogenized Karajan-style music making. Then there was the first performance since its 1983 Paris premiere of Olivier Messiaen's 6½-hour (with intermissions) opera *St. François d'Assise*, directed by Peter Sellars, with the Los Angeles Philharmonic in the pit and the young Finn Esa-Pekka Salonen conducting. There were concerts by the Cleveland (Ohio) Orchestra, St. Petersburg Philharmonic, City of Birmingham (England) Symphony Orchestra, Ensemble Inter-contemporain of Pierre Boulez (*see* BIOGRAPHIES), and William Christie's early-music ensemble, Les Arts Florissants—"hardly," as Edward Rothstein wrote in the *New York Times,* "the usual roundup of

Salzburg suspects." Riccardo Muti made headlines of his own by withdrawing a week and a half before the opening of the *Clemenza di Tito* he was to conduct, protesting the direction of Ursel and Karl-Ernst Herrmann; he was replaced by Gustav Kuhn.

In Seville, Spain, site of Expo 92, the new Teatro de la Maestranza was inaugurated with the opera most closely associated with the city, *Carmen;* Placido Domingo conducted. Between April and October visitors to the Expo could sample performances by New York City's Metropolitan Opera, Milan's La Scala, Paris' Opéra de la Bastille, the Vienna State Opera, the Berlin Philharmonic, the Vienna Philharmonic, the Leipzig (Germany) Gewandhaus Orchestra, the Royal Concertgebouw Orchestra, the Paris Orchestra, the Israel Philharmonic, the St. Petersburg Philharmonic, the Philadelphia Orchestra, and the Montreal Symphony—a list by no means exhaustive. Elsewhere, concert halls returned to use after renovations included Prague's House of Artists (completed in time for the Prague Spring festival) and, after $10 million worth of acoustic reworking, San Francisco's Louise M. Davies Symphony Hall. Yet another round of acoustic modifications, relatively modest this time, was announced for Avery Fisher Hall in New York City, and Munich, Germany's National Theatre was closed for repairs to stage machinery disabled by, of all things, a bacterial infection of its hydraulic fluid.

Having been announced several years beforehand, the highest-visibility job switches among conductors seemed almost anticlimactic. Chief among them were Wolfgang Sawallisch's replacement of Riccardo Muti at the helm of the Philadelphia Orchestra, Esa-Pekka Salonen's installation as music director of the Los Angeles Philharmonic, and Sian Edwards' appointment to succeed Mark Elder as musical director of the English National Opera. Semyon Bychkov was named principal guest conductor of the Maggio Musicale in Florence, starting with the 1993 festival. Mstislav Rostropovich announced his intention to retire from the National Symphony Orchestra (Washington, D.C.) in 1994, and Spiros Argiris resigned as music director of the Spoleto Festivals in both Italy and South Carolina.

The Pulitzer Prize for music occasioned a row when the jury's choice of Ralph Shapey's *Concerto Fantastique* was overturned by the board of directors; the prize was awarded to Wayne Peterson's *The Face of the Night, The Heart of the Dark.* The University of Louisville (Ky.) Grawemeyer Award went to Krzysztof Penderecki's *Adagio for Large Orchestra,* and Alfred Schnittke was awarded the Japan Art Association's Praemium Imperiale.

Deaths included those of the composers John Cage, Olivier Messiaen, William Schuman (*see* OBITUARIES), William Mathias, and Stephen Oliver; conductors Sir Charles Groves, Andrew Schenck, and Roger Wagner; baritone Sir Geraint Evans (*see* OBITUARIES); and pianist Vitya Vronsky-Babin. What would have been the 60th birthday of the eccentric Canadian pianist Glenn Gould—and what *was* the 10th anniversary of his death—was marked by a five-day conference in Toronto. And, after resting for 51 years in a vault at Arlington (Va.) National Cemetery, the remains of pianist-composer-statesman Ignacy Jan Paderewski were returned to his native Poland; U.S. Pres. Franklin Roosevelt had vowed that Paderewski would not return "until Poland is free."

Opera. Among the year's more curious performances was a *Tosca* telecast live from the actual Roman settings described in the libretto. The concept was that of Italian television producer Andrea Andermann, and the principals were Catherine Malfitano (Tosca), Placido Domingo (Cavaradossi), and Ruggero Raimondi (Scarpia); by means of closed-circuit audio-video hookups, they were accompanied by Zubin Mehta and the RAI Symphony Orchestra, housed in a studio.

World premieres during 1992 included William Bolcom's *McTeague* (Lyric Opera, Chicago), Daniel Börtz's *Backanterna* (Stockholm), John Buller's *Bakxai* (English National Opera), Anthony Davis' *Tania,* based on the 1974 kidnapping of publishing heiress Patty Hearst (American Music Theater, Philadelphia), Roberto Gerhard's *La Dueña,* based on Richard Brinsley Sheridan's comedy (Madrid), Philip Glass's *The Voyage* (Metropolitan Opera, New York City), Jonathan Harvey's *The Inquest of Love* and Priti Paintal's *Biko,* the latter based on the life of the South African civil rights leader Steve Biko (both English National Opera commissions), Robert Moran's *Desert of Roses* (Houston [Texas] Grand Opera) and *From the Towers of the Moon* (Minnesota Opera), Wolfgang Rihm's *Die Eroberung von Mexiko* (Hamburg, Germany), Aulis Sallinen's *Kullervo* (Finnish National Opera in Los Angeles), Alfred Schnittke's *Life with an Idiot* (Amsterdam), Bright Sheng's *The Song of Majnun* (Lyric Opera's Center for American Artists, Chicago), Harry Somers' *Mario and the Magician,* based on Thomas Mann's novella (Canadian Opera Company, Toronto), John Tavener's *Mary of Egypt* (Aldeburgh [England] Festival), Andrew Toovey's *Ubu* (Cardiff [Wales] Festival), and Hugo Weisgall's *The Gardens of Adonis* (Opera/Omaha, Neb.).

The Rossini bicentenary sparked revivals in opera houses around the world; among notable discoveries was *Ermione,* which had its first British and U.S. performances at the hands of the San Francisco Opera (in concert version), Opera/Omaha (staged), and the Orchestra of the Age of Enlightenment (concert). In New York City the Lincoln Center for the Performing Arts rounded out its promised survey of Mozart's *gesamtausgabe* with concert performances of the early operas, several of them having their first U.S. hearings; in Cooperstown, N.Y., Glimmerglass Opera presented a provocative *Magic Flute* staged by choreographer-performance artist Martha Clarke.

Orchestras. The New York Philharmonic and the Vienna Philharmonic both celebrated 150th anniversaries in 1992. The Vienna orchestra mainly basked in its history and tradition, and the occasion was marked by the release of huge boxed sets of recordings from both Deutsche Grammophon and Decca (London). The New York orchestra inaugurated an ambitious project of commissioning 36 new works for the sesquicentenary, and, in its second season under its new music director, Kurt Masur, the orchestra began recording at a busy pace not seen since the halcyon days of Leonard Bernstein. In London a new orchestra, the New Queen's Hall Orchestra, was founded to present "authenticist" performances—complete with old-fashioned string *portamento*—of 19th-century music.

The year was notable for a bumper crop of new concerti. In the U.S. there were premieres of concerti by Leslie Bassett (for orchestra, Detroit [Mich.] Symphony), William Bolcom (clarinet, New York Philharmonic), John Harbison (oboe, San Francisco Symphony), Lowell Liebermann (flute, St. Louis [Mo.] Symphony), and Joan Tower (violin, Utah Symphony). The Steinway Foundation commissioned three piano concerti that were premiered together in Washington, D.C., with Rostropovich conducting the National Symphony Orchestra: Lalo Schifrin's Second (*Concerto of the Americas,* played by Cristina Ortiz), Rodion Shchedrin's Fourth (*Sharp Keys,* played by Nikolay Petrov), and Lowell Liebermann's Second (played by Stephen Hough). British audiences had first hearings of concerti by Michael Berkeley (clarinet, English Chamber Orchestra), Robin Holloway (violin, BBC Philharmonic), William Mathias (violin, Hallé

A spaceship prepares to blast off in the year 2092 in *The Voyage*, by Philip Glass with a libretto by David Henry Hwang, which received its premiere at the Metropolitan Opera in New York City. A work about exploration, the opera was commissioned in celebration of the Christopher Columbus quincentenary.
JOHAN ELBERS

[Germany] Orchestra), Dominick Muldowney (violin, Royal Liverpool [England] Philharmonic), and Ronald Stevenson (violin, BBC Scottish Symphony).

Recordings, Publications. In the 10th year since the introduction of the compact disc (CD)—and despite isolated cries that current compact disc prices in the U.S. were undercutting small labels—the recording industry gave at least the appearance of vigorous health. What continued to astonish observers was the flood of lesser-known and even long-forgotten repertory from the 17th through the 20th centuries as long-established record companies exhumed enormous quantities of material from their vaults. In addition to the Vienna Philharmonic retrospectives from DG and Decca, a huge reissue of Leonard Bernstein's Columbia and CBS recordings was under way on their successor label, Sony Classical. Also from Sony Classical came an ambitious Glenn Gould Edition, in both audio and video formats. Between EMI and Pearl, most of Elgar's nearly 15 hours of recordings—the earliest systematic collection of a composer's performances of his own music—were issued on CD. Nikolaus Harnoncourt's quirky recording of the complete Beethoven symphonies, with the Chamber Orchestra of Europe (on Teldec), was named Record of the Year in *Gramophone* magazine's annual awards. And, for the moment, the prize for the most expensive classical recording in history appeared to be won by Sir Georg Solti's all-star Strauss *Die Frau ohne Schatten* on Decca.

Toward the end of the year appeared the long-awaited four-volume *New Grove Dictionary of Opera.* After the better part of 20 years as the highly respected music critic of *The New Yorker* magazine, Andrew Porter returned to England to become principal critic of *The Observer* (London); he was replaced by another Briton, Paul Griffiths. On a sadder note, *Musical America* ceased publication just six years shy of its centenary; its live-music coverage, longtime editor Shirley Fleming, and subscription list were picked up by *The American Record Guide.*   (SCOTT CANTRELL)

Jazz. The first jazz recordings were made in January 1917, by a lively quintet of New Orleans, La., musicians named the Original Dixieland Jazz Band, at a time when most Americans considered jazz a novelty music, a diversion on vaudeville stages. Three-quarters of a century later, with jazz considered an art music, RCA/Bluebird released the band's 1917–21 Victor recordings on compact disc to offi-

cially celebrate the beginning of jazz's recorded history. By way of unofficial celebration, the flood of CD jazz releases continued throughout the year, bewildering in its quantity. Even more than the mid-1970s, the early 1990s were proving to be a golden age of reissued jazz recordings. As a result of international confusion in copyright laws, reissues of early and swing-era jazz especially proliferated; listeners seeking the classic Victor recordings by the 1926–27 Red Hot Peppers of Jelly Roll Morton, for instance, could choose from at least five competing collections, all but one originating in Europe; some were digitally reprocessed, while others appeared to have been dubbed directly from the original 78-rpm discs.

Indeed, it was possible for the alert and wealthy CD buyer to own a fairly comprehensive collection of jazz's major pre-World War II artists, though this material was released onto and then withdrawn from the marketplace with dizzying unpredictability. The major event among 1992's reissues was Count Basie's *The Complete Decca Recordings* in a three-CD set. However, it received stiff competition; for instance, Milestone issued five CDs of its 1920s properties, including music by Morton, the New Orleans Rhythm Kings, King Oliver, Ma Rainey, and Bix Beiderbecke. With Yazoo's two CDs of Charlie Patton, *King of the Delta Blues,* and the seven Tommy Johnson works in Bluebird's *Canned Heat Blues* anthology, two of the three early Mississippi blues giants made it to CD in 1992.

The David Cronenberg film *Naked Lunch* featured much improvising by Ornette Coleman on its sound track, which was among the finest ever recorded for a U.S. film; Milan's sound track CD, including alto saxophonist Coleman, bassist Barre Phillips, drummer Denardo Coleman, and compositions by Coleman and Howard Shore, was the year's major event among new jazz releases. For those who believed that the 1980s and 1990s were the era of the jazz composer, there was evidence in the release of Anthony Davis' opera *X, The Life and Times of Malcolm X,* with jazz improvisers included among the orchestra and singers (Gramavision). There was also evidence in *Sideshow* by Edward Wilkerson, Jr., and his Eight Bold Souls (Arabesque) and in *The Spirits of Our Ancestors* by Randy Weston (Antilles), which included a section of his massive 1984 composition *African Sunrise.* For those who retained faith in pure improvisation, there were the brilliant exploits of multireedman Anthony Braxton in

Willisau (Quartet) 1991 (hat ART) and of unaccompanied woodwind soloist Peter Brötzmann in *No Nothing* (FMP); a happy surprise was the freely improvising trio of saxophonist Tony Bevan, bassist Paul Rogers, and percussionist Steve Noble in *Bigshots* (Incus). Nevertheless, a more balanced view of the year's releases suggested that there were no predominant trends, though the bop revival by young musicians continued its wide popularity; in this connection, it was notable that saxophonist Branford Marsalis began appearing on U.S. television screens nightly, leading the band on NBC's "Tonight" show in the year that his *I Heard You Twice the First Time* (Columbia) became a best-seller.

Another diamond anniversary, that of Dizzy Gillespie's birthday, was celebrated in 1992. It was the first full year of the great bop trumpet pioneer's residency at Queens (N.Y.) College and the year of his acting debut, playing an expatriate jazz trumpeter in Jose Antonio Zorrilla's *The Winter in Lisbon,* for which Gillespie also composed the sound track. In January Gillespie played a monthlong engagement at New York's Blue Note nightclub, joined by a changing cast of important jazz artists; fellow trumpeters Doc Cheatham, Red Rodney, Wynton Marsalis, and others who joined him in the final week were on his *To Diz with Love* CD (Telarc). But after this promising beginning, Gillespie was forced to undergo major surgery in March and then spent much of the rest of the year recuperating.

Among the year's awards were a National Medal of Arts for pianist Billy Taylor and a five-year MacArthur Foundation fellowship, a "genius grant," to soprano saxophonist Steve Lacy. The Lila Wallace-Reader's Digest Foundation disbursed $1 million in grants to present jazz concert and educational programs throughout the U.S. Among the year's festivals, Montreal native son pianist Paul Bley was honoured at four concerts at that city's jazz festival; much of

the JVC Festival in New York City was centred on tributes to leading swing- and bop-era figures.

Edward Blackwell, a giant among jazz drummers for over three decades, played with his new group, the Ed Blackwell Project, and reunited with the American Jazz Quintet, all on tour in 1992, but he died in the autumn. Also dying during the year were blues composer and musician Willie Dixon, pianist bandleader Sammy Price (*see* OBITUARIES), critic Martin Williams, swing-band leader Andy Kirk, and composer-bandleader-multi-instrumentalist Hal Russell.

(JOHN LITWEILER)

Popular. A year of recession in both the U.S. and Britain left the entertainment industry in general, and the music industry in particular, concerned about its future. Popular music had been a major industry for only a relatively short time—since the upheavals and innovations that transformed youth culture during the 1960s—and the mood and interests of many young people had already begun to change by the time the recession began to bite. The CD revolution improved quality but made music more expensive, while the market for single songs virtually collapsed. If there was one notable feature of 1992, it was the realization that all the major artists, including such exponents of carefully promoted outrage and rebellion as Madonna and Prince, had now been around for many years.

In such a climate, in which record companies appeared to be playing it safe by promoting established favourites rather than potential new stars, those who had started out in the 1960s found that they were still in demand. The Rolling Stones signed a new three-album deal for £25 million, and Eric Clapton, who had never seemed to stop working, added still further to his reputation with *Unplugged,* an album that proved that his playing was just as exquisite and emotional when he switched to acoustic guitar.

The Disappearing LP

To a kid brought up on hi-fi and vinyl LPs, the Victrola in Great Aunt Ophelia's parlour resembled a small, cornered dinosaur. The heavy, brittle "78s" it grudgingly played were fossils, their emanations alien to young ears. Now, as suddenly as it galvanized popular culture in the early 1950s, the 33⅓-rpm long-playing record has followed its predecessor to the verge of extinction. Since the U.S. introduction of the compact disc in 1983, the digitally encoded plastic recording has virtually replaced the LP and has taken a substantial bite out of the cassette-tape market.

Proponents of CD technology hail its elimination of the extraneous hiss and crackle associated with analog recording and playback. The pristine CD sound won many early converts among devotees of classical music as recording companies and radio stations increasingly adopted the "cleaner" format. The rock, rhythm and blues, and country music industries were soon to follow. As the cost of CD players fell throughout the 1980s, many consumers expected the cost of CDs to do the same, but the average disc price stabilized at considerably higher than that of corresponding LPs. While the discs themselves are cheaper to manufacture, the format accommodates somewhat lengthier recordings. Low wear and tear and low maintenance requirements—and thus increased longevity—together with crystalline acoustics and the calculated unavailability of LPs, boosted annual CD sales from 800,000

to more than 300 million over the last nine years, while sales of LPs fell from nearly 300 million to less than 5 million.

The relative impacts of consumer preference and production ratios on this trend remain unclear. Inarguably, though, the digitalization of recorded music (including during the same period digitally recorded and digitally remastered LPs) has left some listeners cold. As more LPs go out of print and labels issue only a smattering of new releases on vinyl, the market for used records is booming. LP resale outlets, mail-order services, and auctions have all experienced a steady upturn in their business.

A notably bitter lament for analog recording—and indictment of the CD—is found in a guest editorial written by veteran rock musician Neil Young for *Guitar Player* magazine (May 1992). "We are living in the darkest age of musical sound," writes Young. "I would like to hear guitars again, with the warmth, the highs, the lows, the air, the electricity, the vibrancy of something that's real, instead of just a duplication of the dominant factors." To those who perceive in current recordings a lack of "heart," Young counters, "The real reason is technical. It's not that people don't have souls anymore. All these bands have got huge souls and can't wait to play; they just can't figure out why their albums don't sound as good as some of the things they used to hear."

(JIM CARNES)

Bob Dylan appears in New York City's Madison Square Garden at a tribute organized by Columbia Records to mark his 30 years with the label. Musicians performed Dylan songs at the concert, which lasted nearly four hours and was broadcast on radio and television.
SUZANNE DECHILLO/THE NEW YORK TIMES

In the second year of soft summer concert sales, only two shows consistently sold out large arenas: The Grateful Dead, in its 26th year of touring, and Lollapalooza, 7 bands that played more than 29 U.S. cities. Lollapalooza lasted nine hours and featured the Red Hot Chili Peppers, Pearl Jam, and Soundgarden, as well as a market area that sold T-shirts and crafts and distributed information about voting, the environment, and other issues of current interest.

Peter Gabriel, onetime lead singer with Genesis, released *Us,* his first major solo project in six years, which showed his interest in world music with an adventurous blend of African rhythms, Celtic melodies, and Eastern themes, with elements of funk and gospel added in. All this was blended with highly personal lyrics. During the year Gabriel also celebrated the 10th anniversary of WOMAD, the world music organization that he helped to found, with a series of special concerts involving artists from around the world.

R.E.M. continued its shift from cult heroes to mainstream success with *Automatic for the People,* a moody, doomy, semiacoustic album with typically incomprehensible lyrics, with the notable exception of the angry, political "Ignoreland." U2 also had a good year, touring extensively after the release of *Achtung Baby* at the end of 1991. Nirvana, a band from Seattle, Wash., surprised everyone with the huge success of its second album, *Nevermind,* which popularized so-called grunge-rock—loud, frenetic music that features abrasive guitars and melodic lyrics. Major pop acts found that they had new and unexpected competition in the form of Garth Brooks (*see* BIOGRAPHIES), whose country-rock crossover style showed that country music was one area of the pop spectrum that was still showing healthy development. Country newcomer Billy Ray Cyrus also enjoyed great popularity during the year.

The other growth area was dance music. From the all-electronic house styles in Britain to the hip-hop and rap of black America, most new musicians were concentrating on dance styles rather than guitar pop. Rap's popularity continued to grow, with Boyz II Men's album *Cooleyhigh-harmony* in the number one spot for 22 weeks. Controversy surrounded rap groups Public Enemy, Ice-T, and Sister

Souljah. Three veterans of the 1980s dance scene all had new albums on release and toured extensively to promote them. Michael Jackson's *Dangerous,* with its eclectic blend of hip-hop, dance styles, and rock crossover material, failed to live up to its title. Minneapolis (Minn.)-based Prince released an album that had no title, just a symbol on the cover, with the warning that it "contains language that some people may find offensive." But even Prince's antics were not as outrageous as those of Madonna, who released a book simply entitled *Sex,* which consisted of naked and erotic pictures of herself and others, and an album *Erotica.*

Despite the economic climate, and the tendency of record companies to play it safe by promoting well-established acts, some newcomers did manage to break through. In the U.S., singer-songwriter Tori Amos released *Little Earthquakes,* a startling set of pretty songs with often shocking, personal lyrics. In Britain the surprise of the year was a sudden revival of interest in all things to do with Abba, the easy-listening Swedish supergroup that had stopped recording a decade earlier. The Australian group Bjorn Again became a cult favourite by imitating the songs of the original Bjorn Ulvaeus. Notable deaths during the year included country composer and singer Roger Miller and "champagne music" bandleader Lawrence Welk (*see* OBITUARIES).

(ROBIN DENSELOW)

See also Dance; Motion Pictures; Television and Radio; Theatre.
This article updates the *Macropædia* article The History of Western MUSIC.

Philately and Numismatics

Stamps. The breakup of the U.S.S.R. resulted in separate stamp issues for 11 of the 15 former Soviet republics. Latvia, Lithuania, and Estonia were first, and by August 1992 Turkmenistan had become the 11th. Efforts by the U.K. Stamp Publicity Board to encourage more children to become active collectors had disappointing results, but the senior end of the hobby maintained its strength despite the general economic depression. Important realizations at auction included $154,000 for a cover addressed to Abraham Lincoln, part of the Edwards Western Express sale by Christie's/Robson Lowe (New York), which totaled $968,764. The Peter Robertson Fiji collection made £104,513, £18,700 of which was for a cover bearing a strip of four (1*d,* 6*d,* 9*d,* and 1*s*) Fiji Times Express issue (Christie's/Robson Lowe, London). Stanley Gibbons Auctions (London) achieved a record £6,600 for a used block of four of the Great Britain 1840 2*d* blue, and a Gibbons sale of Far East philately in Hong Kong totaled HK$4.2 million, including HK$74,000 for an 1861 cover from Shanghai to Sydney, Australia.

Eight defendants charged with philatelic fraud in London in 1991 were acquitted after consideration of the distinction between the "open" contracts negotiated by the defendants with certain governments and those negotiated by the Crown Agents with other governments, the latter specifying that all errors and varieties occurring during stamp printing should be destroyed. The eight had been accused of involvement in the production of misprinted stamps with the intention of selling them to collectors as genuine errors.

Major awards at the Fédération Internationale de Philatélic-sponsored exhibition in Tokyo in November 1991 were: Grand Prix d'Honneur, Angelo Lima (Brazil); Grand Prix National, Tsueno Muyakawa (Japan); and four Grand Prix International awards to Luis A. Indarte (Spain), Gerald Ellot (New Zealand), Christian Sundman (Finland), and Augusto Peinada (Colombia). At Granada 92, one of Spain's celebrations of the Columbus quincentenary, three

When the U.S. Postal Service prepared to issue a stamp honouring Elvis Presley, it created two designs—showing him in one as a 1950s rocker (top) and in the other as a middle-aged performer in the 1970s—and, in what the Postal Service claimed would be a profitable marketing scheme, invited the public to choose. Voters overwhelmingly preferred the young Presley.
AP/WIDE WORLD

Spanish competitors secured the major awards: Angela Ruis Vegas (Grand Prix d'Honneur), Luis A. Indarte (Grand Prix International), and José B. Salvans (Grand Prix National). Canada 92 at Montreal was a Youth International that attracted 400 entries from collectors under 21 years old. Genova 92, at Genoa, Italy, was a Thematic International with invited displays on the Columbian theme. The Columbus celebrations inspired stamps from many countries but, uniquely, the issues for the U.S., Italy, Spain, and Portugal were identical except for the inscriptions and currencies.

The British Philatelic Federation Congress was held at Newcastle upon Tyne in September, when four new names were added to the Roll of Distinguished Philatelists: Alberto Bolaffi (Italy; following his grandfather Alberto in 1936, and his father, Guilio, in 1981); Koh Seow Chuan, the first Singaporean signatory; Peter Jaffé (Australia); and Emil Mewes (Germany). The BPF Congress Medal was awarded to Commander George Gibson, and the Lichtenstein Medal of the Collectors Club (of New York) went to Roberto M. Rosende, a specialist in Cuban philately.

The U.K. National Postal Museum acquired (for £10,000) the original woodcut engraved by John Thompson and used to produce the mold from which the Mulready printing plates originated.   (KENNETH F. CHAPMAN)

Coins and Paper Money. Many types of currency made their debut in 1992 following the dissolution of the Soviet Union and other political and economic changes. Russia issued new 1,000- and 5,000-ruble notes, in part to cope with high inflation and to ease a cash shortage created by the country's transition to a free-market economy. Russian-printed bills also circulated in most of the other 14 former Soviet republics, although many of them made plans to introduce their own money. Ukrainian officials created coupons, which replaced the Russian ruble as legal tender in November. In June, Estonia introduced a series of kroon notes, while Lithuania was considering introduction of a litas-denominated currency. Elsewhere, three former Yugoslav republics—Macedonia, Croatia, and Slovenia—issued their own coins or paper bills.

The U.S. printed $100, $50, and $20 Federal Reserve notes with enhanced anticounterfeiting devices. The new bills included microprinting around centre portraits and a polyester thread embedded in the paper, additions expected to make U.S. money more difficult to duplicate accurately on sophisticated colour copiers. Several other countries—including Australia, Austria, Canada, and Finland—had produced currency with elaborate security features, such as holograms or machine-readable coding.

Worldwide sales of gold bullion coins remained at depressed levels throughout much of 1992, the result of recession and a soft market for precious metals. The Gold Institute reported that Australia issued nearly 700,000 troy ounces of gold bullion coins in 1991, much more than its nearest competitor, Canada. (In 1990 Canada had ranked first with sales of about one million troy ounces.) The U.S. American eagle was the most popular silver bullion coin in 1991, as it had been since it was first made in 1986.

The U.S. Senate on February 19 rejected legislation that would have forced the Treasury to put new designs on the "tails sides" of circulating coins. In May a task force of the House Budget Committee discussed a proposal calling for new dollar coins to replace $1 bills. The Federal Reserve concluded that this would save the government nearly $400 million a year, in part because of lower production costs. A dollar coin would last at least 20 years in circulation, while a paper dollar normally wears out in less than 18 months.

In August and September, the U.S. Mint sold to collectors all 500,000 White House silver dollars that it was authorized to make. Congress had set an unusually low mintage ceiling for the 1992-dated dollars, which memorialize the 200th anniversary of the laying of the White House cornerstone. Also in 1992, the U.S. produced coins commemorating U.S. participation in the 1992 Olympic Games and the Columbus quincentenary, as well as proof sets containing silver dimes, quarters, and half-dollars. Such 90% silver sets were last made in 1964. Canada unveiled 12 types of circulating quarters during 1992—each representing one of the country's provinces or territories—to mark the 125th anniversary of Canadian confederation. Canadian citizens were invited to participate in a design competition for the coins, which generated 11,003 entries for the quarters and another 2,871 entries for a "Canada 125" dollar.

The U.S. rare-coin market was little changed in the 12 months ended August 31, according to a *Coin World* price survey that monitored nearly 17,000 coin values. Still, a U.S. $4 gold piece dated 1880 sold for $264,000 in a February auction, and six months later an 1894-S U.S. dime—one of 12 known—brought $165,000 at auction.   (ROGER BOYE)

This article updates the *Macropædia* article COINS AND COINAGE.

Photography

Manufacturers of top-of-the-line 35-mm single-lens-reflex (SLR) cameras in 1992 continued to play a highly competitive game of "Can you top this?" as they brought forth new models with innovative, high-technology features designed to attract professionals and advanced amateurs. Sophisticated applications of electronics enlarged the scope of creative image control but at the cost of increasingly formidable instruction manuals. Many of the year's most highly praised photographic exhibitions were retrospective and historical rather than ground breaking.

Photo Equipment. An outstanding example of the year's highly advanced SLR cameras was the Nikon N90. Similar in size, weight, and general configuration to the Nikon N8008, the N90 provided an identical range of shutter speeds from 30 seconds to ⅛,₀₀₀ second plus B but also many new features, among the most noteworthy being its metering systems for ambient light and flash.

The ambient system included an eight-segment (up from five on the N8008) matrix sensor that provided 1% (of picture area) spot metering, 75% centre-weighted metering, and total picture-area matrix metering with a novel "three-dimensional" measuring capability. The latter's purpose was to detect the region of sharpest focus within the total picture area on the reasonable assumption that this was the part of the picture for which the user wanted optimum exposure. When used with a new series of D (for distance) Nikkor lenses, the N90 could ensure best exposure for the most sharply focused area even when that area was not centred. Flash exposure was controlled with a five-segment sensor array also aided by three-dimensional information. The multiple sensor took one or more preflash readings from an 18% gray shutter curtain, determined in what meter segment the subject was located and at what distance, and supplied the information to the N90's computer, which then determined the amount of flash exposure.

Another example of advanced technology was Canon's remarkable Eye Controlled Focus system for the Canon EOS A2E. It detected where within the viewfinder the user was looking during the instant of exposure and automatically focused on that point. The system, which had to be calibrated for each individual, used four infrared-emitting diodes to send invisible light to the user's eye, which then reflected the light into the camera's viewfinder. There optics formed the light into an image on a CCD (charge-coupled device) sensor that detected the area being observed and guided the autofocusing accordingly.

Minolta introduced the Maxxum 9xi, an impressive professional addition to its well-established Maxxum SLR line. With the fastest top shutter speed ($\frac{1}{12,000}$ second) and flash synchronization ($\frac{1}{300}$ second) of any 35-mm SLR, it also was claimed to have the world's fastest, most accurate autofocusing system, operable even when the film was advanced at 4.5 frames per second.

During the year compact point-and-shoot 35-mm cameras proliferated as manufacturers sought to fill every niche in a market crammed with nearly 200 current models. At their simplest and least expensive they included preloaded single-use (disposable) cameras, which were gaining in popularity among casual users. In this cardboard-and-plastic category Kodak added a Fun Saver TeleFoto 35 equipped with an 85-mm lens, while Fuji introduced a QuickSnap Panorama Flash intended for indoor group portraits.

Among conventional compacts a great variety of fixed-, dual-, and zoom-lens models were introduced, including ultracompact "take me everywhere" designs. An example was the Yashica T4, which comfortably fitted into a shirt pocket and combined the optical quality of a Carl Zeiss-designed 35-mm f/3.5 Tessar T* lens with a one-second to $\frac{1}{700}$-second programmed electronic shutter. Pentax won the European Zoom Camera of the Year 1992–93 award for its IQZoom 90-WR, a splash-proof, water-resistant compact combining a pocketable design with a 38–90-mm f/3.5–7.5 zoom lens and a remote cordless shutter release and zoom control. Top-of-the-line compacts offered features (except for interchangeable lenses) that rivaled advanced SLRs—and with prices to match. An outstanding example was Konica's Hexar, an autofocusing automatic compact with a seven-element 35-mm f/2 lens, a rugged (die-cast metal) body, and the look of a classic range-finder camera.

Enthusiasm for panoramic, or "stretch," pictures grew during the year. The format was achieved by the masking of a standard 24×36-mm frame of 35-mm film to expose a narrow (13-mm-wide) strip across the middle, covering a field of view about 78° across and producing a 90×255-mm ($3\frac{1}{2} \times 10$-in) print. Two new compact cameras with panoramic capability were the Olympus Infinity Zoom 220 Panorama with a 28–56-mm zoom lens and the Nikon Zoom Touch 600 with a 32–85-mm zoom lens. Both models allowed the user to switch between standard 35-mm format and the panoramic format at any time, even in mid roll.

Films from virtually all major manufacturers continued to be modified and improved. Among them Kodak Gold Plus 100 and Gold Plus 200 colour print films were said to provide an enhanced exposure latitude of -2 to $+3$ stops, reduced grain, and increased sharpness and colour saturation. Fuji announced the forthcoming replacement of its Super HG colour print films with a new trio of ISO 100, 200, and 400 Fuji Super G films while also claiming improved grain, sharpness, and colour quality. Polaroid's Polacolor 64 Tungsten was the first instant film balanced for 3,200 K (incandescent) illumination. Ilford's black-and-white 100 Delta film offered extremely fine grain and sharpness and could be used with an unusually wide range of developers.

JOHN KAPLAN

"Beatriz," a photograph of a single mother from Mexico living and working in the U.S., is one of a series on 21-year-olds by John Kaplan. He won the Pulitzer Prize in feature photography for the series.

"Jessie in the Wind" (1989) is one of the photographs of her children taken by Sally Mann over a period of eight years. Although some observers found her images disturbing or even pornographic, a New York show, a traveling exhibit, a new book, and wide publicity created great demand for Mann's photographs.
© SALLY MANN/HOUK FRIEDMAN, N.Y.

The previously announced Kodak Photo CD system became available to consumers. Developed by Eastman Kodak and Philips and licensed to numerous other manufacturers, the system was a technology for transferring conventional silver-halide photographic images onto high-definition compact discs (CDs), which could then be played back on a television set. Photo CD playback units and transfer service became available to the general public, while Kodak also announced a wide range of specialized professional applications of the system for industry, medicine, computer linkage, and archival purposes.

Cultural Trends. The exhibition "On the Edge: Photographs from 100 Years of Vogue" at the New York Public Library (and an accompanying book) provided a feast of changing fashions, visual styles, and social sensibilities in the form of more than 200 photographs by master photographers from Baron Adolphe de Meyer to Deborah Turbeville. "Manuel Alvarez Bravo" at the J. Paul Getty Museum in Malibu, Calif., included recently acquired vintage prints from this warmly humanistic 90-year-old Mexican photographer. "Arnold Newman's Americans" at the National Portrait Gallery in Washington, D.C., displayed 101 of its acquisitions of work by environmental portraiture's most consistently powerful practitioner.

"American Legends: An Exhibition of Recent Works by Yousuf Karsh," the noted portrait photographer who recently closed his world-famous studio in Ottawa, was displayed at New York City's International Center of Photography, as was "Motion and Document—Sequence and Time: Eadweard Muybridge and Contemporary American Photography," an ambitious attempt to trace the influence of this 19th-century pioneer in freezing motion.

"Paul Strand," a retrospective at the Whitney Museum of American Art in New York City, outlined the major stages of this American photographer and filmmaker from innovative formalism and leftist-oriented social documentaries to a latter-day pictorial romanticism. An exhibition jointly curated by the San Francisco Museum of Modern Art and New York City's Metropolitan Museum of Art displayed the gentle but perceptive vision of Helen Leavett, 78, whose street scenes document a time when urban life had a kinder face.

David Bailey's book *If We Shadows* included bizarre and disturbing images made since the early 1980s. *Ancient and Modern* by William Eggleston gave a retrospective look at Eggleston's style of colour documentation. In the cocktail-table-book category, Hiroji Kubota's *A Portrait of America* included spectacular panoramas of the U.S. coast to coast. *Cornell Capa: Photographs*, edited by Capa and Richard Whelan, showed the photojournalistic work of Robert Capa's younger brother and founder of the International Center of Photography.

The staff of the Associated Press won the 1992 Pulitzer Prize for spot news photography with its coverage of events in the former Soviet Union. The Pulitzer for feature photography went to John Kaplan of Block Newspapers for his picture essay on coming of age in America. At the 49th Pictures of the Year competition sponsored by the National Press Photographers Association and the University of Missouri School of Journalism, Christopher Morris, contract photographer for *Time* magazine, was named Magazine Photographer of the Year for his coverage of the Persian Gulf war and the violence in Yugoslavia; the Newspaper Photographer of the Year award went to Randy Olson of the *Pittsburgh* (Pa.) *Press*.

The image "Crying over a Friend's Death in the Gulf War" by David C. Turnley of *Detroit* (Mich.) *Free Press/Black Star* was chosen as the Press Photo of the Year 1991 at the 35th World Press Photo Contest 1992. At the International Center of Photography's eighth annual Infinity Awards program, Swedish photojournalist Lennart Nilsson received the Master of Photography Award for his remarkable medical and scientific photographs, while the Lifetime Achievement Award went to photojournalist and writer Carl Mydans.

Two renowned Japanese photographers died during the year. Taikichi Irie, 86, spent half a century photographing Buddhist images and landscapes in and around Nara, whose historical remains and institutions were rivaled only by those of Kyoto. Jun Miki, 72, was a pioneer in Japan of photography as art and as reporting, joining Time-Life in 1949 and later working as a free-lancer.   (ARTHUR GOLDSMITH)

See also Motion Pictures.

This article updates the *Macropædia* article PHOTOGRAPHY.

Physics

It is a rare event when discoveries in physics are reported in the press. It is rarer still that they are splashed over the front pages. But such was the intensity of coverage given by newspapers around the world, including the *New York Times* and *The Guardian,* to the announcement in April 1992 by a team of scientists led by George Smoot of the Lawrence Berkeley (Calif.) Laboratory of their detection of fluctuations in the cosmic background radiation that fills the universe. What stirred public interest was that the finding related directly back to the origins of galaxies and their organization into large-scale structures. In the words of Smoot, "we have observed the largest and oldest structures in the Universe."

According to the big bang theory, the universe was born about 15 billion years ago in a gigantic explosion. In its early stages of development, the universe was an unimaginably hot and dense cocktail of electromagnetic radiation and charged particles distributed uniformly in space. The radiation was in thermal equilibrium with the matter and had a continuous spectrum of frequencies, known as the blackbody spectrum, that was characteristic of the temperature of the universe at that time. As the universe expanded, its density and temperature dropped, and eventually neutral atoms (predominantly hydrogen) formed. After that time, matter was considerably less well coupled to the cosmic radiation and lost the ability to scatter the radiation at all wavelengths. Consequently, the frequency spectrum that is observed today is a legacy of the time period immediately following the big bang.

Since then, the radiation has changed only in that its characteristic temperature has dropped as the size of the universe has increased. The cosmic radiation was first discovered in 1965 and was found to be uniform in space with a characteristic temperature of 2.7 kelvins (K; −455° F, or −270° C). It was soon realized, however, that the structure observed in the universe today (stars, galaxies, clusters of galaxies, etc.) must have its origin in density fluctuations in the early universe, just as raindrops nucleate around small particles present in clouds. Furthermore, such minute inhomogeneities would have to show up subsequently as temperature fluctuations in the cosmic background. Prior to 1992, attempts to find the fluctuations had managed only to show how tiny they must be. The experiment reported by Smoot and co-workers differed from previous, ground-based ones in that the radiation detectors were in space, mounted aboard the Cosmic Background Explorer (COBE) satellite. Such space-based observations made the true cosmic radiation much easier to discriminate from terrestrial sources of radiation. COBE's data revealed variations of typically 15 microkelvins (15 millionths of a kelvin) on a background of 2.7 K; that is, deviations of less than one part in 100,000.

What was important about the results was not the existence of the temperature fluctuations (few doubted they would be found) but their amplitude, which was much too small to support conventional theories of galaxy formation. On the other hand, proponents of the so-called cold-dark-matter hypothesis claimed that the scale of the fluctuations was in line with their predictions. Dark matter had been proposed as a way to explain the missing-mass problem—the fact that the amount of matter observed in clusters of galaxies is much less than needed to bind them together gravitationally. Dark matter offered a means by which the universe could contain sufficient gravitational energy to override its present expansion and eventually collapse in on itself, thus avoiding what was thought by some to be

a philosophically difficult scenario of a universe with a beginning but no end. Dark matter is purported to be in the form of invisible particles that fill space and exert a gravitational effect on ordinary matter. Some cosmologists suggested that it plays a crucial role in galaxy formation by providing the gravitational fluctuations required for seeding growth without interacting with the cosmic radiation, thus rationalizing the minute amplitude of the observed temperature variations with the existence of stellar matter. The COBE observations gave much-needed information to those attempting to understand the early universe and fueled the search for dark matter.

One possible candidate for dark matter is neutrinos, uncharged elementary particles produced in certain nuclear reactions. This hypothesis remained unproved in 1992 since it was still not known whether neutrinos have mass and thus are able to interact gravitationally. Also unresolved in 1992, despite the results from important new studies, was another long-standing puzzle concerning neutrinos: the solar neutrino deficit. The problem in this case is that an experiment set up in a South Dakota mine and using chlorine atoms to detect neutrinos produced in the Sun's fusion reactions has, for more than two decades, consistently found fewer than half the neutrinos that standard solar models predict. Some theorists argued that the origin of the deficit lies in the Sun itself and that knowledge of conditions inside the Sun—the temperature, for example—is inaccurate. Others started with the fact that there exist three types of neutrinos (electron, muon, and tau neutrinos) and postulated that, if neutrinos do have a small mass, they may transform into each other as they travel through space, so that, for example, what started out from the centre of the Sun as an electron neutrino might reach Earth as a muon neutrino. Because the South Dakota experiment is sensitive only to electron neutrinos, their transformation to other types would help explain the deficit.

More recent experiments employed many tons of the element gallium, which has broader energy sensitivity to electron neutrinos than does chlorine, as detector material. These experiments were again situated deep underground to avoid spurious signals from cosmic-ray–induced background radiation. Solar neutrinos convert some of the gallium into germanium, the rate of conversion being proportional to the flux of incident neutrinos. According to the best models, the rate of detection of solar neutrinos should be around 130 solar neutrino units (SNU), in which one SNU represents one neutrino capture per second for every 10^{36} gallium atoms. In 1990 one gallium experiment called SAGE, run by a Soviet-American team at the Baksan Neutrino Observatory in the Caucasus, reported a detection rate of 20 SNU, but the uncertainty in the figure was at least 20 SNU. A more recent result came from GALLEX, an international collaboration working at the Gran Sasso Laboratory in Italy, which in mid-1992 reported a rate of 83 SNU, again with an uncertainty of more than 20 SNU. Thus it seemed that although these results were still below the theoretical prediction, those from GALLEX were sufficiently close to it (and sufficiently far apart from those from SAGE) to prevent scientists from reaching any firm conclusions. Solar physicists eagerly awaited completion of the next generation of neutrino counters.

The field of high-energy physics, which includes the production of subatomic particles terrestrially in gigantic accelerators, suffered mixed fortunes in 1992. One major new project in the U.S., the Superconducting Super Collider (SSC), a circular accelerator 87 km (54 mi) in circumference to be built in Texas and designed to accelerate protons to enormous speeds and then to collide them, suffered a setback when the U.S. House of Representatives voted to supply only sufficient funds to wind the project down. The SSC was later reprieved by the Senate, but its future remained precarious. On a brighter note, a new high-energy facility, HERA (Hadron Electron Ring Accelerator), located beneath the streets of Hamburg, Germany, began operation. HERA enables electrons and protons in countercirculating beams to collide in such a way as to probe interactions having a spatial scale of 10^{-19} m (about one ten-thousandth the diameter of an atomic nucleus). At such scales a great deal of information was expected to be gained on the quarks and leptons, subatomic particles believed to be the most fundamental constituents of matter. Current wisdom held that quarks, the building blocks of such particles as protons and neutrons, come in six types, of which only five had been directly observed by 1992.

Controversy surrounded the claim by a British group at the University of Oxford that the existence of the sixth quark, the so-called top quark, had already been proved from data taken at Fermi National Accelerator Laboratory near Chicago. The difficulty for scientists in accepting the claimed proof was that it inferred the existence of the top quark only indirectly, from characteristic patterns of other particles generated in high-energy collisions. Much depended on the method of analysis used, and the group that originally took the data did not necessarily accept the approach adopted by the British scientists. It is not difficult to understand the driving force behind such claims. The sixth quark is the last missing piece in currently accepted description of matter, and its discovery would be a truly historic occasion.   (ANDREW T. BOOTHROYD)

This article updates the *Macropædia* articles THE COSMOS; ELECTROMAGNETIC RADIATION; PARTICLE ACCELERATORS; SOLAR SYSTEM: *The Sun;* SUBATOMIC PARTICLES; THE PHYSICAL SCIENCES: *Physics.*

Populations and Population Movements

DEMOGRAPHY

At midyear 1992 world population stood at 5,420,000,000, according to estimates prepared by the Population Reference Bureau. This represented an increase of about 91 million over the previous year. Despite decreases in the birthrate in many less developed countries (LDCs), the number of people added to the world's population had yet to peak. Currently, the number of Earth's inhabitants was rising by nearly one billion each decade. This rise was all the more remarkable in view of the fact that world population numbered only 2.5 billion in 1950, a sum that had taken all of human history to accumulate. The current increase of one billion every 10 years would have been even greater had birthrates not declined in many LDCs after the 1970s.

In 1992, 386,900 babies were born every day and 137,-500 persons died, leading to a daily increase of 249,400. This meant that each month the world's population rose by 7,482,000, equivalent to the population of Bolivia. The overall rate of population growth was estimated to have declined slightly, from about 1.72% in 1991 to about 1.68%. This conclusion, however, was heavily dependent on the availability and reliability of data from LDCs. In particular, the large populations of China and India, which make up almost half the LDC total, exerted heavy statistical weight on world rates. In mid-1992 China's population totaled 1,166,-000,000 and India reached 883 million. The decrease in the world population growth rate noted above was due primarily to a small decline in China's birthrate during 1991 and to a small drop in the more developed countries (MDCs). In China this may have resulted from some couples' postpon-

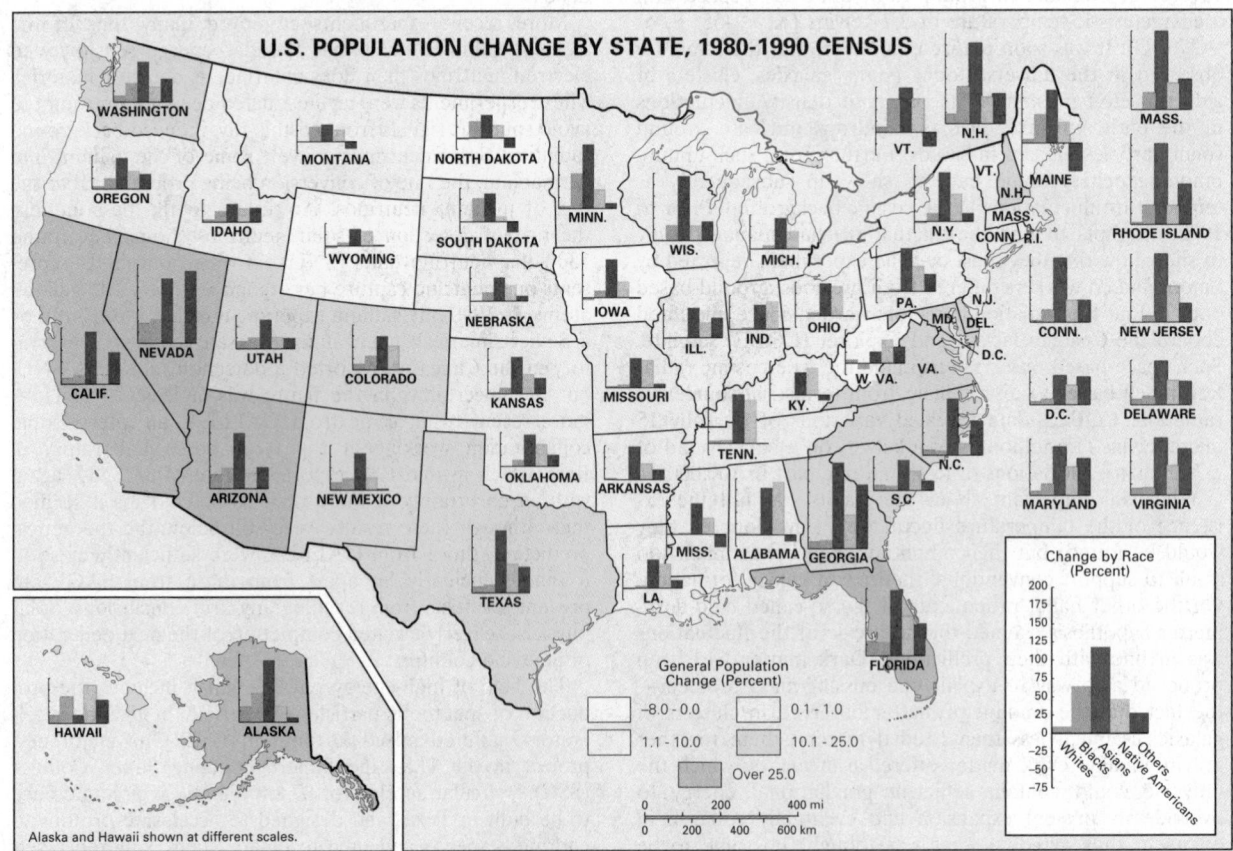

U.S. POPULATION CHANGE BY STATE, 1980-1990 CENSUS

General Population Change (Percent)

−8.0 - 0.0   0.1 - 1.0
1.1 - 10.0   10.1 - 25.0
Over 25.0

Change by Race (Percent)

Alaska and Hawaii shown at different scales.

ing births from the Year of the Sheep to the Year of the Monkey, considered to be more favourable. The decrease in the growth rate in the MDCs was due largely to a drop in the birthrate in the countries of the former U.S.S.R.

Few events in 1992 illustrated the uncertain nature of data from LDCs as dramatically as the release of the census count of Africa's most populous country, Nigeria. This large West African nation was one of the few countries in the world without usable census data, and the November 1991 census was planned as the nation's first reliable count. Previous attempts at censuses had been marred by often grossly inflated figures as the country's states competed for political influence and a larger share of federal revenue. The country's population had been estimated at anywhere from 109 million to 125 million. The actual count was a shockingly low 88.5 million, but doubts remained about the quality of this count as well. The population growth rate of the three billion people living in all LDCs except China remained unchanged from 1991 to 1992 at about 2.3% annually. If maintained, the population of these countries would double in just 30 years. In many countries, decreases in the birthrate were offset by similar declines in the death rate as life expectancy rose and infant mortality fell.

In 1992 the UN issued its latest series of world population projections. World population was put at 6,228,000,000 in 2000 and 8,472,000,000 by 2025. These prognoses, essentially the same as previous UN projections, indicated that rapid population growth would continue for some time. World population would reach the six billion mark early in 1998, just 11 years after reaching five billion. The UN projections assumed a gradually declining birthrate in the LDCs. The UN also issued a long-range-projections series during 1992, projecting world and regional population to the year 2150. The "medium" series, often considered the "most likely" projection, showed world population stabilizing at about 11.5 billion in 2150. A similar projection from the World Bank resulted in an even higher total, 12.5 billion. Such long-range projections are quite risky, and the UN warned that its other series, which showed a possible world population varying anywhere from 6 billion to 28 billion, were equally likely.

Worldwide, nearly all population growth took place in the LDCs. In Japan considerable concern was voiced over low fertility. For women in Japan, the total fertility rate (TFR; the average number of children a woman would bear given that year's rate of childbearing) was only 1.6. Such low fertility leads not only to a decline in population size but also to problems associated with a rising proportion of aged and a decrease in the numbers of young persons entering the labour force. The situation was much the same in Europe. In 1992 the European TFR also stood at 1.6. In northern and western Europe, areas where the birthrate had long been the world's lowest, there were some modest increases in 1992. The TFR in Sweden, which captured attention by rising to 2.1 from a low of 1.6 in the mid-1980s, appeared to have peaked. Surprisingly, fertility was lowest in Italy and Spain, where the TFR stood at a very low 1.3. In the new nations of eastern Europe and the former U.S.S.R., the birthrate tended to fall, possibly in reaction to the uncertain state of the economy and the political situation. The number of births fell by 50% in former East Germany. Throughout Europe, however, the overriding demographic issue in 1992 was not the low birthrate but immigration policy. (See *International Migration,* below.)

In the LDCs declines in national birthrates continued to gather some momentum, although the pattern was uneven. Sub-Saharan Africa, whose countries were among the last to label rapid population growth a problem, showed some

evidence of the beginnings of a birthrate decline. An increasing number of fertility surveys documented this trend, but women in sub-Saharan Africa still averaged over six children each. East and Southeast Asia and Latin America continued to evidence lower birthrates. In both Southeast Asia and Latin America, the TFR was 3.5. The record in South Asia was more uneven. South Asia's TFR stood at 4.3, ranging from 2.4 in Sri Lanka and 3.9 in India to 6.1 in Iran, Nepal, and Pakistan. It appeared that India's birthrate might have begun to decline once again, although very slowly. For Asia as a whole, the TFR was 3.3 including China (where it was 2.2) and 3.9 excluding China. UN projections assumed that much of the momentum in family planning would continue.

In 1992 life expectancy at birth worldwide averaged 63 for males and 67 for females. The corresponding figures for MDCs were 71 and 78 and, for LDCs, 61 and 64. Once again, Japan reported the highest life expectancy, 76 years for men and 82.1 for women. Worldwide, 43% of the population lived in places defined as urban, generally towns with a population of 2,000 or more. The infant mortality rate was 68 infant deaths per 1,000 live births, a rate that varied from 4.6 in Japan to over 100 in many countries of Africa and Asia. One-third of the world's people were under 15 years of age, and 6% were 65 or older, essentially the same as the previous year. In the LDCs, 36% were under 15 and only 4% over 65. In the MDCs, only 21% were under 15 and 12% were over 65. The overall figures masked much variation at the national level. In many countries of Africa, half or even more of the population was below 15, providing a huge potential for future population growth.

In 1992 the U.S. replaced the U.S.S.R. as the world's third most populous country, behind China and India. Russia, the largest of the former Soviet republics at 149.3 million, dropped into sixth place, behind Indonesia (184 million) and Brazil (150 million). The population of the U.S. stood at 255,414,000 on July 1, 1992, including armed forces overseas. This represented an increase of 6,189,000 since the 1990 census. From July 1, 1991, to July 1, 1992, the population grew by about 1.1%. About 2 million of the rise was due to natural increase—births minus deaths—and the remaining 720,000 to immigration.

Birth Statistics. The National Center for Health Statistics reported a provisional 4,111,000 U.S. births in 1991, slightly less than the 4,179,000 births in 1990 (the highest number since 1964). Recent increases in fertility resulted from a somewhat higher proportional increase among women over 30, but rates for all age groups rose. The crude birthrate fell from 16.7 births per 1,000 population in 1990 to 16.2 in 1991, and the U.S. TFR probably fell to 2.0, down from 1990's 2.1. For over a decade, the U.S. TFR had been at a level that would result in a lifetime average of 1.8 children per woman, well below the replacement level.

The total fertility rate was 1.89 among white women in 1989, up from 1.81 the previous year. Comparable figures for blacks were 2.54 and 2.40, respectively. A record 1,094,169 births in 1989 were to unmarried women. The proportion of all births to unmarried women also climbed to a new high, 27.1%. Although the gap between whites and blacks had narrowed somewhat on this measure, black women still had a substantially higher proportion of extramarital births, 65.7% as compared with 19.2% for whites.

Death Statistics. There were 2,165,000 deaths provisionally reported in the U.S. in 1991, compared with 1990's 2,162,000. The crude death rate in 1991 was down slightly from 1990, from 8.6 deaths per 1,000 population to 8.5. The 1991 age-adjusted death rate (year ended November) was the lowest in the country's history, 507.1 deaths per 100,000

World's 25 Most Populous Urban Areas[1]

Rank	City and Country	City proper Population	Year	Metropolitan area Population	Year
1	Tokyo, Japan	8,154,404	1991 est.	29,200,000	1990 est.
2	New York City, U.S.	7,322,564	1990 cen.	18,087,251	1990 cen.
3	Seoul, South Korea	10,627,790	1990 cen.	17,588,000	1989 est.
4	Osaka, Japan	2,613,199	1991 est.	16,210,000	1990 est.
5	São Paulo, Brazil	9,480,427[2]	1991 cen.	15,199,423	1991 cen.
6	Mexico City, Mexico	8,261,951[3]	1990 cen.	14,991,281	1990 cen.
7	Los Angeles, U.S.	3,536,800	1991 est.	14,531,529	1990 cen.
8	Shanghai, China	7,496,509	1990 cen.	13,341,896	1990 cen.
9	Bombay, India	9,909,547	1991 cen.	12,571,720	1991 cen.
10	London, U.K.	6,377,900	1991 cen.	12,275,600	1989 est.
11	Calcutta, India	4,388,262	1991 cen.	10,916,272	1991 cen.
12	Buenos Aires, Arg.	2,960,976	1991 cen.	10,887,355	1991 cen.
13	Beijing, China	5,769,607	1990 cen.	10,819,407	1990 cen.
14	Rio de Janeiro, Brazil	9,600,524[2]	1991 cen.	9,600,525	1991 cen.
15	Paris, France	2,175,110	1990 cen.	9,060,000	1990 cen.
16	Moscow, Russia	8,801,500	1991 est.	8,967,000	1989 cen.
17	Tianjin, China	4,574,689	1990 cen.	8,785,402	1990 cen.
18	Cairo, Egypt	6,452,000	1990 est.	8,761,927	1986 cen.
19	Nagoya, Japan	2,158,784	1991 est.	8,432,000	1990 est.
20	Delhi, India	7,174,755	1991 cen.	8,375,188	1991 cen.
21	Jakarta, Indonesia	[4]		8,254,000	1990 cen.
22	Chicago, U.S.	2,783,726	1990 cen.	8,065,633	1990 cen.
23	Manila, Philippines	1,587,000	1990 cen.	7,832,000	1990 cen.
24	Karachi, Pakistan	5,208,132	1981 cen.	7,702,000	1990 cen.
25	Tehran, Iran	[4]		6,773,000	1990 est.

[1]Ranked by population of metropolitan area.
[2]*Municipio*, an officially delimited area including a central city and adjacent
   urban and rural districts.
[3]Federal District.
[4]Administrative unit within which a separate city proper is not distinguished.

population. The 15 major causes of death accounted for 86% of all deaths. Human immunodeficiency virus infection (AIDS) jumped to the 9th leading cause of death, up from 11th in 1990.

	Causes of death	Estimated rate per 100,000 population
1.	Diseases of the heart	282.2
2.	Malignant neoplasms	203.4
3.	Cerebrovascular diseases	56.4
4.	Accidents and adverse effects	35.2
5.	Chronic obstructive pulmonary diseases	34.6
6.	Pneumonia and influenza	29.3
7.	Diabetes mellitus	19.6
8.	Suicide	11.3
9.	Human immunodeficiency virus infection	11.3
10.	Homicide and legal intervention	10.3
11.	Chronic liver disease and cirrhosis	9.8
12.	Nephritis, nephrotic syndrome, and nephrosis	9.0
13.	Septicemia	7.6
14.	Atherosclerosis	6.8
15.	Certain conditions originating in the perinatal period	6.6

Life Expectancy. Life expectancy at birth in the U.S. reached a record high 75.4 years in 1990. The highest life expectancy was enjoyed by white females, 79.3 years. Next in order were black females 74.5 years, white males 72.6 years, and black males a low 66.0. U.S. life expectancy was equal to the European average but was surpassed by at least 15 other countries.

Infant Mortality. Infant mortality in the U.S. reached another new low in 1991, 8.9 infant deaths per 1,000 live births. Worldwide, the U.S. ranked about 20th out of the world's approximately 220 countries. A wide gap in U.S. infant mortality between whites and blacks remained. In 1989, the latest year for which data were available, infant mortality was 8.2 for whites and 17.7 for blacks. Worldwide, about 9,554,000 infants died, 9,249,000 in the LDCs and 305,000 in the MDCs.

Marriage and Divorce Statistics. There were 2,371,000 marriages in the U.S. in 1991, slightly fewer than the 2,448,-000 in 1990. The marriage rate, 9.4 per 1,000 population, was somewhat lower than 1990's 9.8. The number of divorces rose from 1,175,000 in 1990 to 1,187,000.

Censuses. Census results were reported from Ecuador (9,648,189), Bangladesh (104,766,143), Thailand (54,532,-300), Spain (38,425,679), and New Zealand (3,434,949).

(CARL V. HAUB)

See also World Data.

INTERNATIONAL MIGRATION

The worsening political and economic situation in large parts of the world increased the scale of international migration during 1992. The displacement of millions of people in many instances involved some of the poorest countries of the world. Yemen accepted between 50,000 and 100,000 Somalis fleeing war and famine. Kenya was estimated to have over 230,000 Somali and Ethiopian refugees and, according to the UN High Commissioner for Refugees, had become "a major country of asylum." Bangladesh had received over 300,000 refugees from Myanmar's Rohingya Muslim community. Algeria was sheltering an estimated 50,000 Arab and Tuareg refugees from Mali—adding to the estimated 250,000 refugees in the region since the severe drought hit the Sahara in the mid-1980s. The massive displacement of foreign workers from Kuwait continued to affect population movements in the region. Jordan, for example, had received 250,000–300,000 of the estimated 350,000 Palestinians who fled, or were expelled from, Kuwait.

In 1991 total immigration into Western Europe was more than one million, including around 220,000 ethnic Germans from eastern Europe and the former Soviet Union who were able to migrate to Germany and to acquire immediate citizenship. During the year there were 540,000 asylum-seekers registered, which was nearly twice the 1989 figure and more than three times that of 1987. Germany received 256,000 asylum-seekers, and Austria recorded 27,000, which represented a higher per capita rate than that of Germany. Switzerland received 41,600 applications, and Sweden registered 26,500. The largest industrialized countries spent $7 billion–$8 billion in 1991 on dealing with asylum-seekers from the Third World and eastern Europe. There was an increasing level of racist violence and political activity directed against immigrants, asylum-seekers, and refugees. (*See* RACE RELATIONS.) Western European governments responded with a range of measures designed to limit the rights of asylum for asylum-seekers.

In Germany a controversial law aimed at speeding up asylum procedures and allowing refugees to be housed in "collection camps" came into force on July 1, 1992. The law concentrated power over asylum-seekers and deportations in the central government and stipulated that applications that were "obviously unfounded" had to be dealt with within six weeks, after which unsuccessful applicants would be sent back. The head of Germany's central office for the recognition of refugees resigned in June in protest against the new law. There was controversy over Germany's decision to require visas for Bosnians fleeing the war in former Yugoslavia, as it had not required them for citizens of Croatia and Slovenia. Another controversy flared up over the government's treaty with Romania, signed on September 24, allowing Germany to deport thousands of Romanian refugees, most of whom were Romanies ("Gypsies"), while paying Romania $21 million in "return and reintegration aid." It was estimated that about 20% of the 280,000 foreigners who had sought asylum in Germany in the first 10 months of 1992 came from Romania, and about 60% of these were Romanies.

The British government, which had withdrawn its 1991 Asylum Bill because of the timing of the April 1992 general election, reintroduced the legislation under a new title, the Asylum and Immigration Appeals Bill. It would restrict the right of appeal for visitors refused entry and extend from one year to four the period for which spouses who applied to join their U.K. wives or husbands had to stay married.

The British and Vietnamese governments signed an agreement on May 12, 1992, to forcibly repatriate all Vietnamese boat people in Hong Kong found not to be political refugees. Of the more than 52,000 Vietnamese being held in Hong Kong detention camps as of the end of July, 24,319 were awaiting repatriation, 24,646 still had to go through the screening process, and 3,186 had been classified as legitimate refugees.

In Australia the immigration minister announced a cut in immigration by 25% in 1993, the biggest cut in almost 20 years. In 1992–93 no more than 80,000 immigrants would be allowed in—down from 111,000 for 1991–92—and of the 80,000 more than half, 45,000 places, were to be earmarked for immigrants with relatives already in Australia. Canada's immigration minister introduced proposals in June to speed up the processing of some cases while at the same time giving immigration officers new powers to turn away applicants for refugee status and limiting the right of appeal against Immigration and Refugee Board decisions.

An executive order issued by Pres. George Bush in May that Haitian boat people picked up at sea be returned to Haiti immediately was, in effect, nullified by a federal appeals court and reinstated by the U.S. Supreme Court. However, with President-elect Bill Clinton appearing to take a more lenient view toward the boat people, the direction of U.S. policy was unclear at year's end. It was estimated that about 35,000 Haitians had been picked up by U.S. ships since October 1991.   (LOUIS KUSHNICK)

REFUGEES

As of mid-1992, it was estimated that there were some 17 million refugees worldwide. Although the trend, pattern, and overall magnitude of refugee movements remained comparatively stable, refugee influxes during the year required the establishment of emergency assistance programs as well as care and maintenance assistance provided by the UN High Commissioner for Refugees (UNHCR).

The situation in the Horn of Africa deteriorated dramatically during 1991–92, with thousands of refugees leaving Somalia and southern Ethiopia for Kenya. By the end of May 1992, the refugee population in Kenya had reached 280,000. Events in Somalia also led to the massive return home of some 450,000 Ethiopian refugees, triggering a large-scale repatriation program organized by UNHCR and other UN organizations. Services were also provided to a number of Ethiopian refugees in The Sudan and to some 200,000 Sudanese refugees who had been forced by events to return home unwillingly from western Ethiopia. Djibouti also was host to some 91,500 refugees.

Severe drought and political turmoil contributed to refugee problems in Africa. The already serious situation in Malawi, which was host to one million Mozambican refugees, was exacerbated by the worst drought in living memory. Political turbulence in West Africa, notably in Liberia, led to assistance programs' being set up in neighbouring countries to cope with the flow of refugees. Conflict in Sierra Leone caused refugees to flee to Guinea (175,-000) and Liberia (21,000). UNHCR's intervention was also needed when events in Burundi and Zaire led to refugee outflows.

In Central America the majority of refugees repatriated voluntarily, especially from Costa Rica to Nicaragua, from Mexico to Guatemala, and from various countries to El Salvador. Several refugee camps were closed, including all in Costa Rica and the last remaining one in Honduras. In the region's three main asylum countries, Belize, Costa Rica, and Mexico, UNHCR provided assistance to some 58,000 registered refugees, a figure that was expected to gradually decrease owing to voluntary repatriation. There was also a considerable movement among Haitians seeking asylum in

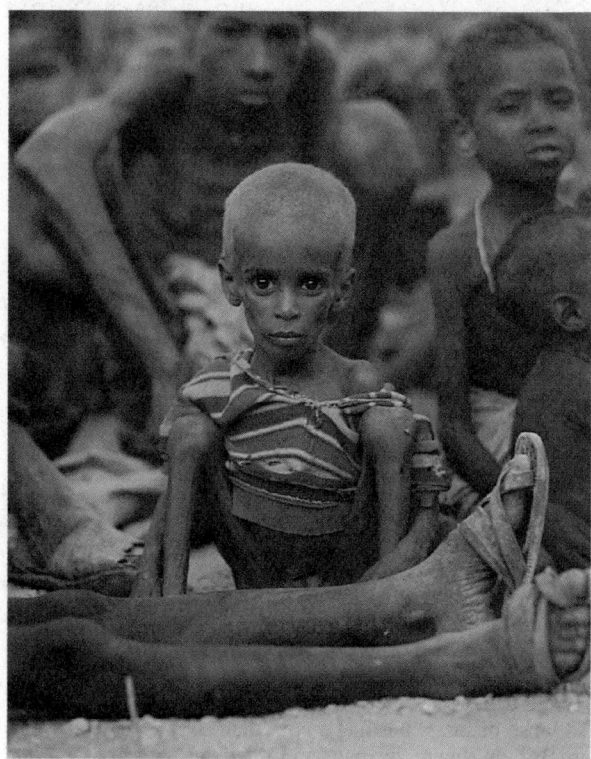

A starving child who has been orphaned waits in a village in Somalia. Suffering from severe famine made even worse by rampant anarchy, thousands of Somalis fled their country in 1992 in an often futile attempt to find food and safety elsewhere.
PETER TURNLEY—BLACK STAR

nearby countries following the overthrow of Haiti's democratically elected government in September 1991.

Following the signing (1991) of a comprehensive political settlement of the Cambodia conflict, a voluntary repatriation of some 370,000 Cambodian refugees and displaced persons began in March 1992. As of September 1, UNHCR had repatriated some 100,000 Cambodians from camps along the Thailand border.

Considerable progress was made in implementing the Comprehensive Plan of Action on Indo-Chinese Refugees adopted in 1989. The number of arrivals of Vietnamese asylum-seekers in Hong Kong and other countries in Southeast Asia dropped following a mass information campaign, announcements of reduced cash assistance, and implementation of a program of returning Vietnamese determined not to be refugees to Vietnam.

Lao refugees continued to repatriate voluntarily, bringing the total since 1980 to 10,000. However, some 64,000 others remained in camps in Thailand. In 1991–92 an increasing number of refugees from Myanmar (Burma) fled to Bangladesh and, as of the end of March 1992, the figure had reached 190,000. During 1991 refugees from Bhutan began arriving in Nepal. As of March 1992, the number had risen to 30,000.

Upheavals in Europe, beginning in 1991, led to enormous changes both in the region and in the response of the international community. The situation in former Yugoslavia produced the largest number of refugees and displaced persons (some two million) since the end of World War II. As of mid-1992, thousands were fleeing daily, not only from the conflict itself but from massive human rights abuses, especially "ethnic cleansing." As the lead UN agency for humanitarian relief, UNHCR took on a large-scale relief operation in collaboration with UNICEF, the World Health

Organization, and the International Committee of the Red Cross.

In Western Europe the numbers of asylum-seekers continued to increase, creating backlogs in asylum applications, a strain on reception centres, and xenophobic and racist attitudes among the local population. As a result, many governments introduced legislation not only to speed up the determination process and harmonize asylum procedures but also to impose more controls and sanctions.

In southwestern Asia over one million Afghan refugees returned home, out of a total of 3.2 million in Pakistan and some three million in Iran. In the second half of 1991, as a result of the Persian Gulf conflict, some 1.8 million Iraqi refugees fled to Iran and Turkey. A large-scale emergency air-transport operation was set up, but by December 1991 some 90% of the refugees had returned to Iraq.   (UNHCR)

This article updates the *Macropædia* article POPULATION.

Publishing

Newspapers. The year 1992 was a gloomy one, dominated by ever deepening recession. With advertising revenue continuing to flag, there was strong competition for sales and heavy reliance on such gimmicks as royal scandal stories and pictures of Madonna.

The death of Robert Maxwell in November 1991 and the collapse of his publishing empire had serious repercussions in Britain, where he had controlled the country's second largest newspaper company, Mirror Group Newspapers, owners of three mass market tabloids, *The Daily Mirror, Sunday Mirror,* and *The People.* This proprietorial power passed to a group of bankers, led by Lloyds Bank, which effectively assumed control over 54% of the newspaper group's equity.

The MGN papers were seen as filling a key role in British public life because of their support, since World War II, of the Labour Party. This political stance was in evidence prior to the U.K. general election in April, when the papers' support of Labour was in marked contrast to the rest of the popular press, dominated by Rupert Murdoch's News International. The latter published *The Sun,* the largest-selling daily, and *The News of the World,* the largest-circulation Sunday paper, both fervent Conservative supporters. After the Conservative victory, *The Sun*'s front page crowed: "It's us wot won it."

In October the MGN board installed a new chief executive, David Montgomery, formerly with Murdoch's midmarket daily tabloid *Today.* Within three weeks he had replaced all three MGN editors, culminating on November 15 with the dismissal of Richard Stott, editor of the *Daily Mirror,* and his replacement by David Banks, recruited at short notice from Murdoch's Australian newspaper chain. This was followed by the instant termination of 100 contract journalists, a move designed to save money. The paper pledged its continuing support to Labour policies, but this was met with skepticism by old hands, who predicted the demise of a great British institution. The papers remained in a state of high tension and might be put up for sale.

One outcome of the battle for circulation was fevered reporting of the woes of the British royal family, an interest fanned by their obvious marital difficulties. This renewed a sharp debate over the conduct of the British press, one of Europe's most unrestrained, and the right of royals and other public figures, including politicians, to some privacy. In November the queen herself, declaring 1992 to have been an "annus horribilis," made a plea for gentler, more understanding treatment. In July the British government asked senior lawyer Sir David Calcutt to reopen his inquiry into British press standards to see how revived self-regulation, under a new Press Complaints Commission and newspaper ombudsmen, was working in practice. The findings were due to be published early in 1993.

Interest in the royal family rose to fever pitch in July with the serialization of Andrew Morton's book *Diana: Her True Story* in Murdoch's *The Sunday Times.* This was followed by publication of two secretly recorded telephone conversations, one purported to be between the princess and her friend James Gilbey, the other between Prince Charles and his friend Camilla Parker-Bowles. The use of secretly recorded phone calls in a third case, involving a government minister, David Mellor, and his lover, Antonia De Sancha, resulted in his resignation from the Cabinet in September. Within Europe generally, there was much comment about the paparazzi—photographers who stalk the stars—fueled by sensational pictures of a topless Duchess of York and her adviser, Texas millionaire John Bryan, at a villa outside Saint-Tropez. The photographs were printed worldwide, but the debate illustrated differences within the European press as the continent moved toward a single market. In Spain an unspoken ban protected the monarchy from invasion or unfriendly comment, while in France the personal lives of politicians were generally off limits. In December a French court ruled that publication of the photographs infringed the country's privacy laws and awarded the duchess and Bryan $130,000 in damages from the magazine *Paris-Match.*

In Spain, unlike the rest of Europe, newspaper sales were experiencing an exceptional boom. *El País,* the country's leading daily, reported that in 1992 Spaniards bought more than 105 papers per 1,000 population. Previously, the average had never risen above 90. (This compared with a European average of 232 daily papers sold per 1,000 population.) In November *El País* expressed its confidence by launching an edition in France.

The editorship of *The Times,* voice of the British establishment, changed hands, with Simon Jenkins succeeded by Peter Stothard. At *The Daily Mail,* Britain's most successful middle-market tabloid, Sir David English was succeeded as editor by Paul Dacre.   (MAGGIE BROWN)

After years of softening readership and sobering financial news, U.S. newspapers began to show scattered signs of renewed vigour. The change was not immediately visible in the bottom line, though advertising and circulation revenues at many dailies did rise slightly, partly because the cost of newsprint remained relatively low. What was apparent was a new sense of purpose in the industry. Having long done little more than worry aloud about how theirs was a declining medium, editors and publishers were beginning to take bold steps to reverse the decline.

"Reinventing" the newspaper became a buzzword in the industry in 1992. A number of major chains, as well as some individual dailies, launched ambitious programs to redesign their pages and redeploy their editorial staffs to plunge into the unfamiliar waters of electronic information. A major motivating factor was the growing likelihood that the nation's giant regional telephone operating companies would enter the information business. Recent court decisions and regulatory actions had cleared the way for the Baby Bells, as they were called, to transmit news and advertising directly to their customers' homes electronically, using telephone lines. At the same time, opinion surveys continued to show that more and more Americans, especially young people, were getting their news from electronic media and losing the newspaper-reading habit.

Typical of the attempts to "reinvent" the newspaper was Gannett's News 2000 program, under which editors of the chain's 81 dailies were ordered to develop local blueprints for making their papers more relevant to readers. At the *Springfield* (Mo.) *News-Leader,* for example, extensive research was conducted to see what readers wanted from the paper, which was accordingly redesigned to include more charts and livelier graphics, shorter stories, and fewer "jumps" of an article from one page to another. The changes, which resembled design features of Gannett's pioneering *USA Today,* were introduced early in 1992. The Knight-Ridder chain's 25/43 Project (named for the commercially important 25-to-43 age group) was launched in 1989 with the chain's *Boca Raton* (Fla.) *News* as a test case. After extensive reader research, the paper shortened stories, added indexes to make news easier to find, and introduced seven alternating daily tabloid sections on themes like "Parent and Child." By 1992 the paper's circulation had risen 10%.

Some dailies, realizing that their newspapers were, in effect, enormous data bases, began to examine the possibility of entering the electronic information business themselves. Several papers began producing newsletters that were delivered by fax. Others introduced telephone services that provided such information as sports scores and stock-price quotations. Still others began offering back issues on the CD-ROM data-storage and retrieval system. Whether all this would halt the medium's slow decline would not be known for years. Critics complained that the movement was producing newspapers with more style but less substance. Other analysts noted that such trends as the rising disinclination of young Americans to read anything and the decline of downtown department stores and their advertising were essentially beyond the newspapers' control.

In any case, "reinvention" had not yet slowed the decline in the total number of newspapers in the U.S. According to the *1992 Editor & Publisher Yearbook,* that figure dropped by 24, to 1,586; 29 dailies ceased publication, and only 5 new ones started. Total circulation fell by 2.6% to 60,-687,125. The nearly two-decade-long trend toward morning publication continued, as did the proliferation of Sunday newspapers. There was a net gain of 12 Sunday papers for the year, although total Sunday circulation declined slightly to about 62 million.

One newspaper that came close to disappearing was the tabloid *New York Daily News,* once the nation's largest daily but crippled in recent years by labour problems, financial difficulties, and declining readership and left rudderless by the death of its owner, Robert Maxwell. At the end of 1992, with the paper on the brink of extinction, it appeared likely that it would be sold to a wealthy real estate developer, Mortimer Zuckerman, who also owned the magazines *U.S. News & World Report* and *The Atlantic Monthly.*

The 1992 Pulitzer Prize for Public Service was awarded to the *Sacramento* (Calif.) *Bee* for Tom Knudson's five-part series on pollution and overdevelopment in the Sierra Nevada. Other Pulitzers went to Lorraine Adams and Dan Malone of the *Dallas* (Texas) *Morning News* (investigative reporting) for a 20-part series on civil rights violations by Texas law-enforcement officials; *New York Newsday* (spot news reporting) for coverage of a fatal New York City subway derailment; *Newsday*'s Patrick J. Sloyan (international reporting) for his dispatches from the postwar Persian Gulf; Jeff Taylor and Mike McGraw of the *Kansas City* (Mo.) *Star* (national reporting) for a critical report on the U.S. Agriculture Department; Deborah Blum of the *Sacramento Bee* (beat reporting) for her science coverage; Howell Raines of the *New York Times* (feature writing) for a reminiscence of his friendship with a family housekeeper during his Alabama boyhood and their meeting more than 30 years later; the *New York Times*'s Anna Quindlen (commentary); Maria Henson of the *Lexington* (Ky.) *Herald-Leader* (editorial writing) for her editorials on the problems of battered women; Signe Wilkinson of the *Philadelphia Daily News* (editorial cartooning); John Kaplan (feature photography) for photo essays in several newspapers depicting how 21-year-olds live across the U.S.; the Associated Press staff (spot news photography) for photos of the attempted coup in Russia; and Robert S. Capers and Eric Lipton of the *Hartford* (Conn.) *Courant* (explanatory journalism) for articles on the U.S. space program. (DONALD MORRISON)

Magazines. Although the trend toward publishing local versions of successful magazines slowed, this did not deter Gruner & Jahr, one of Germany's biggest publishing houses, which spawned editions of its most successful titles throughout Europe. In November it launched *Focus,* a new British men's monthly, brimming with articles about computers and science. It was based on the German mass market *PM* (full title, *Peter Moosleitners' Interesting Magazine*), French and Spanish versions of which had been introduced in the 1980s.

Gloria Steinem launched a British edition of the U.S. feminist magazine *Ms.,* but with a modest initial print run of 30,000 copies. This was in contrast to the spate of soft pornographic magazines for British women. The market was saturated during 1992 with three titles from publisher Northern & Shell: *For Women* (monthly), *Women on Top,* and *Women Only* (both bimonthly), all with initial print runs of 750,000. There was also a launch of a European edition of *Playgirl.* In a recession it seemed that sex still sold.

The humour magazine *Punch,* once a British institution but fallen on evil times, ceased publication. (See *Sidebar.*) (MAGGIE BROWN)

U.S. first cat-elect Socks is hemmed in by photographers outside the governor's mansion in Little Rock, Ark. Despite President-elect Bill Clinton's plea for privacy for his daughter and her cat, the press used catnip to lure Socks within camera range.

The most stunning news of the year in the U.S. magazine world struck when *The New Yorker* named Tina Brown (*see* BIOGRAPHIES), the controversial head of *Vanity Fair,* as its new editor in chief. Speculation spread like wildfire as to how she might change *The New Yorker*'s brand of prestigious, sophisticated journalism. The record breaker of the year was the $55,000 paid at auction for a 1939 comic that featured the debut of Batman; the auction of 250 comics made $1.2 million. The usual sorrowful news for librarians was that the average price of a periodical rose over 12% to $117 in 1992, compared with an average price of $104 in 1991.

Despite the recession gloom, some publishers profited. Amy Dacyczyn's *The Tightwad Gazette,* a monthly newsletter featuring commonsense product advice and tips on saving money, doubled its readership. The editor hoped it would become the *Whole Earth Catalog* of the '90s. Also apparently recession-proof were bridal magazines, all of which reported better-than-average sales.

Defying long odds and a slumping market, several new titles appeared. The bimonthly *Earth* was a first attempt to publish a popular earth science title. *The MultiCultural Review* was a guide for laypersons and librarians trying to develop book and magazine collections for various ethnic groups. Perhaps the most unusual entry—*Journal of Nursing Jocularity*—was a quarterly by and for nurses (as well as many patients) featuring the lighter side of hospital care. Decidedly down-market titles such as *CrimeBeat,* "the news magazine of crime," entered the competition to catch the attention of shoppers in checkout lines.

National Magazine Award winners included *National Geographic* for general interest excellence; *The New Republic,* cited for lucid analysis and sophisticated reporting; *Texas Monthly* for chronicling "the life of a state that was once a nation"; *Vanity Fair* for design; and *Sports Illustrated* for feature writing.

Fighting for attention, profit, and readers, a number of popular magazines once again changed format. *Time,* for example, redesigned its cover and inside layout, and *Mademoiselle* introduced a new logo of white letters against red and added articles to replace fiction. Another approach was to go global. U.S. journals were increasingly being sold abroad, and it was hoped that this would bring millions of dollars to such titles as *Variety* and *Datamation.*

The move to electronic formats proceeded steadily. *Current Clinical Trials,* for example, was a specialized magazine for physicians now available on-line. *People* and *Newsweek* now had audiocassette versions, and *Newsweek* planned a quarterly issue on CD-ROM. The texts of *Penthouse, Compute,* and *Omni* were also available electronically. Jane Austen fans could discuss her novels via an electronic mail journal via a professor at McGill University in Montreal.

After many experiments with alternative procedures, some magazines, including *Time* and *Newsweek,* were going to readers through the mails with the address label printed directly on the cover. Gone were the brown paper kraftwrap and plastic bags. The change spared tons of wasted paper and jammed post office equipment. To appease sensitive or allergic readers who objected to the use of perfumed strips in magazine ads, most advertisers were substituting envelopes that had to be opened to release the fragrance.

(WILLIAM A. KATZ)

Books. The Australian Copyright Amendment Act came into force just in time for the new year. Much gnashing of teeth was noted among U.S. and U.K. publishers at the thought of publishing new titles in Australia within 30 days of original publication elsewhere. Failure to do so would result in forfeiture of copyright of all editions in perpetuity. For the time being, however, the precise meaning of the term *publication* remained subject to dispute.

In July the European Communities (EC) Court of First Instance affirmed a 1988 Commission decision that the Net

---

The Death of *Punch*

Punch was once Britain's best-known humorous magazine, for all that its readers, almost from the beginning, had complained that it was not "as funny as it used to be." It was closed in April 1992 by publishers United Newspapers, after losses of up to a million pounds annually. Its last issue showed Mr. Punch, with Toby and Judy, walking into the sunset, with the caption, "The End." Other *Punch* cartoonists marked the end of an era, stretching back into Victorian England, with characteristic wit: "Mr. Punch, 1841–1992. Not as alive as he used to be" was the tombstone caption on one.

Death came after 150 years of political, commercial, and editorial volatility. *Punch* was born in 1841, in the middle of a general election campaign, and went on to successfully capture the robust spirit of the era for the rising middle classes. But it actually reached a circulation peak of 170,000 in the 1940s, before television had made its inroads and when people still had time for its humorous essays about middle-class life.

In recent years it suffered, along with other weeklies, from a sharp decline in sales: these came to just 33,000 copies a week at the time of closure. Attempts to reposition it during the late 1980s as a more youthful, irreverent magazine for "yuppies" in their 20s, with a new cast of writers, failed to restore circulation and advertising. It had long been known as the magazine most likely to be found in dentists' waiting rooms: it was supposed to calm nerves. But obituarists rushed to point out that *Punch,* in decline, had been afflicted by a failure of humour. For this the writers, not the cartoonists, were blamed. Meanwhile, its satirical role in British society had long been usurped by the ruder biweekly *Private Eye.*

But *Punch* exerted a powerful hold on affections. During 1992 there were several attempts by White Knights wishing to resuscitate the title. As of year's end, they had all foundered. (MAGGIE BROWN)

© PUNCH

Book Agreement (NBA) infringed EC competition rules. Under the ruling, British booksellers would be allowed to reimport U.K.-published books from other EC countries and sell them at a discount. While this ruling did not strike down the NBA in the U.K. as such (although it would need to be reworded), it clearly threatened it indirectly through the effect of intensified competition on prices. The ruling might be appealed to the European Court of Justice. A proposal for a European floor price for books was presented to the Commission by the Federation of European Publishers.

Early in 1992 major U.K. publishers such as Secker & Warburg, Hamish Hamilton, and Chatto & Windus responded to disproportionate declines in hardback sales with a firm commitment to the production of paperback originals. W.H. Smith booksellers also announced its intention to stock first-time authors only in paperback. This raised the issue of whether new books in a paperback format would be reviewed, and also whether glossy paperbacks would end up costing almost as much as hardbacks, as was often the case in Europe.

Do-it-yourself publishing showed signs of taking off. In mid-1992 there were 6,000 DIY publishers in the U.K., and a six-figure total was projected for the end of the decade. As to whether vanity publishing would run riot as a consequence, it had to be borne in mind that, given the low production cost, it was quite possible to make good profits from bizarre subjects by publishing in this way. This might cause the number of published titles to run riot just when the recession had educated major imprints as to the folly of pumping out ever larger numbers of unsalable books.

Publishers' results for 1991, especially the latter half, were surprisingly good, given the severity of the recession. However, some publishers were driven into receivership early in 1992; for example, Biro in France and Harrap in the U.K. (subsequently bought by W & R Chambers, part of the Groupe de la Cité). Layoffs continued to be announced, albeit on a lesser scale than in 1991. The recession proved to have one golden lining in that remainder merchants were able to take advantage of much greater supplies of quite respectable titles, as well as low rents for temporary shops, often in prime retail sites.

As the year progressed, more and more complaints were voiced by U.K. publishers about delays by booksellers in settling their accounts. There were also stories of a sharp increase in unauthorized returns, in some cases of books fit only for scrap. Macmillan caused a stir by offering improved terms for contracts involving "firm orders," and there was ensuing debate as to whether this would result in bookshops' becoming overly conservative in their ordering. U.K. publishers' woes were increased further by evidence that the government had agreed to a uniform value-added-tax (VAT) system that would—albeit after a lengthy period of adjustment—eliminate the current zero rating for books. Despite the recession, Dorling Kindersley opted for an initial stock offering in the autumn to become the largest "pure" publisher on the London Stock Exchange. This optimism was also reflected in the decision by the supermarket group Sainsbury's to join Tesco, Asda, and Safeway in stocking paperback fiction. With Safeway also starting to stock own-brand children's books, publishers could hope for an expansion of the market overall. An interesting development in Germany was the acquisition of 50% of publisher J.C. Bucher Verlag by Heinrich Hugendubel, the largest bookshop group. (PETER J. CURWEN)

Tempered by a weak economy, the U.S. publishing industry began 1992 with an air of caution. At the annual American Booksellers Association convention in May, the focus was on publishing basics, in contrast to past years when excitement centred on a few "big books." Publishers stressed their well-balanced lists of available titles rather than the would-be blockbuster. Plagued by the recession, several companies were forced to reduce staff. By year's end, however, 1992 had had its fair share of highly successful booksellers, book deals of staggering dollar sums, and controversy.

At the close of 1991, Penguin USA dismissed 29 employees. In January, citing a need to "get our operation back in line economically," Farrar, Straus & Giroux laid off 15% of its work force. Later in the year, Bantam Books announced a major streamlining of the company that included trimming staff. Countering these reductions were several multimillion-dollar book deals. Controversial biographer Kitty Kelley, author of *Nancy Reagan: The Unauthorized Biography,* one of the top-selling books of 1991, signed with Warner Books for a reported figure of "over 5 million dollars" for one book. The subject matter was not disclosed. Little, Brown paid $3 million for an illustrated history book, *The West* by Geoffrey C. Ward. Tom Clancy, author of *The Hunt for Red October* and several other tremendously successful novels, received a sum reportedly in the neighbourhood of $13 million–$14 million from Putnam/Berkley for his upcoming book, *Without Remorse.* This was believed to be the most ever paid for a single book. HarperCollins paid over $20 million for a three-book contract with British author Barbara Taylor Bradford, and suspense author Mary Higgins Clark received $35 million in a six-book deal with Simon & Schuster. Pocket Books also paid $2.6 million for the reprint rights to Terry McMillan's novel *Waiting to Exhale,* the highest sum paid for reprint rights since 1987 and a record for the work of an African-American writer.

Waiting to Exhale commanded attention throughout the year and heralded the emergence of multicultural works, previously considered "niche markets," into the mainstream. Several other African-American writers made the best-seller lists for both fact and fiction, including Toni Morrison for her novel *Jazz,* Alice Walker with *Possessing the Secret of Joy,* and, in nonfiction, *The Measure of Our Success: A Letter to My Children and Yours* by Marian Wright Edelman, and *The Autobiography of Malcolm X.* The same held true for books from the gay and lesbian community. The evolution of these categories stemmed from an increase in both quality and quantity of the books and the recognition by publishers and booksellers that these books reached a wide, diverse audience. Ballantine Books launched a multicultural imprint, The World.

Despite the recession, other genres, including children's books, mysteries, and "New Age" books, remained strong. The presidential election campaign spawned a host of books about the candidates, with some H. Ross Perot titles appearing on best-seller lists. Vice presidential candidate Al Gore's environmental book *Earth in the Balance,* published prior to his entering the race, reappeared on best-seller lists as the campaign got under way.

Books by and about celebrities made publishing news. Basketball star Earvin ("Magic") Johnson's book *What You Can Do to Avoid AIDS* provoked controversy when two of the country's largest retailers, K Mart and Walgreen Co., refused to carry it, despite overwhelming support from the bookselling industry and major endorsements by health experts and organizations. As summer approached, "Diana-mania" swept the country with three "tell-all" books about the Princess of Wales. The most ferocious demand was for Andrew Morton's *Diana: Her True Story,* published simultaneously in England and the U.S. October brought two eagerly awaited books: Madonna's *Sex,* a collection of erotic photographs from the controversial star, and *The Senator:*

Shoppers in a book superstore enjoy the coffee bar. The expansion of such stores, which generally stocked 50,000–100,000 titles, continued in the U.S. in 1992, but many long-established independent booksellers and some business analysts were critical of the development.

SAL DIMARCO/THE NEW YORK TIMES

My Ten Years with Ted Kennedy, by Kennedy's former long-time aide Richard E. Burke. Canceled by Putnam because of potential legal problems, *The Senator* was picked up by St. Martin's Press.

Marking the third anniversary of the Iranian religious establishment's "death sentence" against Salman Rushdie, a consortium of publishers and other organizations released a paperback version of *The Satanic Verses,* the book that had so angered Islamic fundamentalists. One of the fastest-selling books of the year was *The Way Things Ought to Be* by the passionately conservative radio and TV talk-show host Rush Limbaugh. In less than four weeks, it sold more than 1.1 million copies. John Grisham, who went from obscurity to publishing fame in less than 18 months, dominated both hardcover and paperback best-seller lists with his three novels, *The Firm, The Pelican Brief,* and *A Time to Kill.*

The continued expansion of the chain superstore (a huge bookstore owned by a major chain, like Barnes & Noble or Waldenbooks) both delighted and concerned publishers. Debate raged over whether superstores increased market share, whether they hurt independent bookstores, and if the rate of growth, still substantial in 1992, was sustainable. The U.S. Supreme Court's decision to overturn New York state's "Son of Sam" law was hailed by publishers. The law, found in violation of the First Amendment, required that a publisher hold the funds due a criminal-author in escrow for five years to give victims of his or her crime a chance to file suit.

The 1992 Pulitzer Prize for fiction went to Jane Smiley for her novel *A Thousand Acres.* The nonfiction award was given to *The Prize: The Epic Quest for Oil, Money, and Power* by Daniel Yergin. In an unusual move, a special prize was awarded to Art Spiegelman (*see* BIOGRAPHIES) for *Maus,* which tells the history of Spiegelman's father, a survivor of the Auschwitz death camp, in comic book form.

Best-sellers for 1991 in the U.S., as reported by *Publishers Weekly,* were, in fiction, *Scarlett: The Sequel to Margaret Mitchell's Gone with the Wind* by Alexandra Ripley (2,148,-225 copies sold), *The Sum of All Fears* by Tom Clancy (1,783,399), and *Needful Things* by Stephen King (1,508,-732). In nonfiction, they were *Me: Stories of My Life* by Katharine Hepburn (800,000), *Nancy Reagan: The Unauthorized Biography* by Kitty Kelley (600,000), and *Uh-oh* by Robert Fulghum (550,403).   (LIZ HARTMAN MUSIKER)

See also Literature.

This article updates the *Macropædia* article PUBLISHING.

Race Relations

Worldwide, the level of racial violence increased during 1992. "Ethnic cleansing" was the euphemism used for the displacement of ethnic groups in former Yugoslavia, while violence against immigrants in Germany and other western European countries became more widespread and disruptive.

Asia. According to the human rights group Americas Watch, the Chinese government's fear of unrest among the four million ethnic Mongolians in the Nei Monggol Autonomous Region (Inner Mongolia) had led to a crackdown and police harassment. Beijing (Peking) was concerned that nationalist influences would spread from neighbouring ex-communist Mongolia. Chinese officials were also apprehensive about nationalist sentiments among the non-Chinese populations in the western region of Xinjiang (Sinkiang). Indonesia was involved in a war against secessionists in its northern province of Aceh, where the situation was seen as similar to that in East Timor but without the presence of British or U.S. media. In Cambodia violence against the Vietnamese population was being held in check, at least temporarily, by the presence of the UN Transitional Authority in Cambodia, but the outlook when UNTAC left was uncertain. The flight of 300,000 Burmese Muslims from Myanmar to Bangladesh increased tensions between those two countries.

Western Europe. A report issued on Aug. 27, 1992, by the German Federal Criminal Office indicated that there had been 1,443 "criminally xenophobic acts" occasioning physical damage to people or property (including 10 deaths) in Germany in the first six months of the year. More than 97% of the perpetrators were under 30, and about half were between 18 and 20. While 67% of the incidents occurred in the 12 western states, some of the worst took place in former East Germany. In Rostock, for five consecutive nights beginning on August 22, some 800 neo-Nazis fire-bombed an apartment building occupied mainly by Romanian Gypsy refugees and Vietnamese contract workers while crowds of onlookers cheered. On August 24 the authorities ordered all refugees out of the city, creating, in effect, Germany's second "foreigner-free" city (the first was Hoyerswerda, following a similar incident in September 1991). Most leading politicians, including Chancellor Helmut Kohl, focused on the need to change Article 16 of the constitution, which guarantees asylum for political refugees. On November 8 more than 350,000 Germans marched in Berlin to protest antiforeigner and anti-Semitic violence, but the demonstration was disrupted by 300 or 400 egg-throwing rioters, described by the police as left-wing radicals.

An opinion poll taken after the violence in Rostock found that 19% of the voters in western Germany and 12% in eastern Germany would vote for "a party to the right of the Christian Democratic Union/Christian Social Union." The neofascist Republican Party won 10.9% of the vote in the April election in Baden-Württemberg and 9.9% in the May election in Berlin. In France the ultraright, antiforeigner National Front (FN) obtained 14% of the vote in the March regional elections—up 4% from the last regional elections in 1986. Exit polls indicated that the FN was making strong inroads into the industrial working class and among young people aged 18–25, a group that was experiencing 28% unemployment. In Italy the ultraright separatists of the Lombard League gained 8.7% of the votes in the April general election and won 55 seats to become the fourth largest party in Parliament.

In the year before the April 1992 general election in the United Kingdom, the Conservative government again raised the issue of immigration. Prime Minister John Major and other prominent party members warned of the threat of economic migrants flooding Britain and Europe. The Asylum Bill, designed to restrict the granting of asylum, was withdrawn just before the election because there was no time to complete its enactment, but it was used as a weapon against Labour, especially by the Tory press, which accused Labour of planning to allow thousands of bogus refugees into the country. It was reintroduced later as the Asylum and Immigration Appeals Bill.

In October the Society of Black Lawyers accused the Council of Legal Education, which trains students for the bar, of operating an examination system that discriminates against blacks. Around 80% of blacks failed the course in 1992, compared with 20% of whites. Only 2% of all serving magistrates were from ethnic minorities; blacks accounted for only 2 of the 451 circuit judges, 6 of the 772 recorders, and none of the lords of appeal, lords justices of appeal, or High Court judges.

A report by the Prison Reform Trust in August declared that racism was rife in the prison service and found that there were too many black prisoners and too few black members of staff. The Commission for Racial Equality, in its second review of the 1976 Race Relations Act published on September 9, called on the government to compel all employers to carry out ethnic monitoring and urged improved enforcement of race relations legislation.

Eastern Europe. The bloody conflicts that followed the breakup of Yugoslavia and the policy of "ethnic cleansing"—expelling those belonging to another ethnic group and taking over their territory—led to the displacement of an estimated 1.4 million people during the year. Ethnic cleansing was practiced by Serbs and Croats against each other and by both against the Muslims of Bosnia and Hercegovina. Most of the fighting during the year took place in Croatia and Bosnia, but there was potential for conflict in the regions of Kosovo and Vojvodina, within Serbia but with populations that were, respectively, 90% Albanian and 18% Hungarian. Elsewhere, there was evidence of bias against Gypsies in Romania and Hungary and against Hungarians in Romania. There was also concern that the forthcoming split between the Czech and Slovak areas of Czechoslovakia would have ominous implications for Slovakia's Hungarian minority.

In the former Soviet Union, armed conflict raged in Moldova between the government, dominated by ethnic Romanians, and the Russian-speakers and Cossacks in the border area between Moldova and Ukraine. The sixth cease-

The Columbus Quincentenary: Celebration or Lament?

It might have been the world's biggest birthday bash: two whole continents celebrating their "discovery." Instead, the quincentennial of Christopher Columbus' fateful first voyage occasioned a spirited debate over the rightful place of the Genoese explorer in history.

Columbus' champions, echoing the classic textbook saga, credit him with discovering the New World and thus ultimately setting the stage for the American Dream. American history, others point out, did not commence from naught the moment the crew of the *Santa Maria* made landfall (probably somewhere in the Bahamas). The ensuing course of Europeanization also met with fresh scrutiny under the new light of multiculturalism.

The honour of having discovered what are now known as the American continents belongs to the first Asians who crossed the frozen sea into Alaska some 15,000 years ago and whose descendants constituted a diverse, stable, well-distributed population by the time Columbus mistook those greeting him for Indians. Even among Europeans, Columbus trailed the Norseman Leif Eriksson (widely held to have reached Nova Scotia) by nearly five centuries.

While quincentenary observances ranging from school pageants to a world's fair (*see* WORLD AFFAIRS [Europe]: *Spain:* Sidebar) explicitly or implicitly promoted the traditional viewpoint, debunkers of what they saw as the Columbus myth used the occasion to air cultural grievances of half a millennium's standing. Indian rights groups on both continents cited slaughter, slavery, and disease as the legacy of European conquest. In response to these concerns, the Canadian government declined to commemorate the anniversary. Most of the protest events culminating on October 12—the official Columbus Day—featured religious ceremonies in tribute to pre-Columbian civilizations. Near Mexico City, indigenous peoples from as far away as Alaska and Peru gathered at the Aztec Pyramids of the Sun and the Moon. Scattered outbreaks of violence mainly took the form of vandalism against monuments honouring Columbus and Queen Isabella of Spain. Spanish institutions incurred damage in several countries. Sit-ins and a small explosion disrupted traffic along the Pan-American Highway in Ecuador and Colombia.

One point in the Columbus story on which traditionalists and revisionists agree is that both sides of the Atlantic were forever transformed by his journey. Outstanding among numerous educational efforts in the Americas and abroad during the "Year of Columbus" was the Smithsonian Institution's major exhibition entitled "Seeds of Change," which used five "seeds"—corn, potatoes, sugar, diseases, and horses—to explore 500 years of cultural "encounter and exchange."

(JIM CARNES)

A television report shows Bosnian men held by Serbs in a prison camp. There was widespread evidence that both Serbs and Croats were practicing "ethnic cleansing," particularly against Muslims in Bosnia and Hercegovina but also in other areas.
ITN

fire agreement between Armenia and Azerbaijan collapsed at the end of September; the undeclared war between the two former Soviet republics had claimed more than 3,000 lives and created half a million refugees. Attempts to establish a cease-fire in the war between Georgian and Abkhazian forces in the northwestern Caucasus also failed. Inside Russia there was violence against Caucasians, chiefly Azerbaijanis. The Institute of Jewish Studies in London reported that probably the most dynamic anti-Semitic movement in the world was flourishing in the former U.S.S.R. (*See* WORLD AFFAIRS [Europe]: *European Affairs*.)

South Africa. The road toward nonracial democracy encountered many dead ends during the year. At the first plenary session of the Convention for a Democratic South Africa (Codesa) in December 1991, the government and the African National Congress (ANC) agreed on a "declaration of intent" committing them to a multiparty political system with "freedom, equality and security for all." There was considerable opposition to the process from the far right of white South Africa, however, and the ruling Nationalist Party suffered a crushing defeat in a by-election in Potchefstroom in February. Pres. F.W. de Klerk then called a "whites-only" referendum to determine the fate of his government. The gamble paid off; in the March 17 referendum, 68.6% of the voters answered "yes" to the question: "Do you support the continuation of the reform process which the state president began on February 2, 1990, and which is aimed at a new constitution through negotiation?" The Codesa process was shaped throughout the year by continuing exposés of government involvement in past and present violence against the ANC and its supporters and by two particularly shocking massacres—in Boipatong and in Bisho in the Ciskei. (*See* WORLD AFFAIRS [Africa South of the Sahara]: *South Africa.*)

United States. The riots in south central Los Angeles in the spring overshadowed other developments in the field of race relations. The disturbances began following the April 29 acquittal, by a suburban jury with no black members, of white police officers who had been videotaped beating a black motorist, Rodney King. The decision crystallized long-simmering anger over racist police practices and bias against blacks and Latinos generally. The violence, which lasted four days, cost 58 lives and billions of dollars in damages. Others besides African-Americans were involved, and much of the looting was carried out by people from outside the area. About 2,400 of the area's 3,600 Korean-owned

stores were damaged or destroyed—at least partly in anger over what was perceived to be widespread disrespect for the African-American community by Korean shopkeepers.

School dropout rates for 16–24-year-old African-Americans had declined from 21.3% in 1972 to 13.6% in 1991, but gross disparities in unemployment rates remained. The unemployment rate for black teenagers was 36.9%, compared with 16.9% for whites in that age group. About one in four African-American men was under the control of the criminal justice system. A study by the National Center on Institutions and Alternatives found that on any given day 56% of African-American men between the ages of 18 and 35 in Baltimore, Md., were either under the control of the criminal justice system or being sought on warrants.

In the presidential election campaign, the tactic of "playing the race card" was less in evidence than in 1988. Democratic candidate Bill Clinton distanced himself from the African-American community, and many observers believed that this, together with his law-and-order record as governor of Arkansas, shielded him from the sort of attack that had been effective against the 1988 Democratic candidate, Michael Dukakis. In the election, Carol Moseley-Braun of Illinois became the first African-American woman and Ben Nighthorse Campbell of Colorado the first Native American to be elected to the Senate. African-Americans increased their representation in the House from 25 to 38.

The federal government proposed a solution to the 110-year-old land dispute between the Navajos and Hopis that would involve transferring 160,000 ha (400,000 ac) of land in Arizona to the Hopis. The settlement, which would require congressional approval, was the subject of considerable controversy at year's end.   (LOUIS KUSHNICK)

Religion

The year's religion news was dominated by concern over issues of abortion, women's role in ministry, homosexuality, ethnic clashes, clergy misconduct, church-state conflicts, religion in the U.S. presidential campaign, and major changes in church leadership.

A 5–4 U.S. Supreme Court ruling in June upheld a woman's right to abortion while allowing states to impose regulations restricting the procedure. The ruling was criticized by both pro-life and pro-choice religious groups. The Presbyterian Church (U.S.A.) moderated its position on abortion and "problem pregnancies," calling abortion an option "of last resort" but adding that the government has "a limited legitimate interest" in regulating it. The middle-of-the-road document, approved by the church's General Assembly, opposed criminal penalties for those seeking or performing abortions.

Debates over homosexuality continued to exacerbate church tensions. Two congregations were expelled from the Southern Baptist Convention, the largest U.S. Protestant denomination, for condoning homosexuality, the first time in the convention's 147-year history that a congregation had been ousted for any reason other than lack of financial support. Another large Protestant body, the United Methodist Church, refused to change its stance that homosexual lifestyles are "incompatible with Christian teaching." The denomination's General Conference did, however, uphold civil rights for homosexuals and receive for study in congregations a commission report that took a relatively open attitude toward gays and lesbians. The General Board of the American Baptist Churches voted in an October mail ballot that homosexual practice is incompatible with a Christian lifestyle. By a 12–1 vote the highest court of the Presbyterian

Church (U.S.A.) nullified the appointment of a practicing lesbian as copastor of a church in Rochester, N.Y.

A request by a largely homosexual denomination, the Universal Fellowship of Metropolitan Community Churches (UFMCC), that it be allowed to endorse UFMCC chaplains to serve in the U.S. armed forces was denied by military officials. The National Council of Churches, a major ecumenical grouping of 32 Protestant and Orthodox churches in the U.S., rejected the UFMCC's request for observer status. The Boy Scouts of America, which bars homosexual youth from participation, came under fire from some religious voices, but the Presbyterian Church (U.S.A.) voted down a resolution that would have asked congregations to expel from their facilities scout troops that refused to include gay youth. The Southern Baptist Convention adopted a statement strongly upholding the Boy Scouts' policy. "Commitment" or "covenant" services for homosexual couples created dissension in some Protestant churches. After one such service in Indianapolis, Ind., United Methodist bishops in Indiana and Michigan directed their clergy to refrain from taking part in such ceremonies. The United Church of Canada decided to leave decisions on same-sex unions to local churches. (See *United Church of Canada,* below.) A new Vatican document issued by the Congregation for the Doctrine of the Faith said restricting the rights of homosexuals was sometimes necessary to protect the common good as represented by the traditional family.

In November the Church of England, the mother church of worldwide Anglicanism, approved legislation to end the exclusion of women from its priesthood. With a two-thirds vote of bishops, clergy, and laity in the church's governing Synod needed for approval, the measure passed by a bare two votes in the lay delegation. The act, which required the approval of England's Parliament and queen, provided that women would continue to be barred from the office of bishop, and a bishop could prevent women priests from serving in his local diocese. The long-debated action provoked talk of schism, and it was expected that some Anglican priests would apply for orders in the Roman Catholic Church. Roman Catholic and Orthodox leaders viewed the decision with dismay, saying that it would delay efforts toward eventual reunion. Meanwhile, Anglican bodies in Australia and southern Africa ordained their first women priests, and the Episcopal Church in the U.S., which had ordained women since 1976, elected its second female bishop. (See *Anglican Communion,* below.)

The world's first female Lutheran bishop, Maria Jepsen of Hamburg, Germany, was elected in April. Two months later, U.S. Lutherans followed suit when April Ulring Larson was elected bishop by the LaCrosse (Wis.) Area Synod of the Evangelical Lutheran Church in America. In United Methodism's July elections of 16 bishops to replace retiring leaders, the church doubled its number of active female bishops from three to six. At their May General Conference, the United Methodists approved a new worship book that included some feminine images for God but stopped short of accepting drafters' language directly addressing the deity as "Mother God." The Reformed Church in America elected its first woman president, Beth Marcus of Holland, Mich., but its more conservative sister church, the Christian Reformed Church, again voted against allowing women to serve in the offices of minister and elder.

U.S. Roman Catholic bishops rejected the fourth draft of their controversial pastoral letter on women, "One in Jesus Christ: A Pastoral Response to the Concerns of Women for Church and Society." Neither liberals nor conservatives were pleased with the compromise document, and some

(continued on page 263)

Eastern Orthodox Christianity: At the Crossroads

BY MARTIN E. MARTY

Orthodox Christianity, in the statistical reckoning of this yearbook, numbers 170,422,000 adherents in 105 countries, making it about one-sixth as large as Catholicism and almost one-half as large as Protestantism. Some 36 million Orthodox live in Europe, while Africa runs a close second, with 28 million members. In North America there are about six million nominal adherents, though estimates suggest that only one million are active on church rolls.

This enormous religious community is much in the news, especially since it had more at stake in the end of the cold war and of communist regimes than any other version of Christianity. The Orthodox like to say that they have lived under the cross of suffering more than the other two main communions or clusters of Christians. For centuries they have been the main Christian presence in the Muslim world, having long ago yielded their historic prominence in Constantinople (Istanbul) to Islamic forces and seen many other Orthodox domains, particularly in the Middle East, pass out of their sphere. In the 20th century, Orthodoxy was the church that the Soviet Union tried to suppress or control for over 70 years. As long as the Middle East and the postcommunist shufflings are in the headlines, Orthodoxy will be strategically placed to make news and be in controversy.

View from the West. Westerners are finding good reason to learn more about Orthodoxy, which makes strong claims to represent the heartland whence Christianity originally issued. Its churches rely on a very strong sense of tradition and are determinedly slow to adapt to modernity. They have led an existence separate from Roman Catholicism since 1054 CE and until the 20th century have been largely remote from and aloof toward Protestantism. Today, both interactions and tensions among Christians are growing, and these will test the fabric of ecumenism, church unity movements, as well as evangelism, efforts to extend the growth of the Christian church.

The Orthodox churches are seen as national and ethnic—though they regard many Western churches as having the same character. They reject the authority of the pope, but they appear to Protestants and the unchurched of the West to be like Catholics because of their more formal ritual and sacramental life.

The Orthodox play a central role in the great late-20th-century drama taking place in the aftermath of communism and the Soviet Union. From 1917 to 1989 the various elements of Orthodoxy led many kinds of existences in the East: from complicity with the regimes to resistance to going underground. It is the first of these strategies that is now most controversial. In the aftermath of the demise of the Soviet Union, and after the opening of KGB files in Moscow in 1991, there were new revelations that confirmed

261

old accusations made by Russian Orthodox dissidents: Orthodox officialdom had in many ways been taken over by the Communist apparatus. Among the faiths there, not only Orthodoxy but—given its large size and close bond with Russian history—especially Orthodoxy had been infiltrated by the Communist Party. When Gleb Yakunin, who was both a member of Parliament and a Russian Orthodox priest who was out of sympathy with his hierarchy, gained access to the religious portions of the party and governmental files, he came away charging that guilty Orthodox leadership was being slow to make changes in the light of exposures about past misdeeds.

Irritants Old and New. Overall, the Orthodox are enjoying their new freedoms and finding some fresh forms of expression. But on the borders between the Eastern (and thus Orthodox) and the Western (chiefly Roman Catholic) church, there have been new and constant aggravations and charges between the communions. These conflicts took away some of the lustre of postcommunist churchly status and threatened to compromise years of positive interchurch engagements. In March 1992, at a gathering in Istanbul of the heads of 12 of the Orthodox churches around the world—only 2 were missing—the leaders complained that Protestant and Catholic missionaries alike were aggressively seeking converts as if the Christian Church had not previously been represented on Orthodox soil. Such proselytizing, charged the Orthodox hierarchy, "poisons the relations among Christians and destroys the road toward their unity."

Particularly irritating were efforts by official Catholicism to win over not just individuals but whole churches. While the most aggressive efforts to convert Orthodox peoples have come from Protestant fundamentalists, evangelicals, and Pentecostals, Orthodoxy has little difficulty interpreting some Vatican moves as invasive. Patriarch Aleksey II of Moscow, on a U.S. visit in November 1991, criticized Pope John Paul II for having appointed bishops for Moscow and elsewhere—to guide proselytizing efforts—without even notifying the Orthodox Holy Synod in Moscow.

Some Orthodox Catholic resentments have roots that are centuries old. After the Council of Brest-Litovsk in 1596, many Byzantine or Eastern churches moved to Roman Catholicism. Under Soviet polity after 1946, many of them were taken over by Orthodoxy, but they are now being turned back to the Catholics. There have been reports of acts of violence in the western Ukraine when these reversions to Catholicism, led by people who had long been underground, occur. Another aggravation going back to 1596: some once-Orthodox churches, keeping many Eastern worship styles, became part of the Roman obedience. They are regarded as Byzantine Churches, Eastern Rite Churches, or "Uniates" by Rome, but they are generally kept at a distance from or disdained by their Orthodox neighbours. The end of communism laid bare the centuries-old discontents seething below the surface in what had been the Soviet Union and in much of the Middle East.

These tensions especially grieve the Polish-born pope, John Paul II, who wanted to dedicate major energies to Catholic-Orthodox entente but who is now regarded in the East as an invader, subverter, or interloper by the more defensive Orthodox. Orthodoxy itself is split, and on postcommunist soil it is the ultranationalist and most anti-Roman Catholic forces that prosper. An International Theological Commission of Catholics and Orthodox, set up in 1979, now sees much of its work set back and its agenda complicated. Some mark of the difficulties that lie ahead was evident in a "Letter to the Bishops of the Catholic Church on Some Aspects of the Church Understood as Communion," issued by the Congregation for the Doctrine of the Faith in the Vatican on June 15. It intended to sound friendly when it spoke of "a certain communion, albeit imperfect," between Orthodoxy and Catholicism. But when the document spelled out what perfect communion looked like, the Orthodox found it dismissive and condescending, as though communion could result only if the Orthodox joined the Roman obedience and accepted "papal infallibility," which the Orthodox find out of the question.

As for the Middle East, turmoil there exposes to view numbers of small but surviving Eastern Christian churches. The growth of Islam led to decline of the four Eastern (Chalcedonian) Orthodox churches in their four patriarchates: Alexandria, Jerusalem, Antioch (now Damascus), and Constantinople. They are honoured more for their history than for their present vitality. An Assyrian, often called Nestorian, Church exists as a very small presence in troubled Iraq and Iran. "Non-Chalcedonian" Oriental Orthodox churches, again with four national styles—Armenian, Coptic, Ethiopian, and Syrian or "Jacobite"—are in the news especially when they come into conflict with assertive Muslims in Ethiopia and Egypt.

Orthodoxy in America. In the United States, Orthodoxy is a significant presence but not a familiar one to most non-Orthodox. The adherents are divided into two broad camps, viewed ethnically as chiefly "Russian" and "Greek." Since 1970 the former, older (in America) body has been called the Orthodox Church in America, or OCA. The "Greek" affiliation is largely associated with a Standing Conference of Orthodox Bishops in America, whose head, Archbishop Iakovos, has been the best-known Orthodox leader and the one who most credibly spoke for "Eastern Orthodoxy" in Western ecumenical circles. The OCA produced the most influential theologians, notably the late Alexander Schmemann and the recently deceased John Meyendorff (see OBITUARIES). It is the OCA that most frequently criticizes Protestant evangelical efforts to "convert Russia" after the fall of the Soviet Union.

From 1950 Orthodox-Protestant interactions had been channeled through the Protestant-dominated National Council of Churches and, secondarily for Americans, through participation in the World Council of Churches. Ten Orthodox denominations are part of a Standing Conference of Canonical Orthodox Bishops in the Americas. In 1990 they were on the point of breaking off all ties with the National Council, in part because they found the NCC lacking in doctrinal clarity. More irritating to the bishops than that vagueness, however, were the council leadership's regular public statements on social issues, often perceived as politically leftist or socially and sexually liberal, with which the majority of the Orthodox were uneasy or even in open disagreement. Matters came to a head in June 1991 when the Greek Orthodox Church of North and South America, 1.9 million members strong, bolted from the council.

After negotiating with NCC General Secretary Joan Campbell, the Orthodox agreed to remain in the council, but they insisted on the right to disagree with its public statements and even to issue minority reports. The language of Orthodox and Protestant relations in the council has varied between "suspension" and the idea of "provisional rejoining." These fairly well represent the larger connections between Orthodox and non-Orthodox in the West. Meanwhile, in the Middle East and the lands of the old Soviet Union, more tense dramas, whose outcomes cannot be foreseen, are unfolding.

Martin E. Marty is Fairfax M. Cone distinguished service professor of the history of modern Christianity at the University of Chicago and a senior editor of The Christian Century.

(continued from page 261)

Catholics suggested that the bishops should abandon the idea of a pastoral on women entirely. The Roman Catholic Church's first new worldwide catechism in more than 400 years was unveiled by the Vatican in November. (See *Roman Catholic Church,* below.)

Atrocities and so-called ethnic cleansing in the territory formerly known as Yugoslavia provoked the outrage of religious communities. The hostilities involved largely Orthodox Serbs, Roman Catholic Croats, and Slav Muslims, mainly in Bosnia and Hercegovina. At the request of the South African Council of Churches, the World Council of Churches (WCC) sent a deputation of "eminent persons" to investigate violence in South Africa and to assess progress toward negotiations for a nonracial government. Five American nuns of the Catholic order known as Adorers of the Blood of Christ, as well as a number of Liberian novices, were murdered in the strife-torn West African nation of Liberia. U.S. churches again withdrew their missionaries from the country.

Western Protestant groups geared up for new evangelistic efforts in the former Soviet Union, organizing congregations in Moscow and other cities and sometimes creating tensions with Orthodox leaders, who took offense at Protestant "proselytizing" in Russian Orthodox territory. There were tensions within the Russian Orthodox Church as well. Before his resignation in April, Metropolitan Filaret of Kiev was accused of collaborating with the former Soviet regime and of violating his monastic vow of celibacy. (See *The Orthodox Church,* below.) The Vatican approved the establishment of a permanent commission to work toward full diplomatic relations with Israel. It had been slow to take steps because of concerns over the status of Palestinians in the occupied territories, of Jerusalem as a holy city, and of Catholics in Israel. In another development, the Vatican and the government of Mexico reestablished full diplomatic relations after a break of 130 years.

Discussions of religion and "family values" as a cornerstone of the Judeo-Christian heritage played a significant role in the U.S. presidential campaign. The Republicans especially emphasized these themes at their convention, where televangelist Pat Robertson made a prominent address. Pres. George Bush criticized the Democrats for omitting the letters "G-O-D" from their platform. Later in the campaign this strategy was downplayed when it did not appear to be attracting voters. After the Democratic victory, however, there were signs of a struggle for power within the GOP between moderates and the religious right. Meanwhile, Democrats also used religious imagery, most notably in the call by candidate Bill Clinton, a Southern Baptist, for a "new covenant."

Many U.S. churches were plagued by red ink. The nation's lagging economy was reflected in congregational offering plates. Many denominations, including Episcopal and Lutheran bodies, were forced to make deep cuts in staff and programs at the national level. The Christian Science Church began selling off or shutting down parts of its troubled electronic media network. The most complete financial accounting ever made by the church, presented at the annual meeting in June, indicated that the church had used $113 million of its unrestricted reserve fund and borrowed $115 million from its pension fund to finance the media empire. Earlier, Harvey W. Wood had resigned as chairman of the church, and there were other changes in the leadership, although critics were not entirely satisfied. The church had expected to receive a $98 million bequest after it published a biography of church founder Mary Baker Eddy by a relative of the legators, but the money was tied up in litigation. The book itself was controversial since many church members believed it was heretical.

The WCC, with a membership of about 300 Protestant and Orthodox bodies in 100 countries, saw a major change of leadership. Uruguayan Methodist cleric Emilio Castro retired as the organization's general secretary, and a German Lutheran theologian, Konrad Raiser, was elected to succeed him. Some church leaders viewed the choice as controversial because of Raiser's desire to focus on broadening the ecumenical movement to embrace non-Christian religions and social movements. In another transition, Frederick W. Franz, president of the Jehovah's Witnesses since 1977, died on December 22 at the age of 99.

In a year when voters were saying "throw the rascals out," Ralph Bohlmann, the respected conservative president of the 2.6 million-member Lutheran Church-Missouri Synod, was unseated in a surprise upset by a still more conservative clergyman, Alvin Barry. (See *Lutheran Communion,* below.) The Presbyterian Church (U.S.A.) General Assembly ousted veteran Stated Clerk James E. Andrews in favour of a relatively unknown regional church official, W. Clark Chamberlain of Houston, Texas. A day later Chamberlain quit, citing "personal reasons," and the assembly reelected Andrews. Later reports revealed that sexual harassment charges had been filed against Chamberlain by a church headquarters staff member, but he was cleared.

The sexual misconduct of clergy emerged as a major problem for both Roman Catholics and Protestants, faced by a rash of news accounts of prominent clerics who had been accused of or had confessed to sexual improprieties. Bishops of the Evangelical Lutheran Church in America endorsed a $350,000 project of prevention and healing, including training events for clergy, seminarians, and church staff. Joseph Cardinal Bernardin took dramatic steps to combat clergy sex abuse in the Catholic archdiocese of Chicago, including an independent board to manage cases, reporting of any allegations to civil authorities, a victim-assistance ministry, a 24-hour toll-free hot line for confidentially lodging complaints, and six years' supervised treatment for errant priests.

The U.S. Supreme Court ruled 5–4 that prayers at public school graduation ceremonies are unconstitutional. The plaintiff in *Lee* v. *Weisman* objected to a prayer offered by a rabbi at his daughter's middle-school graduation. The court said school graduation is one of life's most significant occasions and a student's freedom to absent herself from the exercises was not "in any real sense of the word voluntary." In another ruling the high court said the seals of two Illinois cities, Zion and Rolling Meadows, violated the establishment clause of the First Amendment by displaying crosses and other specifically religious symbols.

In its 1990 decision in *Employment Division* v. *Smith,* a case involving ritual use of peyote by members of the Native American church, the U.S. Supreme Court had overturned the long-standing rule that government can interfere with religious practices only when there is a "compelling state interest." Instead, the court held, laws that infringe such practices can be enforced if they are reasonable and not aimed at a particular religion. In 1992 the court heard arguments in a case concerning laws against animal sacrifice, practiced by Santeria, a religion with African roots that is widespread in the Caribbean. The Santeria church was being supported by several mainstream religious bodies that claimed the new standard was restricting the free practice of religion. A religious freedom restoration bill that would restore the compelling interest test was introduced in the U.S. House of Representatives, but it was blocked by pro-life legislators who feared it would allow women to obtain abortions on religious grounds. (JEAN CAFFEY LYLES)

PROTESTANT CHURCHES

Anglican Communion. An old issue received new attention as debate over the ordination of women dominated the Anglican Communion in 1992. Archbishop of Canterbury George Carey held his first meeting with Pope John Paul II in May. The pope told Carey that he still considered the ordination of women a "grave obstacle" to unity of the two churches, while Carey expressed his conviction that women's ordination was a "proper development" in the church's life. (See *Roman Catholic Church,* below.)

The Church of the Province of Southern Africa, headed by Archbishop Desmond Tutu, became the 11th Anglican province to ordain women as priests. At its August General Synod, a 79% majority approved a measure that led to the ordination of several women in September. In November two more provinces of the Anglican Communion voted to ordain women as priests. On November 11 the measure received the required two-thirds majority in the Church of England's General Synod, although by only two votes among the lay delegates. (See *Introduction,* above.) On November 21 the proposal received the required two-thirds majority at the Anglican Church of Australia's General Synod. Thirteen of the Anglican Communion's 29 self-governing provinces now ordained women. Prior to the vote in the Australian church, three church leaders had brought civil charges against Archbishop Peter Carnely and Bishop Owen Dowling, who had ordained or planned to ordain women. However, an appeals court had ruled in July that the church's internal procedures should resolve the controversy.

In the U.S. the Episcopal Church acquired its second female bishop when Jane Dixon was elected in May as suffragan [assistant] bishop of Washington, D.C. In December 1991 conservative Episcopal leaders

A deacon in the Church of England demonstrates in support of the ordination of women as the General Synod debated the issue. On November 11 the synod voted by narrow margins to admit women as priests.

met in Fresno, Calif., and organized the Episcopal Synod of America, designed to be a nongeographic diocese for traditionalist parishes and clergy. Now called the Missionary Diocese of America (MDA), it still considered itself a part of the Episcopal Church. In April, St. Luke's Church in Richmond, Va., became the first parish to affiliate with the missionary diocese. Donald Davies, MDA leader and bishop, confirmed four persons at the parish in July over the objections of the bishop of Southern Virginia. The Virginia diocese was involved in a legal dispute with the parish over property ownership.

Florence Tim Oi Le, the first woman ever ordained to the Anglican priesthood (by the bishop of Hong Kong in 1944), died in Toronto in February at the age of 84. The archbishop of Canterbury and the Lambeth Conference of bishops never recognized her ordination.

(DAVID E. SUMNER)

Baptist Churches. Southern Baptists continued to furnish the major Baptist story, but with turns and twists from the expected path. After 10 years of political upheaval that had left the fundamentalists in charge of every major board, committee, and commission, it would be expected that a new and clear centrist identity would emerge. Such was not the case. Instead, a number of reaction groups were formed by moderates to duplicate the work of the traditional boards. Schools such as Furman (Greenville, S.C.) and Baylor (Waco, Texas) universities entered into open conflict with the fundamentalists over their academic freedom, long a Baptist tenet.

Black Baptists were having their own troubles. Theodore Jemison, president of the eight million-member National Baptist Convention USA, faced trial in October on federal perjury charges growing out of alleged bribery attempts in the rape trial of the boxer Mike Tyson. Supporters of Jemison maintained that he was trying to uphold young black men in the face of an unfair criminal justice system. A high-ranking African-American official of the predominantly white American Baptist Churches in the U.S.A. (ABC/USA), Aidsand Wright-Riggins, criticized black pastors who rallied around Tyson. Riggins said in a written statement: "This was an opportunity to show concern and bring about healing. Instead, they [Jemison supporters] became voluntary and willing co-participants in the bashing of African American women."

Charles Adams, pastor of the Hartford Memorial Church in Detroit, Mich., and president of the Progressive National Baptist Convention, the other large black Baptist denomination, urged U.S. political candidates to hold as top priorities: job opportunities and training; improved police training; increased minority participation in government; strong civil rights laws; and business ownership by minorities.

Baptists were among the victims of political unrest in Zaire, Myanmar (formerly Burma), and Haiti. In a letter delivered through her husband, Michael Aris, Burmese dissident leader and Nobel Prize winner Daw Aung San Suu Kyi, who had been under house arrest since 1989, thanked the Baptist World Alliance for its "solidarity with and compassion for the people of Burma in their troubles." In response, Denton Lotz, general secretary of the Baptist

World Alliance, assured Aris that Baptists worldwide would "continue to support the just struggle of the people of Burma for justice and freedom."

Frederick Streets of the ABC/USA was named chaplain at Yale University, the first African-American and the first Baptist to so serve.   (NORMAN R. DE PUY)

Christian Church (Disciples of Christ). The 1992 Los Angeles riots drew quick reactions from African-American staff, the general minister and president, and other groups within the Christian Church (Disciples of Christ). It sparked the start of an urban ministry initiative and an October national conference by the Division of Homeland Ministries. The uprising also prompted a book of sermons and addresses delivered after the event: *Dreams on Fire/ Embers of Hope: From the Pulpits of Los Angeles After the Fire.*

In July the church marked the establishment of the Central Pastoral Office for Hispanic Ministries to coordinate ministries with Hispanic Disciples. The Northeastern Regional Assembly defeated a resolution that would lift a moratorium on ordaining homosexual persons. The action was part of a continuing denominational dispute over the suitability of gays and lesbians for ordained ministry.

Two satellite teleconferences helped the church communicate with Disciples across North America in a new way. The March "Season of Prayer" telecast acquainted viewers with the new general minister and president, C. William Nichols.

(CLIFFORD L. WILLIS)

Churches of Christ. Relief in the U.S. and missions in eastern Europe topped concerns of churches of Christ in 1992. Money, supplies, and hundreds of church volunteers arrived in Dade county, Fla., and Louisiana to repair homes and churches damaged by Hurricane Andrew. A prime-time Christian television broadcast, the first U.S. missionaries living in Russia on a long-term basis, a student-faculty exchange program, campaigns in major Russian cities, and food relief were all part of an ongoing effort by churches of Christ in the former Soviet Union.

In India radio evangelist Joshua Gootam's daily broadcasts resulted in 600,000 enrollees in Bible courses. Some 206 church leaders representing 6,545 congregations in 16 African nations met in an evangelism conference in Kenya. More than 100 Korean Christian workers assembled on the campus of Pepperdine University, Malibu, Calif., June 16–19 for the 10th annual Korean Mission Workshop. "One Nation Under God," a nationwide direct mail and advertising campaign, reached more than 102 million homes in the U.S. and elicited over 175,000 responses. The sponsoring church in Cookeville, Tenn., planned a 10-year, worldwide effort.   (M. NORVEL YOUNG)

Church of Christ, Scientist. Healing and regeneration through study of the Bible and the textbook of Christian Science, *Science and Health with Key to the Scriptures* by Mary Baker Eddy, continued to be the church's primary mission. As stated in the president's report at the annual meeting in June: "Healing through prayer, and the love that makes it successful, that's a glue that has kept our movement intact." Also at the annual meeting, members received a financial report more extensive then ever before in response to questions about church finances.

The church experienced increased activity worldwide, notably in Africa and eastern Europe, where the faith could now be celebrated publicly. As the churches developed, they were attracting newcomers. In the former Soviet Union, small groups were beginning to worship together.

In an effort to provide the public with various perspectives on Mrs. Eddy's life, the Christian Science Publishing Society released the first four volumes of a new series of biographies about her.)

(See *Introduction,* above.)

(M. VICTOR WESTBERG)

Church of Jesus Christ of Latter-day Saints. Church membership at the end of 1992 totaled 8.4 million, compared with 5 million in 1982. Of these, 4.5 million were in the U.S. The church had 1,950 stakes (dioceses), 285 missions in 135 countries, and 45,000 missionaries. In 1992 the church celebrated the 150th anniversary of the Relief Society, the organization of Latter-day Saint women. An illustrated coffee-table book, *Something Extraordinary,* and a scholarly history of Mormon women were prepared and published.

The church provided substantial relief to victims of natural disasters throughout the world. Approximately 9,000 members from six states joined in massive cleanup efforts after Hurricane Andrew struck Florida and Louisiana. Substantial shipments of food and medical supplies were sent to the former Soviet Union, eastern Europe, and several locations in Africa. New missions were opened in 1991–92 in Kenya, Uganda, and Congo. Ground was broken for temples in Bountiful, Utah, and Orlando, Fla.

After an exhaustive investigation of the financial resources of the church, the *Arizona Republic* concluded that tithes and other church income were well managed, with "no abuse." First Presidency letters reaffirmed the church's standards of chastity outside marriage and fidelity within marriage, reaffirmed concern over child abuse of all types, opposed gambling and the consumption of alcohol, and joined in a coalition promoting the passage by the U.S. Congress of the religious freedom restoration bill. (See *Introduction,* above.)

(LEONARD J. ARRINGTON)

Jehovah's Witnesses. "While the believers of some confessionals were busy fighting in the Western Ukraine for [control of] their temples and about which religion is true, a grand festival of unity among Christians—the Light Bearers District convention of Jehovah's Witnesses—was being held in Lviv," reported the Ukraine newspaper *Vysoky Zamok* in July 1992. A month earlier delegates from about 30 countries converged on St. Petersburg for the first international convention of the Witnesses in the former Soviet Union. The six conventions held in this former empire were attended by 91,673, with 8,562 baptized.

Three days after Hurricane Andrew caused devastation in Florida, Witnesses sent 305 tons of building materials and 80 tons of food. The *Miami Herald* in August reported: "No one in Homestead [Florida] is slamming doors on the Jehovah's Witnesses this week—even if they still have doors to slam. About 3,000 Witness volunteers have converged on the disaster area, first to help their own, then to help others."

Over a million persons had become Witnesses during the past five years. This 30% increase raised the number of active preachers worldwide to 4,278,820.

(FREDERICK W. FRANZ)

Lutheran Communion. In 1992 Lutherans in the U.S. continued to wrestle with a shortage of funds for work on the national level. Though overall giving to its congregations continued to grow, the amount passed on for work on the national level of the 5.2 million-member Evangelical Lutheran Church in America did not. This led ELCA leaders to warn that even more reductions in national staff and programs might be necessary.

Meanwhile, the 2.6 million-member Lutheran Church—Missouri Synod (also experiencing some financial difficulties on the national level) got a new president. In a 580–568 vote on the fourth ballot, the LCMS national convention elected Alvin Barry, president of an LCMS district in Iowa, over the four-term incumbent, Ralph Bohlmann. Opponents of Bohlmann said he was too permissive on some matters of doctrine and practice.

Two women—Maria Jepsen in Hamburg, Germany, and April Larson in LaCrosse, Wis.—became the first female Lutheran bishops in the world (though at least one other woman had earlier held a comparable position in a Lutheran denomination that does not use the title "bishop").

In countries formerly under communist rule, Lutherans and others continued to try to come to grips with the aftermath, especially revelations that some church people had cooperated with the former state authorities. Silesian Lutherans in Czechoslovakia consecrated a new bishop to replace a predecessor accused of cooperating too much with the Communists, and a regional Lutheran governing body in eastern Germany decided to investigate possible links to the Communist secret service of Horst Gienke, who took early retirement as bishop in late 1989. In Romania an exodus of ethnic Germans meant that a Lutheran church body there lost two-thirds of its membership between 1988 and 1992.

A delegation from the Lutheran World Federation marked a quarter century of official Lutheran-Roman Catholic dialogue by visiting the Vatican. Lutheran and Anglican leaders from eastern and southern Africa met in Zimbabwe to explore closer ties. Nordic and Baltic Lutherans continued to work with Anglicans from England on a common statement on ministry. Roman Catholic and Lutheran theologians in the U.S. were poised to finish their work on another in a long series of common statements, this one on "scripture and tradition." Also in the U.S., theologians proposed that "full communion" be established between the ELCA and the Presbyterian Church (U.S.A.), Reformed Church in America, and United Church of Christ.

(THOMAS HARTLEY DORRIS)

Methodist Churches. Meeting at the World Methodist Council headquarters in Lake Junaluska, N.C., in December 1991, the officers of the WMC adopted a "Vision Statement" that defined some of the tasks and emphases for the quinquennium between World Methodist Conferences. The statement included a commitment "to make the World Methodist Council representative of all Methodists," to explore "whether the organizational shape needs adjustment," to continue the WMC's "involvement in dialogue with other Christian World Communions," to develop the WMC's role "in being available to help in situations of national crisis and dispute within the Methodist Church," and to develop the sense of "a world family." Approval of the statement was one of the first items of business for the Executive Committee of the WMC, which met in Varna, Bulg., in September 1992.

The various standing committees and special committees of the Council met at the same time as the Executive Committee. The Evangelism Committee worked on plans for 2,000 Kingdom Missions around the world during Pentecost 1993 and for an International Christian Youth Conference in 1994. The Ecumenical and Dialogues Committee heard reports of the first "theological conversation" between representatives of the WMC and the Orthodox Church and the first full meeting of the international dialogue between the WMC and the Anglican Consultative Council. The new Education Committee decided to call an international Conference of Methodist college and school presidents, principals, and head teachers.

Zdravko Beslov, the superintendent of the Methodist Church in Bulgaria, was chosen to receive the 1992 Methodist Peace Award. In March a delegation of officers of the WMC visited Rome to meet with the head of the Roman Catholic Congregation for Christian Unity and to have an audience with Pope John Paul II.

The United Methodist Church held its quadrennial General Conference in May in Louisville, Ky. Delegates reaffirmed the church's standard that homosexual practice "is incompatible with Christian teaching," approved a new Book of Worship that includes several references to God as "Mother," and, by a very narrow majority, agreed to continue support for the Religious Coalition for Abortion Rights. In July nearly 170 theologians and pastors from over 20 countries attended the ninth Oxford Institute of Methodist Theological Studies. The theme was "Good News for the Poor in the Wesleyan Tradition."

(JOHN C.A. BARRETT)

Pentecostal Churches. The major international Pentecostal event in 1992 was the meeting of the 16th triennial World Pentecostal Conference (WPC) in Oslo, Norway, in September. With a maximum attendance of 12,500 from 88 nations, it was hailed as the largest religious gathering in Norwegian history. Ray Hughes of the U.S. was reelected to head the WPC for the next three years.

In April the Zion Christian Church (an indigenous African Pentecostal church) held its annual Easter conference in Pietersburg, South Africa. This church, with some six million members, was by far the largest church in South Africa. Almost two million people met to hear Pres. F.W. de Klerk, Nelson Mandela, and Mangosuthu Buthelezi call the nation to peace. Also in April, the International Church of the Foursquare Gospel conducted its 69th annual convention in Van Nuys, Calif. The president of the church, John Holland, reported that 115,000 persons were converted in the church's 3,000 Brazilian congregations in 1991.

In June the worldwide Catholic Charismatic Renewal celebrated its 25th anniversary in Pittsburgh, Pa., the city that saw its birth in 1967. The 17,000 registrants received videotaped messages from Pope John Paul II and Leo Jozel Cardinal Suenens of Belgium. There were over 50 million Catholic charismatics in the world in 1992. The Church of God (Cleveland, Tenn.) General Assembly met in the New Orleans (La.) Superdome in August. Reelected as general overseer was Lamar Vest, who reported that the church surpassed two million members overseas during the year.

(VINSON SYNAN)

Reformed, Presbyterian, and Congregational Churches. "New democratic dispensations for South Africa and Central and Eastern European countries do not automatically hold the promise of economic justice.... The churches are compelled to condemn the absolutist claims of economic systems and examine their devastating effects upon all of God's creation." With this declaration, the World Alliance of Reformed Churches (WARC) initiated a major study process among its member churches on "Faith and Economics." The results would be presented to the next General Council of the WARC, to be held in Debrecen, Hung., in 1997.

Several Reformed church communities continued to experience religious discrimination and persecution. In The Sudan sweeping Arabization and Islamization policies were threatening Christians. The brutal daylight murder of a Christian teacher and the unexplained death of a pastor in prison indicated increasing problems of religious intolerance in Pakistan. In Romania the Reformed Church, composed primarily of ethnic Hungarians, was alarmed by pending laws reinforcing the historic alliance of the Romanian Orthodox Church and the government. In public statements and outspoken sermons, Roman Catholic bishops and leaders of the Church of Central Africa, Presbyterian, in Malawi exposed the reign of terror perpetrated in the country by the government of Pres. H. Kamuzu Banda.

The WARC study on "Reformed Identity" was continuing, with consultations and publications assisting Reformed, Presbyterian, and Congregational churches to consider more deeply what it means to identify oneself as a Christian of the Reformed tradition in an era of Christian and interfaith pluralism. A report on bilateral dialogues between Reformed Christians and eight other Christian communions was released. The WARC initiated a new program entitled "Program to Affirm, Challenge and Transform." Nyambura Njoroge, a female pastor from the Presbyterian Church of East Africa, Kenya, was staffing this program, which promoted the full participation of women as pastors and church leaders.

In 1992 the WARC accepted into membership the National Evangelical Church of Lebanon, the Église Evangélique de Polynésie Française, the Christian Churches of Southern Sumatra, the Iglesia Evangélica Unida de Cristo, and the Fraternidad de Iglesias Evangélicas Costaricenses and recognized the Reformed Christian Church in Croatia, bringing the membership of the WARC to 182 churches in 90 countries representing over 70 million Christians.

The 1992 Templeton Prize for Progress in Religion was awarded to Han Kyung Chik, founder of the Young Nak Presbyterian Church in South Korea.

Religious Society of Friends. The opening of eastern Europe met with a variety of responses from Friends in Europe and North America. A group in the U.S. was translating Quaker materials into Russian. One result was that a small Friends meeting was developing in Moscow. The Quaker United Nations Office in New York worked with the Preparatory Committee for the "Earth Summit" in Rio de Janeiro. A revealing report on child soldiers prepared by the Quaker UN Office in Geneva and Swiss Friends was published in January 1992 by British Quaker Peace and Service. A fifth yearly meeting in Kenya joined the Friends World Committee for Consultation, as did yearly meetings in Burundi and Uganda.

Issues of Christocentricity, biblical authority, and personal behaviour (such as the participation of open gay and lesbian Friends in Quaker communities) came to a head in the Friends United Meeting (FUM), the "orthodox" Quaker group with headquarters in Richmond, Ind. A group of FUM leaders called for a "realignment" of Friends into two groups: those who subscribed to a strict doctrinal statement and those who could not. A conference called to discuss this met with little enthusiasm; later, a "clearness meeting" in March 1992 resulted in the "affirmation of a new life . . . governed by the one God who is present among us to teach us himself."

(THOMAS F. TAYLOR)

Salvation Army. Huge demands on its massive social welfare programs pushed Salvation Army funding to the limit, and finances, together with manpower resources, were stretched still further as the Army responded to the daunting social needs of the people of eastern Europe. A year after reopening the work in Russia, General Eva Burrows, international leader of the Salvation Army, announced far-reaching plans for large reinforcements of officers and lay workers in the area and challenged her territorial commanders to release their best men and women to help in building an indigenous Salvation Army there.

The Army progressed in its development of what were increasingly recognized as some of the most effective and innovative care and prevention initiatives in the field of HIV/AIDS. The Army's AIDS Technical Assistance Team made a presentation to a U.S. Congressional Forum on HIV/AIDS, the purpose of which was to provide a critical evaluation of what does and does not work in the fight against the pandemic.

(MARGARET KIRK)

Seventh-day Adventist Church. The year was notable for developments at the General Conference (central office for the world church) and in several countries. Pres. Robert S. Folkenberg announced four priorities for his administration during the 1990s: fostering assurance of salvation in Christ, global mission, youth involvement, and streamlining of church structures for greater efficiency. After several difficult years, church finances turned upward. During 1991 the General Conference recorded its first operating gain since 1982.

Adventists were able to resume activities in Albania after a lapse of nearly 50 years. In Greece the Supreme Court granted recognition to the church. In a year of famine and natural disasters, the church's relief arm, Adventist Development and Relief Agency (ADRA), received and distributed more food than in any previous year. Besides aiding less developed nations, ADRA distributed 11,000 metric tons of food to Russia. ADRA also expanded its activities to include education and help in view of the AIDS crisis. Adventist volunteers helped coordinate and assist relief efforts for victims of Hurricane Andrew. In one large-scale project, 1,200 volunteers built 25 new churches in 10 weeks in Santo Domingo.

The church continued to grow rapidly, especially in the former U.S.S.R. and eastern Europe. As of Dec. 31, 1991, Adventists resided in 202 countries, and total membership stood at 7,102,976, a 6.63% increase for the year. (WILLIAM G. JOHNSSON)

Unitarian (Universalist) Churches. The Unitarian Universalist Association of Congregations (UUA) was preparing a two-year, 200th-anniversary celebration of Universalism's formal founding in 1793 in Oxford, Mass. In 1961 it merged with the American Unitarian Association to form the UUA. The UUA's annual General Assembly attracted 2,100 attendees to Calgary, Alta., June 25–30, 1992. Its theme was "Building the Global Village." Resolutions adopted dealt with children held unjustly by the U.S. Immigration and Naturalization Service, nonpolluting sources of energy, and universal health care.

A study by the City University of New York revealed that 463,000 Americans designated themselves Unitarian Universalists although only 147,000 adults were enrolled members. A startling 316 persons were studying for the UU ministry although only 80 pulpit vacancies were filled annually. Enrollment in UU religious education classes for youth and children had increased by 39.3% over the past 10 years. Despite the economic recession, the Annual Program Fund and Friends Giving again exceeded their goals.

A primary focus was on training programs to empower UUs to become "effective agents for social change." Another was the establishment of an Office for Racial and Cultural Diversity, a 10-year program to implement racial and multicultural inclusiveness within the denomination and the broader population beyond. The Church of the Larger Fellowship for unconnected UUs, largely in isolated communities, maintained a membership above 2,000. The publishing arm of the denomination, the Beacon Press, received the 1992 New England Publishing Prize of the New England Booksellers Association.

On the occasion of Montreal's 350th anniversary and the 150th anniversary of the Unitarian Church in that city, the 31st annual Canadian Unitarian Council convened there May 15–18. The theme of the meeting was "Making Connections: The Religious Landscape." (JOHN NICHOLLS BOOTH)

The United Church of Canada. The installation of a new moderator at the denomination's 34th General Council in Fredericton, N.B., Aug. 14–22, 1992, proved to be a unique and rich experience for the 400 commissioners (delegates) who elected him. Stan McKay, a Cree Indian by birth, was the first Aboriginal to be elected to the church's highest office. He was currently director of the Dr. Jessie Salteaux Resource

Center in Winnipeg, Man. His installation service included the Native American ritual known as smudging—washing one's head with the smoke of smoldering sweet grass—a traditional rite of purification.

Asked about his main goal during his two-year term, McKay said: "I would hope that our way of relating to one another would be a model of Christian community." Delegates might have had those words in mind when they dealt with a report by the Theology and Faith Committee on *The Authority and Interpretation of Scripture.* A contentious point of whether the Bible is "a" or "the" foundational authority for Christian living was resolved by the simple removal of both articles. The revised wording reads: "God calls us to engage the Bible as foundational authority as we seek to live the Christian life."

Reflecting the atmosphere of that debate, Council issued a statement that adopted a cautious approach to a subject that could have produced bitter division—same-sex relationships. Admitting that "our church is not of one mind on the validity of same-gender covenants," it urged congregations to give "serious consideration to the implications for [our] ministry and mission." At the same time, Council asked the Division of Mission in Canada to make available on request "materials which will enable congregations [and other church bodies] to enter into a process of study and discernment for the welcoming and inclusion of gay men and lesbians in their life and ministry." The statement was approved on a written ballot by a vote of 290–77.   (NORMAN K. VALE)

United Church of Christ. The year 1992 was characterized by continuing activity to strengthen the 1.6 million-member United Church of Christ (UCC). The Coordinating Committee of the all-church planning process, "Toward the 21st Century," shaped a draft statement on church direction to be presented to the 19th General Synod in the summer of 1993. The statement urged the UCC to focus its life around four major themes: A Reflective Church; A Responsive Church; An Inclusive Church; and A Supportive Church. The year also marked the beginning of intensive efforts on behalf of a $30 million fund campaign.

Social concerns addressed throughout the year included continuing involvement in the struggle for freedom in South Africa; in-depth analysis of and involvement in the 500th anniversary of the arrival of Columbus in America; a concern for sexual harassment and abuse in the church; and statements on world events, such as the tragic situation in Bosnia and Hercegovina.

The 18th General Synod had reaffirmed a previous synod's recommendation that a candidate's sexual orientation, in and of itself, not be grounds for denying ordination to the ministry. This and other concerns related to issues of human sexuality were cause for extended deliberation throughout the church. Hearings were held giving members and congregations the opportunity to discuss these issues.

The year was evidenced also by deepening relationships with partner churches in the U.S. and elsewhere; preparation for the first joint gathering of the UCC and the Christian Church (Disciples of Christ) General Synod/Assembly in July 1993 in St. Louis, Mo.; and dialogue with the Evangelical Lutheran Church of America, the Reformed Church in America, and the Presbyterian Church (U.S.A.). The church noted the 100th anniversary of the birth of one of its outstanding theologians, Reinhold Niebuhr.   (PAUL H. SHERRY)

ROMAN CATHOLIC CHURCH

The year 1991 had ended with a special synod on the new situation in Europe created by the collapse of communism and, after initial euphoria, the unleashing of nationalism and anti-Semitism in central and eastern Europe. Protestant and Anglican delegates accepted the papal invitation to attend the synod, but the Orthodox stayed away except for one emissary, deputed to lecture the Catholic bishops on how bad relations had become.

A Catholic-Orthodox conflict on the top level had dangerous consequences on the ground. In March the Orthodox primates released a text denouncing the "proselytism" or "sheep-rustling" to which the ex-communist countries were being exposed. The main target was U.S. televangelists, but the strictures also were aimed at the Roman Catholic Church, which in early 1991 named three apostolic administrators for the vast territory of the Commonwealth of Independent States. The Vatican Secretariat of State huffily replied that the Holy See was merely providing for the pastoral care of those Catholics who had survived Stalin's purges and deportations.

The real problem lay in Ukraine and Romania, where the Orthodox churches denied that the "Uniate" churches recognizing a papal authority had any "theological right to exist." Within 18 months of legalization in 1990, over 3,000 prewar churches were recovered by the Greek Catholics (as the Uniates were known) in Ukraine, and over a thousand Orthodox priests returned to the Roman fold—though what they knew about it was anyone's guess. The pseudo-synod of 1946, at which a few drugged and tortured members of the Ukrainian Catholic Church had abolished themselves and embraced Orthodoxy at gunpoint, was now reversed. In the first free synod, held just before Pentecost in St. George's Cathedral, L'viv (the Ukrainian spelling was revived), the Ukrainian Catholics tried to bond the underground church, the returning exiles, and the "converts" from Orthodoxy. In Belarus there were local objections to Polish missionaries, and the original estimate of two million Catholics was revised downward to 800,000. (See *The Orthodox Church,* below.)

Most ecumenical enterprises, except for purely local ones, ground to a halt. In December 1991 the Final Report hammered out by the Anglican-Roman Catholic International Commission was declared not in accord with the fullness of Catholic faith by Joseph Cardinal Ratzinger's office, the doctrinal watchdog. Both Catholic and Anglican commission members charged that Ratzinger had failed to understand their method, which consisted in "getting behind the Maginot Line of 16th-century controversies" to discover what was held in common today. This setback affected the first visit to Rome of the new archbishop of Canterbury, George Carey, in March. Before setting off, Carey expressed his disagreement with the Catholic "no" to artificial birth control and the Vatican attempt to influence the Rio de Janeiro environmental summit. By the time Carey arrived in Rome, differences over the possible ordination of women in the Church of England made fruitful dialogue impossible.

Carey's attempt to get to know the Catholic Church in Italy—he visited Palermo, Sicily, Venice, and Milan as well as Rome—was more successful. In Milan he met Carlo Maria Cardinal Martini (*see* BIOGRAPHIES), who had emerged as the most influential cardinal in Italy. As president of the Conference of European Bishops, he had an influence that reached out more widely still. He kept in touch with the Russian Orthodox patriarch, Aleksey II, meeting him in Prague in September. The Italian press rashly tipped him as the next pope. Speculation was heightened in July when Pope John Paul II had an operation for the removal of what was described as a benign tumour the size of an orange.

Cardinal Ratzinger continued to produce documents. In June he addressed a letter to Catholic bishops on *koinonia,* or communion—an idea equally dear to the World Council of Churches and the Orthodox. The Ratzinger letter claimed that the "universal Church" preceded the "local churches" and was not just a federation bringing them together. The practical conclusion was that this God-intended unity was guaranteed only by the Petrine Office (as the pope's role is called). The ecumenical partners read that as submission and return to Rome. The Universal Catechism, after nine drafts, was finally completed. Such new sins as terrorism and offenses against ecology were condemned, but the real change was that "grave" sin replaced "mortal" sin, and an attempt was made to understand the psychological factors that could lead to sexual sins. While chastity was recommended to homosexuals, they "should be treated with respect, compassion and delicacy. Unjust discrimination against them is to be avoided." Yet a June letter from Cardinal Ratzinger appeared to condone antigay legislation and caused controversy in the U.S. In the fall a formal statement by the Pontifical Academy of Sciences acknowledged that the church had erred in 1633 when it condemned Galileo for maintaining that the Sun is the centre of the solar system. (See *Introduction,* above.)

In Germany there was a furor over the suspension from the priesthood of Eugen Drewermann, a psychoanalytically trained theologian who gave a mythological interpretation to the New Testament. Some 70% of Germans sided with Drewermann against his archbishop, though this merely proved, said some, how deeply secularization had bitten in former East Germany.

Having convalesced through August and September, Pope John Paul roused himself in October to go to the Dominican Republic for the anniversary of Columbus' landfall. The pope struck a balance between repentance and celebration. Uncertainty about the pope's health—he was 72 May 18—suggested that his pontificate was entering its final phase. (*See* WORLD AFFAIRS [Europe]: *Vatican City.*)

(PETER HEBBLETHWAITE)

THE ORTHODOX CHURCH

From March 13 to 15, 1992, the leaders of the world's canonical Orthodox Churches met at an unprecedented gathering in Constantinople (Istanbul), presided over by the ecumenical patriarch, Bartholomew I. The hierarchs issued a message dealing with Orthodox unity, the ecumenical movement, Uniatism, proselytism, and relations with the Oriental Orthodox.

The breakup of the Soviet Union continued to affect the Orthodox Church in eastern Europe. Ukrainian Metropolitan Filaret of Kiev resigned in April. He was widely criticized for mishandling the Ukrainian Greek Catholic (Uniate) issue and denounced as a KGB collaborator. Filaret was succeeded by Metropolitan Vladimir of Rostov.

In late May the Orthodox Church Assembly in Serbia issued a sternly worded memorandum condemning the Belgrade government's war policies and crimes against human rights. According to a July 1 appeal by the metropolitan of Zagreb-Ljubljana, Jovan, the Orthodox in Slovenia were being devastated by forced conversions, imprisonments of clergy, and property confiscation. Metropolitan Anastasios Yannoulatos was elected by the ecumenical patriarchate on June 24 as archbishop of Tirane to reestablish the hierarchy of the Albanian Orthodox Church. Declared autocephalous in 1937, the Albanian Church had lost all its bishops and clergy under the communists. In March the Bulgarian government and some members of the Holy Synod attempted to remove Patriarch Maxim of the Bulgarian Orthodox Church, claiming that his election 21 years previously had been invalid. The Synod rejected the political action and eventually defrocked the four metropolitans who supported it.

Orthodox-Roman Catholic relations remained tense because of the Uniate question. However, Archbishop Iakovos of the U.S. headed the ecumenical patriarchate's delegation to the Vatican's celebration of the feast of Saints Peter and Paul on June 29, a sign that dialogue would continue. (See *Roman Catholic Church,* above.) In the U.S. the 1991 decision of the Standing Conference of Canonical Orthodox Bishops in the Americas suspending membership in the National Council of Churches was followed, on March 19, by a two-year lifting of the suspension under conditions guaranteeing Orthodox individuality in the Council. The suspension of dialogue with the Episcopal Church was continued.

Father John Meyendorff (*see* OBITUARIES), the leading Orthodox scholar in the U.S., died on July 22. On September 14 the Rev. Thomas Hopko was elected dean of St. Vladimir's Orthodox Theological Seminary, Crestwood, N.Y., to succeed Father Meyendorff. He was the first American-born dean of the school.

Two Serbian jurisdictions, the Serbian Orthodox Church in the U.S.A. and Canada and the New Gracanica Metropolitanate (Free Serbian Orthodox Church), divided since the early 1960s, took a further step toward mending the rift when the former body overwhelmingly approved the reunion of the church at an extraordinary assembly early in the year.   (STANLEY S. HARAKAS)

ORIENTAL ORTHODOX CHURCH

Abuna Paulos, 57, was elected patriarch of the Ethiopian Orthodox Church on July 5, 1992, and enthroned a week later at Addis Ababa's Holy Trinity Cathedral. Imprisoned for seven years under Mengistu Haile Mariam's communist government, he went to the U.S. in 1982 and assumed responsibility for the small but growing Ethiopian

Orthodox community there. On July 10 a funeral service was conducted for the former patriarch Abuna Theophilos, who was murdered by the communists in 1979 but whose death was not revealed until 1991.

It was reported in August that "Jamiat" Islamic militant fundamentalist groups were targeting Coptic Orthodox Christians in Egypt. In May 11 Copts were gunned down by terrorists.

In the U.S. representatives of Armenian and Syrian Orthodox churches met on March 9 to discuss the question of continued membership in the National Council of Churches after the Orthodox bishops suspended membership. (See *The Orthodox Church,* above.) The representatives held that continuing membership would better serve Oriental Church interests. It was decided to resume dialogue with the Roman Catholic Church in the U.S.

(STANLEY S. HARAKAS)

JUDAISM

The year 1991 marked a time of foreboding for American Judaism. Specifically, a National Jewish Population Survey, taken in 1990 and announced in 1991, showed that 57% of Jews married in recent years married spouses who were not born Jewish. Since the life of Judaism centres as much on the home and family as on the synagogue and community, the fact of a high and growing rate of intermarriage called into question the viability of Judaism in the U.S. That question was intensified by the fact that three-quarters of the children of interfaith marriages were not raised as Jews. Commenting on these concerns, Rabbi Joel Zaiman of Baltimore, Md., told his congregation on the New Year (Rosh Hashanah) in 1991, "We are not the first generation of Jews who thought we might be the last generation. . . . Do not worry, Judaism will continue."

Reform Judaism, with a Commission on Reform Jewish Outreach established in 1979, had taken the lead in winning intermarried couples to Judaism. Dru Greenwood, in *Reform Judaism* (fall 1991), said that the goal of conversion of the non-Jewish partner is primary. Since intermarriage is a fact of life, she concluded, "Judaism has to be actively chosen, not only by converts, but also by Jews by birth. All Jews are becoming 'Jews by choice.' " However, a study of the Philadelphia Jewish community could not find a single grandchild of a mixed marriage who considered himself or herself Jewish.

Keen interest in outreach to non-Jews living within the synagogue and Jewish community met criticism in some circles. Rabbi Hillel Goldberg, writing in the *Intermountain Jewish News* (Dec. 13, 1991), pointed to the danger of redefining the life of the community as "multidimensional," by which he meant "embracing Jews, intermarried Jews, their gentile spouses and their non-Jewish children." He said the intermarriage rate in the Colorado Jewish community had reached 72% more than a decade earlier, although everything that people now proposed was tried in Denver. Goldberg alleged that outreach to individuals eliminates "the safeguard of Jewish children socializing in an exclusively Jewish environment." Like Rabbi Zaiman, he recommended outreach as quiet, private, personal, but not a community-wide and dominating program.

His proposal for "inreach to the core Jewish community" rather than outreach to marginal elements stood in striking contrast to the prevailing response to the statistics on demographic decline.

The population study estimated that 625,-000 persons of Jewish descent now followed another religion. Of the children of mixed marriages, more than 40% adopted another religion (primarily Christianity), while 30% professed no religion. On the other side, Orthodox Judaism, certainly the most intense form of Judaic religious observance, had diminished drastically in the two decades since the last study. Under 7% of the surveyed Jewish population identified itself as Orthodox, and Reform or Conservative Jews adopting Orthodoxy accounted for less than 1%. The finding, Irving Greenberg said in *Jerusalem Report* (Sept. 12, 1991), "calls into question the nostalgic magical thinking that a withdrawn right-wing Orthodoxy is the guaranteed saving remnant of the Jewish people."

A contrary view of Judaism in the U.S. emerged in other facts that surfaced in 1991. Admissions to the rabbinical schools rose dramatically: 40% at the (Conservative) Jewish Theological Seminary of America, New York City; 20% at (Reform) Hebrew Union College, Cincinnati, Ohio. Jewish study groups devoted to classical texts multiplied, and Jewish books of a theological character sold in huge numbers—Rabbi David Wolpe's *The Healer of Shattered Hearts: A Jewish View of God* was a best-seller. Egon Mayer, a Brooklyn (N.Y.) College sociologist, suggested (in *U.S. News and World Report,* Oct. 21, 1991) that intermarriage "often triggers a theological search and introspection" that can lead to a clearer and stronger belief in God.

A renewal of spirituality was marked, in the Jewish seminaries, by a commitment to theological issues in place of the political and cultural ones that had predominated. Rabbi Neil Gillman, author of *Sacred Fragments: Recovering Theology for the Modern Jew* and professor at the Jewish Theological Seminary, explained that until recently seminary professors wanted to make the study of Judaism "academically respectable" to a broader society. "No one was prepared to preach about God, prayer, what happens after we die." The curriculum was changed now to "get students to think as religious Jews." This conclusion underlined Rabbi Zaiman's New Year message to his congregation: "Being Jewish involves a decision. What do you believe? . . . Are you willing to sacrifice for those beliefs?"

(JACOB NEUSNER)

BUDDHISM

Nichiren Shoshu Buddhists feuded bitterly during 1992 over control of the wealthy Japanese sect's resources. In November 1991 High Priest Nikken Abe excommunicated the leaders of the sect's 10 million-member lay organization, Soka Gakkai, and ordered it to disband. Abe accused Soka Gakkai of financial misdealings, un-Buddhistic support for UN military projects, inappropriate secularism (such as playing Beethoven's "Ode to Joy" during religious ceremonies), and permitting laypeople to perform sacred functions. Soka Gakkai leaders rallied members' support for independence from the ecclesiastical hierarchy with attacks on the priests' lavish life-styles.

Despite Abe's warning that siding with Soka Gakkai leaders would guarantee rebirth in the Hell of Incessant Suffering, most Soka Gakkai members refused to disband, and pilgrimage to the priests' headquarters, Taisekiji Temple, declined sharply.

Monks of various Japanese sects, represented by the Kyoto Buddhist Association, were also embroiled in debate as Kyoto Hotel began constructing the ancient capital's first skyscraper. Though increasing numbers of pilgrims and tourists in Kyoto had created a need for more hotel rooms, the monks opposed construction of any building taller than Kyoto's tallest Buddhist temple, Toji Pagoda.

Though China's leaders grudgingly permitted a resurgence of folk Buddhism during 1992, they continued to restrain Tibetan Buddhist practices with military force. Their official restoration of Lhasa's Potala Palace neared completion but remained a hollow symbol in the absence of its traditional occupant, the exiled Dalai Lama. In Myanmar opposition leader Daw Aung San Suu Kyi's influential writings on Buddhist democracy circulated though she remained a political prisoner. Beginning in January 1992, military abuses fostered by Buddhist chauvinism forced thousands of ethnic Muslims to flee to Bangladesh.

Buddhist ceremonies fostering environmental consciousness were held throughout Thailand in honour of the fifth-cycle (60th) birthday of Queen Sirikit in August. The trial of Phra Prajak Kutajitto, a Buddhist monk arrested in May 1991 for obstructing logging operations in northeastern Thailand by meditating in targeted forests, remained unresolved.

The remarkable revival of Mongolian Buddhism progressed steadily during 1992. This contrasted sharply with earlier persecution, symbolized by mass graves containing the remains of thousands of Buddhist monks murdered by Stalinists during the late 1930s. A grave was discovered in Moron, near the Soviet border, and reported in October 1991; a second grave was reported in June 1992. Cambodian Buddhists also continued to restore their shattered culture. Late in 1991 Buddhism was named the state religion.   (FRANK E. REYNOLDS; JONATHAN S. WALTERS)

HINDUISM

The year's events were largely dominated by the continuing bitter dispute between Hindus and Muslims in India over the efforts of Hindu nationalists to reclaim and rebuild a 16th-century mosque in Ayodhya, Uttar Pradesh, which they alleged was on the site of an ancient Hindu temple marking the traditional birthplace of the divine hero Rama. The militant Hindu party, the Bharatiya Janata Party (BJP), and its counterpart organization of Hindu fundamentalists, the Vishwa Hindu Parishad (VHP), used the temple dispute to counteract what they perceived to be the evil of secularism in Indian life and favouritism shown the Muslim minority by the central government.

On July 22 the Indian Supreme Court ordered the BJP state government in Uttar Pradesh to stop construction on 1.1 ha (2.77 ac) of land that it had acquired adjacent to the Ayodhya temple/mosque. The VHP urged its supporters to ignore the court's order. At the end of July, Prime Minister P.V. Narasimha Rao negotiated a three-

month truce between the VHP and Muslim leadership, but by autumn the situation had deteriorated. In early December thousands of Hindu militants converged on Ayodhya, and on December 6 they stormed the mosque and destroyed it with hammers and their bare hands. The razing of the mosque set off riots throughout India in which an estimated 1,200 persons were killed. On December 28 the government announced its decision to purchase the site and build both a mosque and a temple on it.

The Ayodhya dispute and increased Hindu militancy gave rise to a new Muslim fundamentalist movement in Kerala. Founded in 1991 by Abdul Nazir Madani, a 27-year-old religious leader, the Islamic Savak Sangh (ISS) claimed in 1992 to have 90,000 members, dedicated to preserving Islam and defending Muslims in India. Repeated incidents of violence over the course of the summer against Hindus and Christians in Kerala were attributed to it.

Fears about the condition of the 12th-century Sri Jagannath temple in Puri were expressed by the temple's Hindu guardians when two massive stones fell 12 m (40 ft) from the vaulting of the inner sanctuary during religious rites honouring Lord Balabhadra on August 13. The Archaeological Survey of India, which had been repairing the temple's interior since 1974, acknowledged that it had not done a complete, detailed examination of the structure's fabric because of the religious prohibition on the use of cameras within the temple. In Mayur Vihar, Uttar Pradesh, the main sanctuary of a new Guruvayoorappan temple, dedicated to Lord Krishna and modeled after the ancient Guruvayoorappan temple in Kerala, was dedicated in traditional rites on August 17. The design of the sanctuary symbolized the deity's mystical anatomy, so that a pilgrimage to the shrine is a form of communion with the god.

(PATRICK H. SULLIVAN)

ISLAM

The year 1992 saw a continuation of the trends that had shaped the Islamic world for some years. Fundamentalist movements remained strong; the breakup of the former Soviet Union affected Muslims from Afghanistan to former Yugoslavia; tensions in the Middle East continued, as did violence in Nigeria, The Sudan, Egypt, the Maghreb, and India, where the destruction of the disputed mosque in Ayodhya by Hindus sparked several days of bloody communal rioting. At the same time, the influence of Islam continued to grow in many parts of the world, including the U.S.

New areas were added to the list of those plagued by religious persecution and violence. Muslim Slavs in Bosnia and Hercegovina were the targets of Serb attacks following the breakup of Yugoslavia. (*See* WORLD AFFAIRS [Europe]: *Bosnia and Hercegovina.*) The Bosnians appealed for help to Muslim countries, and there were reports of arms shipments financed by Middle Eastern nations. Early in the year, Muslim refugees fled to Bangladesh after being expelled from Arakan, a western province of Myanmar. The former Burma, which is overwhelmingly Buddhist, was said to be following a policy of *payatya,* achieving purity in the nation, a concept similar to the "ethnic cleansing" taking place in Bosnia.

In the former U.S.S.R., Muslim volunteers were sought to help the Georgian region of Abkhazia gain independence. Turkey announced it would start broadcasts to the former Soviet Central Asian republics featuring a moderate brand of contemporary Islamic culture as an antidote to Islamic fundamentalist broadcasts from Iran.

Tensions continued over the Dome of the Rock area in Jerusalem, a holy precinct for both Muslims and Jews. The Jordanian government disputed Saudi Arabia's

BARTHOLOMEW—GAMMA LIAISON

With the support of Hindu fundamentalists and their political allies, militants destroy a 16th-century Muslim mosque in Ayodhya, India. Hindus hold the site to be the birthplace of the deity Rama.

Without heat or electricity, a Muslim family in Sarajevo spends an evening together in its apartment. Muslims in Bosnia and Hercegovina continued in 1992 to be targets of Serbian nationalists, with tens of thousands killed or taken hostage or forced to flee their homes.

PETER KULLMANN—THE NEW YORK TIMES

assumption of financial responsibility for repairs to the mosque, including the gilding of the Dome. King Hussein of Jordan sold property in England in order to assume the financial burden. Jordan had had responsibility for the Dome since before the 1967 war, and it was alleged that Saudi support might encourage Israeli intervention. However, the dispute was also seen as fallout from the 1991 Gulf war, when Saudi Arabia and Jordan were at odds over policy. The Saudi government found itself subject to criticism by some of its religious leaders, in part a reflection of its support of the U.S.

The continued growth of Islam in Europe and North America was apparent during the year. In January a Muslim parliament was held in England, convened by Kalim Siddiqi, a militant. Although moderates said the parliament did not speak for them, its occurrence underscored the size and potential influence of the Muslim population. The European Islamic Institute in France began training scholars and directors of Islamic study centres for placement in various European countries. In the U.S. and Canada growth of the Muslim population was led largely by immigration and

conversions within the African-American community. The Muslim Students Association of North America was active in 200 colleges, and eight full-time Muslim imams were serving as chaplains in the U.S. federal prison system. (REUBEN W. SMITH)

WORLD RELIGIOUS STATISTICS

During 1992 some 20 new nations and 10 nonsovereign countries came into existence, mainly through the breakup of the U.S.S.R. (now provisionally termed "Eurasia" in the table) and of Yugoslavia. The former demonstrated what the immediate effect of a newly proclaimed religious liberty could be, as millions flocked into churches, mosques, temples, and synagogues. The latter (especially in Bosnia and Hercegovina) demonstrated just how brutal religious wars could become when opposite sides in civil wars each had a clear religious identity. In a new and frightening development, thousands of churches and mosques were deliberately destroyed in 1992 by rival religionists. It is a startling fact, however, that all the religious carnage and killings of recent months continued to make scarcely a ripple on the global statistical scene, as shown by the table. All religions continued to grow rapidly in membership as world population increased by more than 90 million a year.

(DAVID B. BARRETT)

This article updates the *Macropædia* articles The Buddha and BUDDHISM; CHRISTIANITY; EASTERN ORTHODOXY; HINDUISM; Muhammad and the Religion of ISLAM; JUDAISM; PROTESTANTISM; The Study and Classification of RELIGIONS; ROMAN CATHOLICISM; and *Micropædia* entries on the various denominations.

Adherents of All Religions by Seven Continental Areas, Mid-1992

	Africa	Asia	Europe	Latin America	Northern America	Oceania	Eurasia	World	%	Countries
Christians	327,204,000	285,365,000	413,756,000	435,811,000	239,004,000	22,628,000	109,254,000	1,833,022,000	33.4	270
Roman Catholics	122,907,000	123,597,000	262,638,000	405,623,000	97,022,000	8,208,000	5,590,000	1,025,585,000	18.7	259
Protestants	87,332,000	81,476,000	73,939,000	17,263,000	96,312,000	7,518,000	9,858,000	373,698,000	6.8	246
Orthodox	28,549,000	3,655,000	36,165,000	1,764,000	6,008,000	576,000	93,705,000	170,422,000	3.1	105
Anglicans	26,863,000	707,000	32,956,000	1,300,000	7,338,000	5,719,000	400	74,883,400	1.4	158
Other Christians	61,553,000	75,930,000	8,058,000	9,861,000	32,324,000	607,000	100,600	188,433,600	3.4	118
Muslims	278,250,800	636,976,000	12,574,500	1,350,500	2,847,000	100,500	39,229,400	971,328,700	17.7	184
Nonreligious	1,896,000	691,144,000	52,411,000	17,159,000	25,265,000	3,291,000	85,066,000	876,232,000	16.0	236
Hindus	1,475,000	728,118,000	704,000	884,000	1,269,000	360,000	2,000	732,812,000	13.4	94
Buddhists	21,000	313,114,000	272,000	541,000	558,000	26,000	407,000	314,939,000	5.7	92
Atheists	316,000	161,414,000	17,604,000	3,224,000	1,319,000	535,000	55,898,000	240,310,000	4.4	139
Chinese folk religionists	13,000	186,817,000	60,000	73,000	122,000	21,000	1,000	187,107,000	3.4	60
New-Religionists	21,000	141,382,000	50,000	530,000	1,421,000	10,000	1,000	143,415,000	2.6	27
Tribal religionists	70,588,000	24,948,000	1,000	936,000	41,000	67,000	0	96,581,000	1.8	104
Sikhs	26,000	18,272,000	231,000	8,000	254,000	9,000	500	18,800,500	0.3	21
Jews	337,000	5,587,000	1,469,000	1,092,000	7,003,000	98,000	2,236,000	17,822,000	0.3	134
Shamanists	1,000	10,233,000	2,000	1,000	1,000	1,000	254,000	10,493,000	0.2	11
Confucians	1,000	5,994,000	2,000	2,000	26,000	1,000	2,000	6,028,000	0.1	6
Baha'is	1,496,000	2,680,000	91,000	801,000	365,000	77,000	7,000	5,517,000	0.1	220
Jains	53,000	3,717,000	15,000	4,000	4,000	1,000	0	3,794,000	0.1	11
Shintoists	200	3,220,000	500	500	1,000	500	100	3,222,800	0.1	4
Other religionists	433,000	12,292,000	1,469,000	3,570,000	485,000	4,000	333,000	18,586,000	0.3	182
Total Population	**682,132,000**	**3,231,273,000**	**500,712,000**	**465,987,000**	**279,985,000**	**27,230,000**	**292,691,000**	**5,480,010,000**	**100.0**	**270**

NOTES:
Continents. These follow current UN demographic practice. UN practice began in 1949 by dividing the world into 5 continents; then into 18 regions (1954); then into 8 major continental areas (called macro regions in 1987) and 24 regions (1963); and 7 major areas and 22 regions (1988). (*See* United Nations, *World Population Prospects 1990,* with populations of all continents, regions, and countries covering the period 1950–2025.) The table above therefore now combines its former columns "East Asia" and "South Asia" into one single continental area, "Asia" (which excludes Eurasia [or European Asia], our provisional new term for the former U.S.S.R.).
Countries. The last column enumerates sovereign and nonsovereign countries in which each religion or religious grouping has a significant following.
Rows. The list of religions is arranged by descending order of magnitude of global adherents in 1992 (last two columns but one); similarly for categories within "Christians."
Adherents. As defined and enumerated for each of the world's countries in *World Christian Encyclopedia* (1982), projected to mid-1992, adjusted for recent data.
Christians. Followers of Jesus Christ affiliated with churches (church members, including children: 1,692,466,000) plus persons professing in censuses or polls though not so affiliated.
Other Christians. Catholics (non-Roman), marginal Protestants, crypto-Christians, and adherents of African, Asian, black, and Latin-American indigenous churches.
Muslims. 83% Sunnites, 16% Shi'ites, 1% other schools. The definition excludes former ethnic Muslims who have now abandoned Islam, also followers of syncretistic religions combining Islam with other belief systems. In the U.S., a recent detailed survey showed that most Asian immigrants previously thought to be Muslims are now in fact Christians.
Nonreligious. Persons professing no religion, nonbelievers, agnostics, freethinkers, dereligionized secularists indifferent to all religion.
Hindus. 70% Vaishnavites, 25% Shaivites, 2% neo-Hindus and reform Hindus.
Buddhists. 56% Mahayana, 38% Theravada, 6% Tantrayana.
Atheists. Persons professing atheism, skepticism, disbelief, or irreligion, including antireligious (opposed to all religion).
Chinese folk-religionists. Followers of traditional Chinese religion (local deities, ancestor veneration, Confucian ethics, Taoism, universism, divination, some Buddhist elements).
New-Religionists. Followers of Asian 20th-century New Religions, New Religious movements, radical new crisis religions, and non-Christian syncretistic mass religions, all founded since 1800 and mostly since 1945.
Jews. 84% Ashkenazis, 10% Orientals, 4% Sephardis. The definition includes nonpracticing Jews, underground Jews, and crypto-Jews in Muslim countries.
Confucians. Non-Chinese followers of Confucius and Confucianism, mostly Koreans in Korea.
Other religionists. Including 50 minor world religions and a large number of spiritist religions, New Age religions, quasi religions, pseudoreligions, parareligions, religious or mystic systems, religious and semireligious brotherhoods of numerous varieties.
Total Population. UN medium variant figures for mid-1992, as given in *World Population Prospects 1990* (New York: UN, 1991), pages 136–142. (DAVID B. BARRETT)

Social Security and Welfare Services

Depressed economic conditions, accompanied by high rates of inflation and rapidly increasing levels of unemployment, had a significant impact on social security and welfare programs in 1992. Governments in industrialized countries, already concerned about the effects of future demographic trends on social security, continued to focus on expenditure restraint while examining longer-term options for reform. The former socialist countries in central and eastern Europe embarked on major restructuring of their social protection programs. A number of less developed countries were trying to improve coverage and benefit levels while coping with the pressures of economic restructuring, political turmoil, and widespread drought.

In industrialized countries there was a general concern about the ability of current schemes to assume future financial burdens, and governments were looking at ways to strengthen the basic state plans through private means. In July 1992 Australia introduced a Superannuation Guarantee Levy to supplement the general-revenue-financed age pension system. Switzerland was extending the right of portability, enabling individuals to maintain protection when they moved from one employer to another. Several countries appointed committees to examine the respective roles of the state, employers, and individuals in the provision of retirement incomes. Retirement ages continued to be a focus of attention. Germany's pension-reform law, which went into effect in January, put in place the requirement that, starting in 2001, the normal retirement age for both men and women would be raised gradually to 65. Sweden and Italy also announced that they would increase the retirement age, both to restrain expenditures and to meet possible manpower shortages. Other countries were indirectly affecting the age of retirement by extending the insurance period for pension eligibility.

Health care was another object of reform. New Zealand introduced charges for a variety of hospital and health services and made a number of structural changes in the administration of health care services. Germany announced the introduction of charges and budgetary limitations in an attempt to reduce the growth in expenditure. In Switzerland pilot projects were introduced to examine different cost-containment measures. One involved limiting the patient's choice of doctors to those designated by particular insurance funds. Fundamental reviews of disability and sickness benefits were undertaken by several industrialized countries. In many cases, these payments had been used as a means of early withdrawal from the work force by those who had exhausted their eligibility for unemployment insurance or could not claim an early retirement pension. Sweden, Finland, and The Netherlands introduced major changes to their disability-related payments, placing much greater emphasis on rehabilitation and work force reentry and putting more responsibility on employers. Norway appointed a committee to propose changes to both the invalidity pension and sickness benefit schemes and to examine ways of improving employment opportunities for people with disabilities.

Some interesting developments occurred in the area of survivors' benefits as countries tried to adapt their systems to continuing changes in family structure and increasing participation of women in the labour force. Many countries had already removed the distinction between widows and widowers as regards eligibility for survivors' benefits, and some were extending protection to other single parents. In Israel a Single Parent Families Law, introduced in March, provided income-support benefits for divorced, separated, or single men and women with dependent children in their care; formerly, such benefits were available only to widows. The Netherlands and Denmark announced changes extending eligibility for survivors' pensions to cohabiting males and females, provided they were registered as partners.

Another response to the changing structure of families was the introduction of child-support schemes under which the noncustodial parent had to contribute to the maintenance of the children. The U.K. announced that a new Child Support Agency, to be established in April 1993, would provide a nonadversarial one-stop service for the assessment and collection of child maintenance for all families. Care also became an important issue for industrialized countries with increasing numbers of women in the work force. Besides improving parental leave provisions, many countries were focusing on the emerging need of long-term care for the elderly, particularly with regard to mechanisms for home-based rather than institutional care. In January Norway introduced provisions to ensure that a supplementary pension would be payable to those who stayed home to care for sick or disabled relatives, while Switzerland introduced allowances for household help in addition to the assistance provided for treatment of sick or elderly persons at home.

The continuing rise in unemployment led to the adoption of additional measures in the area of labour-market reform. During 1992 Denmark introduced a series of measures to improve opportunities for the unemployed to undertake vocational training or state-subsidized employment. In France measures went into effect in February 1992 to assist the long-term unemployed, with special emphasis on workers over 50 and unskilled persons aged 16 to 25. Some countries took steps to reduce the opportunities for people to claim benefits illegally.

The economic and political transformation of central and eastern European countries meant a fundamental restructuring of their social security systems. Although the introduction of unemployment insurance was a top priority, reform of pension schemes was also urgent as the real value of benefits deteriorated and serious shortfalls were being experienced in social security accounts. The reform process was still in its early stages, but some countries had already introduced legislation setting out its future direction. Essentially, most countries were proposing a two-tier system with a minimum standard of protection provided by the state and a supplementary scheme providing earnings-related benefits. Specific changes included the creation of social insurance funds separate from the state budget; the introduction of different branches for old-age, disability, work injury, and unemployment and the abolition of favoured-work categories; and the raising of retirement ages (which, with the exception of Poland, were much lower than in other European countries). Legislation establishing the basis for reform was introduced in Bulgaria, Czechoslovakia, Hungary, Poland, and Russia. In Estonia the pensions law that went into effect in January was repealed because of its adverse effect on inflation.

The situation in many less developed countries was reaching crisis proportions as they tried to deal with the effects of structural-adjustment programs, high levels of inflation, and, particularly in Latin America, inadequate resources to finance current commitments. Argentina, Mexico, Panama, Peru, and Uruguay all made major modifications to their social security programs in an attempt to solve their financial problems. In January Argentina replaced its existing schemes with a unified system to be administered by a newly created National Social Security Service. In May

Mexico introduced a retirement savings plan to supplement the benefits of the general pension scheme, while Panama reformed its system in January by raising the contribution rate, modifying the method of calculating pensions, and increasing the retirement age by two years as from January 1995. Peru established a private pension plan in July 1992 as an alternative to the public scheme, and Uruguay announced a new compulsory social security scheme in April.

The African countries continued to increase their contribution rates and earnings ceilings to finance increases in benefits, as well as upgrading the administration of their schemes through new technology. In Asia, Indonesia introduced a new employees' social security system to replace the former provident fund. The new scheme extended coverage to all workers and provided health care coverage as well as old-age, disability, survivors, and work-accident benefits.

(JUDITH E. RAYMOND)

Welfare reform reemerged as a major issue in the U.S. in 1992 as caseloads soared to record highs and concern grew over chronic welfare dependency. New strategies were sought to reduce costs, provide more help, and encourage self-sufficiency and responsible behaviour on the part of welfare recipients.

The renewed push for reform came just four years after passage of the Family Support Act of 1988, the most far-reaching overhaul of the welfare system since it was established in 1935. The 1988 law provided $1 billion a year over a five-year period in matching federal grants to help states set up comprehensive education, training, and employment programs known as JOBS (Job Opportunities and Basic Skills), and it encouraged states to experiment with reforms. The goal was to transform welfare from a system of income maintenance into one that enabled recipients to get off government assistance and into paying jobs. By the end of 1992, every state had a JOBS program in place, and 550,000 persons were participating—ahead of schedule but still representing only one-fourth of eligible adults. Many states, restrained by tight budgets, had not claimed their full share of money for the JOBS program. Although it was too early to assess the full impact of the law, a study by the Manpower Demonstration Research Corporation found that the JOBS program in California was having a positive effect on employment earnings and welfare savings.

Meanwhile, at least 10 states had gotten waivers from Washington to experiment with new approaches to welfare.

In New Jersey additional benefits were denied to women who had more children while on AFDC (Aid to Families with Dependent Children). Wisconsin's "Learnfare" reduced benefits for parents whose children had excessive unexcused absences from school. Maryland required that preschoolers receive their immunizations and school-age children get regular health examinations as a condition of AFDC eligibility. Seven counties in upstate New York encouraged welfare mothers to work by allowing them to keep a large portion of their grants even though they had jobs.

The issue was dealt with by both parties in the fall election campaign. The Republican platform called welfare "the enemy of opportunity and stable family life," and Pres. George Bush pledged to speed up federal approval for state welfare-reform initiatives. Bill Clinton said he would quadruple the amount the government spends on job training for welfare recipients and add $2 billion in tax credits for the working poor, but he also stressed that welfare should be "a second chance, not a way of life." According to David T. Ellwood, a welfare expert at Harvard, a woman receiving AFDC for the first time could expect to stay in the program an average of 6.6 years. About 55% of recipients stayed one to five years, and 45% stayed six years or more. Bipartisan backing for tighter child-support laws was especially strong. Congress passed and the president signed a law imposing federal criminal penalties on parents who failed to meet support-payment obligations to a child living in another state. The most recent figures showed that in 1989 only 58% of women without husbands present had been awarded child support by a state court, and of those who did get awards, only half collected the full amount; 25% received nothing from absent fathers.

The Census Bureau reported that the number of Americans living in poverty reached 35.7 million in 1991, 2.1 million more than in 1990 and the highest figure since 1964. This represented 14.2% of the total U.S. population, and the proportions were much higher among some groups; for example, 32.7% of blacks and 28.7% of Hispanics were poor. The official poverty line in 1991 was $6,932 for a single person and $13,924 for a family of four. The Census Bureau also reported that 35.4 million Americans lacked health insurance in 1991, up from 34.7 million in 1990. Increased poverty and joblessness led to record levels for welfare rolls and costs. After remaining fairly stable during the 1980s, the caseload of AFDC, the basic welfare pro-

A homeless woman stands outside her tent in a campground in Umpqua National Forest in Oregon. During 1992 the U.S. Forest Service agreed to establish a campsite in Umpqua that could accommodate up to 25 homeless people, thus sanctioning a practice that was widespread.

gram, rose by 28% between July 1989 and May 1992, and food-stamp caseloads shot up 37%. As of May 1992, 4.8 million families, or 13.7 million individuals, were receiving AFDC, including 9,279,000 children under age 18—one in every seven.

The annual cost of AFDC was around $25 billion, with approximately 55% coming from the federal government and 45% from states. State welfare costs rose by nearly $2.2 billion from mid-1989 to mid-1992, forcing nine states to cut benefits in 1991 and 31 others to freeze them, according to the Center on Budget and Policy Priorities, a Washington-based research organization. Data compiled by the House Ways and Means Committee showed that the purchasing power of welfare and food-stamp benefits for single mothers had declined by an average of 27% over the last 20 years. As of January 1992 the combined maximum monthly benefits from AFDC and food stamps for a family of three ranged from a low of $412 in Mississippi to a high of $1,184 in Alaska.

Congress did little with welfare reform in 1992, but it did enact some social welfare legislation. The Older Americans Act, which earmarked $1.7 billion for programs to provide the elderly with transportation, employment, and Meals on Wheels, was reauthorized. The largest job-training program, the Job Training Act of 1982, was overhauled to provide for stricter oversight and to target more aid to dropouts and others who have the most trouble getting work. Unemployment benefits were extended twice for the long-term jobless. Both Social Security benefits and taxes were slated to rise again in 1993, but by relatively small amounts. The annual cost-of-living adjustment would give 44 million poor, disabled, and retired Americans on Social Security and Supplemental Security Income (SSI) a 3% boost in benefits, the smallest since 1987. The average monthly check would go up by just $19, to $653 a month. The total cost of the benefit increase was estimated at $8.6 billion. For workers, the payroll tax rate would remain at 7.65% (6.2% for Social Security, 1.45% for Medicare), but the maximum earnings subject to the Social Security tax would rise from $55,500 to $57,600, and the wage base for Medicare would increase from $130,200 to $135,000.   (DAVID M. MAZIE)

See also Education; Health and Disease; Industrial Review: Insurance.

This article updates the Macropædia article SOCIAL WELFARE.

Space Exploration

Worldwide recession and rising program costs started to cut into the ability of nations to support major space programs in 1992. Nevertheless, successes were scored by several missions.

A major event for the U.S. National Aeronautics and Space Administration (NASA) was the surprise resignation in February of Administrator Richard Truly, the first former astronaut ever to direct the agency. Truly was forced to resign as a result of an apparent disagreement with the Bush administration over NASA's direction for the future, especially its plan to continue to depend on the space shuttle. Truly was replaced by Daniel Goldin, a vice president at TRW, Inc.

International Developments. After the breakup of the Soviet Union, its successor, the Commonwealth of Independent States, opened the doors to formerly secret or closed programs and invited international cooperation. In doing so, the CIS was looking for hard currency, and its former rivals were seeking less expensive ways to conduct space missions. At least three U.S. aerospace firms signed

contracts with Russian companies that produce or control the Soyuz spacecraft and Energia heavy-lift launcher, and the European Space Agency (ESA) signed contracts worth more than $5 million. Consequently, it appeared that ESA's Hermes manned shuttle craft, which earlier in 1992 had been reduced to a technology program, might become a joint Russian-European venture, ESA officials said.

NASA also was looking at Russian hardware and established a new office to consider using the Soyuz TM spacecraft as a lifeboat for space station Freedom and using the Progress spacecraft and its automated docking system for resupply missions. During the year the U.S. and Russia signed agreements for the first joint space missions since the Apollo-Soyuz Test Project in 1975. A Russian cosmonaut was to fly on the U.S. space shuttle in October 1993, and a U.S. astronaut was to take part in extended medical experiments aboard the space station Mir in 1994. The shuttle might dock with Mir to retrieve the crew on the latter mission.

Manned Flight. The U.S. space shuttle program in 1992 began with Discovery, launched on January 22. The shuttle carried International Microgravity Laboratory-1 (IML-1) and a seven-person crew (commander Ronald Grabe; pilot Stephen Oswald; mission specialists Norman Thagard, David Hilmers, and William Readdy; and payload specialists Roberta Bondar of Canada and Ulf Merbold of ESA). The mission included experiments on the processing of materials without the effects of gravity and on the influence of weightlessness on the human body. At 14 missions, Discovery became the most experienced shuttle orbiter. The mission ended with a landing at Edwards Air Force Base in California on January 30.

The shuttle orbiter Atlantis carried ATLAS (Atmospheric Laboratory for Applications and Science) and a seven-person crew (commander Charles Bolden; pilot Brian Duffy; mission specialists Michael Foale of Great Britain, Kathryn Sullivan, and David Leestma; and payload specialists Dirk Frimout of ESA and Byron Lichtenberg) into space on March 24. ATLAS consisted of instruments to study the Earth's atmosphere (some first flown on Spacelab 1 in 1983) that NASA intended to refly once a year. The instruments were to be recalibrated each year to ensure accuracy. After many tests, especially of the ozone layer, were performed, Atlantis landed on April 2 at the Kennedy Space Center in Florida.

The new space shuttle Endeavour, with its seven-person crew (commander Daniel Brandenstein; pilot Kevin Chilton; and mission specialists Thomas Akers, Richard Hieb, Bruce Melnik, Kathryn Thornton, and Pierre Thuot), was launched into orbit for the first time on May 7. The high point of the mission was the rescue of an Intelsat 6 communications satellite that was wobbling in a uselessly low orbit. Akers, Hieb, and Thuot captured the satellite by hand after they had failed to do so with high-technology hardware during two days of space walks. After snaring the satellite, the three astronauts were able to attach it to a new upper stage. The mission, which ended on May 16, was the first in which three astronauts walked in space at the same time.

The space shuttle Columbia returned to service on June 25. It carried U.S. Microgravity Laboratory-1 and a seven-person crew (commander Richard Richards; pilot Kenneth Bowersox; mission specialists Bonnie Dunbar, Ellen Baker, and Carl Meade; and payload specialists Lawrence DeLucas and Eugene Trinh). With a two-week flight, it was the longest U.S. mission since the last Skylab crew in 1974. Columbia had been refitted with a special cargo of liquid hydrogen and oxygen tanks to power its fuel cells for missions that might stretch to 16 days. During the flight the

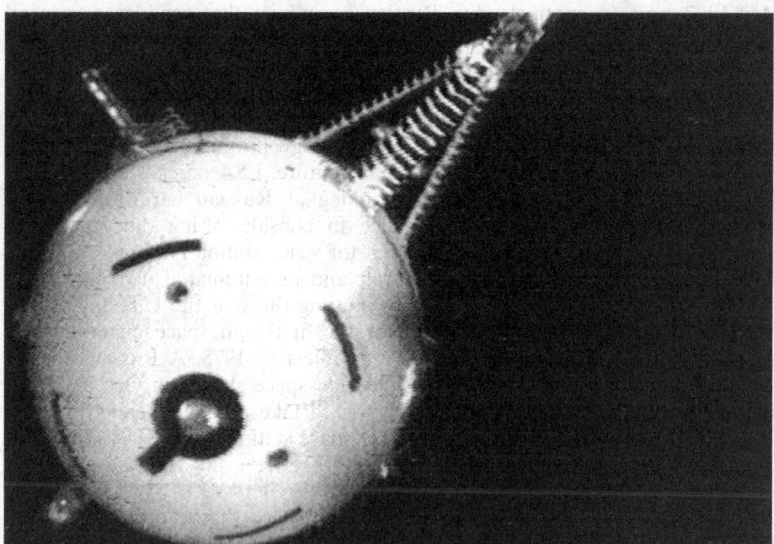

The Italian space agency satellite is tethered to the space shuttle *Atlantis* after its release in August. The satellite was to be unreeled from the shuttle on 20 km (12.5 mi) of Kevlar-and-copper line, which would generate electricity as it cut through the Earth's magnetic field, but because the line was jammed by a small tension-relief nut, only 260 m could be unreeled.
AP/WIDE WORLD

crew burned the first candles ever lighted in space and set fire to wire and plastic foam in tests designed to improve the safety of the craft. *Columbia* landed on July 9 at the Kennedy Space Center.

Atlantis flew again on July 31, with the Tethered Satellite System and the European Retrievable Carrier (EURECA) and a seven-person crew (commander Loren Shriver; pilot Andrew Allen; mission specialists Franklin Chang-Diaz, Claude Nicollier of Switzerland, Jeffrey Hoffman, and Marsha Ivins; and payload specialist Franco Malerba of Italy). The tether was designed to be trolled through the upper atmosphere while the shuttle stayed at a higher altitude. Its 20-km (12.5-mi) Kevlar-and-copper line was to generate electricity as it cut through the Earth's magnetic field, but no more than 260 m (850 ft) of tether would unreel because—postflight inspections showed—a small tension-relief nut jammed the line. The crew also deployed the EURECA, an automated experiment platform that was to be retrieved in 1993. *Atlantis* landed at the Kennedy Space Center on August 8.

Endeavour's second flight for the year, September 12–20, carried Spacelab J and a seven-person crew (commander Robert Gibson; pilot Curtis Brown; mission specialists Mark Lee, Jan Davis, Mae Jemison [*see* BIOGRAPHIES], and Jerome Apt; and payload specialist Mamoru Mohri of Japan). Japan provided more than half the experiments, many of them concerned with the effects of weightlessness on biological organisms.

On October 22 *Columbia* was launched on a 10-day mission with a six-person crew (commander James Wetherbee; pilot Michael Baker; mission specialists Charles Veach, William Shepard, and Tamara Jernigan; and payload specialist Steven MacLean of Canada.) The payload included the second Laser Geodynamics Satellite (LAGEOS II), an Italian satellite studded with laser reflectors; the automated U.S. Microgravity Payload (USMP-1); and an array of technology experiments.

Concluding the U.S. manned flights for 1992, *Discovery* was launched on December 2 on the last secret mission commissioned by the Department of Defense. Its all-military crew consisted of commander David Walker, pilot Robert Cabana, payload specialist Guion Bluford, and mission specialists James Voss and Michael Clifford. The crew deployed a large spy satellite and received laser signals from the ground. *Discovery* landed at Edwards Air Force Base on December 10.

Results from the Space Life Sciences mission flown aboard *Columbia* in June 1991 revealed that the astronauts lost up to 25% of the muscle mass in their thighs and calves during the nine-day flight and regained only half the loss in the same period after landing. Rats carried as test subjects were found to have 57% more nerve synapses in their balance organs than rats have on the ground.

Operations aboard the *Mir* space station continued throughout the year. On March 25 the "time traveler" returned when Sergey Krikalev, launched in May 1991, returned to Earth. Krikalev was to have returned in October 1991, but the breakup of the Soviet Union delayed the trip. First, Russia and the new state of Kazakhstan argued over the fee for launching a spacecraft from the Baikonur Cosmodrome in Kazakhstan, and then the Russians decided to cancel one mission in the fall and leave Krikalev up for a few months more. (On February 23, three people died when construction soldiers at Baikonur rioted over pay, food, and conditions.)

Krikalev and Aleksandr Volkov, who had arrived at *Mir* in October 1991, were replaced by Aleksandr Kalery and Aleksandr Viktorenko, who were launched aboard Soyuz TM-14 on March 17. German scientist Klaus-Dietrich Flade rode with the replacement crew and returned with the old crew. Russia also named a new crew and cosmonauts for the first manned flight of the Buran shuttle, scheduled to take place in 1994.

In the U.S., NASA's space station *Freedom* survived attempts in Congress to slash its funding. During the year it moved into its final design phase.

Interplanetary Probes. Ulysses, the international solar polar probe built by ESA, made a hairpin turn at Jupiter on February 8 and headed for a high pass over the Sun's south pole in 1994. Ulysses found that volcanoes on Jupiter's moon Io had weakened, leaving a "chewed donut" rather than a complete ring of oxygen and sulfur plasma. It also found that the bow shock, where the solar wind strikes Jupiter's magnetosphere, was only halfway as far from the planet as Voyager 1 had recorded in 1979.

Galileo continued to frustrate NASA ground controllers trying to release its stuck main antenna. Several attempts at soaking it in heat or cold yielded no results. Galileo was to make a second flyby of the Earth in December for a final kick onto the outbound leg to Jupiter. ESA's Giotto, which flew past Halley's Comet in 1986, was reawakened for a successful July 10 encounter with Comet Grigg-Skjellerup.

The deep-space record holder continued to send data back to Earth. Pioneer 10, launched in 1972, was more than eight billion kilometres (five billion miles) out into space but still had seven instruments working and indicating they could still detect the solar wind. Closer to home, the Pioneer Venus orbiter, which started mapping the cloud-covered planet in 1978, burned up in the atmosphere in mid-October. The Magellan radar mapper was in poor health, with two erratic transmitters, but had completed its primary objective of charting 80% of the surface of Venus in 1991 and, with its mission extended, the figure was raised to 99%. Budget problems forced NASA to plan on shutting Magellan down after it completed a gravity contour survey in 1993.

NASA on September 25 launched Mars Observer, its first mission to the planet since the Viking landers in the 1970s. This was designed to set the stage for future exploration with a detailed orbital survey of the planet's surface and chemical composition. Mars Observer was to arrive in a lopsided orbit around Mars in August 1993. During the next four months thrusters were to nudge the spacecraft into a lower, 400-km (250-mi) polar orbit that would let it cover the entire surface.

Principal instruments on the Mars Observer included a gamma-ray spectrometer to assay surface chemistry by analyzing radiation scattered back into space, a thermal-emission spectrometer to measure heat radiated from the surface, a pressure modulator infrared radiometer to probe the tenuous atmosphere, a laser altimeter to measure topography precisely, a magnetometer/electron reflectometer to monitor the near-space environment, and an electronic camera. The last instrument, actually a three-in-one camera, was expected to generate the most public interest because it would send back wide-angle and telephoto images of the Martian surface. In low- and moderate-resolution modes, a single picture element would span from 7,500 down to 480 m (24,600–1,570 ft). Areas of interest were to be imaged by the high-resolution camera, which would see details as small as 1.5 m (5 ft) across (it could not be used continuously because it would flood the craft's data system). Among other things, scientists would be looking for signs of water.

Automated Satellites. The Hubble Space Telescope made a comeback with the first images of Jupiter's polar aurora. (In a sense Hubble, in Earth orbit, is the "closest" probe to the planets.) Revelations about problems with Hubble's main mirror in 1990 tarnished the science community's expectations for the craft, but computer enhancement helped it become an observatory superior to the best terrestrial facilities. The Hubble Space Telescope found that embryonic galaxies some 10 billion light-years away may be cannibalizing each other, thus leading to the formation of large galaxies seen in older parts of the universe. (One light-year equals 9.4 trillion km [5.9 trillion mi].)

The Extreme Ultraviolet Explorer was launched June 4 by a Delta rocket on an all-sky survey. It detected at least two new ultraviolet sources. The Advanced X-ray Astrophysics Facility, conceived as a large X-ray telescope, was now expected to fly as imaging and spectroscopy satellites in the late 1990s.

Exploration of the Earth was being conducted by several diverse missions. The Franco-American Ocean Topography Experiment (called Poseidon by the French) was launched August 10 by an Ariane rocket. Poseidon used radar altimeters and microwave scanners to map ocean currents, the height and structure of waves, and other features of the ocean. A U.S. rocket launched the Japanese-built Geotail spacecraft for the International Solar-Terrestrial Physics Program on July 24. Geotail was to study the deep recesses

Soldiers help Russian cosmonaut Sergey Krikalev from his landing craft in Kazakhstan on March 25. He had spent 313 days in space, during which time the Soviet Union had ceased to exist and Leningrad, his hometown, had once again become St. Petersburg.
AP/WIDE WORLD

of the Earth's magnetosphere where it is stretched by the solar wind into deep space.

The first of a new series of "budget" Explorer satellites was launched by a Scout rocket on July 3. The Solar, Anomalous, and Magnetosphere Explorer sampled cosmic rays and other unusual radiation particles in the Earth's near-space environment. The Earth Observing System, once planned as a squadron of large satellite platforms bristling with sensors, was redesigned by NASA to fly as a flotilla of smaller satellites in order to save some $3 billion in costs.

Launch Vehicles. Both Ariane (carrying two communications satellites) and the space shuttle (Spacelab J) achieved their 50th launches in 1992. For the shuttle it was the 25th launch after the *Challenger* tragedy, itself a 25th launch. Plans to build a space launch facility at Cape York, Australia, were under way again; Space Transportation Systems of Australia took over the project from the failed Cape York Space Agency. Russia's Energia-M heavy lift launcher (with almost twice the shuttle's payload capability) was to be marketed by a publicly held company, and Russia planned to test a modified SS-25 missile as a small satellite launcher in December.   (DAVE DOOLING)

See also Astronomy; Earth Sciences; Industrial Review: *Aerospace; Telecommunications;* Military Affairs; Television and Radio.

This article updates the *Macropædia* articles EXPLORATION: *Space Exploration;* TELESCOPES.

The Games of the XXV Olympiad

BY MELINDA C. SHEPHERD

The year 1992 was a watershed in the history of the modern Olympic Games. It was the last time that athletes from the former Soviet Union participated as a single team, the first time in more than 30 years that no country boycotted or was banned from the event, and the last time the Winter and Summer Olympic Games would be held in the same year. The next Winter Games were scheduled for 1994 in Lillehammer, Norway, and the 1996 Summer Games would be held in Atlanta, Ga.

Winter Games. In February 1992 the host city of Albertville, along with several neighbouring towns in the Savoy region of France, welcomed 2,289 athletes (1,801 men and 488 women) from 64 countries to the Winter Olympic Games. Medals were awarded in 57 events, including two sports offered for the first time: freestyle mogul skiing and short-track speed skating. Curling, speed skiing, and two additional freestyle skiing events (aerial and ballet) were demonstration sports. Although the organizers, led by former gold medalist Jean-Claude Killy, were praised for the smooth running of the Games, many participants complained that the sports, spread out over 1,550 sq km (600 sq mi) in 10 different venues, lacked a feeling of camaraderie. Athletes from the former Soviet republics participated as a Unified Team (UT), marching under the Olympic banner instead of a national flag. Meanwhile, there were teams from the newly independent Baltic states, Croatia, and Slovenia.

The flamboyant Alberto Tomba (Italy; *see* BIOGRAPHIES), known to his legion of fans as "La Bomba" Tomba, captured his second consecutive gold medal in giant slalom, making him the first skier to retain his Olympic title in that event. In a dazzling display that was equal parts artistry and athleticism, Kristi Yamaguchi (*see* BIOGRAPHIES) became the first American woman to win the gold in figure skating since Dorothy Hamill in 1976.

Summer Games. The Catalan city of Barcelona, Spain, put on a spectacular show as the host of the Summer Games. With more than 10,000 athletes from 172 teams participating in 257 medal events (159 men's, 86 women's, and 12 mixed), it was the largest sports event in history. There were three new medal sports: badminton, baseball, and women's judo. The former Soviet republics again appeared as the Unified Team, but in Barcelona gold medalists were saluted with their individual national anthems and flags. Namibia, competing for the first time, was joined by returnees South Africa (which sent its first integrated team), Cuba, Nicaragua, Madagascar, Ethiopia, Seychelles, North Korea, and Albania. Although the truncated nation of Yugoslavia was banned, athletes from Serbia and Montenegro were allowed to compete as individuals. Even Somalia and Bosnia and Hercegovina were represented by athletes who had to be escorted to and from their war-torn homelands.

As in 1988, there were athletes ejected for drug abuse and worries over the increasing number of professional athletes. The latter was best exemplified by the U.S. basketball "Dream Team," which comprised one collegian and 11 National Basketball Association stars. There were also complaints over the officiating in boxing, volleyball, weight lifting, and synchronized swimming. However, neither the controversies nor the extreme heat and humidity could make the Games anything less than successful.

Among the outstanding athletes were Belorussian gymnast Vitali Sherbo (*see* BIOGRAPHIES), who led the Unified Team to Olympic gold and won five of the seven individual gold medals awarded, including the all-around title; 32-year-old sprinter Linford Christie (U.K.), heptathlete Jackie Joyner-Kersee (U.S.), and runner Gail Devers (U.S.; *see* BIOGRAPHIES) in track and field; the 13-year-old diving sensation Fu Mingxia (China); Kristina Egerszegi (Hungary; *see* BIOGRAPHIES) and Yevgeny Sadovy (UT) in swimming; and Karen and Sarah Josephson (U.S.; *see* BIOGRAPHIES), twin sisters who dominated synchronized swimming (duet).

HEINZ KLUETMEIER—SPORTS ILLUSTRATED

A replica of a Greek galley appears in the opening ceremonies of the Games of the XXV Olympiad in Barcelona, Spain, on July 25. A record 172 teams participated in the 1992 Summer Games.

Olympic Champions, 1992 Winter Games, Albertville

Alpine Skiing

Men

Downhill	P. Ortlieb (Austria)	1 min 50.37 sec
Slalom	F.C. Jagge (Nor.)	1 min 44.39 sec
Giant slalom	A. Tomba (Italy)	2 min 6.98 sec
Supergiant slalom	K.A. Aamodt (Nor.)	1 min 13.04 sec
Combined event	J. Polig (Italy)	14.58 pt

Women

Downhill	K. Lee-Gartner (Can.)	1 min 52.55 sec
Slalom	P. Kronberger (Austria)	1 min 32.68 sec
Giant slalom	P. Wiberg (Swed.)	2 min 12.74 sec
Supergiant slalom	D. Compagnoni (Italy)	1 min 21.22 sec
Combined event	P. Kronberger (Austria)	2.55 pt

Nordic Skiing

Men

10-km cross-country	V. Ulvang (Nor.)	27 min 36.0 sec
15-km cross-country	B. Daehlie (Nor.)	38 min 1.9 sec
30-km cross-country	V. Ulvang (Nor.)	1 hr 22 min 27.8 sec
50-km cross-country	B. Daehlie (Nor.)	2 hr 3 min 41.5 sec
40-km ski relay	Norway	1 hr 39 min 26.0 sec
90-m ski jump	E. Vettori (Austria)	222.8 pt
120-m ski jump	T. Nieminen (Fin.)	239.5 pt
120-m team ski jump	Finland	644.4 pt
Nordic combined	F. Guy (France)	426.470 pt
Nordic team combined	Japan	1,247.180 pt

Women

5-km cross-country	M. Lukkarinen (Fin.)	14 min 13.8 sec
10-km cross-country	L. Egorova (UT)	25 min 53.7 sec
15-km cross-country	L. Egorova (UT)	42 min 20.8 sec
30-km cross-country	S. Belmondo (Italy)	1 hr 22 min 30.1 sec
20-km ski relay	Unified Team	59 min 34.8 sec

Freestyle Skiing

Men's moguls	E. Grospiron (France)	25.81 pt
Women's moguls	D. Weinbrecht (U.S.)	23.69 pt

Biathlon

Men

10 km	M. Kirchner (Ger.)	26 min 2.3 sec
20 km	Ye. Redkine (UT)	57 min 34.4 sec
30-km relay	Germany	1 hr 24 min 43.5 sec

Women

7.5 km	A. Restzova (UT)	24 min 29.2 sec
15 km	A. Misersky (Ger.)	51 min 47.2 sec
22.5-km relay	France	1 hr 15 min 55.6 sec

Figure Skating

Men	V. Petrenko (UT)	1.5 pt
Women	K. Yamaguchi (U.S.)	1.5 pt
Pairs	N. Mishkutenok and A. Dmitriev (UT)	1.5 pt
Ice dancing	M. Klimova and S. Ponomarenko (UT)	2.0 pt

Speed Skating

Men

500 m	U.-J. Mey (Ger.)	37.14 sec
1,000 m	O. Zinke (Ger.)	1 min 14.85 sec
1,500 m	J. Koss (Nor.)	1 min 54.81 sec
5,000 m	G. Karlstad (Nor.)	6 min 59.97 sec
10,000 m	B. Veldkamp (Neth.)	14 min 12.12 sec

Women

500 m	B. Blair (U.S.)	40.33 sec
1,000 m	B. Blair (U.S.)	1 min 21.90 sec
1,500 m	J. Börner (Ger.)	2 min 5.87 sec
3,000 m	G. Niemann (Ger.)	4 min 19.90 sec
5,000 m	G. Niemann (Ger.)	7 min 31.57 sec

Short-Track Speed Skating

Men

1,000 m	Kim Ki Hoon (S. Korea)	1 min 30.76 sec[1]
5,000 m relay	South Korea	7 min 14.02 sec[1]

Women

500 m	C. Turner (U.S.)	47.04 sec
3,000 m relay	Canada	4 min 36.62 sec

Ice Hockey

Winning team	Unified Team (7–1–0)	

Bobsledding

Two man	Switzerland	4 min 3.26 sec
Four man	Austria	3 min 53.90 sec

Tobogganing (Luge)

Men (single)	G. Hackl (Ger.)	3 min 2.363 sec
Men (double)	S. Krausse and J. Behrendt (Ger.)	1 min 32.053 sec
Women (single)	D. Neuner (Austria)	3 min 6.696 sec

[1]World record.

Olympic Champions, 1992 Summer Games, Barcelona

Archery

	Men		Women	
Individual	S. Flute (France)	110 pt	Cho Youn Jeong (S. Korea)	112 pt
Team	Spain	238 pt	South Korea	236 pt

Badminton

Men's singles	A.B. Kusuma (Indonesia)
Men's doubles	Kim Moon Soo and Park Joo Bong (S. Korea)
Women's singles	S. Susanti (Indonesia)
Women's doubles	Hwang Hye Young and Chung So Young (S. Korea)

Baseball

Winning team	Cuba

Basketball

Men	U.S.	Women	Unified Team

Boxing

48-kg class	R. Marcelo (Cuba)	67-kg class	M. Carruth (Ire.)
51-kg class	Choi Chol Su (N. Korea)	71-kg class	J. Lemus (Cuba)
54-kg class	J. Casamayor (Cuba)	75-kg class	A. Hernandez (Cuba)
57-kg class	A. Tews (Ger.)	81-kg class	T. May (Ger.)
60-kg class	O. de la Hoya (U.S.)	91-kg class	F. Savon (Cuba)
63.5-kg class	H. Vinent (Cuba)	91-kg + class	R. Balado (Cuba)

Canoeing

Men

500-m kayak singles	M. Kolehmainen (Fin.)	1 min 40.34 sec
1,000-m kayak singles	C. Robinson (Australia)	3 min 37.26 sec
500-m kayak pairs	K. Bluhm/T. Gutsche (Ger.)	1 min 29.84 sec
1,000-m kayak pairs	K. Bluhm/T. Gutsche (Ger.)	3 min 16.10 sec
1,000-m kayak fours	Germany	2 min 54.18 sec
Slalom kayak singles	P. Ferrazzi (Italy)	106.89 pt
500-m Canadian singles	N. Bukhalov (Bulg.)	1 min 51.15 sec
1,000-m Canadian singles	N. Bukhalov (Bulg.)	4 min 5.92 sec
500-m Canadian pairs	A. Masseikov/D. Dovgalenok (UT)	1 min 41.54 sec
1,000-m Canadian pairs	U. Papke/I. Spelly (Ger.)	3 min 37.42 sec
Slalom Canadian singles	L. Pollert (Czech.)	113.69 pt
Slalom Canadian pairs	J. Jacobi/S. Strausbaugh (U.S.)	122.41 pt

Women

500-m kayak singles	B. Schmidt (Ger.)	1 min 51.60 sec
500-m kayak pairs	R. Portwich/A. Von Seck (Ger.)	1 min 40.29 sec
500-m kayak fours	Hungary	1 min 38.32 sec
Slalom kayak singles	E. Micheler (Ger.)	126.41 pt

Cycling

Men

Road race	F. Casartelli (Italy)	4 hr 35 min 21 sec
Team time trial	Germany	2 hr 1 min 39 sec
(1-km) time trial	J. Moreno (Spain)	1 min 3.342 sec
4,000-m indiv. pursuit	C. Boardman (U.K.)	3 min 21.649 sec
4,000-m team pursuit	Germany	4 min 8.791 sec
Sprint	J. Fiedler (Ger.)	
50-km points race	G. Lombardi (Italy)	

Women

Road race	K. Watt (Australia)	2 hr 4 min 42 sec
3,000 m indiv. pursuit	P. Rossner (Ger.)	3 min 41.753 sec
Sprint	E. Salumae (Estonia)	

Diving

	Men		Women	
Springboard	M. Lenzi (U.S.)	676.53 pt	Gao Min (China)	572.40 pt
Platform	Sun Shuwei (China)	677.31 pt	Fu Mingxia (China)	461.43 pt

Equestrian

	Individual	Team
3-day event	M. Ryan (Australia)	Australia
Dressage	N. Uphoff (Ger.)	Germany
Jumping	L. Beerbaum (Ger.)	Netherlands

Fencing

	Individual	Team
Men's foil	P. Omnes (France)	Germany
Women's foil	G. Trillini (Italy)	Italy
Épée	E. Srecki (France)	Germany
Sabre	B. Szabo (Hung.)	Unified Team

Field Hockey

Men	Germany	Women	Spain

Gymnastics

Men

Team	Unified Team	585.450 pt
All-around	V. Sherbo (UT)	59.025 pt
Floor exercise	Li Xiaoshuang (China)	9.925 pt
Vault	V. Sherbo (UT)	9.856 pt
Pommel horse	V. Sherbo (UT)	9.925 pt
	Pae Gil Su (N. Korea)	9.925 pt
Rings	V. Sherbo (UT)	9.937 pt
Parallel bars	V. Sherbo (UT)	9.90 pt
Horizontal bar	T. Dimas (U.S.)	9.875 pt

Women

Team	Unified Team	395.666 pt
All-around	T. Gutsu (UT)	39.737 pt
Floor exercise	L. Milosovici (Rom.)	10.00 pt
Vault	L. Milosovici (Rom.)	9.925 pt
	H. Onodi (Hung.)	9.925 pt
Uneven bars	Lu Li (China)	10.00 pt
Balance beam	T. Lyssenko (UT)	9.975 pt
Rhythmic competition	A. Timoshenko (UT)	59.037 pt

Handball

Men	Unified Team	Women	S. Korea

Judo

	Men		Women
60-kg class	N. Gousseinov (UT)	48-kg class	C. Nowak (France)
65-kg class	R. Sampaio (Brazil)	52-kg class	A. Munoz Martinez (Spain)
71-kg class	T. Koga (Japan)	56-kg class	M. Blasco Soto (Spain)
78-kg class	H. Yoshida (Japan)	61-kg class	C. Fleury (France)
86-kg class	W. Legien (Poland)	66-kg class	O. Reve (Cuba)
95-kg class	A. Kovacs (Hung.)	72-kg class	Kim Mi Jung (S. Korea)
95-kg + class	D. Khakhaleichvili (UT)	72-kg + class	Zhuang Xiaoyan (China)

Modern Pentathlon

Individual	A. Skrzypaszek (Pol.)	5,559 pt
Team	Poland	16,018 pt

Rowing

Men

Single sculls	T. Lange (Ger.)	6 min 51.40 sec
Double sculls	Australia	6 min 17.32 sec
Quadruple sculls	Germany	5 min 45.17 sec
Coxed pairs	U.K.	6 min 49.83 sec
Coxless pairs	U.K.	6 min 27.72 sec
Coxed fours	Romania	5 min 59.37 sec
Coxless fours	Australia	5 min 55.04 sec
Eights	Canada	5 min 29.53 sec

Women

Single sculls	E. Lipa (Rom.)	7 min 25.54 sec
Double sculls	Germany	6 min 49.00 sec
Quadruple sculls	Germany	6 min 20.18 sec
Coxless pairs	Canada	7 min 06.22 sec
Coxless fours	Canada	6 min 30.85 sec
Eights	Canada	6 min 02.62 sec

Shooting

Men

Rapid-fire pistol	R. Schumann (Ger.)	885 pt
Free pistol	K. Loukachik (UT)	658 pt
Air pistol	Wang Yifu (China)	684.8 pt
Running game target	M. Jakosits (Ger.)	673 pt
Small-bore rifle, 3 pos.	G. Petikiane (UT)	1,267.4 pt
Small-bore rifle, prone	Lee Eun Chul (S. Korea)	702.5 pt
Air rifle	Y. Fedkin (UT)	695.3 pt
Trap (open event)	P. Hrdlicka (Czech.)	219 pt
Skeet (open event)	Zhang Shan (China)	223 pt

Women

Sport pistol	M. Logvinenko (UT)	684 pt
Air pistol	M. Logvinenko (UT)	486.4 pt
Small-bore rifle, 3 pos.	L. Meili (U.S.)	684.3 pt
Air rifle	Yeo Kab Soon (S. Korea)	498.2 pt

Soccer

Winning team	Spain

Swimming

Men

50-m freestyle	A. Popov (UT)	21.91 sec[1]
100-m freestyle	A. Popov (UT)	49.02 sec
200-m freestyle	Ye. Sadovy (UT)	1 min 46.70 sec[1]
400-m freestyle	Ye. Sadovy (UT)	3 min 45.00 sec[2]
1,500-m freestyle	K. Perkins (Australia)	14 min 43.48 sec[2]
100-m backstroke	M. Tewksbury (Canada)	53.98 sec[1]
200-m backstroke	M. Lopez-Zubero (Spain)	1 min 58.47 sec[1]
100-m breaststroke	N. Diebel (U.S.)	1 min 1.50 sec[1]
200-m breaststroke	M. Barrowman (U.S.)	2 min 10.16 sec[2]
100-m butterfly	P. Morales (U.S.)	53.32 sec
200-m butterfly	M. Stewart (U.S.)	1 min 56.26 sec[1]
200-m individual medley	T. Darnyi (Hung.)	2 min 0.76 sec
400-m individual medley	T. Darnyi (Hung.)	4 min 14.23 sec[1]
4 × 100-m freestyle relay	U.S.	3 min 16.74 sec
4 × 200-m freestyle relay	Unified Team	7 min 11.95 sec[2]
4 × 100-m medley relay	U.S.	3 min 36.93 sec

Women

50-m freestyle	Yang Wenyi (China)	24.79 sec[2]
100-m freestyle	Zhuang Yong (China)	54.64 sec[1]
200-m freestyle	N. Haislett (U.S.)	1 min 57.90 sec
400-m freestyle	D. Hase (Ger.)	4 min 7.18 sec
800-m freestyle	J. Evans (U.S.)	8 min 25.52 sec
100-m backstroke	K. Egerszegi (Hung.)	1 min 0.68 sec
200-m backstroke	K. Egerszegi (Hung.)	2 min 7.06 sec[1]
100-m breaststroke	Ye. Rudkovskaya (UT)	1 min 8.00 sec
200-m breaststroke	K. Iwasaki (Japan)	2 min 26.65 sec
100-m butterfly	Qian Hong (China)	58.62 sec
200-m butterfly	S. Sanders (U.S.)	2 min 8.67 sec
200-m individual medley	Lin Li (China)	2 min 11.65 sec[2]
400-m individual medley	K. Egerszegi (Hung.)	4 min 36.54 sec
4 × 100-m freestyle relay	U.S.	3 min 39.46 sec[2]
4 × 100-m medley relay	U.S.	4 min 2.54 sec[2]
Synchronized swimming-solo	K. Babb-Sprague (U.S.)	191.848 pt
Synchronized swimming-duet	K. Josephson/S. Josephson (U.S.)	192.175 pt

Table Tennis

Men's singles	J.O. Waldner (Swed.)
Men's doubles	Lu Lin/Wang Tao (China)
Women's singles	Deng Yaping (China)
Women's doubles	Deng Yaping/Qiao Hong (China)

Tennis

Men's singles	M. Rosset (Switz.)
Men's doubles	B. Becker/M. Stich (Ger.)
Women's singles	J. Capriati (U.S.)
Women's doubles	G. Fernandez/M.J. Fernandez (U.S.)

Track and Field

Men

100 m	L. Christie (U.K.)	9.96 sec
200 m	M. Marsh (U.S.)	20.01 sec
400 m	Q. Watts (U.S.)	43.50 sec[1]
4 × 100-m relay	U.S.	37.40 sec[2]
4 × 400-m relay	U.S.	2 min 55.74 sec[2]
800 m	W. Tanui (Kenya)	1 min 43.66 sec
1,500 m	F. Cacho (Spain)	3 min 40.12 sec
5,000 m	D. Baumann (Ger.)	13 min 12.52 sec
10,000 m	K. Skah (Morocco)	27 min 46.70 sec
Marathon	Hwang Young Cho (S. Korea)	2 hr 13 min 23 sec
110-m hurdles	M. McKoy (Canada)	13.12 sec
400-m hurdles	K. Young (U.S.)	46.78 sec[2]
Steeplechase	M. Birir (Kenya)	8 min 8.84 sec
20-km walk	D. Plaza Montero (Spain)	1 hr 21 min 45 sec
50-km walk	A. Perlov (UT)	3 hr 50 min 13 sec
High jump	J. Sotomayor (Cuba)	2.34 m
Long jump	C. Lewis (U.S.)	8.67 m
Triple jump	M. Conley (U.S.)	18.17 m
Pole vault	M. Tarasov (UT)	5.80 m
Shot put	M. Stulce (U.S.)	21.70 m
Discus throw	R. Ubartas (Lithuania)	65.12 m
Javelin throw	J. Zelezny (Czech.)	89.66 m[1]
Hammer throw	A. Abduvaliyev (UT)	82.53 m
Decathlon	R. Zmelik (Czech.)	8,611 pt

Women

100 m	G. Devers (U.S.)	10.82 sec
200 m	G. Torrence (U.S.)	21.81 sec
400 m	M.-J. Perec (France)	48.83 sec
4 × 100-m relay	U.S.	42.11 sec
4 × 400-m relay	Unified Team	3 min 20.20 sec
800 m	E. Van Langen (Neth.)	1 min 55.54 sec
1,500 m	H. Boulmerka (Algeria)	3 min 55.30 sec
3,000 m	Ye. Romanova (UT)	8 min 46.04 sec
10,000 m	D. Tulu (Eth.)	31 min 6.02 sec
Marathon	V. Yegorova (UT)	2 hr 32 min 41 sec
100-m hurdles	P. Patoulidou (Greece)	12.64 sec
400-m hurdles	S. Gunnell (U.K.)	53.23 sec
10-km walk	Chen Yueling (China)	44 min 32 sec[1]
High jump	H. Henkel (Ger.)	2.02 m
Long jump	H. Drechsler (Ger.)	7.14 m
Shot put	S. Krivalevra (UT)	21.06 m
Discus throw	M. Marten (Cuba)	70.06 m
Javelin throw	S. Renk (Ger.)	68.34 m
Heptathlon	J. Joyner-Kersee (U.S.)	7,044 pt

Volleyball

Men	Brazil	Women	Cuba

Water Polo

Winning team	Italy

Weight lifting

52-kg class	I. Ivanov (Bulg.)	265 kg
56-kg class	Chun Byung Kwan (S. Korea)	287.5 kg
60-kg class	N. Suleymanoglu (Turkey)	320 kg
67.5-kg class	I. Militossian (UT)	337.5 kg
75-kg class	F. Kassapu (UT)	357.5 kg
82.5-kg class	P. Dimas (Greece)	370.0 kg
90-kg class	K. Kakhiashvili (UT)	412.5 kg
100-kg class	V. Tregubov (UT)	410.0 kg
110-kg class	R. Weller (Ger.)	432.5 kg
110-kg + class	A. Kurlovich (UT)	450.0 kg

Wrestling

	Freestyle	Greco-Roman
48-kg class	Park II (N. Korea)	O. Kucherenko (UT)
52-kg class	Li Hak (N. Korea)	J. Ronningen (Norway)
57-kg class	A. Puerto (Cuba)	An Han Bong (S. Korea)
62-kg class	J. Smith (U.S.)	A. Pirim (Turkey)
68-kg class	A. Fadzaev (UT)	A. Repka (Hung.)
74-kg class	Park Jang (S. Korea)	M. Iskandarian (UT)
82-kg class	K. Jackson (U.S.)	P. Farcas (Hung.)
90-kg class	M. Khadartsev (UT)	M. Bullmann (Ger.)
100-kg class	L. Khabelov (UT)	H. Milian (Cuba)
130-kg class	B. Baumgartner (U.S.)	A. Karelin (UT)

Yachting

Men's 470 class	Spain	Women's Europe	L. Anderson (Nor.)
Women's 470 class	Spain	Flying Dutchman (open)	Spain
Men's sailboard	F. David (France)	Star (open)	U.S.
Women's sailboard	B. Kendall (N.Z.)	Tornado (open)	France
Men's Finn	J. van der Ploeg (Spain)	Soling (open)	Denmark

[1]Olympic record. [2]World record.

Melinda C. Shepherd is Associate Editor of Encyclopædia Britannica Yearbooks.

Sports and Games

AERIAL SPORTS

The first transatlantic balloon race in history, a record-setting 200-person free-fall parachuting formation, and a world-record glider flight across the Mediterranean from France via Spain to Morocco highlighted the year in aerial sports. A Belgian team won the balloon race, which included gas balloons from Belgium, Britain, the United States, The Netherlands, and Germany in flights launched Sept. 16, 1992, from Bangor, Maine, to the European continent. The winning team of Wim Verstraeten of Belgium and Swiss balloonist Bertrand Piccard landed September 21 near Peque, Spain, just over the Portuguese border. Their flight lasted nearly five days (114 hr 27 min) and covered a distance of more than 4,150 km (2,580 mi). They had hoped to fly as far as Italy and break the endurance record of 137 hours set by Ben Abruzzo of the U.S. in the first-ever balloon crossing of the Atlantic in 1978, but bad weather ahead compelled them to curtail their flight once they had reached the continent.

Following, in order, were the balloons from Britain and the U.S. The German and Dutch balloons encountered bad weather and ditched at sea. Their two-man crews were rescued. The Atlantic had been successfully traversed by balloonists only five times. Five balloonists had died in attempts.

The 200-person free-fall parachute "star" was achieved October 23 by a mixed-nationality team jumping from six aircraft at Myrtle Beach, S.C. The new record, presuming confirmation by the Fédération Aéronautique Internationale (FAI), surpassed the briefly held mark of a 150-jumper formation set July 4 at Koksijde, Belgium. That group had the advantage of using only two aircraft—large C-130 military transports—and achieved its formation in just six attempts.

Enjoying clear weather, the South Carolina skydivers made their jump from 5,500 m (18,000 ft). The 200 chutists included four husband-and-wife teams: Kevin and Cynthia Gibson, Amy and Dan Goriesky, James and Robyn Linaberry, and Suzanne and Terry Pike, all Americans.

Two French brothers, Gerard and Jean-Noel Herbaud, became the first ever to fly from France to North Africa in a sailplane and at the same time set a new world distance record for two-place gliders of 1,450 km (900 mi), surpassing the 1,049-km (652-mi) mark set by Hans Werner Grosse and Karin Grosse in 1990. Their mark set records for both straight-line distance and distance to a declared goal.

The world gas balloon championship at Obertraun, Austria, was won October 10 by David Levin (already world hot-air balloon champion) and Jim Schiller of the U.S., scoring 5,798 points. Germany's Thomas Fink and Ranier Hassold took second with 5,732 points, and Austria's Josef Starkbaum and Gert Scholz were third with 5,057.

Nick Saum of the U.S. set a world altitude mark of 5,136 m (16,850 ft) for Class AM balloons in his Saum HGB-14 on January 12. Guy Moyano of Luxembourg set a duration record for hot-air airships of 5 hr 6 min 42 sec flying a Cameron DP-80 on January 25.

A multinational all-women skydiving team organized by Alexis Perry of the U.S. broke world records August 14 at Le Luc, France, by achieving a free-fall parachutist "star" of 100 jumpers. Also in August, French jumpers at Brienne-Le-Château achieved a canopy formation—holding onto one another after chutes were deployed—of 37 people, a world record that lasted only until October 10, when 38 Americans led by Charles Bunch and Lillian Goodin completed a canopy formation at Richland, Wash.

At the world parachuting style and accuracy championship at Trieben, Austria, August 14–23, the men's overall team competition was won by Czechoslovakia with a score of 15. Poland, which also had 15, was given second place. Men's individual accuracy was won by Jindrich Vedmach of Czechoslovakia with a one-centimetre distance from target. Winning the men's style contest was Eric Lauer of France with a 24.87-sec score. The men's individual overall was won by Josef Pavalata of Czechoslovakia with a score of 16.

In women's team overall, Germany scored 4 to take first, China was second with 8, and France was third with 10. Ortai Nuntarom of Thailand was first in women's individual accuracy with a mark of one centimetre. Women's style was won by Denise Barn of Germany with 27.01 sec. In women's individual overall, Nadezhda Kotora of Russia took first with a score of 12.

The first-ever globe-circling general aviation world air race took place during the year with 33 piston and turboprop aircraft (17 from the U.S.) taking off from Geneva on June 20 and finishing July 11 at Cannes, France, after crossing Russia, the Pacific Ocean, North America, and the Atlantic Ocean. Steven Nagorny and Robert Wahl of the U.S., flying a Beech Bonanza with special wingtip tanks, took first place under the handicap scoring system. Bruno Kepler and Nicolas Poncot of Switzerland, in a Piper Cheyenne III, won the turboprop division.   (MICHAEL D. KILLIAN)

AUTOMOBILE RACING

Grand Prix Racing. The Williams-Renault team broke the previous domination of the McLaren-Hondas in international Formula One racing in 1992. At the season opener, the South African Grand Prix at Kyalami on March 1, Britain's Nigel Mansell (see BIOGRAPHIES) and the veteran Italian driver Riccardo Patrese set the pattern, their V10-engined Williams-Renault FW14Bs finishing first and second; 1991 world champion Ayrton Senna of Brazil placed third in a McLaren-Honda. Mansell set the fastest lap, at 191.31 km/h, (161 km = 100 mi). Another sign of things to follow was the fourth place gained by a promising young German, Michael Schumacher, in the much-improved Benetton with a Ford HB V8 engine.

The same pattern occurred in Mexico, where Mansell and Patrese led Schumacher home. Mansell averaged 199.133 km/h for the 304.975-km race, but fastest lap went to the McLaren-Honda of Gerhard Berger (Austria) at 204.761 km/h. For the next Grand Prix, at Interlagos, Brazil, McLaren-Honda tried to return to its 1991 form with the new MP4/7A V12, but Senna retired with electrical malfunctions after only 17 of the 71 laps. The order of finish was the by-now-customary one of Mansell, Patrese, and Schumacher.

The scene changed to Europe in May for the Spanish Grand Prix at Barcelona, but wet weather upset the predicted outcome to some extent. Nevertheless, Mansell was again the winner, and he coped with the changeable conditions with an early fastest lap at 166.682 km/h. Schumacher was second for Benetton. Later that month even the trying heat of Imola, where the San Marino Grand Prix was staged, could not stop Mansell. He won again, followed in by Patrese in his Williams-Renault. Patrese had the fastest lap at 210.687 km/h. The tour then moved to Monaco for the famous street race, where the demands on the drivers were greater than ever before. The race appeared to be another victory for Mansell. He was in the lead with 7 of the 78 laps left, when he thought one of his Goodyear tires had punctured. He stopped, but his mechanics found nothing wrong. He stormed out again, to a quickest lap of 146.795 km/h for the twisting circuit, but it was too late. Senna won by 0.215 second.

Formula One Grand Prix Race Results, 1992

Race	Driver	Average speed (km/h)	Car
South African	N. Mansell	191.31	Williams-Renault
Mexican	N. Mansell	199.133	Williams-Renault
Brazilian	N. Mansell	190.169	Williams-Renault
Spanish	N. Mansell	159.318	Williams-Renault
San Marino	N. Mansell	204.552	Williams-Renault
Monaco	A. Senna	140.298	McLaren-Honda
Canadian	G. Berger	188.765	McLaren-Honda
French	N. Mansell	179.283	Williams-Renault
British	N. Mansell	215.801	Williams-Renault
German	N. Mansell	234.531	Williams-Renault
Hungarian	A. Senna	172.424	McLaren-Honda
Belgian	M. Schumacher	191.387	Benetton-Ford
Italian	A. Senna	235.689	McLaren-Honda
Portuguese	N. Mansell	195.520	Williams-Renault
Japanese	R. Patrese	200.168	Williams-Renault
Australian	G. Berger	171.829	McLaren-Honda

WORLD DRIVERS' CHAMPIONSHIP: Mansell 108 pt, Patrese 56 pt, Schumacher 53 pt, Senna, 50 pt.
CONSTRUCTORS' WORLD CHAMPIONSHIP: Williams-Renault 164 pt, McLaren-Honda 99 pt, Benetton-Ford 91 pt, Ferrari 21 pt.

At Montreal in June, Berger was the winner over Schumacher and also had the fastest lap at 193.679 km/h. In the French Grand Prix at Magny-Cours, a collision between Schumacher and Senna, caused by the former, eliminated both. Patrese set the pace, forcing Mansell to drive hard behind him. Team sense prevailed and the Italian waved Mansell by, so that he scored his 27th Grand Prix victory, equaling Jackie Stewart's record. Mansell drove the fastest lap at 198.721 km/h.

The British Grand Prix at Silverstone was won convincingly by Mansell. Patrese finished second, and Mansell had the fastest lap at 227.891 km/h. At Hockenheim for the German Grand Prix, Mansell was again master, but Patrese lapped fastest on this quick course, at 242.318 km/h, before he spun off. Senna finished second. Then at Budapest for the Hungarian Grand Prix in August, the world championship was clinched for Mansell when he took second behind Senna after suffering a puncture. He recovered to have the fastest lap at 182.418 km/h.

At the Spa circuit late in August, Schumacher won the Belgian Grand Prix for Benetton and also set fastest lap at 220.589 km/h. Mansell finished second. After this great season the position changed in the Italian Grand Prix at Monza, where Mansell went out with hydraulic/gearbox problems after a best lap at 242.455 km/h, and Patrese was fifth. Senna won, and Martin Brundle of Britain in a Benetton was second. Mansell was back on form for the Portuguese Grand Prix at Estoril, but the McLarens were fighting back, Senna achieving the fastest lap at 205.318 km/h and Berger finishing ahead of him, the only driver besides Mansell to make the full 71 laps. Mansell's victory was his ninth of the season, a record for Formula One drivers.

There remained the Grands Prix of Japan and Australia. In the former Patrese won from Berger after Mansell experienced engine failure. Mansell had the fastest lap, at 209.749 km/h. In Australia Mansell was again frustrated; instead of winning his hoped-for 10th victory of 1992, he was rear-ended by Senna, and both were out of the race. This gave Berger a welcome win for McLaren-Honda, with Schumacher only 0.741 second behind him in the Benetton-Ford. Mansell was presumably driving in his last Formula One race, as he planned to drive on the IndyCar circuit in 1993.

Rallies and Other Races. The 1992 Monza 50-km race was won by a Toyota TSO 10 from Peugeot and Spice. At Silverstone the Warwick/Dalmas Peugeot 905 1A scored over Mazda and Lola, and at Le Mans, France, the classic 24-hour race went to the Peugeot 905 LM, from Toyota and another 905 LM. From a 10-car field at Donington, Peugeots finished first and second, and a Toyota was third. Derek Warwick (U.K.) was world champion.

In rally racing the Monte Carlo event was won by Lancia of Italy, from Toyota. Toyota won the winter Swedish Rally from Subaru and Nissan. The Portuguese event was a victory for a Lancia Delta, from a Ford Sierra Cosworth 4 × 4 and two GT4 Toyotas. The winner of the Martini Safari in Kenya was a Toyota Celica Turbo 4 × 4, which beat two Lancia Delta HFs. Lancia took the Tour of Corsica from Ford, and the famous Acropolis Rally went to Didier Auriol's Lancia Delta, with another Lancia Delta second. Toyota won in New Zealand over a Lancia Delta, but in the Argentina Rally a Toyota puncture gave Lancia the victory. In the Finnish Lakes Rally, Lancia won again, over another Lancia. A Lancia Delta Integrale beat two Ford Sierra Cosworth 4 × 4s in Cyprus, and the same order of finish took place in Australia. Mitsubishi won the Ivory Coast event, and the RAC Rally was won by Toyota. Carlos Sainz of

FOCUS ON SPORTS

Al Unser, Jr., races to victory in the Indianapolis 500. He won over Scott Goodyear by only 0.043 second, the smallest margin of victory in the history of the race.

Spain, driving a Toyota, was the world rally drivers' champion for 1992, and Lancia won the manufacturers' award.

(WILLIAM C. BODDY)

U.S. Racing. The closest championship points battle in stock-car history and the closest finish ever in the Indianapolis 500 made 1992 a special year in U.S. auto racing. The retirement of Richard Petty, the National Association for Stock Car Auto Racing's (NASCAR's) greatest driver, after 35 years and the decision of Indy's Michael Andretti and Formula One world champion Nigel Mansell to swap racing venues in 1993 added to the uniqueness.

Late in the Indianapolis 500, it seemed as if Andretti would triumph in his Lola Cosworth Ford, but he suddenly slowed and stopped 11 laps from the end. Seemingly, that left the race to Al Unser, Jr., in a Galmer Chevrolet Special. He had moved steadily up from a 12th-place start to battle Andretti. The excitement was not over, however. Scott Goodyear of Canada, who had started his Lola Chevrolet in 33rd position, closed quickly on Unser, seemingly drawing even as they approached the finish. But Unser spurted across first by 0.043 second to win the $1,244,184 first prize. He set an average speed of 134.479 mph (216.511 km/h).

Although he remained competitive throughout the season, Unser Jr. was not to win again. The battle for the IndyCar championship, however, continued to the final event, which was won by Andretti. But owner-driver Bobby Rahal, in a Lola-Chevrolet, was the year's IndyCar champion. He won four races during the season.

Meanwhile, NASCAR delivered its own surprise ending. Alan Kulwicki, a Wisconsin college graduate who had moved south seven years earlier to race stock cars, completed an amazing late-season stretch run to win the Winston Cup championship and $2,322,561 for the season. Davey Allison had won NASCAR's classic, the Daytona 500, and four other races including the Talladega 500 to take a 30-point lead into the finale at Atlanta, Ga. He crashed during the race, however, leaving the battle for the season crown to Kulwicki and Bill Elliott. Elliott won the race, his fifth major victory, but Kulwicki won the title, 4,078 points to 4,068, by leading more laps before falling back. The first owner-driver champion since 1960, Kulwicki won twice in 1992. Richard Petty did not come close to winning in his final season of racing but nevertheless retired with a record 200 major victories. No one else was close.

A car that was not eligible for International Motor Sports Association (IMSA) Camel series points won IMSA's premier race, the Rolex 24 Hours of Daytona. The Group C Nissan R91, entered by the automaker's Japan factory team and driven by Masa Hasemi, Kaz Hoshino, and Toshio Suzuki, took the lead from the U.S. Nissan company entry after the first lap and led the rest of the way. It set a record for distance, 2,712 mi (4,366 km), and speed, 112.807 mph (181.619 km/h). Top points in the Camel GT championship thus were awarded to the second-place TWR Jaguar of Davy Jones, Scott Pruett, David Brabham, and Scott Goodyear.

(ROBERT J. FENDELL)

BADMINTON

"Something for everyone"—at least among the top countries—best describes the results of the world's premier badminton events during a busy 1992. At Barcelona, Spain, where the sport was contested in the Olympic Games for the first time, two investments paid off in "gold." Indonesia's concentration on singles talent helped Alan Budi Kusuma earn the men's singles gold medal and Susi Susanti the women's singles gold. South Korea's doubles prowess yielded the gold for Park Joo Bong and Kim Moon Soo in the men's competition and for Hwang Hye Young and

Alan Budi Kusuma of Indonesia acknowledges the ovation of the crowd in Barcelona, Spain, after winning the Olympic gold medal in men's singles badminton. Badminton was included in the Olympic Games for the first time in 1992.

AP/WIDE WORLD

Chung So Young in the women's event. Mixed doubles was not contended.

Earlier in the year, at Kuala Lumpur in May, Malaysia celebrated when its men's team upset both China in the semifinals and Indonesia in the final by scores of 3–2 to capture the coveted Thomas Cup for the first time since 1967. The key to the triumph, ironically, may have been China's retired star Yang Yang, now Malaysia's men's singles coach. Both Rashid Sidek at first singles and Foo Kok Keong at second singles performed above expectation for the Malaysian team, as did second doubles team Cheah Soon Kit and Soo Beng Kiang.

China's women's team also gained its share of glory, edging South Korea in a tense final—third singles player Ye Zhaoying stood just three points from defeat against Shim Eun Jung before rallying to win the decisive fifth match—to capture the Uber Cup by a 3–2 score. This was the fifth straight Uber Cup for China, matching Japan's record.

China also achieved a strong showing at the prestigious All-England championships in March, when Liu Jun in men's singles, Tang Jiuhong in women's singles, and Lin Yanfen and Yao Fen in women's doubles emerged victorious. Also at that tournament, Indonesians Eddy Hartono and Rudy Gunawan captured the men's doubles title, and Denmark's Thomas Lund and Pernille Dupont took the mixed—the first European titlists in four years at the All-England meet.

(WARREN K. EMERSON)

BASEBALL

The 1992 major league baseball season was rife with distress signals. Despite significant increases in Baltimore and Montreal, and another four million-plus total in Toronto, overall attendance was down slightly. Television ratings, for regular and postseason games, also sagged. Meanwhile, team owners searched for a new commissioner to replace Fay Vincent, who resigned under pressure.

World Series. The Toronto Blue Jays made Canada's first World Series experience an enjoyable one. They defeated

Final Major League Standings, 1992

AMERICAN LEAGUE
East Division

Club	W.	L.	Pct.	G.B.
Toronto	96	66	.593	–
Milwaukee	92	70	.568	4
Baltimore	89	73	.549	7
Cleveland	76	86	.469	20
New York	76	86	.469	20
Detroit	75	87	.463	21
Boston	73	89	.451	23

West Division

Club	W.	L.	Pct.	G.B.
Oakland	96	66	.593	–
Minnesota	90	72	.556	6
Chicago	86	76	.531	10
Texas	77	85	.475	19
California	72	90	.444	24
Kansas City	72	90	.444	24
Seattle	64	98	.395	32

NATIONAL LEAGUE
East Division

Club	W.	L.	Pct.	G.B.
Pittsburgh	96	66	.593	–
Montreal	87	75	.537	9
St. Louis	83	79	.512	13
Chicago	78	84	.481	18
New York	72	90	.444	24
Philadelphia	70	92	.432	26

West Division

Club	W.	L.	Pct.	G.B.
Atlanta	98	64	.605	–
Cincinnati	90	72	.556	8
San Diego	82	80	.506	16
Houston	81	81	.500	17
San Francisco	72	90	.444	26
Los Angeles	63	99	.389	35

the Atlanta Braves four games to two, winning the clincher on the road before returning home to find an entire nation in a celebratory mood.

The Braves won the opening game 3–1 on October 17 in Atlanta-Fulton County Stadium. Damon Berryhill, a light-hitting catcher, stroked a three-run home run in the sixth inning to support a four-hit pitching effort by Atlanta left-hander Tom Glavine. Jack Morris, the 1991 World Series hero with the triumphant Minnesota Twins, was the losing pitcher. However, the Blue Jays rebounded one night later by rallying to defeat the Braves 5–4. Ed Sprague, a pinch hitter, hit a dramatic two-run home run in the ninth inning off Jeff Reardon, the Braves' third pitcher.

On October 20 a World Series game was played in Canada for the first time, and the Blue Jays enhanced the occasion by beating Atlanta 3–2 before 51,813 in the SkyDome. The Braves, leading 2–1, were tied on Kelly Gruber's home run in the eighth inning. Then, in the ninth, the Blue Jays loaded the bases for Candy Maldonado, who delivered a long single to centre field off Reardon. Duane Ward was Toronto's winning pitcher for the second time in as many games.

In the fourth game, on October 21, veteran left-hander Jimmy Key pitched 7⅔ strong innings, and the Blue Jays edged the Braves again 2–1 to take a commanding lead in the Series, three games to one. Pat Borders, Toronto's hot-hitting catcher, contributed a home run in the third inning, and Devon White singled in the Blue Jays' second run in the seventh.

The Blue Jays were anxious to win the World Series before their loyal fans on October 22, but Morris was unable to handle the assignment again. With the score tied 2–2 in the fifth inning, Deion Sanders singled in the lead run with two out. Then Lonnie Smith launched a grand-slam homer to right field, and the Braves eased to a 7–2 conquest. John Smoltz was the winning pitcher, with relief from Mike Stanton.

On October 24 in Atlanta, the Blue Jays overcame years of frustration and a reputation for postseason misadventures by defeating the Braves 4–3 in 11 innings to clinch the title. The Braves tied the score 2–2 on Otis Nixon's two-out single in the ninth. In the 11th, however, Dave Winfield, a 41-year-old outfielder/designated hitter acquired by Toronto the previous winter to provide leadership, hit a two-out, two-run double to left field off Atlanta's Charlie Leibrandt. The Braves scored a run in their half of the 11th and continued to threaten until Nixon was thrown out at first base while attempting to bunt for a single. The World Series was dominated by pitching. Toronto's team batting average was

.230 and Atlanta's only .220. Borders, with nine hits in 20 at bats for a .450 average, was voted Most Valuable Player for the Series.

Championship Series. The Blue Jays lost the opening game of the American League championship series on October 7 at Toronto, where the Oakland Athletics hit three home runs to beat Morris 4–3. Harold Baines's blast in the ninth inning broke a 3–3 tie. David Cone, obtained in a trade with the New York Mets, stifled the A's the next day 3–1. Toronto won the third game in Oakland 7–5 on October 10, and then, in the turning point of the best-of-seven series, the Blue Jays won 7–6 on October 11 after trailing 6–1. Roberto Alomar, Toronto's brilliant second baseman, tied the game with a two-run homer in the ninth inning against Dennis Eckersley (*see* BIOGRAPHIES), Oakland's usually flawless relief ace.

Venerable Dave Stewart staved off elimination for the A's on October 12 by working a complete 6–2 triumph, but the Blue Jays claimed their first American League pennant since the franchise was granted in 1977 by routing the A's 9–2 in Toronto on October 14. Juan Guzman was the winning pitcher, and Maldonado contributed a three-run homer as Toronto won the series four games to two.

In the National League championship series, the Braves advanced by barely beating the Pittsburgh Pirates for the second consecutive season. The Braves won the first two games at home 5–1 and 13–5. The Pirates took the third game in Pittsburgh 3–2 on October 9 but lost the next night 6–4 to fall behind three games to one. Then, however, the Pirates won the last game in Pittsburgh 7–1 and romped to a 13–4 victory in the sixth game at Atlanta on October 13.

In the deciding game on October 14, the Pirates' best pitcher, Doug Drabek, took a 2–0 lead into the bottom of the ninth inning. But, in a remarkable finish, the Braves scored three runs to steal the pennant from the devastated Pirates 3–2. Ron Gant brought in one run with a sacrifice fly. With two out and the bases loaded, pinch hitter Francisco Cabrera—with just 10 major league at bats during the 1992 season—cracked a single to left field off relief pitcher Stan Belinda. Sid Bream just beat the tag at home plate to register the winning run.

Division Races. The Blue Jays, winner of the American League East division in 1985, 1989, and 1991, won the title again with a record of 96 victories and 66 losses, their 10th consecutive winning season. The Jays were lifted by the arrival of Winfield (26 home runs, 108 runs batted in) and Morris (21 victories, 6 losses). Also, Cone, who joined the team in late August, won four games, the margin by which Toronto won the championship from the second-place Milwaukee Brewers. Oakland, despite having its roster ravaged by injuries, posted a 96–66 record to win the American League West by six games over Minnesota. The achievement merited Manager of the Year honours for Oakland's Tony LaRussa.

The Braves, though trailing Cincinnati by as many as seven games in late May, won the National League West by eight games with a record of 98–64, the best in baseball. The Pirates and their Manager of the Year, Jim Leyland, survived the departure of free-agent slugger Bobby Bonilla (New York Mets), 20-game winner John Smiley (Minnesota), and several members of their bull pen to earn a third National League East crown in succession, by nine games over the Montreal Expos with a record of 96–66.

Regular Season. On September 9 Robin Yount of the Milwaukee Brewers became the 17th player in major league history to amass 3,000 hits. On September 30 George Brett of the Kansas City Royals joined the select group with four hits in a game against the California Angels.

Edgar Martinez of the Seattle Mariners won the American League batting title with a .343 average, and Juan Gonzalez of Texas led the league with 43 home runs. Cecil Fielder of the Detroit Tigers set the pace in runs batted in with 124 and Minnesota's Kirby Puckett in hits with 210. Kenny Lofton of the Cleveland Indians led with 66 stolen bases. Toronto's Morris and Kevin Brown of Texas tied for most victories by a pitcher, 21.

Gary Sheffield of the San Diego Padres led the National League with a .330 batting average. Fred McGriff of San Diego led with 35 home runs. Darren Daulton of Philadelphia had the most runs batted in, 109, while Andy Van Slyke of Pittsburgh tied Atlanta's Terry Pendleton for most hits, 199. Marquis Grissom of Montreal easily won the stolen base derby with 78. Atlanta's Glavine and Greg Maddux of the Chicago Cubs each posted 20 victories. Eckersley (51) and Lee Smith of the St. Louis Cardinals (43) led in saves.

Eckersley won the American League's Cy Young Award for best pitcher and also was named the league's Most Valuable Player. Rookie of the Year in the American League was Pat Listach of Milwaukee. For the National League Barry Bonds of Pittsburgh was voted Most Valuable Player, Maddux won the Cy Young Award, and Eric Karros of Los Angeles was Rookie of the Year.

Other Developments. With the possibility that ongoing strife between management and labour might lead to a lockout before the 1993 season, the climate of baseball was tense throughout 1992. Vincent angered several owners and was taken to court by the Chicago Cubs after he attempted to realign teams in the National League, changing the Cubs and Cardinals to the West while moving Atlanta and Cincinnati to the East. Vincent thought it a good time to make "geographic sense" with two expansion franchises—the Florida Marlins (East) and Colorado Rockies (West)—joining the league in 1993. But he was rebuffed and, sensing that his ability to govern had waned severely, Vincent resigned on Labor Day. Allan ("Bud") Selig, owner of the Milwaukee Brewers, was installed as temporary commissioner.

(ROBERT WILLIAM VERDI)

Cuba's baseball team celebrates its victory over Taiwan, which won it the gold medal in the Olympic Games. Baseball was included in the Olympics for the first time in 1992, and Cuba dominated play by outscoring opponents 95–16.

Latin America. Puerto Rico's Mayagüez Indians, managed by Pat Kelly, took the Caribbean Series, Latin America's top baseball competition, played in Hermosillo, Sonora, Mexico, in February 1992. The road to the title was not easy, however. The Indians dropped their first game to the host team, the Hermosillo Tomato Growers, and later lost a second one against Venezuela's Zulia Eagles. At the end of the official round-robin tournament, they were tied with the Zulia Eagles at four victories apiece.

An additional game was played to break the tie on February 9, and the Indians blanked the Eagles 8–0 behind pitcher Roberto Hernández. Catcher Chad Kreuter of the Indians was voted the Series' Most Valuable Player after batting .450—with three home runs and four runs batted in—over seven games.

In the summer the Mexico City Tigers won the pennant of the AAA Mexican League. In the final championship series they came from two games behind to beat the Owls of the Two Laredos (Nuevo Laredo, Tamaulipas, Mexico, and Laredo, Texas) four games to three.

Cuba continued its domination of international amateur baseball with a national team that could arguably defeat almost any professional Latin-American squad. The most important amateur baseball contest of the year was in the summer Olympic Games in Barcelona, Spain. As usual, Cuba went undefeated as it collected seven victories in the round-robin preliminary stage and two more in the semifinal and final rounds. (SERGIO SARMIENTO)

Japan. The defending champion Seibu Lions of the Pacific League defeated the Central League's Yakult Swallows four games to three to win the Japan Series for the third year in a row and the sixth time in seven years. Lion pitcher Takehiro Ishii, winner of two games, was voted the Most Valuable Player of the Series.

The opening game of the fall classic, played at Tokyo's Jingu Stadium, home of the Swallows, was decided in the bottom of the 12th inning by a home run by Swallow outfielder Toru Sugiura, who pinch-hit for Katsumasa Dobashi. It was the first time in the Series' history that a pinch hitter had hit a home run with the bases loaded to end the game. The Swallows won 7–3.

The next three games were taken by the Lions. They won the second game 2–0 at Jingu Stadium and games three and four, played at Tokorozawa's Seibu Lions' stadium, 6–1 and 1–0.

The fifth game, played in Tokorozawa, went into extra innings with the score tied at 6–6 after nine innings. In the top of the 10th, Swallow shortstop Takahiro Ikeyama hit a home run off Lion reliever Tetsuya Shiozaki, and the Swallows won for the second time.

Back in Tokyo the Swallows won the sixth game, the third to go into extra innings, 8–7, with a home run by right fielder Shinji Hata in the bottom of the 10th inning. In the seventh game the ace hurler of each team, Ishii of the Lions and Yoichi Okabayashi of the Swallows, performed superbly, and the score was 1–1 after nine innings. Then in the top of the 10th, with a runner at third, centre fielder Koji Akiyama hit a sacrifice fly to centre field to score the Series-winning run for the Lions.

Right-hander Ishii, who won 15 games (against 3 losses) for the Lions, was voted the Most Valuable Player of the Pacific League. Yu Takamura, right-hander for the Kintetsu Buffaloes, was the Rookie of the Year in the Pacific League. Jack Howell of the Swallows, who hit .331 and 38 home runs and was the leader in both categories, was voted the Most Valuable Player in the Central League. Teruyoshi Kuji, shortstop for the Hanshin Tigers, was the Central League Rookie of the Year. (TOSHIHIKO SUZUKI)

BASKETBALL

United States. *College.* Late in a regional contest it appeared that Duke's bid for a second straight National Collegiate Athletic Association (NCAA) basketball championship had come to an unhappy end. The Blue Devils were trailing upset-minded Kentucky 103–102 with 2.1 seconds left to play in the Eastern Regional final. The winner would go on to a Final Four berth the following weekend. The loser would take its shattered dreams and go home.

Duke's task seemed impossible: get the ball from underneath its own basket and into the opponents' hoop 29 m (94 ft) away. Incredibly, the defending champions did it. A 23-m (75-ft) inbounds pass somehow found its way into the hands of Christian Laettner, the 2.1-m (6-ft 11-in) Duke centre. Laettner turned and hit a game-winning jump shot that would rank with the greatest clutch moves in tournament history.

After that intense drama the two remaining hurdles seemed both anticlimactic and inevitable. Duke survived a closing flurry of three-point baskets to overcome Indiana 81–78 in the NCAA semifinals before a Hubert H. Humphrey Metrodome throng of 50,379.

In the other April 4 Final Four matchup, Michigan added another chapter to the saga of its "Fabulous Five" by downing stubborn Cincinnati 76–72. The Wolverines' freshman quintet of Jalen Rose, Chris Webber, Juwan Howard, Ray Jackson, and Jimmy King captured the nation's fancy, dominating the headlines in their debut season by talking big and playing bigger.

In the end, however, lack of tourney experience caught up with the Wolverines. Even though Laettner missed six of eight first-half field-goal attempts, Duke's leader came through later in the game, sparking his team to an easy 71–51 victory over Michigan and a repeat championship.

It was the first time a college team had put together back-to-back basketball titles since UCLA did it in 1972 and 1973. This was a personal triumph for Coach Mike Krzyzewski (*see* BIOGRAPHIES), who had masterminded Duke into the Final Four six times in seven years only to fall short in four tries before hitting the jackpot in 1991 and again this time.

Laettner unquestionably was the catalyst, leading all scorers in the final game with 19 points. His three-point basket erased Michigan's 31–30 halftime lead, and the Blue Devils pulled away with dominating defense that keyed a 23–6 outburst during the last seven minutes of the contest. It made Michigan's precocious youngsters wilt, finishing their 25–9

NBA Final Standings, 1991–92					
EASTERN CONFERENCE			**WESTERN CONFERENCE**		
Team	Won	Lost	Team	Won	Lost
Atlantic Division			*Midwest Division*		
*Boston	51	31	*Utah	55	27
*New York	51	31	*San Antonio	47	35
*New Jersey	40	42	Houston	42	40
*Miami	38	44	Denver	24	58
Philadelphia	35	47	Dallas	22	60
Washington	25	57	Minnesota	15	67
Orlando	21	61			
Central Division			*Pacific Division*		
*Chicago	67	15	*Portland	57	25
*Cleveland	57	25	*Golden State	55	27
*Detroit	48	34	*Phoenix	53	29
*Indiana	40	42	*Seattle	47	35
Atlanta	38	44	*L.A. Clippers	45	37
Charlotte	31	51	*L.A. Lakers	43	39
Milwaukee	31	51	Sacramento	29	53

*Gained play-off berth.

campaign on a note of frustration. They shot a woeful 29% from the floor in the closing half, scoring only 20 points in those 20 minutes.

Despite scoring just nine points in the final game, Duke guard Bobby Hurley was named the outstanding player of the NCAA tournament. The Blue Devils, who lost the 1990 championship game to Nevada-Las Vegas (UNLV) and then rebounded to beat Kansas in the 1991 showdown, joined UCLA, Cincinnati, and Ohio State as the only teams to play for the title three straight times. Laettner, named college player of the year, went on to become the only collegiate member of the U.S. "Dream Team," which swept to victory in the 1992 Olympic Games at Barcelona, Spain (*see* below).

Another 1991–92 success story fell just short of complete triumph in the finals of the National Invitation Tournament when Notre Dame lost an 81–76 overtime thriller to Virginia. Coach John MacLeod, returning to college basketball after a long sojourn in the professional ranks, turned things around for the Irish (18–15). But Virginia (20–13) proved too tough in the NIT title clash, overcoming a 39-point barrage by Notre Dame guard Elmer Bennett. The Cavaliers got vital points in overtime from their star, Bryan Stith, who wound up with 24 and the tourney's Most Valuable Player trophy.

The women's NCAA championship was captured by Stanford (30–3) with a convincing 78–62 victory over Western Kentucky. It was the second national title for the Cardinal in three years. Freshman forward Rachel Hemmer paced the victory with 18 points and 15 rebounds, backed up by

AP/WIDE WORLD

The U.S. Olympic basketball team, made up of one college and 11 National Basketball Association stars and called the "Dream Team," receives its gold medals. A change in international rules allowed NBA professionals to participate in the Olympic Games for the first time, and the U.S. team overwhelmingly dominated play.

Val Whiting's 16 points and 13 rebounds. Guard Molly Goodenbour, a veteran of Stanford's 1990 triumph, was named Most Outstanding Player of the tournament.

Professional. Just as everyone expected, magnificent Michael Jordan carried the Chicago Bulls to their second straight National Basketball Association (NBA) championship. This time the Portland Trail Blazers were victimized by a stunning rally that erased a 17-point gap in the decisive contest. Trailing by a seemingly hopeless margin in the sixth game of the NBA finals, the Bulls unleashed a dramatic fourth-quarter rally that overcame the deficit and the Trail Blazers 97–93. It wrapped up the best-of-seven series four games to two.

As they had been able to do throughout the play-offs, the Bulls found the magic touch against Portland when they needed it most. They outscored the tiring Western Conference champions 14–2 in the opening minutes of the fourth period and then turned to 1.98-m (6-ft 6-in) superstar Jordan for the knockout punch. He responded with a dozen of his game-high 33 points in the last six minutes. Jordan became only the second man in league history to earn Most Valuable Player honours for both the regular season and the play-offs and was the first to accomplish that feat for two straight years.

The Bulls rode the same kind of physical and emotional roller coaster throughout the play-offs. They swept the Miami Heat, as expected, in the first round, but things then took an unexpected turn. Proving the adage that repeating is much more than twice as hard as winning the initial championship, the Bulls struggled from there all the way to their June 14 clincher. They came close to getting literally knocked out by the relentless New York Knicks before surviving a take-no-prisoners series that went the seven-game limit.

The Cleveland Cavaliers proved almost as troublesome before losing four games to two. That put the Bulls back into the championship round, though for the first time against Portland. The Blazers, in the finals for the second time in three years, fell short again. The heralded matchup between Jordan and Clyde ("The Glide") Drexler of Portland was a key indicator, with the Bulls' mainstay scoring an average 35.8 points per game to Drexler's 24.8 and outplaying him by an even wider margin.

In August, after playing on the U.S. Olympic team, Boston Celtic star Larry Bird announced his retirement after 13 seasons. Chronic back pain forced him to end a career during which he was named the NBA's Most Valuable Player three times and led the Celtics to three NBA titles.

In September Los Angeles Laker star Earvin ("Magic") Johnson, who had retired from basketball in November 1991, announced that he would play for the Lakers again in the 1992–93 season for a record $14.6 million. But in November, four days before the start of the season, he retired again, apparently because other players objected to his return. (ROBERT G. LOGAN)

World Basketball. The major event for international basketball in 1992 was the Olympic Games competition held in July and August in Barcelona, Spain. The men's tournament was notable for the participation for the first time of players from the U.S. NBA, who made up the U.S. team. With the rules governing professionalism having been redefined by the International Basketball Federation (FIBA) in 1989, it meant that players such as Magic Johnson, Jordan, and Bird, previously ineligible for the team, were able to take their place in Olympic history.

Nicknamed the "Dream Team," the Americans were expected to overpower all their opponents, and this they did throughout the competition. However, Croatia, in the final, proved worthy opponents and even led midway through the first half before eventually losing 117–85.

Lithuania took the bronze medal by defeating the Unified Team 82–78. This match in itself was notable, as it was only earlier in the year that, along with its fellow Baltic nations Estonia and Latvia, Lithuania had been recognized as an independent basketball-playing country. The Unified Team comprised many of the other former Soviet republics, playing together under one banner for the last time.

In the women's tournament the 1988 Olympic champions, the U.S., were beaten in the semifinal by the Unified Team, which went on to defeat China 76–66 in the final. The U.S. took third place by defeating Cuba 88–74.

Also during the year the 16th African championships were won by Angola, which defeated Senegal 71–66 in the final. India won the fifth South Asia Games for men, with Pakistan finishing second, by a score of 83–71, while China won the 14th Asian championship for women, held in Seoul, South Korea, by defeating Korea 89–76 in the final. In the first European championships for men 22 and under, held in Athens, Italy won the championship by defeating Greece in the final 65–63.

Off the court a significant development was a move toward establishing a uniform set of playing rules. Representatives of the FIBA, the NBA, and the NCAA began preliminary discussions with the aim of working toward this goal.

A further item to note was the initiative taken by FIBA with regard to the AIDS virus. The federation ruled that during a game the referee must order any player who is bleeding to leave the playing area. The player can then return to the court only after the bleeding has stopped and the wound has been covered. (MARK HANNEN)

BILLIARD GAMES

Carom Billiards. Torbjorn Blomdahl of Sweden won the second and third of the five World Billiard Association (BWA) 1991 three-cushion billiard international tour stops and then coasted to his third BWA World Cup title. Dick Jaspers of The Netherlands was runner-up, with 21-time world titlist Raymond Ceulemans of Belgium finishing in third place.

Blomdahl also won the 1992 German Open three-cushion championships in Backnang, averaging 1.794 points per inning (PPI). Marco Zanetti of Italy took second place, and Belgium's Ludo Dielis was third. In The Netherlands the Dutch three-cushion championship was won by Jaspers, who defeated fellow Dutchman Raimond Burgman 3–0 in the final match.

The world two-man three-cushion team championship in Viersen, Germany, was won by Japan's team of Nobuaki Kobayashi and Junichi Komori with a combined PPI average of 1.218. Sang Chun Lee and Frank Torres of the U.S. placed second with a 1.129-PPI average, and the Portuguese duo of Jorge Theriaga and Mário Ribeiro finished third, scoring at a 1.096-PPI pace.

Lee, of New York City, won all seven of his matches and averaged 1.591 PPI in the round-robin finals to easily win his second U.S. national three-cushion billiard championship in Chicago. Bill Smith of Chicago was second with a 5–2 record and 0.899-PPI average and planned to join Lee in representing the U.S. in the next world team championship in Europe. Former U.S. national champion George Ashby of Jacksonville, Ill., finished third with a 4–3 record and 0.982 average.

Pocket Billiards. Both major industry publications were in agreement on the best performing players on the professional pocket billiard tour, naming Cecil ("Buddy") Hall of Metropolis, Ill., and Robin Bell of Cypress, Calif., as men's and women's players of the year, respectively. Most of today's high-level tournaments are contested in the version of Rotation called nineball. However, there were a few interesting variations in competitive fare. The Cleveland (Ohio) Open all-around championships sported an unusual format, featuring 14.1 continuous (straight pool), nineball, and tenball divisions, plus a play-off to determine an all-around champion. Johnny Archer of Twin City, Ga., a narrow loser to Hall in Player of the Year voting, won all three divisions and the all-around title. Archer also took nineball titles at the 188-player Last Call for nineball in Las Vegas, Nev.; the 64-player Kupolen Challenge Cup in Borlange, Sweden; the 64-player World Pool-Billiard Association (WPA) nineball championships in Taipei, Taiwan; the 76-player Sands XV Open in Reno, Nev.; and the gigantic 435-player International 9-Ball Classic in St. Charles, Ill. At the 15th U.S. Open 14.1 championships, in New York City, three-time world straight pool titlist Mike Sigel of Baltimore, Md., was the men's division winner.

One-Pocket was played at three major events: the Lexington (Ky.) All-Star, won by Jeff Carter of Chicago; the Legends of One-Pocket in Columbia, S.C., where Shannon Daulton of Kentucky was victorious; and the Legends of One-Pocket in Philadelphia, captured by Sigel.

Aggressive promotion and increasingly accomplished play resulted in a greater demand for women's division competition, particularly at nineball events. The year's major women's titles included: the WPA world meet, won by Franziska Stark of Germany; the 15th U.S. Open 14.1 championships, where Loree Jon Jones of Hillsborough, N.J., triumphed despite a new world record high run of 68 by runner-up Ewa Mataya; the International Classic, topped by Vivian Villarreal of San Antonio, Texas; the McDermott Masters 9-Ball in Las Vegas, won by Bell; the Brunswick Munich Masters in Germany, won by Stacey Hillyard of Sweden; and the Los Angeles Open in Burbank, Calif., where Peg Ledman of Hubertus, Wis., took the title.

Other major men's nineball winners were: Buddy Hall at the Rakm Up Classic in Columbia; Tom Storm of Borlange at the Brunswick Munich Masters; Mike Sigel at the Bicycle Club Invitational 9-Ball Tournament in Bell Gardens, Calif.; and Earl Strickland of Greensboro, N.C., at the McDermott Masters and the Los Angeles Open.   (BRUCE H. VENZKE)

Snooker. Stephen Hendry of Scotland recovered the world professional snooker championship in May 1992 after defeating Jimmy White of England by 18 frames to 14 in the final at Sheffield, England. In February White had won the British Open title at Derby, England, with a 10–7 victory in the final over James Wattana of Thailand, who in an earlier round had made the maximum break of 147. In October at Reading, England, White also gained the Grand Prix title. John Parrott of England, who had beaten White 16–13 in the U.K. final at Preston, England, in December 1991, won the Kent Classic at Beijing (Peking) in August 1992 and the Dubai Classic in October, defeating Hendry in both finals. However, in the Belgian Masters final at Antwerp, Belgium, in November, Parrott was beaten 10–5 by Wattana. White defeated Parrott 16–9 in November to win the U.K. championship at Preston. Neil Mosley of England became the world amateur champion by defeating Leonardo Andam of the Philippines 11–2 in Malta in November. Tom Kollins of Chicago won his second straight U.S. snooker championship at Aurora, Ill., in August.   (SYDNEY E. FRISKIN)

BOWLING

World Tenpins. The 27th Bowling World Cup, held in November 1991 in Beijing (Peking), was once again the top singles tournament in the world. National qualifiers came from 42 different countries. In the men's final Jon Juneau of the U.S. defeated Sweden's Ulf Hämnäs 205–149. Åsa Larsson salvaged Sweden's bowling reputation by beating Pauline Smith of England 190–184 in the women's final.

The 16th South East Asian Games in Manila, also in November 1991, ended international competition in 1991. In men's events the Philippines was the dominating country. It won the doubles, Paeng Nepomuceno the singles, and Paulo Valdez the all-events and masters. Malaysia took the trios title, and Thailand won the five-person team event. In women's competition Poppy Tambis of Indonesia won the singles, Malaysia the doubles, Thailand the trios, and Singapore the five-person team. All-events champion was Pranee Kitipongpithya of Thailand, and the masters champion was Grace Young of Singapore.

At the end of 1991 the world bowling writers voted Canada's Catharina Willis and Taiwan's Yingh-Chieh Ma as the Amateur Bowlers of the Year.

For 1992 the action moved to Europe—and there was no finish to the Finnish gold chain that had begun in the 1991 world championships. First, Tapani Peltola became men's individual cup winner in April in Amsterdam by defeating Ireland's Philip Dunne in a two-game play-off 481–412. Dunne had earlier bowled the cup's first 300. In June at Ålborg, Den., Finland's five-man team won the European team cup by defeating The Netherlands 1,044–975.

Ann Nyström of Sweden downed Dorette Boelens of The Netherlands 418–413 to win the women's individual cup. Denmark beat Germany 921–873 to gain the women's European team cup.   (YRJÖ SARAHETE)

U.S. Tenpins. In a year when nobody on the regular Professional Bowlers Association (PBA) tour took charge, one of the biggest news makers in tenpins was Gene Stus of Detroit, Mich., a competitor in the PBA senior events. Stus, 52, won two of the first nine tournaments, including the Ebonite Senior Championship for the second successive year, and rolled a perfect game on national television. After winning his opening match in the tournament on July 2 at Lakewood, Calif., with a 300, he maintained his composure and bowled 226, 213, and 225 to win the $9,000 first prize.

Marc McDowell of Madison, Wis., captured the PBA's $300,000 Firestone Tournament of Champions in Fairlawn, Ohio, with a 223–193 victory over Don Genalo of Perrysburg, Ohio. McDowell was one of six bowlers on the regular tour with two victories as the year's final tournaments approached.

The American Bowling Congress (ABC) Bud Light Masters Tournament produced another unexpected winner as Ken Johnson of North Richland Hills, Texas, topped David D'Entremont of Parma, Ohio, 235–207 in the final game. Johnson had never won a professional tournament before taking the Masters, staged on the ABC Tournament lanes in Corpus Christi, Texas.

More than 43,000 men competed in the ABC meet. The Regular Division winners were: team, Coors Light of Reading, Pa., 3,344; singles (tie), Bob Youker, Jr., of Syracuse, N.Y., and Gary Blatchford of Phoenix, Ariz., 801; doubles, Gene Stus and David Bernhardt of Detroit, 1,487; all-events, Mike Tucker of Fountain Valley, Calif., 2,158.

In the Women's International Bowling Congress (WIBC) Queens Tournament at Lansing, Mich., Cindy Coburn-Carroll of Buffalo, N.Y., overcame Dana Miller-Mackie of Albuquerque, N.M., 184–170. Open Division winners in the WIBC Championships Tournament were: team, Hoinke Classic of Cincinnati, Ohio, 2,983; singles, Patty Ann of Mayaguez, P.R., 680; doubles, Nancy Fehr of Cincinnati and Lisa Wagner of Palmetto, Fla., 1,325; all-events, Mitsuko Tokimoto of Tokyo, 1,928.   (JOHN J. ARCHIBALD)

BOXING

It seemed that world heavyweight competition had been given a face-lift toward the end of 1992 when Riddick Bowe (U.S.), a 25-year-old from New York City, decisively outpointed Evander Holyfield (U.S.) in 12 rounds at Las Vegas, Nev., to take the heavyweight crown. The new champion was recognized by the World Boxing Council (WBC), World Boxing Association (WBA), and International Boxing Federation (IBF), and few were impressed that the World Boxing Organization (WBO) chose to recognize Michael Moorer (U.S.) as its champion. But the heavyweight situation was again thrown into chaos when Bowe declined to defend his title against the WBC's top contender, Lennox Lewis (England), and consequently was stripped of his crown by the WBC. The WBC decided that Lewis should be declared the new champion but insisted that he had to defend his new title against Tommy Tucker (U.S.). This decision caused more arguments, but Lewis remained the WBC champion at the year's end.

Bowe, standing 1.96 m (6 ft 5 in) and weighing about 106 kg (235 lb), was undefeated after 32 professional contests, with 27 of these won by stoppages. Despite this, he had spent most of his career in the shadows and did not attract world attention until 1992, reaching the very top with the victory over Holyfield in November.

Born in Brooklyn, N.Y., in the tough Brownsville district that produced the talented but trouble-riddled former champion Mike Tyson, Bowe stayed away from drugs and avoided the traps many poor kids fall into. Married with three children, he moved to the middle-class suburbs of Washington, D.C.

Though Holyfield was undefeated in 28 contests before meeting Bowe and had been an outstanding cruiserweight champion, he was never really accepted as a great heavyweight champion and, though 1.88 m (6 ft 2 in) and 93 kg (205 lb), he was regarded as a "small" heavyweight. After winning the heavyweight title in 1990 from James Douglas, the conqueror of Tyson, Holyfield did little to improve his image a year later when George Foreman, a former champion, came out of retirement after 10 years and at the age of 42 took the champion the full 12 rounds. Holyfield did nothing to attract new admirers in June 1992 when another 42-year-old former champion, Larry Holmes, also took him the distance.

Whether or not the 30-year-old Holyfield retired, he had the consolation of becoming one of the richest champions in sports, having grossed around $35 million. He could also derive satisfaction that in courageous defeat he gained more respect than in his triumphs. His downfall threw wide open the plans for heavyweight title fights for 1993. Holyfield's promoter, Dan Duva, convinced that his man would beat Bowe, had journeyed to London to see Lewis flatten Razor Ruddock (Canada) in two rounds of an official WBC final elimination match. Duva had agreed that Holyfield's next defense would be against Lewis in the spring of 1993, but those plans were canceled when Holyfield lost, and Bowe and his management would not make an early decision about the future; they claimed to be thinking of a possible title defense against Foreman, now 43, in Beijing (Peking) and a $20 million payday.

Because Bowe did not defend against Lewis, there were three heavyweight champions recognized by the different organizations. It had taken Tyson, whose career was halted when he was convicted of rape in February, to eliminate the pretenders to the throne and unify the championship.

Boxing's promoters had looked to England because the U.S. was running out of challengers to serve as box-office magnets who could attract millions of dollars from television. The two British fighters hoping to get a crack at the heavyweight title were Frank Bruno and Lennox Lewis. The 30-year-old Bruno had already twice failed against former champions Tim Witherspoon and Tyson but had come back to knock out three carefully picked opponents and become Britain's biggest box-office draw. But Lewis staked first claim with his devastation of Ruddock and at 27 remained undefeated.

Though born in London of Jamaican parents, Lewis was taken to Canada while still a boy and won an Olympic Games gold medal as a super heavyweight for Canada in Seoul, South Korea, in 1984. After turning professional, he returned to England to win the British, Commonwealth, and European titles. Lewis could boast that he stopped Bowe in the super heavyweight Olympic final in Seoul, but the present world champion was only 20 and claimed that he went in against Lewis with a bad right hand.

With Khaosai Galaxy (Thailand) announcing his retirement in December 1991 after defending the WBA super flyweight title 19 times, the unchallenged overall champion of the year was Julio César Chávez (Mexico). Probably Mexico's greatest pugilist ever, the 30-year-old Chávez retained the WBC light welterweight title by stopping Angel Hernández (P.R.) in 5 rounds and Frank Mitchell (U.S.) in 4, by decisively outpointing Hector Camacho (P.R.) over 12, and, for his ninth defense of the title and a remarkable run of 83 contests without defeat, by defeating an outclassed Bruce Pearson (U.S.) in 3 rounds. Next to Chávez, super featherweight Azumah Nelson (Ghana) was the outstanding

World and European Boxing Champions
as of Dec. 31, 1992

Division	WBC[1]	WBA[2]	IBF[3]	WBO[4]	Europe
Heavyweight	L. Lewis (England)	R. Bowe (U.S.)	R. Bowe (U.S.)	M. Moorer (U.S.)	Vacant
Cruiserweight	A. Wamba (France)	B. Czyz (U.S.)	A. Cole (U.S.)	T. Booze (U.S.)	A. Tafer (France)
Light heavyweight	J. Harding (Australia)	V. Hill (U.S.)	C. Williams (U.S.)	L. Barber (U.S.)	Vacant
Super middleweight	N. Benn (England)	M. Nunn (U.S.)	I. Barkley (U.S.)	C. Eubank (England)	V. Nardiello (Italy)
Middleweight	J. Jackson (U.S.)	R. Johnson (U.S.)	J. Toney (U.S.)	G. McClellan (U.S.)	S. Kalambay (Italy)
Light middleweight	T. Norris (U.S.)	J. Vásquez (Arg.)	G. Rosi (Italy)	J.D. Jackson (U.S.)	L. Boudouani (France)
Welterweight	J. McGirt (U.S.)	C. España (Venezuela)	M. Blocker (U.S.)	M. Galloway (U.S.)	L. Proto (France)
Light welterweight	J.C. Chávez (Mexico)	M. East (Phil.)	P. Whitaker (U.S.)	C. González (Mexico)	V. Kayumba (France)
Lightweight	M. González (Mexico)	T. Lopez (U.S.)	Vacant	G. Parisi (Italy)	J.B. Mendy (France)
Super featherweight	A. Nelson (Ghana)	G. Hernández (U.S.)	J. Molina (P.R.)	Jimmi Bredahl (Den.)	R. Tuur (Neth.)
Featherweight	P. Hodkinson (England)	Y. Park (South Korea)	M. Medina (Mexico)	R. Palacio (Colombia)	F. Benichou (France)
Super bantamweight	T. Patterson (U.S.)	W. Vásquez (P.R.)	K. McKinney (U.S.)	D. McKenzie (England)	—
Bantamweight	V. Rabañales (Mexico)	E. Julio (Colombia)	O. Canizales (Mexico)	R. Del Valle (P.R.)	—
Super flyweight	S.K. Moon (South Korea)	K. Onizuka (Japan)	R. Quiroga (U.S.)	Johnny Bredahl (Den.)	—
Flyweight	Y. Arbachakov (Russia)	D. Griman (Venezuela)	F. Sitbanghpacan (Thailand)	P. Clinton (Scotland)	R. Regan (Wales)
Light flyweight	H. González (Mexico)	M. Yuh (South Korea)	M. Carbajal (U.S.)	J. Camacho (P.R.)	—
Straw weight	R. López (Mexico)	H. Ohashi (Japan)	R. Sorvorapin (Thailand)	—	—

[1]World Boxing Council.   [2]World Boxing Association.   [3]International Boxing Federation.   [4]World Boxing Organization.

The referee declares Rafael Lozano of Spain winner in a 6–5 decision over Eric Griffin of the U.S. in a light flyweight match in the Olympic Games. Although it was widely agreed that the scoring, using a new computerized system, was flawed, officials rejected an official protest.
AP/WIDE WORLD

champion. Now 34, Nelson again took on Jeff Fenech (Australia) in Melbourne before 38,000 fans and halted Fenech in eight rounds. Nearly a year earlier the Australian had held Nelson to a draw at Las Vegas, and many observers thought that Fenech should have been given the decision and the title. Nelson settled all arguments in the return bout and followed this up by outpointing Calvin Grove (U.S.) to bring his total to 18 championship fights and the ninth defense of his title.

Others who stood out from the glut of world champion claimants included Moon Sung Kil (South Korea), who remained WBC super flyweight king after seven defenses and lost only one of 17 contests. Thomas ("Hit Man") Hearns (U.S.), who had won five world crowns at different weights, unexpectedly lost his one remaining title, the WBA light heavyweight championship, when outpointed by the IBF super middleweight king, Iran Barkley (U.S.). Barkley relinquished this championship without making a defense in order to concentrate on the super middleweight division. Virgil Hill (U.S.), who had suffered his first and only defeat when losing to Hearns in 1991, regained the WBA light heavyweight crown by outpointing Frank Tate for the vacant championship.

Yury Arbachakov (Russia) made history when he became the first Russian to win a professional boxing title by knocking out WBC flyweight champion Muangchai Kittikssen (Thailand) in eight rounds in Tokyo. Arbachakov later proved his worth with a successful defense against Yunun Chin (South Korea), which also took place in Tokyo. An unusual record was established in Copenhagen when Jimmi and Johnny Bredahl of Denmark became the first brothers ever to win versions of world titles on the same night. Jimmi gained the WBO super featherweight championship with a decision on points against Daniel Londas (France), and Johnny became WBO super flyweight king by outpointing José Quirino (Mexico). They had become world champions after fighting only 28 bouts between them. The Bredahls had both previously won European championships but, to get their achievements in the proper perspective, it must be remembered that WBO championships were less highly regarded than those of the WBC, WBA, and IBF.

By the same reasoning, the claim of Duke McKenzie (England) to have become the first Briton to win three world titles at different weights since Bob Fitzsimmons in 1903 could not be compared with Fitzsimmons' achievement, which took place when there were only seven recognized world titles. In 1992, by contrast, nearly 70 boxers were claiming world titles. McKenzie, after winning and losing the IBF flyweight crown, gained the WBO bantamweight championship only to lose it to Rafael Del Valle (P.R.) on a two-round knockout. It was only the 13th contest for the Puerto Rican. Yet a few months later McKenzie was matched with the WBO super bantamweight champion Jesse Benavides (U.S.) and took this title with a victory on points.

Over the years there had been several official probes into the conduct of professional boxing in the U.S. In 1992 two bills concerning the regulation of the sport were under consideration. One favoured the creation of a Professional Boxing Corporation to work with existing state authorities to arrive at national standards. The other sought to establish minimal health and safety standards through the U.S. Department of Labor. The first bill, financed by a fee on promotions, would set licensing requirements and create national rules governing contracts and conflicts of interest. If either bill were ever passed, it would help to end or ease the unsatisfactory state of the sport aggravated by the many self-appointed ruling bodies.

However, several probes of recent years faded away without action. The last successful investigation took place more than 40 years ago with the Kefauver Commission held in New York City to probe racketeering, extortion, and monopoly. It virtually ended the powerful International Boxing Club, which had a monopoly on the heavyweight championship; sent many involved in racketeering to operate in other states; and sent to prison Frankie Carbo and "Blinky" Palermo, who had controlled some of the richest championships as undercover men.

While the actions of the WBC, WBA, and IBF deserved much criticism, the WBO, the most recent body seeking world boxing power, made some decisions that could only be regarded as incredible and created several titleholders of only moderate skill. Apart from going it alone in the heavyweight scene, declining to recognize Holyfield and Bowe for less creditable champions such as Michael Moorer (U.S.), its current heavyweight king, the WBO came under fire after authorizing a one-sided match for the light flyweight title in which Josue Camacho (P.R.) knocked out a mediocre opponent, Eddie Vallejo (Mexico), in six rounds at San Juan in July. The Puerto Rican Boxing Commission fined them $2,000 for staging the bout without permission.

(FRANK BUTLER)

CHESS

The return, after 20 years of seclusion, of Robert ("Bobby") James Fischer overshadowed the eclipse of Soviet chess in the world individual championships. Yet in the Manila Olympiad (world team championship) Russia struck back to score a remarkable victory for the "Soviet School of Chess."

The feat of eliminating former world titleholder Anatoly Karpov from the championship series was achieved in April by Nigel Short of England at Linares, Spain. Despite losing the first game, Short won convincingly by 6–4 in the scheduled match of 10 games. Karpov was in serious time trouble at many critical points. His loss could be seen as symbolic, as he had been the great chess establishment figure of the U.S.S.R., which had ceased to exist some five months earlier.

At the same time and place, Jan Timman of The Netherlands beat Artur Yusupov of Russia by the same score, to set up a Short-Timman match in Madrid in January 1993 for the new challenger to Garry Kasparov for his world title. Previously, Kasparov had played five matches with Karpov over seven years for the title.

At the Manila Olympiad in June, a young Russian team, headed by Kasparov but lacking Karpov, easily won the 102-country contest, ahead of former Soviet republics Uzbekistan and Armenia and the U.S. England, one of the tournament favourites, finished 10th, equal in points with Georgia and Ukraine. Latvia, restored to membership in the world chess organization Fédération Internationale des Échecs for the first time since 1940, finished in a tie for fifth with Iceland and Croatia. The most remarkable performance came from Bosnia and Hercegovina, which reached 12th place. The team had to play the entire tournament with the four players who chanced to be away from their homeland when it became involved in an armed conflict with Serbia; it was impossible for the two nominated reserves to leave embattled Sarajevo.

Fischer's announced return came as a bombshell in late July after so many projects involving him had fallen through in the 20 years since he beat Boris Spassky in Iceland to take the world title for the U.S. from the U.S.S.R. Fischer agreed to a Yugoslav proposal to play again against Spassky in Montenegro (Sveti Stefan) and Serbia (Belgrade), thereby defying U.S. sanctions against playing in those former Yugoslav states because of their policy of "ethnic cleansing" of minority peoples.

At the press conference at Sveti Stefan on September 1,

Ninth Game of the Bobby Fischer–Boris Spassky Match			
White B. Fischer	Black B. Spassky	White B. Fischer	Black B. Spassky
1 e4	e5	12 Be3	b6
2 Nf3	Nc6	13 a4	0-0-0
3 Bb5	a6	14 a5	Kb7
4 Bxc6	dxc6	15 e5!	Be7
5 0-0	f6	16 Rxd8	Bxd8
6 d4	exd4	17 Ne4!	Kc6?
7 Nxd4	c5	(17...	Bd5 holds on)
8 Nb3	Qxd1	18 axb6	cxb6
9 Rxd1	Bg4	19 Nbxc5!	Bc8
10 f3	Be6	20 Nxa6	fxe5
11 Nc3	Bd6	21 Nb4 +	Black resigned

Fischer made clear his opposition to the sanctions, dismissing a U.S. Treasury Department warning by spitting on it, and gave vent to virulent accusations of cheating in chess. The main culprits in this, he held, were Kasparov, Karpov, and even the Soviet dissident Viktor Korchnoi, who earlier in the year became a Swiss citizen and paid his first visit to his native Russia in 16 years.

Fischer won the first game of the match with Spassky in fine style, then showed signs of rustiness by falling behind after five games. But he gradually improved to reach a 5–2 lead in the Sveti Stefan section. After a nine-day break the match shifted to Belgrade, with Fischer in search of another five wins to clinch the winner's reward, five-eighths of the record $5 million. The match was being played under the old rules, whereby the victory went to the first to win 10 games over a period of time that could be extended as long as necessary. Spassky put up strong resistance despite kidney trouble—he had to take four illness breaks to Fischer's none. Spassky won three games in Belgrade and resisted till the 30th game, when Fischer won as Black in 27 moves to win the match 10 games to 5.

Kasparov was scathing about the quality of the play, claiming that Fischer had undermined his own legend. The year closed amid speculation that Fischer might play 16-year-old Hungarian prodigy Judit Polgar (*see* BIOGRAPHIES) or that Fischer and Kasparov might meet in a big-money contest despite their mutual antipathy. In December Fischer was indicted in the U.S. for violating the International Emergency Economic Powers Act, invoked by U.S. Pres. George Bush to impose sanctions on Yugoslavia. Should Fischer be convicted, he would face a possible sentence of 10 years in prison, a fine of $250,000, and forfeiture of the money he won in the Spassky match.

AP/WIDE WORLD

Bobby Fischer (left) and Boris Spassky begin their nonsanctioned match in Yugoslavia on September 2. In the first public match since he defeated Spassky in 1972 for the world championship, Fischer won 10 games to 5 with 15 draws.

Kasparov scored an impressive tournament victory at Linares in February, enjoying a two-point advantage (almost unprecedented in modern chess) over the next placers. The top finishers in the 12-game contest were Kasparov 10 points; Vasily Ivanchuk (Ukraine) and Timman 8; Karpov 7½; and Viswanathan Anand (India), Boris Gelfand (Belarus), and Valery Salov (Russia) 7.

Short, who had tied for last at Linares, showed more like his true form when he shared first place with Anand at the Euwe Memorial in Amsterdam in May. Short was also being spoken of as a likely opponent for Fischer in 1993.

Another Englishman came to the fore when Michael Adams, whose 21st birthday was November 17, won two strong and well-funded events. These were the SWIFT tournament in Brussels in early July and the Tilburg event in The Netherlands on October 8–28, where no fewer than 110 titled players appeared. In the Tilburg final Adams beat Gelfand in a quick-play tiebreaker. The trend for quicker games became ever more noticeable during the year.

Two of the strongest events of the year were won by Kasparov and Karpov. The former won at Dortmund, Germany, in April but had to share first place with Ivanchuk. The latter dominated at Biel, Switz., in July.

Two severe losses came in 1992 for the chess community. The U.S. veteran Samuel Reshevsky died at the age of 80 at Suffern, N.Y., on April 4, and Mikhail Tal died in a Moscow hospital on June 28 at 55. (*See* OBITUARIES.) The former was a child prodigy who had played professional chess from the 1930s until his 80th year. The latter, nicknamed "the sorcerer of Riga," was famous for winning the world title from Mikhail Botvinnik in 1960.

An unrepresentative British championship in August was won for the second straight year by Julian Hodgson. The U.S. championship in December at Durango, Colo., was won by Patrick Wolff of Somerville, Mass. He and six other players qualified for interzonal competition.

(BERNARD CAFFERTY)

CONTRACT BRIDGE

Many trends previously noticed were confirmed in 1992: the World Bridge Federation (WBF) reported steady growth; the United States failed to reassert at world level the supremacy lost in 1989 (but swept all four events in the newly inaugurated Pan-American championships, contested by 16 nations); women continued to narrow the gap with men; and the use of computers as teaching aids and for visual presentations to audiences was further extended.

By the end of the year, the WBF had 92 national contract bridge organizations. The fastest-growing zonal organization was the European Bridge League, which during 1992 admitted Croatia, Estonia, Georgia, Latvia, Lithuania, Slovenia, and the Commonwealth of Independent States, bringing its total to 37 members. Even before this, Europe's total of registered bridge players—who in most countries were a small fraction of all players—had reached a record 318,146, an increase of 6.5% for the year. The country with the strongest growth was France.

A new record was created in the WBF's most popular event, the Epson Worldwide Bridge Contest. More than 102,000 players competed at more than 2,000 centres, making it the biggest official world contest ever held in any game. An innovation by the World Federation of Tall Towers was the staging of celebrity heats linked by satellite communications.

The ninth World Team Olympiad was held in Salsomaggiore, Italy, with 57 countries in the Open Series and 34 in the Women's. In the Open Series France defeated the U.S. by 250.7 international match points to 171 in a 96-

This deal symbolizes the increased achievement of women in the higher echelons of tournament bridge. It was played by Liz McGowan of Edinburgh, a member of Britain's World Olympiad runner-up squad, in a match against Austria and won her the IBPA's Best-Played Hand of the Year award.

```
                    NORTH
                    ♠ A 10 3
                    ♥ Q 10 4
                    ♦ A 6 5 3
                    ♣ A 5 4
WEST                                    EAST
♠ K Q J 8 7 2                           ♠ 9 6 5 4
♥ J 8 7 3                               ♥ —
♦ 10 9                                  ♦ Q 8 7 4 2
♣ 7                                     ♣ K Q J 9
                    SOUTH
                    ♠ —
                    ♥ A K 9 6 5 2
                    ♦ K J
                    ♣ 10 8 6 3 2
```

Dealer South.
Neither side vulnerable.

SOUTH	WEST	NORTH	EAST
1♥	2♠	Dble	4♠
5♣	Pass	6♥	All pass

Opening lead: ♠K.

McGowan ruffed the spade lead, cashed ♥K, finessed ♥10, and played off ♥Q. She cashed ♠A, throwing a club, entered her hand by finessing ♦J, and played off two more trumps, leaving these cards:

```
                    ♠ 10
                    ♥ —
                    ♦ A 6 5
                    ♣ A 5
♠ Q J 8 7                               ♠ —
♥ —                                     ♥ —
♦ 10                                    ♦ 8 7
♣ 7                                     ♣ K Q 9
                    ♠ —
                    ♥ 2
                    ♦ K
                    ♣ 10 8 6 3
```

South played ♥2, discarding a spade from dummy, and East threw a club. Now South played ace and another club and made the balance. Had East thrown a diamond on the ♥2, all of dummy's diamonds would have become good.

board final. The winning team consisted of Paul Chemla and Michel Perron, Hervé Mouiel and Alain Lévy, Pierre Adad and Maurice Aujaleu, and the nonplaying captain, José Damiani. The losing semifinalists were Sweden and The Netherlands.

In the Women's Series Austria beat Great Britain by 266–218. Members of the winning team were Maria Erhart and Barbara Lindinger, Terry Weigkricht and Doris Fischer, Jovanka Smederevac and Herta Gyimesi, and the nonplaying captain, Ernst Pichler. The losing semifinalists were France and Germany.

For the first time an Open team, Mexico, had more women members than men. Also for the first time, a woman won the annual Best-Played Hand of the Year award presented by the International Bridge Press Association (IBPA). The hand is described above.

Easley Blackwood died at the age of 89 in Indianapolis, Ind., where 60 years earlier he had invented the famous convention for discovering the number of aces held. The simplicity and efficiency of the convention caused it to be spread by word of mouth despite rejection by Ely Culbertson, who dominated the bridge scene and controlled the means of publicity, and indifference on the part of leading players. "Everybody was against me," said Blackwood memorably, "but the public."

(ALBERT G. DORMER)

CRICKET

South Africa returned to international cricket for the first time in 22 years, shrugging off a lengthy absence and a lack of experience by reaching the semifinal of the World Cup, which was won by Pakistan. That represented a triumph for the South Africans, who were given an emotional welcome back into the fold, first by India in a three-match one-day series in late 1991 and then by the West Indies in a five-day Test. South Africa had not played either team before. The South Africans adapted remarkably quickly to the demands of the international game, and had it not been for the controversial rules that came into force in the event of rain, South Africa might have qualified for the World Cup final at its first attempt. Inevitably, with the World Cup held in Australia and New Zealand for the first time, one-day cricket dominated the calendar for much of the year. But a 2–1 victory in a best-of-five Test series in England confirmed Pakistan's status as the best team of the year.

Initially, when they were reinstated as members of the International Cricket Council (ICC), the South Africans were excluded from the World Cup because preparations were thought to be too far advanced. Under pressure from the Australian Cricket Board, which believed that South Africa's presence would increase revenue, the team, captained by K.C. Wessels, was admitted into the nine-nation competition at the last moment. Much of the credit for the return belonged to Ali Bacher, captain of the last South African Test side in 1970 and president of the newly formed United Cricket Board of South Africa. Bacher campaigned long and hard for the development of multiracial cricket in South Africa throughout the years of isolation, but not even he could have realized how quickly his dreams would come true or how ecstatic and emotional the welcome would be. A crowd of over 85,000 packed into the Eden Gardens in Calcutta for South Africa's first-ever international against India, and though the South Africans were predictably rusty and lost the series 2–1, the warmth of the welcome was more important than the result.

Lack of experience also cost South Africa dearly in its one Test of the year. After outplaying the West Indies for most of the four days in Barbados, the South Africans needed just 79 runs to win with 8 wickets in hand on the final morning. But, on an increasingly difficult pitch, they lost 8 for 26, C.A. Walsh producing an inspired spell of fast

bowling to take 4 for 8, and were beaten by 52 runs. Earlier, A.C. Hudson had scored 163.

In the World Cup, Australia, the pretournament favourite, lost three of its first four matches—and failed to qualify for the semifinals. The West Indians also failed to qualify. In one semifinal Pakistan, which had begun the tournament slowly, beat New Zealand, while in the other England beat South Africa in a match that ended in controversy when South Africa's run chase was interrupted by rain just before the end. From needing a plausible 22 runs from 13 balls, South Africa had to score an impossible 21 from one ball under the rules that reduced the competition to a near farce at times. In the final England, led by G.A. Gooch, fell 22 runs short of Pakistan's total of 249 for 6 off 50 overs, and it was Pakistan captain Imran Khan who lifted the trophy aloft. Ironically, in the group match between the two teams, England had bowled Pakistan out for just 74 when rain stopped play. Had it lost that match, Pakistan would not have qualified for the semifinals, but it took full advantage of its reprieve and fully deserved victory.

Before the World Cup, Australia had been in dominant form, beating India 4–0 in the Test series and winning the Benson and Hedges World Series. Captained by A.R. Border and with potentially the strongest batting side in international cricket, Australia proved too powerful. D.C. Boon headed the batting averages for the series with 556 runs (average 79), while fast bowler G.J. McDermott took 31 wickets (average 21.61) to be the leading wicket taker, including match figures of 9 for 101 in the first Test and 10 for 168 in the third. B.R. Reid (12 for 122 in the second) and M.R. Whitney (7 for 27 in the fifth) completed the rout, which was stemmed only in the third Test when R.J. Shastri scored 206 to ensure a draw for India.

The series between England and Pakistan was marred by controversy, first when Pakistan launched a volley of protest at the umpire during the third Test at Old Trafford and later when its two brilliant fast bowlers, Wasim Akram and Waqar Younis, who between them took 43 wickets in the series, were accused of tampering with the ball to make it swing more in the air. In both cases the lack of decisive action by the authorities served only to heighten the furor. On the field Pakistan, led by its new captain, Javed Miandad (see BIOGRAPHIES), was clearly the better team, though it was not until the final Test that its superiority was confirmed. Chasing 138 to win, Pakistan narrowly won the

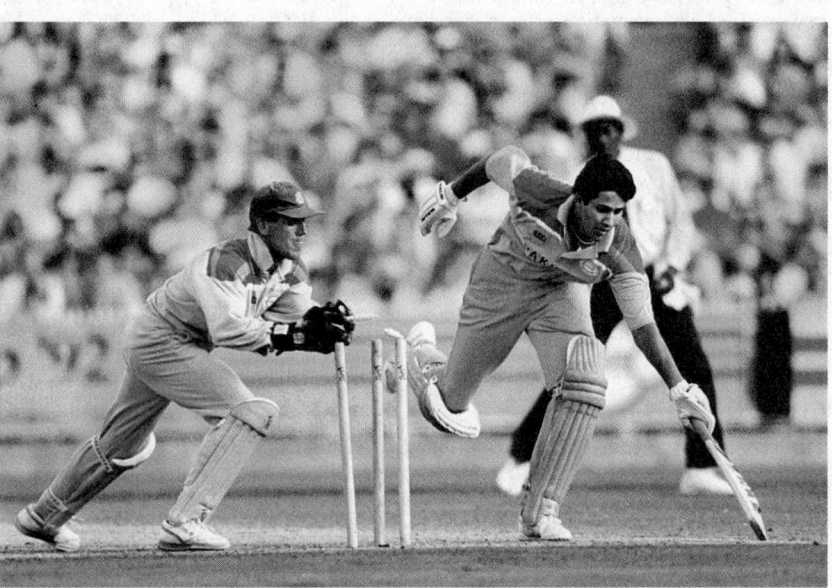

England wicketkeeper Alec Stewart hits the bails but fails to dismiss Pakistan's Inzamam-ul-Haq in the World Cup final in Melbourne, Australia, on March 25. Pakistan went on to win the match by 22 runs.

Test Series Results, September 1991–September 1992

Test	Host country	Ground	Scores	Result
1st	Australia	Brisbane	India 239 and 156; Australia 340 and 58 for 0	Australia won by 10 wkt
2nd	Australia	Melbourne	India 263 and 213; Australia 349 and 128 for 2	Australia won by 8 wkt
3rd	Australia	Sydney	Australia 313 and 173 for 8; India 483	Match drawn
4th	Australia	Adelaide	Australia 145 and 451; India 225 and 333	Australia won by 38 runs
5th	Australia	Perth	Australia 346 and 367 for 6 dec; India 272 and 141	Australia won by 300 runs
1st	Pakistan	Sialkot	Sri Lanka 270 and 137 for 5; Pakistan 423 for 5 dec	Match drawn
2nd	Pakistan	Gujranwala	Pakistan 109 for 2	Match drawn
3rd	Pakistan	Faisalabad	Sri Lanka 240 and 165; Pakistan 221 and 188 for 7	Pakistan won by 3 wkt
1st	New Zealand	Christchurch	England 580; New Zealand 312 and 264	England won by an innings and 4 runs
2nd	New Zealand	Auckland	England 203 and 321; New Zealand 142 and 214	England won by 168 runs
3rd	New Zealand	Wellington	England 305 and 359; New Zealand 432 for 9 dec and 43 for 3	Match drawn
1st	West Indies	Barbados	West Indies 262 and 283; South Africa 345 and 148	West Indies won by 52 runs
1st	England	Edgbaston	Pakistan 446 for 4 dec; England 459 for 7 dec	Match drawn
2nd	England	Lord's	England 255 and 175; Pakistan 293 and 141 for 8	Pakistan won by 2 wkt
3rd	England	Old Trafford	Pakistan 505 for 9 dec and 239 for 5 dec; England 390	Match drawn
4th	England	Headingley	Pakistan 197 and 221; England 320 and 99 for 4	England won by 6 wkt
5th	England	The Oval	England 207 and 174; Pakistan 380 and 5 for 0	Pakistan won by 10 wkt
1st	Sri Lanka	Colombo	Australia 256 and 471; Sri Lanka 547 and 164	Australia won by 16 runs
2nd	Sri Lanka	Colombo	Australia 247 and 296 for 6 dec; Sri Lanka 258 for 9 dec and 136 for 2	Match drawn
3rd	Sri Lanka	Moratuwa	Australia 337 and 271 for 8; Sri Lanka 274 for 9 dec	Match drawn

second Test at Lord's, where Wasim and Waqar, as batsmen this time, putting on 43 for the eighth wicket, guided Pakistan to last-gasp victory from the brink of defeat at 95 for 8. Helped by a century from Gooch, England squared the series in a low-scoring match at Headingley, but at the Oval, Waqar and Wasim took 15 wickets as Pakistan won easily by 10 wickets. Aamir Sohail made 205 in the third Test, while Salim Malik, with 488, was the leading run scorer in the series. In an innings of 73 on his recall for the third test, D.I. Gower surpassed G. Boycott's total of 8,114 runs to become England's highest scorer in Test cricket. In New Zealand earlier in the year, I.T. Botham had played his 100th Test as England became the first visiting team in 13 years to win a Test series in New Zealand.

Sri Lanka, which had played very few Tests in recent years, did its cause no harm with a spirited display in the home series against Australia late in the year. Requiring 181 to win, the home team reached 127 for 2 before collapsing dramatically to 164 all out. Earlier, A.P. Gurusinha (137), A. Ranatunga (127), and R. Kaluwitharana (132 not out) had inspired a massive Sri Lankan total in the first innings. Australia's frantic victory proved decisive, the next two Tests ending in draws, with D.M. Jones (100 not out in the second Test) and Border (106 in the third) scoring centuries for Australia. Sri Lanka would no longer be the newest Test-playing nation after a decision by the ICC to give Zimbabwe Test status. Zimbabwe became the ninth country to play Test cricket.

In domestic cricket Essex, led by Gooch, retained the County Championship title, and Durham, in its first first-class season, finished last. Middlesex, Northamptonshire, and Hampshire won the three one-day competitions. In the future all championship matches would be played over four days as opposed to three. Western Australia won the Sheffield Shield, beating New South Wales by 44 runs in the final. The Red Stripe Cup was won by Jamaica, the Shell Trophy in New Zealand by Central Districts, and South Africa's Castle Cup by Eastern Province.

(ANDREW LONGMORE)

CYCLING

The design of the racing bicycle continued to change during 1992 as technology and the understanding of aerodynamics advanced. The most striking example was seen at the Olympic Games in Barcelona, Spain, where Britain's Christopher Boardman rode a cycle with a solid one-piece carbon fibre frame to victory in the individual 4,000-m pur-

suit. The cycle was developed by the engineering arm of Lotus cars from a 1985 prototype that was banned by the sport's governing body, the Union Cycliste International, until late 1990, when the ruling that frames had to comprise three separate pieces of tubing was revoked.

Boardman beat world champion Jens Lehmann for the gold medal, catching the German one lap from the end of the 16-lap final at the Horta velodrome. Boardman's second-round time of 4 min 24.496 sec was ratified as an outdoor world record, and he went on to set a new mark of 5 min 38.038 sec for 5,000 m on the track at Leicester, England, three weeks later.

1992 Cycling Champions

Event	Winner	Country
WORLD AMATEUR CHAMPIONS—TRACK		
Men		
Tandem sprint	G. Capitano, F. Paris	Italy
Motor paced	C. Podlesch	Germany
Women		
30-km points	I. Haringa	The Netherlands
WORLD PROFESSIONAL CHAMPIONS—TRACK		
Sprint	M. Hübner	Germany
Individual pursuit	M. McCarthy	U.S.
50-km points	B. Risi	Switzerland
Motor paced	P. Steiger	Switzerland
Keirin	M. Hübner	Germany
WORLD AMATEUR CHAMPIONS—ROAD		
Women		
50-km team time trial	J. Bolland, B. Bankaitis-Davis, J. Golay, E. Stephenson	U.S.
WORLD PROFESSIONAL CHAMPION—ROAD		
Individual road race	G. Bugno	Italy
WORLD CHAMPIONS—CYCLO-CROSS		
Amateur	D. Pontoni	Italy
Professional	M. Kluge	Germany
MAJOR PROFESSIONAL ROAD-RACE WINNERS		
Tour de France	M. Indurain	Spain
Tour of Italy	M. Indurain	Spain
Tour of Spain	T. Rominger	Switzerland
Tour of Switzerland	G. Furlan	Italy
Milan–San Remo	S. Kelly	Ireland
Tour of Flanders	J. Durand	France
Paris–Roubaix	G. Duclos-Lassalle	France
Liège–Bastogne–Liège	D. De Wolf	Belgium
Amstel Gold	O. Ludwig	Germany
Wincanton Classic	M. Ghirotto	Italy
Championship of Zürich	V. Ekimov	Estonia
San Sebastian Classic	R. Alcala	Mexico
Paris–Nice	J.-F. Bernard	France
Ghent–Wevelgem	M. Cipollini	Italy
Flèche Wallonne	G. Furlan	Italy
Dunkirk 4-Day	O. Ludwig	Germany
Paris–Brussels	R. Sorensen	Denmark
Grand Prix of Frankfurt	F. Van Den Abbeele	Belgium
Tour of Britain	M. Sciandri	Italy
Milk Race[1]	C. Henry	Ireland

[1]Mixed professional and amateur.

Germany set a world outdoor record of 4 min 8.791 sec on the way to the Olympic 4,000-m team pursuit title. José Moreno won Spain's first-ever Olympic cycling gold medal in the 1,000-m time trial, and Erika Salumae became Estonia's first Olympic champion since 1936 when she retained the women's sprint title she had won for the Soviet Union in 1988.

The 1992 world championships, excluding Olympic events, were also held in Spain. The track competitions took place at the newly constructed Luis Puig Velodrome in Valencia, where Mike McCarthy became the first rider from the U.S. to win the professional 5,000-m pursuit, beating U.S.-based Shaun Wallace of the U.K. by nearly two seconds in the final. Michael Hübner of Germany repeated his 1990 double in the professional sprint and keirin, winning the latter title for the third straight year. The professional road race, held around the coastal resort of Benidorm, was won by the defending champion, Gianni Bugno of Italy, who became the fourth man to take the title in successive years and the first to do so since 1961. The women's team trial was won for the first time by the U.S.

The Tour de France, the major event on the professional cycling calendar, was won for the second successive year by Miguel Indurain of Spain (*see* BIOGRAPHIES). To mark the opening up of Europe's national frontiers, the race visited six other countries on its three-week journey from San Sebastian, Spain, to the finish in the heart of Paris, covering a distance of 3,983 km (2,475 mi).   (JOHN R. WILKINSON)

FIELD HOCKEY

At the summer Olympic Games in Barcelona, Spain, the gold medal for men's hockey was won by Germany with a 2–1 victory over Australia in the final on Aug. 8, 1992. Pakistan gained the bronze medal by defeating The Netherlands 4–3. Behind The Netherlands, in fifth place, was Spain, followed by Great Britain, India, New Zealand, Malaysia, the Unified Team (comprising republics of the former Soviet Union), Argentina, and Egypt. Germany had placed second to Great Britain in the 1988 Olympics. (For additional information on the Olympic Games, *see* Special Report, page 276.)

Germany had earlier defeated Australia 4–0 in the final of the six-nation tournament at Karachi, Pak., in February to gain the Champions Trophy for the fifth time. Pakistan finished third, ahead of The Netherlands, Great Britain, and France. In June Pakistan emerged victorious in a five-nation event at Amsterdam, finishing ahead of Germany, The Netherlands, Great Britain, and Spain. Australia, The Netherlands, Malaysia, and Japan later finished in that order at a four-nation tournament in Kuala Lumpur, Malaysia. Germany reasserted its supremacy at Milton Keynes, England, by winning the Milton Keynes Challenge ahead of Great Britain, Egypt, and Spain.

In women's hockey Spain won the Olympic gold medal for the first time, at Barcelona on August 7, with a 2–1 victory over Germany in the final. Great Britain defeated South Korea 4–3 in overtime for the bronze medal. Australia, winner in the 1988 Olympics, was relegated to fifth place, followed by The Netherlands, Canada, and New Zealand. At a five-nation tournament in June in Amsterdam, The Netherlands won, followed by South Korea, Spain, Germany, and Great Britain. In the Inter-Nations Cup tournament at Singapore in August, the final between France and Scotland ended goalless, but France emerged the winner on penalties. Finishing behind Scotland were India, the Unified Team, Belgium, Italy, Zimbabwe, Malaysia, and Singapore. England won the Home Countries championship at Cork, Ireland, in April. Ireland placed second, Wales third, and Scotland fourth.   (SYDNEY E. FRISKIN)

FOOTBALL

Association Football (Soccer). In June the final tournament of the European championship in Sweden produced a surprising but deserved win for Denmark. The Danes were a late replacement for Yugoslavia, which had been suspended because of the international sanctions imposed on Serbia and Montenegro. Denmark belied the theory that extensive preparation was essential for success at the highest level. With the Danish domestic season recently completed, the players were still fit. They applied themselves with characteristic ability and, despite crippling injuries to key members of the squad, reached the final of a mediocre tournament otherwise devoid of invention and enterprise. The Danes met the powerful Germans in the final, having earlier disposed of the much-fancied French team, which proved to be well past its peak. After withstanding early German pressure, Denmark scored 18 minutes into the contest. Kim Vilfort won a tussle with German defender Andreas Brehme and backheeled the ball down the touchline to Flemming Povlsen. He pulled it back for John Jensen to drive past Bodo Illgner in the German goal. Denmark added a second goal in the 78th minute, after the increasingly frustrated Germans failed to clear a free kick. Claus Christiansen headed the ball down, and Vilfort, with just a suspicion of handling, burst through to score off Illgner's left-hand post to complete a 2–0 win. It was Denmark's first international honour in association football.

European Champions' Cup. Barcelona of Spain beat Sampdoria of Italy 1–0 at Wembley, England, on May 20 to become only the second Spanish club after Real Madrid to win the cup and the third to have achieved success in all three major European competitions, following Juventus of Italy and Ajax of The Netherlands. An absorbing, evenly contested match watched by an enthusiastic crowd of 74,000 went into overtime. The only goal came from a disputed free kick in the 110th minute. Giovanni Invernizzi's tackle on Eusebio Sacristan was judged unfair by German referee Aron Schmidhuber. Hristo Stoichkov of Bulgaria and José-María Bakero set the shot up for Ronald Koeman to drive fiercely beyond the right-hand reach of Sampdoria goalkeeper Gianluca Pagliuca. Thus Koeman, of The Netherlands, became only the second player to win a Champions' Cup medal with different clubs, having gained one with PSV Eindhoven in 1988.

European Cup-Winners' Cup. By beating Monaco of France 2–0 in Lisbon on May 6 before a disappointing attendance of only 16,000, Werder Bremen became the first German team to win the European Cup-Winners' Cup since Hamburg in 1977. There was a distinct contrast in styles; Monaco used the midfield to spring attacks, while the Germans adopted more direct tactics. Klaus Allofs opened the scoring in the 40th minute. A high ball from Frank Neubarth caught the Monaco defense off balance, and Allofs stole in to put the ball under the diving Jean-Luc Ettori. Nine minutes after halftime Allofs put New Zealander Wynton Rufer in to chase a long pass. The Monaco defense expected an offside decision, which never came. Ettori was forced to venture out of his area, and Rufer scored on the untended net.

UEFA Cup. Ajax Amsterdam equaled Juventus' and Barcelona's record of winning the three major European trophies with a victory over Torino, thus breaking the three-year hold of Italian clubs on the trophy. In Turin on April 29 in an exciting first leg, watched by about 65,000, Ajax led from the 16th minute, when Wim Jonk scored unhindered from 23 m (25 yd). Brazilian striker Walter Casagrande tied the score in the 65th minute, but Ajax regained the lead in the 77th minute from a penalty converted by Sweden's

Table I. Association Football National Champions

Nation	League winners	Cup winners
Albania	Vllaznia	Elbasan
Argentina	Newell's Old Boys	
Austria	FK Austria	FK Austria
Belgium	Club Brugge	Antwerp
Bolivia	Bolivar	
Brazil	Flamengo	
Bulgaria	CSKA Sofia	Levski
Chile	Colo Colo	
Colombia	América de Cali	
CIS	CSKA Moscow	Spartak Moscow
Cyprus	Apoel	Apollon
Czechoslovakia	Slovan Bratislava	Sparta Prague
Denmark	Lyngby	Aarhus
Ecuador	Emelec	
El Salvador	Luís Angel Firpo	
England	Leeds United	Liverpool
Faeroe Islands	KI Klakksvik	B36
Finland	Kuusysi Lahti	TPS Turku
France	Marseille	…
Germany	VfB Stuttgart	Hannover 96
Greece	AEK Athens	Olympiakos
Guatemala	Municipal	
Honduras	Motagua	
Hungary	Ferencvaros	Ujpest Dozsa
Iceland	Vikingur	Valur
Ireland	Shelbourne	Bohemians
Italy	AC Milan	Parma
Luxembourg	Avenir Beggen	Avenir Beggen
Malta	Valletta	Hamrun Spartans
Mexico	Léon	
Netherlands, The	PSV Eindhoven	Feyenoord
Northern Ireland	Glentoran	Glenavon
Norway	Viking Stavanger	Stromsgodset
Paraguay	Olimpia	
Peru	Sporting Cristal	
Poland	Lech Poznan	Miedz Legnica
Portugal	FC Porto	Boavista
Romania	Dinamo Bucharest	Steaua Bucharest
Scotland	Rangers	Rangers
Spain	Barcelona	Atletico Madrid
Sweden	IFK Göteborg	IFK Göteborg
Switzerland	Sion	Lucerne
Turkey	Besiktas	Trabzonspor
Uruguay	Defensor	
Venezuela	Minerven	
Wales	—	Cardiff City
Yugoslavia	Red Star Belgrade	Partizan Belgrade

Stefan Pettersson after Dennis Bergkamp had been fouled in the penalty area. But Casagrande tied the game again with only five minutes remaining, and it ended 2–2. A more physical contest in the second leg at Amsterdam on May 13 ended 0–0 in front of 42,000 spectators, and Ajax was awarded the victory because it had scored the most goals away from home.

The breakup of the former Soviet Union and fragmentation of Yugoslavia provided additional members for the Fédération Internationale de Football Association (FIFA), the sport's governing body. Its 48th congress approved an increase to 178 countries.

Olympic Games. Spain won the gold medal at the Olympic Games in Barcelona, Spain, beating Poland 3–2 in a match watched by 95,000, the biggest attendance at any individual event at the 1992 Games. (For additional information on the Olympic Games, *see* Special Report, page 276.)

National Competition. World transfer fee records were broken when Gianluigi Lentini, a winger, was signed by AC Milan from Torino for $24 million. Two other similar moves took Gianluca Vialli from Sampdoria to Juventus in a $22 million deal and Jean-Pierre Papin from Marseille to AC Milan for $10 million. Italian clubs spent more than $436 million on new players during the summer. A new British record was set when Alan Shearer was transferred from Southampton to Blackburn Rovers for £3.6 million.

AC Milan achieved an Italian record for a 34-game series by remaining unbeaten and winning 22 matches in taking the national championship. Its millionaire president, Silvio Berlusconi, continued his policy of adding new players by increasing to six the number of foreigners on the team, even though only three could be used in one game. But with a record 72,000 season-ticket holders, the club had

healthy finances that were the envy of many others. Dinamo Bucharest won 23 of 34 Romanian league games and also stayed undefeated. Besiktas of Turkey won 23 and tied seven, and Malta's Valletta tied three and won 15 of its 18 matches. Rangers achieved its 42nd championship in Scotland, and a national league was instituted in Wales for the first time. On May 5 a temporary stand collapsed in Bastia, Corsica, before the French Cup semifinal between the local team and Marseille, causing at least 14 deaths and more than 700 injuries.

The English Football Association introduced its Premier League, leaving the Football League to administer the three remaining divisions. The new competition received a financial boost from satellite television when BSkyB promised £304 million over five years, though the sponsorship deal's viability appeared to rest precariously on hoped-for increased sales of satellite appliances in recessional times.

Rules. An important rule change at the 106th annual meeting of the International Football Association Board attempted to counter time-wasting tactics by banning intentional passes by defenders to their goalkeeper, preventing him from controlling the ball with his hands in such circumstances. The legislation was also aimed at keeping the game flowing, though the situation had been allowed to develop through overprotection of the goalkeeper.

North America. The Major Soccer League, the long-standing indoor competition of 14 years, folded during the year. This left the U.S. with no nationwide professional soccer league. (JACK ROLLIN)

Latin America. Brazilian soccer teams enjoyed a good year in international play in 1992. São Paulo won the Libertadores de América Cup, South America's club championship. The Brazilian team edged Argentina's Newell's Old Boys in a series of penalty kicks after two inconclusive games that ended in 1–0 victories for each team when playing at home. Meanwhile, Atlético Mineiro, a squad from the state of Minas Gerais, took the first Conmebol Cup—a tournament for teams not qualifying for the Libertadores de América tournament. Atlético won the cup after beating Paraguay's Olimpia 2–0 in Belo Horizonte, Brazil, and losing 1–0 in Asunción, Paraguay.

The surprising winner of the 1991 Libertadores de América Cup, Colo Colo of Chile, did not fare well in its Toyota Inter-Continental Cup match against the European Champions' Cup winner. Yugoslavia's Red Star Belgrade defeated the Chileans 3–0 in December 1991 in Tokyo. São Paulo won the Inter-Continental Cup by defeating Barcelona of Spain in December 1992. In April Colo Colo easily beat Mexico's Puebla, champion of Concacaf—the soccer association in North America, Central America, and the Caribbean—to win the Inter-American Cup.

Latin America's teams performed poorly in the Olympic Games. The region's powerhouses, Brazil, Argentina, and Uruguay, failed to qualify for the tournament, and Colombia and Mexico were eliminated in the preliminary round. Paraguay lost in the quarterfinals.

In national tournaments Boca Juniors of Buenos Aires took Argentina's Torneo de Apertura (Opening Tournament), while Newell's Old Boys became national champion. Flamengo, which won the state championship of Rio de Janeiro in late 1991, gained the Brazilian national title in 1992. In Mexico, León, a team that had not won a national championship in more than 30 years, defeated Puebla in the final play-off series to gain the title. (SERGIO SARMIENTO)

Rugby Football. *Rugby Union.* Following its victory in the final of the World Cup in 1991, Australia confirmed its supremacy in 1992 by beating Scotland, New Zealand, and South Africa. Scotland played two test matches on an eight-

Wade Dooley scores a try for England in its 24–0 win over Wales in the 1992 Five Nations Championship. As it had in 1991, England won all of its matches, the first time a country had had successive grand slams since England accomplished the feat in 1923 and 1924.
DAVID CANNON—ALLSPORT

game tour of Australia in May and June 1992, losing 27–12 in Sydney and 37–13 in Brisbane. In July Australia played host to New Zealand, and a three-test series was staged for the Bledisloe Cup. The Australians made sure of gaining the trophy by winning the first test 16–15 in Sydney and the second 19–17 in Brisbane. There was some consolation for New Zealand, however, when it won the third test 26–23 in Sydney. Each team scored 58 points in the series.

Political changes in South Africa and the merging of the mainly white South African Rugby Football Board with the mainly nonwhite South African Rugby Union—to form a new South African Rugby Football Union—allowed South Africa's Springboks to play official international rugby for the first time in eight years. Both New Zealand and Australia made brief tours of South Africa in August 1992, each playing one test. On August 15 the South Africans lost to New Zealand at Ellis Park, Johannesburg, 27–24, and a week later they were beaten 26–3 by Australia at Newlands, Cape Town.

For the second consecutive year England beat the other four contestants in the Five Nations Championship—a back-to-back grand slam that none of the competitors had achieved since England in 1923 and 1924. England's first Five Nations match, in January 1992, resulted in a 25–7 win over Scotland at Murrayfield in Edinburgh. England then defeated Ireland 38–9 at Twickenham in London and France 31–13 in Paris. In their final match they beat Wales 24–0 at Twickenham. The 118 points that England scored in its four games was a record for the tournament, beating the 102 scored by Wales in 1976. England's fullback, Jonathan Webb, contributed 67 points, beating the record of 60 set by Simon Hodgkinson of England in 1991. He became his country's leading all-time points scorer with 246 in 27 matches, compared with the 240 in 25 matches by Dusty Hare (1974–84).

France, Scotland, and Wales tied for second in the tournament with two wins and two defeats each, while Ireland failed to win a match. After the Five Nations, Ireland toured New Zealand and fared no better. In two tests against the All Blacks, Ireland lost 24–21 in the first, at Dunedin, and 59–6 in the second, at Wellington.

New Zealand highlighted its season in April by playing a three-test series against a world all-star team. The visitors won the first test 28–14 in Christchurch, but the All Blacks came into their own in the other two, winning 54–26 in Wellington and 26–15 in Auckland.

At its 1992 annual meeting the International Rugby Foot-

ball Board upgraded the value of a try from four points to five.

Rugby League. Great Britain made a major tour of Australia in June and July 1992 and was beaten 2–1 in the three-test series. Australia won the first test 22–6 in Sydney, Britain the second 33–10 in Melbourne, and Australia the third 16–10 in Brisbane. The annual home-and-away matches between Great Britain and France resulted in victories for Britain by 30–12 at Perpignan and 36–0 at Hull.

(DAVID FROST)

U.S. Football. *College.* The University of Alabama won its first national championship in college football since 1979 when it defeated the University of Miami (Fla.) 34–13 at the Sugar Bowl in New Orleans, La., on Jan. 1, 1993. The victory made Alabama—at 13–0–0—the only unbeaten and untied team in Division I-A and kept Miami from displacing Alabama's 1979 team as the most recent team with consecutive national championships. Alabama's championship, unanimous in both the writers' and coaches' polls, tied Oklahoma for second place on the all-time title list with six, two behind Notre Dame.

Miami, the 11–1 Big East Conference champion, finished number three behind Atlantic Coast Conference champion Florida State, which also had an 11–1 record after its 27–14 victory over Big Eight champion Nebraska (9–3) in the Orange Bowl. Fourth-ranked Notre Dame (10–1–1) won the Cotton Bowl 28–3 over Southwest Conference champion Texas A&M, which had joined Alabama and Miami with the only perfect regular-season records among major teams but fell to 12–1 and sixth in the coaches' poll and seventh in the writers' poll. Fifth-ranked Michigan (9–0–3 and the Big Ten champion) won the Rose Bowl 38–31 over Pacific Ten champion Washington (9–3).

Alabama and Miami had two of the best defenses in the country. In points allowed, they ranked behind only Arizona's 8.9 per game, with Alabama giving up 9.1 and Miami 11.5. Alabama led the country by allowing averages of 194.2 total yards and 55 rushing yards per game, and it ranked second in pass defense. Miami ranked fifth in pass defense and eighth in rushing and total defense.

Miami also ranked third offensively in passing and ninth in scoring behind quarterback Gino Torretta, who won the Heisman Trophy and Maxwell Award for the outstanding college player. Torretta, the first senior since 1987 to win the Heisman, also won the Davey O'Brien Award for the best quarterback. Before the Sugar Bowl he had a 26–1 record as a starter.

Alabama quarterback Jay Barker (7) hands the ball off to Derrick Lassic in the team's 34–13 victory over Miami (Fla.) in the Sugar Bowl. Lassic was voted the game's outstanding player, and final polls ranked Alabama the top team in college football.
TIM DEFRISCO—ALLSPORT

Trailing Torretta in the Heisman voting were San Diego State sophomore Marshall Faulk, the national rushing leader with 1,630 yd, and Georgia junior Garrison Hearst, the rushing runner-up with 1,547 yd and the touchdown leader with 19 by rushing and 21 overall. Hearst won the Doak Walker Award for the best running back in the country. Reggie Brooks's eight yards per carry for Notre Dame was the best rushing average.

Nebraska was the best rushing team with 328.2 yd per game and 40 touchdowns on the ground. Nebraska also scored 38.8 points per game, second to Fresno State's 40.5. Houston had the most prolific passing offense with national leads of 36 touchdown passes, 407.1 yd passing per game, and 519.5 total yards per game, although its record was 4–7.

Jimmy Klingler's 32 touchdowns and 3,818 yd passing led individual quarterbacks; his 3,768 yd total offense led all players; and teammate Sherman Smith's 103 catches led all receivers. Other individual receiving leaders were California's Sean Dawkins with 14 touchdowns, Wyoming's Ryan Yarborough with 1,351 yd, and Texas Tech's Lloyd Hill with 114.6 yd per game. Michigan's Elvis Grbac led passers with 154.2 rating points and a completion percentage of .663. His runner-up, Marvin Graves of Syracuse, ranked first with 9.49 yd per pass. Torretta's .017 interception percentage was the best.

Joe Allison of Memphis State won the Lou Groza Award for placekicking and led the country with 23 field goals, a .920 percentage on 25 attempts, and 101 kicking points. Other individual leaders were Air Force's Carlton McDonald with eight interceptions, Texas-El Paso's Ed Bunn with a 47.7-yd punting average, Northwestern's Lee Gissendaner with 21.8 yd per punt return, New Mexico State's Fred Montgomery with 32.6 yd per kickoff return, and Pacific's Ryan Benjamin with 2,597 all-purpose yards on runs, catches, and returns.

Florida State linebacker Marvin Jones won the Lombardi Award for the best lineman. Nebraska guard Will Shields won the Outland Trophy for the best interior lineman. Deon Figures of Colorado won the Jim Thorpe Award for the best defensive back. Marshall quarterback Michael Payton won the Walter Payton Award for the most outstanding player in Division I-AA, and Pittsburg (Kan.) State running back Ronald Moore won its Division II equivalent, the Harlon Hill Award.

Other conference champions included Hawaii (11–2) in the Western Athletic, Bowling Green (10–2) in the Mid-

American, and Nevada (7–5) in the Big West. Dartmouth and Princeton tied for the Ivy League championship with 8–2 records in Division I-AA. Charlie Taaffe won that division's Coach of the Year award at The Citadel (11–2), the Southern Conference champion.

Professional. For the first time since the National Football League (NFL) split into six divisions in 1970, none of the defending champions won its division in 1992. Two of those defending champions had played for the 1991 NFL championship when the Washington Redskins defeated the Buffalo Bills 37–24 in the 26th Super Bowl on Jan. 26, 1992, at Minneapolis, Minn.

When it went 9–7 in 1992, Washington became the fifth Super Bowl champion in 11 years to have its won-lost record decline by at least five games. The Redskins and the Bills both qualified for the play-offs among the three runner-up wild-card teams in each conference and, playing first-round games, they became the first pair of Super Bowl teams in 15 years to win play-off games the next season. In Buffalo's 41–38 victory over the Houston Oilers on Jan. 3, 1993, the Bills overcame a third-quarter 35–3 deficit for the biggest comeback in NFL history. The other wild-card teams were New Orleans and Philadelphia in the NFC and Kansas City in the AFC.

San Diego won the American Football Conference (AFC) Western Division for the first time since 1981 and became the first team ever to reach the play-offs after losing its first four games. Pittsburgh won the AFC Central Division for the first time since 1984 under NFL Coach of the Year Bill Cowher. Eastern Division winners Dallas in the National Football Conference (NFC) and Miami in the AFC had not won titles since 1985. NFC Central winner Minnesota had gone two years without winning a division, and San Francisco in the NFC Western Division one year.

Indianapolis failed to reach the play-offs, but its 9–7 record was eight games better than in 1991, tying the record for biggest improvement in one season. Other much-improved teams were San Diego by seven games, Green Bay by five, and Pittsburgh and San Francisco by four.

Six play-off teams from 1991 missed the 12-team field in 1992; five of them had losing records. The biggest declines were Detroit by seven games and Chicago by six. Seattle matched Washington's five-game drop and finished 2–14 with the league's worst offense in total and passing yards and a league-record low of 140 points. Atlanta was one of four teams to decline by four games and ranked last defensively in points, yards, and rushing yards allowed.

San Francisco led the league with 387.2 yd per game and 431 points and had the most passing yards in the NFC. The 49ers' Steve Young led NFL passers with 107 rating points and was the first quarterback ever to top 100 in consecutive seasons. He led the league in each of the rating system's components with a .667 completion percentage, 8.62 yd per pass and percentages of .017 for interceptions and .062 for his league-high 25 touchdowns.

The other teams to lead the NFL in key offensive categories were Buffalo with 152.3 yd rushing per game and Houston with 251.8 yd passing per game. Buffalo also led the AFC in points and total yards with Thurman Thomas' 2,113 yd from scrimmage making him the NFL leader for a record fourth consecutive season. For Houston, Warren Moon led AFC passers with 89.3 rating points, and Haywood Jeffires' 90 receptions made him the first player in 10 years to lead the AFC in catches for three consecutive seasons.

New Orleans and Dallas were the NFL's defensive team leaders. New Orleans allowed league lows of 154.4 yd passing per game and 202 total points and also led the league with both 57 sacks on defense and 15 sacks allowed offensively. Dallas allowed 77.8 yd rushing and 245.8 total yards per game, both best in the NFL. The AFC defensive leaders were Pittsburgh in points, Houston in total yardage, Kansas City in passing yardage, and San Diego and Buffalo in rushing yardage.

Emmitt Smith of Dallas led NFL rushers with 1,713 yd and 18 touchdowns, led all players with 19 total touchdowns, and led the NFC with 2,048 yd from scrimmage. AFC rushing leader Barry Foster of Pittsburgh ran for 1,690 yd and tied Eric Dickerson's eight-year-old record by running for at least 100 yd in 12 games. Heath Sherman's 5.2 yd per carry for Philadelphia led all rushers who had at least 100 attempts and helped the Eagles lead the conference in rushing.

Green Bay wide receiver Sterling Sharpe's 108 catches broke Art Monk's eight-year-old record of 106 and gave him 389 for his career, 31 more than anyone had caught previously in his first five seasons. Sharpe's 1,461 yd receiving and 13 touchdown catches also led the league.

Steve Largent's career receiving records of 819 catches, 13,089 yd, and 100 touchdowns all were broken. Washington's Monk finished the season with 847 catches, Buffalo's James Lofton with 13,821 yd, and San Francisco's Jerry Rice with 103 touchdown catches. Rice also tied a record

by gaining at least 1,000 yd on passes for the seventh consecutive season.

Dan Marino led the league with 4,116 yd passing and the AFC with 24 touchdown passes, extending his NFL record to five seasons with more than 4,000 yd. He helped Miami win six times after it trailed in the fourth quarter, which helped coach Don Shula win his 300th regular-season game, second only to George Halas' 319.

Miami kicker Pete Stoyanovich led the league with 124 points and tied Washington's Chip Lohmiller at 30 field goals. Kansas City's Nick Lowery's .917 field-goal accuracy (22 for 24) was best in the league, as were Greg Montgomery's punting average of 46.9 yd for Houston and Rich Camarillo's net average of 39.6 yd per punt for Phoenix. The kick-return leaders were Phoenix's Johnny Bailey with a 13.2-yd average on punts and New England's Jon Vaughn with 28.2 on kickoffs.

Minnesota's Audray McMillian and Buffalo's Henry Jones tied for the lead in interceptions with eight. Indianapolis rookie Steve Emtman's 90-yd touchdown was the longest interception return in NFL history by a defensive lineman. Philadelphia's Clyde Simmons led the NFL with 19 sacks, and Leslie O'Neal's 17 for San Diego led the AFC.

New York Jet defensive lineman Dennis Byrd suffered a paralyzing neck injury on November 29. A similar injury to Detroit's Mike Utley in 1991 had ended a period of 13 years without a serious spinal cord injury in the NFL.

NFL owners removed videotape replay as an officiating tool after six years of use, but most off-field news was financial. The owners suspended the developmental World League of American Football after the Sacramento Surge defeated the Orlando Thunder 21–17 in the second World Bowl on June 6. They lost costly legal rulings involving pension contributions, restrictions on free agency, and salaries for striking players in 1987 and practicing players in 1989.

The year closed with a tentative labour settlement after players and management had gone more than five years without a collective bargaining agreement in the NFL. The tentative agreement would give most players opportunities for unrestricted free agency after five seasons' experience, reduce the draft of college players from 12 rounds to 7, limit each team's player salaries to 67% of revenue from specified sources, and substantially limit the amount each team could spend on rookies.

Canadian Football. The Calgary Stampeders defeated the Winnipeg Blue Bombers 24–10 in Toronto to win the Grey Cup, the championship of the Canadian Football League (CFL), on Nov. 29, 1992. The game's Most Outstanding Player, Calgary quarterback Doug Flutie, was also the league's Most Outstanding Player for the second year in a row.

Flutie led Calgary to a 13–5 won-lost record that won the Western Division with 607 points and 438.6 yd per game, both league highs. Calgary's Allen Pitts led CFL receivers for the second consecutive year with 103 catches and 1,591 yd. Kicker Mark McLoughlin led the league with 208 points.

Winnipeg won the Eastern Division at 11–7 with league-leading totals of 47 field goals by Troy Westwood and 1,153 yd rushing by Michael Richardson, the CFL's Most Outstanding Rookie. Other award winners were Saskatchewan slotback Ray Elgaard, the Most Outstanding Canadian and runner-up in catches with 91; Ottawa tackle Rob Smith, the Most Outstanding Offensive Lineman; and Edmonton linebacker Willie Pless, the Most Outstanding Defensive Player.

Saskatchewan quarterback Kent Austin was the league leader with 6,225 yd passing and 35 touchdown passes and runner-up to passing efficiency leader Tracy Ham of Ed-

Table II. NFL Final Standings, 1992

AMERICAN CONFERENCE	W	L	T
Eastern Division			
*Miami	11	5	0
*Buffalo	11	5	0
Indianapolis	9	7	0
New York Jets	4	12	0
New England	2	14	0
Central Division			
*Pittsburgh	11	5	0
*Houston	10	6	0
Cleveland	7	9	0
Cincinnati	5	11	0
Western Division			
*San Diego	11	5	0
*Kansas City	10	6	0
Denver	8	8	0
Los Angeles Raiders	7	9	0
Seattle	2	14	0

NATIONAL CONFERENCE	W	L	T
Eastern Division			
*Dallas	13	3	0
*Philadelphia	11	5	0
*Washington	9	7	0
New York Giants	6	10	0
Phoenix	4	12	0
Central Division			
*Minnesota	11	5	0
Green Bay	9	7	0
Tampa Bay	5	11	0
Chicago	5	11	0
Detroit	5	11	0
Western Division			
*San Francisco	14	2	0
*New Orleans	12	4	0
Atlanta	6	10	0
Los Angeles Rams	6	10	0

*Qualified for play-offs.

monton, with 91.5 rating points. Other league leaders were Edmonton's Henry Williams with 2,683 combined yards, Edmonton's Jim Sandusky with 15 touchdown catches, and British Columbia's Jon Volpe with 13 rushing touchdowns.

(KEVIN M. LAMB)

GOLF

Europe's defeat of the United States in the Solheim Cup, the women professional golfers' equivalent of the men's Ryder Cup, was the outstanding golfing performance of 1992. Nor was there the slightest doubt about it, the margin of 11½ to 6½ being thoroughly conclusive.

In recent years the U.S., once the undisputed power in golf, had had several reminders that the balance was shifting. Nick Faldo, Severiano Ballesteros, Sandy Lyle, Bernhard Langer, and Ian Woosnam, all European golfers, had won 14 major championships in as many years. Europe, as a team, had also during the same period won the Ryder Cup twice and tied for it once. Britain's women amateurs also took the Curtis Cup three times in the last four matches, while the men amateurs recorded their first Walker Cup victory on U.S. soil.

But none of these achievements caused a greater surprise than that in the Solheim Cup at Dalmahoy, Edinburgh, which the Americans had won comfortably on its introduction two years earlier at Orlando, Fla. There was little reason to suppose that it would be any different in the first contest to be played on the eastern side of the Atlantic. The United States Ladies' Professional Golf Association (LPGA) tour in 1992 was playing for almost 20 times as much money as its European counterparts ($20.7 million to $1.2 million). The LPGA tour also had a history of more than 40 years behind it; the Women Professional Golfers' European Tour (WPGET), only 13. The recession had also cut deeply into the WPGET calendar in 1992, reducing the number of tournaments to only 12, against 41 in the U.S.

Certainly it had to be conceded that a number of the Europeans—Laura Davies, Helen Alfredsson, Lotte Neumann, Trish Johnson, and Pam Wright among them—improved their ability by playing with some regularity on the U.S. circuit, but it was still an extraordinary performance. It was epitomized by Davies, a former British and U.S. Open champion, who won all three of her matches, two of them with Alison Nicholas, and played not only brilliantly but also with devastating effects on the greens, so often the Achilles heel of European players. Her example on the field of play was an inspiration to the rest of the team, led by Mickey Walker as captain. The fact that Walker's opposite number, Kathy Whitworth, had to return home on the eve of the match because of the death of her mother may have had an unsettling effect on the Americans.

Within a few weeks Sweden, represented by Helen Alfredsson and Lotte Neumann, won the first Sunrise world team championship in Taipei, Taiwan, with a 54-hole score of 445, a stroke ahead of England's Laura Devies and Trish Johnson. The U.S. (Jane Geddes and Meg Mallon) finished third, another six strokes back.

Earlier in the year Britain had also recorded its third Curtis Cup victory in four tournaments by 10–8 at Hoylake, Liverpool, England. It featured a thrilling finish in which all depended on the last of the six singles matches. In that contest Caroline Hall, the English champion, who was only 18 at the time, beat Vicki Goetze, the 1991 U.S. champion, on the 18th hole. Her four-iron second shot to the middle of the green after her opponent had bunkered her approach was one of the most memorable strokes of the year.

At the end of the season, Spain won the women's world amateur team championship, the Espirito Santo trophy, in

Patty Sheehan putts on her way to victory in the U.S. Women's Open. She also won the Ladies' British Open in 1992, the first time a golfer had won both championships in the same year.
FOCUS ON SPORTS

Vancouver, N.Z., when Macarena Campoñanes holed a putt of 2.3 m (8 ft) on the final green. It gave her team a total of 588 for the 54 holes, a stroke ahead of Great Britain and Ireland; New Zealand placed third.

The outstanding golfer of the year was Nick Faldo, who won the British Open championship for a third time at Muirfield, Scotland, and the Johnnie Walker world championship in Jamaica. He also placed second in the U.S. Professional Golfers' Association (PGA) championship, fourth in the U.S. Open, and 13th in the Masters tournament.

Faldo also won four other tournaments in Europe: the Toyota world match-play championship, the European Open, the Irish Open, and the Scandinavian Masters, thereby establishing himself as the clear leader in the Sony world rankings. He also won the PGA European Tour order of merit with earnings of £708,522 and had a stroke average of 69.10 for 60 rounds in 15 tournaments.

Faldo won the British Open in a close contest, even though he had dominated it with opening rounds of 66, 64, and 69 for a four-stroke lead over John Cook of the U.S. With eight holes to play, Faldo was still three strokes ahead, but bogeys on the 11th, 13th, and 14th holes just as Cook was making birdies at the 14th, 15th, and 16th swiftly put him two behind. However, Faldo pulled himself together with a finish of birdie, par, birdie, and par on the last four holes. His final round of 73 for a total of 272 gave him the victory by one stroke from Cook, who missed a very short putt for a birdie at the 17th. Cook, playing in the Open for only the second time, had rounds of 66, 67, 70, and 70 for a total of 273, while José-María Olazábal of Spain was third at 274.

Fred Couples of the U.S. was the dominant player in the early part of the year. He had already won two tournaments and had been second in two others in the U.S. by the time he went to Augusta, Ga., for the Masters in April. His first major title was, therefore, very much according to form. Jeff Sluman and Lanny Wadkins had shared the first-round lead in the Masters with 65s, but Couples, with 69, 67, had moved into third place after 36 holes, a stroke behind Woosnam, the defending champion from Wales, and Craig Parry (Australia), both of whom had scored 69, 66.

Play was suspended because of a thunderstorm in the third round with Parry, after 14 holes, two ahead of Couples, Raymond Floyd, and Ian Baker-Finch, another Australian, who had already shot a 68. Couples closed the difference to a stroke by the start of the final round, and with Parry afflicted by a succession of three-putt holes, he quickly took control. Couples' rounds of 69, 67, 69, 70 for a total of 275 won him the tournament by two strokes from Floyd (69, 68, 69, 71) and by three over Corey Pavin (72, 71, 68, 67).

There had been no more consistent golfer or bigger money winner than Tom Kite of the U.S. A major championship had nevertheless always eluded him. At the age of 42 he at last had his reward when he won the U.S. Open at Pebble Beach, Calif. For the first two days, which were calm and gray, Gil Morgan had been the dominant figure with rounds of 66, 69 for a six-stroke lead. But he shot a 77 in the third, and his advantage was cut to a stroke over Woosnam, Kite, and Mark Brooks. As the skies cleared on the final day, an increasingly strong wind blew off the Pacific. Scores rocketed, and Morgan shot an 81. The early starters had the calmer weather, and a 70 by Colin Montgomerie of Scotland for a total of 288 looked for a time as if it might be good enough to win the tournament. However, Kite, aided by a piece of luck when he chipped in for a two at the exposed short seventh but also playing a lot of controlled golf in very difficult conditions, managed an even-par round for a total of 285 (71, 72, 70, 72) to win by two from Jeff Sluman (73, 74, 69, 71) and three from Montgomerie (70, 71, 77, 70).

Just as Kite's victory was a popular one, so was that of Nick Price of Zimbabwe in the PGA championship at Bellerive Country Club near St. Louis, Mo. He had twice narrowly missed winning the British Open, but some consistent golf on a difficult course at last gave him what was ultimately a comfortable victory. Price had rounds of 70, 70, 68, 70 for a total of 278, three ahead of Faldo (68, 70, 76, 67), Cook (71, 72, 67, 71), Jim Gallagher (72, 66, 72, 71), and Gene Sauers (67, 69, 70, 75).

At the end of the season Couples and Davis Love III brought honour to the U.S. when they won the World Cup of Golf by Philip Morris at La Moraleja, Madrid. Their two-man 72-hole total of 548 was one better than Sweden (Anders Forsbrand and Per-Ulrik Johansson), the defending champions. Couples' further distinction was that he won the Arnold Palmer award as the year's leading U.S. money winner with $1,344,188.

The U.S. had, however, already been beaten in the Alfred Dunhill Cup at St. Andrews, Scotland, losing to the eventual winners, England, in the semifinals. England's victory was a surprise because it was done without Faldo. Instead, the team members were Jamie Spence, David Gilford, and Steve Richardson, who went on to beat Scotland (Colin Montgomerie, Lyle, and Gordon Brand, Jr.) in the final.

Patty Sheehan of the U.S. gained the distinction of becoming the first woman to win both the U.S. and British Open championships in the same year. She had rounds of 69, 72, 70, 69 for a total of 280 at Oakmont, Pa., beating Julie Inkster (72, 68, 71, 69) in a play-off for the U.S. title. It was less close in the British Open at Woburn, Bedfordshire, England, Sheehan winning a championship reduced to 54 holes because of bad weather by three strokes from Corinne Dibnah of Australia. Her scores were 68, 72, 67 for an aggregate of 207.

Dottie Mochrie of the U.S. was leading money winner for the first time on the LPGA tour with $693,335; she won four tournaments. Laura Davies, with three victories and prize money of £66,333, was the leading money winner in Europe.

For the first time since 1957 a Scot, Stephen Dundas, won the British amateur championship. He beat Bradley Drege, from Wales, by seven and six in the final at Carnoustie, Angus, Scotland. The U.S. amateur championship was won by Justin Leonard, who defeated Thomas Scherrer by eight and seven at Muirfield Village, Dublin, Ohio. Later in the year New Zealand took the world amateur team championship for the Eisenhower Trophy in Vancouver, B.C., with a record score of 823 for the four rounds.

Vicki Goetze won the U.S. women's amateur championship when she beat Annika Sorenstam of Sweden by one hole at Kemper Lakes Golf Club in Long Grove, Ill., while Pernille Pedersen became the first Danish golfer to take the British women's amateur championship at Saunton, Devon, England. She defeated Joanne Morley by one hole in the final.   (MICHAEL WILLIAMS)

GYMNASTICS

At the Olympic Games in Barcelona, Spain, in 1992, the men and women gymnasts of the Unified Team, representing republics of the former Soviet Union, again dominated. It was the fourth time since 1952 that the Unified Team/Soviet male gymnasts had won the Olympic team title and the second straight time that they had placed first, second, and third in the all-around event. In the women's team competition the Unified Team took top honours, the 10th time Unified/Soviet women had done so in the 10 Olympics in which they had competed since 1952. The team boycotted the 1984 Olympics in Los Angeles. The U.S. women placed third in the team competition, while the men slipped to sixth.

Vitali Sherbo from Minsk, Belarus, won six gold medals for the Unified Team, the most successful gymnastics performance in the history of the Olympics (*see* BIOGRAPHIES). He triumphed in the team competition and all-around event and then added four individual apparatus gold medals on the parallel bars, pommel horse, rings, and vault. He finished sixth in the floor exercise and did not qualify for the final on the horizontal bar. The all-around women's champion was Tatyana Gutsu, a member of the Unified Team from Ukraine. Overall, the Unified Team accounted for nine gold, five silver, and four bronze medals, of which the men were responsible for six golds, four silvers, and two bronzes.

WILLIAM R. SALLAZ—DUOMO

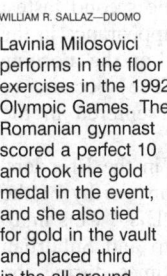
Lavinia Milosovici performs in the floor exercises in the 1992 Olympic Games. The Romanian gymnast scored a perfect 10 and took the gold medal in the event, and she also tied for gold in the vault and placed third in the all-around competition.

In men's competition the other gold medals were won by China, North Korea, and the United States. Trent Dimas of Albuquerque, N.M., won the single gold medal for the U.S., triumphing with a nearly flawless performance on the horizontal bar, the final event on the program. China's winner was Li Xiaoshuang (Li Hsiao-shuang) in the floor exercise, and North Korea's Pae Gil Su tied for first with Sherbo on the pommel horse.

The surprise all-around women's champion, Gutsu, replaced an injured teammate who had qualified with a higher score in the team competition. Placing second was Shannon Miller of Edmond, Okla., and in third place was Romania's Lavinia Milosovici. Milosovici also won gold medals in the floor exercise and the vault.

The other three individual event winners were Hungary's Henrietta Onodi, tying with Milosovici in the vault; Tatyana Lyssenko of the Unified Team on the balance beam; and China's Lu Li on the uneven bars. Only two perfect scores of 10 were awarded, both of them in the women's events. Milosovici scored in the floor exercise and Lu Li on the uneven bars.

In rhythmic gymnastics the gold medalist was the Unified Team's Aleksandra Timoshenko. Spain's Carolina Pascual placed second, and the Unified Team's Oksana Skaldina was third.   (CHARLES ROBERT PAUL, JR.)

HORSE RACING

Thoroughbred Racing and Steeplechasing. *United States and Canada.* Commanding victories in the Santa Anita Derby and the Belmont Stakes during the first half of the year followed by a convincing triumph in the Breeders' Cup Classic in the final start of his career made A.P. Indy the favourite to win 1992 Eclipse Awards as horse of the year and champion three-year-old male. Two other leading horse of the year candidates, Sky Classic and Pleasant Tap, were expected to be honoured as champion turf male and champion older horse, respectively, at the Eclipse Awards ceremony in February 1993.

The remaining division winners were expected to be Paseana, champion older mare; Flawlessly, champion turf female; Saratoga Dew, champion three-year-old filly; Rubiano, champion sprinter; Gilded Time, champion two-year-old colt; and Eliza or Sky Beauty, champion two-year-old filly.

A.P. Indy, which was retired in late November with a career record of 8 wins in 11 starts and earnings of $2,979,-815, was a son of 1977 Triple Crown winner Seattle Slew and a grandson of 1973 Triple Crown winner Secretariat. He was the highest priced yearling sold at auction in 1990, commanding a bid of $2.9 million.

A.P. Indy completed his brilliant racing career on Breeders' Cup Day on October 31 at Gulfstream Park in Florida with a powerful two-lengths come-from-behind victory in the $3 million Classic, a 1¼-mi event in which he defeated the best horses in training, including Pleasant Tap. His smashing win in the Belmont Stakes, in which he tied Easy Goer's 1989 record of 2 min 26 sec for the second fastest Belmont of all time, was A.P. Indy's only appearance in the 1992 Triple Crown races. He was scratched on the morning of the Kentucky Derby (won by Lil E. Tee) because of lameness in his left foreleg and was not entered in the Preakness (won by Pine Bluff).

Although Pleasant Tap finished second in the Breeders' Cup Classic, the five-year-old had a season worthy of the Eclipse Award for champion older horse. His 4 wins in 10 starts included the Jockey Club Gold Cup and Suburban Handicap. He also finished second five times during the year and had earnings of $1,959,914.

Major Thoroughbred Race Winners, 1992

Race	Won by	Jockey
United States		
Acorn	Prospectors Delite	P. Day
Arlington Million	Dear Doctor	C. Asmussen
Beldame	Saratoga Dew	H. McCauley
Belmont	A.P. Indy	E. Delahoussaye
Breeders' Cup Juvenile	Gilded Time	C. McCarron
Breeders' Cup Juvenile Fillies	Eliza	P. Valenzuela
Breeders' Cup Sprint	Thirty Slews	E. Delahoussaye
Breeders' Cup Mile	Lure	M. Smith
Breeders' Cup Distaff	Paseana	C. McCarron
Breeders' Cup Turf	Fraise	P. Valenzuela
Breeders' Cup Classic	A.P. Indy	E. Delahoussaye
Brooklyn	Chief Honcho	R. Romero
Champagne	Sea Hero	J. Bailey
Charles H. Strub Stakes	Best Pal	K. Desormeaux
Coaching Club American Oaks	Turnback The Alarm	C. Antley
Florida Derby	Technology	J. Bailey
Futurity	Strolling Along	C. Antley
Gulfstream Park Handicap	Sea Cadet	A. Solis
Haskell Invitational	Technology	J. Bailey
Hollywood Derby	Paradise Creek	P. Day
Hollywood Futurity	River Special	L. Pincay, Jr.
Hollywood Gold Cup	Sultry Song	J. Bailey
Hollywood Turf Cup	Bien Bien	C. McCarron
Hollywood Turf Handicap	Quest For Fame	G. Stevens
International	Zoman	A. Munro
Iselin Handicap	Jolie's Halo	E. Prado
Jockey Club Gold Cup	Pleasant Tap	G. Stevens
Kentucky Derby	Lil E. Tee	P. Day
Kentucky Oaks	Luv Me Luv Me Not	F. Arguello, Jr.
Man o' War	Solar Splendor	H. McCauley
Meadowlands Cup	Sea Cadet	A. Solis
Metropolitan	Dixie Brass	J. Pezua
Mother Goose	Turnback The Alarm	C. Antley
Oak Tree Invitational	Navarone	P. Valenzuela
Pimlico Special	Strike The Gold	C. Perret
Preakness	Pine Bluff	C. McCarron
Santa Anita Derby	A.P. Indy	E. Delahoussaye
Santa Anita Handicap	Best Pal	K. Desormeaux
Spinster	Fowda	P. Valenzuela
Suburban	Pleasant Tap	E. Delahoussaye
Super Derby Invitational	Senor Tomas	A. Gryder
Travers	Thunder Rumble	H. McCauley
Turf Classic	Sky Classic	P. Day
Whitney	Sultry Song	J. Bailey
Wood Memorial	Devil His Due	M. Smith
Woodward	Sultry Song	J. Bailey
England		
One Thousand Guineas	Hatoof	W.R. Swinburn
Two Thousand Guineas	Rodrigo de Traiano	L. Piggott
Derby	Dr. Devious	J. Reid
Oaks	User Friendly	G. Duffield
St. Leger	User Friendly	G. Duffield
Coronation Cup	Saddlers' Hall	W.R. Swinburn
Ascot Gold Cup	Drum Taps	L. Dettori
Eclipse Stakes	Kooyonga	W. O'Connor
King George VI and Queen Elizabeth Diamond Stakes	St. Jovite	S. Craine
Sussex Stakes	Marling	P. Eddery
International Stakes	Rodrigo de Triano	L. Piggott
Dubai Champion Stakes	Rodrigo de Triano	L. Piggott
France		
Poule d'Essai des Poulains	Shanghai	F. Head
Poule d'Essai des Pouliches	Culture Vulture	T. Quinn
Prix du Jockey-Club	Polytain	L. Dettori
Prix de Diane Hermes	Jolypha	P. Eddery
Prix Royal-Oak	Assessor	T. Quinn
Prix Ganay	Subotica	T. Jarnet
Prix Lupin	Johann Quatz	F. Head
Grand Prix de Paris	Homme de Loi	T. Jarnet
Grand Prix de Saint-Cloud	Pistolet Bleu	D. Boeuf
Prix Vermeille	Jolypha	P. Eddery
Prix de l'Arc de Triomphe	Subotica	T. Jarnet
Grand Critérium	Tenby	P. Eddery
Ireland		
Irish Two Thousand Guineas	Rodrigo de Triano	L. Piggott
Irish One Thousand Guineas	Marling	W.R. Swinburn
Irish Derby	St. Jovite	C. Roche
Irish Oaks	User Friendly	G. Duffield
Irish St. Leger	Mashaallah	S. Cauthen
Irish Champion Stakes	Dr. Devious	J. Reid
Italy		
Derby Italiano	In a Tiff	M.J. Kinane
Gran Premio del Jockey-Club	Silvernesian	L. Piggott
Germany		
Deutsches Derby	Pik Konig	W. Newnes
Grosser Preis von Baden	Mashaallah	J. Reid
Preis der Privatbankiers Merck, Finck & Co.	Platini	M. Rimmer
Geno Europa Preis	Apple Tree	T. Jarnet
Australia		
Melbourne Cup	Subzero	G. Hall

Belmont Stakes winner A.P. Indy, with jockey Eddie Delahoussaye aboard, races to victory in the Breeders' Cup Classic. The three-year-old colt, which had missed the Kentucky Derby and the Preakness Stakes because of injury, was retired to stud at the end of the season.

CHRIS COLE—ALLSPORT

Best Pal dominated the handicap ranks for the first five months of the year. The four-year-old gelding won his first four starts, including the Santa Anita Handicap, before suffering a season-ending injury in the May 9 Pimlico Special. He completed his campaign with $1,672,000 in earnings.

Canadian-bred Sky Classic broke Secretariat's 1973 course record of 2 min 24.8 sec when he won the Turf Classic at Belmont Park in 2 min 24.4 sec, one of his five graded stakes wins in 1992. The five-year-old lost photo-finish decisions in the Arlington Million and the Breeders' Cup Turf. Fraise upset Sky Classic by a nose in the Breeders' Cup Turf to merit consideration for the Eclipse as the champion turf male, but Sky Classic was the winner in their only other two meetings of the year.

The Argentine-bred five-year-old mare Paseana completed her successful 1992 season with a four-length victory in the Breeders' Cup Distaff, her seventh win in nine starts. She dominated her division all year while winning six Grade I stakes, three more than any other horse in the U.S.

Flawlessly clinched honours as champion turf female with her November 29 win in the Matriarch Stakes at Hollywood Park, a race in which she defeated Irish-bred Kostroma and Super Staff. She won three Grade I stakes in five starts in 1992. Although there was no clear-cut leader in the three-year-old-filly division, Saratoga Dew's 8 wins in 11 starts, including the Grade I Beldame Stakes, in which she defeated older rivals, was expected to earn her the Eclipse Award.

Even though he finished third in the six-furlong Breeders' Cup Sprint, Rubiano was undefeated in four starts in seven-furlong races and was expected to earn the Eclipse Award for champion sprinter. His victories included the Carter Handicap. Gilded Time, undefeated in four starts, was the standout in the two-year-old-colt division. He topped off his campaign with a three-quarters-of-a-length victory in the Breeders' Cup Juvenile. Earlier in the year he won Monmouth Park's Sapling Stakes in track record time of 1 min 7.8 sec, the fastest six furlongs ever raced by a two-year-old.

California-based Kent Desormeaux led U.S. jockeys in purse earnings with $14,193,006. If he had not suffered a season-ending spill on December 11 at Hollywood Park in which he suffered several fractures to the head, he would probably have broken Jose Santos' 1988 single-season-earnings record of $14,877,298. Russell Baze led the nation's jockeys in number of victories in 1992, ending the two-year reign of Pat Day. D. Wayne Lukas topped the trainer standings in purse earnings for an unprecedented 10th consecutive year.

Benburb was honoured as Canada's horse of the year and champion three-year-old male. The colt's four wins in seven 1992 starts included the Prince of Wales Stakes, which was the second leg of the Canadian Triple Crown, and the Molson Million, in which he defeated A.P. Indy. In other major Canadian races Alydeed won the Queen's Plate, and Snurge triumphed in the Rothmans Ltd. International.

Canada's remaining Sovereign Awards, voted by a panel of sportswriters, broadcasters, and racing officials from across Canada, went to Deputy Jane West (two-year-old filly); Truth of It All (two-year-old colt); Hope for a Breeze (three-year-old filly); Wilderness Song (older female); Rainbows for life (older male and turf horse); King Corrie (sprinter); Philip England (trainer); and Todd Kabel (jockey).

(JOHN G. BROKOPP)

Europe and Australia. Economic recession began to bite as the European season progressed, although the real state of the sport was hard to gauge because much of it relied on Arab investment. This was particularly true of British racing, whose greatest supporters, the Maktum family, showed their disapproval of the local value-added-tax (VAT) rates by declining to buy yearlings at the annual Newmarket sale. Britain levied 17.5% VAT at the point of sale, compared with 9% in Italy, 7% in Germany, 5.5% in France, and 2.3% in Ireland.

The four Maktum brothers, their relatives, and associates owned about 20% of all the horses in training on the flat in Britain. Sheikh Muhammad, who had the largest share, announced that he would cut his numbers for 1993 and move horses to Germany, as well as increase his representation in Italy and the U.S. He also planned to send quite a few home to Dubai, which was to be part of a racing circuit in the United Arab Emirates from 1993.

Sheikh Muhammad's decision was predictable, since he had too many horses for the opportunities available, but was still a shock to British racing. The sheikh had the most winners during the year in Britain and France, but his greatest rival, Prince Khalid Abdullah, distributed his horses with more success at the highest (Group 1) level. He was among the top three owners in Britain, France, and, under the Juddmonte Farms banner, the U.S.

Jolypha and the English-trained Prix du Moulin winner, All At Sea, were Prince Khalid's leading older horses. His juveniles placed him in a great position for the 1993 season, with the French-trained Zafonic winning three Group 1 events, while the English-trained Armiger and Tenby each won one.

Because Prince Khalid's jockey, Pat Eddery, was often required for his French runners while Steve Cauthen did similar double duty for his principal employer, Sheikh Muhammad, there was a new champion rider on both sides of the Channel. Michael Roberts, already 11 times the leader in South Africa, led in Britain with 206 wins in 1,068 mounts, the first time that anyone had ridden more than 1,000 horses in a season. Thierry Jarnet was the new winner in France.

Richard Hannon was the top British trainer for the first time in both winners and earnings, a remarkable performance considering that he had no Arab-owned horses. Hannon's best were the top sprinter, Mr Brooks, who met a tragic end when he collapsed under a broken foreleg in the homestretch of the Breeders' Cup Sprint; Assessor, winner of the Prix Royal-Oak (French St. Leger); and the speedy two-year-old filly Lyric Fantasy.

Lester Piggott, who rode Mr Brooks in all his races including a second to Lyric Fantasy in the all-aged Keeneland Nunthorpe Stakes, was another of the season's stars. Piggott, who was 57 in November and suffered a fractured clavicle and broken rib in the Breeders' Cup Sprint, accounted for eight European Group 1 victories, a figure equaled only by Pat Eddery. Besides two on Mr Brooks, they included four on Rodrigo de Triano, whose trainer, Peter Chappel-Hyam, also sent out Dr. Devious to win the Epsom Derby in England and the Irish Champion Stakes.

Dr. Devious also contested the Kentucky Derby, finishing seventh, one place in front of the French-trained favourite, Arazi. That colt was a great disappointment on both sides of the Atlantic. But his victory in the Prix du Rond-Point, a Group 2 event over one mile at Longchamp in Paris on October 4, was sufficient to show that he had retained his phenomenal burst of speed.

Dr. Devious beat St. Jovite by two lengths in the English Derby but was 12 lengths second to him in the Irish Derby, only to come back with a short head defeat of the old enemy in the Irish Champion Stakes.

St. Jovite also trounced Saddlers' Hall by six lengths in the King George VI and Queen Elizabeth Diamond Stakes. However, he could finish only fourth, with Dr. Devious sixth, behind Subotica, User Friendly, and Vert Amande, in the Prix de l'Arc de Triomphe. In that race Subotica won his third Group 1 event, all at Longchamp, and became the first horse to beat User Friendly, winner of all her six previous races, including four at the top level.

Polytain was a 37–1 winner of the Prix du Jockey-Club (French Derby) but could not beat a single rival in his two subsequent races. Despite, or because of, the problems at home, British horses won four Irish and two French classics as well as three in Italy, where the Irish took the remaining two. French runners won several big races in Britain, did better than usual in Germany, and prospered in North America during the autumn.

In steeplechasing Party Politics, which changed hands in the days before the race, won the Grand National. Cool Ground, which had beaten the French chaser, The Fellow, by a short head in the Cheltenham Gold Cup, placed 10th. Royal Gait, which raced in Spain and France before finding his way to England, gave Sheikh Muhammad, who had few jumpers, his second Champion Hurdle victory in three years. El Triunfo was a half-length winner of the Grand Steeple-Chase de Paris, and his stable companion, Ubu III, won the Grande Course de Haies d'Auteuil (French Champion Hurdle) 13 days later.

Subzero, winner of the South Australian Derby and Adelaide Cup in May, beat the New Zealand-trained favourite, Veandercross, by 1¾ lengths in Australia's greatest race, the Melbourne Cup. Lee Freedman, who trained the winner, also took Australia's principal weight-for-age race, the W.S. Cox Plate, with Super Impose and the Caulfield Cup with Naturalism, which beat Veandercross by a short head. Freedman equaled the record with 13 Group 1 victories in the 1991–92 season. (ROBERT W. CARTER)

Harness Racing. Artsplace, unbeaten in 16 starts as a four-year-old in 1992, became the second pacer (after Nihilator, $3,225,653) to top $3 million in purse earnings. Artsplace's 1992 earnings of $932,325 took his career bankroll to $3,085,083, whereupon, in October, his retirement to stud was announced. Driven regularly by John Campbell and trained by Canadian Bob McIntosh for U.S. owners George Segal and Brian Monieson, Artsplace posted the world's fastest race mile mark of 1 min 49.4 sec at the Meadowlands in New Jersey in midyear and assured himself of Harness Horse of the Year honours.

Camluck became the second-fastest horse in harness history by pacing a 1-min 48.8-sec mile time trial at the Red Mile in Lexington, Ky., on October 1. The five-year-old son of Cam Fella and Lucky Lady, owned by a Canadian group including trainer Bob McIntosh, was now, in terms of speed, second only to Matt's Scooter, who paced a mile in 1 min 48.4 sec in a time trial at Lexington as a three-year-old in 1988.

Swedish trainer Per Eriksson won the Hambletonian (at $1,380,000 the richest harness race in the world) for the third time when Alf Palema triumphed in the final round at the Meadowlands in August. The three-year-old Speedy Somolli colt clocked 1 min 56.6 sec for driver Micky McNichol. King Conch, also trained by Eriksson, finished second.

Safely Kept, at 30 to 1, scored an upset 1-min 53.2-sec victory in the $1 million North America Cup for pacers at Toronto's Greenwood Raceway in June. Carlsbad Cam, driven by Rod Allen, won the $1 million Meadowlands Pace at the Meadowlands in July in a career-best 1 min 51 sec.

The 1992 International Trot in Yonkers, N.Y., carrying its richest-ever purse of $500,000 in August, was won by Atas Fighter L from Sweden, driven skillfully by Torbjorn Jansson. Winner of $1,129,482 going into the race, Atas Fighter L added $250,000 to that bankroll.

America's Pastime, a previously winless son of Jate Lobell making only his fourth lifetime start, powered to a race-record 1-min 51.8-sec mile in the $778,800 Woodrow Wilson Final for two-year-old pacers at the Meadowlands in August. The colt thus equaled the world record for a two-year-old on a mile track, set two years earlier by Deal Direct.

Lightly-fancied Fake Left won the $556,210 47th edition of the Little Brown Jug for three-year-old pacers at Delaware, Ohio, in September. Driven by Ron Waples, Fake Left won the slowest of three elimination heats, beating Western Hanover, winner of the Messenger Stake and Cane Pace, the first two legs of the pacing Triple Crown.

Five-year-old Verdict Gede from France won the 1992 Prix d'Amerique for trotters, giving driver Jean-Claude Hallais his first victory in his homeland's premier event, raced in January at Vincennes, Paris. Watched by a crowd approaching 40,000, the feature attracted an all-time betting record (galloping or trotting) of nearly F 230 million (roughly $37 million).

New Zealand's Harness Horse of the Year for 1991–92, Christopher Vance, a five-year-old gelding, posted 10 wins in New Zealand and the Sydney Miracle Mile in Australia. The veteran eight-year-old mare Blossom Lady won the 1992 New Zealand Cup. Victory in the Melbourne Inter-Dominion Pacers' Grand Final of 1992 went to the six-year-old Westburn Grant. (RONALD W. BISMAN)

ICE HOCKEY

North America. The National Hockey League (NHL), the major league of ice hockey in the United States and Canada, endured a trying 1991–92 season. The regular season was interrupted by the first players' strike in the league's 75-year history. In the aftermath John Ziegler resigned under pressure after 15 years as the NHL president. On the ice the New York Rangers dominated the regular season, only to see the Pittsburgh Penguins repeat as Stanley Cup play-off champions.

Strike. The club owners said that they lost $9 million during the season, while the players claimed that the owners made $24 million. On April 1, 1992, four days before the scheduled finish of the regular season, the players went on strike. The club owners postponed the 30 remaining regular-season games and the play-offs. Although the players had leverage, Ziegler negotiated a settlement favourable to the owners. The strike ended April 11, and the season resumed the next night.

The players received the right to license photographs of themselves; a $100,000 minimum salary; and increased play-off, insurance, and pension money. However, their union agreed to an expanded 1992–93 season of 84 games (up from 80), achieved only marginal improvement in free-agent compensation, and yielded to the owners' demand for a two-year rather than long-term contract.

Still, the strike angered some club owners. They were already unhappy with Ziegler because he had often been absent during crises and had been unable to generate meaningful television revenue and exposure. Consequently, they forced the 58-year-old lawyer to resign. On June 12, Ziegler agreed to resign as of September 30 and to fulfill the last four years of his $500,000-a-year contract as a consultant. The NHL Board of Governors, made up of the club owners, then elected Bruce McNall, the owner of the Los Angeles Kings, as chairman to replace William Wirtz, the owner of the Chicago Black Hawks. The governors also chose Gil Stein, the NHL's legal counsel, as the league's temporary president. In December the club owners elected Gary Bettman, chief legal officer of the National Basketball Association since 1984, as its first commissioner. Also in December the Walt Disney Co. was awarded an NHL franchise in Anaheim, Calif.

The Season. The New York Rangers won the Patrick Division with the league's best record—50 victories, 25 defeats, and 5 ties for 105 points. The other division winners were the Detroit Red Wings with 98 points, the Vancouver Canucks with 96, and the Montreal Canadiens with 93.

Sixteen of the 22 teams qualified for the play-offs. Pittsburgh eliminated the Rangers four games to two in their division final and entered the final round with seven consecutive victories. Chicago got there with 11 consecutive victories, a play-off record. Pittsburgh then swept Chicago in the final four games to none, and its victory in the last game tied Chicago's fresh record of 11 victories in a row.

It was a stunning play-off triumph for Pittsburgh, which had experienced a troubled regular season. Coach Bob Johnson died of brain cancer on Nov. 26, 1991, and team ownership then changed hands in the play-offs. Mario Lemieux, the team's best player, was slashed by Adam Graves of the Rangers and suffered a broken left hand, but he returned to competition sooner than expected and for the second consecutive year won the Conn Smythe Trophy as the most valuable player in the play-offs.

Stars. The regular-season leaders were Lemieux in scoring (131 points), Brett Hull of the St. Louis Blues in goals (70), Wayne Gretzky of Los Angeles in assists (90), and Patrick

Roy of Montreal in goalkeeping (2.34 goals allowed per game). Mark Messier of the New York Rangers was voted the Hart Memorial Trophy as the league's most valuable player, Brian Leetch of the Rangers the Norris Memorial Trophy as the best defenseman, Pavel Bure of Vancouver the Calder Memorial Trophy as the outstanding rookie, Guy Carbonneau of Montreal the Selke Trophy as the best defensive forward, Gretzky the Lady Byng Memorial Trophy for sportsmanship and gentlemanly play, Roy the Vezina Trophy for goalkeeping, and Pat Quinn of Vancouver the Jack Adams Award as the coach of the year. The all-star team comprised Roy in goal, Ray Bourque of the Boston Bruins and Leetch on defense, Messier at centre, and Kevin Stevens of Pittsburgh and Hull on wing.

Eric Lindros, the most heralded young player since Gretzky a decade earlier, finally found a home. A year after he refused to report to the Quebec Nordiques, who had chosen him first overall in the annual entry draft, Quebec traded him on June 20 to the Philadelphia Flyers and then, 80 minutes later, to the New York Rangers. An arbitrator awarded him to Philadelphia in a deal that gave Quebec five players, a 1993 first-round draft choice, and $15 million. The 19-year-old Lindros then signed a six-year contract with Philadelphia that guaranteed him $20 million, making him the league's highest-paid player.   (FRANK LITSKY)

International. A revised format for the 56th world championship increased the elite number of medal contenders in Pool A from 8 to 12, organized into two groups that played a round-robin tournament; the top four finishers in each group then competed in an elimination tournament for the championship. Sweden retained the title with a 5–2 victory against Finland in the final. Czechoslovakia, the host nation, gained the bronze medal in a third-place play-off against Switzerland. The matches were played in Prague and Bratislava from April 28 to May 10.

The turning point of the tournament was Sweden's 2–0 defeat of the previously unbeaten Russians. The top goal scorer was Finland's Jarkko Varvio, with nine in eight games.

BARTON SILVERMAN/THE NEW YORK TIMES

The Unified Team, made up of players from former Soviet republics, celebrates its victory in the ice hockey finals of the winter Olympic Games. The team, half of which had been drafted by the National Hockey League, defeated Canada 3–1 to take the gold medal.

Three Finns were named to the all-star team: goalkeeper Markus Ketterer, defenseman Timo Jutila, and right winger Varvio; the other all-stars included defenseman Frantisek and centre Petr Hrbek of Czechoslovakia and left winger Mats Sundin of Sweden. Poland was relegated to Pool B in 1993 after losing a last-place play-off to France.

Austria gained promotion to Pool A in 1993 by dominating the Pool B tournament, held in Klagenfurt and Villach, Austria, on April 2–12. The host country won all seven of its round-robin matches, putting the issue beyond doubt with an 8–3 victory over the runners-up from The Netherlands, who never recovered from a five-goal deficit at the end of the first period. Japan gained third place from Denmark by scoring more goals, the two finishing even on points. Antoniius Collard of The Netherlands was the leading scorer in the tournament with 12 goals and 10 assists; he was followed by six Austrians. Yugoslavia finished last and was demoted to Pool C.

Table I. NHL Final Standings, 1992

	Won	Lost	Tied	Points
Prince of Wales Conference				
PATRICK DIVISION				
*New York Rangers	50	25	5	105
*Washington	45	27	8	98
*Pittsburgh	39	32	9	87
*New Jersey	38	31	11	87
New York Islanders	34	35	11	79
Philadelphia	32	37	11	75
ADAMS DIVISION				
*Montreal	41	28	11	93
*Boston	36	32	12	84
*Buffalo	31	37	12	74
*Hartford	26	41	13	65
Quebec	20	48	12	52
Clarence Campbell Conference				
NORRIS DIVISION				
*Detroit	43	25	12	98
*Chicago	36	29	15	87
*St. Louis	36	33	11	83
*Minnesota	32	42	6	70
Toronto	30	43	7	67
SMYTHE DIVISION				
*Vancouver	42	26	12	96
*Los Angeles	35	31	14	84
*Edmonton	36	34	10	82
*Winnipeg	33	32	15	81
Calgary	31	37	12	74
San Jose	17	58	5	39

*Gained play-off berth.

Table II. World Ice Hockey Championships, 1992

Country	Won	Lost	Tied	Goals	Goals against	Points
POOL A, Group A						
Finland	5	0	0	32	8	10
Germany	4	1	0	30	14	8
United States	2	2	1	14	15	5
Sweden	1	2	2	14	12	4
Italy	1	3	1	10	18	3
Poland	0	5	0	8	41	0
POOL A, Group B						
Russia	4	0	1	23	10	9
Czechoslovakia	4	1	0	18	7	8
Switzerland	2	1	2	12	11	6
Canada	2	2	1	15	18	5
Norway	1	4	0	8	16	2
France	0	5	0	8	22	0
POOL B						
Austria	7	0	0	73	4	14
Netherlands, The	5	1	1	53	16	11
Japan	4	3	0	30	24	8
Denmark	4	3	0	23	24	8
Bulgaria	3	4	0	14	38	6
Romania	1	3	3	13	26	5
China	1	5	1	15	50	3
Yugoslavia	0	6	1	7	46	1
POOL C						
Great Britain	5	0	0	62	10	10
North Korea	3	2	0	25	28	6
Australia	2	2	1	24	26	5
Hungary	2	3	0	18	33	4
Belgium	2	3	0	17	24	4
South Korea	0	4	1	18	43	1

Continuing a steady national resurgence, Great Britain, the world and Olympic champion in 1936, comfortably earned promotion by overwhelming the opposition in Pool C at Hull, England, on March 18–24. Averaging more than 12 goals a game in five round-robin matches, the host nation included eight Canadians who now held British passports; one of them, Kevin Conway, was the tournament's top goal scorer with 13. Less experienced nations competed in a second division of Pool C on March 22–29 in Johannesburg, South Africa, the first international ice hockey tournament to be held in that country. Spain clinched the top place by decisively beating South Africa 12–0. Greece finished third, ahead of Israel, Luxembourg, and Turkey.

The same 12 nations that competed in Pool A of the world championships also contested the Olympic Winter Games competition at Méribel, France, on February 8–23. (For results, see Special Report, page 276.) The competition was organized as it was in the world championships, with two groups of six producing eight quarterfinalists. An enthralling cliff-hanger was the quarterfinal between Canada and Germany, won by the Canadians 3–2 on penalty shots after a 3–3 draw and 10 minutes of overtime during which no goals were scored.

In the semifinal Canada defeated Czechoslovakia 4–2, and the Unified Team, comprising several republics of the former Soviet Union, beat the United States 5–2 with three goals in six minutes late in the match. In a play-off for the bronze medal, the U.S. lost 6–1 to Czechoslovakia. In a final that featured two gripping scoreless periods, a 3–1 Unified Team victory over Canada was sealed by a spectacular 7.6-m (25-ft) shot from Vyacheslav Bykov, the Unified Team captain. The competition's leading scorer was Joe Juneau of Canada with 15 points (6 goals and 9 assists), followed by Andrey Khomoutov of the Unified Team and Robert Land of Czechoslovakia with 14 and 13, respectively. The outstanding goalkeeper was Ray LeBlanc of the U.S. The order of positions below the medalists was the U.S. in fourth, followed by Sweden, Germany, Finland, France, Norway, Switzerland, Poland, and Italy.

Djurgarden of Sweden retained the European Cup by beating Dusseldorf of Germany 7–2 in the final at Dusseldorf on Dec. 30, 1991. Dynamo Moscow of Russia finished third by defeating Bern of Switzerland 6–1.

In the second women's world championship, at Tampere, Fin., on April 19–25, Canada retained the title by defeating the U.S. 8–0 in the final. Finland placed third, ahead of Sweden, China, Norway, Denmark, and Switzerland. The International Ice Hockey Federation requested that women's ice hockey be included in the Olympic schedule for Nagano, Japan, in 1998.   (HOWARD BASS)

ICE SKATING

At the international level, the 1991–92 ice skating season was noteworthy for the first participation of athletes representing the Unified Team, which consisted of several of the republics of the former Soviet Union. Despite the glamour of the XVI Olympic Winter Games at Albertville, France, on Feb. 8–23, 1992 (for results, see Special Report, page 276), world championships appeared to be regarded as the year's prime contests.

In October former Olympic figure skating champion John Curry, suffering from AIDS, returned home to England. Three world-class Canadian figure skaters had died of the disease in the previous 12 months.

Figure Skating. The increasing degree of hazardous athleticism in all branches of figure skating caused major competitions to be so affected by injuries that a handful of preseason favourites failed to fulfill their ambitions.

Sprinter Bonnie Blair of the U.S. skates to victory in the 500-m race in the winter Olympic Games. Four days later she won the 1,000-m race, becoming the first American woman in 40 years to win two gold medals in a single winter Olympic competition.

MANNY MILLAN—SPORTS ILLUSTRATED

Kurt Browning's recurrent back troubles handicapped the Canadian's chance to win either a fourth consecutive men's world crown or an Olympic gold medal. A series of physical problems beset Midori Ito's hopes of regaining the women's championship for Japan. A groin injury suffered by Paul Duchesnay marred his Olympic appearance with his sister Isabelle, and the French pair later decided not to defend their world dance title.

Even so, such misfortunes did not detract from the merits of the victors at the 82nd world championships at Oakland, Calif., on March 24–29, when three of the four titles went to Unified Team skaters and all the Olympic gold medalists again won in their respective events. Viktor Petrenko ended his amateur career in triumph, best remembered for a brilliant combination of triple axel and triple toe-loop jumps. Browning, though decisively outpointed, made a commendable effort to achieve the runner-up slot. His compatriot Elvis Stojko, by finishing third, with Browning secured for the first time two places for Canada on the men's world ·podium.

The women's season undeniably belonged to Kristi Yamaguchi of the U.S. (see Biographies), an outstanding jumper who landed five triples in the Olympics and six when retaining her world title, each time succeeding with a Lutz to toe-loop jump combination that no rival attempted. After gaining second place in the Olympics, Ito was unfit to compete in the world event. Nancy Kerrigan of the U.S. followed her Olympic bronze medal with second place at Oakland, ahead of Lu Chen, whose third place at the age of 15 made her one to watch in future years. Her accomplishment reflected the progress that Chinese skaters had made since first competing internationally in 1980.

The pairs season was dominated by the Russians, Natalya Mishkutenok and Artur Dmitriev, whose retention of the world title never appeared to be in doubt. Their triple toe-loop and triple Salchow throws were spectacular highlights, and the smooth flow of their lifts and descents was a delight to behold. They received four perfect scores of six for artistic impression. Isabelle Brasseur and Lloyd Eisler of

Canada, after starting the final competition a close second, made costly errors and were overtaken for the silver by Radka Kovarikova and Renee Novotny of Czechoslovakia, who had managed only fourth place in the Olympics.

The ice dance supremacy of the ever elegant Russian husband-and-wife team Marina Klimova and Sergey Ponomarenko was beyond question throughout the season. They gained their third world title in four years, attaining a technical standard clearly better than their previous best. Another Russian married couple, Maya Usova and Aleksandr Zhulin, though runners-up in Oakland, never posed a serious threat any more than the handicapped Duchesnays could when placing second in the Olympics.

Speed Skating. Roberto Sighel of Italy, who had been runner-up the previous year, captured the overall title in the men's world championship at Calgary, Alta., on March 21–22. Falco Zandstra of The Netherlands placed second, ahead of the Norwegian title defender, Johann Olav Koss. Gunda Niemann of Germany won the women's world championship at Heerenveen, Neth., on March 7–8, followed by Emese Hunyady of Austria and Seiko Hashimoto of Japan.

In the separate world sprint championships at Oslo, Norway, on February 29–March 1, Igor Zhelezovsky of the Unified Team retained the men's crown, and Ye Qiaobo, second the previous season, became the first Chinese women's champion. In the world short-track championships at Denver, Colo., on April 2–4, Ki Hoon Kim and So He Kim, both of South Korea, respectively claimed the men's and women's overall titles. Japan won the men's team relay championship, with France second and Great Britain third, but the Asian dominance was broken in the women's team contest, won by Canada ahead of The Netherlands and France. (HOWARD BASS)

LAWN BOWLS

Both men's and women's world championships—held in different countries every four years—attracted teams from throughout the world to the U.K. in 1992. Many of them were used to the sunbaked surfaces found in their less temperate climates, and they fared indifferently on Britain's slower greens.

At Ayr, Scotland, in June, the seventh women's world event was dominated for two weeks by the home-based players and Irish bowlers. First place in triples and fours enabled Scotland's Senga McCrone, Frances Whyte, Joyce Lindores, Janice Maxwell, and Sarah Gourlay to win the team title. Gold medals in both singles and pairs confirmed the status of Northern Ireland's Margaret Johnston as the world's leading women bowler; she defeated Audrey Rutherford of Australia 25–10 in the singles final. Bowlers north and south of the trouble-torn border constituted the Irish team, and Johnston linked with the republic's Phil Nolan to win the pairs. Scotland finished first, Ireland second, and New Zealand third in the team championship.

Two months later in England, at Worthing, 28 teams competed in the seventh world men's championships. Tony Allcock of England recovered from a 20–14 deficit to defeat Scotland's Richard Corsie 25–20 for the singles title. Jeff Rabkin of Israel won the bronze to add to his country's earlier triples victory, Israel's first world title. The team title, however, went again to Scotland. Corsie and Alex Marshall won the pairs, and Graham Robertson, Angus Blair, and Willie Wood with Marshall as skip took the fours.

For Australia, one of the world's strongest bowling countries, it was a paradoxical year. Though the team failed to win a medal at Worthing, one of the nation's leading players, Ian Schuback, traveled to England in February to become the world indoor champion. (DONALD J. NEWBY)

MOTORBOATING

For most of the drivers competing in American Power Boat Association (APBA)-sanctioned racing events, the 1992 season had its share of ups and downs. On the International Outboard Grand Prix circuit, the eventual winner of the Champ boat class was Mike Seebold of Fenton, Mo., who got off to a bad start at the beginning of the season but was able to pull off the overall victory with three first-place finishes at the end of the season. When the points were finally tallied in the SST-140 class, Mark Trotter of North Charleston, S.C., won the series with only slightly more than 30 points to spare. Racing in the Mod VP class was not nearly as closely contested, however, as Glenn Reynolds of Kingston, Tenn., was able to finish 13th in the season finale and still claim the class crown.

Returning to the sport of Unlimited hydroplane racing after a one-year hiatus, *Miss Budweiser* driver Chip Hanauer had to overcome a roller-coaster ride of a different kind. In spite of two midseason flips, he finished the year with seven victories in nine attempts. He won his sixth overall driving title, while the team earned its 13th national championship. Piloting *The Tide* boat, George Woods ended the season in second place, while Mark Tate and the *Winston Eagle* finished third.

The national high-points championships in Offshore racing went to a new crop of winners in 1992. In the Superboat class Tom Gentry and his *Gentry Eagle* went home with the victory, while *The Executioner* team with driver Alan Fuentes became the new titleholder in the Super Vee class. Beating out the pack for the UIM II crown was Alann Dunteman driving the *Agitator*. William Westberry and his *Spirit of Houston* won the Pro Stock battle, and the Stock class victor was *Sundance Skater*'s Robert Loeffler. In the production classes Art Girard (*Airborne*) won the Offshore D title; Al Hofmann (*Armed & Dangerous*) took the Offshore C crown; Art Lilly (*Heartbeat*) became the victor in Offshore B; and Frank Eiroa (*Frank's Marine*) walked away with the national win in Offshore A.

Breaking ground as a new national series in 1992, the Pro Tunnel Tour crowned champions in three classes. In the SST-100 Gordy Miller earned the overall win, while Todd Bowden was awarded the title in the SST-60 competition, and Rick Hoffman gained the victory in the SST-45.

(RENEE MAHN OLEJNIK)

POLO

True international polo returned in 1992 with the revival of the prestigious Westchester Cup tournament, historically played between the United States and Great Britain. This competition originated in 1886, and the U.S. had tallied nine wins to three for the British before the competition was renewed in 1992. A crowd of more than 20,000 witnessed the contest, played at the Guards Polo Club in Windsor Great Park, England, with Queen Elizabeth II presenting the Tiffany trophy to the U.S., which won 8–7 in two overtime periods.

The Federation of International Polo held the third world championship in April. After worldwide play-offs six teams—Argentina, England, Guatemala, Chile, the U.S., and Mexico—qualified for the finals held in Santiago, Chile. Argentina dominated this round, winning all the games by impressive margins and defeating Chile in the title match 12–7.

At the Argentine Open in Buenos Aires the team of Indios Chapaleufu, all four members of which belonged to the Heguy family, won the championship by defeating Ellerstina 19–13. The U.S. Open was held in Indio, Calif., in Octo- ber. Hanalei Bay, led by the 10-goalers Gracida brothers, dominated the tournament and won the trophy by defeating Fish Creek 13–6. In the U.K. Ellerston White won the Queen's Cup, played at the Guards Polo Club in Windsor, defeating Pendell 10–7. The British Open championship for the Cowdray Park Gold Cup was hotly contested, and the Black Bears won their first Gold Cup by edging Santa Fe 10–9 before a capacity crowd. (ALLAN D. SCHERER)

RODEO

Professional rodeo records tumbled during the $2.6 million National Finals Rodeo (NFR), held Dec. 4–13, 1992, at the Thomas and Mack Center in Las Vegas, Nev. Billy Etbauer of Ree Heights, S.D., claimed his first saddle bronc riding world championship with a performance acknowledged as one of the greatest personal triumphs in the NFR's 34-year history.

Etbauer entered the NFR with $83,144 and the lead in the world title race. When the tournament ended, he had placed nine times in 10 rounds, including five outright victories. His $101,531 in NFR earnings surpassed the previous record of $101,242 set in 1991 by Ty Murray. Etbauer's season earnings totaled $184,675, a record amount for a single season in an individual rodeo event.

World championships in the Professional Rodeo Cowboys Association (PRCA) and Women's Professional Rodeo Association are based on regular-season arena earnings plus prize money won at the season-ending NFR and National Finals Steer Roping competitions. Murray, of Stephenville, Texas, won the world champion all-around cowboy title for the fourth straight year. He was the only cowboy to compete at the NFR in all three roughstock events—saddle bronc riding, bareback riding, and bull riding. His season earnings totaled $225,992, somewhat better than twice the amount earned by all-around runner-up Clay O'Brien Cooper of Gilbert, Ariz.

Cooper and Jake Barnes of Higley, Ariz., stretched the PRCA record for team roping world titles to six following a solid performance at the NFR. The pair entered the rodeo as the second-place team and had to overcome a $20,000 gap that separated them from top-seeded Steve Northcott of Odessa, Texas, and Charles Pogue of Ringling, Okla. Barnes and Cooper outgunned the younger team to win the world title with a year-end total of $83,197 each.

Perennial barrel-racing champion Charmayne Rodman of Galt, Calif., stretched her string of world titles to nine following a hard-fought battle at the NFR. Despite a strong challenge by Twila Haller of Phoenix, Ariz., Rodman maintained her lead through 10 rounds to win the 1992 championship with earnings of $110,868. In so doing, Rodman gained the professional rodeo record for the greatest number of single-event world titles.

Other world titlists for 1992 included Mark Roy of Dalemead, Alta., the first Canadian ever to win a PRCA championship in steer wrestling with $112,103 in season earnings. First-time PRCA champions also included bareback rider Wayne Herman of Dickinson, N.D., who maintained his lead despite sustaining numerous injuries at the NFR and won $122,949, and bull rider Cody Custer of Wickenburg, Ariz., with $149,814, a new bull-riding season-earnings record. Joe Beaver of Huntsville, Texas, achieved his fourth world championship in calf roping with $124,525 in season earnings.

At the National Finals Steer Roping, contested November 27–28 in Guthrie, Okla., Guy Allen of Vinita, Okla., claimed a record seventh world championship in steer roping. His season earnings totaled $44,729.

(GAVIN FORBES EHRINGER)

ROWING

The principal honours in world rowing in 1992 went to Germany, which won a dozen of the 36 titles in men's, women's, lightweight, and junior events. Finishing second was Australia with five titles, followed by Canada and Great Britain with four each, Denmark with three, and Czechoslovakia and Romania with two each. The four remaining winners were Italy, Russia, Slovenia, and the United States.

In the Olympic Games competition at Bañolas, Spain, all but 2 of the 14 titles won in the 1988 Olympics changed hands. Great Britain successfully defended the men's coxless pairs as Steve Redgrave, this time with Matthew Pinsent, won his third successive Olympic gold medal. The British were first at the 500-m mark and then forged steadily farther ahead, showing considerable strength to win by 4.96 sec over Germany.

This was the most decisive verdict in the men's events, the remainder being decided by less than two seconds. Australia—world champions for the two previous years—defeated the U.S. in coxless fours by 1.64 sec and Austria by 1.10 sec in double sculls. Romania was harder pressed to win the coxed fours by 0.97 sec over Germany, which in turn captured the quadruple sculls by defeating Norway and Italy by 1.92 and 2.16 sec, respectively. Thomas Lange defeated Vaclav Chalupa of Czechoslovakia to retain his single sculls gold medal and give Germany its second success.

The biggest surprise, in the best race of the regatta, was the manner in which the young Searle brothers struck gold for Great Britain in coxed pairs. They faced Italy's redoubtable Abbagnale brothers, holders of seven world and two Olympic titles, who were each 10 years older than the Britons. The Italians set a relentless pace to lead Romania by 1.45 sec at 500 m and twice as much at the halfway point. Meanwhile, the Searles, 1.03 sec behind Romania at 500 m, closed the gap to 0.51 sec at the halfway mark and were only 0.12 sec down at 1,500 m, where the Italians were leading by 3.21 sec. Soon afterward, however, the Searle brothers went for the Abbagnales, bringing spectators to their feet with a pulsating finish over the last 30 strokes to overtake the defending champions and win by 1.15 sec.

There was an even tighter finish in eights, the climax to the competition. Canada led most of the way and narrowly denied Romania's determined bid for the title by 0.14 sec.

Canada won three of the women's championships, defeating the U.S. by 1.01 sec in coxless fours, Germany by 1.74 sec in coxless pairs, and Romania by 3.54 sec in eights. Romania also finished second to Germany in double and quadruple sculls, but Elisabeta Lipa collected Romania's second gold medal of the regatta in single sculls.

In the world lightweight championships in Montreal, Denmark won the eights and single sculls, Great Britain retained the coxless fours, and the double and quadruple sculls went to Australia and Italy, respectively. In women's events Germany retained the double sculls against Canada by 0.75 sec, but Denmark and Australia won more comfortably in, respectively, single sculls and coxless fours.

The world junior championships, also held in Montreal, were dominated by Germany with seven gold and seven silver medals in the 14 events. Czechoslovakia won twice, and the remaining titles went to Australia, Great Britain, Russia, Slovenia, and the U.S.

At the Henley Royal Regatta in England, there were only three overseas winners. Canada took the double sculls, while both trophies for quadruple sculls, in open and schools class (new), were won by Sweden. In the 138th University Boat Race, Oxford recorded its 16th win in 17 years.

(KEITH OSBORNE)

SAILING

The year 1992 began with both the challengers' and defenders' America's Cup campaigns getting into full swing. Only 8 of the original 23 challengers who had pledged their intent three years earlier reached the Louis Vuitton series to select the challenger to the U.S. Legal wrangles and world recession had eliminated the others. In the U.S. only two syndicates finally made it to the defender trials, Dennis Conner's low-budget one-boat team and Bill Koch's well-financed group with four boats.

As was to be expected with a new design rule for the America's Cup yachts, design improvements were rapid and expensive as the competition developed. This had to favour the syndicates with the strongest financial backing, and Koch's innovative design team attacked the problems with gusto.

On January 14 the defenders began their round-robin series. With two boats, Koch was expected to hold a big advantage. However, Conner's crew steadily met the challenge as Koch introduced innovations. In the final defender series, Conner managed to contain Koch's $America^3$ to make the score four races each before slipping to defeat in the best-of-13 competition. Koch's veteran skipper, Buddy Melges, who had won almost every major sailing honour except this one, had won the right to defend.

The eight-yacht challenger series began on January 25, and it soon became apparent that, unless something unforeseen happened, New Zealand, Italy, France, and Japan were too strong for Australia, Spain, and Sweden. Qualifying for the final competition were Michael Fay's New Zealand yacht, skippered by ex-American Rod Davis, and Raul Gardini's Italian yacht, skippered by Paul Cayard of the U.S. During this series of races the Italians formally protested about the way the New Zealanders used their bowsprit. Thus by the seventh race Fay's team had seen its 4–1 lead disappear after the controversial annulment of one victory and a loss in race 6; the result was a 3–3 tie. When the Italians won the next race, the New Zealand syndicate's fate was almost sealed. The bowsprit controversy had clearly upset the New Zealand rhythm; consequently, they lost the edge and the challenger spot.

In the competition for the cup, the Italians were physically drained after the dramatic final selection series and, unfortunately, at the first start Cayard jumped the gun and had to restart; after that there was no catching Melges and his crew. The Italians did manage to win the second race by a whisker, but Koch's starting helmsman David Dellenbaugh, who had been outstanding throughout the series, won the next three starts in a row. The U.S. thus retained the America's Cup 4–1.

1992 World Class Boat Champions

Class	Winner	Class	Winner
Cadet	José Conte (Argentina)	Topper	Tim Willis (United Kingdom)
Dragon	Poul-Richard Hoj-Jensen (Denmark)	Tornado	Mitch Booth (Australia)
Flying Dutchman	Paul Foerster (United States)	Youth 420 (girls)	Tracy Haylley (United States)
Flying 15	Rupert Mander (United Kingdom)	Youth 420 (boys)	Sylvian Mizzi (France)
Fireball	Martin Lambrecht (South Africa)	Europe	Severine Blondel (France)
470 (men)	Jordi Calafat (Spain)	Laser	Michael Hare (United States)
470 (women)	Teresa Zabell (Spain)	Boards (boys)	Amir Levinson (Israel)
OK	Bengt Andersson (Sweden)	Boards (girls)	Natasha Sturges (Australia)
Soling	Jochen Schumann (Germany)		

The top competition among small boats in 1992 was the regatta of the Olympic Games off the coast of Spain, with 10 classes in which medals could be won. The host country's team excelled to an extraordinary degree, taking four gold medals (470 men, 470 women, Flying Dutchman, and Finn) and one silver medal (Europe). The U.S. team, as usual, did well with one gold (Star), six silvers (men's sailboard, Flying Dutchman, Finn, 470 men, Soling, and Tornado), and two bronzes (Europe and 470 women). Twelve different countries won medals. (For additional results, *see* Special Report, page 276.)

The world match racing championship was won by Russell Coutts of New Zealand. In defeating Kevin Mahaney of the U.S. in the final, he made up for his disappointments in the America's Cup challenger series and his poor showing in the Olympic regatta. Mahaney, on the other hand, announced his retirement from championship racing, having achieved this second place and a silver medal in the Soling class at the Olympics. (ADRIAN JARDINE)

SKIING

Notwithstanding the worldwide mass media coverage of the XVI Olympic Winter Games, held at Albertville, France, on Feb. 8–23, 1992 (for results, *see* Special Report, page 276), the skiing events, in the minds of many serious followers, were largely overshadowed during the 1991–92 season by separate World Cup series in every major branch of the sport. Each of these series, spread over some four months of contests in many countries, reflected consistency of form and provided a continuity of interest that reached its peak in March.

Alpine Skiing. Paul Accola of Switzerland, who dominated the men's events in the 26th Alpine World Cup series but was less prominent at Albertville, emphasized at the beginning of the season his conviction that World Cup racing mattered most. His versatility was underlined by his placing first in the supergiant slalom, second in the slalom, and third in the giant slalom. By also gaining points in the downhill, he achieved a distinction that only Luxembourg's Marc Girardelli had previously accomplished. Alberto Tomba of Italy (*see* BIOGRAPHIES), outstanding in the slalom with six race victories and also top scorer in the giant slalom, finished second overall, with Girardelli, the defending champion, third.

Petra Kronberger of Austria won her third consecutive women's overall crown, collecting points in all four disciplines for the second time. Her victory was emphatic even though she did not finish first in any discipline. Carole Merle, the runner-up from France, led both the giant slalom and supergiant slalom standings, and third-place Katja Seizinger of Germany narrowly defeated Kronberger in the downhill. Vreni Schneider of Switzerland, fourth overall, was the top scorer in the slalom.

Austrians and Italians won three each of the 10 men's and women's Olympic gold medals, but only one individual—Kronberger—gained two, for slalom and combined. Patrick Ortlieb, youngest of the Austrian squad, defeated Franck Piccard of France by 0.05 sec in the men's downhill. By winning the giant slalom, Tomba became the first Alpine skier to retain an Olympic title, his thrilling finish gaining a two-run aggregate 0.32-sec margin over Girardelli. Kjetil-André Aamodt led Norwegians to three of the top four positions in the supergiant slalom, second-place Girardelli denying them a clean sweep. Sweden's Pernilla Wiberg won the women's giant slalom, while Diann Roffe of the U.S. and Austria's Anita Wachter shared a unique dead heat for the silver medal.

Nordic Events. The 13th Nordic World Cup series for cross-country racing was won by Björn Daehlie of Norway, narrowly clinching the title in the last of 10 meetings after an absorbing season-long rivalry with his second-place compatriot, Vegard Ulvang. Each also won two gold medals in the winter Olympic Games. In women's World Cup competition, Elena Vialbe of the Unified Team (comprising several of the former Soviet republics) retained the title, ahead of Stefania Belmondo of Italy; Ljubov Egorova of the Unified Team finished third. The separate Nordic Combination World Cup went to Fabrice Guy, the first French winner; earlier he had gained an Olympic gold medal in the same event. Klaus Sulzenbacher of Austria was runner-up in the World Cup, with Fred Borre Lundberg of Norway third.

In ski jumping Toni Nieminen, a 16-year-old from Finland, quickly managed to replace the image of his legendary fellow countryman Matti Nykänen. Nieminen not only won the jumping World Cup series but also triumphed in the spectacular 120-m Olympic event and the annual prestigious Austro-German Four Hills Tournament. Next best in the Cup were three Austrians—Werner Rathmayr, Andreas Felder, and fourth-place Ernst Vettori, the Olympic 90-m winner.

Perhaps the most notable accomplishment of the Nordic season was at the Olympics, where, as a member of the winning Unified Team in the women's cross-country relay, Raisa Smetanina, 39, earned a record 10th Olympic medal, became the oldest woman medalist, and was the first to win a medal in five consecutive Games.

SIMON BRUTY—ALLSPORT

Toni Nieminen of Finland jumps 115.5 m to help his team defeat Austria for the gold medal in ski jumping. At age 16, Nieminen became the youngest male to win a gold medal in the history of the winter Olympic Games.

In the Olympic skiing and shooting biathlon, women's events were held for the first time. Anfissa Reztsova of the Unified Team made history as the first woman gold medalist by winning the 7.5 km. In the men's team relay, German veteran Fritz Fischer crossed the finish line first to end the former Soviet Union's 24-year reign in the event.

Freestyle Skiing. The rapid rise in recent years of freestyle skiing was recognized when the moguls were given full Olympic status and the ballet and aerials were contested as demonstration events at Albertville. In the 13th freestyle World Cup series, the men's combined title was captured by Trace Worthington of the U.S., ahead of Hugo Bonatti of Austria and a Canadian, David Belhumeur. Conny Kissling of Switzerland won her 10th consecutive women's combined title, with her compatriot Maja Schmid in second place and Jilly Curry of Great Britain third.

Other Events. Speed skiing came closer to full Olympic inclusion by its acceptance at the Games in Albertville as a demonstration sport at Les Arcs, France. The men's event was won by Michael Prufer, representing the host nation, and the women's by a Finn, Tarja Mulari. (HOWARD BASS)

SQUASH RACKETS

Recent years had started amid speculation that Pakistani Jahangir Khan would not resume his place as the most prolific winner of major squash titles of all time. In 1992 it turned out to be well founded when injury forced him to abort his spring comeback and so not defend the British Open title he had won in each of the preceding 10 years. His absence allowed his countryman Jansher Khan—the three-time World Open champion—to win his first British Open title. He achieved this by beating surprise finalist Chris Robertson of Australia 9–7, 10–9, 9–5. Susan Devoy of New Zealand, who had been similarly dominant in the women's British Open (with seven titles), had suffered an upset loss in 1991 but returned to record her eighth win, beating Martine Le Moignan (England) 9–3, 9–5, 9–3.

In August a record-breaking 24 nations competed in the world men's junior championship in Hong Kong. The domination of English and Australian players was broken in the individual event, with Juha Raumolin of Finland taking the title by defeating Jonathan Power of Canada in the final. In the team championships Australia defeated England 2–1 in the final.

One month later the men's World Open was staged in Johannesburg, South Africa. Rodney Martin of Australia failed to retain his title, losing to fellow Australian Chris Dittmar in the semifinals. Dittmar then fell 3–1 in the final to Jansher Khan.

In Vancouver, B.C., a few weeks later the women's World Open was won by Devoy, who then announced her retirement. The 28-year-old had suffered only a handful of defeats in nearly 10 years, winning eight British Open championships and virtually everything else she entered. In the team competition Australia defeated New Zealand 2–1 in the final to win its third world team title.

(ANDREW SHELLEY)

SWIMMING

The summer Olympic Games in Barcelona, Spain, during July and August 1992 attracted 639 swimmers from 90 nations, the largest number of nations ever to compete. The United States won 11 gold medals, the Unified Team (comprising republics of the former Soviet Union) 6, Hungary 5, and China 4. U.S. male swimmers won 6 of 16 events, and U.S. women won 5 of 15. The U.S won four of five relays. East Germany, which had dominated the 1988 Olympic Games, joined West Germany in a unified German team and went from 11 gold medals to one. In the total medal count the U.S. won 27—11 gold, 9 silver, and 7 bronze; Germany 11—1 gold, 3 silver, 7 bronze; and the Unified Team 10—6 gold, 3 silver, 1 bronze. (For additional results, see Special Report, page 276.)

For the year, 15 world records were set and one equaled in 50-m pools; eight of the new marks were by men, five of them at the Olympic Games. Seven records were set by women, four of them at the Games. The first world record for 1992 was set by Kieren Perkins, an 18-year-old from Brisbane, Australia, in the 800-m freestyle. On February 16 at the New South Wales championships in Sydney, he took 1.25 sec off his mark of 7 min 47.85 sec, clocking 7 min 46.60 sec. On April 3 at the Australian championships in Canberra, Perkins sliced 0.52 sec from the 400-m freestyle record with a time of 3 min 46.47 sec. Two days later he lowered by 1.96 sec the world record for the 1,500-m freestyle with a time of 14 min 48.40 sec.

On July 29 at the Olympics, two world records were set. Yevgeny Sadovy, 19, of Volgograd, swimming for the Unified Team, was timed in the 400-m freestyle at 3 min 45 sec, 1.47 sec faster than the record by Perkins in April. Mike Barrowman, 23, of Potomac, Md., lowered by 0.44 sec his 1991 world record in the 200-m breaststroke with a time of 2 min 10.16 sec. On July 31 two more world records were achieved at the Olympics. Perkins lowered his 1,500-m freestyle by 4.92 sec from 14 min 48.40 sec to 14 min 43.48 sec, and Jeff Rouse, 22, of Fredrickson, Va., set a record in the 100-m backstroke leg of the 4 × 100-m medley relay. With a time of 53.86 sec, Rouse cut 0.07 sec from his mark set in 1991. The U.S. medley team of Rouse, Nelson Diebel, Pablo Morales, and Jon Olson equaled the world record of 3 min 36.93 set by the U.S. team in the 1988 Olympic Games.

Three of the seven world records by women in 1992 were set at the U.S. Olympic Trials at Indianapolis, Ind. On March 1 Jenny Thompson, 19, of Dover, N.H., in a preliminary heat of the 100-m freestyle, achieved a time of 54.48 sec, lowering by 0.25 sec the record set by East Germany's Kristin Otto in 1986. On March 2 Anita Nall, 15, of Towson, Md., the youngest member of the U.S. Olympic team, was timed in 2 min 25.92 sec in a preliminary heat of the 200-m breaststroke, taking 0.79 sec off the world record of 2 min 26.71 sec set by Silke Hörner of East Germany in the 1988 Olympic Games. In the finals Nall went faster by 0.57 sec with a time of 2 min 25.35 sec. At the Olympic Games women from China set two world records. On July 30 Lin Li, 22, won the 200-m individual medley with a time of 2 min 11.65 sec, taking 0.08 sec off the record set by Ute Geweniger of East Germany in 1981. On July 31 in the 50-m freestyle, Yang Wenyi, 20, lowered by 0.19 sec her 1988 record of 24.98 sec with a new time of 24.79 sec. The U.S. won both the 4 × 100-m medley relay and the 4 × 100-m freestyle relay with world records. On July 28 the quartet of Nicole Haislett, Dara Torres, Angel Martino, and Jenny Thompson were timed in 3 min 39.46 sec, chopping 1.11 sec off the mark set by East Germany in 1986. Two days later in the 4 × 100-m medley relay, the foursome of Lea Loveless, Nall, Christine Ahmann-Leighton, and Thompson with a time of 4 min 2.54 sec lowered by 1.15 sec the record set by East Germany in 1988.

Krisztina Egerszegi, 17, of Hungary (see BIOGRAPHIES) was the outstanding woman swimmer of the Olympic Games, setting Olympic records in the 100-m and 200-m backstrokes and winning the 400-m individual medley. The outstanding male swimmer was Yevgeny Sadovy of the Unified Team, winning gold medals in the 200-m and 400-m freestyle and swimming on the record-breaking 4 × 200-m freestyle relay.

In 1991 FINA (Fédération Internationale de Natation Amateur), swimming's governing body, recognized world records set in 25-m pools as of March 3, 1991. During 1992 six world marks were set by men and two by women (*see* Table).

Diving. At the Olympic Games, 38 divers from 31 countries competed in the diving events. On July 29 in the 3-m springboard, Mark Lenzi, 24, of Fredericksburg, Va., came from behind with his last two dives to win the gold medal, upsetting Tan Liangde, 29, of China, the Olympic silver medalist in 1984 and 1988. Lenzi was awarded 9s on a forward 3½ somersault in the pike position and 8.5s on a reverse 1½ with 3½ twists to win by 30.96 points, 676.53 to 645.57. Dmitry Saoutine of the Unified Team gained the bronze, with 627.78. On August 4 Sun Shuwei, 16, of China became the youngest male diver ever to win a gold medal. In the 10-m platform he took the lead on his last compulsory dive and held it for the rest of the competition. He climaxed his performance with a spectacular inward 3½ tuck, the most difficult dive of the tournament, receiving four perfect scores of 10, two 9.5s, and a 9. The total of 99.96 made it the third highest single dive of all time. Shuwei's winning score of 677.31 was 43.68 points greater than that of silver medalist Scott Donie, 23, of Fort Lauderdale, Fla. Bronze medalist Xiong Ni of China scored 600.15.

In the women's events Chinese divers repeated their 1988 Olympic gold medal victories. On August 3 Gao Min, 21, retained the 3-m springboard title. Although she trailed

Fu Mingxia performs one of the dives in the Olympic Games that helped her win the 10-m platform competition by a wide margin. Representing China, Fu was only 13 years old and the second youngest person ever to win an Olympic gold medal.
RONALD C. MODRA—SPORTS ILLUSTRATED

Irina Lashko of the Unified Team by 5.64 points after six dives, Min's last two dives, an inward 2½ pike and a reverse 1½ with 2½ twists, earned mostly 9s, and her final score was 572.40 points to Lashko's 514.14. Brita Pia Baldus of Germany won the bronze medal with 503.07 points. It was the first time in the history of the Olympics that the U.S. failed to win a medal in women's springboard. On July 27 in the platform event, 13-year-old Fu Mingxia of China became the youngest gold medalist in any Olympic sport since 1936, scoring 461.43 points. Her next-to-last dive, a 3½ back tuck, the most difficult of the competition, scored 8s and 8.5s and dispelled any doubt that she would win the gold medal. Yelena Miroshina, 18, of the Unified Team won the silver medal with 411.63 points. Mary Ellen Clark, 29, of Fort Lauderdale won the bronze with 401.91.

Synchronized Swimming. Swimmers from 22 countries entered the Olympic competition August 2–7. In the solo event Kristen Babb-Sprague, 22, of Pleasanton, Calif., upset world champion Sylvie Frechette, 25, of Montreal. After the preliminary event both swimmers were tied going into the compulsory figures competition. Babb-Sprague led Frechette by 0.251 point after the figures. The seven judges registered a split decision, with four of the seven placing Babb-Sprague first. Frechette won the final routine by 0.12 point, not enough to defeat Babb-Sprague for the gold; Babb-Sprague's total was 191.848 points to 191.717 for Frechette. Fumiko Okuno of Japan was the bronze medalist with 187.056. Human error was a deciding factor in the competition. A Brazilian judge intended to give Frechette a 9.7 instead of an 8.7 on one of her figure routines. The judge indicated she wanted to change her score, claiming a malfunctioning touch pad. The 9.7 would have won the gold medal for Frechette with an overall score of 191.887, nipping Babb-Sprague by 0.039 point. The touch pad did not malfunction, however, and the chief referee and panel referee ruled that the judges could not change their scores after they had been made public.

Thirteen nations entered the duet competition. Karen and Sarah Josephson, 28-year-old twins from Bristol, Conn. (*see* BIOGRAPHIES), won the championship for the U.S. The

World Swimming Records Set in 1992

Event	Name	Country	Time
	MEN		
400-m freestyle	Kieren Perkins	Australia	3 min 46.47 sec
400-m freestyle	Yevgeny Sadovy	Unified Team	3 min 45.00 sec
800-m freestyle	Kieren Perkins	Australia	7 min 46.60 sec
1,500-m freestyle	Kieren Perkins	Australia	14 min 48.40 sec
1,500-m freestyle	Kieren Perkins	Australia	14 min 43.48 sec
100-m backstroke	Jeff Rouse	U.S.	53.86 sec
200-m breaststroke	Mike Barrowman	U.S.	2 min 10.16 sec
4 × 200-m freestyle relay	Unified Team (Dimitry Lepikov, Vladimir Pychnenko, Veniamin Taianovitch, Yevgeny Sadovy)	Unified Team	7 min 11.95 sec
4 × 100-m medley relay	U.S. national team (Jeff Rouse, Nelson Diebel, Pablo Morales, Jon Olson)	U.S.	3 min 36.93 sec[1]

[1]Equals world record of U.S. national team, set in Olympic Games, Seoul

	WOMEN		
50-m freestyle	Yang Wenyi	China	24.79 sec
100-m freestyle	Jenny Thompson	U.S.	54.48 sec
200-m breaststroke	Anita Nall	U.S.	2 min 25.92 sec
200-m breaststroke	Anita Nall	U.S.	2 min 25.35 sec
200-m individual medley	Lin Li	China	2 min 11.65 sec
4 × 100 medley relay	U.S. national team (Lea Loveless, Anita Nall, Christine Ahmann-Leighton, Jenny Thompson)	U.S.	4 min 02.54 sec
4 × 100-m freestyle relay	U.S. national team (Nicole Haislett, Dara Torres, Angel Martino, Jenny Thompson)	U.S.	3 min 39.46 sec

World Swimming Records Set in 1992 in 25-m Pools

Event	Name	Country	Time
	MEN		
50-m freestyle	Steve Crocker	U.S.	21.64 sec
1,500-m freestyle	Kieren Perkins	Australia	14 min 32.40 sec
100-m backstroke	Mark Tewksbury	Canada	52.52 sec
100-m backstroke	Mark Tewksbury	Canada	52.50 sec
200-m butterfly	Franck Esposito	France	1 min 54.67 sec
200-m individual medley	Jani Sievinen	Finland	1 min 57.19 sec
	WOMEN		
200-m backstroke	Anna Simcic	New Zealand	2 min 07.11 sec
200-m backstroke	Nicole Livingstone-Stevenson	Australia	2 min 06.78 sec

Josephsons entered the finals with a 2.221-point lead over Penny and Vicky Vilagos, 29-year-old twins from Canada. The Josephsons scored more perfect 10s than any other pair, achieving four 10s for technical merit and four 10s for artistic impression. The Josephsons' final score was 192.175; the Vilagos finished second with 189.394, and Fumiko Okuno and Aki Takayama of Japan won the bronze medal with 186.868.   (ALBERT SCHOENFIELD)

TABLE TENNIS

During the games of the XXV Olympiad held in Barcelona, Spain, Chinese table tennis stars captured three of the four gold medal finals. Deng Yaping needed four games to overcome her compatriot Qiao Hong and win the women's singles title. When the pair had teamed up two days earlier for the women's doubles, they emerged victorious with a four-game victory over another pair from China. In the men's singles Jan-Ove Waldner, a well-known international star from Sweden, was crowned champion. His opponent in the final was Jean-Philippe Gatien of France, who went down to defeat in three straight games.

China again grabbed the spotlight when Lü Lin and Wang Tao captured the men's doubles championship after a five-game battle with Steffen Fetzner and Jörg Rosskopf of Germany. All the Olympic bronze medals were awarded to Korean athletes.

The European championships were decided in Stuttgart, Germany, in April. In the men's team competition Sweden finished first, England second, and Germany third. In the women's division Romania was first, The Netherlands runner-up, and the Unified Team third.

(ARTHUR KINGSLEY VINT)

1992 Table Tennis World Rankings

MEN	WOMEN
1. Jan-Ove Waldner (Sweden)	1. Deng Yaping (China)
2. Jean-Philippe Gatien (France)	2. Qiao Hong (China)
3. Jörgen Persson (Sweden)	3. Hyun Jung Hwa (South Korea)
4. Jörg Rosskopf (Germany)	4. Li Bun Hui (North Korea)
5. Ma Wenge (China)	5. Gao Jun (China)
6. Andrzej Grubba (Poland)	6. Chen Zihe (China)
6. Kim Taek Soo (South Korea)	7. Zhang Qin (China)
8. Jean-Michel Saive (Belgium)	8. Chan Tan Lui (Hong Kong)
9. Li Gun Sang (North Korea)	9. Chai Po Wa (Hong Kong)
10. Yoo Nam Kyu (South Korea)	10. Yu Sun Bok (North Korea)

TENNIS

As John McEnroe and Jimmy Connors, those aging champions, headed into the sunset of their careers, a new generation of players from the United States dominated men's tennis in 1992. For the first half of an Olympic year, Jim Courier looked so invincible there was even talk of the sturdy, broad-shouldered, unsmiling man from Dade City, Fla., completing the grand slam of all four major titles, a feat that many had deemed impossible for anyone in this age of relentless competition. Courier, who could easily have been pitching for his beloved Cincinnati Reds rather than pounding a tennis ball, won the Australian Open convincingly, beating Stefan Edberg of Sweden 6–3, 3–6, 6–4, 6–2 in a reversal of the U.S. Open final the previous year, and then dropped just one set in defending his French Open title in early June.

Courier's run ended emphatically on the first Saturday of Wimbledon, when he was beaten in the third round by Andrey Olhovskiy, a qualifier from Russia ranked 193rd. "Any player can beat anyone on the right day," Courier reflected, a message that Andre Agassi took to heart over the following few days as he swept to the Wimbledon title, his first in grand slam competition, reducing such great grass-

court champions as McEnroe and Boris Becker of Germany to stumbling incompetence by the audacity and power of his service returns. Only the determination of Edberg, who fought for a total of 22 hours to defend his U.S. Open title, thwarted the first sweep of the grand slams by Americans since Don Budge in 1938.

To cap a good year for the U.S., Courier fended off Edberg to gain the number one ranking on the Association of Tennis Professionals (ATP) tour, and the U.S. team, with McEnroe and Agassi to the fore, won back the Davis Cup. In the final in December in Fort Worth, Texas, against Switzerland, Agassi got the U.S. off to a fast start with a 6–1, 6–2, 6–2 triumph over Jakob Hlasek, who had not lost a match in previous Davis Cup rounds. The Swiss, who were competing in their first Davis Cup final, then rallied when Marc Rosset defeated Courier 6–3, 6–7, 3–6, 6–4, 6–4. In the doubles McEnroe and Pete Sampras gave the U.S. a 2–1 lead by defeating Hlasek and Rosset 6–7, 6–7, 7–5, 6–1, 6–2. Courier then avenged his earlier loss and clinched the cup for the U.S. by triumphing over Hlasek 6–3, 3–6, 6–3, 6–4. The fifth match was not played. The victory was the 30th for the U.S. in Davis Cup competition.

Courier's heroics were at first matched and then surpassed by Monica Seles of Yugoslavia in women's competition. Seles, too, went to the green and forbidding lawns of the All England Club at Wimbledon with the Australian and French Open titles safely deposited in her ever increasing collection of grand slam titles. However, still relatively inexperienced on the grass surface and upset by the attention paid to her on-court shrieks, she was a disconsolate figure in the final and was badly beaten by Germany's Steffi Graf, the defending champion. She recovered, though, to win the U.S. Open, thus taking the Australian, French, and U.S. Open titles for the second year in succession at the age of just 18. She also maintained her number one ranking for the whole year, staving off the challenges of Graf; Gabriela Sabatini of Argentina, who won five titles on the Kraft tour in the first half of the year; and Arantxa Sánchez Vicario of Spain.

The year would also be remembered for the retirement from full-time competition of McEnroe, one of the game's greatest and most controversial champions. Though he never seriously threatened to round off his career with his eighth grand slam singles title, McEnroe was still sharp enough to reach the semifinals of Wimbledon, where he first came to prominence as a qualifier in 1977, and to produce the most remarkable result of the year when he outthought and humiliated Becker, the defending champion, 6–4, 6–3, 7–5 in the third round of the Australian Open. By taking the ball impossibly early and putting intolerable pressure on Becker's passing strokes, he shattered the German's nerve to imprint one final stamp of genius on a game he had graced and disgraced in equal measure. McEnroe did not rule out a return at Wimbledon or the U.S. Open, but he decided that he would not play the full tour in 1993.

In Australia, McEnroe's run was ended by Wayne Ferreira of South Africa, while another emerging talent, Richard Krajicek of The Netherlands, reached the semifinals before withdrawing with a sore serving shoulder. In the finals Courier was simply too strong for Edberg, who had just recovered from an injury, while Seles was never seriously troubled by Mary Joe Fernandez of the U.S. in the women's final, winning 6–2, 6–3.

The French Open on the red clay of the Roland Garros stadium near Paris was enlivened by the Gallic heroics of Henri Leconte and by the emergence of Petr Korda, a Czechoslovak left-hander of sublime talent and erratic nature, who reached his first grand slam final but found the

Andre Agassi returns a shot in his 6–7, 6–4, 6–4, 1–6, 6–4 victory at Wimbledon over Goran Ivanisevic of Croatia. It was the first grand slam title of Agassi's career and the first time an American had won the men's Wimbledon since 1984.
DUOMO

occasion, and Courier, overpowering. "He is a machine," Korda said. Once Courier, who had humiliated Agassi in the semifinals, had stemmed an early flow of winners by Korda, he won much as he wished 7–5, 6–2, 6–1, celebrating his triumph with a speech in French that cost him more effort than winning the title itself. The women's final, which lasted 2 hours 43 minutes, produced some breathtaking tennis. In the end, Seles' tenacity was the deciding factor, though Graf saved four match points at 5–3 in the third set, broke back twice when Seles was serving for the title, and faltered only on the sixth match point, the Yugoslav winning 6–2, 3–6, 10–8 amid rising excitement to become the first woman since Hilde Sperling in 1937 to win three successive French Open titles.

A month later the tables were conclusively turned on the centre court at Wimbledon. On a dismal afternoon, punctuated by five breaks for rain, Graf won her fourth Wimbledon title with a 6–2, 6–1 triumph over Seles that was every bit as crushing as the score suggests. Seles had beaten Nathalie Tauziat and Martina Navratilova on the way to the final, but both opponents had complained to the umpire about the grunting sound that Seles made when she hit the ball. Perhaps distracted by the need to be silent, Seles was strangely muted in voice and deed throughout a one-sided final. At the age of 23, Graf had now taken over from Navratilova as the dominant grass-court player of her generation.

Agassi's astonishing triumph not only answered the critics, who had suggested he did not have the nerve to win a grand slam title, but also dispelled the widely held notion that the grass-court game was becoming the exclusive preserve of giants with huge serves. On this fastest of all surfaces, Agassi's speed of hand and eye proved more than a match for the big serves of Becker and Croatia's Goran Ivanisevic. Ivanisevic served an extraordinary 206 aces in seven matches through the tournament, but the final was decided by two double faults in the last game that gave Agassi a 6–7, 6–4, 6–4, 1–6, 6–4 victory and his first grand slam title in only his 13th match on grass. Defending Wimbledon champion Michael Stich of Germany was easily beaten by Sampras in the quarterfinals.

Agassi's adventures, though, were nothing compared with the exploits of Edberg at the U.S. Open in Flushing Meadow, N.Y. Three times the defending champion had to come from behind in the final set—against Krajicek, Ivan Lendl, and Michael Chang—to reach the final. His 6–7,

7–5, 7–6, 5–7, 6–4 semifinal win over Chang, lasting 5 hours 26 minutes, was the longest ever at the U.S. Open and a tribute to the Swede's resilience. In comparison, the final was straightforward, Edberg beating Sampras 3–6, 6–4, 7–6, 6–2 to earn his sixth grand slam title. Earlier, Connors had celebrated his 40th birthday with an emotional victory over Jamie Oncins in a first-round match postponed until Wednesday and carefully stage-managed for U.S. television. There was to be no repeat of the heroics of the previous year as Connors bowed out, perhaps for the last time, to Lendl in the next round. In the women's final Seles beat Sánchez Vicario 6–3, 6–3.

Jennifer Capriati rescued an otherwise disappointing year by winning the Olympic gold medal in Barcelona, Spain, beating defending champion Graf 3–6, 6–3, 6–4 in the final, while the unheralded Rosset, who beat Jordi Arrese of Spain 7–6, 6–4, 3–6, 4–6, 8–6 in the final, won gold in the men's singles. With Hlasek, Rosset also led Switzerland to the final of the Davis Cup, while Germany beat Spain in the final of the Federation Cup. In September the U.S. rejected a plan to revive the Wightman Cup tournament as a Europe versus U.S. match.

In doubles competition Natalya Zvereva of Belarus and Gigi Fernandez of the U.S. were the dominant pair among the women, winning three grand slam titles. Sánchez Vicario and Helena Sukova of Czechoslovakia won the Australian. The men's titles were shared: McEnroe and Stich won Wimbledon with a remarkable 5–7, 7–6, 3–6, 7–6, 19–17 victory in the final over Richey Reneberg and Jim Grabb of the U.S. that lasted one minute over five hours; Australia's Todd Woodbridge and Mark Woodforde took the Australian Open, Hlasek and Rosset the French, and Grabb and Reneberg the U.S.

In February at a Virginia Slims tournament in Chicago, Martina Navratilova won her 158th championship, the most victories by any professional tennis player, man or woman. Arthur Ashe, former U.S. Open and Wimbledon champion, revealed in April that he had contracted AIDS from a blood transfusion.

Financially, tennis continued to be immune from the world recession. Both the ATP tour and the Kraft tour expected to benefit from increased prize money in 1993.

(ANDREW LONGMORE)

AP/WIDE WORLD

Sixteen-year-old Jennifer Capriati of the U.S. celebrates her victory over Steffi Graf of Germany in the tennis finals of the Olympic Games. She upset Graf, two-time gold medal winner, 3–6, 6–3, 6–4.

TRACK AND FIELD SPORTS

In the summer Olympic Games at Barcelona, Spain, in 1992, United States athletes starred in the track and field sports. U.S. men claimed 20 medals, 8 of them gold—as many victory awards as the total of the second highest nation, Kenya (2 gold, 4 silver, 2 bronze). U.S. men also won five silver and seven bronze medals.

The U.S. women claimed 10 medals, their highest total in a nonboycotted Olympics. Four of them were gold—a drop of two from the 1988 Olympics but equal to the number of 1992 winners on the Unified Team, which consisted of republics of the former Soviet Union. U.S. women also won three silvers and three bronzes, but the Unified Team maintained its supremacy with a total of 14 medals.

Men's Olympic Competition. Three world records were set in Barcelona, all by U.S. athletes. Kevin Young became the first man to run the 400-m hurdles in less than 47 seconds as his sensational clocking of 46.78 sec brought the mark down from the 47.02 run in 1983 by the event's one-time master, Edwin Moses, himself a two-time Olympic champion.

The other two records were achieved by U.S. relay teams. The 4 × 100-m squad of Michael Marsh, Leroy Burrell, Dennis Mitchell, and Carl Lewis achieved a stunning 37.40 sec, 0.10 sec faster than a U.S. foursome ran at the 1991 world championships in Tokyo. In the meet-concluding 4 × 400-m relay, the U.S. team clocked 2 min 55.74 sec to better the 2-min 56.16-sec time first run by a U.S. team in 1968 and matched by the 1988 U.S. Olympic winners. Andrew Valmon led off and was followed by Quincy Watts, who had run the second-fastest 400 m ever, 43.50 sec, to win the individual event. But Watts outdid even himself in the relay as he clocked 43.1 sec for his second leg, the fastest relay time ever. Michael Johnson ran a solid third leg before passing to Steve Lewis. The 1988 champion in the 400, Lewis finished second behind Watts in the individual 400 and then blistered a 43.4-sec anchor leg to assure the new relay record.

Michael Marsh and Carl Lewis claimed individual triumphs before their relay victory. At age 31 Lewis became the first three-time winner in the history of the Olympic long jump. His leap of 8.67 m (28 ft 5½ in) edged the 8.64 m (28 ft 4¼ in) by Mike Powell of the U.S., who had defeated Lewis at the 1991 world championships with a world record leap of 8.95 m (29 ft 4½ in).

Lewis' pair of Barcelona victories ran his total of Olympic gold medals to eight, only one short of the record of nine set during the 1920s by Finnish distance runner Paavo Nurmi. In Barcelona, Lewis and Powell were joined on the long-jump victory dais by teammate Joe Greene (8.34 m [27 ft 4½ in]) as the U.S. scored its lone medal sweep of the meet.

The unheralded Marsh, a world-class sprinter but overshadowed during the past three seasons by the domination of Michael Johnson of the U.S., sped through the 200-m dash in 20.01 sec to strike gold. Marsh clocked 19.73 sec in his semifinal race, a U.S. record and just 0.01 off the world mark. But the final was run into a head wind, thus slowing times.

Johnson was rated as one of the "surest" winners before the Olympics, but he did not qualify for the 200-m final. Markedly weakened by a virus he had contracted earlier in the summer, he was eliminated in the semifinals.

The word *upset* could describe many of Barcelona's results. No individual winner from the 1991 world championships was able to gain a gold medal; only Lewis in the long jump repeated from the 1988 Olympics.

Mark Everett runs to victory in the 600-yd event at the Millrose Games, held in Madison Square Garden in New York City in February. His time of 1 min 7.53 sec broke an indoor record that had stood for 22 years.

GEORGE TIEDEMANN—SPORTS ILLUSTRATED

Along with Johnson, Unified Team pole vaulter Sergey Bubka was a heavy favourite, but he failed to clear his opening height in the finals and ignominiously received no placing. However, his teammates Maksim Tarasov and Igor Trandenkov each cleared 5.80 m (19 ft ¼ in) to claim the gold and silver medals, with Tarasov the winner.

Kenya, which had produced four running champions in Tokyo, got only half as many in Barcelona; William Tanui won the 800 m (1 min 43.66 sec), and 20-year-old international newcomer Matthew Birir took the 3,000-m steeplechase (8 min 8.84 sec). Birir led the single medal sweep of a running event as fellow Kenyans Patrick Sang and William Mutwol claimed the silver and bronze.

Another 1-2-3 finish came from the hammer throwers of the Unified Team. Andrey Abduvaliyev became the first athlete from Tajikistan to win an Olympic title when he threw 82.54 m (270 ft 9 in) to defeat Igor Astapkovich from Belarus and Russia's Igor Nikulin. One-two U.S. finishes took place in the triple jump, by Mike Conley at 18.17 m (59 ft 7½ in, the second longest jump ever but not recognized because it was wind aided) and Charlie Simpkins at 17.60 m (57 ft 9 in), and in the shot put, by Mike Stulce at 21.70 m (71 ft 2½ in) and Jim Doehring at 20.96 m (68 ft 9¼ in).

U.S. Olympic Trials. Of the six U.S. men who won individual Olympic titles in Barcelona, only hurdler Young and putter Stulce won their events at the U.S. team selection meet, held in New Orleans, La., in late June. The trials unfailingly produce high levels of tension and competitive excellence as athlete rise—or fall—to the occasion of their one chance to make the U.S. team.

Carl Lewis was hindered by a virus and failed to earn team berths in either the 100 m or 200 m. He had won the 100 and placed first and second in the 200 at the previous two Olympics. Perhaps the most shocking nonqualifier was decathlon star Dan O'Brien, the 1991 world champion, who did not clear a height in the pole vault and finished far down in the final standings. O'Brien claimed some degree of redemption by totaling a world record 8,891 points late in the season.

Jackie Joyner-Kersee of the U.S. performs in the long jump in the course of winning the Olympic gold medal in the heptathlon. Having also taken the event in 1988, she became the only woman to win it twice.

AP/WIDE WORLD

Other Competition. Outside of the Olympic arena, action in 1992 was dominated by vaulter Bubka and Kenyan runner Moses Kiptanui. Bubka set four records, one indoors and three outdoors, and ran his total of world records to an amazing 32. His highest clearance measured 6.13 m (20 ft 1¼ in). Bubka's 16 career records outdoors were the most in an officially recognized event.

Kiptanui, the 1991 world champion in the 3,000-m steeplechase, was hampered by a knee injury at Kenya's Olympic trials and did not make the team. Soon after the Games ended, however, he set world records in the steeplechase (8 min 2.08 sec) and 3,000 m (7 min 28.96 sec)—within three days.

Another 1991 champion who did not fare as well in Barcelona was 1,500-m runner Noureddine Morceli. Finishing only seventh in the tactical Olympic race, the Algerian clocked a world record 3 min 28.86 sec a month later to cut more than one second off the former time.

During the indoor season U.S. competitors starred as sprinter Andre Cason finished the 60-m dash first in 6.45 sec and then 6.41 sec two weeks later for two world records. Danny Everett covered 400 m in 45.02 sec, while Santa Monica (Calif.) Track Club teammate Johnny Gray ran 800 m in 1 min 45.08 sec. Kiptanui and Morceli gave hints of their outdoor records to come, Kiptanui clocking 7 min 37.31 sec for 3,000 m and Morceli 2 min 15.26 sec in the 1,000 m. Christian Plaziat of France set two bests in the heptathlon, the highest totaling 6,418 points.

Outdoors, Steve Backley of the United Kingdom set a javelin record in January of 91.06 m (300 ft 1 in). The record of 96.96 m set in 1991 by Seppo Räty of Finland was disallowed because the type of javelin he used was later banned. In April the Santa Monica Track Club lowered its own 4 × 200-m relay record to 1 min 19.11 sec. The team included eventual Olympic victors Marsh, Burrell, and Lewis. In race walking, records were set on the track at distances of 20 km (1 hr 18 min 35.2 sec by Stefan Johansson of Sweden) and 30 km (2 hr 1 min 44 sec by Maurizio Damilano of Italy).

The outdoor season concluded with the sixth staging of the World Cup, a team competition for national and continental squads. Held in Havana, the first renewal of the meet since 1989 saw Africa's team win the men's championship and the Unified Team women retain their title. The U.S. men placed fifth, the team's lowest ranking in the meet's 15-year history. The American women placed fourth, equal to their best finish ever.

Women's International Competition. As in 1991, women set no individual world records outdoors. Nevertheless, as with the men, the Olympic Games produced electrifying competition. Among many outstanding performances the spotlight fell on two U.S. sprinters, Gail Devers (*see* BI-OGRAPHIES) and Gwen Torrence. Devers, who overcame a debilitating thyroid disease in 1991, stunned the 100-m field as she narrowly won in 10.82 sec. Premeet favourite Torrence ran only fourth in that race and then made not-too-veiled accusations that some of her foes were users of performance-enhancing drugs.

The ensuing controversy did not deter Torrence, who won the 200-m gold medal with a time of 21.81 sec, anchored the U.S. team to the 4 × 100-m relay title at 42.11 sec, and then contributed a leg on the second-place U.S. 4 × 400-m relay.

In her specialty, the 100-m hurdles, Devers barreled along with a wide lead in the final only to smash the final barrier, fall, and barely scramble over the finish in fifth place. The win went to unheralded Paraskevi Patoulidou, who became the first Greek woman ever to win an Olympic track and field medal—let alone a championship gold.

Only three winners at the 1991 world championships repeated in Barcelona: Marie-Jose Pérec of France (400 m), Algeria's Hassiba Boulmerka (1,500 m), and Germany's Heike Henkel (high jump). The lone repeat winner from the 1988 Olympics was U.S. star Jackie Joyner-Kersee, who became the first woman ever to win consecutive Olympic heptathlons. But Joyner-Kersee was beaten in her other strong event, the long jump, by career-long rival Heike Drechsler of Germany, who claimed her first-ever win over Joyner-Kersee in a championship meet.

Lynn Jennings placed third at 10,000 m in a U.S. record time of 31 min 19.89 sec. The race was won by Derartu Tulu of Ethiopia in 31 min 6.02 sec. Elana Meyer of South Africa placed second with 31 min 11.75 sec. Meyer's nation made its return to the Olympic arena for the first time since 1960 following more than three decades of international sports isolation due to its apartheid racial policies.

Another piece of Olympic history was made by the leadoff runner on the winning U.S. team in the 4 × 100-m relay: 35-year-old Evelyn Ashford, who first ran in the Olympics at Montreal in 1976. The 1984 champion in the 100 m, Ashford won her fourth Olympic gold medal on the 1992 relay team.

During the indoor season women's world records were set by Jamaica's Merlene Ottey (6.96 sec for 60 m), Great Britain's Liz McColgan (15 min 3.17 sec for 5,000 m), Henkel (2.07 m [6 ft 9½ in] in the high jump), and Russia's Irina Byelova twice in the pentathlon (4,720 points, then 4,991). Romania's Liliana Nastase totaled 4,726 between Byelova's records.

World 1992 Outdoor Records—Men

Event	Competitor and country	Performance
1,500 m	Noureddine Morceli (Algeria)	3 min 28.86 sec
3,000 m	Moses Kiptanui (Kenya)	7 min 28.96 sec
3,000-m steeplechase	Moses Kiptanui (Kenya)	8 min 2.08 sec
400-m hurdles	Kevin Young (U.S.)	46.78 sec
20,000-m walk	Stefan Johansson (Sweden)	1 hr 18 min 35.2 sec
30,000-m walk	Maurizio Damilano (Italy)	2 hr 1 min 44 sec
4 × 100-m relay	U.S. (Marsh, Burrell, Mitchell, C. Lewis)	37.40 sec
4 × 200-m relay	Santa Monica Track Club (U.S.) (Marsh, Burrell, Heard, C. Lewis)	1 min 19.11 sec
4 × 400-m relay	U.S. (Valmon, Watts, Johnson, S. Lewis)	2 min 55.74 sec
Pole vault	Sergey Bubka (Ukraine)	6.11 m (20 ft ½ in)
Pole vault	Sergey Bubka (Ukraine)	6.12 m (20 ft 1 in)
Pole vault	Sergey Bubka (Ukraine)	6.13 m (20 ft 1¼ in)
Javelin	Steve Backley (U.K.)	91.46 m (300 ft 1 in)
Decathlon	Dan O'Brien (U.S.)	8,891 points

No world records for women were set in 1992.

Cross Country and Marathon Running. Lynn Jennings won her third consecutive women's title at the world cross country championships in leading her U.S. team to second place as Kenya successfully defended its title. Kenya's men dominated the competition, retaining the team crown behind a 1-2 finish by John Ngugi and William Mutwol.

The Olympic marathons were the prime 41.9-km (26-mi) races of the year. The victors in Barcelona were South Korea's Hwang Young Cho (2 hr 13 min 23 sec) and the Unified Team's Valentina Yegorova (2 hr 32 min 41 sec).

The world half-marathon championship was won by yet another Kenyan, Benson Masya, who covered the 21.1-km (13.1-mi) distance in 1 hr 24 sec in leading his nation to the team title. Liz McColgan won the women's title for the U.K. at 1 hr 8 min 53 sec, while Japan won the team championship.

The men's and women's winners of other major marathons in 1992 were: Boston, Ibrahim Hussein (Kenya) 2 hr 8 min 14 sec and Olga Markova (Russia) 2 hr 23 min 43 sec; Rotterdam, Neth., Salvador Garcia (Mexico) 2 hr 9 min 19 sec and Aurora Cunha (Portugal) 2 hr 29 min 14 sec; London, Antonio Pinto (Portugal) 2 hr 10 min 2 sec and Katrin Dörre (Germany) 2 hr 29 min 39 sec; New York, Willie Mtolo (South Africa) 2 hr 9 min 29 sec and Lisa Ondieki (Australia) 2 hr 24 min 40 sec.

(BERT NELSON; JON HENDERSHOTT)

VOLLEYBALL

The United States men's and women's volleyball teams proved that they remained among the elite following bronze medal performances at the 1992 Olympic Games. No other country won medals in both the men's and women's volleyball competition in Barcelona, Spain, and this marked the second time in the past three Olympics that the Americans had accomplished the feat, the other being 1984. Volleyball became one of the main focal points of the Olympics following the controversial reversal of the U.S.-Japan men's match, which the U.S. originally won 3–2. After the Americans lost the match because of a ruling by the International Volleyball Federation that awarded Japan a disputed penalty point, all members of the U.S. team shaved their heads and proceeded to win five consecutive matches, including a 3–1 decision over Olympic favourite Italy. In the match for the gold medal, undefeated Brazil triumphed over The Netherlands 15–12, 15–8, 15–5. The U.S. gained the bronze by defeating Cuba.

In women's Olympic competition, the favoured teams included Cuba, the U.S., the Unified Team (comprising former republics of the Soviet Union), and China. China struggled throughout the tournament and finished a surprising seventh in the eight-team field, while Cuba captured its first Olympic gold medal in women's volleyball by defeating the Unified Team 16–14, 12–15, 15–12, 15–13. The U.S. beat Brazil in the bronze medal match. Paula Weishoff of the U.S. was named the most outstanding player of the competition.

The World League, following its third season, expanded from 10 to 12 countries, and the quality of play continued to improve. The league was divided into three four-team pools, and the season was contested from mid-May through late June, followed by the semifinals and finals in September. Italy claimed its third successive championship by downing Cuba in the final, while the U.S. beat The Netherlands in the bronze medal match. The future also looked bright for women's competition with the implementation of a $1 million Grand Prix tournament beginning in 1993; the format would be similar to that of the World League.

(RICHARD S. WANNINGER)

WEIGHT LIFTING

The Unified Team, composed of former Soviet Union republics, dominated the weight-lifting competition at the Olympic Games at Barcelona, Spain, in 1992. All 10 Unified Team lifters earned medals: five gold, four silver, and one bronze. Bulgaria, in recent years the Soviets' closest rival, finished with one gold, two silvers, and one bronze. The other four gold medals in the 10 weight classes were won by Germany, Greece, South Korea, and Turkey.

In the 1988 Olympics three world records were set in the total lifts, three in the snatch, and one in the clean and jerk. In addition, eight Olympic marks were recorded in the snatch, six in the clean and jerk, and seven in the total lifts. At Barcelona only a single world mark was set: in the snatch. New Olympic records included one in the snatch and one in the clean and jerk. Many observers expressed the opinion that the sharply reduced number of records at Barcelona might be attributed to the nations' aggressive education program against substance abuse, mainly steroids.

Naim Suleymanoglu of Turkey won his second straight Olympic gold medal in the 60-kg (132-lb) class. His total lift of 320 kg (705 lb) was 22 kg less than in 1988. The only other defending champion to repeat was the Unified Team's super heavyweight, Aleksandr Kurlovich. His total lift of 450 kg (992 lb) was 12 kg less than his 1988 effort. Pyrros Dimas of Greece won the 82.5-kg (181.5-lb) crown. This was Greece's first weight-lifting Olympic gold medal since Perikles Kakousis won the since-discontinued two-hand lift in the super heavyweight class in 1904. For a list of the gold medalists in the total lifts, *see* Special Report.

(CHARLES ROBERT PAUL, JR.)

WRESTLING

The Unified Team, consisting of republics of the former Soviet Union, won both the freestyle and Greco-Roman wrestling championships at the Olympic Games in late July and early August 1992 in Barcelona, Spain. In the freestyle competition the Unified Team won three gold, two silver, and two bronze medals. The U.S. finished in second place with three golds, two silvers, and one bronze. The unofficial score was: Unified Team 77 points, U.S. 75 points, and Iran 52 points.

In Greco-Roman wrestling the Unified Team won handily with three golds, three silvers, and three bronzes. Cuba finished second with one gold and two bronzes. Unofficial scores were: Unified Team 90 points, Cuba 43 points, and U.S., Hungary, Poland, and Germany 38 points.

The 62nd U.S. collegiate championships were held March 19–21 in Oklahoma City, Okla. Iowa repeated as champion, winning its 13th team title. Rated as one of the top collegiate teams ever, the Hawkeyes scored 149 points. Oklahoma State finished second with 100.50 points, and Penn State was third with 89.25 points. (MARVIN G. HESS)

This article updates the *Macropædia* article Major Team and Individual SPORTS and *Micropædia* entries on the various sports.

Olympic Games Wrestling Champions, 1992

Weight class	Freestyle	Greco-Roman
48 kg (105.5 lb)	Park Il (N. Korea)	O. Kutherenko (Unified Team)
52 kg (114.5 lb)	Li Hak (N. Korea)	J. Ronningen (Norway)
57 kg (125.5 lb)	A. Puerto (Cuba)	An Han Bong (S. Korea)
62 kg (136.5 lb)	J. Smith (U.S.)	A. Pirim (Turkey)
68 kg (149.5 lb)	A. Fadzyev (Unified Team)	A. Repka (Hungary)
74 kg (163 lb)	Park Jang (S. Korea)	M. Iskandarian (Unified Team)
82 kg (180.5 lb)	K. Jackson (U.S.)	P. Farkas (Hungary)
90 kg (198 lb)	M. Khadartsev (Unified Team)	M. Bullman (Germany)
100 kg (220 lb)	L. Khabelov (Unified Team)	H. Milian (Cuba)
130 kg (286 lb)	B. Baumgartner (U.S.)	A. Karelin (Unified Team)

Sporting Record

ARCHERY

FITA Outdoor World Target Archery Championships

year	men's individual		men's team		women's individual		women's team	
	winner	points	winner	points	winner	points	winner	points
1983	R. McKinney (U.S.)	2,617	United States	7,812	Kim Jin Ho (S.Kor.)	2,616	South Korea	7,704
1985	R. McKinney (U.S.)	2,601	South Korea	7,660	I. Soldatova (U.S.S.R.)	2,595	U.S.S.R.	7,721
1987	V. Esheyev (U.S.S.R.)	329	West Germany	891	Ma Xiangjun (China)	330	U.S.S.R.	884
1989	S. Zabrodsky (U.S.S.R.)	332	U.S.S.R.	985	Kim Soo Nyung (S.Kor.)	338	South Korea	995
1991	S. Fairweather (Australia)	334	South Korea	998	Kim Soo Nyung (S. Kor.)	333	South Korea	1,030

ATHLETICS

World Cup Championship—men

	100 metre	*200 metre*	*400 metre*	*800 metre*	*1,500 metre*
1981	A. Wells (Europe)	M. Lattany (U.S.)	C. Wiley (U.S.)	S. Coe (Europe)	S. Ovett (Europe)
1985	B. Johnson (Americas)	R. Caetano da Silva (Americas)	M. Franks (U.S.)	S. Koskei (Africa)	O. Khalifa (Africa)
1989	L. Christie (Gr.Brit.)	R. Caetano da Silva (Americas)	R. Hernandez (Americas)	T. McKean (Gr.Brit.)	A. Bile (Africa)

	5,000 metre	*10,000 metre*	*Steeplechase*	*110-m hurdles*	*400-m hurdles*
1981	E. Coghlan (Europe)	W. Schildhauer (E.Ger.)	B. Maminski (Europe)	G. Foster (U.S.)	E. Moses (U.S.)
1985	D. Padilla (U.S.)	W. Bulti (Africa)	J. Kariuki (Africa)	T. Campbell (U.S.)	A. Phillips (U.S.)
1989	S. Aouita (Africa)	S. Antibo (Europe)	J. Kariuki (Africa)	R. Kingdom (U.S.)	D. Patrick (U.S.)

	4 × 100 relays	*4 × 400 relays*	*Triple jump*	*High jump*	*Pole vault*
1981	Europe	United States	J. de Oliveira (Americas)	T. Peacock (U.S.)	K. Volkov (U.S.S.R.)
1985	United States	United States	W. Banks (U.S.)	P. Sjoberg (Europe)	S. Bubka (U.S.S.R.)
1989	United States	Americas	M. Conley (U.S.)	P. Sjoberg (Europe)	P. Collet (Europe)

	Long jump	*Shot put*	*Discus throw*	*Hammer throw*	*Javelin throw*
1981	C. Lewis (U.S.)	U. Beyer (E.Ger.)	A. Lemme (E.Ger.)	Yu. Sedykh (U.S.S.R.)	D. Kula (U.S.S.R.)
1985	M. Conley (U.S.)	U. Timmermann (E.Ger.)	G. Kolnootchenko (U.S.S.R.)	Yu. Tamm (U.S.S.R.)	U. Hohn (E.Ger.)
1989	L. Myricks (U.S.)	U. Timmermann (E.Ger.)	J. Schult (E.Ger.)	H. Weis (Europe)	S. Backley (Gr.Brit.)

	Team		*Marathon*		
1981	Europe		1985	A. Salah (Djibouti)	
1985	United States		1987	A. Salah (Djibouti)	
1989	United States		1989	K. Metaferia (Ethiopia)	
			1991	Y. Tolstikov (U.S.S.R.)	

World Cup Championship—women

	100 metre	*200 metre*	*400 metre*	*800 metre*	*1,500 metre*
1981	E. Ashford (U.S.)	E. Ashford (U.S.)	J. Kratochvílová (Europe)	L. Veselkova (U.S.S.R.)	T. Sorokina (U.S.S.R.)
1985	M. Göhr (E.Ger.)	M. Koch (E.Ger.)	M. Koch (E.Ger.)	C. Wachtel (E.Ger.)	H. Korner (E.Ger.)
1989	S. Echols (U.S.)	S. Moller (E.Ger.)	A. Quirot (Americas)	A. Quirot (Americas)	P. Ivan (Europe)

	3,000 metre	*10,000 metre*	*100-m hurdles*	*400-m hurdles*	*4 × 100 relays*
1981	A. Zauber (E.Ger.)	—	T. Anisimova (U.S.S.R.)	E. Neumann (E.Ger.)	East Germany
1985	U. Bruns (E.Ger.)	A. Cunha (Europe)	C. Oschkenat (E.Ger.)	S. Busch (E.Ger.)	East Germany
1989	Y. Murray (Europe)	K. Ullrich (E.Ger.)	C. Oschkenat (E.Ger.)	S. Farmer-Patrick (U.S.)	East Germany

	4 × 400 relays	*High jump*	*Long jump*	*Shot put*	*Discus throw*
1981	East Germany	U. Meyfarth (Europe)	S. Ulbricht (E.Ger.)	I. Slupianek (E.Ger.)	E. Jahl (E.Ger.)
1985	East Germany	S. Kostadinova (U.S.S.R.)	H. Daute Drechsler (E.Ger.)	N. Lisovskaya (U.S.S.R.)	M. Optiz (E.Ger.)
1989	Americas	S. Costa (Americas)	G. Chistyakova (U.S.S.R.)	Zhihong Huang (Asia)	I. Wyludda (E.Ger.)

	Javelin throw	*Team*	*Marathon*		
1981	A. Todorova (Europe)	East Germany	1985	K. Dörre (E.Ger.)	
1985	O. Gavrilova (U.S.S.R.)	East Germany	1987	Z. Ivanova (U.S.S.R.)	
1989	P. Felke (E.Ger.)	East Germany	1989	S. Marchiano (U.S.)	
			1991	R. Mota (Port.)	

Kim Soo Nyung: FITA Outdoor World Target Archery Championships— women's individual (1991)

ROBERT RHODE

For records of previous years, *see* the entry SPORTING RECORD in the *Micropædia*.

World Track-and-Field Championships—men

event	1987	1991
100 m	B. Johnson (Can.)	C. Lewis (U.S.)
200 m	C. Smith (U.S.)	M. Johnson (U.S.)
400 m	T. Schoenlebe (E.Ger.)	A. Pettigrew (U.S.)
800 m	B. Konchellah (Kenya)	B. Konchellah (Kenya)
1,500 m	A. Bile (Som.)	N. Morceli (Alg.)
5,000 m	S. Aouita (Mor.)	Y. Ondieki (Kenya)
10,000 m	P. Kipkoech (Kenya)	M. Tanui (Kenya)
steeplechase	F. Panetta (Italy)	M. Kiptanui (Kenya)
110-m hurdles	G. Foster (U.S.)	G. Foster (U.S.)
400-m hurdles	E. Moses (U.S.)	S. Matete (Zambia)
marathon	D. Wakihuru (Kenya)	H. Taniguchi (Japan)
20-km walk	M. Damilano (Italy)	M. Damilano (Italy)
50-km walk	H. Gauder (E.Ger.)	A. Potashov (U.S.S.R.)
4 × 100 m relay	United States (L. McRae, L. McNeil, H. Glance, C. Lewis)	United States (A. Cason, L. Burrell, D. Mitchell, C. Lewis)
4 × 400 m relay	United States (D. Everett, R. Haley, A. McKay, H. Reynolds)	Great Britain (R. Black, D. Redmond, J. Regis, K. Akabusi)
high jump	P. Sjöberg (Swed.)	C. Austin (U.S.)
pole vault	S. Bubka (U.S.S.R.)	S. Bubka (U.S.S.R.)
long jump	C. Lewis (U.S.)	M. Powell (U.S.)
triple jump	C. Markov (Bulg.)	K. Harrison (U.S.)
shot put	W. Guenther (Switz.)	W. Günthör (Switz.)
discus throw	J. Schult (E.Ger.)	L. Riedel (Ger.)
hammer throw	S. Litvinov (U.S.S.R.)	Y. Sedykh (U.S.S.R.)
javelin throw	S. Raty (Fin.)	K. Kinnunen (Fin.)
decathlon	T. Voss (E.Ger.)	D. O'Brien (U.S.)

H. Henkel: World Track-and-Field Championships—women's high jump (1991)
GRAY MORTIMORE—ALLSPORT

World Track-and-Field Championships—women

event	1987	1991
100 m	S. Gladisch (E.Ger.)	K. Krabbe (Ger.)
200 m	S. Gladisch (E.Ger.)	K. Krabbe (Ger.)
400 m	O. Bryzgina (U.S.S.R.)	M.-J. Pérec (Fr.)
800 m	S. Wodars (E.Ger.)	L. Nurutdinova (U.S.S.R.)
1,500 m	T. Samolenko (U.S.S.R.)	H. Boulmerka (Alg.)
3,000 m	T. Samolenko (U.S.S.R.)	T. Dorovskikh (U.S.S.R.)
10,000 m*	I. Kristiansen (Nor.)	L. McColgan (U.K.)
100-m hurdles	G. Zagorcheva (Bulg.)	L. Narozhilenko (U.S.S.R.)
400-m hurdles	S. Busch (E.Ger.)	T. Ledovskaya (U.S.S.R.)
marathon	R. Mota (Port.)	W. Panfil (Pol.)
10-km walk*	I. Strakhova (U.S.S.R.)	A. Ivanova (U.S.S.R.)
4 × 100 m relay	United States (A. Brown, D. Williams, F. Griffith, P. Marshall)	Jamaica (D. Duhaney, J. Cuthbert, B. McDonald, M. Ottey)
4 × 400 m relay	East Germany (D. Neubauer, K. Emmelmann, P. Mueller, S. Busch)	U.S.S.R. (T. Ledovskaya, L. Dzhigalova, O. Nazarova, O. Bryzgina)
high jump	S. Kostadinova (Bulg.)	H. Henkel (Ger.)
long jump	J. Joyner-Kersee (U.S.)	J. Joyner-Kersee (U.S.)
shot put	N. Lisovskaya (U.S.S.R.)	Huang Zhihong (China)
discus throw	M. Hellmann (E.Ger.)	T. Khristova (Bulg.)
javelin throw	F. Whitbread (U.K.)	Xu Demei (China)
heptathlon	J. Joyner-Kersee (U.S.)	S. Braun (Ger.)

World Cross-Country Championship—men (12,000 m)

year	individual	team
1987	J. Ngugi (Kenya)	Kenya
1988	J. Ngugi (Kenya)	Kenya
1989	J. Ngugi (Kenya)	Kenya
1990	K. Shah (Mor.)	Kenya
1991	K. Shah (Mor.)	Kenya
1992	J. Ngugi (Kenya)	Kenya

World Cross-Country Championship—women (5,000 m)

year	individual	team
1987	A. Sergent (Fr.)	United States
1988	I. Christiansen (Nor.)	U.S.S.R.
1989	A. Sergent (Fr.)	U.S.S.R.
1990	L. Jennings (U.S.)	U.S.S.R.
1991	L. Jennings (U.S.)	Kenya
1992	L. Jennings (U.S.)	Kenya

Boston Marathon

year	men	h:min:s	women	h:min:s
1988	I. Hussein (Kenya)	2:08:43	R. Mota (Port.)	2:24:30
1989	A. Mekonnen (Ethiopia)	2:09:06	I. Kristiansen (Nor.)	2:24:33
1990	G. Bordin (Italy)	2:08:19	R. Mota (Port.)	2:25:23
1991	I. Hussein (Kenya)	2:11:06	W. Panfil (Pol.)	2:24:18
1992	I. Hussein (Kenya)	2:08:14	O. Markova (Russia)	2:23:43

New York Marathon

year	men	h:min:s	women	h:min:s
1988	S. Jones (Wales)	2:08:20	G. Waitz (Nor.)	2:28:07
1989	J. Ikangaa (Tanzania)	2:08:01	I. Kristiansen (Nor.)	2:25:30
1990	D. Wakiihuri (Kenya)	2:12:39	W. Panfil (Pol.)	2:30:45
1991	S. Garcia (Mex.)	2:09:28	L. McColgan (Scot.)	2:27:23
1992	W. Mtolo (S.Afr.)	2:09:29	L. Ondieki (Austl.)	2:24:40

Chicago Marathon

year	men	h:min:s	women	h:min:s
1988	A. Cruz (Mex.)	2:08:57	L. Weidenbach (U.S.)	2:29:17
1989	P. Davies-Hale (U.K.)	2:11:25	L. Weidenbach (U.S.)	2:28:15
1990	M. Pitayo (Mex.)	2:09:41	A. Cunha (Port.)	2:30:11
1991	J. Silva (Braz.)	2:14:33	M. Hamrin-Senorski (Swed.)	2:36:21
1992	J.C. de Souza (Braz.)	2:16:14	L. Somers (U.S.)	2:37:41

W. Mtolo: New York Marathon—men (1992)
STEVEN E. SUTTON—DUOMO

AUTOMOBILE RACING

Indy Car Champions*

year	driver
1987/88	R. Mears
1988/89	E. Fittipaldi
1990	A. Unser, Jr.
1991	Mi. Andretti
1992	B. Rahal

*USAC until 1989.

Indianapolis 500

year	winner	avg. speed in mph
1988	R. Mears	144.809
1989	E. Fittipaldi	167.581
1990	A. Luyendyk	185.984
1991	R. Mears	176.457
1992	A. Unser, Jr.	134.479

International Cup for Formula One Manufacturers

year	car	year	car
1987	Williams/Honda	1990	McLaren/Honda
1988	McLaren/Honda	1991	McLaren/Honda
1989	McLaren/Honda	1992	Williams/Renault

World Championship of Drivers

year	winner	car
1988	A. Senna (Braz.)	McLaren/Honda
1989	A. Prost (Fr.)	McLaren/Honda
1990	A. Senna (Braz.)	McLaren/Honda
1991	A. Senna (Braz.)	McLaren/Honda
1992	N. Mansell (U.K.)	Williams/Renault

Le Mans 24-hour Grand Prix d'Endurance

year	car	drivers
1988	Jaguar	J. Lammers, J. Dumfries, A. Wallace
1989	Mercedes-Benz	J. Mass, M. Reuter, S. Dickens
1990	Jaguar	J. Nielsen, P. Cobb, M. Brundle
1991	Mazda	V. Weidler, J. Herbert, B. Gachot
1992	Peugeot	Y. Dalmas, M. Blundell, D. Warwick

Monte-Carlo Rally

year	car	driver, codriver
1988	Lancia Delta 4WD	Saby, Fauchille
1989	Lancia	Biasion, Siviero
1990	Lancia	Auriol, Ocelli
1991	Toyota Celica	Sainz, Moya
1992	Lancia	Kankkunen

National Association for Stock Car Auto Racing (NASCAR) Winston Cup Champions

year	winner	year	winner
1987	D. Earnhardt	1990	D. Earnhardt
1988	B. Elliott	1991	D. Earnhardt
1989	R. Wallace	1992	A. Kulwicki

Peugeot—Y. Dalmas, M. Blundell, D. Warwick: Le Mans 24-hour Grand Prix d'Endurance (1992)

MAO—VANDYSTADT/ALLSPORT

A. Kulwicki: NASCAR Winston Cup champion (1992)

STEVE SWOPE—SPORTSLIGHT

BADMINTON

World Badminton Championships

year	men's singles	women's singles	men's doubles	women's doubles
1983	I. Sugiarto (Indon.)	Li Lingwei (China)	S. Fladberg, J. Helledie (Den.)	Lin Ying, Wu Dixi (China)
1985	Han Jian (China)	Han Aiping (China)	Park Joo Bong, Kim Moon Soo (S.Kor.)	Han Aiping, Li Lingwei (China)
1987	Yang Yang (China)	Han Aiping (China)	Li Yongbo, Tian Bingyi (China)	Lin Ying, Guan Weizhen (China)
1989	Yang Yang (China)	Li Lingwei (China)	Li Yongbo, Tian Bingyi (China)	Lin Ying, Guan Weizhen (China)
1991	Zhao Jianhua (China)	Tang Jiuhong (China)	Park Joo Bong, Kim Moon Soo (S. Kor.)	Guan Weizhen, Nong Qunhua (China)

All-England Championships—singles

year	men	women
1988	I. Frederiksen (Den.)	Gu Jiaming (China)
1989	Yang Yang (China)	Li Lingwei (China)
1990	Zhao Jianhua (China)	S. Susanti (Indon.)
1991	A. Wiranata (Indon.)	S. Susanti (Indon.)
1992	Liu Jun (China)	Tang Jiuhong (China)

Uber Cup (women)

year	winner	runner-up
1983–84	China	England
1985–86	China	Indonesia
1987–88	China	S.Korea
1989–90	China	S.Korea
1991–92	China	S. Korea

Thomas Cup (men)

year	winner	runner-up
1983–84	Indonesia	China
1985–86	China	Indonesia
1987–88	China	Malaysia
1989–90	China	Malaysia
1991–92	Malaysia	Indonesia

BASEBALL

Toronto Blue Jays: World Series (1992)
RICK STEWART—ALLSPORT

Baseball Hall of Fame

year elected	members
1988	Willie Stargell
1989	Johnny Bench, Carl Yastrzemski
1990	Joe Morgan, Jim Palmer
1991	Rod Carew, Ferguson Jenkins, Gaylord Perry
1992	Rollie Fingers, Tom Seaver

World Series*

year	winning team	losing team	results
1988	Los Angeles Dodgers (NL)	Oakland Athletics (AL)	4–1
1989	Oakland Athletics (AL)	San Francisco Giants (NL)	4–0
1990	Cincinnati Reds (NL)	Oakland Athletics (AL)	4–0
1991	Minnesota Twins (AL)	Atlanta Braves (NL)	4–3
1992	Toronto Blue Jays (AL)	Atlanta Braves (NL)	4–2

*AL—American League; NL—National League.

Japan Series*

year	winning team	losing team	results
1988	Seibu Lions (PL)	Chunichi Dragons (CL)	4–1
1989	Yomiuri Giants (CL)	Kintetsu Buffaloes (PL)	4–3
1990	Seibu Lions (PL)	Yomiuri Giants (CL)	4–0
1991	Seibu Lions (PL)	Hiroshima Tōyō Carp (CL)	4–3
1992	Seibu Lions (PL)	Yakult Swallows (CL)	4–3

*CL—Central League; PL—Pacific League.

BASKETBALL

National Basketball Association (NBA) Championship

season	winner	runner-up	results
1987–88	Los Angeles Lakers	Detroit Pistons	4–3
1988–89	Detroit Pistons	Los Angeles Lakers	4–0
1989–90	Detroit Pistons	Portland Trail Blazers	4–1
1990–91	Chicago Bulls	Los Angeles Lakers	4–1
1991–92	Chicago Bulls	Portland Trail Blazers	4–2

World Amateur Basketball Championship—men

year	winner	runner-up
1984	United States	Spain
1986	United States	U.S.S.R.
1988	U.S.S.R.	Yugoslavia
1990	Yugoslavia	U.S.S.R.
1992	United States	Croatia

World Amateur Basketball Championship—women

year	winner	runner-up
1984	United States	South Korea
1986	United States	U.S.S.R.
1988	United States	Yugoslavia
1990	United States	Yugoslavia
1992	Unified Team	China

Division I National Collegiate Athletic Association (NCAA) Championship—men

year	winner	runner-up	score
1988	Kansas	Oklahoma	83–79
1989	Michigan	Seton Hall	80–79
1990	UNLV	Duke	103–73
1991	Duke	Kansas	72–65
1992	Duke	Michigan	71–51

Division I National Collegiate Athletic Association (NCAA) Championship—women

year	winner	runner-up	score
1988	Louisiana Tech	Auburn	56–54
1989	Tennessee	Auburn	76–60
1990	Stanford	Auburn	88–81
1991	Tennessee	Virginia	70–67
1992	Stanford	Western Kentucky	78–62

National Invitation Tournament (NIT) Championship

year	winner	runner-up	score
1988	Connecticut	Ohio State	72–67
1989	St. John's	St. Louis	73–65
1990	Vanderbilt	St. Louis	74–72
1991	Stanford	Oklahoma	78–72
1992	Virginia	Notre Dame	81–76

Stanford: NCAA Championship—women (1992)
JIM GUND—ALLSPORT

BILLIARDS

World Three-Cushion Championship*

year	winner
1988	T. Blomdahl (Swed.)
1989	T. Blomdahl (Swed.)
1990	L. Dielis (Belg.)
1991	R. Ceulemans (Belg.)
1992	T. Blomdahl (Swed.)

*Amateur until 1988.

World Professional (English) Billiards Champions

year	winner
1988	N. Dagley
1989	M. Russell
1990	M. Russell
1991	M. Russell
1992	G. Sethi

BOWLING

ABC Bowling Championships—Regular Division

year	singles	score	all-events	score
1988	S. Hutkowski	774	R. Steelsmith	2,053
1989	P. Tetreault	813	G. Hall	2,227
1990	R. Hochrein	791	M. Neumann	2,168
1991	E. Deines	826	T. Howery	2,216
1992	Blatchford, Youker (tie)	801	M. Tucker	2,158

WIBC Bowling Championship—Open Division

year	singles	score	all-events	score
1988	M. Meyer-Welty	690	L. Wagner	1,988
1989	L. Anderson	683	N. Fehr	1,911
1990	Carter, Miller-Mackie (tie)	705	C. Norman	1,984
1991	D. Kuhn		D. Kuhn	
1992	P. Ann	680	M. Tokimoto	1,928

FIQ World Bowling Championship—men

year	singles	pairs	triples	fives
1979	G. Bugden (U.K.)	Australia	Malaysia	Australia
1983	T. Cariello (U.S.)	Australia	Sweden	Finland
1987	P. Rolland (Fr.)	Sweden	United States	Sweden
1991	Ying Chieh Ma (Taiwan)	United States	United States	Taiwan

Professional Bowlers Association (PBA) Firestone Tournament of Champions

year	champion	runner-up
1988	M. Williams	T. Westlake
1989	D. Ballard	W.R. Williams
1990	D. Ferraro	T. Westlake
1991	D. Ozio	A. Monacelli
1992	M. McDowell	D. Genalo

FIQ World Bowling Championship—women

year	singles	pairs	triples	fives
1979	L. de la Rosa (Phil.)	Philippines	United States	United States
1983	L. Sulkanen (Swed.)	Denmark	West Germany	Sweden
1987	E. Piccini (Mex.)	United States	United States	United States
1991	M. Beckel (Ger.)	Japan	Canada	South Korea

BOWLS

World Lawn Bowls Championships

year	singles	pairs	triples	fours	team
1984	P. Bellis (N.Z.)	United States	Ireland	England	Scotland
1988	D. Bryant (Eng.)	New Zealand	New Zealand	Ireland	England
1992	T. Allcock (Eng.)	Scotland	Israel	Scotland	Scotland

BOXING

World heavyweight champions—no weight limit

WBA	WBC
James Smith (U.S.; 12/12/86)	James Douglas (U.S.; 2/11/90)
Mike Tyson (U.S.; 3/7/87)	Evander Holyfield (U.S.; 10/26/90)
James Douglas (U.S.; 2/11/90)	Riddick Bowe (U.S.; 11/13/92)
Evander Holyfield (U.S.; 10/26/90)	stripped of title in 1992
Riddick Bowe (U.S.; 11/13/92)	Lennox Lewis (U.K.; 12/14/92)

R. Bowe: WBA heavyweight champion (1992)

DUOMO

World cruiserweight champions—top weight 195 pounds

WBA	WBC
Evander Holyfield (U.S.; 7/12/86)	Evander Holyfield (U.S.; 4/9/88)
gave up title in 1988	gave up title in 1988
Taoufik Belbouli (Fr.)	Carlos de León (P.R.; 5/17/89)
declared vacant in 1989	Massimiliano Duran (Italy; 7/27/90)
Robert Daniels (U.S.; 11/89)	Anaclet Wamba (Fr.; 7/20/91)
Bobby Czyz (U.S.; 3/8/91)	

World junior middleweight champions—top weight 154 pounds (also called super welterweight)

WBA	WBC
Mike McCallum (Jam.; 10/19/84)	Donald Curry (U.S.; 7/8/88)
vacant	René Jacquot (Fr.; 2/11/89)
Julian Jackson (U.S.; 11/21/87)	John Mugabi (Uganda; 7/8/89)
gave up title in 1990	Terry Norris (U.S.; 3/31/90)
Gilbert Dele (Fr.; 2/91)	
Vinny Pazienza (U.S.; 10/11/91)	
vacant	
Julio César Vásquez (Arg.; 12/22/92)	

World light heavyweight champions—top weight 175 pounds

WBA	WBC
Leslie Stewart (Trinidad and	Don Lalonde (Can.; 11/27/87)
Tobago; 5/23/87)	Sugar Ray Leonard (U.S.; 11/7/88)
Virgil Hill (U.S.; 9/5/87)	gave up title in 1988
Thomas Hearns (U.S.; 6/3/91)	Dennis Andries (U.K; 2/89)
Iran Barkley (U.S.; 3/21/92)	Jeff Harding (Australia; 6/24/89)
vacant	Dennis Andries (U.K.; 7/28/90)
Virgil Hill (U.S.; 9/92)	Jeff Harding (Australia; 9/11/91)

World welterweight champions—top weight 147 pounds

WBA	WBC
Tomas Molinares (Colom.; 7/29/88)	Jorge Vaca (Mex.; 10/28/87)
vacant	Lloyd Honeyghan (U.K.; 3/29/88)
Mark Breland (U.S.; 2/4/89)	Marlon Starling (U.S.; 2/4/89)
Aaron Davis (U.S.; 7/8/90)	Maurice Blocker (U.S.; 8/19/90)
Meldrick Taylor (U.S.; 1/19/91)	Simon Brown (Jam.; 3/18/91)
Crisanto España (Venez.; 10/31/92)	James McGirt (U.S.; 11/29/91)

World middleweight champions—top weight 160 pounds

WBA	WBC
Marvin Hagler (U.S.; 9/27/80)	Thomas Hearns (U.S.; 10/29/87)
stripped of title in 1987	Iran Barkley (U.S.; 6/6/88)
Sumbu Kalambay (Italy; 10/23/87)	Roberto Duran (Pan.; 2/24/89)
stripped of title in 1989	stripped of title in 1990
Mike McCallum (Jam.; 5/13/89)	Julian Jackson (U.S.; 11/24/90)
stripped of title in 1991	
Reggie Johnson (U.S.; 4/22/92)	

World junior welterweight champions—top weight 140 pounds (also called super lightweight)

WBA	WBC
Loreto Garza (U.S.; 8/17/90)	Tsuyoshi Hamada (Japan; 7/24/86)
Edwin Rosario (P.R.; 6/15/91)	René Arrendondo (Mex.; 7/22/87)
Akinobu Hiranaka (Japan; 4/10/92)	Roger Mayweather (U.S.; 11/12/87)
Morris East (Phil.; 9/9/92)	Julio César Chávez (Mex.; 5/13/89)

World lightweight champions—top weight 135 pounds

WBA	WBC
Julio César Chávez (Mex.; 11/21/87) gave up title in 1989	José Luis Ramírez (Mex.; 7/19/87)
Edwin Rosario (P.R.; 7/9/89)	Julio César Chávez (Mex.; 10/29/88) gave up title in 1989
Juan Nazario (P.R.; 4/4/90)	Pernell Whitaker (U.S.; 8/20/89)
Pernell Whitaker (U.S.; 8/11/90) gave up title in 1992	gave up title in 1992
Joey Gamache (U.S.; 6/13/92)	Miguel González (Mex.; 8/24/92)
Tony Lopez (U.S.; 10/24/92)	

World junior lightweight champions—top weight 130 pounds (also called super featherweight)

WBA	WBC
Rocky Lockridge (U.S.; 2/26/84)	Julio César Chávez (Mex.; 9/13/84) gave up title
Wilfredo Gómez (P.R.; 5/19/85)	Azumah Nelson (Ghana; 2/29/88)
Alfredo Layne (Pan.; 5/24/86)	
Brian Mitchell (S.Af.; 9/27/86) vacant	
Joey Gamache (U.S.; 6/28/91) gave up title in 1991	
Genaro Hernandez (U.S.; 11/22/91)	

T. Norris (right): WBC junior middleweight champion (1992)

RICHARD MACKSON—SPORTS ILLUSTRATED

World featherweight champions—top weight 126 pounds

WBA	WBC
Eusebio Pedroza (Pan.; 4/15/78)	Azumah Nelson (Ghana; 12/8/84) gave up title in 1988
Barry McGuigan (N.Ire.; 6/8/85)	Jeff Fenech (Australia; 3/7/88) gave up title in 1990
Steve Cruz (U.S.; 6/23/86)	Marcos Villasana (Mex.; 6/2/90)
Antonio Esparragoza (Venez.; 3/6/87)	Paul Hodkinson (U.K.; 11/13/91)
Park Yung Kyun (S.Kor.; 3/30/91)	

World junior bantamweight champions (also called super flyweight)—top weight 115 pounds

WBA	WBC
Watanabe Jiro (Japan; 4/8/82) stripped of title in 1984	Jesús Rojas (Colom.; 8/9/87)
Khaosai Galaxy (Thai.; 11/21/84) gave up title in 1991	Gilberto Román (Mex.; 4/8/88)
Katsuya Onizuka (Japan; 4/10/92)	Nana Konadu (Ghana; 11/7/89)
	Moon Sung Kil (S.Kor.; 1/20/90)

World junior featherweight champions (also called super bantamweight)—top weight 122 pounds

WBA	WBC
Bernardo Pinango (Venez.: 3/5/88)	Jeff Fenech (Australia; 5/8/87) gave up title in 1988
Juan José Estrada (Mex.; 5/28/88)	Daniel Zaragoza (Mex.; 2/29/88)
Jesus Salud (U.S.; 12/11/89) stripped of title in 1990	Paul Banke (U.S.; 4/23/90)
Luís Mendoza (Colom.; 9/11/90)	Pedro Decima (Arg.; 11/5/90)
Raul Pérez (Mex.; 10/7/91)	Kiyoshi Hatanaka (Japan; 2/3/91)
Wilfredo Vásquez (P.R.; 3/27/92)	Daniel Zaragoza (Mex.; 6/14/91)
	Thierry Jacob (Fr.; 3/20/92)
	Tracy Patterson (U.S.; 6/23/92)

World flyweight champions—top weight 112 pounds

WBA	WBC
Jésus Rojas (Venez.; 9/30/89)	Gabriel Bernal (Mex.; 4/9/84)
Lee Yul Woo (S.Kor.; 3/10/90)	Sot Chitalada (Thai.; 10/8/84)
Leopard Tamakuma (Japan; 7/29/90)	Kim Young Kang (S.Kor.; 7/24/88)
Elvis Alvarez (Colom.; 3/14/91)	Sot Chitalada (Thai.; 6/89)
Kim Yong Kang (S.Kor.; 6/1/91)	Muangchai Kittlkasem (Thai.; 2/15/91)
Aquiles Guzmán (Venez.; 9/26/92)	Yury Arbachakov (Russia; 6/23/92)
David Griman (Venez.; 12/92)	

World bantamweight champions—top weight 118 pounds

WBA	WBC
Khaokor Galaxy (Thai.; 5/9/88)	Daniel Zaragoza (Mex.; 5/4/85)
Moon Sung Kil (S.Kor.; 8/14/88)	Miguel Lora (Colom.; 8/9/85)
Khaokor Galaxy (Thai.; 7/9/89)	Raul Pérez (Mex.; 10/29/88)
Luisito Espinosa (Phil.; 10/18/89)	Greg Richardson (U.S.; 2/25/91)
Israel Contreras (Venez.; 10/19/91)	Joichiro Tatsuyoshi (Japan; 9/91) vacant
Eddie Cook (U.S.; 3/15/92)	Victor Rabañales (Mex.; 3/30/92)
Eliecer Julio (Colom.; 10/10/92)	

World junior flyweight champions—top weight 108 pounds

WBA	WBC
Lupe Madera (Mex.; 7/10/83)	German Torres (Mex.)
Francisco Quiroz (Dom.Rep.; 5/19/84)	Lee Yul Woo (S.Kor.)
Joey Olivo (U.S.; 3/29/85)	Humberto Gonzalez (Mex.; 6/89)
Yuh Myung Woo (S.Kor.; 12/8/85)	Rolando Pascua (Phil.; 12/19/90)
Hiroki Ioka (Japan; 12/17/91)	Melchor Cob Castro (Mex.; 3/25/91)
Yuh Myung Woo (S.Kor.; 11/18/92)	Humberto Gonzalez (Mex.; 6/4/91)

CHESS

World Chess Championships—men

year	winner	runner-up
1975	A. Karpov (U.S.S.R.)*	*
1978	A. Karpov (U.S.S.R.)	V. Korchnoy (U.S.S.R.)
1981	A. Karpov (U.S.S.R.)	V. Korchnoy (U.S.S.R.)
1984–85	G. Kasparov (U.S.S.R.)	A. Karpov (U.S.S.R.)
1986	G. Kasparov (U.S.S.R.)	A. Karpov (U.S.S.R.)
1987	G. Kasparov (U.S.S.R.)	A. Karpov (U.S.S.R.)
1990	G. Kasparov (U.S.S.R.)	A. Karpov (U.S.S.R.)

*By default. R. Fischer (U.S.) was stripped of the title for failure to comply with an FIDE ruling, and Karpov was declared the new world champion.

World Chess Championships—women

year	winner	runner-up
1984	M. Chiburdanidze (U.S.S.R.)	I. Levitina (U.S.S.R.)
1986	M. Chiburdanidze (U.S.S.R.)	E. Akhmilovskaya (U.S.S.R.)
1988	M. Chiburdanidze (U.S.S.R.)	N. Ioseliani (U.S.S.R.)
1991	Xie Jun (China)	M. Chiburdanidze (U.S.S.R.)

International Team Chess Championships—men

year	winner	runner-up
1986	U.S.S.R.	United Kingdom
1988	U.S.S.R.	United Kingdom
1989	U.S.S.R.	Yugoslavia
1992	Russia	Uzbekistan

International Team Chess Championships—women

year	winner	runner-up
1982	U.S.S.R.	Romania
1984	U.S.S.R.	Bulgaria
1986	U.S.S.R.	Hungary
1988	Hungary	U.S.S.R.

CONTRACT BRIDGE

Bermuda Bowl

year	winner	runner-up
1987	United States	United Kingdom
1989	Brazil	United States
1991	Iceland	Poland

World Contract Bridge Pair Championship

year	open winner	women's winner	mixed winner
1982	United States	United States	Canada
1986	United States	United States	United States
1990	Brazil	United States	United States

World Team Olympiad

year	open winner	open runner-up	women's winner	women's runner-up
1988	United States	Austria	Denmark	United Kingdom
1992	France	United States	Austria	United Kingdom

CRICKET

All-time First-class Test Cricket Standings (as of Sept. 30, 1992)

	England wins draws losses	Australia w d l	South Africa w d l	West Indies w d l	New Zealand w d l	India w d l	Pakistan w d l	Sri Lanka w d l
England v.	—	88 79 101	46 38 18	24 37 43	33 35 4	30 36 11	14 31 7	3 1 0
Australia v.	101 79 88	—	29 13 11	29 19* 24	10 10 6	24 18* 8	12 13 9	4 3 0
South Africa v.	18 38 46	11 13 29	—	0 0 1	19 6 2	†	†	†
West Indies v.	43 37 24	24 19* 29	1 0 0	—	8 12 4	26 30 6	10 11 7	†
New Zealand v.	4 35 33	6 10 10	2 6 19	4 12 8	—	6 13 12	3 16 13	4 5 0
India v.	11 36 30	8 18* 24	†	6 30 26	12 13 6	—	4 33 7	4 3 1
Pakistan v.	7 31 14	9 13 12	†	7 11 10	13 16 3	7 33 4	—	6 5 1
Sri Lanka v.	0 1 3	0 3 4	†	†	0 5 4	1 3 4	1 5 6	—

*Including one tie.   †No matches.

CURLING

International Olympic Committee President's Cup

year	winner	runner-up
1988	Norway	Canada
1989	Canada	Switzerland
1990	Canada	Scotland
1991	Scotland	Canada
1992	Switzerland	Scotland

World Curling Championship—women

year	winner	runner-up
1988	West Germany	Canada
1989	Canada	Norway
1990	Norway	Scotland
1991	Norway	Canada
1992	Sweden	United States

CYCLING

Tour de France

year	winner	km
1988	P. Delgado (Spain)	3,300
1989	G. LeMond (U.S.)	3,215
1990	G. LeMond (U.S.)	3,399
1991	M. Indurain (Spain)	3,935
1992	M. Indurain (Spain)	3,983

Cycling World Track Championships—women (amateur)

year	sprint	3-km pursuit
1988	E. Salumae (U.S.S.R.)	J. Longo (Fr.)
1989	E. Salumae (U.S.S.R.)	J. Longo (Fr.)
1990	C. Young (U.S.)	J. Longo (Fr.)
1991	I. Haringa (Neth.)	P. Rossner (Ger.)
1992	E. Salumae (Estonia)	P. Rossner (Ger.)

Cycling World Road-Racing Championships

year	men (amateur)	men (professional)	women (amateur)
1988	O. Ludwig (E.Ger.)	M. Fondriest (Italy)	M. Knol (Neth.)
1989	J. Halupczok (Pol.)	G. LeMond (U.S.)	J. Longo (Fr.)
1990	M. Gualdi (Italy)	R. Dhaenens (Belg.)	C. Marsal (Fr.)
1991	V. Pjaksinski (U.S.S.R.)	G. Bugno (Italy)	L. Van Moorsel (Neth.)
1992	F. Casartelli (Italy)	G. Bugno (Italy)	K. Watt (Australia)

M. Indurain: Tour de France (1992)
DUOMO

Cycling World Track Championships—men

year	sprint (amateur)	sprint (professional)	pursuit (amateur)	pursuit (professional)	motor-paced (amateur)	motor-paced (professional)
1988	L. Hesslich (E.Ger.)	S. Pate (Australia)	G. Umaras (U.S.S.R.)	L. Piasecki (Pol.)	V. Colamartino (Italy)	D. Clark (Australia)
1989	B. Huck (E.Ger.)	C. Golinelli (Italy)	V. Ekimov (U.S.S.R.)	C. Sturgess (U.K.)	R. Königshofer (Austria)	G. Renosto (Italy)
1990	B. Huck (E.Ger.)	M. Hübner (E.Ger.)	Ye. Berzin (U.S.S.R.)	V. Ekimov (U.S.S.R.)	R. Königshofer (Austria)	W. Brugna (Italy)
1991	J. Fiedler (Ger.)	not awarded	J. Lehmann (Ger.)	F. Moreau (Fr.)	R. Königshofer (Austria)	D. Clark (Australia)
1992	J. Fiedler (Ger.)	M. Hübner (Ger.)	C. Boardman (U.K.)	M. McCarthy (U.S.)	C. Podlesch (Ger.)	P. Steiger (Switz.)

FENCING

World Fencing Championships—men

year	individual			team		
	foil	épée	sabre	foil	épée	sabre
1988	S. Cerioni (Italy)	A. Schmitt (W.Ger.)	J.-F. Lamour (Fr.)	U.S.S.R.	France	Hungary
1989	A. Koch (W.Ger.)	M. Pereira (Spain)	G. Kirienko (U.S.S.R.)	U.S.S.R.	Italy	U.S.S.R.
1990	P. Omnès (Fr.)	T. Gerull (W.Ger.)	G. Nebald (Hung.)	Italy	Italy	U.S.S.R.
1991	I. Weissenborn (Ger.)	A. Shuvalov (U.S.S.R.)	G. Kirienko (U.S.S.R.)	Cuba	U.S.S.R.	Hungary
1992	P. Omnes (Fr.)	E. Srecki (Fr.)	B. Szabo (Hung.)	Germany	Germany	Unified Team

World Fencing Championships—women

year	individual foil	team foil
1988	A. Fichtel (W.Ger.)	West Germany
1989	O. Velitchko (U.S.S.R.)	West Germany
1990	A. Fichtel (W.Ger.)	Italy
1991	G. Trillini (Italy)	Italy
1992	G. Trillini (Italy)	Italy

Washington Redskins: Super Bowl (1992)
AL TIELEMANS—DUOMO

FIELD HOCKEY

World Cup Field Hockey Championships—men

year	winner	runner-up
1986	Australia	England
1990	The Netherlands	Pakistan

World Cup Field Hockey Championships—women

year	winner	runner-up
1986	The Netherlands	West Germany
1990	The Netherlands	Australia

FOOTBALL

FIFA World Cup

year	result			
1982	Italy	3	West Germany	1
1986	Argentina	3	West Germany	2
1990	West Germany	1	Argentina	0

European Cup-Winners' Cup

season	result			
1987–88	KV Mechelen (Belg.)	1	Ajax Amsterdam	0
1988–89	Barcelona	2	Sampdoria (Italy)	0
1989–90	Sampdoria (Italy)	2	Anderlecht (Belg.)	0
1990–91	Manchester United	2	Barcelona	1
1991–92	Werder Bremen (Ger.)	2	AS Monaco	0

Libertadores de América Cup

year	winner (country)	runner-up (country)	scores
1988	Nacional (Uruguay)	Newell's Old Boys (Arg.)	0–1, 3–0
1989	Nacional of Medellin (Colom.)	Olímpia (Paraguay)	0–2, 2–0, 5–4*
1990	Olímpia (Paraguay)	Barcelona (Ecuador)	2–0, 1–1
1991	Colo Colo (Chile)	Olímpia (Paraguay)	0–0, 3–0
1992	Sao Paulo (Braz.)	Newell's Old Boys (Arg.)	0–1, 1–0, 3–2*

*Winner determined in penalty shootout after tiebreaking game.

The European Cup of Champion Clubs

season	result			
1987–88	PSV Eindhoven (Neth.)*	0	Benfica (Port.)	0
1988–89	A.C. Milan	4	Steaua Bucharest	0
1989–90	A.C. Milan	1	Benfica (Port.)	0
1990–91	Red Star Belgrade*	0	Marseille	0
1991–92	Barcelona	1	Sampdoria (Italy)	0

*Won on penalty kicks.

U.S. Football—professional

Super Bowl

	season	result			
XXII	1987–88	Washington Redskins (NFC)	42	Denver Broncos (AFC)	10
XXIII	1988–89	San Francisco 49ers (NFC)	20	Cincinnati Bengals (AFC)	16
XXIV	1989–90	San Francisco 49ers (NFC)	55	Denver Broncos (AFC)	10
XXV	1990–91	New York Giants (NFC)	20	Buffalo Bills (AFC)	19
XXVI	1991–92	Washington Redskins (NFC)	37	Buffalo Bills (AFC)	24

U.S. Football—college

Heisman Memorial Trophy winner

year	player	school
1987	Tim Brown	Notre Dame
1988	Barry Sanders	Oklahoma State
1989	Andre Ware	Houston
1990	Ty Detmer	Brigham Young
1991	Desmond Howard	Michigan
1992	Gino Torretta	Miami

Rose Bowl

season	result			
1987–88	Michigan St.	20	Southern California	17
1988–89	Michigan	22	Southern California	14
1989–90	Southern California	17	Michigan	10
1990–91	Washington	46	Iowa	34
1991–92	Washington	34	Michigan	14
1992–93	Michigan	38	Washington	31

Orange Bowl

season	result			
1987–88	Miami (Fla.)	20	Oklahoma	14
1988–89	Miami (Fla.)	23	Nebraska	3
1989–90	Notre Dame	21	Colorado	6
1990–91	Colorado	10	Notre Dame	9
1991–92	Miami (Fla.)	22	Nebraska	0
1992–93	Florida St.	27	Nebraska	14

U.S. College Football National Champion

season	champion
1987–88	Miami (Fla.)
1988–89	Notre Dame
1989–90	Miami (Fla.)
1990–91	Colorado* Georgia Tech*
1991–92	Miami (Fla.)* Washington*
1992–93	Alabama

*Tied.

Sugar Bowl

season	result			
1987–88	Auburn	16	Syracuse	16
1988–89	Florida St.	13	Auburn	7
1989–90	Miami (Fla.)	33	Alabama	25
1990–91	Tennessee	23	Virginia	22
1991–92	Notre Dame	39	Florida	28
1992–93	Alabama	34	Miami (Fla.)	13

Cotton Bowl

season	result			
1987–88	Texas A&M	35	Notre Dame	10
1988–89	UCLA	17	Arkansas	3
1989–90	Tennessee	31	Arkansas	27
1990–91	Miami (Fla.)	46	Texas	3
1991–92	Florida State	10	Texas A&M	2
1992–93	Notre Dame	28	Texas A&M	3

Canadian football—professional

Grey Cup

year	result			
1987	Edmonton Eskimos (WFC)	38	Toronto Argonauts (EFC)	36
1988	Winnipeg Blue Bombers (EFC)	22	British Columbia Lions (WFC)	21
1989	Saskatchewan Roughriders (WFC)	43	Hamilton Tiger-Cats (EFC)	40
1990	Winnipeg Blue Bombers (EFC)	50	Edmonton Eskimos (WFC)	11
1991	Toronto Argonauts (EFC)	36	Calgary Stampeders (WFC)	21
1992	Calgary Stampeders (WFC)	24	Winnipeg Blue Bombers (EFC)	10

Rugby Union football

Record of International Test matches 1871 to Nov. 2, 1992

	England wins	draws	losses	Scotland wins	draws	losses	Ireland wins	draws	losses	Wales wins	draws	losses	British Isles wins	draws	losses
England v.	—		—	53	17	39	61	8	36	39	12	47			
Scotland v.	39	17	53	—		—	54	4	45	41	2	53			
Ireland v.	36	8	61	45	4	54	—		—	32	6	57			
Wales v.	47	12	39	53	2	41	57	6	32	—		—			
British Isles* v.	—		—	—		—	—		—	—		—	—		—
South Africa v.	6	1	2	5	0	3	8	1	1	6	1	0	20	6	14
New Zealand v.	13	0	3	13	2	0	11	1	0	12	0	3	24	3	5
Australia v.	12	0	6	7	0	7	7	0	6	7	0	8	3	0	14
France v.	24	7	37	30	3	30	35	5	25	27	3	36			

	South Africa wins	draws	losses	New Zealand wins	draws	losses	Australia wins	draws	losses	France wins	draws	losses
England v.	2	1	6	3	0	13	6	0	12	37	7	24
Scotland v.	3	0	5	0	2	13	7	0	7	30	3	30
Ireland v.	1	1	8	0	1	11	6	0	7	25	5	35
Wales v.	0	1	6	3	0	12	8	0	7	36	3	27
British Isles* v.	14	6	20	5	3	24	14	0	3			
South Africa v.	—		—	20	2	16	21	0	8	12	4	3
New Zealand v.	16	2	20	—		—	65	5	26	23	0	5
Australia v.	8	0	21	26	5	65	—		—	9	2	12
France v.	3	4	12	5	0	23	12	2	9	—		—

*The British Isles ("British Lions") is a combined team from the four "Home Unions" (England, Ireland, Scotland, and Wales).

Five Nations Championship

year	result
1988	Wales*
1989	France
1990	Scotland†
1991	England†
1992	England†

*Triple Crown (all three matches, excluding France) and Grand Slam (all four matches) winner.
†Grand Slam winner.

Rugby League football

Record of Test matches from Jan. 25, 1908, to Sept. 30, 1992

	Great Britain wins	draws	losses	Australia wins	draws	losses	New Zealand wins	draws	losses	France wins	draws	losses
Great Britain v.	—		—	52	4	52	48	3	28	39	3	14
Australia v.	52	4	52	—		—	38	0	22	24	3	12
New Zealand v.	28	3	48	22	0	38	—		—	17	3	11
France* v.	14	3	39	12	3	24	11	3	17	—		—

*France began playing in this series of matches in 1954.

GOLF

British Open Golf Tournament—men

year	winner
1988	S. Ballesteros (Spain)
1989	M. Calcavecchia (U.S.)
1990	N. Faldo (U.K.)
1991	I. Baker-Finch (Australia)
1992	N. Faldo (U.K.)

United States Open Golf Championship—men

year	winner
1988	C. Strange (U.S.)
1989	C. Strange (U.S.)
1990	H. Irwin (U.S.)
1991	P. Stewart (U.S.)
1992	T. Kite (U.S.)

Masters Tournament

year	winner
1987	L. Mize (U.S.)
1988	S. Lyle (Scot.)
1989	N. Faldo (U.K.)
1990	N. Faldo (U.K.)
1991	I. Woosnam (U.K.)
1992	F. Couples (U.S.)

U.S. Professional Golfers' Association (PGA) championship

year	winner
1988	J. Sluman (U.S.)
1989	P. Stewart (U.S.)
1990	W. Grady (Australia)
1991	J. Daly (U.S.)
1992	N. Price (Zimbabwe)

N. Faldo: British Open (1992)
FOCUS ON SPORTS

British Amateur Golf Championship—men

year	winner
1988	C. Hardin (Swed.)
1989	S. Richardson (U.K.)
1990	R. Muntz (Neth.)
1991	R. Willison (U.K.)
1992	S. Dundas (Scot.)

United States Amateur Golf Championship—men

year	winner
1988	E. Meeks (U.S.)
1989	C. Patton (U.S.)
1990	P. Mickelson (U.S.)
1991	M. Voges (U.S.)
1992	J. Leonard (U.S.)

Ladies' British Open Golf Championship

year	winner
1988	C. Dibnah (Australia)
1989	J. Geddes (U.S.)
1990	H. Alfredsson (Swed.)
1991	P. Grice-Whittaker (U.K.)
1992	P. Sheehan (U.S.)

British Ladies Amateur Golf Championship

year	winner
1988	J. Furby (U.K.)
1989	H. Dobson (U.K.)
1990	J. Hall (U.K.)
1991	J. Morley (U.K.)
1992	P. Pedersen (Den.)

United States Women's Open champions

year	winner
1988	L. Neumann (Swed.)
1989	B. King (U.S.)
1990	B. King (U.S.)
1991	M. Mallon (U.S.)
1992	P. Sheehan (U.S.)

United States Women's Amateur Golf Championship

year	winner
1988	P. Sinn (U.S.)
1989	V. Goetze (U.S.)
1990	P. Hurst (U.S.)
1991	A. Fruhwirth (U.S.)
1992	V. Goetze (U.S.)

Ladies' Professional Golf Association (LPGA) champions

year	winner
1988	S. Turner (U.S.)
1989	N. Lopez (U.S.)
1990	B. Daniel (U.S.)
1991	M. Mallon (U.S.)
1992	B. King (U.S.)

Team events

Walker Cup—men (amateur)

year	result	tied	place
1983	United States 13, Britain and Ireland 10	1	Hoylake, Cheshire, Eng.
1985	United States 13, Britain and Ireland 11	2	Pine Valley, N.J., U.S.
1987	United States 16, Britain and Ireland 7	1	Sunningdale, Berkshire, Eng.
1989	Britain and Ireland 9, United States 8	7	Atlanta, Ga., U.S.
1991	United States 14, Britain and Ireland 10	0	Portmarnock, Ire.

World Cup—men (professional)

year	winner
1987	Wales (I. Woosnam and D. Llewellyn)
1988	United States (B. Crenshaw and M. McCumber)
1989	Australia (P. Fowler and W. Grady)
1990	Germany (B. Langer and T. Giedeon)
1991	Sweden (A. Forsbrand and P.-U. Johansson)
1992	United States (F. Couples and D. Love III)

Ryder Cup—men (professional)

year	result	tied	place
1983	United States 13, Great Britain 12	3	Palm Beach Gardens, Fla., U.S.
1985	Europe 16, United States 11	1	Belfry, West Midlands, Eng.
1987	Europe 13, United States 11	4	Dublin, Ohio, U.S.
1989	Europe 14, United States 14	0	Belfry, West Midlands, Eng.
1991	United States 14½, Europe 13½	0	Kiawah Island, S.C., U.S.

Curtis Cup—women (amateur)

year	result	tied	place
1986	Britain and Ireland 11, United States 3	4	Hutchinson, Kan., U.S.
1988	Britain and Ireland 11, United States 7	0	Sandwich, Kent, Eng.
1990	United States 14, Britain and Ireland 4	0	Bernardsville, N.J., U.S.
1992	Britain and Ireland 10, United States 8	0	Hoylake, Merseyside, Eng.

GREYHOUND RACING

British Greyhound Derby

year	winning dog	time (s)	year	winning dog	time (s)
1985	Pagan Swallow	29.04*	1989	Lartigue Note	28.79
1986	Tico	28.69	1990	Slippy Blue	28.70
1987	Signal Spark	28.83	1991	Ballinderry Ash	
1988	Hit the Lid	28.53	1992	Farloe Melody	28.88

*In 1985 the distance was lowered from 500 m to 480 m.

GYMNASTICS

World Gymnastics Championships—men

year	all-around team	all-around individual	horizontal bar	parallel bars
1988*	U.S.S.R.	V. Artyomov (U.S.S.R.)	V. Artyomov (U.S.S.R.)† V. Lyukin (U.S.S.R.)†	V. Artyomov (U.S.S.R.)
1989	U.S.S.R.	I. Korobchinski (U.S.S.R.)	Li Chunyang (China)	V. Artyomov (U.S.S.R.)† Li Jing (China)†
1991	U.S.S.R.	G. Misutin (U.S.S.R.)	R. Buechner (Ger.)† Li Chunyang (China)†	Li Jing (China)
1992*	Unified Team	V. Sherbo (UT)	T. Dimas (U.S.)	V. Sherbo (UT)

year	pommel horse	rings	vault	floor exercise
1988*	D. Bilozerchev (U.S.S.R.)† Z. Borkai (Hung.)† L. Gueraskov (Bulg.)†	H. Behrendt (E.Ger.)† D. Bilozerchev (U.S.S.R.)†	Lou Yun (China)	S. Kharkov (U.S.S.R.)
1989	V. Mogilny (U.S.S.R.)	A. Aguilar (W.Ger.)	J. Behrend (E.Ger.)	I. Korobchinsky (U.S.S.R.)
1991	V. Belenky (U.S.S.R.)	G. Misutin (U.S.S.R.)	You Ok Youl (S.Kor.)	I. Korobchinsky (U.S.S.R.)
1992*	V. Sherbo (UT)† Pae Gil Su (N.Kor.)†	V. Sherbo (UT)	V. Sherbo (UT)	Li Xiaosahuang (China)

*Olympic champions. †Tied.

T. Gutsu: Women's individual all-around world gymnastics champion (1992)
DUOMO

T. Dimas: Men's horizontal bar world gymnastics champion (1992)
WILLIAM R. SALLAZ—DUOMO

World Gymnastics Championships—women

year	all-around team	all-around individual	balance beam
1988*	U.S.S.R.	Y. Shushunova (U.S.S.R.)	D. Silivas (Rom.)
1989	U.S.S.R.	S. Boginskaya (U.S.S.R.)	D. Silivas (Rom.)
1991	U.S.S.R.	K. Zmeskal (U.S.)	S. Boginskaya (U.S.S.R.)
1992*	Unified Team	T. Gutsu (UT)	T. Lyssenko (UT)

year	uneven parallel bars	vault	floor exercise	rhythmic
1988*	D. Silivas (Rom.)	S. Boginskaya (U.S.S.R.)	D. Silivas (Rom.)	M. Lobach (U.S.S.R.)
1989	Fan Di (China)† D. Silivas (Rom.)†	O. Dudnik (U.S.S.R.)	S. Boginskaya (U.S.S.R.)† D. Silivas (Rom.)†	B. Panova (Bulg.)
1991	Kim Gwang Suk (N.Kor.)	L. Milosovici (Rom.)	C. Bontas (Rom.)† O. Chusovitina (U.S.S.R.)†	O. Skaldina (U.S.S.R.)
1992*	Lu Li (China)	L. Milosovici (Rom.)† H. Onodi (Hung.)†	L. Milosovici (Rom.)	A. Timoshenko (UT)

*Olympic champions. †Tied.

HORSE RACING

2,000 Guineas

year	horse	jockey	owner	trainer
1988	Doyoun	W. Swinburn	Aga Khan IV	M. Stoute
1989	Nashwan	W. Carson	H. al-Maktoum	D. Hern
1990	Tirol	M. Kinane	John Horgan	R. Hannon
1991	Mystiko	M. Roberts	Lady Beaverbrook	C. Brittain
1992	Rodrigo de Triano	L. Piggott	R. Sangster	P. Chapple-Hyam

The Derby

year	horse	jockey	owner	trainer
1988	Kahyasi	R. Cochrane	Aga Khan IV	L. Cumani
1989	Nashwan	W. Carson	H. al-Maktoum	D. Hern
1990	Quest for Fame	P. Eddery	K. Abdullah	R. Charlton
1991	Generous	A. Munro	Fahd Salman	P. Cole
1992	Dr Devious	J. Reid	S. Craig	P. Chapple-Hyam

Triple Crown champions—British

year	winner
1915	Pommern
1917	Gay Crusader
1918	Gainsborough
1935	Bahram
1970	Nijinsky

The St. Leger

year	horse	jockey	owner	trainer
1988	Minster Son	W. Carson	Lady Beaverbrook	N. Graham
1989	Michelozzo	S. Cauthen	C. St. George	H. Cecil
1990	Snurge	R. Quinn	M. Arbib	P. Cole
1991	Toulon	P. Eddery	K. Abdullah	A. Fabre
1992	User Friendly	G. Duffield	B. Gredley	C. Brittain

The American Thoroughbred classics

The Kentucky Derby

year	horse	jockey	owner	trainer
1988	Winning Colors	G. Stevens	E. Klein	D.W. Lukas
1989	Sunday Silence	P. Valenzuela	A. Hancock, others	C. Whittingham
1990	Unbridled	C. Perret	F. Genter	C. Nafzger
1991	Strike the Gold	C. Antley	B.G. Brophy, others	N. Zito
1992	Lil E. Tee	P. Day	W.C. Partee	L. Whiting

The Preakness Stakes

year	horse	jockey	owner	trainer
1988	Risen Star	E. Delahoussaye	R. Lamarque, L. Roussel	L. Roussel
1989	Sunday Silence	P. Valenzuela	A. Hancock, others	C. Whittingham
1990	Summer Squall	P. Day	Dogwood Stable	N. Howard
1991	Hansel	J. Bailey	J. Allbritton	F. Brothers
1992	Pine Bluff	C. McCarron	Loblolly Stable	T. Bohannan

The Belmont Stakes

year	horse	jockey	owner	trainer
1988	Risen Star	E. Delahoussaye	R. Lamarque, L. Roussel	L. Roussel
1989	Easy Goer	P. Day	O. Phipps	S. McGaughey
1990	Go and Go	M. Kinane	W. Haeffner	D. Weld
1991	Hansel	J. Bailey	J. Allbritton	F. Brothers
1992	A.P. Indy	E. Delahoussaye	T. Tsurumaki	N. Drysdale

Harness racing

The Hambletonian Trot

year	horse	driver
1988	Armbro Goal	J. Campbell
1989	Park Avenue Joe*	R. Waples
	Probe*	W. Fahy
1990	Harmonius	J. Campbell
1991	Giant Victory	J. Moiseyev
1992	Alf Palema	M. McNicholl

*Tied.

Australian Thoroughbred racing

Melbourne Cup

year	horse	jockey	owner	trainer
1987	Kensei	L. Olsen	Six-man syndicate	L. Bridge
1988	Empire Rose	T. Allan	F.R. & T.J. Bodle	L. Laxon
1989	Tawrrific	R.S. Dye	B.F. Avery, others	D.L. Freedman
1990	Kingston Rule	D. Beadman	Mr. & Mrs. D.H. Hains	J.B. Cummings
1991	Let's Elope	S. King	K.W. White, others	J.B. Cummings
1992	Subzero	G. Hall	D.H.K. Investments	D.L. Freedman

A.P. Indy (second from left): Belmont Stakes (1992)

FOCUS ON SPORTS

Triple Crown champions—U.S.

year	horse
1946	Assault
1948	Citation
1973	Secretariat
1977	Seattle Slew
1978	Affirmed

Lil E. Tee (right): Kentucky Derby (1992)

LARS GELFAN—SPORTSLIGHT

ICE HOCKEY

The Stanley Cup

season	winner	runner-up	games
1987–88	Edmonton Oilers	Boston Bruins	4–0
1988–89	Calgary Flames	Montreal Canadiens	4–2
1989–90	Edmonton Oilers	Boston Bruins	4–1
1990–91	Pittsburgh Penguins	Minnesota North Stars	4–2
1991–92	Pittsburgh Penguins	Chicago Black Hawks	4–0

World Amateur Hockey Championships

year	winner
1988	U.S.S.R.
1989	U.S.S.R.
1990	Sweden
1991	Sweden
1992	Sweden

ICE SKATING

World figure skating champions—women	
year	winner
1988	K. Witt (E.Ger.)
1989	M. Ito (Japan)
1990	J. Trenary (U.S.)
1991	K. Yamaguchi (U.S.)
1992	K. Yamaguchi (U.S.)

World figure skating champions—pairs	
year	winners
1988	E. Valova, O. Vasilyev (U.S.S.R.)
1989	E. Gordeeva, S. Grinkov (U.S.S.R.)
1990	E. Gordeeva, S. Grinkov (U.S.S.R.)
1991	N. Mishkutenok, A. Dmitriev (U.S.S.R.)
1992	N. Mishkutenok, A. Dmitriev (UT)

World figure skating champions—men	
year	winner
1988	B. Boitano (U.S.)
1989	K. Browning (Can.)
1990	K. Browning (Can.)
1991	K. Browning (Can.)
1992	V. Petrenko (UT)

World ice dancing champions	
year	winners
1988	N. Bestemyanova, A. Bukin (U.S.S.R.)
1989	M. Klimova, S. Ponomarenko (U.S.S.R.)
1990	M. Klimova, S. Ponomarenko (U.S.S.R.)
1991	I. Duchesnay, P. Duchesnay (Fr.)
1992	M. Klimova, S. Ponomarenko (UT)

K. Yamaguchi: World figure skating
champion—women (1992)
MIKE POWELL—ALLSPORT

M. Klimova (right) and S. Ponomarenko:
World ice dancing champions (1992)
MIKE POWELL—ALLSPORT

World all-around speed skating champions—men	
year	winner
1988	E. Flaim (U.S.)
1989	L. Visser (Neth.)
1990	J.O. Koss (Nor.)
1991	J.O. Koss (Nor.)
1992	R. Sighel (Italy)

World all-around speed skating champions—women	
year	winner
1988	K. Kania (E.Ger.)
1989	C. Moser (E.Ger.)
1990	J. Börner (E.Ger.)
1991	G. Kleeman (Ger.)
1992	G. Niemann (Ger.)

World Speed Skating Sprint Championships		
year	men	women
1988	D. Jansen (U.S.)	C. Rothenburger (E.Ger.)
1989	I. Zhelezovsky (U.S.S.R.)	B. Blair (U.S.)
1990	Ki Tae Bae (S.Kor.)	A. Hauck (E.Ger.)
1991	I. Zhelezovsky (U.S.S.R.)	M. Garbrecht (Ger.)
1992	I. Zhelezovsky (UT)	Ye Qiaobo (China)

JUDO

World Judo Championships—men			
year	open weights	60 kg	65 kg	71 kg
1983	H. Saito (Japan)	K. Tletseri (U.S.S.R.)	N. Solodukhin (U.S.S.R.)	H. Nakanishi (Japan)
1985	Y. Masaki (Japan)	S. Hosokawa (Japan)	Y. Sokolov (U.S.S.R.)	Keun Ahn Byung (S. Kor.)
1987	N. Ogawa (Japan)	Kim Jae Yup (S.Kor.)	Y. Yamamoto (Japan)	M. Swain (U.S.)
1989	N. Ogawa (Japan)	A. Totikashvili (U.S.S.R.)	D. Becanovic (Yugos.)	T. Koga (Japan)
1991	N. Ogawa (Japan)	T. Koshino (Japan)	G. Quellmalz (Ger.)	T. Koga (Japan)

year	78 kg	86 kg	95 kg	+ 95 kg
1983	N. Hikage (Japan)	D. Ultsch (E.Ger.)	A. Preschel (E.Ger.)	Y. Yamashita (Japan)
1985	N. Hikage (Japan)	P. Seisenbacher (Austria)	H. Sugai (Japan)	Chul Cho Yong (S.Kor.)
1987	H. Okada (Japan)	F. Canu (Fr.)	H. Sugai (Japan)	G. Verichev (U.S.S.R.)
1989	Kim Bying Ju (S.Kor.)	F. Canu (Fr.)	K. Kurtanidze (U.S.S.R.)	N. Ogawa (Japan)
1991	D. Lascau (Ger.)	H. Okada (Japan)	S. Traineau (Fr.)	S. Kosorotov (U.S.S.R.)

T. Murray: Men's World All-Around Rodeo Championship (1992)

KEN LEVINE—ALLSPORT

MOTORBOAT RACING

Gold Cup Championship

year	boat	driver
1988	Miller American	C. Hanauer
1989	Miss Budweiser	T. D'Eath
1990	Miss Budweiser	T. D'Eath
1991	Winston Eagle	M. Tate
1992	Miss Budweiser	C. Hanauer

POLO

Coronation Cup

year	result			
1988	England	8	North America	7
1989	England	7	Australasia	5
1990	England	6	France	5
1991	New Zealand	12	England	10
1992	Not held			

Copa de las Americas

year	winner
1966	Argentina
1969	Argentina
1979	Argentina
1980	Argentina
1988	Argentina

RODEO

Men's World All-Around Rodeo Championship

year	winner	year	winner
1987	L. Feild	1990	T. Murray
1988	D. Appleton	1991	T. Murray
1989	T. Murray	1992	T. Murray

ROWING

World Rowing Championship—men

year	single sculls	min:s	double sculls	min:s	coxed pairs	min:s
1988	T. Lange (E.Ger.)	6:49.86	R. Florijan, N. Rienks (Neth.)	6:21.13	G. Abbagnale, C. Abbagnale (Italy)	6:58.79
1989	T. Lange (E.Ger.)	6:58.14	R. Thorsen, L. Bjoenness (Nor.)	6:23.40	G. Abbagnale, C. Abbagnale (Italy)	6:54.81
1990	Yu. Jensen (U.S.S.R.)	7:22.15	C. Zerbst, A. Jonke (Austria)	6:56.37	G. Abbagnale, C. Abbagnale (Italy)	6:48.30
1991	T. Lange (Ger.)	6:41.29	H.-J. Zwolle, N. Rienks (Neth.)	6:06.14	G. Abbagnale, C. Abbagnale (Italy)	7:34.39
1992	T. Lange (Ger.)	6:51.40	S. Hawkins, P. Antonie (Australia)	6:17.32	J. Searle, G. Searle (U.K.)	6:49.83

year	coxless pairs	min:s	coxed fours	min:s	coxless fours	min:s	eights	min:s
1988	S. Redgrave, A. Holmes (U.K.)	6:36.84	East Germany	6:10.74	East Germany	6:03.11	West Germany	5:46.05
1989	T. Jung, U. Kellner (E.Ger.)	6:39.95	Romania	6:14.90	East Germany	6:06.94	West Germany	5:43.88
1990	T. Jung, U. Kellner (E.Ger.)	7:07.91	East Germany	6:46.73	Australia	5:52.20	West Germany	5:26.62
1991	S. Redgrave, M. Pinsent (U.K.)	6:21.35	Germany	5:58.96	Australia	6:29.69	Germany	5:50.98
1992	S. Redgrave, M. Pinsent (U.K.)	6:27.72	Romania	5:59.37	Australia	5:55.04	Canada	5:29.53

World Rowing Championships—women

year	single sculls	min:s	double sculls	min:s	quadruple sculls	min:s
1988	J. Behrendt (E.Ger.)	7:47.19	B. Peter, M. Schröter (E.Ger.)	7:00.48	East Germany	6:21.06
1989	E. Lipa (Rom.)	7:27.96	J. Sorgers, B. Schramm (E.Ger.)	7:01.71	East Germany	6:16.62
1990	B. Peter (E.Ger.)	7:24.10	K. Boron, B. Schramm (E.Ger.)	8:18.63	East Germany	6:14.08
1991	S. Laumann (Can.)	8:17.58	K. Boron, B. Schramm (Ger.)	6:44.71	Germany	6:55.85
1992	E. Lipa (Rom.)	7:25.54	K. Boron, K. Köppen (Ger.)	6:49.00	Germany	6:20.18

year	coxless pairs	min:s	coxed fours*	min:s	eights	min:s
1988	R. Arba, O. Homeghi (Rom.)	7:28.13	East Germany	6:56.00	East Germany	6:15.17
1989	K. Haaker, J. Zeidler (E.Ger.)	7:26.97	East Germany	6:45.81	Romania	6:07.92
1990	S. Werremeier, I. Althoff (W.Ger.)	8:28.37	Romania	7:51.68	Romania	5:59.26
1991	M. McBean, K. Heddle (Can.)	6:57.42	Canada	6:25.43	Canada	6:28.20
1992	M. McBean, K. Heddle (Can.)	7:06.22	Canada	6:30.85	Canada	6:02.62

*Coxless fours from 1989.

The Diamond Challenge Sculls

year	winner	min:s
1988	H. McGlashan (Melbourne Univ.)	
1989	V. Chalupa (Dukla Praha, Czech.)	7:23*
1990	EFM Verdonk (Koru, N.Z.)	8:21
1991	W. Van Belleghem (Belg.)	†
1992	R. Henderson (Leander R.C.)	7:44

*New record. †Not rowed out.

Grand Challenge Cup

year	winner	min:s
1988	Great Britain Olympic team	
1989	Hansa Dortmund (W.Ger.)	5:58
1990	Hansa Dortmund (W.Ger.)	6:36
1991	Leander and Star R.C.	6:22
1992	University of London	6:04

SKIING

World Nordic (Cross-country) Skiing Championships—men

year	10-km	15-km	30-km	50-km	relay
1987		M. Albarello (Italy)	T. Wassberg (Swed.)	M. De Zolt (Italy)	Sweden
1988		M. Deviatiarov (U.S.S.R.)	A. Prokurorov (U.S.S.R.)	G. Svan (Swed.)	Sweden
1989		G. Svan (Swed.)	V. Smirnov (U.S.S.R.)	G. Svan (Swed.)	Sweden
1991	T. Langli (Nor.)	B. Daehlie (Nor.)	G. Svan (Swed.)	T. Mogren (Swed.)	Norway
1992	V. Ulvang (Nor.)	B. Daehlie (Nor.)	V. Ulvang (Nor.)	B. Daehlie (Nor.)	Norway

World Nordic (Cross-country) Skiing Championships—women

year	5-km	10-km	15-km	20-km	30-km	relay
1987	M. Matikainen (Fin.)	A. Jahren (Nor.)		M.-H. Westin (Swed.)		U.S.S.R.
1988	M. Matikainen (Fin.)	V. Ventsene (U.S.S.R.)		T. Tikhonova (U.S.S.R.)		U.S.S.R.
1989	not held	E. Vialbe (U.S.S.R.)	M. Matikainen (Fin.)		E. Vialbe (U.S.S.R.)	Finland
1991	T. Dybendahl (Nor.)	E. Vialbe (U.S.S.R.)	E. Vialbe (U.S.S.R.)		L. Egorova (U.S.S.R.)	U.S.S.R.
1992	M. Lukkarinen (Fin.)	L. Egorova (UT)	L. Egorova (UT)		S. Belmondo (Italy)	UT

World Nordic Skiing Championships—ski jump

year	70-m hill	90-m hill	120-m hill	team jump	combined	team combined
1987	J. Parma (Czech.)	A. Felder (Austria)		Finland	T. Loekken (Nor.)	West Germany
1988	M. Nykänen (Fin.)	M. Nykänen (Fin.)		Finland	H. Kempf (Switz.)	West Germany
1989	J. Weissflog (E.Ger.)	J. Puikkonen (Fin.)		Finland	T.E. Elden (Nor.)	Norway
1991	H. Kuttin (Austria)	F. Petek (Yugos.)	F. Petek (Yugos.)	Austria	F.-B. Lundberg (Nor.)	Austria
1992		E. Vettori (Austria)	T. Nieminen (Fin.)	Finland	F. Guy (Fr.)	Japan

World Alpine Skiing Championships—slalom

year	men's slalom	men's giant slalom	men's supergiant	women's slalom	women's giant slalom	women's supergiant
1987	F. Woerndl (W.Ger.)	P. Zurbriggen (Switz.)	P. Zurbriggen (Switz.)	E. Hess (Switz.)	V. Schneider (Switz.)	M. Walliser (W.Ger.)
1988	A. Tomba (Italy)	A. Tomba (Italy)	F. Piccard (Fr.)	V. Schneider (Switz.)	V. Schneider (Switz.)	S. Wolf (Austria)
1989	R. Nierlich (Austria)	R. Nierlich (Austria)	M. Hangl ((Switz.)	M. Svet (Yugos.)	V. Schneider (Switz.)	U. Maier (Austria)
1991	M. Girardelli (Lux.)	R. Nierlich (Austria)	S. Eberharter (Austria)	V. Schneider (Switz.)	P. Wiberg (Swed.)	U. Maier (Austria)
1992	F.C. Jagge (Nor.)	A. Tomba (Italy)	K.-A. Aamodt (Nor.)	P. Kronberger (Austria)	P. Wiberg (Swed.)	D. Compagnoni (Italy)

World Alpine Skiing Championships—downhill

year	men	women
1987	P. Müller (Switz.)	M. Walliser (Switz.)
1988	P. Zurbriggen (Switz.)	M. Kichl (W.Ger.)
1989	H. Tauscher (W.Ger.)	M. Walliser (Switz.)
1991	F. Heinzer (Switz.)	P. Kronberger (Austria)
1992	P. Ortlieb (Austria)	K. Lee-Gartner (Can.)

World Alpine Skiing Championships—combined

year	men	women
1987	M. Girardelli (Lux.)	E. Hess (Switz.)
1988	H. Strolz (Austria)	A. Wachter (Austria)
1989	M. Girardelli (Lux.)	T. McKinney (U.S.)
1991	S. Eberharter (Austria)	C. Bournissen (Switz.)
1992	J. Polig (Italy)	P. Kronberger (Austria)

J. Polig: Men's combined world Alpine skiing champion (1992)

MIKE POWELL—ALLSPORT

Alpine World Cup

year	men	women
1988	P. Zurbriggen (Switz.)	M. Figini (Switz.)
1989	M. Girardelli (Lux.)	V. Schneider (Switz.)
1990	P. Zurbriggen (Switz.)	P. Kronberger (Austria)
1991	M. Girardelli (Lux.)	P. Kronberger (Austria)
1992	P. Accola (Switz.)	P. Kronberger (Austria)

Nordic World Cup

year	men	women
1988	G. Svan (Swed.)	M. Matikainen (Fin.)
1989	G. Svan (Swed.)	E. Vialbe (U.S.S.R.)
1990	V. Ulvang (Nor.)	L. Lazutina (U.S.S.R.)
1991	V. Smirnov (U.S.S.R.)	E. Vialbe (U.S.S.R.)
1992	B. Daehlie (Nor.)	E. Vialbe (Russia)

SQUASH RACKETS

British Open Championships—men

year	winner
1987–88	Jah. Khan (Pak.)
1988–89	Jah. Khan (Pak.)
1989–90	Jah. Khan (Pak.)
1990–91	Jah. Khan (Pak.)
1991–92	Jan. Khan (Pak.)

British Open Championships—women

year	winner
1987–88	S. Devoy (N.Z.)
1988–89	S. Devoy (N.Z.)
1989–90	S. Devoy (N.Z.)
1990–91	L. Opie (U.K.)
1991–92	S. Devoy (N.Z.)

World Open Championships—men

year	winner
1988	Jah. Khan (Pak.)
1989	Jan. Khan (Pak.)
1990	Jan. Khan (Pak.)
1991	R. Martin (Australia)
1992	Jan. Khan (Pak.)

World Open Championships—women

year	winner
1987	S. Devoy (N.Z.)
1989	M. Le Moignan (U.K.)
1990	S. Devoy (N.Z.)
1991	not held
1992	S. Devoy (N.Z.)

SWIMMING

World Swimming Championships—men

	freestyle				backstroke	
year	100 m	200 m	400 m	1,500 m	100 m	200 m
1978	D. McCagg (U.S.)	B. Forrester (U.S.)	V. Salnikov (U.S.S.R.)	V. Salnikov (U.S.S.R.)	B. Jackson (U.S.)	J. Vassallo (U.S.)
1982	J. Woithe (E.Ger.)	M. Gross (W.Ger.)	V. Salnikov (U.S.S.R.)	V. Salnikov (U.S.S.R.)	D. Richter (E.Ger.)	R. Carey (U.S.)
1986	M. Biondi (U.S.)	M. Gross (W.Ger.)	R. Henkel (W.Ger.)	R. Henkel (W.Ger.)	I. Polyansky (U.S.S.R.)	I. Polyansky (U.S.S.R.)
1991	M. Biondi (U.S.)	G. Lamberti (Italy)	J. Hoffmann (Ger.)	J. Hoffmann (Ger.)	J. Rouse (U.S.)	M. Lopez Zubero (Spain)

	breaststroke		butterfly		individual medley	
	100 m	200 m	100 m	200 m	200 m	400 m
1978	W. Kusch (W.Ger.)	N. Nevid (U.S.)	J. Bottom (U.S.)	M. Bruner (U.S.)	G. Smith (Can.)	J. Vassallo (U.S.)
1982	S. Lundquist (U.S.)	V. Davis (Can.)	M. Gribble (U.S.)	M. Gross (W.Ger.)	A. Sidorenko (U.S.S.R.)	R. Prado (Braz.)
1986	V. Davis (Can.)	J. Szabo (Hung.)	P. Morales (U.S.)	M. Gross (W.Ger.)	T. Darnyi (Hung.)	T. Darnyi (Hung.)
1991	N. Rozsa (Hung.)	M. Barrowman (U.S.)	A. Nesty (Suriname)	M. Stewart (U.S.)	T. Darnyi (Hung.)	T. Darnyi (Hung.)

	team relays			diving	
	4 × 100-m freestyle	4 × 200-m freestyle	4 × 100-m medley	3-m springboard	platform
1978	United States	United States	United States	P. Boggs (U.S.)	G. Louganis (U.S.)
1982	United States	United States	United States	G. Louganis (U.S.)	G. Louganis (U.S.)
1986	United States	East Germany	United States	G. Louganis (U.S.)	G. Louganis (U.S.)
1991	United States	Germany	United States	K. Ferguson (U.S.)	Sun Shuwei (China)

World Swimming Championships—women

	freestyle				backstroke	
year	100 m	200 m	400 m	800 m	100 m	200 m
1978	B. Krause (E.Ger.)	C. Woodhead (U.S.)	T. Wickham (Australia)	T. Wickham (Australia)	L. Jezek (U.S.)	L. Jezek (U.S.)
1982	B. Meineke (E.Ger.)	A. Verstappen (Neth.)	C. Schmidt (E.Ger.)	K. Linehan (U.S.)	K. Otto (E.Ger.)	C. Sirch (E.Ger.)
1986	K. Otto (E.Ger.)	H. Friedrich (E.Ger.)	H. Friedrich (E.Ger.)	A. Strauss (E.Ger.)	B. Mitchell (U.S.)	C. Sirch (E.Ger.)
1991	N. Haislett (U.S.)	H. Lewis (Australia)	J. Evans (U.S.)	J. Evans (U.S.)	K. Egerszegi (Hung.)	K. Egerszegi (Hung.)

	breaststroke		butterfly		individual medley	
	100 m	200 m	100 m	200 m	200 m	400 m
1978	J. Bogdanova (U.S.S.R.)	L. Kachushite (U.S.S.R.)	J. Pennington (U.S.)	T. Caulkins (U.S.)	T. Caulkins (U.S.)	T. Caulkins (U.S.)
1982	U. Geweniger (E.Ger.)	S. Varganova (U.S.S.R.)	M.T. Meagher (U.S.)	I. Geissler (E.Ger.)	P. Schneider (E.Ger.)	P. Schneider (E.Ger.)
1986	S. Gerasch (E.Ger.)	S. Hörner (E.Ger.)	K. Gressler (E.Ger.)	M.T. Meagher (U.S.)	K. Otto (E.Ger.)	K. Nord (E.Ger.)
1991	L. Frame (Australia)	E. Volkova (U.S.S.R.)	Qian Hong (China)	S. Sanders (U.S.)	Lin Li (China)	Lin Li (China)

	team relays			diving	
	4 × 100-m freestyle	4 × 200-m freestyle	4 × 100-m medley	3-m springboard	platform
1978	United States		United States	I. Kalinina (U.S.S.R.)	I. Kalinina (U.S.S.R.)
1982	East Germany		East Germany	M. Neyer (U.S.)	W. Wyland (U.S.)
1986	East Germany	East Germany	East Germany	Gao Min (China)	Chen Lin (China)
1991	United States	Germany	United States	Gao Min (China)	Fu Mingxia (China)

N. Haislett: World Swimming Championship—
women's 100 m freestyle (1991)

HEINZ KLUETMEIER—SPORTS ILLUSTRATED

TABLE TENNIS

World Table Tennis Championships—men

year	St. Bride's Vase (singles)	Iran Cup (doubles)	Swaythling Cup (team)
1985	Jiang Jialiang (China)	M. Appelgren, U. Carlsson (Swed.)	China
1987	Jiang Jialiang (China)	Chen Longcan, Wei Qingguang (China)	China
1989	J.-O. Waldner (Swed.)	J. Rosskopf, S. Fetzner (W.Ger.)	Sweden
1991	J. Persson (Swed.)	P. Karlsson, T. Von Scheele (Swed.)	Sweden

World Table Tennis Championships—women

year	G. Geist Prize (singles)	W.J. Pope Trophy (doubles)	Corbillon Cup (team)
1985	Cao Yanhua (China)	Dai Lili, Geng Lijuan (China)	China
1987	He Zhili (China)	Hyun Jung Hwa, Yang Young Ja (S.Kor.)	China
1989	Qiao Hong (China)	Qiao Hong, Deng Yaping (China)	China
1991	Deng Yaping (China)	Gao Jun, Chen Zihe (China)	Korea

World Table Tennis Championships—mixed

year	Heydusek Prize
1983	Guo Yuehua, Ni Xialian (China)
1985	Cai Zhenhua, Cao Yanhua (China)
1987	Hui Jun, Geng Lijuan (China)
1989	Yoo Nam Kyu, Hyung Jung Hwa (S.Kor.)
1991	Wang Tao, Liu Wei (China)

Table Tennis World Cup

year	winner
1988	A. Grubba (Pol.)
1989	Ma Wenge (China)
1990	J.-O. Waldner (Swed.)
1991	J. Persson (Swed.)
1992	Ma Wenge (China)

TENNIS

J. Courier: French Open—men's singles (1992)

RICHARD MARTIN—VANDYSTADT/ALLSPORT

Cuba: Women's world volleyball champions (1992)

MITCHELL LAYTON—DUOMO

All-England (Wimbledon) Tennis Championships—singles

year	men	women
1988	S. Edberg (Swed.)	S. Graf (W.Ger.)
1989	B. Becker (W.Ger.)	S. Graf (W.Ger.)
1990	S. Edberg (Swed.)	M. Navratilova (U.S.)
1991	M. Stich (Ger.)	S. Graf (Ger.)
1992	A. Agassi (U.S.)	S. Graf (Ger.)

All-England (Wimbledon) Tennis Championships—doubles

year	men	women
1988	R. Seguso/K. Flach	S. Graf/G. Sabatini
1989	J. Fitzgerald/A. Jarryd	J. Novotna/H. Sukova
1990	R. Leach/J. Pugh	J. Novotna/H. Sukova
1991	J. Fitzgerald/A. Jarryd	L. Savchenko/N. Zvereva
1992	J. McEnroe/M. Stich	G. Fernandez/N. Zvereva

United States Open Tennis Championships—singles

year	men	women
1988	M. Wilander (Swed.)	S. Graf (W.Ger.)
1989	B. Becker (W.Ger.)	S. Graf (W.Ger.)
1990	P. Sampras (U.S.)	G. Sabatini (Arg.)
1991	S. Edberg (Swed.)	M. Seles (Yugos.)
1992	S. Edberg (Swed.)	M. Seles (Yugos.)

United States Open Tennis Championships—doubles

year	men	women
1988	S. Casal/E. Sánchez	G. Fernandez/R. White
1989	J. McEnroe/M. Woodforde	M. Navratilova/H. Mandlikova
1990	P. Aldrich/D. Visser	M. Navratilova/G. Fernandez
1991	J. Fitzgerald/A. Jarryd	P. Shriver/N. Zvereva
1992	J. Grabb/R. Reneberg	G. Fernandez/N. Zvereva

French Open Tennis Championships—singles

year	men	women
1988	M. Wilander (Swed.)	S. Graf (W.Ger.)
1989	M. Chang (U.S.)	A. Sánchez Vicario (Spain)
1990	A. Gomez (Ecu.)	M. Seles (Yugos.)
1991	J. Courier (U.S.)	M. Seles (Yugos.)
1992	J. Courier (U.S.)	M. Seles (Yugos.)

French Open Tennis Championships—doubles

year	men	women
1988	E. Sánchez/A. Gomez	M. Navratilova/P. Shriver
1989	J. Grabb/P. McEnroe	L. Savchenko/N. Zvereva
1990	S. Casal/E. Sánchez	J. Novotna/H. Sukova
1991	J. Fitzgerald/A. Jarryd	G. Fernandez/J. Novotna
1992	J. Hlasek/M.Rosset	G. Fernandez/N. Zvereva

Australian Open Tennis Championships—singles

year	men	women
1988	M. Wilander (Swed.)	S. Graf (W.Ger.)
1989	I. Lendl (Czech.)	S. Graf (W.Ger.)
1990	I. Lendl (Czech.)	S. Graf (W.Ger.)
1991	B. Becker (Ger.)	M. Seles (Yugos.)
1992	J. Courier (U.S.)	M. Seles (Yugos.)

Australian Open Tennis Championships—doubles

year	men	women
1988	R. Leach/J. Pugh	M. Navratilova/P. Shriver
1989	R. Leach/J. Pugh	M. Navratilova/P. Shriver
1990	P. Aldrich/D. Visser	J. Novotna/H. Sukova
1991	S. Davis/D. Pate	P. Fendick/M.J. Fernandez
1992	T. Woodbridge/M.Woodforde	A. Sánchez Vicario/H. Sukova

Davis Cup

year	winner
1987	Sweden
1988	West Germany
1989	West Germany
1990	United States
1991	France
1992	United States

Wightman Cup

year	winner
1987	United States
1988	United States
1989	United States
1990	not held
1991	not held
1992	not held

Federation Cup

year	winner	runner-up	results
1988	Czechoslovakia	U.S.S.R.	2–1
1989	United States	Spain	3–0
1990	United States	U.S.S.R.	2–1
1991	Spain	United States	2–1
1992	Germany	Spain	2–1

VOLLEYBALL

World Volleyball Championships

year	men	women	year	men	women
1982	U.S.S.R.	China	1988	United States	U.S.S.R.
1984	United States	China	1990	Italy	U.S.S.R.
1986	United States	China	1992	Brazil	Cuba

WRESTLING

World Wrestling Championships—Freestyle

year	48 kg	52 kg	57 kg	62 kg	68 kg
1987	Li Jae Sik (N.Kor.)	V. Iordanov (Bulg.)	S. Beloglazov (U.S.S.R.)	J. Smith (U.S.)	A. Fadzaev (U.S.S.R.)
1988	T. Kobayashi (Japan)	M. Sato (Japan)	S. Beloglazov (U.S.S.R.)	J. Smith (U.S.)	A. Fadzaev (U.S.S.R.)
1989	J. Kim (S.Kor.)	V. Jordanov (Bulg.)	S. Yeung (N.Kor.)	J. Smith (U.S.)	B. Bovdayev (U.S.S.R.)
1990	A. Martinez (Cuba)	M. Torkan (Iran)	A. Puerto (Cuba)	J. Smith (U.S.)	A. Fadzaev (U.S.S.R.)
1991	V. Orudzhev (U.S.S.R.)	Z. Jones (U.S.)	S. Smal (U.S.S.R.)	J. Smith (U.S.)	A. Fadzaev (U.S.S.R.)
1992	Park II (N.Kor.)	Li Hak (N.Kor.)	A. Puerto (Cuba)	J. Smith (U.S.)	A. Fadzaev (UT)

year	74 kg	82 kg	90 kg	100 kg	130 kg
1987	A. Varaev (U.S.S.R.)	M. Schultz (U.S.)	M. Khadartsev (U.S.S.R.)	L. Khabelov (U.S.S.R.)	A. Khadartsev (U.S.S.R.)
1988	K. Monday (U.S.)	Han Myang Woo (S. Kor.)	M. Khadartsev (U.S.S.R.)	V. Puscasu (Rom.)	D. Gobedzhishvili (U.S.S.R.)
1989	K. Monday (U.S.)	E. Jabraylov (U.S.S.R.)	M. Khadartsev (U.S.S.R.)	A. Atavov (U.S.S.R.)	A.R. Soleimani (Iran)
1990	R. Sofiyadi (Bulg.)	J. Lohyna (Czech.)	M. Khadartsev (U.S.S.R.)	L. Khabelov (U.S.S.R.)	D. Gobedzhishvili (U.S.S.R.)
1991	A. Khadem (Iran)	K. Jackson (U.S.)	M. Khadartsev (U.S.S.R.)	L. Khabelov (U.S.S.R.)	A. Schroder (Ger.)
1992	Park Jang (S.Kor.)	K. Jackson (U.S.)	M. Khadartsev (UT)	L. Khabelov (UT)	B. Baumgartner (U.S.)

World Wrestling Championships—Greco-Roman style

year	48 kg	52 kg	57 kg	62 kg	68 kg
1987	M. Allakhverdiev (U.S.S.R.)	P. Roque (Cuba)	P. Mourier (France)	J. Vanguelov (Bulg.)	A. Abaev (U.S.S.R.)
1988	V. Maenza (Italy)	J. Ronningen (Nor.)	A. Sike (Hung.)	K. Madzhidov (U.S.S.R.)	L. Dzhulfalakyan (U.S.S.R.)
1989	O. Kucherenko (U.S.S.R.)	A. Ignatenko (U.S.S.R.)	E. Iwanov (Bulg.)	K. Madzhidov (U.S.S.R.)	C. Passarelli (W.Ger.)
1990	O. Kucherenko (U.S.S.R.)	A. Ignatenko (U.S.S.R.)	R. Yildiz (Ger.)	M. Oliveras (Cuba)	I. Doguchiev (U.S.S.R.)
1991	Duk Yong Gooun (S.Kor.)	R. Martínez (Cuba)	R. Yildiz (Ger.)	S. Martynov (U.S.S.R.)	I. Doguchiev (U.S.S.R.)
1992	O. Kucherenko (UT)	J. Ronningen (Nor.)	An Han Bong (S.Kor.)	A. Pirim (Tur.)	A. Repka (Hung.)

year	74 kg	82 kg	90 kg	100 kg	130 kg
1987	J. Salomaki (Fin.)	T. Komaromi (Hung.)	V. Popov (U.S.S.R.)	G. Guedekhaorui (U.S.S.R.)	I. Rostorotsky (U.S.S.R.)
1988	Kim Young Nam (S.Kor.)	M. Mamiashvili (U.S.S.R.)	A. Komchev (Bulg.)	A. Wronski (Pol.)	A. Karelin (U.S.S.R.)
1989	D. Turlykhanov (U.S.S.R.)	T. Komaromi (Hung.)	M. Bullmann (E.Ger.)	G. Himmel (W.Ger.)	A. Karelin (U.S.S.R.)
1990	M. Iskandarian (U.S.S.R.)	P. Farcas (Hung.)	M. Bullmann (Ger.)	S. Demiaschkievish (U.S.S.R.)	A. Karelin (U.S.S.R.)
1991	M. Iskandarian (U.S.S.R.)	P. Farcas (Hung.)	M. Bullmann (Ger.)	H. Milian (Cuba)	A. Karelin (U.S.S.R.)
1992	M. Iskandarian (UT)	P. Farcas (Hung.)	M. Bullmann (Ger.)	H. Milian (Cuba)	A. Karelin (UT)

YACHTING

America's Cup

year	winning yacht	owner	skipper	losing yacht	owner
1977	Courageous (U.S.)	Courageous syndicate	T. Turner	Australia (Australia)	A. Bond and syndicate
1980	Freedom (U.S.)	Maritime College at Fort Schuyler Foundation, Inc.	D. Conner	Australia (Australia)	A. Bond and syndicate
1983	Australia II (Australia)	A. Bond and syndicate	J. Bertrand	Liberty (U.S.)	Maritime College at Fort Schuyler Foundation, Inc.
1987	Stars & Stripes (U.S.)	Sail America syndicate	D. Conner	Kookaburra III (Australia)	K. Parry and syndicate
1988	Stars & Stripes (U.S.)	Sail America syndicate	D. Conner	New Zealand (New Zealand)	M. Fay
1992	America³ (U.S.)	America³ Foundation	B. Koch	Il Moro di Venezia (Italy)	Compagnia della Vela di Venezia

J. Ronningen (left): 52-kg Greco-Roman world wrestling champion (1992)

MIKE POWELL—ALLSPORT

Bermuda Race

year	winning yacht	owner
1984	Pamir	F. Curren, Jr.
1986	Silver Star	D. Clarke
	and Puritan	D. Robinson
1988	Congere	B. Koeppel
1990	Denali	L. Huntington
1992	Constellation	U.S. Naval Academy

Transpacific Race

year	winning yacht	owner
1983	Bravura	I. Loube
1985	Montgomery Street	D. Denning
1987	Merlin	D. Campion
1989	Silver Bullet	J. DeLaura
1991	Chance	R. McNulty

Fastnet Cup

year	winning yacht	owner
1985	Panda	P. Whipp (U.K.)
1987	Irish Independent Pelt	S. Fein (Ire.)
1989	Great News	R. Short (U.S.)
1991	no overall winner	

Television and Radio

For better or worse, television and presidential politics in the United States became intertwined in 1992 as never before as George Bush, Bill Clinton, and Ross Perot discovered that they could use the TV talk-show circuit to circumvent reporters and deliver their messages directly to the American public. Perot led the way, announcing his upstart candidacy on Cable News Network's (CNN's) "Larry King Live" in February. Clinton and Jerry Brown followed with a debate on "Donahue" just before the New York primary in April. And by the last week of the campaign, Clinton and Bush were taking turns on the networks' morning shows. "Candidates have sought out programs with easy access and the best chance of getting easy questions," explained Dan Rather of CBS News. "Western civilization will survive," he added.

Although the networks' reduced coverage of the Democratic and Republican conventions failed to draw big audiences, a series of four televised debates (one of them between the candidates for vice president) in October got very high ratings. After reentering the race on October 1, billionaire Perot spent some $23 million (more than either Clinton or Bush spent on TV during the entire campaign) to air his political "infomercials" in prime time.

The line between political fact and TV fantasy blurred when U.S. Vice Pres. Dan Quayle accused the producers of CBS's "Murphy Brown" of encouraging pregnancies outside of marriage after the show's unwed title character, a successful and wealthy TV newswoman played by Candice Bergen (*see* BIOGRAPHIES), became pregnant. Quayle's comments produced a backlash from those who saw them as an attack on single parenthood.

The same languishing economy that propelled Clinton into the White House produced another year of belt-tightening and slow revenue growth for broadcasting, but there was hope that things would get better. Veronis, Suhler & Associates, a New York City-based investment banking firm, projected that broadcast TV revenues would grow at a rate of 6.3% a year between 1992 and 1996, a significant improvement over the 2.4% annual rate of the previous five years. According to the Radio Advertising Bureau, advertising sales through the first nine months of 1992 were flat. But the trade group believed that a sudden surge in revenues in September—up 8% over September 1991—marked the beginning of a sustained recovery. For the first time in years, it was cable that was being faced with slower growth. This was a result of market saturation and prospects of smaller rate hikes due to the return of stiff regulation.

The soft economy did not slow the inexorable growth of TV and radio outlets in the U.S. In September the Federal Communications Commission (FCC) counted 12,672 radio stations and 1,692 TV stations. According to the A.C. Nielsen Co., 61% (56.6 million) of the 92.1 million homes with television subscribed to cable, and 75.1% had at least one videocassette recorder. The latest Unesco survey (1989) found 524 million radios and 201 million TV sets in the U.S., far more than in any other country and large percentages of the more than 2 billion radios and 900 million TV sets around the world. Japan was second in number of television sets (107.5 million), and China was second in radios (206 million).

Satellite broadcasting, or direct broadcast satellite (DBS) service, might soon be adding its homes and percentages to the media mix in the U.S. Hughes Communications moved ahead with the construction of two high-power satellites with which it and partner United States Satellite Broadcasting planned to beam some 200 channels of TV to subscribers starting in early 1994. Skypix, which had promised to launch an 80-channel satellite broadcasting service in 1992, never did. Its plans unraveled in a flurry of suits and countersuits among investors. By September it was in Chapter 11 bankruptcy.

Programming. NBC's long dominance of prime-time network TV ended as CBS won the 1991–92 season with a 13.8 rating and 23 share, according to Nielsen. The other networks (in order of finish) were: NBC, 12.3/20; ABC, 12.2/20; and Fox, 8.0/13. (A rating is the percentage of the 92.1 million homes with television sets; a share is the percentage of homes with television sets on during a program's time slot.) CBS's top performers were "60 Minutes" and the much-talked-about "Murphy Brown," the first- and third-rated programs of the season, respectively. Despite its third-place finish, ABC placed four situation comedies in the top 10: "Roseanne" (the second-ranked show), "Home Improvement," "Coach," and "Full House." NBC's best was the veteran "Cheers," which came in fourth and whose cancellation was unexpectedly announced in December.

CBS appeared likely to stay atop the ratings in the 1992–93 season, helped along with new entries like "Love & War" and "Hearts Afire." Both seemed to be capturing an audience. Fox and producer Aaron Spelling tried to duplicate their success with "Beverly Hills: 90210," introducing two new youth-oriented ensemble dramas. "Melrose Place" and "The Heights" stumbled in the ratings, however.

The year marked the end of Johnny Carson's reign as the "King of Late Night." After 30 years he relinquished the "Tonight Show" throne in May to comedian Jay Leno (*see* BIOGRAPHIES), who had been the show's permanent guest host. The transition fired up competition for the late-night audience and the $500 million in advertising revenues it attracted. The "Dennis Miller Show" came and went within the year, but "Arsenio" with Arsenio Hall proved a legitimate contender.

CBS duplicated its ratings victory at the 44th annual Emmy awards in August, walking away with 20 statuettes. Its Monday-night "Northern Exposure" led the way with six awards, including that for outstanding drama series. "Murphy Brown" won for outstanding comedy series and best actress (Bergen) and best director (Barnet Kellman) in a comedy series. NBC and ABC each garnered 17 awards; the Public Broadcasting Service, 7; and Fox, 6. "Star Trek: The Next Generation," the only syndicated program to be honoured, took home five Emmies. The cable networks continued to make inroads, picking up 11 awards. Beau Bridges received one for his starring role in HBO's "Without Warning: The James Brady Story," and Christopher Lloyd won the award for best actor in a drama series for his work in the Disney Channel's "Avonlea."

The Sci-Fi Channel and Ted Turner's Cartoon Network were the year's new cable programming services. The former, a mix of movies and such reruns as "Lost in Space" and "Night Gallery," debuted in 10 million cable homes on September 24. The latter appeared in two million homes a week later.

Cable's big hope for the future remained pay-per-view (PPV) television, which allowed subscribers to pay for individual programs or series. But the results of 1992 were disappointing. Sales of NBC's and Cablevision's Triplecast—three channels of extra coverage of the summer Olympic Games—fell far short of projections, contributing to the estimated $100 million that NBC lost on the Games. Cable subscribers were also indifferent to the series of college football games that Showtime and ABC made available in the fall. And early returns from Time Warner's PPV

Texas billionaire Ross Perot (right) makes a point with talk show host Larry King. It was on "Larry King Live" that Perot first announced the conditions under which he would consider running for the presidency, and he appeared on the call-in show several times during the year.

GEORGE BENNETT

trial in New York City, in which subscribers were given a choice of a large number of PPV movies each evening, were inconclusive.

In radio, country music solidified its position as the hottest format, and as country stations multiplied and competition intensified, the format began to splinter. Some stations went with "young country" featuring freewheeling personalities and the music of such new stars as Garth Brooks (*see* BIOGRAPHIES) and Alan Jackson. Others distinguished themselves with "easy country" or "classic country."

Mutual Broadcasting's King and the nationally syndicated Rush Limbaugh, buoyed by the attention paid them by presidential candidates, led a boom in talk radio. According to the 1992 *Broadcasting & Cable Market Place,* the number of stations with talk formats had tripled during the past five years to 875 in 1992. Industry experts estimated that another 500 stations might feature talk for substantial portions of their broadcast days.

When the unprecedented number of baseball free agents sat down to negotiate new contracts in 1993, many might find the big money elusive. The network television money that fueled the upward salary spiral was threatening to dry up. ESPN decided in November to pay a $13 million penalty to avoid a two-year extension (1994 and 1995) of its four-year, $400 million pact with major league baseball that extended through the 1993 season. And in September CBS made it clear that it did not want to extend its $1.1 billion four-year deal, which included rights to the play-offs and World Series and also ran through 1993.

ESPN sustained estimated losses of up to $200 million on the first three years of its baseball deal; CBS lost up to $275 million. CBS and ESPN might bid again for baseball but, given their recent experience, their offers would likely be nowhere near the combined $1.5 billion they put on the table the last time around.

Rivalries between private and public broadcasters and between the terrestrial and satellite channels dominated programming in Europe. Much of the competition centred on the rights to televise major sporting events and came to a head when the competition directorate of the European Communities ordered the European Broadcasting Union, which represented mainly public stations, to stop denying other broadcasters live access to its sports rights. The European Commission also forced the Union of European Football Associations to withdraw all restrictions on the televising of live soccer.

In the United Kingdom the BBC and satellite competitor British Sky Broadcasting (BSkyB) submitted a combined £304 million bid for rights to the English Soccer Premier League, which for the four previous years had gone to the rival commercial Independent Television (ITV) network for only £55 million. BSkyB claimed that some 700,000 viewers had been persuaded to pay to watch Premier games live, twice as many as had been expected. ITV responded by paying £4.8 million for five years of exclusive rights to track and field tournaments in Berlin; Brussels; Oslo, Norway; and Zürich, Switz.; and Channel 4 secured rights to screen Italian league association football (soccer). In The Netherlands the national broadcaster NOS outbid rival RTL 4 to pay $10 million for three seasons of the Dutch soccer league, three times the price paid for its previous contract. RTL 4, in turn, secured exclusive rights to all the home games of the Dutch national soccer team over four years for a fee reported as $12 million.

In Italy state broadcaster RAI lost exclusive rights to national and European soccer cup contests, Formula One motor racing, and the Giro D'Italia cycling race to rival commercial stations controlled by Silvio Berlusconi. RAI's frustrated sports journalists organized a two-day protest.

In France a fierce battle for audience was waged by the commercial channel TF1, whose share of viewers fell sharply during the summer to the public channels Antenne 2 and FR3. Two weekly entertainment programs with TF1's main host, Patrick Sabatier, were taken off the air, and chief political reporter Jean-Luc Mano resigned, claiming that TF1 had delayed broadcasting the results of the referendum on the Maastricht Treaty concerning European unity in order to create an atmosphere of suspense and retain audiences. TF1 finally recovered a majority share of audiences in October. One of its successes was, unexpectedly, "Mystères," a series of real-life unexplained mysteries that attracted 9.5 million viewers and a 42% audience share.

Elsewhere, however, documentary or reality programming was being squeezed out of the schedules. Even in the U.K. a report on cultural trends by the Policy Studies Institute revealed that the amount of time devoted by the BBC to features, documentaries, and current affairs dropped by 148 hours—almost 5%—in 1991. The amount of time devoted to news, however, more than doubled. Significant increases were also evident in the amount of purchased programs, primarily films and popular drama series, up from 16.1% of output to 25.9%.

Soap operas remained an essential element of most broadcasters' programming. The BBC, however, appeared to have lost some of its sure professional touch with "Eldorado," a £10 million three-times-a-week "soap" revolving around the lives of a group of expatriates from different countries living in southern Spain. A holiday village costing £2 million was built in Spain, and a cast of more than 30 characters drawn from six countries was assembled for the series. Despite extensive publicity, though, "Eldorado" failed to draw audiences and received a hostile reception from press and public alike.

Elsewhere, such shows achieved greater success. In New Zealand TVNZ's first five-nights-a-week home-produced series, "Shortland Street," gained a 26% share of audience on its opening night. In Germany a local-language version of the Australian series "The Restless Years," retitled "Gute Zeiten, Schlechte Zeiten" ("Good Times, Bad Times"), drew a respectable two million viewers five times a week. Another Australian soap, "Home and Away," secured a £20 million, three-year contract with the British ITV network, which had feared that satellite rival BSkyB might acquire it.

In regard to television news, dramatic and disturbing pictures came in reports from the conflict in Bosnia and Hercegovina. One of the most remarkable was from Penny Marshall, a reporter with the U.K. news provider ITN. She obtained stark pictures from inside the barbed wire of Serbian internment camps. The report helped heighten international awareness of the human tragedy in Bosnia.

Nevertheless, news and current affairs continued to be threatened almost everywhere by political censorship. In the former Soviet Union demonstrators from the neocommunist movement Trudovaya Rossiya laid siege to the Moscow studios of the Ostankino state broadcaster, accusing the company of being an "empire of lies." The siege was lifted after four days when the station threatened to halt broadcasts of the European soccer championships. In Italy police seized from RAI 3 copies of the documentary program "Gladio," which contained interviews with people who claimed to have information about the murder of former prime minister Aldo Moro in 1978.

In the U.K., what had become a perennial controversy over so-called faction—dramatized documentaries—continued, reaching a peak over two programs, "Civvies" on BBC 1, about an ex-paratrooper adjusting to life outside the army, and "Hostages" on the ITV station Granada, which purported to tell the true story of the British and U.S. hostages held in Lebanon. Four of the hostages portrayed in the program, John McCarthy, Brian Keenan, Terry Waite, and Terry Anderson, signed a joint letter complaining that the program was "insensitive" and a "serious abuse of public trust."

Organization. Feeling the heat from angry consumers and broadcasters, the U.S. Congress overrode a veto by President Bush in October to enact comprehensive cable legislation aimed at holding down subscriber rates and fostering competition to cable. Only time would tell if the measure would achieve its goals, but strict new rate regulation should at least slow the increases in subscriber fees.

Broadcasters had fought hard for the legislation after attaching a provision giving TV stations the choice of either demanding that cable systems carry their signals or negotiating for payments from systems that wanted to carry their signals. Many broadcasters planned to negotiate for payments and a share of cable revenues, which topped $20 billion in 1992. Some industry analysts believed that the broadcasters' take could amount to several hundred million dollars a year. Other likely beneficiaries of the legislation were the prospective DBS providers and other would-be cable competitors. The new law should facilitate their ability to include in their service offerings popular cable programming such as HBO, Showtime, MTV, CNN, and Nickelodeon.

Convinced that the bill was overregulatory, Bush vetoed it. Congress' override marked Bush's first defeat on a veto, breaking a string of 35 successful ones. Bush had issued a deregulatory call to arms in his state of the union address in January, and FCC chairman Alfred Sikes took it to heart. Despite opposition from congressional Democrats, the FCC relaxed rules restricting the number of radio stations a single company could own. Under the liberalized rules, broadcast groups could now own up to 18 AM stations and 18 FM stations nationally and up to 3 stations in the same market.

Also, Sikes led the FCC in relaxing barriers to the involvement of telephone companies in video transmission in hopes of spurring the construction of advanced broadband networks capable of carrying video as well as telephone services. The package of reforms came to be known as "video dialtone," a term that captured Sikes's vision of a time when consumers could order any video program over the telephone network as easily as they now made a phone call. The telephone companies were now allowed to build broadband networks and lease channel capacity to programmers without having to get permission from municipalities and pay local cable franchise fees. They still could not control the programming they transmitted, but they could have a small financial stake in it.

The FCC continued to promote the development of high-definition television (HDTV), an all-new service featuring a wider screen, greater resolution, and superior sound. The agency hoped to have an HDTV standard and a plan to give each TV station a second channel for HDTV broadcasting by the end of 1993. But broadcasters were having second thoughts as they began adding up the cost of converting to HDTV production and transmitting a second signal.

Economic recession and a consequent slowdown in consumer spending overshadowed much of broadcasting developments in Europe in 1992. Spain's RTVE requested a loan of 20 billion pesetas to pay off debts. In France the commercial channel La Cinq collapsed under financial pressures, and new commercial broadcasters in Norway and Sweden struggled to survive with low advertising revenues.

RICHARD CARTWRIGHT—CBS

Actress Candice Bergen, who plays the title role in "Murphy Brown," holds her television baby. The show got a burst of added attention in 1992 when U.S. Vice Pres. Dan Quayle, campaigning for "family values," attacked it for depicting an unmarried mother in a favourable light.

In the United Kingdom there was uncertainty as to whether the proposed Channel 5 would come into existence.

In Portugal the first private channel, SIC, headed by former prime minister Francisco Pinto Balsemão, was launched to a mixed reception from both viewers and advertisers. A second Portuguese private channel, TVi, funded by the Roman Catholic Church and headed by a former minister of education, Robert Carneiro, was scheduled to open on Jan. 1, 1993. Church funding from the Orthodox Church in Cyprus launched Cyprus' first private station, O Logos, in opposition to two state-funded channels, CYBC1 and CYBC2.

Defying the economic climate and the trend toward commercialization, a Franco-German cultural channel, Arte, was launched as Europe's first truly binational, bilingual service and as one with an unashamedly minority appeal. Originally conceived as a cable channel, Arte moved into the terrestrial frequency vacated by the collapse of La Cinq, attracting 500,000 viewers in its first week on the air.

Also against the trend, the French commercial broadcaster TF1 recorded a 13.7% increase in profits in 1991 to F 341 million. The French public broadcasters Antenne 2 and FR3 also reduced their budget deficits, having cut costs and increased advertising revenues. TF1, however, found itself censored and fined F 30 million by the national regulatory body, the CSA, for failing to meet its 1991 quotas for original production.

Elsewhere in Europe, governments backed down from radical proposals to restructure their broadcasting institutions. In Italy a major restructuring that would have entailed the partial privatization of the state broadcaster RAI was shelved, and a new broadcasting bill was postponed. The Dutch government halted plans to sell off the third channel of state broadcaster NOS to private operators. NOS decided, in turn, to revise its programming policies to give each of its three public networks clearer and more distinct identities and provide stronger competition to its successful commercial rival, RTL 4, which had become profitable after only three years of broadcasting.

In the U.K. the BBC awaited government proposals for the future when its royal charter came up for renewal in 1996. The BBC's own proposals in a private internal document leaked to the industry's trade magazine *Broadcast* revealed a controversial strategy to "withdraw from areas which it is no longer able or needed to make an original contribution." This would involve abandoning popular programs such as game shows and imported drama and concentrating on areas other broadcasters might neglect.

In Germany the 15 media authorities suspended all processing of licenses pending a monopolies investigation of the country's commercial broadcasters. This postponed any decision on three proposed new cable and satellite channels. The investigations appeared to be into the market dominance of the Kirch Group, which had an interest in five of the nation's six private channels, and the Bertelsmann Media Group, which had holdings in RTL Plus and the Premiere pay channel. Concern over concentration of media power was also widely expressed throughout Europe following a joint venture between Rupert Murdoch's News Corp. and the French Canal Plus to develop new subscription and PPV TV services and to influence future encryption and transmission standards in Europe.

(MARTIN JACKSON; HARRY A. JESSELL; LAWRENCE B. TAISHOFF)

Amateur Radio. In normal times ham radio tends to be dismissed as a hobbyist's plaything. In times of crisis, however, it emerges as a vital communications link, as it did in the summer of 1992 in the wake of two powerful hurricanes that blasted Miami, Fla., and the Hawaiian island of Kauai. With telephone and other conventional communications networks knocked out, ham operators stepped in to relay lifesaving emergency information or to simply send out reassurances to loved ones from those caught in the storms.

In the scientific arena two of the year's space shuttles were equipped with gear that allowed ham operators throughout the world to talk to the astronauts and relay messages through space. More than 5,000 voice and packet contacts were made with the September flight.

The number of hams continued to grow as more and more people took advantage of the new licensing criteria requiring no Morse code for some classes of operation. According to the American Radio Relay League, there were 580,806 licensed hams at the end of September, up from 529,680 the year before.

(HARRY A. JESSELL; LAWRENCE B. TAISHOFF)

See also Industrial Review: *Advertising; Telecommunications;* Motion Pictures; Music.

This article updates the *Macropædia* article BROADCASTING.

Theatre

Great Britain and Ireland. The Arts Council of Great Britain in 1992 published a document that suggested that the 1980s had been the decade of sponsorship and that the 1990s would be the decade of marketing. This depressing forecast was exacerbated for the theatre community by the resignation in September of the popular minister for the arts, David Mellor, in a personal scandal.

The shock of that news was replaced by the thud of the familiar as the Royal Court, home of new writing, had an indifferent year, and the Royal National Theatre continued, very successfully, to be all sorts of things to all sorts of people. The West End commercial theatre suffered from the recession, bomb scares by the Irish Republican Army, a collapse in the tourist trade, and an alarmingly quick turnover of product that left even the marketing men reeling.

In the year that Marlene Dietrich died (see OBITUARIES), the commercial failure of a new stage version of her breakthrough film, *The Blue Angel*, at the Globe, was a sad indication that audiences were not prepared to pay good money to see a demanding musical play, even if it was directed by Trevor Nunn and first presented by the Royal Shakespeare Company (RSC). This fine show, sensitively adapted by playwright Pam Gems and brilliantly led by Kelly Hunter as the cabaret singer Lola, was one of many musical box-office disasters.

Its fate was unjust. The same could not be said, however, of such catastrophic flops as Cameron Mackintosh's unwise indulgence of moderate talent and inexperience in *Moby Dick*, presented as an end-of-term romp in a girls' school; *Valentine's Day*, a pointless musical elaboration of George Bernard Shaw's *You Never Can Tell;* and *Which Witch*, a witless medieval farrago from Norway with harmonic nods toward Andrew Lloyd Webber. The latter was knighted for his services to the theatre, and he celebrated by adding a few new songs and giving a thorough production overhaul to *Starlight Express*, which entered its ninth year at the Apollo Victoria.

Musicals that rose above the general mediocrity were the Broadway import *Grand Hotel;* a cheerful compilation of Noel Gay songs in the form of a wartime radio show during the London blitz, *Radio Times;* Stephen Sondheim's biliously entertaining cabaret *Assassins,* which received general critical acclaim when it opened the new Warehouse in Covent Garden; and John Kander and Fred Ebb's *Kiss of the Spider Woman,* a blazingly successful transcription of Manuel Puig's novel directed by Harold Prince, starring Chita Rivera as the poisonous movie queen and the resourceful Canadian actor Brent Carver as the imprisoned fantasist.

Spider Woman's fate hung in the balance, as the subject matter was slightly more demanding than that of most musicals. But the *Evening Standard* (ES) award for best musical acknowledged its pioneering spirit and musical complexity; the score was undoubtedly less ingratiating, but no less ambitious, than the same writers' *Cabaret* and *Chicago.*

The West End played host briefly to an incandescent John Malkovich as a lascivious eastern European dissident in Dusty Hughes's *A Slip of the Tongue;* to an on-form but ill-served Albert Finney in Ronald Harwood's *Reflected Glory;* and to John Osborne, who wrote a sequel to *Look Back in Anger* called, self-mockingly, *Déjàvu,* in which a middle-aged Jimmy Porter, played by Peter Egan, railed against the world as a way of shutting out death, not of challenging the old order with new life as in the original play.

Peter O'Toole had been the first choice for Jimmy, but he split with the production after disagreements with the author over cuts. He did not break a contract, as he had never signed one; instead, he continued his extraordinary stage renaissance, begun three years ago in *Jeffrey Bernard Is Unwell,* in *Our Song,* a new West End play by *Jeffrey Bernard* author Keith Waterhouse. O'Toole played an adulterous advertising executive ruminatively recalling an affair with an unsuitable young girl. He was mesmerizing, and he was beautifully partnered by Tara FitzGerald, making a spectacular West End debut after success on television.

There was certainly a general revival of quality production in the West End. John Guare's *Six Degrees of Separation* became as big a talking point in London, surprisingly perhaps, as it had been in New York City, the galvanic Stockard Channing sharing the adulation with Adrian Lester as the supposed son of Sidney Poitier. It quickly moved from the Royal Court into the Duchess. Sir Peter Hall, having lost his base when Jeffrey Archer sold the Playhouse near Charing Cross, joined with producer Bill Kenwright and presented a well-received Oscar Wilde classic, *An Ideal Husband,* starring Martin Shaw, Anna Carteret, and Hannah Gordon. Trevor Nunn assembled an extraordinary galaxy for Shaw's *Heartbreak House* at the Haymarket: Paul Scofield as a bleary-eyed Captain Shotover, with Vanessa Redgrave, Daniel Massey, and Felicity Kendal all prominent. Maureen Lipman and Rosemary Harris seemed likely to give Neil Simon his biggest London hit in years with *Lost in Yonkers.* Graham Greene's *Travels with My Aunt* took lightly to the Wyndham's stage with just four male actors playing all the roles in Giles Havergal's delicious adaptation (first seen at the Glasgow Citizens' in 1989) in which every single word was the novelist's. Finally, Maria Aitken led a spirited revival by Alan Strachan of Noël Coward's classic farce *Hay Fever.*

The RSC continued to struggle in both its London and Stratford-upon-Avon bases. Most of its interesting work seemed to originate in the modern-Elizabethan Swan Theatre in Stratford. Featured there was Antony Sher as an ebullient Tamburlaine, directed by Terry Hands; Peter Hall, the RSC's founder, returned to direct *All's Well That Ends Well;* and Max Stafford-Clark (making his RSC debut) and John Caird succeeded, respectively, with a revamped lost 17th-century comedy, *A Jovial Crew* (by Richard Brome), and an exhilarating, rocky *The Beggar's Opera.*

On the main Stratford stage only Adrian Noble's colourful, balloon-infested version of *The Winter's Tale* (with John Nettles and Gemma Jones) and a spirited *Taming of the Shrew* (with Amanda Harris and Anton Lesser) were generally applauded. The busy Caird laid on a visually sumptuous *Antony and Cleopatra,* designed on a mock-Hollywood set by Sue Blane, but Richard Johnson and Clare Higgins in the title roles misfired badly. In London the RSC's best work was again on the small scale, in the unwelcoming Pit of the Barbican: a superb and impassioned production of *The Dybbuk* with Joanne Pearce as the possessed virgin bride and a fascinating forgotten Aleksandr Ostrovsky backstage drama, *Artists and Admirers.* A play on the main stage by Richard Nelson, *Columbus and the Discovery of Japan,* though wittily written, fell embarrassingly flat in Caird's production and was hastily withdrawn from the schedule. Robert Stephens repeated his Stratford success of the previous year as a bilious, sardonic Falstaff in both parts of Shakespeare's *Henry IV.*

Stephens was unlucky to lose out in the ES best actor stakes to Nigel Hawthorne, but no one could deny that Hawthorne had given the performance of a lifetime in Alan Bennett's *The Madness of George III* at the Royal National Theatre (RNT). The RNT won three more of the seven ES awards: best play, *Angels in America* by Tony Kushner, an American whose full-blooded AIDS-age extravaganza caught the mood of the day and the imagination of the public; best comedy, *The Rise and Fall of Little Voice* by Jim Cartwright, a Royal Court writer, who provided a stunning mother-and-daughter act for Alison Steadman and rising new star Jane Horrocks; and host production, Stephen Daldry's striking reappraisal of J.B. Priestley's repertory war-horse, *An Inspector Calls.*

Along with those prizewinners, the RNT scored other successes. Howard Davies' production of Shaw's *Pygmalion* was one of the year's undoubted highlights, with the return to the front rank of the former RSC champion king-player Alan Howard as Henry Higgins and Frances Barber as Eliza Doolittle. The film script and other variations were incorporated to give the version Shaw himself dreamed of, and the filmic design enabled Eliza's journey to the centre of her identity to be represented physically as well as metaphorically. This gorgeous RNT evening complemented a ferocious small-scale *Uncle Vanya* directed by Sean Mathias in the Cottesloe, with Sir Ian McKellen in the title role, Antony Sher as an electrifying Astrov, Janet McTeer as an intellectually plausible (for a change) Yelena, and Eric Porter as the definitively testy old professor.

The RNT also brought back Théâtre de Complicité in an atmospheric mood piece based on the writings of Bruno Schulz, *The Street of Crocodiles,* and even more memorably welcomed the Canadian director Robert Lepage, first with his own part-autobiographical and staggering solo show about addiction, jazz, and the work of Jean Cocteau, *Needles and Opium,* and then as director of *A Midsummer Night's Dream,* soon rechristened "A Mudsummer Night's Wet Dream" as it applied Jungian psychoanalytic ideas on a Third World mud flat where the entire play was manifested through the bridal bed of Theseus and Hippolyta. The speaking of the lovers was poor, and the extraordinary athletic Puck of Angela Laurier, a circus contortionist, was often incomprehensible. Nor were the mechanicals properly integrated into the interpretative vision. But the event created huge interest and promoted more vigorous argument than any *Dream* since Peter Brook's.

Hampstead Theatre improved slightly on recent seasons with Philip Ridley's *The Fastest Clock in the Universe* (ES most promising playwright), Frank McGuinness' hostage drama *Someone Who'll Watch Over Me* (which transferred briefly to the West End before moving to Broadway) with Stephen Rea and Alec McGowan, and a delightful revival of

John Gay's *The Beggar's Opera* was one of the Royal Shakespeare Company's 1992 productions at Stratford-upon-Avon. The company also presented Richard Brome's *A Jovial Crew*, a Jacobean work that was rarely staged, as well as works by Shakespeare.
CLIVE BARDA

a 1929 Tin Pan Alley comedy by Ring Lardner and George S. Kaufman, *June Moon*.

The most notable London fringe theatres were once again the Almeida in Islington and the Gate in Notting Hill. The first struck up a creative partnership with Harold Pinter, whose trenchant, elliptical *Party Time*, paired with an earlier political play, *Mountain Language*, was an important return to form. Pinter then appeared himself, to great and menacing effect, opposite Paul Eddington in a revival of his own *No Man's Land*. The Almeida also presented Diana Rigg (ES best actress) as *Medea*.

The Gate maintained its extraordinary run—for which it was honoured in the Olivier Awards with the *Observer*'s award for outstanding achievement in memory of Kenneth Tynan—with scorching productions of Euripides' *Hecuba*, Federico García Lorca's *The House of Bernarda Alba*, and the British premiere of Thomas Bernhard's hilariously misanthropic and indiscriminately critical *Elisabeth II*.

The most enterprising regional theatres were the West Yorkshire Playhouse in Leeds and the Leicester Haymarket. The first uncovered the most gifted new director to emerge since Nicholas Hytner and Stephen Daldry; Matthew Warchus staged sumptuous and strikingly intelligent revivals of Calderón's *Life Is a Dream, Fiddler on the Roof*, and Edward Albee's *Who's Afraid of Virginia Woolf?* In Leicester the exploratory productions of Julia Bardsley were tellingly offset against the joyous musical productions of her fellow artistic director, Paul Kerryson.

In Manchester the Royal Exchange mounted the most exciting *Romeo and Juliet* in years, the star-crossed lovers taken by names-to-watch Michael Sheen and Kate Byers. The Glasgow Citizens' Theatre expanded under its own roof, adding two smaller auditoriums to complement the main stage. The most important work remained on the main stage: a wonderful new *Lulu* and a brace of brilliant Philip Prowse productions, of Brecht's *Edward II* and, most thrillingly, of Tennessee Williams' *Sweet Bird of Youth*.

In Ireland the Dublin Theatre Festival struggled with a deficit but won plaudits for bringing American actor Brian Dennehy to town in Eugene O'Neill's *The Iceman Cometh*. Also staged were an insipid, amateurish revival of Dion Boucicault's *The Streets of Dublin*, incongruously starring the English actor Ron Moody, and a disappointing Gate Theatre production of Molière's *Tartuffe* that made no effort in its translation to approximate the rhyming couplets of the original. The most promising new play was *Silverlands* by Antoine O'Flatharta in the Abbey's smaller auditorium; this allegorized the erosion of rural Ireland in a tawdry nightclub setting, where a washed-up country-and-western singer was buffeted about by the new manners and the new music of the urban jungle.

Israel and Greece. The arrival of thousands of Russian Jews in Israel added to the nation's acute unemployment problems. Some Russian actors found work in the Israeli companies, but others formed their own Russian-speaking company, Gesher (meaning "bridge"), which won local funding, rave reviews, and acclaim in New York City. Gesher's production of Tom Stoppard's *Rosencrantz and Guildenstern Are Dead* reinvented a fizzing philosophical apprentice piece as a thoroughgoing European classic. Using Joseph Brodsky's translation, a predominant tango musical motif, and Ennio Mooricone's film score for *The Mission*, Gesher proposed a wonderful, dense, and glinting post-Beckettian view of political imbroglio and emigration. The action was played on a catwalk stage through a small and crowded audience so that the peripheral courtiers were not bypassed by an upstage presentation of *Hamlet* (as is usually the case).

Israeli native drama suffered a bit from the *intifada*, the uprising by Palestinians in the occupied territories. The mood was less brave in contemporary writing than it had been several years earlier, but there were signs of resurgence in Evron's *Jehu*, directed by the brilliant Hanan Snir for the Habimah. In this biblical parable, precise analogies were found with *intifada* brutalities, and the acting was absolutely electrifying.

The biggest cultural event in Greece was the opening of the spectacular new Athens Concert Hall, Greece's first such facility. It promised to be a vibrant staging post for all the arts, with thematically arranged programs, a recording studio, exhibitions, museum and library facilities, and a computer information service on events throughout Europe. The site, a couple of kilometres from the city centre along the road to Marathon, was earmarked in 1956, but financial and political complications delayed the opening until 1992. During the summer Yury Lyubimov and his Taganka Theatre of Moscow premiered an exciting version of Sophocles' *Electra* in the smaller auditorium. Lyubimov's first foray into Greek tragedy was a frenetic, impassioned blast of realpolitik, the House of Atreus represented by rapidly and endlessly revolving doors in the middle of an urban cul-de-sac of corrugated iron. As the temperature rose in Electra's ululations of mourning and revenge, so the doors whirled around with a dangerous celerity. These animated brutal portals were a vivid counterpart to Lyubimov's espionage curtain in the famous Visotsky *Hamlet* and his floating green door in *Crime and Punishment*. They indicated political inevitability, which Alla Demjdova's crazed and fierce Electra challenged with her suffering. (MICHAEL COVENEY)

U.S. and Canada. In 1992 the New York City commercial theatre let itself be deluded by a fantasy of resurrection. After many seasons of declining activity, a sudden burst of production brought out an array of movie stars, including Glenn Close, Richard Dreyfuss, Gene Hackman, Alan Alda, Ben Gazzara, Joan Collins, Judd Hirsch, Jessica Lange, and Alec Baldwin. They succeeded in creating an illusion that the ever dying Broadway theatre, the "Fabulous Invalid," was thriving once again.

Alas, it was only an illusion. By the season's end, most of the plays in which the stars had performed were critical or commercial casualties, and the few successes came from places beyond Broadway. For instance, the Tony award for the season's best play went to *Dancing at Lughnasa* (pronounced "LOO-na-sa"), a drama that originated at Dublin's famed Abbey Theatre and was then transferred to the Royal National Theatre of Great Britain before being taken to New York. Written by the Irish playwright Brian Friel, *Dancing at Lughnasa* is a stirring work, rich in humanity and passion. It is set on an Irish farm in the 1930s, where five repressed sisters discover—through dance music heard on a new radio—a profound sexuality similar to what their uncle discovered in African tribal rituals.

The other new plays were disappointing. Three of the movie stars (Close, Dreyfuss, and Hackman) constituted the entire cast of Ariel Dorfman's *Death and the Maiden,* and they were directed by no less than Mike Nichols. Yet for many, this study of political persecution in a South American country was better served in its low-key original London version than in this glamorous production. Among the new U.S. plays, Alan Alda and Judd Hirsch arrived, respectively, in Neil Simon's *Jake's Women* and Herb Gardner's *Conversations with My Father.* These were both thinly disguised autobiographical plays, and neither was top drawer despite excellent performances by both Hirsch and Alda.

On the other hand, an elaborate revival of the classic *A Streetcar Named Desire* by Tennessee Williams was badly served by Jessica Lange. Although Blanche Du Bois may be the best female part in all U.S. dramatic literature, Lange did not have the professional stage experience to play it. A fine film actress, she was simply unprepared for the theatre and crippled the production. Lost in the wreckage was a superlative performance by Alec Baldwin in the play's other great part, Stanley Kowalski.

As for musicals, again there was only an illusion of a reborn Broadway. In fact, the year's biggest hit was a revival. This was the 1950 classic *Guys and Dolls,* staged with stylish nostalgia by New York's hottest director, Jerry Zaks. Even the Tony award-winning best new musical, *Crazy for You,* was not a new show. Rather, it was a revised version of the 1930 musical hit *Girl Crazy* that also included other music by George and Ira Gershwin. Like so many musical comedies of the period, this one's wonderful songs (including "Embraceable You," "I Got Rhythm," "Bidin' My Time," and "But Not for Me") could not compensate for the flat book and its heavy-handed jokes.

The only brand new musical to enjoy any success was *Jelly's Last Jam,* about the jazz pianist "Jelly Roll" Morton. While this was a dance musical with a dancing star (Gregory Hines), it also dealt with the African-American identity in powerful musical/dramatic ways. Directed by its author, playwright George C. Wolfe, *Jelly's Last Jam* was the most theatrically significant musical on Broadway in 1992.

Thus the euphoria that launched the year gave way, at its end, to a grim reality: the New York commercial theatre was understocked and overpriced. The best that could be said for it was a negative: the British invasion of recent years had finally subsided. The only musical to arrive from across the Atlantic was the small-scale revue *Five Guys Named Moe.* While it was presented by Cameron Mackintosh, the producer of *Phantom of the Opera, Cats, Les Misérables,* and *Miss Saigon* (shows that continued to be New York's biggest hits), this show was not as flamboyant, successful, or good as they.

Yet, paradoxically, the U.S. theatre was healthier than ever before, especially in New York. This was because of continuing activity off-Broadway (led by David Mamet's misogynistic *Oleanna)* and a real renewal in the institutional sector. For instance, New York's Roundabout Theatre, having moved from off-Broadway to the Broadway area, proceeded to attract sellout crowds with professional productions of interesting semiclassics such as Friedrich Dürrenmatt's *The Visit* (in a striking version starring Jane Alexander), Arthur Miller's *The Price* with Eli Wallach, and Tom Stoppard's *The Real Inspector Hound.* A new classics company called the National Actors Theatre was founded by Tony Randall, who promptly scheduled plays by Ibsen (*The Master Builder*), Miller (*The Crucible*), and Georges

JOAN MARCUS

Crazy for You drew on shows, film music, and standards by George and Ira Gershwin. The production won the 1992 Tony award for the best musical, and an original cast recording was released during the year.

Jane Alexander (top left), Madeline Kahn (centre), and Frances McDormand (right) appear in Wendy Wasserstein's *The Sisters Rosensweig* at Lincoln Center in New York City. In the play the sisters gather in London to celebrate a birthday.

MARTHA SWOPE

Feydeau (*A Little Hotel on the Side*). To perform in these classics, Randall engaged a first-rate group of other actors, including Lynn Redgrave, Earle Hyman, and Maryann Plunkett, while appearing himself in the Feydeau. The Vivian Beaumont Theater at Lincoln Center produced a new play by John Guare *(Four Baboons Adoring the Sun)*, while the Circle in the Square presented Al Pacino in Oscar Wilde's rarely performed *Salomé*.

All of this activity provided New York with a rich theatrical menu, and there was similar vitality among the institutional theatres throughout the U.S. At Washington, D.C.'s venerable Arena Stage, for instance, the schedule ranged from adventurous classics like Lorca's *Yerma* to new musicals *(A Wonderful Life* by Sheldon Harnick and the late Joe Raposo) and old ones *(Of Thee I Sing)*. The Seattle (Wash.) Repertory Theatre continued its policy of producing new works by reputable playwrights with Lanford Wilson's *Redwood Curtain*, an appropriate title, certainly, for this Northwest setting. Farther south, the Mark Taper Forum in Los Angeles presented perhaps the most sensational production anywhere in the country: Tony Kushner's two-part *Angels in America* (the plays are separately called *Millennium Approaches* and *Perestroika*, with the connecting subtitle *A Gay Fantasia on National Themes*). The first of the two plays had already been given its world premiere production in San Francisco in 1991 and had opened in early 1992 in London, where it was named the year's best drama. It was scheduled for a New York premiere in 1993.

Chicago seemed to be the hub of America's theatre activity, enjoying a profusion of institutions, from the Goodman Theatre, which won the Tony award for outstanding regional theatre, to the Body Politic, the Pegasus Players, and the Organic Theater Company, and that was merely the city proper; the area's theatre life extended beyond to suburban Park Forest (Illinois Theatre Center), and Evanston (Northlight Theatre) and farther to Rockford (New American Theatre).

In Canada the Stratford (Ont.) Festival completed its 40th season and, while it remained the richest and most aristocratic of North American institutional theatres, even it was not immune from economic constrictions. The number of productions in 1992 was reduced to 11 from the previous

year's 14. Under the artistic directorship of David William, the season's Shakespeare offerings included *The Tempest, Romeo and Juliet, Love's Labour's Lost, The Two Gentlemen of Verona*, and *Measure for Measure*. If any pattern was observable, it was perhaps an avoidance of the less popular chronicle plays. On the other hand, there was nothing timid about William's putting Joe Orton's *Entertaining Mr. Sloane* on the schedule.

Stratford's Canadian kid brother, the Shaw Festival in Niagara-on-the-Lake, Ont., was perhaps more susceptible to a charge of easy programming. This institution had always been limited by the uneven quality of Shaw's output. Its 1992 program fairly balanced the master's obscure *Overruled* with the seldom-done *Widowers' Houses* and the war-horse *Pygmalion*. However, the Broadway musical *On the Town* could hardly be rationalized as being Shavian, and the festival yet again programmed the popular Brandon Thomas farce *Charley's Aunt*.   (MARTIN GOTTFRIED)

See also Dance; Music.

This article updates the *Macropædia* article The History of Western THEATRE.

Transportation

Deepening world recession and lack of agreement in the General Agreement on Tariffs and Trade negotiations meant little growth in trade in 1992, with concomitant stabilization or decline in most sectors of transportation. Although many major infrastructure projects continued, overall levels of vehicle production dropped, and economic constraints generally reduced levels of both urban and intercity traffic.

There were a number of isolated cases where governments were pressing ahead with privatization, but most governments continued to focus on environmental issues, not only in terms of carbon dioxide and global warming but also in terms of other harmful emissions and their effects in urban areas.   (JOHN H. EARP)

AVIATION

Although the world civil aviation industry had recovered from the effects of the Gulf war, it continued in turmoil owing to what Günter Eser, retiring director general of the International Air Transport Association (IATA), called "the four horsemen of the aviation apocalypse—traffic and yields, which are too low, and capacity and unit costs, which are too high." Eser identified a fifth horseman, interest charges and airline debt, "which have become unsustainable." As a result of these factors, airlines were expected to lose some $2.6 billion in 1992 and another $600 million in 1993, bringing total losses in the period 1990–93 to a staggering $9.9 billion. In their efforts to stem the financial hemorrhage, airlines embarked on deep fare-cutting measures, laid off staff (in 1991 alone they shed 51,000 jobs, or 3.4% of the total work force), and delayed taking delivery of many of the new aircraft ordered during the boom years of the late 1980s. By the end of 1992, it was estimated that around 1,000 airliners, many of them newly off the production lines, were parked unproductively in the Arizona desert, awaiting the upturn that the industry continued to predict.

The ripple effect of airline cutbacks was inevitably felt by the manufacturers of airliners and by the companies that lease them to the airlines. Both of the Western world's major civil aircraft manufacturers, Boeing of the U.S. and Airbus Industrie, the European consortium, slowed production rates, and Airbus postponed a go-ahead for a proposed new 120-seat twinjet, the A319. In late 1992, however, Airbus' latest wide-body jet, the twin-engine A330, made its

Northwest Airlines employees in Minneapolis, Minn., also handle ticketing and check-ins for KLM Royal Dutch Airlines, which owns 20% of the U.S. carrier. In 1992 the two airlines won preliminary approval from the U.S. government to merge their operations.
LARRY SALZMAN—THE NEW YORK TIMES

maiden flight, while its long-range, four-engine A340 completed flight trials and went into service with the airlines as 1993 began. At the same time, Boeing pressed ahead with development of its high-capacity 777. Sales did improve in one area, in the Commonwealth of Independent States, as the countries of the former Soviet Union rushed to replace their noisy and unreliable Soviet-made airliners with the high-technology products of the West.

This upheaval took place against changing competition, particularly in Europe and the U.S. The trend in the U.S. continued to be for big carriers to swallow up the small ones. Very few of the 176 new airlines that started up when deregulation began in the late 1970s remained, while eight airlines controlled 90% of the market. Late in 1992 owner Carl Icahn agreed to relinquish control of TWA and to provide the bankrupt carrier with financial support, allowing development of a reorganization plan. Continental, also under Chapter 11 bankruptcy protection, accepted a merger bid from Air Canada. In December the U.S. Department of Transportation gave preliminary permission for Northwest and KLM to operate as a single carrier, but British Airways—which had completed deals with airlines in several other countries—dropped its bid for a share of USAir when the two governments could not agree on opening their markets.

Such developments were eyed with apprehension by many of the airlines within the 12 European Communities nations as the EC prepared to embark, from the beginning of January 1993, on its own form of airline deregulation. Called liberalization, it would enable EC citizens to start new airlines in any EC country, remove virtually all controls on fares, and enable EC airlines to pick up domestic traffic within each others' borders. Having settled its internal aviation affairs, the EC Transport Commission turned its attention to external matters and made the first moves toward having Brussels act on behalf of all 12 member governments in negotiating traffic rights with non-EC countries whose airlines fly into Europe. In particular, the European airlines were anxious to see an "open skies" accord signed with the U.S. that would allow them to buy into U.S. airlines, serve more U.S. destinations, and, in the longer term, have the right to carry domestic passengers within the U.S. Both European and U.S. carriers were increasingly worried over the growing competitiveness of airlines of the Far East, where the recession in the industry did not bite so hard and where wages were lower.

The airline industry in Europe was deeply concerned over whether the aviation infrastructure—airport and airways capacity—could cope with the upsurge in traffic that liberalization was expected to generate. Bernard Attali, the president of Air France and chairman of the IATA executive committee, estimated the annual cost of air traffic control

delays in Europe at $5 billion a year, with 116,000 flight hours lost. European governments moved during 1992 to coordinate their air traffic control systems so the computers that run them would at least be able to "talk" to each other.

Aside from hauling themselves out of the financial red, airlines identified the environment as the most important challenge for 1993. Air transport, they told anybody who cared to listen, uses no more than 5% of the petroleum products consumed worldwide each year, and carbon dioxide emissions from jet engines are responsible for just 1% of the forecast global temperature rise caused by all man-made carbon dioxide.   (ARTHUR REED)

SHIPPING AND PORTS

The recession in the U.S. and Europe cast a gloomy shadow over freight rates, and there was little growth in demand for oil products. Rate levels for bulk carriers over 80,000 deadweight tons (dwt) dropped dramatically during the first quarter of the year, making owners and operators nervous about not seeing a return on their investments. By the middle of the year, 27 vessels over 200,000 dwt were either laid up or had been idle for more than two months. One piece of good news, however, was that the Russian government had allocated $78 million from its foreign reserves to repay overdue freight-shipping debts.

Reorganization and cooperation were of increasing concern in the face of intense world competition. Juan Saez, head of the Committee of EEC Shipbuilders Associations, said that if Europe was to compete with the huge conglomerates of East Asia, yards would have to cooperate on construction as well as design. The same applied to commercial operations, and Denmark's East Asiatic Company planned to invest $473.5 million over the next four years in four 4,000-TEU (20-ft equivalent units) container shops as part of a joint venture with the Ben Line. The cruise market held up in 1992, and recent amendments to national legislation governing the important Alaska cruise trade would ensure that Vancouver, B.C., remained a popular port of call for cruise ships.

Construction of a new DM 90 million ferry terminal at the port of Kiel, Germany, would double the port's terminal area. A new terminal able to handle containerships of up to 1,800-TEU capacity was to be built at the Irish port of Waterford. Plans to expand the Suez Canal were delayed to await new studies on the effect of U.S. maritime safety laws.

The total tonnage of the world fleet in 1992 stood at 444.3 million gross tonnage (gt), an increase of 8.3 million gt (1.9%) over 1991. The principal types of ships in the world fleet trading commercially (gt percentage of the world total in parentheses) were: oil tankers (30.7), ore and bulk carriers (26.4), general cargo (11.0), containerships (6.3), ore/bulk/oil and ore/oil carriers (4.4), liquefied gas carriers

(2.7), oil/chemical tankers (1.5), and chemical tankers (0.9). The principal merchant fleets by flag registry were: Liberia (55.1 million gt), Panama (46.6 million gt), Japan (25.4 million gt), Greece (24.5 million gt), Norway (22.5 million gt), Cyprus (20.3 million gt), The Bahamas (20.1 million gt), China (People's Republic and Taiwan; 20 million gt), U.S. (18.2 million gt), and Russia (15.6 million gt).

(EDWARD CROWLEY)

FREIGHT AND PIPELINES

Despite the downturn in world trade, some sectors, particularly in Asia, continued to grow. Singapore recorded 22% growth in traffic in 1991, to 6,450,000 TEU, and expected to top 15 million by the year 2000. A 26% growth for the first half of 1992 indicated that Hong Kong was likely to regain its title of busiest container port. In Malaysia, Port Kelang was expanded, using a "privatized" container terminal. In Europe, Rotterdam, Neth., led the way in 1991 with 3.7 million TEU and expected to grow to 9 million TEU by 2010 with its Delta Megahub Centre, not dissimilar to the airlines' concept of designated "hubs." Europe was planning for jumbo container vessels and increased use of rail-oriented (intermodal) freight.

There was noticeable growth in river-barge traffic in Europe and in the U.S., with a particularly noteworthy 20% increase in traffic at New Orleans, La. Seventy years after its start, a European east-west canal linking the Rhine and the Danube was completed, at a cost of $3.5 billion.

Although global pipeline construction was expected to fall slightly in 1992, activity in the U.S. was at a 10-year high. Natural-gas pipeline construction led U.S. activities. European gas-line projects still centred on North Sea developments; other projects included a pipeline linking Lisbon to Braga in Portugal and a trans-Mediterranean link from Algeria to Italy. Political upheaval and lack of finance in eastern Europe and the former Soviet Union were delaying much-needed rebuilding and expansion there. In the Middle East, Saudi Aramco embarked on a five-year plan to expand its network, and preliminary discussions were held on the development of a network to transmit Middle Eastern gas to Europe. Turkey was assessing the feasibility of a pipeline to transmit water from the Seyhan and Ceyhan rivers to the Arabian peninsula. In South America both Venezuela and Brazil had major expansion plans for gas and liquid lines, while in Southeast Asia planning continued on a long-distance natural-gas network linking Malaysia to Indonesia and the Philippines.

ROADS AND TRAFFIC

Although car production was down from the all-time high of 1989, the demand for road space continued, epitomized by an 18-hour traffic jam on the Nürnberg-Berlin autobahn during the summer. Authorities were facing the almost impossible task of satisfying traffic demand and, at the same time, reducing emission levels of carbon dioxide and other harmful gases. Increasingly, they were turning to electronic means of controlling traffic, with the DRIVE 2 program in Europe and significant progress in the U.S. on intelligent vehicle highway systems (IVHS).

The use of toll systems to raise capital for investment and to manage urban road space was growing. Scandinavia continued to lead the field in toll-road initiatives. Norway had three active projects (Trondheim, Oslo, and Bergen), while Sweden expected to introduce schemes as soon as a neutral "negotiator" set a fair toll. The revenue would be used to construct tunnels, which were seen as environmentally acceptable. The two-kilometre (1 km = 0.62 mi) immersed tube tunnel in Sydney, Australia, was opened, and Cork, Ireland, planned a similar one-kilometre crossing of the River Lee.

The $150 million Krifast road project, which opened in Norway in 1992, included three firsts: the most slender suspension bridge, the only floating bridge without lateral restraint, and the longest subsea road tunnel. The halfway point of the 6.6-km-long west bridge of Denmark's Store Bælt crossing was reached, although the tunneling work was delayed because of construction difficulties. In Hong Kong work started on the two-kilometre-long Tsing Ma suspension bridge. Work was restarted on the 132-km toll superhighway linking Guangzhou (Canton) with Shenzhen (Shenchen) and Hong Kong. In eastern Europe, the European Bank for Reconstruction and Development was assisting in the promotion of privately financed toll expressways in Vienna and Budapest. Czechoslovakia aimed to link Prague to Nürnberg with a similar toll highway. Pakistan was pressing ahead with 12 privately financed prospects with a value of $500 million.

INTERCITY RAIL

The investment climate for railways in both Europe and North America was highly favourable, with near-record capital improvement plans for 1992. European activity was stimulated by the policies of the EC, preparations for the single European market, and reconstruction in eastern Ger-

MICHAEL L. ABRAMSON

A passenger rail car is rebuilt in a Chicago plant operated by Morrison Knudsen. Beginning in 1990 the company won contracts to build new rail cars or to rehabilitate old ones for a number of U.S. localities.

many. Network expansion, upgrading, and double tracking were reported in many countries. Old routes were being revived for economic reasons (New Zealand, Philippines) or, in some cases, because the end of civil unrest made rehabilitation possible (the Benguela Railway in Angola).

With new east-west lines and electrification schemes in process, investment in rail outstripped that in roads in Germany. The Swiss opened the second Lotschberg tunnel, 16 years in construction, and introduced gauge-adjustable wheels and new low-floor trains. A special excursion train provided the first passenger service across the Alatau Pass in Kazakhstan and presaged an agreement to run a weekly "Silk Road" service between Urumchi, in northwestern China, and the Kazakh capital, Alma-Ata. In the U.S. a commuter line was opened linking Washington, D.C., and Fredericksberg, Va. Russia was reorganizing its rail services, while China was expanding its internal rail services and planning integration with Association of Southeast Asian Nations members.

Freight services were also being expanded. Double stacking of containers was introduced in Australia, Canada, California, and China. The Netherlands and Germany were planning a special high-capacity line to link Rotterdam and the Ruhr, while French National Railways was investigating a high-speed freight depot at Charles de Gaulle Airport. Alitalia joined a lengthening list of airlines operating integrated rail-air services.

High-speed trains continued to gain ground. AVE, Spain's national railway, opened service between Madrid and Seville in time for Expo 92 in Seville. After a 20-year construction period, Italy completed its Direttissima Line between Florence and Rome. Using new aluminum-alloy-bodied Series 300 trains, the world's fastest scheduled service (225 km/h) was established between Kyoto and Nagoya, Japan.

URBAN MASS TRANSIT

The resurgence of urban and suburban transit systems continued, with over a hundred cities planning to spend some $13 billion. Shenzhen announced plans to build a new line (elevated), and Tokyo inaugurated a 12th line. Lines were under construction in Brasília, Brazil; Cairo; Budapest; and St. Louis, Mo., while Tehran expected to complete its first metro line in 1993. The Singapore metro was experimenting with systems for lining up passengers on platforms to cope with heavy demand. Baltimore, Md., and Paris opened light rail transit (LRT) systems. Emphasis on passenger convenience resulted in new low-floor cars operating in Nantes and St.-Étienne, France. A second LRT line was being built in Guadalajara, Mexico, and many other cities, including Hyderabad, India; Curitiba, Brazil; Johannesburg, South Africa; Saarbrücken and Rostock, Germany; and New York City, were planning the early introduction of LRT. Hamburg, Germany, reintroduced trains to its streets, and in Ukraine, where 40 cities were served by trolley buses, a new design for export was being developed.

Lyon, France, opened a fully automated new Line D in September. Chicago's VAL system was being tested, and Honolulu began construction of a 26-km system. Other cities planning the introduction of automated transit included Bratislava, Czech.; Sydney, Australia; and Taipai, Taiwan. The drive to make conventional buses cleaner, quieter, and generally more attractive led to a number of technical developments such as low floors. Express bus services in Göteborg, Sweden, increased patronage there 40%. Integrated ticketing acquired an international dimension with a joint ticket for Copenhagen and Malmö, Sweden. People-mover systems continued to have specialist applications, including access to the Olympic Stadium at Barcelona, Spain. Privati-

zation plans, stalled in Chile, Britain, and Japan, were going ahead in New Zealand, Argentina, and Brazil. Sweden was actively deregulating its railway. (JOHN H. EARP)

See also Energy; Engineering Projects; Environment; Industrial Review: *Aerospace; Automobiles.*

This article updates the *Macropædia* article TRANSPORTATION.

World Affairs

If 1991 had been the year of the fall of the Soviet empire—an event of world historical significance—1992, according to an international agenda decided upon well before, was to be the year of European unity. But events turned out differently, for the year witnessed an upsurge of disunity in Europe as in other parts of the world. At the same time, no end to the global economic recession was in sight, and this, in turn, had important repercussions on the internal political situation in many countries, including Russia, Britain, and even Germany. It contributed to the electoral victory of Bill Clinton in the race for the U.S. presidency. It also cast a long shadow on international relations, which were increasingly preoccupied with economic issues such as world trade, the rate of interest in major countries, and its repercussions elsewhere. The economic plight was nowhere as severe as in the African continent, faced with an annual decline over a lengthy period of 2% of gross national product, rising debts, a small and shrinking share of world trade, and 30 million people facing acute starvation.

The separatist, centrifugal trends were palpable in eastern Europe and the territory of the former Soviet Union. The Czech and Slovak regions, which had once constituted Czechoslovakia, agreed to separate peacefully at year's end, but in Yugoslavia the political struggle turned into a bloody civil war that the United Nations and the European Communities (EC) were powerless to end or even to defuse. Farther east, the main scenes of fighting were Moldova (the former Bessarabia), the Caucasus, and Central Asia. In Central Asia, as in other parts of the Islamic world, Muslim fundamentalism was a destabilizing factor, both domestically and in relations between nations. While such regional affairs per se did not constitute a danger to world peace, there was almost always the danger that small conflicts would spill over and lead to the involvement of greater powers.

It did not take long for observers to realize that a new world order was far from arising from the ruins of the old, and that the end of the cold war, while removing the danger of nuclear confrontation between major powers, had actually given fresh impetus to the proliferation of weapons of mass destruction. It had made the management of local conflicts more difficult.

In December 1991, at a meeting of EC heads of state and government in Maastricht, Neth., a treaty had been agreed upon looking toward a common economic and social policy and a monetary union. It constituted a compromise between European federalists aiming at an eventual political union and more skeptical leaders who wanted to limit cooperation as much as possible to the economic realm. The treaty, signed in February 1992, was called "irreversible" by Chancellor Helmut Kohl of Germany. He added that the Rubicon had been crossed and there was no going back. He was echoed by Italy's foreign minister, who called it a victory for Europe and the most significant step forward since the establishment of the European Economic Community in 1957.

Very shortly, however, the treaty began to unravel. In June a small majority of Danish voters opposed it, and in subsequent discussions and polls it appeared that there was

Changes to Flags of the World

Afghanistan

Albania

Armenia

Azerbaijan

Belarus

Bosnia and Hercegovina

Brazil

Cambodia

Cape Verde

Croatia

Ethiopia

Georgia

Kazakhstan

Kyrgyzstan

Macedonia

Moldova

Mongolia

Russia

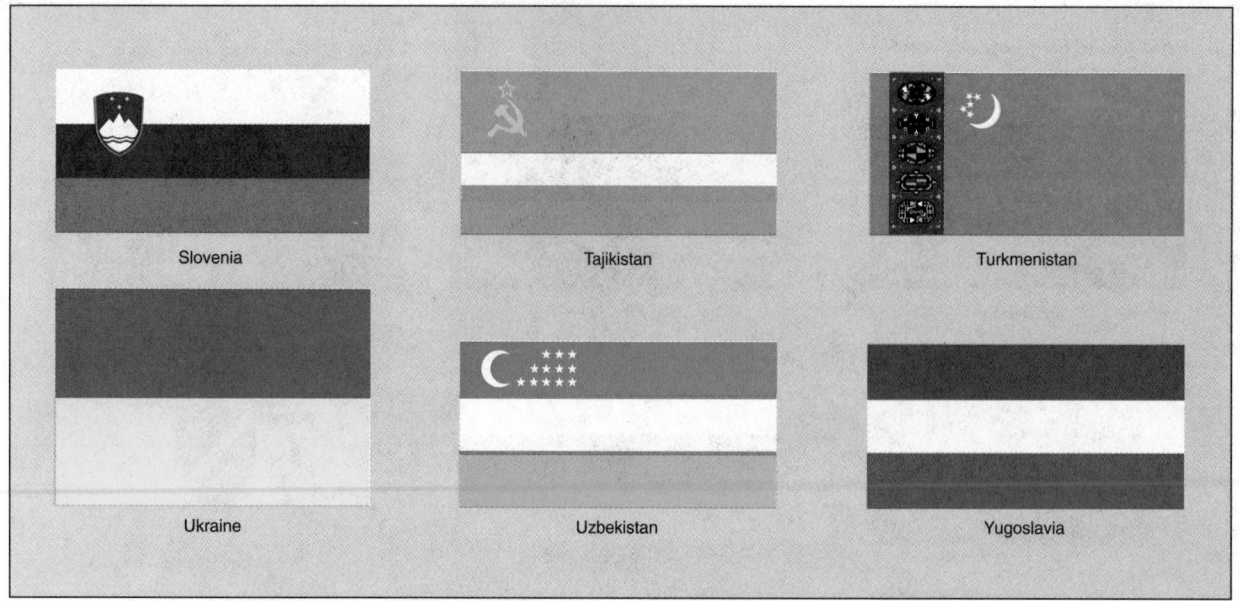

only a small majority—if that—in favour in many European countries. The opposition came from both left and right; it expressed the fear of losing sovereign rights and resentment of the interference of foreign bureaucrats residing in Brussels. The concurrent rise of parties of the extreme right and various xenophobic groups in both western and eastern Europe was part of the same phenomenon. If the technocrats and the political elite in its great majority favoured European union, nationalist passions were running high on the popular level.

The most severe blow, however, came from the financial markets. The European Monetary System (EMS) had existed since 1979; its main function was to provide stability to European currencies. But the economic policies of European countries diverged, since some currencies were overvalued, and speculators saw an opportunity to make quick profits. The result was a series of events in September that led to a de facto devaluation of sterling and the Italian lira, as well as some other European currencies, and to the withdrawal of currency by Britain and Italy from the exchange-rate mechanism of the EMS, at least temporarily. This, in turn, triggered acrimonious exchanges between Britain and Germany, even though all European leaders agreed that, despite these setbacks, efforts would continue to salvage the Maastricht Treaty and some sort of monetary union.

In the circumstances, Europe found it difficult to play an active role in global politics. The talks about trade liberalization, the Uruguay round under the General Agreement on Tariffs and Trade, made very slow progress, with French resistance to cutting farm subsidies a major obstacle. Europe, and the rest of the western world, did not make any significant contribution to the reform process in Russia and the other successor states of the Soviet Union. Russian industrial and agricultural production declined sharply, and inflation grew rapidly—and with it the unpopularity of Pres. Boris Yeltsin's government. In the other successor states there was not even a significant attempt to change the economic, social, and political system.

A plebiscite in South Africa in March 1992 gave a decisive majority to Pres. F.W. de Klerk's policy of revising the constitution and reaching a peaceful settlement with the African National Congress. There were setbacks on the road to power sharing, but there was no denying that, overall, important progress had been made. South Africa

was readmitted to various international bodies from which it had been excluded in the 1960s and '70s.

The Madrid peace talks in 1991 had brought Arabs and Israel to the negotiating table for the first time in decades. This movement gathered speed in multilateral and bilateral peace talks in Washington and elsewhere following the electoral victory in Israel of the Labour Party under Yitzhak Rabin. The negotiations were disrupted after Israel deported more than 400 Palestinians in December. Elsewhere in the Middle East, conflicts continued or became more acute. The results of the Algerian elections—a victory for Muslim fundamentalism—were annulled by the military leadership in January. In Iraq Saddam Hussein continued to fortify his positions despite UN sanctions. Internal conflict continued to rage in various Asian countries—India, Afghanistan, Sri Lanka, and Cambodia. In Africa the chaos in Somalia following the ouster of Muhammad Siyad Barrah (in 1991) claimed tens of thousands of victims and prevented effective help from reaching the millions threatened by starvation.

In a world facing so many internal and external threats, there was a growing conviction that the United Nations should take a more active role in the settlement of disputes, but the UN had neither the financial nor the military resources to play a role of this kind. Two major new initiatives were undertaken during the year. One was the UN Conference on Environment and Development, held in Rio de Janeiro in June in the presence of many world leaders and representatives of some 2,000 nongovernmental organizations. Those attending were concerned with the overconsumption of nonrenewable resources and various other ecological threats, including climate change and the destruction of tropical forests. The other new initiative was the decision, in December, to send troops to Somalia in an attempt to safeguard the delivery of food to the starving population. (See *United Nations*, below.)

(WALTER LAQUEUR)

This article updates the *Macropædia* article 20th-Century INTERNATIONAL RELATIONS.

UNITED NATIONS

UN Summit. On Jan. 31, 1992, 15 heads of government met for the first time as their countries' Security Council representatives and pledged to strengthen UN peacekeeping. They also asked Boutros Boutros-Ghali (*see* BIOGRAPHIES),

World Affairs: Contents

For your convenience this article groups the countries of the world by the geopolitical regions to which they belong. Certain related topics, such as United Nations, Dependent States, and various regional affairs articles (*e.g.,* Latin-American Affairs), are also included. An alphabetical list of these topics appears below, indicating the page where each may be found. Articles on the various countries update the *Macropædia* articles of the same name (except where otherwise noted), as do the more extensive statistical treatments in the *World Data* section.

who began his term as the sixth UN secretary-general on January 1, to suggest ways of preventing incipient disputes from escalating. They did nothing, however, to reduce their collective indebtedness to the UN, which amounted at the time to over $2 billion. Responding to the Council's request, the secretary-general published "An Agenda for Peace" on June 18. It recommended permanent UN armed forces supervised by the Council and an active Military Staff Committee; an "early warning" system to settle disputes before they escalate; authority to stop conflicts in the earliest stages; and additional peacekeeping funds to come from national military budgets and taxes on arms sales and international air travel. The need for stronger and more effective UN forces became increasingly clear as the year passed.

Former Yugoslavia. UN- and European-brokered cease-fire agreements foundered all year on the warring parties' unwillingness to accept outside authority. Nevertheless, on February 21 the Council authorized a UN Protection Force (UNPROFOR) of up to 14,000, which took up positions in two areas of Croatia to protect Serbian minorities. On September 14 the Council approved additional forces from NATO to serve as peacekeepers in Bosnia and Hercegovina. By mid-November UNPROFOR had suffered 300 casualties, including 20 dead. The Council on May 30 imposed economic sanctions on the rump Yugoslavia (Serbia and Montenegro), and on November 16 it imposed a blockade on supplies entering the country.

In June the UN reopened the airport at Sarajevo, the Bosnian capital, for relief missions and began airlifts of food and medicines to 400,000 people trapped in the city by a Serbian siege. On August 13 the Council authorized UN members to do whatever was necessary, even using military force, to ensure delivery of aid to Bosnia. Acting under this authority, French troops exchanged fire with Serbian forces on November 19 while moving food and medicine into Bosanska Krupa, the first Bosnian town outside Sarajevo to receive UN help. Despite repeated attacks on repair crews and installations, UN personnel restored electricity to Sarajevo in October. The Council banned Serbian flights over Bosnia (October 9), asked the secretary-general (November 16) to consider creating security zones for citizens of Bosnia and Hercegovina, and authorized (December 11) the deployment of UN forces to Macedonia to forestall new fighting between Christians and Muslims.

Somalia. Before taking office, Boutros-Ghali said it was disgraceful that the UN had not kept Somalia from disintegrating into bloody anarchy through fighting and famine. Later, he accused Western powers of being more concerned with the "rich man's war" in Yugoslavia than with Somalia. On April 24 the Council authorized 50 military observers to monitor a truce between warring Somali factions, but they were too few to be effective. Muhammad Sahnoun, the secretary-general's personal representative, tried from May on to persuade Somali warlords and countries in the region to allow outside troops to protect food supplies from looters, but he resigned in October accusing the "UN bureaucracy" of lethargy. He charged relief officials (except for the International Committee of the Red Cross, Oxfam, and a few other nongovernmental organizations) with allowing Somalia to descend into a "hell" where possibly 300,000 Somalis, mostly children, had died in 18 months. He complained that 500 Pakistanis airlifted into the country by U.S. planes between September 14 and October 8 were insufficient to guard food supplies and blamed the UN for not supplying impregnable convoys.

On October 29 Boutros-Ghali appointed Ismat Kittani, an Iraqi member of the Secretariat and former General Assembly president (1981), to succeed Sahnoun. On November 25, after one of its ships was attacked, the UN World Food Program suspended relief shipments to Somalia. On November 30 the secretary-general asked the Security Council to launch a military operation to guard relief workers in Somalia, and the Council did so on December 3. The advance guard of a projected 28,000 U.S. troops landed in Somalia December 9. Serving under UN auspices, they were to secure airfields, ports, and roads so aid could be delivered.

Cambodia. On February 28 the Council authorized 22,000 peacekeepers for Cambodia. The fragile peace treaty signed in October 1991 by four warring parties seemed to unravel, however, when the Party of Democratic Kampuchea (the Khmer Rouge), who ruled Cambodia from 1975 to 1979, refused to surrender their arms. Its leaders charged that up to two million Vietnamese settlers in Cambodia were actually disguised troops and warned that it would not take part in UN-sponsored elections in May 1993. On October 13 and again on November 30, the Council unanimously warned that the elections would go forward without the Khmer Rouge if necessary and moved to restrict trade with the Khmer Rouge. On December 22 the Council condemned the Khmer Rouge for detaining several dozen UN peacekeepers during the month, although all were eventually released.

Cyprus. Disillusioned by the failure of Greece and Turkey to resolve their differences over Cyprus after 28 years, Austria, Canada, Denmark, and the U.K. threatened to withdraw their peacekeeping forces. The Council on April 10 pressed the parties to resume negotiating, but without apparent result.

Iraq. No "unfinished business" plagued the UN so much during 1992 as the aftermath of the 1991 Gulf war. Iraq continually obstructed Council efforts to investigate possible nuclear weapons operations within the country and to destroy equipment and buildings for constructing and repairing ballistic missiles.

After conducting 14 inspections and supervising the destruction of surviving nuclear equipment and buildings, the International Atomic Energy Agency reported that Iraq could no longer sustain any nuclear activity. It was not sure, however, that all Scud missiles had been eliminated. On September 7 Iraq agreed to periodic tests of its waters for radioactivity to help ensure that it had not covertly rebuilt nuclear facilities. Such tests, however, would not detect secret but nonoperating underground reactors. The Council refused twice during the year to lift its sanctions on Iraq because Iraq had yet to reveal the names of foreign companies that provided it with nuclear technology or to agree to long-term monitoring of its weapons potential.

On the humanitarian side, the Council tried to prevent continuing harassment of Shi'ites and UN personnel by banning all Iraqi flights south of the 32d parallel after August 27. When, on December 27, Iraq sent a warplane into the no-fly zone, a U.S. plane shot it down. Iraq attempted to stop all international aid programs after June 30, but after the Council voted, on October 2, to take control of $800 million in frozen Iraqi foreign assets to finance relief efforts, Iraq allowed relief shipments to resume. Shipments were

suspended in late December, however, after bombs were found in some relief trucks.

Other Disputes. The UN was supposed to conduct a referendum in the Western Sahara in January to decide whether the inhabitants wanted independence, but it was repeatedly postponed. In August the "Democratic Arab Saharan Republic" abandoned its challenge to Morocco, and on October 16, Morocco, reportedly having flooded the territory with settlers, held local elections there. A UN-sponsored settlement in Angola was endangered when Jonas Savimbi, leader of the National Union for the Total Independence of Angola, challenged his defeat by José Eduardo dos Santos in UN-supervised presidential elections on September 29–30. He alleged fraud, although international observers found none. On November 26 both sides asked UN observers to remain past the original November 30 deadline. On December 16 the Security Council authorized 7,500 troops, police, and civilians to oversee an agreement signed on October 4 that ended the 14-year-old civil war in Mozambique.

In El Salvador on October 16 the government and rebels accepted UN proposals to redistribute 163,000 ha (407,000 ac) of land to 47,500 peasants and to former fighters on both sides, apparently salvaging the endangered peace accords of January 16. UN officials continued to help both sides meet a December 15 deadline for demobilizing the guerrillas, although they were not satisfied with the government's efforts to purge the armed forces of alleged human rights violators. On September 12 the International Court of Justice resolved a complicated border dispute between El Salvador and Honduras dating from 1969. The Council on August 7 unanimously authorized Boutros-Ghali to send UN observers to South Africa to work closely with that country's National Peace Secretariat (representing political parties, trade unions, religious groups, and civic organizations) to end violence there. The Council on March 31 (and again on August 12) ordered UN members to sever airline links and arms sales to and downgrade diplomatic relations with Libya until Col. Mu'ammar al-Qadhdhafi surrendered two suspects in the 1988 bombing of a Pan American airliner over Scotland. It also helped investigate the bombing of a French airliner.

The Council "strongly" condemned Israel on January 6 for deciding to deport 12 Palestinian civilians accused of terrorism from Israeli-occupied territories. It also reaffirmed that the Fourth Geneva Convention (1949) applied to the Israeli-occupied Arab lands. Nonetheless, after six Israeli troopers were killed, Israel deported 415 Palestinians, an act the Council again strongly condemned. On February 20 and November 8 Israeli armoured forces broke through UN barricades in southern Lebanon in "search and destroy" operations designed to stop rocket attacks by Shi'ite Muslim guerrillas; four UN soldiers were wounded in the cross fire. On November 19 the Security Council forbade arms sales to Liberia, hoping to crush a civil war that was endangering West African peacekeepers. By a vote of 59–3 (Israel, Romania, and the U.S.), with 79 abstentions, the General Assembly on November 24 called for the U.S. to end its 30-year embargo against Cuba. The resolution came in response to U.S. legislation penalizing subsidiaries of U.S. companies abroad that trade with Cuba and barring merchant ships that stop at Cuban ports from calling at U.S. ports for six months.

Human Rights. On June 29 and August 13 the Security Council unanimously condemned Serbia for driving out non-Serbs from its territories ("ethnic cleansing") and insisted that the Red Cross have access to prison camps and detention centres. On August 14 the Commission on Human Rights condemned abuses in Bosnia and Hercegovina and sent a special envoy to investigate atrocities. The Security Council, on October 6, unanimously established a war crimes commission to collect evidence of possible atrocities throughout the former Yugoslav federation. In March the Commission on Human Rights criticized 22 countries (especially Iran and Cuba) for human rights abuses and placed others under surveillance. It was also suggested on May 27 that the U.S. might be violating international law by returning Haitian refugees to Haiti without allowing them to appeal for protection and asylum. The U.S. Senate consented in April to U.S. ratification of the International Covenant on Civil and Political Rights, which was adopted by the UN in 1966 and entered into force in 1976. The U.S. became the 104th party to the treaty.

Membership. UN membership stood at 179 at year's end, up from 166 in 1991. The Council admitted San Marino and eight former Soviet republics (Armenia, Azerbaijan, Kazakhstan, Kyrgyzstan, Moldova, Tajikistan, Turkmenistan, and Uzbekistan) on March 2, three former Yugoslav republics (Bosnia and Hercegovina, Croatia, and Slovenia) on May 22, and the former Soviet republic of Georgia on July 31. On September 22 the Assembly, acting on a Security Council recommendation, exercised for the first time its right to bar a sitting member from participating in Assembly work; it ordered the federation of Serbia and Montenegro to apply for the seat previously occupied by the Yugoslav federation because the would-be successors had engaged in "ethnic cleansing" and were not "peace-loving."

Other Activities. The International Narcotics Control Board reported in January that illicit production, trafficking, and abuse of drugs continued to imperil public health in virtually all countries and that drug trafficking gangs in South America, Southeast Asia, and Europe were joining forces. The World Health Organization indicated on February 12 that between 10 million and 12 million people had contracted the human immunodeficiency virus that causes AIDS; that one million children were now infected; that about 90% of new adult infections resulted from heterosexual intercourse; and that AIDS would orphan up to 10 million African children by the turn of the century. (*See* HEALTH AND DISEASE.)

The UN Conference on Environment and Development, held in Rio de Janeiro June 3–14, adopted a biodiversity convention to protect endangered plant and animal species (152 nations signed, with the U.S. a major exception), a global warming treaty (154 nations signed, including the U.S., but only after getting delegates to remove targets for reducing carbon dioxide emissions), a declaration of principles on environmental policy, and guidelines for forestry practices (approved by consensus). The conference urged richer counties to help poorer ones meet higher environmental standards. On November 25 the General Assembly agreed to establish a Sustainable Development Commission to help ensure that states complied with their pledges. (*See* ENVIRONMENT.)

After negotiations spanning a generation, the 39-member Conference on Disarmament in Geneva approved on August 7 a draft treaty banning chemical weapons.

(RICHARD N. SWIFT)

This article updates the *Macropædia* article UNITED NATIONS.

COMMONWEALTH OF NATIONS

Much of the work of the official Commonwealth in 1992 centred on efforts to promote democracy in member countries. Following decisions of the Harare (Zimbabwe) summit of 1991, several governments requested Commonwealth help in monitoring their electoral process as they changed from one-party to multiparty or from military to civilian rule. In

July a team of observers from seven countries, led by Henry Forde, former foreign minister of Barbados, went to Seychelles for multiparty elections setting up a constitutional commission. The Seychelles decision to move to multipartyism had been a direct result of the Harare talks. In October observers from 14 countries led by David Peterson, former premier of Ontario, went to Guyana for the long-postponed elections there, while another team from eight countries was sent to Ghana. Preparations were also begun to send teams to Lesotho and Kenya. Each time, Commonwealth Secretariat officials and legal advisers went in advance to advise on polling arrangements and constitutional procedures.

In the case of Guyana, advance teams of observers were sent three times to check on polling plans. Their attention focused on voter registration, which had been found unsatisfactory, and the election was postponed for several months while improvements were made. After the polling, the observers reported "imperfections" but concluded that these did not undermine the outcome. In Seychelles the Commonwealth report declared that the elections had been "free and fair on the day, notwithstanding some shortcomings." It recommended a fresh look at the voters' list before the presidential elections. The Ghana group declared the November 3 election "free and fair, and free from fear" but accepted that the voters' roll could have been incorrect by over a million. The opposition said the poll had been fraudulent.

The Commonwealth also continued to help the constitutional process in South Africa. In December 1991 a team of observers that included former foreign ministers of three countries (Britain's Sir Geoffrey Howe was one) attended the first meeting of the Convention for a Democratic South Africa (Codesa). Secretary-General Emeka Anyaoku and his officials had meetings with Pres. F.W. de Klerk, Nelson Mandela of the African National Congress, Chief Mangosuthu Buthelezi, leader of the Inkatha Freedom Party, and other party leaders, and in October 1992, 18 observers were sent to South Africa to help arrest the worsening violence. In June Chief Anyaoku pulled off a diplomatic success when he mediated talks in London between the exiled King Moshoeshoe II of Lesotho and the military ruler, Maj. Gen. Elias Ramaema, that led to the king's return home.

The central theme of a meeting of Commonwealth health ministers in Cyprus (October 19–23) was environmental hazards to the health of communities, individuals, and unborn children. Commonwealth finance ministers, meeting, unusually, in New York (September 16–17), suggested setting up a private fund to facilitate privatization and encourage the provision of venture capital within the Commonwealth.

The 40th anniversary of Queen Elizabeth's accession also marked her 40 years as head of the Commonwealth. A golden mace adorned with the flags of the 50 member countries was presented to her. It was paid for by businessmen and industrialists and was to be used at formal Commonwealth occasions in the queen's presence.

Well before the breakup of the Soviet Union, Russians had been showing interest in the way the Commonwealth worked. Thus it was no accident that the association formed after the failed Moscow coup was dubbed, albeit somewhat confusingly, the Commonwealth of Independent States.

(DEREK INGRAM)

COMMONWEALTH OF INDEPENDENT STATES

By the end of its first year the Commonwealth of Independent States (CIS) was still an amorphous body. Established by the three Slavic republics of Russia, Ukraine, and Belarus on Dec. 8, 1991, it was joined later that month by all the other republics of the former Soviet Union except Georgia,

Estonia, Latvia, and Lithuania. The Slavic republics took the initiative because they were among the signatories, in 1922, of the treaty that gave birth to the Soviet Union.

From the beginning there were fundamental disagreements among the members. Russia saw itself as the successor to the U.S.S.R. and therefore the dominant force in the CIS. Ukraine regarded the CIS as an administrative device to cope with the problems that were bound to arise during the transition of the republics to full independence. The issue was complicated by the fact that the Soviet armed forces passed under the control of the CIS with a Russian commander in chief, Marshal Yevgeny Shaposhnikov. Four CIS members, Russia, Ukraine, Belarus, and Kazakhstan, were nuclear powers. By the end of 1992 all tactical nuclear weapons had been transferred to Russia, but not the strategic nuclear weapons. Ukraine wanted "administrative control" over its strategic weapons to ensure that they were not fired on Russian orders. Another bone of contention was control over the Black Sea fleet. Eventually, in June, Presidents Boris Yeltsin of Russia and Leonid Kravchuk of Ukraine had agreed to joint command of the fleet for the forseeable future. Ukraine and Russia had not reached an agreement on a range of economic issues, notably the establishment of a ruble zone with a CIS central bank. Kiev feared Russia's aim was a confederation that would lead to Ukraine's becoming, once again, a "colonial appendage."

By the eighth CIS meeting in Bishkek, Kyrgyzstan, in October, an inner core headed by Russia and an outer core led by Ukraine were forming. Other states in the inner core were Kazakhstan, Kyrgyzstan, Uzbekistan, and Belarus. Those in the outer core, besides Ukraine, were Moldova, Azerbaijan, and Armenia. (However, the Azerbaijani parliament voted that state out of the CIS in September.) Tajikistan was in the throes of civil war, and Turkmenistan appeared to be drifting toward the Middle East. The outer core all intended to introduce their own currencies. All the states had trade deficits with Russia, and this strengthened Moscow's hand. Those Russian politicians who favoured a confederation, effectively led by Russia, were gaining influence by year's end. The Russian military was also strengthening its position outside Russia.

(MARTIN McCAULEY)

POLITICAL PARTIES

The following table is a general guide to the political parties of the world. All countries that were independent on Dec. 31, 1992, are included, although there are a number for which no analysis of political activities can be given. Parties are included in most instances only if represented in parliaments (in the lower house in bicameral legislatures); the last column indicates the number of seats obtained in the last general election (figures in parentheses are those of the penultimate one) and excludes nonelective seats and seats still in dispute. The date of the most recent election follows the name of the country.

The capital letters in the column "Affiliation" show the relative political positions of the parties within each country. There are obvious difficulties involved in labeling parties within the political spectrum of a given country. The key chosen is as follows: F-fascist; ER-extreme right; R-right; CR-centre right; C-centre; CL-centre left; SD-social democratic; S-socialist; L-non-Marxist left; K-Communist; and EL-extreme left. In addition, within some countries there are political organizations that exist chiefly to advance a special interest as distinct from a political orientation. These are represented by lower-case letters as follows: x-parties that have repudiated former Communist affiliation; e-parties based on distinct regional, ethnic, or linguistic identity; r-religious fundamentalist; and g-environmental, or Green.

The numbers in the column "Voting strength" indicate proportions of the valid votes cast for the respective parties, or the percentage of registered voters who went to the polls in single-party states.

(MELINDA C. SHEPHERD)

Political Parties

Country / Name of party	Affiliation	Voting strength (%)	Parliamentary representation
Afghanistan			
Interim government since April 1992	—	—	—
Albania (March 1992)			
Democratic Party	CR	62	92 (75)
Socialist Party	x	25	38 (169)
Other	—	13	10 (6)
Algeria			
Interim government since January 1992	—	—	—
Andorra (April 1992)			
Government Coalition	…	…	17
Opposition	…	…	11
Angola (September 1992)			
Popular Liberation Movement of Angola–Labour Party (MPLA–PT)	x	53.7	129 (203)
National Union for the Total Independence of Angola (UNITA)	—	34.1	70 —
Others	—	12.2	21 —
Antigua and Barbuda (March 1989)			
Antigua Labour Party	C	63.8	15 (16)
United National Democratic Party	C	31.0	1 —
Barbuda People's Movement	—	…	1 —
Barbuda National Party	—	…	— (1)
Argentina (August–December 1991)			
Justicialist National Movement (Peronist)	CR	…	119 (127)
Union of the Democratic Centre	CR	…	12 (11)
Radical Civic Union	CL	…	85 (93)
Others	—	…	38 (24)
Armenia (May–July 1990)			
Supreme Soviet	—	—	260
Australia (March 1990)			
National	R	…	14 (19)
Liberal	C	…	55 (43)
Labor	L	…	78 (86)
Independents	—	…	1 (0)

Country / Name of party	Affiliation	Voting strength (%)	Parliamentary representation
Austria (October 1990)			
Freedom Party	R	16.6	33 (18)
People's Party	C	32.0	60 (77)
Socialist Party	SD	42.8	80 (80)
Greens	Lg	4.8	10 (8)
Azerbaijan (September–October 1990)			
Supreme Soviet	—	—	349
Bahamas, The (August 1992)			
Progressive Liberal Party	C	…	16 (31)
Free National Movement	C	…	33 (16)
Others	—	…	0 (2)
Bahrain			
Emirate, no parties	—	—	—
Bangladesh (February 1991)			
Jatiya Dal	—	11	35 (251)
Nationalist Party	CR	31	166 (18)
Awami League	SD	31	89 —
Islamic Assembly	r	12	21 (5)
Others	—	15	19 (25)
Barbados (January 1991)			
Democratic Labour Party	C	49	18 (24)
Barbados Labour Party	L	44	10 (3)
Belarus (March 1990)			
Supreme Soviet	K	—	272
Belgium (November 1991)			
Vlaams Blok	ERe	6.6	12 (2)
Volksunie	Re	5.9	10 (16)
Front Démocratique des Francophones	Re	1.5	3 (3)
Liberals { Flemish	CR	11.9	26 (25)
{ French	CR	8.2	20 (23)
Social Christians { Flemish	C	16.7	39 (43)
{ French	C	7.8	18 (19)
Socialists { Flemish	SD	12.0	28 (32)
{ French	SD	13.6	35 (40)
Greens { Flemish	g	4.9	7 (6)
{ French	g	5.1	10 (3)
Others	—	7.3	7 (3)

Country / Name of party	Affiliation	Voting strength (%)	Parliamentary representation
Belize (September 1989)			
United Democratic Party	R	49	13 (21)
People's United Party	C	51	15 (7)
Benin (February 1991)			
Union of the Forces of Progress (formerly sole party)	—	…	0
21 other parties	—	…	64
Bhutan			
A monarchy, no parties	—	—	100
Bolivia (May 1989)			
Nationalist Democratic Action	R	25.2	38 (36)
Nationalist Revolutionary Movement	CR	25.6	40 (38)
Conscience of the Fatherland	CL	12.3	9 —
Movement of the Revolutionary Left	L	21.8	33 —
United Left (coalition)	L&EL	8.0	10 —
Bosnia and Hercegovina (December 1990)			
Party of Democratic Action	e	…	86
Serbian Democratic Party	e	…	72
Croatian Democratic Union	e	…	44
Democratic Party of Socialists	x	…	20
Others	—	…	18
Botswana (October 1989)			
Botswana Democratic Party	C	65.0	31 (29)
Botswana People's Party	L	…	— (1)
Botswana National Front	L	27.7	3 (4)
Brazil (October 1990)			
Party of the Brazilian Democratic Movement and allies	CL	…	146
Rightist parties	CR	…	243
Leftist parties	L	…	95
Others	—	…	14
Brunei			
Legislative Council (nonelected)	—	—	—

Political Parties

Country / Name of party	Affiliation	Voting strength (%)	Parliamentary representation
Bulgaria (October 1991)			
Union of Democratic Forces	CL	34.4	110 (144)
Bulgarian Socialist Party	x	33.1	106 (211)
Movement for Rights and Freedom	e	7.5	24 (23)
Bulgarian Agrarian People's Union	—	3.9	0 (16)
Other parties and independents	—	21.1	0 (6)
Burkina Faso (May 1992)			
Organization for Popular Democracy-Labour Movement	—	...	78
Allied parties	—	...	6
Opposition parties	—	...	23
Burundi			
Transitional government since March 1992	—	—	—
Cambodia			
Transitional government since June 1991	—	—	—
Cameroon (March 1992)			
People's Democratic Rally	—	...	88 (180)
National Union for Democracy and Progress	—	...	68 —
Others	—	...	24 —
Canada (November 1988)			
Progressive Conservative	CR	43	170 (211)
Liberal	C	32	82 (40)
New Democratic	SD	20	43 (30)
Others	—	5	0 (1)
Cape Verde (January 1991)			
Movement for Democracy	—	68.5	56 —
African Party for the Independence of Cape Verde	—	31.5	23 (83)
Central African Republic (August 1987)			
Central African Democratic Assembly	—	...	52
Chad			
Transitional government since March 1991	—	—	—
Chile (December 1989)			
National Renovation and allied parties	R	...	48 (48)
Christian Democrats and allied parties	CL	...	72 (69)
Others	—	...	0 (3)
China, People's Republic of (March–April 1988)			
National People's Congress	K	...	2,978
Colombia (October 1991)			
Social Conservative Party	R	...	15 (68)
National Salvation Movement	R	...	12 —
New Democratic Force	R	...	12 —
Liberal Party	C	...	86 (112)
Democratic Alliance–April 19 Movement	L&EL	...	15 (1)
Patriotic Union	EL	...	2 (15)
Others	—	...	19 (1)
Comoros (November–December 1992)			
Federal Assembly	—	...	... (42)
Congo (June–July 1992)			
Pan-African Union for Social Democracy	—	...	39
Congolese Labour Party	x	...	19
Allies of Congolese Labour	—	...	47
Others	—	...	20
Costa Rica (February 1990)			
Social Christian Unity Party	CR	51.3	29 (25)
National Liberation Party	L	47.2	25 (29)
Others	—	1.5	3 (3)
Côte d'Ivoire (November 1990)			
Democratic Party	—	...	163 (175)
Popular Front	—	...	9 —
Others	—	...	3 —
Croatia (August 1992)			
Croatian Party of Rights	ERe	6.4	5
Croatian Democratic Union	e	41.5	85
Croatian People's Party	C	6.9	5
Croatian Social-Liberal Party	CL	18.3	14
Party of Democratic Changes	x	5.8	11
Others	—	20.6	18
Cuba (December 1986)			
Communist Party	K	...	499 (499)
Cyprus			
Greek Zone (May 1991)			
Democratic Rally	R	35.8	20 (19)
Democratic Party (DIKO)	CR	19.5	11 (16)
Socialist Party (EDEK)	CL	10.9	7 (6)
Progressive Party of the Working People	K	30.6	18 (15)
Turkish Zone (May 1990)			
National Unity Party	—	54	34
National Struggle Party	—	44	14
Independents	—	...	2

Country / Name of party	Affiliation	Voting strength (%)	Parliamentary representation
Czechoslovakia (June 1992)			
Civic Democratic Alliance	CR	24	48
Czechoslovak Social Democratic Party	SD	5	10
Movement for a Democratic Slovakia	L	11	24
Left Bloc	xe	10	19
Party of the Democratic Left	xe	5	10
Others	—	45	39
Denmark (December 1990)			
Progress	ER	6.4	12 (16)
Conservative	R	16.0	30 (35)
Liberal Democratic (Venstre)	CR	15.8	29 (22)
Christian People's	CR	2.3	4 (4)
Radical Liberal (Radikale Venstre)	C	3.5	7 (10)
Centre Democrats	C	5.1	9 (9)
Social Democrats	SD	37.4	69 (55)
Socialist People's	S	8.3	15 (24)
Faeroe Islands and Greenland	—	...	4 (4)
Djibouti (December 1992)			
Popular Rally for Progress	—	76.7	65 (65)
New Democratic Party	—	23.3	0 —
Dominica (May 1990)			
Dominica Freedom Party	CR	49.4	11 (15)
Dominica United Workers' Party	C	23.5	6 —
Labour Party	L	26.9	4 (5)
Independents	—	...	0 (1)
Dominican Republic (May 1990)			
Social Christian Reformist Party	CR	...	40 (56)
Dominican Revolutionary Party	L	...	32 (48)
Dominican Liberation Party	L	...	44 (16)
Independent Revolutionary Party	—	...	2 —
Others	—	...	2 —
Ecuador (May 1992)			
Conservative Party	R	...	6 (3)
Republican Unity Party	CR	...	12 —
Social Christian Party	CR	...	21 (16)
Popular Democracy	C	...	5 (7)
Roldosist Party	—	...	13 (13)
Democratic Left	SD	...	7 (14)
Others	—	...	14 (19)
Egypt (December 1990)			
New Wafd Party	R	(Boycotted)	(35)
National Democratic Party	CR	79.6	348 (346)
Socialist Labour Party and allies	L	(Boycotted)	(60)
National Progressive Unionist	L	1.4	6 (0)
Independents	—	...	83 (7)
El Salvador (March 1991)			
Nationalist Republican Alliance (Arena)	R	44	39 (30)
National Conciliation Party	CR	9	9 (7)
Christian Democratic Party	C	28	26 (23)
Democratic Convergence	L	12	8 —
Others	—	7	2 (0)
Equatorial Guinea (July 1988)			
House of People's Representatives	—	...	41
Estonia (September 1992)			
Fatherland coalition	R	...	29
Estonian Popular Front	C	...	15 (43)
Estonian National Independence Party	C	...	10 —
Moderates	—	...	12 —
Safe Home Alliance	x	...	17 —
Others	—	...	18 (62)
Ethiopia			
Transitional government since July 1991	—	—	—
Fiji (May 1992)			
Fijian Political Party	e	...	30
Other Fijians	e	...	7
National Federation (Indian)	e	...	14
Other Indians	e	...	13
Other parties	—	...	6
Finland (March 1991)			
National Coalition Party (Conservative)	R	19.0	40 (53)
Swedish People's	Re	5.4	12 (12)
Centre (including former Liberal) Party	C	24.4	55 (40)
Christian Union	C	3.0	8 (5)
Rural Party	C	4.8	7 (9)
Social Democratic	L	21.7	48 (56)
Left-wing Alliance	S	9.9	19 (20)
Green Party	g	6.7	10 (4)
Others	—	5.2	2 (1)
France (June 1988)			
National Front	ER	...	1 (35)
Rally for the Republic (RPR)	R	...	127 (147)
Union for French Democracy (UDF)	R	...	129 (130)
Diverse right	—	...	16 (14)
Socialist Party	S	...	260 } (207)
Left Radical Movement	SD	...	9 }
Diverse left	—	...	7 (9)

Country / Name of party	Affiliation	Voting strength (%)	Parliamentary representation
Communist Party	L	...	27 (35)
Other	—	...	1
Gabon (September 1990)			
Democratic Party	—	...	66 (111)
Progress Party	—	...	19 —
Rally of Woodcutters	—	...	17 —
Others	—	...	18 —
Gambia, The (March 1987)			
People's Progressive Party	S	...	25 (31)
Others	—	...	11 (5)
Georgia (October 1992)			
Parliament	—	...	234
Germany (December 1990)			
Christian Democratic Union	R	36.7	268
Christian Social Union	R	7.1	51
Free Democratic Party	C	11.0	79
Social Democratic Party	SD	33.5	239
Party of Democratic Socialism	x	2.4	17
Greens/Alliance '90	g	5.1	8
Others	—	4.2	0
Ghana (December 1992)			
Governing party	—	...	189
Others	—	...	11
Greece (April 1990)			
New Democracy Party	CR	46.9	152 (148)
Panhellenic Socialist Movement (Pasok)	S	38.6	124 (128)
Left Alliance	L&K	10.2	21 (21)
Others	—	4.3	4 (3)
Grenada (March 1990)			
Grenada United Labour Party	R	28.3	4 (1)
National Democratic Congress	C	34.6	7 (6)
National Party	C	17.4	2 (5)
New National Party	C	17.2	2 (3)
Guatemala (November 1990)			
National Advancement Party	R	17.3	12
Solidarity Action Movement	CR	24.1	18
Christian Democratic Party	C	17.5	28
National Centre Union	C	25.7	41
Others and independents	—	15.4	17
Guinea			
Transitional government since January 1991	—	—	—
Guinea-Bissau (June 1989)			
African Party for the Independence of Guinea and Cape Verde	—	...	150
Guyana (October 1992)			
United Force	CR	1.2	1 (2)
People's National Congress	Se	43.6	23 (42)
People's Progressive Party	Se	52.3	28 (8)
Working Peoples Alliance	L	1.7	1 (1)
Haiti			
Military control since September 1991	—	—	—
Honduras (November 1989)			
National Party	R	51	71 (63)
Liberal Party	CR	43	55 (67)
Others	—	6	2 (4)
Hungary (March–April 1990)			
Independent Smallholders	R	11.1	43
Hungarian Democratic Forum	CR	42.7	165
Christian Democratic Party	CR	5.4	21
Alliance of Free Democrats	CL	23.8	92
Federation of Young Democrats	L	5.4	21
Hungarian Socialist Party	x	8.5	33
Others	—	1.0	4
Independents	—	1.6	6
Iceland (April 1991)			
Independence Party	R	38.6	26 (18)
Citizens' Party	R	1.2	0 (7)
Progressive (Farmers') Party	C	18.9	13 (13)
Social Democratic Party	SD	15.5	10 (10)
People's Alliance	x	14.4	9 (8)
Women's Alliance	—	8.3	5 (6)
Others	—	3.1	0 (1)
India (May 1991–February 1992)			
Bharatiya Janata	Rr	...	121 (88)
Congress (I)	C	...	245 (192)
Janata Dal	CL	...	58 (141)
Communist parties	K	...	49 (43)
Others	—	...	72 (59)
Indonesia (June 1992)			
Golkar (Functional Groups)	—	68	282 (299)
United Development Party	r	17	62 (61)
Indonesian Democratic Party	—	15	56 (40)
Iran (April–May 1992)			
Consultative Assembly, no parties since 1987	—	...	270
Iraq (April 1989)			
Ba'th Party and others	—	...	250

Political Parties

Country Name of party	Affiliation	Voting strength (%)	Parliamentary representation	
Ireland (November 1992)				
Fianna Fail (Republican)	C	39	67	(77)
Fine Gael (United Ireland)	C	25	45	(55)
Progressive Democrats	C	...	10	(6)
Labour Party	L	19	33	(16)
Democratic Left	S	...	5	(6)
Others	—	...	6	(5)
Israel (June 1992)				
Moledet	ER	...	3	(2)
Tehiya	ER	...	0	(3)
Tzomet	R	...	8	(2)
Shas	Rr	...	6	(6)
Likud	R	...	32	(40)
National Religious	CRr	...	6	(5)
United Torah Judaism (includes Agudat)	—	...	4	(7)
Labour	SD	...	44	(38)
Meretz (includes Mapam)	SD	...	12	(6)
Arab Democratic	e	...	2	(1)
Hadash	K	...	3	(4)
Italy (April 1992)				
Italian Social Movement	F	5.4	34	(35)
Northern League	Re	8.7	55	—
Italian Liberal Party	CR	2.8	17	(11)
Christian Democratic Party	C	29.7	206	(234)
Italian Republican Party	CL	4.4	27	(21)
Italian Social Democratic Party	SO	2.7	16	(17)
Socialist Unity Party	S	13.6	92	(94)
Democratic Party of the Left	x	16.1	107 }	(177)
Communist Refoundation Party	K	5.6	35 }	
Green List	g	2.8	16	(13)
Others	—	10.9	41	(45)
Jamaica (February 1989)				
Jamaica Labour Party	CL	44.1	15	(60)
People's National Party	L	55.8	45	—
Japan (February 1990)				
Liberal-Democratic Party	R	46	275	(300)
Komeito (Clean Government)	C	8	45	(57)
Democratic Socialist Party	SD	5	14	(28)
Japan Socialist Party	S	24	136	(87)
Japan Communist Party	L	8	16	(27)
Others and independents	—	9	26	(13)
Jordan (November 1989)				
Muslim Brotherhood	r	...	20	
Independent Islamic fundamentalists	r	...	12	
Leftist Democratic Bloc	L	...	11	
Others	—	...	17	
Kazakhstan (April 1990)				
Supreme Council	—	...	358	
Kenya (December 1992)				
Kenya African National Union	—	...	100	(188)
Forum for Restoration of Democracy (2 wings)	—	...	62	—
Democratic Party	—	...	23	—
Others	—	...	3	—
Kiribati (May 1991)				
House of Assembly	—	...	39	
Korea, North (April 1990)				
Korean Workers' Party	K	99.8	687	
Korea, South (March 1992)				
United People's Party	—	17.3	31	
Democratic Liberal Party	—	38.5	149	
Democratic Party	—	29.2	97	
Others and independents	—	15.0	22	
Kuwait (October 1992)				
Government supporters	—	...	19	
Fundamental opposition	r	...	19	
Liberal opposition	—	...	12	
Kyrgyzstan				
Supreme Council	—	—	—	
Laos (March 1989)				
Lao People's Revolutionary Party	K	...	65	
Others	—	...	14	
Latvia (March–April 1990)				
Popular Front	—	...	131	
Communist Party	K	...	59	
Others	—	...	11	
Lebanon (August–October 1992)				
Christian members	—	...	64	
Muslim/Druze members	—	...	64	
Lesotho				
Military Council in power from January 1986	—	—	—	
Liberia				
Interim government since November 1990	—	—	—	
Libya				
Military government since Sept. 1, 1969	—	—	—	

Country Name of party	Affiliation	Voting strength (%)	Parliamentary representation	
Liechtenstein (March 1989)				
Progressive Citizens' Party	CR	42.1	12	(7)
Fatherland Union	C	47.2	13	(8)
Lithuania (October–November 1992)				
Democratic Labour Party	x	...	73	
Reform Movement (Sajudis)	—	...	30	
Others	—	...	38	
Luxembourg (June 1989)				
Christian Social People's Party	CR	...	22	(25)
Democratic (Liberal) Party	C	...	11	(14)
Socialist Workers' Party	SD	...	18	(21)
Communist Party	K	...	1	(2)
Five-Sixths Action Committee	—	...	4	(0)
Greens	g	...	4	(2)
Macedonia (November–December 1990)				
Democratic Party for Macedonia National Unity	C	...	37	
League of Communists of Macedonia	x	...	31	
Party for Democratic Prosperity (Albanian)	e	...	25	
Others	—	...	27	
Madagascar				
Transitional government from November 1991	—	—	—	
Malawi (June 1992)				
Malawi Congress Party	—	...	136	(112)
Malaysia (October 1990)				
National Front (Barisan Nasional) Coalition				
United Malays National Organization		...	71	(83)
Allied parties	—	...	56	(65)
Opposition parties	—	...	49	(25)
Independents	—	...	4	(4)
Maldives (November 1989)				
Citizens' Assembly	—	...	40	
Mali (February–March 1992)				
Alliance for Democracy in Mali	—	48.4	76	
Others	—	51.6	40	
Malta (May 1987)				
Nationalist Party	R	51.8	34	(35)
Labour Party	SD	46.5	31	(34)
Marshall Islands (November 1987)				
House of Representatives, no parties	—	—	33	
Mauritania (March 1992)				
Democratic and Social Republican Party	R	85	67	
Others	—	15	12	
Mauritius (September 1991)				
Mauritian Social Movement and allies	CL	...	59	(49)
Opposition parties	CL	...	3	(13)
Mexico (August 1991)				
National Action Party (PAN)	CR	17.7	89	(101)
Institutional Revolutionary Party (PRI)	C	61.4	320	(261)
Democratic Revolutionary Party	L	8.3	41 }	(138)
Others	—	12.5	50 }	
Micronesia (March 1991)				
Congress, no parties		...	14	
Moldova (February–March 1990)				
Supreme Soviet	K	...	380	
Monaco (January 1988)				
National and Democratic Union	—	...	18	(18)
Mongolia (July 1990)				
Mongolian People's Revolutionary Party	x	56.9	71	(33)
Others	—	43.1	5	(20)
Morocco (September 1984)				
Constitutional Union	CR	...	56	
Allied parties	—	...	85	
Opposition parties	—	...	65	
Mozambique (November–December 1986)				
Mozambique Liberation Front (Frelimo)	K	...	250	(210)
Myanmar				
Military government since 1988	—	—	—	
Namibia (November 1989)				
Democratic Turnhalle Alliance	C	28.6	21	
South West Africa People's Organization (SWAPO)	L	57.3	41	
United Democratic Front	—	5.6	4	
Others	—	8.5	6	
Nauru (November 1992)				
Independents	—	...	18	(18)
Nepal (May 1991)				
National Democratic parties	R	12	4	
Nepali Congress Party	C	38	110	

Country Name of party	Affiliation	Voting strength (%)	Parliamentary representation	
Communist parties	K	36	82	
Others and independents	—	14	9	
Netherlands, The (September 1989)				
Christian Democratic Appeal	CR	35.3	54	(54)
People's Party for Freedom and Democracy	CR	14.6	22	(27)
Democrats 66	CL	7.9	12	(9)
Labor Party	SD	31.9	49	(52)
Greens	g	4.1	6	(3)
Others	—	6.2	7	(5)
New Zealand (October 1990)				
National (Conservative) Party	CR	47.8	67	(39)
Labour Party	L	35.1	29	(58)
New Labour Party	L	5.2	1	—
Nicaragua (February 1990)				
National Opposition Union	CR	54.7	51	
Sandinista National Liberation Front	L	40.8	39	
Others	—	4.5	2	
Niger				
Transitional government since August 1991				
Nigeria (July 1992)				
National Republican Convention	CR	...	275	
Social Democratic Party	CL	...	314	
Norway (September 1989)				
Progress Party	R	13.0	22	(2)
Conservative Party	R	22.2	37	(50)
Christian People's Party	CR	8.5	14	(16)
Centre (Agrarian) Party	CR	6.5	11	(12)
Liberal Party	C	3.2	0	(0)
Labour Party	SD	34.3	63	(71)
Socialist Left	S	10.1	17	(6)
Others	—	2.2	1	(0)
Oman				
Independent sultanate, no parties	—	—		
Pakistan (October 1990)				
Islamic Democratic Alliance (IJI)	Rr	37.3	105	(54)
Jamit-i-Ulema-i-Islam	Rr	...	6	(7)
People's Democratic Alliance (includes Pakistan People's Party)	Sr	36.7	45	(93)
Mohajir Qaumi Movement	—	...	15	(13)
Other parties	—	...	14	(11)
Independents	—	...	21	(27)
Panama (May 1989–January 1991)				
Antimilitarist Opposition Democratic Alliance	—	...	55	
National Liberation Coalition	—	...	12	
Papua New Guinea (June 1992)				
Pangu Party	—	...	22	(26)
People's Democratic Movement	—	...	15	(18)
National Party	—	...	2	(12)
Melanesian Alliance	—	...	9	(7)
People's Action Party	—	...	13	(6)
People's Progress Party	—	...	10	(5)
Others	—	...	7	(14)
Independents	—	...	30	(21)
Paraguay (May 1989)				
Colorado Party	R	72.8	48	(48)
Authentic Radical Liberal Party	CL	20.1	19 }	(24)
Other parties	—	...	5 }	
Peru (November 1992)				
Christian Popular Party	R	7.7	8 }	
Liberal Party	R	—	— }	(60)
Popular Action	CR	(Boycotted)	}	
New Majority–Change 90	—	38.6	44	(32)
American Popular Revolutionary Alliance	CL	(Boycotted)		(52)
Others	—	53.7	28	(36)
Philippines (May 1992)				
National People's Coalition	R	...	48	
Liberal Party	C	...	15	
National Union of Christian Democrats	—	...	51	
Democratic Filipino Struggle	—	...	87	
Poland (October 1991)				
Religious parties alliance	CR	26	117	
Confederation for an Independent Poland	CR	8	46	
Democratic Union	CL	12	62	
Solidarity alliance	L	13	49	
Communist alliance	x	21	91	
Others	—	20	95	
Portugal (October 1991)				
Social Democratic Party	C	50.4	135	(148)
Socialist Party	L	29.3	72	(60)
Communist alliance	K	8.8	17	(31)
Other parties	R	11.5	6	(11)
Qatar				
Independent emirate, no parties	—	—		
Romania (September 1992)				
Romanian National Unity Party	ERe	7.7	30	
Greater Romania	e	3.9	16	

Political Parties

Country / Name of party	Affiliation	Voting strength (%)	Parliamentary representation
Democratic Convention of Romania	CR	20.0	82
Democratic National Salvation Front	x	27.7	117
National Salvation Front		10.2	43
Hungarian Democratic Union	e	7.5	27
Others	—	23.0	13
Russia (June 1990)			
Supreme Soviet	—	...	252
Rwanda			
Transitional government since April 1992	—	—	—
Saint Kitts and Nevis (March 1989)			
People's Action Movement	CL	45.3	6 (6)
Nevis Reformation Party	CL	10.9	2 (3)
Labour Party	L	37.4	2 (2)
Concerned Citizens' Movement	—	6.4	1 —
Saint Lucia (April 1992)			
United Workers' Party	C	56.3	11 (9)
St. Lucia Labour Party	CL	43.5	6 (8)
Saint Vincent and the Grenadines (May 1989)			
New Democratic Party	C	66.2	15 (9)
St. Vincent Labour Party	L	30.4	0 (4)
San Marino (May 1988)			
Christian Democrats	CR	...	27 (26)
Socialist Party	S	...	7 (9)
Communist Party	L	...	18 (15)
Socialist Unity Party	EL	...	8 (8)
Other parties	—	...	0 (2)
São Tomé and Príncipe (January 1991)			
Party of Democratic Convergence	C	54.37	33 —
Movement for Liberation	K	30.53	21 (40)
Others	—	15.10	1 —
Saudi Arabia			
Royal government, no parties	—	—	—
Senegal (February 1988)			
Socialist Party	—	71.3	103 (111)
Senegalese Democratic Party	—	24.7	17 (8)
Other parties	—	4.0	0 (1)
Seychelles (December 1987)			
People's Progressive Front	—	...	23 (23)
Sierra Leone			
Military government since May 1992	—	—	—
Singapore (August 1991)			
People's Action Party	CR	61	77 (80)
Democratic Party	CL	12	3 (1)
Workers' Party	L	14	1 (0)
Slovenia (December 1992)			
Liberal Democrats	—	24	...
Christian Democrats	—	15	...
Others	—	61	...
Solomon Islands (February 1989)			
Liberal Party	—	...	4 (1)
United Party	—	...	6 (13)
People's Alliance Party	—	...	14 (12)
Solomone Ano Sagufenua	—	...	0 (4)
Nationalistic Front for Progress	—	...	3 —
Labour Party	—	...	2 —
Independents	—	...	9 (7)
Somalia			
No effective government since January 1991	—	—	—
South Africa (September 1989)			
Herstigte Nasionale Party	ER	...	0 (0)
Conservative Party	R	31.3	39 (22)
National Party	CR	48.6	93 (123)
Democratic (including former Progressive Federal) Party	CL	20.0	33 (21)
Spain (October 1989)			
Popular Party (formerly Alianza Popular)	R	25.8	107 (105)
Democratic and Social Centre	C	7.9	14 (19)
Basque Nationalist Party	Ce	1.2	5 (6)
Convergence and Union (Catalan)	CLe	5.0	18 (18)
Socialist parties	S	39.6	175 (184)
United Left	L	9.0	17 (7)
Herri Batasuna (Basque radicals)	ELe	1.1	.4 (5)
Others	—	...	10 (6)
Sri Lanka (February 1989)			
United National Party	SD	...	125 (140)
Freedom Party	SD	...	67 (8)
Tamil groups	e	...	23 (18)
Communists and others	—	...	10 (2)
Sudan, The			
Transitional government since February 1992	—	—	—
Suriname (May 1991)			
National Democratic Party	—	21.8	12 (3)
Front for Democracy and Development (four-party coalition)	—	54.2	30 (42)
Democratic Alternative '91	—	16.7	9 —
Swaziland (November 1987)			
Transitional government since October 1992	—	—	—
Sweden (September 1991)			
New Democracy	R	6.8	24 —
Christian Democrats	R	7.2	27 (0)
Moderate (Conservative) Party	R	22.1	80 (66)
Centre (Agrarian) Party	CR	8.6	31 (42)
People's (Liberal) Party	C	9.2	33 (44)
Social Democrats	S	38.2	138 (156)
Left (Communist) Party	L	4.5	16 (21)
Greens	g	3.4	0 (20)
Switzerland (October 1991)			
Christian Democrats	R	17.8	37 (42)
Swiss People's	CR	11.8	25 (25)
Radical Democrats	C	20.9	44 (51)
Social Democrats	SD	19.0	41 (41)
Green Party	g	6.4	14 (9)
Others	—	24.1	39 (32)
Syria (May 1990)			
National Progressive Front			
Ba'th Party	—	...	134
Other parties	—	...	32
Independents	—	...	84
Taiwan (December 1992)			
Nationalist (Kuomintang)	—	53	96 (72)
Democratic Progressive Party	—	31	50 (21)
Others and Independents	—	16	15 (8)
Tajikistan			
Transitional government since May 1992	—	—	—
Tanzania (October 1990)			
Revolutionary Party of Tanzania (CCM)	—	...	216 (169)
Thailand (September 1992)			
Democrat Party	—	...	79 (44)
Chart Thai	—	...	77 (74)
Chart Pattana	—	...	60 —
New Aspiration Party	—	...	51 (72)
Palang Dharma	—	...	47 (41)
Social Action Party	—	...	22 (31)
Samakkhi Tham	—	...	— (79)
Others	—	...	24 (18)
Togo			
Transitional government since August 1991	—	—	—
Tonga (February 1990)			
Reformers	—	...	6
Others	—	...	3
Trinidad and Tobago (December 1991)			
People's National Movement	C	45.1	21 (3)
National Alliance for Reconstruction (four parties)	C	24.4	2 (33)
United National Congress	L	29.1	13 —
Tunisia (April 1989)			
National Front (led by the Constitutional Democratic Assembly)	—	80.5	141 (138)
Turkey (October 1991)			
Nationalist Labour Party	ER } 16.9		19 —
Welfare Party	Rr }		43 (0)
True Path Party	CR	27.0	178 (59)
Motherland Party	CR	24.0	115 (292)
Social Democratic Populist	CL } 20.8		66 (99)
People's Labour Party	e }		22 —
Democratic Left Party	CL	10.8	7 (0)
Turkmenistan			
Transitional government since May 1992	—	—	—
Tuvalu (October 1989)			
Parliament, no parties	—	—	12 (12)
Uganda (February 1989)			
National Resistance Council	—	...	168 (98)
Ukraine (March 1990)			
Supreme Soviet	—	...	450
United Arab Emirates			
Federal National Council is appointed	—	—	—
United Kingdom (April 1992)			
Conservative Party	CR	41.9	336 (375)
Liberal Democrats	CL	17.9	20 (22)
Labour Party	L	34.4	271 (229)
Scottish National Party	e	1.9	3 (3)
Plaid Cymru (Welsh Nationalists)	e	0.5	4 (3)
Ulster Unionists (three groups)	e	1.2	13 (13)
Social Democratic and Labour Party (Northern Ireland)	CLe	0.6	4 (3)
Sinn Fein (Northern Ireland)	ELe	0.2	0 (1)
Other	—	1.4	0 (1)
United States (November 1992)			
Republican	CR	...	175 (167)
Democratic	C	...	259 (267)
Other	—	...	1 (1)
Uruguay (November 1989)			
Civic Union	R	...	0 (2)
National (Blanco) Party	C	...	39 (36)
Colorado Party	C	...	30 (40)
New Space	SD	...	9 } (21)
Broad Front	L	...	21 }
Other	—	...	0 (2)
Uzbekistan (February–March 1990)			
Supreme Soviet	—		
Vanuatu (December 1991)			
Union of Moderate Parties	CR	...	19 (20)
National United Party	CR	...	10 —
Vanua'aku }	—	...	17 (26)
Others }	—	...	(0)
Venezuela (December 1988)			
COPEI (Social Christians)	CR	33.33	67 ...
Democratic Action	S	48.26	97 (118)
Movement to Socialism	L	8.96	18 ...
Others	—	9.45	19 ...
Vietnam (July 1992)			
National Assembly	—	...	395
Western Samoa (April 1991)			
Human Rights Protection Party	—	...	30 (27)
Opposition	—	...	14 (19)
Independents	—	...	3 (1)
Yemen			
Transitional government since May 1990	—	—	—
Yugoslavia (December 1992)			
Serbian Radical Party	Fe	...	34 (33)
Socialist Party of Serbia	xe	...	47 (73)
Democratic Party of Socialists of Montenegro	xe	...	26 (23)
Others	—	...	... (6)
Zaire			
Transitional government since March 1990	—	—	—
Zambia (October 1991)			
Movement for Multiparty Democracy	—	75.8	126 —
United National Independence	—	24.2	24 (125)
Zimbabwe (March 1990)			
Zimbabwe African National Union	S	75.4	116
Zimbabwe African National Union/Ndonga	—	0.9	1
Zimbabwe Unity Movement	—	16.6	2

Africa South of the Sahara

AFRICAN AFFAIRS

Much of Africa, from Ethiopia to South Africa, continued in 1992 to suffer from the worst drought of the century, but rains that began to fall near the end of the year gave promise of a return to the economic recovery that had only just begun in 1991. At the end of 1992, 19 countries were still listed by the UN Food and Agriculture Organization as facing exceptional food emergencies. The year was also one of mixed political fortunes, with more governments choosing multiparty democracy but without a letup in the civil wars in The Sudan, Liberia, and Rwanda and with appalling conditions in Somalia. The figures for AIDS continued to rise alarmingly.

Organization of African Unity. The OAU expanded its peacemaking role in the continent. It sent teams of monitors to observe the constitutional talks and to report on political violence in South Africa, to supervise the cease-fire agreement in Rwanda and the first free elections in Angola, and to facilitate peace efforts in Somalia; it also continued its mediation efforts in the civil war in The Sudan.

The question of establishing a permanent African peacekeeping force was on the agenda of the 28th annual summit in Dakar, Senegal, in June, but a final decision was deferred after opposition was voiced to the financing of such an operation as well as its feasibility. Another major discussion was on the need to speed up the process of democratization on the continent, which was widely supported. The election of the first African nominee as secretary-general of the UN, Boutros Boutros-Ghali of Egypt, was followed by a searching discussion on the need for a new world order, initiated by Egyptian Pres. Hosni Mubarak. Support was given to the new independent Commission on Global Cooperation initiated by Shridath Ramphal, former secretary-general of the Commonwealth of Nations, and Ingvar Carlsson, a former prime minister of Sweden.

Concern was expressed by the OAU secretary-general, Salim Ahmad Salim, over the fact that more than half the organization's members had established diplomatic and economic links with South Africa despite the decision to continue a boycott until constitutional talks were completed. But little was said of the fact that an increasing number of OAU members continued to ignore a decision to boycott Israel until the Palestinian question was settled. The new chairman of the OAU was Pres. Abdou Diouf of Senegal.

Southern and Central Africa. The political climate in southern and central Africa was considerably relaxed with the agreement to end the civil war in Mozambique in October and by the holding of the first free elections in Angola since its independence in 1975. Despite initial difficulties, it was hoped that these developments would end two serious conflicts that had destabilized the subcontinent for more than 40 years. The earlier promising talks for a democratic nonracial constitution in South Africa were halted temporarily because of increasing political violence, which was one of the reasons given by the African National Congress for boycotting the Convention for a Democratic South Africa. However, when agreement was reached to end the boycott, Chief Mangosuthu Gatsha Buthelezi's Inkatha Freedom Party caused a new setback by its decision to boycott the talks. Nevertheless, hopes remained alive that an interim government would be formed in early 1993.

The easing of political tensions in the region led to the widening of regional cooperation in trade and other areas of mutual interest, such as electrification. The South African government was invited to participate in regional bodies, such as the Southern African Development Coordination Conference (SADCC), from which it had previously been excluded.

Horn of Africa. The nations in the Horn of Africa, on the Red Sea, continued to give the greatest cause for concern on the continent even though Ethiopia and Eritrea made significant advances toward creating internal stability. But there was no sign of progress toward ending the bloody civil war in The Sudan or the near-genocidal conflict between clans in Somalia, where an estimated 1.5 million people were thought to have perished from starvation and military action. Civil order broke down in the tiny republic of Djibouti, previously an oasis of peace and stability in the Horn, because of ethnic clashes between the Issas, who were linked to Somalia, and the Afars, with links to both Ethiopia and Eritrea. All the efforts to end the fighting between the dominantly southern-led Sudan People's Liberation Army (SPLA) and the government forces foundered on two principal issues: the Khartoum regime's uncompromising commitment to Islamic fundamentalism and its refusal to countenance a multiparty democratic system. While the regime's hold on power continued to strengthen, serious divisions occurred in the SPLA.

The interim government of Ethiopia began to implement its unique approach to constitution making by creating an ethnic federation as a means of facilitating a multiparty democratic system. This experiment was temporarily disrupted by a decision of the Oromo Liberation Front, which claimed to speak for the largest ethnic community in the country, to boycott elections for the first level of a federal government, the regional councils. Meanwhile, Eritrea emerged after 28 years of armed struggle as the most stable part of the region. The victorious Eritrean People's Liberation Front, which formed an interim government, was engaged in rebuilding the shattered economy and in arranging for a referendum to be held in April 1993 to determine whether the territory would become independent.

Inter-African Affairs. Nigeria and Ghana continued to play major roles in supplying troops for the peacekeeping effort in Liberia, which was supported by the 16-nation Economic Community of West African States (ECOWAS). After three years, however, their military intervention had still failed to impose a peace settlement on the country.

Despite repeated denials by Uganda's Pres. Yoweri Museveni, the Rwanda government continued to allege that he had collaborated with a rebel force, operating from Ugandan territory, to overthrow it. East African leaders, acting on the initiative of the OAU, agreed on a peace settlement that included establishment of a coalition government in Rwanda, but the agreement was not honoured. The Sudan accused Kenya, Egypt, Saudi Arabia, and Israel of providing military support to the SPLA. Kenya was among the countries accused by the interim government in Somalia of supporting the ousted military regime of Pres. Muhammad Siyad Barrah. Kenya and Zimbabwe played a crucial role in helping to broker the final agreement between the government in Mozambique and the rebel forces of the Mozambique National Resistance (Renamo).

Inter-African cooperation continued at a regional level. The 10 members of SADCC agreed to continue their organization under the new name of the Southern African Development Community. A tentative beginning was made to reestablish the former East African Community comprising Uganda, Kenya, and Tanzania. The members of ECOWAS continued to meet on a regular basis, but efforts to achieve effective cooperation proved elusive. After a break of four years, the members of the Organization for the Development of the Senegal River—Mauritania, Mali, and Senegal, with Guinea as an observer—held a summit meeting to discuss the future energy and irrigation development of the two huge dams on the Senegal River. A decision was made to go ahead with the project, with special priority given to the Manantali hydroelectric scheme.

Democratization. The movement throughout Africa away from single-party and military rule continued to gain momentum. With the exception of The Sudan, all the sub-Saharan governments embraced the principle of multiparty democracy; Malawi, however, offered only a referendum on the question. Multiparty elections resulted in the defeat of the regimes of Guinea-Bissau and Congo. Four governments survived democratic elections—those in Seychelles, Mauritius, Mauritania, and Cameroon—but the results in the last two were controversial. For the first time in its history, Ethiopia held democratic elections for the first level of its federal government.

In Zaire Pres. Mobutu Sese Seko yielded to a demand by a representative constituent assembly to accept its recommendations for a new government of transition while preparations got under way for democratic elections. Active preparations for multiparty elections began in Tanzania, Ghana, Kenya, and Lesotho.

Because of alleged electoral malpractices, Nigeria canceled its elections for a civilian president. In Togo, the Central African Republic, Guinea, Mauritania, and Mali, constituent assemblies failed to reach agreements. There was only one successful military coup during the year—in Sierra Leone in April.

External Relations. Two major issues dominated relations between sub-Saharan Africa and other nations—debt relief by Western countries and Russia and the terms of international trade, which less developed countries believed discriminated against their exports. This concern was heightened by the approach of the major trading nations to the current round of talks on the General Agreement on Tariffs and Trade. A new issue that seemed likely to affect African relations with the West was a demand by the nonaligned nations for a redistribution of power in the UN through, among other things, the enlargement of the Security Council.

In contrast to previous years, little complaint was heard about foreign intervention in the domestic affairs of the continent. Such intervention as there was—by the U.S. in Angola and Somalia; the Italians, the Portuguese, and the U.S. in Mozambique; and the French in Djibouti—met with general approval. The Sudan, however, complained of intervention by Saudi Arabia and Israel (as well as Egypt and Kenya) on the side of the rebel SPLA. The civil war in Somalia also attracted foreign interests—mainly Iran, Saudi Arabia, and some of the Gulf states. The "Earth Summit" in Rio de Janeiro in June became a forum for confrontation between, especially, African countries and the West because of claims that less developed countries were expected to bear a disproportionate burden of the cost of protecting the environment.

Social and Economic Conditions. Economic recovery failed to maintain its earlier progress because of the severe climatic conditions and the worldwide economic recession, which reduced the demand for, and the price of, export commodities. The outlook for the year was that, on average, the continent would experience a negative growth rate. The 1986 UN Special Session on Africa's Economic Recovery Program had agreed that its success depended, in part, on annual external financial flows of $35 billion, but in the subsequent four years the financial flow in fact declined by about 7% a year. Africa continued to export more capital every year than it received by way of aid and loans. Its debt burden of $270 billion in 1992 was estimated to cost at least $23 billion to service.

Seven African countries—Tanzania, Zambia, Côte d'Ivoire, Kenya, Uganda, Malawi, and Libya—recorded the highest population growth rates in the world during the year, ranging from 3.6 to 3.8%. It was expected that AIDS might reduce, or even reverse, such growth rates by the end of the century.

Famine, war, and disease also accounted for population losses in a number of countries. An estimated 1.5 million Somalis and, possibly, a similar number in Mozambique were believed to be at risk from starvation. Half a million southern Sudanese were not expected to survive without urgent food shipments. The wars in Ethiopia between 1975 and 1990 claimed a million victims, with 61,000 in Eritrea alone. (COLIN LEGUM)

ANGOLA

A republic, Angola is located on the Atlantic coast in southwestern Africa. The small exclave of Cabinda is separated from Angola by a strip of Zaire. Area: 1,246,700 sq km (481,354 sq mi). Pop. (1992 est.): 10,609,000. Cap.: Luanda. Monetary unit: New kwanza, with (Oct. 5, 1992) a par value of 550 New kwanzas to U.S. $1 (free rate of 935 New kwanzas = £1 sterling). President in 1992, José Eduardo dos Santos; prime ministers, Fernando José de Franca Dias van Dunem and, from December 2, Marcolino Moco.

With the nation's first multiparty elections scheduled for September 1992, the year was one of political uncertainty. The U.S. under secretary of state for African affairs, Jeffrey Davidson, after holding talks with Pres. José dos Santos and opposition leader Jonas Savimbi in Luanda in February, said that he felt optimistic about the way the country was moving toward what he hoped would be free, fair, and democratic elections. Other diplomats were more skeptical, fearing that the divisions that had occurred among the leaders of the National Union for the Total Independence of Angola (UNITA) might encourage Savimbi to restart the civil war in order to regain control over his party. Their disquiet became stronger after the defection in February of Gen. Miguel N'Zau Puna, UNITA's spokesman for home affairs, and the party's spokesman for foreign affairs, Tony da Costa Fernandes. The two accused Savimbi of executing members of his own high command, but Savimbi, while admitting that the executions had taken place, claimed that the two defectors had themselves been responsible for them. Meanwhile, in Cabinda, the revival of the Front for the Liberation of the Cabinda Enclave (FLEC) was proving another irritant for the government.

Demobilization of those sections of the two former opposing armies that were not to be incorporated in the new, integrated Angolan army began as agreed on March 31 and continued in spite of occasional delays. There were allegations that Savimbi was secretly keeping a reserve force in those areas where his authority still prevailed, but Savimbi countered by vociferously insisting that free and fair elections were what the country urgently needed. In spite of these skirmishes, an electoral commission was appointed on May 10, and registration of voters began on May 20. The closing date for registration was extended by 10 days to August 10 to allow as many prospective voters as possible to take part.

The forward momentum was maintained in August when the one-party People's Assembly accepted a new, democratic

Officials in Luanda count ballots in Angola's first multiparty elections, held at the end of September. Neither Pres. José Eduardo dos Santos nor rival Jonas Savimbi, head of UNITA, received a majority of votes in the presidential election, threatening the uneasy truce in the country's civil war.

SCOTT DANIEL PETERSON—GAMMA LIAISON

constitution that provided for a multiparty assembly of 223 members. It also agreed that the term *People's* should be removed from the country's official title and that the Republic of Angola should be a secular state with guarantees and safeguards to protect democracy and the rule of law. Eighteen parties contested the elections held on September 29–30, and 12 candidates ran for the presidency. President dos Santos and his party, the Popular Movement for the Liberation of Angola (MPLA), gained the most votes, with Savimbi and UNITA finishing second. The MPLA won 128 seats in the legislature to 71 for UNITA. Because neither dos Santos nor Savimbi received 50% of the vote, a runoff was required. Savimbi, however, charged that the election was fraudulent. Fighting between the government and UNITA broke out in Luanda on October 30, and by late November UNITA reportedly held control over two-thirds of the country. The new parliament was convened on November 26, but the 70 UNITA deputies did not appear. In late December, after repeatedly promising to end the fighting, UNITA once again agreed to a peace plan and the withdrawal of its troops.

On the economic front the government made great efforts to encourage foreign investment in the country. The efforts were rewarded during the year first by the African Development Bank, which offered $75 million to support small and medium-sized farmers, and also by the European Communities, which allocated $140 million to assist in the country's reconstruction program. The French Central Fund for Economic Cooperation followed with a grant of F 17 million for the restoration of the Santa Isabel Mineral Water Sources.   (KENNETH INGHAM)

This article updates the *Macropædia* article SOUTHERN AFRICA: *Angola*.

BENIN

The republic of Benin is on the southern coast of West Africa, on the Gulf of Guinea. Area: 112,600 sq km (43,450 sq mi). Pop. (1992 est.): 4,928,000. Cap.: Porto-Novo (official); Cotonou (de facto). Monetary unit: CFA franc, with (Oct. 5, 1992) a par value of CFAF 50 to the French franc and a free rate of CFAF 238.75 to U.S. $1 (CFAF 405.88 = £1 sterling). President in 1992, Nicéphore Soglo.

In Benin's second year of multiparty government, Pres. Nicéphore Soglo became a major spokesman for democ-

ratization and the need for economic progress in Africa. Speaking in The Netherlands in July 1992, Soglo called for a "Marshall Plan for Africa." At home, the year was marked by continuing discontent among government workers, whose number was to be reduced by 20%. In May, 5,000 public service employees demanded higher wages, better working conditions, the right to strike, and greater press freedom. Later that month, a coup attempt by a few army officers failed, but the ringleaders escaped. The army quelled, without gunfire, a mutiny at Kaba Camp in Natitingou on July 4. It was led by one of the escapees, Captain Tawes, who had been a member of former president Mathieu Kérékou's Presidential Guard.

After a lengthy trial, Kérékou's Malian marabout and former minister of state, Mohammed Cissé, was sentenced to 10 years' imprisonment and fined CFAF 3 million. Cissé and nine others were accused of stealing more than CFAF 2.3 billion. Privatization of state enterprises continued, but at a slower than expected pace, due to the overall weakness of the world economy.   (NANCY ELLEN LAWLER)

This article updates the *Macropædia* article WESTERN AFRICA: *Benin*.

BOTSWANA

A landlocked republic of southern Africa, Botswana is a member of the Commonwealth. Area: 581,730 sq km (224,607 sq mi). Pop. (1992 est.): 1,359,000. Cap.: Gaborone. Monetary unit: pula, with (Oct. 5, 1992) a free rate of 2.08 pula to U.S. $1 (3.54 pula = £1 sterling). President in 1992, Ketumile Masire.

On Jan. 14, 1992, a contingent of 250 U.S. troops arrived in Gaborone to carry out a two-week training exercise with the 4,500-strong Botswana Defence Force, a first in military cooperation between the two countries. In March a major scandal broke when Pres. Ketumile Masire accepted the resignation of one of the country's most powerful and influential figures, the then vice president and minister of local government and lands, Peter Mmusi, as well as that of the minister of agriculture, Daniel Kwelagobe. According to the report of a commission of inquiry chaired by Englishman Kgabo, the vice president had used his authority to ensure that the minister of agriculture obtained land the local authority wished to use for other purposes. The assistant minister of local government and lands, Michael Tshipinare, also resigned. Festus Mogae was made vice president and minister of local government and lands while still keeping his job as minister of finance and development planning. The opposition parties reacted strongly, calling for an early general election. In April, however, Mmusi fought back, claiming that the commission of inquiry had been guilty of irregularities in its investigation.

In 1991 Botswana experienced its first budget deficit since 1982, with the result that in November 1991 the government did not implement promised public-sector pay increases.

(GUY ARNOLD)

This article updates the *Macropædia* article SOUTHERN AFRICA: *Botswana*.

BURKINA FASO

Burkina Faso is a landlocked country of West Africa. Area: 274,400 sq km (105,946 sq mi). Pop. (1992 est.): 9,515,000. Cap.: Ouagadougou. Monetary unit: CFA franc, with (Oct. 5, 1992) a par value of CFAF 50 to the French franc and a free rate of CFAF 238.75 to U.S. $1 (CFAF 405.88 = £1 sterling). President (chairman) of the Popular Front in 1992, Capt. Blaise Compaoré; prime minister from June 16, Youssouf Ouedraogo.

The government of Pres. Blaise Compaoré resisted strong pressure for a national conference in 1992 but, after hard negotiations with leaders of 42 opposition parties, agreed to convene a National Reconciliation Forum. This compromise was thought to be Compaoré's response to the embarrassment of the December 1991 presidential election, in which only 28% of the electorate voted. Three former heads of state and 380 delegates attended the opening of the three-week forum on February 11. Legislative elections, postponed several times, were finally held on May 24, with 27 of the 61 registered parties participating. Compaoré's ruling party, the Organization for Popular Democracy-Labour Movement, won 78 of the 107 seats. Voter turnout was estimated at 34%. The new prime minister, Youssouf Ouedraogo, was an economist who served in the Cabinet of assassinated Pres. Thomas Sankara.

In what some saw as an attempt to improve his international image, Compaoré attended a conference on Liberia, held in Geneva in April. He insisted that Burkina Faso had no interests in that country and was not involved in supporting any rebel forces. (NANCY ELLEN LAWLER)

This article updates the *Macropædia* article WESTERN AFRICA: *Burkina Faso*.

BURUNDI

Burundi is a landlocked republic of central Africa. Area: 27,817 sq km (10,740 sq mi). Pop. (1992 est.): 5,657,000. Cap.: Bujumbura. Monetary unit: Burundi franc, with (Oct. 5, 1992) a free rate of FBu 221.76 to U.S. $1 (FBu 377 = £1 sterling). President in 1992, Maj. Pierre Buyoya; prime minister, Adrien Sibomana.

On Nov. 23, 1991, some 270 people were killed in simultaneous attacks by rebels; these went on for several days in Bujumbura and in the northwestern provinces of Cibitoke and Kayanza, with the result that numbers of (mainly Hutu) refugees fled into Rwanda and Zaire. The attacks occurred while Pres. Pierre Buyoya was on a visit to France and were believed to be the work of the exiled Palipehutu movement. The uprising put at risk Buyoya's cautious moves toward democracy. By Jan. 3, 1992, the death toll was set at 551 and the number of refugees at 10,000 (a European human rights organization claimed that 3,000 had been killed in reprisals by the army and paramilitary groups and that 50,000 had fled). On January 4 the presidents of Burundi, Rwanda, and Zaire, meeting in Mbandaka, Zaire, agreed to reactivate permanent security commissions.

On March 9 a referendum on a draft constitution gave overwhelming support (90% of a 97.05% turnout) to the proposed changes. The constitution, allowing for multiparty politics, was adopted on March 13. On March 4, 30 soldiers, said to be in the pay of former president Jean-Baptiste Bagaza, attempted unsuccessfully to mount a coup. In April former minister Cyprien Mbonimpa was arrested for his alleged involvement; he was a Tutsi hard-liner opposed to Buyoya's policy of having Hutu in the Cabinet.

(GUY ARNOLD)

This article updates the *Macropædia* article CENTRAL AFRICA: *Burundi*.

CAMEROON

A republic of western central Africa, Cameroon lies on the Gulf of Guinea. Area: 465,458 sq km (179,714 sq mi). Pop. (1992 est.): 12,662,000. Cap.: Yaoundé. Monetary unit: CFA franc, with (Oct. 5, 1992) a par value of CFAF 50 to the French franc and a free rate of CFAF 238.75 to U.S. $1 (CFAF 405.88 = £1 sterling). President in 1992, Paul Biya; prime ministers, Sadou Hayatou and, from April 9, Simon Achidi Achu.

Pres. Paul Biya and his Cameroon People's Democratic Movement (RDPC) retained power during the country's first year of multiparty democracy in 1992. On March 1, in the first parliamentary elections in 32 years, the RDPC won 88 seats, ensuring itself a majority by forming an alliance with the Movement for the Defense of the Republic party, which won 6 seats in the north. In the presidential election on October 11, Biya won by an unexpectedly narrow margin—39.98% to 35.97% for his nearest rival, John Fru Ndi, who was subsequently placed under house arrest. There were accusations of fraud and some violent demonstrations, and the U.S. suspended aid worth $14 million. On November 27 Biya reshuffled the Cabinet, reappointing Simon Achidi Achu, who in April had become the country's first Anglophone prime minister.

Concerns about censorship continued. Several independent publications were suspended, and Gen. Benoit Asso'o Emane, supreme commander in Yaoundé, was dismissed in July immediately after publication of a book critical of the Biya regime. The government remained desperately short of funds; the new budget of CFAF 546 billion announced in July would be balanced only by further reductions in expenditures. (NANCY ELLEN LAWLER)

This article updates the *Macropædia* article WESTERN AFRICA: *Cameroon*.

CAPE VERDE

The republic of Cape Verde occupies an island group in the Atlantic Ocean about 620 km (385 mi) off the west coast of Africa. Area: 4,033 sq km (1,557 sq mi). Pop. (1992 est.): 346,000. Cap.: Praia. Monetary unit: Cape Verde escudo, with (Oct. 5, 1992) an official rate of 62.52 escudos to U.S. $1 (106.28 escudos = £1 sterling). President in 1992, Antonio Mascarenhas Monteiro; prime minister, Carlos Veiga.

On Dec. 15, 1991, Cape Verde's first multiparty local elections were held; the ruling Movement for Democracy won control of 10 out of 14 councils, while the African Party for the Independence of Cape Verde won 3. During 1992 the government determined to carry out a program of privatization of existing state companies. Prime Minister Carlos Veiga said that the state bank would be split into two: a conventional central bank and a commercial bank, each to be funded with both local and foreign capital. During the year Cape Verde's tiny economy had a hard time attracting the aid that it needed, but the Arab Bank for Economic

Development in Africa provided a $9 million loan for the construction of air facilities at Praia.

The UN Development Program's Human Development Report of 1992 showed that Cape Verde was managing to do a good deal better than some other small countries with few economic advantages: life expectancy at birth was 67; adult literacy was 53%; and 71% of the population had access to safe water (although only 16% had access to proper sanitation). Approximately 125% of the nation's calorie-intake requirements were fulfilled, and primary and secondary school enrollments totaled 77% of the eligible students. Gross domestic product per capita, at $1,717, was one of the highest in Africa. (GUY ARNOLD)

This article updates the *Macropædia* article WESTERN AFRICA: *Cape Verde*.

CENTRAL AFRICAN REPUBLIC

The Central African Republic is a landlocked state in central Africa. Area: 622,436 sq km (240,324 sq mi). Pop. (1992 est.): 2,930,000. Cap.: Bangui. Monetary unit: CFA franc, with (Oct. 5, 1992) a par value of CFAF 50 to the French franc and a free rate of CFAF 238.75 to U.S. $1 (CFAF 405.88 = £1 sterling). President in 1992, Gen. André Kolingba; prime ministers, Edouard Frank and, from December 4, Timothée Malendoma.

Despite the legalization of opposition parties late in 1991, little progress was made toward genuine democracy in 1992. Pres. André Kolingba resisted strong pressure for convening a national conference, authorizing only a broad "national debate." Opposition parties, the Roman Catholic Church, intellectuals, and trade unions boycotted the debate, which finally opened on August 1. That same day, Jean-Claude Congugo, leader of the opposition Alliance for Democracy and Progress, was killed in Bangui during a clash between pro-democracy demonstrators and security forces. In response, antigovernment leaders declared August 3 a "dead cities day," shutting down the capital. On November 28 President Kolingba announced that legislative and presidential elections would be held in February 1993.

The economy registered few gains. Ranked 142nd out of 160 countries in terms of development, the country experienced virtually no growth in gross domestic product. In July the European Communities agreed to a further three-year aid program amounting to CFAF 35 billion.

(NANCY ELLEN LAWLER)

This article updates the *Macropædia* article CENTRAL AFRICA: *Central African Republic*.

CHAD

Chad is a landlocked republic of central Africa. Area: 1,284,000 sq km (495,755 sq mi). Pop. (1992 est.): 5,961,000. Cap.: N'Djamena. Monetary unit: CFA franc, with (Oct. 5, 1992) a par value of CFAF 50 to the French franc and a free rate of CFAF 238.75 to U.S. $1 (CFAF 405.88 = £1 sterling). President in 1992, Gen. Idriss Deby; prime ministers, Jean Alingue Bawoyeu and, from May 20, Joseph Yodoyman.

At the end of 1991 the government established a commission to determine details of a national conference as the next step toward democratization. On Jan. 3, 1992, France airlifted 450 troops into Chad to reinforce its 1,100-strong garrison in response to news of armed rebels—members of the military wing of the Movement for Development and Democracy (MDD)—advancing into the eastern Lake Chad region. The government claimed to have defeated the rebels on the day the French arrived, and they were withdrawn on January 7, but renewed fighting broke out at the end of the month.

Soldiers tow a tank captured in January from rebels supporting the deposed president of Chad, Hissen Habré. The government of Pres. Idriss Deby, who overthrew Habré in 1990, claimed to have killed more than 400 in putting down the rebellion.
REUTERS/BETTMANN NEWSPHOTOS

A coup attempt was mounted against Pres. Idriss Deby in February, and fighting in N'Djamena resulted in some 12 deaths. The government claimed that French residents were involved, and France repatriated four French aid workers. By May 25, 8 political parties had been recognized. Another coup attempt was mounted on June 18 by the minister of public works and transport, Col. Abbas Koty, but he was forced to flee the country. On June 24 the government signed an agreement with the MDD to end hostilities, but the MDD repudiated it on October 30. (GUY ARNOLD)

This article updates the *Macropædia* article WESTERN AFRICA: *Chad*.

COMOROS

The republic of Comoros is an island state in the Indian Ocean off the east coast of Africa. Area: 1,862 sq km (719 sq mi), excluding the island of Mayotte, which continued to be a de facto dependency of France. Pop. (1992 est.; excluding Mayotte): 497,000. Cap.: Moroni. Monetary unit: Comorian franc, with (Oct. 5, 1992) a par value of CF 50 to the French franc and a free rate of CF 238.75 to U.S. $1 (CF 405.88 = £1 sterling). President in 1992, Said Mohamed Djohar; heads of government, Said Ali Kemal, Mohamed Taki Abdoulkarim to July 4.

On Nov. 19, 1991, the Comoran Union of Progress (Udzima) had withdrawn its support from Pres. Said Mohamed Djohar and gone into opposition, accusing the president of a witch-hunt following the coup attempt of the previous August. On Jan. 6, 1992, Djohar appointed a new coalition government following the signing by 22 political parties (December 31) of a national reconciliation pact that recognized the legitimacy of Djohar's presidency. Udzima was not represented in the new government. The national conference ended its deliberations on April 8 after agreeing on a new constitution and electoral schedule. A referendum to approve the draft constitution was set for May 24. On May 10 Djohar announced a new transitional coalition government, which strengthened the position of Mohamed Said Abdallah Mchangama, leader of the Mwangaza party and son-in-law of Djohar.

The referendum was finally held on June 7, when 74.25% of 213,000 electors voted in favour of the new constitution and only 23.49% voted against. On July 10, owing to a breakdown in relations between Djohar and the head of government, Mohamed Taki Abdoulkarim, Djohar dissolved the transitional government. A coup attempt by junior officers on September 26, when Djohar was out of the country, was put down by loyal troops. The country's first multiparty legislative elections, held November 22 and 29, were marred by violence, and the results in Moroni and Mbeni, where the worst disorders occurred, were canceled. (GUY ARNOLD)

This article updates the *Micropædia* article COMOROS.

CONGO

A republic, Congo is in central Africa on the Atlantic Ocean. Area: 342,000 sq km (132,047 sq mi). Pop. (1992 est.): 2,692,000. Cap.: Brazzaville. Monetary unit: CFA franc, with (Oct. 5, 1992) a par value of CFAF 50 to the French franc and a free rate of CFAF 238.75 to U.S. $1 (CFAF 405.88 = £1 sterling). Presidents in 1992, Col. Denis Sassou-Nguesso and, from August 20, Pascal Lissouba; prime ministers, André Milongo, Stéphane Maurice Bongho-Nouarra from September 2, and, from December 6, Claude Antoine Dacosta.

Congo completed its transformation to a democratic regime in 1992 as relatively peaceful legislative and presidential elections were held after more than a year of civilian rule. Interim Prime Minister André Milongo's transitional government survived an attempted military coup during weeklong violence in early January only to be nearly toppled on January 20 when demonstrators marching in support of Milongo were fired upon by troops who were demanding that he step down. In a referendum on March 15 voters approved a new constitution.

After several postponements legislative elections were held on June 24 and July 19. Pascal Lissouba's Pan-African Union for Social Democracy won 23 of 60 seats in the Senate and 35 of 125 contested seats in the National Assembly. In the first round of internationally supervised presidential elections on August 2, Lissouba led with 36% of the vote, and in the August 16 runoff he won 61% to defeat Bernard Kolelas of the Congolese Movement for Democracy and Integral Development. The new government of Stéphane Maurice Bongho-Nouarra, formed in September, lost a vote of no confidence on October 31. President Lissouba dissolved the legislature and called for new elections, but the move set off widespread demonstrations. On December 6, Claude Antoine Dacosta, an agronomist, was named to head a government of "national union" with the main purpose of preparing for early general elections.

(NANCY ELLEN LAWLER)

This article updates the *Macropædia* article CENTRAL AFRICA: *Congo*.

CÔTE D'IVOIRE

A republic of West Africa, Côte d'Ivoire lies on the Gulf of Guinea. Area: 320,763 sq km (123,847 sq mi). Pop. (1992 est.): 12,951,000. Cap., Abidjan; capital designate, Yamoussoukro. Monetary unit: CFA franc, with (Oct. 5, 1992) a par value of CFAF 50 to the French franc and a free rate of CFAF 238.75 to U.S. $1 (CFAF 405.88 = £1 sterling). President in 1992, Félix Houphouët-Boigny; prime minister, Alassane Ouattara.

The government's failure to discipline high-ranking military officers over the invasion of a student residence hall in May 1991 led to unrest that culminated in a wave of violent protests in February 1992. Hundreds were arrested. Despite claims that the government had planted agents provocateurs among the demonstrators, 75 opposition leaders, including Ivorian Popular Front leader Laurent Gbagbo and human rights activist René Degny Segui, were sentenced to two years' imprisonment under a new law that made organizers of demonstrations responsible for any violence. Martial Ahipeaud, leader of the banned Federation of Students and Scholars, was sentenced to three years' imprisonment and

a heavy fine. The trials and subsequent appeals attracted considerable international interest and led to mass demonstrations in Côte d'Ivoire. Throughout the process, Pres. Félix Houphouët-Boigny remained in Europe on a extended private visit. He returned in late June. In late July he issued an amnesty. The opposition leaders and over 2,000 other prisoners sentenced to less than one year were freed.

Economic woes continued to slow the pace of reform. Coffee and cocoa prices remained at or near record lows. Rumours that the CFA franc would be devalued against the French franc resulted in large transfers of private funds to Europe. In July a dispute with the International Monetary Fund over the need to reduce public expenditure led to a suspension of aid negotiations. (NANCY ELLEN LAWLER)

This article updates the *Macropædia* article WESTERN AFRICA: *Côte d'Ivoire*.

DJIBOUTI

The republic of Djibouti is in the Horn of northeastern Africa on the Gulf of Aden. Area: 23,200 sq km (8,950 sq mi). Pop. (1992 est.): 557,000. Cap.: Djibouti. Monetary unit: Djibouti franc, with (Oct. 5, 1992) a par value of DF 177.72 to U.S. $1 (free rate of DF 302.12 = £1 sterling). President in 1992, Hassan Gouled Aptidon; prime minister, Barkat Gourad Hamadou.

Fighting between forces of the Issa-dominated government and the mainly Afar Front for the Restoration of Unity and Democracy (FRUD), which had broken out in November 1991, continued through January 1992. On Dec. 19, 1991, Pres. Hassan Gouled Aptidon declared that reform in accordance with "democracy, pluralism, or multiparty politics" was possible but would have to be approved in a referendum once the "armed bands operating in the north" had been "chased off national territory." On December 23, 17 Afar deputies walked out of the Chamber of Deputies and demanded talks between the government and the armed opposition. Then, on December 31, 14 Afar deputies resigned from the ruling Popular Rally for Progress, in part because government leaders insisted that the members of FRUD were foreigners. French troops were deployed in Djibouti on Feb. 25, 1992, to keep the peace; on February 28 the rebels declared a unilateral cease-fire and, in response, the government agreed to release the FRUD leader Abbate Edo Adou, who had been imprisoned since December.

During the year a new constitution allowing for multiparty politics but maintaining a strong executive president was overwhelmingly approved in a referendum. In the general election, initially set for November 20 but postponed to December 18, the Popular Rally for Progress retained all 65 legislative seats. (GUY ARNOLD)

This article updates the *Macropædia* article EASTERN AFRICA: *Djibouti*.

EQUATORIAL GUINEA

The republic of Equatorial Guinea consists of Río Muni, on the Atlantic coast of West Africa, and the offshore islands of Bioko and Annobon. Area: 28,051 sq km (10,831 sq mi). Pop. (1992 est.): 367,000. Cap.: Malabo. Monetary unit: CFA franc, with (Oct. 5, 1992) a par value of CFAF 50 to the French franc and a free rate of CFAF 238.75 to U.S. $1 (CFAF 405.88 = £1 sterling). President in 1992, Brig. Gen. Teodoro Obiang Nguema Mbasogo; prime ministers, Capt. Cristino Seriche Bioko and, from March 4, Silvestre Siale Bileka.

On Jan. 23, 1992, Pres. Teodoro Obiang Nguema Mbasogo, whose ruling Democratic Party of Equatorial Guinea had until now been the sole party, appointed a transitional government as the first step toward multiparty politics. During

February, however, a number of members of opposition groups were arrested, including the leader of the Convergence for Social Democracy, Placido Miko. On May 4 the secretary-general of the Union for Democracy and Social Development, Antonio Sibacha, claimed that the opposition activist Feliciano Moto had been beaten to death by presidential guards. In early July five members of the opposition party Popular Union were arrested at Ebebiyin, where they tried to organize a political meeting of their party. Tomas Metcheba Fernandez, secretary-general of the opposition Socialist Party of Equatorial Guinea, in August called for countries of "long-standing democratic tradition" to intervene, militarily if necessary, against the president.

The country's first oil was exported during the year from the Alba well in the north of Bioko near the territorial waters of both Cameroon and Nigeria. Annual production was expected to be 68 million bbl. (GUY ARNOLD)

This article updates the *Macropædia* article WESTERN AFRICA: *Equatorial Guinea*.

ETHIOPIA

The republic of Ethiopia is in the Horn of northeastern Africa, on the Red sea. Area: 1,251,282 sq km (483,123 sq mi). Pop. (1992 est.): 54,077,000. Cap.: Addis Ababa. Monetary unit: birr, with (Oct. 5, 1992) a par value of 5 birr to U.S. $1 (free rate of 8.50 birr = £1 sterling). Interim president in 1992, Meles Zenawi; acting prime minister, Tamirat Laynie.

The interim government dominated by the Ethiopian People's Revolutionary Democratic Front (EPRDF), which had seized power in May 1991, faced increasing difficulties in establishing its promised democratic structure of government. This was to be based on the principle of ethnic federalism, in which each of the major nationalities within the country would have the right to self-government within its own region, while the powers of the central government would be greatly reduced. In accordance with this program, 14 new regions based on nationality were established late in 1991.

At the same time, previously suppressed data from the 1984 national census were published, giving total numbers of people identifying themselves with each nationality at that time. Though the Oromo people, as expected, constituted the largest single group with 29.1% of the total, this was much less than the 40% or more claimed by Oromo nationalists and only slightly more than the 28.3% identifying themselves as Amhara. Other major groups were the Tigrinya-speakers (9.7%), Gurages (4.4%), Somalis (3.8%),

Sidamas (3%), and Welaytas (2.6%). Nine other groups each comprised between 1 and 2% of the total population, and no fewer than 77 had less than 1%. Though these figures were inevitably subject to dispute and were probably inaccurate—especially for northern areas of the country (including Eritrea), where civil war was raging at the time of the census—no more accurate or generally accepted assessment was likely to become available.

The formation of over 60 political organizations, most of which sought to represent nationality groups, greatly complicated the political process. The most important of these groups were first, those associated with the EPRDF, notably the Tigre People's Liberation Front, the Ethiopian People's Democratic Movement (EPDM), and the Oromo People's Democratic Organization (OPDO); and second, the Oromo Liberation Front (OLF). A variety of groups (including EPDM) claimed to represent the Amharas, while OLF's support among Oromos was disputed not only by OPDO but by the Islamic Front for the Liberation of Oromia, which operated in the Harar region in eastern Ethiopia. Although OLF representatives had been included in the interim government formed in 1991, their relations with EPRDF remained tense, and fighting between them took place early in the year.

An open breach was prompted by Ethiopia's first multiparty elections, for officials at the district level, which took place on June 21. OLF boycotted the elections, accusing the EPRDF government of intimidation, and disrupted the polls, especially in western parts of the country; Western observers who had been monitoring the elections withdrew from these areas. The elections were postponed in three eastern regions where the security situation was also precarious. The cochair of the observer delegation, U.S. Rep. Donald Payne, stated that the elections could not be described as "completely free and fair." Even in Addis Ababa, where conditions were peaceful, EPRDF supporters won an implausibly large share of the votes.

On June 23 OLF withdrew its representatives from the interim government and also withdrew its organization from Addis Ababa, in an evident prelude to the resumption of civil war. Though open hostilities were averted, following Western diplomatic pressure, the situation remained tense. As a result, the planned state funeral of Emperor Haile Sellassie on July 23, the centenary of his birth, was postponed.

Famine continued to affect millions of Ethiopians, with the greatest need in the southeastern part of the country, where refugees flooded in from the civil war in neighbour-

JANE PERLEZ—THE NEW YORK TIMES

In a part of Eritrea where the Ethiopian government had granted land to their Bedouin tribe for settlement, Rashaida women prepare coffee. A referendum on the independence of Eritrea was scheduled for 1993.

ing Somalia and access was restricted by fighting between rival Oromo groups in the region around Harar. In August relief organizations in the area reported that thousands of people had died, while several relief workers were killed by mines and bandits. Some 7.8 million people, about one-sixth of the country's population, were said to be at risk from famine, and an appeal for 1.4 million tons of food aid was only partially successful. Though peaceful conditions prevailed in the north, famine relief was impeded by transport delays from the port at Aseb and distribution problems on the spot. Large numbers of internally displaced people and farmers returning from the previous government's ill-advised resettlement schemes in the south and west placed further strains on relief services. In September the Ethiopian birr, which had been held at 2.05 birr to the U.S. dollar since the 1950s, was devalued to 5 birr = $1.

The northern region of Eritrea had effectively become self-governing from May 1991, pending a referendum on the territory's independence that was due to be held in April 1993. In contrast to the rest of Ethiopia, the whole of Eritrea appeared to be firmly under the control of the Eritrean People's Liberation Front (EPLF) led by Issayas Afewerke, which enjoyed considerable support. The EPLF-led Provisional Government of Eritrea (PGE) launched a campaign of reconstruction after the 30-year war. The economy remained at a very low level, however, and Eritrea continued to be highly dependent on relief food. Relations with international organizations and other donors were affected by Eritrea's anomalous international status; the territory was not independent, but the PGE refused to acknowledge that it was even formally part of Ethiopia. The PGE was nonetheless closely involved in attempts to achieve a peaceful political settlement in Ethiopia while also maintaining good relations with The Sudan.

(CHRISTOPHER S. CLAPHAM)

This article updates the *Macropædia* article EASTERN AFRICA: *Ethiopia.*

GABON

Gabon is a republic of central Africa, on the Atlantic Ocean. Area: 267,667 sq km (103,347 sq mi). Pop.: in 1992 estimates ranged from 800,000 to 1,450,000 (UN est., 1,253,000). Cap.: Libreville. Monetary unit: CFA franc, with (Oct. 5, 1992) a par value of CFAF 50 to the French franc and a free rate of CFAF 238.75 to U.S. $1 (CFAF 405.88 = £1 sterling). President in 1992, Omar Bongo; prime minister, Casimir Oyé Mba.

During 1992 Pres. Omar Bongo remained firmly in control after weathering Gabon's stormy transition to multiparty democracy. His Gabonese Democratic Party held a strong majority in the National Assembly, while the main opposition parties expended most of their energies attacking each other over differences in ideology and charges of betraying the revolution. In August Bongo's government easily survived a no-confidence vote over what the opposition said were unwarranted delays in announcing the date of new municipal elections. Although a serious clash between security forces and striking teachers on March 23 resulted in the death of one demonstrator, there had been no other major political disturbances in the country since June 1990. Radio and television were still state controlled, but independent newspapers, while few in number, seemed to be enjoying unprecedented freedom.

This calm and stability under democratization clearly improved the nation's international image. France even held joint military exercises with the Gabonese army in June. Over $300 million in development aid was promised by donors, including the European Communities, the World

Bank, and the Arab Development Bank. The highly profitable Africa One, the most popular music radio station on the continent, was expected to begin broadcasting on a Paris band.

(NANCY ELLEN LAWLER)

This article updates the *Macropædia* article CENTRAL AFRICA: *Gabon.*

GAMBIA, THE

A republic and member of the Commonwealth, The Gambia extends from the Atlantic Ocean along the lower Gambia River in West Africa; it is surrounded by Senegal. Area: 10,689 sq km (4,127 sq mi). Pop. (1992 est.): 921,000. Cap.: Banjul. Monetary unit: dalasi, with (Oct. 5, 1992) a free rate of 8.42 dalasis to U.S. $1 (14.31 dalasis = £1 sterling). President in 1992, Sir Dawda Jawara.

On Feb. 14, 1992, Pres. Sir Dawda Jawara announced that presidential and legislative elections would be held on April 29. He dissolved the House of Representatives three days later. Although the previous December Jawara had announced that he would step down as president, he changed his mind under pressure from his People's Progressive Party (PPP). In the elections Jawara obtained 58.4% of the votes, and he was sworn in for his fifth term of office on May 11. His nearest presidential rival, Sheriff Mustapha Dibba, leader of the National Convention Party (NCP), obtained 22% of the votes. In the legislative elections the PPP won 25 of the 36 seats in the House of Representatives, the NCP won 6, the Gambia People's Party won 2, and 3 seats went to independents. Jawara announced a new government on May 11 in which he promoted Saihou S. Sabally from minister of economic affairs to vice president.

About 1,300 refugees from fighting in the Casamance region of Senegal fled across the border into The Gambia during July. In August President Jawara went on a four-day official visit to Tehran, Iran. The budget for 1992–93, at 249 million dalasis, represented a 15% increase over that for the previous year.

(GUY ARNOLD)

This article updates the *Macropædia* article WESTERN AFRICA: *The Gambia.*

GHANA

A republic of West Africa and member of the Commonwealth, Ghana lies on the Gulf of Guinea. Area: 238,533 sq km (92,098 sq mi). Pop. (1992 est.): 15,237,000. Cap.: Accra. Monetary unit: cedi, with (Oct. 5, 1992) a free rate of 485.29 cedis to U.S. $1 (825 cedis = £1 sterling). Chairman of the Provisional National Defense Council in 1992, Jerry John Rawlings.

The year in Ghana was dominated by the move to multiparty politics. On March 6, 1992 (Independence Day), Flight Lieut. Jerry Rawlings, chairman of the Provisional National Defense Council (PNDC), set out a timetable for a return to civilian rule with Jan. 7, 1993, as the target date for inauguration of the Fourth Republic. The timetable included a referendum on the draft constitution (April 28), the lifting of the ban on political parties (May 18), presidential elections (November 3), and legislative elections (December 29).

In the April referendum 90% of the voters in a 60% turnout approved the draft constitution. The ban on parties was lifted on May 17, although opposition groups challenged the legislation regarding the formation and conduct of parties. At the end of August it became clear that Rawlings did intend to run for the presidency (a matter that had been the subject of intense interest and debate) as the candidate for the National Democratic Congress. On November 6 it was announced that Rawlings had won 58.3% of the vote in the presidential election, making him the winner without the need for a runoff. However, the result was disputed by the opposition parties. The opposition boycotted the legislative elections, with the result that Rawlings' supporters won almost all of the 200 seats.   (GUY ARNOLD)

This article updates the *Macropædia* article WESTERN AFRICA: *Ghana.*

GUINEA

The republic of Guinea is located in West Africa, on the Atlantic Ocean. Area: 245,857 sq km (94,926 sq mi). Pop. (1992 est.): 7,232,000. Cap.: Conakry. Monetary unit: Guinean franc, with (Oct. 5, 1992) a free rate of GF 811 to U.S. $1 (GF 1,378 = £1 sterling). President in 1992, Brig. Gen. Lansana Conté.

Guinea's transition to multiparty democracy made some progress in 1992 as a result of continuing popular protest. On February 14, Pres. Lansana Conté narrowly escaped from a burning car that was set afire by student demonstrators. On April 3, bowing to intense pressure from opposition political forces, Western aid donors, and general discontent with the sagging economy, the president declared that constitutional rule would begin. No elections, however, were scheduled. It was increasingly possible that Conté would be unable to resist opposition calls for a national conference. The returned exile Alpha Condé, leader of the Rally of the Guinean People, who once had been condemned to death in absentia by the Sekou Touré regime, appeared to have a large following in all sectors of the country except the president's coastal strongholds.

Austerity measures demanded by the International Monetary Fund had a severe impact on the urban economy. All citizens, including the poor, had to pay for basic services such as water, electricity, schools, and medicine. While beneficial to Guinean farmers, the sharp rise in food prices added to the internal tensions. The volatility of the political environment continued to dampen international investors' enthusiasm for participation in the economy, although a major electrification project had been underwritten by a consortium of Western development agencies.

(NANCY ELLEN LAWLER)

This article updates the *Macropædia* article WESTERN AFRICA: *Guinea.*

GUINEA-BISSAU

A republic of West Africa, Guinea-Bissau lies on the Atlantic Ocean. Area: 36,125 sq km (13,948 sq mi). Pop. (1992 est.): 1,015,000. Cap.: Bissau. Monetary unit: Guinea-Bissau peso, with (Oct. 5, 1992) a free rate of 4,491 pesos to U.S. $1 (8,485 pesos = £1 sterling). President in 1992, João Bernardo Vieira; prime minister, Carlos Correia.

On Nov. 18, 1991, the Supreme Court ended 17 years of one-party rule when it legalized the opposition Democratic Front led by Aristides Menezes, a former dissident member of the ruling African Party for the Independence of Guinea and Cape Verde (PAIGC). On December 27 the court legalized two new political parties, the Resistance Party of Guinea-Bissau (Bafata Movement) and the Social Democratic Front, and at least two others were preparing to contest power. Also on December 27, Pres. João Bernardo Vieira appointed Carlos Correia (minister of state for rural development and agriculture) to the restored post of prime minister. On March 9, 1992, dates were set for multiparty presidential and legislative elections on November 15 and December 13, respectively, but they were later postponed to March 1993. When the authorities gave permission for

an opposition demonstration to take place on March 7 (the first such occasion in Guinea-Bissau), an estimated 30,-000 people took part and listened to speakers denouncing PAIGC corruption.

A drop of 58% in cereal production in 1991 forced Guinea-Bissau to seek food aid. However, export-crop production rose by 19% over the year, with 18,251 metric tons of cashew nuts accounting for 86.5% of exports. The increase was attributed to privatization of the trade sector and the freeing of prices. The country's first private newspaper appeared, the weekly *Expresso-Bissau.*   (GUY ARNOLD)

This article updates the *Macropædia* article WESTERN AFRICA: *Guinea-Bissau.*

KENYA

A republic and member of the Commonwealth, Kenya is in eastern Africa, on the Indian Ocean. Area: 582,646 sq km (224,961 sq mi), including 11,230 sq km of inland water. Pop. (1992 est.): 26,985,000. Cap.: Nairobi. Monetary unit: Kenya shilling, with (Oct. 5, 1992) a free rate of 33.84 shillings to U.S. $1 (57.53 shillings = £1 sterling). President in 1992, Daniel arap Moi.

The year 1992 began badly for the ruling Kenya African National Union (KANU). Mwai Kibaki, formerly vice president and one of five ministers who had resigned in December 1991 alleging mismanagement of the economy and election rigging by the government, announced the formation of the Democratic Party on January 8. The new party won considerable support in the Central province. There were those who asked why Kibaki and others had been content to serve the government for so long, but Kibaki's soundly based economic program had wide appeal. Later in the month, the Forum for the Restoration of Democracy (FORD), the only opposition party so far registered, held a mass meeting in Nairobi; estimates of the attendance varied between 100,000 and 250,000. The party leader, Jaramogi Oginga Odinga, called on Pres. Daniel arap Moi to dissolve the National Assembly immediately and to hold elections.

Early in March riots broke out in Nairobi when police attempted to break up a hunger strike led by mothers of political prisoners. The popularity of the government was in no way enhanced by newspaper pictures of Wangari Maathi, an environmentalist and a leading woman politician, being carried to a car after being beaten by police. In the wake of the riots, although not as a result of them, the government published a bill aimed at drastically reducing the powers of the president. There was further trouble in the west, where intermittent fighting between the Kalenjin, Kisii, and Luo groups led to accusations that the president was deliberately encouraging ethnic conflict. In September opposition leaders in the west complained that the government was supporting some of those involved in the fighting and called for a UN peacekeeping force.

The government did not take kindly to the violent criticisms of some of its opponents. In April the U.S.-based Lawyers Committee for Human Rights called for an end to the harassment of Kenyan lawyers who, among other things, had protested the confiscation of a copy of the magazine *Society* in January. The committee also urged that all periodicals be allowed to circulate freely in line with the provisions of the Kenyan constitution.

The economy was facing problems as serious as those on the political front, due in part to mismanagement but also to the fall in coffee prices on the world market. The influx of scores of thousands of refugees from the civil war in Somalia and from Ethiopia and The Sudan into the northeastern part of the country placed another heavy burden on the already overstrained food supply. In conditions

Kenyans wait in line to vote in that country's first multiparty elections to be held in a quarter century. Early returns from the voting, held on December 29, indicated that Pres. Daniel arap Moi would retain power.

BETTY PRESS—PICTURE GROUP

exacerbated by drought, food was having to be imported on a considerable scale. The government of The Netherlands offered Kenya 3.7 million shillings to help with the drilling of boreholes in the refugee camps, where water was dangerously short. In June, Moi issued an appeal for help in feeding Kenya's own drought victims as well as the refugees, whose number had by then risen to nearly half a million. In response, the UN World Food Program launched an airlift to deliver wheat to the affected areas.

In May formal relations were reopened with South Africa, and a month later Moi became the first African head of state to visit South Africa in 21 years. The president's position at home also took a turn for the better as a result of divisions among the leaders of FORD. Elections within the party, due to be held on August 1, were boycotted by everyone except the Luo, who were supporting Oginga Odinga's bid to retain the party leadership. On October 28 Moi dissolved the National Assembly five months early, and legislative and presidential elections were held December 29. Early returns indicated that Moi had been reelected and that KANU had won 100 seats (12 of the 188 seats were appointive and would presumably also go to KANU). The two branches of FORD (31 seats each) and the Democratic Party (23) disputed the results. (KENNETH INGHAM)

This article updates the *Macropædia* article EASTERN AFRICA: *Kenya*.

LESOTHO

A monarchy of southern Africa and member of the Commonwealth, Lesotho forms a landlocked enclave within South Africa. Area: 30,355 sq km (11,720 sq mi). Pop. (1992 est.): 1,854,000. Cap.: Maseru. Monetary unit: loti (plural: maloti), at par with the South African rand, with (Oct. 5, 1992) a free rate of 2.84 maloti to U.S. $1 (4.82 maloti = £1 sterling). King, Letsie III; chairman of the Military Council in 1992, Maj Gen. Elias Phisoana Ramaema.

At the end of 1991 Lesotho signed agreements worth $525 million with European banks to fund part of its huge hydroelectric development. One of the biggest civil engineering projects in the world, it was expected to cost $3 billion by the year 2020. As of 1992 Lesotho was dependent on South Africa for 98% of its electricity, but the next phase of the project (the Muela hydroelectric plant) was expected to save Lesotho $9.6 million a year in electricity bills when

completed in 1996. During the year Lesotho established full diplomatic relations with South Africa, the third African country—after Côte d'Ivoire and Kenya—to do so.

Lesotho suffered during the year from the drought that was afflicting all of southern Africa. As a result, the nation expected to produce only 54% of its normal output of grain.

In July the former king, Moshoeshoe II, returned home to an emotional welcome after two years in exile. The government requested the Commonwealth Secretariat to provide assistance during its return to multiparty politics, and a Commonwealth mission visited Lesotho in March.

(GUY ARNOLD)

This article updates the *Macropædia* article SOUTHERN AFRICA: *Lesotho*.

LIBERIA

The republic of Liberia is located in West Africa, on the Atlantic Ocean. Area: 99,067 sq km (38,250 sq mi). Pop. (1992 est.): 2,780,000 (including Liberian refugees temporarily residing in surrounding countries estimated to number about 600,000). Cap.: Monrovia. Monetary unit: Liberian dollar, at par with the U.S. dollar, with a free rate (Oct. 5, 1992) of L$1.70 to £1 sterling. President of the interim government in 1992, Amos Sawyer.

Despite the peace agreement of October 1991 (which was to be implemented in 60 days), 1992 continued to be a deeply troubled year for Liberia. The agreement was rejected by the United Liberation Movement of Liberia for Democracy (ULIMO), whose leader, Raleigh Seekie, said on March 4 that his forces would continue to fight. In January the interim government of Amos Sawyer introduced new currency, but the two main rebel groups (Charles Taylor's National Patriotic Forces of Liberia [NPFL] and Prince Yormie Johnson's rival Independent National Patriotic Forces of Liberia) refused to recognize it and dismissed the move as politically motivated. The currency reform was only part of a package of sanctions aimed at depriving the rebels of fuel, alcohol, tobacco, and other items so as to force the NPFL to conform to the 1991 peace accord.

On January 13 an election commission was sworn in to organize free and fair elections for mid-1992, but on January 15 the deadline for the rebels to lay down their arms and place themselves in camps passed without compliance. In early April the Economic Community of West African States (ECOWAS) Committee of Five on Liberia met in

Geneva with Sawyer and Taylor and confirmed the 1991 peace accord. It was agreed that ECOMOG, the ECOWAS peacekeeping force, should establish a buffer zone along thsaverder with Sierra Leone, where forces loyal to the former president, Samuel Doe, were based. At first Taylor would not accept the agreement, but on April 29 he announced that he would dissolve his government and withdraw his troops from within 3 km (1.8 mi) of the Sierra Leone border. ECOMOG began to deploy troops in areas controlled by the NPFL, and in June six Senegalese soldiers serving with the peacekeeping force were killed in NPFL-held territory. The fragile half-peace appeared to be shattered in August, when fierce fighting occurred between the NPFL and the Sierra Leone-based fighters loyal to former president Doe. Some of the worst fighting of the civil war took place in October and early November as Taylor's forces laid siege to Monrovia and ECOMOG used Nigerian aircraft to bomb rebel positions outside the city. Among those killed, presumably by Taylor's forces, were five American nuns. ECOWAS ordered a trade embargo on NPFL-controlled territory (about 95% of the country), and on November 19 the UN Security Council called for a "general and complete" arms embargo and directed Secretary-General Boutros Boutros-Ghali to send a special representative to report on the conflict. (GUY ARNOLD)

This article updates the *Macropædia* article WESTERN AFRICA: *Liberia*.

MADAGASCAR

The republic of Madagascar occupies the island of the same name and minor adjacent islands in the Indian Ocean off the southeast coast of Africa. Area: 587,041 sq km (226,658 sq mi). Pop. (1992 est.): 12,803,000. Cap.: Antananarivo. Monetary unit: Malagasy franc, with (Oct. 5, 1992) a free rate of FMG 1,512 to U.S. $1 (FMG 2,570 = £1 sterling). President in 1992, Didier Ratsiraka; prime minister, Guy Razanamasy; president of the High State Authority (chief of transitional regime), Albert Zafy.

The formation of a new coalition government under Guy Razanamasy as prime minister at the end of 1991 was seen as the prelude to a fresh approach to politics; his coalition included members of the opposition Committee of Active Forces, who received 14 out of 36 portfolios (earlier they had refused to take part in a coalition). A High State Authority for the Transition to the Third Republic was set up, as well as a National Committee for Economic and Social Recovery.

While moving toward a new political era, Madagascar faced major economic problems, some of them also a matter of transition to a free-market economy. The Madagascar free zone established in Antananarivo in 1989 was designed to help foreign investors work in partnership with local enterprises; it was hoped that investors would be attracted by the quality of the local labour force and its low costs.

At the end of July 1992, in what seemed to be a growing custom, four members of an armed opposition group, apparently part of a breakaway faction of the Committee of Active Forces, briefly seized the radio station in Antananarivo and declared a coup. After the security forces had regained control, the prime minister announced that the electoral calendar would be respected. In the first round of the presidential election, on November 25, Albert Zafy, the president of the High State Authority, fell just short of receiving a majority, with Ratsiraka a distant second. The results were marred by irregularities, however, and the second round was postponed to Feb. 10, 1993. Reportedly, the budget for all elections had been used up, and new funds would have to be found. (GUY ARNOLD)

MALAWI

A republic and member of the Commonwealth, Malawi is a landlocked state in eastern Africa. Area: 118,484 sq km (45,747 sq mi). Pop. (1992 est.): 9,484,000 (excluding Mozambican refugees estimated to number about 950,000). Cap.: Lilongwe (legislature meets in Zomba). Monetary unit: Malawi kwacha, with (Oct. 5, 1992) a free rate of 3.93 kwacha to U.S. $1 (6.69 kwacha = £1 sterling). President in 1992, Hastings Kamuzu Banda.

In March 1992, the government belatedly acknowledged that Malawi, in common with most other countries in southern Africa, had been gravely affected by drought. The effects of the acute shortage of food resulting from a bad harvest were exacerbated by the presence of almost a million refugees from Mozambique, for whom provision had to be made.

Opponents of Pres. Hastings Banda, emboldened by the economic crisis, pressed for a change of government. In March Banda's critics met in Lusaka, Zambia, and called for an end to a constitutional situation in which the Malawi Congress Party was the sole legal political organization. Chakufwa Chihana, a trade union official, agreed to return to Malawi and present the views of the meeting, but on his arrival in Lilongwe he was immediately arrested. Although he was released on bail in July, he was detained again after criticizing the government publicly and in December was sentenced to two years' hard labour. On March 8, eight Roman Catholic bishops also aroused the anger of the government by signing a pastoral letter condemning its fihuman rights record, and in May there were widespread strikes by workmen demanding higher pay. Parliamentary elections held in June aroused so little enthusiasm that 45 of the 141 seats were uncontested. In October the president announced a referendum on multiparty politics but said he was convinced it would expose "lies" about the extent of support for a change. (KENNETH INGHAM)

This article updates the *Macropædia* article SOUTHERN AFRICA: *Malawi*.

MALI

Mali is a landlocked republic of West Africa. Area: 1,248,574 sq km (482,077 sq mi). Pop. (1992 est.): 8,464,000. Cap.: Bamako. Monetary unit: CFA franc, with (Oct. 5, 1992) a par value of CFAF 50 to the French franc and a free rate of CFAF 238.75 to U.S. $1 (CFAF 405.88 = £1 sterling). President of the Transitional Committee for the Salvation of the People to June 8, 1992, Lieut. Col. Amadou Toumani Touré; president from June 8, Alpha Oumar Konaré; prime ministers, Soumana Sacko and, from June 9, Younoussí Touré.

Early in 1992 local and legislative multiparty elections were held. On April 26, Alpha Konaré won 70% of the vote in the second round of the presidential election; he was inaugurated on June 8. His Alliance for Democracy in Mali (ADEMA) won 76 of 116 seats in the National Assembly.

In August the Cabinet granted immunity to Amadou Touré, leader of the transitional government. The action was seen as a gesture of appreciation for his role in the restoration of democracy. By contrast, the twice-postponed trial of former president Moussa Traoré and 32 colleagues resumed on November 26. Despite a national peace pact signed by representatives of the government and the Tuaregs on April 11, violence continued to plague the area along the Mali-Mauritania frontier.

The announcement on July 7 that CFAF 5.7 billion were missing from the Treasury underscored Mali's continuing financial woes. The World Bank and the International Monetary Fund (IMF) agreed in August to grant CFAF 16 billion toward the implementation of a structural adjustment program. In June the IMF had granted $22 million for economic- and financial-reform programs.

(NANCY ELLEN LAWLER)

This article updates the *Macropædia* article WESTERN AFRICA: *Mali.*

MAURITANIA

The republic of Mauritania is on the Atlantic coast of West Africa. Area: 1,030,700 sq km (398,000 sq mi). Pop. (1992 est.): 2,108,000. Cap.: Nouakchott. Monetary unit: ouguiya, with (Oct. 5, 1992) a free rate of 75.95 ouguiya to U.S. $1 (129.11 ouguiya = £1 sterling). President of the Military Committee for National Salvation and prime minister to April 18, 1992, Col. Maaouya Ould Sidi Ahmed Taya; president from April 18, Taya; prime minister from April 18, Sidi Mohamed Ould Boubacar.

Col. Maaouya Ould Sidi Ahmed Taya defeated three opponents in presidential elections on Jan. 24, 1992. He took 63% of the vote, nearly double that of his nearest opponent, Ahmed Ould Daddah. After the arrest of 160 election protesters, the opposition Union of Democratic Forces-New Era called for a boycott of the March legislative elections, and voter turnout was less than 40%. Taya's Democratic and Social Republican Party won 67 of 79 seats. (For tabulated results, see *Political Parties,* above.) On April 20 the new prime minister, Sidi Mohamed Ould Boubacar, announced his Cabinet. All were civilians except the minister of defense, Col. Ahmed Ould Minnih.

Full diplomatic relations with Senegal, broken in 1989, were restored in April. Relations with Mali remained satisfactory. At least 10 Tuaregs, members of the Azawad Arab Islamic Front based in Mali, were arrested in Nouakchott.

The economy remained stagnant, and international donors continued to provide food aid. The International Monetary Fund agreed to finance a three-year economic and financial development program, conditional on the government's devaluing the currency and raising food prices. Widespread demonstrations broke out in October, when a 28% devaluation against the U.S. dollar provoked a 40% increase in the price of basic foodstuffs.   (NANCY ELLEN LAWLER)

This article updates the *Macropædia* article WESTERN AFRICA: *Mauritania.*

MAURITIUS

The republic of Mauritius, a member of the Commonwealth, occupies an island in the Indian Ocean about 800 km (500 mi) east of Madagascar and includes the island dependencies of Rodrigues, Agalega, and Cargados Carajos Shoals. Area: 2,040 sq km (788 sq mi). Pop. (1992 est.): 1,081,000. Cap.: Port Louis. Monetary unit: Mauritian rupee, with (Oct. 5, 1992) a free rate of Mau Rs 14.60 to U.S. $1 (Mau Rs 24.82 = £1 sterling). Queen until March 12, 1992, Elizabeth II; governor-general until March 12, Sir Veerasamy Ringadoo; presidents, Ringadoo from March 12 and, from June 30, Cassam Uteem; prime minister, Aneerood Jugnauth.

On March 12, 1992, Mauritius formally severed its association with the British crown to become a republic within the Commonwealth; the last governor-general, Veerasamy Ringadoo, became interim president for three months. The guest of honour at the ceremony was India's prime minister, P.V. Narasimha Rao, who emphasized the strong ties between the two countries (68% of Mauritians are of Indian origin). Rao announced an Indian contribution of Mau Rs 200 million for an India-Mauritius Fund to promote joint ventures and indicated India's desire for expanded trade links. During 1991 the Mauritian economy slowed to a growth rate of only 4% (from more than 6% in 1990), but 1992 was generally expected to be a good year, with an

estimated growth rate of 6.5% following a modest recovery in the sugar industry and expansion in the tourist trade. Sectors of the economy that grew during the year were construction, finance, and some industries in the export-processing zone.

The country's new president, Cassam Uteem, elected by the National Assembly on June 30, called for harder work if the country was to join the ranks of the industrialized nations. He urged an improvement in manufacturing standards, as otherwise the economy would be "left behind."

In 1966 Britain gave the island of Diego Garcia in the Chagos Archipelago (a part of Mauritius and then still a colony) to the U.S. for 50 years to be used as a military base, and the 1,800 islanders were forcibly moved to Mauritius. This "lease" of the island was part of cold war strategy, but with the end of the cold war the question arose as to when and whether the island would be returned to Mauritius, which had constantly asked for it. As of the end of 1992, however, the U.S. was showing no sign of being willing to relinquish control of Diego Garcia.   (GUY ARNOLD)

This article updates the *Micropædia* article MAURITIUS.

MOZAMBIQUE

The republic of Mozambique is located in eastern Africa, on the Indian Ocean. Area: 812,379 sq km (313,661 sq mi). Pop. (1992 est.): 14,842,000 (excluding Mozambican refugees estimated to number about 1.2 million). Cap.: Maputo. Monetary unit: metical, with (Oct. 5, 1992) a free rate of 2,712 meticais to U.S. $1 (4,611 meticais = £1 sterling). President in 1992, Joaquim Chissanó; prime minister, Marío de Graça Machungo.

On Oct. 4, 1992, three days after the date originally planned, a cease-fire agreement was signed in Rome by Pres. Joaquim Chissanó on behalf of the government and Afonso Dhlakama, leader of the Mozambique National Resistance (Renamo). This was the culmination of two years of intermittent discussions between the warring parties organized by the Roman Catholic Church and was made possible by the tireless mediation of Pres. Robert Mugabe of Zimbabwe. Others who played a role in urging Dhlakama to participate were the South African government and Tiny Rowland, chairman of Lonrho, a company that had considerable interests in Mozambique. Perhaps the dominant factor, however, was the devastating impact of the drought, which threatened the lives of millions of the population and made it virtually impossible for either side to continue the war much longer.

The year had not begun auspiciously. Early in January Renamo rebels attacked the town of Macia, killing 50 people and wounding another 25. This was part of Renamo's continuing campaign to dislocate the country, an endeavour in which the rebels seemed to be achieving a considerable measure of success; an international index published in May placed Mozambique at the head of a table of human misery. That opinion was reinforced by a World Bank claim that the country had the world's lowest per capita gross national product. The government itself had already admitted that the standard of living had fallen even further during the last two years, and it was a disappointment when the aid package offered by Sweden in May proved, at about £39.5 million, to be some £8 million less than in 1991. Even the report that gold production had increased in 1991 and that there was a prospect of $10 million of foreign investment in the mining industry in 1992 was offset by the knowledge that serious problems remained because of the difficulty of maintaining obsolete equipment, the shortage of funds to operate the mines, the lack of spare parts, and the danger involved in transporting the ore to the ports.

Joaquim Chissanó (left), president of Mozambique, embraces Afonso Dhlakama, leader of the Mozambique National Resistance (Renamo), at their meeting on August 5. On October 4 the two signed a cease-fire accord aimed at ending 16 years of civil war.

LIVIO ANTICOLI—GAMMA LIAISON

Faced with the knowledge that the country would have to import one million tons of corn to meet the basic requirements of the people, and being fully aware that the inhabitants of Renamo-held territory would have no hope of gaining access to such supplies even if they became available elsewhere, Dhlakama announced on July 4 that he was tired of the war that his rebel forces had waged against the government since 1976. After talks with South African Pres. F.W. de Klerk and later with President Mugabe, he said that a solution could be found to a conflict that was bad for both Mozambique and the surrounding region. Chissanó, who had been calling for a settlement throughout the year, welcomed the statement, and on August 7 he and Dhlakama signed a joint declaration in Rome stating that the two sides would sign a general peace agreement by October 1. Doubts remained, however, as to whether Dhlakama had sufficient control over the scattered units of Renamo, each with its own virtually independent commander, to guarantee fulfillment of his side of any agreement.

Those doubts were reinforced when Dhlakama arrived late in Rome to sign the agreement and then only after setting out a number of preconditions that seemed to verge on deliberate delaying tactics. Nevertheless, the agreement was signed on October 4. President Chissanó optimistically declared that a new era had begun. Dhlakama, even more optimistically, promised that his men would stop fighting within 24 hours. On December 16, with the timetable agreed to under terms of the peace accord falling behind schedule, the UN Security Council decided to send a peacekeeping force of some 7,500 troops, police, and civilians to oversee the disarming of the rival forces and to organize elections. The UN force would also take over the task of protecting the transport corridors across Mozambique to Central Africa.   (KENNETH INGHAM)

This article updates the *Macropædia* article SOUTHERN AFRICA: *Mozambique.*

NAMIBIA

A republic and member of the Commonwealth, Namibia is in southern Africa, on the Atlantic Ocean; it surrounds the 1,124-sq km South African exclave of Walvis Bay (the future joint administration of Walvis Bay by South Africa and Namibia was announced in August 1992). Area: 823,144 sq km (317,818 sq mi). Pop. (1992 est.): 1,431,000. Cap.: Windhoek. Monetary unit: Namibian dollar, at par with the South African rand (also legal currency) from June 1992, with (Oct. 5, 1992) a commercial rate of R 2.84 to U.S. $1 (R 4.82 = £1 sterling). President in 1992, Sam Nujoma; prime minister, Hage Geingob.

Namibia's second full year of independence passed without major developments. On the one hand, this signified the success of the government's policy of reconciliation after two decades of war, including the unification of the defense force. On the other hand, there were signs, with the passing of the euphoria of independence, of growing realization of the obstacles to raising the living standards of most of the population—including an increasingly stagnant economy and a lack of the foreign investment promised at the time of independence.

Gross domestic product grew by 3.2% in 1990 and a healthy 5.1% in 1991 (largely because of the fishing and diamond industries), but the economy slowed down seriously in 1992 as a result of the country's severest drought of the century and a weakening of the uranium and diamond markets. During 1991 there was a 21% drop in real fixed capital outlays. The Rossing uranium mine, previously a major export earner, laid off 750 workers in 1991 to operate at 50% capacity, though it signed new contracts with Japan during 1992. Other planned projects included a copper mine and a sugar agribusiness scheme in the Caprivi area.

By midyear it was estimated that half the economically active population was unemployed. While 16,500 entered the labour market each year, only 3,000–4,000 new jobs were being created. In Ovamboland, home of 600,000 people, there were only 6,000 formal jobs. Surveys also showed that 90% of Namibians earned less than R 750 a year. Some 60% of the population was illiterate, and 74% of the arable land was in the hands of 4,000 mainly white farmers. The rate of inflation rose to 20.4% by March 1992 (11.9% in 1990).

During the year, agreement was reached between the Namibian and South African governments for the joint administration of the previously South African enclave of Walvis Bay. Namibia also signed an agreement with South Africa for the repayment over 17 years from April 1995 of an outstanding debt of R 827 million.

(MARTIN LEGASSICK)

This article updates the *Macropædia* article SOUTHERN AFRICA: *Namibia.*

NIGER

Niger is a landlocked republic of West Africa. Area: 1,186,408 sq km (458,075 sq mi). Pop. (1992 est.): 8,281,000. Cap.: Niamey. Monetary unit: CFA franc, with (Oct. 5, 1992) a par value of CFAF 50 to the French franc and a free rate of CFAF 238.75 to U.S. $1 (CFAF 405.88 = £1 sterling). President in 1992, Gen. Ali Saibou; prime minister, Amadou Cheiffou.

The year 1992 was dominated by the desperate state of the economy and the widening Tuareg rebellion. In February mutinous soldiers took over a radio station and closed Niamey Airport. More than 3,000 of them and the entire civil service had not been paid for two months. A threatened general strike to protest the mutiny set for March 4 was narrowly averted following an appeal by Laouali Moutari, secretary-general of the National Trade Union Federation. Prime Minister Amadou Cheiffou dissolved the transitional government on March 23. In July hundreds of students demonstrated over nonpayment of grants, taking Minister of Education Boube Gado hostage.

Hostilities continued between the government and the Tuareg Liberation Front of Air and Azawad (FLAA). In mid-August the army retaliated for a series of rebel attacks on tourists and security forces by seizing 43 Tuaregs, including the prefect of Agades, Moctar El Incha. In all, 186 Tuaregs were arrested. A new democratic constitution was overwhelmingly approved in a referendum in December. The World Bank refused to finance Niger's CFAF 54 billion budget deficit, and China suspended diplomatic relations on July 30.   (NANCY ELLEN LAWLER)

This article updates the *Macropædia* article WESTERN AFRICA: *Niger.*

NIGERIA

A republic and member of the Commonwealth, Nigeria is located in West Africa, on the Gulf of Guinea. Area: 923,768 sq km (356,669 sq mi). Pop. (1992 est.): 89,666,000. Cap.: Abuja. Monetary unit: naira, with (Oct. 5, 1992) a free rate of 18.42 naira to U.S. $1 (31.31 naira = £1 sterling). President and chairman of the Armed Forces Ruling Council in 1992, Maj. Gen. Ibrahim Babangida.

On Jan. 1, 1992, Pres. Ibrahim Babangida presented the federal budget with projected expenditure for the year of 27,594,000,000 naira, a substantial increase from the 1991 figure of 22,123,000,000. Economic growth had slowed during 1991 owing to declining oil prices. Foreign exchange earnings for the year were estimated at $8,988,000,000, of which $2,227,000,000 (just under 25%) would be required for debt servicing. A new National Council of Ministers was sworn in on January 13 following a decision to reduce the number of ministries from 27 to 20. On January 24 the chairman of the National Electoral Commission (NEC), Humphrey Nwosu, set the dates for the elections for a return to civilian rule: November 7 for the National Assembly and December 5 for the president. The first month of the year was marked by religious rioting in Katsina state follow-

AP/WIDE WORLD

South African Pres. F.W. de Klerk (left) meets with Ibrahim Babangida, president of Nigeria, in Abuja in April. Babangida invited de Klerk to Nigeria after South African whites had voted in March to support their president's policy of ending apartheid.

ing the arrest of 263 people described by the governor as Islamic fundamentalists; at least 10 people were killed.

On March 19 the results of the November 1991 census were published. They revealed a total population of 88,514,-501 Nigerians, between 20 million and 30 million below the figures that had been widely used for years by the World Bank and the UN. The northern states had a population of 46.9 million; the southern states, 41.3 million. The reduced figure meant an alteration upward of estimated per capita income from $250 to $360. During March the central bank of Nigeria effectively devalued the naira when the exchange rate against the U.S. dollar was increased from 10.6 naira to 17.8 naira. The devaluation, which was in line with International Monetary Fund (IMF)/World Bank prescriptions for the economy, was made in an effort to obtain rescheduling of Nigeria's external debt of about $35 billion. Dates for the elections to the National Assembly were advanced to July from November.

Ethnic violence erupted in Taraba state during March, when about 100 people were killed in fighting between the Jukun and Tiv people. Nominally over farming rights, such violence had first occurred in October 1991. A total of 5,000 people were thought to have been killed altogether, while 30,000 had become refugees. Mismanagement caused Nigeria to face an expensive fuel crisis in April when the Warri refinery cut output owing to power-supply problems and the Port Harcourt refinery cut back during maintenance. As a result, Nigeria (the world's 13th largest crude petroleum producer) was obliged to import oil from Europe.

In the legislative elections on July 4, the Social Democratic Party (SDP) won 52 of the 91 Senate seats (less than the two-thirds majority required for altering the constitution or reversing presidential vetoes), while the National Republican Convention (NRC) won 37 seats. Two seats had to be contested again. In the House of Representatives the SDP won 314 seats and the NRC 275, while 4 seats from the total of 593 had to be recontested. In general, NRC support came from the Muslim Hausa-speaking states of northern Nigeria. Only 25% of the electorate voted; voters abstained in protest against both the imposed party system and the open ballot, whereby voters lined up behind images of those they intended to support.

On August 7 the NEC canceled the results of the first round of presidential primaries because of widespread allegations of irregularities and corruption, and all further rounds were suspended. However, on August 24 the NEC announced new primaries for September. The process of choosing presidential candidates was again suspended on October 6 following further allegations of malpractices by some of the 23 candidates. On October 9 the vice president, Augustus Aikhomu, said that Jan. 1, 1993, had been set for the handover to civilian rule, but this was subsequently postponed to August 27. On January 2 the Armed Forces Ruling Council and the Council of Ministers were to be replaced by a National Defense and Security Council and a civilian Transitional Council, in effect extending military rule by eight months.   (GUY ARNOLD)

This article updates the *Macropædia* article WESTERN AFRICA: *Nigeria.*

RWANDA

The landlocked republic of Rwanda is situated in central Africa. Area: 26,338 sq km (10,169 sq mi). Pop. (1992 est.): 7,347,000. Cap.: Kigali. Monetary unit: Rwanda franc, with (Oct. 5, 1992) a free rate of RF 140.21 to U.S. $1 (RF 239.15 = £1 sterling). President in 1992, Maj. Gen. Juvénal Habyarimana; prime ministers, Sylvestre Nsanzimana and, from April 2, Dismas Nsengiyaremye.

On Dec. 30, 1991, Prime Minister Sylvestre Nsanzimana, who had been appointed by Pres. Juvénal Habyarimana the previous October, named a new transitional government drawn mainly from the ruling National Republican Movement for Democracy and Development (MRNDD), with one member from the Christian Democratic Party. Other opposition parties refused representation in the government unless the prime minister was appointed from outside the MRNDD. On March 14, 1992, however, three opposition parties signed a protocol of understanding with the MRNDD in what appeared to be the prelude to a unity government. On April 2 the president replaced Nsanzimana with Dismas Nsengiyaremye of the Republican Democratic Movement, and on April 16 he named a 19-member transitional government drawn from five parties.

In June representatives of the government and the rebel Rwandan Patriotic Front (FPR) met in Paris and agreed to a cease-fire, and a formal accord ending the civil war was signed in August. However, the country continued to be troubled by violations of the truce. Further talks in October resulted in an agreement envisioning a transitional Cabinet, including members of all political parties and the FPR, that would share power with the president.   (GUY ARNOLD)

This article updates the *Macropædia* article CENTRAL AFRICA; *Rwanda.*

SÃO TOMÉ AND PRÍNCIPE

The republic of São Tomé and Príncipe comprises two main islands and several smaller islets that straddle the Equator in the Gulf of Guinea, off the west coast of Africa. Area: 1,001 sq km (386 sq mi). Pop. (1992 est.): 126,000. Cap.: São Tomé. Monetary unit: dobra, with (Oct. 5, 1992) a free rate of 239.58 dobras to U.S. $1 (407.28 dobras = £1 sterling). President in 1992, Miguel Trovoada; prime ministers, Daniel Lima dos Santos Daio and, from May 16, Norberto José d'Alva Costa Alegre.

On April 22, 1992, Pres. Miguel Trovoada dismissed the government of Prime Minister Daniel Lima dos Santos Daio, which had held office since January 1991, and invited the ruling Party of Democratic Convergence (PCD) to form a new government. The party claimed the dismissal was unconstitutional, but Daio had criticized the president, and on April 8 some 7,000 people had converged on the presidential palace to demand the dismissal of his government. Daio was blamed for the state of the economy following implementation of a structural adjustment program agreed on with the International Monetary Fund and the World Bank.

On May 16 a new prime minister, Norberto José d'Alva Costa Alegre, named his government. New funds for the structural adjustment program were promised during August by the World Bank and the African Development Bank, and donors meeting in July in Geneva agreed to a measure of debt relief and food aid. A clash between army and police followed the arrest by the police of two soldiers. A new illegal industry appeared to consist of stripping the bells from old colonial churches and delivering them to foreign antique dealers in yachts off the coast.   (GUY ARNOLD)

This article updates the *Macropædia* article CENTRAL AFRICA: *São Tomé and Príncipe.*

SENEGAL

The republic of Senegal is located in West Africa, on the Atlantic Ocean; it surrounds the country of The Gambia. Area: 196,712 sq km (75,951 sq mi). Pop. (1992 est.): 7,691,000. Cap.: Dakar. Monetary unit: CFA franc, with (Oct. 5, 1992) a par value of CFAF 50 to the French franc and a free rate of CFAF 238.75 to U.S. $1 (CFAF 405.88 = £1 sterling). President in 1992, Abdou Diouf; prime minister, Habib Thiam.

Senegal played a prominent role in inter-African affairs in 1992 as host to the meetings of the Organization of African Unity (OAU) and the Economic Community of West African States (ECOWAS). Pres. Abdou Diouf was also elected president of the OAU. In an effort to halt the Liberian civil war, Senegal sent a peacekeeping force of 3,000 soldiers to serve with the ECOWAS monitoring group (ECOMOG). In October Diouf called for an international conference to try to end the armed conflict in Somalia. Democratic Party leader Abdoulaye Wade resigned as minister of state in the National Unity government on October 18. He was expected to be a candidate in the presidential elections set for February 1993.

Full diplomatic relations with Mauritania, broken off in 1989, were resumed in April. In June Diouf led a large delegation of ministers on an official visit to Paris, where he intensified his efforts to attract more foreign investment to Africa. He stressed concern that the continent was becoming "marginalized." Together with the presidents of Burkina Faso, Côte d'Ivoire, and Gabon, Diouf met with Pres. François Mitterrand of France in August to allay widespread fears that the CFA franc would be devalued. These rumours had fueled a large flight of capital from Francophone Africa to Europe.

In January a peace commission composed of government representatives and members of the separatist Movement of Democratic Forces of Casamance (MFDC) was created. Rebellion in Casamance intensified, however, and more than 1,000 refugees fled to The Gambia. There were numerous clashes between security forces and rebels. The most serious occurred on September 1. The army reported that 50 rebels were killed in the village of Kaguitt near the Guinea-Bissau border; the MFDC claimed that 100 people died. As a result, polls in Casamance would not be open for the 1993 elections.   (NANCY ELLEN LAWLER)

This article updates the *Macropædia* article WESTERN AFRICA: *Senegal.*

SEYCHELLES

A republic and member of the Commonwealth, the Seychelles consists of about 100 islands in the Indian Ocean, 1,450 km (900 mi) from the east coast of Africa. Area: 453 sq km (175 sq mi). Pop. (1992 est.): 71,000. Cap.: Victoria. Monetary unit: Seychelles rupee, with (Oct. 5, 1992) a free rate of SR 4.83 to U.S. $1 (SR 8.30 = £1 sterling). President in 1992, France-Albert René.

In an extraordinary congress on Dec. 3, 1991, the Seychelles People's Progressive Front (FPPS) voted to legalize opposition parties. Both Britain and France had linked further aid to a return to democracy. Former president James Mancham returned to Seychelles from exile on April 12, 1992, and had talks with Pres. France-Albert René on April 21. Elections for a commission to draft a new constitution were held July 23–26, the first multiparty elections since the 1977 coup that brought René to power. The 23-member commission was dominated by René's FPPS, which won 58.4% of the vote and 14 seats; the Democratic Party, led by Mancham, won 8 seats and, under the "best losers" system, the Seychelles Party of Wavel Ramkalawan (an Anglican clergyman whose party started as an underground movement in 1991) got one. The proposed constitution was presented to the voters on November 15, but it gained only 53.7% of the vote, short of the 60% needed for approval. The opposition groups and the Roman Catholic Church had called for a "no" vote, claiming that the new constitution would perpetuate one-party rule and failed to protect human rights.

In July, South Africa paid the Seychelles R 8 million

as compensation for the abortive coup attempt of 1981, in which South African mercenaries had taken part.

(GUY ARNOLD)

This article updates the *Micropædia* article SEYCHELLES.

SIERRA LEONE

A republic of West Africa and member of the Commonwealth, Sierra Leone lies on the Atlantic Ocean. Area: 71,740 sq km (27,699 sq mi). Pop. (1992 est.): 4,373,000. Cap.: Freetown. Monetary unit: leone, with (Oct. 5, 1992) a free rate of 493.38 leones to U.S. $1 (838.75 leones = £1 sterling). President to April 30, 1992, Maj. Gen. Joseph Saidu Momoh; chairman of the National Provisional Ruling Council (later the Supreme Council of State) from May 1 and head of state from May 7, Capt. Valentine E.M. Strasser.

A military coup by 30 mutinous soldiers on April 30, 1992, forced Pres. Joseph Momoh to flee to Guinea. The rebels, who were led by Capt. Valentine Strasser, established a National Provisional Ruling Council (NPRC), demanded settlement of back pay and improved conditions, and claimed that the Momoh government had brought the country to "permanent poverty and a deplorable life." On May 1 Strasser was named chairman of the NPRC, and later he was made head of state and minister of defense. The NPRC was made up of 23 members representing all ethnic groups. A Cabinet of 19 was appointed, including 6 civilians and 2 senior members of the previous government. On May 4 the NPRC dissolved the House of Representatives and suspended all political activities.

The new government gave high priority to ending its border war with rebel forces from Liberia while at the same time insisting that it would respect Sierra Leone's obligations to the Organization of African Unity and the Economic Community of West African States, including its involvement in ECOWAS' peacekeeping force in Liberia. On July 14 Strasser announced that the NPRC was to become the Supreme Council of State, while the Cabinet would become the Council of Secretaries of State. At year's end up to 26 persons were reportedly executed for involvement in an abortive coup on December 28.   (GUY ARNOLD)

This article updates the *Macropædia* article WESTERN AFRICA: *Sierra Leone*.

SOMALIA

A republic in the Horn of northeastern Africa, the Somali Democratic Republic, or Somalia, lies on the Gulf of Aden and the Indian Ocean. Area: 637,000 sq km (246,000 sq mi). Pop. (1992 est.): 7,872,000 (including Somali refugees in neighbouring countries estimated to number about one million). Cap.: Mogadishu. Monetary unit: Somali shilling, with (Oct. 5, 1992) a free rate of 2,615 Somali shillings to U.S. $1 (4,446 Somali shillings = £1 sterling). President (interim) in 1992, Ali Mahdi Muhammad; prime minister, Umar Arteh Ghalib.

In what was described as "the worst humanitarian disaster in the world today," drought and vicious interclan warfare and banditry combined in 1992 to produce a famine that threatened 1.5 million people in Somalia with starvation. This led to an enormous exodus of refugees; in September the UN High Commissioner for Refugees estimated the number at more than one million, most of them in Ethiopia, Kenya, Djibouti, and Yemen.

Somalia was effectively divided into separate regions, each dominated by a clan or alliance of clans. The northwest, ruled by the Somali National Movement (SNM) based mainly on the Isaaq clan, failed to gain any international recognition for its secessionist state of "Somaliland." The northeast was dominated by the Somali Salvation Democratic Front (SSDF) based on the Majerteen clan. In the south leaders fought to reassemble and then control the Somali state, while the rank and file fought for land. The United Somali Congress (USC) split into two factions, which fought for control of the capital, Mogadishu. One was headed by interim president Ali Mahdi Muhammad and was based on the Abgal clan; the other, consisting mainly of the Habar Gadir clan, was led by the capable and ambitious Gen. Muhammad Farah Aydid. A UN-sponsored cease-fire agreement reached on February 14 and signed on March 3 led to the cessation of the use of heavy artillery, but random violence continued.

In April the forces of former president Muhammad Siyad Barrah attempted a comeback but were repulsed by Aydid and his allies. Barrah sought refuge in Nigeria, where Pres. Ibrahim Babangida granted him temporary asylum. In June, 10 organizations, including the SNM, SSDF, and Ali Mahdi's USC, met in Bahir Dar, Eth., and agreed on peaceful cooperation. They were not joined, however, by Aydid and his allies, and this signaled a lining up of the various factions into two groups. One consisted of the Abgal-USC, the SSDF, and related groups, including Barrah's clan; the other comprised a Habar Gadir-USC/Somali Patriotic Movement (SPM) alliance with other southern groups, headed by Aydid, which took the name of the Somali National Alliance (SNA). By the end of the year Aydid and the SNA controlled nearly all of the south.

After the UN agencies pulled out of the country in January 1991, humanitarian aid in Somalia was provided by voluntary groups, especially the International Red Cross. But this was inadequate. The principal problems were looting and demands from the various factions to be paid in kind for their protection of the aid. From January the UN, urged by Secretary-General Boutros Boutros-Ghali, attempted to mediate the conflict and to provide aid. On January 23 the Security Council passed a resolution calling for an arms embargo. (However, smuggling, added to the huge amount of weapons already in the country, maintained the supply.) In April the Security Council authorized the dispatch of 50 military observers to monitor the cease-fire.

Boutros-Ghali proposed a plan that on July 27 was adopted by the Security Council; as well as an international food airlift, it entailed sending 500 armed peacekeepers to protect relief workers and providing supplies to the existing four political zones through their four main ports of Berbera, Boosaaso, Mogadishu, and Kismaayo. A resolution on August 28 deployed a UN force of 750 for each zone to protect food shipments. However, strong opposition, especially from General Aydid, held up the deployment of the UN troops. By November, though the initial 500 had reached Mogadishu, they remained inactive.

A U.S. offer of the use of ground troops to safeguard the delivery of food was accepted by the UN on December 3. The first of an expected 28,000 U.S. troops landed in Mogadishu six days later, and by late December some 7,000 U.S. and 2,000 allied forces were in the country. The port and airport of Mogadishu and seven other relief zones had been secured and the delivery of supplies speeded up, but sporadic fighting and looting continued outside the secure areas as well as in Mogadishu itself. Ali Mahdi and Aydid met and agreed to end the fighting, although the extent of their control over the various factions was doubtful. U.S. Pres. George Bush visited Somalia at New Year's. Bush had promised a speedy withdrawal of U.S. troops as soon as the situation was secure enough for UN forces to take over, but at year's end it was unclear when this would be.

(VIRGINIA R. LULING)

This article updates the *Macropædia* article EASTERN AFRICA: *Somalia*.

SOUTH AFRICA
The Republic

South Africa occupies the southern tip of Africa, with the Atlantic Ocean to the west and the Indian Ocean to the east. It includes the 1,124-sq km exclave of Walvis Bay surrounded by Namibia (a future joint administration of Walvis Bay between South Africa and Namibia was announced in August 1992) and partially surrounds the four republics of Bophuthatswana, Ciskei, Transkei, and Venda (whose independence from South Africa is not recognized by the international community). Area: 1,123,226 sq km (433,680 sq mi). Pop. (1992 est.): 32,063,000. (Area and population figures exclude the four republics.) Executive cap., Pretoria; judicial cap., Bloemfontein; legislative cap., Cape Town. Monetary unit: South African rand, with (Oct. 5, 1992) a financial rate of R 4.83 to U.S. $1 (R 8.21 = £1 sterling) and a commercial rate of R 2.84 to U.S. $1 (R 4.82 = £1 sterling). State president in 1992, Frederik W. de Klerk.

The Republic. *Domestic Affairs.* The year 1992 opened on an optimistic note following the Convention for a Democratic South Africa (Codesa) held on Dec. 20–21, 1991, at which 19 major political organizations, including the government and the African National Congress (ANC), committed themselves to negotiating an undivided, democratic, and peaceful South Africa. But for much of the year this commitment was undermined by the failure of Codesa II in mid-May to reach further agreement and by escalating political violence, of which the most publicized incidents were the massacres in Boipatong (June 17) and Bisho (September 7).

By July it was estimated that some 7,000 had died in such violence since Pres. F.W. de Klerk's proposal of a negotiated settlement in February 1990. Police figures claimed 1,181 such deaths in the first six months of 1992, compared with 2,240 in all of 1991. The Human Rights Commission claimed 2,762 dead to the end of September 1992. The commission's assignments of responsibility for the violence became a source of controversy. The South African Institute of Race Relations (SAIRR) accused it of pro-ANC bias, while the SAIRR was in turn accused of bias toward Mangosuthu Gatsha Buthelezi's Inkatha Freedom Party (IFP).

The role of the government in promoting the violence remained controversial. In April police captain Brian Mitchell and four black police officers were found guilty of the murder of 11 and attempted murder of 2 others in a massacre in December 1988 in Natal, where they were assisting the IFP. In July a leading pathologist who had investigated the deaths of people held in jail claimed that 90% were caused by the police. The first government-issued accounts in May of the Goldstone Commission's interim report into the causes of political violence attributed it purely to conflict between the ANC and the IFP, but in November the commission released documentary evidence of "dirty tricks" sanctioned by top members of the military. On December 19, in what amounted to a retreat from previous statements, de Klerk dismissed or suspended 23 officers, including 6 generals, for "illegal or unauthorized activities and malpractices."

On March 17 a whites-only referendum was held to decide whether the reform process should continue. This followed the defeat of the National Party (NP) by the more right-wing Conservative Party (CP) in a white by-election in Potchefstroom in February. In the referendum 68.7% voted yes in a poll of 85.8%, the highest in the country's history. Only in one of 15 regions, the Northern Transvaal, did the no vote have a majority.

The negotiation process and the results of the referendum contributed to shake-ups and realignments in political parties from right to left. In April the CP expelled two of its MPs who were advocating entering Codesa to negotiate

for a small "Volkstaat" (white homeland); one of them later admitted his responsibility for bombing a black school in 1991. In August another five CP MPs resigned to form the Afrikaner Volksunie (AV), committed to negotiating a homeland in the Northern Transvaal.

The NP, for its part, secured control of the Coloured (mixed race) House of Representatives in the tricameral Parliament through the defection of Labour Party (LP) MPs and also made inroads in the (Indian) House of Delegates. In June the NP for the first time won a by-election against the LP among Coloured voters in Kimberley, though with a very low voter turnout. In pursuit of a new nonracial image, de Klerk visited the large Coloured township of Mitchell's Plain in Cape Town in April, though he had to retreat in the face of opposition. Spokesmen at midyear NP provincial congresses nevertheless claimed that the party and its allies could win a majority in one-person, one-vote elections.

Five Democratic Party (DP) MPs were suspended from the party in April for holding meetings with the ANC; soon afterward they joined the ANC as its first MPs. One of these, Jan van Eck, was suspended from Parliament in June for accusing former president P.W. Botha of sanctioning assassinations, but he was readmitted in the October session.

Further allegations surfaced concerning the involvement of Winnie Mandela, wife of ANC leader Nelson Mandela, in corruption and murder. In April Nelson Mandela announced his separation from her, and she resigned as head of the ANC's social welfare department. Though reelected as chairperson of the Witwatersrand ANC Women's League in May, she resigned from all ANC positions in September. In October the ANC published a report admitting to the practice of torture and other atrocities during the 1980s in the Angolan camps of its military wing, Umkhonto We Sizwe (MK).

The breakdown of Codesa II in mid-May revolved around differences between the government and the ANC over procedures for the adoption of a new constitution, in particular the percentages required for approval of measures by a constitution-making body. Other unresolved questions were a demand by the IFP for separate representation at Codesa for the Zulu monarchy and KwaZulu government and insistence by the South African and Bophuthatswana governments that reincorporation of the independent homelands would not be automatic.

On May 31 an ANC policy conference adopted a comprehensive document on economic and social policy, based on a mixed economy, and also endorsed a program of mass action for an end to violence and Bantustan repression and in favour of an interim government and a democratically elected sovereign constituent assembly. This campaign, led by the tripartite alliance of the ANC, Congress of South African Trade Unions (COSATU), and South African Communist Party (SACP), was initiated in marches and occupations of government buildings in June and July and reached its peak in a general strike of three million–four million on August 3–4. The campaign coincided with an upturn in industrial strikes, in which those of radio and television workers, Toyota workers, and health workers alone involved the loss of 750,000 workdays. In August 100,000 metal and engineering workers went on strike for four weeks in the second largest wage strike in the country's history.

The momentum of mass action was fueled by the massacre of at least 42 people, including women and children, by pro-Inkatha hostel dwellers in Boipatong township in the Vaal Triangle on June 17, the day following the 16th commemoration of the 1976 Soweto massacre. On Soweto Day itself de Klerk had addressed the KwaZulu Legislative Assembly to provide assurances that he would defend

African National Congress members flee machine-gun fire from soldiers in Ciskei, one of the black republics in South Africa. The demonstrators marched on the capital on September 7 to protest military rule in the republic.
GREG MARINOVITCH—SYGMA

federalism and the role of chiefs in a new constitution. Following this massacre the ANC suspended bilateral talks with the government and participation in Codesa until the government ended what it termed its "campaign of terror" and committed itself to negotiations for real democracy.

During July and August and in the context of UN concern (*see* below), the government made a number of concessions, including the disbandment of notorious units in the South African Defence Force, the retirement of a number of police generals, and the appointment (later in the year) of the first black police generals. At the same time, government and big business denounced the mass action campaign, while the government appeared to be pressing forward toward constitutional agreement with those Codesa parties supporting its federalist proposals, particularly the Bophuthatswana, Ciskei, and KwaZulu governments.

In August a match against the All Blacks marked the reentry of Springboks to international rugby. The waving of the South African flag and singing of the anthem "Die Stem" by the white crowd, however, contrary to prior agreements, caused an outcry. More serious was the massacre in Bisho on September 7, with at least 24 killed and 198 injured by units of the Ciskei Defence Force (*see* below). This took place during a march from South Africa to the Ciskei capital, part of a targeting by the mass action campaign of the repressive homeland governments of Ciskei, Bophuthatswana, and KwaZulu, with the aim of establishing rights of free political activity or (in the eyes of many) overthrowing those regimes. The massacre led to accusations and counteraccusations by the Ciskei government, the ANC, and the South African government. The Goldstone Commission reported that, despite ANC violations of agreements concerning the march, there was no justification for the opening of fire by the Ciskei Defence Force.

Rapprochement between the government and the ANC was resumed in a meeting between de Klerk and Nelson Mandela on September 26, the groundwork for which was believed to have been prepared by UN mediation, including that of special envoy Cyrus Vance. This meeting agreed on the need for a democratically elected constitution-making body acting as an interim parliament under an interim constitution, with a government of national unity. It also agreed that the constitution-making body should be bound by prin-

ciples decided in advance. This idea was also contained in a draft "Transition to Democracy Act" published by the ANC in September. Measures were agreed on for preventing political violence, including bans on carrying dangerous weapons in public. Additional political prisoners were released, most notably Barend Strydom of the ultraright and Robert McBride, an MK activist who had bombed a white Durban bar frequented by police.

Buthelezi immediately declared he was breaking off negotiations with the government in protest against the bilateral deals between it and the ANC. Inkatha organized mass marches in Johannesburg and Durban in October, and the civil war in Natal escalated. Equally controversial was the government's decision to interpret the September 26 agreement as endorsing a general amnesty for all those, including state personnel, who had violated the law for political reasons in the past.

In a keynote speech to a special session of Parliament in October, de Klerk stated that the principles that must bind a constitution-making body included "strong and entrenched regional government" and "power-sharing at the level of the executive." He ruled out so-called sunset clauses, which provided only for an interim period of "power sharing." What the NP meant by "strong regional government" had been spelled out at a conference of pro-federalists in September: a national government responsible only for defense, foreign affairs, and constitutional planning, with regional governments having responsibility for all other matters, including taxation. A form of federalism was also the policy of the DP and was endorsed by the South African Congress of Business at its conference in October. In the same month, a conference was held by the KwaZulu, Ciskei, and Bophuthatswana governments with the CP and AV to explore matters of common concern. The government planned further bilateral talks with the ANC, Inkatha, and other parties during the remainder of the year. Optimistic observers believed that it would be possible to reconvene a Codesa-like multilateral gathering early in 1993, including also such previous nonparticipants as the Pan-Africanist Congress (PAC), with which the government had been having talks since August, the AV, and possibly the CP.

Foreign Affairs. The resumption of normalized relations between South Africa and other countries continued during the year. Japan restored full diplomatic relations in January. Germany and Denmark lifted most sanctions in March, though the Dutch prime minister and foreign minister postponed a visit. The European Communities ended its oil embargo and sporting and cultural sanctions in April. The only EC sanctions remaining were those on the export of arms-related equipment and other military and nuclear cooperation measures.

The breakdown of negotiations and escalation of political violence led to a debate on South Africa in the UN Security Council in July, at which, among others, Foreign Minister Pik Botha, Nelson Mandela, and Gatsha Buthelezi spoke. Resolution 765 called for an end to the violence, the resumption of negotiations, and a measure of UN involvement in achieving this, the first outcome of which was the appointment of U.S. diplomat Cyrus Vance as special envoy. It was also decided to send UN observers to monitor the conduct of police and participants during mass demonstrations. The UN secretary-general and a high-level EC delegation visited the country during the year.

Economy. The economic downswing that began in March 1989 continued, making this South Africa's longest recession since 1904–08. Gross domestic product (GDP) fell by 0.6% in 1991 (the biggest drop since 1985) and, aggravated by drought, by an annualized 2.5% in the first six months of 1992 and faster in the third quarter. Decline in gross fixed domestic investment continued, by 19% from the end of 1989 to the second quarter of 1992. In 1991 manufacturing investment fell by 11%.

There were severe repercussions on employment, with far sharper cuts than in previous recessions. In November 1992 it was estimated that 250,000 jobs had been lost since September 1989, of which 100,000 were in mining.

Continued inflation, together with the need to sustain surpluses on the current account of the balance of payments (to pay off foreign debt and compensate for capital outflows), caused tight fiscal policies to be retained. Inflation, at a peak annualized rate of 16.8% in October 1991, had dropped to 13.5% in September 1992. But food-price inflation (averaging 28.3% in 1991) was at a record level of 30.4% in August. At the start of the year the bank rate was 17%, but two cuts of 1% each were made in March and June.

Bophuthatswana

The republic of Bophuthatswana consists of seven discontinuous, landlocked geographic units, entirely surrounded by South Africa except for one unit that borders Botswana on the northwest. Area: 44,000 sq km (16,988 sq mi). Pop. (1992 est.): 2,056,000. Cap.: Mmabatho. Monetary unit: South African rand. President in 1992, Lucas Mangope.

Ciskei

Bordering the Indian Ocean in the south, Ciskei is surrounded on land by South Africa. Area: 7,760 sq km (2,996 sq mi). Pop. (1992 est.): 854,000. Cap.: Bisho. Monetary unit: South African rand. Chairman of the Military Committee and of the Council of State in 1992, Brig. Joshua Oupa Gqozo.

Transkei

Bordering the Indian Ocean and surrounded on land by South Africa, Transkei comprises three discontinuous geographic units, two of which are landlocked and one of which borders Lesotho. Area: 43,653 sq km (16,855 sq mi). Pop. (1992 est.): 3,303,000. Cap.: Umtata. Monetary unit: South African rand. Head of the Military Council in 1992, Maj. Gen. Bantu Holomisa.

Venda

The landlocked republic of Venda is located in extreme northeastern South Africa. Area: 7,176 sq km (2,771 sq mi). Pop. (1992 est.): 567,000. Cap.: Thohoyandou. Monetary unit: South African rand. Head of state in 1992, Col. Gabriel Ramushwana.

The Homelands. The question of their place in a future South Africa dominated the year for the homelands. There were sharp divergences between the pro-ANC policies of the Transkei government and the increasingly hostile anti-ANC stance taken by the governments of Ciskei and Bophuthatswana. Venda was relatively quiet.

The government of Ciskei, headed by Brig. Joshua Oupa Gqozo, became a focus for regional mass action by the ANC early in the year. On March 1 Gqozo claimed that the ANC had a plan to overthrow him. During that month, however, the Ciskei government signed the National Peace Accord and reached agreement with the ANC on the defusing of tensions. Then, with the launching of the national mass action campaign by the ANC, a march from the eastern Cape Province to the Ciskei capital, Bisho, took place on August 8.

On September 7 another march took place in an atmosphere of high tension. The eventual agreement was that the march could proceed to a sports stadium in Bisho but not any farther. However, some marchers attempted to proceed farther through a gap in fencing arrangements, and the Ciskei Defence Force opened fire on the march as a whole. Gqozo claimed that the troops had first been fired on by marchers. The ANC denied this and blamed the South African government for the massacre. The government and the DP blamed the ANC's mass action campaign. The Ciskei government appointed a commission of inquiry headed by Chief Justice B. de V. Pickard.

Bophuthatswana Pres. Lucas Mangope was, like Gqozo, an uncompromising opponent of the ANC, declaring his wish to preserve the "independence" of his territory. His government refused to release the report of the Handler Commission investigating corruption in the area. An amendment to the Internal Security Act during the year prohibited nonregistered political organizations from holding meetings and, together with a higher level of political arrests than in South Africa, was interpreted as repression of the ANC. After student demonstrations the University of Bophuthatswana campus was closed indefinitely in October.

In September 3,000 Transkei Defence Force troops detained 23 senior officers in a controversy over wages and conditions in the armed forces. Maj. Gen. Bantu Holomisa intervened personally to sort out the situation.

(MARTIN LEGASSICK)

This article updates the *Macropædia* article SOUTHERN AFRICA: *South Africa*.

SUDAN, THE

A republic of North Africa, The Sudan has a coastline on the Red Sea. Area: 2,503,890 sq km (966,757 sq mi). Pop. (1992 est.): 29,971,000. Cap.: Khartoum. Monetary unit: Sudanese pound, with (Oct. 5, 1992) a free rate of LSd 99.82 to U.S. $1 (LSd 169.70 = £1 sterling), and the Sudanese dinar (currency circulated alongside the Sudanese pound from May 18), with a free rate of 9.98 dinars to U.S. $1 (16.97 dinars = £1 sterling). President of the Revolutionary Command Council for National Salvation and prime minister in 1992, Lieut. Gen. Omar Hassan Ahmad al-Bashir.

When representatives of the government and of the two factions of the Sudanese People's Liberation Army (SPLA) met to hold discussions in Abuja, Nigeria, from late May

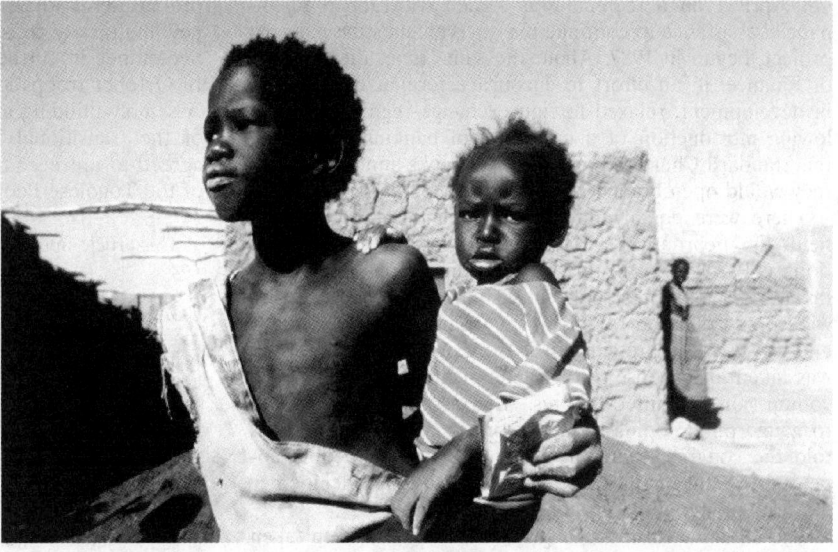

A Sudanese boy carries his younger brother in a southern refugee camp. Fighting between the Islamic government of The Sudan and the largely Christian and animist rebels of the south created a huge number of refugees, many of them children.

MIKE GOLDWATER—NETWORK/MATRIX

to early June 1992, there was a glimmer of hope that there might be an end to the hostilities that had torn the country apart. The deep divisions between them were soon revealed, however. In March the government, backed by troops sent from Iran, had launched an offensive against the SPLA in southern Sudan that met with considerable success, although it did not break the rebel siege of Juba. Against this background, government spokesmen in Abuja could afford to appear intransigent, although it was they who accused the rebels of inflexibility, obstinacy, and rigidity. In a vaguely worded statement of general principles, they reaffirmed the government's commitment to a united Sudan with equal treatment for all citizens of the country. It was prepared, they said, to recognize the nation's plural society and to guarantee freedom of belief and religious observance. All this was acceptable to John Garang's section of the SPLA, but there remained the vital question as to whether the Shari'ah (Islamic law) would form the basis of the country's legal system. No agreement could be reached if the answer, as seemed certain, was in the affirmative. Equally adamant were the representatives of Riek Machar's breakaway rebel group, who ruled out any accommodation with the government, insisting on the right of southern Sudan to determine its own political destiny.

Consequently, the war continued, with seven million people suffering as a result of food shortages and three million displaced persons seeking refuge wherever they could. Relations with both Iran and Iraq were strengthened, and the government criticized the Western attempt to impose a "no-fly" zone in southern Iraq, underlining its commitment to the Arab and Islamic cause. (KENNETH INGHAM)

SWAZILAND

Swaziland is a landlocked monarchy of southern Africa and a member of the Commonwealth. Area: 17,364 sq km (6,704 sq mi). Pop. (1992 est.): 826,000. Administrative cap., Mbabane; royal and legislative cap., Lobamba. Monetary unit: lilangeni (plural: emalangeni), at par with the South African rand, with (Oct. 5, 1992) a free rate of 2.84 emalangeni to U.S. $1 (4.82 emalangeni = £1 sterling). King, Mswati III; prime minister in 1992, Obed Dlamini.

As 1992 opened, there were few real signs that Swaziland was prepared to do more than make gestures toward greater democratization of its political system. King Mswati III called on exiles (mainly political opponents of the regime)

to return home to help work out a new political direction for the country. Prime Minister Obed Dlamini pledged that Swaziland would not lag behind other nations in light of the political changes taking place in Africa. However, Swaziland's record on human rights came under scrutiny following publication of the 1991 UN Development Program's Human Rights Index and reports of the U.S. Senate and House Foreign Relations committees, all of which found much to criticize. In October the king dissolved Parliament and announced plans for a new constitution and multiparty elections, to be held in 1993.

Although the economy was doing reasonably well, it faced three main problems: population growth, rising unemployment, and low agricultural productivity. Swaziland was host to large numbers of Mozambican refugees, and they were coming to be seen as easy targets to blame for the country's rising crime rate. (GUY ARNOLD)

This article updates the *Macropædia* article SOUTHERN AFRICA: *Swaziland*.

TANZANIA

The republic of Tanzania, a member of the Commonwealth, consists of Tanganyika, on the east coast of Africa, and Zanzibar, just off the coast in the Indian Ocean, which includes Zanzibar Island, Pemba Island, and small islets. Area: 942,799 sq km (364,017 sq mi). Pop. (1992 est.): 25,809,000. Cap.: government in process of being transferred from Dar es Salaam to Dodoma. Monetary unit: Tanzania shilling, with (Oct. 5, 1992) a free rate of 319.44 shillings to U.S. $1 (543.04 shillings = £1 sterling). President in 1992, Ali Hassan Mwinyi; prime minister, John Malecela.

The year 1992 began with the prospect of an agreement with Indonesia to exploit the natural gas deposits found on the island of Songo in the 1970s but undeveloped owing to lack of funds. In February a meeting of foreign ministers of Tanzania, Uganda, and Kenya in Nairobi, Kenya, agreed to revive regional cooperation. Their decision was confirmed with the signing of an agreement on February 15 by representatives of the three countries. This was followed in April by a meeting of Tanzanian and Ugandan Energy Ministry officials, who resolved to strengthen relations in the energy sector. Their immediate concern was to review the progress being made in providing the Kagera region in the west with hydroelectric power from Masaka in Uganda and to look at the problem of compensation for people whose property was destroyed or damaged by the installation of power lines.

On April 1 an agreement was signed with Japan for financial assistance to continue the government's antimalarial project, begun in 1987. About the same time, the Ministry of Finance, in an effort to encourage foreign involvement in development, relaxed foreign exchange regulations. Following introduction of a new code of banking behaviour, the Standard Chartered and Barclays banks announced that they would open branches in Tanzania.

There were equally interesting stirrings in the political field. On February 18 a special congress of the Revolutionary Party of Tanzania (CCM) unanimously voted in favour of a multiparty political system. There had been no widespread demand for pluralism from within the country and no sustained pressure for it from outside. The decision was taken in response to the recommendations of a special commission appointed by Pres. Ali Hassan Mwinyi in 1991 to gauge public opinion on constitutional matters. Mwinyi told the congress that only about 20% of the people appeared to want a multiparty system but that in a democracy minority opinions should not be ignored.

The initiative for this change of direction had been taken in 1990 by former president Julius Nyerere, who, some thought, was worried lest, unchallenged, the CCM might stray too far from the socialist path. However, the underlying factor that swayed the congress was the fear of Zanzibari separatist movements. Nyerere himself argued during the debate that any new party must be both socialist and national, while Pres. Salmin Amour of Zanzibar declared that any multiparty formula that permitted the island to go its own way would be unacceptable. The congress supported this view and reinforced the ruling against Zanzibari separatism by insisting that political parties should be not only national but secular, thereby checking separatist movements operating under the guise of religious groups. These decisions were endorsed by the parliament and by the Zanzibari authorities. There was pressure for new elections to be held before the end of the year, but the CCM wanted the present parliament to remain in office until the end of its term in 1995.　(KENNETH INGHAM)

This article updates the *Macropædia* article EASTERN AFRICA: *Tanzania*.

TOGO

A republic of West Africa, Togo is situated on the Bight of Benin. Area: 56,785 sq km (21,925 sq mi). Pop. (1992 est.): 3,701,000. Cap.: Lomé. Monetary unit: CFA franc, with (Oct. 5, 1992) a par value of CFAF 50 to the French franc and a free rate of CFAF 238.75 to U.S. $1 (CFAF 405.88 = £1 sterling). President in 1992, Gnassingbe Eyadema; prime minister, Joseph Kokou Koffigoh.

The democratization process in Togo was under siege throughout 1992. Local and municipal elections scheduled for May were postponed indefinitely. The army made determined efforts to restore the powers that were stripped from Pres. Gnassingbe Eyadema during the 1991 national conference. In May assassins shot and seriously wounded probable presidential candidate Gilchrist Olympio and killed 10 others. Massive demonstrations erupted, and protesters called for the resignation of both President Eyadema and Prime Minister Joseph Koffigoh. On July 23 opposition leader Tavio Amorin was wounded in an ambush. When his death was announced on July 30, a huge strike shut down Lomé.

In an apparent attempt to disrupt the forthcoming constitutional referendum, armed raiders looted the National Centre for Studies and Data Processing on August 8. Koffigoh named a new Cabinet on September 14, 24 hours after

pro-Eyadema soldiers seized the radio station. Although the new multiparty constitution was overwhelmingly ratified on September 25, further elections were postponed indefinitely. In October troops loyal to Eyadema occupied the National Assembly building and held the chairman and 38 members of the transitional legislature hostage until the chairman agreed to unfreeze the assets of Eyadema's party, the Rally of the Togolese People, dissolved in 1991.

(NANCY ELLEN LAWLER)

This article updates the *Macropædia* article WESTERN AFRICA: *Togo*.

UGANDA

A landlocked republic and member of the Commonwealth, Uganda is located in eastern Africa. Area: 241,040 sq km (93,070 sq mi), including 44,000 sq km of inland water. Pop. (1992 est.): 17,194,000. Cap.: Kampala. Monetary unit: Uganda shilling, with (Oct. 5, 1992) a priority rate of 1,192 shillings to U.S. $1 (2,026 shillings = £1 sterling). President in 1992, Yoweri Museveni; prime minister, George Cosmas Adyebo.

On March 28, 1992, Pres. Yoweri Museveni announced a number of changes in the arrangement of government departments. Most important was the merging of the Finance and Economic Planning ministries, aimed at avoiding the mistakes that had dogged all previous efforts to implement the national recovery plan. The former planning minister, Joshua Mayanja-Nkangi, was to head the new, enlarged ministry. Three months later, on June 30, the minister introduced his budget for the forthcoming year. Prominent among his aims were a growth rate in gross domestic product of at least 5% and a reduction in the rate of inflation to 15% by June 1993. On the same day, the minister of public service and Cabinet affairs, Sam Sebagereka, said that, as part of the retrenchment program in the public sector, 4,832 civil servants would be laid off by July 1, 1992, and another 1,507 who had reached the age of retirement would be asked to retire immediately. The army was also reducing its personnel. Earlier in the year, the Bank of Uganda had increased interest rates, while maximum lending rates were raised from 38 to 40% for development projects and from 42 to 44% for commercial borrowers.

In the north, where opposition to the government had been strongest, a reconstruction program was launched by the president on July 4. The program, which was funded by the World Bank and a number of other donors and aid agencies, would cost $93.6 million and was aimed in the first instance at repairing roads and improving the supply of electricity to the region. In a second phase, the population of the area would be encouraged to increase production so as to take full advantage of the new infrastructure and help to repay its cost. A number of other countries and the Arab Bank for Economic Development in Africa also offered financial or technical assistance. Donor agencies in Paris promised $830 million for the 1992–93 financial year while at the same time calling for improvements in macroeconomic management.

Bearing in mind the extent to which the destruction of the forests had contributed to desiccation, erosion, and drought in many parts of the continent, a national tree-planting campaign was launched on April 7. President Museveni called on every Ugandan to plant trees and urged the Ministry of Water, Energy, and Environment Protection to devise alternative sources of fuel.

In the diplomatic field, the signing of a security agreement with Rwanda on August 8 brought hopes of an end to the border clashes and disputes that had strained relations between the two countries for several years. A meeting of the foreign ministers of Uganda, Kenya, and Tanzania in February laid the foundations for the revival of some of the joint activities formerly carried out by the East African Community. In July, Museveni visited Nigeria and had discussions with Pres. Ibrahim Babangida; a joint communiqué was issued expressing the two presidents' determination to strengthen still further the links between their two countries.

At home Museveni still set his face firmly against the revival of political parties, which he called a divisive element at a time when the country needed a period of rehabilitation and convalescence. His views were reinforced by a resolution of the National Resistance Council stating that party activities should remain suspended until completion of the ongoing constitution-making process.

(KENNETH INGHAM)

This article updates the *Macropædia* article EASTERN AFRICA: *Uganda*.

ZAIRE

The republic of Zaire is located in central Africa with a short coastline on the Atlantic Ocean. Area: 2,345,095 sq km (905,446 sq mi). Pop. (1992 est.): 41,151,000. Cap.: Kinshasa. Monetary unit: zaïre, with (Oct. 5, 1992) a free rate of 962,941 zaïres to U.S. $1 (1,637,000 zaïres = £1 sterling). President in 1992, Mobutu Sese Seko; first state commissioners (prime ministers), Nguza Karl-I-Bond and, from August 15, Etienne Tshisekedi.

The meeting of the national conference studying constitutional change in Zaire was suspended on Jan. 19, 1992, by Prime Minister Nguza Karl-I-Bond, who claimed that the opposition parties were overrepresented. A small group of soldiers demanding that the conference be reconvened and calling for the resignation of Pres. Mobutu Sese Seko and the prime minister briefly seized the radio station in Kinshasa on January 23, but their revolt was put down by troops loyal to the president. The 12 members of the European Communities had already suspended aid in protest against Nguza's action, and France responded to the mutiny by urging the resumption of the national conference as the only way to restore calm.

On February 16 young Roman Catholic clergymen took the lead in organizing what was intended to be a peaceful protest after the morning service. Senior clergy did not support the protest, and the demonstration had been banned by the government the previous day. When the protest went ahead, led by priests and opposition politicians and calling for the immediate resumption of the national conference, members of the security forces opened fire on the marchers and killed a number of them. Joseph Ileo, leader of the opposition Christian Social Democratic Party, was among those injured. Several foreign governments, notably France, Belgium, and the U.S., condemned the government's action and stressed once more the need to reconvene the national conference. Nguza expressed regret for the killings— the government said there had been 16 or 17, although opposition spokesmen claimed that the number was much greater—but pointed out that the march had been illegal. There was further embarrassment for the government, however, when the UN Human Rights Commission, which had been carrying out its own inquiry into the killing of students in Lubumbashi in May 1990, reported that the death toll in that conflict had been between 12 and 14. This was considerably fewer than the 100 claimed by Amnesty International and other organizations but significantly more than the one casualty acknowledged by the government. Undeterred by criticism, however, security forces disrupted a series of pro-conference marches organized by church groups on March 1.

The International Monetary Fund expressed concern about the decline in the country's debt repayments while noting that other creditors had received better treatment. Additional measures to recover overdue payments were threatened if Zaire did not cooperate more actively. In the U.S. warning was given that if Zaire did not pay $400,000 in rent due for offices occupied by its mission to the UN, the diplomats would be evicted not only from the premises but from the country.

On April 6 the national conference resumed its deliberations after discussions between Mobutu, Nguza, and the conference chairman designate, Archbishop Laurent Monsengwo Pasinya. On the previous day the leaders of the opposition Sacred Union coalition had refused to meet Mobutu at Mbandaka, 1,300 km (800 mi) northeast of Kinshasa, claiming that it was unsafe for them to make the journey.

On April 17 the conference declared itself sovereign. Its agenda included drafting a new constitution to be submitted to a referendum, organizing a period of transition leading up to elections, setting up new executive bodies to put its decisions into effect, and defining a new role for the armed forces. On April 20 Monsengwo was elected head of the conference bureau. In June he said that a transitional government should be established by the end of July, by which time a plan for a new constitution and an electoral calendar would be ready. He added that most speakers at the conference agreed that Mobutu should stay in office during the transitional period but only if he were to rule and not govern. Having set up a number of commissions to make recommendations on different subjects, the plenary session of the conference was suspended for three weeks, and during that period, on June 30, Mobutu marked the 32nd anniversary of Zaire's independence by broadcasting a call to his fellow countrymen to bring back their financial assets from overseas. Coming from one who was believed to have millions of dollars invested in European banks and in property in several European countries, this was considered by many to be an ironic appeal.

On July 23 Monsengwo announced that Mobutu had agreed to the setting up of a High Council of the Republic to oversee the implementation of the conference's decisions and had conceded that the conference might elect a prime minister. Nguza, however, rejected the conference's proposal to change the country's name back to Congo. Mobutu, apparently still accommodating, pledged cooperation with Etienne Tshisekedi, who was elected prime minister by the conference in mid-August, and Tshisekedi in turn carefully avoided naming hard-line opponents of the president when he appointed his Cabinet. This did not mean an end to the struggle. Four days after Tshisekedi's election there were violent ethnic confrontations in Shaba (formerly Katanga) province between supporters of Tshisekedi and Nguza in which at least five people were reported to have been killed. Nguza had a strong following in Shaba, where the people were hostile to their neighbours in Kasai, Tshisekedi's home province. Moreover, on August 31 Mobutu appointed Nguza minister of state to the presidency, a move that was unpopular with the opposition parties. The national conference ended December 6, having elected Monsengwo as president of the High Council of the Republic. On December 11 Mobutu announced that he was suspending the council, and the following day troops briefly occupied the office of the prime minister. Mobutu's opponents said his action was illegal and that they would ignore it.

(KENNETH INGHAM)

This article updates the *Macropædia* article CENTRAL AFRICA: *Zaire*.

ZAMBIA

A landlocked republic and member of the Commonwealth, Zambia is in eastern Africa. Area: 752,614 sq km (290,586 sq mi). Pop. (1992 est.): 8,303,000. Cap.: Lusaka. Monetary unit: kwacha, with (Oct. 5, 1992) a free rate of 196.65 kwacha to U.S. $1 (334.31 kwacha = £1 sterling). President in 1992, Frederick Chiluba.

On Jan. 6, 1992, the United National Independence Party (UNIP) announced that it had accepted Kenneth Kaunda's resignation as party leader. He had said two weeks earlier that he wished to devote himself to international problems. Seven months later, following a reversal in May, Kaunda again said that he would resign, and Kebby Musokotwane was elected president at an extraordinary party congress in October. Kaunda had not had an easy time since his party's election defeat, often being met with jeers and hostility when making a public appearance.

Pres. Frederick Chiluba (*see* BIOGRAPHIES), by contrast, remained a popular leader, although criticism was leveled at some of his ministers. His policies, determined largely by the need to reestablish Zambia's credibility in the eyes of potential aid donors, aroused protest in some areas because of the economic pressures they imposed on employees in the public sector as well as on agricultural workers. The pace was set by both students and staff of the University of Zambia, the former demanding increases in their grants and the latter protesting against what they regarded as wholly inadequate salary increases. The discontent was fueled by rocketing inflation, which had stood at 400% when the new government took office. Chiluba's problems were exacerbated by a drought that led to a serious shortage in the supply of corn (maize), the principal food crop.

Prompt action on all fronts put an end to the threat of famine but did not reduce the general hardship that the people were forced to endure, although Zambia's position as a recipient of aid improved markedly. An arrangement whereby three million bags of corn were purchased from the U.S. provided assurance that there would be no acute shortage of food, although this position was temporarily threatened when railway workers went on strike in March after rejecting pay increases of 100%. The devaluation of the kwacha by 30% in January resulted in a sharp increase in prices for many commodities, and the raising of the bank rate to 47% made borrowing difficult. But these stiff measures helped to convince external observers that the government was getting a grip on the economy and, as a result, offers of assistance began to pour in. Following negotiations in March with the World Bank in Paris, Western donors pledged $400 million in aid, thereby marking the end of Zambia's suspension as a recipient of aid after it had reneged on its debt payments in 1991. (KENNETH INGHAM)

This article updates the *Macropædia* article SOUTHERN AFRICA: *Zambia.*

ZIMBABWE

A republic and member of the Commonwealth, Zimbabwe is a landlocked state in eastern Africa. Area: 390,759 sq km (150,873 sq mi). Pop. (1992 est.): 9,871,000. Cap.: Harare. Monetary unit: Zimbabwe dollar, with (Oct. 5, 1992) a free rate of Z$5.08 to U.S. $1 (Z$8.63 = £1 sterling). President in 1992, Robert Mugabe.

The prolonged drought that affected many countries in southern Africa created serious problems for Zimbabwe. Corn (maize), the nation's staple food, of which there was normally a considerable surplus for export, was in short supply. The shortage was only partly due to the drought, however. In the expectation of another good harvest and ignoring warnings from experts that this was a wildly inaccurate forecast, it was decided in 1991 to sell off at low prices the country's ample reserves in order to save on storage costs. This error in judgment had a marked effect on the popularity of the government, and criticism mounted when the need to buy corn from overseas imposed a heavy strain on other parts of the economy. White commercial farmers were angered by Pres. Robert Mugabe's claim that they were hoarding corn to feed their workers and their cattle. Earlier the government had given way after widespread international protest and discussions between Mugabe and Lewis Preston, president of the World Bank, and had amended the Land Acquisition Act (passed by Parliament on March 19) to allow for compensation for land acquired compulsorily from white farmers and to permit the courts to vary the government's assessment of the value of confiscated land if it were deemed to be unfair.

The corn shortage brought about another change when Vice Pres. Joshua Nkomo, who had been appointed acting head of state in Mugabe's absence on holiday in April, authorized the transport minister, Denis Norman, to meet his opposite number in South Africa to try to sort out

LOUISE GUBB—JB PICTURES

Carcasses of animals litter barren fields in Zimbabwe. It was estimated that Zimbabwe lost half of its cattle from starvation as parts of southern Africa suffered from severe drought.

the delays in transporting corn imported via South Africa. Since independence Mugabe had forbidden his ministers to have any contact with the South African government. In June Norman signed an accord in Pretoria, South Africa, to facilitate drought relief in Zimbabwe, the first formal agreement between the two countries since Mugabe came to power in 1980.

Corn was not the only victim of the drought. The output of sugar was reduced to less than a quarter of what had been anticipated, and the shortfall in the coffee crop was almost equally severe. Overall, agricultural production was expected to fall 35% according to the predictions of John Nkomo, minister of labour, manpower planning, and social welfare. The gross domestic product for 1992–93 was at first expected to decline by about 10%, but this figure was doubled by later estimates; such a fall was expected to cause thousands to lose their jobs.

Some of the most remote rural areas were initially worst hit by shortages, but by August Bulawayo, the country's second largest city, was suffering acutely from a shortage of water. Industry was especially badly hit when, after an earlier agreement to import electricity from Zambia and Zaire to avoid power cuts, continuing water shortages made it necessary in September—as a temporary measure, it was hoped—to reduce supplies of electricity; this increased still further the threat of unemployment.

The cancellation of a £211 million order for Russian MiG-29 aircraft brought some relief to the economy. The reason given for the cancellation was the reduction in tension between Zimbabwe and South Africa. Also, in spite of a ruling by the Convention on International Trade in Endangered Species, it was decided to sell the country's ivory stock, amounting to some 25,000 metric tons.

Dissatisfaction with the government induced a number of lawyers, former judges, economists, and businessmen to form the Forum for Democratic Reform in May. None of those involved had played a prominent role in the country's politics, and they all dissociated themselves from the parties formed recently by politicians of the preindependence era, who now lacked credibility. They stressed, however, that the forum was not itself a political party, but they hoped that, by opening up the debate on the country's political and economic future, they would encourage the formation of political parties with coherent programs.

In two or three areas there was some progress on the economic front. Early in the year leading businessmen from Zimbabwe and South Africa signed an agreement aimed at reducing obstacles to trade and improving business links between the two countries. A month later, in February, the Arab Bank for Economic Development in Africa granted a loan of $8,820,000 in support of an energy-production project, and in April an agreement was signed with Canada that was designed to attract Canadian investment in manufacturing and mining. There was a significant increase, too, in the number of tourists visiting Zimbabwe, which was threatening to challenge Kenya as African's leading country in that area.

President Mugabe suffered a great loss with the death of his wife, Sally, in January. A Ghanaian, she had supported her husband vigorously through the years of struggle for majority rule in Zimbabwe, although during that time they spent only 6 of their 19 married years together. After independence she was not always readily accepted as first lady by some members of her adopted country because of her foreign origin, but she played her role with warmth and graciousness. (KENNETH INGHAM)

This article updates the *Macropædia* article SOUTHERN AFRICA: *Zimbabwe*.

Middle East and North Africa

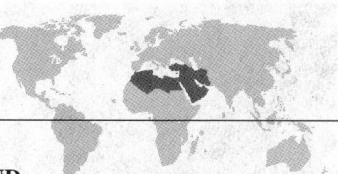

MIDDLE EASTERN AND NORTH AFRICAN AFFAIRS

After a year of sporadic but hopeful progress in the U.S.-backed Arab-Israeli talks, the Middle East peace process was put on hold at the end of 1992 by the expulsion from Israel of some 415 Muslim fundamentalists. Refused admission by Lebanon, the men ended the year camped in tents in the frigid mountains of Israeli-controlled southern Lebanon, their situation threatening to become a worldwide public-relations disaster for Prime Minister Yitzhak Rabin's six-month-old Israeli government. Prior to the expulsion crisis, some gains for peace had been made, although the defeat of Pres. George Bush in the U.S. election in November was generally viewed as a setback for the Arabs. Meanwhile, Arab unity remained a distant dream as negotiations between Egypt, Syria, and the six conservative Arab states belonging to the Gulf Cooperation Council (GCC) faltered.

The expulsion row had escalated quickly. The deportees were allegedly members of the fundamentalist movements Hamas and Islamic Jihad but included distinguished academics and doctors. Hamas was in many ways Israel's own creation. In 1976, when other Palestinian political organizations in the occupied territories were banned, Shin Bet, Israel's domestic intelligence service, issued a permit to Sheikh Ahmed Yassin, a 56-year-old religious leader paralyzed from the neck down, to found a nonmilitant Islamic group. The Israelis saw Yassin as a counterbalance to the more popular Palestine Liberation Organization (PLO); instead they created a new guerrilla group in the fertile breeding grounds of the Palestinian refugee camps in the occupied territories.

Much of Hamas' funding and military training came from Iran, but after 1991 Saudi Arabia also provided support, following its abandonment of the PLO over the latter's backing for Iraq in the Iraq-Kuwait war. Hamas led and dominated the Arab resistance in the occupied territories during 1992. In a 10-day period in December, Hamas murdered four Israeli soldiers in ambushes in Gaza and Hebron. The government retaliated with mass arrests and curfews and finally sealed off the occupied territories, but it failed to find any gunmen. Hamas then changed its tactics by seizing a hostage, part-time border policeman Nissim Toledano, whose body was dumped on the Jericho road on December 16 when the Israelis missed a deadline for the release of Hamas' leader, serving a life sentence for the murder of four collaborators. The Israeli response was to round up suspected fundamentalist sympathizers, and on December 17 each man was given $50 worth of Lebanese currency, a thin coat, and a blanket and taken, blindfolded and handcuffed, to a frosty hillside between an Israeli-controlled "security zone" in southern Lebanon and the Lebanese border. Lebanon had previously admitted a few deportees from Israel, but in this case Beirut ordered its army to block entry.

The following day Israeli troops shot dead six Palestinians, including a young child, as riots broke out in the occupied territories. Rabin's centre-left government ignored a UN Security Council demand that it let the deported Palestinians back, while the Israeli Supreme Court upheld the government's actions (which were under fire from, among others, the left-wing Meretz Party). Rabin signaled renewed

Israeli Prime Minister Yitzhak Rabin (left) meets with Egyptian Pres. Hosni Mubarak in Cairo in July. It was the first meeting between Israeli and Egyptian leaders in six years.
REUTERS/BETTMANN

interest in links with hard-line Israeli parties that opposed concessions in the peace process. Arab foreign ministers, meeting on December 24, condemned the expulsions but stopped short of declaring that the peace process was finished. At year's end both Israel and Lebanon were denying relief groups access to the deportees, although the men were reportedly receiving some food and other assistance from local villagers.

Middle East Peace. Rabin's electoral victory on June 23 had aroused expectations in the Arab world of an acceleration of the peace process, though these were tempered by knowledge of the new prime minister's past as an Israeli military chief. By early June the peace process begun in Madrid in October 1991 had appeared to be reaching a dead end, and the return to power of Prime Minister Yitzhak Shamir would have ensured its death. After his defeat Shamir admitted that he intended to delay the talks until the occupied territories were filled with Jewish settlers. In his inaugural speech on July 13, Rabin expressed support for the peace process, offering to go to any Arab capital to discuss peace. His statement was welcomed by Egypt, but there was widespread Arab concern over Rabin's failure to mention the "land for peace" principle, stipulated in UN Resolutions 242 of 1967 and 338 of 1983. Syria criticized Rabin's offer to engage in autonomy talks with the Palestinians as "divide and rule" tactics.

Radical Arabs declared that the new Israeli government made no difference to the prospects for peace. Palestinian leader George Habbash said that the only change would be in Israel's domestic politics, while Lebanon's Hezbollah—whose leader, Abbas Mussawi (*see* OBITUARIES), was assassinated in February, along with his wife and child, by Israeli special forces—said the war would continue. The Rabin government showed some evidence of a mood of compromise when it freed 800 Palestinian detainees and canceled 11 deportation orders prior to the resumption of the Middle East peace talks on August 24. Rabin's hold on the Knesset (parliament) was precarious; only 62 of the 120 members belonged to his coalition, including 12 from Meretz. His pledge to bring about a peace agreement in nine months seemed hollow, but within a month of the election he took a substantial step when Israel's housing minister, Benjamin Ben-Eliezer, announced a limited freeze on the construction of settlements in the occupied territories; future settlements, he stated, could be built only on security grounds. This

announcement led President Bush to end the freeze on $10 billion in loan guarantees to Israel, imposed February 24, when Bush said U.S. approval was contingent on a halt to new settlements.

Israel's negotiating position appeared to rest on a return to the Camp David proposals of 1978, with Israel having control over all its borders and all security arrangements in the West Bank and Gaza Strip; 100,000 settlers in the occupied territories; and no change in the status of Jerusalem. Counterproposals by the Palestinians were regarded as a "blueprint for an independent state." Israel had repeatedly stated that it had three objectives: a more formal and guaranteed Arab recognition of its right to exist; cessation of the state of war between itself and the Palestinians, on the one hand, and its Arab neighbours on the other; and the conclusion of formal peace treaties with the Palestinians and its Arab neighbours, similar to the one that it had with Egypt.

U.S. President-elect Bill Clinton's pro-Israel comments during his election campaign caused some concern that there would be a slowdown in the peace process. Clinton said he would be prepared to support the loan guarantees, regardless of Jewish settlements in occupied Arab land, and called for closer military ties with Israel and even for the release of Israeli spies held in U.S. prisons. As a candidate, he was vocal in his criticism of U.S. military support for Arab states such as Saudi Arabia and Kuwait, echoing Israel's complaint that the weapons could be used against it. Arabs were shaken by the extent of the efforts of all three major candidates to please Israel. One of the pledges by the Bush administration to American Jewish leaders was to make a new effort to end the 40-year-old Arab boycott of Israel. It seemed unlikely that the U.S. commitment to Egypt would change under Clinton, however, particularly as Pres. Hosni Mubarak was steering his country toward a more market-based economy. Similarly, maintaining relations with Syria, Jordan, Morocco, and the GCC countries was likely to prove a key to U.S. economic, political, and military influence in the Arab world.

It was reported in February that in a secret ceremony in November 1991, PLO leader Yasir Arafat, aged 62, married his aide Suha Tawil, aged 28, a Palestinian Christian from Ramalla. He had long claimed to be wedded only to the Palestinian struggle. Arafat narrowly escaped death on April 7 when his Soviet-made Antonov transport aircraft crashed in the desert while he was en route to a PLO training camp at Sarra in southeastern Libya. The U.S. denied having any role in the subsequent search operation but was nevertheless thanked by senior PLO official Bassem Abu Sherif. The incident came during a period of decline in the PLO's leadership of the Palestinian cause, but the December expulsions resulted in a call by left-wingers in Israel, including the Meretz Party, for a dialogue with Arafat's group.

Inter-Arab Dialogue. The signatories to the 1991 Damascus Declaration, Egypt, Syria, and the GCC states, met in Doha, Qatar, on September 9 and agreed to set up a ministerial commission to speed the flow of aid to the two non-Gulf Arab states. The commission would oversee a $6.6 million fund established by Saudi Arabia, Kuwait, Oman, Bahrain, Qatar, and the United Arab Emirates (U.A.E.). The final communiqué, however, made no mention of a more substantial issue—the dispatch of Egyptian and Syrian troops to the Gulf to form the vanguard of a Gulf security force. It appeared that the idea had been dropped in the face of stiff Gulf opposition and lack of Syrian support, despite the interest shown by the GCC's Western allies. On September 30 the GCC was plunged into crisis by a border clash between Saudi Arabia and Qatar, with the result that—despite a last-minute settlement mediated by President Mubarak—its December summit in Abu Dhabi was a strained affair, with real questions arising over the 11-year-old organization's future.

The GCC states were divided over relations with Iraq, with Kuwait and Saudi Arabia adamantly opposed to any resumption of diplomatic links. Qatar announced in early November that it was returning its ambassador to Baghdad, while Oman had retained its envoy in the Iraqi capital throughout the Kuwait occupation crisis. GCC Secretary-General Abdullah Bishara took a predictably hard line on enforcement of the UN embargo against Iraq when speaking to reporters at Spain's Expo 92 in July, calling for greater pressure on Iraq to force it to free Kuwaitis held since the Gulf war. In Doha on October 28 the GCC under secretary for economic affairs, Abdullah al-Quwaiz, outlined a timetable toward a Gulf common market—four years to tackle trade issues and seven years for those related to currency rates, share ownership, and the establishment of banks in member states.

GCC links with the European Communities (EC) were boosted in June by the nomination as GCC ambassador to the EC of Musthaq Abdullah, former Omani envoy to Beijing (Peking). Gulf politicians remained highly critical of the EC's proposed energy tax, designed to reduce carbon dioxide emissions, which they claimed would be harmful to the global economy and discourage the search for more crude oil reserves. The GCC secretary-general—due to retire at the end of 1992 and to be replaced by the U.A.E. ambassador to the UN—was especially critical of the tax at a meeting between GCC and EC foreign ministers in Kuwait on May 16. The impasse threatened to delay the conclusion of a free-trade agreement between the two blocs. A South African trade delegation visited Bahrain in May at the start of a GCC tour aimed at promoting business links with the region. The Gulf states had no diplomatic ties with Pretoria, but after the whites-only referendum in March rejected apartheid, commerce began to flourish. The South African airline Flitestar started weekly flights to Bahrain and Dubayy in October, with reciprocal rights granted to the regional carrier Gulf Air.

At the GCC summit in December 1991 in Kuwait, it had been made clear that the Arabs failed to see Iran as a full partner in their security arrangements. In 1992 GCC links with Iran were further fragmented by a dispute between Tehran and the U.A.E. concerning sovereignty over Abu Musa and Greater and Lesser Tunb, a group of Arab-owned islands close to the Iranian littoral. Iran expelled several U.A.E. citizens from the islands and on September 10 declared its sovereignty over them. On September 24 U.A.E. Pres. Sheikh Zaid sought intervention from Pres. Hafez al-Assad of Syria, but the issue remained unresolved. Arab fears were subsequently intensified by Iran's purchase for $750 million of three Russian submarines, despite an offer by the U.S. to give GCC navies antisubmarine warfare training. On November 3 the U.S. Navy deployed a nuclear-powered submarine to the Gulf. Regardless of these difficulties, in May Qatar had welcomed Iranian Vice Pres. Hassan Habibi, who signed agreements on air traffic, customs, and exchange of news, and trade continued to boom between Iran and Kuwait, the U.A.E., and Oman. In June, Doha, in a move that angered Tehran, confirmed a 10-year defense pact with the U.S., a step previously taken by Kuwait and Bahrain.

In a rare expression of Arab unity, the Arab Satellite Communications organization (Arabsat) on September 30 awarded a $258 million contract to a U.S. company for the launch of two communications satellites by the French rocket Ariane. Much less successful was the opening on March 26 by Israel of telephone links to 10 Arab states—Jordan, Saudi Arabia, Lebanon, Bahrain, Qatar, the U.A.E., Morocco, Algeria, Tunisia, and Yemen. Jordanian Minister of Communications Jamal Sariri slammed down the phone after receiving a direct call from the offices of the daily newspaper *Yediot Ahronot* in Tel Aviv.

North African Affairs. The reverberations of the assassination of Algerian Pres. Muhammad Boudiaf (*see* OBITUARIES), a veteran of the struggle against colonialism, on June 29 resulted in a crackdown elsewhere on Islamic fundamentalists. Egypt, where fundamentalist power was growing, declared three days of mourning for Boudiaf in a strong sign of support for Algeria's High State Council. Boudiaf had been brought to power in January in a military takeover. With victory for the fundamentalist Islamic Salvation Front in the second round of elections, scheduled for January 16, appearing almost certain, the military had forced the resignation of Pres. Chadli Bendjedid and set up the High State Council, which canceled the elections. The outcome of the Algerian crisis was seen as integral to regional stability. Tunisia's Foreign Minister Habib Ben Yahya commented on January 15: "When security prevails in Algeria, this means stability for the whole region."

Libya cautiously criticized the military takeover in Algiers but moved into a confrontation of its own with the West and moderate Arab states over its refusal to hand over two suspects wanted for the 1988 terrorist bombing of a jet over Scotland. On April 15 the UN Security Council imposed sanctions, including a ban on air travel and weapons sales and exclusions of some Libyan diplomats, until the government showed by "concrete measures" that it no longer supported terrorist action. Of the Arab states, only Iraq and The Sudan failed to comply with the UN edict, but Tunisia expressed concern over the effect of the sanctions on regional tourism. Tripoli news reports claimed soon afterward that the government was demolishing training camps used by the Abu Nidal Palestinian guerrilla group. Tripoli had previously handed over information about its links with the terrorist Irish Republican Army at a meeting between British and Libyan officials in Geneva.

In response to the political upheavals in the region, Morocco put a revised constitution to a referendum in September. The favourable outcome gave more power to both government and parliament. King Hassan, on the throne since 1961, remained the supreme authority, "inviolate and sacred." Despite these apparent concessions to liberalization, Morocco was defiant over its plan to hold general elections in the Western Sahara. Foreign Minister Abdellatif Filali said in September that the elections "cannot be linked in any way to the projected referendum under the UN settlement plan." The 19-year-old Polisario guerrilla cause was set back by the defection on August 11 of Ibrahim Hakim, former Polisario foreign minister and ambassador to Algeria. He declared the next day that the UN initiative was dead and that a solution had to be found inside Morocco. King Hassan mounted a major diplomatic initiative in the autumn to convene an Arab minisummit to tackle such issues as territorial disputes. He also sought to calm the anger felt by the Gulf states toward Jordan over its backing of Iraq during the Kuwait occupation crisis.

(JOHN WHELAN)

ALGERIA

Algeria is a republic of North Africa on the Mediterranean Sea. Area: 2,381,741 sq km (919,595 sq mi). Pop. (1992 est.): 26,401,000. Cap.: Algiers. Monetary unit: Algerian dinar, with (Oct. 5, 1992) a free rate of 20.51 dinars to U.S. $1 (34.87 dinars = £1 sterling). President in 1992, Col. Chadli Bendjedid until January 11; chairmen of the High State Council, Muhammad Boudiaf from January 11 to June 29 and, from July 2, Ali Kafi; prime ministers, Sid Ahmed Ghozali and, from July 8, Belaid Abdessalam.

Throughout 1992 Algeria was dominated by the consequences of the December 1991 elections. In the first round of the elections, held on Dec. 26, 1991, the Front Islamique du Salut (FIS) won a majority of the vote. However, before the second round could take place, the Algerian armed forces forced Pres. Chadli Bendjedid to resign. The elections were canceled on Jan. 11, 1992, and a state of emergency was declared.

The new army-backed regime, headed by the High State Council (HSC), invited a longstanding political exile, Muhammad Boudiaf, who had spent the previous 28 years in Morocco, to become its head. The security services dismantled the FIS, arresting 9,000 militants who were then interned in camps in the Sahara; on March 4 the FIS was banned. In retaliation, extremist elements associated with the FIS began an urban terrorist campaign against the new

regime, particularly targeting the security services, and by October more than 150 security personnel had been killed.

Boudiaf, rejecting the purely titular role originally offered to him by the HSC, began to try to rebuild Algeria's damaged democratic experiment. Although legislative elections had been postponed for at least a year, Boudiaf appointed a 60-man Consultative Council in April and then tried to create a new mass political movement, the Assemblé Patriotique. He also announced a campaign against the corruption that had been widespread during the latter part of the Bendjedid regime. The first major corruption trial, that of former army general Mustapha Beloucif, was due to begin in July, but on June 29 Boudiaf was assassinated in Annaba.

Boudiaf's assassin, although described by the authorities as a Islamicist sympathizer, was a member of his personal bodyguard and the direct responsibility of the interior minister, Gen. Larbi Belkhair. Most Algerians therefore assumed that the assassination had been the work of elements within the regime that felt threatened by the anticorruption drive. Boudiaf's successor, Ali Kafi, was seen as a more pliant tool in the army's hands, but the new prime minister—Sid Ahmed Ghozali was replaced just after the assassination—was not. Belaid Abdessalam was a veteran politician who had been responsible for the government-sponsored development drive under Pres. Houari Boumedienne in the 1970s. He soon made it clear that he was determined to stamp out urban terrorism, instituting special courts and severe punishments in October. At the same time, the door was left open to the banned FIS to cooperate with the government when its two leaders, Abbassi Madani and Ali Belhadj, who had been arrested in June 1991, were sentenced in July to 12-year prison terms rather than to death, as had been expected.

The Abdessalam government continued the nation's economic policy. Although the new prime minister was anxious to slow down the proposed privatization program, he encouraged private foreign investment. The oil sector alone attracted $4.2 billion of foreign investment in 1992. The regime also made it clear that, apart from $1.5 billion of commercial debt that was refinanced in early 1992, Algeria would continue to service its $25 billion foreign debt.

(GEORGE JOFFÉ)

This article updates the *Macropædia* article NORTH AFRICA: *Algeria*.

The body of Muhammad Boudiaf, head of Algeria's High State Council, lies in state in Algiers after he was assassinated by a bodyguard on June 29. It was not clear if his death had been the work of Islamic fundamentalists or of political rivals.

BAHRAIN

The monarchy (emirate) of Bahrain consists of a group of islands in the Persian Gulf between the Qatar Peninsula and Saudi Arabia. Area: 692 sq km (267 sq mi). Pop. (1992 est.): 531,000. Cap.: Manama. Monetary unit: Bahrain dinar, with (Oct. 5, 1992) a free rate of 0.38 dinar to U.S. $1 (0.65 dinar = £1 sterling). Emir in 1992, Isa ibn Sulman al-Khalifah; prime minister, Khalifah ibn Sulman al-Khalifah.

The festering territorial dispute with Qatar over islands, sandbanks, and reefs close to the Qatari mainland entered a new phase with moves at the International Court of Justice. On July 3, 1992, Qatar rejected a demand by Bahrain to present a joint petition and said it would proceed with a unilateral bid to recover the Hawar Islands through ICJ arbitration. Bahrain wanted to widen the case to include a look at its own claim to part of the Qatari mainland around the northwestern town of Zubara.

On June 20 Bahrain became the first Arab Gulf state to urge better relations with Iraq since the liberation of Kuwait in February 1991. The Bahraini prime minister, Sheikh Khalifah ibn Sulman al-Khalifah, said it was time for a new chapter in relations. In July Crown Prince Sheikh Hamad ibn Isa al-Khalifah asserted that the Gulf Cooperation Council was capable of building a million-man army and also commented on his country's closer ties with Iran. In June an Iranian team visited Bahrain to study the island's free-trade and offshore-banking policies. Iran had historically made claims to ownership of Bahrain.

On October 2 the South African airline Flitestar inaugurated its first service to the Gulf with a Johannesburg–Bahrain route. Following South Africa's whites-only referendum in March that abandoned apartheid, commercial relations had opened with some of the Gulf states.

Massive processions took place in Bahrain over a period of five days following the death in al-Kufah, Iraq, on August 8 of the Shi'ite divine Grand Ayatollah Abolqassem al-Khoei (*see* OBITUARIES). On December 16 the emir announced that he would appoint a consultative council to allow greater citizen participation.   (JOHN WHELAN)

This article updates the *Macropædia* article ARABIA: *Bahrain*.

CYPRUS

An island republic and member of the Commonwealth, Cyprus is in the eastern Mediterranean Sea. Island area: 9,251 sq km (3,572 sq mi). Island pop. (1992 est.): 756,000. Area of the Turkish Republic of Northern Cyprus (TRNC), proclaimed unilaterally (1983) in the occupied northern third of the island (controlled by Turkish Cypriots since 1974): 3,355 sq km (1,295 sq mi); pop. (1992 est.): 176,000. Cap.: Nicosia. Monetary unit: Cyprus pound, with (Oct. 5, 1992) a free rate of £C 0.42 to U.S. $1 (£C 0.72 = £1 sterling). President in 1992, George Vassiliou. President of TRNC in 1992, Rauf Denktash.

UN Secretary-General Boutros Boutros-Ghali spent much of 1992 trying to get Greek and Turkish Cypriot leaders to inch a last few steps forward—all that seemed necessary to establish a federal republic and end 30 years of ethnic division on the island. UN-sponsored talks had centred on a federal solution. They were stalled by disagreements over the powers of the central government, demilitarization, and the territory to be held by both sides. Another problem was Turkey's rejection of UN Security Council resolutions demanding the withdrawal of an estimated 35,000 Turkish troops and 45,000 mainland settlers from the Turkish-occupied north and the return there of some 200,000 Greek Cypriot refugees. Hopes for progress centred on Ankara's new preoccupation with the Central Asian republics and the

Balkans. Greek Foreign Minister Michalis Papaconstantinou quoted Turkish Prime Minister Suleyman Demirel as "repeatedly saying he is fed up spending money on Cyprus."

UN efforts collapsed in August after several rounds of fruitless talks in New York, but Turkish Cypriot leader Rauf Denktash and Pres. George Vassiliou agreed to meet in New York in October. The UN blamed Denktash for the stalemate. The October 26 talks got off to a grim start when Denktash walked out because conference documents failed to title him "president"—a bid for equal billing with the internationally recognized Vassiliou. After a procedural compromise, the talks staggered on until mid-November with no breakthroughs. The two leaders merely signed reports on their positions and went home, agreeing only to meet again in March 1993. One possible spur to action had already been hinted at. Boutros-Ghali said countries participating in the UN peacekeeping force on Cyprus had declared their intention to withdraw or reduce their contingents, totaling about 2,140 men. UNFICYP had kept the two sides at a safe distance since the 1974 war.

Economically, the Greek Cypriot south recovered from the tourism drought of the Gulf war period. Up to one and a half million tourists were expected to pack foreign exchange coffers by the end of the year. The unrecognized north continued to stagnate, mostly making do on Turkey's increasingly reluctant handouts. Cyprus continued rapid development of its new high-tech industries. Digital Equipment Corp. of the U.S. opened a subsidiary to market, sell, and service its products. Some 500 former Yugoslav companies were added to the growing offshore company register, but the central bank had to act quickly to regulate them after evidence surfaced that some were breaking UN sanctions against Serbia. In September, Cyprus opened its first university; 90% of the first 500 students were women because of compulsory army conscription for male school-leavers.

(THOMAS O'DWYER)

EGYPT

A republic of North Africa, Egypt has coastlines on the Mediterranean and Red seas. Area: 997,739 sq km (385,229 sq mi). Pop. (1992 est.): 55,979,000. Cap.: Cairo. Monetary unit: Egyptian pound, with (Oct. 5, 1992) a free rate of LE 3.34 to U.S. $1 (LE 5.68 = £1 sterling). President in 1992, Hosni Mubarak; prime minister, Atef Sedki.

Egypt was shaken by a rising tide of Islamic fundamentalist violence in 1992, aimed at ruining the tourist trade, while Cairo was shattered by an earthquake on October 12 measuring 5.9 on the Richter scale. The government maintained its commitment to liberalizing the economy but failed to consolidate its alliance with Syria and the conservative Gulf Cooperation Council (GCC) states; there was only desultory progress toward greater cooperation through the Damascus Declaration of 1991. The arrival in office as UN secretary-general of Egyptian diplomat Boutros Boutros-Ghali (*see* BIOGRAPHIES) was a boost for his country's prestige, but this received a blow from the assassination in Cairo in June of Egyptian writer and social reformer Farag Foda.

Many Egyptians expected a rapid expansion of democracy after the Gulf war, when some 35,000 Egyptians fought alongside Americans and other Westerners to drive the Iraqi army from Kuwait. This did not happen, though officials insisted in the government media that they were building democracy and broadening political participation. Pres. Hosni Mubarak told the semiofficial daily *al-Ahram* in February: "Constitutional amendments will not achieve people's hopes for more jobs, more production, more income and better services. Amendments are not a priority."

An Egyptian family watches Sheikh Metu'ali Sher'awi, a fundamentalist whose daily television program was very popular. Islamic fundamentalism continued to gain support in Egypt and in other Middle Eastern countries.
JOSEF POLLEROSS—JB PICTURES

Nevertheless, in local and provincial council elections on November 3, Muslim fundamentalists made limited gains. Fighting under the banner of the Socialist Labour Party, the Muslim Brotherhood won more than 35 seats, but the ruling National Democratic Party was not seriously threatened. The Brotherhood and most opposition groups had boycotted the last parliamentary elections in 1990, but this time they concentrated on what were widely regarded as Egypt's biggest problems: corruption, police brutality, government incompetence, failing education and health services, unemployment, housing, bureaucracy, and patronage.

Indeed, Egypt marked the 40th anniversary of the Egyptian army's 1952 coup d'état on July 23 with the legacy of Gamal Abdel Nasser largely dismantled. Celebrations were notably low key, although President Mubarak gave a speech on July 22 defending "the July revolution that remains a source of noble values urging social justice." Leading novelist Naguib Mahfouz, winner of the 1988 Nobel Prize for Literature, blamed the revolution for the economic climate that Egypt was struggling to escape.

Domestic Affairs. The Cairo earthquake killed 552 persons and injured more than 6,500. The epicentre was about 30 km (20 mi) southwest of the capital, near the village of al-Fayyum. The disaster served to highlight a lack of planning standards and building controls in Cairo over the past 20 years. Many of the dead were trapped in the wreckage of tenement blocks with more stories than the prescribed limits. Fundamentalist Islamic groups were quick to offer shelter and blankets for homeless families. The total bill for reconstruction and compensation to the victims was expected to reach $660 million, with Saudi Arabia, Kuwait, the United Arab Emirates, and Libya making donations.

The earthquake was less troublesome to the Mubarak regime than religiously inspired violence. Not since the troubled autumn of 1981 had extremists mounted such a sustained challenge to the government. The banned organization al-Jama'a al-Islamiya called for the destruction of Egypt's Pharaonic monuments as "pagan sites" and claimed responsibility for armed attacks on tourists. The violence was concentrated in a 210-km (130-mi) stretch of the Nile from al-Minya south to Sawhaj, about 560 km (350 mi) south of Cairo. On October 21 militants ambushed a tourist bus near the militant stronghold of Dayrut, killing a British woman and wounding two men. Tourism Minister Fouad Sultan said in November that Interpol statistics showed

Egypt to be one of the countries suffering the least from violence. The terrorists were hiding under the "cloak of religion," and he believed they would have little effect on the growth in visitors from Arab countries and Europe. In the year ended June 30 Egypt drew some three million visitors, including 150,000 Americans, and earned $3 billion in foreign exchange from tourism. Hoteliers claimed occupancy rates of 100% in Cairo and 98% in Luxor, Aswan, and the Sinai Peninsula.

Violence also erupted in the quiet town of Idku (population 250,000), nestled between the Mediterranean and the Nile Delta, when at least three people were killed in August. Unlike the troubled province of Asyut in Upper Egypt, where religious militants and security forces fought almost daily, sectarian violence was virtually unknown in Idku. The riots were sparked by reports that a local man had died under police torture. Hundreds of young men poured into the streets and set fire to local council offices and other government property but left shops alone.

Farag Foda was killed in Cairo in June by the same organization that claimed responsibility for the assassination in 1990 of the speaker of the People's Assembly, Rifaat al-Mahgoub. Foda's guiding belief was that any Egyptian government should be neutral as between the major monotheist faiths. Partly as a response to the outrage, the authorities continued a vigorous purge of extremists. On July 1 police arrested 16 suspects in one sweep and 6 in another in Asyut province. In the preceding three weeks, sectarian violence and clashes between the police and extremists had left 12 dead and 24 wounded. In another aspect of the crackdown, demonstrating a readiness to quell permissiveness as well as religious extremism, the writer 'Alaa Hamid was sentenced to a year in prison for attacking Islam and "encouraging promiscuity." Hamid also faced an eight-year jail term for blasphemy.

In line with a reform plan agreed upon with the International Monetary Fund (IMF), Egypt was obliged to cut subsidies on many basic items. The 1992–93 budget presented to the People's Assembly on May 6 embodied these subsidy cuts and held down increases in salaries and military spending to the level of inflation. The budget proposed a modest cut in the deficit to the equivalent of $2.8 billion. Cairo residents saw electricity bills triple in 1992, but following the October earthquake prices on basic food items were slashed by up to 20%. The first IMF program, a standby facility of $372 million, ended in November. According to the terms of debt forgiveness, a new agreement on further reforms was due to be in force by the beginning of 1993. In June a long-delayed land-reform bill was passed by the People's Assembly; reversing 40 years of strict rent controls, it enabled landlords to triple rents and buy tenants off their land. The measure would affect some 500,000 families who used some of the richest agricultural land for subsistence plots, paying annual rents that averaged $110 a hectare. Egypt was a net exporter of food until the 1970s, but as a result of the population explosion it now suffered a yawning food gap, importing about 70% of its needs.

Foreign Affairs. Egypt reacted positively to Yitzhak Rabin's victory in the Israeli general election in June. President Mubarak's top political adviser, Osama al-Baz, expressed the hope that the outcome would "give a strong push to the peace process." Yet the peace talks, stalled in December following the expulsion from Israel of more than 400 Islamic fundamentalists, were secondary to other problems for the Cairo government. President Mubarak returned to Egypt on August 12 apparently empty-handed after two days of meetings in Tripoli with Mu'ammar al-Qadhdhafi on the Libyan leader's crisis with the West over the bombing of a Pan Am jet over Scotland in 1988. Mubarak was engaged in high-level international diplomacy for most of the year trying to avoid the imposition of harsh penalties on a country where more than one million Egyptians lived or worked. A border dispute with The Sudan concerning mineral rights in the Halaib triangle erupted after The Sudan granted a Canadian oil company exploration rights in late 1991. Three days of talks in Khartoum took place between the two sides in the spring. Relations between the two countries, traditionally strong, had been soured by Khartoum's backing of Iraq in the Gulf war, although Mubarak had initially backed the leaders of the military junta in The Sudan when they seized power in 1989.

Egypt's hopes of securing a dominant role in regional affairs through the Damascus Declaration, an alliance of the six GCC states, Egypt, and Syria, received a major setback when foreign ministers meeting September 9–10 in Doha, Qatar, declined to support Cairo's suggestion of a permanent rapid deployment force. The strike force would be composed of soldiers from all eight states, but with Egyptian and Syrian troops forming a vanguard. The oil-rich Gulf states did, however, agree to establish a ministerial council with Egypt and Syria to speed up the flow of economic aid to those two countries. The ministerial commission would oversee the work of a $6.5 billion fund paid for by the GCC and largely subscribed by Saudi Arabia. It was a response to criticism from Cairo and Damascus that promised Gulf aid was often slow to materialize.   (JOHN WHELAN)

IRAN

The Islamic republic of Iran is in southwestern Asia on the Caspian and Arabian seas and the Persian Gulf. Area: 1,638,057 sq km (632,457 sq mi). Pop. (1992 est., including about 2 million Afghan refugees): 59,570,000. Cap.: Tehran. Monetary unit: Iranian rial, with (Oct. 5, 1992) an official exchange rate of 63.71 rials to U.S. $1 (108.30 rials = £1 sterling) and a free rate of 1,458 rials to U.S. $1 (2,479 rials = £1 sterling). *Rahbar* (spiritual leader) in 1992, Ayatollah Sayyed Ali Khamenei; president, Hojatolislam Hashemi Ali Akbar Rafsanjani.

Strict scrutiny of the Islamic credentials of candidates in the April 1992 general elections for the Majlis (national assembly) enabled disqualification of the more radical applicants. The outcome of the election was predictable given the close management of proceedings, and two-thirds of the 270-man assembly supported the president. Hard-line groups lost

seats, including those led by former Majlis speaker Mehdi Karrubi and Ali Akbar Mohtashemi, a principal radical leader. The turnout of voters was approximately 50%.

In May there was an outbreak of rioting in urban areas across Iran, with Meshed, Shiraz, Tabriz, and Arak the most affected. In Meshed rioting persisted for several days, and there were a number of deaths. Eight people were executed in Meshed and Shiraz for taking part. Ostensibly, the rioting arose from clashes between municipal officials and illegal squatters, but in fact it took on the form of general antigovernment demonstrations. Despite an improved rate of economic expansion in recent years, the poorer sections of the population remained severely deprived. Deepening apathy toward the regime was being contained only by repression. In the aftermath of the Meshed riots the *bassij* volunteer forces were given absolute legal powers to break up demonstrations and arrest suspected troublemakers. Toward year's end political difficulties arose from disputes over economic policy between Pres. Hashemi Rafsanjani and the hard-liners, who opposed the president's wish for rapid implementation of a five-year plan using borrowed funds and technology from abroad. The president appeared unable to overcome the hard-liners' objections, and the thrust toward firmer political control and economic growth lost momentum.

Abroad, the regime began the year with great optimism that Iran could reap cultural and political gains from the disintegration of the U.S.S.R. Efforts were made to establish economic ties with Transcaucasia and Central Asia through multilateral regional trade groupings as well as bilateral agreements. The Iranian authorities promised the new republics that rail and pipeline facilities could transit Iranian territory to ports on the Persian Gulf and offered cultural and Islamic support. Despite the signing of trade agreements with individual republics, Iranian influence in the region was slow to take root, although construction of a railway from Meshed to the frontier with Turkmenistan was begun.

Relations with Iraq failed to improve. On April 5 Iranian military jets attacked opposition Mujahedin-e Khalq bases on Iraqi territory, and one Iranian aircraft was shot down. The Mujahedin mounted demonstrations against Iranian embassies and official offices abroad in retaliation for the raid. Difficulties arose with other Arab states, the most severe with the United Arab Emirates over the status of Abu

A woman in Tehran casts her ballot in the Iranian parliamentary elections held in April. In the first national elections since 1989, supporters of the president, Hojatolislam Hashemi Ali Akbar Rafsanjani, won an overwhelming majority of the seats.

Musa island in April, when the Iranian military commander on Abu Musa expelled U.A.E. workers. The problem recurred in the fall when the U.A.E. reopened the issue of the two islands of Greater and Lesser Tunb, like Abu Musa seized by Iran in 1971.

Iran's links with the developed world were under strain during the year. A tit-for-tat expulsion of diplomats occurred with the U.K.; France and Switzerland became embroiled in a dispute over the role of Iranian diplomats in the murder of the exiled Iranian politician Shahpur Bakhtiar in Paris in 1991; and Germany was banned from attending the Tehran book fair.

Growth in gross domestic product (GDP) was reported at 10% for the year to March 20, 1992, but the outlook for the rest of the year was poor. Inflation remained at 20% and unemployment at two million. Above all, the Iranian rial was devalued against most hard currencies, falling to 1,458 rials = U.S. $1 by October, as compared with the official rate of 63 rials. Oil revenues were forecast at $15 billion, 7% below 1991 revenues. Imports rose to $30 billion and, with lower capital inflows in the form of loans and investments, there were difficulties with foreign payments at midyear.

(KEITH S. MCLACHLAN)

IRAQ

A republic of southwestern Asia, Iraq has a short coastline on the Persian Gulf. Area: 435,052 sq km (167,975 sq mi). Pop. (1992 est.): 18,838,000. Cap.: Baghdad. Monetary unit: Iraqi dinar, with (Oct. 5, 1992) a par value of 0.35 dinar to U.S. $1 (free rate of 0.59 dinar = £1 sterling); a truer value of the dinar was on the black market, where in late September more than 40 dinars = U.S. $1 (about 70 dinars = £1 sterling). President in 1992, Saddam Hussein; prime minister, Muhammad Hamzah az-Zubaydi.

Pres. Saddam Hussein came under growing pressure from the Gulf war allies with the imposition of a no-fly zone south of the 32nd parallel in late August 1992. UN sanctions remained in force throughout the year, and a UN boundary commission awarded disputed territory to Kuwait. Opposition to the Ba'th Party leadership gathered strength with a meeting of rebel groups on Iraqi soil on October 27. Iraqi incursions into the no-fly zone in late December may have aimed to test American resolve during the transition between U.S. administrations.

The Iraqi regime's reputation for lawlessness was undiminished. On December 7 an assassin gunned down in Amman Moayyed al-Janabi, an atomic scientist seeking to defect to the U.K. Baghdad sentenced four westerners to seven-year prison terms for allegedly entering Iraq illegally. It was also alleged to be holding more than 450 "prisoners-of-war" from Kuwait in prisons and police cells, releasing only a trickle of Kuwaiti nationals during the course of the year. On August 27 the Kuwaiti government denied that 71 recently released persons were former POWs, claiming instead that they were Kuwaitis and other nationalities whose families still lived in Iraq.

The year was marked by a series of confrontations with the UN. On March 11 Deputy Prime Minister Tariq Aziz told the Security Council that Baghdad was ready to make a full and complete disclosure of all weapons programs covered by Council resolutions and to enter immediate technical talks. He insisted, nevertheless, that destruction be limited to equipment used to produce banned weapons. Iraq's intransigence was shown in a protracted game of cat and mouse with UN inspectors seeking to enter the Agriculture Ministry building in Baghdad in search of information on the regime's chemical weapons program. On July 29 the inspectors, having been denied access for several weeks, finally left after a predictably fruitless search.

The decision to deploy Aziz, a Christian, as Iraq's international voice was a shrewd move by the regime, as was the nomination in September of Nizar Hamdoun, former Iraqi ambassador to Washington, as Iraq's envoy to the UN. In further government changes in late July, Ahmad Hussein was replaced as foreign minister by Muhammad Saeed as-Sahhaf, who was ambassador to Italy during the Gulf crisis. Hussein took over at Finance, while hard-liner Humam 'Abd al-Khaliq came to the Higher Education Ministry to keep the lid on the universities.

On July 17, the 24th anniversary of the Ba'thist revolution, the president warned his people that they should not expect any early lifting of the economic blockade imposed in August 1990. With factories and businesses closed because of the UN embargo, unemployment soared; diplomats estimated the jobless rate at 40% in Baghdad and higher in the provinces. On April 1 the Baghdad Stock Exchange opened for the first time in more than 50 years, but there was little demand for shares, and trading was virtually nonexistent.

On April 16 the UN Iraq-Kuwait border demarcation commission awarded six oil wells in the Rumaylah oil field and part of the Umm Qasr port to Kuwait, a verdict confirmed in August by the Security Council. Iraq disputed the

REUTERS/BETTMANN

Iraqi shoppers buy food at a street market in Baghdad. A fall in the value of the Iraqi dinar in 1992 led to reduced imports and sharply higher food prices.

decision, and diplomats feared that years of hostility could result from the rulings. On January 7 Iraq detained two Kuwaiti policemen who strayed across the poorly marked border, setting a pattern that was to be repeated throughout the year. Iraqi troops, backed by tanks and artillery, launched a war of attrition in southern Iraq on April 21, according to the Tehran-based Supreme Council for the Islamic Revolution in Iraq. The attacks were concentrated on marshes near the towns of Basra, Amarah, and Nasiriyah, centres of the Shi'ite rebellion crushed by the Iraqi army in 1991, when thousands of dissidents and army deserters had taken refuge in the wetlands. At the same time, Iraqi engineers began work on a Russian-designed canal called the Leader's River. Opposition sources claimed its purpose was to drain the marshes and destroy the rebels' cover. A visit by journalists on August 25 revealed that only 11 km (7 mi) needed to be dug before the waters would begin flowing down the 565-km (350-mi) waterway from Baghdad to Basra. In December, Saddam Hussein announced that the canal had been completed. By the time the allies imposed their no-fly zone, the London-based Iraqi National Congress was claiming that 300 sorties a day were being mounted by the Ba'thist forces against the rebels, who were effectively encircled by units of the Iraqi regular army. Late in the year there were signs that Iraq was growing restive. On December 27 a U.S. plane shot down an Iraqi MiG fighter that had entered the no-fly zone, although Iraq claimed it was "over our national territory." The U.S. was reportedly building up its forces in the area.

The death in Kurah in August of 93-year-old Grand Ayatollah Abolqassem al-Khoei (see OBITUARIES) was a blow for Saddam Hussein, since the cleric had been a useful tool for placating Shi'ite religious opinion about the government's intentions toward the rebels.   (JOHN WHELAN)

ISREAL

A republic of southwestern Asia, Israel is situated on the Mediterranean Sea. Area: 20,700 sq km (7,992 sq mi), not including territory occupied in the June 1967 war. Pop. (1992 est.): 5,239,000. Cap.: Jerusalem (but see Israel table in World Data section). Monetary unit: New (Israeli) sheqel, with (Oct. 5, 1992) a free rate of 2.49 sheqalim to U.S. $1 (4.24 sheqalim = £1 sterling). President in 1992, Chaim Herzog; prime ministers, Yitzhak Shamir and, from July 13, Yitzhak Rabin.

The year 1992 was a singular one in modern Israel's experience. Political life, the economy, and the general outlook were—for once—dominated by the apparently real prospect of peace and not by threats of war. By the end of October, the bilateral peace talks with Syria, Lebanon, and the Jordanian-Palestinian delegation that began in October 1991 had completed seven rounds of negotiations before they adjourned to await the outcome of the U.S. presidential election. The talks had focused the attention of governments and people on the opportunities—and difficulties—of making peace as a preferred option to the devastation and human tragedy of war, which they had but recently witnessed in Iraq and Kuwait. This provided a new and powerful incentive to persevere in the often seemingly insurmountable difficulties of the "peace process." The talks hit a snag on December 17, however, when Israel expelled some 415 Palestinians to a desolate buffer zone in southern Lebanon and rejected international pleas to reconsider the action or to allow humanitarian aid to be sent to the stranded men through Israeli territory. (See Middle Eastern and North African Affairs, above.)

There were also other factors that had greatly assisted the desire for peace in Israel and among its Arab neigh-

bours, not least the Palestinians. All of them were looking to the U.S. for economic help, political support, and, in some cases, military aid. The U.S. was the only surviving superpower that had the capacity and will to provide this help. The former Soviet Union was no longer a pertinent factor. Europe had not yet become one. The cold war was no more. The perceived entrance ticket to American benevolence was a demonstrative determination to end the Arab-Israeli conflict by a negotiating process leading to the peaceful coexistence of Israel and the Arab states.

This had presented the Likud-dominated coalition government under Prime Minister Yitzhak Shamir with a real dilemma. During the first half of the year (until the general election on June 23), it had to contend with a built-in assumption—almost an article of faith—that no peace terms acceptable to the Shamir government were possible in view of the prevailing Arab and U.S. attitudes. Therefore, maintaining the existing preferred condition, a political status quo, became the main objective of the peace talks for the Likud government's negotiating teams; "stalling" was elevated into a fine art.

This understandably antagonized the administration of U.S. Pres. George Bush and led it to take political and economic sanctions, especially by delaying consideration of Israel's request for loan guarantees totaling $10 billion intended to assist the settling of an estimated million new Jewish immigrants from the former Soviet Union expected over the next five years. Relations with the Bush administration were further exacerbated by the Likud government's embarking on an escalation of a Jewish settlement presence in the occupied territory of the West Bank. It was clearly intended to preempt any stronger U.S. intervention or a change of government in Jerusalem.

This policy by the Shamir government of stalling in the talks while settling Jews in the West Bank was grist to Arab mills. It provided Syrian and Palestinian negotiators with justification for their own lack of movement while they hoped and waited for the U.S. to intervene and pressure Israel to make the concessions demanded by the Arab side. By the end of May, as the Israeli general election campaign entered its final phase, the peace process was getting nowhere. The Arab leaders gave voice to their hope that a new Labour government led by Yitzhak Rabin would be more forthcoming and concede on Arab demands.

Other factors during the run-up to the election were to have a powerful impact on its outcome. While outwardly maintaining a facade of strength, the Shamir administration began to disintegrate as Shamir's rivals began to stake their claims to the party leadership. Some powerful ministers pursued illegal, uncoordinated, and unauthorized policies. Much of this surfaced on April 27, just eight weeks before the general election. The state comptroller, Miriam Ben-Porat, published a report that accused the Ministry of Housing and Construction of executing an ill-planned and sometimes illegal campaign to build housing for immigrants and, additionally, wasting millions of dollars. The report accused senior ministry officials of abusing expense accounts and offering preferential contracts to companies associated with Likud members. Other agencies of the government were also severely criticized in Ben-Porat's independent review.

Four weeks later the governor of the Bank of Israel personally handed the bank's report to Shamir. It was a devastating document criticizing the government for failing either to generate sustainable growth or to provide jobs for the new immigrants. This point was reinforced by a Jewish Agency report on June 1, which noted that only 3,360 immigrants from the former Soviet Union had arrived during May 1992, compared with 16,000 in May 1991. On the eve of the election it became known that unemployment during the first quarter of 1992 had risen by 24% to 11.6%.

Even so, the election result stunned Likud and the right-wing parties generally. Some foreign observers described it as an "earthquake," which had displaced the ruling Likud elite that had wielded power for 15 years. This was true, but it was not the only change that followed the election. There were others of no lesser significance. It had been Israel's most democratic election yet. The new Labour Party leader, Yitzhak Rabin, had been chosen not by a party caucus but by some 100,000 registered Labour Party members in a nationwide primary election. The same applied to Labour's nominated slate of candidates for election to the Knesset (parliament), which had many more new faces, younger faces, and women to back the old guard at the head. With Rabin as prime minister and Shimon Peres as foreign minister, it was an energetic and able combination.

In the new Knesset, Labour held 44 seats to Likud's 32. Fifteen parties did not win any seats. (For tabulated results, see *Political Parties,* above.) Rabin's first Cabinet, which was presented on July 13, was carefully crafted, with the left-wing party Meretz and Sephardi religious Shas canceling out each other's influence on domestic political issues. More important, the Cabinet's consensus on the policy to be pursued in the peace negotiations was directed by Rabin personally, with all his authority as prime minister and minister of defense. This accorded with Rabin's conviction that central control and freedom of action were essential to the successful conduct of the disparate peace negotiations. He won Peres' approval for the central authority to be vested in the prime minister. Rabin alone, because of his personal standing as a soldier-statesman, could launch daring diplomatic peace initiatives that would have the support of his Cabinet and of a majority of Israel's Jewish population—4.4 million, or about 85% of Israel's total population. At the same time, Rabin reiterated that he would not countenance any concession that might jeopardize Israel's essential security. So as not to encourage false hopes or rouse undue fears, Rabin elaborated Israel's peace with security policy—a theme that he continued to emphasize with ever increasing precision in a series of major speeches to the Knesset.

As the negotiations proceeded, however, it became evident that the fundamental difference between Israel and the Arab understanding of UN Security Council Resolution 242—which was supposed to be the basis of the peace

process—had become a serious hindrance to any real further progress. Israel maintained—with U.S. support—that UN Resolution 242 set out the parameters for a "negotiated" peace settlement based on a mutually agreed Israeli withdrawal from some territory and "the establishment of agreed and secure boundaries." The Arab interpretation of Resolution 242 was that its mandatory terms had to be "implemented" as a precondition before there could be any peace negotiation. Syria and the Palestinians insisted that Israel would have to withdraw first and fully from all territories occupied in 1967 (the West Bank, the Gaza Strip, the Golan Heights, and Jerusalem) before any question of peace or secure boundaries could be negotiated. It was a position totally unacceptable to the Rabin government, as it had been to previous Israeli governments of whatever composition and however peace oriented. It was this albatross of Resolution 242 that had hung over the seven rounds of the peace process after the Madrid peace initiative.

However, these were not the only problems facing the new Rabin government as it sought to rearrange Israel's economic priorities. Considering the worldwide recession and Israel's own massive immigration of Soviet Jews (another 80,000 to 120,000 were expected in 1993), the economy showed considerable buoyancy. Unemployment declined in 1992 and was expected to fall further in 1993, despite the influx of immigrants. The economy's growth rate was 6% in 1992; exports were up by 14%; and the budget proposals announced on October 28 showed that spending was kept under control. The government allocated 18.3% of budget expenditures to military consumption, 16.7% to civilian consumption, a massive 29.2% to debt repayment, 9.9% to investment, and 25.9% to transfer payments.

The biggest change that had come over Israel was that it had as its prime minister a national leader who was prepared to deal with Israel's economic and political priorities realistically, who was not afraid of unpopularity and opposition from the nationalist and religious right-wing parties, and who had reestablished Israel's traditional good relations with the U.S. But central to the new Israel that emerged from the elections of 1992 was the fact that the Rabin government's policies were essentially its own and not U.S. inspired, as had been the case with the Madrid peace initiative. As a former soldier, Rabin was not given to encouraging pipe dreams about peace. He saw what was going on in the Arab camp and had reached a conclusion

Supporters of the Palestine Liberation Organization wave banners during elections on July 13 in a town in the West Bank. On the same day, Israel's new prime minister, Yitzhak Rabin, proposed a five-year interim period of autonomy for the West Bank and Gaza Strip, during which time talks on a permanent agreement would be held.

similar to Shamir's that, as yet, Syria and the Palestinians were not ready for formal peace on terms acceptable to Israel. However, Rabin's response to this threatening deadlock was the opposite of Shamir's: he took the initiative; he won the support of the U.S. and of the international community; and he put the onus of rejecting peace offers on the Syrians and the Palestinians. By November 1992 a new political map in the Middle East appeared to be in the making, but Rabin lost much of that goodwill with his decision to deport 415 Palestinian fundamentalists. The Israeli Supreme Court refused to overturn the order, but the government acknowledged that 10 of the deportees should not have been expelled.   (JON KIMCHE)

JORDAN

A constitutional monarchy, Jordan is located in southwestern Asia and has a short coastline on the Gulf of Aqaba. Area: 88,946 sq km (34,342 sq mi). Pop. (1992 est.): 3,636,000. Cap.: Amman. Monetary unit: Jordan dinar, with (Oct. 5, 1992) an official rate of 0.66 dinar to U.S. $1 (1.12 dinars = £1 sterling). King, Hussein I; prime minister in 1992, Sharif Zaid ibn Shaker.

King Hussein underwent what was described as successful cancer surgery in the U.S. on Aug. 20, 1992. His return to Jordan on September 24 was followed two days later by his first official encounter with Palestinian notables from the Israeli-occupied territories since July 1988, when Jordan cut legal and administrative ties with the West Bank and passed responsibility for it to the Palestine Liberation Organization.

The meeting highlighted the monarch's significant role in the Arab-Israeli peace talks that had opened in Madrid in October 1991. The Palestinians were part of the Jordanian delegation to the talks, which aimed at ending the state of war between Israel and its Arab foes in return for territory seized by the Jewish state. Roughly half of Jordan's 3.6 million people were from Palestinian families who fled or were driven out of their homeland during the Arab-Israeli wars.

The monarch also received a welcome home message from Iraqi Pres. Saddam Hussein. After Iraq's August 1990 invasion of Kuwait, the king had tried to mediate a diplomatic solution, but his neutral stance was overshadowed by widespread popular support for Saddam, painting Jordan as pro-Iraq. As a result, the Jordanian government lost traditional friends in the West and bankrollers in the Gulf states, which halted a $1,250,000,000 annual aid program to Jordan. On March 12 King Hussein met U.S. Pres. George Bush for talks, and bilateral relations were described as back to normal. Six months later joint military exercises were carried out by Jordanian and U.S. defense forces.

In August Saudi Arabia barred imports of Jordanian fruit and vegetables, alleging that shipments had been contaminated. However, some observers saw this as continuing evidence of a chill in relations between the two countries. King Hussein was involved in a dispute with King Fahd of Saudi Arabia as to who should have the honour of paying for repairs to the Dome of the Rock in Jerusalem, one of Islam's holiest shrines. This was resolved when the Jordanian monarch paid $8,250,000 from his private coffers for the repairs, to be carried out by a contractor from Northern Ireland. King Fahd had wanted the work done under the auspices of Unesco.

The loss of some traditional markets placed the Jordanian economy under increasing strain. Finance Minister Basil Jardaneh announced on August 30 that his government had agreed in principle with the London Club of commercial creditors to reduce some $1.2 billion of debt, but he gave no details. Jordan, burdened with a total foreign debt of $7.2 billion, had agreed with the Paris Club of official creditors

Tank trucks carry petroleum products from Iraq to Amman, Jordan. In return for much-needed fuel, Jordan continued in 1992 to overlook violations of the UN embargo against Iraq, although late in the year it responded to U.S. pressure by tightening controls.
BARRY IVERSON—TIME MAGAZINE

earlier in 1992 to reschedule some $800 million originally due for repayment between 1991 and 1993.

In August a law was passed legalizing political parties for the first time since they were banned in 1957, marking another step in a democratization process that started in 1989. In April martial law was lifted, and in June the National Charter was approved. Up to 60 political parties had applied for licenses, among them the Islamic Action Front, which demanded a society based on Islam with strict observance of Shari'ah law, and the free-market Progress and Justice Party led by Adnan Abu Odeh, who on March 26 was named Jordan's permanent representative to the UN.

The elections scheduled for November 1993 would be the first multiparty ballot since 1956. In the current assembly 33 seats were held by MPs who were identified with the Muslim Brotherhood or Islamic fundamentalism, but in the northern city of Irbid, Islamic candidates suffered an unexpected defeat in local elections held during the summer. During the year the fundamentalist MPs urged the government to close all 10 of the Christian-owned breweries in Jordan. On November 20 two fundamentalist MPs were among those released from prison in a general amnesty to mark the king's birthday. The pair had been sentenced to 20 years' hard labour for possession of illegal weapons and plotting to overthrow the government.   (JOHN WHELAN)

KUWAIT

A constitutional monarchy (emirate), Kuwait is in the northeastern Arabian Peninsula, on the Persian Gulf. Area: 17,818 sq km (6,880 sq mi). Pop. (1992 est.): 1,190,000. Cap.: Kuwait City. Monetary unit: Kuwaiti dinar, with (Oct. 5, 1992) an official rate of 0.29 dinar to U.S. $1 (0.50 dinar = £1 sterling). Emir, Sheikh Jabir al-Ahmad al-Jabir as-Sabah; prime minister in 1992, Crown Prince Sheikh Saad al-Abdullah as-Salim as-Sabah.

The general election on Oct. 5, 1992, for 50 seats in the National Assembly resulted in successes for Islamic candidates and for independents who supported their demand for a return to Shari'ah (Islamic) law. On October 17 Prime Minister Sheikh Saad formed a new Cabinet that included six antigovernment deputies. Two key appointments were Foreign Minister Sheikh Sabah al-Ahmad as-Sabah, who held the portfolio when the Iraqis invaded in 1990, and a newcomer, Oil Minister Ali Ahmad al-Baghli. The prime

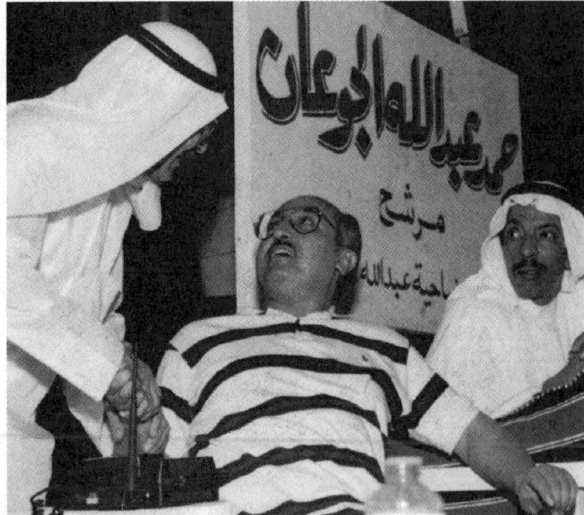

Hamad al-Jou'an (centre), an opposition candidate, accepts congratulations after winning a seat in the parliamentary elections held in Kuwait on October 5. The opposition won a comfortable majority, and Islamic candidates more than doubled their number of seats.
AP/WIDE WORLD

minister, initially reluctant to continue, recalled the talented Kuwaiti ambassador to the U.S., Sheikh Saud Nasser as-Sabah, as information minister.

The assembly elected independent Ahmad as-Saadoun, speaker of the parliament dissolved in 1986, as its speaker, while another stalwart nationalist from former assemblies, Ahmad Baqr, was voted in as secretary. Opposition MPs now commanded 31 seats in the assembly, after a 90% turnout of the 81,500 all-male electorate. The franchise was restricted to Kuwaitis whose families were resident before 1920. Within days of the election an independent MP introduced a draft bill to allow women to vote and to cut the age of majority to 18 from 21. The U.S. State Department said the election was the most open Kuwait had ever staged. Old-fashioned campaigning had gripped the city for weeks, with signs and placards featuring candidates plastered on every available site.

Security and border matters were major issues facing the government. Kuwait signed bilateral defense cooperation agreements with the U.K. on February 11 and with France later in the year. Defense Minister Sheikh Ali Sabah as-Salim as-Sabah hinted in early October at a similar deal with Russia. A UN boundary-demarcation commission ruled that six oil wells formerly exploited by Iraq were Kuwaiti territory and gave Kuwait part of the Umm Qasr port at the head of the Gulf. Nevertheless, incidents in the border area continued. The Iraqis seized a British catering worker and three Swedish engineers for allegedly illegally entering Iraq from Kuwait. The emir of Kuwait, Sheikh Jabir, toured Latin-American countries in late May and subsequently visited Australasia to thank governments that supported the liberation of Kuwait but also to publicize the plight of several hundred Kuwaiti hostages still held in Iraqi detention centres.

The pace of economic recovery quickened after the extinction in November 1991 of the last oil fires. On Oct. 29, 1992, the new oil minister forecast that 1993 third-quarter oil production would reach two million barrels a day, in excess of the level attained in August 1990. He also emphasized the new government's desire to use foreign expertise while increasing the number of Kuwaitis involved in the oil sector.   (JOHN WHELAN)

This article updates the Macropædia article ARABIA: Kuwait.

LEBANON

A republic of southwestern Asia, Lebanon is situated on the Mediterranean Sea. Area: 10,230 sq km (3,950 sq mi). Pop. (1992 est.): 2,803,000 (including Palestinian refugees estimated to number about 400,000). Cap.: Beirut. Monetary unit: Lebanese pound, with (Oct. 5, 1992) a free rate of LL 2,473 to U.S. $1 (LL 4,204 = £1 sterling). President in 1992, Elias Hrawi; prime ministers, Omar Karami, Rashid as-Solh from May 13, and, from October 31, Rafiq al-Hariri.

The first general election since May 1972, starting on Aug. 23, 1992, led to a polarization of Lebanon's political and religious groups. Most of the Christians boycotted the polls, demanding that voting be postponed until after Syrian troops were withdrawn. The Maronites, who dominated Lebanon from independence in 1943 until the outbreak of civil war in the 1970s, considered that the new parliament was heavily tilted toward Syria and would make Lebanon a Syrian satellite. Syria, Lebanon's undisputed master, maintained 40,000 troops in the country under a 1976 Arab League mandate.

The new legislature of 128 members was scheduled to meet for the first time on October 15, when the interim Cabinet headed by Sunni Muslim Prime Minister Rashid as-Solh would step down. Polling for the last five seats took place on October 11 in the Keserwan area north of Beirut, with one of the seats being won by Faris Bouez, son-in-law of Pres. Elias Hrawi. Polling for these five seats in the Maronite heartland had been originally scheduled for August 30, but all but one candidate withdrew at the last moment amid massive Christian protests. Bouez had been minister of expatriate affairs until he resigned in August.

The new National Assembly, while made up mostly of pro-Syrian members, included for the first time pro-Iranian Hezbollah fundamentalists. All 22 candidates on the "Liberation List" offered by Hezbollah, the secular Amal movement, and their Syrian-backed allies were elected. Hezbollah's triumph followed a landslide in eastern Lebanon and a strong showing in Beirut, which gave it a total of eight seats in the new assembly. On September 13 President Hrawi ended two days of talks with Pres. Hafez al-Assad of Syria at Latakia, Syria, where they agreed to press ahead with the U.S.-sponsored Arab-Israeli peace talks. There was no hint of a serious attempt to address the question of Syria's withdrawal from Lebanon, despite a series of meetings between the two countries in November.

Political tension mounted in February when the government produced an economic austerity package with a ceiling on borrowing. Small banks came under pressure, and on March 6 the General Confederation of Lebanese Workers staged the first in a series of strikes. By May 4 the value of the Lebanese pound had fallen to 2,000 to the U.S. dollar. Two days later the government was plunged into crisis with the resignation of the 16-month-old administration of Prime Minister Omar Karami.

The return of the 66-year-old Sunni lawyer as-Solh, premier in 1974–75, as caretaker prime minister sparked a round of political infighting; Druze leader Walid Jumblatt staged a boycott, and the head of the Maronite forces, Samir Geagea, resigned. Housing Minister Suleiman Tony Franjieh quit on June 16 to protest courtesies offered by the government to Geagea. On June 8 Georges Saadeh, the minister of posts and telecommunications, was reelected chairman of the Phalangist Party, defeating Geagea and avoiding a boycott of the as-Solh Cabinet. On October 22 the president named Rafiq al-Hariri, a 48-year-old billionaire entrepreneur with strong business ties to Saudi Arabia, as the new prime minister.

On June 17 the last two Western hostages in Lebanon held by Shi'ite factions, the German aid workers Thomas Kemptner and Heinrich Strübig, were released, freeing a grant of $212 million in European Communities aid. In December Lebanon refused to accept or give aid to 415 Palestinians camped along its southern border, declaring that the men, who had been expelled from Israel, were that country's responsibility.

The death on July 23 at age 82 of former president Suleiman Franjieh (*see* OBITUARIES) marked the end of an era. He was the last of his generation of *zaims,* or feudal lords, who held power after independence. (JOHN WHELAN)

LIBYA

A socialist country of North Africa, Libya lies on the Mediterranean Sea. Area: 1,757,000 sq km (678,400 sq mi). Pop. (1992 est.): 4,447,000. Cap.: Tripoli (policy-making body meets in Surt). Monetary unit: Libyan dinar, with (Oct. 5, 1992) a free rate of 0.26 dinar to U.S. $1 (0.44 dinar = £1 sterling). De facto chief of state in 1992, Col. Mu'ammar al-Qadhdhafi; secretary of the General People's Congress (nominal chief of state), 'Abd ar-Razig as-Sawsa'; secretary of the General People's Committee (premier), Abu Zaid Umar Dourda.

Libya's isolation was reinforced in 1992 by the imposition on April 15 of an embargo on all international flights to and from its airport. The move came as the U.S., Britain, and France maneuvered to force the Libyan government to make the two Libyans suspected of planting the bomb that downed the Pan Am flight over Lockerbie, Scotland, in December 1988 subject themselves to relevant courts, preferably in Scotland or alternatively in the U.S. According to the Libyan media, Libyan leader Col. Mu'ammar al-Qadhdhafi was prepared to allow them to go abroad if they themselves were willing, but he was overruled by the country's General People's Congress. Qadhdhafi also suggested that the trial be conducted at the International Court of Justice in The Hague, where Libya had achieved success in border arbitration in the 1980s. The UN ruled against the use of its court on the grounds that the court was not competent to hear "criminal action." By the end of 1992 there had been no resolution of the disagreement.

Meanwhile, the embargo caused great inconvenience and probably had more domestic political impact than the serious but much less obvious accumulated impairment of the Libyan oil industry and of the country's airlines, deprived in both cases of the means to maintain and expand capacity by an accompanying UN embargo on parts and equipment. The posture of the Libyan government in regard to the embargoes was nonconfrontational throughout the year. For example, it was reported in June that information on former Libyan links with the Irish Republican Army had been provided to the British government, but this gesture was not sufficient to remove the sanctions. The Libyan leader attempted to indicate his commitment to improved relations with the West by closing down the Abu Nidal training camps and expelling the staff, who went mainly to The Sudan, Lebanon, and Iraq.

The Libyan economy continued to strengthen compared with the 1980s, when low oil prices and production reduced oil earnings. There were few constraints on domestic consumption, but the economy was not strong enough to assume development spending at the rates possible in the oil-rich 1970s. Unfortunately for small exporters such as Libya, the world oil market was steered assertively during the latter part of the 1990–91 Gulf crisis and afterward to accord with Saudi and U.S. interests. An important new law passed in June called for accelerated privatization to further strengthen the economy.

A sign of the Libyan cash-flow predicament in 1992 was its approach to the African Development Bank for a loan to enable it to begin the second phase of the Great Man-Made River to bring water from southwestern Libya to al-Jifarah and Tripoli in the north. The allocation of water to agriculture, at a delivered cost of about $1 per cubic metre, was a controversial issue, especially because the water supplies in the coastal cities of Libya were in disarray as a result of seawater intrusion into the coastal aquifers; the intrusion was a consequence of the overuse of scarce groundwater in agriculture during the past three decades. Other evidence of the urgency of addressing the problems associated with ensuring future national income was the talks between Libyan officials and U.S. oil companies. Nothing came of these talks during the year, as there were some painful points of dispute concerning the loss of assets by the companies during the period of nationalizations and the breaking off of U.S.-Libyan relations in the early 1980s.

The border dispute with Chad went to the International Court, and relations with Chad improved as the two nations signed a wide-ranging agreement for mutual cooperation. However, Libya's relations with neighbouring Arab countries continued to improve. Large numbers of Egyptians and people from other nations of North Africa came without restriction to seek work in Libya, and the exchange of produce and consumer goods, especially across the Tunisian border, was lively. (J.A. ALLAN)

This article updates the *Macropædia* article NORTH AFRICA: *Libya*.

MOROCCO

A constitutional monarchy of North Africa, Morocco has coastlines on the Atlantic Ocean and the Mediterranean Sea. Area: 458,730 sq km (177,117 sq mi). Pop. (1992 est.): 26,239,000. (Area and population figures refer to Morocco as constituted prior to the purported division of Western Sahara between Morocco and Mauritania and the subsequent Moroccan occupation of the Mauritanian zone in 1979.) Cap.: Rabat. Monetary unit: dirham, with (Oct. 5, 1992) a free rate of 7.94 dirhams to U.S. $1 (13.50 dirhams = £1 sterling). King, Hassan II; prime ministers in 1992, Azzedine Laraki and, from August 11, Mohamed Karim Lamrani (interim).

The army-backed coup in Algeria was of considerable interest to the Moroccan government at the start of 1992, both because of Muhammad Boudiaf's assumption of supreme office there and because of its own determination to liquidate the Western Sahara issue as soon as possible. Boudiaf's sympathies for Morocco were expected to help in this respect, and his assassination in late June cast a cloud over Moroccan-Algerian relations. His successors, however, did not seem ready to renew active support for the Polisario Front, the Western Saharan national liberation movement.

Although Morocco had accepted the UN-sponsored cease-fire in Western Sahara in September 1991 and the deployment of a UN peacekeeping force, MINURSO, it raised objections to the proposed voting lists for the UN-organized referendum on self-determination, arguing that an additional 120,000 names should be added to the 74,000 voters derived from Spain's 1974 census of the territory. At the start of 1992, as Morocco joined the UN Security Council for a two-year term, the UN itself accepted many of Morocco's objections, against furious opposition from the Polisario Front; the new UN secretary-general, Boutros Boutros-Ghali, called on both sides to remove the remaining obstacles to the referendum within three months. This period was later extended, although the UN warned that MINURSO would be withdrawn if no agreement could be reached by the end of 1992. Late in the year the UN attempted to organize a meeting of tribal chiefs from Western Sahara to consider the list of names, but the Polisario Front objected to some of the chiefs scheduled to attend.

Morocco equally demonstrated its impatience with the long-drawn-out referendum process by warning that it would extend the electoral process to Western Sahara in 1992 whether or not the referendum had been held and the final status of the territory thereby established. Consequently, in September Western Sahara was included in a nationwide referendum on a new constitution, and in October Morocco's municipal elections also were contested there. Legislative elections were postponed until early 1993.

The new constitution reflected some of the demands of Morocco's opposition parties for political reforms by allowing the majority party after the elections to assume governmental power and select its own Cabinet; previously the king had appointed the Cabinet ministers. King Hassan, however, reserved the right of terminating parliament for himself. Guarantees for human rights were also written into the new constitution in an attempt to ward off further international criticism of Morocco's human rights record. The referendum on the constitutional changes was boycotted by the new opposition front, the Democratic Bloc. The opposition did not, however, boycott the subsequent elections.

(GEORGE JOFFÉ)

This article updates the *Macropædia* article NORTH AFRICA: *Morocco*.

OMAN

The sultanate of Oman occupies the southeastern part of the Arabian Peninsula, facing the Persian Gulf, the Gulf of Oman, and the Arabian Sea. A small part of the country lies to the north and is separated from the rest of Oman by the United Arab Emirates. Area: 306,000 sq km (118,150 sq mi). Pop. (1992 est.): 1,640,000. Cap.: Muscat. Monetary unit: rial Omani, with (Oct. 5, 1992) a par value of 0.38 rial to U.S. $1 (free rate of 0.65 rial = £1 sterling). Sultan and prime minister in 1992, Qabus ibn Sa'id.

On Oct. 31, 1992, it was announced that Sultan Qabus had signed a border-delineation agreement with Pres. Ali Abdallah Salih of Yemen, ending a 25-year dispute. It marked a period of cautious Omani diplomacy with states normally considered hostile to the Gulf Cooperation Council (GCC) bloc; Oman also retained its ambassador in Baghdad and continued a dialogue with Iran on trade and political issues.

Within the GCC, Oman continued to press for a unified GCC army of 100,000 men, a proposal discussed by Oman's chief of staff, Gen. Khamis al-Kalbani, when he visited Kuwait (the 1992 president of the GCC) on January 18. The momentum for the proposal slowed, however, when Kuwait and Qatar signed bilateral defense treaties with the U.S.

Petroleum Minister Sa'id ash-Shanfari said in April that the sultanate would expand oil production in late 1992 to 750,000 bbl a day and forecast that his country would produce at that level for 10 years. On February 8 he signed a memorandum with the Royal Dutch/Shell group for detailed research on exploiting Oman's gas reserves, now totaling 480 billion cu m (17 trillion cu ft). On June 17 Oman entered into a partnership with Kazakhstan to help the landlocked former Soviet republic build a pipeline for its potentially large oil exports. The deal was Oman's first foreign venture in its bid to find fresh sources of revenue.

Archaeologists made two sensational finds in the southern Dhofar region. In February the lost city of Ubar—known as Iran the "city of towers" in the Qur'an—was unearthed. Then in May, Juris Zarins, chief archaeologist of a U.S.-British-Omani expedition, announced another new find, Saffara Metropolis at the base of the al-Qara Mountains

at a site with the modern name of Ayn Humran. It was marked on the maps of Claudius Ptolemy, the Alexandrian geographer of the 2nd century.   (JOHN WHELAN)

This article updates the *Macropædia* article ARABIA: *Oman*.

QATAR

A monarchy (emirate) on the Arabian Peninsula, Qatar occupies a desert peninsula on the west coast of the Persian Gulf. Area: 11,427 sq km (4,412 sq mi). Pop. (1992 est.): 520,000. Cap.: Doha. Monetary unit: Qatar riyal, with (Oct. 5, 1992) a free rate of 3.67 riyals to U.S. $1 (6.25 riyals = £1 sterling). Emir and prime minister in 1992, Sheikh Khalifah ibn Hamad ath-Thani.

A surprise Saudi attack on a Qatari border post at Khofous on Sept. 30, 1992, in which two Qatari soldiers died, plunged Qatar into its deepest crisis since the removal of the previous emir in 1972. The Saudis occupied the post, claiming it was 14 km (8½ mi) inside their territory. They also said the tension had been brought about by nomadic Bedouins. The Qatar government retaliated by unilaterally suspending a 1965 border agreement with Riyadh. Saudi Arabia called for the two countries to choose a mutually acceptable mediator, but in a further move the Qataris threatened to take the dispute to the International Court of Justice (ICJ) at The Hague. On October 28 the Qatar government, in a deliberate snub to the Saudis, sent its ambassador back to Baghdad in breach of the Gulf Cooperation Council (GCC) boycott against Iraq. Talks were also opened at senior level with Tehran. Much of Qatar's anger originated in what was seen in Doha as unspoken Saudi backing for Bahrain in a long-standing dispute over the Hawar islands off the Qatari peninsula. Qatar had taken this dispute to the ICJ in July 1991, but diplomats said the court might take until 1995 to decide competence. In December the border dispute with Saudi Arabia was settled in time for Qatar, which had boycotted recent GCC meetings, to attend the summit in Abu Dhabi on December 21.

On September 1 the emir announced a major government reshuffle that created two superministries to manage the economy. The most significant change was the appointment of Abdullah ibn Hamad al-Attiyah as energy and industry minister to oversee the government's massive investment in gas and petrochemical projects. In early June Qatar became the third Gulf state to sign a defense pact with the U.S.

(JOHN WHELAN)

This article updates the *Macropædia* article ARABIA: *Qatar*.

SAUDI ARABIA

The kingdom of Saudi Arabia occupies four-fifths of the Arabian Peninsula, with coastlines on the Red Sea and the Persian Gulf. Area: 2,240,000 sq km (865,000 sq mi). Pop. (1992 est.): 15,267,000. Cap.: Riyadh. Monetary unit: Saudi Arabian riyal, with (Oct. 5, 1992) an official rate of 3.79 riyals to U.S. $1 (6.44 riyals = £1 sterling). King and prime minister in 1992, Fahd.

King Fahd entered his second decade as monarch with a fresh commitment to political reform, but he also faced open attack from conservative elements in the religious establishment. In foreign affairs, the kingdom was quick to recognize the independence of the Muslim republics of the former Soviet Union, and it gave economic and political backing to beleaguered Bosnia and Hercegovina. Economic prosperity returned in the aftermath of the Gulf war thanks to steady energy prices.

Fahd had come to power in 1982 with a reputation as a reformer, but it was only on March 1, 1992, that the monarch fulfilled his promise with three major decrees. He provided for the establishment of an advisory 60-member

King Fahd holds one of his regular audiences for Saudi citizens. In March the king announced that a Consultative Council would be formed, and he also made changes to the country's basic laws so as to balance demands of conservatives and of those wanting modernization.
FRANÇOIS GUENET—ODYSSEY/MATRIX

Consultative Council (*majlis ash-shura*) and ordered a devolution of power to local assemblies, established a "basic law" giving weight to civil as well as religious legislation, and set down rules for the royal succession that brought into the equation hundreds of second-generation princes, hitherto sidelined by the king's 30 or so surviving brothers.

The changes had become inevitable after the Gulf war brought new influences into the kingdom with the arrival of 500,000 allied troops. However, the promised deadline of six months after the decree for the first meeting of the *majlis ash-shura* was not met. On September 23, the 60th anniversary of the founding of the kingdom, the king swore in former justice minister Sheikh Muhammad ibn Ibrahim ibn Jubair as the *majlis ash-shura*'s first speaker. Fahd also ordered Interior Minister Prince Naif to carry out an overhaul of current laws to bring them into line with the "basic law."

Despite support for these measures from within the as-Sa'ud family, Fahd faced a backlash at the end of 1992. A petition signed by 107 leading scholars and clerics was presented to the government calling for strict adherence to Islamic law and accusing the authorities of wasting billions of dollars funding "atheistic regimes." In late November Fahd dismissed seven members of the council of senior ulema (religious scholars) who had used illness as an excuse for failing to attend a meeting called to condemn the petition. The king named 17 younger clerics to replace them and to broaden the council. The council interprets the Qur'an—the constitution of the kingdom—and makes religious pronouncements. In the past it had been used by the ruling as-Sa'ud family to validate their decisions.

Until the dismissals, Fahd had been trying to placate the orthodox strain in the kingdom, giving greater authority to the religious police and refusing to allow women to drive automobiles. The petition was a virtual declaration of war. Its authors blamed the government for the "total chaos of the economy and society, administrative corruption, widespread bribery, favouritism and the extreme feebleness of the courts." It also lambasted the lack of political freedoms and alleged "torture by the security services and the police." At a ceremony in late March to mark the 1992 Faisal Foundation prizes, Prince Khalid ibn Faisal, son of the late king, praised his uncle's reforms, distinguishing them as "neither Oriental nor Occidental" but instead constituting a "reaffir-

mation of the Islamic foundation of Saudi government and life." Since they were begun in the late 1970s, the King Faisal International Prizes had been awarded to 74 scholars from 24 countries, including 9 Americans.

Saudi Arabia's primacy in Islamic diplomacy was underlined by Foreign Minister Prince Sa'ud al-Faisal's confident declaration of support for Bosnia and Hercegovina at the Islamic Conference summit in Jiddah in early December. He threatened to supply weapons to Bosnian Muslims unless the UN acted to end the bloodshed in the former Yugoslav republic. After civil war broke out in Bosnia in the spring, King Fahd conducted an intensive political campaign to pressure Belgrade and the Serbs to end what Muslims regarded as "aggression" against Bosnia. In June the monarch launched a national fund-raising effort to provide aid to Bosnia, giving $8 million from his own purse. On February 22 Prince Sa'ud signed protocols establishing diplomatic links with the Muslim former Soviet republics of Tajikistan, Turkmenistan, and Uzbekistan. All the Muslim republics were being actively courted by Saudi Arabia, Iran, and Turkey. Speaking in the Turkmen capital of Ashkhabad, Prince Sa'ud said, "As a Muslim country, we feel fully linked with the peoples of this Islamic region which stood by Islam and the Muslims throughout history." He promised aid from the Saudi Fund for Development, a soft loans agency.

Saudi Arabia's relations with three of its neighbours took a turn for the worse. In April the Riyadh authorities wrote to Yemen-based Western oil companies telling them they were exploring for oil inside Saudi territory in the Hadhramaut region. The crisis further strained relations between the two states, already tense because of Yemen's pro-Iraq stand during the Gulf war. Talks took place in November but came to no conclusion. In September Saudi Arabia barred imports of Jordanian fruit and vegetables, alleging contamination but in reality as a reprisal against Amman's sympathies with Baghdad. These tussles paled into insignificance, however, when on September 30 Saudi forces attacked a Qatari border post at Khofous, which some maps placed inside Saudi territory, killing two of its occupants and then seizing it the following day. Qatar unilaterally abrogated a 1965 border agreement, plunging into crisis not only its relationship with the kingdom but also the political balance of the Saudi-led Gulf Cooperation Council (GCC). Qatar withdrew from a number of GCC events and angered the Saudis by deciding to restore diplomatic links with Iraq, but tensions eased with the signing of a new border agreement in December.

The Saudis also faced a period of uncertainty over their relationship with Washington after Pres. George Bush's defeat in the U.S. presidential election. On September 11 the Bush administration approved the sale of 72 F-15 fighter aircraft to Saudi Arabia, but President-elect Bill Clinton said that before he could endorse the sale he would have to be certain that Israel would retain its military superiority in the region. Saudi Arabia was seeking to double the size of its 70,000-strong regular forces. During the Gulf war its air force flew more than 10,000 sorties. On February 22 the Saudi forces ended military exercises code-named South Storm, the largest ever held in the kingdom.

Notwithstanding these setbacks, the Saudi economy enjoyed boom conditions. The 1992 budget announced on January 2 was, at $48.2 billion, significantly higher than two years earlier and hinted at renewed economic growth. Fahd said the priorities were military and economic development as well as education. As if to demonstrate the kingdom's new strength, Saudi Aramco, the national oil company, in February announced plans to borrow $2.9 billion from foreign banks in two separate loans. In other measures, the Saudi authorities in February announced that foreign partners in the eight joint-venture banks would have to start paying tax on their retained profits.   (JOHN WHELAN)

This article updates the *Macropædia* article ARABIA: *Saudi Arabia.*

SYRIA

A republic of southwestern Asia, Syria is on the Mediterranean Sea. Area: 185,180 sq km (71,498 sq mi). Pop. (1992 est.): 12,958,000. Cap.: Damascus. Monetary unit: Syrian pound, with (Oct. 5, 1992) a par value (official rate) of LS 11.22 to U.S. $1 (LS 19.08 = £1 sterling) and a promotion rate of LS 20.96 to U.S. $1 (LS 35.64 = £1 sterling). President in 1992, Gen. Hafez al-Assad; prime minister, Mahmoud Zuabi.

Syria in 1992 took a predictably hard line with Israel despite the change in government in Tel Aviv. In January Syria boycotted multilateral Middle East peace talks in Moscow. However, at peace talks in Washington, D.C., in September, Foreign Minister Farouk ash-Shara insisted that his government was ready for "total peace" with Israel.

At home Pres. Hafez al-Assad was sworn in for another seven-year term on March 12. Vowing to continue recent political and economic reforms, he said that greater efforts would be made to improve the living conditions of Syrians. While reaffirming his commitment to peace talks, Assad was critical of Israel and U.S. policy toward that nation. Reacting to Israeli Prime Minister Yitzhak Rabin's speech in July after his election victory, he expressed the view that Israel's offer to engage in talks concerning autonomy with the Palestinians reflected a "divide and rule" approach by Tel Aviv, designed to split Arab ranks.

In other spheres Syria played a dominant role in regional politics, mediating between Egypt and Iran in July when Foreign Minister ash-Shara visited Cairo and in September between Iran and the United Arab Emirates when U.A.E. Pres. Sheikh Zaid ibn Sultan an-Nahayan visited Damascus to protest Iran's seizure of U.A.E. islands in the Persian Gulf. In August the foreign minister of Turkey visited Syria to clear up misunderstandings concerning the opening of the Ataturk Dam on the Euphrates River, and both nations confirmed their adherence to the 1987 bilateral water-sharing agreement.

In a minor Cabinet reshuffle in June, 19 new ministers entered the 36-member administration. The new appointees reflected the continued emphasis on gradual economic reform and liberalization. The most senior government posts remained unchanged, but Nadir Nabulsi, former chairman of the al-Furat Petroleum Co., was named oil minister, and a second woman, Saliha Sanqar, entered the administration as minister of higher education. The Cabinet was dominated by the Arab Socialist Ba'th Party, with 24 of the 36 positions.

Although Syria had not embraced a free-market economy and appeared to be reluctant to follow Egypt's path in adopting International Monetary Fund/World Bank development programs, it embarked on its own style of reforms based on the free-market model. The 1992 budget was 37% above that of the previous year and followed the pattern of recent years when cost cutting was the theme in order to halt spiraling inflation. Syria's participation in the Gulf war led to an injection of some $2 billion from Saudi Arabia, as well as new loans from Germany and Japan.

In early November the London-based daily *al-Hayat* reported that Syria had struck a new weapons deal with Russia that would provide Damascus with a number of sophisticated Sukhoi and MiG interceptors, tanks, and antimissile systems. The deal, concluded earlier in the year, was part of a $2 billion weapons cooperation accord signed in 1991.

Syria would begin receiving the hardware in 1993. North Korea's army chief of staff, Vice-Marshal Chi Koang, visited Syria in October, and reports circulated that the Syrians were buying Scud-C missiles.

Addressing the 250-member parliament on March 12, Assad said that the role of the Progressive Front, which included several political parties, would be streamlined. More political parties could also be established. Nevertheless, Syria remained in difficulties with its Western trading partners over its human rights record. In mid-January the European Parliament voted to block disbursement of aid to Damascus. During a trial that ended in early March, 14 civil rights activists were sentenced to terms of prison ranging from 3 to 10 years. Partly as a response to the criticism of its human rights record, Syria in April lifted all travel restrictions on Syrian Jews and cooperated with Turkey in opposing Kurdish guerrilla operations. On April 20 Elie and Salim Souad, the last two detained Syrian Jews, were freed, and in July it emerged that Syrian Jews no longer were required to have the Arabic *moussawi* ("Jew") stamped on their identity cards. In December the U.S. claimed Syria was again refusing exit permits to Jews, but this was denied by the Syrian ambassador to the U.S. in a letter to the civil rights leader Jesse Jackson.   (JOHN WHELAN)

TUNISIA

A republic of North Africa, Tunisia lies on the Mediterranean Sea. Area: 154,530 sq km (59,664 sq mi). Pop. (1992 est.): 8,413,000. Cap.: Tunis. Monetary unit: Tunisian dinar, with (Oct. 5, 1992) a free rate of 0.84 dinar to U.S. $1 (1.43 dinars = £1 sterling). President in 1992, Gen. Zine al-Abidine Ben Ali; prime minister, Hamed Karoui.

The major concern of Pres. Zine al-Abidine Ben Ali in 1992 was to counter the efforts of Islamic fundamentalists, particularly those connected with the Nahda movement led by Rachid Ghannouchi. A January army-backed coup in neighbouring Algeria was greeted with relief in Tunis, particularly because it came hard on the heels of the expulsion of 29 Nahda activists from Algeria the previous month. Tunisia remained aloof from The Sudan, refusing to restore diplomatic relations because of that country's support for the Nahda. At the same time, Tunisian statesmen toured the Middle East, warning of the political dangers of Islamic movements. Relations with Egypt were reinforced when Pres. Hosni Mubarak, during an April visit to Tunis, joined Ben Ali in warning of the Islamic danger.

A Ministry of Islamic Affairs was created in early 1992, even though the Nahda's domestic network had been dismantled. Great media emphasis was placed on Ben Ali's piety. According to the government, some 400 Nahda militants were being held in prison. Amnesty International, which published a damning report on Tunisia's human rights record in early 1992, reported that 8,000 militants were being held in 1991. The courts were also severe in dealing with criminal acts by Islamists. In August heavy prison sentences were meted out to 171 Nahda members convicted by a military court of plotting to overthrow the government. Ten of them were tried in absentia, including Ghannouchi, who eventually ended up in Britain after a sojourn in The Sudan. In an attempt to bolster its human rights record, Tunisia established a special government department to protect these rights. This move was tarnished, however, by official harassment of Tunisia's human rights organization and by new legal measures designed to limit its effectiveness.

Despite its sympathy with Iraq during the 1991 Gulf war, Tunisia refused Iraqi requests in February to return five of its civilian airliners and funds frozen as a result of UN sanctions. Tunisia also reluctantly observed UN sanctions imposed in April against Libya after its attempts at mediation had failed.

Tunisia's economic future showed improvement as a result of bumper cereal and olive harvests in 1991. Gross domestic product growth for 1992 was set at an ambitious 6.5%, and economic reform continued. Poverty, however, continued to be widespread, with 544,000 persons (65% of them in urban areas) being defined by the government as poverty-stricken. The World Bank also approved a $250 million structural adjustment loan, which was cofinanced by the European Communities.   (GEORGE JOFFÉ)

This article updates the *Macropædia* article NORTH AFRICA: *Tunisia*.

TURKEY

A republic of Asia Minor and southeastern Europe, Turkey has coastlines on the Aegean, Black, and Mediterranean seas. Area: 779,452 sq km (300,948 sq mi), including 23,764 sq km in Europe. Pop. (1992 est.): 58,584,000. Cap.: Ankara. Monetary unit: Turkish lira, with (Oct. 5, 1992) a free rate of 7,511 liras to U.S. $1 (12,768 liras = £1 sterling). President in 1992, Turgut Ozal; prime minister, Suleyman Demirel.

The coalition government formed by Suleyman Demirel, leader of the centre-right True Path Party, with Erdal Inonu's Social Democratic Populist Party (SHP) as a junior partner, continued the policy initiated by Pres. Turgut Ozal of establishing Turkey as a bastion of stability in a troubled region. Turkey's willingness to work with the U.S. in promoting stability was stressed by Prime Minister Demirel when he conferred with Pres. George Bush in Washington on Feb. 11, 1992. A similar message was conveyed to French Pres. François Mitterrand when the latter went to Ankara on April 13. Demirel visited the Turkic republics of the former Soviet Union between April 27 and May 3 and Moscow on May 25–26.

On June 25 Turkey was host to the first summit meeting of the Black Sea economic cooperation region, a project that had been launched by President Ozal. The summit, which brought together the leaders of Turkey, Russia, Ukraine, Moldova, Georgia, Armenia, Azerbaijan, Romania, Bulgaria, Albania, and Greece, was followed by Turkish attempts to help find a peaceful solution to the dispute between Armenia and Azerbaijan over Nagorno-Karabakh. Turkey also played an active part in efforts to halt the bloodshed in Bosnia and Hercegovina, but its advocacy of threatening the Serbs with air strikes did little to ease the position of Bosnian Muslims. The Black Sea summit allowed Demirel to confer with his Greek counterpart, Konstantinos Mitsotakis, but once again the conclusion of a friendship pact was postponed pending solution of the Cyprus dispute.

At home, the government's parliamentary majority was reduced by defections from the SHP, while the opposition was weakened by President Ozal's efforts to wrest control of the Motherland Party, which he had founded, from the hands of its current leader, Mesut Yilmaz. The first rift in the ranks of the Social Democrats occurred over the Kurdish issue. After the government intensified military measures to counter the terrorist campaign of the separatist Kurdish Workers' Party (PKK), 18 radical Kurdish members of Parliament, who had been elected on the SHP ticket in October 1991, resigned and rejoined the—predominantly Kurdish—People's Labour Party. Then in September, after Parliament revoked a law passed in 1980 banning all political parties existing at the time, the SHP's precursor, the Republican People's Party, was reconstituted and elected Inonu's rival

Bodies of Kurdish terrorists are laid out for identification after Turkish government forces defeated their attack on an army post in the southeastern part of the country. More than 200, most of them Kurds, were killed in the fighting, which took place at the end of September.
AJANSI—GAMMA LIAISON

Deniz Baykal as its leader. Baykal and 17 other members of Parliament thereupon resigned from the SHP, while former prime minister Bulent Ecevit lost four members of his small Democratic Left Party.

The Kurdish campaign caused over 1,000 casualties in 1992. The worst incident occurred on September 29 when some 23 members of the security forces and up to 200 terrorists were killed in an attack on a post guarding the Iraqi frontier. The government responded by launching ground and air operations both within the country and across the frontier. At the same time, it reached agreement with the governments of Syria and Iran, and with leaders of the Iraqi Kurds, to deny the terrorists facilities across the border. Masoud Barzani and Jalal Talabani, the two main leaders of the Iraqi Kurds, visited Ankara, and in October forces under their command attacked PKK camps in northern Iraq. By late November more than half the PKK forces had reportedly been killed, wounded, or captured.

After stagnating in 1991, the economy grew by over 6% in the first half of 1992. The new government's promise to halt the rise in prices could not be fulfilled, and the consumer price index rose by 44% in the first eight months. Nevertheless, a good export performance and the revival of tourism after the Gulf war led to an increase in foreign currency reserves, and Turkey was able to service its foreign debt of some $50 billion and to attract fresh foreign investment. The first two power units of the Ataturk dam on the Euphrates, the centrepiece of the vast southeast Anatolia project, were commissioned on July 25.   (ANDREW MANGO)

UNITED ARAB EMIRATES

Consisting of Abu Dhabi, Ajman, Dubayy, al-Fujayrah, Ra's al-Khaymah, ash-Shariqah, and Umm al-Qaywayn, the United Arab Emirates is a federation of seven largely autonomous emirates located on the eastern Arabian Peninsula. Area: 77,700 sq km (30,000 sq mi). Pop. (1992 est.): 1,989,000. Provisional cap.: Abu Dhabi. Monetary unit: United Arab Emirates dirham, with (Oct. 5, 1992) an official rate of 3.71 dirhams to U.S. $1 (6.30 dirhams = £1 sterling). President in 1992, Sheikh Zaid ibn Sultan an-Nahayan; prime minister, Sheikh Maktum ibn Rashid al-Maktum.

Diplomacy to settle the Iranian annexation of Abu Musa and Greater and Lesser Tunb, three islands near the Strait of Hormuz, met with deadlock during 1992. The crisis started in late April when Iran refused several hundred expatriates the right to return to the jointly administered Abu Musa island, sovereignty over which was shared with ash-Shariqah, one of the seven U.A.E. emirates, under a 1971 accord. Ra's al-Khaymah, another full member of the U.A.E., had owned the two Tunb islands, which Iran annexed to its Hormozgan province. Two days later, talks were held in the U.A.E. between Iranian Foreign Ministry officials and their U.A.E. counterparts, but little progress was made toward resolving the issue. The Iranian action appeared to have been motivated by fears that the U.A.E. was planning to allow the U.S. to establish a military base in the Gulf.

Despite the political tension with Iran, the U.A.E. enjoyed a mild economic boom following the end of the Kuwait crisis. By October nearly 450 companies had enlisted in the Jebel Ali Free Zone outside Dubayy.   (JOHN WHELAN)

This article updates the *Macropædia* article ARABIA: *United Arab Emirates*.

YEMEN

A republic of the southwestern Arabian Peninsula, Yemen has coastlines on the Red Sea, the Gulf of Aden, and the Arabian Sea. Area: 531,869 sq km (205,356 sq mi), including 59,770 sq km of undemarcated area bordered by Saudi Arabia claimed by the former Yemen Arab Republic (North Yemen). Pop. (1992 est.): 12,147,000. Cap.: San'a'. Monetary units: Yemeni dinar, with (Oct. 5, 1992) a par value of 0.46 dinar to U.S. $1 (free rate of 0.79 dinar = £1 sterling), and Yemen rial, with (Oct. 5, 1992) a par value of 16.50 rials to U.S. $1 (free rate of 28 rials = £1 sterling). President in 1992, Gen. Ali Abdallah Salih; prime minister, Haidar Abu Bakr al-Attas.

Elections scheduled for the fall of 1992 were postponed by the government until April 27, 1993, because of a rising pattern of violence, which targeted leaders of the two main parties. A transitional period for the Yemen merger between the conservative north and the former Marxist south had been scheduled to expire on November 22, after multiparty parliamentary elections were held.

Yemen was wracked by bombings and attacks on leading politicians, including two of the five members of the ruling Presidential Council. On April 26, Justice Minister 'Abd al-Wasei Salam was shot in the leg and eye. On July 17 gunmen tried to kill Anis Hassan Yahya, a member of the Socialist Party politburo whose brother was shot dead on June 15. Southern Yemen's three million people, outnumbered three to one by the northerners, were reportedly storing weapons for a showdown. Because of Yemen's strained ties with Saudi Arabia, which began when Yemen backed Iraq in the Gulf war, there was speculation that the Saudis might be backing the northern activists. Saudi Arabia denied the allegation but cut all financial aid to Yemen and withdrew the residence permits of more than 850,000 Yemeni workers. In mid-December a protest in Ta'izz against rising prices escalated into three days of rioting in San'a' and other cities that left some 13 dead. It was reported that Prime Minister Haidar Abu Bakr al-Attas had resigned but that the resignation had been rejected.

In the fall Yemen and Saudi Arabia opened the first direct talks concerning a long-standing border dispute. At a meeting in early November, Saudi Arabia suggested that a joint commission hire an international company to re-mark the disputed area. In May Saudi Arabia warned six foreign oil companies with exploration rights near the unmarked border that they were violating Saudi territory.

In October, Yemen and Oman ratified a border-demarcation agreement, ending a 25-year-old dispute between the two neighbours.   (JOHN WHELAN)

This article updates the *Macropædia* article ARABIA: *Yemen*.

East Asia

CHINA

The People's Republic of China is situated in eastern Asia, with coastlines on the Yellow Sea and the East and South China seas. Area: 9,572,900 sq km (3,696,100 sq mi), including Tibet and excluding Taiwan. (See *Taiwan*, below.) Pop. (1992 est., excluding Taiwan): 1,165,888,000. Cap.: Beijing (Peking). Monetary unit: renminbi yuan, with (Oct. 5, 1992) an official rate of 5.63 yuan to U.S. $1 (9.57 yuan = £1 sterling). President in 1992, Yang Shangkun (Yang Shang-k'un); premier, Li Peng (Li P'eng).

The pace of economic reform quickened in China in 1992, but Deng Xiaoping (Teng Hsiao-p'ing), the country's 88-year-old paramount leader, remained adamantly opposed to political liberalization. At its long-awaited 14th congress in October, the Communist Party of China (CPC) revamped the nation's leadership and charted a path to a socialist market economy. The political process of succession, however, was not expected to be known until Deng no longer held the reigns of power.

Reaffirming their commitment to socialism with Chinese characteristics, China's leaders decried the collapse of Soviet communism, but at the same time they presided over a country that, particularly along its dynamic southern and eastern edges, was evolving ever further from classic definitions of socialism. Instead of being a homogeneous country in which a unified party-state bureaucracy commanded a centrally planned economy through administrative fiat, China was becoming a more complex and variegated society in which regional, economic, and social differences tended to weaken the nation's political cohesiveness. The erosion of political idealism turned attention away from societal goals and toward individual and familial enrichment. Meanwhile, an export-oriented strategy of rapid economic development increased China's international interdependence. China steered a careful foreign-policy course pending the further buildup of its national power.

Domestic Affairs. During a January inspection tour in the south, Deng urged acceleration of China's market-oriented economic reforms and strongly defended his policy of opening to the world. Quickly responding to these cues, the March plenum of the CPC's Central Committee confirmed Deng's immense political authority and personal prestige by translating his terse pronouncements into official policy. CPC General Secretary Jiang Zemin (Chiang Tse-min) further elaborated Deng's directives in his report to the 14th party congress in October. Implicitly acknowledging that the paramount leader's time was growing short, Jiang paid lavish tribute to Deng as "the chief architect of our socialist reform" who displayed "his great political courage by blazing a new path to socialism" and manifested "his great theoretical courage by opening new perspectives for Marxism."

Deng's radically reductionist interpretation of Marxism considered nothing as sacrosanct except the Communist Party's monopoly on political power. That monopoly was said to guarantee social stability, but in reality it merely preserved the privileges of the party elite. Jiang outlined his idea of political reform as meaning "a socialist democracy suited to Chinese conditions and in no respect a Western, multiparty, parliamentary system." Nevertheless, his report and other official documents envisioned the further expansion of China's private economic sector, the eventual elimination of state subsidies to inefficient Maoist-era industrial dinosaurs, and the management of the economy through financial, fiscal, and monetary policies rather than through direct administrative controls.

The leadership changes effected by the 14th congress of the 52 million-strong CPC represented at least a partial victory for party reformers. Zhu Rongji (Chu Jung-chi), China's moderate 63-year-old economic overlord, Hu Jintao (Hu Chin-t'ao), the 49-year-old party secretary of Tibet, and Gen. Liu Huaqing (Liu Hua-ch'ing), a 76-year-old military professional, joined holdovers Jiang, Premier Li Peng (Li P'eng), Qiao Shi (Ch'iao Shih), and Li Ruihuan (Li Jui-huan) on the seven-member Political Bureau Standing Committee, from which conservatives Yao Yilin (Yao Yi-lin) and Song Ping (Sung P'ing) retired. The Political Bureau itself expanded to 22 (including alternates) as 8 elderly members retired and 14 younger officials, most proponents of reform, joined its ranks. Almost half of the 189 voting and 130 alternate members of the 14th Central Committee were newly elected, representing a better-educated generation of mostly middle-aged party technocrats.

Gen. Yang Shangkun (Yang Shang-k'un), China's 85-year-old president, lost his seat on the Political Bureau, while his younger half-brother Gen. Yang Baibing (Yang Pai-ping) was removed from the powerful Central Military Commission and given a face-saving seat on the Political Bureau. Continuing military influence in Chinese politics was demonstrated, however, by the armed forces' growing share of the national budget and the considerable autonomy enjoyed by military industries and weapons exporters. The Central Advisory Commission—a rest home for elderly hard-liners under its 87-year-old chairman, Chen Yun (Ch'en Yün)—was abolished outright. On the day after the congress ended, Deng, appearing frail, emerged from seclusion to exchange greetings with the delegates and expressed satisfaction with their work.

The stalemate over political reform in China was symbolized by the Central Committee's decision, on the eve of the party congress, to let stand the 1989 verdict on former party chief Zhao Ziyang (Chao Tzu-yang), purged after the 1989 Tiananmen (T'ien-an-men) massacre. Rehabilitation of Zhao would have presaged the "reversal of verdicts" on the crushed democracy movement, but this was not likely to come until Deng passed from the scene. Continuing their campaign against political dissent, Chinese courts publicly pronounced sentence on a score of pro-democracy activists for various "counterrevolutionary activities." The longest sentence, seven years, was meted out to Zhao's former top aide Bao Tong (Pao T'ung). Chinese authorities encouraged pro-democracy activists to return from abroad, but when student leader Shen Tong (Shen T'ung), testing the limits of this promise, tried to organize a Beijing branch of his Democracy for China Fund, he was arrested, detained for two months, and sent back to the U.S.

There was no letup in the systematic abuse of political prisoners, who were variously kept in unspeakable conditions of solitary confinement, beaten and tortured, routinely denied medical assistance, roughly force-fed if on hunger strikes, and cut off from their families, which were also subjected to punitive state actions. Such abuses were detailed by the international human rights organizations Amnesty International and Asia Watch. They also reported systematic Chinese mistreatment of Tibetan political prisoners. Beijing (Peking) attempted to counter this unfavourable publicity by issuing a government White Paper late in 1991 that portrayed the Chinese prison system as a model of humane treatment.

Beijing's chronic aversion to political liberalization was also evidenced in Hong Kong, where the efforts of Hong Kong's new governor, Chris Patten (*see* BIOGRAPHIES), to further democratize the British colony's Legislative Council elections elicited harsh denunciations from Chinese officials, including Lu Ping (Lu P'ing), director of the Hong Kong and Macao Affairs Office. Beijing even threatened to scrap the landmark 1984 Sino-British agreement on the transfer of sovereignty to China in 1997, which guaranteed the maintenance of Hong Kong's distinctive way of life, and to invalidate all contracts signed by the territorial government but not approved by the Chinese government unless Patten backed down. But, strongly supported by Hong Kong public opinion as well as by British Prime Minister John Major, Patten showed no signs of being intimidated.

A mass riot in early August in Shenzhen (Shen-chen), where a million people vainly queued for the chance to buy stocks on the booming local exchange, provided an ironic comment on the official slogan that "Only socialism can save China." Police used tear gas to disperse 50,000 rioters whose hopes of striking it rich were frustrated by speculators and manipulative brokers. An epidemic of capitalist

The Political Bureau Standing Committee, which sets policy for China, poses for a formal photograph. Elected at the 14th party congress in October, the committee included three new members and was expected to continue the country's free-market economic reforms.

fever gripped everyone from high officials, who profited from corrupt business deals, to ordinary Chinese with dollar signs in their eyes.

Jiang, in his report to the 14th party congress, boosted previous predictions for growth of the country's gross national product in the 1990s from 6 to 8–9% per annum, but the economy exceeded even these figures by growing at 10.6% in the first half of the year. An official 11.7% rate of inflation during the same period resuscitated familiar fears about the effects of too-rapid growth and a possible repetition of the politically destabilizing inflationary pressures of 1987–88 that preceded the 1989 protest movement. Workers leery of the effects of privatization and marketization on wages and job security had already periodically engaged in wildcat strikes and various kinds of job actions. Although the private and cooperative sectors consistently outperformed state industries, the latter continued to absorb the bulk of capital investment even in Guangdong (Kwangtung) province, where the annual growth rate was a spectacular 20%.

Foreign Affairs. Confounding predictions that it would become isolated or marginalized in the post-cold war world, China hewed to its independent foreign policy line in 1992, carefully balancing international cooperation with unilateral pursuit of its long-term national interests. During a year in which relations with its neighbours took centre stage, Beijing improved its strategic and diplomatic position in Asia, boosting its claim to being a great world power. At the same time, China's leaders were concerned about a long-term threat to their regime from what they viewed as the hegemonic aspirations of the U.S., the world's sole surviving superpower. They pointed to the continuing struggle between socialism and capitalism and to growing conflicts among developed capitalist states as proof that even though "one cold war had ended, two more cold wars had begun." But rather than seek security in isolation, China intensified its interactions with the rest of the world in order to accelerate the pace of its domestic economic development. As the world's limited stock of moral outrage was exhausted by fresh horrors in Bosnia and Somalia, memories of the 1989 Tiananmen massacre continued to fade, facilitating Beijing's strategy of engagement

Jiang, Li Peng, and Yang Shangkun all made successful overseas tours in 1992, while Emperor Akihito of Japan, South Korean Pres. Roh Tae Woo, Indian Pres. Ramaswamy Venkataraman, and Russian Pres. Boris Yeltsin paid historic visits to China. Chinese helmsmen cautiously navigated through the wreckage of the former Soviet Union, but Taiwan's open-handed courtship of the newly independent republics complicated China's relations with these nations. Beijing barely averted a trade war with Washington in mid-October, and the victory of Democrat Bill Clinton over Pres. George Bush in the U.S. presidential election heightened China's anxieties about the future of Sino-American relations.

In August China completed the circle of its diplomatic relations in East Asia by establishing official ties with South Korea, a country with which it already enjoyed substantial trade and cultural relations. Hobbled by its long-term connection with North Korea, Beijing had hesitated to take this final step, but the collapse of the Soviet Union, which had been North Korea's patron, resolved China's doubts. While Seoul increased pressure on Pyongyang to accelerate the pace of Korean reunification, China managed to rob Taiwan of its most important diplomatic partner and attract more Korean investment. China's cordial welcome to Roh signaled the further weakening of Beijing's ties to its old North Korean comrades.

Earlier in the year, China, which had long been an active player in Middle East politics and an ardent supporter of the Palestinians, finally established diplomatic relations with Israel. This step, reportedly taken with the blessing of Palestine Liberation Organization leader Yasir Arafat, enabled China to participate in the ongoing Middle East peace process.

The October visit of Emperor Akihito, the first ever by a Japanese monarch, reinforced an already close relationship that was, however, still haunted by the angry ghosts of the 1937–45 Sino-Japanese War. Reciprocating Jiang's April visit to Tokyo, the emperor emphasized Japan's cultural indebtedness to China, but he stopped short of formally apologizing for Japan's wartime atrocities. The reiteration in February by the National People's Congress (NPC) of China's claims to sovereignty over the Diaoyu (Tiao-yü) islets northeast of Taiwan with their potentially oil-rich continental shelf waters elicited objections from Japan. Tokyo also laid claim to the territory that it called the Senkaku Islands. Good Sino-Japanese relations were too important to both sides, however, for these conflicting claims to escalate any time soon into a serious dispute.

The same could not be said about Beijing's claims to the islands and territorial waters of the South China Sea. The NPC not only reiterated these claims but declared China's right to employ military force in defense of its sovereignty. In May China contracted with a U.S. oil-prospecting firm (Crestone Energy Corp.) for a concession area midway between an existing Vietnamese-let concession and the uninhabited Spratly Islands, where five nations (China, Taiwan, Vietnam, the Philippines, and Malaysia) had staked territorial claims. Beijing's growing air and naval capabilities in the South China Sea strengthened its position vis-à-vis rival claimants. The situation represented an important test of China's intentions toward Vietnam as well as toward the Association of Southeast Asian Nations (ASEAN) states, which favoured a peaceful resolution of the problem. The use of force would not only confirm Asian fears of China as a rising expansionist power but would also seriously damage China's prospects for eventual peaceful reunification with Taiwan.

The disintegration of the Soviet Union at the end of 1991 presented China with an entirely new constellation of states and political forces along its northern and Inner Asian frontiers. After several centuries of eastward expansion, Russia had retreated from Asia, if only partially and temporarily, leaving China as the dominant continental power. But Beijing's satisfaction was tempered by the unsettling influence that Muslims in the independent Central Asian republics (Kazakhstan, Kyrgyzstan, Tajikistan, Turkmenistan, and Uzbekistan) might exert on discontented Muslims in China's northwest provinces (Xinjiang [Sinkiang], Gansu [Kansu], and Ningxia [Ningsia]). Late in 1991 China extended diplomatic recognition to Russia and the other post-Soviet republics. By developing good relations with the smaller shards of the Soviet Union, China apparently hoped to contain any future resurgence of Russian imperial power. Meanwhile, as flocks of petty Russian traders descended on China's abundantly stocked markets hunting for bargains, Chinese officials shopped for high-tech Soviet arms and military equipment, including high-performance aircraft and avionics. Less pleasing to China, because it bolstered Taiwan's international status, was the enormous interest the post-Soviet republics expressed in Taiwan as a developmental model, trading partner, foreign investor, and source of technical and economic assistance.

Chinese leaders were chagrined by the failure of President Bush to win reelection because they considered him more

A policeman in Shenzhen (Shen-chen) attempts to control a crowd waiting to buy shares on the city's stock exchange. In 1992, for the first time, the communist government allowed private citizens to hold stock in companies.
REUTERS/BETTMANN

sympathetic to Chinese interests. While clearly signaling its desire for good relations with the Democratic administration of Bill Clinton after he assumed office in January 1993, China feared that the new president might toughen U.S. policy toward China. In September Bush infuriated Beijing by approving the sale to Taiwan of up to 150 F-16 fighters and high-performance helicopters. France then rushed to sell Taiwan 60 Mirage fighters, further provoking Beijing's ire. In December China retaliated by ordering France to close its consulate in Guangzhou.

China's trade practices and human rights abuses remained contentious issues in U.S.-China relations. The U.S. Congress, however, failed to override Bush's veto of legislation that would have linked the extension of China's most-favoured-nation status (MFN) to improvements in its human rights record. Beijing also criticized the Chinese Student Protection Act, which was signed into law by Bush and indefinitely extended the visas of Chinese students who feared reprisals should they go home. China similarly objected to an assertion in Congress that the U.S. had an interest in Hong Kong's future. China implicitly acknowledged the complexity of current political realities by muffling warnings about the dangers of U.S. political subversion while increasing its surveillance of foreign journalists.

Beijing signed important trade agreements with Washington in January and October that partially met longstanding U.S. demands for protection of intellectual property rights and greater market opening. In exchange the U.S. supported China's application to join the General Agreement on Tariffs and Trade. China's 1992 trade surplus with the U.S. grew again to a projected $15 billion (according to U.S. figures); only Japan had a larger trade surplus with the U.S. Trying to ward off protectionism, Beijing stepped up purchases of U.S. agricultural and industrial commodities and allowed the U.S. insurance giant American International Group to set up shop in Shanghai. The major threat to Sino-American trade remained the possible loss of China's MFN status. Beijing continued to resist every effort to associate its observance of human rights with an extension of its MFN status. It also vowed to retaliate against U.S. goods if it lost that status. Such remarks did not appear to constitute a major menace because China depended on the U.S. market to absorb one-quarter of its consumer and light-industrial exports.

On the whole, in the realm of foreign affairs, Chinese leaders followed Deng's Sphinxlike injunctions to hold one's ground, calmly observe developments, hide one's capacities while biding one's time, and refrain from being a leader. This prescription for a low-profile foreign policy was premised on the belief that internal stability (meaning continued communist rule) could be maintained and that time favoured the growth of Chinese power because rapid development expanded the economic and military instruments available to the Chinese state. (STEVEN I. LEVINE)

JAPAN

A constitutional monarchy in the northwestern Pacific Ocean, Japan comprises an archipelago with four main islands (Hokkaido, Honshu, Kyushu, and Shikoku), the Ryukyus (including Okinawa), and lesser adjacent islands. Area: 377,835 sq km (145,883 sq mi). Pop. (1992 est.): 124,330,000. Cap.: Tokyo. Monetary unit: yen, with (Oct. 5, 1992) a free rate of 119.56 yen to U.S. $1 (203.25 yen = £1 sterling). Emperor, Akihito; prime minister in 1992, Kiichi Miyazawa.

On Jan. 24, 1992, in a major policy speech at the opening session of the Diet, Prime Minister Kiichi Miyazawa urged Japan to make a greater contribution to the international community. The charge presaged the government's six-month struggle to enact legislation that would, in effect, reinterpret Japan's constitution. In June, over strenuous opposition, the governing Liberal-Democratic Party (LDP)—in alliance with centrist parties—finally put through the law permitting the Self-Defense Forces (SDF) to participate in UN peacekeeping operations overseas, and in September the dispatch of a contingent to Cambodia was approved. On the domestic front, success eluded the government's handling of a sharp recession, marked mainly by deflation of the "bubble economy" and a collapse of averages on the Tokyo Stock Exchange (TSE). The Miyazawa Cabinet continued to be weakened by a series of money-for-favours scandals, which reached into the top level of the LDP. In July the party did, however, score a slim victory in the crucial election for the (upper) House of Councillors.

Japanese troops prepare to depart in September to join a United Nations peacekeeping mission in Cambodia. For the first time since the end of World War II, Japanese military forces would be stationed outside Japan but for noncombat duties only.
KAKU KURITA—GAMMA LIAISON

Domestic Affairs. In December 1991 support for Miyazawa's Cabinet, which had come to power the preceding October, had reached a high of 50% of respondents, according to the Kyodo News Service poll. In March the level plunged to 24.1%. Meanwhile, in January, Miyazawa practically handed over control of the party to LDP Vice Pres. Shin Kanemaru (also chairman of the faction identified with former prime minister Noboru Takeshita). Michio Watanabe, head of the fourth largest faction, assumed the posts of deputy prime minister and foreign minister.

When the Diet reconvened in January, seats in the (lower) House of Representatives were apportioned as follows: LDP 278, Social Democratic Party of Japan (SDPJ) 138, Komeito (Clean Government Party) 46, Japan Communist Party (JCP) 16, Democratic Socialist Party (DSP) 14, independents and minor parties 10, vacancies 10 (total 512). Seats in the upper house were distributed as follows: LDP 115, SDPJ 73, Komeito 20, JCP 14, Rengo (Japan Trade Union Confederation) 11, DSP 10, independents and minor parties 8, vacancies 1 (total 252).

From the beginning of the session, the Diet was mired down in consideration of the UN peacekeeping bill and maneuvers toward the July upper house election. Early results in by-elections to fill upper house vacancies did not augur well for the LDP; in February and in March, party nominees in Nara and Miyagi prefectures lost to Rengo-backed candidates who opposed the UN legislation. In late March, however, an LDP candidate won in Gunma prefecture, and by June support for the Miyazawa Cabinet had rallied to the 32.4% level (Kyodo).

The showdown on the peacekeeping legislation began in the upper house. At 2 AM on June 9, four days and nights after the plenary session was convened, the law was passed in the House of Councillors by an alliance of LDP, Komeito, and DSP members. On June 15 the government turned down a collective resignation request by 141 opposition members of the lower house. After hours of delay, the LDP proposal became law. The newspaper *Asahi Shimbun* editorialized that the move "was sparked by calls from the United States" and ignored majority public opinion. The battle was not over. Peacekeeping overseas immediately became the most important single issue in the election.

The campaign for the triennial election began on July 8, with 600 candidates vying for 126 seats (half of the upper house). To avoid the peacekeeping issue, the LDP emphasized a five-year plan labeled "In Pursuit of Lifestyle Superpower." SDPJ Chairman Makoto Tanabe sought an alliance with the DSP, despite differences over the UN bill. Koshiro Ishida, head of Komeito, discounted his party's support of the peacekeeping bill and emphasized the need for an economy more reliant on domestic demand. Presidium Chairman Tetsuzo Fuwa of the JCP declared the government's peacekeeping law unconstitutional. Morihiro Hosokawa, a former member of the upper house and governor of Kumamoto, withdrew from the LDP and formed the Japan New Party specifically for the July election, stating that he hoped to eliminate bureaucratic government.

On July 26 the LDP rebounded from the defeat of three years before by winning 69 of 127 contested upper house seats. The party (with a total of 108 seats), in alliance with Komeito (24) and the DSP (7), maintained a working majority (139) over other opposition forces (113). Hosokawa's new party won only four seats. The future of Rengo, which won no seats, was uncertain. Prime Minister Miyazawa told reporters that the LDP "victory" signaled public approval of his peacekeeping law. The record low turnout (50.72%), however, indicated apathy.

Public indifference turned to anger over yet another brace of "money-politics" scandals. In February former prime minister Zenko Suzuki and Jun Shiozaki, former head of the Management and Coordination Agency, had testified under oath in the Diet that they and the Miyazawa faction were not directly involved in bribery by the Kyowa Corp., a bankrupt steel-frame maker. The same month prosecutors arrested the head of a major trucking company, Tokyo Sagawa Kyubin, for allegedly passing more than $4 billion through firms linked with a crime syndicate. The press identified some 100 politicians who were named as recipients of Sagawa "donations," but evidence was not clear until after the July election. On August 27 Kanemaru, the LDP's chief power broker, resigned from the party vice presidency and also as head of the Takeshita faction. Kanemaru admitted that he had received $4 million from the arrested president of Sagawa. Miyazawa's grip on power was loosened, and the media began speculation as to a successor. On December 11 Miyazawa reshuffled his Cabinet, hours after the Takeshita faction had split. The breakaway group was headed by Tsutomu Hata, who was replaced as finance minister by Yoshiro Hayashi.

The Economy. Debate on peacekeeping delayed the Diet's adoption of a budget. On April 9, eight days after the start of the fiscal year, the lower house passed a 72,220,000,000,000 yen budget, a 2.7% increase over fiscal year 1991.

The Organization for Economic Cooperation and Development estimated Japan's inflation-adjusted growth in gross national product (GNP) on an annual basis at 2.25% in the January–June period. It predicted that growth would be only 1.8% in 1992, the first growth rate below 2% since 1974. The TSE also reflected a sharp recession; on April 7 the 225-issue Nikkei gauge fell below the 18,000 level, and on June 22 it plunged below the psychological 16,000 floor. On August 18 the Nikkei closed at 14,309, the lowest level in six years five months. In 1989 it had peaked at 38,916. By October 27 it had recovered to 17,185.26.

In December 1991, on the eve of U.S. Pres. George Bush's Tokyo visit, the Bank of Japan had lowered the official discount rate by 0.5 points to 4.5%. Another cut to 3.75% came on April 1, and yet another on July 27 to 3.25%, the lowest level in two years. On August 28 the government announced a comprehensive package of measures totaling 10.7 trillion yen to stimulate the economy and consolidate domestic demand, the largest such program ever undertaken. The total would be equivalent to 2.3% of GNP, including 8.6 trillion yen in public works. A supplementary budget to finance the package was introduced in the fall extraordinary Diet. Among advanced industrial democracies, Japan continued to enjoy a modest consumer price inflation rate (0.1% monthly change in July) and a low percentage of the work force unemployed (October, 2.2%).

Foreign Affairs. On January 9 Under Secretary General Yasushi Akashi (*see* BIOGRAPHIES), the highest ranking Japanese UN official, was appointed to head the UN Transitional Authority in Cambodia (UNTAC). Like Sadako Ogata, the UN high commissioner for refugees, he had studied in the U.S. and was a member of the first generation to reach adulthood in postwar Japan. Akashi helped organize a one-day conference on Cambodia in Tokyo on June 22, attended by Prince Norodom Sihanouk, Khmer Rouge leader Khieu Samphan, and representatives of 32 nations. The result was the tenuous Tokyo Declaration on the Cambodian Peace Process. Akashi's success, however, depended on the outcome of the peacekeeping debate. When the government bill was passed on June 15, he stressed the need for Japan to join UN operations immediately, but severe restrictions had been placed in the law by the centrist parties. These included the prime minister's responsibility for decisions, his accountability to the legislature, and a freeze on the dispatch of SDF forces until the Diet approved each case. On September 6 the Miyazawa Cabinet officially approved a plan to send some 1,800 SDF and civilian police personnel to the mainland. Engineering troops would begin the repair of roads and bridges around Phnom Penh. It would be the first appearance of Japanese forces in a combat zone (and the first in Asia) since the Pacific War (World War II).

Former prime minister Takeshita represented Japan at the "Earth Summit" held in Rio de Janeiro June 3–14. He advocated a Japanese contribution of $31.2 billion (20–30% of a total world goal of $125 billion) for the environment.

Japan's current account surplus in fiscal 1991, according to the Finance Ministry, more than doubled to reach a total of $90 billion. At least part of the surplus was assigned to official development assistance (ODA), which rose 20% to $11 billion (0.32% of GNP) during the year. Japan thus became the world's number one aid donor. On May 15 Japan provided $400 million in aid to central and eastern Europe to help in free-market reforms, and in June it was announced that Japan would contribute $83.8 million to drought-stricken Africa. On September 22 Foreign Minister Watanabe, addressing the UN General Assembly in New York City, gave broad hints that Japan, because of its economic status and increased UN activities, deserved a seat on the Security Council.

Diplomatic exchanges with the U.S. continued to focus on trade issues. President Bush visited Tokyo January 7–10 with a delegation that was headed by Commerce Secretary Robert Mosbacher and included 20 U.S. businessmen. Miyazawa and Bush signed a two-part economic "global partnership" calling on Japan to make sacrifices to aid the ailing U.S. economy. Concessions included a promise that Japanese automakers would increase imports of American parts to $19 billion by 1995. Japanese officials criticized the pact as an example of "managed trade," while the chief executives of America's "Big Three" (Ford, General Motors, and Chrysler), who were in the U.S. delegation, were disgruntled over the small effect on the trade balance. The *Asahi Shimbun* referred to the visit as "less than a success," given the emphasis on trade friction, Bush's need to win a second term, and the president's embarrassing illness at a state dinner.

In June the Industrial Council issued a report assessing Japan's top 10 trade partners. It singled out the U.S. as having the worst record, characterized by unilateral action (for example, sanctions under section 301 of the U.S. Trade Act of 1974). The General Agreement on Tariffs and Trade, the council concluded, should be the forum for settling trade disputes. In July government and steel industry officials expressed disappointment over petitions filed with the U.S. Trade Commission by 12 American companies. They alleged dumping of steel exports, despite the fact that several of the Japanese firms named in the petitions had close business ties with U.S. counterparts. Talks on the Structural Impediments Initiative, begun in 1990, continued in August. While media attention focused on Japanese trade restrictions, Ministry of International Trade and Industry officials complained that little or no action had taken place in the U.S. Tokyo urged Washington to cut the budget deficit, increase private savings, and improve industrial competitiveness.

Relations between Tokyo and Moscow remained stranded on the shoals of a territorial dispute. Japan continued to protest Russian occupation of—and a military buildup on—what it called the "Northern Territories," originally Japanese

Japanese Prime Minister Kiichi Miyazawa and U.S. Pres. George Bush meet in Tokyo on January 8. Discussions centred on economic issues, including policies to stimulate growth in the world economy and U.S. efforts to gain greater access to Japanese markets.

islets northeast of Hokkaido. A formal peace treaty ending World War II awaited resolution of the problem. Soviet ground troops in the region had begun a withdrawal in May 1991. In December 1991 Russian Foreign Minister Andrey Kozyrev proposed a solution in tune with a 1956 declaration, which provided a return of two of the four islands, matched by a peace treaty. In a two-day meeting in Tokyo, March 20–21, Kozyrev urged Japan to extend aid to the new Russian state or miss the opportunity to settle the dispute. On July 7, at their Munich (Germany) summit, the Group of Seven major industrial powers (G-7) called on Russia to settle the problem on the basis of "law and justice." In talks with Foreign Minister Watanabe on September 2 in Moscow, however, Russian Pres. Boris Yeltsin warned that Japanese pressure would be counterproductive, and on September 9 Yeltsin announced cancellation of his long-expected visit to Tokyo, scheduled for September 13. In October Japan sharply rejected Yeltsin's suggestion that Russia return two of the islands.

Jiang Zemin (Chiang Tsi-min), general secretary of the Chinese Communist Party, made a five-day visit to Tokyo April 4–8, meeting with Prime Minister Miyazawa and Emperor Akihito. The emperor and empress traveled to Beijing (Peking) October 23–28, the first visit by a Japanese emperor. Despite some worries, the trip passed without incident. The year marked the 20th anniversary of normalization of relations between Japan and China.

Prime Minister Miyazawa was in Seoul, South Korea, in January to start an "action plan" to redress the $8 billion (1991) Japanese trade surplus. It was agreed to establish a foundation in each country to facilitate technology transfers. In June South Korean Trade and Industry Minister Hann Bong Soo met with Watanabe in Tokyo to finalize the program. South Korea, however, was critical of a Japanese government study of the use of Korean "comfort women" by Imperial Army troops during World War II. The Korean foreign minister welcomed Tokyo's apology and admission of an official role in forcing the women into prostitution but called the report "incomplete." Although Japan had supported separate UN membership for both Koreas in 1991, Tokyo had only informal relations with the North. Normalization of contacts was set back when North Korea's ambassador to China, Chu Chang Jun, stated that Japan was "not qualified" for a permanent seat on the UN Security Council.   (ARDATH W. BURKS)

KOREA, DEMOCRATIC PEOPLE'S REPUBLIC OF

A socialist republic of northeastern Asia on the northern half of the peninsula of Korea, the Democratic People's Republic of Korea (North Korea) borders the Sea of Japan, the Yellow Sea, and the Republic of Korea at roughly the 38th parallel. Area: 122,762 sq km (47,400 sq mi). Pop. (1992 est.): 22,227,000. Cap.: Pyongyang. Monetary unit: won, with (Oct. 5, 1992) a free rate of 2.15 won to U.S. $1 (3.65 won = £1 sterling). President in 1992, Marshal Kim Il Sung; chairmen of the Council of Ministers (premiers), Yon Hyong Muk and, from December 11, Kang Song San.

North Korea's diplomatic agenda in 1992 was largely dominated by high-level talks with South Korea. North Korean Premier Yon Hyong Muk and his South Korean counterpart, Chung Won Shik, met alternately in Pyongyang and Seoul throughout the year to implement the historic inter-Korea accords drafted in December 1991. The 25-point nonaggression and reconciliation treaty and a declaration for a nonnuclear peninsula were exchanged by the two premiers in Pyongyang on February 19.

Implementation of the accords, however, stalled over the issue of North Korea's nuclear program. South Korea and the U.S. believed that the North was developing nuclear weapons at a suspected nuclear reprocessing plant at Yongbyon, about 90 km (56 mi) north of Pyongyang. North Korea refused to allow joint inspections unless U.S. military bases were also open for inspection.

However, North Korea did make some concessions on the nuclear issue. In January it signed a nuclear safeguards accord with the International Atomic Energy Agency (IAEA). The North Korean legislature ratified the treaty on April 9. On May 4 the nation's Atomic Energy Ministry gave a 100-page document to the IAEA describing four nuclear reactors that it said would be opened to international inspection. North Korea said that all four were research reactors and denied that they were reprocessing plutonium for nuclear weapons.

The director general of the IAEA, Hans Blix, visited the Yongbyon nuclear facility in May, along with an IAEA inspection team. North Korean officials told them that the facility was a "radio chemical research laboratory" and revealed that they had succeeded in producing "a tiny amount" of plutonium. Blix confirmed that it was a large-scale reprocessing plant and that construction was 80% complete. North Korean officials insisted the plant was only for research. In December a dramatic report surfaced in Moscow that Russian troops had stormed a jet about to take off for Pyongyang with 36 senior weapons specialists on board. The scientists were reportedly hired by North Korea to work on its nuclear weapons program.

Pres. Kim Il Sung turned 80 on April 15, and his son and heir apparent, Kim Jong Il, was 50 on February 16. North Korean representatives told U.S. officials in January that Kim Jong Il had taken charge of foreign policy. However, there were no public announcements regarding the long-anticipated transfer of power from father to son. On December 11 Kim Il Sung dismissed Prime Minister Yon Hyong Muk, replacing him with Kang Song San, a Moscow-trained economics expert. On December 29 China, Pyongyang's largest trading partner, announced that beginning in 1993 North Korea would have to pay cash for all trade rather than barter. The economy continued its downward slide, with increasing reports of shortages.

(JOSEPH L. NAGY)

This article updates the *Macropædia* article KOREA: *North Korea*.

KOREA, REPUBLIC OF

A republic of northeastern Asia on the southern half of the peninsula of Korea, the Republic of Korea (South Korea) borders the Sea of Japan, the Korea Strait, the Yellow Sea, and the Democratic People's Republic of Korea at roughly the 38th parallel. Area: 99,263 sq km (38,326 sq mi). Pop. (1992 est.): 43,663,000. Cap.: Seoul. Monetary unit: won, with (Oct. 5, 1992) a free rate of 795 won to U.S. $1 (1,352 won = £1 sterling). President in 1992, Roh Tae Woo; prime ministers, Chung Won Shik and, from October 7, Hyun Soong Jong.

A presidential election and reconciliation with China were watershed events for South Korea in 1992. The December 18 presidential poll was the nation's second peaceful transfer of power and the first in which all the candidates were civilians. In what was widely acknowledged to be a free and fair election, ruling Democratic Liberal Party candidate Kim Young Sam captured 41.4% of the vote, followed by opposition stalwart Kim Dae Jung with 33.4% and political newcomer Chung Ju Yung with 16.1%. Kim Young Sam was to take office on Feb. 25, 1993, succeeding Pres. Roh Tae Woo.

Kim Young Sam, 64, had managed a remarkable transformation from outsider to insider. A longtime campaigner

Kim Tal Hyon (left), a deputy premier of North Korea, and Choi Gak Kyu, a deputy prime minister of South Korea, meet in Seoul on July 19. Throughout the year the two governments continued high-level talks to implement the accords reached in December 1991.

REUTERS/BETTMANN

for democracy, he and Kim Dae Jung ran against Roh in 1987, splitting the opposition vote. In 1990 Kim Young Sam merged his party with Roh's ruling party. In return, he was awarded the party's presidential nomination. For Kim Dae Jung, 67, of the main opposition Democratic Party, it was apparently the end of a political career that spanned 40 years. After his defeat he resigned from the National Assembly and as party leader.

Chung, the 76-year-old founder of the country's second largest industrial conglomerate, Hyundai, was the surprise entry. A critic of Roh's government, he resigned as Hyundai's honorary chairman and formed the United People's Party in January. It gained a firm political foothold in the March 24 parliamentary elections, winning 31 seats in the 299-member assembly. The polls were a setback for Roh. His Democratic Liberal Party won 149 seats, one short of a majority, and was forced to woo several independents to keep control of the National Assembly. Kim Dae Jung's Democratic Party took 97 seats, with independents winning 22.

Chung had frequent clashes with the government. His family and several Hyundai subsidiaries had been ordered to pay a record $181 million in back taxes and penalties in November 1991. In April 1992 seven Hyundai executives, including Chung's son Chung Mong Hun, were arrested for tax evasion. Through it all, Chung continued to criticize the government for its economic policies.

President Roh came under fire for postponing elections for local mayors and provincial governors that had been scheduled for June 30. He said that the government could not afford to hold three elections in one year. Opposition leaders accused him of attempting to give the ruling party an edge in the December presidential polls. The appointed local administrators were considered loyal to the ruling party.

The crowning achievement of Roh's last year in office came on August 24, when South Korea and China established full diplomatic relations. Roh said that this diplomatic breakthrough removed the "last external constraint to reunification of the peninsula." The agreement, signed in Beijing (Peking) by South Korean Foreign Minister Lee Sang Ock and his Chinese counterpart, Qian Qichen (Ch'ien Ch'i-ch'en), ended 40 years of hostility between the two powers. China had come to North Korea's aid in the 1950–53 Ko-

rean War. Since taking office, Roh had pursued a "Northern Policy" aimed at improving ties with South Korea's communist neighbours. His goal was to win over North Korea's allies and seek their help in encouraging North Korea to go to the bargaining table. South Korea established diplomatic relations with the Soviet Union in 1990. With the breakup of the Soviet Union, China remained North Korea's last major communist ally.

President Roh clearly hoped that China would mediate between the North and the South. However, in his historic visit to Beijing on September 27–30, he failed to get a clear commitment from China. Pres. Yang Shangkun (Yang Shang-k'un) of China said that international pressure on North Korea over the nuclear issue was "undesirable." But he did note that the Chinese government expected North Korea to refrain from developing nuclear weapons and to open its plants to international inspection.

The agreement to open relations with China required that South Korea break off ties with Taiwan. President Roh said he hoped that unofficial relations would soon be established. The official response from Taiwan, however, was swift and sharp. It suspended landing rights for South Korean airlines and canceled South Korea's preferential treatment in import quotas and construction contracts.

As the December election neared, Roh and his party were hit by several political scandals. The government was forced in September to cancel a lucrative contract for South Korea's second mobile telephone network. The license had been awarded to a consortium led by Sunkyong, the country's fifth largest business group. However, the opposition claimed that Sunkyong had received favoured treatment because President Roh's only daughter was married to the son of Sunkyong's chairman. Ruling party presidential candidate Kim Young Sam, worried that the scandal would hurt his election chances, persuaded the president to cancel the deal. The contract would be reconsidered after the election.

Roh was severely embarrassed later in September when a former county official, Han Joon Soo, admitted buying votes on behalf of Democratic Liberal Party candidates in the parliamentary election in March. Roh moved quickly to limit the damage the scandal might cause his party. He allowed Kim Young Sam to take over as president of the Democratic Liberal Party, and on October 7 he appointed a caretaker prime minister to assure the fairness of the presidential poll. The National Assembly overwhelmingly approved his choice of university president Hyun Soong Jong to replace Chung Won Shik as prime minister.

(JOSEPH L. NAGY)

This article updates the *Macropædia* article KOREA: *South Korea*.

MONGOLIA

A landlocked republic between the U.S.S.R. and China in eastern Asia, Mongolia was formerly known as Outer Mongolia. Area: 1,566,500 sq km (604,800 sq mi). Pop. (1992 est.): 2,182,000. Cap.: Ulaanbaatar (Ulan Bator). Monetary unit: tugrik, with (Oct. 5, 1992) a par value of 40 tugriks to U.S. $1 (68 tugriks = £1 sterling) and a free rate of 120 tugriks to U.S. $1 (204 tugriks = £1 sterling). President in 1992, Punsalmaagiyn Ochirbat; prime ministers, Dashiyn Byambasüren and, from July 21, Puntsagiyn Jasray.

In accordance with its new (fourth) constitution, which came into force in February 1992, Mongolia abandoned the name "people's republic" and the star on its flag and adopted a new national emblem embodying traditional symbols. The People's Great Hural (assembly) and Little Hural (indirectly elected legislature) were replaced by the Mongolian Great Hural, a single chamber with a four-year term. In general elections for its 76 seats, 293 candidates stood in the 26 constituencies. With 80 candidates, the Mongolian People's Revolutionary Party (MPRP) received 56.7% of the ballot, and other parties (excluding independents) around 40%. The outcome of the election was disproportionate, however, the MPRP taking 70 seats (71, if a pro-MPRP independent is included). The remainder went to the Mongolian Democrats (2), Social-Democrats, National Progress Party, and United Party.

At its first session in July, the Great Hural elected its chairman, Natsagiyn Bagabandi (who could stand in for Pres. Punsalmaagiyn Ochirbat), and approved Puntsagiyn Jasray as prime minister. Jasray took about a month to form his Cabinet. Reappointments to provide continuity included Choyjilsürengiyn Pürevdorj (deputy prime minister for industry), Lieut. Gen. Shagalyn Jadambaa (defense), and Tserenpiliyn Gombosuren (foreign relations).

The drive for privatization and a market economy continued, but Jasray's team faced problems of falling production, declining foreign trade, growing indebtedness, food rationing, and rising crime. Russia's failure to deliver oil for several months disrupted road, rail, and air transport and halted coal extraction, so power stations had to cut electricity supplies and were unable to stockpile for the winter. However, in May representatives of the International Monetary Fund and other international organizations and donor countries, meeting in Tokyo, raised another $320 million in short- and medium-term aid. Meanwhile, the final stage of the withdrawal of Russian troops from Mongolia was completed on schedule.   (ALAN J.K. SANDERS)

TAIWAN

Taiwan, which consists of the island of Taiwan and surrounding islands off the coast of China, is the seat of the Republic of China (Nationalist China). Area: 36,179 sq km (13,969 sq mi), including the island of Taiwan and its 86 outlying islands, 22 in the Taiwan group and 64 in the Pescadores group. Pop. (1992 est.): 20,727,000. (Area and population figures include the Quemoy and Matsu groups, which are administered as an occupied part of Fujian [Fukien] province.) Cap.: Taipei. Monetary unit: New Taiwan dollar, with (Oct. 5, 1992) a free rate of NT$25.26 to U.S. $1 (NT$42.95 = £1 sterling). President in 1992, Lee Tenghui; president of the Executive Yuan (premier), Hau Pei-tsun.

The world again paid close attention to the remarkable economic power of Taiwan (the Republic of China) during 1992. Many countries, including Russia and other former Soviet republics, established or upgraded unofficial relations with Taiwan, a pint-sized economic giant that ranked among the 10 leading capital exporters in the world. Even a relatively modest economic growth of 6.5% facilitated the implementation of Pres. Lee Teng-hui's blueprint for carefully managed democratization. Per capita income surpassed $10,000.

The December 19 elections were the first since the Republic of China moved to Taiwan in 1949 in which an entirely new Legislative Yuan was chosen by all the voters. The ruling Nationalist Party (Kuomintang; KMT), with 53% of the vote and 96 of the 161 seats, won a smaller majority than had been expected, while the Democratic Progressive Party (DPP) gained 31% and 50 seats. Most of the remainder went to independents. Once again, such issues as the economy, taxes, and environmental pollution bulked larger in the eyes of the electorate than the emotionally charged question of Taiwan independence. This election and the 1991 election for the National Assembly were both significant milestones in Taiwan's democratic transformation.

When the second National Assembly convened on March 20 to consider revising the constitution, the rambunctious DPP minority proposed an amendment that would have mandated direct popular election of the president. The KMT, unable to reconcile different views within its own ranks, deferred a decision until 1995, a year before the president's term was due to expire. With conservatives blocking more fundamental changes, the National Assembly passed eight KMT-initiated amendments that reduced the powers of the Control Yuan, cut from six to four years the terms of the president and National Assembly members, and approved direct popular election of Taiwan's provincial governors and county magistrates. Taiwan's harsh sedition law was also significantly moderated, and public advocacy of fundamental political changes, including Taiwan independence, was legalized. Several leading dissidents were released from prison and others allowed to return from exile. Although the government no longer considered banning the DPP for advocating an independent Republic of Taiwan, Premier Hau Pei-tsun warned that a proclamation of independence would be suicidal in view of Beijing's (Peking's) threats to use force to preserve Taiwan's status as a province of China. Positioning itself for eventual negotiations with the People's Republic of China (PRC) over reunification, the government defined China as "one country and two areas." Meanwhile, trade, investment, tourism, and cultural exchanges between Taiwan and the PRC continued to expand under the joint management of Taiwan's Straits Exchange Foundation and the PRC's Association for Relations Across the Taiwan Strait.

In September U.S. Pres. George Bush reversed a longstanding policy by approving the sale to Taiwan of up to 150 F-16 fighter planes. President Lee's flexible diplomacy scored new successes. Russia, Ukraine, and other former Soviet republics established economic and cultural links with Taiwan. Taiwan was finally granted observer status at the General Agreement on Tariffs and Trade, albeit on terms it disliked. In August long-term ally South Korea switched diplomatic recognition to the PRC, a loss hardly balanced by the resumption of relations with Niger.

Despite the rapid appreciation of the Taiwan dollar, local traders continued to prosper, and the central bank became the largest buyer of U.S. Treasury bills. The island's foreign exchange reserves reached $90 billion at midyear. Legislation tightening protection of intellectual property rights warded off threatened U.S. trade sanctions. The problems that Taiwan faced, including environmental pollution and rapid social changes, were largely a by-product of its prosperity.   (STEVEN I. LEVINE)

South and Central Asia

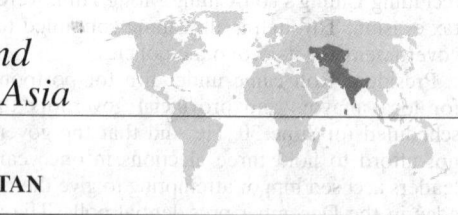

AFGHANISTAN

Afghanistan is a landlocked republic in central Asia. Area: 652,225 sq km (251,825 sq mi). Pop. (1992 est.): 18,052,000 (excluding Afghan refugees estimated to number about 2.4 million in Pakistan and 2 million in Iran). Cap.: Kabul. Monetary unit: afghani, with (Oct. 5, 1992) a free rate of 58.38 afghanis to U.S. $1 (99.25 afghanis = £1 sterling). President to April 15, 1992, Mohammad Najibullah; acting president from April 15, Abdul Rahim Hatef; interim presidents, Sibgatullah Mojadedi from April 28 and, from June 28, Burhanuddin Rabbani; prime ministers, Fazal Haq Khaliqyar to April 15 and, from July 6 to August 15, Abdul Sabur Farid Kuhestani.

Pres. Mohammad Najibullah's Communist regime collapsed on April 16, 1992, but 14 years of civil war, which had claimed two million lives and forced at least five million people out of the country, left the nation divided and almost in ruins. When peace seemed imminent, fighting among the various guerrilla groups, divided along ethnic and sectarian lines, brought on a new struggle. Najibullah took refuge in the UN office after a failed attempt to escape. Kabul, once a bustling city of 1.5 million people, looked like a ghost town after the takeover by Islamic resistance forces. Throughout the year, the city was the centre of battles between forces friendly to the new government and the renegade Islamic Party, which was expelled from the government in a dispute over power sharing.

Caretaker President Sibgatullah Mojadedi, a 70-year-old former Islamic philosophy teacher, surrendered power on June 28 to Burhanuddin Rabbani, who headed a 10-member Supreme Leadership Council of guerrilla chiefs. The changeover did not end the bloodshed, however. The most serious fighting broke out after the Islamic Party, led by firebrand fundamentalist Gulbuddin Hekmatyar, rained thousands of rockets on the city from hilltop positions on the southeastern outskirts, bringing more destruction than had taken place in the 14-year war between Soviet-backed Communist regimes and the Muslim resistance. The government also faced a serious challenge from an Iranian-backed alliance of Shi'ite Muslims. The Unity Party, a coalition of eight Shi'ite Muslim parties that enjoyed the moral and financial backing of Iran, demanded that the interim government honour past promises to share power. The Unity Party claimed to represent 35% of Afghanistan's population, mostly the downtrodden Hazaras living in the central highlands, the country's poorest and most neglected region.

A U.S. State Department report accused both the rebels and their former Communist enemies of torturing prisoners, executing political opponents, and trampling on human rights. The report said arbitrary killings and other acts of violence against suspected opponents of the Kabul regime continued. France, Italy, and Bulgaria closed their embassies and withdrew their diplomats in August, joining the exodus from Kabul under bombardment. The U.S., Britain, Germany, Japan, and Austria had withdrawn their diplomats in February 1989, just weeks before Moscow ended its nine-year occupation of the country. Also in August, the last three non-Afghan UN officials slipped out of Kabul by car to Pakistan, leaving Najibullah's fate unresolved. The ruling group wanted to try Najibullah for his role in the civil war and for the death or disappearance of hundreds of thousands of Afghans while he commanded the once-feared secret police. Pakistan sealed its border with Afghanistan, stranding thousands of Afghan refugees who had fled the rocket attacks on Kabul. This policy was a dramatic reversal for Pakistan, which for 14 years had provided a haven for some three million refugees and had helped arm the Islamic rebels. Another two million refugees had fled to Iran.

Afghanistan's growing poppy cultivation remained a concern for the West and especially for the U.S., which wanted a guarantee that production would be cut before aid was given. Guerrilla commanders were heavily involved in the lucrative poppy trade. Even the most conservative estimates expected the poppy harvest in Afghanistan to reach at least 500 metric tons, which translates into at least 50 tons of heroin. This was almost five times the production level in neighbouring Pakistan, which had become the transit route for heroin out of Afghanistan and Iran.

On December 30 a national council, composed of 1,335 delegates from throughout the country, met in Kabul and elected Rabbani to a two-year term as president. Most of the rebel groups boycotted the meeting, and the city was shelled from the hills as the voting was in progress.

(DILIP GANGULY)

BANGLADESH

A republic and member of the Commonwealth, Bangladesh is in the northeastern part of the Indian subcontinent, on the Bay of Bengal. Area: 143,998 sq km (55,598 sq mi). Pop. (1992 est.): 110,602,000. Cap.: Dhaka. Monetary unit: taka, with (Oct. 5, 1992) an official rate of 39 taka to U.S. $1 (66.30 taka = £1 sterling). President in 1992, Abdur Rahman Biswas; prime minister, Khaleda Zia.

Democracy, which had returned to Bangladesh in 1991 after 15 years of rule by the army and military-backed governments, took root in 1992 despite economic hardships and sporadic trade union strife. The most striking feature of the year was the absence of any major political discord. Prime Minister Khaleda Zia and the opposition, led by her longtime rival, Sheikh Hasina Wajeb of the Awami League, grappled with political issues inside the 330-seat Parliament instead of on the streets. With 170 seats in Parliament, Zia's government on August 30 defeated a no-confidence motion moved by the opposition accusing her administration of nonperformance in curbing lawlessness. The military did not interfere with the government.

Floods and cyclones, the country's two most common killers, spared Bangladesh in 1992. The year before, a cyclone roaring in from the Bay of Bengal had pounded the southern coast, killing at least 131,000 people and causing losses amounting to $1.7 billion. The absence of major flooding and cyclones did not leave the country problem free, however. Persecution by the military junta in neighbouring Myanmar (Burma) sent some 265,000 Muslim refugees fleeing into Bangladesh. Despite foreign aid for the refugees totaling $13.9 million, they remained a heavy burden on the meagre resources of Bangladesh, where per capita income stood at $176. The refugees, who were living in 19 camps in the southern leech-infested teakwood forests, refused to return until the human rights situation in Myanmar improved. A repatriation pact, signed in April, and eight rounds of talks between the two governments failed to persuade them to return. The refugee issue chilled Bangladesh-Myanmar relations at the beginning of the year, when both sides mobilized troops along the 280-km (175-mi) frontier.

The government unveiled a $1.7 billion deficit budget for the 1992–93 fiscal year, which began in July. The shortage would be met through loans and grants, mainly from western nations. With inflation standing at 10% and food prices remaining more or less stable, Zia's government had time to concentrate on consolidating democracy.

In September the government passed an ordinance meant to stop campus terrorism. Student power was formidable in Bangladesh, where universities produced the activists of the national political parties. The offenses covered by the law included extortion, blocking transport, hijacking, theft, abduction, sexual harassment, intimidating people, and damaging vehicles and other public and private property. On November 2 police in Dhaka clashed with students protesting legislation aimed at cheating on examinations.

Bangladesh achieved some success in improving relations with India. A small land corridor that Dhaka needed to give it access to two enclaves was handed over by India in June, ending an 18-year dispute. Zia visited New Delhi in May. Pakistan agreed to repatriation of 250,000 Pakistani nationals, stranded in Bangladesh since 1971 when Dhaka gained independence from Pakistan. Zia visited the United States in March and met with Pres. George Bush.

Muslim refugees from Myanmar (Burma) work to create living facilities in neighbouring Bangladesh. Hundreds of thousands of Muslims fled their homes to escape persecution by the Myanmar government and army, but in doing so they created severe problems for Bangladesh.

CHRISTOPHER LANGRIDGE—SYGMA

A formal agreement between the government and the Chakma insurgents in the Chittagong Hill Tracts was signed in November. Chakma rebels, who were mainly Buddhist, had been fighting a sporadic bush war for 17 years in an attempt to gain more political and economic power. At least 4,000 people had been killed in army crackdowns, rebel attacks, and reprisal killings by settlers. The government tacitly encouraged Muslims to settle in the hills on the grounds that this would ease pressure on the overpopulated plains. More than 111 million Bangladeshis were packed into an area the size of Greece.

Islamic fundamentalism also evoked concern in Bangladesh, where about 90% of the people were Muslims. The Islamic Assembly emerged as the fourth largest party in Parliament with 21 seats. (DILIP GANGULY)

BHUTAN

The monarchy of Bhutan is a landlocked state situated in the eastern Himalayas between China and India. Area: 47,000 sq km (18,150 sq mi). Pop. (1992 est.): 1,511,000 (official projection based on 1980 census includes some 600,000–700,000 Nepalese residents purportedly declared stateless by the Bhutanese government in late 1990, more than 75,000 of whom are now refugees in Nepal). Cap.: Thimphu. Monetary unit: ngultrum, at par with the Indian rupee (which is also in use), with (Oct. 5, 1992) an official rate of 28.29 ngultrums to U.S. $1 (48.10 ngultrums = £1 sterling). Druk gyalpo (king) in 1992, Jigme Singye Wangchuk.

After three years of trying to overcome a pro-democracy uprising, Bhutan suffered a potentially more devastating revolt in 1992. Some 70,000 Nepalese civil servants, soldiers, and policemen fled Bhutan, and several top technocrats joined the exodus, creating a near vacuum in some parts of the government. Most Cabinet posts were held by the indigenous Drukpa majority, to which King Jigme Singye Wangchuk belonged, but hands-on managerial posts often were held by Nepalese. The Nepalese said that they were waging a pro-democracy campaign against Bhutan's absolute monarchy; they claimed that 53% of Bhutan's residents were Nepalese.

The Bhutanese government called the pro-democracy campaign "antinational activities . . . A terrorist movement" and said that Nepalese militants had killed 33 people and kidnapped 174 others since the revolt started in early 1988.

Bhutan's actions against the pro-democracy activists drew criticism. Representatives of the U.S.-based Refugees International, the agency dealing with early refugee warning, visited refugee sites in Nepal in July. (DILIP GANGULY)

INDIA

A federal republic of southern Asia and member of the Commonwealth, India is situated on a peninsula extending into the Indian Ocean with the Arabian Sea to the west and the Bay of Bengal to the east. Area: 3,165,596 sq km (1,222,243 sq mi), including the Indian-administered portion of Jammu and Kashmir. Pop. (1992 est.): 889.7 million, including Indian-administered Jammu and Kashmir. Cap.: New Delhi. Monetary unit: Indian rupee, with (Oct. 5, 1992) a free rate of Rs 28.29 to U.S. $1 (Rs 48.10 = £1 sterling). Presidents in 1992, Ramaswamy Venkataraman and, from July 25, Shankar Dayal Sharma; prime minister, P.V. Narasimha Rao.

Domestic Affairs. The year 1992 ended on a grim note with Hindu-Muslim riots erupting throughout the country following demolition of the Babri Mosque in Ayodhya, Uttar Pradesh, by Hindu militants on December 6. Hindu groups for some years had campaigned to build a temple for Lord Rama at the site, maintaining that the mosque had been built by the Mughal emperor Babar over a temple that marked Rama's birthplace. The Bharatiya Janata Party (BJP), Vishwa Hindu Parishad, and other extremist Hindu organizations served notice that they would start *kar seva* ("manual service") on the spot on December 6. The Supreme Court decreed that this action should be confined to symbolic prayer, and the Uttar Pradesh government, the BJP, and others gave a solemn assurance that the court's order would be obeyed. At the same time, thousands of volunteers were massed at the site, and on the appointed day they pulled down the 464-year-old mosque, with no interference from the state police. Religious clashes broke out in a number of cities, mainly Bombay, Ahmedabad, Kanpur, and Jaipur, and by December 12 the death toll had reached 1,150. There were demonstrations in Muslim countries expressing solidarity with the Muslims of India.

The union government reacted swiftly. On the night of December 6 it dismissed the BJP-run state government of Uttar Pradesh and imposed president's rule. On the evening of December 7 it announced its decision to outlaw

Hindu and Muslim fundamentalist parties and to rebuild the mosque, and on December 8 the BJP leaders L.K. Advani and Murli Manohar Joshi were arrested. On December 15 the BJP state governments of Madhya Pradesh, Rajasthan, and Himachal Pradash were also dissolved. The National Front and leftist parties demanded the resignation of Prime Minister P.V. Narasimha Rao, but the ruling Congress (I) rallied around him.

Congress continued to be without a majority in Parliament, but the government was adjudged to have consolidated its hold. This was due partly to the ineptitude of opposition parties and partly to the success of the Congress in attracting groups and individuals from other parties. The government comfortably survived a vote of no confidence on July 17, securing 267 votes to 215. The Janata Dal was the main victim of the process of attrition; an influential group headed by Ajit Singh seceded and was formally expelled. The BJP was weakened by the dissension and by the lacklustre performance of its four state governments. The Communist parties lost their elan with the worldwide setback to communism and their own dogged alliance with a fading V.P. Singh. In Gujarat the chief minister, Chimanbhai Patel, joined the Congress along with his regional party. The Congress held its organizational election after a decade and a half.

Punjab continued to be disturbed by the activities of secessionists. However, the government was able to hold elections to the state legislative assembly in February. (These had been postponed at the last minute at the time of the general election in 1991.) Most of the Akali factions boycotted the poll, and the turnout of voters was only 24.23%. The Congress secured 87 of the 117 seats in the legislature and formed a ministry under Beant Singh. It also won 12 out of 13 seats in the Lok Sabha. Municipal elections were held in the state in September, and voter participation was considerably higher. Militants declared a hartal (a cessation of work or business) in October when the assassins of Gen. A.S. Vaidya, the former chief of army staff, were executed.

Jammu and Kashmir remained unsettled. Attempts by units of the Jammu and Kashmir Democratic Alliance to cross over from Pakistan were thwarted by Pakistan in January and March and again in October. Another disturbed area was the Telingana region of Andhra Pradesh, where extremist groups, popularly referred to as Naxalites, resorted to killing landowners and government officials. Trouble continued in the northeast, and the Bodo tribes renewed their demand for a separate state. An additional political problem that government had to face was the revived demand for the formation of a new state of Jharkhand, consisting of areas from Bihar, Madhya Pradesh, Uttar Pradesh, and West Bengal, to serve as a homeland for tribal people. The strong actions taken against terrorists came under attack from human rights groups, and it was decided to establish a national human rights commission.

Andhra Pradesh had a change in leadership, with N. Janardhan Reddy stepping down from the chief ministership in October after the state high court set aside his orders for sanctioning some new medical and dental colleges. He was succeeded by K. Vijaya Bhaskara Reddy, union minister for law and company affairs. In November the chief minister of Karnataka, S. Bangarappa, relinquished office and M. Veerappa Moily took his place. Foreign Minister Madhav Sinh Solanki resigned after admitting that he had passed on to the Swiss foreign minister a letter from a lawyer relating to the Bofors kickback case. In July five new ministers of state and a deputy minister were inducted into the union Council of Ministers. R. Venkataraman, at the end of his five-year term as the country's president, was succeeded on July 25 by Shankar Dayal Sharma. In the election for the post, Sharma had defeated G.G. Swell by 675,864 electoral college votes to 346,485. K.R. Narayanan was elected vice president, filling the place vacated by Sharma.

The constitution was amended to give the status of a union territory to the capital region of Delhi and to place three more languages, Konkani, Manipuri, and Nepali, in the eighth schedule (of languages that the union is required to develop and promote).

The year began on a dismal note for Bombay with the deaths of at least 91 slum dwellers from drinking adulterated liquor during New Year's revelry. A similar tragedy claimed 210 lives in Orissa in May. As many as 47 people died in a stampede during ritual bathing in the temple town of Kumbakonam in February. Among notables who died during the year were the filmmaker Satyajit Ray (*see* OBITUARIES) and former vice president M. Hidayatullah. A technological achievement was the successful launching of an Indian-built communications satellite from Kourou in French Guiana.

On November 16 the Supreme Court upheld the legality of the order passed by the V.P Singh government in 1990 reserving 27% of government jobs for "socially and

Muslim youths demonstrate against the Indian government, charging that it had failed to prevent demolition of a mosque in Ayodhya. The destruction of the mosque by Hindu fundamentalists in December led to Muslim-Hindu riots throughout India and also created a government crisis.

educationally backward classes." The court added, however, that the better off among these classes should be excluded from the benefit. It set aside the announcement of the Rao government reserving a further 10% for the poor sections of castes considered socially advanced.

The Economy. The union budget, presented on February 29, introduced partial convertibility of the rupee and allowed the import of gold; relaxed the income-tax structure, raising the exemption limit and fixing a ceiling of 40%; and abolished control over capital issues. Total income was estimated at Rs 113,698,000,000 and total expenditure at Rs 119,087,000,000; it was the first time in years that the deficit had been brought down to 5%. There was a marginal increase in the allocations for welfare and defense. The tax on cigarettes and cement was increased. Although petroleum products were not touched in the budget, their prices were raised in September, as were the support prices of cereals. The rate of inflation, which had touched 16.2% in the middle of 1991, fell to 7.4% in September but rose again to 9.3% on October 3. The foreign exchange reserves, which at one stage had dropped to a low of $600 million, rose to $6 billion on October 23. Iron and steel prices were decontrolled in January. New areas of the economy and several public-sector undertakings, notably those producing steel, chemicals, fertilizer, and machine tools, were thrown open to private participation. The opposition criticized these decisions as more knuckling under to the World Bank and the International Monetary Fund..

All this effort at deregulation was overshadowed by the gigantic stock swindle known as the scam. A group of brokers and bankers had collaborated to manipulate stock market operations, using funds belonging mainly to public-sector undertakings. Share prices shot up on the Bombay Stock Exchange; the index rose from 3100 on February 29 to 4400 on April 24 before the bubble burst. Two prominent brokers, Harshad Mehta and Bhupen Dalal, were arrested, as were the executives of several Indian and foreign banks and financial institutions. A Reserve Bank of India estimate put the sum involved at Rs 30,786,000,000, a figure that was later revised upward to Rs 35,428,000,000. There were allegations of involvement and connivance against politicians and officials. P. Chidambaram, the minister of commerce, resigned, volunteering the information that his wife had bought shares in one of Harshad Mehta's companies. A member of the planning commission, V. Krishnamurthi, was arrested. A joint parliamentary committee was constituted under the chairmanship of Ram Niwas Mirdha to go into the entire affair, and a special court also was appointed.

In May the National Development Council gave approval to the eighth five-year plan (1992–97). It envisaged an aggregate investment of Rs 7,980,000,000,000, including a public-sector outlay of Rs 4,340,000,000,000, with an annual growth rate of 5.6%.

Foreign Affairs. The precipitate dissolution of the Soviet Union meant the loss of a dependable supporter in international diplomacy and a source of military supplies that did not have to be paid for in hard currency. The concept of nonalignment also had to be redefined with the disappearance of the "Second World." Relations were quickly established with the individual countries of the Commonwealth of Independent States. The defense minister visited Russia, where agreements were reached on defense supplies and trade. The prime minister visited the United States, and the two countries undertook joint military exercises in May. The prime minister addressed the UN Security Council in New York City, the "Earth Summit" in Rio de Janeiro, and the summit meeting of nonaligned countries in Jakarta, Indon., and had four meetings with the prime minister

of Pakistan. An important development was the conclusion of an extradition treaty with Britain with respect to terrorists.

Among prominent visitors to India were the presidents of Kazakhstan, Kyrgyzstan, Maldives, Malta, Mauritius, Namibia, Portugal, Sri Lanka, Turkmenistan, and Ukraine, Chairman Yasir Arafat of the Palestine Liberation Organization, and the prime minister of Bangladesh. President Venkataraman paid a state visit to China. India accorded full diplomatic recognition to Israel in January and established a diplomatic mission. A strip of land called Tin Bigha was given to Bangladesh on lease in perpetuity to enable that country to have access to its enclaves in India.

(H.Y. SHARADA PRASAD)

KAZAKHSTAN

A republic of Central Asia, Kazakhstan borders Russia on the west and north, China on the east, Kyrgyzstan on the southeast, Uzbekistan and the Aral Sea on the south, and Turkmenistan and the Caspian Sea on the southwest. Area: 2,717,300 sq km (1,049,200 sq mi). Pop. (1992 est.): 17,008,000. Cap.: Alma-Ata (Kazakh: Almaty). Monetary unit: ruble, with (Oct. 5, 1992) a free rate of 316.82 rubles = U.S. $1 (538.59 rubles = £1 sterling). President in 1992, Nursultan Nazarbayev; prime minister, Sergey Tereshchenko.

Kazakhstan declared itself an independent republic on Dec. 16, 1991, the last of the Soviet republics to do so. This underlined the reluctance with which the republic viewed the breakup of the Soviet Union. Pres. Nursultan Nazarbayev, who was also first secretary of the Kazakh Socialist Party (KSP; formerly the Kazakh Communist Party [KCP]), had strongly supported Soviet Pres. Mikhail Gorbachev's proposal for a Union of Soviet Sovereign States and ensured that Kazakhstan would be a member of the inner core in the Commonwealth of Independent States.

Nazarbayev was acutely sensitive to the risk of interethnic conflict within the republic. Although Kazakhs were the largest ethnic group, they formed only 40% of the population, and Russians were almost as numerous. Nearly a million Germans, making up almost 6% of the population, played a key role in agriculture and industry. Ukrainians accounted for just over 5%. After the first native Kazakh head of the KCP was removed in December 1986 by Gorbachev and accused of corruption and nepotism, he was replaced by a Russian, Gennady Kolbin. This led to ethnic riots in Alma-Ata and other cities. Nazarbayev, an ethnic Kazakh, took over in June 1989. Acutely aware of the ethnic tinderbox the republic had become, he provided strong leadership that might be characterized as enlightened authoritarianism. He was the only candidate in the December 1991 presidential election. His position was stronger than that of Pres. Boris Yeltsin in Russia. He ensured that the name of the newly independent state would be the Republic of Kazakhstan and not the Kazakh Republic. He named a Russian prime minister. In June 1992 a draft constitution made Kazakh the official state language and guaranteed political pluralism.

A multiparty system soon emerged with parties ranging from a Communist Party, consisting of mainly Russian-speaking Communists who had parted company with Nazarbayev, to a "fascist party" of Kazakh national independence. There were also an Islamic party, a German party, and various Russian Cossack organizations.

Kazakhstan was harshly affected by the price liberalization that began in Russia in January 1992. The Kazakhs did not have the ministerial expertise or the financial know-how to cope easily, and the leadership did not exhibit much enthusiasm for the market reforms being instituted in Rus-

Nursultan Nazarbayev (left), president of Kazakhstan, talks to Leonid Kravchuk, president of Ukraine and host of the March meeting of the Commonwealth of Independent States (CIS) in Kiev. During 1992 Kazakhstan tended to align itself with Russia against Ukraine in the CIS.
REUTERS/BETTMANN

sia. It preferred a gradual approach to the market and was actively studying the South Korean and Chinese models, which involved a strong role for the state and an absence of democracy in the Western sense. Kazakh industry had been plagued by shortages and had suffered the same decline as Russia's. Kazakhstan was developing its own oil industry and signed agreements with the U.S. oil company Chevron in May and with a consortium of British Gas and Agip, the Italian state-owned oil company, in July. Agriculture fared better in 1992. The harvest was good, and grain deliveries to the state reached planned levels. State and collective farms that sold more than planned deliveries to the state would receive 60% of the price in U.S. dollars.

Kazakhstan increased its international standing by joining the UN, the International Monetary Fund, and the Conference on Security and Cooperation in Europe (CSCE). Nazarbayev traveled widely to promote the republic. His visits resulted in the signing of several treaties and the promotion of economic cooperation. His first foreign trip as president was to Britain in December 1991. In March 1992 he visited China, and diplomatic relations were established. He warned at the UN that the problem of water in the Central Asian region could become a source of "dangerous conflict" and appealed for help in overcoming the environmental disasters of the Aral Sea and the Semipalatinsk (Semey) nuclear testing range. He also called for an Asia security conference along the lines of the CSCE. On a trip to Washington, D.C., in May, he agreed to remove all strategic nuclear weapons from Kazakhstan within two years. In November he signed oil, transport, and finance agreements with Iran. (MARTIN MCCAULEY)

This article updates the *Macropædia* article CENTRAL ASIA: *Kazakhstan*.

KYRGYZSTAN

A landlocked republic of Central Asia, Kyrgyzstan borders Kazakhstan to the north, China to the southeast, Tajikistan to the south and west, and Uzbekistan to the west. Area: 198,500 sq km (76,600 sq mi). Pop. (1992 est.): 4,533,000. Cap.: Bishkek (until 1991 called Frunze). Monetary unit: ruble, with (Oct. 5, 1992) a free rate of 316.82 rubles = U.S. $1 (538.59 rubles = £1 sterling). President in 1992, Askar Akayev; prime minister, Tursunbek Chyngyshev.

In 1992, its first full year as an independent republic, Kyrgyzstan (formerly Kirgizia) took its place in the international community as a member of the UN, the International Monetary Fund (IMF), and the Conference on Security and Cooperation in Europe. The republic remained a member of the inner core of the new Commonwealth of Independent States, however, and was closely linked to Russia, on which it was economically dependent.

Pres. Askar Akayev was first elected president by the Supreme Soviet in October 1990, replacing the conservative Communist leader Absamat Masaliyev after bloody ethnic conflicts between Kyrgyz and Uzbeks in Osh oblast the previous June. The republic was the first to condemn unequivocally the attempted coup against the Soviet government in August 1991, and the defeat of the coup consolidated Akayev's victory over the conservatives. Kirgizia declared its independence on August 31, and Akayev was elected president in October. Akayev, who had no Communist Party background, was supported by the Democratic Movement of Kyrgyzstan and had wide backing among the democratic opposition. He was concerned with balancing the various ethnic groups and insisted that Kyrgyzstan belonged to all the peoples of the republic and not only to the Kyrgyz, who made up almost 53% of the population. Russians constituted some 22% of the populace, with Uzbeks accounting for another 13%.

In July 1992 the government adopted a shock-therapy economic program drafted by Akayev and the IMF. There were few Kyrgyz qualified to take over the running of industry and a modern banking and financial system, so movement toward privatization and a free-market economy had been slow. Relations with China were established, and an agreement was signed to deliver electricity to Xinjiang (Hsin-chiang), just across the border, where there was a Kyrgyz community. (MARTIN MCCAULEY)

This article updates the *Macropædia* article CENTRAL ASIA: *Kyrgyzstan*.

MALDIVES

A republic and member of the Commonwealth in the Indian Ocean, Maldives consists of about 2,000 small islands southwest of the southern tip of India. Area: 298 sq km (115 sq mi). Pop. (1992 est.): 230,000. Cap.: Male. Monetary unit: rufiyaa, with (Oct. 5, 1992) a free rate of 10.92 rufiyaa to U.S. $1 (18.57 rufiyaa = £1 sterling). President in 1992, Maumoon Abdul Gayoom.

Opposition to the regime of Pres. Maumoon Gayoom continued in 1992 and was centred on accusations of corruption, which came especially from young foreign-educated Maldivians. In 1991 the government had imposed press censorship in its efforts to dampen down demands for a fully elected Majlis (legislature).

By 1992 an estimated 30% of all foreign currency earnings came from tourism. Thus, despite the ongoing problems in Sri Lanka, visa restrictions on tourists and visitors from that country were lifted at the end of 1991 following a visit to

Colombo by President Gayoom when he attended the sixth annual summit of the South Asian Association for Regional Co-operation (SAARC).

Considering its tiny size and limited resources, Maldives had achieved a number of economic advances over the past decade. By 1992 it had a per capita income of $420. The mortality rate per 1,000 was reduced to 85 (for children under five), and 70% of the population had access to safe water, compared with only 5% in 1980. But the average daily caloric intake was still only 80% of requirements.

(GUY ARNOLD)

This article updates the *Micropædia* article MALDIVES.

NEPAL

A constitutional monarchy, Nepal is a landlocked country in the Himalayas between India and the Tibetan Autonomous Region of China. Area: 147,181 sq km (56,827 sq mi). Pop. (1992 est.): 19,795,000. Cap.: Kathmandu. Monetary unit: Nepalese rupee, with (Oct. 5, 1992) a free rate of NRs 46.55 to U.S. $1 (NRs 79.13 = £1 sterling). King, Birendra Bir Bikram Shah Dev; prime minister in 1992, Girija Prasad Koirala.

Democracy, which in 1991 in Nepal replaced one of the last monarchies of the world, established deeper roots in 1992, but the Nepali Congress Party government faced new challenges of street protests and political violence. At least seven people died in police gunfire in Kathmandu in April when a mob of 2,000, protesting price increases and corruption, turned violent. The demonstration was sponsored by the United Nepal Communist Party, the largest opposition group. The Nepali Congress Party held its first national convention in February. Former prime minister Krishna Prasad Bhattarai was unanimously elected party president.

P.V. Narasimha Rao paid a visit to Nepal in October, the first by an Indian prime minister in 15 years. He and Prime Minister Girija Prasad Koirala discussed cooperation on trade and water resources.

The government opened eight new Himalayan peaks to climbers, raising the number of the nation's mountains accessible to climbers to 222. But in a bid to discourage climbers from attempting the world's loftiest peak, it increased the fee for Mt. Everest to $50,000 from $10,000.

In 1992 Nepal experienced its two worst air crashes when 113 people died in the crash of a Thai Airways jetliner on July 31, and 167 were killed when a Pakistani Airbus crashed on September 28.   (DILIP GANGULY)

PAKISTAN

A federal republic and a member of the Commonwealth, Pakistan is in the northwestern part of the Indian subcontinent, on the Arabian Sea. Area: 796,095 sq km (307,374 sq mi), excluding the 83,716-sq mi Pakistani-controlled section of Jammu and Kashmir. Pop. (1992 est., including some 2.4 million Afghan refugees and 3 million residents of Pakistani-controlled Jammu and Kashmir): 130,129,000. Cap.: Islamabad. Monetary unit: Pakistan rupee, with (Oct. 5, 1992) a free rate of PRs 25.06 to U.S. $1 (PRs 42.60 = £1 sterling). President in 1992, Ghulam Ishaq Khan; prime minister, Nawaz Sharif.

An unprecedented flood in September 1992 left at least 2,000 people dead, hundreds missing, and thousands hurt in Pakistan. The financially strapped nation obtained food, shelter, and medicine, mostly from Islamic countries, for the three million people left homeless by the floods, caused by continuous monsoon rains that began on September 8 and pounded the north and east for three straight days. Overflowing rivers flooded three of the nation's five provinces, including Punjab, its farm belt. Estimates put the damage at more than $1 billion.

Former prime minister Benazir Bhutto (centre) defies a ban by leading a march on November 18 in Islamabad against the Pakistani government, which she charged with electoral fraud and other crimes. The government denied her charges and later banned her from the capital.
PANJIAR—INDIA TODAY/SIPA

Prime Minister Nawaz Sharif faced growing opposition during the year as he tried to thread the middle path between right-wing Islamic fundamentalists and social democrats. Pakistan's influential fundamentalist Party of Islam withdrew its support from Sharif's coalition of eight parties in the National Assembly, accusing him of reneging on a promise to convert Pakistan into a rigid Islamic society. Sharif's governing coalition, known by its Urdu-language initials, IJI (Islam-e Jamhoori Ittehad, or Islamic Democratic Alliance), remained a bewildering combination of parties espousing widely different ideologies—from secular socialism to Islamic fundamentalism. Although the Party of Islam had only 6 seats in the 217-member National Assembly, it was considered to be the country's best organized party. Analysts doubted if the Party of Islam's withdrawal would affect Sharif's stability, but they said that it would make him vulnerable and heavily dependent on other coalition partners.

Sharif during the year launched an ambitious economic reform program by privatizing dozens of state-owned businesses, ranging from banks to sugar mills. The government in May unveiled a 278-page economic report, which recorded a healthy 6.5% growth rate, a 13% increase in exports, and a rising stock market. The comfortable climb in exports was, however, offset by a 21% increase in imports. Also, Sharif faced a huge hurdle after a court decision, in keeping with the Islamic code of conduct, outlawed bank interest earlier in the year. The economic survey cautioned the nation about the $320 million increase in military costs. Pakistan, however, continued to build its armed forces and arsenals. The government during the year indirectly confirmed what the U.S. had long claimed—that Pakistan had the components to build an atomic bomb.

That issue clouded Pakistan's relations with the U.S., which had considered Pakistan to be an ally in the region. The U.S. had suspended financial assistance and said that aid would not be resumed until Pakistan destroyed all its nuclear weapons components and promised not to make them again. Pakistan refused, claiming that this would leave the country vulnerable to a possible attack by India, which had exploded a nuclear device in 1977. Pakistan remained at odds with India over Kashmir, which demanded independence from India. Hindu temples across Pakistan were attacked in December, following the destruction of the Babri Mosque in India by Hindu militants.

The government's international problems were compounded by widespread sectarian violence within Pakistan. Sandbag bunkers became part of Karachi's landscape in 1992 after the government ordered a crackdown in July to weed out bandits who had terrorized southern Sindh province for more than a decade. Some 50,000 troops took part in the operation to disarm criminals, who were blamed for some 3,000 politically motivated murders in the province during the last decade. London-based Amnesty International, however, accused the government of keeping hundreds of people under arbitrary detention in Sindh. The province was the base of the Pakistan People's Party, the main opposition party, headed by former prime minister Benazir Bhutto. A "long march" through the country by Bhutto late in the year drew large crowds. (DILIP GANGULY)

SRI LANKA

A republic and member of the Commonwealth, Sri Lanka occupies an island in the Indian Ocean off the southeast coast of peninsular India. Area: 65,610 sq km (25,332 sq mi). Pop. (1992 est.): 17,464,000. Legislative cap., Sri Jayawardenepura Kotte; administrative cap., Colombo. Monetary unit: Sri Lanka rupee, with (Oct. 5, 1992) a free rate of SL Rs 44.06 to U.S. $1 (SL Rs 74.90 = £1 sterling). President in 1992, Ranasinghe Premadasa; prime minister, Dingiri Banda Wijetunge.

Pres. Ranasinghe Premadasa's efforts to end the Tamil separatist war in Sri Lanka floundered in 1992 as the island republic was again wracked by the savage guerrilla uprising. At least 20,000 people had died in the decade-old insurrection. Tamils, who make up 18% of Sri Lanka's 17.5 million people, were fighting for secession of the northeastern part of the island, where they are a majority.

The rebels carried out numerous attacks during the year. On August 8 nine senior Sri Lankan military officers, including the army's northern commander, Maj. Gen. Denzil Kobbekaduwa, were killed in a land mine explosion. Some 140 people, mostly Muslims, were massacred in raids on three northern villages in October, and on November 16 a motorcycle suicide bomber killed Sri Lanka's naval commander, Vice Adm. Clancy Fernando, and three aides in Colombo. On March 16 more than 10,000 demonstrators began a 290-km (180-mi), 18-day march for peace.

On April 5 a group of World War II veterans who had served in Sri Lanka unveiled a plaque to mark the 50th anniversary of the defense of the country by British and allied forces against the Japanese. Britain granted freedom to Sri Lanka in 1948.

President Premadasa successfully thwarted political threats during the year. On March 19 the government by a majority of 66 votes defeated an opposition no-confidence motion in Parliament. The motion, submitted by four opposition parties, accused the government of corruption. On September 1 the Supreme Court unanimously dismissed a petition to invalidate President Premadasa's 1988 election, ending a three-year court battle. The five-member bench ruled that former prime minister Sirimavo Bandaranaike, leader of the opposition Freedom Party, had failed to prove that intimidation swung the December 1988 election in Premadasa's favour.

During the year the government faced charges of human rights violations. On April 9 the attorney general filed charges against a former deputy inspector general, Premadasa Udugampola, who claimed knowledge of 1,079 political killings by government-backed death squads to suppress both the Tamil uprising and the movement by the nationalist Sinhalese organization People's Liberation Front opposing the government's handling of the Tamil war.

On June 6 at least 10 people died when 50 cm (20 in) of rain lashed Colombo. More than 150,000 people were affected by the rain, the heaviest recorded in the city since 1876.

On August 7 the Australian cricket team arrived in Sri Lanka for a five-week tour. This ended a five-year boycott of the country by Test-playing nations. (DILIP GANGULY)

TAJIKISTAN

A landlocked republic of Central Asia, Tajikistan borders Kyrgyzstan on the north, Uzbekistan on the north and west, Afghanistan on the south, and China on the east. Area: 143,100 sq km (55,300 sq mi). Pop. (1992 est.): 5,568,000. Cap.: Dushanbe. Monetary unit: ruble, with (Oct. 5, 1992) a free rate of 316.82 rubles to U.S. $1 (538.59 rubles = £1 sterling). Presidents in 1992, Rakhmon Nabiyev, Akbarshah Iskandarov (acting) from September 7, and, from November 20, Imomali Rakhmonov (acting; from November 27 title was chairman of the Supreme Soviet); prime ministers, Akbar Mirzoyev and, from September 24, Abdumalek Abdulajanov (acting to early December).

Power in Tajikistan splintered during the republic's first year of independence, with armed bands fighting one another in the southern part of the country. Some of those fighting were supporters of Pres. Rakhmon Nabiyev, who was a bastion of communist orthodoxy, while others favoured the Islamic Revival Party (IRP) and the democratic opposition. The fall of Kabul, Afghanistan, to Islamic insurgents directly affected Tajikistan, with arms being smuggled across the frontier. Russian and Uzbek frontier troops, who were called in, were incapable of stopping the flow.

After Nabiyev's election as president in November 1991, there was relative calm until March 1992. In April, after almost a month of demonstrations in Dushanbe, some concessions were made, but the demonstrators demanded Nabiyev's resignation, the dissolution of the Supreme Soviet, multiparty elections, and a new constitution. On May 11 an agreement was signed establishing a government of national reconciliation, but the next day fighting again broke out. Nabiyev was forced to resign on September 7, and Akbarshah Iskandarov, speaker of the Supreme Soviet, became acting president at the head of a government dominated by Islamic and democratic parties. In October fighting spread to Dushanbe, which was briefly held by forces loyal to Nabiyev. On November 20 the Supreme Soviet, meeting in the northern city of Khojand, away from the strife-torn capital, replaced Iskandarov with Imomali Rakhmonov, a former Communist from the southern Kulyab region. On November 27 presidential rule was abolished and Tajikistan was named a parliamentary republic. The new government, controlled by former Communists, seized Dushanbe on December 10, but fighting continued. Thousands of refugees fled toward Afghanistan, and many reportedly drowned attempting to cross the Amu Darya. (MARTIN MCCAULEY)

This article updates the *Macropædia* article CENTRAL ASIA: *Tajikistan.*

TURKMENISTAN

A republic of Central Asia, Turkmenistan borders Uzbekistan on the northeast, Kazakhstan on the northwest, the Caspian Sea on the west, Iran on the southwest, and Afghanistan on the southeast. Area: 488,100 sq km (188,500 sq mi). Pop. (1992 est.): 3,859,000. Cap.: Ashkhabad (Turkmen: Ashgabat). Monetary unit: ruble, with (Oct. 5, 1992) a free rate of 316.82 rubles to U.S. $1 (538.59 rubles = £1 sterling). President in 1992, Saparmuryad Niyazov; prime minister, Khan A. Akhmedov.

On May 18, 1992, Turkmenistan, which had declared its independence from the Soviet Union on Oct. 27, 1991, became the first Central Asian state to adopt a new constitution. The supreme body would be the Khalk Maslahaty (People's Council), with a 50-seat elected Majlis as the working parliament. The constitution guaranteed political pluralism, but ethnic and religious political parties were proscribed. It also guaranteed the right to private ownership of land and other property. On June 21 Saparmuryad Niyazov, who had been elected president by the Supreme Soviet on Oct. 27, 1990, was confirmed in office as the only candidate in the republic's first presidential election. Niyazov's rule was authoritarian and he brooked no opposition. Democratic opposition was weak, and power rested almost entirely with the president and the former Communist Party apparatus.

During 1992 Turkmenistan played a less and less active role in the Commonwealth of Independent States (CIS). Economically it developed closer ties with Iran, and new air and railway links between the two countries were planned. During the CIS summit in October, there were complaints that the Turkmen-Iran frontier was open, thus permitting Iranians unfettered access to Central Asia.

Several foreign companies were exploring for natural gas and oil around the Caspian Sea, and in November the Turkmen government signed an agreement with a U.S.–Turkish consortium to build a natural gas pipeline to Europe. In October Turkmenistan and Ukraine signed several treaties, including one on natural gas supplies. Ukraine agreed to pay the equivalent of 60% of the world price for natural gas.   (MARTIN MCCAULEY)

This article updates the *Macropædia* article CENTRAL ASIA: *Turkmenistan*.

UZBEKISTAN

A republic of Central Asia, Uzbekistan borders the Aral Sea to the north, Kazakhstan to the north and west, Turkmenistan to the southwest, Afghanistan to the south, and Tajikistan and Kyrgyzstan to the east. Area: 447,400 sq km (172,700 sq mi). Pop. (1992 est.): 21,363,000. Cap.: Tashkent (Uzbek: Toshkent). Monetary unit: ruble, with (Oct. 5, 1992) a free rate of 316.82 rubles to U.S. $1 (538.59 rubles = £1 sterling). President in 1992, Islam Karimov; prime minister from January 8, Abdulkhashim Mutalov.

The republic's first direct election of a president on Dec. 29, 1991, resulted in a stunning victory (86%) for Islam Karimov, formerly first secretary of the Uzbek Communist Party. The only other candidate, Muhammad Solikh of the Erk ("Freedom") Democratic Party, polled 12%. Karimov was supported by the People's Democratic Party (formerly the Communist Party). The main opposition party, the Birlik ("Unity") People's Movement, was not permitted to field a candidate, while the Party of Islamic Rebith (PIR) could not be registered since there was a ban on parties based on a religious platform. The presidential election was accompanied by a referendum on the declaration of independence adopted by the Uzbek Supreme Soviet in August 1991. This time 98% of the electors were in favour, almost the same figure as had voted for Uzbekistan to remain within a renewed Soviet Union in March 1991. As president, Karimov had a policy of ensuring that Uzbekistan remained a stable, secular state. This involved incremental political and social change, tightly administered from the centre. As a concession to the Muslims, he placed one hand on the Qur'an and the other on the Uzbek constitution when he was sworn in as president on Jan. 4, 1992.

Birlik claimed a membership of 1.5 million, and its nationalist and Islamic appeal was proving more and more attractive. Solikh's Erk (with perhaps 5,000 members) had split from Birlik, but repression welded them together again. Birlik, Erk, and the PIR all advocated a secular Uzbek government but with Islam occupying a central position in public life. Birlik had been collaborating with a business group that favoured a faster transition to the market. They were unhappy that the government's legislation on privatization, private banking, foreign investment, and other reforms was still only on paper.

Demonstrations in Dushanbe, Tajikistan, in April and May led the opposition to form a coalition. This so alarmed Karimov that he moved against them. Birlik's headquarters were closed and its leaders arrested and beaten. The Supreme Soviet amended the criminal code to impose more severe penalties for antigovernment activity, increase the powers of the police, and provide for the registration of political parties. The state also promoted the formation of new political parties such as the Party of the Heirs of Timur, to attract those interested in Uzbek history, and the Social Progress Party, which received much positive coverage in the official press. Another significant move was the campaign to rehabilitate Sharaf Rashidov, first party secretary from 1959 to 1983. He had been discredited as the key figure in a massive cotton scandal, but he was now presented as having defended Uzbekistan from predatory Moscow. In order to

Islam Karimov, president of Uzbekistan, tours a factory in Beijing during his visit to China in March. The two countries established diplomatic relations in 1992 and reached other agreements.

raise Uzbekistan's foreign profile, Karimov welcomed U.S. Secretary of State James Baker and the Saudi foreign minister, Prince Saud al-Faisal, to Tashkent in February. He afterward traveled to Helsinki, Fin., to sign the Conference on Security and Cooperation in Europe accords. A visit to Beijing (Peking) led to diplomatic relations with China.

Uzbek living standards were among the lowest in Central Asia. It was thought that gross domestic product might fall 20% in 1992, and there were about two million unemployed. Price reforms in Russia in January forced Uzbekistan to follow suit. The republic intended to introduce its own currency, but it was still dependent on Russia and the ruble zone. While most consumer goods could be purchased only with coupons, the state gave in to strikes and protests, thus fueling inflation. In May the government ordered the state bank to provide another 4.5 billion rubles as credit to industrial enterprises. About 60% of Uzbekistan's annual gold production of 70 tons went to pay for oil, food, and spare parts from Russia. Although oil was discovered at Mingbulak, development would require foreign investment. About 85% of the arable land was under cotton, but it was difficult to cut this back in favour of diversified crops because cotton was needed for export. Private leasing of land was only just beginning. The republic had enough grain to last until the end of 1992. (MARTIN MCCAULEY)

This article updates the Macropædia article CENTRAL ASIA: Uzbekistan.

Southeast Asia

SOUTHEAST ASIAN AFFAIRS

In 1992 concerns about security took centre stage for regional leaders. The departure of U.S. forces from their last base in the Philippines, Subic Bay Naval Station, led to fears that other powers would want to fill the perceived vacuum. Fueling unease was new tension over the long-disputed Spratly Islands in the South China Sea. Washington, however, continued to insist that it remained a Pacific power, and officials said U.S. forces would continue to patrol the region. The Americans were leaving the Philippines following a 1991 vote by the Senate in Manila against a new bases treaty. An initial agreement on a three-year phaseout had broken down, and all but a handful of U.S. forces had left the country by September 20.

In part, Washington's confidence was due to support from other countries within the region. Singapore announced in January that it would be host to a small but important logistical headquarters unit previously based at Subic. The move meant that an additional 150–200 U.S. military personnel would join some 75 already stationed in Singapore. The island republic had agreed in 1990 to accept limited numbers of U.S. naval vessels and fighter aircraft and to store spare parts. As always, however, the Singaporeans were quick to allay any fears on the part of neighbours Indonesia and Malaysia that the U.S. presence constituted a "base," and the two accepted that it was not.

Indeed, Malaysia also warmed up to the U.S. presence, despite its longtime official support for the nuclear-free Zone of Peace, Freedom and Neutrality proposed by the Association of Southeast Asian Nations (ASEAN). When U.S. Pres. George Bush passed through Singapore en route

to Japan in January, Malaysia announced that it would allow the U.S. to use its Lumut naval base for maintenance of frigates and smaller warships. In April, shortly before the first U.S. vessels arrived, Malaysian Defense Minister Najib Abdul Razak summed up a widely held view: "It is in our interest to see that there will not be a vacuum in the region after the U.S. withdrawal from the Philippines, as it may result in a new area of conflict with a new power configuration." Soon afterward, U.S. Defense Secretary Dick Cheney gave the standard American litany on a visit to Canberra: "The bottom line is there will not be any reduction in the U.S. commitment to the region." Nonetheless, increased regional concern was evident at a January 27–28 summit in Singapore of the leaders of ASEAN, which groups Brunei, Indonesia, Malaysia, the Philippines, Singapore, and Thailand. They resolved to "seek avenues to engage member states in new areas of cooperation in security matters." Previously, the association had studiously avoided discussing defense issues.

By July, security dominated talks at the annual meeting of ASEAN foreign ministers and a postministerial meeting that included the U.S., Japan, China, and Russia. In February, China had put into law its claim to the Spratlys, parts of which were also claimed by Vietnam, Malaysia, the Philippines, and Brunei. Taiwan claimed them as well in the name of China. The Chinese legislation also covered the Paracels, disputed with Vietnam. In May, China had signed an oil-exploration deal in the Spratlys with a U.S. company, angering Vietnam. In early July, Beijing (Peking) troops had planted a marker on another atoll claimed by Vietnam. Although mostly mere specks of rock, the strategic islets were thought to harbour major resources. The ASEAN ministers urged "restraint" over the Spratlys and issued a declaration calling for negotiations among all claimants. China guardedly endorsed "some basic principles" in the declaration. Nevertheless, suspicion about Chinese intentions in the region remained a major talking point. Repeated reports that Beijing wanted to buy an aircraft carrier from Ukraine did nothing to quiet such concerns, and a number of countries in the region were noticeably upgrading their armed forces.

The Spratly issue was one of several irritants between China and Vietnam. The two had made a great show of normalizing relations in 1991, but tensions soon returned. There were some minor skirmishes along their common border early in the year. Then in August and September, Chinese naval patrols began seizing Vietnamese ships headed from Hong Kong to northern Vietnam along China's south coast. China accused the Vietnamese of smuggling luxury goods, but the unprecedented action was also seen as a means of putting political pressure on Vietnam while asserting Chinese power in the South China Sea. Reformist Vietnam was increasingly less isolated, however. Brunei became the last ASEAN member to open diplomatic relations with Hanoi. Japan resumed giving official aid after a 14-year suspension and called on the U.S. to normalize relations. A number of top regional officials visited, including Malaysian Prime Minister Datuk Seri Mahathir bin Mohamad and former Singapore prime minister Lee Kuan Yew. Vietnamese Prime Minister Vo Van Kiet said his country would like to join ASEAN. Laos and Cambodia also made overtures. Mahathir said he hoped Indochina would be part of ASEAN "within the next five years."

In Cambodia's case, much would depend on the success of the UN in preparing the country for elections in 1993. Under terms of the Paris peace accords signed in 1991, some 19,500 military and police personnel from 44 countries took up positions throughout Cambodia as part of the UN Transitional Authority in Cambodia. However, the massive operation was seriously hampered by the refusal of the Khmer Rouge guerrilla faction to disarm, and the UN imposed trade sanctions against the group. Myanmar also indicated interest in joining ASEAN, but that seemed a considerably more distant prospect. While Myanmar's neighbours had long preferred "constructive engagement" to criticism in dealing with the military government's severe internal repression, Muslim-dominated Malaysia spoke out against Yangon's forcible expulsion of some 265,000 Muslims, known as Rohingyas, from the northern state of Arakan into neighbouring Bangladesh. The replacement in April of Senior Gen. Saw Maung as the country's leader by Gen. Than Shwe led to some easing of internal restrictions, but it did little to stem the flow of international denunciations of the regime.

Malaysia's international assertiveness, which included a strong call for action to aid Muslims in Bosnia, raised hackles in Indonesia. Mahathir was seen in some quarters as having "stolen the show" when Jakarta was host to the nonaligned summit in September. Jakarta was upset when Malaysian television ran footage of the 1991 crackdown on demonstrators in East Timor, though the Malaysian information minister moved quickly to reassure the Indonesians that this had resulted from a "very serious mistake" in the newsroom. Jakarta was also unhappy about Malaysia's decision not to repatriate Indonesians who had fled troubled Aceh province. Even so, the two upgraded military cooperation, and Indonesia praised Malaysia for giving visas to some 320,000 mainly Indonesian illegal immigrants.

Indonesia, Malaysia, and Singapore confronted the twin issues of piracy and safety in the Strait of Malacca. The shipping industry complained strongly of an upsurge in attacks by pirates, who seemed to be based in Indonesia. While Jakarta denied allegations of official involvement, joint patrols by Indonesia and Singapore led to a drop in reported incidents. The shipping industry also called on littoral governments, including Thailand, to improve safety in the strait. Collisions there were running at a rate of about one a month; one, involving a tanker, resulted in a serious oil spill.

Economies in the region continued to boom, although Singapore registered a slowdown by its own high-growth standards. The Philippines was buoyed by the election of Pres. Fidel Ramos, who pledged to get the country moving again, but a serious crime wave made foreign investors cautious. The bloody crackdown on demonstrators in Thailand slowed the economy for a time, but it soon bounced back with the appointment of an interim government and the subsequent holding of new elections.

The ASEAN summit approved creation of an ASEAN Free Trade Area with a virtual phasing out of tariffs over 15 years. Later, economics ministers agreed to compress the timetable to 7–10 years. The summit leaders gave short shrift to Malaysia's proposal for an East Asian Economic Caucus, which had been fiercely opposed by the U.S. on the grounds that it could become a trade bloc. Washington's favoured trade vehicle, the Asia-Pacific Economic Cooperation (APEC) forum, which would include the U.S., Canada, and Australia along with East Asia, got a boost when members agreed to site a secretariat in Singapore.

The spread of satellite television brought new choices to many viewers, although some countries, notably Malaysia, banned use of the dishes needed to receive it. The Hong Kong-based STAR service offered five channels visible across the region. Indonesia's Palapa satellite became the vehicle for several U.S. cable services, and an Australian channel aimed at the region was announced.

(BERTON WOODWARD)

BRUNEI

The sultanate of Brunei is located on the northern coast of the island of Borneo, on the South China Sea. Area: 5,765 sq km (2,226 sq mi). Pop. (1992 est.): 268,000. Cap.: Bandar Seri Begawan. Monetary unit: Brunei dollar, with (Oct. 5, 1992) a free rate of B$1.60 to U.S. $1 (B$2.71 = £1 sterling). Sultan and prime minister in 1992, Sir Muda Hassanal Bolkiah Mu'izzadin Waddaulah.

The Oct. 5, 1992, celebration of the 25th anniversary of the sultan's accession to the throne proved to be one of the country's biggest events since independence in 1984. A number of regional leaders and international representatives attended, in tacit recognition of the financial power of the tiny oil-rich nation. Despite some predictions that the sultan might use the occasion to announce constitutional changes, he chose to reemphasize his creed of "Malay-Muslim-Monarchy." This set out a religious and cultural foundation for the 600-year-old system of absolute rule by the royal family.

In February the sultanate established diplomatic relations with Vietnam. The warming of relations with the reform-minded communist regime followed the watershed opening of ties with China in late 1991. Brunei was the last member of the Association of Southeast Asian Nations to establish relations with Beijing (Peking). About one-fifth of Brunei's population was Chinese, but many were denied citizenship. A Brunei delegation arrived in Hanoi in early July to discuss agreements on shipping and telecommunications. At about the same time, Singapore Prime Minister Goh Chok Tong, during a visit to Bandar Seri Begawan, announced that Brunei businessmen could join a Singapore trade mission to Vietnam to look into possible joint ventures there. In September Brunei joined the Non-Aligned Movement at its summit in Jakarta, Indon.   (BERTON WOODWARD)

This article updates the *Micropædia* article BRUNEI.

CAMBODIA (KAMPUCHEA)

A "state" of Southeast Asia, Cambodia occupies the southwestern part of the Indochinese Peninsula, on the Gulf of Thailand. Area: 181,916 sq km (70,238 sq mi). Pop. (1992 est.): 8,974,000. Cap.: Phnom Penh. Monetary unit: riel, with (Oct. 5, 1992) an official rate of 1,508 riels to U.S. $1 (2,564 riels = £1 sterling), and a free rate of 2,250 riels to U.S. $1 (3,825 riels = £1 sterling). Chairman of the Supreme National Council (head of state) in 1992, Prince Norodom Sihanouk.

The UN-overseen peace process got under way in January 1992, when the former head of UN disarmament affairs, Yasushi Akashi (*see* BIOGRAPHIES), was appointed head of the UN Transitional Authority in Cambodia (UNTAC), and a UN force was sanctioned to clear mines along the border with Thailand. In February the Security Council approved the UNTAC operation, to include 16,000 soldiers and 3,600 police, as well as administrators and a contingent to prepare for elections due in April or May 1993. The cost was about $2 billion. Akashi and Lieut. Gen. John Sanderson, the UNTAC military commander, arrived with the first UN troops in March.

However, the Khmer Rouge faction refused to cooperate with UNTAC. It launched cease-fire-breaking operations near Kompong Thom in northern central Cambodia in January and continued fighting despite UN-brokered cease-fires in March and May. In Pailin the group refused access to UN troops verifying the cease-fire and, in May, to Akashi and General Sanderson themselves. When the UN began regrouping the estimated 200,000 Cambodian troops in June

A member of the United Nations peacekeeping mission patrols a road in Cambodia. Despite the settlement reached in October 1991, it was not clear that the UN mission would succeed in maintaining the cease-fire.
JACQUES LANVIN—SYGMA

in advance of demobilizing 70% of them, as required by the Paris peace accord, the Khmer Rouge refused. Its leaders said the UN had not verified that all Vietnamese troops had left Cambodia. They also demanded the dismantling of the Phnom Penh government, which ran the administration alongside UNTAC, or at least some participation in the government for themselves. In early December the UN embargoed log and gem exports from and oil supplies to Khmer Rouge-held areas. The Khmer Rouge replied by taking a number of UN hostages in various places, releasing them quickly but complaining that they were provoking the faction by intruding. The repatriation of the 370,000 refugees from the Thai border began in March despite the delays in the peace process, and by August 100,000 had returned.

In Phnom Penh in January, the Supreme National Council (SNC), Cambodia's sovereign body made up of members of all four Cambodian factions, agreed on freedom of the press and the freedom to form parties. However, Tea Bun Long, an official who had criticized government corruption, was killed in an attack, and Oung Phan, the former transport minister arrested in 1990 for trying to form an opposition party, was injured in another. The government quickly introduced harsher penalties and set up a Ministry of National Security, but two more government critics were attacked in March. The government freed some prisoners early in the year, bringing the total released since the peace accord in October 1991 to 453, but it said another 1,000 were still in jail.

Exploratory talks were held in Washington in April on Cambodia's reentry to the International Monetary Fund, to which it owed $58 million, and the Asian Development Bank, to which it owed about $2 million. At a conference in Tokyo in June, 33 countries and 12 international organizations pledged $880 million for Cambodia's reconstruction. Thailand remained Cambodia's biggest investor, with 43 Thai companies granted licenses for projects by April and at least six banks having permission to operate. In May four foreign oil companies began surveying the coast of Cambodia, and two more were allocated blocks for exploration. A UN report in July said inflation was running at an annual rate of 100%.

The U.S., which was to pay a third of the UNTAC budget, lifted its 16-year trade and aid embargo on Cambodia in January, and the two countries cooperated on looking for

Americans missing in the Vietnam war. In March, Hun Sen of the SNC visited Washington. Cambodia received visits in January from the Italian foreign minister, who promised $25 million in aid, and from a British minister of state, who announced that Britain was doubling its aid to $20 million. Chinese Foreign Minister Qian Qichen (Ch'ien Ch'i-ch'en) arrived in February, the first visit by a high Chinese official since 1978. Chea Sim, head of the Cambodian People's Party, returned the visit in July.   (JUDITH L. CLARKE)

This article updates the *Macropædia* article Mainland SOUTH-EAST ASIA: *Cambodia.*

INDONESIA

A republic of Southeast Asia, Indonesia consists of the major islands of Sumatra, Java, Kalimantan (Indonesian Borneo), Celebes (Indonesian: Sulawesi), and Irian Jaya (West New Guinea) and more than 13,000 smaller islands and islets. Area: 1,919,317 sq km (741,052 sq mi). Pop. (1992 est.): 184,796,000. Cap.: Jakarta. Monetary unit: rupiah, with (Oct. 5, 1992) a free rate of 2,071 rupiah to U.S. $1 (3,520 rupiah = £1 sterling). President in 1991, Suharto.

Through 1992 President Suharto, the armed forces, and the ruling Golkar organization found their dominance and prestige in Indonesian politics somewhat in decline. An inquiry into the November 1991 massacre in East Timor revealed that soldiers had used "excessive force" against a peaceful funeral crowd of 2,000. Investigators reported that about 50 died in the shooting, a sharp contrast to the initial military estimate of 19. Some witnesses claimed that as many as 200 had been killed. Six senior officers were dismissed or disciplined, and eight other men were court-martialed. The army urged more development in East Timor and a tougher line against groups resisting integration into Indonesia. Meanwhile, a top Irian Jaya rebel surrendered as neighbouring Papua New Guinea cracked down on border camps.

In another challenge to the armed forces, two academics in June suggested in the parliament that the military should no longer have 100 appointed seats, arguing that its involvement in government was not necessary for stability. Generals disagreed, and Suharto praised the army in his Independence Day speech. But he also remarked that the number of military seats was open to negotiation. Currently, 100 military men and 400 elected officials constituted the House of People's Representatives. They and 500 appointed representatives formed the People's Consultative Assembly, which elected the president every five years. Suharto was expected to win another term in March 1993, but there was a move in Golkar to trim his powers. In April the assembly won the right to draft a national policy blueprint normally done by Suharto, whose biggest challenge came when several international publications detailed the monopolies, loans, and contracts granted to his children by the government. The World Bank, while praising Indonesia's development, criticized the monopolies. Parliament investigated the clove monopoly held by a Suharto son, and the textile industry resisted his move for an export levy.

This issue, more open campaigning, and the army's neutrality contributed to Golkar's less than impressive showing in the June elections. Golkar won 68% of the vote and 282 seats, down from 73% and 299 seats in 1987. The biggest gain was made by the Indonesian Democratic Party, a nationalist-Christian coalition, which garnered 56 seats. The remaining 62 seats went to the United Development Party, informally aligned with the nation's Muslim majority. For many months Golkar had courted Indonesia's largest Muslim organization, Nahdatul Ulama, whose members numbered 20 million.

The economy grew steadily as Jakarta implemented further liberalization. Batam Island near Singapore continued to boom as part of a "growth triangle" linking the two with Malaysia's Johore state. Government banks were allowed to expand operations beyond development lending. A new round of sweeping tariff cuts came in July, along with rules enabling foreigners to wholly own industrial firms.

Without Suharto's support, however, technocrats made little headway against monopolies, and controls still hampered business. Moreover, the continuing tight-money policy pushed some big corporate groups into financial difficulty and kept the stock market sluggish. Still, the overall outlook was positive. The World Bank forecast that by the year 2000 Indonesia would be a solid middle-income country with per-capita income exceeding $1,000.

On the international front, Indonesia tussled with The Netherlands and Portugal over its human rights record. It barred local development organizations from receiving Dutch funding and got the World Bank to form a new grouping of aid donors to replace the one headed by The Netherlands. Portugal, East Timor's colonial ruler before its annexation by Indonesia in 1976, blocked a proposed economic pact between the European Communities and the Association of Southeast Asian Nations, which included Indonesia. Despite such difficulties, Jakarta pushed for constructive dialogue between rich and less developed nations during the Non-Aligned Movement summit in September.

On December 12 a powerful earthquake killed nearly 2,500 people on the island of Flores and destroyed 80% of the city of Maumere.   (RICARDO L. SALUDO)

LAOS

A landlocked republic, Laos is in the northern part of the Indochinese Peninsula. Area: 236,800 sq km (91,400 sq mi). Pop. (1992 est.): 4,409,000. Cap.: Vientiane. Monetary unit: kip, with (Oct. 5, 1992) an official rate of 714 kip to U.S. $1 (1,213 kip = £1 sterling). Presidents in 1992, Kaysone Phomvihan to November 21 and, from November 25, Nouhak Phoumsavan; chairman of the Council of Ministers (prime minister), Gen. Khamtai Siphandon.

Fighting on a small scale between government forces and anticommunist rebels broke out in January 1992 100 km (c. 60 mi) west of Vientiane and continued for three days. Hundreds of refugees fled into Thailand's Loei province.

Most of the resistance forces were Hmong tribesmen, but some of the leaders were Lao officials of the pre-1975 royal government. Thai army intelligence reckoned that Gen. Vang Pao commanded about 1,000 men, led in the field by his brother, Vang Fung, and that two other resistance movements, led by Li Lau and Pa Kou, had 5,000 between them. Some analysts considered these numbers exaggerated. Thailand undertook to prosecute rebel officers intruding across its border and to use its influence with the U.S. to stop Hmong immigrants from providing financial support to antigovernment forces. Vang Fung was deported by Bangkok to the U.S. in October. Thailand and Laos agreed that all Laotian refugees—about 18,000 at the start of the year—would be repatriated, and thousands were sent back.

Pres. Kaysone Phoumvihan (see OBITUARIES), the country's leader since 1975 and head of the Communist Party since 1955, died November 21. He was 71. His funeral was attended by Indochina leaders and Thailand's Crown Prince Maha Vajiralongkorn and Princess Maha Chakri Sirindhorn, both making a second visit in the year. Kaysone was succeeded as president by his old revolutionary comrade Nouhak Phoumsavan, 78, the National Assembly president, and as party chairman by Khamtai Siphandon, who stayed on as prime minister. The three had worked together closely for decades, and no major changes were expected. In March U.S. Assistant Secretary of State Richard Solomon visited and announced new aid in food and cash. The head of the U.S. mission in Laos was upgraded to full ambassador.

The eighth plenary session of the second Supreme People's Assembly in mid-March approved a budget of 205 billion kip. The ninth plenary session in August decreed elections for 85 seats in the reformed National Assembly. They were held in December, but the tally was not complete at year's end. A major furor erupted over the theft in July of $2 million of UN money that was to be delivered in Vientiane. Investigations led to the arrest of two Thai police major generals, two colonels, and a number of officials of both Thailand and Laos. Most of the money was recovered.

The economy performed well, boosted by market-opening measures, and gross domestic product growth of 4% was expected. Investment in transport and communications infrastructure increased substantially. The Australian government was building a bridge across the Mekong near Vientiane, and a Vietnamese state enterprise won the contract to upgrade the 167-km (104-mi) highway from Louangphrabang, the old royal capital, to Vientiane. The government announced that foreign investment for the first six months had reached $77 million.   (ROBERT WOODROW)

This article updates the *Macropædia* article Mainland SOUTHEAST ASIA: *Laos.*

MALAYSIA

A federal constitutional monarchy of Southeast Asia and member of the Commonwealth, Malaysia consists of the former Federation of Malaya at the southern end of the Malay Peninsula (excluding Singapore) and Sabah and Sarawak on the northern part of the island of Borneo. Area: 330,442 sq km (127,584 sq mi). Pop. (1992 est.): 18,630,000. Cap.: Kuala Lumpur. Monetary unit: ringgit, with (Oct. 5, 1992) a free rate of 2.51 ringgit to U.S. $1 (4.26 ringgit = £1 sterling). Paramount ruler in 1992, with the title of *yang di-pertuan agong,* Tuanku Azlan Muhibbudin Shah ibni al-Marhum Yusuff Ghafarullahu-Lahu Shah; prime minister, Datuk Seri Mahathir bin Mohamad.

Tensions between the powerful United Malays National Organization (UMNO) and the country's nine hereditary rulers and two opposition-led state governments dominated Malaysian politics in 1992. The rulers enjoy royal privileges under the constitutional monarchy. Every five years they elect from among themselves Malaysia's paramount ruler. But under state and federal constitutions, royals must restrict their political and business activities.

In February, however, UMNO, dominant partner in the ruling Barisan Nasional (National Front) coalition, formally complained of royal interference in politics and business. Among its allegations were pressure on state-level officials, attempts to influence appointments, and commercial activities. Concern had been building since the 1990 general elections, when UMNO's loss of the state of Kelantan to Parti Islam sa-Malaysia (Pas), a Muslim political group, was partly blamed on royal support. In April the Sultan of Kelantan stirred controversy further by refusing to pay taxes on a new sports car. In July, however, after months of discussions, most of the royals approved a proclamation affirming the constitutional limits.

Kelantan also played a role in a public debate between UMNO and Pas. The Islamic party had declared its intention to gradually implement *hudud*, Muslim criminal punishments, in the state. They include amputation of hands for repeated theft and stoning for adultery. In April Prime Minister Datuk Mahathir challenged Pas to impose *hudud* immediately, contending that the party was just using the issue to appear more Islamic. Even Pas's opposition allies expressed concern. The party said that by the end of 1992 it would be ready to propose constitutional changes allowing *hudud*. Parliament was not likely to approve them. But Pas also planned state legislation enforcing Muslim penalties.

The state of Sabah in northeastern Borneo was also ruled by a party that was part of the federal-level opposition. Led by state Chief Minister Joseph Pairin Kitingan, Parti Bersatu Sabah (PBS, or Sabah United Party) came to power in 1985 with support from Kadazans, the state's largest ethnic group. It later joined Barisan but left the coalition five days before the 1990 national election. The following year Pairin's brother was detained for allegedly plotting to pull Sabah out of Malaysia, and Pairin was charged with corruption. Saying that the state's rights had been eroded over the years, Pairin's government sought to review the terms of its entry into the federation in 1963. Tensions between UMNO and PBS led to an economic slowdown in Sabah.

Most of Malaysia's economy remained strong, though it was slowing from 1991's overheated pace. Johor Baharu, the capital of Johor state, gained from an industrial "growth triangle" linking it with Singapore and Indonesia's Batam Island, but Japan and Taiwan, the main sources of investment in recent years, brought in less capital. Industrial growth was slowed by a lack of manpower and the limitations of Malaysia's infrastructure. A crackdown on illegal immigrants showed just how many extra hands were needed, and a power failure blacked out a huge swath of the peninsula in September.

Despite tensions at home, Mahathir achieved prominence as a spokesman for the less developed nations. At the "Earth Summit" in Rio de Janeiro, he strongly opposed Western antilogging groups. He also pushed hard for an East Asian economic grouping to deal with trade blocs in Europe and the Western Hemisphere and for Muslim support for Bosnia and Hercegovina in its conflict with Serbia. His vigorous approach caused some irritation, however. Indonesia appeared peeved at the high profile Malaysia achieved in raising the Bosnia problem at the Non-Aligned Movement summit in Jakarta, Indon., in September. Relations with Australia were also strained by an Australian feature film on alleged atrocities by Malaysians against Vietnamese refugees.

(RICARDO L. SALUDO)

This article updates the *Macropædia* article Mainland SOUTHEAST ASIA: *Malaysia.*

MYANMAR (BURMA)

Myanmar (Burma until May 26, 1989) is a republic of Southeast Asia with coastlines on the Bay of Bengal and the Andaman Sea. Area: 676,577 sq km (261,228 sq mi). Pop. (1992 est.): 43,466,000. Cap.: Yangon (Rangoon). Monetary unit: kyat, with (Oct. 5, 1992) a free rate of 6.65 kyats to U.S. $1 (11.31 kyats = £1 sterling). Chairmen of the State Law and Order Restoration Council in 1992, Gen. Saw Maung and, from April 23, Gen. Than Shwe; prime minister from April 24, Gen. Than Shwe.

Gen. Saw Maung, 63-year-old head of a military junta widely criticized for widespread human rights abuses in Myanmar, resigned as its chairman in April 1992 after suffering from a nervous disorder. Gen. Than Shwe, deputy chairman and army commander, succeeded Saw Maung, who with a group of military officers had seized power in 1988 after suppressing a nationwide pro-democracy uprising.

The government, disregarding international appeals, continued to deprive its citizens of basic human rights. It toned

REUTERS/BETTMANN

A Karen guerrilla surveys a graveyard where fellow soldiers, killed by government troops, lie buried. Fighting between the Karens and the brutal military government of Myanmar continued in 1992.

down its campaign of terror, however, and late in September lifted a martial law decree imposed in 1989; no longer would civilians be tried by military tribunals.

The government held meetings with civilian politicians to prepare for a national convention to formulate guidelines for a new constitution. No concrete proposal came out of the conferences, but the dialogue represented a softening in approach by the government. It had suspended talks with the opposition after losing to the National League for Democracy in May 1990 elections.

The government refused to free Nobel Peace Prize winner Aung San Suu Kyi, held under house arrest in Yangon since July 1989, and it did not rule out the possibility that she might be put on trial. It did, however, release more than 200 political prisoners and allowed Suu Kyi's family to visit her in detention. In December it denied her husband's assertion that she was on a hunger strike.

Predominantly Buddhist Myanmar's relations with Bangladesh chilled after 265,000 of the country's Muslims emigrated to Islamic Bangladesh to escape persecution. A Myanmar patrol attacked a Bangladesh border outpost, killing two soldiers. Myanmar said that the refugees were illegal immigrants.   (DILIP GANGULY)

This article updates the *Macropædia* article Mainland SOUTHEAST ASIA: *Myanmar.*

PHILIPPINES

Situated in the western Pacific Ocean off the southeast coast of Asia, the republic of the Philippines consists of an archipelago of about 7,100 islands. Area: 300,000 sq km (115,800 sq mi). Pop. (1992 est.): 63,609,000. Cap.: Manila (lower house of the legislature meets in Quezon City). Monetary unit: Philippine peso, with (Oct. 5, 1992) a free rate of 24.29 pesos to U.S. $1 (41.30 pesos = £1 sterling). Presidents in 1992, Corazon Aquino and, from June 30, Fidel V. Ramos.

Fidel V. Ramos (*see* BIOGRAPHIES) became president of the Philippines on June 30, 1992, after winning just 23.6% of the vote in a May 11 election victory over six opponents. He succeeded Corazon C. Aquino, who had supported his candidacy. As head of the corrupt and brutal Philippine Constabulary, Ramos, a career military officer, had enforced martial law for Pres. Ferdinand E. Marcos after 1972. However, he turned against Marcos in 1986 and supported the popular uprising that brought Aquino to power. He served

as defense minister under Aquino, helping her survive seven coup attempts.

Only 70% of eligible voters cast ballots. A former judge who campaigned against corruption, Miriam Defenso Santiago, finished second behind Ramos with 19.7% of the vote. Eduardo Cojuangco, Jr., who grew wealthy as a crony of Marcos, got 18.2%, and Marcos' widow, Imelda, got 10.3%. Under a ticket-splitting system, Cojuangco's running mate, Joseph Estrada, a former movie star, was elected vice president. Ramos' opponents gained control of Congress.

Ramos was the first Protestant president of a country that is 84% Roman Catholic. The archbishop of Manila, Jaime Cardinal Sin, had urged voters to back Catholics who had opposed Marcos, but he pledged to support the new administration. Popular opposition to traditional politicians helped Ramos. So did support from businessmen who feared a return of the business monopolies Cojuangco had run for Marcos.

Ramos named a Cabinet that represented his former military colleagues, his business supporters, and some old politicians. The main problem facing the government was continuing economic weakness. Half of the country's 64 million people lived below a low poverty line. With unemployment around 10%, an estimated 1.2 million persons worked abroad. The political stability demonstrated by the May 11 elections encouraged economic investment. A financing package signed by the government and commercial banks on July 23 reduced the country's immediate foreign debt as a percentage of exports. This freed more resources for such pressing infrastructure needs as increased electrical-generation facilities. On August 10 the government announced the end of most restrictions on foreign exchange, thus encouraging trade.

Crime and corruption hampered business, however. Kidnapping syndicates seized relatives of rich businessmen for ransom. A director of the American Chamber of Commerce, Michael Barnes, was kidnapped January 17 in daylight in Manila's main business district. He was released 61 days later in a police raid in which 14 members of a breakaway faction of Communist guerrillas, the New Peoples Army, were killed. The NPA killed 41 soldiers in an ambush on Mindanao island on February 15 in a continuing struggle that included atrocities by both sides. Nationwide, however, the guerrillas were on the defensive. Their strength was estimated to have declined since the mid-1980s from 18,000 or

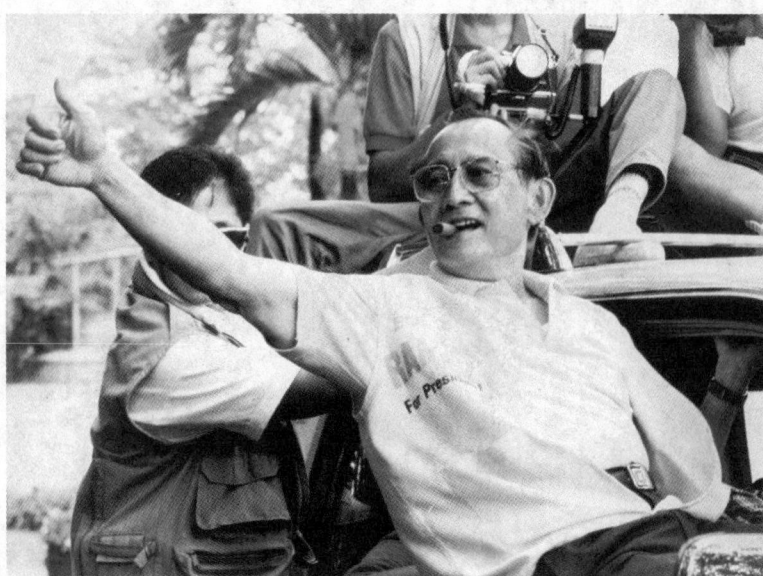

REUTERS/BETTMANN

Fidel Ramos, who had the support of Pres. Corazon Aquino, campaigns for the presidency of the Philippines. A retired army general and a member of a prominent political family, Ramos won the office in elections held on May 11.

more to fewer than 13,000. Ramos sought to eliminate the 23-year-old communist insurgency. On his recommendation, Congress passed a law lifting the ban on the Communist Party of the Philippines. Ramos released two captured NPA leaders and reached agreement for formal peace talks. On December 23 Gregorio Honasan, a former lieutenant colonel who had led several of the coup attempts against Aquino, emerged from hiding to sign a peace agreement between the government and his clandestine Reform the Armed Forces Movement.

The Mt. Pinatubo volcano, which had caused more than 700 deaths and devastated a wide area northwest of Manila in 1991, began erupting again in late August 1992. At least 72 persons were killed by lava and mud flows. Following the Philippines' refusal in 1991 to renew for 10 years U.S. use of military facilities there, the U.S. Navy turned the Subic Bay naval base over to the Philippines on September 30. Some 40,000 Filipino workers at the big base lost their jobs.

(HENRY S. BRADSHER)

SINGAPORE

Singapore, a republic of Southeast Asia and member of the Commonwealth, occupies a group of islands, the largest of which is Singapore, at the southern extremity of the Malay Peninsula. Area: 622 sq km (240 sq mi). Pop. (1992 est.): 2,792,000. Monetary unit: Singapore dollar, with (Oct. 5, 1992) a free rate of S$1.60 to U.S. $1 (S$2.71 = £1 sterling). President in 1992, Wee Kim Wee; prime minister, Goh Chok Tong.

In the wake of opposition gains in the August 1991 elections, Singapore's ruling People's Action Party had stepped back from Prime Minister Goh Chok Tong's liberal style. The PAP's tighter rein continued through 1992. On January 3 the government banned the manufacture and sale of chewing gum. Officials cited the litter and nuisance it caused, including instances when commuter-train doors were stuck shut. Violators faced fines of $1,200–$6,100 and a year in prison. In May the prime minister said that voters who "chose the wrong party" must be made to feel "worse off." Under a $10 billion, 15-year program to upgrade housing, Goh announced that among estates of equal priority the government would first refurbish those in wards where a majority had voted for the PAP. In July the government said that more kindergartens would be opened in PAP wards, while places for schoolchildren in opposition constituencies would be reduced 10%. Opposition leaders claimed that these moves were intended to sway voters in by-elections expected shortly. In a by-election in the Marine Parade constituency in December, the PAP won 73% of the vote.

The government's tougher line extended to the media. A pay-TV satellite channel began broadcasting, but imported material was censored. In August the *Business Times* was raided after publishing economic data allegedly leaked from a government office. Its editor and three other staffers were questioned, as were economic officials and foreign executives.

Several days after the raid, Senior Minister Lee Kuan Yew said he doubted that leaked data would have been published if he were still prime minister. He added that foreign analysts would likely not have questioned the nation's high-savings policy. Boosted by compulsory pension contributions, Singapore's 47% savings rate was probably the world's highest. But, with the economy slowing as a result of sluggish exports, foreign economists urged that savings be reduced to spur consumer spending and business investment.

There was also concern that Singapore's assets were not reaping the best returns. Some overseas enterprises had yet to pay off, including one by a state investment company chaired by Lee. Nonetheless, strategic investments abroad were expected to continue, especially those intended to obtain technology, gain footholds in Asia, and promote Singapore as a source of high-value services.

(RICARDO L. SALUDO)

This article updates the *Macropædia* article Mainland SOUTHEAST ASIA: *Singapore*.

THAILAND

Thailand is a constitutional monarchy in Southeast Asia, on the Andaman Sea and the Gulf of Thailand. Area: 513,115 sq km (198,115 sq mi). Pop. (1992 est.): 56,801,000. Cap.: Bangkok. Monetary unit: baht, with (Oct. 5, 1992) an official rate of 25.18 baht to U.S. $1 (42.80 baht = £1 sterling). King, Bhumibol Adulyadej; prime ministers in 1992, Anand Panyarachun, Suchinda Kraprayoon from April 7, Anand from June 10, and Chuan Leekpai from September 23.

Elections for the 360-seat National Assembly were held March 22, 1992, under a new constitution drafted by the military junta that had overthrown Prime Minister Chatichai Choonhavan a year earlier. Samakkhi Tham (Unification Virtue), a party formed by supporters of junta leaders Suchinda Kraprayoon, the army commander, and Kaset Rojananin, the air force chief, won 79 seats and formed a coalition with the same parties that had been ousted by the generals on grounds of corruption. Meanwhile, Prime Minister Anand Panyarachun, who had been appointed by the military after the 1991 coup, was praised for the efficiency and honesty of his interim government.

The new parliamentary majority's first choice for prime minister, Narong Wongwan, withdrew after Washington confirmed that a U.S. visa had recently been denied to him on grounds of suspected involvement in the drug trade. The coalition then picked General Suchinda, who immediately resigned from the army and was sworn in by King Bhumibol Adulyadej (*see* BIOGRAPHIES) on April 7. The appointment angered democracy activists, who took to the streets. Huge crowds gathered daily around Ratchadamnoen Avenue, Bangkok's ceremonial thoroughfare. Chamlong Srimuang, leader of the Buddhist-aligned Palang Dharma party, galvanized the crowd May 4 with his vow to starve himself to death unless Suchinda stepped down. As tension mounted, confrontations between troops and demonstrators became progressively more ugly. A number of people were killed by rifle fire on May 18 and 19, but the death toll was not satisfactorily established. It was widely believed that hundreds of people had been killed by soldiers and their bodies disposed of secretly, but by September only 38 families had claimed compensation.

Chamlong was arrested and more than a thousand demonstrators were detained. With the nation on the edge of chaos, the king intervened on May 20. In televised comments to a kneeling Suchinda and Chamlong, he asked them to resolve their differences. Immediately the troubles subsided, and within a week Suchinda had resigned. Former army commander Chaovalit Yongchaiyut and Democrat Party leader Chuan Leekpai tried without success to form a government by splitting the government coalition. After changing the constitution to make it mandatory for future prime ministers to come from the ranks of elected parliamentarians, the National Assembly was dissolved. On June 10 Anand was recalled as interim prime minister, and a new election was called for September 13. Anand replaced the army and air force commanders. He also removed military men from traditional ex-officio positions as chairmen of state enterprises. Samakkhi Tham dissolved.

A supporter presents flowers to Chuan Leekpai (centre), chosen in September as prime minister of a coalition government in Thailand. A lawyer who had held posts in previous Thai governments, Chuan vigorously opposed military involvement in politics.
AP/WIDE WORLD

The September 13 elections were judged free and fair. The opposition parties secured 185 of the 360 seats, barely enough to govern, and Social Action, a party in the old coalition, was brought in to strengthen the majority. The Democrats nearly doubled their representation to 78 seats, and Chuan was sworn in as prime minister. A career politician of humble origins and modest means, Chuan insisted that Cabinet ministers make their assets public. Among its first acts, the new parliament rescinded an amnesty decree promulgated by the Suchinda Cabinet just before it resigned. The intention was to allow prosecution of generals who might have given shoot-to-kill orders in May, but it could also be interpreted as reinstating the arrest of Chamlong. Chuan vowed that the government would not interfere with the functions of the courts. It was feared that arrests of serving officers could promote new tensions.

The economy continued its strong growth of the past few years. Gross national product was expected to rise 8%. Tourism, however, was badly affected by the May troubles.

(ROBERT WOODROW)

This article updates the *Macropædia* article Mainland SOUTH-EAST ASIA: *Thailand.*

VIETNAM

The socialist republic of Vietnam occupies the eastern part of the Indochinese Peninsula in Southeast Asia and is bounded on the south and east by the South China Sea. Area: 329,566 sq km (127,246 sq mi). Pop. (1992 est.): 69,052,000. Cap.: Hanoi. Monetary unit: dong, with (Oct. 5, 1992) a free rate of 10,881 dong to U.S. $1 (18,497 dong = £1 sterling). Chairman of the State Council to September 22, 1992, Vo Chi Cong; president from September 23, Le Duc Anh; chairman of the Council of Ministers (prime minister after September 24), Vo Van Kiet.

In April 1992 the National Assembly adopted a new constitution to replace the one in use since 1980. The Council of State and Council of Ministers were abolished. The post of president was created, a more powerful position than the old chairman of the State Council, and provision was made for the prime minister, chosen by the president and confirmed by the assembly, to choose a Cabinet from among assembly members. The constitution confirmed the free-market economy and the continued leadership of the Communist Party, but it reduced the party's role to one of guidance. It also guaranteed foreign investors' assets against nationalization. In July there were general elections to the assembly's 395 seats—reduced from 496—from among 601 candidates. In

September the assembly elected former defense minister Le Duc Anh, 72, as president and voted for Vo Van Kiet, 69, to continue as prime minister. Kiet's Cabinet closely resembled the earlier Council of Ministers.

The economy boomed in 1992. In December it was announced that gross national product growth for 1992 was 5.3%, and annual inflation was officially put at 15% for the year. Industrial growth was up by 14.5–15% compared with 1991. The trade surplus was expected to be $75 million for the year (there had been a deficit in 1991). Inflation was reined in by tighter monetary control and reduction of credit to state enterprises. The dong increased in value as the state bank sold gold and foreign currency to shore it up. However, cheap goods smuggled from China flooded the market from the second quarter of the year, forcing some industries to close. In late September the Commerce Ministry banned the import of 17 commodities, including garments and textiles.

Taiwan and Hong Kong remained the biggest foreign investors in Vietnam. Singapore was its largest trading partner. Officials said in August that overseas projects worth $3.5 billion had been approved since foreign investment was allowed in 1988, though only $900 million had actually been used. In January six foreign banks were given the go-ahead to open branches in Vietnam, and licenses were issued to some during the year. Also in January, five concessions for oil exploration off southern Vietnam were given in principle to foreign firms. Vietnam and Malaysia agreed on joint development of oil in territory claimed by both, and a similar agreement was made with Thailand. Four more oil-exploration blocks were handed out to overseas companies in June. In July Hanoi signed a treaty of amity and cooperation with the Association of Southeast Asian Nations, a preliminary step to joining the group. The European Commission agreed to release more aid for returning refugees and their communities, and in May Hanoi agreed to the forced repatriation of Vietnamese who had fled to Hong Kong but were judged to be economic rather than political refugees. Vietnam announced in June that it had sent its first official delegation to the Vatican. Communist Party leader Do Muoi visited India in September. In November Japan announced an end to its aid embargo with a $370 million low-interest loan. Diplomatic ties with South Korea were established in December.

The Russians confirmed in January that their last big warship had left the Cam Ranh naval base. All Soviet military advisers were said to have departed in May—there had been 1,000 after the 1979 war with China. Chinese Foreign Minister Qian Qichen (Ch'ien Ch'i-ch'en) visited Hanoi in February, the highest-level Chinese leader to go there since the 1979 war. In March Vietnam and China signed agreements on air, rail, postal, and shipping links, and in April the border was officially opened. An air service started between Guangzhou (Canton) and Hanoi in May. However, Vietnam was upset by China's granting of a concession for oil exploration to a U.S. company in the disputed Spratly Islands in the South China Sea (May 8) and by its landing of troops on one of the islands (June 4). Hanoi also accused China of moving their common border in several places. An international conference on the Spratlys was held in Indonesia in early July, and all sides agreed to settle the matter by negotiation. In September Vietnam objected to oil exploration by China in the Gulf of Tonkin and to the detention by Chinese ships since August of Vietnam-bound cargo vessels leaving Hong Kong. Two sets of talks were held in October, when the oil-exploration platform was removed. Chinese Premier Li Peng (Li P'eng) visited Vietnam at the end of November, the first trip by a Chinese premier

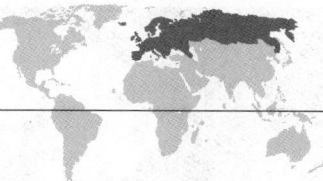

in 21 years, and the two countries agreed to expand trade and increase efforts to resolve their disputes.

Vietnam's intensified cooperation with the U.S. in the search for American soldiers missing in action during the Vietnam war was rewarded with increased aid from Washington. In October Hanoi agreed to release all the information it had on the matter, photographs, and personal effects of U.S. servicemen. Some 5,000 photographs from the Vietnam military archives were handed over to the U.S. All remaining detainees in the reeducation camps set up in 1975 were released in April, and it was announced that 40,000–50,000 had resettled in the U.S. Washington eased its trade embargo on Vietnam in April to allow telephone lines to be set up between the U.S. and Vietnam (the links were opened only in November, when the U.S. agreed not to impound payment for the service) and to permit the sale of essential materials such as food and books. Later it allowed restricted use in Vietnam of aircraft made in the U.S. or with U.S.-made parts. In December U.S. companies were allowed to hire staff in Vietnam and to sign contracts to start after the lifting of the embargo.

An antigovernment group was captured in April in southern Vietnam, and another was jailed in May. Reports of the capture of two other subversive groups surfaced during that month. In eastern Cambodia some 400 members of FULRO, the Vietnamese Montagnard resistance group, surrendered to UN forces in August; they did not know the war was over. In September the country's first hijacking took place when an émigré from the U.S. took over a Vietnamese plane above Ho Chi Minh City and dropped antigovernment leaflets. He parachuted from the plane but was captured. (JUDITH L. CLARKE)

This article updates the *Macropædia* article Mainland SOUTHEAST ASIA: *Vietnam.*

A man in Vietnam loads cases of Coca-Cola onto his motorbike. Although the U.S. government officially maintained its trade embargo against Vietnam, many products from various parts of the world found their way into the country.

Europe

EUROPEAN AFFAIRS

Western Europe. The agreement reached in December 1991 at Maastricht, Neth., on the Treaty on European Union and the Treaty of Economic and Monetary Union by the heads of state and government of the 12 member states (and signed by the 12 foreign ministers in February 1992) augured well for the future of the European Communities (EC; comprising the European Economic Community [EEC], the European Coal and Steel Community [ECSC], and Euratom). There was little to indicate the scale of the problems ahead. Despite Britain's cautious insistence on an "opt-out" clause allowing it to decide at a later date whether to join its partners in full monetary union, as well as on the right to opt out of the protocol on social and employment policies, the ratification process of the 12 member states was expected to be complete by the end of the year.

Work was speeded up on the creation of a European Economic Area (EEA) with the seven European Free Trade Association (EFTA) nations (Austria, Norway, Sweden, Finland, Switzerland, Iceland, and Liechtenstein). This was to serve as an interim measure before admission of those of the six that wanted full membership in the EC. Agreement to enlargement was considered by most member states and the European Parliament—which would have the final say on the admission of new members—to be dependent on the full ratification of the two treaties designed to strengthen the integration of the member states. Legal arguments over the EEA were resolved in the EC's own European Court of Justice in April, and the agreement allowing 40 million Scandinavians, Austrians, and Swiss access to the EC's internal market was initialed on April 14. Although the Swiss government had announced plans to apply for EC membership, Swiss voters unexpectedly rejected the EEA in a referendum on December 6. The remaining EFTA nations declared they would continue negotiations as planned.

In a surprise result Danish voters in June reversed the decision of their own Folketing (parliament) and rejected the Maastricht Treaty, as the two documents had become known. They did so by a narrow majority: of a population of some five million, 50.7% voted against and 49.3% in favour. The difference of only some 46,000 votes left the Community in shock but able to convince itself that once the 11 other member states had ratified the treaties, Denmark would be persuaded to find a formula for a second referendum. Pres. François Mitterrand then followed the Danish rejection with a controversial decision to hold a referendum in France. The September vote was preceded by deepening concern as the issue of union became inextricably linked with the popularity of the French government and of Mitterrand himself.

Before the French went to the polls, crisis overtook the exchange-rate mechanism (ERM), the agreement locking most European currencies inside agreed fluctuation limits. The money markets were rocked as Britain left the ERM and Italy dropped out temporarily only a few days after devaluing the lira by 7%. With its first step toward the goal of monetary union under tremendous strain, the EC watched a fierce battle for votes in France. The result of the national referendum was a tiny majority in favour. The result—51.05% for and 48.95% against—left governments of the member states and Jacques Delors, the president

German Chancellor Helmut Kohl (left) meets with French Pres. François Mitterrand in Paris following the French voters' narrow approval of the Maastricht Treaty on September 20. Germany and France continued to take the lead in 1992 in pressing for European unity.
REUTERS/BETTMANN

of the European Commission in Brussels, in no doubt that there was considerable hostility to the Maastricht Treaty.

Prime Minister John Major of Britain called an emergency summit in Birmingham in October to discuss the two crises. Against a background of deepening recession, the summit also considered the dispute with the U.S. over aspects of the Uruguay round of negotiations in the General Agreement on Tariffs and Trade (GATT). Increasingly bitter bilateral negotiations had followed the collapse of a full 108-nation GATT meeting in Brussels in December 1990. The U.S. and the EC had failed to agree on a new multifibre agreement or aspects of market access for insurance, banking, and other services, but their main disagreement was over agriculture. By October the U.S. side was threatening to impose a $1 billion package of trade sanctions on EC imports. The draft list mainly affected French, Italian, and Irish farm and dairy produce. It clearly reflected the U.S. view that these three countries were the main culprits behind objections to any agreement that might affect the reformed common agricultural policy (CAP).

This had been agreed to in May by the EC agriculture ministers after two years of difficult negotiations. The first major reform in the CAP since it was created, the legislation shifted the emphasis of EC support away from food production toward direct income support, which meant paying farmers not to produce. However, the agreement did not go far enough for the U.S., which objected to the EC's high levels of export subsidies—refunds to make up the difference to its farmers if world prices fell. It also challenged the way the EC was supporting the production of oilseeds. With France now stridently objecting to any compromise on the CAP reform and taking an increasingly anti-American line, the special summit instructed the EC agriculture commissioner, Ray MacSharry of Ireland, and the external trade commissioner, Frans Andriessen of The Netherlands, to resume negotiations.

Attention was now focused on the British Parliament, where opposition to the Maastricht Treaty was mounting. Former prime minister Margaret Thatcher, recently created baroness and elevated to the House of Lords, vocally opposed ratification. She was joined by one of her former Cabinet ministers, Norman (now Lord) Tebbit. With his party split over Europe and the British economy in trouble,

Major was under intense criticism for his handling of the ERM affair, which had led to a lowering of the value of the pound sterling by more than 12%. Speculation against weaker currencies in the ERM continued, and in the weeks following sterling's withdrawal, the German Bundesbank was forced to support the French franc against devaluation. By the latter part of November the ERM was again in crisis, with Spain and Portugal forced to devalue the peseta and escudo, respectively, by 6%. The outgoing Fianna Fail government in Ireland was battling to stop the slide of its own punt, and the Danish krone was coming under pressure following devaluation of the Swedish krona and the Finnish markka. Inevitably, there was anxious debate about whether the financial turmoil would require the deferment or even the abandonment of plans for full economic and monetary union by 1997.

Meanwhile, the Community pressed on with plans for dismantling frontier controls and passport checks at borders. Once again the U.K., while supporting the creation of a single internal market from Jan. 1, 1993, was reluctant to abolish checks on people, arguing that as an island Britain was a special case. As a result of the Danish referendum and the evidence of French opposition to European integration, Delors called for more openness to allay the public's fears about the EC. There was also widespread agreement on the need to reduce the secrecy surrounding the Council of Ministers and to increase the powers of the European Parliament. This was a theme taken up by Prime Minister Major when he took over the six-month rotating presidency of the EC from Portugal in July. He identified completion of the single market, agreement on the future financing of Community programs, and preparations for enlargement as priorities.

Despite this assurance, the Community was split on the levels of funding it would need for the forthcoming five years. Delors' proposal to increase funding by 30% was criticized by the finance ministers, meeting in Luxembourg in June, as inappropriate at a time of recession and mounting unemployment. Delors pointed out that the CAP reform voted in May was costlier than that originally proposed by the Commission. By the time of the special summit in Birmingham, Danish Prime Minister Poul Schlüter, who was

(continued on page 422)

Europe's Single Market

BY GREGORY F. TREVERTON

The European Communities' Maastricht Treaty, agreed in December 1991 at the Maastricht (Neth.) summit, capped Europe's progress toward a single market, due to begin Jan. 1, 1993. The treaty marked a stunning success, the EC's most far-reaching progress since the Treaty of Rome 35 years earlier, all the more striking in light of the "Europessimism" of the mid-1980s.

Yet during 1992 Europe came down from its Maastricht high. In June, Denmark narrowly voted down the Maastricht Treaty in a referendum, and in September a French referendum, originally expected to be no contest, produced a bare "oui"—the same week that chaos in currency markets all but exploded the EC's exchange rate cooperation.

The votes betokened resentment against ceding national sovereignty to "faceless Eurocrats" in Brussels. The Community is suffering from what the president of its Commission (and thus the paramount Eurocrat), Jacques Delors, calls a "democratic deficit" just as it confronts the challenges not only of Maastricht but of expanding in Europe's west and reaching out to its east.

The Single Market and the Maastricht Treaty. In principle, the single market program and Maastricht are separate, the latter the next step in integration beyond the former. In practice, though, the specific backlash against Maastricht is also a broader backlash against "Brussels"—the centralizing of standards and regulations in the EC, which seems to threaten symbols near and dear to the hearts of Europeans, from British sausage to German beer and Spanish tildes.

The single market began in 1985, when the Community had become mired in a series of tiresome arguments about Britain's share of the joint budget. In the Single European Act of 1986, the EC's leaders adopted an ambitious program for the free movement of goods, services, people, and capital throughout the Community. The program came to comprise some 300 regulations, drawn up by the EC's Commission, negotiated with member states, and eventually adopted into national legislation by all 12 EC members. By Jan. 1, 1993, some nine-tenths of those regulations would have been enacted by all 12.

Before 1992's backlash, concern about the single market centred on "sins of omission," what was left out. One exclusion was agriculture—the EC's common agricultural policy, which gobbles up two-thirds of the EC budget, raises consumer prices, and produces surpluses that, in turn, make for continuous wrangling with other agricultural exporters, especially the United States. A second exclusion was defense procurement. In other areas, individual nations were allowed to opt out of particular regulations, at least for a limited time. Britain, for instance, argued that it could not risk admitting potential terrorists, and the Community was far from dismantling all its border controls.

Gregory F. Treverton is a senior fellow of the Council on Foreign Relations; his books include America, Germany, and the Future of Europe.

Now, however, "sins of commission"—or perhaps Commission—have come to the fore. The principle of the single market was reciprocity—if a bank was chartered in Britain or a health standard was acceptable in Germany, the bank could operate in or the German product be exported to all the other member countries. In some areas—telecommunications, for example—common EC standards were imperative, and they had the effect of handicapping the member states whose standards were *not* the ones adopted.

More to the point, reciprocity and its twin principle—infelicitously labeled "subsidiarity" in Eurospeak—have their limits. The idea of both is to let the level of government closest to the people decide as much as possible. In practice, though, when does Germany's law on beer purity become a nontariff barrier on imports from its partners or, more pointedly, when do laxer safety regulations in Spain give it a competitive advantage? The drive to set more and more standards in Brussels is almost irresistible and the backlash against that standardization almost inevitable.

The Next Test: EMU. Maastricht's centrepiece was the economic and monetary union (EMU). The treaty's political half, European political union, or EPU, was modest—somewhat less scope for national vetoes in the Community's board of directors, the Council of Ministers; a little more role for the European Parliament, now mostly a talk shop. Maastricht called boldly for a common EC foreign and defense policy but left the task to cooperation among member governments, not to the supranational Brussels machinery. And the Community's difficulties in dealing with Yugoslavia's civil war—in particular, the open water between Germany and France—demonstrated just how far Europe is from a "common" foreign policy.

In contrast, EMU offered the concrete prospect, by 1999 at the latest, of a common European currency and central bank. Yet even before the September crisis, there were signs of cooling on the idea, not least in Germany, Europe's core economy. Why, Germans asked, should they give up their cherished Deutsche Mark, the symbol of their postwar success, for a European currency, mere "Esperanto money"? Now the EC states are linked in a European monetary system around the Deutsche Mark; in effect, the German Bundesbank sets interest rates for all EC members without having to share any real power over decisions with them.

Thus several times in 1991 and 1992 the Bundesbank could drive up interest rates for purely German reasons—keeping the lid on German inflation despite the huge fiscal transfers needed to jump start eastern Germany. The action put upward pressure on interest rates in its EC partners, whose currencies are tied to the Deutsche Mark. Their difficulty, alas, was not inflation but recession, and so Germany's solution became their problem.

This exchange-rate mechanism, or ERM, came to crisis in September when, under pressure, Germany finally agreed to reduce interest rates but then produced only a sliver of cuts. Speculation against the weaker currencies, the British pound and the Italian lira in particular, forced them to devalue against the Deutsche Mark, and Britain and Italy dropped out of the ERM.

Even before September, economic and monetary union seemed far from assured. For Germany, moving to such a union, along with a European central bank (or EuroFed), would mean sharing decision-making with less inflation-phobic partners, like Italy, and so Germany had insisted that the EuroFed be just as anti-inflation as the Bundesbank. Maastricht set strict criteria for "convergence" among member countries, toward small budget deficits and low rates of inflation; indeed, the criteria are so strict that Germany itself does not now qualify to participate in the new system.

Logically, one response to the September crisis would be to move immediately to a common currency; then speculation would have no weak currencies to target. But a common currency requires roughly common economic policies; when recession hit the U.S. oil patch, that part of the country could not "devalue" its currency to spur economic recovery. And the EC nations are hardly in step economically—a fact obscured when Margaret Thatcher was British prime minister by her railing against EMU as an unacceptable transfer of sovereignty.

Maastricht went further than the political traffic in Europe would bear. So, while Europe will one day have a common currency—if for no other reason than that, to the private-sector concerns that drove the single market, multiple currencies, like multiple markets, are a nuisance—that day will not come soon.

Challenges Beyond Maastricht. As it argues over the next steps in its integration, the EC is stretched both westward and eastward. To the west, it faces an imminent widening to take in the countries of the European Free Trade Association (EFTA). In October 1991 the EC and EFTA agreed to form a European Economic Area (EEA). The idea, originally proposed by the Community to fend off pressure from the EFTA nations for full membership, was more takeover than merger, for EFTA is to assume existing EC rules governing matters from antitrust to the environment without much say in framing them.

Not surprisingly, EEA looked to the EFTA nations like "taxation without representation," so Austria, Sweden, Finland, and Norway applied for full EC membership. These rich EFTA countries easily qualify for full EC membership on economic grounds. Yet all of them—save NATO member Norway—were neutrals when there was something to be neutral about, and they would bring to the Community quite different traditions and practices.

To the east of the Community, states will not soon be ready for full EC membership but hanker for tighter political association with anything "European"—the Council of Europe, NATO, the Western European Union, but above all the Community. French Pres. François Mitterrand floated the idea of a confederated Europe built around the EC, but no one has picked up the suggestion.

What eastern Europe needs is access to the EC market; what it hopes for is full membership in the club in the long run, and not too long at that. For their part, the EC nations understand that their choice is between accepting eastern Europe's goods now or its people in the form of immigrants not much later. But accepting those goods is still perplexing, for those imports will fall in sectors that are already bones of contention in the existing Community—textiles, coal, steel, and agriculture.

Spurred by the attempted Moscow coup in 1991, the EC proposed to phase out over six years tariffs against products from Hungary, Czechoslovakia, and Poland, thereby creating a free-trade zone, and to begin negotiations with Romania and Bulgaria. The proposal was modest, for special restrictions still applied to the four sensitive sectors, but the Community granted "asymmetry"—beginning its tariff cuts before the eastern Europeans had to start theirs. Nevertheless, France held up the agreement over Polish exports of process beef, a tiny sliver of exports.

Europe's single market is an impressive achievement, and Maastricht remains an equally impressive goal. Yet progress to it will be in fits and starts, given the pressure on the Community from both east and west, and in the process the EC almost certainly will become what it has sought to avoid: a Community of different speeds, tiers, and forms of association, perhaps with variations by the issue at hand.

(continued from page 420)

scheduled to take up the six-month presidency in January, was giving notice that, before holding a second referendum some time in 1993, his country would want special arrangements for Denmark that would be legally binding. Notably, the Danes rejected participation in European defense and monetary union. They also rejected the provision in the Treaty of Political Union for the creation of European citizenship.

On November 4, after an often rowdy debate in the House of Commons, Major succeeded in getting a three-vote majority for a motion supporting continuation of the Maastricht Treaty ratification process. A surprise assurance that the bill would not be put before the Commons until after the second Danish referendum led to widespread protests from the Commission and other member states. The decision to delay the treaty, possibly to the autumn of 1993, was described by Mitterrand as unacceptable. He was stiffly rebuked in a terse statement from Number 10 Downing Street, which said that the issue was for Britain to decide. During the latter months of 1992 there was much speculation about possible alternative avenues for European integration if the Maastricht Treaty failed. There were persistent—but never fully authenticated—reports that a group of "core" EC countries, including France, Germany, and the Benelux nations, might forge a "fast track" monetary union on their own within the EC.

The Community leadership looked more positive in October, when Major and Delors were hosts to a meeting of the prime ministers of Poland, Hungary, and the soon-to-be-divided Czech and Slovak republics, which had formed a free-trade zone, Visegrad. Both EC leaders welcomed the meeting as a demonstration of support for the newly democratizing countries of eastern and central Europe. They agreed that the Community should encourage intensified practical cooperation with the countries of the Visegrad group, looking toward eventual EC membership for the four former Soviet satellite states.

The EC summit in Edinburgh on December 11–12 proved to be somewhat less contentious than had been anticipated, thanks in large part to Major's deft handling and persistence. At the summit, the last before the arrival of the single market on Jan. 1, 1993, the 12 member nations agreed to exempt Denmark from certain key elements of the Maastricht Treaty, thus allowing the Danes to schedule another referendum in early 1993. Agreement was also reached on a new, seven-year budget, the allotment of seats in an enlarged European Parliament, and a common foreign policy, particularly in regard to eastern Europe.

On November 13 the two EC negotiators returned from Washington, D.C., to announce that they had concluded a bilateral agreement with the United States resolving their differences in the stalled GATT talks. The Uruguay round was due to be completed in Geneva in December against a continuing background of furious protest from French farmers.

During the year the EC shared with the UN an unenviable responsibility for the search for peace in Yugoslavia. Two former British foreign secretaries headed the UN-sponsored peace delegation: Lord Carrington (formerly Peter Carington), who resigned in August, and Lord Owen (formerly David Owen). The Community provided several hundred cease-fire monitors as well as armed peacekeeping forces. There was discussion about extending the role of those forces to peace enforcement. The nine-nation Western European Union (WEU) took an active role in these discussions. During the year it expanded its membership to include Greece; Denmark and Ireland were granted observer status; and Turkey, Norway, and Iceland became associates. Agreement was reached clarifying the relationship of the WEU to both NATO and the EC. Most member states supported a gradual incorporation of the WEU into the Community as its defense and security arm.

(JOHN PALMER)

Central and Eastern Europe. By common consent 1992 was not a good year for central and eastern Europe, if one measured positive and negative developments by the criteria of political stability and movement toward economic well-being. The underlying problem was similar throughout the postcommunist area. The transformation of communist rule into market-based democracies was encountering obstacles with which no one had reckoned and which were in many ways becoming structural. (*See* ECONOMIC AFFAIRS: *Special Report.*)

The most visible expression of this was the rise of nationalism as the single, overriding approach to all political difficulties. In every postcommunist country a nationalist view of the world increasingly came to dominate the concerns of the nation's leaders, and the rise of nationalism encountered popular sympathy in societies that were politically inexperienced and not fully able to separate myth from reality.

The core of the problem was that nationhood was an effective instrument for the definition of the identity of a community but had little to say as to how that community should be governed. However, excessive emphasis on nationhood did act as a major obstacle to democratic practice, largely because it made compromise very difficult if not actually impossible to achieve. While one can bargain over the allocation of resources—this is the standard fare of Western politics—bargaining over questions of identity is virtually impossible.

The communist legacy played a malign role in this respect. The communist system did everything in its power to block the emergence of independent institutions, as this development would have threatened the Communist Party's political monopoly. Consequently, when communism collapsed, these systems were left without any experience of operating through institutions worthy of the name.

Thus, for anyone brought up under communism—which included the overwhelming majority of people in central and eastern Europe—institutions were a facade, a pretence, while the real decisions were made elsewhere. Rather than rely on institutions, someone who wanted something done would turn to a personal contact. This attitude could hardly be expected to disappear overnight, and so politics in these postcommunist nations remained throughly personalized.

The significance of all this was that political parties, national legislatures, and the legal system remained as much coteries of friends as they did bodies intended to represent interests and to structure power; even when they did seek to act on the basis of impersonal criteria, most people did not believe they were doing so. Because these institutions were not regarded as authentic, people took the view that power was being exercised covertly; one result of this was the growth of conspiracy theories.

It is a common feature of such theories that those who hold them believe that every outcome has a cause and that it was deliberate; chance, accident, or mishap has no role to play in this view of the world. This helped explain the deep distrust and lack of goodwill in postcommunist politics and the unwillingness of political leaders to accept that a degree of neutrality, a kind of attitude where a person's intentions are not automatically subjected to question, was essential for democracy. The spreading of this attitude had another consequence, however. Political problems could not, of course, be solved by the kind of relatively simplistic remedies proposed, such as "sack the former communists and everything will be fine," a widespread viewpoint. The insistence on such measures by a large number of political leaders made genuine remedies, such as urgent economic restructuring, that much more difficult to adopt.

STATES OF THE FORMER U.S.S.R. AND CIS AFFILIATION

Nationalism became a part of this political equation because belonging to a national community was believed to be an authentic experience, and it was an easy step from there to assume that ever larger doses of nationalism would be sufficient to solve all existing problems. When this did not happen, failure was attributed to the machinations of hostile, alien elements, thereby completing the vicious circle of suspicion and hatred.

This theoretical and psychological background made it possible to explain the deep-rootedness of the postcommunist crisis. In this connection a number of specific issues require closer attention. Obviously, the impact of the conflict in the former Yugoslavia with its application of the principle of "ethnic cleansing" in Croatia and in Bosnia and Hercegovina was studied closely by nationalists elsewhere. Wherever an ethnic minority existed, it tended to be singled out by the majority as the alien scapegoat to which responsibility for current problems could be attributed. The fact that this had nothing whatever to do with reality seemed to trouble no one.

In concrete terms the Turkish minority in Bulgaria, the Hungarian minorities in Romania and Slovakia, the Gypsies in Hungary, and the Germans in Poland were all exposed potentially or actually to this threat. Furthermore, the acceptance of the principle of national self-determination and the independence of the post-Soviet, the post-Yugoslav, and the forthcoming Czech and Slovak republics encouraged others to look in the same direction.

The economic situation in the region was, to put it mildly, unhelpful. Communism collapsed at least in part because it had reached the end of the road economically. The postcommunists, however, were unable to do much to improve the situation, partly through inexperience and partly through lack of resources. That, in turn, exacerbated the popular mood of discontent and resentment and made some political leaders more responsive to radical rhetoric.

Finally, the attitude of the West—also beset by inexperience and quailing at the prospect of sorting out the massive economic and political problems of the postcommunist world—was ambivalent. Western hesitations in the face of this multiple crisis made it easier for authoritarians in central and eastern Europe to pursue their aims and caused democrats to become disheartened.

There were some positive signs, however. The fear of war, while very real, kept the neighbours of the former Yugoslavia out of the conflict, although the anomalous status of Macedonia (unrecognized by virtually everyone) and the threat of a major upheaval in Kosovo (a province in Serbia where the majority of the people were of Albanian descent) remained in force. Russia, the former imperial superpower but now out of the area, embarked on a policy of reestablishing better relations. In Poland, in the Czech lands, in Hungary, and in Slovenia, there were some indications that economic reform, especially the growth of private-sector activity, was beginning to make an impact. Overall, however, the negatives continued to outweigh the positives during the year.   (GEORGE SCHÖPFLIN)

See also Economic Affairs; Military Affairs.

ALBANIA

A republic in the western Balkan Peninsula of southeastern Europe, Albania is situated on the Adriatic Sea. Area: 28,748 sq km (11,100 sq mi). Pop. (1992 est.): 3,357,000. Cap.: Tirane. Monetary unit: lek, with (Oct. 5, 1992) a free rate of 109.81 leks to U.S. $1 (186.67 leks = £1 sterling). Presidents in 1992, Ramiz Alia and, from April 9, Sali Berisha; chairmen of the Council of Ministers (premiers), Vilson Ahmeti and, from April 13, Aleksander Meksi.

Albania took a big leap into Western-style democracy in the March 22, 1992, elections with the landslide victory of the Democratic Party over the Socialist Party (the former Communists). The results were a reversal of those of March 31, 1991, when the Communists had managed to retain power. The Democrats won 62% of the votes and achieved an overall majority with 92 of the 140 seats in the parliament. On April 9 the charismatic Sali Berisha became Albania's first democratically elected president in seven decades when he replaced the veteran Communist Ramiz Alia. The first non-Communist government, consisting of 18 ministers and headed by Aleksander Meksi, was elected on April 13. Its stated priority was to establish law and order and transform the paralyzed economy through a reform program emphasizing a free-market economy and privatization.

Four months after its March defeat, the Socialist Party made impressive gains in the country's first democratic local elections. In the July 26 balloting, the Democratic Party won 43.16% of the vote, only 2% more than the 41.32% cast for the Socialists. Continued economic hardships, general apathy, and a split within the Democratic Party also contributed to its poor showing. It held local administrative control in most large cities, while the Socialists controlled much of the countryside. The split grew into a rift in November when a group of reform-minded Democrats broke away and formed a new party, the Democratic Alliance.

By fall there were signs that the country's economic and political situation was on the mend, though ordinary Albanians still faced a daily struggle to make ends meet. While there was no repetition of the previous year's mass exodus to Italy, many people continued to flee to Greece. The traumatic experience of 1991 had sensitized Italy to Albania's plight. Operation Pelican, a massive Italian humanitarian aid program, continued throughout 1992.

Albania made considerable progress in foreign relations. President Berisha and other senior government officials visited a number of countries, and Albania became a full member of several international organizations and expressed an interest in joining NATO.   (LOUIS ZANGA)

This article updates the *Macropædia* article BALKAN STATES: *Albania*.

ANDORRA

A landlocked independent coprincipality of Europe, Andorra is in the Pyrenees Mountains between Spain and France. Area: 468 sq km (181 sq mi). Pop. (1992 est.): 57,100. Cap.: Andorra la Vella. Monetary units: French franc and Spanish peseta. Coprinces: the president of the French Republic and the bishop of Urgel, Spain, represented by their *veguers* (provosts) and *batlles* (prosecutors); chief executive in 1992, Oscar Ribas Reig. An elected General Council of 28 members elects the first syndic, in 1992 Albert Gelabert.

In January 1992 the country experienced the first popular demonstration in its 714-year history as Andorrans took to the streets to protest the political paralysis within the General Council of the Valleys (parliament). The reformist government headed by Oscar Ribas Reig had attempted to introduce a new constitution that, among other things, would legalize political parties and trade unions and guarantee civil rights. Blocked by the conservative opposition, Ribas resigned as president of the Executive Council (head of government). On January 30 the General Council dissolved itself and scheduled general elections for April 5.

In the hotly contested elections, 82% of the 8,592 eligible voters went to the polls. (Some 80% of Andorra's population consists of foreigners.) For the first time political parties, though officially illegal, campaigned on Andorra's year-old national television stations, and women candidates ran for the first time in all seven parishes. The reformists, led by Ribas, won 17 of the 28 seats in the parliament, and Ribas was sworn in as head of government on May 4. The major task of the new government was to complete work on a new constitution that would give the country a modern political and legal framework. When completed, the constitution would be submitted to the voters in a referendum.

(ANNE ROBY)

This article updates the *Micropædia* article ANDORRA.

ARMENIA

A landlocked republic of Transcaucasia, Armenia borders Georgia to the north, Azerbaijan to the east, Iran to the south, the Azerbaijani exclave of Nakhichevan to the southwest, and Turkey to the west. Area: 29,800 sq km (11,500 sq mi). Pop. (1992 est.) 3,426,000. Cap.: Yerevan. Armenia claims the predominantly Armenian-populated Nagorno-Karabakh region, which has been part of Azerbaijan since 1923. Monetary unit; ruble, with (Oct. 5, 1992) a free rate of 316.82 rubles = U.S. $1 (538.59 rubles = £1 sterling). President in 1992, Levon Ter-Petrosyan; prime minister, Gagik Arutyunyan.

During 1992 the Armenians gained their main military objectives in Nagorno-Karabakh—free air and land access to that disputed enclave in Azerbaijan and a halt to the indiscriminate bombardment by the ethnic Azeri forces of Armenian towns and villages there. The capture of Khojali in late February was a major turning point for the Armenians because it gave them access to the only airfield in the region, thus permitting them to ferry in supplies vitally needed to continue the war. The loss of Khojali and the subsequent bloody fighting was a great blow to the Azeris and led to a frenzied search for scapegoats. The main victim was Ayaz Mutalibov, the ex-Communist president of Azerbaijan. He had talked much about defending Azeri interests in Nagorno-Karabakh but had done little to improve the military situation. One reason for this was apparently his concern that a powerful Azeri fighting force might slip beyond his control.

Mutalibov was forced out by the powerful Popular Front of Azerbaijan, whose candidate, Abulfez Elchibey, was eventually elected president. A major priority for the new president was to defend Azeri interests in Nagorno-Karabakh. However, Elchibey soon came to the conclusion that the fighting in the disputed enclave was in no one's interest and tried to find a diplomatic solution. The Armenian president, Levon Ter-Petrosyan, also saw the advantages of bringing the conflict to an end. It was crippling Armenia economically and had cut the country off from its main sources of energy. Armenia had always denied that it was directly involved in the fighting, and so Ter-Petrosyan was willing to enter into officially sponsored attempts to bring about peace. He signed various documents, but they had little effect on the hostilities since there was no way to enforce the peace settlement.

The Azeris accused Russia of aiding Armenia militarily in Nagorno-Karabakh, but there was little hard evidence to back this up. After taking the enclave, the Armenians secured a land link from it through part of Azerbaijan to Armenia, and this led to international criticism. The enclave renamed itself the Republic of Nagorno-Karabakh and requested Armenian recognition. President Ter-Petrosyan came under considerable pressure from the opposition to accede to this request but repeatedly refused to do so, arguing that Armenia should not be the first nation to extend recognition. Despite the moderate leaderships in Armenia and Azerbaijan, no solution emerged.

The nationalist Dashnaktsutyun Party dominated the Nagorno-Karabakh parliament and disagreed strongly with Ter-Petrosyan, who was willing to accept autonomy and free access from Armenia for the enclave. The danger for Armenia was that Azerbaijan, which was larger and more populous than Armenia, might build up its forces to the point where it could successfully challenge Armenian military control of Nagorno-Karabakh. The conflict was also causing economic hardship for Armenia. The energy blockade from Azerbaijan forced a slowdown in manufacturing. In February only 10% of Armenia's industrial capacity was operating, and in October it was only 18%. During the first half of the year, national income was about half that of the previous year. The republic planned to introduce its own currency in tandem with the ruble, but there was little likelihood of this occurring in the near future. The state bank of Armenia had no foreign reserves, and money due after the collapse of the Soviet Union was frozen in the Bank for Foreign Trade (Vneshekonom Bank) in Moscow.

Foreign Minister Raffi Hovannisyan was indefatigable in his attempts during the year to break the state out of the isolation in which it found itself. However, in October he was asked by the president to resign in an apparent policy dispute; he was replaced a month later by Arman Kirakosyan. Armenia remained within the Commonwealth of Independent States but claimed that it benefited little from this. (MARTIN MCCAULEY)

This article updates the *Macropædia* article TRANSCAUCASIA: *Armenia*.

AUSTRIA

The republic of Austria is a landlocked state of central Europe. Area: 83,859 sq km (32,378 sq mi). Pop. (1992 est.): 7,857,000. Cap.: Vienna. Monetary unit: Austrian Schilling, with (Oct. 5, 1992) a free rate of 9.86 Schillings to U.S. $1 (16.76 Schillings = £1 sterling). Presidents in 1992, Kurt Waldheim and, from July 8, Thomas Klestil; chancellor, Franz Vranitzky.

Presidential elections were held in Austria in the spring of 1992, and the People's Party (ÖVP) candidate, Thomas Klestil, was elected in the second round with 57% of the votes. As a result of the international isolation of Pres. Kurt Waldheim, who had been accused of past Nazi associations, the new president was faced with a need to address a backlog of diplomatic contacts. Shortly after Klestil took office, Israel once again sent an ambassador to Vienna.

The new political situation in Europe changed the character of any possible threat to Austria's security and to its defense against such threats. There were plans to make the federal army smaller but more efficient in order to protect against any local conflicts in neighbouring regions that might threaten Austria's borders. To this end the basic mobilization force would be reduced to 120,000 troops, a permanent rapid-deployment force of 15,000 would be created, and the basic military service would be more flexibly regulated. The abolition of universal military service and the creation of a professional army were not considered.

Austria's neutrality was again the subject of heavy debate. Even though political reality had superseded the original reasons behind neutrality, it remained a popular policy, and no one was willing to expressly renounce it. Therefore, as long as no system of collective security existed in Europe, the constitutional law regarding neutrality would remain standing, and the politics of neutrality would be adapted to new developments. This would eliminate any obstacles to Austria's bid for membership in the European Communities (EC). Meanwhile, negotiations concerning EC membership were being energetically pursued by the government. In spite of government propaganda, however, the people's euphoria over the EC was reserved. In mid-1992 a poll showed only

Thomas Klestil (second from right) appears at ceremonies during his inauguration as the new president of Austria on July 8. A career diplomat, Klestil was the candidate of the conservative People's Party.

PETER KURZ—GAMMA LIAISON

a slim majority of Austrians in favour of EC membership. A national referendum on the issue was anticipated.

In June the 32-year-old controversy over the status of Südtirol (South Tyrol) came to an end when Austria and Italy announced the completion of a 1969 package containing 137 individual measures that would guarantee Südtirol's autonomy. In the future the issue could be taken before the International Court of Justice and the panels of the Conference on Security and Cooperation in Europe.

In early 1992 Austria formally recognized Slovenia, Croatia, and 11 republics of the former Soviet Union. The flow of refugees from the Balkans swelled to such numbers that visa requirements had to be introduced. By September Austria was harbouring more than 57,000 refugees from former Yugoslavia, the highest burden per capita in Europe. Vienna, Salzburg, and Kärnten (Carinthia) had to cease admitting refugees. In the same month, there was a terrorist attack on a refugee camp. The popularly financed charity organization "Neighbour in Despair," which had raised some $36 million in aid, received high international recognition.

In order to stem the overflow of economic refugees into Austria while at the same time preserving the ability to help those who were genuine victims of persecution, the government enacted a new, stricter asylum law. More laws were planned by which the rate of immigration would be regulated to between 20,000 and 30,000 per year, while Jörg Haider's right-wing Freedom Party launched an initiative aimed at ending all immigration. Neo-Nazism, anti-Semitism, right-wing radicalism, and xenophobia were vigorously combated by the authorities in 1991–92. New legislation amended the country's anti-Nazi laws and reduced mandatory sentences, thus making the laws more responsive to social realities and making convictions easier.

The international economic recession was only weakly felt in Austria. For 1992 an increase in economic growth of 1.7–2.2% was expected. The summer of 1992 was extremely hot and dry, causing significant crop damage and prolonged environmental harm, especially to forests and to the water table, which was steadily lowering. In November the magnificent Hofburg Palace in Vienna was badly damaged in a fire, but the priceless Lippizaner horses stabled there escaped injury.   (ELFRIEDE DIRNBACHER)

AZERBAIJAN

A republic of Transcaucasia, Azerbaijan borders Russia on the north, the Caspian Sea on the east, Iran on the south, Armenia on the west, and Georgia on the northwest. The 5,500-sq km exclave of Nakhichevan to the southwest is separated from Azerbaijan proper by a strip of Armenia. Area (including Nakhichevan): 86,600 sq km (33,400 sq mi). Pop. (1992 est.): 7,237,000. Cap.: Baku (Azerbaijani: Baky). Monetary unit: manat, with (Oct. 5, 1992) a free rate of 31.68 manat = U.S. $1 (53.86 manat = £1 sterling); the manat replaced the ruble as legal tender from August 14, with a value set at 1 manat = 10 rubles. Presidents in 1992, Ayaz Mutalibov to March 6, Yagub Mamedov (acting) to May 14, Mutalibov (reinstated) to May 15, Isa Gambarov (acting) from May 18, and, from June 16, Abulfez Elchibey; prime ministers, Gasan Hasanov to April 7, Firuz Mustafayev (acting), and, from June, Rakhim Guseynov.

The four-year-old conflict in Nagorno-Karabakh had a major influence on Azerbaijan's politics during the year. In March the fall of Khojali, one of the few towns still held by Azerbaijani forces, led to a furious search for scapegoats. The bloodletting that followed the town's capture inflamed passions to the point where demonstrations eventually forced Ayaz Mutalibov, the former Communist Party leader, to resign. He had done little to organize a viable fighting force to combat the better led and organized Armenians. The Azerbaijan Popular Front (APF), headed by Abulfez Elchibey, maintained that one reason for his lax attitude was his fear that a powerful Azerbaijani army would escape his control. Mutalibov was succeeded by Yagub Mamedov, another ex-Communist and former rector of the Institute of Medicine. The fall of Shusha, the centre of Azerbaijani cultural identity in Nagorno-Karabakh, in May led to his fall and the brief return of Mutalibov, whose supporters argued that only he could unite the nation in its darkest hour. The APF strongly disagreed and organized massive demonstrations that swept Mutalibov away. Isa Gambarov, an orientalist and member of the APF presidium, took over until a presidential election was held. This took place on June 7 and was won by Elchibey. In November criminal charges were filed against Mutalibov, and Azerbaijan called on Russia to extradite him.

Since new parliamentary elections were not held, the old parliament elected in 1990 and dominated by Communists remained in place. However, an inner core, more representative of contemporary politics, enjoyed considerable prestige. New structures were formed to permit the democratically elected president to exercise power. A group of presidential advisers was appointed, and the key members, mostly from the ranks of the APF and its supporters, formed an inner circle that ultimately wielded political influence. Elchibey promoted APF supporters, but since they lacked administrative experience they sometimes proved less skilled than their Communist predecessors. The clan nature of politics in Azerbaijan resulted in the promotion of family members, though not all who believed they had a claim to preferment secured posts. The "official" opposition, the Party for National Independence, led by Etibar Mamedov, had support from businessmen and several academics.

Elchibey rapidly came to the conclusion that the conflict in Nagorno-Karabakh benefited no one and sought a diplomatic solution. Pres. Levon Ter-Petrosyan of Armenia was like-minded, and attempts were made to reach a settlement. However, the Dashnaktsutiun Party, which dominated the Nagorno-Karabakh parliament, would settle for nothing less than independence. To this end it proclaimed the Republic of Nagorno-Karabakh and sought but failed to gain international recognition. By year's end Azerbaijanis were stating that the only solution to the crisis was a military one.

Azerbaijan's parliament formally voted the republic out of the Commonwealth of Independent States, but its industry remained inextricably linked to Russia. A separate currency was introduced, the central bank had few reserves and no stabilization fund, but like several other ex-Soviet republics, Azerbaijan believed a separate currency was necessary to underline economic independence. The republic's oil and natural gas reserves presaged a better future, and several international companies, including British Petroleum, concluded agreements to explore for oil. Progress on privatization was slow, and natural resources such as oil and gas would remain in state ownership. The republic was heavily dependent on Turkey for foreign banking transactions.

(MARTIN McCAULEY)

This article updates the *Macropædia* article TRANSCAUCASIA: *Azerbaijan*.

BELARUS

A landlocked republic of eastern Europe, Belarus borders Latvia on the north, Russia on the north and east, Ukraine on the south, Poland on the west, and Lithuania on the northwest. Area: 207,600 sq km (80,200 sq mi). Pop. (1992 est.): 10,321,000. Cap.: Minsk. Monetary unit: Belarus rubel (a transitional quasi currency), with (Oct. 5, 1992) a free rate of 31.68 rubels = U.S. $1 (53.86 rubels = £1 sterling); introduced May 25 (at a rate of 1 rubel = 10 Soviet rubles). Chairman of the Supreme Soviet in 1992, Stanislau Shushkevich; prime minister, Vyacheslau Kebich.

Belarus had been one of the founding members of the Commonwealth of Independent States (CIS) on Dec. 8, 1991, together with Russia and Ukraine. However, the declaration of independence by Ukraine on Dec. 1, 1991, complicated the key relationship between Russia and Ukraine from the beginning, and Belarus, which came into existence only under Soviet rule as the Belorussian S.S.R., had to tread warily. Belarus had its own language and literature, but affairs of state were conducted in Russian. As a multiethnic state, it was still in the process of building a national identity. The Belarus leadership, all former Communists, led by Stanislau Shushkevich, decided not to adopt a presidential form of government. Hence the Supreme Soviet, elected in 1990 when Mikhail Gorbachev still headed the Soviet Union, became the supreme organ of state power, and Shushkevich, as chairman or speaker of the Supreme Soviet, became head of state.

The question of what policy Belarus was to pursue within the CIS divided the leadership throughout 1992. Should it side with Russia and favour the emergence of a confederation of equal states—in other words, a successor state to the Soviet Union? Or should it regard the CIS as a purely transitional arrangement and establish closer links with the rest of Europe? Eventually it became clear that Vyacheslau Kebich, the head of government, favoured the former option while Shushkevich took the latter view. This was highlighted in July after a joint session of the Belarus and Russian governments in Moscow, at which 21 military, economic, and other agreements were signed, involving a "high level of real integration" of the two states. Yegor Gaidar, the Russian acting prime minister, saw the accords as a move in the direction of a confederation within the CIS, and Kebich

Sheepherders vote in Azerbaijan's first multiparty presidential election, held on June 7. The election was won by Abulfez Elchibey, a prominent dissident and nationalist since the 1970s and leader of the Popular Front.

agreed with this evaluation. However, Shushkevich immediately contradicted his prime minister and declared that the documents were contrary to CIS and Belorussian law.

Shushkevich's views had evolved to the point where he regarded the CIS as an interim arrangement lasting 10–15 years, enough time to permit Belarus to develop into an associate member or even full member of the European Communities (EC). He spoke of the establishment of an eastern European economic community, again an organization that would smooth access to the EC. Belarus actively participated in international organizations (it was a founding member of the UN), becoming a member of the International Monetary Fund and the World Bank. At the Bishkek (Kyrgyzstan) CIS summit in October, an inner core consisting of Russia, Belarus, Kazakhstan, and Kyrgyzstan emerged, with Ukraine and the others in an outer core.

Belarus issued its own rubel notes in May, and from November only the Belarus rubel was accepted as legal tender. However, the republic lacked banking expertise, and its central bank had no hard currency reserves or stabilization fund to back up its currency. During the first half of 1992 industrial production fell by 14%, mainly owing to the disruption of trade with the other former Soviet republics. Gross domestic product was expected to drop by at least 16%, with no sign of an upturn in 1993. Belorussian industry was closely integrated with Russian industry, while large tracts of its agricultural land had been contaminated by fallout from the Chernobyl nuclear accident. Kebich stated that privatization would take about eight years, but industrial managers were well represented in the parliament and could be expected to protect their interests.

Belarus was one of the four nuclear powers of the former U.S.S.R., but it had announced its intention to become nuclear free. Agreement was reached in July about the coordination of military policy with Russia. The last tactical nuclear warhead left Belorussian territory in May; all long-range nuclear weapons would be transferred to Russia over the next seven years. Russia was to be responsible for the cost of the strategic forces, but Belarus would pay for Russia's huge conventional forces remaining on its soil. The Belorussian Popular Front opposition in parliament severely criticized the accords as being too conciliatory to Russia. Meanwhile, Belarus and Poland settled their differences in June and, among other things, recognized each other's frontiers.   (MARTIN MCCAULEY)

BELGIUM

A constitutional monarchy, the Benelux country of Belgium is situated on the North Sea coast of northwestern Europe. Area: 30,528 sq km (11,787 sq mi). Pop. (1992 est.) 10,021,000. Cap. Brussels. Monetary unit: Belgian franc, with (Oct. 5, 1992) a free rate of BF 28.85 to U.S. $1 (BF 49.05 = £1 pound sterling). King, Baudouin I; prime ministers in 1992, Wilfried Martens and, from March 7, Jean-Luc Dehaene.

In spite of its election defeat in November 1991, the Social Christian and Socialist coalition remained in power under a new prime minister, Jean-Luc Dehaene (*see* BIOGRAPHIES). Two major objectives were the reform of the state structures and the reduction of the budget deficit to the norms of the Maastricht Treaty. Although opinion polls indicated that only 13.8% of the population deemed the first of these important, the dialogue between political representatives of the French- and Flemish-speaking communities was resumed without the Liberals, who had been excluded. Again the discussions ended in deadlock.

In September the prime minister called a meeting of top politicians from his coalition to end the stalemate. An agreement, yet to be approved by a two-thirds parliamentary majority, was found that would turn Belgium into a truly federal state. Henceforth, voters residing in Flanders and Wallonia would each elect their own assembly; the federal government would be limited to 15 ministers. The House of Representatives would have no more than 150 members and the Senate only 71, as against the current 212 and 183, respectively. Forty senators would be directly elected by the voters, 21 designated by the regional assemblies, and 10 co-opted. The Flemish Assembly would number 124 members, including 6 from the Brussels region; the Walloon Assembly would have 75 members, the Council of the French Community 94 (75 from Wallonia and 19 from the Brussels region). The Brussels regional council would retain its 75 members, and the council of the German community its 25. Deviation from the principle of territoriality, also agreed on, would be possible only when a regional assembly decided by a two-thirds majority to allow a directly elected senator to take part in their discussions in an advisory role. It was implied that this senator would have to relinquish all his other elected mandates.

The partition of the bilingual Brabant province was also agreed on. Furthermore, the regions, including Brussels, could raise their own taxes. In Brussels the tax yields would be turned over in an 80/20 proportion to the two regional community commissions. Radio and TV taxes collected in Flanders and Wallonia were to be transferred to the two communities. Parliamentary elections would henceforth be held every four years, and a change of government could take effect only when a majority in the parliament gave it approval. The regional assemblies would be elected for a five-year period. The powers of the Senate were to be curtailed, but it would be competent to rule on conflicts of interest between the regional assemblies. First reactions from the opposition were not entirely negative, but approval would require the government to make certain changes.

The "convergence plan" in the Maastricht Treaty imposed a reduction of the Belgian budget deficit to 3% of the gross national product by 1996. The 1992 budget provided for a deficit of 5.6%, with heavier taxes and the abrogation of tax deductions but hardly any cuts in expenditure. Unemployment continued to climb. At the end of September nearly 420,000 people were without a job (50,000 more than in September 1991).

In Wallonia, Socialists and Social Christians again teamed up to form the regional government, headed by Guy Spitaels, outgoing chairman of the French Socialists. In Flanders proportional representation determined the structure of the executive body, now led by Social Christian Luc Van den Brande. A new law allowed longtime residents or those born in Belgium of foreign parents to obtain their naturalization papers more quickly.   (JAN R. ENGELS)

BOSNIA AND HERCEGOVINA

A republic of the western Balkans, Bosnia and Hercegovina borders Croatia on the north, southwest, and south, the Adriatic Sea on the south (via a narrow extension), and Yugoslavia on the east. Area: 51,129 sq km (19,741 sq mi). Pop. (1992 est. based on prewar projection): 4,397,000. Cap.: Sarajevo. De facto monetary unit: Yugoslav dinar, with (Oct. 5, 1992) a free rate of 225.41 dinars to U.S. $1 (383.20 dinars = £1 sterling); Bosnia was not supplied with dinars by Yugoslav authorities from June 1992. President in 1992, Alija Izetbegovic; prime ministers, Jure Pelivan and, from November 9, Mile Akmadzic.

At a referendum on Feb. 29 and March 1, 1992, 63% of the population of Bosnia and Hercegovina voted for independence from Yugoslavia, but most Serbs boycotted the vote.

On April 6 the European Communities (EC) recognized the new republic, and the U.S. followed suit on April 7. Bosnia and Hercegovina joined the UN on May 22.

Armed conflict started on March 3 with the Serb shelling of Bosanski Brod in northern Bosnia. By the middle of March, fighting had spread to all parts of the republic, with the Yugoslav army fighting alongside the Serb irregulars. On March 27 Serb leaders proclaimed the creation of a Serbian Republic of Bosnia and Hercegovina, with a constitution that declared it to be a constitutive part of Yugoslavia. Thousands of refugees (mainly Muslim but also Croat) began fleeing into Croatia to escape the so-called ethnic cleansing policy directed against non-Serbs. This included regular massacres, rapes, mass expulsions, and imprisonment in brutal internment camps. On July 3 the predominantly Croat region of western Hercegovina proclaimed itself an autonomous region under the name of Herceg-Bosna, prompting international criticism that Croatia, too, wanted Bosnia's partition.

Although Yugoslavia denied being directly involved in the fighting, the UN Security Council blamed Serbia as the chief culprit for the conflict and ordered sanctions against it and Montenegro (see *Yugoslavia,* below). A peace conference in London on August 26–27 failed to achieve a cease-fire, and on September 14 the Security Council authorized sending additional UN troops to Bosnia. By December Serb nationalist forces occupied some 70% of Bosnia, with a smaller area under Croatian control. UN-sponsored peace talks began in Geneva, but there was little progress, and the Muslim population in Sarajevo, which had been under siege for eight months, faced severe food shortages and disease. Islamic countries gave the EC and the U.S. a deadline of Jan. 15, 1993, after which, they said, they would act to help Bosnia if the West had not done so.   (K.F. CVIIC)

This article updates the *Macropædia* article BALKAN STATES: *Bosnia and Hercegovina.*

BULGARIA

The republic of Bulgaria is on the eastern Balkan Peninsula of southeastern Europe, along the Black Sea. Area: 110,994 sq km (42,855 sq mi). Pop. (1992 est.): 8,985,000. Cap.: Sofia. Monetary unit: lev, with (Oct. 5, 1992) a free rate of 25.29 leva to U.S. $1 (43 leva = £1 sterling). President in 1992, Zhelyu Zhelev; prime ministers, Filip Dimitrov and, from December 30, Lyuben Berov.

On May 7, 1992, Bulgaria celebrated its admission to the European Council. In domestic affairs there was less reason for satisfaction. In January incumbent Zhelyu Zhelev, backed by the Union of Democratic Forces, needed a second round of voting to defeat socialist-sponsored Velko Valkanov in the presidential election. Zhelev was concerned over the rigours of the government's anti-Communist policies and economic reforms, which he subjected to stinging criticism in the summer. Measures taken against former Communists included the Restitution Act of April 9, restoring to its former owners or their descendants property nationalized between 1947 and 1962. Former premier Andrei Lukanov was arrested in July on charges of peculation. Later in the year, former dictator Todor Zhivkov and former premier Georgy Atanasov were given prison sentences of 7 and 10 years, respectively, for similar offenses.

Economic reform also alarmed the two main trade union organizations, the Confederation of Independent Trade Unions in Bulgaria and Podkrepa ("Support"). The principal items of the reform program were price liberalization, pay restraint, the breaking up of cooperative farms, and, in April, a bill to privatize state industries. The unions were especially angered by elimination of the tripartite commis-

sion of government, employers, and unions. In May Prime Minister Filip Dimitrov demanded the resignation of Defense Minister Dimitar Ludzhev, who championed closer cooperation with the unions. Ludzhev fought a rearguard action but was finally forced to leave on May 20, when Dimitrov reshuffled his Cabinet and reorganized a number of ministries. In the summer, strikes by workers at the vital Neftochim oil refinery, by medical workers, and by transport workers in Sofia forced the government to grant a 14% increase in salaries for state employees.

The Turkish areas were particularly hard hit in economic terms, and this complicated Dimitrov's relations with the Movement for Rights and Freedoms (MRF), the mainly Turkish party on which he depended for a parliamentary majority. Although it stood by the government to defeat a censure motion in July, in September the MRF demanded and secured the removal of the president of the assembly, Stefan Savov. Dimitrov rightly warned that this was a dress rehearsal for an assault on the Cabinet. On October 28 Dimitrov resigned after the MRF joined the Bulgarian Socialist Party to pass a vote of no confidence. At year's end Lyuben Berov, a non-Turk nominated by the MRF, was named prime minister.

In foreign affairs Bulgaria recognized all the secessionist republics of former Yugoslavia in January. It continued its efforts to establish friendly official relations with Turkey despite a series of disputes over fishing rights in Bulgarian waters.   (RICHARD J. CRAMPTON)

This article updates the *Macropædia* article BALKAN STATES: *Bulgaria.*

CROATIA

A republic of the northwestern Balkans, Croatia is an elongated crescent-shaped country to the north, west, and southwest of Bosnia and Hercegovina. Its extensive Adriatic coastal region on the southwest includes nearly 1,200 islands and islets. Area: 56,538 sq km (21,829 sq mi). Pop. (1992 est.) 4,808,000. Cap.: Zagreb. Monetary unit: Croatian dinar, with (Oct. 12, 1992) a free rate of 365.67 dinars to U.S. $1 (622.95 dinars = £1 sterling). President in 1992, Franjo Tudjman; prime ministers, Franjo Greguric and, from September 8, Hrvoje Sarinic.

Nearly one-third of Croatia's territory—the region round Knin in the south and parts of Western and Eastern Slavonia in the north—remained under Serbian control throughout 1992. Under an agreement brokered in January by UN special envoy Cyrus Vance, those regions were placed under the protection of a 14,000-strong UN force pending the final regulation of their status. Croatia was recognized by 11 European Communities (EC) members on January 15 (Germany had already recognized it on Dec. 23, 1991) and by the United States on April 15. It became a member of the UN on May 22.

On August 2 Croatia held its first postcommunist presidential and parliamentary elections. Franjo Tudjman was reelected as president with a 56.7% majority. His closest rival, Drazen Budisa of the Croatian Social-Liberal Party (HSLS), won 21.9%. Tudjman's party, the Croatian Democratic Union (HDZ), won 41.5% of votes and 85 out of the total of 138 seats in the Croatian legislature. The Social-Liberals won 18.3% of votes and 14 seats. The extreme nationalist Croatian Party of Rights (HSP), which had organized its own paramilitary formations, won 5%. On October 17 parliamentary immunity of three HSP deputies was lifted to allow for legal proceedings against them. On December 27 it was announced that elections for the upper house of the legislature, in which the regions were represented, would be held on Feb. 7, 1993. Under an agreement President Tudjman signed with Dobrica Cosic, president of

Croats celebrate in Zagreb on January 15 after it was announced that the members of the European Communities, along with Austria and Switzerland, had recognized the independence of Croatia and Slovenia. The two former republics of Yugoslavia had earlier voted for independence.
FUTY—SIPA

Yugoslavia, Serb forces withdrew from the region south of Dubrovnik prior to its demilitarization; they had ended their siege of the city by the end of October.

Croatia's biggest economic and social problem in 1992 was the presence on its soil of a large number of refugees, both those from its own currently Serb-occupied territories and from Bosnia. At the end of the year, Croatia had in its charge some 750,000 displaced persons, of whom roughly 500,000 were from Bosnia. Croatia's main source of hard-currency income—tourism—began to revive in 1992, but industrial output was 20% lower than in 1991 and unemployment reached 20%. War damage was roughly estimated at $21 billion. However, exports in the first 10 months of 1992 totaled $3.8 billion, 28.9% above that in the first 10 months of 1991. On December 15 Croatia was received into the European Bank for Reconstruction and Development in London. The International Monetary Fund began to consider Croatia's application for membership on December 14.   (K.F. CVIIC)

This article updates the *Macropædia* article BALKAN STATES: *Croatia*.

CZECHOSLOVAKIA

The federal republic of Czechoslovakia is a landlocked state of central Europe. Area: 127,899 sq km (49,382 sq mi). Pop. (1992 est.): 15,605,000. Cap.: Prague. Monetary unit: koruna, with (Oct. 5, 1992) a commercial rate of 26.56 koruny to U.S. $1 (45.16 koruny = £1 sterling). President in 1992, Vaclav Havel until July 20; federal premiers, Marian Calfa until June 26 and, from July 1, Jan Strasky.

The year 1992 proved at least as momentous for Czechoslovakia as 1989 had been with the collapse of communism. It was the year when the Czechs and Slovaks agreed that they would cease to live in one state and would break up the federation at the end of December. Numerous factors underlay this move, some of them conscious and deliberate, the others the result of accident and chance.

The federal and regional parliamentary elections of June 5–6 brought matters to a head. They were fought over several issues, but what was crucial was that these issues were quite different in the two parts of the country. In the Czech lands of Bohemia and Moravia, the dominant issue was the speed and extent of economic change, focusing especially on the introduction of privatization. The leader of the most successful political party to arise from the ruins of Civic Forum, the movement that had taken over from the Communists in 1989, was Vaclav Klaus, the minister

of finance and leader of the Civic Democratic Party. Klaus favoured rapid and far-reaching privatization coupled with the closing down of bankrupt, uneconomical factories. This alone was calculated to make the Slovaks uneasy, given that the Slovak economy was in a much worse state than that in the Czech lands.

Czech-Slovak disagreements went far beyond this, however. At heart these concerned matters of power and status, coupled with an atmosphere of mutual suspicion and distrust. The Slovaks were convinced that the Czechs refused to understand their need for a much more high-profile status within the federation and resented what they saw as their permanent second-class position. The lack of trust was far-reaching and thoroughgoing, to the extent that by 1992 there was a general lack of goodwill on the part of many, though not all, Slovaks.

The Czechs, on the other hand, increasingly came to view the Slovaks as parasites who were never satisfied with the continuous transfer of resources to their much poorer eastern third of the country, whose demands were inexhaustible, and whose agendas were undermining the Czechs' own aspirations. For many Czechs this attitude was crystallized by the paralysis of federal institutions in 1991–92, when the Slovaks enjoyed a blocking veto thanks to arrangements inherited from the Communist period. The old Communist legislature was, of course, completely irrelevant for the running of the nation, and the pseudodemocratic rules by which it was governed were never intended to be taken seriously.

The elections, then, proved to be the watershed. While Klaus's preeminence and thus the desirability of his program of rapid economic transformation was confirmed in the Czech lands, in Slovakia Vladimir Meciar emerged as equally dominant. His Movement for a Democratic Slovakia gained over 30% of the national vote and was assured of the support of the Slovak National Party (around 8% of the vote) in his attempt to secure a special status for Slovakia. It was, however, unclear whether Meciar intended that his negotiations result in Slovak independence; indeed, there was considerable evidence that he, and Slovak opinion, were taken aback when Klaus insisted that the options were either a relatively tightly organized federal state or full independence. Thus Meciar's bluff was called, and on Jan. 1, 1993, the two parts of the country officially separated.

The implications of the separation were absorbed only slowly in the two regions. For the new Czech Republic there were clear security considerations in having a weak neighbour to the east. To this should be added the problems of disentangling the shared political, economic, military, and other institutions of Czechoslovakia. A customs union and a formal agreement on the division of property were expected to ease some of the economic problems, and a separate agreement provided for the free movement of people. Also, there were more than 300,000 Slovaks living in the Czech lands, while about 50,000 Czechs lived in Slovakia. The existence of these two minorities was expected to be a further complication.

There were psychological aspects that did not augur well for the future of Czech society. The marriage with the Slovaks had been put together in 1918 in order to counterbalance the large number of ethnic Germans in the new state; most of the German minority was expelled after 1945, and from this perspective the Czechs believed that they no longer needed the Slovaks. However, it seemed certain that the new Czech nation would be under very strong German influence economically, geographically, and, to an extent, culturally, and there were signs that for many Czechs this was highly unwelcome. The symptoms of a marked Czech nationalist current were palpable by year's end.

Other political issues included the adoption on December 16 of a new constitution for the Czech state, which would govern the relationship between Bohemia and Moravia-Silesia; the pursuit of ambitious privatization plans; and the downturn in the economy. The latter increased inflation and the fear of growing unemployment.

Matters were significantly worse in Slovakia. This was caused by the fear of the unknown and the inexperience of the Slovak leaders; the acute economic difficulties of the new nation; the rising tension between Slovakia and Hungary over the Gabcikovo-Nagymaros dam project (which the Hungarians wanted to cancel but the Slovaks insisted on pursuing); and the approximately 565,000-strong Hungarian minority, which was acutely concerned about its future in Slovakia. At the same time, the Slovak economy was in rather poor condition, with unemployment above 10% and an industrial structure that relied on arms production and other, less viable, economic enterprises.

In a broad historical perspective, however, it is worth stressing that the divorce between the Czech lands and Slovakia proceeded in an orderly and calm manner, quite unlike the disintegration of Yugoslavia. This held out some hope that relations between the two new countries would be relatively civilized.   (GEORGE SCHÖPFLIN)

DENMARK

A constitutional monarchy of north central Europe, Denmark lies between the North and Baltic seas. Area: 43,093 sq km (16,638 sq mi), excluding the Faeroe Islands and Greenland. Pop. (1992 est.): 5,167,000. Cap.: Copenhagen. Monetary unit: Danish krone, with (Oct. 5, 1992) a free rate of 5.46 kroner to U.S. $1 (9.29 kroner = £1 sterling). Queen, Margrethe II; prime minister in 1992, Poul Schlüter.

The year 1992 would go down in history as one of the most exciting in Denmark since the end of World War II. It was the year when Denmark—generally dismissed as a Scandinavian backwater by the outside world—made front-page headlines by rejecting the Maastricht Treaty on closer European political union in a June referendum. The surprise vote—a knife-edge 50.7 to 49.3% "no"—sent shock waves across the European Communities (EC), severely denting support for tighter European cohesion in some of the other 11 EC member states—notably the U.K.—and delaying ratification of the treaty. Only some 46,000 votes separated rejectionists from supporters of the treaty in a poll that saw almost 83% of Denmark's four million-strong electorate turn out to vote.

The Danes' defiant "no" to Maastricht was very much a protest against an elitist political establishment that used scare campaigns to force bemused voters to ballot "yes." Although most politicians and a sizable majority of five of the eight parties in the Folketing (parliament)—as well as trade, commerce, business, finance, and industry, and most labour organizations—urged Danish voters to acquiesce, the rejectionists, many of them women and members of the opposition Social Democrats, saw closer political union as a threat to Danish sovereignty and national identity. Along with Britain, Denmark had long been a lukewarm member of the EC. Danish suspicions of increased bureaucracy in Brussels, the threat of a newly reunited Germany on its doorstep, and fear of what many saw as French machinations were also issues that turned Danes against the treaty at a time of uncertainty and unrest in Europe.

When the wave of nationalism and general euphoria sparked by the "no" vote died down, Denmark's minority Conservative-Liberal government produced a White Paper in October outlining eight possible solutions to the deadlock

LEE MALIS—GAMMA LIAISON

Vaclav Klaus (centre), Czech prime minister, greets citizens after talks in June with his Slovak counterpart, Vladimir Meciar. The Czech and Slovak republics agreed during the year to dissolve their union on Jan. 1, 1993.

Opponents of the Maastricht Treaty speak in front of a poster urging Danes to vote "nej" ("no"). In a setback for closer European union, voters in Denmark narrowly rejected the treaty in a referendum held on June 2.
FRANCIS DEAN—SYGMA

with the rest of the EC over Maastricht. Conservative Prime Minister Poul Schlüter—celebrating a decade in power—insisted that the treaty could not be ratified without Denmark. The options listed in the White Paper ranged from scrapping the treaty altogether to Denmark's ratifying the existing pact with a clause that would permit it to reconsider its position at a later juncture. Also mooted were the possibilities of Denmark's securing special status within the EC—a form of associate membership—or footnotes to Maastricht allowing the Danes to opt out of areas they disliked, such as joint defense policy, economic and monetary union, EC citizenship, and police and legal cooperation. The White Paper's contents formed the basis for hectic autumn talks between the government and the six opposition parties in the Folketing, as well as grass-roots rejectionist groups, on a consensus proposal for Denmark's future role in Europe. The EC summit in Edinburgh in December agreed to exempt Denmark from key points in the treaty, paving the way for another referendum in early 1993.

Adding to Denmark's jubilant summer—the hottest since 1874—was the Danish association football team's sensational David and Goliath-style 2–0 victory over Germany in the finals of the European championship in Göteborg, Sweden—an event that triggered the greatest festivity seen in Copenhagen since Denmark's liberation from Nazi occupation in World War II. Denmark was eligible for the championships only because Yugoslavia had been barred. The economy continued to revive, becoming one of Europe's strongest with impressive balance of payments and trade surpluses and ultralow inflation. Unemployment—at over 300,000, or 11% of the work force—remained at a record high, however, fueling a major state budget deficit.

(CHRISTOPHER FOLLETT)

ESTONIA

A republic of northern Europe, Estonia borders the Baltic Sea on the west and north. Area: 45,100 sq km (17,413 sq mi). Pop. (1992 est.): 1,592,000. Cap.: Tallinn. Monetary unit: kroon, with (Oct. 5, 1992) a par value (from June 20, 1992) of 8 krooni to 1 DM (free rates of 11.26 krooni = U.S. $1 and 19.14 krooni = £1 sterling). Chairman of the Supreme Council in 1992, Arnold Ruutel, replaced from October 5 by president, Lennart Meri; prime ministers, Edgar Savisaar until January 30, Tiit Vahi, and, from October 8, Mart Laar.

The first free elections for over half a century were held on Sept. 20, 1992, and resulted in a victory for the right-wing parties, which obtained just over half of the 101 seats

in the Riigikogu (parliament). Only Estonian citizens were permitted to vote. This excluded about 38% of the population, mainly Russians. In the presidential election held the same day, Arnold Ruutel polled 41.8% of the votes, and Lennart Meri of the Fatherland coalition got 29.5%. Since no candidate had achieved more than 50%, it was left to the Riigikogu to elect the president. On October 5 Meri obtained 59 votes and duly took office.

The economic situation he faced was dire, with inflation raging and gross domestic product expected to drop 20% during the year. In June a new currency, the kroon, was introduced and tied to the German mark. Russia agreed to troop withdrawals—there were an estimated 15,000 Russian troops in Estonia—but halted withdrawals on October 29.

(MARTIN MCCAULEY)

This article updates the *Macropædia* article BALTIC STATES: *Estonia*.

FINLAND

The republic of Finland is in northern Europe, on the Gulf of Bothnia and the Gulf of Finland. Area: 338,145 sq km (130,559 sq mi). Pop. (1992 est.): 5,033,000. Cap.: Helsinki. Monetary unit: Finnish markka, with (Oct. 5, 1992) a free rate of 4.53 markkaa to U.S. $1 (7.70 markkaa = £1 sterling). President in 1992, Mauno Koivisto; prime minister, Esko Aho.

Finland was shaken in 1992 by accusations that Urho Kekkonen, its president from 1956 to 1981, received campaign financing from Moscow, and that the Kremlin had acted politically to secure his election. Kekkonen was a moving power behind the Conference on Security and Cooperation in Europe, which held its latest summit in Helsinki in July. Rumours that Kekkonen, who died in 1986, was too intimate with Soviet leaders had flourished throughout his career, prompting the coining of the word *Finlandization* to depict the situation of a country that was overly compliant to the wishes of a powerful neighbour. Open allegations had been few, however, until Andrey Smirnov, a head of department at the Russian Foreign Ministry, told a political affairs society in Helsinki in October that the Kremlin instructed Finnish Communists in 1956 to switch their votes in the electoral college to ensure Kekkonen's elevation to the presidency. In the same month the publication of documents, reportedly from the Moscow archives of the Soviet Communist Party, revealed that Kekkonen's senior fund-raiser in his 1962 re-election campaign had petitioned the Kremlin for cash on more than one occasion and had received it. A book by the Finnish researcher Hannu Rautkallio, also published in October, alleged that a diplomatic note from Moscow that helped to secure Kekkonen's reelection in 1962 was made to order for that purpose.

Kekkonen's official biographer, who had sole access to his own records, rejected the evidence as flimsy and the documents as suspect. Supporters of the former president protested the attacks on Kekkonen's character, though they did not always reject the substance of the charges. "I have no admiration for his working methods, but one must remember the historical context," a former senior diplomat who served under Kekkonen said. A former prominent politician, who broke away from Kekkonen's Agrarian Union and founded his own party, went on record in much blunter terms, telling a newspaper, "Kekkonen was a prisoner of Moscow who had a certain amount of leeway. He was a prisoner on probation."

In November the European Commission spelled out the terms under which Finland could negotiate membership in the European Communities (EC). Finland had set 1995 as the target date for its accession, but the Commission said that talks on bringing the country's heavily subsidized agriculture and regions into line with the Community's own policies could prove difficult. The Commission also suggested that Finland would have to commit itself more firmly to the defense system envisaged for the EC, but Finnish ministers insisted the country would maintain its own independent and nonaligned defense. In August a senior Finnish official told the country's ambassadors that Finland would have to consider asking for membership in NATO because of the theoretical possibility of a future threat from Russia, with which Finland shares a 1,270-km (800-mi) border. Finland, meanwhile, ratified the treaty under which the EC and the countries of the European Free Trade Association, to which Finland belongs, were scheduled to set up a joint European Economic Area agreement from the beginning of 1993. The EEA would allow free movement in goods, capital, services, and labour.

The country plunged deeper into debt, and the government had to support the major banks. In September the government was forced to allow the Finnish markka to float, and it fell by around 12% against most major foreign currencies. This was the second downrating of the markka in a year, following a devaluation by a similar amount the preceding November. Nevertheless, the government said trade in goods and services was running strongly in surplus in 1992 and would largely offset the current account deficit in the next few years.   (EDWARD M. SUMMERHILL)

FRANCE

A republic of western Europe, France includes the island of Corsica in the Mediterranean Sea and has coastlines on the English Channel, the Mediterranean, and the Atlantic Ocean. Area: 543,965 sq km (210,026 sq mi). Pop. (1992 est.): 57,289,000. Cap.: Paris. Monetary unit: franc, with (Oct. 5, 1992) a free rate of F 4.78 to U.S. $1 (F 8.12 = £1 sterling). President in 1992, François Mitterrand; prime ministers, Edith Cresson and, from April 2, Pierre Bérégovoy.

If 1992 was not the end of an era, it could very well begin to appear to be so. François Mitterrand had been president for more than 11 years—the longest reign of the Fifth Republic—but he was seriously ill, and he had never been more unpopular. France seemed to hesitate about which path to take; if it rejected the ruling Socialist Party (PS), it hardly appeared tempted by the opposition from the right. Therefore, 1993, with its March parliamentary elections, ran the risk of being a critical year.

Domestic Affairs. By chance, the French had not voted since 1989. This electoral pause accentuated a feeling of hidden unrest, which fed off political and financial scandals and the government's apparent opposition to progress. In local elections (regional, district, and senatorial) and in the referendum on the Maastricht Treaty, the French voters expressed subtle choices in 1992 that were difficult to interpret for the future.

In the regional elections in March, the fall of the PS was remarkable; the president's party received 18.3% of the votes, compared with nearly 30% in previous elections. But the conservative opposition—made up of the Union for French Democracy (UDF) and the Gaullist Rally for the Republic (RPR)—also lost ground, receiving only 33% of the votes. (A muster of only a third of the electorate was not much for parties that aspired to govern.) The country's third largest force was completely new, as the Greens gathered nearly 15% of the votes cast. Jean-Marie Le Pen's extreme right-wing National Front grabbed less than 14%, far from the 20% it had hoped for.

The fallout from these elections was not long in coming. A week later Edith Cresson was forced to resign from her post as prime minister. The first woman appointed to this position had failed. Commentators observed that Cresson, with her many blunders, had missed her chance. Furthermore, her colleagues, who hardly liked her, strove to complicate her task. One of them, Finance Minister Pierre Bérégovoy (see BIOGRAPHIES), was chosen as her successor. The appointment of this simply dressed, self-taught man was initially well received. His working-class origins reassured the left, and his economic ideas reassured the right. A good speech before the National Assembly won him a favourable opinion. He stopped the majority of the reforms and projects that had stirred up public opinion, and he loudly announced his intention to "fight against corruption." The opposition, which upon his appointment had been quick to recall that two of his Cabinet members had been involved in financial scandals, momentarily left him a clear field. The star of the new government was Bernard Tapie, a controversial businessman and president of the Olympique association football club in Marseille. Appointed minister of urban affairs, he faced problems in the suburbs, which were shaken by violent crises, provoked by the formidable mix of unemployment, insecurity, and resistance to immigration. Less than two months after joining the government, he was charged by an examining magistrate with misuse of public funds and fraud in relation to a business concern with a former business partner who was a member of the RPR. The prime minister requested and received Tapie's resignation.

Two social crises and a threat placed the new prime minister in a difficult position. In July a reform launched by Cresson took effect: the establishment of a license for automobile drivers based on points. It was believed that this measure would be well received by a nation ravaged by driving accidents (11,000 deaths on the roads in 1990), but the truck drivers' lobby would not accept the measure. At a time of major vacation travel, truck drivers blocked the roads, paralyzing access to several large cities. To underscore his determination, Bérégovoy sent an unarmed tank to clear a roadblock on the north highway. In August and September prison guards went on strike after the murder of several guards by prisoners during an escape. The threats arose from the reform of the European Communities (EC) common agricultural policy (CAP). French farmers and the agricultural community in general rose up against these measures. The impact of this rural grumbling was soon evident in the results of the referendum on the Maastricht Treaty. It also explained the noticeably tougher position taken by the French government in the General Agreement on Tariffs and Trade negotiations later in the year.

Ratification of the Maastricht Treaty was the big event of the year. Upon his return from The Netherlands in December 1991, Mitterrand had presented this agreement on television as "one of the most important events of the century." The president, aware of both the historical and the political implications of the treaty, tried to take advantage of it to regain the domestic initiative and to attempt to reverse a political trend that was largely against him. He announced his intention to run for reelection on the same day the Danish "no" vote on the treaty was announced, thus dividing the opposition. Since French public opinion was clearly for the European side, the issue seemed a simple one, but as the weeks passed the percentage of those favouring "yes" decreased in the polls, from 65 to 48%. On June 23 the National Assembly and the Senate, meeting in a rare joint session at Versailles, voted 592–73 (216 abstained) to approve the constitutional reforms that would allow ratification. On September 20 the French electorate ratified the treaty by referendum, but by a very small margin: 51.05 to 48.95%.

This narrow margin of victory constituted a rejection of the head of the state by the public. According to the polls, Mitterrand's popularity stood at less than 30%. Parliamentary opposition, which was for the most part pro-Europe, during the campaign increased its appeals to the president to announce his withdrawal in the case of a "no" vote. Bérégovoy put an end to the debate when he announced: "The president will remain in place no matter what happens." Therefore, numerous supporters of the treaty preferred to vote "no" rather than give their vote to Mitterrand. However, one incident perhaps changed the course of events. Shortly after a brilliant performance, televised from the Sorbonne, in which he debated one of the leaders of the "no" faction, Philippe Séguin of the RPR, Mitterrand was admitted to the hospital for prostate surgery. A week later his doctors announced that the president was suffering from cancer. Public compassion led to an increase in popularity for Mitterrand, which undoubtedly contributed to the "yes" victory, but rather quickly the image of a seriously ill president weakened the executive office.

Even more than the president, it was French society that appeared to be ill. A form of melancholy, not to say nervous depression, seized France. Uncertainty spread at the very moment that the country's economic situation was without doubt one of the most enviable among the developed countries. Political and financial scandals undermined French society to an unprecedented extent in 1992. On January 14 an examining magistrate carried out an unprecedented search of the Socialist Party's headquarters. Meanwhile, the party suffered other problems. Its former treasurer, Henri Emmanuelli, who had become president of the National Assembly, was charged with corruption and influence peddling—the third person in the government to be caught this way. Some other elected officials were charged for secret financial practices undertaken during their election campaigns. If the centralizing of its finances placed the PS under a spotlight, other incidents affected the opposition. The former mayor of Nice, Jacques Médecin, after having taken refuge in Uruguay, was sentenced to a year in prison for misusing public funds. François Léotard, who was honorary president of the Republican Party and mayor of Frejus, resigned from his posts after being charged with "interference and corruption." An exchange agent, threatened with charges after certain problems arose involving his company, declared that he had financed in part the presidential campaigns of Valéry Giscard d'Estaing in 1974 and 1981.

Pierre Bérégovoy, appointed prime minister of France on April 2, addresses the National Assembly. Formerly finance minister, Bérégovoy was charged with restoring public confidence in the Socialist government of Pres. François Mitterrand.
REUTERS/BETTMANN

These financial scandals, serious as they might have been, did not have the repercussions that the "scandal of the contaminated blood" had. About 1,300 hemophiliacs had been infected with the AIDS virus through blood transfusions. The failure to perform screening tests on donors and to use decontaminated products for hemophiliacs before the autumn of 1985 was at the heart of the tragedy. Bad management may have been to blame, as well as a poor understanding of the disease, but the distribution of blood supplies that were known to be contaminated deeply shocked the public. In October officials at the national blood transfusion centre and other administrative officials were convicted by a Paris tribunal. The families of those infected asked that the government officials in power at the time be judged as well; among them was Laurent Fabius, then prime minister, who later became the head of the PS. After much controversy, it was decided that Fabius and two other former ministers would appear before the High Court (a court composed of members of parliament, which had never met under the Fifth Republic and which had the task of judging crimes of "high treason"). Meanwhile, Luc Montagnier (see BIOGRAPHIES), whose team at the Pasteur Institute first isolated the virus, was enmeshed in other AIDS-related controversies.

The Economy. Despite a serious political and psychological crisis, the economy was not doing too badly. Prices in 1991 increased only 3.1%, compared with 5% in Germany, and predictions for 1992 indicated a similar rate of inflation. With a deficit in 1991 of F 30 billion, versus F 50 billion in 1990, the balance of trade was expected to be favourable for the first time since 1984. This good news was due in part to an increase in exports to Germany and to successful performances by the automobile and aerospace industries. In the first quarter of 1992 the gross national product rose by 1%, sustaining the hope of strong growth. It would probably reach only the rate of 2% for the year, but many countries would envy such results. The budget projected a growth rate of 2.6% in 1993. Only the unemployment figures were bad. In April unemployment exceeded 10%, and the psychological barrier of three million unemployed remained unbroken only with the help of government artifice.

Society creaked dangerously, however, as the farmers' anger roared and the trade-union structures were shaken. The only independent union still in existence in France, the Federation of National Education, exploded into different political tendencies. Several officials in charge of groups of affiliated trade unions were replaced.

Faced with this, Cresson's government practiced an industrial policy that resulted in different outcomes. The merger of the industrial activities of the Commission for Nuclear Energy and the electric utility Thomson SA created much doubt. This large, high-tech utility group would probably be led back to more modest ambitions under Bérégovoy. In the same manner, Cresson set up a reform of the regulations for dock workers, which should improve conditions at French ports that were handicapped by excessive trade-union burdens.

Bérégovoy had made the defense of a strong franc the axis of his policy during the six years that he headed the Ministry of Economy and Finance. His successor in that post, Michel Sapin, had to fight hard in 1992 to save the national currency. On July 16 the Bundesbank triggered a destabilization of the financial markets by raising the German discount rate from 8 to 8.75%. On September 17 the British pound and the Italian lira were forced to pull out of the EC exchange-rate mechanism and float. The French vote on the Maastricht Treaty three days later, far from calming the game, set it off again, and it was the turn of the French currency, traditionally one of the strongest in Europe, to be attacked the next day. Chancellor Helmut Kohl promised that Germany would help support the franc, but at year's end it remained under pressure.

Foreign Affairs. The year 1991 ended with an embarrassing setback for French diplomacy. At the opening of the Middle East peace conference in Madrid, it was obvious that France was absent, despite the fact that Roland Dumas, minister of foreign affairs, had justified French participation in the Gulf war with the fact that it would give France a seat at the negotiating table. In January a scandal erupted with the arrival in Paris, for medical treatment, of the Palestinian leader George Habash. Considered one of the principal persons responsible for Palestinian terrorism, Habash was examined by doctors and returned to Tunisia three days later. Cresson survived a parliamentary no-confidence vote over the affair, but several high-level officials were penalized.

The big event of 1992 was more than ever the changing structure of Europe. Joint French-German initiatives had increased during 1991, in preparation for the December 9–10 summit at Maastricht, Neth., but this French-German cohesion had limits. At the time of the summit, the EC members did not want to look into the serious situation taking place in Yugoslavia. One week later the EC foreign affairs ministers met, at France's request, in order to define the "criteria for the recognition of the new states of eastern Europe and in the Soviet Union." The EC agreed that on Jan. 15, 1992, it would recognize the Yugoslav republics that met those conditions, but Germany broke ranks and recognized Slovenia and Croatia on Dec. 23, 1991.

The Yugoslav crisis rebounded in Bosnia and Hercegovina in 1992. The discovery of open graves and concentration camps once again raised the question of outside military intervention. Although some of the French were in favour of it, Mitterrand acted with great cautiousness. At the EC summit in Lisbon in June, the focus was again on the Balkans. At the end of the meeting, having barely informed his partners, Mitterrand flew to Sarajevo, Bosnia. This action was a controversial one, but the risky and dramatic six-hour visit caused the air blockade to be lifted; within hours French planes loaded with relief supplies had been sent to Sarajevo. The president was accompanied only by Bernard Kouchner, minister of humanitarian action and founder of the medical charity Médecins sans Frontières. Kouchner also accompanied Mitterrand's wife, Danièlle, to visit Kurds in Iraq, where they narrowly escaped a murder attempt. If French traditional diplomacy was not able to prevail at the Madrid conference, French humanitarian diplomacy met with some success elsewhere.   (CHRISTIAN SAUVAGE)

See also *Dependent States,* below.

GEORGIA

A republic of Transcaucasia, Georgia borders Russia on the north and northeast, Azerbaijan on the southeast, Armenia and Turkey on the south, and the Black Sea on the west. Area: 69,700 sq km (26,900 sq mi). Pop. (1992 est.) 5,482,000. Cap.: Tbilisi. Monetary unit: ruble, with (Oct. 5, 1992) a free rate of 316.82 rubles = U.S. $1 (538.59 rubles = £1 sterling). President to January 6, Zviad Gamsakhurdia; coleaders of Military Council from January 6, Tengiz Kitovani and Dzhaba Ioseliani; chairman of State Council (president) from March 10, Eduard Shevardnadze; chairman of parliament (president) from November 6, Shevardnadze; prime minister from January 6, Tengiz Sigua.

Georgian leader Eduard Shevardnadze (centre) is surrounded by guards as he leaves his helicopter on a tour of an Abkhaz village. Shevardnadze accused Russia of fomenting unrest among the Abkhaz, who were fighting to secede from Georgia.

The overthrow of the democratically elected president, Zviad Gamsakhurdia, in January 1992 after a bloody and bitter struggle led to a search for legitimacy by his successors. The return of Eduard Shevardnadze (*see* BIOGRAPHIES) from Moscow in March as chairman of the State Council promised to resolve this problem. Eventually elections in October resulted in a clear victory for Shevardnadze as leader. However, no single party or alliance won the parliamentary elections that were taking place at the same time, and the government remained a fragile coalition.

Shevardnadze's position was dependent partly on the military men who had brought him to power in March. The key figures were Tengiz Kitovani, and Dzhaba Ioseliani, coleaders of the Military Council. Several times during the year Shevardnadze's attempts to reach agreement in Georgia's regions of South Ossetia, Mingrelia, and Abkhazia appeared to have been sabotaged by these men. The South Ossetians, mainly Muslim, wished to join their conationals in North Ossetia, which was part of Russia. Sporadic fighting continued for months, with Kitovani believing he could impose a military solution and Ruslan Khasbulatov, the chairman of the Russian parliament, threatening to annex South Ossetia. In June, however, Russian and Georgian leaders signed an agreement to provide a tripartite peace force (Russian, Georgian, and North Ossetian) to impose a buffer zone in South Ossetia. At the same time, Russia recognized Georgia's independence. In December Shevardnadze placed all government ministers under martial law because of the deteriorating situation in Abkhazia.   (MARTIN MCCAULEY)

This article updates the *Macropædia* article TRANSCAUCASIA: *Georgia*.

GERMANY

Germany is in central Europe, on the North and Baltic seas. Area: 356,957 sq km (137,822 sq mi). Pop. (1992 est.): 80,293,-000. Cap. designate, Berlin; seat of government, Bonn. Monetary unit: Deutsche Mark, with (Oct. 5, 1992) a free rate of DM 1.41 to U.S. $1 (DM 2.39 = £1 sterling). President in 1992, Richard von Weizsäcker; chancellor, Helmut Kohl.

In 1992 the full scale of the problems and costs of German unification finally became apparent. The worries of the previous year about the weakening of the economy became fears that Germany was heading rapidly toward recession. Growth turned out to be well below expectations. Caught between falling tax revenues from western Germany and urgent demands for ever higher subsidies to the struggling ex-Communist eastern part of the country, Chancellor Helmut Kohl's centre-right coalition was forced for the second time to abandon its pledge that taxes would not be raised to pay for unity. Popular dissatisfaction with the government especially, and all the main political parties in general, grew sharply during the year, a reaction not just to the economic malaise but also to the politicians' seeming inability to tackle a series of problems, the most acute of which was a record number of economic refugees seeking asylum in Germany. Acts of xenophobic violence increased, and support for extreme-right parties grew sharply in state elections.

Abroad, the German government dedicated most of its efforts to preventing the Maastricht Treaty on European economic and political union from collapsing. This effort was complicated by an unexpected cooling of the German population's traditionally strong support for European integration. With its plan to ease the constitutional restrictions on deploying troops abroad still blocked by the opposition Social Democrats (SPD), the government tested the limits of what was politically possible by sending troops to participate in the monitoring of UN sanctions against Serbia.

Domestic Affairs. The year opened with a new law enabling ordinary citizens to examine whatever personal files the Stasi, the secret police of former East Germany, may have had on them. Some 10,000 people applied in the first week alone. Many were devastated to find they had been spied on by close friends and, in some cases, by members of their own family. Former East German leader Erich Honecker, who had been living in the Chilean embassy in Moscow since 1991, was extradited to Berlin in July on charges of manslaughter and corruption. The trial began in November despite motions that Honecker was too ill from terminal cancer to stand trial.

The economic tensions that were to dominate the year soon came to the fore as the western German pay round got under way. (Wages in the east were being raised separately to western levels by 1994.) The opening move came from the 130,000 steelworkers. Theirs was, in fact, a delayed claim from the 1991 wage round, so even though the economy had slowed down rapidly in the meantime, the steelworkers were eager to do well out of the unification boom of 1990 and early 1991 and demanded a 10.5% increase. A strike was barely averted in the early hours of February 3

Police shield Richard von Weizsäcker (centre), president of Germany, at a rally held in Berlin on November 8 to condemn violence against foreigners, largely attributed to neo-Nazis. At the rally left-wing radicals disrupted the president's speech and pelted him with various objects.

when employers, overriding government appeals for wage restraint, settled for a 6.4% raise. No sooner was the deal struck than industry, the government, and the unions began arguing over whether this delayed 1991 steel accord had a "pilot function" for the impending 1992 bargaining round. Pointing to inflation near 5%—high by German standards—Kohl's government recommended settlements below 5%. Unemployment in Germany had soared in January to well over three million. The greatest increase was in eastern Germany, where the termination of numerous short-time work contracts caused the sudden loss of 515,000 jobs. Hidden unemployment in eastern Germany covered about two million people, kept out of the statistics by a panoply of job-creation and maintenance schemes, early-retirement programs, and the fact that many formerly employed women had dropped out of the market.

Kohl suffered a personal blow at the end of March when a longtime party friend, the Christian Democrat defense minister, Gerhard Stoltenberg, was obliged to resign over revelations of illegal shipments of tanks to Turkey. The public outcry was further fueled by simultaneous publicity surrounding the use of German armaments by Turkish forces against the Kurds, in defiance of a German ban. The 63-year-old Stoltenberg was replaced by 49-year-old Volker Rühe, general secretary of Christian Democratic Union (CDU). The entry into the Cabinet of Rühe, well known internationally from his years as the CDU's foreign-policy expert, symbolized an important generational change in German politics as senior positions were taken over by those less constrained than the immediate postwar generation about defending what they saw as Germany's interests.

The extent of popular disaffection with the chancellor and his Christian Democrats was underscored by the results of elections in two federal states (*Länder*) on April 5. In both Baden-Württemberg and Schleswig-Holstein, economic uncertainty and anger over the unchecked flood of asylum-seekers into the country, placing massive strains on municipal housing resources and social security budgets, produced strong gains for the extreme right. Twenty years of Christian Democratic predominance in Baden-Württemberg ended as support for the antiforeigner Republicans soared to 11%. Unwilling to work with the extremists, the CDU was obliged to form a "grand coalition" with the Social Democrats, who had also lost heavily. In Schleswig-Holstein the Social Democrats, headed by their national leader, Björn Engholm, just managed to hold onto their absolute majority by one seat in the parliament, while the extreme-right German People's Union made strong gains. The results of both elections were interpreted as a sign that people were fed up with the main parties. With no more elections due until 1994, Kohl said he would use the coming 18 "free months" to sort out Germany's main problems.

His first test came soon enough, in the form of a showdown with the public-sector trade unions, representing 2.3 million workers. Although the unions had indicated they were prepared to accept an independent arbitrator's compromise of a 5.4% wage increase, Kohl wanted to push the first deal of the 1992 pay round below the psychologically important 5% barrier. Saying that Germans were living beyond their means, he set the tone for a confrontation that was unusually bitter by German industrial relations standards. Following an overwhelming "yes" vote in the strike ballots, the unions started industrial action, their first in 18 years, on April 27, hitting transport, postal, and refuse services. The drama of the first day of the strike was heightened by the announcement of the retirement of Germany's foreign minister, Hans-Dietrich Genscher. Consistently the country's most popular politician and for two decades the

pivot of every German Cabinet, the 65-year-old Genscher said he would be bowing out on May 17, 18 years to the day after he first became foreign minister. For many Germans, the departure of the man whose name had become synonymous with constant striving to improve relations with Communist eastern Europe amounted to the passing of an era. Genscher's replacement was the 55-year-old justice minister, Klaus Kinkel. Known for his plain speaking, he quickly came to represent, along with Rühe, the new generation of German leaders.

The strike fronts hardened rapidly as the public-sector unions stepped up industrial action, hitting airports and harbours. Rubbish piled up on street corners as people cycled to work to avoid huge traffic jams. On the 11th day the strike ended, the government having settled for a deal just above the arbitrator's 5.4% it had initially rejected. Kohl, whose anti-inflationary 5% barrier had been smashed, admitted the deal "contained severe risks for the German economy." The militant mood of workers was further demonstrated when a strong majority of the public-sector union members rejected the settlement as insufficient. Even though the public-sector union leadership chose not to resume the strike, other unions took this as a sign of rank-and-file determination to ignore warnings about inflation and unemployment.

The prospect that the temperature of Germany's hot industrial spring would rise steadily to the boiling point was finally averted when, on May 18, IG Metall, the country's biggest union, pulled back from its strike threat and settled for a 5.4% wage deal. Importantly, the settlement covered 21 months, setting a benchmark increase of only 3% in 1993. Although the government's hopes of keeping wage increases below 5% had been dashed, the compromise was widely welcomed as proof of the resilience of Germany's consensual industrial relations system. Before long, however, warnings about the effects of the wage increases on employment turned into a steady stream of job-cut announcements by the household names of German industry.

The hardening mood of popular frustration with the political establishment was captured in dramatic terms in June by Pres. Richard von Weizsäcker, who criticized the main political parties for "an overall failure of intellectual and moral leadership." People still had not been told the true extent of the sacrifices needed to make unification work, he said. An opinion poll found what it described as an "epidemic of mistrust of politicians": over 60% of western Germans no longer trusted their politicians, as against 39% 10 years previously. In eastern Germany 64% said they had lost faith in their politicians.

Following months of debate, members of the Bundestag (parliament) voted on June 26 to extend former East Germany's liberal abortion regime, allowing abortion on demand within the first three months of pregnancy, to all of Germany. In former West Germany abortion was illegal unless recommended by doctors on medical and psychological grounds. The new pan-German regime was due to come into force on Jan. 1, 1993, but the Constitutional Court, after an appeal by conservative MPs, ordered suspension of the new legislation pending a ruling as to whether it was unconstitutional. By July opinion polls were revealing that, for the first time, more western Germans claimed unification filled them with alarm rather than joy. A majority also said they wanted the massive subsidies to eastern Germany—running at DM 170 billion in 1992—to be cut back. In the east, support for unification remained strong, but disillusionment over the failure of the long-promised economic recovery to appear was overwhelming, creating social tension.

One of the most sinister manifestations of this tension—the continuing incidents of violence against foreigners—

exploded with shocking intensity in late August in the depressed eastern port city of Rostock. Hundreds of extreme-right youths laid siege to a refugee hostel, housing mainly Romanian asylum-seekers and Vietnamese contract workers, and were cheered on by thousands of local onlookers. It was the beginning of five nights of street battles with police, who were accused of incompetence in not rapidly stamping out the violence. The climax came when the residents were bused to safety and the thugs stormed the hostel and burned it while police looked on helplessly. As the government renewed its calls for the opposition to abandon its resistance to toughening the generous asylum clause in the constitution, the Rostock events sparked a recrudescence of xenophobic attacks across the country, especially in the east. In November two neo-Nazi youths were charged with murder and arson after they confessed to the firebombing of a house in which three Turkish immigrants were killed. There was a 70% increase in violence against foreigners over 1991. Opinion polls showed mounting intolerance toward foreigners and a growing sympathy for the antiforeigner line of extreme-right parties, though most Germans strongly disapproved of the violence. There were no signs that the political logjam over the asylum problem was loosening—some 450,000 refugees were expected to enter Germany in 1992, up from the nearly 260,000 in 1991.

In the middle of October the governing coalition of Christian Democrats, Christian Social Union, and Free Democrats ended over a year of internal argument and presented to the Bundestag its joint proposals for toughening the asylum regulations. It proposed basing the new law on the Geneva Convention for Refugees, which in turn would be qualified by a number of strict conditions, enabling the immediate expulsion of "clearly unjustified" applicants. The Social Democrats remained badly divided over whether to support the government's plans, but in December the SPD agreed to a revised asylum law. It was hoped that this—and the banning of several neo-Nazi militant groups—would ease the situation.

By September the rumblings of dissatisfaction with Kohl's leadership had turned into the beginnings of a palace coup. The vehicle for the challenge was the call, mainly by eastern CDU parliamentarians, for a special tax on western Germans to raise more funds for investing in the east. Headed by the party's number two—and the man widely regarded as the chancellor-in-waiting—Wolfgang Schäuble, the rebels appeared to be seeking common ground with the opposition Social Democrats for a possible "grand coalition" government. For several days Kohl's fate hung in the balance, until he vigorously reasserted his authority. In an address to the Bundestag on September 9, Kohl poured scorn on suggestions of his imminent demise. On October 1 he celebrated 10 years as chancellor, and 19 years as chairman of the Christian Democrats, with his position in the party as strong as ever, largely because of the absence of any alternatives.

Kohl had originally intended the Christian Democrats' annual congress, which took place in Düsseldorf in late October, to be a celebration of Europe, but he found it overwhelmed by the economic crisis. In a dramatic "hour of truth" speech, he told delegates that tax increases would be unavoidable in 1995, to cover the massive debts from former East Germany that would then fall on the Bonn budget. But, he warned, if people did not accept real wage cuts and sharp savings in public spending, tax increases would come "much sooner and be much steeper." The chancellor's gloomy message was reinforced by the autumn report on the economy from Germany's five leading economic institutes. Western Germany was expected to grow by 0.5% in 1993, but only if a series of optimistic conditions were fulfilled.

In early November the government decided to borrow more money to plug some of the DM 20 billion gap in its proposed budget for 1993 while it tried to agree on substantial cuts in spending.

On October 8 one of Germany's most revered elder statesmen, Willy Brandt (see OBITUARIES), died of cancer at the age of 78. The architect of *Ostpolitik* and the only postwar German politician to win the Nobel Peace Prize, the former Social Democratic chancellor was mourned by Germans of all generations and parties. On October 19 police found the decomposing body of 44-year-old Petra Kelly (see OBITUARIES), a founder of the German Greens and the country's best known environmental activist, in her house in Bonn. She apparently had been shot three weeks previously by her 69-year-old companion and fellow campaigner, Gert Bastian, who then turned his gun on himself. No explanation was found, shrouding in mystery the violent deaths of two leading pacifists who had become alienated from the Green movement in recent years.

Foreign Affairs. The year began with Germany answering criticisms from its European Communities (EC) partners and the U.S. that the now united country was throwing its weight around internationally. Cause of the tension was the reluctant decision by the EC, under strong German pressure in late 1991, to recognize the independence of Slovenia and Croatia. Chancellor Kohl said it was only natural that Germany now enjoyed more influence, and it was a state of affairs that Germans themselves and their partners had to get used to.

To his great dismay, Kohl found that no sooner had the Maastricht Treaty on European economic and political union been agreed in December 1991 than a bout of worried second thoughts swept Germany, characterized mainly by fear of losing the Deutsch Mark for the unknown quantity of a common European currency. Opinion polls showed a strong rise in Euro-skepticism as Germans, long regarded as among the most pro-European, suddenly wanted integration to proceed more slowly and the government to be more forceful in defending national interests. Kohl, personally committed to European union, found his task complicated by conservative nationalists in his own coalition, the opposition SPD, and the governments of the *Länder,* all maneuvering to make political capital out of popular misgivings about Maastricht.

The appointment of Rühe as defense minister paved the way for Germany's pulling out of the four-nation European Fighter Aircraft project. Rühe said the fighter was too expensive and belonged to a bygone cold war era. Despite efforts by the Italian, Spanish, and British governments to negotiate cost reductions, Rühe insisted that the project be dropped, contributing to strains in Anglo-German relations, in particular, during the course of the year. The appointment of Kinkel as foreign minister in April brought no immediate change of substance but some shift to a more forthright, plain-speaking style. Kinkel made clear Germany's interest in acquiring a permanent voice on the UN's Security Council, either by itself or through a new common EC seat. Still unable, because of SPD opposition, to lift the constitutional restrictions on troop deployments abroad, Kinkel nonetheless adopted an increasingly tough approach toward the Yugoslav conflict.

The narrow Danish rejection of the Maastricht Treaty in a referendum on June 2 gave a boost to the Euro-skeptics in Germany while Kohl placed his government at the forefront of efforts to save the plan for European integration. Responding to popular worries over excessive Brussels bureaucracy and a loss of national identity, Kohl abandoned his former rhetoric about a United States of

Garbage piles up in the streets of Frankfurt in early May during a strike by German public workers. After an 11-day strike that disrupted garbage collection, transportation, and postal services, the workers won a wage increase slightly above the German inflation rate.
PATRICK PIEL—GAMMA LIAISON

Europe and began emphasizing the need for a Europe "united in diversity," with each country and region retaining its identity, free from unnecessary external meddling. The *Länder* threatened to block ratification of Maastricht in the upper house, the Bundesrat, where they were represented, unless the government conceded a substantial increase in the regions' powers to influence the day-to-day shaping of Germany's EC policies. During the course of difficult negotiations, the government had to give some ground, but it managed to limit effective state influence to areas such as culture, education, and certain financial matters. In July, Germany dispatched a destroyer and three reconnaissance aircraft to assist the monitoring of UN sanctions against Serbia. Rühe described this as a "new situation" for Germany, which was participating militarily for the first time in an international mission that was not purely humanitarian. The Social Democrats protested the move but did not block it.

September was marked by unprecedented turbulence in the European currency system, which produced intense criticism of Germany by those countries, notably Britain and Italy, that felt the Bundesbank's high-interest-rate policy had contributed considerably to their problems and forced them to pull the pound and lira, respectively, out of the exchange-rate mechanism. Relations between London and Bonn reached a low point. The close French vote in favour of Maastricht in the referendum on September 20 saved the treaty from complete collapse, and Kohl urged his colleagues to move full steam ahead toward European union. The simmering row with Britain was brought to a boil again over German plans to celebrate the 50th anniversary of the V2 rocket bomb. Hugely embarrassed, Kohl's government called off the official ceremony.

The opening of the Maastricht ratification debate in Bonn on October 8 saw the government obliged to make heavy concessions to the Euro-skeptics in order to guarantee the treaty's safe passage. The Bundestag was assured it would vote again in 1996 on whether Germany should enter the final phase of European monetary union. The move was widely interpreted as a German parliamentary veto, casting some doubt on the strength of Germany's commitment to Maastricht in future years. (JOHN EISENHAMMER)

GREECE

The republic of Greece occupies the southern part of the Balkan Peninsula and several adjoining island groups in southeastern Europe, in and between the Ionian and Aegean seas. Area: 131,957 sq km (50,949 sq mi). Pop. (1992 est.): 10,288,000. Cap.: Athens. Monetary unit: drachma, with (Oct. 5, 1992) a free rate of 181.40 drachmas to U.S. $1 (308.38 drachmas = £1 sterling). President in 1992, Konstantinos Karamanlis; prime minister, Konstantinos Mitsotakis.

Two major issues preoccupied Greece almost exclusively through 1992: the conservative government's belated efforts to redress the economy through drastic but unpopular reforms and its determination to stop the new "Republic of Macedonia," across its northern borders, from using a name held to be part of the ancient Greek heritage. Under Greek pressure, the European Communities (EC) reluctantly agreed at its June summit meeting in Lisbon to withhold recognition of this state, born out of Yugoslavia's dismemberment, until its leaders adopted a name acceptable to Greece. On the economic front, the government of Konstantinos Mitsotakis put through a painful package of institutional reforms and austerity measures to bring the debt-ridden economy under control. Its determination to enforce this onerous program despite the explosive social tensions it unleashed won praise from the EC. However, both the economic upheaval and the Macedonian issue imperiled, at different times, the internal unity of the ruling New Democracy Party.

Efforts to seek an accommodation over the name *Macedonia* culminated in two abortive bilateral meetings, one in Athens on January 3, the other in Lisbon on April 20. The Greeks demanded elimination of *Macedonia* (and any adjective derived from it) from the official title of the neighbouring state on the grounds that it implied irredentist aspirations toward the adjacent Greek province of the same name. The nascent state categorically rejected anyone's right to dictate its name. Emotions ran high in Greece, where a massive protest rally in Salonika on February 14 was followed by a boycott of Italian and Dutch products on the premise that those countries were hostile to the Greek cause. The government distanced itself from these extreme positions. On April 13 Mitsotakis dismissed his foreign minister, Antonis Samaras, whom he held responsible for the jingoistic line, but the wave of nationalism sweeping the nation forced the government to uphold Samaras' policy of no compromise.

Greece's objections did not stop Turkey, Bulgaria, and Russia from extending diplomatic recognition to the new state, but Mitsotakis persuaded the EC to withhold recognition. U.S. Pres. George Bush also refrained from upsetting Athens, though Washington's concern over eventual destabilization of the region was made clear to the Greeks. Relations with Albania remained tense as the two sides traded accusations of maltreatment of their ethnic groups in each other's territory. Efforts to improve relations with Turkey led to negotiations on the text of a friendship treaty, but progress was blocked by the continuing difficulty in devising a settlement on the future of Cyprus. Greece tried to obtain security guarantees against the perceived threat from Turkey by joining the Western European Union. In April the WEU agreed to take Greece, as a member of the EC, under its wing, but only on condition that Turkey obtain associate membership and that the WEU treaty's guarantee of military help in case of attack against one of its members not be operative in case of conflict between members or associate members.

More than a million Greek citizens fill central Athens on December 10 to protest other countries' recognition of the former Yugoslav republic of Macedonia as an independent republic with that name. In deference to Greece, members of the European Communities agreed to withhold recognition.
ARGYROPOULOS—SIPA

New strains emerged within the ruling party as the result of a controversial stabilization package launched by the government's new economy minister, Stefanos Manos. Its aim was to enable Greece to catch up with its European partners and meet the convergence criteria of the Maastricht Treaty, which the Greek parliament ratified by an impressive 286–8 vote on July 31. Under this package public-sector wages were frozen for the year, all appointments in the overstaffed public administration were suspended, prices were freed, substantial new taxes were levied, and the privatization of state enterprises was speeded up. U.S. Internal Revenue Service experts were brought in to advise on methods to combat widespread tax evasion, and the country's pension system was drastically reformed. The result was one of the worst spates of strikes, mass protest rallies, and violent street demonstrations the country had experienced in decades, climaxed by an unsuccessful attempt on the life of the finance minister by the elusive terrorist organization 17 November. Labour unrest gradually petered out as the reforms were passed by the razor-thin government majority in parliament. The return to market-economy practices pushed up the inflation index by an average 15.5% in 1992, and unemployment rose sharply to almost 10% of the work force.

Criticism of the reforms came mainly from within New Democracy. With elections due in 1994, many felt the party could not afford the heavy political cost of these unpopular measures. However, fears that any defection might cause the government to fall and force early elections stopped the dissenters short of withdrawing their confidence from it. In early December Mitsotakis sacked his entire Cabinet.

Andreas Papandreou, leader of the Panhellenic Socialist Movement (Pasok), the main opposition party, was exonerated in January of charges relating to the Bank of Crete embezzlement scandal, but two of his ministers received heavy prison sentences. The conviction of one of the ministers prompted a by-election in a suburban constituency of Athens, which other parties refused to challenge. Pasok received a boost when its candidate raised the socialist majority by more than one-third, but as the government went ahead with its reforms, there were complaints from Pasok rank and file that Papandreou's style of opposition was ineffectual. An opinion poll in October pointed to Giorgos Yennimatas, the party's parliamentary spokesman,

as the likeliest successor to the party leadership, whereupon Papandreou stripped him of his job as spokesman.

In October the government gave its consent to a generous settlement of tax and property problems of former king Constantine, who had lived in London since losing his throne in 1974. The deal left him with two royal summer palaces in his native country, fueling speculation that he might be planning to settle again in Greece.

(MARIO MODIANO)

HUNGARY

A republic, Hungary is a landlocked state in central Europe. Area: 93,033 sq km (35,920 sq mi). Pop. (1992 est.): 10,318,000. Cap.: Budapest. Monetary unit: forint, with (Oct. 5, 1992) a free rate of 76.77 forints to U.S. $1 (130.52 forints = £1 sterling). President in 1992, Arpad Goncz; chairman of the Council of Ministers (prime minister), Jozsef Antall.

In many respects, the year 1992 was spent in marking time. The political decision-making machinery, instead of being employed in attempts to ease the increasingly serious economic burden, was engaged in debates over issues of status, prestige, and identity. In a sense, this was an unavoidable consequence of the devastation caused by 40 years of communism and the need to reconstruct society in a new image, but in the interim the nation was perturbed as the standard of living dropped.

The political party system, while at first sight reasonably stable, in reality exhibited a good deal of fluidity, and the level of underlying tension was shown by the election fever that increasingly came to dominate the minds of the nation's leaders by the third quarter of the year, although elections were not due until 1994. The parties of the government coalition, led by the Hungarian Democratic Forum, proved unpopular with the electorate, which demonstrated its dislike of the government by voting for the opposition at by-elections. The Independent Smallholders' Party split into two factions, with the party outside the National Assembly generally backing the minority, making them rather ineffectual coalition partners.

The Forum itself was split by the document produced by one of the party deputy presidents, the populist Istvan Csurka, in August. Csurka attacked his own party and the leadership of Jozsef Antall for having been too lenient with the opposition, for not having introduced radical changes to eliminate the remnants of communism, and for not having established proper control over the media. As his critics, both inside and outside the Forum, pointed out, Csurka's proposals, had they been accepted, would have amounted to an end to the democratic institutions that were set up after the collapse of communism. Csurka's tract was widely assailed, but the party leadership distanced itself from its propositions only cautiously, presumably fearful that a direct attack on Csurka might split the party.

The opposition was likewise in some disarray. The opposition party, the Alliance of Free Democrats, remained divided between its formerly dissident wing and its pragmatists, and the two branches found it difficult to resolve their differences. In the autumn Ivan Peto, a member of the former dissident wing, was elected as leader of the parliamentary faction, replacing the pragmatist Peter Tolgyessy. Among the voters, however, the Free Democrats remained unpopular, and they were unable to capitalize on the government's difficulties. More surprisingly, the Federation of Young Democrats also found it hard to convert support in the opinion polls to success in the by-elections. Although the Young Democrats led the popularity contest, it was the former Communist party, the Hungarian Socialist Party, that consistently outperformed all the others in terms of votes. This was attributable, at least in part, to the superiority of the former Communists' organizational abilities and experience under the old regime.

The by-elections were also revealing in another respect—popular apathy or distaste for politics. Turnouts were low to very low; several elections had to be repeated because they failed to reach the required level of participation, one or two up to six times. The explanation for this apathy was to be sought in the population's inability to understand the function of politics in a democracy—a continuing debate about the distribution of power—coupled with the failure of the political leaders (and their predecessors) to educate the public on this topic.

The fate of the electronic media was an acute case in point. The government took the view that the media should represent its views rather than those of the opposition, and it launched a series of bitter attacks on radio and television executives because it believed that they were treating it unfairly. The government clearly rejected the argument that the function of the media was to criticize as much as it was to report. By the end of the year, however, the government seemed to be winning. The head of television was suspended on vague charges of incompetence, and more importantly, the budgets of both television and radio were brought directly under the office of the prime minister, thereby effectively ensuring that their future independence was in question.

The most important institution to counterbalance the government, the Constitutional Court, made a number of important decisions during the year. It threw out the bill on retroactive legislation aimed at highly placed Communists and set a deadline for passing a new media law, guaranteeing the independence of radio and television. Because passage of the media law required a two-thirds majority in the National Assembly, the government could enact it only with the consent of the opposition, and the antagonism between the two was such that this degree of agreement was inconceivable.

The economy continued to fare badly. Output declined; industrial production was particularly poor during the first half of the year, though there was some improvement later. Unemployment was rising, but inflation seemed to have leveled off. The one positive sign was that foreign investment maintained its high level, and Hungary continued to attract about half of all the Western funds going to central and eastern Europe. According to preliminary estimates, well over $1 billion flowed into the country during the year. Meanwhile, there were plans to expand privatization.

In foreign affairs there was no serious change in the broad direction of forging closer relations with the West and keeping out of trouble locally. The latter was increasingly difficult because of the war in former Yugoslavia. Hungary gave shelter to perhaps 100,000 refugees from the conflict, was anxious about the fate of the roughly 350,000 ethnic Hungarians in Serbia, was subjected to a vitriolic propaganda campaign by the Serbian press, and was fearful of a possible Serbian attack. It was partly to this end that a new radar system was installed and an arms deal was signed with Russia during Russian Pres. Boris Yeltsin's visit to Hungary in November.

(GEORGE SCHÖPFLIN)

FILIP HORVAT—SABA

Billboards mark the site of a General Motors plant in Hungary. The U.S. company began development in eastern Europe in the late 1980s and in 1992 produced the first automobile in Hungary in a quarter century.

ICELAND

Iceland is an island republic in the North Atlantic Ocean, near the Arctic Circle. Area: 102,819 sq km (39,699 sq mi). Pop. (1992 est.): 261,000. Cap.: Reykjavík. Monetary unit: Icelandic króna, with (Oct. 5, 1992) a free rate of 54.51 krónur to U.S. $1 (92.67 krónur = £1 sterling). President in 1992, Vigdís Finnbogadóttir; prime minister, Davíd Oddsson.

Iceland went through a deep recession in 1992, with the gross national product (GNP) declining by 3% in real terms, the sharpest fall in decades. Unemployment, almost nonexistent for years, rose to more than 3%. Inflation, however, which had run at double-digit rates for decades, declined to 1½%, well below the Organization for Economic Cooperation and Development average.

The main cause of the recession was the sharp reduction in the fish catch due to declining stocks. The fish stocks had been dwindling for years, while the fish catch had kept up with an ever increasing fishing fleet. The decline in stocks had been particularly steep in the past two years, and the government had been forced to lower catch quotas severely. The stock of cod, the most important species, had fallen to its lowest level in decades, and the government had been forced to reduce the cod catch quota by nearly one-fourth. In addition, world markets for aluminum and ferrosilicon, the two primary metals produced in Iceland, were going through a severe slump. These developments led to a drop in exports of some 2% in 1992 and a current account deficit amounting to around 3½% of GNP. A small recovery was expected in 1993, but the pace of growth would be restrained by the limited scope for export growth.

Faced with these difficulties, Prime Minister Davíd Oddsson's government was determined to pursue a market-oriented economic policy that called for curbing the fiscal deficit and the current account deficit. It succeeded in slowing inflation and stabilizing the exchange rate but, faced with dwindling fish stocks, it still had to grapple with a low rate of growth and a sluggish economy. Toward the autumn of 1992, with unemployment rising rapidly, the government decided that it should implement reflationary measures and allow the fiscal deficit to expand in order to stimulate domestic demand and thus reduce unemployment. New public construction projects were set in motion for that purpose.

Iceland, along with the other European Free Trade Association nations, had reached agreement with the European Communities (EC) in October 1991 on the establishment of a European Economic Area (EEA). The EEA agreement was hotly debated by the Althing (parliament) in a special summer session. Concessions on fisheries from the EC that Iceland sought but that had yet to be negotiated made passage of the EEA agreement difficult. However, the agreement appeared to have majority support in the Althing, but no legislative action was taken on it before the end of the year.

Iceland's efforts to attract an aluminum plant had been frustrated in 1991 by reduced aluminum prices in world markets. In late 1992 exploratory talks on a new aluminum plant in Iceland began between the Icelandic government and Kaiser Aluminum of the U.S., but at year's end it was still too early to tell whether these talks would produce tangible results.

In mid-February Oddsson paid an official visit to Israel. The visit was overshadowed by accusations of war crimes allegedly committed by an 81-year-old naturalized Icelandic citizen, Estonian by birth, who had immigrated to Iceland 40 years earlier. The crimes, allegedly committed during World War II, had come to light through research by the Wiesenthal Institute in Tel Aviv. The Icelandic government responded by appointing a committee of inquiry, which turned in its report in October. The committee concluded that it would be impossible to prove the allegations after so much time had elapsed and that, in any case, extradition to Estonia would not be legally possible. It recommended that no further action be taken in the matter.

(BJÖRN MATTHÍASSON)

IRELAND

The republic of Ireland, separated from Great Britain by the North Channel, the Irish Sea, and St. George's Channel, shares its island with Northern Ireland to the northeast. Area: 70,285 sq km (27,137 sq mi). Pop. (1992 est.): 3,519,000. Cap.: Dublin. Monetary unit: Irish pound (punt), with (Oct. 5, 1992) a free rate of £Ir 0.54 to U.S. $1 (£Ir 0.91 = £1 sterling). President in 1992, Mary Robinson; prime ministers, Charles Haughey and, from February 11, Albert Reynolds.

After 12 years as leader of the ruling Fianna Fail party, Charles Haughey was forced to resign in 1992 and was replaced by Albert Reynolds (see BIOGRAPHIES). The circumstances were dramatic. After a series of scandals Reynolds, who had been finance minister during the previous two years, challenged Haughey as leader, was dismissed, together with the minister for the environment, Padraig Flynn, and then was defeated in the subsequent vote. There followed revelations from Sen. Sean Doherty that Haughey had been directly involved in the telephone tapping of two prominent political journalists during 1982. Haughey had always denied this, but these revelations, combined with a series of business scandals that had been linked to the prime minister at the end of the previous year, forced his resignation. On his election as prime minister to replace Haughey, Reynolds promptly sacked 8 of 12 serving Fianna Fail ministers in a move unprecedented in the nation's history for its severity. Some saw it as guaranteeing a continuation of the divisions and animosities that had plagued Fianna Fail for the past 12 years.

Reynolds established a coalition government consisting of Fianna Fail and the Progressive Democrats. However, the Progressive Democrats left the coalition when Reynolds did not apologize to their leader, Des O'Malley, for accusing him of being "reckless, irresponsible, and dishonest" in his testimony on Ireland's beef industry. On November 5, without the support of the Progressive Democrats, Reynolds lost a confidence vote in the Dail (parliament). As a result, a general election was called for November 25, the same day as three national referenda on abortion (see below). Final results gave Fianna Fail 67 seats in the 168-member Dail to 45 for Fine Gael and 33 for Labour. Reynolds sought to establish a Fianna Fail-Labour coalition, but at the year's end this had not been achieved, and Reynolds, though formally voted out of office, remained prime minister.

At the outset of 1992, 269,200 people were unemployed (20% of the labour force), the highest figure in the history of Ireland but one that increased steadily to nearly 300,000 at year's end. This catastrophe, together with a sustained preoccupation about abortion in the nation, dominated political life throughout the year.

The abortion issue derived from the case of a 14-year-old girl, pregnant as a result of rape, who was refused permission through a High Court injunction to travel to England for an abortion. This stemmed from a 1983 referendum that established a constitutional ban on abortion in Ireland. In addition, there was no right to freedom of information on abortion. The parents took the case to the Supreme Court, where the judges, by a majority of 4 to 1, overthrew the High Court decision on the basis of the fundamental and personal rights provisions of the constitution and taking into account the girl's suicide threats. The case attracted attention and outrage abroad and left the strong "pro-life" movement at home to face the unacceptable fact that limited abortion rights were now legal for Irish women virtually up to full term. They at once called for another referendum to roll back the Supreme Court decision.

With little public realization of the fact, a right-wing, pro-life senator had managed to persuade Haughey to have an abortion protocol included in the Maastricht Treaty on closer political and economic union within Europe. As this protocol had now been reinterpreted by the Supreme Court ruling, it threw the electorate into confusion over Maastricht generally. Despite the best efforts of the government to concentrate people's minds on the financial benefits of closer union within the European Communities (EC), more time was spent debating the implications of the abortion protocol than on the broader issues. However, there was wide recognition of the benefits of greater European union, and in the June 18 referendum on Maastricht, 69% voted in favour and 31% against.

In the autumn the government headed into a potentially divisive referendum campaign on the abortion issues. It decided to put three separate questions on abortion to the nation's 2.5 million voters on November 25. Every voter was to receive a separate ballot paper on the so-called substantive issue of abortion itself, as well as on abortion information and travel rights. In the election the voters rejected the substantive issue but approved providing abortion information and allowing travel rights.

The University of Dublin, Ireland's oldest, which had been founded by Queen Elizabeth I, celebrated its quatercentenary. Distinguished past alumni, including Jonathan Swift, Samuel Beckett, and the president of Ireland, Mary Robinson, were honoured.

The Beef Tribunal, a judicial investigation into malpractices in the country's largest single industry, beef processing, continued throughout the year, with both the former and present prime ministers as witnesses. Among other revelations was the sale to Iraq of beef misrepresented as to source and ritual slaughter, as well as unsanctioned insurance arrangements putting huge sums of public money at risk. In May the most radical overhaul of the common agricultural policy (CAP) in its 30-year history was agreed to by the EC farm ministers. While agricultural economists were predicting that Irish consumers would gain by £100 million annually, there were sharp disagreements between farming organizations and the minister for agriculture over the benefits of the CAP reform package. Irish ministers continued to participate through the year in talks with their British counterparts, and with leaders of the political parties in Northern Ireland, in an attempt to pursue fresh initiatives on the devolution of power.

In May an American woman, Annie Murphy, revealed that the father of her 17-year-old son was the popular Roman Catholic bishop of Galway, Eamonn Casey, and that she had been receiving maintenance payments from him. Amid a storm of controversy, and following the discovery that church funds had been borrowed to finance the payments, the bishop resigned.

President Robinson traveled to Somalia in October—the first head of state to visit the famine-stricken areas—and then held discussions with the UN secretary-general in New York City on what could be done to relieve the plight of starving millions.   (MAVIS ARNOLD)

See also *United Kingdom,* below.

ITALY

A republic of southern Europe, Italy occupies the Apennine Peninsula, Sicily, Sardinia, and a number of smaller islands in the Mediterranean Sea. Area: 301,277 sq km (116,324 sq mi). Pop. (1992 est.): 57,158,000. Cap.: Rome. Monetary unit: Italian lira, with (Oct. 5, 1992) a free rate of 1,315 lire to U.S. $1 (2,236 lire = £1 sterling). Presidents in 1992, Francesco Cossiga to April 28 and, from May 28, Oscar Luigi Scalfaro; prime ministers, Giulio Andreotti to April 24 and, from June 28, Giuliano Amato.

It was a year when virtually all sectors of public life seemed to have slipped their moorings. Starting with the April 1992 parliamentary elections, the first to be held since 1987, the two parties that had governed Italy in various coalitions for nearly 30 years, the Christian Democrats (CD) and the Socialists, suffered serious setbacks at the polls. The former retained the position it had held since 1948 as the nation's number one party, but it dropped below its longtime minimum reserve of 30% of the vote. The results were a shock to both parties and a surprise to most outside political observers.

Some of the parties' losses could be explained by the rising support given to the Lombard League, a populist party created in Lombardy five years earlier and now with clone parties in other regions, mostly in northern Italy. The voters in April's parliamentary election made the Lombard League the first party in Milan, the second-ranking party in northern Italy, and (in combination with allied parties under the joint name Northern League) the fourth party in the nation. From two MPs in parliament—one of them the party's founder, Umberto Bossi—the league's roster had risen to 55. At a local election in Mantua five months later, the league garnered more than one-third of the votes. But subsequent events—could they have been registered on a Richter scale for measuring political earthquakes—would have indicated even greater devastation for the CD and the Socialists.

Rumours of corruption and even indictments are not new to political parties anywhere, and for the party that had been in a ruling position in Italy for 46 years (Mussolini and fascism endured only 22 years), it was inevitable that the opportunities for corruption were great. As 1992 drew to a close, more than 160 politicians, including 70 MPs and former Cabinet ministers, were under investigation for corruption and demanding bribes. Some were imprisoned. At the local level, entire city councils were handcuffed and packed off to jail. The charges were mostly related to the awarding of public works projects.

It all began when the owner of a small building-cleaning firm complained to the Milan police that he was fed up with paying a certain party go-between for the contract to clean a charity hospital. The carabinieri, and a magistrate named Antonio Di Pietro, laid a trap for the party functionary, using marked lira banknotes for the 14 million lire kickback. The man was arrested and told he would be detained until he confessed to that and similar acts of corruption and named others. This led to the resignation of Milan's mayor. Judge Di Pietro did not rest; he and his colleagues began ordering more arrests in other cities. The suspects, if they agreed to a partial confession, claimed that the bribes they demanded were solely for the good of the party coffers. In some cases, those coffers were to be found in Swiss banks. Some ex-Communist hands were involved, but the vast majority of corruption charges directly touched the two governing parties.

Di Pietro became a national hero. Bettino Craxi, who had expected to be returned to the office of prime minister

Demonstrators take to the streets of Milan in September to protest the economic policies of the new coalition government headed by Giuliano Amato. Proposed spending cuts and tax increases were intended to treat Italy's economic ills, which included enormous debt.
ALBERTO CALCINAI—SIPA

(which he held in 1983–87), further blotted his copybook by suggesting that Di Pietro was part of a plot against the parties being engineered by right-wing industrialists. His own position as Socialist leader was put in jeopardy by that foolish move. The Christian Democrats, for their part, suggested that the snowballing corruption allegations were somehow the work of Italy's Freemasons, known in some Roman Catholic circles as Satan's agents.

It was worth recalling that Italy's 1948 constitution gave juridical status to political parties, whereas in other countries they are free and even loose associations. In 1974 the parliament granted annual subsidies to the parties, the amount to be based on their percentage of votes at the last national election. The avowed purpose was to curtail bribery and corruption. By 1988 the state subsidies for the Christian Democrats and the Communists were, respectively, 25.5 billion lire and 17.7 billion lire, with lesser parties receiving lesser shares of the total handout of 150 billion lire. Clearly, it was not quite enough. In 1987 the small Radical Party had sponsored a referendum to abolish the subvention law. Fifty-six percent of those voting were in favour, but the total turnout at the polls was not sufficient to achieve the result sought. Still, it might have sounded an alarm bell to the parties. Scenes outside parliament in 1992 with crowds shouting "Thieves, thieves!" at the entering MPs might thus have been avoided.

After the April 5 elections, Pres. Francesco Cossiga, two months short of his full seven-year term, suddenly announced his resignation. His public behaviour, particularly his barbed insults directed at his own CD party, among others, led some people to think he had gone off the rails. His departure on April 25 was, for all, a relief, but it caused a legal delay in forming a new government. The office of head of state had to be filled before a new prime minister could be named to succeed Giulio Andreotti. In the interim, parliament elected the presidents of the two houses: Giovanni Spadolini of the Republican Party was reelected head of the Senate, and Giorgio Napolitano, a leading figure in the ex-Communist Party (renamed the Democratic Party of the Left), was elected president of the Chamber of Deputies. For nearly two months Italy was in the unusual position of being without either a president or a new government. On May 25 Oscar Luigi Scalfaro was elected in the joint

session of parliament to be the new head of state. He was a 73-year-old ramrod-straight *galant 'uomo,* as virtually all the press instantly dubbed him—a term that is moderately stronger than "gentleman." He entered the political fracas with the stern vigour of a Catholic Seneca.

By the end of June a coalition government had been formed, headed by Giuliano Amato (*see* BIOGRAPHIES), a 54-year-old Socialist who had entered politics only in 1983, when he was elected to the parliament from his native Turin. Previously, he had been a professor of law at Rome University. He strove to fill his Cabinet with "new faces," but the faces were not altogether new. He said Italy had become a welfare state and as such was generous and inefficient to the point of risking bankruptcy, and he repeated many times that Italy was "on the edge of an economic abyss." Most experts outside parliament agreed. In September he announced drastic cost-cutting and revenue-raising measures that would save the treasury 93 trillion lire (approximately $75 billion). Civil service wages were frozen, and pensionable ages rose from 60 to 65 for men and from 55 to 60 for women.

In October Amato announced what he described as a "minimum tax" program for Italy's 6.1 million self-employed, a category of people who traditionally file income-tax returns that put one-third of them below the poverty line of 7.2 million lire a year. (The classic example, often cited, was that of a trader who reported an income lower than that of his hired clerks.) The Amato scheme could turn out to be unconstitutional, since it was to be based on what a mythical "Tax-Meter" estimated that a butcher, for example, must earn. Other indicators of income were to be telephone bills, possession of sailboats and fast cars, and domestic help in the home. If this "life-style" gauge of taxation succeeded, Amato might secure 70% of the additional revenue he said he had to find. The stark fact was that Italy had Europe's biggest public deficit, expected to be more than $150 billion by year's end, and it would not go away without drastic measures.

The expected union-organized marches and demonstrations against the new taxes took place throughout Italy, even though most Italians might well have been convinced that the economic situation was indeed dire. Moreover, Amato asked parliament to grant him "emergency powers," which would permit him to rule by decree, not by law, and threatened to resign if parliament refused. His resignation would have thrown the country into even greater turmoil, and Amato knew it. Calling another election early in 1993 could mean handing over the government to the Lombard League and its cohorts. Guido Carli, for years governor of the Bank of Italy and a sometime Cabinet minister, said that Italy's financial crisis "is the product of the populist nature of the political parties. This has allowed a system of public finances where free handouts are widespread . . . and where citizens never pay what they should for services they receive." Getting people to pay for what they took to be their due would be about as easy for the Amato government as carrying out its plan of changing the electoral laws— which would require parliament's approval and would put a large number of MPs out of work. In October and November the Chamber of Deputies and the Senate, respectively, approved Amato's austerity budget. In both houses many legislators were not present for the vote.

The Mafia, possibly the most solvent of Italy's major industries, upgraded its criminal activities in 1992 by killing, two months apart, the two Sicilian magistrates who allegedly were closing in on its real leaders. The murders of Giovanni Falcone (*see* OBITUARIES) and his wife and of Paolo Borsellino and his five bodyguards horrified the country. Both killings allegedly had required high-tech assistance from the American branch of the Mafia, as well as insider information within U.S. and Italian law-enforcement agencies. Earlier, the Mafia had killed a former Palermo mayor and MP, Salvo Lima, considered to be Andreotti's political arm in the Sicilian capital. Investigators said that Lima was assassinated for having failed to protect the Mafia from police and political interference as he had promised. Andreotti, seven times prime minister, was named by President Cossiga to be a lifetime senator, the highest political honour that can be bestowed. No one was prepared to say that the "old fox" of Italian politics would not attempt a comeback to centre stage.   (GEORGE ARMSTRONG)

LATVIA

A republic of northern Europe, Latvia is on the eastern shore of the Baltic Sea. Area: 64,610 sq km (24,946 sq mi). Pop. (1992 est.): 2,685,000. Cap.: Riga. Monetary unit: Latvian ruble (transition currency from May 1992 at par with the Russian ruble), with (Oct. 5, 1992) a free rate of 316.82 rubles to U.S. $1 (538.59 rubles = £1 sterling). Chairman of the Supreme Council in 1992, Anatolijs Gorbunovs; prime minister, Ivars Godmanis.

The government experienced much tension in 1992 as a result of the very difficult economic situation, but it managed to survive. Living standards slumped, and gross domestic product was expected to drop by up to 30%. Some factories had to stop production owing to a lack of energy and raw materials. The liberalization of prices in Russia in January was a rude shock. By October inflation was running at a monthly rate of 15%. The ruble ceased to be legal tender in July, and the government announced plans to introduce a new currency, the lat.

Russia agreed to pull out troops by the end of 1994 if Latvia would amend legislation that affected ethnic Russians and abandon territorial and financial claims against Russia. Only 52% of the population were ethnically Latvian, and they wished to preserve the ethnic identity of the state by denying citizenship to Russians. Meanwhile, Latvia forged closer links with Scandinavia, especially Sweden, and with Germany.   (MARTIN MCCAULEY)

This article updates the *Macropædia* article BALTIC STATES: *Latvia*.

LIECHTENSTEIN

A landlocked constitutional monarchy of central Europe, Liechtenstein is united with Switzerland by a customs and monetary union. Area: 160 sq km (62 sq mi). Pop. (1992 est.): 29,600. Cap.: Vaduz. Monetary unit: Swiss franc, with (Oct. 5, 1992) a free rate of Sw F 1.23 to U.S. $1 (Sw F 2.09 = £1 sterling). Sovereign prince, Hans Adam II; head of government in 1992, Hans Brunhart.

In June 1992, 56.3% of voters in Liechtenstein rejected a proposed referendum to lower the voting age from 20 to 18. The turnout was 36.5% of the electorate. During the year, the tiny principality flexed its muscles when the head of government, Hans Brunhart, demanded that Czechoslovakia return the confiscated ancestral home and estates (some 1,600 sq km [617 sq mi]) of Liechtenstein's reigning monarch, Prince Hans Adam II. The land had been appropriated by Czechoslovakia between its independence in 1918 and the Communist takeover in 1945, without recompense to Liechtenstein for its estates and castles, estimated to be worth billions of dollars. Though Liechtenstein threatened to take its case to the International Court of Justice in The Hague, it faced complications when Czechoslovakia announced that it would break up on Jan. 1, 1993.

Liechtenstein's reputation as a tax haven was underscored in June when it was disclosed that the late publishing magnate Robert Maxwell had set up illegal bank accounts for Soviet KGB and Communist Party officials during the 1980s.   (KAREN SPARKS)

This article updates the *Micropædia* article LIECHTENSTEIN.

LITHUANIA

A republic of northern Europe, Lithuania is on the southeastern shore of the Baltic Sea. Area: 65,301 sq km (25,213 sq mi). Pop. (1992 est.): 3,802,000. Cap.: Vilnius. Monetary unit: Lithuanian coupon or talonas (a transitional quasi currency) replaced the ruble from October 1. Presidents of the Supreme Council in 1992, Vytautas Landsbergis and, from November 25, Algirdas Brazauskas; prime ministers, Gedimanas Vagnorius, Aleksandras Abisala from July 21, and, from December 2, Bronislovas Lubys.

Parliamentary elections in 1992 produced a shock result, with former Communists securing an absolute majority in the legislature and announcing that they intended to develop a more pragmatic relationship with Moscow. In the first round, on October 25, the Lithuanian Democratic Labour Party (LDLP), headed by Algirdas Brazauskas, the former Communist Party leader, obtained 44.7% of the vote, while the nationalist Lithuanian Reform Movement (Sajudis) won only 19.8%. In the second round, on November 15, the LDLP was again the clear winner, with 73 of the 141 seats to Sajudis' 30.

The LDPD favoured a slower move to a market economy. It intended to form a coalition government, not wishing to be held solely responsible for the country's economic misery.   (MARTIN MCCAULEY)

This article updates the *Macropædia* article BALTIC STATES: *Lithuania*.

LUXEMBOURG

The Benelux country of Luxembourg is a landlocked constitutional monarchy in western Europe. Area: 2,586 sq km (999 sq mi). Pop. (1992 est.): 387,000. Cap.: Luxembourg. Monetary unit: Luxembourg franc, at par with the Belgian franc, with (Oct. 5, 1992) a free rate of Lux F 28.85 to U.S. $1 (Lux F 49.05 = £1 sterling). Grand duke, Jean; prime minister in 1992, Jacques Santer.

On July 2, 1992, Luxembourg became the second member country to ratify the European Communities (EC) Treaty on European Union. The parliament voted 51–6 to approve the Maastricht Treaty, which called for the unification of the economic, political, and security policies of the 12 EC countries. Ireland had ratified the treaty in June, while Denmark had rejected it. All 12 EC member nations would have to ratify the pact before it could take effect.

Luxembourg's approval came after heated debate over a provision that would allow voting rights to foreigners. Finally, the parliament agreed to negotiate an exemption to the provision allowing citizens of one of the EC countries who lived in a different nation the right to vote and stand for office in local elections. This was a major concern in Luxembourg, where about one-third of the country's nearly 400,000 inhabitants were foreigners, mostly EC nationals from Italy and Portugal.

A Luxembourg court ruling in July delayed a proposed settlement to creditors of the failed Bank of Credit and Commerce International. Regulators had shut down the scandal-ridden bank a year earlier. The bank's main holding company had been based in Luxembourg, although the majority shareholder was the emirate of Abu Dhabi, United Arab Emirates. On February 21, Abu Dhabi offered a settlement that included $1.7 billion in cash in addition to the proceeds of the liquidation to pay off the bank's creditors and depositors. Although this would repay creditors only some 30 to 40% of losses, on October 22 the court agreed to the plan to let the payout begin.   (ANNE ROBY)

MACEDONIA

A landlocked republic of the central Balkans, Macedonia borders Yugoslavia to the north, Bulgaria to the east, Greece to the south, and Albania to the west. Area: 25,713 sq km (9,928 sq mi). Pop. (1992 est.): 2,050,000. Cap.: Skopje. Monetary unit: denar (transitional quasi currency introduced April 1992), with (Oct. 5, 1992) a par value of 360 denars = DM 1 (508 denars = U.S. $1 and 863 denars = £1 sterling). President in 1992, Kiro Gligorov; prime minister from August 17, Branko Crvenkovski.

Unlike Bosnia and Hercegovina, Croatia, and Slovenia, Macedonia remained unrecognized throughout 1992 by the European Communities (EC) and the United States (though it was recognized by Bulgaria, Russia, and Turkey). The main reason was Greece's objection that the name of the new state was the same as that of its own northern province of Macedonia and thus—in Greece's view—a potential vehicle of Slav Macedonian expansionism. By the end of January Macedonia complained that it was being subjected to an economic blockade both by Greece and by Serbia and appealed to the EC for help. At a meeting in April, however, EC members appeared to accept Greece's objections and instituted a search for a compromise name. Greece refused to accept any mention—even as an adjective—of the word *Macedonia* in the republic's name and also refused to take as sufficient reassurance a special clause in the preamble to the Macedonian constitution disclaiming any territorial ambitions.

Clashes between members of the Albanian minority in Skopje and Macedonian police on November 6 led to the death of one Albanian and the wounding of four. Fears of a deteriorating internal situation that might lead to an international conflict prompted EC governments to offer economic aid to Macedonia in November and caused the UN Security Council to send UN monitors to Macedonia.   (K.F. CVIIC)

This article updates the *Macropædia* article BALKAN STATES: *Macedonia*.

MALTA

The republic of Malta, a member of the Commonwealth, comprises the islands of Malta, Gozo, and Comino in the Mediterranean Sea between Sicily and Tunisia. Area: 316 sq km (122 sq mi). Pop. (1992 est.): 360,000. Cap.: Valletta. Monetary unit: Maltese lira, with (Oct. 5, 1992) an official rate of 0.30 lira to U.S. $1 (0.51 lira = £1 sterling). President in 1992, Censu Tabone; prime minister, Eddie Fenech Adami.

In the general election held on Feb. 22, 1992, six months before the end of the government's five-year term in office, the Nationalist Party, led by Prime Minister Eddie Fenech Adami, was again returned with an increased majority. Following the election, the Malta Labour Party, the one-party parliamentary opposition, elected Alfred Sant as its new leader. The general government policy continued to be one of liberalization, in line with Malta's aspiration to become a full member of the European Communities. Import barriers were reduced, and the future introduction of a value-added tax was announced.

Queen Elizabeth II visited the island in May. Her visit was climaxed by the inauguration of the Siege Bell Monument to commemorate those who fell in World War II in the defense of the "Island Fortress of Malta." The 50th anniversary of the award of the George Cross to the Maltese people was also celebrated.

Tourism, the island's main industry, registered an all-time high of one million visitors. There was a move to upgrade the industry by attracting more affluent tourists, which included the provision of five-star hotels. Malta was also being developed as a hub for cruise liners, while a modern international airport was inaugurated in February. The banking sector was improving its services to cater to an international clientele. The Bank of Valletta International Limited emerged in October as Malta's first offshore bank. There was a steady increase in business at the free port and in the number of ships that were registered under the Malta flag, and a cable television system was launched.

(ALBERT GANADO)

MOLDOVA

A landlocked republic of the extreme northeastern Balkans, Moldova borders Ukraine on the north, northeast, and southeast and Romania on the west. Area: 33,700 sq km (13,000 sq mi). Pop. (1992 est.) 4,394,000. Cap.: Chisinau. Monetary unit: ruble, with (Oct. 5, 1992) a free rate of 316.82 rubles = U.S. $1 (538.59 rubles = £1 sterling). President in 1992, Mircea Snegur; prime ministers, Valeriu Muravschi and, from July 1, Andrei Sangheli.

Fighting continued sporadically during the year in the region of Moldova east of the Dniester River, which was seeking independence. Russians and Ukrainians together formed a majority in that region, which occupies the eastern part of Moldova, and the Russian 14th Army was also stationed there. The latter provided arms and often troops to the insurgents, helping them to defeat the Moldovan army in several battles, notably that for Bendery in June. The Russian army was not wholly under the command of Moscow. A convention signed by Pres. Boris Yeltsin of Russia and Moldovan Pres. Mircea Snegur resulted in a cease-fire in July.

During the year Moldova moved closer to unification with Romania, though some feared that this eventuality would fuel the desire of the Slav separatists to join Russia. Moldova remained nominally within the Commonwealth of Independent States throughout 1992. The economic situation was difficult, and the nation's financial leaders hoped that membership in the International Monetary Fund and World Bank would lead to hard currency loans.

(MARTIN MCCAULEY)

This article updates the *Macropædia* article BALKAN STATES: *Moldova.*

MONACO

A sovereign principality on the northern Mediterranean coast, Monaco is bounded on land by the French département of Alpes-Maritimes. Area: 1.95 sq km (0.75 sq mi). Pop. (1992 est.): 30,300. Monetary unit: French franc, with (Oct. 5, 1992) a free rate of F 4.78 to U.S. $1 (F 8.12 = £1 sterling). Chief of state, Prince Rainier III; minister of state in 1992, Jacques Dupont.

The thriving economy of Monaco pushed the tiny principality to seek to expand its territory. Having already reclaimed 16 ha (40 ac) of land from the sea, in April the government announced a plan to build a floating suburb comprising pontoons. Apartments and office space for some 2,000 people would be constructed over the pontoons, with space for parking in the submerged section. The floating structure would be linked to Fontvieille, the suburb developed on the reclaimed land. In addition, it was announced that the France–Italy railway line would be placed underground to provide more space.

Tourism, which represented about 25% of the gross domestic product, continued to thrive. Of the 3.5 million visitors each year, some 240,000 remained for overnight stays. The banking industry continued to prosper with some 40 banks, twice the number of 10 years earlier. Monaco's status as a tax haven (except for citizens of France) had attracted a wealth of international deposits.

In July the Vatican announced that it had annulled the first marriage of Princess Caroline to Philippe Junot of France. The ruling would allow the princess to remarry in the Roman Catholic Church. (ANNE ROBY)

This article updates the *Micropædia* article MONACO.

NETHERLANDS, THE

A constitutional monarchy of northwestern Europe, The Netherlands, a Benelux country, is on the North Sea. Area: 41,863 sq km (16,163 sq mi). Pop. (1992 est.): 15,163,000. Cap., Amsterdam; seat of government, The Hague. Monetary unit: Netherlands guilder, with (Oct. 5, 1992) a free rate of 1.58 guilders to U.S. $1 (2.69 guilders = £1 sterling). Queen, Beatrix; prime minister in 1992, Ruud Lubbers.

On Feb. 7, 1992, the formal signing of the Treaty on European Union took place in Maastricht in the southern part of The Netherlands. The ceremony marked the culmination of the summit conference of government leaders of the 12 European Communities (EC) countries, held Dec. 9–10, 1991, in Maastricht. During this conference, chaired by Dutch Prime Minister Ruud Lubbers, agreement was reached to establish a framework and time schedule for initiating a European Union. (See *European Affairs,* above.) In November the lower house of the Dutch parliament approved the treaty by acclamation. A month later Dutch farmers marched in protest against an EC-U.S. agriculture accord.

On February 28 the Dutch government decided to take part in UN peacekeeping operations in Yugoslavia. Initially, there were about 300 Dutch troops in the UN Protection Force (UNPROFOR) for Yugoslavia, but the number had grown to 700 by November 1. This brought to seven the international peacekeeping operations in which The Netherlands was taking part, five of them under the aegis

of the UN and two under the EC. The most significant Dutch contribution was the participation of 800 troops in the UN Transitional Authority in Cambodia. Peacekeeping actions, the end of the cold war, and the political need to lower defense costs led to a parliamentary debate on the maintenance of a system of general conscription. Minister of Defense Relus ter Beek was preparing for a possible transition to a small professional army.

At its general conference on March 13–14, the Labour Party (PvdA) elected a new, two-headed leadership. The chairmanship was taken over by Felix Rottenberg and Ruud Vreeman, who declared that their main mission was to steer the party out of crisis "by seeking the people." The crisis resulted from the party's responsibility, as a member of the governing coalition, for 1991 government measures reducing social security benefits, especially disability benefits. Besides being the object of numerous protests, the party had lost a significant number of members and had been forced to reorganize its management and finances.

On September 15—the traditional third Tuesday in September, or Prinsjesdag—Queen Beatrix gave her speech opening the new parliamentary year. In the budget estimates, the government declared that important goals such as reduction of the deficit were being reached. On the other hand, there was concern over the slowdown in the growth of employment. The government forecast further spending cuts in the long term to help insulate the Dutch economy from the international recession. The position of the government within the parliament was very stable, thanks to strong support for the government parties, the Christian Democratic Appeal and the PvdA.

In the evening of October 4 an Israeli El Al Boeing 747 cargo plane lost two of its engines shortly after takeoff from Schiphol Airport and crashed in Amsterdam. The jet demolished two 10-story apartment buildings, wiped out 80 apartments, and caused a huge fire. The accident was the worst air crash ever to occur in The Netherlands. The people living in the building were mainly of African (Ghanaian) and Caribbean origin (Netherlands Antilles and Suriname). A number were illegal immigrants, and this, together with the fact that many of the victims could not be found or were burned beyond recognition, made estimation of the casualties very difficult. At first, officials expected that 250 to 300 had been killed, but later estimates were revised to the astonishingly low figure of about 70 people, including three Israeli crew members and a passenger; only 31 of the victims could be identified. A week after the disaster more than 20,000 citizens joined in a moving memorial service. Among those present were Prime Minister Lubbers, Crown Prince Willem-Alexander, Suriname's Pres. Ronald Venetiaan, Prime Minister Maria Liberia-Peters from the Antilles, and Israeli and Ghanaian representatives.

(KLAAS J. HOEKSEMA)

See also *Dependent States,* below.

NORWAY

A constitutional monarchy of northern Europe, Norway occupies the western part of the Scandinavian Peninsula, with coastlines on the Skagerrak, the North Sea, the Norwegian Sea, and the Arctic Ocean. Area: 323,878 sq km (125,050 sq mi), excluding the Svalbard Archipelago and Jan Mayen Island. Pop. (1992 est.): 4,283,000. Cap.: Oslo. Monetary unit: Norwegian krone, with (Oct. 5, 1992) a free rate of 5.75 kroner to U.S. $1 (9.78 kroner = £1 sterling). King, Harald V; prime minister in 1992, Gro Harlem Brundtland.

In many ways, the Norwegian economic scene remained sombre in 1992. The unemployment rate reached 7.5% by the end of September, and the number of bankruptcies was up compared with a year earlier. The world recession kept demand and prices for key Norwegian exports low. The kroner value per barrel of oil exported fell with the decline in the value of the U.S. dollar, the currency in which oil is traded on world markets. Although oil and gas output from the fields on Norway's shelf rose significantly during the year—to an estimated 130 million tons of oil equivalents, from 118 million tons in 1991—the value of petroleum exports, including pipeline transport, was expected to be 2.3 billion kroner below the 1991 total of 98.3 billion kroner. On the other hand, investment in oil- and gas-production installations and pipelines remained at a high level. The minority Labour government's budget for 1993, introduced on October 6, foresaw a real rise in these investments of more than 25% from 1991 to 1993 and said this alone would boost domestic demand by about 1.5% of the gross national product.

In the troubled banking and financial sector, an important event was the failure of an ambitious and costly bid by the country's largest insurance group, UNI Storebrand, to take over a Swedish insurance concern, Skandia. The venture cost the group several billion kroner, and in August it had to be put under public administration—the equivalent of going bankrupt. This created serious problems on the Norwegian securities market, as did the failure, soon afterward, of a major finance company, Investa. The Bank of Norway cushioned the impact by reaffirming its commitment to provide liquidity support to mortgage companies and by extending this commitment to include finance companies.

The Norwegian krone weathered the September turmoil on European currency markets considerably better than many other currencies. When the Swedish krona came under severe pressure in September, the Bank of Norway was able to maintain the krone's value with far less drastic interest rate increases than those seen in Sweden. On December 10, however, Norway allowed the krone to float because of "the general lack of trust in fixed exchange rates on the markets." It suffered a 5% devaluation against other European currencies.

In June, Prime Minister Gro Harlem Brundtland said Norway would resume commercial catching of minke whales in 1993. The announcement provoked heated criticism from environmentalists around the world, coupled with threats to boycott Norwegian products. Previous Norwegian governments had been unwilling to risk such boycotts, despite strong pressure from the whale boat owners in northern Norway. Many saw Brundtland's move as a bid to win back the goodwill of northern Norwegian fishermen, who were critical of the government's plans to make Norway a member of the European Economic Area (EEA). The EEA treaty, which would link the European Communities (EC) and the European Free Trade Association in a 19-nation single market, effective Jan. 1, 1993, would give EC fishermen increased access to Norway's fishery resources.

Fishermen were not alone in their opposition to the treaty. All the country's green organizations were against it because as an EEA member Norway would have to accept EC environmental standards and regulations—in many cases less stringent than Norwegian ones. Because the EEA treaty would introduce free movement of labour within the 19-nation market, offshore unions feared it might lead to "social dumping"—the import of workers from EEA countries where unions were weak and pay and conditions poorer than in Norway. Norway ratified the treaty in late October. Brundtland saw Norwegian accession to the EEA as only a stopgap solution to what she called "the problem of Norway's relationship with the new Europe," and she planned to put the matter of full EC membership to a vote.

On November 19, with her backing, the Norwegian Storting (parliament) voted to apply to join the EC. (FAY GJESTER)
See also *Dependent States,* below.

POLAND

A republic of eastern Europe, Poland is on the Baltic Sea. Area: 312,683 sq km (120,727 sq mi). Pop. (1992 est.): 38,429,000. Cap.: Warsaw. Monetary unit: zloty, with (Oct. 5, 1992) a free rate of 14,199 zlotys to U.S. $1 (25,139 zlotys = £1 sterling). President in 1992, Lech Walesa; prime ministers, Jan Olszewski, Waldemar Pawlak from June 5, and, from July 8, Hanna Suchocka.

Midway through 1992 the prognosis for political stability and economic recovery in Poland was not good. Jan Olszewski's government, formed after the October 1991 general elections, had been ousted on the night of June 4 amid rumours of military coups and accusations of secret police links that reached up to Pres. Lech Walesa himself. This maneuver was carried out by a coalition of forces that were held together by little more than opposition to the incumbents. The president's choice as the next prime minister was Waldemar Pawlak, the young leader of the ex-Communist Polish Peasant Party (PSL). Faced with the prospect of political leadership slipping away from the post-Solidarity alliance, the traditional right-of-centre Christian National Union (ZChN) and the Democratic Union (UD) of Tadeusz Mazowiecki, along with four other parties (including Jan Bielecki's Liberals), buried their differences and put Hanna Suchocka (*see* BIOGRAPHIES), Poland's first female prime minister, into office.

Her government survived for the rest of the year largely because no acceptable alternative existed. As the main Solidarity parties, such as the Centre Agreement (PC) and the UD, continued to splinter—adding to the complexity of Poland's political scene, which now contained no fewer than 159 political parties—the ex-Communists became the single largest parliamentary grouping. They were accompanied in opposition by the right-wing Confederation for an Independent Poland (KPN) from the other end of the political spectrum. Meanwhile, various ex-parliamentary groupings and new coalitions, such as the Movement for the Republic, which included the victims of the June 4 ouster, were seeking to establish themselves. The role of the Roman Catholic Church remained controversial, with continuing conflict over such issues as religious education, church property, the role of the clergy in industrial disputes, and abortion.

Despite the industrial unrest that swept through parts of the country in late summer, Poland's economic performance contained some hopeful elements. The industrial and building sector registered low but discernible growth in the second and third quarters of the year, and the rate of increase in unemployment dropped slightly. The total number of unemployed was expected to reach 2.7 million, or 14.7% of the work force, by year's end.

The government moved to introduce a package of jobs measures that included retraining, increased public works, reform of employment exchanges, and incentives for investment in especially depressed areas. Meanwhile, productivity improved, and earnings from exports rose 11.8% while imports remained steady. Inflation at the end of the third quarter stood at 46% on an annual basis. Agricultural production, badly hit by prolonged drought, recorded a 14% decline overall. With between 60 and 80% of the population considering their material situation to be worse than in 1989, the last year of the Communist government, Suchocka's Cabinet prepared a set of social security measures to monitor and alleviate poverty.

Hanna Suchocka, the first woman to serve as prime minister of Poland, attends a meeting of Solidarity in Gdansk. In early July, after a stalemate of five weeks, a coalition of parties in the Sejm (parliament) agreed to support Suchocka for the position.

WOJTEK LASKI—SIPA

However, all areas of state activity were threatened by a budget crisis and the government's continuing inability to pass appropriate legislation. The 1992 budget deficit was forecast at 8–9% of gross domestic product, and it was difficult to see how it could be lower in 1993. Pensions in particular were seen as prime targets for the cuts being forced on the government by International Monetary Fund (IMF) pressures, and they provided a flash point in the budget debates in the Sejm (parliament). On November 6 the Sejm voted to accept the government's plan to increase sales taxes and reduce spending. The IMF approved of the vote and on November 24 agreed to allow Poland to draw on about $700 million; the IMF approval also meant that Poland's international debt would be substantially reduced by creditor nations. In mid-December more than 300,000 coal miners went on strike in protest against low wages and a government reorganization that would eliminate 180,000 jobs in 10 years. On December 31 the government signed an agreement with the strikers that called for a quick bailout of indebted mines and additional state subsidies.

The government embarked on a controversial "pact for the state enterprise," to be negotiated between the unions and the government. Employees of privatized enterprises would receive 10% of the shares in the enterprise free, while 60% would be distributed to national investment funds run by foreign experts for sale to Polish citizens. The government was banking on considerable budget revenues from this exercise. There were in 1992 1.6 million nonagricultural private enterprises in Poland employing 65% of building workers, 85% of retail-trade employees, and a third of industrial employees.

In foreign relations, a treaty with Ukraine was ratified and one with Latvia was proposed, while relations with Lithuania improved. Incidents involving German citizens and the increased visibility of the German minority sparked discussions on regionalization and greater local autonomy. Silesia in particular might look to Germany if Warsaw did not act to alleviate its disastrous environmental situation. Both German and Polish nationalist groups were making political capital from such incidents as Wehrmacht graffiti and vandalism of town signs and gravestones.

The main emphasis in Polish foreign policy remained the establishment of closer links with the European Communities (EC), following the 1991 agreement on associate membership, and improved ties with the other Visograd Triangle

countries (Hungary and Czechoslovakia) in the form of a free-trade zone starting in 1993. The latter was seen as a step toward EC membership. The departure of most of the ex-Soviet military—some 6,000 personnel remained to oversee the transit of troops from Germany—left an enormous (and still incompletely assessed) legacy of environmental despoliation. Furthermore, the military installations left behind by the departing Russians were in the wrong place. The perceived threat to Poland was now in the east rather than the west, a point underlined by the instability in the former Soviet Union and the increase in foreign nationals using Poland as a transit point to the West.

(GEORGE KOLANKIEWICZ)

PORTUGAL

A republic of southwestern Europe, metropolitan Portugal is on the Atlantic coast of the Iberian Peninsula, which it shares with Spain. Area: 92,389 sq km (35,672 sq mi), including the Azores and Madeira island groups/archipelagoes in the Atlantic. Pop. (1992 est.): 9,848,000. Cap.: Lisbon. Monetary unit: Portuguese escudo, with (Oct. 5, 1992) a free rate of 125.74 escudos to U.S. $1 (213.75 escudos = £1 sterling). President in 1992, Mario Soares; prime minister, Anibal Cavaco Silva.

Apart from a Cabinet reshuffle in March, when the minister of education, Antonio Couto dos Santos, was replaced by Gomes Durão, the government's attention in 1992 was focused overseas as a result of Portugal's presidency of the European Communities (EC). The end of the six-month term in June was marked by a meeting of EC heads of state and of government and the issuing of the Lisbon Declaration, which covered efforts made to complete the single market, reform the common agricultural policy (CAP), and reach agreement on structural funding and EC budget reform.

Shortly before Portugal handed over the presidency of the EC to the U.K., the EC finance ministers reached agreement on key aspects of the investment services directive, paving the way for the creation of an EC-wide market in financial services. After Jan. 1, 1993, banks and stockbrokers would have the right to establish branches in any member nation once they had authorization from that nation. A minimum capital of 5 million European Currency Units was required.

As well as a better sense of integration with Europe, EC membership also brought substantial financial benefits to Portugal, with transfers of EC funds totaling about 550 billion escudos and another 900 billion escudos promised by the end of 1993. Because there was broad consensus between the Social Democrats and the Socialist Party on the EC, Portugal decided not to hold a referendum on the Maastricht Treaty but instead to leave approval to the Assembly. Both parties believed that between them they could engineer the two-thirds majority needed to pass various minor changes to the constitution required by the treaty. On December 10 the Assembly ratified the treaty by a vote of 207–22.

The government during the year concentrated on efforts to modernize the nation's economy, focusing on long-overdue reforms to the civil and health services, with the latter to be partly privatized. Although the Socialist Party should have been leading the opposition to the measures, its job was complicated by the fact that many of its policies were similar to those of the Social Democrats. After its defeat in the 1991 elections, the Socialist Party elected Antonio Guterres as secretary-general, with the hope that he would revitalize the party's fortunes. However, the honeymoon was short-lived, and the factions continued their infighting. In

March the Christian Democrats also replaced their leader when Manuel Monteiro was elected president; the party won only 4.4% of the vote in the 1991 elections.

After five years of spectacular growth, Portugal's economy began to slow in 1991, and the trend continued in 1992, providing an uncomfortable reminder of how vulnerable the nation remained to changes in conditions abroad. Both investment and exports stagnated as the crises in agriculture and the textiles sector deepened. Public expectations had to adjust abruptly. Especially in the public sector, strikes took place against government efforts to keep wage increases to levels compatible with the official 8% inflation target for 1992. To this end the government agreed to a 10% raise in the basic public-sector wage. The level of the increase made it difficult for the private sector to settle for less and put further pressure on Portugal's firms to remain competitive. There were signs that the government was toughening its stance; it introduced a law in the Assembly making it more difficult to organize a strike.

The 1993 budget aimed to reduce the deficit from above 5% of gross domestic product to under 4%. Public expenditure was set to fall in real terms, as would wages in the public sector if the government was successful in persuading the unions to accept 5.5% pay raises in support of the target of reducing inflation to 5–7% in 1993. The government planned to cut current expenditure by 5% and continue its streamlining of the civil and health services; the police and armed services were also to be reduced in size. All those measures fomented predictable protests, but the government, secure in its majority, pressed on, calculating that there would be enough time to rebuild popularity before general elections in 1995.

On October 6 Portugal's first private television station, SIC (Sociedade Independente de Communicação), began transmissions. Headed by former prime minister Pinto Balsemão, it was competing directly with Portugal's two government-owned TV networks in terms of timing, programs, and content. In 1993 TVI (TV Independente) was scheduled to start transmissions.   (MICHAEL WOOLLER)

See also *Dependent States,* below.

ROMANIA

A republic on the Balkan Peninsula in southeastern Europe, Romania has a coastline on the Black Sea. Area: 237,500 sq km (91,699 sq mi). Pop. (1992 est.): 23,332,000. Cap.: Bucharest. Monetary unit: leu, with (Oct. 5, 1992) a free rate of 440.65 lei to U.S. $1 (749.10 lei = £1 sterling). President in 1992, Ion Iliescu; prime ministers, Theodor Stolojan and, from November 4, Nicolae Vacaroiu.

Romania, a byword for political turbulence since the overthrow of Nicolae Ceausescu in December 1989, presented an image of relative stability throughout 1992. The government headed by Theodor Stolojan vigorously applied the economic reform program recommended by the International Monetary Fund (IMF), reducing state subsidies on consumer goods by 25% on May 1 and by another 15% on September 1. Under an agreement signed with the IMF at the beginning of June, the Romanian government declared it would restrict the monthly rate of inflation to 1.5% by December 1992, halt the decline in economic activity, and continue to implement rapid economic reform. Despite parliamentary elections in September, the reformist momentum was maintained. Oil subsidies were further reduced in October, and a highly optimistic target for controlling inflation was set. Although privatization was one of the main planks of the reform program, the government's performance was checkered. More than 30% of confiscated lands remained

Romanian gypsies take up life in a rural camp in the northern part of the country after a rape led villagers to drive them from their homes. Gypsies in Romania and elsewhere continued to be subject to attacks in 1992 and were often being forced into extreme poverty.
JUDITH INGRAM—THE NEW YORK TIMES

in the hands of the state, and no new measures were taken to return nationalized property to original owners. Despite Romania's incoherent fiscal legislation, foreign investment rose by $118 million in the first half of 1992, bringing the total to $387 million since January 1990.

The country's economic difficulties were aggravated by the UN embargo against Serbia, which Romanian officials estimated would reduce revenues to industry, transport, and agriculture by $550 million. After allegations arose that Romania had broken those UN sanctions, Pres. Ion Iliescu and Prime Minister Stolojan invited Western observers to check Romanian compliance. At the end of September, U.S. and British customs inspectors arrived in the country.

The principal changes in the political scene included a split in the ruling National Salvation Front (FSN), which occurred at the FSN's convention on March 30. This resulted in the creation of a breakaway party called the Democratic National Salvation Front (FDSN) and in the formation of an effective alliance of opposition parties known as the Democratic Convention (DC). In the February local elections the DC won control of several major cities but, at the same time, the ultranationalist and xenophobic Romanian National Unity Party (PUNR) made significant gains, returning mayors to the Transylvanian cities of Cluj and Baia Mare. After the PUNR mayor of Cluj, Gheorghe Funar, issued an order on April 28 severely curtailing the constitutional right of freedom of assembly and Pres. Iliescu failed to address this violation, questions were raised about Iliescu's commitment to establishing a genuine democracy. Funar's unchecked abuse of human rights, notably his instruction to remove Hungarian-language signs from public buildings in Cluj, and Iliescu's tolerance of these measures were considered major reasons why in September the U.S. House of Representatives, by a vote of 283 to 88, rejected a recommendation to grant Romania most-favoured-nation status.

On April 25–26 the deposed monarch, King Michael, was allowed to make a brief visit to his country after an absence of 45 years. (He had set foot in the country for less than 12 hours in 1990.) His attendance at Easter mass in Suceava drew a crowd of several hundred thousand people. The king's popularity prompted the National Liberal Party (NLP) to try to persuade him to stand as a candidate in the September presidential elections. The unsuccessful move was widely seen as an attempt to split the opposition vote to help Iliescu. The electorate's verdict on this strategy resulted in the failure of the NLP to win any seats in the Assembly of Deputies or the Senate.

The joint parliamentary and presidential elections held on September 27 confirmed the gains made by the DC in the February local elections, but they were not enough to prevent Iliescu, a former Communist, from being returned as president for a second four-year term and his party, the breakaway FDSN, from becoming the largest single party in Parliament, with 114 seats in the Assembly of Deputies. The DC won 82 seats, and the FSN came in third with 43 seats. A notable outcome of the elections was the strong showing of extremist parties. The ultranationalist PUNR and the Great Romania Party won 30 and 16 seats, respectively. In the October 11 runoff ballot for the presidency, Iliescu won 61% of the vote, and his challenger, Emil Constantinescu of the DC, captured 39%. The FDSN, however, did not have a sufficient plurality to govern in its own right, and feverish discussions were held with smaller parties, including the FSN, in order to form a coalition. The elections left the extremist parties with considerable bargaining power, which they sought to exercise, while Iliescu was concerned with finding a prime minister, notably one who would signal to the West the new government's continuing commitment to the policies of economic reform recommended by the World Bank and the IMF. On November 3 Nicolae Vacaroiu, an official in the Ministry of Economy and Finance, was asked by the president to form a government.

(DENNIS J. DELETANT)

This article updates the *Macropædia* article BALKAN STATES: *Romania*.

RUSSIA

Russia is a federal republic occupying eastern and northeastern Europe and all of northern Asia. Area: 17,075,400 sq km (6,592,800 sq mi). Pop. (1992 est.): 149,469,000. Cap.: Moscow. Monetary unit: ruble, with (Oct. 5, 1992) a free rate of 316.82 rubles = U.S. $1 (538.59 rubles = £1 sterling). President in 1992, Boris Yeltsin; chairman of the Council of Ministers (prime minister) to June 15, Yeltsin; acting chairmen of the Council of Ministers (acting prime ministers) from June 15, Yegor Gaidar and, from December 14, Viktor Chernomyrdin.

Economic decline dominated Russian politics during 1992. In January price liberalization was introduced, but by the end of the year inflation had risen to about 30% monthly, money supply and budget deficits were out of control, the ruble had declined from 120 to the U.S. dollar in January to over 400 in November, convertibility of the ruble was off the agenda, the International Monetary Fund (IMF) was reluctant to get involved in the economic morass, privatization had hardly touched industry, and Pres. Boris Yeltsin was retreating from market reforms. The euphoria that had greeted the collapse of communism and the rise of Yeltsin had been dissipated amid a grim struggle for existence. Democracy and market forces by year's end were

perceived by the overwhelming majority of the population as devices to enable politicians, entrepreneurs, mafiosi, and the quick-witted to get rich. Politics had become a bore to most people. Yeltsin's popularity rating was down sharply as public anger welled up against him, for he had promised that no one would lose out during the transition to a market economy.

Nevertheless, by the end of the year the political situation had stabilized as Yeltsin cut deals with the industrialist opponents of the rapid transition to the market. There were hopes that the rapid depreciation of the ruble would be slowed down and that the IMF would play a more interventionist role in the economy. On the other hand, a vibrant, dynamic entrepreneurial culture was developing in Moscow and in many other parts of the country. These businesspeople concentrated on trade, however, while the manufacturing entrepreneurial culture was slow to emerge.

The Commonwealth of Independent States. The founding of the Commonwealth of Independent States (CIS) on Dec. 8, 1991, by Russia, Ukraine, and Belarus was motivated by two key considerations: to remove Pres. Mikhail Gorbachev by dissolving the U.S.S.R. and to provide an organization to permit the disentangling of the successor states from the old empire. Originally everyone appeared to agree that the goal was divorce. Misunderstandings that surfaced from the very beginning between Russia and Ukraine, however, led to bitter feuds during 1992. Russia never clearly defined its understanding of the CIS. Although the latter was not a state and had no government or secretariat, the former Soviet armed forces were under its command. Russia, which viewed itself as the successor state to the U.S.S.R., acquired the Soviet Union's seat on the UN Security Council and took over all Soviet embassies and properties abroad. The ruble was the currency of the CIS, and since all printing presses were in Russia, only it could emit currency. A Russian marshal was commander in chief of the CIS armed forces, but he was subordinate to Yeltsin. Russia did not clearly delineate its frontiers, and it was unclear whether a Russian nation existed. There were about 25 million ethnic Russians living in the other republics. Should Russia defend their interests, or should they come to some modus vivendi with the dominant ethnic majority in each state? This dilemma was never resolved, as there were conflicting views within the Russian leadership. The military and the

EPIX/SYGMA

Russian citizens show their support for Pres. Boris Yeltsin outside the Constitutional Court in Moscow, which was debating the legality of his 1991 ban of the Soviet and Russian Communist parties. In November the court upheld the ban but left certain related questions unresolved.

conservatives favoured an interventionist policy since they had not given up hope that a modified Soviet Union could again come into existence.

There were several CIS summits during the year, each in a different capital, and by the end of the year the CIS had coalesced into an inner and an outer core. The inner group (Russia, Belarus, Kazakhstan, Kyrgyzstan, and Uzbekistan) was dominated by Moscow and its interests. A major problem for Moscow was that, whereas the Russian central bank controlled currency emission, each national bank could issue ruble credits to its enterprises to pay for Russian imports. The concept of one economic space, or ruble zone, broke down as Russian inflation flowed into other states. The outer core (Ukraine, Moldova, Armenia, Azerbaijan, Turkmenistan, and Tajikistan) fragmented during the year. Ukraine left the ruble zone in November; the Moldovan and Azerbaijani parliaments failed to ratify their states' adherence to the CIS; Tajikistan was engulfed in a civil war; and Turkmenistan was forging closer links with Iran and Turkey. Russia signed many agreements with Kazakhstan, which underlined the close relations that Pres. Nursultan Nazarbayev of Kazakhstan was sedulously cultivating. In July Russia signed 21 military, economic, and other agreements with Belarus, involving a "high level of integration" of the two states and establishing the outline of a single political and economic space. Yegor Gaidar, acting Russian prime minister, viewed these as moves toward a confederation. However, Stanislau Shushkevich, the Belorussian head of state, contradicted this assessment and regarded membership in the CIS as temporary. Relations with Ukraine plumbed the depths during the year, with observers speaking of a "cold war" between the two powers and even the possibility of armed conflict. Various agreements were reached, but they always unraveled until Yeltsin and Ukrainian Pres. Leonid Kravchuk met in June and struck a wide-ranging deal. The Black Sea Fleet was withdrawn from CIS command and placed under joint Russian-Ukrainian command for three years.

Russia became involved in various other ethnic conflicts during 1992. The most serious were in Georgia, where South Ossetia and Abkhazia struggled for their independence from Tbilisi and called for Russian support. Eventually a tripartite peacekeeping force composed of Russians, Ossetians, and Georgians imposed a buffer zone in South Ossetia. Also, Russia recognized Georgia's independence for the first time. In September Russia and Georgia signed an agreement recognizing Abkhazia as part of Georgia, to the great disappointment of the separatists. Russian policy was confused at times, with Yeltsin consistently avoiding military intervention while the speaker of the Russian parliament threatened that Russia would annex South Ossetia. The Russian military in the region did not appear to be entirely under Yeltsin's control and wanted a more belligerent stance. In Moldova the Transdnistria republic's calls for recognition were ignored by Russia until June, when Russia performed a volte-face and sided with the separatists. Relations with Checheno-Ingushetia, nominally with Russia, were often tense. Russian troops were engaged in sporadic fighting in Tajikistan.

Domestic Politics. The Russian Federation came into existence on March 31 when the federal treaty was signed by 18 of the 20 sovereign republics within the federation, the Russian *krais* (territories) and oblasts, and the cities of Moscow and St. Petersburg. Tatarstan and Checheno-Ingushetia declined to sign. Tatarstan aimed to negotiate a separate agreement with the Russian Federation. Chechnia's goal was independence. The federal government was responsible for foreign policy, defense, and protection of human rights and ethnic minorities. Russian became the official language of the federation, although republics could also have their own official languages. Despite the treaty, regionalism was waxing stronger in Russia—oil-rich Tyumen oblast in western Siberia and Sakhalin Island in the Far East, for example, were determined to gain greater autonomy from Moscow.

Yeltsin rejected the opportunity to establish his own party after the failed hard-line coup in August 1991. He believed that he should be above party politics. This left him dependent on support from various parties and organizations, grouped in Democratic Russia. Its main platform was anticommunism, but it began to fall apart when confronted with such divisive issues as privatization. Gradually the conservative forces regained confidence and reorganized themselves. The Communists claimed that the ban on their party in 1991 was unconstitutional, and the government took the issue to the Constitutional Court. The state tried to use the proceedings to demonstrate, among other things, that the Communist Party had turned the state into an instrument of its power and that it had financed foreign Communist parties and terrorist organizations out of the state budget. In November the court ruled that the ban was constitutional. The Russian procurator's office began an investigation of the perpetrators of the attempted coup and tried but failed to call Gorbachev as a witness. By the end of the year it was too late to stage a trial of the accused since conservative opposition had become too strong. The same trend was visible in the Supreme Soviet, the parliament. The speaker, Ruslan Khasbulatov, consistently attempted to strengthen the authority of parliament by demanding that the government be subordinate to it and not to the president. Parliament, elected in March 1990 and containing a majority of former Communists, acted independently of the president on several occasions. For example, it declared invalid the transfer of the Crimea to Ukraine by Nikita Khrushchev in 1954. In October 1992, however, Yeltsin banned the parliament's private army, which had been under Khasbulatov's control.

At the Congress of People's Deputies (over 1,000 strong and from which the 252 members of the Supreme Soviet were elected) in April, the conservative forces strongly attacked the reform program presented by Gaidar, then finance minister, and won concessions from the president.

BILL SWERSEY—GAMMA LIAISON

Dishes are offered for sale at a street market in Moscow. It was estimated that in the city of Moscow alone nearly 10,000 traders were using such markets to sell goods, many of them imported, to earn a living or to supplement family income.

Three former leading Soviet officials joined the government. A centre-right coalition, Civic Union, formed during the summer. It combined four groups: the Democratic Party of Russia, led by Nikolay Travkin; the People's Party of Free Russia, headed by Vice Pres. Aleksandr Rutskoy; the Renewal Union, led by Arkady Volsky; and Smena (Change). Volsky was the spokesman for the Union of Industrialists and Entrepreneurs, which was dominated by the military-industrial complex. Civic Union became an influential faction within parliament. To the right of Civic Union was Russian Unity, a broad coalition of conservatives and former Communists who opposed market reform and wished to bring about Yeltsin's resignation. Political parties in the Western sense had not yet developed—their memberships were very small, and there was little party discipline. The precise relationship between Yeltsin and his Cabinet remained unclear. In order to stave off demands for the resignation of the government, Yeltsin cut various deals with the Civic Union just before the Congress of People's Deputies met in December. Market reforms would be slowed down, and the state would support the restructuring of key sectors of the economy.

During its December session the congress clashed with Yeltsin on a number of issues, and the conflict came to a head on December 9 when the congress refused to confirm Gaidar as prime minister. In an angry speech the next day Yeltsin described the congress as a "fortress of conservative and reactionary forces"; the congress responded by voting to take control of the parliamentary army. On December 12 Yeltsin and Khasbulatov agreed on a compromise that included the following provisions: (1) a national referendum on framing a new Russian constitution would be held in April 1993; (2) most of Yeltsin's emergency powers were extended until the referendum; (3) the congress asserted its right to nominate and vote on its own choices for prime minister; and (4) the congress gained the right to reject the president's choices to head the Defense, Foreign Affairs, Interior, and Security ministries. Yeltsin nominated Viktor Chernomyrdin to be prime minister on December 14, and the congress confirmed him.

The Economy. Yeltsin had to choose between two economic policy options: Gregory Yavlinksy's package, which envisaged the cooperation of most states, a common currency, and coordination of fiscal policy; or Gaidar's proposal that Russia proceed with liberalization and stabilization without consulting the other republics. Yeltsin chose the latter, and Gaidar's program was launched in January. It broke the pact signed by Russia and nine other republics in November 1991, which had envisaged common action. Liberalization resulted in rapid price increases that forced all the other republics to follow suit. Their central banks began to expand credit to support their industry and trade. It became clear that the common currency, the ruble, was destroying the common economic space as states put up trade barriers to protect their own goods. Russian enterprises were prevented from exporting freely to save themselves, and the Russian government kept the domestic prices of key export goods, such as oil, well below world levels. It sold licenses for their export, and this inevitably led to massive corruption. Stabilization involved a tight monetary policy (control of the money supply and interest rates). No fixed exchange rate for the ruble was set, and reducing the budget deficit was a key priority—it had climbed to 30% of gross national product in 1991. Structural change involved privatization, but this would affect only shops and other small-scale activities. It would take about two years to organize medium and large-scale privatizations. Prices were not really free. Foreign trade was not liberalized significantly. Export quotas and taxes were imposed, and imports were centralized. However, the state quickly discovered it could not collect export taxes since exporters left their hard-currency earnings in foreign banks. Russia's ability to impose cross-border taxes turned out to be very limited. Inflation declined from 220% in January to 9% in August. The money supply grew by 9–14% monthly.

The CIS grain harvest was 182.4 million metric tons, which was not sufficient to cover the grain needs of the region. The number of private farmers grew rapidly to reach approximately 140,000 in Russia, but they cultivated only 2% of the total land. An estimated 3,000 private farms in the CIS had folded owing to high prices and shortages. During 1992 gross domestic product and industrial output were expected to drop 15%.

Foreign Policy. A vigorous debate developed between those who believed that Russia should identify with western Europe and North America and those who thought it should be a bridge between Europe and Asia. The former, headed by Foreign Minister Andrey Kozyrev, had the better of the argument. Yeltsin traveled far and wide to cultivate support for his policies, taking in most of the Group of Seven countries. In November he signed a bilateral treaty in Britain—the first between the two states since 1766—which was to provide a framework for a raft of other accords. In South Korea, also in November, he pledged to abandon military support for North Korea. The elusive prize, a pot of money, was denied him. The IMF promised $24 billion but provided less than $2 billion. On December 29 Russia and the U.S. announced that they had agreed on the text of the second Strategic Arms Reduction Treaty (START II). The pact would reduce each nation's nuclear arsenal by about two-thirds.   (MARTIN McCAULEY)

SAN MARINO

The republic of San Marino is a landlocked enclave in northeastern Italy. Area: 61 sq km (24 sq mi). Pop. (1992 est.): 23,600. Cap.: San Marino. Monetary unit: Italian lira, with (Oct. 5, 1992) a free rate of 1,315 lire to U.S. $1 (2,236 lire = £1 sterling). The republic is governed by two *capitani reggenti*, or coregents, appointed every six months by a popularly elected Great and General Council. Executive power rests with the Congress of State, headed by the coregents and composed of three secretaries of state and seven ministers.

The admission of San Marino to the UN made 1992 a year of historic importance. Presented by Austria and Spain and endorsed by 100 member states, the proposal to admit the world's oldest republic to full membership was accepted unanimously. UN Secretary-General Boutros Boutros-Ghali expressed particular sympathy for the hopes and aspirations of the small countries of the world.

The republic's active presence in international affairs was also felt at the January meeting of the Conference on Security and Cooperation in Europe, which acknowledged membership of the ex-Soviet republics. On that occasion the secretary of state for foreign and political affairs, Gabriele Gatti, exchanged invitations for official visits with the representative of Slovenia. In September San Marino joined the International Monetary Fund.

Economic activities benefited from an agreement signed with the European Communities late in 1991 that put San Marino on an equal footing with full EC member states in regard to tariffs and trade. In the same period, a bilateral agreement signed with Italy gave the republic greater freedom in minting currency, which circulates freely in Italian national territory. Another highlight in bilateral relations was the official visit of the coregents early in 1992 to Pope John Paul II.

In March the Social Democrats, having withdrawn from their alliance with the Progressive Democratic (formerly Communist) Party, formed a coalition government with the majority Christian Democrats.   (GREGORY O. SMITH)

This article updates the *Micropædia* article SAN MARINO.

SLOVENIA

A republic of the extreme northwestern Balkans, Slovenia borders Austria to the north, Hungary to the east, Croatia to the southeast and south, the Adriatic Sea to the southwest, and Italy to the west. Area: 20,256 sq km (7,821 sq mi). Pop. (1992 est.): 1,985,000. Cap.: Ljubljana. Monetary unit: tolar, with (Oct. 12, 1992) a free rate of 84.65 tolars to U.S. $1 (144.65 tolars = £1 sterling). President in 1992, Milan Kucan; prime ministers, Lojze Peterle and, from May 14, Janez Drnovsek.

On Jan. 15, 1992, Slovenia, along with Croatia, was recognized as an independent nation by the European Communities (EC), and it was received into the UN on May 22. In December Slovenia signed an agreement on economic and commercial cooperation with the EC, similar to the one the former Yugoslavia had had. Slovenia's reputation abroad remained good throughout the year despite two events: the murder on June 7 of Ivan Kramberger, an amiable eccentric and a member of the Homeland Peasant Party; and the relatively strong public popularity of Zmago Jelincic, a leader of Slovenian nationalists whose main platform was "Slovenia for the Slovenes."

Slovenia entered 1992 with a steadily growing political crisis in the fairly broad governing coalition presided over by Lojze Peterle, the Christian Democratic Party leader. The Peterle government fell on a vote of no confidence on April 22, and Peterle was replaced as prime minister on May 14 by Janez Drnovsek, a leader of the Liberal Democrat Party and a Slovene member of the old Yugoslav Collective Presidency during the period before the collapse of Yugoslavia. Foreign Minister Dimitrij Rupel and Interior Minister Igor Bavcar, who had resigned from the Peterle Cabinet, decided to serve under Drnovsek.

Some 76% of the electorate turned out in the nation's first Western-style multiparty elections, held on December 6. The incumbent president, Milan Kucan of the Party of Democratic Reform (the former Communists), was reelected to a five-year term with a majority of 63.8%. In the legislative elections, eight parties gained seats in the National Assembly. Drnovsek's Liberal Democrats took the largest number of seats, with 23.7% of the vote, followed by the Christian Democrats (14.5%), the Associated List (13.5%), and the right-wing Slovene National Party (9.8%). Drnovsek then formed a new coalition government.

Thanks to its tough monetary policy, Slovenia managed to keep its inflation rate low. However, industrial production fell in 1992 by 30% and employment by 20% compared with 1991. The annual inflation rate was 117%, which was low in comparison with other nations in eastern and central Europe. Slovenia's exports totaled $3 billion in the period from January to December 1992, and imports were worth $2.9 billion. Slovenia continued its cooperation with Austria and Italy during the year, though there was some irritation with the latter because of anti-Slovene propaganda from Trieste, in particular. Relations with Croatia were strained because of a number of disputes, ranging from those about fishing rights in territorial waters to those over whether the Slovenes or the Croats had the right to look after certain Roman Catholic parishes on the Croat-Slovene border.
                                        (K.F. CVIIC)

This article updates the *Macropædia* article BALKAN STATES: *Slovenia*.

SPAIN

A constitutional monarchy of southwestern Europe with coastlines on the Bay of Biscay, the Atlantic Ocean, and the Mediterranean Sea, Spain shares the Iberian Peninsula with Portugal; it includes the Balearic and Canary island groups, in the Mediterranean and the Atlantic, respectively, and enclaves in northern Morocco. Area: 504,783 sq km (194,898 sq mi). Pop. (1992 est.): 39,085,000. Cap.: Madrid. Monetary unit: Spanish peseta, with (Oct. 5, 1992) a free rate of 100.47 pesetas to U.S. $1 (170.80 pesetas = £1 sterling). King, Juan Carlos I; prime minister in 1992, Felipe González Márquez.

The year 1992 was a special one for Spain, marked by the Olympic Games at Barcelona, the Universal Exposition in Seville, the celebrations of Columbus' landfall in Ibero-America 500 years earlier, and Madrid acting as cultural capital of Europe. (See *Sidebar*.) In the political sphere, Felipe González Márquez and the Socialists (PSOE) celebrated 10 years in power. Spain's economy was affected by a slowdown in demand from overseas, although it continued to grow at a faster rate than its European Communities (EC) partners. However, it was generally accepted that conditions would become tougher as the European single market took effect and regional aid from EC funds became conditional on continuing economic convergence with EC partners and compliance with tough new environmental laws. In the autumn the Cortes (parliament) overwhelmingly ratified the Maastricht Treaty on European economic and political union.

The Basque and Catalan regional governments continued to strive for greater transfers of power. The Basque terrorist organization Euzkadi ta Azkatasuna (ETA) made sporadic attacks on military and civilian targets, but it kept to its offer of a truce during the Olympic Games despite the refusal of the Madrid government to enter negotiations with it. Roundups of ETA leaders in France and heavy police surveillance during the Games gave the government's policy more credibility than had appeared possible at the start of the year. Ongoing political malaise was deepened by corruption scandals in the public and financial sectors. After a highly public row with González, Jordi Pujol, the head of Catalonia's regional government, withdrew the offer of his nationalist party's support in the Cortes, making PSOE accommodation with the Basque Nationalist Party more likely.

González' intention was to continue the policies needed to maintain Spain's tie with the European Monetary Union. However, tightening an already slowing economy had implications for unemployment, at 17.5% already the highest in the EC. The leading trade unions threatened work stoppages in November and December to protest government efforts to freeze public-sector salaries, but in November Madrid backed away from its plans to impose stiff rules on the unions. This enabled González to reach the government's first agreement with the unions since the December 1988 general strike. The unions promised to maintain essential services in 17 sectors in case of strike action. To get the agreement, however, the government was forced to drop clauses from a controversial law on strikes that would have led to automatic dismissal of strikers who failed to provide minimum services during a work stoppage.

The peseta was devalued by 5% during the European currency crisis in September, and the government instituted special exchange controls. Economy Minister Carlos Solchaga stated that the option of withdrawing from the European exchange-rate mechanism, following the lead of the Italian lira and British pound sterling, was not a valid one for the peseta. The secretary of state for the economy,

Pédro Pérez, commented that the effects of the devaluation on Spain's inflation rate were difficult to predict. The official target for inflation in 1992 was 6.4%, as against 5.5% in 1991.

A massive exodus of foreign investors in late September, combined with the Treasury's failure to attract buyers at its debt auction, disposed both the government and the central bank to agree that an increase in the official interest rate might be needed to offset the effects of the exchange controls on foreign investment. In early October the central bank attempted to boost confidence by partially lifting the exchange controls. The bank removed controls on nonresident peseta deposits and loans but retained a 100% deposit for nonresidents on currency swap and forward operations, which the authorities viewed as purely speculative. The bank also lowered obligatory deposit requirements on foreign currency held by Spanish institutions. These measures failed to stabilize the currency, however, and on November 22 the government devalued the peseta by a further 6% and lifted the exchange controls entirely.

In the year to August 1992, the budget deficit rose 84% to 1.4 trillion pesetas from 755 billion in the corresponding period a year earlier. Spending on the Olympics and the Seville Expo accounted for 20% of expenditure. Solchaga increased the personal income tax to produce 11% more income for the state, and value-added tax (VAT) rates were raised by two percentage points. At the same time, the minister imposed a hiring freeze on the civil service and limited pay raises to 4%. The 1993 budget was the most restrictive in 20 years. The central government's deficit was targeted at 2.57% of gross domestic product, against 2.6% for 1992. Current expenditure would rise 9.5%, with capital expenditure on nondefense items up 6.2% and defense spending down by 10.7%. Although inflation appeared to be coming under control, core inflation remained high and was picking up. The greatest increase was in the services component, which rose 11.4% in the year to September, but this was cushioned by much slower rises in seasonal food and industrial prices.

At the end of October, González celebrated 10 years in power by announcing his intention to stand for reelection in 1993 at a massive PSOE rally in Madrid's main bullring. The day before, nearly 1,000 out-of-work steelworkers who had walked from the Basque country and Asturias were joined

Seville and Barcelona—Spain's Big Year

By many accounts, the real star of the 1992 Olympic Games was the host city, Barcelona. Similarly, as Expo 92 showcased the achievements of some 110 nations, it presented romantic, elemental Seville to the world. With 1992 marking the quincentennial of Columbus' Spanish-sponsored first transatlantic voyage, it was no coincidence that Spain was host to the two biggest international celebrations of the year. The Seville Expo—the largest Universal Exposition ever and the first to be held in 20 years—skirted the controversy surrounding Columbus (see RACE RELATIONS: Sidebar) by selecting as its theme the generic "Age of Discoveries." The Olympics provided further fanfare for the Year of Spain while incorporating only a brief reference to the explorer into the opening festivities.

The most striking—and the most lasting—feature of both events was the architecture. True to the world's fair tradition, many countries held national competitions for pavilion design and erected bold, innovative structures that were themselves main attractions. Tadao Ando of Japan, for example, created a grand "temple" billed as the world's largest all-wooden building. Britain, by contrast, took a somewhat futuristic approach in its glass-and-steel box featuring solar power and a "water wall." The U.S. entry, caught in a congressional tug-of-war over funding, borrowed a pair of geodesic domes from a traveling trade fair. Among the national treasures, products, and curiosities on display, Chile's authentic 60-ton iceberg was especially popular under the Andalusian sun.

All of Seville became the backdrop for such cultural events as operas, ballets, and art exhibitions. Despite several setbacks, including the near-destruction of its centrepiece "Pavilion of Discoveries" by fire two months before the opening, Expo 92 delivered on its promise to energize impoverished southern Spain. After closing on October 12, the fair was to be converted to a science and technology park. The city's improved infrastructure and historic restoration were a further legacy.

The Catalan capital in the northeast staged its extravaganza with the advantage of economic prosperity. Since the days of Antoni Gaudí in the late 19th century, Barcelona had been considered a design mecca. Television coverage of the Games revealed to international audiences a city of vibrant culture, broad boulevards, and imaginative architecture. Preparation of the sports complexes combined renovation (the 1929 Olympic Stadium) with new construction (most notably the Palau Sant Jordi indoor stadium). New transportation and communications facilities, beaches, and promenades gave once insular yet urbane Barcelona the amenities of a state-of-the-art resort.

As the tallying began, it appeared that for both Seville and Barcelona the increasingly high-stakes gamble of acting as host to such events had paid off handsomely—for them and for Spain.   (JIM CARNES)

SUSAN MAY TELL—SABA

A monorail carries passengers through Expo 92 in Seville, Spain. A record 110 countries participated in the world's fair, which was called "The Age of Discoveries" in commemoration of the quincentenary of Columbus' voyage to the Americas.

by another 10,000 protesters outside the Ministry for Industry. INI, the state industrial holding company, announced plans to eliminate another 20,000 jobs over four years.

(MICHAEL WOOLLER)

SWEDEN

A constitutional monarchy of northern Europe, Sweden occupies the eastern side of the Scandinavian Peninsula, with coastlines on the North and Baltic seas and the Gulf of Bothnia. Area: 449,964 sq km (173,732 sq mi). Pop. (1992 est.): 8,673,000. Cap.: Stockholm. Monetary unit: Swedish krona, with (Oct. 5, 1992) a free rate of 5.35 kronor to U.S. $1 (9.10 kronor = £1 sterling). King, Carl XVI Gustaf; prime minister in 1992, Carl Bildt.

Sweden was faced with its most serious economic crisis in more than half a century during 1992. In September the country's currency—the krona—came under enormous international financial pressure as capital flowed out of the country in expectation of a devaluation. But unlike a number of other European countries in that month, Sweden did not succumb to the turbulence on the money markets. On the contrary, the nation rallied round a defense of the krona. Two unprecedented agreements were reached between the Swedish centre-right coalition government led by Prime Minister Carl Bildt and the main Social Democratic opposition. All sides agreed there had to be sweeping cuts in government spending programs and tax increases in order to eliminate Sweden's rising structural budget deficit over the next two years. The political parties also accepted the need for measures to reduce the cost burden on Swedish industry to improve its international competitiveness.

There was overwhelming support for these crisis measures among the Swedish people, even though they would mean a further squeeze on living standards and probably a rise in the level of registered unemployment, already the highest since World War II. The historic compromises of September 1992 marked an important watershed in modern Swedish politics. They signaled to the outside world that the country was prepared to carry out radical changes in its social and economic system to meet the conditions of the open, global economy. However, the pressures continued to mount, and on November 19 the Riksbank finally abandoned its efforts to defend the krona and allowed the currency to float downward.

On Jan. 1, 1993, Sweden would become part of the 19-nation European Economic Area—a single integrated market stretching from the Arctic Circle to the Mediterranean. During 1992 it was preparing for formal negotiations to join the European Communities (EC). The consensus among the main political parties in support of Sweden's membership in the EC held firm, despite signs of growing doubt among the Swedish people, particularly after the Danes' narrow "no" vote in June to the Maastricht Treaty on European economic and political union. Bildt and other party leaders insisted that Sweden had to prepare itself to become part of the inner fast lane of any emerging two-speed Europe.

In 1992 Sweden finally abandoned its commitment to the concept of neutrality in foreign and defense policy. In its autumn 1992 statement to the Riksdag (parliament), the government did not even use the word to describe its future strategy toward the outside world. This did not mean that Sweden would join an existing military alliance, but it did suggest that the country would be ready to accept a defense posture inside the EC based on collective security. Certainly it seemed there would be no danger of neutrality's becoming an obstacle to full EC membership for Sweden.

Foreign exchange employees in Sweden cope with the decision of the country's central bank on September 9 to raise marginal rates on loans to commercial banks to 75%. The rate was later temporarily raised even higher, to 500%, in an effort to maintain the value of the krona.
CHARLIE GUSTAVSSON—REPORTAGEBILD/PHOTOREPORTERS

The economic recession deepened during 1992, with a fall in growth, rising unemployment, a slump in production and investment, and a growing number of bankruptcies. The country's banks faced mounting credit-loss difficulties that began to hurt their operating profits and forced the government to provide an open-ended guarantee to support the financial system with taxpayers' money. At the start of the year it had been hoped that a slow recovery would begin in 1992, but this proved overoptimistic, mainly because of the weak revival in the U.S., the intractable slump in Britain, and growing difficulties in Germany—all Sweden's main export markets. Inevitably, the gloom affected the popularity of Bildt's coalition government. Its electoral support declined, and the Social Democrats saw a rapid improvement in their position. However, with the next general election not due until Sept. 18, 1994, observers believed there was plenty of time for a government revival. At year's end Sweden was still in the grip of its worst recession since the early 1930s, and the cooperative spirit that had been evident in September had dissipated as the Social Democrats refused to support another round of austerity measures.

(ROBERT G. TAYLOR)

SWITZERLAND

A landlocked federal state in west central Europe, Switzerland consists of a confederation of 26 cantons (6 of which are demi-cantons). Area: 41,293 sq km (15,943 sq mi). Pop. (1992 est.): 6,911,000. Administrative cap., Bern; judicial cap., Lausanne. Monetary unit: Swiss franc, with (Oct. 5, 1992) a free rate of Sw F 1.23 to U.S. $1 (Sw F 2.09 = £1 sterling). President in 1992, René Felber.

Switzerland was shaken to its political core—and positively galvanized—when the December 6 national referendum resulted in rejection of the European Economic Area (EEA) draft agreement, grouping the 12 member countries of the European Communities (EC) with the 7 nations of the European Free Trade Association (EFTA), including the Swiss. The agreement, endorsed by the federal government, approved by the parliament, backed by industry and banks, and supported by all those of the younger generation who regarded themselves as "true" Europeans, had been scheduled to come into force on Jan. 1, 1993. The other EFTA nations, which had virtually taken for granted Swiss participation in the enlarged market of 380 million consumers, had to amend provisions of the agreement, so delaying its application until later in the year.

But the "no"—by only 50.3% of the votes cast—was simply not taken as the final answer, especially in French-speaking Suisse Romande (western Switzerland), which had voted massively in favour. The refusal, most pronounced in the smaller rural cantons where residents speak their own distinctive dialect of Swiss-German, was seen as due to EEA opponents exploiting deep-seated sentiments relating to patriotism, traditional neutrality, and continued stability while avoiding detailed informed discussion of potential benefits from the treaty.

As emotions cooled and second thoughts prevailed, attention turned to the implications of the country's thus isolating itself from the mainstream of European integration. In the week following the referendum, opinion polls in Zürich and Bern, both of which had returned smaller majorities against the EEA, were already indicating a switch of up to 60% support for it. Much was made of the fact that more than one referendum had previously been required until the Swiss electorate came round to accepting major change. It became apparent that reaction to the negative vote, in the form of the sharp stimulus given to consideration of the near future, was altogether salutary, even perhaps a blessing in disguise. Since establishing procedures for a second vote on the EEA was unlikely to take less than a year, efforts were directed to closing ranks and limiting the damage. One of the first moves was to provisionally freeze Switzerland's application for full EC membership.

Prior to the December referendum, forecasts had pointed to recession, severe in Swiss experience, continuing for a third year. After the "no" vote, predictions became gloomier; growth in gross national product in 1993 was expected to be a mere 0.3%, while the number of unemployed was expected to rise from 115,000 to 150,000 (almost 5%), about half under age 30. This compared with almost zero unemployment only two years earlier and did not include thousands of temporary foreign workers returning to their own countries. For more than three decades, they had, in effect, represented a safety valve available in the event of labour market shrinkage. Job losses, particularly in the construction sector, consequent upon recession were added to those resulting from widespread restructuring, a greater use of automation, and the effects of large Swiss enterprises having shifted a proportion of their capacity outside the country. As a result, they were collectively employing more people abroad than they were at home.

The growing incidence of insolvencies and foreclosures proceeded against a backdrop of federal government indebtedness: Sw F 4 billion–Sw F 5 billion deficit in the 1993 budget, with the likelihood of Sw F 2 billion–Sw F 3.5 billion annual deficits for some years to come. This forecast was predicated on 2% economic growth in conjunction with reduced state expenditure, including cuts in the long-standing civil defense program. The cuts, however, did not touch the Sw F 138 million narrowly approved by the parliament for the construction—already well advanced—of a bunker inside a mountain as crisis accommodation for the Federal Council (Cabinet) and essential services. Its advocates pointed to events in former Yugoslavia. A similar argument was being used in support of the government's hotly criticized intention of buying 34 F/A-18 advanced fighter aircraft from the U.S.   (ALAN McGREGOR)

UKRAINE

A republic of eastern Europe, Ukraine borders Russia to the north and east, the Black Sea to the south, Romania and Moldova to the southwest, and Hungary, Czechoslovakia, and Poland to the west. Area: 603,700 sq km (233,100 sq mi). Pop. (1992 est.): 52,135,000. Cap.: Kiev (Ukrainian: Kyyiv). Monetary unit: ruble, with (Oct. 5, 1992) a free rate of 316.82 rubles = U.S. $1 (538.59 rubles = £1 sterling); from November 13 the Ukrainian coupon (the de facto quasi currency) replaced the ruble as legal tender. President in 1992, Leonid Kravchuk; prime ministers, Vitold Fokin (acting) to September 30, Valentyn Symonenko from October 2, and, from October 13, Leonid Kuchma.

In a referendum on Dec. 1, 1991, 90.3% of the population voted for the independence of Ukraine. On the same day, Leonid Kravchuk, a former Communist, scored a decisive victory in the presidential election, securing 61.6% of the votes cast. A week later Ukraine, Belarus, and Russia established the Commonwealth of Independent States (CIS), which eight of the other former republics joined by year's end. Kravchuk's primary aim was to demolish the U.S.S.R. and to be rid of Soviet Pres. Mikhail Gorbachev. A secondary aim was to establish an administrative body whose function was to serve as a "committee for liquidating the old structures." From the Ukrainian point of view, the CIS was not a state or a subject in international law because the sovereignty of the old union had passed completely to the successor countries. However, Moscow began to regard the CIS itself as a successor state to the U.S.S.R. and to assume that its interests coincided with those of Russia. Ukraine was angered by Russia's taking control of all ex-Soviet embassies and property abroad and the U.S.S.R.'s seat on the UN Security Council. There was also concern over the nuclear weapons left on Ukrainian territory after the Soviet breakup. Although Ukraine transferred its tactical nuclear weapons to Russia, by year's end the country had not signed the Strategic Arms Reduction Treaty. The government was particularly concerned over the burdensome cost of dismantling the remaining strategic weapons in its possession.

Kravchuk consolidated his power in 1992. The Supreme Soviet, elected in March 1990, had a solid majority of former Communists, and all attempts by the opposition to dissolve it and hold new elections failed. Although the number of Kravchuk loyalists in the parliament ranged from only 80 to 110 of the 450 delegates, the opposition remained fragmented. Most opposition parties were weak, and since they were all formed after the 1990 elections, their influence in the parliament was minimal. The process of coalescing into coalitions began in earnest in 1992. The extreme right was too fractious to enter into a coalition. The conservative right, which in August formed the Congress of National Democratic Forces, had 20 member organizations and about 40 delegates. Rukh (the Ukrainian Popular Movement) split, and Vyacheslav Chornovil dominated the new grouping. Chornovil, Kravchuk's most vociferous opponent, had a political base in western Ukraine with limited support elsewhere. About 46 delegates supported him. The centre-left coalition formed New Ukraine (52 delegates) in January. It supported market reform, the maintenance of the CIS, privatization, and "capitalism with a human face." Its most prominent representative was Volodymyr Lanovy, minister for privatization and deputy prime minister, but Kravchuk sacked him in July. The extreme left, all former Communists, called for the return of the U.S.S.R. and the planned economy. As many as 90 delegates supported it.

Although only 22.1% of the Ukrainian population were ethnic Russians, for about a third Russian was the mother

Workers in Kiev, Ukraine, load a nuclear warhead onto a truck for transport to Russia, where it was to be dismantled. Although tactical nuclear weapons were transferred, Ukraine later tied the surrender of intercontinental nuclear missiles to increased Western aid.

REUTERS/BETTMANN

tongue. The Ukrainian leadership had to present itself as acting for the whole population, rather than the ethnic Ukrainian majority. The Donets Basin (called Donbass), dominated by coal mining and by Russians, saw many strikes against declining living and working standards during the year. Russians, who accounted for 67% of the population of the Crimea, attempted to gain independence from Ukraine in May. This was greeted with uproar in Kiev, and it encouraged the Crimean Ukrainians to organize and counter the move. Kravchuk had another card to play: support for the returning Crimean Tatars, who had dominated the peninsula until deported by Stalin in 1945 for allegedly collaborating with the German army. The Tatars began to mobilize, and the Crimea returned to the Ukrainian fold after cutting a deal with Kravchuk.

The Crimea was also the scene of the struggle over the Black Sea Fleet. Both Ukraine and Russia claimed control, and a bitter conflict ensued. Kravchuk and Russian Pres. Boris Yeltsin compromised in June and agreed to joint command for three years. The most serious territorial threat to Ukraine was posed by Romania, which requested the return of Chernivtsi province and southern Bessarabia. Moldova also sought the return of these regions, in which Romanians/Moldavians were in a minority. The conflict in Transdnistria (the breakaway Dniester republic), under way since 1990, intimately involved Ukraine since the Slav majority sought military and political support from Kiev. Although Ukraine had supported Moldova, in June Kravchuk performed a spectacular volte-face and came out in support of an autonomous Dniester region within Moldova. This appeared to be part of a wide-ranging deal by Kravchuk and Yeltsin that saw, among other things, Russian concessions in the

Crimea and on the Black Sea Fleet, Ukraine changing sides in the Dniester republic and supporting the Russian position, open frontiers between Russia and Ukraine, the right of Ukraine to introduce its own currency, and some foreign embassies to be ceded to Ukraine.

If the relationship with Russia was the most important issue for the leadership during the year, there were other acute problems, primarily economic. In November Prime Minister Leonid Kuchma informed the parliament that the economic situation was catastrophic. Gross national product had declined by 18%; the budget deficit was a staggering 44% of gross domestic product; and the price of wholesale goods had increased 22-fold since the beginning of the year. He announced an ambitious reform program. There was to be "forced" privatization, sweeping tax reforms, and the promotion of agriculture. Ukraine left the ruble zone in November, but the new currency, the hryvnya, could not be introduced, as there was no stabilization fund to back it up. Coupons were issued as legal tender in the interim. A major reason for the move was to escape Russian hyperinflation, running at 2,000% annually. Given that about 95% of enterprises were integrated into the Russian economy and that Ukraine was dependent on Russia for oil, timber, and other products, disengaging from Moscow would be painful and slow.   (MARTIN McCAULEY)

UNITED KINGDOM

A constitutional monarchy in northwestern Europe and member of the Commonwealth, the United Kingdom comprises the island of Great Britain (England, Scotland, and Wales) and Northern Ireland, together with many small islands. Area: 244,110 sq km (94,251 sq mi), including 3,218 sq km of inland water but excluding the crown dependencies of the Channel Islands and Isle of Man. Pop. (1992 est.): 57,730,000. Cap.: London. Monetary unit: pound sterling, with (Oct. 5, 1992) a free rate of £0.59 to U.S. $1 (U.S. $1.70 = £1 sterling). Queen, Elizabeth II; prime minister in 1992, John Major.

Domestic Affairs. On March 11, 1992, Prime Minister John Major (*see* BIOGRAPHIES) finally ended speculation about the date of the U.K.'s general election and announced that polling day would be April 9. The victory of his Conservative Party (*see* Sidebar), albeit by a much-reduced majority, seemed to enhance Major's authority—not least because the result confounded the opinion polls.

Major reshuffled his Cabinet significantly after the election. He appointed his main rival for the Conservative leadership in November 1990, Michael Heseltine, as president of the Board of Trade—in effect, the minister responsible for reviving British industry. He switched Kenneth Clarke from Education to the Home Office, and promoted a close personal friend, David Mellor, to the new post of secretary of the national heritage, responsible for broadcasting, newspapers, the arts, and sport. Among the ministers who retained their existing portfolios were Norman Lamont (chancellor of the Exchequer) and Douglas Hurd (foreign secretary).

For the first few weeks after the election, everything seemed to go Major's way. There were signs of a revival in consumer confidence and in the housing market. On May 7 the Conservatives made sweeping gains in local council elections throughout England. On May 21 the House of Commons voted 336 to 92 in favour of the European Communities (amendment) bill. This was the first step in the long process toward ratifying the Maastricht Treaty agreed among EC leaders in December 1991.

By September the short-lived recovery had petered out, and problems were beginning to mount. The U.K.'s withdrawal from the European exchange-rate mechanism (ERM; *see Economic Affairs,* below) dealt a damaging blow to public and business confidence in Major's administration in general and Lamont in particular. Major resisted widespread calls—not least from normally loyal pro-Tory newspapers—to dismiss Lamont. However, he was unable to resist demands for Mellor's resignation. Tabloid newspapers had published lurid accounts of an affair between Mellor and an actress, and he was named as having accepted a free holiday from the family of a prominent member of the Palestine Liberation Organization. The significance of his resignation on September 24 was not that a sexual indiscretion was bound to destroy a politician's career. On February 5, Paddy Ashdown, the leader of the Liberal Democrats, admitted to having had an affair with his secretary some years earlier. His candid admission won him praise and boosted his public popularity. In Mellor's case, however, ever more sleazy disclosures reduced the minister to a figure of fun, and Major's continued support for him called the prime minister's own judgment into question.

Major's handling of other issues also attracted criticism. The trickiest of these concerned Europe. A minority of Tory MPs, collectively known as the Euro-skeptics, opposed the Maastricht Treaty. Their resistance was bolstered by the Danish voters' decision in a referendum on June 2 to reject the treaty. Sterling's departure from the ERM helped their campaign yet further. When the Conservatives met in Brighton on October 6–9 for their annual conference, the hostility of a large section of the party to the treaty was evident. That hostility was amplified by a strongly anti-Maastricht newspaper article by Major's predecessor, Baroness Thatcher, and by uncompromising speeches by two former party chairmen, Kenneth Baker and Lord Tebbit. (Margaret Thatcher and Norman Tebbit had been given life peerages following the general election.)

Rather than let the matter fester, Major decided to bring the issue to a head in the House of Commons in a debate on November 4. Twenty-six Conservative MPs voted against the government and another 6 abstained, but 19 of the 20 Liberal Democrat MPs voted with the government, whose European policy survived by just three votes—319 to 316. The price of the government's victory was a concession to agree to delay the Maastricht legislation so that it would not become law until after a second Danish referendum.

While the arguments about Europe raged, the government was forced to retreat on another policy. On October 13, Heseltine announced that 31 of British Coal's remaining 50 pits would be closed, with the loss of 30,000 jobs. This decision aroused an unprecedented backlash, not only from the Labour Party and the trade unions but also from a wide range of energy experts, business people, and Conservative MPs. By October 21, when the House of Commons debated the issue, Heseltine had been forced to concede demands for a wide-ranging review of the U.K.'s energy policy. Pending this review, no pit would be closed irrevocably. On December 21 the High Court ruled that the original decision to close the pits was unlawful, as British Coal had failed to consult Britain's miners. This judgment added to ministers' embarrassment.

Pressure on the government intensified further when three businessmen were acquitted on November 9 of selling arms-making equipment to Iraq in contravention of an arms ban. The three defendants had argued that government ministers had privately helped them to break the law by circumventing the ban. As a result, shipments to Iraq had continued until just a few days before Iraq's invasion of Kuwait in August 1990. A former minister of defense procurement, Alan Clark, gave evidence at the trial that confirmed ministerial support for the company, Matrix Churchill.

The government's troubles gave John Smith (*see* BIOGRAPHIES) an opportunity to settle in as the Labour Party's new leader. On April 13, four days after the general election, Neil Kinnock announced his decision to step down. Kinnock had fought and lost two elections as party leader. Smith, shadow chancellor until the election, defeated Bryan Gould, his only opponent, by 91–9%. Margaret Beckett, previously shadow chief secretary and hence number two in Smith's shadow treasury team, was elected deputy leader.

During 1992 the media chronicled the breakdown of the marriage of the Prince and Princess of Wales. A book published in June—*Diana: Her True Story* by a British journalist, Andrew Morton—said that their marital problems had provoked several suicide attempts by the princess. Although Morton had not interviewed the princess, it quickly became clear that he had spoken to several of her closest friends and that she had, tacitly at least, authorized their disclosures. The stories about the couple, amplified by aggressive reporting by tabloid newspapers, added to the pressures on the royal family, which had seen the divorce of the Princess Royal (the Prince of Wales's sister) and the separation of the Duke and Duchess of York earlier in 1992. Finally, on December 9, Buckingham Palace announced that the Prince and Princess of Wales would separate. This announcement completed what the Queen described as an "annus horribilis" in a rare public comment on her troubles during a speech on the occasion of her 40th anniversary on the throne. Not only had every one of the first marriages of her children ended in separation, she also had to contend

REUTERS/BETTMANN

Prime Minister John Major greets citizens after the Conservative Party won Britain's elections on April 9. Despite recession and dissatisfaction among the electorate, the Conservatives won their fourth straight victory against the Labour Party.

with a fire that destroyed much of the interior of Windsor Castle on November 20. The government agreed to finance the castle's restoration, in line with established policy toward the royal castles, leaving the Queen to pay only for the furnishings that had been destroyed within her private apartments. Controversy over whether the Queen should make a greater contribution was only partly softened by an announcement six days later that she had volunteered to give up her tax-free status. The one undoubted source of joy to the royal family in the final weeks of a difficult year was the Princess Royal's wedding on December 12 to Comdr. Timothy Laurence, a former equerry (aide) to the Queen.

Economic Affairs. The U.K. economy remained in recession for the second consecutive year. By the third quarter of 1992, the U.K. was suffering its longest recession since World War II. One part of the U.K.'s problem was that sterling's membership in the ERM prevented interest rates from falling as far and as fast as industry wanted. At the start of 1992, the Bank of England's base rate stood at 10.5%. It was reduced to 10% in May, but with inflation at around 4%, this meant that real interest rates stood at a historically high 6%.

The government's determination to protect sterling's position was undermined by a massive speculative attack on the pound in September. On September 3, Lamont sought to deter currency dealers by borrowing £7,250,000,000 in Deutsche Marks. On September 10, Major told a meeting of Scottish industrialists: "There is to be no devaluation, no realignment. . . . I was under no illusions when I took Britain into the ERM. I said then membership was no soft option. The soft option, the devaluer's option, the inflationary option would be a betrayal of our future."

Speculative attacks on sterling intensified just four days later, following the devaluation of the Italian lira. By the morning of September 16—a day that subsequently became known as "black Wednesday"—pressure on the pound was so intense that Lamont authorized the Bank of England to raise its base rate to 12%. Three hours later, when this failed to revive sterling, interest rates were raised a further three points. Finally, at 7:30 PM, Lamont announced that the U.K. was suspending its ERM membership forthwith.

The following day base rates were reduced once more to 10%. Over the following weeks a succession of interest rate reductions followed. By mid-November the base rate was down to 7%, and sterling was trading at around DM 2.40—almost 20% below the DM 2.95 midpoint rate at which sterling had joined the ERM in October 1990. On October 8, Lamont announced that the government was abandoning its previous target of zero inflation; instead, it would seek to keep inflation at or below the EC average. Major and Lamont subsequently signaled a shift of emphasis in economic policy, toward a greater commitment to growth and measures to combat rising unemployment, which stood at 2.9 million, or more than 10% of the labour force.

Foreign Affairs. The U.K. took over the presidency of the European Communities on July 1, but Major's domestic problems regarding the Maastricht Treaty and sterling's withdrawal from the ERM largely thwarted his attempts to use the presidency to project the U.K. as coequal with France and Germany as the "big three" leaders of the EC.

U.K. Election

In the teeth of recession, and despite opinion-poll forecasts that he would lose power, on April 9, 1992, John Major led the U.K. Conservative Party to its fourth consecutive election victory. His overall majority was reduced sharply to 21, compared with 101 in 1987, but this was wholly explained by switches in support among the opposition parties. The Conservatives' own percentage share remained virtually unaltered and, because of a higher turnout, Major's party became the first in U.K. history to exceed 14 million votes. (For tabulated results, see *Political Parties,* above.)

The election was essentially a lesser-of-two-evils battle between two parties struggling to overcome their shortcomings. The Conservatives were handicapped by the weakness of the U.K.'s economy and by the party's reputation for neglecting public services, such as health and education. Labour, on the other hand, was seen as a tax-raising party, and its leader, Neil Kinnock, was widely depicted as lacking the personal qualities needed in a prime minister.

Throughout the campaign, the opinion polls appeared to show that the Conservatives' failings weighed more heavily with voters than Labour's. Of the five polls published during the last 48 hours before election day, three showed Labour narrowly ahead, one showed the two main parties level, and one showed the Conservatives ahead by just half of a percentage point. In the event, the result—a nearly eight-point Conservative victory over Labour—mocked the pollsters more comprehensively than in any major Western democracy since the U.S. presidential election of 1948.

Subsequent research indicated that although the Conservatives did benefit from a small last-minute swing, the polls underestimated government support throughout the campaign. The Conservatives played their one strong card with skill and tenacity—John Major's personal popularity. This owed much to his quiet, apparently unassuming manner and consensual style, which contrasted strongly with the abrasive reputation of his predecessor, Margaret Thatcher. The Conservatives also attacked Labour relentlessly as a tax-and-spend party that would increase the income taxes of an average family by £1,200 a year.

Labour retorted that this was a lie and that only the highest-earning 10% of workers would pay extra tax. But the Conservative claims, endorsed with exceptional vigour by most mass-circulation newspapers, were sufficiently widely believed to persuade key groups of middle-income voters to stick with the Conservatives.

The minor parties enjoyed mixed fortunes. The Liberal Democrats, fighting their first election since the merger of the Liberal Party and the Social Democrats in 1988, never managed to capitalize fully on the weaknesses of the two main parties. Although they captured the seat of Chris Patten, the Conservative Party chairman, they ended up with two fewer MPs than their parent parties had won in 1987.

The Scottish Nationalists failed to achieve the breakthrough that seemed likely at one stage and ended up with three MPs, the same as in 1987; the Welsh Nationalists, Plaid Cymru, gained one seat. In Northern Ireland, Gerry Adams lost the only seat being defended by Sinn Fein, the political arm of the Provisional IRA.

(PETER KELLNER)

A London store forced to close down offers its merchandise at sale prices. Britain continued to suffer from what was by some measures the worst economic slowdown since the 1930s, with unemployment rates increasing steadily for two and a half years.

JOHN STURROCK—NETWORK/MATRIX

Two EC summits were held during the U.K. presidency—at Birmingham on October 16 and at Edinburgh on December 11–12. The Birmingham summit mainly concerned attempts to define "subsidiarity"—the principle enshrined in the Maastricht Treaty whereby decisions would be taken as close as possible to the people they affected. The Edinburgh summit demonstrated Major's patient negotiating skills, as he defied predictions of the summit's failure and secured compromise agreements on a range of thorny issues, including the EC's future budget and Denmark's right to opt out of some features of the Maastricht Treaty.

Two other foreign policy issues dominated British concerns during the year. On August 18 the government decided to send 1,800 troops to the former Yugoslavia as part of a UN force protecting aid convoys. On August 26, as part of its EC presidency, the U.K. was host to a peace conference in London. The conference achieved little in the short term, but the parties to the conflict accepted the appointment of former foreign secretary David Owen (later Lord Owen) as the EC's chief mediator, as successor to Lord Carrington.

The U.K.'s new governor of Hong Kong, Chris Patten (*see* BIOGRAPHIES), attempted to secure Chinese acceptance of greater democracy for the colony ahead of its transfer to China in 1997. When Patten visited Beijing (Peking) in October, however, the Chinese refused to negotiate any change in previous agreements. A joint Sino-British declaration in 1984 had agreed that Hong Kong's capitalist character would be preserved for at least 50 years and that basic human rights, including freedom of speech, would be respected. Patten sought China's agreement to go further and admit greater, and more democratic, autonomy for Hong Kong.

Northern Ireland. On January 27, Peter Brooke, the U.K.'s Northern Ireland secretary, announced that he was abandoning attempts he had first made in 1991 to hold roundtable negotiations among the four main constitutional parties in the province—the Ulster Unionists, the Democratic Unionists, the Alliance Party, and the Social Democratic and Labour Party. The impending general election

was one factor; the parties did not wish to reveal their hands in a way that might jeopardize their own support—or to prejudge possible shifts in U.K. policy after the election.

A fresh attempt to start talks was made by Brooke's successor, Sir Patrick Mayhew, who was appointed on April 11 in the aftermath of the election. On April 27, as a gesture to the Unionists, Mayhew persuaded the Irish government to suspend the regular Anglo-Irish conference meetings. This paved the way for a resumption of all-party talks on April 29. On July 6 the four parties met with the U.K. and Irish governments in London; afterward the U.K. and Irish prime ministers issued a joint statement indicating that the 1985 Anglo-Irish agreement (disliked intensely by the Unionists) might be replaced by a "new and more broadly-based agreement or structure." Talks continued until November 10, but they concluded with little visible progress.

Terrorist action continued throughout the year both in Northern Ireland and, spasmodically, on the U.K. mainland. (*See* CRIME, LAW ENFORCEMENT, AND PENOLOGY.) On April 10, the day after the general election, a 45-kg (100-lb) car bomb exploded in the financial heart of the City of London, killing 3 people and injuring more than 90 others. Mainland terrorism was caused overwhelmingly by the Irish Republican Army, but within Northern Ireland violence was caused by terrorists from both communities. On August 10, Mayhew outlawed the Ulster Defense Association, a Protestant paramilitary organization. The UDA had acknowledged responsibility for 14 killings during the first seven months of the year.   (PETER KELLNER)

See also *Commonwealth of Nations,* above; *Dependent States,* below.

VATICAN CITY STATE

The independent sovereignty of Vatican City State is surrounded by but is not part of Rome. As a state with territorial limits, it is properly distinguished from the Holy See, which constitutes the worldwide administrative and legislative body for the Roman Catholic Church. Area: 44 ha (109 ac). Pop. (1992 est.): 750. As sovereign pontiff, John Paul II is the chief of state. Vatican City is administered by a pontifical commission of five cardinals headed by the secretary of state, in 1992 Angelo Cardinal Sodano.

The historic recognition of Croatia and Slovenia in January 1992 opened a year of intense international activity. In subsequent months the Vatican established diplomatic relations with a host of new nations, including the new eastern European countries of Armenia, Azerbaijan, Bosnia and Hercegovina, Georgia, Moldova, and Ukraine. It also reestablished relations with Mexico after a 125-year rift. Pope John Paul II took the occasion of the UN Conference on Environment and Development in Rio de Janeiro to reiterate from Rome his continued support of environmental issues. His concern for world issues was also stated during a visit to the Vatican by officials from the International Labour Organization.

The Vatican witnessed the escalation of violence in Bosnia with intense concern. Its many appeals for peace were accompanied by the clarification that it would remain extraneous to decisions involving military operations. On the ecclesiastical front, the pope reorganized the Polish church, creating new dioceses and ecclesiastical provinces and appointing several bishops and archbishops.

The pope's week-long July visit to Angola and São Tomé and Príncipe was his ninth to Africa and his 55th pastoral visit outside Italy. In Italy the pontiff traveled extensively in the city of Rome and other parts of the country. In the northeast, on the border with troubled eastern Europe, he warned against the dangers of exaggerated nationalism.

The pontiff, who turned 72 in May, was hospitalized in the summer for major surgery. His speedy recovery was announced by his own voice only four days after surgery, when he recited the weekly Angelus prayer via Vatican Radio.

(GREGORY O. SMITH)

See also RELIGION: *Roman Catholic Church.*
This article updates the *Micropædia* article VATICAN CITY.

YUGOSLAVIA

A federal republic of the northern and central Balkans, Yugoslavia borders Hungary to the north, Romania to the northeast, Bulgaria to the southeast, Macedonia and Albania to the south, the Adriatic Sea to the southwest, and Croatia and Bosnia and Hercegovina to the west. Area: 102,173 sq km (39,449 sq mi). Pop. (1992 est.): 10,394,000. Cap.: Belgrade. Monetary unit: Yugoslav dinar, with (Oct. 5, 1992) a free rate of 225.41 dinars to U.S. $1 (383.20 dinars = £1 sterling). President from June 15, 1992, Dobrica Cosic; prime minister from July 14, Milan Panic.

In December 1991 four of the six constituent Yugoslav republics applied for international recognition as independent states. The two remaining republics, Serbia and Montenegro, re-formed into a new Yugoslavia, which came into being on April 27, 1992, when the rump Yugoslav Federal Assembly, originally elected in 1986, adopted the constitution of a "third Yugoslavia" as a successor to the pre-1941 royalist and the post-1945 Titoist nation.

Hostilities that had begun in Croatia in 1991 were largely superseded in 1992 by widespread fighting between Bosnian Muslims and Yugoslav-backed Serb nationalists in Bosnia and Hercegovina. On March 27 Bosnian Serb leaders proclaimed the creation of a Serbian Republic of Bosnia and Hercegovina, with a constitution that declared it to be part of Yugoslavia. Serbia officially distanced itself from the war in April by relinquishing formal control over the Yugoslav army in Bosnia, which renamed itself the Army of the Serbian Republic of Bosnia and Hercegovina. Western governments, however, continued to single out Serbia (and its leader since 1986, Slobodan Milosevic) as the instigator of the war in Bosnia and showed their disapproval of its

policy by refusing to accept the new rump Yugoslavia as a continuation of the old country. On May 30 the UN Security Council formally accused Serbia (along with Montenegro) of aggression and adopted a resolution imposing comprehensive sanctions against it to include a trade embargo (excluding essential medical material), a ban on all civilian air traffic in and out of Serbia, a freeze on all Serbian assets abroad, the expulsion of Yugoslav diplomats, and other measures. In October the Security Council passed a resolution banning all flights over Bosnia except those on UN-endorsed humanitarian missions.

The Milosevic regime managed to beat the blockade partially. Russia officially supported UN sanctions against Yugoslavia, but its government had to take into account strong attacks on concessions allegedly being made by Pres. Boris Yeltsin to U.S. policy in the Balkans. Serbia also got moral and material support from the Greek government. Much of the oil that managed to get to Belgrade despite the UN-imposed embargo went via Greece, apparently with its tacit support. The rest was transported via the Danube, with Romania's collusion, or through Bulgaria. Nevertheless, the effects of Western sanctions against Yugoslavia continued to be felt. In the first 11 months of 1992, industrial output was 20% below that of the corresponding period of 1991. Shortages were widespread, and inflation was running at an annual rate of 3,000%.

The election of Dobrica Cosic, a respected writer and former dissident as well as a strong Serbian nationalist, as new Yugoslavia's president in June inspired hopes of a political change among those opposed to Milosevic. There were large demonstrations against Milosevic in Belgrade and other cities in March and again in June. But elections in Serbia and Montenegro on May 31 produced, in an admittedly low poll (60% in Serbia and 50% in Montenegro), a 68% majority for the ruling Socialist (formerly Communist) Party. Hopes that a real change might after all be on the way were boosted on July 14 when Milan Panic (*see* BIOGRAPHIES), a Serb who had immigrated to California, was appointed federal prime minister. Panic embarked on a series of international visits aimed at having the UN sanctions lifted. In Belgrade he took an antiwar stand and began to attack Milosevic. He even sacked a senior Milosevic supporter from the federal government.

The democratic opposition was defeated at the combined parliamentary and presidential elections held on December 20. Milosevic was comfortably reelected as Serbian president, routing Panic, who stood against him. Milosevic's party, however, failed to win an overall majority. The second largest postelection party was the Radical Party of Vojislav Seselj, an extremist politician who had led raids against the civilian population in both Croatia and Bosnia. A well-known extremist, Zeljko Raznjetovic ("Arkan"), leader of the notorious White Tigers, was elected in Kosovo, where Albanians had boycotted the election. (Albanians in Kosovo had held their own unofficial election on May 24 and subsequently proclaimed an independent republic with a government-in-exile in western Europe. Unrest in Kosovo continued despite local Albanian leaders' attempts to contain it for fear that provocations might lead to Serb "ethnic cleansing" on the Bosnian model.)

On December 29 Panic lost a unanimous parliamentary vote of no confidence. The Federal Assembly then named Radoje Kontic to serve as interim prime minister, but Panic refused to step down under a constitutional rule that allowed him to remain as caretaker until the new parliament could replace him in early 1993. (K.F. CVIIC)

This article updates the *Macropædia* article BALKAN STATES: *Yugoslavia.*

COUNTRIES OF FORMER YUGOSLAVIA AND AREAS OF ETHNIC CONTROL (LATE NOVEMBER)

AUSTRIA
HUNGARY
SLOVENIA
Ljubljana
Zagreb
CROATIA
ROMANIA
VOJVODINA
Novi Sad
Bihac
Orasje
BOSNIA AND HERCEGOVINA
Belgrade
Travnik
Tuzla
Vares
SERBIA
Sarajevo
Srebrenica
Gorazde
YUGOSLAVIA
Mostar
ADRIATIC SEA
MONTENEGRO
Pristina
KOSOVO
BULGARIA
ITALY
Podgorica
Skopje
MACEDONIA
ALBANIA
GREECE

AREAS OF CONTROL
Serbian
Croatian
Bosnian
Bosnian and Croatian
Boundary of former Yugoslavia
Republic boundaries
Autonomous province boundaries
• Capital cities

0   50   100 mi
0   50   100   150 km

North America

CANADA

Canada is a federal parliamentary state and member of the
Commonwealth covering North America north of conterminous
United States and east of Alaska. Area: 9,970,610 sq km (3,849,-
674 sq mi). Pop. (1992 est.): 27,737,000. Cap.: Ottawa. Monetary
unit: Canadian dollar, with (Oct. 5, 1992) a free rate of Can$1.25
to U.S. $1 (Can$2.13 = £1 sterling). Queen, Elizabeth II; governor-general in 1992, Ramon Hnatyshyn; prime minister, Brian
Mulroney.

Domestic Affairs. In the long search for a new constitution for Canada, a national referendum was held on Oct.
26, 1992, to decide whether new arrangements worked out
earlier would satisfy the aspirations of Canadians living in
French-speaking Quebec as well as in other parts of the
country. The movement to renew the Canadian federal
structure was led by the government of Prime Minister
Brian Mulroney, which had sponsored an earlier formula
for change, the Meech Lake accord. That accord had died
in 1990 when it had failed to gain the support of all 10
provinces.

The Mulroney government put forward a second plan
for constitutional change in September 1991. The "Canada
Round" proposals differed from Meech Lake in addressing
the desires of other regions of Canada as well as Quebec.
It also met the concerns of aboriginal people by promising
them an assured role in shaping their future. The Meech
Lake accord had been widely criticized as the product of secretive closed-door bargaining by the prime minister and the
10 provincial premiers. The Mulroney government promised
that the new proposals would be subject to an unparalleled
measure of consultation with the citizens of Canada. A joint
committee drawn from the Senate and House of Commons
began the public process in the last months of 1991 but
soon became bogged down in partisan differences. The government, trying a new tack, sponsored five three-day policy
conferences in January and February 1992 to discuss constitutional renewal. The meetings brought together members
of the joint committee, provincial, territorial, and aboriginal
representatives, academics, spokesmen for interest groups,
and ordinary citizens.

The policy conferences brought out clearly the constitutional priorities of the various regions. The west, especially
Alberta, pressed for a "Triple-E Senate," one that would
be elected, equal in provincial representation, and effective.
This demand arose from the west's unhappiness with the
appointed Senate, in which western provinces were underrepresented. Ontario, with a New Democratic (social democratic) government in office, argued for a social charter in
the reformed constitution protecting medicare, education,
and basic human services. Quebec's response, crucial to the
success of the federal government's plan, was equivocal. In
March the governing Liberal Party moved from its historic
federalist position to adopt a report that spelled out a semi-
autonomous Quebec within a loose Canadian federation.
While this document pleased the younger, more nationalist
wing of the party, it did not find favour with the party's
leader, Premier Robert Bourassa. Careful not to reject the
report openly, Bourassa assumed a more conciliatory tone,
arguing for a renewed federalism and emphasizing the costly
disruption that would result from Quebec's separation. He

later stated that he might transform a referendum on Quebec's sovereignty, which he was obligated by law to hold by
Oct. 26, 1992, into a vote on the province's participation in
a new federal structure.

A new constitutional round began in Ottawa on March
12, with the federal government, all the provinces but Quebec, the two federal territories, and representatives of the
four principal native groups present. The first meeting took
an important decision that was stimulated by Ontario's premier, Bob Rae. The initiative in constitutional reform would
not be left solely in the hands of the federal government
but would be shared with the provinces, the territories, and
the four national aboriginal groups. The object would be to
reach a "multilateral consensus" on reform. The meetings
that followed were chaired by Ottawa's minister for constitutional affairs, Joe Clark, an Albertan whom Mulroney had
succeeded as leader of the Progressive Conservative Party
in 1983. Clark showed great tenacity of purpose in presiding
over a long series of exhaustive discussions. By July 7, after
27 days of meetings in seven different cities, a breakthrough
had been achieved on the principal points in dispute.

With the tentative set of arrangements, the "multilateral
consensus," before him, Mulroney judged that the time was
ripe for the premiers of the provinces to meet with him.
Bourassa now agreed to attend, and the first meeting was
held at the prime minister's summer residence at Harrington Lake, north of Ottawa, on August 4. The results were
encouraging, and in the following days a series of sessions
was held in the capital. The prime minister, provincial
premiers, territorial leaders, and aboriginal representatives
steadily advanced to agreement on contentious issues. An
early deal on a modified Senate provided momentum that
led the group to settlements on aboriginal self-government,
power sharing, and cooperation in a new economic and
social union. Approval for a final package of changes was
announced in the early evening of August 22. The meeting
then adjourned to Charlottetown, Prince Edward Island,
where the initial agreement on terms for confederation had
been reached in 1864, to review the final text of the document. At the same time, all governments and the aboriginal
leaders committed themselves to a nationwide referendum
on the proposals, to be held on the date specified by Quebec
for its referendum, October 26. Bourassa agreed that the
question used in the national plebiscite would also be asked
of Quebecers. When announced a few days later it was, in
Rae's words, "short, sharp, direct, blunt and unequivocal":
"Do you agree that the Constitution of Canada should be
renewed on the basis of the agreement reached on August
28, 1992?" In the first national referendum to be held in
Canada in 50 years, the country's destiny was to be decided
through a 22-word question.

The accord of August 28 drew on the September 1991
proposals of the federal government as well as the later
agreements reached among the federal, provincial, and territorial governments and aboriginal leaders. It opened with
a Canada Clause expressing fundamental values shared by
the whole country. Within this list was Quebec's position as
a "distinct society" based on the province's French-speaking
majority, unique culture, and civil law tradition.

The most far-reaching changes were those proposed for
the Senate and House of Commons. The Senate would be
reduced from its current 104 members to 62. There would
be six senators from each province and one from each of
the territories. The new body's powers to approve legislation
would depend on the category of the legislation. The defeat
or amendment of ordinary legislation by the Senate would
trigger a joint-sitting process with the Commons in which a
simple majority would prevail. Senators would have the right

to approve senior appointments to federal agencies. While the changes in the Senate brought equality of representation to all the provinces, House of Commons changes confirmed the dominance of the larger provinces through the principle of representation by population. Ontario and Quebec would each be assigned 18 additional seats, British Columbia 4, and Alberta 2. These 42 additional members, the number lost in the Senate, would bring the total membership of the House of Commons to 337 seats. Quebec would be guaranteed no fewer than 25% of the seats in the House of Commons, a number corresponding to its proportion of the Canadian population. Other provisions limited the federal spending power in fields of provincial jurisdiction. Exclusive provincial jurisdiction would be recognized in the areas of forestry, mining, tourism, recreation, housing, and municipal and urban affairs. Aboriginal peoples were recognized as having an inherent right to self-government.

With the support of the federal government in Ottawa, the governments of all 10 provinces and the two federal territories, as well as major native groups, the proposals appeared to have a good prospect of approval. Forces arrayed against the proposals included the separatist Parti Québécois in Quebec and its allies in the federal Parliament, the Bloc Québécois. The Reform Party, a western voice speaking against the domination of central Canada, opposed the proposals and called for a moratorium on further constitutional discussions. Interest groups, such as those urging women's rights, claimed that the proposals did not go far enough in advancing those rights. Former prime minister Pierre Trudeau castigated the Charlottetown arrangements as giving too many concessions to Quebec nationalists whose goal was to destroy Canada.

On October 26 Canadians decisively turned down, by a 54–45% margin, the constitutional changes proposed by their governments. Four provinces and one territory (Newfoundland, Prince Edward Island, New Brunswick, Ontario (very narrowly), and the Northwest Territories) voted "yes" for the Charlottetown accord; six provinces and one territory (Nova Scotia, Quebec, the four western provinces, and the Yukon Territory) voted "no." Seventy-five percent of eligible voters cast their ballots.

There were many reasons for the failure of the accord. In Quebec it was seen as not transferring sufficient new powers to the province. In Ontario many felt that it imposed difficulties in implementing new social programs. In the west there was concern over the vagueness of the sections dealing with aboriginal self-government and the cost of assistance to native peoples. For British Columbia, where the "no" vote was stronger than anywhere else, there was a belief that the province had not received its rightful representation in Parliament and that Quebec had been unfairly protected through its guarantee of 25% of House of Commons seats. A problem fundamental to constitution-making in Canada was also revealed. The west viewed Canada as a federation of 10 equal provinces with no special treatment for Quebec. To the older provinces—Quebec, Ontario, and the Atlantic provinces—Canada resulted from a partnership of two founding peoples, English and French, with two languages and two societies. To everyone's surprise, even many Indians living on reserves rejected the accord, convinced that it contained too many obstacles to the achievement of their desired goal of self-government.

Did the defeat of the constitutional proposals represent a victory for Quebec separatism? To Jacques Parizeau, leader of the Parti Québécois, the answer was clear. "This time we said what we didn't want, the next time we'll say what we want." Yet Parizeau had deliberately refrained from emphasizing independence as his goal in the campaign, and the "no" vote was not as large as the 60% of Quebecers who had rejected sovereignty linked with an economic association with the rest of Canada in the 1980 referendum. Many federalists, unhappy over aspects of the accord, had voted with the sovereigntists in the Quebec contest. Polls showed support for sovereignty had declined since 1980 and that Bourassa the federalist, not Parizeau the separatist, was the most popular politician in Quebec. Quebec's "no" did not mean an endorsement of independence.

Although political leaders believed that an opportunity had been lost, most agreed that a broad negative vote across the country was preferable to a split between Quebec and the rest of Canada. Clearly another vote would be needed in Quebec to provide a final pronouncement on sovereignty.

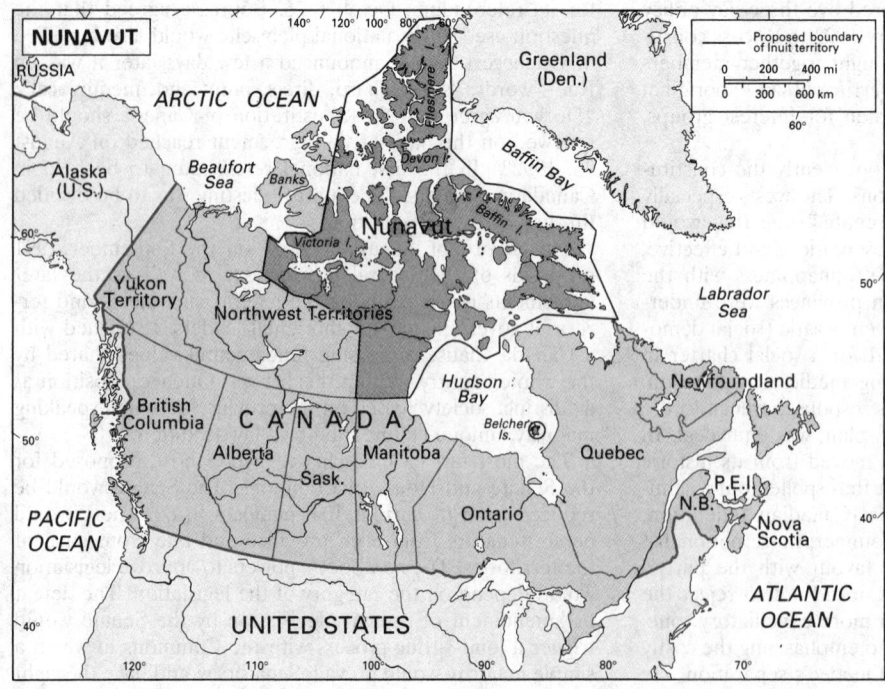

Nunavut ("our land") encompasses 350,000 sq km (135,000 sq mi) of the Northwest Territories. In November Inuit voters accepted an agreement with the Canadian government that would establish the territory of Nunavut by the end of the century.

Mulroney, unbowed by his defeat, announced that he would lead the Progressive Conservatives into an expected 1993 election, and that meanwhile he would make the improvement of the economy his top priority.

There were no Cabinet changes following Prime Minister Mulroney's sweeping reorganization of his Cabinet in April 1991. A Bloc Québécois (separatist) member resigned from the House of Commons in August. As of September 30, party standings in the 295-seat Commons were: Progressive Conservatives 158; Liberals 81; New Democratic Party 44; Bloc Québécois 8; Reform Party 1; Independent Conservative 1; Independent 1; vacancy 1.

The Yukon Territory held an election on October 19. Government leader Tony Penikett and his New Democratic Party administration, trying for a third term in office, were narrowly defeated by the conservative Yukon Party under John Ostashek. The new government was sworn in on November 7. In Alberta, Ralph Klein was sworn in as premier on December 14. Klein, who had been environment minister, replaced Donald Getty, who had announced his resignation in September.

The Economy. The sluggish global economy in 1992 was reflected in Canada, where the beginnings of a recovery were slow and halting. First-quarter growth was estimated at 1.1%; the second quarter was weaker at 0.7%. Merchandise exports and imports rose to record levels in the summer but had little impact on the overall economy, which was weakened by slow consumer spending. Unemployment was disturbingly high at 11.6% of the labour force during the summer months as industries attempted to restructure to meet competition. For the whole country the gross domestic product (GDP), on a seasonally adjusted annual basis, stood at $684.3 billion at the end of June. The only economic bright spots were to be found in historically low inflation and interest rates. In August the consumer price index showed a 1.2% increase from a year earlier, a rate comparable to those experienced in the early 1960s, and the Bank of Canada lending rate in late September was standing at 5.6%. Yet the lower rates did not appear to stimulate demand in consumer spending or the housing market.

Finance Minister Donald Mazankowski presented his first budget on February 25. In providing tax cuts and modest reductions in some areas of government expenditure, it appeared to set the stage for a general election, expected in 1993. Mazankowski reduced the income tax surtax on higher personal incomes in two steps, one beginning on July 1, 1992, the other on Jan. 1, 1993. In an effort to jump start the housing industry, the government agreed that up to $20,000 could be withdrawn tax free from an individual's retirement savings plan to buy or build a house in the year ending on March 1, 1993. The money had to be repaid into the retirement fund over the next 15 years. Forty-six agencies, boards, and state corporations were to be eliminated, merged, or privatized in a move to reduce expenditures. Spending for 1992–93 was projected at $159.6 billion, with revenues at $132.1 billion. The resulting deficit, $27.5 billion, was expected to be about $4 billion less than that occurring in the 1991–92 budget year. Revenues were down because of the recession, but lower interest rates also reduced the cost of carrying the public debt. On December 2, Mazankowski announced sharp cuts in spending, including a two-year wage freeze for all federal employees.

Foreign Affairs. Canada sent peacekeepers to the UN force monitoring the cease-fire in strife-torn Yugoslavia; 1,200 Canadian troops arrived in March, to be stationed in Croatia and in Sarajevo, where a force of 600 spent a month in July attempting to open the airport to relief flights. Later it was announced that another 1,200 troops would be as-

signed to UN tasks in the former Yugoslavia, and 750 men, as well as three large transport aircraft, were to be sent to Somalia in October to deliver and guard badly needed food supplies. Altogether, over 4,200 Canadians were serving in UN peacekeeping missions in countries from Cambodia to El Salvador in late 1992. On September 10 a naval supply ship left Halifax carrying carpenters, plumbers, and material to aid in the rebuilding of schools in south Florida after the onslaught of Hurricane Andrew.

A long-standing dispute with France over fishing zones around the tiny French islands of St. Pierre and Miquelon off the south coast of Newfoundland was settled by an international panel decision of June 10. The islands' fishermen were given access to a zone 24 nautical miles wide south and west of the islands, as well as to a strip 200 mi long and 10.5 mi wide reaching in a southerly direction to the open sea. France had claimed 13,703 square nautical miles in the Gulf of St. Lawrence; by the decision it gained control of 2,537 square miles.

After 14 months of tough negotiations, Canada, the U.S., and Mexico reached agreement late on August 11 on a North American Free Trade Agreement (NAFTA). The treaty, still to be ratified in the three countries, would create a free-trade zone encompassing some 364 million people, the largest in the world. For Canada NAFTA was seen as building on the Canada-U.S. agreement of 1989 (FTA). The new treaty would raise the North American content for duty-free automobiles from the 50% level of the FTA to 62.5% for cars and light trucks, 60% for parts alone. Under the pact, Canada would obtain protection from foreign imports for its poultry and dairy farmers and, along with Mexico, the right to screen incoming U.S. investment. NAFTA would also introduce technical improvements in the valuable dispute-settlement process contained in the earlier FTA. The North American commercial agreement was expected to become a controversial issue in a forthcoming election in Canada. Several provinces and the trade union movement were unhappy with it, fearing the loss of jobs to the low-cost Mexican economy. The unpopularity of the Mulroney government was also expected to make the selling of NAFTA a difficult task.   (D.M.L. FARR)

UNITED STATES

The United States of America is a federal republic composed of 50 states, 49 of which are in North America and one of which consists of the Hawaiian Islands. Area: 9,372,571 sq km (3,618,770 sq mi), including 205,856 sq km of inland water but excluding the 156,492 sq km of the Great Lakes that lie within U.S. boundaries. Pop. (1992 est.): 255,414,000. Cap.: Washington, D.C. Monetary unit: U.S. dollar, with (Oct. 5, 1992) a free rate of U.S. $1.70 to £1 sterling. President in 1992, George Bush.

With the cold war over, the 1991 Persian Gulf war a fast-fading memory, and no major foreign policy crises on the horizon, Americans were able to focus on domestic concerns in 1992. Chief among these were the sluggish economy and the quadrennial presidential election. Indeed, the two turned out to be virtually inseparable. After 12 years of Republican rule—8 under Ronald Reagan and 4 under George Bush (see BIOGRAPHIES)—Americans in 1992 voted resoundingly for change. Bill Clinton (see BIOGRAPHIES), the 46-year-old Democratic governor of the relatively small state of Arkansas, was elected the country's 42nd president. More than 100 million Americans voted in the election, or nearly 55% of registered voters; that was the best turnout in nearly two decades and a measure of how deeply Americans were concerned about the problems, mostly domestic, that their country faced. (See Special Report.)

Carol Moseley-Braun (left), the first African-American woman elected to the U.S. Senate, talks to prospective voters. A local Democratic official in Illinois, she upset the two-term incumbent in the primary and then went on to become one of four new women in the Senate.
BARBARA KASHIAN

The Economy. On the surface the U.S. seemed to be reasonably prosperous. Inflation and interest rates remained encouragingly low; by late 1992, consumer prices had risen less than 4% over the previous year, and the prime bank lending rate spent most of the year around 6%. Gross domestic product (GDP), the total amount of all goods and services produced in the U.S., had fallen in late 1990 and early 1991 but rose throughout 1992. While that growth was generally lower than in the boom years of the late 1980s, it was high enough to signal that the downturn of 1990–91 would not become a dreaded "double dip" recession. In the third quarter, GDP rose by a strong 3.9%.

Nonetheless, many Americans remained deeply pessimistic about the future; most measures of consumer confidence were well below 1991 levels. One explanation was that some secondary but highly visible measures of economic health were frightening. Unemployment remained intractably high throughout the year, at one point hitting 7.8% of the work force, and several large U.S. manufacturers had announced massive retrenchments. General Motors, the biggest industrial company in the world, was in the midst of a plan to close 21 assembly plants and drop 74,000 employees after posting a loss of nearly $4.5 billion in 1991, the largest ever recorded by a U.S. company. IBM, a mainstay of the U.S. economy since the dawn of the computer age, was eliminating 20,000 management-level jobs—a sign that even middle-class Americans were vulnerable. Real wages remained lower than they had been a decade earlier; the median weekly pay of a U.S. worker was about $391, or $18 less than in 1979, adjusted for inflation. Meanwhile, Americans watched in despair as their highways, bridges, parks, and schools deteriorated for lack of public funds, and their local taxes rose as the Reagan and Bush administrations shifted the burden for many programs from the federal government to states and municipalities. The $3.8 trillion national debt also frightened many Americans. So did the $341 billion federal budget deficit projected for 1993, which many people felt could be reduced only through higher taxes or painful reductions in federal spending, or both.

Foreign Affairs. In the aftermath of the Gulf war, the U.S. quickly wound down its military presence in the Middle East and turned over to the UN the job of policing Iraq's compliance with the treaty that ended the war. The U.S. did, however, provide warplanes to help enforce a no-fly zone over Iraq and support relief efforts to Iraq's rebellious Kurds. Meanwhile, a controversy simmered quietly over the role that U.S. officials and businesses had played in building up the Iraqi military before the war. There were allegations of U.S. complicity in illegal sales of arms and sensitive technology to Iraq, and even President Bush did not escape suspicion. Statements by a number of U.S. officials indicated that he had known more about secret U.S. dealings with both Iraq and Iran during their 10-year war than he had previously acknowledged. A Senate subcommittee did, however, exonerate Reagan campaign officials of charges that they had conspired with Iran to delay the release of U.S. hostages in Tehran until after the 1980 election in order to help prevent the reelection of Jimmy Carter. One high-ranking Reagan administration official, former defense secretary Caspar Weinberger, was indicted for lying to investigators about the government's role in providing arms to Iran, but he and five other officials were granted full pardons by Bush on December 24.

The U.S.-brokered peace talks between Israel and its Arab neighbours continued fitfully. The discussions stalemated late in the year, partly because of Israel's controversial expulsion of 415 Palestinians and partly because the U.S.—preoccupied with the election campaign and other domestic matters—relaxed its pressure on the two sides to keep talking. Diplomats, though, were generally optimistic that the negotiations would eventually bring results. A major reason for that view was the defeat of the hard-line Israeli government led by the Likud coalition and its replacement by a more flexible regime led by the Labour Party.

The Bush administration, mindful of the cost of U.S. involvement in the civil war in Vietnam nearly three decades earlier, was notably reluctant to intervene in the civil war in Yugoslavia, despite the urging of many of Bush's critics, who wanted the U.S. to do more to help embattled Bosnia and Hercegovina. One place the U.S. was not reluctant to intervene was Somalia. In December, Bush sent the first of an anticipated 28,000 U.S. troops to help distribute food to that country's starving population and to prevent local warlords from hijacking relief deliveries. The effort had broad support in Congress, in part because the administration indicated that the troops would not face intense danger and would possibly be home in early 1993. Observers in Somalia, however, believed that the American presence would have to last far longer if order was to be restored and maintained.

The U.S. was remarkably aloof toward the new democracies of eastern Europe and the former Soviet Union, whose liberation from communism had for decades been a primary aim of U.S. foreign policy. The Bush administration declined to make any significant commitments of financial aid to help those countries in the difficult transition to capitalist economies. President Bush did, however, join with Russian Pres. Boris Yeltsin to complete a new Strategic Arms Reduction Treaty, START II, scheduled to be signed on Jan. 3, 1993.

In a world newly devoid of superpower military rivalry, it appeared that economic competition might fill the vacuum. The U.S. and Japan continued their grousing over commercial matters, though not as loudly as in past years. More ominously, a major trade war momentarily loomed between the U.S. and the European Communities over subsidies to the EC's oilseed farmers. After negotiations to resolve the dispute failed, mostly because of French intransigence, the U.S. announced a 200% tariff on French white wine and other European products. U.S. and European negotiators appeared to have resolved the dispute at year's end.

Closer to home, President Bush, Canadian Prime Minister Brian Mulroney, and Mexican Pres. Carlos Salinas de Gortari signed the North American Free Trade Agreement (NAFTA), which would eliminate trade barriers among their countries. Environmentalists and trade union leaders in Canada and the U.S. feared that NAFTA would prompt companies to move jobs to less prosperous Mexico in search of lower wages and looser environmental regulations. In any event, the agreement would have to be ratified by the three countries' legislatures. In the U.S. that prospect looked favourable. Even Bill Clinton had declined to make a serious issue of NAFTA during the campaign.

Domestic Affairs. The seemingly insoluble question of race hung over much of U.S. public life throughout the year. A major focus of the debate was the rioting that erupted in Los Angeles after a jury with no black members acquitted four policemen in the beating of a black motorist, Rodney King, that had been captured on videotape by a bystander. The tape, seen by millions of Americans on television newscasts, showed what appeared to be indefensible brutality on the part of the policemen, yet the jury accepted their arguments that the force they used was justified. Outraged by the finding, thousands of Los Angeles residents, most of whom were African-American and Hispanic, took to the streets. Businesses and homes were burned, and dozens of people—many of them black—were killed. Property damage was put in the hundreds of millions of dollars.

The riots focused national attention on social and economic conditions in Los Angeles and other U.S. cities and prompted closer examination of long-standing complaints among blacks that police routinely mistreated them. Such complaints, along with allegations of mismanagement, served to hasten the retirement of Daryl Gates after 14 years as chief of the Los Angeles Police Department and his replacement by an African-American, Willie Williams (*see* BIOGRAPHIES). The four Los Angeles policemen were later indicted on federal civil rights charges for their role in the beating. King, partially recovered from his injuries, made a moving plea for racial amity at a press conference during the riots. "Can we all get along?" he asked.

The question resurfaced in dozens of incidents elsewhere. In New York City, racial tensions were high after a black man was acquitted of charges in the stabbing death of a Hasidic Jewish rabbinical student; the student was killed apparently in retaliation for the death of a black child who had been hit by a car that was part of a Hasidic Jewish motorcade. In Detroit, Mich., four policemen were charged with murder and manslaughter in the killing of a black motorist, but in this case the city remained calm. Law-enforcement organizations in Texas and elsewhere threatened a boycott of Time Warner Inc. after one of the company's record labels released "Cop Killer," a recording by rap music artist Ice-T, which they claimed would encourage violence toward police.

One event that was expected to fan flames of racial misunderstanding probably had the opposite effect: the release late in the year of *Malcolm X,* director Spike Lee's film biography of the Black Muslim leader. The more than three-hour-long movie was almost universally praised by audiences and critics as a thoughtful examination of black self-determination in America, and expectations of violence at the film's opening proved groundless. *Malcolm X* sold nearly $10 million worth of tickets in its first weekend in theatres. A vigorous merchandising campaign by Lee and other entrepreneurs had millions of Americans, including many whites, wearing hats and other articles of clothing emblazoned with the letter X.

A number of states tried to enforce various restrictions on abortion in 1992, with 24-hour waiting periods and requirements that parents of minors give consent among the most common. The U.S. Supreme Court upheld several such rules in a closely watched Pennsylvania case, reasoning that restrictions were acceptable if they did not place an "undue burden" on women. Using that standard, however, the court struck down a requirement that women seeking an abortion notify their husbands. Significantly, the Pennsylvania decision let stand the basic right to abortion, as established by the court in 1973 in *Roe* v. *Wade.* That reaffirmation surprised many legal experts, who had expected the court to overturn *Roe* v. *Wade,* especially since the panel's membership had shifted toward the right under the weight of several Reagan-Bush appointments. The court in 1992 also refused to reinstate an abortion law, the country's most restrictive, that had been adopted in the U.S. territory of Guam but quashed by a lower court. However, antiabortion forces did generally have an ally in the Bush administration;

After more than 50 years of production, a factory on the waterfront of Hoboken, N.J., shut down in the spring. The closing of facilities and elimination of jobs, called downsizing, continued in the U.S. in 1992.

A block of stores in south-central Los Angeles stands destroyed by the looting and arson that accompanied riots at the end of April. Although the disorder began in protest against the verdict in the Rodney King trial, it was generally agreed that inadequate police leadership and planning were to blame for allowing the crowds to get out of control.

LESTER STONE—WOODFIN CAMP & ASSOCIATES

the government moved to restrict the use of fetal tissue for research purposes and forbade government-funded clinics from even discussing abortion with patients (the so-called gag rule). The Clinton administration was expected to reverse those actions.

Gay activists pressed vociferously for equal rights for homosexuals and increased government funding for research on AIDS, which continued to devastate the homosexual population and had begun making inroads among heterosexuals as well. Several localities adopted "gay rights" measures, and a number of others acted resolutely to oppose such legislation. In the most publicized case, Colorado vot-

ers adopted an amendment to the state constitution that outlawed measures supportive of homosexual rights, and several Hollywood actors called for a boycott of the state in protest. Late in the year, a judge ordered the U.S. Navy to reinstate Petty Officer Keith Meinhold, a 12-year veteran who had been discharged after announcing on national television that he was gay. President-elect Clinton promised that he would end the long-standing prohibition against homosexuals in the armed forces, prompting senior officials in the military to protest that such a move would be harmful to discipline in the armed forces.   (DONALD MORRISON)

See also *Dependent States,* below.

Church Membership in the United States

Religious body	Total clergy	Inclusive membership	Religious body	Total clergy	Inclusive membership
Baha'i Faith	...	110,000	Jehovah's Witnesses	None	858,367
Baptist bodies			Jews	6,500	5,981,000
American Baptist Association	1,760	250,000	Latter Day Saints (Mormons)		
American Baptist Churches in the U.S.A.	8,356	1,535,971	Church of Jesus Christ of Latter-day Saints	31,059	4,267,000
Baptist Bible Fellowship, International	4,500	1,405,900	Reorganized Church of Jesus Christ of L.D.S.	16,666	189,524
Baptist General Conference	1,700	134,717	Lutherans		
Baptist Missionary Association of America	2,557	229,166	Evangelical Lutheran Church in America	17,402	5,240,739
Conservative Baptist Association of America	1,324	210,000	Lutheran Church—Missouri Synod	8,301	2,602,849
Free Will Baptists	2,900	197,206	Wisconsin Evangelical Lutheran Synod	1,607	420,039
General Baptists (General Association of)	1,384	74,156	Mennonites		
Liberty Baptist Fellowship	3,500	180,000	Mennonite Church	2,545	92,517
National Baptist Convention of America	28,574	2,668,799	Old Order Amish Church	3,140	70,650
National Baptist Convention, U.S.A., Inc.	27,500	5,500,000	Methodists		
National Primitive Baptist Convention	636	250,000	African Methodist Episcopal Church	6,550	2,210,000
Primitive Baptists	...	72,000	African Methodist Episcopal Zion Church	2,686	1,200,000
Progressive National Baptist Convention	863	521,692	Christian Methodist Episcopal Church	2,650	718,922
Regular Baptist Churches, General Association of	...	168,068	Free Methodist Church of North America	1,805	74,313
Southern Baptist Convention	64,500	15,038,409	United Methodist Church	38,359	8,904,824
Christian and Missionary Alliance	2,385	279,207	Wesleyan Church	2,499	111,992
Christian Brethren	500	98,000	North American Old Roman Catholic Church	150	62,611
Christian Congregation	1,455	109,919	Pentecostals		
Church of the Brethren	1,541	148,253	Assemblies of God	30,524	2,181,502
Church of God (Anderson, Ind.)	3,504	205,884	Church of God	2,737	75,890
Church of the Nazarene	9,363	573,834	Church of God (Cleveland, Tenn.)	6,585	620,393
Churches of Christ—Christian Churches			Church of God in Christ	10,426	3,709,661
Christian Church (Disciples of Christ)	6,899	1,039,692	Church of God in Christ, International	1,600	200,000
Christian Churches and Churches of Christ	6,596	1,070,616	Church of God of Prophecy	10,151	72,904
Churches of Christ	...	1,683,346	Full Gospel Fellowship of Churches and Ministers, Intl.	850	65,000
Community Churches, International Council of	...	250,000	International Church of the Foursquare Gospel	4,505	199,385
Congregational Christian Churches, Natl. Assn. of	650	90,000	Pentecostal Church of God	1,634	91,300
Eastern Churches			Pentecostal Holiness Church, International	2,095	119,073
Antiochian Orthodox Christian Archdiocese of N. Am.	325	350,000	United Pentecostal Church, International	7,464	500,000
Apostolic Catholic Assyrian Ch. of the East, N. Am. Dioc.	109	120,000	Polish National Catholic Church of America	141	282,411
Armenian Apostolic Church of America	29	150,000	Presbyterians		
Armenian Church of America, Diocese of the	61	450,000	Cumberland Presbyterian Church	799	98,891
Coptic Orthodox Church	49	165,000	Evangelical Presbyterian Church	313	52,645
Greek Orthodox Archdiocese of N. and S. America	655	1,950,000	Presbyterian Church in America	2,073	223,935
Orthodox Church in America	531	1,000,000	Presbyterian Church (U.S.A.)	20,338	3,788,009
Romanian Orthodox Episcopate of America	81	65,000	Reformed bodies		
Russian Orthodox Church Outside of Russia	168	55,000	Christian Reformed Church in North America	1,119	226,163
Serbian Orth. Ch. in the U.S.A. and Canada	82	67,000	Reformed Church in America	1,729	326,850
Ukrainian Orthodox Church in the U.S.A.	131	87,745	United Church of Christ	9,635	1,599,212
Episcopal Church	14,878	2,446,050	Roman Catholic Church	53,088	58,568,015
Evangelical Covenant Church of America	1,267	89,735	Salvation Army	5,184	445,566
Evangelical Free Church of America	1,863	192,352	Seventh-day Adventist Church	4,582	717,446
Friends United Meeting	585	54,945	Triumph the Church and Kingdom of God in Christ	1,375	54,307
Independent Fundamental Churches of America	1,510	78,174	Unitarian Universalist Association	1,210	191,543

Table includes churches reporting a membership of 50,000 or more and represents the latest information available.
Source: National Council of the Churches of Christ in the U.S.A., *Yearbook of American and Canadian Churches* (1992).

(ALICE M. JONES)

The U.S. Presidential Election

BY DONALD MORRISON

If anyone had told George Bush in early 1991 that he would be out of a job in little more than a year, he would surely have scoffed. Bush (see BIOGRAPHIES) was still taking bows for his leadership role in the coalition of industrial democracies that won the 1991 Gulf war and for presiding over the collapse of communism in eastern Europe and the Soviet Union. His approval rating at one point hit 90%, the highest ever recorded for a president. Yet while Bush was scoring well in opinion polls, other surveys detected a deepening pessimism, a sense that the country had gone off the rails. Two-thirds of Americans in one 1991 poll thought that many of the people running their government were crooked. Three-quarters of respondents in another survey felt that the political system was dominated by professional politicians who did not understand the problems of ordinary people.

That attitude was fed by a seemingly endless series of disclosures about lavish congressional perquisites, the influence of special interests on legislation and on regulatory decisions, the deterioration of government services even as taxes increased, and the standoff between the Republican White House and the Democratic-controlled Congress. As a measure of that political "gridlock," President Bush had vetoed some three dozen major bills since taking office, and congressional Democrats had been unable to muster the required two-thirds majority to overturn a single one of those vetoes. (On October 5 Congress finally managed to override Bush's veto of a cable-TV bill.) In nearly all cases, the bills embodied popular reforms but contained a tax increase of some sort, and Bush was leery of breaking a promise of his that had since become famous: "Read my lips. No new taxes." Bush made that vow in 1988 but sidestepped it in 1990 to allow a budget agreement with Congress, a move that angered his more conservative supporters.

Bush was also unfortunate to be president in a time of high anxiety over the economy. The country's savings and loans were devastated, and commercial banks were shaky. Real estate values had dropped. Real household income had barely changed in a decade, and it had held steady largely because both spouses were now working. America seemed to be losing ground in competitiveness and living standards to its European and Asian trading partners. Young Americans could no longer count on a better life than their parents enjoyed.

The Primary Season. As worried as many voters were about the future, Bush's personal popularity was so high that not many leading Democrats were willing to challenge his bid for reelection. Michael Dukakis, the party's unsuccessful candidate in 1988, made it clear that he would not run in 1992—not that many Democrats wanted him to. A perennial favourite, New Jersey's Sen. Bill Bradley, declined to run and was thought to be waiting until 1996. Yet the lure of the presidency remained so strong that, one by one, possible Democratic candidates began to emerge. Among them:

- Paul Tsongas, a former U.S. senator from Massachusetts who had left politics in 1984 after being diagnosed as having cancer and was now calling himself fully recovered
- Bob Kerrey, a U.S. senator from Nebraska who had received the Medal of Honor for his military service in Vietnam
- Douglas Wilder, the governor of Virginia and one of the country's most senior African-American officeholders
- Mario Cuomo, the governor of New York, known for his thoughtfulness, liberal views, and gifts as an orator
- Jerry Brown, a former California governor with a reputation as an unconventional—some said flaky—intellect
- Tom Harkin, a U.S. senator from Iowa with populist leanings and solid backing from organized labour
- Bill Clinton (see BIOGRAPHIES), the governor of Arkansas and a leading member of the party's centrist faction

Tsongas was first out of the gate, but he was soon eclipsed by Kerrey, designated the front-runner by virtue of his youth, war record, and Hollywood patina (he had for a time dated actress Debra Winger). The field narrowed slightly when Wilder dropped out of the race, recognizing that, as a black who was not well known outside his region, he had only a faint chance of winning. In one of the campaign's biggest surprises, Mario Cuomo, expected to become the favourite as soon as he declared his candidacy, announced that he would not run.

As the first primary—in New Hampshire on February 18—approached, Clinton's well-organized and well-financed campaign propelled him to the fore. Then a former lounge singer named Gennifer Flowers was quoted in the *Star,* a tabloid newspaper, as claiming she had had a 12-year affair with the governor. To contain the damage, Clinton and his wife, Hillary, appeared together to affirm the strength of their marriage. Polls showed that only a tiny proportion of Americans believed Flowers' story and that an overwhelming majority thought that the press had no business prying into a candidate's personal life. Nonetheless, Clinton's character had been introduced as a campaign issue. A *Wall Street Journal* story raised questions about his efforts to avoid military service in the Vietnam war era, and this time the candidate's responses were confusing and, to some minds, evasive. His standing in the polls began to slip. Tsongas won New Hampshire with 33% of the vote to Clinton's 25%.

Clinton fought back, winning the Georgia primary (with 57% to 24% for Tsongas). Kerrey, running out of money and not winning enough primaries, dropped out. So, for similar reasons, did Harkin. On the heavy primary day of March 10, "Super Tuesday," Clinton swept the South and the border states to emerge as the odds-on favourite. Tsongas withdrew and several months later underwent additional treatment for cancer. Clinton's only remaining rival, Jerry Brown, was conducting a low-cost, low-key campaign and was not a serious threat.

The Campaign. At the Democratic national convention, a relatively placid affair held in New York City, Clinton was officially designated the party's standard-bearer. As his vice presidential running mate, he chose Tennessee senator Al Gore (see BIOGRAPHIES), 44, who had campaigned for the presidency in 1988 but chose to sit out this race. Though Gore brought little in the way of geographic balance to the all-Southern ticket, he was young, photogenic, politically moderate, and articulate on a wide range of issues, especially the environment. His book on that subject, *Earth in the Balance: Ecology and the Human Spirit,* hit the bestseller lists for the second time after his nomination. In another departure from standard political practice, the two candidates spent much of their time in the ensuing weeks campaigning together, accompanied by their wives, on a series of bus trips through the American heartland. The tactic, which highlighted their mutual youthfulness and affability, was judged a success by Democratic strategists.

The Republicans, meanwhile, were facing some unexpected turbulence. Pat Buchanan, a political commentator and former speech writer for Pres. Richard Nixon, decided to run against Bush for the Republican nomination. Though dismissed by many politicians as a right-wing crank, Buchanan racked up a respectable 37% of the Republican vote in the New Hampshire primary, against Bush's 53%. The challenger made similar strong showings in other states, though not enough to give Bush serious trouble at the Republican national convention in Houston, Texas. Buchanan did, though, convince Bush strategists that he spoke for the party's conservative base, and he was allowed to deliver a major televised speech at the convention. That address, with its appeals to racial, religious, and cultural intolerance, stirred the delegates but evidently frightened many TV viewers. It also ran long, forcing the ever popular former president Ronald Reagan to appear after many Americans had gone to bed. Republican strategists later blamed the Buchanan speech, and other convention manifestations of ideological rigidity, for helping drive voters away.

Vice President Dan Quayle (see Biographies) remained another problem for the Republican ticket, though not, as it turned out, as serious a one as in 1988. Then his relative inarticulateness and lack of poise had made him the butt of jokes. He had become a more polished public figure in the ensuing four years, though he retained his gift for attracting controversy. In one speech early in the 1992 campaign, he criticized the fictional heroine of the CBS television network's popular "Murphy Brown" show for deciding to have a baby even though she was not married. Quayle's remark was consistent with the emerging Republican campaign theme of "family values," and it played well with voters concerned about the decline of the nuclear family and of morality in general. But the episode also alienated fans of the highly rated show and, some said, made the vice president look faintly ridiculous. Confused White House officials alternately disavowed and supported Quayle's remark. Quayle gained more attention when, in an appearance at a New Jersey elementary school, he insisted that the word *potato* was spelled with a final "e." It was rumoured that White House insiders tried to have him removed from the ticket, but he survived the coup, campaigned strenuously for Bush, performed creditably in the single vice presidential debate, and emerged from the election as a formidable contender for the Republican presidential nomination in 1996.

A larger problem for Bush—and, as it turned out, for Clinton—was H. Ross Perot (see Biographies), a Texas billionaire who had made a fortune in the computer industry. Denouncing Washington incompetence and promising vigorous action to reduce the immense national debt, Perot poured millions of dollars of his own money into his campaign and organized armies of "volunteers"—many of them paid—who got him on the ballot in all 50 states. Americans responded positively to Perot's folksy forthrightness, and he began scoring impressively in opinion polls. But in July, toward the end of the Democratic convention, he abruptly dropped out of the race, citing his general agreement with Clinton on economic matters.

With the election season approaching its crucial autumn phase, Bush began to trail far behind Clinton in the polls, and the president's reelection team was hampered by dissension and lack of direction. Jim Baker, Bush's longtime friend and former White House chief of staff, was persuaded to leave his post as secretary of state and run the campaign,

but he did not take over officially until shortly before the troubled convention. After the "family values" theme failed to improve the president's fortunes significantly, his strategists shifted to more direct attacks on Clinton's character and to the assertion that he would raise taxes. But the Clinton campaign, evidently having learned from Dukakis' fatal stoicism, responded quickly to the charges. Perot, haunted perhaps by accusations that he was a quitter, took advantage of the Bush-Clinton slanging to reenter the race. The first of his half-hour "infomercials"—commercials disguised as news programs—was seen by 16 million viewers.

All three candidates appeared on popular TV talk shows, but the campaign's best TV ratings were won by the three presidential debates. Bush, though at first reluctant to participate, eventually saw the debates as a chance to boost his sagging fortunes. He managed a draw at best. In the first debate, in St. Louis, Mo., Perot stole the show with his down-home informality and sharp one-liners. In the second, held before a panel of ordinary citizens in Richmond, Va., the candidates heard complaints that the campaign had grown too negative; Bush wisely avoided negative comments but missed an opportunity to make an issue of Clinton's trustworthiness. In the third debate, at East Lansing, Mich., Bush finally seemed focused and forceful, but it was too late.

In the campaign's final days, the president, hammering away at the issues of trust and taxes, did manage to gain ground. Clinton continued to focus on economic issues, heeding the advice of a well-publicized sign posted at his Little Rock, Ark., campaign headquarters: "The economy, stupid." Ironically, that issue was helping Perot. Clinton advisers, who had previously assumed that Perot was taking votes mostly from Bush, began to fear the Texan would cripple their man as well. Perot, however, hurt his credibility in the final weeks by making unsubstantiated charges about an attempt on his life by foreign terrorists and a plot by Republicans to disrupt his daughter's wedding.

The Vote. When the votes were in, Clinton had won the election with 43% of the vote to Bush's 38%. Perot received a remarkably strong 19%, the best showing for a third presidential candidate since 1912. Clinton carried 32 states and the District of Columbia to 18 for Bush and none for Perot, and the electoral college vote was Clinton 370, Bush 168. The Democratic recovery of the White House did not, however, translate into comparable gains in Congress. Though the party would control both chambers, as before, it lacked the numbers needed to prevent Republicans from filibustering.

The election did clearly establish 1992 as what many called "the year of the woman." The number of female U.S. senators rose from two to six, and the number of women in the House of Representatives increased from 28 to 47; an overwhelming majority of them were Democrats. Similarly encouraging for women was the prominent role, as strategist and surrogate candidate, that Hillary Clinton, a lawyer well-versed on many issues, notably childrens' rights, had played in her husband's campaign.

At age 46, Bill Clinton would become the youngest president since 43-year-old John F. Kennedy took office in 1961. Clinton was also the first member of the large and influential demographic group born after World War II—the baby boomers—to occupy the Oval Office. Al Gore, at 44 not quite as young as Dan Quayle when he became vice president in 1988, was also a genuine baby boomer. To paraphrase a famous line by Kennedy, the torch had indeed passed to a new generation.

Donald Morrison is assistant managing editor of Entertainment Weekly *magazine and former senior editor of* Time *magazine.*

Developments in the States in 1992

The states maintained their role on the front lines of social policy as the federal government's goal of shifting responsibility to state governments continued to be felt and congressional gridlock worsened. State governments, having taken the lead on such issues as health care, family leave, education, and the environment for the past 12 years, had reason to believe that things might change with the election of Bill Clinton, an activist governor and former chairman of the National Governors' Association. There was optimism in some quarters, concern in others, that the federal government would once again take a more active role in governing.

Party Strengths. The November elections yielded mixed results, with only modest changes in party strengths. The Democrats added to their majorities in statehouses, but Republicans took control of both legislative chambers in three additional states. Nevertheless, a dramatic transfer of power seemed assured by an enormous influx of new legislators, many of them members of minority groups.

Democrats won 8 of the 12 gubernatorial contests, for a net gain of 2, giving them a total of 30, compared with 18 Republicans and 2 independents. All four Democratic incumbents were reelected, including Evan Bayh of Indiana, at 36 the country's youngest governor. Democrats picked up seats in Delaware, Missouri, and North Carolina, where former governor James Hunt won a comeback victory. Republicans held on to governorships in Montana, New Hampshire, and Utah and picked up a seat in North Dakota, where businessman Edward Schafer won the seat of retiring Democratic governor George Sinner. Democrats controlled both houses of the legislature in 25 states, while Republicans held 9 and 15 others were split. (Nebraska has a unicameral, nonpartisan legislature.)

More than 2,000 newcomers were elected to legislatures, a turnover rate of more than 25%, the largest in more than a decade. The anti-incumbent movement claimed a significant number of victims among legislative leaders; more than 80 leaders decided against running for reelection, and 9 others from seven states were tossed out by the voters.

While all three women gubernatorial candidates lost, the number of women winning elective office at the state level continued its steady growth. The Center for the American Woman and Politics reported that women would constitute 20% of state legislators in 1993, an 11% gain from 1992. Seventy-one women also held statewide elected office, 20% of the total.

New women executives included four lieutenant governors, four attorneys general, two secretaries of state, and three treasurers. Washington state had the most women in executive office, including attorney general, lands commissioner, schools superintendent, and insurance commissioner. Women were elected to the highest court in five states and, in Indiana, Pam Carter became the nation's first black female attorney general.

Government Structures, Powers. Voters nationwide made a record number of decisions, with more than 200 initiatives and referenda on the ballot. Term limits won in all 14 states where they were on the ballot. Arizona, Arkansas, California, Florida, Michigan, Missouri, Montana, Nebraska, North Dakota, Ohio, Oregon, South Dakota, Washington, and Wyoming joined Colorado, which had approved term limits in 1990. As a result, 181 members of the next Congress would go to Washington, D.C., with the spectre of term limits over them, although a future court challenge could determine whether states have the right to limit congressional terms. Eleven states also limited the terms of state officeholders.

In Oregon voters rejected an initiative defining homosexuality as "abnormal, wrong, unnatural and perverse," but in Colorado a constitutional amendment rescinded gay-rights ordinances in Aspen, Boulder, and Denver. Soon afterward, groups from around the U.S. promised to ban events in the state, and many threatened to do their skiing elsewhere.

Many people thought the most critical and far-reaching issue facing voters was Proposition 161, known as the "California Death with Dignity Act." The state would have become the only jurisdiction in the world to sanction physician-assisted suicide for terminally ill patients. Despite the backing of some physicians, the American Civil Liberties Union, and the Gray Panthers, among others, opponents argued that the law's safeguards would not give adequate protection to patients. The measure failed (as had a similar one the year before in Washington), but the issue was not likely to go away.

Voters in Colorado, Illinois, Kansas, Missouri, and New Mexico endorsed constitutional amendments to create victims' bills of rights. In Colorado a school-choice proposal giving parents vouchers worth up to $2,400 per child for public or private school was overwhelmingly defeated. Arizona finally recognized Martin Luther King, Jr., Day as an official paid state holiday. And Iowa voters nullified a section of their state constitution that disqualified anyone who had participated in a duel from holding public office.

Finances. The slow national recovery from recession did little to ease the budget crisis in the states. Despite the largest collective tax increase in 20 years in 1991, most states remained hard-pressed to balance their budgets. The year began with 31 states expecting shortfalls as a result of the sluggish economy, even as half the states reported that expenses for mandated social programs were well above estimates. As taxpayer resistance to still more taxes blossomed into full-scale revolt, the states were forced to resort to painful cuts in spending.

State workers were a favourite target of budgeteers. Twenty-one states reduced the number of government jobs during the year; 18 reduced employee benefits; and one-third eliminated pay raises. New Jersey laid off 1,500 state workers in October, a 2% reduction in its work force. Massachusetts and Michigan also experienced sizable layoffs.

The most notable budget crisis of the year was in California, where a recession far more virulent than the national average decimated state coffers and plunged the Golden State into fiscal chaos. Confronted with a $10.7 billion deficit, Democratic legislators pushed for higher taxes, lower welfare payments, and reduced subsidies to local jurisdictions, while Republican Gov. Pete Wilson proposed massive spending cuts, particularly in health, welfare, environmental, and educational programs. The state ran out of cash in July and issued more than $2 billion in IOUs to creditors. After several banks refused to honour the IOUs in August, a compromise was reached in September that required major cuts in spending on social programs.

Because it was an election year, tax increases for 1992 were relatively small. Even so, state taxes were raised by an estimated $5.3 billion, roughly one-quarter of the total raised the previous year. Of that amount, nearly half was raised by the taxation of enterprises associated with health care. Twenty-seven states raised taxes for fiscal 1993, while 10 reduced them. Nine states raised taxes by more than 5%. Personal income taxes rose in 11 states, corporate taxes in 8, and sales taxes in 10. Ten states increased excise taxes on fuel and motor vehicles; Alabama and Maryland hiked their gasoline taxes by a hefty five cents per gallon. Maryland and the District of Columbia raised taxes by 20 cents per pack of cigarettes. West Virginia was the only state to enact a reduction in income-tax rates.

Several jurisdictions raised revenues by broadening their tax bases. Florida started taxing pest-control and security services, while Maryland included building-cleaning, credit-reporting, and security services. Dry cleaning and laundry were subject to taxes in the District of Columbia, as were local government purchases in Minnesota. Dismaying its farmers, Nebraska imposed a $4-per-ton tax on fertilizer. As concern over the environment became more popular politically, 17 states increased their taxes and fees on waste and environmental services; nine states imposed new taxes on solid- and hazardous-waste-disposal activities.

Despite the ocean of red ink, 10 states managed net decreases in taxation totaling $1.4 billion. The New Jersey legislature repealed a one-cent increase in the sales tax engineered previously by Gov. James Florio and then overrode his veto. In Pennsylvania and Massachusetts personal-income-tax surcharges were allowed to expire.

Taxpayers predictably demonstrated their irritation at being asked to raise their tax burdens by beating back several such attempts at the polls in November. In Oklahoma a tax on health-care providers was trounced, and a proposal to raise the sales tax by 1% to fund education was rejected in Colorado, whose voters approved an initiative requiring all future tax increases to be approved by the voters. And in California voters defeated Proposition 167, the so-called Robin Hood Amendment that would have drastically increased business taxes and income taxes on the state's wealthiest wage earners.

The most creative new tax was enacted in Minnesota, which began charging a 2% levy on gross revenues of any hospital in the U.S. that treated at least 20 Minnesotans. Neighbouring states were particularly incensed by the tax, which seemed destined for a test of its constitutionality in the courts.

Education. The 20-year struggle to devise an equitable plan for funding education in Texas continued. According to the Texas

Education Agency, the state spent $2,337 per student per year in the poorest district, compared with $56,791 per student in the wealthiest. The legislature's most recent plan was declared unconstitutional, and the state was given a court-imposed deadline of June 1993 to come up with an alternate funding scheme.

A long-awaited U.S. Supreme Court ruling in a Mississippi school-desegregation case might lead to a reexamination of desegregation settlements in more than 15 other states. This was the first time the Supreme Court had dealt with desegregation at the college level, and the decision might inadvertently create problems for historically black colleges. The suit was brought by African-American students seeking increased funding for Mississippi's three black colleges. In ruling for the plaintiffs, the Supreme Court returned the case to a lower court, saying the burden of proof was on the state to "prove that it has undone its prior segregation." But the lower court's proposed remedy effectively closed two of the three black colleges and infuriated civil rights activists less interested in integrating higher education than in preserving and improving existing black colleges.

Maryland became the first state to require students to perform community service as a prerequisite for graduation. Many private schools throughout the U.S. had similar requirements, but only a handful of cities, including Atlanta, Ga., and Detroit, Mich., had community service programs in their public schools as a condition for receiving a high-school diploma. Activities such as working in soup kitchens, homeless shelters, or senior citizen centres were acceptable choices for fulfilling the requirement, as were tutoring fellow classmates or helping with recycling projects. The goal of community service—to create a sense of personal and social responsibility, increase self-esteem, and generally get in touch with reality—failed to impress most student and teacher associations or the 22 of Maryland's 24 school districts that opposed the requirement.

A local school board in a working-class section of Queens, New York City, adamantly refused to accept part of a 443-page multicultural curriculum entitled *Children of the Rainbow*. In the section on "Fostering Positive Attitudes Toward Sexuality," first-grade teachers were encouraged to "include references" to lesbians and gays. A reading list included such titles as *Heather Has Two Mommies* and *Daddy's Roommate*. Board members and parents were enraged at what they considered a violation of their rights and the outright promotion of a gay life-style. New York City had 31 other school boards, all of which accepted the curriculum as it was or with minor modifications.

Health and Welfare. The number of families on welfare in the U.S. reached a record high of nearly five million, with some estimates adding almost 2,000 children a day to the rolls. New Jersey signed into law a major overhaul of its welfare system, with the most dramatic feature a cap on family size. The state no longer would grant an extra $64 per month to a woman on welfare who had another child. The plan also made it possible for women to marry and not lose their benefits. As part of the New Jersey legislature's budget cuts, general assistance

benefits of $140 a month would be limited to six months each year. In a ruling hailed by advocates of the homeless, a Florida judge ordered Miami to create two arrest-free "safe zones" where homeless people would be able to sleep, bathe, eat, and sit without getting arrested or harassed by the police. The judge said that it was a violation of their constitutional rights to arrest the homeless for "harmless, involuntary, life-sustaining acts."

The National Governors' Association declared that the Medicaid system had become "unmanageable for governors and states." Oregon proposed a plan that would have extended benefits to 120,000 additional poor people—primarily women and children—through a system of rationing. The plan ranked 709 medical conditions according to their procedures' costs and benefits. Anything ranked lower than 587th would no longer be covered by Medicaid. The plan was rejected by the federal government because it deviated from Medicaid law, but it nevertheless drew wide attention and support.

Connecticut, California, Indiana, and New York began cosponsoring the sale of long-term nursing home insurance. The idea was to let elderly residents keep up to $50,000 in assets and still qualify for Medicaid—provided they bought the insurance first.

Pennsylvania became the first state to furnish information on patient death rates of surgeons who performed coronary bypass surgery. It was learned that the two most expensive hospitals had the highest death rates, while the least expensive had the lowest.

Abortion. The hot political issue of abortion failed to dominate the presidential campaign as activists on both sides had hoped. The Supreme Court's decision in a Pennsylvania case gave a little to each group, keeping *Roe* v. *Wade* legal while upholding restrictions such as a 24-hour waiting period and parental consent for minors. Polls showed that most Americans found the decision an acceptable compromise.

Parental consent came under attack in several states. In California a law requiring unmarried women under 18 to obtain permission from a parent or a judge before having an abortion was ruled unconstitu-

tional. A judge in Ohio struck down as unconstitutional a law stating that women wanting an abortion would have to get counseling 24 hours before the procedure and be informed about fetal development. In Virginia the governor vetoed a parental-notification bill for unmarried women under 18, and a Michigan judge ruled that state's parental consent law for women 17 and younger unenforceable as written. The governor of Kansas signed into law a bill requiring an eight-hour waiting period after medical counseling and parental notification.

Mississippi became the first state to enforce a 24-hour waiting period. There were some 10 other states with laws on the books that had not yet been enforced. A referendum in Maryland was approved guaranteeing a woman's right to an abortion until the fetus was viable outside the womb, and voters in Arizona defeated a constitutional amendment that would have banned most abortions.

Laws and Justice. Pennsylvania became the last state to adopt a law giving terminally ill patients the right to die. All states now recognized some form of living will, and many recognized a family's right to decide for someone who had not signed a living will.

Hours before the governor of Michigan signed legislation banning physician-assisted suicide, retired pathologist Jack Kevorkian helped two acutely ill women end their lives, bringing to eight the number of patients who had asked and received his help since 1990. Known as Dr. Death, Kevorkian faced murder charges in two deaths, but the case was dropped because Michigan had no law against assisted suicide. The new bill imposed a 15-month ban while a commission studied the issue. A survey conducted by the American Society of Internal Medicine revealed that one in five physicians said that he or she had deliberately taken action to cause a patient's death.

In a case that drew national attention, a 12-year-old Florida boy became the first child in the U.S. to hire an attorney and sue to sever his relationship with his natural mother. The boy, Gregory Kingsley, wanted a "divorce" from his mother so that his foster parents could adopt him. He had spent much of his life in foster care and had lived

PETER FREDIN—GAMMA LIAISON

Gay rights supporters in Denver protest a measure passed by Colorado voters on November 3 to prohibit legislation giving antidiscrimination protection to homosexuals. Several groups throughout the U.S. vowed to boycott the state unless the measure was overturned.

with his mother only seven months out of the last eight years. His father relinquished his parental rights, but Gregory's mother contested the case. The judge sided with Gregory—who also asked that his name be changed to Shawn—in what appeared to be the first time family rights had been ended because of legal action brought by a child. Legal experts said that this was a natural evolution in the way that society and the legal system viewed the rights of children. Only a century earlier, children had been considered chattel with no rights at all.

In a New York courtroom, the definition of family continued its evolution. A surrogate court judge, saying that "a child who receives proper nutrition, adequate schooling and supportive shelter is among the fortunate, whatever the source," approved the adoption of a six-year-old boy by the lesbian partner of the child's mother. The women, who were both employed, had lived as a couple for 14 years.

Massachusetts proposed the toughest law in the nation to help locate parents who owed child support and to punish those who did not pay. Massachusetts would become the first state to garnishee insurance reimbursement checks and to suspend or revoke drivers' licenses of those who did not keep their court dates and who had outstanding arrest warrants. The state would also have the power to revoke professional licenses.

The New Jersey Supreme Court ruled that, in towns without salaried public defenders, attorneys in private practice had to provide free legal service to criminal defendants. This would apply even to those lawyers who did not practice criminal law. New Jersey also became the first state to require students to wear seat belts on school buses.

Prisons. In fiscal 1992 states spent more than $15 billion to operate prison systems. Though operating costs in fiscal 1993 were expected to increase only 5%, spending on construction was expected to double to $4 billion as 112 new prisons opened to house 75,000 more inmates. With punishment programs second only to health costs as the fastest growing part of state budgets, lawmakers were rethinking the human and financial cost of recent trends toward tougher criminal laws, especially mandatory minimum sentencing statutes. Nearly every state had begun experimenting with alternatives to prison for nonviolent offenders. These included drug treatment and vocational and educational programs.

Thirty-one prisoners on death row were executed in 1992, the highest number since the 1976 reinstatement of capital punishment. More than one-third (12) took place in Texas. Arizona, California, Delaware, and Wyoming carried out their first executions since the reinstatement.

According to the Centers for Disease Control and Prevention, the incidence of tuberculosis was three times higher among prison inmates than in the general population. Contributing factors included overcrowding, delays in diagnosis, and a lack of facilities for isolating patients.

Native Americans in prison in Colorado would now find it easier to call for divine intervention. Colorado became the third state, joining Arizona and New Mexico, to allow prayer services by traditional Indian religious practitioners. Prisoners would be able to worship with sacred items such as

sage, cedar, and sweet grass. Drums, eagle feathers, tobacco, and the use of sweat lodges would also be allowed.

Gambling. In 1992 some form of legalized gambling existed in every state except Utah and Hawaii. The gambling industry had grown faster than the general economy in almost every year since 1982. But along with the benefits of more revenue and jobs came a variety of problems. On canyon roads near the three gambling towns of Black Hawk, Cripple Creek, and Central City in Colorado, it was estimated that in 1992 there was a threefold increase in drunk driving arrests and citations over the previous year. The three towns were also put on the list of most endangered historic landmarks by the National Park Service because of demolition and new construction related to gambling. Local authorities in the three towns were ordered by the Colorado Department of Health to increase the capacity of their sewage-treatment plants, which had become overloaded and were spilling pollutants into mountain streams. In Iowa the riverboat gambling town of Fort Madison borrowed $2.6 million for riverfront improvements, but before they could be completed, the two floating casinos sailed off to Mississippi, leaving hundreds of people out of work and the local government badly in debt.

In a move that critics feared could turn New Orleans into the Las Vegas of the South, the Louisiana legislature approved a bill that would allow construction of a large casino near the French Quarter. The project was strongly backed by Gov. Edwin W. Edwards, whose love of gambling was legendary but whose past indictment and subsequent acquittal on charges of fraud and racketeering left some citizens a bit wary. Opponents of the plan—derided as "do-gooders" by the governor—argued that, among other things, Louisiana already had plenty of other forms of legalized gambling, including betting on cockfights in rural areas of the state. The truly compulsive gambler could applaud the legislature in New Jersey, where a law was passed allowing casinos in Atlantic City to stay open 24 hours on weekends and holidays.

Environment. Environmentalists had cause to cheer the election of vice presidential candidate Sen. Al Gore of Tennessee. Referred to as "the Ozone man" by U.S. Pres. George Bush during the campaign, Gore was an ardent supporter of environmental issues.

Governors from 12 Northeastern and Middle Atlantic states and the mayor of the District of Columbia signed an agreement to develop a regional plan that would put them in compliance with the Clean Air Act of 1990. The states would face fines if they were unable to reduce ground-level ozone, the main element in urban smog. Controls to minimize motor-vehicle emissions and standards for stationary sources of nitrogen oxides were also adopted.

The decline of California's San Francisco Bay and its estuary was called "one of the worst environmental calamities of the American West." The estuary in 1992 supplied drinking water to 20 million people and irrigation for millions of hectares of agricultural land. New pumping rules and water standards were implemented to revitalize the bay and reverse ecological damage. California also established regu-

lations mandating the elimination of hydrocarbons in household products. More than 2,600 products, such as laundry starch and aerosol cooking sprays, were affected. Though many were already in compliance, it was estimated that consumer products accounted for 10% of nonautomotive emissions of hydrocarbons.

A New Jersey law to reduce pollution by heavy metals banned most household batteries now in use because of their high mercury content. Manufacturers were required to eliminate mercury from dry cells by the end of 1995 and to establish collection programs for used batteries. Rechargeable products would also have to be redesigned so that batteries could be removed before the product was discarded. The measure, one of the toughest in the nation, would prevent potentially deadly pollutants from entering the waste stream.

In Oklahoma a 22-year-old nuclear factory with a history of violations was finally closed. The plant, which processed uranium for fuel rods and military shells, had experienced numerous accidents, including fires and leakage of toxic gas. Uranium was discovered leaking into underground waters at levels 35,000 times higher than federal law allowed.

Equal Rights. Gay Americans had much to celebrate this election year. President-elect Clinton made unprecedented campaign promises to further the rights of homosexuals and to step up the federal government's fight against AIDS. A spokesman for the National Gay and Lesbian Task Force declared, "We have moved from political outsider and social pariah to political partner and Washington insider."

Republican Gov. Pete Wilson of California signed into law a measure banning job discrimination based on sexual orientation for state and private employees. Religious organizations and businesses with fewer than five employees were exempt. The law was similar to the one Wilson had vetoed in 1991. California thus joined Wisconsin, Massachusetts, Hawaii, Connecticut, Vermont, and New Jersey in adding sexual orientation to the factors covered in job-discrimination laws.

In Massachusetts, Republican Gov. William Weld approved visitation rights for gay couples in prisons and state hospitals and granted gay state employees the same spousal bereavement rights as heterosexual couples. In Kentucky the state Supreme Court struck down the state's antisodomy law, saying that the law violated the constitutional privacy rights of gays. Kentucky was one of eight states with laws prohibiting sexual acts between people of the same sex. In Texas a district judge overturned the Dallas police department's policy barring homosexuals from serving as police officers. Dallas was the only major city to have such a policy.

Iowa voters rejected a two-sentence referendum granting equal constitutional rights to women. The first sentence would have added the words "and women" to the preamble declaring Iowa men "free and equal." The second reference banned discrimination based on gender. Groups from the religious right campaigned strongly against the measure. North Carolina and New York joined 27 other states giving employment-protection to people who smoked off the job.   (MELANIE ANNE COOPER)

Latin America and the Caribbean

LATIN-AMERICAN AFFAIRS

The year 1992, which marked the 500th anniversary of Christopher Columbus' arrival in the Americas, turned out to be a particularly turbulent one in large areas of Latin America. Perhaps the most dramatic events were registered in Venezuela, Peru, and Brazil.

Political Developments. In Venezuela there were two failed attempts by the military (on February 4 and November 27) to seize power from the government of Pres. Carlos Andrés Pérez. Both were led by members of the Revolutionary Bolivarist Movement, whose inspirational leader was Lieut. Col. Hugo Chávez (imprisoned after the February coup attempt).

Peru's president, Alberto Fujimori, acted to suspend the country's constitution on April 5, in effect imposing a "self coup," following challenges by the legislature to his free-market reforms. When it became clear that the country risked international isolation if democratic procedures were not reinstated, Fujimori announced that polls to elect an 80-member constituent assembly would be held later in the year. During the period from May to September, the terrorist organization Sendero Luminoso (Shining Path) stepped up its bombing campaign in the capital, Lima, adding to the government's difficulties. On September 13 the authorities captured the Sendero leader, Abimael Guzmán. He was sentenced to life imprisonment on October 27, but this did not deter the movement from taking fresh action. Meanwhile, disquiet within the country's military resulted in an assassination attempt on Fujimori on November 13—barely a week before the assembly elections (which went ahead as planned and produced a majority of pro-government members).

In Brazil allegations in May of an influence-peddling racket devised by Pres. Fernando Collor de Mello's former campaign treasurer, Paulo César Farias, led to a congressional inquiry during July–August that produced evidence that Collor, close family members, and associates were also involved. This did not prevent Collor from scoring an important personal success when serving as host to the UN "Earth Summit" in Rio de Janeiro during June. However, on September 29 more than a two-thirds majority of Congress voted for an impeachment trial of the president. This was conducted by the Senate during October–December. In the interim, from October 2 Vice Pres. Itamar Franco became acting president, with a new government team, and he was expected to be sworn in as president after the Senate verdict on Collor. On December 29, just as the Senate was beginning the decisive session of the impeachment hearings, Collor resigned. Hours later Franco was sworn in as president.

The year got off to a promising start in regard to bringing sustained peace to El Salvador, which had been riven by civil war for some 12 years. An accord was reached at a Central American summit held in Mexico City on January 15 and chaired by Mexican Pres. Carlos Salinas de Gortari. However, an October 31 deadline, by which time the leftwing Farabundo Martí National Liberation Front was to demobilize, was missed, and the deadline was extended to mid-December. On September 11 a World Court ruling ended a long-running dispute between El Salvador and Honduras.

In Nicaragua the administration of Pres. Violeta Barrios de Chamorro encountered further difficulties in restructuring many of the country's institutions (especially the security forces), which remained dominated by individuals from the Sandinista period. Earlier in the year this situation had jeopardized relations with, and aid from, the United States, but the position was gradually rectified from about May onward.

Despite the increased economic hardship occasioned by the collapse of the former Soviet Union, Cuba's Pres. Fidel Castro remained firm in his commitment to retaining political control in the hands of a single (Communist) party. During the year it became clear that some ground was being given in favour of more democratic practices, with direct elections and secret ballots being introduced for municipal offices and provincial assemblies. The authorities were also attempting to attract more foreign investors. On November 24 a UN General Assembly resolution (supported by some 59 nations, including Mexico and Canada) called for an end to the U.S. trade embargo against Cuba. Implementing this would fall to the new Democrat-led administration of Bill Clinton.

Little progress was made in 1992 toward securing the return of Haiti's democratically elected Pres. Jean-Bertrand Aristide—in exile since September 1991—although the military-backed government was prepared to allow partial elections for 9 of 27 Senate seats in late December. In the latter part of the year, associates of the deposed leader were working within the Organization of American States and the UN, and in discussions with advisers of the incoming U.S. Clinton administration, to find a solution that might overcome the obstacles to Aristide's return and to resolve difficulties posed by large numbers of Haitian asylum-seekers in the U.S.

In presidential elections held in Ecuador in two rounds (May 17 and July 5), Sixto Durán Ballén (*see* BIOGRAPHIES) of the new Republican Unity Party defeated Jaime Nebot of the Social Christian Party as well as eclipsing the former ruling party, the Democratic Left. Durán began his four-year term on August 10, but the swift introduction of a series of free-market reforms (including extensive privatization) and economic-adjustment measures was not well received, and a one-day general strike was held on September 23.

Guyana's twice-postponed general election was held on October 5. It resulted in victory for Cheddi Jagan's People's Progressive Party, but not before there had been rioting and violence, largely perpetrated by supporters of the former ruling People's National Congress. In Jamaica Prime Minister Michael Manley retired at the end of March owing to health problems and was replaced by former finance minister Percival Patterson (who had been removed from office in a Cabinet reshuffle in January).

The year began fairly positively for Colombia's president, César Gaviria, with the ruling Liberal Party winning an overall majority in local elections in early March. But the situation deteriorated from April, when the government declared a state of economic emergency on account of electric power shortages. During subsequent months peace talks with guerrilla groups lapsed, imprisoned Medellín drug baron Pablo Escobar escaped (July 22), and the general political situation deteriorated. This was compounded after Gaviria again declared a state of emergency on November 8, in a bid to fight so-called Marxist rebels. In late November members of the ex-guerrilla M-19 movement—which, having demobilized to become a political party in 1989, had previously supported the government—withdrew from the government.

Representatives of the governments of Argentina and Brazil shake hands at the signing of the Tlatelolco Treaty in Mexico City on August 26. The treaty, which would prohibit nuclear weapons in Latin America and the Caribbean, was signed by 11 countries.
AP/WIDE WORLD

In Uruguay the fortunes of the government of Luis Lacalle and the ruling National (Blanco) Party were mixed, with Cabinet resignations in January and increasing opposition activity to block key planks of the party's economic-reform program. Not least, on December 13 a national referendum on privatization resulted in heavy defeat for the government, which had favoured privatizing some state-controlled firms.

Economic Affairs. Concerning economic developments, 1992 was expected to produce average growth of the region's gross domestic product (GDP) of 3–4%, with inflation declining to well under the roughly 300% of 1991. Among the major economies, by the final quarter of the year, increases in the GDP were more than 10% in Chile, over 9% in Venezuela, 6–7% in Argentina, and close to 3% in Mexico. Brazil was the main exception, with a deep recession continuing in the nation's industries throughout the year and zero to negative growth expected overall. On the other hand, Brazil was running a strong trade surplus ($12,890,000,000 by the end of October), while Mexico was expected to end the year with a deficit of more than $18 billion. Argentina's trade position also moved toward a $1 billion annual deficit, and Chile's surplus was cut to about $850 million, both results largely influenced by a high level of imports.

The region's foreign debt remained high (more than $420 billion in nominal terms), although further progress was made toward converting the commercial debt of Argentina and Brazil into bonds. Agreement in principle on an arrangement covering $31 billion (including $8 billion of arrears) was reached between Argentina and its bankers on April 6, and there was a similar accord (covering $44 billion) for Brazil on July 9. Neither deal had been completed by the end of 1992, but initial signings had begun for Argentina (and progress made on assembling up to $3.2 billion of collateral), with a view to the new bonds being issued in April and May 1993. Completion of the Brazil deal was set back by political circumstances, although a Senate panel had approved the bank terms at the beginning of December prior to a vote by the full Senate in 1993. More hurdles also had to be overcome in regard to renegotiating the country's $2.1 billion International Monetary Fund standby accord (which was agreed to in late January but which lapsed from May). Banks also appeared to have made progress in debt talks late in the year with officials from Peru and Ecuador.

On the trade front, important progress was made in regard to the North American Free Trade Agreement between Mexico, the U.S., and Canada. The accord was agreed to in principle by July 13, and initial signings were made on December 17 prior to ratification by the legislature of each country. In early November the 13 members of the Caribbean Community and Common Market (Caricom) agreed to cut external tariffs from 1993. The Andean Pact was beset by division earlier in the year but appeared closer to consensus in the final quarter. Differences between Argentina and Brazil (and the political difficulties in Brazil in the second half of the year) hindered further progress on the Southern Cone Common Market (Mercosur) arrangements, although there was time to rectify this by the end of 1994, when full integration was scheduled to begin.

(SUSAN CUNNINGHAM)

ANTIGUA AND BARBUDA

A constitutional monarchy and member of the Commonwealth, Antigua and Barbuda comprises the islands of Antigua, Barbuda, and Redonda in the eastern Caribbean Sea. Area: 442 sq km (171 sq mi). Pop. (1992 est.): 64,000. Cap.: Saint John's. Monetary unit: Eastern Caribbean dollar, with (Oct. 5, 1992) a par value of EC$2.70 to U.S. $1 (free rate of EC$4.59 = £1 sterling). Queen, Elizabeth II; governor-general in 1992, Sir Wilfred E. Jacobs; prime minister, Vere Cornwall Bird.

The Antigua and Barbuda government was under continuing political pressure in 1992, as opponents of the 82-year-old prime minister, Vere Bird, sought to drive him from office on the basis of an alleged "check scandal." The disclosure that Bird had deposited an EC$67,000 government check to his own bank account sparked several opposition protest demonstrations during the year, starting in February. Bird explained that he was being repaid legitimately by the government for money he had lent to a woman entitled to government-assisted medical attention overseas. This did not satisfy the three main opposition parties, which banded together as the United Progressive Party (UPP). A UPP-inspired general strike in April closed most businesses. Bird was sufficiently moved by the protests to announce he would step down as Antigua Labour Party leader before the 1994 general election, but the party failed to elect a successor.

The Barbudans, meanwhile, indicated in August that they might "secede" from the union if their needs did not receive more attention. On the economic front, the country's debt burden remained high, at $328.6 million, equivalent to 74% of gross domestic product. (DAVID RENWICK)

This article updates the *Macropædia* article THE WEST INDIES: *Antigua and Barbuda.*

ARGENTINA

The federal republic of Argentina occupies the eastern section of the Southern Cone of South America, along the Atlantic Ocean. Area: 2,780,400 sq km (1,073,518 sq mi). Pop. (1992 est.): 33,070,000. Cap.: Buenos Aires. Monetary unit: peso, with (Oct. 5, 1992) an official rate of 0.99 peso to U.S. $1 (1.68 pesos = £1 sterling). President in 1992, Carlos Saúl Menem.

Domestic Affairs. By the standards of recent years, Argentine affairs were characterized by a high degree of stability during most of 1992. This was due in large measure to the underlying calm on the economic front that resulted from the convertibility plan established in April 1991 by Economy Minister Domingo Cavallo. The continuation of this plan, which was incorporated into law and obliged the government to back the issue of currency with dollar reserves, provided the platform for further reform and deregulation of the economy and reduced the potential for significant disruption by the organized labour movement or the main opposition Radical Civic Union (UCR). The country also benefited from steps taken to minimize the scope for military interference in the country's political process since Carlos Menem became president in July 1989.

Menem also managed to avert bad publicity from the continuing saga of corruption scandals affecting close aides and family members; his sister-in-law and former secretary, Amira Yoma, was given a prison sentence in August for involvement in the laundering of funds derived from drug trafficking. Only one major Cabinet change had taken place by late October, the replacement of Justice Minister Leon Carlos Arslanian on September 8 by Menem's legal secretary, Jorge Maioriano. In December, however, Menem dismissed Home Minister José Luis Manzano, Labour Minister Rodolfo Diaz, and Education Minister Antonio Salonia.

Signals from Menem early in the year suggested that he might move toward revision of the constitution during 1992, at least partly in order to secure passage of an amendment that would permit him to run for president again in 1995. However, this idea was dropped, particularly after Avelino Porto, the pro-Menem candidate in the Senate election in Buenos Aires, was beaten by a substantial margin in June by his UCR rival, Fernando de la Rúa. Porto won only some 30% of the vote, against almost 50% for de la Rúa. While Porto had not been expected to win, the magnitude of the defeat was taken to indicate a high degree of dissatisfaction with government policies and corruption among voters in the country's most economically advanced area.

Soon after the Buenos Aires vote, it was made clear that constitutional changes would not be sought in the short term; instead the aim would be to deepen the reform process. This would include enacting proposals to reform pension provisions, making changes in labour law, further streamlining public-sector employment, and making adjustments to the judicial system. There remained a strong contingent within the ruling Peronist (Partido Justicialista, PJ) movement, however, that wished to see Menem reelected, and this could revive constitutional reform moves during 1993.

By the final quarter of 1992 both the UCR and dissident members of the General Workers Confederation (CGT) appeared to be stepping up their opposition to certain aspects of government plans. In late September the UCR announced that it would no longer attend periodic discussions convened by Menem with the aim of winning consensus for reform measures, while during October the CGT threatened a work stoppage to protest against government policies (an earlier planned strike in July was averted when the authorities successfully negotiated with CGT leaders). On November 9 the CGT called a one-day general strike.

The Economy. Having succeeded in bringing about sustained stability to the economy from the start of the second quarter of 1991, along with a fairly robust recovery that provided growth of some 5% in gross domestic product (GDP) and relatively low annual inflation (84%, down from 1,344% in 1990) in the same year, Cavallo proceeded to extend his program of reforms during 1992. A 6.5% growth rate was officially envisioned for the year, with the consumer boom that had been based on imported goods during 1991 giving way to more solidly based domestic investment and output growth by 1993. In dollar terms GDP was initially projected at $153 billion for 1992, but an alternative method of calculation by the country's central bank published in early October indicated that the true figure could be closer to $228 billion. Inflation, meanwhile, was kept under control, with monthly rates for consumer price rises registering 3% or less during the first nine months of 1992 and with an accumulated increase to the end of September of 15.2% and an annual rate of 18%. Wholesale prices, however, had increased only 5.6% as of the end of September.

Efforts to boost tax revenues and reduce tax evasion were evident throughout the year. The key moves were the increase in the value-added tax (VAT) from 16 to 18% on March 1, 1992, along with a new tax on assets held abroad, and, in June, the extension of VAT to bank loans. The measures proved effective in improving tax revenues and diminishing the Treasury's reliance on income from the privatization program, which also continued. Among the main projects of the latter were the sale of a 30% government stake in the telecommunications concern, Telecom de Argentina, in March 1992 and the disposal of parts of the Buenos Aires electricity concern, Segba, at various times during the year. Congressional approval was given in late September for the sale of the state oil concern, YPF, which could begin in early 1993. Further changes designed to simplify the tax regime (and in some cases reduce or phase out taxes) were announced in early October. They included: the phasing out of the stamp duty on capital goods; the reduction of federal taxes on fuels used by both rural and industrial producers; a call for provincial governments to eliminate business taxes on gross revenues and replace energy and financial taxes with new provincial sales taxes; and simpler tax and customs procedures for exporters.

In July 1992, when the government published its draft budget for 1993 (projecting growth of 4.5% and annual inflation down to 5.3%), the authorities expected a budget surplus for 1992 equivalent to $3 billion (rising to $3.4 billion in 1993). It was unclear by mid-October whether this surplus would be achieved, although there had been no contraindications from, for example, the regular monitoring of the economy by the International Monetary Fund (IMF), with which Argentina had a $3 billion extended financing facility (approved at the end of March).

Success in obtaining the IMF facility helped underpin the conclusion of a debt-rescheduling deal with foreign commercial banks. It covered some $23 billion that would be restructured under two bond options (par and discount), with each bond maturing in 30 years, and arrangements for dealing with $8 billion of arrears (apart from a cash payment of $400 million, the remainder was to be covered by 12-year past-due-interest bonds). After bank options were lodged in early August, it became clear that there was an unequal distribution between the par and discount bonds in the proportion 80–20 (reflecting the better returns that banks expected from par bonds). It had been hoped that, in order to have a workable deal and ensure that pledged collateral needed to back the bond issues would be disbursed, the mix would have been closer to 50–50. Subsequently, banks were approached to review their options and, at the annual IMF–World Bank meetings in Washington, D.C., in late September, there was agreement that an acceptable mix would be 65% for the par bonds and 35% for the discounts. By the third week of October some progress had been made toward this goal, and on December 7 the banks agreed to accept the 65–35% mix. Having rescheduled part of its debt with Paris Club creditors in September 1991, Argentina reached an additional accord in late July to restructure some $8,730,000,000.

Argentina's foreign trade position was less favourable during 1992 than in 1991 (when there was a $4.3 billion surplus) or 1990 (when the surplus was almost $8.3 billion). For the period from January to May there was a surplus of $700 million, compared with $2.4 billion for the same period of 1991. The authorities were projecting an annual 1992 surplus of $1,320,000,000 based on exports of $12,-

320,000,000 and imports of $11 billion, with little change envisioned for 1993.

Argentina's less competitive exchange rate, especially with neighbouring Brazil, with which it was linked in the Mercosur pact (along with Uruguay and Paraguay), contributed in large measure to the falling trade surplus. As of the end of July, Argentina had incurred a $600 million deficit in its trade with Brazil. President Menem remained committed to the Mercosur common market, which was scheduled to become fully operative in January 1995, but during a state visit to Mexico in mid-October, he was understood to be exploring ways in which links might be enhanced with the North American free-trade area.

(SUSAN M. CUNNINGHAM)

BAHAMAS, THE

A constitutional monarchy and member of the Commonwealth, The Bahamas comprises an archipelago of about 700 islands in the North Atlantic Ocean just southeast of the United States. Area: 13,939 sq km (5,382 sq mi). Pop. (1992 est.): 264,000. Cap.: Nassau. Monetary unit: Bahamian dollar, with (Oct. 5, 1992) a par value of B$1 to U.S. $1 (free rate of B$1.70 = £1 sterling). Queen, Elizabeth II; governor-general in 1992, Clifford Darling; prime ministers, Sir Lynden O. Pindling and, from August 21, Hubert Ingraham.

One of the biggest upsets in Caribbean politics took place in The Bahamas in August 1992 when Prime Minister Sir Lynden Pindling's Progressive Liberal Party was swept from power after 25 years, to be replaced by the Free National Movement, led by Hubert Ingraham (*see* BIOGRAPHIES). Ingraham's policies were not markedly different from Pindling's, but there was a slightly stronger emphasis on free markets and privatization. He said he would maintain a nonresident diplomatic relationship with Cuba but that The Bahamas' interests lay with North America and the Caribbean. In November Pindling resigned as leader of his party.

Only four days after the election, Hurricane Andrew slammed into The Bahamas, doing $250 million worth of damage and leaving 1,700 people homeless. A government-

Hubert Ingraham, head of the Free National Movement and new prime minister of The Bahamas, speaks to supporters after elections on August 19. His party defeated the Progressive Liberal Party of Sir Lynden Pindling, which had ruled the country for 25 years.

sponsored Hurricane Relief Committee was set up to coordinate rehabilitation efforts.

Two major development projects were announced: a German-financed ship-repair yard at Freeport and a $30 million Japanese-backed citrus-processing plant at Abaco. In April the Bahamas Appeal Court ruled that a prominent Nassau lawyer, Nigel Bowe, could be extradited to the U.S. to face drug charges. The 10,000th international business company formed under liberalized legislation that took effect in 1990 was registered in July.   (DAVID RENWICK)

This article updates the *Macropædia* article The WEST INDIES: *The Bahamas*.

BARBADOS

The constitutional monarchy of Barbados, a member of the Commonwealth, occupies the most easterly island in the southern Caribbean Sea. Area: 430 sq km (166 sq mi). Pop. (1992 est.): 259,000. Cap.: Bridgetown. Monetary unit: Barbados dollar, with (Oct. 5, 1992) a par value of BDS$2.01 to U.S. $1 (free rate of BDS$3.42 = £1 sterling).Queen, Elizabeth II; governor-general in 1992, Dame Nita Barrow; prime minister, Erskine Sandiford.

Barbados entered 1992 under an International Monetary Fund adjustment program, which included reductions in the civil service salary bill, higher interest rates, cuts in unemployment benefits, and divestment of state enterprises. Devaluation of the Barbados dollar was avoided at the insistence of the Democratic Labour Party (DLP) government, which obtained $64.9 million in credits from the Fund to stabilize foreign reserves.

The economy remained depressed. Sugar production, after hitting a 60-year record low in 1991, plunged even further, to about 55,000 metric tons in 1992. The British multinational consultancy firm Booker Tate, called in to manage the industry, recommended the closing of one of the three remaining sugar factories and restructuring of the industry's debt. A U.S. State Department advisory in April, warning U.S. tourists about increased crime in Barbados, affected visitor arrivals. The British government took a similar step a month later.

Harold Blackman resigned as minister of state in the Finance Ministry in April and proceeded to launch a scathing attack on the DLP leadership. In September the Barbados Mutual Life Assurance company was given the green light to take over local assets of the scandal-ridden Bank of Credit and Commerce International.   (DAVID RENWICK)

This article updates the *Macropædia* article The WEST INDIES: *Barbados*.

BELIZE

A constitutional monarchy and member of the Commonwealth, Belize is on the Caribbean coast of Central America. Area: 22,965 sq km (8,867 sq mi). Pop. (1992 est.): 196,000. Cap.: Belmopan. Monetary unit: Belize dollar, with (Oct. 5, 1992) a par value of BZ$2 to U.S. $1 (free rate of BZ$3.40 = £1 sterling). Queen, Elizabeth II; governor-general in 1992, Dame Minita Gordon; prime minister, George Cadle Price.

In his 1992 budget Prime Minister George Price forecast continued growth and budgeted a total of BZ$335.1 million, a 14.6% increase over the previous year. Expenditures included rural electrification and a hydroelectric power project. Leading growth sectors in 1992 were construction, transport and communications, utilities, and tourism. Belize also became a member of the Inter-American Development Bank.

Belize opened its doors to 100 Haitian refugees during

the year. Because the population of Belize was predominantly Hispanic, 100 Belizeans were included in the Haitian resettlement area to encourage ethnic mix. In November the Congress of Guatemala voted to approve the decision by Guatemala's president to recognize Belizean independence.

In February members who had been expelled or had resigned from the opposition United Democratic Party (UDP) announced the formation of a new political party, the National Alliance for Belizean Rights (NABR), which was coordinated by Philip Goldson. Both the UDP and the NABR protested the publication by Guatemala of a map that advertised oil concession bids in an area that included part of Belize's exclusive economic zone and part of its territorial waters. (INES T. BAPTIST)

This article updates the *Macropædia* article CENTRAL AMERICA: *Belize*.

BOLIVIA

Bolivia is a landlocked republic in central South America. Area: 1,098,581 sq km (424,164 sq mi). Pop. (1992 est.): 7,739,000. Administrative cap., La Paz; judicial cap., Sucre. Monetary unit: boliviano, with (Oct. 5, 1992) a free rate of 4 bolivianos to U.S. $1 (6.80 bolivianos = £1 sterling). President in 1992, Jaime Paz Zamora.

Municipal elections held in December 1991 were described by Pres. Jaime Paz Zamora as the "cleanest on record," and the poll passed off peacefully. The government coalition won only 31.5% of the vote, but this was higher than any other political grouping. The two populist parties did well, with the Civic Solidarity Union gaining 26.9% of the overall vote. The government coalition nominated Gen. Hugo Banzer as its presidential candidate in the general election due in May 1993.

The year began shakily with a national strike on Jan. 2, 1992, led by the Confederation of Bolivian Workers, protesting the government's privatization program. Internal transport was paralyzed as workers blocked roads and held demonstrations throughout the country. The government, nevertheless, continued its program, with the most interest being shown in the energy sector. Seven groups of private operators were exploring for oil in all nine of Bolivia's departments, and nine companies were negotiating new contracts. The sale of Lloyd Aéreo Boliviano, the national carrier, was also encouraged by the government.

The economy was boosted by gas exports to Argentina and a new gas pipeline to Brazil, to open by the end of the year. Inflation was expected to drop to 12%. Growth of gross domestic product was announced at 3.8%, down from the 4.1% registered in 1991 but higher than the 1990 index of 2.6%.

On January 24 an agreement was signed by President Paz and Pres. Alberto Fujimori of Peru allowing Bolivia access to the Pacific. Bolivia has been landlocked since it lost its coastline to Chile in the 1879 War of the Pacific. Bolivian companies would now be able to use the Peruvian port of Ilo, and movement of individuals between the two countries would be freer. In return, Bolivia promised to help Peru gain access to the Atlantic through Brazil via the Bolivian border town of Puerto Suárez. The Bolivians saw Ilo as the springboard for exports to the Pacific Rim countries.

In the campaign against cocaine, Bolivia fell 1,000 ha (2,470 ac) short of its target of eradicating 7,000 ha (17,290 ac) in 1991. A U.S. embassy official in La Paz announced that $6.2 million of the $66 million allocated for drug-related campaigns would be withheld because of the shortfall. Joint operations between Bolivian and U.S. officials to destroy the drug-trafficking network had been hampered

by mutual accusations. Relations were soured by rumours that U.S. soldiers were building a secret base for the Drug Enforcement Agency in the Beni district. The Bolivian government responded to criticism by claiming that seven prominent drug traffickers had surrendered between July and November 1991, under protection from its guarantee of nonextradition to the U.S. By May 1992, however, only 1,000 ha of coca fields had been destroyed; at that rate only half of the 1991 goal would be achieved by the end of the year. (HUW CLOUGH)

BRAZIL

Brazil is a federal republic in eastern South America on the Atlantic Ocean. Area: 8,511,996 sq km (3,286,500 sq mi). Pop. (1992 est.): 151,381,000. Cap.: Brasília. Monetary unit: cruzeiro, with (Oct. 5, 1992) a free rate of 6,558 cruzeiros to U.S. $1 (11,149 cruzeiros = £1 sterling). Presidents in 1992, Fernando Collor de Mello and, from October 2, Itamar Franco.

Domestic Affairs. The year 1992 proved to be a turbulent one for Pres. Fernando Collor de Mello, who began his third year of office in March. As had been evident for some time, Collor was increasingly on a collision course with the legislature, which added to his difficulties in pushing ahead with reform. Then, during late May, allegations made by his younger brother, Pedro, triggered what became known as "Collorgate." In a nutshell, the allegations were that the president was involved in (or knew of) a multimillion-dollar influence-peddling and corruption scheme orchestrated by Paulo Cesar Farias, who had been Collor's campaign treasurer in 1989. Further revelations regarding the affair continued in the following months, and a congressional inquiry into Farias' dealings was begun. The findings of the inquiry, whose report was completed in late August, were sufficient to merit impeachment proceedings of Collor by Congress. The lower house of Congress on September 29 voted 441–38 to impeach the president. Also, on November 12 the attorney general's office moved separately to launch criminal proceedings against Collor. The impeachment trial of the president by the Senate began on December 29. Only minutes after it started, Collor resigned, and Vice Pres. Itamar Franco was sworn in as president. The Senate then banned Collor from public office for eight years.

Franco had taken the reins of the presidency on October 2. A seasoned politician who had been at odds with Collor for some time, he moved to appoint a new, multiparty Cabinet, whose composition was intended to help guarantee congressional support for urgent economic measures. Among them was a revised package of fiscal reforms that needed approval before the end of 1992 to avert a budget collapse in 1993. Collor had submitted a detailed package of fiscal reforms in July, but these required several constitutional amendments. Given the poor state of his relations with Congress and the unfolding ramifications of "Collorgate," it proved impossible to pass these measures. Franco acted to decentralize the power of the Economy "superministry," which had been established by Collor, by returning to the pre-1990 format of separate Finance, Planning, and Industry/Commerce ministries. He also adopted a style that allowed for more consultation with Congress than had been evident under Collor. He signaled, for example, that Congress would be asked to review proposals to privatize certain large state-owned concerns, and in December he suspended the privatization program for three months. Subsequently, his finance minister, Gustavo Krause, resigned.

Municipal elections took place throughout the country in October and November. Left-of-center parties made the greatest gains.

Brazil's Pres. Fernando Collor de Mello and his wife, Rosane Collor, leave the presidential palace in Brasília on October 2 after his powers were suspended for 180 days. On December 29, minutes after his impeachment trial began, Collor resigned.
ALEXANDRE SASSAKI—GAMMA LIAISON

The nation was shocked in December when Daniela Pérez, the star of a popular television soap opera, was found murdered near Rio de Janeiro. Guilherme de Pádua, the actor who played her jealous boyfriend on the soap opera, was charged with the crime.

The Economy. Throughout 1992 Brazil's economy remained largely in recession, with manufacturing (which had registered declines in both 1990 and 1991) being particularly hard hit. Until October the economy was managed along orthodox lines under the control of Economy Minister Marcílio Marques Moreira (who had been appointed in May 1991 after the departure of Zélia Cardoso de Mello). Moreira, however, was constrained by the effect of measures specified under previous plans (including the need to return, until September 1992, some $1.5 billion–$2 billion per month of new cruzado assets frozen in 1990). It thus proved difficult to moderate the high interest rates and to reduce inflation, which was well above 20% per month from January through October (26.07% in the latter month). The growth of gross domestic product for 1992 was officially expected to be negative (about −0.2%) following a rise of 0.93% in 1991 (the 1991 rate was revised downward in November from the 1.1% previously indicated). A strong performance from agriculture helped offset what would otherwise have been a much worse result for 1992.

A new economic team under Finance Minister Gustavo Krause and Planning Minister Paulo Haddad, which took over in early October, initially provided policy continuity, with no radical new plans envisioned. As noted above, the immediate priority was to prepare revised proposals for fiscal reform, although there were strong indications that social welfare measures would also be introduced. Fiscal reforms were submitted to Congress in early November. They involved the introduction of some new taxes (including a financial transactions tax and excise taxes) and the elimination of others, with the aim of boosting revenue for 1993 by

up to $16 billion. Other measures, involving changes that aimed to improve the fiscal base over the long term, were also expected following the submission of revised proposals for the $224 billion 1993 budget to Congress. It was far from clear whether Congress would fully approve the various measures, but some compromise plan seemed likely. On December 31 President Franco introduced his new economic program. Among its major provisions were increased wages for government workers, at least a doubling of the minimum wage, and the creation of four million new jobs during the next two years.

Concerning the external sector, the trade position continued to improve significantly, with an accumulated surplus of $11.6 billion in the nine months to the end of September (up from $9 billion in the same period of 1991) based on exports of $26.1 billion and imports of $14,560,000,000. The country's international reserves also increased rom about $8.5 billion at the end of 1991 to $18.9 billion by the end of August and were estimated at about $22 billion in late October. The upturn in capital inflows was encouraged earlier in the year when Brazil in January reached an accord with the International Monetary Fund for a $2.1 billion standby loan and in February achieved a rescheduling deal with the Paris Club of official creditors. In July there was an agreement in principle on a rescheduling of $44 billion of bank debt; a Senate panel approved the agreement on December 10.

(SUSAN M. CUNNINGHAM)

CHILE

The republic of Chile extends along the Pacific coast of the Southern Cone of South America. Area: 756,626 sq km (292,135 sq mi), not including Chile's Antarctic claim. Pop. (1992 est.): 13,599,000. Cap.: Santiago (national); Valparaíso (legislative). Monetary unit: Chilean peso, with (Oct. 5, 1992) a free rate of 384.90 pesos to U.S. $1 (654.33 pesos = £1 sterling). President in 1992, Patricio Aylwin Azócar.

Former president Augusto Pinochet underwent heart surgery in May 1992, but by the end of the month he had fully recovered and reassumed command of the army, the post that under the constitution he could hold until 1997. One of the reforms to the constitution proposed by Pres. Patricio Aylwin consisted of measures to reduce the autonomy of the armed services, which they had conferred on themselves before handing over the government to civilians in 1990.

Currently, the president was not allowed to interfere in military discipline. Though he formally held the title of supreme commander, his powers were limited to approving promotions. Pinochet's defense for this state of affairs was that since the armed services have an overriding duty to defend the constitution, they must be beyond the control of politicians who might threaten it. President Aylwin stated that if the Senate, where the ruling coalition lacked a majority, passed the reform, he would not use his new power to interfere in military affairs. Aylwin also promised that senators appointed for eight years by the previous regime would be allowed to complete their terms.

In municipal elections on June 28, the ruling Coalition of Parties for Democracy polled 53.3% of the vote, against 29.8% for the right-wing National Renovation Party and the Independent Democratic Union combined. The populist Centre-Centre Union received 8% of the poll, and the Communist Party 7%. President Aylwin claimed the result gave him a clear mandate to proceed with constitutional reform. However, the right wing warned that it would not allow the president to steamroller the country into constitutional change while it retained control of the Senate.

On January 23 the official exchange rate was reduced

from 395.4 pesos to 374.99 pesos to the U.S. dollar. This produced a 4% drop in the parallel rate to 375.64 pesos = U.S. $1. The move was aimed at stemming foreign exchange losses of $150 million over two years, caused by the inflow of hot money seeking Chile's high interest rates. At the same time, the government raised its savings targets by 50% to $930 million to help lower inflation and sustain the exchange rate. The stock exchange was a main beneficiary of the government's decision to revalue the peso and introduce looser exchange controls, and trading volume doubled. The consensus forecast was for a rise of 50% in real share values, compared with 124% in 1991. However, the peso move was hurting the prospects of large exporting conglomerates such as those operating in the timber products, fish meal, steel, and sugar sectors. Bank profits were also expected to suffer as interest rates and corporate profits fell. Many of Chile's exporting companies were perceived to have reached the limits of expansion within Chile and would have to become multinational in order to expand further.

Chile had invested more than $800 million over the past two years in Argentine assets, which were cheap compared with their Chilean equivalents. Chilean pension fund managers also hoped to expand into Argentina, despite a critical International Labour Organization review of their domestic performance. Chile had privatized its pension system 11 years earlier and was considered to be in the vanguard in this regard, but Chilean fund managers could invest only 10% of their assets overseas. As a result, the high inflow of money, amounting to $200 million monthly, was depressing domestic returns.

Chile's privatization program had been halted in 1990 with the return to democracy. The Aylwin administration had not probed alleged irregularities in the sales, despite the resentment of many Chileans over the way the firms had been traded under the military regime. Many employees had been encouraged to trade their shares for ownership rights in investment societies. The shares, in turn, were used as collateral for loans that allowed managers to buy controlling stakes in companies. Employees' shares in profits were then used to repay the collateralized loans. The Chilean experience pointed to the need for effective legislation to protect the rights of employees compelled to take shares instead of pay.

Since 1976 Codelco, the state-owned copper corporation, had provided a fifth of state revenues, but the government had reinvested only 0.2% of profits back into the firm. Largely as a result of this policy, Codelco could contribute only $870 million to revenues in 1991, compared with almost $2 billion in 1989. To reverse the trend, Codelco obtained Treasury approval to invest $2.8 billion over the next five years to develop new mines and to modernize. Codelco officials conceded that full autonomy for the company was too explosive an issue to be raised in the final two years of the Aylwin administration. However, they believed that this had to be a goal in the longer term if Codelco was to gain the trust of foreign partners. A step in the right direction was a recent law allowing Codelco to form joint ventures, though by presidential decree the firm was to "aim for majority control." This did not go down well with prospective multinational partners, who preferred to have majority control over their major investments. Codelco's managers saw the reform as a key to the copper sector's long-term development. It would allow the state company to seek partners when it did not have the resources to develop mines on its own. Codelco owned one-third of the mining prospects in Chile, but investment restrictions had limited exploration and expansion. Part of the problem was that the firm was so important to the economy that its managers, the

government, the unions, and the army were all struggling for control over it. The army received 10% of copper sales, or $300 million indexed to 1989. More than 70% of this was spent on salaries. The army had 22,000 officers and noncommissioned officers to only 30,000 soldiers.

On November 10 retired general Manuel Contreras and Col. Pedro Espinoza, heads of the secret police during the military regime, were charged with the murder in 1976 of Orlando Letelier, a government minister during the 1970–73 presidency of Salvador Allende.   (MICHAEL WOOLLER)

COLOMBIA

A republic in northwestern South America, Colombia has coastlines on the Caribbean Sea and the Pacific Ocean. Area: 1,141,748 sq km (440,831 sq mi). Pop. (1992 est.): 33,392,000. Cap.: Bogotá. Monetary unit: Colombian peso, with (Oct. 5, 1992) a free rate of 625 pesos to U.S. $1 (1,062 pesos = £1 sterling). President in 1992, César Gaviria Trujillo.

On July 22, 1992, Pablo Escobar, leader of the Medellín drug cartel, escaped from prison in an operation that exposed the government's weakness against the powerful crime network. Escobar reportedly sauntered out of Envigado prison, 220 km (135 mi) northwest of Bogotá, amid orchestrated confusion during his transfer to a high-security military prison. Six people were killed in the escape. In the subsequent investigation, 7 government officials and 26 prison guards were dismissed. Escobar remained at large, and the government turned down his offer to surrender again under "certain conditions."

Peace talks in Tlaxcala, Mexico, between the government and guerrilla organizations collapsed in March following news of the death in captivity of a former minister, Argelino Durán Quintero, who had been kidnapped by guerrillas in January. Subsequently, Pres. César Gaviria Trujillo announced that peace talks would not be resumed; hope of reaching a political agreement with the guerrilla groups had been abandoned, and army action was now aimed at "wiping them out." Some of the fiercest fighting in months broke out at the end of May in Antioquia province, resulting in the deaths of an estimated 40 guerrillas and 20 soldiers. On November 8 Gaviria declared a state of emergency to combat increased violence by guerrillas and drug traffickers.

A state of emergency was declared on April 23 because of a serious energy shortage. Hydroelectric power, on which the country is heavily dependent, was strictly rationed as a result of the worst drought on record. El Niño, the warm-water current that surges through the Pacific every few years causing severe local climatic effects, was cited as the official cause of the drought. Critics, however, blamed corruption and incompetence in the energy sector and the failure to invest in coal-generated power as a safeguard against such hazards. A sharp increase in the destruction of tropical rain forest was also blamed for the dramatic drop in rainfall.

At the beginning of July, President Gaviria announced the first major Cabinet reshuffle of the year, prompted by mass resignations of ministers. The new Cabinet maintained a coalition balance, including representatives of the April 19 Movement Democratic Alliance (M-19), the party of the left-wing guerrilla group disbanded in 1991. However, after Gaviria declared the state of emergency in November, the M-19 representatives resigned.

The tax-reform bill, in much-watered-down form, was finally approved by Congress at the end of June. The value-added tax was raised from 12 to 14%, and income tax was increased from 30 to 37.5%. The government continued its economic liberalization program. Lower tariffs had stimulated a boom in imports, with 20% growth in 1992.

Pablo Escobar appears with his wife and children in this photograph taken in prison by a fellow inmate. Head of the Medellín drug cartel, Escobar escaped from prison on July 22 but later offered to surrender to the Colombian government under certain conditions.

GAMMA LIAISON

In April, Americas Watch, a U.S. human rights group, described the situation in Colombia as "appalling." It categorized 3,760 murders, out of a total of 24,033 in 1991, as "politically motivated," an increase, on average, of 3,500 over the previous four years. The victims included those killed in conflicts between the armed forces and guerrillas and in "social cleansing" campaigns, as well as murders of left-wing activists, union leaders, and members of the judiciary. Americas Watch credited efforts made toward peace but emphasized the obstacles of military and police intransigence. Nevertheless, military intervention did not seem likely. There was a civilian minister of defense, Rafael Pardo, and the consistent growth of the Colombian economy would work to the disadvantage of potential plotters.

(HUW CLOUGH)

COSTA RICA

The Central American republic of Costa Rica has coastlines on the Caribbean Sea and the Pacific Ocean. Area: 51,100 sq km (19,730 sq mi). Pop. (1992 est.): 3,161,000. Cap.: San José. Monetary unit: Costa Rican colón, with (Oct. 5, 1992) an official rate of 135.17 colones to U.S. $1 (230.54 colones = £1 sterling). President in 1992, Rafael Angel Calderón Fournier.

Costa Rican exporters hoped to benefit from the easing of foreign exchange restrictions in February 1992. This move, which also floated the colón against the dollar and legalized the black market in dollars, combined with other measures to continue the process of opening up trade under the International Monetary Fund Structural Adjustment. In July, Japan withdrew its $100 million commitment to the $300 million third phase of the Fund. It was unhappy with the progress of the program, especially as regards tax reform and social development.

Costa Rica was in the forefront of those claiming that the European Communities' proposal to protect exports from former colonies, at the expense of Latin-American growers,

was contrary to the rules of the General Agreement on Tariffs and Trade. Production of bananas, Costa Rica's main foreign exchange earner, had been expanded in expectation of greater access to EC markets after liberalization of Community trade rules at the end of 1992. Initial negotiations to find a compromise under GATT in September failed. Costa Rica's second largest export crop, coffee, also faced problems as the International Coffee Organization was unable during the year to achieve consensus between producers and purchasers.

In June the Legislative Assembly approved a plan for construction of a rail link between Parismina on the Caribbean coast and Cuajiniquil on the Pacific that would complement the Panama Canal. (BEN BOX)

This article updates the *Macropædia* article CENTRAL AMERICA: *Costa Rica*.

CUBA

The socialist republic of Cuba comprises the island of Cuba and several thousand smaller islands and cays in the Caribbean Sea. Area: 110,861 sq km (42,804 sq mi). Pop. (1992 est.): 10,848,000. Cap.: Havana. Monetary unit: Cuban peso, with (Oct. 5, 1992) an official rate of 0.76 pesos to U.S. $1 (1.29 pesos = £1 sterling). President of the Councils of State and Ministers in 1992, Fidel Castro Ruz.

The Cuban economy experienced another difficult year in 1992 as the government strove to increase foreign trade and investment to generate much-needed foreign exchange. Since the breakup of the Eastern European bloc and especially the Soviet Union, Cuba had had to secure new trading partners, and its exports and imports had fallen dramatically. Compared with about $8 billion in 1989, exports were expected to be only $4 billion in 1992, while crucial oil purchases were reported as falling from 13 million metric tons in 1989, when subsidized by the Soviet Union, to 6 million metric tons in 1992, when bought at market prices. Though Cuba maintained links with several republics of the former Soviet Union for the sale of sugar, contracts were also signed with several Arab countries: Algeria, Tunisia, Lebanon, Libya, and Yemen. A trade protocol was signed with China for the export of nickel, sugar, citrus, and medical products in return for food and medicine and spare parts for the sugar industry.

By 1992 tourism had become the major foreign exchange earner. About 500,000 visitors were expected during the year, up from 400,000 in 1991, and with the help of foreign investment, an additional 3,000–4,000 hotel rooms per year were scheduled to be built by 1995. The industry was given a boost when the board of directors of the Caribbean Tourism Organization approved Cuba's application for membership in July.

The domestic economy was still severely affected by the loss of Soviet support. Power cuts of 3–4 hours a day remained the norm, while shortages of fuel and spare parts led to further cuts in railway services. Supplies of basic goods such as cooking fat and soap were poor, and there was increased use of wood and charcoal for cooking. The sugar harvest started six weeks late and was expected to be less than 7.5 million metric tons, down from 7.6 million in 1991. Although the sugar mills use the sugarcane product bagasse as fuel, there were fuel shortages for the vehicles that were used to cut and transport the cane. A massive effort to cut down on food imports pushed supplies of farm produce up by 11% compared with the first quarter of 1991. Thousands of workers were displaced from their office or factory jobs and went to work in the fields to grow food crops. Tourism receipts were up by 23%. Nickel production

Cuban men work on the engine of a 1956 Chevrolet in order to keep the automobile in running condition. The country continued to suffer economic difficulties in 1992, many of them related to loss of aid from former Soviet-bloc countries.

ROB CRANDALL—PICTURE GROUP

was expected to be 35,000 metric tons in 1992, up from 34,-000 metric tons in 1991, and was forecast to rise to 100,000 metric tons by the end of the decade with the modernization and upgrading of three plants and a fourth being brought into operation.

The decline in living standards led to resentment against the Castro regime; dissidence increased, but it was not sufficient to destabilize the government. In January three exiles were put on trial following their capture in Cárdenas when they landed with weapons and explosives, intent on sabotage and local recruitment. The three were found guilty of terrorism, sabotage, and enemy propaganda and were sentenced to death. Two of them later had their sentences commuted to 30 years' imprisonment, but one, Eduardo Díaz Betancourt, was executed. In February two men were executed for murdering three policemen while trying to steal a boat in which to escape from the country; four men and three women involved in the episode were jailed for between 4 and 30 years.

In March the UN Commission on Human Rights adopted a U.S.-sponsored resolution criticizing Cuba's human rights record. Twenty-three countries voted for the resolution, including such former allies as Russia, Bulgaria, Czechoslovakia, and Hungary. However, Grenada subsequently announced that Cuba had satisfied all conditions for a normalization of diplomatic relations, which had been in abeyance since the 1983 Grenadian crisis.

The U.S. intensified its economic pressure on Cuba to achieve political reforms. U.S. Pres. George Bush authorized the U.S. telephone comany AT&T to install a new telephone cable between the U.S. and Cuba, for which Cuba received a fee of $620,000, but this rare exception to the blockade was made because of claimed benefits from an increased flow of information to Cuba. The link was severed in August, however, when Hurricane Andrew destroyed AT&T equipment. A Cuba democracy bill debated in the U.S. Congress would prohibit U.S. subsidiaries in other nations from trading with Cuba. The bill would also authorize the president to cut off aid, trade, or debt relief to any country that provided assistance to Cuba. Several countries reported unwanted U.S. pressure on them to cease trading with Cuba. In November the UN General Assembly voted 59–3 with 79 abstentions in favour of a resolution calling on the U.S. to end its embargo of Cuba.

Constitutional reforms were approved by the National Assembly in July as a result of the recommendations made at the fourth party Congress in October 1991. Direct secret voting for members of the National Assembly would replace the previous method of election by municipal and regional councils; the first direct election was likely to take place in 1993. A major change allowed private investment in certain state companies; also, the state monopoly on trade was ended, and foreign ownership of property in joint venture enterprises was recognized.   (SARAH CAMERON)

This article updates the *Macropædia* article The WEST INDIES: *Cuba.*

DOMINICA

An island republic within the Commonwealth, Dominica is in the eastern Caribbean Sea. Area: 750 sq km (290 sq mi). Pop. (1992 est.): 71,500. Cap.: Roseau. Monetary unit: Eastern Caribbean dollar, with (Oct. 5, 1992) a par value of EC$2.70 to U.S. $1 (free rate of EC$4.59 = £1 sterling). President in 1992, Clarence Augustus Seignoret; prime minister, Eugenia Charles.

The major public issue in Dominica in 1992 was whether the government should "sell" citizenship to businessmen from Taiwan and Hong Kong as a means of encouraging much-needed foreign investment. A Taiwanese jewelry manufacturer was the first to be granted a Dominica passport in return for $35,000 worth of investment, but opposition parties were hostile to the concept, arguing that it would gain little for the country in the long term.

Demonstrations led by the official opposition United Workers Party, which began in May, finally forced the Dominica Freedom Party government to announce adjustments to the policy in September. The $35,000 requirement remained, but the investment would have to be maintained for at least 10 years, and an extra $25,000 would have to be deposited in a special fund. In April ground was broken for a new 250-room hotel, which the government hoped would be financed by funds from "economic citizens." The goal was 800 such citizens within the next few years.

Michael Douglas, leader of the Dominica Labour Party,

died of cancer in April. He had led the DLP for seven years. The 1992–93 budget in June called for EC$229.8 million in public spending, but no new taxes were imposed.

(DAVID RENWICK)

This article updates the *Macropædia* article The WEST INDIES: *Dominica.*

DOMINICAN REPUBLIC

The Dominican Republic covers the eastern two-thirds of the Caribbean island of Hispaniola, which it shares with Haiti. Area: 48,443 sq km (18,704 sq mi). Pop. (1992 est.): 7,471,000. Cap.: Santo Domingo. Monetary unit: Dominican peso, with (Oct. 5, 1992) a free rate of 12.71 pesos to U.S. $1 (21.60 pesos = £1 sterling). President in 1992, Joaquín Balaguer.

Celebrations for the 500th anniversary of Columbus' landing on Hispaniola on Oct. 12, 1992, culminated in the inauguration of the massive Faro a Colón (Columbus Lighthouse). (*See* RACE RELATIONS: *Sidebar.*) Violent demonstrations against the celebrations took place in September and October. Plainclothes secret police killed the head of the Dominican Committee for Human Rights during a march on September 30, and 10 of them were later arrested.

Divisions in the opposition Dominican Liberation Party (PLD) exploded when 47 of its high-ranking members resigned following the expulsion of a leading trade unionist and deputy for Santo Domingo. Nélsida Marmolejos had criticized the PLD's stance on the proposed new Labour Code. Several other members of the PLD were later suspended or expelled. They subsequently formed a new party, the Alliance for Democracy, and expressed their willingness to form a broad front to vote Pres. Joaquín Balaguer out of office in 1994. The Labour Code was approved by both houses of Congress and ratified by the president in May. One of its controversial points gave unions the right to organize in free-trade zones.

Allegations were made by the U.S. Drug Enforcement Agency that high-ranking Dominican officials were engaged in drug trafficking. The president denied any knowledge of involvement by members of his staff.   (SARAH CAMERON)

This article updates the *Macropædia* article The WEST INDIES: *Dominican Republic.*

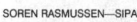
SOREN RASMUSSEN—SIPA

The Columbus Lighthouse, built to commemorate the 500th anniversary of the landing of Christopher Columbus, looms over Santo Domingo. A project of Dominican Pres. Joaquín Balaguer, it was criticized for both its expense and its symbolism.

ECUADOR

The republic of Ecuador is in western South America, on the Pacific Ocean. Area: 270,667 sq km (104,505 sq mi), including the Galápagos Islands. Pop. (1992 est.): 10,607,000. Cap.: Quito. Monetary unit: sucre, with (Oct. 5, 1992) a par value of 2,000 sucres to U.S. $1 (free rate of 3,400 sucres = £1 sterling). Presidents in 1992, Rodrigo Borja Cevallos and, from August 10, Sixto Durán Ballén.

On Aug. 10, 1992, Sixto Durán Ballén (*see* BIOGRAPHIES), a former mayor of Quito, took office as president after winning 58% of the vote in a July 5 runoff election. In the first round of voting on May 17, Durán, the candidate of a newly formed conservative coalition, Republican Unity Party (PUD), captured just 36% of the vote. Second place went to Jaime Nebot, president of the Social Christian Party (PSC), with 26%, followed by Abdalá Bucaram Ortiz, director of the Roldosist Party (PRE), with 21%. After his elimination in the first round, Bucaram advised his supporters to vote for Durán, who claimed victory in 19 of the 21 provinces in the second round. The May 17 elections for the 77-seat Congress resulted in the PSC's gaining 21 seats, the PRE 13, and the PUD 12. The Conservative Party, allies of the PUD, won six seats. Mirroring the poor performance in simultaneous local elections, centre and left-wing parties fared badly. (For tabulated results, see *Political Parties,* above.)

Though the president lacked a working majority in Congress, he sought to build a national consensus by relying on two right-wing parties as well as support from business, indicating his espousal of free-market policies. Three weeks after his inauguration, Durán sanctioned a 26.2% devaluation of the sucre and eliminated energy price subsidies, forcing gasoline price increases of 300%. In late September the United Workers Front called a national strike in protest. Cities throughout Ecuador experienced unrest, with demonstrations and looting in Guayaquil and a riot in Quito. Public sector workers also staged strikes protesting government reforms in health care and the judiciary.

At the November OPEC meeting, Ecuador withdrew from the 13-member oil cartel, citing a need to economize on annual dues of $1.5 million and expressing disappointment over OPEC's failure to benefit smaller producers.

(MICHAEL WOOLLER)

EL SALVADOR

The republic of El Salvador is situated on the Pacific coast of Central America. Area: 21,041 sq km (8,124 sq mi). Pop. (1992 est.): 5,460,000. Cap.: San Salvador. Monetary unit: Salvadoran colón, with (Oct. 5, 1992) an offical rate of 8.58 colones to U.S. $1 (14.62 colones = £1 sterling). President in 1992, Alfredo Cristiani.

The year began auspiciously with the Jan. 16, 1992, signing of the peace accord between the government and the rebel Farabundo Martí National Liberation Front (FMLN), ending 12 years of a civil war that had cost about 80,000 lives, displaced one million people, and caused material losses estimated at $1 billion. A detailed timetable was drawn up for the gradual demobilization of the guerrilla forces, the elimination of the National Guard and the Treasury Police, the reduction of the armed forces, and political and economic reforms that would enable the FMLN members to be incorporated into civilian life.

There were delays in complying with the deadlines. On June 30, two months behind schedule, the UN mission in El Salvador confirmed the demobilization of the first 20%

Citizens in San Salvador celebrate the signing on January 16 of a peace treaty between the government of El Salvador and the Farabundo Martí National Liberation Front. It was hoped that the accord would end the country's brutal 12-year civil war.

CINDY KARP—BLACK STAR

of the FMLN forces. Under pressure from the UN and the U.S., the government and the FMLN agreed to a new timetable for the demobilization. The FMLN leadership criticized the government for wanting the rebel forces to disarm while failing to institute the reforms or fulfill its obligations to guarantee security for the ex-combatants and grant them land, financing, technical assistance, and farm equipment. By August 20, however, the FMLN had concentrated all its forces in the 15 agreed-upon sites. The demobilization was finally completed on December 14, and a ceremony in San Salvador the next day marked the formal end of the civil war.

The founder and leader of the ruling right-wing Nationalist Republican Alliance (Arena), Roberto d'Aubuisson (*see* OBITUARIES), died on February 20. He was a hard-line anti-Communist and had been linked with many political murders. His death was expected to lead to a battle for power within his party.   (SARAH CAMERON)

This article updates the *Macropædia* article CENTRAL AMERICA: *El Salvador.*

GRENADA

A constitutional monarchy within the Commonwealth, Grenada (with its dependency, the Southern Grenadines) is in the eastern Caribbean Sea. Area: 345 sq km (133 sq mi). Pop. (1992 est.): 90,900. Cap.: Saint George's. Monetary unit: Eastern Caribbean dollar, with (Oct. 5, 1992) a par value of EC$2.70 to U.S. $1 (free rate of EC$4.59 = £1 sterling). Queen, Elizabeth II; governors-general in 1992, Sir Paul Scoon and, from August 6, Reginald Palmer; prime minister, Nicholas Brathwaite.

The governing National Democratic Congress party spent most of the year fending off criticism of its "structural adjustment" program, designed to stabilize the economy without direct International Monetary Fund intervention. The program included a reduction in the size of the civil service and the sell-off of government enterprises. The prospect of

layoffs did nothing to improve the mood of public-sector employees, who forced the government to settle a 1990–92 wage claim, at a cost of EC$10.8 million.

In February, Parliament passed the highly controversial Traders and Professional Licenses Act, requiring professional people, including journalists, to pay fees ranging from EC$100 to EC$100,000. The act was strongly attacked by professional associations. Winifred Strachan, sole remaining opposition Grenada United Labour Party member in Parliament, was expelled from the party in March for "blatant disloyalty" and "substandard performance."

The government announced during the year that Cuba had "satisfied all conditions" for a resumption of diplomatic relations with Grenada. In August, Reginald Palmer, a former senior public servant, was appointed governor-general to succeed Sir Paul Scoon.   (DAVID RENWICK)

This article updates the *Macropædia* article The WEST INDIES: *Grenada.*

GUATEMALA

A republic of Central America, Guatemala has coastlines on the Caribbean Sea and the Pacific Ocean. Area: 108,889 sq km (42,042 sq mi). Pop. (1992 est.): 9,442,000. Cap.: Guatemala City. Monetary unit: quetzal, with (Oct. 5, 1992) a free rate of 5.32 quetzales to U.S. $1 (9.04 quetzales = £1 sterling). President in 1992, Jorge Serrano Elías.

The new year began with extensive political maneuvering for the election of the president of Congress and Supreme Court justices. Edmond Mulet Lessieur of the National Centrist Union was elected to the presidency of Congress amid allegations of vote selling, although the last-minute support of Pres. Jorge Serrano Elías also influenced the outcome. Nine justices were elected to the Supreme Court for six-year terms. Later in the year, following many scandals and allegations of criminal activities, a congressional commission recommended an end to secret hearings for all legal proceedings against congressmen.

AP/WIDE WORLD

Villagers from Pujujil carry the newly exhumed bodies of residents who had disappeared in 1981, reportedly after having been killed by the Guatemalan military. The government continued to be criticized throughout the world in 1992 for its record on human rights.

Human rights came to the fore at the beginning of 1992 when several human rights groups released their figures for abuses in 1991. The government launched a campaign in Europe to convince the world that human rights were under control, prior to the convening in February of the UN Commission on Human Rights meeting that would lead to reduced levels of aid if Guatemala's record was condemned. The U.S. State Department Human Rights Report, released in February, blamed the Guatemalan security forces for the majority of human rights violations, although it noted that the overall situation had improved. A report by the UN human rights adviser stated, however, that there had not been any substantial decrease in criminal violence and that many of the crimes were clearly politically motivated. The UN Commission on Human Rights decided not to appoint a permanent observer in Guatemala but to maintain a special adviser to visit several times a year. A second UN report in August again condemned Guatemala for consistently violating human rights.

Discussions were held during the year between the government and the rebel alliance Guatemalan National Revolutionary Unity. A few accords were reached, but the guerrillas continued military operations.   (SARAH CAMERON)

This article updates the *Macropædia* article CENTRAL AMERICA: *Guatemala*.

GUYANA

A republic and member of the Commonwealth, Guyana is situated in northeastern South America, on the Atlantic Ocean. Area: 215,083 sq km (83,044 sq mi). Pop. (1992 est.): 748,000. Cap.: Georgetown. Monetary unit: Guyana dollar, with (Oct. 5, 1992) a free rate of G$125.27 to U.S. $1 (G$212.96 = £1 sterling). Presidents in 1992, Desmond Hoyte and, from October 9, Cheddi Jagan; prime ministers, Hamilton Green and, from October 9, Sam Hinds.

Cheddi Jagan, 74, a U.S.-trained dentist and longtime major political figure on the Guyana scene, was returned to office after 28 years in opposition in the Oct. 5, 1992, general election. Jagan's People's Progressive Party (PPP) won 52.3% of the vote under Guyana's system of proportional representation, compared with 43.6% for then president Desmond Hoyte's People's National Congress (PNC). Jagan became president and his running mate, Sam Hinds, prime minister. The PPP had 28 of the 53 directly elected seats in Parliament, and the PNC had 23. The Working People's Alliance and the United Force obtained one seat each.

Jagan had quietly abandoned the Marxism-Leninism with which he had long been associated, and the new government would encourage private initiative, though it would also slow the state enterprise divestment program. Jagan said he would review all privatization deals made after March 1992, including that for the sugar industry. The PNC had sold off 14 state companies by mid-1992, earning G$1 billion.

The market-oriented policies pursued by the PNC in its last years in office had helped boost production. Some 32,-000 troy ounces of gold were mined in the first six months of 1992, and annual sugar output reached 225,000 metric tons, compared with 162,753 in 1991. A G$500 note was put into circulation in July for the first time, reflecting the high inflation. Guyana signed a tax information exchange agreement with the U.S. in July.   (DAVID RENWICK)

HAITI

The republic of Haiti occupies the western one-third of the Caribbean island of Hispaniola, which it shares with the Dominican Republic. Area: 27,700 sq km (10,695 sq mi). Pop. (1992 est.): 6,764,000. Cap.: Port-au-Prince. Monetary unit: gourde, with (Oct. 5, 1992) a free rate of 9.98 gourdes to U.S. $1 (16.97 gourdes = £1 sterling). President in 1992, Joseph Nerette (interim) until June 19; prime ministers, Jean-Jacques Honorat (interim) and, from June 19, Marc Bazin.

Marc Bazin, a former World Bank economist and presidential candidate in the December 1990 elections, was sworn in as prime minister of Haiti on June 19 under a tripartite agreement made by the army, administration, and parliamentary leaders. Officially his mandate was to negotiate a settlement with the deposed president, Jean-Bertrand Aristide, who had won 67% of the vote, compared with Bazin's 14%. The figurehead president, Joseph Nerette, resigned after Bazin's inauguration, leaving the post vacant for the return of Aristide. The ceremony was boycotted by all diplomats except for the papal nuncio, the Vatican being the only state to recognize the army-backed regime.

Representatives of the army-backed regime and of Aristide met in September and agreed that 18 representatives of the Organization of American States (OAS) should go to Haiti and monitor human rights violations. Michael Manley, the former prime minister of Jamaica, was named as "facil-

A refugee being returned to Haiti is carried onshore from a U.S. Coast Guard cutter. The U.S. government began repatriating Haitian refugees in 1992 on the grounds that they were economic refugees and thus not eligible for political asylum.

itator" for the OAS mission, in which two monitors would be stationed in each province.

Prime Minister Bazin appeared before parliament in August to hear reports of repression and abuse, which he called shocking but failed to condemn. Tens of thousands of people applied to the U.S. for political asylum, and people flooded into Florida by boat. Amnesty International accused the U.S. of flouting international law because it repatriated Haitian refugees without examining their cases and determining whether they were at risk of human rights abuses in their own country. The U.S. held that they were economic refugees and therefore not entitled to asylum.

(SARAH CAMERON)

This article updates the *Macropædia* article The WEST INDIES: *Haiti*.

HONDURAS

A republic of Central America, Honduras has coastlines on the Caribbean Sea and the Pacific Ocean. Area: 112,088 sq km (43,277 sq mi). Pop. (1992 est.): 4,996,000. Cap.: Tegucigalpa. Monetary unit: lempira, with (Oct. 5, 1992) a free rate of 6 lempiras to U.S. $1 (10.20 lempiras = £1 sterling). President in 1992, Rafael Leonardo Callejas.

In March 1992 Congress passed the Agriculture Modernization Law, designed to encourage foreign investment and promote crop development. Its provision allowing farmers to sell cooperative land received through agrarian reform was criticized for eliminating the remaining benefits of the reform designed to give land to poor peasants. In May officials from the armed forces and the National Agrarian Institute (INA) began to evict campesino groups who had invaded 25,000 ha (61,750 ac) of fallow land in 10 departments two weeks earlier. The campesinos complained that the suspension of agrarian reform and the freezing of credits by the National Agriculture Bank had made their lives onerous. After negotiations, it was agreed that new occupations of land would be suspended and the INA would discuss resolving disputes on a case-by-case basis.

The emergence of "parallel" leadership boards of trade unions caused splits within the labour movement. Allegations were made that the parallel boards were a government strategy to weaken the unions so that privatization and firing could take place with little opposition. Political violence continued with a series of assassinations of leaders from both the right and left in July. On March 30 the Nicaraguan National Assembly repealed law 99, thereby dropping the country's lawsuit in the International Court of Justice against the government of Honduras for supporting, housing, and training *contras* during the Nicaraguan civil war.

The Honduran Ecological Association accused the transnational fruit companies of using harmful pesticides on their plantations. Labourers who handled the pesticides had developed skin disorders or cancer or had become sterile. Preliminary investigations indicated that there had been misuse of toxins and inadequate protection for workers.

(SARAH CAMERON)

This article updates the *Macropædia* article CENTRAL AMERICA: *Honduras*.

JAMAICA

A constitutional monarchy within the Commonwealth, Jamaica occupies an island in the Caribbean Sea. Area: 10,991 sq km (4,244 sq mi). Pop. (1992 est.): 2,445,000. Cap.: Kingston. Monetary unit: Jamaica dollar, with (Oct. 5, 1992) a free rate of J$21.89 to U.S. $1 (J$37.21 = £1 sterling). Queen, Elizabeth II; governor-general in 1992, Howard Cooke; prime ministers, Michael Manley and, from March 30, Percival J. Patterson.

Percival J. Patterson speaks at his inauguration on March 30 as prime minister of Jamaica. He replaced Michael Manley, also of the People's National Party, who resigned for reasons of health after having headed the Jamaican government for several years.
NAJLAH FEANNY—SABA

The lengthy Manley political dynasty came to an end in March 1992 when 67-year-old Michael Manley, who had followed his father, Norman, as head of the People's National Party (PNP), bowed out of politics, citing ill health. He had been leader of the PNP for 23 years and prime minister for several five-year terms. The succession passed to Percival J. Patterson, who said he would maintain the current PNP policy of economic deregulation, divestment of state enterprises, and encouragement of private initiative.

Gun battles between supporters of the two main political parties, the PNP and the Jamaica Labour Party (JLP), led by Edward Seaga, continued in the early part of the year, following the death in prison of a well-known JLP activist, Lester Coke, also known as Jim Brown, and the murder of his son. At least eight people died. Sugar workers went on strike for two weeks in March; civil servants threatened to stop work in protest against the proposed loss of 8,000 jobs; and demonstrators blocked roads and burned tires when bus fares and school fees went up in September.

In June the central bank set up a currency stabilization fund to support the weak Jamaican dollar. Patterson met Venezuelan Pres. Carlos Andrés Pérez in September and obtained an increase, to 13,000 bbl per day, in the oil Jamaica could buy at subsidized prices. He later negotiated an oil-supply agreement with Nigeria.   (DAVID RENWICK)

This article updates the *Macropædia* article The WEST INDIES: *Jamaica*.

MEXICO

A federal republic of North America, Mexico has coastlines on the Pacific Ocean, the Gulf of Mexico, and the Caribbean Sea. Area: 1,958,201 sq km (756,066 sq mi). Pop. (1992 est.): 84,439,-000. Cap.: Mexico City. Monetary unit: Mexican peso, with (Oct. 5, 1992) a free rate of 3,013 pesos to U.S. $1 (5,122 pesos = £1 sterling). President in 1992, Carlos Salinas de Gortari.

Gubernatorial elections were held during July and August 1992 in 8 of Mexico's 31 states. The ruling Institutional Revolutionary Party (PRI) retained control of all except Chihuahua, the largest and richest state in the country. Francisco Barrio Terrazas of the right-wing National Action Party (PAN) won there. It was only the second time in over 60 years that PRI had lost a state election. However, the ruling party defeated the candidate of the left-wing Democratic Revolutionary Party (PRD) in Michoacán, the stronghold of PRD leader Cuauhtémoc Cárdenas Solórzano. In Durango the PRI candidate, Maximiliano Silerio, won by a slim majority. PAN and PRD had tried to force PRI out by combining their votes, and their defeat drove enraged opposition supporters onto the streets, claiming fraud. Order was restored when PRI conceded several towns to PAN in return for its candidate's dropping his claim to the state governorship. On August 29 some 40,000 people led by Cárdenas gathered in the main square of Mexico City, demanding changes in the electoral system and protesting the controversial elections. Absenteeism was as high as 70% in some states, and mutual accusations of cheating were rife among all participating parties. Continued demonstrations in Michoacán caused the newly elected PRI governor to step down on October 6.

On November 8 elections for governor took place in Puebla, Sinaloa, and Tamaulipas. PRI candidates were declared the winners in all three, but the opposition parties charged fraud, challenged the results, and held protest demonstrations. An electoral commission office in Matamoros, Tamaulipas, was looted and burned on November 10. In elections in the states of Oaxaca and Tlaxcala on November 8, PRI candidates were victorious, with few charges of fraud.

Economic growth was healthy during the year. An overall rise of 3% in the gross domestic product (GDP) was forecast. Inflation was predicted to average 14.5% for 1992, down from 18.8% in 1991. Proceeds from the privatization campaign totaled $14.5 billion over the first three years, most of which had gone toward paying off the national debt. In June the Finance Ministry released figures showing that the debt amounted to 28.4% of the country's total GDP, a significant drop from 35.6% at the end of 1991. In November the government submitted an austerity budget for 1993 in which total spending would decline 0.2%.

At the end of August the government announced the privatization of 60 companies, including mining, gas suppliers, fertilizer manufacturers, and gasoline (petrol) service stations. Amid growing labour unrest, trade unions criticized the program, claiming that over 100,000 workers had lost their jobs since 1982 either directly or indirectly as a result of privatization. Several industries were hit by damaging strikes during the year, including textiles, farming, fishing, and the state oil industry.

On August 12, after 14 months of negotiation, agreement was reached on a North American Free Trade Agreement (NAFTA) between Mexico, Canada, and the U.S. However, the details of NAFTA would not be officially confirmed until it was signed and ratified by the three governments. Mexico was thought to have won important concessions for its oil industry and agriculture, considered vulnerable sectors. Many Mexicans remained concerned, nevertheless, about being exploited for cheap unskilled labour. Jan. 1, 1994, was set as the target date for enactment of the treaty.

Pres. Carlos Salinas de Gortari made several Cabinet changes, prompting speculation over likely candidates to be his successor in the 1994 presidential election. Under the Mexican constitution no president could be reelected. Pedro Aspe Armella, previously the finance minister, took over the newly merged Ministries of Finance and Planning and Budget, the two most important economic departments, making him the front-runner. Another likely successor was the PRI president, Luis Donaldo Colosio, made minister of the Secretariat of Urban Development and Ecology. This put him in charge of the important Solidaridad program. Genaro Borrego Estrade, governor of Zacatecas, was the new PRI president, and Beatriz Paredes, Tlaxcala state governor, was appointed PRI secretary-general.

On April 22 a series of sewer-line explosions destroyed more than 20 blocks of a working-class district in the city of Guadalajara, leaving an estimated 200 people dead and 1,500 injured. The government moved swiftly, sending in emergency rescue teams and bulldozers to clear the rubble. A preliminary report ordered by President Salinas showed that gasoline had leaked out of a pipeline into a parallel sewage pipeline, ultimately causing the explosions. It also confirmed that local authorities had not taken adequate precautions when residents had complained of strong gasoline odours several days earlier. The attorney general's report laid the blame for the incident on local government, the water board, and Pemex, the state oil company; 11 officials were charged with criminal negligence, and most were imprisoned. The Jalisco state governor, Guillermo Cosio, was forced to resign.

For several weeks during March and April, air pollution

Workers in Juárez, Mexico, sew clothes for a U.S. company. Many economists believed that the proposed North American Free Trade Agreement would encourage additional U.S. companies to move some of their manufacturing operations to low-wage Mexico.

in Mexico City rose to dangerously high levels. Schools were closed, some 200 plants cut output by 75%, and 300,000 cars were forced to stay off the roads. Long-term measures announced by the government included the conversion of 144,000 freight and public transport vehicles to natural gas or liquid petroleum gas by 1994. Industries in the capital also agreed to cut toxic emissions by the end of 1993. According to a local environmental protection agency (Asociacion de Lucha Metropolitana para el Mejoramiento Ambiental), as many as two million inhabitants of Mexico City suffered from serious respiratory problems.   (HUW CLOUGH)

NICARAGUA

A republic of Central America, Nicaragua has coastlines on the Caribbean Sea and the Pacific Ocean. Area: 130,682 sq km (50,457 sq mi). Pop. (1992 est.): 4,131,000. Cap.: Managua. Monetary unit: córdoba oro, with (Oct. 5, 1992) a par value of 5 córdobas oro to U.S. $1 (free rate of 8.50 córdobas oro = £1 sterling). President in 1992, Violeta Barrios de Chamorro.

In April 1992 the Cerro Negro volcano erupted, spewing ash over a large area in the west; 10,000 persons were evacuated, and there was considerable damage in the province of León, where the roofs of houses collapsed under the weight of black sand. At the beginning of September a powerful earthquake offshore spawned a series of tidal waves up to 13.75 m (45 ft) high, which swept over Nicaragua's Pacific coast. At least 105 people were drowned and several hundred more were injured or reported missing, while more than 4,200 were left homeless. Towns all along the coast suffered damage, though the extent of the destruction would take some time to evaluate. Pres. Violeta Chamorro launched an international appeal for aid, and the U.S. pledged $5 million in disaster relief. The U.K. sent $100,000.

At the instigation of Sen. Jesse Helms (Rep., N.C.), the U.S. Senate Foreign Relations Committee suspended $116 million in aid in June. A report by Republican staff members of the committee, released in early September, recommended continuing the freeze on U.S. aid on the grounds that the country was still controlled by Sandinistas. The report called for the removal of the army commander, Gen. Humberto Ortega, and other Sandinista army officers, the appointment of new judges, and the return of property expropriated by the Sandinistas when they were in office. The Nicaraguan government rejected the report as full of lies, stating that the aid freeze threatened economic recon-

struction and that without it Nicaragua would be unable to meet its international reserve target agreed upon with the International Monetary Fund.

Under obvious U.S. pressure, the president subsequently announced measures to speed up the settlement of expropriated property claims. All 5,000 claims were to be settled in favour of the former owners; they would receive land if unoccupied or compensation, largely in the form of shares in state companies to be privatized; no property would be returned to the Somoza family, which formerly ruled Nicaragua, or its close associates.

On December 30 President Chamorro reacted to an increasing conflict between the executive and the legislature by ordering the police to occupy the National Assembly building and seize its assets and documents fot safekeeping. An interim commission was appointed to manage the assembly's affairs until the election of new assembly leaders on Jan. 9, 1993.   (SARAH CAMERON)

This article updates the *Macropædia* article CENTRAL AMERICA: *Nicaragua*.

PANAMA

A republic of Central America, Panama lies between the Caribbean Sea and the Pacific Ocean on the Isthmus of Panama. Area: 75,517 sq km (29,157 sq mi). Pop. (1992 est.): 2,515,000. Cap.: Panama City. Monetary unit: balboa, at par with the U.S. dollar, with a free rate (Oct. 5, 1992) of 1.70 balboas to £1 sterling. President in 1992, Guillermo Endara Galimany.

In January 1992 the human rights group Americas Watch released a report on Panama's human rights record in 1991, which concluded that there had been little improvement in the country's penal and judicial systems since the 1989 invasion by the United States. The report drew attention to the length of time prisoners were detained before trial, often up to five years, and noted that at least 80% of those in jail had not been convicted and in many cases had not even been formally charged.

Pres. Guillermo Endara Galimany announced a new antiterrorist force, to be called the Elite Tactical Weapons Unit, to combat Panama's rising crime and terrorism. The unit would be specially trained to deal with attempts to overthrow the government. On February 7 the president held a press conference to announce the success of the unit in foiling a conspiracy to stage such a coup. Critics regarded the unit as a smoke screen to distract attention from the economic and social problems affecting the country and also

REUTERS/BETTMANN

Surrounded by security agents, U.S. Pres. George Bush (lower left) and Panamanian Pres. Guillermo Endara (lower right) rub their eyes after tear gas fired at demonstrators in Panama City on June 11 drifted back to where they were to address a rally. Bush was in Panama to commemorate the 1989 U.S. invasion that toppled Gen. Manuel Noriega, but the demonstration prevented the two leaders from making their speeches.

as an excuse to enlarge the armed forces and to increase repression of the civilian population.

In February U.S. Secretary of Defense Richard Cheney paid an official visit to Panama to inspect military bases where about 10,000 U.S. troops were stationed. According to the treaty on the Panama Canal, all U.S. troops were to be removed from Panama by the end of 1999, when the canal was to be officially handed over to the Panamanian government. Many groups within Panama, however, feared that the loss of U.S. troops would mean unemployment for thousands of workers. A movement to press for a referendum on the issue gathered force, spurred on by the increasing instability in the country and the perceived inability of the administration to manage or defend the canal. The treaty could be renegotiated only by mutual consent based on a popular referendum in Panama or in the event that Panama was determined by the U.S. to be incapable of effectively defending the Canal Zone. However, despite surveys showing that a large percentage of the population supported the U.S. military presence, thousands protested against the June visit of U.S. Pres. George Bush, and there were several violent attacks against the U.S. military. Angry demonstrators protested that the U.S. promise of reparation and reconstruction after the invasion had never been fulfilled, and hundreds of Panamanians were still homeless as a result of the war. President Bush was unable to deliver his public address, and police had to disperse the protesting crowd with tear gas.

On November 15 Panamanians voted in a national referendum on a package of 58 reform measures proposed by the government. Only 40% of the eligible voters went to the polls, and 64% of them rejected the package. The most controversial of the measures was one that would have abolished the armed forces. Citing the "no" vote and the mass abstentions as a rejection of the government, opposition leaders called for the election of a national constituent assembly to draw up a new constitution. (SARAH CAMERON)

This article updates the *Macropædia* article CENTRAL AMERICA: *Panama*.

PARAGUAY

Paraguay is a landlocked republic of central South America. Area: 406,752 sq km (157,048 sq mi). Pop. (1992 est.): 4,519,000. Cap.: Asunción. Monetary unit: guaraní, with (Oct. 5, 1992) a free rate of 1,543 guaraníes to U.S. $1 (2,624 guaraníes = £1 sterling). President in 1992, Gen. Andrés Rodríguez.

Pressure from the army forced the ruling Colorado Party to paper over its internal strife and helped it gain an emphatic victory in the December 1991 elections for a constituent assembly; this guaranteed the government a major role in the drafting of a new constitution. On June 15 the assembly approved a measure whereby Pres. Andrés Rodríguez was included in the constitutional ban on reelection bids by serving presidents. The inclusion of Rodríguez in the prohibition was taken by him as an attack on his family, his honour, and his word as a soldier that he would not run for reelection in 1993. The president refused to attend the final session of the constituent assembly on June 18. A series of protests by his supporters fueled fears of a military coup, fears that were laid to rest only when Rodríguez finally swore allegiance to the new constitution in a ceremony on June 22.

On December 27 the Colorado Party chose Luis María Argaña as its candidate for president in the elections scheduled for May 9, 1993. Argaña, who had served as president of the Supreme Court under Gen. Alfredo Stroessner, received 48% of the vote to 41% for second-place Juan Carlos

Wasmosy. Charging vote fraud, Wasmosy announced that he would challenge the results. The candidate of the opposition, led by the Authentic Radical Liberals, was Domingo Laíno. (MICHAEL WOOLLER)

PERU

The republic of Peru is located in western South America, on the Pacific Ocean. Area: 1,285,216 sq km (496,225 sq mi). Pop. (1992 est.): 22,454,000. Cap.: Lima. Monetary unit: nuevo sol, with (Oct. 5, 1992) a free rate of 1.52 nuevos soles to U.S. $1 (2.58 nuevos soles = £1 sterling). President in 1992, Alberto Fujimori; prime ministers, Alfonso de los Heros and, from April 6, Oscar de la Puente Raygada.

On April 5, 1992, Pres. Alberto Fujimori carried out an *autogolpe* (self-coup) when he closed Congress, sacked judiciary authorities, and set up a new government of "national emergency and reconstruction." The president blamed Congress for blocking his efforts to strengthen the economy and quash guerrilla activities. Congress condemned the move and raised fears that Fujimori was being used as a puppet of the armed forces prior to a military takeover. However, no blood was shed in the initial confusion, and the army showed support for the president by its restraint. On November 13, however, a small group of army officers tried to seize the national palace and kill Fujimori. Loyalist soldiers routed the rebels, and some 25 army officers were later arrested.

Fujimori attempted to appease international concern by promising constitutional reforms and new elections. In elections for the new Democratic Constituent Congress on November 22, parties supporting Fujimori won some 38% of the vote but nonetheless gained an absolute majority. Most of the major opposition parties boycotted the election, charging that the Congress would be only a rubber stamp for Fujimori.

Several friendly nations that had previously promised loans to Peru—Germany, France, and Japan—held back on their pledges, and Spain withdrew from the agreement altogether. The Inter-American Development Bank (IDB), however, removed its block on new loans to Peru, which had been suspended after the events of April 5.

The economy appeared to be set for a modest recovery at the beginning of the year, with the government's severe austerity measures bringing inflation down to 2.8% in August, the lowest since December 1985. But during the year industrial output declined, with a particular slump in July. Agricultural production rose in 1991 but was nipped in the bud in 1992 by disastrous effects of El Niño (a warm current that sweeps through the Pacific every few years, provoking severe climatic reactions on land). Unseasonably heavy rains flooded the north of the country, while the south suffered severe drought.

The government declared that one of its highest priorities was to wipe out Sendero Luminoso (Shining Path) and Movimiento Revolucionario Tupac Amarú, whose activities had spread throughout Peru. Reports emerged that prisons were being used as indoctrination centres for the guerrilla groups. In early May the police tried to restore order in the Miguel Castro prison on the outskirts of Lima. When they attempted to move female detainees to another prison, some 35 members of the Shining Path and 2 policemen were killed in the ensuing conflict. In July a series of car bombs exploded in Lima, causing many casualties and marking the worst spate of violence in the capital in many years. On September 12 police arrested Abimael Guzman, leader of the Shining Path, in a raid on a house in Lima. The capture of Guzman after 12 years in hiding was at-

Abimael Guzman, leader of the Shining Path, remains defiant in a jail cell in Lima. The head of the terrorist group that had threatened the Peruvian government for more than a decade, he was arrested on September 12 and in early October was sentenced to life imprisonment.
SYGMA

tributed to Dincote, Peru's counterterrorist police force.

Guzman was taken before a top-secret military tribunal and charged with terrorist offenses related to an unofficial total of about 22,500 deaths since the inception of the guerrilla war in 1980. In early October he was found guilty of treason and sentenced to life imprisonment. The loss of Guzman and the later arrests of other leaders were the worst setbacks in the Shining Path's history. However, the guerrillas were thought to be well organized into self-contained cells and capable of quickly finding new leadership.

The police, meanwhile, stepped up security in the capital, bracing themselves for a backlash reaction to Guzman's sentence. Nevertheless, a spate of terrorist attacks did break out, mainly in and around Lima, leaving at least one person dead and several injured.   (HUW CLOUGH)

SAINT KITTS AND NEVIS

A constitutional monarchy and member of the Commonwealth, St. Kitts and Nevis comprises the islands of St. Kitts and Nevis in the eastern Caribbean Sea. Area: 269 sq km (104 sq mi). Pop. (1992 est.): 43,100. Cap.: Basseterre. Monetary unit: Eastern Caribbean dollar, with (Oct. 5, 1992) a par value of EC$2.70 to U.S. $1 (free rate of EC$4.59 = £1 sterling). Queen, Elizabeth II; governor-general in 1992, Sir Clement Arrindell; prime minister, Kennedy A. Simmonds.

The dismissal of Deputy Prime Minister Michael Powell in April 1992 brought crowds into the streets of Basseterre in protest. Powell was a popular politician, but his relationship with Kennedy Simmonds, the prime minister and leader of the governing People's Action Movement (PAM), had been strained for some time. The results of the Nevis local election in June did little to lift PAM's spirits. Its coalition partner, the Nevis Reformation Party, was defeated 3–2 by the Concerned Citizens Movement (CCM), which had established itself at the national level in the 1989 election by winning one seat in the federal parliament. The CCM victory removed, for the moment, the threat of Nevis' secession from the federation.

Shortly after the election, Nevis was jolted by the discovery of the body of the deputy governor-general, Weston Parris. He was found floating in the sea near his home in Charlestown.

There was some cheerful news on the economic front when the sugar crop closed in midyear at 20,159 metric tons, well above the 19,000-ton target. The British government helped boost economic development by providing £900,000 for three new road projects, including a new bypass to the east of Basseterre.   (DAVID RENWICK)

This article updates the *Macropædia* article The WEST INDIES: *Saint Kitts and Nevis.*

SAINT LUCIA

A constitutional monarchy and member of the Commonwealth, St. Lucia is the second largest of the Windward Islands in the eastern Caribbean Sea. Area: 617 sq km (238 sq mi). Pop. (1992 est.): 135,000. Cap.: Castries. Monetary unit: Eastern Caribbean dollar, with (Oct. 5, 1992) a par value of EC$2.70 to U.S. $1 (free rate of EC$4.59 = £1 sterling). Queen, Elizabeth II; governor-general in 1992, Stanislaus A. James; prime minister, John Compton.

The United Workers Party (UWP), led by John Compton, was returned to office yet again in April 1992, with an 11–6 majority in the House of Assembly and 56.3% of the vote. The Saint Lucia Labour Party (SLP) remained the official opposition. Compton had been prime minister since 1982. Prior to independence, he was head of successive governments during the period 1964 to 1979. In June, Compton presented the first budget of his new administration. It envisaged expenditure of EC$490.7 million, with EC$219.2 million earmarked for capital development.

Despite its defeat at the polls, the SLP reelected Julian Hunte as its leader in July, ignoring calls for his removal. An inquiry into reports of malpractice and irregularities in the operations of the Castries City Council was launched in midyear. In August, Compton promised an "all-out offensive" against drug traffickers, following revelations that schoolchildren were being suborned into the drug trade.

The Royal Caribbean Cruise Line, one of the main cruise ship operators in the region, dropped Saint Lucia from its itinerary after the cruise visitor tax was raised from $2 to $10. Compton accused the line of "singling-out" Saint Lucia for "discriminatory action."   (DAVID RENICK)

This article updates the *Macropædia* article The WEST INDIES: *Saint Lucia.*

SAINT VINCENT AND THE GRENADINES

A constitutional monarchy within the Commonwealth, St. Vincent and the Grenadines comprises the islands of St. Vincent and the northern Grenadines in the eastern Caribbean Sea. Area: 389 sq km (150 sq mi). Pop. (1992 est.): 109,000. Cap.: Kingstown. Monetary unit: Eastern Caribbean dollar, with (Oct. 5, 1992) a par value of EC$2.70 to U.S. $1 (free rate of EC$4.59 = £1 sterling). Queen, Elizabeth II; governor-general in 1992, David Jack; prime minister, James Fitz-Allen Mitchell.

The EC$274.4 million budget presented in January 1992 included a capital spending component of EC$104.8 million, to be financed principally from external sources. The largest capital project in the country's recent history was completed in May, when the new EC$55 million airport opened for business in Bequia. The airport was named after the prime minister, James F. Mitchell, who represented the island in Parliament.

Plans for an even bigger project, a $75 million boatyard and marina near Kingstown, were approved by Parliament at midyear. It would be a joint venture between the government (49%) and an Italian company (51%). The West Deutsche Landesbank pledged funding to the extent of $50.3 million to the operating company, Caribbean Charter and Yacht Yard Holdings Ltd. The company would receive duty-free concessions during the construction stage, a 15-year tax break, and free repatriation of profits. Forty Vincentians were to receive training in Italy.

Ivy Joshua, the first elected female member of the St. Vincent and the Grenadines legislature, died in August at the age of 67. She was the wife of the late Ebenezer Joshua, the country's first chief minister. (DAVID RENWICK)

This article updates the Macropædia article The WEST INDIES: Saint Vincent and the Grenadines.

SURINAME

The republic of Suriname is in northeastern South America, on the Atlantic Ocean. Area: 163,820 sq km (63,251 sq mi), not including a 17,635-sq km area disputed with Guyana. Pop. (1992 est.): 404,000. Cap.: Paramaribo. Monetary unit: Suriname guilder, with (Oct. 5, 1992) a par value of 1.79 guilders to U.S. $1 (free rate of 3.03 guilders = £1 sterling). President in 1992, Ronald Venetiaan; prime minister, Jules Adjodhia.

In May 1992 the two main guerrilla groups, Ronnie Brunswijk's Surinamese Liberation Army or Jungle Commando and Thomas Sabajo's Tucayana Amazonas, announced a cessation of hostilities against the government, and in early August a draft peace treaty was signed by the government, these groups, and some smaller guerrilla factions. The agreement included a general amnesty and integration of the guerrillas into the civilian police. A disarmament meeting took place on August 24 at Moengo, where Brunswijk, who had led a seven-year insurgency, was the first to hand over his weapons to an observer from the Organization of American States.

On March 21 the government asked the National Assembly to remove articles in the constitution that allowed the army to act in a way "that did not stand with the functioning of a democratic Constitutional State." On February 3 Pres. Ronald Venetiaan visited U.S. Pres. George Bush, who reportedly promised assistance in case of another military coup in Suriname. In The Netherlands on June 18, Venetiaan and Dutch Prime Minister Ruud Lubbers signed an agreement providing for the resumption of Dutch aid, suspended during the period of military rule. The Dutch government promised some 1 billion guilders over the next five years. (KLAAS J. HOEKSEMA)

TRINIDAD AND TOBAGO

A republic and member of the Commonwealth, Trinidad and Tobago consists of two islands in the Caribbean Sea off the coast of Venezuela. Area: 5,128 sq km (1,980 sq mi). Pop. (1992 est.): 1,261,000. Cap.: Port of Spain. Monetary unit: Trinidad and Tobago dollar, with (Oct. 5, 1992) a par value of TT$4.25 to U.S. $1 (free rate of TT$7.23 = £1 sterling). President in 1992, Noor Mohammad Hassanali; prime minister, Patrick Manning.

The People's National Movement (PNM) government presented the first budget of its new administration in January 1992, setting expenditures for the year at TT$7.9 billion. Income tax rates were increased, and the corporation tax was restored to 45%.

Prime Minister Patrick Manning met U.S. Pres. George Bush and other U.S. government officials in Washington, D.C., in May. Cooperation between the two countries in combating the drug trade was discussed.

Following its decisive defeat in the December 1991 elections, the National Alliance for Reconstruction (NAR) elected a new leader, Carson Charles. The previous leader, A.N.R. Robinson, who had been prime minister during 1986–91, resigned shortly after the election.

The 114 members of the Jamaat al Muslimeen group that stormed Parliament and held the prime minister and several other government ministers hostage for five days in July–August 1990 were released from jail in July. A High Court judge upheld the validity of the amnesty they had been granted by the acting president in an effort to avoid bloodshed. The government appealed part of the judgment.

Local government elections in September confirmed the PNM's popularity. The party regained total control of four boroughs and was victorious in six of the nine regional councils. However, the NAR retained control of the Tobago House of Assembly in elections on December 7.

Efforts were under way at the year's end to merge the two government-owned oil companies, Trintoc and Trintopec, at the instigation of international lending agencies. The integrated company was expected to have 6,000 employees and assets of TT$3.2 billion. (DAVID RENWICK)

This article updates the Macropædia article The WEST INDIES: Trinidad and Tobago.

URUGUAY

A republic of eastern South America, Uruguay lies on the Atlantic Ocean. Area: 176,215 sq km (68,037 sq mi). Pop. (1992 est.): 3,130,000. Cap.: Montevideo. Monetary unit: Uruguayan new peso, with (Oct. 5, 1992) a free rate of 3,271 new pesos to U.S. $1 (5,561 new pesos = £1 sterling). President in 1992, Luis Alberto Lacalle.

The Inter Union Assembly and the National Confederation of Workers (PIT-CNT) called another general strike in January 1992 as part of its ongoing protest against the economic policies of Pres. Luis Lacalle; the PIT-CNT confederation had previously organized a 36-hour general strike in December 1991 following the award of a 12% pay raise to public sector workers that the confederation described as wholly insufficient.

On February 27 Finance Minister Lic Ignacio de Posadas announced the third most severe stage in the fiscal readjustment program designed to bring Uruguay back into line with its agreement with the International Monetary Fund and international banks. Partly as a result of a Cabinet reshuffle in which Posadas became finance minister, the Battlismo Radical faction pulled out of the governing coalition.

By mid-February the opposition left-wing Frente Amplio and the PIT-CNT had gathered the necessary 12,000 signatures required for a special poll to be held in their campaign to slow the government's privatization program and preserve PIT-CNT jobs. The poll was duly held on July 5, but only 458,818 actually voted, as compared with the 581,069 in favour (25% of the electorate) required for a referendum on the issue to be forced. Another referendum on the issue took place in December, and the government again lost.

(MICHAEL WOOLLER)

VENEZUELA

A republic of northern South America, Venezuela lies on the Caribbean Sea. Area: 912,050 sq km (352,144 sq mi). Pop. (1992 est.): 20,184,000. Cap.: Caracas. Monetary unit: bolívar, with (Oct. 5, 1992) a free rate of 69.49 bolívares to U.S. $1 (118.14 bolívares = £1 sterling). President in 1992, Carlos Andrés Pérez.

At 2 AM on Feb. 4, 1992, Pres. Carlos Andrés Pérez appeared on national television and announced that an attempted military coup had been thwarted. The uprising had begun a few hours earlier at the José Leonardo Chirinos paratroops regiment base in the city of Maracay. Even as the president spoke, sporadic gunfire continued to erupt in the capital. Later another rebel unit took control of the city of

Alleged troublemakers are rounded up in early February during an attempted coup against the Venezuelan government. In spite of grievances among military officers and discontent among the populace over economic and other problems, the government put down the February uprising and a second coup attempt in November.
BILL GENTILE—SIPA

Maracaibo. By daybreak, however, loyal government troops had regained the upper hand, and at midday the leader of the rebels, Lieut. Col. Hugo Chávez Frías, surrendered and made an appeal on television for any remaining forces to follow suit.

In the aftermath 133 officers were arrested for their part in the uprising. The rebels belonged to the radical Bolivarist Revolutionary Movement (MRB). Their activities began during the 1989 riots, when they circulated pamphlets around army barracks, accusing the military leadership of corruption and calling for a coup. Military unrest had been growing for some months, since the emergence of scandals linking high-ranking officers to drug traffickers and financial profiteering. But despite warnings from the ministry of defense, no one really believed that the military would challenge the 34-year period of civilian rule.

Public condemnation of the rebels was muted. However, there was increased support for opposition leaders, particularly former president Rafael Caldera of the Social Christian Party (COPEI). The government announced a series of reforms in the wake of the uprising, including an inquiry into corruption within the armed forces, an increase in the minimum wage, an increase in low-cost housing expenditures, and lower interest rates to stimulate the private sector of the economy.

On February 25 a Cabinet reshuffle was announced, and dominant figures within the leading Democratic Action party were appointed. The defense minister, Gen. Fernando Ochoa Antich, was appointed foreign minister during Cabinet changes in June. He was the first military figure to hold the post in the civilian government, and his appointment was viewed as a concession to disgruntled army factions. After the government defeated a move to cut short its term by a year, the next presidential elections were scheduled for December 1993.

On November 27 rebellious units of the air force along with leftist groups staged the year's second coup attempt. Air attacks were made on the office of President Pérez, and two air bases were captured. After 12 hours of heavy fighting in Caracas, the rebels were defeated. In December a court-martial ordered the arrest of 240 soldiers and civilians for their part in the attack, in which at least 170 died.

Regional elections took place in December. Preliminary returns indicated that the governing Democratic Action Party won only 6–8 of the 22 governor's seats; in 1989 it had won 11 of the 20.

Despite continuing political unrest, the economy was reasonably healthy. In June the gross domestic product was 8.5% higher than in the same period of 1991. Unemploy-

ment fell from 8.7% at the end of 1991 to 8.4% by mid-1992 and, following 1991 growth, per capita income increased to $2,600. On the down side, oil exports fell by $14 million compared with the first six months of 1991. For the first time since 1976, when the oil industry was nationalized, private oil companies were offered 20-year contracts for exploration of marginal fields. Any oil produced, however, would have to be processed by Petróleos de Venezuela (PDVSA), the state oil company.

A government reform package, announced in August, included a freeze on public-sector pay at 1992 levels, a $369 million cut in spending on PDVSA, a cut in internal government spending, a ban on new weapons systems for the armed forces, and the privatization of Alcasa, a state aluminum producer.   (HUW CLOUGH)

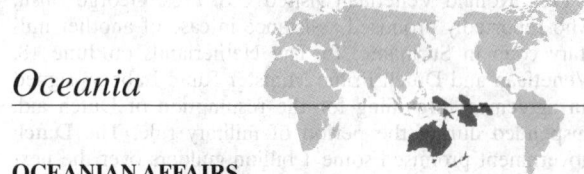

Oceania

OCEANIAN AFFAIRS

Regional organizations played a prominent role in Oceanian affairs in 1992, with environmental concerns an underlying theme. The South Pacific Forum, now with 15 members that were independent or self-governing states, met in Honiara, Solomon Islands, in July. The meeting was chaired by Solomon Mamaloni, prime minister of Solomon Islands. This was the last Forum meeting to be attended by Sir Robert Rex, premier of Niue, who had attended his first Forum meeting as an observer in 1973 and had the longest unbroken record of attendance at the Forum of any Pacific leader. Absent from the meeting for the first time was Ratu Sir Kamisese Mara, former prime minister of Fiji, who had been a founding member of the Forum in 1971 and had served since that time, except for a break after the Fiji coups of 1987. Mara was a strong advocate of informal discussion rather than formal business in the Forum and had urged recognition of the "Pacific Way" of discussion, compromise, and consensus in decision making. During the year, the region marked the death of Sir Robert Muldoon (see OBITUARIES), former New Zealand prime minister. As a member of the Forum, Muldoon was a strong advocate of regional trade and the Forum Shipping Line, though he sometimes drew criticism because of perceived racism in the immigration policies of his government.

The Forum welcomed an Australian-funded program to monitor climate change in the region and to evaluate the impact of global warming on sea levels, freshwater supplies, and the frequency of cyclonic storms. Several of the independent nations were represented at the "Earth Summit" in Rio de Janeiro in June and were among the first to sign the Conventions on Climate Change and Biodiversity. Any significant rise in sea levels would raise questions about the viability of maintaining populations on many low-lying Pacific Islands. The Forum expressed continuing concern over the destruction of chemical weapons by the U.S. at Johnston Atoll and was critical of proposals to dispose of toxic waste in the Pacific Islands. The concern was by no means allayed by the visit to Johnston Atoll of a team of scientists representing Forum countries.

The Forum joined in criticism of Japan's proposal to ship plutonium from Europe by a route that would pass close to a number of member countries. France's announcement that it would suspend its nuclear testing program for 1992 was welcomed, and the Forum called for the U.S., the U.K., and France to sign the protocols of the South Pacific Nuclear Free Zone Treaty (the Rarotonga Treaty) of 1985. Despite protests from China, the Forum recognized Taiwan as a dialogue partner—one of those nations from outside the region that are invited to hold talks with Forum members. The invitation recognized the growing role of Taiwan in the region's economies. New Caledonia's Kanak Liberation Front was denied observer status on the grounds that it did not meet the normal requirement of representing a nation that had achieved self-government or was on the verge of independence.

The Forum also expressed disappointment over delays in establishing the Joint Commercial Commission proposed during talks between U.S. Pres. George Bush and Forum leaders in Hawaii in 1991. The leaders were concerned that no funds had been forthcoming from the U.S. and expressed doubt as to whether the venture could survive on private funding alone. By the end of the year, a director (Jioji Kotobalavu of Fiji) had been appointed, and there were plans to draw up detailed terms of reference and to establish a headquarters organization in Hawaii in association with the East-West Center. It was intended that the commission would promote economic development through the private sector.

Earlier in the year, the inaugural summit of smaller Pacific Island states was held in Rarotonga, Cook Islands, and was attended by the Cook Islands, Kiribati, Nauru, Niue, and Tuvalu. Kiribati, with some 74,700 inhabitants, had more than twice the population of the other states put together. The summit explored possible sources of development capital for very small states, expressed concern over the reduction of the Forum Line's feeder service, looked at the possibilities of sharing technologies for black pearl production, and considered the amalgamation of their respective exclusive economic zones to facilitate negotiations over the licensing of commercial fishing.

Plans for a regional approach to environmental issues came a step closer when the South Pacific Regional Environmental Program produced a draft plan that would provide for the coordination of efforts to deal with short-term problems—like disaster relief—and to plan for longer-term developments related to global warming—including the management of freshwater resources, reef protection, and the development of building standards to meet hurricane conditions. The program was also concerned with broader issues such as the protection of rain forest.

The South Pacific Commission (SPC) had a troubled year. Originally designed to coordinate the social and economic development activities of the colonial powers, the SPC had remained an important point of contact for island nations, especially those not eligible for membership in the South Pacific Forum. However, the organization had been troubled by financial and management difficulties. The facilities in Noumea, New Caledonia, needed replacement, but there was difficulty in reaching agreement between the French and New Caledonian governments, which wanted to rebuild on a new (and less desirable) site in Noumea, and many of the region's governments, which wanted to rebuild on the current site or remove to another Pacific capital. Fiji offered to meet the $13.6 million cost of moving the organization to Suva. A compromise was reached—to rebuild in Noumea, with costs to be met by France and Australia—but not without acrimony. The new secretary-general-elect, Jacques Iekawe of New Caledonia, died before taking over the position from Atanraoi Baiteke of Kiribati.

Fiji, Kiribati, Papua New Guinea, Solomon Islands, and Vanuatu combined to participate in Expo 92 in Seville, Spain. They planned a Pacific Village with buildings representing various regional building styles, but the spectacular exhibit was destroyed by fire just days before Expo opened. This left little time to make alternative arrangements, though New Zealand and other adjoining pavilions made space and facilities available. It was hoped that the publicity from Expo participation would promote tourism development. The Tourism Council of the South Pacific won the award for the Most Effective Corporate Image among 3,000 exhibits from 140 countries at the World Travel mart in London. Within the region, there was widespread participation in, and publicity for, the Pacific Arts Festival in Rarotonga in October.   (BARRIE MACDONALD)

AUSTRALIA

A federal parliamentary state (formally a constitutional monarchy) and member of the Commonwealth, Australia occupies the smallest continent and includes the island state of Tasmania. Area: 7,682,300 sq km (2,966,200 sq mi). Pop. (1992 est.): 17,562,000. Cap.: Canberra. Monetary unit: Australian dollar, with (Oct. 5, 1992) a free rate of $A 1.38 to U.S. $1 ($A 2.35 = £1 sterling). Queen, Elizabeth II; governor-general in 1992, Bill Hayden; prime minister, Paul Keating.

Domestic Affairs. The prospect of a snap general election hung over Australian politics in 1992. The two party leaders, Prime Minister Paul Keating (see BIOGRAPHIES) and the leader of the opposition, John Hewson, jockeyed for supremacy in the public opinion polls. Hewson expected Keating to call an early election because Australia's economic position was continually worsening, but Keating continued to work for an improvement in living standards and a lowering of the high unemployment rate as essential prerequisites before going to the electorate. The yearlong political uncertainty frayed the nerves of both leaders. Hewson's major problem was that he had decided to approach the next election promising a new tax instead of following tradition and letting the government fail through its own ineptitude.

Throughout the year, Keating's personal popularity remained low. He recorded the lowest-ever popularity rating for an incoming prime minister in his first Morgan Gallup Poll, 25%—a figure that matched the lowest rating ever recorded by a prime minister in office, Sir William McMahon in 1972. Nor was the Australian Labor Party (ALP) helped by former prime minister Bob Hawke's behaviour on leaving Parliament. Hawke's decision to resign his seat of Wills in February 1992 left the ALP facing the prospect of a swing to the conservatives in the by-election as voters in the formerly safe Labor seat deserted the leader who had deserted them. The voters of Wills, however, were fed up with both major parties and returned an independent, Phil Cleary, whose local popularity was based on his ability as a football coach. Cleary was only the seventh independent member of Parliament since federation in 1901.

During the by-election campaign, there was considerable negative public comment on deals organized by the International Management Group on the ex-prime minister's behalf when Hawke retired from Parliament. These included television appearances, free accommodation, and free clothing and tailoring advice. Hawke also reneged on his promise not to undermine his successor. He attacked Keating for raising impossible public expectations in his economic predictions as well as for dressing personal staff at the official Canberra residence of the prime minister, the Lodge, in morning suits. Hawke commented that for nearly nine years while he was prime minister the standard garb had been an ordinary Aussie suit. "You," he said, addressing Keating, "have put them into morning suits, the uniform of the British butlering class—just a mite hypocritical mate."

The prime minister was far more concerned about the damage done to his party by a scandal involving Sen. Graham Richardson, one of the key figures behind Keating's career. Richardson was forced to resign as a minister over his relationship with a relative by marriage, who was arrested in the Marshall Islands on a forgery charge while involved in a business migration program designed to attract Asian investors to the Marshall Islands. Senator Richardson denied any wrongdoing but decided to step down to avoid long-term damage to the ALP. "I owe the party too much to contribute in any way to inhibiting its chances of electoral success," he said. Keating reluctantly accepted Richardson's resignation but refused to condemn him, saying only that his relationship with his relative had been unfortunate rather than improper. The ALP's troubles were compounded by the resignation of Premier John Bannon of South Australia, who took political responsibility for the losses of a state-owned bank, and the landslide victory of the conservative opposition in state elections in Victoria in October.

The battle between Hewson and Keating was marked by personal bitterness. In April, Hewson accused the speaker of the Parliament, Leo McLeay, of subverting the political process by denying the opposition a fair go. Hewson described McLeay as a national disgrace who had allowed the House of Representatives to become a shambles and said

that members of the New South Wales right-wing faction, to which both Keating and McLeay belonged, were "the nearest thing this country's had to the Mafia in decades." Keating replied that Hewson's remarks were a deliberate, unjustified slur that would do nothing but lower the esteem in which the Parliament was held by the public, and he asked Hewson to repeat his remarks outside Parliament so that action could be taken against him in the courts. Hewson declined to take up Keating's challenge, instead responding that Keating could dish it out but not take it. He described Keating as a nasty, mean school-yard bully "squealling and whingeing and whining and sniffling," but he admitted that the threats of legal action had confined his debate on the alleged Mafia links to the parliamentary arena, where he was protected from litigation by parliamentary privilege.

So low was public esteem for its political leaders that a man who planned to kill Hewson by shooting him with a shotgun received only a suspended jail sentence and a fine. Clifton Moss told a Canberra court that he had thought, "If I done Hewson in, Keating might have to go out of Government, so I'd get two birds in one stone."

Foreign Affairs. As the new Labor prime minister, Keating determined to distance himself from his predecessor by a high-profile interest in the Pacific and Australia's northern neighbours. Keating gave high priority to making overseas trips to Indonesia, Papua New Guinea (P.N.G.), and Japan. Australia's support for the P.N.G. against secessionist guerrillas was a sensitive issue, particularly when a range of witnesses claimed that Australian-supplied helicopters were being used to attack targets in Bougainville. Australia asked the P.N.G. to provide a detailed response to the allegations, but Keating himself used the Australia-P.N.G. link to cement his domestic popularity at home. Australia also criticized P.N.G. incursions into the Solomon Islands.

Australian foreign policy toward the U.K. hardened—also, cynics said, for domestic political reasons. Relations with Britain were soured by Keating's behaviour during a visit by Queen Elizabeth II in February. Keating took the opportunity of the royal tour to call for the establishment of an Australian republic and accused Britain of abandoning Australia and Southeast Asia to the Japanese in World War II. The British prime minister, John Major, was forced to caution the British press about a reciprocal attack on Keating and Australia. Keating touched a particularly raw nerve when he put his arm round the queen while guiding her through a crowded reception, inspiring such British tabloid

Demonstrators in Sydney protest policies of U.S. Pres. George Bush on the occasion of his visit to Australia at the beginning of the year. As part of his trip to several Pacific countries, Bush spent four days in Australia.

headlines as "Hands off our Queen" and "An insult to 27,000 heroes."

In a lengthy reassessment of Australia's constitutional relationship with the U.K., Keating told the queen that attitudes had changed during her 40-year reign. "The men who sat in the Australian Parliament on your first visit— and they were practically all men in those days—had memories of Empire," Keating said. This was an altogether different generation, reflecting the profound changes in the two countries and the relationship between them. Just as Great Britain some time ago sought to make its future secure in the European Communities, so Australia now sought partnerships with the countries in its own regions. The diplomatic editor of *The Times* observed that Keating had been accused of lese-majesty for so rudely bringing up the issue of republicanism to the queen's face. The prime minister's wife, Annita Keating, declined to curtsey to the queen, and neither the queen nor the Duke of Edinburgh was willing to hold or pat a koala, the duke going so far as to comment, "Oh no, I couldn't, I might catch a ghastly disease."

Keating, unrepentant, said in Parliament that he learned at school about self-respect and self-regard for Australia, not about cultural cringing to a country that had decided not to defend the Malay Peninsula, not to worry about Singapore, and not to give Australia back its troops to keep the country free from Japanese domination. In October it was announced that, by agreement with the queen, Australian citizens would no longer be nominated for knighthoods or other British honours. In December the Cabinet decided to remove any reference to the queen from the country's oath of allegiance, and legislation amending the Citizenship Act was to be introduced in Parliament.

Keating inflamed a new brand of aggressive nationalism by calling for a new Australian flag. He told Parliament that he regarded the Australian flag as an ambiguous representation of his nation and that he believed the flag should be changed. During the debate, he stirred up public opinion by continuing to put forth arguments about such historical matters as the fall of Singapore. Hewson accused Keating of using the flag as a diversion from unemployment. He amplified this by saying that Keating had a particularly limited formal education and was an illegitimate prime minister who had not been properly elected. He accused Keating of making a mockery of himself and Australia by speaking about the flag in Indonesia and of distorting history to defend his position. Keating responded vigorously by calling the opposition "snivellers, crawlers and lick-spittles to forces abroad."

Relationships with the U.S. were harmed when Pres. George Bush used the U.S. Export Enhancement Program to subsidize grain exports into markets that Australian farmers traditionally considered theirs. Stephen Censky, the acting administrator of the U.S. Foreign Agricultural Service, rejected Australian assertions that Bush had gone back on his promise that the U.S. would try to minimize damage caused by its wheat subsidies. The *Adelaide Advertiser,* in an editorial called "U.S. becomes our grim reaper," commented that although the U.S. action was infuriating, there was no merit in trying to flex Australia's undersized muscles by tying other bilateral agreements, such as joint bases or airline access, to trade issues. Australia welcomed the decision by President Bush to discontinue production of plutonium and highly enriched uranium for nuclear weapons. Foreign Minister Gareth Evans praised Bush for taking a historic step in preventing the further proliferation of nuclear weapons and applauded Bush's increased contribution to the International Atomic Energy Agency's safeguards budget.

Dealers at the Australian Futures Exchange in Sydney look over a paper giving the latest economic news. The Australian government announced several initiatives, including a program to create jobs, to cope with the country's continuing recession.
AFP

A tragic disaster that could have severely damaged Australia's relationship with the U.S. was narrowly averted in July when a U.S. warship threatened to shoot down a Qantas passenger jet, even though its pilot had clearly identified the plane as being on a routine commercial flight. The incident involved the USS *Cowpens,* a Ticonderoga-class guided missile cruiser and a sister ship to the USS *Vincennes,* which shot down an Iranian A-300 Airbus over the Persian Gulf in 1988, killing all 290 passengers and crew. When the pilot of the Qantas Boeing 747-400, two and a half hours into its journey from Los Angeles to Sydney, heard a U.S. naval warship instruct him to leave the area or be fired upon, he immediately diverted his course and radioed the U.S. Federal Aviation Authority in Los Angeles before being given clearance by *Cowpens* to resume the flight to Australia. Both the U.S. Navy and the Australian Bureau of Air Safety investigated the incident. The U.S. apologized, and diplomats from both countries tried to minimize the incident's importance.

Relations with Malaysia improved in 1992. The controversial ABC television series "Embassy" toned down its perceived anti-Muslim bias and then ceased production. More important, two days of talks were held in July 1992 between the Australia-Malaysia and Malaysia-Australia Business Councils. To signal better relations, Malaysia's minister for international trade and industry, Dato'Seri Rafidah Aziz, joined Australia's minister for trade and overseas development, John Kerin, at the seminar. The meeting's concluding statement referred to the resolution of recent difficulties in bilateral relations, clearing the way for increased trade and investment.

Despite high levels of migration from Yugoslavia, Australia did not experience local repercussions from the civil war in the migrants' homeland. The government banned the use of ethnic names for sporting teams, and community leaders from both the Serbian and Croatian groups played down the ethnic rivalry. The president of the Serbian Youth Club in Sydney's western suburbs, Stephen Damjanovic, explained that the Serbs were trying to keep things calm. "We tell the kids to just forget what happened back in Yugoslavia; we live in Australia now." As part of his strategy of focusing attention on Australia's immediate region, Paul Keating attended the 23rd South Pacific Forum Meeting in Honiara, Solomon Islands, on July 8–9. The Forum, which meets annually at head-of-government level, discussed environmental, trade and investment, and law-enforcement and nuclear issues. (See *Oceanian Affairs,* above.)

The Economy. While the ALP was successful in reducing Australia's inflation rate, unemployment continued to rise, reaching the worst levels since the Great Depression of the 1930s. By July 1992 the unemployment rate stood at 11.1%, or 963,500 people. All states had jobless rates above 10%, with South Australia continuing to have the highest, 12.5%. The youth unemployment rate (15- to 19-year-olds) jumped from 34.1% to 35.8%. The government's policy of reducing interest rates to stimulate the economy appeared to have little effect.

Both Keating and Hewson proposed new solutions to Australia's economic woes. Keating's One Nation package, presented in February, cut sales tax on new cars, relaxed foreign investment guidelines, and increased family allowances. At the centre of Hewson's Fightback plan was the imposition of a new goods and services tax (GST). Both leaders projected a rosy future, Keating promising to "kick start" the economy, provide an extra 800,000 jobs, upgrade roads and railways, and compel increased pension contributions by employers.

Treasurer John Dawkins (*see* BIOGRAPHIES) made unemployment relief the major target of government policy in the August budget. With a general election due in 1993, the government saw reducing unemployment as crucial to its hope of retaining office. Accordingly, the budget pledged $A 742 million in 1992 and $A 467 million in 1993 to attack the unemployment crisis. The target was to return 800,000 Australians to work with a grass-roots-level job-creation program. The major initiative was a $A 345 million local capital works program involving 411 local government councils, situated in areas that were home to 70% of Australia's unemployed. Priority would be given to getting long-term unemployed adults back to work, and Dawkins promised sensible projects, not painting rocks or putting up pine-log fencing. The budget also attempted to fund a $A 1.6 billion overhaul of the public health system by increasing the Medicare levy from 1.25% of taxable income to 1.4%. The government decided to raise revenue by selling off Australia's uranium stockpile and privatizing the merged airline created by the amalgamation of QANTAS and Australian Airlines. The pension for single persons was slightly increased to $A 312 a fortnight by January 1993. In another popular move, the environment minister, Ros Kelly, said that the government would spend $A 1.5 million to attack feral animals hunting native species.

Shortly after the budget was introduced, the Australian dollar fell to a five-year low against the U.S. dollar and lost even more ground against other major currencies. Hewson blamed the budget and commented that the dollar's plunge would lead to higher inflation and a cut in living standards. Dawkins, on the other hand, argued that the dollar's fluctuation was caused by Germany's high interest rates and concern about the U.S. economy. The Reserve Bank of Australia spent over $A 1 billion on August 25 trying to prop up the dollar, which reached a 12-year low against the German Deutsche Mark, and intervened to defend the dollar again in early December. Dawkins, meanwhile, was being investigated for possible irregularities in connection with loans to the former Labour government of Victoria.

The fallout from the boom-and-bust phenomenon of the 1980s continued. In June, John Elliott, the man behind the Foster's Brewing Group and a person once touted as a future prime minister, had his investment group forced into receivership by Australia's biggest company, BHP. Alan Bond of America's Cup fame was imprisoned in May 1992. He had been declared bankrupt on April 14 after months of haggling over the responsibility for a $A 255 million debt to the Hongkong and Shanghai Banking Corporation and

Tricontinental. Bond was convicted of dishonest financial dealings and sentenced to two and a half years in prison, but the conviction was quashed on appeal, and a second trial ended in acquittal. (A.R.G. GRIFFITHS)

See also *Dependent States,* below.

FIJI

The republic of Fiji occupies an island group in the South Pacific Ocean. Area: 18,274 sq km (7,056 sq mi). Pop. (1992 est.): 748,-000. Cap.: Suva. Monetary unit: Fiji dollar, with (Oct. 5, 1992) a free rate of F$1.51 to U.S. $1 (F$2.57 = £1 sterling). President in 1992, Ratu Sir Penaia Ganilau; prime ministers, Ratu Sir Kamisese Mara and, from June 2, Sitiveni Rabuka.

The interim government of Ratu Sir Kamisese Mara, installed after the coups of 1987, remained in power until elections were held in May 1992. In its budget for 1992, the government introduced a 10% value-added tax, adjusted income and company taxes, and made further adjustments to protect lower-income earners. The government expected a net deficit of $15.3 million, or 1% of gross domestic product (GDP). Because of a decline in tourism and sugar production and a prolonged strike at the Vatukoula gold mine, GDP fell by 0.4% in 1991.

In elections in May, Maj. Gen. Sitiveni Rabuka, leader of the two coups in 1987, became prime minister as leader of the Fijian Political Party, which supported affirmative action to protect the interests of indigenous Fijians. The new constitution guaranteed ethnic Fijians a preponderance of seats in the legislature and reserved the presidency, prime ministership, and other key positions for ethnic Fijians. In the election most Indian votes went to the National Federation Party and to the Fiji Labour Party, which enjoyed a degree of multiracial support.

The election brought the retirement from politics of Mara, who, except for brief periods in 1977 and 1987, had led Fiji since independence in 1970. He had also been a founder and leading member of the South Pacific Forum.

(BARRIE MACDONALD)

This article updates the *Macropædia* article PACIFIC ISLANDS: *Fiji.*

KIRIBATI

A republic in the western Pacific Ocean and member of the Commonwealth, Kiribati comprises the former Gilbert Islands, Banaba (Ocean Island), the Line Islands, and the Phoenix Islands. Area: 811 sq km (313 sq mi). Pop. (1992 est.): 74,700. Cap.: Bairiki, on Tarawa. Monetary unit: Australian dollar, with (Oct. 5, 1992) a free rate of $A 1.38 to U.S. $1 ($A 2.35 = £1 sterling). President (*beretitenti*) in 1992, Teatao Teannaki.

A number of new economic initiatives were taken in Kiribati during 1992. The Asian Development Bank funded a development plan for the Northern Line Islands, which contain most of the country's land but are some 3,200 km (2,000 mi) to the east of the Gilbert Islands, where most of the people live. Continuing resettlement from the Gilberts was envisioned, together with developments in fisheries, agriculture, and tourism. Further steps were taken to establish a garment industry in the Gilbert group, with some 40,000 garments produced under a training program. Exported garments were to have preferential access to Australian and New Zealand markets under the South Pacific Regional Free Trade Agreement. Using aid and technical assistance from China, Kiribati began upgrading its main airport at Bonriki, Tarawa, with improved navigational aids and facilities for night landing; it would be able to accommodate Boeing 737s.

In political developments, the minister of public works and energy, Nei Koriri Teaiwa Tenieu, the only woman member of the Maneaba ni Maungatabu (legislature), was forced to resign after she was found guilty of improper electoral practice. (BARRIE MACDONALD)

This article updates the *Macropædia* article PACIFIC ISLANDS: *Kiribati*.

MARSHALL ISLANDS

A republic in the central Pacific Ocean, the Marshall Islands comprises two 1,300-km (800-mi)-long parallel chains of coral atolls. Area: 181 sq km (70 sq mi). Pop. (1992 est.): 50,000. Cap.: Majuro. Monetary unit: U.S. dollar, with (Oct. 5, 1992) a free rate of U.S. $1.70 to £1 sterling. President in 1992, Amata Kabua.

In general elections in November 1991, several Cabinet ministers were defeated, but Amata Kabua was reelected president by the Nitijela (legislature) in January 1992. Kabua's new government announced that it would expand social services and shift the emphasis of development from urban centres to rural areas and outer islands. Priority would be given to agriculture, fisheries, and tourism projects that would generate revenue. The government also announced that it would seek an additional $74 million from the U.S. as compensation for nuclear testing that had been conducted by the U.S. and for development projects that were left incomplete at the time of the Marshall Islands' independence. Under the Compact of Free Association, the Marshall Islands received 75% of its revenue from the U.S. in the form of aid and defense payments. The Marshall Islands also received its first loan—$6,950,000 for fisheries development—from the Asian Development Bank.

In January the first personal compensation payments were made for illness caused by U.S. nuclear testing. Some 300 individuals received $10.9 million. A study was scheduled for measuring radiation on Rongelap Island, which was damaged by fallout from a 1954 test. The islanders disputed U.S. government claims that the southern islets of their atoll were safe for resettlement.

Under the Historic Preservation Act of 1991, the government established a research code, imposed controls on access and modifications to historic sites, established procedures for the handling of human remains discovered by archaeologists, and banned the export of artifacts. (BARRIE MACDONALD)

This article updates the *Macropædia* article PACIFIC ISLANDS: *Marshall Islands*.

MICRONESIA, FEDERATED STATES OF

A republic in the western Pacific Ocean, the Federated States of Micronesia comprises more than 600 islands and islets in the Caroline Islands archipelago. Area: 701 sq km (271 sq mi). Pop. (1992 est.): 114,000. Cap.: Palikir, on Pohnpei. Monetary unit: U.S. dollar, with (Oct. 5, 1992) a free rate of U.S. $1.70 to £1 sterling. President in 1992, Bailey Olter.

The Federated States of Micronesia was admitted to the United Nations in 1991. In his first address to the General Assembly, Pres. Bailey Olter praised the role of the United States in helping his country move toward self-determination. He raised environmental issues important to Pacific Islands nations and was critical of continuing nuclear testing. After talks in Washington, D.C., between Olter and U.S. Pres. George Bush, a planned tuna-fishing industry for the Federated States of Micronesia was granted concessionary tariffs for the U.S. market and exempted from import-quota requirements.

Sustained drought in the island state of Chuuk (formerly Truk) caused severe problems with the supply of domestic water and brought an increase in waterborne diseases. As a result, President Olter sought additional assistance from the U.S. In keeping with the close relationship that existed between the two countries under the Compact of Free Association, President Bush declared a state of emergency in Chuuk to facilitate the granting of emergency aid. The unusual climatic conditions were blamed on the El Niño weather pattern over the Pacific Ocean.

(BARRIE MACDONALD)

This article updates the *Macropædia* article PACIFIC ISLANDS: *Micronesia*.

NAURU

An island republic within the Commonwealth, Nauru lies in the Pacific Ocean about 1,900 km (1,200 mi) east of New Guinea. Area: 21 sq km (8 sq mi). Pop. (1992 est.): 9,600. Cap.: Yaren. Monetary unit: Australian dollar, with (Oct. 5, 1992) a free rate of $A 1.38 to U.S. $1 ($A 2.35 = £1 sterling). President in 1992, Bernard Dowiyogo.

In its dispute with Australia before the International Court of Justice in The Hague, Nauru made some progress in 1992. Nauru claimed that Australia, acting as the administrator of Nauru, allowed phosphate mining to occur in a way that breached the basic obligation of trusteeship. In response, Australia raised a number of objections to the court's dealing with the case. On June 26 the court ruled that the Australian objections were unsound and decided to proceed to hear the merits of Nauru's claim for compensation for the phosphate lands. Commenting on the judgment, Nauru Pres. Bernard Dowiyogo said that, in a year when so much emphasis had been placed on the world environment, it was a joy to see that Nauru's environmental problems were being given proper recognition. On a sadder note, an era in Nauruan history ended in July when former president Hammer DeRoburt, Nauru's elder statesman, who had led the nation to independence, died in Melbourne, Australia (*see* OBITUARIES). (A.R.G. GRIFFITHS)

This article updates the *Macropædia* article PACIFIC ISLANDS: *Nauru*.

NEW ZEALAND

New Zealand, a constitutional monarchy and member of the Commonwealth in the South Pacific Ocean, consists of North and South islands and Stewart, Chatham, and other minor islands. Area: 270,534 sq km (104,454 sq mi). Pop. (1992 est.): 3,481,000. Cap.: Wellington. Monetary unit: New Zealand dollar, with (Oct. 5, 1992) a free rate of $NZ 1.84 to U.S. $1 ($NZ 3.13 = £1 sterling). Queen, Elizabeth II; governor-general in 1992, Dame Catherine Tizard; prime minister, Jim Bolger.

On Sept. 19, 1992, in the first part of a two-part referendum, a turnout of about 50% of New Zealand voters declared an 84.5% preference for change from their first-past-the-post method of electing members of Parliament. Offered the opportunity to indicate which of five options they would prefer, 70.3% voted for mixed member proportional (MMP) representation. In this system each voter would have two votes: one to choose an individual electorate MP and the other to be expressed for a political party, which would have the opportunity to nominate additional MPs on the basis of the proportion of votes received nationwide. Voters had been warned that coalitions between parties might be needed to form a government under this system.

The government announced that the second part of the referendum would be held in conjunction with regular general elections, due toward the end of 1993. At that time voters would make a binding choice between MMP and the traditional system. Details of the alternative system would be added, such as the size of electorates and of Parliament and whether MMP would continue the traditional guarantee of four Maori electorates. By late 1993 MMP proponents would have an opportunity to lobby for specific details, and the incumbents would have more opportunity to work together to improve Parliament's image.

Many observers saw the size of the rejection of the status quo as a condemnation of Cabinet conniving, caucus impotency, and parliamentary bickering in a single-chamber system where two parties dominated and the winners usually had an ample cushion of seats, although they might represent less than half the total vote. A Royal Commission on Electoral Reform had recommended some form of MMP. If a new system was confirmed, it could be in place for general elections in 1996. At the 1993 elections the government was also expected to inquire whether the electorate wanted the restoration of an upper house, abolished as ineffectual in 1950.

As a backdrop to the voting, New Zealanders faced unemployment at 15%, which owed something to a continuing economic restructuring process, the bite of some user-paid health services in a new era of privatization of state services, and inflation, which edged out of its straitjacket to 1.1%. The Bank of New Zealand was acquired by National Australia Bank, while a "no-frills" federal budget moved some business leaders to comment that they were "bored to cheers." Meanwhile, the winter was so bleak that power resources were stretched beyond capacity and more than a million sheep disappeared under the snow.

Cabinet strategist Minister of Labour Bill Birch guided various follow-ups to the previous Labour administration's policy of deregulation and to its corporatism of state services. These included user-paid health services and the breakdown of industrywide unionism in favour of a single-plant focus. Industrial reforms in New Zealand even became an election issue in an Australian state (Victoria) and a bone of contention in Canberra. In September the New Zealand Reserve Bank said the economy appeared to be becoming "increasingly well-grounded and broad-based," and the country's Institute of Economic Research forecast gross domestic product growth of 2.7% during the five years to March 1997.

In the contentious field of equal race opportunities, the government and representatives of most Maori tribes signed a compensation agreement aimed at ending a 150-year-old dispute over commercial fishing rights. The government caucus expelled its most recalcitrant member, former Maori affairs minister Winston Peters. Members of Parliament of all persuasions closed ranks to pay tribute to Sir Robert Muldoon, who died in his sleep on August 5 (*see* OBITUARIES). (JOHN A. KELLEHER)

See also *Dependent States,* below.

PAPUA NEW GUINEA

A constitutional monarchy and member of the Commonwealth, Papua New Guinea is situated in the southwestern Pacific Ocean and comprises the eastern part of the island of New Guinea, the islands of the Bismarck, Kiriwina (Trobriand), Louisiade, and D'Entrecasteaux groups, Muyua (Woodlark) Island and other nearby islands, and parts of the Solomon Islands, including Bougainville. Area: 462,840 sq km (178,704 sq mi). Pop. (1992 est.): 3,834,000. Cap.: Port Moresby. Monetary unit: kina, with (Oct. 5, 1992) a free rate of 0.97 kina to U.S. $1 (1.65 kinas = £1 sterling). Queen, Elizabeth II; governor-general in 1992, Wiwa Korowi; prime ministers, Rabbie Namaliu to June 13 and, from July 17, Paias Wingti.

Papua New Guinea faced an election year in 1992 against a background of disturbances in Bougainville and the Solomons. In April the Bougainville leader Tony Anugu, who had negotiated establishment of the South Bougainville Interim Authority with Papua New Guinea authorities Sir Michael Somare and Father John Momis, was murdered. Government troops launched a major offensive on Bougainville in October, and at the end of the month it was announced that the rebel stronghold of Arawa had fallen.

Prime Minister Rabbie Namaliu was defeated in the June general election, and Paias Wingti, elected prime minister on the casting vote of the speaker of Parliament on July 17, was given responsibility for preventing the spread of the relatively small revolutionary secessionist movement. The new prime minister announced his 27-member Cabinet after taking office. It included the leaders of the two parties in his coalition government, Sir Julius Chan and John Nilkare, as well as leading independent MPs who played a major role in electing him to office. Somare became leader of the opposition. In December Namaliu was charged with misappropriating government funds. (A.R.G. GRIFFITHS)

This article updates the *Macropædia* article PACIFIC ISLANDS: *Papua New Guinea.*

SOLOMON ISLANDS

A constitutional monarchy and member of the Commonwealth, the Solomon Islands comprises a 1,450-km (900-mi) chain of islands and atolls in the western Pacific Ocean. Area: 28,370 sq km (10,954 sq mi). Pop. (1992 est.): 339,000. Cap.: Honiara. Monetary unit: Solomon Islands dollar, with (Oct. 5, 1992) a free rate of SI$2.97 to U.S. $1 (SI$5.04 = £1 sterling). Queen, Elizabeth II; governor-general in 1992, Sir George Lepping; prime minister, Solomon Mamaloni.

During 1992 Solomon Islands became embroiled in border disputes with neighbouring Papua New Guinea. The island of Bougainville, geographically and culturally part of the Solomons chain but constitutionally part of Papua New Guinea, tried to secede because of the closure, by terrorist activity since 1989, of a major copper mine. A blockade of the island by Papua New Guinea was breeched from Solomon Islands, leading to incursions across the border by Papua New Guinean troops, who attacked civilians and destroyed fuel stores. In October the UN secretary-general announced an inquiry into these incidents.

After a substantial improvement in export earnings in 1991, especially for fish products and copra, the government issued a 1992 budget with appropriations of $91 million. Priority was given to expenditure on fisheries and forestry, industrial development, and a rural health program. Public service expenditure increased to cover a salary rise of 16%, and new payroll and wholesale taxes were introduced. The central bank warned of rising government debt levels and imposed controls on the use of overseas funds.

In July Solomon Islands was host to the South Pacific Forum, which primarily discussed environmental issues. (BARRIE MACDONALD)

This article updates the *Macropædia* article PACIFIC ISLANDS: *Solomon Islands.*

TONGA

A constitutional monarchy and member of the Commonwealth, Tonga is an island group in the Pacific Ocean east of Fiji. Area: 780 sq km (301 sq mi). Pop. (1992 est.): 97,300. Cap.: Nuku'alofa. Monetary unit: pa'anga, with (Oct. 5, 1992) a free rate of 1.38 pa'anga to U.S. $1 (2.35 pa'anga = £1 sterling). King, Taufa'ahau Tupou IV; prime minister in 1992, Baron Vaea.

Agriculture remained the principal economic activity of Tonga, where most land was held by the nobility but allotted to commoners for cultivation. Several proposals for developing new sources of revenue had failed to win the support of segments of Tongan society.
PHILIP QUIRK—WILDLIGHT

In association with foreign investors, Tonga took another step toward its objective of becoming a major provider of satellite services for the Pacific region with the announcement that its first satellite would be launched early in 1993. The economy continued to improve, with inflation down from 17% in 1990 to 7.4% in 1991. Foreign reserves at the end of 1991 were 5% higher than in 1990, largely owing to remittances from Tongans overseas, tourism receipts, and revenue from squash exports to Japan, which in 1991 accounted for almost two-thirds of all export earnings.

Business interests unsuccessfully opposed legislation to impose a 0.7% currency tax on all foreign exchange transactions; the measure was also seen as an attempt to tax personal remittance income. In anticipation of general elections in 1993, there were preliminary moves toward the formation of a political party that would represent the interests of commoners; Tonga's parliament was dominated by hereditary nobles and Cabinet ministers appointed by the king.

In an attempt to protect rare native species, a 16-km (10-mi) strip of coastline on the island of 'Eua was declared a national park, and limits were imposed on public access.

(BARRIE MACDONALD)
This article updates the *Macropædia* article PACIFIC ISLANDS: *Tonga*.

TUVALU

A constitutional monarchy within the Commonwealth, Tuvalu comprises nine main islands and their associated islets and reefs in the western Pacific Ocean. Area: 24 sq km (9 sq mi). Pop. (1992 est.): 9,500. Cap.: Fongàfale, on Funafuti Atoll. Monetary unit: Australian dollar, with (Oct. 5, 1992) a free rate of $A 1.38 to U.S. $1 ($A 2.35 = £1 sterling). Queen, Elizabeth II; governor-general in 1992, Toaripi Lauti; prime minister, Bikenibeu Paeniu.

Tuvalu, which is composed of low-lying coral islands, was one of the first nations to sign the Climate Change and Biodiversity conventions at the "Earth Summit" in Rio de Janeiro in June 1992. Prime Minister Bikenibeu Paeniu made an impassioned plea on behalf of small island states like his own, which faced serious environmental problems because of the actions of industrialized powers. If global warming were to cause some of the extreme consequences

that were predicted, many if not all of Tuvalu's islands could become uninhabitable.

The Tuvalu Trust Fund, intended to assist in meeting the recurrent costs of government, showed an annual return of 11% over its first four years. In a new development Tuvalu received significant French aid to rebuild classrooms that had been destroyed by storms on the main island of Funafuti. The new school was opened by the French ambassador. Tuvalu joined Unesco and received its first grant, for the development of a national archives and library.

After a Taiwanese fishing vessel was detained for encroaching on Tuvalu's exclusive economic zone, a fine of $75,000 was imposed. Under a bilateral agreement Taiwanese vessels had been licensed to fish in the zone until 1989, but the agreement was not renewed at that time.

(BARRIE MACDONALD)
This article updates the *Macropædia* article PACIFIC ISLANDS: *Tuvalu*.

VANUATU

The republic of Vanuatu, a member of the Commonwealth, comprises 12 main islands and some 60 smaller ones in the southwestern Pacific Ocean. Area: 12,190 sq km (4,707 sq mi). Pop. (1992 est.): 154,000. Cap.: Vila. Monetary unit: vatu, with (Oct. 5, 1992) a free rate of 112.94 vatu to U.S. $1 (192 vatu = £1 sterling). President in 1992, Fred Timakata; prime minister, Maxime Carlot Korman.

A general election in December 1991 launched a new era in Vanuatu's politics in 1992. In August 1991 the ruling Vanuaaku Party, led by Father Walter Lini since Vanuatu's independence in 1980, dismissed him as president of the party. When Lini lost a vote of no confidence, he was replaced as prime minister by Donald Kalpokas. In the election 19 seats were won by the francophone Union of Moderate Parties (UMP), which then formed a coalition with Lini and his newly formed National United Party (10 seats), leaving the Vanuaaku Party (12 seats) in opposition. (For tabulated results, see *Political Parties*, above.) The new government was formed by Maxime Carlot of UMP in alliance with Lini.

Soon after the election, the new prime minister was given the honorific title of Korman by his home village. With the change of government, there were allegations of politically motivated dismissals from the public service, countered by an insistence that the officials in question had refused to follow directions from incoming ministers. The new government moved quickly to normalize relations with France after years of friction over diplomatic representation, aid, and alleged interference in Vanuatu's politics.

(BARRIE MACDONALD)
This article updates the *Macropædia* article PACIFIC ISLANDS: *Vanuatu*.

WESTERN SAMOA

A constitutional monarchy and member of the Commonwealth, Western Samoa occupies an island group in the South Pacific Ocean. Area: 2,831 sq km (1,093 sq mi). Pop. (1992 est.): 160,000. Cap.: Apia. Monetary unit: Western Samoa tala, with (Oct. 5, 1992) a free rate of 2.44 tala to U.S. $1 (4.15 tala = £1 sterling). Head of state (*O le Ao o le Malo*) in 1992, Malietoa Tanumafili II; prime minister, Tofilau Eti Alesana.

Addressing the UN General Assembly in October 1991, Prime Minister Tofilau Eti Alesana had delivered a regional perspective on a number of international issues. He raised concern over the effect of climate change on small island countries, attacked attempts to dump toxic waste in the Pacific Islands, and called on the major world powers to join the comprehensive nuclear test ban treaty. Later, he met with Pres. George Bush.

In December 1991, less than two years after the devastation of Typhoon Ofa, Typhoon Val struck Western Samoa, killing 12 people and causing extensive damage. As a result, gross domestic product was expected to fall by 4–6% in 1992. The government shifted development emphasis from agriculture to tourism, with plans for growth of 9.4% a year in visitor numbers.

Western Samoa's national team competed in the rugby World Cup in Europe as an outsider, but its success in reaching the quarterfinals and its flamboyant play won media attention and greatly enhanced awareness of Samoa and its people. The games were broadcast to crowds in a football stadium in Apia, the capital, through a satellite television link and were followed by a decision to establish a limited television service for the country.   (BARRIE MACDONALD)

This article updates the *Macropædia* article PACIFIC ISLANDS: *Western Samoa*.

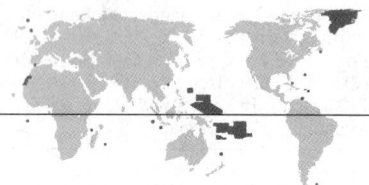

Dependent States

Europe and the Atlantic. In 1992 the Falkland Islands/Islas Malvinas commemorated the 10th anniversary of the Falklands War between Argentina and the U.K. with a four-day program attended by Baroness Thatcher, who, as Prime Minister Margaret Thatcher, had authorized the deployment of British forces. In the intervening decade the economy of the Falklands had improved dramatically, largely because of revenues from licenses issued to foreign trawlers fishing for squid in surrounding waters. The islands suffered a serious financial loss in 1992, however, after Argentina began issuing cheaper, less restrictive licenses. British officials filed a protest with the Argentine government. In December the Hongkong & Shanghai Banking Corp. took control of the Falklands' only trading operation.

Gibraltar continued to seek an end to its colonial status in 1992. José Bossano, Gibraltar's chief minister and the leader of the crown colony's fight for self-determination within the European Communities (EC), was overwhelmingly reelected early in the year. He met with British Foreign Secretary Douglas Hurd in November. The Isle of Man, compelled to bring its laws into line with EC directives, decriminalized homosexual acts in 1992. Local tradition got a boost in September when the Manx language was taught in two of the island's schools for the first time since it fell out of use early in the century. Manx was to be introduced in the remaining schools in 1993. In September a 500-page report on the 1982 collapse of the Isle of Man Savings and Investment Bank was finally released. The report blamed the collapse on a lack of regulation by Manx authorities. After the report's release, two bank officials were given suspended sentences for conspiracy to defraud.

Caribbean. Construction of the largest hotel project ever undertaken in the Caribbean commenced in Puerto Rico during the year. The 926-room El Conquistador Hotel and Country Club was located at Las Croabas, 48 km (30 mi) east of San Juan. It was expected to be ready for occupancy by September 1993.

In the Cayman Islands the government signed an agreement allowing U.S. court orders for confiscation of illegal

drug profits to be registered and enforced in the Caymans. Agreement was also reached with the U.S. for the building of a radar station with a range of 240 nautical miles, bringing most of Cuba within its range. A $20 million recapitalization plan was announced during the year for the technically insolvent Caymans Airways.

In regional council elections in Guadeloupe in March, the leader of the right-wing group Objectif Guadeloupe, Lucette Michaux-Cherry, was elected council president, with support from two socialist parties. The opposite situation occurred in Martinique, where the presidency fell to a Communist, Émile Capgras, despite the fact that the right-wing party obtained the largest single block of seats.

Coastal Oil of Texas started moving its marketing headquarters to Aruba from Bermuda during the year and began preparations for doubling the size of its refinery, formerly owned by Exxon Corp. By contrast, the future of the Isla refinery in Curaçao, in the Netherlands Antilles, became uncertain. The Venezuelan state oil company, PDVSA, which had a lease on the refinery into 1994, indicated its reluctance to renew it unless Curaçao and Amsterdam agreed to share part of the $279 million cost of upgrading the plant.

It was a bad year for Bermuda's bread-and-butter industry, tourism, with visitor arrivals falling by 2.3%, to 222,827, in the first six months. In the summer a strike by the island's main labour union further aggravated the situation. Meanwhile, the government announced it was spending $78 million on capital projects to boost employment. Lord Waddington (formerly British Home Secretary David Waddington) was named to succeed Sir Desmond Langley as governor.

Following a visit to British dependencies in the Caribbean, Mark Lennox-Boyd, parliamentary under secretary of state in the British Foreign and Commonwealth Office, said a board of management would be installed by the U.K. to speed up spending on development and welfare projects for the Caribbean. The British Virgin Islands was paid $1.8 million by the U.S. Drug Enforcement Administration during the year, as an installment on assets taken from convicted drug dealers.

Pacific. Although still a self-governing state in free association with New Zealand, the Cook Islands continued to extend its international relationships. It accepted $1 million

Apra Harbor, Guam's main port, shows extensive damage caused by Typhoon Omar, which struck the island in August with winds up to 385 km/h (240 mph). Of the several storms that reached Guam in 1992, Omar hit most directly and was by far the most destructive.

in French aid to upgrade utilities and received an Asian Development Bank loan of $1.5 million for private-sector developments in tourism, agriculture, fisheries, and light industry. At a meeting of the bank's board of governors, however, Prime Minister Sir Geoffrey Henry was critical of lending policies for small states, maintaining that the bank took too narrow a view of a country's assets and prospects. In May most of the government centre at Avarua, Rarotonga, was destroyed by arson.

Niue continued to feel the effects of New Zealand's decision to cut economic assistance. It faced a deficit of $1.5 million, and there were layoffs in the public sector, which had 500 members for a resident population of 2,500 (three-quarters of all Niueans lived in New Zealand). Following a referendum, Niue was to have its own Court of Appeal, and its High Court and Land Court would be combined. The residential qualification for voting was increased from 3 to 12 months. On December 12, 83-year-old Prime Minister Sir Robert Rex died. Rex had been leader of the Niuean government from 1966 (prime minister from 1974) and was the longest serving premier in the South Pacific.

When France announced the suspension of nuclear tests in French Polynesia, Pres. Gaston Flosse expressed concern because nearly one-fifth of employment and economic activity in the territory was directly related to the testing program. French spending and assistance was $1,030,000,-000 a year, giving a per capita income of $1,840, among the highest in Oceania. In New Caledonia there were signs of a split within the pro-independence Kanak Liberation Front over whether to explore an accommodation with "moderate" (pro-French) elements. A new nickel mine, which was expected to handle a million tons of ore a year for 15 years, opened at Kopeto on the central west coast.

In the Republic of Palau (Belau) a Supreme Court procedural ruling caused the cancellation of a proposed seventh constitutional referendum to remove antinuclear provisions and thus approve a Compact of Free Association with the U.S. In the November 4 election the voters approved a referendum proposal to allow passage of constitutional amendments by a simple majority, rather than the 75% majority required in the past. At the same time, Vice Pres. Kuniwo Nakamura was elected president.

In August Typhoon Omar caused serious damage on Guam; one person was killed, more than 130 were injured, and 5,000 were made homeless. Another typhoon, Brian,

Chris Patten (right), recently appointed governor of Hong Kong, visits Beijing (Peking) in October. Angered by his policies, including proposals to broaden the franchise and to build an expensive new airport, high-level Chinese officials snubbed Patten on his trip.
AFP

did little damage in October, but on November 3 Typhoon Elsie forced a postponement of the U.S. general election on the island. In American Samoa, Star-Kist Foods announced plans for a $20 million investment in the expansion and upgrading of its Pago Pago tuna cannery. Star-Kist, which was the largest private-sector employer in American Samoa, was responding to the local government's promise of tax advantages. The deal was jeopardized, however, by proposed U.S. legislation that would increase the minimum wage.

East Asia. In British-run Hong Kong the most important event of 1992 was the change of governor. Late in 1991 London had announced that Sir David Wilson (later Lord Wilson) would be replaced. Subsequent press leaks made it clear that Prime Minister John Major had been unhappy with the way Wilson conducted negotiations with China over construction of a new airport in Hong Kong.

In April 1992, after the Conservatives won reelection in Britain, Major announced that his close friend party chairman Chris Patten (see BIOGRAPHIES) would be the new governor. When Patten arrived in Hong Kong in July, the contrast was striking between his glad-handing style as a professional politician and the aloof reserve of the long line of diplomats who had preceded him. The contrast became substantive when Patten delivered his maiden policy speech on October 7. Along with an expansive social program, he announced a series of "proposals" for a more democratic Hong Kong. These immediately drew scathing denunciations from Beijing (Peking)-controlled local newspapers. China had already made clear that it would brook no change to arrangements for direct election in 1995 of 20 of the 60 legislative councillors, whose terms would span the 1997 return of sovereignty over the territory to China. Patten, however, proposed to broaden the number of people who could vote in the council's 30 so-called functional constituencies—mainly professional, business, and other sectoral groupings—and to define nine in such a way that they would effectively enfranchise all working people. He also moved to democratize an "election committee" that would choose the last 10 councils.

When Patten visited Beijing later in October, he was snubbed at the highest level. The head of the Hong Kong and Macau Affairs Office, Lu Ping (Lu P'ing), insisted that Patten's reforms contravened the post-1997 Basic Law. Tensions increased in late November, when the Hong Kong

Dependent States[1]	
Australia	**Portugal**
Christmas Island	Macau
Cocos (Keeling) Islands	**United Kingdom**
Norfolk Island	Anguilla
Denmark	Bermuda
Faeroe Islands	British Virgin Islands
Greenland	Cayman Islands
France	Falkland Islands
French Guiana	Gibraltar
French Polynesia	Guernsey
Guadeloupe	Hong Kong
Martinique	Isle of Man
Mayotte	Jersey
New Caledonia	Montserrat
Réunion	Pitcairn Island
Saint Pierre and Miquelon	Saint Helena
Wallis and Futuna	Turks and Caicos Islands
Netherlands, The	**United States**
Aruba	American Samoa
Netherlands Antilles	Guam
New Zealand	Northern Marianas
Cook Islands	Palau
Niue	Puerto Rico
Tokelau	Virgin Islands (of the U.S.)
Norway	
Jan Mayen	
Svalbard	

[1]Excludes territories (1) to which Antarctic Treaty is applicable in whole or in part, (2) without permanent civilian population, (3) without internationally recognized civilian government (Western Sahara, Gaza Strip), or (4) representing unadjudicated unilateral or multilateral territorial claims.

government announced plans to proceed with the new airport without Chinese approval. Despite the political turmoil, the Hong Kong stock market reached an all-time high in November.

Meanwhile, in neighbouring Macau, a £465 million international airport was expected to open on schedule in 1995. In elections held on September 20, a new and complex voting system helped pro-China candidates to expand their representation to half of the eight directly elected seats in the 23-member Legislative Assembly, at the expense of liberals. The Portuguese-run enclave was due to be returned to China in 1999.   (BARRIE MacDONALD; DAVID RENWICK; MELINDA C. SHEPHERD; BERTON WOODWARD)

This article updates the *Macropædia* articles HONG KONG; PACIFIC ISLANDS; The WEST INDIES.

Polar Regions

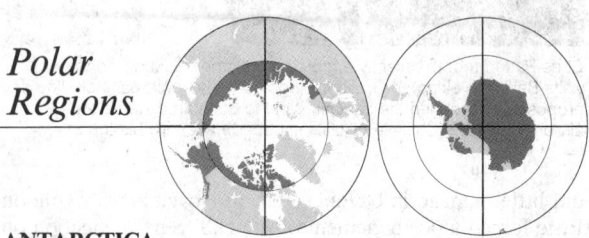

ANTARCTICA

One of Earth's least known areas—even by Antarctic standards—is the ice-covered southern portion of the Weddell Sea. Yet the Weddell Sea is the major producer of the cold, nutrient-rich bottom water that moves as far as the Northern Hemisphere before upwelling to influence climate and nurture fisheries.

On June 4, 1992, U.S. and Russian scientists completed a 117-day occupation of a camp on Weddell Sea ice—the first staffed research station ever established on sea ice of the southern ocean and the first human presence in the area since 1915. The expedition provided a unique opportunity to study the region's biological and physical development. The resultant data suggest that scientists will have to alter their views of how the region fits into the global climate system.

The camp was set up on an ice floe 2 m (6½ ft) thick and less than five square kilometres (two square miles) in area. On February 6 the Russian icebreaker *Academic Federov* delivered the scientists and their instruments, support personnel, camp buildings, and supplies, sticking to U.S. and Soviet plans made years before despite difficulties posed by the concurrent breakup of the former Soviet Union. The floe, driven by winds and ocean currents, drifted some 640 km (400 mi) from south to north while the scientists worked from it. Adding value to data collected at the camp itself, two helicopters made numerous research sorties tens of kilometres to either side of the floe's track. The new U.S. research icebreaker *Nathaniel B. Palmer,* performing its first mission after its completion in March by a shipbuilding firm in Louisiana, rotated crews in April at about the midpoint of the floe's drift. The June recovery of the expeditioners and their camp was made by the U.S. and Russian icebreakers, working together.

The researchers studied formation and movement of sea ice, ocean currents beneath it, atmospheric conditions above it, and the rich marine plant and animal life under and in it. The entire western rim of the Weddell Basin was mapped in great detail, a remarkable achievement considering the region was essentially unexplored before the 1992 expedition. Among other discoveries, the continental slope off the Antarctic Peninsula was found to be 100 km (62 mi) farther

west than previously thought, a fundamental topographical difference that would change understanding of ocean circulation. The scientists obtained clues that might explain the mystery of why the western Weddell is covered by ice all year, unlike areas to the east where ice melts in summer and remains thin even in winter.

The floe generally followed the path that Ernest Shackleton's ship *Endurance* took involuntarily in 1915. *Endurance,* trying to land a party for an expedition across Antarctica, had been trapped in ice and, over nine months, had been carried 915 km (570 mi) north, where the ice crushed and sank it. Shackleton and his crew escaped by dragging boats over the ice to open water and rowing to Elephant Island. The party was rescued after Shackleton and a small crew sailed to a settlement on South Georgia Island.

Antarctica today holds 90% of the world's ice—35 million cu km (8.4 million cu mi) of it. Most scientists agree that a continental Antarctic ice sheet first existed about 40 million years ago, when Antarctica moved to its polar position and separated from Australia and South America. Antarctica has been isolated ever since, so there was no particular reason to suspect that the size of the ice sheet had changed greatly. However, recent discoveries indicate that the ice sheet has been dynamic these last 40 million years and perhaps even disappeared for a while. The time scales for the changes range from millions of years to mere decades. The influence of the changes on both global climate and sea level could be significant within the next decades or century, although predictions could not yet be made with confidence.

Among the examples of recent research indicating change over various time scales, geologists in 1991 reported finding rocks in the Transantarctic Mountains containing three million-year-old fossil leaves. The find means the ice sheet has not changed much in the last two million years, but the present ice sheet is not typical of ice sheets over the last 38 million years. Other investigators found that the Sirius Group, a geologic formation widely distributed in the Transantarctic Mountains, contains diatom floras, suggesting open marine conditions in interior East Antarctica as recently as about three million years ago. Other work showed that, within the last 2½ million years, intensified cooling in the Northern Hemisphere resulted in a reduction of the Antarctic ice sheet by about a third of its volume, equal to a rise in sea level of about 40 m (130 ft).

Turning from millions to thousands of years ago, radiocarbon dating of tiny fossils in marine sediment cores drilled off East Antarctica showed that, at and around glacial maximum 18,000 years ago, grounded ice sheets extended to the Antarctic continental shelf edge—hundreds of kilometres north of present-day ice sheets. Ice shelves and ice tongues formerly occupied areas that in the last 4,000 years have been open ocean. The record was now complete enough for scientists to state with confidence that climatic warming in the Antarctic makes the ice sheets bigger, not smaller. That may seem odd, but in a cold climate it appears that higher temperatures put more moisture into the air and thus cause more snowfall.

Dropping from thousands to tens of years ago, a survey along a 700-km (435-mi) segment of East Antarctica documented changes in the net rate of snow accumulation since 1806. The rate increased significantly after a minimum around 1960, leading to recent rates about 20% above the long-term mean. Shorter-term accumulation data from across a large part of Antarctica suggest the increase since 1960 has been widespread. This increase in accumulation rate should contribute to a lowering of sea level of 1 to 1.2 mm (0.039 to 0.047 in) per year, although a tripled rate of iceberg calving in 1986 and 1987—from the annual average

A balloon carrying an ozonesonde, which measures concentrations of atmospheric ozone, is sent aloft from the South Pole on November 19. The measurements were part of a research project being conducted by the U.S. National Oceanic and Atmospheric Administration to study the behaviour of the thinning ozone layer over the Antarctic.

BERNARD G. MENDONCA/NOAA-CLIMATE MONITORING AND DIAGNOSTICS LABORATORY, BOULDER, COLORADO

of 1,450 to more than 7,000 cu km (348 to more than 1,680 cu mi)—if continued could change that prediction.

The involvement of Antarctic ice in man-induced climate change was the subject of much study and, as yet, uncertainty. Nevertheless, the oxygen-isotope record in ice cores from Greenland and Antarctica indicates that changes in the amounts of greenhouse gases have amplified the effects of glacial-to-interglacial climate changes. A National Academy of Sciences report on the role of land ice in sea-level change stated that the Antarctic ice sheet may be growing at a rate equivalent to about 0.6 mm (0.024 in) per year of sea-level fall. On the other hand, it says that the rate of iceberg discharge may have been underestimated, so the ice sheet may be close to balance. The report notes that a warmer climate may cause warmer ocean water to intrude under Antarctica's floating ice shelves, causing the ice streams that enter the shelves to accelerate. This process could deplete the ice sheet enough to raise sea level by 0.3 m (c. 1 ft) by the year 2100. Complete disintegration of the West Antarctic Ice Sheet, which would raise sea level 6 m (c. 20 ft), was seen as unlikely for centuries or millennia. Increased accumulation, if it happens, could contribute to sea level fall by 0.1 to 0.5 m (0.3 to 1.6 ft) in the next hundred years. In short, the Antarctic ice sheet presents an enormous scientific challenge, but the consequences of its future actions are of such significance that a considerable amount of scientific study continued to be given to it.

In other news, ozone in the stratosphere over Antarctica (the ozone hole) reached new record low levels in October 1992, probably because of the discharge of dust and aerosols from the Mt. Pinatubo volcano in the Philippines after its June 1991 eruption. On October 7 the U.S. Senate approved the Antarctic Treaty protocol that prohibits mining on the continent and strengthens environmental protection measures. The Senate sent the measure to the president, who would have to deposit the treaty papers to complete the ratification process. The U.S. finished removing waste that had accumulated at McMurdo Station over many years and opened a new $23 million research centre at the station, Antarctica's largest. Plans were under way to send a robot named Dante, developed by Carnegie Mellon University in Pittsburgh, Pa., into the crater of the Mt. Erebus volcano early in 1993. (GUY G. GUTHRIDGE)

This article updates the *Macropædia* article ANTARCTICA.

ARCTIC REGIONS

The dominant theme for 1992 was the growing internationalization of the circumpolar north. The focus was on empowerment of indigenous peoples and sustainable development activities. With the opening up of the former Soviet Union, the Russian Inuit participated in the sixth general assembly of the Inuit Circumpolar Conference (ICC), held in July in Inuvik, N.W.T. For the first time since its inception in 1977, the ICC could claim to represent all of the Inuit, estimated at about 117,000 people living in Russia, Alaska, Canada, and Greenland. Twenty representatives from the newly formed Republic of Chukotka on the easternmost peninsula of Siberia reported on their experiences living in a largely unregulated industrialized economy, their concerns for the Arctic environment, and their strong desire to work with the concept of sustainable development.

Over 40 resolutions were passed by the assembly. Included were resolutions concerning recognition of the inherent right of native self-government, which was being considered in the constitutional discussions taking place in Canada; the desire of some Alaskan Inuit to secede from the state of Alaska; opposition to the establishment of quotas on bowhead and other whales by the International Whaling Commission; recognition of traditional Inuit environmental knowledge; and economic development suggestions such as the establishment of an Inuit free-trade zone across the Arctic. After serving a six-year term as president of the ICC, Mary Simon, a Canadian, was succeeded by Eileen MacLean, an Inuk from Alaska who was also a member of the Alaskan House of Representatives.

There was increasing evidence that the Inuit already had established themselves as important contributors to the environmental decision-making process in the Arctic. In October the *Toronto Globe and Mail* reported on voluntary agreements being drafted by the Exploration and Production Forum, an umbrella organization representing the world's major oil companies, that would establish drilling standards for the Arctic. Land-use maps for the western Arctic were being developed as a joint effort by Canadian federal and territorial governments. All eight Arctic nations—Canada, Russia, the U.S., Sweden, Norway, Finland, Iceland, and Greenland—had signed the Finnish Initiative, which, besides seeking means to safeguard the Arctic ecosystem, was

Scientists, working on the Greenland Ice Sheet 645 km (400 mi) above the Arctic Circle, cut through an ice core believed to reveal many thousands of years of past life. They were part of the five-year Greenland Ice Sheet Project 2, designed to study volcanic, solar, and climatic activity.

AP/WIDE WORLD

institutionalizing ways in which governments, the Inuit, and other indigenous peoples could develop forums for the exchange of information and for discussion. Momentum was also building for the establishment of an international Arctic council that would act as a sort of mini-UN where governments and indigenous peoples could meet to consider key environmental questions facing the Arctic. These initiatives complemented the declaration of friendship and cooperation with regard to Arctic environmental protection that was signed in February by Russian Pres. Boris Yeltsin and Canadian Prime Minister Brian Mulroney.

The fall issue of *Cultural Survival* reported that after years of plummeting oil, diamond, and gold production, Russia hoped to renew the exploitation of Siberia's natural resources and encourage foreign investment. Many major companies from the U.S., Canada, and Japan were showing interest in joint-venture petrochemical, forestry, and natural-gas projects. The new economic and political climate in Siberia also was stimulating interest in tourism investments, ranging from remote salmon-fishing lodges to the creation of opportunities for big-game hunting. Questions were being raised about the environmental consequences of resource development under the former Soviet Union; in some areas three-fourths of the land had been rendered useless for hunting, fishing, or reindeer herding.

Thirty indigenous Siberian groups, totaling an estimated 4% of the population, were claiming to be the rightful owners of Siberia's wealth and were demanding a voice in any future development activities. Some groups were proposing to establish designated "zones of life," which would be set aside for traditional activities, fully protected from industrial exploitation. Siberia's indigenous peoples were receiving advice in connection with royalty negotiations and other practical business matters from native groups in North America who had gained relevant experience during the settlement of land claims in Canada and Alaska.

In May the *New York Times* reported that the state of Alaska was suing the federal government to allow it to export North Slope crude oil. Alaska's attorney general claimed that Congress had exceeded its constitutional powers by limiting sales to domestic markets and that the wellhead price of the oil had been devalued as a result. Alaska was seeking $2.5 billion in damages for the state revenues it claimed to have lost because of the export ban. The North Slope produced 1.8 million bbl of oil a day, and it was reported that 85% of Alaska's operating budget came from the oil industry in the form of royalties, taxes, and other fees. The *New York Times* also reported that Norway, Finland, and Sweden were considering financial assistance to Moscow in order to ensure the environmental security of the Russian-Norwegian border area. A nearby Russian nickel smelter, one of the largest in the world, was identified as the source of the high levels of sulfur dioxide affecting the whole Scandinavian region.

In May the residents of Arctic Canada voted in favour of redrawing the map of the Northwest Territories to mark off the western boundary of a new territory called Nunavut, meaning "our land" in the Inuit language. The vote appeared to clear the way for final settlement of a massive land claim that would eventually create a new territory of 2.2 million sq km (850,000 sq mi), roughly one-fifth of Canada's total landmass. In November the Inuit voted in favour of ratification of the claim, which would provide the 17,500 Inuit with $1.5 billion over 14 years, outright ownership of over 350,000 sq km (135,100 sq mi) of land, and the right to hunt, fish, and trap anywhere in the territory. The new territory, scheduled to be created by 1999, would effectively be run by Canada's first aboriginal government, since the Inuit represented 85% of the population.

Canada launched its first northern television network in January. "Television Northern Canada" broadcast to a possible audience of 100,000 people distributed in 94 communities from the Yukon to Baffin Island and Labrador. The station broadcast for 12 hours daily in 10 native languages, as well as in English, on topics of interest to its northern audience. Programs included, for example, information shows discussing native self-government and hunting skills and sports shows featuring dogsled racing.

Tourism in the form of adventure tours, wildlife viewing, and cultural activities continued to gain considerable attention in the Arctic. In August the Canadian minister of the environment announced that a new national park—to be called Aulavik from the Inuvialuit word meaning "where people travel"—would be established on Banks Island in the western Arctic. The area of the park, covering more than 12,000 sq km (4,600 sq mi), is characterized by deep canyons, desertlike badlands, and archaeological sites with evidences of human occupation dating back 3,400 years. In August the *Kapitan Khlebnikov* became the first tourist-carrying Russian icebreaker to travel legally through Canada's Northwest Passage. The 52 passengers made it through the virtually impassable Northwest Passage thanks to the incredible power of the 150-m (492-ft)-long, 26,000-hp icebreaker. The *Globe and Mail* reported that while the North Pole was enjoying a tourism boom, controversy was arising as to whether adventure-seeking tourists should make deposits to help cover the costs in case rescue operations were needed.

The year marked the 50th anniversary of the Alaska Highway. Formerly known as the "Alaska Military Highway" or the "Alcan Highway," it was built in 1942 in response to the Japanese threat in the Pacific following the bombing of Pearl Harbor. The highway begins in Dawson Creek, B.C., and spans 2,446 km (1,520 mi) to Fairbanks, Alaska.

(KENNETH DE LA BARRE)

This article updates the *Macropædia* article The ARCTIC.

Major Revisions from the 1993 *Macropædia*

This section of the *Britannica Book of the Year* consists of articles or parts of articles reprinted from the *Macropædia*. The articles appearing here have been selected from among those recently revised or rewritten and have been chosen for their general interest or their timeliness.

Four of the articles that have been chosen from the 1993 printing are wholly new: the sections on the recent history of *South Africa* from SOUTHERN AFRICA and of the UNION OF SOVIET SOCIALIST REPUBLICS; the section (in part) on *Organized Labour* from WORK AND EMPLOYMENT; and the biography of FREDERICK

the Great; the section on the recent history of CENTRAL ASIA has been extensively revised.

Subscribers desiring update sheets to put in their encyclopaedia to indicate that an article has been revised or added, and owners of older sets wishing information about the exact article being replaced by the reprints, should address their requests to Editorial Yearbooks, Encyclopædia Britannica, Inc., 310 South Michigan Avenue, Chicago, IL 60604. There is no charge for the article update sheets, but you must tell us the copyright year of your set of *Encyclopædia Britannica*.

Central Asia

The Mongol epoch. The creation of the Mongol empire by Genghis Khan was a great feat of political and military skill that left a lasting imprint on the destinies of both Asia and Europe. The geographic basis of Genghis' power, the northwestern parts of which later became known as Mongolia, had been the centre of such Turkic empires as those of the Turks and Uighurs. There are no indications of the time and the manner in which the Mongols took over this region.

Creation of the Mongol empire. It is probable that Turks were incorporated in the nascent Mongol empire. In a series of tribal wars that led to the defeat of the Merkits and the Naimans, his most dangerous rivals, Genghis gained sufficient strength to assume, in 1206, the title of khan. Acting in the tradition of previous nomad empires of the region, Genghis' aggressive policies were directed primarily against China, then ruled in the north by the Chin (Juchen) dynasty. His western campaigns were set in motion quite accidentally by a senseless attack on Mongol forces by the fugitive Naiman prince Küchlüg, and they maintained their momentum through the pursuit of 'Alā' ad-Dīn Muḥammad of Khwārezm, who in 1218 ordered the execution of Mongol envoys seeking to establish trade relations. As a result, many of the flourishing cities of Khwārezm, Khorāsān, and Afghanistan were destroyed, and by 1223 Mongol armies had crossed the Caucasus. Although an important Russo-Kipchak force was defeated on May 31, 1223, at the battle of the Kalka, the Mongols did not make a definite thrust into eastern Europe until the winter of 1236–37. The fall of Kiev in December 1240— with incalculable consequences for Russian history—was followed by a Mongol invasion of Hungary in 1241–42. Although victorious against the forces of King Béla IV, the Mongols evacuated Hungary and withdrew to southern and central Russia. Ruled by Batu (d. 1255 or 1256), the Mongols of eastern Europe (the so-called Golden Horde)

became a major factor in that region and exerted a decisive influence on the development of the Russian states.

Simultaneously with these western campaigns, Genghis' successor Ögödei (reigned 1229–41) intensified Mongol pressure in China. Korea was occupied in 1231, and in 1234 the Chin dynasty succumbed to Mongol attacks. The establishment of the Mongol Yüan dynasty in China (1260–1368) was accomplished by the great khan Kublai (ruled 1260–94), a grandson of Genghis.

Mongol rule. The great khan Möngke (ruled 1251–59), who had sent his brother Kublai to conquer China, entrusted another of his brothers, Hülegü, with the task of consolidating the Mongol hold on Iran. In 1258 Hülegü occupied Baghdad and put an end to the 'Abbāsid Caliphate. He laid the foundations of a Mongol state in Iran, known as the Il-Khanate (because the il-khan was subordinate to the great khan in faraway Mongolia or China), which embraced, in addition to the Iranian plateau, much of Iraq, northern Syria, and eastern and central Anatolia and which, under Abaqha (ruled 1265–82), Arghun (ruled 1284–91), Ghāzān (ruled 1295–1304), and Öljeitü (ruled 1304–17), became both powerful and highly civilized. Although practically independent, the il-khans of Iran (Persia) remained loyal to Möngke and Kublai, but with the passing of Kublai, the drift toward full independence grew stronger. With Ghāzān's decision to make Islām the state religion—a gesture intended to gain the confidence of the majority of his subjects—a big step toward integration in the purely Iranian (as opposed to Mongol) tradition was taken. A lengthy conflict that opposed the il-khans to the Mamlūks of Egypt was not resolved until 1323, when a peace was concluded between the sultan al-Malik an-Nāṣir and Abū Sa'īd (ruled 1316–35), the last effective il-khan. After Abū Sa'īd's death the Il-Khanate, no longer held together by Mongol efficiency, disintegrated.

Mongol thrust into eastern Europe

In Iran and China the Mongol rulers, who increasingly linked their destinies with those of their sedentary subjects, inevitably began to lose their Mongol identity. But in the Central Asian heartland the descendants of Chaghatai and Ögödei, sons of Genghis, maintained traditional steppe polities geared to the interests of their nomad followers and increasingly opposed to the policies of the great khan in China and his ally, the il-khan, in Iran. After Möngke's death in 1259 there was a struggle between his two younger brothers, Kublai and Arigböge. The steppe candidate, Arigböge, lost in his bid for supreme power to the older Kublai, and further attempts to reestablish the centre of Mongol power in the Central Asian heartland also failed.

The most active and successful proponent of this policy was Kaidu, a grandson of Ögödei, who made several attempts to carve out an empire for himself in the heartland from lands ruled by other Mongol princes. In the course of time, he extended his control over most of the Semirechye, Kashgaria, and Transoxania, and in 1269 he even assumed the title of great khan. Chaghatai's descendants, enfeoffed with the territories stretching from Bishbaliq in the Dzungarian Basin westward to Samarkand, were to some extent victims of Kaidu's ambitions but for lack of better alternatives lent him their support. After Kaidu's death in 1301, however, the Chaghataid khan Duwa hastened to make peace with his Mongol kin in both Iran and China.

Thereafter the Chaghataid khanate, coterminous with the Central Asian heartland, enjoyed a checkered fortune. For the next 30 years it remained united, but during the 1330s and '40s it split into a western and an eastern khanate, the former consisting of the area between the Syr Darya and the Amu Darya, together with much of what is today Afghanistan, while the latter comprised the Semirechye and Kashgaria. The Chaghataid khans who ruled in the western khanate, where they usually resided in Bukhara, openly espoused Islām and a Muslim life-style, as did perhaps the majority of their followers. Northeast of the Syr Darya, the Chaghataid rulers of the eastern khanate endeavoured to maintain the nomadic traditions of their Genghiskhanid ancestors with a considerable degree of success. They continued to locate their headquarters in the Ili or Chu valley, while amirs of the important Mongol Dughlat clan, with whom the Chaghataids were closely linked through marriage alliances, ruled the Tarim Basin on their behalf from Kashgar. To the inhabitants of Transoxania and Iran, the eastern Chaghataid khanate was known as Mughulistān (literally, "Land of the Mongols"), and its inhabitants, unflatteringly, as Jāṭs (literally, "Robbers").

During the last third of the 14th century, the western Chaghataid khanate passed under the control of the Barlas Turk Timur (d. 1405; known in the west as Tamerlane), while the eastern khanate went through a protracted period of political instability but also gradual Islāmization. Under a succession of vigorous rulers—Esen Buga (d. 1462), Yunus (d. 1487), and Ahmad (d. 1503)—the eastern khanate held its own, ringed as it was by Oyrat foes in Dzungaria, the Kyrgyz in the Tien Shan, and the Kazakhs in the Semirechye. But decline did set in, temporarily postponed during the reign of Ahmad's able son Sultan Sa'īd Khān (reigned 1514–33), who ruled from Kashgar. By the beginning of the 17th century, however, the Chaghataid khans in the east had become mere figureheads, with the towns under the quasi-theocratic rule of a family of Khwājahs originating from Bukhara, while the countryside was dominated by rival Kyrgyz confederacies. The line seems to have died out obscurely before the end of the century.

Developments within the most enduring Mongol successor state, that of the Golden Horde, with its headquarters at Sarai on the lower Volga, followed a rather different course. Its Islāmization, begun under Batu's brother Berke (reigned 1257–67), led to tensions with the il-khans but resulted in the forging of strong links with the Mamlūks of Egypt. The Mamlūks were themselves Kipchak Turks from the Kipchak steppes of southern Russia over which the khans of the Golden Horde ruled. The prosperity of the Golden Horde under Ghiyath ad-Dīn Muḥammad Özbeg (Uzbeck or Öz Beg) between about 1312 and about 1341 stands in sharp contrast to the disintegrating

Il-Khanate and Chaghataid khanate, yet it had its own problems, both internal and external. From within, the growing and unavoidable antagonism between the Turko-Mongol ruling class, Turkish-speaking and now Muslim, and their Christian Russian subjects was exacerbated by the ceaseless dissensions among the members of the ruling house and the military elite, increasingly referred to by their Slav neighbours as Tatars. In foreign policy, the peace concluded in 1323 between the il-khans and the Mamlūks weakened the Golden Horde's influence in Egypt, while the establishment of the Ottomans on the Dardanelles (1354) put a virtual end to commercial relations between the Volga and Nile valleys. Perhaps the gravest political mistake of the rulers of the Golden Horde was their failure to recognize that the West—with which, through the Russians, they had excellent links—offered a more fertile ground for further expansion than the sunbaked deserts of Turkestan. The khans of the Golden Horde, instead of controlling the Russian and Lithuanian princes, increasingly relied upon their help in internal and dynastic struggles that were rending the khanate. While their attention was drawn southward and eastward, they overlooked the rise of dangerous enemies—Russian and Lithuanian—in their rear. The policies of the khan Tokhtamysh (reigned 1376–95) differed from those of his predecessors. Hereditary ruler of the White Horde, its pastures located in western Siberia and extending to the lower reaches of the Syr Darya, he was able to enlarge his power base by uniting its resources with those of the Golden Horde, of which he eventually made himself master. He thus introduced fresh "steppe power" into the Golden Horde at a time when it was no longer the force it had once been (in 1380 the Muscovites had inflicted a crushing, if temporary, defeat on the horde at Kulikovo Pole). Furthermore, instead of seeking the assistance of petty eastern European princes, he hitched his wagon to the rising star of Timur, with whose support he reasserted Mongol supremacy in Russia. After Tokhtamysh's death the Golden Horde survived under the aegis of an able usurper, Edigü, but after Edigü's death in 1419 a process of disintegration set in. The core territories of the former Golden Horde, centred on the Volga-Don steppes, became known as the "Great Horde," while outlying regions seceded to form independent khanates based on Kazan and Astrakhan on the Volga, the Crimea, western Siberia, and the Nogai steppe east of the lower Volga. All eventually fell victim to dynastic feuds, internecine rivalry, and Muscovite expansionism. Thus, in the case of the Kazan khanate, its founder Ulugh Muḥammad (reigned c. 1437–45) bequeathed the throne to his able son Maḥmud (or Maḥmutek), who reigned with conspicuous success between 1445 and 1462. Maḥmud's brothers, however, fled for sanctuary to Vasily II of Moscow, who set up a puppet khanate for one of them (Kasim) at Gorodets-on-the-Oka (thereafter renamed Kasimov). The khanate of Kasimov was to be a thorn in Kazan's flesh until the latter's extinction in 1552. Kasimov itself survived as a political fiction until about 1681, by which time the last khans had abandoned Islām for Christianity.

In 1502 the Great Horde was extinguished and its lands annexed by the khan of the Crimea, Mengli Girai, who had already placed himself under Ottoman suzerainty in 1475. Kazan fell to the troops of Ivan IV of Moscow in 1552, and Astrakhan was annexed two years later. The khanate of Sibir (western Siberia), after a stubborn resistance, submitted to Boris Godunov, the regent for Ivan's son Fyodor (reigned 1584–98). Only the khanate of the Crimea was left, separated from Muscovy by the still-unconquered Ukrainian steppe and enjoying some protection because of its status as an Ottoman vassal. It survived for two more centuries, until Catherine the Great's conquest in 1783. Its capital, Bakhchisaray, long a centre of Tatar culture, was to take on a new life in the late 19th century as the home of the Tatar national revival associated with the name of Ismail Bey Gasprinski.

Timur.   While the Golden Horde was beginning to enter its long decline in the late 14th century, the demise of Chaghataid rule in the area between the Amu Darya and Syr Darya was taking place as a result of the rise of

Mongol khanates of the steppes

The Golden Horde

Demise of the Golden Horde

Timur and his descendants

Timur. Timur first united under his leadership the Turko-Mongol tribes located in the basins of the two rivers. With the assistance of these tribes he expanded into the neighbouring regions of Khorāsān, Sīstān, Khwārezm, and Mughulistān before embarking upon extensive campaigning in what are now Iran and Iraq, eastern Turkey, and the Caucasus region. In addition, he launched two successful attacks on his erstwhile protégé, Tokhtamysh, ruler of the Golden Horde. In 1398–99 Timur invaded northern India and sacked Delhi, and between 1399 and 1402 he turned westward again to harry the Egyptian Mamlūks in Syria and the Ottoman sultan Bayezid I, whom he captured in battle near Ankara. At the time of his death at Otrar on the Syr Darya in 1405, Timur was leading his forces on an invasion of China. He never assumed openly the full attributes of sovereignty, contenting himself with the title of amir while upholding the fictional authority of a series of puppet khans of the line of Chaghatai, to whom he claimed kinship by marriage; in consequence he styled himself *güregen,* meaning son-in-law (*i.e.,* of the Chaghataid khan). Timur seems to have lacked the innate administrative capacity or the foresight of Genghis Khan, and after Timur's death his conquests were disputed among his numerous progeny. In the ensuing struggles his fourth son, Shāh Rukh (reigned 1407–47), emerged victorious. He abandoned his father's capital of Samarkand for Herāt in Khorāsān (now in western Afghanistan), where he ruled in great splendour, leaving his son, Ulūgh Beg, as his deputy in the former capital. Ulūgh Beg's rule in Samarkand between 1409 and 1447 probably brought a considerable measure of tranquility to the long-troubled region. Himself an enthusiastic astronomer and the builder of a celebrated observatory, he ensured that during his lifetime Samarkand would be a major centre of scientific learning, especially in astronomy and mathematics. He was killed in 1449.

Throughout the second half of the 15th century, the western part of Central Asia was divided into a number of rival principalities ruled by descendants of Timur, among which Bukhara and Samarkand were the most important. The courts of these rulers witnessed an extraordinary cultural florescence in literature, the arts, and architecture, with Chaghatai Turkish, a dialect derived partly from Khakani, the language spoken at the Karakhanid court (and a precursor of modern Uzbek), emerging as a flexible vehicle for sophisticated literary expression. These Timurid epigones, however, were locked in unceasing rivalry with each other and were unable to combine against intruders from beyond their frontiers. By the close of the century, therefore, all the Timurid possessions in Central Asia had passed into the hands of the Uzbeks.

The Uzbeks. The early history of the Uzbek people (whose rulers were descendants of a younger brother of Batu, khan of the Golden Horde) is wrapped in obscurity, but by the middle of the 15th century they had migrated from their original homeland, east of the Ural Mountains, southeast toward the lower Syr Darya, whence, under their

Rise of the Uzbeks

leader, Abū'l-Khayr Khan, they began to threaten the Timurids across the river. However, before Abū'l-Khayr Khan could undertake a full-scale invasion, he was killed in battle in 1468 by two rebellious kinsmen who, refusing to recognize his assertion of paramountcy, had defected, together with their tribal followers, and placed themselves under the nominal suzerainty of the Chaghataid khan of Mughulistān. Their descendants were to become the Kazakh hordes of later centuries.

With the death of Abū'l-Khayr Khan, the fortunes of the Uzbeks temporarily declined, only to be revived under the leadership of his grandson, Muḥammad Shaybānī, who by 1500 had made himself master of Samarkand as well as of the Syr Darya and Amu Darya basins and was advancing into Khorāsān (Herāt fell to him in 1507) when he was defeated and killed in 1510 by Shah Ismā'īl Safavi. He had, however, changed the course of Central Asian history. By the time of his death, all the lands between the Syr Darya and Amu Darya were in Uzbek hands, and so they were to remain. Throughout the 16th century, Muḥammad Shaybānī's kinsmen ruled over a powerful and aggressive khanate from their capital at Bukhara. They continued

Muḥammad Shaybānī's feud with the Iranian Safavids, articulated along Shī'ite-versus-Sunnite lines, and with the Mughal dynasty in India, whose founder, the Timurid Babur, had been driven out of Central Asia by Shaybānī. In contrast, friendly, if sporadic, ties with the Ottomans were maintained by way of the Volga-Don steppes. Unlike the Ottomans, Safavids, and Mughals, however, the Uzbeks had only limited access to firearms, which placed them at a considerable disadvantage with their rivals.

During Shaybānid rule, and even more under the Ashtarkhanids (also known as the Tuquy-Timurids or Jānids) who succeeded them during the 1600s, Central Asia experienced a decline in prosperity compared to the preceding Timurid period, due in part to a marked falling-off in the transcontinental caravan trade following the opening of new oceanic trade routes. In the 1700s the basins of the Amu Darya and Syr Darya passed under the control of three Uzbek khanates claiming legitimacy in their descent from the Genghiskhanids. These were, from west to east, the Qungrāts based on Khiva in Khwārezm (1717–1920), the Mangits in Bukhara (1753–1920), and the Mings in Kokand (c. 1710–1876), in the upper valley of the Syr Darya. During this same period, east of the Pamirs, Kashgaria was torn apart by the rivalries of Khwājahs and Kyrgyz; in the Semirechye the Kazakhs were locked in conflict with the Mongol Oyrats and Dzungars; while between the Aral and Caspian seas the Turkmens roamed the northern borders of Iran, enslaving the sedentary population and transporting it to Bukhara to labour in the oases. The time was ripe for Russian intervention, made easier by the intruders' possession of cannon and firearms.

THE MODERN PERIOD: THE AGE OF DECADENCE

From the beginnings of recorded history, pastoral nomadism, practiced on a grandiose scale, was the economic basis of the great Central Asian empires. Once the domestication of the horse was sufficiently advanced to allow for its use in warfare, the superiority of the mounted archer over the foot soldier or the war chariot was never effectively challenged.

The waning of nomadic military power. When headed by capable leaders, well-trained and disciplined mounted troops were almost invincible. The sedentary civilizations could not, by their very nature, put aside for breeding purposes pastures sufficiently large to sustain a cavalry force that could equal that of the pastoral nomads; hence the latter's military superiority remained a constant for about 2,000 years of Eurasian history.

At its highest degree of development, Central Asian nomad society constituted a very sophisticated and highly specialized social and economic structure, advanced but also highly vulnerable because of its specialization and the lack of diversification of its economy. Geared almost entirely to the production of war matériel—*i.e.,* the horse—when not engaged in warfare, it was unable to provide the people with anything but the barest necessities of life. To ensure their very existence, Central Asian empires had to wage war and obtain through raids or tribute the commodities they could not produce. When, owing to circumstances such as severe weather decimating the horse herds or inept leadership, raids against other peoples became impossible, the typical Central Asian nomad state had to disintegrate to allow its population to fend for itself and secure the necessities for a subsistence. Hunting and pastoral nomadism both need vast expanses to support a thinly scattered population that does not naturally lend itself to strong, centralized political control. The skill of a Central Asian leader consisted precisely in the gathering of such dispersed populations and in providing for them on a level higher than they had been accustomed to. There was but one way to achieve this: successful raids on other, preferably richer, peoples. The military machinery was dependent on numbers, which then precluded self-sufficiency. In case of prolonged military reverses, the nomadic aggregation of warriors had to disband because it was only in dispersion that, without recourse to war, they were economically autonomous.

In the course of the 15th century, the steppe territory

Social and economic structure of nomad society

suitable for great horse herds began to shrink. In the east the Yung-lo emperor of the Ming led five major campaigns against the Mongols (1410–24), all successful but none decisive. Yet when, under the leadership of Esen Taiji (1439–55), the Mongol Oyrats pushed as far as Peking, they found the city defended by cannon, and they withdrew. In the Middle East, as noted above, the Ottoman and Ṣafavid gunpowder empires barred the road to the no-longer-invincible nomad cavalry, and, along the western borders of Central Asia, the Russians were soon to start on their decisive and irresistible march across Central Asia to the borders of China, India, and Iran.

The Russian conquests.   Their most spectacular advance into Central Asia carried the Russians eastward through the forest belt, where the hunting and fishing populations offered little resistance and where the much-coveted furs of Siberia could be found in abundance. Acting on behalf of the Stroganov family of entrepreneurs, in 1578 or 1581 the Cossack Yermak crossed the Urals and defeated the Shaybānid prince Kuchum, who alone represented organized political power in Siberia.

The Russian advance from west to east across Siberia, motivated by commercial rather than political considerations, remains unparalleled in history for its rapidity. The native Finno-Ugrians—Samoyed or Tungus hunters accustomed to paying their fur tribute—were little concerned with the nationality of the tax collectors and found dealing with the Russians no more unpleasant than with Turks or Mongols. Russian penetration was marked by the building of small forts, such as Tobolsk (1587) near the former capital of Kuchum, Tara (1594) on the Irtysh River, and Narym (1596) on the upper Ob River. The Yenisey was reached in 1619, and the town of Yakutsk on the Lena was founded in 1632. About 1639 the first small group of Russians reached the Pacific in the neighbourhood of present-day Okhotsk. About 10 years later, Anadyrsk was founded on the shores of the Bering Sea, and, by the end of the century, Kamchatka was annexed. When advanced Russian parties reached the Amur River about the middle of the 17th century, they entered the Chinese sphere of interest. Although some clashes occurred, restraint on both sides led to the signing of the treaties of Nerchinsk (1689) and Kiakhta (1727), which remained in force until 1858. To this day, the border delineated at Kiakhta has not been altered substantially.

The thorniest question to be dealt with in the early Russo-Chinese negotiations concerned the Mongols—wedged between the two Great Powers—who, in the course of the 16th and 17th centuries, reasserted their control over most of the steppe belt. In the 15th century the western Mongols, or Oyrats, had become quite powerful under Esen Taiji but, under the strong leadership of Dayan Khan (ruled 1470–1543) and his grandson Altan Khan (1543–83), the eastern Mongols—and more precisely the Khalkha tribe—gained ascendancy. In 1552 Altan took possession of what was left of Karakorum, the old Mongol capital. Altan's reign saw the conversion of a great many Mongols to the tenets of the Yellow Hat sect of Tibetan Buddhism, a religion that, until the 1920s, played a major role in Mongol life. The attempts of Ligdan Khan (reigned 1604–34) to unite the various Mongol tribes failed not only because of internal dissensions but also on account of the rising power of the Manchus, to whom he was forced to surrender. The active Central Asian policy of China's Ch'ing (Manchu) dynasty brought a lasting transformation in the political structure of the region.

More distant from China, the Oyrats could pursue a more independent course. One of their tribes, the Dzungars, under the leadership of Galdan (Dga'-ldan; ruled 1676–97), created a powerful state that remained a serious menace to China until 1757, when the Ch'ien-lung emperor defeated their last ruler, Amursana, and thus put an end to the last independent Mongol state prior to the creation, in 1921, of Outer Mongolia (the Khalkha princes had submitted to the Manchus in 1691).

The treaties of Nerchinsk and Kiakhta established the northern border of the Chinese zone of influence, which included Mongolia. In the wars against the Dzungars, the Chinese established their rule over East Turkestan

and Dzungaria. China's western boundary remained undefined, but it ran farther west than it does today and included Lake Balkhash and parts of the Kazakh steppe.

Wedged between the Russian and Chinese empires, unable to break through the stagnant but solid Ottoman and Ṣafavid barriers, the Turkish nomads of the steppe lying east of the Volga and the Caspian Sea and south of Russian-occupied Siberia found themselves caught in a trap from which there was no escape. If there is cause for surprise, it lies in the lateness rather than in the fact of the ultimate Russian conquest.

(DENIS SINOR; GAVIN R.G. HAMBLY)

West of the Uzbek khanates, between the Aral and Caspian Sea, were the nomad Turkmens, notorious robbers who roamed the inhospitable land. The Kazakhs, who since the 17th century divided into three "hordes," nomadized between the Volga and the Irtysh. During the 16th and 17th centuries, they fought Oyrats and Dzungars but succeeded in holding their own, and in 1771 Ablai, ruler of the "Middle Horde," located west of Lake Balkhash, was confirmed as ruler both by China and Russia. Yet Russian expansion, motivated by the urge to get closer to the Indian Ocean, forced the Kazakhs to yield. Although some Kazakh leaders, such as the sultan Kinesary, put up spirited resistance (1837–47), the line of the Syr Darya was reached by the Russians toward the middle of the 19th century.

The Uzbek khanate of Kokand was annexed in 1876; those of Khiva and Bukhara became Russian protectorates in 1873 and 1868, respectively. The conquest of the Turkmens in the last quarter of the 19th century defined Russia's (now Turkmenistan's) southern frontier with Iran and Afghanistan.

Under Russian rule.   The Russian conquests in Central Asia had given the tsars control of a vast area of striking geographic and human diversity, acquired at relatively little effort in terms of men and money. The motives for the conquest had not been primarily economic; peasant colonization of the virgin steppes and the systematic cultivation of cotton were later developments. The factors that determined the Russian advance into the area were complex and interrelated. They included the historic pull of the frontier, the thirst for military glory on the part of the officer corps, and the fear of further British penetration into Central Asia from across the Indus, as well as the infectious rhetoric of imperialism common to the age. From the outset, Russia's objectives as a colonial power were strictly limited: to maintain "law and order" at minimum cost and to disturb as little as possible the traditional way of life of its new subjects. Such an approach was favoured by the remoteness of the area and its isolation even from the rest of the Muslim world. It was improbable that an almost wholly illiterate population, its prejudices formed by a venal and obscurantist 'ulamā' (class of Muslim theologians and scholars), could offer any concerted resistance to the Russian presence; and such, indeed, proved to be the case. The Russians, like other colonial powers, did experience an occasional uprising, generally of a very localized character, but the overwhelming military superiority displayed by the Russians at the time of the initial conquest, the inability of the inhabitants of the khanates to offer effective resistance, and the heavy-handedness with which subsequent insurrection or insubordination was dealt with ensured minimal opposition. Finally, by preserving the titular sovereignty of the amir of Bukhara and the khan of Khiva, they left a substantial part of the population, especially the urban classes, most deeply devoted to the Islāmic way of life, under traditionally minded Muslim rulers.

Tsarist rule.   Yet the Russians, whether intentionally or not, became agents of change throughout the area in much the same way as any other colonial power. The economy was gradually realigned to meet the Russian need for raw materials and new markets. This required the construction of railroads: by 1888 the Trans-Caspian Railroad had reached Samarkand; between 1899 and 1905 the Orenburg-Tashkent Railroad was completed; the Turkestan-Siberian Railroad came later, begun just before World War I and not completed until 1930. In Tashkent

Russian advance into Siberia

Motives for conquest

and Samarkand new European suburbs were laid out at a distance from the walled native cities, but, as in the case of the newly established garrison towns, such islands of European life required local services and supplies. Nor did the Russians wholly ignore the welfare of their new subjects. An effort was made, halfheartedly at first, to put down the indigenous slave trade; irrigation projects were initiated; and bilingual elementary education was cautiously introduced. As elsewhere in colonial Asia, the work of Russian scholars studying the literature, history, and antiquities of the Central Asian peoples aroused upon the part of a numerically small but influential Russian-educated elite, especially among the Kazakhs, nostalgic awareness of a colourful past and a sense of national, or cultural, identity.

Kazakh
response to
Russian
rule

Of the major racial groups in Central Asia—Uzbeks, Kazakhs, Turkmens, Tajiks, and Kyrgyz—the Kazakhs were the first to respond to the impact of Russian culture. Their early contacts with their new masters had in the main been carried out through intermediaries—Kazan Tatars, who, paradoxically, had contributed to strengthening the Kazakhs' awareness of being part of a greater Muslim world community and their sense of being a "nation" rather than a welter of tribes and clans. Moreover, through the Tatars they were exposed to current Pan-Turkish and Pan-Islāmic propaganda. In the 1870s the Russians countered Tatar influence by establishing bilingual Russian-Kazakh schools, from which emerged a westernized elite of considerable distinction.

Kazakh unrest. This Russo-Kazakh "dialogue" was, however, doomed to founder on the rock of the government's policy of settling peasants from European Russia and Ukraine on the Kazakh steppe, where agricultural settlement on an extensive scale could be undertaken only by curtailing the area available for grazing by the nomads' livestock and by restricting their seasonal migrations. As early as 1867–68 the northwestern fringes of the Kazakh steppe had been the scene of violent protests at the presence of colonists, but it was not until the last decade of the century that the movement got fully under way with the arrival of upward of one million peasants, resulting in the inevitable expropriation of Kazakh grazing grounds and in savage conflict between the Kazakhs and the intruders. Finally in 1916, during World War I, the Kazakhs, driven to desperation by the loss of their lands and by the ruthlessness of the wartime administration, rose up in protest against a decree conscripting the non-Russian subjects of the empire for forced labour. The rebellion assumed the character of a popular uprising, in which many colonists and many more Kazakhs and Kyrgyz were massacred. The revolt was put down with the utmost savagery, and more than 300,000 Kazakhs are said to have sought refuge across the Chinese frontier.

The
Kazakh
republic

With the collapse of tsarist rule, the westernized Kazakh elite formed a party, the Alash Orda, as a vehicle through which to express their aspirations for regional autonomy. Having found during the Russian Civil War that the anticommunist "Whites" were implacably opposed to their aspirations, the Kazakhs cast in their lot with the "Reds." After the war the Kazakhs were granted their own republic, in which, for the first few years, the leaders of the Alash Orda maintained a fairly dominant position and were active in protecting Kazakh interests. After 1924, however, direct confrontation with the Communist Party became more intense, and in 1927–28 the Alash Orda leaders were liquidated as "bourgeois nationalists." The history of the Kazakhs in the first half of the 20th century was bleak indeed—expropriation of their grazing lands under the tsars, the bloody uprising and reprisals of 1916, the losses in the civil war and in the famine in 1921, the purges of the intelligentsia in 1927–28, collectivization during the 1930s, and further peasant colonization after World War II.

In Transoxania, divided between the administration of the Russian governor-general of Turkestan, based on Tashkent, and that of the amir of Bukhara and the khan of Khiva, opposition to colonial domination was centred in the most conservative elements of a profoundly Islāmic society—the '*ulamā*' and the inhabitants of the

bazaar. Nonetheless, the Russians favoured, for reasons of expediency, the preservation of the traditional social framework and endeavoured, with only partial success, to insulate the inhabitants of the region from contact with the more "advanced" Muslims of the empire—the Volga and Crimean Tatars. In this they were aided by the fact that the virtual absence of European colonization provided no fuel for popular resentment comparable to that felt by the Kazakhs; and, in consequence, the westernized products of the bilingual Russian-Uzbek educational system, concerned primarily with reform of the Islāmic way of life, regarded the Muslim "ultras" as their most dangerous opponents.

If the main influence in shaping the outlook of the Kazakh intelligentsia was the educational system imported from European Russia, the catalyst in the case of the Uzbeks was knowledge of the educational reforms and the Pan-Turkish ideology of the Crimean Tatar renaissance of the late 19th century. The Uzbek reformers, known as Jadidists, advocated the introduction of a modern educational system as a prerequisite for social change and cultural revitalization; and, despite intense opposition from the clerical classes, they opened their first school in Tashkent in 1901 and by 1914 had established more than 100. After 1908, influenced by the Young Turks of the Ottoman Empire, the Young Bukharans and the Young Khivans worked for a program of radical institutional change in the ramshackle governments of the khanates. It may be doubted, however, whether by 1917 the Uzbek intelligentsia had made any substantial impact outside a fairly narrow circle of like-minded persons.

Soviet rule. Neither before nor after the Russian Revolution of 1917 were the nationalist aspirations of the Muslims of Central Asia compatible with the interests of the Russian state or those of the European population of the region. This was demonstrated once and for all when the troops of the Tashkent Soviet crushed a short-lived Muslim government established in Kokand in January 1918. Indeed, the Soviet authorities in Central Asia regarded the native intelligentsia, even the most "progressive" of them, with lively and (from their point of view) justifiable apprehension. At the same time, there was the problem of an active resistance on the part of conservative elements, which was anti-Russian as much as anticommunist. Having extinguished the khanate of Khiva in 1919 and that of Bukhara in 1920, local Red Army units found themselves engaged in a protracted struggle with the Basmachis—guerrillas operating in the mountains in the eastern part of the former khanate of Bukhara. Not until 1925 did the Red Army gain the upper hand.

Thereafter, Central Asia was increasingly integrated into the Soviet system through a planned economy and improved communications, through the communist institutional and ideological framework of control, and, for young males, through compulsory service in the Red Army. The economy of the region became further distorted to meet the needs of the central planners. Traditional religion, values, and culture were suppressed, but in such areas as education, health care, and welfare Central Asians benefited to a degree from their forced participation in the system. Eventually the Soviets developed an ingenious strategy for neutralizing the two common denominators most likely to unite Central Asians against continuing control from Moscow: Islāmic culture and Turkish ethnicity. After a protracted period of trial and error, their ultimate solution was the creation of five Soviet socialist republics: the Kazakh S.S.R. (now Kazakhstan) in 1936, the Kirgiz S.S.R. (now Kyrgyzstan) in 1936, the Tadzhik S.S.R. (now Tajikistan) in 1929, the Turkmen S.S.R. (now Turkmenistan) in 1924, and the Uzbek S.S.R. (now Uzbekistan) in 1924. The plan was to will into being five new nations whose separate development under close surveillance and firm tutelage from Moscow would preempt the emergence of a "Turkestani" national identity and such comcomitant ideologies as Pan-Turkism or Pan-Islāmism. To some extent, this ethno-engineering reflected colonial conceptions of the peoples of Central Asia dating back to tsarist times. Thus the Kazakhs, whose absorption into the Russian Empire had been a

Creation
of Soviet
republics

gradual process extending from the early 18th to the early 19th century, were perceived as wholly separate from the Uzbeks south of the Syr Darya, whose territories had been annexed during the middle decades of the 19th century. As speakers of an Iranian language, the Tajiks could be clearly distinguished from their Turkish-speaking neighbours, while the Russian perception of the nomadic Turkmens, whom they had conquered during the closing years of the 19th century, set them apart from the sedentary Uzbeks. Similarly, the Kyrgyz of the Issyk-Kul region (whom the Russians of tsarist times had confusingly designated "Kara-Kirgiz," while applying the name "Kirgiz" to the Kazakhs) were declared to be distinct from their Kazakh neighbours. Thus, the colonial experience and 19th-century Russian ethnological and anthropological fieldwork were, when appropriate, enlisted by the Soviets to serve very different ideological ends. Inevitably, the boundaries of these artificial creations willed into being by Soviet fiat did not reflect the ethnic and cultural patterns of Central Asia, and all five republics contained substantial minority populations (among them, immigrants from European Russia), a situation which, with the coming of independence in 1991, was fraught with the likelihood of future conflicts. To ensure the success of this design for stabilizing Central Asia under Soviet rule, school textbooks, scholarly research and publishing, and cultural policies in general were devised to stress, on the one hand, the particular and unique experience of each republic and, on the other, the enduring benefits of the Russian connection, which paradoxically required that the tsarist conquests and their consequences be represented as an overwhelming boon to Central Asians. Great significance was given to language policy, with strenuous efforts being made to emphasize the linguistic differences among the various Turkish languages spoken in the republics, clear evidence of intent to divide and rule.

During the last two decades of Soviet history, the remoteness and economic backwardness of Central Asia meant that this region felt less intensely the winds of change beginning to blow through metropolitan Russia, Ukraine, or the Baltic republics, although from 1979 Soviet intervention in neighbouring Afghanistan produced ripple effects across the frontier. Historians, however, may conclude that the most significant aspects of the history of Central Asia under the Soviets were the extent to which its peoples managed to retain their traditional cultural heritage under the most debilitating circumstances. Now that all five are independent sovereign states, their future destinies will be of more than regional significance. They (or some of them) may continue to maintain significant economic links with Russia and various other former Soviet republics, or they may form some kind of economic common market or seek to give substance to old dreams of a united Turkestan. What is certain is that Central Asia will no longer be the backwater that it became when the age of European maritime discovery brought to an end the centuries-old transcontinental caravan trade.

(GAVIN R.G. HAMBLY)

Frederick the Great

Frederick II the Great, third king of Prussia from 1740 to 1786, ranks among the two or three dominant figures in the history of modern Germany. Under his leadership Prussia became one of the great states of Europe. Its territories were greatly increased and its military strength displayed to striking effect. From early in his reign Frederick achieved a high reputation as a military commander, and the Prussian army rapidly became a model admired and imitated in many other states. He also emerged quickly as a leading exponent of the ideas of enlightened government, which were then becoming influential throughout much of Europe; indeed, his example did much to spread and strengthen those ideas. Notably, his insistence on the primacy of state over personal or dynastic interests and his religious toleration widely affected the dominant intellectual currents of the age. Even more than his younger contemporaries, Catherine II the Great of Russia and Joseph II in the Habsburg territories, it was Frederick who, during the mid-18th century, established in the minds of educated Europeans a notion of what "enlightened despotism" should be. His actual achievements, however, were sometimes less than they appeared on the surface; indeed, his inevitable reliance on the landowning officer (Junker) class set severe limits in several respects to what he could even attempt. Nevertheless, his reign saw a revolutionary change in the importance and prestige of Prussia, which was to have profound implications for much of the subsequent history of Europe.

Early life. Frederick was born on Jan. 24, 1712, in Potsdam, near Berlin. He was the eldest surviving son of Frederick William I, king of Prussia, and Sophia Dorothea of Hanover, daughter of George I of Britain. Frederick's upbringing and education were strictly controlled by his father, who was a martinet as well as a paranoiac. Encouraged and supported by his mother and his sister Wilhelmina, Frederick soon came into bitter conflict with his father. Frederick William I deeply despised the artistic and intellectual tastes of his son and was infuriated by Frederick's lack of sympathy with his own rigidly puritanical and militaristic outlook. His disappointment and contempt took the form of bitter public criticism and even outright physical violence, and Frederick, beaten and humiliated by his father, often over trifling details of behaviour, took refuge in evasion and deceit. This personal and family feud culminated spectacularly in 1730, when Frederick was imprisoned in the fortress of Küstrin after planning unsuccessfully to flee initially to France or Holland. Lieutenant Hans Hermann von Katte, the young officer who had been his accomplice in the plan, was executed in Frederick's presence, and there was for a short time a real possibility that the prince might share his fate. During the next year or more Frederick, as a punishment, was employed as a junior official in local administration and deprived of his military rank. The effects of this terrible early life are impossible to measure with accuracy, but there is little doubt that the violent and capricious bullying of his father influenced him deeply.

In 1733, after a partial reconciliation with his father,

Tension between father and son

By courtesy of the Staatliche Museen zu Berlin

Frederick II, portrait by Antoine Pesne (1683–1757). In the Gemäldegalerie, Berlin.

Frederick was married to a member of a minor German princely family, Elizabeth Christine of Brunswick-Bevern, for whom he never cared and whom he systematically neglected. In the following year he saw active military service for the first time under the great Austrian commander Eugene of Savoy against the French army in the Rhineland. In the later 1730s, in semiretirement in the castle of Rheinsberg near Berlin and able for the first time to give free rein to his own tastes, he read voraciously, absorbing the ideas on government and international relations that were to guide him throughout his life. These years were perhaps the happiest that Frederick ever experienced. However, his relations with his father, though somewhat improved, remained strained.

Accession to the throne and foreign policy. Frederick William I died on May 31, 1740, and Frederick, on his accession, immediately made it clear to his ministers that he alone would decide policy. Within a few months he was given a chance to do so in a way that revolutionized Prussia's international position. The Holy Roman emperor Charles VI, of the Austrian house of Habsburg, died on October 20, leaving as his heir a daughter, the archduchess Maria Theresa, whose claims to several of the heterogeneous Habsburg territories were certain to be disputed. Moreover, her army was in a poor state, the financial position of the Habsburg government very difficult, and her ministers mediocre and in many cases old. Frederick, however, thanks to his father, had a fine army and ample funds at his disposal. He therefore decided shortly after the emperor's death to attack the Habsburg province of Silesia, a wealthy and strategically important area to which the Hohenzollerns, the ruling family of Prussia, had dynastic claims, though weak ones. The most important threat to his plans was Russian support for Maria Theresa, which he hoped to avert by judicious bribery in St. Petersburg and by exploiting the confusion that was likely to follow the imminent death of the empress Anna. He also hoped that Maria Theresa would cede most of Silesia in return for a promise of Prussian support against her other enemies, but her refusal to do so made war inevitable.

Invasion of Silesia

The first military victory of Frederick's reign was the battle of Mollwitz (April 1741), though it owed nothing to his own leadership; in October Maria Theresa, now threatened by a hostile coalition of France, Spain, and Bavaria, had to agree to the Convention of Klein-Schnellendorf, by which Frederick was allowed to occupy the whole of Lower Silesia. However, the Habsburg successes against the French and Bavarians that followed so alarmed Frederick that early in 1742 he invaded Moravia, the region south of Silesia, which was under Austrian rule. His rather incomplete victory at Chotusitz in May nonetheless forced Maria Theresa to cede almost all of Silesia by the Treaty of Berlin of 1742 in July. This once more allowed Habsburg forces to be concentrated against France and Bavaria, and 1743 and the early months of 1744 saw Maria Theresa's position in Germany become markedly stronger. Frederick, again alarmed by this, invaded Bohemia in August 1744 and rapidly overran it. However, by the end of the year lack of French support and threats to his lines of communication had forced him to retreat. Moreover, the elector Augustus III (king of Poland and the elector of Saxony) now joined Maria Theresa in attacking him in Silesia. He was rescued from this threatening situation by the prowess of his army; victories at Hohenfriedberg in June 1745 and at Soor in September were followed by a Prussian invasion of Saxony. The Treaty of Dresden, signed on Dec. 25, 1745, finally established Prussian rule in Silesia and ended for the time being the complex series of struggles that had begun five years earlier.

Silesia was a valuable acquisition, being more developed economically than any other major part of the Hohenzollern dominions. Moreover, military victory had now made Prussia at least a semigreat power and marked Frederick as the most successful ruler in Europe. He was well aware, however, that his situation was far from secure. Maria Theresa was determined to recover Silesia, and the peace she signed with France and Spain at Aix-la-Chapelle in 1748 allowed her to accelerate significant improvements in the administration of her territories and the organization of her army. Frederick's alliance with France, which dated from an agreement of June 1741, was based merely on mutual hostility toward the Habsburgs and had never been effective. More serious, anti-Prussian feeling was now running high in Russia, where both the empress Elizabeth, who had ascended the throne in 1741, and her chancellor, Aleksey Bestuzhev-Ryumin, bitterly disliked Frederick. Moreover, Great Britain, under George II, seeking an effective continental ally against France, seemed to be moving closer to Maria Theresa and Elizabeth. In September 1755 Britain signed an agreement with Russia by which Russia, in return for British subsidies, was to provide a large military force in its Baltic provinces to protect, if necessary, the electorate of Hanover, ruled by George II, against possible French or Prussian attack. Frederick was deeply alarmed by this: a hostile Austro-Russian alliance backed by British money seemed to threaten the destruction of Prussia. In January 1756 he attempted to escape from this menacing situation by an agreement with Britain for the neutralization of Germany in the Anglo-French colonial and naval war that had just begun. This, however, deeply antagonized Louis XV and the French government, who saw the agreement as an insulting desertion of France, Frederick's ostensible ally. The result was the signature in May of a Franco-Austrian defensive alliance. This did not in itself threaten Frederick, but he soon became convinced that a Russo-Austrian attack on him, with French support, was imminent. He determined to forestall his enemies and, in a daring move, invaded Saxony in August 1756 and marched on into Bohemia. This action has been more actively debated by historians than any other event of Frederick's reign because it raised in an acute form the general issue regarding the morality of preventive military action. Though Frederick took the offensive and thus unleashed a great military struggle, there is no doubt that he was by 1756 seriously threatened, indeed, even more seriously than he himself realized, and that his enemies, most of all the empress Elizabeth, meant to destroy Prussia's newly won international status.

Invasion of Saxony and Bohemia

The Seven Years' War, on which he embarked thus soon became a life-and-death struggle. In 1757 France, Sweden, Russia, and many of the smaller German states joined the ranks of his opponents, while the Prussian invasion of Bohemia collapsed after a serious defeat at Kolín in June. Brilliant victories over the French and Austrian armies, respectively, at Rossbach and Leuthen in November and December partially reestablished Frederick's position, but it still remained extremely precarious. Ruthless exploitation of every available resource (notably of much of Saxony, which was under Prussian military occupation during most of the war), debasement of the currency, and a British subsidy that he received in 1758–62 allowed Frederick with increasing difficulty to keep up the unequal struggle. More than anything, however, he was helped by the complete failure of his enemies to cooperate effectively, while a partly British and British-financed army in western Germany from 1758 onward neutralized the French military effort. Nevertheless, the strain was immense; in October 1757 a cabinet order suspended all payment of salaries and pensions to Prussian civil servants and judges apart from diplomats serving abroad. Frederick could still win victories in the field, as, for example, at Zorndorf (August 1758) against the Russians at heavy cost or at Liegnitz and Torgau (August and November 1760) against the Austrians. But he also suffered serious defeats at Hochkirch in October 1758 and above all at the hands of a Russian army at Kunersdorf in August 1759. This disaster temporarily reduced him to despair and thoughts of suicide; if it had been effectively followed up by his adversaries, he could not have continued the struggle. As the forces he could put in the field dwindled and resistance grew among his subjects to the unprecedented burdens imposed by the war (in 1760 the landowners of Brandenburg refused to contribute further), the Prussian position became increasingly difficult; by 1761 it was desperate. However, the death in January 1762 of the empress Elizabeth, the most bitter of all Frederick's enemies, completely changed the situation. Her successor, Peter III, a fanatical admirer of Prussia and Frederick,

The
Treaty of
Hubertus-
burg

signed an armistice in May, followed by a Russo-Prussian peace treaty. This turn of events ended Maria Theresa's hopes of recovering Silesia. The Treaty of Hubertusburg (Feb. 15, 1763), which ended the war in Germany, left the province in Frederick's hands. Prussia had survived, and its military reputation was now greater than ever. The cost had been enormous, however. The Prussian army had lost 180,000 men during the struggle, and some Prussian provinces had been completely devastated.

Henceforth Frederick was determined to avoid another such conflict: the alliance with Russia that he signed in 1764 and which lasted until 1780 was directed largely to this end. Nevertheless, he still firmly opposed any growth of Habsburg power in Germany, and in July 1778 a new Austro-Prussian struggle broke out over the efforts of the emperor Joseph II, the son of Maria Theresa, to gain a large part of Bavaria. This War of the Bavarian Succession was half-hearted and short-lived, and the Treaty of Teschen ending it in May 1779 was a severe check to Joseph's ambitions and a diplomatic victory for Frederick. But this new conflict showed unmistakably that Austro-Prussian rivalry stemming from the events of 1740–41 was now a deeply ingrained fact of German political life. Fear of Habsburg ambitions continued to haunt Frederick to the end of his reign. His last significant achievement was to inspire the formation, in July 1785, of the League of Princes (Fürstenbund), which united a number of German states—the most important being Hanover, Saxony, and the archbishopric of Mainz—in successful opposition to Joseph II and his renewed efforts to acquire the whole of Bavaria in exchange for the Austrian Netherlands.

The first
partition of
Poland

The most important foreign policy development in the second half of Frederick's reign was the first partition of Poland, in 1772. By this Prussia gained the Polish province of West Prussia (though without the great commercial city of Danzig), and thus Brandenburg and Pomerania, the core of the monarchy, became linked with the theretofore isolated East Prussia. This gave the state a much greater territorial coherence and more defensible frontiers. It also moved its geographic centre decisively to the east and sharpened the social and political differences that tended to separate it from the states of western Europe.

Frederick had always hoped for territorial gains of this kind, and, as the weakness and confusion of the internally divided Polish republic increased during the 1760s, the possibilities of realizing them grew. In 1769 he tried indirectly to interest Catherine II of Russia in a partition but in vain. By January 1771, however, faced by strong Austrian opposition to her expansionist ambitions in southeastern Europe, the empress had changed her mind. The visit to St. Petersburg in that month of Frederick's younger brother Prince Henry played a decisive role in making a partition possible; the Habsburg government, which had hoped to recover Silesia or gain territory in the Balkans, was persuaded to join in the process. Frederick bears much of the responsibility for the partition, for he alone of the monarchs who took part had consciously desired it. Since both Russia and Austria were persuaded to follow a policy that was largely Prussian in inspiration, it ranks as perhaps his greatest diplomatic success.

Domestic policies. In administrative, economic, and social policy Frederick's attitudes were essentially conservative. Much of what he did in these areas was little more than a development of policies pursued by his father. He justified these policies in terms of the rationalizing rhetoric of "enlightened despotism," whereas the devoutly Protestant Frederick William I had done so in terms of religious obligation, but many of the objectives, and the means used to attain them, were the same. Frederick, in spite of his appalling personal relationship with his father, admired him as a ruler and freely acknowledged the debt he owed him. "Only his care," he wrote during the Seven Years' War, "his untiring work, his scrupulously just policies, his great and admirable thriftiness and the strict discipline he introduced into the army which he himself had created, made possible the achievements I have so far accomplished."

Like Frederick William I, Frederick thought of kingship as a duty. To him it entailed obligations to be met only by untiring and conscientious work. It was his duty to protect his subjects from foreign attack, to make them prosperous, to give them efficient and honest administration, and to provide them with laws that were simple and adapted to their wants and their particular temperament. In order to achieve these objectives, the ruler must sacrifice his own interests and any purely personal or family feeling. *Raison d'état,* the needs of the state, took precedence over these and also over the immediate comfort and happiness of his subjects. The ruler could carry out his duties effectively only if he kept the reins of government firmly in his own hands. His rule must be personal. He must not rely on ministers who were likely to be influenced by selfish ambitions or factional feeling and who might well keep important information from their master if they were allowed to. Personal rule alone could produce the unity and consistency essential to any successful policy. In his *Anti-Machiavel,* a somewhat conventional discussion of the principles of good government published in 1740 just before his accession, Frederick wrote that there were two sorts of princes—those who ruled in person and those who merely relied on subordinates. The former were "like the soul of a state" and "the weight of their government falls on themselves alone, like the world on the back of Atlas," whereas the second group were mere phantoms. Yet he would have rejected outright, and on the whole with justification, any suggestion that he ruled as a despot. On the contrary, he would have claimed that his power, however great, was exercised only within limits set by law and that the obligations inherent in his position made it impossible for him to govern in an arbitrary way.

Concept of
rulership

The insistence that any effective monarchical rule must be intensely personal had obvious potential dangers. As Frederick grew older, these showed themselves with increasing clarity. His whole psychology was hostile to the development in the Prussian administration or army of any real originality, new ideas, or willingness to take initiatives or accept individual responsibilities. He fostered among those who served him a tendency to play safe and to perform their duties conscientiously but to do no more than that. Under him the Prussian administration was the most honest and hardworking in Europe. Its achievements, however, stemmed from the impetus supplied from above by the king rather than from any creative force inherent in the system itself. The provincial War and Domains Chambers established by Frederick William I in 1722 remained very important, and their number grew from 9 to 12. The General Directory, again created by Frederick William, as the main organ of central government with wide-ranging powers, acquired under Frederick several new departments (for commerce and manufactures in 1740, for mines and metallurgy in 1768, for forestry a few years later) but tended, as the reign went on, to become ossified and to lose a good deal of its former importance. The administration of Silesia after its acquisition in the 1740s was notably efficient, and its resources helped greatly in carrying Frederick through the dark days of the Seven Years' War. But tradition and continuity rather than innovation were the hallmarks of the Prussian administration under him; many of what new departures there were (for example, an effort in 1770 to introduce a system of state examinations for entry into the civil service) were not very effective. Many of the truly successful innovations were in the judicial system, where the reforming efforts of Samuel von Cocceji resulted in all judges in higher and appellate courts being appointed only after they had passed a rigorous examination. Cocceji also inspired the establishment in 1750 of a new Superior Consistory to supervise church and educational affairs and began the process of legal codification that culminated after Frederick's death in the issue of the Prussian Common Law (Das Allgemeine Preussische Landrecht) of 1794, one of the most important 18th-century efforts of this kind. Yet Frederick's unwillingness ever to admit a mistake or change his mind tended, as he grew older, to make the processes of government increasingly rigid and inflexible. The government's refusal to adapt and adjust, which was already visible during the monarch's later years, culminated in the Prussian collapse of 1806 before the armies of Napoleon.

The Prussian army

The overriding objective of Frederick's rule was to increase the power of the state. His desire to foster education and cultural life was sincere, but these humanitarian goals were secondary compared with the task of building a great army and gaining the financial resources needed to maintain it. The army was the pivot around which all else turned, and the administrative system existed essentially to recruit, feed, equip, and pay it. In proportion to the resources available to support it, its size was unequaled anywhere in Europe. In 1740 Frederick inherited a standing army of 83,000 men; when he died, this figure had risen to 190,000 (though of these only about 80,000 were Prussian subjects). Under him it remained a force of peasants and of numerous foreign recruits obtained often by outright kidnapping, officered by landowners. In Prussia the army was recruited almost entirely in the countryside; the function of townsmen was to pay for it through their taxes, not to serve in it. Up to a point Frederick tried to protect the peasants and the soldiers against the demands of the Junker landlord-officers. In 1749 and 1764 he issued decrees limiting the obligations of the peasant to his lord, and in 1748 he ordered officers not to treat their men "like serfs"; but these were essentially efforts to prevent the plight of the peasant from becoming so desperate that he would be driven into flight and thus jeopardize the supply of recruits. Throughout Frederick's reign, army service was for the majority of his subjects the most onerous of all the burdens imposed by the state. In order to finance the great army, heavy demands were made on territories that for the most part were poor. Nothing, however, seemed more important to the monarch than amassing a large reserve of cash to be used for the recruitment of men in case of war. The financial demands that a serious conflict would make were constantly on his mind, and the desperate struggles of 1756–62 confirmed him in his beliefs.

Much of the tax system, based on the excise (largely a tax on food) paid by the towns and the contribution (a complex property tax) raised in the countryside, supplemented by the profits of the extensive royal domains, remained essentially unchanged. Still, Frederick experimented with a number of new taxes, notably with a new system of taxing tobacco and some less important commodities (introduced in 1766 under the supervision of a French entrepreneur, Le Haye de Launay), but these innovations did not bring about significant changes. Indeed, many of Frederick's fiscal policies were ill-judged; for example, the maintenance of a great reserve of cash, which removed from circulation much of the liquid capital of a poor society, was economically damaging. Yet strict control of expenditure and relatively efficient tax collection meant that the government, unlike many others of the age, was never hamstrung by lack of money.

Economic policies

Frederick's economic policies were squarely in the mercantilist tradition. "The foundation of trade and manufactures," he wrote in his *Testament Politique* of 1752, "is to prevent money leaving the country and to make it come in." The direct and simplistic way in which these ideas were sometimes applied can be seen in an order of 1747 forbidding individuals to take more than 300 thalers in specie out of their territories. So far as possible Prussia was to avoid importing foreign manufactured goods, and to this end domestic producers were to be helped by privileges and even outright grants of money. Exports were to be encouraged in the same way. In particular, much money was spent on efforts to develop a substantial silk industry, with generally disappointing results. By the end of the reign textiles of all kinds accounted for two-thirds of Prussia's industrial production, and the textile industry employed about 90 percent of the industrial labour force, but this situation owed little to Frederick's economic policies. Efforts to foster the production of porcelain—which, like silk, was one of the industrial status symbols of a number of 18th-century rulers—were also costly and not very effective. A small number of favoured industrialists, notably David Splitgerber and Johann Ernst Gotzkowsky in the 1750s, benefited by these policies, but for Prussia as a whole they were largely a misuse of resources. Other new creations such as the Maritime Trading Company (Seehandlung), a government-backed corporation set up in 1772 to develop overseas trade, and even the Royal Bank of Berlin, established in 1765, were also marginal to the economic life of Frederick's territories, which, except to some extent in Silesia, in the area around Berlin, and in the little county of Mark in western Germany, continued to be based on agriculture.

Some of the state's programs, however, achieved real success, though sometimes at high cost. Most important was the sustained effort, in the 1760s and '70s, to attract immigrants and to settle them on waste or depopulated land; this settlement program formed the central feature of the *rétablissement,* the making good of the losses of the Seven Years' War. During Frederick's reign more than 300,000 settlers were attracted to Prussia from other parts of Europe—a substantial addition to a population that in 1740 had numbered only about 2,200,000. In addition, the army provided a large market for arms and woolen cloth for uniforms and thus did something to stimulate economic growth. Moreover, in peacetime the soldiers served with their regiments only for a few months of the year, spending the remaining part in agriculture or some urban employment. The fact that they were in this way integrated into society helped to offset the burden that so great a military effort placed on the economy.

The importance of the nobility

Frederick's social policies were as conservative as his economic ones. He considered the nobility the most important class in Prussian society. From it were drawn the majority of the army officers and virtually all the higher-ranking ones. It also produced the majority of his officials and all his ministers and completely dominated local government in the countryside. In Frederick's eyes, the nobility alone of all the social groups had a sense of personal honour and responsibility. The continued existence of the state depended on it, and the regime could not function without its cooperation. Thus its interests were always to be safeguarded. In particular, it was not to be diluted by the grant of noble status to self-made bourgeois, and land owned by noble families was to be protected against purchase by members of the urban middle class, however wealthy. Frederick stated these ideas repeatedly in his voluminous writings on statecraft, notably in the political testaments of 1752 and 1768 drawn up for his successor. Given this attitude, it is not surprising that his reign saw little practical improvement for the peasantry, much of which, in Pomerania, Brandenburg, and East Prussia, was still personally unfree, owing labour services to noble landowners. In principle, Frederick sincerely disliked serfdom. In practice, however, he realized that any rapid move against it risked the disruption of Prussia's agricultural life and the erosion of the position of the all-important nobility. His efforts to improve the lot of his peasant subjects were therefore little more than gestures. As part of his commitment to stimulate recovery from the losses of the Seven Years' War, he tried to abolish serfdom in Prussian Pomerania and also to give the peasantry of Upper Silesia greater security of tenure, but none of this had much practical effect because he never contemplated any significant change in the social order.

Frederick prided himself on being, among rulers, the leading representative of the high culture of his day. He was a prolific writer on contemporary history and politics; his *Histoire de mon temps* (1746) is still a source of some value for the period it covers. He produced large quantities of mediocre poetry and composed music. He invited to Prussia several of the leading French intellectuals of the age, notably Voltaire (with whom he soon quarrelled). But here again his outlook was essentially conservative. Culture to him meant French culture: he wrote and spoke French by preference, using German only when necessary. He had no interest in the profound intellectual stirrings occurring in Germany. Berlin under him never became an important intellectual centre. Gotthold Ephraim Lessing, perhaps the greatest German writer of the mid-18th century, described Prussia as "the most slavish country in Europe," and Carl Philipp Emanuel Bach, the most distinguished of the musicians serving Frederick, did so rather reluctantly. Frederick's religious tolerance, however, was

Enlight-
ened
reforms

genuine: it was one of the things that helped to mark him in the eyes of contemporaries as a truly enlightened ruler. The abolition of judicial torture, one of his first acts as king, also showed his genuine belief in this aspect of enlightened reform. On an even more fundamental level, the General Education Regulations (General-Landschul-Reglement) of 1763 attempted to create a system of universal primary education throughout the Prussian monarchy. Lack of resources limited its practical effect, but it was the most ambitious effort of the kind theretofore seen anywhere in Europe.

Significance of Frederick's reign. Both by his accomplishments and by his example Frederick deeply influenced the course of German history. In the struggles of the 1740s and '50s he weakened still further the tottering structure of the Holy Roman Empire. The bitter Austro-Prussian rivalry that he began was to be a dominant political force in Germany and central Europe for well over a century. Not until the final Prussian victory over Austria in 1866 was the long contest for leadership in Germany finally resolved. For his share in creating the division of the German world Frederick was later attacked, sometimes bitterly, by a number of historians who saw him as having prevented the emergence of a united Great Germany that included all the major German-speaking areas of Europe. Certainly, he had no sympathy, and indeed no understanding, for the embryonic German nationalism. The efforts

of some writers of the 19th and 20th centuries to present him as a forerunner of German national unity are quite misleading. His renewed attack on Maria Theresa of Austria in 1744, for example, frustrated an Austrian invasion of Alsace and its possible return from French to German control, and during the Seven Years' War he offered more than once to cede to France territory in western Germany in the hope of breaking up the coalition that threatened him. Moreover, by his part in the first partition of Poland he helped to create an important common interest with Russia: thenceforth both states had as one of their major objectives the suppression, or at least the strict control, of Polish nationalist aspirations. For generations to come this was to be a factor turning Prussia's attention to eastern Europe and making it less Western in some of its political attitudes than might otherwise have been the case. Yet in many ways Frederick deserved the admiration that later generations, especially in Germany, increasingly felt for him. For all his social and intellectual conservatism he never ceased to feel himself in sympathy with the enlightened intellectual currents and political strivings of the age and with their tolerant and humanitarian aspects. Building on the foundations laid by his father, he consolidated a Prussian ethos of duty, effort, and discipline that, despite some serious negative features, was to become for several generations one of the major political traditions of Europe.

(MATTHEW SMITH ANDERSON)

Southern Africa

South Africa

In the first two decades of the Union, segregation became a distinctive feature of South African political, social, and economic life. It was promoted as actively under the South African Party (1910–24) as it was in the years when J.B.M. Hertzog was premier (1924–39). New statutes provided for racial separation in industrial, territorial, administrative, and residential spheres. It is less than helpful to explain this barrage of legislation as the product of reactionary attitudes inherited from the past. Rather, segregation represented efforts to regulate class and race relations during a period of rapid industrialization, a set of mechanisms for achieving both economic development and the maintenance of white supremacy. Indeed, the central institutions of 20th-century segregation—migrant labour, reserves, compounds, and urban locations—took shape around the gold-mining industry.

The 1911 Mines and Works Act and its 1926 successor reserved certain jobs in mining and the railways for white workers. The Natives Land Act of 1913 defined 8 percent of South Africa as African "reserves" and prohibited any purchase or lease of land by Africans outside the reserves. The law also restricted the terms of tenure under which Africans might live on white-owned farms. The Native (Urban Areas) Act of 1923 provided for segregating urban residential space and created "influx controls" to reduce access to cities by Africans. In 1926 Hertzog published bills proposing simultaneously to increase reserve areas and remove African voters in the Cape from the common roll. These aims were realized in legislation 10 years later. . . .

For Africans, segregation meant restricted mobility, diminished opportunities, more stringent controls, and a general sense of exclusion. Economic conditions in the reserves were deteriorating, on white farms the terms of tenancy became more onerous, and the urban slums provided a harsh alternative for those who left the land. The middle-class leadership of the African National Congress (ANC) had pressed for the extension of the Cape franchise to other provinces. By 1926 it was evident that even this slender link to central political institutions was under threat of severance. These conditions prepared the ground in which the first mass-based African political organiza-

tion flourished. The Industrial and Commercial Workers Union (ICU) was until 1926 a Cape-based union with African and Coloured members drawn mainly from urban areas. It became a mass-based vehicle of rural protest, drawing scores of thousands of supporters from African tenants on white farms. The ICU linked innumerable local rural grievances with a generalized call for land and liberation. By 1929 the ICU was a spent force; unable to meet the expectations it raised in the countryside, it fell apart into several feuding factions.

The mushroom growth of the ICU stimulated radicalism in other organizations. Some ANC leaders, especially Josiah Gumede (president, 1927–30), moved leftward in the late 1920s. The Communist Party of South Africa, founded in 1921, was at first active almost solely within white trade unions, but from 1925 it recruited African members more energetically, and in 1928–29 it called for black majority rule and closer cooperation with the ANC.

These political challenges to white supremacy were reflected in the 1929 general election. For the first time since union, questions of "native policy" dominated white electoral politics. Afrikaner nationalists made "black peril" and "communist menace" their rallying cry. It was not to be the last such occasion. (COLIN J. BUNDY)

The 1930s. The central theme in the history of South Africa since 1930 is the creation and eventual unraveling of the most stringent system of racial segregation and discrimination that the world has known. British troops and South Africans of European descent had completed the conquest of the indigenous Africans by the end of the 19th century, and by 1930 Great Britain had ceased to interfere in South African affairs. The local whites, who never formed more than 21 percent of the total population and were fewer than 14 percent by the 1990s, dominated the South African economy as well as the parliamentary institutions that they had inherited from Great Britain, at the expense of the Africans, Coloureds, and Indians. By 1976 white South Africans had constructed a rigid racial system known as apartheid (separateness), which caused untold misery and poverty and had become notorious throughout the world. The apartheid system then began to fall apart as a result of internal resistance and fundamental changes in the distribution and exercise of power in the neighbouring states and the world beyond. By the 1990s white and black South Africans were groping toward a more egalitarian order, a profoundly difficult enterprise in a society that had become ridden with divisions and violence.

In the early 1930s the South African cabinet was composed of members of the National Party, which held a majority of the seats in the House of Assembly and drew its main support from Afrikaner farmers and intellectuals. The major parliamentary opposition was the South African Party—the party of most of the English-speaking whites, who formed about 45 percent of the white population and included the major industrialists. In 1931 the Hertzog government achieved a major goal when the British Parliament passed the Statute of Westminster, which removed the last vestiges of British legal authority over South Africa. In 1934 the South African Parliament made that decision watertight in South African law by enacting the Status of the Union Act. Meanwhile, the Hertzog government had been losing support through its mismanagement of the problems created by the Great Depression, and in 1933 the prime minister decided to form a coalition with his rival Jan Smuts, the leader of the South African Party. A year later, the two organizations merged to form the United Party, with Hertzog as prime minister and Smuts his deputy.

The two parties and the two leaders had a common interest in favouring the enfranchised population, nearly all of whom were white, at the expense of the unenfranchised, all of whom were black. They agreed in providing massive support for white farmers; in assisting whites to rise above poverty, by providing them with jobs protected from black competition; in endorsing the mining industries' continued use of migrant African workers; in excluding Africans from participation in the conciliation machinery for settling industrial disputes; and in trying to curb the movement of Africans from the reserves into the towns. Furthermore, in 1936, with an overwhelming majority, Parliament removed from the ordinary voters' rolls those relatively few Africans who were qualified to vote; in return, it entitled them to choose three white people to represent them in the House of Assembly, and it created a Native Representative Council with advisory powers.

After 1933, with the improvement in the international economy as the Western powers recovered from the depression, the white farmers prospered; new secondary industries were established; and South Africans of all races began to flock to the towns. South Africa was transformed from an overwhelmingly rural country, producing primary commodities for export and importing manufactured consumption goods, into a country with a diverse and nearly self-sufficient economy. But, although the standard of living of most whites improved greatly from this expansion, there was scarcely any improvement in the lives of Africans, Coloureds, and Asians. The government did add some land to the reserves, but these never exceeded 13 percent of the area of the country, and their condition was deteriorating through overpopulation and soil erosion, making it necessary for a high proportion of the men to work for wages outside the reserves, on the white farms or in the towns. There they were in an unfriendly world. African and Coloured farm labourers, scattered in small groups throughout the agricultural areas, were the most deprived of all South Africans. In the towns, life was insecure for Africans, and wages were low. In the gold-mining industry, the real wages of Africans declined by 15 percent between 1911 and 1941, when white miners were paid 12 times as much as Africans.

The education of Africans was left to Christian missions, whose resources, augmented by small government grants, enabled them to find places for only a small proportion of the African population. Missionaries did, however, run numerous schools, including some excellent high schools that took a few pupils through to the university matriculation level. Missionaries also were the dominant influence in the South African Native College at Fort Hare, which they had founded in 1916 and which included degree courses. These institutions educated a small but increasing number of Africans, who secured jobs as teachers, in the lower reaches of the civil service, or as clergy (especially in

The Statute of Westminster

Role of mission schools

the independent churches, which had broken away from mainstream white churches). Frustrated by the fact that whites did not treat them as equals, some of them took part in opposition politics in the ANC. However, the ANC and two parallel movements—the African Political Organization (a Coloured group) and the South African Indian Congress—had little popular support and exerted scarcely any influence over the main course of events. Their leaders were mission-educated men who had liberal goals and used strictly constitutional methods, such as petitions to the authorities. The radical African ICU had collapsed by 1930; and the Communist Party of South Africa, founded in 1921, made little headway among Africans at that time.

World War II. When Britain declared war on Germany on Sept. 3, 1939, the United Party split. Hertzog proposed that South Africa should be neutral, but Smuts opted for joining Britain. Smuts's faction narrowly won the crucial parliamentary debate, the Hertzogites left the United Party, Smuts became prime minister, and South Africa declared war on Germany.

South Africa made significant contributions to the Allied war effort. Some 135,000 white South Africans fought in the East and North African and Italian campaigns, and 70,000 Africans and Coloureds served as labourers and transport drivers. South African platinum, uranium, and steel were valuable resources and, during the many months while the Mediterranean was closed to the Allies, Durban and Cape Town provisioned a vast number of ships en route from Britain to Suez.

The war was an economic bonanza for South Africa. Stimulated by the reduction of imports, the manufacturing and service industries expanded rapidly, and the flow of Africans and others to the towns, already under way since 1933, became a flood. By the war's end, there were more Africans than whites in the towns. These Africans set up vast squatter camps on the outskirts of the white cities, improvising shelters from whatever materials they could find. They also began to flex their political muscles. They boycotted a Witwatersrand bus company that tried to raise fares; they formed trade unions; and, in 1946, 74,000 African gold miners went on strike for higher wages and improved living conditions.

The government suppressed that strike brutally but had no clear program for the future. White intellectuals proposed a series of reforms within the segregation framework, and the government and private industry made a few concessions, easing the industrial colour bar, increasing African wages, and relaxing the pass laws. But the government failed to discuss these problems with black representatives. It lost credibility in the eyes of educated Africans in 1946 when it snubbed the Native Representative Council for criticizing its handling of the miners' strike and calling for the removal of discriminatory legislation.

Meanwhile, Afrikaners had created a series of ethnic organizations to promote their interests, including an economic association, a federation of Afrikaans cultural associations, and the Broederbond, a secret society of Afrikaner cultural leaders. In 1934 Daniel F. Malan, a former Dutch Reformed minister, had refused to follow Hertzog's Nationalists when they fused with the South African Party to form the United Party. Instead, he formed a new Purified National Party, which became the official parliamentary opposition. During the war, many Afrikaners welcomed the early German victories—some of them committed acts of sabotage—but Malan's party adhered to constitutional methods and gradually gained support from Afrikaner clergy and intellectuals as well as from Afrikaans cultural and economic associations.

The United Party, which had won a general election in 1943 by a large majority, approached the 1948 election complacently. But its policy statements were equivocal on race relations, while the National Party claimed that the government's weakness was threatening white supremacy and produced a statement that used the word apartheid to describe a program of tightened segregation and discrimination. With the support of a tiny fringe group, Malan's National Party won the election by a narrow margin.

Apartheid. After winning the 1948 election, the National Party rapidly consolidated its control over the state,

Afrikaner political organizations

and in subsequent years it won a series of elections with increased majorities. In 1956 Parliament removed the Coloured voters from the common voters' rolls. To do that, the government packed the Senate with its nominated supporters to gain the two-thirds majority in a joint session of both houses required by the constitution. The 1956 law also entitled Coloured people to elect four whites to represent them in Parliament, but that arrangement did not last long. In 1969 the government abolished those seats. That made the electorate exclusively white. Indians had never had parliamentary representation, and the seats of white representatives of Africans were abolished in 1960.

The Republic of South Africa

In 1961, with the approval of a majority of the white voters in a referendum the previous October (but without consultation with any Africans, Coloureds, or Indians), South Africa became a republic. The government had hoped that the country would follow a 1947 precedent, when India became a republic but continued to be a member of the British Commonwealth; but, meeting criticism from other Commonwealth members, it withdrew South Africa from that loose association.

At home, the government vigorously furthered its ethnic goals. It made it compulsory for white children to attend schools that were conducted in their home language, either Afrikaans or English (except for the few who went to private schools). It advanced Afrikaners to top positions in the civil service, the army, the police, and the state corporations, such as the South African Broadcasting Corporation, which had a monopoly of radio services. It also awarded official contracts to Afrikaner banks and insurance companies. These methods raised the living standards of Afrikaners toward those of English-speaking white South Africans.

Except for a recession during the early 1960s, the economy grew rapidly until the late 1970s. By that time, with a mixture of public and private enterprise, South Africa possessed a modern infrastructure, which was by far the most advanced in Africa: efficient financial institutions; a national network of roads as well as railways; modernized port facilities in Cape Town and Durban; and, besides the long-established diamond-, gold-, and coal-mining industries, a wide range of factories. The private sector was dominated by two great interlocking giants: the Anglo American Corporation of South Africa, founded by Ernest Oppenheimer in 1917, and De Beers Consolidated Mines. They formed the core of one of the world's most powerful networks of mining, industrial, and financial companies, employing 800,000 workers on six continents. State corporations controlled industries that were vital to national security, notably ARMSCOR (Armaments Corporation of South Africa), which produced high-quality military equipment, and SASOL (South African Coal, Oil, and Gas Corporation), which alleviated South Africa's lack of petroleum resources by converting coal to gasoline and diesel fuel. This burgeoning economy was buoyant enough to sustain the cost of a drastic program of social engineering. The man who played the major part in transforming apartheid from an election slogan into practice was Hendrik F. Verwoerd. Born in The Netherlands, Verwoerd immigrated with his parents to South Africa when he was a child. He became a nominated senator in 1948, minister of native affairs in 1950, and prime minister from 1958 to 1966, when a deranged man assassinated him in Parliament. According to Verwoerd, the South African population comprised four distinct racial groups (white, African, Coloured, and Asian), each with an inherent culture; whites were the "civilized" group and, as such, entitled to control the state.

Program of Hendrik Verwoerd

Parliament passed a plethora of laws to give effect to these ideas. The Population Registration Act (1950) classified every South African by race. There were laws to prohibit interracial marriage or sex. Other laws and regulations segregated South Africans in every sphere of life: in buses, taxis, and hearses; in cinemas, restaurants, and hotels; in trains and railway waiting rooms. When a court declared that separate amenities should be equal, Parliament passed a special law to override it. Under the Group Areas Act (1950), the cities and towns were divided into segregated residential and business areas, and the government removed thousands of Coloureds and Indians from areas classified for white occupation.

A vast bureaucracy, staffed largely by party loyalists, administered apartheid, aided by a mass of coercive laws. The Suppression of Communism Act of 1950 defined communism and its aims sweepingly and empowered the government to detain anyone it deemed likely to further any communist aims. Later laws gave the police the right to arrest and detain people without trial and without access to families or lawyers and left the courts with scarcely any means to intervene.

Africans were treated as "tribal" people, domiciled in the reserves under hereditary chiefs and bound to live there except when they were working for whites. In 1951 the government abolished the Native Representative Council. Then it began to consolidate the scattered reserves into 8 (eventually 10) distinct territories, designating each of them as the "homeland" of a specific African ethnic community. It also manipulated homeland politics so that compliant chiefs controlled the administrations of most of those territories. Claiming to match the decolonization process that was taking place in tropical Africa, the government devolved powers onto those administrations and eventually encouraged them to become "independent." Between 1976 and 1981 four accepted independence: Transkei, Bophuthatswana, Venda, and Ciskei. However, like the other homelands, they were economic backwaters, dependent on subsidies from Pretoria, and not a single foreign government recognized them.

The "homelands"

Conditions in the homelands rapidly deteriorated, partly because they had to accommodate vast numbers of additional Africans. Attempting to reverse the flood of Africans into the towns, the government strengthened the pass laws, making it illegal for an African to be in a town for more than 72 hours without a job in a white home or business. By 1983, in particularly brutal series of forced removals, it had ejected more than 3.5 million Africans from the towns and from white rural areas (including lands they had occupied for generations) and dumped them in the reserves.

The government also established direct control over the education of Africans. In the Bantu Education Act of 1953, it took African schools away from the missions. Then, to meet the expanding economy's increasing demand for semiskilled black labour, it created more African schools, especially in the lower grades, but subjected the students to stringent discipline and prescribed syllabi and textbooks that endorsed official policies.

A 1959 law prohibited the established universities from accepting black students, except with special permission on an individual basis. Instead, the government created five new ethnic university colleges—one for Coloureds, one for Indians, one for Zulus, and one for Sotho, Tswana, and Venda students, plus a medical school for Africans—and transformed the South African Native College at Fort Hare, which missionaries had founded primarily but not exclusively for Africans, into a state college solely for Xhosa students. It staffed these ethnic colleges with white supporters of the National Party and subjected the students to stringent controls.

Resistance to apartheid. Apartheid imposed appallingly heavy burdens on most South Africans. The economic gap between the wealthy few, nearly all of whom were white, and the poor masses, virtually all of whom were African, Coloured, or Indian, was larger than in any other country. The whites were well fed, well housed, and well cared for; Indians, Coloureds, and especially Africans suffered from widespread poverty, malnutrition, and disease. Consequently, despite the growth of the national economy, for most South Africans life was a struggle for day-to-day survival.

Nevertheless, during the 1950s the previously moribund ANC came to life under a vigorous president, Albert Lutuli, and three younger men—Oliver Tambo and Nelson Mandela, who ran a joint law practice in Johannesburg, and Walter Sisulu. In cooperation with the South African Indian Congress, which had also been revitalized, they organized a passive resistance campaign in 1952, when thousands of volunteers defied discriminatory laws. Three years later, in conjunction with Indians, Coloureds, and sympathetic whites, they convened a mass meeting (Congress of the People) that adopted the Freedom Charter, asserting that "South Africa belongs to all who live in it, black or white, and no Government can justly claim authority unless it is based on the will of the people." The government broke up the meeting and subsequently arrested 156 people and charged them with high treason. None was found guilty, but the trial dragged on until 1961, when the last of the accused were released.

In 1959 a group of Africans led by Robert Sobukwe, a language teacher at the University of the Witwatersrand, believing that the alliances with white, Coloured, and Indian organizations had impeded the struggle for African liberation, broke away from the ANC and founded the Pan-Africanist Congress (PAC). On March 21, 1960, the PAC launched a fresh campaign. Thousands of unarmed Africans invited arrest by presenting themselves at police stations without passes; and at Sharpeville, near Johannesburg, the police opened fire on such a crowd, killing 69 and wounding 178 Africans, most of whom were shot in the back as they were running away. Thousands of workers then went on strike, and in Cape Town 30,000 Africans marched in a peaceful protest to the centre of the city. The government reestablished control by force: it mobilized the army, outlawed the ANC and the PAC, and arrested more than 11,000 people under emergency regulations.

These events led to the change in the strategy of the congresses. Previously, they had confined themselves to non-violent methods. After Sharpeville, however, the ANC and PAC leaders and some of their white sympathizers came to the conclusion that black people would never overcome apartheid by peaceful means alone. Violence, they concluded, was a necessary and legitimate means of resistance to the violence of an illegitimate regime. However, although their military units detonated several bombs in government buildings during the next few years, they did not pose a serious threat to the state, which had a virtual monopoly of modern weapons. By 1964 the government had captured many of the leaders, including Mandela and Sobukwe, and sentenced them to long terms of imprisonment on Robben Island, in Table Bay four miles from Cape Town. Hundreds of others fled the country. Oliver Tambo presided over an exiled ANC executive in Zambia.

A new phase of resistance began in 1973, when black trade unions organized a series of strikes for higher wages and improved working conditions. Moreover, Steve Biko and other African students founded a Black Consciousness Movement that appealed to Africans to take pride in their own culture. That ideology was immensely attractive to young Africans. On June 16, 1976, thousands of children in Soweto, the African township outside Johannesburg, demonstrated against the government's insistence that they should be taught in Afrikaans rather than in English. Police opened fire, touching off a nationwide cycle of protest and repression. Once again the government reestablished control by force. Within a year, it had banned many more organizations and the police had killed more than 500 people, including Biko. Those events received worldwide execration. In 1973 the UN General Assembly had declared apartheid to be "a crime against humanity," and in 1977 the UN Security Council unanimously voted a mandatory embargo on the export of arms to South Africa.

The unraveling of apartheid. By 1978 the illusion that apartheid would bring peace to South Africa was shattered. Most of the homelands were economic and political disasters. Their only significant export was labour, and most of their leaders were corrupt and unpopular. The national economy was in recession. Skilled whites were emigrating and inflation was running high. Moreover, the global environment was changing. The Portuguese had handed over the government of Angola and Mozambique to Africans in 1974–75, and the writing was on the wall for Ian Smith's white regime in Rhodesia (which would come under African control as Zimbabwe in 1980). Increasingly isolated as the last bastion of white racial domination, South Africa had become the focus of global denunciation.

By that time, the National Party was passing under the control of a new class of urban Afrikaners—businessmen and intellectuals who, like their English-speaking white counterparts, believed that reforms should be introduced to appease foreign and domestic critics. The first attempt to give effect to their ideas occurred after Pieter W. Botha, who had been a National Party politician throughout his adult life, succeeded Balthazar J. Vorster as prime minister in 1978. Botha's administration applied a mixture of carrots and sticks. It repealed the bans on interracial sex and marriage; it desegregated many hotels, restaurants, trains, and buses; it removed the reservation of skilled jobs for whites; and it repealed the pass laws. Provided that black trade unions registered, they were entitled to access to a new industrial court and permitted to strike. Also, a new constitution created separate parliamentary bodies for Indians and for Coloureds and vested great powers in an executive president, namely P.W. Botha.

However, the Botha reforms stopped short of making any real change in the distribution of power. The white parliamentary chamber could override the Coloured and Indian chambers on matters of national significance, and all Africans remained disenfranchised. The Group Areas Act and the Land Acts maintained residential segregation. Schools and health and welfare services for Africans, Indians, and Coloureds remained segregated and inferior, and most nonwhites, especially Africans, were still desperately poor. Moreover, Botha used the State Security Council—which was dominated by military officers—rather than the cabinet as his major policy-making body, and he embarked on a massive military buildup.

In 1979, in an effort to limit South Africa's economic domination of the region, South Africa's black neighbours formed the Southern African Development Coordinating Conference (SADCC), but it made little progress. Most of the export trade of the region continued to pass through South Africa to South African ports, and South Africa provided employment for 280,000 migrant workers from neighbouring countries. Botha also used South Africa's military strength to restrain those countries from pursuing antiapartheid policies. He kept South West Africa/Namibia under South African domination, sent military raids into every other southern African state, and assisted the Renamo rebels in Mozambique and the UNITA faction in its civil war in Angola.

During the 1980s the conservative British and American administrations of Margaret Thatcher and Ronald Reagan, respectively, faced increasingly vociferous pressures for sanctions against South Africa. In 1986 a high-level Commonwealth mission went to South Africa in an unsuccessful effort to persuade the government to suspend its military actions in the townships, release political prisoners, and stop destabilizing neighbouring countries. Later that year, American public resentment of South Africa's racial policies was strong enough for the U.S. Congress to pass a Comprehensive Anti-Apartheid Act over a presidential veto, banning new investments and loans, ending air links, and prohibiting the importation of many commodities. Other governments took similar actions.

Meanwhile, in 1983, 1,000 black and white representatives of 575 community bodies, trade unions, sporting bodies, and women's and youth organizations launched the United Democratic Front. There followed a vast escalation of strikes, boycotts, and attacks on black police and urban councilors. Under strong pressure from white hawks, the Botha government decided to resist those pressures. In 1985 it applied a state of emergency in many parts of the country; a year later it declared a nationwide state of emergency and embarked on a savage attempt to eliminate all opposition. For three years police and soldiers patrolled the African townships in armed vehicles, destroying black squatter camps and detaining and abusing thousands of Africans, while the army also continued its forays into neighbouring countries. A rigid censorship tried to conceal those actions by banning television, radio, and newspaper coverage. The resort to brute force did not create stability. By 1989 the apartheid regime was in crisis. Clergy such as Anglican Archbishop Desmond Tutu defied the emergency regulations; strikes continued, including a massive strike by the National Union of Mineworkers; and saboteurs caused an increasing number of deaths and injuries. The South African economy was severely strained by the costs of administering apartheid, of military adventurism, and of sanctions. The gross domestic product was decreasing, inflation was above 14 percent per annum, and there was a dearth of investment capital. Moreover, in 1988 the army had suffered a military setback in Angola, after which the government signed an accord paving the way for the removal of Cuban troops from Angola and the UN-supervised independence of Namibia in 1990. In these circumstances, many whites came to realize that there was no stopping the incorporation of Africans into the South African political system.

In 1989 P.W. Botha stepped down first as party leader and then as president. To succeed him, the National Party parliamentary caucus elected Frederik W. de Klerk. The Transvaal leader of the party, de Klerk was 21 years younger than Botha and more sensitive to the dynamics of a world where racism was anathema and democracy was on the rise in eastern Europe and the Soviet Union. On Feb. 2, 1990, de Klerk announced a radical program. Shortly afterward he released Mandela, a skillful and charismatic leader, from prison and lifted the state of emergency. During 1991 Parliament abolished the Group Areas Act and the Land Acts; political prisoners were freed and their colleagues returned from exile.

Both de Klerk and Mandela, who was elected president of the ANC in 1991 (since his predecessor, Tambo, was in poor health), were committed to negotiations that should lead to the introduction of a new South African constitution, though they differed about the membership of a constitution-making body and about the substance of such a document. Both of them, however, were hard put to hold their followers together. De Klerk was losing

the support of white conservatives, who were unwilling to forfeit their power and privileges; Mandela's freedom of maneuver was constrained by radical members of the ANC, who included communists, as well as by the PAC and another splinter group, the Azanian People's Organization (AZAPO), which feared a sellout.

The negotiation process was marred by massive violence, especially in Natal and in the industrial heart of the country in the southern Transvaal. African society was riddled with fissures—some ethnic, some regional, and some related to class and generational differences. In particular, there were conflicts between supporters of the ANC and supporters of Inkatha, a well-organized ethnic movement led by Chief Mangosuthu Buthelezi, chief minister of KwaZulu, the Zulu homeland; but such clashes merged into warfare between rival African gangs and anomic violence. The government assisted Inkatha financially, and right-wing whites, with or without links to the police or the army, were determined to prevent the erosion of white supremacy and provoked some of those conflicts.

Whatever the outcome of the negotiation process, apartheid will cast a long shadow over South Africa. Most living South Africans have suffered profound psychological damage from hunger, insecurity, and social disruption. Africans, Coloureds, and Indians expect that a new regime will improve their health, their education, and their housing and provide them with employment at adequate wages and with decent working conditions. It will be extremely difficult for the country to generate enough wealth to satisfy such expectations. South Africans and their governments will have to grapple with the legacy of apartheid for years to come.   (LEONARD MONTEATH THOMPSON)

Constitutional negotiations

Union of Soviet Socialist Republics

THE INTERREGNUM: ANDROPOV AND CHERNENKO

Toward the end of his life, Brezhnev lost control of the country. Regionalism became stronger as the centre faltered. When Brezhnev died on Nov. 10, 1982, he was succeeded as party leader by Yury Andropov, although his chosen successor was Konstantin Chernenko. Andropov had been head of the KGB from 1967 to May 1982. He then slipped into the Central Committee secretariat after Mikhail Suslov, the dry, severe guardian of ideological rectitude, died. Without this move he could not have become party leader. By June 1983 Andropov had also become president of the U.S.S.R. and chairman of the defense council—all the posts that Brezhnev had filled.

Andropov was the best-informed man in the U.S.S.R. and set about reforming the country. He was a cautious reformer, believing that there was nothing fundamentally wrong with the socialist system. He believed that more discipline, energy, and initiative would turn things around. Corruption, absenteeism, and alcoholism were rife and were his special concerns. The retail trade system and transportation were targeted and felt his reforming zeal. His leadership style was in sharp contrast to that of the opulent, pompous Brezhnev. He cut back privilege and met workers on the shop floor. Andropov's antialcohol campaign was well conceived but it led to a sharp fall in government revenue. His industrial and agricultural policy was quite sensible but ineffective, since the economy was already in terminal decline.

Reformers under Andropov

Under Andropov a group of cautious reformers rose to prominence. These included Mikhail Gorbachev, Yegor Ligachev, and Nikolay Ryzhkov. Andropov wanted Gorbachev to succeed him and added a paragraph to this effect to his report to a Central Committee plenum that did not convene until after his death on Feb. 9, 1984. Instead the 72-year-old, terminally ill Konstantin Chernenko was eased into the top party post and later became president of the U.S.S.R. and chairman of the defense council. The aging Politburo had plumped for a nonreformer, a throwback to Brezhnevism. However, Gorbachev became "second"

secretary, with responsibility for chairing Politburo meetings when Chernenko was away or unfit—which turned out to be quite often. But Chernenko did set a precedent: he became the first politician to succeed as party leader after having previously failed. Party privilege again grew under Chernenko. The military did not have things all their own way. The able, dynamic chief of staff, Marshal Nikolay Ogarkov, was moved sideways and replaced by Marshal Sergey Akhromeyev, another formidable soldier. Ogarkov was blamed for his aggressive promotion of the SS-20 missile program and for the shooting down of a Korean jet, Flight 007, with 269 passengers and crew on board, after it had strayed into Soviet airspace in September 1983. The incident caused an international furor and increased tension between NATO and the Warsaw Pact countries.

THE GORBACHEV ERA

Gorbachev's succession. There appears to have been a tacit agreement among Politburo members that on Chernenko's death Gorbachev would take over. But some of them were having second thoughts. Grigory Romanov, Central Committee secretary for the military economy and previously party boss in Leningrad, and Viktor Grishin, Moscow party leader, both decided to try for the highest office in the land, that of party leader. Ligachev later confirmed that a power struggle had taken place and that the Soviet foreign minister Andrey Gromyko, the party control commission chairman Mikhail Solomentsev, and the KGB boss Viktor Chebrikov had ensured that Gorbachev outmaneuvered Grishin. Ligachev, even though he was not at that time a member of the Politburo, later claimed that he had played a significant role in Gorbachev's election through his role as Central Committee secretary in charge of organizational work. He carefully selected the Central Committee members who were invited to a hastily convened plenum on March 11, 1985, that confirmed Gorbachev as leader. About a third of the membership was not present. Ligachev became "second" secretary since the Politburo empowered him to chair Central Committee secretariat meetings. He was also to be in control of cadres and ideology. The normal practice was for the general secretary to head the secretariat. Hence Gorbachev started with a considerable handicap, since all personnel changes would be the subject of intense bargaining and horse trading. Gorbachev turned out to be a skillful horse trader. In April 1985 Ligachev became a full member of the Politburo and was replaced as cadres chief by Georgy Razumovsky. Gorbachev's nominee was Aleksandr Yakovlev, who became secretary for propaganda and overseer of the media. *Glasnost* His task was to expand *glasnost* ("openness") and protect creative writers and journalists against Ligachev's ire. Gorbachev managed to make Yakovlev a full member of the Politburo by June 1987. He was a strategic ally in the battle to restructure the Soviet political and economic system. In July 1985 Romanov left the Politburo and secretariat, and Boris Yeltsin, first party secretary in Sverdlovsk, and Lev Zaikov, party boss in Leningrad province, joined. Yeltsin appears to have been an appointee of Gorbachev and Zaikov Ligachev. In July Gorbachev managed to get Gromyko elected president and Eduard Shevardnadze appointed as foreign minister and a full member of the Politburo. In September the octogenarian Tikhonov made way for Nikolay Ryzhkov as prime minister. At the 27th Party Congress in February–March 1986 there were wholesale changes. Yeltsin became a candidate member of the Politburo on becoming Moscow party leader. Gorbachev's brief to him was to clean up the notoriously corrupt Moscow apparat. Grishin had been known as "the Godfather." About 52 percent of the newly elected Central Committee were new appointees. The new moderate reform team was in place.

Economic and social reforms. When Gorbachev took office in March 1985 he was clear about his policy preferences. In a speech on Dec. 10, 1984, he spoke of the need to effect "deep transformations in the economy and the whole system of social relations," to carry through the policies of *perestroika* ("restructuring" of economic management), the "democratization of social and economic life," and *glasnost*. He underlined the need for greater social justice, a more important role for local soviets, and more participation by workers at the workplace. His goal was to set in motion a revolution controlled from above. He did not wish to undermine the Soviet system, only to make it more efficient. The leading role of the party and the central direction of the economy were to stay. Under Andropov he had attended seminars by such radical scholars as Tatyana Zaslavskaya and Abel Aganbegyan. He accepted Zaslavskaya's main point that the "command-administrative system" was dragging the country down and would ruin it if not dismantled.

Initially Gorbachev continued Andropov's reforms. He insisted on acceleration of economic growth and spoke of "perfecting" the system. Machine building was given preference as light and consumer goods took second place. There was to be more technical innovation and worker discipline. He was enthusiastic about the antialcohol campaign and was dubbed the "mineral water general secretary." All this produced few positive results. He overlooked the obvious point that workers require greater incentives if they are to give of their best. His policy led to a fall in the consumer goods available, and agriculture did not blossom. At the 27th Party Congress Gorbachev spoke of the need for far-reaching reforms to get the economy going. The first clear evidence that Gorbachev and his *Yeltsin's* supporters had moved to the offensive against the ex- *criticisms* isting party order surfaced at the congress. The centre *of the* of contention was Boris Yeltsin, who shocked delegates *party* by strongly criticizing the privileges of the party apparat. Among his targets were the special shops for the elite, which also had been denounced in a *Pravda* article just before the congress. Ligachev responded by vitriolically attacking the *Pravda* article and the raising of the issue in the first place. Gromyko supported him. The battle lines had been drawn. Thereafter Ligachev would be the principal defender of the rights of the party apparat and of the existing order in general.

Glasnost was put to the test on April 26, 1986, when

a reactor at the Chernobyl nuclear plant exploded. Gorbachev waited 18 days before going on television to give an account of the worst nuclear disaster in history. Chernobyl had a profoundly negative effect on the population's thinking about nuclear power and provided a powerful stimulus to the growth of a Green (environmental) movement. Afterward the regime became much more open about natural disasters, drug abuse, and crime. *Glasnost* took hold and produced much greater freedom of expression and open criticism of the political order. Gorbachev sought to win over the intelligentsia by bringing the dissident physicist Andrey Sakharov and his wife, Yelena Bonner, back to Moscow from exile in Gorky. The intelligentsia's support was perceived to be critical if the battle with the bureaucracy was to be won.

Perestroika concentrated initially on economic reform. Enterprises were encouraged to become self-financing, cooperatives were set up by groups of people as businesses, and land could be leased to allow family farming. But the bureaucrats who ran the economy rightly feared that these activities would undermine their privileges and power. Cooperatives were heavily taxed, supplies were difficult to procure, and the public was often hostile. Lessees of land had to be very resilient to succeed.

Political restructuring. A major problem for Gorbachev was that there was no agreement at the top as to what *perestroika, glasnost,* and democratization should achieve. The radical reformers, Gorbachev, Yakovlev, and Shevardnadze, were outflanked by the moderate reformers, Ligachev, Ryzhkov, and others. The problem was compounded by an apparent lack of clarity in Gorbachev's own thinking. He was never able to construct a coherent goal and the means of reaching it. His frustrations with the party apparat led him to formulate a very radical solution—to emasculate it. He wanted to exclude it from day-to-day involvement in the management of the economy and to end its dominance over the state legislature and party affairs. The secretariat had been the party's brain, and all key decisions had been taken there. Gorbachev wanted to end the party officials' domination of *End* the soviets. He achieved this remarkable feat at the 19th *of the* Party Conference in June 1988. The party thereby lost *party's* its dominant role at the centre of the political process *dominance* but gained its revenge on Gorbachev by consolidating its power at the periphery, where the weak soviets were no match for it. Hence there was a centrifugal flow of power from the centre to the periphery. This process had been under way since the death of Stalin, and the removal of Khrushchev had underlined the influence of local party officials. The Brezhnev era further added to the flow of power to the periphery.

Elections to the U.S.S.R. Congress of People's Deputies, which replaced the U.S.S.R. Supreme Soviet as the highest organ of state power, took place in March 1989. About 88 percent of the deputies were communists, but by then the Communist Party was no longer a monolithic party. The congress elected from among its members a bicameral legislature (called the Supreme Soviet), each house having 271 members. Gorbachev chaired the proceedings. Boris Yeltsin became a member of the Supreme Soviet after another deputy stood down in his favour. Yeltsin had been sacked as Moscow party leader and from his Politburo membership in November 1987 after a furious row with Ligachev. Gorbachev chose not to back him up. Thus began the titanic struggle between Gorbachev and Yeltsin that was to result in Gorbachev's political destruction. As a deputy Yeltsin had a national platform for the first time and used it very skillfully. The main focus of his attacks were party privilege, the lack of success of *perestroika,* the need for market reforms, and personal criticism of Gorbachev's leadership.

The new pattern at the top was repeated in each republic. Congresses were elected and Supreme Soviets emerged from them. Local soviet elections also took place in early 1990 and led to many shocks. Communist officials, encouraged by Gorbachev to stand, were often defeated even when standing as the only candidate. In order to be elected, a deputy needed more than 50 percent of the votes cast. *Glasnost* permitted non-Russian nationalities to voice their opposition to Russian and communist domination and led to a growth of nationalism and regionalism. This was exacerbated by economic decline. In the Baltic republics, especially, many argued that they could run their economic affairs better than Moscow. Interethnic strife and conflict intensified and sometimes resulted in bloodshed. The conflict in Nagorno-Karabakh, an Armenian-dominated enclave in Azerbaijan, was the most violent and bitter. The newly-elected Supreme Soviets could claim to speak for the population. This was especially true in the Baltic. Multiparty politics became legitimate in 1990, when Article 6 of the constitution, which had guaranteed a communist monopoly, was removed. Hundreds, indeed thousands of informal associations and then parties sprang up in the receptive climate of *glasnost* and democratization. Popular fronts, most noticeably in the Baltic, united all those opposing Moscow rule and seeking independence. As these fronts dominated the Supreme Soviets they could pass declarations of sovereignty. In March 1990 Lithuania went further and declared itself independent. In May 1990 Yeltsin became, despite Gorbachev's bitter opposition, chairman of the Russian Supreme Soviet. The following month the Russian S.F.S.R. declared itself a sovereign state. It claimed that its laws took precedence over Soviet laws. Gorbachev ruled this invalid. This was the pattern in every republic that had declared itself sovereign. It was known as the "war of laws." As a consequence, the survival of the U.S.S.R. became an issue.

Gorbachev soon tired of the "new-look" U.S.S.R. Supreme Soviet and cast his net even wider in his search for a model. He eventually chose an executive presidency based on a mixture of the U.S. and French presidencies. Following U.S. custom he needed a vice president. Unfortunately he chose Gennady Yanayev—the Kazakh leader Nursultan Nazarbayev and Shevardnadze having turned down the job. The U.S.S.R. Council of Ministers was abolished and replaced by a cabinet of ministers subordinate to the president. On paper Gorbachev had achieved his ambition: he was chief decision maker and indeed a constitutional dictator. His authority, or his ability to make decisions, had never been higher. However, the power that accompanies the post of president in the United States and France was not transmitted to him. His power or ability to have his decisions implemented declined daily.

The impetus for reform came from the politically active part of the Communist Party and society. However, opposition to *perestroika* was fiercest among the same group. The reformers knew that the party and state apparat were past masters at blocking reforms that they perceived to be inimical to their interests. The only way to drive through a reform was to use a battering ram. During the first three years Gorbachev launched a series of reforms. Each time he encountered opposition from party conservatives, he retreated and sought another route to advance. According to Yakovlev, one of the architects of *perestroika* and its main theorist, the revolution from above reached a critical point at the 19th Party Conference in June 1988. There Gorbachev was presented with a stark choice: to advance and transform *perestroika* into a "genuinely popular democratic revolution, go all the way and afford society total freedom" or to pull back, remain a communist reformer, and stay within the well-known milieu of the bureaucracy. Yakovlev saw various dangers facing *perestroika:* it could be suffocated by Stalinist reaction or Brezhnevite conservatism or be highjacked by officials mouthing its slogans while they redistributed power among themselves. The choice was between genuine or controlled democracy. In early 1988 Fyodor Burlatsky was a member of a small group under the chairmanship of Anatoly Lukyanov. The latter proposed a two-stage approach to the election of a Supreme Soviet. Legal authority was to be vested in local soviets, but the relationship between the party and the soviets was left vague. Burlatsky proposed direct elections of the Supreme Soviet, president, and vice president, but everyone opposed this except Yakovlev. Gorbachev could have effected a political revolution but, true to his low-risk strategy, chose Lukyanov's proposal. This was a fatal mistake. Had Gorbachev stood for election as president, he might have won. He would then have become the

people's president. Instead he had himself elected by the U.S.S.R. Congress of People's Deputies, a body dominated by communists. Unfortunately for Gorbachev he had opened Pandora's box. Social and political forces awakened by *perestroika* could not be regulated from above. If Gorbachev would not claim them as his constituency, then others would. The Communist Party resisted the march toward democracy and lost its more radical members. They set up their own groups and challenged the party head-on. Boris Yeltsin emerged as the most likely leader of the radical constituency. His election as chairman of the Russian parliament in May 1990 proved to be a turning point for Gorbachev. Yeltsin became a pole of attraction for frustrated, radical, especially economic, reformers. Gorbachev's greatest mistakes were made in economic policy.

Economic policy. The economic stagnation of the late Brezhnev era was the result of various factors: the exhaustion of easily available resources, especially raw materials, and the growing structural imbalance of the economy due to the distorting effects of the incentive system, which paralyzed initiative and dissuaded people from doing an honest day's work. Under *perestroika* the economy moved from stagnation to crisis, and this deepened as time passed. Hence the policies of *perestroika* must carry much of the blame for the economic catastrophe that resulted. Gorbachev admitted in 1988 that the first two years had been wasted since he was unaware of the depth of the crisis when he took over. This is an extraordinary statement for a party leader to make. Either he had paid little attention to the underlying trends of the economy or no one at the top was aware of the real situation. The latter is probably more accurate, since the state planning commission, Gosplan, had no model of how the economy functioned. The Soviet gross national product (GNP) was almost stagnant during the first four years of *perestroika* and did not fall. Unemployment remained at about 4 percent of the labour force, almost all in the labour-surplus areas of Central Asia and the Caucasus. Open inflation remained low until 1989. Underlying trends, however, pointed to systemic failure. Shortages, endemic to all planned economies, became serious from the mid-1980s. By mid-1990 more than 1,000 basic consumer goods were very seldom on sale. Rationing became widespread, with most goods being sold at the point of work. Queueing became the national pastime: a 1990 estimate put it at 30–40 million man-, or rather woman-, hours a year. The only thing that was not in short supply was money. This was due to a rapidly growing budget deficit, first evident in 1987. Then the Law on State Enterprises, effective from January 1988, permitted managers to increase wages to cope with the tight labour situation. These increases were far in excess of productivity growth. The State Bank lost control of monetary growth. The plan for 1990 was a growth of 10 billion rubles, but it turned out to be about 28 billion rubles. Social benefits, amounting to about a quarter of the gross family income, were always modest by international standards. However, in 1990 they increased by 21 percent as a result of the U.S.S.R. Congress of People's Deputies voting to increase a whole raft of benefits, noticeably pensions. Since there were no resources to meet this extra expenditure, the budget deficit grew, as did the money supply. The kolkhoz, the comparatively free market in which peasants sold their surplus produce, is a rough guide to price trends: prices between 1985 and 1988 increased by less than 1 percent annually, but in 1989 they jumped 9.5 percent and in 1990 by 29 percent.

Responsibility for the budget deficit rested fairly and squarely on the shoulders of the Gorbachev leadership. Traditionally the budget deficit had been 2 or 3 percent of GNP. The years 1985 and 1986 changed all that. Gorbachev's desire to achieve faster growth—the policy advocated by Aganbegyan, his chief economic adviser, was acceleration—resulted in the 12th Five-Year Plan (1986–90) being returned three times to Gosplan with instructions to raise targets. In 1986 the budget deficit rose to 6 percent of GNP. The Gorbachev leadership did not mention the subject in public until 1988. By then the deficit had risen to more than 10 percent. The result of all this was to throw the industrial sector into imbalance from 1985 onward. The Law on the State Enterprise further aggravated the problem.

Between 1985 and 1987 the Gorbachev leadership increased investment and defense expenditure, while at the same time state revenue was declining owing to a fall in alcohol sales and lower prices for export goods. From 1988 the situation became dire. In 1991 the economy was facing total collapse. The government found it increasingly difficult to intervene decisively. The Law on the State Enterprise reduced the power of the ministries, and simultaneously the number of officials was cut back sharply. Those who remained were overwhelmed by the work load. Since there was no effective control from Moscow, rising nationalism, ethnic strife, and regionalism fragmented the economy into dozens of mini-economies. Many republics sought independence, others sovereignty, and they all pursued policies of economic autarky. Barter was widespread. Ukraine introduced coupons, and Moscow issued ration cards.

Foreign trade suffered. Lower oil prices and economic fragmentation caused the hard currency debt to rise from U.S. $25.6 billion at the end of 1984 to about $80 billion at the end of 1991. Imports from the West were cut back sharply between 1985 and 1987. These were almost exclusively consumer goods and not capital goods, which often could not be installed. The public vented its frustration. This led to a complete reversal, and imports from the West rose by almost 50 percent between 1987 and 1989. As a consequence, by 1989 the Soviets could no longer service their hard currency debt on time.

Recalculations of Soviet economic performance by Soviet statisticians widened the gap between the Soviet and U.S. economies. The official view was that the Soviet national income was about 64 percent of the U.S. level in 1988. Gorbachev, in a speech in October 1990, implied that the real figure was about 40 percent. Another estimate put the real level at about 46 percent in 1970, declining to 40 percent in 1987.

Gorbachev received much advice on how to solve the Soviet Union's economic crisis. There were two basic solutions: the socialist solution and the market solution. The Ryzhkov group favoured central planning, more efficient administration, and greater decision-making powers for enterprises and farms. State ownership of the means of production would continue. They called it a "regulated market economy." The radicals, led by Stanislav Shatalin, Nikolay Petrakov, and Grigory Yavlinsky, wanted a move toward a free-market economy. This involved private ownership of enterprises, land, services, and so on. It also meant the freeing of prices. Gorbachev could not make up his mind and always tried to persuade the two groups to pool their resources and arrive at a compromise. The radicals thought they had convinced Gorbachev in the autumn of 1990 to introduce a 500-day program that would have implemented a market economy, but he changed his mind and sided with the conservatives. This was a fatal mistake. It left him without a viable economic policy, and the right felt that if they applied enough pressure he would always abandon radical solutions.

One of the reasons Gorbachev shied away from the market was price liberalization. He would not risk sharp price rises because of the fear of social unrest. Despite the abundant evidence of the seriousness of the situation in 1988, the critical year, Gorbachev and other leading communists refused to draw the necessary lessons. At the 19th Party Conference in June 1988 Leonid Abalkin pointed out that the country was still suffering from stagnation. Gorbachev and others criticized him and adopted a motion claiming that the economic decline had been halted. The election of the U.S.S.R. Congress of People's Deputies made it virtually impossible for the Gorbachev leadership to adopt austerity measures. The popular mood was one of spend, spend, spend. Gorbachev paid only cursory attention to the economy until late 1989. A charitable explanation for this would be that he was concentrating on political reform. A less charitable one would be that he lacked the intellectual capacity to grasp the seriousness of the economic crisis. Gorbachev was never able to construct a

viable economic policy or to put in place a mechanism for the implementation of economic policy.

Foreign policy. Like Khrushchev, Gorbachev was more popular abroad than at home. He proved a brilliant diplomat and for the first time bridged the gulf between a Soviet communist leader and the Western public. He was friendly, accessible, and a skilled performer on television. It was the message the West had been waiting decades to hear. His "new political thinking" consisted of removing ideology from foreign and security policy-making and arguing that all states were interdependent. If they did not unite, the whole planet would be in danger. He proposed the elimination of all nuclear weapons by the year 2000 and the establishment of a system of comprehensive security, a military doctrine that stressed reasonable sufficiency and recognized the complexity of the modern world. He signaled a change in the U.S.S.R.'s attitude toward the United Nations in December 1988 when, in a speech to the UN General Assembly, he praised its role in promoting international peace and security. He announced a reduction of 500,000 in the Soviet armed forces over the following two years, including the reduction of the number of divisions in Europe and Asia, as well as pulling back many tanks. The Soviet General Staff, which exercised a monopoly over defense and security policy, was not altogether convinced of the wisdom of such a move. Throughout the Gorbachev era the General Staff was more conservative than the national leader and became bolder in its opposition as time passed. It effectively sabotaged the Conventional Forces in Europe (CFE) Treaty.

Gorbachev, ably aided by Shevardnadze, set out to end the "new Cold War" that had broken out in the late 1970s. A key reason for this was that the new leadership had come to the conclusion that the defense burden was crippling the Soviet Union.

The first Reagan-Gorbachev summit took place in Geneva in November 1985. A joint statement proposed a 50 percent reduction in the superpowers' nuclear arsenal. The next summit took place at Reykjavík, Ice., in October 1986. The Soviets came very well prepared and demanded agreement on all their points. The discussions broke down over the Strategic Defense Initiative (SDI; a proposed U.S. system that would intercept attacking ballistic missiles), which the Americans were not willing to abandon. The third summit, held in Washington, D.C., in December 1987, was historic. It produced an agreement to eliminate a whole category of nuclear weapons: land-based intermediate- and shorter-range missiles. This was the Intermediate-Range Nuclear Forces (INF) Treaty, signed by Reagan and Gorbachev at their final summit in Moscow in May–June 1988. Serious differences still existed, however, especially over verification of the implementation of the treaties. Reagan and Gorbachev did not discuss SDI at the Washington and Moscow summits: the Soviets had made their stand at Reykjavík and lost.

One of the agreements reached at the Geneva summit concerned the withdrawal of Soviet troops from Afghanistan. The last soldier left in February 1989. Brezhnev had blundered into Afghanistan, and the U.S.S.R. had paid a heavy price in soldiers (almost 14,000), matériel, and foreign hostility.

Relations between Gorbachev and Reagan's successor, George Bush, were good, and there were several summits. These produced two historic agreements: the CFE treaty, signed in November 1990, and the START treaty, signed in July 1991. But opposition by the Soviet General Staff undermined the CFE Treaty, and the dissolution of the U.S.S.R. in August 1991 halted progress on the START treaty. The new relationship between the superpowers resulted in Shevardnadze voting for military action against Iraq in the UN. This was painful for Moscow, because Iraq had been an ally.

Gorbachev was a hit everywhere he went in Europe. This was especially so in West Germany, where he received a rapturous welcome in 1989. In eastern Europe the tumultuous events of 1989 were possible because Gorbachev did not permit the intervention of the military to keep communist regimes in power. He promoted *perestroika* in the region, believing that it would benefit socialism.

Central planning versus free market

Ending the Cold War

He undermined Erich Honecker in East Germany and accelerated the collapse of that country. He was opposed to the unification of Germany but was forced in the end to accept it.

Gorbachev's visit to China in 1989 was almost a fiasco and deeply disturbed the Chinese leadership. Many Chinese were attracted to *perestroika,* but the aged leadership ruthlessly suppressed those calling for political reform.

One of the objects of Soviet foreign policy had been to strengthen socialism around the world. By 1990 it was abundantly clear that this mission had failed. The U.S.S.R.'s only allies were underdeveloped Third World states such as Angola, Ethiopia, and Cuba. These were all liabilities, requiring more and more aid to stay afloat.

The attempted coup. Rumours of a coup against Gorbachev were rife in Moscow throughout the spring and summer of 1991. The military, the KGB, and conservative communists were alarmed at the turn of events. They wanted strong central leadership in order to keep the Soviet Union communist and together. Gorbachev had little to fear from the Communist Party. He had sharply reduced the power of the Politburo at the 28th Party Congress in June 1990 but had had to concede the emergence of a Russian Communist Party. This was dominated by the party apparat and turned out to be a toothless tiger. As it eventually transpired, a coup was organized by the KGB and was timed to prevent the signing of a union treaty on August 20 that would have strengthened the republics and weakened the centre.

On Aug. 18, 1991, a delegation visited Gorbachev at his summer dacha at Foros in the Crimea. The delegation demanded Gorbachev's resignation and replacement by Gennady Yanayev, the vice president. When Gorbachev refused, he was held prisoner while the coup leaders, called the Extraordinary Commission and guided by KGB boss Vladimir Kryuchkov, declared that Gorbachev had been obliged to resign for reasons of health. As the commission tried to take over the country, Yeltsin arrived at the Russian parliament building, from where, beginning on August 19, he declared the putsch an attempt to crush Russia, called for the return of Gorbachev, and appealed for popular support. Lack of decisiveness on the part of the coup leaders led to more and more support for the Russian president; even some soldiers and tank units turned to defend the parliament building, and some top military officers sided with Yeltsin. There were only three fatalities in Moscow before the coup collapsed on August 21.

There were many reasons why the coup should have succeeded. Many were disenchanted with the course of *perestroika.* The military was depressed about the withdrawal from eastern Europe and about declining defense expenditure and loss of status at home. Several republican leaders, including those in Azerbaijan, Tajikistan, Turkmenistan, and Uzbekistan, came out in support of the coup. Most others prevaricated, while the lone condemnatory voice from the beginning was that of Askar Akayev, the president of the Kirghiz S.S.R. (now Kyrgyzstan). Why then did it fail? Astonishingly, it was poorly planned and executed. The lessons of the brilliant coup of General

Wojciech Jaruzelski in Poland in December 1981 were ignored. The fatal tactical error was the failure to identify and deploy loyal troops. It was assumed that orders would be obeyed. Troops had moved ruthlessly against civilians in Tbilisi, Georgia, in April 1989; in Baku, Azerbaijan, in January 1990; and in Vilnius, Lithuania, in January 1991—to name only a few instances when coercion was used. What was different this time was that troops who were overwhelmingly Russian were being ordered to move against Russians. The crucial weakness of the plotters was their inability to understand the radical political and social transformation that had occurred in the U.S.S.R. since 1985. It was no longer possible simply to announce that Gorbachev had retired for "health" reasons. Yeltsin and the democrats seized the opportunity afforded by the incompetent plotters to organize very effective resistance in Moscow. Anatoly Sobchak did the same in St. Petersburg (formerly Leningrad). Probably a majority in the provinces supported the coup, but its fate was decided in the cities. There were significant divisions among top military and KGB officers. World statesmen condemned the coup and warned that all aid would be cut off.

The attempted coup destroyed Gorbachev politically. The republics rushed to be free of Moscow's control before another coup succeeded. The three Baltic republics successfully seceded from the union, as did many others. The key republic was Ukraine, politically and economically number two. It voted for independence on Dec. 1, 1991. Russia, Ukraine, and Belorussia (now renamed Belarus) on Dec. 8, 1991, in Minsk, Belarus, declared that the Soviet Union had ceased to exist and founded a loose grouping known as the Commonwealth of Independent States (CIS). On December 21 in Alma Ata, Kazakhstan, 11 states signed a protocol formally establishing the CIS. Of the former Soviet republics, Estonia, Latvia, Lithuania, and Georgia refused to join. Gorbachev resigned as Soviet president on December 25, and all Soviet institutions ceased to function at the end of 1991. The main benefactor was Russia. It assumed the U.S.S.R.'s seat on the UN Security Council, and all Soviet embassies became Russian embassies. The Soviet armed forces were placed under CIS command, but it was only a matter of time before each successor state formed its own armed forces. Russia, Ukraine, Belarus, and Kazakhstan became nuclear powers, but all, except Russia, declared their goal to be the destruction of their nuclear arms.

The Soviet experiment, begun in 1917, had ended in failure. The high moral goals that it had set for itself were never realized. Indeed, countless crimes had been committed in the attempt. Stalin perceived that the U.S.S.R. could only be kept together by a strong central hand that was willing to use coercion. Attempts at democratization under Khrushchev began a slow unraveling of the empire. Gorbachev merely accelerated the breakup by promoting *glasnost.* He confirmed that a communist system cannot become democratic. When democracy triumphs, communism departs the stage. Economic failure was the key reason for the U.S.S.R.'s collapse. The socialist alternative to the market economy turned out to be an illusion.

(MARTIN MCCAULEY)

Resentment among the military and secret police

Secession of the republics

Work and Employment

Great Britain, Australia, and New Zealand

ORIGINS IN BRITAIN

British trade unionism has a long and continuous history. Medieval guilds, which regulated craft production, clearly differed in function from trade unions, in that guilds were combinations of both masters and workers while modern unions emerged to serve workers' interests alone. However, aspects of guild regulation—as in matters relating to apprenticeship—were incorporated into the objectives of

early unionism, so that some continuity may be discerned between the decay of the one form of organization and the emergence of the other. Examples of the trade-union form of organization are hard to trace before the late 17th century; but during the following hundred years, combinations, as they were known to contemporaries, became widespread, emerging among groups of handicraft workers such as tailors, carpenters, and printers. Their emergence at this period was a result of the development of manufacturing and commerce on a capitalist basis. The number of handicraft workers within the economy was expanding, yet for such workers the prospect of making the transition from journeyman to master was diminishing. Both the rising demand for their labour and their emerging status as permanent employees were essential elements in this early development of labour organization. An additional factor, related to the rise of capitalism, was the progressive withdrawal of the state from wage regulation in particular and from labour-market intervention more generally. This was confirmed by the repeal, in 1813 and 1814, of legislation that had provided for the fixing of wages by justices and had stipulated apprenticeship requirements for entry into a trade. The state's withdrawal from labour-market regulation raised with some urgency the issue of the legality of trade unions. Under the Combination Acts of 1799 and 1800, a general prohibition had been placed upon them, in addition to the restraints imposed by the common law of conspiracy. Such a general prohibition now appeared anomalous and unjust, and it was indeed removed by legislation in 1824 and 1825. Common law impediments remained.

Craft orientation of early industrial unions

In the ensuing period, unions multiplied. As in the previous century, they were typically local in scope and craft in composition. Even in the emerging mechanized and factory-based sector, the relatively unsophisticated technology and managerial organization required the employment of skilled tradesmen, and these were assimilated into combinations based on the craft pattern of organization; engineers, boilermakers, and cotton spinners are examples. Yet, at this stage, the structure of unionism was still sufficiently fluid to permit widespread experimentation. During the 1830s there developed a movement toward "general unionism," directed both at establishing organization nationally and at drawing the various organized trades into alliance with one another. The pioneer in this movement was the cotton spinners' leader, John Doherty, but much of its impetus derived from Robert Owen, whose ideal of cooperative as against capitalist production found widespread support. The most ambitious Owenite union project was the Grand National Consolidated Trades Union of 1833–34, designed to embrace the whole of labour though in practice focused on London tailors and shoemakers. Inherently unstable, as were the other broad labour formations of the period, this union did not expire without leaving an enduring legacy. Six Dorsetshire agricultural labourers—the Tolpuddle Martyrs—were convicted and sentenced to transportation to Australia for swearing a secret oath in connection with the union. The union mounted a major campaign on their behalf, and this episode is still cherished by the modern labour movement as symbolic of its early struggle.

CRAFT UNIONISM IN THE 19TH CENTURY

British settlers brought their customs with them to Australia and New Zealand, and, accordingly, early unions there corresponded closely to the pattern of the home country. The penal character of the settlements established in Australia from the late 18th century was hardly conducive to forming workers' combinations, but the transition from convict to free settlement brought the first signs of union activity. Local societies of craftsmen were operating in the 1830s and '40s, ostensibly for the purpose of providing friendly benefits for their members but in practice for trade purposes as well. Groups involved in these societies included printers, tailors, building craftsmen, and engineers. With the expansion of the economy from the 1850s, such groups formed the basis for permanent trade unions. The emerging pattern was one of craft unionism, in which Australian unions, like their counterparts in Britain, sought to restrict entry into and regulate working conditions within their respective trades. In Britain, during the middle decades of the century, a number of such unions developed their organization on a national basis. The most famous were the Amalgamated Society of Engineers and the Amalgamated Society of Carpenters and Joiners, constituted in 1851 and 1860, respectively. In Australia the main impetus to the national organization of trades came later, with the federation of the separate colonies in 1901.

In both countries, as unions consolidated their organization on independent and sectional lines, collaboration became a means of securing common legislative objectives rather than concerting industrial activity. This was classically the case with the British Trades Union Congress (TUC), an annual union assembly initiated in 1868 with a view to lobbying the legislature through a standing Parliamentary Committee. The model was followed in Australia, where, beginning in 1879, a number of Intercolonial Trade Union Congresses were held, partly with a view to encouraging the formation of parliamentary committees in each of the self-governing colonies. Such political activity certainly achieved a further clarification of the unions' legal status. Legislation removing various remaining impediments was passed in Britain in 1871 and 1875; similar measures followed in all the Australian colonies between 1876 and 1902 and in New Zealand in 1878. Though the three societies differed in many respects, their broadly liberal character had, so far, proved accommodating to trade unionism. In Britain especially, unions had themselves contributed to this effect. As highly visible, stable, and professionally administered organizations, the national craft unions of the mid-19th century contrasted with the more secretive and volatile unions of the preceding era.

Formation of the Trades Union Congress

THE CRISIS OF THE 1890S: NEW UNIONS AND POLITICAL ACTION

The late 19th century brought major labour upheavals that decisively influenced the further development of unionism in all three countries. In Britain, a tendency for unionism to expand beyond its narrow craft confines, apparent in the early 1870s, was curtailed during the depression of the mid-1880s. In the business upswing of 1888–92, the formation of new unions of less skilled workers was resumed, this time with the aid of socialist activists. The movement received an enormous stimulus through the victory of London dockers in their great strike of 1889, secured in the last resort by Australian financial support—a gesture from the New World to the Old. However, in 1890 employers in the maritime sector counterattacked against new unions of seamen and dockers, and the new union established in the gas industry also suffered major setbacks. Even certain craft unions experienced stronger resistance from employers, who were alarmed by the injection of a greater militancy into union behaviour at a time when they faced increased foreign competition in their established markets. Following a national lockout in 1897–98, the Amalgamated Society of Engineers was obliged to accept the introduction of new machinery and payment systems on employers' terms. In both the maritime and engineering industries, employers had asserted their power by combining in national federations. Perhaps most serious of all for the unions, employer reaction spilled over into the courts, where a series of judicial rulings, culminating in the Taff Vale judgment of 1901, undermined the legislation of the 1870s.

The Taff Vale judgment

A crisis in labour relations was also reached in Australia and New Zealand in 1890. From 1870, the craft character of unionism in those countries had also been modified by the emergence of national industrially based unions in the mining, shipping, and pastoral industries. The most notable examples in Australia were the Miners' Association and the Shearers' Union; these extended their organization to New Zealand, where union development closely paralleled that in Australia. Greater scale and militancy in labour organization, clearly apparent by the late 1880s, drew forth a corresponding response from employers, leading to major confrontations in the early 1890s. The first was the great maritime strike of 1890, involving seamen and wharf labourers in both Australia and New Zealand and also extending to shearers and coal miners. These new unions, however, had embarked on a trial of strength with associated employers at a time when the economy had turned against them, boom turning into prolonged depression. In conditions of heavy unemployment, the maritime strike was broken, and there followed further defeats for the shearers in 1891 and 1894 and for the miners in 1892.

Industrial defeats led unions to turn to politics with greater urgency than before. In New Zealand they gave their support to the Liberal Party, which won a historic victory in December 1890. The Liberals' social and economic reforms that followed attracted attention throughout the developed world, but they also may have delayed the emergence of labour as an independent political force, since the modern Labour Party emerged as late as 1916 and did not form a government for the first time until 1935. In Britain also the break with Liberalism came slowly, but interest in direct labour representation quickened in the 1890s, leading at the turn of the century to a political alliance between unions and moderate socialist groups. The Labour Party so created remained in the shadow of the Liberals until after World War I, but thereafter it developed rapidly to assume office for the first time in 1924. The link between the industrial defeats of the 1890s and direct union involvement in politics was most clearly manifest in Australia. By 1900, Labour parties had emerged in four of the colonies, consisting of affiliated trade unions and electorate branches. The federation of the colonies in the following year led to the formation of a national parliamentary party, and by the end of 1915 Labour governments were in office at the federal level and in five of the six states. Despite differences in timing, the experience of all three countries was remarkably similar, with enhanced union interest in politics from the 1890s leading to the formation of Labour parties and, ultimately, Labour governments. However, the outcomes of such political involvement, in regard to the unions' situation within the wider society, diverged widely between New Zealand and Australia on the one hand and Britain on the other.

COMPULSORY ARBITRATION AND UNION GROWTH IN AUSTRALASIA

To remedy their industrial weakness, unions in Australasia turned to the state and the law for support, through the installation of systems of compulsory arbitration that would oblige employers to deal with them. It was the Liberal government in New Zealand that enacted the first effective measure. The Industrial Conciliation and Arbitration Act of 1894 was drafted by that government's most radical member, William Pember Reeves, a socialist among liberals. Addressing the problem of employers' noncompliance with arbitration decisions, Reeves devised a system in which participation was voluntary for unions but compulsory for employers. A union that chose to register under the act could bring any employer before the Arbitration Court, whose awards had legal force.

Following the New Zealand legislation, compulsory arbitration was introduced in Australia at both the state and federal level. The major landmarks were the Acts of 1900 and 1901 in Western Australia and New South Wales, respectively, and the federal statute of 1904. The new system was not installed without a struggle; employer opposition was strong, and it was overborne only by a combination of political forces that included Liberals and the new Labour parties. The New Zealand experiment also attracted attention in Britain. Within the TUC, support came from weaker, newer unions that had not yet achieved employer recognition and saw compulsory arbitration as a means of enforcing it. The temporary operation of such a system in World War I did indeed have this effect, but at the turn of the century most unions were skeptical. Legally enforced collective agreements would entail closer involvement with the judiciary, and British judges were regarded as incapable of delivering impartial rulings on labour issues. Following the 1901 Taff Vale judgment, union support for the Labour Party developed rapidly, with a view to securing maximum freedom from judicial interference. In the 1906 Trade Disputes Act, British unions secured the legal immunities they desired, and the principle of legal abstention remained fundamental to the conduct of British labour relations to the 1970s.

In a different social setting, Australasian unions believed that compulsory arbitration would work to their advantage, and so it proved. In 1890 there was little to suggest that the propensity to unionize was exceptionally high in

these countries, but 20 years later Australia was the most highly unionized country in the world, and union coverage had been greatly extended in New Zealand as well. Apart from a slight drop in the early 1920s, growth in union membership in Australia was virtually unchecked until 1927, the proportion of the work force organized rising from 9 to 47 percent. Compulsory arbitration explicitly recognized and protected unions, and under it even the weakest unions could force employers to have the pay and working conditions of their employees fixed by an arbitration court. This capacity drew in recruits, and in both countries growth was further encouraged by the practice of handing down arbitration awards that conferred preference in employment on union members. In the case of New Zealand, a 1936 amendment to the legislation of 1894 provided for compulsory union membership—a change that led to a dramatic increase in union coverage. In Australia a further crucial development came in 1907, with the Arbitration Court's judgment in the Harvester case. This ruling held that a living wage was a first charge upon industry, and it set a basic wage for unskilled labour at a level substantially higher than existing rates—an approach to wage determination that unions could certainly live with. Within both countries, however, the degree of dependence of unions upon legal support varied. Unions with a small or scattered membership (and there were many such) were almost wholly dependent; but for larger and more concentrated organizations, a real alternative existed in the shape of direct bargaining and strike action.

In the years immediately before and after World War I, that alternative found increasing support in unions of miners, railway men, and wharf workers, where, as in Britain, the syndicalist ideology of direct action had acquired some influence. Syndicalist rejection of parliamentary politics, and hostility to the state in all its forms, was given particular edge in the context of compulsory arbitration. In New Zealand a militant Federation of Labour developed in opposition to the arbitration system, and in 1912–13 a violent confrontation occurred in ports and mining towns, but the strikes were broken by employers (now mobilized in defense of arbitration), farmers, and the government. It was significant that the majority of unions valued their registration under the Arbitration Act too highly to affiliate with the Federation of Labour. In Australia, compulsory arbitration also survived an increased advocacy and practice of strike action. During and after the war the idea of the "One Big Union," which would unify existing organizations and maximize striking power, gained a certain currency. It seems to have delayed the emergence of an Australian counterpart to the TUC, toward which the intercolonial congresses of the previous century had been moving. Eventually hopes of realizing the grander plan faded, and the Australian Council of Trade Unions (ACTU) was formed in 1927. Though some of the impetus behind the ACTU's emergence came from those who saw it as an instrument for the coordination of strike activity, in practice its survival owed much to the function it performed within the federal arbitration system in representing unions in basic wage and other national test cases.

UNION EXPANSION UNDER A VOLUNTARY SYSTEM

In Britain the broadening of unionism's membership base was underpinned by the spread of employer recognition and voluntary collective bargaining procedures, and it was the union leaders' faith in this process that encouraged them to believe that they could dispense with political and legal support. The engineers' defeat in 1898 did not lead to a withdrawal of employer recognition, and by this stage collective bargaining had spread beyond the crafts into coal mining and cotton manufacturing. However, unlike the craft, coal, and cotton unions, those of more recent origin still faced an uphill struggle. In the maritime, railway, and gas industries recognition was commonly denied, but the willingness of the new unions to recruit across occupational boundaries contributed to their survival. During the years after 1910 it was the unions constituted on a general or multioccupational basis that grew most rapidly. Of the three largest unions of the second half of the 20th

New Zealand's Industrial Conciliation and Arbitration Act

The Harvester case in Australia

The "new unions" of the 1890s

century, two—the Transport and General Workers Union and the General and Municipal Workers Union—were direct descendants of new unions of 1889.

Though union membership growth was a marked feature of the early 20th century in Britain, as in Australasia, its upward course was less steady and more vulnerable to shifts in the economic cycle. In the full-employment years of 1910–20 it was explosive, accompanied by an escalation of industrial militancy in mining, railways, docks, and elsewhere. As in the former colonies, such militancy was tinged with syndicalism. But growth was halted abruptly in 1920, with membership at 45 percent of the work force, and in conditions of heavy unemployment there followed a long decline into the early 1930s. Though unemployment checked growth in the other countries as well, the contraction in British union coverage, to 22.6 percent, was particularly severe. Despite the shrinking membership, industrial conflict took time to abate, as employers' efforts to force down wages were met with determined resistance. In 1921, with the creation of a General Council, the TUC had equipped itself to coordinate industrial action, and this power was put to the test in 1926 when a general strike was called in support of the Miners Federation. Conflict on this scale inevitably pitted unions against state, and it was this wider aspect of the dispute that in the end caused the TUC, committed as it was to constitutional modes of action, to call the strike off. Government, for its part, having established what it regarded as the boundaries of legitimate action and having confirmed them in legislation in 1927, was not inclined to intervene further to restrict union activity. Nor did employers move to de-recognize unions.

TRADE UNIONISM AFTER WORLD WAR II: AN EROSION OF STRENGTH

In conditions of full employment and inflation following World War II, the respective industrial relations systems of both Britain and Australasia came under strain. In the case of compulsory arbitration, unions that had once clung to the system when they were weak now chafed at its restrictions when their strength was recovered. At an early stage there were confrontations involving traditionally militant mining and wharf unions. With the Cold War then at its height, Communist influence within such unions called forth drastic countermeasures by governments, and the 1949 coal strike and 1951 wharf strike, in Australia and New Zealand, respectively, were decisively defeated. As in the past, however, the majority of unions were not drawn into open opposition to arbitration. Nonetheless, though the "adventurist" phase of Communist-inspired militancy was over, more general tendencies toward direct bargaining and strike activity persisted in both countries.

Crisis in the compulsory arbitration system Established as an alternative to industrial conflict, compulsory arbitration always faced in practice the problem of how to deal with strikes. A crisis was reached in Australia in the 1960s, when unions were fined for strikes with increasing frequency. The imprisonment of a union official in 1969, in an attempt to recover payment, led to a wave of protest and to the tacit abandonment of penal sanctions. The episode was revealing. It was the system's flexibility, its capacity to adapt to variations in the balance of industrial power over time and between different industries, that had contained the unions within it. Indeed, flexibility (and complexity) became such marked characteristics of the system that doubt grew as to its continued usefulness. In the 1980s the Australian government commissioned a complete review, yet the Hancock Report that emerged recommended no fundamental modification. Compulsory arbitration had been woven deeply into the fabric of national life in both countries, and in the process unions had been integrated more completely than in other democracies.

In postwar Britain, enhanced union power was widely blamed for inflation and for overmanning and disruption in industry. Between 1945 and 1951, when the Labour Party was in government and the wartime ban on strikes continued, integration between state and unions was unusually close. Government acted to break a series of dock strikes, without general union opposition, in a situation that closely paralleled that in Australasia. Through the 1950s and '60s, however, unions and government drifted into opposition. The wartime experiment in compulsory arbitration had struck no deep roots and was abandoned, while the return to purely voluntary bargaining was increasingly perceived as damaging in its economic consequences. Under full employment, shop steward organization spread rapidly through industry and was associated with a growing tendency toward unofficial, or "wildcat," strike activity. The voluntary institutions of British industrial relations appeared to be breaking down, and they were subjected to searching review by a Royal Commission on Trade Unions and Employers' Associations appointed in 1965. The largely voluntary remedies proposed by the commission did not satisfy governments, which were intent on urgent action. In 1969 a Labour government proposed legal restraints on unofficial strikers, enforceable by fines—a development even less welcome to British unions than to those in Australia. The proposals were withdrawn, but the successor Conservative government introduced a new legal code in the Industrial Relations Act of 1971, which included laws on unfair industrial practices and on legally binding agreements. These and various other provisions were to be enforced by a special Industrial Relations Court—in effect reversing the entire British tradition of legal abstention. Even then, unions refused to be contained within the tight legal framework that had been created, and this government was besieged by a renewed industrial militancy that not only rendered its legislation inoperable but also brought it to electoral defeat on the issue of the enforcement of statutory controls on wage bargaining.

In all three countries, profound shifts in the structure of the employed population during the later 20th century eroded the traditional membership base of unions. In following these shifts toward white-collar, female, and service-sector employment, unions endeavoured to match strides with the rapidly changing composition of the work force—just as, earlier in the century, they had broken through the divide separating skilled from unskilled manual labour. However, though their composition was modified profoundly, with greatly increased representation of white-collar and female employees, they could not keep pace. Union coverage of the work force in Britain recovered to its 1920 level in 1948, then surged forward in the 1970s to pass 50 percent for the first time. From a peak in 1979, however, it fell away. Closer integration with the state may have afforded Australasian unions better protection against the adverse consequences of structural change, but this is uncertain. Australian union coverage peaked at 60 percent in 1954; subsequent decline was checked in the early 1970s, but by the late 1980s coverage may have been as low as 42 percent. Higher levels of unemployment from the 1970s reinforced the trend, associated as they were with a rapid contraction of employment in union strongholds in manufacturing, mining, and the docks. In Britain this contraction was accelerated by a series of union defeats, the most drastic of which was inflicted upon the National Union of Mineworkers in the great strike of 1984–85. Legal restrictions on British unions, attempted in the 1970s, were reintroduced in the following decade. But if the political and industrial climate had turned more sharply against British than Australasian unions, the problem of adaptation to change remained a common one. (JOHN CHRISTOPHER LOVELL)

Changing structure of the work force

The United States and Canada

ORIGINS OF CRAFT UNIONISM

Trade unionism in North America had its beginnings in a transition during the late 18th century from a mutualist/dependent to a free wage-labour system. As journeymen artisans moved out of what has been called "economic clientage" to master craftsmen, they found their interests in conflict with those of their employers. Only through collective effort could workers enforce the list of "prices" they established for their work and defend their trades against cheap and diluted labour. The first identifiable labour strike dates from 1768, when journeymen tailors in New York City stopped work to resist a pay cut. Sustained labour organization began with the Federal Society of Journeymen Cordwainers (shoemakers) in Philadelphia in 1794. The first sign of a labour movement—that is, organizational activity exceeding the narrow sectional interests of particular crafts—appeared in Philadelphia, where the various craft bodies joined in 1827 to form the Mechanics' Union of Trade Societies. In Canada, these developments were slower to emerge: the first craft locals appeared in Montreal in 1827 and in Toronto in 1832, and the earliest city central came only in 1871, with the formation of the Toronto Trades Assembly. The first national union of locals in a single trade to survive, the National Typographical Union, was formed in 1852 in the United States. Like other national unions that followed, it chartered locals in Canada as well; this led to its renaming in 1869 as the International Typographical Union— a designation that became common in North American unionism.

National and international unions

Rooted as it was in the preindustrial trades, this early trade unionism did not lose its essential craft character with the onset of industrialization. Mule spinners, molders, machinists, and iron puddlers and rollers were employing new skills, and they functioned in a factory context, but they had much the same collective concerns as did traditional craftsmen and fitted readily into the emergent trade-union structure. On the railroads, too, the key jobs were defined as operating "crafts." Even with the quickening pace of industrialism, then, North American trade unionism in the 19th century was overwhelmingly a movement of skilled workers.

But job consciousness, powerful though it was, by no means constituted the sole, or even predominant, inspiration for collective activity. Historical research on working-class life has demonstrated that labour consciousness was a complex phenomenon, rooted in distinctive structures of culture, community, and ideology as well as in craft identity. American workers of the Jacksonian era adhered to a conception of artisan republicanism, which celebrated producerist values and the republican ideals of the American Revolution. Counter to this vision ran the corrosive impact of emergent industrial capitalism, which, in the view of the Philadelphia Workingmen's Party, created "invidious distinctions [and] unjust and unnatural inequalities" by dividing Americans into "two distinct classes, the rich and the poor." Beginning with workingmen's parties in the 1830s, a series of labour-reform movements fought a running battle for "equal rights." In the 1860s, this was the task of the National Labor Union and, after its decline, of the Knights of Labor. On their face, these reform movements seemed to cut athwart trade unionism, insofar as they aspired to the cooperative commonwealth rather than simply to a higher wage, appealed broadly to all "producers" rather than strictly to wage workers, and thought of themselves as broadly inclusive political and educational movements. But contemporaries saw no contradiction here: trade unions tended to workers' day-to-day needs, labour reform to their higher hopes. While the two were accepted as strands of a single labour movement, however, it was well understood that they were strands that had to be kept operationally apart.

During the 1880s, that functional separation began to break down. The international craft unions, having by now emerged as the dominant element in the trade-union structure, became less tolerant of challenges to their jurisdictions and internal lines of authority. For its part, despite a robust labour-reform rhetoric, the Knights of Labor began to act increasingly like a rival trade-union movement, carrying on strikes and organizing workers along industrial rather than craft lines. When the Knights rejected a proposal reaffirming the historic separation of trade-union and labour-reform functions, the alarmed internationals joined in December 1886 and formed the American Federation of Labor (AFL). The immediate aim was to drive the Knights from the industrial field, and, thanks largely to the Knights' own confusion and to employers' counterattacks, this was speedily accomplished. But more important in the long run was the permanent stamp that the AFL made on the American labour movement. This

was partly institutional: the AFL legitimized the emergent trade-union structure that gave preeminence to the rule of the internationals. But equally significant was the enunciation of a guiding labour philosophy—"pure and simple" unionism—under the aegis of Samuel Gompers and his circle of Marxist trade unionists. Labour reform was thenceforth denied any further role in the struggle of American workers. The weapons in that struggle were to be defined as economic and not political; the participants would be strictly wage workers organized along occupational lines; and the objective of trade unionism became exclusively the incremental achievement of higher wages and better working conditions.

"Pure-and-simple" unionism

In Canada these American events had very considerable consequences. Given the sparse settlement and small industrial base, Canadian unions found it difficult to build a national structure of their own. An attempt initiated by the Toronto Trades Assembly in 1873 soon failed. It was also natural, given the colonial (after 1867, dominion) ties to Britain, for Canadian workers to look to English unions, and at least two groups—the carpenters and engineers—in fact built up sizable Canadian memberships after 1850. But the much more compelling links were to the United States, partly because labour markets in many skilled trades ignored the national boundaries and partly because the American unions were the readiest source of institutional assistance. By the end of the 1880s, as many as half the organized workers in Canada were in locals affiliated to internationals with headquarters in the United States. And it was this segment of Canadian labour that was mainly responsible for forming, parallel to the AFL, the Trades and Labor Congress (TLC) in 1886.

For some years, the TLC followed its own bent. The Knights of Labor had been highly successful in Canada, notably in Quebec. After virtually disappearing from the United States in the early 1890s, the Knights remained a considerable force in Canada, and, although strictly excluded from the AFL, were made welcome in the TLC. As late as 1901, moreover, its president was proposing that the Canadian branches break their links with the internationals, form their own national unions, and turn the TLC into a wholly Canadian movement. But in 1902 just the opposite transpired. The TLC expelled the Knights and adopted the AFL principle of opposition to dual unionism, which meant that the Canadian branches of the internationals gained a virtual monopoly on trade-union representation in the TLC. It became, in effect, the Canadian wing of the American movement. Responding to Canadian political conditions, the TLC was somewhat more flexible than the AFL on issues of independent labour politics and state intervention, but, on the whole, American pure-and-simple unionism exerted the commanding influence on Canadian unionism in these years.

Only in Quebec did a very different tradition assert itself. Here, following a lockout of boot and shoe workers in 1900, the Roman Catholic church stepped in and, in accordance with the papal encyclical *Rerum Novarum* (1891), encouraged the unionization of Quebec workers. The result was a vigorous French Catholic movement, the Confédération des Travailleurs Catholiques du Canada, which stands as a unique instance of confessional unionism in North America. Only after World War II did Quebec unionism shed its links to the church and evolve into a secular movement.

CHALLENGES TO PURE-AND-SIMPLE UNIONISM

In the American West, pure-and-simple unionism was challenged in 1905 by the Industrial Workers of the World (IWW). The IWW had two sources. One was the socialist left wing, which had concluded that the AFL could not be captured and made over into the necessary trade-union base for socialist electoral politics. The second was a western brand of working-class radicalism forged by a decade of industrial war in the western mining states. The two groups proved incompatible, and the IWW, dominated by radicals from the Western Federation of Miners, drove out the socialists and committed itself to a syndi-

The Industrial Workers of the World

calist version of class war, in which political action was excluded. Struggle would centre on direct industrial action and ultimately on the revolutionary general strike, and out of that would emerge a workers' society organized on the basis of industrial unions. The IWW led a number of important strikes in the east between 1907 and 1913, but its main theatre of operations was among western workers, including Canadians, in metal mining, lumber, transportation, and agriculture. During World War I, however, the IWW was violently suppressed, and it never regained the organizational momentum of its peak years between 1914 and 1917.

The Canadian version of western syndicalism sprang into life in 1919, just as the IWW was expiring. This was the One Big Union (OBU), which had its roots in a postwar labour disaffection from conventional trade unionism that was especially pronounced in western Canada. Structured more along geographic than along the industrial-union lines of the IWW, the OBU had its moment of glory in the Winnipeg General Strike of 1919, and for a few years thereafter it virtually displaced the TLC as the dominant movement in the four western provinces. The OBU, despite its swift collapse, left behind a significant regional legacy: thereafter, the western provinces would persistently be the site of a more progressive, politically active brand of Canadian trade unionism.

The syndicalist challenge stemmed, to some degree, from the failing fortunes of pure-and-simple unionism in the early decades of the 20th century. The essence of that formulation had been to locate labour's struggle firmly in the industrial arena. But the struggle for collective bargaining proved to be much harder than Gompers and other trade unionists had anticipated. Where competitive pressures were severe enough, as in bituminous coal mining, not even the most innovative and determined of union efforts at market control proved sufficient—hence the collapse of the United Mine Workers of America (UMWA) in the 1920s. Elsewhere, as in the metal-fabricating industries, the problem was the speed of technological innovation and, in particular, the perfection of mass-production methods, which undercut the role of craft workers. Scientific management, moreover, demanded strict supervisory control over the workplace and hence posed a profound threat to customary patterns of workers' autonomy in the labour process (see above, *History of the organization of work*). When an effort to find common ground in the Murray Hill agreement (1900) between the International Association of Machinists and the National Metal Trades Association failed within a year, the die was cast: a quarter-century of bitter industrial warfare ensued. Labour's fortunes varied at different times and places, but the end result was unquestionably an arrested labour movement, with union penetration settling at roughly 10 percent of the nonagricultural labour force. As welfare capitalism took hold in the New Era of the 1920s, the more advanced sectors of the industrial economy seemed quite beyond the reach of the AFL.

ESTABLISHMENT OF INDUSTRIAL UNIONISM

Progress under the New Deal With the onset of the Great Depression in 1929, the balance of forces in the United States shifted dramatically. To begin with, national politics became more favourable to organized labour. Partly for ideological reasons, partly because of labour's increasing influence on the Democratic Party, Franklin Roosevelt's New Deal proved much more responsive to trade-union demands than had the Republican administrations of the post-World War I era. By now, moreover, key union leaders—most important, John L. Lewis of the UMWA and Sidney Hillman of the Amalgamated Clothing Workers of America—had defined what the labour movement most required from the state: protection of the rights of workers to organize and engage in collective bargaining. These rights were asserted in principle under Section 7(a) of the National Industrial Recovery Act (NIRA) of 1933 and then made thoroughly effective by passage of the National Labor Relations Act in 1935. More commonly known as the Wagner Act, the latter legislation prohibited employers from interfering with the right of workers to organize and from dominating the organizations they established. It also defined the procedures by which, through majority rule, workers selected their bargaining agents; required employers to bargain with such agents to the end of reaching contractual agreements; and set up, through the National Labor Relations Board, quasi-judicial mechanisms for enforcement of the law. American employers lost the enormous power advantages they had enjoyed in the struggle over collective bargaining, but in exchange the labour movement conceded the highly prized independence from the state that was a core element of pure-and-simple unionism. Under the Wagner Act, collective bargaining remained "free"—that is, the terms of agreements were not to be mandated by the state—but the framework itself came securely under the aegis of state regulation.

At the same time, the New Deal moved to mitigate the market pressures that had driven the antiunionism of American employers. The NIRA legislation, through codes of fair competition, was designed to enable industries to cartelize their depression-ridden markets. The exchange was entirely deliberate—granting representational rights to workers as a price for granting market controls to industry. As the basis of New Deal economic policy, this attempt at industrial stabilization lasted only two years, but the underlying linkage of labour rights and market benefits survived invalidation of the NIRA by the Supreme Court in 1935.

The Wagner Act contained an explicit economic rationale: collective bargaining would generate the mass purchasing power essential for sustained economic growth. This, in turn, prefigured the Keynesian economic policy that, by managing demand, became the government's way of underwriting the New Deal's collective bargaining system after World War II. With federal macroeconomic policy (as specified by the Employment Act of 1946) responsible for maintaining long-term demand, and price competition firmly controlled by the restored oligopolistic structures of the major industries (or, as in the transportation and communications sectors, by direct state regulation), the market-driven basis for American antiunionism seemed to have run its course in the postwar era.

Much the same could be said for the labour-process basis for antiunionism in the key mass-production sectors. By the 1930s, the Taylorist crisis over job control had passed; what remained at issue was no longer whether managers had the authority to control the labour process but only how they would exercise it. There were compelling reasons, almost systemic in nature, for the formalization of labour-relations policies. For example, where tasks were subdivided and precisely defined, job classification necessarily followed, and from that in turn came the principle of pay equity. Time-and-motion study—another pillar of Taylorist management—meant objective, testable standards for setting the pace of work. Corporate commitment to this formalized system was imperfect, however, and broke down disastrously in the early years of the Great Depression. Rank-and-file fury over job insecurity and intolerable speedups, plus pressure from New Deal agencies and the labour movement, forced management's hand. Consequently, between 1933 and 1936—before collective bargaining actually began—all the key elements of the modern workplace regime fell more or less into place: specified, uniform rights for workers (beginning with seniority and pay equity); a formal procedure to adjudicate grievances arising from those rights; and a structure of shop-floor representation to implement the grievance procedure. Corporate employers would have much preferred to keep this regime under nonunion conditions. Indeed, it had taken shape in the course of their efforts to implant so-called employee representation plans (*i.e.,* company unions) that they had hoped would satisfy the requirements of New Deal labour policy. But when that strategy failed, managers were prepared to have their workplace regimes incorporated into contractual relationships with independent unions within the terms of the Wagner Act.

To fulfill its part in this process, the labour movement had first of all to adopt an industrial-union (*i.e.,* plantwide) structure appropriate to mass-production industry. The

Collective bargaining and control over the work process

The
Congress of
Industrial
Organiza-
tions

problem was that the AFL was committed to a craft structure and, under its constitutional rules, lacked the means
to compel member unions to cede jurisdictions they held
over craft workers in the mass-production sector to the
emerging industrial unions. This impasse was broken only
by a split within the AFL in 1935, leading to the formation of the rival Congress of Industrial Organizations
(CIO) under the leadership of John L. Lewis. Even then,
once the CIO unions scored their dramatic unionizing
victories in rubber, auto, and steel of 1936 and 1937, a
second condition had to be met: the CIO unions had to
demonstrate their capacity to enforce the contractual provisions of workplace due process and discipline a turbulent
rank and file. World War II brought this second phase to
completion. Under close wartime regulation, institutional
relations between the CIO and corporate industry were
solidified, and, after a strike wave tested the parameters of
this relationship in the immediate postwar period, there
ensued a system of industrywide collective bargaining that
endured for the next 40 years.

The industrial-union struggle spilled over from the United
States into Canada. At the insistence of the AFL, the TLC
expelled the Canadian branches of the CIO internationals
in 1939. The next year these CIO unions joined the remnants of the All-Canadian Congress of Labour, which had
formed in 1927 on the dual principles of industrial unionism and Canadian nationalism, to create the Canadian
Congress of Labour (CCL) in affiliation with the American
CIO. Only during World War II, however, did organizational realities begin to catch up with these superstructural
developments. Although stirred by events south of the border, the Canadian movement did not experience a comparable surge of organization during the Great Depression.
Only in February 1944 did the wartime administration of
W.L. Mackenzie King issue Order in Council P.C. 1003,
granting to Canadian workers collective-bargaining rights
that American workers already enjoyed under the Wagner
Act. The Canadian version, however, allowed for a greater
degree of public intervention in the bargaining process.
Investigative and cooling-off provisions in labour disputes
were already a cornerstone of Canadian policy (going
back to Mackenzie King's Industrial Disputes Investigative Act of 1907), and wartime conditions demanded a
no-strike provision (linked to the mandatory inclusion
of binding arbitration of grievances in union contracts),
which likewise became a permanent feature of Canadian
labour-relations law. During the war decade, the Canadian mass-production sector was rapidly organized by
CIO unions.

By the early 1950s the organizational situation was similar on both sides of the border. In both countries, one-
third of the nonagricultural labour force was unionized.
In both countries, the industrial-union federations peaked
at roughly two-thirds the size of their longer established
craft rivals. At the onset of the Cold War, an internal
crisis over Communist participation gripped the labour
movements of both countries. Although somewhat different in its details, the outcome was identical on both sides
of the border—the expulsion of Communist-dominated
unions in 1949 and 1950. And when the American unions
settled their differences and merged into the AFL–CIO in
1955, the Canadian federations followed suit the next year
by uniting in the Canadian Labour Congress (CLC). At
that point, 70 percent of all Canadian unionists belonged
to international unions with headquarters in the United
States. The 1950s can be said to mark the apex of this
historical tendency toward an integrated Canadian-Amer-
ican movement.

DECLINE AND DIVERGENCE

Beginning in the 1960s, the fortunes of the two movements
diverged. In the United States, market pressures steadily
eroded the postwar collective-bargaining system. In auto,
steel, and clothing, the problem was intensifying foreign
competition; in communications, trucking, railroads, and
airlines, it was federal deregulation in the 1970s; and
elsewhere, as in mining, retailing, and meat processing,
a host of nonunionized domestic competitors entered the
field. Meanwhile, a structural shift occurred toward a ser-

Economic
pressures
on
unionized
industries

vice economy, narrowing the established union base in
the goods-producing sectors: production workers made up
30 percent of the nonagricultural U.S. labour force in
1950 but only 22 percent in 1976. The economic troubles
that then set in—declining productivity and a slowing
growth rate, inflation, the harsh recession of 1982—had a
devastating impact on the American movement. Between
1975 and 1984, four million members were lost, and the
unionized share of the labour force shrank from 28.9
percent to below 20 percent. If not for public-employee
unions, which added two million members between 1956
and 1976, the U.S. labour movement would have found
itself in an even more parlous state, as unionization
in the private sector slipped to close to pre-New Deal
levels.

Canada's economy was comparably hard hit in these
years, yet unions north of the border fared far better.
Indeed, they grew steadily after the mid-1960s, and, with
3.5 million members by the early 1980s, claimed over 40
percent of the Canadian labour force—more than twice
the union density in the United States. How is this remarkable divergence to be explained?

The decline of the American movement occurred within
an increasingly hostile political environment. In Canada,
on the other hand, a changing party system enhanced
labour's place in Canadian public life. In 1961, with the
backing of Canadian labour, the New Democratic Party
(NDP) was formed as a social-democratic rival to the
Liberal and Progressive Conservative parties. As it made
headway, the NDP changed the landscape of Canadian
politics. For its part, Canadian organized labour, by abandoning the nonpartisanship espoused by the AFL–CIO,
not only gained political muscle but also became a progressive force in the nation's public life. It assumed the
mantle of what has been called "social unionism"—in
stark contrast to the political marginalization of the AFL–
CIO that followed the collapse of the Democratic New
Deal coalition in the late 1960s.

Beginning with passage of the Taft-Hartley Act of 1947,
which applied unfair-labour-practice provisions to unions
and in a variety of ways weakened their economic and
organizational power, labour law in the United States
became steadily more burdensome to the labour movement. By contrast, Canadian federal and provincial law
retained, and even deepened, its pro-union bias. Nor was
there any Canadian counterpart to U.S. President Ronald
Reagan's decision in 1981 to break a strike by federal air-
traffic controllers—an act of enormous symbolic importance that legitimized the resurgence of antiunionism in
corporate America. Antiunionism gained no such public
legitimacy in Canada. Underlying this was a factor emphasized by the sociologist Seymour Martin Lipset: that
collectivist values inhering in Canadian political culture
granted the labour movement a legitimacy it never quite
achieved in the more entrepreneurial nation south of
the border.

As these divergences became more marked, the "international" character of the North American movement began
to wane. Public-employee unionism—even more prominent a recent development in Canada than in the United
States—would have sufficed in itself to push the Canadian
movement in an independent direction, but Canadian
branches in the private sector as well began to break
loose, some by seeking greater autonomy within their
international unions, but others—including those of communications workers, paper workers, woodworkers, and
auto workers—by splitting off and becoming independent.
A dwindling share of the Canadian movement—less than
35 percent by 1990—retained ties to the AFL–CIO. Two
developments offered some prospect for reviving the in-
tegrationist bent of the North American movement: first,
the creation of a common U.S.-Canadian economic market and, second, the deepening crisis in Canada over an
independent Quebec. But, in the main, events of the 1970s
and '80s merely underscored the very different dynamics
that were driving the Canadian and American trade-union
movements and that seemed to be carrying them farther
apart along separate paths of national development.

Indepen-
dent
Canadian
labour
movement

(DAVID BRODY)

Western Europe

CHARACTERISTICS OF THE CONTINENTAL LABOUR MOVEMENT

The history of unionism on the European continent differs significantly in several respects from that in Britain and the United States. First, industrial development came later and proceeded faster than in Britain, with plants and enterprises starting on a large scale and often using the most advanced technology. This disconnected European unions from medieval craft traditions and prevented the establishment of a system of craft unions representing only workers with a specific skill. Early attempts at craft unionism were soon absorbed into broad and encompassing industrial unions, which organized all workers in an industry or country regardless of skill and employment status. These unions represented primarily the interests of workers in large establishments who had no particular skills to defend and whose employers exercized firm control over the organization of work, or they represented workers in industries such as railways, mining, and electricity supply, in which labour relations were a matter of public interest and concern. Not being able to monopolize an indispensable skill and thereby realize their interests at the workplace and through the market alone, workers in such industries needed unions capable of mobilizing mass solidarity across occupational boundaries. As a consequence, western European union movements have usually formed strong national confederations capable of representing their affiliates in political bargaining with the government; maintained weak or nonexistent division between skilled and unskilled, and often between blue-collar and white-collar, members or affiliates; contained a small number of large, instead of a large number of small, individual unions; conducted comprehensive industrywide collective bargaining with a tendency to reduce or eliminate wage differentials by sector, employer, skill, or occupation; and pursued a universalistic social policy—on such issues as social insurance, health care, and occupational safety—that takes the place of enterprise- or group-specific "voluntary" regulations characteristically negotiated by more narrowly defined, sectional unions.

A second distinction of trade unionism in western Europe emerged in the area of managerial prerogative. Since many continental industries started at new sites and on a large scale, they were less burdened with a legacy of local management and craft autonomy than were British enterprises. Because of the more unitary and centralized organization of European firms, a distinction between management and labour and the right of management to manage were from the beginning more securely established, and shop-floor contestation between management and labour over the organization of the labour process became much less central to European than to British and American industrial relations. Representing both unskilled and skilled workers in large establishments, western European industrial unions were never committed to defending job demarcations among skilled and between skilled and unskilled workers. This enabled especially the more politically powerful union movements to accept managerial prerogative and high flexibility in internal labour markets. In fact, their lack of commitment to any specific division of labour on the shop floor later enabled European unions to support and promote comprehensive public and private labour-market policies of general upgrading of skills and jobs. And while effective centralized control over the shop floor was ceded to management from the beginning, that control was later available to share with politically powerful unions if and when these were willing to seek legislation on "industrial democracy." "Cooperative" union participation in management then became possible, because industrial unions had no history of resisting large-scale organization as such, were not beholden to any particular group of workers, and had no principal interest in curtailing firms' internal flexibility.

A third defining characteristic of trade-union history in western Europe is in the area of political power. Unable to afford the laissez-faire liberalism of Victorian Britain, European states early on took an active role in the regulation of labour markets, often siding with capital in support of rapid accumulation. At a time when the doctrines of voluntarism and state abstention became established in British industrial relations, unions were regarded by European ruling elites as a threat to both national unity and economic progress. In these circumstances, "pure-and-simple" unionism was impossible. European unions had little choice but to define themselves as political movements—at least until conditions for independent, economic unionism had been created—and in fact they typically started out as industrial arms of political parties, usually socialist or Roman Catholic. Where political unionism was of the Roman Catholic kind, it aimed at establishing an autonomous space for cooperative industrial self-governance of workers and employers, free from interference by the modern nation-state. Where the guiding political doctrine was Socialist or, after 1917, Communist, the objective was to gain control over the state in order to use its growing interventionist capacities for fundamental social transformation in the interest of workers. Finally, where political unionism was syndicalist or anarchist, its ultimate goal was to replace the state with a political organization based on the workplace and on relations between associated producers.

Just as craft unionism gives rise to fragmentation by occupation, so political unionism may breed fragmentation along party lines, and by the end of the 19th century almost all continental European union movements outside Scandinavia were ideologically divided. In order to overcome these divisions, unions had to extricate themselves from the control of allied political parties, and European industrial-political unionism became most powerful where unions managed to escape political division, overcome it to form unified organizations, or coordinate their policies. Where organizational unity was accomplished, it enabled political unionism to become an independent economic and political force, continuing universalist traditions of comprehensive social reform without being subservient to any particular party or government strategy. Especially in northern and northwestern Europe, unions became established participants in national politics, functioning in a wide variety of policy areas as recognized quasi-public or para-governmental intermediary institutions.

FROM WORLD WAR I TO 1968: THE INSTITUTIONALIZATION OF UNIONS AND COLLECTIVE BARGAINING

By the early 20th century western European unions were making slow but steady progress toward expanding their membership, extending the range of collective bargaining, consolidating their organizations, and winning legal and political recognition. The breakthrough, however, came with World War I. Wartime mobilization brought tight labour markets, rapid expansion of mass production, long working days, hazardous working conditions in arms and ammunition factories, and soaring profits for employers. It also ushered in state intervention and economic planning on an unprecedented scale. As the war dragged on, national elites found themselves compelled to include labour leaders in the governance of the war economy as managers of rising shop-floor discontent. Typically, union cooperation was gained in exchange for promises of democratization, union recognition, and redress of social inequities after the war.

Ironically, the position of moderate union leaders in national war coalitions was strengthened by objection among workers to the war and to the sacrifices demanded of them. All over Europe, autonomous movements of shop-floor workers' councils emerged, continuing labour's prewar tradition of pacifism and internationalism. Workers' councils not only opposed the governments that organized the war and the employers that profited from it but they also rejected the leadership of collaborationist unions and social-democratic political parties. Rather than parliamentary social democracy, their objective was a syndicalist political order founded on and controlled by councils of industrial workers. Especially toward the end of the war, council movements succeeded in organizing major strikes in a number of countries, and in Russia the Bolsheviks overthrew the tsar with a program of soviet (that is, "coun-

Politicized unionism

National confederations and industrywide bargaining

Syndicalism

cil") democracy (see below *Eastern Europe*). All of this enabled moderate union leaders to extract more promises and commitments from governments, military leaders, and employers for the time after the war.

Faced with overexpanded economies, huge national debts, a radicalized and assertive working class, and the threat of revolutionary internationalism inspired and supported by the Soviet Union, employers and political elites after 1918 were eager to close ranks with the moderate labour leaders who had assumed quasi-governmental responsibility during the war. In country after country, unions obtained major concessions, such as universal suffrage and parliamentary democracy, the right to strike, legal support of union organization and industrywide collective bargaining, the extension of industrial agreements to nonunionized firms and sectors, the eight-hour working day, a wide range of social benefits, joint councils of unions and employers to oversee key industries, and works councils to represent workers at the workplace. Often these were conceded as elements of comprehensive social pacts—like the Stinnes-Legien Agreement in Germany—that were negotiated between national organizations of capital and labour and underwritten by the government, apparently foreshadowing a continuing role of unions in the governance of national economies.

In most European countries, the bulk of the concessions made in the immediate aftermath of the war were withdrawn in subsequent years. Increasingly, the stabilization of western Europe's war-torn economies came to be perceived as possible only at the expense of workers and unions, with the fight against inflation seeming to require wage cuts, longer hours, curtailment of union rights, sharp reductions in public spending, and the resulting high unemployment. As domestic conflicts intensified, the political right found confirmed its old doubts about the compatibility of social order and national unity with democracy and free trade unions, and even the moderate left came again to question the compatibility of democracy and full employment with capitalism. The Great Depression of the early 1930s, in particular, brought large-scale unemployment and made deep inroads in the organizational strength and political influence of unions, in many countries abolishing the fragile postwar gains in the institutionalization of union rights and collective bargaining.

By the end of the 1920s at the latest, national political systems in Europe began to drift sharply apart. First in Italy and most dramatically in Germany, Fascist or conservative-authoritarian regimes either outlawed unions altogether—often driving their leaders from their countries, incarcerating them, or assassinating them—or turned them into appendages of an ever-more powerful state apparatus. Authoritarian responses to class conflict and economic crisis were encouraged by an international environment that seemed to offer little opportunity for shared economic growth and few if any alternatives to nationalist protection and preparation for renewed military hostilities.

In Sweden, on the other hand, the electoral victory of the Social Democrats in 1932 paved the way for the first successful attempt to achieve full employment by Keynesian means under political democracy and free collective bargaining within a capitalist economy. After intense industrial and social conflict in the 1920s, the Social Democrats were able to unite their country behind a platform of state-led expansion, an extensive social-welfare policy, social equality, and institutionalized autonomy for responsible, centralized, and comprehensive collective bargaining. In 1938, the peak associations of business and labour concluded the Saltsjöbaden Agreement, in which, while affirming the rights of unions to strike and of employers to lock out in retaliation, they pledged to use these measures only as a last resort and in consideration of their effect on third parties. Swedish unions, having moved into a secure position of industrial strength in which their actions inevitably affected the performance of the national economy, accepted responsibility for economic growth and monetary stability in exchange for a number of concessions: a complementary social and labour-market policy; the cooperation of employers in a reduction of pay differentials; progressive taxation; expansion of employment in

Collective bargaining in Sweden

the public sector; and equal participation of women in the work force. Given such economic and political strength, Swedish unions were prepared to accept employers' claims to an almost unlimited right to manage. As World War II drew closer, therefore, Germany and Sweden represented opposite ends of a wide spectrum of western European politics and industrial relations.

It was only after 1945, under the leadership of the two victorious democracies, the United States and Britain, that unions and collective bargaining became firmly established throughout western Europe. In some countries, business and traditional elites were discredited by their collaboration with Fascist regimes or the German occupation. In others, joint resistance during the war had laid the ground for close postwar cooperation. Everywhere, the presence of Soviet Communism as an apparent alternative to capitalism seemed to make it imperative to include moderate labour movements in the reconstruction. And not least, the United States, as the architect of a system of free trade intended to be immune against the nationalism of the interwar years, needed to ensure that competing economies were saddled with the same social costs that it had incurred under the New Deal.

Modern western Europe thus came to be built on a "historical compromise" between capital and labour. Among the concessions gained by the latter were a firm commitment to parliamentary democracy; a welfare state establishing a basic floor of income and services for all citizens; a commitment of governments, of whatever political complexion, to an active full-employment policy; and the right of unions to free collective bargaining. In return, moderate labour movements pledged to pursue political reform only by constitutional means, renouncing in particular the use of the strike for political purposes; tolerated private property in the means of production; accepted a free-market economy with little or no public intervention in price formation; and agreed in principle to observe the right of management to manage. By the end of the 1950s at the latest, most European unions had, explicitly or implicitly, come to accept the terms of this bargain.

This second postwar settlement marked the beginning of the longest uninterrupted period of peace and prosperity in European history. Embedded in an international free-trade regime guaranteed and dominated by the United States, it helped accelerate the spread from America to Europe of "Fordist" modes of production and accumulation: the mass manufacture of standardized consumer durables in factories that used Taylorist methods of work organization and were operated by large, vertically integrated, and increasingly multinational corporations. By helping to expand and maintain the purchasing power of mass consumers, European unions also played an important part in the stabilization of economic growth. Moreover, by concentrating their activities on macroeconomic wage bargaining and redistributive social policies at the national level, political-industrial unions left managers the freedom to introduce new technologies and to rationalize the labour process in pursuit of higher productivity and profitability.

The "historical compromise"

BREAKUP OF THE POSTWAR SETTLEMENT: INFLATION, NEOCORPORATISM, AND RESTRUCTURING

An inherent problem of the post-World War II settlement was that, with governments guaranteeing full employment and free collective bargaining, inflation could be contained only if unions resisted using their artificially increased bargaining power to win wage gains in excess of productivity increases. This required, at the minimum, effective control of national unions over the shop floor. While European industrial unions were much more successful in this than their British counterparts, by the end of the 1960s even their hold on their members began to slip. In part this was caused by a general rise in inflation imported from the United States. When unions continued to exercise wage restraint in increasingly overheated national economies, a new generation of workers that had not lived through the Great Depression and had never experienced unemployment turned against their leaders. All over Europe, massive waves of unofficial strikes occurred in 1968 and 1969, organized from the shop floor in defiance of na-

The strike wave of 1968–69

tional union policy and throwing moderate "income policies" into disarray. More subtle factors also contributed to this outbreak. By concentrating on macroeconomic matters during a period of aggressive rationalization and fast productivity growth, industrial unions had left workers with little protection at the workplace. Growing discontent with an ever more perfect Taylorist organization of work, workers found no official representation in an industrial-relations system that had accepted managerial prerogative in the workplace in exchange for the recognition and political status of unions, full employment, growing wages, and a comprehensive welfare state. Remarkably, such discontent emerged strongly even in countries, such as Italy and France, where unions were weak and the shop floor was ruled by employer paternalism, and Germany and Sweden, where union distance from the "qualitative" issues of the workplace was part of a general union strategy of economywide solidarity and egalitarianism.

During the 1960s it had come to be widely believed in Europe that worker militancy was a matter of the past and that strikes in particular were withering away. This made the shock of 1968 and '69 all the more profound, and in the immediate aftermath employers and national governments accepted high wage increases and inflation rates in order to avoid further confrontations with workers. This lasted well into 1973 and 1974, the years of the first oil crisis, when governments continued to assign high priority to full employment without touching unions' right to free collective bargaining. Instead, economic stabilization was sought by bringing unions still further into the centre of policy making, increasing rather than curtailing their power and responsibility and helping them strengthen their organizations so that national union leaders could manage shop-floor discontent more effectively. This brought about a new political configuration that came to be known as "neocorporatism."

Essentially a tripartite social contract involving government, business, and labour, neocorporatism sought to restore full employment through moderate wage demands (often entailing losses in real wages and distributive position), in return for which unions were granted influence over policies relating to subjects such as unemployment insurance, employment protection, early retirement, working hours, old-age pensions, health insurance, housing, taxation, public-sector employment, vocational training, regional aid, and subsidies to declining industries. In addition, governments and employers agreed to a variety of means to help industrial unions strengthen their workplace **Industrial** organizations so they could better absorb worker discon-**democracy,** tent. One important means was legislation on industrial **or "co-** democracy. "Codetermination," as it was called in Ger-**determina-** many and Sweden, provided workers with quasi-constitu-**tion"** tionalized shop-floor representation on nonwage matters, such as work organization, that industrial unions had been unable or unwilling to address before 1968. Thus, in order to prevent a return of the representation gap of the 1960s and channel the energies of workplace unionists into economically innocuous activities, governments in a number of countries allowed industrial democracy to make significant inroads into managerial discretion. For this and other reasons, neocorporatism increasingly alienated European employers, but unions, backed by and working through the new or expanded institutions of industrial democracy, often succeeded in increasing their membership density during the 1970s.

The second oil shock in 1979 heralded fundamental changes in European economic policy and industrial relations. Faced with persistently high unemployment, an increasingly integrated world capital market and a rapid loss of competitive position to Japan, European governments gradually abandoned their attempts at bargained national accommodation with organized labour and gave preference to supply-side policies of competitive restructuring. An important factor in this restructuring was the advance of microelectronic technology. Unlike the dedicated technology of the Fordist period, microelectronics allowed for a variety of alternative, "flexible" ways of organizing production in response to different product strategies, local organizational structures and cultures, and available work skills. For unions to play a role in the reorganization of productive relations that was made possible (and necessary) by the new technologies, they had to decentralize their organizational and political capacities and create a strong union presence in the workplace.

Other factors also militated toward the decentralization of unions and industrial relations. As the work force became increasingly heterogenous, its interests were less easily subsumed under the blue-collar egalitarianism that had dominated union policies since the interwar and immediate postwar years. In particular, during the 1960s and '70s pay differentials had been reduced to the point where many skilled and white-collar workers were no longer willing to be represented by comprehensive, "solidaristic" collective bargaining. Class-based solidarity was further attenuated by growing employment in the public sector—often under privileged conditions that in the leaner 1980s were perceived by private-sector workers as coming at their expense. As a result, national unions found it more difficult to unite their members behind common demands. Where centralized wage bargaining did not actually break up—as it did in Sweden—union leaders came under pressure to give groups inside their organizations greater freedom to express and pursue their special interests.

During the 1980s most western European unions came **Adaptation** to realize that the survival of the high-wage and high-**to the** welfare economies that they had been so instrumental **changing** in creating depended less on political bargains with the **workplace** government and national employers' associations than on participating in this restructuring toward a flexible, highly skilled, innovative economy capable of producing customized and quality-competitive goods and services. This seemed to require cooperative workplace relations, flexible internal labour markets, extensive training and retraining of workers, and a fundamental reorganization of work. This last involved a blurring of the distinction between conception and execution or between indirect and direct, nonmanual and manual, and managerial and nonmanagerial work; decentralization of decision making; flatter hierarchies; and broader and overlapping job descriptions and skill profiles.

Never having depended for their strength on job control, European unions found it easier to adapt to the "post-Fordist" forms of industrial organization than did their British or American counterparts. Still, adaptation required that unions decentralize their organizations and insert themselves into the workplace in a way that jeopardized neither productive cooperation nor their own independence. For this, industrial unions that could avail themselves of established systems of industrial democracy and codetermination seem to have been particularly well placed. Indeed, German and Scandinavian unions in particular may actually have contributed to the quality-competitive restructuring of their economies by, on the one hand, foreclosing employers' options of hiring low-wage and low-skill labour and, on the other hand, exerting pressures and creating opportunities at the workplace for the de-Taylorization of work organization and the general upgrading of production. Especially important in this context were the unions' roles in labour-market policy and vocational training.

By adjusting to the requirements of productive flexibility at the workplace, then, most Scandinavian unions increased their membership density, while Belgian, German, and in part Italian unions maintained their strength. In France, Spain, and to an extent The Netherlands and Austria, on the other hand, unions were left behind by rapid industrial modernization and went into precipitous decline.   (WOLFGANG STREECK)

CONTRIBUTORS

Adelman, Kenneth L. Vice President, Institute for Contemporary Studies; Syndicated Columnist. Author of *Getting the Job Done* and others.
ECONOMIC AFFAIRS: Special Report

Aers, Vivianne L. Editor and Publisher. Publishing Consultant, *World Fishing*.
AGRICULTURE AND FOOD SUPPLIES: *Fisheries*

Allaby, Michael. Writer and Lecturer. Author of *Ecology Facts; A Guide to Gaia*.
ENVIRONMENT (*in part*)

Allan, J.A. Professor of Geography, School of Oriental and African Studies, University of London.
WORLD AFFAIRS: *Libya*

Amedeo, Michael. Writer, Encyclopædia Britannica Educational Corp.; Free-lance Entertainment Writer, *Chicago Sun-Times*.
BIOGRAPHIES (*in part*)

Anderson, D.F. Director, Department of Economic Affairs, International Iron & Steel Institute, Brussels. Author of *Steel Demand Forcasting* and others.
INDUSTRIAL REVIEW: *Iron and Steel*

Anderson, Matthew Smith. Emeritus Professor of International History, University of London. Author of *Europe in the Eighteenth Century, 1713–1783* and others.
Macropædia: FREDERICK THE GREAT

Archibald, John J. Retired Feature Writer, *St. Louis* (Mo.) *Post-Dispatch;* Adjunct Professor, Washington University, St. Louis; Member of Professional Bowlers Association Hall of Fame.
SPORTS AND GAMES: *Bowling (in part)*

Armstrong, George. Rome Correspondent, *The Economist*.
WORLD AFFAIRS: *Italy*

Arnold, Guy. Free-lance Writer. Author of *Modern Nigeria; Aid in Africa;* and others.
WORLD AFFAIRS: *Botswana; Burundi; Cape Verde; Chad; Comoros; Djibouti; Equatorial Guinea; Gambia, The; Ghana; Guinea-Bissau; Lesotho; Liberia; Madagascar; Maldives; Mauritius; Nigeria; Rwanda; São Tomé and Príncipe; Seychelles; Sierra Leone; Swaziland*

Arnold, Mavis. Free-lance Journalist, Dublin.
WORLD AFFAIRS: *Ireland*

Arrington, Leonard J. Formerly Church Historian, Church of Jesus Christ of Latter-day Saints.
RELIGION: *Church of Jesus Christ of Latter-day Saints*

Balaban, Avraham. Professor of Modern Hebrew Literature, University of Florida, Gainesville. Author of *Between God and Beast: An Examination of Amos Oz's Prose*.
LITERATURE: *Hebrew*

Bannen, James T. Political Consultant and Free-lance Writer.
BIOGRAPHIES (*in part*)

Baptist, Ines T. Free-lance Writer.
WORLD AFFAIRS: *Belize*

Barford, Michael F. Editor and Director, *Tabacosmos*, London.
CONSUMER AFFAIRS: Sidebar; INDUSTRIAL REVIEW: *Tobacco*

Barrett, David B. Missions Researcher, Foreign Mission Board, U.S. Southern Baptist Convention; Church Missionary Society, Church of England.
RELIGION: *World Religious Statistics*

Barrett, John C.A. Headmaster, The Leys School, Cambridge, England; Secretary, British Committee, World Methodist Council. Author of *Family Worship in Theory and Practice*.
RELIGION: *Methodist Churches*

Bass, Howard. Journalist and Broadcaster; Ice Hockey Correspondent, *Daily Telegraph*, London; Skiing and Skating Correspondent, *Daily Mail*, London. Author of 16 books on winter sports.

BIOGRAPHIES (*in part*); SPORTS AND GAMES: *Ice Hockey (in part); Ice Skating; Skiing*

Bickelhaupt, David L. Professor Emeritus, Faculty of Finance, College of Business, Ohio State University, Columbus.
INDUSTRIAL REVIEW: *Insurance*

Bird, Thomas E. Director, Council for the Study of Ethics and Public Policy, Queens College, City University of New York.
LITERATURE: *Yiddish*

Bisman, Ronald W. North Island Editor, *New Zealand Harness Racing Weekly*. Author of *Salute to Trotting; Harness Heroes*.
SPORTS AND GAMES: *Horse Racing (in part)*

Bleibtreu, Hermann K. Professor of Anthropology, University of Arizona.
ANTHROPOLOGY

Boddy, William C. Editor, *Motor Sport*. Full Member, Guild of Motoring Writers.
SPORTS AND GAMES: *Automobile Racing (in part)*

Boden, Edward. Publications Adviser, British Veterinary Association; formerly Editor, *Veterinary Record*.
HEALTH AND DISEASE: *Veterinary Medicine*

Booth, John Nicholls. Lecturer and Writer. Author of *The Quest for Preaching Power*.
RELIGION: *Unitarian (Universalist) Churches*

Boothroyd, Andrew T. University Lecturer and Fellow of Oriel College, Oxford Department of Physics, Clarendon Laboratory, University of Oxford, England.
PHYSICS

Boswall, Jeffery. Senior Lecturer in Biological Imaging, University of Derby, England.
LIFE SCIENCES: *Ornithology*

Box, Ben. Editor, Trade and Travel Publications (*South American Handbook* and others).
WORLD AFFAIRS: *Costa Rica*

Boye, Roger. Coin Columnist, *Chicago Tribune*.
PHILATELY AND NUMISMATICS: *Coins and Paper Money*

Boylan, Patrick J. Professor and Head, Department of Arts Policy and Management, City University, London. Author of *Museums 2000: Politics, People, Professionals and Profit* and others.
MUSEUMS (*in part*)

Bradsher, Henry S. Foreign Affairs Writer.
WORLD AFFAIRS: *Philippines*

Braidwood, Robert J. Professor Emeritus of Old World Prehistory, Oriental Institute and Department of Anthropology, University of Chicago. Author of *Prehistoric Men*.
ARCHAEOLOGY: *Eastern Hemisphere*

Brazee, Rutlage J. Geophysical Consultant.
EARTH SCIENCES: *Geophysics*

Brecher, Kenneth. Professor of Astronomy and Physics, Boston University. Coauthor and coeditor of *Astronomy of the Ancients*.
ASTRONOMY

Brody, David. Professor of History, University of California at Davis. Author of *Workers in Industrial America: Essays on the Twentieth Century Struggle* and others.
Macropædia: WORK AND EMPLOYMENT (*in part*)

Brokopp, John G. Specialist in publicity, public relations, and writing about horse racing.
SPORTS AND GAMES: *Horse Racing (in part)*

Brown, Heidi C.D. Technical Information Officer, British Glass Manufacturers Confederation, Sheffield, England.
INDUSTRIAL REVIEW: *Glass*

Brown, Maggie. Media Editor, The Independent Newspapers, London.
PUBLISHING: *Magazines (in part); Newspapers (in part);* Sidebar

Bundy, Colin J. Professor of History and Director, Institute of Historical Research, University of the Western Cape, Bellville, South Africa.

Author of *Rise and Fall of the South African Peasantry*.
Macropædia: SOUTHERN AFRICA (*in part*)

Burdin, Joel L. Coordinator of Educational Administration, Frostburg (Md.) State University.
EDUCATION (*in part*)

Burks, Ardath W. Emeritus Professor of Asian Studies, Rutgers University.
WORLD AFFAIRS: *Japan*

Butler, Frank. Former Sports Editor, *News of the World*, London. Author of *The Good, the Bad and the Ugly: A Story of Boxing*.
SPORTS AND GAMES: *Boxing*

Cafferty, Bernard. Editor, *British Chess Magazine*; Chess Columnist, *The Sunday Times*, London.
SPORTS AND GAMES: *Chess*

Cameron, Sarah. Free-lance Writer and Editor, Trade and Travel Publications.
WORLD AFFAIRS: *Cuba; Dominican Republic; El Salvador; Guatemala; Haiti; Honduras; Nicaragua; Panama*

Campbell, Robert. Architect and Architecture Critic. Author of *Cityscapes of Boston;* Coauthor of *American Architecture of the 1980s*.
ARCHITECTURE

Cantrell, Scott. Classical Music Editor, *Kansas City* (Mo.) *Star*.
MUSIC: *Classical*

Carnes, Jim. Free-lance Writer; formerly Associate Editor, *Encyclopædia Britannica*.
AGRICULTURE AND FOOD SUPPLIES: Sidebar; ART EXHIBITIONS AND ART SALES: Sidebar; BIOGRAPHIES (*in part*); MUSIC: Sidebar; RACE RELATIONS: Sidebar; WORLD AFFAIRS: *Spain:* Sidebar

Carter, Robert W. Journalist, London.
SPORTS AND GAMES: *Horse Racing (in part)*

Chapman, Kenneth F. Former Editor, *Stamp Collecting* and *Philatelic Magazine*.
PHILATELY AND NUMISMATICS: *Stamps*

Chappell, Duncan. Director, Australian Institute of Criminology.
CRIME, LAW ENFORCEMENT, AND PENOLOGY: *Crime; Law Enforcement*

Chapple, Abby. Writer and Consultant, Consumer Communications, Annapolis, Md.
INDUSTRIAL REVIEW: *Furniture*

Cheuse, Alan. Writing Faculty, English Department, George Mason University, Fairfax, Va.; Book Commentator, National Public Radio. Author of *The Light Possessed* and others.
LITERATURE: *English (in part)*

Clapham, Christopher S. Professor of Politics and International Relations, University of Lancaster, England. Author of *Transformation and Continuity in Revolutionary Ethiopia*.
WORLD AFFAIRS: *Ethiopia*

Clarke, Judith L. Lecturer, Department of Journalism, Baptist College, Hong Kong.
WORLD AFFAIRS: *Cambodia; Vietnam*

Clarke, R.O. Lecturer and Consultant on Industrial Relations, London.
LABOUR–MANAGEMENT RELATIONS

Cleveland, William A. Editor, Britannica World Data and *Britannica Atlas*.
MINING

Clough, Huw. Free-lance Translator and Writer on Iberia and Latin America.
WORLD AFFAIRS: *Bolivia; Colombia; Mexico; Peru; Venezuela*

Cogle, T.C.J. Consultant, *Electrical Review*, London.
INDUSTRIAL REVIEW: *Electrical*

Cook, Kevin G. Global Publications Officer, International Organization of Consumers Unions, Santiago, Chile.
CONSUMER AFFAIRS (*in part*)

Cooper, Melanie Anne. Senior Editorial Assistant, *Newsweek* magazine.

WORLD AFFAIRS: *United States:* Developments in the States in 1992

Costin, Stanley H. British Correspondent, *Nykytekstiili,* Finland, and *Textilia,* The Netherlands.
FASHION AND DRESS *(in part)*

Coveney, Michael. Theatre Critic, *The Observer.* Author of *Maggie Smith: A Bright Particular Star* and others.
THEATRE *(in part)*

Crampton, Richard J. Fellow, St. Edmund Hall, Oxford, England; formerly Professor of East European History, University of Kent at Canterbury. Author of *Bulgaria 1878–1918: A History* and others.
WORLD AFFAIRS: *Bulgaria*

Crowley, Edward. Technical Journalist; Director, Technical Writing Services.
INDUSTRIAL REVIEW: *Shipbuilding;* TRANSPORTATION *(in part)*

Cunningham, Susan M. Economic and Political Analyst; Free-lance Writer. Author of *Latin America Since 1945* (in preparation).
WORLD AFFAIRS: *Argentina; Brazil; Latin-American Affairs*

Curwen, Peter J. Reader in Business Policy, Sheffield Business School, England. Author of *The U.K. Publishing Industry* and others.
PUBLISHING: *Books (in part)*

Cviic, K.F. East European Specialist, Royal Institute of International Affairs, London.
WORLD AFFAIRS: *Bosnia and Hercegovina; Croatia; Macedonia; Slovenia; Yugoslavia*

Czerwinski, Edward J. Professor of Slavic and Comparative Literature, State University of New York at Stony Brook. Author of *Contemporary Polish Theater and Drama (1956–1984);* Area Editor, *Theater Companies of the World.*
LITERATURE: *Eastern European (in part); Russian (in part)*

Davis, Donald A. Editor, *Drug & Cosmetic Industry* and *Cosmetic Insider's Report.*
INDUSTRIAL REVIEW: *Pharmaceuticals*

Deam, John B. Technical Director, AMT—The Association for Manufacturing Technology, McLean, Va.
INDUSTRIAL REVIEW: *Machinery and Machine Tools*

de la Barre, Kenneth. Director, Katimavik, Montreal.
WORLD AFFAIRS: *Arctic Regions*

Deletant, Dennis J. Senior Lecturer in Romanian Studies, University of London. Author of *Colloquial Romanian; Romania* (World Bibliographical Series).
WORLD AFFAIRS: *Romania*

Denselow, Robin. Rock Music Critic, *The Guardian,* London; Current Affairs Reporter, BBC Television. Author of *When the Music's Over: The Politics of Pop.*
MUSIC: *Popular*

De Puy, Norman R. Minister, American Baptist Churches; Editor and Publisher, *Cabbages and Kings* newsletter.
RELIGION: *Baptist Churches*

Deshayes, Marie-Jose. Head of Documentation Service, International Vine and Wine Office, Paris.
INDUSTRIAL REVIEW: *Beverages (in part)*

Dicks, Geoffrey R. Associate Professor, London Business School. Author of *Sources of World Financial and Banking Information.*
INDUSTRIAL REVIEW: *Introduction*

Dirnbacher, Elfriede. Austrian Civil Servant.
WORLD AFFAIRS: *Austria*

Dixon, Bernard. Science Writer; Consultant. European Editor, *Bio/Technology;* Editor, *Medical Science Research.* Author of *Health and the Human Body* and others.
HEALTH AND DISEASE: *Mental Health; Overview (in part)*

Dooling, Dave. Consultant and Writer, D² Associates, Huntsville, Ala.
SPACE EXPLORATION

Dormer, Albert G. Bridge Correspondent, *The Times,* London. Coauthor of *Complete Book of Bridge* and others.
SPORTS AND GAMES: *Contract Bridge*

Dorris, Thomas Hartley. Communications Director, Life and Peace Institute, Uppsala, Sweden.
RELIGION: *Lutheran Communion*

Earp, John H. Director, Halcrow Fox and Associates, Bristol, England.
TRANSPORTATION *(in part)*

Ehringer, Gavin Forbes. Rodeo Columnist, *Western Horseman,* Colorado Springs, Colo.
SPORTS AND GAMES: *Rodeo*

Eisenhammer, John. Chief Correspondent on Germany, *The Independent,* London.
WORLD AFFAIRS: *Germany*

Elliot, Betsy Rossen. Associate Editor, *Compton's Encyclopedia.*
BIOGRAPHIES *(in part);* ENGINEERING PROJECTS: Sidebar

Emerson, Warren K. Writer and Photographer.
SPORTS AND GAMES: *Badminton*

Engels, Jan R. Retired Director, Centre Paul Hymans.
WORLD AFFAIRS: *Belgium*

Farr, D.M.L. Professor Emeritus of History, Carleton University, Ottawa.
WORLD AFFAIRS: *Canada*

Fendell, Robert J. Newspaper Writer on automotive topics. Author of *How to Make Your Car Last* and others.
SPORTS AND GAMES: *Automobile Racing (in part)*

Finkelstein, Ellen. Senior Copy Editor, Encyclopædia Britannica, Inc.
BIOGRAPHIES *(in part)*

Flagg, Gordon. Senior Editor, *American Libraries* magazine.
LIBRARIES *(in part)*

Follett, Christopher. Denmark Correspondent, *The Times,* London; Danish Correspondent, Radio Sweden; Newscaster, Radio Denmark; Free-lance Correspondent, Reuters. Author of *Fodspor paa Cypern.*
WORLD AFFAIRS: *Denmark*

Franz, Frederick W. President, Watch Tower Bible and Tract Society of Pennsylvania.
RELIGION: *Jehovah's Witnesses*

Friday, Elbert W., Jr. Assistant Administrator for Weather Services, National Oceanic and Atmospheric Administration.
EARTH SCIENCES: *Meteorology*

Fridovich, Irwin. James B. Duke Professor of Biochemistry, Duke University Medical Center, Durham, N.C.
LIFE SCIENCES: *Molecular Biology (in part)*

Fridovich-Keil, Judith L. Assistant Professor of Medical Genetics, Emory University School of Medicine, Atlanta, Ga.
LIFE SCIENCES: *Molecular Biology (in part)*

Friskin, Sydney E. Hockey Correspondent, *The Times,* London.
SPORTS AND GAMES: *Billiard Games (in part); Field Hockey*

Frost, David. Rugby Union Writer, *The Guardian,* London.
SPORTS AND GAMES: *Football (in part)*

Gaddum, Anthony H. Chairman, H. T. Gaddum and Company Ltd., Silk Merchants, Macclesfield, Cheshire, England; Deputy Vice President, International Silk Association.
INDUSTRIAL REVIEW: *Textiles (in part)*

Ganado, Albert. Lawyer, Malta.
WORLD AFFAIRS: *Malta*

Ganguly, Dilip. Senior Correspondent, The Associated Press (USA), South Asia Bureau, New Delhi, India.
WORLD AFFAIRS: *Afghanistan; Bangladesh; Bhutan; Myanmar; Nepal; Pakistan; Sri Lanka*

Gibbons, Anne R. Free-lance Writer.
LIFE SCIENCES: *Entomology*

Gibbons, J. Whitfield. Professor of Zoology, University of Georgia's Savannah River Ecology Laboratory, Aiken, S.C.
LIFE SCIENCES: *Zoology*

Gjester, Fay. Free-lance Journalist and Editor; Oslo Correspondent, *Petroleum Economist* and *Offshore Engineer,* London.
WORLD AFFAIRS: *Norway*

Goldblatt, Howard C. Professor of Chinese, University of Colorado, Boulder. Author of *Chinese Literature for the 1980s* and others.
LITERATURE: *Chinese*

Goldsmith, Arthur. Editor-at-Large, *Popular Photography,* New York City.
PHOTOGRAPHY

Goodwin, Noël. Free-lance Writer and Broadcaster. Associate Editor and Music Editor, *Dance & Dancers.*
DANCE *(in part)*

Gottfried, Martin. Drama Critic, New York City. Author of *All His Jazz: The Life and Death of Bob Fosse; More Broadway Musicals.*
THEATRE *(in part)*

Greeman, Adrian Lee. Editor, *Ground Engineering.*
ENGINEERING PROJECTS: *Bridges*

Green, Anthony L. Senior Copy Editor, Encyclopædia Britannica, Inc.
BIOGRAPHIES *(in part)*

Greskovic, Robert J. Free-lance Dance Writer. Coauthor of *Balanchine's Teaching and Technique* (in preparation).
DANCE *(in part)*

Griffiths, A.R.G. Senior Lecturer in History, Flinders University of South Australia. Author of *Contemporary Australia.*
BIOGRAPHIES *(in part);* WORLD AFFAIRS: *Australia; Nauru; Papua New Guinea*

Grossman, Joel W. Archaeologist.
ARCHAEOLOGY: *Western Hemisphere.*

Guthridge, Guy G. Manager, Polar Information Program, U.S. National Science Foundation.
WORLD AFFAIRS: *Antarctica*

Hambly, Gavin R.G. Professor of History, University of Texas at Dallas. Coauthor and editor of *Central Asia.*
Macropædia: CENTRAL ASIA *(in part)*

Hannen, Mark. Competitions Officer, English Basket Ball Association.
SPORTS AND GAMES: *Basketball (in part)*

Harakas, Stanley S. Archbishop Iakovos Professor of Orthodox Theology, Holy Cross Greek Orthodox School of Theology, Brookline, Mass. Author of *Toward Transfigured Life: The "Theoria" of Eastern Orthodox Ethics.*
RELIGION: *The Orthodox Church; Oriental Orthodox Church*

Hartman, Kathleen. Picture Archivist, Encyclopædia Britannica, Inc.
BIOGRAPHIES *(in part)*

Haub, Carl V. Demographer, Population Reference Bureau, Washington, D.C.
POPULATIONS AND POPULATION MOVEMENTS: *Demography*

Havard-Williams, P. Professor of Library and Information Studies, University of Botswana. Emeritus Professor, Loughborough University, Leicestershire, England.
LIBRARIES *(in part)*

Hawkland, William D. Chancellor Emeritus of Law and Boyd Professor, Louisiana State University.
LAW: *Court Decisions*

Hebblethwaite, Peter. Vatican Affairs Writer, *National Catholic Reporter,* Kansas City, Mo.
BIOGRAPHIES *(in part);* RELIGION: *Roman Catholic Church*

Hébert, Pierre. Professor *titulaire,* University of Sherbrooke, Que.
LITERATURE: *French (in part)*

Hendershott, Jon. Associate Editor, *Track & Field News* magazine. Author of *Track's Greatest Women.*
SPORTS AND GAMES: *Track and Field Sports (in part)*

Hendershott, Myrl C. Professor of Oceanography, Scripps Institution of Oceanography, La Jolla, Calif.
EARTH SCIENCES: *Oceanography*

534 **Contributors**

Hess, Marvin G. Executive Vice President, National Wrestling Coaches Association.
SPORTS AND GAMES: *Wrestling*

Hoeksema, Klaas J. Staff Member, Institute for Polytechnics, Amsterdam.
WORLD AFFAIRS: *Netherlands, The; Suriname*

Hope, Thomas W. Chairman, Hope Reports, Inc., Rochester, N.Y.
MOTION PICTURES *(in part)*

Hunnings, Neville March. Editorial Director, European Law Centre, Sweet & Maxwell, London. Editor, *Common Market Law Reports.*
LAW: *International Law*

IEIS. International Economic Information Services, London.
ECONOMIC AFFAIRS: *World Economy; Stock Exchanges (in part)*

Ingham, Kenneth. Emeritus Professor of History, University of Bristol, England. Author of *Politics in Modern Africa: The Uneven Tribal Dimension* and others.
WORLD AFFAIRS: *Angola; Kenya; Malawi; Mozambique; Sudan, The; Tanzania; Uganda; Zaire; Zambia; Zimbabwe*

Ingram, Derek. Editor, Gemini News Service, London. Author of *Commonwealth for a Colour-Blind World; The Imperfect Commonwealth.*
WORLD AFFAIRS: *Commonwealth of Nations*

Jackson, Martin. Publisher and Editor in Chief, *Broadcast* magazine, London.
TELEVISION AND RADIO *(in part)*

Jardine, Adrian. Company Director. Member, Guild of Yachting Writers.
SPORTS AND GAMES: *Sailing*

Jaspert, W. Pincus. Technical and Editorial Consultant. International Editor, *American Printer* and *World-Wide Printer.* Author of *State of the Art* (4th ed.) and others.
INDUSTRIAL REVIEW: *Printing*

Jessell, Harry A. Senior Editor, *Broadcasting* magazine, Washington, D.C.
TELEVISION AND RADIO *(in part)*

Joffé, George. Journalist and Writer on North African and Middle Eastern Affairs.
WORLD AFFAIRS: *Algeria; Morocco; Tunisia*

Johnsson, William G. Editor, *Adventist Review.* Author of *Behold His Glory* and others.
RELIGION: *Seventh-day Adventist Church*

Jones, Alice M. Editorial Associate, *Yearbook of American and Canadian Churches.*
WORLD AFFAIRS: *United States (table)*

Jones, D.A.N. Novelist and Critic. Author of *Parade in Pairs; Never Had It So Good.*
LITERATURE: *Introduction; United Kingdom*

Jones, W. Glyn. Professor of European Literature, University of East Anglia, Norwich, England.
LITERATURE: *Danish*

Joseph, Lou. Free-lance Science Writer, Chicago.
HEALTH AND DISEASE: *Dentistry*

Jotischky, Helma. Principal Research Officer, Paint Research Association, London.
INDUSTRIAL REVIEW: *Paints and Varnishes*

Katz, William A. Professor, School of Information Science and Policy, State University of New York, Albany.
PUBLISHING: *Magazines (in part)*

Kelleher, John A. New Zealand Journalist. Formerly Editor, *The Dominion* and *Dominion Sunday Times,* Wellington, New Zealand.
WORLD AFFAIRS: *New Zealand*

Kellman, Jerold L. President, Gabriel House, Inc.
BIOGRAPHIES *(in part)*

Kellner, Peter. Political Commentator, BBC Television. Author of *The Civil Servants: An Inquiry into Britain's Ruling Class* and others.
BIOGRAPHIES *(in part)*; WORLD AFFAIRS: *United Kingdom; United Kingdom: Sidebar*

Kennedy, Richard M. Agricultural Economist, Agriculture and Trade Analysis Division of the Economic Research Service, U.S. Department of Agriculture.
AGRICULTURE AND FOOD SUPPLIES *(in part)*

Kieffer, Sandra Marie. Illustrations Permissions Coordinator, Encyclopædia Britannica, Inc.
BIOGRAPHIES *(in part)*

Kilian, Michael D. Washington Columnist, *Chicago Tribune.* Author of *Flying Can Be Fun; Heavy Losses.*
SPORTS AND GAMES: *Aerial Sports*

Kimche, Jon. Formerly Editor, *New Middle East; Afro-Asian Affairs,* London. Author of *Palestine or Israel* and others.
WORLD AFFAIRS: *Israel*

Kind, Joshua B. Professor of Art History, Northern Illinois University, De Kalb. Author of *Rouault; Geometry as Abstract Art.*
MUSEUMS *(in part)*

Kirk, Margaret. United Kingdom Press Officer, Salvation Army.
RELIGION: *Salvation Army*

Kloos, Jean Clark Cameron. Consultant, Timber Research and Development Association.
INDUSTRIAL REVIEW: *Wood Products*

Knox, Richard A. Managing Editor, *Power Technology International* and *Power Generation Technology.*
INDUSTRIAL REVIEW: *Nuclear Industry*

Kolankiewicz, George. Lecturer in Sociology, University of Essex, England; Research Coordinator, Research Initiative on East-West Studies, U.K. Economic and Social Research Council. Coauthor of *Social Groups in Polish Society* and others.
WORLD AFFAIRS: *Poland*

Kroll, Thomas E. Visiting Assistant Professor, Roosevelt University, Chicago; President, Thomas Kroll Associates. Author of *Introduction to Telecommunications.*
INDUSTRIAL REVIEW: *Microelectronics; Telecommunications*

Kushnick, Louis. Senior Lecturer, Department of American Studies, University of Manchester, England.
POPULATIONS AND POPULATION MOVEMENTS: *International Migration;* RACE RELATIONS

LaFleur, Virginia M. LaFleur & Associates, Editorial & Graphic Design.
BIOGRAPHIES *(in part)*

Lamb, Kevin M. Special Projects Writer, *Dayton* (Ohio) *Daily News.* Author of *Quarterbacks, Nickelbacks & Other Loose Change.*
BIOGRAPHIES *(in part)*; SPORTS AND GAMES: *Football (in part)*

Laqueur, Walter. Chairman, International Research Council, Center for Strategic & International Studies, Washington, D.C. Author of *Europe in Our Time.*
WORLD AFFAIRS: *Introduction*

Larsson, Gerd. Japan Correspondent, *Dagens Industri.*
BIOGRAPHIES *(in part)*

Laskey, Elizabeth. Senior Copy Editor, Encyclopædia Britannica, Inc.
BIOGRAPHIES *(in part)*

Lawler, Nancy Ellen. Professor of Economics, Oakton Community College, Des Plaines, Ill. Author of *Soldiers of Misfortune* and others.
WORLD AFFAIRS: *Benin; Burkina Faso; Cameroon; Central African Republic; Congo; Côte d'Ivoire; Gabon; Guinea; Mali; Mauritania; Niger; Senegal; Togo*

Legassick, Martin. Lecturer, History Department, University of the Western Cape, South Africa.
WORLD AFFAIRS: *Namibia; South Africa*

Legum, Colin. Associate Editor (1947–81), *The Observer;* Editor, *Africa Contemporary Record* and *Third World Reports,* London.
BIOGRAPHIES *(in part)*; WORLD AFFAIRS: *African Affairs*

Lennox-Kerr, Peter. Editor, *High Performance Textiles* and *OE Report;* European Editor, *Textile World.* Author of *World Fibres Book.*
INDUSTRIAL REVIEW: *Textiles (in part)*

Levine, Lisbeth. Fashion Editor, *Chicago Sun-Times.*
FASHION AND DRESS *(in part)*

Levine, Steven I. Scholar in Residence, Asian-Pacific Studies Institute, Duke University, Durham, N.C. Author of *Anvil of Victory: The Communist Revolution in Manchuria* and others.
WORLD AFFAIRS: *China; Taiwan*

Litsky, Frank. Sportswriter, *New York Times.*
SPORTS AND GAMES: *Ice Hockey (in part)*

Litweiler, John. Jazz Critic; Contributor to *Down Beat, Chicago Tribune,* and other publications. Author of *The Freedom Principle: Jazz after 1958.*
MUSIC: *Jazz*

Logan, Robert G. Sportswriter, *Daily Herald,* Arlington Heights, Ill. Author of *Cubs Win!* and others.
SPORTS AND GAMES: *Basketball (in part)*

Longmore, Andrew. Free-lance Sportswriter, *The Times,* London; formerly Assistant Editor, *The Cricketer.*
BIOGRAPHIES *(in part)*; SPORTS AND GAMES: *Cricket; Tennis*

Lovell, John Christopher. Senior Lecturer in Economic and Social History, University of Kent at Canterbury, England. Author of *British Trade Unions 1875–1933* and others.
Macropædia: WORK AND EMPLOYMENT *(in part)*

Luling, Virginia R. Social Anthropologist.
WORLD AFFAIRS: *Somalia*

Lyles, Jean Caffey. News Director, United Methodist News Service, Evanston, Ill.; Editor-at-Large, *The Christian Century.*
RELIGION: *Introduction*

McBride, Gail W. Free-lance Medical Writer and Editor; formerly Medical News Editor, *Journal of the American Medical Association.*
HEALTH AND DISEASE: *Overview (in part);* HEALTH AND DISEASE: Sidebar

McCauley, Martin. Senior Lecturer in Politics, School of Slavonic and East European Studies, University of London.
Macropædia: UNION OF SOVIET SOCIALIST REPUBLICS; WORLD AFFAIRS: *Armenia; Azerbaijan; Belarus; Commonwealth of Independent States; Estonia; Georgia; Kazakhstan; Kyrgyzstan; Latvia; Lithuania; Moldova; Russia; Tajikistan; Turkmenistan; Ukraine; Uzbekistan*

McClure, Amanda. Editorial Coordinator, *Compton's Encyclopedia.*
BIOGRAPHIES *(in part)*

Macdonald, Barrie. Professor of History, Massey University, Palmerston North, N.Z.
WORLD AFFAIRS: *Dependent States (in part); Fiji; Kiribati; Marshall Islands; Micronesia, Federated States of; Oceanian Affairs; Solomon Islands; Tonga; Tuvalu; Vanuatu; Western Samoa*

McGregor, Alan. Geneva Correspondent, *The Times,* London; Swiss Radio International, Bern; ABC, Australia; and RNZ, New Zealand.
WORLD AFFAIRS: *Switzerland*

McLachlan, Keith S. Professor, School of Oriental and African Studies, University of London.
WORLD AFFAIRS: *Iran*

Mallett, H.M.F. Editor, *Wool Record Weekly Market Report,* Bradford, England.
INDUSTRIAL REVIEW: *Textiles (in part)*

Mango, Andrew. Foreign Affairs Analyst.
WORLD AFFAIRS: *Turkey*

Mars, Deborah A. Editorial Coordinator, CMME, *Compton's Encyclopedia.*
BIOGRAPHIES *(in part)*

Martin, Marvin. Free-lance Writer.
BIOGRAPHIES *(in part)*; LIFE SCIENCES: Sidebar

Marty, Martin E. Fairfax M. Cone Distinguished Service Professor of the History of Modern Christianity, University of Chicago.
RELIGION: Special Report

Mateja, James L. Auto Editor, Columnist, and Financial Reporter, *Chicago Tribune.* Author of *Used Cars: Finding the Best Buy.*
INDUSTRIAL REVIEW: *Automobiles (in part)*

Mathews, John H. Copy Editor, Encyclopædia Britannica, Inc.
BIOGRAPHIES *(in part)*

Matthíasson, Björn. Economist, Ministry of Finance, Iceland.

WORLD AFFAIRS: *Iceland*
Maunder, Michael. Head of Conservation Unit, Living Collections Department, Royal Botanic Gardens, Kew, England.
BOTANICAL GARDENS AND ZOOS (in part)
Mazie, David M. Staff Writer, *Reader's Digest;* Free-lance Writer.
SOCIAL SECURITY AND WELFARE SERVICES *(in part)*
Mazze, Edward Mark. Professor of Marketing, School of Business Administration, Temple University, Philadelphia.
CONSUMER AFFAIRS *(in part);* INDUSTRIAL REVIEW: *Advertising*
Mermel, T.W. Consultant; formerly Chairman, Committee on World Register of Dams, International Commission on Large Dams.
ENGINEERING PROJECTS: *Dams; Dams table*
Millikin, Sandra. Architectural Historian.
ART EXHIBITIONS AND ART SALES: *Art Exhibitions*
Modiano, Mario. Athens Correspondent (1952–90), *The Times,* London.
WORLD AFFAIRS: *Greece*
Moragne, Edward Paul. Index Supervisor, Encyclopædia Britannica, Inc.
BIOGRAPHIES *(in part)*
Morris, Jacqui M. Editor, *Oryx* magazine.
ENVIRONMENT *(in part)*
Morrison, Donald. Assistant Managing Editor, *Entertainment Weekly* magazine.
PUBLISHING: *Newspapers (in part);* WORLD AFFAIRS: *United States; United States: Special Report*
Mumtaz, Khawar. Coordinator, Shirkat Gah—Women's Resource Centre, Lahore, Pakistan. Author of *Women of Pakistan: Two Steps Forward, One Step Back.*
ANTHROPOLOGY: Special Report
Murray, Lorraine. Assistant Editor, Encyclopædia Britannica, Inc.
BIOGRAPHIES *(in part)*
Musiker, Liz Hartman. Free-lance Public Relations Writer; formerly Associate Director of Publicity, Simon & Schuster.
PUBLISHING: *Books (in part)*
Myers, Susan Marts. Project Editor, Educational Foundation of the National Restaurant Association.
BIOGRAPHIES *(in part)*
Nagy, Joseph L. Senior Editor, *Asiaweek* magazine, Hong Kong.
WORLD AFFAIRS: *Korea, Democratic People's Republic of; Korea, Republic of*
Naylor, Ernest. Lloyd Roberts Professor of Marine Zoology, University College of North Wales.
LIFE SCIENCES: *Marine Biology*
Neher, Stephen. Assistant Editor, Britannica World Data.
INDUSTRIAL REVIEW: *Beverages (in part)*
Nelson, Bert. Editor, *Track and Field News.* Author of *Olympic Track and Field.*
SPORTS AND GAMES: *Track and Field Sports (in part)*
Netschert, Bruce C. Retired Vice President, National Economic Research Associates, Inc., Washington, D.C.
ENERGY
Neusner, Jacob. Distinguished Research Professor of Religious Studies, University of South Florida. Author of *Transformation of Judaism.*
RELIGION: *Judaism*
Newby, Donald J. Bowls Correspondent, *Daily Telegraph,* London; formerly Editor, *World Bowls.* Author of various bowls publications.
SPORTS AND GAMES: *Lawn Bowls*
Newton, Carolyn D. Free-lance Writer and Editor.
NOBEL PRIZES *(in part)*
Niesz, Dale E. Director, Center for Ceramic Research, Rutgers University.
INDUSTRIAL REVIEW: *Ceramics*
Norman, Geraldine. Art Market Correspondent, *The Independent,* London. Author of *Nineteenth*

Century Painters and Painting; Coauthor of *The Fake's Progress.*
ART EXHIBITIONS AND ART SALES: *Art Sales*
Oberman, Bonnie. Writer and Editor.
NOBEL PRIZES *(in part)*
O'Donoghue, Michael. Curator, Science Reference Library, London; Lecturer in Gemmology, City of London Polytechnic.
INDUSTRIAL REVIEW: *Gemstones*
O'Dwyer, Thomas. Foreign Editor, *Jerusalem Post;* Writer on East Mediterranean and Middle East affairs.
WORLD AFFAIRS: *Cyprus*
Olejnik, Renee Mahn. Executive Editor, American Power Boat Association.
SPORTS AND GAMES: *Motorboating*
Olney, P.J.S. Director, Federation of Zoos of Great Britain and Ireland. Editor, *International Zoo Yearbook.*
BOTANICAL GARDENS AND ZOOS *(in part)*
Olson, Kay Melchisedech. Executive Editor, *Flower & Garden* magazine, Kansas City, Mo.
GARDENING *(in part)*
Osborne, Keith. Editor, *British Rowing Almanack* (since 1960). Author of *Boat Racing in Britain, 1715–1975.*
SPORTS AND GAMES: *Rowing*
Osterbind, Carter C. Associate, Gerontology Center, and Professor Emeritus of Economics, University of Florida.
INDUSTRIAL REVIEW: *Building and Construction*
Palmer, John. European Editor, *The Guardian,* Brussels.
WORLD AFFAIRS: *European Affairs (in part)*
Parker, Sandy. Publisher of weekly newsletter on fur industry; Copublisher, *Fur World.*
INDUSTRIAL REVIEW: *Furs*
Pasco, Adam Gerhold. Editor, *BBC Gardeners' World* magazine; formerly Editor, *Garden News, Garden Answers,* and *Greenhouse* magazines.
GARDENING *(in part)*
Paul, Charles Robert, Jr. Consultant, U.S. Olympic Committee, Colorado Springs, Colo.
SPORTS AND GAMES: *Gymnastics; Weight Lifting*
Penfold, Robin C. Free-lance Writer on industrial topics. Formerly Editor, *Shell Petrochemicals.* Author of *A Journalist's Guide to Plastics.*
INDUSTRIAL REVIEW: *Plastics*
Perlinska, Agnieszka. Ph.D. Candidate in Department of Comparative Literature, New York University.
LITERATURE: *Eastern European (in part); Russian (in part)*
Pertile, Lino. Professor of Italian, University of Edinburgh, Scotland.
LITERATURE: *Italian*
Petherick, Karin. Reader in Swedish, University of London.
LITERATURE: *Swedish*
Pfeffer, Irving. Attorney. Author of *The Financing of Small Business.*
ECONOMIC AFFAIRS: *Stock Exchanges (in part)*
Pinfold, Geoffrey M. Director, NCL Stewart Scott Ltd., London. Author of *Reinforced Concrete Chimneys and Towers.*
ENGINEERING PROJECTS: *Buildings*
Poirié, François. Writer and Critic. Author of *La Passade légendaire; Ils dansent.*
LITERATURE: *French (in part)*
Prasad, H.Y. Sharada. Formerly Information Adviser to the Prime Minister of India.
WORLD AFFAIRS: *India*
Prince, Greg W. Senior Editor, *Beverage World.*
INDUSTRIAL REVIEW: *Beverages (in part)*
Ranger, Robin. Vice President, Ranger Associates Inc., Washington, D.C. Author of *Arms and Politics 1958–1978; Arms Control in a Changing Political Context.*
MILITARY AFFAIRS; MILITARY AFFAIRS: Special Report
Rapp, Susan. Associate Science Editor, *Compton's Encyclopedia.*
BIOGRAPHIES *(in part)*
Raymond, Judith E. Research Officer, Research and Documentation Branch, ISSA.

SOCIAL SECURITY AND WELFARE SERVICES *(in part)*
Rebelo, L.S. Reader Emeritus, Department of Portuguese Studies, King's College, University of London.
LITERATURE: *Portuguese (in part)*
Reed, Arthur. Senior Editor, Europe, *Air Transport World.* Author of *Britain's Aircraft Industry;* Coauthor of *RAE Farnborough.*
TRANSPORTATION *(in part)*
Reid, J.H. Professor of Contemporary German Studies, University of Nottingham, England. Author of *Writing Without Taboos: The New East German Literature* and others.
LITERATURE: *German*
Reid, Philip D. Louise C. Harrington Professor of Biological Sciences, Smith College, Northampton, Mass.
LIFE SCIENCES: *Botany*
Renwick, David. Free-lance Journalist.
WORLD AFFAIRS: *Antigua and Barbuda; Bahamas, The; Barbados; Dependent States (in part); Dominica; Grenada; Guyana; Jamaica; Saint Kitts and Nevis; Saint Lucia; Saint Vincent and the Grenadines; Trinidad and Tobago*
Reynolds, Frank E. Professor of the History of Religions and Buddhist Studies, Divinity School, University of Chicago.
RELIGION: *Buddhism (in part)*
Riggs, Thomas. Free-lance Writer.
BIOGRAPHIES *(in part)*
Robinson, David. Film Critic, *The Times,* London. Author of *A History of World Cinema; Chaplin: His Life and Art.*
MOTION PICTURES *(in part)*
Roby, Anne. Associate Editor, Compton's Encyclopedia.
WORLD AFFAIRS: *Andorra; Luxembourg; Monaco*
Rollin, Jack. Association Football Columnist, *Sunday Telegraph,* London. Editor, *Rothmans Football Yearbook.* Author of *World Cup 1930–1990* and others.
BIOGRAPHIES *(in part);* SPORTS AND GAMES: *Football (in part)*
Rutherford, Andrew. Reader, Faculty of Law, University of Southampton, England. Author of *Criminal Justice and the Pursuit of Decency* and others.
CRIME, LAW ENFORCEMENT, AND PENOLOGY: *Prisons and Penology*
Saeki, Shoichi. Professor of Literature, Chuo University, Tokyo. Author of *Japanese Autobiographies.*
LITERATURE: *Japanese*
Sakauchi, Rinzo. Editor, *Britannica International Yearbook,* Tokyo.
INDUSTRIAL REVIEW: *Automobiles (in part)*
Salisbury, Jonathan M. Publisher, *World Toy News,* U.K.
INDUSTRIAL REVIEW: *Games and Toys*
Saludo, Ricardo L. Senior Editor, *Asiaweek* magazine, Hong Kong.
WORLD AFFAIRS: *Indonesia; Malaysia; Singapore*
Sanders, Alan J.K. Lecturer in Mongolian Studies, School of Oriental and African Studies, University of London. Author of *Mongolia: Politics, Economics and Society.*
WORLD AFFAIRS: *Mongolia*
Sarahete, Yrjö. General Secretary, Fédération Internationale des Quilleurs, Helsinki.
SPORTS AND GAMES: *Bowling (in part)*
Sarmiento, Sergio. Editor in Chief, Spanish- and Portuguese-language publications, Encyclopædia Britannica Publishers, Inc.
SPORTS AND GAMES: *Baseball (in part); Football (in part)*
Sauvage, Christian. Editor in Chief, Agence Presse Hachette; Chief of Political Service, *Journal du Dimanche.* Author of *Les Giscardiens.*
WORLD AFFAIRS: *France*
Scherer, Allan D. Director, United States Polo Association; Editor, *Polo Newsletter.*
SPORTS AND GAMES: *Polo*
Schoenfield, Albert. Member, U.S. Swimming Olympic International Committee (1989–92).

Formerly Publisher, *Swimming World.* Honouree, International Swimming Hall of Fame.
SPORTS AND GAMES: *Swimming*

Schöpflin, George. Lecturer in East European Political Institutions, London School of Economics and School of Slavonic and East European Studies, University of London.
WORLD AFFAIRS: *Czechoslovakia; European Affairs (in part); Hungary*

Seddon, Stephen S. Index Editor, Encyclopædia Britannica, Inc.
BIOGRAPHIES *(in part)*

Shackleford, Peter. Chief of Environment, Planning, and Finance, World Tourism Organization, Madrid.
INDUSTRIAL REVIEW: *Tourism*

Shelley, Andrew. Events Manager, Squash Rackets Association, England.
SPORTS AND GAMES: *Squash Rackets*

Shepherd, Melinda C. Associate Editor, Encyclopædia Britannica Yearbooks.
SPORTS AND GAMES: Special Report; WORLD AFFAIRS: *Dependent States (in part); Political Parties (in part)*

Sherman, Francine Shonfeld. Assistant Editor, *Compton's Encyclopedia.*
BIOGRAPHIES *(in part);* ENVIRONMENT: Sidebar

Sherry, Paul H. President, United Church of Christ, Cleveland, Ohio.
RELIGION: *United Church of Christ*

Sinor, Denis. Distinguished Professor Emeritus of Uralic and Altaic Studies and of History, Indiana University, Bloomington. Author of *Inner Asia* and others.
Macropædia: CENTRAL ASIA *(in part)*

Smith, Donald. Editor, *Rubber World* magazine, Akron, Ohio.
INDUSTRIAL REVIEW: *Rubber*

Smith, Gregory O. Dean of Academic Affairs, American University of Rome.
WORLD AFFAIRS: *San Marino; Vatican City State*

Smith, Hedrick. Writer, Author, Lecturer, TV Commentator, and Documentarian. Author of *The Power Game: How Washington Works; The New Russians;* and others.
Commentary: THE NOT – SO – NEW WORLD ORDER

Smith, Reuben W. Dean, Graduate School, and Professor of History, University of the Pacific, Stockton, Calif.
RELIGION: *Islam*

Sorkin, Beverly E. Copy Editor, Encyclopædia Britannica, Inc.
BIOGRAPHIES *(in part)*

Sparks, Karen. Senior Editor, Encyclopædia Britannica Yearbooks.
WORLD AFFAIRS: *Liechtenstein*

Stephens, Sarah. Executive Secretary for Cooperation and Witness, World Alliance of Reformed Churches.
RELIGION: *Reformed, Presbyterian, and Congregational Churches*

Stern, Irwin. Senior Lecturer in Portuguese, Columbia University, New York City.
LITERATURE: *Portuguese (in part)*

Stewart, Ian. Professor of Mathematics, University of Warwick, England. Author of *Does God Play Dice?; Game, Set, and Math.*
MATHEMATICS

Støverud, Torbjørn. Honorary Research Fellow, University College, London.
LITERATURE: *Norwegian*

Streeck, Wolfgang. Professor of Sociology and Industrial Relations, University of Wisconsin, Madison. Coeditor of *New Technology and Industrial Relations.*
Macropædia: WORK AND EMPLOYMENT *(in part)*

Sullivan, H. Patrick. Dean Emeritus of the College and Professor of Religion, Vassar College, Poughkeepsie, N.Y.
RELIGION: *Hinduism*

Summerhill, Edward M. Staff Member, Reuters; Free-lance Writer, Finnish News Agency.
WORLD AFFAIRS: *Finland*

Sumner, David E. Author of *The Episcopal*

Church's History: 1945–1985. Columnist; Contributor to Episcopal Church periodicals.
RELIGION: *Anglican Communion*

Suzuki, Toshihiko. Senior Editor, Dobunshoin International, Tokyo.
SPORTS AND GAMES: *Baseball (in part)*

Swan, Russ. Editor, *World Highways,* Nottingham, England.
ENGINEERING PROJECTS: *Roads*

Swift, Richard N. Professor Emeritus of Politics, New York University, New York City.
WORLD AFFAIRS: *United Nations*

Synan, Vinson. Chairman, North American Renewal Service Committee. Author of *The Holiness-Pentecostal Movement.*
RELIGION: *Pentecostal Churches*

Taggart, Charles Johnson. Free-lance Writer.
BIOGRAPHIES *(in part)*

Taishoff, Lawrence B. Chairman, *Broadcasting* magazine, Washington, D.C.; Adviser, Cahners Consumer/Entertainment Publishing Division.
TELEVISION AND RADIO *(in part)*

Tateishi, Kay K. Free-lance Writer and Translator.
BIOGRAPHIES *(in part)*

Taylor, Robert G. Nordic Correspondent, *Financial Times,* London. Author of *The Fifth Estates: Britain's Unions in the Modern World* and others.
WORLD AFFAIRS: *Sweden*

Taylor, Thomas. General Secretary of Friends World Committee for Consultation.
RELIGION: *Religious Society of Friends*

Thomas, Robert Murray. Professor of Education and Head, Program in International Education, University of California at Santa Barbara. Author of *International Comparative Education* and others.
EDUCATION *(in part)*

Thompson, Leonard Monteath. Charles H. Stillé Professor Emeritus of History, Yale University; Director, Yale Southern African Research Program. Author of *The Political Mythology of Apartheid.*
Macropædia: SOUTHERN AFRICA *(in part)*

Treverton, Gregory F. Senior Fellow, Council on Foreign Relations, New York City. Author of *Covert Action* and others.
WORLD AFFAIRS: *European Affairs:* Special Report

UNHCR. The Office of the United Nations High Commissioner for Refugees.
POPULATIONS AND POPULATION MOVEMENTS: *Refugees*

Utt, Roger L. Editor, *Puerta del Sol,* Madrid; formerly Assistant Professor of Spanish, Department of Romance Languages and Literatures, University of Chicago.
LITERATURE: *Spanish (in part)*

Vale, Norman K. Retired Director of News Services, The United Church of Canada.
RELIGION: *The United Church of Canada*

Van Haveren, Bruce P. Adjunct Professor, Department of Earth Resources, Colorado State University, Fort Collins, Colo. Author of *Water Resource Measurements: A Handbook.*
EARTH SCIENCES: *Hydrology*

Venzke, Bruce H. Associate Editor, *Pool & Billiard Magazine.* Member, Statistics and Records Committee, Billiard Congress of America; President, Billiard Congress of Wisconsin.
SPORTS AND GAMES: *Billiard Games (in part)*

Verdi, Robert William. Sports Columnist, *Chicago Tribune.*
SPORTS AND GAMES: *Baseball (in part)*

Vint, Arthur Kingsley. Counselor, International Table Tennis Federation.
SPORTS AND GAMES: *Table Tennis*

Wallis, Shani. Editorial Consultant, *Tunnels & Tunnelling* magazine, London.
ENGINEERING PROJECTS: *Tunnels*

Walters, Jonathan S. Assistant Professor of Religion, Whitman College, Walla Walla, Wash.
RELIGION: *Buddhism (in part)*

Wanninger, Richard S. Director of Media Re-

lations, United States Volleyball Association.
SPORTS AND GAMES: *Volleyball*

Warner, Edward S. Editor, *Advanced Wireless Communications* magazine.
INFORMATION PROCESSING AND INFORMATION SYSTEMS *(in part);* INFORMATION PROCESSING AND INFORMATION SYSTEMS: Sidebar

Warren, J. Robert. Executive Editor, *Chemical Business.*
INDUSTRIAL REVIEW: *Chemicals*

Way, Diane Lois. Historical Researcher.
BIOGRAPHIES *(in part)*

Weinthal, John R. Writer on the auto industry.
INDUSTRIAL REVIEW: *Automobiles (in part)*

Westberg, M. Victor. Manager, Committees on Publication, The First Church of Christ, Scientist, Boston.
RELIGION: *Church of Christ, Scientist*

Whelan, John. Consultant Editor, *Sawt Al Kuwait* and *New Arabia,* London.
WORLD AFFAIRS: *Bahrain; Egypt; Iraq; Jordan; Kuwait; Lebanon; Middle Eastern and North African Affairs; Oman; Qatar; Saudi Arabia; Syria; United Arab Emirates; Yemen*

Whitney, Barbara. Copy Supervisor, Encyclopædia Britannica, Inc.
BIOGRAPHIES *(in part)*

Wilkinson, John R. Sportswriter, Coventry Newspapers Ltd., U.K.
SPORTS AND GAMES: *Cycling*

Williams, Michael. Golf Correspondent, *Daily Telegraph,* London.
SPORTS AND GAMES: *Golf*

Williams, Raymond Leslie. Professor of Spanish, University of Colorado, Boulder.
LITERATURE: *Spanish (in part)*

Willis, Clifford L. Director of News and Information, Office of Communication, Christian Church (Disciples of Christ).
RELIGION: *Christian Church (Disciples of Christ)*

Wilson, Michael. Free-lance Aviation Writer and Consultant; Associate Editor, *Prophecy Today.*
INDUSTRIAL REVIEW: *Aerospace*

Woodrow, Robert. Assistant Managing Editor, *Asiaweek* magazine, Hong Kong.
WORLD AFFAIRS: *Laos; Thailand*

Woods, Elizabeth. Writer. Author of *If Only Things Were Different (I): A Model for a Sustainable Society* and others.
LITERATURE: *English (in part)*

Woods, Michael. Science Editor, *Toledo* (Ohio) *Blade.*
CHEMISTRY

Woodward, Berton. Assistant Managing Editor, *Asiaweek* magazine, Hong Kong.
WORLD AFFAIRS: *Brunei; Dependent States (in part); Southeast Asian Affairs*

Woollen, Anthony. Editor (1959–79), *Food Manufacture,* London. Editor, *Food Industries Manual* (20th ed.).
AGRICULTURE AND FOOD SUPPLIES: *Food Processing*

Wooller, Michael. Economist and Researcher on Iberia and South America.
WORLD AFFAIRS: *Chile; Ecuador; Paraguay; Portugal; Spain; Uruguay*

Wyllie, Peter John. Division of Geological and Planetary Sciences, California Institute of Technology.
EARTH SCIENCES: *Geology and Geochemistry*

Yamadori, Yuji. Director, Research and International Affairs, Japan Information Processing Development Center.
INFORMATION PROCESSING AND INFORMATION SYSTEMS *(in part)*

Young, M. Norvel. Chancellor Emeritus, Pepperdine University, Malibu, Calif. Author of *Preachers of Today.*
RELIGION: *Churches of Christ*

Zanga, Louis. Analyst, RFE/RL Research Institute, Munich, Germany.
WORLD AFFAIRS: *Albania*

1993
Britannica
World Data

Encyclopædia Britannica, Inc.
Chicago
Auckland/Geneva/London/Madrid/Manila/Paris/Rome
Seoul/Sydney/Tokyo/Toronto

CONTENTS

INTRODUCTION

Britannica World Data provides a statistical portrait of some 220 countries and dependencies of the world, at a level appropriate to the size and importance of each. It contains 195 country statements (the "Nations of the World" section), ranging in length from one to four pages, and permits, in the development of more than a score of major thematic tables (the "Comparative National Statistics" section), simultaneous comparisons among all of these larger countries and 26 additional smaller dependent states.

The entrance of more than a score of newly independent countries onto the world stage during 1990 and 1991 has displaced a number of smaller dependent states for which pages had been provided in past editions of *Britannica World Data* (despite its increased length this year). These new countries, by virtue of their population, economic importance, and independent status, must, naturally, be assigned coverage commensurate with their importance, but, their present status being only recently acquired, most have not yet been assimilated by the information systems of international organizations like the UN. Thus, certain information provided will remain in the form published by the country itself, rather than the more-familiar international consensus presentation available for older states. Further, this year the "World and regional summaries" table has been made permanent, the "Religion" table restored, and a new "Communications" table added.

Updated annually, *Britannica World Data* can be consulted as a separate work of reference developing a particular body of subject matter, but it is particularly intended as direct, structured support for many of Britannica's other reference works—encyclopaedias, yearbooks, atlases—at a level of detail that their editorial style or space requirements do not permit.

Like the textual, graphic, or cartographic modes of expression of these other products, statistics possess their own inherent editorial virtues and weaknesses. Two principal goals in the creation of *Britannica World Data* were up-to-dateness and comparability, each possible separately, but not always possible to combine. If, for example, research on some subject is completed during a particular year (x), figures may be available for 100 countries for the preceding year ($x - 1$), for 140 countries for the year before that ($x - 2$), and for 180 countries for the year before that ($x - 3$).

Which year should be the basis of a thematic compilation for 220 countries so as to give the best combination of up-to-dateness and comparability? And, should $x - 1$ be adopted for the thematic table, ought up-to-dateness in the country table (for which year x is already available) be sacrificed for agreement with the thematic table? In general, the editors have opted for maximum up-to-dateness in the country statistical boxes and maximum comparability in the thematic tables, so as to take the best advantage of late information, published and unpublished.

Comparability, however, also resides in the meaning of the numbers compiled, which may differ greatly from country to country. The headnotes to the thematic tables explain many of these definitional problems; the Glossary serves the same purpose for the country statistical pages. Since the researcher or editor does not always find a neat, unambiguous choice between a datum compiled on two different bases (say, railroad track length, or route length), one of which is wanted and the other not, a choice must often be made between the latest official national data (which may be incomplete, published only after a delay of several years, politically suspect, compiled on the wrong basis [for international comparability], or may refer to some time period other than a standard Gregorian calendar year) and some external figure, often only an estimate, compiled by an international organization (such as the UN, FAO, or IMF), on the desired basis, but often at a considerable remove from the country's own most recent data. When no recent official data exist, the tables may show unofficial estimates, a range (of published opinion), analogous data, or no data at all. For certain subjects, especially population, the editors have prepared their own estimates.

The published basis of the information compiled is the statistical collections of Encyclopædia Britannica, Inc., some of the principal elements of which are enumerated in the Bibliography. All of these sources are held, and updated continuously for editorial use, in Britannica's editorial offices. The publications themselves are issued in some 75 languages in common use among the countries of the world; the information contained in them is supplemented by unpublished data received in correspondence from the countries concerned. Usual holdings for a country with a well-developed statistical and publishing program may include any of the following kinds of documents: the national statistical abstract; the constitution; the most recent censuses of population; periodic or occasional reports on vital statistics, social indicators, agriculture, mining, labour, manufacturing, wholesale and retail trade, finance and banking, development planning, foreign trade, transportation, and communications.

The great majority of the social, economic, and financial data contained in this work should not be interpreted in isolation. Interpretive text of long perspective, such as that of the *Encyclopædia Britannica* itself; political, geographic, and topical maps, such as those in the *Britannica Atlas;* and recent analysis of political events and economic trends, such as that contained in the articles of the *Book of the Year,* will all help to supply balance, physical framework, and analytic focus that numbers alone cannot provide. By the same token, study of those sources will be made more concrete by use of *Britannica World Data* to supply up-to-date geographic, demographic, and economic data to illuminate the methodology of those works.

GLOSSARY

A number of terms that are used to classify and report data in the "Nations of the World" section require some explanation.

Those italicized terms that are used regularly in the country compilations to introduce specific categories of information (*e.g., birth rate, budget*) appear in this glossary in italic boldface type, followed by a description of the precise kind of information being offered and how it has been edited and presented.

All other terms are printed here in roman boldface type. Many terms have quite specific meanings in statistical reporting, and they are so defined here. Other terms have less specific application as they are used by different countries or organizations. Data in the country compilations based on definitions markedly different from those below will usually be footnoted.

Terms that appear in small capitals in certain definitions are themselves defined at their respective alphabetical locations.

Terms whose definitions are marked by an asterisk (*) refer to data supplied only in the larger two- to four-page country compilations.

access to services, a group of measures indicating a population's level of access to public services, including electrical power, treated public drinking water, sewage removal, and fire protection.*

activity rate, *see* participation/activity rates.

age breakdown, the distribution of a given population by age, usually reported here as percentages of total population in 15-year age brackets. When substantial numbers of persons do not know, or state, their exact age, distributions may not total 100.0%.

area, the total surface area of a country or its administrative subdivisions, including both land and inland (nontidal) water area. Land area is usually calculated from "mean low water" on a "plane table," or flat, basis.

area and population, a tabulation usually including the first-order administrative subdivisions of the country (such as the states of the United States), with capital (headquarters, or administrative seat), area, and population. When these subdivisions are especially numerous or, occasionally, nonexistent, a regional, electoral, census, or other nonadministrative scheme of subdivisions has been substituted.

associated state, *see* (free) association; *see* state.

atheist, in statements of religious affiliation, one who professes active opposition to religion; "nonreligious" refers to those professing only no religion, nonbelief, or doubt.

balance of payments, a financial statement for a country for a given period showing the balance among: (1) transactions in goods, services, and income between that country and the rest of the world, (2) changes in ownership or valuation of that country's monetary gold, SPECIAL DRAWING RIGHTS, and claims on and liabilities to the rest of the world, and (3) unrequited transfers and counterpart entries needed (in an accounting sense) to balance transactions and changes among any of the foregoing types of exchange that are not mutually offsetting. The United Nations *System of National Accounts* (SNA) provides a framework for international comparability in classifying such transactions, but detail of local law as to what constitutes a transaction, the basis of its valuation, and the size of a transaction visible to fiscal authorities all result in differences in the meaning of a particular national statement.*

balance of trade, the net value of all international goods trade of a country, usually excluding reexports (goods received only for transshipment), and the percentage that this net represents of total trade.

Balance of trade refers only to the "visible" international trade of goods as recorded by customs authorities and is thus a segment of a country's BALANCE OF PAYMENTS, which takes all visible and invisible trade with other countries into account. (Invisible trade refers to imports and exports of money, financial instruments, and services such as transport, tourism, and insurance.) A country has a favourable balance of trade when the value of exports exceeds that of imports.

barrel (bbl), a unit of liquid measure. The barrel conventionally used for reporting crude petroleum and petroleum products is equal to 42 U.S. gallons, or 159 litres. The number of barrels of crude petroleum per metric ton, ranging typically from 6.45 to 8.13, depends upon the specific gravity of the petroleum. The world average is roughly 7.33 barrels per ton.

birth rate, the number of live births annually per 1,000 of midyear population. Birth rates for individual countries may be compared with the world annual average of 27 births per 1,000 population between 1985 and 1990.

budget, the annual receipts and expenditures of a central government for its activities only; does not include state, provincial, or local governments or semipublic (parastatal, quasi-nongovernmental) corporations unless other-

---

Abbreviations

Measurements

cu m	cubic metre(s)
kg	kilogram(s)
km	kilometre(s)
kW	kilowatt(s)
kW-hr	kilowatt-hour(s)
metric ton-km	metric ton-kilometre(s)
mi	mile(s)
passenger-km	passenger-kilometre(s)
passenger-mi	passenger-mile(s)
short ton-mi	short ton-mile(s)
sq km	square kilometre(s)
sq m	square metre(s)
sq mi	square mile(s)
troy oz	troy ounce(s)
yr	year(s)

Political Units and International Organizations

CACM	Central American Common Market
Caricom	Caribbean Community and Common Market
CFA	Communauté Financière Africaine
CFP	Comptoirs Françaises du Pacifique
CUSA	Customs Union of Southern Africa
E.Ger.	East Germany
EEC	European Economic Community
FAO	United Nations Food and Agriculture Organization
IMF	International Monetary Fund
OECS	Organization of Eastern Caribbean States
U.A.E.	United Arab Emirates
U.K.	United Kingdom
U.S.	United States
U.S.S.R.	Union of Soviet Socialist Republics
W.Ger.	West Germany

Months

Jan.	January	Oct.	October
Feb.	February	Nov.	November
Aug.	August	Dec.	December
Sept.	September		

Miscellaneous

AIDS	Acquired Immune Deficiency Syndrome
avg.	average
c.i.f.	cost, insurance, and freight
commun.	communications
CPI	consumer price index
est.	estimate(d)
excl.	excluding
f.o.b.	free on board
GDP	gross domestic product
GNP	gross national product
govt.	government
incl.	including
mo.	month(s)
n.a.	not available (in text)
n.e.s.	not elsewhere specified
NMP	net material product
no.	number
pl.	plural
pos.	position
pub. admin.	public administration
PVC	Polyvinyl Chloride
SDR	Special Drawing Right
SITC	Standard International Trade Classification
svcs.	services
teacher tr.	teacher training
transp.	transportation
voc.	vocational
$	dollar (of any currency area)
£	pound (of any currency area)
...	not available (in tables)
—	none, less than half the smallest unit shown, or not applicable (in tables)

wise specified. Figures for budgets are limited to ordinary (recurrent) receipts and expenditures, wherever possible, and exclude capital expenditures, *i.e.,* funds for development and other special projects originating as foreign-aid grants or loans.

When both a recurrent and a capital budget exist for a single country, the former is the budget funded entirely from national resources (taxes, duties, excises, etc.) that would recur (be generated by economic activity) every year. It funds the most basic governmental services, those least able to suffer interruption. The capital budget is usually funded by external aid and may change its size considerably from year to year.

capital, usually, the actual seat of government and administration of a state. When more than one capital exists, each is identified by kind; when interim arrangements exist during the creation or movement of a national capital, the de facto situation is described.

Anomalous cases are annotated, such as those in which (1) the de jure designation under the country's laws differs from actual local practice (*e.g.,* Benin's designation of one capital in constitutional law, but another in actual practice), (2) international recognition does not validate a country's claim (as with the proclamation by Israel of a capital on territory not fully recognized as part of Israel), or (3) both a state and a capital have been proclaimed on territory recognized as part of another state (as with the Turkish Republic of Northern Cyprus).

capital budget, *see* budget.

causes of death, as defined by the World Health Organization, "the disease or injury which initiated the train of morbid events leading directly to death, or the circumstances of accident or violence which produced the fatal injury." This principle, the "underlying cause of death," is the basis of the medical judgment as to cause; the statistical classification system according to which these causes are grouped and named is the *International List of Causes of Death,* the latest revision of which is the Ninth. Reporting is usually in terms of events per 100,000 population. When data on actual causes of death are unavailable, information on morbidity, or illness rate, usually given as reported cases per 100,000 of infectious diseases (notifiable to WHO as a matter of international agreement), may be substituted.

chief of state/head of government, paramount national governmental officer(s) exercising the highest executive and/or ceremonial roles of a country's government. In general usage, the chief of state is the formal head of a national state. The primary responsibilities of the chief of state may range from the purely ceremonial—convening legislatures and greeting foreign officials—to the exercise of complete national executive authority. The head of government, when this function exists separately, is the officer nominally charged (by the constitution) with the majority of actual executive powers, though they may not in practice be exercised, especially in military or single-party regimes in which effective power may reside entirely outside the executive governmental machinery provided by the constitution. A prime minister, for example, usually understood to be the head of government, may in practice exercise only cabinet-level authority.

In communist countries an official identified as the chief of state may be the chairman of the policy-making organ, and the official given as the head of government the chairman of the nominal administrative/executive organ.

c.i.f. (trade valuation): *see* imports.

colony, an area annexed to, or controlled by, an independent state but not an integral part of it; a non-self-governing territory. A colony has a charter and may have a degree of self-government. A crown colony is a colony originally chartered by the British government.

commonwealth (U.K. and U.S.), a self-governing political entity that has regard to the common weal, or good; usually associated with the United Kingdom or United States. Examples include the Commonwealth of Nations (composed of independent states [from 1931 onward]), Puerto Rico since 1952, and the Northern Marianas since 1979.

communications, collectively, the means available for the public transmission of information within a country. Data are provided for daily newspapers, their number and total circulation, and the per capita rate of circulation implied by that total; for radio, television, and telephone receivers, total numbers and rates of availability are supplied. Telephone receiver data refer to the number of sets (stations) having access to the public switched network. Data for a few countries refer to the number of "main lines" through which subscribers' equipment is connected to the network.

constant prices, an adjustment to the members of a financial time series to eliminate the effect of inflation year by year. It consists of referring all data in the series to a single year so that "real" change may be seen.

constitutional monarchy, *see* monarchy.

consumer price index (CPI), also known as the retail price index, or the cost-of-living index, a series of index numbers assigned to the price of a selected "basket," or assortment, of basic consumer goods and services in a country or region to measure changes over time in prices paid by a typical household for those goods and services. Items included in the CPI are ordinarily determined by governmental surveys of typical household expenditures and are assigned weights relative to their proportion of those expenditures. Index values are period averages unless otherwise noted.

coprincipality, *see* monarchy.

current prices, the valuation of a financial aggregate as of the year reported.

daily per capita caloric intake (supply), the calories equivalent to the known average daily supply of foodstuffs for human consumption in a given country divided by the population of the country (and the proportion of that supply provided, respectively, by vegetable and animal sources). The daily per capita caloric intake of a country may be compared with the corresponding recommended minimum daily requirement. The latter is calculated by the Food and Agriculture Organization of the United Nations from the age and sex distributions, average body weights, and environmental temperatures in a given region to determine the calories needed to sustain a person there at normal levels of activity and health. The daily per capita caloric requirement ranges from 2,200 to 2,500.

de facto population, for a given area, the population composed of those actually present at a particular time, including temporary residents and visitors (such as immigrants not yet granted permanent status, "guest" or expatriate workers, refugees, or tourists), but excluding legal residents temporarily absent.

de jure population, for a given area, the population composed only of those legally resident at a particular time, excluding temporary residents and visitors (such as "guest" or expatriate workers, refugees, or tourists), but including legal residents temporarily absent.

deadweight tonnage, the maximum weight of cargo, fuel, fresh water, stores, and persons that may safely be carried by a ship. It is customarily measured in long tons of 2,240 pounds each, equivalent to 1.016 metric tons. Deadweight tonnage is the difference between the tonnage of a fully loaded ship and the fully unloaded tonnage of that ship.

See also gross ton.

death rate, the number of deaths annually per 1,000 of midyear population. Death rates for individual countries may be compared with the world annual average of 10 deaths per 1,000 population between 1985 and 1990.

density (of population), usually, the DE FACTO POPULATION of a country divided by its total area. Special adjustment is made for inland water or other uninhabitable areas, *e.g.,* excluding the lake area of Finland.

department, a first-order civil administrative subdivision. The *overseas department* (France) is an overseas subdivision of the French Republic, almost equivalent to a department of metropolitan France, with elected representation in the French Parliament.

Dependent states[1]

Australia	**Portugal**
Christmas Island	Macau
Cocos (Keeling) Islands	**United Kingdom**
Norfolk Island	Anguilla
Denmark	Bermuda
Faeroe Islands	British Virgin Islands
Greenland	Cayman Islands
France	Falkland Islands
French Guiana	Gibraltar
French Polynesia	Guernsey
Guadeloupe	Hong Kong
Martinique	Isle of Man
Mayotte	Jersey
New Caledonia	Montserrat
Réunion	Pitcairn Island
Saint Pierre and Miquelon	Saint Helena and Dependencies
Wallis and Futuna	Turks and Caicos Islands
Netherlands, The	**United States**
Aruba	American Samoa
Netherlands Antilles	Guam
New Zealand	Northern Mariana Islands
Cook Islands	Palau
Niue	Puerto Rico
Tokelau	Virgin Islands (of the U.S.)
Norway	
Jan Mayen	
Svalbard	

[1]Excludes territories (1) to which Antarctic Treaty is applicable in whole or in part, (2) without permanent civilian population, (3) without internationally recognized civilian government (Western Sahara, Gaza Strip), or (4) representing unadjudicated unilateral or multilateral territorial claims.

dependent state, constitutionally or statutorily organized political entity outside of and under the jurisdiction of an independent state (or a federal element of such a state) but not formally annexed to it (*see* Table).

direct taxes, taxes levied directly on firms and individuals, such as taxes on income, profits, and capital gains. The *immediate* incidence, or burden, of direct taxes is on the firms and individuals thus taxed; direct taxes on firms may, however, be passed on to consumers and other economic units in the form of higher prices for goods and services, blurring the distinction between direct and indirect taxation.

distribution of income/wealth, the portion of personal income or wealth accruing to households or individuals comprising each respective decile (tenth) or quintile (fifth) of a country's households or individuals.*

divorce rate, the number of legal, civilly recognized divorces annually per 1,000 population.

doubling time, the number of complete years required for a country to double its population at its current rate of natural increase.

earnings index, a series of index numbers comparing average wages in a collective industrial sample for a country or region with the same industries at a previous period to measure changes over time in those wages. It is most commonly reported for wages paid on a daily, weekly, or monthly basis; annual figures represent averages of these shorter periods. The scope of the earnings index varies from country to country; the index is often limited to earnings in manufacturing industries. The index for each country applies to all wage earners in a designated group and ordinarily takes into account basic wages (overtime is normally distinguished), bonuses, cost-of-living allowances, and contributions toward social security. Some countries include payments in kind. Contributions toward social security by employers are usually excluded, as are social security benefits received by wage earners.

economically active population, *see* population economically active.

education, tabulation of the principal elements of a country's educational establishment, classified as far as possible according to the country's own system of primary, secondary, and higher levels (the usual age limits for these levels being identified in parentheses), with total number of schools (physical facilities) and of teachers and students (whether full- or part-time). The student-teacher ratio is calculated whenever available data permit.

educational attainment, the distribution of the population age 25 and over with completed educations by the highest level of formal education attained or completed; it must sometimes be reported, however, for age groups still in school or for the economically active only.

emirate, empire, *see* monarchy.

enterprise, a legal entity formed to conduct a business, which it may do from more than one establishment (place of business or service point).

ethnic/linguistic composition, ethnic, racial, or linguistic composition of a national population, reported here according to the most reliable breakdown available, whether published in official sources (such as a census) or in external analysis (when the subject is not addressed in national sources).

exchange rate, the value of one currency compared with another, or with a standardized unit of account such as the SPECIAL DRAWING RIGHT, or as mandated by local statute when one currency is "tied" by a par value to another. Rates given usually refer to free market values when the currency itself is traded.

exports, material goods legally leaving a country (or customs area) and subject to customs regulations. The total value and distribution by percentage of the major items (in prefer-

ence to groups of goods) exported are given, together with the distribution of trade among major trading partners (usually single countries or trading blocs). Valuation of goods exported is free on board (f.o.b.) unless otherwise specified. The value of goods exported and imported f.o.b. is calculated from the cost of production and excludes the cost of transport.

external debt, public and publicly guaranteed debt with a maturity of more than one year owed to nonnationals of a country and repayable in foreign currency, goods, or services. The debt may be an obligation of a national or subnational governmental body (or an agency of either), of an autonomous public body, or of a private debtor that is guaranteed by a public entity. The debt is usually either outstanding (contracted) or disbursed (drawn).

external territory (Australia), *see* territory.

federal, consisting of first-order political subdivisions that are prior to and independent of the central government in certain functions.

federal republic, *see* republic.

federation, a union of coequal political entities that retain some degree of autonomy within the union.

fertility rate, *see* total fertility rate.

financial aggregates, tabulation of seven-year time series, providing principal measures of the financial condition of a country, including: (1) the exchange rate of the national currency against the U.S. dollar, the pound sterling, and the International Monetary Fund's SPECIAL DRAWING RIGHT (SDR), (2) the amount and kind of international reserves (holdings of SDRs, gold, and foreign currencies) and reserve position of the country in the IMF, and (3) principal economic rates and prices (central bank discount rate, government bond yields, and industrial stock [share] prices). For BALANCE OF PAYMENTS, the origin in terms of component balance of trade items and balance of invisibles (net) is given.*

fish catch, the live-weight equivalent of the aquatic animals (including fish, crustaceans, mollusks, etc., but excluding whales, seals, and other aquatic mammals) caught in freshwater or marine areas by national fleets and landed in domestic or foreign harbours for commercial, industrial, or subsistence purposes.

f.o.b. (trade valuation): *see* exports.

food, see daily per capita caloric intake.

form of government/political status, the structure of a country's administration provided for in normal constitutional operation—whether or not suspended by extralegal military or civil action, although such de facto administrations are identified—together with the number of members (elected, appointed, and ex officio) for each legislative house, named according to its English rendering. Dependent states (*see* Table) are classified according to the status of their political association with the administering country.

(free) association, late stage in the process by which U.K. and U.S. dependencies achieve independence; it usually implies a relation between a largely self-governing dependency and its administering power that is capable of termination in full independence at the instance of the dependent state, though always in consultation with the administering power.

global social product, *see* material product.

gross domestic product (GDP), the total value of the final goods and services produced by residents and nonresidents within a given country during a given year. The GDP excludes the value of net income earned abroad, which is included in the GROSS NATIONAL PRODUCT (GNP). Unless otherwise noted, the value is given in current prices of the year indicated.

gross national product (GNP), the total value of final goods and services produced both from within a given country *and* from external (foreign) transactions in a given year. Unless

otherwise noted, the value is given in current prices of the year indicated. GNP is equal to GROSS DOMESTIC PRODUCT adjusted by net factor income from abroad, which is the income residents receive from abroad for factor services (labour, investment, and interest) less similar payments made to nonresidents who contribute to the domestic economy.

gross ton, volumetric unit of measure (equaling 100 cu ft [2.83 cu m]) of the permanently enclosed volume of a ship, above and below decks available for cargo, stores, or passenger accommodation. Net, or register, tonnage exempts certain nonrevenue spaces—such as those devoted to machinery, bunkers, crew accommodations, and ballast—from the gross tonnage. *See also* deadweight tonnage.

head of government, see chief of state/head of government.

health, a group of measures including number of accredited physicians currently practicing or employed and their ratio to the total population; total hospital beds and their ratio; and INFANT MORTALITY RATE.

household income and expenditure, data for average size of a HOUSEHOLD (by number of individuals) and median household income. Sources of income and expenditures for major items of consumption are given as percentages.

In general, household income is the amount of funds, usually measured in monetary units, received by the members (generally those 14 years old and over) of a household in a given time period. The income can be derived from (1) wages or salaries, (2) nonfarm or farm SELF-EMPLOYMENT, (3) transfer payments, such as pensions, public assistance, unemployment benefits, etc., and (4) other income, including interest and dividends, rent, royalties, etc. The income of a household is expressed as a gross amount before deductions for taxes. Data on expenditure refer to consumption of personal or household goods and services; they normally exclude savings, taxes, and insurance; practice with regard to inclusion of credit purchases differs markedly.

household, economically autonomous individual or group of individuals living in a single dwelling unit. A family household is one composed principally of individuals related by blood or marriage.

immigration, usually, the number and origin of those immigrants admitted to a nation in a legal status that would eventually permit the granting of the right to settle permanently or to acquire citizenship.*

imports, material goods legally entering a country (or customs area) and subject to customs regulations; excludes financial movements. The total value and distribution by percentage of the major items (in preference to groups of goods) imported are given, together with the direction of trade among major trading partners (usually single countries), trading blocs (such as the European Economic Community), or customs areas (such as Belgium-Luxembourg). The value of goods imported is given free on board (f.o.b.) unless otherwise specified; f.o.b. is defined above under EXPORTS.

The principal alternate basis for valuation of goods in international trade is that of cost, insurance, and freight (c.i.f.); its use is restricted to imports, as it comprises the principal charges needed to bring the goods to the customs house in the country of destination. Because it inflates the value of imports relative to exports, more countries have, latterly, been estimating imports on an f.o.b. basis as well.

incorporated territory (U.S.), *see* territory.

independent, of a state, autonomous and controlling both its internal and external affairs. Its date usually refers to the date from which the country was in effective control of these affairs within its present boundaries, rather than the date independence was proclaimed or the date recognized as a de jure act by the former administering power.

indirect taxes, taxes levied on sales or transfers of selected intermediate goods and services, including excises, value-added taxes, and tariffs, that are ordinarily passed on to the ultimate consumers of the goods and services. Figures given for individual countries are limited to indirect taxes levied by their respective central governments unless otherwise specified.

infant mortality rate, the number of children per 1,000 live births who die before their first birthday. Total infant mortality includes neonatal mortality, which is deaths of children within one month of birth.

invisibles (invisible trade), *see* balance of trade.

kingdom, *see* monarchy.

labour force, portion of the POPULATION ECONOMICALLY ACTIVE comprising those most fully employed or attached to the labour market (the unemployed are considered to be "attached" in that they usually represent persons previously employed seeking to be reemployed), particularly as viewed from a short-term perspective. It normally includes those who are self-employed, employed by others (whether full-time, part-time, seasonally, or on some other less than full-time basis), and, as noted above, the unemployed (both those previously employed and those seeking work for the first time). In the "gross domestic product and labour force" table, the majority of the labour data provided refer to population economically active, since PEA represents the longer-term view of working population and, thus, subsumes more of the marginal workers who are often missed by shorter-term surveys.

land use, distribution by classes of vegetational cover or economic use of the land area only (excluding inland water, for example, but not marshland), reported as percentages.

leisure, the principal uses or reported preferences in the use of the individual's free time for recreation, rest, or self-improvement.*

life expectancy, the number of years a person born within a particular population group (age cohort) would be expected to live, based on actuarial calculations.

literacy, the ability to read and write a language with some degree of competence; the precise degree constituting the basis of a particular national statement is usually defined by the national census and is often tested by the census enumerator. Elsewhere, particularly where much adult literacy may be the result of literacy campaigns rather than passage through a formal educational system, definition and testing of literacy may be better standardized.

major cities, usually the five largest cities proper whose population is at least one-tenth that of the primate (largest) city; fewer will be listed if the size disparity is very great or there are fewer urban localities in the country. For multipage tables, 10 or more will be listed without regard for the size of the primate city.* All populations will refer to the most specific administrative or demographically defined city proper, unless a municipality or METROPOLITAN AREA is specified.

manufacturing, mining, and construction enterprises/retail sales and service enterprises, a detailed tabulation of the principal industries in these sectors, showing for each industry the number of enterprises and employees, wages in that industry as a percentage of the general average wage, and the value of that industry's output in terms of value added or turnover.*

marriage rate, the number of legal, civilly recognized marriages annually per 1,000 population.

material (or social) product, in the national accounting systems of the socialist countries, the aggregate (sometimes "global") value of all "productive" economic activity, generally omitting personal (nonpublic) services, finan-

cial activities, and the like that in conventional Western national accounts would contribute to the GROSS DOMESTIC PRODUCT, a more comprehensive measure that includes not only material output but also every identifiable service element of a national economy. Socialist countries that are members of the International Monetary Fund have begun, however, to report gross domestic, and national, product according to the *System of National Accounts* that forms the basis of international standardization of national accounts.

material well-being, a group of measures indicating the percentage of households or dwellings possessing certain goods or appliances, including automobiles, telephones, television receivers, refrigerators, air conditioners, and washing machines.*

merchant marine, the privately or publicly owned ships registered with the maritime authority of a nation (limited to those in Lloyd's of London statistical reporting of 100 or more GROSS TONS) that are employed in commerce, whether or not owned or operated by nationals of the country.

metropolitan area, a city and the region of dense, predominantly urban, settlement around the city; the population of the whole usually has strong economic and cultural affinities with the central city.

military expenditure, the apparent value of all identifiable military expenditure by the central government on hardware, personnel, pensions, research and development, etc., reported here both as a percentage of the GNP, with a comparison to the world average, and as a per capita value in U.S. dollars.

military personnel, *see* total active duty personnel.

mobility, the rate at which individuals or households change dwellings, usually measured between censuses and including international as well as domestic migration.*

monarchy, a government in which the CHIEF OF STATE holds office, usually hereditarily and for life, but sometimes electively for a term. The state may be a coprincipality, emirate, empire, kingdom, principality, sheikhdom, or sultanate. The powers of the monarch may range from absolute (*i.e.,* he or she both reigns and rules) through various degrees of limitation of authority to nominal, as in a constitutional monarchy, in which the titular monarch reigns but others, as elected officials, effectively rule.

monetary unit, currency of issue, or that in official use in a given country; name, spelling, and abbreviation in English according to International Monetary Fund recommendations or local practice; name of the lesser, usually decimal, monetary unit comprising the main currency; and valuation in U.S. dollars and U.K. pounds sterling, usually according to market or commercial rates.

See also exchange rate.

natural increase, also called natural growth, or the balance of births and deaths, the excess of births over deaths in a population; the rate of natural increase is the difference between the BIRTH RATE and the DEATH RATE of a given population. Natural increase is added to the balance of migration to calculate the total growth of that population.

net material product, *see* material product.

nonreligious, *see* atheist.

official language(s), that (or those) prescribed for actual day-to-day conduct and publication of a country's official business. Other languages may have local protection, may be permitted in legal action (such as a trial), or may be "national languages," for the protection of which special provisions have been made, but these are not deemed official.

official name, the local official form(s), short or long, of a country's legal name(s) taken from the country's constitution or from other

official documents. The English-language form is usually the protocol form in use by the country, the U.S. Department of State, and the United Nations.

official religion, generally, any religion prescribed or given special status or protection by the constitution or legal system of a country. Identification as such is not confined to constitutional documents utilizing the term explicitly.

organized territory (U.S.), *see* territory.

overseas department (France), *see* department.

overseas territory (France), *see* territory.

parliamentary state, *see* state.

part of a realm, a dependent political entity with some degree of self-government and having a special status above that of a colony (*e.g.,* the prerogative of rejecting for local application any law enacted by the motherland).

participation/activity rates, measures defining differential rates of economic activity within a population. Participation rate refers to the percentage of those employed or economically active who possess a particular characteristic (sex, age, etc.); activity rate refers to the fraction of the total population who *are* economically active.

passenger-miles, or **passenger-kilometres,** aggregate measure of passenger carriage by a specified means of transportation, equal to the number of passengers carried multiplied by the number of kilometres each is transported. Figures given for countries are often calculated from ticket sales and ordinarily exclude passengers carried free of charge.

people's republic, *see* republic.

place of birth/national origin, if the former, numbers of native- and foreign-born population of a country by actual place of birth; if the latter, any of several classifications, including those based on origin of passport at original admission to country, on cultural heritage of family name, on self-designated (often multiple) origin of (some) ancestors, and on other systems for assigning national origin.*

political status, *see* form of government/political status.

population, the number of persons present within a country or other civil entity at the date of a census of population, survey, cumulation of a civil register, or other enumeration. Unless otherwise specified, populations given are DE FACTO, referring to those actually present, rather than DE JURE, those legally resident but not necessarily present on the referent date. If a time series, noncensus year, or per capita ratio referring to a country's total population is cited, it will usually refer to midyear of the calendar year indicated. Populations for cities will usually refer to the city proper, *i.e.,* the legally bounded corporate entity, or the most compact, contiguous, demographically urban portion of the entity defined by the local authorities. Occasionally it has been necessary to provide city figures for METROPOLITAN AREAS when the relevant civil entity at the core of a major agglomeration had an unrepresentatively small population.

population economically active, the total number of persons (above a set age for economic labour, usually 10–15 years) in all employment statuses—self-employed, wage- or salary-earning, part-time, seasonal, unemployed, etc. The International Labour Organisation defines the economically active as "all persons of either sex who furnish the supply of labour for the production of economic goods and services." National practices vary as regards the treatment of such groups as armed forces, inmates of institutions, persons seeking their first job, seasonal workers and persons engaged in part-time economic activities. In some countries, all or part of these groups may be included among the economically active, while in other countries the same groups may be treated as inactive. In general, however, the data on economically active population do not include students, women occupied solely in domestic duties, retired persons, persons living entirely on their own means, and persons wholly dependent upon others.

See also labour force.

population projection, the expected population in the years 2000 and 2010, embodying the country's own projections wherever possible. Estimates of the future size of a population are usually based on assumed levels of fertility, mortality, and migration. Projections in the tables, unless otherwise specified, are medium (*i.e.,* most likely) variants, whether based on external estimates by the United Nations, World Bank, or U.S. Department of Commerce or on those of the country itself.

price and earnings indexes, tabulation comparing the change in the CONSUMER PRICE INDEX over a period of seven years with the change in the general labour force's EARNINGS INDEX for the same period.

principality, *see* monarchy.

production, the physical quantity or monetary value of the output of an industry, usually tabulated here as the most important items or groups of items (depending on the available detail) of primary (extractive) and secondary (manufactured) production. When a single consistent measure of value, such as VALUE ADDED, can be obtained, this is given, ranked by value; otherwise, and more usually, quantity of production is given.

public debt, the current outstanding debt of all periods of maturity for which the central government and its organs are obligated. Publicly guaranteed private debt is excluded. For many developing countries, only figures for long-term EXTERNAL DEBT are available.

quality of working life, a group of measures including weekly hours of work (including overtime); rates per 100,000 for job-connected injury, illness, and mortality; coverage of labour force by insurance for injury, permanent disability, and death; workdays lost to labour strikes and stoppages; and commuting patterns (length of journey to work in minutes and usual method of transportation).*

railroads, mode of transportation by self-driven or locomotive-drawn cars over fixed rails. Length-of-track figures ordinarily include the total length of all mainline and spurline running track and exclude switching sidings and yard track. Route length, when given, does not compound multiple running tracks laid on the same trackbed.

recurrent budget, *see* budget.

religious affiliation, distribution of practicing or nominal religionists, as a percentage of total population. This usually assigns to children the religion of their parents.

republic, a state with elected leaders and a centralized presidential form of government, local subdivisions being subordinate to the national government. A *federal republic* (as distinguished from a unitary republic) is a republic in which power is divided between the central government and the constituent subnational administrative divisions (*e.g.,* states, provinces, or cantons) in whom the central government itself is held to originate, the division of power being defined in a written constitution and jurisdictional disputes usually being settled in a court; sovereignty usually rests with the authority that has the power to amend the constitution. A *people's republic,* in the dialectics of Communism, is the first stage of development toward a communist state, the second stage being a *socialist republic.* A *soviet republic* is a republic governed by an elected soviet (council). A *unitary republic* (as distinguished from a federal republic) is a republic in which power is held by a central authority and not derived from constituent subdivisions.

retail price index, *see* consumer price index.

retail sales and service enterprises, *see* manufacturing, mining, and construction enterprises/retail sales and service enterprises.

roundwood, wood obtained from removals from forests, felled or harvested (with or without bark), in all forms.

rural, *see* urban–rural.

self-employment, work in which income derives from direct employment in one's own business, trade, or profession, as opposed to work in which salary or wages are earned from an employer.

self-governing, of a state, in control of its internal affairs in degrees ranging from control of most internal affairs (though perhaps not of public order or of internal security) to complete control of all internal affairs (*i.e.,* the state is autonomous) but having no control of external affairs or defense. In this work the term self-governing refers to the final stage in the successive stages of increasing self-government that generally precede independence.

service/trade enterprises, *see* manufacturing, mining, and construction enterprises/retail sales and service enterprises.

sex distribution, ratios, calculated as percentages, of male and female population to total population.

sheikhdom, *see* monarchy.

social deviance, a group of measures, usually reported as rates per 100,000, for principal categories of socially deviant behaviour, including specified crimes, alcoholism, drug abuse, and suicide.*

social participation, a group of measures indicative of the degree of social engagement displayed by a particular population, including rates of participation in such activities as elections, voluntary work or memberships, trade unions, and religion.*

social security, public programs designed to protect individuals and families from loss of income owing to unemployment, old age, sickness or disability, or death and to provide other services such as medical care, health and welfare programs, or income maintenance.

socialist republic, *see* republic.

sources of income, *see* household income and expenditure.

soviet republic, *see* republic.

Special Drawing Right (SDR), a unit of account utilized by the International Monetary Fund (IMF) to denominate monetary reserves available under a quota system to IMF members to maintain the value of their national currency unit in international transactions.*

state, in international law, a political entity possessing the attributes of: territory, permanent civilian population, government, and the capacity to conduct relations with other states. Though the term is sometimes limited in meaning to fully independent and internationally recognized states, the more general sense of an entity possessing a *preponderance* of these characteristics is intended here. It is, thus, also a first-order civil administrative subdivision, especially of a federated union. An *associated state* is an autonomous state in free association with another that conducts its external affairs and defense. A *parliamentary state* is an independent state of the Commonwealth that is governed by a parliament and that may recognize the British monarch as its titular head.

structure of gross domestic product and labour force, tabulation of the principal elements of the national economy, according to standard industrial categories, together with the corresponding distribution of the labour force (when possible POPULATION ECONOMICALLY ACTIVE) that generates the GROSS DOMESTIC PRODUCT.

sultanate, *see* monarchy.

territory, a noncategorized political dependency; a first-order administrative subdivision; a dependent political entity with some degree of self-government, but with fewer rights and less autonomy than a colony since there is no charter. An *external territory* (Australia) is a territory situated outside the area of the country. An *incorporated territory* (U.S.) is a part of the United States with nonvoting representation in the Congress but with most constitutional provisions extended to its inhabitants (*e.g.,* Alaska until 1959). An *organized territory* (U.S.) is a territory for which a system of laws and a settled government have been provided by an act of the United States Congress. An *overseas territory* (France) is an overseas subdivision of the French Republic with elected representation in the French Parliament, having individual statutes, laws, and internal organization adapted to local conditions. An *unincorporated territory* (U.S.) is a dependency of the United States with limited self-government, whose inhabitants can claim the fundamental but not all of the procedural rights (*e.g.,* trial by jury) guaranteed by the United States Constitution.

ton-miles, or ***ton-kilometres,*** aggregate measure of freight hauled by a specified means of transportation, equal to tons of freight multiplied by the miles (or kilometres) each ton is transported. Figures are compiled from waybills (nationally) and ordinarily exclude mail, specie, passengers' baggage, the fuel and stores of the conveyance, and goods carried free.

total active duty personnel, full-time active duty military personnel (excluding militias and part-time, informal, or other paramilitary elements), with their distribution by percentages among the major services.

total fertility rate, the sum of the current age-specific birth rates for each of the child-bearing years (usually 15–49). It is the probable number of births, given present fertility data, that would occur during the lifetime of each woman should she live to the end of her child-bearing years.

tourism, service industry comprising activities connected with domestic and international travel for pleasure or recreation; confined here to international travel and reported as expenditures in U.S.$ by tourists of all nationalities visiting a particular country and, conversely, the estimated expenditures of that country's nationals in all countries of destination.

transfer payments, *see* household income and expenditure.

transport, all mechanical methods of moving persons or goods. Data reported for national establishments include: for railroads, length of track and volume of traffic for passengers and cargo (but excluding mail, etc.); for roads, length of network and numbers of passenger cars and of commercial vehicles, *i.e.,* trucks and buses; for merchant marine, the number of vessels of more than 100 gross tons and their total deadweight tonnage; for air transport, traffic data for passengers and cargo, and the number of airports with scheduled flights.

unincorporated territory (U.S.), *see* territory.

unitary republic, *see* republic.

urban-rural, social characteristic of local or national populations, defined by predominant economic activities, "urban" referring to a group of largely nonagricultural pursuits, "rural" to agriculturally oriented employment patterns. The distinction is usually based on the country's own definition of urban, which may depend only upon the size (population) of a place or upon factors like employment, administrative status, density of housing, etc.

value added, also called value added by manufacture, the gross output value of a firm or industry minus the cost of inputs—raw materials, supplies, and payments to other firms—required to produce it. Value added is the portion of the sales value or gross output value that is actually created by the firm or industry. Value added generally includes labour costs, administrative costs, and operating profits.

The Nations of the World

Afghanistan

Official name: Da Afghānestān Jamhawrīyat (Pashto); Jomhūrī-ye Afghānestān (Dari) (Republic of Afghanistan).
Form of government[1]: 50-member coalition of political factions (30 mujahideen commanders, 10 clerics, and 10 members nominated by the mujahideen factions).
Chief of state: interim President.
Head of government: Prime Minister.
Capital: Kabul (Kābol).
Official languages: Pashto; Dari (Persian).
Official religion: Islam.
Monetary unit: 1 afghani (Af) = 100 puls (puli); valuation (Oct. 5, 1992) 1 U.S.$ = Af 58.38; 1 £ = Af 99.25.

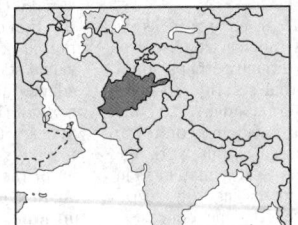

Area and population	area		population
	sq mi	sq km	1988 estimate
Regions			
Eastern	28,664	74,240	2,050,400
North-central	20,461	52,994	2,584,400
North-east	29,911	77,468	1,478,400
North-west	50,581	131,005	2,157,100
South-central	32,963	85,375	1,215,700
South-east	12,546	32,494	4,252,000
Western	76,699	198,649	1,666,400
TOTAL	251,825	652,225	15,404,400

Demography

Population (1992): 18,052,000.
Density (1992): persons per sq mi 71.7, persons per sq km 27.7.
Urban-rural (1990): urban 18.2%; rural 81.8%.
Sex distribution (1990): male 51.42%; female 48.58%.
Age breakdown (1990): under 15, 42.0%; 15–29, 27.3%; 30–44, 15.8%; 45–59, 10.1%; 60–74, 4.2%; 75 and over, 0.6%.
Population projection: (2000) 25,088,000; (2010) 30,627,000.
Doubling time: 29 years.
Ethnic composition (1983): Pashtun 52.3%; Tadzhik 20.3%; Uzbek 8.7%; Hazāra 8.7%; Chahar Aimak 2.9%; Turkmen 2.0%; Baluchi 1.0%; other 4.1%.
Religious affiliation (1989): Sunnī Muslim 74%; Shīʿī Muslim 25%; other 1%.
Major cities (1988): Kabul 1,424,400; Kandahār (Qandahār) 225,500; Herāt 177,300; Mazār-e Sharīf 130,600.

Vital statistics

Birth rate per 1,000 population (1991): 43.7 (world avg. 26.4).
Death rate per 1,000 population (1991): 20.0 (world avg. 9.2).
Natural increase rate per 1,000 population (1991): 23.7 (world avg. 17.2).
Total fertility rate (avg. births per childbearing woman; 1991): 6.3.
Life expectancy at birth (1991): male 44.0 years; female 43.0 years.
Major causes of death per 100,000 population: n.a.; however, in 1982, injuries and poisoning, infectious and parasitic diseases, and diseases of the respiratory system were the leading causes of death reported in hospitals.

National economy

Budget (1987–88). Revenue: Af 79,800,000,000 (1984–85; tax revenue 45.4%, nontax revenue 54.6%). Expenditures: Af 105,800,000,000 (1981–82; governmental ministries 50.0%, developmental budget 31.9%, foreign-debt service 13.9%, surplus 1.6%).
Production (metric tons except as noted). Agriculture, forestry, fishing (1990): wheat 1,925,000, corn (maize) 800,000, grapes 450,000, rice 430,000, potatoes 300,000, barley 250,000; livestock (number of live animals) 13,500,000 sheep, 2,150,000 goats, 1,650,000 cattle, 1,300,000 asses, 400,000 horses, 265,000 camels, 7,000,000 chickens; roundwood 6,465,000 cu m; fish catch (1989) 1,500. Mining and quarrying (1989): salt 10,000; copper 5,000; gypsum 3,000; barite 2,000. Manufacturing (by production value in Af '000,000,000; 1987–88): pharmaceutical products 462.5; food products 203.0; industrial chemicals (including fertilizers) 123.4; cement 104.0; textiles 15.6; salt 15.4. Construction (Af '000,000; 1985): 1,094. Energy production (consumption): electricity (kW-hr; 1990) 1,128,000,000 (1,128,000,000); coal (metric tons; 1990) 143,000 (143,000); petroleum products (metric tons; 1990) 4,000 (603,000); natural gas (cu m; 1990) 2,934,000,000 (1,888,000,000).
Population economically active (1989–90)[2]: total 6,009,000; activity rate of total population 38.0% (participation rates [1985]: ages 10–59, 43.1%; female 7.9%; unemployed 3.0%).

Price index (1985 = 100)							
	1985	1986	1987	1988	1989	1990	1991
Consumer price index	100.0	96.8	115.7	138.7	242.9	344.7	540.0

Household size. Average household size (1979)[2]: 6.2.
Tourism: receipts (1988) U.S.$1,000,000; expenditures (1987) U.S.$1,000,000.
Public debt (external, outstanding; 1989): U.S.$4,964,000,000.
Gross national product (1988): U.S.$3,100,000,000 (U.S.$220 per capita).

Structure of gross domestic product and labour force	1989–90		1981–82	
	in value Af '000,000[3]	% of total value	labour force	% of labour force
Agriculture	65,600	52.6	2,194,770	57.3
Manufacturing, mining, and public utilities	35,600	28.5	466,860	12.2
Construction	7,200	5.8	48,880	1.3
Transp. and commun.	4,400	3.5	65,650	1.7
Trade	9,900	7.9	126,100	3.3
Public administration			79,260	2.1
Public services	2,000	1.6	204,940	5.3
Other			642,360	16.8
TOTAL	124,700	100.0[4]	3,828,820	100.0

Land use (1989): forested 2.9%; meadows and pastures 46.0%; agricultural and under permanent cultivation 12.4%; other 38.7%.

Foreign trade

Balance of trade (current prices)						
	1985	1986	1987	1988	1989	1990
Af '000,000	−23,863	−33,826	−17,917	−19,642	−24,217	−27,000
% of total	29.4%	37.8%	25.7%	33.0%	50.4%	53.2%

Imports (1990): U.S.$768,700,000 (1989–90; machinery 37.7%, basic manufactures 18.3%, minerals and fuels 10.9%). *Major import sources* (1989): U.S.S.R. 55.5%; Japan 7.8%; Singapore 7.5%; India 5.4%; South Korea 2.2%.
Exports (1990): U.S.$235,100,000 (dried fruits and nuts 42.7%, carpets and rugs 16.5%, wool and hides 7.7%, cotton 1.1%). *Major export destinations* (1989): U.S.S.R. 72.6%; W.Ger. 3.5%; E.Ger. 2.1%; Saudi Arabia 1.7%.

Transport and communications

Transport. Railroads (1988): length 6 mi, 10 km. Roads (1988): total length 11,930 mi, 19,200 km (paved 47%). Vehicles (1989): passenger cars 31,800; trucks and buses 30,900. Merchant marine: none. Air transport (1989): passenger-mi 120,981,000, passenger-km 194,700,000; short ton-mi cargo 9,843,000[5], metric ton-km cargo 14,370,000[5]; airports (1992) 1.
Communications. Daily newspapers (1989): total number 16; total circulation 108,400[6]; circulation per 1,000 population 7.3[6]. Radio (1991): 1,400,000 receivers (1 per 12 persons). Television (1991): 100,000 receivers (1 per 169 persons). Telephones (1984): 31,200 (1 per 443 persons).

Education and health

Education (1988–89)	schools	teachers	students	student/ teacher ratio
Primary	553	16,756	586,014	35.0
Secondary	819	5,715	271,000	47.4
Voc., teacher tr.	33	556	8,537	15.4
Higher	5	198	1,491	7.5

Educational attainment (1980). Percentage of population age 25 and over having: no formal schooling 88.5%; some primary education 6.8%; complete primary 0.3%; some secondary 1.2%; postsecondary 3.2%. *Literacy* (1990): percentage of total population age 15 and over literate 29.4%; males 44.1%; females 13.9%.
Health: physicians (1987) 2,957 (1 per 4,797 persons); hospital beds (1981–82) 6,875 (1 per 2,054 persons); infant mortality rate (1991) 164.0.
Food (1984–86): daily per capita caloric intake 2,290 (vegetable products 90%, animal products 10%); 91% of FAO recommended minimum requirement.

Military

Total active duty personnel (1991): 45,000 (army 88.9%, air force 11.1%).
Military expenditure as percentage of GNP (1984): 9.1% (world 5.6%); per capita expenditure U.S.$24.

---

[1]On April 16, 1992, the Soviet-installed president, Najibullah, was overthrown by a coalition of Muslim rebels and replaced by the 50-member interim council. [2]Based on settled population only. [3]At prices of 1978–79. [4]Detail does not add to total given because of rounding. [5]Excludes mail. [6]Circulation for 13 dailies only.

Albania

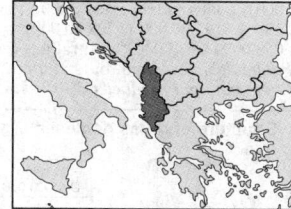

Official name: Republika e Shqipërisë (Republic of Albania).
Form of government: multiparty republic with one legislative house (People's Assembly [140])[1].
Chief of state: President.
Head of government: Prime Minister.
Capital: Tiranë.
Official language: Albanian.
Official religion: none.
Monetary unit: 1 lek = 100 qindars; valuation (Oct. 5, 1992)
1 U.S.$ = 109.81 leks;
1 £ = 186.67 leks.

Area and population

Provinces	Capitals	area sq mi	area sq km	population 1990 estimate
Berat	Berat	396	1,027	180,489
Dibër	Peshkopi	605	1,568	153,775
Durrës	Durrës	327	848	251,029
Elbasan	Elbasan	572	1,481	248,676
Fier	Fier	454	1,175	251,115
Gjirokastër	Gjirokastër	439	1,137	67,392
Gramsh	Gramsh	268	695	44,791
Kolonjë	Ersekë	311	805	25,291
Korçë	Korçë	842	2,181	218,219
Krujë	Krujë	234	607	109,876
Kukës	Kukës	514	1,330	104,731
Lezhë	Lezhë	185	479	63,505
Librazhd	Librazhd	391	1,013	73,871
Lushnjë	Lushnjë	275	712	137,830
Mat	Burrel	397	1,028	78,754
Mirditë	Rrëshen	335	867	51,701
Përmet	Përmet	359	929	40,419
Pogradec	Pogradec	280	725	73,333
Pukë	Pukë	399	1,034	50,286
Sarandë	Sarandë	424	1,097	89,456
Shkodër	Shkodër	976	2,528	241,549
Skrapar	Çorovoda	299	775	47,605
Tepelenë	Tepelenë	315	817	51,022
Tiranë	Tiranë	478	1,238	374,483
Tropojë	Bajram	403	1,043	45,965
Vlorë	Vlorë	621	1,609	180,725
TOTAL		11,100[2]	28,748	3,255,891[2]

Demography

Population (1992): 3,357,000.
Density (1992): persons per sq mi 302.4, persons per sq km 116.8.
Urban-rural (1990): urban 35.2%; rural 64.8%.
Sex distribution (1990): male 51.40%; female 48.60%.
Age breakdown (1990): under 15, 32.6%; 15–29, 28.5%; 30–44, 19.1%; 45–59, 11.6%; 60–74, 6.3%; 75 and over, 1.9%.
Population projection: (2000) 3,796,000; (2010) 4,315,000.
Doubling time: 37 years.
Ethnic composition (1989): Albanian 98.0%; Greek 1.8%; Macedonian 0.1%; other 0.1%.
Religious affiliation (1992): a significant portion of the population are non-religious; believers identify themselves as: Muslim 65%; Orthodox 20%; Roman Catholic 13%; other 2%.
Major cities (1990): Tiranë 243,000; Durrës 85,400; Elbasan 83,300; Shkodër 81,800; Vlorë 73,800.

Vital statistics

Birth rate per 1,000 population (1990): 25.2 (world avg. 27.1).
Death rate per 1,000 population (1990): 5.6 (world avg. 9.8).
Natural increase rate per 1,000 population (1990): 19.6 (world avg. 17.3).
Total fertility rate (avg. births per childbearing woman; 1991): 2.9.
Marriage rate per 1,000 population (1990): 8.9.
Divorce rate per 1,000 population (1990): 0.8.
Life expectancy at birth (1989–90): male 69.3 years; female 75.4 years.
Major causes of death per 100,000 population: n.a.; however, in 1983 the leading causes of death were cardiovascular diseases, diseases of the respiratory system, malignant neoplasms (cancers), diseases of the digestive system, and injuries.

National economy

Budget (1990). Revenue: 9,650,000,000 leks (1989; surplus from state enterprises 77.6%, social insurance 9.9%, other 12.5%). Expenditures: 9,600,-000,000 leks (economy 51.4%, social and cultural services 31.7%, defense 10.7%, administration 1.8%).
Public debt (1991): U.S.$350,000,000.
Tourism (1990): number of tourist arrivals 30,000; receipts from visitors, n.a.
Production (metric tons except as noted). Agriculture, forestry, fishing (1991): wheat 300,000, vegetables and melons 248,000, sugar beets 205,000, corn (maize) 180,000, potatoes 65,000, grapes 52,000, barley 26,000, sorghum 25,000, olives 18,000, oats 18,000, sunflower seeds 14,000, tobacco 12,000; livestock (number of live animals) 1,600,000 sheep, 1,000,000 goats, 650,000 cattle, 170,000 pigs, 100,000 horses, 76,000 mules and asses; roundwood (1990) 2,330,000 cu m; fish catch (1989) 11,961. Mining and quarrying (1991): ferronickel ore 1,273,000; chromite ore 612,000; copper 565,500; salt 52,000; bauxite 8,000. Manufacturing (1989): cement 754,000; distillate fuel oils 380,000; metallurgical coke 290,000; phosphate fertilizers 165,000; ammonium nitrate 109,000; rolled steel 93,000; sulfuric acid 92,000; urea 92,-

000; caustic soda 82,000; raw sugar 48,000; soda ash 27,000; machinery and equipment 486,000,000 leks; spare parts 485,000,000 leks; footwear 6,103,000 pairs; heavy cloth 12,000,000 metres; beer 228,000 hectolitres; cigarettes 6,184,000 units; radio receivers 30,000 units; television receivers 23,000 units. Construction (1989): 16,061 units. Energy production (consumption): electricity (kW-hr; 1990) 4,100,000,000 (3,450,000,000); coal (metric tons; 1990) 2,400,000 (2,640,000); crude petroleum (barrels; 1990) 19,123,000 (19,123,-000); petroleum products (metric tons; 1990) 1,200,000 (1,200,000); natural gas (cu m; 1990) 397,000,000 (397,000,000).
Gross national product (1987): U.S.$4,030,000,000 (U.S.$1,300 per capita).

Structure of net material product and labour force

	1989 value	% of total value	labour force[3]	% of labour force[3]
Agriculture	...	32.7	423,000	50.5
Manufacturing, mining, public utilities	...	44.6	199,000	23.8
Construction	...	6.4	60,000	7.2
Transp. and commun.			24,000	2.9
Trade			41,000	4.9
Pub. admin., defense	...	16.3	62,000	7.4
Services				
Other			28,000	3.3
TOTAL	...	100.0	837,000	100.0

Population economically active (1985): total 1,398,000; activity rate of total population 45.8% (participation rates: ages 15–64, 74.5%; female 41.0%; unemployed [1992] as much as 50.0%).
Household income and expenditure. Average household size (1989) 4.7; income per household: n.a.; sources of income: n.a.; expenditure: n.a.
Land use (1990): forested 38.2%; meadows and pastures 14.7%; agricultural and under permanent cultivation 25.8%; other 21.3%.

Foreign trade

Balance of trade (current prices)

	1985	1986	1987	1988	1989
'000,000 leks	− 414	65	0	− 509	− 589
% of total	8.7%	8.2%	0	8.6%	8.4%

Imports (1989): 3,792,000,000 leks (machinery and transport equipment 28.2%; fuels, minerals, and metals 26.0%; raw materials of plant and animal origin 17.9%; chemicals and related products 12.1%; consumer goods 7.8%; food and live animals 7.2%). *Major import sources* (1982): U.S.S.R. and eastern European countries 35.6%; European Economic Community countries 28.7%; United States 4.6%; Japan 2.8%.
Exports (1989): 3,203,000,000 leks (crude minerals and metalliferous ores 41.3%; food and food preparations 17.2%; consumer goods 9.8%; fuels 7.7%; electricity 5.3%). *Major export destinations:* Czechoslovakia 11.4%; Bulgaria 10.3%; East Germany 9.2%; Romania 9.1%; Italy 7.9%; Poland 6.7%; China 5.6%; West Germany 4.9%; Yugoslavia 4.9%; Austria 4.1%; Hungary 3.7%; Greece 3.0%; Sweden 2.9%.

Transport and communications

Transport. Railroads (1989): length 425 mi, 684 km; passenger-mi 467,705,000, passenger-km 752,000,000; short ton-mi cargo 462,000,000, metric ton-km cargo 674,000,000. Roads (1991): total length 11,465 mi, 18,450 km (paved 40%). Vehicles (1991): passenger cars 16,000; trucks and buses 32,900. Merchant marine (1990): vessels (100 gross tons and over) 24; total deadweight tonnage 80,954. Air transport: passengers, n.a.; cargo, n.a.; airports (1992) with scheduled flights 1.
Communications. Daily newspapers (1989): total number 2; total circulation 135,000; circulation per 1,000 population 42. Radio (1991): total number of receivers 525,000 (1 per 6.3 persons). Television (1991): total number of receivers 246,220 (1 per 13 persons). Telephones: n.a.

Education and health

Education (1990)

	schools	teachers	students	student/ teacher ratio
Primary (age 6–13)	1,726	28,798	557,000	19.3
Secondary (age 14–17)	47	2,318	68,000	29.3
Voc., teacher tr.	466	7,390	138,000	18.7
Higher	8	1,806	27,000	15.0

Educational attainment (1979). Percentage of population age 25 and over having: primary education 74.7%; secondary 20.9%; higher 4.4%. *Literacy* (1989): virtually 100%.
Health (1989): physicians 5,570 (1 per 574 persons); hospital beds 18,226 (1 per 176 persons); infant mortality rate per 1,000 live births (1990) 28.3.
Food (1980–82): daily per capita caloric intake 3,060 (vegetable products 87%, animal products 13%); 127% of FAO recommended minimum requirement.

Military

Total active duty personnel (1992): 40,000 (army 67.5%, navy 5.0%, air force 27.5%). *Military expenditure as percentage of GNP* (1989): 4.1% (world 5.4%); per capita expenditure U.S.$50.

[1]A transitional constitution was adopted on April 29, 1991. [2]Detail does not add to total given because of rounding. [3]State sector only.

Algeria

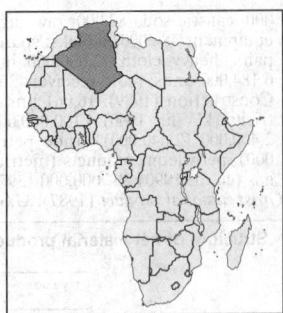

Official name: al-Jumhūrīyah
al-Jazā'irīyah ad-Dīmuqrāṭīyah
ash-Sha'bīyah (Arabic) (Democratic
and Popular Republic of Algeria).
Form of government: military-
dominated extraconstitutional
administration with one interim
legislative body (National
Consultative Council [60]).
Chief of state: President assisted by
High State Council.
Head of government: Prime Minister.
Capital: Algiers.
Official language: Arabic.
Official religion: Islam.
Monetary unit: 1 Algerian dinar
(DA) = 100 centimes; valuation (Oct.
5, 1992) 1 U.S.$ = DA 20.51;
1 £ = DA 34.87.

Population (1987[1] census)

Wilāyat	population	Wilāyat	population
Adrar	217,678	Médéa	652,863
Aïn Defla	537,256	Mila	511,605
Aïn Temouchent	274,990	Mostaganem	505,932
Alger	1,690,191	M'Sila	604,693
Annaba	455,888	Naâma	113,700
Batna	752,617	Oran	932,473
el-Bayadh	153,254	Ouargla	284,454
Béchar	185,346	el-Oued	376,909
Bejaïa	700,952	Oum el-Bouaghi	403,936
Biskra	430,202	Relizane	544,877
Blida	702,188	Saïda	235,494
Bordj Bou Arreridj	424,828	Sétif	1,000,694
Bouira	526,900	Sidi bel-Abbès	446,277
Boumerdes	650,975	Skikda	622,510
ech-Chleff	684,192	Souk Ahras	296,077
Constantine	664,303	Tamanrasset	95,822
Djelfa	494,494	et-Tarf	275,315
Ghardaïa	216,140	Tébessa	410,233
Guelma	353,309	Tiaret	575,794
Illizi	18,930	Tindouf	16,428
Jijel	472,312	Tipaza	620,151
Khenchela	246,541	Tissemsilt	228,120
Laghouat	212,388	Tizi Ouzou	936,948
Mascara	566,901	Tlemcen	714,862
		TOTAL	23,038,942

Demography

Area: 919,595 sq mi, 2,381,741 sq km.
Population (1992): 26,401,000.
Density (1992): persons per sq mi 28.7, persons per sq km 11.1.
Urban-rural (1990): urban 51.7%; rural 48.3%.
Sex distribution (1990): male 50.14%; female 49.86%.
Age breakdown (1990): under 15, 43.6%; 15–29, 28.7%; 30–44, 14.2%; 45–59,
8.1%; 60–74, 4.1%; 75 and over, 1.3%.
Population projection: (2000) 32,584,000; (2010) 40,288,000.
Doubling time: 28 years.
Ethnic composition (1983): Arab 82.6%; Berber 17.0%; other 0.4%.
Religious affiliation (1980): Sunnī Muslim 99.1%; Roman Catholic 0.5%;
other 0.4%.
Major cities (1987): Algiers 1,507,241; Oran 628,558; Constantine 440,842;
Annaba 305,526; Batna 181,601.

Vital statistics

Birth rate per 1,000 population (1988): 31.0 (world avg. 27.1); legitimacy rate,
n.a.; marriage, however, is nearly universal.
Death rate per 1,000 population (1988): 6.0 (world avg. 9.8).
Natural increase rate per 1,000 population (1988): 25.0 (world avg. 17.3).
Total fertility rate (avg. births per childbearing woman; 1990): 5.1.
Marriage rate per 1,000 population (1990): 5.9.
Divorce rate per 1,000 population (1985): 2.1[2].
Life expectancy at birth (1990–95): male 65.0 years; female 67.3 years.
Notified cases of infectious diseases per 100,000 population (1986): measles
15.2; typhoid fever 12.5; dysentery 11.8.

National economy

Budget (1992). Revenue: DA 328,400,000,000 (ordinary receipts 39.1%, hydrocarbons 60.9%). Expenditures: DA 327,900,000,000 (administrative 62.2%,
capital 37.8%).
Tourism (1990): receipts from visitors U.S.$64,000,000; expenditures by na-
tionals abroad U.S.$149,000,000.
Production (metric tons except as noted). Agriculture, forestry, fishing (1991):
barley 1,751,000, wheat 1,741,000, potatoes 1,000,000, tomatoes 500,000,
grapes 260,000, dates 215,000, oranges 190,000; livestock (number of live animals) 13,350,000 sheep, 3,800,000 goats, 1,443,000 cattle; roundwood (1990)
2,162,000 cu m; fish catch (1990) 91,093. Mining and quarrying (1990): iron
ore 2,700,000[3]; phosphates 1,128,000; barite 53,078; gypsum 49,000; zinc
7,984; silver 96,500 troy oz[3]. Manufacturing (1990): cement 6,337,000; flour
and semolina 2,588,000; bricks 1,679,000; crude steel 767,000; pig iron and
ferroalloys 1,095,000[4]; edible oils 338,000; sugar 209,000; trucks 4,291 units.
Construction (annual average; 1981–87): residential 22,400 units. Energy production (consumption): electricity (kW-hr; 1990) 15,994,000,000 (15,934,000,-

000); coal (metric tons; 1990) 10,000 (1,210,000); crude petroleum (barrels;
1990) 319,300,000 (172,650,000); petroleum products (metric tons; 1990) 41,-
058,000 (6,813,000); natural gas (cu m; 1990) 66,680,000,000 (25,439,000,000).
Public debt (external, outstanding; 1990): U.S.$24,316,000,000.
Gross national product (1990): U.S.$51,585,000,000 (U.S.$2,060 per capita).

Structure of gross domestic product and labour force

	1987		1990	
	in value DA '000,000	% of total value	labour force	% of labour force
Agriculture	38,180	14.9	907,490	15.9
Crude pet., nat. gas	45,310	17.7	55,000	1.0
Other mining	1,100	0.4	...	...
Manufacturing	34,950	13.6	646,390	11.3
Public utilities	3,525	1.4 }	651,370	11.4
Construction	44,290	17.3 }		
Transp. and commun.	12,975	5.1	252,230	4.4
Trade	36,490	14.2	444,970	7.8
Finance and services }	12,890	5.0	1,558,910	27.3
Pub. admin., defense }				
Other	26,515[5]	10.4[5]	1,194,640[6]	20.9[6]
TOTAL	256,225	100.0	5,711,000	100.0

Population economically active (1990): total 5,711,000; activity rate of population 22.8% (1987; participation rates: ages 15–64, 44.3%; female 9.2%;
unemployed 21.4%).

Price and earnings indexes (1985 = 100)

	1984	1985	1986	1987	1988	1989	1990
Consumer price index	90.5	100.0	112.4	120.7	127.9	139.8	163.0
Earnings index	...	...	...	...	...	...	...

Household income and expenditure. Average household size (1987) 6.9; income
per household: n.a.; sources of income: n.a.; expenditure (1979–80): food
and beverages 55.7%, housing and household durable goods 18.1%, clothing
and footwear 9.2%, transportation and communications 6.7%, recreation
3.4%, medical care and health 3.1%.
Land use (1990): forested 2.0%; meadows and pastures 13.1%; agricultural
and under permanent cultivation 3.2%; other (mostly desert) 81.7%.

Foreign trade

Balance of trade (current prices)

	1985	1986	1987	1988	1989	1990
DA '000,000	+15,073	–6,567	+4,959	+4,115	–3,118	+27,374
% of total	13.3%	8.2%	6.8%	4.5%	2.3%	13.6%

Imports (1990): DA 87,018,000,000 (industrial equipment 61.2%, food and
beverages 19.4%, consumer products 4.6%). *Major import sources:* France
23.1%; Italy 12.3%; United States 11.5%; Germany 11.3%; Spain 6.2%;
Japan 4.6%.
Exports (1990): DA 114,392,000,000 (mineral fuels and lubricants 96.8%).
Major export destinations: Italy 20.5%; United States 19.2%; France 17.3%;
Spain 6.0%; Germany 2.1%.

Transport and communications

Transport. Railroads (1990): route length 2,668 mi, 4,293 km; passenger-km
2,991,000,000; metric ton-km cargo 2,690,000,000. Roads (1991): total length
90,000 km (paved 70%). Vehicles (1990): passenger cars 750,000; trucks and
buses 500,000. Merchant marine (1991): vessels (100 gross tons and over)
148; total deadweight tonnage 1,093,363. Air transport (1987)[7]: passenger-
km 2,248,000,000; metric ton-km cargo 10,622,000; airports (1992) 25.
Communications. Daily newspapers (1990): total number 6; total circulation
1,400,000; circulation per 1,000 population 56. Radio (1991): 5,500,000 receivers (1 per 4.7 persons). Television (1991): 1,600,000 receivers (1 per 16
persons). Telephones (1990): 1,085,200 (1 per 23 persons).

Education and health

Education (1990–91)

	schools	teachers	students	student/ teacher ratio
Primary (age 6–11)	12,240[8]	145,555	4,189,000	28.8
Secondary (age 12–18)	2,913[8]	120,886	2,175,000	18.0
Voc., teacher tr.	71[9]	6,138	165,182[8]	29.4[10]
Higher	15[9]	17,581[11]	250,813	12.3[11]

Educational attainment (1989). Percentage of economically active population
age 16 and over having: no formal schooling 38.2%; Qur'anic education
0.9%; primary education 20.8%; secondary education 11.1%; vocational
19.7%; higher 9.3%. *Literacy* (1987): total population age 15 and over
literate 6,281,000 (49.6%); males literate 4,019,000 (63.4%); females literate
2,262,000 (35.8%).
Health: physicians (1990) 23,550 (1 per 1,062 persons); hospital beds (1988)
60,514 (1 per 393 persons); infant mortality rate per 1,000 live births (1990–
95) 61.0.
Food (1988–90): daily per capita caloric intake 2,944 (vegetable products 89%,
animal products 11%); 123% of FAO recommended minimum requirement.

Military

Total active duty personnel (1992): 139,000 (army 86.3%, navy 5.0%, air force
8.7%). *Military expenditure as percentage of GNP* (1989): 5.1% (world 4.9%);
per capita expenditure U.S.$94.

[1]March 20. [2]Algerian population only. [3]1989. [4]1988. [5]Customs duties. [6]Includes
1,141,278 unemployed, of whom 862,117 were not previously employed. [7]Air Algérie
international traffic only. [8]1989–90. [9]1981–82. [10]1987–88. [11]1988–89.

Andorra

Official name: Principat (Co-Principat) or Senyoriu (Co-Senyoriu) d'Andorra; les Valls d'Andorra (Principality [or Co-Principality] of Andorra; the Valleys of Andorra).
Form of government: co-principality with one nonpartisan[1] legislative house (General Council of the Valleys [28]).
Chiefs of state: President of France; Bishop of Urgel, Spain.
Head of government: Chief executive.
Capital: Andorra la Vella.
Official language: Catalan.
Official religion: Roman Catholicism.
Monetary unit: There is no local currency of issue; the French franc and Spanish peseta are both in circulation. 1 franc (F) = 100 centimes; 1 peseta (Pta) = 100 céntimos.
Valuation (Oct. 5, 1992)
1 U.S.$ = F 4.78, 1 £ = F 8.12;
1 U.S.$ = Ptas 100.47,
1 £ = Ptas 170.80.

Area and population		area		population
		sq mi	sq km	1990 census
Parishes	**Capitals**			
Andorra la Vella	Andorra la Vella	49[2]	127[2]	20,437
Canillo	Canillo	74	191	1,513
Encamp	Encamp }			7,489
La Massana	La Massana	25	65	4,386
Les Escaldes–Engordany	—	2	2	12,996
Ordino	Ordino	33	85	1,414
Sant Julià de Lòria	Sant Julià de Lòria	2	2	6,272
TOTAL		181	468	54,507

Demography

Population (1992): 57,100.
Density (1992): persons per sq mi 315.5, persons per sq km 122.0.
Urban-rural (1990): urban 62.5%; rural 37.5%.
Sex distribution (1990): male 53.14%; female 46.86%.
Age breakdown (1990): under 15, 17.4%; 15–29, 26.4%; 30–44, 27.0%; 45–59, 15.4%; 60–74, 10.1%; 75 and over, 3.7%.
Population projection: (2000) 73,000; (2010) 100,000.
Doubling time: 82 years.
Ethnic composition (1990): Spanish 49.7%; Andorran 28.6%; French 7.6%; Portuguese 7.2%; British 1.9%; other 5.0%.
Religious affiliation (1990): Roman Catholic 90.0%; other 10.0%.
Major cities (1990): Andorra la Vella 20,437; Les Escaldes 12,996; Encamp 7,489.

Vital statistics

Birth rate per 1,000 population (1990): 12.2 (world avg. 27.1).
Death rate per 1,000 population (1990): 3.7 (world avg. 9.8).
Natural increase rate per 1,000 population (1990): 8.5 (world avg. 17.3).
Total fertility rate (avg. births per childbearing woman; 1991): 1.3.
Marriage rate per 1,000 population (1990): 3.0.
Divorce rate per 1,000 population: n.a.
Life expectancy at birth (1990): male 74.0 years; female 81.0 years.
Major causes of death per 100,000 population: n.a.; however, health problems are those of a developed country—cardiovascular disease, hypertension, malignant neoplasms (cancers).

National economy

Budget (1990). Revenue: Ptas 12,470,000,000 (excise taxes on imported consumer goods and gasoline 87.4%). Expenditures: Ptas 21,370,000,000 (current expenditures 41.1%, of which education and culture 10.6%, tourism and exports 6.1%; development expenditures 55.9%, of which public services 49.1%).
Production (value of recorded exported products in Ptas '000 except as noted). Agriculture (1990): cattle 214,600, sheep and goats 11,200, horses and mules 5,800, tobacco 2,100, milk 1,600, sugar 1,200, natural honey 600. Quarrying (1990): marble 32,000. Manufacturing (1990): wearing apparel for men and boys 1,269,000; mineral water 435,700; electrical machinery and apparatus for industry 145,400; sports clothing 142,100; plastic products 61,400; scrap paper and pasteboard 43,300. Construction (1984): 90 buildings totaling 83,834 sq m were authorized for construction. Energy production (consumption): electricity (kW-hr; 1989) 140,000,000 (340,000,000[3]); coal, none (n.a.); crude petroleum, none (n.a.); petroleum products (metric tons; 1986) none (95,349); natural gas, none (n.a.).
Population economically active (1989): total 24,734; activity rate of total population 55.1% (participation rates: ages 15–64, 74.3%; female 45.6%; unemployed, none).

Price and earnings indexes (1985 = 100)[4]							
	1985	1986	1987	1988	1989	1990	1991
Consumer price index	100.0	108.8	114.5	120.0	128.2	136.8	144.9
Earnings index	...	...	...	...	...	...	...

Gross national product (at current market prices; 1988): U.S.$837,000,000 (U.S.$16,600 per capita)[5].

Structure of labour force		
	1989	
	labour force	% of labour force
Agriculture	291	1.2
Mining	...	...
Manufacturing	2,719	11.0
Construction	2,914	11.8
Public utilities	...	...
Transportation and communications	...	...
Trade	5,984	24.2
Restaurants, hotels	4,698	18.9
Finance, real estate, insurance	1,331	5.4
Pub. admin., defense	2,553	10.3
Other	4,127	16.7
Unknown	117	0.5
TOTAL	24,734	100.0

Land use (1989): forested 23.7%; meadows and pastures 44.2%; agricultural and under permanent cultivation 4.0%; other 28.1%.
Household income and expenditure. Average household size: n.a.; income per household: n.a.; sources of income: n.a.; expenditure: n.a.
Public debt: n.a.
Tourism: receipts from tourist arrivals, n.a.; expenditures by nationals abroad, n.a.; number of tourist arrivals (1988) approximately 12,000,000 annually, most of whom do not stay overnight; number of hotel rooms (1987) 35,000.

Foreign trade[6]

Balance of trade (current prices)						
	1985	1986	1987	1988	1989	1990
Ptas '000,000	...	−71,871	−73,200	−78,988	−89,007	−117,280
% of total	...	96.9%	93.8%	93.4%	94.2%	95.5%

Imports (1990): Ptas 120,023,000,000 (electrical and electronic equipment 11.9%, transport equipment 9.8%, wearing apparel 6.7%, nonelectrical machinery and equipment 5.0%, perfumes and cosmetics 4.8%, alcoholic beverages 4.6%, tobacco products 4.3%). *Major import sources:* France 36.7%; Spain 32.6%; Germany 7.0%; Japan 6.2%; Italy 3.2%.
Exports (1990): Ptas 2,743,000,000 (wearing apparel 52.1%, mineral water 15.9%, live cattle 7.8%, electrical and electronic equipment 7.3%, paper and paper products 2.9%). *Major export destinations:* France 64.1%; Spain 29.1%; Germany 3.5%; Portugal 1.4%.

Transport and communications

Transport. Railroads: none; however, both French and Spanish railways stop near the border. Roads (1990): total length 138 mi, 220 km (paved 80%). Vehicles (1989): passenger cars 31,571; trucks and buses 4,193. Merchant marine: vessels (100 gross tons and over) none. Airports (1992) with scheduled flights: none.
Communications. Daily newspapers (1991): total number 1; circulation 3,000; circulation per 1,000 population 54. Radio (1991): total number of receivers 10,000 (1 per 5.5 persons). Television (1989): total number of receivers 6,000 (1 per 8.6 persons). Telephones (1982): 17,719 (1 per 2.1 persons).

Education and health

Education (1990–91)	schools	teachers	students	student/teacher ratio
Primary (age 6–11)	...	...	...	...
Lower secondary (age 11–14)	12	...	2,303	...
Voc., teacher tr.	6	...	1,455	...
Higher	...	...	802[7, 8]	...

Educational attainment (mid-1980s). Percentage of population age 15 and over having: no formal schooling 5.5%; primary education 47.3%; secondary education 21.6%; postsecondary education 24.9%; unknown 0.7%. *Literacy* (1987): total population literate (virtually 100%).
Health (1989): physicians 107 (1 per 486 persons); hospital beds 122 (1 per 417 persons); infant mortality rate per 1,000 live births (1988–90 avg.) 4.9.
Food (1987–89)[9]: daily per capita caloric intake 3,508 (vegetable products 64%, animal products 36%); 141% of FAO recommended minimum requirement.

Military

Total active duty personnel (1990): none. France and Spain are responsible for Andorra's external security; a 100-man police force maintains domestic security.

[1]Election laws of 1985 provided for the creation of political parties. [2]Andorra la Vella includes Les Escaldes–Engordany and Sant Julià de Lòria. [3]Approximately 200,000,000 kW-hr of electricity are imported from Spain. [4]In Spanish pesetas. [5]Trade, tourism (including winter-season sports, fairs, and festivals), and the banking system (of some importance as a tax haven for foreign financial investment and transactions) are the primary sources of GNP. [6]Official statistics do not reflect what is thought to be extensive smuggling. [7]Students attending universities in other countries. [8]1988–89. [9]Composite values derived from Spanish and French food data.

Angola

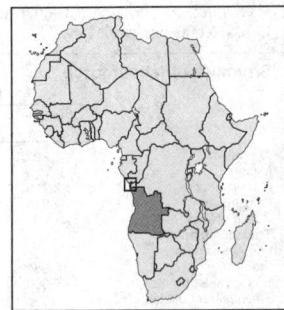

Official name: República de Angola (Republic of Angola).
Form of government: multiparty[1] republic with one legislative house (National Assembly [220]).
Head of state and government: President.
Capital: Luanda.
Official language: Portuguese.
Official religion: none.
Monetary unit: 1 New kwanza[2] (NKz) = 100 lwei; valuation (Oct. 5, 1992) 1 U.S.$ = NKz 550.00; 1 £ = NKz 935.00.

Area and population		area		population
		sq mi	sq km	1992 estimate[3]
Provinces	**Capitals**			
Bengo	Caxito	12,112	31,371	171,000
Benguela	Benguela	12,273	31,788	660,000
Bié	Kuito	27,148	70,314	1,153,000
Cabinda	Cabinda	2,807	7,270	168,000
Cunene	N'Giva	34,495	89,342	235,000
Huambo	Huambo	13,233	34,274	1,562,000
Huíla	Lubango	28,958	75,002	887,000
Kuando Kubango	Menongue	76,853	199,049	134,000
Kuanza Norte	N'Dalatando	9,340	24,190	385,000
Kuanza Sul	Sumbe	21,490	55,660	660,000
Luanda	Luanda	934	2,418	1,717,000
Lunda Norte	Lucapa	39,685	102,783	297,000
Lunda Sul	Saurimo	17,625	45,649	156,000
Malanje	Malanje	37,684	97,602	911,000
Moxico	Lwena	86,110	223,023	325,000
Namibe	Namibe	22,447	58,137	120,000
Uíge	Uíge	22,663	58,698	863,000
Zaire	M'Banza Kongo	15,494	40,130	205,000
TOTAL		481,354[4]	1,246,700	10,609,000

Demography

Population (1992): 10,609,000.
Density (1992): persons per sq mi 22.0, persons per sq km 8.5.
Urban-rural (1990): urban 28.3%; rural 71.7%.
Sex distribution (1991): male 48.80%; female 51.20%.
Age breakdown (1992): under 15, 45.0%; 15–29, 25.6%; 30–44, 15.1%; 45–59, 8.8%; 60 and over, 5.5%.
Population projection: (2000) 13,400,000; (2010) 18,082,000.
Doubling time: 25 years.
Ethnic composition (1983): Ovimbundu 37.2%; Mbundu 21.6%; Kongo 13.2%; Luimbe-Nganguela 5.4%; Nyaneka-Humbe 5.4%; Chokwe 4.2%; Luvale (Luena) 3.4%; Luchazi 2.4%; Ambo (Ovambo) 2.4%; Lunda 1.2%; Mbunda 1.2%; Portuguese 0.5%; mestizo 0.5%; other 0.4%.
Religious affiliation (1980): Christian 90.0%, of which Roman Catholic 68.7%; Protestant 19.8%; traditional beliefs 9.5%; other 0.5%.
Major cities: Luanda (1988) 1,134,000; Huambo (1983) 203,000; Benguela (1983) 155,000; Lobito (1983) 150,000; Lubango (1984) 105,000.

Vital statistics

Birth rate per 1,000 population (1990–95): 46.6 (world avg. 26.4).
Death rate per 1,000 population (1990–95): 18.6 (world avg. 9.2).
Natural increase rate per 1,000 population (1990–95): 28.0 (world avg. 17.2).
Total fertility rate (avg. births per childbearing woman; 1990–95): 6.3.
Marriage rate per 1,000 population (1972): 4.5.
Divorce rate per 1,000 population: n.a.
Life expectancy at birth (1990–95): male 44.9 years; female 48.1 years.
Major causes of death per 100,000 population (1973): accidents, poisoning, and violence 89.0; infectious and parasitic diseases 73.2; diseases of the respiratory system 24.6; diseases of the circulatory system 19.2; malignant neoplasms (cancers) 6.5.

National economy

Budget (1991). Revenue: NKz 186,383,000,000 (1989; tax revenue 82.8%, of which petroleum taxes 53.1%, income and property taxes 11.6%, domestic production taxes 9.5%, import duties 6.3%; nontax revenue 17.2%). Expenditures: NKz 275,468,000,000 (defense and internal security 36.9%; administration 23.9%; education 17.5%; health 7.5%; energy 3.6%; other 10.6%).
Public debt (external, outstanding; 1988): U.S.$1,356,000,000[5].
Tourism: receipts from visitors, n.a.; expenditures by nationals abroad, n.a.
Production (metric tons except as noted). Agriculture, forestry, fishing (1991): cassava 1,850,000, sugarcane 335,000, corn (maize) 299,000, bananas 280,000, sweet potatoes 170,000, millet 61,000, dry beans 48,000, palm oil 40,000, peanuts (groundnuts) 20,000, coffee 6,000; livestock (number of live animals) 3,100,000 cattle, 990,000 goats, 495,000 pigs, 280,000 sheep, 6,000,000 chickens; roundwood (1990) 6,448,000 cu m; fish catch (1990) 77,389. Mining and quarrying (1991): diamonds 960,000 carats. Manufacturing (1990): fresh meat 91,000[6]; bread 45,000; corn flour 35,000; wheat flour 22,000; laundry soap 7,556; sugar 3,190[7]; pasta 3,190[7]; leather shoes 132,000 pairs[7]; beer 410,000 hectolitres; soft drinks 69,050 hectolitres[7]; matches 6,357,000 boxes[7]. Construction (value in NKz '000,000; 1986): residential 608; nonresidential 1,977. Energy production (consumption): electricity (kW-hr; 1990) 1,840,-000,000 (1,840,000,000); coal, none (none); crude petroleum (barrels; 1991) 180,205,000 ([1990] 11,506,000); petroleum products (metric tons; 1990) 1,311,000 (349,000); natural gas (cu m; 1990) 166,576,000 (166,576,000).

Gross national product (at current market prices; 1989): U.S.$6,010,000,000 (U.S. $620 per capita).

Structure of gross domestic product and labour force				
	1991		1987	
	in value NKz '000,000[8]	% of total value	labour force	% of labour force
Agriculture	28,558	10.3	2,741,000	71.4
Mining	160,750	58.2		
Manufacturing	6,935	2.5		
Construction	5,235	1.9		
Finance	2,360	0.9	384,000	10.0
Trade	16,803	6.1		
Public utilities	818	0.3		
Transportation and communications	6,255	2.3		
Pub. admin., defense	48,391	17.5	714,000	18.6
Services				
Other	...	...		
TOTAL	276,105	100.0	3,839,000	100.0

Population economically active (1987): total 3,839,000; activity rate of total population 41.9% (participation rates [1985]: ages 15–64, 71.8%; female 39.7%; unemployed, n.a.).
Price and earnings indexes: n.a.
Household income and expenditure. Average household size (1980) 4.8; annual income per household: n.a.; sources of income: n.a.; expenditure: n.a.
Land use (1990): forested 41.7%; meadows and pastures 23.3%; agricultural and under permanent cultivation 2.7%; other 32.3%.

Foreign trade

Balance of trade (current prices)						
	1986	1987	1988	1989	1990	1991
U.S.$'000,000	+206	+953	+1,081	+1,191	+1,276	+2,080
% of total	8.6%	26.6%	28.1%	25.1%	25.1%	43.6%

Imports (1991): U.S.$1,347,000,000 (current consumption goods 50.2%, capital goods 20.2%, intermediate consumption goods 18.9%, transport equipment 6.8%). *Major import sources:* Portugal 29.8%; United States 10.5%; France 9.7%; Japan 7.8%; Brazil 7.3%.
Exports (1991): U.S.$3,427,000,000 (mineral fuels 89.8%, diamonds 5.5%). *Major export destinations:* United States 56.6%; Germany 5.6%; Brazil 4.9%; The Netherlands 4.2%; United Kingdom 3.4%; Belgium-Luxembourg 3.3%.

Transport and communications

Transport. Railroads (1988): route length 1,739 mi, 2,798 km; passenger-mi 203,000,000, passenger-km 326,000,000; short ton-mi cargo 1,178,000,000, metric ton-km cargo 1,720,000,000. Roads (1990): total length 45,118 mi, 72,611 km (paved 11%). Vehicles (1990): passenger cars 130,000; trucks and buses 45,000. Merchant marine (1991): vessels (100 gross tons and over) 111; total deadweight tonnage 122,403. Air transport (1985)[9]: passenger-mi 606,000,000, passenger-km 975,000,000; short ton-mi cargo 23,200,000, metric ton-km cargo 33,900,000; airports (1992) with scheduled flights 16.
Communications. Daily newspapers (1984): total number 4; total circulation 111,500; circulation per 1,000 population 13.5. Radio (1991): total number of receivers 450,000 (1 per 23 persons). Television (1991): total number of receivers 50,000 (1 per 206 persons). Telephones (1991): 78,000 (1 per 132 persons).

Education and health

Education (1988–89)	schools	teachers	students	student/ teacher ratio
Primary (age 7–10)	6,308[10]	31,953	1,607,906	33.4
Secondary (age 11–16)	5,276[10]	3,870[11]	154,381	...
Voc., teacher tr.	...	539[12]	6,087	...
Higher	1[10]	316[10]	4,965[10]	15.7[10]

Educational attainment: n.a. Literacy (1990): percentage of population age 15 and over literate 41.7%; males literate 55.6%; females literate 28.5%.
Health (1990): physicians 662 (1 per 15,136 persons); hospital beds 11,857 (1 per 845 persons); infant mortality rate per 1,000 live births (1990–95) 127.0.
Food (1985): daily per capita caloric intake 1,969 ([1979–81] vegetable products 92%, animal products 8%); (1984) 84% of FAO recommended minimum requirement.

Military

Total active duty personnel (1992): 127,500[13] (army 94.1%, navy 1.2%, air force 4.7%). *Military expenditure as percentage of GNP* (1984): 14.3% (world 5.7%); per capita expenditure U.S.$119.

[1]Multiparty system approved in March 1991; elections were held on Sept. 29–30, 1992; presidential results were inconclusive and a definitive runoff election was to take place in the near future. [2]The New kwanza was valued at a 2:1 ratio to the Old kwanza as of March 1991. [3]Unified national estimates and projections based on sample surveys, partial censuses, and analysis of provincial vital statistics. [4]Detail does not add to total given because of rounding. [5]Includes external long-term debt not guaranteed by the government. [6]1988. [7]1989. [8]At official prices of 1980. [9]TAAG Airline only. [10]1985–86. [11]1981–82. [12]1984–85. [13]In 1988, about 52,000 Cuban troops and other Soviet-bloc advisers and technicians were assisting government forces. On July 20, 1988, an agreement was reached between South Africa, Cuba, Angola, and the United States calling for the withdrawal of all foreign troops over a period of 27 months. As of 1992 there were only 416 observers and advisers remaining.

Antigua and Barbuda

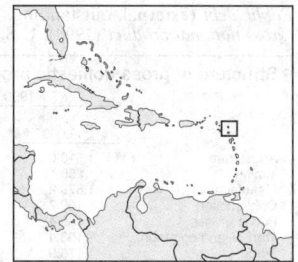

Official name: Antigua and Barbuda.
Form of government: constitutional monarchy with two legislative houses (Senate [17]; House of Representatives [17]).
Chief of state: British Monarch represented by Governor-General.
Head of government: Prime Minister.
Capital: Saint John's.
Official language: English.
Official religion: none.
Monetary unit: 1 East Caribbean dollar (EC\$) = 100 cents; valuation (Oct. 5, 1992) 1 U.S.\$ = EC\$2.70; 1 £ = EC\$4.59.

Area and population	area		population
			1991
Parishes[1]	sq mi	sq km	census
Saint George	10.2	26.4	...
Saint John's	26.2	67.9	...
Saint Mary	25.1	65.0	...
Saint Paul	17.7	45.8	...
Saint Peter	12.8	33.2	...
Saint Phillip	16.0	41.4	...
Islands[1]			
Barbuda	62.0	160.6	[2]
Redonda	0.5	1.3	[3]
TOTAL	170.5	441.6	63,880[4]

Demography

Population (1992): 64,000.
Density (1992): persons per sq mi 375.4, persons per sq km 144.9.
Urban-rural (1990): urban 32.0%; rural 68.0%.
Sex distribution (1985): male 48.00%; female 52.00%.
Age breakdown (1985): under 15, 37.2%; 15–29, 30.8%; 30–44, 12.8%; 45–59 11.5%; 60–74, 6.4%; 75 and over, 1.3%.
Population projection: (2000) 64,000; (2010) 64,000.
Doubling time: 58 years.
Ethnic composition (1988): black 89.0%; mixed 10.0%; other (mostly British, Portuguese, and Lebanese) 1.0%.
Religious affiliation (1980): Anglican 44.5%; other Protestant (largely Moravian, Methodist, and Seventh-day Adventist) 41.6%; Roman Catholic 10.2%; Rastafarian 0.7%; other 3.0%.
Major cities (1986): Saint John's 36,000; Codrington 1,200[5].

Vital statistics

Birth rate per 1,000 population (1991): 18.0 (world avg. 26.4); (1988) legitimate 23.4%; illegitimate 76.6%.
Death rate per 1,000 population (1991): 6.0 (world avg. 9.2).
Natural increase rate per 1,000 population (1991): 12.0 (world avg. 17.2).
Total fertility rate (avg. births per childbearing woman; 1991): 1.7.
Marriage rate per 1,000 population (1988): 4.9.
Divorce rate per 1,000 population (1988): 0.2.
Life expectancy at birth (1991): male 70.0 years; female 74.0 years.
Major causes of death per 100,000 population (1988): diseases of the circulatory system 237.5; malignant neoplasms (cancers) 44.5; diseases of the respiratory system 44.5; endocrine and metabolic disorders 25.4; ill-defined conditions 68.6.

National economy

Budget (1990). Revenue: EC\$237,700,000 (current revenue 95.1%, of which consumption taxes 24.2%, import duties 18.4%, taxes on goods and services 17.4%, nontax revenue 13.1%; development revenue 3.5%). Expenditures: EC\$227,100,000 (current expenditures 91.9%; development expenditures 8.1%).
Production (metric tons except as noted). Agriculture, forestry, fishing (1988): sugarcane 4,000[6], mangoes 1,000[6], melons 672, limes 249, eggplant 248, pumpkins 233, sweet potatoes 219, "Antiguan Black" pineapples 126, ginger 98, sea island cotton lint 36; livestock (number of live animals; 1990): 18,000 cattle, 13,000 sheep; roundwood, n.a.; fish catch (1990) 2,200 (of which spiny lobster 200). Mining and quarrying: crushed stone for local use. Manufacturing (1988): rum 4,000 hectolitres; wine and vodka 2,000 hectolitres; other manufactures include garments, household appliances, and soft drinks; electronic components are assembled for reexport. Construction (1988): gross value of building applications EC\$221,800,000. Energy production (consumption): electricity (kW-hr; 1990) 95,000,000 (95,000,000); coal, none (none); crude petroleum, none (none); petroleum products (metric tons; 1990) negligible (98,000); natural gas, none (none).
Population economically active (1985): total 32,254; activity rate of total population 42.6% (participation rates: over age 16 [1983] 56.2%; female 40.1%; unemployed, n.a.[7]).

Price and earnings indexes (1987 = 100)							
	1984	1985	1986	1987	1988	1989	1990
Consumer price index	93.7	94.6	96.5	100.0	103.4	108.9	117.3
Weekly earnings index[8]	...	...	...	100.0	110.0	122.1	...

Household income and expenditure. Average household size (1984) 3.5; income per household: n.a.; sources of income: n.a.; expenditure (1974)[9]: food

and nonalcoholic beverages 42.9%, housing 23.3%, transportation 10.0%, clothing and footwear 7.5%, energy 5.5%, alcoholic beverages and tobacco 3.6%, other 7.2%.
Gross national product (at current market prices; 1990): U.S.\$363,000,000 (U.S.\$4,600 per capita).

Structure of gross domestic product and labour force				
	1988[10]		1982	
	in value EC\$'000,000	% of total value	labour force[11]	% of labour force[11]
Agriculture, fishing	32.1	4.4	2,090	9.0
Quarrying	16.8	2.3	60	0.3
Manufacturing	24.1	3.3	1,718	7.4
Construction	95.9	13.0	2,577	11.1
Public utilities	31.3	4.2	340	1.5
Transportation and communications	110.8	15.0	2,575	11.1
Trade, restaurants, and hotels	183.9	24.9	5,201	22.4
Finance, real estate	103.7	14.1	778	3.3
Pub. admin., defense	125.3	17.0 }	7,883	33.9
Services	49.5	6.7 }		
Other	−35.8[12]	−4.9[12]	—	—
TOTAL	737.6	100.0	23,222	100.0

Land use (1990): forested 11.0%; meadows and pastures 9.0%; agricultural and under permanent cultivation 18.0%; other 62.0%.
Public debt (external, outstanding; end of 1990): U.S.\$268,300,000.
Tourism (1990): receipts from visitors U.S.\$258,000,000; expenditures by nationals abroad U.S.\$16,000,000.

Foreign trade[13]

Balance of trade (current prices)						
	1986	1987	1988	1989	1990	1991
EC\$'000,000	−507	−614	−757	−854	−790	−771
% of total	82.8%	85.4%	82.2%	83.3%	81.5%	81.7%

Imports (1987): EC\$667,000,000 (basic manufactures 27.0%, machinery and transport equipment 26.8%, food 12.3%, mineral fuels and lubricants 9.9%). *Major import sources* (1989)[14]: United States 27.0%; United Kingdom 16.0%; Canada 4.0%; OECS 3.0%; Italy 3.0%.
Exports (1987): EC\$53,000,000 (reexports 57.5%, domestic exports 42.5%). *Major export destinations* (1989)[14]: United States 41.0%; United Kingdom 19.0%; Germany 19.0%.

Transport and communications

Transport. Railroads[15]. Roads (1988): total length 724 mi, 1,165 km (paved 33%). Vehicles (1990): passenger cars 13,500; trucks and buses 3,500. Merchant marine (1991): vessels (100 gross tons and over) 241; total deadweight tonnage 811,176. Air transport (1990)[16]: passenger-mi 110,000,000, passenger-km 177,000,000; metric ton-km cargo, none; airports (1992) with scheduled flights 2.
Communications. Daily newspapers: none[17]. Radio (1991): total number of receivers 75,000 (1 per 0.9 persons). Television (1991): total number of receivers 28,000 (1 per 2.3 persons). Telephones (1988): 7,400 (1 per 11 persons).

Education and health

Education (1988–89)				
	schools	teachers	students	student/ teacher ratio
Primary (age 5–10)	45	414	9,097[18]	20.4[18]
Secondary (age 11–16)	13	273	4,413[18]	13.8[18]
Voc., teacher tr. }	2	85	927	10.9
Higher }				

Educational attainment: n.a. *Literacy* (1985): total population age 15 and over literate 45,000 (90.0%).
Health (1987): physicians (1988) 48 (1 per 1,333 persons); hospital beds 373 (1 per 207 persons); infant mortality rate per 1,000 live births 21.2.
Food (1988–90): daily per capita caloric intake 2,307 (vegetable products 64%, animal products 36%); 98% of FAO recommended minimum requirement.

Military

Total active duty personnel (1990): an almost 100-member defense force is part of the Eastern Caribbean regional security system. *Military expenditure as percentage of central government current expenditure* (1990–91): 1.4%[19].

[1]Community councils on Antigua and the local government council on Barbuda are the actual organs of local government. [2]1990 estimate was 1,100. [3]Uninhabited. [4]Preliminary de facto census adjusted for underenumeration. [5]1982. [6]1991. [7]Labour shortage of mid-1980s has eased. 1990 unemployment increased, particularly in the depressed construction sector. No official data; a noticeable shortage of skilled and semiskilled workers in 1988–89 indicated a low unemployment rate. [8]Construction only. [9]Weights of consumer price index components. [10]At factor cost. [11]Wage earners and self-employed only. [12]Less imputed bank service charges. [13]Exports f.o.b.; imports c.i.f. [14]Estimated percentages. [15]48 mi (78 km) of privately owned track are mostly nonoperative. [16]Caribbean Airline LIAT (airline jointly operated by 11 Caricom governments that is headquartered in Antigua). [17]Three weekly newspapers and one twice-weekly newspaper had a total circulation of 12,200 in 1990. [18]1987–88. [19]May not agree with military expenditure as percentage of GNP because of different bases used.

Argentina

Official name: República Argentina (Argentine Republic).
Form of government: federal republic with two legislative houses (Senate [46]; Chamber of Deputies [254]).
Head of state and government: President.
Capital: Buenos Aires.
Official language: Spanish.
Official religion: Roman Catholicism.
Monetary unit: 1 peso (pl. pesos)[1] (Ps) = 100 centavos; valuation (Oct. 5, 1992) 1 U.S.$ = Ps 0.99; 1 £ = Ps 1.68.

Area and population

Provinces	Capitals	area sq mi	area sq km	population 1991 census[2]
Buenos Aires	La Plata	118,754	307,571	12,538,007
Catamarca	Catamarca	39,615	102,602	264,940
Chaco	Resistencia	38,469	99,633	799,302
Chubut	Rawson	86,752	224,686	356,445
Córdoba	Córdoba	63,831	165,321	2,764,176
Corrientes	Corrientes	34,054	88,199	780,778
Entre Ríos	Paraná	30,418	78,781	1,021,042
Formosa	Formosa	27,825	72,066	363,035
Jujuy	San Salvador de Jujuy	20,548	53,219	513,213
La Pampa	Santa Rosa	55,382	143,440	260,041
La Rioja	La Rioja	34,626	89,680	220,910
Mendoza	Mendoza	57,462	148,827	1,400,142
Misiones	Posadas	11,506	29,801	787,514
Neuquén	Neuquén	36,324	94,078	385,606
Río Negro	Viedma	78,384	203,013	506,314
Salta	Salta	60,034	155,488	863,688
San Juan	San Juan	34,614	89,651	526,263
San Luis	San Luis	29,633	76,748	286,379
Santa Cruz	Río Gallegos	94,187	243,943	159,726
Santa Fe	Santa Fe	51,354	133,007	2,782,809
Santiago del Estero	Santiago del Estero	52,645	136,351	670,388
Tucumán	San Miguel de Tucumán	8,697	22,524	1,142,321
Other federal entities				
Distrito Federal	Buenos Aires	77	200	2,960,976
Tierra del Fuego	Ushuaia	8,329	21,571	69,450
TOTAL		1,073,518[3]	2,780,400	32,423,465

Demography

Population (1992): 33,070,000.
Density (1992): persons per sq mi 30.8, persons per sq km 11.9.
Urban-rural (1990): urban 86.2%; rural 13.8%.
Sex distribution (1991): male 48.90%; female 51.10%.
Age breakdown (1990): under 15, 29.9%; 15–29, 23.2%; 30–44, 19.5%; 45–59, 14.2%; 60–74, 9.9%; 75 and over, 3.3%.
Population projection: (2000) 36,461,000; (2010) 40,687,000.
Doubling time: 63 years.
Ethnic composition (1986): European 85%; mestizo, Amerindian, and other 15%.
Religious affiliation (1990): Roman Catholic 91.0%; other 9.0%.
Major cities (1991): Buenos Aires 2,960,976 (Greater Buenos Aires 12,582,-321); Córdoba 1,179,067; Rosario 1,078,374[4]; La Plata 542,567.

Vital statistics

Birth rate per 1,000 population (1991): 20.0 (world avg. 26.4); (1982) legitimate 67.5%; illegitimate 29.8%; unknown 2.7%.
Death rate per 1,000 population (1991): 9.0 (world avg. 9.2).
Natural increase rate per 1,000 population (1991): 11.0 (world avg. 17.2).
Total fertility rate (avg. births per childbearing woman; 1991): 2.7.
Marriage rate per 1,000 population (1983): 6.0.
Life expectancy at birth (1991): male 68.0 years; female 74.0 years.
Major causes of death per 100,000 population (1987): circulatory diseases 357.7; cancers 140.4; accidents 53.0; respiratory diseases 52.5.

National economy

Budget (1988). Revenue: Ps 10,285,400[1] (social-security taxes 42.2%, excise taxes 14.4%, import duties 7.1%, general sales tax 6.0%, property tax 5.7%, income taxes 4.2%, export duties 2.3%). Expenditures: Ps 12,011,000[1] (social security 38.9%, economic services 20.5%, education 9.3%, transportation and communications 9.1%, defense 8.6%, debt service 7.4%).
Land use (1990): forested 21.6%; meadows and pastures 52.0%; agricultural and under permanent cultivation 9.9%; other 16.5%.
Production (metric tons except as noted). Agriculture, forestry, fishing (1991): sugarcane 19,000,000, soybeans 11,250,000, wheat 9,000,000, corn (maize) 7,768,000, sunflower seeds 3,970,000, potatoes 2,600,000, sorghum 2,251,000, grapes 2,000,000, tomatoes 720,000; livestock (number of live animals) 50,-080,000 cattle, 27,552,000 sheep; roundwood (1990) 10,819,000 cu m; fish catch (1990) 555,571. Mining and quarrying (1990): silver 289,357 troy oz; gold 29,579 troy oz[5]. Manufacturing (by value of production in U.S.$'000; 1988): textiles 2,884,000; motor vehicles 2,620,000; metal products 2,348,000; iron and steel 2,151,000; industrial chemicals 2,095,000; electrical machinery 1,485,000; beverages 1,459,000. Construction (authorized; 1984): 10,606,800 sq m. Energy production (consumption): electricity (kW-hr; 1990) 50,907,-000,000 (51,743,000,000); coal (metric tons; 1990) 270,000 (1,407,000); crude petroleum (barrels; 1990) 177,181,000 (170,933,000); petroleum products (metric tons; 1990) 20,890,000 (17,065,000); natural gas (cu m; 1990) 27,563,-492,000 (30,526,276,000).

Public debt (external, outstanding; 1990): U.S.$45,558,000,000.
Gross national product (1990): U.S.$76,491,000,000 (U.S.$2,370 per capita).

Structure of gross domestic product and labour force

	1990 in value A '000,000[1,6]	1990 % of total value	1980 labour force	1980 % of labour force
Agriculture	1,518.0	16.7	1,200,992	12.0
Mining	259.1	2.9	47,171	0.5
Manufacturing	1,878.2	20.7	1,985,995	19.9
Construction	169.7	1.9	1,003,175	10.1
Public utilities	489.4	5.4	103,256	1.0
Transp. and commun.	1,103.4	12.2	460,476	4.6
Trade	1,176.9	13.0	1,702,080	17.0
Finance	760.5	8.4	395,704	4.0
Pub. admin., defense Services	} 1,708.1	18.8	2,399,039	24.0
Other	...	...	691,302	6.9
TOTAL	9,063.4[3]	100.0	9,989,190	100.0

Population economically active (1989): total 12,141,440; activity rate of total population 38.0% (participation rates: ages 15–64, 59.5%; female 33.4%; unemployed [1987] 5.2%).

Price and earnings indexes (1985 = 100)

	1985	1986	1987	1988	1989	1990	1991
Consumer price index	100.0	210.3	468.7	1,948	62,162	1,495,000	4,062,000
Hourly earnings index[7]	100.0	206.9	423.3	...	...	...	...

Household size and expenditure. Average household size (1991) 3.2; expenditure (1985–86): food 38.2%, transportation 11.6%, housing 9.3%, energy 9.0%, clothing and footwear 8.0%, health 7.9%, recreation and culture 7.5%, education 2.6%, other 5.9%.
Tourism (1990): receipts U.S.$903,000,000; expenditures U.S.$1,171,000,000.

Foreign trade[8]

Balance of trade (current prices)

	1986	1987	1988	1989	1990	1991
U.S.$'000,000	+2,446	+1,000	+4,051	+5,706	+8,627	+4,572
% of total	21.7%	8.5%	29.3%	42.5%	53.7%	23.6%

Imports (1989): U.S.$4,203,194,000 (machinery and transport equipment 31.5%, of which electrical machinery 8.2%, transport equipment 5.8%; chemicals 25.8%; petroleum and products 8.8%; iron and steel products 6.6%; plastics 5.3%). *Major import sources:* U.S. 20.9%; Brazil 17.2%; W.Ger. 9.4%; Italy 5.8%.
Exports (1989): U.S.$9,579,271,000 (animal feed 14.9%; cereals 10.6%; iron and steel 10.2%; vegetable and animal oils 9.1%; machinery and transport equipment 6.5%; chemicals 5.7%). *Major export destinations:* U.S. 12.0%; Brazil 11.7%; The Netherlands 10.3%; U.S.S.R. 8.7%; W.Ger. 4.3%; China 4.2%; Chile 3.8%.

Transport and communications

Transport. Railroads (1989): route length (1988) 34,115 km; passenger-km 10,651,000,000; metric ton-km cargo 8,453,000,000. Roads (1986): total length 131,338 mi, 211,369 km (paved 27%). Vehicles (1989): passenger cars 4,088,000; commercial vehicles and buses 1,512,000. Merchant marine (1991): vessels (100 gross tons and over) 490; total deadweight tonnage 2,540,776. Air transport (1991)[9]: passenger-km 8,078,000,000; metric ton-km cargo 174,994,000; airports (1992) 49.
Communications. Daily newspapers (1988): total number 194; total circulation 2,748,400[10]; circulation per 1,000 population 88[10]. Radio (1991): 21,582,456 receivers (1 per 1.5 persons). Television (1991): 7,165,000 receivers (1 per 4.5 persons). Telephones (1989): 3,921,629 (1 per 8.1 persons).

Education and health

Education (1987)

	schools	teachers	students	student/ teacher ratio
Primary (age 6–12)	21,025	252,259	4,906,907	19.5
Secondary (age 13–17)[11]	1,987[12]	111,421	773,615	6.9
Vocational	3,117[12]	150,885	1,207,200	8.0
Higher	1,540	69,985[13]	902,882[13]	12.9[13]

Educational attainment (1980). Percentage of population age 25 and over having: no formal schooling 6.0%; less than primary education 32.0%; primary 34.6%; secondary 20.5%; higher 6.9%. *Literacy* (1990): percentage of total population age 15 and over literate 95.3%; males literate 95.5%; females literate 95.1%.
Health: physicians (1987) 96,000 (1 per 326 persons); hospital beds (1987) 150,000 (1 per 205 persons); infant mortality rate (1991) 31.0.
Food (1988–90): daily per capita caloric intake 3,068 (vegetable products 69%; animal products 31%); 131% of FAO recommended minimum requirement.

Military

Total active duty personnel (1992): 65,000 (army 53.8%, navy 30.8%, air force 15.4%). *Military expenditure as percentage of GNP* (1989): 3.4% (world 4.9%); per capita expenditure: U.S.$58.

[1]On Jan. 1, 1992, the austral was replaced by the peso at a ratio of 10,000:1. [2]Preliminary. [3]Detail does not add to total given because of rounding. [4]*Municipio.* [5]1989. [6]At 1970 prices. [7]Skilled workers in manufacturing only. [8]Import figures are f.o.b. in balance of trade and c.i.f. in commodities and trading partners. [9]Aerolineas Argentina only. [10]For 109 newspapers in 1986 only. [11]Secondary includes teacher training. [12]1984. [13]1986.

Armenia

Official name: Hayastani Hanrape-
tut'yun (Republic of Armenia).
Form of government: unitary multiparty
republic with a single legislative body
(Supreme Council [260]).
Head of state: President.
Head of government: Prime Minister.
Capital: Yerevan.
Official language: Armenian.
Official religion: none.
Monetary unit: 1 ruble = 100 kopecks;
valuation (Oct. 5, 1992) free rate,
1 U.S.$ = 316.82 rubles;
1 £ = 538.59 rubles.

Area and population		area		population
Administrative subdivisions	Capitals	sq mi	sq km	1987 estimate
Cities[1]				
Gyumri	—	...	...	228,400
Kirovakan	—	...	...	169,400
Yerevan	—	...	...	1,184,500
Rural districts				
Abovyani	Abovyan	313	810	108,200
Akhuryani	Akhuryan	223	577	39,500
Amasiayi	Amasia	235	609	19,300
Anii	Maralik	166	429	19,700
Aparani	Aparan	228	591	19,900
Aragatsi	Tsaghkahovit	148	382	14,100
Ararati	Vedi	540	1,399	85,100
Artashati	Artashat	200	517	95,500
Art'iki	Art'ik	187	484	44,800
Ashtaraki	Ashtarak	267	692	36,400
Azizbekovi	Azizbekov	453	1,172	17,000
Baghramyani	Baghramyan	175	453	16,100
Ejmiadzini	Ejmiadzin	141	366	121,000
Ghap'ani	Ghap'an	529	1,371	61,500
Ghukasyani	Ghukasyan	211	547	9,800
Gorisi	Goris	290	752	38,000
Gugark'i	Gugark'	297	770	31,000
Hoktemberyani	Hoktemberyan	163	423	109,900
Hrazdani	Hrazdan	366	948	78,600
Ijevani	Ijevan	516	1,336	46,600
Kalininoyi	Kalinino	266	690	39,100
Kamoyi	Kamo	269	697	56,400
Krasnoselski	Krasnoselsk	269	697	27,900
Martunu	Martuni	458	1,185	67,900
Masisi	Masis	70	182	64,400
Meghru	Meghri	256	664	15,100
Nairii	Yeghvard	133	344	47,200
Noyemberyani	Noyemberyan	208	538	29,700
Sevani	Sevan	152	393	42,700
Shamshadini	Berd	318	824	34,200
Sisiani	Sisian	664	1,719	34,600
Spitaki	Spitak	212	549	46,300
Step'anavani	Step'anavan	246	637	36,500
T'alini	T'alin	421	1,091	35,100
T'umanyani	Alaverdi	433	1,121	58,200
Vardenisi	Vardenis	444	1,151	60,200
Yeghegnadzori	Yeghegnadzor	438	1,134	35,400
TOTAL		11,506[2]	29,800[2]	3,411,900[2]

Demography

Population (1992): 3,426,000.
Density (1992): persons per sq mi 297.8, persons per sq km 115.0.
Urban-rural (1991): urban 69.5%; rural 30.5%.
Sex distribution (1991): male 49.10%; female 50.90%.
Age breakdown (1990): under 15, 30.3%; 15–29, 25.7%; 30–44, 20.8%; 45–59, 13.6%; 60–69, 6.4%; 70 and over, 3.2%.
Population projection: (2000) 3,968,000; (2010) 4,445,000.
Doubling time: 44 years.
Ethnic composition (1989): Armenian 93.3%; Azerbaijani 2.6%; other 4.1%.
Religious affiliation: believers are predominantly Armenian Apostolic.
Major cities (1991): Yerevan 1,283,000; Gyumri 163,000[3]; Kirovakan 76,000[3].

Vital statistics

Birth rate per 1,000 population (1990): 22.5 (world avg. 27.1); (1989) legitimate 92.1%; illegitimate 7.9%.
Death rate per 1,000 population (1990): 6.2 (world avg. 9.8).
Natural increase rate per 1,000 population (1990): 16.3 (world avg. 17.3).
Total fertility rate (avg. births per childbearing woman; 1989): 2.6.
Marriage rate per 1,000 population (1989): 8.0.
Divorce rate per 1,000 population (1989): 1.2.
Life expectancy at birth (1990): male 67.9 years; female 73.4 years.
Major causes of death per 100,000 population (1990): circulatory diseases 305.9; cancers 98.3; accidents and violence 55.6; respiratory diseases 50.3.

National economy

Budget (1992). Revenue: 9,556,000,000 rubles (tax revenue 97.4%, of which value-added tax 49.2%, income tax 34.0%, excise taxes 10.5%; nontax revenue 2.6%). Expenditures: 10,746,000,000 rubles (education 29.9%; national economy 23.7%; health 18.3%; police 5.3%; defense 2.3%).
Production (metric tons except as noted). Agriculture, forestry, fishing (1991): vegetables (except potatoes) 457,000, milk 403,200, potatoes 316,000, wheat 310,000, grapes 200,000, meat 141,200, geraniums 8,500, tobacco 2,200, wool 2,100; livestock (number of live animals) 1,172,200 sheep, 640,000 cattle, 9,352,300 poultry; roundwood 44,100 cu m; fish catch, n.a. Mining and

quarrying (1990): gold, copper, molybdenum. Manufacturing (1990): cement 1,466,000; chemical fibres 9,351; paper 7,500; synthetic rubber 1,441; furniture 99,700,000 rubles; cotton fabrics 31,600,000 sq m; silk fabrics 16,000,000 sq m; wool fabrics 4,900,000 sq m; carpets 1,300,000 sq m; watches 3,000,000 pieces; car tires 1,009,000 units; metal-cutting equipment 8,559 units; construction materials 826,000 cu m; leather shoes 18,740,000 pairs; wine 419,-100 hectolitres; cognac 61,400 hectolitres. Construction (1990): n.a. Energy production (consumption): electricity (kW-hr; 1991) 9,500,000,000 (1990; 12,076,000,000); coal (metric tons; 1990) 50,000 (570,000); crude petroleum, none (n.a.); petroleum products (metric tons; 1990) 292,000 (4,346,000); natural gas (cu m; 1990) 170,000,000 (4,882,000,000).
Gross national product (1991): 12,329,000,000 rubles (3,500 rubles per capita)[4].

Structure of gross domestic product and labour force				
	1990			
	in value '000,000 rubles	% of total value	labour force	% of labour force
Agriculture	3,166	25.7	117,300	5.7
Manufacturing, mining }	5,959	48.3	397,900	19.4
Public utilities			55,300	2.7
Construction	1,800	14.6	161,600	7.9
Transp. and commun.	274	2.2	88,000	4.3
Trade	689	5.6	88,100	4.3
Finance	—	—	17,800	1.0
Pub. admin., defense	—	—	7,900	0.4
Services	—	—	413,300	20.2
Other	441	3.6	697,200[5]	34.1[5]
TOTAL	12,329	100.0	2,044,400	100.0

Household income and expenditure. Average household size (1989) 4.7; income per household (1990) 11,100 rubles; sources of income (1990): salaries and wages 74.8%, social benefits 8.0%, agricultural income 4.9%, other 12.3%; expenditure (1990) 8,100 rubles: food 47.3%, clothing 17.4%, taxes 8.1%, services 7.1%, household furnishings 6.6%, other 13.5%.
Population economically active (1990): total 2,044,400; activity rate of total population 57.2% (participation rates [1989]: ages 16–59 [male], 16–54 [female] 79.9%; female [1990] 49.4%; unemployed [1990] 3.6%).

Price and earnings indexes (1985 = 100)						
	1985	1986	1987	1988	1989	1990
Consumer price index	100.0	102.0	103.0	103.0	104.0	112.0
Monthly earnings index	100.0	102.3	105.9	109.2	121.9	133.7

Land use (1988): forest 14.4%; pasture 35.2%; agriculture 21.6%; other 28.8%.

Foreign trade

Balance of trade (current prices)						
	1985	1986	1987	1988	1989	1990
'000,000 rubles	20	374	−135	−1,110	−1,207	−1,039
% of total	0.2%	3.5%	1.6%	12.8%	14.1%	12.7%

Imports (1990): 4,662,000,000 rubles (light-industrial products 25.0%, machine-building and metalworking machinery 20.9%, food 16.2%, chemical products 7.9%, agricultural imports 6.2%, energy products [except electricity] 6.1%). *Major import sources:* Russia 30.0%; Ukraine 18.7%; Belarus 7.2%.
Exports (1990): 3,523,000,000 rubles (light-industrial products 42.6%, machine-building and metalworking machinery 23.5%, food industry 11.7%, chemical products 6.0%). *Major export destinations:* Russia 60.9%; Ukraine 12.2%; Kazakhstan 11.1%; Uzbekistan 4.1%; Turkmenistan 3.3%.

Transport and communications

Transport. Railroads (1991): length 823 km; (1990) passenger-km 316,000,000; metric ton-km cargo 4,884,000,000. Roads (1991): total length 7,700 km (paved 99%). Vehicles (1988): passenger cars 230,100; trucks and buses, n.a. Merchant marine: vessels (100 gross tons and over) n.a.; total deadweight tonnage, n.a. Air transport (1990): passenger km 5,556,900,000; metric ton-km cargo 49,000,000; airports (1992) 2.
Communications. Daily newspapers (1991): total number 82; total circulation 1,678,000; circulation per 1,000 population 469. Radio (1991): 642,000 receivers (1 per 5.6 persons). Television (1991): 722,000 receivers (1 per 5.0 persons). Telephones (1991): 595,300 (1 per 6.0 persons).

Education and health

Education (1990–91)				
	schools	teachers	students	student/ teacher ratio
Primary (age 6–13) Secondary (age 14–17) }	1,397	53,400	597,900	11.2
Voc., teacher tr.	70	...	45,900	...
Higher	14	...	68,400	...

Educational attainment (1989). Percentage of population age 25 and over having: primary education or no formal schooling 7.4%; some secondary 18.6%; completed secondary and some postsecondary 57.7%; higher 13.8%.
Health (1990): physicians 14,519 (1 per 246 persons); hospital beds 30,482 (1 per 117 persons); infant mortality rate per 1,000 live births 18.6.

Military

Total active duty personnel (1992): c. 50,000 (army 100%). *Military expenditure as percentage of GNP:* n.a.; per capita expenditure, n.a.

[1]18 additional cities of republic jurisdiction exist. [2]Total includes 1,556 sq km (601 sq mi) and 86,700 persons not distributed by administrative subdivision. [3]1989; reduced in population by evacuation following Dec. 7, 1988, earthquake. [4]No equivalent U.S.$ value is offered, as Soviet GNP data are very speculative. [5]Includes self-employed and unemployed.

Australia

Official name: Commonwealth of
 Australia.
Form of government: federal
 parliamentary state (formally a
 constitutional monarchy) with two
 legislative houses (Senate [76]; House
 of Representatives [148]).
Chief of state: British Monarch
 represented by Governor-General.
Head of government: Prime Minister.
Capital: Canberra.
Official language: English.
Official religion: none.
Monetary unit: 1 Australian dollar
 ($A) = 100 cents; valuation (Oct. 5,
 1992) 1 U.S.$ = $A 1.38;
 1 £ = $A 2.35.

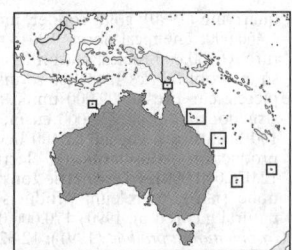

Area and population		area		population
				1992[1]
States	**Capitals**	sq mi	sq km	estimate
New South Wales	Sydney	309,500	801,600	5,962,400
Queensland	Brisbane	666,900	1,727,200	3,021,700
South Australia	Adelaide	379,900	984,000	1,458,000
Tasmania	Hobart	26,200	67,800	470,300
Victoria	Melbourne	87,900	227,600	4,452,200
Western Australia	Perth	975,100	2,525,500	1,658,000
Territories				
Australian Capital				
Territory	Canberra	900	2,400	295,100
Northern Territory	Darwin	519,800	1,346,200	168,600
TOTAL		2,966,200	7,682,300	17,486,300

Demography

Population (1992): 17,562,000.
Density (1992): persons per sq mi 5.9, persons per sq km 2.3.
Urban-rural (1986): urban 85.4%; rural 14.6%.
Sex distribution (1992): male 49.92%; female 50.08%.
Age breakdown (1992): under 15, 21.7%; 15–29, 23.7%; 30–44, 23.5%; 45–59,
 15.5%; 60–74, 11.0%; 75 and over, 4.6%.
Population projection: (2000) 19,705,000; (2010) 22,125,000.
Doubling time: 87 years.
Ethnic composition (1986): white 95.2%; aboriginal 1.5%; Asian 1.3%; other
 2.0%.
Religious affiliation (1986): Christian 73.0%, of which Roman Catholic 26.1%,
 Anglican Church of Australia 23.9%, other Protestant 17.4% (Uniting
 Church and Methodist 7.6%, Presbyterian 3.6%), Orthodox 2.7%; Muslim
 0.7%; Buddhist 0.5%; Jewish 0.4%; no religion 12.7%; other 12.7%.
Major cities (1991): Sydney 3,698,500; Melbourne 3,153,500; Perth 1,930,100[2];
 Brisbane 1,327,000; Adelaide 1,049,900[2]; Newcastle 432,600; Canberra 310,-
 000[2, 3]; Gold Coast 274,200[4]; Wollongong 239,900; Hobart 183,600[2].
Place of birth (1989): 78.2% native-born; 21.8% foreign-born, of which Europe 14.3% (United Kingdom 7.2%[5], Italy 1.6%, Yugoslavia 1.0%, Greece
 1.0%, East and West Germany 0.7%, other Europe 2.8%), Asia and Middle
 East 3.9%, New Zealand 1.9%, Africa and the Americas 1.5%, other 0.2%.
Mobility (1988). Population age 15 and over living in the same residence
 as in 1987: 84.1%; different residence, same state 14.4%; different state
 or territory 1.5%.
Households (1988–89). Total number of households 5,420,400. Average household size 2.8; (1986) 1 person 19.5%, 2–3 persons 47.1%, 4–5 persons 28.2%,
 6 or more persons 5.2%. Family households (1987): 4,145,500 (70.5%);
 nonfamily 1,736,000 (29.5%).
Immigration (1990–91): permanent immigrants admitted 121,690, from United
 Kingdom and Ireland 18.0%, Hong Kong 11.1%, Vietnam 10.9%, New
 Zealand 6.1%, China 5.5%, Philippines 5.3%, Malaysia 4.7%, India 4.2%,
 Sri Lanka 2.7%, Lebanon 2.4%. Refugee arrivals (1990): 10,339.

Vital statistics

Birth rate per 1,000 population (1991): 14.8 (world avg. 26.4); (1989) legiti-
 mate 80.0%; illegitimate 20.0%.
Death rate per 1,000 population (1991): 6.9 (world avg. 9.2).
Natural increase rate per 1,000 population (1991): 8.1 (world avg. 17.2).
Total fertility rate (avg. births per childbearing woman; 1991): 1.9.
Marriage rate per 1,000 population (1991): 6.6.
Divorce rate per 1,000 population (1991): 2.6.
Life expectancy at birth (1990): male 73.8 years; female 79.9 years.
Major causes of death per 100,000 population (1990): diseases of the circu-
 latory system 318.0; cancers 180.0; diseases of the respiratory system 53.0;
 accidents, poisoning, and violence 46.0; diseases of the digestive system 24.0;
 endocrine, nutritional, and metabolic diseases 19.0.

Social indicators

Educational attainment (1991). Percentage of population age 15 to 69 having:
 no formal schooling 0.3%; incomplete secondary education 42.3%, of which
 completed secondary 30.3%[6]; postsecondary, technical, or other certificate/
 diploma 33.4%; university 9.2%.
Quality of working life (1990–91). Average workweek: 35.7 hours (16%
 overtime). Annual rate per 100,000 workers for: injury or accident, n.a.;
 industrial illness, n.a.; death, n.a. Proportion of employed persons insured
 for damages or income loss resulting from: injury 100%; permanent dis-

ability 100%; death 100%. Average days lost to labour stoppages per 1,000
 workdays (1990): 0.5. Means of transportation to work (1986): private automobile 69.4%; public transportation 10.1%; motorcycle and bicycle 3.2%;
 foot 6.6%; other 10.7%. Discouraged job seekers among persons not in the
 labour force (considered by employers to be too young or too old, having
 language or training limitations, or no vacancies in line of work; 1991):
 1.5% of labour force.

Distribution of family income (1990)[7]

percentage of family income by decile									
1	2	3	4	5	6	7	8	9	10 (highest)
1.4%	3.1%	4.2%	5.5%	6.9%	8.6%	10.6%	13.3%	17.2%	29.2%

Access to services (1976). Proportion of dwellings having access to: electricity
 99.5%; bathroom 96.0%; flush toilet 92.2%; kitchen 97.9%; public sewer
 73.4%.
Social participation. Eligible voters participating in last national election
 (1990): n.a.; voting is compulsory. Population age 16 and over participating
 in voluntary work: n.a. Trade union membership in total work force (1990):
 41.0%. Practicing religious population in total affiliated population: n.a.
Social deviance (1988–89). Offense rate per 100,000 population for: murder
 and attempted murder 4.2; sexual assault 53.3; assault 401.9; auto theft
 760.4; burglary and housebreaking 1,969.4; fraud and forgery 760.4. Incidence per 100,000 in general population of: alcoholism, n.a.; drug offenses
 (1985) 388.2; suicide (1989) 13.1.
Material well-being (1983). Households possessing: automobile 86.0%; telephone 85.0%; refrigerator 99.6%; air conditioner 32.3%; washing machine
 91.7%; hot water 98.7%; central heating 3.9%; swimming pool 10.1%.

National economy

Gross national product (1990): U.S.$290,522,000,000 (U.S.$17,080 per capita).

Structure of gross domestic product and labour force

	1990–91			
	in value $A '000,000	% of total value	labour force	% of labour force
Agriculture	10,991	3.3	433,800	5.2
Mining	16,829	5.0	96,000	1.2
Manufacturing	51,408	15.4	1,167,400	14.0
Construction	29,345	8.8	571,300	6.9
Public utilities	12,199	3.7	104,200	1.2
Transportation and communications	27,861	8.4	541,500	6.5
Trade	47,149	14.2	1,620,900	19.4
Finance	74,451	22.4	897,300	10.8
Pub. admin., defense	13,030	3.9	362,600	4.3
Services	58,280	17.5	1,993,300	23.9
Other	−8,756[8]	−2.6[8]	548,300[9]	6.6[9]
TOTAL	332,787	100.0	8,336,600	100.0

Budget (1991–92). Revenue: $A 96,776,000,000 (1990–91; income tax 69.3%,
 of which individual 52.3%, corporate 17.0%; excise duties and sales tax
 23.5%). Expenditures: $A 101,508,000,000 (1989–90; social security and wel-
 fare 36.4%; transfers to state governments 26.2%; interest on public debt
 8.5%; transfers to the non-budget sector 2.8%).
Public debt (1990): $A 126,688,000,000[10].
Tourism (1990): receipts from visitors U.S.$3,797,000,000; expenditures by
 nationals abroad U.S.$4,120,000,000.

Manufacturing, mining, and construction enterprises (1989–90)[11]

	no. of estab-lishments[13]	no. of employees	Avg. annual wages[12] as a % of all wages[13]	annual turnover ($A '000,000)
Manufacturing				
Food, beverages, and tobacco	3,735	171,700	95.0	33,256
Basic metal products	595	67,100	131.6	20,578
Machinery and equipment	4,142	134,600	102.0	15,902
Transport equipment	1,599	106,000	101.9	16,677
Chemical, petroleum, and coal products	949	51,700	124.8	18,883
Paper, printing, and publishing	3,398	106,800	107.1	13,590
Fabricated metal products	4,827	104,900	94.5	12,778
Miscellaneous manufacturing	2,626	64,000	95.3	8,059
Wood, wood products, and furniture	4,849	83,600	82.3	8,287
Nonmetallic mineral products	1,501	42,800	112.5	7,856
Clothing and footwear	2,311	65,800	74.5	5,052
Textiles	717	29,000	93.2	4,126
Mining				
Coal, oil, and gas	141	32,697[13] }	150.5[14]	9,910.6[13]
Metallic minerals	231	31,980[13]		9,447.2[13]
Nonmetallic minerals[15]	1,047	9,157		989
Construction	98,100	395,000[13]	104.0[16]	46,756[13]

Production (gross value in $A '000 except as noted). Agriculture, forestry,
 fishing (1990–91): livestock slaughtered—cattle 3,707,500, poultry 741,500,
 pigs 635,000, sheep and lambs 335,700; wool 4,607,000, wheat 1,950,500,
 cotton 821,000, sugarcane 698,500, barley 568,600, grapes 428,000, potatoes
 377,100, bananas 220,300, apples 186,800, tomatoes 172,300, oranges 162,300,
 oats 147,900, rice 138,500, sorghum 121,300, carrots 77,100, tobacco 76,300,
 onions 76,200, pears 75,500, peaches 48,100, cauliflower 40,400, pineapples
 36,700, corn (maize) 32,700; livestock (number of live animals) 162,774,000
 sheep, 23,430,000 cattle, 2,530,000 pigs, 63,000,000 poultry; roundwood (1990)
 20,326,000 cu m; fish catch (1990) 210,400 metric tons. Mining and quarrying (metric tons [tons of contained metal]; 1990–91): iron ore 111,415,000;
 bauxite 41,751,000; zinc 969,000; lead 562,000; copper 327,000; tin 5,668; gold
 240,769 kg; diamonds 30,751,000 carats. Manufacturing (metric tons except

as noted; 1990–91): cement 6,110,000; pig iron 5,600,000; iron and steel slabs 2,521,000; beef and veal 1,730,000; sulfuric acid 986,000; lamb and mutton 673,000; pork 310,000; textile floor coverings 42,837,000 sq m; woven cotton cloth 35,687,000 sq m; woven woolen cloth 7,641,000 sq m; beer 19,110,000 hectolitres; electric motors 2,480,000 units; motor vehicles 329,000 units; colour television receivers 167,000 units. Construction (buildings completed, by value in $A '000; 1990–91): new dwellings 11,170,600; alterations and additions to dwellings 2,131,300; nonresidential 13,727,800.

Retail and service enterprises (1987–88)

	no. of establishments	no. of employees	total wages and salaries ($A '000,000)	annual turnover ($A '000,000)
Retail[17]				
Motor vehicle dealers, gasoline and tire dealers	38,395	213,900	2,572	38,166
Food stores	51,652	340,900	2,461	33,644[18]
Department and general stores	655	101,100	1,175	9,734[18]
Clothing, fabrics, and furniture stores	25,817	101,500	965	8,324[18]
Household appliances and hardware stores	15,122	62,200	629	7,809[18]
Services				
Real estate agents	5,741	42,196	835	2,201
Architectural services	4,534	17,717	354	1,030
Surveying services	1,104	6,872	116	309
Engineering and technical services	5,190	28,326	682	1,716
Legal services	6,459	55,363	500	3,069
Accounting services	6,048	49,479	503	2,334
Computing services	3,691	24,067	585	1,628
Advertising services	2,390	16,048	423	4,675
Debt collecting and credit reporting services	234	2,658	52	142
Pest control services	565	2,902	44	135
Cleaning services	4,181	44,322	330	622
Security/protection and business services	1,087	25,483	365	839

Energy production (consumption): electricity (kW-hr; 1990) 154,571,000,000 (154,571,000,000); coal (metric tons; 1990) 205,666,000 (96,054,000); crude petroleum (barrels; 1990) 198,278,000 (202,072,000); petroleum products (metric tons; 1990) 30,423,000 (32,559,000); natural gas (cu m; 1990) 20,090,-000,000 (17,282,000,000).
Population economically active (1990–91): total 8,418,400; activity rate of total population 49.0% (participation rates: ages 15–64, 73.6%; female 41.7%; unemployed 9.3%).

Price and earnings indexes (1985 = 100)

	1986	1987	1988	1989	1990	1991	1992[19]
Consumer price index	109.1	118.3	126.9	136.5	146.4	151.1	152.7
Weekly earnings index	107.8	113.4	121.2	131.0	142.2	149.4	155.3

Household income and expenditure. Average household size (1989): 2.8; average annual income per household (1989) $A 33,100 (U.S.$26,230); sources of income (1989–90): wages and salaries 62.6%, transfer payments 11.0%, self-employment 7.4%, other 19.0%; expenditure (1989–90): food and beverages 20.9%, housing 17.9%, transportation and communications 15.0%, recreation and education 12.8%, health 7.0%, household durable goods 6.9%, clothing and footwear 5.8%, energy 2.1%, other 11.6%.

Financial aggregates

	1986	1987	1988	1989	1990	1991	1992[20]
Exchange rate, $A 1.00 per:							
U.S. dollar	0.67	0.70	0.78	0.79	0.78	0.78	0.75
£	0.46	0.43	0.44	0.48	0.44	0.44	0.39
SDR	0.54	0.51	0.64	0.60	0.54	0.53	0.52
International reserves (U.S.$)							
Total (excl. gold; '000,000)	7,246	8,744	13,598	13,780	16,264	16,534	14,304
SDRs ('000,000)	332	389	334	307	311	290	282
Reserve pos. in IMF ('000,000)	231	268	275	322	349	351	354
Foreign exchange ('000,000)	6,684	8,107	12,989	13,150	15,605	15,894	13,667
Gold ('000,000 fine troy oz)	7.93	7.93	7.93	7.93	7.93	7.93	7.93
% world reserves	0.8	0.8	0.8	0.8	0.8	0.8	0.9
Interest and prices							
Central bank discount (%)	16.93	14.95	13.20	17.23	15.24	11.0	6.25
Govt. bond yield (%)	14.0	13.17	12.18	15.14	13.46	9.94	5.65
Industrial share prices (1985 = 100)	134.8	193.4	164.6	176.6	167.0	168.4	182.2
Balance of payments (U.S.$'000,000)							
Balance of visible trade	−1,841	+264	−696	−3,446	+366	+3,510	...
Imports, f.o.b.	24,264	26,749	33,892	40,329	38,966	38,500	...
Exports, f.o.b.	22,423	27,014	33,196	36,883	39,332	42,010	...
Balance of invisibles	−7,368	−7,582	−9,401	−13,885	−15,093	−13,362	...
Balance of payments, current account	−9,209	−7,318	−10,097	−17,331	−14,724	−9,852	...

Land use (1990): meadows and pastures 54.6%; agricultural and under permanent cultivation 6.4%; other 39.0%[21].

Foreign trade

Balance of trade (current prices)

	1986	1987	1988	1989	1990	1991
$A '000,000	−1,945	−726	−258	−4,100	1,194	4,141
% of total	2.8%	1.0%	3.0%	4.1%	1.2%	4.0%

Imports (1990–91): $A 48,919,000,000 (machinery 28.8%, of which office machines and automatic data-processing equipment 6.9%; transport equipment 15.6%, of which road motor vehicles 9.1%; basic manufactures 15.1%, of which textile yarn and fabrics 3.7%, paper and paper products 2.4%, nonferrous metals 0.8%; chemicals and related products 10.5%; mineral fuels

and lubricants 6.4%; food and live animals 3.9%; crude materials [inedible] excluding fuels 2.5%; beverages and tobacco 0.8%). Major import sources: U.S. 23.5%; Japan 18.1%; U.K. 6.7%; Germany 6.4%; New Zealand 4.4%; Taiwan 3.6%; China 3.1%; Italy 2.8%; South Korea 2.6%; France 2.5%.
Exports (1990–91): $A 52,455,000,000 (crude materials excluding fuels 24.3%, of which metalliferous ores and metal scrap 14.8%, textile fibres and their waste 6.9%; mineral fuels and lubricants 20.4%, of which coal, coke, and briquettes 12.4%, petroleum, petroleum products, and natural gas 8.0%; food and live animals 18.1%, of which meat 6.1%, cereals 5.0%; machinery and transport equipment 8.7%; chemicals 2.6%). Major export destinations: Japan 27.5%; U.S. 11.0%; South Korea 6.2%; Singapore 5.3%; New Zealand 4.9%; Taiwan 3.7%; U.K. 3.4%; Hong Kong 3.0%; Indonesia 2.7%.

Trade by commodity group (1990–91)

		imports		exports	
SITC Group		$A '000,000	%	$A '000,000	%
00	Food and live animals	1,916	3.9	9,494	18.1
01	Beverages and tobacco	395	0.8	303	0.6
02	Crude materials, excluding fuels	1,220	2.5	12,772	24.3
03	Mineral fuels, lubricants, and related materials	3,129	6.4	10,705	20.4
04	Animal and vegetable oils, fat, and waxes	129	0.3	132	0.3
05	Chemicals and related products, n.e.s.	5,114	10.5	1,390	2.6
06	Basic manufactures	7,398	15.1	6,372	12.1
07	Machinery and transport equipment	21,698	44.4	4,551	8.7
08	Miscellaneous manufactured articles	6,954	14.2	1,336	2.5
09	Goods not classified by kind	966	2.0	5,400	10.3
TOTAL		48,919	100.0[22]	52,455	100.0[22]

Direction of trade (1990–91)

	imports		exports	
	$A '000,000	%	$A '000,000	%
Africa	115	0.2	491	0.9
Asia	19,498	39.9	31,273	59.6
Japan	8,854	18.1	14,443	27.5
South America	447	0.9	332	0.6
North and Central America	12,689	25.9	6,681	12.7
United States	11,478	23.5	5,790	11.0
Europe	12,938	26.4	8,396	16.0
EEC	10,678	21.8	6,340	12.1
U.S.S.R.	52	0.1	377	0.7
Other Europe	2,208	4.5	1,679	3.2
Oceania	2,859	5.8	3,780	7.2
New Zealand	2,150	4.4	2,566	4.9
Other	373	0.8	1,502	2.9
TOTAL	48,919	100.0[22]	52,455	100.0[22]

Transport and communications

Transport. Railroads (1990)[23]: route length 22,050 mi, 35,486 km; passenger-mi 1,359,051,000[24], passenger-km 2,187,120,000[24]; short ton-mi cargo 36,-533,000,000[25], metric ton-km cargo 53,338,000,000[25]. Roads (1990): total length 503,474 mi, 810,264 km (paved 36%). Vehicles (1990): passenger cars 7,672,300; trucks and buses 2,104,300. Merchant marine (1991): vessels (100 gross tons and over) 714; total deadweight tonnage 3,644,985. Air transport (1989–90): passenger-km 23,018,400,000, passenger-km 37,044,500,000; short ton-mi cargo 1,414,600,000, metric ton-km cargo 2,065,300,000; airports (1990) with scheduled flights 441.
Communications. Daily newspapers (1988): total number 71; total circulation 6,689,000; circulation per 1,000 population 405. Radio (1991): 20,000,000 receivers (1 per 0.9 persons). Television (1991): 7,000,000 receivers (1 per 2.5 persons). Telephones (1985): 8,727,000 (1 per 1.8 persons).

Education and health

Education (1991)

	schools	teachers	students	student/teacher ratio
Primary (age 6–12) }	9,980	96,779	1,786,529	18.5
Secondary (age 13–17) }		102,753	1,288,608	12.5
Vocational[26]	234[27]	52,587[27]	951,598[28]	...
Higher[29]	95	25,916	420,640	16.2

Literacy (1980): percentage of total population age 15 and over literate 99.5%.
Health (1991): physicians (1986) 36,610 (1 per 438 persons); hospital beds (1990) 86,036 (1 per 199 persons); infant mortality rate per 1,000 live births 7.1.
Food (1988–90): daily per capita caloric intake 3,302 (vegetable products 63%, animal products 37%); 124% of FAO recommended minimum requirement.

Military

Total active duty personnel (1992): 67,900 (army 44.6%, navy 22.5%, air force 32.9%). Military expenditure as percentage of GNP (1989): 2.3% (world 4.9%); per capita expenditure U.S.$368.

[1]March 1. [2]1990. [3]Includes Queanbeyan. [4]Includes part of Tweed Shire. [5]Includes both Northern Ireland and Republic of Ireland. [6]Completed highest level of secondary school available. [7]December 1990. [8]Less imputed bank service charges. [9]Unemployed. [10]Net foreign debt. [11]Excludes operations of single-establishment enterprises employing fewer than four persons. [12]Excludes the drawings of working proprietors. [13]1988–89. [14]1986–87. [15]1987–88. [16]1985. [17]1985–86. [18]1985. [19]First quarter. [20]July. [21]Urban areas, state forests and mining leases, unoccupied land (mainly desert). [22]Detail does not add to total given because of rounding. [23]Government railways only. [24]1978–79. [25]1989–90. [26]Includes special education. [27]1986. [28]1988. [29]1989.

Austria

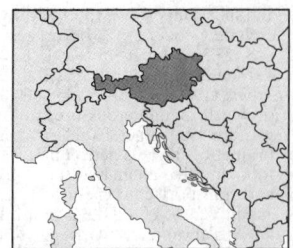

Official name: Republik Österreich
(Republic of Austria).
Form of government: federal multi-
party republic with two legislative
houses (Federal Council [63];
National Council [183]).
Chief of state: President.
Head of government: Chancellor.
Capital: Vienna.
Official language: German.
Official religion: none.
Monetary unit: 1 Schilling (S) = 100
Groschen; valuation (Oct. 5, 1992)
1 U.S.$ = S 9.86; 1 £ = S 16.76.

Area and population

States	Capitals	area sq mi	area sq km	population 1991 census
Burgenland	Eisenstadt	1,531	3,966	273,541
Kärnten	Klagenfurt	3,681	9,533	552,421
Niederösterreich	Sankt Pölten	7,403	19,174	1,480,927
Oberösterreich	Linz	4,626	11,980	1,340,076
Salzburg	Salzburg	2,762	7,154	483,880
Steiermark	Graz	6,327	16,388	1,184,593
Tirol	Innsbruck	4,883	12,648	630,358
Vorarlberg	Bregenz	1,004	2,601	333,128
Wien (Vienna)	—	160	415	1,533,176
TOTAL		32,378[1]	83,859	7,812,100

Demography

Population (1992): 7,857,000.
Density (1992): persons per sq mi 242.7, persons per sq km 93.7.
Urban-rural (1991): urban 53.9%; rural 46.1%.
Sex distribution (1990): male 47.86%; female 52.14%.
Age breakdown (1990): under 15, 17.4%; 15–29, 23.9%; 30–44, 20.8%; 45–59,
17.5%; 60–74, 13.3%; 75 and over, 7.1%.
Population projection: (2000) 8,091,000; (2010) 8,201,000.
Doubling time: not applicable; population is stable.
Ethnic composition (national origin; 1981): Austrian 96.1%; Yugoslav 1.7%;
Turkish 0.8%; German 0.5%; other 0.9%.
Religious affiliation (1981): Roman Catholic 84.3%; nonreligious and athe-
ist 6.0%; Evangelical (Lutheran) 5.6%; Muslim 1.0%; Jewish 0.1%; other
(mostly Christian) 1.9%; unknown 1.1%.
Major cities (1991): Vienna 1,533,176; Graz 232,155; Linz 202,855; Salzburg
143,971; Innsbruck 114,996.

Vital statistics

Birth rate per 1,000 population (1991): 12.0 (world avg. 26.4); (1990) legiti-
mate 76.4%; illegitimate 23.6%.
Death rate per 1,000 population (1991): 10.6 (world avg. 9.2).
Natural increase rate per 1,000 population (1991): 1.4 (world avg. 17.2).
Total fertility rate (avg. births per childbearing woman; 1990): 1.4.
Marriage rate per 1,000 population (1991): 5.6.
Divorce rate per 1,000 population (1990): 2.1.
Life expectancy at birth (1990): male 72.5 years; female 79.0 years.
Major causes of death per 100,000 population (1990): diseases of the circu-
latory system 552.3, of which ischemic heart diseases 210.6, cerebrovascular
disease 145.1; malignant neoplasms (cancers) 250.4.

National economy

Budget (1990). Revenue: S 629,410,000,000 (tax revenue 90.7%, of which social-security contributions 36.4%, value-added tax 17.1%, individual income
tax 15.4%; nontax revenue 8.6%). Expenditures: S 694,016,000,000 (social
security and welfare 45.2%; health 12.9%; education 9.2%; transportation
and communications 6.0%; defense 2.5%).
National debt (end of year 1990): S 867,150,000,000.
Production (metric tons except as noted). Agriculture, forestry, fishing
(1990): silage 4,289,000, sugar beets 2,494,000, corn (maize) 1,620,000, barley
1,521,000, wheat 1,404,000, potatoes 794,000, grapes 400,000, rye 396,000,
apples 338,000, turnips 171,000, pears 100,000; livestock (number of live
animals) 3,688,000 pigs, 2,584,000 cattle, 13,139,000 chickens; roundwood
17,280,000 cu m; fish catch (1989) 5,000. Mining and quarrying (1990): iron
ore 2,124,000[2], magnesite 1,179,000, zinc ore 24,200, high-grade graphite
22,700. Manufacturing (value added in S '000,000,000; 1988): machinery
and equipment 58.1, of which electrical 31.9; ferrous and nonferrous base
metals 37.6; chemicals and chemical products 25.6; beverages and tobacco
23.7; transport equipment 17.3; food products 17.0. Construction (dwellings
completed; 1990): residential 3,618,000 sq m; nonresidential, n.a. Energy
production (consumption): electricity (kW-hr; 1991) 51,480,000,000 ([1990]
49,951,000,000); coal (metric tons; 1991) 2,424,000 ([1990] 6,282,000); crude
petroleum (barrels; 1991) 9,093,000 ([1990] 56,925,000); petroleum products
(metric tons; 1990) 7,900,000 (9,869,000); natural gas (cu m; 1991) 1,322,-
000,000 ([1990] 5,858,000,000).
Land use (1989): forested 38.7%; meadows and pastures 24.4%; agricultural
and under permanent cultivation 18.5%; other 18.4%.
Tourism (1990): receipts from visitors U.S.$13,017,000,000; expenditures by
nationals abroad U.S.$7,476,000,000.
Population economically active (1990): total 3,522,900; activity rate of total
population 45.6% (participation rates: ages 15–64, 67.7%; female 40.9%;
unemployed 5.8%[3]).

Price and earnings indexes (1985 = 100)

Price and earnings indexes (1985 = 100)

	1986	1987	1988	1989	1990	1991	1992
Consumer price index	101.7	103.1	105.1	107.8	111.3	115.0	118.7[4]
Monthly earnings index	104.5	107.8	111.8	116.7	125.1	131.6	...

Gross national product (at current market prices; 1990): U.S.$147,016,000,000
(U.S.$19,240 per capita).

Structure of gross domestic product and labour force

	1990 in value S '000,000	% of total value	labour force	% of labour force
Agriculture	56,200	3.1	270,900	7.7
Mining	475,740	26.6	11,900	0.3
Manufacturing			950,500	27.0
Construction	124,470	7.0	301,300	8.6
Public utilities	45,430	2.5	40,700	1.2
Transportation and communications	110,880	6.2	221,500	6.3
Trade, restaurants	293,460	16.4	660,300	18.7
Finance, real estate	298,580	16.7	224,800	6.4
Pub. admin., defense	246,890	13.8	805,900	22.9
Services	72,130	4.0		
Other	65,620[5]	3.7[5]	35,100	1.0
TOTAL	1,789,390[1]	100.0	3,522,900	100.0[1]

Household income and expenditure. Average household size (1990) 2.5; net
income per household[6] (1989) S 228,240 (U.S.$17,250); sources of income
(1989): wages and salaries 55.3%, transfer payments 24.6%, other 20.1%;
expenditure (1989): food and beverages 18.0%, transportation 16.5%, housing 13.6%, cafe and hotel expenditures 11.8%, clothing and footwear 9.7%.

Foreign trade[7]

Balance of trade (current prices)

	1985	1986	1987	1988	1989	1990
S '000,000	−57,570	−47,480	−51,520	−47,910	−62,180	−65,190
% of total	7.5%	6.5%	7.0%	5.9%	6.8%	6.5%

Imports (1990): S 566,230,000,000 (machinery and transport equipment 37.9%,
of which passenger cars 7.0%, electrical machinery and apparatus 6.6%;
chemicals and related products 9.9%; food products 4.6%; crude petroleum
and petroleum products 4.0%). *Major import sources:* Germany 44.0%; Italy
9.1%; Japan 4.5%; Switzerland 4.3%; France 4.2%; United States 3.6%.
Exports (1990): S 466,070,000,000 (machinery and transport equipment 37.5%,
of which electrical machinery and apparatus 6.9%, internal-combustion
piston engines 4.5%; chemicals and related products 8.5%; iron and steel
6.5%; paper and paper products 5.9%). *Major export destinations:* Germany
37.4%; Italy 9.8%; Switzerland 6.9%; France 4.8%; United Kingdom 3.9%;
United States 3.2%.

Transport and communications

Transport. Railroads (1991): length (1990) 4,137 mi, 6,658 km; passenger-
mi 5,570,000,000[8], passenger-km 8,964,000,000[8]; short ton-mi cargo 8,811,-
000,000[8], metric ton-km cargo 12,864,000,000[8]. Roads (1990): total length
66,598 mi, 107,180 km (paved 100%). Vehicles (1990): passenger cars
2,991,284; trucks and buses 261,906. Merchant marine (1991): vessels (100
gross tons and over) 32; total deadweight tonnage 233,613. Air transport
(1991): passenger-mi 1,773,000,000, passenger-km 2,853,000,000; short ton-
mi cargo 36,400,000, metric ton-km cargo 53,100,000; airports (1992) with
scheduled flights 6.
Communications. Daily newspapers (1991): total number 27; total circulation
3,477,625; circulation per 1,000 population 445. Radio (1991): total receivers
4,700,000 (1 per 1.7 persons). Television (1991): total receivers 2,688,000 (1
per 2.9 persons). Telephones (1990): 4,541,000 (1 per 1.7 persons).

Education and health

Education (1990–91)

	schools	teachers	students	student/ teacher ratio
Primary (age 6–10)	3,386	29,404	371,971	12.7
Secondary (age 11–18)	2,013	57,548	436,931	7.6
Voc., teacher tr.[9]	939	18,915	171,164	9.0
Higher[9]	88	13,013	199,845	15.4

Educational attainment (1990). Percentage of population age 25 and over
having: compulsory education (through lower secondary) 39.3%; terminal
vocational at secondary level 44.4%; nonterminal general secondary or vocational 10.3%; higher 6.0%. *Literacy:* virtually 100%.
Health (1991): physicians 23,238 (1 per 334 persons); hospital beds 75,068 (1
per 103 persons); infant mortality rate per 1,000 live births 7.5.
Food (1987–89): daily per capita caloric intake 3,496 (vegetable products 62%,
animal products 38%); 133% of FAO recommended minimum requirement.

Military

Total active duty personnel (1991): 44,000 (army 86.4%; navy, none; air force
13.6%). *Military expenditure as percentage of GNP* (1989): 1.1% (world 4.9%);
per capita expenditure U.S.$184.

---

[1]Detail does not add to total given because of rounding. [2]1991. [3]Average of March
1, 1991–Feb. 29, 1992. [4]April. [5]Value-added tax plus import duties (S 169,090,000,-
000) less imputed bank service charges (S 103,470,000,000). [6]Two-person households
without children only. [7]Import figures are f.o.b. in balance of trade and c.i.f. in
commodities and trading partners. [8]Federal railways only. [9]1989–90.

Azerbaijan

Official name: Azärbayjan Respublikasi (Azerbaijani Republic).
Form of government: federal multiparty republic with a single legislative body (Parliament [360]).
Head of state: President.
Head of government: Prime Minister.
Capital: Baku (Azerbaijani: Baky).
Official language: Azerbaijani.
Official religion: none.
Monetary unit (until Aug. 15, 1992):
1 ruble = 100 kopecks;
valuation (Oct. 5, 1992) free rate,
1 U.S.$ = 316.82 rubles; 1 £ = 538.59 rubles. From Aug. 15, 1992, a new currency, the manat, replaced the ruble; valuation (Oct. 5, 1992)
1 U.S.$ = 31.68 manats; 1 £ = 53.86 manats.

Area and population

		area		population
		sq mi	sq km	1991 estimate
Republics	**Capitals**			
Nagorno Karabakh	Stepanakert	1,700	4,400	193,300
Nakhichevan	Nakhichevan	2,100	5,500	305,700
Regions under republican jurisdiction	—	29,600	76,700	4,924,300
Cities				
Baku (City Soviet)	—	...	...	1,713,300
TOTAL		33,400	86,600	7,136,600

Demography

Population (1992): 7,237,000.
Density (1992): persons per sq mi 216.4, persons per sq km 83.6.
Urban-rural (1990): urban 53.5%; rural 46.5%.
Sex distribution (1989): male 50.05%; female 49.95%.
Age breakdown (1989): under 15, 32.8%; 15–29, 29.7%; 30–44, 16.8%; 45–59, 12.8%; 60–74, 5.7%; 75 and over, 2.2%.
Population projection: (2000) 8,324,000; (2010) 9,445,000.
Doubling time: 35 years.
Ethnic composition (1989): Azerbaijani 82.7%; Russian 5.7%; Armenian 5.6%; Lezgin 2.4%; Avar 0.6%; Ukrainian 0.5%; Tatar 0.4%; other 2.1%.
Religious affiliation (1991): Shīʿī Muslim 70%; Sunnī Muslim 30%.
Major cities (1991): Baku 1,080,500; Gyandzha (formerly Kirovabad) 282,200; Sumgait 236,200; Mingechaur 90,900; Nakhichevan 61,700.

Vital statistics

Birth rate per 1,000 population (1990): 26.4 (world avg. 27.1); (1989) legitimate 97.5%; illegitimate 2.5%.
Death rate per 1,000 population (1990): 6.2 (world avg. 9.8).
Natural increase rate per 1,000 population (1990): 20.2 (world avg. 17.3).
Total fertility rate (avg. births per childbearing woman; 1989): 2.8.
Marriage rate per 1,000 population (1989): 6.7.
Divorce rate per 1,000 population (1989): 1.7.
Life expectancy at birth (1990): male 66.9 years; female 74.8 years.
Major causes of death per 100,000 population (1989): diseases of the circulatory system 292.4; diseases of the respiratory system 88.9; malignant neoplasms (cancers) 72.1; accidents, poisoning, and violence 42.1; infectious and parasitic diseases 42.1; diseases of the digestive system 25.6; diseases of the nervous system 9.7; endocrine and metabolic disorders 8.6.

National economy

Budget (1991). Revenue: 7,197,500,000 rubles (tax revenue 76.4%, of which turnover tax 38.6%, enterprise profits tax 21.1%, individual income tax 8.3%, sales tax 8.0%; nontax revenue 23.6%, of which stabilization fund 10.9%). Expenditures: 8,373,900,000 rubles (social welfare and culture 54.9%, of which education 24.7%, pensions 16.0%, health 9.2%; national economy 25.5%; government administration 3.7%).
Public debt (external, outstanding): n.a.
Production (metric tons except as noted). Agriculture, forestry, fishing (1991): grain 1,348,000, grapes 1,152,000, vegetables (except potatoes) 820,000, cotton 540,000, fruit (except grapes) 496,000, potatoes 191,000, watermelon 68,000, tobacco 56,000, tea 27,000; livestock (number of live animals; 1990) 5,258,200 sheep and goats, 1,934,800 cattle, 190,600 pigs; roundwood 56,-000 cu m; fish catch, n.a. Mining and quarrying (1989): iron ore 718,200. Manufacturing (1991): sulfuric acid 552,000; crude steel 462,000; steel pipes 411,000; mineral fertilizers 189,000; caustic soda 171,000; sulfonal 118,000; detergents 76,100; soap 24,800; pesticides 6,700; electric motors 3,761,000 units; transformers 1,883,000 units; metal goods 724,000 units; pumping equipment 462,000 units; refrigerators 354,200 units; air conditioners 295,000 units; children's furniture 259,000 units; bicycles 103,000 units; ventilators 93,000 units; drilling equipment 73,000 units; footwear 17,600,000 pairs; carpets and rugs 2,710,000 sq m; canned foods 710,400,000 cans; bricks 1,172,-000,000 pieces; roof tiles 78,000,000 pieces; reinforced concrete 1,089,000,000 cu m. Construction (1989): 2,700,000 sq m. Energy production (consumption): electricity (kW-hr; 1991) 23,300,000,000 (n.a.); coal, n.a. (n.a.); crude petroleum (barrels; 1991) 86,100,000 (n.a.); petroleum products (metric tons; 1991) 15,192,900 (7,079,100); natural gas (cu m; 1991) 11,655,000,000 (n.a.).

Gross national product (at current market prices; 1991): 17,752,000,000 rubles (2,500 rubles per capita)[1].

Structure of net material product and labour force

	1991		1990	
	in value '000,000 rubles	% of total value	labour force	% of labour force
Agriculture	4,636	26.1	1,047,000	32.3
Mining	}			
Manufacturing	9,625	54.2		
Public utilities	}			
Construction	1,877	10.6		
Transportation and communications	519	2.9	2,195,000	67.7
Trade	383	2.2		
Finance	—	—		
Pub. admin., defense	—	—		
Services	—	—		
Other	712	4.0		
TOTAL	17,752	100.0	3,242,000	100.0

Population economically active (1990): total 3,242,000; activity rate of total population 45.4% (participation rates [1989]: ages 16–59 [male], 16–54 [female] 71.8%; female [1989] 42.6%; unemployed 3.7%).

Price and earnings indexes (1985 = 100)

	1985	1986	1987	1988	1989	1990
Consumer price index	100.0					
Monthly earnings index	100.0	99.0	101.2	104.9	109.8	119.6

Land use: n.a.
Tourism: receipts from visitors, n.a.; expenditures by nationals abroad, n.a.
Household income and expenditure. Average household size (1989) 4.8; income per household: n.a.; sources of income: n.a.; expenditure: n.a.

Foreign trade

Balance of trade (current prices)

	1987	1988	1989	1990	1991
'000,000 rubles	1,209	1,110	1,933	678	1,190
% of total	...	...	...	...	5.1%

Imports (1991): 11,009,800,000 rubles (food products 26.0%; machinery and equipment 18.2%; nonferrous metals 11.8%; textiles 11.0%; oil and gas 8.2%; ferrous metals 8.2%; chemicals and petrochemicals 5.8%; agricultural products 4.4%; timber, pulp, and paper 3.3%; building materials 1.4%). *Major import sources:* former Soviet republics 80.3%, of which Russia 56.1%, Ukraine 28.3%, Kazakhstan 5.3%, Belarus 2.8%, Estonia 1.4%; other countries 19.7%.
Exports (1991): 12,199,500,000 rubles (food products 31.9%; textiles 18.6%; machinery and equipment 17.7%; oil and gas 11.9%; chemicals and petrochemicals 9.5%; nonferrous metals 3.1%; ferrous metals 2.3%; agricultural products 2.3%; building materials 0.3%). *Major export destinations:* former Soviet republics 93.9%, of which Russia 59.7%, Ukraine 13.1%, Turkmenistan 4.5%, Kazakhstan 4.1%, Uzbekistan 2.6%, Baltic republics 2.1%; other countries 6.1%.

Transport and communications

Transport. Railroads (1991): length 1,299 mi, 2,090 km; passenger-mi 3,025,-400,000, passenger-km 4,868,900,000; cargo traffic, n.a. Roads (1991): total length 22,800 mi, 36,700 km (paved 87%). Vehicles (1988): passenger cars 235,600; trucks and buses, n.a. Merchant marine: vessels (100 gross tons and over) n.a.; total deadweight tonnage, n.a. Air transport (1990): passenger-mi 3,025,400,000, passenger-km 4,868,900,000; cargo traffic, n.a.; airports (1992) with scheduled flights 1.
Communications. Daily newspapers (1990): total number 168; total circulation 520,000,000; circulation per 1,000 population 73. Radio and television (1990): total number of receivers 1,257,000 (1 per 5.7 persons). Telephones (1991): n.a.

Education and health

Education (1990–91)

	schools	teachers	students	student/ teacher ratio
Primary (age 6–13)	} 4,521	...	1,449,000	...
Secondary (age 14–17)				
Voc., teacher tr.	...	...	...	...
Higher	17	...	105,100	...

Educational attainment (1989). Percentage of population age 25 and over having: primary education or no formal schooling 12.2%; some secondary 19.2%; completed secondary and some postsecondary 58.1%; higher 10.5%.
Literacy: n.a.
Health (1990): physicians 28,000 (1 per 255 persons); hospital beds 72,700 (1 per 98 persons); infant mortality rate per 1,000 live births 23.0.
Food: daily per capita caloric intake, n.a.

Military

Total active duty personnel (1992): 5,000 (army 100%, navy[2], air force, none). *Military expenditure as percentage of GNP* (1991): c. 12.5% (world c. 5.4%); per capita expenditure U.S.$230.

[1]No equivalent U.S.$ value is offered, as Soviet GNP data are very speculative. [2]Azerbaijan shares a portion of the Caspian Flotilla.

Bahamas, The

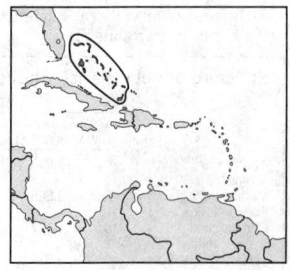

Official name: The Commonwealth of
The Bahamas.
Form of government: constitutional
monarchy with two legislative
houses (Senate [16]; House of
Assembly [49]).
Chief of state: British Monarch
represented by Governor-General.
Head of government: Prime Minister.
Capital: Nassau.
Official language: English.
Official religion: none.
Monetary unit: 1 Bahamian dollar
(B$) = 100 cents; valuation
(Oct. 5, 1992) 1 Bahamian
dollar = U.S.$1.00 = £1.70.

Area and population

Islands and Island Groups[2]	area[1] sq mi	area[1] sq km	population 1990 census
Abaco, Great and Little	649	1,681	10,034
Acklins	192	497	405
Andros	2,300	5,957	8,180
Berry Islands	12	31	628
Bimini Islands	9	23	1,639
Cat Island	150	388	1,698
Crooked and Long Cay	93	241	412
Eleuthera	187	484	7,993
Exuma, Great, and Exuma Cays	112	290	3,556
Grand Bahama	530	1,373	40,898
Harbour Island	3	8	1,219
Inagua, Great and Little	599	1,551	985
Long Island	230	596	2,954
Mayaguana	110	285	312
New Providence	80	207	172,196
Ragged Island	14	36	89
Rum Cay	30	78	53
San Salvador	63	163	465
Spanish Wells	10	26	1,372
Other uninhabited cays and rocks	9	23	—
TOTAL	5,382	13,939[3]	255,095[4]

Demography

Population (1992): 264,000.
Density (1992): persons per sq mi 49.1, persons per sq km 18.9.
Urban-rural (1990): urban 64.3%; rural 35.7%.
Sex distribution (1990): male 49.00%; female 51.00%.
Age breakdown (1985): under 15, 38.0%; 15–29, 27.9%; 30–44, 17.9%; 45–59,
10.5%; 60–74, 4.8%; 75 and over, 0.9%.
Population projection: (2000) 298,000; (2010) 337,000.
Doubling time: 48 years.
Ethnic composition (1988): black 80.0%; mixed 10.0%; white 10.0%.
Religious affiliation (1980): non-Anglican Protestant 55.2%, of which Baptist
32.1%, Methodist 6.1%, Church of God (Anderson Ind.) 5.7%; Anglican
20.1%; Roman Catholic 18.8%; other 5.9%.
Major cities (1990): Nassau 172,196[5]; Freeport/Lucaya 26,574; Marsh Harbour
3,611; Bailey Town 1,490; Dunmore Town (Harbour Island) 1,219.

Vital statistics

Birth rate per 1,000 population (1990): 19.2 (world avg. 26.4); (1988) legiti-
mate 42.3%, illegitimate 57.7%.
Death rate per 1,000 population (1990): 4.5 (world avg. 9.2).
Natural increase rate per 1,000 population (1990): 14.7 (world avg. 17.2).
Total fertility rate (avg. births per childbearing woman; 1991): 2.2.
Marriage rate per 1,000 population (1989): 8.5.
Divorce rate per 1,000 population (1989): 1.1.
Life expectancy at birth (1991): male 69.0 years; female 76.0 years.
Major causes of death per 100,000 population (1988): heart diseases 98.1;
malignant neoplasms (cancers) 94.4; cerebrovascular disease 45.2; accidents
40.3; diabetes mellitus 36.6.

National economy

Budget (1991–92). Revenue: B$508,866,000 (import taxes 51.2%, stamp taxes
11.5%, departure taxes 8.1%, fines and forfeits 7.3%, business and professional licenses 5.2%). Expenditures: B$563,377,000 (education 19.5%, health
14.6%, interest on public debt 12.2%, general administration 11.1%, public
order 10.1%, tourism 8.0%, defense 3.3%).
Public debt (September 1991): U.S.$829,500,000.
Production (value of production in B$'000 except as noted). Agriculture,
forestry, fishing (1990): marine products landed at Nassau (mostly crayfish,
groupers, conchs) 56,400[6], fruits and vegetables 22,800, poultry products
18,400, beef and mutton 300; roundwood 115,000 cu m. Mining and quarrying (1991): salt 9,400; aragonite 3,600. Manufacturing (1991): pharmaceuticals 94,200; rum 35,700. Construction (gross value of buildings started
in B$'000,000; 1991): residential 111; nonresidential 20. Energy production
(consumption): electricity (kW-hr; 1990) 950,000,000 (950,000,000); coal,
none (none); crude petroleum, none (none); petroleum products (metric
tons; 1990) negligible (435,000); natural gas, none (none).
Tourism (1991): receipts from visitors (1991) U.S.$1,222,000,000; expenditures by
nationals abroad (1990) U.S.$196,000,000.
Gross national product (1990): U.S.$2,913,000,000 (U.S.$11,510 per capita).

Structure of gross domestic product and labour force

	1986 in value B$'000,000	1986 % of total value	1989 labour force	1989 % of labour force
Agriculture, fishing	90	4.5	4,970	3.9
Mining			360	0.3
Manufacturing	206	10.3	4,210	3.3
Public utilities			1,570	1.2
Construction	61	3.1	9,880	7.8
Transportation and communications	219	10.9	8,880	7.0
Trade, restaurants	524	26.2	36,300	28.5
Finance, real estate	245	12.2	8,580	6.7
Pub. admin., defense	342	17.1	35,750	28.1
Services	315	15.7		
Other	—	—	16,900[7]	13.3[7]
TOTAL	2,003[3]	100.0	127,400	100.0[3]

Population economically active (1989): total 127,400; activity rate of total population 51.2% (participation rates: ages 15–64 [1980] 70.5%; female 47.3%;
unemployed 11.7%).

Price and earnings indexes (1985 = 100)

	1986	1987	1988	1989	1990	1991	1992[8]
Consumer price index[9]	105.4	111.7	116.4	122.7	128.4	137.5	145.3
Earnings index	...	...	...	...	...	...	...

Household income and expenditure. Average household size (1990) 3.8; income per household (1989) B$22,515 (U.S.$22,515); sources of income: n.a.;
expenditure (1988)[10]: food and beverages 19.8%, housing 19.2%, transportation and communications 18.9%, household furnishings 10.2%, education
7.8%.
Land use (1989): forested 32.4%; meadows and pastures 0.2%; agricultural
and under permanent cultivation 1.0%; other 66.4%.

Foreign trade[11]

Balance of trade (current prices)

	1985	1986	1987	1988	1989	1990
B$'000,000	– 350	– 588	– 309	– 99	– 534	– 327
% of total	6.0%	9.8%	5.4%	2.4%	9.4%	5.9%

Imports (1990): B$2,920,000,000 (crude petroleum and petroleum products
65.2%, machinery and transport equipment 6.7%, food 5.3%). *Major import
sources* (1989): Saudi Arabia 40.2%; United States 33.6%; Nigeria 7.5%;
Iraq 2.4%; Venezuela 2.2%.
Exports (1990): B$2,593,000,000 (mineral fuels [mostly crude petroleum]
64.6%, chemicals [mostly pharmaceuticals] 17.5%, food [mostly crayfish
and fish] 2.1%, beverages [mostly rum] 1.0%). *Major export destinations*
(1989): United States 78.8%; Puerto Rico 14.0%; Canada 1.6%; United
Kingdom 0.9%.

Transport and communications

Transport. Railroads: none. Roads (1990): total length of paved roads 2,094
mi, 3,370 km. Vehicles (1989): passenger cars 69,000; trucks and buses
14,000. Merchant marine (1991): vessels (100 gross tons and over) 973; total
deadweight tonnage 28,798,214. Air transport (1990): passenger-mi 214,000,-
000, passenger-km 345,000,000; short ton-mi cargo 205,000, metric ton-km
cargo 300,000; airports (1992) with scheduled flights 24.
Communications. Daily newspapers (1991): total number 3; total circulation
35,000; circulation per 1,000 population 135. Radio (1991): total receivers
200,000 (1 per 1.3 persons). Television (1991): total receivers 50,000 (1 per
5.2 persons). Telephones (1991): 144,570 (1 per 1.8 persons).

Education and health

Education (1990–91)

	schools	teachers	students	student/ teacher ratio
Primary (age 5–10)	100[12]	1,409[13]	27,264[12]	20.9[13]
Secondary (age 11–17)	37[12]	1,555[13]	23,616[12]	19.1[13]
Higher[14]	1	300	2,200	7.3

Educational attainment: n.a. Literacy (1986): total population age 15 and over
literate 139,000 (95.0%).
Health (1988): physicians 303 (1 per 809 persons); hospital beds 1,009 (1 per
243 persons); infant mortality rate per 1,000 live births (1990) 26.3.
Food (1987–89): daily per capita caloric intake 2,791 (vegetable products 65%,
animal products 35%); 115% of FAO recommended minimum requirement.

Military

Total active duty personnel (1991): 850[15]. *Military expenditure as percentage of
GNP*[16] (1989): 0.2% (world 4.9%); per capita expenditure U.S.$23.

---

[1]Land area only of individual islands or island groups. [2]Family (Out) Islands (all
islands other than New Providence) are administered by commissioners assigned by
the central government. Extent of commissioner districts varies from part of an island
to island groups. [3]Detail does not add to total given because of rounding. [4]Includes
seven people not accounted for by island. [5]Population cited is for New Providence
Island. [6]1991. [7]Includes 1,990 not adequately defined and 14,910 unemployed. [8]April.
[9]New Providence Island only. [10]Domestic purchases by resident households only; data
for expenditures in restaurants and hotels are not available. [11]Imports c.i.f.; exports
f.o.b. [12]Data exclude 86 combined primary/secondary schools with 10,739 students.
[13]1986–87; includes combined primary/secondary schools. [14]College of The Bahamas
only. [15]Naval defense force (excludes 1,700 police). [16]Includes police.

Bahrain

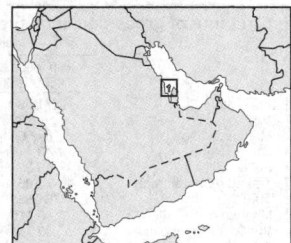

Official name: Dawlat al-Baḥrayn
 (State of Bahrain).
Form of government: monarchy
 (emirate) with a cabinet appointed by
 the Emir.
Chief of state: Emir.
Head of government: Prime Minister.
Capital: Manama.
Official language: Arabic.
Official religion: Islam.
Monetary unit: 1 Bahrain dinar
 (BD) = 1,000 fils; valuation (Oct. 5,
 1992) 1 BD = U.S.$2.63 = £1.54.

Area and population

	area		population
Regions	sq mi	sq km	1981 census
al-Gharbīyah	60.2	156.0	14,503
al-Hadd	2.2	5.6	7,111
Jidd (Judd) Ḥafṣ	8.3	21.6	33,693
al-Manāmah	9.9	25.6	121,986
al-Muḥarraq	5.9	15.2	61,853
ar-Rifāʿ	112.6	291.6	28,150
ash-Shamālīyah	14.2	36.8	22,117
Sitrah	11.0	28.6	22,993
al-Wusṭā	13.6	35.2	16,776
Towns with special status			
Hammād	5.1	13.1	...
Madīnat ʿĪsā	4.8	12.4	21,275
Islands			
Hawār and other	19.5	50.6	341
TOTAL	267.3[1]	692.4[1, 2]	350,798[3]

Demography

Population (1992): 531,000[3].
Density (1992): persons per sq mi 1,986.5, persons per sq km 766.9.
Urban-rural (1990): urban 83.0%; rural 17.0%.
Sex distribution (1990): male 59.30%; female 40.70%.
Age breakdown (1990): under 15, 32.7%; 15–29, 24.5%; 30–44, 30.0%; 45–59, 9.7%; 60–74, 2.7%; 75 and over, 0.4%.
Population projection: (2000) 654,000; (2010) 825,000.
Doubling time: 29 years.
Ethnic composition (1981): Bahraini Arab 68.0%; Persian, Indian, and Pakistani 24.7%; other Arab 4.1%; European 2.5%; other 0.7%.
Religious affiliation (1981): Muslim 85.0% (Shīʿī 60.0% and Sunnī 40.0%); Christian 7.3%; other 7.7%.
Major cities (1988): al-Manāmah 151,500; al-Muḥarraq 78,000; Jidd Ḥafṣ 48,000; ar-Rifāʿ 45,530[4]; Madīnat ʿĪsā 39,783[4].

Vital statistics

Birth rate per 1,000 population (1991): 27.9 (world avg. 26.4); legitimate, n.a.; illegitimate, n.a.
Death rate per 1,000 population (1991): 3.7 (world avg. 9.2).
Natural increase rate per 1,000 population (1991): 24.2 (world avg. 17.2).
Total fertility rate (avg. births per childbearing woman; 1990): 4.7.
Marriage rate per 1,000 population (1989): 6.2.
Divorce rate per 1,000 population (1989): 1.5.
Life expectancy at birth (1991): male 71.0 years; female 76.0 years.
Major causes of death per 100,000 population (1988): diseases of the circulatory system 110.0; malignant neoplasms (cancers) 34.1; accidents and violence 23.7; diseases of the respiratory system 15.0; endocrine, nutritional, and metabolic diseases 14.6; diseases of the digestive system 3.8; infectious and parasitic diseases 2.4; diseases of the nervous system 2.2.

National economy

Budget (1990). Revenue: BD 440,000,000 (petroleum company dividends and oil field receipts 56.8%, tax revenue 33.2%, grants and loans 10.0%). Expenditures: BD 540,000,000 (public utilities 15.2%, defense 13.5%, education 10.1%, health 8.0%, transfer and loan repayments 7.0%, roads 5.0%).
Public debt (external, outstanding; 1989)[5]: U.S.$1,240,000,000.
Population economically active (1988): total 192,900; activity rate of total population 40.8% (participation rates: 15 and over, 62.3%; female 13.7%; unemployed 10.0%).

Price and earnings indexes (1985 = 100)

	1985	1986	1987	1988	1989	1990	1991
Consumer price index	100.0	97.7	96.0	96.3	97.7	98.6	99.4
Earnings index	...	...	...	...	...	...	...

Production (metric tons except as noted). Agriculture, forestry, fishing (1991): fruit (excluding melons) 21,000, cow's milk 19,000, dates 16,000, tomatoes 5,000, hen's eggs 2,750, onions 1,000, cucumbers 1,000; livestock (number of live animals) 16,000 goats, 15,000 cattle, 9,000 sheep 1,000 camels, 1,000,000 chickens; fish catch (1990) 8,287. Manufacturing (barrels; 1990): gas oil 27,619,000; fuel oil 23,287,700; naphtha 13,809,000; kerosene 3,419,000; liquefied petroleum gas 2,330,000; heavy lubricant distillate 2,027,000; petroleum bitumen 986,000; other manufactures include methanol, aluminum metal, plastics, and paper products. Construction (permits issued; 1987): residential 7,207; nonresidential 1,367. Energy production (consumption): electricity (kW-hr; 1990) 3,490,000,000 (3,490,000,000); coal, none (n.a.); crude petroleum (barrels; 1990) 15,449,000 (90,560,000); petroleum products (metric tons; 1990) 10,362,000 (797,000); natural gas (cu m; 1990) 5,151,000,000 (5,151,000,000).
Gross national product (at current market prices; 1989): U.S.$3,120,000,000 (U.S.$6,380 per capita).

Structure of gross domestic product and labour force

	1989		1986	
	value in BD '000,000	% of total value	labour force	% of labour force
Agriculture	15.8	1.2	3,654	2.0
Mining	236.4	17.5	6,374	3.5
Manufacturing	239.8	17.8	14,364	7.8
Construction	87.6	6.5	38,444	21.0
Public utilities	27.8	2.1	3,869	2.1
Transp. and commun.	152.5	11.3	17,236	9.4
Trade	137.0	10.2	24,634	13.5
Finance	213.5	15.8	7,693	4.2
Pub. admin., defense	299.6	22.2	...	...
Services	70.4	5.2	66,911	36.5
Other	−132.9	−9.9	...	...
TOTAL	1,347.5	100.0[2]	183,179	100.0

Households. Average household size (1986) 6.5; income per household: n.a.; sources of income: n.a.; expenditure (1984): food and tobacco 33.3%, housing 21.2%, household durable goods 9.8%, transportation and communications 8.5%, recreation 6.4%, clothing and footwear 5.9%, education 2.7%, health 2.3%, energy and water 2.2%.
Land use (1990): meadows and pastures 5.6%; agricultural and under permanent cultivation 2.9%; built-on and wasteland (mostly sand plains and salt marshes) 91.5%.
Tourism: receipts from visitors (1989) U.S.$83,900,000; expenditures by nationals abroad (1988) U.S.$65,000,000.

Foreign trade[6]

Balance of trade (current prices)

	1985	1986	1987	1988	1989	1990
BD '000,000	+19.3	+12.3	−5.7	+28.2	+3.1	+162.0
% of total	0.9%	0.7%	0.3%	1.6%	1.4%	6.1%

Imports (1990): BD 1,236,500,000 (crude petroleum products 54.3%, non-petroleum products 45.7%). *Major import sources* (1989): Saudi Arabia 49.5%; Japan 10.4%; United States 7.8%; United Kingdom 7.6%; Italy 6.6%; Australia 3.5%; West Germany 3.3%; The Netherlands 1.9%; France 1.4%; India 1.0%; South Korea 0.9%.
Exports (1990): BD 1,398,500,000 (petroleum products 79.0%, aluminum products 5.6%). *Major export destinations* (1989): United States 25.7%; United Arab Emirates 19.3%; Japan 11.9%; India 10.8%; Canada 9.9%; Singapore 6.1%; Saudi Arabia 2.9%; Réunion 1.3%; Djibouti 1.2%.

Transport and communications

Transport. Railroads: none. Roads (1988): total length 1,624 mi, 2,614 km (paved, 75%). Vehicles (1990): passenger cars 104,585; trucks and buses 23,501. Merchant marine (1991): vessels (100 gross tons and over) 93; total deadweight tonnage 262,041. Air transport (1990)[7]: passenger-mi 963,000,000, passenger-km 1,549,000,000; short ton-mi cargo 30,300,000, metric ton-km cargo 44,300,000; airports (1992) with scheduled flights 1.
Communications. Daily newspapers (1989): total number 3; total circulation 58,500; circulation per 1,000 population 116. Radio (1991): total number of receivers 250,000 (1 per 2.1 persons). Television (1991): total number of receivers 185,952 (1 per 2.8 persons). Telephones (1989): 140,000 (1 per 3.5 persons).

Education and health

Education (1987–88)

	schools	teachers	students	student/ teacher ratio
Primary (age 6–11)	131	3,673	60,519	16.5
Secondary (age 12–17)	35	1,563	33,148	21.2
Voc., teacher tr.	9	707	7,478	10.6
Higher	4	539	5,529	10.3

Educational attainment (1981). Percentage of population age 10 and over having: no formal education 27.2%; knowledge of reading and writing 26.3%; primary education 24.9%; secondary 13.3%; higher 8.3%. *Literacy* (1990): percentage of population age 15 and over literate 77.4%; males literate 82.1%; females literate 69.3%.
Health (1987): physicians 664 (1 per 713 persons); hospital beds 1,445 (1 per 328 persons); infant mortality rate per 1,000 live births (1991) 17.0.
Food: n.a.

Military

Total active duty personnel (1992): 6,150 (army 81.3%, navy 8.1%, air force 10.6%). *Military expenditure as percentage of GNP* (1989): 6.5% (world 4.9%); per capita expenditure U.S.$389.

---

[1]Total area includes numerous small uninhabited islands and dependencies of Bahrain. [2]Detail does not add to total given because of rounding. [3]The 1991 census, conducted in December, recorded a total population of 518,243. [4]1987. [5]Includes long-term private debt not guaranteed by the government. [6]Import figures are f.o.b. in balance of trade and c.i.f. for commodities and trading partners. [7]One-fourth apportionment of international flights of Gulf Air (jointly administered by the governments of Bahrain, Oman, Qatar, and the United Arab Emirates).

Bangladesh

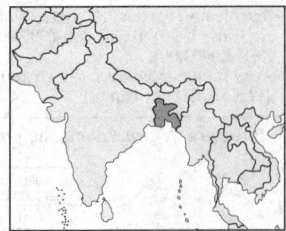

Official name: Gana Prajātantrī Bangladesh (People's Republic of Bangladesh).
Form of government: unitary multiparty republic with one legislative house (Parliament [330[1]]).
Chief of state: President.
Head of government: Prime Minister.
Capital: Dhākā.
Official language: Bengali.
Official religion: Islam.
Monetary unit: 1 Bangladesh taka (Tk) = 100 paisa; valuation (Oct. 5, 1992) 1 U.S.$ = Tk 39.00; 1 £ = Tk 66.30.

Area and population

Divisions[2]	Administrative centres	area sq mi	area sq km	population 1991 census[3]
Chittagong	Chittagong	17,535	45,415	27,096,904
Dhākā	Dhākā	11,881	30,772	32,270,994
Khulna	Khulna	12,963	33,574	19,966,590
Rājshāhi	Rājshāhi	13,219	34,237	25,431,655
TOTAL		55,598	143,998	104,766,143

Demography

Population (1992): 110,602,000.
Density (1992): persons per sq mi 1,989.3, persons per sq km 768.1.
Urban-rural (1989): urban 24.4%; rural 75.6%.
Sex distribution (1991): male 51.47%; female 48.53%.
Age breakdown (1988): under 15, 42.3%; 15–29, 26.0%; 30–44, 16.2%; 45–59, 8.6%; 60 and over, 5.0%; unknown, 1.9%.
Population projection: (2000) 128,043,000; (2010) 153,761,000.
Doubling time: 32 years.
Ethnic composition (1983): Bengali 97.7%; tribal (Chakmā, Gāro, Khāsi, Santāl, etc.) 1.0%; other 1.3%.
Religious affiliation (1981): Muslim 86.6%; Hindu 12.1%; Buddhist 0.6%; Christian 0.3%; other 0.4%.
Major cities (1991)[4]: Dhākā 6,105,160; Chittagong 2,040,663; Khulna 877,388; Rājshāhi 517,136; Mymensingh 185,517[5].

Vital statistics

Birth rate per 1,000 population (1990): 32.8 (world avg. 27.1).
Death rate per 1,000 population (1990): 11.3 (world avg. 9.8).
Natural increase rate per 1,000 population (1990): 21.5 (world avg. 17.3).
Total fertility rate (avg. births per childbearing woman; 1991): 4.9.
Marriage rate per 1,000 population (1989): 10.9.
Divorce rate per 1,000 population: n.a.
Life expectancy at birth (1990): male 56.4 years; female 55.4 years.
Major causes of death (1976; percentage of recorded deaths): diseases of the respiratory system 25.7%, of which tuberculosis 4.8%; malignant neoplasms (cancers) 19.8%; infectious intestinal diseases 15.5%; diseases of the liver and kidney 11.4%; diseases of the circulatory system 5.9%; virus fevers 4.5%; childbirth-related causes 4.4%; diabetes 3.6%.

National economy

Budget (1990–91). Revenue: Tk 80,505,000,000 (customs duties 29.2%, excise duties 26.1%, dividends and profits from public enterprises 9.2%, sales tax 9.1%, business tax 9.0%, income taxes 3.1%, stamps [nonjudicial] 2.5%, post and telegraph 2.3%). Expenditures: Tk 73,902,000,000 (employee compensation 38.3%, transfer payments 35.1%, goods and services 20.7%, capital formation 5.9%).
Public debt (external, outstanding; 1990): U.S.$11,226,000,000.
Production (metric tons except as noted). Agriculture, forestry, fishing (1991): paddy rice 28,575,000, sugarcane 7,290,000, wheat 1,004,000, jute 977,000, bananas 620,000, pulses 507,000, oilseeds 378,000[6], condiments and spices 322,000[6], jackfruit 254,000[6], mangoes 160,000, pineapples 130,000, tea 38,000; livestock (number of live animals) 23,500,000 cattle, 22,000,000 goats, 900,000 sheep, 810,000 buffalo, 60,000,000 chickens, 12,000,000 ducks; roundwood (1990) 30,936,000 cu m; fish catch (1990) 847,830. Mining and quarrying (1988–89): marine salt 415,000; industrial limestone 29,457. Manufacturing (1990–91): chemical fertilizers 1,533,419; jute manufactures 433,800; cement 332,000[6]; sugar 246,109; iron and steel 129,310; newsprint 49,510; paper 43,092; glass sheet 1,217,000 sq m; cotton yarn 270,000 bales; matches 10,230,000 gross boxes. Construction: n.a. Energy production (consumption): electricity (kW-hr; 1990) 8,057,000,000 (8,057,000,000); coal (metric tons; 1990) none (558,000); crude petroleum (barrels; 1990) 142,000 (8,690,000); petroleum products (metric tons; 1990) 777,000 (1,849,000); natural gas (cu m; 1990) 4,392,000,000 (4,392,000,000).
Land use (1990): forested 14.3%; meadows and pastures 4.6%; agricultural and under permanent cultivation 70.1%; other 11.0%.
Household income. Average household size (1991) 5.3; average annual income per household (1985–86) Tk 30,933 (U.S.$1,035); sources of income (1985–86): self-employment 50.8%, wages and salaries 26.1%, transfer payments 0.5%, other 22.6%; expenditure (1985–86): food and drink 63.3%, housing and rent 8.8%, fuel and light 8.4%, clothing and footwear 5.9%, other 13.6%.
Gross national product (at current market prices; 1990): U.S.$22,579,000,000 (U.S.$200 per capita).

Structure of gross domestic product and labour force

	1989–90 in value Tk '000,000	1989–90 % of total value	1985–86 labour force	1985–86 % of labour force
Agriculture	271,790	36.9	17,685,000	57.2
Mining	89	—	5,000	—
Manufacturing	64,506	8.7	3,059,000	9.9
Construction	43,110	5.8	649,000	2.1
Public utilities	8,824	1.2	45,000	0.1
Transp. and commun.	75,061	10.2	1,329,000	4.3
Trade	61,583	8.4	3,894,000	12.6
Finance	15,110	2.1	371,000	1.2
Public admin., defense	32,764	4.4	3,863,000	12.5
Services and other	164,734	22.3		
TOTAL	737,571	100.0	30,900,000	100.0[7]

Population economically active (1985–86): total 30,900,000; activity rate of total population 30.4% (participation rates: over age 10, 45.6%; female 8.2%; unemployed 1.1%[8]).

Price and earnings indexes (1985 = 100)

	1985	1986	1987	1988	1989	1990	1991
Consumer price index	100.0	111.0	121.6	133.0	146.3	158.1	169.5
Daily earnings index[9]	100.0	125.8	148.4	158.1	164.5	180.6	...

Tourism (1990): receipts from visitors U.S.$11,000,000; expenditures by nationals abroad U.S.$78,000,000.

Foreign trade

Balance of trade (current prices)

	1986	1987	1988	1989	1990	1991
Tk '000,000	−47,222	−47,948	−39,386	−63,910	−55,550	−48,564
% of total	46.9%	46.6%	32.5%	43.1%	32.4%	28.2%

Imports (1990–91): Tk 122,840,000,000 (textile yarn, fabrics, and made-up articles 15.2%; machinery and transport equipment 10.7%; petroleum and petroleum products 9.8%; chemicals 4.3%; iron and steel 2.8%; dairy products and eggs 2.3%). *Major import sources* (1989–90): Japan 9.1%; United States 7.2%; India 6.7%; Hong Kong 5.3%; China 5.0%; West Germany 4.7%; United Kingdom 4.2%; Singapore 4.1%.
Exports (1990–91): Tk 59,560,000,000 (ready-made garments 47.2%; jute manufactures 16.9%; fish and prawns 10.2%; hides, skins, and leather 8.3%; raw jute 7.2%; tea 2.4%). *Major export destinations* (1989–90): United States 32.3%; Italy 7.2%; United Kingdom 6.2%; West Germany 4.9%; Singapore 4.8%; Japan 4.2%; Belgium 4.0%; U.S.S.R. 3.5%.

Transport and communications

Transport. Railroads (1989–90): route length 1,706 mi, 2,745 km; passenger-mi 3,150,000,000, passenger-km 5,070,000,000; short ton-mi cargo 440,000,000, metric ton-km cargo 643,000,000. Roads (1990): total length 120,100 mi, 193,283 km (paved 4%). Vehicles (1990): passenger cars 41,401; trucks and buses 53,200. Merchant marine (1991): vessels (100 gross tons and over) 308; total deadweight tonnage 620,415. Air transport (1990)[10]: passenger-mi 1,368,000,000, passenger-km 2,201,000,000; short ton-mi cargo 64,318,000, metric ton-km cargo 93,903,000; airports with scheduled flights (1992) 7.
Communications. Daily newspapers (1990): total number 55; total circulation 1,212,000; circulation per 1,000 population 11. Radio (1991): 4,500,000 receivers (1 per 25 persons). Television (1991): 350,000 receivers (1 per 320 persons). Telephones (1990): 205,500 (1 per 519 persons).

Education and health

Education (1989–90)

	schools	teachers	students	student/ teacher ratio
Primary (age 6–10)	45,283	186,872	11,286,000	60.4
Secondary (age 11–17)	10,579	126,883	2,949,000	23.2
Voc., teacher tr.	151	2,049	24,000	11.7
Higher	459	16,564	548,492	33.1

Educational attainment (1981). Percentage of population age 25 and over having: no formal schooling 70.4%; primary education 24.1%; secondary 4.2%; postsecondary 1.3%. *Literacy* (1990): total population age 15 and over literate 35.3%; males literate 47.1%; females literate 22.0%.
Health (1990): physicians 19,387 (1 per 5,500 persons); hospital beds 33,376 (1 per 3,195 persons); infant mortality rate 94.0.
Food (1988–90): daily per capita caloric intake 2,037 (vegetable products 97%, animal products 3%); 88% of FAO recommended minimum requirement.

Military

Total active duty personnel (1992): 107,000 (army 86.9%, navy 7.0%, air force 6.1%). *Military expenditure as percentage of GNP* (1989): 1.6% (world 4.9%); per capita expenditure U.S.$3.

---

[1]Includes 30 seats reserved for women. [2]Geographic reorganization at the district level took place in 1984; each division is now divided into the following number of new districts: Chittagong 15, Dhākā 17, Khulna 16, and Rājshāhi 16. [3]Unadjusted results. [4]Metropolitan population. [5]Municipal population. [6]1989–90. [7]Detail does not add to total given because of rounding. [8]Excluding underemployment. [9]Skilled wage earnings in manufacturing. [10]Bangladesh Biman only.

Barbados

Official name: Barbados.
Form of government: constitutional monarchy with two legislative houses (Senate [21]; House of Assembly [28]).
Chief of state: British Monarch represented by Governor-General.
Head of government: Prime Minister.
Capital: Bridgetown.
Official language: English.
Official religion: none.
Monetary unit: 1 Barbados dollar (BDS$) = 100 cents; valuation (Oct. 5, 1992) 1 U.S.$ = BDS$2.01; 1 £ = BDS$3.42.

Area and population	area		population
Parishes[1]	sq mi	sq km	1990 census
Christ Church	22	57	44,993
St. Andrew	14	36	6,426
St. George	17	44	18,390
St. James	12	31	20,827
St. John	13	34	10,206
St. Joseph	10	26	7,619
St. Lucy	14	36	9,454
St. Michael[2]	15	39	97,517
St. Peter	13	34	10,388
St. Philip	23	60	19,755
St. Thomas	13	34	11,508
TOTAL	166	430[3]	257,083

Demography

Population (1992): 259,000.
Density (1992): persons per sq mi 1,560, persons per sq km 602.3.
Urban-rural (1990): urban 37.9%; rural 62.1%.
Sex distribution (1990): male 47.74%; female 52.26%.
Age breakdown (1990): under 15, 24.1%; 15–29, 27.0%; 30–44, 22.1%; 45–59, 11.4%; 60 and over, 15.4%.
Population projection: (2000) 266,000; (2010) 274,000.
Doubling time: 92 years.
Ethnic composition (1988): black 80.0%; mixed 16.0%; white 4.0%.
Religious affiliation (1980): Anglican 39.7%; other Protestant 25.6%, of which Pentecostal 7.6%, Methodist 7.1%; nonreligious 17.5%; Roman Catholic 4.4%; not stated 2.7%; other 10.1%.
Major cities (1990): Bridgetown 6,070 (urban area 97,517); no other bounded localities exist.

Vital statistics

Birth rate per 1,000 population (1991): 16.4 (world avg. 26.4); (1979) legitimate 26.9%; illegitimate 73.1%.
Death rate per 1,000 population (1991): 8.8 (world avg. 9.2).
Natural increase rate per 1,000 population (1991): 7.6 (world avg. 17.2).
Total fertility rate (avg. births per childbearing woman; 1990): 1.8.
Marriage rate per 1,000 population (1989): 7.3.
Divorce rate per 1,000 population (1989): 1.6.
Life expectancy at birth (1990–95): male 72.9 years; female 77.9 years.
Major causes of death per 100,000 population (1988): diseases of the circulatory system 338.9, of which cerebrovascular disease 103.9, ischemic heart diseases 89.5; malignant neoplasms (cancers) 160.7; endocrine and metabolic disorders 79.8.

National economy

Budget (1991–92). Revenue: BDS$990,384,000[4] (tax revenue 93.2%, of which consumption taxes 23.1%, personal income taxes 16.9%, company taxes 10.8%, import duties 8.8%; nontax revenue 6.8%). Expenditures: BDS$1,043,865,000 (current expenditure 88.3%, of which education 18.9%, debt charges 15.7%, health 13.3%, general public services 12.9%, economic services 12.0%, defense 2.4%; development expenditure 11.7%).
Production (metric tons except as noted). Agriculture, forestry, fishing (1991): raw sugar 55,000[5], sweet potatoes 2,040, yams 1,989, carrots 1,340, onions 726, tomatoes 403, cucumbers 321; livestock (number of live animals; 1990) 56,000 sheep, 49,000 pigs, 34,000 goats, 18,000 cattle; roundwood, n.a.; fish catch (1989) 2,558. Manufacturing (value added in BDS$'000; 1991): food, beverages, and tobacco (mostly sugar, molasses, rum, cigarettes, and beer) 116,700; paper products, printing, and publishing 30,000; metal products and assembly-type goods (mostly electronic components) 24,700; textiles and wearing apparel 17,100. Construction (value added in BDS$; 1991): 161,900,000. Energy production (consumption): electricity (kW-hr; 1991) 527,000,000 ([1990] 468,000,000); coal, none (none); crude petroleum (barrels; 1991) 454,000 ([1990] 2,091,000); petroleum products (metric tons; 1990) 267,000 (266,000); natural gas (cu m; 1991) 23,000,000 ([1990] 29,000,000).
Population economically active (1991): total 122,500; activity rate of total population 47.5% (participation rates: ages 15 and over, 65.2%; female 57.4%; unemployed 17.2%).

Price and earnings indexes (1985 = 100)							
	1985	1986	1987	1988	1989	1990	1991
Consumer price index	100.0	101.3	104.7	109.8	116.6	120.2	127.7
Hourly earnings index	100.0	104.2	106.0	113.8	116.9	122.7	...

Household income and expenditure. Average household size (1980) 3.7; income per household (1988) BDS$13,455 (U.S.$6,690); sources of income: n.a.; expenditure (1978–79): food 43.2%, housing 13.1%, household operations 9.6%, alcohol and tobacco 8.4%, fuel and light 6.2%, clothing and footwear 5.1%, transportation 4.6%, other 9.8%.
Gross national product (at current market prices; 1990): U.S.$1,680,000,000 (U.S.$6,540 per capita).

Structure of gross domestic product and labour force				
	1991		1990	
	in value BDS$'000,000	% of total value	labour force	% of labour force
Agriculture, fishing	161.0	4.8	6,700	5.4
Mining	18.6[7]	0.6[7]	[8]	[8]
Manufacturing	230.8	6.8	13,300	10.7
Construction	161.9	4.8	10,300[8]	8.3[8]
Public utilities	99.8[7]	2.9[7]	1,400	1.1
Transportation and communications	254.2	7.5	17,800[9]	14.3[9]
Trade, restaurants	890.9	26.3	20,800	16.7
Finance, real estate	435.5	12.8	3,800	3.0
Pub. admin., defense	530.1	15.6	25,500	20.4
Services	109.7	3.2	21,800	17.5
Other	500.0[10]	14.7[10]	3,400	2.7
TOTAL	3,392.6[3]	100.0	124,800	100.0[3]

Public debt (1991): U.S.$948,000,000.
Tourism (1990): receipts from visitors U.S.$500,200,000; expenditures by nationals abroad U.S.$47,400,000.
Land use (1989): forested, negligible; meadows and pastures 9.0%; agricultural and under permanent cultivation 77.0%; other 14.0%.

Foreign trade[11]

Balance of trade (current prices)						
	1986	1987	1988	1989	1990	1991
BDS$'000,000	−521.0	−631.2	−703.9	−856.7	−858.8	−984.6
% of total	32.0%	50.4%	49.8%	53.4%	50.5%	53.6%

Imports (1991): BDS$1,396,140,000 (retained imports 87.8%, of which machinery 16.7%, food and beverages 16.1%, construction materials 6.4%, chemicals 5.4%, fuels 4.8%; reexported imports 12.2%). *Major import sources* (1990): United States 33.2%; Trinidad and Tobago 11.0%; United Kingdom 10.6%; Canada 5.7%; Japan 5.3%.
Exports (1991): BDS$411,553,000 (domestic exports 58.7%, of which sugar 13.1%, chemicals 10.0%, electrical components 8.3%, clothing 4.3%, molasses 1.3%; reexports 41.3%, of which mineral fuels 28.3%). *Major export destinations* (1990): United Kingdom 16.5%; United States 12.3%; Trinidad and Tobago 8.7%; Jamaica 6.2%; offshore ships' stores and bunkers 29.9%.

Transport and communications

Transport. Railroads: none. Roads (1989): total length 977 mi, 1,573 km (paved 95%). Vehicles (1990): passenger cars 38,832; trucks and buses 8,628[12]. Merchant marine (1991): vessels (100 gross tons and over) 35; total deadweight tonnage 7,781. Air transport (1990): passenger arrivals 668,700, passenger departures 647,800; cargo unloaded 8,928 metric tons, cargo loaded 6,072 metric tons; airports (1992) with scheduled flights 1.
Communications. Daily newspapers (1991): total number 2; total circulation 41,405; circulation per 1,000 population 160. Radio (1991): total number of receivers 200,000 (1 per 1.3 persons). Television (1991): total number of receivers 69,350 (1 per 3.7 persons). Telephones (1989): 107,707 (1 per 2.4 persons).

Education and health

Education (1989–90)	schools	teachers	students	student/ teacher ratio
Primary (age 3–11)[13]	104	1,602	29,539	18.4
Secondary (age 12–16)	33	1,406	21,259	15.1
Vocational[14]	8	79	996	12.6
Higher[15]	1	153	1,314	8.6

Educational attainment (1980). Percentage of population age 25 and over having: no formal schooling 0.8%; primary education 63.5%; secondary 32.3%; higher 3.3%. *Literacy* (1985): total population age 15 and over literate[16] 180,000 (98.0%).
Health: physicians (1986) 243 (1 per 1,042 persons); hospital beds (1987) 2,111 (1 per 121 persons); infant mortality rate per 1,000 live births (1991) 11.8.
Food (1987–89): daily per capita caloric intake 3,247 (vegetable products 70%, animal products 30%); 134% of FAO recommended minimum requirement.

Military

Total active duty personnel (1989): 154 (paramilitary marine and coast guard components only). *Military expenditure as percentage of GNP* (1988): 0.7% (world 5.0%); per capita expenditure U.S.$41.

---

[1]Parishes and city of Bridgetown have no local administrative function. [2]Includes city of Bridgetown. [3]Detail does not add to total given because of rounding. [4]Current revenue only. [5]1992. [6]May. [7]Mining excludes natural gas; Public utilities includes natural gas. [8]Construction includes Mining. [9]Includes tourism services. [10]Net indirect taxes. [11]Import figures are f.o.b. in balance of trade and c.i.f. in commodities and trading partners. [12]Includes taxis. [13]Includes preprimary. [14]1987–88. [15]University of the West Indies, Cave Hill campus. [16]National literacy standard based solely on school attendance. Functional literacy may be appreciably lower.

Belarus

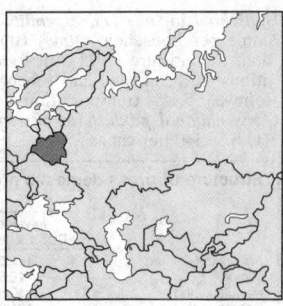

Official name: Respublika Belarus
(Republic of Belarus).
Form of government: unitary multiparty
republic with a single legislative body
(Supreme Council [360[1]]).
Head of state: President.
Head of government: Prime Minister.
Capital: Minsk.
Official language: Belorussian.
Official religion: none.
Monetary unit: 1 ruble = 100 kopecks;
valuation (Oct. 5, 1992) free rate,
1 U.S.$ = 316.82 rubles;
1£ = 538.59 rubles[2].

Area and population

Provinces	Capitals	area sq mi	area sq km	population 1991[3] estimate
Brest	Brest	12,500	32,300	1,483,700
Homel (Gomel)	Homel	15,600	40,400	1,628,400
Hrodno (Grodno)	Hrodno	9,700	25,000	1,188,700
Mahilyoŭ (Mogilyov)	Mahilyoŭ	11,200	29,000	1,269,400
Minsk (Mensk)	Minsk	15,700	40,800	3,256,000
Vitebsk	Vitebsk	15,500	40,100	1,434,200
TOTAL		80,200	207,600	10,260,400

Demography

Population (1992): 10,321,000.
Density (1992): persons per sq mi 128.8, persons per sq km 49.7.
Urban-rural (1991): urban 67.1%; rural 32.9%.
Sex distribution (1990): male 47.00%; female 53.00%.
Age breakdown (1989): under 15, 23.0%; 15–29, 22.4%; 30–44, 20.6%; 45–59, 18.0%; 60–74, 11.5%; 75 and over, 4.5%.
Population projection: (2000) 10,572,000; (2010) 10,894,000.
Doubling time: not applicable; doubling time exceeds 100 years.
Ethnic composition (1989): Belorussian 77.9%; Russian 13.2%; Polish 4.1%; Ukrainian 2.9%; Jew 1.1%; other 0.8%.
Religious affiliation: believers are predominantly Belorussian Orthodox; there is a Roman Catholic minority.
Major cities (1991): Minsk 1,633,600; Homel 503,300; Vitebsk 369,200; Mahilyoŭ 363,000; Hrodno 284,800.

Vital Statistics

Birth rate per 1,000 population (1990): 13.9 (world avg. 27.1); legitimate 91.0%; illegitimate 9.0%.
Death rate per 1,000 population (1990): 10.7 (world avg. 9.8).
Natural increase rate per 1,000 population (1990): 3.2 (world avg. 17.3).
Total fertility rate (avg. births per childbearing woman; 1989): 2.0.
Marriage rate per 1,000 population (1989): 9.6
Divorce rate per 1,000 population (1989): 3.4.
Life expectancy at birth (1990): male 63.9 years; female 74.7 years.
Major causes of death per 100,000 population (1989): diseases of the circulatory system 563.7; malignant neoplasms (cancers) 167.6; accidents and violence 96.5; diseases of the respiratory system 79.8; diseases of the digestive system 21.3; diseases of the nervous system 7.8; infectious and parasitic diseases 7.5; endocrine and metabolic disorders 5.8.

National economy

Budget (1992). Revenue: 87,400,000,000 rubles (share in profits of state and cooperative enterprises 58.1%, state social insurance 31.9%, taxes on individuals 6.0%). Expenditures: 95,700,000,000 rubles (national economy 63.5%, social welfare and culture 32.7%, health 18.0%, education and science 14.6%, law enforcement 0.9%).
Public debt (external, outstanding): n.a.
Tourism: receipts from visitors, n.a.; expenditures by nationals abroad, n.a.
Production (metric tons except as noted). Agriculture, forestry fishing (1991): potatoes 8,958,000, grain 6,296,000, sugar beets 1,147,000, other vegetables 894,000, fruit 494,000, flax fibre 76,000; livestock (number of live animals) 6,377,000 cattle, 4,703,000 pigs, 380,000 sheep and goats, 50,000,000 poultry; roundwood 6,700,000 cu m; fish catch, n.a. Mining and quarrying (1989): peat 2,341,000. Manufacturing (1991): fertilizers 5,000,000; cement 2,173,000; crude steel 1,127,000; synthetic fibres 443,000; paper 207,000; television receivers 1,103,000 units; cameras 965,000 units; radio receivers 932,000 units; bicycles 811,000 units; electric bulbs 301,000 units; motorcycles 214,000 units; tractors 95,000 units; metal-cutting lathes 14,800 units; elevators 12,600 units. Construction (1989): 5,490,000 sq m. Energy production (consumption): electricity (kW-hr; 1991) 38,700,000,000 (51,744,000,000); coal (1991) none (1,500,000); crude petroleum (barrels; 1991) 10,995,000 (n.a.); petroleum products (1991) n.a. (n.a.); natural gas (cu m; 1991) 210,000,000 (15,400,000,000).
Population economically active (1990): total 5,149,000; activity rate of total population 50.2% (participation rates [1989]: ages 16–59 [male], 16–54 [female] 91.4%; female [1990] 46.7%; unemployed [1990] 2.9%).

Price and earnings indexes (1985 = 100)

	1985	1986	1987	1988	1989
Consumer price index	100.0	102.4	103.5	104.2	105.8
Monthly earnings index	100.0	103.9	109.4	119.5	131.3

Gross national product (at current market prices; 1990): 28,017,000,000 rubles (2,700 rubles per capita)[4].

Structure of net material product and labour force

	1990 in value '000,000 rubles	1990 % of total value	1990 labour force	1990 % of labour force
Agriculture	8,206	29.3	985,000	18.9
Mining } Manufacturing } Public utilities }	12,333	44.0	1,593,000	30.9
Construction	3,293	11.8	570,000	11.0
Transportation and commununications	1,423	5.1	238,000	4.6
Trade	1,552	5.5	382,000	7.4
Finance	—	—	...	...
Public administration, defense	—	—	1,281,000	25.2
Services	—	—	...	...
Other	1,210	4.3	100,000	2.0
TOTAL	28,017	100.0	5,149,000	100.0

Land use (1989): forested 32.7%; meadows and pastures 15.2%; agricultural and under permanent cultivation 45.4%; other 6.7%.
Household income and expenditure. Average household size (1989) 3.2; income per household (1991) 8,000 rubles; sources of income (1989): wages and salaries 71.6%, pensions and stipends 20.4%, other 8.0%; expenditure (1989): consumer goods 30.6%, food 29.0%, housing 2.7%, taxes 2.7%, other 35.0%.

Foreign trade

Balance of trade (current prices)

	1987	1988	1989	1990	1991
'000,000,000 rubles	1.2	2.1	1.0	−0.8	−1.8
% of total	3.3%	5.6%	2.5%	2.1%	2.3%

Imports (1991): 40,064,700,000 rubles (1990; machine building and metalworking machinery 35.1%, consumer goods 13.7%, chemical and petrochemical products 12.3%, oil and natural gas 8.6%, processed food 7.7%, ferrous metals 7.0%, agricultural products 5.1%). *Major import sources:* former Soviet republics 75.1%; foreign countries 24.9%.
Exports (1991): 38,264,700,000 rubles (machine building and metalworking machinery 46.0%, consumer goods 17.8%, chemical and petrochemical products 12.7%, oil and natural gas 7.6%, processed food 5.4%, agricultural products 1.3%). *Major export destinations:* former Soviet republics 90.7%; foreign countries 9.3%.

Transport and communications

Transport. Railroads (1990): length 3,472 mi, 5,587 km; (1989) passenger-mi 10,268,000,000, passenger-km 16,525,000,000; (1989) short ton-mi cargo 57,034,000, metric ton-km cargo 81,734,000,000. Roads (1990): total length 29,900 mi, 48,100 km (paved 94%). Vehicles (1988): passenger cars 498,700; trucks and buses, n.a. Merchant marine: vessels (100 gross tons and over) n.a.; total deadweight tonnage, n.a. Air transport (1989): passenger-mi 3,575,000,000, passenger-km 5,754,000,000; short ton-mi cargo 34,000,000, metric ton-km cargo 49,000,000; airports (1991) with scheduled flights 1.
Communications. Daily newspapers (1989): total number 220; total circulation 2,674,000; circulation per 1,000 population 260. Radio (1990): total number of receivers 7,987,000 (1 per 1.3 persons). Television (1990): total number of receivers 3,122,000 (1 per 3.3 persons). Telephones (1990): 1,635,100 (1 per 6.3 persons).

Education and health

Education (1989–90)

	schools	teachers	students	student/ teacher ratio
Primary (age 6–13)	2,760 }	121,600	1,474,000	12.1
Secondary (age 14–17)	2,611 }			
Voc., teacher tr.	145	...	299,000	...
Higher	33	...	189,400	...

Educational attainment (1989). Percentage of population age 25 and over having: primary education or no formal schooling 23.0%; some secondary 16.8%; completed secondary and some postsecondary 49.4%; higher 10.8%.
Literacy: total population age 15 and over literate, n.a.; males literate, n.a.; females literate, n.a.
Health (1990): physicians 41,400 (1 per 248 persons); hospital beds 135,100 (1 per 76 persons); infant mortality rate per 1,000 live births 11.9.
Food: daily per capita caloric intake, n.a.

Military

Total active duty personnel (1992): 125,000[5] (army 76%, air force 24%). *Military expenditure as percentage of GNP:* n.a.; per capita expenditure, n.a.

---

[1]Includes 88 nonelective seats. [2]A parallel system of coupons was introduced in January 1992 to facilitate the transition from the ruble to national currency, but by year's end, no switch was imminent. [3]January 1. [4]No equivalent U.S.$ value is offered, as Soviet GNP data are very speculative. [5]To be reduced to 90,000 upon formation of a National Armed Forces.

Belgium

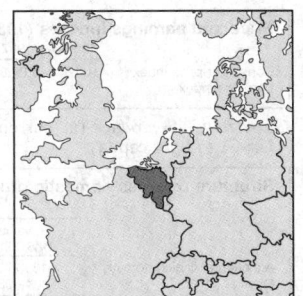

Official name: Koninkrijk België (Dutch); Royaume de Belgique (French) (Kingdom of Belgium).
Form of government: constitutional monarchy with two legislative houses (Senate [185[1]]; House of Representatives [212]).
Chief of state: Monarch.
Head of government: Prime Minister.
Capital: Brussels.
Official languages: Dutch; French; German.
Official religion: none.
Monetary unit: 1 Belgian franc (BF) = 100 centimes; valuation (Oct. 5, 1992) 1 U.S.\$ = BF 28.85, 1 £ = BF 49.05.

Area and population		area		population
		sq mi	sq km	1991 census
Provinces	Capitals			
Antwerp	Antwerp	1,107	2,867	1,605,167
Brabant	Brussels	1,296	3,358	2,245,890
East Flanders	Ghent	1,151	2,982	1,335,793
Hainaut	Mons	1,462	3,786	1,278,791
Liège	Liège	1,491	3,862	999,646
Limburg	Hasselt	935	2,422	750,435
Luxembourg	Arlon	1,714	4,440	232,813
Namur	Namur	1,415	3,666	423,317
West Flanders	Brugge	1,214	3,144	1,106,829
TOTAL		11,787[2]	30,528[2]	9,978,681

Demography

Population (1992): 10,021,000.
Density (1992): persons per sq mi 850.2, persons per sq km 328.3.
Urban-rural (1991): urban 96.6%; rural 3.4%.
Sex distribution (1991): male 48.86%; female 51.14%.
Age breakdown (1991): under 15, 18.1%; 15–29, 21.8%; 30–44, 22.5%; 45–59, 16.9%; 60–74, 14.1%; 75 and over, 6.6%.
Population projection: (2000) 10,236,000; (2010) 10,512,000.
Doubling time: not applicable; doubling time exceeds 100 years.
Nationality (1991): Belgian 91.0%; Italian 2.4%; Moroccan 1.4%; French 0.9%; Turkish 0.8%; Dutch 0.6%; other 2.9%.
Religious affiliation (1980): Roman Catholic 90.0%; Muslim 1.1%; Protestant 0.4%; nonreligious and atheist 7.5%; other 1.0%.
Major cities (1991): Brussels 136,424 (954,045[3]); Antwerp 467,518; Ghent 230,246; Charleroi 206,214; Liège 194,596.

Vital statistics

Birth rate per 1,000 population (1990): 12.4 (world avg. 27.1); (1987) legitimate 90.8%; illegitimate 9.2%.
Death rate per 1,000 population (1990): 10.5 (world avg. 9.8).
Natural increase rate per 1,000 population (1990): 1.9 (world avg. 17.3).
Total fertility rate (avg. births per childbearing woman; 1985–90): 1.6.
Marriage rate per 1,000 population (1990): 6.5.
Divorce rate per 1,000 population (1990): 2.0.
Life expectancy at birth (1988–90): male 72.4 years; female 79.1 years.
Major causes of death per 100,000 population (1987): diseases of the circulatory system 457.2, of which cerebrovascular disease 105.8; malignant neoplasms (cancers) 272.4.

National economy

Budget (1990). Revenue: BF 1,751,087,000,000 (direct taxes 41.7%; value-added, stamp, and similar duties 10.2%; customs and excise duties 7.6%). Expenditures: BF 2,080,656,000,000 (government departments 27.6%; public debt 24.5%; pension 10.1%; defense 4.5%).
Public debt (1990): U.S.\$233,179,000,000.
Production (metric tons except as noted). Agriculture, forestry, fishing (1990): sugar beets 6,200,000[4], potatoes 1,750,000[4], wheat 1,527,000[4], barley 625,-000[4], tomatoes 231,000[4], apples 223,000[4], corn (maize) 60,000[4], oats 60,000[4]; livestock[4] (number of live animals) 6,350,000 pigs, 3,069,000 cattle, 195,000 sheep, 21,000 horses; roundwood 4,682,000 cu m[4]; fish catch (1989) 39,854, of which European plaice (flounder) 14,416, Atlantic cod 5,324, common sole 4,317. Mining and quarrying (1990): quartz 223,000; barite 35,000; marble 481 cu m. Manufacturing (value added in BF '000,000; 1988): metal products and machinery 325,048; food, beverages, and tobacco 205,912; chemicals and chemical products 179,349; pig iron, steel, and nonferrous metals 105,524; paper, printing, and publishing 77,767; furniture and fixtures 61,960; textiles 56,784; building materials 53,918; clothing and footwear 24,298. Construction (1990): residential 31,754,800 cu m; nonresidential 52,061,700 cu m. Energy production (consumption): electricity (kW-hr; 1990) 70,215,000,000 (66,491,000,000); coal (metric tons; 1990) 2,357,000 (16,911,000); petroleum (barrels; 1990) none (184,657,000); petroleum products (metric tons; 1990) 23,671,000 (16,522,000); natural gas (cu m; 1990) 14,142,000 (12,111,500,000).
Household income and expenditure. Average household size (1981) 2.7; sources of income (1990): wages and salaries 50.4%, transfer payments 20.2%, property income 18.2%, self-employment 11.2%; expenditure (1990): food 22.0%, housing 16.1%, transportation and communications 13.5%, health 11.5%, household durable goods 9.4%, clothing and footwear 7.8%.
Gross national product (at current market prices; 1990): U.S.\$154,688,000,000 (U.S.\$15,440 per capita).

Structure of gross domestic product and labour force				
	1990		1989	
	in value BF '000,000	% of total value	labour force	% of labour force
Agriculture	124,326	1.9	100,962	2.5
Mining	16,819	0.3	} 778,404	18.8
Manufacturing	1,457,107	22.2		
Construction	380,990	5.8	225,348	5.4
Public utilities	198,917	3.0	42,581	1.0
Transp. and commun.	529,006	8.0	252,455	6.1
Trade	} 2,125,645	32.3	685,116	16.5
Finance			315,664	7.6
Pub. admin., defense	} 1,928,020	29.3	1,311,297	31.7
Services				
Other	−184,180[5]	−2.8[5]	432,483[6]	10.4[6]
TOTAL	6,576,650	100.0	4,144,310	100.0

Population economically active (1989): total 4,144,310; activity rate of total population 41.7% (participation rates: ages 15–64, n.a.; female 41.2%[7]; unemployed 9.3%).

Price and earnings indexes (1985 = 100)							
	1985	1986	1987	1988	1989	1990	1991
Consumer price index	100.0	101.3	102.9	104.1	107.3	111.0	114.6
Hourly earnings index	100.0	102.8	104.8	105.6	111.6	116.4	122.3

Land use[4] (1989): forested 21.3%; meadows and pastures 20.8%; agricultural and under permanent cultivation 25.0%; other 32.9%.
Tourism (1990): receipts from visitors U.S.\$3,575,000,000; expenditures by nationals abroad U.S.\$5,664,000,000.

Foreign trade[4]

Balance of trade (current prices)						
	1986	1987	1988	1989	1990	1991
BF '000,000	+96,800	+124,300	+96,400	+177,300	+61,200	+21,700
% of total	1.6%	2.0%	1.4%	2.3%	0.8%	0.3%

Imports (1990): BF 4,011,589,000,000 (machinery and transport equipment 25.5%, of which road vehicles and parts 9.3%; chemicals and chemical products 11.4%; mineral fuels and lubricants 8.0%, of which petroleum and petroleum products 5.7%; food and live animals 7.8%; nonindustrial [gem] diamonds 6.6%). *Major import sources:* Germany 17.8%[8]; The Netherlands 17.5%; France 15.9%; U.K. 8.3%; U.S. 4.6%.
Exports (1990): BF 3,944,466,000 (machinery and transport equipment 27.3%, of which passenger cars 11.5%; chemicals and chemical products 13.9%, of which plastics 5.1%; food and live animals 8.3%; iron and steel 8.0%; nonindustrial [gem] diamonds 6.4%; textile yarns and fabrics 5.4%; petroleum and petroleum products 3.1%). *Major export destinations:* France 20.2%; Germany 15.1%[8]; The Netherlands 13.6%; U.K. 8.7%; Italy 6.6%; U.S. 4.3%.

Transport and communications

Transport. Railroads (1990): route length 2,162 mi, 3,479 km; passenger-mi 4,063,000,000, passenger-km 6,539,000,000; short ton-mi cargo 5,720,000,000, metric ton-km cargo 8,352,000,000. Roads (1988): total length 79,749 mi, 128,345 km (paved 96%). Vehicles (1991): passenger cars 3,970,317; trucks and buses 596,452. Merchant marine (1991): vessels (100 gross tons and over) 268; total deadweight tonnage 305,267. Air transport (1990): passenger-mi 4,705,000,000, passenger-km 7,572,000,000; short ton-mi cargo 471,994,000, metric ton-km cargo 689,100,000; airports (1992) with scheduled flights 4.
Communications. Daily newspapers (1990): total number 35; total circulation 3,153,000[9]; circulation per 1,000 population 316[9]. Radio (1991): 4,520,590 receivers (1 per 2.2 persons). Television (1991): 4,200,000 receivers (1 per 2.4 persons). Telephones (1990): 5,173,000 (1 per 1.9 persons).

Education and health

Education (1989–90)	schools	teachers[10]	students	student/ teacher ratio
Primary (age 6–12)	4,577	71,064[11]	752,024	...
Secondary (age 12–18)[12]	2,069	114,628	809,759	...
Voc., teacher tr.	489	14,548	136,003	...
Higher	21	10,517	108,420	...

Educational attainment (1977). Percentage of population age 25 and over having: less than secondary education 64.4%; lower secondary 16.0%; upper secondary 10.0%; vocational 3.7%; teacher's college 2.1%; university 3.8%.
Literacy (1988): virtually 100% literate.
Health: physicians (1990) 33,442 (1 per 298 persons); hospital beds (1988) 91,170 (1 per 108 persons); infant mortality rate per 1,000 live births (1988–90) 6.9.
Food[4] (1987–89): daily per capita caloric intake 3,947 (vegetable products 61%, animal products 39%); 150% of FAO recommended minimum requirement.

Military

Total active duty personnel (1991): 85,450 (army 73.4%, navy 5.3%, air force 21.3%). *Military expenditure as percentage of GNP* (1989): 2.5% (world 4.9%); per capita expenditure U.S.\$392.

[1]Includes one ex officio member from the royal family. [2]Detail does not add to total given because of rounding. [3]Région Bruxelloise. [4]Includes Luxembourg. [5]Includes imputed bank service charges. [6]Includes 384,018 unemployed and 48,465 persons working abroad. [7]1988. [8]For January through September only. [9]For 25 newspapers only. [10]1987–88. [11]Includes preschool teachers. [12]Secondary includes some Voc., teacher tr.

Belize

Official name: Belize.
Form of government: constitutional monarchy with two legislative houses (Senate [8[1]]; House of Representatives [28[2]]).
Chief of state: British Monarch represented by Governor-General.
Head of government: Prime Minister.
Capital: Belmopan.
Official language: English.
Official religion: none.
Monetary unit: 1 Belize dollar (BZ$) = 100 cents; valuation (Oct. 5, 1992) 1 U.S.$ = BZ$2.00[3]; 1 £ = BZ$3.40.

Area and population

Districts	Capitals	area sq mi	area sq km	population 1990 estimate
Belize	Belize City	1,663	4,307	56,131
Cayo	San Ignacio	2,006	5,196	35,194
Corozal	Corozal	718	1,860	28,217
Orange Walk	Orange Walk	1,790	4,636	29,462
Stann Creek	Dangriga	986	2,554	18,061
Toledo	Punta Gorda	1,704	4,413	17,275
TOTAL		8,867	22,965[4]	184,340[5]

Demography

Population (1992): 196,000.
Density (1992): persons per sq mi 22.1, persons per sq km 8.5.
Urban-rural (1990): urban 51.6%; rural 48.4%.
Sex distribution (1989): male 50.67%; female 49.33%.
Age breakdown (1989): under 15, 44.6%; 15–29, 28.0%; 30–44, 12.4%; 45–59, 7.4%; 60–74, 5.1%; 75 and over, 2.5%.
Population projection: (2000) 230,000; (2010) 269,000.
Doubling time: 21 years.
Ethnic composition (1980): Creole (predominantly black) 39.7%; mestizo (Spanish-Indian) 33.1%; Mayan Indian 9.5%; Garifuna (black-Carib Indian) 7.6%; white 4.2%; East Indian 2.1%; other or not stated 3.8%.
Religious affiliation (1980): Roman Catholic 62.0%; Protestant 30.6%, of which Anglican 11.8%, Methodist 6.0%, Mennonite 4.0%, Seventh-day Adventist 2.9%; nonreligious 1.2%; other 6.2%.
Major cities (1990): Belize City 43,621; Orange Walk 10,410; San Ignacio/Santa Elena 7,989; Corozal 7,268; Belmopan 5,256.

Vital statistics

Birth rate per 1,000 population (1990): 38.1 (world avg. 27.1); legitimate 43.2%; illegitimate 56.8%.
Death rate per 1,000 population (1990): 5.0 (world avg. 9.8).
Natural increase rate per 1,000 population (1990): 33.1 (world avg. 17.3).
Total fertility rate (avg. births per childbearing woman; 1991): 4.7.
Marriage rate per 1,000 population (1990): 6.6.
Divorce rate per 1,000 population (1990): 0.4.
Life expectancy at birth (1991): male 67.0 years; female 72.0 years.
Major causes of death per 100,000 population (1988): ischemic heart diseases 61.2; diseases of the respiratory system 52.3; accidents 50.6; malignant neoplasms (cancers) 40.0; cerebrovascular disease 33.9; nutritional deficiencies 20.6.

National economy

Budget (1991–92). Revenue: BZ$247,589,000 (current revenue 88.3%, of which taxes on international trade 44.2%, taxes on income and profits 16.4%; nontax revenue 17.0%; grants 9.9%; development revenue 1.8%). Expenditures: BZ$291,653,000 (current expenditures 54.6%; development expenditures 45.4%).
Production (metric tons except as noted). Agriculture, forestry, fishing (1990): sugarcane 1,114,000[6], oranges 48,600[6, 7], grapefruits 28,700[6, 7], bananas 25,500, corn (maize) 18,700, rice 4,600, coconuts 3,000, red kidney beans 2,600, cocoa 167, honey 72; livestock (number of live animals) 51,000 cattle, 26,000 pigs, 1,000,000 chickens; roundwood 188,000 cu m; fish catch (1989) 1,229, of which lobsters 537, freshwater and marine fish 367, shrimp 202, conchs 123. Mining and quarrying (1988): limestone 600,000; sand and gravel 500,000. Manufacturing (1990): sugar 101,900[6]; molasses 53,900[6]; flour 10,450; fertilizer 9,980; orange concentrate 33,600 hectolitres[6]; beer 31,600 hectolitres; grapefruit concentrate 14,800 hectolitres[6]; cigarettes 100,400,000 units; garments (mostly jeans, overalls, and shirts) 3,492,000 units. Construction (publicly financed buildings under construction; 1991): residential 180 units; nonresidential, n.a. Energy production (consumption): electricity (kW-hr; 1990–91) 97,300,000 (85,800,000); coal, none (none); crude petroleum, none (none); petroleum products (metric tons; 1990) none (83,000); natural gas, none (none).
Public debt (external, outstanding; 1991): U.S.$142,800,000.
Household income and expenditure. Average household size (1990) 4.8; income per household: n.a.; sources of income: n.a.; expenditure (1980): food and beverages 51.5%, clothing and footwear 11.1%, household furnishings 10.1%, transportation and communications 6.5%, energy and water 6.0%, health care 3.4%, housing 2.3%, other 9.1%.
Population economically active (1983–84): total 47,325; activity rate of total population 29.6% (participation rates: ages 15–64 [1980] 63.0%; female 32.5%; unemployed, n.a.).

Price and earnings indexes (1985 = 100)

	1986	1987	1988	1989	1990	1991	1992[8]
Consumer price index	100.8	102.8	106.1	108.3	111.8	118.0	121.9
Earnings index	...	...	...	...	...	...	...

Gross national product (at current market prices; 1990): U.S.$373,000,000 (U.S.$1,970 per capita).

Structure of gross domestic product and labour force

	1990 in value BZ$'000[9]	1990 % of total value	1983–84 labour force	1983–84 % of labour force
Agriculture, fishing, forestry	139,722	22.8	13,065	27.6
Mining	4,103	0.7	81	0.2
Manufacturing	77,027	12.6	4,192	8.9
Construction	52,924	8.6	1,994	4.2
Public utilities	15,564	2.5	611	1.3
Transportation and communications	72,535	11.9	2,035	4.3
Trade, restaurants	101,053	16.5	4,558	9.6
Finance, real estate, insurance	64,618	10.6	570	1.2
Pub. admin., defense	70,591	11.5	6,268	13.2
Services	46,308	7.6	7,326	15.5
Other	−32,472[10]	−5.3[10]	6,625[11]	14.0[11]
TOTAL	611,973	100.0	47,325	100.0

Land use (1989): forested 44.4%; meadows and pastures 2.1%; agricultural and under permanent cultivation 2.5%; other 51.0%.
Tourism (1990): receipts from visitors U.S.$91,000,000; expenditures by nationals abroad U.S.$8,000,000.

Foreign trade[12]

Balance of trade (current prices)

	1986	1987	1988	1989	1990	1991
BZ$'000,000	−41.5	−54.2	−96.6	−143.1	−126.0	−216.3
% of total	9.0%	11.6%	17.2%	22.3%	19.6%	31.2%

Imports (1990): BZ$422,500,000 (manufactured goods 29.4%; machinery and transport 23.5%; food 20.6%; fuels 12.9%; chemicals and chemical products 9.6%). *Major import sources:* United States 54.6%; United Kingdom 9.9%; Mexico 8.5%; The Netherlands 4.0%; Japan 4.0%.
Exports[13] (1990): BZ$258,100,000 (domestic exports 81.0%, of which sugar 33.1%, orange concentrate 13.6%, garments 11.1%, bananas 7.6%, fish, crustaceans, and mollusks 5.8%; reexports 19.0%). *Major export destinations:* United States 42.6%; United Kingdom 34.4%; Mexico 9.7%; Canada 3.6%; Jamaica 3.5%.

Transport and communications

Transport. Railroads: none. Roads (1990): total length 1,600 mi, 2,575 km (paved 13%). Vehicles (1990): passenger cars 11,040; trucks and buses (1989) 2,328. Merchant marine (1990): vessels (100 gross tons and over) 3; total deadweight tonnage 305. Air transport (1990)[14]: passenger arrivals 130,933, passenger departures 134,681; cargo loaded 227 metric tons, cargo unloaded 1,392 metric tons. Airports (1992) with scheduled flights 8.
Communications. Daily newspapers: none[15]. Radio (1991): total number of receivers 100,000 (1 per 1.9 persons). Television (1991): total number of receivers 12,000 (1 per 16 persons). Telephones (1990): 15,917[16] (1 per 12 persons).

Education and health

Education (1990–91)

	schools	teachers	students	student/ teacher ratio
Primary (age 5–14)	236	1,698	44,645	26.3
Secondary (age 14–18)	29	564	7,904	14.0
Voc., teacher tr.	} 8	37[17]	1,726	31.6[17]
Higher				

Educational attainment (1980). Percentage of population age 25 and over having: no formal schooling 10.7%; primary education 75.3%; secondary 11.7%; higher 2.3%. *Literacy* (1991): total population age 15 and over literate 99,000 (93%).
Health (1990): physicians 121 (1 per 1,543 persons); hospital beds 604 (1 per 309 persons); infant mortality rate per 1,000 live births 35.0.
Food (1987–89): daily per capita caloric intake 2,660 (vegetable products 69%, animal products 31%); 118% of FAO recommended minimum requirement.

Military

Total active duty personnel (1991): 665 (army 90.2%, maritime wing 7.5%, air wing 2.3%); British troops 1,500. *Military expenditure as percentage of GNP* (1989): 3.0% (world 4.9%); per capita expenditure U.S.$54.

---

[1]Excludes president of the Senate, who may be elected by the Senate from outside its appointive membership. [2]Excludes speaker of House of Representatives, who may be elected by the House from outside its elected membership. [3]The Belize dollar is officially pegged to the U.S. dollar. [4]Detail does not add to total given because of rounding. [5]1991 census totaled 190,792. [6]1990–91. [7]Commercial production. [8]May. [9]At factor cost. [10]Less imputed bank service charges. [11]Unemployed. [12]Import figures are f.o.b. in balance of trade and c.i.f. in commodities and trading partners. [13]*Exports* (1991): BZ$238,100,000 (domestic exports 79.6%, of which sugar 35.0%, garments 14.7%, orange concentrate 6.6%, bananas 5.9%, lobster 5.2%; reexports 20.4%). [14]Belize International Airport only. [15]Four weekly newspapers had a total circulation in 1990 of 26,500. [16]Number of lines. [17]1988–89.

Benin

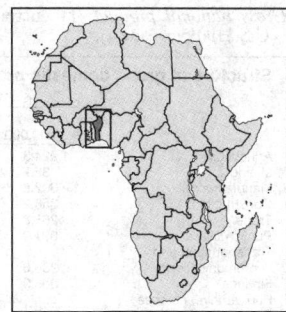

Official name: République du Bénin
  (Republic of Benin).
Form of government: multiparty
  republic with one legislative house
  (National Assembly [64]).
Head of state and government:
  President.
Capitals[1]: Porto-Novo (official);
  Cotonou (de facto).
Official language: French.
Official religion: none.
Monetary unit: 1 CFA franc
  (CFAF) = 100 centimes; valuation
  (Oct. 5, 1992) 1 U.S.$ = CFAF 238.75;
  1 £ = CFAF 405.88.

Area and population

Provinces	Capitals	area sq mi	area sq km	population 1987 estimate
Atacora	Natitingou	12,050	31,200	622,000
Atlantique	Cotonou	1,250	3,200	909,000
Borgou	Parakou	19,700	51,000	630,000
Mono	Lokossa	1,450	3,800	610,000
Ouémé	Porto-Novo	1,800	4,700	806,000
Zou	Abomey	7,200	18,700	731,000
TOTAL		43,450	112,600	4,308,000

Demography

Population (1992): 4,928,000.
Density (1992): persons per sq mi 113.4, persons per sq km 43.8.
Urban-rural (1985): urban 26.5%; rural 73.5%.
Sex distribution (1988): male 48.83%; female 51.17%.
Age breakdown (1988): under 15, 49.3%; 15–29, 24.5%; 30–44, 14.2%; 45–59, 7.4%; 60–74, 3.7%; 75 and over, 0.9%.
Population projection: (2000) 6,369,000; (2010) 8,745,000.
Doubling time: 21 years.
Ethnic composition (1979): Fon 39.2%; Yoruba (Nago) 11.9%; Adja 11.0%; Bariba 8.5%; Somba (Otomary) 6.5%; Fulani (Peul) 5.6%; Djougou 3.0%; Dendi 2.1%; other 3.7%.
Religious affiliation (1980): traditional beliefs 61.4%; Christian 23.1%, of which Roman Catholic 18.5%, Protestant 2.8%; Muslim 15.2%; other 0.3%.
Major cities (1985): Cotonou 402,290; Porto-Novo 163,260; Parakou 66,000[2]; Abomey 54,000[2]; Kandi 53,000[2].

Vital statistics

Birth rate per 1,000 population (1991): 49.0 (world avg. 26.4).
Death rate per 1,000 population (1991): 16.0 (world avg. 9.2).
Natural increase rate per 1,000 population (1991): 33.0 (world avg. 17.2).
Total fertility rate (avg. births per childbearing woman; 1991): 7.0.
Marriage rate per 1,000 population (1980–85): 12.8.
Divorce rate per 1,000 population (1980–85): 0.8.
Life expectancy at birth (1991): male 49.0 years; female 52.0 years.
Major causes of death per 100,000 population (1986): n.a.; however, of the 184,310 reported cases of infectious diseases (notifiable to the World Health Organization): 82.0% were malaria, 4.2% dysentery, 4.0% measles, 2.6% pneumonia, 2.2% chicken pox, 1.4% mumps, 1.3% schistosomiasis.

National economy

Budget (1992). Revenue: CFAF 136,500,000,000 (1991; current receipts 93.2%, of which fiscal receipts and customs duties 85.8%, other current receipts 7.4%; aid 3.9%; loans 2.9%). Expenditures: CFAF 203,800,000,000 (1991; general administration 39.1%, of which personnel costs 27.9%, material costs 11.1%; internal-debt service 22.6%; public-investment program 22.2%; external public-debt service 9.3%; social security 4.7%; highway fund 1.1%; other expenses 1.0%).
Production (metric tons except as noted). Agriculture, forestry, fishing (1991): yams 1,206,000, cassava 889,000, corn (maize) 390,000, seed cotton 167,000, sorghum 106,000, tomatoes 73,000, peanuts (groundnuts) 69,000, dry beans 48,000, millet 26,000, sweet potatoes 24,000, coconuts 20,000, paddy rice 18,000, bananas 13,000, mangoes 12,000, oranges 12,000, palm kernels 9,000, karité (a butter from the nut of the shea tree) 7,000[3], pineapples 3,000, coffee beans 1,000, cacao beans 900[4], tobacco 322[3]; livestock (number of live animals) 1,080,000 goats, 970,000 sheep, 955,000 cattle, 730,000 pigs, 25,000,-000 chickens; roundwood (1990) 5,038,000 cu m; fish catch (1989) 38,292. Mining and quarrying (1986): marine salt 100, limestone is mined for use in cement. Manufacturing (1988): cement 300,000; meat 61,000; sugar 52,000[5]; cotton fibre 37,456[6]; palm oil and palm kernel oil 7,850[6]. Construction: n.a. Energy production (consumption): electricity (kW-hr; 1990) 5,000,000 (200,000,000); coal, none (none); crude petroleum (barrels; 1990) 1,999,000 (negligible); petroleum products (metric tons; 1990) none (136,000); natural gas, none (none).
Population economically active (1986): total 1,447,000; activity rate of total population 34.5% (participation rates: ages 15–64, 60.2%; female 35.6%; unemployed, n.a.).

Price and earnings indexes (1985 = 100)

	1984	1985	1986	1987	1988	1989	1990
Consumer price index[7]	...	...	...	...	...	...	...
Hourly earnings index[8]	100.0	100.0	100.0	100.0	100.0	100.0	100.0

Land use (1990): forested 31.4%; meadows and pastures 4.0%; agricultural and under permanent cultivation 16.8%; other 47.8%.
Tourism (1988): receipts from visitors U.S.$15,000,000; expenditures by nationals abroad U.S.$8,000,000.
Gross national product (at current market prices; 1990): U.S.$1,716,000,000 (U.S.$360 per capita).

Structure of gross domestic product and labour force

	1986 in value CFAF '000,000	1986 % of total value	1979 labour force	1979 % of labour force
Agriculture	200,183	39.8	673,732	61.1
Mining and manufacturing	28,335	5.6	84,475	7.7
Public utilities	4,282	0.9	2,509	0.2
Construction	24,564	4.9	13,329	1.2
Trade	96,637	19.2	234,130	21.2
Transportation and communications	48,100	9.6	23,535	2.1
Finance and services	34,476	6.9	} 71,713	} 6.5
Pub. admin., defense	39,321	7.8		
Other	26,768	5.3		
TOTAL	502,666	100.0	1,103,423	100.0

Household income and expenditure. Average household size (1979) 5.4; income per household (1983) U.S.$240; sources of income: self-employment 73.7%, wages and salaries 26.3%; expenditure: n.a.
Public debt (external, outstanding; 1990): U.S.$1,092,000,000.

Foreign trade[9]

Balance of trade (current prices)

	1984	1985	1986	1987	1988	1989
CFAF '000,000	−81,830	−100.47	−98.23	−61.23	−80.84	−59.00
% of total	46.2%	42.9%	55.5%	13.3%	14.5%	40.7%

Imports (1990): U.S.$438,800,000 (1987; manufactured goods 38.5%, of which cotton yarn and fabric 10.5%, chemical products 5.6%; food products 23.5%, of which cereals 17.1%; machinery and transport equipment 13.5%, of which transport equipment 5.0%, nonelectrical equipment 4.9%, electrical equipment 3.6%; beverages and tobacco 7.6%). *Major import sources* (1989): India 23.4%; France 15.9%; The Netherlands 5.0%; Côte d'Ivoire 4.6%; Thailand 4.6%; United States 3.7%; West Germany 3.4%; Italy 3.2%; Taiwan 2.9%; Korea 2.7%.
Exports (1990): U.S.$93,300,000 (1987; cotton 55.6%; energy 27.5%; food products 4.3%, of which cocoa beans 0.9%, coffee 0.7%; palm kernel oil and palm oil 3.8%; manufactured goods 1.7%). *Major export destinations* (1989): Portugal 15.2%; Italy 9.9%; Thailand 9.6%; Taiwan 9.0%; United States 7.4%; Niger 6.2%; France 6.1%.

Transport and communications

Transport. Railroads (1992): length 359 mi, 578 km; passenger-mi 86,754,000[5], passenger-km 139,610,000[5]; short ton-mi cargo 2,748,000[5], metric ton-km cargo 4,012,000[5]. Roads (1986): total length 4,626 mi, 7,445 km (paved 11%). Vehicles (1989): passenger cars 22,000; trucks and buses 12,000. Merchant marine (1991): vessels (100 gross tons and over) 12; total deadweight tonnage 210. Air transport (1990)[10]: passenger-mi 144,363,000, passenger-km 232,329,000; short ton-mi cargo 26,971,000, metric ton-km cargo 39,374,000; airports (1992) with scheduled flights 1.
Communications. Daily newspapers (1990): total number 1; total circulation 12,000; circulation per 1,000 population 2.6. Radio (1991): total number of receivers 350,000 (1 per 14 persons). Television (1991): total number of receivers 16,346 (1 per 292 persons). Telephones (1988): 16,195 (1 per 279 persons).

Education and health

Education (1988)

	schools	teachers	students	student/ teacher ratio
Primary	2,879	13,821	482,451	34.9
Secondary[11]	151	2,711	90,184	33.3
Voc., teacher tr.[11]	13	687	6,879	10.0
Higher	13[11]	625[12]	8,883[12]	14.2[12]

Educational attainment (1979). Percentage of population age 25 and over having: no formal schooling 89.2%; primary education 8.3%; some secondary 1.4%; secondary 0.8%; postsecondary 0.3%. *Literacy* (1990): total percentage of population age 15 and over literate 23.4%; males literate 31.7%; females literate 15.6%.
Health: physicians (1986) 363 (1 per 11,306 persons); hospital beds (1982) 4,902 (1 per 749 persons); infant mortality rate per 1,000 live births (1991) 119.0.
Food (1987–89): daily per capita caloric intake 2,245 (vegetable products 95%, animal products 5%); 98% of FAO recommended minimum requirement.

Military

Total active duty personnel (1992): 4,350 (army 87.4%, navy 4.6%, air force 8.0%). *Military expenditure as percentage of GNP* (1989): 2.0% (world 4.9%); per capita expenditure U.S.$7.

[1]Porto-Novo is the official capital established under the constitution, but Cotonou, where the president and most government ministers reside, is de facto capital. [2]1982. [3]1989–90. [4]1986–89. [5]1986. [6]Export figures. [7]No consumer price index is published, but inflation was estimated by the World Bank at an annual average of 8.0% during 1980–88. [8]January. [9]Figures do not include unaccountable reexports of black-market goods, which originate mainly in Nigeria and amounted to an estimated 90% of Benin's actual exports in 1981. [10]Air Afrique only. [11]1987–88. [12]1989.

Bhutan

Official name: Druk-Yul (Kingdom of Bhutan).
Form of government: constitutional[1] monarchy with one legislative house (National Assembly [150[2]]).
Head of state and government: Monarch (*druk gyalpo*).
Capital: Thimphu.
Official language: Dzongkha (a Tibetan dialect).
Official religion: Mahāyāna Buddhism.
Monetary unit: 1 ngultrum[3] (Nu) = 100 chetrum; valuation (Oct. 5, 1992) 1 U.S.$ = Nu 28.29; 1 £ = Nu 48.10.

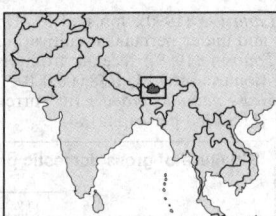

Area and population[4]

Districts	Capitals	area sq mi	area sq km	population[5] 1985 estimate
Bumthang	Jakar	1,150	2,990	23,900
Chirang	Damphu	310	800	108,800
Chhukha	Chhukha	...	...	...
Dagana	Dagana	540	1,400	28,400
Gaylegphug	Gaylegphug	1,020	2,640	111,300
Ha	Ha	830	2,140	16,700
Lhuntshi	Lhuntshi	1,120	2,910	39,600
Mongar	Mongar	710	1,830	73,200
Paro	Paro	580	1,500	45,600
Pema Gatsel	Pema Gatsel	150	380	37,100
Punakha	Punakha	2,330	6,040	33,600
Samchi	Samchi	830	2,140	172,100
Samdrup Jongkhar	Samdrup Jongkhar	900	2,340	73,100
Shemgang	Shemgang	980	2,540	44,500
Tashigang	Tashigang	1,640	4,260	177,700
Thimphu	Thimphu	630	1,620	58,700
Tongsa	Tongsa	570	1,470	26,000
Wangdi Phodrang	Wangdi Phodrang	1,160	3,000	47,200
TOTAL		18,150[6, 7]	47,000[6, 7]	1,285,300[8]

Demography[4]

Population (1992): 1,511,000.
Density (1992): persons per sq mi 83.3, persons per sq km 32.1.
Urban-rural (1985): urban 13.1%; rural 86.9%.
Sex distribution (1988): male 50.97%; female 49.03%.
Age breakdown (1988): under 15, 40.3%; 15–29, 26.4%; 30–44, 16.5%; 45–59, 10.5%; 60–74, 5.2%; 75 and over, 1.1%.
Population projection: (2000) 1,812,000; (2010) 2,266,000.
Doubling time: 32 years.
Ethnic composition (1983): Bhutiã (Ngalops) 62.5%; Nepalese (Gurung) 17.7%; Sharchops 13.2%; other 6.6%.
Religious affiliation (1980): Buddhist 69.6%; Hindu 24.6%; Muslim 5.0%; other 0.8%.
Major cities (1985): Thimphu 20,000; Phuntsholing 10,000[9].

Vital statistics[4]

Birth rate per 1,000 population (1991): 39.0 (world avg. 26.4); legitimate, n.a.; illegitimate, n.a.
Death rate per 1,000 population (1991): 19.0 (world avg. 9.2).
Natural increase rate per 1,000 population (1991): 20.0 (world avg. 17.2).
Total fertility rate (avg. births per childbearing woman; 1991): 5.9.
Marital status of population 15 years and over (1985): married 71.2%; single 19.7%; widowed 7.5%; divorced 1.6%.
Divorce rate per 1,000 population: n.a.
Life expectancy at birth (1989): male 49.2 years; female 47.8 years.
Major causes of death per 100,000 population (1987): n.a.; however, major health problems include diarrhea and dysentery, respiratory tract infections, parasitic worms, skin infections, malaria, and nutritional deficiencies.

National economy[4]

Budget (1991–92). Revenue: Nu 1,855,900,000 (internal revenue 64.3%, grants from UN and other international agencies 24.1%, grants from government of India 11.5%). Expenditures: Nu 1,960,200,000 (current expenditures 52.4%, capital expenditures 47.6%).
Public debt (external, outstanding; 1990): U.S.$89,000,000.
Production (metric tons except as noted). Agriculture, forestry, fishing (1991): oranges 62,000, rice 43,000, corn (maize) 40,000, potatoes 33,000, sugarcane 12,000, green peppers and chilies 7,000, millet 7,000, wheat 5,000, apples 5,000, barley 4,000, pulses 2,000; livestock (number of live animals) 413,000 cattle, 73,000 pigs, 59,000 sheep, 38,000 goats; roundwood 3,224,000 cu m; fish catch 1,000. Mining and quarrying (1989): limestone 100,000; dolomite 50,000; gypsum 10,000. Manufacturing (value in Nu; 1980–81): distillery products 47,000,000; cement 36,000,000; chemical products 19,000,000; processed food 14,000,000; forest products 3,000,000. Construction (number of buildings completed; 1977–78): residential 10; nonresidential (guest house) 1. Energy production (consumption): electricity (kW-hr; 1990) 1,564,000,000 (172,000,000); coal (metric tons; 1990) 2,000 (18,000); crude petroleum, none (n.a.); petroleum products (metric tons; 1990) none (26,000); natural gas, none (n.a.).
Household income and expenditure. Average household size (1980): 5.4; income per household: n.a.; sources of income: n.a.; expenditure (1979): food 72.3%, clothing 21.2%, energy 3.7%, household durable goods 0.7%, personal effects and other 2.1%.

Gross national product (at current market prices; 1990): U.S.$273,000,000 (U.S.$190 per capita).

Structure of gross domestic product and labour force

	1989 in value Nu '000,000	1989 % of total value	1984 labour force	1984 % of labour force
Agriculture	1,924.3	44.9	580,000[10]	87.2
Mining	35.7	0.8		
Manufacturing	302.5	7.1		
Construction	358.2	8.4		
Trade	268.8	6.3	6,000[10]	0.9
Public utilities	391.0	9.1		
Transportation and communications	235.6	5.5		
Finance	306.9	7.2		
Pub. admin., defense	525.1	12.3	23,000[10]	3.4
Services			56,000[10]	8.5[11]
Other	−67.0[12]	−1.6[12]		
TOTAL	4,281.1	100.0	664,000	100.0

Population economically active (1984): total 664,000; activity rate of total population 52.7% (participation rates: ages 15–64, 94.8; female 55.0; unemployed 6.5).

Price and earnings indexes (1985 = 100)

	1985	1986	1987	1988	1989	1990	1991
Consumer price index	100.0	110.0	115.3	127.5	139.0	154.1	172.3
Earnings index	...	...	...	...	...	...	...

Land use (1990): forested 55.5%; meadows and pastures 5.8%; agricultural and under permanent cultivation 2.8%; other 35.9%.
Tourism (1990): receipts from visitors U.S.$2,000,000; expenditures by nationals abroad, n.a.

Foreign trade

Balance of trade (current prices)

	1985–86	1986–87	1987–88	1988–89	1989–90	1990–91
Nu '000,000	−769.6	−858.3	−482.7	−833.3	−545.4	−606.9
% of total	58.6%	50.1%	25.3%	28.6%	18.2%	17.9%

Imports (1988)[13]: Nu 1,108,700,000 (petroleum products 7.7%, motor vehicles and parts 6.9%, rice 6.2%, machinery parts 3.2%, iron and steel products 1.8%, fabrics 1.4%). *Major import source* (1988–89): India 64.0%.
Exports (1988)[13]: Nu 989,770,000 (electricity 34.1%; timber and wood manufactures 24.5%, fruit and vegetables 13.0%, cement 11.2%, nonmetallic mineral manufactures 9.7%, alcoholic beverages 1.8%). *Major export destination* (1988–89): India 93.2%.

Transport and communications

Transport. Railroads: none. Roads (1990): total length 1,600 mi, 2,500 km (paved 72%). Vehicles (1988): passenger cars 2,590; trucks and buses 1,367. Merchant marine: none. Air transport (1986): passenger-mi 2,722,000, passenger-km 4,381,000; metric ton-km cargo, n.a.; airports (1992) with scheduled flights 1.
Communications. Daily newspapers: none[14]. Radio (1991): total number of receivers 22,000 (1 per 67 persons). Television (1983): total number of receivers 200 (1 per 6,180 persons). Telephones (1986): 1,945 (1 per 675 persons).

Education and health[4]

Education (1988)

	schools	teachers	students	student/ teacher ratio
Primary (age 7–11)	150	1,513	42,446	28.1
Secondary (age 12–16)	30	695	16,350	23.5
Voc., teacher tr.	5			
Higher	2	150	1,761	11.7

Educational attainment: n.a. *Literacy* (1977): total population age 15 and over literate 124,000 (18.0%); males literate 98,000 (31.0%); females literate 26,000 (9.0%).
Health (1988): physicians 142 (1 per 9,686 persons); hospital beds 932 (1 per 1,476 persons); infant mortality rate per 1,000 live births (1990) 128.2.
Food (1975–77): daily per capita caloric intake 2,058 (vegetable products 98%, animal products 2%); 89% of FAO recommended minimum requirement.

Military

Total active duty personnel (1992): about 5,500 (army 100%).

---

[1]There is no formal constitution, but a form of constitutional monarchy is in place. [2]Includes 50 nonelective seats. [3]Indian currency is also accepted legal tender; the ngultrum is at par with the Indian rupee. [4]The population data used in this compilation, which is based on the now repudiated 1980 census, should be viewed with extreme care, as the actual 1992 population could range from 850,000 to 1,600,000. [5]Rural only. [6]2,700 sq mi (7,000 sq km) are not included in the district area totals. [7]Includes Chhukha area. [8]Includes urban population; includes Chhukha population. [9]1982. [10]Derived value. [11]Includes 6.5% with no occupation. [12]Imputed bank service charges. [13]Trade data with India only. [14]A weekly newspaper is published from Thimphu in Dzongkha, Nepalese, and English, circulation (1989) 10,500.

Bolivia

Official name: República de Bolivia (Republic of Bolivia).
Form of government: unitary multiparty republic with two legislative houses (Chamber of Senators [27]; Chamber of Deputies [130]).
Head of state and government: President.
Capitals: La Paz (administrative); Sucre (judicial).
Official languages: Spanish, Aymara, Quechua.
Official religion: Roman Catholicism.
Monetary unit: 1 boliviano (Bs) = 100 centavos; valuation (Oct. 5, 1992) 1 U.S.$ = Bs 4.00; 1 £ = Bs 6.80.

Area and population		area		population
		sq mi	sq km	1990 estimate
Departments	**Capitals**			
Beni	Trinidad	82,458	213,564	278,000
Chuquisaca	Sucre	19,893	51,524	498,000
Cochabamba	Cochabamba	21,479	55,631	1,098,000
La Paz	La Paz	51,732	133,985	2,409,000
Oruro	Oruro	20,690	53,588	461,000
Pando	Cobija	24,644	63,827	59,000
Potosí	Potosí	45,644	118,218	967,000
Santa Cruz	Santa Cruz	143,098	370,621	1,237,000
Tarija	Tarija	14,526	37,623	315,000
TOTAL		424,164	1,098,581	7,322,000

Demography

Population (1992): 7,739,000.
Density (1992): persons per sq mi 18.2, persons per sq km 7.0.
Urban-rural (1990): urban 51.4%; rural 48.6%.
Sex distribution (1990): male 49.29%; female 50.71%.
Age breakdown (1988): under 15, 41.1%; 15–29, 25.9%; 30–44, 17.0%; 45–59, 9.5%; 60–74, 4.7%; 75 and over, 1.3%, unknown 0.5%.
Population projection: (2000) 9,668,000; (2010) 12,700,000.
Doubling time: 24 years.
Ethnic composition (1982): mestizo 31.2%; Quechua 25.4%; Aymara 16.9%; white 14.5%; other 12.0%.
Religious affiliation (1980): Roman Catholic 92.5%; Baha'i 2.6%; other 4.9%.
Major cities (1989): La Paz 669,400; Santa Cruz 529,200; Cochabamba 403,600; El Alto 307,400; Oruro 176,700; Potosí 110,700.

Vital statistics

Birth rate per 1,000 population (1988): 42.8 (world avg. 27.1).
Death rate per 1,000 population (1988): 14.1 (world avg. 9.8).
Natural increase rate per 1,000 population (1988): 28.7 (world avg. 17.3).
Total fertility rate (avg. births per childbearing woman; 1987): 6.1.
Marriage rate per 1,000 population (1980): 4.8.
Divorce rate per 1,000 population: n.a.
Life expectancy at birth (1987): male 51.0 years; female 55.0 years.
Major causes of death per 100,000 population: n.a.; however, major health problems include diseases of the respiratory system, gastrointestinal infections, measles, diphtheria, malaria, and tetanus.

National economy

Budget (1990). Revenue: Bs 2,112,100,000 (income of government enterprises 40.4%, taxes on goods and services 31.6%, social-security contributions 8.8%, property taxes 7.4%, taxes on international trade 7.3%, income taxes 4.9%). Expenditures: Bs 2,530,200,000 (education 18.0%, social security 17.7%, defense 14.1%, public services 12.7%, transportation and communications 8.1%, public order and safety 6.6%, health 2.3%).
Public debt (external, outstanding; 1990): U.S.$3,649,000,000.
Production (metric tons except as noted). Agriculture, forestry, fishing (1990): sugarcane 2,100,000, potatoes 534,000, bananas and plantains 496,000, corn (maize) 325,000, cassava 299,000, soybeans 232,000, rice 207,000, oranges and tangerines 113,000, wheat 51,000; livestock (number of live animals) 12,-500,000 sheep, 5,950,000 cattle, 2,400,000 goats, 2,220,000 pigs, 630,000 asses, 320,000 horses; roundwood 1,597,000 cu m; fish catch (1989) 6,024. Mining and quarrying (metric tons of pure metal; 1991): zinc 95,032; lead 20,520; tin 12,588; antimony 8,533[1]; silver 231,000 kilograms; gold 3,595 kilograms[1]. Manufacturing (value added in Bs; 1986)[2]: food products 1,234,700; beverages 876,700; textiles 283,900; printing and publishing 264,100; chemicals 222,100; paper and paper products 172,000; leather and leather products 134,600. Construction (1985)[3]: residential dwellings 226. Energy production (consumption): electricity (kW-hr; 1990) 1,955,000,000 (1,961,000,000); coal (metric tons; 1990) none (none); crude petroleum (barrels; 1990) 7,093,000 (7,384,000); petroleum products (metric tons; 1990) 1,016,000 (999,000); natural gas (cu m; 1990) 3,033,000,000 (745,000,000).
Population economically active (1990): total 2,275,847; activity rate of total population 31.1% (participation rates: ages 15–64, 54.5%; female 23.8%; unemployed 19.0%).

Price and earnings indexes (1985 = 100)							
	1985	1986	1987	1988	1989	1990	1991
Consumer price index	100.0	376.3	431.2	500.1	575.2	674.7	819.4
Monthly earnings index	100.0	365.5	527.6	642.3	760.4	...	...

Gross national product (at current market prices; 1990): U.S.$4,526,000,000 (U.S.$620 per capita).

Structure of gross domestic product and labour force				
	1990		1988	
	in value Bs '000,000[4]	% of total value	labour force[5]	% of labour force[5]
Agriculture	25,097	20.7	868,800	42.3
Mining	18,340	15.1	64,200	3.1
Manufacturing	16,250	13.4	179,700	8.7
Construction	3,297	2.7	110,000	5.4
Public utilities	1,165	1.0	18,900	0.9
Transportation and communications	10,361	8.5	108,300	5.3
Trade	15,617	12.9	259,500	12.6
Finance	15,070	12.4	32,600	1.6
Pub. admin., defense } Services	15,376	12.7	375,100	18.3
Other	743[6]	0.6[6]	36,200	1.8
TOTAL	121,316	100.0	2,053,300	100.0

Household income and expenditure. Average household size (1988): 4.6; average annual income per household: n.a.; sources of income: n.a.; expenditure (1979): food 41.4%, housing 12.5%, transportation and communications 12.5%, clothing and footwear 9.7%, household durable goods 8.9%, health 4.5%, recreation 3.1%, education 1.2%.
Tourism (1990): receipts from visitors U.S.$98,000,000; expenditures by nationals abroad U.S.$60,000,000.
Land use (1989): forested 51.3%; meadows and pastures 24.6%; agricultural and under permanent cultivation 3.2%; other 20.9%.

Foreign trade[7]

Balance of trade (current prices)						
	1986	1987	1988	1989	1990	1991
U.S.$'000,000	−36.9	−85.4	+99.2	+301.8	+326.6	+59.0
% of total	3.2%	7.0%	9.0%	22.5%	21.4%	3.6%

Imports (1989): U.S.$621,600,000 (capital goods 39.6%, of which capital goods for industry 24.0%, transport equipment 13.7%; raw materials 39.2%, of which raw materials for industry 32.0%; consumer goods 20.8%, of which durable consumer goods 11.5%, nondurable consumer goods 9.3%). *Major import sources:* United States 21.2%; Brazil 19.1%; Argentina 15.2%; Japan 11.9%; Chile 6.2%; West Germany 5.3%; Peru 2.3%.
Exports (1989): U.S.$821,200,000 (natural gas 26.0%; zinc 16.1%; tin 15.4%; silver 7.2%; soybeans 6.6%; gold 5.4%; timber 5.4%; sugar 2.4%; hides and skins 2.1%). *Major export destinations:* Argentina 27.9%; United Kingdom 14.0%; United States 13.2%; Belgium 8.5%; Chile 7.6%; Brazil 5.8%; Peru 5.4%; West Germany 4.5%.

Transport and communications

Transport. Railroads (1990): route length 2,269 mi, 3,652 km; passenger-mi 241,000,000, passenger-km 388,000,000; short ton-mi cargo 370,500,000, metric ton-km cargo 540,900,000. Roads (1988): total length 25,875 mi, 41,642 km (paved 4%). Vehicles (1988): passenger cars 83,741; trucks and buses 150,898. Merchant marine (1991): vessels (100 gross tons and over) 1; total deadweight tonnage 15,765. Air transport (1990): passenger-mi 795,000,000, passenger-km 1,280,000,000; short ton-mi cargo 21,896,000, metric ton-km cargo 31,968,000; airports (1992) with scheduled flights 19.
Communications. Daily newspapers (1988): total number 16; total circulation 353,000[8]; circulation per 1,000 population 51[8]. Radio (1991): total number of receivers 4,000,000 (1 per 1.9 persons). Television (1991): total number of receivers 610,000 (1 per 12 persons). Telephones (1989): 194,180 (1 per 37 persons).

Education and health

Education (1986–87)				
	schools	teachers	students	student/ teacher ratio
Primary (age 6–13)	9,758	51,376	888,182	17.3
Secondary (age 14–17)	724	8,258	211,519	25.6
Voc. teacher tr.	47	1,805	15,947	8.8
Higher	10	3,555	97,153	27.3

Educational attainment (1988). Percentage of population age 25 and over having: no formal schooling 25.6%; some primary 23.2%; primary education 23.5%; some secondary 7.0%; secondary 13.5%; some higher 2.6%; higher 3.6%; not specified 1.0%. *Literacy* (1990): total population age 15 and over literate 77.5%; males literate 84.7%; females literate 70.7%.
Health (1987): physicians 3,174 (1 per 2,124 persons); hospital beds 9,824 (1 per 686 persons); infant mortality rate per 1,000 live births (1988) 102.0.
Food (1987–89): daily per capita caloric intake 1,968 (vegetable products 85%, animal products 15%); 82% of FAO recommended minimum requirement.

Military

Total active duty personnel (1991): 31,000 (army 74.2%, navy 12.9%, air force 12.9%). *Military expenditure as percentage of GNP* (1989): 4.3% (world 4.9%); per capita expenditure U.S.$26.

[1]1989. [2]Establishments with 20 or more employees. [3]National government sponsored only. [4]In 1980 prices. [5]Population 10 years and over. [6]Net import duties. [7]Import figures are f.o.b. in balance of trade and c.i.f. for commodities and trading partners. [8]Circulation refers to 12 dailies only.

Bosnia and Hercegovina

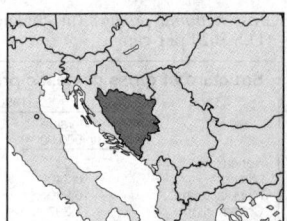

Official name: Republika Bosna i Hercegovina (Republic of Bosnia and Hercegovina).
Form of government: multiparty republic with bicameral legislature (National Assembly [240]).
Chief of state: President.
Head of government: Prime Minister.
Capital: Sarajevo.
Official language: Serbo-Croatian.
Official religion: none.
Monetary unit: 1 New Yugoslav dinar (Din) = 100 paras; valuation (Oct. 5, 1992) 1 U.S.$ = Din 225.41; 1 £ = Din 383.20.

Area and population (1991 census)

Districts	area sq km[1]	population	Districts	area sq km[1]	population
Banja Luka	1,232	195,139	Livno	994	39,526
Banovići	176	26,507	Ljubinje	326	4,162
Bihać	689	70,896	Ljubuški	289	27,182
Bijeljina	734	96,796	Lopare	429	32,400
Bileća	633	13,269	Lukavac	350	56,830
Bosanska Dubica	499	31,577	Maglaj	384	43,294
Bosanska Gradiška	762	60,062	Modriča	297	35,413
Bosanska Krupa	780	58,212	Mostar	1,300	126,067
Bosanski Brod	234	33,962	Mrkonjič Grad	679	27,379
Bosanski Novi	554	41,541	Neum	230	4,268
Bosanski Petrovac	853	15,552	Nevesinje	923	14,421
Bosanski Šamac	219	32,835	Odžak	205	30,651
Bosansko Grahovo	780	8,303	Olovo	408	16,901
Bratunac	793	33,575	Orašje	166	28,201
Brčko	493	87,332	Posušje	372	16,659
Breza	83	17,266	Prijedor	834	112,470
Bugojno	366	46,843	Prnjavor	631	46,894
Busovača	145	18,883	Prozor	477	19,601
Čajniče	275	8,919	Pucarevo	232	30,624
Capljina	249	27,852	Rogatica	664	21,812
Čazin	381	63,406	Rudo	344	11,572
Čelinac	365	18,666	Sanski Most	984	60,119
Čitluk	181	14,709	Sarajevo	2,049	525,980
Derventa	516	56,328	Šekovići	195	9,639
Doboj	684	102,546	Šipovo	470	15,553
Donji Vakuf	338	24,232	Skender Vakuf	360	19,416
Foča	1,270	40,513	Sokolac	723	14,833
Fojnica	308	16,227	Srbac	447	21,660
Gacko	736	10,844	Srebrenica	527	37,211
Glamoč	1,096	12,421	Srebrenik	249	40,769
Goražde	383	37,505	Stolac	541	18,845
Gornji Vakuf	402	25,130	Tešanj	223	48,390
Gračanica	387	59,050	Teslić	846	59,632
Gradačac	405	56,378	Titov Drvar	950	17,079
Grude	218	15,976	Tomislavgrad	967	29,261
Han Pijesak	342	6,346	Travnik	563	70,402
Jablanica	289	12,664	Trebinje	1,205	30,879
Jajce	398	44,903	Tuzla	307	131,861
Kakanj	462	55,857	Ugljevik	199	25,641
Kalesija	272	41,795	Vareš	356	22,114
Kalinovik	732	4,657	Velika Kladuša	304	52,921
Kiseljak	165	24,081	Višegrad	448	21,202
Kladanj	325	16,028	Visoko	242	46,130
Ključ	850	37,233	Vitez	156	27,728
Konjic	1,101	43,636	Vlasenica	532	33,817
Kotor Varoš	574	36,670	Zavidovići	540	57,153
Kreševo	149	6,699	Zenica	500	145,577
Kupres	622	10,728	Žepče	210	22,840
Laktaši	387	29,910	Živinice	281	54,653
Lištica	388	26,437	Zvornik	500	81,111
			TOTAL	51,129[2]	4,365,639

Demography

Population (1992): 4,397,000.
Density (1992): persons per sq mi 222.7, persons per sq km 86.0.
Urban-rural (1981): urban 36.2%; rural 63.8%.
Sex distribution (1981): male 49.73%; female 50.27%.
Age breakdown (1981): under 15, 27.5%; 15–29, 29.0%; 30–44, 19.2%; 45–59, 15.8%; 60–74, 6.3%; 75 and over, 1.9%.
Population projection: (2000) 4,601,000; (2010) 4,871,000.
Doubling time: 90 years.
Ethnic composition (1981): Bosnian 39.5%; Serb 32.0%; Croat 18.4%; Montenegrin 0.3%; Gypsy 0.2%; other 9.6%.
Religious affiliation (1991): most believers are Sunnī Muslims, Serbian Orthodox, or Roman Catholic.
Major cities (1991)[3]: Sarajevo 525,980; Banja Luka 195,139; Zenica 145,577; Tuzla 131,861.

Vital Statistics

Birth rate per 1,000 population (1990): 14.1 (world avg. 27.1).
Death rate per 1,000 population (1990): 6.4 (world avg. 9.8).
Natural increase rate per 1,000 population (1990): 7.7 (world avg. 17.3).
Total fertility rate (avg. births per childbearing woman): n.a.
Marriage rate per 1,000 population (1989): 8.0.
Divorce rate per 1,000 population (1989): 0.5.
Life expectancy at birth (1980–82): male 68.0 years; female 73.0 years.
Major causes of death per 100,000 population (1989): diseases of the circulatory system 344.1; malignant neoplasms (cancers) 122.6; accidents, violence, and poisoning 47.1; diseases of the respiratory system 29.0; diseases of the digestive system 29.2.

National economy

Budget. Revenue: n.a. Expenditures: n.a.
Tourism (1991): total tourist nights 2,360,000.
Production (metric tons except as noted). Agriculture, forestry, fishing (1991): corn (maize) 763,000, wheat 413,000, potatoes 358,000, plums 78,000, grapes 34,000; livestock (number of live animals) 1,317,000 sheep, 853,000 cattle, 617,000 pigs, 10,607,000 poultry; roundwood (1990) 5,379,000 cu m; fish catch (1990) 3,606, all freshwater. Mining (1990): iron ore 6,756,000; bauxite 1,702,000; lead-zinc ore 608,000. Manufacturing (1990): crude steel 1,421,-000; pig iron 1,284,000; alumina 735,000; rolled wire 580,000; steel bars 467,000. Construction (residential units constructed; 1990): 26,568. Energy production (consumption): electricity (kW-hr; 1990) 14,632,000,000 (12,557,-000,000); coal (metric tons; 1990) 17,926,000 (n.a.); petroleum products (metric tons; 1990) 2,320,000 (n.a.).
Gross national product (1990): U.S.$10,667,000,000 (U.S.$2,454 per capita).

Structure of gross material product and labour force

	1989		1990	
	in value Din '000,000	% of total value	labour force[4]	% of labour force[4]
Agriculture	2,963	10.9	39,053	3.8
Mining Manufacturing }	15,589	57.6	496,190	48.3
Construction	1,918	7.1	74,861	7.3
Public utilities	403	1.5	22,345	2.2
Transp. and commun.	1,600	5.9	68,798	6.7
Trade	3,777	13.9	130,914	12.8
Finance			38,686	3.8
Pub. admin., defense Services Other }	834	3.1 }	155,411	15.1
TOTAL	27,084	100.0	1,026,258	100.0

Population economically active (1991): total 992,000; activity rate of total population 22.7% (participation rates: ages 15–64, n.a.; female [1990] 37.7%).

Price and earnings indexes (1985 = 100)

	1984	1985	1986	1987	1988	1989	1990[5]
Consumer price index	58	100	188	400	1,188	16,169	109,000
Monthly earnings index[6]	99	100	106	99	86	109	87

Land use (1990): forest 47.9%; pasture 31.0%; agricultural 15.5%; other 5.6%.
Household income and expenditure. Average household size (1991) 3.4; income per household (1990) Din 72,850 (U.S.$6,437); sources of income (1990): wages 53.2%, transfers 18.2%, self-employment 12.0%, other 16.6%; expenditure (1988): food 41.3%, clothing 8.3%, fuel and lighting 7.8%, housing 7.8%, transportation 6.0%, beverages and tobacco 5.7%, household durable goods 4.1%, education and entertainment 3.5%, health care 3.4%.

Foreign trade

Balance of trade (current prices)

	1985	1986	1987	1988	1989	1990
Din '000,000	−4	2	15	77	962	2,141
% of total	4.5%	1.2%	6.2%	9.2%	7.4%	4.8%

Imports (1990): Din 21,130,000,000 (mineral fuels 31.6%; raw materials and semifinished goods 26.8%; basic manufactures 17.5%; consumer goods 13.3%, of which food and tobacco 3.6%). *Major import sources:* n.a.
Exports (1990): Din 23,271,000,000 (machinery 20.8%; chemicals 9.4%; clothing 9.2%; furniture 5.0%). *Major export destinations:* n.a.

Transport and communications

Transport. Railroads (1990): length 646 mi, 1,039 km; passengers transported 11,197,000; cargo transported 35,054,000 tons. Roads (1991): total length 13,153 mi, 21,168 km (paved 54%). Vehicles (1990): passenger cars 438,080; trucks and buses 50,578. Airports (1992) with scheduled flights 1.
Communications. Daily newspapers (1990): total number 3; circulation 161,-000; circulation per 1,000 population 37. Radio (1989): number of receivers 904,000 (1 per 4.8 persons). Television (1989): number of receivers 844,000 (1 per 5.1 persons). Telephones (1990): 727,316 (1 per 6.0 persons).

Education and health

Education (1990–91)

	schools	teachers	students	student/ teacher ratio
Primary (age 7–14)	2,205	23,369	539,875	23.1
Secondary (age 15–18)	238	9,030	172,063	19.1
Higher	44	2,802	37,541	13.4

Educational attainment (1981). Percentage of population age 15 and over having: less than full primary education 49.5%; primary 24.2%; secondary 21.7%; postsecondary and higher 4.3%. *Literacy* (1981): total population age 10 and over literate 2,962,400 (85.5%); males 96.5%; females 76.6%.
Health (1990): physicians (1989) 6,929 (1 per 624 persons); hospital beds 19,858 (1 per 219 persons); infant mortality rate per 1,000 live births 15.2.

Military

Total active duty personnel (1992): 67,000 (army 100%). *Military expenditure as percentage of GNP:* n.a.

[1]One sq km is equal to approximately 0.3861 sq mi. [2]Detail adds to 554 sq km more than total given; the reason for the discrepancy is unknown. [3]Populations refer to municipal areas, not cities proper. [4]Excludes 28,000 workers in the private sector. [5]On Jan. 1, 1990, the new dinar, equal to 10,000 old dinars, was introduced. [6]Based on worker real net personal income.

Botswana

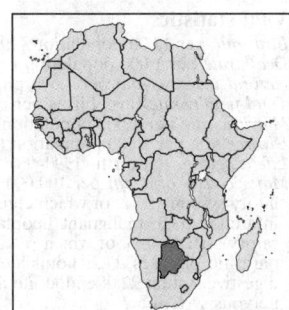

Official name: Republic of Botswana.
Form of government: multiparty republic with one legislative body[1] (National Assembly [40[2]]).
Head of state and government: President.
Capital: Gaborone.
Official language: English[3].
Official religion: none.
Monetary unit: 1 pula (P) = 100 thebe; valuation (Oct. 5, 1992) 1 U.S.$ = P 2.08; 1 £ = P 3.54.

Area and population		area		population
				1991
Districts	Capitals	sq mi	sq km	census[4]
Barolong	...	425	1,100	18,365
Central	Serowe	57,039[5]	147,730[5]	284,264
Ghanzi	Ghanzi	45,525	117,910	24,695
Kgalagadi	Tsabong	41,290	106,940	30,873
Kgatleng	Mochudi	3,073	7,960	57,168
Kweneng	Molepolole	13,857	35,890	169,835
North East	Masunga	1,977	5,120	43,361
North West				
Chobe	Kasane	8,031	20,800	14,186
Ngamiland	Maun	42,135	109,130	94,322
Ngwaketse	Kanye	10,568	27,370	129,474
Serowe/Palapye	...	5	5	111,300
South East	Ramotswa	687[5]	1,780[5]	31,101
Towns[6]				
Francistown	—	31	79	65,026
Gaborone	—	37	97	133,791
Jwaneng	—	39	100	11,199
Lobatse	—	12	30	25,992
Orapa	—	4	10	8,853
Palapye	—	8	21	17,131
Selebi-Pikwe	—	19	50	39,769
Sowa		...	...	2,220
Tlokweng	—	10	26	12,366
TOTAL		224,607	581,730	1,325,291

Demography

Population (1992): 1,359,000.
Density (1992): persons per sq mi 6.1, persons per sq km 2.3.
Urban-rural (1991): urban 24.1%; rural 75.9%.
Sex distribution (1987): male 47.70%; female 52.30%.
Age breakdown (1987): under 15, 48.2%; 15–29, 25.9%; 30–44, 13.4%; 45–59, 7.3%; 60–74, 3.9%; 75 and over, 1.3%.
Population projection: (2000) 1,782,000; (2010) 2,500,000.
Doubling time: 20 years.
Ethnic composition (1983): Tswana 75.5%; Shona 12.4%; San (Bushman) 3.4%; Khoikhoin (Hottentot) 2.5%; Ndebele 1.3%; other 4.9%.
Religious affiliation (1980): traditional beliefs 49.2%; Protestant 29.0%; African Christian 11.8%; Roman Catholic 9.4%; other 0.6%.
Major cities (1991): Gaborone 133,791; Francistown 65,026; Selebi-Pikwe 39,769; Molepolole 36,928; Kanye 31,341.

Vital statistics

Birth rate per 1,000 population (1990–95): 43.9 (world avg. 26.4); (1986) legitimate 28.8%; illegitimate 71.2%.
Death rate per 1,000 population (1990–95): 9.5 (world avg. 9.2).
Natural increase rate per 1,000 population (1990–95): 34.4 (world avg. 17.2).
Total fertility rate (avg. births per childbearing woman; 1989): 5.0.
Marriage rate per 1,000 population (1986): 0.3%.
Life expectancy at birth (1989): male 52.7 years; female 59.3 years.
Major causes of death (as percentage of total registered deaths; 1986): diseases of the circulatory system 17.3%; infectious and parasitic diseases 16.6%; malignant neoplasms (cancers) 13.4%; diseases of the respiratory system 12.2%; endocrine, nutritional, and metabolic diseases 6.1%.

National economy

Budget (1992–93). Revenue: P 4,160,600,000 (mineral royalties 44.7%, customs and excise taxes 24.4%, nontax revenue 19.2%, other [nonmineral] income taxes 8.9%). Expenditures: P 4,051,400,000 (recurrent expenditure 51.1%, development expenditure 34.9%, net lending 13.0%).
Population economically active (1984–85): total 367,949; activity rate of total population 37.0% (participation rates: ages 15–64, 72.7%; female 54.6%; unemployed [1986] 19.2%).

Price and earnings indexes (1985 = 100)							
	1985	1986	1987	1988	1989	1990	1991
Consumer price index	100.0	110.0	120.8	130.9	146.0	162.7	181.8
Earnings index[7]	100.0	114.3	125.0	133.9	148.2	164.3	...

Production (metric tons except as noted). Agriculture, forestry, fishing (1991): cereals 45,000 (of which sorghum 38,000, corn [maize] 4,000, millet 1,000), vegetables and melons 16,000, pulses 14,000, fruits 11,000, roots and tubers 7,000, seed cotton 3,000, cotton seed 2,000, peanuts (groundnuts) 1,000; livestock (number of live animals) 2,844,000 cattle, 2,301,000 goats, 349,000 sheep, 151,000[8] mules and asses, 25,000[8] horses; roundwood (1990) 1,389,000 cu m; fish catch (1990) 1,900. Mining and quarrying (1991): diamonds 16,506,000 carats; copper 20,576; nickel 19,294; cobalt 212. Manufacturing

(value added in P '000,000; 1986–87): food products 161.9; textiles 46.0; chemicals 20.8; wood products 10.3; paper and paper products 5.5. Construction (1985): residential 70,200 sq m; nonresidential 80,700 sq m. Energy production (consumption): electricity (kW-hr; 1991) 929,000,000 (929,000,000); coal (metric tons; 1991) 850,000 (n.a.); crude petroleum, none (n.a.).
Public debt (external, outstanding; 1991): U.S.$393,700,000.
Tourism (1990): receipts U.S.$65,000,000; expenditures U.S.$39,000,000.
Gross national product (1990): U.S.$2,561,000,000 (U.S.$2,040 per capita).

Structure of gross domestic product and labour force				
	1990–91		1989	
	in value P '000,000	% of total value	labour force[9]	% of labour force
Agriculture	361.3	5.2	6,500	3.3
Mining	2,873.0	41.6	7,800[10]	3.9
Manufacturing	276.9	4.0	23,300	11.7
Construction	393.4	5.7	29,300	14.8
Public utilities	160.9	2.3	2,100	1.1
Transp. and commun.	175.6	2.5	8,100	4.1
Trade	983.0	14.2	35,700	18.0
Finance and business services	354.8	5.1	13,200	6.6
Pub. admin., defense	1,284.2	18.6		
Services	166.0	2.4	72,500	36.5
Other	−117.5	−1.7		
TOTAL	6,911.6	100.0[11]	198,500	100.0

Household income and expenditure (1985–86). Average household size 5.0; average annual income per household P 3,910 (U.S.$2,080); sources of income: wages and salaries 59.9%, transfers 30.8%, self-employment 9.3%; expenditure: food, beverages, and tobacco 39.4%, household durable goods 14.0%, rent and services 13.3%, transportation 13.1%, clothing 5.6%, health 2.3%.
Land use (1990): forested 19.3%; meadows and pastures 58.2%; agricultural and under permanent cultivation 2.4%; other 20.1%.

Foreign trade[12]

Balance of trade (current prices)						
	1986	1987	1988	1989	1990	1991
P '000,000	+458.9	+1,322.1	+813.1	+1,278.4	+493.1	+362.5
% of total	16.7%	32.8%	17.8%	21.1%	8.0%	5.1%

Imports (1991): P 3,490,000,000 (1990; transport equipment 19.2%; machinery and electrical goods 18.5%; food, beverages, and tobacco 14.1%; chemical and rubber products 8.5%; metal and metal products 8.4%; textiles and footwear 8.4%; mineral fuels 6.4%; wood and paper 4.3%). Major import sources (1988): Customs Union of Southern Africa 77.4%; European countries 10.2%, of which U.K. 6.1%; U.S. 2.3%.
Exports (1991): P 3,673,000,000 (diamonds 80.1%; copper-nickel matte 6.8%; beef products 4.0%). Major export destinations (1988): European countries 85.9%, of which U.K. 1.1%; African countries 13.5%; U.S. 0.3%.

Transport and communications

Transport. Railroads (1991): length 551 mi, 887 km; passenger-km 257,000,000[13]; metric ton-km cargo 964,000[14]. Roads (1989): total length 9,300 mi, 15,000 km (paved 13%). Vehicles (1989): passenger cars 17,000; trucks and buses 28,000. Merchant marine: none. Air transport (1991)[15]: passenger-km 71,818,000; metric ton-km cargo 642,000; airports (1992) 8.
Communications. Daily newspapers (1990): total number 1; total circulation 35,000; circulation per 1,000 population 2.4. Radio (1991): total receivers 1,100,000 (1 per 1.2 persons). Television (1987): total receivers 8,000 (1 per 145 persons). Telephones (1990): 47,917 (1 per 26 persons).

Education and health

Education (1991)	schools	teachers	students	student/ teacher ratio
Primary (age 6–13)	654	9,708	308,840	31.8
Secondary (age 14–18)	169	3,743	68,137	18.2
Voc., teacher tr.	40	759	7,057	9.3
Higher	1	370	3,352	9.1

Educational attainment (1981). Percentage of population age 25 and over having: no formal schooling 54.7%; some primary education 31.0%; complete primary 9.4%; some secondary 3.1%; complete secondary 1.3%; postsecondary 0.5%. Literacy (1990): total population over age 15 literate 486,500 (73.6%); males literate (83.7%); females literate (65.1%).
Health: physicians (1986) 156 (1 per 7,185 persons); hospital beds (1984) 2,367 (1 per 440 persons); infant mortality rate (1985–90) 67.0.
Food (1988–90): daily per capita caloric intake 2,260 (vegetable products 86%, animal products 14%); 97% of FAO recommended minimum requirement.

Military

Total active duty personnel (1992): 6,100 (army 98.4%, navy, none [landlocked], air force 1.6%). Military expenditure as percentage of GNP (1989): 2.8% (world 4.9%); per capita expenditure U.S.$52.

[1]In addition, the House of Chiefs, a 15-member body consisting of chiefs, subchiefs, and associated members, serves in an advisory capacity to the government. [2]Including four specially elected members and two nonelective seats. [3]Tswana is the national language. [4]Preliminary. [5]Areas for Central district and South East district include the area for Serowe/Palapye. [6]Areas are included with respective district totals; population figures are not included with district totals. [7]Excludes government sector. [8]1989. [9]Formal sector only. [10]13,516 Tswana were employed in South African mines in 1990. [11]Detail does not add to total given because of rounding. [12]Import figures are f.o.b. in balance of trade and c.i.f. in commodities and trading partners. [13]1986–87. [14]1989–90. [15]Air Botswana only.

Brazil

Official name: República Federativa
do Brasil (Federative Republic
of Brazil).
Form of government: multiparty
federal republic with 2 legislative
houses (Senate [81]; Chamber of
Deputies [503]).
Chief of state and government:
President.
Capital: Brasília.
Official language: Portuguese.
Official religion: none.
Monetary unit: 1 cruzeiro[1] (Cr$) = 100
centavos; valuation (Oct. 5, 1992)
1 U.S.$ = Cr$6,558;
1 £ = Cr$11,149.

Area and population

States	Capitals	area sq mi	area sq km	population 1991 census[2]
Acre	Rio Branco	59,343	153,698	417,437
Alagoas	Maceió	11,238	29,107	2,512,515
Amapá[3]	Macapá	54,965	142,359	289,050
Amazonas	Manaus	605,390	1,567,954	2,088,682
Bahia	Salvador	218,912	566,979	11,801,810
Ceará	Fortaleza	56,253	145,694	6,353,346
Espírito Santo	Vitória	17,658	45,733	2,598,231
Goiás[4]	Goiânia	131,339	340,166	4,024,547
Maranhão	São Luís	127,242	329,556	4,922,339
Mato Grosso	Cuiabá	348,040	901,421	2,020,581
Mato Grosso do Sul	Campo Grande	138,021	357,472	1,778,494
Minas Gerais	Belo Horizonte	226,497	586,624	15,746,200
Pará	Belém	481,405	1,246,833	5,084,726
Paraíba	João Pessoa	20,833	53,958	3,200,620
Paraná	Curitiba	76,959	199,324	8,415,659
Pernambuco	Recife	39,005	101,023	7,109,626
Piauí	Teresina	97,017	251,273	2,581,054
Rio de Janeiro	Rio de Janeiro	16,855	43,653	12,584,108
Rio Grande do Norte	Natal	20,528	53,167	2,413,618
Rio Grande do Sul	Pôrto Alegre	108,369	280,674	9,127,611
Rondônia	Pôrto Velho	92,039	238,379	1,130,400
Roraima[3]	Boa Vista	86,880	225,017	215,790
Santa Catarina	Florianópolis	36,803	95,318	4,536,433
São Paulo	São Paulo	95,852	248,256	31,192,918
Sergipe	Aracaju	8,441	21,863	1,492,400
Tocantins[4]	Palmas	107,075	277,322	920,133
Federal District				
Distrito Federal	Brasília	2,237	5,794	1,596,174
Disputed areas[5]		1,306	3,382	
TOTAL		3,286,500[6,7]	8,511,996[6,7]	146,154,502

Demography

Population (1992): 151,381,000.
Density (1992): persons per sq mi 46.1, persons per sq km 17.8.
Urban-rural (1990): urban 74.9%; rural 25.1%.
Sex distribution (1990): male 49.87%; female 50.13%.
Age breakdown (1990): under 15, 35.2%; 15–29, 28.0%; 30–44, 19.3%; 45–59, 10.4%; 60–74, 5.5%; 75 and over, 1.5%.
Population projection: (2000) 173,850,000; (2010) 200,067,000.
Doubling time: 38 years.
Ethnic composition (1980): Brazilian white 53.0%, of which Portuguese 15.0%, Italian 11.0%, Spanish 10.0%, German 3.0%; mulatto 22.0%; mestizo 12.0%; black 11.0%; Japanese 0.8%; Amerindian 0.1%; other 1.1%.
Religious affiliation (1980): Roman Catholic 87.8%, of which Spiritist Catholic 15.7%[8], Evangelical Catholic 9.0%[9]; Protestant (mostly Assemblies of God, other Pentecostal, and Baptist) 6.1%; Afro-American Spiritist 2.0%[10]; Spiritist 1.7%[11]; nonreligious 1.0%; atheist 0.4%; Buddhist 0.3%; Jewish 0.2%; other 0.5%.
Major cities (municipio [metropolitan area]; 1991)[12]: São Paulo 9,480,427 (15,-199,423); Rio de Janeiro 5,336,179 (9,600,524); Salvador 2,056,013 (2,472,-131); Belo Horizonte 2,048,861 (3,461,905); Fortaleza 1,758,334 (2,294,524); Brasília 1,596,274; Recife 1,290,149 (2,859,469); Curitiba 1,290,142 (1,975,-624); Nova Iguaçu[13] 1,286,337 (3,015,960); Pôrto Alegre 1,262,631 (3,015,960); Belém 1,246,435 (1,334,460).

Other principal *municipios* (1991)

	population		population		population
Campinas	846,084	Maceió	628,209	São Bernardo	
Campo Grande	525,612	Manaus	1,010,558	do Campo[15]	565,171
Contagem[14]	448,822	Natal	606,541	São Gonçalo[13]	747,891
Duque de Caxias[13]	664,643	Niterói[13]	416,123	São João de	
Goiânia	920,838	Osasco[15]	563,419	Meriti[13]	425,038
Guarulhos[15]	781,499	Ribeirão		São José dos	
Jaboatão dos		Prêto	430,805	Campos	442,728
Guararapes[16]	482,434	Santo André[15]	613,672	São Luís	695,780
João Pessoa	497,214	Santos	428,526	Teresina	598,449

Place of birth/national origin (1980): 99.07% native-born; 0.93% foreign-born, of which Portugal 0.33%, Japan 0.12%, Italy 0.09%, Spain 0.08%.
Mobility (1980). Population living in same residence: less than 1 year 19.3%, 1–3 years 19.5%, 3–6 years 22.1%.
Families (1989). Average family size 3.9; 1–2 persons 25.8%, 3 persons 20.8%, 4 persons 21.3%, 5–6 persons 22.5%, 7 or more persons 9.6%.
Immigration (1982–84): permanent immigrants admitted 7,673, from Portugal 28.4%, Uruguay 8.7%, Argentina 8.2%.

Vital statistics

Birth rate per 1,000 population (1990–95): 26.1 (world avg. 26.4).
Death rate per 1,000 population (1990–95): 7.5 (world avg. 9.2).
Natural increase rate per 1,000 population (1990–95): 18.6 (world avg. 17.2).
Total fertility rate (avg. births per childbearing woman; 1991): 3.1.
Marriage rate per 1,000 population (1988): 6.7.
Divorce rate per 1,000 population (1988): 0.6.
Life expectancy at birth (1990–95): male 63.5 years; female 69.1 years.
Major causes of death per 100,000 population (1986[17]): diseases of the circulatory system 156.2, of which cerebrovascular disease 53.3, acute myocardial infarction 33.3; malignant neoplasms (cancers) 52.4; diseases of the respiratory system 48.3, of which pneumonia 25.5; accidents 39.9; infectious and parasitic diseases 37.2; homicide and other violence 29.3; diseases of the digestive system 22.0; endocrine and metabolic diseases 13.0; diseases of the nervous system 6.7.

Social indicators

Educational attainment (1989). Percentage of population age 10 and over having: no formal schooling or less than one year of primary education 18.7%; incomplete primary 56.9%; complete primary 6.9%; incomplete secondary 11.9%; complete secondary or higher 5.5%; unknown 0.1%.

Distribution of income (1988)[18]

percentage of national income by decile

1	2	3	4	5	6	7	8	9	10 (highest)
0.7	1.7	2.2	3.4	3.9	5.0	6.8	9.9	15.9	50.5

Quality of working life. Average workweek (1986): 79.9% of the labour force works 40 or more hours per week. Annual estimated rate per 100,000 insured urban workers (1987) for: injury or accident 4,030; industrial illness, n.a.; death 22. Proportion of labour force participating in national social insurance system (1988): 48.1%. Proportion of employed population receiving minimum wage (1987): 52.0%.
Access to services (1986). Proportion of households having access to: electricity (1989) 86.9%, of which urban households having access 97.2%, rural households having access 53.2%; safe public (piped) water supply 69.9%, of which urban households having access 88.7%, rural households having access 11.6%; public sewage collection 58.5%, of which urban households having access 75.2%, rural households having access 6.5%; public fire protection, n.a.
Social participation. Eligible voters participating in last (October 1990) national election: *c.* 64%; although voting is mandatory, about 15% of the electorate did not vote and about 25% of those who did spoiled their ballots or cast blank votes. Trade union membership in total work force (1980): 10–15%. Practicing religious population in total affiliated population: most men, and in particular Portuguese-Brazilian men, attend Mass only on special occasions. They believe religion is the domain and duty of women.
Social deviance. The incidence of crime is not accurately reported. Crimes resulting in imprisonment (1989): 150,460, of which murder 7.0%; assault 10.8%; theft, burglary, and housebreaking 26.5%; robbery and extortion 11.5%; narcotics trafficking 6.1%; narcotics usage 5.6%. Suicide (1988): 4,700.
Leisure. Favourite leisure activities include: playing soccer, rehearsing all year in neighbourhood samba groups for celebrations of Carnival, and competing in water sports, volleyball, and basketball.
Material well-being (1989). Households possessing: radio receiver 83.4% (urban 85.9%, rural 75.0%); television receiver 72.6% (urban 83.3%, rural 37.6%); refrigerator 63.1%[19] (urban 75.4%, rural 25.1%); automobile, n.a.; telephone, n.a.

National economy

Gross national product (at current market prices; 1990): U.S.$402,788,000,000 (U.S.$2,680 per capita).

Structure of gross domestic product and labour force

	1990 in value U.S.$'000,000[20]	1990 % of total value	1989 labour force[18, 21]	1989 % of labour force
Agriculture	30,075	9.2	14,034,900	22.5
Mining	6,225	1.9 }	9,653,000	15.4
Manufacturing	87,915	27.0 }		
Construction	22,953	7.0	3,786,900	6.1
Public utilities	8,893	2.7	929,300	1.5
Transportation and communications	18,559	5.7	2,273,700	3.6
Trade	23,630	7.2	7,436,000	11.9
Finance, real estate	80,954	24.8	1,936,500	3.1
Pub. admin., defense	27,677	8.5 }	18,822,700[22]	30.1[22]
Services	−11,755	−3.6 }		
Other	31,070[23]	9.5[23]	3,640,200[24]	5.8[24]
TOTAL	326,195[6]	100.0[6]	62,513,200	100.0

Budget (1991). Revenue: Cr$52,810,000,000,000 (current receipts 62.5%, of which social contributions 31.7% [including social security 17.0%], taxes 23.7% [including income taxes 11.9%]; development receipts 37.5%). Expenditures: Cr$52,810,000,000,000 (current expenditures 55.6%, of which transfers to parastatal[25] organizations 19.2%; development expenditures 44.4%, of which amortization of domestic debt 24.7%).
Public debt (external, outstanding; 1990): U.S.$85,600,000,000.
Production ('000 metric tons except as noted; 1991). Agriculture, forestry, fishing: sugarcane 262,057, cassava 24,878, corn (maize) 23,638, soybeans 14,768, oranges 17,488[28], rice 9,503, bananas 5,488[28], wheat 3,420, coffee 2,998, dry beans 2,880, tomatoes 2,311, potatoes 2,117, seed cotton 1,851, papayas 1,650[28], grapes 786[28], tangerines and clementines 640[28], lemons and limes 490[28], tobacco leaves 422[28], cocoa 348[28], cashews 169[28], palm oil 69[28];

livestock (number of live animals; 1990) 140,000,000 cattle, 33,200,000 pigs, 21,000,000 sheep, 6,100,000 horses; roundwood (1990) 259,243,000 cu m; fish catch (1989) 850, of which freshwater fishes 210. Mining and quarrying (1991): iron ore 150,000; bauxite 10,310; manganese 1,967; kaolin (clay) 840; zinc (metal content) 134; copper (metal content) 37; tin (metal content) 29; gold 2,833,000 troy oz; diamonds 550,000 carats[29]. Manufacturing (value added in U.S.$'000,000; 1988): food products 11,007; nonelectrical machinery 10,195; electrical machinery 8,823; iron and steel 8,126; textiles 7,443; transport equipment 7,257; pharmaceuticals, cosmetics, and soaps 7,158; industrial chemicals 7,078; refined petroleum 6,910; fabricated metal products 4,631; nonmetallic mineral products 3,872; paper and paper products 3,617; wearing apparel (excluding footwear) 3,160; plastics 3,049. Construction (new buildings authorized[30]; 1987): residential 20,090,000 sq m; nonresidential 8,180,000 sq m.

Manufacturing enterprises (1985)

	no. of enterprises	number of labourers	wages of labourers as a % of avg. of all mfg. wages	value added in producer's prices (in U.S.$'000,000)
Chemical products (incl. refined petroleum, excl. pharmaceuticals)	5,066	287,742	191.7	11,668
Fabricated metals, iron and steel, and nonferrous metals	18,964	565,036	117.1	8,229
Food products	43,034	733,199	68.4	8,149
Nonelectrical machinery	11,088	552,163	146.5	6,337
Electrical machinery	4,573	315,767	138.5	5,392
Transport equipment	4,184	341,621	154.8	4,313
Textiles	5,570	351,360	75.1	4,185
Clothing and footwear	23,200	655,234	49.6	3,466
Nonmetallic mineral products	28,974	365,643	65.7	2,866
Paper and paper products	2,107	132,948	120.7	1,977
Plastics	2,975	146,151	85.1	1,505
Rubber products	1,421	71,656	136.3	1,248
Publishing and printing	9,053	164,523	100.1	1,208
Pharmaceuticals	930	49,048	173.7	1,110
Wood and wood products (excl. furniture)	17,129	218,059	48.4	1,091
Furniture	13,759	186,467	...	965
Beverages	2,798	77,167	...	835

Population economically active (1988)[18, 21]: total 61,047,954; activity rate of total population 43.2% (participation rates: over age 15, 63.6%; female 35.1%; unemployed [late 1991] 10.5%).

Price and earnings indexes (1985 = 100)

	1987	1988	1989	1990	1991	1992[26]
Consumer price index	808	6,325	87,722	2,665,000	14,412,000	108,952,000
Monthly earnings index[27]	617	4,767	71,588	1,499,000	...	...

Tourism (1990): receipts from visitors U.S.$1,444,000,000; expenditures by nationals abroad U.S.$1,559,000,000.

Retail trade enterprises (1985)

	no. of enterprises	total no. of employees	annual wage as a % of all trade wages	annual value of sales in U.S.$'000,000
General merchandise stores (including food products)	16,690	370,813	83.4	11,566
Vehicles, new and used; parts	38,900	268,989	123.9	10,473
Gas stations	21,751	169,831	100.0	8,831
Food, beverages, and tobacco	275,593	682,211	64.1	7,581
Clothing, footwear, and apparel	129,228	564,120	77.5	6,861
Hardware, appliances, and construction materials	48,166	268,817	90.4	5,548
Domestic goods, equipment, kitchenware, and antiques	28,830	194,214	102.5	4,119
Pharmaceutical and cosmetic products	43,929	185,901	82.5	3,115
Agricultural and industrial equipment and machinery	9,451	73,809	141.2	2,799
Books, magazines, newspapers	13,636	56,167	82.3	661

Household income and expenditure. Average household size (1985) 4.3; income per household of families having income (1986[18, 32]) 21,802 cruzados (U.S.$2,922); sources of income: n.a.; expenditure: n.a.

Financial aggregates[33]

	1987	1988	1989	1990	1991	1992[34]
Exchange rate, cruzeiros per:						
U.S. dollar	0.07	0.77	11.1	177.1	1,069	2,849
£	0.13	1.39	18.2	341.4	1,999	5,187
SDR	0.10	1.03	15.0	251.9	1,529	3,978
International reserves (U.S.$)						
Total (excl. gold; '000,000)	6,299	6,972	7,535	7,441	8,033	18,963
SDRs ('000,000)	—	—	—	11	13	16
Reserve pos. in IMF ('000,000)	—	—	—	—	—	—
Foreign exchange ('000,000)	6,299	6,971	7,535	7,430	8,020	18,947
Gold ('000,000 fine troy oz)	2.43	2.73	2.98	4.57	2.02	2.83
% world reserves	0.26	0.29	0.32	0.49	0.21	0.30
Interest and prices						
Central bank discount (%)	401	2,282	38,341	1,088	2,494	1,099
Govt. bond yield (%)	...	...	...	...	...	...
Industrial share prices	...	...	...	...	...	...
Balance of payments (U.S.$'000,000)						
Balance of visible trade	+11,173	+19,184	+16,120	+10,753	+10,596	...
Imports, f.o.b.	15,052	14,605	18,263	20,661	21,054	...
Exports, f.o.b.	26,225	33,789	34,383	31,414	31,650	...
Balance of invisibles	−12,678	−15,009	−15,087	...	...	...
Balance of payments, current account	−1,450	+4,159	+1,025	...	...	...

Energy production (consumption): electricity (kW-hr; 1991) 248,636,000,000 (246,999,000,000[28]); coal (metric tons; 1990) 4,595,000 (15,436,000); crude petroleum (barrels; 1991) 236,056,000 (430,410,000[28]); petroleum products (metric tons; 1990) 49,778,000 (48,204,000); natural gas (cu m; 1990) 3,596,-000,000 (3,484,000,000); carburant alcohol (hectolitres; 1989–90) 119,617,000 (110,000,000[31]).

Land use (1989): forested 65.4%; meadows and pastures 20.1%; agricultural and under permanent cultivation 9.3%; other 5.2%.

Foreign trade[35]

Balance of trade (current prices)

	1986	1987	1988	1989	1990	1991
U.S.$'000,000	+8,305	+11,173	+19,184	+16,120	+11,052	+10,622
% of total	22.8%	27.1%	39.6%	30.6%	21.3%	20.2%

Imports (1990): U.S.$20,362,000,000 (raw materials 31.1%, capital goods 29.1%, fuels and lubricants 26.0%, consumer goods 13.8%). *Major import sources:* United States 21.1%; Germany 8.6%; Saudi Arabia 6.8%; Argentina 6.7%; Japan 6.0%; Iraq 5.0%; Iran 4.5%; Italy 3.1%; France 2.7%; Uruguay 2.6%; Switzerland 2.3%; Chile 2.3%.

Exports (1990): U.S.$31,414,000,000 (soya products 9.1%, boiler equipment 7.9%, iron ore 7.7%, transport equipment 6.8%, iron and steel fabricated products 5.2%, orange juice 4.7%, coffee beans 4.0%, paper and cellulose 3.9%, footwear 3.8%, electrical and electronic equipment 3.2%, crude aluminum 2.8%, tobacco leaves 1.8%). *Major export destinations:* United States 24.5%; The Netherlands 7.9%; Japan 7.5%; Germany 5.7%; Italy 5.1%; Belgium-Luxembourg 3.1%; United Kingdom 3.0%; France 2.9%; Spain 2.2%; Argentina 2.0%; South Korea 1.7%.

Transport and communications

Transport. Railroads (1990): route length 18,721 mi, 30,129 km; passenger-mi 8,431,000,000, passenger-km 13,569,000,000; short ton-mi cargo 82,267,-000,000, metric ton-km cargo 120,108,000,000. Roads (1990): total length 1,037,780 mi, 1,670,148 km (paved 10%). Vehicles (1988): passenger cars 14,995,837; trucks and buses 1,609,764. Merchant marine (1991): vessels (100 gross tons and over) 669; total deadweight tonnage 9,855,446. Air transport (1991)[36]: passenger-mi 17,294,000,000, passenger-km 27,832,000,000; short ton-mi cargo 1,729,000,000, metric ton-km cargo 2,525,000,000; airports (1992) with scheduled flights 100.

Communications. Daily newspapers (1990): total number 208; total circulation 7,892,712[37]; circulation per 1,000 population 54[37]. Radio (1991): total number of receivers 60,000,000 (1 per 2.6 persons). Television (1991): total number of receivers 30,000,000 (1 per 5.1 persons). Telephones (1990): 14,125,396 (1 per 10 persons).

Education and health

Education (1990)

	schools	teachers	students	student/teacher ratio
Primary (age 7–14)	208,934	1,260,501	28,943,619	23.0
Secondary (age 15–18)	10,160	243,246	3,498,777	14.4
Higher	918	145,585	1,540,080	10.6

Literacy (1989)[38]: total population age 15 and over literate 76,052,856 (81.2%); males literate 37,022,807 (81.8%); females literate 39,030,049 (80.6%).
Health (1987): physicians 206,382 (1 per 685 persons); hospital beds 496,140 (1 per 285 persons); infant mortality rate per 1,000 live births (1991) 68.0.
Food (1987–89): daily per capita caloric intake 2,722 (vegetable products 85%, animal products 15%); 114% of FAO recommended minimum requirement.

Military

Total active duty personnel (1991): 296,700 (army 66.1%, navy 16.8%, air force 17.1%). *Military expenditure as percentage of GNP* (1988): 1.3% (world 5.1%); per capita expenditure U.S.$40.

[1]The cruzeiro replaced the new cruzado at a rate of one to one on March 16, 1990. The new cruzado (NCz$) had replaced the old cruzado at a rate of 1,000 old to 1 new on Jan. 15, 1989. [2]Preliminary figures. [3]Amapá and Roraima territories were raised to the status of states on Jan. 1, 1990. [4]Tocantins state was created from northern Goiás on Oct. 5, 1988. [5]Area in dispute between Ceará and Piauí. [6]Detail does not add to total given because of rounding. [7]Land area excluding inland water is 3,265,076 sq mi (8,456,508 sq km). [8]Spiritist Catholics actively and regularly practice medium religions; about 60,000,000 Roman Catholics defer to spiritist dogma and participate in organized spiritism occasionally. [9]Evangelical Catholics are officially regarded as Roman Catholic but are affiliated to Protestant churches. [10]Non-Christian followers of Afro-Brazilian syncretistic religions ("low spiritism"). [11]Non-Christian followers of Kardecism ("high spiritism"). [12]First population cited refers to the *municipio*, an officially delimited area including a central city and adjacent urban and rural districts; second (parenthetical) figure refers to the metropolitan area, defined as the adjoining predominantly urban *municipios* that are economically dependent on the central city. [13]*Municipio* within Rio de Janeiro metropolitan area. [14]*Municipio* within Belo Horizonte metropolitan area. [15]*Municipio* within São Paulo metropolitan area. [16]*Municipio* within Recife metropolitan area. [17]Estimates based on about 75 percent of total deaths. [18]Excludes rural economically active population of Acre, Amapá, Amazonas, Pará, Rondônia, Roraima, and Tocantins states. [19]1985. [20]At constant prices of 1988. [21]Excludes persons not employed regularly on a weekly basis. [22]Includes restaurants and hotels. [23]Indirect taxes less subsidies. [24]Includes 1,749,000 (2.8%) activities not adequately defined and 1,891,200 (3.0%) unemployed. [25]Formally, a nongovernmental organization created by the state. [26]June. [27]Minimum wage. [28]1990. [29]1989. [30]Urban construction only for 74 cities. [31]Estimated amount used as automobile fuel. [32]Prices of September 1985. [33]End-of-period figures. [34]May. [35]Import figures are f.o.b. in balance of trade and commodities and c.i.f. in trading partners. [36]Transbrasil, VARIG, Cruzeiro do Sul, and VASP airlines only. [37]185 newspapers only. [38]By official estimate; functional literacy, however, may be as low as 42.0% of total population over age 15.

Brunei

Official name: Negara Brunei
 Darussalam (State of Brunei, Abode
 of Peace).
Form of government: monarchy
 (sultanate)[1].
Head of state and government: Sultan.
Capital: Bandar Seri Begawan.
Official language: Malay[2].
Official religion: Islam.
Monetary unit: 1 Brunei dollar
 (B$) = 100 cents; valuation (Oct. 5,
 1992) 1 U.S.$ = B$1.60;
 1 £ = B$2.71.

Area and population

Districts	Capitals	area sq mi	area sq km	population 1991 census
Belait	Kuala Belait	1,052	2,724	53,087
Brunei and Muara	Bandar Seri Begawan	220	571	170,357
Temburong	Bangar	504	1,304	7,695
Tutong	Tutong	450	1,166	29,724
TOTAL		2,226	5,765	260,863

Demography

Population (1992): 268,000.
Density (1992): persons per sq mi 120.4, persons per sq km 46.5.
Urban-rural (1982): urban 63.6%; rural 36.4%.
Sex distribution (1989): male 51.65%; female 48.35%.
Age breakdown (1989): under 15, 36.1%; 15–29, 31.3%; 30–44, 20.6%; 45–59,
 7.9%; 60–69, 2.5%; 70 and over, 1.6%.
Population projection: (2000) 334,000; (2010) 432,000.
Doubling time: 27 years.
Ethnic composition (1987): Malay 68.7%; Chinese 18.1%; other indigenous
 5.2%; Indian and other 8.0%.
Religious affiliation (1986): Muslim 66.5%; Buddhist 11.8%; Christian 8.9%;
 other religions 3.7%; nonreligious 9.1%.
Major cities (1981): Bandar Seri Begawan 52,300[3]; Seria 23,511; Kuala Belait
 19,281; Tutong 6,161.

Vital statistics

Birth rate per 1,000 population (1991): 29.0 (world avg. 26.4); (1982) legiti-
 mate 99.6%; illegitimate 0.4%.
Death rate per 1,000 population (1991): 3.0 (world avg. 9.2).
Natural increase rate per 1,000 population (1991): 26.0 (world avg. 17.2).
Total fertility rate (avg. births per childbearing woman; 1991): 3.7.
Marriage rate per 1,000 population (1989): 7.2.
Divorce rate per 1,000 population (1987): 0.8.
Life expectancy at birth (1989): male 72.6 years; female 76.4 years.
Major causes of death per 100,000 population: cardiovascular disease
 32.7; malignant neoplasms (cancers) 27.0; cerebrovascular disease 19.4; con-
 ditions originating from perinatal period 15.9; pneumonia 12.4; bronchitis,
 emphysema, and asthma 11.0; motor vehicle accidents 11.0; tuberculosis 4.9;
 signs, symptoms, and other ill-defined conditions 99.4.

National economy

Budget (1988). Revenue: B$2,486,800,000 (indirect taxes 60.0%, government
 property 33.6%[4], commercial receipts 6.2%). Expenditures: B$2,721,400,000
 (current expenditure 71.5%, development expenditure 13.8%).
Public debt (external, outstanding): none.
Tourism (1990): receipts from visitors U.S.$35,000,000; expenditures by na-
 tionals abroad, n.a.
Production (metric tons except as noted). Agriculture, forestry, fishing (1991):
 coconuts 1,045,000[5], vegetables and melons 8,000, fruits (excluding melons)
 5,000, eggs 3,000, rice 1,000, cassava 1,000, pineapples 1,000; livestock (number of live animals) 14,000 pigs, 10,000 buffalo, 1,000 cattle, 2,000,000 chickens; roundwood (1990) 294,000 cu m; fish catch (1990) 2,307. Mining and
 quarrying (1991): other than petroleum and natural gas (see below), none
 except sand and gravel for construction. Manufacturing (1989): gasoline
 133,000; diesel oils 88,000; jet fuels 21,000; kerosene 12,000; naphtha 5,000.
 Construction (number of buildings completed; 1984): residential 195; nonresidential 5. Energy production (consumption): electricity (kW-hr; 1990)
 1,215,000,000 (1,215,000,000); coal, none (none); crude petroleum (barrels;
 1990) 55,050,000 (n.a.); petroleum products (metric tons; 1990) 693,000
 (530,000); natural gas (cu m; 1990) 10,464,000,000 (2,391,000,000).
Population economically active (1986): total 86,395; activity rate of total
 population 37.8% (participation rates: ages 15–64, 60.4%; female 30.7%;
 unemployed 6.1%).

Price and earnings indexes (1985 = 100)

	1983	1984	1985	1986	1987	1988	1989
Consumer price index	94.8	97.7	100.0	101.8	103.1	104.3	105.7
Monthly earnings index[6]	108.0	99.1	100.0	87.9	...	...	...

Household income and expenditure. Average household size (1986) 5.8; income per household: n.a.; sources of income: n.a.; expenditure (1977):
 food 45.1%, transportation and communications 17.2%, recreation, education, and cultural services 8.9%, household furnishings 8.3%, clothing and
 footwear 6.1%, rent and utilities 5.0%.

Gross national product (at current market prices; 1989): U.S.$3,302,000,000[7]
 (U.S.$13,290 per capita).

Structure of gross domestic product and labour force

	1988 in value B$'000,000	1988 % of total value	1986 labour force	1986 % of labour force
Agriculture	135.2	2.2	3,059	3.5
Mining	2,179.9	36.1 }	6,006	7.0
Manufacturing	561.4	9.3 }		
Construction	154.5	2.6	9,424	10.9
Public utilities	81.1	1.3	2,042	2.4
Transportation and communications	293.1	4.9	6,883	8.0
Trade	746.8	12.4	8,022	9.3
Finance			4,330	5.0
Services }	1,993.5	33.0	38,557	44.6
Other	−111.0	−1.8	8,072[8]	9.3[8]
TOTAL	6,034.5	100.0	86,395	100.0

Land use (1991): forested 42.7%; meadows and pastures 1.1%; agricultural
 and under permanent cultivation 1.3%; other 54.9%.

Foreign trade

Balance of trade (current prices)

	1984	1985	1986	1987	1988	1989
B$'000,000	+5,482	+5,184	+2,540	+2,655	+2,012	+1,334
% of total	67.3%	65.8%	46.7%	49.6%	40.9%	22.0%

Imports (1989): B$1,722,800,000 (1986; machinery and transport equipment
 38.0%, manufactured goods 21.1%, food and live animals 14.4%, miscellaneous manufactured articles 10.6%, chemicals 7.0%, beverages and tobacco
 5.9%, crude materials 1.2%, mineral fuels 1.0%). Major import sources
 (1988): ASEAN 43.4%, of which Singapore 36.3%, Malaysia 4.9%; EEC
 40.3%; United States 6.8%; Japan 5.9%.
Exports (1989): B$3,693,500,000 (crude petroleum 46.9%, natural gas 44.6%,
 petroleum products 4.9%, other 3.6%). Major export destinations (1988):
 Japan 51.9%; South Korea 15.0%; ASEAN 14.5%, of which Thailand 7.7%,
 Singapore 5.1%; EEC 13.8%.

Transport and communications

Transport. Railroads[9] (1990): length 12 mi, 19 km. Roads (1989): total length
 1,366 mi, 2,199 km (paved 50%). Vehicles (1990): passenger cars 100,114;
 trucks and buses 11,973. Merchant marine (1991): vessels (100 gross tons
 and over) 48; total deadweight tonnage 348,016. Marine transport (1988):
 cargo loaded 14,500,000 metric tons, cargo unloaded 1,210,000 metric tons.
 Air transport (1990): passenger-mi 278,000,000, passenger-km 448,000,000;
 short ton-mi cargo 6,751,000, metric ton-km cargo 9,857,000; airports (1992)
 with scheduled flights 1.
Communications. Daily newspapers (1991): none. Radio (1991): total number
 of receivers 100,000 (1 per 2.6 persons). Television (1991): total number
 of receivers 100,000 (1 per 2.6 persons). Telephones (1989): 49,036 (1
 per 5.1 persons).

Education and health

Education (1989–90)

	schools	teachers	students	student/ teacher ratio
Primary (age 5–11)	162	2,912	49,611	17.0
Secondary (age 12–20)	19	1,713	19,761	11.5
Voc., teacher tr.	6	326	1,565	4.8
Higher	2	214	1,110	5.2

Educational attainment (1981). Percentage of population age 25 and over
 having: no formal schooling 32.1%; primary education 28.3%; secondary
 30.1%; postsecondary and higher 9.4%. Literacy (1986): total population age
 15 and over literate 121,281 (85.1%); males literate 67,714 (90.9%); females
 literate 53,567 (78.7%).
Health (1989): physicians 171 (1 per 1,469 persons); hospital beds 893 (1 per
 281 persons); infant mortality rate per 1,000 live births 9.0.
Food (1988–90): daily per capita caloric intake 2,854 (vegetable products 80%,
 animal products 20%); 128% of FAO recommended minimum requirement.

Military

Total active duty personnel (1992): 4,450[10] (army 80.9%, navy 12.4%, air force
 6.7%). Military expenditure as percentage of GNP (1983): 5.8% (world 6.1%);
 per capita expenditure U.S.$1,200.

[1]A nonelective 21-member body advises the sultan on legislative matters. [2]All official
documents that must be published by law in Malay are, however, also required to
be issued in an official English version as well. [3]1988 metropolitan area population
estimate. [4]In 1983 more than 98% of state revenue was derived from exports of
oil and gas. [5]1985. [6]Nonagricultural sectors only. [7]GDP data. [8]Mostly unemployed.
[9]Privately owned. [10]All services form part of the army.

Bulgaria

Official name: Republika Bŭlgaria (Republic of Bulgaria).
Form of government: unitary multiparty republic with one legislative body (Parliament [240]).
Chief of state: President.
Head of government: Chairman of the Council of Ministers (Premier).
Capital: Sofia.
Official language: Bulgarian.
Official religion: none.
Monetary unit: 1 lev (leva) = 100 stotinki; valuation (Oct. 5, 1992) 1 U.S.$ = 25.29 leva; 1 £ = 43.00 leva.

Area and population		area		population
				1992[1]
Regions	Capitals	sq mi	sq km	estimate
Burgas	Burgas	5,659	14,657	878,000
Khaskovo	Khaskovo	5,364	13,892	1,054,000
Lovech	Lovech	5,849	15,150	1,048,000
Mikhaylovgrad	Mikhaylovgrad	4,095	10,607	653,000
Plovdiv	Plovdiv	5,262	13,628	1,290,000
Ruse (Razgrad)	Ruse	4,186	10,842	837,000
Sofiya	Sofia (Sofiya)	7,328	18,978	1,004,000
Varna	Varna	4,606	11,929	991,000
City Commune				
Sofiya	Sofia (Sofiya)	506	1,311	1,220,000
TOTAL		42,855	110,994	8,975,000[2]

Demography

Population (1992): 8,985,000[2].
Density (1992): persons per sq mi 209.7, persons per sq km 81.0.
Urban-rural (1992): urban 68.2%; rural 31.8%.
Sex distribution (1992): male 49.23%; female 50.77%.
Age breakdown (1991): under 15, 20.2%; 15–29, 20.8%; 30–44, 21.4%; 45–59, 18.3%; 60–74, 14.4%; 75 and over, 4.8%.
Population projection: (2000) 9,007,000; (2010) 9,035,000.
Doubling time: not applicable; population is declining.
Ethnic composition (1989)[2]: Bulgarian 85.3%; Turkish 8.5%; Gypsy 2.6%; Macedonian 2.5%; Armenian 0.3%; Russian 0.2%; other 0.6%.
Religious affiliation (1982): atheist 64.5%; Eastern Orthodox 26.7%; Muslim 7.5%; Protestant 0.7%; Roman Catholic 0.5%; other 0.1%.
Major cities (1991[1]): Sofia 1,220,914; Plovdiv 379,083; Varna 320,636; Burgas 226,121; Ruse 209,762.

Vital statistics

Birth rate per 1,000 population (1991): 10.7 (world avg. 26.4); (1990) legitimate 88.0%; illegitimate 12.0%.
Death rate per 1,000 population (1991): 12.2 (world avg. 9.2).
Natural increase rate per 1,000 population (1991): −1.5 (world avg. 17.2).
Total fertility rate (avg. births per childbearing woman; 1991): 1.6.
Marriage rate per 1,000 population (1991): 5.6.
Divorce rate per 1,000 population (1989): 1.5.
Life expectancy at birth (1989–91): male 68.0 years; female 74.7 years.
Major causes of death per 100,000 population (1990): diseases of the circulatory system 743.3; malignant neoplasms (cancers) 168.4; diseases of the respiratory system 71.8; accidents, poisoning, and violence 61.9; diseases of the digestive system 36.6; endocrine and metabolic disorders 19.2.

National economy

Budget (1991). Revenue: 62,967,000,000 leva (1988; national economy 92.0%, other 8.0%). Expenditures: 70,476,500,000 leva (1988; economy 47.2%, education and health 18.8%, social security 17.1%, administration and other 16.9%).
Public debt (external, outstanding; 1990): U.S.$10,964,000,000.
Tourism (1989): receipts from visitors U.S.$362,000,000.
Production (metric tons except as noted). Agriculture, forestry, fishing (1991): wheat 4,503,000, corn (maize) 2,718,000, barley 1,495,000, sugar beets 868,000, grapes 741,000, tomatoes 623,000, potatoes 503,000, sunflower seeds 423,000, apples 161,000; livestock (number of live animals; 1992) 6,703,000 sheep, 3,141,000 pigs, 1,310,000 cattle; roundwood 3,984,000 cu m; fish catch (1990) 56,143. Mining and quarrying (contained metal; 1991): iron ore 182,000; manganese 6,900. Manufacturing (1991): cement 2,687,000; crude steel 1,615,000; pig iron 971,000; fertilizers 797,300; paper 159,900; cotton fabrics 124,400 sq m; beer 4,968,000 hectolitres; wine 1,915,000 hectolitres; wearing apparel 25,587,000 pieces; television sets 107,500 units; trucks 2,755 units. Construction (1991): residential 1,318,246 sq m. Energy production (consumption): electricity (kW-hr; 1991) 38,917,000,000 (45,700,000,000[3]); coal (metric tons; 1991) 28,451,000 (28,451,000); crude petroleum (barrels; 1990) 440,000 (60,100,000); petroleum products (metric tons; 1990) 6,177,000 (4,967,000); natural gas (cu m; 1990) 117,000,000 (9,135,000,000).
Household income and expenditure. Average household size (1982) 3.3; income per household (1988) 7,762 leva (U.S.$9,240); sources of income (1991): wages and salaries 45.4%, self-employment in agriculture 21.4%, transfer payments 16.7%; expenditure (1991): food 47.4%, clothing 8.6%, housing 7.3%, transportation 6.7%, recreation 6.0%, education and culture 3.2%, household durable goods 3.0%, health care 1.8%.
Gross national product (1991): U.S.$37,136,000,000[4] (U.S.$4,124 per capita).

Structure of gross domestic product and labour force				
	1991			
	in value '000,000 leva	% of total value	labour force[5]	% of labour force
Agriculture	17,876	12.9	659,530	19.0
Manufacturing, mining	69,208	50.0	1,216,852	35.1
Construction			248,249	7.2
Transp. and commun.			259,848	7.5
Trade			308,095	8.9
Public utilities, housing	51,316	37.1	80,331	2.3
Pub. admin., defense			670,768	19.4
Services			...	...
Other			22,772	0.7
TOTAL	138,400	100.0	3,466,445	100.0[6]

Population economically active (1985): total 4,686,140; activity rate of total population 52.4% (participation rates: ages 15–64, 75.7%; female 47.7%; unemployed [1992] 14.0%).

Price and earnings indexes (1985 = 100)						
	1985	1986	1987	1988	1989	1990	1991
Consumer price index	100.0	103.5	103.6	104.1	106.7	...	...
Monthly earnings index	100.0	105.2	109.7	118.0	128.0	168.7	426.2

Land use (1990): forested 35.0%; meadows and pastures 18.1%; agricultural and under permanent cultivation 37.6%; other 9.3%.

Foreign trade

Balance of trade (current prices)						
	1986	1987	1988	1989	1990	1991
'000,000 leva	−1,022.6	−265.3	+489.4	+877.1	+244.6	+12,235.9
% of total	3.6%	1.0%	1.7%	3.3%	1.2%	11.9%

Imports (1991): 45,132,400,000 leva (machinery and equipment 38.9%; fuels, mineral raw materials, and metals 15.8%; chemical products and rubber 5.1%; consumer goods 4.4%). *Major import sources:* U.S.S.R. 43.2%; Germany 7.0%; Austria 4.7%; Italy 4.2%; United Kingdom 3.6%.
Exports (1991): 57,368,300,000 leva (machinery and equipment 30.6%; consumer goods 22.3%; food and beverages 15.3%; chemicals and rubber 10.9%; fuels, minerals, and metals 10.5%). *Major export destinations:* U.S.S.R. 49.8%; Germany 4.8%; United States 3.4%; Italy 2.7%; Greece 2.2%; Libya 2.1%; Poland 2.1%.

Transport and communications

Transport. Railroads (1991): track length 4,106 mi, 6,607 km; passenger-mi 4,838,000,000, passenger-km 7,785,000,000; short ton-mi cargo 5,950,000,000, metric ton-km cargo 8,685,000,000. Roads (1991): length 22,943 mi, 36,922 km (paved 92%). Vehicles (1990): cars 1,300,000; trucks and buses 200,000. Merchant marine (1992): vessels (100 gross tons and over) 226; deadweight tonnage 1,962,345. Air transport (1990): passenger-mi 1,663,000,000, passenger-km 2,677,000,000; short ton-mi cargo 21,200,000, metric ton-km cargo 31,000,000; airports (1992) with scheduled flights 3.
Communications. Daily newspapers (1988): total number 17; total circulation 2,396,000; circulation per 1,000 population 267. Radio (1992): 1,856,900 receivers (1 per 4.8 persons). Television (1991): 2,300,000 receivers (1 per 3.9 persons). Telephones (1989): 2,515,100 (1 per 3.6 persons).

Education and health

Education (1991–92)				
	schools	teachers	students	student/ teacher ratio
Primary (age 6–14) Secondary (age 15–17)	3,439	72,719	1,068,206	14.7
Voc., teacher tr.	503	18,167	254,480	14.0
Higher	86	23,960	175,557	7.3

Educational attainment (1983). Percentage of employed population having: postsecondary vocational certificate 15.6%; 4-year college 7.5%. *Literacy* (1980): total population age 15 and over literate 95.5%.
Health (1991): physicians 26,757 (1 per 337 persons); hospital beds 87,764 (1 per 103 persons); infant mortality rate per 1,000 live births (1991) 16.7.
Food (1987–89): daily per capita caloric intake 3,683 (vegetable products 75%, animal products 25%); 147% of FAO recommended minimum requirement.

Military

Total active duty personnel (1992): 107,000 (army 70.1%, navy 9.3%, air force 20.6%). *Military expenditure as percentage of GNP* (1991): 7.0% (world 5.0%); per capita expenditure U.S.$199.

---

[1]January 1. [2]Excludes adjustment for immigration to Turkey of some 300,000 Bulgarian Turks in 1989 and subsequent return of about 50,000. [3]1990. [4]External estimates vary; GNP may be as low as U.S.$20 billion. [5]State sector only. [6]Detail does not add to total given because of rounding.

Burkina Faso

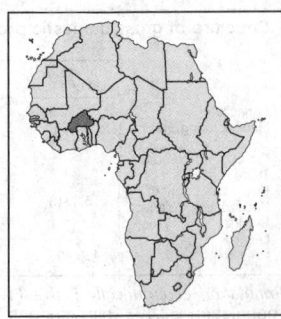

Official name: Burkina Faso
(Burkina Faso).
Form of government: multiparty
republic with one legislative house
(National Assembly [107][1]).
Chief of state: President.
Head of government: Prime Minister.
Capital: Ouagadougou.
Official language: French.
Official religion: none.
Monetary unit: 1 CFA franc
(CFAF) = 100 centimes; valuation
(Oct. 5, 1992) 1 U.S.$ = CFAF 238.75;
1 £ = CFAF 405.88.

Area and population		area		population
				1985
Provinces	Capitals	sq mi	sq km	census
Bam	Kongoussi	1,551	4,017	162,575
Bazéga	Kombissiri	2,051	5,313	303,941
Bougouriba	Diébougou	2,736	7,087	220,895
Boulgou	Tenkodogo	3,488	9,033	402,236
Boulkiemde	Koudougou	1,598	4,138	365,223
Comoé	Banfora	7,102	18,393	249,967
Ganzourgou	Zorgho	1,578	4,087	195,652
Gnagna	Bogandé	3,320	8,600	229,152
Gourma	Fada N'Gourma	10,275	26,613	294,235
Houet	Bobo-Dioulasso	6,438	16,672	581,722
Kadiogo	Ouagadougou	451	1,169	459,826
Kénédougou	Orodara	3,207	8,307	139,973
Kossi	Nouna	5,088	13,177	332,960
Kouritenga	Koupéla	628	1,627	198,486
Mouhoun	Dédougou	4,032	10,442	288,735
Nahouri	Pô	1,484	3,843	105,509
Namentenga	Boulsa	2,994	7,755	198,890
Oubritenga	Ziniaré	1,812	4,693	304,265
Oudalan	Gorom Gorom	3,879	10,046	106,194
Passoré	Yako	1,575	4,078	223,830
Poni	Gaoua	4,000	10,361	235,480
Sanguie	Réo	1,994	5,165	217,277
Sanmatenga	Kaya	3,557	9,213	367,724
Sèno	Dori	5,202	13,473	228,905
Sissili	Léo	5,303	13,736	244,919
Soum	Djibo	5,154	13,350	186,812
Sourou	Tougan	3,663	9,487	268,108
Tapoa	Diapaga	5,707	14,780	158,859
Yatenga	Ouahigouya	4,746	12,292	536,578
Zoundwéogo	Manga	1,333	3,453	155,777
TOTAL		105,946	274,400	7,964,705

Demography

Population (1992): 9,515,000.
Density (1992): persons per sq mi 89.8, persons per sq km 34.7.
Urban-rural (1988): urban 8.6%; rural 91.4%.
Sex distribution (1990): male 48.10%; female 51.90%.
Age breakdown (1990): under 15, 49.1%; 15–29, 23.6%; 30–44, 13.3%; 45–59, 8.3%; 60–74, 4.5%; 75 and over, 1.2%.
Population projection: (2000) 11,884,000; (2010) 15,549,000.
Doubling time: 23 years.
Ethnic composition (1983): Mossi 47.9%; Mande 8.8%; Fulani 8.3%; Lobi 6.9%; Bobo 6.8%; Senufo 5.3%; Grosi 5.1%; Gurma 4.8%; Tuareg 3.3%; other 2.8%.
Religious affiliation (1980): traditional beliefs 44.8%; Muslim 43.0%; Christian 12.2%, of which Roman Catholic 9.8%, Protestant 2.4%.
Major cities (1985): Ouagadougou 441,514; Bobo-Dioulasso 228,668; Koudougou 51,926; Ouahigouya 38,902; Banfora 35,319.

Vital statistics

Birth rate per 1,000 population (1990–95): 47.0 (world avg. 26.4).
Death rate per 1,000 population (1990–95): 17.1 (world avg. 9.2).
Natural increase rate per 1,000 population (1990–95): 29.9 (world avg. 17.2).
Total fertility rate (avg. births per childbearing woman; 1990–95): 6.5.
Life expectancy at birth (1990–95): male 47.6 years; female 50.9 years.
Major causes of morbidity (percentage of reported cases of infectious disease; 1984): measles 39.6%; malaria 12.4%; tetanus 5.7%; diarrheal diseases 5.3%.

National economy

Budget (1990). Revenue: CFAF 114,800,000,000 (1989; import duties 30.5%, value-added taxes 17.4%, personal income taxes 13.0%, excise taxes 10.8%, other 9.6%). *Expenditures:* CFAF 139,700,000,000 (1989; education 18.4%, defense 16.8%, debt service 8.7%, health 6.9%, social security 4.1%).
Production (metric tons except as noted). Agriculture, forestry, fishing (1991): sorghum 1,113,000, millet 757,000, sugarcane 350,000, corn (maize) 296,000, pulses 271,000, seed cotton 176,000, peanuts (groundnuts) 152,000, rice 50,000, cassava 30,000, sweet potatoes 24,000, sesame 8,000; livestock (number of live animals) 6,137,000 goats, 3,339,000 sheep, 2,900,000 cattle, 22,000,000 chickens; roundwood (1990) 875,000 cu m; fish catch (1990) 7,006. Mining and quarrying (1988): manganese 15,000; phosphates 3,000[2]; gold 3,049 kg[3]. Manufacturing (1988): flour 24,000; soap 11,200; cotton yarn 238[2]; bicycle and motorcycle tires 3,812,000 units; motorcycles and bicycles 66,000 units; footwear 470,000 pairs; beer 401,000 hectolitres; soft drinks 131,000 hectolitres. Construction (value added in CFAF; 1987): 2,800,000,000. Energy production (consumption): electricity (kW-hr; 1990) 155,000,000 (155,000,000); petroleum, none (n.a.); petroleum products (metric tons; 1990) none (175,000).

Gross national product (1990): U.S.$2,955,000,000 (U.S.$330 per capita).

Structure of gross domestic product and labour force				
	1987		1985	
	in value CFAF '000,000	% of total value	labour force	% of labour force
Agriculture	200,479	45.8	3,739,000	92.3
Mining	89	0.1		
Manufacturing	63,216	14.5	113,000	2.8
Construction	2,800	0.6		
Public utilities	6,645	1.5		
Transp. and commun.	19,349	4.4		
Finance	18,862	4.3		
Trade	53,801	12.3	199,000	4.9
Pub. admin., defense	65,226	14.9		
Services	...	...		
Other	6,865	1.6	...	...
TOTAL	437,332	100.0	4,051,000	100.0

Tourism: receipts (1990) U.S.$9,000,000; expenditures U.S.$35,000,000.
Public debt (external, outstanding; 1990): U.S.$935,000,000.
Population economically active: total (1985) 4,051,000; activity rate 51.0% (participation rates: over age 15, 83.0%; female 49.1%; unemployed 0.9%).

Price and earnings indexes (1985 = 100)						
	1986	1987	1988	1989	1990	1991
Consumer price index	97.4	94.8	98.6	98.8	97.8	102.5[4]
Hourly earnings index[5]	100.0	100.0	114.0	114.6	114.6	114.6

Household income and expenditure. Average household size (1985) 6.2; average annual income per household CFAF 303,000 (U.S.$640); sources of income: n.a.; expenditure (1985)[6]: food 38.7%; transportation 18.6%; electricity and fuel 13.7%; beverages 9.0%; health 5.2%; housing 5.1%.
Land use (1990): forested 24.3%; meadows and pastures 36.5%; agricultural and under permanent cultivation 13.0%; other 26.2%.

Foreign trade

Balance of trade (current prices)					
	1985	1986	1987	1988	1989	1990
CFAF '000,000	−82.91	−80.25	−55.23	−63.31	−91.40	−78.70
% of total	57.1%	58.3%	37.2%	43.0%	39.9%	32.2%

Imports (1988): CFAF 134,944,000,000 (machinery and transport equipment 28.1%, of which road transport equipment 11.0%, electrical machinery 5.8%; manufactured goods 26.5%; chemicals 11.8%; cereals 9.2%; petroleum products 7.3%; dairy products 3.9%; raw materials 2.6%; grease and lubricants 1.0%). *Major import sources* (1990): France 30.5%; Côte d'Ivoire 29.9%; Italy 4.7%; Japan 4.0%; Germany 3.3%; The Netherlands 3.1%.
Exports (1988): CFAF 41,947,000,000 (raw cotton 45.3%; manufactured goods 33.7%; machinery and equipment 6.0%; live animals 4.0%; vegetable food products 2.0%). *Major export destinations* (1990): France 29.5%; Taiwan 12.9%; Portugal 8.2%; Italy 7.6%; Japan 5.7%; Tunisia 5.0%.

Transport and communications

Transport. Railroads (1984)[7]: route length[8] 308 mi, 495 km; passenger-km 679,790,000; metric ton-km cargo 469,675,000. Roads (1991): total length 8,161 mi, 13,134 km (paved 12%[2]). Vehicles (1990): passenger cars 12,000; trucks and buses 13,000. Merchant marine: none. Air transport (1988): passenger-km 208,567,000; metric ton-mi cargo 35,223,000; airports (1992) 2.
Communications. Daily newspapers (1991): total number 2; total circulation 8,500; circulation per 1,000 population 0.9. Radio (1991): 200,000 receivers (1 per 46 persons). Television (1991): 41,500 receivers (1 per 223 persons). Telephones (1988): 15,000 (1 per 569 persons).

Education and health

Education (1989–90)	schools	teachers	students	student/ teacher ratio
Primary	2,362	8,572	472,979	55.2
Secondary	113[9]	1,700[9]	82,931	33.7[9]
Vocational	18[2]	341	8,055	23.6
Higher	1[2]	205	5,675	27.7

Educational attainment. Percentage of population age 10 and over having: no formal schooling 86.1%; some primary 7.3%; general secondary 2.2%; specialized secondary and postsecondary 3.8%; other 0.6%. *Literacy* (1990): percentage of total population age 15 and over literate 18.2%; males 27.9%; females 8.9%.
Health: physicians (1988) 280 (1 per 29,914 persons); hospital beds (1984) 5,580 (1 per 1,359 persons); infant mortality rate (1990–95) 127.0.
Food (1988–90): daily per capita caloric intake 2,219 (vegetable products 96%, animal products 4%); 94% of FAO recommended minimum requirement.

Military

Total active duty personnel (1992): 7,200 (army 97.2%; navy, none; air force 2.8%). *Military expenditure as percentage of GNP* (1988): 2.7% (world 5.0%); per capita expenditure U.S.$7.

[1]Ruling political party defeated a fragmented opposition (26 other political parties) at multiparty legislative elections of May 1992. [2]1986. [3]Officially marketed gold only; does not include substantial illegal production. [4]Third quarter. [5]January 1; index refers to the *S.M.I.G. (salaire minimum interprofessionnel guaranti)*, a form of minimum professional wage. [6]Weights of consumer price index components; Ouagadougou only. [7]Passenger-km and metric ton-km cargo figures are based on traffic between Abidjan, Côte d'Ivoire, and Ouagadougou. [8]1989. [9]1987–88.

Burundi

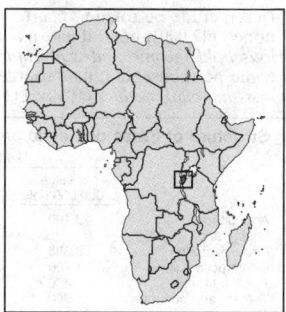

Official name: Republika y'u Burundi (Rundi); République du Burundi (French) (Republic of Burundi).
Form of government: transitional government[1].
Head of state and government: President assisted by Prime Minister.
Capital: Bujumbura.
Official languages: Rundi; French.
Official religion: none.
Monetary unit: 1 Burundi franc (FBu) = 100 centimes; valuation (Oct. 5, 1992) 1 U.S.$ = FBu 221.76; 1 £ = FBu 377.00.

Area and population

Provinces	Capitals	area sq mi	area sq km	population 1990 census[2]
Bubanza	Bubanza	420	1,089	225,849
Bujumbura	Bujumbura	509	1,319	596,185
Bururi	Bururi	952	2,465	392,910
Cankuzo	Cankuzo	759	1,965	142,194
Cibitoke	Cibitoke	631	1,636	282,625
Gitega	Gitega	764	1,979	564,127
Karuzi	Karuzi	563	1,457	301,651
Kayanza	Kayanza	476	1,233	443,677
Kirundo	Kirundo	658	1,703	404,564
Makamba	Makamba	757	1,960	240,741
Muramvya	Muramvya	593	1,535	440,283
Muyinga	Muyinga	709	1,836	385,518
Ngozi	Ngozi	569	1,474	483,814
Rutana	Rutana	756	1,959	198,011
Ruyigi	Ruyigi	903	2,339	254,117
TOTAL LAND AREA		10,019	25,949	
INLAND WATER		721	1,867	
TOTAL		10,740	27,816	5,356,266

Demography

Population (1992): 5,657,000.
Density (1992)[3]: persons per sq mi 564.6, persons per sq km 218.0.
Urban-rural (1986): urban 7.5%; rural 92.5%.
Sex distribution (1990): male 48.55%; female 51.45%.
Age breakdown (1990): under 15, 45.1%; 15–29, 27.0%; 30–44, 15.6%; 45–59, 7.5%; 60–74, 3.9%; 75 and over, 0.9%.
Population projection: (2000) 7,036,000; (2010) 8,824,000.
Doubling time: 22 years.
Ethnic composition (1983): Rundi 97.4%, of which Hutu 81.9%, Tutsi 13.5%; Twa Pygmy 1.0%; other 1.6%.
Religious affiliation (1980): Christian 85.5%, of which Roman Catholic 78.3%, Protestant 4.9%, Anglican 2.2%; traditional beliefs 13.5%; Muslim 0.9%; other 0.1%.
Major cities (1990): Bujumbura 226,628; Gitega 95,300[4]; Ngozi 20,000[5].

Vital statistics

Birth rate per 1,000 population (1991): 47.0 (world avg. 26.4).
Death rate per 1,000 population (1991): 15.0 (world avg. 9.2).
Natural increase rate per 1,000 population (1991): 32.0 (world avg. 17.2).
Total fertility rate (avg. births per childbearing woman; 1991): 6.9.
Marriage rate per 1,000 population: n.a.
Divorce rate per 1,000 population: n.a.
Life expectancy at birth (1991): male 50.0 years; female 54.0 years.
Major causes of death (percentage of reported deaths, 1990)[6]: diarrheal diseases 32.4%; malaria 25.2%; AIDS 17.6%; measles 13.4%; pulmonary tuberculosis 5.6%.

National economy

Budget (1991). Revenue: FBu 32,719,100,000 (customs duties 25.4%, excise duties 16.2%, property tax 11.7%, administrative receipts 8.8%, income tax 7.7%). Expenditures: FBu 36,883,400,000 (goods and services 55.1%, subsidies and transfers 20.6%, public debt 11.0%).
Public debt (external, outstanding; 1990): U.S.$940,000,000.
Tourism (1990): receipts from visitors U.S.$4,000,000; expenditures by nationals abroad U.S.$16,000,000.
Production (metric tons except as noted). Agriculture, forestry, fishing (1990): bananas 1,547,000, cassava 670,000, sweet potatoes 500,000, dry beans 330,000, corn (maize) 167,900, yams and taros 131,000, sorghum 88,000, peanuts (groundnuts) 87,000, rice 37,000, coffee 30,000, palm kernels 14,200, millet 10,000, wheat 8,600, sugarcane 8,000, cotton lint 2,000; livestock (number of live animals) 848,000 goats, 450,000 cattle, 420,000 sheep, 4,000,000 chickens; roundwood (1989) 4,083,000 cu m; fish catch 17,335. Mining and quarrying (1989): peat 14,200; kaolin clay 4,305; lime 202; gold 579 troy oz. Manufacturing (1991): beer 1,083,831 hectolitres; carbonated beverages 147,968 hectolitres; cigarettes 450,015,000 units; blankets 275,969 units; footwear 296,168 pairs. Construction: n.a. Energy production (consumption): electricity (kW-hr; 1991) 100,700,000 (130,000,000); coal, none (n.a.); crude petroleum, none (n.a.); petroleum products (metric tons; 1990) none (61,000); natural gas, none (n.a.); peat (metric tons; 1990) 11,000 (11,000).
Land use (1989): forested 2.6%; meadows and pastures 35.6%; agricultural and under permanent cultivation 52.1%; other 9.7%.
Gross national product (at current market prices; 1990): U.S.$1,151,000,000 (U.S.$210 per capita).

Structure of gross domestic product and labour force

	1991 in value FBu '000,000[7]	1991 % of total value	1979 labour force	1979 % of labour force
Agriculture	105,535.5	48.5	2,246,200	93.1
Mining	} 2,217.5	} 1.0	1,400	0.1
Public utilities			1,700	0.1
Manufacturing	26,160.5	12.0	36,700	1.5
Construction	8,922.5	4.1	14,700	0.6
Transportation and communications	6,650.8	3.1	6,400	0.2
Trade	19,770.6	9.1	20,900	0.9
Finance	...	...	1,300	0.1
Pub. admin., defense	24,084.6	11.1	5,700	0.2
Services	3,844.4	1.8	75,000	3.1
Other	20,362.4	9.3	3,100	0.1
TOTAL	217,548.8	100.0	2,413,100	100.0

Population economically active (1986): total 2,653,951; activity rate of total population 55.5% (participation rates: ages 15–64, 88.7%; female 52.7%; unemployed, n.a.).

Price and earnings indexes (1985 = 100)

	1985	1986	1987	1988	1989	1990	1991[8]
Consumer price index	100.0	101.8	109.3	114.0	127.3	136.3	155.4
Monthly earnings index[9]	100.0	100.5	101.8	...	...	...	...

Household income and expenditure. Average household size (1990) 4.6; income per household: n.a.; sources of income: n.a.; expenditure[10]: food 59.6%, clothing and footwear 11.1%, furniture and household goods 6.0%, energy and water 5.8%, housing 4.4%, other 13.1%.

Foreign trade[11]

Balance of trade (current prices)

	1986	1987	1988	1989	1990	1991
FBu '000,000	−864	−12,273	−7,136	−13,719	−26,583	−28,144
% of total	2.2%	37.0%	16.6%	35.8%	51.0%	45.8%

Imports (1991): FBu 44,786,500,000 (machinery and transport equipment 34.9%, food and food products 11.6%, mineral oil 11.0%, construction materials 6.0%). Major import sources: Belgium-Luxembourg 14.5%; Iran 11.0%; France 9.8%; Japan 8.4%; Germany 8.2%; China 5.9%; Italy 3.6%.
Exports (1991): FBu 16,642,900,000 (coffee 81.0%, tea 9.1%, animal hides and skins 2.6%, cotton fabric 1.5%). Major export destinations (1990): Germany 13.7%; United States 11.7%; France 9.6%; United Kingdom 7.3%; Finland 6.2%; Zaire 3.2%; Kenya 2.2%.

Transport and communications

Transport. Railroads: none. Roads (1991): total length 3,900 mi, 6,300 km (paved 16%). Vehicles (1990): passenger cars 12,698; trucks and other vehicles 12,793. Merchant marine (1979): vessels (100 gross tons and over) 1; total gross tonnage 385. Air transport (1991)[12]: passenger arrivals 35,735, departures 36,247; cargo loaded 1,821 short tons (1,652 metric tons), unloaded 4,611 short tons (4,183 metric tons); airports (1992) with scheduled flights 2.
Communications. Daily newspapers (1991): total number 1; total circulation 20,000; circulation per 1,000 population 3.6. Radio (1991): total number of receivers 500,000 (1 per 11 persons). Television (1991): total number of receivers 4,500 (1 per 1,221 persons). Telephones (1990): 8,737 (1 per 611 persons).

Education and health

Education (1989–90)

	schools	teachers	students	student/ teacher ratio
Primary (age 6–11)	1,299[4]	9,246	601,599	65.1
Secondary (age 12–18)	114	2,153	38,864	18.1
Higher	10[4]	556	3,279	5.9

Educational attainment: n.a. Literacy (1990): percentage of total population age 15 and over literate 50.0%; males literate 60.1%; females literate 39.8%.
Health (1990): physicians 168 (1 per 31,777 persons); hospital beds 10,370 (1 per 515 persons); infant mortality rate per 1,000 live births 111.0.
Food (1987–89): daily per capita caloric intake 1,995 (vegetable products 98%, animal products 2%); 86% of FAO recommended minimum requirement.

Military

Total active duty personnel (1991): 5,700 (army 96.5%, navy 0.9%, air force 2.6%). Military expenditure as percentage of GNP (1989): 2.6% (world 4.9%); per capita expenditure U.S.$5.

[1]Multiparty system approved by constitutional amendment of March 1992; multiparty elections scheduled for March 1993. [2]Preliminary. [3]Based on land area. [4]1986. [5]1982. [6]Data shown is for five provinces only. [7]Estimate. [8]November. [9]Nonagricultural employees in Bujumbura only; includes family allowances. [10]Weights of consumer price index components. [11]Import figures are f.o.b. in balance of trade and c.i.f. in commodities and trading partners. [12]Figures for Bujumbura airport only.

Cambodia

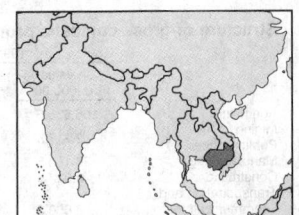

Official name: Roat Kampuchea (State
of Kampuchea; conventionally: State
of Cambodia)[1].
Form of government: UN-supervised
transitional administration with
one legislative house (National
Assembly [117]).
Heads of state and government: Head
of UN Transitional Authority in
Cambodia (for United Nations);
Chairman of Supreme National
Council assisted by Delegation Heads
(for Cambodia).
Capital: Phnom Penh.
Official language: Khmer.
Official religion: Buddhism.
Monetary unit: 1 riel = 100 sen;
valuation (Oct. 5, 1992)
1 U.S.$ = 1,508 riels; 1 £ = 2,564 riels.

Area and population

Provinces	Capitals	area		population
		sq mi	sq km	1987 estimate
Bântéay Méanchey	...	2	2	2
Bătdâmbâng	Bătdâmbâng	7,353	19,044	837,000
Kâmpóng Cham	Kâmpóng Cham	4,053	10,498	1,244,000
Kâmpóng Chhnăng	Kâmpóng Chhnăng	2,131	5,520	257,000
Kâmpóng Saôm	Kâmpóng Saôm	27	69	61,000
Kâmpóng Spoe	Kâmpóng Spoe	2,709	7,016	396,000
Kâmpóng Thum	Kâmpóng Thum	4,730	12,251	441,000
Kâmpôt	Kâmpôt	3,808	9,862	412,000
Kândal	...	1,472	3,813	838,000
Kaôh Kŏng	Krŏng Kaôh Kŏng	4,301	11,140	30,000
Krâchéh	Krâchéh	4,283	11,094	182,000
Môndól Kiri	Senmonorom	5,517	14,288	18,000
Ŏtdâr Méanchey	...	3	3	3
Phnom Penh	Phnom Penh	18	46	564,000
Poŭthĭsăt	Poŭthĭsăt	4,900	12,692	204,000
Preăh Vihéar	Phnum Tbéng Meanchey	5,541	14,350	80,000
Prey Vêng	Prey Vêng	1,885	4,883	782,000
Rôtânôkiri	Lumphăt	4,163	10,782	52,000
Siĕmréab	Siĕmréab	4,207	10,897	555,000
Stœ̆ng Trêng	Stœ̆ng Trêng	4,328	11,229	46,000
Svay Riĕng	Svay Riĕng	1,145	2,966	340,000
Takêv	Takêv	1,474	3,818	618,000
TOTAL LAND AREA		68,045	176,238	
INLAND WATER		2,192	5,678	
TOTAL		70,238[4]	181,916	7,957,000

Demography

Population (1992): 8,974,000.
Density (1992)[5]: persons per sq mi 131.9, persons per sq km 50.9.
Urban-rural (1990): urban 12.0%; rural 88.0%.
Sex distribution (1990): male 50%; female 50%.
Age breakdown (1990): under 15, 34.9%; 15–29, 29.6%; 30–44, 21.0%; 45–59,
9.6%; 60–74, 4.3%; 75 and over, 0.6%.
Population projection: (2000) 10,448,000; (2010) 11,988,000.
Doubling time: 28 years.
Ethnic composition (1979): Khmer 94.1%; Chinese 3.1%; Cham 2.3%; other
(Thai, Lao, Kola, and Vietnamese) 0.5%.
Religious affiliation (1980): Buddhist 88.4%; Muslim 2.4%; other 9.2%.
Major cities (1987): Phnom Penh 800,000[6]; Bătdâmbâng 45,000; Kâmpóng
Cham 33,000; Pursat 16,000; Kâmpóng Chhnăng 15,000.

Vital statistics

Birth rate per 1,000 population (1989): 41.8 (world avg. 27.1); legitimate, n.a.;
illegitimate, n.a.
Death rate per 1,000 population (1989): 16.9 (world avg. 9.8).
Natural increase rate per 1,000 population (1989): 24.9 (world avg. 17.3).
Total fertility rate (avg. births per childbearing woman; 1989): 4.6.
Marriage rate per 1,000 population: n.a.
Divorce rate per 1,000 population: n.a.
Life expectancy at birth (1989): male 46.5 years; female 49.4 years.
Major causes of death per 100,000 population (registered deaths only; 1966):
tuberculosis of the respiratory system 154; all accidents other than vehicle
accidents 111; malaria 55; pneumonia 51.

National economy

Budget (1990). Revenue: international assistance 40.0%; state enterprises
25.0%; taxes 25.0%, of which import duties 17.5%, commerce 7.0%; other
national sources 10.0%. Expenditures: n.a.
Public debt (external, outstanding; 1988): U.S.$704,000,000[7].
Production (metric tons except as noted). Agriculture, forestry, fishing (1991):
rice 2,400,000, sugarcane 238,000, bananas 120,000, roots and tubers 112,-
000 (of which cassava 62,000, sweet potatoes 35,000), corn (maize) 50,000,
beans 45,000, rubber 30,000, soybeans 16,000; livestock (number of live
animals) 2,150,000 cattle, 1,610,000 pigs, 760,000 buffalo, 12,000,000 poultry;
roundwood (1990) 5,929,000 cu m; fish catch 105,000. Mining and quarrying
(1989): salt 40,000. Manufacturing (value of production in '000,000 riels;
1988): cigarettes 1,064.5; food 116.9; chemical products (including rubber)
83.5; light industries (including textiles) 63.2; mechanical equipment and
parts 46.8; building materials 4.5. Construction: n.a. Energy production
(consumption): electricity (kW-hr; 1990) 70,000,000 (70,000,000); coal, n.a.

(n.a.); crude petroleum, n.a. (n.a.); petroleum products (metric tons; 1990)
none (147,000); natural gas, n.a. (n.a.).
Household income and expenditure. Average household size (1980) 5.6; income per household: n.a.; sources of income: n.a.; expenditure: n.a.
Gross national product (1990): U.S.$1,066,000,000 (U.S.$130 per capita).

Structure of gross domestic product and labour force

	1966		1989	
	in value '000,000 riels	% of total value	labour force	% of labour force
Agriculture	13,100	40.9	2,632,000	70.4
Mining and manufacturing	3,300	10.3		
Construction	1,700	5.3		
Public utilities	400	1.3		
Transp. and commun.	700	2.2	1,104,000	29.6
Trade	7,300	22.8		
Public admin., defense	3,900	12.2		
Services	1,600	5.0		
TOTAL	32,000	100.0	3,736,000	100.0

Population economically active (1989): total 3,736,000; activity rate of total
population 44.6% (participation rates: ages 15–64 [1985] 71.4%; female
40.5%; unemployed, n.a.).

Price and earnings indexes (1970 = 100)

	1967	1968	1969	1970	1971	1972	1973
Consumer price index	79.5	84.1	89.4	100.0	172.0	215.2	556.1
Earnings index							

Land use (1990): forested 75.8%; meadows and pastures 3.3%; agricultural
and under permanent cultivation 17.3%; other 3.6%.
Tourism (1989): total number of tourist arrivals 3,272.

Foreign trade

Balance of trade (current prices)

	1983	1984	1985	1986	1987	1988
U.S.$'000,000	− 96	− 98	− 105	...	...	− 115
% of total	88.2%	87.1%	80.9%	...	...	64.2%

Imports (1988): U.S.$147,000,000 (1985; machinery and transport equipment
36.9%, of which transport equipment 10.9%; petroleum and petroleum
products 30.2%; woven cotton fabrics 3.6%; synthetic fabrics 2.5%; cotton
yarn 2.3%; basic manufactures 1.5%; chemicals 1.2%). *Major import sources*
(1985): U.S.S.R. 93.5%; Japan 1.5%; France 1.1%; Australia 1.1%; United
Kingdom 0.6%.
Exports (1988): U.S.$32,000,000 (1985; rubber 82.9%; basic manufactures
5.1%; miscellaneous manufactured articles 3.0%). *Major export destinations*
(1985): U.S.S.R. 88.2%; United States 2.9%; Japan 2.9%.

Transport and communications

Transport. Railroads (1988): length 403 mi, 649 km; passenger-mi 33,554,000[8],
passenger-km 54,000,000[8]; short ton-mi cargo 6,850,000[8], metric ton-km
cargo 10,000,000[8]. Roads (1989): total length 9,200 mi, 14,800 km (paved
18%). Vehicles (1988): passenger cars 4,000; trucks and buses 7,100. Merchant marine (1991): vessels (100 gross tons and over) 3; total deadweight
tonnage 3,839. Air transport (1977): passenger-mi 26,098,800, passenger-
km 42,000,000; short ton-mi cargo 274,000, metric ton-km cargo 400,000;
airports (1992) with scheduled flights 1.
Communications. Daily newspapers (1991): total number 1; total circulation
25,000; circulation per 1,000 population 2.8. Radio (1991): 800,000 receivers
(1 per 11 persons). Television (1991): 70,000 receivers (1 per 125 persons).
Telephones (1991): 2,900[9] (1 per 3,300 persons).

Education and health

Education (1990–91)

	schools	teachers	students	student/ teacher ratio
Primary (age 6–10)	4,617	40,821	1,321,573	32.4
Secondary (age 11–16)	463	13,105[10]	248,966	24.7[10]
Voc., teacher tr.[11]	13	278	7,334	26.4
Higher	7	180[12]	6,640	13.5[12]

Educational attainment: n.a. *Literacy* (1980): total population age 15 and
over literate 48%.
Health (1988): physicians 303 (1 per 27,000 persons); hospital beds 12,953[13]
(1 per 632[13] persons); infant mortality rate per 1,000 live births (1989) 131.
Food (1986–88): daily per capita caloric intake 2,174 (vegetable products 95%,
animal products 5%); 81% of FAO recommended minimum requirement.

Military

Total active duty personnel (1992): 85,000[14] (army 94.1%, navy 4.7%, air
force 1.2%). *Military expenditure as percentage of GNP:* n.a.; per capita
expenditure, n.a.

[1]A peace agreement signed Oct. 23, 1991, by Cambodia's Supreme National Council
(SNC; composed of its four domestic political factions) and 18 nations provided for
transfer of administrative control, which took place in March 1992, to the United
Nations Transitional Authority in Cambodia (UNTAC). Cambodian sovereignty, however, would be retained by the SNC until UN-supervised free elections are held.
[2]Included with Bătdâmbâng. [3]Included with Siĕmréab. [4]Detail does not add to total
given because of rounding. [5]Based on land area. [6]1989. [7]Includes long-term debt
not guaranteed by the government. [8]1981. [9]Number of telephone lines. [10]1988–89.
[11]1983–84. [12]University of Phnom Penh only. [13]Public hospitals only. [14]Figures are
based on estimates and exclude provincial and paramilitary forces.

Cameroon

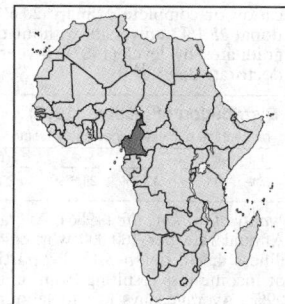

Official name: République du Cameroun (French); Republic of Cameroon (English).
Form of government: unitary multiparty[1] republic with one legislative house (National Assembly [180]).
Chief of state: President.
Head of government: Prime Minister.
Capital: Yaoundé.
Official languages: French; English.
Official religion: none.
Monetary unit: 1 CFA franc (CFAF) = 100 centimes; valuation (Oct. 5, 1992) 1 U.S.$ = CFAF 238.75; 1 £ = CFAF 405.88.

Area and population

Provinces	Capitals	area sq mi	area sq km	population 1987 census
Adamoua	Ngaoundéré	23,979	62,105	495,200
Centre	Yaoundé	26,655	69,035	1,651,600
Est	Bertoua	42,086	109,002	517,200
Extrême-Nord	Maroua	12,477	32,316	1,855,700
Littoral	Douala	7,810	20,229	1,354,800
Nord	Garoua	26,134	67,686	832,200
Nord-Ouest	Bamenda	6,722	17,409	1,237,400
Ouest	Bafoussam	5,360	13,883	1,339,800
Sud	Ebolowa	18,200	47,137	373,800
Sud-Ouest	Buea	9,540	24,709	838,000
LAND AREA		178,963	463,511	
INLAND WATER		751	1,947	
TOTAL		179,714	465,458	10,495,700

Demography

Population (1992): 12,662,000.
Density (1992)[2]: persons per sq mi 70.8, persons per sq km 27.3.
Urban-rural (1990): urban 41.2%; rural 58.8%.
Sex distribution (1991): male 49.88%; female 50.12%.
Age breakdown (1991): under 15, 46.4%; 15–29, 24.4%; 30–44, 15.1%; 45–59, 8.6%; 60 and over, 5.5%.
Population projection: (2000) 16,701,000; (2010) 23,665,000.
Doubling time: 21 years.
Ethnic composition (1983): Fang 19.6%; Bamileke and Bamum 18.5%; Duala, Luanda, and Basa 14.7%; Fulani 9.6%; Tikar 7.4%; Mandara 5.7%; Maka 4.9%; Chamba 2.4%; Mbum 1.3%; Hausa 1.2%; French 0.2%; other 14.5%.
Religious affiliation (1980): Roman Catholic 35%; Protestant 18%; animist 25%; Muslim 22%.
Major cities (1987): Douala 810,000; Yaoundé 649,000; Garoua 142,000; Maroua 123,000; Bafoussam 113,000.

Vital statistics

Birth rate per 1,000 population (1990–95): 47.3 (world avg. 26.4).
Death rate per 1,000 population (1990–95): 13.3 (world avg. 9.2).
Natural increase rate per 1,000 population (1990–95): 34.0 (world avg. 17.2).
Total fertility rate (avg. births per childbearing woman; 1990–95): 6.9.
Life expectancy at birth (1990–95): male 53.5 years; female 56.5 years.
Major causes of death per 100,000 population: n.a.; however, major health problems include measles, malaria, tuberculosis of respiratory system, anemias, meningitis, and intestinal obstruction and hernia.

National economy

Budget (1991–92). Revenue: CFAF 545,000,000,000 (direct taxes 36.0%; customs duties 28.3%; petroleum royalties 22.0%). Expenditures: CFAF 545,000,000,000 (current expenditure 69.4%, of which education 13.0%, defense 8.8%, administration 4.6%, health 4.5%, finance 3.1%).
Gross national product (at current market prices; 1990): U.S.$11,233,000,000 (U.S.$940 per capita).

Structure of gross domestic product and labour force

	1987 in value CFAF '000,000	1987 % of total value	1985 labour force	1985 % of labour force
Agriculture	1,096	23.5	2,900,871	74.0
Mining	515	11.0	1,793	0.1
Manufacturing	510	10.9	174,498	4.5
Construction	275	5.9	66,684	1.7
Public utilities	52	1.1	3,522	0.1
Transp. and commun.	210	4.5	51,688	1.3
Trade	508	10.9	154,014	3.9
Finance	554	11.8	8,009	0.2
Public admin., defense	318	6.8 }	292,922	7.5
Services	104	2.2 }		
Other	530[3]	11.3[3]	263,634	6.7
TOTAL	4,671[4]	100.0[4]	3,917,635	100.0

Household income and expenditure. Average household size (1980) 5.2; average annual income per household (1983)[5] U.S.$420; sources of income: n.a.; expenditure (1983)[5]: food 33.6%, clothing and footwear 16.3%, housing 14.6%, transportation and communications 10.5%, recreation 5.1%, health 5.0%.
Tourism (1990): receipts from visitors U.S.$21,000,000; expenditures by nationals abroad U.S.$283,000,000.

Population economically active (1987): total 4,269,000; activity rate of total population 39.4% (participation rates [1985]: ages 15–69, 66.3%; female 38.5%; unemployed, n.a.).

Price and earnings indexes (1985 = 100)

	1983	1984	1985	1986	1987	1988	1989
Consumer price index	88.7	98.7	100.0	107.7	114.2	124.0	124.0
Earnings index	...	...	...	...	...	...	...

Production (metric tons except as noted). Agriculture, forestry, fishing (1991): sugarcane 1,400,000, cassava 1,230,000, plantains 860,000, bananas 520,000, vegetables and melons 453,000, corn (maize) 450,000, sweet potatoes 154,000, peanuts (groundnuts) 110,000, palm oil 105,000, cacao 95,000, rice 90,000, yams 80,000, millet 63,000, palm kernels 42,000; livestock (number of live animals) 4,700,000 cattle, 3,550,000 goats, 3,550,000 sheep, 1,414,000 pigs; roundwood (1990) 14,216,000 cu m; fish catch (1990) 77,664. Mining and quarrying (1989): marble 200,000; pozzolana 130,000; aluminum 91,716; limestone 57,000; tin ore and concentrate 5. Manufacturing (1988): cement 586,000; palm oil 98,000; wheat flour 49,000; soap 23,400; footwear 1,733,000 pairs; sawn wood 568,000 cu m; beer 5,622,000 hectolitres; soft drinks 1,172,000 hectolitres. Construction (1983): residential 230,400 sq m; nonresidential 51,100 sq m. Energy production (consumption): electricity (kW-hr; 1990) 2,705,000,000 (2,705,000,000); coal (metric tons; 1990) 1,000 (1,000); crude petroleum (barrels; 1990) 61,098,000 (14,374,000); petroleum products (metric tons; 1990) 1,813,000 (1,760,000); natural gas, none (n.a.).
Public debt (external, outstanding; 1991): U.S.$5,007,000,000.
Land use (1990): forested 52.7%; meadows and pastures 17.8%; agricultural and under permanent cultivation 15.1%; other 14.4%.

Foreign trade[6]

Balance of trade (current prices)

	1985	1986	1987	1988	1989	1990
CFAF '000,000,000	−140.8	−265.1	−228.3	−68.8	+40.3	+141.5
% of total	17.9%	32.8%	32.1%	11.1%	5.2%	14.8%

Imports (1987): CFAF 526,186,000,000 (machinery and transport equipment 35.6%, of which road-transport equipment and parts 12.3%; motor-vehicle tires 5.5%; iron and steel 4.6%; flour products 3.4%; chemical products 3.2%; nonmetallic minerals 2.8%; paper and paper products 2.6%; plastic products 2.5%). *Major import sources* (1990): France 32.9%; Germany 10.6%; Japan 5.7%; Belgium-Luxembourg 5.5%; Italy 5.2%; United States 4.7%; The Netherlands 3.4%; Guinea 3.3%; United Kingdom 3.0%.
Exports (1990): CFAF 570,000,000,000 (crude petroleum 54.2%; cacao 10.5%; coffee 10.0%; sawn wood and logs 7.9%; cotton 5.8%). *Major export destinations:* France 32.7%; United States 14.9%; The Netherlands 14.4%; Italy 7.8%; Germany 4.2%; Spain 4.2%; Korea 3.3%; China 1.9%; Equatorial Guinea 1.9%.

Transport and communications

Transport. Railroads (1989–90): route length 686 mi, 1,104 km; passenger-mi 284,000,000, passenger-km 457,000,000; short ton-mi cargo 514,000,000, metric ton-km cargo 751,000,000. Roads (1987): total length 32,444 mi, 52,214 km (paved 6%). Vehicles (1987): passenger cars 78,272; trucks and buses 43,868. Merchant marine (1991): vessels (100 gross tons and over) 45; total deadweight tonnage 39,722. Air transport (1985): passenger-mi 360,000,000, passenger-km 580,000,000; short ton-mi cargo 76,000,000, metric ton-km cargo 111,000,000; airports (1992) with scheduled flights 5.
Communications. Daily newspapers (1991): 1; total circulation 66,000; circulation per 1,000 population 5.4. Radio (1991): total number of receivers 2,000,000 (1 per 6.1 persons). Television (1991): total number of receivers 5,000 (1 per 2,448 persons). Telephones (1988): 60,770 (1 per 185 persons).

Education and health

Education (1989–90)

	schools	teachers	students	student/ teacher ratio
Primary (age 6–14)	6,549	37,804	1,946,301	51.4
Secondary (age 15–24)	388[7]	11,400	366,528	32.2
Voc., teacher tr.	220[7]	6,267	90,633	14.5
Higher[7]	5	975	19,586	20.1

Educational attainment (1976). Percentage of population age 15 and over having: no schooling 51.1%; primary education 41.7%; some postprimary 0.2%; secondary 5.7%; some postsecondary 0.3%; higher 0.2%; other 0.8%.
Literacy (1990): percentage of total population age 15 and over literate 54.1%; males literate 66.3%; females literate 42.6%.
Health: physicians (1986) 833 (1 per 12,540 persons); hospital beds (1984–85) 26,832 (1 per 377 persons); infant mortality rate (1990–95) 86.0.
Food (1988–90): daily per capita caloric intake 2,208 (vegetable products 93%, animal products 7%); 95% of FAO recommended minimum requirement.

Military

Total active duty personnel (1992): 7,700 (army 85.7%, navy 10.4%, air force 3.9%). *Military expenditure as percentage of GNP* (1989): 1.3% (world 4.9%); per capita expenditure U.S.$14.

---

[1]Multiparty legislative elections were held on March 1, 1992. Presidential elections were held on Oct. 11, 1992; the results have not been made official. [2]Based on land area. [3]Indirect taxes, less subsidies. [4]Detail does not add to total given by source. [5]Capital city only. [6]Import figures are f.o.b. in balance of trade and c.i.f. for commodities and trading partners. [7]1986–87.

Canada

Official name: Canada.
Form of government: federal multiparty parliamentary state with two legislative houses (Senate [104[1]]; House of Commons [295]).
Chief of state: Queen of Canada (British Monarch).
Representative of chief of state: Governor-General.
Head of government: Prime Minister.
Capital: Ottawa.
Official languages: English; French.
Official religion: none.
Monetary unit: 1 Canadian dollar (Can$) = 100 cents; valuation (Oct. 5, 1992) 1 U.S.$ = Can$1.25; 1 £ = Can$2.13.

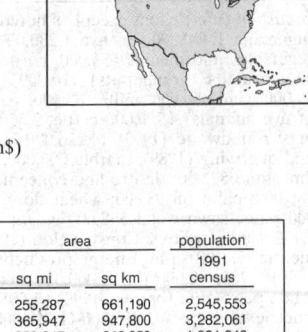

Area and population		area		population
				1991
Provinces	Capitals	sq mi	sq km	census
Alberta	Edmonton	255,287	661,190	2,545,553
British Columbia	Victoria	365,947	947,800	3,282,061
Manitoba	Winnipeg	250,947	649,950	1,091,942
New Brunswick	Fredericton	28,355	73,440	723,900
Newfoundland	St. John's	156,649	405,720	568,474
Nova Scotia	Halifax	21,425	55,490	899,942
Ontario	Toronto	412,581	1,068,580	10,084,885
Prince Edward Island	Charlottetown	2,185	5,660	129,765
Quebec	Quebec	594,860	1,540,680	6,895,963
Saskatchewan	Regina	251,866	652,330	988,928
Territories				
Northwest Territories	Yellowknife	1,322,909	3,426,320	57,649
Yukon Territory	Whitehorse	186,661	483,450	27,797
TOTAL		3,849,672	9,970,610	27,296,859

Demography

Population (1992): 27,737,000.
Density[2] (1992): persons per sq mi 7.8, persons per sq km 3.0.
Urban-rural (1990): urban 77.1%; rural 22.9%.
Sex distribution (1991): male 49.28%; female 50.72%.
Age breakdown[3] (1991): under 15, 20.9%; 15–29, 22.9%; 30–44, 24.9%; 45–59, 15.3%; 60–74, 11.2%; 75 and over, 4.8%.
Population projection: (2000) 31,214,000; (2010) 36,182,000.
Doubling time: 91 years.
Ethnic origin (1986): British 34.4%; French 25.7%; German 3.6%; Italian 2.8%; Ukrainian 1.7%; Amerindian and Inuktitut (Eskimo) 1.5%; Chinese 1.4%; Dutch 1.4%; multiple origin and other 27.5%[4].
Religious affiliation (1981): Roman Catholic 46.5%; Protestant 41.2%; Eastern Orthodox 1.5%; Jewish 1.2%; Muslim 0.4%; Hindu 0.3%; Sikh 0.3%; nonreligious 7.4%; other 1.2%.
Major metropolitan areas (1991): Toronto 3,893,046; Montreal 3,127,242; Vancouver 1,602,502; Ottawa-Hull 920,857; Edmonton 839,924; Calgary 754,033; Winnipeg 652,354; Quebec 645,550; Hamilton 599,760; London 381,522.

Other metropolitan areas (1991)					
	population		population		population
Chicoutimi-Jonquière	160,928	Regina	191,692	Sherbrooke	139,194
Halifax	320,501	St. Catharines–Niagara	364,552	Sudbury	157,613
Kitchener	356,421	St. John's	171,859	Trois Rivières	136,303
Oshawa	240,104	Saskatoon	210,023	Victoria	287,897
				Windsor	262,075

Place of birth (1986): 84.2% native-born; 15.8% foreign-born, of which United Kingdom 3.2%, other European 6.6%, Asian countries 3.2%, other 2.8%.
Mobility (1986). Population living in the same residence as in 1981: 56.3%; different residence, same municipality 24.2%; same province, different municipality 13.5%; different province 4.0%; different country 2.0%.
Households (1990). Total number of households 9,624,000. Average household size 2.8; (1985) 1 person 20.5%, 2 persons 30.8%, 3 persons 18.0%, 4 persons 18.8%, 5 persons 8.1%, 6 or more persons 3.8%. Family households: 6,635,000 (73.8%), nonfamily 2,356,670 (26.2%, of which 1 person 21.5%).
Immigration (1989): permanent immigrants admitted 191,886, from Asia 49.8%, Europe 27.1%, Central and South America 12.7%, Africa 6.4%, United States 3.6%, other 0.4%; refugee arrivals (1986) 18,282.

Vital statistics

Birth rate per 1,000 population (1989): 14.9 (world avg. 27.1); (1985) legitimate 83.8%; illegitimate 16.2%.
Death rate per 1,000 population (1989): 7.3 (world avg. 9.8).
Natural increase rate per 1,000 population (1989): 7.6 (world avg. 17.3).
Total fertility rate (avg. births per childbearing woman; 1986): 1.7.
Marriage rate per 1,000 population (1989): 7.3.
Divorce rate per 1,000 population (1989): 3.2.
Life expectancy at birth (1985–87): male 73.3 years; female 80.0 years.
Major causes of death per 100,000 population (1989): diseases of the circulatory system 296.2; malignant neoplasms (cancers) 195.7; diseases of the respiratory system 61.6; accidents and violence 52.7.

Social indicators

Educational attainment (1986). Percentage of population age 25 and over having: no formal schooling, negligible; less than complete primary education or complete primary 20.6%; secondary 35.0%; postsecondary vocational 25.1%; university without degree 8.3%; completed university 11.0%; graduates by level (1987): 4-year higher degree 101,960, master's 15,790, doctorate 2,385.

Distribution of income (1987)				
percentage of national income by quintile				
1	2	3	4	5 (highest)
5.7%	11.8%	17.7%	24.6%	40.2%

Quality of working life (1986). Average workweek: 38.8 hours (3.1% overtime). Annual rate per 100,000 workers for (1988): injury, accident, or industrial illness 4,580; death 5.1[5]. Proportion of labour force insured for damages or income loss resulting from: injury 99%; permanent disability 99%; death 99%. Average days lost to labour stoppages per 1,000 employee-workdays (1989): 1.6. Average duration of journey to work (1983): 23 minutes[6] (17.3% public transportation, 72.8% automobile, 9.9% other). Rate per 1,000 workers of discouraged (unemployed no longer seeking work; 1983): 10.5.
Access to services (1988). Proportion of households having access to: electricity 100.0%; public water supply 99.8%; public sewage collection 99.3%; public fire protection (1978) 90.4%.
Social participation. Eligible voters participating in last national election (1988): 75.9%. Population over 18 years of age participating in voluntary work (1987): 27.0%. Union membership in total work force (1990): 29.9%. Practicing religious population in total affiliated population: 92.7%.
Social deviance (1989). Offense rate per 100,000 population for: violent crime 949; property crime 5,507, of which auto theft 382, burglary and housebreaking 1,330; homicide 2.5. Incidence per 100,000 in general population of: alcoholism 2,285; drug and substance abuse 258; suicide (1988) 13.5.
Leisure (1989). Favourite leisure activities (hours weekly): television 23.4; social time 10.7[7]; reading 3.5[7]; recreation and culture 2.7[7].
Material well-being (1988). Households possessing: automobile 88.3%, of which two or more 25.1%; telephone 98.5%[8]; radio 99.1%[8]; television receiver 99.0%[8]; refrigerator 99.6%; central air conditioner 24.6%[9]; automatic washing machine 77.0%; cable television 69.0%; videocassette recorder 58.8%[9]; microwave oven 63.4%[9].

National economy

Gross national product (1990): U.S.$542,774,000,000 (U.S.$20,450 per capita).

Structure of gross domestic product and labour force				
	1990			
	in value Can$'000,000	% of total value	labour force	% of labour force
Agriculture	14,800	2.2	580,000	4.2
Mining	26,200	3.9	194,000	1.4
Manufacturing	120,200	17.9	2,198,000	16.1
Construction	44,300	6.6	923,000	6.8
Public utilities	27,600	4.1		
Transportation and communications	57,100	8.5	1,010,000	7.4
Trade	77,200	11.5	2,428,000	17.8
Finance	106,100	15.8	786,000	5.7
Pub. admin., defense	43,600	6.5	878,000	6.4
Services	154,500	23.0	3,575,000	26.1
Other			1,109,000[10]	8.1[10]
TOTAL	671,600	100.0	13,681,000	100.0

Budget (1991–92). Revenue: Can$128,500,000,000 (income taxes 58.5%; sales tax 21.8%; import duties 3.4%). Expenditures: Can$159,000,000,000 (public debt interest 27.2%; transfers to households 25.5%; other, including defense, 21.3%).
National debt (1990): Can$311,971,000,000.
Tourism (1990): receipts from visitors U.S.$6,374,000,000; expenditures by nationals abroad U.S.$8,390,000,000.

Manufacturing, mining, and construction enterprises (1988)			
	no. of establishments	no. of employees	hourly wages as a % of avg. of all wages[11]	annual value added (Can$'000,000)
Manufacturing				
Food and beverages	3,600	232,000	90.3	17,020
Transport equipment	1,519	207,000	119.4	15,970
Chemicals and related products	1,623	101,000	114.8	12,830
Paper and related products	701	119,000	125.3	12,270
Primary metals	517	109,000	127.1	10,330
Machinery	4,749	156,000	101.3	8,640
Electrical and electronics products	1,382	129,000	105.0	8,120
Printing, publishing, and related products	5,618	134,000	105.4	7,830
Metal fabricating	3,857	141,000	96.5	7,610
Wood	2,889	113,000	93.8	5,850
Rubber and plastic	1,537	90,000	91.8	4,770
Nonmetallic mineral products	1,409	57,000	...	4,440
Clothing	3,269	125,000	56.5	3,750
Textiles	1,364	79,000	82.3	3,610
Petroleum and coal products	158	17,000	...	3,160
Furniture and fixtures	2,616	66,000	73.5	2,430
Tobacco products industries	19	6,000	90.5	1,020
Mining	1,340	118,000	149.3	25,910
Construction	...	800,000	112.3	28,182

Production (metric tons except as noted). Agriculture, forestry, fishing (1991): wheat 32,822,000, barley 12,463,000, corn (maize) 7,319,000, rapeseed 4,303,-000, potatoes 2,781,000, vegetables 2,061,000 (of which tomatoes 649,000, carrots 290,000, cabbage 155,000, onions 123,000), oats 1,894,000, soybeans 1,406,000, sugar beets 1,065,000, linseed 691,000, apples 526,000, hops 480,000, dry peas 406,000, rye 354,000, lentils 354,000; livestock (number of live animals) 12,369,000 cattle, 10,516,000 pigs, 780,000 sheep, 114,000,000 chickens;

roundwood (1990) 155,475,000 cu m; pelts 2,580,809 units; fish catch (1990) 1,544,423. Mining and quarrying (1991): iron ore 35,961,000; zinc 1,079,912; copper 773,640; lead 239,558; nickel 189,161; molybdenum 11,292; uranium 7,813; silver 1,240; gold 5,496,700 troy oz. Manufacturing (1990): wood pulp 25,350,000; crude steel 21,684,000; cement 11,076,000; newsprint 9,068,000; pig iron 7,344,000; sulfuric acid 3,898,000[11]; caustic soda 1,769,000[11]; synthetic rubber 197,000[12]; road motor vehicles[9] 1,933,599 units, of which passenger cars 983,897 units, trucks and vans 949,702 units; washing machines and dryers 830,520 units[11]; refrigerators 568,960 units[11]; footwear 33,661,000 pairs[9]; beer 235,470,000 hectolitres[12]. Construction (building permits; 1989): residential Can$21,705,800,000; nonresidential Can$18,339,300,000.

Service enterprises (1988)

	no. of enter- prises	no. of employees[13]	weekly wages as a % of all wages	annual sales (Can$'000,000)
Retail trade				
Motor vehicle dealers	...	79,800	...	35,917
Food stores	...	213,400	...	35,187
Service stations	...	63,700	...	14,612
Department stores	...	[14]	...	13,271
Clothing stores	...	50,200	...	7,486
Pharmacies	...	52,400	...	7,459
Furniture and appliance stores	...	62,100	...	4,447
Automotive stores	...	31,500	...	3,767
General merchandise	...	231,700[14]	...	3,109
Sporting goods	...	...	...	2,669
General stores	...	[14]	...	2,415
Hardware stores	...	17,300	...	1,824
Shoe stores	...	18,400	...	1,599
Jewelry stores	...	14,000	...	1,215
Variety stores	...	45,100	...	1,057

Energy production (consumption): electricity (kW-hr; 1990) 481,791,000,000 (481,336,000,000); coal (metric tons; 1990) 68,331,000 (49,180,000); crude petroleum (barrels; 1990) 569,044,000 (521,017,000); petroleum products (metric tons; 1990) 87,126,000 (75,473,000); natural gas (cu m; 1990) 104,560,000,000 (63,357,000,000).
Population economically active (1990): total 13,681,000; activity rate of total population 51.4% (participation rates: ages 15–64, 76.6%[9]; female 44.3%[9]; unemployed 8.1%).

Price and earnings indexes (1985 = 100)

	1985	1986	1987	1988	1989	1990	1991
Consumer price index	100.0	104.2	108.7	113.1	118.7	124.4	131.4
Monthly earnings index	100.0	103.1	105.8	110.7	116.8	123.4	...

Household income and expenditure (1988). Average household size 2.8; average annual income per family Can$41,238 (U.S.$33,508); sources of income (1989): wages and salaries 65.4%, transfer payments 14.1%, self-employment 7.2%, other 13.3%; expenditure (1989): housing 22.3%[15], food 16.3%, transportation and communications 15.3%, household durable goods 10.2%, recreation 8.6%, clothing 5.8%, health 4.4%, education 2.8%.

Financial aggregates

	1986	1987	1988	1989	1990	1991	1992[16]
Exchange rate, Can$ per:							
U.S. dollar	1.39	1.33	1.23	1.18	1.17	1.14	1.19
£	2.04	2.18	2.19	1.94	2.08	2.03	2.09
SDR	1.69	1.84	1.60	1.52	1.65	1.65	1.64
International reserves (U.S.$)							
Total (excl. gold; '000,000)	3,251	7,277	15,391	16,055	17,845	16,252	14,897
SDRs ('000,000)	247	399	1,369	1,377	1,526	1,582	1,525
Reserve pos. in IMF ('000,000)	686	661	505	528	517	592	585
Foreign exchange ('000,000)	2,318	6,218	13,517	14,150	15,802	14,079	12,787
Gold ('000,000 fine troy oz)	19.72	18.52	17.14	16.10	14.76	12.96	12.21
% world reserves	2.12	2.12	1.81	1.71	1.56	1.38	1.30
Interest and prices							
Central bank discount (%)	8.49	8.66	11.17	12.47	11.78	8.00	7.00
Govt. bond yield (%)	9.52	9.95	10.22	9.92	10.85	9.76	9.51
Industrial share prices (1985 = 100)	111.1	131.5	121.8	140.1	126.1	127.9	125.8[17]
Balance of payments (U.S.$'000,000)							
Balance of visible trade,	7,676	8,960	9,422	6,732	9,952	7,545	...
of which:							
Imports, f.o.b.	81,350	89,092	106,637	116,284	119,093	120,080	...
Exports, f.o.b.	89,027	98,052	116,058	123,016	129,046	127,625	...
Balance of invisibles	−16,050	−17,659	−20,571	−24,479	−30,665	−30,593	...
Balance of payments, current account	−8,190	−8,754	−11,237	−17,480	−18,815	−23,374	...

Land use (1990): forested 38.9%; meadows and pastures 3.1%; agricultural and under permanent cultivation 5.0%; built-on, wasteland, and other 53.0%.

Foreign trade

Balance of trade (current prices)

	1986	1987	1988	1989	1990	1991
Can$'000,000,000	7.7	9.0	9.4	6.7	10.0	7.5
% of total	4.5%	4.8%	4.2%	2.8%	4.0%	3.0%

Imports (1990): Can$135,921,700,000 (road motor vehicles and parts 19.8%; chemicals 6.1%; food, feed, beverages, and tobacco 5.9%; crude petroleum 3.9%; nonferrous metals 1.9%; iron and steel 1.9%). *Major import sources:* United States 64.5%; Japan 7.0%; United Kingdom 3.6%; West Germany 2.8%; France 1.8%; South Korea 1.7%; Taiwan 1.5%; Italy 1.4%; Mexico 1.3%; Norway 1.2%.
Exports (1990): Can$140,989,300,000 (road motor vehicles and parts 23.4%; crude materials 13.7%, of which crude petroleum 3.9%, natural gas 2.0%;

food 7.6%, of which wheat 2.4%; newsprint 4.6%; wood pulp 4.3%; lumber 3.7%; industrial machinery 3.0%; petroleum and coal products 2.4%; aluminum 2.1%; office equipment 1.9%). *Major export destinations:* United States 74.9%; Japan 5.5%; United Kingdom 2.4%; West Germany 1.6%; South Korea 1.0%; China 1.1%; The Netherlands 1.1%; France 0.9%; Belgium 0.8%; Iran 0.8%.

Trade by commodities (1989)

SITC Group	imports U.S.$'000,000	%	exports U.S.$'000,000	%
00 Food and live animals	6,769.3	5.0	9,264.5	6.7
01 Beverages and tobacco	690.9	0.5	404.8	0.3
02 Crude materials, excluding fuels	4,872.4	3.6	21,535.4	15.7
03 Mineral fuels, lubricants, and related materials	6,373.1	4.7	12,583.6	9.2
04 Animal and vegetable oils, fats, and waxes	...	...	...	...
05 Chemicals and related products, n.e.s.	8,261.4	6.1	7,106.0	5.2
06 Basic manufactures	17,814.3	13.2	23,119.3	16.9
07 Machinery and transport equipment	70,622.9	52.4	52,768.4	38.5
08 Miscellaneous manufactured articles	15,210.0	11.3	5,044.1	3.7
09 Goods not classified by kind	4,207.8	3.1	5,132.1	3.7
TOTAL	134,935.7[18]	100.0[18]	137,347.4[18]	100.0[18]

Direction of trade (1990)[19]

	imports Can$'000,000	%	exports Can$'000,000	%
Africa	1,104.9	0.8	1,106.1	0.7
Asia	19,589.4	11.9	15,511.4	10.1
Americas	91,560.0	65.6	113,869.2	74.3
United States	86,983.8	62.0	111,298.7	72.7
Mexico	1,730.4	1.2	569.4	0.4
South America	2,172.6	1.6	1,312.6	0.9
Europe	19,947.6	14.3	14,065.8	9.2
EEC	15,574.4	11.2	11,629.5	7.6
U.S.S.R.	185.5	0.1	1,126.0	0.7
Other Europe	4,187.7	3.0	1,310.2	0.9
Oceania	1,183.1	0.6	1,049.0	0.7
TOTAL	139,643.8	100.0	153,175.2	100.0

Transport and communications

Transport. Railroads (1990): length (1988) 56,771 mi, 91,365 km; passenger-mi 724,500,000, passenger-km 1,166,000,000; short ton-mi cargo 163,978,000,000, metric ton-km cargo 239,404,000,000. Roads (1989): total length 546,514 mi, 879,530 km (paved 32%). Vehicles (1989): passenger cars 12,811,318; trucks and buses 3,458,368. Merchant marine (1991): vessels (100 gross tons and over) 1,204; total deadweight tonnage 2,928,808. Air transport (1990): passenger-mi 29,461,000,000, passenger-km 47,413,000,000; short ton-mi cargo 3,568,800,000, metric ton-km cargo 5,210,400,000; airports (1992) with scheduled flights 106.
Communications. Daily newspapers (1991): total number 105; total circulation 5,114,700; circulation per 1,000 population 187. Radio (1991): total number of receivers 22,577,806 (1 per 1.2 persons). Television (1991): total number of receivers 15,709,000 (1 per 1.7 persons). Telephones (1987): 20,126,490 (1 per 1.3 persons).

Education and health

Education (1990–91)

	schools	teachers	students	student/ teacher ratio
Primary (age 6–14) } Secondary (age 14–18)	15,507	286,375	5,129,060	17.9
Postsecondary and higher	270	63,570	856,520	13.5

Literacy (1975): total population age 14 and over literate 16,185,000 (95.6%); males literate 8,003,000 (95.6%); females literate 8,182,000 (95.7%).
Health (1989): physicians 58,470 (1 per 449 persons); hospital beds 183,775 (1 per 143 persons); infant mortality rate per 1,000 live births 7.1.
Food (1988–90): daily per capita caloric intake 3,242 (vegetable products 68%, animal products 32%); 122% of FAO recommended minimum requirement.

Military

Total active duty personnel (1992): 84,000 (army 26.2%, navy 20.2%, air force 26.7%, not identified by service 26.9%). *Military expenditure as percentage of GNP* (1989): 2.0% (world 4.9%); per capita expenditure U.S.$413.

[1]On Sept. 27, 1990, Prime Minister Brian Mulroney, under a previously unused constitutional provision, requested and obtained from Queen Elizabeth II the appointment of 8 temporary members to the Senate, increasing its membership to 112; reduced to 110 as of April 1992. [2]Based on land area of 3,558,096 sq mi (9,215,430 sq km). [3]Excludes 45,000 population in Indian reserves and settlements. [4]Includes 4.6% who are of both French and British origin. [5]1987. [6]Urban areas. [7]1981. [8]1990. [9]1989. [10]Unemployed. [11]1986. [12]1988. [13]1984. [14]Department and General stores included with General merchandise. [15]Includes energy and utilities. [16]April. [17]March. [18]Detail does not add to total given because of rounding. [19]Totals and subtotals include Can$6,258,800,000 in imports and Can$7,573,700,000 in exports (4.7% of all foreign trade; mostly special transactions) not distributable by region.

Cape Verde

Official name: República de Cabo
Verde (Republic of Cape Verde).
Form of government: multiparty[1]
republic with one legislative house
(National People's Assembly [79]).
Chief of state: President.
Head of government: Prime Minister.
Capital: Praia.
Official language: Portuguese.
Official religion: none.
Monetary unit: 1 escudo
(C.V.Esc) = 100 centavos; valuation
(Oct. 5, 1992) 1 U.S.$ = C.V.Esc 62.52;
1 £ = C.V.Esc 106.28.

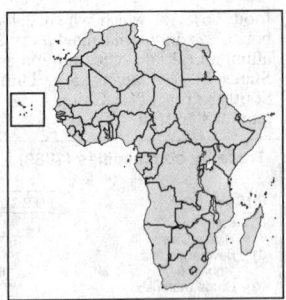

Area and population

Island Groups Islands/Counties[2] Counties	Capitals	area sq mi	area sq km	population 1990 census[3]
Leeward Islands		696[4]	1,803	217,237
Brava	Nova Sintra	26	67	6,980
Fogo	São Filipe	184	476	33,860
Maio	Porto Inglês	104	269	4,964
Santiago		383	991	171,433
Praia	Praia	153	396	82,874
Santa Catarina	Assomada	94	243	37,274
Santa Cruz	Pedra Badejo	58	149	26,732
Tarrafal	Tarrafal	78	203	24,553
Windward Islands		861[4]	2,230	119,561
Boa Vista	Sal Rei	239	620	3,457
Sal	Santa Maria	83	216	7,998
Santo Antão		300	779	43,272
Paúl	Pombas	21	54	7,926
Porto Novo	Porto Novo	215	558	14,838
Ribeira Grande	Ponta do Sol	64	167	20,508
São Nicolau	Ribeira Brava	150	388	13,577
São Vicente	Mindelo	88	227	51,257
TOTAL		1,557	4,033	336,798

Demography

Population (1992): 346,000.
Density (1992): persons per sq mi 222.2, persons per sq km 85.8.
Urban-rural (1990): urban 29.7%; rural 70.3%.
Sex distribution (1990): male 48.00%; female 52.00%.
Age breakdown (1987): under 15, 44.5%; 15–29, 31.5%; 30–44, 9.1%; 45–59, 7.6%; 60 and over, 7.3%.
Population projection: (2000) 383,000; (2010) 436,000.
Doubling time: 29 years.
Ethnic composition (1986): mixed 71%; black 28%; white 1%.
Religious affiliation (1991): Roman Catholic 93.2%; Protestant and other 6.8%.
Major cities (1990): Praia 61,707; Mindelo 47,080; São Filipe 5,616.

Vital statistics

Birth rate per 1,000 population (1987): 32.1 (world avg. 27.1); (1975) legitimate 55.2%; illegitimate 44.8%.
Death rate per 1,000 population (1987): 7.7 (world avg. 9.8).
Natural increase rate per 1,000 population (1987): 24.4 (world avg. 17.3).
Total fertility rate (avg. births per childbearing woman; 1990–95): 5.3.
Marriage rate per 1,000 population (1988): 3.2.
Divorce rate per 1,000 population: n.a.
Life expectancy at birth (1987): male 63.0 years; female 67.0 years.
Major causes of death per 100,000 population (1987): enteritis and other diarrheal diseases 97.4; heart disease 77.9; malignant neoplasms (cancers) 47.9; pneumonia 46.4; accidents, poisoning, and violence 44.0.

National economy

Budget. Revenue (1987): C.V.Esc 3,428,939,000 (indirect taxes 38.2%, of which import duties 15.4%; direct taxes 21.2%, of which taxes from industry 7.2%; receipts from petroleum 3.1%). Expenditures (1986): C.V.Esc 2,798,000,000 (current expenditure 90.8%, of which salaries 43.6%, transfer payments 26.8%; capital expenditure 9.2%).
Public debt (external, outstanding; 1991): U.S.$147,000,000.
Tourism: n.a.
Land use (1990): forested 0.2%; meadows and pastures 6.2%; agricultural and under permanent cultivation 9.7%; other 83.9%.
Production (metric tons except as noted). Agriculture, forestry, fishing (1991): sugarcane 13,000, fruits (except melons) 11,000, coconuts 10,000, pulses 9,000, sweet potatoes 8,000, vegetables (including melons) 6,000, bananas 5,000, cassava 4,000, potatoes 4,000, dates 2,000; livestock (number of live animals) 110,000 goats, 86,000 pigs, 12,000 cattle; roundwood, n.a.; fish catch (1990) 8,600. Mining and quarrying (1989): salt 3,000. Manufacturing (C.V.Esc; 1987): cigars 232,253,000; flour 176,677,000; cocoa powder 94,439,000[5]; canned fish 78,401,000; bread 35,530,000[5]; alcoholic beverages 25,972,000; soft drinks 7,419,000 litres. Construction (1982): residential C.V.Esc 365,800,000; nonresidential C.V.Esc 1,700,000. Energy production (consumption): electricity (kW-hr; 1990) 36,000,000 (36,000,000); coal, none (none); crude petroleum, none (none); petroleum products (metric tons; 1990) none (27,000); natural gas, none (none).
Gross national product (at current market prices; 1990): U.S.$331,000,000 (U.S.$890 per capita).

Structure of gross domestic product and labour force

	1986 in value C.V.Esc '000,000	1986 % of total value	1980 labour force	1980 % of labour force
Agriculture	2,730.7	10.3	22,144	33.2
Manufacturing	2,279.9	8.6	1,871	2.8
Public utilities	377.7	1.4	336	0.5
Mining	135.7	0.5	535	0.8
Construction	4,124.5	15.6	18,873	28.3
Transportation and communications	3,489.0	13.2	3,411	5.1
Pub. admin., defense	4,388.9	16.6	2,128	3.2
Trade	5,625.4	21.3	3,930	5.9
Finance	1,723.3	6.5	226	0.4
Services	446.1	1.7		
Other	1,110.5	4.2	13,156	19.8
TOTAL	26,431.6[4]	100.0[4]	66,610	100.0

Population economically active (1980): total 66,610; activity rate of total population 22.5% (participation rates: ages 15–64, 42.9%; female 30.5%; unemployed, n.a.).

Price and earnings indexes (1985 = 100)

	1983	1984	1985	1986	1987	1988
Consumer price index	85.1	95.4	100.0	110.5	115.5	120.3
Earnings index	...	...	...	...	...	...

Household income and expenditure. Average household size (1980) 4.3; income per household: n.a.; sources of income: n.a.; expenditure (1986)[6]: food 63.4%, clothing and footwear 9.2%, beverages and tobacco 6.7%, other 20.7%.

Foreign trade

Balance of trade (current prices)

	1984	1985	1986	1987	1988	1989
C.V.Esc '000,000	−6,799	−7,081	−8,240	−6,714	−7,416	−8,179
% of total	94.1%	87.1%	92.1%	85.6%	93.8%	88.6%

Imports (1988): C.V.Esc 7,652,000,000 (foodstuffs and beverages 27.2%, machinery and apparatus 16.0%, transport equipment 12.4%, nonmetallic mineral products 11.5%, metal products 8.5%). *Major import sources:* Portugal 33.7%; The Netherlands 10.8%; Japan 5.8%; West Germany 5.2%; Brazil 5.0%; Sweden 4.9%.
Exports (1988): C.V.Esc 236,000,000 (bananas 36.7%, frozen tuna 30.5%, spiny lobster 9.4%, canned tuna 3.1%, refined sugar 3.0%). *Major export destinations:* Portugal 41.5%; Spain 30.3%; France 7.3%; The Netherlands 4.8%; Italy 4.3%.

Transport and communications

Transport. Railroads: none. Roads (1987): total length 3,489 mi, 5,615 km (paved 29%). Vehicles (1988): passenger cars 13,027; trucks and buses 4,356. Merchant marine (1991): vessels (100 gross tons and over) 41; total deadweight tonnage 31,471. Air transport (1987): passenger-mi 76,403,000, passenger-km 122,959,000; (1985) short ton-mi cargo 1,606,000, metric ton-km cargo 2,345,000; airports (1992) with scheduled flights 8.
Communications. Daily newspapers: none. Radio (1991): total number of receivers 50,000 (1 per 6.8 persons). Television (1987): total number of receivers 5,000 (1 per 65 persons). Telephones (1988): 7,840 (1 per 42 persons).

Education and health

Education (1987–88)

	schools	teachers	students	student/ teacher ratio
Primary (age 7–12)	545	1,892	62,727	33.2
Secondary (age 13–17)	16[7]	191	5,740	30.1
Voc., teacher tr.	3[7]	77	673	8.7
Higher	...	...	...	...

Educational attainment (1980). Percentage of population age 25 and over having: no formal schooling or incomplete primary education 84.2%; complete primary 12.4%; secondary 1.7%; higher 0.5%; unknown 1.2%. *Literacy* (1985): total population age 15 and over literate 73,500 (47.4%); males literate 42,500 (61.4%); females literate 31,000 (38.6%).
Health (1987): physicians 77 (1 per 4,208 persons); hospital beds 625 (1 per 550 persons); infant mortality rate per 1,000 live births (1988) 51.0.
Food (1988–90): daily per capita caloric intake 2,778 (vegetable products 88%, animal products 12%); 118% of FAO recommended minimum requirement.

Military

Total active duty personnel (1992): 1,300 (army 76.9%, navy 15.4%, air force 7.7%). *Military expenditure as percentage of GNP* (1981): 12.1% (world 5.5%); per capita expenditure U.S.$43.

[1]Constitution revised Sept. 28, 1990, to adopt a multiparty system; first multiparty elections took place on Jan. 13, 1991. [2]Island/county areas are coterminous except Santiago and Santo Antão islands. [3]Preliminary results. [4]Detail does not add to total given because of rounding. [5]1986. [6]Praia only. [7]1986–87.

Central African Republic

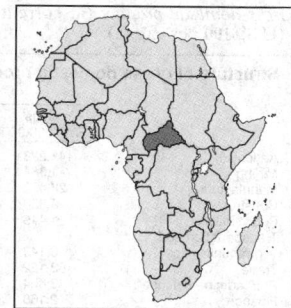

Official name: République Centrafricaine (Central African Republic).
Form of government: republic[1] with a bicameral Congress that meets as two chambers, an upper (Economic and Regional Council[2]) and a lower (National Assembly [52]).
Chief of state: President.
Head of government: Prime Minister.
Capital: Bangui.
Official languages: French; Sango.
Official religion: none.
Monetary unit: 1 CFA franc (CFAF) = 100 centimes; valuation (Oct. 5, 1992) 1 U.S.$ = CFAF 238.75; 1 £ = CFAF 405.88.

Area and population

Prefectures	Capitals	area sq mi	area sq km	population 1988 census
Bamingui-Bangoran	Ndélé	22,471	58,200	28,643
Basse-Kotto	Mobaye	6,797	17,604	194,750
Haut-Mbomou	Obo	21,440	55,530	27,113
Haute-Kotto	Bria	33,456	86,650	58,838
Kemo	Sibut	6,642	17,204	82,884
Lobaye	Mbaïki	7,427	19,235	169,554
Mambere-Kadei	Berbérati	11,661	30,203	230,364
Mbomou	Bangassou	23,610	61,150	119,252
Nana-Gribizi	Kaga-Bandoro	7,721	19,996	95,497
Nana-Mambere	Bouar	10,270	26,600	191,970
Ombella-Mpoko	Boali	12,292	31,835	180,857
Ouaka	Bambari	19,266	49,900	208,332
Ouham	Bossangoa	19,402	50,250	262,950
Ouham-Pendé	Bozoum	12,394	32,100	287,653
Sangha-Mbaere	Nola	7,495	19,142	65,961
Vakaga	Birao	17,954	46,500	32,118
Autonomous commune				
Bangui	Bangui	26	67	451,690
TOTAL		240,324	622,436	2,688,426

Demography

Population (1992): 2,930,000.
Density (1992): persons per sq mi 12.2, persons per sq km 4.7.
Urban-rural (1990): urban 46.7%; rural 53.3%.
Sex distribution (1988): male 49.14%; female 50.86%.
Age breakdown (1988): under 15, 43.2%; 15–29, 27.5%; 30–44, 15.0%; 45–59, 9.2%; 60–74, 4.1%; 75 and over, 0.8%; unknown 0.2%.
Population projection: (2000) 3,528,000; (2010) 4,449,000.
Doubling time: 24 years.
Ethnic composition (1983): Banda 28.6%; Baya (Gbaya) 24.5%; Ngbandi 10.6%; Azande 9.8%; Sara 6.9%; Mbaka 4.3%; Mbum 4.1%; Kare 2.4%; French 0.1%; other 8.7%.
Religious affiliation (1985): Protestant 40.0%; Roman Catholic 28.0%; traditional 24.0%; Muslim 8.0%.
Major cities (1988)[3]: Bangui 451,690; Bambari 52,092; Bouar 49,166; Berbérati 45,432; Bossangoa 41,877.

Vital statistics

Birth rate per 1,000 population (1990–95): 45.1 (world avg. 26.4); legitimate, n.a.; illegitimate, n.a.
Death rate per 1,000 population (1990–95): 16.3 (world avg. 9.2).
Natural increase rate per 1,000 population (1990–95): 28.8 (world avg. 17.2).
Total fertility rate (avg. births per childbearing woman; 1988): 6.1.
Marriage rate per 1,000 population: n.a.
Divorce rate per 1,000 population: n.a.
Life expectancy at birth (1990–95): male 48.0 years; female 53.0 years.
Morbidity (as percentage of reported cases of illness; 1984): malaria 13.3%; dysentery, enteritis, and other intestinal diseases 12.5%; respiratory diseases 9.9%, of which pneumonia 2.7%.

National economy

Budget (1991). Revenue: CFAF 49,820,000,000 (fiscal receipts 87.3%; nonfiscal receipts 12.7%). Expenditures: CFAF 87,060,000,000 (current expenditure 53.5%; capital expenditure 46.5%, of which grants from abroad 32.6%).
Public debt (external, outstanding; 1990): U.S.$548,000,000.
Tourism (1990): receipts from visitors U.S.$9,000,000; expenditures by nationals abroad U.S.$41,000,000.
Production (metric tons except as noted). Agriculture, forestry, fishing (1991): cassava 520,000, yams 200,000, peanuts (groundnuts) 106,000, corn (maize) 100,000, bananas 93,000, plantains 68,000, seed cotton 63,000, oranges 50,000, sorghum 40,000, cottonseed 19,000, coffee 17,000, rice 15,000, pulses 15,000, cotton lint 11,000; livestock (number of live animals) 2,677,000 cattle, 1,270,-000 goats, 426,000 pigs, 3,000,000 chickens; roundwood (1990) 3,490,000 cu m; fish catch (1989) 13,000. Mining and quarrying (1990): diamonds 414,789 carats[4]; gold 7,745 troy oz. Manufacturing (value of production in CFAF '000,000; 1989): food, beverages, and tobacco 15,456; wood products 9,156; textiles, wearing apparel, and leather products 8,343; chemical products 3,555; metal products 2,199. Construction (1990)[5]: residential 14,700 sq m; nonresidential 11,200 sq m. Energy production (consumption): electricity

(kW-hr; 1990) 92,600,000 (65,000,000); coal, none (none); crude petroleum, none (none); petroleum products (metric tons; 1990) none (65,000); natural gas, none (none).
Land use (1990): forested 57.4%; meadows and pastures 4.8%; agricultural and under permanent cultivation 3.2%; other 34.6%.
Gross national product (at current market prices; 1990): U.S.$1,194,000,000 (U.S.$390 per capita).

Structure of gross domestic product and labour force

	1990 in value CFAF '000,000[6]	1990 % of total value	1987 labour force	1987 % of labour force
Agriculture	123,990	39.8	907,000	65.8
Mining	10,740	3.5		
Manufacturing	29,570	9.5		
Construction	5,670	1.8	94,000	6.8
Public utilities	1,360	0.4		
Transp. and commun.				
Trade	118,750	38.2	377,000	27.4
Finance, real estate				
Pub. admin., defense				
Other	21,110[7]	6.8[7]	...	...
TOTAL	311,190	100.0	1,378,000	100.0

Population economically active (1987): total 1,378,000; activity rate of total population 48.9% (participation rates [1985]: ages 15–64, 81.6%; female 47.0%; unemployed, n.a.).

Price and earnings indexes (1985 = 100)

	1985	1986	1987	1988	1989	1990	1991
Consumer price index[8]	100.0	102.2	95.1	91.3	92.0	91.9	89.8[9]
Earnings index	...	...	...	...	...	...	...

Household income and expenditure. Average household size (1988) 4.7; average annual income per household CFAF 91,985 (U.S.$435); sources of income: n.a.; expenditure (1983)[5]: food 70.5%, clothing 9.5%, energy 6.5%, transportation and communications 4.1%, recreation 1.3%, health 1.0%.

Foreign trade

Balance of trade (current prices)

	1985	1986	1987	1988	1989	1990
CFAF '000,000	−5,327	−57,089	−17,174	−18,346	−6,009	−10,917
% of total	6.1%	55.4%	18.0%	22.5%	6.3%	17.9%

Imports (1990): CFAF 35,889,000,000 (general manufactures 36.2%; food products 24.3%, of which wheat flour 5.9%; motor cars 9.2%; pharmaceuticals 7.1%). *Major import sources:* France 46.6%; Cameroon 11.2%; Germany 7.0%; Japan 5.8%; Congo 3.8%.
Exports (1990): CFAF 24,972,000,000 (diamonds 66.2%; wood 13.4%; coffee 13.0%; cotton 2.6%; gold 2.0%). *Major export destinations:* Belgium-Luxembourg 65.9%; France 22.8%; Switzerland 5.0%; Germany 1.2%.

Transport and communications

Transport. Railroads: none. Roads (1990): total length 14,564 mi, 23,438 km (paved 2%). Vehicles (1989): passenger cars 10,782; trucks and buses 8,051. Merchant marine: vessels (100 gross tons and over) none. Air transport (1990)[10]: passenger-mi 144,362,000, passenger-km 232,329,000; short ton-mi cargo 12,119,000, metric ton-km cargo 17,694,000; airports (1992) with scheduled flights 1[11].
Communications. Daily newspapers (1990): total number 1; total circulation 200; circulation per 1,000 population 0.1. Radio (1991): 550,000 receivers (1 per 5.3 persons). Television (1988): 7,000 receivers (1 per 393 persons). Telephones (1991): 4,100[12] (1 per 716 persons).

Education and health

Education (1989–90)

	schools	teachers	students	student/ teacher ratio
Primary (age 6–11)	1,003	3,581	323,661	90.4
Secondary (age 12–18) Vocational	46	1,149	47,212	41.1
Higher[13]	1	134	2,534	18.9

Educational attainment (1975). Percentage of population age 15 and over having: no formal schooling 73.5%; primary education 22.8%; lower secondary 3.0%; upper secondary 0.6%; higher 0.1%. *Literacy* (1990): total population age 15 and over literate 37.7%; males literate 51.8%; females literate 24.9%.
Health: physicians (1988) 154 (1 per 17,292 persons); hospital beds (1990) 4,052 (1 per 689 persons); infant mortality rate per 1,000 live births (1991) 219.0.
Food (1987–89): daily per capita caloric intake 2,004 (vegetable products 90%, animal products 10%); 89% of FAO recommended minimum requirement.

Military

Total active duty personnel (1992): 3,800 (army 92.1%; navy, none; air force 7.9%). *Military expenditure as percentage of GNP* (1989): 1.7% (world 4.9%); per capita expenditure U.S.$6.

---

[1]Multiparty system was announced July 1991, but multiparty elections had not been held as of August 1992. [2]Number of seats not available. [3]Population of Bangui is census figure; other figures are estimates. [4]About an equal amount is smuggled out of the country annually. [5]Bangui only. [6]At constant prices of 1984. [7]Import duties plus value-added taxes. [8]Indigenous households in Bangui only. [9]Average of third quarter. [10]Total traffic of Air Afrique, an airline shared by 10 West African countries. [11]International air service only. [12]Number of subscribers. [13]University of Bangui only; 1991.

Chad

Official name: Jumhūrīyah Tshad (Arabic); République du Tchad (French) (Republic of Chad).
Form of government: transitional regime[1].
Chief of state: President[1].
Head of government: Prime Minister[1].
Capital: N'Djamena.
Official languages: Arabic; French.
Official religion: none.
Monetary unit: 1 CFA franc (CFAF) = 100 centimes; valuation (Oct. 5, 1992) 1 U.S.$ = CFAF 238.75; 1 £ = CFAF 405.88.

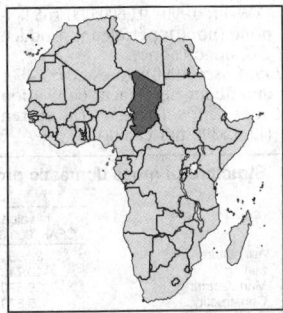

Area and population		area		population
		sq mi	sq km	1992 estimate
Préfectures	**Capitals**			
Batha	Ati	34,285	88,800	470,900
Biltine	Biltine	18,090	46,850	238,400
Borkou-Ennedi-Tibesti	Faya Largeau	231,795	600,350	119,200
Chari-Baguirmi	N'Djamena	32,010	82,910	924,000
Guéra	Mongo	22,760	58,950	280,200
Kanem	Mao	44,215	114,520	268,200
Lac	Bol	8,620	22,320	178,800
Logone Occidental	Moundou	3,357	8,695	399,400
Logone Oriental	Doba	10,825	28,035	417,300
Mayo-Kebbi	Bongor	11,625	30,105	941,900
Moyen-Chari	Sarh	17,445	45,180	709,400
Ouaddaï	Abéché	29,436	76,240	465,000
Salamat	Am Timan	24,325	63,000	143,000
Tandjilé	Laï	6,965	18,045	405,300
TOTAL		495,755[2]	1,284,000	5,961,000

Demography

Population (1992): 5,961,000.
Density (1992): persons per sq mi 12.0, persons per sq km 4.6.
Urban-rural (1990): urban 32.0%; rural 68.0%.
Sex distribution (1990): male 49.31%; female 50.69%.
Age breakdown (1990): under 15, 42.8%; 15–29, 26.0%; 30–44, 15.9%; 45–59, 9.6%; 60–74, 4.8%; 75 and over, 0.9%.
Population projection: (2000) 7,337,000; (2010) 9,491,000.
Doubling time: 28 years.
Ethnic composition (1983): Sara, Bagirmi, and Kreish 30.5%; Sudanic Arab 26.1%; Teda (Tubu) 7.3%; Mbum 6.5%; Masalit, Maba, and Mimi 6.3%; Tama 6.3%; Mubi 4.2%; Kanuri 2.3%; Hausa 2.3%; Masa 2.3%; Kotoko 2.1%; other 3.8%.
Religious affiliation (1989): Muslim 40.4%; Christian 33.0%; traditional beliefs 26.6%.
Major cities (1992): N'Djamena 687,800; Sarh 129,600; Moundou 117,500; Abéché 95,800; Koumra 48,700.

Vital statistics

Birth rate per 1,000 population (1990–95): 43.3 (world avg. 26.4); legitimate, n.a.; illegitimate, n.a.
Death rate per 1,000 population (1990–95): 17.9 (world avg. 9.2).
Natural increase rate per 1,000 population (1990–95): 25.4 (world avg. 17.2).
Total fertility rate (avg. births per childbearing woman; 1990): 6.0.
Marriage rate per 1,000 population: n.a.
Divorce rate per 1,000 population: n.a.
Life expectancy at birth (1990–95): male 45.9 years; female 49.1 years.
Major causes of death per 100,000 population: n.a.; however, major diseases include malaria, sleeping sickness, leprosy, venereal diseases, and tuberculosis.

National economy

Budget (1991–92). Revenue: CFAF 34,800,000,000 (1990; goods and services tax 33.2%, customs duties 28.8%, income tax 28.0%). Expenditures: CFAF 48,890,000,000 (1990; administrative 65.0%, defense 23.9%).
Public debt (external, outstanding; 1990): U.S.$417,000,000.
Tourism (1990): receipts from visitors U.S.$12,000,000; expenditures by nationals abroad U.S.$36,000,000.
Production (metric tons except as noted). Agriculture, forestry, fishing (1991): sugarcane 370,000, cassava 342,000, millet 302,000, yams 248,000, seed cotton 170,000, peanuts (groundnuts) 115,000, rice 86,000, pulses 60,000, sweet potatoes 48,000, corn (maize) 44,000, dates 32,000, mangoes 32,000, potatoes 18,000, onions 14,000, sesame seeds 12,000; livestock (number of live animals) 4,400,000 cattle, 2,923,000 goats, 1,983,000 sheep, 565,000 camels, 4,000,000 chickens; roundwood 4,033,000 cu m; fish catch (1990) 115,000. Mining and quarrying: clay, natron, tungsten, bauxite, and gold. Manufacturing (1988): beef and veal 53,000; refined sugar 27,000; salted, dried, or smoked fish 19,000[3]; goat meat 8,000; cattle hides 7,500; sheepskins and goatskins 3,318; mutton and lamb 1,000; wheat flour 1,000[4]; woven cotton fabrics 13,075,000 metres[4]; beer 117,000 hectolitres[5]; cigarettes 14,200,000 packets. Construction: n.a. Energy production (consumption): electricity (kW-hr; 1990) 82,000,000 (82,000,000); coal, none (n.a.); crude petroleum, none (n.a.); petroleum products (metric tons; 1990) none (71,000); natural gas, none (n.a.).
Household income and expenditure (1980). Average household size 3.9; average annual income per household CFAF 96,806 (U.S.$458); sources of income: n.a.; expenditure (1983)[6]: food 45.3%, health 11.9%, energy 5.8%, clothing 3.3%.

Gross domestic product (at current market prices; 1990): U.S.$1,074,000,000 (U.S.$190 per capita).

Structure of gross domestic product and labour force				
	1987			
	in value CFAF '000,000	% of total value	labour force	% of labour force
Agriculture	141,228	41.3	1,439,000	77.4
Mining	1,384	0.4		
Manufacturing	26,472	7.8		
Construction	5,326	1.6	117,000	6.3
Public utilities	1,445	0.4		
Transportation and communications	6,143	1.8		
Trade	83,122	24.3		
Pub. admin., defense	43,404	12.7	303,000	16.3
Finance	2,168	0.6		
Services	3,308	1.0		
Other	27,565[7]	8.1[7]	...	...
TOTAL	341,565	100.0	1,859,000	100.0

Population economically active (1989): total 1,934,000; activity rate of total population 34.9% (participation rates [1987]: over age 10, 51.2%; female 21.6%; unemployed, n.a.).

Price and earnings indexes (1985 = 100)							
	1984	1985	1986	1987	1988	1989	1990
Consumer price index	95.2	100.0	87.0	84.6	95.4	89.8	90.3
Earnings index	...	...	...	...	...	...	...

Land use (1990): forested 10.1%; meadows and pastures 35.7%; agricultural and under permanent cultivation 2.6%; built-on, wasteland, and other 51.6%.

Foreign trade

Balance of trade (current prices)						
	1985	1986	1987	1988	1989	1990
CFAF '000,000	−41,205	−39,713	−48,277	−50,646	−27,437	−26,241
% of total	34.3%	36.8%	42.1%	37.7%	21.7%	20.3%

Imports (1990): CFAF 77,743,000,000 (1983; petroleum products 16.8%; cereal products 16.8%; pharmaceutical products and chemicals 11.5%; machinery and transport equipment 8.5%, of which transport equipment 7.3%; electrical equipment 5.7%; textiles 2.9%; raw and refined sugar 2.3%). *Major import sources* (1989): France 36.2%%; United States 20.4%; Cameroon 18.4%; Italy 5.6; West Germany 3.7%.
Exports (1990): CFAF 51,502,000,000 (1983; raw cotton 91.1%; live cattle and frozen bovine meat 1.8%; hides and skins 0.4%). *Major export destinations* (1989): Portugal 21.0%; West Germany 16.9%; Japan 13.3%; France 9.9%; Spain 8.4%.

Transport and communications

Transport. Railroads: none. Roads (1983): total length 24,855 mi, 40,000 km (paved 1%). Vehicles (1989): passenger cars 8,000; trucks and buses 6,000. Merchant marine: vessels (100 gross tons and over) none. Air transport (1990): passenger-mi 144,044,000, passenger-km 232,329,000; short ton-mi cargo 12,119,000, metric ton-km cargo 17,694,000; airports (1992) with scheduled flights 1.
Communications. Daily newspapers (1987): total number 1; total circulation 1,500; circulation per 1,000 population 0.3. Radio (1991): total number of receivers 1,250,000 (1 per 4.7 persons). Television (1987): total number of receivers 5,000 (1 per 1,050 persons). Telephones (1988): 9,856 (1 per 555 persons).

Education and health

Education (1989–90)				
	schools	teachers	students	student/ teacher ratio
Primary (age 6–12)	1,868	7,327	492,231	67.2
Secondary (age 13–19)	66[8]	1,422	54,751	38.5
Voc., teacher tr.	25[3]	285[8]	3,819	15.1[8]
Higher	4[9]	59	2,969	50.3

Educational attainment: n.a. *Literacy* (1990): percentage of total population age 15 and over literate 29.8%; males literate 42.2%; females literate 17.9%.
Health: physicians (1980) 94 (1 per 47,640 persons); hospital beds (1978) 3,553 (1 per 1,190 persons); infant mortality rate per 1,000 live births (1990–95) 122.
Food (1987–89): daily per capita caloric intake 1,791 (vegetable products 92%, animal products 8%); 75% of FAO recommended minimum requirement.

Military

Total active duty personnel (1992): 25,200 (army 99.2%; navy, none; air force 0.8%). *Military expenditure as percentage of GNP* (1989): 5.6% (world 4.9%); per capita expenditure U.S.$8.

[1]The military regime that overthrew the constitutional government in December 1990 adopted a 30-month national charter (transitional constitution) in February 1991. The appointed 31-member Provisional Council of the Republic established by the national charter is a consultative body only. A new constitution and multiparty elections are expected in late 1993. The Prime Minister was made head of government in May 1992. [2]Detail does not add to total given because of rounding. [3]1987. [4]1983. [5]1986. [6]Capital city only. [7]Indirect taxes less subsidies. [8]1988–89. [9]1989.

Chile

Official name: República de Chile
 (Republic of Chile).
Form of government: multiparty
 republic with two legislative
 houses (Senate [48[1]]; Chamber of
 Deputies [120]).
Head of state and government:
 President.
Capital: Santiago[2].
Official language: Spanish.
Official religion: none.
Monetary unit: 1 peso (Ch$) = 100
 centavos; valuation (Oct. 5, 1992)
 1 U.S.$ = Ch$384.90;
 1 £ = Ch$654.33.

Area and population

Regions	Capitals	area[3] sq mi	area[3] sq km	population 1992 census[4]
Aisén del General Carlos				
Ibáñez del Campo	Coihaique	42,095	109,025	82,071
Antofagasta	Antofagasta	48,820	126,444	407,409
Araucanía	Temuco	12,300	31,858	774,959
Atacama	Copiapó	29,179	75,573	230,786
Bío-Bío	Concepción	14,258	36,929	1,729,920
Coquimbo	La Serena	15,697	40,656	502,460
Libertador General				
Bernardo O'Higgins	Rancagua	6,319	16,365	688,385
Los Lagos	Puerto Montt	25,868	66,997	953,330
Magallanes y la				
Antártica Chilena	Punta Arenas	50,979	132,034	143,058
Maule	Talca	11,700	30,302	834,053
Santiago,				
Región Metropolitana de	Santiago	5,926	15,349	5,170,293
Tarapacá	Iquique	22,663	58,698	341,112
Valparaíso	Valparaíso	6,331	16,396	1,373,967
TOTAL		292,135	756,626	13,231,803

Demography

Population (1992): 13,599,000[4].
Density (1992): persons per sq mi 46.6, persons per sq km 18.0.
Urban-rural (1990): urban 84.6%; rural 15.4%.
Sex distribution (1992): male 49.13%; female 50.87%.
Age breakdown (1991): under 15, 30.6%; 15–29, 27.6%; 30–44, 20.9%; 45–59, 12.0%; 60–74, 6.7%; 75 and over, 2.2%.
Population projection: (2000) 15,272,000; (2010) 17,182,000.
Doubling time: 41 years.
Ethnic composition (1983): mestizo 91.6%; Indian (mostly Araucanian) 6.8%; others (mainly European) 1.6%.
Religious affiliation (1982): Roman Catholic 80.7%; Protestant 6.1%; Jewish 0.2%; atheist and nonreligious 12.8%; other 0.2%.
Major cities (1991): Greater Santiago 5,342,900; Viña del Mar 312,300; Concepción 311,500; Valparaíso 296,000; Talcahuano 251,100.

Vital statistics

Birth rate per 1,000 population (1990): 23.3 (world avg. 27.1); legitimate 65.7%; illegitimate 34.3%.
Death rate per 1,000 population (1990): 6.0 (world avg. 9.8).
Natural increase rate per 1,000 population (1990): 17.3 (world avg. 17.3).
Total fertility rate (avg. births per childbearing woman; 1990): 2.6.
Marriage rate per 1,000 population (1990): 7.5.
Divorce rate per 1,000 population (1987): 0.4.
Life expectancy at birth (1985–90): male 68.1 years; female 75.1 years.
Major causes of death per 100,000 population (1990): diseases of the circulatory system 163.7; malignant neoplasms (cancers) 107.5; diseases of the respiratory system 73.1; accidents and adverse effects 72.8.

National economy

Budget (1988). Revenue: Ch$1,534,290,000,000 (sales and value-added taxes 29.0%, nontax revenue 24.1%, income taxes 23.3%, import and export duties 9.8%, social security contributions 6.0%, stamp taxes 4.2%). Expenditures: Ch$1,620,440,000,000 (social security and welfare 29.8%, education 10.1%, economic services 8.8%, defense 8.4%, public services 7.2%, health 5.9%).
Public debt (external, outstanding; 1990): U.S.$10,366,000,000.
Production (metric tons except as noted). Agriculture, forestry, fishing (1990): sugar beets 2,326,000, wheat 1,718,000, potatoes 829,000, corn (maize) 823,000, oats 205,000, rice 136,000, rapeseed 53,000; livestock (number of live animals) 6,650,000 sheep, 3,250,000 cattle, 1,450,000 pigs; roundwood 18,708,000 cu m; fish catch (1991) 6,166,000. Mining (1991): iron 8,464,000; copper 1,857,144; manganese 44,041; zinc 30,275; molybdenum 14,433; silver 669,484 kilograms; gold 28,823 kilograms. Manufacturing (1991): cement 2,250,800; cellulose 798,000; refined sugar 353,300[5]; newsprint 172,900; noodles 55,200; carbonated drinks 7,197,000 hectolitres; tires 1,824,900 units; pressed-fibre panels 9,082,900 sq m; flat glass 5,730,300 sq m. Construction[6] (1990): residential 4,495,400 sq m; nonresidential 1,747,900 sq m. Energy production (consumption): electricity (kW-hr; 1990) 18,372,000,000 (18,372,000,000); coal (metric tons; 1991) 2,579,000 ([1990] 3,720,000); crude petroleum (barrels; 1990) 6,320,000 (44,676,000); petroleum products (metric tons; 1990) 6,105,000 (6,448,000); natural gas (cu m; 1991) 4,067,200,000 (4,067,200,000).
Land use (1989): forested 11.8%; meadows and pastures 18.0%; agricultural and under permanent cultivation 6.0%; other 64.2%.
Gross national product (1990): U.S.$25,504,000,000 (U.S.$1,940 per capita).

Structure of gross domestic product and labour force

	1991 in value Ch$'000,000[7]	1991 % of total value	1990 labour force	1990 % of labour force
Agriculture	44,500	8.7	883,300	17.8
Mining	37,000	7.3	106,200	2.1
Manufacturing	104,500	20.5	761,300	15.4
Construction	29,600	5.8	328,900	6.6
Public utilities	12,800	2.5	22,600	0.5
Transp. and commun.	37,400	7.4	324,800	6.6
Trade	94,200	18.5	829,600	16.8
Finance			213,200	4.3
Pub. admin., defense				
Services[8]	149,100	29.3	1,207,500	24.4
Other			273,200[9]	5.5[9]
TOTAL	509,100	100.0	4,950,700[10]	100.0

Population economically active (1990): total 4,950,700; activity rate of total population 36.6% (participation rates: ages 15–64 56.9%; female 34.9%; unemployed 5.6%).

Price and earnings indexes (1985 = 100)

	1985	1986	1987	1988	1989	1990	1991
Consumer price index	100.0	119.5	143.2	164.3	192.2	242.0	295.0
Monthly earnings index	100.0	122.5	146.1	178.6	212.7	287.9	349.0

Household income and expenditure. Average household size (1992) 4.1; average annual income per family (household; 1985)[11] Ch$440,738 at June prices (U.S.$2,840); sources of income (1976): wages and salaries 40.8%, transfer payments 8.0%, self-employment and other 51.2%; expenditure (1989): food 27.9%, clothing 22.5%, housing 15.2%, transportation 6.4%.
Tourism (1990): receipts from visitors U.S.$548,000,000; expenditures by nationals abroad U.S.$426,000,000.

Foreign trade[12]

Balance of trade (current prices)

	1986	1987	1988	1989	1990	1991
U.S.$'000,000	+1,620	+1,704	+2,822	+2,391	+2,308	+2,363
% of total	23.7%	20.1%	25.0%	17.1%	15.5%	15.3%

Imports (1991): U.S.$7,685,800,000 (intermediate goods 57.8%; capital goods 23.9%; consumer goods 14.8%). *Major import sources:* U.S. 20.6%; Brazil 9.1%; Japan 8.4%; Argentina 7.2%; Germany 6.5%; France 3.1%; Nigeria 2.6%; Venezuela 2.6%.
Exports (1991): U.S.$9,048,400,000 (mining 48.5%; industrial products 36.6%, of which paper and paper products 4.9%, chemical and petroleum products 3.9%; fruits and vegetables 11.0%). *Major export destinations:* Japan 18.2%; U.S. 17.6%; Germany 7.8%; Brazil 4.9%; U.K. 4.5%; Taiwan 4.4%; France 4.3%; The Netherlands 4.0%.

Transport and communications

Transport. Railroads (1990): route length 2,778 mi, 4,470 km; passenger-km 1,076,000,000; metric ton-km cargo 1,572,000,000. Roads (1990): total length 49,457 mi, 79,593 km (paved 14%). Vehicles (1989) passenger cars 690,000; trucks and buses 300,000. Merchant marine (1991): vessels (100 gross tons and over) 387; total deadweight tonnage 874,999. Air transport (1990): passenger-km 2,980,000,000; metric ton-km cargo 689,844,000; airports (1992) with scheduled flights 16.
Communications. Daily newspapers (1990): total number 34; total circulation 890,800[13]; circulation per 1,000 population 68[13]. Radio (1991): 4,250,000 receivers (1 per 3.1 persons). Television (1989): 3,200,000 receivers (1 per 4.1 persons). Telephones (1988): 866,663 (1 per 15 persons).

Education and health

Education (1989)

	schools	teachers	students	student/ teacher ratio
Primary (age 6–13)	8,101	55,268	1,987,758	36.0
Secondary (age 14–17)	1,694[14]	...	607,709	...
Vocational	1,262[14]	...	134,301	...
Higher[14]	201	15,131[15]	233,148	...

Educational attainment (1982). Percentage of population age 25 and over having: no formal schooling 9.4%; primary education 56.6%; secondary 26.9%; higher 7.1%. *Literacy* (1990): total population age 15 and over literate 93.4%; males 93.5%; females 93.2%.
Health (1990): physicians 14,334 (1 per 919 persons); hospital beds 43,297 (1 per 304 persons); infant mortality rate (1989) 17.1.
Food (1987–89): daily per capita caloric intake 2,553 (vegetable products 83%, animal products 17%); 105% of FAO recommended minimum requirement.

Military

Total active duty personnel (1991): 91,800 (army 58.8%, navy 27.2%, air force 14.0%). *Military expenditure as percentage of GNP* (1989): 3.4% (world 4.9%); per capita expenditure: U.S.$61.

[1]Includes 10 nonelective seats. [2]Legislative bodies meet in Valparaíso. [3]Excludes the territory of Antártica Chilena and "inland" (actually tidal) water areas. [4]Preliminary figures not adjusted for undercount; 1992 midyear based on precensus demographic analysis, [5]1989. [6]Construction approved and already begun only. [7]In constant prices of 1977. [8]Services includes restaurants and hotels. [9]Includes 46,100 unemployed persons not previously employed. [10]Detail does not add to total given because of rounding. [11]Greater Santiago area. [12]Import figures are f.o.b. in balance of trade and c.i.f. for commodities and trading partners. [13]Circulation for 32 newspapers only. [14]1988. [15]1984.

China

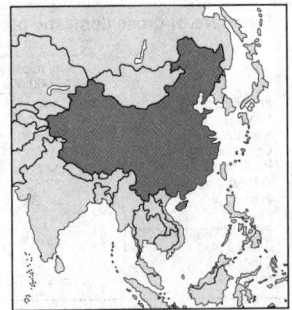

Official name: Chung-hua Jen-min Kung-ho-kuo (People's Republic of China).
Form of government: single-party people's republic with one legislative house (National People's Congress [2,978]).
Chief of state: President.
Head of government: Premier.
Capital: Peking (Beijing).
Official language: Mandarin Chinese.
Official religion: none.
Monetary unit: 1 Renminbi (yuan) (Y) = 10 jiao = 100 fen; valuation (Oct. 5, 1992) 1 U.S.$ = Y 5.63; 1 £ = Y 9.57.

Area and population[1, 2]

Provinces	Capitals	area sq mi	area sq km	population 1990 census
Anhwei (Anhui)	Ho-fei (Hefei)	54,000	139,900	56,180,813
Chekiang (Zhejiang)	Hang-chou (Hangzhou)	39,300	101,800	41,445,930
Fukien (Fujian)	Fu-chou (Fuzhou)	47,500	123,100	30,048,224
Hainan (Hainan)	Hai-k'ou (Haikou)	13,200	34,300	6,557,482
Heilungkiang (Heilongjiang)	Harbin	179,000	463,600	35,214,873
Honan (Henan)	Cheng-chou (Zhengzhou)	64,500	167,000	85,509,535
Hopeh (Hebei)	Shih-chia-chuang (Shijiazhuang)	78,200	202,700	61,082,439
Hunan (Hunan)	Ch'ang-sha (Changsha)	81,300	210,500	60,659,754
Hupeh (Hubei)	Wu-han (Wuhan)	72,400	187,500	53,969,210
Kansu (Gansu)	Lan-chou (Lanzhou)	141,500	366,500	22,371,141
Kiangsi (Jiangxi)	Nan-ch'ang (Nanchang)	63,600	164,800	37,710,281
Kiangsu (Jiangsu)	Nanking (Nanjing)	39,600	102,600	67,056,519
Kirin (Jilin)	Ch'ang-ch'un (Changchun)	72,200	187,000	24,658,721
Kwangtung (Guangdong)	Canton (Guangzhou)	76,100	197,100	62,829,236
Kweichow (Guizhou)	Kuei-yang (Guiyang)	67,200	174,000	32,391,066
Liaoning (Liaoning)	Shen-yang (Shenyang)	58,300	151,000	39,459,697
Shansi (Shanxi)	T'ai-yüan (Taiyuan)	60,700	157,100	28,759,014
Shantung (Shandong)	Chi-nan (Jinan)	59,200	153,300	84,392,827
Shensi (Shaanxi)	Sian (Xi'an)	75,600	195,800	32,882,403
Szechwan (Sichuan)	Ch'eng-tu (Chengdu)	219,700	569,000	107,218,173
Tsinghai (Qinghai)	Hsi-ning (Xining)	278,400	721,000	4,456,946
Yunnan (Yunnan)	K'un-ming (Kunming)	168,400	436,200	36,972,610
Autonomous regions				
Inner Mongolia (Nei Monggol)	Hu-ho-hao-t'e (Hohhot)	454,600	1,177,500	21,456,798
Kwangsi Chuang (Guangxi Zhuang)	Nan-ning (Nanning)	85,100	220,400	42,245,765
Ningsia Hui (Ningxia Hui)	Yin-ch'uan (Yinchuan)	25,600	66,400	4,655,451
Sinkiang Uighur (Xinjiang Uygur)	Wu-lu-mu-ch'i (Urumqi)	635,900	1,646,900	15,155,778
Tibet (Xizang)	Lhasa	471,700	1,221,600	2,196,010
Municipalities				
Peking (Beijing)	—	6,500	16,800	10,819,407
Shanghai (Shanghai)	—	2,400	6,200	13,341,896
Tientsin (Tianjin)	—	4,400	11,300	8,785,402
TOTAL		3,696,100[3]	9,572,900[3]	1,133,682,501[4]

Demography

Population (1992): 1,165,888,000.
Density (1992): persons per sq mi 315.4, persons per sq km 121.8.
Urban-rural (1990): urban 26.2%; rural 73.8%.
Sex distribution (1990): male 51.60%; female 48.40%.
Age breakdown (1990): under 15, 27.7%; 15–29, 31.0%; 30–44, 20.7%; 45–59, 12.0%; 60–74, 6.9%; 75 and over, 1.7%.
Population projection: (2000) 1,291,894,000; (2010) 1,387,729,000.
Doubling time: 54 years.
Ethnic composition (1990): Han (Chinese) 91.96%; Chuang 1.37%; Manchu 0.87%; Hui 0.76%; Miao 0.65%; Uighur 0.58%; Yi 0.58%; Tuchia 0.50%; Mongolian 0.42%; Tibetan 0.41%; Puyi 0.23%; Tung 0.22%; Yao 0.18%; Korean 0.17%; Pai 0.14%; Hani 0.11%; Kazakh 0.10%; Tai 0.09%; Li 0.09%; other 0.51%.
Religious affiliation (1980): nonreligious 59.2%; Chinese folk-religionist 20.1%; atheist 12.0%; Buddhist 6.0%; Muslim 2.4%; Christian 0.2%; other 0.1%.
Major cities (1990): Shanghai 7,496,509; Peking 5,769,607; Tientsin 4,574,689; Shen-yang 3,603,712; Wu-han 3,284,229; Canton 2,914,281; Harbin 2,443,398; Chungking (Chongqing) 2,266,772; Nanking 2,090,204; Sian 1,959,044; Ta-lien (Dalian) 1,723,302; Ch'eng-tu 1,713,255; Ch'ang-ch'un 1,679,270; T'ai-yüan 1,533,884; Tsinan 1,480,915; Ch'ing-tao (Qingdao) 1,459,195; An-shan (Anshan) 1,203,986; Fu-shun 1,202,388; Lan-chou 1,194,640; Cheng-chou 1,159,679; Tzu-po (Zibo) 1,138,074; K'un-ming 1,127,411.
Households (1990). Average rural household size 4.8; urban household size 3.5. Family households (1990): 277,390,000 (99.4%); collective 1,671,000 (0.6%).

Vital statistics

Birth rate per 1,000 population (1991): 19.7 (world avg. 26.4).
Death rate per 1,000 population (1991): 6.7 (world avg. 9.2).
Natural increase rate per 1,000 population (1991): 13.0 (world avg. 17.2).
Total fertility rate (avg. births per childbearing woman; 1991): 2.3.
Marriage rate per 1,000 population (1990): 8.4.
Divorce rate per 1,000 population (1990): 0.7.

Life expectancy at birth (1990): male 68.6 years; female 71.8 years.
Major causes of death per 100,000 population (percentage distribution; 1990)[5]: malignant neoplasms (cancers) 21.9%; diseases of the circulatory system 20.8%; diseases of the respiratory system 15.8%; diseases of the heart 15.8%; injuries and poisoning 6.9%; digestive diseases 4.0%.

Social indicators

Educational attainment (1982). Percentage of population age 25 and over having: no schooling and incomplete primary 44.5%; completed primary 32.7%; completed junior secondary 16.1%; completed senior secondary 5.6%; postsecondary 1.1%.

Distribution of urban household income (1990)

by per capita income group (avg. Y 1,523)

Y 600 and under	Y 601–Y 1,200	Y 1,201–Y 1,800	over Y 1,800
7.3%	40.0%	30.4%	22.3%

Quality of working life (1991). Average workweek: 48 hours. Annual rate per 100,000 workers for: injury or accident, n.a.; industrial illness, n.a.; death, n.a. Funds for pensions and social welfare relief (1990): Y 47,240,000,000. Average days lost to labour stoppages per 1,000 workdays: n.a. Average duration of journey to work: n.a. Method of transport: n.a. Rate per 1,000 workers of discouraged (unemployed no longer seeking work): n.a.
Access to services. Proportion of communes having access to electricity (1979) 87.1%. Percentage of urban population with: safe public water supply (1990) 89.2%; public sewage collection, n.a.; public fire protection, n.a.
Social participation. Eligible voters participating in last national election: n.a. Population participating in voluntary work: n.a. Trade union membership in total labour force (1988): 18.9%. Practicing religious population in total affiliated population: n.a.
Social deviance. Annual reported arrest rate per 100,000 population (1986) for: property violation 20.7; infringing personal rights 7.2; disruption of social administration 3.3; endangering public security[6] 1.0.
Leisure. Favourite leisure activities: n.a.
Material well-being (1990). Urban families possessing (number per family): bicycles 1.9; televisions 1.1; sewing machines 0.7; wristwatches 0.7; radios 0.5. Rural families possessing (number per family): wristwatches 1.7; bicycles 1.2; sewing machines 0.6; radios 0.5; televisions 0.4.

National economy

Gross national product (at current market prices; 1990): U.S.$415,884,000,000 (U.S.$370 per capita).

Structure of gross national product and labour force

	1990 in value Y '000,000,000	% of total value	labour force ('000)[7]	% of labour force
Agriculture	502.4	34.1	341,770	60.2
Mining	...	...	1,000	0.2
Manufacturing	698.1	47.3	96,970	17.1
Construction	84.8	5.7	24,610	4.3
Public utilities	...	...		
Transp. and commun.	95.6	6.5	14,690	2.6
Trade	94.4	6.4	29,370	5.2
Finance	...	...	2,180	0.4
Pub. admin.	...	...	10,790	1.9
Services	...	...	28,040	4.9
Other	...	...	17,980	3.2
TOTAL	1,475.3	100.0	567,400	100.0

Budget (1990). Revenue: Y 331,260,000,000 (taxes 85.2%; funds collected for energy and transport projects 5.6%). Expenditures: Y 345,220,000,000 (capital construction 21.0%; culture, education, public health 17.9%; subsidies 11.0%; defense 8.4%).
Public debt (external, outstanding; 1990): U.S.$52,550,000,000.
Tourism: receipts from visitors (1991) U.S.$2,840,000,000; expenditures by nationals abroad (1990) U.S.$470,000,000.

Retail and service enterprises (1990)

	no. of enter-prises	no. of employees	annual wage as a % of all wages	annual gross output value (Y '000,000)
Retail trade	8,709,000	20,914,000	...	...
Grocery stores	162,000	1,162,000	...	...
Department stores	159,000	1,793,000	...	...
Other food shops	109,000	733,000	...	...
Agricultural supplies stores	88,000	436,000	...	...
Electrical appliances stores	72,000	715,000	...	...
Household supplies stores	66,000	344,000	...	...
Grain and oil shops	63,000	647,000	...	...
Textile stores	36,000	247,000	...	...
Drugstores	27,000	210,000	...	...
Bookstores	26,000	127,000	...	...
Coal stores	14,000	167,000	...	...
Service trade	1,639,000	4,027,000	...	...
Repair shops	669,000	1,004,000	...	...
Barbershops	422,000	670,000	...	...
Hotels	171,000	1,308,000	...	...
Photo studios	89,000	205,000	...	...

Production (metric tons except as noted). Agriculture, forestry, fishing (1991): grains—rice 187,450,000, wheat 95,003,000, corn (maize) 93,350,000, sorghum 5,615,000, millet 4,501,000, barley 3,000,000; oilseeds—rapeseed 7,436,000, peanuts (groundnuts) 6,060,000, sunflower seed 1,250,000; fruits and nuts—watermelons 6,280,000, oranges 5,385,000, apples 4,816,000, cantaloupes 3,135,000, walnuts 153,000; other—sweet potatoes 107,-

190,000, sugarcane 73,103,000, potatoes 35,533,000, seed cotton 16,989,000, sugar beets 16,237,000, soybeans 9,807,000, cabbage 8,103,000, tomatoes 5,690,000, cucumbers 4,148,000, tobacco leaves 3,121,000, eggplant 2,383,-000, tea 566,000; livestock (number of live animals) 363,975,000 pigs, 112,820,000 sheep, 97,378,000 goats, 81,407,000 cattle, 21,635,000 water buffalo, 11,198,000 asses, 10,174,000 horses, 2,077,000,000 chickens, 369,000,000 ducks; roundwood (1990) 277,015,000 cu m; fish catch (1990) 12,095,363. Mining and quarrying (1991): metals (metal content of ores)—copper 560,-000, zinc 550,000, lead 300,000, tungsten 30,000, tin 26,000; other metals—iron ore 170,000,000, bauxite 2,500,000, manganese ore 1,600,000[8], silver 125,000[8], gold 90,000[8]; nonmetals—salt 25,530,000, gypsum 8,300,000, phosphates 4,100,000[8], barite 1,750,000, fluorite 1,700,000, talc 1,600,000, graphite 200,000[8], asbestos 150,000. Manufacturing (1991): cement 248,000,000; rolled steel 55,470,000; chemical fertilizer 19,880,000; paper and paperboard 14,300,-000; sulfuric acid 13,140,000; sugar 6,310,000; cotton yarn 4,500,000; woolen fabrics 300,000,000 m; bicycles 36,270,000 units; television sets 26,220,000 units; household washing machines 6,830,000 units; household refrigerators 4,760,000 units; automobiles 713,000 units. Construction (1990): residential 862,888,000 sq m; nonresidential 215,038,000 sq m. Distribution of industrial production (percentage of total value of output by sector; 1978 [1990]): state-operated enterprises 80.6% (67.2%); collectives 19.2% (28.1%); privately operated enterprises 0.2% (4.7%). Retail sales (percentage of total sales by sector; 1978 [1990]): state-operated enterprises 90.5% (43.7%); collectives 7.4% (34.9%); privately operated enterprises 2.1% (21.4%).

Manufacturing and mining enterprises (1990)

	no. of enterprises	no. of employees[9]	annual wages as a % of avg. of all wages[10]	annual gross output value (Y '000,000)
Manufacturing				
Machinery, transport equipment, and basic manufactures,	104,757	17,620,000	96.7	440,189
of which,				
Industrial equipment	6,542	9,890,000	...	34,125
Transport equipment	10,925	...	...	71,387
Electronic goods	4,637	1,570,000	...	58,419
Measuring equipment	3,508	...	...	11,012
Textiles,	24,584	7,450,000	95.5	229,108
of which,				
Cotton	9,303	...	...	126,136
Foodstuffs,	40,207	4,430,000	87.5	126,584
of which,				
Grains and edible oils	12,373	...	...	32,822
Processed meat	...	...	...	...
Tobacco manufactures	317	...	...	51,199
Chemicals,	40,966	6,720,000	92.1	275,529
of which,				
Organic chemicals	6,417	...	...	46,568
Plastics	14,238	1,000,000	...	34,982
Building materials,	53,120	3,900,000	93.0	89,057
of which,				
Brick, tile, other	...	...	...	...
Cement (all forms)	5,383	856,000[11]	...	28,986
Secondary forest products (including paper and stationery)	30,977	2,320,000	96.1	57,331
Primary forest products	1,059	1,190,000	114.3	9,207
Mining				
Nonferrous and ferrous metals	3,759	940,000	107.6	14,010
Crude petroleum	33	760,000	...	42,720
Coal	9,601	5,390,000	119.8	45,753

Energy production (consumption): electricity (kW-hr; 1990) 618,000,000,000 (619,460,000,000); coal (metric tons; 1990) 1,080,000,000 (1,064,500,000); crude petroleum (barrels; 1990) 1,010,892,000 (800,515,000); petroleum products (metric tons; 1990) 85,877,000 (85,109,000); natural gas (cu m; 1990) 15,258,000,000 (15,258,000,000).

Financial aggregates[12]

	1987	1988	1989	1990	1991	June 1992[13]
Exchange rate, Y per:						
U.S. dollar	3.72	3.72	4.72	5.22	5.43	5.46
£	6.96	6.73	7.58	10.06	10.16	10.36
SDR	5.28	5.01	6.21	7.43	7.77	7.82
International reserves (U.S.$)						
Total (excl. gold; '000,000)	16,305	18,541	17,960	29,586	43,674	46,124
SDRs ('000,000)	640	586	540	562	577	594
Reserve pos. in IMF ('000,000)	429	407	398	430	433	433
Foreign exchange	15,236	17,548	17,022	28,594	42,664	45,097
Gold ('000,000 fine troy oz)	12.7	12.7	12.7	12.7	12.7	12.7
% world reserves	1.3	1.3	1.4	1.4	1.4	1.4
Interest and prices						
Central bank discount (%)	...	...	...	...	...	...
Govt. bond yield (%)	...	...	...	...	...	...
Industrial share prices	...	...	...	...	...	...
Balance of payments (U.S.$ '000,000)						
Balance of visible trade,	−1,661	−5,315	−5,620	+9,165	+8,743	...
of which:						
Imports, f.o.b.	−36,395	−46,369	−48,840	−42,354	−50,176	...
Exports, f.o.b.	34,734	41,054	43,220	51,519	58,919	...
Balance of invisibles	1,961	1,513	1,303	2,833	5,022	...
Balance of payments, current account	300	−3,802	−4,317	+11,998	+13,765	...

Household income and expenditure. Average household size (1990) 4.0; rural household 4.8, urban household 3.5. Average annual income per household, Y 4,644; rural household Y 4,436, urban household Y 5,230. Sources of income: rural household (1990)—income from household businesses 82.3%, income from the collective 9.6%, rural new economic associations 0.4%, other 7.7%; urban household[9] (1990)—time wages 59.3%, subsidies 20.8%, bonuses and piece-rate wages 19.9%. Expenditure (1990): rural household—food 54.9%, housing 12.9%, personal effects 11.9%, clothing 8.4%, fuel 4.5%, cultural activities 2.8%; urban household—food 54.2%, clothing

13.4%, personal effects 10.1%, cultural activities 8.8%, fuel 3.1%, medicines 1.5%, rent 0.7%.
Population economically active (1987): total 584,569,200; activity rate of total population 54.7% (participation rates: over age 15, 76.8%; female 49.7%; unemployed 2.0%[14]). Urban work force by sector of employment, 1978 (1990): state-run enterprises 74,500,000 (103,460,000); collectives 20,000,000 (35,490,-000); self-employment or privately run enterprises 150,000 (8,343,000).

Price and earnings indexes (1985 = 100)

	1984	1985	1986	1987	1988	1989	1990
Consumer price index	89.4	100.0	107.0	116.4	140.5	163.4	165.5
Annual earnings index[15]	84.8	100.0	115.8	127.1	152.2	168.6	186.4

Land use (1990): forested 13.6%; meadows and pastures 42.9%; agricultural and under permanent cultivation 10.4%; other 33.1%.

Foreign trade[16]

Balance of trade (current prices)

	1986	1987	1988	1989	1990	1991
Y '000,000	−28,930	−990	−11,810	−6,600	+62,570	+69,470
% of total	11.8%	0.3%	3.2%	1.7%	12.0%	10.2%

Imports (1990): U.S.$53,345,000,000 (machinery and transport equipment 31.6%; products of textile industries, rubber and metal products 16.7%; chemical and related products 12.5%; inedible raw materials 7.7%; food and live animals 6.3%; mineral fuels and lubricants 2.4%). *Major import sources:* Hong Kong 26.7%; Japan 14.2%; United States 12.3%; West Germany 5.5%; U.S.S.R. 4.0%; France 3.1%; Canada 2.8%; United Kingdom 2.6%; Australia 2.5%; Italy 2.0%; Singapore 1.6%.
Exports (1990): U.S.$62,091,000,000 (products of textile industries, rubber and metal products 20.3%; food and live animals 10.6%; machinery and transport equipment 9.0%; mineral fuels and lubricants 8.4%; chemicals and allied products 6.0%; inedible raw materials 5.7%). *Major export destinations:* Hong Kong 42.9%; Japan 14.5%; United States 8.3%; U.S.S.R. 3.6%; West Germany 3.3%; Singapore 3.2%; The Netherlands 1.5%; Italy 1.3%; Thailand 1.3%; United Kingdom 1.0%; France 1.0%.

Transport and communications

Transport. Railroads (1990): length 41,973 mi, 67,549 km; (1991) passenger-mi 175,700,000,000, passenger-km 282,700,000,000; short ton-mi cargo 751,-500,000,000, metric ton-km cargo 1,097,200,000,000. Roads (1990): total length 638,985 mi, 1,028,348 km (paved 86%). Vehicles (1990): passenger cars 1,664,010; trucks and buses 4,171,855. Merchant marine (1991): vessels (100 gross tons and over) 2,382; total deadweight tonnage 21,109,995. Air transport (1991): passenger-mi 18,700,000,000, passenger-km 30,100,000,000; short ton-mi cargo 685,000,000, metric ton-km cargo 1,000,000,000; airports (1992) with scheduled flights 90.
Communications. Daily newspapers (1988): total number 78; total circulation 39,597,000[17]; circulation per 1,000 population 37[17]. Radio (1990): total number of receivers 121,211,690 (1 per 9.4 persons). Television (1991): total number of receivers 126,000,000 (1 per 9.1 persons). Telephones (1990): 12,735,400 (1 per 89 persons).

Education and health

Education (1990)

	schools	teachers	students	student/ teacher ratio
Primary (age 7–13)	938,394	6,332,000	142,136,000	22.4
Secondary (age 13–17)	87,631	3,033,000	45,860,000	15.1
Secondary specialized	13,146	459,000	5,194,000	11.3
Higher	1,075	395,000	2,063,000	5.2

Literacy (1990): total population age 15 and over literate 636,112,000 (77.7%); males literate 364,687,000 (87.0%); females literate 271,425,000 (68.0%).
Health (1991): physicians 1,780,000 (1 per 646 persons); hospital beds 2,689,-000 (1 per 428 persons); infant mortality rate per 1,000 live births 33.0.
Food (1988–90): daily per capita caloric intake 2,641 (vegetable products 89%, animal products 11%); 112% of FAO recommended minimum requirement.

Military

Total active duty personnel (1992): 3,030,000 (army 75.9%, navy 8.6%, air force 15.5%). *Military expenditure as percentage of GNP* (1989): 3.7% (world 4.9%); per capita expenditure U.S.$20.

[1]Names of the provinces, autonomous regions, and municipalities are stated in conventional form, followed by Pinyin transliteration; names of capitals are stated in conventional form or Wade-Giles transliteration, followed by Pinyin transliteration. [2]Data for Taiwan, Quemoy, and Matsu are excluded. [3]Includes 4,600 sq mi (11,900 sq km) not shown separately. [4]Total includes servicemen not assigned to any political division. [5]Based on urban sample population. [6]Excludes arrests for anti-Communist activities. [7]Social labour force. [8]1989. [9]In state-owned and collective-owned industries only. [10]1979. [11]1984. [12]Exchange rates and international reserves are end-of-year figures. [13]End-of-month figures for exchange rates and international reserves. [14]Rate of waiting for employment in cities and towns. [15]Average annual wage in industrial establishments in urban areas. [16]Imports and exports f.o.b. [17]Circulation data based on 58 dailies.

Colombia

Official name: República de Colombia
(Republic of Colombia).
Form of government: unitary,
multiparty republic with two
legislative houses (Senate [102];
House of Representatives [161]).
Head of state and government:
President.
Capital: Santafé de Bogotá, D.C.
Official language: Spanish.
Official religion: none.
Monetary unit: 1 peso (Col$) = 100
centavos; valuation (Oct. 5, 1992)
1 U.S.$ = Col$625; 1 £ = Col$1,062.

Area and population

Departments	Capitals	area sq mi	area sq km	population 1992 estimate
Amazonas	Leticia	42,342	109,665	52,874
Antioquia	Medellín	24,561	63,612	4,467,914
Arauca	Arauca	9,196	23,818	96,972
Atlántico	Barranquilla	1,308	3,388	1,703,968
Bolívar	Cartagena	10,030	25,978	1,451,726
Boyacá	Tunja	8,953	23,189	1,274,393
Caldas	Manizales	3,046	7,888	909,848
Caquetá	Florencia	34,349	88,965	309,506
Casanare	Yopal	17,236	44,640	176,826
Cauca	Popayán	11,316	29,308	933,643
Cesar	Valledupar	8,844	22,905	799,875
Chocó	Quibdó	17,965	46,530	350,934
Córdoba	Montería	9,660	25,020	1,115,142
Cundinamarca	Santafé de Bogotá, D.C.	8,735	22,623	1,658,751
Guainía	Puerto Inírida	27,891	72,238	13,092
Guaviare	Guaviare	16,342	42,327	63,886
Huila	Neiva	7,680	19,890	777,876
La Guajira	Riohacha	8,049	20,844	347,538
Magdalena	Santander	8,953	23,188	979,747
Meta	Villavicencio	33,064	85,635	564,276
Nariño	Pasto	12,845	33,268	1,163,436
Norte de Santander	Cúcuta	8,362	21,658	1,006,919
Putumayo	Mocoa	9,608	24,885	221,872
Quindío	Armenia	712	1,845	414,524
Risaralda	Pereira	1,598	4,140	735,700
San Andrés y Providencia	San Andrés	17	44	41,581
Santander	Bucaramanga	11,790	30,537	1,642,579
Sucre	Sincelejo	4,215	10,917	611,421
Tolima	Ibagué	9,097	23,562	1,193,450
Valle	Cali	8,548	22,140	3,335,827
Vaupés	Mitú	25,200	65,268	34,428
Vichada	Puerto Carreño	38,703	100,242	19,370
Special District				
Santafé de Bogotá, D.C.		613	1,587	4,921,642
TOTAL		440,831[1]	1,141,748	33,391,536

Demography

Population (1992): 33,392,000.
Density (1992): persons per sq mi 75.7, persons per sq km 29.2.
Urban-rural (1985): urban 67.2%; rural 32.8%.
Sex distribution (1990): male 49.64%; female 50.36%.
Age breakdown (1990): under 15, 36.1%; 15–29, 30.2%; 30–44, 18.7%; 45–59, 8.9%; 60–74, 4.7%; 75 and over, 1.4%.
Population projection: (2000) 38,218,000; (2010) 44,279,000.
Doubling time: 36 years.
Ethnic composition (1985): mestizo 58.0%; white 20.0%; mulatto 14.0%; black 4.0%; mixed black-Indian 3.0%; Amerindian 1.0%.
Religious affiliation (1991): Roman Catholic 93.8%; other 6.2%.
Major cities (1992): Santafé de Bogotá, D.C., 4,921,642; Cali 1,624,401; Medellín 1,581,364; Barranquilla 1,018,763; Cartagena 688,306.

Vital statistics

Birth rate per 1,000 population (1983–88): 27.9 (world avg. 27.1).
Death rate per 1,000 population (1983–88): 7.4 (world avg. 9.8).
Natural increase rate per 1,000 population (1983–88): 20.5 (world avg. 17.3).
Total fertility rate (avg. births per childbearing woman; 1981–86): 3.4.
Life expectancy at birth (1990–95): male 66.4 years; female 72.3 years.
Major causes of death per 100,000 population (1990)[2]: homicide with firearms 101.0; malignant neoplasms (cancers) 82.6; ischemic heart disease 70.4; accidents 49.0; infectious and parasitic diseases 25.5.

National economy

Budget (1990). Revenue: Col$3,265,691,000,000 (indirect taxes 40.3%, credit resources 26.6%, direct taxes 25.2%). Expenditures: Col$2,502,705,000,000 (finance and public credit 20.8%, education 18.8%, defense 11.6%, public works and transportation 7.2%, health 6.2%, agriculture 6.0%).
Public debt (external, outstanding; 1990): U.S.$15,637,000,000.
Tourism (1990): receipts U.S.$362,000,000; expenditures U.S.$515,000,000.
Production (metric tons except as noted). Agriculture (1991): sugarcane 27,577,000, plantains 2,706,000, potatoes 2,372,000, rice 1,739,000, bananas 1,630,000, corn (maize) 1,274,000, coffee (green) 870,000, sorghum 809,000; roundwood (1990) 19,384,000 cu m; fish catch (1990) 101,119; livestock (number of live animals) 24,875,000 cattle, 3,708,000 vicuña, 2,745,000 sheep, 1,440,000 pigs. Mining and quarrying (1991): iron ore 595,952; gold 1,016,625 troy oz; silver 258,386 troy oz. Manufacturing (value added in Col$'000,000; 1989): processed food 490,322; beverages 373,927; textiles 310,239; chemical products 205,208; machinery and electrical apparatus

164,743; basic steel 142,791; metal products 137,920; transport equipment 126,916. Construction (1991)[3]: residential 6,598,079 sq m; nonresidential 1,952,344 sq m. Energy production (consumption): electricity (kW-hr; 1990) 36,000,000,000 (36,000,000,000); coal (metric tons; 1990) 19,000,000 (5,300,-000); crude petroleum (barrels; 1990) 156,946,000 (96,168,000); petroleum products (metric tons; 1990) 10,645,000 (7,835,000); natural gas (cu m; 1990) 5,656,773,000 (5,656,773,000).
Gross national product (1990): U.S.$40,805,000,000 (U.S.$1,240 per capita).

Structure of gross domestic product and labour force

	1990 in value Col$'000,000	1990 % of total value	1980 labour force	1980 % of labour force
Agriculture	3,453,677	16.7	2,412,413	28.5
Mining	1,563,091	7.6	49,740	0.6
Manufacturing	4,331,964	20.9	1,136,735	13.4
Construction	1,168,935	5.7	242,191	2.9
Public utilities	586,285	2.8	44,233	0.5
Transp. and commun.	1,909,763	9.2	352,623	4.2
Trade	2,910,372	14.1	1,261,633	14.9
Finance	2,262,141	11.0	278,210	3.2
Pub. admin., defense	1,634,235	8.0 }	1,998,460	23.6
Services	975,422	4.7 }		
Other	−141,545[4]	−0.7[4]	690,762[5]	8.2[5]
TOTAL	20,654,340	100.0	8,467,000	100.0

Population economically active (1985): total 9,558,000; activity rate 34.3% (participation rates: over age 12, 49.4%; female 32.8%; unemployed 4.3%).

Price and earnings indexes (1985 = 100)

	1985	1986	1987	1988	1989	1990	1991
Consumer price index	100.0	118.9	146.6	187.8	236.3	305.1	397.9
Monthly earnings index[6]	100.0	104.0	103.6	103.1	105.0	...	...

Household income and expenditure. Avg. household size (1985) 4.7; sources of income (1988): wages 46.7%, self-employment 37.7%, transfer payments 8.5%; expenditure (1989): food 34.3%, transportation 15.6%, housing 8.2%, health care 6.6%, household durable goods 6.3%, clothing 6.0%.
Land use (1990): forested 48.4%; pastures 38.9%; agricultural 5.2%; other 7.5%.

Foreign trade[7]

Balance of trade (current prices)

	1986	1987	1988	1989	1990	1991
U.S.$'000,000	+1,537.6	+735.0	+505.4	+729.9	+1,621.0	+2,720.1
% of total	17.7%	8.6%	5.3%	6.8%	13.6%	23.2%

Imports (1991)[8]: U.S.$4,909,397,000 (machinery 25.3%, chemicals 11.0%, transport equipment 7.4%, steel products 6.9%, crude petroleum 6.0%, plastic products 3.9%). *Major import sources:* U.S. 37.7%; Japan 9.6%; Germany 9.5%; Venezuela 5.1%; Brazil 3.6%; France 3.6%; Switzerland 2.8%.
Exports (1991)[8]: U.S.$7,265,702,000 (petroleum and petroleum products 28.8%, coffee 18.4%, textile apparel 7.7%, fruits 6.1%, flowers 3.9%, iron and steel 2.4%). *Major export destinations:* U.S. 40.5%; Germany 11.0%; Venezuela 3.4%; France 3.1%; The Netherlands 3.0%; Peru 2.8%.

Transport and communications

Transport. Railroads (1991): route length (1987) 3,236 km; passenger-km 79,-231,000; metric ton-km cargo 298,277,000. Roads (1989): total length 129,117 km (paved 8%). Vehicles (1989): cars 936,000; trucks and buses 364,000. Merchant marine (1991): vessels (100 gross tons and over) 100; deadweight tonnage 466,146. Air transport (1991): passenger-km 4,501,528,000; metric ton-km cargo 945,453,000; airports (1992) 63.
Communications. Daily newspapers (1992): 31; circulation 1,440,700; circulation per 1,000 population 23. Radio (1989): 4,400,000 receivers (1 per 7.3 persons). Television (1991): 5,500,000 receivers (1 per 6.1 persons). Telephones (1990): 2,909,243 (1 per 11 persons).

Education and health

Education (1989)

	schools	teachers	students	student/teacher ratio
Primary (6–10)	39,634	140,681	4,205,657	30.0
Secondary (11–16)[9]	6,134[10]	114,839	2,282,816	19.9
Higher	235[11]	51,725	474,787	9.2

Educational attainment (1985). Percentage of population age 25 and over having: no schooling 15.3%; primary education 50.1%; secondary 25.4%; higher 6.8%; not stated 2.4%. *Literacy* (1990): population age 15 and over literate 86.7%; males literate 87.5%; females literate 85.9%.
Health: physicians (1988) 29,353 (1 per 1,079 persons); hospital beds (1983) 46,651 (1 per 612 persons); infant mortality rate (1990–95) 37.0.
Food (1988–90): daily per capita caloric intake 2,453 (vegetable products 84%, animal products 16%); 106% of FAO recommended minimum requirement.

Military

Total active duty personnel (1992): 139,000 (army 86.3%, navy 8.6%, air force 5.1%). *Military expenditure as percentage of GNP* (1989): 2.1% (world 4.9%); per capita expenditure U.S.$24.

[1]Detail does not add to total given because of rounding. [2]Estimates based on about 75% of total deaths. [3]Construction permits issued for 11 urban centres. [4]Net imputed bank service charges. [5]Includes unemployed. [6]Real wages in the industrial sector. [7]Import figures are f.o.b. in balance of trade and c.i.f. in commodities and trading partners. [8]Estimate. [9]Secondary includes vocational and teacher training. [10]1988. [11]1987.

Comoros[1]

Official name: Jumhurīyat al-Qumur al-Ittihādīyah al-Islāmīyah (Arabic); République Fédéral Islamique des Comores (French) (Federal Islamic Republic of the Comoros).
Form of government: federal Islamic republic[2].
Head of state and government: President.
Capital: Moroni.
Official languages: Arabic; French.
Official religion: Islam.
Monetary unit: 1 Comorian franc (CF) = 100 centimes; valuation (Oct. 5, 1992) 1 U.S.$ = CF 238.75; 1 £ = CF 405.88.

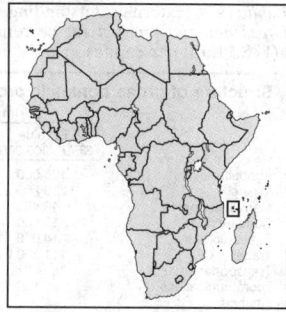

Structure of gross domestic product and labour force

	1991		1980	
	in value CF '000,000	% of total value	labour force	% of labour force
Agriculture, fishing	26,095	37.0	53,063	53.3
Mining	...	...	62	0.1
Manufacturing	3,161	4.5	3,946	4.0
Construction }	1,382	2.0	3,267	3.3
Public utilities }			129	0.1
Transportation and communications	...	...	2,118	2.1
Trade, restaurants, hotels	...	...	1,873	1.9
Finance, insurance	...	...	237	0.2
Public admin., defense }	3,128	4.4	2,435	2.5
Services }			4,646	4.7
Other	36,722	52.1	27,687[12]	27.8[12]
TOTAL	70,488	100.0	99,463	100.0

Area and population

		area		population
Governorates/Islands[3]	Capitals	sq mi	sq km	1990 estimate[4]
Mohéli (Mwali)	Fomboni	112	290	24,557
Grande Comore (Njazidja)	Moroni	443	1,148	249,053
Anjouan (Nzwani)	Mutsamudu	164	424	192,667
TOTAL		719	1,862	466,277

Demography

Population (1992): 497,000.
Density (1992): persons per sq mi 691.2, persons per sq km 266.9.
Urban-rural (1990): urban 27.8%; rural 72.2%.
Sex distribution (1989): male 49.95%; female 50.05%.
Age breakdown (1989): under 15, 45.8%; 15–29, 27.9%; 30–44, 13.3%; 45–59, 8.3%; 60–74, 3.8%; 75 and over, 0.9%.
Population projection: (2000) 659,000; (2010) 933,000.
Doubling time: 20 years.
Ethnic composition (1980): Comorian (a mixture of Bantu, Arab, and Malagasy peoples) 96.9%; Makua (a Bantu people from East Africa) 1.6%; French 0.4%; other 1.1%.
Religious affiliation (1990): Sunnī Muslim 99.4%; Roman Catholic 0.6%.
Major cities (1988): Moroni 22,000; Mutsamudu 14,000; Domoni 7,147[5]; Fomboni 7,000; Ouani 6,936[5].

Vital statistics

Birth rate per 1,000 population (1991): 47.0 (world avg. 26.4).
Death rate per 1,000 population (1991): 12.0 (world avg. 9.2).
Natural increase rate per 1,000 population (1991): 35.0 (world avg. 17.2).
Total fertility rate (avg. births per childbearing woman; 1991): 7.0.
Marriage rate per 1,000 population: n.a.
Divorce rate per 1,000 population: n.a.
Life expectancy at birth (1991): male 54.0 years; female 59.0 years.
Major causes of death per 100,000 population: n.a.; however, major diseases include malaria (afflicts 80% of the adult population), tuberculosis, leprosy, and kwashiorkor (a nutritional deficiency disease).

National economy

Budget (1991). Revenue: CF 23,102,700,000 (grants 43.8%; tax revenue 32.9%; loans 14.3%; nontax revenue 9.0%). Expenditures: CF 26,162,800,000 (current expenditures 71.8%, of which interest on the debt 9.0%; development expenditures 28.2%, of which debt amortization 10.9%).
Production (metric tons except as noted). Agriculture, forestry, fishing (1991): bananas 51,000, coconuts 50,000[6,7], cassava 46,150, pulses 7,000[6,7], corn (maize) 3,570, rice 3,050, cloves 1,200, vanilla 207, copra 103[8,9], ylang-ylang 50, other export crops grown in small quantities include coffee, cinnamon, and tuberoses; livestock (number of live animals; 1991) 125,000 goats[6], 47,-000 cattle[6], 14,000 sheep[6]; roundwood, n.a.; fish catch (1989) 4,500[6]. Mining and quarrying: sand and gravel for local construction. Manufacturing: products include processed vanilla and ylang-ylang, cement, handicrafts, soaps, soft drinks, woodwork, and clothing. Construction: n.a. Energy production (consumption): electricity (kW-hr; 1991) 24,400,000 (16,000,000[7]); coal, none (none); crude petroleum, none (none); petroleum products (metric tons; 1990) none (22,000); natural gas, none (none).
Population economically active (1985): total 117,216; activity rate of total population 29.6% (participation rates: ages 15–64, 53.1%; female 26.2%; unemployed [1987] 36.0%).

Price and earnings indexes (1985 = 100)

	1984	1985	1986	1987	1988	1989	1990
Consumer price index[10]	93.7	100.0	106.8	111.1	114.0	117.6	122.3
Earnings index	...	...	...	...	...	...	...

Tourism (1990): receipts from visitors U.S.$2,600,000; expenditures by nationals abroad U.S.$4,800,000.
Public debt (external, outstanding; 1990): U.S.$170,000,000.
Household income and expenditure. Average household size (1985) 5.6; income per household: n.a.; sources of income: n.a.; expenditure (1983)[11]: food and beverages 56.0%, energy 14.4%, clothing and footwear 10.0%, transportation and communications 6.6%, health care 5.0%, recreation 3.0%, tobacco 3.0%, other 2.0%.
Gross national product (at current market prices; 1990): U.S.$227,000,000 (U.S.$480 per capita).

Land use (1990)[6]: forested 15.7%; meadows and pastures 7.0%; agricultural and under permanent cultivation 44.8%; other 32.5%.

Foreign trade[13]

Balance of trade (current prices)

	1986	1987	1988	1989	1990	1991
CF '000,000	−5,796	−12,075	−9,249	−7,767	−9,157	−9,371
% of total	29.1%	63.4%	42.0%	40.1%	48.4%	40.0%

Imports (1991): CF 16,399,000,000 (rice 12.3%, petroleum products 10.7%, vehicles 9.9%, meat and fish 7.7%, cement 5.6%, iron and steel 2.9%, unspecified commodities 41.5%). *Major import sources*[7,14]: France 56.0%; Belgium-Luxembourg 11.0%; Japan 5.0%; Bahrain 4.0%; Singapore 3.0%.
Exports (1991): CF 7,028,000,000 (vanilla 63.8%, cloves 15.5%, ylang-ylang 14.1%). *Major export destinations*[7,14]: France 56.0%; United States 20.0%; Germany 16.0%; Japan 3.0%; Portugal 2.0%.

Transport and communications

Transport. Railroads: none. Roads (1987): total length 466 mi, 750 km (paved 53%). Vehicles (1987): passenger cars, 1,000; trucks and buses, 4,000. Merchant marine (1991): vessels (100 gross tons and over) 7; total deadweight tonnage 3,980. Air transport[15]: passenger arrivals and departures (1985) 33,000; cargo loaded and unloaded (1983) 172 metric tons; airports (1992) with scheduled flights 4.
Communications. Daily newspapers: none[16]. Radio (1991): total number of receivers 50,000 (1 per 9.6 persons). Television (1988): total number of receivers 100 (1 per 4,332 persons). Telephones (1991): 3,641[17] (1 per 132 persons).

Education and health

Education (1989–90)

	schools	teachers	students	student/ teacher ratio
Primary (age 6–11)[18]	257	1,777	64,737	36.4
Secondary (age 12–18)	...	557	14,472	26.0
Higher	...	32	248	7.8

Educational attainment (1980). Percentage of population age 25 and over having: no formal schooling 56.7%; Qur'anic school education 8.3%; primary 3.6%; secondary 2.0%; higher 0.2%; not specified 29.2%. *Literacy* (1980): total population age 15 and over literate 82,053 (46.3%); males literate 46,586 (54.2%); females literate 35,467 (39.0%).
Health: physicians (1984) 31 (1 per 12,237 persons); hospital beds (1982) 813 (1 per 437 persons); infant mortality rate per 1,000 live births (1991) 87.0.
Food (1987–89)[6]: daily per capita caloric intake 1,895 (vegetable products 95%, animal products 5%); 81% of FAO recommended minimum requirement.

Military

Total active duty personnel (1990): 700–800 (army 100%). *Military expenditure as percentage of GNP* (1987): 1.9% (world 5.4%); per capita expenditure U.S.$7.

[1]Excludes Mayotte, a *collectivité territoriale* ("territorial collectivity") of France, unless otherwise indicated. [2]The transitional government formed in May 1992 (the fifth government in 27 months) was dissolved July 1992. The constitution of 1978 has not been officially suspended (as of September 1992), but the legislature was dissolved March 1992; legislative elections were scheduled for November 1992. [3]Island names in French and Comorian Swahili, respectively. [4]Mid-September. [5]1980. [6]Includes Mayotte. [7]1990. [8]Commercial production only. [9]1989. [10]GDP price deflator. [11]Weights of consumer price index components. [12]Not adequately defined. [13]Imports c.i.f.; exports f.o.b. [14]Estimated figures. [15]Air Comores only. [16]Weekly newspapers: 2; total circulation not available. [17]Number of subscribers. [18]1987–88.

Congo

Official name: République du Congo
　(Republic of the Congo).
Form of government[1]: multiparty
　republic with two legislative houses
　(Senate [60]; National Assembly
　[125]).
Chief of state: President.
Head of government: Prime Minister.
Capital: Brazzaville.
Official language: French.
Official religion: none.
Monetary unit: 1 CFA franc (CFAF) =
　100 centimes; valuation (Oct. 5,
　1992) 1 U.S.$ = CFAF 238.75;
　1 £ = CFAF 405.88.

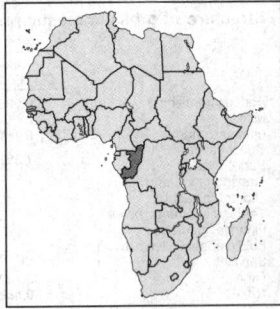

Area and population		area		population
				1992
Regions	Capitals	sq mi	sq km	estimate
Bouenza	Madingou	4,733	12,258	177,357
Cuvette	Owando	28,900	74,850	151,839
Kouilou	Pointe-Noire	5,270	13,650	89,296
Lékoumou	Sibiti	8,089	20,950	74,420
Likouala	Impfondo	25,500	66,044	70,675
Niari	Loubomo	10,007[2]	25,918[2]	120,077
Plateaux	Djambala	14,826	38,400	119,722
Pool	Kinkala	13,110	33,955	182,671
Sangha	Ouesso	21,542[3]	55,795[3]	35,961
Communes				
Brazzaville	—	39	100	937,579
Loubomo	—	7	18	83,605
Mossendjo	—	2[2]	5[2]	16,405
Nkayi	—	3	8	42,465
Ouesso	—	2[3]	5[3]	16,171
Pointe-Noire	—	17	44	576,206
TOTAL		132,047	342,000	2,694,449

Demography

Population (1992): 2,692,000.
Density (1992): persons per sq mi 20.4, persons per sq km 7.9.
Urban-rural (1990): urban 40.5%; rural 59.5%.
Sex distribution (1990): male 48.89%; female 51.11%.
Age breakdown (1990): under 15, 46.1%; 15–29, 25.8%; 30–44, 14.4%; 45–59,
　8.5%; 60–74, 4.2%; 75 and over, 1.0%.
Population projection: (2000) 3,511,000; (2010) 4,934,000.
Doubling time: 21 years.
Ethnic composition (1983): Kongo 51.5%; Teke 17.3%; Mboshi 11.5%; Mbete
　4.8%; Punu 3.0%; Sango 2.7%; Maka 1.8%; Pygmy 1.5%; other 5.9%.
Religious affiliation (1980): Roman Catholic 53.9%; Protestant 24.9%; African
　Christian 14.2%; traditional beliefs 4.8%; other 2.2%.
Major cities (1992): Brazzaville 937,579; Pointe-Noire 576,206; Loubomo 83,-
　605; Nkayi 42,465; Mossendjo 16,405.

Vital statistics

Birth rate per 1,000 population (1990–95): 46.1 (world avg. 26.4); legitimate,
　n.a.; illegitimate, n.a.
Death rate per 1,000 population (1990–95): 13.2 (world avg. 9.2).
Natural increase rate per 1,000 population (1985–90): 32.9 (world avg. 17.2).
Total fertility rate (avg. births per childbearing woman; 1990): 6.6.
Marriage rate per 1,000 population: n.a.
Divorce rate per 1,000 population: n.a.
Life expectancy at birth (1990–95): male 52.1 years; female 57.3 years.
Morbidity (reported cases of infectious disease per 100,000 population; 1988):
　diarrhea 1,144; malaria 874; gonorrhea 160; schistosomiasis 133; hookworm
　69.5.

National economy

Budget (1990). Revenue: CFAF 209,400,000,000 (petroleum revenue 58.6%;
　nonpetroleum receipts 40.9%; aid 0.5%). Expenditures: CFAF 268,800,-
　000 (current expenditure 81.5%, of which salaries 29.6%, interest 29.6%,
　transfers, subsidies, goods, and services 22.4%; restructuring expenditure
　7.9%; capital expenditure 7.3%; net lending 3.3%).
Tourism: receipts from visitors (1990) U.S.$7,000,000; expenditures by nation-
　als abroad (1988) U.S.$126,000,000.
Production (metric tons except as noted). Agriculture, forestry, fishing (1991):
　cassava 780,000, sugarcane 450,000, pineapples 117,000, plantains 80,000,
　bananas 40,000, peanuts (groundnuts) 27,000, corn (maize) 25,000, avocados
　23,000, palm oil 17,000, yams 12,000, cacao beans 12,000, coffee 1,000; live-
　stock (number of live animals) 272,000 goats, 108,000 sheep, 68,000 cattle;
　roundwood (1990) 3,644,000 cu m; fish catch (1989) 19,106. Mining and
　quarrying (1988): zinc concentrate 2,300; lead 1,400; gold 500 troy oz. Man-
　ufacturing (1988): raw sugar 31,000; wheat flour 16,000; cement 15,000; jet
　fuel 12,000; soap 1,500; cigarettes 770; mineral water 28,948,000 hectolitres;
　beer 744,000 hectolitres; soft drinks 178,000 hectolitres; veneer sheets 56,000
　cu m; footwear 296,000 pairs. Construction: n.a. Energy production (con-
　sumption): electricity (kW-hr; 1990) 398,000,000 (461,000,000); coal, none
　(none); crude petroleum (barrels; 1990) 56,103,000 (3,946,000); petroleum
　products (metric tons; 1990) 567,000 (546,000); natural gas (cu m; 1990)
　2,306,000 (2,306,000).
Land use (1990): forested 62.0%; meadows and pastures 29.3%; agricultural
　and under permanent cultivation 0.5%; other 8.2%.

Public debt (external, outstanding; 1990): U.S.$3,355,000,000.
Gross national product (at current market prices; 1990): U.S.$2,296,000,000
　(U.S.$1,010 per capita).

Structure of gross domestic product and labour force				
	1989		1984	
	in value CFAF '000,000[4]	% of total value	labour force	% of labour force
Agriculture	106,900	13.8	291,365	51.7
Mining	216,200	28.0	7,324	1.3
Manufacturing	48,400	6.2	38,080	6.8
Construction	13,900	1.8	23,621	4.2
Public utilities	14,000	1.8	2,641	0.5
Trade	111,300	14.4	65,775	11.7
Transportation and communications	70,100	9.1	27,807	4.9
Finance			2,866	0.5
Pub. admin., defense	192,700	24.9 }	83,629	14.9
Services			19,826	3.5
Other				
TOTAL	773,500	100.0	562,934	100.0

Population economically active (1989): total 765,000; activity rate of total pop-
　ulation 34.8% (participation rates [1984]: ages 15–64, 54.0%; female 45.6%;
　unemployed 2.3%[5]).

Price and earnings indexes (1985 = 100)							
	1984	1985	1986	1987	1988	1989	1990
Consumer price index	94.2	100.0	102.5	104.8	108.6	113.1	115.2
Earnings index	...	...	...	...	...	...	...

Household income and expenditure. Average household size (1984) 5.2; in-
　come per household: n.a.; sources of income: n.a.; expenditure: n.a.

Foreign trade[6]

Balance of trade (current prices)						
	1984	1985	1986	1987	1988	1989
CFAF '000,000,000	+333.0	+295.7	+64.8	+26.0	+87.2	+155.0
% of total	43.1%	40.3%	16.2%	9.1%	23.5%	36.3%

Imports (1989): CFAF 136,020,000,000 (1988: machinery and transport equip-
　ment 33.2%, of which machinery 22.4%, transport equipment 10.8%; food,
　beverages, and tobacco 21.3%; chemicals and chemical products 12.5%;
　metal manufactures 7.6%; basic manufactures 3.4%). *Major import sources:*
　France 48.1%; Cameroon 6.4%; Italy 6.1%; West Germany 4.2%; Zaire
　4.1%; The Netherlands 3.9%.
Exports (1989): CFAF 291,000,000,000 (1988: petroleum and petroleum prod-
　ucts 76.7%; wood and wood products 15.6%; diamonds 2.1%; iron and
　steel 0.1%). *Major export destinations:* United States 42.9%; France 16.1%;
　Belgium-Luxembourg 8.3%; Italy 7.8%; The Netherlands 7.2%; Spain 6.2%.

Transport and communications

Transport. Railroads (1989): length 494 mi, 795 km; passenger-mi 270,000,000,
　passenger-km 434,000,000; short ton-mi cargo 320,000,000, metric ton-km
　cargo 467,000,000. Roads (1985): total length 6,835 mi, 11,000 km (paved
　5%). Vehicles (1989): passenger cars 26,000; trucks and buses 20,000. Mer-
　chant marine (1991): vessels (100 gross tons and over) 22; total deadweight
　tonnage 10,840. Air transport (1990)[7]: passenger-mi 144,276,000, passenger-
　km 232,329,000; short ton-mi cargo 26,971,000, metric ton-km cargo 39,374,-
　000; airports (1992) with scheduled flights 14.
Communications. Daily newspapers (1990): total number 2; total circulation
　16,000; circulation per 1,000 population 6.9. Radio (1991): total number of
　receivers 250,000 (1 per 9.3 persons). Television (1991): total number of
　receivers 5,786 (1 per 404 persons). Telephones (1987): 19,239 (1 per 111
　persons).

Education and health

Education (1989–90)				
	schools	teachers	students	student/ teacher ratio
Primary (age 6–13)	1,604	7,704	492,595	63.9
Secondary (age 14–18)	238[8]	4,774	165,840	34.7
Voc., teacher tr.[8]	60	1,965	20,722	10.5
Higher[8]	12	641	10,310	16.1

Educational attainment (1974)[9]. Percentage of population age 15 and over
　having: secondary education 30.0%, of which males 37.0%, females 23.0%.
Literacy (1990): total population age 15 and over literate 56.6%; males
　literate 70.0%; females literate 43.9%.
Health (1989): physicians 567 (1 per 3,873 persons); hospital beds 4,817 (1
　per 456 persons); infant mortality rate per 1,000 live births (1990–95) 65.
Food (1987–89): daily per capita caloric intake 2,603 (vegetable products 93%,
　animal products 7%); 117% of FAO recommended minimum requirement.

Military

Total active duty personnel (1992): 10,850 (army 92.2%, navy 3.2%, air force
　4.6%). *Military expenditure as percentage of GNP* (1987): 5.1% (world 5.4%);
　per capita expenditure U.S.$50.

---

[1]Transitional government ended August 1992. [2]Mossendjo is included with Niari.
[3]Ouesso is included with Sangha. [4]At constant prices of 1978. [5]Previously employed
only. [6]Import figures f.o.b. in balance of trade and trading partners, c.i.f. in commodities. [7]Air Afrique only. [8]1988–89. [9]For the commune of Brazzaville only.

Costa Rica

Official name: República de Costa Rica (Republic of Costa Rica).
Form of government: unitary multiparty republic with one legislative house (Legislative Assembly [57]).
Head of state and government: President.
Capital: San José.
Official language: Spanish.
Official religion: Roman Catholicism.
Monetary unit: 1 Costa Rican colón (₡) = 100 céntimos; valuation (Oct. 5, 1992) 1 U.S.$ = ₡135.17; 1 £ = ₡230.54.

Area and population

Provinces	Capitals	area sq mi	area sq km	population 1991[1] estimate
Alajuela	Alajuela	3,766	9,753	539,375
Cartago	Cartago	1,207	3,125	340,298
Guanacaste	Liberia	3,915	10,141	242,681
Heredia	Heredia	1,026	2,657	243,679
Limón	Limón	3,548	9,188	219,485
Puntarenas	Puntarenas	4,354	11,277	338,384
San José	San José	1,915	4,959	1,105,844
TOTAL		19,730[2]	51,100	3,029,746

Demography

Population (1992): 3,161,000.
Density (1992): persons per sq mi 160.2, persons per sq km 61.9.
Urban-rural (1990): urban 54.0%; rural 46.0%.
Sex distribution (1990): male 50.54%; female 49.46%.
Age breakdown (1990): under 15, 36.2%; 15–29, 28.5%; 30–44, 19.4%; 45–59, 9.5%; 60–74, 5.0%; 75 and over, 1.4%.
Population projection: (2000) 3,711,000; (2010) 4,366,000.
Doubling time: 29 years.
Ethnic composition (1985): European 87.0%; mestizo 7.0%; black/mulatto 3.0%; East Asian (mostly Chinese) 2.0%; Amerindian 1.0%.
Religious affiliation (1990): Roman Catholic 88.5%; other (mostly Protestant) 11.5%.
Major cities (1988): San José 294,167[3] (metropolitan area 1,040,000[3]); Desamparados 50,860[4]; Limón 43,158[5]; Alajuela 41,390; Puntarenas 35,166.

Vital statistics

Birth rate per 1,000 population (1990): 27.4 (world avg. 27.1); (1984) legitimate 62.8%; illegitimate 37.2%.
Death rate per 1,000 population (1990): 3.8 (world avg. 9.8).
Natural increase rate per 1,000 population (1990): 23.6 (world avg. 17.3).
Total fertility rate (avg. births per childbearing woman; 1990): 3.0.
Marriage rate per 1,000 population (1989): 7.4.
Divorce rate per 1,000 population (1988): 0.9.
Life expectancy at birth (1990–95): male 72.9 years; female 77.6 years.
Major causes of death per 100,000 population (1989): diseases of the circulatory system 110.1; malignant neoplasms (cancers) 81.2; diseases of the respiratory system 37.8; accidents, poisoning, and violence 22.1; diseases of the digestive system 20.3.

National economy

Budget (1990). Revenue: ₡120,720,000,000 (tax revenue 85.2%, of which social-security contributions by employers 19.9%, customs duties 13.1%, general sales taxes 13.1%, excises 12.7%; nontax revenue 14.4%). Expenditures: ₡133,920,000,000 (health 26.3%; education 19.0%; social security 13.8%; general public services 9.3%; public order and security 6.8%; defense, none).
Public debt (external, outstanding; 1990): U.S.$2,832,000,000.
Gross national product (at current market prices; 1990): U.S.$5,342,000,000 (U.S.$1,910 per capita).

Structure of gross domestic product and labour force

	1990 in value ₡'000,000	% of total value	labour force	% of labour force
Agriculture, fishing	83,807	16.1	270,371	24.4
Mining }	99,999	19.2	1,842	0.2
Manufacturing			192,429	17.4
Construction	17,079	3.3	70,753	6.4
Public utilities	16,706	3.2	12,779	1.2
Transp. and commun.	25,777	4.9	42,368	3.8
Trade, restaurants	104,607	20.0	167,268	15.1
Finance, real estate	63,295	12.1	34,893	3.1
Public administration	79,442	15.2 }	257,982	23.3
Services	31,508	6.0 }		
Other	—	—	57,755[6]	5.2
TOTAL	522,219[2]	100.0	1,108,440	100.0[2]

Production (metric tons except as noted). Agriculture, forestry, fishing (1990): sugarcane 2,400,000, bananas 1,530,000, rice 207,000, coffee 170,000, pineapples 150,000, oranges 86,000, plantains 85,000, corn (maize) 72,000, palm oil 58,000, cacao beans 4,000, other products include other tropical fruits, cut flowers, and ornamental plants grown for export; livestock (number of live animals) 1,762,000 cattle, 224,000 pigs, 4,000,000 chickens; roundwood 4,127,000 cu m; fish catch (1989) 20,410, of which shrimps 8,890. Mining and quarrying (1989): gold 11,300 troy oz[7]. Manufacturing (value added

in ₡'000,000; 1989): food products 24,211; alcoholic and nonalcoholic beverages 9,444; petroleum products 4,508; paper and paper products 3,186; plastics 2,951; electrical machinery 2,729; industrial chemicals 2,646. Construction (buildings constructed; 1989): 1,914,000 sq m. Energy production (consumption): electricity (kW-hr; 1990) 3,609,000,000 (3,772,000,000); coal, none (none); crude petroleum (barrels; 1990) none (3,057,000); petroleum products (metric tons; 1990) 372,000 (904,000); natural gas, none (none).
Population economically active (1990): total 1,108,440; activity rate of total population 39.5% (participation rates: ages 15–69, 59.6%; female 28.7%; unemployed [1991] 5.5%).

Price and earnings indexes (1985 = 100)

	1986	1987	1988	1989	1990	1991	1992
Consumer price index	111.8	130.7	157.9	184.9	219.0	281.9	345.1[8]
Monthly earnings index[9]	114.2	128.5	147.5	176.1	212.1	...	...

Tourism (1990): receipts from visitors U.S.$275,000,000; expenditures by nationals abroad U.S.$148,000,000.
Family income and expenditure: average household size (1990) 4.7; income per urban family (1983) ₡181,416 (U.S.$4,415), income per rural family ₡98,328 (U.S.$2,393); sources of income: n.a.; expenditure (1974)[10]: food 40.8%, housing 12.3%, clothing and footwear 10.0%, education and recreation 9.2%, household furnishings 8.2%, energy 6.6%, other 12.9%.
Land use (1989): forested 32.1%; meadows and pastures 45.4%; agricultural and under permanent cultivation 10.4%; other 12.1%.

Foreign trade[11]

Balance of trade (current prices)

	1986	1987	1988	1989	1990	1991
U.S.$'000,000	+83.5	−90.7	−28.3	−136.4	−372.6	−83.3
% of total	3.9%	3.8%	1.1%	4.6%	11.3%	2.6%

Imports (1991): U.S.$1,852,700,000 (basic manufactures for industry 38.0%; nondurable consumer goods 16.3%; capital goods for industry 15.1%; refined petroleum and derivatives 9.9%). *Major import sources:* United States 43.2%; Venezuela 6.6%; Japan 6.0%; Mexico 4.7%; Guatemala 4.4%.
Exports (1991)[12]: U.S.$1,590,300,000 (nontraditional exports 53.0%, of which garments 26.4%; bananas 25.1%; coffee 16.6%; beef 1.6%). *Major export destinations:* United States 43.8%; Germany 11.0%; Belgium-Luxembourg 4.8%; Italy 4.6%; Guatemala 3.7%.

Transport and communications

Transport. Railroads: route length (1990) 402 mi, 647 km; (1988) passenger-mi 35,200,000, passenger-km 56,600,000; (1987) short ton-mi cargo 102,700,000, metric ton-km cargo 150,000,000. Roads (1990): total length 22,093 mi, 35,556 km (paved 15%). Vehicles (1990): passenger cars 168,814; trucks and buses 95,066. Merchant marine (1991): vessels (100 gross tons and over) 29; total deadweight tonnage 10,060. Air transport (1991)[13]: passenger-mi 658,000,000, passenger-km 1,059,000,000; short-ton mi cargo 24,755,000, metric ton-km cargo 36,141,000; airports (1992) with scheduled flights 9.
Communications. Daily newspapers (1990): total number 6; total circulation 307,800; circulation per 1,000 population 102. Radio (1991): total number of receivers 255,000 (1 per 12 persons). Television (1991): total number of receivers 611,000 (1 per 5.1 persons). Telephones (1990): 398,300 (1 per 7.0 persons).

Education and health

Education (1990)

	schools	teachers	students	student/ teacher ratio
Primary (age 7–12)	3,268	13,651	435,205	31.9
Secondary (age 13–17)	179	5,808	125,738	21.6
Vocational	77	2,076	28,593	13.8
Higher[14]	4	6,451	57,789	9.0

Educational attainment (1984). Percentage of economically active population age 25 and over having: no formal schooling 8.3%; incomplete primary education 28.6%; complete primary 26.3%; secondary 22.6%; postsecondary and higher 14.2%. *Literacy* (1990): total population age 15 and over literate 1,798,000 (92.8%); males literate 913,000 (92.6%); females literate 885,000 (93.1%).
Health (1990): physicians (1989) 3,686 (1 per 798 persons); hospital beds 6,178 (1 per 454 persons); infant mortality per 1,000 live births 15.3.
Food (1987–89): daily per capita caloric intake 2,791 (vegetable products 84%, animal products 16%); 125% of FAO recommended minimum requirement.

Military

Military expenditure as percentage of GNP (1989): 0.4% (world 4.9%); per capita expenditure U.S.$7. The army was officially abolished in 1948. Paramilitary and police forces had 7,500 members in 1991.

---

[1]January 1. [2]Detail does not add to total given because of rounding. [3]1990. [4]Within San José metropolitan area. [5]1984. [6]Includes 41,778 unemployed persons previously employed. [7]Gold purchased by central bank from placer deposits and mines; actual production estimated to be at least twice this amount. [8]June. [9]Minimum wage. [10]Based on survey of selected low- and middle-income families in San José only. [11]Import figures are f.o.b. in balance of trade and c.i.f. for commodities and trading partners. [12]Exports (1990): U.S.$1,457,400,000 (nontraditional exports 54.1%, of which nontraditional manufactures [including garments, electronic components, fish products, and jewelry] 43.5%; nontraditional agricultural products [mostly tropical fruits, ornamental plants, and cut flowers] 10.6%). [13]Lacsa (Costa Rican Airlines). [14]Universities only.

Côte d'Ivoire

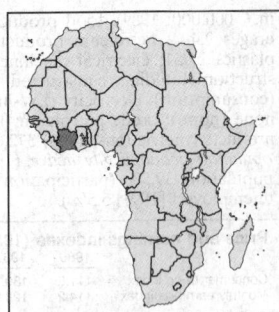

Official name: République de Côte d'Ivoire (Republic of Côte d'Ivoire [Ivory Coast][1]).
Form of government: multiparty republic with one legislative house (National Assembly [175]).
Chief of state: President.
Head of government: Prime Minister.
Capital: Abidjan (de facto; legislative).
Capital designate: Yamoussoukro (de jure; administrative).
Official language: French.
Official religion: none.
Monetary unit: 1 CFA franc (CFAF) = 100 centimes; valuation (Oct. 5, 1992) 1 U.S.$ = CFAF 238.75; 1 £ = CFAF 405.88.

Area and population

Departments[2]	Capitals	area sq mi	area sq km	population 1975 census
Abengourou	Abengourou	2,664	6,900	177,692
Abidjan	Abidjan	5,483	14,200	1,389,141
Aboisso	Aboisso	2,413	6,250	148,823
Adzopé	Adzopé	2,019	5,230	162,837
Agboville	Agboville	1,486	3,850	141,970
Biankouma	Biankouma	1,911	4,950	75,711
Bondoukou	Bondoukou	6,382	16,530	296,551
Bongouanou	Bongouanou	2,151	5,570	216,907
Bouaflé	Bouaflé	2,189	5,670	164,817
Bouaké	Bouaké	9,189	23,800	808,048
Bouna	Bouna	8,290	21,470	84,290
Boundiali	Boundiali	3,048	7,895	96,449
Dabakala	Dabakala	3,734	9,670	56,230
Daloa	Daloa	4,483	11,610	265,529
Danané	Danané	1,776	4,600	170,249
Dimbokro	Dimbokro	3,293	8,530	258,116
Divo	Divo	3,058	7,920	202,511
Ferkessedougou	Ferkessedougou	6,845	17,728	90,423
Gagnoa	Gagnoa	1,737	4,500	174,018
Guiglo	Guiglo	5,463	14,150	137,672
Issia	Issia	1,386	3,590	104,081
Katiola	Katiola	3,637	9,420	77,875
Korhogo	Korhogo	4,826	12,500	276,816
Lakota	Lakota	1,054	2,730	76,105
Man	Man	2,722	7,050	278,659
Mankono	Mankono	4,116	10,660	82,358
Odienné	Odienné	7,954	20,600	124,010
Oumé	Oumé	927	2,400	85,486
Sassandra	Sassandra	6,768	17,530	116,644
Séguéla	Séguéla	4,340	11,240	75,181
Soubré	Soubré	3,193	8,270	75,350
Tingréla	Tingréla	849	2,200	35,829
Touba	Touba	3,367	8,720	77,786
Zuénoula	Zuénoula	1,093	2,830	98,792
TOTAL		123,847[3]	320,763	6,702,866

Demography

Population (1992): 12,951,000.
Density (1992): persons per sq mi 104.6, persons per sq km 40.4.
Urban-rural (1990): urban 40.4%; rural 59.6%.
Sex distribution (1990): male 50.93%; female 49.07%.
Age breakdown (1990): under 15, 48.2%; 15–29, 24.7%; 30–44, 12.0%; 45–59, 8.5%; 60 and over, 6.6%.
Population projection: (2000) 17,600,000; (2010) 25,503,000.
Ethnic composition (1975): Akan 41.4%; Kru 16.7%; Voltaic 15.7%; Malinke 14.9%; Southern Mande 10.2%; other 1.1%.
Religious affiliation (1988): Muslim 38.0%; Christian 27.5%; animist 17.0%; atheist 13.4%; other 4.1%.
Major cities (1984): Abidjan 2,168,000[4]; Bouaké 220,000; Yamoussoukro 120,000; Gagnoa 93,500[5]; Daloa 59,500.

Vital statistics

Birth rate per 1,000 population (1990–95): 50.0 (world avg. 26.4).
Death rate per 1,000 population (1990–95): 13.2 (world avg. 9.2).
Natural increase rate per 1,000 population (1990–95): 36.8 (world avg. 17.2).
Total fertility rate (avg. births per childbearing woman; 1991): 7.4.
Life expectancy at birth (1990–95): male 52.8 years; female 56.2 years.
Major causes of death per 100,000 population: n.a.; however, the major infectious diseases include malaria, dysentery, yaws, pneumonia, leprosy.

National economy

Budget (1992). Revenue: CFAF 556,000,000,000 (1990; customs duties 32.0%, excise tax 27.4%, income taxes 16.6%). Expenditures: CFAF 556,000,000,000 (1989; education 29.8%, public services 21.3%, agriculture 11.5%).
Public debt (external, outstanding; 1990): U.S.$10,050,000,000.
Tourism (1990): receipts U.S.$48,000,000; expenditures U.S.$246,000,000.
Production (metric tons except as noted). Agriculture, forestry, fishing (1991): yams 2,559,000, sugarcane 1,600,000, cassava 1,435,000, plantains 1,110,000, cacao beans 710,000, rice 690,000, coconuts 515,000, corn (maize) 510,000, coffee 240,000; livestock (number of live animals) 1,150,000 sheep, 1,064,000 cattle, 905,000 goats; roundwood (1990) 12,654,000 cu m; fish catch (1990) 108,935. Mining and quarrying (1991): diamonds 280,000 carats. Manufacturing (1986): cement 770,000; beer 1,300,000 hectolitres; carbonated beverages 495,000 hectolitres; synthetic fibres 5,000,000 metres. Construction (in CFAF; 1984): 62,000,000,000. Energy production (consumption): elec-

tricity (kW-hr; 1990) 2,365,000,000 (2,365,000,000); coal, none (n.a.); crude petroleum (barrels; 1990) 2,301,000 (17,305,000); petroleum products (metric tons; 1990) 1,426,000 (1,426,000).
Gross national product (1990): U.S.$8,920,000,000 (U.S.$730 per capita).

Structure of gross domestic product and labour force

	1990 in value CFAF '000,000,000	1990 % of total value	1985 labour force	1985 % of labour force
Agriculture	974.2	36.2	2,452,000	60.5
Manufacturing, construction, mining, and public utilities	547.9	20.3	409,000	10.1
Trade, finance, transp. and commun., pub. admin., defense, and services	811.8	30.2	1,192,000	29.4
Other	359.0	13.3	—	—
TOTAL	2,692.9	100.0	4,053,000	100.0

Population economically active (1990): total 4,577,000; activity rate 38.2% (participation rates [1985]: ages 15–64, 71.4%; female 34.7%).

Price and earnings indexes (1985 = 100)

	1984	1985	1986	1987	1988	1989	1990[6]
Consumer price index	98.2	100.0	107.3	107.7	115.2	116.4	116.2
Hourly earnings index[7]	100.0	100.0	100.0	100.0	100.0	100.0	100.0

Household income and expenditure. Average household size (1980) 4.5; average annual income per household CFAF 500,000; sources of income: self-employment 49.9%, wages 44.9%, transfers and other resources 5.2%; expenditure (1985)[8]: food 38.8%, transportation 16.5%, housing 11.9%, clothing 10.5%, energy and water 8.0%.
Land use (1990): forested 23.2%; meadows and pastures 40.9%; agricultural and under permanent cultivation 11.6%; other 24.3%.

Foreign trade

Balance of trade (current prices)

	1985	1986	1987	1988	1989	1990
U.S.$'000,000	+1,351.1	+1,547.5	+1,118.3	+1,078.1	+1,067.4	+1,417.0
% of total	32.3%	32.1%	23.4%	24.1%	23.5%	29.4%

Imports (1990): CFAF 499,000,000,000 (1989; food and food products 21.0%; crude petroleum 20.3%; machinery and transport equipment 16.4%, of which nonelectrical machinery 8.1%, transport equipment 4.6%, electrical machinery 3.6%; chemicals 14.8%). *Major import sources* (1988): France 28.7%; Nigeria 16.0%; W.Ger. 5.4%; Italy 5.3%; The Netherlands 4.7%.
Exports (1990): CFAF 799,000,000,000 (1989; food products 59.7%, of which cocoa beans and products 41.0%, coffee and coffee products 10.7%, fish products 2.0%; energy products 9.6%; cotton and cotton cloth 5.4%). *Major export destinations* (1989): The Netherlands 22.5%; France 13.6%; W.Ger. 7.5%; U.S. 6.6%; Italy 5.9%; U.S.S.R. 5.9%; Belgium-Luxembourg 4.3%.

Transport and communications

Transport. Railroads (1991): route length 660 km; passenger-km 1,021,000,000[9]; metric ton-km cargo 578,000,000[9]. Roads (1988): total length 41,900 mi, 67,500 km (paved 7%). Vehicles (1989): passenger cars 168,000; trucks and buses 91,000. Merchant marine (1991): vessels (100 gross tons and over) 51; total deadweight tonnage 98,618. Air transport (1990)[10]: passenger-km 84,427,000; metric ton-km cargo 7,638,000; airports (1992) 7.
Communications. Daily newspapers (1990): total number 2; total circulation 130,000; circulation per 1,000 population 11. Radio (1991): 1,500,000 receivers (1 per 8.3 persons). Television (1991): 810,000 receivers (1 per 15 persons). Telephones (1991): 87,300 (1 per 143 persons).

Education and health

Education (1985)

	schools	teachers	students	student/ teacher ratio
Primary (age 7–12)	5,796	33,500	1,214,511	36.3
Secondary (age 13–19)	218[11]	4,569[11]	260,330	...
Voc., teacher tr.	38[11]	1,947[12]	25,328[5]	...
Higher	1[11]	1,204[13]	19,660[4]	...

Educational attainment (1975). Percentage of population age 6 and over having: no formal schooling 75.3%; primary education 17.3%; secondary 5.1%; higher 0.5%. *Literacy* (1990): percentage of population age 15 and over literate 53.8%; males literate 66.9%; females literate 40.2%.
Health (1982): physicians 502 (1 per 17,847 persons); hospital beds 10,062 (1 per 891 persons); infant mortality rate per 1,000 live births (1990–95) 87.
Food (1987–89): daily per capita caloric intake 2,580 (vegetable products 94%, animal products 6%); 112% of FAO recommended minimum requirement.

Military

Total active duty personnel (1992): 7,100 (army 77.5%, navy 9.8%, air force 12.7%). *Military expenditure as percentage of GNP* (1989): 1.5% (world 4.9%); per capita expenditure U.S.$11.

---

[1]From 1986, Côte d'Ivoire has requested that the French version of the country's name be utilized as the official protocol version in all languages. [2]Fifteen additional departments were created in 1985, for which separate data are not available. [3]Detail does not add to total given because of rounding. [4]1990. [5]1986. [6]December. [7]January 1; index refers to the S.M.I.G. (*salaire minimum interprofessionel garanti*), a form of minimum professional wage. [8]Weights of consumer price index components. [9]1987; traffic includes Burkina Faso. [10]Air Ivoire only. [11]1979–80. [12]1981. [13]1982.

Croatia

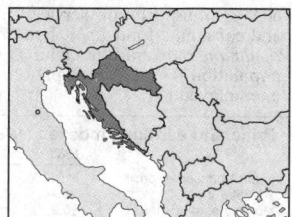

Official name: Republika Hrvatska (Republic of Croatia).
Form of government: multiparty republic with a two-chambered legislature (Chamber of Districts [n.a.]; Chamber of Deputies [138]).
Head of state: President.
Head of government: Prime Minister.
Capital: Zagreb.
Official language: Croatian.
Official religion: none.
Monetary unit: Croatian dinar (HrD)[1]; valuation (Oct. 12, 1992)
1 U.S.$ = HrD 365.67;
1 £ = HrD 622.95.

Area and population (1991 census)

Districts	area sq km[2]	population	Districts	area sq km[2]	population
Beli Manastir	1,147	54,265	Nova Gradiška	969	60,749
Benkovac	640	33,378	Novi Marof	283	29,254
Biograd na moru	232	17,661	Novska	585	24,696
Bjelovar	732	66,039	Obrovac	509	11,557
Brač	395	13,824	Ogulin	1,077	29,095
Buje	368	23,877	Omiš	379	25,784
Buzet	319	7,439	Opatija	310	29,799
Čabar	280	5,169	Orahovica	436	15,631
Čakovec	724	119,866	Osijek	659	165,253
Čazma	455	15,263	Otočac	1,117	24,992
Cres-Lošinj	513	11,796	Ozalj	278	14,787
Crikvenica	440	19,154	Pag	285	7,612
Đakovo	833	52,954	Pakrac	567	27,589
Daruvar	610	30,092	Pazin	532	19,006
Delnice	713	17,848	Petrinja	390	35,565
Donja Stubica	249	30,760	Ploče	169	13,008
Donji Lapac	606	8,054	Podravska Slatina	781	31,227
Donji Miholjac	471	20,365	Poreč	350	22,988
Drniš	840	24,169	Pregrada	150	16,939
Dubrovnik	979	71,419	Pula	574	85,326
Duga Resa	561	30,485	Rab	115	9,562
Dugo Selo	223	19,693	Rijeka	523	206,229
Đurđevac	680	40,901	Rovinj	291	19,727
Dvor	505	14,555	Šenj	658	9,205
Garešnica	419	18,442	Šibenik	1,020	85,002
Glina	543	23,040	Sinj	1,077	60,210
Gospić	1,674	29,049	Sisak	1,052	84,348
Gračac	1,016	10,434	Slavonska Požega	1,249	71,745
Grubišno Polje	435	14,206	Slavonski Brod	1,065	114,249
Hvar	312	11,459	Slunj	802	18,962
Imotski	606	39,052	Solin	472	27,402
Ivanec	345	41,680	Split	149	207,147
Ivanić-Grad	380	25,592	Sveti Ivan Zelina	216	17,152
Jastrebarsko	632	32,422	Titova Korenica	1,150	11,393
Karlovac	637	81,319	Trogir	250	22,168
Kaštela	250	32,286	Valpovo	360	33,108
Klanjec	119	10,917	Varaždin	375	94,373
Knin	1,079	42,954	Vinkovci	1,024	98,445
Koprivnica	715	61,052	Virovitica	642	46,661
Korčula	336	19,651	Vis	101	4,354
Kostajnica	365	14,851	Vojnić	237	8,236
Krapina	182	26,382	Vrbovec	514	28,074
Križevci	548	39,248	Vrbovsko	280	7,528
Krk	428	16,402	Vrginmost	447	16,599
Kutina	596	39,520	Vrgorac	284	7,497
Labin	386	25,983	Vukovar	606	84,189
Lastovo	53	1,228	Zabok	221	36,309
Ludbreg	223	21,848	Zadar	1,121	136,572
Makarska	226	21,041	Zagreb	1,705	933,914
Metković	279	22,818	Zlatar-Bistrica	343	31,291
Našice	675	40,829	Županja	815	49,026
			TOTAL	56,538	4,784,265

Demography

Population (1992): 4,808,000.
Density (1992): persons per sq mi 220.2, persons per sq km 85.0.
Urban-rural (1981): urban 50.8%; rural 49.2%.
Sex distribution (1981): male 48.40%; female 51.60%.
Age breakdown (1981): under 15, 20.9%; 15–29, 23.3%; 30–44, 20.2%; 45–59, 19.9%; 60–74, 11.0%; 75 and over, 3.9%.
Population projection: (2000) 4,960,000; (2010) 5,157,000.
Doubling time: not applicable; doubling time exceeds 100 years.
Ethnic composition (1981): Croat 75.1%; Serb 11.6%; Magyar 0.6%; Slovene 0.5%; Bosnian 0.5%; other 11.7%.
Religious affiliation (1991): Roman Catholic 76.5%; Eastern Orthodox 11.1%; Muslim 1.2%; other 11.2%[3].
Major cities (1991)[4]: Zagreb 930,753; Split 206,559; Rijeka 205,842; Osijek 164,589; Zadar 134,669.

Vital statistics

Birth rate per 1,000 population (1990): 11.9 (world avg. 27.1); legitimate, n.a.; illegitimate, n.a.
Death rate per 1,000 population (1990): 11.4 (world avg. 9.8).
Natural increase rate per 1,000 population (1990): 0.5 (world avg. 17.3).
Total fertility rate (avg. births per childbearing woman): n.a.
Marriage rate per 1,000 population (1989): 6.1.
Divorce rate per 1,000 population (1989): 1.1.
Life expectancy at birth (1980–82): male 67.0 years; female 74.0 years.
Major causes of death per 100,000 population (1989): diseases of the circulatory system 581.5; malignant neoplasms (cancers) 222.2; accidents, violence, and poisoning 86.5; diseases of the digestive system 54.7.

National economy

Production (metric tons except as noted). Agriculture, forestry, fishing (1991): corn (maize) 2,540,000, wheat 1,495,000, potatoes 656,000, grapes 431,000, plums 43,000; livestock (number of live animals) 1,620,000 pigs, 757,000 cattle, 753,000 sheep, 16,512,000 poultry; roundwood (1990) 4,877,000 cu m; fish catch (1990) 45,333, of which freshwater 10,432. Mining and quarrying (1990): lime 437,000; bauxite 309,000; gypsum 100,000; refined silver 2,500. Manufacturing (1990): nitrogenous fertilizers 1,172,000; crude steel 424,000; hot rolled iron slabs 184,000; detergents 110,000; polyvinyl chloride powder 105,000. Construction (residential units constructed; 1990): 18,565. Energy production (consumption): electricity (kW-hr; 1990) 9,043,000,000 (15,442,-000,000); coal (metric tons; 1990) 173,000 (n.a.); crude petroleum (barrels; 1990) 14,719,000 (n.a.); petroleum products (metric tons; 1990) 8,471,000 (n.a.); natural gas (cu m; 1990) 1,989,000,000 (n.a.).
Gross national product (1990): U.S.$20,900,000,000 (U.S.$4,399 per capita).

Structure of gross material product and labour force

	1989		1990	
	in value Din '000,000	% of total value	labour force[5]	% of labour force[5]
Agriculture	6,276	11.2	69,156	4.6
Mining }	27,299	48.7	595,489	39.4
Manufacturing }				
Construction	3,896	6.9	118,656	7.9
Public utilities	588	1.0	36,601	2.4
Transp. and commun.	5,256	9.4	124,943	8.3
Trade	10,848	19.4	238,075	15.8
Finance			60,980	4.0
Pub. admin., defense }	1,894	3.4	265,591	17.6
Services }				
Other				
TOTAL	56,057	100.0	1,509,491	100.0

Population economically active (1991): total 1,327,000; activity rate of total population 27.7% (participation rates: ages 15–64, n.a.; female [1990] 44.0%).

Price and earnings indexes (1985 = 100)

	1984	1985	1986	1987	1988	1989	1990[6]
Consumer price index	57	100	193	430	1,270	16,500	114,000
Annual earnings index[7]	100	100	109	100	93	114	93

Land use (1990): forest 36.5%; pasture 36.0%; agricultural 23.5%; other 4.0%.
Household income and expenditure. Average household size (1991) 2.9; income per household (1990) Din 165,813 (U.S.$14,650); sources (1990): self-employment 40.8%, wages 40.2%, transfers 12.1%, other 6.9%; expenditure (1988): food 34.2%, transportation 9.3%, clothing 8.6%, housing 8.3%, energy 7.6%, drink and tobacco 5.1%, durable goods 4.5%, health care 4.3%.

Foreign trade

Balance of trade (current prices)

	1985	1986	1987	1988	1989	1990
Din '000,000	−10	−32	−31	−155	−3,774	−16,692
% of total	7.1	16.0	7.9	10.2	18.1	20.2

Imports (1990): Din 49,728,000,000 (raw materials and semifinished goods 29.9%, consumer goods 24.2%, mineral fuels 19.2%, basic manufactures 13.4%, machinery 9.1%). *Major import sources:* n.a.
Exports (1990): Din 33,036,000,000 (machinery 29.7%, chemicals 11.3%, food 9.2%, clothing 8.5%). *Major export destinations:* n.a.

Transport and communications

Transport. Railroads (1990): passengers transported 35,762,000; cargo transported 27,867,000 tons. Roads (1991): total length 19,932 mi, 32,071 km (paved 73%). Vehicles (1990): passenger cars 865,516; trucks and buses 72,043. Merchant marine (1990): fishing vessels 369. Airports (1991) 1.
Communications. Daily newspapers (1990): 9; total circulation 715,000; circulation per 1,000 population 150. Radio (1989): 1,226,000 receivers (1 per 3.9 persons). Television (1989): 1,063,000 receivers (1 per 4.5 persons). Telephones (1990): 1,101,451 (1 per 4.3 persons).

Education and health

Education (1990–91)

	schools	teachers	students	student/teacher ratio
Primary (age 7–14)	2,588	27,197	497,790	18.3
Secondary (age 15–18)	229	13,121	215,425	16.4
Higher	60	6,633	70,781	10.7

Educational attainment (1981). Percentage of population age 15 and over having: less than full primary education 45.4%; primary 19.2%; secondary 28.3%; post-secondary and higher 6.4%. *Literacy* (1981): total population age 10 and over literate 3,734,000 (94.4%); males 97.5%; females 91.6%.
Health (1990): physicians (1989) 10,160 (1 per 466 persons); hospital beds 35,603 (1 per 133 persons); infant mortality rate per 1,000 live births 10.0.

Military

Total active duty personnel (1991): n.a.; however, the Croatian National Guard was formed in April 1991. *Military expenditure as percentage of GNP:* n.a.

[1]The Croatian dinar was introduced on Dec. 23, 1991, at parity with the Yugoslav dinar (Din), which it replaced as Croatia's official currency. [2]One sq km is equal to approximately 0.3861 sq mi. [3]Includes a significant minority of adherents of the Croatian Old Catholic Church, as well as small communities of Protestant Christians and Jews. [4]Populations refer to municipal areas, not cities proper. [5]Excludes 58,000 workers in the private sector. [6]On Jan. 1, 1990, the new dinar, equal to 10,000 old dinars (Din), was introduced. [7]Based on worker real net personal income.

Cuba

Official name: República de Cuba (Republic of Cuba).
Form of government: unitary socialist republic with one legislative house (National Assembly of the People's Power [510]).
Head of state and government: President.
Capital: Havana.
Official language: Spanish.
Official religion: none.
Monetary unit: 1 Cuban peso (CUP) = 100 centavos; valuation (Oct. 5, 1992)
1 U.S.$ = 0.76 CUP;
1 £ = 1.29 CUP.

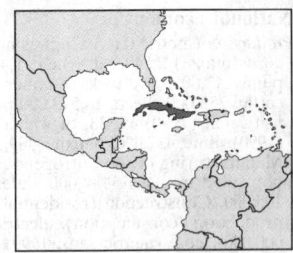

Area and population

Provinces	Capitals	area sq mi	area sq km	population 1989[1] estimate
Camagüey	Camagüey	6,174	15,990	732,056
Ciego de Avila	Ciego de Avila	2,668	6,910	358,059
Cienfuegos	Cienfuegos	1,613	4,178	358,589
Ciudad de la Habana[2]	—	281	727	2,077,938
Granma	Bayamo	3,232	8,372	781,331
Guantánamo	Guantánamo	2,388	6,186	491,422
Holguín	Holguín	3,591	9,301	982,722
La Habana[3]	Havana	2,213	5,731	636,889
Las Tunas	Las Tunas	2,544	6,589	485,136
Matanzas	Matanzas	4,625	11,978	602,996
Pinar del Río	Pinar del Río	4,218	10,925	684,725
Sancti Spíritus	Sancti Spíritus	2,604	6,744	424,243
Santiago de Cuba	Santiago de Cuba	2,382	6,170	980,002
Villa Clara	Santa Clara	3,345	8,662	801,456
Special municipality				
Isla de la Juventud	Nueva Gerona	926	2,398	71,097
TOTAL		42,804	110,861	10,468,661

Demography

Population (1992): 10,848,000.
Density (1992): persons per sq mi 253.4, persons per sq km 97.9.
Urban-rural (1990): urban 72.8%; rural 27.2%.
Sex distribution (1990): male 50.35%; female 49.65%.
Age breakdown (1989): under 15, 23.3%; 15–29, 31.7%; 30–44, 19.5%; 45–59, 13.7%; 60 and over, 11.8%.
Population projection: (2000) 11,502,000; (2010) 12,181,000.
Doubling time: 63 years.
Ethnic composition (1981): white 66.0%; mixed 21.9%; black 12.0%.
Religious affiliation (1980): nonreligious 48.7%; Roman Catholic 39.6%; atheist 6.4%; Protestant 3.3%; Afro-Cuban syncretist 1.6%; other 0.4%.
Major cities (1989[1]): Havana 2,077,938; Santiago de Cuba 397,024; Camagüey 278,958; Holguín 222,794; Guantánamo 197,868.

Vital statistics

Birth rate per 1,000 population (1991): 18.0 (world avg. 26.4).
Death rate per 1,000 population (1991): 7.0 (world avg. 9.2).
Natural increase rate per 1,000 population (1991): 11.0 (world avg. 17.2).
Total fertility rate (avg. births per childbearing woman; 1991): 1.9.
Marriage rate per 1,000 population (1990): 8.3.
Divorce rate per 1,000 population (1990): 3.5.
Life expectancy at birth (1991): male 73.0 years; female 78.0 years.
Major causes of death per 100,000 population (1988): diseases of the circulatory system 291.4; malignant neoplasms (cancers) 127.8; accidents, violence, and suicide 81.5; diseases of the respiratory system 58.1; endocrine and metabolic diseases 22.9.

National economy

Budget (1990). Revenue: CUP 12,463,200,000. Expenditures: CUP 14,448,400,000 (capital investment 37.7%; education and public health 20.4%; social, cultural, and scientific activities 17.3%; defense, internal security 9.5%; housing, community services 6.0%).
Production (metric tons except as noted). Agriculture, forestry, fishing (1991): sugarcane 74,000,000, oranges and tangerines 615,000, rice 430,000, grapefruit 332,000, bananas and plantains 320,000, cassava 300,000, tomatoes 260,000, sweet potatoes 250,000, potatoes 180,000, tobacco leaves 44,000; livestock (number of live animals) 4,920,000 cattle, 1,900,000 pigs, 28,000,000 chickens; roundwood (1990) 3,134,000 cu m; fish catch (1990) 188,188. Mining and quarrying (1989): chromite 50,600; nickel (metal content of ores) 46,500[4]. Manufacturing (in CUP '000,000; 1989): processed food (excluding fish and refined sugar) 1,843; refined sugar 1,610; nonelectrical machinery 709; fuels 655; beverages and tobacco products 521; chemicals and chemical products 445; construction materials 440; textiles (excluding ready-made clothing) 287. Construction (gross value of construction in CUP '000,000; 1989): residential 227; nonresidential 872. Energy production (consumption): electricity (kW-hr; 1990) 16,245,000,000 (16,245,000,000); coal (metric tons; 1990) none (200,000); crude petroleum (barrels; 1990) 5,482,000 (49,889,000); petroleum products (metric tons; 1990) 6,694,000 (10,416,000); natural gas (cu m; 1990) 30,753,000 (30,753,000).
Household income and expenditure. Average household size (1981) 4.2; average annual income per household (1982) CUP 3,680 (U.S.$4,330); sources of income (1982): wages and salaries 57.3%, bonuses and other payments 42.7%; personal consumption (1988) food 26.7%, other retail purchases 60.8%, transportation services 5.4%, energy 2.5%, value of self-produced and consumed food 1.5%, household repairs 1.2%, other 1.9%.
Population economically active (1988): total 4,570,236; activity rate of total population 43.7% (participation rates: over age 15, 56.9%; female 36.1%; unemployed 6.0%).

Price and earnings indexes (1985 = 100)

	1983	1984	1985	1986	1987	1988	1989
Implicit consumer price deflator index	94.9	98.0	100.0	101.4	102.8	103.1	...
Monthly earnings index[5]	95.9	99.0	100.0	100.1	98.1	99.6	100.0

Public debt (hard currency to the West; 1989): U.S.$6,800,000,000.
Tourism (1990): receipts from visitors U.S.$246,000,000; expenditures by nationals abroad U.S.$48,000,000.
Gross national product (at current market prices; 1990): U.S.$20,900,000,000 (U.S.$2,000 per capita).

Structure of global social product and labour force

	1989 in value CUP '000,000	% of total value	labour force[5]	% of labour force
Agriculture	4,273	15.9	721,100	20.4
Mining[6]	1,039	3.9		
Manufacturing	10,617	39.4	767,500	21.8
Public utilities	733	2.7		
Construction	2,510	9.3	344,300	9.8
Transp. and commun.	2,151	8.0	235,900	6.7
Finance, insurance	—	—	21,700	0.6
Trade	5,401	20.1	395,300	11.2
Public administration	—	—	151,700	4.3
Services	—	—	835,700	23.7
Other	191	0.7	53,400	1.5
TOTAL	26,915	100.0	3,526,600	100.0

Land use (1990): forested 25.1%; meadows and pastures 27.1%; agricultural and under permanent cultivation 30.3%; other 17.5%.

Foreign trade[7]

Balance of trade (current prices)

	1984	1985	1986	1987	1988	1989
CUP '000,000	−1,751	−2,043	−2,275	−2,181	−2,062	−2,732
% of total	13.8%	14.6%	17.6%	16.8%	15.7%	20.2%

Imports (1989): CUP 8,124,200,000 (mineral fuels and lubricants 32.4%, machinery and transport equipment 31.2%, food and live animals 11.4%, basic manufactures 10.3%, chemicals 6.5%, inedible crude materials 3.8%). *Major import sources:* U.S.S.R. 68.0%; East Germany 4.4%; China 3.1%; Czechoslovakia 2.7%; Spain 2.3%; Argentina 2.2%.
Exports (1989): CUP 5,392,000,000 (sugar 73.2%, minerals and concentrates 9.2%, citrus and other agricultural products 3.9%, fish products 2.4%, raw tobacco and tobacco products 1.6%). *Major export destinations:* U.S.S.R. 59.9%; East Germany 5.3%; China 4.0%; Bulgaria 3.3%; Czechoslovakia 2.5%.

Transport and communications

Transport. Railroads (1989): length 3,009 mi, 4,843 km; passenger-km 2,891,000,000; metric ton-km cargo 2,416,200,000. Roads (1986): total length 28,928 mi, 46,555 km (paved 27%). Vehicles (1988): passenger cars 241,300; trucks and buses 208,400. Merchant marine (1991): vessels (100 gross tons and over) 401; total deadweight tonnage 1,009,484. Air transport (1991): passenger-km 3,070,000,000; metric ton-km cargo 34,794,000; airports with scheduled flights (1992) 11.
Communications. Daily newspapers (1989): total number 19; total circulation 1,269,700; circulation per 1,000 population 121. Radio (1991): 3,500,000 receivers (1 per 3.1 persons). Television (1991): 2,500,000 receivers (1 per 4.3 persons). Telephones (1990): 609,974 (1 per 18 persons).

Education and health

Education (1989–90)

	schools	teachers	students	student/ teacher ratio
Primary (age 6–11)	9,417	71,887	885,500	12.3
Secondary (age 12–17)	2,175	108,560	1,073,100	9.9
Voc., teacher tr.	618	30,252	312,000	10.3
Higher	35	24,499	242,400	9.9

Educational attainment (1981). Percentage of population age 25 and over having: no formal schooling or some primary education 39.6%; completed primary 26.6%; secondary 29.6%; higher 4.2%. *Literacy* (1985): total population age 15 and over literate 7,200,000 (96.0%).
Health (1989): physicians 34,752 (1 per 303 persons); hospital beds 74,407 (1 per 141 persons); infant mortality rate per 1,000 live births 11.1.
Food (1988–90): daily per capita caloric intake 3,129 (vegetable products 78%, animal products 22%); 135% of FAO recommended minimum requirement.

Military

Total active duty personnel (1992): 175,500 (army 82.6%, navy 7.7%, air force 9.7%). *Military expenditure as percentage of GNP* (1989): 3.9% (world 4.9%); per capita expenditure: U.S.$131.

[1]January 1. [2]Province coextensive with the city of Havana. [3]Province bordering the city of Havana on the east, south, and west. [4]Includes cobalt. [5]State sector only; excludes military and unemployed. [6]Mining includes metallurgy and refined petroleum products. [7]Imports c.i.f.; exports f.o.b.

Cyprus

Island of Cyprus

Area: 3,572 sq mi, 9,251 sq km.
Population (1992): 756,000[1].

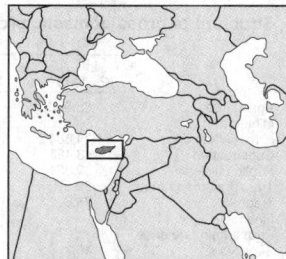

Two de facto states currently exist on the island of Cyprus: the Republic of Cyprus (ROC), predominantly Greek in character, occupying the southern two-thirds of the island, which is the original and still the internationally recognized de jure government of the whole island; and the Turkish Republic of Northern Cyprus (TRNC), proclaimed unilaterally Nov. 15, 1983, on territory originally secured for the Turkish Cypriot population by the July 20, 1974, intervention of Turkey. Only Turkey recognizes the TRNC, and the two ethnic communities have failed to reestablish a single state. Provision of separate data below does not imply recognition of either state's claims but is necessitated by the continuing lack of unified data.

Republic of Cyprus

Official name: Kipriakí Dimokratía (Greek); Kıbrıs Cumhuriyeti (Turkish) (Republic of Cyprus).
Form of government: unitary multiparty republic with a unicameral legislature (House of Representatives [80[2]]).
Head of state and government: President.
Capital: Nicosia.
Official languages: Greek; Turkish.
Monetary unit: 1 Cyprus pound (£C) = 100 cents; valuation (Oct. 5, 1992) 1£C = U.S.$2.38 = £1.39.

Area and population

Districts	Capitals	area		population[3]
		sq mi	sq km	1990[4] estimate
Famagusta	Famagusta	...	...	28,700
Larnaca	Larnaca	433	1,121	94,400
Limassol	Limassol	538	1,393	166,900
Nicosia	Nicosia	...	...	230,800
Paphos	Paphos	539	1,396	47,700
TOTAL		2,276[5]	5,896[5]	568,500

Demography

Population (1992): 580,000[3].
Urban-rural (1990): urban 68.5%; rural 31.5%.
Age breakdown (1990): under 15, 25.8%; 15–29, 23.7%; 30–44, 22.0%; 45–59, 14.6%; 60–74, 9.8%; 75 and over, 4.1%.
Ethnic composition: Greek Cypriot *c.* 95%; other *c.* 5%.
Religious affiliation (1990): Cypriot Orthodox 82.0%; Maronite 1.5%; other 16.5%.
Major urban areas (1990): Nicosia 168,800; Limassol 132,100.

Vital statistics

Birth rate per 1,000 population (1991): 18.6 (world avg. 26.4).
Death rate per 1,000 population (1991): 8.8 (world avg. 9.2).
Natural increase rate per 1,000 population (1991): 9.8 (world avg. 17.2).
Life expectancy at birth (1985–89): male 73.9 years; female 78.3 years.

National economy

Budget (1990). Revenue[6]: £C 578,500,000 (income taxes 25.5%, import duties 16.9%, excises 14.1%). Expenditures: £C 765,600,000 (development expenditures 10.9%).
Tourism: receipts (1991) U.S.$1,070,000; expenditures (1990) U.S.$162,000,000.
Household expenditure (1990): food 19.3%, transportation 14.3%, household goods and operations 10.1%, hotel expenditures 9.4%.
Gross national product (1990): U.S.$5,633,000,000 (U.S.$8,040 per capita).

Structure of gross domestic product and labour force

	1991			
	in value £C '000,000	% of total value	labour force	% of labour force
Agriculture	166.5	6.3	34,400	12.3
Mining	7.4	0.3	700	0.2
Manufacturing	388.3	14.6	48,200	17.3
Construction	273.0	10.3	23,200	8.3
Public utilities	52.0	2.0	1,300	0.5
Transp. and commun.	231.6	8.7	15,400	5.5
Trade	497.0	18.8	60,500	21.7
Finance, insurance	424.6	16.0	16,900	6.0
Pub. admin., defense	328.0	12.4 }	54,100	19.4
Services	160.0	6.0 }		
Other	122.0	4.6	24,600[7]	8.8[7]
TOTAL	2,650.4	100.0	279,300	100.0

Production. Agriculture (value of production in £C'000,000; 1990): potatoes 30.8, milk 23.3, pork 17.6, sheep and goat meat 17.4, citrus fruits 16.1, grapes 15.9, poultry 15.8, barley 11.1. Manufacturing (value added in £C'000,000;

1989): wearing apparel 45.9; food 44.2; beverages 29.3; cement, bricks, and tiles 28.7. Energy production: electricity (kW-hr; 1990) 1,974,000,000.

Foreign trade

Imports (1991): £C 1,215,800,000 (consumer goods 24.6%; transport equipment 12.6%; capital goods 10.5%; mineral fuels 10.3%). *Major import sources:* U.K. 13.0%; Japan 11.4%; Italy 10.1%; Germany 9.6%; U.S. 7.9%.
Exports (1991): £C 441,800,000 (domestic exports 54.9%, of which clothing 15.6%, potatoes 6.4%; reexports 45.1%). *Major export destinations:* U.K. 21.0%; Lebanon 12.7%; Greece 8.4%; Germany 5.2%; ships' stores 8.6%.

Transport and communications

Transport. Roads (1989): total length 9,824 km (paved 43%). Vehicles (1989): cars 171,000; trucks and buses 68,800. Merchant marine (1991): vessels 1,359; deadweight tonnage 36,526,992. Air transport (1991)[8]: passenger-km 2,252,000,000; metric ton-km cargo 32,158,000; airports (1992) 1.
Communications. Daily newspapers (1990): 11; total circulation 91,469; circulation per 1,000 population 161. Television (1991): 234,000 receivers (1 per 2.5 persons). Telephones (1988): 303,822 (1 per 1.8 persons).

Education and health

Education (1989–90)

	schools	teachers	students	student/ teacher ratio
Primary (age 5–12)	378	2,824	60,841	21.5
Secondary (age 12–18)	94[9]	3,145	40,073	12.7
Vocational	12[9]	465	3,146	6.8
Higher	26	481	5,852	12.2

Educational attainment (1989). Percentage of population age 20 and over having: no formal schooling 6%; higher education 14%. *Literacy* (1989): population age 15 and over literate 95%; male 98%; female 92%.
Health (1989): physicians 1,172 (1 per 480 persons); hospital beds 3,397 (1 per 166 persons); infant mortality rate per 1,000 live births (1991) 9.8.

Turkish Republic of Northern Cyprus

Official name: Kuzey Kıbrıs Türk Cumhuriyeti (Turkish) (Turkish Republic of Northern Cyprus).
Capital: Lefkoşa (Nicosia).
Official language: Turkish.
Monetary unit: 1 Turkish lira (LT) = 100 kurush; valuation (Oct. 5, 1992) 1 U.S.$ = LT 7,511; 1£ = LT 12,768.

Area and population

Districts	Administrative centres	area		population
		sq mi	sq km	1989 estimate
Lefkoşa (Nicosia)	Lefkoşa	...	...	78,772
Gazimagosa (Famagusta)	Gazimagosa	...	...	64,190
Girne (Kyrenia)	Girne	247	640	26,310
TOTAL		1,295	3,355	169,272[1]

Population (1992): 176,000 (Lefkoşa 39,496[10]; Gazimagosa 20,516[10]).
Ethnic composition (1985): Turkish 98.7%; other 1.3%.

Structure of gross domestic product and labour force

	1991			
	in value LT '000,000,000	% of total value	labour force	% of labour force
Agriculture	207	9.1	19,094	26.1
Mining and manufacturing	279	12.3	6,845	9.3
Construction	133	5.9	7,518	10.3
Public utilities	35	1.5	1,202	1.6
Transp. and commun.	214	9.4	5,728	7.8
Trade	462	20.4	6,942	9.5
Finance, real estate	152	6.7	2,016	2.8
Pub. admin.	442	19.5	15,979	21.8
Services	144	6.4	6,776	9.3
Other	199[11]	8.8[11]	1,079[12]	1.5[12]
TOTAL	2,267	100.0	73,179	100.0

Budget (1991)[13]. Revenue: LT 713,000,000,000 (local taxes 51.2%, loans 23.9%, foreign aid 13.4%). Expenditures: LT 713,000,000,000 (current expenditure 84.6%, development expenditure 10.3%, defense 5.1%).
Imports (1991): U.S.$301,100,000 (machinery and transport equipment 21.4%, food 14.4%). *Major import sources:* Turkey 47.5%; U.K. 15.2%.
Exports (1991): U.S.$52,500,000 (citrus fruits 42.8%). *Major export destinations:* U.K. 67.4%; Turkey 13.9%.

Education (1989–90)

	schools	teachers	students	student/ teacher ratio
Primary (age 7–12)	150	790	16,488	20.9
Secondary (age 13–18)	36	849	15,885	18.7
Vocational	10	257	2,544	9.9
Higher	4	201	5,240	26.1

Health (1989): physicians 250 (1 per 677 persons); hospital beds 1,042 (1 per 162 persons); infant mortality rate per 1,000 live births (1987–89 avg.) 6.3.

[1]Includes "settlers" from Turkey in the TRNC; excludes 30,000 Turkish military in the TRNC, 4,200 British military in the Sovereign Base Areas in the ROC, and 2,300 UN peacekeeping forces. [2]Twenty-four seats reserved for Turkish Cypriots are not occupied. [3]Population excludes British and UN military forces. [4]January 1. [5]Area includes 73 sq mi (256 sq km) of British military Sovereign Base Areas and *c.* 107 sq mi (*c.* 278 sq km) of the UN Buffer Zone. [6]Current revenue only. [7]Includes 8,300 unemployed. [8]Cyprus Airways. [9]1988–89. [10]1989. [11]Customs duties. [12]Unemployed. [13]Eleven months only.

Czechoslovakia[1]

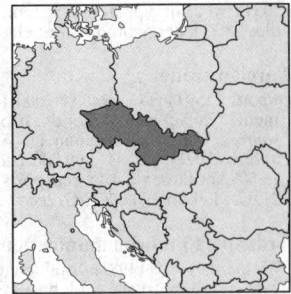

Official name: Česká a Slovenská Federativní Republika (Czech); Česká a Slovenská Federatívna Republika (Slovak) (Czech and Slovak Federal Republic).
Form of government: federal republic with one legislative house (Federal Assembly [300][2]).
Chief of state: President.
Head of government: Premier.
Capital: Prague.
Official languages: Czech; Slovak.
Official religion: none.
Monetary unit: 1 koruna (Kčs) = 100 halura; valuation (Oct. 5, 1992) 1 U.S.$ = Kčs 26.56; 1 £ = Kčs 45.16.

Area and population		area		population
Republics				**1991**
Regions	Capitals	sq mi	sq km	census[3]
Czech Republic	Prague			
Jihočeský	České Budějovice	4,380	11,345	697,334
Jihomoravský	Brno	5,802	15,028	2,048,867
Severočeský	Ustí nad Labem	3,019	7,819	1,173,681
Severomoravský	Ostrava	4,273	11,067	1,961,508
Středočeský	Prague	4,245	10,994	1,112,374
Východočeský	Hradec Králové	4,340	11,240	1,232,646
Západočeský	Plzeň	4,199	10,875	860,311
Slovak Republic	Bratislava			
Stredoslovenský	Banská Bystrica	6,943	17,982	1,609,806
Východoslovenský	Košice	6,252	16,193	1,505,495
Západoslovenský	Bratislava	5,595	14,492	1,712,181
Capital Cities				
Prague	—	192	496	1,212,010
Bratislava		142	368	441,453
TOTAL		49,382	127,899	15,567,666

Demography

Population (1992): 15,605,000.
Density (1992): persons per sq mi 316.0, persons per sq km 122.0.
Urban-rural (1990): urban 77.5%; rural 22.5%.
Sex distribution (1991): male 48.69%; female 51.31%.
Age breakdown (1991): under 15, 22.5%; 15–29, 22.1%; 30–44, 22.8%; 45–59, 15.9%; 60–74, 11.9%; 75 and over, 4.8%.
Population projection: (2000) 15,829,000; (2010) 16,114,000.
Doubling time: not applicable; population growth is negligible.
Ethnic composition (1991): Czech 54.1%; Slovak 31.0%; Moravian 8.7%; other 6.2%.
Religious affiliation (1991): Roman Catholic 46.4%; nonreligious and atheist 29.5%; Slovak Evangelical 2.1%; Evangelical Church of Czech Brethren 1.2%; Greek Catholic 1.2%; other 19.6%.
Major cities (1991): Prague 1,212,010; Bratislava 441,453; Brno 387,986; Ostrava 327,553; Košice 234,840.

Vital statistics

Birth rate per 1,000 population (1990): 13.4 (world avg. 27.1); (1988) legitimate 92.7%; illegitimate 7.3%.
Death rate per 1,000 population (1990): 11.7 (world avg. 9.8).
Natural increase rate per 1,000 population (1990): 1.7 (world avg. 17.3).
Total fertility rate (avg. births per childbearing woman; 1990): 2.0.
Marriage rate per 1,000 population (1990): 8.4.
Divorce rate per 1,000 population (1990): 2.6.
Life expectancy at birth (1989): male 68.9 years; female 75.1 years.
Major causes of death per 100,000 population (1990): diseases of the circulatory system 648.3; malignant neoplasms (cancers) 245.7; accidents, poisonings, and violence 82.9; diseases of the respiratory system 60.0; diseases of the digestive system 50.4; endocrine and metabolic diseases 19.8.

National economy

Budget (1990). Revenue: Kčs 463,524,000,000 (receipts from enterprises 75.1%; taxes 0.5%). Expenditures: Kčs 455,900,000,000 (education, health, social welfare, and culture 29.6%; national economy 19.9%; defense 9.2%).
Public debt (external, outstanding; 1990): U.S.$7,300,000,000[4].
Tourism (1990): receipts from visitors U.S.$470,000,000; expenditures by nationals abroad U.S.$636,000,000.
Production (metric tons except as noted). Agriculture, forestry, fishing (1991): wheat 6,205,000, sugar beets 5,515,000, barley 3,793,000, potatoes 2,713,000; livestock (number of live animals; 1991) 6,350,000 pigs, 4,168,000 cattle, 466,000 sheep, 33,021,000 chickens; roundwood 13,332,000 cu m; fish catch (1990) 22,407. Mining and quarrying (1991): iron ore 1,760,000; lead-zinc ore 780,000; copper ore 580,000. Manufacturing (1991): crude steel 12,071,000; rolled steel 9,267,000; cement 8,299,000; flour 1,107,000; plastic and resins 943,839; sulfuric acid 682,000; phosphate fertilizers 168,329; beer 20,578,000 hectolitres; other alcoholic beverages 1,434,000 hectolitres; refrigerators and freezers 514,745 units; road motor vehicles 176,554 units. Construction (dwellings completed; 1991): 38,211 units. Energy production (consumption): electricity (kW-hr; 1990) 89,345,000,000 (92,645,000,000); coal (metric tons; 1990) 108,291,000 (108,291,000); crude petroleum (barrels; 1990) 834,186 (99,096,381); petroleum products (metric tons; 1990) 8,670,000 (8,454,000); natural gas (cu m; 1990) 702,911,000 (12,491,000,000).
Gross national product (1990): U.S.$124,334,000,000 (U.S.$8,000 per capita).

Structure of gross domestic product and labour force

	1989			
	in value Kčs '000,000	% of total value	labour force	% of labour force
Agriculture	66,592	10.5	906,000	11.0
Mining and manufacturing	374,585	59.2	2,954,000	36.0
Construction	63,423	10.0	799,000	9.7
Public utilities	2,321	0.4	—	—
Transp. and commun.	32,392	5.1	513,000	6.3
Trade	76,802	12.1	886,000	10.8
Finance	—	—	5	5
Pub. admin., defense	}		115,000	1.4
Services	16,718	2.6	1,515,000[5]	18.5[5]
Other			513,000[6]	6.3[6]
TOTAL	632,833	100.0[7]	8,201,000	100.0

Population economically active (1991): total 7,758,785; activity rate of total population 49.8% (participation rates [1987]: working age 88.2%; female 46.1%; unemployed, n.a.).

Price and earnings indexes (1985 = 100)							
	1986	1987	1988	1989	1990	1991	1992[8]
Consumer price index	100.5	100.6	100.7	102.1	112.3	177.2	193.1
Monthly earnings index	100.0	101.5	103.5	106.0	108.3	112.4	131.5

Household income and expenditure. Average household size (1991) 2.9; income per household (1987) Kčs 82,750 (U.S.$15,240); sources of income (1991): wages and salaries 55.3%, transfer payments 13.7%, other 31.0%; expenditure (1987): food 26.1%, services 11.7%, clothing and footwear 8.7%.
Land use (1990): agricultural 40.7%; forested 36.8%; meadows and pastures 13.1%; other 9.4%.

Foreign trade

Balance of trade (current prices)						
	1986	1987	1988	1989	1990	1991
Kčs '000,000	−1,974	−2,192	+3,978	+2,828	−22,945	+27,489
% of total	0.5%	0.5%	0.9%	0.7%	5.0%	2.5%

Imports (1991): Kčs 293,696,000,000 (mineral fuels and lubricants 29.8%, machinery and transport equipment 28.0%, chemicals 9.8%, crude materials 9.2%, food and live animals 5.7%). *Major import sources:* U.S.S.R. 31.8%; Germany 20.3%; Austria 7.9%; Poland 4.9%; Italy 3.3%; Switzerland 2.4%; France 2.3%; Yugoslavia 2.1%.
Exports (1991): Kčs 321,185,000,000 (consumer goods 30.5%, machinery and transport equipment 28.0%, chemicals 10.6%, food and live animals 7.7%, mineral fuels and lubricants 4.2%). *Major export destinations:* Germany 25.1%; U.S.S.R. 19.4%; Poland 7.3%; Austria 5.8%; Yugoslavia 5.0%; Hungary 4.4%; Italy 4.4%; United Kingdom 1.9%.

Transport and communications

Transport. Railroads (1991): length 8,147 mi, 13,111 km; passenger-mi 11,969,000,000, passenger-km 19,263,000,000; short ton-mi cargo 31,027,000,000, metric ton-km cargo 49,933,000,000. Roads (1991): total length 45,486 mi, 73,203 km (paved 90%). Vehicles (1990): passenger cars 3,242,262; trucks and buses 333,336. Merchant marine (1991): vessels (100 gross tons and over) 24; total deadweight tonnage 577,789. Air transport (1990): passenger-mi 1,459,000,000, passenger-km 2,348,000,000; short ton-mi cargo 39,537,000, metric ton-km cargo 57,723,000; airports (1992) with scheduled flights 7.
Communications. Daily newspapers (1990): total number 48; total circulation (1988) 5,100,000; circulation per 1,000 population 327. Radio (1991): 10,500,000 receivers (1 per 1.5 persons). Television (1991): 5,720,000 receivers (1 per 2.7 persons). Telephones (1991): 4,278,081 (1 per 3.6 persons).

Education and health

Education (1989–90)	schools	teachers	students	student/ teacher ratio
Primary (age 6–14)	6,206	98,038	1,961,742	20.0
Secondary (age 15–18)	884	36,273	452,696	12.5
Voc., teacher tr.	979	50,612	404,275	8.0
Higher	42	25,350	143,866	5.7

Educational attainment (1980). Percentage of adult population having: less than full primary education 1.2%; primary and less than full secondary 52.6%; full secondary 41.2%; higher 5.0%. *Literacy* (1990): total population age 15 and over literate 12,051,091 (100%); males literate 5,782,691 (100%); females literate 6,268,400 (100%).
Health (1991): physicians 50,014 (1 per 311 persons); hospital beds 154,970 (1 per 100 persons); infant mortality rate per 1,000 live births (1990) 11.3.
Food (1988–90): daily per capita caloric intake 3,574 (vegetable products 67%, animal products 33%); 145% of FAO recommended minimum requirement.

Military

Total active duty personnel (1992): 116,800 (army 61.6%, navy, none, air force 38.4%). *Military expenditure as percentage of GNP* (1989): 6.8% (world 4.9%); per capita expenditure U.S.$534.

[1]Agreement was reached in 1992 to divide the two federal republics of Czechoslovakia, the Czech republic and the Slovak republic, into two independent countries on Jan. 1, 1993. [2]Usually meets in two separate bodies (Chamber of Nations [150]; Chamber of the People [150]). [3]Preliminary. [4]Hard-currency debt to the West. [5]Services includes Finance. [6]Includes women on maternity leave. [7]Detail does not add to total given because of rounding. [8]June.

Denmark

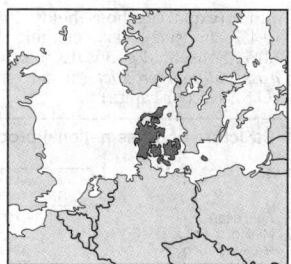

Official name: Kongeriget Danmark (Kingdom of Denmark).
Form of government: parliamentary state and constitutional monarchy with one legislative house (Folketing [179]).
Chief of state: Danish Monarch.
Head of government: Prime Minister.
Capital: Copenhagen.
Official language: Danish.
Official religion: Evangelical Lutheran.
Monetary unit: 1 krone (Dkr; plural kroner) = 100 øre; valuation (Oct. 5, 1992) 1 U.S.$ = Dkr 5.46; 1 £ = Dkr 9.29.

Area and population[1]

Counties	Capitals	area sq mi	area sq km	population 1992 estimate[2]
Århus	Århus	1,761	4,561	605,447
Bornholm	Rønne	227	588	45,541
Frederiksborg	Hillerød	520	1,347	344,559
Fyn	Odense	1,346	3,486	463,241
København	—	203	526	603,179
Nordjylland	Ålborg	2,383	6,173	485,787
Ribe	Ribe	1,209	3,131	219,800
Ringkøbing	Ringkøbing	1,874	4,853	268,398
Roskilde	Roskilde	344	891	220,129
Sønderjylland	Åbenrå	1,520	3,938	250,756
Storstrøm	Nykøbing Falster	1,312	3,398	256,987
Vejle	Vejle	1,157	2,997	332,707
Vestsjælland	Sorø	1,152	2,984	285,098
Viborg	Viborg	1,592	4,122	229,559
Communes				
Copenhagen (København)	—	34	88	464,566
Frederiksberg	—	3	9	86,372
TOTAL		16,638[3]	43,093[3]	5,162,126

Demography

Population (1992): 5,167,000.
Density (1992): persons per sq mi 310.6, persons per sq km 119.9.
Urban-rural (1990): urban 84.8%; rural 15.2%.
Sex distribution (1992): male 49.29%; female 50.71%.
Age breakdown (1992): under 15, 17.0%; 15–29, 22.4%; 30–44, 21.9%; 45–59, 18.4%; 60–74, 13.3%; 75 and over, 7.0%.
Population projection: (2000) 5,184,000; (2010) 5,171,000.
Doubling time: not applicable; population is stable.
Ethnic composition (1990): Danish 97.1%; Asian 1.2%, of which Turkish 0.5%; other Scandinavian 0.4%; British 0.2%; Yugoslav 0.2%; other 0.9%.
Religious affiliation (1991): Evangelical Lutheran 88.9%; Roman Catholic 0.6%; other Protestant 0.5%; other Christian 0.4%; other 9.6%.
Major cities (1990): Greater Copenhagen 1,337,114; Århus 200,188; Odense 138,986; Ålborg 113,599; Frederiksberg 85,611[4].

Vital statistics

Birth rate per 1,000 population (1990): 12.4 (world avg. 27.1); legitimate 54.9%; illegitimate 45.1%.
Death rate per 1,000 population (1990): 11.9 (world avg. 9.8).
Natural increase rate per 1,000 population (1990): 0.5 (world avg. 17.3).
Total fertility rate (avg. births per childbearing woman; 1990): 1.7.
Marriage rate per 1,000 population (1990): 6.1.
Divorce rate per 1,000 population (1990): 2.7.
Life expectancy at birth (1989–90): male 72.0 years; female 77.7 years.
Major causes of death per 100,000 population (1990): ischemic heart disease 303.4; malignant neoplasms (cancers) 292.3; cerebrovascular disease 108.3.

National economy

Budget (1990). Revenue: Dkr 319,389,000,000 (individual income taxes 30.4%, general sales taxes 24.2%, nontax entrepreneurial and property income 10.6%, excise duties 9.6%). Expenditures: Dkr 320,143,000,000 (current expenditure 96.5%, development expenditure 3.5%).
National debt (end of year; 1990): Dkr 546,564,000,000.
Tourism (1991): receipts from visitors U.S.$3,475,000,000; expenditures by nationals abroad U.S.$3,377,000,000.
Population economically active (1990): total 2,912,428; activity rate of total population 56.7% (participation rates: ages 15–64, 82.7%; female 46.1%; unemployed 11.0%[5]).

Price and earnings indexes (1985 = 100)

	1986	1987	1988	1989	1990	1991	1992[6]
Consumer price index	103.7	107.8	112.7	118.1	121.2	124.1	127.3
Hourly earnings index	105.6	115.9	123.2	128.1	133.1	138.3	...

Household income and expenditure. Average household size (1991) 2.2; income per household (1988) Dkr 199,354 (U.S.$29,613); principal sources of income (1988)[7]: wages and salaries 48.2%, self-employment 33.6%, transfers 18.2%; expenditure (1990): housing 21.6%, food, beverages, and tobacco 20.9%, transportation and communications 16.4%, recreation and education 10.5%, household furnishings 6.3%.
Production (in Dkr '000,000 except as noted). Agriculture, forestry, fishing (value added; 1991): pork 15,281, milk 11,991, beef 4,308, barley 3,853, wheat 3,515, flowers and plants 2,563, oilseeds 1,953, furs 1,088; roundwood (1990)

2,107,000 cu m; fish catch 1,625,000 metric tons. Mining and quarrying (1990): sand and gravel 28,100,000 cu m; chalk and limestone 2,600,000 cu m. Manufacturing (value added; 1990): nonelectrical machinery and apparatus 18,895; food other than meat 16,580; metal products 11,376; paints, soaps, and pharmaceuticals 9,515; processed meat 8,617; electrical machinery and apparatus 8,161; industrial chemicals 6,842. Construction (buildings completed; 1991): residential 1,736,000 sq m; nonresidential 4,509,000 sq m. Energy production (consumption): electricity (kW-hr; 1990) 24,396,-000,000 (32,772,000,000); coal (metric tons; 1990) none (10,012,000); crude petroleum (barrels; 1990) 46,088,000 (55,749,000); petroleum products (metric tons; 1990) 7,570,000 (7,823,000); natural gas (cu m; 1990) 3,249,000,000 (2,116,000,000).
Gross national product (1990): U.S.$113,515,000,000 (U.S.$22,090 per capita).

Structure of gross domestic product and labour force

	1991 in value Dkr '000,000[8]	1991 % of total value	1990 labour force	1990 % of labour force
Agriculture, fishing	29,483	4.1	155,856	5.4
Mining	8,615	1.2	2,467	0.1
Manufacturing	135,875	19.0	579,065	19.9
Construction	41,424	5.8	201,461	6.9
Public utilities	13,485	1.9	20,349	0.7
Transp. and commun.	68,577	9.6	197,642	6.8
Trade, restaurants	97,184	13.6	428,685	14.7
Finance, real estate	143,363	20.0	256,824	8.8
Pub. admin., defense	157,371	22.0 }	1,018,504	35.0
Services	39,999	5.6 }		
Other	−18,434[9]	−2.6[9]	51,575[10]	1.8[10]
TOTAL	716,939[3]	100.0[3]	2,912,428	100.0[3]

Land use (1989): forested 11.6%; meadows and pastures 5.2%; agricultural and under permanent cultivation 60.3%; other 22.9%.

Foreign trade[11]

Balance of trade (current prices)

	1986	1987	1988	1989	1990	1991
Dkr '000,000	−4,830	+8,891	+19,061	+18,764	+26,404	+31,753
% of total	1.4%	2.6%	5.4%	4.8%	6.5%	7.5%

Imports (1990): Dkr 195,781,000,000 (electrical and nonelectrical machinery and equipment 21.9%, food products 10.2%, transport equipment 9.7%). *Major import sources:* Germany 22.8%; Sweden 11.6%; U.K. 7.6%; U.S. 6.2%; The Netherlands 5.8%; France 5.3%.
Exports (1990): Dkr 216,444,000,000 (machinery and instruments 24.2%, live swine or pork 5.9%, fish and fish products 5.8%, textiles and clothing 4.5%, drugs and medicine 3.6%). *Major export destinations:* Germany 19.8%; Sweden 12.8%; U.K. 10.7%; France 6.0%; Norway 5.7%; U.S. 5.0%.

Transport and communications

Transport. Railroads (1990): length 1,763 mi, 2,838 km; passenger-mi 3,139,-000,000, passenger-km 5,051,000,000; short ton-mi cargo 1,234,000,000, metric ton-km cargo 1,801,000,000. Roads (1991): total length 44,156 mi, 71,063 km (paved 100%). Vehicles (1990): passenger cars 1,590,345; trucks and buses 301,350. Merchant marine (1991)[12]: vessels (100 gross tons and over) 1,290; total deadweight tonnage 8,221,093. Air transport (1990)[13]: passenger-mi 2,646,000,000, passenger-km 4,258,000,000; short ton-mi cargo 84,354,000, metric ton-km cargo 123,155,000; airports (1992) with scheduled flights 12.
Communications. Daily newspapers (1991): total number 48; total circulation 1,851,000; circulation per 1,000 population 359. Radio (1991): 2,235,000 receivers (1 per 2.3 persons). Television (1991): 3,000,000 receivers (1 per 1.7 persons). Telephones (1989): 4,397,776 (1 per 1.2 persons).

Education and health

Education (1990–91)

	schools	teachers	students	student/ teacher ratio
Primary/lower secondary (age 7–15)[14]	3,000	62,700[15]	632,174	10.7[15]
Upper secondary (age 16–18)	157	7,500[15]	71,876	9.6[15]
Vocational[16]	352	...	240,267	
Higher	94	...	126,221	

Educational attainment (1990). Percentage of population age 25–69 having: primary education 3.0%; completed lower secondary 23.4%; completed upper secondary or vocational 48.0%; advanced vocational 5.0%; undergraduate 7.4%; graduate 3.9%; unknown 9.3%. *Literacy:* virtually 100%.
Health (1990): physicians 14,277 (1 per 360 persons); hospital beds 29,104 (1 per 177 persons); infant mortality rate per 1,000 live births 7.5.
Food (1987–89): daily per capita caloric intake 3,622 (vegetable products 54%, animal products 46%); 135% of FAO recommended minimum requirement.

Military

Total active duty personnel (1991): 29,400 (army 60.9%, navy 17.0%, air force 22.1%). *Military expenditure as percentage of GNP* (1989): 2.2% (world 4.9%); per capita expenditure U.S.$426.

---

[1]Excludes the Faeroe Islands and Greenland. [2]January 1. [3]Detail does not add to total given because of rounding. [4]Within Greater Copenhagen. [5]Average of June 1, 1991–May 31, 1992. [6]May. [7]Excludes interest and dividends. [8]At factor cost. [9]Imputed bank service charges (Dkr 23,527,000,000) less other producers (Dkr 5,093,000,000). [10]Includes 41,334 activities not adequately defined. [11]Import figures are f.o.b. in balance of trade and c.i.f. in commodities and trading partners. [12]Includes the Faeroe Islands and Greenland. [13]Danish share of Scandinavian Airlines System; scheduled air service only. [14]Includes preprimary. [15]1988–89. [16]Includes higher vocational.

Djibouti

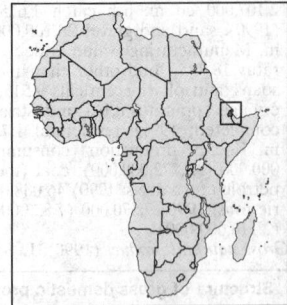

Official name: Jumhūrīyah Jībūtī (Arabic); République de Djibouti (French) (Republic of Djibouti).
Form of government: multiparty republic with one legislative house (National Assembly [65]).
Head of state and government: President.
Capital: Djibouti.
Official languages: Arabic; French.
Official religion: none.
Monetary unit: 1 Djibouti franc (DF) = 100 centimes; valuation (Oct. 5, 1992) 1 U.S.$ = DF 177.72; 1 £ = DF 302.12.

Area and population

Districts	Capitals	area[1] sq mi	sq km	population 1982 estimate
'Alī Sabīḥ (Ali-Sabieh)	'Alī Sabīḥ	925	2,400	15,000
Dikhil	Dikhil	2,775	7,200	30,000
Djibouti	Djibouti	225	600	200,000
Obock	Obock	2,200	5,700	15,000
Tadjoura (Tadjourah)	Tadjoura	2,825	7,300	30,000
TOTAL		8,950	23,200	335,000[2]

Demography

Population (1992): 557,000.
Density (1992): persons per sq mi 62.2, persons per sq km 24.0.
Urban-rural (1990): urban 80.7%; rural 19.3%.
Sex distribution (1990): male 50.37%; female 49.63%.
Age breakdown (1990): under 15, 45.2%; 15–29, 24.9%; 30–44, 16.1%; 45–59, 9.0%; 60 and over, 4.8%.
Population projection: (2000) 706,000; (2010) 949,000.
Doubling time: 24 years.
Ethnic composition (1983): Somali 61.7%, of which Issa 33.4%, Gadaboursi 15.0%, Issaq 13.3%; Afar 20.0%; Arab (mostly Yemeni) 6.0%; European 4.0%; other (refugees) 8.3%.
Religious affiliation (1988): Sunnī Muslim 96%; Christian 4%, of which Roman Catholic 2%, Protestant 1%, Orthodox 1%.
Major city and towns (1989): Djibouti 450,000[3]; 'Alī Sabīḥ 4,000; Tadjoura 3,500; Dikhil 3,000.

Vital statistics

Birth rate per 1,000 population (1990–95): 45.8 (world avg. 26.4).
Death rate per 1,000 population (1990–95): 16.4 (world avg. 9.2).
Natural increase rate per 1,000 population (1990–95): 29.4 (world avg. 17.2).
Total fertility rate (avg. births per childbearing woman; 1990): 6.6.
Marriage rate per 1,000 population (1982): 6.7.
Divorce rate per 1,000 population (1982): 1.9.
Life expectancy at birth (1990–95): male 47.4 years; female 50.7 years.
Major causes of death (percentage of total deaths; 1984)[4]: diarrhea and acute dehydration 16.0%; malnutrition 16.0%; poisoning 11.0%; tuberculosis 6.0%; acute respiratory disease 6.0%; malaria 6.0%; anemia 6.0%; heart disease 2.0%; kidney disease 1.0%; other ailments 19.0%; no diagnosis 11.0%.

National economy

Budget (1989). Revenue: DF 23,900,000,000 (1988; current receipts 93.3%, of which indirect taxes 60.6%, direct taxes 21.5%, nontax revenue 11.2%; external development receipts 6.0%). Expenditures: DF 24,300,000,000 (1988; wages and salaries 57.7%; goods and services 27.9%; development expenditures 3.9%).
Public debt (external, outstanding; 1990): U.S.$150,000,000.
Tourism: receipts from visitors (1990) U.S.$6,000,000; expenditures by nationals abroad, n.a.
Production (metric tons except as noted). Agriculture, forestry, fishing (1991): vegetables and melons 22,000, of which tomatoes 1,000, eggplant (1985–86) 66; livestock (number of live animals) 504,000 goats, 420,000 sheep, 170,000 cattle, 60,000 camels, 8,000 asses; fish catch (1989) 470, of which snapper 120, grouper 100, carangids 50. Mining and quarrying: mineral production limited to locally used construction materials and evaporated salt. Manufacturing (1988): detail n.a.; main items produced include furniture, nonalcoholic beverages, meat and hides, light electromechanical goods, and mineral water. Construction (1989): 53,900 sq m. Energy production (consumption): electricity (kW-hr; 1990) 175,000,000 (175,000,000); coal, none (n.a.); crude petroleum, none (n.a.); petroleum products (metric tons; 1990) none (123,000); natural gas, none (n.a.).
Population economically active (1985): total 161,000; activity rate of total population 44.5% (participation rates: over age 10, 65.2%; female 39.1%; unemployed [1987] c. 40–50%).

Price and earnings indexes (1985 = 100)

	1983	1984	1985	1986	1987	1988	1989
Consumer price index[5]	...	116.6	100.0	116.4	121.3	129.0	132.9
Earnings index[6]	...	...	...	...	...	...	...

Household income and expenditure. Average household size[7] (1985) 7.2; income per household: n.a.; sources of income (1976): wages and salaries 51.6%, self-employment 36.0%, transfer payments 10.5%, other 1.9%; expen-

diture (expatriate households; 1984): food 50.3%, energy 13.1%, recreation 10.4%, housing 6.4%, clothing 1.7%, personal effects 1.4%, health care 1.0%, household goods 0.3%, other 15.4%.
Gross national product (at current market prices; 1986): U.S.$216,600,000[8] (U.S.$475 per capita).

Structure of gross national product and labour force

	1986 in value DF '000,000	1986 % of total value	1987 labour force	1987 % of labour force
Agriculture	1,079	3.1	127,000	76.9
Mining	—	—		
Manufacturing	924	2.6	14,000	8.5
Construction	752	2.1		
Public utilities	3,506	10.0		
Transportation and communications	4,873	13.9		
Trade	3,803	10.8		
Finance	807	2.3	24,000	14.6
Pub. admin., defense	10,505	29.9		
Services	655	1.9		
Other	8,209[9]	23.4[9]		
TOTAL	35,113	100.0	165,000	100.0

Land use (1990): forested 0.3%; meadows and pastures 9.1%; agricultural and under permanent cultivation[10]; built-on, wasteland, and other 90.6%.

Foreign trade[11]

Balance of trade (current prices)

	1985	1986	1987	1988	1989	1990
DF '000,000	−33,182	−29,847	−31,511	−31,655	−30,497	−33,763
% of total	87.0%	80.4%	88.0%	79.4%	77.5%	79.3%

Imports (1990): DF 38,183,000,000 (food and beverages 27.0%; textiles and footwear 11.8%; machinery and electrical machinery 8.0%; khat [a narcotic leaf] 7.8%; fossil fuels 7.1%; chemical products 5.7%; metals and metal products 4.5%; raw tobacco and tobacco products 2.7%). *Major import sources:* France 29.3%; Ethiopia 11.3%; Japan 5.4%; Italy 5.3%; Saudi Arabia 5.0%; United States 3.2%.
Exports (1990): DF 4,420,000,000 (1989; unspecified special transactions 62.3%, of which live animals [including camels] 36.1%, food and food products 5.9%). *Major export destinations:* France 49.0%; Italy 3.6%; Somalia 1.7%; Saudi Arabia 1.1%.

Transport and communications

Transport. Railroads (1989): length 66 mi, 106 km; passenger-mi 182,000,000, passenger-km 293,000,000; short ton-mile cargo 81,700,000[12], metric ton-km cargo 119,300,000[12]. Roads (1989): total length 1,906 mi, 3,067 km (paved 10%). Vehicles (1989): passenger cars 13,000; trucks and buses 2,000. Merchant marine (1991): vessels (100 gross tons and over) 8; total deadweight tonnage 350. Air transport (1989)[13]: passenger arrivals 64,000, passenger departures 66,000; cargo loaded 1,100 metric tons, cargo unloaded 7,100 metric tons; airports (1992) with scheduled flights 3.
Communications. Weekly newspapers (1990): total number 1; total circulation 4,000; circulation per 1,000 population 7.6. Radio (1991): total number of receivers 30,000 (1 per 18 persons). Television (1991): total number of receivers 14,000 (1 per 39 persons). Telephone subscribers (1989): 5,100 (1 per 100 persons).

Education and health

Education (1989–90)

	schools	teachers	students	student/ teacher ratio
Primary (age 6–11)	66	707	30,778	43.5
Secondary (age 12–18)	32	319[14]	8,912	...
Voc., teacher tr.				
Higher[15]	—	—	161	—

Educational attainment: n.a. *Literacy* (1987): percentage of population age 20 and over literate 33.7%.
Health (1989): physicians 97 (1 per 5,258 persons); hospital beds[16] 1,383 (1 per 369 persons); infant mortality rate per 1,000 live births (1990–95) 112.
Food: n.a.

Military

Total active duty personnel (1992): 3,200[17] (army 93.8%, navy 3.1%, air force 3.1%). *Military expenditure as percentage of GNP* (1984): 9.0% (world 5.6%); per capita expenditure U.S.$67.

[1]Original figures are those given in sq km; sq mi equivalent is rounded to appropriate level of generality. [2]Including 45,000 not distributed by district. [3]Not including 20,000 people categorized as transients. [4]Infants and children to age 10, district of Djibouti only. [5]European expatriate community only. [6]Minimum monthly wage remained constant between 1980 and 1986. [7]City of Djibouti only. [8]Estimate based on per capita GNP. [9]Import duties, less imputed bank service charge. [10]In 1988–89 only 1,005 acres (407 hectares) of land were cultivated. [11]The value of imports includes merchandise destined for Ethiopia and northern Somalia; that of exports excludes reexports coming from those areas. In 1980 the value of reexports from Ethiopia and northern Somalia was approximately five times greater than the value of domestic exports. Import figures are c.i.f. [12]Based on total weight of Ethiopian exports and imports transported to and from the port of Djibouti. [13]Djibouti International Airport only. [14]Public schools only. [15]1983–84. [16]Public health only. [17]Excludes 4,000 French troops.

Dominica

Official name: Commonwealth of Dominica.
Form of government: multiparty republic with one legislative house (House of Assembly [31][1]).
Chief of state: President.
Head of government: Prime Minister.
Capital: Roseau.
Official language: English.
Official religion: none.
Monetary unit: 1 East Caribbean dollar (EC$) = 100 cents; valuation (Oct. 5, 1992) 1 U.S.$ = EC$2.70; 1 £ = EC$4.59.

Area and population

	area		population
			1991
Parishes[2]	sq mi	sq km	census
St. Andrew	69	179	11,106
St. David	49	127	6,977
St. George	21	54	20,365
St. John	23	60	4,990
St. Joseph	46	119	6,183
St. Luke	4	10	1,552
St. Mark	4	10	1,943
St. Patrick	32	83	8,929
St. Paul	26	67	7,495
St. Peter	11	29	1,643
TOTAL	290[3, 4]	750[3, 4]	71,183[5]

Demography

Population (1992): 71,500.
Density (1992): persons per sq mi 246.6, persons per sq km 95.3.
Urban-rural: n.a.
Sex distribution (1991): male 50.04%; female 49.96%.
Age breakdown (1989): under 15, 35.1%; 15–29, 28.1%; 30–44, 14.5%; 45–59, 9.5%; 60 and over, 11.7%; unknown, 1.1%.
Population projection: (2000) 80,000; (2010) 92,000.
Doubling time: 47 years.
Ethnic composition (1981): black 91.2%; mixed race 6.0%; Amerindian 1.5%; white 0.5%; not stated 0.6%; other 0.2%.
Religious affiliation (1981): Roman Catholic 76.9%; Protestant 15.5%, of which Methodist 5.0%, Seventh-day Adventist 3.2%, Pentecostal 2.9%; other 7.6%.
Major towns (1991): Roseau 15,853; Portsmouth 3,621; Marigot 2,919; Atkinson 2,518; Mahaut 2,372.

Vital statistics

Birth rate per 1,000 population (1990): 22.3 (world avg. 27.1); (1980) legitimate 35.0%; illegitimate 65.0%.
Death rate per 1,000 population (1990): 7.1 (world avg. 9.8).
Natural increase rate per 1,000 population (1990): 15.2 (world avg. 17.3).
Total fertility rate (avg. births per childbearing woman; 1991): 2.6.
Marriage rate per 1,000 population (1990): 3.2.
Divorce rate per 1,000 population: n.a.
Life expectancy at birth (1991): male 73.0 years; female 79.0 years.
Major causes of death per 100,000 population (1990): diseases of the circulatory system 273.5, of which ischemic heart diseases 120.8, hypertensive disease 88.8; malignant neoplasms (cancers) 116.6; endocrine, metabolic, and nutritional disorders 51.4; diseases of the respiratory system 43.0; infectious and parasitic diseases 37.5.

National economy

Budget (1991–92). Revenue: EC$209,700,000 (current revenue 69.5%; other revenue [sale of government assets, loans, and foreign aid] 30.5%). Expenditures: EC$209,700,000 (current expenditures 66.1%[6]; development expenditures 33.9%, of which communications 11.5%, education 4.7%, water and sewerage 4.3%).
Gross national product (1990): U.S.$160,000,000 (U.S.$1,940 per capita).

Structure of gross domestic product and labour force

	1991		1989	
	in value EC$'000,000[7]	% of total value	labour force	% of labour force
Agriculture	101.6	25.5	7,900	25.8
Mining	3.8	1.0 }	3,400	11.1
Manufacturing	27.4	6.9 }		
Construction	29.1	7.3	2,800	9.2
Public utilities	12.9	3.2	300	1.0
Transportation and communications	64.8	16.3	1,600	5.2
Trade, hotels, restaurants	52.6	13.2	3,700	12.1
Finance, real estate, insurance	58.5	14.7	800	2.6
Pub. admin., defense	72.5	18.2 }	5,800	19.0
Services	4.2	1.1 }		
Other	−29.5[8]	−7.4[8]	4,300[9]	14.1[9]
TOTAL	397.9	100.0	30,600	100.0[4]

Population economically active (1989): total 30,600; activity rate of total population 37.5% (participation rates: ages 15–64, 62.3%; female 41.8%; unemployed [1992] 15.0%).

Price and earnings indexes (1985 = 100)

	1985	1986	1987	1988	1989	1990	1991
Consumer price index	100.0	103.0	108.0	110.4	117.3	121.6	128.8
Earnings index	...	...	...	...	...	...	...

Public debt (external, outstanding; end of 1991): U.S.$83,900,000.
Household income and expenditure. Average household size (1981) 4.3; income per household: n.a.; expenditure (1984)[10]: food and nonalcoholic beverages 43.1%, housing and utilities 16.1%, clothing and footwear 6.5%, alcoholic beverages and tobacco 2.0%, other 32.3%.
Production. Agriculture, forestry, fishing (value of production in EC$'000; 1991): bananas 39,600, root crops 32,800 (of which yams 9,800, dasheens 9,200, tanias 6,400, cassava 4,300), coconuts 4,600, plantains 3,700, grapefruit 3,500, oranges 3,300, cinnamon 2,400; livestock (number of live animals) 10,000 goats, 9,000 cattle, 8,000 sheep; roundwood, n.a.; fish catch (1990) 700 metric tons. Mining and quarrying (1989): pumice and volcanic ash (1990) 100,000 metric tons. Manufacturing (1990): coconut-based soaps 9,586 metric tons[11]; pasta products 156 metric tons; edible coconut oil 2,904 hectolitres; rum (1987) 2,614 hectolitres; bottled spring water 323,000 cases; other products include electronic components and garments. Construction (value of starts; 1990): U.S.$29,800,000. Energy production (consumption): electricity (kW-hr; 1990) 36,900,000 (30,700,000); coal, none (none); crude petroleum, none (none); petroleum products (metric tons; 1990) none (19,-000); natural gas, none (none).
Tourism: receipts from visitors (1991) U.S.$30,000,000; expenditures by nationals abroad (1990) U.S.$4,000,000.
Land use (1990): forested 41.0%; meadows and pastures 3.0%; agricultural and under permanent cultivation 23.0%; other 33.0%.

Foreign trade[12]

Balance of trade (current prices)

	1985	1986	1987	1988	1989	1990
EC$'000,000	−72.6	−33.5	−49.6	−86.3	−167.2	−169.8
% of total	32.1%	12.5%	16.1%	22.3%	40.7%	36.4%

Imports (1990): EC$318,400,000 (machinery and transport equipment 26.1%; basic manufactures 24.5%; food 17.3%; chemicals and chemical products 11.1%). *Major import sources:* United States 27.0%; United Kingdom 14.4%; Trinidad and Tobago 9.2%; St. Lucia 4.2%; Germany 3.1%; unspecified countries 26.5%.
Exports (1990): EC$148,600,000 (domestic exports 95.8%, of which bananas 55.9%, coconut-based laundry and toilet soaps 21.4%, plantains 1.3%, bay oil 1.3%; reexports 4.2%). *Major export destinations:* United Kingdom 49.6%; Jamaica 12.2%; United States 9.2%; Italy 7.1%; Trinidad and Tobago 2.6%.

Transport and communications

Transport. Railroads: none. Roads (1988): total length 470 mi, 756 km (paved, n.a.). Vehicles (1991): passenger cars 4,696; trucks and buses 4,616. Merchant marine (1991): vessels (100 gross tons and over) 7; total deadweight tonnage 3,153. Air transport (1991): passenger arrivals 43,312, passenger departures, n.a.; cargo unloaded 259 metric tons, cargo loaded 415 metric tons; airports (1992) with scheduled flights 2.
Communications. Daily newspapers: none[13]. Radio (1991): 45,000 receivers (1 per 1.9 persons). Television (1991): 5,200 receivers (1 per 16 persons). Telephones (1991): 12,404 (1 per 5.8 persons).

Education and health

Education (1990–91)

	schools	teachers	students	student/teacher ratio
Primary	65	626	14,427	23.0
Secondary	13	199	4,374	22.0
Higher	2	38[14]	388	9.5[14]

Educational attainment (1981). Percentage of population age 25 and over having: no formal schooling 6.6%; primary education 80.6%; secondary 11.1%; higher 1.7%. *Literacy* (1986): total population age 15 and over literate, c. 49,000 (94.4%).
Health (1990): physicians 37 (1 per 1,947 persons); hospital beds 292 (1 per 247 persons); infant mortality rate per 1,000 live births 18.4.
Food (1988–90): daily per capita caloric intake 2,911 (vegetable products 79%, animal products 21%); 120% of FAO recommended minimum requirement.

Military

Total active duty personnel (1990): none[15].

[1]Includes 10 nonelective seats. Nine of the 10 nonelective seats are potentially elective according to the constitution. [2]Dominica is divided into 10 parishes for statistical purposes only. Local government is based on village or town councils. [3]Includes inland water area. [4]Detail does not add to total given because of rounding. [5]Preliminary figure; excludes institutionalized population. [6]Current expenditures (1990–91): EC$135,500,000, of which general administration 17.8%, education 16.6%, health 12.9%, public debt 9.7%, police 8.1%, defense, none. [7]At factor cost. [8]Less imputed service charges. [9]Activities not specified. [10]Weights of consumer price index components. [11]Coconut-based soap products were the main contributor to total value added of manufacturing sector in 1990. [12]Imports c.i.f.; exports f.o.b. [13]Weekly newspapers (1990): total number 2; total circulation 5,050; circulation per 1,000 population 14. [14]1989–90. [15]300-member police force includes a coast guard unit.

Dominican Republic

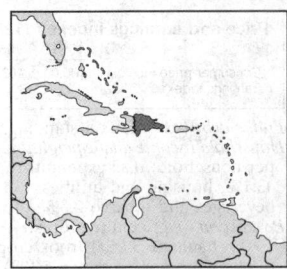

Official name: República Dominicana
(Dominican Republic).
Form of government: multiparty
republic with two legislative
houses (Senate [30]; Chamber of
Deputies [120]).
Head of state and government:
President.
Capital: Santo Domingo.
Official language: Spanish.
Official religion: none[1].
Monetary unit: 1 Dominican peso
(RD$) = 100 centavos; valuation
(Oct. 5, 1992) 1 U.S.$ = RD$12.71;
1 £ = RD$21.60.

Area and population		area		population
				1990
Provinces	Capitals	sq mi	sq km	estimate
Azua	Azua	938	2,430	195,420
Bahoruco (Baoruco)	Neiba	531	1,376	87,376
Barahona	Barahona	976	2,528	152,405
Dajabón	Dajabón	344	890	64,123
Duarte	San Francisco de Macorís	499	1,292	261,725
El Seíbo	El Seíbo	641	1,659	97,590
Espaillat	Moca	386	1,000	182,248
Hato Mayor	Hato Mayor	514	1,330	77,823
Independencia	Jimaní	719	1,861	43,077
La Altagracia	Higüey	1,191	3,084	111,241
La Estrelleta	Elías Piña	690	1,788	72,651
La Romana	La Romana	209	541	169,223
La Vega	La Vega	916	2,373	303,047
María Trinidad Sánchez	Nagua	506	1,310	125,148
Monseñor Nouel	Bonao	388	1,004	124,794
Monte Cristi	Monte Cristi	768	1,989	92,678
Monte Plata	Monte Plata	841	2,179	174,799
Pedernales	Pedernales	373	967	18,896
Peravia	Baní	626	1,622	186,810
Puerto Plata	Puerto Plata	726	1,881	229,738
Salcedo	Salcedo	206	533	110,216
Samaná	Samaná	382	989	73,002
San Cristóbal	San Cristóbal	604	1,564	320,921
San Juan	San Juan	1,375	3,561	266,628
San Pedro de Macorís	San Pedro de Macorís	450	1,166	197,862
Sánchez Ramírez	Cotuí	453	1,174	140,635
Santiago	Santiago de los Caballeros	1,205	3,122	704,835
Santiago Rodríguez	Sabaneta	394	1,020	61,570
Santo Domingo[2]	—	570	1,477	2,411,895
Valverde	Mao	220	570	111,470
TOTAL		18,704[3]	48,443[3]	7,169,846

Demography

Population (1992): 7,471,000.
Density (1992): persons per sq mi 399.4, persons per sq km 154.2.
Urban-rural (1990): urban 60.4%; rural 39.6%.
Sex distribution (1990): male 50.82%; female 49.18%.
Age breakdown (1990): under 15, 37.9%; 15–29, 29.9%; 30–44, 17.6%; 45–59, 9.1%; 60–74, 4.4%; 75 and over, 1.1%.
Population projection: (2000) 8,621,000; (2010) 9,903,000.
Doubling time: 35 years.
Ethnic composition (1990): mixed 70%; white 15%; black 15%.
Religious affiliation (1990): Roman Catholic 90.8%; other 9.2%.
Major urban centres (1989): Santo Domingo 2,200,000; Santiago de los Caballeros 467,000; La Vega 189,000; San Pedro de Macorís 137,000.

Vital statistics

Birth rate per 1,000 population (1991): 27.0 (world avg. 26.4).
Death rate per 1,000 population (1991): 7.0 (world avg. 9.2).
Natural increase rate per 1,000 population (1991): 20.0 (world avg. 17.2).
Total fertility rate (avg. births per childbearing woman; 1991): 3.1.
Marriage rate per 1,000 population (1987): 2.3.
Divorce rate per 1,000 population (1987): 0.8.
Life expectancy at birth (1991): male 65.0 years; female 69.0 years.
Major causes of death per 100,000 population (1985): diseases of the circulatory system 100.3; infectious and parasitic diseases 51.4; diseases of the respiratory system 35.4; accidents, poisoning, and violence 33.7.

National economy

Budget (1991). Revenue: RD$10,427,000,000 (tax revenue 89.6%, of which import duties 42.2%, income taxes 22.6%, taxes on goods and services 21.8%; grants and loans 4.7%; nontax revenue 2.5%). Expenditures: RD$9,-996,000,000 (development expenditure 53.1%; current expenditure 46.9%).
Public debt (external, outstanding; 1990): U.S.$3,343,000,000.
Tourism (1990): receipts from visitors U.S.$750,000,000; expenditures by nationals abroad U.S.$144,000,000.
Production (metric tons except as noted). Agriculture, forestry, fishing (1991): sugarcane 6,930,000, plantains 750,000[4], unhusked rice 435,800, bananas 395,000[4], mangoes 150,000[4], tomatoes 148,900, coffee cherries 110,400, cacao 44,100, beans 43,700, raw tobacco 23,700, raw cotton 7,000; livestock (number of live animals; 1990) 2,240,000 cattle, 431,000 pigs; roundwood (1990) 982,000 cu m; fish catch (1989) 21,800. Mining (1991): ferronickel 75,800; gold 101,600 troy oz. Manufacturing (value of production in RD$'000,000; 1986[5]): food products 1,515; alcoholic beverages 558; refined petroleum 505; cigarettes 215; cement 158. Construction (value of authorized construction in RD$'000,000; 1987): residential 352; nonresidential 253. Energy production

(consumption): electricity (kW-hr; 1991) 3,094,000,000 (2,229,000,000); coal, none (none); crude petroleum (barrels; 1990) none (10,262,000); petroleum products (metric tons; 1990) 1,258,000 (1,735,000); natural gas, none (none).
Gross national product (1990): U.S.$5,847,000,000 (U.S.$820 per capita).

Structure of gross domestic product and labour force				
	1991		1981	
	in value RD$'000,000[6]	% of total value	labour force	% of labour force
Agriculture	526	15.3	420,463	22.0
Mining	116	3.4	4,743	0.2
Manufacturing	554	16.1	224,437	11.7
Construction	249	7.2	80,850	4.3
Public utilities	57	1.7	13,891	0.7
Transp. and commun.	297	8.6	40,470	2.1
Trade	504	14.6	192,181	10.0
Finance, real estate	452	13.1	22,369	1.2
Pub. admin., defense	352	10.2 }	363,125	18.9
Services	338	9.8 }		
Other	—	—	552,859[7]	28.9
TOTAL	3,445	100.0	1,915,388	100.0

Population economically active (1981): total 1,915,388; activity rate of total population 33.9% (participation rates: ages 15–64, 53.6%; female 28.9%; unemployed [December 1991] 30.0%).

Price and earnings indexes (1985 = 100)							
	1985	1986	1987	1988	1989	1990	1991
Consumer price index	100.0	109.7	127.2	183.7	267.1	425.9	655.3
Monthly earnings index[8]	100.0	117.4	132.9	199.5	258.2	...	...

Household income and expenditure. Average household size (1981) 5.1; average income: n.a.; sources of income: n.a.; expenditure (1976–77)[9]: food, beverages, and tobacco 51.7%, housing 23.9%, clothing and footwear 6.0%.
Land use (1989): forested 12.8%; meadows and pastures 43.2%; agricultural and under permanent cultivation 29.9%; other 14.1%.

Foreign trade[10]

Balance of trade (current prices)						
	1986	1987	1988	1989	1990	1991
U.S.$'000,000	−629.6	−880.2	−718.3	−1,039.4	−1,058.3	−1,070.5
% of total	30.4%	38.2%	28.8%	36.0%	41.9%	44.8%

Imports (1991): U.S.$1,728,800,000 ([11]crude petroleum and pet. products 18.8%, machinery 16.1%, motor vehicles 12.0%, foodstuffs 8.5%). *Major import sources* (1990): U.S. 43.5%; Venezuela 12.0%; Japan 10.6%; Mexico 8.5%.
Exports (1991): U.S.$658,300,000[12] (ferronickel 33.5%, raw sugar 20.1%, coffee 6.6%, gold alloy 6.0%, cacao 4.8%). *Major export destinations:* U.S. 56.0%; The Netherlands 15.1%; Puerto Rico 7.7%; Japan 3.6%; Belgium 3.1%.

Transport and communications

Transport. Railroads:[13]. Roads (1989): total length 17,000 km (paved 17%). Vehicles (1989): passenger cars 114,000; trucks and buses 72,000. Merchant marine (1991): vessels (100 gross tons and over) 29; total deadweight tonnage 11,322. Air transport (1988)[14]: passenger-km 247,880,000; metric ton-km cargo 3,965,000; airports (1992) 5.
Communications. Daily newspapers (1990): total number 9; total circulation 267,000; circulation per 1,000 population 37. Radio (1991): 1,150,000 receivers (1 per 6.4 persons). Television (1991): 728,000 receivers (1 per 10 persons). Telephones (1988): 292,733 (1 per 24 persons).

Education and health

Education (1989–90)				student/
	schools	teachers	students	teacher ratio
Primary (age 7–14)[15]	4,854	21,850	1,032,055	47.2
Secondary (age 15–18)[16]	...	9,963	426,962	42.9
Teacher tr.[16]	...	108	3,602	...
Higher[17]	7	5,319	86,504	16.3

Educational attainment (1981). Percentage of population age 25 and over having: no formal schooling 48.0%; incomplete primary education 31.7%; complete primary 4.0%; secondary 14.0%; higher 2.3%. *Literacy* (1990): total population age 15 and over literate, *c.* 3,710,000 (83.3%); males literate, *c.* 1,922,000 (84.8%); females literate, *c.* 1,788,000 (81.8%).
Health: physicians (1988) 7,332 (1 per 934 persons); hospital beds (1987) 13,169 (1 per 508 persons); infant mortality rate (1991) 60.0.
Food (1987–89): daily per capita caloric intake 2,342 (vegetable products 89%, animal products 11%); 104% of FAO recommended minimum.

Military

Total active duty personnel (1991): 23,200 (army 64.7%, navy 17.2%, air force 18.1%). *Military expenditure as percentage of GNP* (1989): 0.8% (world 4.9%); per capita expenditure U.S.$7.

[1]Roman Catholicism is the state religion per concordat with Vatican City. [2]National district. [3]Total includes 63 sq mi (163 sq km) of offshore islands not shown separately. [4]1990. [5]Traditional manufacturing only; in 1991, 26 free zones employed 142,300 people manufacturing assorted goods (mostly ready-made garments) for reexport. [6]At prices of 1970. [7]Not adequately defined (421,628) and those seeking work for first time (131,231). [8]Minimum wage. [9]Weights of consumer price index components. [10]Excludes free zones. [11]Percentage breakdown is for 1986 based on U.S.$1,351,700,-000. [12]1990 reexports of free zones were estimated to equal U.S.$550,000,000. [13]Most track serves the sugar and mining industries only, except for 142 km for public transport. [14]CDA (Dominicana) Airlines only. [15]Public schools only. [16]1986–87. [17]1990–91; universities only.

Ecuador

Official name: República del Ecuador (Republic of Ecuador).
Form of government: unitary multiparty republic with one legislative house (National Congress [77]).
Head of state and government: President.
Capital: Quito.
Official language: Spanish.
Official religion: none.
Monetary unit: 1 Sucre (S/.) = 100 centavos; valuation (Oct. 5, 1992) 1 U.S.$ = S/. 2,000; 1 £ = S/. 3,400.

Area and population

Regions Provinces	Capitals	area sq mi	sq km	population 1990 census
Amazonica				
Morona-Santiago	Macas	11,164	28,915	84,216
Napo	Tena	12,899	33,409	103,387
Pastaza	Puyo	11,398	29,520	41,811
Sucumbíos[1]	Nueva Loja	7,186	18,612	76,952
Zamora-Chinchipe	Zamora	7,985	20,681	66,167
Costa				
El Oro	Machala	2,312	5,988	412,572
Esmeraldas	Esmeraldas	5,875	15,216	306,628
Guayas	Guayaquil	8,070	20,902	2,515,146
Los Ríos	Babahoyo	2,415	6,254	527,559
Manabí	Portoviejo	7,104	18,400	1,031,927
Insular				
Galápagos	Puerto Baquerizo Moreno	3,093	8,010	9,785
Sierra				
Azuay	Cuenca	2,973	7,701	506,090
Bolívar	Guaranda	1,256	3,254	155,088
Cañar	Azogues	1,509	3,908	189,347
Carchi	Tulcán	1,428	3,699	141,482
Chimborazo	Riobamba	2,176	5,637	364,682
Cotopaxi	Latacunga	2,041	5,287	276,324
Imbabura	Ibarra	1,925	4,986	265,499
Loja	Loja	4,167	10,793	384,698
Pichincha	Quito	6,409	16,599	1,756,228
Tungurahua	Ambato	1,118	2,896	361,980
TOTAL		104,505[2]	270,667	9,648,189[3]

Demography

Population (1992): 10,607,000.
Density (1992): persons per sq mi 101.5, persons per sq km 39.2.
Urban-rural (1990): urban 55.4%; rural 44.6%.
Sex distribution (1990): male 49.71%; female 50.29%.
Age breakdown (1990): under 15, 38.8%; 15–29, 28.5%; 30–44, 17.3%; 45–59, 9.0% 60–74, 4.7%, 75 and over, 1.7%.
Population projection: (2000) 12,417,000; (2010) 14,467,000.
Doubling time: 25 years.
Ethnic composition (1989): Amerindian 40.0%; mestizo 40.0%; white 15.0%; black 5.0%.
Religious affiliation (1986): Roman Catholic 93.5%; other 6.5%.
Major cities (1990): Guayaquil 1,508,844; Quito 1,100,847; Cuenca 194,981; Machala 144,197; Portoviejo 132,937.

Vital statistics

Birth rate per 1,000 population: (1988) 35.4[4] (world avg. 27.1); (1982) legitimate 67.9%; illegitimate 32.1%.
Death rate per 1,000 population (1988): 7.6[4] (world avg. 9.8).
Natural increase rate per 1,000 population (1988): 27.8[4] (world avg. 17.3).
Total fertility rate (avg. births per childbearing woman; 1985–90): 4.7.
Marriage rate per 1,000 population (1986): 6.2[4, 5].
Divorce rate per 1,000 population (1988): 0.4[4, 5].
Life expectancy at birth (1985–90): male 63.4 years; female 67.6 years.
Major causes of death per 100,000 population (1988): circulatory diseases 83.7; accidents, poisonings, and violence 63.7; infectious and parasitic diseases 61.1; respiratory diseases 56.2; neoplasms (cancers) 48.4.

National economy

Budget (1990). Revenue: S/. 1,363,149,000,000 (income from petroleum 50.6%, production and sales tax 17.2%, import duties 12.3%, income taxes 6.1%). Expenditures: S/. 1,411,109,000,000 (debt service 36.8%, public services 21.2%, education 15.8%, health 7.0%, transport and communications 5.2%).
Production (metric tons except as noted). Agriculture, forestry, fishing (1990): sugarcane 5,700,000, bananas 2,817,000, plantains 972,000, rice 760,000, corn (maize) 400,000, potatoes 398,000, soybeans 133,000, cacao 95,000; livestock (number of live animals) 4,361,000 cattle, 4,180,000 pigs, 1,350,000 sheep, 55,000,000 chickens; roundwood 10,157,000 cu m; fish catch (1989) 723,624. Mining and quarrying (1988): limestone 3,000,000; gold 305,000 troy oz. Manufacturing (value added in S/. '000,000; 1988): food products 94,726, of which beverages (including liquors) 11,504; textiles 30,180; chemical products 25,192; metal products 15,777. Construction (in S/.[6]; 1985): residential 31,-391,900,000; nonresidential 2,916,100,000. Energy production (consumption): electricity (kW-hr; 1990) 6,327,000,000 (6,327,000,000); crude petroleum (barrels; 1990) 106,494,000 (42,473,000); petroleum products (metric tons; 1990) 6,022,000 (4,713,000); natural gas (cu m; 1990) 99,998,000 (99,998,000).
Tourism (1990): receipts U.S.$193,000,000; expenditures U.S.$176,000,000.
Public debt (external, outstanding; 1990): U.S.$9,858,000,000.
Gross national product (1990): U.S.$10,112,000,000 (U.S.$960 per capita).

Structure of gross domestic product and labour force

	1990			
	in value[7] S/. '000,000	% of total value	labour force	% of labour force
Agriculture	31,525	17.4	1,035,712	30.8
Mining	30,404	16.8	20,870	0.6
Manufacturing	21,554	11.9	370,338	11.0
Construction	5,914	3.3	196,716	5.9
Public utilities	2,984	1.7	12,660	0.4
Transp. and commun.	15,438	8.5	131,084	3.9
Trade	26,854	14.8	476,730	14.2
Finance	19,574	10.8	81,357	2.4
Pub. admin., defense } Services	27,046	15.0	838,129	24.9
Other	–341	–0.2	196,171[8]	5.8[8]
TOTAL	180,952	100.0	3,359,767	100.0[2]

Population economically active (1990): total 3,359,767; activity rate of total population 34.8% (participation rates: ages 15–64, 56.6%; female 30.0%; unemployed [1989] 8.0%).

Price and earnings indexes (1985 = 100)

	1985	1986	1987	1988	1989	1990	1991
Consumer price index	100.0	123.0	159.3	252.1	442.8	657.6	978.0
Hourly earnings index[9]	100.0	141.2	170.6	258.8	376.5	...	...

Household income and expenditure. Average household size (1982) 5.1; average annual income per household (1982) S/. 28,747 (U.S.$956); sources of income (1989): self-employment 74.9%, wages 17.4%, transfer payments 4.5%, interest, dividends, and rent 3.2%; expenditure (1989): food and tobacco 37.7%, clothing 12.1%, transportation and communications 11.7%, household furnishings 8.8%, housing and utilities 5.1%, health care 4.1%.
Land use (1989): forested 40.5%; meadows and pastures 18.4%; agricultural and under permanent cultivation 9.6%; other 31.5%.

Foreign trade[10]

Balance of trade (current prices)

	1986	1987	1988	1989	1990	1991
U.S.$'000,000	+603.4	+232.2	+674.8	+719.7	+1,077.7	+736.0
% of total	16.0%	6.1%	18.2%	18.0%	24.7%	14.1%

Imports (1990): U.S.$1,861,745,000 (industrial raw materials 43.6%, industrial capital goods 20.2%, transport equipment 11.0%, consumer goods 9.6%, agricultural raw materials 4.6%). *Major import sources* (1989): United States 33.9%; European Economic Community 21.5%; Latin American Integration Association 20.9%; Japan 8.2%.
Exports (1990): U.S.$2,722,182,000 (crude petroleum 46.5%, bananas 17.2%, shrimp 12.5%, petroleum products 5.5%, coffee 3.8%, cacao 2.7%). *Major export destinations* (1989): United States 54.6%; Latin American Integration Association 13.3%; European Economic Community 8.8%; Andean Group 7.8%; Japan 2.5%.

Transport and communications

Transport. Railroads (1988): route length 965 km; passenger-km 63,300,000; metric ton-km cargo 8,180,000. Roads (1988): total length 37,636 km (paved 17%). Vehicles (1987): passenger cars 272,282; trucks and buses 41,231. Merchant marine (1991): vessels (100 gross tons and over) 158; deadweight tonnage 525,645. Air transport (1990): passenger-km 1,243,000,000; metric ton-km cargo 63,200,000; airports (1992) 14.
Communications. Daily newspapers (1988): total number 26; total circulation 887,000[11]; circulation per 1,000 population 87[11]. Radio (1991): 3,000,000 receivers (1 per 3.5 persons). Television (1991): 780,000 receivers (1 per 15 persons). Telephones (1989): 691,460 (1 per 14 persons).

Education and health

Education (1989–90)

	schools[12]	teachers	students	student/ teacher ratio
Primary (age 4–12)	16,146	60,608	1,843,819	30.4
Secondary (age 12–18)[13, 14] }	2,207	36,730	504,481	13.7
Vocational[14]		16,838	260,850	15.5
Higher	21	12,856	206,541	16.1

Educational attainment (1982). Percentage of population age 25 and over having: no schooling 25.4%; incomplete primary 17.0%; complete primary 34.1%; some secondary 8.1%; secondary 7.9%; postsecondary 7.6%. *Literacy* (1990): total population age 10 and over literate 6,402,011 (89.8%); males 3,217,497 (91.6%); females 3,184,514 (88.0%).
Health (1988): physicians (1984) 11,033 (1 per 826 persons); hospital beds 16,726 (1 per 610 persons); infant mortality rate per 1,000 live births 63.0.
Food (1987–89): daily per capita caloric intake 2,518 (vegetable products 85%, animal products 15%); 110% of FAO minimum requirement.

Military

Total active duty personnel (1991): 57,800 (army 86.5%, navy 8.3%, air force 5.2%). *Military expenditure as percentage of GNP* (1989): 1.7% (world 4.9%); per capita expenditure U.S.$16.

[1]Created on Feb. 11, 1989. [2]Detail does not add to total given because of rounding. [3]Total includes 70,621 persons not shown separately. [4]Excluding nomadic Indian tribes. [5]Based on incomplete registration. [6]Authorized construction. [7]At constant 1975 prices. [8]Includes unemployed persons not previously employed. [9]General minimum wage. [10]Import figures are f.o.b. in balance of trade and c.i.f. for commodities and trading partners. [11]Circulation refers to 23 daily newspapers only. [12]1986–87. [13]Includes teacher training. [14]1987–88.

Egypt

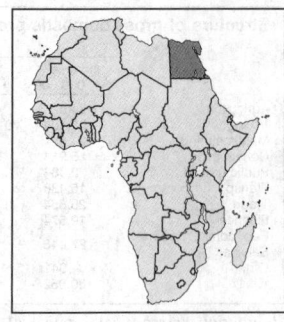

Official name: Jumhūrīyah Miṣr al-'Arabīyah (Arab Republic of Egypt).
Form of government: republic with one legislative house (People's Assembly [454[1]]).
Chief of state: President.
Head of government: Prime Minister.
Capital: Cairo.
Official language: Arabic.
Official religion: Islam.
Monetary unit: 1 Egyptian pound (LE) = 100 piastres = 1,000 millièmes; valuation (Oct. 5, 1992)
1 U.S.$ = LE 3.34; 1 £ = LE 5.68.

Area and population

Regions Governorates	Capitals	area sq mi	area sq km	population 1990 estimate
Desert				
al-Baḥr al-Aḥmar	al-Ghurdaqah	78,643	203,685	108,000
Maṭrūḥ	Marsā Maṭrūḥ	81,897	212,112	182,000
Janūb Sīnā'	aṭ-Ṭūr	12,796	33,140	33,000
Shamāl Sīnā'	al-'Arīsh	10,646	27,574	196,000
al-Wādī al-Jadīd	al-Kharijah	145,369	376,505	126,000
Lower Egypt				
al-Buḥayrah	Damanhūr	3,911	10,130	3,602,000
ad-Daqahlīyah	al-Manṣūrah	1,340	3,471	3,828,000
Dumyāṭ	Dumyāṭ	227	589	808,000
al-Gharbīyah	Ṭanṭā	750	1,942	3,113,000
al-Ismā'īlīyah (Ismailia)	—	557	1,442	623,000
Kafr ash-Shaykh	Kafr ash-Shaykh	1,327	3,437	1,968,000
al-Minūfīyah	Shibīn al-Kawm	592	1,532	2,449,000
al-Qalyūbīyah	Banhā	387	1,001	2,868,000
ash-Sharqīyah	az-Zaqāzīq	1,614	4,180	3,766,000
Upper Egypt				
Aswān	Aswān	262	679	883,000
Asyūṭ	Asyūṭ	600	1,553	2,456,000
Banī Suwayf	Banī Suwayf	510	1,322	1,586,000
al-Fayyūm	al-Fayyūm	705	1,827	1,720,000
al-Jīzah	al-Jīzah	32,878	85,153	4,265,000
al-Minyā	al-Minyā	873	2,262	2,916,000
Qinā	Qinā	715	1,851	2,493,000
Sawhāj	Sawhāj	597	1,547	2,689,000
Urban				
Būr Sa'īd (Port Said)	—	—	72	461,000
al-Iskandarīyah (Alexandria)	—	1,034	2,679	3,170,000
al-Qāhirah (Cairo)	—	83	214	6,452,000
as-Suways (Suez)	—	6,888	17,840	392,000
TOTAL		385,229	997,739	53,153,000

Demography

Population (1992): 55,979,000.
Density (1992): persons per sq mi 145.3, persons per sq km 56.1.
Urban-rural (1986): urban 43.9%; rural 56.1%.
Sex distribution (1990): male 51.14%; female 48.86%.
Age breakdown (1986): under 15, 41.8%; 15–29, 26.1%; 30–44, 16.2%; 45–59, 10.4%; 60–74, 4.7%; 75 and over, 0.8%.
Population projection: (2000) 65,556,000; (2010) 77,251,000.
Doubling time: 24 years.
Ethnic composition (1983): Egyptian 99.8%; other 0.2%.
Religious affiliation (1990): Sunnī Muslim c. 90%; Christian c. 10%[2].
Major cities (1990): Cairo 6,452,000; Alexandria 3,170,000; al-Jīzah 2,156,000; Shubrā al-Khaymah 811,000; al-Maḥallah al-Kubrā 385,300[3].

Vital statistics

Birth rate per 1,000 population (1990): 32.2 (world avg. 27.1).
Death rate per 1,000 population (1990): 7.5 (world avg. 9.8).
Natural increase rate per 1,000 population (1990): 24.7 (world avg. 17.3).
Total fertility rate (avg. births per childbearing woman; 1987): 5.4.
Marriage rate per 1,000 population (1990): 8.4.
Divorce rate per 1,000 population (1990): 1.5.
Life expectancy at birth (1989): male 59.0 years; female 60.0 years.
Major causes of death per 100,000 population (1987): diseases of the circulatory system 314.4; diseases of the respiratory system 140.7; infectious and parasitic diseases 98.9; malignant neoplasms (cancers) 22.0.

National economy

Budget (1992–93). Revenue: LE 53,389,000,000 (general taxes 48.8%, of which sales taxes 13.9%, customs duties 10.1%; oil revenue 8.1%; Suez Canal fees 5.8%). Expenditures: LE 62,533,000,000 (debt servicing 31.4%; wages and salaries 16.0%; defense 7.4%; pensions and benefits 5.4%).
Public debt (external, outstanding; 1990): U.S.$40,660,000,000.
Tourism (1990): receipts U.S.$1,994,000,000; expenditures U.S.$166,000,000.
Production (metric tons except as noted). Agriculture, forestry, fishing (1991): sugarcane 11,095,000, corn (maize) 5,270,000, wheat 4,483,000, rice 3,152,000, oranges 1,600,000, tomatoes 1,592,000, sorghum 655,000, dry onions 493,000, cotton (lint) 294,000; livestock (number of live animals) 4,900,000 sheep, 4,500,000 goats, 3,500,000 cattle, 2,550,000 buffalo, 2,000,000 asses, 200,000 camels, 35,000,000 chickens; roundwood (1990) 2,248,000 cu m; fish catch (1990) 312,950. Mining and quarrying (1989–90): iron ore 2,405,000; phosphate rock 1,505,000; salt 1,125,000. Manufacturing (1990–91): cement 16,650,000; nitrate fertilizers 4,650,000; reinforcing iron 1,560,000; phosphate fertilizers 1,450,000; sugar 973,000; soap 383,000; cotton yarn 305,000; glass sheets 24,000; refrigerators 386,000 units; washing machines 290,000 units.

Construction (1989–90): urban residential units 155,785. Energy production (consumption): electricity (kW-hr; 1990) 39,550,000,000 (39,550,000,000); coal (metric tons; 1990) n.a. (1,340,000); crude petroleum (barrels; 1990) 340,700,000 (166,700,000); petroleum products (metric tons; 1990) 23,210,000 (19,197,000); natural gas (cu m; 1990) 6,433,000,000 (6,433,000,000).
Gross national product (1990): U.S.$31,381,000,000 (U.S.$600 per capita).

Structure of gross domestic product and labour force

	1990–91 in value LE '000,000[4]	1990–91 % of total value	1986 labour force	1986 % of labour force
Agriculture	9,820	19.6	5,160,500	42.7
Mining	} 10,923	} 21.8	37,000	0.3
Manufacturing			1,872,400	15.5
Construction	2,514	5.0	571,200	4.7
Public utilities	1,922[5]	3.8[5]	92,400	0.8
Transp. and commun.	4,992	10.0	595,900	4.9
Trade	} 12,062	} 24.0	1,027,300	8.5
Finance			121,900	1.0
Pub. admin., defense	5,719	11.4 }	} 2,616,000	} 21.6
Services	2,225	4.4 }		
TOTAL	50,177	100.0	12,094,600	100.0

Population economically active (1990–91): total 14,760,000; activity rate of total population 27.4% (participation rates: ages 15–64 [1986] 45.1%; female [1986] 14.6%; unemployed 8.4%).

Price and earnings indexes (1985 = 100)

	1985	1986	1987	1988	1989	1990	1991
Consumer price index	100.0	123.9	148.3	174.4	211.5	247.0	295.9
Annual earnings index	100.0	108.8	114.7	...	...	...	...

Household income and expenditure. Average household size (1986): 4.9; sources of income: n.a.; expenditure (1974–75)[6]: food 49.7%, clothing 14.2%, housing 12.4%, transportation 5.2%, tobacco 4.9%, recreation 1.3%.
Land use (1990): pasture 0.6%; agricultural 2.6%; other 96.8%.

Foreign trade

Balance of trade (current prices)

	1986	1987	1988	1989	1990	1991
LE '000,000	−5,193.0	−7,117.0	−10,684.8	−9,228.1	−15,389.3	−10,932.2
% of total	55.8%	54.1%	57.2%	45.6%	52.5%	31.7%

Imports (1990–91): LE 21,849,200,000 (machinery and transport equipment 20.4%; foodstuffs 14.2; chemical products 10.2%; base metals 7.1%). *Major import sources* (1988): U.S. 11.9%; West Germany 11.0%; France 8.4%; Italy 7.0%; Japan 5.0%.
Exports (1990–91): LE 8,606,100,000 (petroleum and petroleum products 50.7%; cotton yarn, textiles, and fabrics 13.6%; raw cotton 2.1%). *Major export destinations* (1988): U.S.S.R. 12.2%; Italy 11.1%; The Netherlands 6.9%; U.S. 6.3%; France 5.8%; West Germany 4.2%; Saudi Arabia 3.2%.

Transport and communications

Transport. Railroads (1990–91): length 5,489 mi, 8,831 km; passenger-km 43,185,000,000; metric ton-km cargo 3,162,000,000. Roads (1989): total length 28,300 mi, 45,500 km (paved 68%). Vehicles (1989): passenger cars 826,915; trucks and buses 550,649. Merchant marine (1991): vessels (100 gross tons and over) 444; total deadweight tonnage 1,852,457. Inland water (1990): Suez Canal, number of transits 17,664; metric ton cargo 271,881,000. Air transport (1990)[7]: passenger-km 5,230,009,000; metric ton-km cargo 131,572,000; airports (1992) 10.
Communications. Daily newspapers (1990): total number 17; total circulation 3,307,100[8]; circulation per 1,000 population 62[8]. Radio (1991): 14,000,000 receivers (1 per 3.9 persons). Television (1991): 3,750,000 receivers (1 per 15 persons). Telephones (1987): 1,455,000 (1 per 34 persons).

Education and health

Education (1989–90)

	schools	teachers	students	student/ teacher ratio
Primary (age 6–11)[9]	14,767	241,119	6,155,100	25.5
Secondary (age 12–17)[9]	6,558	155,941[10]	3,867,760[11]	...
Voc., teacher tr.	519[11]	72,237	1,015,809	14.1
Higher[12]	12	33,106[13]	656,179	...

Educational attainment (1986). Percentage of population age 15 and over having: no formal education 70.6%, of which literate 14.7%; primary and secondary 25.3%; higher 4.1%. *Literacy* (1990): total population age 15 and over literate 15,470,000 (48.4%); males 62.9%; females 33.8%.
Health (1987): physicians 26,988 (1 per 1,816 persons); hospital beds (1990) 107,880 (1 per 493 persons); infant mortality rate 49.6.
Food (1988–90): daily per capita caloric intake 3,310 (vegetable products 92%, animal products 8%); 132% of FAO recommended minimum.

Military

Total active duty personnel (1992): 410,000 (army 70.7%, navy 4.9%, air force 24.4%). *Military expenditure as percentage of GNP* (1989): 5.0% (world 4.9%); per capita expenditure U.S.$67.

---

[1]Includes 10 nonelective seats. [2]According to the 1986 census, the Christian population of Egypt was 5.9% of the total; this figure is considered by many authorities to underestimate the Christian population by as much as 60%. [3]1986. [4]At prices of 1986–87. [5]Includes housing. [6]Urban only. [7]Egypt Air only. [8]Based on 12 dailies only. [9]Data exclude 1,147 primary and 1,057 secondary schools in the El Azhar education system. [10]1987–88. [11]1983. [12]1988–89; universities only. [13]Excludes El Azhar University.

El Salvador

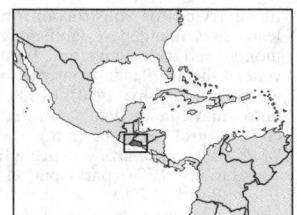

Official name: República de El Salvador (Republic of El Salvador).
Form of government: republic with one legislative house (Legislative Assembly [84]).
Chief of state and government: President.
Capital: San Salvador.
Official language: Spanish.
Official religion: none[1].
Monetary unit: 1 colón ($\mathcal{C}$) = 100 centavos; valuation (Oct. 5, 1992) 1 U.S.$ = $\mathcal{C}$8.58 1 £ = $\mathcal{C}$14.62.

Area and population

Departments	Capitals	area sq mi	area sq km	population 1987 estimate
Ahuachapán	Ahuachapán	479	1,240	286,140
Cabañas	Sensuntepeque	426	1,104	207,573
Chalatenango	Chalatenango	779	2,017	267,201
Cuscatlán	Cojutepeque	292	756	228,965
La Libertad	Nueva San Salvador	638	1,653	464,724
La Paz	Zacatecoluca	473	1,224	292,009
La Unión	La Unión	801	2,074	361,737
Morazán	San Francisco (Gotera)	559	1,447	244,550
San Miguel	San Miguel	802	2,077	502,113
San Salvador	San Salvador	342	886	1,150,531
San Vicente	San Vicente	457	1,184	226,524
Santa Ana	Santa Ana	781	2,023	510,565
Sonsonate	Sonsonate	473	1,226	384,078
Usulután	Usulután	822	2,130	453,586
TOTAL		8,124	21,041	5,580,296[2]

Demography

Population (1992): 5,460,000[2].
Density (1992): persons per sq mi 672.1, persons per sq km 259.5.
Urban-rural (1991): urban 44.4%; rural 55.6%.
Sex distribution (1990): male 49.02%; female 50.98%.
Age breakdown (1990): under 15, 44.4%; 15–29, 27.6%; 30–44, 13.4%; 45–59, 8.9%; 60–74, 4.6%; 75 and over, 1.1%.
Population projection: (2000) 6,604,000; (2010) 8,099,000.
Doubling time: 26 years.
Ethnic composition (1988): mestizo (white and Indian) 89.0%; Indian 10.0%; white 1.0%.
Religious affiliation (1990): Roman Catholic 91.8%; Protestant (mostly evangelical or fundamentalist) 8.2%.
Major cities (1987)[3]: San Salvador 481,397; Santa Ana 232,210; San Miguel 183,449; Mejicanos 112,066; Delgado 98,234.

Vital statistics

Birth rate per 1,000 population (1991): 34.0 (world avg. 26.4); (1988) legitimate 32.0%; illegitimate 68.0%.
Death rate per 1,000 population (1991): 7.0 (world avg. 9.2).
Natural increase rate per 1,000 population (1991): 27.0 (world avg. 17.2).
Total fertility rate (avg. births per childbearing woman; 1991): 4.0.
Marriage rate per 1,000 population (1988): 4.3.
Divorce rate per 1,000 population (1988): 0.5.
Life expectancy at birth (1991): male 63.0 years; female 68.0 years.
Major causes of death per 100,000 population (1988): diseases of the circulatory system 70.5; accidents and violence 49.3; infectious and parasitic diseases 41.8; ill-defined conditions 309.4.

National economy

Budget (1990–91). Revenue: $\mathcal{C}$5,284,000,000 (indirect taxes 49.0%, of which domestic taxes on goods and services 33.6%, import duties 11.0%, export duties 4.5%; development income 25.4%; direct taxes 22.1%, of which income taxes 17.2%). Expenditures: $\mathcal{C}$5,322,000,000 (current expenditure 77.5%; development expenditure 18.8%; debt amortization 3.7%).
Public debt (external, outstanding; 1990): U.S.$1,758,000,000.
Production (value added in $\mathcal{C}$'000,000 except as noted). Agriculture, forestry, fishing (1990): coffee 1,652, corn (maize) 528, aviculture 282, beans 225, sugarcane 209, fish catch 205, maicillo (variety of millet) 133, forest products 77, tobacco 54, rice 50, bananas 36,000 metric tons; livestock (number of live animals) 1,193,000 cattle, 450,000 pigs, 5,000,000 chickens. Mining and quarrying (1990): very limited amounts of gold, silver, and limestone. Manufacturing (1990): food products 2,890; beverages 1,134; petroleum products 482; textiles 437; chemical products 412; nonmetallic mineral products 395; clothing and footwear 316; tobacco products 307. Construction (1990): private residential 515; private nonresidential 169; total public 388. Energy production (consumption): electricity (kW-hr; 1990–91) 2,234,000,000 (2,007,000,000); coal, none (none); crude petroleum (barrels; 1990) none (4,918,000); petroleum products (metric tons; 1990) 620,000 (711,000); natural gas, none (none).
Household income and expenditure. Average household size (1978) 5.1; income per household: n.a.; sources of income: n.a.; expenditure (1978): food and beverages 39.7%, household furnishings 12.7%, transportation 10.9%, clothing and footwear 9.5%.
Tourism (1990): receipts U.S.$70,000,000; expenditures U.S.$104,000,000.
Population economically active (1990)[4]: total 982,802; activity rate of total population 42.0% (participation rates: ages 15–64, 66.6%; female 44.7%; unemployed 10.0%[5]).

Price and earnings indexes (1985 = 100)

	1986	1987	1988	1989	1990	1991	1992
Consumer price index	131.9	164.7	197.3	232.1	287.8	329.2	346.9[6]
Annual earnings index[7]	114.4	114.4	129.7	129.7	...	...	...

Gross national product (at current market prices; 1990): U.S.$5,767,000,000 (U.S.$1,100 per capita).

Structure of gross domestic product and labour force

	1990 in value $\mathcal{C}$'000,000	% of total value	labour force[4]	% of labour force[4]
Agriculture	4,599	11.2	80,212	8.1
Mining	65	0.2	734	0.1
Manufacturing	7,647	18.6	213,145	21.7
Construction	1,072	2.6	63,540	6.5
Public utilities	793	2.0	5,838	0.6
Transportation and communications	1,897	4.6	50,631	5.2
Trade	14,290	34.8	253,637	25.8
Finance, real estate	3,290	8.0	24,890	2.5
Public admin., defense	3,129	7.6 }		264,991	27.0
Services	4,275	10.4 }		
Other	—	—	25,184	2.5
TOTAL	41,057	100.0	982,802	100.0

Land use (1990): forested 5.0%; meadows and pastures 29.4%; agricultural and under permanent cultivation 35.4%; other 30.2%.

Foreign trade[8]

Balance of trade (current prices)

	1986	1987	1988	1989	1990	1991
$\mathcal{C}$'000,000	−899.5	−2,015.6	−1,991.1	−3,717.4	−5,184.0	−6,607.9
% of total	10.6%	25.4%	24.6%	40.0%	37.0%	41.0%

Imports (1990): $\mathcal{C}$9,594,800,000 (mineral fuels 20.0%, of which crude petroleum 9.7%; chemical products 14.5%; transport equipment 7.4%; nonelectrical machinery and equipment 6.9%; paper and paper products 4.6%). Major import sources: United States 42.6%; Guatemala 11.5%; Mexico 7.7%; Venezuela 6.3%; Japan 3.5%.
Exports (1990): $\mathcal{C}$4,410,800,000 (coffee 45.3%; pharmaceuticals 3.6%; raw sugar 3.5%; cotton yarn 3.1%; cardboard boxes 2.7%). Major export destinations: United States 33.2%; Guatemala 17.3%; Germany 15.7%; Costa Rica 8.2%; The Netherlands 8.0%.

Transport and communications

Transport. Railroads (1990): route length 374 mi, 602 km; passenger-mi 3,718,000, passenger-km 5,983,000; short ton-mi cargo 25,713,000, metric ton-km cargo 37,540,000. Roads (1989): total length 7,764 mi, 12,495 km (paved 14%). Vehicles (1990): passenger cars 80,000; trucks and buses 80,000. Merchant marine (1991): vessels (100 gross tons and over) 12; total deadweight tonnage 3,220[9]. Air transport (1990)[10]: passenger-mi 662,000,-000, passenger-km 1,066,000,000; short ton-mi cargo 3,182,000, metric ton-km cargo 4,645,000; airports (1992) with scheduled flights 1.
Communications. Daily newspapers (1991): total number 6; total circulation 255,100; circulation per 1,000 population 47. Radio (1991): total number of receivers 1,935,000 (1 per 2.8 persons). Television (1991): total number of receivers 500,000 (1 per 11 persons). Telephones (1989): 124,000 (1 per 42 persons).

Education and health

Education (1989)

	schools	teachers	students	student/ teacher ratio
Primary (age 7–15)	4,160	23,318	1,016,181	40.1
Secondary (age 16–18) }	468	...	28,370	28.2[11]
Vocational			66,708	
Higher[12, 13]	6	2,637	51,277	19.4

Educational attainment (1980). Percentage of population over age 10 having: no formal schooling 30.2%; primary education 60.7%; secondary 6.9%; higher 2.3%. Literacy (1990): total population age 15 and over literate, c. 2,127,000 (73.0%); males literate, c. 1,048,000 (76.2%); females literate, c. 1,079,000 (70.0%).
Health: physicians (1991) 4,080 (1 per 1,322 persons); hospital beds (1989) 5,343 (1 per 973 persons); infant mortality rate per 1,000 live births (1991) 47.0.
Food (1984–86): daily per capita caloric intake 2,152 (1979–81; vegetable products 88%, animal products 12%); 94% of FAO recommended minimum requirement.

Military

Total active duty personnel (1992): 49,700 (army 80.5%, navy 2.6%, air force 4.8%, paramilitary 12.1%). Military expenditure as percentage of GNP (1989): 4.0% (world 4.9%); per capita expenditure U.S.$48.

[1]Roman Catholicism, although not official, enjoys special recognition in the constitution. [2]1987 population estimate includes 526,334 registered emigrants leaving El Salvador between July 1971 and June 1987; 1992 population estimate excludes registered emigrants. [3]Municipio population, including registered emigrants leaving since 1971. [4]Urban areas only, excluding 72,735 unemployed persons previously employed. [5]Underemployed rate equals 29.0%. [6]April. [7]Minimum wages in manufacturing and services in San Salvador department. [8]Import c.i.f., exports f.o.b. [9]1989. [10]TACA International Airlines. [11]1988. [12]1990. [13]Universities only.

Equatorial Guinea

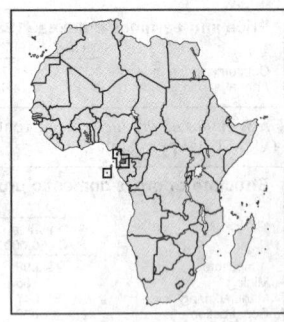

Official name: República de Guinea
Ecuatorial (Republic of Equatorial
Guinea).
Form of government[1]: transitional
government with one legislative house
(House of Representatives of the
People [41[2]]).
Chief of state: President.
Head of government: Prime Minister.
Capital: Malabo.
Official language: Spanish.
Official religion: none.
Monetary unit[3]: 1 CFA franc
(CFAF) = 100 centimes; valuation
(Oct. 5, 1992) 1 U.S.$ = CFAF 238.75;
1 £ = CFAF 405.88.

Area and population

Regions	area		population
	sq mi	sq km	1987 estimate
Provinces			
Insular	785[4]	2,034	70,280
Annobón	7	17	2,360
Bioko Norte	300	776	56,600
Bioko Sur	479	1,241	11,320
Continental	10,045[4]	26,017	259,950
Centro-Sur	3,834	9,931	55,970
Kie-Ntem	1,522	3,943	74,050
Litoral	2,573	6,665	75,640
Wele-Nzas	2,115	5,478	54,290
TOTAL	10,831[4]	28,051	330,230

Demography

Population (1992): 367,000.
Density (1992): persons per sq mi 33.9, persons per sq km 13.1.
Urban-rural (1987): urban 31.0%; rural 69.0%.
Sex distribution (1983): male 48.25%; female 51.75%.
Age breakdown (1983): under 15, 41.7%; 15–29, 25.1%; 30–44, 15.7%; 45–59, 11.2%; 60–74, 5.3%; 75 and over, 1.0%.
Population projection: (2000) 448,000; (2010) 573,000.
Doubling time: 26 years.
Ethnic composition (1983): Fang 82.9%; Bubi 9.6%; Ndowe 3.8%; Annobonés 1.5%; Bujeba 1.4%; other 0.8%.
Religious affiliation (1980): Christian (mostly Roman Catholic) 88.8%; traditional beliefs 4.6%; atheist 1.4%; Muslim 0.5%; other 0.2%; none 4.5%.
Major cities (1983): Malabo 30,418; Bata 24,308; Ela-Nguema 6,179; Campo Yaunde 5,199; Los Angeles 4,079.

Vital statistics

Birth rate per 1,000 population (1990): 43.0 (world avg. 27.1); legitimate, n.a.; illegitimate, n.a.
Death rate per 1,000 population (1990): 16.0 (world avg. 9.8).
Natural increase rate per 1,000 population (1990): 27.0 (world avg. 17.3).
Total fertility rate (avg. births per childbearing woman; 1990): 5.5.
Marriage rate per 1,000 population: n.a.
Divorce rate per 1,000 population: n.a.
Life expectancy at birth (1990): male 48.0 years; female 52.0 years.
Major causes of death per 100,000 population: n.a.; however, major diseases include malaria (affecting about 60% of the population), cholera, leprosy, trypanosomiasis (sleeping sickness), and waterborne (especially gastrointestinal) diseases.

National economy

Budget (1990). Revenue: CFAF 7,520,000,000 (fiscal receipts 68.4%; other receipts 31.6%). Expenditures: CFAF 8,105,000,000 (current expenditure 85.9%, of which interest 28.6%, salaries 26.1%; capital expenditure 14.1%).
Public debt (external, outstanding; 1990): U.S.$220,000,000.
Gross national product (at current market prices; 1990): U.S.$136,000,000 (U.S.$330 per capita).

Structure of gross domestic product and labour force

	1989		1983	
	in value CFAF '000,000	% of total value	labour force	% of labour force
Agriculture, forestry	22,991	53.6	59,390	57.9
Manufacturing, mining	545	1.3	1,616	1.6
Construction	2,402	5.6	1,929	1.9
Public utilities	1,277	3.0	224	0.2
Transportation and communications	823	1.9	1,752	1.7
Trade	3,594	8.4	3,059	3.0
Finance	...	...	409	0.4
Pub. admin., defense	7,367	17.2	8,377	8.2
Services	3,924	9.1	25,809	25.2
Other				
TOTAL	42,923	100.0[4]	102,565	100.0[4]

Production (metric tons except as noted). Agriculture, forestry, fishing (1991): roots and tubers 81,000 (of which cassava 46,000, sweet potatoes 35,000), bananas 17,000, coconuts 8,000, cacao beans 7,000, coffee 7,000, palm oil 5,000, palm kernels 3,000; livestock (number of live animals) 36,000 sheep, 8,000 goats, 5,000 pigs, 5,000 cattle; roundwood (1990) 607,000 cu m; fish catch (1990) 4,000. Mining and quarrying: details n.a.; however, in addition

to quarrying for construction materials, unexploited deposits of iron ore, lead, zinc, manganese, and molybdenum are present; traces of gold, diamonds, and radioactive ores have also been located. Manufacturing (1990): veneer sheets 10,000. Construction: n.a. Energy production (consumption): electricity (kW-hr; 1990) 18,000,000 (18,000,000); coal, none (n.a.); crude petroleum[5], none (n.a.); petroleum products (metric tons; 1990) none (37,-000); natural gas, none (n.a.).
Population economically active (1983): total 102,565; activity rate of total population 39.2% (participation rates: ages 15–64, 66.7%; female 35.7%; unemployed 24.2%).

Price and earnings indexes (1985 = 100)

	1985	1986	1987	1988	1989	1990
Consumer price index	100.0	82.0	72.0	73.0	78.0	78.0
Earnings index	...	...	...	...	...	...

Household income and expenditure. Average household size (1980) 4.5; income per household: n.a.; sources of income: n.a.; expenditure: n.a.
Tourism: tourism is a government priority but remains undeveloped.
Land use (1990): forested 46.2%; meadows and pastures 3.7%; agricultural and under permanent cultivation 8.2%; built-on, wasteland, and other 41.9%.

Foreign trade

Balance of trade (current prices)

	1985	1986	1987	1988	1989
CFAF '000,000	–3,819	–6,822	–3,426	–2,949	–4,083
% of total	15.5%	22.2%	12.8%	9.5%	12.1%

Imports (1989): U.S.$58,200,000 (1984; machinery and transport equipment 25.4%, of which motor vehicles and parts 16.7%; fuels and lubricants 20.1%; food and live animals 19.4%, of which fish 5.1%; manufactured goods 11.0%, of which electrical machinery and apparatus 6.2%; beverages and tobacco products 4.9%). *Major import sources* (1985): Spain 30.2%; France 23.6%; Italy 14.6%; The Netherlands 4.8%; West Germany 4.1%; Belgium-Luxembourg 3.0%; China 2.4%; United States 1.9%; Japan 1.7%; Norway 1.5%; United Kingdom 1.1%; Switzerland 0.9%.
Exports (1989): U.S.$36,900,000 (food and live animals 57.0%, of which cocoa 42.4%; fuels and lubricants 19.5%; wood 19.4%; manufactured goods 2.8%). *Major export destinations* (1985): The Netherlands 37.6%; Spain 31.5%; West Germany 16.4%; Italy 5.0%; France 2.2%; Switzerland 1.4%; Portugal 1.3%; Belgium-Luxembourg 0.7%; Greece 0.3%.

Transport and communications

Transport. Railroads: none. Roads (1989): total length 1,667 mi, 2,682 km (paved 19%). Vehicles (1990): passenger cars 5,500; trucks and buses 3,500. Merchant marine (1991): vessels (100 gross tons and over) 2; total deadweight tonnage 6,699. Air transport (1985): passenger-mi 4,000,000, passenger-km 7,000,000; short ton-mi cargo 700,000, metric ton-km cargo 1,000,000; airports (1992) with scheduled flights 1.
Communications. Daily newspapers (1988): total number 2; total circulation 1,000[6]; circulation per 1,000 population 3.0[6]. Radio (1991): total number of receivers 100,000 (1 per 3.6 persons). Television (1991): total number of receivers 2,500 (1 per 143 persons). Telephones (1987): 2,000 (1 per 163 persons).

Education and health

Education (1987–88)

	schools	teachers	students	student/ teacher ratio
Primary (age 6–11)	703	1,065	61,009	57.3
Secondary (age 12–17)	9	319	9,226	28.9
Voc., teacher tr.[7]	...	...	...	...
Higher	5	133	1,542	11.6

Educational attainment (1983). Percentage of population age 15 and over having: no schooling 35.4%; some primary education 46.6%; primary 13.0%; secondary 2.3%; postsecondary 1.1%; not specified 1.6%. *Literacy* (1983): percentage of total population age 15 and over literate 62.2%; males literate 77.8%; females literate 48.6%.
Health: physicians (1987) 90 (1 per 3,622 persons); hospital beds (1982) 3,200 (1 per 89 persons); infant mortality rate per 1,000 live births (1985–90) 127.
Food (latest): daily per capita caloric intake 2,230; 68% of FAO recommended minimum requirement.

Military

Total active duty personnel (1992): 1,300 (army 84.6%, navy 7.7%, air force 7.7%). *Military expenditure as percentage of GNP* (1981): 1.8% (world 5.8%); per capita expenditure U.S.$9.

[1]A new constitution establishing a multiparty system was approved in a national referendum on Nov. 17, 1991. [2]Forty-one unopposed candidates elected July 10, 1988. Number of seats in legislative house per constitution is to range between a minimum of 45 and a maximum of 60. [3]As of Jan. 1, 1985, Equatorial Guinea became a member of the franc zone, substituting the CFA franc for the previous monetary unit, the ekwele (EK, plural bipkwele), effectively devaluing the latter by 82%. [4]Detail does not add to total given because of rounding. [5]Equatorial Guinea's offshore prospective oil-lease areas totaled about 13,450 sq km. [6]Circulation for one daily newspaper only. [7]Efforts are being undertaken to provide the training necessary to qualify nondegree teachers for service. Also, teacher-training schools are to be expanded in order to increase the number of primary-school teachers.

Estonia

Official name: Eesti Vabariik (Republic of Estonia).
Form of government: unitary multiparty republic with a single legislative body (Parliament [101]).
Chief of state: President.
Head of government: Prime Minister.
Capital: Tallinn.
Official language: Estonian.
Official religion: none.
Monetary unit (until June 18–20, 1992):
1 ruble = 100 kopecks; valuation (Oct. 5, 1992) 1 U.S.$ = 316.82 rubles;
1 £ = 538.59 rubles. After June 20:
1 kroon (EEK) = 100 senti;
valuation (Oct. 5, 1992; official)
1 U.S.$ = EEK 11.26;
1 £ = EEK 19.14.

Area and population

| Cities of republic jurisdiction | Capitals | area | | population |
		sq mi	sq km	1991 estimate
Kohtla-Järve	—	25	64	90,300
Narva	—	39	101	87,900
Pärnu	—	14	35	58,600
Sillamäe	—	4	10	20,900
Tallinn	—	71	183	502,400
Tartu	—	15	39	115,300
Counties				
Harju	Keila	1,601	4,147	108,100
Hiiumaa	Kärdla	395	1,023	11,500
Ida-Viru	...	1,233	3,194	23,900
Järva (Paide)	Paide	1,013	2,624	43,600
Jõgeva	Jõgeva	1,005	2,604	42,900
Lääne (Haapsalu)	Haapsalu	933	2,417	34,300
Lääne-Viru (Rakvere)	Rakvere	1,332	3,451	79,700
Pärnu	Pärnu	1,842	4,771	42,700
Põlva	Põlva	836	2,164	36,100
Rapla	Rapla	1,135	2,939	39,800
Saare (Kingissepa)	Kuressaare	1,126	2,917	40,700
Tartu	Tartu	1,186	3,071	49,300
Valga	Valga	789	2,044	42,500
Viljandi	Viljandi	1,381	3,578	65,700
Võru	Võru	890	2,305	45,600
TOTAL		**17,458[1,2]**	**45,215[2]**	**1,581,800**

Demography

Population (1992): 1,592,000.
Density (1992): persons per sq mi 91.3, persons per sq km 35.2.
Urban-rural (1991): urban 71.6%; rural 28.4%.
Sex distribution (1990): male 46.82%; female 53.18%.
Age breakdown (1989): under 15, 22.2%; 15–29, 21.4%; 30–44, 21.0%; 45–59, 18.5%; 60–74, 11.7%; 75 and over, 5.1%.
Population projection: (2000) 1,629,000; (2010) 1,699,000.
Doubling time: not applicable; population is stable.
Ethnic composition (1989): Estonian 61.5%; Russian 30.3%; Ukrainian 3.1%; Belorussian 1.8%; Finnish 1.1%; other 2.2%.
Religious affiliation: believers are predominantly Evangelical Lutheran, with Orthodox and Baptist minorities.
Major cities (1991): Tallinn 499,800; Tartu 115,400; Narva 82,300; Kohtla-Järve 76,800; Pärnu 54,200.

Vital statistics

Birth rate per 1,000 population (1990): 14.1 (world avg. 27.1); (1989) legitimate 25.2%; illegitimate 74.8%.
Death rate per 1,000 population (1990): 12.3 (world avg. 9.8).
Natural increase rate per 1,000 population (1990): 1.8 (world avg. 17.3).
Total fertility rate (avg. births per childbearing woman; 1990): 1.8.
Marriage rate per 1,000 population (1989): 8.0.
Divorce rate per 1,000 population (1989): 3.8.
Life expectancy at birth (1990): male 64.9 years; female 74.9 years.
Major causes of death per 100,000 population (1988): diseases of the circulatory system, males 897.5 (females 596.2); malignant neoplasms (cancers) 291.9 (141.7); accidents, poisoning, and violence 160.7 (51.8); diseases of the respiratory system 45.8 (15.8).

National economy

Budget (1989). Revenue: 2,236,600,000 rubles (turnover tax 35.5%; state participation in business enterprises 17.9%; personal income tax 12.9%). Expenditures: 2,141,300,000 rubles (economy 55.8%; social and cultural affairs 37.5%, of which education 17.5%, social welfare and pensions 12.2%, health 7.6%).
Public debt (external, outstanding; 1991): $650,000,000.
Tourism (1990): tourist arrivals, 200,000.
Production (metric tons except as noted). Agriculture, forestry, fishing (1989): grains 967,400, potatoes 864,200, vegetables 142,800, fruits and berries 74,-900; livestock (number of live animals) 1,080,400 pigs, 806,100 cattle, 140,200 sheep and goats, 6,922,500 poultry; roundwood 1,319,000 cubic m; fish catch, n.a. Mining and quarrying: minerals exploited include oil shale, limestone, and dolomite. Manufacturing (1989): sulfuric acid 552,400; mineral fertilizers 214,000; paper 137,000; cellulose 92,000; excavating machinery 1,645 units; beer 892,700 hectolitres; vodka 149,000 hectolitres; other manufactures include wire and cable, wood veneers, petrochemicals, building materials,

textiles, and clothing. Construction (1989): new residential 589,000 sq m. Energy production (consumption): electricity (kW-hr; 1989) 17,600,000,000 (n.a.); oil shale (metric tons; 1989) 23,300,000 (25,899,000); coal (metric tons; 1989) none (315,000); crude petroleum, none (n.a.); natural gas (cu m; 1989) none (1,301,000).
Gross domestic product (1991): 16,750,000,000 rubles (10,555 rubles per capita)[3].

Structure of gross domestic product and labour force

| | 1989 | | | |
	in value '000,000 rubles	% of total value	labour force	% of labour force
Agriculture	1,132.4	25.3	100,000	12.3
Manufacturing, mining	1,957.2	43.7	270,000	33.2
Construction	488.2	10.9	73,000	9.0
Trade	621.3	13.9	75,000	9.2
Transp. and commun.	278.4	6.2	73,000	9.0
Pub. admin., defense, finance	—	—	23,000	2.8
Services	—	—	182,000	22.4
Other	—	—	15,000	1.8
TOTAL	4,477.5	100.0	814,000	100.0[1]

Population economically active (1989): total 850,500; activity rate of total population 54.3% (participation rates: ages 15–59/55[4], 63.4%; female, n.a.; unemployed, n.a.).

Price and earnings indexes (1985 = 100)

	1985	1986	1987	1988	1989	1990	1991
Consumer price index	100.0	107.2	110.8	115.3	120.7	141.4	297.0
Monthly earnings index	100.0	102.7	106.5	115.9	125.6	...	...

Household income and expenditure. Average household size (1989) 3.1; average annual income per household: n.a.; sources of income: n.a.; expenditure: n.a.
Land use (1989): forested 42.6%; meadows and pastures, n.a.; agricultural and under permanent cultivation 32.5%, of which arable 21.6%; other 24.9%.

Foreign trade

Balance of trade (current prices)

	1988	1989
'000,000 rubles	−700	−700
% of total	10.4%	10.1%

Imports (1989): 3,820,000,000 rubles (principal commodities include machine tools and other capital goods, transportation equipment including tram cars). *Major import sources:* Commonwealth of Independent States- (CIS-) member countries and Georgia (former U.S.S.R.) 84.6%; non-CIS countries 15.4% (including Germany, Hungary, Czechoslovakia, France, and Japan).
Exports (1989): 3,120,000,000 rubles (textiles, cement, processed foods [especially dairy, confectionery, and fish], paper, footwear, electronic goods, and mining equipment). *Major export destinations:* CIS countries and Georgia 92.9%; non-CIS countries 7.1% (including some 80 countries in 1990).

Transport and communications

Transport. Railroads: (1990) length 638 mi, 1,026 km; (1989) passenger-mi 971,000,000, passenger-km 1,562,000,000; short ton-mi cargo 5,212,000,000, metric ton-km cargo 7,609,000,000. Roads (1989): total length 28,000 mi, 45,000 km (paved 98%). Vehicles (1988): passenger cars 198,300; trucks and buses, n.a. Merchant marine (1991): vessels (1,000 gross tons and over) 65; total deadweight tonnage 516,866. Air transport: (1990) passenger-mi 773,-000,000, passenger-km 1,244,300,000; (1989) short ton-mi cargo 6,200,000, metric ton-km cargo 9,000,000; airports (1992) with scheduled flights 1.
Communications. Daily newspapers: total number, n.a.; total circulation, n.a.; circulation per 1,000 population, n.a. Radio (1989): total number of receivers 926,000 (1 per 1.7 persons). Television (1989): total number of receivers 605,000 (1 per 2.6 persons). Telephones (1989): 354,000 (1 per 4.5 persons).

Education and health

Education (1989–90)

	schools	teachers	students	student/ teacher ratio
Primary Secondary }	606	17,952	227,560	12.7
Voc., teacher tr.	36	6,495	19,915	3.1
Higher	6	2,977	26,279	8.8

Educational attainment (1989). Percentage of persons age 15 and over having: primary or less 19.9%; incomplete secondary 21.0%; complete secondary 22.9%; vocational 17.2%; some higher 1.4%; higher 10.8%. *Literacy:* n.a.; however, primary and secondary education are compulsory.
Health (1990): physicians 7,200 (1 per 219 persons); hospital beds 19,000 (1 per 82.6 persons); infant mortality rate per 1,000 live births (1989) 14.7.
Food: daily per capita caloric intake, n.a.

Military

Total active duty personnel (1992): 2,000. *Military expenditure as a percentage of GNP:* n.a. Until 1991, the U.S.S.R. was responsible for Estonia's external security; about 9,000 Soviet military personnel remained in Estonia at year-end 1992.

---

[1]Detail does not add to total given because of rounding. [2]Total includes 592 sq mi (1,534 sq km) not distributed by administrative subdivision, largely the Estonian portion of Lake Peipus. [3]No equivalent U.S.$ value is offered, as Soviet GNP data are very speculative. [4]Males retire at age 59, females at 55.

Ethiopia

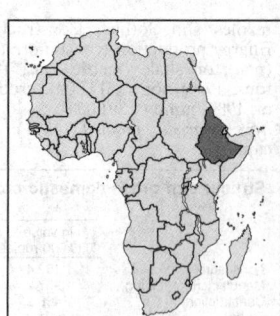

Official name: YeĒtiyop'iya (Ethiopia [Transitional Government of]).
Form of government[1]: transitional regime with one legislative house (Council of Representatives [87]).
Chief of state and government: President (EPRDF [Ethiopian People's Revolutionary Democratic Front] Chairman) assisted by Prime Minister.
Capital: Addis Ababa.
Official Language: Amharic.
Official religion: none.
Monetary unit: 1 Ethiopia birr (Br) = 100 cents; valuation (Oct. 5, 1992) 1 U.S.$ = Br 5.00; 1 £ = Br 8.50.

Area and population

Regions	Capitals	area sq mi	area sq km	population 1992 estimate
Addis Ababa	...	2,003	5,188	2,556,627
Arsi	Asela	9,155	23,710	2,093,932
Asosa	...	8,906	23,067	554,439
Bale	Goba	25,996	67,330	1,031,924
Borena	...	36,301	94,018	702,567
Eastern Gojam	...	5,381	13,936	1,649,609
Eastern Harerge	...	34,981	90,600	2,693,116
Eastern Shewa	...	4,924	12,754	993,015
Gambela	...	10,064	26,065	189,322
Ilubabor	Mefa	12,905	35,059	3,025,995
Kefa	Jima	15,476	40,083	1,115,429
Metekel	...	11,768	30,481	404,254
Northern Gonder	...	23,946	62,020	1,977,742
Northern Omo	...	11,553	29,923	2,958,706
Northern Shewa	...	10,436	27,030	2,494,940
Northern Welo	...	11,906	30,835	1,574,021
Sidamo	Awasa	8,009	20,742	2,892,758
Southern Gonder	...	6,594	17,079	1,813,623
Southern Omo	...	8,494	22,000	261,429
Southern Shewa	...	6,486	16,799	3,141,382
Southern Welo	...	7,993	20,702	2,597,609
Welega	Nekemte	16,460	42,632	2,595,640
Western Gojam	...	6,675	17,289	2,145,529
Western Harerge	...	12,814	33,188	1,439,358
Western Shewa	...	8,964	23,218	2,849,357
Autonomous regions				
Aseb	...	26,945	69,786	477,819
Dire Dawa	...	11,291	29,244	505,031
Eritrea	Asmera	36,170	93,679	3,317,611
Ogaden	...	69,239	179,327	880,915
Tigray	Mekele	20,656	53,498	2,910,967
TOTAL		483,122[2]	1,251,282	53,844,666

Demography

Population (1992): 53,845,000.
Density (1992): persons per sq mi 111.5, persons per sq km 43.0.
Urban-rural (1992): urban 11.2%; rural 88.8%.
Sex distribution (1992): male 49.93%; female 50.07%.
Age breakdown (1992): under 15, 46.5%; 15–29, 22.8%; 30–44, 15.6%; 45–59, 8.9%; 60–74, 4.5%; 75 and over, 1.7%.
Population projection: (2000) 67,525,000; (2010) 90,572,000.
Ethnolinguistic composition (1983): Amhara 37.7%; Galla (Oromo) 35.3%; Tigrinya 8.6%; Gurage 3.3%; Ometo (Omotic) 2.7%; Sidamo 2.4%.
Religious affiliation (1980): Ethiopian Orthodox 52.5%; Muslim 31.4%; traditional beliefs 11.4%; other Christian 4.5%; other 0.2%.
Major cities (1988): Addis Ababa 1,673,060; Asmera 331,029; Dire Dawa 117,734; Gonder 95,000; Nazret 90,975.

Vital statistics

Birth rate per 1,000 population (1990–95): 48.4 (world avg. 26.4).
Death rate per 1,000 population (1990–95): 18.3 (world avg. 9.2).
Natural increase rate per 1,000 population (1990–95): 30.1 (world avg. 17.2).
Total fertility rate (avg. births per childbearing woman; 1990–95): 6.8.
Life expectancy at birth (1990–95): male 45.4 years; female 48.7 years.
Major causes of death (1987–88)[3]: infectious and parasitic diseases 33.1%; respiratory diseases 15.7%; digestive system diseases 10.7%.

National economy

Budget (1989–90). Revenue: Br 3,093,000,000 (taxes 73.0%, of which income and profit tax 31.5%, excise tax 15.2%, import duties 13.8%, export duties 1.8%; nontax revenue 27.0%). Expenditures: Br 4,976,000,000 (general services 48.5%; economic development 21.3%, of which agriculture 5.3%; social services 12.7%, of which education 7.9%, public health 2.6%).
Tourism (1990): receipts U.S.$25,000,000; expenditures U.S.$10,000,000.
Production (metric tons except as noted). Agriculture, forestry, fishing (1991): wheat 4,483,000, corn (maize) 1,590,000, sugarcane 1,530,000, barley 965,000, sorghum 805,000, pulses 763,000, potatoes 384,000, yams 261,000, millet 260,000, coffee 168,000, seed cotton 63,000; livestock (number of live animals) 30,000,000 cattle, 23,000,000 sheep, 18,000,000 goats, 8,410,000 horses, mules, and asses, 1,060,000 camels; roundwood (1990) 42,549,000 cu m; fish catch (1989) 4,263. Mining and quarrying (1989): cement 400,000; limestone 150,000; salt 110,000; gold 24,000 troy oz; platinum 48 troy oz. Manufacturing (gross value in Br '000[4]; 1989–90): food and beverages 750,000; textiles 403,000; leather and shoes 233,000; cigarettes 100,000; chemicals 97,000. Construction (authorized; 1987–88[5]): residential 260,251 sq m; nonresiden-

tial 63,346 sq m, of which commercial 16,994 sq m. Energy production (consumption): electricity (kW-hr; 1990) 906,000,000 (906,000,000); coal, none (n.a.); crude petroleum (barrels; 1990) n.a. (5,263,000); petroleum products (metric tons; 1990) 640,000 (807,000); natural gas, n.a. (n.a.).
Land use (1990): forested 24.6%; meadows and pastures 40.8%; agricultural and under permanent cultivation 12.7%; other 21.9%.
Gross national product (1990): U.S.$6,015,000,000 (U.S.$120 per capita).

Structure of gross domestic product and labour force

	1989–90 in value Br '000,000	1989–90 % of total value	1985 labour force	1985 % of labour force
Agriculture	4,699.6	41.1	14,982,000	78.1
Mining	21.7	0.2		
Manufacturing	1,265.4	11.1		
Construction	415.5	3.6	1,630,000	8.5
Public utilities	171.2	1.5		
Transp. and commun.	826.1	7.2		
Trade	1,098.3	9.6		
Finance	407.9	3.6		
Pub. admin., defense	1,436.7	12.5	2,570,000	13.4
Services	853.9	7.5		
Other	239.9	2.1		
TOTAL	11,436.2	100.0	19,182,000	100.0

Public debt (external, outstanding; 1991): U.S.$3,496,000,000.
Population economically active (1987): total 19,814,900; activity rate of total population 43.1% (participation rates: ages 15–64 [1985] 73.5%; female 35.2%; unemployed [1990] 44.2%).

Price and earnings indexes (1985 = 100)

	1985	1986	1987	1988	1989	1990	1991
Consumer price index	100.0	90.2	88.0	94.2	101.6	106.8	145.0
Earnings index	...	...	...	...	...	...	...

Household income and expenditure. Average household size (1984) 4.5; income per household (1981–82) Br 1,728 (U.S.$835); sources of income: (1981–82): self-employment 79.5%, wages and salaries 0.2%, other 20.3%; expenditure (1988): food 66.7%, fuel and power 15.9%, clothing and footwear 6.8%, health care 3.1%, education 2.5%, household goods 2.1%.

Foreign trade

Balance of trade (current prices)

	1985	1986	1987	1988	1989	1990
Br '000,000	−1,367.0	−981.2	−1,124.7	−1,081.2	−747.6	−1,271.6
% of total	49.8%	34.3%	43.3%	60.8%	29.1%	50.8%

Imports (1989–90): Br 1,831,000,000 (machinery [including aircraft] 16.7%, petroleum and petroleum products 12.3%, metal and metal wares 11.5%, road transport equipment 10.4%, food and beverages 7.2%). *Major import sources* (1989): Italy 14.0%; U.S.S.R. 13.6%; W.Ger. 10.8%; U.K. 8.9%.
Exports (1989–90): Br 736,817,000 (coffee 55.0%, hides 18.1%, pulses 4.8%, petroleum products 3.6%). *Major export destinations* (1989): W.Ger. 23.2%; U.S. 14.4%; U.S.S.R. 9.3%; Italy 6.6%; Saudi Arabia 6.6%.

Transport and communications

Transport. Railroads (1989)[6]: length 782 km; passenger-km 297,000,000; metric ton-km cargo 128,000,000. Roads (1991): total length 27,972 km (paved 15%). Vehicles (1991): passenger cars 37,799; trucks and buses 15,539. Merchant marine (1991): vessels (100 gross tons and over) 27; total deadweight tonnage 84,326. Air transport (1989): passenger-km 1,607,940,000; metric ton-km cargo 167,940,000; airports (1992) 29.
Communications. Daily newspapers (1991): 3; circulation 47,000; circulation per 1,000 population 0.9. Radio (1991): 9,000,000 receivers (1 per 5.8 persons). Television (1991): 100,000 receivers (1 per 518 persons). Telephones (1989): 153,010 (1 per 320 persons).

Education and health

Education (1988)

	schools	teachers	students	student/ teacher ratio
Primary (age 7–12)	8,584[7]	65,993	2,855,846	43.3
Secondary (age 13–18)	1,209[7]	21,220	874,000	41.2
Voc., teacher tr.	...	763	8,243	10.8
Higher	11[8]	1,699	31,204	18.4

Educational attainment: n.a. *Literacy* (1980)[9]: total population age 15 and over literate 1,000,000 (4.8%); males (9.3%); females (0.5%).
Health (1986–87): physicians 1,241 (1 per 36,660 persons); hospital beds 11,745 (1 per 3,873 persons); infant mortality rate (1990–95) 122.0.
Food (1979–81): daily per capita caloric intake 2,149 (vegetable products 93%, animal products 7%); (1984) 72% of FAO recommended minimum.

Military

Total active duty personnel (1992): the armed forces were demobilized when the government was overthrown in May 1991. *Military expenditure as percentage of GNP* (1989): 12.8% (world 4.9%); per capita expenditure U.S.$15.

---

[1]The central government was overthrown in May 1991, and a transitional government was formed in July 1991. A referendum on Eritrean independence was to be held in 1993. [2]Detail does not add to total given because of rounding. [3]Percentage of illnesses in a sample population of hospital outpatients. [4]At constant prices of 1978–79. [5]Addis Ababa only. [6]Includes 62 mi (100 km) of the Chemin de Fer Djibouti-Ethiopien (CDE) in Djibouti; excludes 190 mi (306 km) of Northern Ethiopia Railway, not in use since 1978. [7]1985–86. [8]1983–84. [9]Adult illiteracy was 37% in 1987.

Fiji

Official name: Sovereign Democratic Republic of Fiji[1].
Form of government: republic with two legislative houses (Senate [34[2]]; House of Representatives [70]).
Chief of state: President.
Head of government: Prime Minister.
Capital: Suva.
Official language: English.
Official religion: none.
Monetary unit: 1 Fiji dollar (F$) = 100 cents; valuation (Oct. 5, 1992) 1 U.S.$ = F$1.51; 1 £ = F$2.57.

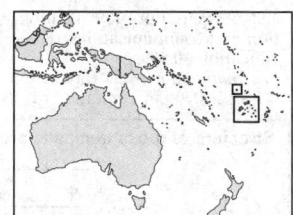

Area and population

Divisions Provinces[3]	Capitals	area sq mi	area sq km	population 1986 census
Central	Suva			
Naitasiri	—	643	1,666	100,227
Namosi	—	220	570	4,836
Rewa	—	105	272	97,442
Serua	—	320	830	13,356
Tailevu	—	369	955	44,249
Eastern	Levuka			
Kadavu	—	185	478	9,805
Lau	—	188	487	14,203
Lomaiviti	—	159	411	16,066
Rotuma	—	18	46	2,688
Northern	Labasa			
Bua	—	532	1,379	13,986
Cakaudrove	—	1,087	2,816	40,433
Macuata	—	774	2,004	74,735
Western	Lautoka			
Ba	—	1,017	2,634	197,633
Nadroga-Navosa	—	921	2,385	54,431
Ra	—	518	1,341	31,285
TOTAL		7,056	18,274	715,375

Demography

Population (1992): 748,000.
Density (1992): persons per sq mi 106.0, persons per sq km 40.9.
Urban-rural (1986): urban 38.7%; rural 61.3%.
Sex distribution (1989): male 50.65%; female 49.35%.
Age breakdown (1989): under 15, 37.9%; 15–29, 28.6%; 30–44, 18.3%; 45–59, 9.9%; 60–74, 4.0%; 75 and over, 1.3%.
Population projection: (2000) 826,000; (2010) 917,000.
Doubling time: 32 years.
Ethnic composition (1991): Fijian 48.9%; Indian 46.2%[4]; other 4.9%.
Religious affiliation (1986): Christian 52.9%; Hindu 38.1%; Muslim 7.8%; Sikh 0.7%; other 0.5%.
Major cities (1986): Suva 69,665; Lautoka 28,728; Lami 8,601; Nadi 7,679; Ba 6,518.

Vital statistics

Birth rate per 1,000 population (1990): 24.8 (world avg. 27.1); (1978) legitimate 82.7%; illegitimate 17.3%.
Death rate per 1,000 population (1990): 4.9 (world avg. 9.8).
Natural increase rate per 1,000 population (1990): 19.9 (world avg. 17.3).
Total fertility rate (avg. births per childbearing woman; 1988): 3.1.
Marriage rate per 1,000 population (1986): 8.8.
Divorce rate per 1,000 population (1979): 0.7.
Life expectancy at birth (1986): male 61.0 years; female 65.2 years.
Major causes of death per 100,000 population (1986): diseases of the circulatory system 181.5; malignant neoplasms (cancers) 51.7; accidents, poisonings, and violence 48.6; diseases of the respiratory system 43.7; birth trauma 34.5; diabetes mellitus 33.9; infectious and parasitic diseases 25.2.

National economy

Budget (1990). Revenue: F$538,203,000 (customs duties and port dues 41.5%; income taxes, estate taxes, and gift duties 40.5%; fees, royalties, and sales 7.6%). Expenditures: F$500,659,000 (departmental expenditure 70.8%; public-debt charges 24.4%; pensions and gratuities 4.8%).
Production (metric tons except as noted). Agriculture, forestry, fishing (1990): sugarcane 4,016,000, paddy rice 32,147, copra 19,005, ginger 5,500; livestock (number of live animals) 160,000 cattle, 75,000 goats, 12,000 pigs; roundwood 307,000 cu m; fish catch (1989) 32,784. Mining and quarrying (1990): gold 4,116 kilograms; silver 779 kilograms. Manufacturing (1990): refined sugar 408,000; cement 77,900; flour 24,733; stock feed 22,212; coconut oil 11,615; soap 6,614; beer 193,600 hectolitres; paint 21,880 hectolitres. Construction (1990): residential 22,000 sq m; nonresidential 24,000 sq m. Energy production (consumption): electricity (kW-hr; 1990) 435,000,000 (435,000,000); coal (metric tons; 1990) none (14,000); crude petroleum, none (n.a.); petroleum products (metric tons; 1990) none (219,000); natural gas, none (n.a.).
Population economically active (1986): total 241,160; activity rate of total population 33.7% (participation rates: ages 15–64, 56.0%; female 21.2%; unemployed [1990] 6.4%).

Price and earnings indexes (1985 = 100)

	1986	1987	1988	1989	1990	1991	1992[5]
Consumer price index	101.8	107.6	120.2	127.7	138.1	147.1	150.9
Daily earnings index	100.0	105.3	103.3	...	...	...	...

Gross national product (at current market prices; 1990): U.S.$1,316,000,000 (U.S.$1,770 per capita).

Structure of gross domestic product and labour force

	1989 in value F$'000	1989 % of total value	1986 labour force	1986 % of labour force
Agriculture	325,502	19.6	106,305	44.1
Mining	55,625	3.3	1,345	0.5
Manufacturing	174,564	10.5	18,106	7.5
Construction	66,342	4.0	11,786	4.9
Public utilities	55,036	3.3	2,154	0.9
Transportation and communications	169,224	10.2	13,151	5.4
Trade	379,141	22.8	26,010	10.8
Finance	216,158	13.0	6,016	2.5
Pub. admin., defense } Services	305,200	18.4	36,619	15.2
Other	−85,392[6]	−5.1[6]	19,668[7]	8.2[7]
TOTAL	1,661,400	100.0	241,160	100.0

Public debt (external, outstanding; 1990): U.S.$297,000,000.
Household income and expenditure. Average household size (1986) 5.7; income per household (1980) F$2,837 (U.S.$3,546); sources of income (1973): wages and salaries 81.5%, self-employment 9.1%, other 9.4%; expenditure (1988): food 31.3%, housing and energy 11.9%, transportation and communications 11.3%, clothing and footwear 10.2%, household durable goods 7.8%.
Tourism (1990): receipts from visitors U.S.$230,000,000; expenditures by nationals abroad U.S.$32,000,000.
Land use (1989): forested 64.9%; agricultural and under permanent cultivation 13.1%; meadows and pastures 3.3%; other 18.7%.

Foreign trade

Balance of trade (current prices)

	1986	1987	1988	1989	1990	1991
F$'000,000	−124.7	−131.4	−61.76	−253.87	−251.32	−279.57
% of total	16.6%	16.4%	5.6%	18.7%	14.1%	20.1%

Imports (1990): F$1,015,562,000 (machinery and transport equipment 31.1%; durable manufactures 22.4%; mineral fuels 14.2%; food, beverages, and tobacco 12.4%; miscellaneous manufactured consumer articles 9.5%; chemicals 7.4%). *Major import sources:* Australia 28.4%; New Zealand 16.7%; United States 13.3%; Japan 11.3%; Singapore 6.1%; Taiwan 4.1%; Hong Kong 3.0%.
Exports (1990)[8]: F$659,017,000 (sugar 37.0%; gold 10.4%; fish 6.9%; timber 6.6%; molasses 1.3%; coconut oil 0.7%). *Major export destinations*[9]: United Kingdom 29.2%; Australia 18.8%; New Zealand 17.0%; United States 10.3%; Japan 5.5%; Malaysia 4.7%; Singapore 3.4%.

Transport and communications

Transport. Railroads[10] (1990): length 370 mi, 595 km. Roads (1991): total length 2,996 mi, 4,821 km (paved 13%). Vehicles (1990): passenger cars 40,253; trucks and buses 27,589. Merchant marine (1991): vessels (100 gross tons and over) 62; total deadweight tonnage 49,590. Air transport (1990)[11]: passenger-mi 548,000,000, passenger-km 882,000,000; short ton-mi cargo 17,356,000, metric ton-km cargo 25,339,000; airports (1992) with scheduled flights 17.
Communications. Daily newspapers (1988): total number 2; total circulation 40,000; circulation per 1,000 population 56. Radio (1991): total number of receivers 450,000 (1 per 1.6 persons). Television (1990): total number of receivers 10,000 (1 per 73 persons). Telephones (1990): 72,584 (1 per 10 persons).

Education and health

Education (1990)

	schools	teachers	students	student/ teacher ratio
Primary (age 5–15)	672[12]	4,272	143,553	33.6
Secondary (age 16–19)	140[12]	2,684	52,536	19.6
Voc., teacher tr.	44[12]	369	3,290	8.9
Higher	5[13]	320[12]	2,211[12]	6.9[12]

Educational attainment (1986). Percentage of population age 25 and over having: no formal schooling 28.3%; primary only 19.1%; some secondary 44.1%; secondary 4.1%; postsecondary 3.3%; other 1.1%. *Literacy* (1986): total population age 15 and over literate 87.0%; males literate 90.0%; females literate 84.0%.
Health (1990): physicians 300 (1 per 2,438 persons); hospital beds 1,747 (1 per 413 persons); infant mortality rate per 1,000 live births (1988) 27.0.
Food (1987–89): daily per capita caloric intake 2,871 (vegetable products 82%, animal products 18%); 126% of FAO recommended minimum requirement.

Military

Total active duty personnel (1991): 5,000 (army 94.0%; navy 6.0%; air force, none). *Military expenditure as percentage of GNP* (1989): 2.2% (world 4.9%); per capita expenditure: U.S.$35.

[1]The official name recognized by the constitution of 1990; "Republic of Fiji" is also used in many official documents. [2]All seats are appointed. [3]The provinces are autonomous only with respect to local affairs. [4]The emigration of the Indian population after the coup in 1987 has resulted in the reemergence of a Fijian majority. [5]May. [6]Includes unclassified activities and imputed bank service charges. [7]Not stated and unemployed. [8]Excludes reexports, valued at F$105,227,000. [9]Based on exports of local products only. [10]Owned by the Fiji Sugar Corporation. [11]Air Pacific only. [12]1986. [13]1983.

Finland

Official name: Suomen Tasavalta
(Finnish); Republiken Finland
(Swedish) (Republic of Finland).
Form of government: multiparty
republic with one legislative house
(Parliament [200]).
Chief of state: President.
Head of government: Prime Minister.
Capital: Helsinki.
Official languages: Finnish; Swedish.
Official religion: none[1].
Monetary unit: 1 markka (Fmk) = 100
penniä; valuation (Oct. 5, 1992)
1 U.S.$ = Fmk 4.53; 1 £ = Fmk 7.70.

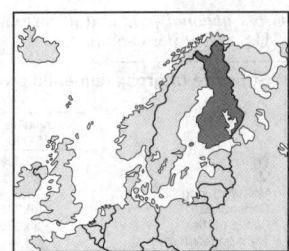

Area and population		land area		population
		sq mi	sq km	1992[2] estimate
Provinces	**Capitals**			
Häme	Hämeenlinna	6,309	16,341	685,757
Keski-Suomi	Jyväskylä	6,266	16,230	254,429
Kuopio	Kuopio	6,374	16,509	257,495
Kymi	Kouvola	4,163	10,783	335,174
Lappi	Rovaniemi	35,930	93,057	201,590
Mikkeli	Mikkeli	6,310	16,342	207,655
Oulu	Oulu	21,957	56,868	442,580
Pohjois-Karjala	Joensuu	6,866	17,782	177,150
Turku ja Pori	Turku	8,818	22,839	730,287
Uusimaa	Helsinki	3,822	9,898	1,262,752
Vaasa	Vaasa	10,199	26,416	446,704
Autonomous Province				
Åland (Ahvenanmaa)	Mariehamn (Maarianhamina)	590	1,527	24,847
TOTAL LAND AREA		117,604	304,592	
INLAND WATER		12,955	33,553	
TOTAL		130,559	338,145	5,026,420

Demography

Population (1992): 5,033,000.
Density (1992)[3]: persons per sq mi 42.8, persons per sq km 16.5.
Urban-rural (1992): urban 61.7%; rural 38.3%.
Sex distribution (1991): male 48.54%; female 51.46%.
Age breakdown (1991): under 15, 19.3%; 15–29, 20.5%; 30–44, 24.6%; 45–59,
17.1%; 60–74, 12.9%; 75 and over, 5.6%.
Population projection: (2000) 5,064,000; (2010) 5,036,000.
Doubling time: not applicable; population is stable.
Linguistic composition (1991): Finnish 93.5%; Swedish 5.9%; other 0.6%.
Religious affiliation (1990): Evangelical Lutheran 88.1%; Finnish (Greek) Or-
thodox 1.1%; nonaffiliated 9.9%; other 0.9%.
Major cities (1992[2]): Helsinki 496,311 (metropolitan area 837,918); Espoo
175,806[4]; Tampere 174,266; Turku 159,541; Vantaa 157,920[4].

Vital statistics

Birth rate per 1,000 population (1991): 13.1 (world avg. 26.4); (1987) legiti-
mate 80.8%; illegitimate 19.2%.
Death rate per 1,000 population (1991): 9.8 (world avg. 9.2).
Natural increase rate per 1,000 population (1991): 3.3 (world avg. 17.2).
Total fertility rate (avg. births per childbearing woman; 1991): 1.7.
Marriage rate per 1,000 population (1989): 5.0.
Divorce rate per 1,000 population (1989): 2.9.
Life expectancy at birth (1989): male 70.8 years; female 78.9 years.
Major causes of death per 100,000 population (1989): ischemic heart diseases
283.4; malignant neoplasms (cancers) 196.6; cerebrovascular disease 117.7;
diseases of the respiratory system 67.2; accidents 58.0.

National economy

Budget (1991). Revenue: Fmk 157,655,000,000 (tax revenue 87.5%, of which
sales taxes 35.7%, income and property taxes 27.4%, excise duties 12.4%;
nontax revenue 12.5%). Expenditures: Fmk 157,653,000,000 (social security
20.0%; education 18.4%; health 8.4%; transportation and communications
7.7%; administration 7.4%; agriculture 6.8%; defense 5.7%).
National debt (end of December 1990): Fmk 54,000,000,000.
Tourism (1991): receipts from visitors U.S.$1,236,000,000; expenditures by
nationals abroad U.S.$2,745,000,000.
Production (metric tons except as noted). Agriculture, forestry, fishing (1991):
silage 4,642,000, barley 1,778,000, oats 1,155,000, sugar beets 1,043,000, potatoes 672,000, carrots 38,700, strawberries 9,200, cut flowers 76.4 hectares;
livestock (number of live animals) 1,315,000 cattle, 1,290,000 pigs, 236,700
reindeer[5,6]; roundwood (1990) 41,647,000 cu m; fish catch (1990) 97,391.
Mining and quarrying (1991): zinc concentrate 107,000; gold 70,700 troy oz.
Manufacturing (value added in Fmk '000,000; 1990): pulp paper and paperboard 14,247; food, beverages, and tobacco products 12,840; nonelectrical
machinery 12,655; printing and publishing 8,060; wood furniture and other
wood products 7,995; electrical machinery 6,867; fabricated metal products
6,755. Construction (1990): residential 22,230,000 cu m; nonresidential 34,-
050,000 cu m. Energy production (consumption): electricity (kW-hr; 1991)
55,068,000,000 (65,261,000,000[6]); coal (metric tons; 1990) none (6,227,000);
crude petroleum (barrels; 1990) none (67,883,000); petroleum products
(metric tons; 1990) 9,043,000 (8,627,000); natural gas (cu m; 1990) none
(2,695,000,000).
Household income and expenditure. Average household size (1988) 2.3; income per household Fmk 140,600 (U.S.$33,614); sources of income: wages
and salaries 65.6%, transfer payments 21.4%, self-employment 8.1%, other

4.9%; expenditure (1990): food, beverages, and tobacco 22.5%, transportation and communications 18.0%, housing and energy 17.8%, recreation and
education 10.5%.
Gross national product (at current market prices; 1990): U.S.$129,823,000,000
(U.S.$26,070 per capita).

Structure of gross domestic product and labour force				
	1990			
	in value Fmk '000,000	% of total value	labour force	% of labour force
Agriculture, fishing	15,463	3.4 }	213,000	8.3
Forestry	13,090	2.9 }		
Mining	1,365	0.3	4,000	0.2
Manufacturing	99,826	21.8	539,000	20.9
Public utilities	10,959	2.4	28,000	1.1
Construction	44,551	9.7	221,000	8.6
Transp. and commun.	37,566	8.2	183,000	7.1
Trade, restaurants	51,610	11.3	402,000	15.6
Finance, real estate	88,152	19.3	205,000	8.0
Pub. admin., defense	82,069	17.9 }	766,000	29.7
Services	31,461	6.9 }		
Other	–18,562	–4.1	15,000	0.6
TOTAL	457,550	100.0	2,576,000	100.0[7]

Population economically active (1990): total 2,576,000; activity rate of total
population 51.7% (participation rates: ages 15–64, 76.3%; female 47.1%;
unemployed [August 1991–July 1992] 11.0%).

Price and earnings indexes (1985 = 100)							
	1986	1987	1988	1989	1990	1991	1992[8]
Consumer price index	102.9	107.1	112.6	120.0	127.3	132.6	135.9
Hourly earnings index	106.9	114.4	124.7	135.7	148.2	157.4	...

Land use (1990): forested 76.2%; meadows and pastures 0.4%; agricultural
and under permanent cultivation 8.0%; other 15.4%.

Foreign trade[9]

Balance of trade (current prices)						
	1986	1987	1988	1989	1990	1991
Fmk '000,000	+8,411	+4,845	+6,136	+2,928	+2,799	+9,141
% of total	5.4%	2.8%	3.5%	1.5%	1.4%	5.6%

Imports (1991): Fmk 87,720,000,000 (raw materials 48.4%; consumer goods
24.2%; mineral fuels 10.8%). *Major import sources:* Germany 16.9%; Sweden
12.3%; Russia 8.5%; United Kingdom 7.7%; United States 6.9%; Japan
6.0%.
Exports (1991): Fmk 92,876,000,000 (paper, paper products, and graphic arts
32.0%; metal products and machinery 31.4%; wood products including
furniture 7.5%). *Major export destinations:* Germany 15.4%; Sweden 13.9%;
United Kingdom 10.4%; United States 6.1%; France 5.9%; The Netherlands
5.0%; Russia 4.9%.

Transport and communications

Transport. Railroads: route length (1991) 3,646 mi, 5,867 km; passenger-mi
1,645,000,000, passenger-km 2,647,000,000; short ton-mi cargo 5,230,000,000,
metric ton-km cargo 7,635,000,000. Roads (1990): total length 47,477 mi, 76,-
407 km (paved 61%). Vehicles (1990): passenger cars 1,926,326, trucks and
buses 271,082. Merchant marine (1991): vessels (100 gross tons and over)
266; total deadweight tonnage 875,858. Air transport (1991)[10]: passenger-
mi 6,116,000,000, passenger-km 9,842,000,000; short ton-mi cargo 95,539,000,
metric ton-km cargo 139,484,000; airports (1992) 25.
Communications. Daily newspapers (1990): total number 54; total circulation
2,595,909; circulation per 1,000 population 521. Radio (1991): 4,950,000 receivers (1 per 1.0 person). Television (1991): 1,900,000 receivers (1 per 2.6
persons). Telephones (1991)[11]: 2,670,000 (1 per 1.9 persons).

Education and health

Education (1990–91)	schools	teachers	students	student/ teacher ratio
Primary (age 7–15)[12]	4,845	42,165[13]	583,676	13.9[13]
Secondary (age 16–18)[14]	464	6,178[13]	101,625	16.1[13]
Voc. (incl. higher)	593	...	164,249	
Higher	20	7,744[13]	110,646	14.0[13]

Educational attainment (1990). Percentage of population age 25 and over
having: incomplete upper-secondary education 50.5%; complete upper-
secondary or vocational 38.6%; some postsecondary 4.3%; undergraduate
2.1%; graduate 4.1%; postgraduate 0.4%. *Literacy:* virtually 100%.
Health (1989): physicians 9,871 (1 per 503 persons); hospital beds 66,616 (1
per 75 persons); infant mortality rate per 1,000 live births 6.0.
Food (1988–90): daily per capita caloric intake 3,066 (vegetable products 59%,
animal products 41%); 113% of FAO recommended minimum requirement.

Military

Total active duty personnel (1992): 32,800 (army 83.2%, navy 7.6%, air force
9.2%). *Military expenditure as percentage of GNP* (1989): 1.6% (world 4.9%);
per capita expenditure U.S.$360.

---

[1]The Evangelical Lutheran and Finnish (Greek) Orthodox churches have special
recognition. [2]January 1. [3]Based on land area only. [4]Within metropolitan Helsinki.
[5]Excluding calves. [6]1990. [7]Detail does not add to total given because of rounding.
[8]April. [9]Import figures are f.o.b. in balance of trade and c.i.f. in commodities and
trading partners. [10]Finnair only. [11]Main lines. [12]Includes lower-secondary. [13]1989–90.
[14]Excludes lower-secondary.

France

Official name: République Française (French Republic).
Form of government: republic with two legislative houses (Parliament; Senate [321], National Assembly [577]).
Chief of state: President.
Head of government: Prime Minister.
Capital: Paris.
Official language: French.
Official religion: none.
Monetary unit: 1 franc (F) = 100 centimes; valuation (Oct. 5, 1992) 1 U.S.$ = F 4.78; 1 £ = F 8.12.

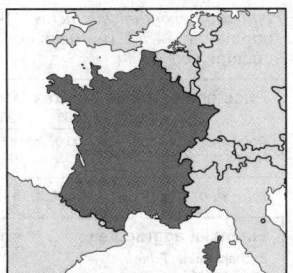

Area and population

Regions Departments	Capitals	area sq mi	area sq km	population 1991 estimate
Alsace				
Bas-Rhin	Strasbourg	1,836	4,755	958,000
Haut-Rhin	Colmar	1,361	3,525	673,900
Aquitaine				
Dordogne	Périgueux	3,498	9,060	387,500
Gironde	Bordeaux	3,861	10,000	1,223,600
Landes	Mont-de-Marsan	3,569	9,243	313,100
Lot-et-Garonne	Agen	2,070	5,361	306,900
Pyrénées-Atlantiques	Pau	2,952	7,645	581,300
Auvergne				
Allier	Moulins	2,834	7,340	356,900
Cantal	Aurillac	2,211	5,726	158,300
Haute-Loire	Le Puy	1,922	4,977	206,800
Puy-de-Dôme	Clermont-Ferrand	3,077	7,970	598,800
Basse-Normandie				
Calvados	Caen	2,142	5,548	621,300
Manche	Saint-Lô	2,293	5,938	480,900
Orne	Alençon	2,356	6,103	292,900
Bretagne				
Côtes-d'Armor	Saint-Brieuc	2,656	6,878	538,300
Finistère	Quimper	2,600	6,733	839,800
Ille-et-Vilaine	Rennes	2,616	6,775	804,200
Morbihan	Vannes	2,634	6,823	623,100
Bourgogne				
Côte-d'Or	Dijon	3,383	8,763	496,200
Nièvre	Nevers	2,632	6,817	232,600
Saône-et-Loire	Mâcon	3,311	8,575	558,500
Yonne	Auxerre	2,868	7,427	324,600
Centre				
Cher	Bourges	2,793	7,235	322,000
Eure-et-Loir	Chartres	2,270	5,880	399,700
Indre	Châteauroux	2,622	6,791	237,300
Indre-et-Loire	Tours	2,366	6,127	532,100
Loiret	Orléans	2,616	6,775	585,900
Loir-et-Cher	Blois	2,449	6,343	307,100
Champagne-Ardenne				
Ardennes	Charleville-Mézières	2,019	5,229	295,700
Aube	Troyes	2,318	6,004	289,400
Haute-Marne	Chaumont	2,398	6,211	203,400
Marne	Châlons-sur-Marne	3,151	8,162	559,600
Corse				
Corse-du-Sud	Ajaccio	1,550	4,014	119,300
Haute-Corse	Bastia	1,802	4,666	131,700
Franche-Comté				
Doubs	Besançon	2,021	5,234	485,200
Haute-Saône	Vesoul	2,070	5,360	229,300
Jura	Lons-le-Saunier	1,930	4,999	249,600
Territoire de Belfort	Belfort	235	609	134,400
Haute-Normandie				
Eure	Évreux	2,332	6,040	519,800
Seine-Maritime	Rouen	2,424	6,278	1,226,200
Île-de-France				
Essonne	Évry	696	1,804	1,096,300
Hauts-de-Seine	Nanterre	68	176	1,393,400
Paris	Paris	40	105	2,152,200
Seine-et-Marne	Melun	2,284	5,915	1,102,100
Seine-Saint-Denis	Bobigny	91	236	1,388,000
Val-de-Marne	Créteil	95	245	1,219,300
Val-d'Oise	Pontoise	481	1,246	1,064,900
Yvelines	Versailles	882	2,284	1,320,000
Languedoc-Roussillon				
Aude	Carcassonne	2,370	6,139	301,000
Gard	Nîmes	2,260	5,853	591,700
Hérault	Montpellier	2,356	6,101	805,500
Lozère	Mende	1,995	5,167	72,700
Pyrénées-Orientales	Perpignan	1,589	4,116	367,100
Limousin				
Corrèze	Tulle	2,261	5,857	237,500
Creuse	Guéret	2,149	5,565	130,700
Haute-Vienne	Limoges	2,131	5,520	353,500
Lorraine				
Meurthe-et-Moselle	Nancy	2,024	5,241	711,500
Meuse	Bar-le-Duc	2,400	6,216	195,900
Moselle	Metz	2,400	6,216	1,011,400
Vosges	Épinal	2,268	5,874	385,200
Midi-Pyrénées				
Ariège	Foix	1,888	4,890	136,700
Aveyron	Rodez	3,373	8,736	269,300
Gers	Auch	2,416	6,257	174,700
Haute-Garonne	Toulouse	2,436	6,309	938,500
Hautes-Pyrénées	Tarbes	1,724	4,464	224,800
Lot	Cahors	2,014	5,217	156,100
Tarn	Albi	2,223	5,758	343,400
Tarn-et-Garonne	Montauban	1,435	3,718	201,400
Nord-Pas-de-Calais				
Nord	Lille	2,217	5,742	2,533,000
Pas-de-Calais	Arras	2,576	6,671	1,435,000

Area and population (continued)

Regions Departments	Capitals	area sq mi	area sq km	population 1991 estimate
Pays de la Loire				
Loire-Atlantique	Nantes	2,631	6,815	1,058,100
Maine-et Loire	Angers	2,767	7,166	708,900
Mayenne	Laval	1,998	5,175	278,700
Sarthe	Le Mans	2,396	6,206	514,600
Vendée	La Roche-sur-Yon	2,595	6,720	512,000
Picardie				
Aisne	Laon	2,845	7,369	537,600
Oise	Beauvais	2,263	5,860	733,200
Somme	Amiens	2,382	6,170	548,300
Poitou-Charentes				
Charente	Angoulême	2,300	5,956	342,300
Charente-Maritime	La Rochelle	2,650	6,864	528,700
Deux-Sèvres	Niort	2,316	5,999	346,300
Vienne	Poitiers	2,699	6,990	380,900
Provence–Alpes–Côte d'Azur				
Alpes-de-Haute-Provence	Digne	2,674	6,925	132,400
Alpes-Maritimes	Nice	1,660	4,299	983,600
Bouches-du-Rhône	Marseille	1,964	5,087	1,764,100
Hautes-Alpes	Gap	2,142	5,549	114,200
Var	Toulon	2,306	5,973	828,300
Vaucluse	Avignon	1,377	3,567	471,800
Rhône-Alpes				
Ain	Bourg-en-Bresse	2,225	5,762	477,400
Ardèche	Privas	2,135	5,529	278,800
Drôme	Valence	2,521	6,530	417,100
Haute-Savoie	Annecy	1,694	4,388	577,600
Isère	Grenoble	2,869	7,431	1,025,300
Loire	Saint-Étienne	1,846	4,781	747,100
Rhône	Lyon	1,254	3,249	1,516,500
Savoie	Chambéry	2,327	6,028	351,400
TOTAL		210,026	543,965	56,893,200

Demography

Population (1992): 57,289,000.
Density (1992): persons per sq mi 272.8, persons per sq km 105.3.
Urban-rural (1990): urban 74.3%; rural 25.7%.
Sex distribution (1990): male 48.68%; female 51.32%.
Age breakdown (1990): under 15, 19.1%; 15–29, 22.6%; 30–44, 22.8%; 45–59, 15.6%; 60–74, 12.8%; 75 and over, 7.1%.
Population projection: (2000) 59,245,000; (2010) 61,784,000.
Doubling time: not applicable; doubling time exceeds 100 years.
Ethnolinguistic composition (1982): French (mother tongue) 93.2%, of which fully or substantially bilingual in Occitan 2.7%, German (mostly Alsatian) 2.3%, Breton 1.0%, Catalan 0.4%; Arabic 2.6%; other 4.2%.
Religious affiliation (1980): Roman Catholic 76.4%; other Christian 3.7%; atheist 3.4%; Muslim 3.0%; other 13.5%.
Major cities (1990): Paris 2,152,423 (metropolitan area 9,060,257); Marseille 800,550 (1,231,082); Lyon 415,487 (1,262,223); Toulouse 358,688 (608,430); Nice 342,439 (475,507); Strasbourg 252,338 (338,483); Nantes 244,995 (492,-255); Bordeaux 210,336 (685,456); Montpellier 207,996 (236,788).
National origin (1990): French 93.6%; Portuguese 1.1%; Algerian 1.1%; Moroccan 1.0%; Italian 0.4%; Spanish 0.4%; Turkish 0.3%; other 2.1%.
Mobility (1982). Population living in same residence as in 1975: n.a.; same region 91.7%; different region 5.8%; different country 2.5%.
Households (1990). Average household size 2.6; 1 person 27.1%, 2 persons 29.6%, 3 persons 17.7%, 4 persons 15.7%, 5 persons 6.7%, 6 persons or more 3.2%. Family households: 14,118,940 (72.1%); nonfamily 5,471,460 (27.9%, of which 1-person 24.6%).
Immigration (1989): permanent immigrants admitted 53,240, from Morocco 25.6%, Turkey 10.0%, Tunisia 5.9%, Germany 2.1%, Portugal 1.7%.

Vital statistics

Birth rate per 1,000 population (1991): 13.3 (world avg. 26.4); (1990) legitimate 69.9%; illegitimate 30.1%.
Death rate per 1,000 population (1991): 9.2 (world avg. 9.2).
Natural increase rate per 1,000 population (1991): 4.1 (world avg. 17.2).
Total fertility rate (avg. births per childbearing woman; 1991): 1.8.
Marriage rate per 1,000 population (1991): 4.9.
Divorce rate per 1,000 population (1990): 1.9.
Life expectancy at birth (1991): male 73.0 years; female 81.1 years.
Major causes of death per 100,000 population (1990): heart disease and other circulatory diseases 307.6; malignant neoplasms (cancers) 250.0; respiratory diseases 67.1; digestive tract diseases 47.7.

Social indicators

Educational attainment (1990). Percentage of population age 25 and over having: primary 22.1%; lower secondary 7.8%; higher secondary and vocational 29.4%; postsecondary 11.6; undeclared attainment 29.1%.

Distribution of income (1984)

percentage of household income by quintile				
1	2	3	4	5 (highest)
7.1%	12.3%	17.1%	23.2%	40.3%

Quality of working life. Average workweek (1990): 39.1 hours. Annual rate per 100,000 workers (1990) for: injury or accident 3,013; accidents in transit to work 338 (deaths 3.1); industrial illness 16.6[1]; death 4.8[1]. Proportion of labour force insured for damages or income loss resulting from: injury, permanent disability, or death, n.a. Average days lost to labour stoppages per 1,000 workers (1989): 33.1. Average length of journey to work (1990): 8.7 mi (14 km)[2].
Social deviance. Offense rate per 100,000 population (1990) for: murder 4.4; rape 7.7[1]; other assault 86.5[3]; theft (including burglary and housebreaking) 4,302.7[4]. Incidence per 100,000 in general population of: alcoholism

(deaths related to alcoholism; 1985) 63.6; drug and substance abuse, n.a.; suicide (1988) 20.8.

Access to services (1990). Proportion of dwellings having: central heating 78.9%; piped water 99.7%; indoor plumbing 93.5%; natural gas (1982) 48.9%.

Social participation. Eligible voters participating in last national election: 78.0%. Population over 15 years of age participating in voluntary associations: 28.0%.

Leisure (1987–88). Participation rate for favourite leisure activities: watching television 82%; reading magazines 79%; listening to radio 75%; entertaining relatives 64%; visiting relatives 61%; attending fairs/expositions 56%.

Material well-being (1991). Households possessing: automobile 75.0%; television receiver 95.0%, of which colour 88.0%; videocassette recorder 37.0%; refrigerator 97.5%[1]; washing machine 86.5%[1].

National economy

Gross national product (at current market prices; 1990): U.S.$1,099,750,000,-000 (U.S.$19,480 per capita).

Structure of gross domestic product and labour force

	1991			
	in value F '000,000	% of total value	labour force	% of labour force
Agriculture	387,668	5.7	1,839,100	7.5
Mining } Manufacturing	1,255,989	18.4	4,022,900	16.5
Construction	355,635	5.3	1,599,100	6.5
Public utilities	150,962	2.2	162,600	0.7
Transp. and commun.	391,367	5.9	1,302,300	5.2
Trade	1,027,170	15.2	3,936,200	16.1
Finance	286,926	4.2	601,900	2.4
Pub. admin., defense	1,078,848	15.9	5,640,300	23.1
Services	1,570,464	23.3	3,190,100	13.1
Other	261,488[5]	3.9[5]	2,203,000[6]	8.9[6]
TOTAL	6,766,517	100.0	24,497,500	100.0

Budget (1991). Revenue: F 1,445,049,000,000 (value-added taxes 44.4%, direct contributions 39.0%, customs taxes 9.0%). Expenditure: F 1,559,959,000,000 (current expenditures 80.9%, defense 13.0%, capital expenditure 6.1%).

Manufacturing enterprises (1991)

	no. of enter- prises	no. of employees	annual salaries as a % of avg. of all salaries	annual value added (F '000,000)
Food products	55,197	569,100	87	190,443
Electrical machinery	15,620	453,400	118	156,885
Transport equipment	4,293	543,500	108	154,115
Mechanical equipment	32,134	437,900	104	122,101
Iron and steel	27,847	453,000	96	119,642
Petroleum refineries	180	51,400	174	112,454
Printing, publishing	30,359	238,800	125	78,109
Textiles and wearing apparel	29,701	340,900	78	68,417
Rubber products	5,875	210,600	94	55,748
Industrial chemicals	1,442	120,000	128	51,734
Paper and paper products	1,916	104,000	102	34,773
Metal products	442	90,400	103	34,331
Glass products	1,536	54,400	104	17,246
Footwear	4,236	69,500	75	13,877

Production (metric tons except as noted). Agriculture, forestry, fishing (1991): wheat 34,483,000, sugar beets 29,280,000, corn (maize) 12,787,000, barley 10,651,000, grapes 7,020,000, potatoes 6,300,000, sunflower seeds 2,563,-000, rapeseed 2,286,000, apples 2,000,000, tomatoes 858,000, oats 733,000, cauliflower 596,000, peaches 450,000, sorghum 388,000, pears 280,000, rye 216,000, soybeans 150,000; livestock (number of live animals) 21,446,000 cattle, 12,239,000 pigs, 11,490,000 sheep, 1,236,000 goats; roundwood (1990) 44,718,000 cu m; fish catch (1990) 896,841. Mining and quarrying (1990): iron ore 2,617,000[7]; potash salts 1,400,000; bauxite 490,000; zinc 23,760[7]; lead 840[7]; gold 135,000 troy oz[7]. Manufacturing (1990): cement 26,508,000; crude steel 16,800,000; pig iron 14,412,000; sulfuric acid 4,187,000[1]; aluminum 535,-200; rubber products 521,800, of which tires 61,368,000 units[1]; automobiles 3,214,800 units. Construction (dwelling units completed; 1991) 258,900.

Retail trade enterprises (1988)

	no. of enter- prises	no. of employees	weekly wages as a % of all wages	annual turnover (F '000,000)
Large food stores	3,955	356,006	...	470,805
Small food stores	89,024	232,533	...	115,766
butcher shops	43,353	131,099	...	60,835
Clothing stores	72,677	202,405	...	100,163
Pharmacies	21,356	117,955	...	82,089
Department stores	1,492	62,021	...	52,601
Furniture stores	7,757	54,435	...	47,427
Electrical and electronics stores	11,190	59,158	...	36,784
Publishing and paper	22,017	53,373	...	26,035
Gas, coal, and other energy products	3,418	14,855	...	19,426

Energy production (consumption)[8]: electricity (kW-hr; 1990) 419,584,000,000 (374,146,000,000); coal (metric tons; 1990) 13,251,000 (28,656,000); crude petroleum (barrels; 1990) 22,172,000 (529,972,000); petroleum products (metric tons; 1990) 68,293,000 (74,621,000); natural gas (cu m; 1990) 3,130,800,000 (34,341,000,000).

Household income and expenditure. Average household size (1991) 2.6; average annual income per household (1991) F 205,400 (U.S.$37,720). Sources of income (1990): wages and salaries 52.4%, social security 26.1%, self-employment 21.2%; expenditure (1990): food 19.3%, housing 19.3%, transportation and communications 16.7%, health 9.4%, recreation 7.6%, clothing 6.5%.

Tourism (1990): receipts from visitors U.S.$21,651,000,000; expenditures by nationals abroad U.S.$13,476,000,000.

Population economically active (1992): total 24,832,000; activity rate of total population 54.7% (participation rates: ages 15–64, 65.5%[1]; female 43.3%; unemployed 9.2%).

Price and earnings indexes (1985 = 100)

	1985	1986	1987	1988	1989	1990	1991
Consumer price index	100.0	102.5	105.9	108.8	112.6	116.4	120.2
Hourly earnings index	100.0	104.5	109.4	112.8	118.1	119.9	125.0

Public debt (1991): F 1,800,600,000,000 (U.S.$319,136,000,000).

Financial aggregates

	1987	1988	1989	1990	1991	1992[9]
Exchange rate, F per:						
U.S. dollar	5.34	6.06	5.79	5.13	5.18	4.77
£	9.99	10.96	9.30	9.89	9.67	8.49
SDR	7.58	8.15	7.80	7.30	7.41	7.01
International reserves (U.S.$)						
Total (excl. gold; '000,000)	33,049	25,364	24,611	36,778	31,284	31,662[10]
SDRs ('000,000)	1,502	1,390	1,329	1,283	1,326	1,311
Reserve pos. in IMF ('000,000)	1,914	1,615	1,414	1,428	1,666	1,739
Foreign exchange	29,634	22,359	28,910	21,868	28,292	28,471[10]
Gold ('000,000 fine troy oz)	81.85	81.85	81.85	81.85	81.85	81.89[10]
% world reserves	8.7	8.7	8.7	8.7	8.7	8.8[10]
Interest and prices						
Central bank discount (%)	9.50	9.50	9.50	9.50	9.50	9.50
Govt. bond yield (%)	9.43	9.06	8.79	9.96	9.05	8.71
Industrial share prices (1985 = 100)	177.6	162.1	234.9	207.7	220.8	244.2
Balance of payments (U.S.$'000,000)						
Balance of visible trade	−8,667	−8,537	−10,651	−13,667	−10,139	...
Imports, f.o.b.	150,325	168,726	181,412	220,339	217,233	...
Exports, f.o.b.	141,658	160,188	170,761	206,672	207,084	...
Balance of invisibles	4,221	3,742	5,031	−105	3,991	...
Balance of payments, current account	−4,446	−4,795	−5,620	−13,772	−6,148	...

Land use (1990): forested 26.9%; meadows and pastures 20.7%; agricultural and under permanent cultivation 34.7%; other 17.7%.

Foreign trade

Balance of trade (current prices)

	1986	1987	1988	1989	1990	1991
F '000,000,000	−3.0	−30.7	−32.8	−44.2	−51.3	−81.5
% of total	0.2%	1.7%	1.6%	1.9%	2.1%	3.2%

Imports (1991): F 1,302,876,000,000 (machinery 24.7%; agricultural products 11.4%; transport equipment 10.2%, of which automobiles 5.7%; fuels 9.5%). *Major import sources:* Germany 18.1%; Italy 10.9%; U.S. 9.1%; Belgium-Luxembourg 8.4%; U.K. 7.6%; The Netherlands 5.1%; Spain 5.1%; Japan 4.1%.

Exports (1991): F 1,221,408,000,000 (machinery 26.7%; agricultural products 15.8%; transport equipment 13.6%, of which automobiles 6.8%). *Major export destinations:* Germany 18.3%; Italy 10.8%; U.K. 8.8%; Belgium-Luxembourg 8.8%; Spain 6.7%; U.S. 6.3%; The Netherlands 4.9%.

Transport and communications

Transport. Railroads (1991): route length 21,173 mi, 34,074 km; passenger-mi 38,618,000,000, passenger-km 62,150,000,000; short ton-mi cargo 35,264,-000,000, metric ton-km cargo 51,484,000,000. Roads (1991): total length 503,300 mi, 810,000 km (paved [1985] 92%). Vehicles (1991): passenger cars 23,810,000; trucks and buses 5,192,000. Merchant marine (1991): vessels (100 gross tons and over) 910; total deadweight tonnage 5,677,689. Air transport (1991)[11]: passenger-mi 20,236,392,000, passenger-km 32,567,378,000; short ton-mi cargo 4,580,493,000, metric ton-km cargo 6,687,407,000; airports (1992) with scheduled flights 64.

Communications. Daily newspapers (1989): number 114; circulation 9,961,-300[12]; circulation per 1,000 population 176[12]. Radio (1991): 49,000,000 receivers (1 per 1.2 persons). Television (1991): 29,300,000 receivers (1 per 1.9 persons). Telephones (1987)[13]: 33,357,900 (1 per 1.7 persons).

Education and health

Education (1990–91)

	schools	teachers	students	student/ teacher ratio
Primary (age 6–10)	44,131	309,876	4,062,246	13.1
Secondary (age 11–18) } Voc., teacher tr.	11,325	413,304	5,402,300	13.1
Higher	1,062[14]	53,110	1,698,643	32.0

Literacy (1980): total population literate 41,112,000 (98.8%); males literate 19,933,000 (98.9%); females literate 21,179,000 (98.7%).

Health (1991): physicians 152,096 (1 per 374 persons); hospital beds (1990) 702,184 (1 per 81 persons); infant mortality rate 7.3.

Food (1988–90): daily per capita caloric intake 3,593 (vegetable products 61%, animal products 39%); 143% of FAO recommended minimum requirement.

Military

Total active duty personnel (1992): 431,700 (army 60.4%, navy 15.0%, air force 21.2%, other 3.4%). *Military expenditure as percentage of GNP* (1989): 3.7% (world 4.9%); per capita expenditure U.S.$628.

[1]1989. [2]Distance measured "as the bird flies." [3]Including rape. [4]1991. [5]Includes value-added taxes, customs duties, and imputed bank service charges. [6]Unemployed. [7]Metal content of ores. [8]All energy statistics include Monaco. [9]September, unless otherwise marked. [10]August. [11]Air France and UTA only. [12]89 newspapers only. [13]Does not include public telephones. [14]1988–89.

Gabon

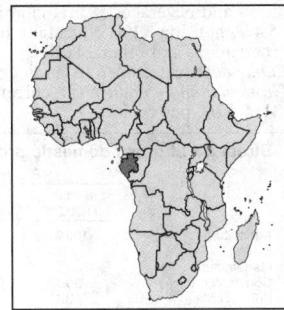

Official name: République Gabonaise
(Gabonese Republic).
Form of government: multiparty[1]
republic with one legislative house
(National Assembly [120]).
Chief of state: President.
Head of government: Prime Minister.
Capital: Libreville.
Official language: French.
Official religion: none.
Monetary unit: 1 CFA franc
(CFAF) = 100 centimes; valuation
(Oct. 5, 1992) 1 U.S.$ = CFAF 238.75;
1 £ = CFAF 405.88.

Area and population

Provinces	Capitals	area sq mi	area sq km	population 1978 estimate[2]
Estuaire	Libreville	8,008	20,740	359,000
Haut-Ogooué	Franceville	14,111	36,547	213,000
Moyen-Ogooué	Lambaréné	7,156	18,535	49,000
Ngounié	Mouila	14,575	37,750	118,000
Nyanga	Tchibanga	8,218	21,285	98,000
Ogooué-Ivindo	Makokou	17,790	46,075	53,000
Ogooué-Lolo	Koulamoutou	9,799	25,380	49,000
Ogooué-Maritime	Port-Gentil	8,838	22,890	194,000
Woleu-Ntem	Oyem	14,851	38,465	166,000
TOTAL		103,347[3]	267,667	1,300,000[3-]

Demography

Population (1992)[2]: 1,253,000.
Density (1992)[2]: persons per sq mi 12.1, persons per sq km 4.7.
Urban-rural (1990): urban 45.7%; rural 54.3%.
Sex distribution (1990): male 49.23%; female 50.77%.
Age breakdown (1990): under 15, 32.5%; 15–29, 30.4%; 30–44, 15.3%; 45–59, 12.9%; 60–74, 7.3%; 75 and over, 1.6%.
Population projection[2]: (2000) 1,612,000; (2010) 2,052,000.
Doubling time: 26 years.
Ethnic composition (1983): Fang 35.5%; Mpongwe 15.1%; Mbete 14.2%; Punu 11.5%; other 23.7%.
Religious affiliation (1980): Christian 96.2%, of which Roman Catholic 65.2%, Protestant 18.8%, African indigenous 12.1%; traditional religion 2.9%; Muslim 0.8%; other 0.1%.
Major cities (1988): Libreville 352,000; Port-Gentil 164,000; Franceville 75,000.

Vital statistics

Birth rate per 1,000 population (1990–95): 43.4 (world avg. 26.4).
Death rate per 1,000 population (1990–95): 16.0 (world avg. 9.2).
Natural increase rate per 1,000 population (1990–95): 27.4 (world avg. 17.2).
Total fertility rate (avg. births per childbearing woman; 1990): 5.8.
Marriage rate per 1,000 population: n.a.
Divorce rate per 1,000 population: n.a.
Life expectancy at birth (1990–95): male 51.9 years; female 55.2 years.
Major causes of death per 100,000 population: n.a.; however, major diseases include malaria, measles, shigellosis (infection with dysentery), trypanosomiasis, and tuberculosis.

National economy

Budget (1992). Revenue: CFAF 398,000,000,000 (oil revenues 50.0%; customs duties 18.6%; other revenues 31.4%). Expenditures: CFAF 375,000,000,000 (current expenditure 80.3%, of which running costs 58.4%, public debt 21.9%; capital expenditure 19.7%).
Tourism (1990): receipts from visitors U.S.$4,000,000; expenditures by nationals abroad U.S.$143,000,000.
Production (metric tons except as noted). Agriculture, forestry, fishing (1991): roots and tubers 430,000, cassava 250,000, plantains 240,000, sugarcane 210,000, corn (maize) 20,000, peanuts (groundnuts) 16,000, bananas 9,000, palm oil 4,900, cacao beans 2,000, coffee 2,000; livestock (number of live animals) 165,000 sheep, 162,000 pigs, 81,000 goats, 28,000 cattle, 2,000,000 chickens; roundwood (1990) 3,789,000 cu m; fish catch (1990) 22,000. Mining and quarrying (1991): manganese 1,600,000; uranium 710[4]. Manufacturing (1989): cement 117,000; flour 25,976; refined sugar 20,905; beer 460,200 hectolitres; soft drinks 297,200 hectolitres; cigarettes 17,800,000 packs[5]; textiles CFAF 2,420,000,000[5]. Construction: n.a. Energy production (consumption): electricity (kW-hr; 1990) 915,000,000 (915,000,000); crude petroleum (barrels; 1990) 103,328,000 (13,602,000); petroleum products (metric tons; 1990) 620,000 (426,000); natural gas (cu m; 1990) 304,526,000 (304,526,000); fuelwood (cu m; 1990) 2,567,000 (2,567,000).
Land use (1990): forested 77.6%; meadows and pastures 18.2%; agricultural and under permanent cultivation 1.8%; other 2.4%.
Population economically active (1990): total 518,000; activity rate of total population 44.2% (participation rates [1985]: ages 15–64, 68.2%; female 38.4%; unemployed, n.a.).

Price and earnings indexes (1985 = 100)

	1984	1985	1986	1987	1988	1989	1990
Consumer price index	93.2	100.0	106.3	105.3	95.0	101.6	110.4
Earnings index	...	...	...	...	...	...	...

Gross national product (at current market prices; 1990): U.S.$3,654,000,000 (U.S.$3,220 per capita).

Structure of gross domestic product and labour force

	1990 in value CFAF '000,000	1990 % of total value	1983 labour force[6]	1983 % of labour force[6]
Agriculture, forestry, fishing	123,200	11.4	14,118	10.2
Mining	518,400	47.8	3,919	2.9
Manufacturing	54,500	5.0	4,123	3.0
Construction	67,800	6.2	13,154	9.5
Public utilities	23,400	2.2	7	7
Transportation and communications	88,100	8.1	7	7
Trade	131,100	12.1	3,732	2.7
Finance			7	7
Pub. admin., defense			42,678	31.0
Services	78,200[8]	7.2[8]	7	7
Other, including taxes on imports			56,143[7]	40.7[7]
TOTAL	1,084,600[3]	100.0	137,867	100.0

Public debt (external, outstanding; 1990): U.S.$2,889,000,000.
Household income and expenditure. Average household size (1980) 4.0; income per household: n.a.; sources of income (1983): private sector 73.4%, public sector 26.6%; expenditure (1983)[9]: food and tobacco 54.7%, clothing and footwear 17.5%, housing 13.0%, transportation and communications 6.3%.

Foreign trade

Balance of trade (current prices)

	1985	1986	1987	1988	1989	1990
CFAF '000,000	+500,000	+140,000	+170,000	+120,400	+274,400	+267,800
% of total	39.2%	18.9%	28.2%	20.3%	36.3%	35.6%

Imports (1989): CFAF 241,800,000,000 (machinery and mechanical equipment 29.2%, food and agricultural products 14.6%, transport equipment 12.5%, manufactured products 12.1%, metal and metal products 11.2%, chemical products 5.4%, mining products 1.6%). *Major import sources:* France 46.3%; Cameroon 9.7%; The Netherlands 5.5%; United States 5.4%; Japan 4.1%; West Germany 3.7%; United Kingdom 2.9%; Italy 2.4%; Belgium-Luxembourg 1.9%.
Exports (1989): CFAF 509,600,000,000 (crude petroleum and petroleum products 70.8%, manganese ore and concentrate 11.6%, wood 9.4%, uranium ore and concentrate 4.1%). *Major export destinations:* France 36.2%; United States 26.1%; The Netherlands 6.2%; Japan 3.3%; Côte d'Ivoire 2.9%; Italy 2.3%.

Transport and communications

Transport. Railroads (1992): length 414 mi, 668 km; passenger-mi 21,000,000[10], passenger-km 34,000,000[10]; short ton-mi cargo 126,000,000[10], metric ton-km cargo 184,000,000[10]. Roads (1987): total length 4,286 mi, 6,898 km (paved 11%). Vehicles (1989): passenger cars 19,000; trucks and buses 15,000. Merchant marine (1991): vessels (100 gross tons and over) 28; total deadweight tonnage 29,956. Air transport (1990)[11]: passenger-mi 276,679,000, passenger-km 445,273,000; short ton-mi cargo 17,863,000, metric ton-km cargo 26,079,000; airports (1992) with scheduled flights 18.
Communications. Daily newspapers (1988): total number 1; total circulation 15,000; circulation per 1,000 population 14. Radio (1991): total number of receivers 250,000 (1 per 4.8 persons). Television (1991): total number of receivers 40,000 (1 per 30 persons). Telephones (1991): 19,000 (1 per 64 persons).

Education and health

Education (1987)

	schools	teachers	students	student/ teacher ratio
Primary	992	4,229	195,049	46.1
Secondary	51[12]	1,512	32,922	21.8
Voc., teacher tr.	29[12]	759	15,352	20.2
Higher[13, 14]	1	363	2,896	8.0

Educational attainment: n.a. *Literacy* (1990): total population age 15 and over literate 60.7%; males literate 73.5%; females literate 48.5%.
Health (1984): physicians 565 (1 per 2,000 persons); hospital beds 10,980 (1 per 103 persons); infant mortality rate per 1,000 live births (1990–95) 94.0.
Food (1984–86): daily per capita caloric intake 2,700 (vegetable products 88%, animal products 12%); (1984) 104% of FAO recommended minimum requirement.

Military

Total active duty personnel (1992): 4,750 (army 68.4%, navy 10.5%, air force 21.1%), not including 500 French troops. *Military expenditure as percentage of GNP* (1989): 4.5% (world 4.9%); per capita expenditure U.S.$132.

---

[1]Transitional constitution approved May 22, 1990; first multiparty elections held September 1990 through March 1991. [2]Population distribution is based on country estimate, which is substantially higher than estimates from external sources (such as the United Nations and the World Bank), which form the basis of the 1992 estimate. [3]Detail does not add to total given because of rounding. [4]1990. [5]1984. [6]Official government figures for salaried workers only, not including traditional agricultural workers; agricultural workers (FAO estimate, 1986) totaled 370,000 (71.0% of the labour force). [7]Public utilities, Transportation and communications, Finance, and Service employees included with Other. [8]Less imputed bank service charges. [9]Libreville only. [10]1987. [11]Air Gabon only. [12]1984–85. [13]Universities only. [14]1988.

Gambia, The

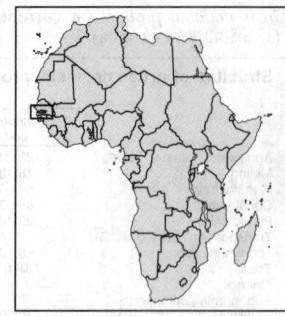

Official name: Republic of The Gambia.
Form of government: multiparty republic with one legislative house (House of Representatives [50[1]]).
Head of state and government: President.
Capital: Banjul.
Official language: English.
Official religion: none.
Monetary unit: 1 dalasi (D) = 100 butut; valuation (Oct. 5, 1992)
1 U.S.$ = D 8.42; 1 £ = D 14.31.

Area and population

| | | area | | population |
Divisions	Capitals	sq mi	sq km	1983 census[2]
Kombo St. Mary[3, 4]	Kanifing	29	76	101,504
Lower River	Mansakonko	625	1,618	55,263
MacCarthy Island	Kuntaur/Georgetown	1,117	2,894	126,004
North Bank	Kerewan	871	2,256	112,225
Upper River	Basse	799	2,069	111,388
Western	Brikama	681	1,764	137,245
City				
Banjul[4]	—	5	12	44,188
TOTAL		4,127	10,689	687,817

Demography

Population (1992): 921,000.
Density[5] (1992): persons per sq mi 277.0, persons per sq km 106.9.
Urban-rural (1988): urban 21.5%; rural 78.5%.
Sex distribution (1990): male 49.36%; female 50.64%.
Age breakdown (1990): under 15, 44.1%; 15–29, 24.8%; 30–44, 16.1%; 45–59, 10.1%; 60 and over, 4.9%.
Population projection: (2000) 1,132,000; (2010) 1,446,000.
Doubling time: 28 years.
Ethnic composition (1983): Malinke 40.4%; Fulani 18.7%; Wolof 14.6%; Dyola 10.3%; Soninke 8.2%; other 7.8%.
Religious affiliation (1983): Muslim 95.4%; Christian 3.7%; traditional beliefs and other 0.9%.
Major cities/urban areas (1986): Serekunda 102,600[3]; Banjul 44,188[4, 6] (Greater Banjul 145,692[4, 6]); Brikama 24,300; Bakau 23,600[3]; Farafenni 10,168[6].

Vital statistics

Birth rate per 1,000 population (1990–95): 44.9 (world avg. 26.4); legitimate, n.a.; illegitimate, n.a.
Death rate per 1,000 population (1990–95): 19.5 (world avg. 9.2).
Natural increase rate per 1,000 population (1990–95): 25.4 (world avg. 17.2).
Total fertility rate (avg. births per childbearing woman; 1990–95): 6.2.
Marriage rate per 1,000 population: n.a.
Divorce rate per 1,000 population: n.a.
Life expectancy at birth (1990–95): male 43.4 years; female 46.6 years.
Major causes of death per 100,000 population: n.a.; however, major infectious diseases include malaria, gastroenteritis and dysentery, pneumonia and bronchitis, measles, schistosomiasis, and whooping cough.

National economy

Budget (1991–92). Revenue: D 827,000,000 (tax revenue 71.5%, of which import duties and excises 62.4%, income taxes 9.0%; nontax revenue and grants 28.5%). Expenditures: D 704,400,000 (administrative expenses 31.1%; goods and services 23.4%; interest payments 21.2%; transportation and communications 11.2%; agriculture 5.8%; public services 4.6%; education and culture 3.5%).
Production (metric tons except as noted). Agriculture, forestry, fishing (1990): peanuts (groundnuts) 75,000, millet 50,000, paddy rice 20,000, corn (maize) 15,000, cassava 6,000, pulses (mostly beans) 4,000, palm oil 2,500, palm kernels 2,000, seed cotton 1,000; livestock (number of live animals) 400,000 cattle, 200,000 goats, 170,000 sheep; roundwood 928,000 cu m; fish catch (1989) 17,619, of which inland water 2,700, Atlantic Ocean 14,919. Mining and quarrying: sand and gravel are excavated for local use. Manufacturing (value of production in D '000; 1982): processed food, including peanut and palm kernel oil 62,878; beverages 10,546; textiles 3,253; chemicals and related products 1,031; nonmetals 922; printing and publishing 358; leather 150. Construction: n.a. Energy production (consumption): electricity (kW-hr; 1990) 67,000,000 (67,000,000); coal, none (none); crude petroleum, none (none); petroleum products (metric tons; 1990) none (61,000); natural gas, none (none).
Population economically active (1983): total 325,623; activity rate of total population 47.3% (participation rates: ages 15–64 78.2%; female 46.3%; unemployed, n.a.).

Price and earnings indexes (1985 = 100)

	1985	1986	1987	1988	1989	1990	1991
Consumer price index	100.0	156.6	193.4	216.0	233.9	262.5	285.0
Daily earnings index[7]	100.0	104.6	90.2	...	...	...	...

Tourism (1990): receipts from visitors U.S.$26,000,000; expenditures by nationals abroad U.S.$8,000,000.
Household income and expenditure. Average household size (1983) 8.3; income per household: n.a.; sources of income: n.a.; expenditure[8] (1986):

food and beverages 58.0%, clothing and footwear 17.5%, energy and water 5.4%, housing 5.1%, education, health, transportation and communications, recreation, and other 14.0%.
Public debt (external, outstanding; 1990): U.S.$352,000,000.
Gross national product (at current market prices; 1990): U.S.$229,000,000 (U.S.$260 per capita).

Structure of gross domestic product and labour force

| | 1990–91[9] | | 1983 | |
	in value D'000,000	% of total value	labour force	% of labour force
Agriculture	109.7	23.6	239,940	73.7
Mining	—	—	66	0.0
Manufacturing	32.1	6.9	8,144	2.5
Construction	30.1	6.5	4,373	1.3
Public utilities	3.1	0.7	1,233	0.4
Transportation and communications	85.0	18.3	8,014	2.5
Trade	171.7	37.0	16,551	5.1
Finance	33.0	7.1	4,577	1.4
Public administration	56.5	12.2	8,295	2.5
Services	15.0	3.2	9,381	2.9
Other	−71.9[10]	−15.5[10]	25,049[11]	7.7[11]
TOTAL	464.3	100.0	325,623	100.0

Land use (1989): forested 16.2%; meadows and pastures 9.0%; agricultural and under permanent cultivation 17.8%; built-on area, wasteland, and other 57.0%.

Foreign trade[12]

Balance of trade (current prices)

	1986	1987	1988	1989	1990	1991
D '000,000	−497.0	−615.9	−530.7	−1,023.0	−1,252.4	−1,292.0
% of total	51.3%	52.3%	40.6%	72.1%	66.1%	63.9%

Imports (1990–91): D 1,759,374,000 (food 30.4%; basic manufactures 18.1%; machinery and transport equipment 14.7%; mineral fuels and lubricants 10.7%; chemicals and related products 6.8%). *Major import sources* (1990): United Kingdom 17.2%; China 13.9%; France 10.9%; Germany 8.5%; Hong Kong 8.5%; Belgium-Luxembourg 5.7%.
Exports (1990–91): D 332,189,000 (reexports 59.1%[13]; domestic exports 40.9%, of which peanuts 12.4%, fish and fish preparations 9.1%, peanut meal 1.9%). *Major export destinations* (1990): Belgium-Luxembourg 44.8%; New Zealand 35.4%; Guinea 4.0%; United Kingdom 3.0%; France 3.0%; Switzerland 2.4%.

Transport and communications

Transport. Railroads: none. Roads (1990): total length 1,483 mi, 2,386 km (paved 32%). Vehicles (1989): passenger cars 5,500; trucks and buses 1,000. Merchant marine (1991): vessels (100 gross tons and over) 9; total deadweight tonnage 1,651. Air transport (1989): passenger arrivals and departures 203,353; cargo 2,128 metric tons; airports (1992) with scheduled flights 1.
Communications. Daily newspapers (1988): total number 1; total circulation 1,000; circulation per 1,000 population 1.2. Radio (1991): total number of receivers 175,000 (1 per 5.2 persons). Television: none. Telephones (1991): 11,000 (1 per 80 persons).

Education and health

Education (1989)

	schools	teachers	students	student/teacher ratio
Primary (age 8–14)	232	2,451	73,620	30.0
Secondary (age 15–21)	11	281	3,624	12.9
Secondary vocational	18	540	12,982	24.0
Postsecondary[14]	9	177	1,489	8.4

Educational attainment (1973). Percentage of population age 20 and over having: no formal schooling 90.8%; primary education 6.2%; secondary 2.6%; higher 0.4%. *Literacy* (1990): total population age 15 and over literate 27.2%; males literate 39.0%; females literate 16.0%.
Health (1989): physicians 48 (1 per 17,604 persons); hospital beds (1981) 756 (1 per 865 persons); infant mortality rate per 1,000 live births (1990–95) 132.
Food (1987–89): daily per capita caloric intake 2,351 (vegetable products 94%, animal products 6%); 99% of FAO recommended minimum requirement.

Military

Total active duty personnel (1991): 900. *Military expenditure as percentage of GNP* (1989): 0.7% (world 4.9%); per capita expenditure U.S.$1.

---

[1]Includes 5 indirectly elected chiefs and 9 nonelective seats. [2]Preliminary. [3]Kombo St. Mary includes the fast-growing urban areas of Serekunda and Bakau. [4]Kombo St. Mary and Banjul city make up Greater Banjul. [5]Based on land area, which is 8,613 sq km (3,325 sq mi). [6]1983. [7]December; nonagricultural employees only. [8]Low-income population in Banjul and Kombo St. Mary only; weights of consumer price index components. [9]At factor cost in constant prices of 1976–77. [10]Indirect taxes less subsidies. [11]Not adequately defined. [12]Imports c.i.f.; exports f.o.b. [13]Mostly unofficial trade with Senegal. [14]1984–85.

Georgia

Official name: Sakartvelos Respublikis
  (Republic of Georgia).
Form of government: multiparty
  republic with a single legislative body
  (Parliament [234]).
Head of state: Chairman of State
  Council (president).
Head of government: Prime Minister.
Capital: Tbilisi.
Official language: Georgian.
Official religion: none.
Monetary unit: 1 ruble = 100 kopecks;
  valuation (Oct. 5, 1992)
  free rate, U.S.$ = 316.82 rubles;
  1 £ = 538.59 rubles.

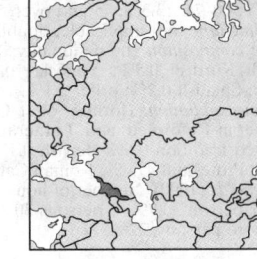

Area and population

		area		population
				1991[1]
Regions	Capitals	sq mi	sq km	estimate
Abkhaz	Sukhumi	3,300	8,600	533,800
Adzhar	Batumi	1,200	3,000	381,500
South Ossetia[2]	Tskhinvali	1,500	3,900	
Regions under republican jurisdiction	—	20,900	54,200	4,548,900
TOTAL		26,900	69,700	5,464,200

Demography

Population (1992): 5,482,000.
Density (1992): persons per sq mi 203.7, persons per sq km 78.7.
Urban-rural (1991): urban 56.2%; rural 43.8%.
Sex distribution (1989): male 47.2%; female 52.8%.
Age breakdown (1989): under 15, 24.8%; 15–29, 24.1%; 30–44, 19.2%; 45–59,
  17.5%; 60–74, 10.8%; 75 and over, 3.6%.
Population projection: (2000) 5,777,000; (2010) 6,101,000.
Doubling time: 77 years.
Ethnic composition (1989): Georgian 70.1%; Armenian 8.1%; Russian 6.3%;
  Azerbaijani 5.7%; Ossetes 3.0%; Greek 1.9%; Abkhazian 1.8%; other 3.1%.
Religious affiliation: believers are predominantly Georgian Orthodox (65%);
  minorities include Muslims (11%), Russian Orthodox (10%), and Armenian
  Orthodox (8%).
Major cities (1991): Tbilisi 1,283,000; Kutaisi 238,200; Rustavi 161,900; Batumi
  137,500; Sukhumi 120,000.

Vital statistics

Birth rate per 1,000 population (1990): 17.0 (world avg. 27.1); (1989) legiti-
  mate 82.3%; illegitimate 17.7%.
Death rate per 1,000 population (1990): 8.4 (world avg. 9.8).
Natural increase rate per 1,000 population (1990): 8.6 (world avg. 17.3).
Total fertility rate (avg. births per childbearing woman; 1989): 2.1.
Marriage rate per 1,000 population (1989): 7.2.
Divorce rate per 1,000 population (1989): 1.3.
Life expectancy at birth (1990): male 69.0 years; female 76.3 years.
Major causes of death per 100,000 population (1989): diseases of the cir-
  culatory system 553.2; diseases of the respiratory system 513.0; malignant
  neoplasms (cancers) 98.6; accidents, poisoning, and violence 58.2; diseases
  of the digestive system 32.1; infectious and parasitic diseases 13.5; endocrine
  and metabolic disorders 12.0; diseases of the nervous system 4.1.

National economy

Budget (1991). Revenue: 5,741,000,000 rubles (turnover tax 36.2%, profit tax
  25.3%, individual income tax 11.5%). Expenditures: 6,879,000,000 rubles
  (national economy 48.5%, social and cultural affairs 43.5%, government
  administration 3.6%, other 4.4%).
Public debt (external, outstanding): n.a.
Tourism: receipts from visitors, n.a.; expenditures by nationals abroad, n.a.
Production (metric tons except as noted). Agriculture, forestry, fishing (1990):
  grain 693,100,000, grapes 691,100, fruit (other than grapes) 592,200, crude tea
  501,700, vegetables (other than potatoes) 443,200, potatoes 293,800, citrus
  fruit 283,100, sugar beets 30,600, sunflower seeds 7,700; livestock (number
  of live animals; 1990) 1,834,000 sheep and goats, 1,427,000 cattle, 1,028,000
  pigs, 24,002,100 poultry; roundwood, n.a.; fish catch 104,000. Mining and
  quarrying (1990): manganese ore 1,316,000. Manufacturing (1990): crude
  steel 1,316,000; rolled ferrous metals 1,109,000; rolled steel 1,105,000; milk
  702,500; canned food 677,000; steel tubes 499,000; mineral fertilizers 130,-
  000; meat and sausage 96,200; synthetic resins and plastics 40,000; synthetic
  fibres 32,300; paper 28,200; soap 12,100; bricks 328,000,000 pieces; cement
  tiles 26,400,000 pieces; footwear 13,300,000 pairs; knitwear 49,600,000 units;
  magnetic stations 137,000 units; colour television sets 50,000 units; machine
  tools 1,565 units; prefabricated concrete structures 1,761,000 cu m; ceramic
  tiles 830,000 cu m; silk fabrics 45,000,000 sq m; cotton fabrics 34,100,000 sq
  m; wool fabrics 9,800,000 sq m; carpets 800,000 sq m; grape wine 1,628,300
  hectolitres; beer 947,700 hectolitres; cognac 216,500 hectolitres; vodka and
  liqueurs 82,200 hectolitres. Construction (1990): 1,313,000,000,000 rubles.
  Energy production (consumption): electricity (kW-hr; 1990) 14,200,000,000
  (n.a.); coal (metric tons; 1991) 700,000 (n.a.); crude petroleum (barrels;
  1991) 1,327,000 (n.a.); petroleum products (metric tons; 1990) 3,308,400
  (n.a.); natural gas (cu m; 1991) 44,900,000 (n.a.).

Gross national product (at current market prices; 1990): 10,865,700,000 rubles
  (2,000 rubles per capita)[3].

Structure of net domestic product and labour force

	1990		1988	
	in value '000,000 rubles	% of total value	labour force	% of labour force
Agriculture	4,045.8	37.2	640,300	26.0
Mining		...	...	...
Manufacturing	3,800.3	35.0	738,800	30.0
Public utilities			147,800	6.0
Construction	1,194.1	11.0	...	...
Transportation and communications	531.6	4.9	197,000	8.0
Trade	612.7	5.6	172,400	7.0
Finance	—	—	—	—
Public administration, defense	—	—	73,900	3.0
Services	—	—	492,500	20.0
Other	681.2	6.3	—	—
TOTAL	10,865.7	100.0	2,462,700	100.0

Population economically active (1990): total 2,834,000; activity rate of total
  population 51.9% (participation rates [1989]: ages 16–59 [male], 16–54 [fe-
  male] 90.1%; female 45.9%; unemployed 3.5%).

Price and earnings indexes (1985 = 100)

	1985	1986	1987	1988	1989	1990
Consumer price index	100.0	...	...	...	...	...
Monthly earnings index	100.0	101.8	105.7	111.4	126.4	144.4

Land use (1990): forested 0.4%; meadows and pastures 28.6%; agricultural
  and under permanent cultivation 1.2%; other 69.8%.
Household income and expenditure. Average household size (1989) 4.1; income per household: n.a.; sources of income (1988): wages and salaries
  71.4%, pensions and stipends 10.8%, income from personal plots 7.3%,
  other 10.5%; expenditure (1988): food and beverages 38.3%, clothing and
  footwear 14.8%, social and cultural 9.2%, furniture and household utensils
  5.9%, building materials 2.0%, utilities 0.3%.

Foreign trade

Balance of trade (current prices)

	1988	1989	1990	1991
'000,000 rubles	−592	−385	−855	−1,154
% of total	4.8%	3.1%	6.7%	8.6%

Imports (1991): 7,266,000,000 rubles (machinery and equipment 18.4%, light-
  industry products 16.5%, food 14.6%, oil and gas 9.6%, chemicals 9.6%,
  ferrous metals 4.1%, nonferrous metallurgical products 3.3%). *Major import
  sources:* former Soviet republics 89.6%; other countries 10.4%.
Exports (1991): 6,112,000,000 rubles (food 34.5%, light-industry products
  19.3%, machinery and metalworking equipment 13.7%, ferrous metallurgy
  5.8%, chemicals 3.5%, building materials 1.1%). *Major export destinations:*
  former Soviet republics 98.0%; other countries 2.0%.

Transport and communications

Transport. Railroads (1990): length 976 mi, 1,570 km; (1989) passenger-mi
  10,600,000, passenger-km 17,000,000; cargo traffic, n.a. Roads (1989): length
  21,000 mi, 33,900 km (paved 87%). Vehicles (1988): passenger cars 427,400;
  trucks and buses, n.a. Merchant marine: vessels (1,000 gross tons and over)
  54; total deadweight tonnage 1,108,068. Air transport (1989): passenger-mi
  3,290,500,000, passenger-km 5,295,600,000; short ton-mi cargo, n.a., metric
  ton-km cargo, n.a.; airports (1992) with scheduled flights 1.
Communications. Daily newspapers (1989): total number 147; total circulation
  3,677,000; circulation per 1,000 population 671. Radio and television (1990):
  total number of receivers 3,760,000 (1 per 1.5 persons). Telephones: n.a.

Education and health

Education (1989–90)

	schools	teachers	students	student/ teacher ratio
Primary (age 6–13)	3,788	...	924,700	...
Secondary (age 14–17)				
Voc., teacher tr.	...	...	...	...
Higher	19	...	93,100	...

Educational attainment (1989). Percentage of population age 25 and over
  having: primary education or no formal schooling 12.3%; some secondary
  15.2%; completed secondary and some postsecondary 57.4%; higher 15.1%.
Literacy: total population age 15 and over literate, n.a.; males literate, n.a.;
  females literate, n.a.
Health (1990): physicians 32,100 (1 per 170 persons); hospital beds 60,000 (1
  per 90 persons); infant mortality rate per 1,000 live births 15.9.
Food: daily per capita caloric intake, n.a.

Military

Total active duty personnel (1992): 13,000 (army, n.a., navy, n.a., air force, n.a.).
  Military expenditure as percentage of GNP: n.a.; per capita expenditure, n.a.

---

[1]January 1. [2]In December 1990 the Supreme Soviet of the Republic of Georgia abolished the South Ossetian autonomous oblast. [3]No equivalent U.S.$ value is offered,
as Soviet GNP data are very speculative.

Germany

Official name: Bundesrepublik Deutschland (Federal Republic of Germany).
Form of government: federal multiparty republic with two legislative houses (Federal Council [68]; Federal Diet [662]).
Chief of state: President.
Head of government: Chancellor.
Seat of government: Bonn (Berlin is capital-designate).
Official language: German.
Official religion: none.
Monetary unit: 1 Deutsche Mark (DM) = 100 Pfennige; valuation (Oct. 5, 1992) 1 U.S.$ = DM 1.41; 1 £ = DM 2.39.

Area and population

States Administrative districts	Capitals	area sq mi	area sq km	population 1991[1] estimate
Baden-Württemberg	Stuttgart	13,804[2]	35,751[2]	9,822,000[2]
Freiburg	Freiburg	3,613	9,357	1,977,900
Karlsruhe	Karlsruhe	2,671	6,919	2,532,500
Stuttgart	Stuttgart	4,076	10,558	3,683,100
Tübingen	Tübingen	3,443	8,918	1,628,600
Bayern	Munich	27,241	70,554[2]	11,448,800
Mittelfranken	Ansbach	2,798	7,246	1,598,900
Niederbayern	Landshut	3,989	10,331	1,078,100
Oberbayern	Munich	6,768	17,529	3,801,400
Oberfranken	Bayreuth	2,792	7,231	1,074,900
Oberpfalz	Regensburg	3,742	9,691	1,009,000
Schwaben	Augsburg	3,858	9,993	1,627,500
Unterfranken	Würzburg	3,294	8,532	1,259,000
Berlin	—	343	889	3,433,700
Brandenburg	Potsdam	11,219	29,056	2,578,300
Bremen	Bremen	156	404	681,700
Hamburg	Hamburg	292	755	1,652,400
Hessen	Wiesbaden	8,152[2]	21,114	5,763,300
Darmstadt	Darmstadt	2,875	7,445	3,547,200
Giessen	Giessen	2,078	5,381	1,003,300
Kassel	Kassel	3,200	8,288	1,212,800
Mecklenburg-Vorpommern	Schwerin	9,096	23,559	1,924,000
Niedersachsen	Hannover	18,282	47,351[2]	7,387,200[2]
Braunschweig	Braunschweig	3,126	8,097	1,639,800
Hannover	Hannover	3,492	9,045	2,060,700
Lüneburg	Lüneburg	5,889	15,252	1,491,300
Weser-Ems	Oldenburg	5,775	14,958	2,195,500
Nordrhein-Westfalen	Düsseldorf	13,155[2]	34,070	17,349,700
Arnsberg	Arnsberg	3,088	7,999	3,732,000
Detmold	Detmold	2,516	6,517	1,895,400
Düsseldorf	Düsseldorf	2,042	5,288	5,220,500
Köln	Köln	2,844	7,365	4,025,300
Münster	Münster	2,664	6,901	2,476,500
Rheinland-Pfalz	Mainz	7,664	19,849	3,763,500
Koblenz	Koblenz	3,125	8,093	1,402,100
Rheinhessen-Pfalz	Mainz	2,637	6,830	1,877,400
Trier	Trier	1,902	4,926	484,000
Saarland	Saarbrücken	992	2,570	1,073,000
Sachsen	Dresden	7,081	18,341	4,764,300
Sachsen-Anhalt	Magdeburg	7,956	20,607	2,874,000
Schleswig-Holstein	Kiel	6,074	15,731	2,626,100
Thüringen	Erfurt	6,275	16,251	2,611,300
TOTAL		137,782	356,854[2]	79,753,200[2]

Demography

Population (1992): 80,293,000.
Density (1992): persons per sq mi 582.6, persons per sq km 224.9.
Urban-rural (1990): urban 85.3%; rural 14.7%.
Population projection: (2000) 83,231,000; (2010) 87,056,000.
Major cities (1990): Berlin 3,420,600; Hamburg 1,640,100; Munich 1,219,600; Cologne 950,200; Frankfurt am Main 641,300; Essen 626,100; Dortmund 597,400; Stuttgart 575,600; Düsseldorf 575,100; Leipzig 513,600.

Other principal cities (1990)

City	population	City	population	City	population
Aachen	239,200	Hannover	509,800	Nürnberg	490,500
Augsburg	254,300	Heidelberg	135,800	Oberhausen	223,400
Bergisch		Heilbronn	115,100	Offenbach am	
Gladbach	103,700	Herne	177,400	Main	114,400
Bielefeld	317,200	Hildesheim	104,800	Oldenburg	142,900
Bochum	395,100	Ingolstadt	103,600	Osnabrück	161,200
Bonn	289,500	Jena	102,700	Paderborn	118,600
Bottrop	118,200	Karlsruhe	272,800	Pforzheim	111,900
Braunschweig	257,600	Kassel	193,400	Potsdam	139,700
Bremerhaven	129,900	Kiel	244,800	Recklinghausen	124,600
Chemnitz	296,300	Koblenz	108,200	Regensburg	120,900
Cottbus	126,400	Krefeld	242,600	Remscheid	122,800
Darmstadt	138,300	Leverkusen	159,800	Reutlingen	102,800
Dresden	493,200	Lübeck	214,400	Rostock	248,800
Duisburg	533,600	Ludwigshafen		Saarbrücken	191,200
Erfurt	210,500	am Rhein	161,100	Salzgitter	113,600
Erlangen	101,500	Magdeburg	279,900	Schwerin	127,800
Freiburg		Mainz	178,000	Siegen	108,300
im Breisgau	189,300	Mannheim	308,400	Solingen	164,300
Furth	102,000	Moers	104,200	Ulm	109,900
Gelsenkirchen	292,200	Mönchenglad-		Wiesbaden	258,500
Gera	129,700	bach	258,000	Witten	105,100
Göttingen	120,900	Mülheim		Wolfsburg	127,600
Hagen	213,500	an der Ruhr	177,600	Wuppertal	381,100
Halle an der Saale	311,400	Münster	255,600	Würzburg	126,700
Hamm	178,200	Neuss	144,600	Zwickau	115,600

Sex distribution (1991): male 48.27%; female 51.73%.
Age breakdown (1991): under 15, 16.2%; 15–29, 22.2%; 30–44, 21.3%; 45–59, 19.9%; 60–74, 13.3%; 75 and over, 7.1%.
Doubling time: not applicable; doubling time exceeds 100 years.
Ethnic composition (by nationality; 1990): German 93.4%; Turkish 2.1%, of which Kurdish 0.5%; Yugoslav 0.8%; Italian 0.7%; Greek 0.4%; Polish 0.4%; Spanish 0.2%; other 2.1%.
Religious affiliation: (former West Germany; 1987) Roman Catholic 42.9%; Lutheran-Reformed and Lutheran traditions 41.6%; Muslim 2.7%; Reformed tradition 0.6%; Jewish 0.1%; other 12.9%; (former East Germany; 1990) Protestant 47.0%; Roman Catholic 7.0%; unaffiliated and other 46.0%.
Households (1990). Number of households 34,827,000; average household size 2.3; 1 person 33.7%, 2 persons 30.2%, 3 persons 17.5%, 4 persons 13.4%, 5 or more persons 5.2%.

Vital statistics

Birth rate per 1,000 population (1990): 11.4 (world avg. 27.1); legitimate 89.5%; illegitimate 10.5%.
Death rate per 1,000 population (1990): 11.6 (world avg. 9.8).
Natural increase rate per 1,000 population (1990): −0.2 (world avg. 17.3).
Total fertility rate (avg. births per childbearing woman; 1989)[3]: 1.5.
Marriage rate per 1,000 population (1990): 6.5.
Divorce rate per 1,000 population (1990): 1.6.
Life expectancy at birth: (former West Germany; 1986–88) male 72.2 years; female 78.7 years; (former East Germany; 1987–88): male 69.8 years; female 75.9 years.
Major causes of death per 100,000 population (1990): diseases of the circulatory system 508.6; malignant neoplasms (cancers) 260.3, of which stomach, colon, and rectum 57.9, bronchial, lung, and tracheal 43.3; diseases of the respiratory system 66.8, of which pneumonia 22.3, chronic bronchitis 18.7; chronic liver disease and cirrhosis 21.9.

Social indicators

Educational attainment (1989)[3]. Percentage of population age 25 and over having: less than full primary education 0.9%; primary and lower (junior) secondary 67.2%; primary and intermediate secondary 17.7%; vocational postsecondary and certification for higher education 14.2%, of which postsecondary vocational degree 6.6%, university graduates (all levels) 5.7%.
Quality of working life[3]. Average workweek (1990): 39.7 hours. Annual rate per 100,000 workers (1986) for: injuries or accidents at work 5,911; deaths, including commuting accidents 8.0. Proportion of labour force insured for damages or income loss resulting from: injury, virtually 100%; permanent disability, virtually 100%; death, virtually 100%. Average days lost to labour stoppages per 1,000 workers (1990): 1.3.

Distribution of income (1984)[3]

percentage of household income by quintile

1	2	3	4	5 (highest)
6.8	12.7	17.8	24.0	38.7

Access to services[3]. Proportion of dwellings (1987) having: electricity, virtually 100%; piped water supply, virtually 100%; flush sewage disposal 98.3%; public fire protection, virtually 100%.
Social participation. Eligible voters participating in last (December 1990) national election 77.8%. Trade union membership in total work force (1990): 37.7%. Practicing religious population (1989)[3]: 5% of Protestants and 25% of Catholics "regularly" attend religious services.
Social deviance (1990)[3]. Offense rate per 100,000 population for: murder and manslaughter 4; sexual abuse 59, of which child molestation 20, rape and forcible sexual assault 14; robbery 56; assault and battery 106; larceny 4,258. Incidence per 100,000 in general population (late 1970s) of: alcoholism 2,500 to 3,000; drug and substance abuse 650; suicide 19[4].
Material well-being (1988)[3]. Households possessing: automobile 67.8%; telephone 93.2%; colour television receiver 87.4%; refrigerator, virtually 100%; washing machine 85.7%; home freezer 51.7%.

Recreational and leisure activities
(Monthly household expenditures, 1990; medium income)[3]

Activity	DM	percentage
Vacations	159	25.0
Expenditures for motor vehicles	85	13.3
Sporting and camping equipment and sporting events	83	13.0
Televisions, radios, and their fees	79	12.4
Books, newspapers, and magazines	53	8.3
Gardening and pets	45	7.1
Games and toys	30	4.7
Photographic and movie-making equipment and film	17	2.7
Visits to theatre and cinema	15	2.4
Tools	7	1.1
Other activities	64	10.0
TOTAL	637	100.0

National economy

Budget (1991). Revenue: DM 1,240,982,000,000 (1990; taxes 54.9%, social-security contributions 39.3%). Expenditures: DM 1,345,921,000,000 (1990; current transfers 43.0%, consumption 41.1%, debt interest payments 5.9%).
Total national debt (1992)[3, 5]: DM 596,760,000,000.
Production (value of production in DM except as noted; 1990–91). Agriculture[3], forestry, fishing: cereal grains 5,090,000,000, fruits 3,024,000,000, sugar beets 2,322,000,000, flowers and ornamental plants 2,260,000,000, grapes for wine 2,035,000,000, vegetables 1,561,000,000, nurseries 1,380,000,000, oilseed crops 1,231,000,000, potatoes 921,000,000; livestock: dairy cattle

13,922,000,000; pigs 9,221,000,000, beef cattle 8,121,000,000, chicken eggs 1,694,000,000, poultry 1,264,000,000; roundwood (1990) 75,021,000 cu m; fish catch (metric tons; 1990) 390,744. Mining and quarrying (metric tons; 1991): potash 26,105,000; iron ore 84,000; zinc 49,900; lead 7,300. Manufacturing (value added at factor cost in DM; 1990)[3]: capital equipment 298,827,000,-000, of which machinery 81,106,000,000, electrical equipment 79,700,000,000, transport equipment 67,761,000,000; chemicals (including pharmaceuticals) 57,187,000,000; food and beverages 34,552,000,000; calculators and computers 22,713,000,000; plastics and other synthetic products 18,042,000,000; iron founding 14,031,000,000; furniture and other wood products 12,821,000,000; stone and ceramic products 11,750,000,000; textiles 11,666,000,000; printing and copy machines 11,410,000,000; precision instruments 9,205,000,000; office equipment 8,441,000,000; clothing 7,534,000,000; paper and cardboard products 7,320,000,000; musical instruments and toys 3,392,000,000; fine pottery and ceramic products 2,482,000,000. Construction (1990)[3]: residential 4,848,000 sq m; nonresidential 35,906,000 sq m.

Service enterprises (1989)[3]

	no. of enterprises	no. of employees	weekly wage as a % of all wages	annual turnover (DM '000,000)
Gas	115	23,000	...	22,397
Water	162	19,000	...	3,947
Electrical power	471	238,000	...	123,848
Transport				
air	176	49,000	...	16,416
buses	5,724	149,000	...	11,858[4]
rail[6]	1	9,394	...	1,361
shipping	1,810	10,445	...	...
Communications				
press	2,481	248,000	...	32,797
film[7]	615	3,000	...	836
Postal services	17,616	515,190	...	52,050
Hotels and restaurants[8]	114,167	651,600	...	42,736
Wholesale trade	36,605	1,018,00	...	861,112
Retail trade[6]	159,794	2,153,000	...	524,565

Energy production (consumption): electricity (kW-hr; 1990) 572,002,000,-000 (573,302,000,000); hard coal (metric tons; 1990) 76,354,000 (85,032,-000); lignite (metric tons; 1990) 387,531,000 (389,427,000); crude petroleum (barrels; 1990) 26,328,000 (706,847,000); petroleum products (metric tons; 1990) 88,267,000 (108,827,000); natural gas (cu m; 1990) 19,010,000,000 (64,499,000,000).

Manufacturing, mining, and construction enterprises (1990)[3]

	no. of enterprises	no. of tradesmen and professionals	wages as a % of avg. of all wages[9]	annual gross production value (DM '000,000)
Manufacturing	38,367	7,252,000	101.4	1,804,566
of which				
Road motor vehicles	1,858	884,000	112.1	252,546
Machinery (nonelectric)	5,313	1,072,000	105.5	210,364
Machinery and appliances (electric)	2,967	1,109,000	103.1	210,102
Chemical	1,208	606,000	127.7	198,943
Food and beverages	3,942	477,000	84.5	179,081
Petroleum and natural gas	50	[10]	160.5	[10]
Calculators, computers	2,181	332,000	92.4	61,338
Plastics	2,043	271,000	87.0	54,782
Iron and steel	100	189,000	105.6	51,693
Textiles	1,226	208,000	101.2	40,313
Wood and wood products	2,126	206,000	86.5	37,897
Mining and quarrying	84	170,000	107.1	27,666
Construction	15,664	966,000	83.8	136,792

Gross national product (at current market prices; 1990)[3]: U.S.$1,495,679,000,-000 (U.S.$24,170 per capita).

Structure of gross domestic product and labour force[3]

	1991 in value DM '000,000	% of total value	labour force	% of labour force
Agriculture	30,180	1.2	930,000	3.0
Public utilities, mining	73,980	2.8	460,000	1.5
Manufacturing	780,330	30.0	9,100,000	29.8
Construction	145,470	5.6	1,970,000	6.4
Transp. and commun.	139,230	5.4	1,649,000	5.4
Trade	219,970	8.5	3,892,000	12.7
Finance, real estate	321,090	12.4	915,000	3.0
Services	450,360	17.3	5,955,000	19.5
Pub. admin., defense	271,160	10.4	4,302,000	14.1
Other (productive)	64,290	2.5	1,402,000	4.6
Other (accounting)	103,250	4.1	—	—
TOTAL	2,599,310	100.0[2]	30,575,000	100.0

Population economically active (1991): total 39,011,000; activity rate of total population 49.3% (participation rates [1989]: ages 15–64, 67.9%[3]; female [1990] 39.8%[3]; unemployed [1991] 6.7%).

Price and earnings indexes (1985 = 100)[3]

	1986	1987	1988	1989	1990	1991	1992
Consumer price index	99.9	100.1	101.4	104.2	107.0	110.7	116.1[11]
Hourly earnings index	103.5	107.6	111.1	112.4	116.5	122.5	130.2

Household income and expenditure[3]. Average household size (1990) 2.3; average annual income per household (1989) DM 50,948 (U.S.$30,008); sources of take-home income (1989): wages 81.9%, self-employment 10.3%, transfer payments 7.8%; expenditure (1989): food 23.8%, rent 20.9%, transportation 15.5%, entertainment and education 10.7%, household operations and maintenance 8.7%, clothing and footwear 8.0%.
Tourism (1990)[3]: receipts from visitors U.S.$10,683,000,000; expenditures by nationals abroad U.S.$29,836,000,000.

Financial aggregates[12]

	1986	1987	1988	1989	1990	1991	1992 (Oct.)
Exchange rate, DM per:							
U.S. dollar	1.9408	1.5815	1.7803	1.6978	1.4940	1.5160	1.5370
£	2.8617	2.9598	3.2215	2.7258	2.8804	2.8360	2.4116
SDR	2.3740	2.2436	2.3957	2.2312	2.1255	2.1685	2.1609
International reserves (U.S.$)							
Total (excl. gold; '000,000)	51,734	78,756	58,528	60,709	67,902	63,001	88,400
SDRs ('000,000)	2,020	1,964	1,857	1,804	1,880	1,917	1,937
Reserve pos. in IMF ('000,000)	3,848	3,900	3,346	3,043	3,056	3,567	3,448
Foreign exchange	45,866	72,893	53,324	55,862	62,967	57,517	83,015
Gold ('000,000 fine troy oz)	95.18	95.18	95.18	95.18	95.18	95.18	95.18
% world reserves	9.99	10.05	10.04	10.10	10.12	10.13	10.22[13]
Interest and prices							
Central bank discount (%)	3.5	2.5	3.5	6.0	6.0	8.0	8.3
Govt. bond yield (%)	5.9	5.8	6.1	7.1	8.9	8.6	7.5
Industrial share prices (1985 = 100)[14]	135.2	124.5	104.0	133.0	152.8	135.8	122.2[13]
Balance of payments (U.S.$'000,000,000)							
Balance of visible trade	+55.75	+70.21	+79.78	+77.74	+71.70	+23.53	+13.20[15]
Imports, f.o.b.	175.27	208.28	228.85	247.22	319.61	354.49	182.18[15]
Exports, f.o.b.	231.02	278.49	308.63	324.96	391.31	378.02	195.38[15]
Balance of invisibles	−15.67	−23.92	−29.13	−20.09	−25.44	−43.01	−25.35[15]
Balance of payments, current account	+40.09	+46.28	+50.65	+57.65	+46.27	−19.48	−12.15[15]

Land use (1990): forest 29.8%; pasture 16.1%; agriculture 35.5%; other 18.6%.

Foreign trade

Balance of trade (current prices)[3]

	1986	1987	1988	1989	1990	1991
DM '000,000,000	+123.45	+127.88	+139.23	+147.85	+118.90	+15.31
% of total	13.3%	13.8%	13.9%	13.0%	9.9%	1.2%

Imports (1991)[3]: DM 633,054,000,000 (machinery and transport equipment 35.1%, of which transport equipment 10.2%, electrical machinery other than office equipment 8.1%, office equipment 4.4%; chemicals and chemical products 8.4%, of which organic chemical products 2.1%, unfabricated plastics 1.7%; food and beverages 8.3%, of which fruits and vegetables 3.2%, meat and meat products 1.3%, milk and milk products 0.9%; mineral fuels 8.1%, of which crude petroleum and petroleum products 6.2%, natural gas 1.6%; clothing and wearing apparel 6.2%; thread, yarn, and finished spinning goods 3.1%; iron and steel 3.1%). Major import sources: France 12.2%; The Netherlands 9.7%; Italy 9.3%; Belgium-Luxembourg 7.1%; United Kingdom 6.6%; United States 6.6%; Japan 6.2%; Austria 4.2%; Switzerland 3.9%.
Exports (1991)[3]: DM 648,363,000,000 (machinery and transport equipment 49.0%, of which transport equipment 15.4%, electrical machinery other than office equipment 9.0%, office equipment 2.4%; chemicals and chemical products 12.7%, of which organic chemical products 2.7%, unfabricated plastics 2.2%, medical and pharmaceutical products 1.6%). Major export destinations: France 13.1%; Italy 9.2%; United Kingdom 7.6%; The Netherlands 8.4%; Belgium-Luxembourg 7.3%; United States 6.3%; Austria 5.9%; Switzerland 5.7%; Spain 4.0%; Japan 2.5%; Sweden 2.3%.

Transport and communications

Transport. Railroads (1990): length 56,397 mi, 90,760 km; passengers carried 1,134,000,000[3]; passenger-mi 27,706,000,000[3], passenger-km 44,588,000,000[3]; short ton-mi cargo 43,058,000,000[3], metric ton-km cargo 62,864,000,000[3]. Roads (1989)[3]: total length 308,614 mi, 496,652 km (paved 99%). Vehicles (1990): passenger cars 35,512,000; trucks and buses 2,764,000. Merchant marine (1991): vessels (100 gross tons and over) 1,522; total deadweight tonnage 7,323,603. Air transport (1989)[3]: passengers carried 56,000,000; passenger-mi 22,566,000,000, passenger-km 36,316,000,000; short ton-mi cargo 2,630,000,000, metric ton-km cargo 3,840,000,000; airports (1992) with scheduled flights 40.
Communications. Daily newspapers (1990)[3]: total number 350; total circulation 25,088,000; circulation per 1,000 population 401. Radio (1991): 32,000,-000 receivers (1 per 2.5 persons). Television (1991): 45,150,000 receivers (1 per 2.1 persons). Telephones (1989): 43,095,000 (1 per 1.8 persons).

Education and health

Education (1990–91)

	schools	teachers	students	student/teacher ratio
Primary (age 6–10) } Secondary (age 10–19)	38,294	493,004	8,962,461	18.2
Voc., teacher tr.	8,110	116,343	2,557,881	22.0
Higher	312	370,134[3]	1,782,738	4.4[3]

Health (1991): physicians 244,238 (1 per 324 persons); dentists 54,972 (1 per 1,441 persons); hospital beds 833,055 (1 per 95 persons); infant mortality rate per 1,000 live births 7.5.
Food (1987–89): daily per capita caloric intake 3,648 (vegetable products 64%, animal products 36%); 137% of FAO recommended minimum requirement.

Military

Total active duty personnel (1992): 447,000 (army 70.6%, navy 7.9%, air force 21.4%). Military expenditure as percentage of GNP (1989)[3]: 2.8% (world 4.9%); per capita expenditure U.S.$544.

[1]January 1. [2]Detail does not add to total given because of rounding. [3]Former West Germany only. [4]1987. [5]August. [6]1988. [7]1984. [8]1986. [9]1989. [10]Data withheld for reasons of confidentiality. [11]October. [12]End-of-period figures unless footnoted otherwise. [13]September. [14]Period averages. [15]Through June.

Ghana

Official name: Republic of Ghana.
Form of government: military regime[1].
Head of state and government:
  Chairman of the Provisional
  National Defense Council[1].
Capital: Accra.
Official language: English.
Official religion: none.
Monetary unit: 1 cedi (₵) = 100
  pesewas; valuation (Oct. 5, 1992)
  1 U.S.$ = ₵485.29; 1 £ = ₵825.00.

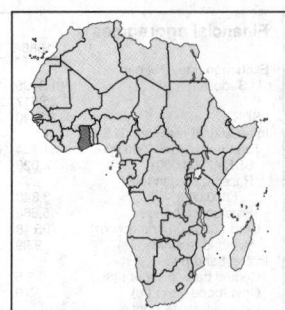

Area and population

Regions	Capitals	area sq mi	area sq km	population 1988 estimate[2]
Ashanti	Kumasi	9,417	24,389	2,308,100
Brong-Ahafo	Sunyani	15,273	39,557	1,332,200
Central	Cape Coast	3,794	9,826	1,262,200
Eastern	Koforidua	7,461	19,323	1,855,800
Greater Accra	Accra	1,253	3,245	1,580,000
Northern	Tamale	27,175	70,384	1,285,900
Upper East	Bolgatanga	3,414	8,842	853,200
Upper West	Wa	7,134	18,476	483,600
Volta	Ho	7,942	20,570	1,338,200
Western	Sekondi-Takoradi	9,236	23,921	1,278,300
TOTAL		92,098[3]	238,533	13,577,500

Demography

Population (1992): 15,237,000.
Density (1992): persons per sq mi 165.4, persons per sq km 63.9.
Urban-rural (1990): urban 33.0%; rural 67.0%.
Sex distribution (1990): male 49.64%; female 50.36%.
Age breakdown (1984): under 15, 45.0%; 15–29, 26.4%; 30–44, 14.6%; 45–59, 8.1%; 60–74, 4.1%; 75 and over, 1.8%.
Population projection: (2000) 18,733,000; (2010) 24,253,000.
Doubling time: 22 years.
Ethnolinguistic composition (1983): Akan 52.4%; Mossi 15.8%; Ewe 11.9%; Ga-Adangme 7.8%; Gurma 3.3%; Yoruba 1.3%; other 7.5%.
Religious affiliation (1980): Christian 62.6%, of which Protestant 27.9%, Roman Catholic 18.7%, African indigenous 16.0%; traditional beliefs 21.4%; Muslim 15.7%, of which Ahmadīyah 7.9%; other 0.3%.
Major cities (1988): Accra 949,100; Kumasi 385,200; Tamale 151,100; Tema 110,000; Sekondi-Takoradi 103,600.

Vital statistics

Birth rate per 1,000 population (1985–90): 44.4 (world avg. 27.1); legitimate, n.a.; illegitimate, n.a.
Death rate per 1,000 population (1985–90): 13.1 (world avg. 9.8).
Natural increase rate per 1,000 population (1985–90): 31.3 (world avg. 17.3).
Total fertility rate (avg. births per childbearing woman; 1985–90): 6.4.
Life expectancy at birth (1985–90): male 52.2 years; female 55.8 years.
Major causes of death per 100,000 population: n.a.; however, major infectious diseases include malaria, tuberculosis, leprosy, trypanosomiasis (sleeping sickness), and onchocerciasis (river blindness).

National economy

Budget (1990). Revenue: ₵267,347,000,000 (income taxes 19.3%, of which corporate 12.2%, personal 4.1%; import duties 13.5%; grants and loans 10.4%; export duty on cocoa 9.8%). Expenditures: ₵254,473,000,000 (current expenditures 79.1%, of which education 25.5%, debt service 10.7%, health 10.1%, social security and welfare 7.2%, defense 3.5%, transportation and communications 1.3%; capital expenditures 20.9%).
Public debt (external, outstanding; 1990): U.S.$2,770,000,000.
Production (metric tons except as noted). Agriculture, forestry, fishing (1990): roots and tubers 4,409,000 (of which cassava 2,717,000, yams 877,000, taro 815,000), cereals 845,000 (of which corn [maize] 553,000, sorghum 136,000, rice 81,000, millet 75,000), bananas and plantains 799,000, cocoa 284,400, coconuts 200,000[4], green peppers 146,000, peanuts (groundnuts) 113,000, sugarcane 110,000[4], oranges 50,000[4], lemons and limes 30,000[4], palm kernels 30,000[4], pulses 14,300; livestock (number of live animals) 2,600,000 goats, 2,433,000 sheep, 1,250,000 cattle, 614,000 pigs, 10,000,000 chickens; roundwood 17,169,000 cu m; fish catch (1989) 361,734 (of which anchovies 76,348). Mining and quarrying (1991): bauxite 324,313; manganese ore 319,777; gold 26,310 kg; diamonds 687,736 carats. Manufacturing (1990): cement 678,600; kerosene, gasoline, and diesel fuel 526,100; wheat flour 108,422; soap 35,065; cocoa cake, cocoa butter, and cocoa liquor 23,208; margarine 3,560; iron rods 382; toothpaste 213; textiles 29,500,000 metres; soft drinks 3,350,000 hectolitres; beer 628,000 hectolitres; evaporated milk 208,000 hectolitres; ice cream 9,930 hectolitres; cigarettes 1,805,000,000 units. Construction (value added in ₵'000; 1988): 26,446,700. Energy production (consumption): electricity (kW-hr; 1991) 6,108,688,000 ([1990] 5,003,000,000); coal (metric tons; 1990) none (3,000); crude petroleum (barrels; 1990) none (7,433,000); petroleum products (metric tons; 1990) 503,000 (609,000); natural gas, none (n.a.).
Household income and expenditure. Average household size (1983) 4.9; average annual income per household (1978) ₵9,600 (U.S.$[5]); sources of income: n.a.; expenditure (1978): food and beverages 57.4%, clothing and footwear 14.3%, housing and energy 11.5%, transportation and communications 3.3%, health care 1.3%.

Gross national product (1990): U.S.$5,824,000,000 (U.S.$390 per capita).

Structure of gross domestic product and labour force

	1990 in value ₵'000,000	1990 % of total value	1984 labour force	1984 % of labour force
Agriculture	972,323.8	47.9	3,310,967	59.4
Mining	35,824.2	1.8	26,828	0.5
Manufacturing	187,523.9	9.2	588,418	10.5
Construction	62,210.7	3.1	64,686	1.2
Public utilities	36,612.4	1.6	15,437	0.3
Transp. and commun.	89,417.2	4.4	122,806	2.2
Trade	385,808.8	19.0	792,147	14.2
Finance	78,421.2	3.9	27,475	0.5
Pub. admin., defense	172,012.8	8.5	97,548	1.7
Services	2,158.4	0.1	376,168	6.7
Other	9,372.9[6]	0.5[6]	157,624[7]	2.8[7]
TOTAL	2,031,686.3	100.0[3]	5,580,104	100.0

Tourism (1990): receipts from visitors U.S.$82,000,000; expenditures by nationals abroad U.S.$13,000,000.
Population economically active (1984): total 5,580,104; activity rate of total population 45.4% (participation rates: over age 15, 82.5%; female 51.2%; unemployed 2.8%).

Price and earnings indexes (1985 = 100)

	1985	1986	1987	1988	1989	1990	1991
Consumer price index	100.0	124.6	174.2	228.8	286.5	393.2	464.1
Monthly earnings index	100.0	167.3	258.4	...	...	...	...

Land use (1989): forested 35.4%; meadows and pastures 21.7%; agricultural and under permanent cultivation 11.8%; other 31.1%.

Foreign trade

Balance of trade (current prices)

	1984	1985	1986	1987	1988	1989
₵'000,000	+637.1	−4,070.0	+11,578.0	+7,594.0	+32,080	−49,087
% of total	1.6%	5.8%	8.1%	2.6%	8.5%	8.2%

Imports (1989): ₵346,218,000,000 (1987; machinery and transport equipment 28.1%; mineral fuels and lubricants 14.0%; chemicals 12.0%; food and live animals 5.2%; beverages and tobacco 0.4%). *Major import sources* (1987): United Kingdom 41.4%; Nigeria 13.2%; West Germany 11.5%; United States 11.1%; Japan 4.3%; France 3.8%.
Exports (1989): ₵274,784,000,000 (1986; food and live animals 60.4%, of which cocoa 53.9%; logs and sawn timber 17.9%; gold 15.5%; manganese ore 1.1%; industrial diamonds 0.7%). *Major export destinations* (1987): United Kingdom 27.0%; United States 18.6%; The Netherlands 13.5%; U.S.S.R. 9.2%; Japan 9.0%; West Germany 8.3%.

Transport and communications

Transport. Railroads (1990): route length[4] 592 mi, 953 km; passenger-mi 172,400,000, passenger-km 277,500,000; short ton-mi cargo 86,920,000, metric ton-km cargo 126,900,000. Roads (1985): total length 17,600 mi, 28,300 km (paved 20%). Vehicles (1986): passenger cars 60,000; trucks and buses 46,000. Merchant marine (1991): vessels (100 gross tons and over) 160; total deadweight tonnage 120,958. Air transport (1990): passenger-mi 253,270,-000, passenger-km 407,600,000; short ton-mi cargo 45,753,000, metric ton-km cargo 66,798,000; airports (1992) with scheduled flights 3.
Communications. Daily newspapers (1989): total number 3; total circulation 180,000; circulation per 1,000 population 13. Radio (1991): 3,142,000 receivers (1 per 4.7 persons). Television (1991): 175,000 receivers (1 per 85 persons). Telephones (1989): 77,105 (1 per 189 persons).

Education and health

Education (1988–89)

	schools	teachers	students	student/ teacher ratio
Primary (6–12)	9,634	65,826	1,705,843	25.9
Secondary (13–20)	5,702[8]	43,112	763,167	17.7
Voc., teacher tr.	137[8]	2,317	30,221	13.0
Higher	3	1,160[9]	9,582[10]	

Educational attainment (1984). Percentage of population age 25 and over having: no formal schooling 60.4%; primary education 7.1%; middle school 25.4%; secondary 3.5%; vocational and other postsecondary 2.9%; higher 0.6%. *Literacy* (1990): total population age 15 and over literate 4,960,000 (60.4%); males literate 2,835,000 (70.0%); females literate 2,125,000 (50.9%).
Health: physicians (1989) 628 (1 per 22,452 persons); hospital beds (1991) 18,477 (1 per 791 persons); infant mortality rate per 1,000 live births (1985–90) 90.
Food (1987–89): daily per capita caloric intake 2,246 (vegetable products 95%, animal products 5%); 98% of FAO minimum recommended requirement.

Military

Total active duty personnel (1991): 11,900 (army 84.0%, navy 9.3%, air force 6.7%). *Military expenditure as percentage of GNP* (1989): 0.6% (world 4.9%); per capita expenditure U.S.$2.

---

[1]Following the approval by referendum of a multiparty constitution in April 1992, an 11-year ban on political parties was lifted; presidential elections were scheduled for November 1992. [2]January 1. [3]Detail does not add to total given because of rounding. [4]1989. [5]Unofficial 1978 exchange rate (7.5 to 9.9 times the official rate) does not permit meaningful conversion into other currencies. [6]Import duties less imputed bank service charges. [7]Unemployed only. [8]1985–86. [9]1986–87. [10]1990–91.

Greece

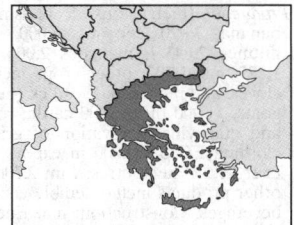

Official name: Ellinikí Dimokratía
(Hellenic Republic).
Form of government: unitary multiparty
republic with one legislative house
(Greek Chamber of Deputies [300]).
Chief of state: President.
Head of government: Prime Minister.
Capital: Athens.
Official language: Greek.
Official religion: Eastern Orthodox.
Monetary unit: 1 drachma (Dr) = 100
lepta; valuation (Oct. 5, 1992)
1 U.S.$ = Dr 181.40; 1 £ = Dr 308.38.

Area and population

Regions		area sq mi	area sq km	population 1991 census
Anatolikí Makedhonía kaí Thráki	(Eastern Macedonia and Thrace)	5,466	14,157	570,261
Attikí	(Attica)	1,470	3,808	3,522,769
Dhytikí Ellás	(Western Greece)	4,382	11,350	702,027
Dhytikí Makedhonía	(Western Macedonia)	3,649	9,451	292,751
Iónioi Nísoi	(Ionian Islands)	891	2,307	191,003
Ípiros	(Epirus)	3,553	9,203	339,210
Kedrikí Makedhonía	(Central Macedonia)	7,393	19,147	1,737,623
Kríti	(Crete)	3,218	8,336	536,980
Nótion Aiyaíon	(Southern Aegean)	2,041	5,286	257,522
Pelopónnisos	(Peloponnesos)	5,981	15,490	605,663
Stereá Ellás	(Central Greece)	6,004	15,549	578,876
Thessalía	(Thessaly)	5,420	14,037	731,230
Vóreion Aiyaíon	(Northern Aegean)	1,481	3,836	198,241
TOTAL		50,949	131,957	10,264,156

Demography

Population (1992): 10,288,000.
Density (1992): persons per sq mi 201.9, persons per sq km 78.0.
Urban-rural (1990): urban 62.5%; rural 37.5%.
Sex distribution (1991): male 49.00%; female 51.00%.
Age breakdown (1988): under 15, 19.8%; 15–29, 22.1%; 30–44, 19.8%; 45–59,
19.2%; 60–74, 13.1%; 75 and over, 6.0%.
Population projection: (2000) 10,406,000; (2010) 10,463,000.
Doubling time: not applicable; doubling time exceeds 100 years.
Ethnic composition (1983): Greek 95.5%; Macedonian 1.5%; Turkish 0.9%;
Albanian 0.6%; other 1.5%.
Religious affiliation (1980): Christian 98.1%, of which Greek Orthodox 97.6%,
Roman Catholic 0.4%, Protestant 0.1%; Muslim 1.5%; other 0.4%.
Major cities (1991): Athens 748,110; Thessaloníki 377,951; Piraiévs 169,622;
Pátrai 155,180; Peristérion 145,854.

Vital statistics

Birth rate per 1,000 population (1990): 10.1 (world avg. 27.1); legitimate
97.8%; illegitimate 2.2%.
Death rate per 1,000 population (1990): 9.2 (world avg. 9.8).
Natural increase rate per 1,000 population (1990): 0.9 (world avg. 17.3).
Total fertility rate (avg. births per childbearing woman; 1989): 1.8.
Marriage rate per 1,000 population (1990): 5.8.
Divorce rate per 1,000 population (1989): 0.6.
Life expectancy at birth (1985): male 72.6 years; female 77.6 years.
Major causes of death per 100,000 population (1990): malignant neoplasms
(cancers) 189.4; cerebrovascular disease 178.7; diseases of pulmonary circu-
lation and other forms of heart disease 163.3; ischemic heart disease 118.2.

National economy

Budget (1990). Revenue: Dr 5,552,996,000,000[1] (indirect and excise taxes
33.4%, direct taxes 14.6%, European Community 0.7%). Expenditures: Dr
4,878,495,000,000 (1989; health and social insurance 20.4%, defense 10.2%,
education and culture 9.0%, police and other sectors 2.6%).
Public debt (1990): U.S.$12,852,900,000.
Tourism (1990): receipts from visitors U.S.$2,575,000,000; expenditures by
nationals abroad U.S.$1,088,000,000.
Production (metric tons except as noted). Agriculture, forestry, fishing (1990):
sugar beets 2,500,000, tomatoes 2,124,000, corn (maize) 1,700,000, grapes
1,600,000, wheat 1,580,000, olives 1,300,000, potatoes 1,100,000, oranges 610,-
000, barley 400,000, cotton 234,000, onions 165,000, tobacco 132,000, rice
100,000; livestock (number of live animals) 10,353,000 sheep, 5,904,000 goats,
1,160,000 pigs, 715,000 cattle, 168,000 asses, 27,000,000 chickens; roundwood
3,289,000 cu m; fish catch 128,867. Mining and quarrying (1990): bauxite
2,612,000; nickel ore 2,090,000; iron ore 474,700[2, 3]; zinc ore 51,500[3]; lead
ore 37,360[3]; manganese 11,500[3, 4]. Manufacturing (value added in Dr; 1990):
food, beverages, and tobacco 316,918,000,000; chemicals 226,054,000,000;
textiles 222,603,000,000; transport equipment 119,562,000,000; paper and
printing 104,770,000,000; clothing and footwear 99,948,000,000. Construction
(cu m authorized; 1989): residential 43,461,793; nonresidential 13,509,174.
Energy production (consumption): electricity (kW-hr; 1990) 35,002,000,000
(35,713,000,000); coal (metric tons; 1990) 51,896,000 (53,119,000); crude
petroleum (barrels; 1990) 5,549,000 (105,449,000); petroleum products (metric tons; 1990) 15,464,000 (13,165,000); natural gas (cu m; 1990) 101,278,000
(101,278,000).
Household income and expenditure. Average household size (1982) 3.3; income per household (1982) Dr 252,300 (U.S.$3,777); sources of income
(1989): property and entrepreneurial income 43.4%, wages and salaries
38.4%, transfer payments 17.9%, other 0.3%; expenditure (1989): food,

beverages, and tobacco 37.9%, transportation 13.4%, clothing and footwear
9.3%, housing 8.4%, other 31.0%.
Gross national product (1990): U.S.$60,245,000,000 (U.S.$6,000 per capita).

Structure of gross domestic product and labour force

	1990 in value Dr '000,000	1990 % of total value	1988 labour force	1988 % of labour force
Agriculture	1,446,955	15.7	972,000	24.5
Mining	136,673	1.5	22,500	0.6
Manufacturing	1,498,727	16.3	706,500	17.8
Construction	629,302	6.8	231,700	5.8
Public utilities	251,534	2.7	34,900	0.9
Transp. and commun.	702,314	7.6	241,900	6.1
Trade	1,387,653[5]	15.0[5]	600,800	15.2
Finance		[5]	160,400	4.0
Pub. admin., defense	1,811,243	19.6 }	685,700	17.3
Services	766,879	8.3 }		
Other	583,813[6]	6.3[6]	304,400[7]	7.7[7]
TOTAL	9,215,096[8]	100.0[8]	3,960,800	100.0[8]

Population economically active (1988): total 3,960,800; activity rate of total
population 39.6% (participation rates: ages [1985] 15–64, 57.5%; female
36.8%; unemployed 7.7%).

Price and earnings indexes (1985 = 100)

	1985	1986	1987	1988	1989	1990	1991
Consumer price index	100.0	123.0	143.2	162.5	184.9	222.6	265.9
Hourly earnings index	100.0	112.7	123.5	146.3	176.3	210.5	...

Land use (1989): forested 20.0%; meadows and pastures 40.2%; agricultural
and under permanent cultivation 30.0%; other 9.8%.

Foreign trade

Balance of trade (current prices)

	1986	1987	1988	1989	1990	1991
Dr '000,000,000	−614.8	−688.4	−861.4	−1,199.2	−1,613.3	−1,886.1
% of total	28.0%	28.1%	33.8%	30.8%	44.3%	37.3%

Imports (1991): Dr 3,921,522,300,000 (machinery and transport equipment
32.9%, of which automobiles 7.1%; food, beverages, and tobacco 12.7%,
of which dairy products 1.1%, meat products 1.0%, coffee 0.3%; chemical
products 10.4%, of which medicinal and pharmaceutical products 0.5%;
crude petroleum 6.3%). *Major import sources:* Germany 19.4%; Italy 14.2%;
France 7.8%; Japan 6.6%; The Netherlands 6.0%; United Kingdom 5.4%;
United States 4.3%; Belgium-Luxembourg 3.4%.
Exports (1991): Dr 1,579,967,200 (food, beverages, and tobacco 27.9%, of
which tobacco 4.0%, olive oil 2.4%, olives 1.1%; clothing and footwear
21.5%; petroleum products 7.8%; textiles 4.1%; furs and raw skins 0.9%).
Major export destinations: Germany 23.9%; Italy 16.7%; France 7.5%; United
Kingdom 6.8%; United States 5.7%; The Netherlands 3.4%.

Transport and communications

Transport. Railroads (1990): route length[2] 1,540 mi, 2,479 km; passenger-mi
939,500,000[9], passenger-km 1,512,000,000[9]; short ton-mi cargo 443,000,000,
metric ton-km cargo 648,000,000. Roads (1990): total length 80,800 mi, 130,-
000 km (paved 79%). Vehicles (1990): passenger cars 1,691,070; trucks and
buses 781,320. Merchant marine (1991): vessels (100 gross tons and over)
1,863; total deadweight tonnage 41,691,685. Air transport (1990): passenger-
mi 4,824,000,000, passenger-km 7,764,000,000; short ton-mi cargo 84,158,000,
metric ton-km cargo 122,868,000; airports (1992) with scheduled flights 33.
Communications. Daily newspapers (1989): total number 147; total circulation
1,162,100[10]; circulation per 1,000 population, n.a. Radio (1991): 4,085,492
receivers (1 per 2.5 persons). Television (1991): 2,300,000 receivers (1 per
4.5 persons). Telephones (1989): 4,522,834 (1 per 2.2 persons).

Education and health

Education (1987–88)

	schools	teachers	students	student/ teacher ratio
Primary (age 6–12)	8,178	39,125	868,335	22.2
Secondary (age 12–18)	2,765[11]	44,887	708,549	15.8
Voc., teacher tr.	506[11]	7,435	117,193	15.8
Higher	82[11]	12,760	189,173	14.8

Educational attainment (1981). Percentage of population age 25 and over having: no formal schooling (illiterate) 11.4%; some primary education 16.8%;
completed primary 44.1%; lower secondary 6.0%; higher secondary 13.5%;
some postsecondary 2.5%; a degree from institution of higher education
4.9%. *Literacy* (1990): total population age 15 and over literate 7,550,000
(93.2%); males literate 3,925,000 (97.6%); females literate 3,625,000 (89.1%).
Health: physicians (1987) 33,290 (1 per 300 persons); hospital beds (1989) 51,-
448 (1 per 197 persons); infant mortality rate per 1,000 live births (1990) 9.7.
Food (1987–89): daily per capita caloric intake 3,793 (vegetable products
76%, animal products 24%); 143% of FAO minimum.

Military

Total active duty personnel (1991): 158,500 (army 71.3%, navy 12.3%, air
force 16.4%). *Military expenditure as percentage of GNP* (1989): 5.9% (world
4.9%); per capita expenditure U.S.$309.

---

[1]Includes Dr 2,728,065,000,000 of domestic borrowing. [2]1988. [3]Metal content of
ore. [4]1987. [5]Trade includes finance. [6]Income from ownership of buildings. [7]Includes
303,500 unemployed. [8]Detail does not add to total given because of rounding. [9]1989.
[10]For 33 dailies only. [11]1986–87.

Grenada

Official name: Grenada.
Form of government: constitutional monarchy with two legislative houses (Senate [13]; House of Representatives [15[1]]).
Chief of state: British Monarch represented by Governor-General.
Head of government: Prime Minister.
Capital: St. George's.
Official language: English.
Official religion: none.
Monetary unit: 1 East Caribbean dollar (EC$) = 100 cents; valuation (Oct. 5, 1992) 1 U.S.$ = EC$2.70; 1 £ = EC$4.59.

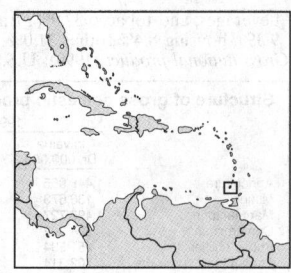

Area and population

		area		population
Local Councils	Principal towns	sq mi	sq km	1991 census[2]
Carriacou	Hillsborough	14[3]	37[3]	4,595
Petite Martinique	...	3	3	720
St. Andrew	Grenville	35	91	23,531
St. David	...	18	47	10,703
St. George	...	26[4]	67[4]	24,719
St. John	Gouyave	15	39	8,547
St. Mark	Victoria	9	23	3,785
St. Patrick	Sauteurs	17	44	9,652
Town				
St. George's	—	4	4	4,439
TOTAL		134	348	90,691

Demography

Population (1992): 90,900.
Density (1992): persons per sq mi 678.4, persons per sq km 261.2.
Urban-rural (1991)[5]: urban 32.2%; rural 67.8%.
Sex distribution (1991): male 49.35%; female 50.65%.
Age breakdown (1988): under 15, 35.9%; 15–29, 28.5%; 30–44, 14.2%; 45–59, 8.5%; 60 and over, 11.3%; not stated, 1.6%.
Population projection: (2000) 92,000; (2010) 94,000.
Doubling time: 28 years.
Ethnic composition (1991): black 82.0%; mixed 13.0%; white 1.0%; other 4.0%.
Religious affiliation (1980): Roman Catholic 59.3%; Protestant 34.5%, of which Anglican 17.1%, Seventh-day Adventist 5.7%, Pentecostal 3.9%; other 6.2%.
Major localities (1991): St. George's 4,439; Gouyave 2,980[6]; Grenville 2,100[6]; Victoria 2,000[6].

Vital statistics

Birth rate per 1,000 population (1989): 33.0 (world avg. 27.1); (1979) legitimate 22.5%; illegitimate 77.5%.
Death rate per 1,000 population (1989): 8.3 (world avg. 9.8).
Natural increase rate per 1,000 population (1989): 24.7 (world avg. 17.3).
Total fertility rate (avg. births per childbearing woman; 1990): 3.0.
Marriage rate per 1,000 population: n.a.
Divorce rate per 1,000 population: n.a.
Life expectancy at birth (1991): male 69.0 years; female 74.0 years.
Major causes of death per 100,000 population (1984): diseases of the circulatory system 290.3; malignant neoplasms (cancers) 90.5; endocrine and metabolic diseases 62.9; diseases of the respiratory system 54.1; accidents and violence 47.9; diseases of the digestive system 39.5.

National economy

Budget (1992). Revenue: EC$223,000,000 (current revenue 76.7%; development revenue 23.3%, of which foreign grants 11.9%, foreign loans 6.3%). Expenditures: EC$229,000,000 (current expenditures 77.3%, of which education 15.2%, public debt service 12.5%, health 11.7%, communications and public works 9.6%; development expenditures 22.7%).
Public debt (external, outstanding; 1990): U.S.$82,100,000.
Tourism: receipts from visitors (1991) U.S.$38,500,000; expenditures by nationals abroad (1990) U.S.$7,000,000.
Gross national product (at current market prices; 1990): U.S.$199,000,000 (U.S.$2,120 per capita).

Structure of gross domestic product and labour force

	1990		1988	
	in value EC$'000,000[7]	% of total value	labour force	% of labour force
Agriculture	47.1	15.4	5,560	14.3
Quarrying	1.3	0.4	111	0.3
Manufacturing	18.4	6.0	2,835	7.3
Construction	37.0	12.1	3,531	9.1
Public utilities	8.0	2.6	389	1.0
Transportation and communications	47.0	15.3	1,696	4.4
Trade, restaurants	62.1	20.2	5,421	13.9
Finance, real estate	33.3	10.9	778	2.0
Pub. admin., defense	54.8	17.9 }	5,949	15.3
Services	11.4	3.7 }		
Other	−13.7[8]	−4.5[8]	12,650[9]	32.5[9]
TOTAL	306.7	100.0	38,920	100.0[10]

Production (metric tons except as noted). Agriculture, forestry, fishing (1990): bananas 7,920, coconuts 7,000, sugarcane 6,000, roots and tubers 3,000, nutmeg 2,643[11], mangoes 2,000, avocados 2,000, grapefruit 2,000, cacao 1,875, mace 227, other crops include soursop, sapodilla plums, cinnamon, cloves, and pimiento; livestock (number of live animals) 15,000 sheep, 11,000 goats, 11,000 pigs, 5,000 cattle; roundwood, n.a.; fish catch 1,710[12]. Mining and quarrying: excavation of gravel for local use. Manufacturing (1989): clothing EC$3,800,000 in export sales; flour EC$2,100,000 in export sales; beer 21,000 hectolitres; rum 2,700 hectolitres[13]; cigarettes 23,000,000 units; other products include edible coconut oil, paints, retread tires, and aerated beverages. Construction: n.a. Energy production (consumption): electricity (kW-hr; 1990) 51,000,000 (51,000,000); coal, none (none); crude petroleum, none (none); petroleum products (metric tons; 1990) none (39,000); natural gas, none (none).
Household income and expenditure. Average household size (1991) 3.7; income per household (1988) EC$7,097 (U.S.$2,629); sources of income: n.a.; expenditure (weights of current price index components): food 59.0%, clothing and footwear 8.0%, housing 6.5%, household furnishings 6.5%, fuel and light 6.0%, transportation 4.0%, alcohol and tobacco 2.5%, other 7.5%.
Population economically active (1988): total 38,920; activity rate of total population 39.9% (participation rates: ages 15–65, 72.7%; female 48.6%; unemployed [1992] more than 30.0%).

Price and earnings indexes (1985 = 100)

	1984	1985	1986	1987	1988	1989	1990
Consumer price index	97.5	100.0	100.5	99.7	106.2	110.0	114.1
Earnings index[14]	...	...	...	...	...	...	...

Land use (1989): forested 8.8%; meadows and pastures 3.0%; agricultural and under permanent cultivation 38.2%; other 50.0%.

Foreign trade[15]

Balance of trade (current prices)

	1985	1986	1987	1988	1989	1990
U.S.$'000,000	−46.9	−54.7	−56.7	−59.4	−72.5	−82.9
% of total	51.2%	48.7%	47.1%	47.5%	56.1%	61.0%

Imports (1990): U.S.$109,500,000 (food 25.4%, machinery and transport equipment 22.4%, basic manufactures 18.8%, chemicals and chemical products 9.0%). *Major import sources*[16]: United States 28.0%; Trinidad and Tobago 17.0%; United Kingdom 11.0%; Hong Kong 6.0%; Barbados 4.0%.
Exports (1990): U.S.$26,600,000 (nutmeg 25.1%, bananas 16.0%, cocoa beans 12.1%, mace 4.3%, fresh fruit 3.2%). *Major export destinations*[16]: United Kingdom 23.0%; United States 21.0%; Trinidad and Tobago 12.0%; Germany 5.0%; The Netherlands 4.0%.

Transport and communications

Transport. Railroads: none. Roads (1991): total length 700 mi, 1,127 km (paved 51%). Vehicles: n.a. Merchant marine (1991): vessels (100 gross tons and over) 3; total deadweight tonnage 484. Air transport (1990)[17]: passenger arrivals 109,212, passenger departures 110,595; cargo loaded 970 metric tons, cargo unloaded 467 metric tons; airports (1992) with scheduled flights 2.
Communications. Daily newspapers (1991): none[18]. Radio (1991): total number of receivers 80,000 (1 per 1.1 persons). Television (1991): total number of receivers 30,000 (1 per 3.0 persons). Telephones (1990): 10,930 (1 per 8.3 persons).

Education and health

Education (1989–90)

	schools	teachers	students	student/ teacher ratio
Primary (age 5–11)[19]	57	768	20,730	27.0
Secondary (age 12–16)	19	337	6,798	20.2
Vocational	...	...	...	...
Higher	2	91	559	6.1

Educational attainment (1981). Percentage of population age 25 and over having: no formal schooling 2.2%; primary education 87.8%; secondary 8.5%; higher 1.5%. *Literacy* (1988): total population age 15 and over literate 49,000 (85.0%).
Health (1990): physicians 56 (1 per 1,617 persons); hospital beds 325 (1 per 279 persons); infant mortality rate per 1,000 live births (1991) 29.0.
Food (1987–89): daily per capita caloric intake 2,657 (vegetable products 81%, animal products 19%); 110% of FAO recommended minimum requirement.

Military

Total active duty personnel (1990):[20]. *Military expenditure as percentage of GNP:* n.a.; per capita expenditure, n.a.

---

[1]Excludes the speaker who may be elected from outside its elected membership. [2]Preliminary. [3]Carriacou includes Petite Martinique. [4]St. George local council includes St. George's town. [5]Urban defined as St. George's town and St. George local council. [6]1979. [7]At prices of 1984. [8]Less imputed bank service charges. [9]Includes 1,752 persons in activities not adequately defined and 10,898 unemployed. [10]Detail does not add to total given because of rounding. [11]1991. [12]1989. [13]1986. [14]Wages in public service increased by an average of 22% between 1988 and 1990. [15]Imports c.i.f.; exports f.o.b. [16]Estimated percentages. [17]Point Salines airport. [18]Weekly newspapers (1991): total number 4; total circulation 12,000. [19]Includes preprimary. [20]The 632-member police force includes a paramilitary unit.

Guadeloupe

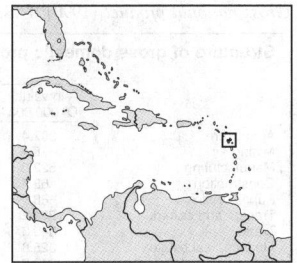

Official name: Département de la Guadeloupe (Department of Guadeloupe).
Political status: overseas department (France) with two legislative houses (General Council [42]; Regional Council [41]).
Chief of state: President of France.
Heads of government: Commissioner of the Republic (for France); President of the General Council (for Guadeloupe); President of the Regional Council (for Guadeloupe).
Capital: Basse-Terre.
Official language: French.
Official religion: none.
Monetary unit: 1 franc (F) = 100 centimes; valuation (Oct. 5, 1992) 1 U.S.$ = F 4.88; 1 £ = F 8.12.

Area and population

Arrondissements	Capitals	area		population
		sq mi	sq km	1990 census
Basse-Terre[1]	Basse-Terre	332	861	151,979
Pointe-à-Pitre[2]	Pointe-à-Pitre	297	769	192,643
Saint-Martin–Saint-Barthélemy[3]	Marigot	29	75	33,556
TOTAL		687[4]	1,780[4]	378,178[5]

Demography

Population (1992): 400,000.
Density (1992): persons per sq mi 582.2, persons per sq km 234.2.
Urban-rural (1990): urban 48.4%; rural 51.6%.
Sex distribution (1991): male 48.88%; female 51.12%.
Age breakdown (1991): under 15, 24.8%; 15–29, 29.5%; 30–44, 21.4%; 45–59, 12.5%; 60–74, 8.3%; 75 and over, 3.5%.
Population projection: (2000) 442,000; (2010) 507,000.
Doubling time: 52 years.
Ethnic composition (1980): Creole (mulatto) 77.0%; black 10.0%; Guadeloupe mestizo (French–East Asian) 10.0%; white 2.0%; other 1.0%.
Religious affiliation (1990): Roman Catholic 93.2%; other 6.8%.
Major communes (1990): Les Abymes 62,809; Saint-Martin 28,524; Pointe-à-Pitre 26,083 (141,000[6,7]); Le Gosier 20,708; Basse-Terre 14,000 (53,000[6]).

Vital statistics

Birth rate per 1,000 population (1990): 19.4 (world avg. 27.1); legitimate 38.9%; illegitimate 61.1%.
Death rate per 1,000 population (1990): 6.0 (world avg. 9.8).
Natural increase rate per 1,000 population (1990): 13.4 (world avg. 17.3).
Total fertility rate (avg. births per childbearing woman; 1990): 2.3.
Marriage rate per 1,000 population (1990): 5.2.
Divorce rate per 1,000 population (1990): 1.2.
Life expectancy at birth (1991): male 70.0 years; female 77.0 years.
Major causes of death per 100,000 population (1987): diseases of the circulatory system 216.0; malignant neoplasms (cancers) 118.0; accidents and violence 74.6; diseases of the digestive system 40.7; diseases of the respiratory system 29.1.

National economy

Budget (1991). Revenue: F 1,964,000,000 (receipts from French central government and local administrative bodies 38.2%, new loans 21.5%, subsidies for investments 10.6%, taxes on motor fuels 7.4%). Expenditures: F 1,964,-000,000 (capital investments and works 30.8%, health and social services 23.1%, debt amortization 7.4%).
Public debt (external, outstanding; 1988[8]): U.S.$41,000,000.
Tourism (1990): receipts from visitors U.S.$231,000,000; expenditures by nationals abroad, n.a.
Production (metric tons except as noted). Agriculture, forestry, fishing (1990): sugarcane 373,000, bananas 50,000, yams 12,000, sweet potatoes 7,000, plantains 5,000, tomatoes 4,000, pineapples 3,000, limes 2,000, melons 2,000, mangoes 2,000, eggplants 1,000, oranges 1,000, foliage and plants 60[9,10], cut flowers 29[9,10]; livestock (number of live animals) 84,000 goats, 65,000 cattle, 29,000 pigs; roundwood 17,000 cu m; fish catch (1989) 8,360. Mining and quarrying (1988): pozzolana 240,000. Manufacturing (1990): cement 291,144; rum 72,133 hectolitres; raw sugar 53,200[11]; other products include clothing, wooden furniture and posts, and metalware. Construction (buildings authorized): residential (1985) 239,000 sq m; nonresidential (1991) 217,761 sq m. Energy production (consumption): electricity (kW-hr; 1991) 824,000,000 (727,000,000); coal, none (none); crude petroleum, none (none); petroleum products (metric tons; 1990) none (336,000); natural gas, none (none).
Household income and expenditure. Average household size (1991) 3.4; income per household (1980) F 72,898 (U.S.$16,142); sources of income (1980): wages and salaries 76.8%, rent 4.0%, other 19.2%; expenditure (1984–85): food and beverages 29.8%, housing, household furnishings, and energy 26.3%, transportation and communications 13.3%, clothing and footwear 8.2%, other 22.4%.
Gross national product (at current market prices; 1987): U.S.$1,170,000,000 (U.S.$3,200 per capita).

Structure of gross domestic product and labour force

	1982		1986	
	in value F '000,000	% of total value	labour force	% of labour force
Agriculture	742	10.1	9,379	7.2
Mining and manufacturing	389	5.3	6,072	4.7
Construction	345	4.7	8,825	6.8
Public utilities	−50	−0.7	763	0.6
Transportation and communications	355	4.8	4,006	3.1
Trade	1,249	17.0	9,561	7.4
Finance, real estate	728	9.9	18,736	14.5
Pub. admin., defense	2,333	31.7 }	31,388	24.3
Services	1,105	15.0 }		
Other	162	2.2	40,641[12]	31.4[12]
TOTAL	7,358	100.0	129,371	100.0

Population economically active (1990): total 172,418; activity rate of total population 45.6% (participation rates: ages 15–64, 68.0%; female 45.5%; unemployed 31.1%).

Price and earnings indexes (1985 = 100)[13]

	1986	1987	1988	1989	1990	1991	1992[14]
Consumer price index	101.3	104.9	106.9	109.9	114.0	116.0	117.6
Monthly earnings index[15]	100.4	102.0	105.0	107.0	112.2	114.4	115.8

Land use (1989): forested 40.8%; meadows and pastures 16.0%; agricultural and under permanent cultivation 17.2%; other 26.0%.

Foreign trade

Balance of trade (current prices)

	1986	1987	1988	1989	1990	1991
F '000,000	−4,709	−5,665	−6,260	−6,995	−8,439	−8,209
% of total	75.9%	83.4%	77.5%	83.8%	86.3%	79.8%

Imports (1990): F 9,106,619,000 (consumer goods 27.0%; food and agriculture products 19.6%; machinery and equipment 16.5%; transport vehicles and parts 10.0%). *Major import sources:* France 65.6%; other EEC 12.8%; United States 4.1%; Japan 2.2%; Martinique 2.0%.
Exports (1990): F 667,880,000 (agricultural products 77.2%, of which bananas 30.1%, sugar 29.4%, consumer goods 6.7%; machinery and equipment 6.4%). *Major export destinations:* France 75.9%; Martinique 14.0%; other EEC 5.3%; French Guiana 3.6%.

Transport and communications

Transport. Railroads: none. Roads (1988): total length 1,301 mi, 2,093 km (paved [1986] 80%). Vehicles (1985): passenger cars 95,962; trucks and buses 28,134. Merchant marine (1990): vessels (100 gross tons and over) 13; deadweight tonnage, n.a. Air transport (1991)[16]: passenger arrivals 653,545, passenger departures 668,720; cargo loaded 7,434 metric tons, cargo unloaded 4,765 metric tons; airports (1992) with scheduled flights 5.
Communications. Daily newspapers (1991): total number 1; total circulation 25,000; circulation per 1,000 population 63. Radio (1991): total number of receivers 100,000 (1 per 4.0 persons). Television (1991): total number of receivers 150,000 (1 per 2.6 persons). Telephones (1991): 123,080 (1 per 3.2 persons).

Education and health

Education (1990–91)[17]

	schools	teachers	students	student/teacher ratio
Primary (age 6–10)	222	2,064	39,290	19.0
Secondary (age 11–17) }	75	3,237[18]	49,846[18]	15.4[18]
Vocational				
Higher[18, 19]	1	...	2,373	...

Educational attainment (1982). Percentage of population age 25 and over having: no formal schooling 10.7%; primary education 54.6%; secondary 29.5%; higher 5.2%. *Literacy* (1982): total population age 15 and over literate 225,400 (90.1%); males literate 108,700 (89.7%); females literate 116,700 (90.5%).
Health: physicians (1986) 491 (1 per 682 persons); hospital beds (1987) 3,391 (1 per 99 persons); infant mortality rate per 1,000 live births (1990) 10.0.
Food (1987–89): daily per capita caloric intake 2,720 (vegetable products 81%, animal products 19%); 112% of FAO recommended minimum requirement.

Military

Total active duty personnel (1991): 8,800 French troops[20].

[1]Comprises Basse-Terre 327 sq mi (848 sq km), pop. 149,943, and Îles des Saintes 5 sq mi (13 sq km), pop. 2,036. [2]Comprises Grande-Terre 228 sq mi (590 sq km), pop. 177,570; Marie-Galante 61 sq mi (158 sq km), pop. 13,463; La Désirade 8 sq mi (20 sq km), pop. 1,610; and the uninhabited Îles de la Petite-Terre. [3]Comprises the French part of Saint-Martin 20 sq mi (52 sq km), pop. 28,518; Saint-Barthélemy 8 sq mi (21 sq km), pop. 5,038; and the small, uninhabited island of Tintamarre. [4]Total area includes 29 sq mi (75 sq km) not allocated by arrondissement. [5]Preliminary; final 1990 census total was 386,987. [6]Urban agglomeration. [7]Includes Les Abymes. [8]Includes external long-term private debt not guaranteed by the government. [9]1989. [10]Export only. [11]1991. [12]Unemployed. [13]Base and indexes are end of year unless footnoted. [14]End of March. [15]Based on minimum-level wage of public employees. [16]Pointe-à-Pitre airport only. [17]Public schools only. [18]1988–89. [19]University of Antilles–French Guiana, Guadeloupe campus. [20]Includes Martinique and French Guiana.

Guatemala

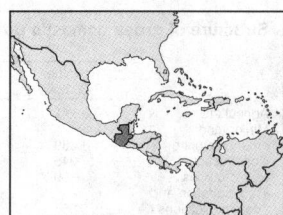

Official name: República de Guatemala (Republic of Guatemala).
Form of government: republic with one legislative house (Congress of the Republic [116]).
Head of state and government: President.
Capital: Guatemala City.
Official language: Spanish.
Official religion: none.
Monetary unit: 1 Guatemalan quetzal (Q) = 100 centavos; valuation (Oct. 5, 1992) 1 U.S.$ = Q 5.32; 1 £ = Q 9.04.

Area and population

Departments	Capitals	area sq mi	area sq km	population 1992 estimate[1]
Alta Verapaz	Cobán	3,354	8,686	610,714
Baja Verapaz	Salamá	1,206	3,124	189,510
Chimaltenango	Chimaltenango	764	1,979	353,877
Chiquimula	Chiquimula	917	2,376	257,355
El Progreso	Guastatoya (Progreso)	742	1,922	110,687
Escuintla	Escuintla	1,693	4,384	558,497
Guatemala	Guatemala City	821	2,126	2,074,462
Huehuetenango	Huehuetenango	2,857	7,400	740,371
Izabal	Puerto Barrios	3,490	9,038	336,971
Jalapa	Jalapa	797	2,063	195,849
Jutiapa	Jutiapa	1,243	3,219	362,215
Petén	Flores	13,843	35,854	266,793
Quetzaltenango	Quetzaltenango	753	1,951	573,651
Quiché	Santa Cruz del Quiché	3,235	8,378	593,158
Retalhuleu	Retalhuleu	717	1,856	246,067
Sacatepéquez	Antigua Guatemala	180	465	185,488
San Marcos	San Marcos	1,464	3,791	723,075
Santa Rosa	Cuilapa	1,141	2,955	273,519
Sololá	Sololá	410	1,061	249,761
Suchitepéquez	Mazatenango	969	2,510	371,726
Totonicapán	Totonicapán	410	1,061	306,144
Zacapa	Zacapa	1,039	2,690	164,737
TOTAL		42,042[2]	108,889	9,744,627

Demography

Population (1992): 9,442,000[1].
Density (1992): persons per sq mi 224.6, persons per sq km 86.7.
Urban-rural (1992): urban 38.3%; rural 61.7%.
Sex distribution (1989): male 49.00%; female 51.00%.
Age breakdown (1989): under 15, 46.2%; 15–29, 24.7%; 30–44, 15.1%; 45–59, 8.4%; 60–74, 4.4%; 75 and over, 1.2%.
Population projection: (2000) 11,809,000; (2010) 15,242,000.
Doubling time: 22 years.
Ethnic composition (1987): Amerindian 45%; Ladino (Hispanic/Amerindian) 45%; white 5%; black 2%; other mixed race and Chinese 3%.
Religious affiliation (1986): Roman Catholic c. 75%, of which Catholic/traditional syncretist c. 25%; Protestant (mostly fundamentalist) c. 25%.
Major cities (1992): Guatemala City 1,114,432; Mixco 368,940[3]; Villa Nueva 134,372; Chinautla 55,492; Amatitlan 35,714.

Vital statistics

Birth rate per 1,000 population (1989): 39.4 (world avg. 27.1).
Death rate per 1,000 population (1989): 7.3 (world avg. 9.8).
Natural increase rate per 1,000 population (1989): 32.1 (world avg. 17.3).
Total fertility rate (avg. births per childbearing woman; 1990): 5.4.
Marriage rate per 1,000 population (1988): 5.4.
Divorce rate per 1,000 population (1988): 0.2.
Life expectancy at birth (1985–90): male 59.7 years; female 64.4 years.
Major causes of death per 100,000 population (1984): infectious and parasitic diseases 211.5; diseases of the respiratory system 145.7, of which pneumonia 112.4; diseases of the circulatory system 57.2; malnutrition 45.3; homicide and other violence 35.1; ill-defined conditions 72.6.

National economy

Budget (1991). Revenue: Q 4,296,100,000 (tax revenue 81.2%, of which tax on goods and services 34.8%, income taxes 24.6%, customs duties 16.5%; nontax revenue 18.1%). Expenditures: Q 4,312,000,000 (1990: education 14.3%; defense 12.7%; transportation 8.2%; health 8.1%; agriculture 3.7%).
Tourism (1990): receipts from visitors U.S.$185,000,000; expenditures by nationals abroad U.S.$139,000,000.
Land use (1990): forested 34.6%; meadows and pastures 12.9%; agricultural and under permanent cultivation 17.4%; other 35.1%.
Production (metric tons except as noted). Agriculture, forestry, fishing (1991): sugarcane 9,797,000, corn (maize) 1,150,000, bananas 470,000, coffee 195,000, tomatoes 128,000, dry beans 110,000, seed cotton 110,000, sorghum 80,000, cottonseed 60,000, plantains 55,000; livestock (number of live animals) 1,695,000 cattle, 1,110,000 pigs, 675,000 sheep; roundwood (1990) 7,822,000 cu m; fish catch (1990) 6,894. Mining and quarrying (1990): iron ore 6,370; antimony ore 1,400. Manufacturing (value added in Q '000,000; 1989[3]): food products 138.0; beverages 66.2; clothing and footwear 47.6; textiles 43.2; metal products 30.2. Construction (value of buildings authorized in Q '000,000; 1991)[4]: residential 170.2; nonresidential 127.5. Energy production (consumption): electricity (kW-hr; 1990) 2,325,000,000 (2,325,000,000); crude petroleum (barrels; 1990) 1,262,000 (4,975,000); petroleum products (metric tons; 1990) 598,000 (962,000).

Gross national product (1990): U.S.$8,309,000,000 (U.S.$900 per capita).

Structure of gross domestic product and labour force

	1991 in value Q '000,000[3]	1991 % of total value	1989 labour force	1989 % of labour force
Agriculture	902.4	25.8	1,416,499	48.9
Mining	8.4	0.2	5,241	0.2
Manufacturing	522.0	14.9	388,301	13.4
Construction	68.7	2.0	114,246	3.9
Public utilities	88.0	2.5	11,784	0.4
Transp. and commun.	284.2	8.1	72,493	2.5
Trade	840.3	24.0	374,690	12.9
Finance, real estate	325.8	9.3	38,115	1.3
Pub. admin., defense	249.3	7.1 }	417,065	14.4
Services	212.2	6.1 }		
Other	—	—	59,882[5]	2.1[5]
TOTAL	3,501.3	100.0	2,898,316	100.0

Public debt (external, outstanding; 1990): U.S.$2,100,000,000.
Population economically active (1989): total 2,898,316; activity rate of total population 33.5% (participation rates: age 15–64, 59.1%; female 25.5%; unemployed 2.9%[6]).

Price and earnings indexes (1985 = 100)

	1985	1986	1987	1988	1989	1990	1991
Consumer price index	100.0	136.9	153.8	170.5	189.9	268.1	357.1
Annual earnings index[7]	100.0	117.0	144.2	193.1	229.0	263.5	333.6

Household income and expenditure. Average household size (1989) 5.4; income per household (1989): Q 4,306 (U.S.$1,529); sources of income: n.a.; expenditure (1981): food 64.4%, housing and energy 16.0%, transportation and communications 7.0%, household furnishings 5.0%, clothing 3.1%.

Foreign trade[8]

Balance of trade (current prices)

	1986	1987	1988	1989	1990	1991
U.S.$000,000	+185.2	−345.8	−391.5	−389.2	−207.4	−197.3
% of total	9.6%	14.9%	16.1%	14.9%	8.0%	7.5%

Imports (1990): U.S.$1,648,798,600 (primary and intermediate materials for industry 40.3%; capital goods 19.4%; nondurable consumer goods 12.8%; petroleum 10.0%). *Major import sources:* United States 39.5%; Venezuela 7.2%; Mexico 6.7%; Japan 6.0%; West Germany 5.6%.
Exports (1990): U.S.$1,162,970,100 (coffee 27.8%; sugar 10.4%; bananas 6.0%; vegetables 3.6%; fish, crustaceans, and mollusks 2.8%). *Major export destinations:* United States 38.7%; El Salvador 12.4%; Costa Rica 6.3%; West Germany 5.5%; Honduras 3.3%.

Transport and communications

Transport. Railroads (1990)[9]: route length 570 mi, 917 km; passenger-km 10,099,000; metric ton-km cargo 42,700,000. Roads (1990): total length 8,297 mi, 13,352 km (paved 26%). Vehicles (1990): passenger cars 130,000; trucks and buses 100,000. Merchant marine (1991): vessels (100 gross tons and over) 7; total deadweight tonnage 947. Air transport (1990)[10]: passenger-km 213,000,000; metric ton-km cargo 9,000,000; airports (1992) 2.
Communications. Daily newspapers (1988): total number 8; total circulation 186,500[11]; circulation per 1,000 population 22[11]. Radio (1991): 400,000 receivers (1 per 23 persons). Television (1991): 475,000 receivers (1 per 19 persons). Telephones (1990): 250,000 (1 per 36 persons).

Education and health

Education (1989)

	schools	teachers	students	student/ teacher ratio
Primary (age 7–12)	8,840	33,666	1,235,509	36.7
Secondary (age 13–18) } Voc., teacher tr.	1,541	17,313	297,437	17.2
Higher	5	4,346	69,532	16.0

Educational attainment (1989). Percentage of population age 25 and over having: no formal schooling 50.0%; incomplete primary education 21.6%; complete primary 16.2%; secondary 9.2%; higher 3.0%. *Literacy* (1989): total population age 15 and over literate 2,809,000 (60.3%); males literate 1,544,000 (69.7%); females literate 1,265,000 (51.7%).
Health (1987): physicians 3,579 (1 per 2,356 persons); hospital beds 13,667 (1 per 602 persons); infant mortality rate per 1,000 live births (1989) 43.6.
Food (1988–90): daily per capita caloric intake 2,254 (vegetable products 94%, animal products 6%); 103% of FAO recommended minimum requirement.

Military

Total active duty personnel (1992): 44,600 (army 94.2%, navy 2.7%, air force 3.1%). *Military expenditure as percentage of GNP* (1989): 1.6% (world 4.9%); per capita expenditure U.S.$15.

---

[1]Population of departments and cities taken from official projections based on 1973–81 intercensal growth rates and subsequent vital (birth and death) rates; 1992 national population estimate based on demographic surveys taken in October 1986–August 1987 and April–July 1989. [2]Detail does not add to total given because of rounding. [3]At prices of 1958. [4]Private construction in Guatemala City metro area only. [5]Includes 1,924 persons in activities not adequately defined and 57,958 officially unemployed. [6]Officially unemployed; 63% of economically active population is estimated to be underemployed. [7]Based on employees entitled to social security. [8]Import figures are f.o.b. in balance of trade and c.i.f. for commodities and trading partners. [9]Guatemala Railways only. [10]Aviateca Airlines only. [11]Five newspapers only.

Guinea

Official name: République de Guinée (Republic of Guinea).
Form of government: transitional[1] government (composed of a 15-member Transitional Committee for National Recovery).
Head of state and government: President (and Head of Transitional Committee for National Recovery)[1].
Capital: Conakry.
Official language: French.
Official religion: none.
Monetary unit: 1 Guinean franc (GF) = 100 cauris; valuation (Oct. 5, 1992) 1 U.S.$ = GF 811; 1 £ = GF 1,378.

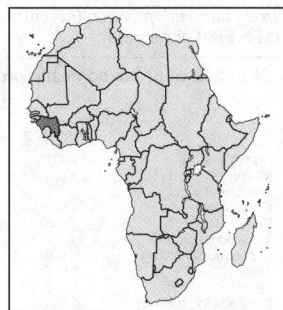

Area and population

Regions	Capitals	area sq mi	area sq km	population 1983 census
Beyla	Beyla	6,738	17,452	161,347
Boffa	Boffa	1,932	5,003	141,719
Boké[2]	Boké	3,881	10,053	225,207
Conakry	Conakry	119	308	705,280
Coyah (Dubréka)	Coyah	2,153	5,576	134,190
Dabola	Dabola	2,317	6,000	97,986
Dalaba	Dalaba	1,313	3,400	132,802
Dinguiraye	Dinguiraye	4,247	11,000	133,502
Faranah[2]	Faranah	4,788	12,400	142,923
Forécariah	Forécariah	1,647	4,265	116,464
Fria	Fria	840	2,175	70,413
Gaoual	Gaoual	4,440	11,500	135,657
Guéckédou	Guéckédou	1,605	4,157	204,757
Kankan	Kankan	7,104	18,400	229,861
Kérouané	Kérouané	3,070	7,950	106,872
Kindia	Kindia	3,409	8,828	216,052
Kissidougou	Kissidougou	3,425	8,872	183,236
Koubia	Koubia	571	1,480	98,053
Koundara	Koundara	2,124	5,500	94,216
Kouroussa	Kouroussa	4,647	12,035	136,926
Labé	Labé	973	2,520	253,214
Lélouma	Lélouma	830	2,150	138,467
Lola	Lola	1,629	4,219	106,654
Macenta	Macenta	3,363	8,710	193,109
Mali	Mali	3,398	8,800	210,889
Mamou	Mamou	2,378	6,160	190,525
Mandiana	Mandiana	5,000	12,950	136,317
Nzérékoré	Nzérékoré	1,460	3,781	216,355
Pita	Pita	1,544	4,000	227,912
Siguiri	Siguiri	7,626	19,750	209,164
Télimélé	Télimélé	3,119	8,080	243,256
Tougué	Tougué	2,394	6,200	113,272
Yomou	Yomou	843	2,183	74,417
TOTAL		94,926[3]	245,857	5,781,014

Demography

Population (1992): 7,232,000.
Density (1992): persons per sq mi 76.2, persons per sq km 29.4.
Urban-rural (1990): urban 25.6%; rural 74.4%.
Sex distribution (1990): male 50.17%; female 49.83%.
Age breakdown (1990): under 15, 46.7%; 15–29, 25.9%; 30–44, 15.0%; 45–59, 8.0%; 60 and over, 4.4%.
Population projection: (2000) 8,879,000; (2010) 11,451,000.
Doubling time: 27 years.
Ethnic composition (1983): Fulani 38.6%; Malinke 23.2%; Susu 11.0%; Kissi 6.0%; Kpelle 4.6%; other 16.6%.
Religious affiliation (1988): Muslim 85.0%; traditional beliefs 5.0%; Christian 1.5%; other 8.5%.
Major cities (1983): Conakry 705,280; Kankan 88,760; Labé 65,439; Kindia 55,904.

Vital statistics

Birth rate per 1,000 population (1991): 47.0 (world avg. 26.4).
Death rate per 1,000 population (1991): 21.0 (world avg. 9.2).
Natural increase rate per 1,000 population (1991): 26.0 (world avg. 17.2).
Total fertility rate (avg. births per childbearing woman; 1990): 6.5.
Life expectancy at birth (1990–95): male 44.0 years; female 45.0 years.
Major causes of death per 100,000 population: n.a.; however, major diseases include malaria, venereal disease, tuberculosis, and measles.

National economy

Budget (1992). Revenue: GF 415,200,000,000 (mineral sector 46.3%; other 53.7%). Expenditures: GF 593,100,000,000 (capital spending 52.3%; current expenditure 47.7%, of which personnel 22.4%, services 14.7%).
Public debt (external, outstanding; 1990): U.S.$2,249,000,000.
Tourism: n.a.
Production (metric tons except as noted). Agriculture, forestry, fishing (1991): roots and tubers 732,000 (of which cassava 450,000, yams 106,000), rice 628,000, vegetables and melons 420,000, plantains 408,000, sugarcane 225,000, citrus fruit 163,000, bananas 110,000, corn (maize) 79,000, pulses 62,000, peanuts (groundnuts) 52,000, palm kernels 40,000, pineapples 38,000, coconuts 18,000, eggs 13,860, coffee 8,000; livestock (number of live animals) 1,800,000 cattle, 518,000 sheep, 464,000 goats, 33,000 pigs, 13,000,000 chickens; roundwood 4,034,000 cu m; fish catch (1990) 32,000. Mining and quarrying (1991): bauxite 17,500,000[4]; alumina 640,000; diamonds 200,000

carats; gold 2,500 kg. Manufacturing (value of production in GF '000; 1985): corrugated and sheet iron 571,081; plastics 462,242; tobacco products 375,154; cement 326,138; printed matter 216,511; fruit juice 75,763; beer 69,934; matches 22,449. Construction: n.a. Energy production (consumption): electricity (kW-hr; 1990) 518,000,000 (518,000,000); coal, none (n.a.); crude petroleum, none (n.a.); petroleum products (metric tons; 1990) none (341,000); natural gas, none (n.a.).
Gross national product (at current market prices; 1990): U.S.$2,756,000,000 (U.S.$480 per capita).

Structure of gross domestic product and labour force

	1990 in value GF '000,000,000	1990 % of total value	1987 labour force	1987 % of labour force
Agriculture	551	27.8	2,246,000	76.3
Mining	474	23.9		
Manufacturing	71	3.6	327,000	11.1
Construction	111	5.6		
Public utilities	16	0.8		
Transp. and commun.	71	3.6		
Trade	434	21.9		
Finance			371,000	12.6
Pub. admin., defense	222	11.2		
Services				
Other	32	1.6	...	...
TOTAL	1,982	100.0	2,944,000	100.0

Population economically active (1990): total 2,476,000; activity rate of total population 43.0% (participation rates [1985]: ages 15–64, 76.2%; female 40.8%; unemployed, n.a.).

Price index (1988 = 100)

	1988[5]	1989[5]	1990[5]
Consumer price index	100.0	126.0	160.1

Household income and expenditure. Average household size (1983) 6.7; average annual income per capita (1984) GS 7,660 (U.S.$305); sources of income: n.a.; expenditure (1985): food 61.5%, health care 11.2%, clothing and footwear 7.9%, housing and energy 7.3%, transportation 5.1%.
Land use (1990): forested 59.3%; meadows and pastures 25.0%; agricultural and under permanent cultivation 3.0%; other 12.7%.

Foreign trade[6]

Balance of trade (current prices)

	1985	1986	1987	1988	1989	1990	1991
U.S.$'000,000	+111	+147	+120	+10	+146	+177	+33.2
% of total	11.0%	12.6%	9.6%	0.7%	10.6%	11.8%	2.7%

Imports (1990): U.S.$693,000,000 (1988; intermediate goods 33.7%, capital goods 13.1%, petroleum products 10.5%, food products 9.8%, consumer goods 9.7%). *Major import sources:* France 36.0%; U.S. 9.0%; Belgium-Luxembourg 9.0%; Germany 6.0%; Italy 5.0%.
Exports (1990): U.S.$788,000,000 (bauxite 56.9%, alumina 20.7%, diamonds 8.9%, gold 5.8%, coffee 4.5%, fish 1.8%). *Major export destinations:* U.S. 23.0%; France 14.0%; Germany 14.0%; Spain 13.0%; Ireland 9.0%.

Transport and communications

Transport. Railroads (1992): route length 411 mi, 662 km. Roads (1988): total length 17,600 mi, 28,400 km (paved 4%). Vehicles (1989): passenger cars 13,000; trucks and buses 13,000. Merchant marine (1991): vessels (100 gross tons and over) 26; total deadweight tonnage 2,827. Air transport (1986): passenger-mi 17,873,000, passenger-km 28,764,000; short ton-mi cargo 1,684,000, metric ton-km cargo 2,458,000; airports (1992) with scheduled flights 1.
Communications. Daily newspapers (1988): 1; total circulation 13,000; circulation per 1,000 population 2.0. Radio (1991): 200,000 receivers (1 per 35 persons). Television (1991): 65,000 receivers (1 per 108 persons). Telephones (1990): 19,602 (1 per 355 persons).

Education and health

Education (1989)

	schools	teachers	students	student/ teacher ratio
Primary (age 7–12)	2,442	8,113	310,064	38.2
Secondary (age 13–18)	225[7]	3,868	71,346	18.4
Voc., teacher tr.	35[7]	635[7]	7,313	5.2[7]
Higher	10[7]	805[8]	6,245[8]	7.8[8]

Educational attainment: n.a. *Literacy* (1990): percentage of total population age 15 and over literate 24.0%; males 34.9%; females 13.4%.
Health (1988): physicians 672 (1 per 9,732 persons); hospital beds 3,382 (1 per 1,934 persons); infant mortality rate per 1,000 live births (1990–95) 134.
Food (1988–90): daily per capita caloric intake 2,242 (vegetable products 96%, animal products 4%); 97% of FAO recommended minimum requirement.

Military

Total active duty personnel (1992): 9,700 (army 87.6%, navy 4.1%, air force 8.3%). *Military expenditure as percentage of GNP* (1988): 1.2% (world 5.1%); per capita expenditure U.S.$4.

---

[1]Transitional government established January 1991 was to end with multiparty elections scheduled for December 1992. [2]The provinces of Boké and Faranah were abolished by presidential decree in January 1988. [3]Detail does not add to total given because of rounding. [4]1990. [5]December. [6]Imports c.i.f.; exports f.o.b. [7]1987–88. [8]Universities only.

Guinea-Bissau

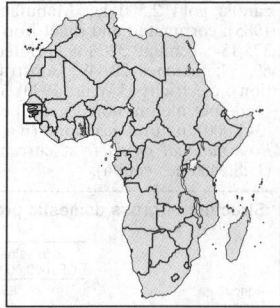

Official name: República da Guiné-Bissau (Republic of Guinea-Bissau).
Form of government: transitional regime with one legislative house (National People's Assembly [150])[1].
Chief of state: President.
Head of government: Prime Minister.
Capital: Bissau.
Official language: Portuguese.
Official religion: none.
Monetary unit: 1 Guinea-Bissau peso (PG) = 100 centavos; valuation (Oct. 5, 1992) 1 U.S.$ = PG 4,491; 1 £ = PG 8,485.

Area and population		area		population
Regions	**Capitals**	sq mi	sq km	1979 census[2]
Bafatá	Bafatá	2,309	5,981	115,656
Biombo[3]	Bissau	324	840	51,796
Bolama	Bolama	1,013	2,624	25,449
Cacheu	Cacheu	1,998	5,175	127,514
Gabú	Gabú	3,533	9,150	103,683
Oio	Farim	2,086	5,403	131,271
Quinara	Fulacunda	1,212	3,138	35,567
Tombali	Catió	1,443	3,736	55,088
Autonomous Sector				
Bissau[3]	—	30	78	107,281
TOTAL		13,948	36,125	753,305

Demography

Population (1992): 1,015,000.
Density (1992): persons per sq mi 72.8, persons per sq km 28.1.
Urban-rural (1990): urban 19.9%; rural 80.1%.
Sex distribution (1990): male 49.17%; female 50.83%.
Age breakdown (1990): under 15, 40.9%; 15–29, 24.9%; 30–44, 16.7%; 45–59, 10.9%; 60–74, 5.6%; 75 and over, 1.0%.
Population projection: (2000) 1,200,000; (2010) 1,480,000.
Doubling time: 29 years.
Ethnic composition (1979): Balante 27.2%; Fulani 22.9%; Malinke 12.2%; Mandyako 10.6%; Pepel 10.0%; other 17.1%.
Religious affiliation (1992): traditional beliefs 54%; Muslim 38%; Christian 8%.
Major cities (1979): Bissau 125,000[4]; Bafatá 13,429; Gabú 7,803; Mansôa 5,390; Catió 5,179.

Vital statistics

Birth rate per 1,000 population (1991): 42.0 (world avg. 26.4); legitimate, n.a.; illegitimate, n.a.
Death rate per 1,000 population (1991): 18.0 (world avg. 9.2).
Natural increase rate per 1,000 population (1991): 24.0 (world avg. 17.2).
Total fertility rate (avg. births per childbearing woman; 1990): 6.0.
Marriage rate per 1,000 population: n.a.
Divorce rate per 1,000 population: n.a.
Life expectancy at birth (1990–95): male 41.9 years; female 45.1 years.
Major causes of death per 100,000 population: n.a.; however, major diseases include tuberculosis of the respiratory system, whooping cough, typhoid fever, cholera, bacillary dysentery and amebiasis, malaria, pneumonia, and meningococcal infections.

National economy

Budget (1988). Revenue: PG 36,338,000,000 (tax revenue 43.7%, of which excise tax 15.4%, export duties 14.1%; grants from abroad 38.5%; nontax revenue 17.8%). Expenditures (1987): PG 48,822,000,000 (economic affairs 40.0%, of which agriculture, forestry, and fishing 20.1%; general public services 25.5%; health 5.4%; education 5.2%; defense 4.4%).
Public debt (external, outstanding; 1992): U.S.$556,000,000.
Production (metric tons except as noted). Agriculture, forestry, fishing (1991): rice 118,000, fruits 50,000, roots and tubers (sweet potatoes and cassava) 50,000, plantains 33,000, coconuts 25,000, peanuts (groundnuts) 20,000, millet 20,000, vegetables 20,000, cashews 20,000, corn (maize) 13,000, sorghum 11,000, palm kernels 10,000, sugarcane 6,000, copra 5,000, seed cotton 3,000; livestock (number of live animals) 410,000 cattle, 293,000 pigs, 245,000 sheep, 208,000 goats, 1,000,000 chickens; roundwood (1990) 567,000 cu m; fish catch (1990) 5,400. Mining and quarrying: extraction of construction materials only. Manufacturing (in PG '000,000; 1982): beverages 143.7, of which beer 122.3, orangeade and lemonade 16.5; clothing 14.0[5]; peanut oil 7.0; palm oil 2.4. Construction (value added in Esc[6]; 1987): 520,000,-000. Energy production (consumption): electricity (kW-hr; 1989) 15,000,000 (15,000,000); coal, none (none); crude petroleum, none (none); petroleum products (metric tons; 1989) none (48,000); natural gas, none (none).
Population economically active (1990): total 450,000; activity rate of total population 46.7% (participation rates: ages 15–64 [1979] 41.0%; female 3.6%; unemployed, n.a.).

Price and earnings indexes (1985 = 100)							
	1983	1984	1985	1986	1987	1988	1989
Consumer price index	35.4	60.4	100.0	82.0	72.0	73.0	78.0
Annual earnings index	50.8	75.6	100.0	129.9	...	...	...

Gross national product (at current market prices; 1990): U.S.$176,000,000 (U.S.$180 per capita).

Structure of gross domestic product and labour force				
	1987		1979	
	in value Esc '000,000	% of total value	labour force	% of labour force
Agriculture	15,401	51.7	153,069	71.9
Mining	412	1.4	162	0.1
Manufacturing			2,905	1.4
Construction	520	1.7	1,667	0.8
Public utilities	598	2.0	162	0.1
Transportation and communications	120	0.4	2,372	1.1
Trade	5,416	18.2	5,085	2.4
Finance	1,362	4.6	162	0.1
Pub. admin., defense	4,523	15.2	26,194	12.3
Services	1,420	4.8		
Other	—		21,232[7]	10.0[7]
TOTAL	29,772	100.0	213,010	100.0[8]

Tourism: n.a.
Land use (1990): forested 38.1%; meadows and pastures 38.4%; agricultural and under permanent cultivation 11.9%; other 11.6%.
Household income and expenditure. Average household size (1981) 4.1; income per household: n.a.; sources of income: n.a.; expenditure: n.a.

Foreign trade

Balance of trade (current prices)						
	1983	1984	1985	1986	1987	1988
U.S.$'000,000	−49.8	−42.7	−51.4	−43.1	−29.3	−37.4
% of total	74.0%	55.1%	68.9%	69.2%	63.0%	54.0%

Imports (1988): U.S.$53,300,000 (transport equipment 28.7%, building materials 17.9%, foodstuffs 8.6%, fuel and lubricants 8.6%, other 36.2%). *Major import sources* (1989): Italy 27.3%; Portugal 23.0%; Thailand 7.6%; The Netherlands 7.2%; France 4.3%; Senegal 4.2%; U.S.S.R. 3.0%.
Exports (1988): U.S.$15,900,000 (cashews 52.8%, peanuts [groundnuts] 11.3%, frozen fish 3.1%). *Major export destinations* (1989): Portugal 34.4%; Spain 19.2%; France 18.1%; Japan 6.7%; The Netherlands 6.1%; Italy 6.0%; Belgium-Luxembourg 4.5%.

Transport and communications

Transport. Railroads: none. Roads (1989): total length 2,175 mi, 3,500 km (paved 15%). Vehicles (1989): passenger cars 3,200; trucks and buses 2,400. Merchant marine (1991): vessels (100 gross tons and over) 19; total deadweight tonnage 1,846. Air transport (1985): passenger-mi 6,000,000, passenger-km 9,000,000; short ton-mi cargo 700,000, metric ton-km cargo 1,000,000; airports (1992) with scheduled flights 2.
Communications. Daily newspapers (1990): total number 2; total circulation 12,000; circulation per 1,000 population 12. Radio (1991): total number of receivers 35,000 (1 per 28 persons). Television: n.a. Telephones (1987): 7,000 (1 per 130 persons).

Education and health

Education (1988)	schools	teachers	students	student/ teacher ratio
Primary (age 7–13)	632[9]	3,065[9]	79,035	24.6[9]
Secondary (age 13–18)	12[10]	824[10]	5,505	7.8[10]
Voc., teacher tr.	4[9]	107	825	7.7

Educational attainment (1979). Percentage of population age 7 and over having: no formal schooling or knowledge of reading and writing 90.4%; primary education 7.9%; secondary 1.0%; technical 0.5%; higher 0.2%.
Literacy (1990): total population age 15 and over literate 211,200 (36.5%); males literate 138,800 (50.2%); females literate 72,400 (24.0%).
Health: physicians (1985) 122 (1 per 7,164 persons); hospital beds (1983) 1,593 (1 per 526 persons); infant mortality rate per 1,000 live births (1990–95) 140.
Food (1984–86): daily per capita caloric intake 2,278 (vegetable products 93%, animal products 7%); 84% of FAO recommended minimum requirement.

Military

Total active duty personnel (1992): 7,200 (army 94.4%, navy 4.2%, air force 1.4%). *Military expenditure as percentage of GNP* (1987): 2.4% (world 5.4%); per capita expenditure U.S.$4.

[1]Constitution was amended in June 1991, opposition parties legalized in November 1991, transitional government to exist until January 1993. [2]Preliminary. [3]Biombo region excludes Bissau city. [4]1988. [5]Production figure for first three quarters only. [6]Esc is the abbreviation for Portuguese escudo. [7]Not adequately defined. [8]Detail does not add to total given because of rounding. [9]1987. [10]1986.

Guyana

Official name: Co-operative Republic of Guyana.
Form of government: unitary multiparty republic with one legislative house (National Assembly [65[1]]).
Head of state and government: President.
Capital: Georgetown.
Official language: English.
Official religion: none.
Monetary unit: 1 Guyana dollar (G$) = 100 cents; valuation (Oct. 5, 1992) 1 U.S.$ = G$125.27; 1 £ = G$212.96.

Area and population		area		population
Administrative Regions	**Capitals**	sq mi	sq km	1986 estimate[2]
Region 1 (Barima/Waini)	Mabaruma	7,853	20,339	18,516
Region 2 (Pomeroon/Supenaam)	Anna Regina	2,392	6,195	41,966
Region 3 (Essequibo Islands/West Demerara)	Vreed-en-Hoop	1,450	3,755	102,760
Region 4 (Demerara/Mahaica)	Paradise	862	2,233	310,758
Region 5 (Mahaica/Berbice)	Fort Wellington	1,610	4,170	55,556
Region 6 (East Berbice/Corentyne)	New Amsterdam	13,998	36,255	148,967
Region 7 (Cuyuni/Mazaruni)	Bartica	18,229	47,213	17,941
Region 8 (Potaro/Siparuni)	Mahdia	7,742	20,052	5,672
Region 9 (Upper Takutu/Upper Essequibo)	Lethem	22,313	57,790	15,338
Region 10 (Upper Demerara/Berbice)	Linden	6,595	17,081	38,598
TOTAL		83,044	215,083	756,072

Demography

Population (1992): 748,000.
Density (1992): persons per sq mi 9.0, persons per sq km 3.5.
Urban-rural (1990): urban 34.5%; rural 65.5%.
Sex distribution (1990): male 49.50%; female 50.50%.
Age breakdown (1990): under 15, 33.4%; 15–29, 33.2%; 30–44, 18.8%; 45–59, 8.7%; 60–74, 4.6%; 75 and over, 1.3%.
Population projection: (2000) 728,000; (2010) 807,000.
Doubling time: 44 years[3].
Ethnic composition (1980): East Indian 51.4%; black (African Negro and Bush Negro) 30.5%; mixed 11.0%; Amerindian 5.3%, of which Carib 3.7%, Arawak 1.4%; Chinese 0.2%; white (mostly Portuguese) 0.1%; other 1.5%.
Religious affiliation (1980): Christian 42.4%, of which Protestant 30.5% (including Anglican 14.3%), Roman Catholic 11.4%; Hindu 37.1%; Muslim 8.7%; nonreligious 3.7%; other and not stated 8.1%.
Major cities (1985): Georgetown 150,368[4]; Linden 35,000; New Amsterdam 25,000; Corriverton 13,718[5]; Bartica 6,223[5].

Vital statistics

Birth rate per 1,000 population (1991): 23.0 (world avg. 26.4); (1980) legitimate 61.4%; illegitimate 38.6%.
Death rate per 1,000 population (1991): 7.0 (world avg. 9.2).
Natural increase rate per 1,000 population (1991): 16.0 (world avg. 17.2).
Total fertility rate (avg. births per childbearing woman; 1991): 2.7.
Marriage rate per 1,000 population: n.a.
Divorce rate per 1,000 population: n.a.
Life expectancy at birth (1991): male 61.0 years; female 68.0 years.
Major causes of death per 100,000 population (1984): diseases of the circulatory system 202.5, of which cerebrovascular disease 79.0; diseases of the digestive system 74.0; accidents and violence 56.5; diseases of the respiratory system 39.8; malignant neoplasms (cancers) 37.1.

National economy

Budget (1991–92). Revenue: G$14,407,000,000 (current revenue 95.9%, of which consumption taxes 27.0%, income taxes on companies 21.9%, import duties 9.5%, nontax revenue 5.8%; development revenue 4.1%, of which external grants 3.3%). Expenditures: G$16,185,000,000 (current expenditure 86.3%, of which interest payments on debt 32.6%, education subsidies and grants 2.1%; development expenditure 13.7%).
Public debt (external, outstanding; 1991): U.S.$1,112,000,000.
Production (metric tons except as noted). Agriculture, forestry, fishing (1991): raw sugar 162,600, rice 150,800, coconuts 48,000, roots and tubers 32,000, plantains 23,000, bananas 20,000, oranges 15,000; livestock (number of live animals) 210,000 cattle, 185,000 pigs, 120,000 sheep; roundwood (1990) 225,000 cu m; fish catch 43,900, of which shrimps and prawns 7,900. Mining and quarrying (1991): bauxite 1,346,000; gold 59,400 troy oz; diamonds 21,900 carats. Manufacturing (1991): flour 35,300; rum 162,600 hectolitres; beer and stout 124,100 hectolitres; cigarettes 307,000,000 units; refrigerators 7,971 units; pharmaceuticals 14,900,000 tablets; other products include cotton cloth and dyed and printed fabrics. Construction: n.a. Energy production (consumption): electricity (kW-hr; 1990) 220,000,000 (220,000,000); coal, none (none); crude petroleum, none (none); petroleum products (metric tons; 1990) none (207,000); natural gas, none (none).
Household income and expenditure. Average household size (1980) 5.1; income per household: n.a.; sources of income: n.a.; expenditure (1970)[6]: food, beverages, and tobacco 42.5%, rent and water 21.4%, clothing and footwear 8.6%, education and recreation 6.4%, fuel and light 5.2%, other 15.9%.
Gross national product (at current market prices; 1990): U.S.$293,000,000 (U.S.$370 per capita).

Structure of gross domestic product and labour force

	1991		1980	
	in value G$'000,000[7]	% of total value	labour force	% of labour force
Agriculture, fishing	879	25.0	50,316	20.4
Mining	380	10.8	9,669	3.9
Manufacturing	409[8]	11.6[8]	28,980	11.8
Construction	251	7.1	7,024	2.8
Public utilities	[8]	[8]	2,850	1.2
Transportation and communications	290	8.3	9,412	3.8
Trade	301	8.6	15,231	6.2
Finance, real estate	266	7.6	2,944	1.2
Pub. admin., defense	609	17.3	29,948	12.1
Services	131	3.7	29,295	11.9
Other	—	—	61,002[9]	24.7[9]
TOTAL	3,516	100.0	246,671	100.0

Population economically active (1987): total 270,074; activity rate of total population 35.7% (participation rates: ages 15–64, 60.4%; female 29.9%; unemployed [end of 1991] 13.5%).

Price and earnings indexes (1985 = 100)

	1983	1984	1985	1986	1987	1988	1989[10]
Consumer price index	69.4	86.9	100.0	107.9	138.9	194.4	380.7
Earnings index	...	...	...	...	...	...	...

Tourism: receipts from visitors (1990) U.S.$30,000,000; expenditures by nationals abroad, n.a.
Land use (1990): forested 83.2%; meadows and pastures 6.2%; agricultural and under permanent cultivation 2.5%; other 8.1%.

Foreign trade[11]

Balance of trade (current prices)

	1986	1987	1988	1989	1990	1991
G$'000,000	−52.7	+93.5	+197.2	−776.9	−1,691.4	−4,596.2
% of total	2.6%	1.8%	4.4%	5.9%	7.4%	7.2%

Imports (1991): G$34,274,900,000 (capital goods 40.6%; fuels and lubricants 21.9%; consumer goods 19.2%). *Major import sources*[12]: United States 34.0%; United Kingdom 14.0%; Trinidad and Tobago 12.0%; Japan 6.0%; Canada 5.0%.
Exports (1991): G$29,678,700,000 (domestic exports 95.7%, of which sugar 35.3%, bauxite 30.2%, gold 7.8%, rice 7.1%, shrimps 6.8%, timber 1.5%; reexports 4.3%). *Major export destinations*[12]: United States 30.0%; United Kingdom 27.0%; Canada 8.0%; Japan 6.0%; The Netherlands 4.0%.

Transport and communications

Transport. Railroads[13]: length (1990) 55 mi, 88 km. Roads (1990): total length 3,540 mi, 5,697 km (paved 11%). Vehicles (1990): passenger cars 24,000; trucks and buses 9,000. Merchant marine (1991): vessels (100 gross tons and over) 81; total deadweight tonnage 10,951. Air transport (1990)[14]: passenger-mi 134,000,000, passenger-km 216,000,000; short ton-mi cargo 1,900,000, metric ton-km cargo 2,800,000; airports (1992) with scheduled flights 1[15].
Communications. Daily newspapers (1991): total number 2; total circulation 40,000; circulation per 1,000 population 53. Radio (1991): total number of receivers 310,000 (1 per 2.4 persons). Television (1991): total number of receivers 40,000 (1 per 19 persons). Telephones (1990): 16,003 (1 per 47 persons).

Education and health

Education (1989–90)

	schools	teachers	students	student/teacher ratio
Primary (age 6–11)	423	3,948[16]	134,679[16]	...
Secondary (age 12–17)	93	2,700[16]	73,418[16]	27.2[16]
Voc., teacher tr.	8	176	5,388	30.6
Higher[17]	1	370	2,169	5.8

Educational attainment (1980). Percentage of population age 25 and over having: no formal schooling 8.1%; primary education 72.8%; secondary 17.3%; higher 1.8%. *Literacy* (1990): total population age 15 and over literate, c. 490,000 (96.4%); males literate, c. 245,000 (97.5%); females literate, c. 245,000 (95.4%).
Health: physicians (1989) 111 (1 per 6,809 persons); hospital beds (1987) 2,204 (1 per 341 persons); infant mortality rate per 1,000 live births (1991) 51.0.
Food (1988–90): daily per capita caloric intake 2,495 (vegetable products 86%, animal products 14%); 110% of FAO recommended minimum requirement.

Military

Total active duty personnel (1992): 2,000[18] (army 85.0%, navy 5.0%, air force 10.0%). *Military expenditure as percentage of GNP* (1989): 2.7% (world 4.9%); per capita expenditure U.S.$8.

---

[1]Includes 12 indirectly elected seats. [2]Sample survey. [3]Net migration nearly equals natural-increase rate. [4]1986. [5]1980. [6]Weights of consumer price index components for Georgetown, New Amsterdam, and Linden only. [7]At prices of 1988. [8]Manufacturing includes Public utilities. [9]Represents "not stated." [10]June. [11]Imports c.i.f.; exports f.o.b. [12]Estimated figures. [13]The two railways are privately owned and are used to transport minerals. [14]Scheduled traffic only. [15]International only; the number of domestic airports with scheduled air service is not available. [16]1986–87. [17]University of Guyana. [18]Excludes 2,000 paramilitary.

Haiti

Official name: Repiblik Dayti (Haitian Creole): République d'Haïti (French) (Republic of Haiti).
Form of government: military-dominated extraconstitutional regime with two legislative houses (Senate [27]; Chamber of Deputies [83]).
Chief of state: President[1].
Head of government: Prime Minister.
Capital: Port-au-Prince.
Official languages: Haitian Creole; French.
Official religion: none[2].
Monetary unit: 1 gourde (G) = 100 centimes; valuation (Oct. 5, 1992) 1 U.S.\$ = G 5.00; 1 £ = G 16.97.

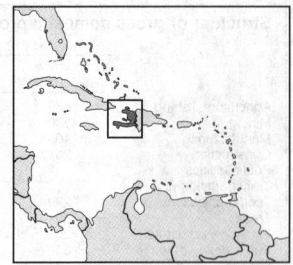

Area and population

Departements	Capitals	area[3]		population
		sq mi	sq km	1992 estimate
Artibonite	Gonaïves	1,924	4,984	961,447
Centre	Hinche	1,419	3,675	467,514
Grande Anse	Jérémie	1,278	3,310	616,151
Nord	Cap-Haïtien	813	2,106	724,084
Nord-Est	Fort-Liberté	697	1,805	239,734
Nord-Ouest	Port-de-Paix	840	2,176	395,442
Ouest	Port-au-Prince	1,864	4,827	2,285,044
Sud	Les Cayes	1,079	2,794	630,007
Sud-Est	Jacmel	781	2,023	444,323
TOTAL		10,695	27,700	6,763,746

Demography

Population (1992): 6,764,000.
Density (1992): persons per sq mi 632.4, persons per sq km 244.2.
Urban–rural (1990): urban 29.6%; rural 70.4%.
Sex distribution (1990): male 49.07%; female 50.93%.
Age breakdown (1990): under 15, 40.2%; 15–29, 27.7%; 30–44, 16.3%; 45–59, 9.6%; 60–74, 4.9%; 75 and over, 1.3%.
Population projection: (2000) 8,003,000; (2010) 8,876,000.
Doubling time: 25 years.
Ethnic composition (1985): black 95.0%; mulatto 4.9%; white 0.1%.
Religious affiliation (1982): Roman Catholic 80.3%[4]; Protestant 15.8%, of which Baptist 9.7%, Pentecostal 3.6%; nonreligious 1.2%; other 2.7%.
Major cities (1992): Port-au-Prince 752,600 (metropolitan area 1,255,078); Carrefour 241,223[5]; Delmas 200,251[5]; Cap-Haïtien 92,122; Gonaïves 63,291.

Vital statistics

Birth rate per 1,000 population (1991): 43.0 (world avg. 26.4).
Death rate per 1,000 population (1991): 15.0 (world avg. 9.2).
Natural increase rate per 1,000 population (1991): 28.0 (world avg. 17.2).
Total fertility rate (avg. births per childbearing woman; 1991): 6.3.
Marriage rate per 1,000 population (1980): 0.7[6].
Divorce rate per 1,000 population (1980): 0.1[6].
Life expectancy at birth (1991): male 52.0 years; female 55.0 years.
Major causes of death per 100,000 population (1982)[7]: infectious and parasitic diseases 46.0; diseases of the circulatory system 11.9; diseases associated with malnutrition 8.5; diseases of the respiratory system 8.3; endocrine and metabolic disorders 8.0; ill-defined conditions 115.2.

National economy

Budget (1990–91). Revenue: G 1,382,000,000 (general sales taxes 18.3%; import duties 16.2%; income taxes 14.8%; excises 12.5%). Expenditures: G 1,999,000,000 (current expenditures 93.1%, of which extrabudgetary 31.2%; development expenditure 6.9%).
Tourism (1990–91): receipts from visitors U.S.\$66,000,000; expenditures by nationals abroad U.S.\$33,000,000.
Public debt (external, outstanding; 1991): U.S.\$745,000,000.
Production (metric tons except as noted). Agriculture, forestry, fishing (1991): sugarcane 3,100,000, sweet potatoes 380,000, mangoes 280,000, plantains 280,000, bananas 220,000, corn (maize) 145,000, rice 120,000, sorghum 70,000, dry beans 55,000, coffee 37,000, oranges 29,000, sisal 10,000, cacao 5,000; livestock (number of live animals) 1,400,000 cattle, 1,200,000 goats, 930,000 pigs; roundwood (1990) 5,840,000 cu m; fish catch (1990) 7,500. Mining and quarrying (1989–90): limestone 287,000. Manufacturing (1991–92): cement 178,600; flour 44,500; essential oils (mostly amyris, neroli, and vetiver) 86; cigarettes 920,000 units; articles assembled for reexport (value of production in G '000,000) 632, of which garments 294, sports equipment and toys 100, electronic components 90, luggage and handbags 25. Construction: n.a. Energy production (consumption): electricity (kW-hr; 1990–91) 399,000,000 (308,000,000); coal, none (none); crude petroleum, none (none); petroleum products (metric tons; 1990) none (203,000); natural gas, none (none).
Population economically active (1990): total 2,679,140; activity rate of total population 41.1% (participation rates: ages 15–64, 64.8%; female 40.0%; unemployed [1989] unofficially 60.0%).

Price and earnings indexes (1985 = 100)

	1986	1987	1988	1989	1990	1991	1992
Consumer price index	103.3	91.5	95.2	101.8	123.7	142.8	150.7[8]
Annual earnings index	100.0	100.0	100.0	108.4	...	...	...

Household income and expenditure. Average household size (1982) 4.4; average annual income of wage earners (1984): urban (G 1,545 [U.S.\$309]), rural (G 629 [U.S.\$126]); expenditure (1976): food and beverages 77.9%[9], housing 8.3%, household furnishings 4.0%, clothing and footwear 3.2%.
Gross national product (1990): U.S.\$2,400,000,000 (U.S.\$370 per capita).

Structure of gross domestic product and labour force

	1989–90		1990	
	in value G '000,000[10]	% of total value	labour force	% of labour force
Agriculture	1,753	33.8	1,535,444	57.3
Mining	5	0.1	24,012	0.9
Manufacturing	783	15.1	151,387	5.6
Construction	264	5.1	28,001	1.0
Public utilities	55	1.0	2,577	0.1
Transp. and commun.	108	2.1	20,691	0.8
Trade, restaurants	888	17.1	352,970	13.2
Finance, real estate	311	6.0	5,057	0.2
Pub. admin., defense	618	11.9	155,347	5.8
Services	176	3.4 }		
Other	230[11]	4.1[11]	403,654[12]	15.1[12]
TOTAL	5,191	100.0	2,679,140	100.0

Land use (1990): forested 1.4%; meadows and pastures 18.0%; agricultural and under permanent cultivation 32.8%; other 47.8%.

Foreign trade[13, 14]

Balance of trade (current prices)

	1986–87	1987–88	1988–89	1989–90	1990–91	1991–92
G '000,000	−808.4	−805.8	−806.3	−862.8	−1,159.2	−1,605.0
% of total	27.3	30.6	34.6	35.1	40.7	59.8

Imports (1991–92): G 2,143,900,000 (food and live animals 22.7%, basic manufactures 16.4%, machinery and transport equipment 14.1%, mineral fuels 13.9%). *Major import sources* (1989–90): United States 46.1%; Caribbean area 11.8%; France 7.4%; Japan 7.1%; Canada 6.6%.
Exports (1991–92)[15]: G 538,900,000 (local manufactures—mostly processed foods, electrical equipment, textiles, and clothing—70.7%, coffee 10.5%, wood and sisal handicrafts 5.7%, sugar 3.0%, sisal and twine 2.3%, essential oils 1.9%). *Major export destinations* (1989–90): United States 47.8%; France 10.7%; Italy 10.1%; Belgium 9.7%; Caribbean area 6.8%.

Transport and communications

Transport. Railroad (1990)[16]: route length 50 mi, 80 km. Roads (1988): total length 2,485 mi, 4,000 km (paved 15%). Vehicles (1989): passenger cars 32,000; trucks and buses 21,000. Merchant marine (1991): vessels (100 gross tons and over) 3; total deadweight tonnage 429. Air transport (1990)[17]: passenger arrivals 282,063, passenger departures 296,172; cargo unloaded 13,236 metric tons, cargo loaded 11,152 metric tons; airports (1992) with scheduled flights 2.
Communications. Daily newspapers (1990): total number 4; total circulation 44,500; circulation per 1,000 population 6.9. Radio (1991): total number of receivers 3,000,000 (1 per 2.2 persons). Television (1991): total number of receivers 25,000 (1 per 265 persons). Telephones (1990): 82,000 (1 per 79 persons).

Education and health

Education (1989–90)

	schools	teachers	students	student/ teacher ratio
Primary (age 6–12)	5,625[18]	24,238	1,148,400	47.4
Secondary (age 13–18)	686	13,262	197,400	14.9
Voc., teacher tr.[18]	36	491	3,012	6.1
Higher[19, 20]	1	500	6,300	12.6

Educational attainment (1982). Percentage of population age 25 and over having: no formal schooling 76.9%; primary education 15.2%; secondary 7.2%; higher 0.7%. *Literacy* (1990): total population age 15 and over literate 2,096,900 (53.0%); males literate 1,128,000 (59.1%); females literate 968,000 (47.4%).
Health (1989): physicians 944 (1 per 6,083 persons); hospital beds 4,566 (1 per 1,258 persons); infant mortality rate per 1,000 live births (1991) 106.0.
Food (1988–90): daily per capita caloric intake 2,005 (vegetable products 89%, animal products 11%); 89% of FAO recommended minimum requirement.

Military

Total active duty personnel (1992): 7,400 (army 94.6%, navy 3.4%, air force 2.0%). *Military expenditure as percentage of GNP* (1989): 1.9% (world 4.9%); per capita expenditure U.S.\$7.

---

[1]Office declared vacant June 1992. [2]Roman Catholicism has special recognition. [3]Estimated. [4]About 80% of all Roman Catholics also practice voodoo. [5]Within Port-au-Prince metropolitan area. [6]Registered only. [7]Public health facilities only. [8]Average of first quarter. [9]Excludes alcoholic beverages. [10]At prices of 1976. [11]Import duties. [12]Includes 63,975 not adequately defined and 339,679 officially unemployed. [13]Import figures c.i.f., export figures f.o.b. for fiscal year ending September 30; Organization of American States trade embargo went into effect October 1991. [14]The import and export value of preassembled and assembled U.S.-made components is excluded. Virtually all components used in the export assembly plants are imported. [15]Export value (1991–92) of assembled components equals G 632,000,000 (garments comprise 46.5% of total, sports equipment and toys 15.8%, electronic components 14.2%). [16]The only railway is privately owned and used to transport sugarcane. [17]Port-au-Prince Airport only. [18]1988–89. [19]State University of Haiti only. [20]1990–91.

Honduras

Official name: República de Honduras (Republic of Honduras).
Form of government: multiparty republic with one legislative house (Congress [128]).
Head of state and government: President.
Capital: Tegucigalpa[1].
Official language: Spanish.
Official religion: none.
Monetary unit: 1 Honduran lempira (L) = 100 centavos; valuation (Oct. 5, 1992) 1 U.S.$ = L 6.00; 1 £ = L 10.20.

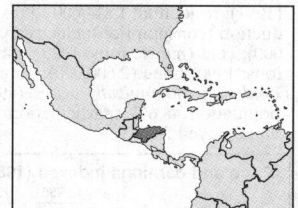

Area and population

Departments	Administrative centres	area sq mi	area sq km	population 1991 estimate
Atlántida	La Ceiba	1,641	4,251	255,000
Choluteca	Choluteca	1,626	4,211	309,000
Colón	Trujillo	3,427	8,875	164,000
Comayagua	Comayagua	2,006	5,196	257,000
Copán	Santa Rosa de Copán	1,237	3,203	226,000
Cortés	San Pedro Sula	1,527	3,954	706,000
El Paraíso	Yuscarán	2,787	7,218	277,000
Francisco Morazán	Tegucigalpa	3,068	7,946	878,000
Gracias a Dios	Puerto Lempira	6,421	16,630	37,000
Intibucá	La Esperanza	1,186	3,072	130,000
Islas de la Bahía	Roatán	100	261	24,000
La Paz	La Paz	900	2,331	112,000
Lempira	Gracias	1,656	4,290	180,000
Ocotepeque	Nueva Ocotepeque	649	1,680	77,000
Olancho	Juticalpa	9,402	24,351	309,000
Santa Bárbara	Santa Bárbara	1,975	5,115	291,000
Valle	Nacaome	604	1,565	121,000
Yoro	Yoro	3,065	7,939	355,000
TOTAL		43,277	112,088	4,708,000

Demography

Population (1992): 4,996,000.
Density (1992): persons per sq mi 115.4, persons per sq km 44.6.
Urban-rural (1991): urban 41.1%; rural 58.9%.
Sex distribution (1988): male 49.59%; female 50.41%.
Age breakdown (1990): under 15, 44.6%; 15–29, 28.3%; 30–44, 14.4%; 45–59, 7.8%; 60–74, 3.9%; 75 and over, 1.0%.
Population projection: (2000) 6,249,000; (2010) 7,872,000.
Doubling time: 23 years.
Ethnic composition (1987): mestizo 89.9%; Amerindian 6.7%; black (including Black Carib) 2.1%; white 1.3%.
Religious affiliation (1986): Roman Catholic 85.0%; Protestant (mostly fundamentalist, Moravian, and Methodist) 10.0%; other 5.0%.
Major cities (1989): Tegucigalpa 608,100[2]; San Pedro Sula 300,400; La Ceiba 71,600; El Progreso 63,400; Choluteca 57,400.

Vital statistics

Birth rate per 1,000 population (1991): 39.0 (world avg. 26.4); legitimate, n.a.; illegitimate, n.a.
Death rate per 1,000 population (1991): 8.0 (world avg. 9.2).
Natural increase rate per 1,000 population (1991): 31.0 (world avg. 17.2).
Total fertility rate (avg. births per childbearing woman; 1991): 5.3.
Marriage rate per 1,000 population (1983): 4.9.
Divorce rate per 1,000 population (1983): 0.4.
Life expectancy at birth (1989): male 63.0 years; female 67.0 years.
Major causes of death per 100,000 population (1983): diseases of the circulatory system 48.4; infectious and parasitic diseases 46.6; accidents and violence 42.2; diseases of the respiratory system 26.3.

National economy

Budget (1991). Revenue: L 5,902,000,000 (current revenue 82.1%, of which taxes on production and consumption 17.2%, import duties 11.6%, income taxes 10.6%; capital revenue 17.9%). Expenditures: L 5,902,000,000 (current expenditure 63.8%; public-debt service 19.2%; capital expenditure 17.0%).
Public debt (external, outstanding; 1990): U.S.$2,992,000,000.
Production (metric tons except as noted). Agriculture, forestry, fishing (1990): sugarcane 2,700,000, bananas 1,100,000, corn (maize) 539,000, plantains 170,000, coffee 118,000, palm oil 72,700, sorghum 65,000, dry beans 54,000, rice 44,000; livestock (number of live animals) 3,514,000 cattle, 734,000 pigs; roundwood 6,165,000 cu m; fish catch (1989) 18,322, of which shrimp and lobster 5,735. Mining and quarrying (1989): zinc concentrate 28,000; lead (metal content) 5,400. Manufacturing (1991): cement 693,000; raw sugar 385,-000; wheat flour 217,000; beer 671,000 hectolitres; milk 507,000 hectolitres; cigarettes 2,528,000,000 units. Construction (value of private construction in L '000,000; 1991)[3]: residential 139.3; nonresidential 100.3. Energy production (consumption): electricity (kW-hr; 1990) 1,105,000,000 (1,268,000,000); coal, none (none); crude petroleum (barrels; 1990) none (1,942,000); petroleum products (metric tons; 1990) 245,000 (511,000); natural gas, none (none).
Household income and expenditure. Average household size (1988) 5.4; income per household: n.a.; sources of income (1985): wages and salaries 58.8%, transfer payments 1.8%, other 39.4%; expenditure (1986): food 44.4%, utilities and housing 22.4%, clothing and footwear 9.0%, household furnishings 8.3%, health care 7.0%, transportation and communications 3.0%, other 5.9%.
Gross national product (at current market prices; 1990): U.S.$3,023,000,000 (U.S.$590 per capita).

Structure of gross domestic product and labour force

	1991 in value L '000,000[4]	% of total value	labour force	% of labour force
Agriculture	3,262	22.8	702,900	46.1
Mining	269	1.9	4,100	0.3
Manufacturing	2,424	17.0	179,600	11.8
Construction	623	4.4	88,700	5.8
Public utilities	476	3.3	10,300	0.7
Transportation and communications	770	5.4	42,800	2.8
Trade	1,857	13.0	156,500	10.3
Finance, real estate	2,051	14.4	27,900	1.8
Public admin., defense	1,050	7.3	} 310,500	20.4
Services	1,507	10.5		
TOTAL	14,289	100.0	1,523,300	100.0

Population economically active (1991): total 1,523,300; activity rate of total population 31.0% (participation rates: ages [1984] 15–64, 53.6%; female [1984] 16.7%; unemployed [1990] 40.0%).

Price and earnings indexes (1985 = 100)

	1985	1986	1987	1988	1989	1990	1991
Consumer price index	100.0	104.4	106.9	111.8	122.8	151.4	202.8
Weekly earnings index[5]	100.0	100.0	100.0	100.0	100.0	100.0	...

Land use (1989): forested 29.9%; meadows and pastures 22.8%; agricultural and under permanent cultivation 16.2%; other 31.1%.
Tourism: receipts from visitors (1990) U.S.$29,000,000; expenditures by nationals abroad (1989) U.S.$40,000,000.

Foreign trade[6]

Balance of trade (current prices)

	1986	1987	1988	1989	1990	1991
L '000,000	+124.7	−99.0	−47.3	+5.4	−29.8	+11.9
% of total	3.8%	2.8%	1.3%	0.1%	0.8%	0.7%

Imports (1991): U.S.$879,800,000 (machinery and transport equipment 25.9%, mineral fuels 18.8%, chemical products 15.8%, plastics and resins 7.8%, base-metal products 7.4%). *Major import sources:* United States 40.5%; Japan 9.0%; Mexico 7.3%; Venezuela 6.6%; The Netherlands 6.0%.
Exports (1991): U.S.$808,100,000 (bananas 42.3%, coffee 19.2%, shrimp and lobsters 12.8%, lead and zinc 4.7%, roundwood 2.0%). *Major export destinations:* United States 53.8%; Germany 8.7%; Belgium 7.0%; Japan 5.4%; Italy 3.6%.

Transport and communications

Transport. Railroads (1988): length (1990) 583 mi, 939 km; passenger-km 7,900,000; metric ton-km cargo 385,700,000. Roads (1990): total length 7,066 mi, 11,371 km (paved 21%). Vehicles (1990): passenger cars 88,982; trucks and buses 18,049. Merchant marine (1991): vessels (100 gross tons and over) 846; total deadweight tonnage 1,225,100. Air transport (1990): passenger-mi 321,000,000, passenger-km 516,000,000; short ton-mi cargo 2,000,000, metric ton-km cargo 3,000,000; airports (1992) with scheduled flights 9.
Communications. Daily newspapers (1989): total number 6; total circulation 218,000; circulation per 1,000 population 49. Radio (1991): total number of receivers 1,800,000 (1 per 2.6 persons). Television (1991): total number of receivers 200,000 (1 per 24 persons). Telephones (1991): 94,147 (1 per 46 persons).

Education and health

Education (1991)

	schools	teachers	students	student/ teacher ratio
Primary (age 7–13)	7,487	25,854	923,902	35.7
Secondary (age 14–19)	540	8,517	132,953	15.6
Voc., teacher tr.	5[7]	581[7]	47,727	13.7[7]
Higher	5	2,740	34,333	12.5

Educational attainment (1988). Percentage of population age 10 and over having: no formal schooling 33.4%; primary education 50.1%; secondary education 13.4%; higher 3.1%. *Literacy* (1990): total population age 15 and over literate 2,082,000 (73.1%); males literate 1,078,000 (75.5%); females literate 1,004,000 (70.6%).
Health (1991): physicians (1990) 2,900 (1 per 1,586 persons); hospital beds 5,303 (1 per 818 persons); infant mortality rate per 1,000 live births 48.0.
Food (1987–89): daily per capita caloric intake 2,229 (vegetable products 89%, animal products 11%); 99% of FAO recommended minimum.

Military

Total active duty personnel (1991): 17,500 (army 82.3%, navy 5.7%, air force 12.0%). *Military expenditure as percentage of GNP* (1989): 3.2% (world 4.9%); per capita expenditure U.S.$33.

[1]Tegucigalpa and adjacent city of Comayagüela jointly form the capital according to the constitution. [2]Population cited is for Central District (Tegucigalpa and Comayagüela). [3]Tegucigalpa, San Pedro Sula, and 10 other urban centres. [4]At factor cost. [5]Official minimum wages in all sectors. Minimum wages were fixed from June 1981 to Jan. 1, 1990, when new minimum wages were introduced. [6]Import figures are f.o.b. in balance of trade and c.i.f. for commodities and trading partners. [7]1989.

Hong Kong

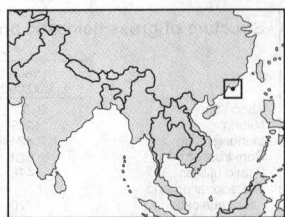

Official name: Hsiang Kang (Chinese); Hong Kong (English).
Political status: Crown Colony (United Kingdom)[1] with one legislative house (Legislative Council [60[2]]).
Chief of state: British Monarch.
Head of government: Governor.
Capital: none[3].
Official languages: Chinese; English.
Official religion: none.
Monetary unit: 1 HK dollar (HK$) = 100 cents; valuation (Oct. 5, 1992) 1 U.S.$ = HK$7.75; 1 £ = HK$13.17.

Area and population	area[4]		population
Area	sq mi	sq km	1991 census
Hong Kong Island	30.9	79.9	1,250,993
Kowloon	16.4	42.6	2,030,683
New Territories	367.7	952.3	2,374,818
Marine	—	—	17,620
TOTAL	415.0	1,074.8	5,674,114

Demography

Population (1992): 5,799,000.
Density (1992): persons per sq mi 13,980.8, persons per sq km 5,398.1.
Urban–rural (1992): urban 100.0%.
Sex distribution (1991): male 51.14%; female 48.86%.
Age breakdown[5] (1991): under 15, 20.9%; 15–24, 15.2%; 25–44, 37.5%; 45–54, 8.8%; 55–64, 8.9%; 65 and over, 8.7%.
Population projection: (2000) 6,167,000; (2010) 6,660,000.
Doubling time: 87 years.
Ethnic composition[6] (nationality; 1991): Chinese 94.9%; Filipino 1.2%; British 1.2%; other 2.7%.
Religious affiliation (1991): predominantly Buddhist and Taoist; however, there are about 258,000 Protestants, 253,000 Roman Catholics, 50,000 Muslims, and 12,000 Hindus.
Major cities: no bounded localities exist within Hong Kong.

Vital statistics

Birth rate per 1,000 population (1991): 12.0 (world avg. 26.4); legitimate (1985) 94.5%; illegitimate 5.5%.
Death rate per 1,000 population (1991): 5.0 (world avg. 9.2).
Natural increase rate per 1,000 population (1991): 7.0 (world avg. 17.2).
Total fertility rate (avg. births per childbearing woman; 1988): 1.4.
Marriage rate per 1,000 population (1991): 7.3.
Divorce rate per 1,000 population (1991): 1.2.
Life expectancy at birth (1991): male 75.0 years; female 81.0 years.
Major causes of death per 100,000 population (1991): malignant neoplasms (cancers) 151.8; diseases of the circulatory system 138.2; diseases of the respiratory system 80.0; accidents and poisonings 31.6; diseases of the genitourinary system 22.3; diseases of the digestive system 20.9.

National economy

Budget (1991–92). Revenue: HK$112,020,000,000 (earnings and profit taxes 39.6%; indirect taxes 28.4%, of which entertainment and stamp duties 15.6%, duties 6.2%; capital revenue 11.9%). Expenditures: HK$112,982,000,000 (education 17.1%; general services support 13.7%; transport and public works 13.5%; law and order 13.2%; housing 11.5%; health 10.0%; social welfare 6.0%; culture and recreation 5.2%).
Public debt: n.a.
Gross domestic product (at current market prices; 1991): U.S.$71,303,000,000 (U.S.$12,500 per capita).

Structure of gross domestic product and labour force				
	1990			
	in value HK$'000,000	% of total value	labour force	% of labour force
Agriculture	1,441	0.3	23,500	0.9
Mining	209	—	600	—
Manufacturing	88,825	15.8	761,400	27.7
Construction	30,730	5.5	229,100	8.3
Public utilities	12,623	2.3	18,700	0.7
Transp. and commun.	49,504	8.8	272,300	9.9
Trade	127,575	22.8	713,000	25.9
Finance, insurance, and real estate	168,877	30.1	210,200	7.7
Pub. admin., defense, and services	82,472	14.7	514,900	18.7
Other	−1,727[7]	−0.3[7]	4,400	0.2
TOTAL	560,529	100.0	2,748,100	100.0

Production (metric tons except as noted). Agriculture, forestry, fishing (1991): vegetables 105,000, fruits and nuts 3,950, milk 1,670, field crops 1,260, eggs 84,500,000 units; livestock (number of live animals) 314,000 pigs[8], 820 cattle, 6,000,000 chickens[9]; roundwood (1990) 193,000 cu m; fish catch (1989) 242,680. Mining and quarrying (1990): clay and kaolin 16,587; feldspar 3,820. Manufacturing (value added in HK$; 1989): wearing apparel 19,194,000,000; basic metals and fabricated metal products 16,544,000,000; textiles 14,297,000,000; electrical and electronic products 12,694,000,000; publishing and printed material 7,477,000,000; plastic products 6,931,000,000. Construction

(1991): residential 1,814,000 sq m; nonresidential 2,166,000 sq m. Energy production (consumption): electricity (kW-hr; 1990) 28,938,000,000 (27,141,000,000); coal (metric tons; 1990) none (8,932,000); petroleum products (metric tons; 1990) none (2,600,000); natural gas (cu m; 1990) none (385,800,000).
Population economically active (1991): total 2,796,000; activity rate of total population 48.6% (participation rates: over age 15, 63.4%; female 48.0%; unemployed 2.1%).

Price and earnings indexes (1985 = 100)							
	1985	1986	1987	1988	1989	1990	1991
Consumer price index	100.0	102.9	108.6	116.6	128.4	140.8	157.3
Daily earnings index[10]	100.0	110.2	123.5	141.8	166.3	187.8	182.0

Household income and expenditure (1991). Average household size 3.4; monthly income per household: HK$9,964 (U.S.$1,282); sources of income: n.a.; expenditure (1989–90): food 34.2%, housing 25.6%, transportation and vehicles 7.6%, clothing and footwear 7.5%, durable goods 3.8%.
Tourism (1991): receipts from visitors U.S.$4,929,000,000; expenditures by nationals abroad, n.a.
Land use (1991): forested 20.5%; agricultural and under permanent cultivation 6.2%; fish ponds 1.5%; built-on, scrublands, and other 71.8%.

Foreign trade

Balance of trade (current prices)						
	1986	1987	1988	1989	1990	1991
HK$'000,000	+575	+86	−5,717	+7,728	−2,656	−13,096
% of total	0.1%		0.6%	0.7%	0.2%	0.1%

Imports (1991): HK$778,981,950,000 (machinery and transport equipment 29.1%, of which electrical machinery 10.2%, telecommunications equipment 7.7%; textile yarn and fabrics 12.1%; apparel and accessories 8.6%; chemicals and related products 7.7%; food and live animals 5.1%; photographic apparatus, watches, and clocks 4.9%). *Major import sources:* China 37.7%; Japan 16.4%; Taiwan 9.6%; United States 7.6%; South Korea 4.5%; Singapore 4.0%; Germany 2.1%; United Kingdom 2.1%.
Exports (1991): HK$231,045,280,000[11] (clothing accessories and apparel 32.8%; watches and clocks 6.9%; textile fabrics 6.8%; telecommunications equipment 5.0%; computer components 4.9%; jewelry 2.8%; metal products 2.1%; articles of artificial resins and plastics 1.8%; toys and dolls 1.8%). *Major export destinations:* United States 27.2%; China 23.5%; Germany 8.4%; United Kingdom 5.9%; Japan 5.0%; Singapore 3.8%; Taiwan 2.6%.

Transport and communications

Transport. Railroads (1990): route length 21 mi, 34 km; passenger-mi 1,573,000,000, passenger-km 2,532,000,000; short ton-mi cargo 49,000,000, metric ton-km cargo 72,000,000. Roads (1991): total length 950 mi, 1,529 km (paved 100%). Vehicles (1991): passenger cars 236,747; trucks and buses 132,595. Merchant marine (1991): vessels (100 gross tons and over) 355; total deadweight tonnage 10,023,958. Air transport (1991): passenger arrivals 7,412,000, passenger departures 7,602,000; airports (1992) with scheduled flights 1.
Communications. Daily newspapers (1987): total number (1990) 69; total circulation 3,189,000[12]; circulation per 1,000 population 602[12]. Radio (1991): total number of receivers 3,000,000 (1 per 1.9 persons). Television (1991): total number of receivers 1,749,000 (1 per 3.4 persons). Telephones (1990): 3,279,000 (1 per 1.8 persons).

Education and health

Education (1990–91)	schools	teachers[13]	students	student/ teacher ratio[13]
Primary (age 6–11)	681	19,625	524,919	27.3
Secondary (age 12–18)	489	19,419	433,208	25.0
Vocational	34[14]	2,488	30,833[14]	18.5
Higher	11	1,422	67,373	32.4

Educational attainment (1991). Percentage of population age 15 and over having: no formal schooling 12.8%; primary education 25.2%; secondary 45.8%; matriculation 4.9%; nondegree higher 5.4%; higher degree 5.9%.
Literacy (1985): total population age 15 and over literate 3,668,000 (88.1%); males literate 2,040,000 (94.7%); females literate 1,628,000 (80.9%).
Health (1991): physicians 6,545[15] (1 per 896 persons); hospital beds 25,277 (1 per 232 persons); infant mortality rate per 1,000 live births (1991) 7.0.
Food (1987–89): daily per capita caloric intake 2,817 (vegetable products 71%, animal products 29%); 123% of FAO recommended minimum requirement.

Military

Total active duty personnel (1990): 6,800[16] (army 86.8%; navy 8.8%; air force 4.4%). *Military expenditure as percentage of GNP* (1984): 0.6% (world 5.9%); per capita expenditure U.S.$39.

[1]On July 1, 1997, Hong Kong will revert to China as a Special Administrative Region in which the existing socioeconomic system would remain unchanged for a period of 50 years. [2]Includes 21 nonelective seats. [3]Victoria, for some time, had been regarded as the capital because it is the seat of the British administration of the Crown Colony. [4]Excludes the surface areas of reservoirs. [5]Excludes transients and Vietnamese refugees. [6]Excludes about 59,900 Vietnamese refugees, about 1% of the population. [7]Indirect taxes less subsidies. [8]Excludes local pigs not slaughtered in abattoirs. [9]1989. [10]In manufacturing. [11]Excludes reexports valued at HK$534,840,850,000. [12]Thirty-five newspapers only. [13]1987–88. [14]1989–90. [15]Registered personnel; all may not be present and working in the country. [16]British forces with a few locally enlisted personnel.

Hungary

Official name: Magyar Köztársaság (Republic of Hungary).
Form of government: unitary multi-party republic with one legislative house (National Assembly [394[1]]).
Chief of state: President.
Head of government: Prime Minister.
Capital: Budapest.
Official language: Hungarian.
Official religion: none.
Monetary unit: 1 forint (Ft) = 100 fillér; valuation (Oct. 5, 1992) 1 U.S.$ = Ft 76.77; 1 £ = Ft 130.52.

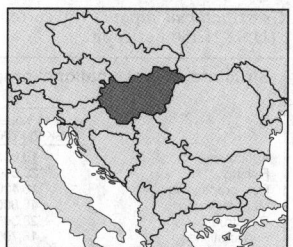

Area and population

Counties	Capitals	area sq mi	area sq km	population 1991 estimate[2]
Bács-Kiskun	Kecskemét	3,229	8,362	543,199
Baranya	Pécs	1,732	4,487	418,025
Békés	Békéscsaba	2,175	5,632	409,226
Borsod-Abaúj-Zemplén	Miskolc	2,798	7,247	756,926
Csongrád	Szeged	1,646	4,263	438,315
Fejér	Székesfehérvár	1,688	4,373	422,048
Győr-Sopron	Győr	1,549	4,012	424,017
Hajdú-Bihar	Debrecen	2,398	6,211	549,204
Heves	Eger	1,404	3,637	333,377
Jász-Nagykun-Szolnok	Szolnok	2,165	5,607	424,430
Komárom-Esztergom	Tatabánya	869	2,251	314,014
Nógrád	Salgótarján	982	2,544	225,738
Pest	Budapest[3]	2,469	6,394	951,057
Somogy	Kaposvár	2,331	6,036	343,315
Szabolcs-Szatmár-Bereg	Nyíregyháza	2,293	5,938	568,830
Tolna	Szekszárd	1,430	3,704	252,872
Vas	Szombathely	1,288	3,337	275,470
Veszprém	Veszprém	1,810	4,689	381,685
Zala	Zalaegerszeg	1,461	3,784	305,059
Capital City				
Budapest[3]		203	525	2,018,035
TOTAL		**35,920**	**93,033**	**10,354,842**

Demography

Population (1992): 10,303,000.
Density (1992): persons per sq mi 286.8, persons per sq km 110.7.
Urban-rural (1990): urban 61.9%; rural 38.1%.
Sex distribution (1991): male 48.02%; female 51.98%.
Age breakdown (1991): under 15, 19.9%; 15–29, 20.5%; 30–44, 22.6%; 45–59, 18.0%; 60–74, 13.6%; 75 and over, 5.4%.
Population projection: (2000) 10,057,000; (2010) 9,758,000. During the intercensal period 1980–90, the population declined at an average annual rate of 0.3%.
Ethnic composition (nationality; 1987): Magyar 96.6%; German 1.6%; Slovak 1.1%; other 0.7%.
Religious affiliation (1989): Christian 87.9%, of which Roman Catholic 64.1%, Protestant 23.3%, Orthodox 0.5%; Jewish 0.9%; atheist and nonreligious 11.2%.
Major cities (1991): Budapest 2,018,035; Debrecen 213,927; Miskolc 194,033; Szeged 176,135; Pécs 170,023.

Vital statistics

Birth rate per 1,000 population (1990): 12.1 (world avg. 27.1); legitimate 86.9%; illegitimate 13.1%.
Death rate per 1,000 population (1990): 14.0 (world avg. 9.8).
Natural increase rate per 1,000 population (1990): −1.9 (world avg. 17.3).
Total fertility rate (avg. births per childbearing woman; 1990): 1.8.
Marriage rate per 1,000 population (1990): 6.4.
Divorce rate per 1,000 population (1990): 2.4.
Life expectancy at birth (1990): male 65.1 years; female 73.7 years.
Major causes of death per 100,000 population (1990): diseases of the circulatory system 736.8; malignant neoplasms (cancers) 301.2; accidents and self-inflicted injuries 125.0.

National economy

Budget (1990). Revenue: Ft 1,279,000,000,000 (payments by enterprises 42.0%, turnover tax 19.9%, income tax 9.9%). Expenditures: Ft 1,279,700,000,000 (social security 26.8%, education 9.4%, health 6.2%, defense 5.6%).
Production (metric tons except as noted). Agriculture, forestry, fishing (1990): wheat 6,198,000, sugar beets 4,743,000, corn (maize) 4,500,000, barley 1,368,000, potatoes 1,226,000, grapes 863,000, sunflower seeds 699,000[4], rye 232,000; livestock (number of live animals) 8,000,000 pigs, 1,865,000 sheep, 1,571,000 cattle, 50,502,000 poultry; roundwood 6,604,000 cu m; fish (1989) catch 37,517. Mining and quarrying (1990): limestone 6,572,000; bauxite 2,559,000; manganese ore 117,200. Manufacturing (1990): cement 3,933,000; crude steel 2,963,000; rolled steel 2,176,000; pig iron 1,693,000; alumina 826,-000; chemical fertilizers 748,700; cotton fabrics 267,000,000 sq m[4]; leather footwear 24,300,000 pairs; buses 7,994 units; diesel motors 7,150 units. Construction (in Ft '000,000; 1990): residential 17,126[5]. Energy production (consumption): electricity (kW-hr; 1990) 28,411,000,000 (39,538,000,000); coal (metric tons; 1990) 17,578,000 (17,891,000); crude petroleum (barrels; 1990) 13,206,000 (42,353,000); petroleum products (metric tons; 1990) 6,931,000 (7,550,000); natural gas (cu m; 1990) 4,399,400,000 (10,446,000,000).
Tourism (1990): receipts from visitors U.S.$1,023,400,000; expenditures by nationals abroad U.S.$614,135,000.
Gross national product (1990): U.S.$30,047,000,000 (U.S.$2,780 per capita).

Structure of gross domestic product and labour force

	1990 in value Ft '000,000,000	% of total value	labour force[2]	% of labour force[2]
Agriculture	258.6	12.4	685,600	15.1
Mining and manufacturing	552.3	26.5	1,384,900	30.4
Construction	105.4	5.1	308,100	6.8
Public utilities	22.6	1.1	74,700	1.6
Transp. and commun.	143.0	6.9	385,700	8.5
Trade	262.5	12.6	494,700	10.9
Services	391.0	18.8	1,096,000	24.1
Other	345.5[6]	16.6[6]	119,600[7]	2.6[7]
TOTAL	2,080.9	100.0	4,549,300	100.0

Public debt (external, outstanding; 1991): U.S.$18,112,000,000.
Population economically active (1990[2]): total 4,549,300; activity rate of total population 43.8% (participation rates: working age 77.5%[4]; female 44.6%; unemployed 1.8%).

Price and earnings indexes (1985 = 100)

	1984	1985	1986	1987	1988	1989	1990
Consumer price index	93.5	100.0	105.3	113.9	132.3	155.0	198.7
Monthly earnings index	91.2	100.0	107.4	117.0	129.9	152.0	182.1

Household income and expenditure. Average household size (1990) 2.7; income per household (1988) Ft 176,150 (U.S.$3,500); sources of income (1989): wages 55.2%, social income 36.8%; expenditure (1989): food and beverages 41.5%, housing 11.9%, clothing 7.6%, household durable goods 7.4%, transportation and communications 7.1%, culture and recreation 7.1%.
Land use (1990): forested 18.2%; meadows and pastures 12.7%; agricultural and under permanent cultivation 56.9%; other 12.2%.

Foreign trade[8]

Balance of trade (current prices)

	1985	1986	1987	1988	1989	1990
Ft '000,000,000	+22.6	−11.8	−5.0	+40.2	+56.2	+67.7
% of total	2.8%	1.4%	0.6%	4.1%	5.2%	5.9%

Imports (1990): Ft 544,921,000,000 (machinery and transport equipment 34.6%, of which road vehicles 7.2%, electrical equipment 4.7%; chemicals and chemical products 14.9%; mineral fuels 14.2%, of which petroleum 9.0%). *Major import sources:* U.S.S.R. 19.1%; W.Ger. 17.4%; Austria 10.0%; E.Ger. 5.9%; Czechoslovakia 4.7%; Italy 4.1%; Switzerland 3.1%; U.S. 2.6%; Poland 2.4%.
Exports (1990): Ft 603,636,000,000 (machinery and transport equipment 25.6%, of which road vehicles 6.9%, electrical equipment 4.5%; food and live animals 19.8%, of which meat and meat products 8.7%; chemicals and chemical products 12.4%). *Major export destinations:* U.S.S.R. 20.2%; W.Ger. 16.9%; Austria 7.5%; Italy 5.9%; Yugoslavia 4.7%; Czechoslovakia 4.1%; U.S. 3.5%; E.Ger. 3.1%.

Transport and communications

Transport. Railroads (1990): length 8,221 mi, 13,230 km; passenger-mi 7,085,-000,000, passenger-km 11,403,000,000; short ton-mi cargo 11,474,000,000, metric ton-km cargo 16,752,000,000. Roads (1990): total length 18,480 mi, 29,741 km (paved 99%). Vehicles (1990): passenger cars 1,912,200; trucks and buses 223,900. Merchant marine (1991): vessels (100 gross tons and over) 17; total deadweight tonnage 151,036. Air transport (1990): passenger-mi 1,053,000, passenger-km 1,695,000; short ton-mi cargo 5,754,000, metric ton-km cargo 8,408,000; airports (1992) with scheduled flights 1.
Communications. Daily newspapers (1990): total number 29; total circulation 2,759,300; circulation per 1,000 population 266. Radio (1991): 6,000,000 (1 per 1.7 persons). Television (1991): 4,214,949 (1 per 2.5 persons). Telephones (1991): 1,871,687 (1 per 5.5 persons).

Education and health

Education (1989–90)

	schools	teachers	students	student/teacher ratio
Primary (age 6–13)	3,527	90,602	1,183,600	13.1
Secondary (age 14–17)	675	21,425	273,511	12.8
Vocational	299	6,842	201,702	29.5
Higher	57	16,319	100,868	6.2

Educational attainment (1984). Percentage of population age 7 and over having: no formal schooling 1.3%; primary education 65.5%; secondary 27.1%; higher 6.1%. *Literacy* (1984): total population age 15 and over literate 8,269,850 (98.9%); males literate 3,934,250 (99.2%); females literate 4,335,600 (98.6%).
Health (1990): physicians 33,905 (1 per 306 persons); hospital beds 105,097 (1 per 99 persons); infant mortality rate per 1,000 live births (1990) 14.8.
Food (1987–89): daily per capita caloric intake 3,638 (vegetable products 63%; animal products 37%); 138% of FAO recommended minimum.

Military

Total active duty personnel (1991): 86,500 (army 76.8%, air force 23.2%).
Military expenditure as percentage of GNP (1989): 6.3% (world 4.9%); per capita expenditure U.S.$391.

---

[1]Includes 8 nonelective seats. [2]January 1. [3]Budapest has separate county status. The area and population of the city are excluded from the larger county (Pest), which it administers. [4]1989. [5]Includes hotel construction. [6]Other material activities and balance of taxes on products. [7]Includes 82,000 unemployed and employed not allocated by activity. [8]Import figures are f.o.b. in balance of trade and c.i.f. for commodities and trading partners.

Iceland

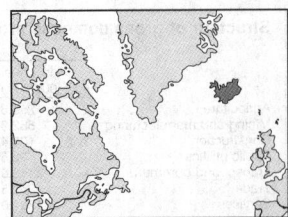

Official name: Lýdhveldidh Ísland
(Republic of Iceland).
Form of government: unitary multiparty
republic with one legislative house
(Althing [63][1]).
Chief of state: President.
Head of government: Prime Minister.
Capital: Reykjavík.
Official language: Icelandic.
Official religion: Evangelical Lutheran.
Monetary unit: 1 króna (ISK) = 100
aurar; valuation (Oct. 5, 1992)
1 U.S.$ = ISK 54.51; 1 £ = ISK 92.67.

Area and population

Regions[2]	Administrative centres	area sq mi	area sq km	population 1991[3] estimate
Austurland	Egilsstadhir	8,491	21,991	13,180
Höfudhborgarsvædhi	Reykjavík	765[4]	1,982[4]	149,482
Nordhurland eystra	Akureyri	8,636	22,368	26,382
Nordhurland vestra	Saudhárkrókur	5,055	13,093	10,340
Sudhurland	Selfoss	9,735	25,214	20,548
Sudhurnes	Keflavík	4	4	15,357
Vestfirdhir	Ísafjördhur	3,657	9,470	9,756
Vesturland	Borgarnes	3,360	8,701	14,532
TOTAL		39,699	102,819	259,577

Demography

Population (1992): 261,000.
Density[5] (1991): persons per sq mi 8.5, persons per sq km 3.3.
Urban-rural (1990): urban 91.0%; rural 9.0%.
Sex distribution (1991): male 50.14%; female 49.86%.
Age breakdown (1991): under 15, 24.7%; 15–29, 24.7%; 30–44, 22.4%; 45–59, 13.4%; 60–74, 10.2%; 75 and over, 4.6%.
Population projection: (2000) 276,000; (2010) 293,000.
Doubling time: 65 years.
Ethnic composition (1991): Icelandic 93.9%; Danish 1.3%; persons born in or citizens of the United States 0.7%; Swedish 0.5%; German 0.4%; other 3.2%.
Religious affiliation (1991): Protestant 96.2%, of which Evangelical Lutheran 92.2%, other Lutheran 3.1%; Roman Catholic 1.0%; nonreligious 1.4%; other 1.4%.
Major cities (1991): Reykjavík 99,623 (urban area 148,858); Kópavogur 16,677[6]; Hafnarfjördhur 15,623[6]; Akureyri 14,436; Keflavík 7,566.

Vital statistics

Birth rate per 1,000 population (1991): 17.6 (world avg. 26.4); (1990) legitimate 44.8%; illegitimate 55.2%.
Death rate per 1,000 population (1991): 6.9 (world avg. 9.2).
Natural increase rate per 1,000 population (1991): 10.7 (world avg. 17.2).
Total fertility rate (avg. births per childbearing woman; 1990): 2.3.
Marriage rate per 1,000 population (1990): 4.5.
Divorce rate per 1,000 population (1990): 1.9.
Life expectancy at birth (1989–90): male 75.7 years; female 80.3 years.
Major causes of death per 100,000 population (1990): diseases of the circulatory system 292.9, of which ischemic heart diseases 171.4, cerebrovascular disease 70.2; malignant neoplasms (cancers) 178.0; diseases of the respiratory system 79.6.

National economy

Budget (1991). Revenue: ISK 99,953,000,000 (sales tax 39.0%, income tax 19.3%, import duties 10.6%, taxes on alcohol and tobacco 6.5%). Expenditures: ISK 112,487,000,000 (health and welfare 44.9%, education 15.7%, general services 10.4%, interest on public debt 8.8%).
Production (metric tons except as noted). Agriculture, forestry, fishing (1991): milk (1990) 110,000, potatoes 15,100, silage 962,900 cu m; livestock (number of live animals) 510,800 sheep, 77,700 cattle, 74,100 horses; fish catch 991,000 (of which cod 294,700, capelin 250,600, redfish 100,500, lobster and shrimp 44,800). Mining and quarrying (1991): diatomite 23,000. Manufacturing (value added in ISK '000,000; 1989): food products 20,068; graphic arts 4,201; fabricated metal products and machinery 4,167; wood furniture 1,964; nonmetallic mineral products 1,646. Construction (number of buildings completed; 1988): residential 1,728; nonresidential 649. Energy production (consumption): electricity (kW-hr; 1990) 4,610,000,000 (4,610,000,000); coal (metric tons; 1990) none (70,000); crude petroleum, none (none); petroleum products (metric tons; 1990) none (637,000); natural gas, none (none).
Land use (1989): forested 1.2%; meadows and pastures 22.7%; agricultural and under permanent cultivation 0.1%; other 76.0%.
Population economically active (1989): total 128,053; activity rate of total population 50.7% (participation rates: 15–64, 78.6%; female [1984] 39.5%; unemployed [June 1991–July 1992] 2.1%).

Price and earnings indexes (1985 = 100)

	1986	1987	1988	1989	1990	1991	1992[7]
Consumer price index	120.6	143.4	181.3	221.7	254.3	268.5	280.9
Hourly wages index	132.6	188.3	238.4	270.2	291.0	313.9	326.2

Tourism (1991): receipts from visitors U.S.$223,600,000; expenditures by nationals abroad U.S.$272,100,000.

Gross national product (at current market prices; 1990): U.S.$5,456,000,000 (U.S.$21,150 per capita).

Structure of gross national product and labour force

	1990 in value ISK '000,000[8]	% of total value	labour force	% of labour force
Agriculture	10,000	3.1	6,029	4.7
Fishing	29,200	9.1	7,086	5.6
Fish processing	15,400	4.8	7,659	6.0
Manufacturing	45,600	14.2	15,625	12.3
Construction	28,300	8.8	12,379	9.8
Public utilities	15,700	4.9	1,110	0.9
Transportation and communications	26,700	8.3	8,411	6.6
Trade	36,600	11.4	18,105	14.3
Finance, real estate	53,000	16.5	9,977	7.9
Pub. admin., defense	53,300	16.6	22,751	17.9
Services	21,500	6.7	9,333	7.4
Other	−14,100[9]	−4.4[9]	8,393[10]	6.6[10]
TOTAL	321,200[11]	100.0	126,858	100.0

Public debt (external, outstanding; end of 1991): U.S.$1,929,000,000.
Household income and expenditure. Average household size (1985) 2.9; average net income for persons filing tax returns (1989) ISK 939,000 (U.S.$16,462); sources of income (1989)[12]: wages and salaries 74.2%, transfer payments 16.1%, self-employment 2.4%, other 7.3%; expenditure (1987): food and beverages 21.1%, transportation and communications 18.6%, housing 11.2%, household furnishings 11.1%, clothing and footwear 10.4%, expenditures in restaurants and hotels 8.5%, recreation 8.2%.

Foreign trade[13]

Balance of trade (current prices)

	1986	1987	1988	1989	1990	1991
ISK '000,000	+3,356	−2,617	−576	+7,280	+4,540	−647
% of total	3.9%	2.4%	0.5%	4.8%	2.5%	0.4%

Imports (1991): ISK 101,538,000,000 (consumer goods 21.2%; capital goods [except transport equipment] 19.6%; transport equipment 14.6%; fuels and lubricants 8.3%; food and beverages 8.2%). *Major import sources:* Germany 13.0%; United States 10.3%; The Netherlands 10.0%; Denmark 8.6%; United Kingdom 8.2%; Sweden 7.6%; Japan 7.4%.
Exports (1991): ISK 91,560,000,000 (marine products 80.0%, of which frozen cod fillets 17.6%, uncured salted fish 11.7%, fresh whole fish chilled or on ice 9.6%, frozen shrimp 6.8%; aluminum 8.8%; ferrosilicon 1.9%). *Major export destinations:* United Kingdom 23.4%; United States 12.6%; Germany 12.1%; France 10.1%; Japan 7.9%; Spain 4.8%.

Transport and communications

Transport. Railroads: none. Roads (1990): total length 7,070 mi, 11,378 km (paved 20%). Vehicles (1991): passenger cars 120,862; trucks and buses 16,012. Merchant marine (1991): vessels (100 gross tons and over) 392; total deadweight tonnage 118,478. Air transport (1991)[14]: passenger-mi 1,147,000,000, passenger-km 1,846,000,000; short ton-mi cargo 23,713,000, metric ton-km cargo 34,620,000; airports (1992) with scheduled flights 21.
Communications. Daily newspapers (1991): total number 6; total circulation 147,500; circulation per 1,000 population 572. Radio (1991): total number of receivers 155,000 (1 per 1.7 persons). Television (1991): total number of receivers 76,250 (1 per 3.4 persons). Telephones (1990): 130,000[15] (1 per 2.0 persons).

Education and health

Education (1990–91)

	schools	teachers	students	student/ teacher ratio
Primary (age 7–12)[16]	265[17]	3,200[17]	58,642[17]	18.3[17]
Secondary (age 13–20)				
Voc., teacher tr.				
Higher	5	369[18]	5,450	14.0[18]

Educational attainment: n.a. *Literacy:* virtually 100%.
Health: physicians (1989) 675 (1 per 373 persons); hospital beds (1988) 2,490 (1 per 100 persons); infant mortality rate per 1,000 live births (1991) 5.5.
Food (1987–89): daily per capita caloric intake 3,518 (vegetable products 62%, animal products 38%); 132% of FAO recommended minimum requirement.

Military

Total active duty personnel (1991): 130 coast guard personnel; NATO-sponsored U.S.-manned Iceland Defense Force (1991): 3,000 (navy 60.0%, air force 40.0%). *Military expenditure as percentage of GNP* (1989): none (world average 4.9%).

---

[1]Usually meets as two separate bodies (Upper House [21]; Lower House [42]). [2]Regions have limited administrative authority. [3]December 1. [4]Höfudhborgarsvædhi includes Sudhurnes. [5]Population density calculated with reference to 30,748 sq mi (79,638 sq km) non-wasteland area (area free of glaciers and lava fields). [6]Within Reykjavík urban area. [7]July. [8]Data estimated from percentage distribution of sectors. [9]Net of imputed bank service charges and changes in value of stock. [10]Includes 2,255 unemployed. [11]GDP (1990) equals ISK 335,900,000,000. [12]For persons filing tax returns. [13]Import figures are f.o.b. in balance of trade and c.i.f. in commodities and trading partners. [14]Icelandair only. [15]Number of subscribers. [16]Includes preprimary. [17]1988–89. [18]Based on data for 4 schools only.

India

Official name: Bhārat (Hindī); Republic of India (English).
Form of government: multiparty federal republic with two legislative houses (Council of States [245][1], House of the People [545][2]).
Chief of state: President.
Head of government: Prime Minister.
Capital: New Delhi.
Official languages: Hindī; English.
Official religion: none.
Monetary unit: 1 Indian rupee (Re, plural Rs) = 100 paise; valuation (Oct. 5, 1992) 1 U.S.$ = Rs 28.29; 1 £ = Rs 48.10.

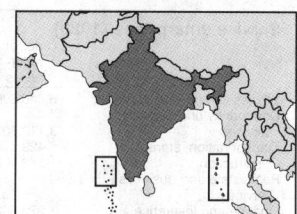

Area and population

States	Capitals	area sq mi	area sq km	population 1991 census[3]
Andhra Pradesh	Hyderābād	106,204	275,068	66,354,559
Arunāchal Pradesh	Itānagar	32,333	83,743	858,392
Assam	Dispur	30,285	78,438	22,294,562
Bihār	Patna	67,134	173,877	86,338,853
Goa	Panaji	1,429	3,702	1,168,622
Gujarāt	Gāndhīnagar	75,685	196,024	41,174,343
Haryāna	Chandīgarh	17,070	44,212	16,317,715
Himāchal Pradesh	Shimla	21,495	55,673	5,111,079
Jammu and Kashmir	Srīnagar	38,830	100,569	7,718,700[4]
Karnātaka	Bangalore	74,051	191,791	44,806,468
Kerala	Trivandrum	15,005	38,863	29,032,828
Madhya Pradesh	Bhopāl	171,215	443,446	66,135,862
Mahārāshtra	Bombay	118,800	307,690	78,748,215
Manipur	Imphāl	8,621	22,327	1,826,714
Meghālaya	Shillong	8,660	22,429	1,760,626
Mizorām	Āīzawl	8,140	21,081	686,217
Nāgāland	Kohīma	6,401	16,579	1,215,573
Orissa	Bubaneshwar	60,119	155,707	31,512,070
Punjab	Chandīgarh	19,445	50,362	20,190,795
Rājasthān	Jaipur	132,140	342,239	43,880,640
Sikkim	Gangtok	2,740	7,096	405,505
Tamil Nādu	Madras	50,216	130,058	55,638,318
Tripura	Agartala	4,049	10,486	2,744,827
Uttar Pradesh	Lucknow	113,673	294,411	139,031,130
West Bengal	Calcutta	34,267	88,752	67,982,732
Union Territories				
Andaman and Nicobar Islands	Port Blair	3,185	8,249	279,111
Chandīgarh	Chandīgarh	44	114	640,725
Dādra and Nagar Haveli	Silvassa	190	491	138,401
Damān and Diu	Damān	43	112	101,439
Delhi	Delhi	572	1,483	9,370,475
Lakshadweep	Kavaratti	12	32	51,681
Pondicherry	Pondicherry	190	492	807,045
TOTAL		1,222,243[5]	3,165,596[5]	844,324,222

Demography

Population (1992): 889,700,000[6].
Density (1992)[5]: persons per sq mi 727.9, persons per sq km 281.1.
Urban-rural (1991): urban 25.7%; rural 74.3%.
Sex distribution (1991): male 51.85%; female 48.15%.
Age breakdown (1990): under 15, 36.5%; 15–29, 27.5%; 30–44, 17.8%; 45–59, 11.1%; 60–74, 5.9%; 75 and over, 1.2%.
Population projection: (2000) 1,041,543,000; (2010) 1,223,483,000.
Doubling time: 34 years.
Linguistic composition (1981)[7]: Hindī (lingua franca) 45.00%; Hindī (including associated languages and dialects) 38.77%; Telugu 7.96%; Bengali 7.56%; Marāthī 7.28%; Tamil 6.56%; Urdū 5.18%; Gujarātī 4.87%; Kannada 3.95%; Malayālam 3.81%; Oriyā 3.36%; Punjābī 2.73%; English (lingua franca) 2.50%; Assamese 1.64%[8]; Bhīlī/Bhilodī 0.65%; Santhālī 0.62%; Kashmīrī 0.47%; Gondī 0.29%; Sindhī 0.29%; Konkani 0.23%; Dogrī 0.22%; Tulu 0.20%; Kurukh 0.19%; Nepālī 0.18%; Khandeshī 0.17%; Manipurī 0.13%; other 2.69%.
Place of birth (foreign born; 1981): other Asia 7,875,399, of which Bangladesh 4,170,524, Pakistan 2,736,038, Nepal 501,292, Sri Lanka 211,514, Myanmar 134,783; Africa 42,726; Europe 13,046; United States and Canada 5,923.
Major cities (urban agglomerations; 1991): Greater Bombay 9,909,547 (12,571,720); Delhi 7,174,755 (8,375,188); Calcutta 4,388,262 (10,916,272); Madras 3,795,028 (5,361,468); Hyderābād 3,005,496 (4,280,261); Ahmadābād 2,872,865 (3,297,655); Bangalore 2,650,659 (4,086,548); Kānpur 1,958,282 (2,111,284); Nāgpur 1,622,225; Lucknow 1,592,010; New Delhi 294,149[9].

Other principal cities (1991)

	population		population		population
Āgra	899,195	Indore	1,086,673	Rājkot	556,137
Allahābād	806,447	Jabalpur	739,961	Rānchi	598,498
Amritsar	709,456	Jaipur	1,454,678	Sholāpur	
Aurangābād	572,634	Jalandhar (Jullundur)	519,530	(Solāpur)	603,870
Bareilly	583,473	Jodhpur	648,621	Srīnagar	586,038[10]
Bhopāl	1,063,662	Kalyān	1,014,062	Sūrat	1,496,943
Chandīgarh	502,992	Kota	536,444	Thāne (Thāna)	796,620
Cochin (Kochi)	564,038	Ludhiāna	1,012,062	Trivandrum	523,733
Coimbatore	853,402	Madurai	951,696	Vadodara	
Farīdabād	613,828	Meerut	752,078	(Baroda)	1,021,084
Guwāhāti	577,591	Nāshik (Nāsik)	646,896	Vārānasi	
Gwalior	692,982	Patna	916,980	(Benares)	925,962
Howrah (Hāora)	946,732	Pimpri-Chinchwad	515,962	Vijayawāda	701,351
Hubli-Dhārwād	647,640	Pune	1,559,558	Vishākhapatnam	750,024

Religious affiliation (1981)[11]: Hindu 82.64%; Muslim 11.35%; Christian 2.43%; Sikh 1.97%; Buddhist 0.71%; Jain 0.48%; Zoroastrian 0.01%; other 0.41%.
Mobility (1981). Population living in same district but at different residence as in 1971: 47,604,000; different district, same state 22,557,000; different state 10,860,000; moved outside the country 1,179,000.
Households (1981)[11]. Total households 119,230,710. Average household size 5.6; 1 person 5.6%, 2 persons 8.3%, 3 persons 11.0%, 4 persons 14.6%, 5 persons 15.9%, 6 or more persons 44.6%. Average number of rooms per household 2.0; no exclusive room 0.6%, 1 room 44.7%, 2 rooms 28.6%, 3 rooms 12.2%, 4 rooms 6.3%, 5 rooms 2.7%, 6 or more rooms 3.1%, unspecified number of rooms 1.8%. Average number of persons per room 2.8. Shelterless (homeless) population estimated (1987) at more than 100,000,000.
Emigration (1987 estimation): persons living abroad 12,697,000 (accepting foreign citizenship 8,200,000), of which in Nepal (1980) 3,800,000 (2,388,000); Malaysia 1,170,000 (1,029,000); Middle Eastern countries 1,064,000 (102,000); Sri Lanka 1,028,000 (457,000); South Africa 850,000 (850,000); United Kingdom 789,000 (395,000); Mauritius 701,000 (700,000); United States 500,000 (287,000); Trinidad and Tobago 430,000 (430,000); Fiji 339,000 (339,000); Myanmar 330,000 (50,000); Canada 229,000 (129,000).

Vital statistics

Birth rate per 1,000 population (1990): 29.9[12] (world avg. 27.1).
Death rate per 1,000 population (1990): 9.6[12] (world avg. 9.8).
Natural increase rate per 1,000 population (1990): 20.3[12] (world avg. 17.3).
Total fertility rate (avg. births per childbearing woman; 1991): 3.7.
Marital status of male (female) population age 25 and over (1981): single 6.4% (1.1%); married 87.4% (79.4%); widowed 5.7% (18.8%); divorced or separated 0.5% (0.7%).
Life expectancy at birth (1986–91): male 58.1 years; female 59.1 years.
Major causes of death (rural areas only; 1990)[13]: senility 24.4%[14]; infectious and parasitic diseases 18.0%; diseases of the respiratory system 15.7%; diseases of the circulatory system 10.9%; accidents and injuries 6.9%; prematurity at birth 4.9%; diseases of the digestive system 3.7%; cancers 3.4%; anemias 3.2%; suicide 1.6%; diseases of the nervous system 1.3%; diabetes 0.7%.

Social indicators

Educational attainment (1981)[11]. Percentage of population age 25 and over having: no formal schooling (illiterate) 64.8%; no formal schooling (literate) 1.0%; some primary education 7.1%; completed primary 10.9%; some secondary 6.2%; completed secondary 7.1%; higher vocational 0.4%; completed undergraduate degree 2.5%.

Distribution of income (1983)

percentage of household income by quintile

1	2	3	4	5 (highest)
8.1%	12.3%	16.3%	22.0%	41.3%

Quality of working life. Average workweek (1989): 42 hours. Rate of fatal (nonfatal) injuries per 100,000 workers: industrial workers (1987) 14 (4,140); miners (1987) 31 (169); railway workers (1987–88) 17 (1,188). Employees covered under Employee's State Insurance Scheme (1989) 6,807,000; number of beneficiaries 26,411,000. Average days lost to labour stoppages per 1,000 workdays (1989): 20.
Access to services. Proportion of villages having access to electricity (1990) 83.4%; proportion of urban (rural) population having access to (1990): safe water supply 84.0% (74.0%), safe sewage disposal 46.0% (2.0%).
Social participation. Eligible voters participating in last (May/June 1991) national election: 53%. Verified trade union membership in total work force (1986): less than 5% (about 10,000,000 workers).
Social deviance (1984). Offense rate per 100,000 population for: murder 3.4; dacoity (gang robbery) 1.4; theft and housebreaking 43.7; rape 0.8. Rate of suicide per 100,000 population (1990): 6.9.
Leisure (1987). Favourite leisure activities in urban areas: listening to the radio, watching television, reading periodicals, and attending the cinema.
Material well-being (1983). Households possessing: automobile 0.8%; telephone 2.3%; television receiver 1.6%; radio receiver 17.2%.

National economy

Gross national product (1990): U.S.$294,816,000,000 (U.S.$350 per capita).

Structure of gross domestic product and labour force

	1989–90[15] in value Rs '000,000,000	1989–90[15] % of total value	1981[11] labour force	1981[11] % of labour force
Agriculture	1,232.6	31.2	172,713,291	66.4
Mining	86.5	2.2	1,301,632	0.5
Manufacturing	740.6	18.8	26,554,517	10.2
Construction	220.2	5.6	3,864,104	1.5
Public utilities	86.6	2.2	989,490	0.3
Transp. and commun.	277.9	7.0	6,206,697	2.4
Trade, restaurants	506.2	12.8	12,638,204	4.9
Finance, real estate	341.1	8.6	1,822,229	0.7
Pub. admin., defense	237.4	6.0 }	18,514,810	7.1
Services	222.3	5.6 }		
Other			15,670,144[16]	6.0[16]
TOTAL	3,951.4	100.0	260,275,118	100.0

Budget (1991–92). Revenue: Rs 1,002,493,000,000 (tax revenue 63.6%, of which excise taxes 26.8%, customs duties 25.8%, corporation taxes 6.7%; nontax revenue 36.4%, of which economic services 20.1%, interest receipts 11.0%). Expenditures: Rs 1,141,032,000,000 (interest payments and debt servicing 24.1%; grants to state governments 13.2%; transportation 12.6%; defense 10.2%; agriculture 5.5%; social services 3.3%).

Public debt (external, outstanding; 1991): U.S.$62,585,000,000.
Production (in '000 metric tons except as noted). Agriculture, forestry, fishing (1991): sugarcane 240,290, rice 110,945, wheat 54,522, potatoes 15,254, sorghum 10,800, mangoes 9,700, millet 9,000, corn (maize) 8,200, peanuts (groundnuts) 7,000, coconuts 6,550, bananas 6,400, cassava 5,600, chick-peas 5,196, rapeseed 5,152, seed cotton 5,106, dry beans 4,052, cottonseed 3,404, tomatoes 3,100, palm oil 2,800, soybeans 2,100, oranges 1,890, cotton lint 1,700, barley 1,642, jute 1,620, apples 1,020, sunflower seed 850, lentils 835, sesame seed 800, tea 730, chilies 609[17], tobacco 560, turmeric 340[17], ginger 154[17], black pepper 43[17]; livestock (number of live animals) 198,400,000 cattle, 112,000,000 goats, 77,000,000 water buffalo, 55,740,000 sheep; roundwood (1990) 274,460,000 cu m; fish catch (1990) 3,619, of which freshwater fish 1,371. Mining and quarrying (1990): limestone 64,116[18]; iron ore (metal content) 29,469; bauxite 4,618; dolomite 2,520[18]; manganese 1,404; chromite 1,084; magnesite 476[18]; zinc concentrate 79; copper (metal content) 65; gold 59,700 troy oz.; diamonds 16,500 carats[18]. Manufacturing (1990–91): cement 46,609; steel ingots 14,194; refined sugar 11,808; finished steel 11,118; nitrogenous fertilizers 7,068; paper and paperboard 2,062; jute manufactures 1,388; soda ash 1,384; aluminum 443; nylon and polyester yarns 261; electric motors 5,850,000 horsepower; bicycles 6,768,000 units; motorcycles and scooters 1,865,000 units; diesel engines 1,795,000 units; passenger cars and jeeps 221,000 units; passenger buses and trucks 146,000 units; cotton cloth 12,738,000,000 metres[18]; computers, Rs 8,200,000,000[19]; gold jewelry, Rs 7,200,000,000[20]; silk goods, Rs 6,760,000,000[20]. Construction (value in Rs; 1984) residential 87,010,000,000; nonresidential 40,730,000,000.

Manufacturing enterprises (1986–87)[21]

	no. of factories	no. of persons engaged	avg. wages as a % of avg. of all wages	annual value added (Rs '000,000)[15]
Chemicals and chemical products,	6,335	524,000	148.9	30,455
of which industrial chemicals	1,017	86,000	166.4	7,207
drugs and medicine	1,374	120,000	167.2	7,117
fertilizers and pesticides[22]	546	80,000	180.2	5,920
Textiles (excl. clothing)	11,761	1,429,000	90.6	29,451
Iron and steel	5,251	571,000	130.7	20,561
Food products	17,299	956,000	54.3	19,531
Transport equipment,	3,120	487,000	147.3	18,959
of which motor vehicles	1,567	183,000	169.2	11,033
Nonelectrical machinery/apparatus	7,254	412,000	130.7	17,551
Electrical machinery/apparatus,	3,888	339,000	147.6	16,446
of which radios and televisions	992	93,000	124.7	3,664
Refined petroleum	17	16,000	312.3	9,573
Bricks, tiles, cement	7,184	345,000	67.8	8,478
Metal products	5,978	178,000	96.5	5,257
Paper and paper products	1,720	130,000	98.3	3,982
Printing and publishing	3,201	147,000	106.6	3,959
Tobacco products	6,716	346,000	29.6	3,795
Beverages	447	46,000	89.8	2,094
Plastic products	1,953	59,000	76.2	1,975
Professional and scientific goods	737	47,000	115.2	1,738
Petroleum, coal derivatives	470	33,000	136.6	1,625

Energy production (consumption): electricity (kW-hr; 1991–92) 286,700,000,000 ([1990] 286,940,000,000); coal (metric tons; 1991–92) 229,000,000 ([1990] 218,939,000); crude petroleum (barrels; 1991–92) 230,584,000 ([1990] 379,980,000); petroleum products (metric tons; 1990) 39,456,000 (44,766,000); natural gas (cu m; 1991) 13,792,000,000 ([1990] 10,303,000,000).

Financial aggregates[23]

	1986	1987	1988	1989	1990	1991	1992[24]
Exchange rate, Rs per:							
U.S. dollar	13.12	12.88	14.95	17.03	18.07	25.83	25.89
£	19.35	24.10	27.05	27.35	34.84	48.33	47.13
SDR	16.05	18.27	20.12	22.39	25.71	36.95	36.15
International reserves (U.S.$)							
Total (excl. gold; '000,000)	6,396	6,454	4,899	3,859	1,521	3,627	5,570
SDRs ('000,000)	356	159	96	113	316	46	112
Reserve pos. in IMF ('000,000)	596	691	656	640	—	—	1
Foreign exchange ('000,000)	5,444	5,603	4,148	3,105	1,205	3,580	5,458
Gold ('000,000 fine troy oz)	10,449	10,449	10,449	10,449	10,692	11,282	11,282
% world reserves	1.1	1.1	1.1	1.1	1.1	1.2	1.2
Interest and prices							
Central bank discount (%)	10.0	10.0	10.0	10.0	10.0	12.0	12.0
Advance (prime) rate (%)	16.5	16.5	16.5	16.5	16.5	17.9	19.0
Industrial share prices (1985 = 100)[25]	122.1	111.9	115.0	173.8	241.3	325.1	...
Balance of payments (U.S.$'000,000)							
Balance of visible trade	−5,438	−5,777	−6,581	−6,110	...	...	...
Imports, f.o.b.	15,686	17,661	20,091	22,254	...	...	...
Exports, f.o.b.	10,248	11,884	13,510	16,144	...	...	...
Balance of invisibles	+841	+585	−567	−716	...	...	...
Balance of payments, current account	−4,597	−5,192	−7,148	−6,826	...	...	...

Population economically active (1981)[11]: total 260,275,118; activity rate of total population 39.1% (participation rates: over age 15, 60.7%; female 27.0%; unemployed[26] [March 1990] 13.1%).

Price and earnings indexes (1984 = 100)

	1986	1987	1988	1989	1990	1991	1992[24]
Consumer price index	114.8	124.9	136.6	145.1	158.1	180.0	198.6
Monthly earnings index[27]	...	...	162.0	179.5			

Household income and expenditure. Average household size[28] (1981) 5.5; income per household: n.a.; sources of income (1984–85): salaries and wages 42.2%, self-employed 39.7%, interest 8.6%, profits and dividends 6.0%, rent 3.5%; expenditure (1988–89): food and beverages 52.1%, clothing and footwear 12.2%, transportation and communications 8.4%, housing 6.6%, household furnishings 4.4%, energy 4.3%.

Service enterprises (1980)

	no. of enterprises	no. of employees	annual value added (Rs '000,000)[17]
Wholesale and retail trade	6,046,200	10,228,700	412,450
Community and personal services	3,177,700	13,128,800	205,880
Transportation, storage	429,800	1,551,200	202,750
Construction	152,000	451,200	198,560
Real estate and business services	...	...	150,670
Finance and insurance	273,500	1,570,800	132,270
Electricity, gas, and steam	33,700	363,500	64,260
Communications	98,900	530,900	37,690
Restaurants and hotels	807,000	2,080,500	24,690

Land use (1990): forested 22.4%; meadows and pastures 4.1%; agricultural and under permanent cultivation 56.9%; other 16.6%.
Tourism: receipts from visitors (1990–91) U.S.$1,362,000,000; expenditures by nationals abroad (1990) U.S.$425,000,000.

Foreign trade[29, 30]

Balance of trade (current prices)

	1985–86	1986–87	1987–88	1988–89	1989–90	1990–91
Rs '000,000	−67,571	−53,990	−43,326	−49,417	−40,213	−61,163
% of total	23.4%	17.7%	12.1%	10.9%	6.8%	8.6%

Imports (1990–91): Rs 432,596,000,000 (mineral fuels and lubricants 25.0%; nonelectrical machinery and apparatus 15.4%; pearls and precious and semiprecious stones [mostly diamonds] 8.6%; iron and steel 5.1%; electrical machinery and apparatus 4.0%; transport equipment 3.8%; organic chemicals 3.7%). *Major import sources:* U.S. 12.1%; Germany 8.0%; Japan 7.5%; U.K. 6.7%; Saudi Arabia 6.7%; Belgium 6.3%; U.S.S.R. 5.9%; United Arab Emirates 4.4%.
Exports (1990–91): Rs 326,120,000,000 (pearls, precious and semiprecious stones [mostly diamonds], and jewelry 16.0%; ready-made garments 12.4%; machinery, transport equipment, and metal manufactures including iron and steel 12.0%; leather and leather manufactures 7.8%; chemicals and chemical products 7.1%; cotton yarn and fabrics 6.3%; iron ore 3.3%; tea 3.2%). *Major export destinations:* U.S.S.R. 16.1%; U.S. 14.7%; Japan 9.3%; Germany 7.8%; U.K. 6.5%; Belgium 3.8%; Hong Kong 3.3%; Italy 3.1%.

Transport and communications

Transport. Railroads (1990–91): route length 38,752 mi, 62,366 km; passenger-mi 183,700,000,000, passenger-km 295,700,000,000; short ton-mi cargo 166,200,000,000, metric ton-km cargo 242,700,000,000. Roads (1990–91): total length 1,266,000 mi, 2,037,000 km (paved 49%). Vehicles (1990): passenger cars 2,391,000; trucks and buses 1,396,000. Merchant marine (1991): vessels (100 gross tons and over) 890; total deadweight tonnage 10,528,528. Air transport (1990)[31]: passenger-mi 10,264,000,000, passenger-km 16,518,000,000; short ton-mi cargo 454,003,000, metric ton-km cargo 662,832,000; airports (1992) with scheduled flights 98.
Communications. Daily newspapers (1989): total number 2,281; total circulation 17,000,000[32]; circulation per 1,000 population 21[32]. Radio (1991): 55,000,000 receivers (1 per 16 persons). Television (1990): 20,000,000 receivers (1 per 44 persons). Telephones (1990): 5,485,872 (1 per 157 persons).

Education and health

Education (1989–90)

	schools	teachers	students	student/ teacher ratio
Primary (age 6–10)	550,700	1,601,717	97,318,114	60.8
Secondary (age 11–17)	214,380	2,311,837	49,402,664	21.4
Higher[17]	6,600	242,000	3,820,000	15.8

Literacy (1990): total population age 15 and over literate 261,200,000 (48.2%); males literate 173,200,000 (61.8%); females literate 88,000,000 (33.7%).
Health: physicians 365,000 (1 per 2,337 persons); hospital beds 649,417 (1 per 1,314 persons); infant mortality rate 80.0[12].
Food (1988–90): daily per capita caloric intake 2,229 (vegetable products 93%, animal products 7%); 101% of FAO recommended minimum requirement.

Military

Total active duty personnel (1992): 1,265,000 (army 87.0%, navy 4.3%, air force 8.7%). *Military expenditure as percentage of GNP* (1989): 3.1% (world 4.9%); per capita expenditure U.S.$10.

[1]Council of States can have a maximum number of 250 members; a maximum of 12 of these members may be nominated by the president. [2]Includes 2 nonelective seats. [3]Revised preliminary. [4]Census not conducted; population based on projection of 1989 official estimate. [5]Excludes 46,976 sq mi (121,667 sq km) of territory claimed by India as part of Jammu and Kashmir but occupied by Pakistan or China. [6]UN estimate based on revision of population projection completed in 1990. [7]Mother tongue unless otherwise noted. [8]Percentage based on 1971 census. [9]Within Delhi urban agglomeration. [10]1981 census. [11]Excludes Assam. [12]Based on a sample registration scheme. [13]Percentage breakdown based on 21,028 deaths recorded at 1,305 nationally dispersed primary-health-centre villages. [14]Deceased over age 60 with no apparent sickness. [15]At factor cost. [16]Not adequately defined. [17]1988–89. [18]1989–90. [19]1990 value of production. [20]1991–92 value of exports. [21]Establishments with 10 or more workers using electrical power or 20 or more workers not using electrical power. [22]1985–86. [23]End of period unless otherwise noted. [24]May. [25]Annual average. [26]Applicants registered at employment exchanges. [27]Public sector only. [28]Excludes shelterless population. [29]Import figures are f.o.b. in balance of trade and c.i.f. in commodities and trading partners. [30]Fiscal year beginning April 1st. [31]Air India and Indian Airlines only. [32]1987.

Indonesia

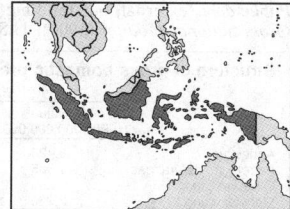

Official name: Republik Indonesia
  (Republic of Indonesia).
Form of government: unitary multiparty
  republic with two legislative houses
  (House of People's Representatives
  [500[1]]; People's Consultative
  Assembly [1,000[2]]).
Head of state and government:
  President.
Capital: Jakarta.
Official language: Bahasa Indonesia.
Official religion: monotheism.
Monetary unit: 1 Indonesian rupiah
  (Rp) = 100 sen; valuation (Oct. 5,
  1992) 1 U.S.$ = Rp 2,071;
  1 £ = Rp 3,520.

Area and population

Metropolitan district	Capitals	area sq mi	area sq km	population 1990 census[3]
Jakarta Raya	Jakarta	228	590	8,254,000
Provinces				
Bali	Denpasar	2,147	5,561	2,778,000
Bengkulu	Bengkulu	8,173	21,168	1,179,000
Irian Jaya	Jayapura	162,928	421,981	1,641,000
Jambi	Jambi	17,297	44,800	2,016,000
Jawa Barat	Bandung	17,877	46,300	35,381,000
Jawa Tengah	Semarang	13,207	34,206	28,522,000
Jawa Timur	Surabaya	18,502	47,921	32,504,000
Kalimantan Barat	Pontianak	56,664	146,760	3,239,000
Kalimantan Selatan	Banjarmasin	14,541	37,660	2,598,000
Kalimantan Tengah	Palangkaraya	58,919	152,600	1,396,000
Kalimantan Timur	Samarinda	78,162	202,440	1,877,000
Lampung	Tanjung Karang	12,860	33,307	6,006,000
Maluku	Ambon	28,767	74,505	1,856,000
Nusa Tenggara Barat	Mataram	7,790	20,177	3,370,000
Nusa Tenggara Timur	Kupang	18,485	47,876	3,269,000
Riau	Pakanbaru	36,510	94,561	3,306,000
Sulawesi Selatan	Ujung Pandang	28,101	72,781	6,982,000
Sulawesi Tengah	Palu	26,921	69,726	1,711,000
Sulawesi Tenggara	Kendari	10,690	27,686	1,350,000
Sulawesi Utara	Menado	7,345	19,023	2,479,000
Sumatera Barat	Padang	19,219	49,778	3,999,000
Sumatera Selatan	Palembang	40,034	103,688	6,277,000
Sumatera Utara	Medan	27,331	70,787	10,256,000
Timor Timur	Dili	5,743	14,874	748,000
Special autonomous districts				
Aceh	Banda Aceh	21,387	55,392	3,416,000
Yogyakarta	Yogyakarta	1,224	3,169	2,913,000
TOTAL		741,052	1,919,317	179,323,000

Demography

Population (1992): 184,796,000.
Density (1992): persons per sq mi 249.4, persons per sq km 96.3.
Urban-rural (1991): urban 31.4%; rural 68.6%.
Sex distribution (1990): male 49.88%; female 50.12%.
Age breakdown (1989): under 15, 37.0%; 15–29, 28.1%; 30–44, 17.8%; 45–59, 10.9%; 60–74, 5.3%; 75 and over, 0.9%.
Population projection: (2000) 211,288,000; (2010) 238,174,000.
Doubling time: 34 years.
Ethnolinguistic composition (1980): Javanese 40.1%; Sundanese 15.3%; Bahasa Indonesian 12.0%; Madurese 4.8%; other 27.8%.
Religious affiliation (1985): Muslim 86.9%; Christian 9.6%, of which Roman Catholic 3.1%; Hindu 1.9%; Buddhist 1.0%; other 0.6%.
Major cities (1985): Jakarta 7,829,000; Surabaya 2,345,000; Medan 2,110,000; Bandung 1,633,000; Semarang 1,269,000.

Vital statistics

Birth rate per 1,000 population (1991): 32.2 (world avg. 26.4).
Death rate per 1,000 population (1991): 11.7 (world avg. 9.2).
Natural increase rate per 1,000 population (1991): 20.5 (world avg. 17.2).
Total fertility rate (avg. births per childbearing woman; 1991): 3.7.
Marriage rate per 1,000 population (1988–89): 7.4.
Divorce rate per 1,000 population (1988–89): 0.8.
Life expectancy at birth (1991): male 55.6 years; female 58.9 years.
Major causes of death: n.a.; however, major diseases include tuberculosis, malaria, dysentery, cholera, and plague.

National economy

Budget (1991–92). Revenue: Rp 50,555,000,000,000 (royalties from energy production 29.7%, aid for development 20.5%, value-added tax 16.3%, income tax 15.9%, nontax revenues 5.6%, import duties 5.1%). Expenditures: Rp 50,555,000,000,000 (development 39.6%, debt service 28.4%, civil service 15.3%, subsidies for autonomous regions 9.2%).
Public debt (external, outstanding; 1990): U.S.$44,314,000,000.
Tourism (1990): receipts U.S.$1,879,000,000; expenditures U.S.$886,000,000.
Production (metric tons except as noted). Agriculture, forestry, fishing (1990): rice 44,490,000, sugarcane 25,503,000, cassava 17,064,000, corn 6,741,000, palm oil 1,937,000, rubber 1,300,000, copra 1,250,000; livestock (number of live animals) 10,800,000 goats, 10,300,000 cattle, 5,700,000 sheep, 3,400,000 buffalo; roundwood 171,532,000 cu m; fish catch 3,131,000. Mining and quarrying (1991): nickel ore 2,300,000; bauxite 1,240,000; copper ore[4] 656,520; iron ore[4] 173,242; tin ore[4] 30,061; silver 89,690 kg. Manufacturing (1990):

cement 15,972,000; fertilizer 6,991,000; paper 165,620[5]; cigarettes 13,941,-870,000 units[5]. Energy production (consumption): electricity (kW-hr; 1990) 44,260,000,000 (44,260,000,000); coal (metric tons; 1990) 7,327,000 (3,499,-000); crude petroleum (barrels; 1990) 531,993,000 (273,139,000); petroleum products (metric tons; 1990) 32,150,000 (24,641,000); natural gas (cu m; 1990) 40,453,000,000 (11,155,000,000).
Gross national product (1990): U.S.$101,151,000,000 (U.S.$560 per capita).

Structure of gross domestic product and labour force

	1990 in value Rp '000,000,000	1990 % of total value	1989 labour force	1989 % of labour force
Agriculture	43,062	21.7	41,097,381	54.0
Mining	28,748	14.5	...	...
Manufacturing	38,602	19.5	6,496,655	8.5
Construction	10,828	5.5	...	...
Public utilities	1,258	0.6	...	...
Transp. and commun.	11,041	5.6	...	...
Trade	32,154	16.2	10,777,639	14.2
Finance, real estate	13,073	6.6	}	
Pub. admin., defense	12,801	6.5	} 11,725,261	15.4
Services	6,434	3.3	}	
Other	...	...	5,991,820[6]	7.9[6]
TOTAL	198,001	100.0	76,088,756	100.0

Population economically active: total (1989) 76,088,756; activity rate 43.5% (participation rates: ages 15–64, 68.6%; female 39.9%; unemployed 2.9%).

Price and earnings indexes (1985 = 100)

	1985	1986	1987	1988	1989	1990	1991
Consumer price index	100.0	105.8	115.6	124.9	133.0	142.9	156.1
Monthly earnings index[7]	100.0	108.4	114.7	...	...	...	...

Household income and expenditure. Average household size (1990) 4.5; income per household: n.a.; sources of income (1976): wages 42.1%, self-employment 41.5%, transfer payments 2.5%; expenditure (1987): food 61.3%, housing and utilities 17.1%, clothing 5.1%, durable goods 3.0%.
Land use (1989): forested 62.6%; meadows and pastures 6.5%; agricultural and under permanent cultivation 11.7%; other 19.2%.

Foreign trade

Balance of trade (current prices)

	1986	1987	1988	1989	1990	1991
U.S.$'000,000	+5,249	+5,625	+7,419	+7,229	+6,240	+6,075
% of total	21.5%	19.6%	23.5%	19.6%	13.8%	11.6%

Imports (1991): U.S.$25,868,800,000 (machinery and transport equipment 45.0%, chemicals 13.3%, mineral fuels 9.0%, crude materials 8.3%). *Major import sources:* Japan 24.5%; U.S. 13.1%; Germany 8.0%.
Exports (1991): U.S.$29,142,000,000 (crude petroleum 19.5%, natural gas 14.3%, plywood 9.9%, garments 7.9%, preparation rubber 3.3%). *Major export destinations:* Japan 36.9%; U.S. 12.0%; Singapore 8.3%.

Transport and communications

Transport. Railroads (1990): length 6,583 km; passenger-km 9,288,000,000; metric ton-km cargo 3,192,000,000. Roads (1988): length 250,314 km (paved 43%). Vehicles (1991): passenger cars 1,372,673; trucks and buses 1,533,152. Merchant marine (1991): vessels (100 gross tons and over) 1,991; deadweight tonnage 3,130,834. Air transport (1991): passenger-km 12,707,924,000; metric ton-km cargo 423,900,000; airports (1992) 116.
Communications. Daily newspapers (1988): total number 60; total circulation 3,716,000; circulation per 1,000 population 22. Radio (1991): 22,000,000 receivers (1 per 8.2 persons). Television (1991): 11,000,000 receivers (1 per 16 persons). Telephones (1989): 1,015,275 (1 per 172 persons).

Education and health

Education (1989–90)[8]

	schools	teachers	students	student/teacher ratio
Primary (age 7–12)	146,558	1,140,886	26,528,590	23.3
Secondary (age 13–18)	28,745	703,099	8,473,299	12.1
Voc., teacher tr.	3,880	111,448	1,410,073	12.7
Higher[9]	792	115,359	1,179,489	10.2

Educational attainment (1985). Percentage of population age 25 and over having: no schooling 30.3%; less than complete primary 32.2%; primary 22.8%; some secondary 6.4%; secondary 7.1%; higher 1.2%. *Literacy* (1987): total population age 15 and over literate 80,233,132 (77.6%); males literate 43,062,304 (85.6%); females literate 37,170,828 (70.0%).
Health: physicians (1988–89) 23,367 (1 per 7,427 persons); hospital beds (1989–90) 118,585 (1 per 1,490 persons); infant mortality rate per 1,000 live births (1991) 90.
Food (1987–89): daily per capita caloric intake 2,708 (vegetable products 97%, animal products 3%); 125% of FAO recommended minimum.

Military

Total active duty personnel (1991): 278,000 (army 76.3%, navy 15.1%, air force 8.6%). *Military expenditure as percentage of GNP* (1989): 1.7% (world 4.9%); per capita expenditure U.S.$9.

[1]Includes 100 nonelective seats reserved for the military. [2]Includes the 500 members of the House of People's Representatives plus 500 other delegates. [3]Preliminary results. [4]Concentrates. [5]1988. [6]Includes unemployed. [7]Based on daily average wages of agricultural estate workers. [8]Refers to schools under the Department of Education and Culture only. [9]1987–88.

Iran

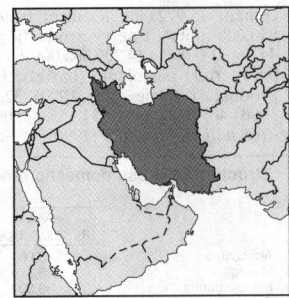

Official name: Jomhūrī-ye Eslamī-ye Irān (Islamic Republic of Iran).
Form of government: unitary Islamic republic with one legislative house (Islamic Consultative Assembly [270]).
Supreme leader: Rahbar (religious guide).
Head of state and government: President.
Capital: Tehrān.
Official language: Farsī (Persian).
Official religion: Islam.
Monetary unit: 1 rial (Rls); valuation (free rate; Oct. 5, 1992)
1 U.S.$ = Rls 1,458; 1£ = Rls 2,479.

Area and population

Provinces	Capitals	area sq mi	area sq km	population 1986 census
Āzārbāyjān-e Gharbī	Orūmīyeh	14,517	37,599	1,971,677
Āzārbāyjān-e Sharqī	Tabrīz	25,421	65,842	4,114,084
Bākhtarān	Bākhtarān	9,121	23,622	1,462,965
Būshehr	Būshehr	9,792	25,360	612,183
Chahār Maḥāll va Bakhtīārī	Shahr Kord	5,722	14,820	631,179
Eṣfahān	Eṣfahān	40,852	105,805	3,294,916
Fārs	Shīrāz	48,505	125,627	3,193,769
Gīlān	Rasht	5,722	14,820	2,081,037
Hamadān	Hamadān	7,508	19,445	1,505,826
Hormozgān	Bandar ʿAbbās	25,243	65,379	762,206
Īlām	Īlām	7,369	19,086	382,091
Kermān	Kermān	71,690	185,675	1,622,958
Khorāsān	Mashhad	121,887	315,687	5,280,605
Khūzestān	Ahvāz	25,688	66,532	2,681,978
Kohkīlūyeh va Būyer Aḥmadī	Yāsūj	5,289	13,699	411,828
Kordestān	Sanandaj	10,756	27,858	1,078,415
Lorestān	Khorramābād	11,027	28,560	1,367,029
Markazī	Arāk	11,402	29,530	1,082,109
Māzandarān	Sarī	18,010	46,645	3,419,346
Semnān	Semnān	35,345	91,544	417,035
Sīstān va Balūchestān	Zāhedān	70,066	181,471	1,197,059
Tehrān	Tehrān	10,896	28,221	8,712,087
Yazd	Yazd	24,704	63,984	574,028
Zanjān	Zanjān	14,047	36,382	1,588,600
TOTAL LAND AREA		630,578[1]	1,633,189[1]	
INLAND WATER		1,880[2]	4,868[2]	
TOTAL		632,457[1]	1,638,057	49,445,010

Demography

Population (1992): 59,570,000.
Density (1992): persons per sq mi 94.2, persons per sq km 36.4.
Urban-rural (1990): urban 56.7%; rural 43.3%.
Sex distribution (1990): male 51.15%; female 48.85%.
Age breakdown (1990): under 15, 43.8%; 15–29, 26.9%; 30–44, 15.2%; 45–59, 8.3%; 60–74, 4.8%; 75 and over, 1.0%.
Population projection: (2000) 71,894,000; (2010) 91,537,000.
Doubling time: 20 years.
Ethnic composition (1983): Persian 45.6%; Azerbaijani 16.8%; Kurdish 9.1%; Gīlakī 5.3%; Luri 4.3%; Māzandarānī 3.6%; Baluchi 2.3%; Arab 2.2%; Bakhtiari 1.7%; Turkmen 1.5%; Armenian 0.5%; other 7.1%.
Religious affiliation (1986): Muslim 98.3% (Shīʿī 90.5%; Sunnī 7.8%); Bahāʾī 0.8%; Christian 0.7%; Zoroastrian 0.1%; Jewish 0.1%.
Major cities (1986): Tehrān 6,042,584; Mashhad 1,463,508; Eṣfahān 986,753; Tabriz 971,482; Shīrāz 848,289.

Vital statistics

Birth rate per 1,000 population (1991): 44.0 (world avg. 26.4).
Death rate per 1,000 population (1991): 9.0 (world avg. 9.2).
Natural increase rate per 1,000 population (1991): 35.0 (world avg. 17.2).
Total fertility rate (avg. births per childbearing woman; 1991): 6.5.
Marriage rate per 1,000 population (1988): 6.9.
Life expectancy at birth (1991): male 64.0 years; female 65.0 years.
Major causes of death per 100,000 population (1987–88)[3]: diseases of the circulatory system 298.8; accidents 175.3; malignant neoplasms (cancers) 77.5; diseases of the respiratory system 67.4; diseases of early infancy 58.1.

National economy

Budget (1990–91). Revenue: Rls 4,009,700,000,000 (taxes 40.5%, oil and gas 27.2%). Expenditures: Rls 5,595,800,000,000 (current expenditure 70.8%, development expenditure 29.2%).
Production (metric tons except as noted). Agriculture, forestry, fishing (1991): wheat 8,900,000, sugar beets 3,950,000, barley 3,600,000, rice 2,100,000, sugarcane 2,000,000, grapes 1,650,000, apples 1,350,000, oranges 1,270,000, dates 570,000, pistachios 170,000; livestock (head) 45,000,000 sheep, 23,500,000 goats, 6,900,000 cattle; roundwood 6,727,000 cu m[4]; fish catch 250,000[4]. Mining and quarrying (value of production in Rls ʾ000,000; 1987): gravel and sand 12,653; marble, granite, and travertine 11,225; copper 9,427. Manufacturing (value added, in Rls ʾ000,000; 1987–88): textiles (excluding wearing apparel) 232,000; bricks, tiles, and cement 225,600; tobacco products 161,900; food products 148,300; nonelectrical machinery 95,600; iron and steel 75,500. Construction (1988–89): 21,375,000 sq m[5]. Energy production (consumption): electricity (kW-hr; 1990–91) 59,102,000,000 (45,107,000,000); coal (metric tons; 1990) 1,300,000 (1,700,000); crude petroleum (barrels; 1991) 1,207,000,000 (261,500,000[4]); petroleum products (metric tons; 1990) 34,560,000 (40,114,000); natural gas (cu m; 1990–91) 25,600,000,000 (23,500,000,000).

Public debt (external, outstanding; December 1990): U.S.$9,021,000,000.
Gross national product (1990): U.S.$139,120,000,000 (U.S.$2,450 per capita).

Structure of gross domestic product and labour force

	1990–91 in value Rls ʾ000,000,000	1990–91 % of total value	1986 labour force	1986 % of labour force
Agriculture	6,423	18.2	3,190,761	24.9
Petroleum, natural gas	1,385	3.9 }	32,370	0.3
Other mining	250	0.7 }		
Manufacturing	3,220	9.1	1,451,330	11.3
Construction	1,853	5.3	1,206,264	9.4
Public utilities	299	0.8	91,044	0.7
Transp. and commun.	2,639	7.5	630,546	4.9
Trade, restaurants	10,185	28.9	875,458	6.8
Finance, real estate	4,537	12.9	114,288	0.9
Pub. admin., defense	3,656	10.4 }	3,049,753	23.8
Services	838	2.4 }		
Other			2,178,477[6]	17.0[6]
TOTAL	35,285	100.0[1]	12,820,291	100.0[1]

Tourism (1990): receipts U.S.$62,000,000; expenditures U.S.$396,000,000.
Population economically active (1986): total 12,820,291; activity rate 25.9% (particip. rates: ages 15–64, 51.3%; female 10.2%; unemp. [1992] 25–30%).

Price and earnings indexes (1985 = 100)

	1986	1987	1988	1989	1990	1991	1992[7]
Consumer price index	118.4	152.3	195.9	239.7	258.0	302.2	368.4
Monthly earnings index	96.6	104.6	...	...	...	...	...

Household income and expenditure. Average household size (1986) 5.1; income per urban household (1988) Rls 1,339,970 (U.S.$19,536); sources of urban income (1988): wages 37.4%, self-employment 30.5%, other 32.1%; expenditure (1988–89): food and hotels 47.5%, housing and energy 23.9%.
Land use (1990): forested 11.0%; meadows and pastures 26.9%; agricultural and under permanent cultivation 9.2%; other 52.9%.

Foreign trade

Balance of trade (current prices)

	1985	1986	1987	1988	1989	1990
U.S.$000,000	+2,745	−719	+2,330	−409	+2,148	+807
% of total	11.1%	4.2%	11.8%	2.5%	10.0%	2.7%

Imports (1990): U.S.$14,354,000,000 ([8]nonelectrical machinery and apparatus 20.9%; iron and steel 9.7%; grains and derivatives 6.9%; transportation equipment 6.8%). Major import sources: Germany 20.0%; Japan 12.4%; Italy 8.5%; U.K. 5.3%; France 4.6%; Turkey 4.3%.
Exports (1990): U.S.$15,161,000,000 ([9]crude petroleum, petroleum products, and natural gas 91.3%; carpets 3.0%; pistachios 1.6%; copper bars 0.5%; caviar 0.3%). Major export destinations: Japan 20.8%; Italy 9.5%; France 8.2%; The Netherlands 6.1%; Brazil 6.1%; Belgium-Luxembourg 5.8%.

Transport and communications

Transport. Railroads (1990): route length 2,779 mi, 4,473 km; (1989–90) passenger-km 4,752,000,000; metric ton-km cargo 7,963,000,000. Roads (1989): length 95,273 mi, 153,327 km (paved 34%). Vehicles: passenger cars (1989–90) 2,008,000; trucks and buses 472,000. Merchant marine (1991): vessels (100 gross tons and over) 401; total deadweight tonnage 8,382,930. Air transport (1990)[10]: passenger-km 5,561,000,000; metric ton-km cargo 113,653,000; airports (1992) with scheduled flights 18.
Communications. Daily newspapers (1990): 13; circulation 728,000[11]; circulation per 1,000 population 13[11]. Radio (1991): 11,500,000 receivers (1 per 5.0 persons). Television (1991): 2,250,000 receivers (1 per 26 persons). Telephones (1989): 2,104,000 (1 per 26 persons).

Education and health

Education (1989–90)

	schools	teachers	students	student/ teacher ratio
Primary (age 7–11)	56,537	361,878	8,817,145	24.4
Secondary (age 12–18)	15,834[12]	240,102	4,456,342	18.6
Vocational	1,088[12]	23,297	212,100	9.1
Higher	85[12]	20,515[13]	315,657[13]	15.4[13]

Educational attainment (1986). Percentage of population age 25 and over having: no formal schooling 12.8%; primary education 40.4%; secondary 38.0%; higher 7.8%; not specified and not reported 1.0%. Literacy (1990): total population age 15 and over literate 18,200,000 (54.0%); males literate 11,600,000 (64.5%); females literate 6,600,000 (43.3%).
Health (1988–89): physicians 18,350 (1 per 2,882 persons); hospital beds 81,000 (1 per 653 persons); infant mortality rate (1991) 66.0.
Food (1986–88): daily per capita caloric intake 3,317 (vegetable products 90%, animal products 10%); 130% of FAO recommended minimum requirement.

Military

Total active duty personnel (1992): 528,000 (revolutionary guard corps 32.2%, army 57.8%, navy 3.4%, air force 6.6%). Military expenditure as percentage of GNP (1989): 2.2%[14] (world 4.9%); per capita expenditure U.S.$158[14].

---

[1]Detail does not add to total given because of rounding. [2]Area of Lake Urmia. [3]21 cities only. [4]1990. [5]Completed private construction, urban areas only. [6]Includes 1,818,756 unemployed. [7]May. [8]Based on 1988–89 data totaling U.S.$8,177,000,000. [9]Based on 1990–91 estimate totaling U.S.$15,800,000,000. [10]Iran Air. [11]Circulation based on seven dailies only. [12]1987–88. [13]1988–89. [14]Defense costs are highly tentative; barter and counter-trade agreements are excluded.

Iraq

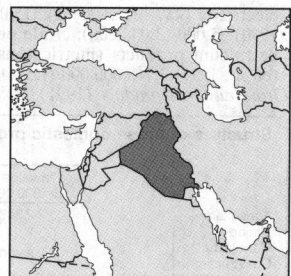

Official name: al-Jumhūrīyah al-ʿIrāqīyah (Republic of Iraq).
Form of government: unitary multiparty[1] republic with one legislative house (National Assembly [250]).
Head of state and government: President.
Capital: Baghdad.
Official language: Arabic[2].
Official religion: Islam.
Monetary unit: 1 Iraqi dinar (ID) = 20 dirhams = 1,000 fils; valuation (Oct. 5, 1992) 1 ID = U.S.$2.86[3]; 1 ID = £1.69.

Area and population

Governorates	Capitals	area[4] sq mi	area[4] sq km	population 1991 estimate
al-Anbār	ar-Ramādī	53,208	137,808	865,500
Bābil	al-Hillah	2,163	5,603	1,221,100
Baghdād	Baghdad	1,572	4,071	3,910,900
al-Baṣrah	Basra	7,363	19,070	1,168,800
Dhī Qār	an-Nāṣirīyah	4,981	12,900	1,030,900
Diyālā	Baʿqūbah	6,828	17,685	1,037,600
Karbalāʾ	Karbalāʾ	1,944	5,034	567,600
Maysān	al-ʿAmārah	6,205	16,072	524,200
al-Muthannā	as-Samāwah	19,977	51,740	350,000
an-Najaf	an-Najaf	11,129	28,824	666,400
Nīnawā	Mosul	14,410	37,323	1,618,700
al-Qādisiyah	ad-Dīwānīyah	3,148	8,153	595,600
Ṣalāḥ ad-Dīn	Tikrīt	9,407	24,363	772,200
at-Taʾmīm	Kirkūk	3,737	9,679	605,900
Wāsiṭ	al-Kūt	6,623	17,153	605,700
Kurdish Autonomous Region[5]				
Dahūk	Dahūk	2,530	6,553	309,300
Irbīl	Irbīl	5,820	15,074	928,400
as-Sulaymānīyah	as-Sulaymānīyah	6,573	17,023	1,124,200
LAND AREA		167,618	434,128	
INLAND WATER		357	924	
TOTAL		167,975	435,052	17,903,000

Demography

Population (1992): 18,838,000.
Density (1992): persons per sq mi 112.1, persons per sq km 43.3.
Urban-rural (1991): urban 70.4%; rural 29.6%.
Sex distribution (1991): male 50.28%; female 49.72%.
Age breakdown (1991): under 15, 44.5%; 15–29, 28.9%; 30–44, 14.1%; 45–59, 7.3%; 60–74, 3.9%; 75 and over, 1.3%.
Population projection: (2000) 23,947,000; (2010) 30,834,000.
Doubling time: 18 years.
Ethnic composition (1983): Arab 77.1%; Kurd 19.0%; Turkmen 1.4%; Persian 0.8%; Assyrian 0.8%; other 0.9%.
Religious affiliation (1990): Shīʿī Muslim 61.5%; Sunnī Muslim 34.0%; Christian 3.7%, of which Eastern-rite Roman Catholic 2.5%, Nestorian 0.8%, Orthodox 0.4%; Yazīdī syncretist 0.8%.
Major cities (1985): Baghdad (1987) 3,844,608; Basra 616,700; Mosul 570,926; Irbīl 333,903; as-Sulaymānīyah 279,424.

Vital statistics

Birth rate per 1,000 population (1991): 46.0 (world avg. 26.4).
Death rate per 1,000 population (1991): 7.0[6] (world avg. 9.2).
Natural increase rate per 1,000 population (1991): 39.0 (world avg. 17.2).
Total fertility rate (avg. births per childbearing woman; 1990): 6.2.
Marriage rate per 1,000 population (1990): 8.1.
Life expectancy at birth (1991)[7]: male 46.0 years; female 57.0 years.
Major causes of death. During the 1980s there were high war casualties and high incidences of trachoma, influenza, and measles. The 1991 war resulted in 70,000–90,000 postwar civilian deaths from gastroenteritis, typhoid, deprivation of medical care, and malnutrition.

National economy

Budget (1992). Revenue: ID 13,935,000,000. Expenditures: ID 13,935,000,000. Details of the 1992 and 1993 proposed budgets were not released by the National Assembly. Special emphasis was to be placed on the reconstruction of the infrastructure.
Tourism (1989): receipts U.S.$59,000,000; expenditures, n.a.
Public debt (external, outstanding; 1988): U.S.$75,000,000,000.
Production (metric tons except as noted). Agriculture, forestry, fishing (1991): wheat, 1,476,000, barley 768,000, tomatoes 438,000, watermelons 394,000, dates 375,000, grapes 470,000[8], cucumbers 298,000, corn (maize) 297,000, rice 189,000, oranges 180,000[8]; livestock (number of live animals; 1990) 9,600,000 sheep, 1,675,000 cattle, 80,000,000 chickens; roundwood (1990) 155,000 cu m; fish catch 16,100. Mining and quarrying (1989): sulfur 1,270,000; phosphate rock 1,300,000; gypsum 450,000. Manufacturing (value added in U.S.$'000,000; 1987): petroleum products 1,359; industrial chemicals 852; nonmetal mineral products 701; food 384; textiles 293; machinery and transport equipment 289, of which transport equipment 79; tobacco 175; beverages 142; printing and publishing 112; metal products 101. Construction (buildings authorized; 1991): residential 4,558,000 sq m; nonresidential 410,000 sq m. Energy production (consumption): electricity (kW-hr; 1990) 29,478,000,000 (26,132,000,000); coal, none (none); crude petroleum (barrels; 1991) 99,800,-

000 ([1990] 137,700,000); petroleum products (metric tons; 1990) 17,430,000 (10,191,000); natural gas (cu m; 1990) 3,203,000,000 (1,153,000,000).
Gross national product (1990): U.S.$73,000,000,000[9] (U.S.$4,110 per capita).

Structure of gross domestic product and labour force

	1990 in value ID '000,000[10]	1990 % of total value	1987 labour force	1987 % of labour force
Agriculture	5,119	20.3	493,006	12.4
Mining	2,981	11.8	45,137	1.4
Manufacturing	2,578	10.2	266,961	6.7
Construction	2,012	8.0	341,186	8.6
Public utilities	220	0.9	36,236	0.9
Transp. and commun.	2,119	8.4	224,271	5.6
Trade	4,071	16.1	215,605	5.4
Finance, real estate	2,669	10.6	27,015	0.7
Pub. admin., defense, and services	3,472	13.7	1,954,816	49.4
Other	—	—	352,112	8.9
TOTAL	25,241	100.0	3,956,345	100.0

Population economically active (1987): total 3,956,345; activity rate of total population 24.2% (participation rates: over age 15, 43.1%; female 11.6%; unemployed 4.6%).

Price and earnings indexes (1985 = 100)

	1983	1984	1985	1986	1987	1988
Consumer price index	89.0	95.9	100.0	101.3	115.5	140.2
Earnings index	...	...	...	...	...	...

Household income and expenditure. Average household size (1986) 7.8; income per household: n.a.; sources of income (1988): self-employment 33.9%, wages and salaries 23.9%, transfers 23.0%, rent 18.6%; expenditure (1988): food and beverages 50.2%, housing and energy 19.9%, clothing and footwear 10.6%.
Land use (1990): forested 4.3%; meadows and pastures 9.1%; agricultural and under permanent cultivation 12.5%; built-on, wasteland, and other 74.1%.

Foreign trade[11]

Balance of trade (current prices)

	1984	1985	1986	1987	1988	1989
ID '000,000	+282	+966	−1,124	+2,006	−198	+1,782
% of total	1.3%	4.4%	6.9%	12.5%	1.1%	8.0%

Imports (1990): U.S.$4,834,000,000 (machinery and transport equipment 30.3%, food and live animals 27.9%, chemical and pharmaceutical products 8.8%). *Major import sources:* United States 13.6%; Germany 8.5%; Japan 8.2%; United Kingdom 6.7%; France 5.8%.
Exports (1990): U.S.$10,353,000,000 (1989): fuels and other energy 99.5%, food and agricultural raw materials 0.5%). *Major export destinations:* U.S. 28.5%; Brazil 9.9%; Turkey 9.8%; Japan 7.8%; The Netherlands 7.4%.

Transport and communications

Transport. Railroads (1991): route length 1,484 mi, 2,389 km; passenger-mi 271,000,000, passenger-km 436,000,000; short ton-mi cargo 223,000,000, metric ton-km cargo 326,000,000. Roads (1989): total length 28,305 mi, 45,554 km (paved 84%). Vehicles (1991): passenger cars 744,252; trucks and buses 295,744. Merchant marine (1991): vessels (100 gross tons and over) 138; total deadweight tonnage 1,589,925. Air transport (1992): no scheduled service[12].
Communications. Daily newspapers (1990): total number 5; total circulation 572,000; circulation per 1,000 population 32. Radio (1991): 3,500,000 receivers (1 per 5.2 persons). Television (1991): 1,000,000 receivers (1 per 18 persons). Telephones (1990): 712,109 (1 per 25 persons).

Education and health

Education (1991–92)

	schools	teachers	students	student/ teacher ratio
Primary (age 6–11)	8,875	127,578	3,316,036	26.0
Secondary (age 12–17)	2,746	43,937	1,084,715	24.7
Voc., teacher tr.	296	9,957	152,903	15.4
Higher	20	10,520	197,786	18.8

Educational attainment: n.a. Literacy (1990): total population age 15 and over literate 6,030,000 (59.7%); males literate 3,570,000 (69.8%); females literate 2,460,000 (49.3%).
Health (1991): physicians 9,366 (1 per 1,922 persons); hospital beds (1990) 31,227 (1 per 568 persons); infant mortality rate per 1,000 live births 80.0[7].
Food (1991)[7]: daily per capita caloric intake 2,300–2,400; 93–97% of FAO recommended minimum requirement.

Military

Total active duty personnel (1992): 382,500 (army 91.9%, navy 0.3%, air force 7.8%). *Military expenditure as percentage of GNP* (1990): 18.2% (world, n.a.); per capita expenditure U.S.$749.

---

[1]Multipartyism authorized by a September 1991 law. [2]Kurdish is official in the Kurdish Autonomous Region only. [3]Official pegged rate; black market rate was about 18 Iraqi dinars per U.S.$ in May 1992. [4]Excluding Iraqi–Saudi Arabia Neutral Zone. [5]De facto self-government as of May 1992 elections. [6]Excludes war-related deaths. [7]Postwar estimate. [8]1990. [9]By mid-1992 the UN embargo was estimated to have reduced the GNP by at least 50%. [10]At factor cost. [11]Import figures are f.o.b. in balance of trade and c.i.f. for commodities and trading partners. [12]UN sanctions stopped international service from March 1991; lack of spare parts ended domestic service from June 1992.

Ireland

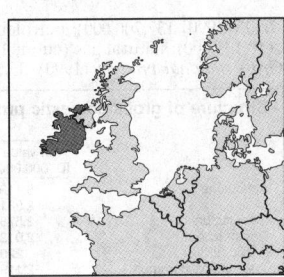

Official name: Éire (Irish); Ireland[1] (English).
Form of government: unitary multiparty republic with two legislative houses (Senate [60[2]]; House of Representatives [166]).
Chief of state: President.
Head of government: Prime Minister.
Capital: Dublin.
Official languages: Irish; English.
Official religion: [3].
Monetary unit: 1 Irish pound (£Ir) = 100 new pence; valuation (Oct. 5, 1992) 1 £Ir = U.S.$1.85 = £1.10.

Area and population	area		population
			1991
Provinces Counties	sq mi	sq km	census[4]
Connacht	6,611	17,122	422,909
Galway[5]	2,293	5,940	180,304
Leitrim	581	1,525	25,297
Mayo	2,084	5,398	110,696
Roscommon	951	2,463	51,876
Sligo	693	1,796	54,736
Leinster	7,580	19,633	1,860,037
Carlow	346	896	40,946
Dublin[5]	356	922	1,024,429
Kildare	654	1,694	122,516
Kilkenny	796	2,062	73,613
Laoighis	664	1,719	52,325
Longford	403	1,044	30,293
Louth	318	823	90,707
Meath	902	2,336	105,540
Offaly	771	1,998	58,448
Westmeath	681	1,763	61,882
Wexford	908	2,351	102,045
Wicklow	782	2,025	97,293
Munster	9,315	24,127	1,008,443
Clare	1,231	3,188	90,826
Cork[5]	2,880	7,460	409,814
Kerry	1,815	4,701	121,719
Limerick[5]	1,037	2,686	161,856
Tipperary North Riding	771	1,996	57,829
Tipperary South Riding	872	2,258	74,791
Waterford[5]	710	1,838	91,608
Ulster	3,093	8,012	232,012
Cavan	730	1,891	52,756
Donegal	1,865	4,830	127,994
Monaghan	498	1,291	51,262
TOTAL LAND AREA	26,600	68,895[6]	
INLAND WATER	537	1,390	
TOTAL	27,137	70,285	3,523,401

Demography

Population (1992): 3,519,000.
Density (1992): persons per sq mi 129.7, persons per sq km 50.1.
Urban-rural (1990): urban 57.1%; rural 42.9%.
Sex distribution (1991): male 49.74%; female 50.26%.
Age breakdown (1986): under 15, 28.9%; 15–29, 24.7%; 30–44, 18.8%; 45–59, 12.8%; 60–74, 10.7%; 75 and over, 4.1%.
Population projection: (2000) 3,492,000; (2010) 3,458,000.
Doubling time: not applicable; doubling time exceeds 100 years.
Ethnic composition (1981): more than 94% Irish nationality.
Religious affiliation (1981): Roman Catholic 93.1%; Church of Ireland (Anglican) 2.8%; Presbyterian 0.4%; other 3.7%.
Major cities[7] (1991): Dublin 477,675; Cork 127,024; Limerick 52,040; Galway 50,842; Waterford 40,345.

Vital statistics

Birth rate per 1,000 population (1991): 15.7 (world avg. 26.4); (1990) legitimate 85.5%; illegitimate 14.5%.
Death rate per 1,000 population (1991): 9.0 (world avg. 9.2).
Natural increase rate per 1,000 population (1991): 6.7 (world avg. 17.2).
Total fertility rate (avg. births per childbearing woman; 1990–95): 2.4.
Life expectancy at birth (1985–87): male 71.0 years; female 76.7 years.
Major causes of death per 100,000 population (1990): heart and circulatory diseases 413.7, of which ischemic heart disease 231.6; malignant neoplasms (cancers) 203.9; respiratory disease 79.1, of which pneumonia 58.3.

National economy

Budget (1991): Revenue: £Ir 9,311,000,000 (income taxes 36.8%, value-added tax 22.9%, excise taxes 19.6%). Expenditures: £Ir 9,076,000,000 (debt service 25.9%, social welfare 19.9%, health 14.8%, education 13.3%, defense 4.1%).
Public debt (1991): U.S.$46,184,000,000.
Tourism (1990): receipts U.S.$1,447,000,000; expenditures U.S.$1,159,000,000.
Production (metric tons except as noted). Agriculture, forestry, fishing (1990): sugar beets 1,480,000, barley 1,380,000, potatoes 633,000, wheat 625,000, oats 104,000, milk 52,400,000 hectolitres; livestock (number of live animals) 8,691,000 sheep, 6,997,000 cattle, 1,046,000 pigs; roundwood 1,527,000 cu m; fish catch (1989) 245,000. Mining and quarrying (1991): gypsum 342,800; zinc ore 186,800[8]; lead ore 40,200[8]. Manufacturing (value added in £Ir; 1988): metals and engineering goods 2,831,600,000; food products 1,609,100,000; chemical products 1,101,600,000; nonmetallic mineral products 388,200,000; paper, printing, and publishing 378,600,000; textiles 173,600,000. Construction (1990): residential 5,887,000 sq m. Energy production (consumption):

electricity (kW-hr; 1990) 14,515,000,000 (14,515,000,000); coal (metric tons; 1990) 35,000 (3,034,000); crude petroleum (barrels; 1990) none (13,308,000); petroleum products (metric tons; 1990) 1,456,000 (3,716,000); natural gas (cu m; 1991) 3,763,000,000 ([1990] 3,671,000,000).
Gross national product (1991): U.S.$41,354,000,000 (U.S.$11,740 per capita).

Structure of gross domestic product and labour force				
	1990			
	in value £Ir '000,000	% of total value	labour force	% of labour force
Agriculture	2,337	10.1	167,000	12.8
Mining			8,000	0.6
Manufacturing	8,530	37.0	223,000	17.1
Construction			76,000	5.8
Public utilities			13,000	1.0
Transp. and commun.	4,426	19.2	68,000	5.2
Trade			225,000[9]	17.3[9]
Pub. admin., defense	1,363	5.9	64,000	4.9
Services			282,000	21.6
Finance	6,396	27.8	9	9
Other			179,000[10]	13.7[10]
TOTAL	23,052	100.0	1,305,000	100.0

Population economically active (1990): total 1,305,000; activity rate of total population 37.0% (participation rates: ages 15–64, 59.2%[11]; female 30.5%[11]; unemployed 13.7%).

Price and earnings indexes (1985 = 100)							
	1985	1986	1987	1988	1989	1990	1991
Consumer price index	100.0	103.8	107.1	109.4	113.8	117.6	121.4
Weekly earnings index	100.0	107.5	113.0	118.3	123.1	127.3	133.4

Household income and expenditure. Average household size (1983) 3.9; income per household: n.a.; sources of income (1987): wages and salaries 58.6%, self-employment 13.3%, interest and dividends 8.2%; expenditure (1988): food 39.1%, rent and household goods 18.6%, transportation 12.6%.
Land use (1989): forest 5.0%; pasture 68.1%; agricultural 13.8%; other 13.1%.

Foreign trade

Balance of trade (current prices)						
	1986	1987	1988	1989	1990	1991
£Ir '000,000	1,164	2,004	2,574	2,880	2,458	2,784
% of total	6.6%	10.3%	11.7%	11.0%	9.4%	10.2%

Imports (1990): £Ir 12,455,800,000 (machinery and transport equipment 35.9%, chemicals 12.4%, food 9.0%, petroleum and petroleum products 6.4%, beverages and tobacco 1.2%). *Major import sources:* U.K. 42.2%; U.S. 14.5%; Germany 8.3%; Japan 5.6%; France 4.6%.
Exports (1990): £Ir 14,336,200,000 (machinery and transport equipment 31.3%, food 19.9%, chemical products 15.9%, beverages and tobacco 2.3%). *Major export destinations:* U.K. 33.7%; Germany 11.7%; France 10.5%; U.S. 8.2%.

Transport and communications

Transport. Railroads (1990): length 2,814 km; passenger-km 1,224,000,000; metric ton-km cargo 589,000,000. Roads (1991): length 57,354 mi, 92,303 km (paved 94%). Vehicles (1990): passenger cars 796,408; trucks and buses 147,213. Merchant marine (1991): vessels (100 gross tons and over) 187; total deadweight tonnage 203,038. Air transport (1990): passenger-km 3,804,000,000; metric ton-km cargo 431,618,000; airports (1992) 11.
Communications (1991). Daily newspapers: 7; total circulation 632,300; circulation per 1,000 population 179. Radios: 2,000,000 (1 per 1.8 persons). Televisions: 991,000 (1 per 3.6 persons). Telephones (1990): 916,207 (1 per 3.8 persons).

Education and health

Education (1989–90)	schools	teachers	students	student/ teacher ratio
Primary (age 6–11)	3,428	20,321[12]	560,833	...
Secondary (age 12–18)	493	11,630	213,788	18.4
Voc., teacher tr.	352	7,118	129,702	18.2
Higher	43	3,934[13]	61,323	16.0[13]

Educational attainment (1981). Percentage of population age 25 and over having: primary education 52.3%; secondary 23.3%; some postsecondary 16.5%; university or like institution 7.9%. *Literacy* (1987): virtually 100% literate.
Health (1990): physicians (1984) 5,180 (1 per 681 persons); hospital beds 13,709[14] (1 per 257 persons); infant mortality rate 8.0.
Food (1987–89): daily per capita caloric intake 3,779 (vegetable products 63%, animal products 37%); 151% of FAO recommended minimum requirement.

Military

Total active duty personnel (1991): 12,900 (army 86.8%, navy 7.0%, air force 6.2%). *Military expenditure as percentage of GNP* (1989): 1.6% (world 4.9%); per capita expenditure U.S.$128.

---

[1]As provided by the constitution; the 1948 Republic of Ireland Act provides precedent for this longer formulation of the official name but, per official sources, "has not changed the usage *Ireland* as the name of the state in the English language." [2]Includes 11 nonelective seats. [3]Though a 1973 amendment to the Irish constitution deleted sections that had given "special position" to the Roman Catholic Church, much doctrinal language remains. [4]Preliminary. [5]Includes county borough(s). [6]Detail does not add to total given because of rounding. [7]County boroughs. [8]Metal content of ores. [9]Trade includes Finance. [10]Unemployed. [11]1988. [12]National schools only. [13]1988–89. [14]Acute-care public hospitals only.

Israel

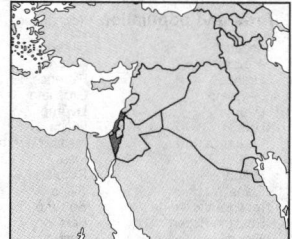

Official name: Medinat Yisra'el (Hebrew); Isrā'īl (Arabic) (State of Israel).
Form of government: multiparty republic with one legislative house (Knesset [120]).
Chief of state: President.
Head of government: Prime Minister.
Capital: Jerusalem is the proclaimed capital of Israel (from Jan. 23, 1950) and the actual seat of government, but recognition of its status as capital by the international community has largely been withheld pending final settlement of territorial and other issues through peace talks between Israel and the Arab parties concerned.
Official languages: Hebrew; Arabic.
Official religion: none.
Monetary unit: 1 New (Israeli) sheqel (NIS) = 100 agorot; valuation (Oct. 5, 1992) 1 U.S.$ = NIS 2.49; 1 £ = NIS 4.24.

Area and population		area[1]		population
				1990[2]
Districts	Capitals	sq mi	sq km	estimate
Central (Ha Merkaz)	Ramla	479	1,242	969,800
Haifa (Hefa)	Haifa	330	854	612,600
Jerusalem (Yerushalayim)	Jerusalem	215	557	556,000
Northern (Ha Zafon)	Tiberias	1,347	3,490	762,700
Southern (Ha Darom)	Beersheba	5,555	14,387	541,900
Tel Aviv	Tel Aviv–Yafo	66	170	1,043,600
TOTAL		7,992	20,700	4,486,600

Demography

Population (1992): 5,239,000.
Density (1992)[1]: persons per sq mi 655.5, persons per sq km 253.1.
Urban-rural (1990): urban 89.9%; rural 10.1%.
Sex distribution (1989): male 49.87%; female 50.13%.
Age breakdown (1989): under 15, 31.7%; 15–29, 24.8%; 30–44, 20.0%; 45–59, 11.2%; 60–74, 8.5%; 75 and over, 3.8%.
Population projection: (2000) 6,275,000; (2010) 6,581,000.
Doubling time: 47 years.
Ethnic composition (1991): Jewish 82.0%; Arab and other 18.0%.
Religious affiliation (1990): Jewish 81.5%; Muslim (mostly Sunnī) 14.4%; Christian 2.3%; Druze and other 1.8%.
Major cities (1990): Jerusalem 504,100; Tel Aviv–Yafo 321,700; Haifa 223,600; Holon 148,400; Bat Yam 133,200.

Vital statistics

Birth rate per 1,000 population (1991): 21.4 (world avg. 26.4); (1988)[3] legitimate 98.8%; illegitimate 1.2%.
Death rate per 1,000 population (1991): 6.3 (world avg. 9.2).
Natural increase rate per 1,000 population (1991): 15.1 (world avg. 17.2).
Total fertility rate (avg. births per childbearing woman; 1990): 2.8.
Marriage rate per 1,000 population (1990): 6.6.
Divorce rate per 1,000 population (1990): 1.3.
Life expectancy at birth (1988): male 73.9 years; female 77.5 years.
Major causes of death per 100,000 population (1988): diseases of the circulatory system 275.9; malignant neoplasms (cancers) 123.7; accidents 44.0; diseases of the respiratory system 43.5.

National economy

Budget (1990–91). Revenue: NIS 63,517,000,000 (income tax and property tax 22.9%, internal loans 22.0%, value-added tax 14.6%, external loans 14.1%). Expenditures: NIS 63,517,000,000 (debt 20.4%, defense 19.7%, interest on loans 15.3%, labour and social welfare 8.2%, education and culture 7.4%).
Public debt (1989): U.S.$74,215,700,000.
Production (metric tons except as noted). Agriculture, forestry, fishing (1991): oranges 567,000, grapefruit 384,000, tomatoes 245,000, potatoes 220,000, wheat 160,000, watermelons 100,000, seed cotton 58,000; livestock (number of live animals) 375,000 sheep, 331,000 cattle, 115,000 goats, 100,000 pigs, 24,-000,000 chickens; roundwood (1990) 113,000 cu m; fish catch (1990) 26,114. Mining and quarrying (1990): phosphate rock 2,400,000; potash 2,200,000; phosphoric acid 200,000; bromine compounds 127,000. Manufacturing (1990): cement 2,868,000; sulfuric acid 153,800; polyethylene 106,599; cardboard 92,864; paper 41,159; chlorine 36,342; ammonium sulfate 35,441; wine 12,795,000 litres. Construction (1990): residential 2,900,000 sq m; nonresidential 1,070,000 sq m. Energy production (consumption): electricity (kW-hr; 1990) 20,730,000 (20,340,000); coal (metric tons; 1990) none (3,708,000); crude petroleum (barrels; 1990) 94,300 (59,412,000); petroleum products (metric tons; 1990) 7,633,000 (7,590,000); natural gas (cu m; 1990) 30,317,000 (30,317,000).
Land use (1990): forested 5.5%; meadows and pastures 7.2%; agricultural and under permanent cultivation 21.5%, other 65.8%.
Population economically active (1991)[4]: total 1,770,500; activity rate of total population 35.3% (participation rates: over age 15, 51.7%; female 41.1%; unemployed 10.6%).

Price and earnings indexes (1985 = 100)							
	1985	1986	1987	1988	1989	1990	1991[5]
Consumer price index	100	148	178	206	248	291	368
Monthly earnings index	100	161	212	258	312	366	442

Tourism (1990): receipts from visitors U.S.$1,382,000,000; expenditures by nationals abroad U.S.$1,485,000,000.
Gross national product (1990): U.S.$50,866,000,000 (U.S.$10,970 per capita).

Structure of gross domestic product and labour force				
	1989		1991	
	in value NIS '000,000	% of total value	labour force	% of labour force
Agriculture	1,922	3.1	55,500	3.1
Manufacturing, mining	11,937	19.2	339,700	19.2
Construction	3,319	5.3	96,200	5.4
Public utilities	1,649	2.7	16,800	0.9
Transp. and commun.	5,582	9.0	96,600	5.5
Trade	7,174	11.6	224,000	12.7
Finance	14,344	23.1	160,800	9.1
Public and community services	2,545	4.1	468,300	26.4
Services }	13,625	21.9	114,900	6.6
Other }			197,700[6]	11.2[6]
TOTAL	62,097	100.0	1,770,500	100.0[7]

Household income and expenditure (1989). Average household size 3.6; monthly income per household (1988)[8] NIS 2,937 (U.S.$1,496); sources of income (1988)[8]: salaries and wages 87.9%, allowances and assistance 9.7%, self-employment 2.3%; expenditure (1991): food, beverages, and tobacco 25.4%, housing 20.0%, household durable goods 6.8%, clothing 5.8%, energy 3.8%, transportation 3.6%.

Foreign trade

Balance of trade (current prices)						
	1986	1987	1988	1989	1990	1991
U.S.$'000,000	−2,352.1	−3,253.8	−2,841.8	−2,358.1	−3,504.0	−5,473.3
% of total	14.5%	16.6%	13.1%	10.0%	13.1%	19.6%

Imports (1991): U.S.$16,688,400,000 (investment goods 18.3%; diamonds 16.2%; consumer goods 11.2%; fuel and lubricants 8.8%). *Major import sources:* U.S. 19.3%; Germany 11.9%; Belgium 11.1%; Switzerland 8.5%; U.K. 8.3%; Italy 6.5%; Japan 4.3%; France 4.2%.
Exports (1991): U.S.$11,215,100,000 (machinery 28.9%; worked diamonds 27.4%; chemicals 13.0%; textiles 7.6%; food, beverages, and tobacco 4.8%; rubber and plastic 3.4%). *Major export destinations:* U.S. 30.2%; Japan 7.4%; U.K. 7.1%; Germany 6.0%; Belgium 5.8%; France 4.9%; The Netherlands 4.6%; Hong Kong 4.5%; Italy 4.2%.

Transport and communications

Transport. Railroads (1990): route length 323 mi, 520 km; (1989–90) passenger-mi 94,858,000, passenger-km 152,660,000; short ton-mi cargo 710,700,000, metric ton-km cargo 1,037,600,000. Roads (1989): total length 8,075 mi, 12,-996 km (paved 100%). Vehicles (1990): passenger cars 786,266; trucks and buses 157,886. Merchant marine (1991): vessels (100 gross tons and over) 58; total deadweight tonnage 654,170. Air transport (1990)[9]: passenger-mi 4,363,000,000, passenger-km 7,021,000,000; short ton-mi cargo 568,856,000, metric ton-km cargo 830,516,000; airports (1992) with scheduled flights 7.
Communications. Daily newspapers (1989): total number 28; total circulation 1,611,000; circulation per 1,000 population 350. Radio (1991): 2,250,000 receivers (1 per 2.2 persons). Television (1991): 1,200,000 receivers (1 per 4.1 persons). Telephones (1990): 2,425,000 (1 per 2.0 persons).

Education and health

Education (1989–90)	schools	teachers	students	student/ teacher ratio
Primary (age 6–13)	1,989	37,768[10]	611,671	...
Secondary (age 14–17)	710	43,548	393,508	9.0
Vocational	383	...	110,967	...
Higher	7	6,479[11]	67,750	...

Educational attainment (1987). Percentage of population age 25 and over having: no formal schooling 6.5%; primary education 21.7%; secondary 48.3%; postsecondary, vocational, and higher 23.5%. *Literacy* (1983): total population age 15 and over literate 2,542,403 (91.8%); males literate 1,312,-258 (95.0%); females literate 1,230,145 (88.7%).
Health (1989): physicians[12] 11,895 (1 per 345 persons); hospital beds 28,399 (1 per 162 persons); infant mortality rate per 1,000 live births (1989) 9.0.
Food (1988–90): daily per capita caloric intake 3,220 (vegetable products 79%, animal products 21%); 125% of FAO recommended minimum.

Military

Total active duty personnel (1992): 176,000 (army 76.1%, navy 5.7%, air force 18.2%). *Military expenditure as percentage of GNP* (1989): 12.8% (world 4.9%); per capita expenditure U.S.$1,323.

---

[1]Excluding West Bank, Gaza Strip, Golan Heights, and East Jerusalem. [2]January 1. De jure; includes population of East Jerusalem. [3]Jewish population only. [4]Excludes armed forces; includes Israelis in occupied territories. [5]November. [6]Mostly unemployed. [7]Detail does not add to total given because of rounding. [8]Urban population only. [9]El Al only. [10]Teaching posts financed by Ministry of Education and Culture only. [11]1987–88. [12]1987.

Italy

Official name: Repubblica Italiana
(Italian Republic).
Form of government: republic with
two legislative houses (Senate [325[1]];
Chamber of Deputies [630]).
Chief of state: President.
Head of government: Prime Minister.
Capital: Rome.
Official language: Italian.
Official religion: none.
Monetary unit: 1 lira (Lit, plural
lire) = 100 centesimi; valuation (Oct.
5, 1992) 1 U.S.$ = Lit 1,315;
1 £ = Lit 2,236.

Area and population

Regions Provinces	Capitals	area sq mi	area sq km	1991 census
Abruzzi	L'Aquila	4,168	10,794	1,249,388
Chieti	Chieti	999	2,587	379,689
L'Aquila	L'Aquila	1,944	5,034	301,296
Pescara	Pescara	473	1,225	291,115
Teramo	Teramo	752	1,948	277,288
Basilicata	Potenza	3,858	9,992	591,897
Matera	Matera	1,331	3,447	200,519
Potenza	Potenza	2,527	6,545	391,378
Calabria	Catanzaro	5,823	15,080	2,010,195
Catanzaro	Catanzaro	2,026	5,247	711,526
Cosenza	Cosenza	2,568	6,650	730,081
Reggio di Calabria	Reggio di Calabria	1,229	3,183	568,588
Campania	Naples	5,249	13,595	5,625,575
Avellino	Avellino	1,078	2,792	430,210
Benevento	Benevento	800	2,071	291,036
Caserta	Caserta	1,019	2,639	825,294
Napoli	Naples	452	1,171	3,023,366
Salerno	Salerno	1,900	4,922	1,055,669
Emilia-Romagna	Bologna	8,542	22,123	3,984,055
Bologna	Bologna	1,429	3,702	943,269
Ferrara	Ferrara	1,016	2,632	363,451
Forlì	Forlì	1,123	2,910	618,670
Modena	Modena	1,039	2,690	611,883
Parma	Parma	1,332	3,449	401,952
Piacenza	Piacenza	1,000	2,589	271,167
Ravenna	Ravenna	718	1,859	351,296
Reggio nell'Emilia	Reggio nell'Emilia	885	2,292	422,367
Friuli-Venezia Giulia	Trieste	3,029	7,845	1,216,398
Gorizia	Gorizia	180	467	139,315
Pordenone	Pordenone	878	2,273	279,784
Trieste	Trieste	82	212	267,118
Udine	Udine	1,889	4,893	530,181
Lazio	Rome	6,642	17,203	5,145,763
Frosinone	Frosinone	1,251	3,239	478,393
Latina	Latina	869	2,251	475,633
Rieti	Rieti	1,061	2,749	145,848
Roma	Rome	2,066	5,352	3,764,298
Viterbo	Viterbo	1,395	3,612	281,591
Liguria	Genoa	2,092	5,418	1,701,788
Genova	Genoa	709	1,836	961,276
Imperia	Imperia	446	1,155	218,616
La Spezia	La Spezia	341	882	230,835
Savona	Savona	596	1,545	291,061
Lombardia	Milan	9,211	23,857	8,940,594
Bergamo	Bergamo	1,066	2,760	943,584
Brescia	Brescia	1,846	4,782	1,062,416
Como	Como	798	2,067	799,050
Cremona	Cremona	684	1,771	328,279
Mantova	Mantova	903	2,339	371,472
Milano	Milan	1,066	2,762	3,957,547
Pavia	Pavia	1,145	2,965	496,924
Sondrio	Sondrio	1,240	3,212	174,781
Varese	Varese	463	1,199	806,541
Marche	Ancona	3,743	9,693	1,446,751
Ancona	Ancona	749	1,940	445,877
Ascoli Piceno	Ascoli Piceno	806	2,087	364,220
Macerata	Macerata	1,071	2,774	298,371
Pesaro e Urbino	Pesaro	1,117	2,892	338,283
Molise	Campobasso	1,713	4,438	320,916
Campobasso	Campobasso	1,123	2,909	230,380
Isernia	Isernia	590	1,529	90,536
Piemonte	Turin	9,807	25,399	4,338,262
Alessandria	Alessandria	1,375	3,560	441,225
Asti	Asti	583	1,511	209,348
Cuneo	Cuneo	2,665	6,903	552,722
Novara	Novara	1,388	3,594	505,399
Torino	Turin	2,637	6,830	2,254,622
Vercelli	Vercelli	1,159	3,001	374,946
Puglia	Bari	7,470	19,348	3,970,525
Bari	Bari	1,980	5,129	1,507,059
Brindisi	Brindisi	710	1,838	402,639
Foggia	Foggia	2,774	7,185	685,804
Lecce	Lecce	1,065	2,759	783,714
Taranto	Taranto	941	2,437	591,309
Sardegna	Cagliari	9,301	24,090	1,645,192
Cagliari	Cagliari	2,662	6,895	770,113
Nuoro	Nuoro	2,720	7,044	267,281
Oristano	Oristano	1,016	2,631	155,474
Sassari	Sassari	2,903	7,520	452,324
Sicilia (Sicily)	Palermo	9,926	25,709	4,989,871
Agrigento	Agrigento	1,175	3,042	472,800
Caltanissetta	Caltanissetta	822	2,128	273,978
Catania	Catania	1,371	3,552	1,036,480
Enna	Enna	989	2,562	185,008
Messina	Messina	1,254	3,248	690,882
Palermo	Palermo	1,927	4,992	1,233,359
Ragusa	Ragusa	623	1,614	281,779
Siracusa	Siracusa	814	2,109	397,328
Trapani	Trapani	951	2,462	418,257

Area and population (continued)

Toscana	Florence	8,877	22,992	3,599,085
Arezzo	Arezzo	1,248	3,232	315,874
Firenze	Florence	1,498	3,879	1,217,454
Grosseto	Grosseto	1,739	4,504	216,535
Livorno	Livorno	468	1,213	342,130
Lucca	Lucca	684	1,773	378,350
Massa-Carrara	Massa-Carrara	447	1,157	199,057
Pisa	Pisa	945	2,448	394,277
Pistoia	Pistoia	373	965	270,054
Siena	Siena	1,475	3,821	265,354
Trentino-Alto Adige	Bolzano	5,258	13,618	934,731
Bolzano-Bozen	Bolzano	2,857	7,400	478,617
Trento	Trento	2,401	6,218	456,114
Umbria	Perugia	3,265	8,456	822,972
Perugia	Perugia	2,446	6,334	598,181
Terni	Terni	819	2,122	224,791
Valle d'Aosta	Aosta	1,259	3,262	117,208
Veneto	Venice	7,090	18,364	4,452,667
Belluno	Belluno	1,420	3,678	211,140
Padova	Padova	827	2,142	846,711
Rovigo	Rovigo	691	1,789	246,784
Treviso	Treviso	956	2,477	745,991
Venezia	Venice	950	2,460	839,847
Verona	Verona	1,195	3,096	810,079
Vicenza	Vicenza	1,051	2,722	752,115
TOTAL		116,324	301,277	57,103,833

Demography

Population (1992): 57,103,000.
Density (1992): persons per sq mi 491.4, persons per sq km 189.7.
Urban-rural (1991): urban 67.1%; rural 32.9%.
Sex distribution (1991): male 48.61%; female 51.39%.
Age breakdown (1988): under 15, 17.8%; 15–29, 24.1%; 30–44, 20.1%; 45–59, 18.6%; 60–74, 13.5%; 75 and over, 5.9%.
Population projection: (2000) 57,274,000; (2010) 56,270,000.
Doubling time: n.a.; population stable.
Ethnolinguistic composition (1983): Italian 94.1%; Sardinian 2.7%; Rhaetian 1.3%; other 1.9%.
Religious affiliation (1980): Roman Catholic 83.2%; nonreligious 13.6%; atheist 2.6%; other 0.6%.
Major cities (1991): Rome 2,791,354; Milan 1,432,184; Naples 1,206,013; Turin 991,870; Palermo 734,238; Genoa 701,032; Bologna 411,803; Florence 408,-403; Catania 364,176; Bari 353,032; Venice 317,837.
National origin (1980): Italian 98.8%; foreign-born 1.2%, of which Austrian 0.4%, French 0.2%, Slovene 0.2%, Albanian 0.1%, other 0.3%.
Mobility (1981). Population living in the same residence as in 1976: 92.4%.
Households. Average household size (1986) 2.8; composition of households: 1 person 21.1%, 2 persons 24.4%, 3 persons 22.5%, 4 persons 22.0%, 5 or more persons 10.0%. Family households (1983): 15,205,000 (85.3%); nonfamily 2,617,000 (14.7%), of which 1-person 13.0%.
Immigration (1989): immigrants admitted 81,201, from Europe 48.2%, of which West Germany 16.2%, Switzerland 7.8%; Africa 14.0%; Argentina 9.3%; Asia 9.2%; U.S. 5.4%.

Vital statistics

Birth rate per 1,000 population (1990): 9.8 (world avg. 27.1); legitimate 93.7%; illegitimate 6.3%.
Death rate per 1,000 population (1990): 9.3 (world avg. 9.8).
Natural increase rate per 1,000 population (1990): 0.5 (world avg. 17.3).
Total fertility rate (avg. births per childbearing woman; 1985–90): 1.4.
Marriage rate per 1,000 population (1990): 5.4.
Divorce rate per 1,000 population (1990): 0.4.
Life expectancy at birth (1988): male 73.2 years; female 79.7 years.
Major causes of death per 100,000 population (1988): diseases of the circulatory system 411.8; malignant neoplasms (cancers) 248.3; diseases of the respiratory system 60.1; diseases of the digestive system 51.8.

Social indicators

Educational attainment (1981). Percentage of population age 25 and over having: no formal schooling 19.3%[2]; primary education 47.4%; lower secondary 18.0%; upper secondary 11.2%; higher 4.1%.

Distribution of income (1986) percent of household income by quintile				
1	2	3	4	5 (highest)
6.8	12.0	16.7	23.5	41.0

Quality of working life. Average workweek (1985): 36.6 hours. Annual rate per 100,000 workers (1988) for: injury or accident 3,697; industrial illness 405[3]; death 5.7. Percentage of labour force insured for damages or income loss (1982) resulting from: injury 100%; permanent disability 100%; death 100%. Number of working days lost to labour stoppages (1989): 4,436,143. Average duration of journey to work: n.a. Rate per 1,000 workers of discouraged (unemployed no longer seeking work; 1982): 0.9.
Material well-being. Rate per 1,000 of population possessing (1990): telephone 555; automobile 439[4]; television 258[4] (colour 188[4]). Households possessing (1979): television 72%; refrigerator 91%; washing machine 88%.
Social participation. Eligible voters participating in last national election (1987): 88.5%. Population participating in voluntary work: n.a. Trade union membership in total workforce (1984): c. 70%. Practicing religious population in total affiliated population (1980): 65.7%, of which weekly 28.0%.
Social deviance (1990). Offense rate per 100,000 population for: murder 2.6; rape 2.4; assault 111.4; theft, including burglary and housebreaking 2,731.
Access to services (1981). Proportion of dwellings having access to: electricity 99.5%; safe water supply 98.7%; toilet facilities 98.5%; bath facilities 86.4%.

Leisure (1988). Favourite leisure activities (as percentage of household spending on culture): sporting events 19.0%; cinema 18.5%; theatre 13.7%.

National economy

Gross national product (1990): U.S.$970,619,000,000 (U.S.$16,850 per capita).

Structure of gross domestic product and labour force

	1990			
	in value 000,000,000 lire	% of total value	labour force	% of labour force
Agriculture	41,131	3.1	1,895,000	7.9
Mining }	289,951	22.2	229,000	1.0
Manufacturing			4,757,000	19.7
Construction	76,583	5.9	1,859,000	7.7
Public utilities	64,823	5.0	...	...
Transp. and commun.	76,321	5.8	1,146,000	4.8
Trade	244,344	18.7	4,537,000	18.8
Finance	157,215	12.0	895,000	3.7
Pub. admin., defense	166,675	12.8 }	5,986,000	24.9
Services	173,736	13.3 }		
Other	16,054[5]	1.2[5]	2,771,000[6]	11.5[6]
TOTAL	1,306,833	100.0	24,075,000	100.0

Budget (1990). Revenue: Lit 404,048,000,000,000 (income taxes 37.7%, of which individual 30.9%, corporate 6.7%; value-added and excise taxes 30.0%; social-security taxes 29.5%; property taxes 1.4%). Expenditures: Lit 459,616,000,000,000 (1988) social security and welfare 39.7%; debt service 16.3%; health 11.8%; education and culture 9.7%; transportation 7.4%; defense 3.8%).
Public debt (1990): U.S.$1,033,000,000,000.
Tourism (1990): receipts U.S.$19,738,000,000; expenditures U.S.$13,826,000,000.

Manufacturing, mining, and construction enterprises (1987)

	no. of enterprises[7]	no. of employees[8]	hourly wages as a % of avg. of all wages[9]	annual value added (Lit '000,000,000)
Manufacturing				
Machinery (nonelectrical)	3,873	376,000	98.0	18,030
Industrial chemicals	1,082	212,000	119.7	15,600
Transport equipment	730	309,000	117.7	14,598
Electrical machinery	1,554	272,000	112.1	13,490
Textiles	3,279	230,000	84.4	10,961
Pottery, ceramics, and glass	2,180	166,000	...	9,558
Food products	1,640	150,000	92.2	8,120
Iron and steel	1,024	183,000	122.6	7,739
Metal products	2,620	172,000	86.7	7,198
Printing, publishing	985	85,000	103.2	5,592
Wearing apparel	2,423	170,000	75.0	5,397
Plastic products	1,328	79,000	84.4	4,613
Paper and paper products	672	60,000	102.2	3,709
Petroleum and gas	17	6,000	136.6	2,400
Mining and quarrying	348	21,000	...	3,206
Construction	326,000[10]	1,849,000	...	53,465

Production (metric tons except as noted). Agriculture, forestry, fishing (1991): sugar beets 13,085,000, wheat 9,289,000, grapes 9,230,000, corn (maize) 6,208,000, tomatoes 6,069,000, potatoes 2,227,000, apples 1,793,000, soybeans 1,774,000, peaches 1,389,000, barley 1,325,000, olives 685,000; livestock (number of live animals) 11,575,000 sheep, 9,520,000 pigs, 8,647,000 cattle, 138,000,000 chickens; roundwood (1990) 8,038,000 cu m; fish catch (1990) 336,941. Mining and quarrying (1990): rock salt 3,750,000; feldspar 1,590,000; potash 661,000; zinc 80,000; magnesium 65,000; barite 37,000; lead 23,000. Manufacturing (1990): cement 40,544,149; crude steel 25,466,928; pig iron 11,852,303; sulfuric acid 3,260,636; plastics 3,130,426; caustic soda 1,145,307; textiles 496,195; wine 61,680,000 hectolitres[4]; beer 11,502,571 hectolitres[11]; olive oil 5,813,000 hectolitres[4]; 4,349,188 washing machines; 3,971,645 refrigerators; 3,018,097 motorized road vehicles, of which 1,873,278 automobiles, 884,216 motorcycles, scooters, and mopeds, 260,601 trucks and buses; 2,324,641 televisions, of which 2,322,602 colour. Construction (1990): residential 84,111,031 cu m; commercial, industrial, and other 97,878,223 cu m.

Service enterprises (1990)

	no. of enterprises[9]	no. of employees	hourly wage as a % of all wages	annual value added (Lit '000,000,000)
Public utilities	1,398	230,000[4]	...	53,292[4]
Transportation }	132,164	1,146,000	...	76,321
Communications				
Finance	89,092	895,000	...	157,215
Wholesale and retail trade	1,495,702	4,537,000	...	244,344
Pub. admin., services		5,986,000	...	166,675

Energy production (consumption): electricity (kW-hr; 1990) 216,891,000,000 (251,546,000,000); coal (metric tons; 1990) 1,014,000 (20,768,000); crude petroleum (barrels; 1990) 31,805,000 (529,827,000); petroleum products (metric tons; 1990) 81,468,000 (88,543,000); natural gas (cu m; 1990) 15,792,000,000 (40,699,000,000).
Population economically active (1990): total 24,075,000; activity rate of total population 41.8% (participation rates: ages 14–64, 56.7%; female 37.2%; unemployed 10.9%).

Price and earnings indexes (1985 = 100)

	1985	1986	1987	1988	1989	1990	1991
Consumer price index	91.6	105.9	110.9	116.5	123.8	131.8	140.1
Earnings index	90.0	104.8	111.6	118.4	125.6	134.7	147.9

Household income and expenditure (1988). Average household size 2.9; average annual income per household (1984) Lit 19,692,000 (U.S.$11,208);

sources of income (1987): salaries and wages 43.5%, property income and self-employment 36.6%, transfer payments 19.9%; expenditure (1990): food and beverages 23.5%, transportation and communications 16.4%, housing 14.9%, recreation and education 6.9%.

Financial aggregates

	1987	1988	1989	1990	1991	1992[12]
Exchange rate, Lit per:						
U.S. dollar	1,296.1	1,301.6	1,372.1	1,198.1	1,240.6	1,129.9
£	2,124.2	2,318.7	2,249.8	2,138.1	2,195.1	2,168.3
SDR	1,658.8	1,757.2	1,669.6	1,607.8	1,645.5	1,615.9
International reserves (U.S.$)						
Total (excl. gold; '000,000)	30,214	34,715	46,720	62,927	48,679	26,764
SDRs ('000,000)	948	949	998	1,037	930	922
Reserve pos. in IMF ('000,000)	1,447	1,266	1,444	1,714	2,255	2,253
Foreign exchange ('000,000)	27,765	32,500	44,278	60,176	45,495	23,589
Gold ('000,000 fine troy oz)	66.67	66.67	66.67	66.67	66.67	66.67
% world reserves	7.1	7.1	7.1	7.1	7.1	7.1
Interest and prices						
Central bank discount (%)	12.00	12.50	14.21	12.50	12.00	12.00[13]
Govt. bond yield (%)	9.65	10.16	10.72	11.51	10.10	10.07
Industrial share prices (1985=100)	224.6	185.1	214.2	194.3	152.8	10.74[13]
Balance of payments (U.S.$'000,000)						
Balance of visible trade	−338	−1,362	−2,167	724	−895	...
Imports, f.o.b.	−116,516	−128,816	−142,285	−169,216	−169,701	...
Exports, f.o.b.	116,178	128,048	140,118	169,940	168,806	...
Balance of invisibles	−550	−3,619	−6,403	3,555	2,020	...
Balance of payments, current account	−1,272	−6,190	−10,886	−14,222	−21,451	...

Land use (1990): forested 22.4%; meadows and pastures 16.2%; agricultural and under permanent cultivation 39.4%; other 22.0%.

Foreign trade

Balance of trade (current prices)

	1986	1987	1988	1989	1990	1991
Lit '000,000,000	+6,592	−6,533	−1,012	−3,358	+724	−1,913
% of total	2.3%	2.2%	0.3%	0.8%	0.2%	0.4%

Imports (1990): Lit 217,721,629,000,000 (machinery and transport equipment 32.2%, of which transport equipment 12.8%, precision machinery 5.8%; chemicals and chemical products 15.3%; metal and semiprocessed metal 10.7%; food and live animals 6.6%; crude petroleum 6.7%; textiles 4.1%). *Major import sources*: W.Ger. 21.2%; France 14.2%; The Netherlands 5.7%; U.K. 5.2%; U.S. 5.1%; Switzerland 4.6%.
Exports (1990): Lit 203,556,674,000,000 (machinery and transport equipment 41.8%, of which automobiles 4.9%, electrical machinery 4.6%, precision machinery 4.0%; chemicals and chemical products 10.0%; textiles 8.7%; wearing apparel 8.2%, of which shoes 3.3%; metal and processed metal 6.7%). *Major export destinations*: W.Ger. 19.0%; France 16.4%; U.S. 7.6%; U.K. 7.1%; Spain 4.9%.

Transport and communications

Transport. Railroads (1990): length[14] 12,153 mi, 19,559 km; passenger-mi 28,282,000,000, passenger-km 45,516,000,000; short ton-mi cargo 14,589,000,000, metric ton-km cargo 21,300,000,000. Roads (1988): total length 187,904 mi, 302,403 km (paved 100%). Vehicles (1989): passenger cars 24,307,000; trucks and buses 2,082,000. Merchant marine (1991): vessels (100 gross tons and over) 1,652; total deadweight tonnage 11,720,041. Air transport (1990)[15]: passenger-mi 14,139,000,000, passenger-km 22,754,000,000; short ton-mi cargo 800,287,000, metric ton-km cargo 1,168,400,000; airports (1992) 30.
Communications. Daily newspapers (1989): total number 72; total circulation 9,262,400; circulation per 1,000 population 161. Radio (1991): 14,817,197 receivers (1 per 3.9 persons). Television (1991): 17,000,500 receivers (1 per 3.4 persons). Telephones (1990): 32,037,396 (1 per 1.8 persons).

Education and health

Education (1990–91)

	schools	teachers	students	student/ teacher ratio
Primary (age 6–10)	24,337	195,017	3,060,562	15.7
Secondary (age 11–18)	9,992	113,562	2,275,582	20.0
Voc., teacher tr.	7,910	134,193	2,860,983	21.3
Higher[16]	49	53,213	1,222,645	22.9

Literacy (1990): total population age 15 and over literate 47,507,000 (97.1%); males literate 22,832,000 (97.8%); females literate 24,675,000 (96.4%).
Health (1988): physicians 255,110 (1 per 225 persons); hospital beds 424,417 (1 per 135 persons); infant mortality rate per 1,000 live births (1990) 8.5.
Food (1988–90): daily per capita caloric intake 3,498 (vegetable products 74%, animal products 26%); 139% of FAO recommended minimum requirement.

Military

Total active duty personnel (1992): 354,000 (army 64.9%, navy 13.6%, air force 21.5%). *Military expenditure as percentage of GNP* (1989): 2.4% (world 4.9%); per capita expenditure U.S.$360.

[1]Includes 10 nonelective seats. [2]More than two-thirds are age 55 and over. [3]1978. [4]1988. [5]Imputed bank charges less duties on imports. [6]Includes 2,621,000 unemployed. [7]Enterprises with 20 or more persons engaged. [8]Total number of persons engaged. [9]1981. [10]All enterprises (1982). [11]1987. [12]July. [13]June. [14]1989. [15]Alitalia only. [16]1988–89.

Jamaica

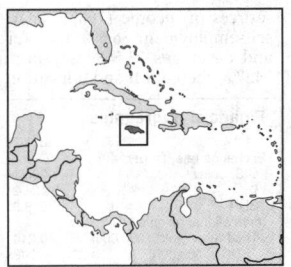

Official name: Jamaica.
Form of government: constitutional monarchy with two legislative houses (Senate [21]; House of Representatives [60]).
Chief of state: British Monarch represented by governor-general.
Head of government: Prime Minister.
Capital: Kingston.
Official language: English.
Official religion: none.
Monetary unit: 1 Jamaica dollar (J$) = 100 cents; valuation (Oct. 5, 1992) 1 U.S.$ = J$21.89; 1 £ = J$37.21.

Area and population

Parishes	Capitals	area sq mi	area sq km	population 1991 census
Clarendon	May Pen	462	1,196	212,324
Hanover	Lucea	174	450	65,958
Kingston	1	8	22	2
Manchester	Mandeville	321	830	164,979
Portland	Port Antonio	314	814	76,067
Saint Andrew	1	166	431	643,801[2]
Saint Ann	Saint Ann's Bay	468	1,213	149,015
Saint Catherine	Spanish Town	460	1,192	361,535
Saint Elizabeth	Black River	468	1,212	144,118
Saint James	Montego Bay	230	595	156,152
Saint Mary	Port Maria	236	611	107,993
Saint Thomas	Morant Bay	287	743	84,266
Trelawny	Falmouth	338	875	71,646
Westmoreland	Savanna-la-Mar	312	807	128,213
TOTAL		4,244	10,991	2,366,067

Demography

Population (1992): 2,445,000.
Density (1992): persons per sq mi 576.1, persons per sq km 222.5.
Urban-rural (1990): urban 52.3%; rural 47.7%.
Sex distribution (1991): male 50.00%; female 50.00%.
Age breakdown (1991): under 15, 33.0%; 15–29, 31.1%; 30–44, 16.7%; 45–59, 9.2%; 60 and over, 10.0%.
Population projection: (2000) 2,602,000; (2010) 2,813,000.
Doubling time: 36 years.
Ethnic composition (1982): black 74.7%; mixed black 12.8%; East Indian 1.3%; other 11.2%, of which not stated 9.5%.
Religious affiliation (1982): Protestant 55.9%, of which Church of God 18.4%, Baptist 10.0%, Anglican 7.1%, Seventh-day Adventist 6.9%, Pentecostal 5.2%; Roman Catholic 5.0%; nonreligious or atheist 17.7%; not stated 11.2%; other 10.2%, of which Rastafarian *c.* 5.0%.
Major cities (1991): Kingston 103,771[3] (metropolitan area 643,801); Spanish Town 92,383; Montego Bay 83,446; Portmore 73,400[4]; May Pen 46,785.

Vital statistics

Birth rate per 1,000 population (1991): 24.7 (world avg. 26.4); (1987) legitimate 14.9%, illegitimate 85.1%.
Death rate per 1,000 population (1991): 5.5 (world avg. 9.2).
Natural increase rate per 1,000 population (1991): 19.2 (world avg. 17.2).
Total fertility rate (avg. births per childbearing woman; 1990): 2.4.
Marriage rate per 1,000 population (1990): 5.4.
Divorce rate per 1,000 population (1990): 0.3.
Life expectancy at birth (1990–95): male 71.4 years; female 75.8 years.
Major causes of death per 100,000 population (1984): diseases of the circulatory system 217.2; malignant neoplasms (cancers) 90.9; diseases of the respiratory system 35.7; endocrine and metabolic disorders 33.6.

National economy

Budget (1991–92). Revenue J$14,496,400,000 (tax revenue 79.1%, of which income taxes 32.7%, consumption taxes 19.8%, stamp duties 7.1%; nontax revenue 7.4%). Expenditures: J$17,422,800,000 (current expenditure 60.6%, of which debt interest 24.2%; development expenditure 39.4%).
Public debt (external, outstanding; 1990): U.S.$3,673,000,000.
Tourism: receipts from visitors (1990) U.S.$764,000,000; expenditures by nationals abroad (1989) U.S.$54,000,000.
Production (metric tons except as noted). Agriculture, forestry, fishing (1991): sugarcane 2,732,000, yams 186,100, vegetables 101,200, bananas 75,300, citrus fruits 43,000, plantains 26,700, coffee 9,200, legumes 8,400, cacao beans 4,374, pimientos 1,752; livestock (number of live animals; 1990) 440,000 goats, 290,-000 cattle, 240,000 pigs; roundwood 215,000 cu m; fish catch (1989) 10,605. Mining and quarrying (1991): crude bauxite 4,249,000, alumina 3,004,000; gypsum 136,800. Manufacturing (1991): sugar 232,200; flour 149,300; poultry meat 37,000; beer and stout 595,300 hectolitres; rum 187,200 hectolitres; cigarettes 1,215,000,000 units. Construction (1990): residential units completed 3,292[5]; factory space completed 6,989 sq m. Energy production (consumption): electricity (kW-hr; 1990) 2,730,000,000 (2,730,000,000); coal, none (none); crude petroleum (barrels; 1990) none (6,643,000); petroleum products (metric tons; 1990) 850,000 (1,405,000); natural gas, none (none).
Land use (1989): forested 17.2%; meadows and pastures 17.5%; agricultural and under permanent cultivation 24.8%; other 40.5%.
Gross national product (at current market prices; 1990): U.S.$3,606,000,000 (U.S.$1,510 per capita).

Structure of gross domestic product and labour force

	1991 in value J$'000,000	% of total value	labour force	% of labour force
Agriculture	2,412	5.7	247,700	23.0
Mining	4,816	11.4	5,300	0.5
Manufacturing	7,704	18.2	95,600	8.9
Construction	5,565	13.1	54,900	5.1
Public utilities	1,079	2.6	6,200	0.6
Transp. and commun.	3,650	8.6	35,800	3.3
Trade	8,766	20.7	173,500	16.1
Pub. admin., defense	2,879	6.8 }		
Finance, real estate	5,472	12.9 }	283,000	26.3
Services	2,010	4.7 }		
Other	−1,986[6]	−4.7[6]	174,600[7]	16.2[7]
TOTAL	42,367	100.0	1,076,600	100.0

Population economically active (1991): total 1,076,600; activity rate of total population 44.4% (participation rates: ages 14–64, 71.6%[8]; female 47.4%; unemployed 15.7%).

Price and earnings indexes (1985 = 100)

	1985	1986	1987	1988	1989	1990	1991
Consumer price index	100.0	115.1	122.8	132.9	152.0	185.3	280.0
Monthly earnings index	...	...	...	...	...	...	...

Household income and expenditure. Average household size (1982) 4.3; average annual income per household (1988) J$8,356 (U.S.$1,525); sources of income (1989): wages and salaries 66.1%, self-employment 19.3%; transfers 14.6%; expenditure (1988)[9]: food and beverages 55.6%, housing 7.9%, fuel and other household supplies 7.4%, health care 7.0%, transportation 6.4%, clothing and footwear 5.1%, household furnishings 2.8%, other 7.8%.

Foreign trade[10]

Balance of trade (current prices)

	1985	1986	1987	1988	1989	1990
U.S.$'000,000	−437	−248	−357	−357	−606	−468
% of total	27.7%	17.4%	20.1%	16.8%	23.3%	16.8%

Imports (1991): J$20,830,000,000 (raw materials 63.5%, of which fuels 18.1%; capital goods 21.6%, of which machinery and apparatus 12.5%; consumer goods 14.8%). *Major import sources* (1990): United States 45.0%; Canada 6.4%; United Kingdom 5.7%; Venezuela 5.5%; Mexico 5.4%.
Exports (1991): J$13,079,000,000 (alumina 47.4%; bauxite 9.9%; raw sugar 7.6%; bananas 3.9%; rum 1.3%; coffee 1.1%). *Major export destinations* (1990): United States 30.4%; United Kingdom 17.3%; Canada 13.5%; The Netherlands 10.0%; U.S.S.R. 3.6%.

Transport and communications

Transport. Railroads (1989): route length 211 mi, 339 km; passenger-mi 22,460,000, passenger-km 36,146,000; short ton-mi cargo 71,505,000, metric ton-km cargo 104,395,000. Roads (1991): total length 10,212 mi, 16,435 km (paved 29%). Vehicles (1989): passenger cars 93,000; trucks and buses 16,000. Merchant marine (1991): vessels (100 gross tons and over) 12; total deadweight tonnage 21,317. Air transport (1991)[11]: passenger-mi 805,758,-000, passenger-km 1,296,745,000; short ton-mi cargo 14,893,000, metric ton-km cargo 21,743,000; airports (1992) with scheduled flights 6.
Communications. Daily newspapers (1991): total number 3; total circulation 130,400; circulation per 1,000 population 53. Radio (1991): 1,500,000 receivers (1 per 1.6 persons). Television (1991): 484,000 receivers (1 per 5.0 persons). Telephones (1991): 192,100 (1 per 13 persons).

Education and health

Education (1990–91)[12]

	schools	teachers	students	student/ teacher ratio
Primary (age 6–11)[13]	790	9,693	385,041	48.7
Secondary (age 12–16)	127	7,721	151,304	19.6
Voc., teacher tr.	17[14]	821	14,898	18.1
Higher	15[15]	1,047[16]	19,173[14]	17.9[16]

Educational attainment (1982). Percentage of population age 25 and over having: no formal schooling 3.2%; some primary education 79.8%; some secondary 15.0%; complete secondary and higher 2.0%. *Literacy* (1990): total population age 15 and over literate 1,630,000 (98.4%); males literate 800,000 (98.2%); females literate 830,000 (98.6%).
Health (1990): physicians[17] 407 (1 per 5,904 persons); hospital beds 5,130 (1 per 468 persons); infant mortality rate per 1,000 live births (1989) 27.0.
Food (1987–89): daily per capita caloric intake 2,622 (vegetable products 84%, animal products 16%); 117% of FAO recommended minimum requirement.

Military

Total active duty personnel (1991): 3,350 (army 89.5%; coast guard 5.4%; air force 5.1%). *Military expenditure as percentage of GNP* (1989): 1.1% (world 4.9%); per capita expenditure U.S.$14.

[1]The parishes of Kingston and Saint Andrew are jointly administered from the Half Way Tree section of Saint Andrew. [2]Kingston included with Saint Andrew. [3]City of Kingston is coextensive with Kingston parish. [4]1982. [5]80% public sector. [6]Less imputed service charges. [7]Includes 168,700 unemployed. [8]1990. [9]Weights of consumer price index components. [10]Import figures are f.o.b. in balance of trade and c.i.f. in commodities and trading partners. [11]Air Jamaica only. [12]Public schools only. [13]Includes lower-secondary students at all-age schools. [14]1989–90. [15]1988–89. [16]1987–88. [17]Public health only.

Japan

Official name: Nihon (Japan).
Form of government: constitutional monarchy with a National Diet consisting of two legislative houses (House of Councillors [252]; House of Representatives [512]).
Chief of state: Emperor.
Head of government: Prime Minister.
Capital: Tōkyō.
Official language: Japanese.
Official religion: none.
Monetary unit: 1 yen (¥) = 100 sen; valuation (Oct. 5, 1992) 1 U.S.$ = ¥119.56; 1 £ = ¥203.25.

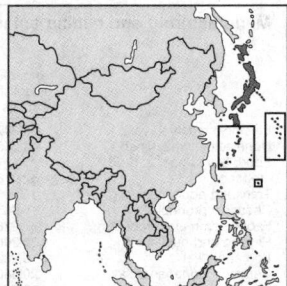

Area and population

Regions Prefectures	Capitals	area sq mi	area sq km	population 1991[1] estimate
Chūbu				
Aichi	Nagoya	1,984	5,139	6,724,000
Fukui	Fukui	1,619	4,192	824,000
Gifu	Gifu	4,091	10,596	2,072,000
Ishikawa	Kanazawa	1,621	4,198	1,166,000
Nagano	Nagano	5,245	13,585	2,160,000
Niigata	Niigata	4,857	12,579	2,474,000
Shizuoka	Shizuoka	3,001	7,773	3,686,000
Toyama	Toyama	1,642	4,252	1,121,000
Yamanashi	Kōfu	1,723	4,463	858,000
Chūgoku				
Hiroshima	Hiroshima	3,269	8,467	2,858,000
Okayama	Okayama	2,738	7,092	1,929,000
Shimane	Matsue	2,559[2]	6,629[2]	778,000
Tottori	Tottori	1,349[2]	3,494[2]	616,000
Yamaguchi	Yamaguchi	2,358	6,107	1,569,000
Hokkaidō				
Hokkaidō (Territory)	Sapporo	32,247	83,520	5,649,000
Kantō				
Chiba	Chiba	1,989	5,151	5,614,000
Gumma	Maebashi	2,454	6,356	1,974,000
Ibaraki	Mito	2,353	6,094	2,870,000
Kanagawa	Yokohama	928	2,403	8,044,000
Saitama	Urawa	1,467	3,799	6,483,000
Tochigi	Utsunomiya	2,476	6,414	1,947,000
Kinki				
Hyōgo	Kōbe	3,236	8,381	5,437,000
Mie	Tsu	2,231	5,778	1,802,000
Nara	Nara	1,425	3,692	1,389,000
Shiga	Ōtsu	1,551	4,016	1,234,000
Wakayama	Wakayama	1,824	4,725	1,076,000
Kyūshū				
Fukuoka	Fukuoka	1,916	4,963	4,831,000
Kagoshima	Kagoshima	3,539	9,167	1,792,000
Kumamoto	Kumamoto	2,860	7,408	1,843,000
Miyazaki	Miyazaki	2,986	7,735	1,167,000
Nagasaki	Nagasaki	1,588	4,113	1,557,000
Ōita	Ōita	2,447	6,338	1,235,000
Saga	Saga	942	2,440	877,000
Ryukyu				
Okinawa	Naha	871	2,255	1,229,000
Shikoku				
Ehime	Matsuyama	2,190	5,672	1,513,000
Kagawa	Takamatsu	727	1,883	1,023,000
Kōchi	Kōchi	2,744	7,107	821,000
Tokushima	Tokushima	1,601	4,146	830,000
Tohoku				
Akita	Akita	4,484[3]	11,613[3]	1,223,000
Aomori	Aomori	3,714[3]	9,619[3]	1,477,000
Fukushima	Fukushima	5,322	13,784	2,108,000
Iwate	Morioka	5,898	15,277	1,415,000
Miyagi	Sendai	2,815	7,292	2,264,000
Yamagata	Yamagata	3,601	9,327	1,257,000
Metropolis				
Tōkyō[4]	Tōkyō	836	2,166	11,887,000
Urban prefectures				
Kyōto[5]	Kyōto	1,781	4,613	2,604,000
Ōsaka[5]	Ōsaka	722	1,869	8,737,000
TOTAL		145,883[6,7]	377,835[6,7]	124,043,000[7]

Demography

Population (1992): 124,310,000.
Density (1992): persons per sq mi 852.1, persons per sq km 328.3.
Urban-rural (1990): urban 77.4%; rural 22.6%.
Sex distribution (1992): male 49.09%; female 50.91%.
Age breakdown (1992): under 15, 17.3%; 15–29, 22.0%; 30–44, 21.9%; 45–59, 20.2%; 60–69, 10.2%; 70 and over, 8.4%.
Population projection: (2000) 126,894,000; (2010) 129,410,000.
Doubling time: not applicable; doubling time exceeds 100 years.
Composition by nationality (1990): Japanese 99.2%; Korean 0.6%; Chinese and other 0.2%.
Place of birth (1991): 99.2% native-born; 0.8% foreign-born (mainly Korean).
Immigration (1990): permanent immigrants/registered aliens admitted 984,500, from North and South Korea 69.3%, Taiwan, Hong Kong, and China 14.0%, Philippines 4.0%, United States 3.5%, United Kingdom 0.9%, Malaysia 0.4%, Canada 0.4%, France 0.3%, West Germany 0.3%, Australia 0.3%, other 6.6%.
Major cities (1991): Tōkyō 8,154,404; Yokohama 3,250,887; Ōsaka 2,613,199; Nagoya 2,158,784; Sapporo 1,696,056; Kōbe 1,488,619; Kyōto 1,458,563; Fukuoka 1,249,320; Kawasaki 1,187,034; Hiroshima 1,090,048; Kita-Kyūshū 1,021,816.

Other principal cities (1991)

	population		population		population
Akashi	275,399	Kakogawa	242,608	Okazaki	311,906
Akita	303,805	Kanazawa	444,024	Ōmiya	410,694
Amagasaki	498,038	Kashiwa	308,447	Otsu	262,953
Aomori	287,297	Kasugai	268,506	Sagamihara	542,000
Asahikawa	361,631	Kawagoe	308,082	Sakai	808,072
Chiba	834,545	Kawaguchi	443,985	Sasebo	243,960
Fujisawa	354,679	Kōchi	317,877	Sendai	930,520
Fukui	253,470	Koriyama	316,833	Shimonoseki	261,388
Fukushima	279,127	Koshigaya	288,489	Shizuoka	472,666
Fukuyama	367,322	Kumamoto	630,926	Suita	343,696
Funabashi	535,572	Kurashiki	415,476	Takamatsu	329,777
Gifu	410,619	Machida	352,500	Takatsuki	360,770
Hachiōji	474,698	Maebashi	287,710	Tokorozawa	307,174
Hakodate	308,289	Matsudo	458,893	Tokushima	263,887
Hamamatsu	549,962	Matsuyama	446,979	Toyama	322,470
Higashi-Ōsaka	517,237	Miyazaki	289,080	Toyohashi	343,064
Himeji	457,579	Nagano	348,791	Toyonaka	408,305
Hirakata	392,392	Nagasaki	443,823	Toyota	337,122
Hiratsuka	248,363	Naha	303,480	Urawa	427,690
Ibaraki	254,542	Nara	351,985	Utsunomiya	430,967
Ichihara	262,739	Neyagawa	257,097	Wakayama	396,620
Ichikawa	443,378	Niigata	487,856	Yamagata	249,615
Ichinomiya	263,912	Nishinomiya	426,711	Yao	278,022
Iwaki	356,746	Ōita	412,860	Yokkaichi	277,502
Kagoshima	536,895	Okayama	597,238	Yokosuka	434,957

Religious affiliation (1989): Shintō and related religions 39.5%; Buddhism 38.3%; Christian 3.9%; other 18.3%.
Households (1992). Total households 42,458,000; average household size (1990) 3.0; composition of households (1985) 1 person 20.8%, 2 persons 18.4%, 3 persons 17.9%, 4 persons 23.6%, 5 persons 11.0%, 6 persons 5.2%, 7 or more persons 2.9%. Family households (1985) 30,021,000 (79.0%); nonfamily 7,967,000 (21.0%), of which 1-person 7,900,000 (20.8%).

Type of household (1988)

Total number of dwelling units: 37,413,000

	number of dwellings	percentage of total
by kind of dwelling		
exclusive entry (do not share bathroom or kitchen)	34,701,000	92.8
combined with nondwelling	2,712,000	7.3
detached house	23,311,000	62.3
apartment building	11,409,000	30.5
tenement (substandard or overcrowded building)	2,490,000	6.7
other	203,000	0.5
by legal tenure of householder		
owned	22,948,000	61.3
rented	14,015,000	37.5
other	450,000	1.2
by kind of amenities		
flush toilet	24,300,000	65.0
bathroom	34,126,000	91.2
by year of construction		
prior to 1945	2,701,000	7.3
1945–70	11,487,000	31.1
1971–80	13,543,000	36.8
1981–83	3,564,000	9.7
1984–88	5,556,000	15.1

Mobility (1980). Population living in same residence from birth 24.0%; different residence established prior to October 1975, 44.0%; different residence established after October 1975, 32.0%, of which: same prefecture 24.1%; different prefecture 7.7%.

Vital statistics

Birth rate per 1,000 population (1991): 9.9 (world avg. 26.4); (1985) legitimate 99.0%; illegitimate 1.0%.
Death rate per 1,000 population (1991): 6.7 (world avg. 9.2).
Natural increase rate per 1,000 population (1991): 3.2 (world avg. 17.2).
Total fertility rate (avg. births per childbearing woman; 1990): 1.5.
Marriage rate per 1,000 population (1991): 6.0[8]; median age at first marriage (1987) men 28.3 years, women 25.6 years.
Divorce rate per 1,000 population (1991)[8]: 1.4.
Life expectancy at birth (1990): male 75.9 years; female 81.8 years.
Major causes of death per 100,000 population (1991): malignant neoplasms (cancers) 180.5; heart diseases 136.3; cerebrovascular diseases 95.6; pneumonia and bronchitis 61.6; accidents and adverse effects 26.8; senility without mention of psychosis 18.7; suicide 16.0; nephritis, nephrotic syndrome, and nephrosis 13.7; cirrhosis of the liver 13.6; diabetes mellitus 7.8; hypertensive diseases 7.3.

Social indicators

Educational attainment (1980). Percentage of population aged 15 years and over having: no schooling 0.3%; primary and lower secondary education 38.5%; higher secondary 38.0%; junior college and technical college 5.7%; university and postgraduate 8.0%; still in school 9.5%.

Distribution of income (1989)

percentage of average household income by quintile

1	2	3	4	5 (highest)
10.9	15.5	18.7	23.3	31.6

Quality of working life. Average workweek (1991): 45.0 hours. Annual rate of industrial deaths per 100,000 workers (1989): 2.8. Proportion of labour force insured for damages or income loss resulting from injury, permanent disability, and death (1991): 50.1%. Average man-days lost to labour stoppages per 1,000,000 workdays (1990): 8.9. Average duration of journey to work (1988)[9]: 26.8 minutes (1983; 26.7% private automobile, 67.4% public transportation, 5.5% taxi, 0.4% other). Rate per 1,000 workers of discouraged (unemployed no longer seeking work; 1982): 69.7.

Access to services (1989). Proportion of households having access to: gas supply 64.6%; safe public water supply 94.0%; public sewage collection 89.4%.
Social participation. Eligible voters participating in last national election (1990): 73.3%. Population 15 years and over participating in social service activities on a voluntary basis (1987): 25.2%. Trade union membership in total work force (1990): 25.2%.
Social deviance (1989). Offense rate per 100,000 population for: homicide 1.1; rape 1.3; robbery 1.3; larceny and theft 1,203.7. Incidence in general population of: alcoholism, n.a.; drug and substance abuse, n.a. Rate of suicide per 100,000 population (1989): 21.1.

Leisure/use of personal time

Discretionary daily activities (1986)
(Population age 15 years and over)

	weekly average hrs./min.
Total discretionary daily time	5:47
of which	
Hobbies and amusements	0:31
Sports	0:10
Learning (except schoolwork)	0:12
Social service	0:02
Voluntary social organizations and associations	0:28
Radio, television, newspapers, and magazines	2:18
Rest and relaxation	1:21
Other activities	0:45

Major leisure activities (1986)
(Population age 15 years and over)

	Percentage of participation		
	Male	Female	Total
Hobbies and amusements	89.4	86.8	88.0
Sports	84.0	69.1	76.3
Light exercises	30.4	32.9	31.6
Swimming	31.5	21.0	26.1
Bowling	29.6	18.8	24.0
Learning (except schoolwork)	37.0	34.1	35.5
Travel			
Domestic	76.1	70.4	73.1
Foreign	5.8	3.7	4.7

Material well-being (1991). Households possessing: automobile 79.5%; telephone, virtually 100%; colour television receiver 99.3%; refrigerator 98.9%; air conditioner 68.1%; washing machine 99.4%; vacuum cleaner 98.7%; videocassette recorder 71.5%; camera 86.8%; microwave oven 75.6%; compact disc player 41.0%.

National economy

Gross national product (at current market prices; 1990): U.S.$3,140,948,000,-000 (U.S.$25,430 per capita).

Structure of gross domestic product and labour force

	1990		1991	
	in value ¥'000,000,000	% of total value	labour force	% of labour force
Agriculture, fishing	10,482	2.6	4,270,000	6.6
Mining	957	0.2	60,000	0.1
Manufacturing	125,205	31.3	15,500,000	23.8
Construction	35,212	8.8	6,040,000	9.3
Public utilities	14,503	3.6	330,000	0.5
Transportation and communications	25,761	6.4	3,780,000	5.8
Trade	55,301	13.8	14,330,000	22.0
Finance	65,398	16.3	2,630,000	4.1
Pub. admin., defense	26,106	6.5	1,990,000	3.1
Services	64,633	16.1	14,460,000	22.2
Other	−22,959[10]	−5.7[10]	1,660,000[11]	2.6[11]
TOTAL	400,599	100.0[7]	65,050,000	100.0[7]

Budget (1992)[12]. Revenue: ¥72,218,011,000,000 (income tax 37.8%; corporation tax 25.1%; public bonds 10.1%; liquor and tobacco tax 2.8%; stamp duties 2.3%; customs duties 1.2%). Expenditures: ¥72,218,011,000,000 (national debt 22.8%; transfers to local governments 21.8%; social security 17.6%; public works 11.1%; culture, education, and science promotion 7.9%; national defense 6.3%; pensions 2.5%; economic cooperation 1.3%; measures for energy 0.9%; foodstuff control 0.5%; small-enterprise assistance 0.3%).
Public debt (1991): U.S.$1,250,000,000,000.
Population economically active (1991): total 65,050,000; activity rate of total population 52.4% (participation rates: ages 15 and older 63.8%; female 40.8%; unemployed 2.1%).

Price and earnings indexes (1985 = 100)

	1986	1987	1988	1989	1990	1991	1992[13]
Consumer price index	100.6	100.7	101.4	103.7	106.9	110.4	112.8
Monthly earnings index	102.9	105.0	108.6	112.1	116.3	120.4	124.6

Household income and expenditure (1990)[14]. Average household size 3.7; average annual income per household ¥6,585,200 (U.S.$48,900); sources of income (1987): wages and salaries 57.8%, transfer payments 20.0%, self-employment 12.1%, other 10.1%; expenditure (1991): food 19.3%, transportation 8.1%, reading and recreation 7.6%, clothing and footwear 5.7%, housing 4.2%, fuel, light, and water charges 4.1%, education 4.0%, furniture and household utensils 3.2%, medical care 2.0%.

Manufacturing and mining enterprises (1988)

	no. of establishments	avg. no. of persons engaged	annual wages as a % of avg. of all contract wages	annual value added (¥'000,000,000)
Electrical machinery	35,347	1,891,000	95.4	17,158
Nonelectrical machinery	44,855	1,118,000	120.9	10,677
Food, beverages, and tobacco	52,076	1,214,000	76.4	9,900
Transport equipment	15,033	889,000	126.6	9,917
Chemical products	5,363	391,000	143.9	10,089
Fabricated metal products	51,276	816,000	98.7	6,613
Printing and publishing	30,206	540,000	124.2	5,449
Iron and steel	6,282	338,000	150.5	5,613
Ceramic, stone, and clay	20,846	455,000	100.0	4,711
Plastic products	19,551	417,000	91.7	3,401
Textiles	32,204	559,000	72.6	3,035
Paper and paper products	11,672	280,000	103.0	2,809
Apparel products	32,218	572,000	50.9	1,972
Precision instruments	7,353	246,000	101.2	1,777
Nonferrous metal products	4,244	163,000	122.2	1,836
Lumber and wood products	21,167	261,000	77.3	1,535
Furniture and fixtures	17,517	229,000	82.6	1,527
Rubber products	5,760	168,000	102.4	1,408
Petroleum and coal products	1,061	34,000	159.9	1,062
Leather products	5,808	77,000	72.1	413
Mining	780	29,000	136.5	227

Energy production (consumption): electricity (kW-hr; 1990) 857,273,000,000 (857,273,000,000); coal (metric tons; 1990) 8,277,000 (113,113,000); crude petroleum (barrels; 1990) 3,977,000 (1,395,000,000); petroleum products (metric tons; 1990) 155,331,000, of which (by volume) diesel 31.5%, heavy fuel oil 26.4%, gasoline 20.0%, kerosene and jet fuel 14.3%, naphtha 4.8% (182,155,000); natural gas (cu m; 1990) 2,073,000,000 (51,391,000,000). Composition of energy supply by source (1989): crude oil and petroleum products 57.9%, coal 17.2%, natural gas 10.0%, nuclear power 8.9%, hydroelectric power 4.6%, other 1.4%. Domestic energy demand by end use (1989): mining and manufacturing 45.0%, residential and commercial 24.3%, transportation 22.9%, agriculture, forestry, and fisheries 3.5%, other 4.3%.
Tourism (1990): receipts from visitors U.S.$3,578,000,000; expenditures by nationals abroad U.S.$24,928,000,000.

Financial aggregates

	1986	1987	1988	1989	1990	1991	1992[13]
Exchange rate[15], ¥ per:							
U.S. dollar	159.10	123.50	125.85	143.45	134.40	125.20	126.81
£	247.22	237.05	228.29	226.21	258.41	234.21	238.20
SDR	194.61	175.20	169.36	188.52	191.21	179.09	179.61
International reserves (U.S.$)							
Total (excl. gold; '000,000)	42,257	80,973	96,728	83,957	78,501	72,059	70,502
SDRs ('000,000)	2,218	2,463	2,936	2,447	3,042	2,579	2,649
Reserve pos. in IMF ('000,000)	2,382	2,853	3,278	3,518	5,971	7,722	7,597
Foreign exchange ('000,000)	37,657	75,657	90,514	77,992	69,487	61,758	60,256
Gold ('000,000 fine troy oz)	24.23	24.23	24.23	24.23	24.23	24.23	24.23
% world reserves	2.5	2.6	2.6	2.6	2.6	2.6	2.6
Interest and prices							
Central bank discount (%)[15]	3.00	2.50	2.50	4.25	6.00	4.50	3.75
Govt. bond yield (%)	4.94	4.21	4.27	5.05	7.36	6.53	5.14
Industrial share prices (1985=100)	132.9	196.4	213.9	257.8	218.8	184.9	130.3
Balance of payments (U.S.$'000,000,000)							
Balance of visible trade	92.8	96.4	95.0	76.9	63.6	103.1	...
Imports, f.o.b.	112.8	128.2	164.8	192.7	216.8	203.5	...
Exports, f.o.b.	205.6	224.6	259.8	269.6	280.4	306.6	...
Balance of invisibles	−4.9	−5.7	−11.3	−15.6	−22.2	−17.7	...
Balance of payments, current account	85.8	87.0	79.6	57.0	35.9	72.9	...

Production (metric tons except as noted). Agriculture, forestry, fishing (1991): rice 12,005,000, sugar beets 3,750,000, potatoes 3,700,000, cabbages 3,000,000, sugarcane 2,200,000, mandarin oranges 2,040,000, sweet potatoes 1,460,000, onions 1,299,000, apples 1,046,000, cucumbers 980,000, raw sugar 915,000, wheat 860,000, tomatoes 770,000, watermelons 750,-000, carrots 709,000, eggplants 570,000, pears 420,000, pumpkins 303,000, grapes 300,000, barley 268,000, soybeans 260,000, strawberries 218,000, peaches 193,000, dry beans 150,000, green beans 98,000, tea 90,000, tobacco leaves 71,000, green peas 60,000, cow's milk 8,180,000, hen's eggs 2,466,000; livestock (number of live animals) 11,335,000 pigs, 4,863,000 cattle (of which 33% dairy cows), 34,000 goats, 32,000 sheep, 24,000 horses, 335,000,000 poultry; roundwood (1990) 29,813,000 cu m; fish catch (1990) 10,353,555, of which sardines 3,678,229, Alaska pollack 871,408, Japanese scallops 421,709, mackerel 273,005, oysters 248,793, Keta salmon 223,273, squid 219,524, crabs 48,932, river eels 38,855, carp 22,611. Mining and quarrying (1991): limestone 206,780,000; silica stone 18,472,000; dolomite 5,318,000; silica sand 4,331,000; pyrophyllite 904,000; pyrophyllite clay 325,000; zinc 133,004; lead 18,329; copper 12,413; tungsten 465; silver 170,700 kg; gold 8,300 kg. Manufacturing (1991): crude steel 109,649,000; semifinished steel 102,727,000; cement 89,564,000; hot-rolled steel products 87,982,000; pig iron 79,985,000; paper pulp 11,556,500; sulfuric acid 7,057,-100; plastic products 5,516,800; compound fertilizers 2,803,100; spun yarn 939,100; synthetic fabrics 2,591,760,000 sq m; cotton fabrics 1,603,280,000 sq m; finished products (in number of units) 477,216,000 watches and clocks, 69,371,000 electronic desk calculators, 26,058,000 videocassette recorders, 18,164,000 telephones, 17,657,000 35-mm cameras, 13,438,000 colour television receivers, 9,753,100 passenger cars, 7,447,900 bicycles, 6,981,000 vacuum cleaners, 5,587,000 automatic washing machines, 5,212,000 electric refrigerators, 4,547,000 facsimile machines, 4,282,000 microwave ovens, 4,178,-000 stereo recorders, 3,028,600 motorcycles, 2,654,700 photocopy machines, 1,456,800 typewriters. Construction (floor area started; 1990): residential 155,868,000 sq m; nonresidential 127,560,000 sq m.

Retail and wholesale trade and services (1988)

	no. of establish-ments	avg. no. of em-ployees	annual sales (¥'000,000,000)
Retail trade	1,619,752	6,851,000	114,840
Food and beverages	653,637	2,586,000	35,679
Grocery	77,717	669,000	14,308
Liquors	107,746	317,000	5,656
General merchandise	4,015	405,000	15,971
Department stores	1,911	394,000	15,700
Gasoline service stations	73,581	385,000	9,562
Motor vehicles and bicycles	89,374	514,000	13,779
Apparel and accessories	236,581	800,000	12,268
Furniture and home furnishings	166,042	602,000	10,223
Eating and drinking places[16]	838,449	2,055,000	9,720
Wholesale trade	436,421	4,332,000	446,484
General merchandise	824	56,000	76,346
Machinery and equipment	94,775	1,079,000	89,583
General machinery except electrical	46,084	461,000	29,326
Motor vehicles and parts	15,365	208,000	23,485
Minerals and metals	21,041	240,000	44,447
Farm, livestock, and fishery products	41,071	416,000	55,926
Food and beverages	54,996	536,000	39,904
Textiles, apparel, and accessories	42,235	486,000	33,313
Building materials	59,877	396,000	26,993
Chemicals	16,924	166,000	19,514
Drugs and toilet goods	18,525	258,000	15,566
Medical services[16]	171,986	2,026,000	...
Educational services[16]	84,512	2,065,000	...

Land use (1990): forested 66.7%; meadows and pastures 1.7%; agricultural and under permanent cultivation 12.2%; other 19.4%.

Foreign trade[17]

Balance of trade (current prices)

	1986	1987	1988	1989	1990	1991
¥'000,000,000	+15,519	+12,107	+11,903	+11,235	+10,398	+13,093
% of total	28.2%	22.2%	21.3%	17.4%	14.3%	18.3%

Imports (1991): ¥31,900,200,000,000 (mineral fuels, lubricants, and related materials 23.1%, of which crude petroleum and petroleum products 16.0%; machinery and transport equipment 18.1%; food, beverages, and tobacco 14.6%; crude materials excluding fuels 11.5%). *Major import sources:* United States 22.5%; China 6.0%; Australia 5.5%; Indonesia 5.4%; South Korea 5.2%; Germany 4.5%; Saudi Arabia 4.3%; Taiwan 4.0%; Canada 3.3%; France 2.5%.

Exports (1991): ¥42,359,900,000,000 (motor vehicles 17.4%; office machinery 7.1%; chemicals 5.6%, of which plastic materials 1.5%; iron and steel products 4.3%; scientific and optical equipment 4.1%; power-generating machinery 2.6%; textiles and allied products 2.5%; tape recorders 2.3%; vessels 2.1%; metalworking machinery 1.4%; radio receivers 1.0%; televison receivers 0.7%). *Major export destinations:* United States 29.1%; Germany 6.6%; South Korea 6.4%; Taiwan 5.8%; Hong Kong 5.2%; Singapore 3.9%; United Kingdom 3.5%; Thailand 3.0%; Canada 2.3%; Australia 2.1%.

Trade by commodity group (1991)

SITC group	imports U.S.$'000,000	%	exports U.S.$'000,000	%
00 Food and live animals	34,698	14.7	1,718	0.5
01 Beverages and tobacco				
02 Crude materials, excluding fuels	24,645[18]	10.4[18]	1,875[18]	0.6[18]
03 Mineral fuels, lubricants, and related materials	54,756	23.1	1,397	0.4
04 Animal and vegetable oils, fats, and waxes	18	18	18	18
05 Chemicals and related products, n.e.s.	16,910	7.1	17,195	5.5
06 Basic manufactures	18,757	7.9	22,247	7.1
07 Machinery and transport equipment	35,550	15.0	171,595	54.6
08 Miscellaneous manufactured articles	32,573	13.8	80,606	25.6
09 Goods not classified by kind	18,848	8.0	17,892	5.7
TOTAL	236,737	100.0	314,525	100.0

Direction of trade (1991)

	imports U.S.$'000,000	%	exports U.S.$'000,000	%
Africa	1,873	0.8	3,576	1.1
Asia	102,357	43.2	117,301	37.2
South America	8,096	3.4	9,975	3.2
North America and Central America	64,619	27.3	102,883	32.7
United States	53,317	22.5	91,538	29.1
other North and Central Am.	11,302	4.8	11,345	3.6
Europe	43,142	18.2	71,801	22.8
EEC	31,792	13.4	59,158	18.8
Russia	3,317	1.4	2,114	0.7
other Europe	8,033	3.4	10,529	3.3
Oceania	16,650	7.0	9,209	2.9
TOTAL	236,737	100.0[7]	314,525	100.0[7]

Transport and communications

Transport. Railroads (1991): length 23,690 mi, 38,125 km; rolling stock (1985) locomotives 3,177, passenger cars 46,192, freight cars 40,951; passengers carried 22,581,000,000; passenger-mi 242,976,000,000, passenger-km 391,032,-000,000; short ton-mi cargo 18,732,000,000, metric ton-km cargo 27,348,-000,000. Roads (1991): total length 693,207 mi, 1,115,609 km (paved 70%). Vehicles (1991): passenger cars 37,076,065; trucks 22,688,131; buses 248,258. Merchant marine (1991): vessels (100 gross tons and over) 10,063; total deadweight tonnage 39,691,692. Air transport (1990): passengers carried 70,528,000; passenger-mi 59,268,000,000, passenger-km 95,383,000,000; short ton-mi cargo 9,063,562,000, metric ton-km cargo 13,232,579,000; airports (1992) with scheduled flights 71. Shares of domestic passenger traffic by mode of transportation (1989): automobiles and light motor vehicles 54.2%; railway 32.4%; buses 13.1%; ships 0.2%; airplanes 0.1%.

Distribution of traffic (1988)

	cargo carried ('000,000 tons)	% of national total	passengers carried ('000,000)	% of national total
Road	5,578.6	90.6	34,679.0	47.4
Rail (intercity)	83.0	1.3	20,748.0	28.4
Urban transport	—	—	17,538.0	24.0
road	—	—	8,538.0	11.7
rail	—	—	9,000.0	12.3
Inland water	493.0	8.0	154.0	0.2
Air	0.8	0.0	53.0	0.1
TOTAL	6,155.4	100.0[7]	73,172.0	100.0[7]

Communications. Daily newspapers (1991): total number 124; total circulation 72,536,000; circulation per 1,000 population 585. Radio (1991): 97,000,000 receivers (1 per 1.3 persons). Television (1991): 80,000,000 receivers (1 per 1.5 persons). Telephones (1990): 54,443,000[19] (1 per 2.3 persons).

Other communications media (1989)

Print	titles	Electronic	traffic ('000)
Books (new)	39,698	Telegram	44,040
of which		Domestic	43,380
Social sciences	9,518	International	660
Fiction	8,354	Telex	20,610
Engineering	3,500		
Art	3,359		
Natural sciences	2,763		
History	2,561	**Post**	
Philosophy	1,779	Mail	21,361,000
Magazines/journals	3,864	Domestic	21,077,000
Weekly	110	International	284,000
Monthly	2,642	Parcels	302,800
		Domestic	298,000
Cinema		International	4,800
Feature films (greater than 1,600 m)	255		

Radio and television broadcasting (1990): total radio stations 1,241, of which commercial 390; total television stations 35,183[20], of which commercial 17,866. Commercial broadcasters' broadcasting hours (by percentage of programs; 1989): reports—radio 14.1%, television 18.7%; education—radio 5.2%, television 12.1%; culture—radio 16.3%, television 24.2%; entertainment—radio 63.5%, television 43.2%; music—radio 0%, television 0%; sports—radio 0%, television 0%; other—radio 0.9%, television 1.8%. Advertisements (daily average; 1989): radio 167, television 294.

Education and health

Education (1991)

	schools	teachers	students	student/teacher ratio
Primary (age 6–11)	24,798	445,000	9,157,000	20.6
Secondary (age 12–17)	16,793	573,000	10,644,000	18.6
Higher	1,169	151,000	2,763,000	18.3

Literacy: total population age 15 and over literate, virtually 100%.

Health (1990): physicians 210,197 (1 per 588 persons); dentists 73,041 (1 per 1,691 persons); nurses 365,298[21] (1 per 336[21] persons); pharmacists 130,604 (1 per 946 persons); midwives 24,056[22] (1 per 5,082[22] persons); hospital beds 1,677,000 (1 per 74 persons), of which (1989) general 72.9%, mental 22.2%, tuberculosis 3.3%, other 1.6%; infant mortality rate per 1,000 live births (1991) 4.6.

Food (1989–90): daily per capita caloric intake 2,921 (vegetable products 79%, animal products 21%); 125% of FAO recommended minimum.

Military

Total active duty personnel (1992): 246,000 (army 63.4%, navy 17.9%, air force 18.7%). *Military expenditure as percentage of GNP* (1989): 1.0% (world 4.9%); per capita expenditure U.S.$231.

[1]October 1; preliminary. [2]Excludes Lake Naka (38 sq mi [98 sq km]), which is part of both Shimane and Tottori prefectures. [3]Excludes Lake Towada (23 sq mi [60 sq km]), which is part of both Akita and Aomori prefectures. [4]Part of Kantō geographical region. [5]Part of Kinki geographical region. [6]1987 survey; includes Lake Naka and Lake Towada. [7]Detail does not add to total given because of rounding. [8]Figures relate only to Japanese nationals in Japan. [9]Applies to passengers carried within metropolitan areas only. [10]Import duties and statistical discrepancy less imputed bank service charge. [11]Includes 1,360,000 unemployed. [12]Initial budget. [13]June. [14]Worker's household. [15]End of period. [16]1985. [17]Import figures are f.o.b. in balance of trade and c.i.f. in commodities and trading partners. [18]Crude materials includes Animal and vegetable oils, fats, and waxes. [19]Number of subscribers. [20]Includes satellite broadcasting. [21]1989. [22]1987.

Jordan

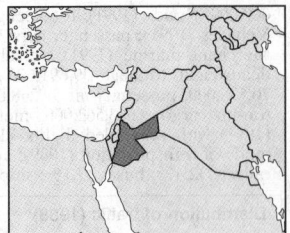

Official name: al-Mamlakah al-Urdunnīyah al-Hāshimīyah (al-Urdun) (Hashemite Kingdom of Jordan).
Form of government: constitutional monarchy[1] with two legislative houses (Senate [40 appointed by king]; House of Deputies [80]).
Chief of state: King.
Head of government: Prime Minister (on king's authority).
Capital: Amman.
Official language: Arabic.
Official religion: Islam.
Monetary unit: 1 Jordan dinar (JD) = 1,000 fils; valuation (Oct. 5, 1992) JD 1.00 = U.S.$1.52 = £0.89.

Area and population

Governorates	Capitals	area sq mi	area sq km	population 1991[2] estimate
'Ammān	Amman	4,097	10,612	1,444,400
al-Balqā'	aş-Şalt	425	1,100	235,300
Irbid	Irbid	985	2,551	814,600
al-Karak	al-Karak	1,548	4,010	140,000
Ma'ān	Ma'ān	13,954	36,141	113,200
al-Mafraq	al-Mafraq	10,475	27,129	127,200
aṭ-Ṭafīlah	aṭ-Ṭafīlah	850	2,202	47,400
az-Zarqā'	az-Zarqā'	2,008	5,201	530,900
TOTAL		34,342	88,946	3,453,000

Demography

Population (1992): 3,636,000.
Density (1992): persons per sq mi 105.9, persons per sq km 40.9.
Urban-rural (1990): urban 68.0%; rural 32.0%.
Sex distribution (1990): male 51.46%; female 48.54%.
Age breakdown (1990): under 15, 43.6%; 15–29, 31.6%; 30–44, 12.0%; 45–59, 8.3%; 60–74, 3.4%; 75 and over, 1.1%.
Population projection: (2000) 4,790,000; (2010) 6,760,000.
Doubling time: 17 years.
Ethnic composition (1983): Arab 99.2%, of which Palestinian *c.* 50.0%; Circassian 0.5%; Armenian 0.1%; Turk 0.1%; Kurd 0.1%.
Religious affiliation (1980): Sunnī Muslim 93.0%; Christian 4.9%; other 2.1%.
Major cities (1989): Amman 936,300; az-Zarqā' 318,055; Irbid 167,785; ar-Ruşayfah 72,580; aş-Şalt 47,585.

Vital statistics

Birth rate per 1,000 population (1991): 45.7 (world avg. 26.4).
Death rate per 1,000 population (1991): 4.7 (world avg. 9.2).
Natural increase rate per 1,000 population (1991): 41.0 (world avg. 17.2).
Total fertility rate (avg. births per childbearing woman; 1991): 7.1.
Marriage rate per 1,000 population (1990): 10.0.
Divorce rate per 1,000 population (1990): 1.5.
Life expectancy at birth (1991): male 70.0 years; female 73.0 years.
Major causes of death per 100,000 population: n.a.; however, major diseases include tuberculosis, typhoid, paratyphoid fevers, salmonella, hepatitis, and dysentery; nonvenereal syphilis is widespread in the southern desert region.

National economy

Budget (1992). Revenue: JD 1,163,000,000 (1991; direct and indirect taxes 77.8%, foreign grants and loans 22.2%). Expenditures: JD 1,270,000,000 (1988; administration 42.9%, defense and security 25.8%, economic development 15.2%, social welfare 13.2%, transportation and communications 2.8%).
Production (metric tons except as noted). Agriculture, forestry, fishing (1991): tomatoes 300,000, citrus fruit 159,000, watermelons 57,000, cucumbers 50,000, eggplants 45,000, potatoes 45,000, wheat 40,000, olives 40,000, grapes 40,000, squash 30,000, onions 27,000, barley 25,000, green peppers 20,000, cauliflower 20,000; livestock (number of live animals) 1,400,000 sheep, 500,000 goats, 29,000 cattle, 18,000 camels, 47,000,000 chickens; roundwood (1989) 9,000 cu m; fish catch 62. Mining and quarrying (1990): phosphate ore 5,925,000; potash 1,400,000. Manufacturing (value of production in JD '000; 1989): petroleum refining 240,660; chemicals 207,199; food products 115,932; plastic and plastic products 40,947; paper and paper products 33,088; furniture and wood products 31,594; textiles 22,865; electrical machinery 18,541; clothing 12,285; transport equipment 2,587. Construction (1989)[3]: 1,816,630 sq m. Energy production (consumption): electricity (kW-hr; 1990) 3,688,000,000 (3,688,000,000); coal, none (n.a.); crude petroleum (barrels; 1990) 118,000 (19,846,000); petroleum products (metric tons; 1990) 2,540,000 (2,997,000); natural gas, none (n.a.).
Public debt (external, outstanding; 1990): U.S.$7,513,000,000.
Population economically active (1988): total 521,815; activity rate of total population 17.7% (participation rates: over age 15 [1986] 39.0%; female 10.9%; unemployed [1989] 20.0%).

Price and earnings indexes (1985 = 100)

	1985	1986	1987	1988	1989	1990	1991
Consumer price index	100.0	100.0	99.8	106.4	133.8	155.4	168.1
Earnings index	...	...	...	...	...	...	...

Tourism (1989): receipts from visitors U.S.$551,000,000; expenditures by nationals abroad U.S.$424,000,000.
Household income and expenditure. Average household size (1984) 6.9; income per household (1979) JD 1,820 (U.S.$6,055); sources of income: n.a.; expenditure (1986): food and beverages 37.8%; housing and energy 6.3%; transportation 5.8%; clothing and footwear 5.5%; household durable goods 4.8%; health care 4.0%; education 3.3%; other goods and services 32.5%.
Gross national product (at current market prices; 1990): U.S.$3,924,000,000 (U.S.$1,240 per capita).

Structure of gross domestic product and labour force

	1989 in value JD '000,000	1989 % of total value	1990 labour force	1990 % of labour force
Agriculture	143.5	6.9	38,266	7.3
Mining	161.3	7.7 }	53,468	10.2
Manufacturing	308.7	14.8 }		
Construction	129.1	6.2	51,895	9.9
Public utilities	52.8	2.5	6,815	1.3
Transportation and communications	307.4	14.7	44,557	8.5
Trade	187.6	9.0	52,944	10.1
Finance	353.1	16.9	16,774	3.2
Pub. admin., defense	415.2	19.8 }		
Services	78.3	3.7 }	259,478	49.5
Other	−46.6[4]	−2.2[4]		
TOTAL	2,090.4	100.0	524,197	100.0

Land use (1990): forested 0.8%; meadows and pastures 8.9%; agricultural and under permanent cultivation 4.5%; wasteland (mostly desert), built-on, and other 85.8%.

Foreign trade

Balance of trade (current prices)[5]

	1985	1986	1987	1988	1989	1990
JD '000,000	−645	−500	−499	−528	−457	−829
% of total	50.9%	49.4%	44.1%	40.9%	26.4%	37.0%

Imports (1990): JD 1,535,400,000 (food and live animals 22.8%, of which cereals 9.6%; mineral fuels 18.1%; machinery and appliances 8.6%; aircraft and aircraft parts 5.5%; clothing and textiles 1.8%; aluminum and aluminum products 1.0%). *Major import sources:* United States 16.1%; Iraq 14.7%; France 5.3%; Germany 5.2%; United Kingdom 4.8%; Saudi Arabia 4.3%; Italy 3.6%; Japan 2.9%; Belgium-Luxembourg 2.7%.
Exports (1990): JD 706,100,000 (phosphate fertilizers 23.8%; nonmetallic minerals, plastering material, and cement 23.0%; fruits and vegetables 6.3%; synthetic fibres 2.2%; iron and steel products 2.1%). *Major export destinations:* India 21.1%; Iraq 19.4%; Saudi Arabia 7.6%; Indonesia 5.0%; Ethiopia 3.8%; United Arab Emirates 3.5%; China 2.9%.

Transport and communications

Transport. Railroads (1988): route length 490 mi, 788 km; passengers, 31,304; short ton-mi cargo 493,000,000[6], metric ton-km cargo 720,000,000[6]. Roads (1990): total length 3,733 mi, 6,007 km (paved 100%). Vehicles (1990): passenger cars 173,077; trucks and buses 65,687. Merchant marine (1991): vessels (100 gross tons and over) 4; total deadweight tonnage 135,473. Air transport (1990): passenger-mi 1,729,000,000, passenger-km 2,782,000,000; short ton-mi cargo 173,754,000, metric ton-km cargo 253,676,000; airports (1992) with scheduled flights 2.
Communications. Daily newspapers (1990): total number 5; total circulation 230,000; circulation per 1,000 population 73. Radio (1991): 700,000 receivers (1 per 4.7 persons). Television (1991): 250,000 receivers (1 per 13 persons). Telephones (1989): 280,092 (1 per 11 persons).

Education and health

Education (1989–90)

	schools	teachers	students	student/ teacher ratio
Primary (age 6–14)	2,983	21,073	590,275	28.0
Secondary (age 15–17)	622	10,264[7]	357,754	11.5[7]
Voc., teacher tr.	30	2,135	26,525	12.4
Higher	55[7]	3,435	69,389	20.2

Educational attainment (1979). Percentage of population age 14 and over having: no formal schooling 47.9%; primary education 19.8%; secondary 26.4%; higher 5.9%. *Literacy* (1990): percentage of population age 15 and over literate 80.1%; males literate 89.3%; females literate 70.3%.
Health (1991): physicians 4,246 (1 per 813 persons); hospital beds (1987) 5,672 (1 per 502 persons); infant mortality rate per 1,000 live births 38.0.
Food (1984–86): daily per capita caloric intake 2,498 (vegetable products 89%, animal products 11%); 120% of FAO recommended minimum requirement.

Military

Total active duty personnel (1992): 99,400 (army 85.5%, navy 0.4%, air force 14.1%). *Military expenditure as percentage of GNP* (1989): 12.7% (world 4.9%); per capita expenditure U.S.$175.

---

[1]Political parties legalized July 1992; November 1993 legislative elections will be multiparty. [2]January 1. [3]Private sector only. [4]Less imputed bank service charges. [5]Includes reexports. [6]1987. [7]1988–89.

Kazakhstan

Official name: Qazaqstan Respublikasï (Republic of Kazakhstan).
Form of government: unitary multiparty republic with a single legislative body (Parliament [360]).
Head of state: President.
Head of government: Prime Minister.
Capital: Alma-Ata (Kazakh: Almaty).
Official language: Kazakh.
Official religion: none.
Monetary unit: 1 ruble = 100 kopecks; valuation (Oct. 5, 1992) free rate, 1 U.S.$ = 316.82 rubles; 1 £ = 538.59 rubles.

Area and population

Provinces[1]	Capitals	area sq mi	area sq km	population 1991 estimate
Akmola	Akmola	35,600	92,100	885,400
Aktyubinsk	Aktyubinsk	115,300	298,700	752,900
Alma-Ata (Almaty)	Alma-Ata (Almaty)	40,600	105,100	2,153,700
Atyrau	Atyrau	43,800	113,500	447,100
Dzhambul	Auliye-Ata (Dzhambul)	55,700	144,200	1,056,400
Dzhezkazgan	Dzhezkazgan	121,000	313,400	496,200
East Kazakhstan	Ust-Kamenogorsk	37,600	97,300	949,000
Karaganda	Karaganda	45,500	117,900	1,339,900
Kokchetav	Kokchetav	30,200	78,100	669,400
Kustanay	Kustanay	44,200	114,500	1,074,400
Kzyl-Orda	Kzyl-Orda	88,100	228,100	664,900
Mangistau	Aktau	63,800	165,100	331,700
North Kazakhstan	Petropavlosk	17,100	44,300	610,400
Pavlodar	Pavlodar	49,200	127,500	956,900
Semipalatinsk	Semipalatinsk	69,300	179,600	841,900
South Kazakhstan	Chimkent	44,900	116,300	1,879,200
Taldy-Kurgan	Taldy-Kurgan	45,700	118,500	731,000
Turgay	Arkalyk	43,200	111,900	304,600
West Kazakhstan	Uralsk	58,400	151,200	648,000
TOTAL		1,049,200	2,717,300	16,793,100[2]

Demography

Population (1992): 17,008,000.
Density (1992): persons per sq mi 16.2, persons per sq km 6.3.
Urban-rural (1991): urban 57.6%; rural 42.4%.
Sex distribution (1989): male 48.50%; female 51.50%.
Age breakdown (1989): under 15, 31.9%; 15–29, 26.3%; 30–44, 19.4%; 45–59, 13.2%; 60–74, 6.9%; 75 and over, 2.3%.
Population projection: (2000) 19,006,000; (2010) 21,748,000.
Doubling time: 50 years.
Ethnic composition (1989): Kazakh 39.7%; Russian 37.8%; German 5.8%; Ukrainian 5.4%; Uzbek 2.0%; Tatar 2.0%; other 7.3%.
Religious affiliation: believers are predominantly Sunnī Muslims (Ḥanafīyah); there is a Christian minority (mainly Russian Orthodox and Baptist).
Major cities (1991): Alma-Ata (Almaty) 1,156,200; Karaganda 608,600; Chimkent 438,800; Semipalatinsk 344,700; Pavlodar 342,500.

Vital statistics

Birth rate per 1,000 population (1990): 21.7 (world avg. 27.1); (1989) legitimate 88.0%; illegitimate 12.0%.
Death rate per 1,000 population (1990): 7.7 (world avg. 9.8).
Natural increase rate per 1,000 population (1990): 14.0 (world avg. 17.3).
Total fertility rate (avg. births per childbearing woman; 1989): 2.8.
Marriage rate per 1,000 population (1989): 10.0.
Divorce rate per 1,000 population (1989): 2.8.
Life expectancy at birth (1990): male 64.2 years; female 73.2 years.
Major causes of death per 100,000 population (1989): diseases of the circulatory system 333.9; malignant neoplasms (cancers) 131.1; accidents, poisoning, and violence 99.9; diseases of the respiratory system 79.4; diseases of the digestive system 24.6; infectious and parasitic diseases 24.6; endocrine and metabolic disorders 6.3; diseases of the nervous system 6.1.

National economy

Budget (1992). Revenue: 83,806,000,000 rubles (tax revenue 77.7%, of which value-added tax 30.8%, corporate tax 16.5%, tax for investment fund 9.7%, excise tax 8.4%, tax for geological work 3.0%, property tax 1.5%; nontax revenue 22.0%; grants 0.3%). Expenditures: 94,511,000,000 rubles (national economy 31.8%; education 22.7%; social security transfers 16.7%; health 11.5%).
Public debt (external, outstanding): n.a.
Tourism: receipts from visitors, n.a.; expenditures by nationals abroad, n.a.
Production (metric tons except as noted). Agriculture, forestry, fishing (1989): seed cotton 315,200,000, grain 20,356,000, corn 19,851,000, wheat 11,654,000, potatoes 1,783,000, vegetables (other than potatoes) 1,254,000, sugar beets 1,118,000, forage 258,000, fruit (other than grapes) 118,200, sunflower seeds 105,000, grapes 48,200, hay 21,394; livestock (number of live animals; 1990) 36,222,700 sheep and goats, 9,818,400 cattle, 3,264,200 pigs, 1,618,800 horses, 142,500 camels; roundwood 2,337,000 cu m; fish catch, n.a. Mining and quarrying (1990): iron ore 23,846,000; chrome 3,660,000; manganese 169,400. Manufacturing (1991): steel 6,377,000; rolled ferrous metals 4,660,000; mineral fertilizers 1,515,000; textiles 248,708,000 sq m; carpets 2,017,000 sq m; shoes 35,410,000 pairs; bulldozers 11,280 units; excavators 577 units. Construction (1989): residential 8,800,000 rubles. Energy production (consumption): electricity (kW-hr; 1991) 86,128,000,000 (118,805,000,000); coal (metric

tons; 1991) 130,315,000 (n.a.); crude petroleum (barrels; 1990) 188,500,000 (n.a.); petroleum products (metric tons; 1991) 18,007,000 (n.a.); natural gas (cu m; 1991) 7,885,000,000 (n.a.).
Gross national product (at current market prices; 1990): 34,961,000,000 rubles (2,100 rubles per capita)[3].

Structure of net material product and labour force

	1990 in value '000,000 rubles	1990 % of total value	1989 labour force[4]	1989 % of labour force[4]
Agriculture	13,937	39.9	1,220,100	18.8
Manufacturing, mining }	9,647	27.6	1,392,800	21.4
Public utilities			247,500	3.8
Construction	5,337	15.3	765,900	11.8
Transportation and communications	3,256	9.3	697,900	10.7
Trade	1,602	4.6	531,600	8.2
Finance	—	—	39,900	0.6
Public administration, defense	—	—	95,900	1.5
Services	—	—	1,502,900	23.1
Other	1,182	3.4	...	...
TOTAL	34,961	100.0[2]	6,494,500	100.0[2]

Population economically active (1990): total 8,267,000; activity rate of total population 49.2% (participation rates [1989]: ages 16–59 [male], 16–54 [female] 80.4%; female 54.0%; unemployed 2.2%).

Price and earnings indexes (1985 = 100)

	1985	1986	1987	1988	1989	1990	1991
Consumer price index	100.0	101.9	103.7	103.7	104.1	123.4	191.5
Monthly earnings index	100.0	103.3	106.9	115.1	125.3	142.3	215.6

Land use (1989): forested 6.3%; meadows and pastures 68.7%; agricultural and under permanent cultivation 13.1%; other 11.9%.
Household income and expenditure. Average household size (1989) 4.0; income per household: n.a.; sources of income (1989): salaries and wages 81.4%, social benefits 7.1%, other 11.5%; expenditure (1989): food 29.6%, consumer goods 30.0%, taxes 9.9%, housing 2.6%.

Foreign trade

Balance of trade (current prices)

	1991
'000,000 rubles	−4,324
% of total	10.9%

Imports (1991): 19,780,000,000 rubles (commodity detail, n.a.). *Major import sources:* former Soviet republics.
Exports (1991): 15,486,000,000 rubles (1989; raw materials and consumer goods 96.1%, machinery and equipment 3.8%). *Major export destinations:* former Soviet republics 66.3%; other countries 33.7%.

Transport and communications

Transport. Railroads (1990): length 9,040 mi, 14,550 km; (1989) passenger-mi 12,900,000,000, passenger-km 18,800,000,000; short ton-mi cargo 208,500,000, metric ton-km cargo 409,600,000. Roads (1990): total length 102,464 mi, 164,900 km (paved 64%). Vehicles (1988): passenger cars 734,800; trucks and buses, n.a. Merchant marine: vessels (100 gross tons and over) n.a.; total deadweight tonnage, n.a. Air transport (1990): passenger-mi 8,259,200,000, passenger-km 13,291,200,000; short ton-mi cargo 62,000,000, metric ton-km cargo 90,000,000; airports (1992) with scheduled flights 5.
Communications. Newspapers (1989): total number 450; total circulation 6,700,000; circulation per 1,000 population 405. Radio and television receivers (1991): total number of receivers 4,781,000 (1 per 3.5 persons). Telephones (1990): 1,967,000 (1 per 8.5 persons).

Education and health

Education (1989–90)

	schools	teachers	students	student/ teacher ratio
Primary (age 7–13) } Secondary (age 14–17)	8,064	...	3,021,070	...
Voc., teacher tr.	...	...	...	...
Higher	55	...	285,600	...

Educational attainment (1989). Percentage of population age 25 and over having: primary education or no formal schooling 16.2%; some secondary 19.8%; completed secondary and some postsecondary 54.1%; higher 9.9%.
Literacy: total population age 15 and over literate, n.a.; males literate, n.a.; females literate, n.a.
Health (1990): physicians 68,900 (1 per 244 persons); hospital beds 227,800 (1 per 74 persons); infant mortality rate per 1,000 live births 26.4.
Food: daily per capita caloric intake, n.a.

Military

Total active duty personnel (1992): about 62,000 under joint Commonwealth of Independent States- (CIS-) Kazakh control (army forces include air forces). *Military expenditure as percentage of GNP:* n.a.; per capita expenditure, n.a.

---

[1]Local government was directly subordinated to the President in January 1992. [2]Detail does not add to total given because of rounding. [3]No equivalent U.S.$ value is offered, as Soviet GNP data are very speculative. [4]State sector only.

Kenya

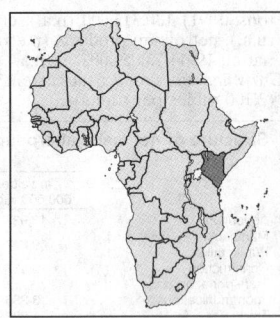

Official name: Jamhuri ya Kenya (Swahili); Republic of Kenya (English).
Form of government: unitary[1] republic with one legislative house (National Assembly [202[2]]).
Head of state and government: President.
Capital: Nairobi.
Official languages: Swahili; English.
Official religion: none.
Monetary unit: 1 Kenya shilling (K Sh) = 100 cents; valuation (Oct. 5, 1992) 1 U.S.$ = K Sh 33.84; 1 £ = K Sh 57.53.

Area and population

Provinces	Provincial headquarters	area sq mi	sq km	population 1990 estimate
Central	Nyeri	5,087	13,176	3,691,700
Coast	Mombasa	32,279	83,603	2,150,400
Eastern	Embu	61,734	159,891	4,367,900
North Eastern	Garissa	48,997	126,902	640,600
Nyanza	Kisumu	6,240	16,162	4,322,700
Rift Valley	Nakuru	67,131	173,868	5,356,900
Western	Kakamega	3,228	8,360	2,836,700
Special area				
Nairobi	—	264	684	1,504,900
TOTAL		224,961[3]	582,646	24,871,800

Demography

Population (1992): 26,985,000.
Density (1992): persons per sq mi 120.0, persons per sq km 46.3.
Urban-rural (1991): urban 25.3%; rural 74.7%.
Sex distribution (1992): male 49.92%; female 50.08%.
Age breakdown (1992): under 15, 49.6%; 15–29, 27.3%; 30–44, 13.0%; 45–59, 6.7%; 60–74, 2.9%; 75 and over, 0.5%.
Population projection: (2000) 37,505,000; (2010) 56,629,000.
Doubling time: 19 years.
Ethnic composition (1979): Kenyan 98.8% (Kikuyu 20.9%, Luhya 13.8%, Luo 12.8%, Kamba 11.3%, Kalenjin 10.8%, other Kenyan 29.2%); other 1.2%.
Religious affiliation (1980): Christian 73.0%, of which Protestant 26.5%, Roman Catholic 26.4%, African Indigenous 17.6%, Orthodox 2.5%; traditional beliefs 18.9%; Muslim 6.0%; other 2.1%.
Major cities (1984): Nairobi 1,504,900[4]; Mombasa 425,600; Kisumu 167,100; Nakuru 101,700; Machakos 92,300[5].

Vital statistics

Birth rate per 1,000 population (1990–95): 47.0 (world avg. 26.4).
Death rate per 1,000 population (1990–95): 9.7 (world avg. 9.2).
Natural increase rate per 1,000 population (1990–95): 37.3 (world avg. 17.2).
Total fertility rate (avg. births per childbearing woman): 6.8.
Life expectancy at birth (1990–95): male 59.0 years; female 63.0 years.
Major causes of death per 100,000 population: n.a.; however, major infectious diseases include AIDS, malaria, gastroenteritis, venereal diseases, diarrhea and dysentery, trachoma, amebiasis, and schistosomiasis.

National economy

Budget (1991–92). Revenue: K Sh 66,066,000,000 (indirect taxes 49.5%, of which sales tax 29.1%, custom and excise duties 19.0%; direct taxes 24.0%; grants 15.5%; nontax revenue 8.6%). Expenditures: K Sh 70,650,000,000 (recurrent expenditure 69.1%; development expenditure 30.9%).
Production (metric tons except as noted). Agriculture, forestry, fishing (1991): sugarcane 5,350,000, corn (maize) 2,250,000, cassava 650,000, sweet potatoes 590,000, plantains 350,000, potatoes 300,000, pineapple 245,000, pulses 240,000, wheat 210,000, bananas 210,000, tea 204,000, sorghum 140,000, coffee 90,000, coconuts 76,000, millet 63,000, seed 39,000, tomatoes 31,000, seed cotton 31,000, barley 20,000, cottonseed 20,000, cashew nuts 15,000, copra 13,000, sunflower seeds 5,000; livestock (number of live animals) 13,700,000 cattle, 8,100,000 goats, 6,550,000 sheep; roundwood (1990) 35,580,000 cu m; fish catch (1990) 142,417, of which freshwater fish 94.5%. Mining and quarrying (1989): soda ash 240,880; salt 103,220; fluorite 95,181; limestone 32,167; garnet 127 kg. Manufacturing (1989): cement 1,316,400; sugar 431,000; wheat flour 189,000; beer and stout 3,154,000 hectolitres; mineral water 1,698,000 hectolitres; alcoholic beverages 12,741 hectolitres; paint 7,499 hectolitres. Construction (1986): residential 136,000 sq m; nonresidential 180,000 sq m. Energy production (consumption): electricity (kW-hr; 1990) 3,044,000,000 (3,215,000,000); coal (metric tons; 1990) none (151,000); crude petroleum (barrels; 1990) none (15,899,000); petroleum products (metric tons; 1990) 2,088,000 (1,467,000).
Public debt (external, outstanding; 1990): U.S.$4,507,000,000.
Household income and expenditure. Average household size (1980) 6.2; average annual income per household: n.a.; sources of income: n.a.; expenditure (1980): food 46.5%, housing 10.0%, furniture and utensils 9.4%, transportation 8.4%, clothing and footwear 7.7%, energy 2.6%, health 2.2%, education 1.0%.
Population economically active (1985): total 8,389,000; activity rate of total population 40.7% (participation rates: ages 15–64, 76.2%; female 40.9%; unemployed, n.a.).

Price and earnings indexes (1985 = 100)

	1985	1986	1987	1988	1989	1990	1991
Consumer price index	100.0	104.0	109.4	118.4	130.7	145.3	166.8
Monthly earnings index[6]	100.0	57.9	64.5	68.3	97.2	...	...

Gross national product (at current market prices; 1990): U.S.$8,958,000,000 (U.S.$370 per capita).

Structure of gross domestic product and labour force

	1990 in value K Sh '000,000	1990 % of total value	1989 labour force[7]	1989 % of labour force
Agriculture	48,829.0	24.3	257,100	18.9
Mining	487.8	0.2	4,100	0.3
Manufacturing	19,748.0	9.8	182,300	13.4
Construction	13,743.2	6.9	67,400	5.0
Public utilities	2,510.6	1.3	22,400	1.7
Transp. and commun.	11,963.4	6.0	69,400	5.1
Trade	18,952.6	9.5	110,300	8.1
Finance	27,722.8	13.8	63,700	4.7
Pub. admin., defense	26,465.0	13.2 }	582,300	42.8
Services	2,271.2	1.1 }		
Other	27,978.8[8]	13.9[8]		
TOTAL	200,652.0[3]	100.0	1,359,000	100.0

Tourism (1990): receipts from visitors U.S.$443,000,000; expenditures by nationals abroad U.S.$38,000,000.
Land use (1990): forested 4.1%; meadows and pastures 66.9%; agricultural and under permanent cultivation 4.3%; other 24.7%.

Foreign trade[9]

Balance of trade (current prices)

	1986	1987	1988	1989	1990	1991
K Sh '000,000	−3,271	−9,063	−11,137	−18,131	−18,164	−11,890
% of total	7.7%	22.3%	22.6%	31.3%	27.7%	16.4%

Imports (1990): K Sh 51,024,100,000 (machinery and transport equipment 42.2%, crude petroleum 14.7%, manufactured goods 14.6%, chemicals 13.3%, food and live animals 6.1%). *Major import sources:* U.K. 18.5%; Japan 9.1%; U.S. 9.1%; West Germany 7.9%; France 5.8%; Italy 4.7%; The Netherlands 3.4%; India 1.8%.
Exports (1990): K Sh 24,397,600,000[10] (tea 25.9%, coffee [not roasted] 18.4%, petroleum products 12.4%, fruits and vegetables 12.2%, soda ash 2.0%). *Major export destinations:* U.K. 18.1%; West Germany 10.4%; The Netherlands 5.7%; Uganda 5.2%; U.S. 3.4%.

Transport and communications

Transport. Railroads (1989–90): route length 1,885 mi, 3,034 km; passenger-mi 427,700,000, passenger-km 688,300,000; short ton-mi cargo 1,369,100,000, metric ton-km cargo 1,998,800,000. Roads (1988): total length 34,000 mi, 54,700 km (paved 15%). Vehicles (1989): passenger cars 133,000; trucks and buses 149,000. Merchant marine (1991): vessels (100 gross tons and over) 30; total deadweight tonnage 11,649. Air transport (1991)[11]: passenger-mi 918,790,000, passenger-km 1,478,652,000; short ton-mi cargo 119,723,000, metric ton-km cargo 174,792,000; airports (1992) with scheduled flights 16.
Communications. Daily newspapers: total number (1991) 5; total circulation 328,000[12]; circulation per 1,000 population 13[12]. Radio (1991): 4,200,000 receivers (1 per 6.2 persons). Television (1991): 260,000 receivers (1 per 100 persons). Telephones (1989): 357,251 (1 per 67 persons).

Education and health

Education (1989–90)

	schools	teachers	students	student/ teacher ratio
Primary (age 5–11)	14,691	163,609	5,389,300	32.9
Secondary (age 12–17)	2,654	28,056	640,735	22.8
Voc., teacher tr.[13]	24	1,332[14]	15,456	13.4[14]
Higher	15	...	29,231	...

Educational attainment (1979). Percentage of population over age 25 having: no formal schooling 58.6%; primary education 32.2%; some secondary 7.9%; complete secondary and higher 1.3%. *Literacy* (1985): total population over age 15 literate 5,758,000 (59.2%); males literate 3,311,000 (69.6%); females literate 2,447,000 (49.2%).
Health (1989): physicians 3,266 (1 per 7,313 persons); hospital beds 32,534 (1 per 734 persons); infant mortality rate per 1,000 live births (1990–95): 63.0.
Food (1988–90): daily per capita caloric intake 2,064 (vegetable products 86%, animal products 14%); 89% of FAO recommended minimum requirement.

Military

Total active duty personnel (1992): 24,200 (army 84.7%, navy 5.0%, air force 10.3%). *Military expenditure as percentage of GNP* (1989): 2.7% (world 4.9%); per capita expenditure U.S.$9.

[1]Multiparty system approved on Dec. 3, 1991; elections to follow in March 1993. [2]Includes 14 nonelective seats. [3]Detail does not add to total given because of rounding. [4]1990. [5]1983. [6]Manufacturing employees only. [7]Employed persons only. [8]Indirect taxes less subsidies and imputed bank service charges. [9]Import figures are f.o.b. in balance of trade and c.i.f. in commodities and trading partners. [10]Includes K Sh 239,000,000 reexports. [11]Kenya Airways only. [12]Circulation for four newspapers only. [13]Teacher training only. [14]1987–88.

Kiribati

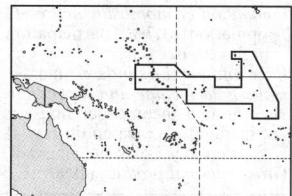

Official name: Republic of Kiribati.
Form of government: unitary republic with one legislature (House of Assembly [41[1]]).
Head of state and government: President.
Capital: Bairiki, on Tarawa Atoll.
Official language: English.
Official religion: none.
Monetary unit: 1 Australian Dollar ($A) = 100 cents; valuation (Oct. 5, 1992) 1 U.S.$ = $A 1.38; 1 £ = $A 2.35.

Area and population		area[2]		population
Island Groups				1990
Islands	**Capitals**	sq mi	sq km	census
Gilberts Group	Bairiki Islet	110	286[3]	67,471
Abaiang	Tuarabu	7	18	5,314
Abemama	Kariatebike	11	27	3,218
Aranuka	Takaeang	5	12	1,002
Arorae	Roreti	3	9	1,440
Banaba	Anteeren	2	6	284
Beru	Taubukinberu	7	18	2,909
Butaritari	Butaritari	5	13	3,786
Kuria	Tabontebike	6	16	985
Maiana	Tebangetua	6	17	2,184
Makin	Makin	3	8	1,762
Marakei	Rawannawi	5	14	2,863
Nikunau	Rungata	7	19	2,048
Nonouti	Teuabu	8	20	2,766
Onotoa	Buariki	6	16	2,112
Tabiteuea North	Utiroa	10	26	3,275
Tabiteuea South	Buariki	5	12	1,325
Tamana	Bakaka	2	5	1,396
Tarawa North	Abaokoro	6	15	3,648
Tarawa South	Bairiki	6	16	25,154
Line Group	Kiritimati	192	496	4,782
Northern		167	432	—
Kiritimati (Christmas)	London	150	388	2,537
Tabuaeran (Fanning)	Paelau	13	34	1,309
Teraina (Washington)	Washington	4	10	936
Southern		25	64	—
(Caroline, Flint, Malden, Starbuck, Vostok)				
Phoenix Group	Kanton	11	29	45
(Birnie, Enderbury, Kanton [Canton], McKean, Manra [Sydney], Nikumaroro [Gardner], Orona [Hull], Rawaki [Phoenix])				
TOTAL		313	811	72,298

Demography

Population (1992): 74,700.
Density[4] (1992): persons per sq mi 266.8, persons per sq km 102.9.
Urban-rural (1990): urban 34.8%; rural 65.2%.
Sex distribution (1990): male 49.46%; female 50.54%.
Age breakdown (1990): under 15, 40.3%; 15–29, 27.5%; 30–44, 17.3%; 45–59, 9.2%; 60–74, 4.8%; 75 and over, 0.9%.
Population projection: (2000) 87,100; (2010) 103,000.
Doubling time: 33 years.
Ethnic composition (1990): I-Kiribati 97.4%; mixed (part I-Kiribati and other) 1.5%; Tuvaluan 0.5%; European 0.2%; other 0.4%.
Religious affiliation (1990): Roman Catholic 53.5%; Kiribati Protestant (Congregational) 39.1%; Bahā'ī 2.4%; Seventh-day Adventist 1.9%; Mormon 1.7%; other 1.4%.
Major cities (1990): Urban Tarawa 25,154.

Vital statistics

Birth rate per 1,000 population (1991): 33.0 (world avg. 26.4); legitimate, n.a.; illegitimate, n.a.
Death rate per 1,000 population (1991): 12.0 (world avg. 9.2).
Natural increase rate per 1,000 population (1991): 21.0 (world avg. 17.2).
Total fertility rate (avg. births per childbearing woman; 1991): 4.2.
Marriage rate per 1,000 population (1988): 5.2.
Divorce rate per 1,000 population: n.a.
Life expectancy at birth (1991): male 52.0 years; female 58.0 years.
Major causes of death per 100,000 population: n.a.; however, the leading causes of morbidity include influenza, diarrhea, sores and skin diseases, conjuctivitis, dental disorders, ear diseases, anemia and malnutrition, parasitic infestations, and fish poisoning.

National economy

Budget (1989). Revenue: $A 20,648,000 (1988; nontax revenue 46.0%, of which reserve fund drawdown 32.1%, fishing licenses 9.8%; tax revenue 28.4%, of which import duties 9.4%, income tax 4.9%; development revenue 25.6%). Expenditures: $A 20,648,000 (1988; education 16.1%; development 15.9%; health 13.0%; natural resources 7.3%; communications 7.0%; public works 6.6%).
Production (metric tons except as noted). Agriculture, forestry, fishing (1991): coconuts 63,000, roots and tubers 8,000 (of which taro 2,000), copra 8,000, vegetables and melons 5,000, bananas 4,000; livestock (number of live animals) 9,000 pigs, 191,000 chickens[5]; fish catch (1990) 30,000. Mining

and quarrying: none. Manufacturing (1988): processed copra 14,406; other important products are processed fish, baked goods, clothing, and handicrafts. Energy production (consumption): electricity (kW-hr; 1990) 7,000,000 (7,000,000); coal: none (n.a.); crude petroleum: none (n.a.); petroleum products (metric tons; 1990) none (7,000); natural gas: none (n.a.).
Gross national product (at current market prices; 1990): U.S.$54,000,000 (U.S.$760 per capita).

Structure of gross domestic product and labour force				
	1989		1990	
	in value $A '000	% of total value	labour force	% of labour force
Agriculture, fishing	10,939	24.5	23,137[6]	71.0[6]
Mining	—	—	—	—
Manufacturing	836	1.9	622	1.9
Construction	1,760	3.9	339	1.0
Public utilities	775	1.7	301	0.9
Transp. and commun.	6,344	14.2	921	2.8
Trade	6,050	13.5	1,341	4.1
Finance	3,410	7.6	441	1.4
Pub. admin., defense	11,276	25.2	2,123	6.5
Services	1,205	2.7	2,286	7.0
Other	2,120	4.8	1,097[7]	3.4[7]
TOTAL	44,715	100.0	32,610	100.0

Public debt (external, outstanding; 1988): U.S.$12,000,000.
Population economically active (1990): total 32,610; activity rate of total population 45.1% (participation rates: over age 15, 75.6%; female 46.4%; unemployed 2.8%).

Price and earnings indexes (1985 = 100)							
	1984	1985	1986	1987	1988	1989	1990
Consumer price index	95.1	100.0	107.8	111.8	113.8	120.8	126.9
Earnings index	...	...	...	...	...	...	...

Household income and expenditure. Average household size (1990) 6.4; income per household: n.a.; sources of income (1978): wages 69.7%, self-employment 21.4%, transfer payments 6.0%, other 2.9%; expenditure (1982): food 50.0%, tobacco and alcohol 8.0%, clothing 8.0%, transportation 8.0%, housing, energy, and household operation 7.5%.
Tourism (1990): receipts from visitors U.S.$2,000,000; expenditures by nationals abroad, n.a.
Land use (1990): forested 2.8%; agricultural and under permanent cultivation 52.1%; other 45.1%.

Foreign trade

Balance of trade (current prices)						
	1985	1986	1987	1988	1989	1990
$A '000	−15,525	−18,956	−22,274	−21,515	−22,161	−30,765
% of total	56.2%	79.2%	79.5%	61.7%	63.3%	80.7%

Imports (1990): $A 34,446,000 (food 26.6%, machinery and transport equipment 19.1%, manufactured goods 11.8%, mineral fuels 10.7%, chemicals 5.1%, beverages and tobacco 4.4%, crude materials 2.8%). *Major import sources:* Australia 33.3%; Japan 23.6%; Fiji 19.3%; United States 6.6%; New Zealand 5.6%; China 4.4%; Hong Kong 1.3%.
Exports (1990): $A 3,681,000 (copra 27.8%, fish and fish preparations 27.1%, seaweed 19.6%, reexports 18.3%). *Major export destinations:* The Netherlands 21.1%; Denmark 19.6%; Fiji 18.7%; United States 15.4%; Marshall Islands 7.5%.

Transport and communications

Transport. Roads (1991): total length 398 mi, 640 km (paved 5%). Vehicles (1985): passenger cars 307; trucks and buses 130. Merchant marine (1991): vessels (100 gross tons and over) 7; total deadweight tonnage 2,685. Air transport (1990): passenger-mi 5,331,000, passenger-km 8,579,000; short ton-mi cargo 514,000, metric ton-km cargo 750,000; airports (1992) with scheduled flights 18.
Communications. Daily newspapers: none. Radio (1991): total number of receivers 10,000 (1 per 7.3 persons). Television: none. Telephones (1988): 1,304 (1 per 53 persons).

Education and health

Education (1989)	schools	teachers	students	student/ teacher ratio
Primary (age 6–13)	110	507	14,321	28.2
Secondary (age 14–18)	9	142	2,293	16.1
Voc., teacher tr.	6	94	610	6.5
Higher[8]	—	—	—	—

Educational attainment (1990)[9]. Percentage of population age 15 and over having: no schooling 4.0%; primary 54.3%; secondary 39.4%; higher 2.1%; not stated 0.2%. *Literacy* (1985): total population age 15 and over literate 90%.
Health (1986): physicians 16 (1 per 4,104 persons); hospital beds 283 (1 per 232 persons); infant mortality rate per 1,000 live births (1991) 63.0.
Food (1988–90): daily per capita caloric intake 2,517 (vegetable products 89%, animal products 11%); 110% of FAO recommended minimum requirement.

[1]Includes two nonelective members. [2]Includes uninhabited islands. [3]Detail does not add to total given because of rounding. [4]Density based on inhabited island areas (280 sq mi, 726 sq km) only. [5]1982. [6]Includes 20,568 persons engaged in "village work" (subsistence agriculture or fishing). [7]Includes 900 unemployed. [8]85 students overseas. [9]For population in the cash sector of the labour force.

Korea, North

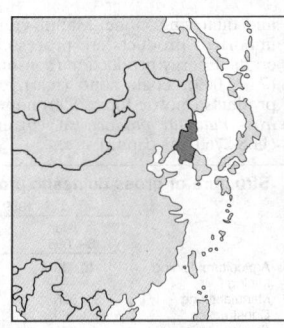

Official name: Chosŏn Minjujuŭi
In'min Konghwaguk (Democratic
People's Republic of Korea).
Form of government: unitary
single-party republic with one
legislative house (Supreme People's
Assembly [687]).
Chief of state: President.
Head of government: Premier.
Capital: P'yŏngyang-si.
Official language: Korean.
Official religion: none.
Monetary unit: 1 won = 100
chon; valuation (Oct. 5, 1992)
1 U.S.$ = 2.15 won; 1 £ = 3.65 won.

Area and population

		area		population[1]
				1987
Provinces	**Capitals**	sq mi	sq km	estimate
Chagang-do	Kanggye	6,551	16,968	1,156,000
Hamgyŏng-namdo	Hamhŭng	7,324	18,970	2,547,000
Hamgyŏng-pukto	Ch'ŏngjin	6,784	17,570	2,003,000
Hwanghae-namdo	Haeju	3,090	8,002	1,914,000
Hwanghae-pukto	Sariwŏn	3,092	8,007	1,409,000
Kangwŏn-do	Wŏnsan	4,306	11,152	1,227,000
P'yŏngan-namdo	P'yŏngsan	4,470	11,577	2,653,000
P'yŏngan-pukto	Sinŭiju	4,707[2]	12,191[2]	2,380,000
Yanggang-do	Hyesan	5,528	14,317	628,000
Special cities				
Kaesŏng-si	—	485	1,255	331,000
Namp'o-si	—	291	753	715,000
P'yŏngyang-si	—	772	2,000	2,355,000
Special district				
Hyangsan-chigu	—	2	2	28,000
TOTAL		47,400	122,762	19,346,000

Demography

Population (1992): 22,227,000.
Density (1992): persons per sq mi 468.9, persons per sq km 181.1.
Urban-rural (1990): urban 59.8%; rural 40.2%.
Sex distribution (1990): male 49.36%; female 50.64%.
Age breakdown (1990): under 15, 29.4%; 15–29, 33.8%; 30–44, 20.4%; 45–59, 10.6%; 60–74, 4.7%; 75 and over, 1.1%.
Population projection: (2000) 25,491,000; (2010) 28,491,000.
Doubling time: 37 years.
Ethnic composition (1989): Korean 99.8%; Chinese 0.2%.
Religious affiliation (1980): atheist or nonreligious 67.9%; traditional beliefs 15.6%; Ch'ŏndogyo 13.9%; Buddhist 1.7%; Christian 0.9%.
Major cities (1987): P'yŏngyang-si 2,355,000; Hamhŭng 701,000; Ch'ŏngjin 520,000; Namp'o 370,000; Sunch'ŏn 356,000.

Vital statistics

Birth rate per 1,000 population (1991): 24.3 (world avg. 26.4).
Death rate per 1,000 population (1991): 5.5 (world avg. 9.2).
Natural increase rate per 1,000 population (1991): 18.8 (world avg. 17.2).
Total fertility rate (avg. births per childbearing woman; 1991): 2.5.
Marriage rate per 1,000 population (1987): 9.3.
Divorce rate per 1,000 population (1987): 0.2.
Life expectancy at birth (1991): male 66.0 years; female 72.0 years.
Major causes of death per 100,000 population (1986): diseases of the circulatory system 224.9; malignant neoplasms (cancers) 69.0; diseases of the digestive system 51.6; diseases of the respiratory system 46.7; injuries and poisonings 38.2; infectious and parasitic diseases 19.4.

National economy

Budget (1990). Revenue: 35,656,000,000 won (1984; turnover tax 55.0%, payments by state enterprises 30.0%). Expenditures: 35,656,000,000 won (national economy 67.5%, social and cultural affairs 18.8%, defense 12.1%, administration 1.6%).
Public debt (external, outstanding; 1990): U.S.$6,780,000,000.
Production (metric tons except as noted). Agriculture, forestry, fishing (1990): rice 5,500,000, corn (maize) 4,400,000, potatoes 2,100,000, sweet potatoes 505,000, soybeans 455,000, cabbages 420,000, wheat 220,000, barley 150,000, pears 115,000, peaches 105,000, watermelons 96,000, tomatoes 70,000, cucumbers and gherkins 65,000, tobacco leaves 65,000, oats 60,000, millet 60,000; livestock (number of live animals) 3,200,000 pigs, 1,300,000 cattle, 385,000 sheep, 295,000 goats, 21,000,000 chickens; roundwood 4,692,000 cu m; fish catch (1989) 1,700,100. Mining and quarrying (1989): iron ore 9,500,000; magnesite (metal content) 1,500,000; phosphate rock 500,000; sulfur 230,000; zinc 210,000; lead (metal content) 80,000; fluorite 40,000; graphite 35,000; copper 12,000; silver 1,600,000 troy oz; gold 160,000 troy oz. Manufacturing (1988): cement 8,200,000; pig iron 5,800,000; crude steel 4,200,000; chemical fertilizers 4,000,000; steel semimanufactures 3,400,000[3]; meat 290,000; television sets 240,000 units[4]; machine tools 27,000 units; tractors 24,500 units; cars 20,000 units[4]; refrigerators 10,000 units[3]; textile fabrics 535,000,000 m. Construction: n.a. Energy production (consumption): electricity (kW-hr; 1990) 53,500,000 (53,500,000); coal (metric tons; 1990) 53,700,000 (56,150,000); crude petroleum (barrels; 1990) none (20,588,000); petroleum products (metric tons; 1990) 2,770,000 (3,390,000); natural gas, none (n.a.).

Population economically active[5] (1987): total 12,517,000; activity rate of total population 61.7% (participation rates: ages 15–64, n.a.; female, n.a.; unemployed, n.a.).
Price and earnings indexes: n.a.
Household income and expenditure. Average household size (1987) 4.8; average annual income per household (1980) 3,677 won (U.S.$4,275); sources of income: n.a.; expenditure[6] (1984): food 46.5%; clothing 29.9%; furniture 3.8%; energy 3.3%; housing 0.6%.
Gross national product (1990): U.S.$23,100,000,000 (U.S.$1,079 per capita).

Structure of gross domestic product and labour force

	1982			
	in value '000,000 won	% of total value	labour force	% of labour force
Agriculture	...	...	3,276,000	44.1
Mining and manufacturing	...	...		
Construction	...	...	2,790,000	33.0
Public utilities	...	...		
Transportation and communications	...	...	418,000	4.9
Trade	...	...		
Finance	...	...		
Pub. admin., defense	...	...	1,521,000	18.0
Services	...	...		
Other	...	...		
TOTAL	11,800	100.0	8,455,000	100.0

Land use (1989): forested 74.5%; meadows and pastures 0.4%; agricultural and under permanent cultivation 16.6%; other 8.5%.
Tourism (1986): total number of tourist arrivals 85,000.

Foreign trade

Balance of trade (current prices)

	1985	1986	1987	1988	1989	1990
U.S.$'000,000,000	−0.4	−0.3	−0.7	−0.7	−0.5	−0.8
% of total	18.7%	8.1%	16.3%	12.7%	22.9%	19.2%

Imports (1990): U.S.$2,540,000,000 (crude petroleum, coal and coke, industrial machinery and transport equipment [including trucks], industrial chemicals, textile yarn and fabrics, and grain are among the major imports). *Major import sources* (1985): U.S.S.R. 36.1%; China 18.8%; Japan 13.2%; western European countries 4.0%; Hong Kong 3.5%.
Exports (1990): U.S.$1,720,000,000 (minerals [including lead, magnesite, zinc], metallurgical products [iron and steel, nonferrous metals], cement, agricultural products [including fish, grain, fruit and vegetables, tobacco], and manufactured goods [textile fabrics, clothing] are among the major exports). *Major export destinations* (1985): U.S.S.R. 43.6%; Japan 15.1%; China 13.4%; western European countries 4.3%; Australia 3.3%; Hong Kong 3.1%.

Transport and communications

Transport. Railroads (1989): length 3,122 mi, 5,024 km; passengers, n.a.; cargo, n.a. Roads (1988): total length 14,290 mi, 23,000 km (paved 2%). Vehicles (1988): passenger cars 248,000. Merchant marine (1991): vessels (100 gross tons and over) 98; total deadweight tonnage 749,181. Air transport (1979): passenger-mi 52,200,000, passenger-km 84,000,000; short ton-mi cargo 1,370,000, metric ton-km cargo 2,000,000; airports (1992) with scheduled flights 1.
Communications. Daily newspapers (1987): total number 16; total circulation 3,000,000[7]; circulation per 1,000 population 140[7]. Radio (1991): total number of receivers 3,750,000 (1 per 5.8 persons). Television (1991): total number of receivers 250,000 (1 per 87 persons). Telephones (1988): 30,000[8] (1 per 700 persons).

Education and health

Education (1987)

	schools	teachers	students	student/ teacher ratio
Primary (age 6–9)	4,792[4]	...	1,492,000	...
Secondary (age 10–15)			2,655,000	...
Voc., teacher tr.	473[4]	...	220,000	...
Higher	281[4]	9,244[9]	301,000	...

Educational attainment (1987–88). Percentage of population age 16 and over having attended or graduated from postsecondary-level school: 13.7%. *Literacy* (1984): 99%.
Health (1989): physicians 57,690 (1 per 370 persons); hospital beds 290,590 (1 per 74 persons); infant mortality rate per 1,000 live births (1991) 30.0.
Food (1987–89): daily per capita caloric intake 2,797 (vegetable products 92%, animal products 8%); 120% of FAO recommended minimum requirement.

Military

Total active duty personnel (1991): 1,111,000 (army 90.0%, navy 3.7%, air force 6.3%). *Military expenditure as percentage of GNP* (1989): 20.0% (world 4.9%); per capita expenditure U.S.$285.

---

[1]Civilian population only. [2]P'yŏngan-pukto includes special district of Hyangsan-chigu. [3]1984. [4]1986. [5]The Democratic People's Republic of Korea categorizes economically active as including students in higher education, retirees, and heads of households, as well as those in the civilian labour force. [6]Workers and clerical workers only. [7]Four dailies only. [8]Number of telephone lines. [9]1982.

Korea, South

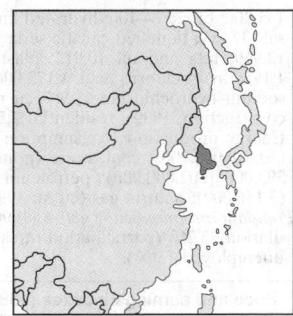

Official name: Taehan Min'guk
(Republic of Korea).
Form of government: unitary multiparty
republic with a National Assembly
(299 members).
Chief of state: President.
Head of government: Prime Minister.
Capital: Seoul.
Official language: Korean.
Official religion: none.
Monetary unit: 1 won (W) = 100 chon;
valuation (Oct. 5, 1992)
1 U.S.$ = W 795; 1 £ = W 1,352.

Area and population		area		population
Provinces	Capitals	sq mi	sq km	1990 census[1]
Cheju-do	Cheju	705	1,825	514,000
Chŏlla-namdo	Kwangju	4,561	11,812	2,523,000
Chŏlla-pukto	Chŏnju	3,109	8,053	2,070,000
Ch'ungch'ŏng-namdo	Taejŏn	3,211	8,317	2,028,000
Ch'ungch'ŏng-pukto	Ch'ŏngju	2,872	7,437	1,414,000
Kangwŏn-do	Ch'unch'ŏn'	6,524	16,898	1,592,000
Kyŏnggi-do	Suwŏn	4,158	10,769	6,154,000
Kyŏngsang-namdo	Masan	4,545	11,771	3,679,000
Kyŏngsang-pukto	Taegu	7,507	19,443	2,866,000
Special cities				
Inch'ŏn-si	Inch'ŏn	121	313	1,818,000
Kwangju-si	Kwangju	193	501	1,145,000
Pusan-si	Pusan	203	526	3,798,000
Sŏul-t'ŭkpyŏlsi	Seoul	234	605	10,628,000
Taegu-si	Taegu	176	456	2,229,000
Taejŏn-si	Taejŏn	207	537	1,062,000
TOTAL		38,326	99,263	43,520,000

Demography

Population (1992): 43,663,000.
Density (1992): persons per sq mi 1,139.3, persons per sq km 439.9.
Urban-rural (1990): urban 74.4%; rural 25.6%.
Sex distribution (1992): male 50.34%; female 49.66%.
Age breakdown (1990): under 15, 25.4%; 15–29, 29.9%; 30–44, 23.2%; 45–59, 13.7%; 60–74, 6.2%; 75 and over, 1.6%.
Population projection: (2000) 46,789,000; (2010) 49,683,000.
Doubling time: 70 years.
Ethnic composition (1990): Korean 99.9%; other 0.1%.
Religious affiliation (1991): religious[2] 54.0%, of which Buddhist 27.6%, Protestant 18.6%, Roman Catholic 5.7%, Confucian 1.0%, Wonbulgyo 0.3%, Ch'ondogyo 0.2%, other 0.6%; nonreligious 46.0%.
Major cities (1990): Seoul 10,628,000; Pusan 3,798,000; Taegu 2,229,000; Inch'ŏn 1,818,000; Kwangju 1,145,000.

Vital statistics

Birth rate per 1,000 population (1991): 15.5 (world avg. 26.4).
Death rate per 1,000 population (1991): 5.8 (world avg. 9.2).
Natural increase rate per 1,000 population (1991): 9.7 (world avg. 17.2).
Total fertility rate (avg. births per childbearing woman; 1990): 1.6.
Marriage rate per 1,000 population (1989): 7.3.
Divorce rate per 1,000 population (1989): 1.1.
Life expectancy at birth (1990): male 67.4 years; female 75.4 years.
Major causes of death per 100,000 population (1990): diseases of the circulatory system 133.1; malignant neoplasms (cancers) 89.6; accidents, poisonings, and violence 68.8; diseases of the digestive system 36.1; diseases of the respiratory system 13.8.

National economy

Budget (1990). Revenue: W 26,818,000,000,000 (income taxes 33.3%, taxes on goods and services 32.8%, nontax revenue 11.1%, customs duties 10.4%). Expenditures: W 26,278,000,000,000 (defense 25.8%, education 19.6%, economic development 17.0%, social security and welfare 9.7%).
Public debt (external, outstanding; 1990): U.S.$18,152,000,000.
Production (metric tons except as noted). Agriculture, forestry, fishing (1990): rice 7,786,000, cabbages 3,214,000, apples 629,000, oranges 493,000, garlic 417,000, barley 416,000, dry onions 407,000, soybeans 233,000; livestock (number of live animals) 4,801,000 pigs, 2,051,000 cattle, 62,000,000 chickens; roundwood (1989) 6,803,000 cu m; fish catch 3,274,506. Mining and quarrying (1991): iron ore 563,000; graphite 85,953; zinc ore 44,985; lead ore 17,197; tungsten ore 1,867. Manufacturing (1991): cement 39,167,000; crude steel 26,879,620; pig iron 18,546,017; animal feed 10,864,517; chemical fertilizers 2,753,090; synthetic fabrics 3,281,499,000 sq m; television receivers 15,514,793 units; passenger cars 1,131,792 units. Construction (1991): residential 59,060,000 sq m; nonresidential 46,124,000 sq m. Energy production (consumption): electricity (kW-hr; 1990) 118,738,000,000 (118,738,000,000); coal (metric tons; 1990) 17,217,000 (43,405,000); crude petroleum (barrels; 1990) none (306,321,000); petroleum products (metric tons; 1990) 36,325,000 (40,597,000); natural gas (cu m; 1990) none (3,243,000,000).
Household income and expenditure (1992)[3]. Average household size (1990) 3.8; income per household W 15,516,000 (U.S.$19,800); sources of income: wages 84.2%, other 15.8%; expenditure: food and beverages 28.4%, education and recreation 14.7%, clothing and footwear 8.2%, transportation and communications 8.2%, health care 5.5%, household durable goods 5.1%, energy 5.0%, housing 3.6%, other 21.3%.

Gross national product (at current market prices; 1990): U.S.$231,132,000,000 (U.S.$5,400 per capita).

Structure of gross domestic product and labour force				
	1990			
	in value W '000,000,000	% of total value	labour force	% of labour force
Agriculture	15,444.5	9.1	3,292,000	17.8
Mining	783.7	0.5	81,000	0.4
Manufacturing	49,499.1	29.2	4,847,000	26.2
Construction	21,835.0	12.9	1,339,000	7.2
Public utilities	3,682.1	2.2	71,000	0.4
Transp. and commun.	12,100.5	7.1	922,000	5.0
Trade	19,156.3	11.3	3,920,000	21.2
Finance	23,358.4	13.8	935,000	5.1
Pub. admin., defense	13,419.8	7.9	} 2,630,000	14.2
Services	11,172.5	6.6		
Other	−750.4[4]	−0.4[4]	451,000[5]	2.4[5]
TOTAL	169,701.4[6]	100.0[6]	18,487,000[6]	100.0[6]

Population economically active (1990): total 18,487,000; activity rate 43.1% (participation rates: ages 15 and over, 60.0%; female 40.4%; unemployed 2.4%).

Price and earnings indexes (1985 = 100)							
	1985	1986	1987	1988	1989	1990	1991
Consumer price index	100.0	102.8	105.9	113.9	119.9	130.2	142.8
Monthly earnings index	100.0	108.2	119.2	137.7	166.7	192.3	...

Tourism (1990): receipts from visitors U.S.$3,559,000,000; expenditures by nationals abroad U.S.$3,166,000,000.
Land use (1989): forested 65.7%; meadows and pastureland 0.9%; agricultural and under permanent cultivation 21.5%; other 11.9%.

Foreign trade

Balance of trade (current prices)						
	1986	1987	1988	1989	1990	1991
U.S.$'000,000	+4,237	+6,940	+8,510	+2,875	−701	−3,968
% of total	7.4%	9.8%	10.6%	3.6%	0.8%	3.6%

Imports (1991): U.S.$81,524,900,000 (machinery and transport equipment 33.3%, manufactured goods 16.3%, mineral fuels and lubricants 15.6%, inedible crude materials 10.9%, chemicals 10.0%). *Major import sources:* Japan 25.9%; United States 23.2%; Germany 4.5%; Saudi Arabia 4.0%; Australia 3.7%; Canada 2.3%; Malaysia 2.3%; United Kingdom 1.9%.
Exports (1991): U.S.$71,870,100,000 (machinery and transport equipment 41.6%, manufactured goods 22.0%, chemicals 4.4%, food and live animals 2.9%, mineral fuels 2.1%). *Major export destinations:* United States 25.8%; Japan 17.2%; Hong Kong 6.6%; Germany 4.4%; Singapore 3.8%; United Kingdom 2.5%; Canada 2.3%; Taiwan 2.2%.

Transport and communications

Transport. Railroads (1990): length 4,012 mi, 6,456 km; passenger-km 29,868,000,000; metric ton-km cargo 13,476,000,000. Roads (1988): total length 34,659 mi, 55,778 km (paved 61%). Vehicles (1990): passenger cars 2,074,922; trucks and buses 1,308,385. Merchant marine (1991): vessels (100 gross tons and over) 2,136; total deadweight tonnage 12,227,135. Air transport (1990): passenger-km 18,708,000,000; metric ton-km cargo 2,494,000,000; airports (1992) with scheduled flights 12.
Communications. Daily newspapers (1990): total number 81; total circulation 13,000,000[7]; circulation per 1,000 population 309[7]. Radio (1991): 42,000,000 receivers (1 per 1.0 persons). Television (1991): 8,700,000 receivers (1 per 5.0 persons). Telephones (1990): 12,814,000 (1 per 3.3 persons).

Education and health

Education (1991)	schools	teachers	students	student/ teacher ratio
Primary (age 6–13)	6,245	138,200	4,758,505	34.4
Secondary (age 14–19) } Vocational	4,198	187,620	4,443,242	23.7
Higher	560	43,821	1,518,512	34.7

Educational attainment (1990). Percentage of population age 6 and over having: primary education or less 33.7%, of which no formal schooling (1985) 14.3%; some secondary and secondary 52.1%; postsecondary 14.2%. *Literacy* (1990): total population age 15 and over literate 96.3%; males literate 99.1%; females literate 93.5%.
Health (1990): physicians 42,554 (1 per 1,007 persons); hospital beds 99,843 (1 per 429 persons); infant mortality rate per 1,000 live births 12.8.
Food (1987–89): daily per capita caloric intake 2,853 (vegetable products 87%, animal products 13%); 121% of FAO recommended minimum requirement.

Military

Total active duty personnel (1991): 750,000 (army 86.7%, navy 8.0%, air force 5.3%). *Military expenditure as percentage of GNP* (1989): 4.3% (world 4.9%); per capita expenditure: U.S.$214.

---

[1]Census data are preliminary. [2]Refers to persons who have received commandments, accepted baptism, or entered a faith and who participate in a religious function regularly or put the religious idea into practice. [3]Excludes farm households. [4]Import duties less imputed bank service charges. [5]Unemployed. [6]Detail does not add to total given because of rounding. [7]Circulation for 1988.

Kuwait

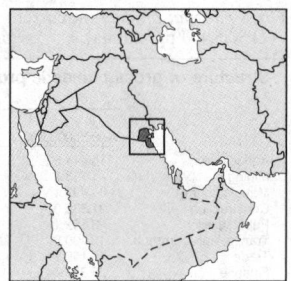

Official name: Dawlat al-Kuwayt (State of Kuwait).
Form of government: Constitutional monarchy with one legislative house (National Assembly [50]).
Head of state and government: Emir, assisted by Prime Minister.
Capital: Kuwait City.
Official language: Arabic.
Official religion: Islam.
Monetary unit: 1 Kuwaiti dinar (KD) = 1,000 fils; valuation (Oct. 5, 1992) 1 KD = U.S.$3.45 = £2.00.

Area and population

Governorates[2]	Capitals	area[1] sq mi	area[1] sq km	population 1985 census
al-Aḥmadī	al-Aḥmadī	1,984	5,138	301,513
al-Farwānīyah	al-Farwānīyah			416,644
al-Jahrāʾ	al-Jahrāʾ	4,372	11,324	241,285
Capital	Kuwait City	38	98	241,356
Ḥawallī	Ḥawallī	138	358	496,503
Islands[3]	—	347	900	...
TOTAL		6,880[4]	17,818	1,697,301

Demography

Population (1992): 1,190,000.
Density (1992): persons per sq mi 173.0, persons per sq km 66.8.
Urban-rural (1990): urban 95.6%; rural 4.4%.
Sex distribution (1990): male 56.50%; female 43.50%.
Age breakdown (1990): under 15, 35.5%; 15–29, 24.6%; 30–44, 27.2%; 45–59, 10.3%; 60–74, 2.1%; 75 and over, 0.3%.
Population projection: (2000) n.a.; (2010) n.a.
Doubling time: n.a.
Ethnic composition (1991): Kuwaiti Arab 51.6%; non-Kuwaiti Arab 45.3%; Asian 3.1%.
Religious affiliation (1986): Muslim 90.0%, of which Sunnī 63.0%, Shīʿah 27.0%; Christian 8.0%; Hindu 2.0%.
Major cities (1985): as-Sālimīyah 153,220; Ḥawallī 145,215; al-Jahrāʾ 111,165; al-Farwānīyah 68,665; Kuwait City 44,224.

Vital statistics

Birth rate per 1,000 population (1989): 25.9 (world avg. 27.1); legitimate, n.a.; illegitimate, n.a.
Death rate per 1,000 population (1989): 2.3 (world avg. 9.8).
Natural increase rate per 1,000 population (1989): 23.6 (world avg. 17.3).
Total fertility rate (avg. births per childbearing woman; 1989): 3.9.
Marriage rate per 1,000 population (1989): 5.4.
Divorce rate per 1,000 population (1989): 1.5.
Life expectancy at birth (1989): male 72.0 years; female 76.0 years.
Major causes of death per 100,000 population (1987): circulatory diseases 73.6; accidents, poisoning, and violence 31.4; malignant neoplasms (cancers) 25.5; respiratory diseases 16.5; endocrine, nutritional, and metabolic diseases 6.9; infectious and parasitic diseases 6.7; diseases of the digestive system 4.9; diseases of the nervous system 1.3.

National economy

Budget (1991–92). Revenue: KD 870,000,000 (oil revenue 80.5%). Expenditures: KD 6,087,000,000 (defense 43.4%; electricity, water, and public utilities 7.6%; education 7.5%; administrative services 3.9%; health 3.1%; transportation and communications 1.2%).
Public debt (external, outstanding; 1989): U.S.$610,000,000[5].
Tourism (1990): receipts from visitors U.S.$80,000,000; expenditures by nationals abroad U.S.$2,315,000,000.
Gross national product (at current market prices; 1989): U.S.$33,089,000,000 (U.S.$16,150 per capita).

Structure of gross domestic product and labour force

	1989 in value KD '000,000	1989 % of total value	1988 labour force	1988 % of labour force
Agriculture	46.0	0.7	8,756	1.3
Mining (oil sector)	2,773.0	40.9	6,028	0.9
Manufacturing	974.0	14.4	50,160	7.2
Construction	155.0	2.3	107,404	15.4
Public utilities	−43.0	−0.6	6,908	1.0
Transportation and communications	272.0	4.0	36,938	5.3
Trade	555.0	8.2	79,882	11.4
Finance			22,132	3.2
Pub. admin., defense	2,047.0	30.2	370,238	53.0
Services				
Other			10,472	1.5
TOTAL	6,779.0	100.0[4]	698,918	100.0[4]

Production (metric tons except as noted). Agriculture, forestry, fishing (1990): tomatoes 34,000, cucumbers and gherkins 20,000, onions 20,000, eggplants 2,000, pumpkins and squash 1,000, garlic 1,000; livestock (number of live animals) 200,000 sheep, 25,000 goats, 18,000 cattle, 6,000 camels, 21,000,000 chickens; fish catch 4,500. Mining and quarrying (1988): sulfur 360,000; lime 65,000. Manufacturing (1989): cement 1,107,700; ammonia 808,400; flour

145,200; bread 84,100; hydrated lime 51,802; metal pipes 41,800; bran 41,600; salt 37,859; liquefied caustic soda 17,879; chlorine gas 15,850; asbestos pipes 12,969; fats and oil 10,912; plastic pipes 4,903; detergents 2,800; biscuits 1,195; hydrochloric acid 1,173,000 gallons; hydrogen gas 5,011,000 cu m; sodium hydrochloride 11,987 cu m. Construction (floor area approved for construction; 1989): residential 2,563,000 sq m; nonresidential 416,000 sq m.
Energy production (consumption): electricity (kW-hr; 1990) 20,610,000,000 (20,610,000,000); coal, none (none); crude petroleum (barrels; 1990) 432,-393,000 (202,800,000); petroleum products (metric tons; 1990) 27,325,000 (3,156,000); natural gas (cu m; 1990) 5,227,139,000 (7,277,299,000).
Population economically active (1990): total 722,495; activity rate of total population 37.2% (participation rates [1988]: ages 15–64, 56.1%; female 18.8%; unemployed 1.9%).

Price and earnings indexes (1985 = 100)

	1984	1985	1986	1987	1988	1989	1990[6]
Consumer price index	98.5	100.0	101.0	101.6	103.1	106.6	108.7
Earnings index	...	...	...	...	...	...	...

Household income and expenditure. Average household size (1986) 7.4; annual income per household (1973[7]) KD 4,246 (U.S.$12,907); sources of income: wages and salaries 53.8%, self-employment 20.8%, other 25.4%; expenditure (1988): food, beverages, and tobacco 28.1%, housing and energy 15.5%, transportation 13.7%, household appliances 11.2%, clothing and footwear 8.1%, education and recreation 5.2%, health 0.7%.
Land use (1990): forested 0.1%; meadows and pastures 7.5%; agricultural and under permanent cultivation 0.2%; other, built-up, and wasteland 92.2%.

Foreign trade

Balance of trade (current prices)

	1984	1985	1986	1987	1988	1989
KD '000,000	+1,861.9	+1,618.1	+664.2	+996.8	+679.5	+1,774
% of total	34.5%	33.7%	18.7%	26.9%	18.6%	35.6%

Imports (1989): KD 1,849,410,000 (machinery and transport equipment 29.5%, manufactured goods 22.1%, food and live animals 17.3%, miscellaneous manufactured articles 17.2%, chemical products 7.7%, fuels 1.0%). *Major import sources:* United States 14.6%; Japan 11.4%; West Germany 7.8%; United Kingdom 6.4%; Italy 5.7%; South Korea 3.9%; France 3.6%.
Exports (1989): KD 3,378,000,000 (crude petroleum and petroleum products 92.2%). *Major export destinations:* Japan 18.8%; The Netherlands 9.2%; United States 8.4%; Pakistan 5.9%; Singapore 4.6%; India 4.2%; Italy 4.1%; Denmark 3.5%; Taiwan 3.3%.

Transport and communications

Transport. Railroads: none. Roads (1990): total length 2,655 mi, 4,273 km (paved 100%). Vehicles (1990): passenger cars 499,388; trucks and buses 110,663. Merchant marine (1991): vessels (100 gross tons and over) 197; total deadweight tonnage 2,293,230. Air transport (1991): passenger-mi 1,185,994,000, passenger-km 1,908,264,000; short ton-mi cargo 197,624,000, metric ton-km cargo 288,526,000; airports (1992) with scheduled flights 1.
Communications. Daily newspapers (1992): total number 9; total circulation 655,000; circulation per 1,000 population 550. Radio (1989): total number of receivers 1,100,000 (1 per 1.9 persons). Television (1989): total number of receivers 800,000 (1 per 2.6 persons). Telephones (1988): 281,771 (1 per 6.9 persons).

Education and health

Education (1991–92)

	schools	teachers	students	student/ teacher ratio
Primary (age 6–9)	203[8]	10,310	189,560	18.4
Secondary (age 10–17)	315[8]	21,585	270,580	12.5
Voc., teacher tr.	34	617	2,872	4.7
Higher[9]	1	1,181	17,988	15.2

Educational attainment (1988). Percentage of population age 10 and over having: no formal schooling 33.2%; primary education 18.4%; some secondary 22.7%; complete secondary 14.6%; higher 11.1%. *Literacy* (1990): percentage of total population age 15 and over literate 73.0%; males literate 77.1%; females literate 66.7%.
Health (1989): physicians 2,949 (1 per 695 persons); hospital beds 6,104[10] (1 per 336 persons); infant mortality rate per 1,000 live births (1989) 14.0.
Food (1987–89): daily per capita caloric intake 3,146 (vegetable products 75%, animal products 25%); 130% of FAO recommended minimum requirement.

Military

Total active duty personnel (1992): 11,700 (army 68.4%, navy 10.2%, air force 21.4%). *Military expenditure as percentage of GNP* (1989): 6.2% (world 4.9%); per capita expenditure U.S.$692.

---

[1]Area of governorates reflects conditions prior to Amiri Decree No. 156 of 1988, which established al-Farwānīyah governorate. [2]Governorates have no administrative function. [3]Bubian Island 333 sq mi (863 sq km) and Warba Island 14 sq mi (37 sq km). [4]Detail does not add to total given because of rounding. [5]Includes external long-term debt not guaranteed by the government. [6]May. [7]Kuwaiti households only. [8]1990–91. [9]1988–89. [10]Public hospitals only.

Kyrgyzstan

Official name: Kyrgyzstan Respublikasy (Republic of Kyrgyzstan).
Form of government: unitary multiparty republic with a single legislative body (Parliament [350]).
Head of state: President.
Head of government: Prime Minister.
Capital: Bishkek (Frunze).
Official language: Kyrgyz.
Official religion: none.
Monetary unit: 1 ruble = 100 kopecks; valuation (Oct. 5, 1992) free rate, 1 U.S.$ = 316.82 rubles; 1 £ = 538.59 rubles.

Area and population		area		population
				1991
Provinces	Capitals	sq mi	sq km	estimate
Chu	Kara-Balta	7,200	18,700	791,200
Dzhalal-Abad	Dzhalal-Abad	15,200	39,500	782,200
Issyk-Kul	Issyk-Kul	16,800	43,500	426,400
Naryn	Naryn	18,300	47,300	259,900
Osh	Osh	14,700	38,100	1,322,600
Talas	Talas	4,400	11,400	198,600
City of republic subordination				
Bishkek (Frunze)	—	...	...	641,400
TOTAL		76,600	198,500	4,422,200[1]

Demography

Population (1992): 4,533,000.
Density (1992): persons per sq mi 58.9, persons per sq km 22.8.
Urban-rural (1991): urban 38.1%; rural 61.9%.
Sex distribution (1990): male 48.90%; female 51.10%.
Age breakdown (1989): under 15, 37.5%; 15–29, 27.0%; 30–44, 16.3%; 45–59, 10.9%; 60–74, 6.2%; 75 and over, 2.1%.
Population projection: (2000) 5,403,000; (2010) 6,545,000.
Doubling time: 32 years.
Ethnic composition (1989): Kyrgyz 52.4%; Russian 21.5%; Uzbek 12.9%; Ukrainian 2.5%; German 2.4%; Tatar 1.6%; other 6.7%.
Religious affiliation: believers are predominantly Sunnī Muslim (Ḥanafīyah).
Major cities (1991): Bishkek (Frunze) 631,300; Osh 218,700; Dzhalal-Abad 74,200; Tokmak 71,200; Przhevalsk 64,300.

Vital statistics

Birth rate per 1,000 population (1990): 29.3 (world avg. 27.1); (1989) legitimate 87.3%; illegitimate 12.7%.
Death rate per 1,000 population (1990): 7.0 (world avg. 9.8).
Natural increase rate per 1,000 population (1990): 22.3 (world avg. 17.3).
Total fertility rate (avg. births per childbearing woman; 1989): 3.8.
Marriage rate per 1,000 population (1989): 9.7.
Divorce rate per 1,000 population (1989): 1.9.
Life expectancy at birth (1990): male 64.5 years; female 72.8 years.
Major causes of death per 100,000 population (1989): diseases of the circulatory system 284.2; diseases of the respiratory system 143.7; malignant neoplasms (cancers) 73.2; accidents, poisoning, and violence 86.0; infectious and parasitic diseases 31.4; diseases of the digestive system 28.7; diseases of the nervous system 7.9; endocrine and metabolic disorders 5.3.

National economy

Budget (1992). Revenue: 11,967,000,000 rubles (tax revenue 95.4%, of which value-added tax 42.9%, excise duties 27.2%, enterprise profits tax 22.7%, individual income tax 1.8%; nontax revenue 4.6%, of which highway fees 1.7%, privatization fees 0.8%). Expenditures: 17,053,000,000 rubles (social welfare and culture 55.9%, of which education 24.8%, social security 15.8%, health 13.4%; national economy 19.2%; interest obligations 12.9%; law enforcement 3.6%).
Public debt (external, outstanding): n.a.
Production (metric tons except as noted). Agriculture, forestry, fishing (1989): grain 1,654,800, vegetables (other than potatoes) 585,300, potatoes 324,300, fruit (other than grapes) 79,400, seed cotton 74,000, grapes 33,300; livestock (number of live animals; 1990) 10,485,900 sheep and goats, 1,213,900 cattle, 440,500 pigs; roundwood 6,000 cu m; fish catch, n.a. Mining and quarrying (1989): n.a. Manufacturing (1989): cement 1,165,900; milk 1,148,000; meat 239,400; wool 38,200; eggs 699,700,000 units. Construction (1989): residential 1,435,000 sq m. Energy production (consumption): electricity (kW-hr; 1991) 14,903,000,000 (n.a.); coal (metric tons; 1989) 3,997,000 (n.a.); crude petroleum (barrels; 1989) 1,685,900 (n.a.); petroleum products, n.a. (n.a.); natural gas (cu m; 1989) 1,102,500,000 (n.a.).
Land use: forested, n.a.; meadows and pastures, n.a.; agricultural and under permanent cultivation, n.a.; other, n.a.
Household income and expenditure. Average household size (1989) 4.2; income per household (1989) 6,100 rubles; sources of income (1989): wages and salaries 71.2%, pensions and stipends 7.8%, other 21.0%; expenditure (1989): food 33.5%, consumer goods 30.9%, taxes 8.0%, alcohol 2.6%, housing 2.2%.
Gross national product (at current market prices; 1989): 5,238,000,000 rubles (1,200 rubles per capita)[2].

Structure of net material product and labour force				
	1991		1989	
	in value '000,000 rubles	% of total value	labour force[3]	% of labour force[3]
Agriculture	4,058.0	36.4	474,000	33.2
Mining }				
Manufacturing }	5,054.0	45.3	400,000	28.0
Public utilities }				
Construction	864.0	7.7	...	...
Transportation and communications	307.0	2.8	78,600	5.5
Trade	—	—	92,900	6.5
Finance	—	—	40,000	2.8
Public administration, defense			...	...
Services	869.0	7.8	288,100	20.2
Other	—	—	55,300	3.9
TOTAL	11,152.0	100.0	1,428,900	100.0[1]

Population economically active (1990): total 1,894,000; activity rate of total population 42.8% (participation rates [1989]: ages 16–59 [male], 16–54 [female], 81.3%; female 48.6%; unemployed 2.6%).

Price and earnings indexes (1985 = 100)					
	1985	1986	1987	1988	1989
Consumer price index	100.0	101.0	102.0	102.0	104.0
Monthly earnings index	100.0	102.3	105.4	112.9	121.4

Tourism: receipts from visitors, n.a.; expenditures by nationals abroad, n.a.

Foreign trade

Balance of trade (current prices)					
	1987	1988	1989	1990	1991
'000,000 rubles	−458	−435	−813	−417	−958
% of total	9.9%	7.9%	13.8%	7.9%	8.2%

Imports (1991): 5,373,000,000 rubles (light-industrial products 23.0%, machinery and equipment 22.0%, chemicals 10.5%, oil and gas 10.1%, food 8.1%, ferrous metals 5.4%, nonferrous metals 5.2%, pulp and paper 3.3%, building materials 1.5%). *Major import sources:* former Soviet republics.
Exports (1991): 6,331,000,000 rubles (machinery and equipment 33.2%, light-industrial products 30.0%, food 18.0%, nonferrous metals 7.8%, electricity 3.0%, agricultural products 2.8%). *Major export destinations:* former Soviet republics.

Transport and communications

Transport. Railroads (1990): length 490 mi, 789 km; passengers 1,364,000; short ton cargo 113,100. Roads (1990): total length 11,900 mi, 19,100 km (paved 86%). Vehicles (1988): passenger cars 173,800; trucks and buses, n.a. Merchant marine: vessels (100 gross tons and over) n.a.; total deadweight tonnage, n.a. Air transport (1990): passenger-mi 2,304,200,000, passenger-km 3,708,300,000; short ton-mi cargo, n.a.; metric ton-km cargo, n.a.; airports (1992) with scheduled flights 1.
Communications. Daily newspapers (1990): total number 128; total circulation 1,622,000; circulation per 1,000 population 367. Radio and television (1990): total number of receivers 747,900 (1 per 5.9 persons). Telephones (1990): 307,100 (1 per 14 persons).

Education and health

Education (1989–90)	schools	teachers	students	student/ teacher ratio
Primary (age 6–13)	465 }		931,300	12.6
Secondary (age 14–17)	1,334 }	74,100		
Voc., teacher tr.	109	...	38,923	...
Higher	9	...	59,265	...

Educational attainment (1989). Percentage of population age 19 and over having: primary education 4.7%; some secondary 20.9%; completed secondary 44.4%; some postsecondary 19.3%; higher 10.7%. *Literacy:* total population age 15 and over literate, n.a.; males literate, n.a.; females literate, n.a.
Health (1990): physicians 16,100 (1 per 275 persons); hospital beds 52,600 (1 per 84 persons); infant mortality rate per 1,000 live births 30.0.
Food: daily per capita caloric intake, n.a.

Military

Total active duty personnel (1992): under joint Commonwealth of Independent States- (CIS-) Kyrgyz control 8,000 (army 100%). *Military expenditure as percentage of GNP:* n.a.; per capita expenditure, n.a.

[1]Detail does not add to total given because of rounding. [2]No equivalent U.S.$ value is offered, as Soviet GNP data are very speculative. [3]State sector only.

Laos

Official name: Sathalanalat
  Paxathipatai Paxaxôn Lao (Lao
  People's Democratic Republic).
Form of government: unitary
  single-party people's republic with
  one legislative house (National
  Assembly[1] [79]).
Chief of state: President.
Head of government: Prime Minister.
Capital: Vientiane.
Official language: Lao.
Official religion: none.
Monetary unit: 1 kip (KN) = 100 at;
  valuation (Oct. 5, 1992)
  1 U.S.$ = KN 714; 1 £ = KN 1,213.

Area and population

		area		population
				1985
Provinces	Capitals	sq mi	sq km	census
Attapu	Attapu	...	...	69,631
Bokeo	Houayxay	...	...	54,925
Bolikhamxay	Pakxan	...	...	122,300
Champasak	Pakxé	...	...	403,041
Houaphan	Xam Nua	...	...	209,921
Khammouan	Thakhek	...	...	213,462
Louang Namtha	Louang Namtha	...	...	97,028
Louangphrabang	Louangphrabang	...	...	295,475
Oudomxay	Xay	...	...	187,115
Phôngsali	Phôngsali	...	...	122,984
Saravan	Saravan	...	...	187,515
Savannakhét	Savannakhét	...	...	543,611
Vientiane	Vientiane	...	...	264,277
Xaignabouri	Xaignabouri	...	...	223,611
Xékong	Thong	...	...	50,909
Xiangkhoang	Phônsavan	...	...	161,589
Municipalities				
Vientiane	—	...	...	377,409
TOTAL		91,400	236,800	3,584,803

Demography

Population (1992): 4,409,000.
Density (1992): persons per sq mi 48.2, persons per sq km 18.6.
Urban-rural (1990): urban 19.0%; rural 81.0%.
Sex distribution (1990): male 50.25%; female 49.75%.
Age breakdown (1990): under 15, 43.7%; 15–29, 26.0%; 30–44, 16.2%; 45–59, 9.2%; 60–74, 4.2%; 75 and over, 0.7%.
Population projection: (2000) 5,435,000; (2010) 6,710,000.
Doubling time: 28 years.
Ethnic composition (1983): Lao-Lu (Lao) 67.0%; Lao-Theng (Mon-Khmer) 16.5%; Lao-Tai (Tai) 7.8%; Lao-Soung (Miao [Hmong] and Man [Yao]) 5.2%; other 3.5%.
Religious affiliation (1980): Buddhist 57.8%; tribal religionist 33.6%; Christian 1.8%, of which Roman Catholic 0.8%, Protestant 0.2%; Muslim 1.0%; atheist 1.0%; Chinese folk-religionist 0.9%; none 3.8%; other 0.1%.
Major cities (1985): Vientiane 178,203; Savannakhét 96,652; Louangphrabang 68,399; Pakxé 47,323.

Vital statistics

Birth rate per 1,000 population (1991): 37.0 (world avg. 26.4).
Death rate per 1,000 population (1991): 15.0 (world avg. 9.2).
Natural increase rate per 1,000 population (1991): 22.0 (world avg. 17.2).
Total fertility rate (avg. births per childbearing woman; 1991): 5.0.
Marriage rate per 1,000 population: n.a.
Divorce rate per 1,000 population: n.a.
Life expectancy at birth (1990): male 48.3 years; female 51.3 years.
Major causes of death per 100,000 population: n.a; however, during the 1980s bronchitis, influenza, pneumonia, malaria, and diarrhea were among the country's major health problems.

National economy

Budget (1990). Revenue: KN 58,245,000,000 (taxes 76.0%, nontax revenue 24.0%). Expenditures: KN 131,957,000,000 (current expenditure 49.9%, capital expenditure 50.1%).
Public debt (external, outstanding; 1990): U.S.$1,052,000,000.
Tourism (1989): total number of tourist arrivals 2,631.
Population economically active (1989): total 1,888,000; activity rate of total population 49.0% (participation rates [1985]: ages 15–64, 84.2%; female 45.3%; unemployed, n.a.).

Price and earnings indexes (1985 = 100)

	1982	1983	1984	1985	1986[2]
Consumer price index	30.1	39.6	60.5	100.0	136.2
Earnings index	...	...	...	...	...

Production (metric tons except as noted). Agriculture, forestry, fishing (1991): rice 1,400,000, sweet potatoes 220,000, sugarcane 97,000, cassava 66,000, corn (maize) 60,000, onions 42,000, potatoes 33,000, pineapples 32,000, melons 32,000, oranges 22,000, bananas 18,000; livestock (number of live animals) 1,390,000 pigs, 1,100,000 water buffalo, 865,000 cattle, 143,000 goats, 45,000 horses, 8,000,000 chickens; roundwood (1989) 3,972,000 cu m; fish catch (1989) 20,000. Mining and quarrying (1989): gypsum 104,000; rock salt 7,950;

tin (metal content) 281; gemstones (mainly sapphires) 32,825 carats. Manufacturing (1986): domestic animal feed 5,000; cement 5,000; washing powder 2,500; plastic products 191; textiles 97,900 sq m; clothing 883,000 pieces; cigarettes 16,000,000 packets; rubber tires and tubes 883,000 units; ceramic articles 87,000 units; beer and soft drinks 26,000 hectolitres; fish sauce 2,300 hectolitres. Construction: n.a. Energy production (consumption): electricity (kW-hr; 1990) 870,000,000 (363,000,000); coal (metric tons; 1981) 1,000 (1,000); crude petroleum, n.a. (n.a.); petroleum products (metric tons; 1990) none (74,000); natural gas, n.a. (n.a.).
Gross national product (at current market prices; 1990): U.S.$848,000,000 (U.S.$200 per capita).

Structure of gross domestic product and labour force

	1989		1989	
	in value KN '000,000	% of total value	labour force	% of labour force
Agriculture	191,667	57.4	1,359,000	72.0
Manufacturing	32,940	9.9		
Mining	1,048	0.3		
Construction	12,499	3.7		
Public utilities	6,517	2.0		
Transportation and communications	14,683	4.4	529,000	28.0
Trade	34,344	10.3		
Finance	4,986	1.5		
Pub. admin., defense	11,250	3.4		
Services	23,743	7.1		
Other				
TOTAL	333,675[3]	100.0	1,888,000	100.0

Household income and expenditure. Average household size (1985) 6.0; average annual income per household KN 3,710 (U.S.$371); sources of income: n.a.; expenditure: n.a.
Land use (1990): forested 53.6%; meadows and pastures 3.4%; agricultural and under permanent cultivation 3.8%; other 39.2%.

Foreign trade[4]

Balance of trade (current prices)

	1984	1985	1986	1987	1988	1989
U.S.$'000,000	−118.0	−139.0	−131.0	−154.0	−125.0	−162.0
% of total	39.8%	56.3%	54.4%	55.4%	49.8%	58.7%

Imports (1989): U.S.$219,000,000 (important imports include cereals, other food products, petroleum products, agricultural and general machinery, and transport equipment). *Major import sources:* Thailand 55.1%; Japan 22.0%; China 4.0%; Hong Kong 0.5%.
Exports (1989): U.S.$57,000,000 (1988; wood 47.6%, electricity 17.5%, coffee 12.7%, tin 3.2%). *Major export destinations:* Thailand 37.4%; China 11.6%; Japan 7.3%; Hong Kong 0.6%.

Transport and communications

Transport. Railroads: none. Roads (1990): total length 8,681 mi, 13,971 km (paved 21%). Vehicles (1989): passenger cars 17,000; trucks and buses 3,500. Merchant marine (1991): vessels (100 gross tons and over) 1; total deadweight tonnage 1,469. Air transport (1986): passenger-mi 11,000,000, passenger-km 18,000,000; short ton-mi cargo 1,370,000, metric ton-km cargo 2,000,000; airports (1992) with scheduled flights 12.
Communications. Daily newspapers (1989): total number 3; total circulation 30,500; circulation per 1,000 population 7.7. Radio (1991): total number of receivers 425,000 (1 per 10 persons). Television (1991): total number of receivers 32,000 (1 per 134 persons). Telephones (1985): 8,136 (1 per 450 persons).

Education and health

Education (1988–89)

	schools	teachers	students	student/ teacher ratio
Primary (age 6–10)	8,330	19,438	571,630	29.4
Secondary (age 11–16)	750	9,752	124,169	12.7
Voc., teacher tr.	117[5]	2,049[6]	16,293[6]	8.0[5]
Higher	9	503	5,253	10.4

Educational attainment: n.a. *Literacy* (1985): total population age 15 and over literate 83.9%; males literate 92.0%; females literate 75.8%.
Health (1985): physicians 558 (1 per 6,495 persons); hospital beds 9,815 (1 per 369 persons); infant mortality rate per 1,000 live births (1991) 124.
Food (1984–86): daily per capita caloric intake 2,190 (vegetable products 90%, animal products 10%); 101% of FAO recommended minimum requirement.

Military

Total active duty personnel (1992): 37,000 (army 89.2%, navy 1.4%, air force 9.4%). *Military expenditure as percent of GNP* (1984): 10.5% (world 5.7%); per capita expenditure U.S.$16.

---

[1]Formerly known as the Supreme People's Assembly. [2]January–June. [3]Detail does not add to total given because of rounding. [4]Import figures are c.i.f. in balance of trade and commodities. [5]1984–85. [6]1987–88.

Latvia

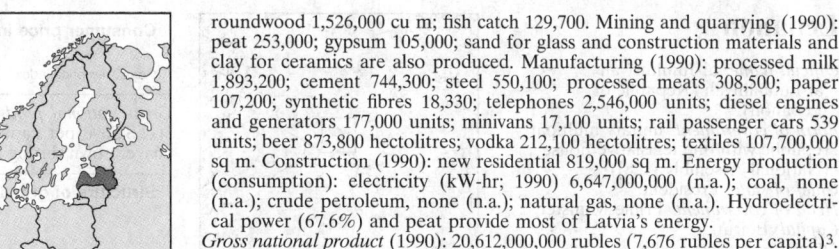

Official name: Latvijas Republika (Republic of Latvia).
Form of government: unitary multiparty republic with a single legislative body (Supreme Council [201]).
Chief of state: Chairman of the Supreme Council.
Head of government: Prime Minister.
Capital: Rīga.
Official language: Latvian.
Official religion: none.
Monetary unit: (until May 7, 1992)
1 (Soviet) ruble = 100 kopecks;
valuation (Oct. 5, 1992)
1 U.S.$ = 316.82 rubles; 1£ = 538.59 rubles.
Latvian ruble (LR)[1] introduced May 7, 1992, at par with Soviet ruble and circulated parallel with it; on July 20, LR became sole legal tender, floating against all currencies; valuation not available.

Area and population		area		population
		sq mi	sq km	1991 estimate
Cities of republic jurisdiction	**Capitals**			
Daugavpils	—	28	72	129,000
Jelgava	—	23	60	74,500
Jūrmala	—	39	100	66,500
Liepāja	—	23	60	114,900
Rēzekne	—	7	17	43,200
Rīga	—	114	295	910,200
Ventspils	—	18	46	50,400
Rural districts				
Aizkraukle	Aizkraukle	988	2,558	44,900
Alūksne	Alūksne	867	2,246	28,700
Balvi	Balvi	920	2,384	33,500
Bauska	Bauska	727	1,884	55,800
Cēsis	Cēsis	1,182	3,062	64,400
Daugavpils	Daugavpils	975	2,526	46,000
Dobele	Dobele	649	1,680	45,200
Gulbene	Gulbene	724	1,876	30,200
Jēkabpils	Jēkabpils	1,158	2,998	62,300
Jelgava	Jelgava	623	1,613	39,100
Krāslava	Krāslava	883	2,288	41,200
Kuldīga	Kuldīga	966	2,503	40,800
Liepāja	Liepāja	1,386	3,589	54,700
Limbaži	Limbaži	1,005	2,602	41,200
Ludza	Ludza	991	2,566	41,600
Madona	Madona	1,293	3,348	49,600
Ogre	Ogre	701	1,816	66,100
Preiļi	Preiļi	788	2,042	45,300
Rēzekne	Rēzekne	1,025	2,654	43,200
Rīga	Rīga	1,194	3,094	153,300
Saldus	Saldus	824	2,134	39,700
Talsi	Talsi	1,061	2,748	49,900
Tukums	Tukums	949	2,457	59,200
Valka	Valka	944	2,444	37,300
Valmiera	Valmiera	918	2,377	63,200
Ventspils	Ventspils	954	2,471	15,400
TOTAL		24,946[2]	64,610	2,680,500

Demography

Population (1992): 2,685,000.
Density (1992): persons per sq mi 107.8, persons per sq km 41.6.
Urban-rural (1991): urban 71.1%; rural 28.9%.
Sex distribution (1990): male 46.60%; female 53.40%.
Age breakdown (1990): under 15, 21.5%; 15–29, 21.5%; 30–44, 20.6%; 45–59, 18.9%; 60–74, 12.2%; 75 and over, 5.3%.
Population projection: (2000) 2,768,000; (2010) 2,853,000.
Ethnic composition (1989): Latvian 52.0%; Russian 34.0%; Belorussian 4.5%; Ukrainian 3.5%; Polish 2.3%; Lithuanian 1.3%; Jewish 0.9%; other 1.5%.
Religious affiliation: believers are predominantly Evangelical Lutheran, Russian Orthodox, or Roman Catholic.
Major cities (1991): Rīga 910,200; Daugavpils 129,000; Liepāja 114,900; Jelgava 74,500; Jūrmala 66,500.

Vital statistics

Birth rate per 1,000 population (1990): 14.1 (world avg. 27.1); legitimate 83.1%; illegitimate 16.9%.
Death rate per 1,000 population (1990): 13.0 (world avg. 9.8).
Natural increase rate per 1,000 population (1990): 1.1 (world avg. 17.3).
Total fertility rate (avg. births per childbearing woman; 1989–90): 2.0.
Marriage rate per 1,000 population (1990): 8.8.
Divorce rate per 1,000 population (1990): 4.0.
Life expectancy at birth (1990): male 64.2 years; female 74.6 years.
Major causes of death per 100,000 population (1990): diseases of the circulatory system 756.5; malignant neoplasms (cancers) 207.2; accidents, poisoning, and violence 138.9; diseases of the respiratory system 44.0.

National economy

Budget (1990). Revenue: 4,575,100,000 rubles (turnover tax 46.4%; state participation in economic enterprises 25.6%). Expenditures: 4,376,500,000 rubles (economic affairs 54.8%; social affairs 31.6%, of which education and science 13.8%, social security 10.4%, health 7.3%).
Production (metric tons except as noted). Agriculture, forestry, fishing (1990): grains 1,622,000, potatoes 1,016,000, sugar beets 439,100, vegetables 169,400, fruits and berries 31,900, flax fibre 3,000; livestock (number of live animals) 1,401,000 pigs, 535,000 dairy cattle, 165,000 sheep, 10,321,000 poultry;

roundwood 1,526,000 cu m; fish catch 129,700. Mining and quarrying (1990): peat 253,000; gypsum 105,000; sand for glass and construction materials and clay for ceramics are also produced. Manufacturing (1990): processed milk 1,893,200; cement 744,300; steel 550,100; processed meats 308,500; paper 107,200; synthetic fibres 18,330; telephones 2,546,000 units; diesel engines and generators 177,000 units; minivans 17,100 units; rail passenger cars 539 units; beer 873,800 hectolitres; vodka 212,100 hectolitres; textiles 107,700,000 sq m. Construction (1990): new residential 819,000 sq m. Energy production (consumption): electricity (kW-hr; 1990) 6,647,000,000 (n.a.); coal, none (n.a.); crude petroleum, none (n.a.); natural gas, none (n.a.). Hydroelectrical power (67.6%) and peat provide most of Latvia's energy.
Gross national product (1990): 20,612,000,000 rubles (7,676 rubles per capita)[3].

Structure of net material product and labour force				
	1990			
	in value '000,000 rubles	% of total value	labour force	% of labour force
Agriculture	1,980	22.7	218,700	15.5
Manufacturing and mining	4,213	48.3	426,200	30.3
Construction	697	8.0	144,500	10.3
Transportation and communications	650	7.4	103,200	7.3
Trade	1,191	13.6	128,300	9.1
Pub. admin., defense, and finance	—	—	} 387,800	} 27.5
Services	—	—		
Other	—	—		
TOTAL	8,731	100.0	1,408,700	100.0

Population economically active (1990): total 1,408,700; activity rate of total population 52.5%; (participation rates: ages 16–59/55[4], 93.4%; female, n.a.; unemployed, n.a.).

Price and earnings indexes (1985 = 100)							
	1985	1986	1987	1988	1989	1990	1991
Consumer price index	100.0	105.4	110.0	114.6	120.6	133.7	350.3
Monthly earnings index	100.0	102.8	106.6	115.9	127.6	148.5	...

Household income and expenditure. Average household size (1989) 3.1; average annual income per household: n.a.; sources of income (1990): wages and salaries 75.7%, pensions and transfers 8.5%, self-employment 3.8%, other 12.0%; expenditure: n.a.

Foreign trade

Balance of trade (current prices)			
	1988	1989	1990
'000,000 rubles	−700	−617	−784
% of total	6.7%	5.4%	6.5%

Imports (1990): 6,358,000,000 rubles (industrial goods 88.1%, of which machinery and metalworking equipment 28.2%). *Major import sources* (1989): Commonwealth of Independent States- (CIS-) member countries and Georgia (former U.S.S.R.) 75.0%, non-CIS countries 25.0%.
Exports (1990): 5,574,000,000 rubles (industrial goods 87.9%, of which machinery and metalworking equipment 27.2%, consumer goods 21.5%). *Major export destinations* (1989): CIS countries and Georgia 93.2%, non-CIS countries 6.8%.

Transport and communications

Transport. Railroads (1990): length 1,489 mi, 2,397 km; passenger-km 5,366,000,000; metric-km cargo 18,538,000,000. Roads (1990): total length 79,100 km (paved 49%). Vehicles (1990): passenger cars 271,500; trucks and buses 14,116. Merchant marine (1991): cargo vessels 87; total deadweight tonnage, n.a. Air transport (1990): passenger-km 3,357,000,000; metric ton-km cargo 22,000,000; airports (1992) 1.
Communications. Total newspapers (1990): total number 172; total circulation 4,396,000; circulation per 1,000 population 1,637. Radio (1990): 1.4 receivers per household. Television (1990): 1.2 receivers per household. Telephones (1990): 732,000 (1 per 3.7 persons).

Education and health

Education (1990–91)	schools	teachers	students	student/ teacher ratio
Primary } Secondary }	962	32,200	352,450	10.9
Voc., teacher tr.	57	...	36,100	...
Higher	10	...	46,000	...

Educational attainment (1989). Percentage of persons age 15 and over having: primary or less 18.7%; incomplete secondary 23.4%; complete secondary 46.4%; some higher 11.5%. *Literacy:* approximately 98%.
Health (1990): physicians 13,240 (1 per 202.7 persons); hospital beds 39,500 (1 per 67.9 persons); infant mortality rate per 1,000 live births 13.7.

Military

Total active duty personnel (1992): 2,550. *Military expenditure:* n.a. Until 1991, the U.S.S.R. was responsible for Latvia's external security; about 40,000 of its troops remained in Latvia at year-end 1992.

---

[1]Interim currency unit until its eventual replacement by a new national currency, the lats, when the LR exchange rate has stabilized. [2]Detail does not add to total given because of rounding. [3]No equivalent U.S.$ value is offered, as Soviet GNP data are very speculative. [4]Males retire at age 59, females at 55.

Lebanon

Official name: al-Jumhūrīyah
al-Lubnānīyah (Republic of
Lebanon).
Form of government: unitary multiparty
republic with one legislative house
(National Assembly [128])[1].
Chief of state: President.
Head of government: Prime Minister.
Capital: Beirut.
Official language: Arabic.
Official religion: none.
Monetary unit: 1 Lebanese pound
(LL) = 100 piastres; valuation
(Oct. 5, 1992) 1 U.S.$ = LL 2,473;
1 £ = LL 4,204.

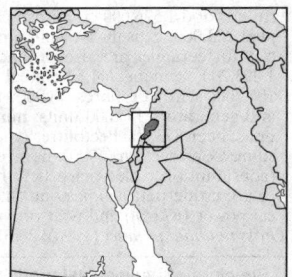

Area and population

Governorates	Capitals	area sq mi	area sq km	population 1970 estimate
Bayrūt	Beirut (Bayrūt)	7	18	474,870
al-Biqāʿ	Zaḥlah	1,653	4,280	203,520
Jabal Lubnān	Bʿabdā	753	1,950	833,055
al-Janūb	Sidon (Ṣaydā)	772	2,001	249,945
ash-Shamāl	Tripoli (Ṭarābulus)	765	1,981	364,935
TOTAL		3,950	10,230	2,126,325

Demography

Population (1992): 2,803,000.
Density (1992): persons per sq mi 709.6, persons per sq km 274.0.
Urban-rural (1990): urban 83.7%; rural 16.3%.
Sex distribution (1990): male 48.57%; female 51.43%.
Age breakdown (1990): under 15, 36.1%; 15–29, 30.5%; 30–44, 15.8%; 45–59, 9.7%; 60–74, 6.1%; 75 and over, 1.8%.
Population projection: (2000) 3,327,000; (2010) 3,898,000.
Doubling time: during the 1970–75 prewar period the average growth rate was 2.6%; however, the dislocation of the population by the civil war between 1976 and 1991 rendered both the absolute size and principal components of population change (births, deaths, migration) highly problematic.
Ethnic composition (1983): Lebanese 82.6%; Palestinian 9.6%; Armenian 4.9%; Syrian, Kurd, and other 2.9%.
Religious affiliation: no official data exist subsequent to the 1932 census, when Christians (predominantly Maronite Roman Catholic) were a slight majority; it is thought that Muslims today constitute the majority but by what margin is highly uncertain. Unofficial and CIA estimates (1984/1986) indicated that the main religious groups were distributed as follows: Shīʿī Muslim 32/41%; Maronite Christian 24.5/16%; Sunnī Muslim 21/27%; Druze 7/7%; Greek Orthodox 6.5/5%; Greek Catholic 4/3%; Armenian Christian 4%/n.a.; other 1/1%.
Major cities (1990): Beirut 1,500,000; Tripoli 160,000; Zaḥlah 45,000; Sidon (Ṣaydā) 38,000; Tyre 14,000.

Vital statistics

Birth rate per 1,000 population (1990–95): 29.6 (world avg. 26.4).
Death rate per 1,000 population (1990–95): 7.7 (world avg. 9.2).
Natural increase rate per 1,000 population (1990–95): 21.9 (world avg. 17.2).
Total fertility rate (avg. births per childbearing woman; 1990–95): 3.4.
Life expectancy at birth (1990–95): male 61.5 years; female 69.0 years.
Major causes of death: normally, cardiovascular and gastrointestinal diseases, including typhoid fever and dysentery; but violence and acts of war were also among the principal causes of mortality between 1975 and 1991.

National economy

Budget (1992). Revenue: LL 1,470,000,000,000 (1986; income taxes 49.6%, customs 31.5%). Expenditures: LL 1,470,000,000,000 (1990; debt service 22.9%, defense 16.0%, public works and transportation 7.0%, education 5.0%).
Public debt (external, outstanding; 1990): U.S.$248,000,000.
Production (metric tons except as noted). Agriculture, forestry, fishing (1991): oranges 270,000, potatoes 200,000, grapes 200,000, tomatoes 200,000, apples 195,000, sugar beets 90,000, cucumbers 75,000, lemons and limes 65,000, onions 50,000, tangerines, mandarins, and clementines 50,000; opium poppies were an increasingly important cash crop in the late 1980s; livestock (number of live animals) 400,000 goats, 205,000 sheep, 57,000 cattle, 24,-000,000 chickens; roundwood 467,000 cu m; fish catch (1990) 1,500. Mining and quarrying (1989): lime 10,000; salt 3,000; gypsum 2,000. Manufacturing (1988): cement 907,000; wheat flour 190,000[2]; paper and paperboard 37,000; petroleum refining is also significant. Construction (1987): 4,938,000 sq m. Energy production (consumption): electricity (kW-hr; 1990) 4,735,000,-000 (4,777,000,000); coal, n.a. (none); crude petroleum (barrels; 1990) n.a. (9,265,000); petroleum products (metric tons; 1990) 1,192,000 (2,781,000); natural gas, none (n.a.).
Household income and expenditure. Average household size (1987) 5.0; average annual income per household (1985) LL 120,000 (U.S.$6,630; in constant prices, about 75% of 1966 income levels); sources of income (1974): wages and salaries 27.9%, transfers 3.0%, other 69.1%; expenditure (1966)[3]: food 42.8%, housing 16.8%, clothing 8.6%, health care 7.2%.
Tourism (1980): number of tourist arrivals 135,548[4].
Population economically active (1986): total 693,812; activity rate of total population 25.1% (participation rates: over age 15, 39.9%; female 21.7%; unemployed [1991] reported by the national trade union at 30% but perhaps as low as 7–8% according to a 1987 study of 60,000 households).

Consumer price index (1985 = 100)

	1981	1982	1983	1984	1985	1986	1987
Consumer price index	40.6	48.7	51.9	61.0	100.0	204.6	1,030.6

Gross national product (at current market prices; 1985): U.S.$1,800,000,000 (U.S.$690 per capita); though estimates are very uncertain, the GNP may have grown during 1985–88, perhaps regaining 83% of its prewar value.

Structure of gross domestic product and labour force

	1987 in value U.S.$'000,000[5]	1987 % of total value	1986 labour force	1986 % of labour force
Agriculture	287	8.7	132,211	19.1
Mining	—	—	694	0.1
Manufacturing	483	14.7	123,647	17.8
Construction	158	4.8	43,357	6.2
Public utilities	28	0.8	6,668	1.0
Transp. and commun.	[6]	[6]	48,242	7.0
Trade	1,127	34.2	114,706	16.5
Finance	286	8.7	24,224	3.5
Pub. admin., defense	171	5.2 }	200,063	28.8
Services	756[6]	22.9[6] }		
TOTAL	3,296	100.0	693,812	100.0

Land use (1990): forested 7.7%; meadows and pastures 1.0%; agricultural and under permanent cultivation 28.9%; wasteland and other areas 62.4%.

Foreign trade

Balance of trade (current prices)

	1982	1983	1984	1985	1986	1987
LL '000,000	−9,890	−12,461	−13,987	−25,581	−59,090	−269,311
% of total	48.5%	69.0%	64.9%	61.8%	60.6%	50.4%

Imports (1987): LL 402,027,000,000 (1982; consumer goods 40.0%, machinery and transport equipment 35.0%, petroleum products 20.0%). *Major import sources:* Italy 10.7%; Turkey 8.5%; France 8.1%; West Germany 5.9%.
Exports (1987): LL 132,716,000,000 (1985; jewelry 10.2%, clothing 5.2%, pharmaceutical products 4.9%, metal products 4.8%). *Major export destinations:* Saudi Arabia 8.7%; Switz. 7.6%; Jordan 6.0%; Kuwait 5.4%; U.S. 5.2%.

Transport and communications

Transport. Railroads (1982)[7]: length (1986) 417 km; passenger-km 8,570,000; metric ton-km cargo 42,010,000. Roads (1987): total length 7,370 km (paved 85%). Vehicles (1985): passenger cars 300,000; trucks and buses 49,560. Merchant marine (1991): vessels (100 gross tons and over) 164; total deadweight tonnage 424,646. Air transport (1990)[8]: passenger-km 1,503,227,000; metric ton-km cargo 24,037,000; airports (1992) with scheduled flights 2.
Communications. Daily newspapers (1986): total number 39; total circulation 572,734[9]; circulation per 1,000 population 211.6[9]. Radio (1991): 2,150,000 receivers (1 per 1.3 persons). Television (1991): 838,037 receivers (1 per 3.3 persons). Telephones (1987): 150,400 (1 per 18.4 persons).

Education and health

Education (1984–85)

	schools	teachers	students[10]	student/ teacher ratio
Primary (age 5–9)	2,130	22,810[11]	399,029	...
Secondary (age 10–16)	1,405[11]	21,344[11]	279,849	...
Voc., teacher tr.	181[11]	3,506	30,407	10.6
Higher	18[11]	7,460	70,510	9.5

Educational attainment (1970). Percentage of population age 25 and over having: no formal schooling 45.6%, of which, ability to read and write 35.6%; incomplete primary education 28.5%; complete primary 10.8%; incomplete secondary 7.1%; complete secondary 4.9%; higher 3.1%. *Literacy* (1990): total population age 15 and over literate, c. 1,538,800 (80.1%); males literate, c. 798,100 (87.8%); females literate, c. 739,100 (73.1%).
Health (1986): physicians 3,509 (1 per 771 persons); hospital beds (1982) 11,-400 (1 per 263 persons); infant mortality rate per 1,000 live births (1990) 44.0.
Food (1979–81): daily per capita caloric intake 2,995 (vegetable products 84%, animal products 16%); 120% of FAO recommended minimum requirement.

Military

Total active duty personnel (1992): Lebanese national armed forces 36,900 (army 96.7%, navy 1.1%, air force 2.2%). External regular military forces include: UN peacekeeping force in Lebanon 5,900; Syrian army 30,000. Most civilian militias were disbanded after the civil war ended in 1991. According to external analysts, however, the following factions were still active in 1992, though on a much reduced scale[12]: Palestine Liberation Organization (all factions) 9,800; Druze (Progressive Socialist Party) 4,000; Shīʿī Muslim (pro-Iran Hezbollah [Party of God]) 3,000; Maronite Christian (Lebanese Forces [Phalange]) 3,000; Shīʿī Muslim (pro-Syrian Amal) 2,000. *Military expenditure as percentage of GDP* (1990): 4.2% (world, n.a.); per capita expenditure: U.S.$52.

[1]The current legislature was elected between August and October 1992; one-half of its membership is Christian and one-half Muslim/Druse. [2]1983. [3]Weights based on consumer price index components. For capital city only. [4]Approximately one-fourth the annual prewar rates of the early 1970s. [5]Because of the instability of the Lebanese pound, the domestic economy reportedly became increasingly "dollarized" as more transactions were quoted or paid in dollars during the late 1980s and early '90s. [6]Services includes Transportation and communications. [7]Apart from a short section near Beirut, no track is currently in use. [8]MEA-Airliban international flights only. [9]For 20 newspapers only. [10]1986–87. [11]1981–82. [12]Active personnel.

Lesotho

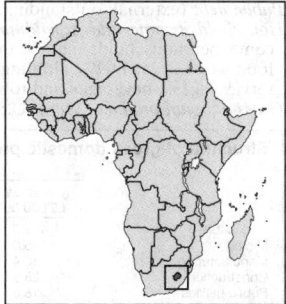

Official name: Lesotho (Sotho); Kingdom of Lesotho (English).
Form of government: monarchy assisted by a Military Council[1].
Chief of state: King.
Head of government: Chairman of the Military Council.
Capital: Maseru.
Official languages: Sotho; English.
Official religion: Christianity.
Monetary unit: 1 loti (plural maloti [M]) = 100 lisente; valuation (Oct. 5, 1992) 1 U.S.$ = M 2.84; 1 £ = M 4.82.

Area and population

Districts	Capitals	area sq mi	area sq km	population 1987 estimate
Berea	Teyateyaneng	858	2,222	199,600
Butha-Buthe	Butha-Buthe	682	1,767	103,000
Leribe	Hlotse	1,092	2,828	264,600
Mafeteng	Mafeteng	818	2,119	200,600
Maseru	Maseru	1,652	4,279	319,100
Mohale's Hoek	Mohale's Hoek	1,363	3,530	168,600
Mokhotlong	Mokhotlong	1,573	4,075	76,600
Qacha's Nek	Qacha's Nek	907	2,349	65,600
Quthing	Quthing	1,126	2,916	113,200
Thaba-Tseka	Thaba-Tseka	1,649	4,270	106,800
TOTAL		11,720	30,355	1,617,700

Demography

Population (1992): 1,854,000.
Density (1992): persons per sq mi 158.2, persons per sq km 61.1.
Urban-rural (1988): urban 18.9%; rural 81.1%.
Sex distribution (1987): male 48.15%; female 51.85%.
Age breakdown (1987): under 15, 40.7%; 15–29, 25.2%; 30–44, 16.6%; 45–59, 10.7%; 60–74, 5.5%; 75 and over, 1.3%.
Population projection: (2000) 2,282,000; (2010) 2,958,000.
Doubling time: 24 years.
Ethnic composition (1983): Sotho 99.7%; other 0.3%.
Religious affiliation (1980): Roman Catholic 43.5%; Protestant (mostly Lesotho Evangelical) 29.8%; Anglican 11.5%; other Christian 8.0%; traditional beliefs 6.2%; other 1.0%.
Major urban centres (1986): Maseru 109,382; Maputsoe 20,000; Teyateyaneng 14,251; Mafeteng 12,667; Hlotse 9,595.

Vital statistics

Birth rate per 1,000 population (1990–95): 40.2 (world avg. 26.4); legitimate, n.a.; illegitimate, n.a.
Death rate per 1,000 population (1990–95): 11.0 (world avg. 9.2).
Natural increase rate per 1,000 population (1990–95): 29.2 (world avg. 17.2).
Total fertility rate (avg. births per childbearing woman; 1990–95): 5.8.
Marriage rate per 1,000 population: n.a.
Divorce rate per 1,000 population: n.a.
Life expectancy at birth (1990–95): male 54.0 years; female 63.0 years.
Major causes of death per 100,000 population: n.a.; however, major diseases include malaria, typhoid fever, and infectious and parasitic diseases.

National economy

Budget (1990–91). Revenue: M 820,500,000 (tax revenue 75.0%, of which customs receipts 43.2%, sales tax 13.8%, income tax 4.5%, company tax 3.1%; grants 25.0%). Expenditures: M 835,000,000 (recurrent expenditure 53.1%, of which personal emoluments 21.0%, interest payments 9.8%, subsidies and transfers 5.4%, other goods and services 16.9%; capital expenditure 46.9%).
Production (metric tons except as noted). Agriculture, forestry, fishing (1991): corn (maize) 95,000, fruit 19,000, sorghum 18,000, roots and tubers 8,000, peas 4,000, beans 3,000; livestock (number of live animals) 1,475,000 sheep, 1,065,000 goats, 540,000 cattle, 129,000 asses, 122,000 horses, 75,000 pigs, 1,000,000 chickens; roundwood (1990) 613,000 cu m; fish catch (1990) 30. Mining and quarrying (1988): sand and gravel 50,000 cu m. Manufacturing (total value added; 1990): M 180,800,000, of which food and beverages 47.2%, textiles, apparel, and leather 39.8%, chemical products 2.1%, printing and publishing 2.0%, iron and steel products 1.6%, furniture and fixtures 1.2%. Construction (total value added; 1990): M 259,700. Energy production (consumption): electricity (kW-hr; 1988) 1,000,000 (n.a.); coal, none (n.a.); petroleum, none (n.a.); natural gas, none (n.a.).
Public debt (external, outstanding; 1991): U.S.$376,440,000.
Tourism (1990): receipts from visitors U.S.$17,000,000; expenditures by nationals abroad U.S.$15,000,000.
Population economically active (1985–86): total 716,270; activity rate of total population 45.7% (participation rates: ages 15–64, 79.8%; female 45.5%; unemployed [1988] 23%).

Price and earnings indexes (1985 = 100)

	1985	1986	1987	1988	1989	1990	1991
Consumer price index	100.1	118.0	131.9	147.0	168.6	188.2	221.5
Earnings index	...	...	...	...	...	...	...

Household income and expenditure. Average household size (1986) 4.8; average annual income per household (1986–87) M 2,832 (U.S.$1,297); sources of income (1986–87): transfer payments 44.7%, self-employment 27.8%, wages and salaries 22.4%, other 5.1%; expenditure (1986–87): food 33.4%,

clothing 21.9%, household durable goods 13.2%, education and recreation 5.2%, housing 4.8%, transportation 4.7%.
Gross national product (at current market prices; 1990): U.S.$832,000,000 (U.S.$470 per capita).

Structure of gross domestic product and labour force

	1990 in value M '000,000	1990 % of total value	1985–86 labour force	1985–86 % of labour force
Agriculture	204.3	14.7	474,171	66.2
Mining	6.0	0.4	6,446	0.9
Manufacturing	180.8	13.0	19,339	2.7
Construction	259.7	18.7	31,516	4.4
Public utilities	9.2	0.7	1,433	0.2
Transp. and commun.	51.6	3.7	5,014	0.7
Trade	97.0	7.0	22,204	3.1
Finance	71.0	5.1	3,581	0.5
Pub. admin., defense	210.4	15.1	17,907	2.5
Services	107.6	7.7	126,780	17.7
Other	194.0[2]	13.9[2]	7,879	1.1
TOTAL	1,391.4[3]	100.0	716,270[4]	100.0[4]

Land use (1990): meadows and pastures 65.9%; agricultural and under permanent cultivation 10.5%; other 23.6%.

Foreign trade[5]

Balance of trade (current prices)

	1985	1986	1987	1988	1989	1990
M '000,000	−746.9	−834.6	−830.5	−1,106.3	−1,072.1	−1,517.0
% of total	88.2%	87.8%	81.4%	79.2%	75.8%	83.2%

Imports (1990): M 1,670,700,000 (1985; manufactured goods [excluding chemicals, machinery, and transport equipment] 44.1%, of which clothing 9.3%, footwear 4.2%, blankets and traveling rugs 3.8%; food and live animals 18.2%, of which cereals [all forms] 6.1%, sugar [all forms] 2.3%; machinery and transport equipment 15.5%, of which trucks and vans 2.0%; petroleum products 7.3%). *Major import sources:* Customs Union of Southern Africa 94.1%; Asia 2.9%; Europe 2.6%, of which European Economic Community 2.5%; the Americas 0.2%.
Exports (1990): M 153,740,000 (miscellaneous manufactured goods 58.7%; food and live animals, of which cornmeal 3.9%; crude materials 10.1%, of which wool 9.5%; beverages and tobacco 1.9%; chemicals 1.4%). *Major export destinations:* Customs Union of Southern Africa 59.5%; Europe 20.2%, of which European Economic Community 19.6%; the Americas 18.5%; Asia 0.4%.

Transport and communications

Transport. Railroads (1991): length 1.6 mi, 2.6 km. Roads (1988): total length 2,930 mi, 4,715 km (paved 12%). Vehicles (1986): passenger cars 6,363; trucks and buses 15,379. Merchant marine: vessels (100 gross tons and over) none. Air transport (1990): passenger-mi 8,027,000, passenger-km 12,918,-000; short ton-mi cargo 55,500, metric ton-km cargo 81,000; airports (1992) with scheduled flights 1.
Communications. Daily newspapers (1990): total number 3; total circulation 9,000; circulation per 1,000 population 5. Radio (1991): total number of receivers 420,000 (1 per 4.3 persons). Television (1991): total number of receivers 50,000 (1 per 36 persons). Telephones (1988): 28,583 (1 per 56 persons).

Education and health

Education (1989–90)

	schools	teachers	students	student/teacher ratio
Primary (age 6–12)	1,190	6,452	351,652	54.5
Secondary (age 13–17)	175	2,213	45,064	20.4
Voc., teacher tr.	10	201	2,348	11.7
Higher	1	133	1,273	9.6

Educational attainment (1986–87). Percentage of population age 10 and over having: no formal education 22.9%; primary 52.8%; secondary 23.2%; higher 0.6%. *Literacy* (1985): total population age 15 and over literate 655,400 (73.6%); males literate 273,800 (62.4%); females literate 381,600 (84.5%).
Health: physicians 103 (1 per 15,728 persons); hospital beds 2,409 (1 per 672 persons); infant mortality rate per 1,000 live births (1990–95) 89.
Food (1988–90): daily per capita caloric intake 2,121 (vegetable products 93%, animal products 7%); 93% of FAO recommended minimum requirement.

Military

Total active duty personnel (1992): 2,000[6]. *Military expenditure as percentage of GNP* (1987): 2.2% (world 5.4%); per capita expenditure U.S.$10.

[1]Traditional monarchy under control of military since February 1990. [2]Indirect taxes less imputed bank service charges. [3]Detail does not add to total given because of rounding. [4]Approximately 110,000 to 120,000 persons (45% of Lesotho's adult male labour force) were employed in South Africa in 1987. [5]Import figures are f.o.b. in balance of trade and c.i.f. in commodities and trading partners. [6]Royal Lesotho Defence Force.

Liberia

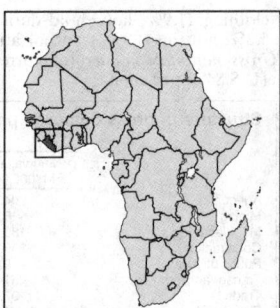

Official name: Republic of Liberia.
Form of government: interim extraconstitutional administration with one interim legislative house (Interim National Assembly [51])[1].
Head of state and government: President.
Capital: Monrovia.
Official language: English.
Official religion: none.
Monetary unit: 1 Liberian dollar (L$) = 100 cents; valuation (Oct. 5, 1992) 1 U.S.$ = L$1.00; 1 £ = L$1.70.

Area and population		area		population
		sq mi	sq km	1986 estimate
Counties	**Capitals**			
Bong	Gbarnga	3,127	8,099	268,100
Grand Bassa	Buchanan	3,382	8,759	166,900
Grand Cape Mount	Robertsport	2,250	5,827	83,900
Grand Gedeh	Zwedru	6,575	17,029	109,000
Grand Kru[2]	Barclayville	3	3	3
Lofa	Voinjama	7,475	19,360	261,000
Margibi[4]	Kakata	1,260	3,263	104,000
Maryland	Harper	2,066[3]	5,351[3]	137,700[3]
Montserrado	Bensonville	1,058	2,740	582,400
Nimba	Sanniquellie	4,650	12,043	325,700
Sinoe	Greenville	3,959	10,254	65,400
Territories				
Bomi	Tubmanburg	755	1,955	67,300
Rivercess	Rivercess City	1,693	4,385	39,900
TOTAL		38,250	99,067[5]	2,221,300[6]

Demography

Population (1992): 2,780,000[7].
Density (1992): persons per sq mi 72.7, persons per sq km 28.1.
Urban-rural (1990): urban 45.9%; rural 54.1%.
Sex distribution (1990): male 50.60%; female 49.40%.
Age breakdown (1984): under 15, 43.2%; 15–29, 28.2%; 30–44, 14.7%; 45–59, 7.7%; 60–74, 4.4%; 75 and over, 1.8%.
Population projection: (2000) 3,602,000; (2010) 4,933,000.
Doubling time: 22 years.
Ethnic composition (1984): Kpelle 19.4%; Bassa 13.8%; Grebo 9.0%; Gio 7.8%; Kru 7.3%; Mano 7.1%; other 35.6%.
Religious affiliation (1984): Christian 67.7%; Muslim 13.8%[8]; traditional beliefs and other 18.5%.
Major cities (1974): Monrovia 421,058[9]; Buchanan 23,999; Congo Town 21,495; Yekepa 14,189; Tubmanburg 14,089.

Vital statistics

Birth rate per 1,000 population (1990–95): 46.7 (world avg. 26.4).
Death rate per 1,000 population (1990–95): 14.1 (world avg. 9.2).
Natural increase rate per 1,000 population (1990–95): 32.6 (world avg. 17.2).
Total fertility rate (avg. births per childbearing woman; 1990–95): 6.7.
Marriage rate per 1,000 population: n.a.
Divorce rate per 1,000 population: n.a.
Life expectancy at birth (1990–95): male 54.0 years; female 57.0 years.
Major causes of death per 100,000 population (1985)[10]: complications during pregnancy 632.6[9]; malaria 79.8; pneumonia 64.2; anemia 50.2; malnutrition 23.4; measles 12.7.

National economy

Budget (1990). Revenue: L$391,000,000 (1989; income and profits taxes 33.9%; import duties and consular fees 29.6%; excise tax 12.7%; property taxes 1.9%). Expenditures: L$460,000,000 (1988; current expenditure 91.1%, of which wages and salaries 34.1%, interest on public debt 13.1%, goods and services 7.8%, subsidies and grants 5.1%; development expenditure 8.9%).
Tourism: receipts from visitors (1986) U.S.$6,000,000; expenditures by nationals abroad, n.a.
Population economically active (1984): total 704,321; activity rate 33.5% (participation rates: ages 15–64, 56.3%; female 41.0%; unemployed 12.5%).

Price and earnings indexes (1985 = 100)							
	1983	1984	1985	1986	1987	1988	1989
Consumer price index	99.4	100.6	100.0	103.6	108.8	119.3	130.6
Earnings index	...	...	...	...	...	...	...

Production (metric tons except as noted). Agriculture, forestry, fishing (1991): cassava 300,000, sugarcane 225,000, rice 110,000, bananas 80,000, plantains 33,000, sweet potatoes 18,000, yams 15,000, natural rubber 9,000, oranges 7,000, pineapples 7,000, green coffee 2,000, cacao beans 2,000; livestock (number of live animals) 220,000 sheep, 220,000 goats, 120,000 pigs, 38,000 cattle, 4,000,000 chickens; roundwood (1990) 6,056,000 cu m; fish catch (1990) 16,000. Mining and quarrying (1989): iron ore 7,007,000; diamonds 350,000 carats[11]; gold 23,600 troy oz. Manufacturing (1986): cement 96,350; palm oil 35,000; cigarettes 91,235,200 units; soft drinks 115,092 hectolitres; beer 105,547 hectolitres. Construction: n.a. Energy production (consumption): electricity (kW-hr; 1990) 565,000,000 (565,000,000); coal, none (n.a.); crude petroleum, none (n.a.); petroleum products (metric tons; 1990) none (144,000); natural gas, none (n.a.).

Public debt (external, outstanding; 1990): U.S.$1,126,000,000.
Household income and expenditure. Average household size (1983) 4.3; income per household: n.a.; sources of income: n.a.; expenditure (1963)[12]: food 34.4%, rent 14.9%, clothing and footwear 13.8%, household goods and services 6.1%, beverages and tobacco 5.7%, fuel and light 5.0%.
Gross national product (1988): U.S.$975,200,000 (U.S.$400 per capita).

Structure of gross domestic product and labour force				
	1988		1984	
	in value L$'000,000	% of total value	labour force	% of labour force
Agriculture	412.0	35.6	481,177	68.3
Mining	115.0	9.9	17,500	2.5
Manufacturing	80.4	6.9	10,699	1.5
Construction	28.8	2.5	4,072	0.6
Public utilities	18.8	1.6	2,878	0.4
Transp. and commun.	79.1	6.8	13,986	2.0
Trade	64.2	5.5	46,850	6.6
Finance	136.1	11.8	2,117	0.3
Pub. admin., defense	109.1	9.4 }	61,168	8.7
Services	35.5	3.1 }		
Other	79.3[13]	6.8[13]	63,874[14]	9.1[14]
TOTAL	1,158.3	100.0[5]	704,321	100.0

Land use (1990): forested 18.0%; meadows and pastures 58.9%; agricultural and under permanent cultivation 3.9%; other 19.2%.

Foreign trade

Balance of trade (current prices)						
	1983	1984	1985	1986	1987	1988
L$'000,000	+73.8	+137.6	+189.4	+201.1	+115.9	+160.6
% of total	9.4%	17.1%	27.8%	33.1%	17.9%	25.4%

Imports (1988): L$447,000,000 (machinery and transport equipment 31.1%, petroleum and petroleum products 22.7%, basic manufactures 16.4%, food and live animals 16.4%, chemicals 5.8%). *Major import sources* (1986): United States 32.2%; West Germany 9.7%; Japan 8.4%; United Kingdom 7.6%; The Netherlands 6.3%; Spain 2.5%; Belgium-Luxembourg 2.5%.
Exports (1988): L$398,400,000 (iron ore 55.1%, rubber 28.0%, logs and timber 8.4%, diamonds 2.1%, gold 1.8%, coffee 1.5%). *Major export destinations* (1986): West Germany 32.2%; United States 19.3%; Italy 15.7%; France 8.8%; Belgium-Luxembourg 5.8%; The Netherlands 4.4%; Spain 4.1%.

Transport and communications

Transport. Railroads (1990)[15]: route length 304 mi, 490 km; short ton-mi cargo 1,746,000,000[11, 16], metric ton-km cargo 2,549,000,000[11, 16]. Roads (1987): total length 5,011 mi, 8,064 km (paved 9%). Vehicles (1990): passenger cars 8,000; trucks and buses 4,000. Merchant marine (1991): vessels (100 gross tons and over) 1,605; total deadweight tonnage 93,640,340. Air transport (1980): passenger-mi 10,600,000, passenger-km 17,000,000; short ton-mi cargo 68,000, metric ton-km cargo 100,000; airports (1992) 1.
Communications. Daily newspapers (1990): total number 1[17]; total circulation 30,000; circulation per 1,000 population 11.5. Radio (1991): 600,000 receivers (1 per 4.5 persons). Television (1991): 45,000 receivers (1 per 60 persons). Telephones (1988): 8,736 (1 per 278 persons).

Education and health

Education (1980)	schools	teachers	students	student/ teacher ratio
Primary (age 6–12)	1,651	9,099	227,431	25.0
Secondary (age 13–18)	419	1,129	51,666	45.8
Voc., teacher tr.	6	63	2,322	36.9
Higher	3	472[18]	5,095[18]	10.8[18]

Educational attainment (1974). Percentage of population age 25 and over having: no grade completed 87.1%; some primary education 4.8%; complete primary 1.5%; some secondary 5.1%; higher 1.5%. *Literacy* (1990): total population age 15 and over literate 547,800 (39.5%); males literate 350,200 (49.8%); females literate 197,600 (28.8%).
Health: physicians (1983) 221 (1 per 9,324 persons); hospital beds (1981) 3,000 (1 per 653 persons); infant mortality rate (1985–90) 87.0.
Food (1988–90): daily per capita caloric intake 2,259 (vegetable products 96%, animal products 4%); 98% of FAO recommended minimum requirement.

Military

Total active duty personnel (1992): as a result of the civil war, the Armed Forces of Liberia (AFL) has ceased to exist. *Military expenditure as percentage of GNP* (1987): 3.8% (world 5.4%); per capita expenditure U.S.$17.

[1]The government of Pres. Samuel K. Doe ended with his death Sept. 9, 1990. Subsequently, Doe's surviving forces, two principal insurrectionist groups, and a five-power occupying force raised by ECOWAS (the Economic Community of West African States) created an interim caretaker administration in November 1990. The National Patriotic Reconstruction Assembly, a guerrilla organization opposed to ECOWAS, effectively controlled 95% of Liberia in April 1992. [2]New county created from Kru Coast and Sasstown territories and part of Maryland county. [3]Figures for Grand Kru included in Maryland. [4]New county created from Marshall and Gibi territories. [5]Detail does not add to total given because of rounding. [6]Includes 10,000 persons not accounted for. [7]Includes Liberian refugees residing in surrounding countries, estimated to number about 600,000. [8]Some external sources estimate the Muslim population to exceed 30%. [9]1984. [10]Hospital inpatient morbidity rates. [11]1988. [12]Monrovia only. [13]Import duties less imputed bank service charges. [14]Includes 34,991 unemployed. [15]For iron-ore transport only. [16]Lamco and Bong Mining Company railroads only. [17]In 1990, owing to the civil war, the publication of a number of newspapers was suspended. [18]1987.

Libya

Official name: al-Jamāhīrīyah al-ʿArabīyah al-Lībīyah ash-Shaʿbīyah al-Ishtirākīyah (Socialist People's Libyan Arab Jamahiriya).
Form of government: socialist state with one policy-making body (General People's Congress [750]).
Chief of state: Muʿammar al-Qadhdhāfī (de facto)[1]; Secretary of General People's Congress (de jure).
Head of government: Secretary of the General People's Committee (prime minister).
Capital: Tripoli[2].
Official language: Arabic.
Official religion: Islam.
Monetary unit: 1 Libyan dinar (LD) = 1,000 dirhams; valuation (Oct. 5, 1992) 1 Libyan dinar = U.S.$3.85 = £2.27.

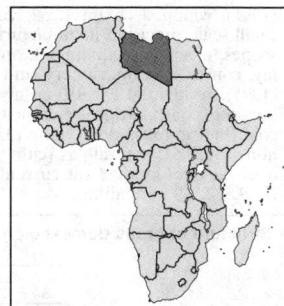

Area and population

Baladīyāt	Capitals	area sq mi	area sq km	population 1988 estimate
Banghāzī	Banghāzī	5,800	15,000	512,200
al-Jabal al-Akhḍar	al-Bayḍā'	14,300	37,000	308,300
al-Jabal al-Gharbī	Gharyān	33,600	87,000	204,300
Khalīj Surt	Surt	145,200	376,000	382,100
al-Kufrah	al-Kufrah	186,900	484,000	23,800
Margib	al-Khums	11,200	29,000	408,900
Marzūq	Marzūq	135,100	350,000	45,200
Nikāt al-Khums	Zuwārah	39,000	101,000	196,000
Sabhā	Sabhā	31,700	82,000	121,700
Ṭarābulus	Tripoli (Ṭarābulus)	1,200	3,000	1,083,100
Ṭubruq	Ṭubruq	32,400	84,000	110,900
Wādī al-Ḥaiṭ	Awbārī	40,500	105,000	49,600
az-Zāwiyah	az-Zāwiyah	1,500	4,000	326,500
TOTAL		678,400	1,757,000	3,772,600

Demography

Population (1992): 4,447,000.
Density (1992): persons per sq mi 6.6, persons per sq km 2.5.
Urban-rural (1990): urban 70.2%; rural 29.8%.
Sex distribution (1987): male 52.37%; female 47.63%.
Age breakdown (1987): under 15, 47.2%; 15–29, 24.8%; 30–44, 15.7%; 45–59, 8.4%; 60 and over, 3.9%.
Population projection: (2000) 5,559,000; (2010) 6,990,000.
Doubling time: 18 years.
Ethnic composition (1984): Libyan Arab and Berber 89.0%; other 11.0%.
Religious affiliation (1982): Sunnī Muslim 97.0%; other 3.0%.
Major cities (1988): Tripoli 591,100; Banghāzī 446,250; Miṣrātah 121,700.

Vital statistics

Birth rate per 1,000 population (1988): 46.0 (world avg. 27.1).
Death rate per 1,000 population (1988): 7.0 (world avg. 9.8).
Natural increase rate per 1,000 population (1988): 39.0 (world avg. 17.3).
Total fertility rate (avg. births per childbearing woman; 1990): 6.6.
Marriage rate per 1,000 population (1981): 4.3.
Divorce rate per 1,000 population (1981): 1.1.
Life expectancy at birth (1990–95): male 61.6 years; female 65.0 years.
Major causes of death per 100,000 population: n.a.; however, the major causes of death during the 1980s were pneumonia, dysentery and diarrhea, cardiovascular disease, accidents, and malignant neoplasms (cancers).

National economy

Budget (1990–91). Revenue: LD 2,640,000,000 (current revenue 55.7%, of which oil revenues 31.0%, income taxes 24.0%, customs duties 17.0%, stamp duties 4.2%; capital revenue 44.3%). Expenditures: LD 2,640,000,000 (current expenditures 55.7%, of which allocations to municipal people's committees 39.4%, education and scientific research 4.3%, health 2.7%; capital expenditures 44.3%, of which agriculture and land reclamation 13.6%, industry 5.3%).
Production (metric tons except as noted). Agriculture, forestry, fishing (1991): watermelons 210,000, tomatoes 170,000, wheat 150,000, potatoes 148,000, barley 145,000, oranges 95,000, onions 85,000, dates 75,000, olives 70,000, almonds 34,000; livestock (number of live animals) 5,500,000 sheep, 1,200,-000 goats, 150,000 cattle, 150,000 camels, 55,000,000 chickens; roundwood (1990) 643,000 cu m; fish catch (1990) 7,800. Mining and quarrying (1989): lime 260,000; gypsum 180,000; salt 12,000. Manufacturing (1989): cement 3,500,000; methanol 620,000; urea 450,000; canned fruits and vegetables 380,000; ammonia 300,000; shoes 6,000,000 pairs; blankets 400,000 units. Construction (gross value in LD; 1982): residential 127,051,000; nonresidential 200,877,000. Energy production (consumption): electricity (kW-hr; 1990) 19,000,000,000 (19,000,000,000); coal (metric tons; 1990) none (5,000); crude petroleum (barrels; 1990) 492,750,000 (80,300,000); petroleum products (metric tons; 1990) 13,200,000 (7,163,000); natural gas (cu m; 1990) 9,513,000,000 (8,273,000,000).
Population economically active (1987): total 1,005,000; activity rate of total population 25.0% (participation rates: ages 10 and over, 37.6%; female 6.9%; unemployed, n.a.).

Price and earnings indexes (1980 = 100)

	1980	1981	1982	1983	1984	1985	1986
Consumer price index	100.0	...	137.6	152.2	165.8	...	...
Earnings index	...	...	...	...	...	...	...

Gross national product (at current market prices; 1989): U.S.$23,333,000,000 (U.S.$5,310 per capita).

Structure of gross domestic product and labour force

	1989 in value LD '000,000	% of total value	labour force	% of labour force
Agriculture	395.5	5.5	191,600	19.2
Mining and quarrying	2,008.0	27.8	23,700	2.4
Manufacturing	560.5	7.8	92,200	9.3
Construction	920.0	12.7	156,300	15.7
Public utilities	152.5	2.1	28,500	2.9
Transportation and communications	440.0	6.1	78,500	7.9
Trade	490.5	6.8	52,800	5.3
Finance, insurance	622.0	8.6	15,000	1.5
Pub. admin., defense	1,543.5	21.4	308,000	31.0
Services	91.0	1.2	48,300	4.8
TOTAL	7,223.5	100.0	994,900	100.0

Public debt (long-term debt; 1988): U.S.$182,000,000[3].
Household income and expenditure. Average household size (1980) 5.1; income per household: n.a.; sources of income: n.a.; expenditure (1977): food 37.2%, housing and energy 32.2%, transportation 9.4%, education and recreation 8.5%, clothing 6.9%, health care 3.3%.
Land use (1990): forested 0.4%; meadows and pastures 7.6%; agricultural and under permanent cultivation 1.2%; desert and built-up areas 90.8%.
Tourism (1990): receipts from visitors U.S.$6,000,000; expenditures by nationals abroad U.S.$424,000,000.

Foreign trade[4]

Balance of trade (current prices)

	1984	1985	1986	1987	1988	1989
U.S.$'000,000	+2,555	+4,583	+1,246	+364	−537	+2,253
% of total	13.1%	28.5%	12.3%	3.3%	4.8%	17.3%

Imports (1989): U.S.$5,497,000,000 (foodstuffs 42.3%, agricultural goods 18.5%, medical goods 12.4%, capital goods 12.4%). *Major import sources:* Italy 21.2%; West Germany 12.2%; United Kingdom 6.8%; France 6.2%.
Exports (1989): U.S.$7,750,000,000 (crude petroleum 96.8%). *Major export destinations:* Italy 57.8%; West Germany 26.6%; Spain 13.8%; France 8.3%; United Kingdom 3.0%.

Transport and communications

Transport. Railroads: none. Roads (1987): total length 11,992 mi, 19,300 km (paved 56%). Vehicles (1989): passenger cars 448,000; trucks and buses 322,000. Merchant marine (1991): vessels (100 gross tons and over) 129; total deadweight tonnage 1,469,747. Air transport (1990)[5]: passenger-mi 1,222,963,000, passenger-km 1,968,172,000; short ton-mi cargo 7,080,000, metric ton-km cargo 10,336,000; airports (1992) with scheduled flights 11.
Communications. Daily newspapers (1990): total number 1; circulation 40,000; circulation per 1,000 population 9.5. Radio (1991): total number of receivers 1,000,000 (1 per 4.3 persons). Television (1991): total number of receivers 500,000 (1 per 8.7 persons). Telephones (1988): 500,000 (1 per 8.0 persons).

Education and health

Education (1987–88)

	schools	teachers[6]	students	student/ teacher ratio[6]
Primary (age 6–12)	2,744[7]	41,515	974,295	19.0
Secondary (age 13–18)	1,555[7]	30,524	389,530	12.2
Teacher tr.	195[7, 8]	3,051	70,335	10.0
Higher	6	...	40,365	...

Educational attainment (1973). Percentage of population age 25 and over having: no formal schooling (illiterate) 72.7%; incomplete primary education 18.8%; complete primary 3.5%; secondary 4.0%; higher 1.0%. *Literacy* (1990): percentage of total population age 15 and over literate 63.8%; males literate 75.4%; females literate 50.4%.
Health: physicians (1984) 5,272 (1 per 690 persons); hospital beds (1982) 16,051 (1 per 207 persons); infant mortality rate per 1,000 live births (1985–90) 82.0.
Food (1988–90): daily per capita caloric intake 3,293 (vegetable products 86%, animal products 14%); 140% of FAO recommended minimum requirement.

Military

Total active duty personnel (1992): 85,000 (army 64.7%, navy 9.4%, air force 25.9%). *Military expenditure as percentage of GNP* (1989): 14.9% (world 4.9%); per capita expenditure U.S.$808.

[1]No formal titled office exists. [2]Policy-making body (General People's Congress) meets in Surt. [3]Includes external long-term debt not guaranteed by the government. [4]Imports c.i.f. [5]Libyan Arab Airlines. [6]1984–85. [7]1982–83. [8]Includes vocational.

Liechtenstein

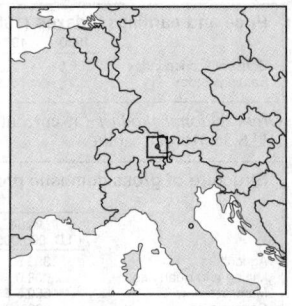

Official name: Fürstentum
  Liechtenstein
  (Principality of Liechtenstein).
Form of government: constitutional
  monarchy with one legislative house
  (Diet [25]).
Chief of state: Prince.
Head of government: Head of the
  Government.
Capital: Vaduz.
Official language: German.
Official religion: none.
Monetary unit: 1 Swiss franc
  (Sw F) = 100 centimes; valuation (Oct.
  5, 1992) 1 U.S.$ = Sw F 1.23;
  1 £ = Sw F 2.09.

Area and population

Communes	area		population
	sq mi	sq km	1992 estimate[1]
Balzers	7.6	19.6	3,752
Eschen	4.0	10.3	3,138
Gamprin	2.4	6.1	1,003
Mauren	2.9	7.5	2,919
Planken	2.0	5.3	312
Ruggell	2.9	7.4	1,516
Schaan	10.3	26.8	5,035
Schellenberg	1.4	3.5	835
Triesen	10.2	26.4	3,586
Triesenberg	11.5	29.8	2,403
Vaduz	6.7	17.3	4,887
TOTAL	61.8[2]	160.0	29,386

Demography

Population (1992): 29,600.
Density (1992): persons per sq mi 479.6, persons per sq km 185.2.
Urban-rural: n.a.
Sex distribution (1992): male 48.92%; female 51.08%.
Age breakdown (1992): under 15, 19.4%; 15–29, 24.8%; 30–44, 25.4%; 45–59,
  16.8%; 60–74, 9.5%; 75 and over, 4.1%.
Population projection: (2000) 33,300; (2010) 38,500.
Doubling time: 89 years.
National composition (1992): Liechtensteiner 62.5%; Swiss 15.6%; Austrian
  7.6%; German 3.7%; other 10.6%.
Religious affiliation (1992): Roman Catholic 86.3%; Protestant 7.9%; other
  5.8%.
Major cities (1990): Schaan 4,930; Vaduz 4,874.

Vital statistics

Birth rate per 1,000 population (1991): 14.2 (world avg. 26.4); legitimate
  92.3%; illegitimate 7.7%.
Death rate per 1,000 population (1991): 6.4 (world avg. 9.2).
Natural increase rate per 1,000 population (1991): 7.8 (world avg. 17.2).
Total fertility rate: n.a.
Marriage rate per 1,000 population (1991): 6.3.
Divorce rate per 1,000 population (1991): 1.2.
Life expectancy at birth (1991): male 69.5 years; female 73.6 years.
Major causes of death per 100,000 population (1991): diseases of the cir-
  culatory system 277.9, of which heart disease 178.0 (including ischemic
  heart disease 102.7); malignant neoplasms (cancers) 154.1; diseases of the
  respiratory system 41.1; accidents, poisoning, and acts of violence 30.8 (including suicide 6.8).

National economy

Budget (1991). Revenue: Sw F 439,394,370 (taxes and interest 67.6%; post,
  telephone, and telegraph 15.7%; other revenue sources include real estate capital-gains taxes and death and estate taxes). Expenditures: Sw F
  436,001,034 (financial affairs 40.9%; education 15.0%; post, telephone, and
  telegraph 12.4%; social affairs 11.6%).
Public debt: none.
Tourism (1991): 71,211 tourist arrivals; receipts from visitors, n.a.; expenditures by nationals abroad, n.a.
Population economically active (1991[3]): total 14,698; activity rate of total
  population 50.0% (participation rates: ages 15–64, 70.8%; female 37.8%;
  unemployed 0.1%).

Price and earnings indexes (December 1982 = 100)

	1986	1987	1988	1989	1990	1991	1992[4]
Consumer price index[5]	108.2	109.7	111.8	115.4	121.6	128.7	133.7
Monthly earnings index							

Household income and expenditure. Average household size (1980) 3.0; income per household: n.a.; sources of earned income (1987): wages and
  salaries 92.9%, self-employment 7.1%; expenditure (1986)[6]: food 21.3%,
  rent 18.0%, education and self-improvement 16.3%, transportation 13.3%,
  health 7.7%, clothing 6.6%.
Production (metric tons except as noted). Agriculture, forestry, fishing (1991):
  silo corn (maize) 27,880[7], milk 13,146, potatoes 1,040[7], wheat 460[7], barley
  416[7]; livestock (number of live animals) 6,204 cattle, 3,543 pigs, 2,689 sheep;
  commercial timber 10,333 cu m. Mining and quarrying: n.a. Manufacturing

(1991): whipped cream 1,252; yogurt 77; cheese 6; wine 789.8 hectolitres;
small-scale precision manufacturing includes optical lenses, electron micro-
scopes, electronic equipment, and high-vacuum pumps; metal manufacturing, construction machinery, and ceramics are also important. Construction
(1991): residential 256,930 cu m; nonresidential 271,094 cu m. Energy production (consumption): electricity (kW-hr; 1991) 153,777,000 (224,944,000);
coal (metric tons; 1991) none (35); petroleum products (metric tons; 1991)
none (56,505); natural gas (cu m; 1991) none (15,755,000).
Gross national product (at current market prices; 1990): *c.* U.S.$940,000,000
(U.S.$32,790 per capita).

Structure of gross domestic product and labour force

	1988		1991	
	in value Sw F '000	% of total value	labour force	% of labour force
Agriculture	...	...	346	2.4
Mining	...	...	57	0.4
Manufacturing	...	...	4,811	32.7
Construction	...	...	1,217	8.3
Public utilities	...	...	182	1.2
Transportation and communications	...	...	454	3.1
Trade	...	...	1,666	11.3
Finance, insurance, real estate	...	...	1,052	7.2
Pub. admin., defense	...	...	609	4.1
Services	...	...	4,195	28.5
Other	...	...	109[8]	0.7[8]
TOTAL	1,700,000	100.0	14,698	100.0[2]

Land use (latest): forested 34.8%; meadows and pastures 15.7%; agricultural
  and under permanent cultivation 24.3%; other 25.2%.

Foreign trade

Balance of trade (current prices)

	1986	1987	1988	1989	1990	1991
Sw F '000,000	+761.6	+737.6	+745.2	+742.8	+757.1	+822.8
% of total	44.4%	42.0%	37.3%	29.8%	27.8%	31.4%

Imports (1991): Sw F 898,280,000 (machinery and transport equipment 29.2%;
  limestone, cement, and other building materials 13.7%; metal products
  10.8%; unrefined and semifabricated metal 6.1%; chemical products 6.0%;
  food, beverages, and tobacco 2.2%, of which fruits and vegetables 0.2%;
  wood and cork 1.1%). *Major import sources:* n.a.
Exports (1991): Sw F 1,721,100,000 (machinery and transport equipment
  47.3%; metal products 18.0%; other finished goods 13.8%; chemical products
  8.1%; limestone, cement, and other building materials 6.9%). *Major export
  destinations:* European Economic Community countries 45.4%; Switzerland
  14.8%; other European Free Trade Association countries 5.5%.

Transport and communications

Transport. Railroads (1990): length 11.5 mi, 18.5 km; passenger and cargo
  traffic, n.a. Roads (1989): total length 201 mi, 323 km. Vehicles (1990):
  passenger cars 16,891; trucks and buses 1,673. Merchant marine: none. Air
  transport: none.
Communications. Daily newspapers (1990): total number 2; total circulation
  17,195; circulation per 1,000 population 598. Radio (1990): total number
  of receivers 10,279 (1 per 2.8 persons). Television (1990): total number of
  receivers 9,787 (1 per 2.9 persons). Telephones (1991): 17,499 (1 per 1.7
  person).

Education and health

Education (1990–91)

	schools	teachers	students	student/ teacher ratio
Primary (age 7–12)	14	115	1,892	16.4
Secondary (age 13–19)	8	80	1,092	13.6
Vocational[9]	1	74[10]	147	...

Educational attainment (1980). Percentage of population age 25 and over
  having: no formal schooling 0.2%; primary and lower secondary education
  47.6%; higher secondary and vocational 41.0%; some postsecondary 6.6%;
  university 4.6%. *Literacy:* virtually 100%.
Health: physicians (1991) 29 (1 per 1,007 persons); hospital beds (1985) 100
  (1 per 269 persons); infant mortality rate per 1,000 live births (1985–89) 7.0.
Food (1987–89)[11]: daily per capita caloric intake 3,530 (vegetable products 62%, animal products 38%); 133% of FAO recommended minimum
  requirement.

Military

Total active duty personnel: none. *Military expenditure as percentage of GNP:*
  none.

---

[1]January 1. [2]Detail does not add to total given because of rounding. [3]December 31.
[4]May. [5]The index is for Switzerland, which is united with Liechtenstein in a customs
and monetary union. [6]Household expenditures are taken from a 1986 Swiss sample
survey; a similarity of consumption patterns is assumed. [7]1987. [8]Includes 80 unclassi-
fiable and 29 unemployed persons. [9]1988–89. [10]Includes part-time teachers. [11]Figures
are derived from statistics for Switzerland and Austria.

Lithuania

Official name: Lietuvos Respublika (Republic of Lithuania).
Form of government: unitary multi-party republic with a single legislative body, the Diet (141)[1].
Head of state and government: Chairman of the Diet[1].
Capital: Vilnius.
Official language: Lithuanian.
Official religion: none.
Monetary unit (until Sept. 30, 1992): 1 ruble = 100 kopecks; valuation (Oct. 5, 1992) 1 U.S.$ = 316.82 rubles; 1£ = 538.59 rubles. Coupons were introduced Oct. 1, 1992, to permit eventual replacement of the ruble by a new national currency, the lit.

Area and population		area		population
		sq mi	sq km	1989 estimate
Cities of republic jurisdiction				
Alytus	—	1	3	73,100
Birštonas	—	5	12	4,100
Druskininkai	—	8	22	22,500
Kaunas	—	46	120	422,600
Klaipėda	—	27	71	204,000
Marijampolė	—	8	20	50,500
Neringa	—	35	90	2,500
Palanga	—	27	69	19,400
Panevėžys	—	12	30	126,500
Šiauliai	—	27	69	145,000
Vilnius	—	110	286	582,400
Regions	**Capitals**			
Akmenė	Naujoji Akmenė	407	1,055	37,800
Alytus	Alytus	545	1,411	32,700
Anykščiai	Anykščiai	681	1,765	38,300
Biržai	Biržai	570	1,476	38,600
Ignalina	Ignalina	581	1,505	59,000
Jonava	Jonava	364	944	54,000
Joniškis	Joniškis	445	1,152	32,900
Jurbarkas	Jurbarkas	582	1,507	40,200
Kaišiadorys	Kaišiadorys	451	1,169	40,200
Kaunas	Kaunas	588	1,522	85,500
Kėdainiai	Kėdainiai	647	1,677	69,400
Kelmė	Kelmė	660	1,710	42,900
Klaipėda	Gargždai	527	1,366	45,000
Kretinga	Kretinga	385	997	44,100
Kupiškis	Kupiškis	417	1,080	25,900
Lazdijai	Lazdijai	595	1,542	33,400
Marijampolė	Marijampolė	599	1,551	49,200
Mažeikiai	Mažeikiai	390	1,009	61,200
Molėtai	Molėtai	528	1,368	27,300
Pakruojis	Pakruojis	508	1,316	30,700
Panevėžys	Panevėžys	849	2,199	41,900
Pasvalys	Pasvalys	498	1,289	36,800
Plungė	Plungė	653	1,691	53,900
Prienai	Prienai	443	1,148	39,500
Radviliškis	Radviliškis	631	1,635	54,800
Raseiniai	Raseiniai	607	1,573	46,100
Rokiškis	Rokiškis	697	1,806	47,800
Šakiai	Šakiai	623	1,613	41,600
Šalčininkai	Šalčininkai	578	1,498	41,500
Šiauliai	Šiauliai	701	1,815	49,900
Šilalė	Šilalė	459	1,188	31,700
Šilutė	Šilutė	866	2,243	69,000
Širvintos	Širvintos	350	906	21,500
Škuodas	Škuodas	352	911	26,600
Švenčionys	Švenčionys	653	1,692	37,800
Tauragė	Tauragė	455	1,179	52,600
Telšiai	Telšiai	556	1,439	59,200
Trakai	Trakai	640	1,657	81,700
Ukmergė	Ukmergė	539	1,395	52,500
Utena	Utena	475	1,229	52,300
Varėna	Varėna	933	2,416	38,500
Vilkaviškis	Vilkaviškis	497	1,286	52,200
Vilnius	Vilnius	855	2,215	93,800
Zarasai	Zarasai	515	1,334	25,900
TOTAL		25,213[2]	65,301[2]	3,690,000

Demography

Population (1992): 3,802,000.
Density (1992): persons per sq mi 150.8, persons per sq km 58.2.
Urban-rural (1992): urban 68.8%; rural 31.2%.
Sex distribution (1992): male 47.38%; female 52.62%.
Age breakdown (1989): under 15, 22.6%; 15–29, 23.8%; 30–44, 20.0%; 45–59, 17.9%; 60–74, 10.9%; 75 and over, 4.8%.
Population projection: (2000) 3,935,000; (2010) 4,110,000.
Ethnic composition (1989): Lithuanian 79.6%; Russian 9.4%; Polish 7.0%; Belorussian 1.7%; other 2.3%.
Religious affiliation (1986): believers are mainly Roman Catholic.
Major cities (1992): Vilnius 596,900; Kaunas 433,600; Klaipėda 208,300; Šiauliai 149,000; Panevėžys 132,300.

Vital statistics

Birth rate per 1,000 population (1991): 15.0 (world avg. 26.4).
Death rate per 1,000 population (1991): 10.9 (world avg. 9.2).
Natural increase rate per 1,000 population (1991): 4.1 (world avg. 17.2).
Life expectancy at birth (1990): male 66.6 years; female 76.3 years.
Major causes of death per 100,000 population (1990): circulatory diseases 604; cancers 189; accidents 140; respiratory diseases 45.

National economy

Budget (1990). Revenue: 4,674,300,000 rubles (turnover tax 34.6%; profits of state enterprises 25.5%; individual income tax 10.9%). Expenditures: 4,491,400,000 rubles (national economy 56.5%; social and cultural affairs 37.9%, of which education 16.9%).
Production (metric tons except as noted). Agriculture, forestry, fishing (1991): grains 3,347,500, corn (maize) 1,712,200, potatoes 1,508,300, sugar beets 811,200; livestock (head; 1992) 2,196,600 cattle, 2,179,900 pigs, 16,994,000 poultry; roundwood 1,443,000 cu m; fish catch 317,000. Mining and quarrying (1986): limestone, dolomite, and clay are quarried for construction and manufacturing. Manufacturing (value of production, '000,000 rubles; 1991): processed foods 11,147; light industry 7,627; machinery and metalworking equipment 6,557; paper and pulp products 2,066; construction materials 1,864. Construction (1991): residential construction 1,015,000 sq m. Energy production (consumption): electricity (kW-hr; 1991) 29,363,000,000 (16,613,600,000).
Gross national product (1991): 56,661,000,000 rubles (15,084 rubles per capita)[3].

Structure of gross national product and labour force				
	1991			
	in value '000,000 rubles	% of total value	labour force[4]	% of labour force[4]
Agriculture, forestry	11,122	19.6	337,500	17.8
Manufacturing, mining	37,200	65.7	566,900	29.9
Construction	3,520	6.2	182,700	9.6
Transp. and commun.	1,380	2.4	132,500	7.0
Trade			188,600	9.9
Finance, pub. admin., defense	3,439	6.1	43,800	2.3
Services, public utilities			412,500	21.7
Other			33,100	1.7
TOTAL	56,661	100.0	1,897,600	100.0[5]

Population economically active (1991): total 2,112,200; activity rate of total population 56.2% (participation rates: ages 16–60/55[6], 89.9%; female 53.8%; unemployed [1991] 105,000–140,000 [c. 5–6.6%]).

Price and earnings indexes (1985 = 100)							
	1985	1986	1987	1988	1989	1990	1991
Consumer price index							
Monthly earnings index[4]	100.0	102.6	107.4	117.4	128.4	149.2	387.9

Household income and expenditure. Average household size (1989) 3.2; sources of income (1991): wages 60.6%, self-employment in agriculture 18.5%, pensions and grants 14.3%, other 6.6%; expenditures (1991): food 36.0%, clothing and footwear 15.9%, taxes 9.5%, furniture and household goods 8.3%.
Land use (1990): forest 28%; pasture 17%; agricultural 35%; other 20%.

Foreign trade

Imports (1991): 8,728,800,000 rubles (from Commonwealth of Independent States [CIS]: machinery 21.2%, petroleum and gas 16.4%, light industry 16.2%, chemicals 12.3%, foodstuffs 9.9%). Major import sources: CIS-member countries 82.7%, of which Russia 49.6%, Ukraine 10.4%; Latvia 4.7%; EEC 2.8%.
Exports (1991): 12,300,100,000 rubles (to CIS: food products 31.5%, light industry 28.5%, machinery 20.0%). Major export destinations: CIS countries 85.1%, of which Russia 56.5%, Ukraine 11.4%; Latvia 6.7%; Estonia 2.3%; EEC 2.1%.

Transport and communications

Transport. Railroads: length (1991) 3,033 km; (1991) passenger-km 3,225,000,000; metric ton-km cargo 17,748,000,000. Roads (1991): total length 44,500 km (paved 80%). Merchant marine: n.a. Air transport (1991): passenger-km 2,432,000,000; metric ton-km cargo 15,000,000; airports (1992) 3.
Communications. Daily newspapers (1983): number 12; circulation (1990) all newspapers 5,780,000; circulation per 1,000 population 1,547. Radio (1987): 3,082,000 receivers (1 per 1.2 persons). Television (1987): 1,272,000 receivers (1 per 2.9 persons). Telephones (1991): 870,500 (1 per 4.3 persons).

Education and health

Education (1991–92)	schools	teachers	students	student/ teacher ratio
Primary Secondary	2,147	42,897	509,800	11.9
Voc., teacher tr.	108	4,870	46,200	9.5
Higher	14	9,003[7]	60,500	7.3[7]

Educational attainment (1979). Percentage of persons having: incomplete primary 12.5%; complete primary 31.7%; incomplete secondary 23.1%; complete secondary 25.0%; higher 7.7%. Literacy: n.a.
Health (1991): physicians 14,464 (1 per 262 persons); hospital beds 45,900 (1 per 82 persons); infant mortality rate 14.3.

Military

Total active duty personnel (1992): 7,000. The U.S.S.R. was responsible for Lithuania's external security until 1991; about 15,000 Soviet troops remained in Lithuania at year-end 1992. A Lithuanian military force of about 7,000 was under development in 1992.

[1]A constitution providing for a presidential form of government was approved by referendum Oct. 25, 1992, with elections scheduled for early 1993. [2]Total includes 12 sq mi (30 sq km) not distributed by administrative subdivision. [3]No U.S.$ value is offered, as Soviet GNP data are very speculative. [4]State sector only. [5]Detail does not add to total given because of rounding. [6]Males retire at age 60, females at 55. [7]1987–88.

Luxembourg

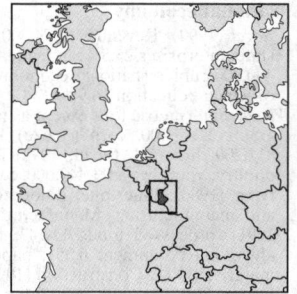

Official name: Groussherzogtum
Lëtzebuerg (Luxemburgian);
Grand-Duché de Luxembourg
(French); Grossherzogtum
Luxemburg (German) (Grand Duchy
of Luxembourg).
Form of government: constitutional
monarchy with two legislative houses
(Council of State [21]; Chamber of
Deputies [60]).
Chief of state: Grand Duke.
Head of government: Prime Minister.
Capital: Luxembourg.
Official language: none: Luxemburgian
(national); French (used for
most official purposes); German
(lingua franca).
Official religion: none.
Monetary unit: 1 Luxembourg franc
(Lux F) = 100 centimes; valuation
(Oct. 5, 1992) 1 U.S.$ =
Lux F 28.85; 1 £ = Lux F 49.05.

Area and population	area		population
Districts **Cantons**	sq mi	sq km	1991 census
Diekirch	447	1,157	56,896
Clervaux	128	332	10,263
Diekirch	92	239	23,258
Redange	103	267	11,073
Vianden	21	54	2,720
Wiltz	102	265	9,582
Grevenmacher	203	525	42,837
Echternach	72	186	11,726
Grevenmacher	82	211	18,113
Remich	49	128	12,998
Luxembourg	349	904	284,329
Capellen	77	199	31,817
Esch	94	243	116,389
Luxembourg (Ville et Campagne)	92	238	116,988
Mersch	86	224	19,135
TOTAL	999	2,586	384,062

Demography

Population (1992): 387,000.
Density (1992): persons per sq mi 387.4, persons per sq km 149.6.
Urban-rural (1991): urban 85.9%; rural 14.1%.
Sex distribution (1991): male 48.78%; female 51.22%.
Age breakdown (1989): under 15, 17.1%; 15–29, 22.3%; 30–44, 23.3%; 45–59,
18.5%; 60–74, 12.8%; 75 and over, 6.0%.
Population projection: (2000) 395,000; (2010) 403,000.
Doubling time: not applicable; population stable.
Ethnic composition (nationality; 1990): Luxemburger 72.5%; Portuguese 9.0%;
Italian 5.4%; French 3.4%; Belgian 2.5%; German 2.4%; other 4.8%.
Religious affiliation (1989): Roman Catholic 94.6%; Protestant 1.1%; other
4.3%.
Major cities (1991): Luxembourg 75,377; Esch-sur-Alzette 24,012; Differdange
15,699; Dudelange 14,677; Pétange 12,345.

Vital statistics

Birth rate per 1,000 population (1990): 12.9 (world avg. 27.1); legitimate
87.1%; illegitimate 12.9%.
Death rate per 1,000 population (1990): 9.9 (world avg. 9.8).
Natural increase rate per 1,000 population (1990): 3.0 (world avg. 17.3).
Total fertility rate (avg. births per childbearing woman; 1990): 1.6.
Marriage rate per 1,000 population (1990): 6.1.
Divorce rate per 1,000 population (1990): 2.0.
Life expectancy at birth (1985–87): male 70.6 years; female 77.9 years.
Major causes of death per 100,000 population (1990): circulatory diseases
465.9, of which cerebrovascular disease 163.4, ischemic heart disease and
myocardial infarction 130.7; malignant neoplasms (cancers) 253.8; accidents
and suicide 62.3, of which suicide 17.8.

National economy

Budget (1992). Revenue: Lux F 116,375,800,000 (income and excise taxes
55.7%, customs taxes 11.6%). Expenditures: Lux F 114,914,000,000 (social
security 20.8%, education 11.7%, transportation 9.0%, administration 7.2%,
defense 2.6%, debt service 1.8%).
Public debt (1990): U.S.$348,000,000.
Production (metric tons except as noted). Agriculture, forestry, fishing (1990):
barley 59,200, wheat 37,000, potatoes 24,900, oats 16,000, wine grapes 15,100;
livestock (number of live animals; 1991) 219,544 cattle, 66,592 pigs; roundwood (1987) 327,600 cu m. Mining and quarrying (1987): metal ores, none;
sand and gravel 956,810; gypsum 420,000; crushed stone 344,841. Manufacturing (1990): steel ingots and castings 3,560,000; pig iron 2,645,000; milk
282,800; meat products 21,900; wine 151,100 hectolitres. Construction (1990):
residential and semiresidential 490,958 sq m; nonresidential 171,530 sq m.
Energy production (consumption): electricity (kW-hr; 1990) 1,374,000,000
(5,242,000,000); coal (metric tons; 1990) none (197,000); crude petroleum,
none (n.a.); petroleum products (metric tons; 1990) none (1,462,000); natural gas (cu m; 1990) none (461,286,000).

Gross national product (at current market prices; 1990): U.S.$10,875,000,000
(U.S.$28,770 per capita).

Structure of gross domestic product and labour force				
	1990			
	in value Lux F '000,000	% of total value	labour force	% of labour force
Agriculture	5,880	2.0	5,851	3.7
Mining	269	0.1 }	30,561	19.2
Manufacturing	76,277	26.2 }		
Construction	20,409	7.0	13,590	8.5
Public utilities	5,817	2.0	1,434	0.9
Transp. and commun.	19,871	6.8	10,448	6.5
Trade	47,737	16.4	31,666	19.8
Finance	38,380	13.2	19,521	12.2
Pub. admin., defense	40,829	14.0 }	43,472	27.2
Services	44,270	15.2 }		
Other	−8,234[1]	−2.9[1]	3,166	2.0
TOTAL	291,505	100.0	159,709	100.0

Population economically active (1990): total 159,709; activity rate of total
population 46.8% (participation rates: ages 15–64, 60.6%; female 34.8%;
unemployed 1.6%).

Price and earnings indexes (1985 = 100)							
	1985	1986	1987	1988	1989	1990	1991
Consumer price index	100.0	100.3	100.2	101.7	105.1	109.0	112.4
Hourly earnings index	100.0	106.0	106.5	108.9	114.7	...	...

Household income and expenditure. Average household size (1991) 2.6; income per household (1982) Lux F 751,800 (U.S.$16,455); sources of income
(1987): wages and salaries 88.6%, self-employment 9.1%, transfer payments
2.3%; expenditure (1989): transportation and communications 18.4%, food
and beverages 14.6%, housing 14.6%, household goods and furniture 10.6%,
health 7.9%, clothing and footwear 6.6%.
Tourism (1989): receipts from visitors U.S.$286,000,000.
Land use (1988): forested 34.3%; meadows and pastures 27.3%; agricultural
and under permanent cultivation 21.5%; other 16.9%.

Foreign trade

Balance of trade (current prices)						
	1986	1987	1988	1989	1990	1991
Lux F '000,000	−13,390	−24,530	−20,549	−31,200	−40,200	−62,800
% of total	3.9%	7.0%	5.2%	6.8%	8.7%	13.4%

Imports (1991): Lux F 277,110,000,000 (metal products, machinery, and
transport equipment 48.7%, of which transport equipment 14.2%; mineral
products 11.9%; chemical products 7.8%; food and beverages 4.5%). *Major
import sources:* Belgium 39.2%; Germany 30.0%; France 11.9%; The Netherlands 4.1%; Italy 2.1%; U.S. 2.0%.
Exports (1991): Lux F 214,353,000,000 (metal products, machinery, and transport equipment 56.9%, of which transport equipment 7.5%; plastic materials
and rubber manufactures 12.6%; textile yarn, fabrics, and related products
6.0%; chemical products 5.0%; food, beverages, and tobacco 3.6%). *Major
export destinations:* Germany 29.6%; France 17.3%; Belgium 17.1%; The
Netherlands 5.1%; U.K. 5.1%; Italy 4.4%; U.S. 3.3%.

Transport and communications

Transport. Railroads (1990): route length 168 mi, 271 km; passenger-mi 164,-
000,000, passenger-km 264,000,000; short ton-mi cargo 490,000,000, metric
ton-km cargo 720,000,000. Roads (1990): total length 3,163 mi, 5,091 km
(paved 99%). Vehicles (1991): passenger cars 191,588; trucks and buses
19,535. Merchant marine (1991): vessels (100 gross tons and over) 51; total deadweight tonnage 2,854,324. Air transport (1990): passenger arrivals
484,278, departures 489,000; short ton-mi cargo 606,902,000[2], metric ton-km
cargo 886,062,000[2]; airports (1992) with scheduled flights 1.
Communications. Daily newspapers (1990): total number 5; total circulation
130,000; circulation per 1,000 population 340. Radio (1991): 230,000 receivers
(1 per 1.7 persons). Television (1991): 100,000 receivers (1 per 3.8 persons).
Telephones (1990): 183,700 (1 per 2.1 persons).

Education and health

Education (1990–91)	schools	teachers	students	student/ teacher ratio
Primary (age 6–11)[3]	...	1,764[4]	26,612	...
Secondary (age 12–18)	...	}	7,594	...
Voc., teacher tr.	...	1,922[7]	11,430	...
Higher	...	}	4,957	

Educational attainment: n.a. Literacy (1990): virtually 100% literate.
Health (1990): physicians 766 (1 per 498 persons); hospital beds 4,483 (1 per
85 persons); infant mortality rate per 1,000 live births 7.3.
Food (1987–89): daily per capita caloric intake[5] 3,947 (vegetable products
61%, animal products 39%); 150% of FAO recommended minimum.

Military

Total active duty personnel (1991): 800 (army 100.0%). *Military expenditure
as percentage of GNP* (1988): 1.0% (world 5.0%); per capita expenditure
U.S.$235.

[1]Imputed bank service charges. [2]1987. [3]Public schools only. [4]1989–90. [5]Figures for
Belgium-Luxembourg.

Macau

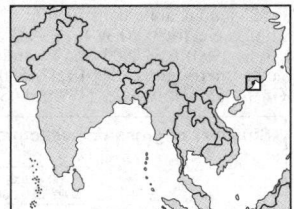

Official name: Ao-men (Chinese);
Macau (Portuguese).
Political status: special territory[1]
(Portugal) with one legislative house
(Legislative Assembly [23[2]]).
Head of state and government:
Governor.
Capital: Macau.
Official languages[1]: Chinese
(Cantonese); Portuguese.
Official religion: Roman Catholicism.
Monetary unit: 1 pataca[3] = 100 avos;
valuation (Oct. 5, 1992)
1 U.S.$ = 7.97 patacas; 1 £ = 13.54
patacas.

Area and population

Districts Parishes	Capital	area sq mi	area sq km	population 1991 census
Islands		4.4	11.3	10,314
Nossa Senhora Carmo (Taipa)	—	1.6	4.1	7,168
São Francisco Xavier (Coloane)	—	2.8	7.2	3,146
Macau	Macau	2.6[4]	6.7	342,548
Nossa Senhora Fátima	—	1.0	2.7	126,224
Santo António	—	0.4	1.1	108,654
São Lázaro	—	0.2	0.6	32,622
São Lourenço	—	0.4	0.9	45,814
Sé	—	0.5	1.4	29,234
Marine Area	—	—	—	2,831
TOTAL		6.9[4]	18.0	355,693

Demography

Population (1992): 367,000.
Density (1992): persons per sq mi 53,188, persons per sq km 20,389.
Urban-rural (1991): urban, virtually 100%[5].
Sex distribution (1991): male 48.49%; female 51.51%.
Age breakdown (1991): under 15, 24.6%; 15–29, 26.9%; 30–44, 29.4%; 45–59,
9.5%; 60–74, 7.3%; 75 and over, 2.3%.
Population projection: (2000) 493,000; (2010) 713,000.
Doubling time: 58 years.
Nationality (1991): Chinese 68.2%; Portuguese 27.9%; English 1.8%; other
2.1%.
Religious affiliation (1981): Buddhist 45.1%; Christian 8.7%, of which Roman
Catholic 7.4%, Protestant 1.3%; nonreligious 45.8%; other 0.4%.
Major city (1991): Macau 342,548.

Vital statistics

Birth rate per 1,000 population (1990): 15.3 (world avg. 27.1); legitimate, n.a.;
illegitimate, n.a.
Death rate per 1,000 population (1990): 3.3 (world avg. 9.8).
Natural increase rate per 1,000 population (1990): 12.0 (world avg. 17.3).
Total fertility rate (avg. births per childbearing woman; 1988): 1.5.
Marriage rate per 1,000 population (1990): 4.0.
Divorce rate per 1,000 population (1990): 0.1.
Life expectancy at birth (1988): male 75.1 years; female 80.3 years.
Major causes of death per 100,000 population (1990): diseases of the cir-
culatory system 145.2; malignant neoplasms (cancers) 73.1; diseases of the
respiratory system 52.5; accidents, poisoning, and violence 31.8; diseases of
the digestive system 14.5; infectious and parasitic diseases 11.9; diseases of
the genitourinary system 10.6; obstetric and perinatal disorders 8.0; endocrine and metabolic disorders 7.2.

National economy

Budget (1990). Revenue: 5,997,823,000 patacas (recurrent receipts 68.6%,
autonomous agency receipts 17.1%, capital receipts 14.2%). Expenditures:
5,489,985,000 patacas (recurrent payments 56.3%, capital payments 25.0%,
autonomous agency expenditures 18.7%).
Tourism (1990): number of tourist arrivals 5,942,200.
Land use (1991): built-on area, wasteland, and other 100.0%.
Gross domestic product (at current market prices; 1990): U.S.$3,685,000,000
(U.S.$8,000 per capita).

Structure of labour force

	1990 labour force	1990 % of labour force
Agriculture	...	...
Mining	...	...
Manufacturing	72,050	32.6
Construction	19,330	8.7
Public utilities	2,538	1.1
Transportation and communications	10,349	4.7
Trade	47,708	21.6
Finance	7,550	3.4
Public administration	...	...
Services	...	...
Other	61,701	27.9
TOTAL	221,226	100.0

Production (metric tons except as noted). Agriculture, forestry, fishing (1991):
grapes 3,000, eggs 645; livestock (number of live animals) 1,000 pigs; fish
catch 2,530. Mining and quarrying (1982): granite 656,920. Manufacturing
(output in '000,000 patacas; 1989): wearing apparel 6,315; textiles 2,766;
paper and paper products 246; leather products 212; electrical appliances
202; printing and publishing 138; food products 135; metal products 126.
Construction (1990): residential 696,100 sq m; nonresidential 225,500 sq
m. Energy production (consumption): electricity (kW-hr; 1990) 790,000,000
(879,000,000); coal (metric tons) none (none); crude petroleum (barrels)
none (none); petroleum products (metric tons; 1990) none (335,000); natural
gas, none (n.a.).
Public debt (long-term, external; 1988): U.S.$190,000,000.
Population economically active (1990): total 221,226; activity rate of total
population 64.9% (participation rates [1981]: over age 10, 61.5%; female
37.1%; unemployed 3.9%).

Price and earnings indexes (1985 = 100)

	1984	1985	1986	1987	1988	1989	1990
Consumer price index[6]	96.6	100.0	102.0	106.7	115.1	125.1	135.1
Earnings index	...	...	...	...	...	...	...

Household income and expenditure. Average household size (1980): 4.8; income per household: n.a.; sources of income: n.a.; expenditure (1981–82):
food 42.0%, housing 22.8%, education, health, and other services 8.1%,
clothing and footwear 7.3%, transportation 4.9%, energy 4.9%, household
durable goods 2.9%.

Foreign trade

Balance of trade (current prices)

	1985	1986	1987	1988	1989	1990
'000,000 patacas	+1,002	+1,312	+2,216.4	+1,632.0	+1,314.7	+1,295.1
% of total	7.5%	8.2%	10.9%	7.2%	5.2%	5.0%

Imports (1990): 12,343,101,000 patacas (raw materials 60.3%, capital goods
11.0%, foodstuffs 9.0%, fuels and lubricants 4.7%). *Major import sources:*
Hong Kong 42.2%; China 17.8%; Japan 11.5%; European Economic Community 8.4%; Taiwan 7.1%; United States 5.1%.
Exports (1990): 13,638,192,000 patacas (textiles and garments 69.5%, toys
9.8%, hides and skins 2.4%, wool and woolen articles 2.1%, artificial
flowers 1.9%). *Major export destinations:* United States 36.2%; European
Economic Community 34.3%; Hong Kong 13.0%; China 4.5%; Japan 3.1%;
Australia 1.4%.

Transport and communications

Transport. Railroads: none. Roads (1988): total length 60 mi, 97 km (paved
100%). Vehicles (1990): passenger cars 27,639; trucks and buses 5,335.
Merchant marine (1990): vessels 6; total gross tonnage 3,512. Air transport:
none.
Communications. Daily newspapers (1990): total number 10; total circulation
242,000[7]; circulation per 1,000 population 568[7]. Radio (1991): total number
of receivers 250,000 (1 per 1.9 persons). Television (1991): total number of
receivers 70,000 (1 per 6.8 persons). Telephones (1990): 96,353 (1 per 3.4
persons).

Education and health

Education (1989–90)

	schools	teachers	students	student/ teacher ratio
Primary (age 6–11)	69	1,104	32,639	29.6
Secondary (age 12–18)	22	918	16,862	18.4
Teacher tr.	3	20	294	14.7
Higher	7	624	7,838	12.6

Educational attainment (1981). Percentage of economically active population
age 10 and over having: no formal schooling 13.8%; primary education
22.6%; some secondary 27.2%; complete secondary 20.5%; some postsecondary 13.0%; higher 2.9%. *Literacy* (1981): total population age 10 and
over literate 127,359 (61.3%); males literate 80,102 (76.4%); females literate
47,257 (46.2%).
Health (1990): physicians 329 (1 per 1,176 persons); hospital beds 1,183 (1
per 327 persons); infant mortality rate per 1,000 live births 8.4.
Food (1988–90): daily per capita caloric intake 2,294 (vegetable products 76%,
animal products 24%); 100% of FAO recommended minimum requirement.

Military

Total active duty personnel (1990): the Portuguese garrison has been replaced
by a paramilitary force of 1,800 men drawn from the Chinese residents only.

---

[1]A new Organic Law (constitution), effective May 10, 1990, made Chinese co-official
(with Portuguese) and changed the territory's status to special territory. [2]Enlarged to
23 seats by 1990 Organic Law from previous 17 seats. [3]The pataca free-floats with the
Hong Kong dollar and has a parity of 1.03 patacas = HK$1.00. [4]Detail does not add
to total given because of rounding. [5]0.8% of Macau's population live on sampans and
other vessels. [6]Excluding rent. [7]1986.

Macedonia

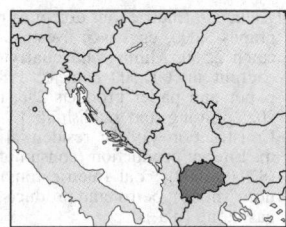

Official name: Republika Makedonija
  (Republic of Macedonia).
Form of government: multiparty
  republic with a unicameral legislature
  (Assembly [120]).
Head of state: President.
Head of government: Prime Minister.
Capital: Skopje.
Official language: Macedonian.
Official religion: none.
Monetary unit: Denar; valuation
  (Oct. 5, 1992) 1 Yugoslav dinar
  (Din) = Denar 2.25; 1 U.S.$ = Denar
  508; 1 £ = Denar 863.

Area and population (1991 census)

Districts	area sq km[1]	population	Districts	area sq km[1]	population
Berovo	806	20,395	Negotino	734	23,246
Bitolj	1,798	122,173	Ohrid	1,069	65,531
Brod	924	11,671	Prilep	1,675	98,327
Debar	274	26,266	Probištip	326	16,556
Delčevo	589	25,531	Radoviš	735	30,975
Demir Hisar	443	12,078	Resen	739	23,203
Gevgelija	757	35,055	Škopje	1,818	563,301
Gostivar	1,341	116,107	Štip	815	51,947
Kavadarci	1,132	41,852	Struga	507	62,950
Kičevo	854	55,157	Strumica	952	94,517
Kočani	570	50,122	Sveti Nikole	649	21,569
Kratovo	376	11,329	Tetovo	1,080	180,654
Kriva Palanka	720	25,601	Titov Veles	1,536	67,535
Kruševo	239	12,620	Valandovo	331	12,264
Kumanovo	1,212	135,529	Vinica	432	19,903
			TOTAL	25,713[2]	2,033,964

Demography

Population (1992): 2,050,000.
Density (1992): persons per sq mi 206.5, persons per sq km 79.7.
Urban-rural (1981): urban 53.9%; rural 46.1%.
Sex distribution (1981): male 50.71%; female 49.29%.
Age breakdown (1981): under 15, 29.1%; 15–29, 27.1%; 30–44, 19.6%; 45–59, 14.8%; 60–74, 7.1%; 75 and over, 2.2%.
Population projection: (2000) 2,157,000; (2010) 2,298,000.
Doubling time: 70 years.
Ethnic composition (1981): Macedonian 67.0%; Albanian 19.8%; Turkish 4.5%; Serb 2.3%; Gypsy 2.3%; Bosnian 2.1%; other 2.0%.
Religious affiliation (1991): most believers are Christians and are predominantly adherents of the Eastern Orthodox Church; other Christians include members of the Macedonian Orthodox Church and the Roman Catholic Church; there is also a substantial Islamic community and a small Jewish community.
Major cities (1991)[3]: Skopje 563,301; Tetovo 180,654; Kumanovo 135,529; Bitolj (Bitola) 122,173.

Vital statistics

Birth rate per 1,000 population (1990): 16.9 (world avg. 27.1).
Death rate per 1,000 population (1990): 7.0 (world avg. 9.8).
Natural increase rate per 1,000 population (1990): 9.9 (world avg. 17.3).
Total fertility rate (avg. births per childbearing woman): n.a.
Marriage rate per 1,000 population (1989): 7.9.
Divorce rate per 1,000 population (1989): 0.5.
Life expectancy at birth (1980–82): male 68.0 years; female 72.0 years.
Major causes of death per 100,000 population (1989): diseases of the circulatory system 346.2; malignant neoplasms (cancers) 102.4; diseases of the respiratory system 49.8; accidents, violence, and poisoning 34.5; diseases of the digestive system 18.2.

National economy

Budget. Revenue: n.a. Expenditures: n.a.
External debt: U.S.$850,000,000.
Tourism (1991): total tourist nights 2,766,000.
Production (metric tons except as noted). Agriculture, forestry, fishing (1991): wheat 341,000, grapes 258,000, corn (maize) 141,000, potatoes 135,000, plums 29,000; livestock (number of live animals) 2,297,000 sheep, 287,000 cattle, 179,000 pigs, 5,729,000 poultry; roundwood (1990) 1,063,000 cu m; fish catch (1990) 1,572 (all freshwater). Mining and quarrying (1990): copper ore 3,706,000; lead-zinc ore 1,357,000; kaolin and dolomite 467,000; gypsum 54,000; lime 47,000; iron ore 44,000; refined silver 15,000; sand and gravel 194,000 cu m. Manufacturing (1990): rolled zinc products 6,907,000; hot rolled iron slabs 619,000; steel plates 507,000; crude steel 247,000; fermented tobacco 26,481; hydrochloric acid 24,000; refined lead 22,000; soap and detergents 21,000; refined zinc 17,000; cotton yarn 15,000; household ceramics 8,872; husked rice 8,715; fancy candies 7,392; aluminum ingots 5,500; zinc alloys 5,000; woolen yarn 5,000; chocolate products 2,903; glues 2,700; cosmetics 2,225; knitted underwear 2,075; knitted outerwear 2,034; cheese 1,149; rubber goods 348; cocoa powder 41; cotton fabric 40,000,000 sq m; ready-made underwear 30,000,000 sq m; ready-made outerwear 20,000,000 sq m; woolen fabric 9,000,000 sq m; silk fabric 5,900,000 sq m; upper shoe leather 2,259,000 sq m; domestic animal fur 851,000 sq m; carpets 555,000 sq m; leather outerwear 446,000 sq m; wine 634,000 hectolitres; brandy 39,000 hectolitres; leather footwear 6,638,000 pairs; silver and gold jewelry 994 kg; refrigerators 156,000 units; toys 85,000 units; buses 953 units. Construction

(residential units constructed; 1990): 10,189. Energy production (consumption): electricity (kW-hr; 1990) 5,755,000,000 (5,369,000,000); coal (metric tons; 1990) 6,635,000 (n.a.); crude petroleum, none (n.a.); petroleum products (metric tons; 1990) 1,472,500 (n.a.); natural gas, none (n.a.).
Gross national product (1990): U.S.$4,856,000,000 (U.S.$2,399 per capita).

Structure of gross domestic product and labour force

	1989		1990	
	in value Din '000,000	% of total value	labour force	% of labour force
Agriculture	2,105	16.8	42,184	8.3
Mining and manufacturing	6,979	55.6	213,169	42.0
Construction	709	5.7	47,637	9.4
Public utilities	166	1.3	10,476	2.1
Transp. and commun.	543	4.3	26,249	5.2
Trade	1,807	14.4	63,593	12.5
Finance			14,422	2.8
Public admin., defense	240	1.9	89,597	17.7
Services				
Other				
TOTAL	12,549	100.0	507,327[4]	100.0[4]

Population economically active (1991): total 493,000; activity rate of total population 24.2% (participation rates: ages 15–64, n.a.; female [1990] 37.7%; unemployed, n.a.).

Price and earnings indexes (1985 = 100)

	1984	1985	1986	1987	1988	1989	1990[5]
Consumer price index	58	100	189	406	1,190	16,200	113,000
Annual earnings index[6]	104	100	106	100	92	120	100

Land use (1990): forested 37.4%; meadows and pastures 25.9%; agricultural and under permanent cultivation 15.6%; other 21.1%.
Household income and expenditure. Average household size (1991) 3.9; income per household (1990) Din 75,556 (U.S.$6,676); sources of income (1990): wages and salaries 57.7%, self-employment 17.1%, transfer payments 16.2%, other 9.0%; expenditure (1988): food 37.5%, clothing and footwear 7.8%, fuel and light 7.8%, transportation and communications 6.5%, housing 5.7%, drink and tobacco 4.9%, household durable goods 4.2%, education and entertainment 3.3%, health care 3.0%.

Foreign trade

Balance of trade (current prices)

	1985	1986	1987	1988	1989	1990
Din '000,000	−8	−10	−11	−51	−596	−6,047
% of total	22.3%	21.0%	10.0%	12.9%	11.9%	31.6%

Imports (1990): Din 12,601,000,000 (raw materials and semifinished goods 33.2%; consumer goods 28.4%, of which food, beverages, and tobacco 14.8%, clothing and footwear 4.9%, medicine and pharmaceuticals 0.6%; mineral fuels 19.1%; basic manufactures 10.7%; machinery 6.7%, of which electrical motors 1.0%; transport equipment 0.5%). *Major import sources:* n.a.
Exports (1990): Din 6,555,000,000 (clothing and footwear 20.7%; machinery and transport equipment 14.2%, of which transport equipment 1.3%; chemicals 4.6%; food 3.6%; textiles 2.2%; medicine and pharmaceuticals 0.8%; furniture 0.5%). *Major export destinations:* n.a.

Transport and communications

Transport. Railroads (1990): length 431 mi, 693 km; passengers transported 4,406,000; cargo transported 6,377,000 tons. Roads (1991): total length 6,582 mi, 10,591 km (paved 48%). Vehicles (1990): passenger cars 230,993; trucks and buses 22,594. Merchant marine: n.a. Air transport: n.a.; airports (1992) with scheduled flights 1.
Communications. Daily newspapers (1990): total number 2; total circulation 52,000; circulation per 1,000 population 26. Radio (1989): total number of receivers 449,000 (1 per 4.5 persons). Television (1989): total number of receivers 385,000 (1 per 5.2 persons). Telephones (1990): 356,837 (1 per 5.7 persons).

Education and health

Education (1990–91)

	schools	teachers	students	student/ teacher ratio
Primary (age 7–14)	1,063	12,987	268,963	20.7
Secondary (age 15–18)	90	4,200	74,886	17.8
Higher	27	2,101	26,413	12.6

Educational attainment (1981). Percentage of population age 15 and over having: less than full primary education 45.3%; primary 28.1%; secondary 21.2%; postsecondary and higher 5.1%; unknown 0.3%. *Literacy* (1981): total population age 10 and over literate 1,365,000 (89.1%); males literate 729,000 (94.2%); females literate 636,000 (83.8%).
Health (1990): physicians (1989) 4,331 (1 per 464 persons); hospital beds 11,804 (1 per 171 persons); infant mortality rate per 1,000 live births 35.3.

Military

Total active duty personnel (1992): 20,000 (army 100%). *Military expenditure as percentage of GNP:* n.a.; per capita expenditure, n.a.

[1]One sq km is equal to approximately 0.3861 sq mi. [2]Total includes 280 sq km of inland water not distributed in above districts. [3]Populations refer to municipal areas, not cities proper. [4]Excludes 15,000 workers in the private sector. [5]On Jan. 1, 1990, the new Yugoslav dinar, equal to 10,000 old dinars, was introduced. [6]Based on worker real net personal income.

Madagascar

Official name: Repoblika Demokratika Malagasy (Malagasy); République Démocratique de Madagascar (French) (Democratic Republic of Madagascar).
Form of government: transitional regime[1].
Chief of state: President.
Chief of transitional regime: President of the High State Authority.
Head of government: Prime Minister.
Capital: Antananarivo.
Official languages: Malagasy; French.
Official religion: none.
Monetary unit: 1 Malagasy franc (FMG) = 100 centimes; valuation (Oct. 5, 1992) 1 U.S.$ = FMG 1,512; 1 £ = FMG 2,570.

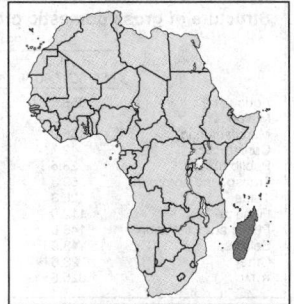

Area and population

Provinces	Capitals	area		population
		sq mi	sq km	1990 estimate[2]
Antananarivo	Antananarivo	22,503	58,283	3,998,000
Antsirañana	Antsirañana	16,620	43,046	750,000
Fianarantsoa	Fianarantsoa	39,526	102,373	2,539,000
Mahajanga	Mahajanga	57,924	150,023	1,314,000
Toamasina	Toamasina	27,765	71,911	1,663,000
Toliara	Toliara	62,319	161,405	1,740,000
TOTAL		226,658	587,041	12,004,000

Demography

Population (1992): 12,804,000.
Density (1992): persons per sq mi 56.5, persons per sq km 21.8.
Urban-rural (1990): urban 21.9%; rural 78.1%.
Sex distribution (1990): male 49.97%; female 50.03%.
Age breakdown (1990): under 15, 45.6%; 15–29, 26.7%; 30–44, 15.0%; 45–59, 7.7%; 60–69, 3.3%; 70 and over, 1.7%.
Population projection: (2000) 16,627,000; (2010) 22,827,000.
Doubling time: 22 years.
Ethnic composition (1983): Malagasy 98.9%, of which Merina 26.6%, Betsimisaraka 14.9%, Betsileo 11.7%, Tsimihety 7.4%, Sakalava 6.4%; Antandroy 5.3%; Comorian 0.3%; Indian and Pakistani 0.2%; French 0.2%; Chinese 0.1%; other 0.3%.
Religious affiliation (1980): Christian 51.0%, of which Roman Catholic 26.0%, Protestant 22.8%; traditional beliefs 47.0%; Muslim 1.7%; other 0.3%.
Major cities (1990): Antananarivo 802,400; Toamasina 145,400; Fianarantsoa 124,500; Mahajanga 122,000.

Vital statistics

Birth rate per 1,000 population (1990–95): 44.9 (world avg. 26.4); legitimate, n.a.; illegitimate, n.a.
Death rate per 1,000 population (1990–95): 12.6 (world avg. 9.2).
Natural increase rate per 1,000 population (1990–95): 32.3 (world avg. 17.2).
Total fertility rate (avg. births per childbearing woman; 1989): 5.9.
Marriage rate per 1,000 population: n.a.
Divorce rate per 1,000 population: n.a.
Life expectancy at birth (1990–95): male 54.0 years; female 57.0 years.
Major causes of death per 100,000 population: n.a.; however, major causes of death include communicable diseases and respiratory diseases.

National economy

Budget (1992). Revenue: FMG 1,315,000,000,000 (1987; taxes 80.2%, of which import duties 14.9%, excises 14.8%, income tax 12.5%; other receipts 19.8%). Expenditures: FMG 1,315,000,000,000 (1987; current expenditure 77.3%, of which education 12.3%, defense 7.5%, health 4.2%, agriculture 1.8%, public works 0.7%).
Tourism (1990): receipts from visitors U.S.$29,000,000; expenditures by nationals abroad U.S.$34,000,000.
Production (metric tons except as noted). Agriculture, forestry, fishing (1991): cassava 2,290,000, rice 2,200,000, sugarcane 1,970,000, sweet potatoes 487,000, potatoes 273,000, bananas 218,000, mangoes 205,000, corn (maize) 150,000, taro 99,000 oranges 84,000, coconuts 84,000, coffee 80,000, pineapples 50,000, beans 37,000, seed cotton 35,000, peanuts (groundnuts) 30,000; livestock (number of live animals) 10,265,000 cattle, 1,461,000 pigs, 1,283,000 goats, 753,000 sheep, 22,000,000 chickens; roundwood (1990) 8,096,000 cu m; fish catch (1990) 106,740. Mining and quarrying (1989): chromite concentrate 152,600; salt 35,000; graphite 16,000; mica 600; gold 2,894 troy oz[3]. Manufacturing (1987): sugar 101,216; cement 44,490; soap 14,563; vegetable oils 7,956; cigarettes 2,669; chewing tobacco 878; beer 240,257 hectolitres. Construction (1986)[4]: residential 19,700 sq m; nonresidential 5,700 sq m. Energy production (consumption): electricity (kW-hr; 1990) 566,000,000 (566,000,000); coal (metric tons; 1990) none (13,000); crude petroleum (barrels; 1990) none (1,209,000); petroleum products (metric tons; 1990) 152,000 (292,000); natural gas, none (n.a.).
Household income and expenditure. Average household size (1980) 4.7; average annual income per household, n.a.; sources of income (1975)[5]: wages and salaries 58.8%, self-employment 14.1%, other 27.1%; expenditure (1983)[6]: food 60.4%, fuel and light 9.1%, clothing and footwear 8.6%, household goods and utensils 2.4%.

Gross national product (at current market prices; 1990): U.S.$2,710,000,000 (U.S.$230 per capita).

Structure of gross domestic product and labour force

	1987			
	in value U.S.$'000,000[7]	% of total value	labour force	% of labour force
Agriculture	981	42.0	3,651,000	77.9
Manufacturing	276	11.8		
Mining	6	0.3		
Construction	88	3.8	462,000	9.9
Public utilities	26	1.1		
Transportation and communications	188	8.0		
Trade	299	12.8		
Finance	183	7.8	574,000	12.2
Services				
Pub. admin., defense	289	12.4		
TOTAL	2,336	100.0	4,687,000	100.0

Population economically active (1987): total 4,687,000; activity rate of total population 44.3% (participation rates [1985]: ages 15–64, 74.9%; female 44.2%; unemployed [1982] 0.6%).

Price and earnings indexes (1985 = 100)

	1985	1986	1987	1988	1989	1990	1991
Consumer price index	100.0	114.5	131.7	167.0	182.1	203.6	221.1
Earnings index	...	...	...	...	...	...	...

Land use (1990): forested 26.7%; meadows and pastures 58.5%; agricultural and under permanent cultivation 5.3%; other 9.5%.
Public debt (external, outstanding; 1990): U.S.$3,669,000,000.

Foreign trade

Balance of trade

	1986	1987	1988	1989	1990	1991
FMG '000,000,000	+14.8	+85.9	−39.9	+50.8	−244.5	−62.1
% of total	3.6%	13.8%	4.9%	5.3%	21.0%	5.1%

Imports (1991): FMG 796,700,000,000 (1989; machinery 13.6%; vehicles and parts 10.4%; electrical equipment 7.3%; rice 7.2%; crude petroleum 5.5%; pharmaceutical products 3.2%; fats, waxes, and oils 2.5%). *Major import sources:* France 27.7%; Japan 4.8% Iran 4.5%; Bahrain 4.4%; Germany 4.1%; Italy 2.9%; United States 2.8%.
Exports (1991): FMG 559,070,000,000 (1989; coffee 25.2%; vanilla 13.4%; cloves and clove oil 10.2%; sugar 7.8%; shrimps 7.5%). *Major export destinations:* France 27.4%; United States 12.4%; Japan 9.5%; Germany 8.5%; Italy 7.0%; Réunion 5.1%; Singapore 4.7%; United Kingdom 3.5%.

Transport and communications

Transport. Railroads (1990): route length 655 mi, 1,054 km; passenger-mi 121,750,000, passenger-km 195,938,000; short ton-mi cargo 144,040,000, metric ton-km cargo 210,295,000. Roads (1989): total length 33,700 mi, 54,200 km (paved 10%). Vehicles (1990): passenger cars 46,636; trucks and buses 33,156. Merchant marine (1991): vessels (100 gross tons and over) 86; total deadweight tonnage 90,710. Air transport (1990): passenger-mi 318,601,000, passenger-km 512,739,000; short ton-mi cargo 52,515,000, metric ton-km cargo 76,670,000; airports (1992) with scheduled flights 50.
Communications. Daily newspapers (1990): total number 5; total circulation 53,000[8]; circulation per 1,000 population 4[8]. Radio (1991): total number of receivers 1,500,000 (1 per 8.3 persons). Television (1991): total number of receivers 130,000 (1 per 95 persons). Telephones (1988): 43,600 (1 per 258 persons).

Education and health

Education (1989–90)

	schools	teachers	students	student/ teacher ratio
Primary (age 6–13)	13,555	37,932	1,512,322	39.9
Secondary (14–18)	1,142[9]	14,382	331,238	23.0
Voc., teacher tr.	61[10]	1,630	17,674	10.8
Higher	5[9]	960	37,046	38.6

Educational attainment: n.a. *Literacy* (1990): percentage of total population age 15 and over literate 80.2%; males literate 87.7%; females literate 72.9%.
Health: physicians (1985) 1,189 (1 per 8,610 persons); hospital beds (1982) 20,800 (1 per 442 persons); infant mortality rate per 1,000 live births (1990–95) 110.
Food (1988–90): daily per capita caloric intake 2,156 (vegetable products 89%, animal products 11%); 95% of FAO recommended minimum requirement.

Military

Total active duty personnel (1992): 21,000 (army 95.2%, navy 2.4%, air force 2.4%). *Military expenditure as percentage of GNP* (1989): 1.5% (world 4.9%); per capita expenditure U.S.$3.

[1]Legislature dissolved November 1991; elections pending November 1992. [2]Based on official 1985 projections. [3]1988. [4]Capital city only. [5]Malagasy households only. [6]Weights of consumer price index components in Antananarivo only; housing not included. [7]At factor cost. [8]For four newspapers only. [9]1988–89. [10]1987–88.

Malaŵi

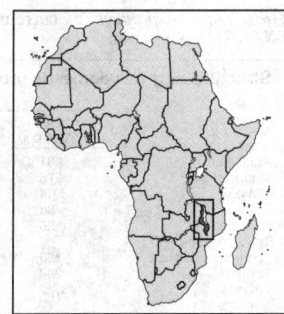

Official name: Republic of Malaŵi.
Form of government: single-party republic with one legislative house (National Assembly [146[1]]).
Head of state and government: President.
Capital: Lilongwe[2].
Official language: English[3].
Official religion: none.
Monetary unit: 1 Malaŵi kwacha (MK) = 100 tambala; valuation (Oct. 5, 1992) 1 U.S.$ = MK 3.93; 1 £ = MK 6.69.

Area and population		area		population
Regions **Districts**	**Capitals**	sq mi	sq km	1987 census[4]
Central	Lilongwe	13,742	35,592	3,116,038
Dedza	Dedza	1,399	3,624	410,847
Dowa	Dowa	1,174	3,041	322,112
Kasungu	Kasungu	3,042	7,878	322,854
Lilongwe	Lilongwe	2,378	6,159	986,411
Mchinji	Mchinji	1,296	3,356	248,161
Nkhotakota	Nkhotakota	1,644	4,259	157,083
Ntcheu	Ntcheu	1,322	3,424	359,618
Ntchisi	Ntchisi	639	1,655	120,697
Salima	Salima	848	2,196	188,255
Northern	Mzuzu	10,398	26,931	907,121
Chitipa	Chitipa	1,353	3,504	96,842
Karonga	Karonga	1,141	2,955	147,096
Mzimba	Mzimba	4,027	10,430	432,437
Nkhata Bay	Nkhata Bay	1,579	4,090	136,044
Rumphi	Rumphi	2,298	5,952	94,702
Southern	Blantyre	12,260	31,753	3,959,448
Blantyre	Blantyre	777	2,012	587,893
Chikwawa	Chikwawa	1,836	4,755	319,781
Chiradzulu	Chiradzulu	296	767	210,736
Machinga	Machinga	2,303	5,964	514,569
Mangochi	Mangochi	2,422	6,272	495,876
Mulanje	Mulanje	1,332	3,450	638,326
Mwanza	Mwanza	886	2,295	121,267
Nsanje	Nsanje	750	1,942	201,311
Thyolo	Thyolo	662	1,715	431,539
Zomba	Zomba	996	2,580	438,150
TOTAL LAND AREA		36,400	94,276[5]	
INLAND WATER		9,347	24,208	
TOTAL		45,747	118,484	7,982,607

Demography

Population (1992): 9,484,000[6].
Density (1992)[7]: persons per sq mi 260.5, persons per sq km 100.6.
Urban-rural (1989): urban 14.6%; rural 85.4%.
Sex distribution (1990): male 48.74%; female 51.26%.
Age breakdown (1989): under 15, 48.1%; 15–29, 25.5%; 30–44, 14.3%; 45–59, 8.0%; 60–74, 3.5%; 75 and over, 0.6%.
Population projection: (2000) 12,493,000; (2010) 17,069,000.
Doubling time: 20 years.
Ethnic composition (1983): Maravi (including Nyanja, Chewa, Tonga, and Tumbuka) 58.3%; Lomwe 18.4%; Yao 13.2%; Ngoni 6.7%; other 3.4%.
Religious affiliation (1980): Christian 64.5%, of which Protestant 33.7%, Roman Catholic 27.6%; traditional beliefs 19.0%; Muslim 16.2%; other 0.3%.
Major cities (1987): Blantyre 333,120; Lilongwe 223,318; Mzuzu 44,217.

Vital statistics

Birth rate per 1,000 population (1990–95): 55.4 (world avg. 26.4).
Death rate per 1,000 population (1990–95): 19.0 (world avg. 9.2).
Natural increase rate per 1,000 population (1990–95): 36.4 (world avg. 17.2).
Total fertility rate (avg. births per childbearing woman; 1990–95): 7.6.
Marriage rate per 1,000 population (1977): 7.8.
Divorce rate per 1,000 population (1977): 1.4.
Life expectancy at birth (1990–95): male 48.4 years; female 49.7 years.
Major causes of death per 100,000 population (1986)[8]: infectious and parasitic diseases 711, of which malaria 270, diarrheal diseases 148, measles 128; malnutrition 267; diseases of the respiratory system 265, of which pneumonia 234; anemia 224.

National economy

Budget (1991). Revenue: MK 1,239,009,000 (recurrent revenue 76.7%, of which income tax 34.0%, surtax 25.3%). Expenditures: MK 1,547,000,000 (recurrent expenditures 73.2%, of which debt payment 7.8%; development expenditure 26.8%).
Public debt (external, outstanding; 1990): U.S.$1,530,000,000.
Production (metric tons except as noted). Agriculture (1991): sugarcane 1,800,000, corn (maize) 1,590,000, potatoes 340,000, cassava 168,000, plantains 145,000, tobacco 125,000, bananas 90,000, dry beans 82,000, peanuts (groundnuts) 64,000, tea 41,000, sorghum 19,000; livestock (number of live animals) 1,150,000 cattle, 1,100,000 goats, 280,000 pigs, 230,000 sheep; roundwood (1990) 8,215,000 cu m; fish catch (1990) 80,000. Mining and quarrying (1989): limestone 105,000; cement 70,000. Manufacturing (value added in MK '000; 1986): chemicals 30,805; textiles 19,630; food products 11,988; beverages 11,988; tobacco 9,480; printing and publishing 9,250. Construction (value in MK; 1990): 26,950,000[9]. Energy production (consumption): electricity (kW-hr; 1990) 587,000,000 (587,000,000); coal (metric tons; 1990) none (19,000); petroleum products (metric tons; 1990) none (145,000).
Gross national product (1990): U.S.$1,662,000,000 (U.S.$200 per capita).

Structure of gross domestic product and labour force

	1991		1987	
	in value MK '000,000[10]	% of total value	labour force	% of labour force
Agriculture	358.5	34.9	2,699,900	81.8
Mining	...	...	1,662	0.1
Manufacturing	135.0	13.2	95,594	2.9
Construction	42.7	4.2	52,101	1.6
Public utilities	23.6	2.3	6,808	0.2
Transp. and commun.	59.3	5.7	16,726	0.5
Trade	128.3	12.5	103,203	3.1
Finance	112.0	10.9	7,142	0.2
Public administration	146.8	14.3 }	137,142	4.2
Services	43.9	4.3 }		
Other	–23.6[11]	–2.3[11]	179,920[12]	5.4[12]
TOTAL	1,026.5	100.0	3,300,198	100.0

Population economically active (1987): total 3,300,198; activity rate 41.7% (participation rates: ages 15–64, 84.6%; female 51.5%; unemployed 5.4%).

Price and earnings indexes (1985 = 100)							
	1985	1986	1987	1988	1989	1990	1991
Consumer price index	100.0	114.0	142.7	191.1	214.9	240.3	270.7
Monthly earnings index	100.0	109.4	129.9	145.8	169.7	...	...

Household income and expenditure (1979–80). Average household size 4.5[13]; income per household MK 1,934 (U.S.$2,419); sources of income: wages 83.3%, household enterprise 6.0%; expenditure (1985)[14]: food 32.9%, transportation 17.6%, housing 13.3%, clothing and footwear 10.7%.
Tourism (1990): receipts from visitors U.S.$8,000,000; expenditures by nationals abroad U.S.$13,000,000.
Land use (1990): forested 38.6%; meadows and pastures 19.6%; agricultural and under permanent cultivation 25.7%; other 16.1%.

Foreign trade[15]

Balance of trade (current prices)						
	1986	1987	1988	1989	1990	1991
MK '000,000	+175.5	+222.7	+139.4	–96.1	+180.1	+140.9
% of total	23.4%	22.1%	10.1%	6.1%	8.7%	5.6%

Imports (1991): MK 1,975,799,000 (1989; basic manufactures 40.6%, machinery and equipment 14.9%, transport equipment 14.3%, consumer goods 11.1%, building and construction materials 5.7%). *Major import sources* (1989): South Africa 36.8%; U.K. 17.1%; W.Ger. 6.3%; Japan 6.3%.
Exports (1991): MK 1,299,330,000 (tobacco 75.6%, tea 8.0%, sugar 6.1%, cotton 2.6%). *Major export destinations* (1989): U.K. 21.0%; U.S. 12.8%; W.Ger. 10.5%; South Africa 9.7%.

Transport and communications

Transport. Railroads (1988–89): route length 495 mi, 797 km; passenger-km 111,609,000; metric ton-km cargo 70,649,000. Roads (1989): total length 7,590 mi, 12,215 km (paved 22%). Vehicles (1989): passenger cars 16,118, trucks and buses 17,394. Merchant marine (1991): vessels (100 gross tons and over) 1; total deadweight tonnage 300. Air transport (1990)[16]: passenger-km 79,000,000; metric ton-km cargo 14,273,000; airports (1992) 5.
Communications. Daily newspapers (1991): total number 1; total circulation 25,000; circulation per 1,000 population 2.7. Radio (1991): total number of receivers 1,060,000 (1 per 8.6 persons). Television (1991): total number of receivers, n.a. Telephones (1990): 50,180 (1 per 176 persons).

Education and health

Education (1989–90)				
	schools	teachers	students	student/ teacher ratio
Primary (age 6–13)	2,624	20,580	1,325,453	64.4
Secondary (age 14–18)	94	1,096	29,326	26.8
Teacher tr., voc.	13	250	3,679	14.7
Higher	4	235	2,685	11.4

Educational attainment (1987). Percentage of population age 5 and over having: no formal education 54.9%; primary education 41.7%; secondary and higher 3.4%. *Literacy* (1987): total population age 15 and over literate 41.6%.
Health: physicians (1984) 262 (1 per 27,094 persons); hospital beds (1987) 12,617 (1 per 627 persons); infant mortality rate per 1,000 live births (1990–95) 138.0.
Food (1988–90): daily per capita caloric intake 2,049 (vegetable products 97%, animal products 3%); 88% of FAO recommended minimum requirement.

Military

Total active duty personnel (1992): 10,750 (army 97.7%, marines 0.9%, air force 1.4%). *Military expenditure as percentage of GNP* (1989): 2.3% (world 4.9%); per capita expenditure U.S.$4.

[1]Excludes 5 seats (of 141 elective) left vacant at the June 1992 elections (candidates were disqualified before the election) and includes 10 nonelective seats appointed by the president. [2]Some government offices (including parliament) remain in the former capital, Zomba. [3]Chewa is the national language. [4]Preliminary. [5]Detail does not add to total given because of rounding. [6]Excludes refugees, estimated to number about 950,000 in 1992. [7]Based on land area. [8]Estimates based on reported inpatient deaths in hospitals, constituting an estimated 8% of total deaths. [9]Cities of Blantyre, Lilongwe, and Mzuzu only. [10]At constant prices of 1978. [11]Less imputed bank service charges. [12]Includes 179,263 unemployed persons. [13]Based on sample survey of the city of Blantyre. [14]Weights of consumer price index components, cities of Blantyre and Lilongwe only. [15]Import figures are f.o.b. in balance of trade and c.i.f. in commodities and trading partners. Reexports included in balance of trade, excluded from commodities and trading partners. [16]Air Malaŵi only.

Malaysia

Official name: Malaysia.
Form of government: federal constitutional monarchy with two legislative houses (Senate [69[1]]; House of Representatives [180]).
Chief of state: Yang di-Pertuan Agong (Paramount Ruler).
Head of government: Prime Minister.
Capital: Kuala Lumpur.
Official language: Malay.
Official religion: Islam.
Monetary unit: 1 ringgit, or Malaysian dollar (M$) = 100 cents; valuation (Oct. 5, 1992) 1 U.S.$ = M$2.51; 1 £ = M$4.26.

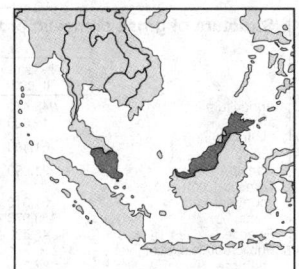

Area and population			area		population
Regions States		Capitals	sq mi	sq km	1990 census[2]
East Malaysia					
Sabah		Kota Kinabalu	28,425	73,620	1,470,200[3]
Sarawak		Kuching	48,050	124,449	1,669,000
West Malaysia					
Johor		Johor Baharu	7,331	18,986	2,106,500
Kedah		Alor Setar	3,639	9,426	1,412,800
Kelantan		Kota Baharu	5,769	14,943	1,220,100
Melaka		Melaka	637	1,650	583,500
Negeri Sembilan		Seremban	2,565	6,643	723,800
Pahang Darul Makmur		Kuantan	13,886	35,965	1,054,800
Perak		Ipoh	8,110	21,005	2,222,200
Perlis		Kangar	307	795	187,700
Pulau Pinang		Pinang	398	1,031	1,142,200
Selangor Darul Ehsan		Shah Alam	3,072	7,956	1,978,000
Terengganu		Kuala Terengganu	5,002	12,955	752,000
Federal Territories					
Kuala Lumpur		—	94	243	1,232,900
Labuan		—	35	91	3
TOTAL LAND AREA			127,320	329,758	
INLAND WATER			264	684	
TOTAL			127,584	330,442	17,755,700

Demography

Population (1992): 18,630,000.
Density (1992): persons per sq mi 146.0, persons per sq km 56.4.
Urban-rural (1985): urban 38.2%; rural 61.8%.
Sex distribution (1990): male 50.40%; female 49.60%.
Age breakdown (1990): under 15, 36.8%; 15–29, 28.6%; 30–44, 18.7%; 45–59, 9.8%; 60 and over, 6.1%.
Population projection: (2000) 22,140,000; (2010) 25,986,000.
Doubling time: 30 years.
Ethnic composition (1990): Malay and other indigenous (Orang Asli, or Bumiputera) 61.7%; Chinese 29.7%; Indian 8.1%; other nonindigenous 0.5%.
Religious affiliation (1980): Muslim 52.9%; Buddhist 17.3%; Chinese folk-religionist 11.6%; Hindu 7.0%; Christian 6.4%; other 4.8%.
Major cities (1980): Kuala Lumpur 1,209,800[4]; Ipoh 293,849; Pinang 248,241; Johor Baharu 246,395; Petaling Jaya 207,805.

Vital statistics

Birth rate per 1,000 population (1990): 28.0 (world avg. 27.1).
Death rate per 1,000 population (1990): 4.6 (world avg. 9.8).
Natural increase rate per 1,000 population (1990): 23.4 (world avg. 17.3).
Total fertility rate (avg. births per childbearing woman; 1989): 3.5.
Marriage rate per 1,000 population (1979): 1.7.
Divorce rate per 1,000 population (1979): 0.02.
Life expectancy at birth (1989): male 68.8 years; female 73.3 years.
Major causes of death per 100,000 population (1989): diseases of the circulatory system 63.1; accidents, homicide, and other violence 36.0; infectious and parasitic diseases 33.1; malignant neoplasms (cancers) 31.9; obstetric and perinatal causes 22.6; senility and ill-defined conditions 149.3.

National economy

Budget (1991). Revenue: M$30,246,000,000 (income tax 37.8%, nontax revenue 28.0%, import duties 10.6%, sales taxes 8.4%). Expenditures: M$29,040,000,000 (social services 27.4%, security 14.3%, administration 9.7%, economic services 8.5%).
Production (metric tons except as noted). Agriculture, forestry, fishing (1990): palm oil 6,094,700, rice 1,650,000, rubber 1,420,000, bananas 505,000, cacao beans 250,000, pineapples 211,000; livestock (number of live animals) 2,380,000 pigs, 652,000 cattle, 310,000 goats, 185,000 buffalo, 150,000 sheep, 145,000,000 chickens; roundwood 44,629,000 cu m; fish catch 604,128. Mining and quarrying (1990): bauxite 398,180; iron ore 293,186; copper concentrates 101,931; tin concentrates 28,468. Manufacturing (1990): cement 5,881,000; poultry feed 1,165,805; fertilizer 921,111; refined sugar 800,913; standard rubber 800,739; iron and steel bars 785,142; processed latex 255,947; plywood 1,197,385 cu m; radio receivers 37,019,000 units; television receivers 2,168,817 units; passenger cars 130,908 units. Construction (buildings completed; 1986)[5]: residential 8,809,100 sq m; nonresidential 959,900 sq m. Energy production (consumption): electricity (kW-hr; 1990) 24,723,000,000 (24,666,000,000); coal (metric tons; 1990) 120,000 (1,860,000); crude petroleum (barrels; 1990) 229,444,000 (68,922,000); petroleum products (metric tons; 1990) 8,924,000 (13,452,000); natural gas (cu m; 1990) 12,756,000,000 (3,402,000,000).
Gross national product (1991): U.S.$44,944,000,000 (U.S.$2,470 per capita).

Structure of gross domestic product and labour force				
	1990			
	in value M$'000,000[6]	% of total value	labour force[7]	% of labour force
Agriculture	14,829	18.8	1,837,600	27.8
Mining	7,688	9.7	39,100	0.6
Manufacturing	21,381	27.0	1,290,200	19.5
Construction	2,788	3.5	426,900	6.4
Public utilities	1,511	1.9	45,900	0.7
Transp. and commun.	5,489	6.9	285,400	4.3
Trade	8,700	11.0	1,239,400	18.7
Finance	7,650	9.7	231,300	3.5
Pub. admin., defense	8,459	10.7	850,200	12.8
Services	1,656	2.1	375,000	5.7
Other	−1,048[8]	−1.3[8]	...	...
TOTAL	79,103	100.0	6,621,000	100.0

Public debt (external, outstanding; 1990): U.S.$15,835,000,000.
Tourism (1990): receipts from visitors U.S.$1,657,000,000; expenditures by nationals abroad U.S.$4,473,000,000.
Population economically active (1990): total 7,046,500; activity rate of total population 39.7% (participation rates: ages 15–64, 66.5%; female [1980] 33.6%; unemployed 6.0%).

Price index (1985 = 100)							
	1985	1986	1987	1988	1989	1990	1991
Consumer price index	100.0	100.7	101.6	103.6	106.5	109.3	114.1

Household income and expenditure. Average household size (1980) 5.2; annual income per household (1987) M$12,890 (U.S.$5,120); sources of income: n.a.; expenditure (1983): food 28.7%, transportation 20.9%, recreation and education 11.0%, housing 10.2%, household durable goods 7.7%, clothing and footwear 4.3%, health 2.5%.
Land use (1989): forested 58.1%; meadows and pastures 0.1%; agricultural and under permanent cultivation 14.9%; other 26.9%.

Foreign trade[9]

Balance of trade (current prices)						
	1986	1987	1988	1989	1990	1991
M$'000,000	+10,480	+11,864	+16,048	+12,725	+7,947	+3,165
% of total	17.1%	17.1%	17.0%	10.3%	5.3%	1.7%

Imports (1990): M$79,118,600,000 (machinery and transport equipment 50.2%, manufactured goods 15.8%, chemicals 8.5%, food 5.8%, mineral fuels 5.1%, inedible crude materials 3.2%). *Major import sources:* Japan 24.1%; U.S. 16.8%; Singapore 15.0%; U.K. 5.5%; Taiwan 5.5%; West Germany 4.3%; Australia 3.7%.
Exports (1990): M$79,646,400,000 (thermionic valves and tubes 14.7%, crude petroleum 13.4%, sawn logs and timber 8.9%, palm oil 4.6%, natural rubber 3.8%, liquefied natural gas 3.3%). *Major export destinations:* Singapore 22.8%; U.S. 16.9%; Japan 15.8%; South Korea 4.6%; U.K. 3.9%; West Germany 3.9%; Thailand 3.5%; Hong Kong 3.2%.

Transport and communications

Transport. Railroads (1990): track length 1,381 mi, 2,222 km; passenger-km 1,836,000,000[10]; metric ton-km cargo 1,404,000,000[10]. Roads (1989): total length 32,623 mi, 52,501 km (paved 68%). Vehicles (1990): passenger cars 1,845,618; trucks and buses 407,133. Merchant marine (1991): vessels (100 gross tons and over) 508; total deadweight tonnage 2,541,933. Air transport (1990): passenger-km 11,909,395,000; metric ton-km cargo 575,372,000; airports (1992) with scheduled flights 38.
Communications. Daily newspapers (1988): total number 47; circulation 2,462,000[11]; circulation per 1,000 population 145[11]. Radio (1991): 3,500,000 receivers (1 per 5.2 persons). Television (1991): 2,000,000 receivers (1 per 9.1 persons). Telephones (1990): 2,022,581 (1 per 8.8 persons).

Education and health

Education (1990)	schools	teachers	students	student/ teacher ratio
Primary (age 7–12)	6,828	120,025	2,447,206	20.4
Secondary (age 13–19)	1,261	69,493	1,335,377	19.2
Voc., teacher tr.	81	3,902	39,187	10.0
Higher[4]	43	10,697	108,845	10.2

Educational attainment (1980). Percentage of population age 25 and over having: no formal schooling 36.6%; primary education 42.1%; secondary 19.4%; higher 1.9%. *Literacy* (1990 est.): total population age 15 and over literate 78.4%; males literate 86.5%; females literate 70.4%.
Health (1989): physicians 6,577 (1 per 2,638 persons); hospital beds 38,003 (1 per 457 persons); infant mortality rate per 1,000 live births (1990) 12.6.
Food (1987–89): daily per capita caloric intake 2,754 (vegetable products 85%, animal products 15%); 123% of FAO recommended minimum.

Military

Total active duty personnel (1991): 127,900 (army 82.1%, navy 8.2%, air force 9.7%). *Military expenditure as percentage of GNP* (1989): 2.9% (world 4.9%); per capita expenditure U.S.$60.

---

[1]Includes 43 nonelective seats. [2]Preliminary results. [3]Sabah state includes Labuan federal territory. [4]1989. [5]Results of the Central Bank Survey of four major towns: Kuala Lumpur, Shah Alam, Kelang, and Seberang Prai. [6]At constant prices of 1978. [7]Employed only. [8]Net bank service charges. [9]Import figures are f.o.b. in balance of trade. [10]Peninsular Malaysia and Singapore. [11]Circulation for 45 dailies.

Maldives

Official name: Divehi Jumhuriyya (Republic of Maldives).
Form of government: republic with one legislative house (People's Council [48[1]]).
Head of state and government: President.
Capital: Male.
Official language: Divehi.
Official religion: Islam.
Monetary unit: 1 Maldivian Rufiyaa (Rf) = 100 laari; valuation (Oct. 5, 1992) 1 U.S.$ = Rf 10.92; 1 £ = Rf 18.57.

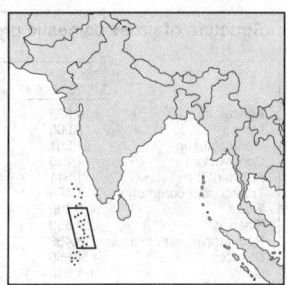

Structure of gross domestic product and labour force

	1991		1990	
	in value Rf '000[5]	% of total value	labour force	% of labour force
Agriculture[6]	248,410	23.7	14,117	25.0
Mining	19,800	1.9	496	0.9
Manufacturing }	61,190	5.8	8,441	15.0
Public utilities }			445	0.8
Construction	91,090	8.7	3,151	5.6
Transportation and communications	61,310	5.8	5,321	9.4
Trade	183,070	17.5	8,884	15.7
Finance	43,520	4.2	1,058	1.9
Public administration, defense	85,380	8.1 }	11,848	21.0
Services	254,320	24.3 }		
Other	...	...	2,674	4.7
TOTAL	1,048,090	100.0	56,435	100.0

Population economically active (1990): total 56,435; activity rate of total population 26.5% (participation rates: ages 15–64, 50.2%; female 19.9%; unemployed 0.9%).
Land use (1990): forested 3.3%; meadows and pastures 3.3%; agricultural and under permanent cultivation 10.0%; built-on, wasteland, and other 83.4%.

Area and population[2]

		area		population
Administrative atolls	Capitals	sq mi	sq km	1990 census
Haa-Alifu	Dhidhdhoo	...	...	12,031
Haa-Dhaalu	Nolhivaranfaru	...	...	12,890
Shaviyani	Farukolhu Funadhoo	...	...	9,022
Noonu	Manadhoo	...	...	8,437
Raa	Ugoofaaru	...	...	11,303
Baa	Eydhafushi	...	...	7,716
Lhaviyani	Naifaru	...	...	7,224
Kaafu	Male	...	...	61,856
Alifu	Mahibadhoo	...	...	9,027
Vaavu	Felidhoo	...	...	1,579
Meemu	Muli	...	...	4,186
Faafu	Magoodhoo	...	...	2,614
Dhaalu	Kudahuvadhoo	...	...	4,199
Thaa	Veymandhoo	...	...	8,189
Laamu	Hithadhoo	...	...	9,101
Gaafu-Alifu	Viligili	...	...	7,295
Gaafu-Dhaalu	Thinadhoo	...	...	10,417
Gnyaviyani	Foah Mulah	...	...	6,160
Seenu	Hithadhoo	...	...	15,177
TOTAL		115	298	213,215[3]

Demography

Population (1992): 230,000.
Density (1992): persons per sq mi 2,000.0, persons per sq km 771.8.
Urban-rural (1990): urban 25.9%; rural 74.1%.
Sex distribution (1990): male 51.28%; female 48.72%.
Age breakdown (1990): under 15, 46.9%; 15–29, 26.7%; 30–44, 12.3%; 45–59, 9.0%; 60–74, 4.0%; 75 and over, 0.8%; not stated, 0.3%.
Population projection: (2000) 287,000; (2010) 369,000.
Doubling time: 19 years.
Ethnic composition: the majority is principally of Sinhalese and Dravidian extraction; Arab, African, and Negrito influences are also present.
Religious affiliation: virtually 100% Sunnī Muslim.
Major cities (1990): Male 55,130.

Vital statistics

Birth rate per 1,000 population (1991): 46.0 (world avg. 26.4); legitimate, n.a.; illegitimate, n.a.
Death rate per 1,000 population (1991): 9.0 (world avg. 9.2).
Natural increase rate per 1,000 population (1991): 37.0 (world avg. 17.2).
Total fertility rate (avg. births per childbearing woman; 1991): 6.6.
Marriage rate per 1,000 population (1990): 10.6.
Divorce rate per 1,000 population (1990): 7.9.
Life expectancy at birth (1990): male 66.0 years; female 64.1 years.
Major causes of death per 100,000 population: n.a.; however, waterborne diseases (including gastroenteritis, cholera, and typhoid fever) are principal health problems, as are malaria, shigellosis, filariasis, leprosy, and tuberculosis.

National economy

Budget (1992). Revenue: Rf 1,021,000,000 (1990; nontax revenue 34.8%, import duties 25.5%, foreign grants 18.2%, tourism tax 15.3%). Expenditures: Rf 1,512,400,000 (economic development 23.9%, atoll development 21.6%, education 14.7%, public order and safety 7.7%, health 7.3%).
Public debt (external, outstanding; 1990): U.S.$66,000,000.
Production (metric tons except as noted). Agriculture, forestry, fishing (1991): vegetables and melons 19,000, coconuts 13,000, fruits (excluding melons) 10,000, roots and tubers (including cassava, sweet potatoes, and yams) 8,000, copra 2,000; fish catch (1990) 78,250. Mining and quarrying: coral for construction materials. Manufacturing: details n.a.; however, major industries include boat building and repairing, coir yarn and mat weaving, coconut and fish processing, lacquer work, garment manufacturing, and handicrafts. Construction: n.a. Energy production (consumption): electricity (kW-hr; 1990) 29,000,000 (29,000,000); coal, none (n.a.); petroleum products (metric tons; 1990) none (31,000); natural gas, none (n.a.).
Tourism (1990): receipts from visitors U.S.$85,000,000; expenditures by nationals abroad U.S.$19,000,000.
Household income and expenditure. Average household size (1990) 7.1; income per household: n.a.; sources of income: n.a.; expenditure (1981)[4]: food and beverages 61.8%, housing equipment 17.0%, clothing 8.0%, recreation and education 5.9%, transportation 2.6%, health 2.5%, rent 1.6%.
Gross national product (at current market prices; 1990): U.S.$96,000,000 (U.S.$440 per capita).

Foreign trade[7]

Balance of trade (current prices)

	1986	1987	1988	1989	1990	1991
U.S.$'000,000	− 33,459	− 47,932	− 54,977	− 50,963	− 65,114	− 83,500
% of total	40.5%	43.8%	40.7%	36.3%	38.5%	43.7%

Imports (1990): Rf 1,315,406,000 (food, beverages, and tobacco 28.9%; basic manufactures 24.5%; machinery and transport equipment 21.7%; mineral fuels 15.8%; chemicals 4.8%). *Major import sources* (1988): Japan 12.4%; Sri Lanka 9.2%; West Germany 4.3%; United Kingdom 3.6%.
Exports (1990): Rf 502,717,000 (apparel and clothing 27.6%; frozen skipjack tuna 26.3%; canned fish 25.2%; dried skipjack tuna 10.7%). *Major export destinations:* United States 24.4%; United Kingdom 18.5%; Thailand 18.1%; Sri Lanka 13.0%; Japan 8.5%; Singapore 4.9%.

Transport and communications

Transport. Railroads: none. Roads: total length, n.a. Vehicles (1990): passenger cars 623; trucks and buses 813. Merchant marine (1991): vessels (100 gross tons and over) 42; total deadweight tonnage 61,371. Air transport (1990): passenger arrivals 217,953, passenger departures 217,841; cargo loaded 2,263 metric tons, cargo unloaded 7,711 metric tons; airports (1992) with scheduled flights 1.
Communications. Daily newspapers (1986): total number (1987) 2; total circulation 2,000; circulation per 1,000 population 11. Radio (1990): total number of receivers 26,532 (1 per 8.1 persons). Television (1991): total number of receivers 4,750 (1 per 47 persons). Telephones (1989): 3,462 (1 per 60 persons).

Education and health

Education (1986)

	schools	teachers	students	student/ teacher ratio
Primary (age 6–11)	243	1,138	41,812	36.7
Secondary (age 11–18)	9	291	3,581	12.3
Voc., teacher tr.	10	52	462	8.9
Higher	—	—	—	—

Educational attainment (1990). Percentage of population age 15 and over having: no standard passed 25.6%; primary standard 37.2%; middle standard 25.9%; secondary standard 6.3%; preuniversity 3.4%; higher 0.4%; not stated 1.2%. *Literacy* (1985): total population age 15 and over literate 90,189 (90.4%); males literate 47,412 (90.6%); females literate 42,777 (90.1%).
Health (1990): physicians 40 (1 per 5,377 persons); hospital beds[8] 167 (1 per 1,288 persons); infant mortality rate per 1,000 live births 34.
Food (1984–86): daily per capita caloric intake 2,033 (vegetable products 91%, animal products 9%); 92% of FAO recommended minimum requirement.

Military

Total active duty personnel: Maldives maintains a single security force numbering about 700–1,000; it performs both army and police functions.

[1]Includes eight nonelective seats. [2]Maldives is divided into 19 administrative districts corresponding to atoll groups; arrangement shown here is from north to south; total area excludes 34,634 sq mi (89,702 sq km) of tidal waters. [3]Includes 4,792 people in resort and industrial islands. [4]Weights of consumer price index components. [5]At 1985 prices. [6]Primarily fishing. [7]Import figures are f.o.b. in balance of trade and c.i.f. for commodities and trading partners. [8]In government establishments only.

Mali

Official name: République du Mali
  (Republic of Mali).
Form of government: multiparty[1]
  republic with one legislative house
  (National Assembly [129[2]]).
Chief of state: President.
Head of government: Prime Minister.
Capital: Bamako.
Official language: French.
Official religion: none.
Monetary unit: 1 CFA franc
  (CFAF) = 100 centimes; valuation
  (Oct. 5, 1992) 1 U.S.$ = CFAF 238.75;
  1 £ = CFAF 405.88.

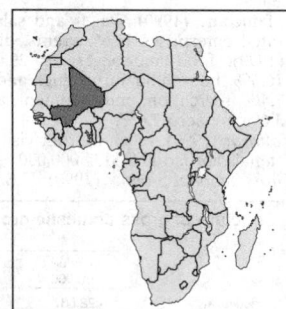

Area and population

Regions	Capitals	area sq mi	area sq km	population 1992 estimate
Gao	Gao	124,326	322,002	392,000
Kayes	Kayes	46,233	119,743	1,172,000
Koulikoro	Koulikoro	37,007	95,848	1,358,000
Mopti	Mopti	30,508	79,017	1,358,000
Ségou	Ségou	25,028	64,821	1,482,000
Sikasso	Sikasso	27,135	70,280	1,432,000
Tombouctou	Timbuktu (Tombouctou)	191,743[3]	496,611[3]	451,000
District				
Bamako	Bamako	97	252	819,000
TOTAL		482,077	1,248,574	8,464,000

Demography

Population (1992): 8,464,000.
Density (1992): persons per sq mi 17.6, persons per sq km 6.8.
Urban-rural (1992): urban 24.9%; rural 75.1%.
Sex distribution (1992): male 48.83%; female 51.17%.
Age breakdown (1987): under 15, 46.1%; 15–29, 23.9%; 30–44, 15.0%; 45–59, 8.9%; 60–74, 4.9%; 75 and over, 1.2%.
Population projection: (2000) 9,790,000; (2010) 11,744,000.
Doubling time: 23 years.
Ethnic composition (1983): Bambara 31.9%; Fulani 13.9%; Senufo 12.0%; Soninke 8.8%; Tuareg 7.3%; Songhai 7.2%; Malinke 6.6%; Dogon 4.0%; Dyula 2.9%; Bobo 2.4%; Arab 1.2%; other 1.8%.
Religious affiliation (1983): Muslim 90%; traditional beliefs 9%; Christian 1%.
Major cities (1987): Bamako 646,163; Ségou 88,877; Mopti 73,979; Sikasso 73,050; Gao 54,874.

Vital statistics

Birth rate per 1,000 population (1991): 51.0 (world avg. 26.4); legitimate, n.a.; illegitimate, n.a.
Death rate per 1,000 population (1991): 21.0 (world avg. 9.2).
Natural increase rate per 1,000 population (1991): 30.0 (world avg. 17.2).
Total fertility rate (avg. births per childbearing woman; 1991): 7.0.
Marriage rate per 1,000 population (1990)[4]: 0.4.
Divorce rate per 1,000 population: n.a.
Life expectancy at birth (1991): male 45.0 years; female 47.0 years.
Major causes of death per 100,000 population: n.a.; morbidity ([notified cases of illness] by cause as a percentage of all reported infectious disease; 1985): malaria 62.1%; measles 10.3%; amebiasis 10.3%; syphilis and gonococcal infections 6.0%; influenza 4.9%; other principal causes in 1989 included polio and conditions originating in the perinatal period.

National economy

Budget (1991). Revenue: CFAF 225,000,000,000 (fiscal receipts 49.1%, non-fiscal receipts 14.4%). Expenditures: CFAF 230,800,000,000 (capital expenditure 43.6%, current expenditure 42.4%).
Public debt (external, outstanding; 1991): U.S.$2,576,000,000.
Tourism (1990): receipts from visitors U.S.$37,000,000; expenditures by nationals abroad U.S.$67,000,000.
Population economically active (1987): total 2,722,000; activity rate of total population 31.9% (participation rates: over age 10, 48.3%; female 15.3%; unemployed 1.3%[5]).

Price and earnings indexes (1985 = 100)

	1985	1986	1987	1988	1989	1990	1991
Consumer price index[6]	100.0	96.3	88.5	92.7	93.7	94.6	97.3
Hourly earnings index[7]	100.0	100.0	100.0	100.0	100.0	100.0	100.0

Production (metric tons except as noted). Agriculture, forestry, fishing (1991): millet 713,206, sorghum 656,000, rice 400,075, seed cotton 317,530, corn (maize) 207,799, peanuts (groundnuts) 176,344, wheat 19,911, dry beans 17,057, sweet potatoes 12,576, cassava 1,147; livestock (number of live animals; 1990) 12,172,000 goats and sheep, 4,996,000 cattle, 575,000 asses, 245,000 camels, 77,000 horses, 56,000 pigs; roundwood (1990) 5,569,000 cu m; fish catch 29,534. Mining and quarrying (1991): limestone 25,000[8]; phosphate 8,000; gold 5,352 kg. Manufacturing (1991): cotton fibre 46,396; sugar 29,040; cement 10,953; soft drinks 64,750 hectolitres; beer 37,754 hectolitres; shoes 127,000 pairs; cigarettes 141,757 cartons. Construction: n.a. Energy production (consumption): electricity (kW-hr; 1991) 241,941,000 (1990; 214,000,000); coal, none (n.a.); crude petroleum, none (n.a.); petroleum products (metric tons; 1990) none (134,000); natural gas, none (n.a.).

Gross national product (at current market prices; 1990): U.S.$2,292,000,000 (U.S.$270 per capita).

Structure of gross domestic product and labour force

	1991 in value CFAF '000,000	1991 % of total value	1987 labour force	1987 % of labour force
Agriculture	320,169	45.6	2,243,000	82.4
Mining	10,326	1.5		
Manufacturing	48,260	6.8	68,000	2.5
Construction	27,920	4.0		
Public utilities	9,432	1.3		
Transp. and commun.	30,974	4.4		
Trade	109,131	15.5		
Finance	8,202	1.2	411,000	15.1
Pub. admin., defense	105,185	15.0		
Services				
Other	33,026[9]	4.7[9]	...	...
TOTAL	702,625	100.0	2,722,000	100.0

Household income and expenditure. Average household size (1987) 5.6; average annual income per household: n.a.; sources of income: n.a.; expenditure: n.a.
Land use (1989): forested 5.7%; meadows and pastures 24.6%; agricultural and under permanent cultivation 1.7%; other 68.0%.

Foreign trade[10]

Balance of trade (current prices)

	1984	1985	1986	1987	1988	1989
CFAF '000,000,000	−71.5	−131.7	−100.5	−70.2	−79.0	−70.1
% of total	28.6%	45.4%	41.4%	31.0%	33.0%	28.6%

Imports (1990): CFAF 187,735,000,000 (machinery, appliances, and transport equipment 29.3%; food products 12.7%; chemicals 9.2%; petroleum products 9.1%). *Major import sources* (1987): France 24.7%; Côte d'Ivoire 21.8%; West Germany 7.7%; Italy 5.0%; Senegal 4.2%; Spain 3.6%; The Netherlands 3.5%; Belgium-Luxembourg 2.7%; United States 2.3%; Hong Kong 2.3%; United Kingdom 2.0%; Japan 1.8%; China 1.3%; Switzerland 0.6%.
Exports (1990): CFAF 101,920,000,000 (raw cotton and cotton products 44.9%; live animals 24.0%; gold and diamonds 12.5%). *Major export destinations* (1987): France 11.2%; United Kingdom 9.5%; West Germany 7.7%; Morocco 7.6%; Belgium-Luxembourg 5.7%; Algeria 5.7%; Portugal 5.6%; Spain 5.0%; The Netherlands 4.4%; Réunion 4.1%; Tunisia 3.1%.

Transport and communications

Transport. Railroads (1990): route length (1988) 401 mi, 646 km; passenger-mi 304,155,000, passenger-km 489,491,000; short ton-mi cargo 187,176,000, metric ton-km cargo 273,273,000. Roads (1987): total length 11,185 mi, 18,000 km (paved 8%). Vehicles (1987): passenger cars 29,436; trucks and buses 7,556. Merchant marine: vessels (100 gross tons and over) none. Air transport (1983): passenger-mi 68,000,000, passenger-km 110,000,000; short ton-mi cargo 411,000, metric ton-km cargo 600,000; airports (1992) with scheduled flights 1.
Communications. Daily newspapers (1991): total number 1; total circulation 40,000; circulation per 1,000 population 4.9. Radio (1991): total number of receivers 150,000 (1 per 55 persons). Television (1991): total number of receivers 10,000 (1 per 830 persons). Telephones (1990): 11,165 (1 per 730 persons).

Education and health

Education (1989–90)

	schools	teachers	students	student/teacher ratio
Primary (age 6–14)	1,320	7,581	323,354	42.7
Secondary (age 15–17)[11]	331	3,411	51,818	15.2
Higher[12]	7	499	5,792	11.6

Educational attainment (1976). Percentage of adult population age 25 and over having: no formal schooling 95.4%; primary education 3.8%; secondary 0.6%; postsecondary and higher 0.2%. *Literacy* (1990): percentage of total population age 15 and over literate 32.0%; males literate 40.8%; females literate 23.9%.
Health (1983): physicians 349 (1 per 20,602 persons); hospital beds 4,215 (1 per 1,706 persons); infant mortality rate per 1,000 live births (1991) 114.
Food (1987–89): daily per capita caloric intake 2,234 (vegetable products 94%, animal products 6%); 95% of FAO recommended minimum requirement.

Military

Total active duty personnel (1991): 7,300 (army 94.5%, air force 5.5%). *Military expenditure as percentage of GNP* (1989): 2.0% (world 4.9%); per capita expenditure U.S.$5.

---

[1]New constitution approving a multiparty system was adopted Feb. 14, 1992; multiparty legislative elections of February–March 1992 were boycotted by most opposition parties. [2]Includes 13 seats for Malians abroad. [3]Area for Tombouctou region is estimated as residue between total reported area and the remainder of the regions. [4]Bamako only. [5]Urban areas only; estimated. [6]General price index. [7]Minimum hourly wages of industrial workers. [8]1987. [9]Less imputed bank service charges. [10]Imports c.i.f. [11]Excludes vocational. [12]1985–86.

Malta

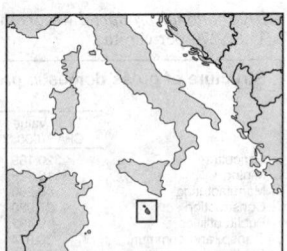

Official name: Repubblika ta' Malta (Maltese); Republic of Malta (English).
Form of government: unitary multiparty republic with one legislative house (House of Representatives [65]).
Chief of state: President.
Head of government: Prime Minister.
Capital: Valletta.
Official languages: Maltese; English.
Official religion: Roman Catholicism.
Monetary unit: 1 Maltese lira (Lm) = 100 cents = 1,000 mils; valuation[1] (Oct. 5, 1992) 1 Lm = U.S.$3.33 = £1.96.

Area and population	area		population
			1991
Census regions[2]	sq mi	sq km	estimate[3]
Gozo and Comino	27	70	26,064
Inner Harbour	6	15	101,749
Northern	30	78	33,718
Outer Harbour	12	32	102,976
South Eastern	20	53	45,035
Western	27	69	46,368
TOTAL	122	316[4]	355,910

Demography

Population (1992): 360,000.
Density (1992): persons per sq mi 2,950.8, persons per sq km 1,139.2.
Urban-rural (1985): urban 85.3%; rural 14.7%.
Sex distribution (1991): male 49.40%; female 50.60%.
Age breakdown (1991): under 15, 23.2%; 15–29, 21.7%; 30–44, 24.2%; 45–59, 16.1%; 60–74, 10.8%; 75 and over, 4.0%.
Population projection: (2000) 377,000; (2010) 393,000.
Doubling time: 93 years.
Ethnic composition (by nationality; 1980): Maltese 95.7%; British 2.1%; other 2.2%.
Religious affiliation (1980): Roman Catholic 97.3%; Anglican 1.2%; other 1.5%.
Major cities (1990): Birkirkara 20,963; Qormi 19,092; Hamrun 13,677; Sliema 13,541; Valletta 9,196.

Vital statistics

Birth rate per 1,000 population (1990): 15.2 (world avg. 27.1); legitimate 98.2%; illegitimate 1.8%.
Death rate per 1,000 population (1990): 7.7 (world avg. 9.8).
Natural increase rate per 1,000 population (1990): 7.5 (world avg. 17.3).
Total fertility rate (avg. births per childbearing woman; 1985–90): 1.9.
Marriage rate per 1,000 population (1990): 7.0.
Divorce rate per 1,000 population: n.a.
Life expectancy at birth (1990): male 73.7 years; female 78.1 years.
Major causes of death per 100,000 population (1990): diseases of the circulatory system 387.9; malignant neoplasms (cancers) 160.4; diseases of the respiratory system 59.7; endocrine, nutritional, and metabolic diseases of the blood and blood-forming organs 41.2; diseases of the digestive system 29.4; accidents, poisonings, and violence 27.4.

National economy

Budget (1992). Revenue: Lm 351,100,000 (customs and excise taxes 23.6%, national insurance and Central Bank contributions 20.6%, income tax 19.2%, Central Bank profits 5.1%). Expenditures: Lm 330,800,000 (national insurance benefits 41.1%, education 12.3%, health 9.8%, debt service 4.7%).
Public debt (1990): U.S.$565,407,000.
Production (wholesale value in Lm except where noted). Agriculture, forestry, fishing (1990): vegetables 4,396,800 (of which tomatoes 737,600, melons 530,800, cauliflower 347,600, carrots 208,100, onions 186,700), fruits 799,000 (of which peaches 167,300, strawberries 156,000), potatoes 533,000; livestock (number of live animals) 101,000 pigs, 21,000 cattle, 6,000 sheep, 5,000 goats, 1,000,000 chickens; fish catch (metric tons; 1990) 726.6. Quarrying (1989): 1,334,000. Manufacturing (1989): textiles and wearing apparel 33,226,000, of which clothing 25,069,000, textiles 4,298,000, footwear 3,859,000; machinery and transport equipment 33,215,000; food and beverages 29,744,000; printing and publishing 11,184,000; wood, cork, and furniture 8,562,000; chemicals 5,205,000; plastics 2,836,000; tobacco products 2,268,000. Construction (1989): 15,957,000. Energy production (consumption): electricity (kW-hr; 1990) 1,100,000,000 (1,100,000,000); coal (metric tons; 1990) none (300,000); crude petroleum, none (n.a.); petroleum products (metric tons; 1990) none (320,000); natural gas, none (n.a.).
Population economically active (1990): total 132,283; activity rate of total population 37.4% (participation rates: ages 15–64 [1985] 45.9%; female 25.4%; unemployed 3.8%).

Price and earnings indexes (1987 = 100)							
	1985	1986	1987	1988	1989	1990	1991
Consumer price index	97.6	99.5	100.0	101.1	101.8	104.8	107.5
Annual earnings index	...	...	100.0	103.8	106.9	108.6	117.8

Household income and expenditure. Average household size (1985) 3.3; average annual income per household (1982) Lm 4,736 (U.S.$11,399); sources

---

of income (1990): wages and salaries 47.7%, professional and unincorporated enterprises 16.6%, rents, dividends, and interest 13.2%; expenditure (1990): food and beverages 29.0%, transportation and communications 16.6%, household furnishings and operations 7.6%, clothing and footwear 7.4%, recreation, entertainment, and education 7.4%, housing 5.5%, health 3.6%, tobacco 3.6%.
Tourism (1990): receipts from visitors U.S.$496,000,000; expenditures by nationals abroad U.S.$134,000,000.
Gross national product (1990): U.S.$2,342,000,000 (U.S.$6,630 per capita).

Structure of gross domestic product and labour force				
	1990			
	in value Lm '000	% of total value	labour force	% of labour force
Agriculture	22,537	3.5	3,255	2.5
Manufacturing	175,634	27.0	35,469	26.8
Mining	22,882	3.5	809	0.6
Construction			5,849	4.4
Public utilities	5	5	1,857	1.4
Transportation and communications	37,131	5.7	9,191	7.0
Trade	93,772	14.4	12,912	9.8
Finance	93,336[6]	14.4[6]	4,901	3.7
Pub. admin., defense	146,099[5]	22.5[5]	43,159	32.6
Services	58,200	9.0	9,794	7.4
Other	...	...	5,087[7]	3.8[7]
TOTAL	649,591	100.0	132,283	100.0

Land use (1989): agricultural and under permanent cultivation 40.6%; other (infertile clay soil with underlying limestone) 59.4%.

Foreign trade[8]

Balance of trade (current prices)						
	1986	1987	1988	1989	1990	1991
Lm '000,000	− 167.6	− 184.3	− 168.1	− 169.0	− 172.8	− 214.5
% of total	31.7%	30.6%	26.3%	22.3%	18.3%	21.1%

Imports (1990): Lm 620,511,000 (machinery and transport equipment 45.8%, of which electrical equipment 28.4%, transport equipment 7.5%; semimanufactured goods 19.4%; food and live animals 8.7%; chemicals and chemical products 6.9%; mineral fuels 5.1%; nonfuel materials 2.0%; beverages and tobacco 1.2%). *Major import sources:* Italy 32.6%; U.K. 14.9%; W.Ger. 11.7%; France 7.1%; Japan 3.7%; U.S. 3.3%; The Netherlands 2.8%.
Exports (1990): Lm 357,890,000 (machinery and transport equipment 44.6%, of which electrical equipment 41.5%, transport equipment 3.1%; clothing and footwear 16.4%; semimanufactured goods 8.3%; reexports 8.1%; food and live animals 1.9%; beverages and tobacco 0.6%). *Major export destinations:* Italy 37.3%; W.Ger. 21.3%; U.K. 8.6%; France 7.3%; Libya 4.6%; U.S. 3.8%.

Transport and communications

Transport. Railroads: none. Roads (1990): total length 990 mi, 1,593 km (paved 91%). Vehicles (1990): passenger cars 104,863; trucks and buses 19,951. Merchant marine (1991): vessels (100 gross tons and over) 702; total deadweight tonnage 11,852,963. Air transport (1990): passenger-mi 561,113,-000, passenger-km 903,025,000; short ton-mi cargo 3,275,000, metric ton-km cargo 4,781,000; airports (1992) with scheduled flights 1.
Communications. Daily newspapers (1989): total number 3; total circulation 67,000; circulation per 1,000 population 192. Radio (1991): 90,000 receivers (1 per 4.0 persons). Television (1991): 146,107 receivers (1 per 2.4 persons). Telephones (1991): 191,000 (1 per 1.9 persons).

Education and health

Education (1989–90)	schools	teachers	students	student/ teacher ratio
Primary (age 5–10)	91	1,798	37,016	20.6
Secondary (age 11–17)	33	1,374	24,800	18.0
Voc., teacher tr.	32	748	7,037	9.4
Higher	1	244	2,511	10.3

Educational attainment (1967). Percentage of economically active population having: no formal schooling 10.8%; primary education 60.4%; lower secondary 3.4%; upper secondary 17.6%; technical secondary 3.9%; postsecondary and higher 3.9%. *Literacy* (1985): total population age 15 and over literate 250,419 (96.0%); males literate 121,899 (96.2%); females literate 128,520 (95.9%).
Health (1991): physicians 805 (1 per 444 persons); hospital beds 3,326 (1 per 107 persons); infant mortality rate per 1,000 live births (1990) 11.3.
Food (1987–89): daily per capita caloric intake 3,238 (vegetable products 72%, animal products 28%); 131% of FAO recommended minimum requirement.

Military

Total active duty personnel (1991): 1,650 (army 100%). *Military expenditure as percentage of GNP* (1989): 1.1% (world 4.9%); per capita expenditure U.S.$62.

---

[1]The Maltese lira is tied to the currencies of several principal trading partners. [2]Although Gozo is administered separately, the island of Malta has no first-order administrative subdivisions; data are reported according to census regions. [3]January 1. [4]Detail does not add to total given because of rounding. [5]Pub. admin., defense includes Public utilities. [6]Finance includes income from property. [7]Unemployed only. [8]Import figures are f.o.b. in balance of trade and c.i.f. for commodities and trading partners.

Marshall Islands

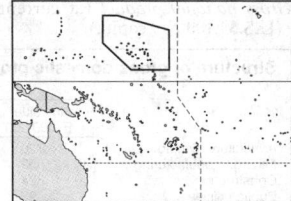

Official name: Majōl (Marshallese);
Republic of the Marshall Islands
(English).
Form of government: unitary republic
with two legislative houses (House of
Iroij [12][1]; Nitijela [33]).
Head of state and government:
President.
Capital: Majuro.
Official languages: Marshallese
(Kajin-Majōl); English.
Official religion: none.
Monetary unit: 1 U.S. dollar
(U.S.$) = 100 cents; valuation
(Oct. 5, 1992) 1 £ = U.S.$1.70.

Area and population

Election districts	area sq mi	area sq km	population 1988 census
Ailinglaplap	5.67	14.69	1,715
Ailuk	2.07	5.36	488
Arno	5.00	12.95	1,656
Aur	2.17	5.62	438
Bikini	2.32	6.00	10
Ebon	2.22	5.75	741
Enewetak and Ujelang	2.93	7.59	715
Jabat	0.22	0.57	112
Jaluit	4.38	11.34	1,709
Kili	0.36	0.93	602
Kwajalein	6.33	16.39	9,311
Lae	0.56	1.45	319
Lib	0.36	0.93	115
Likiep	3.97	10.28	482
Majuro	3.75	9.71	19,664
Maloelap	3.79	9.82	796
Mejit	0.72	1.86	445
Mili	6.15	15.93	854
Namorik	1.07	2.77	814
Namu	2.42	6.27	801
Rongelap	3.07	7.95	0
Ujae	0.72	1.86	448
Utrik	0.94	2.43	409
Wotho	1.67	4.32	90
Wotje	3.16	8.18	646
Other atolls	4.05	10.49	0
TOTAL	70.07	181.48[2]	43,380

Demography

Population (1992): 50,000.
Density (1992): persons per sq mi 714.3, persons per sq km 275.8.
Urban-rural (1988): urban 64.5%; rural 35.5%.
Sex distribution (1988): male 51.13%; female 48.87%.
Age breakdown (1988): under 15, 51.0%; 15–29, 24.5%; 30–44, 14.6%; 45–59, 5.5%; 60–74, 3.6%; 75 and over, 0.8%.
Population projection: (2000) 68,400; (2010) 100,000.
Doubling time: 18 years.
Ethnic composition (1988): Marshallese 96.9%; Pacific islanders 1.7%; Filipino 0.5%; other 0.9%.
Religious affiliation (1973): Protestant 90.1%; Roman Catholic 8.5%; other 1.4%.
Major cities (1988): Dalap-Uliga-Darrit 14,649; Ebeye 8,324.

Vital statistics

Birth rate per 1,000 population (1991): 47.0 (world avg. 26.4).
Death rate per 1,000 population (1991): 8.0 (world avg. 9.2).
Natural increase rate per 1,000 population (1991): 39.0 (world avg. 17.2).
Total fertility rate (avg. births per childbearing woman; 1991): 7.1.
Marriage rate per 1,000 population: n.a.
Divorce rate per 1,000 population: n.a.
Life expectancy at birth (1988): male 59.6 years; female 62.6 years.
Major causes of death per 100,000 population (1985): respiratory diseases 109.1; circulatory diseases 70.9; accidents, injuries, and violence 49.1; endocrine and metabolic disorders 38.2; infections and parasitic diseases 35.5; malignant neoplasms (cancers) 32.7; nervous-system disorders 27.3; digestive diseases 13.6.

National economy

Budget (1984). Revenue[3]: U.S.$30,292,000 (U.S. government grants 62.5%, income tax 10.1%, import tax 8.6%, fees and sales 4.0%). Expenditures: U.S.$22,233,000 (U.S. government grants 25.1%, health services 19.5%, public works and social programs 13.6%, education 12.5%, transportation and communications 7.5%, internal security 3.3%).
Public debt (external, outstanding): n.a.
Production (metric tons except as noted). Agriculture, forestry, fishing (1985): copra 4,066; other crops include breadfruit, cassava, and a variety of tropical fruits; livestock comprises mostly swine and poultry; roundwood, n.a.; fish catch 47,880[4, 5]. Mining and quarrying: quarrying of sand and aggregate for local construction only. Manufacturing: n.a.; however, copra and coconut oil are the most important products; the manufacture of handicrafts and personal items (clothing, mats, boats, etc.) by individuals is also important. Construction: n.a. Energy production (consumption): electricity (kW-hr; 1984) 7,576,260 (n.a.); coal, none (n.a.); petroleum, oil, and lubricants (barrels; 1984) 35,820 (n.a.); natural gas, none (n.a.).

Gross domestic product (at current market prices; 1989): U.S.$63,000,000 (U.S.$1,500 per capita).

Structure of gross domestic product and labour force

	1981 in value U.S.$'000	1981 % of total value	1988 labour force	1988 % of labour force
Agriculture	32.5	0.1	2,150	18.7
Mining	...	...	2	—
Manufacturing	75.3	0.3	945	8.2
Public utilities	...	...	82	0.7
Construction	2,235.6	7.4	1,076	9.4
Transportation and communications	1,762.7	5.9	537	4.7
Trade, restaurants, hotels	25,151.0	83.7	1,394	12.1
Finance, insurance, real estate	510.5	1.7	833	7.3
Public administration	...	... }	3,035	26.4
Services	36.0	0.1		
Other	199.9	0.7	1,434[6]	12.5[6]
TOTAL	30,053.0[2]	100.0[2]	11,488	100.0

Land use (1989)[7]: forested 22.5%; meadows and pastures 13.5%; agricultural and under permanent cultivation 33.1%; other 30.9%.
Household income and expenditure. Average household size (1988) 8.7; income per household (1979) U.S.$3,366; sources of income: n.a.; expenditure (latest): food 57.7%, housing 15.6%, clothing 12.0%, personal effects and other 14.7%.
Population economically active (1988): total 11,488; activity rate of total population 26.5% (participation rates: over age 14, 54.1%; female 30.1%; unemployed 12.5%).

Price and earnings indexes (1985 = 100)

	1983	1984	1985	1986	1987	1988	1989
Consumer price index	96.9	100.6	100.0	108.5	105.1	109.0	108.0
Earnings index	...	...	...	...	...	...	...

Tourism (1986): receipts from visitors U.S.$366,832; expenditures by nationals abroad, n.a.

Foreign trade

Balance of trade (current prices)

	1984	1985	1986	1987	1988
U.S.$'000,000	−19.7	−37.1	−39.3	...	−31.7
% of total	62.4%	84.5%	84.5%	...	88.3%

Imports (1988): U.S.$33,800,000 (food, agricultural raw materials, mineral ores[8], and concentrates 45.5%; fuels and other energies 10.7%; manufactured goods[9] 43.7%). *Major import sources:* United States 51.3%; Japan 17.6%.
Exports (1988): U.S.$2,100,000 (food and agricultural raw materials [includes coconut oil, live animals, preserved fish, coral, shells] 100%). *Major export destinations* (1983): United States 79.4%; other 20.6%.

Transport and communications

Transport. Railroads: none. Roads: n.a. Vehicles (1984): passenger cars 763; trucks and buses 80. Merchant marine (1991): vessels (100 gross tons and over) 40; total deadweight tonnage 2,800,000. Air transport: n.a.; airports (1992) with scheduled flights 24.
Communications. Daily newspapers (1991): there are no dailies, only weeklies, of which there are two with a total circulation of over 10,000. Radio (1990): total number of receivers, n.a.; but there are two radio stations. Television (1990): total number of receivers, n.a.; but there are two television stations. Telephones (1988): 800 (1 per 53 persons).

Education and health

Education (1988–89)

	schools	teachers	students	student/ teacher ratio
Primary (age 6–14)	89[10]	538	10,940	20.3
Secondary (age 15–18)	7[10]	95	1,862	19.6
Voc., teacher tr.	...	...	...	...
Higher	...	...	...	...

Educational attainment (1988). Percentage of population age 25 and over having: no grade completed 5.1%; elementary education 43.2%; secondary 39.7%; higher 11.4%; not stated 0.6%. *Literacy* (latest): total population age 15 and over literate 19,377 (91.2%); males literate 9,993 (92.4%); females literate 9,384 (90.0%).
Health (1985): physicians 17 (1 per 2,217 persons); hospital beds 54 (1 per 698 persons); infant mortality rate per 1,000 live births (1991) 53.0.
Food (1986–88): daily per capita caloric intake, n.a.

Military

Under the 1984 Compact of Free Association, the United States provides for the defense of the Republic of the Marshall Islands.

---

[1]House of Iroij is an advisory body only. [2]Detail does not add to total given because of rounding. [3]Recurrent. [4]1982. [5]Includes 9,440 metric tons caught by Japanese vessels; local tonnage refers to fish landed at Dalap-Uliga-Darrit only. [6]Includes 1,432 unemployed. [7]Data are for the former Trust Territory of the Pacific Islands. [8]Excludes precious stones. [9]Includes precious stones. [10]1985–86.

Martinique

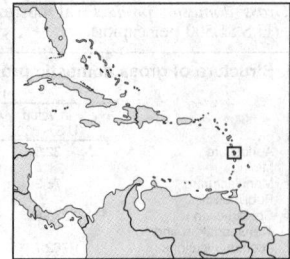

Official name: Département de
la Martinique (Department of
Martinique).
Political status: overseas department
(France) with two legislative houses
(General Council [45]; Regional
Council [41]).
Chief of state: President of France.
Heads of government: Commissioner
of the Republic (for France);
President of the General Council
(for Martinique); President of the
Regional Council (for Martinique).
Capital: Fort-de-France.
Official language: French.
Official religion: none.
Monetary unit: 1 franc (F) = 100
centimes; valuation (Oct. 5, 1992)
1 U.S.$ = F 4.78; 1 £ = F 8.12.

Area and population

Arrondissements	Capitals	area sq mi	area sq km	population 1990 census
Fort-de-France	Fort-de-France	147	381	187,275
Le Marin	Le Marin	158	409	93,411
La Trinité	La Trinité	131	338	78,893
TOTAL		436	1,128	359,579

Demography

Population (1992): 369,000.
Density (1992): persons per sq mi 846.3, persons per sq km 327.1.
Urban-rural (1990): urban 80.5%; rural 19.5%.
Sex distribution (1990): male 48.36%; female 51.64%.
Age breakdown (1990): under 15, 23.1%; 15–29, 28.9%; 30–44, 20.5%; 45–59,
13.5%; 60–74, 9.7%; 75 and over, 4.3%.
Population projection: (2000) 404,000; (2010) 452,000.
Doubling time: 60 years.
Ethnic composition (1983): mulatto 93.7%; French (metropolitan and Mar-
tinique white) 2.6%; East Indian 1.7%; other 2.0%.
Religious affiliation (1987): Roman Catholic 87.9%; other (mostly Seventh-
day Adventist, Jehovah's Witness, syncretist, and nonreligious) 12.1%.
Major urban areas (1990): Fort-de-France 100,072; Le Lamentin 30,026;
Schoelcher 19,825[1]; Sainte-Marie 19,683; Le Robert 17,675.

Vital statistics

Birth rate per 1,000 population (1990): 17.8 (world avg. 27.1); legitimate
33.7%; illegitimate 66.3%.
Death rate per 1,000 population (1990): 6.1 (world avg. 9.8).
Natural increase rate per 1,000 population (1990): 11.7 (world avg. 17.3).
Total fertility rate (avg. births per childbearing woman; 1989): 1.9.
Marriage rate per 1,000 population (1990): 4.3.
Divorce rate per 1,000 population (1990): 0.7.
Life expectancy at birth (1989): male 71.0 years; female 77.0 years.
Major causes of death per 100,000 population (1988): diseases of the circula-
tory system 210.4; malignant neoplasms (cancers) 127.9; accidents, poison-
ing, and violence 40.3; diseases of the digestive system 34.0; endocrine and
metabolic disorders 28.4.

National economy

Budget (1991). Revenue: F 1,755,000,000 (general receipts from French central government and local administrative bodies 49.2%, tax receipts 29.2%,
new loans 11.6%, public-works subsidies 6.0%). Expenditures: F 1,755,000,-
000 (health and social assistance 35.0%, improvements to public works
and property 34.0%, other administrative services 16.2%, debt amortization
3.3%).
Public debt (external, outstanding; 1987)[2]: U.S.$30,000,000.
Production (metric tons except as noted). Agriculture, forestry, fishing (1990):
bananas 246,000, sugarcane 205,000, pineapples 24,000, yams 13,000, plantains 9,000, cucumbers 4,000, sweet potatoes 4,000, tomatoes 3,000, melons
2,390[3], avocados 1,000, limes 862, flowers and foliage 183[3], pimientos
170[3]; livestock (number of live animals) 78,000 sheep, 49,000 pigs, 35,000
cattle; roundwood 12,000 cu m; fish catch 3,500. Mining and quarrying
(1988): pumice 132,000; sand and gravel for local construction. Manufacturing (1990): cement 277,400; processed pineapples 10,900; sugar 6,698; rum
84,800 hectolitres; other products include clothing, fabricated metals, and
yawls and sails. Construction (buildings authorized; 1990): residential, n.a.;
nonresidential 274,400 sq m. Energy production (consumption): electricity
(kW-hr; 1990) 657,000,000 (581,000,000); coal, none (none); crude petroleum
(barrels; 1990) none (5,406,000); petroleum products (metric tons; 1990)
601,200 (601,200); natural gas, none (none).
Household income and expenditure. Average household size (1990) 3.3; income
per household (1979) F 70,009 (U.S.$17,415); sources of income (1979):
wages and salaries 74.2%, rent 4.8%, other 21.0%; expenditure (1984–85):
food and beverages 31.9% (of which poultry and meat 7.9%), housing,
household furnishings, and energy 24.7%; transportation and communications 14.2%; clothing and footwear 7.2%; other 22.0%.
Tourism (1990): receipts from visitors U.S.$240,000,000; expenditures by na-
tionals abroad, n.a.

Gross national product (at current market prices; 1987): U.S.$1,429,000,000
(U.S.$4,100 per capita).

Structure of gross domestic product and labour force

	1982 in value F '000,000	1982 % of total value	1986 labour force	1986 % of labour force
Agriculture, fishing	720	8.1	10,364	7.1
Mining, manufacturing	552	6.2	5,769	4.0
Construction	324	3.6	6,894	4.7
Public utilities	96	1.1	1,303	0.9
Transportation and communications	390	4.4	5,870	4.0
Trade, restaurants, hotels	1,541	17.4	12,399	8.5
Finance, real estate, insurance	630	7.1	19,296	13.2
Pub. admin., defense, services	4,267	48.1	32,894	22.6
Other	354	4.0	51,135[4]	35.0[4]
TOTAL	8,874	100.0	145,924	100.0

Population economically active (1990): total 164,870; activity rate of total population 44.5% (participation rates [1986]: ages 15–64, 67.4%; female 50.6%;
unemployed [1990] 32.1%).

Price and earnings indexes (1985 = 100)[5]

	1985	1986	1987	1988	1989	1990	1991[6]
Consumer price index	100.0	102.6	106.3	108.8	112.4	116.8	118.3
Monthly earnings index[7]	100.0	100.9	103.0	106.1	108.9	111.3	114.2

Land use (1988): forested 36%; meadows and pastures 19%; agricultural and
under permanent cultivation 19%; other 26%.

Foreign trade[8]

Balance of trade (current prices)

	1985	1986	1987	1988	1989	1990	1991
F '000,000	−4,593	−4,569	−5,544	−6,551	−6,732	−7,970	−7,934
% of total	61.2%	60.4%	70.4%	73.7%	73.5%	72.7%	78.4%

Imports (1991): F 9,027,309,000 (1990; food products 18.1%, transport equipment 17.2%, machinery 14.5%, mineral fuels 10.9%, chemical products 8.8%,
metal manufactures 6.5%). *Major import sources:* France 62.1%; United
States 2.8%; Venezuela 1.1%; Guadeloupe 1.1%; unspecified 32.9%.
Exports (1991): F 1,092,807,000 (1990; bananas 40.4%, refined petroleum
15.9%, rum 8.9%, fertilizer 3.9%, melons 2.3%). *Major export destinations:*
France 57.1%; Guadeloupe 32.6%; French Guiana 6.5%.

Transport and communications

Transport. Railroads: none. Roads (1989): total length 1,050 mi, 1,690 km
(paved [1988] 75%). Vehicles (1985): passenger cars 135,269; trucks and
buses 7,328. Merchant marine (1990): vessels (100 gross tons and over)
6; total deadweight tonnage, n.a. Air transport (1990): passenger arrivals
610,584, passenger departures 616,537; cargo unloaded 6,944 metric tons,
cargo loaded 7,269 metric tons; airports (1992) with scheduled flights 1.
Communications. Daily newspapers (1990): total number 1; total circulation
30,000; circulation per 1,000 population 83. Radio (1991): total number of
receivers 60,000 (1 per 6.1 persons). Television (1991): total number of
receivers 45,000 (1 per 8.1 persons). Telephones (1989): 124,931 (1 per 2.9
persons).

Education and health

Education (1988–89)

	schools	teachers	students	student/ teacher ratio
Primary (age 6–11)	210	2,004	32,986	16.4
Secondary (age 12–18)	} 75[9]	} 2,745[9]	31,234	} 16.5[9]
Vocational			8,035	
Higher	1	40[9]	2,743	30[9]

Educational attainment (1982). Percentage of population age 25 and over having: no formal schooling 9.8%; primary education 62.7%; secondary 21.2%;
higher 6.3%. *Literacy* (1982): total population age 15 and over literate 206,-
807 (92.5%); males literate 97,538 (91.8%); females literate 109,269 (93.2%).
Health (1990): physicians (1989) 623 (1 per 573 persons); hospital beds 3,572
(1 per 101 persons); infant mortality rate per 1,000 live births 7.1.
Food (1988–90): daily per capita caloric intake 2,768 (vegetable products 75%,
animal products 25%); 114% of FAO recommended minimum requirement.

Military

Total active duty personnel (1991): 8,800 French troops[10].

---

[1]Preliminary figure. [2]Includes external long-term private debt not guaranteed by
the government. [3]Production for export only. [4]Unemployed. [5]All figures are end-of-
year unless otherwise footnoted. [6]March. [7]Based on minimum-level wage of public
employees. [8]Imports c.i.f.; exports f.o.b. [9]1986–87. [10]Includes troops stationed in
Guadeloupe and French Guiana.

Mauritania

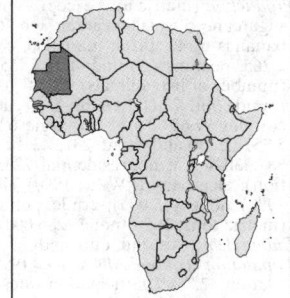

Official name: al-Jumhūrīyah
al-Islāmīyah al-Mūrītānīyah (Arabic)
(Islamic Republic of Mauritania).
Form of government: republic[1] with
two legislative houses (Senate [56];
National Assembly [79]).
Head of state and government:
President.
Capital: Nouakchott.
Official languages: Arabic.
Official religion: Islam.
Monetary unit: 1 Mauritanian Ouguiya
(UM) = 5 khoums; valuation (Oct. 5,
1992) 1 U.S.$ = UM 75.95;
1 £ = UM 129.11.

Area and population

Regions	Capitals	area sq mi	area sq km	population 1988 census
el-'Açâba	Kiffa	13,900	36,000	167,123
Adrar	Atar	83,100	215,300	61,043
Brakna	Aleg	14,000	37,100	192,157
Dakhlet Nouadhibou	Nouadhibou	11,600	30,000	63,030
Gorgol	Kaédi	5,400	14,000	184,359
Guidimaka	Sélibaby	4,000	10,000	116,436
Hodh ech-Chargui	Néma	64,000	166,000	212,203
Hodh el-Gharbi	'Ayoûn el-'Atroûs	22,000	57,000	159,296
Inchiri	Akjoujt	19,000	49,000	14,613
Tagant	Tidjikdja	36,000	93,000	64,908
Tiris Zemmour	Fdérik	98,600	255,300	33,147
Trarza	Rosso	26,000	67,000	202,596
District				
Nouakchott	Nouakchott	400	1,000	393,325
TOTAL		398,000	1,030,700	1,864,236

Demography

Population (1992): 2,108,000.
Density (1992): persons per sq mi 5.3, persons per sq km 2.0.
Urban-rural (1988): urban 39.1%; rural 60.9%.
Sex distribution (1990): male 49.41%; female 50.59%.
Age breakdown (1990): under 15, 44.6%; 15–29, 25.8%; 30–44, 15.5%; 45–59,
9.1%; 60–74, 4.2%; 75 and over, 0.7%.
Population projection: (2000) 2,665,000; (2010) 3,572,000.
Doubling time: 22 years.
Ethnic composition (1983): Moor 81.5% (about half Arab-Berber and half
African Sudanic); Wolof 6.8%; Tukulor 5.3%; Soninke 2.8%; Fulani 1.1%;
other 2.5%.
Religious affiliation (1980): Muslim 99.4%; Christian 0.4%; other 0.2%.
Major cities (1988): Nouakchott 393,325; Nouadhibou 59,198; Kaédi 30,515;
Kiffa 29,292; Rosso 27,783.

Vital statistics

Birth rate per 1,000 population (1991): 49.6 (world avg. 26.4); legitimate, n.a.;
illegitimate, n.a.
Death rate per 1,000 population (1991): 17.5 (world avg. 9.2).
Natural increase rate per 1,000 population (1991): 32.1 (world avg. 17.2).
Total fertility rate (avg. births per childbearing woman; 1991): 7.2.
Marriage rate per 1,000 population: n.a.
Divorce rate per 1,000 population: n.a.
Life expectancy at birth (1991): male 44.0 years; female 50.0 years.
Morbidity (notified cases of infectious disease per 100,000 population; 1984):
enteritis and diarrhea 10,566; conjunctivitis 7,080; malaria 2,897; scarlet fever
2,476; measles 714.0; chicken pox 306.4.

National economy

Budget (1991). Revenue: UM 22,063,000,000 (tax revenue 75.3%, of which
import and export duties 30.2%, value-added tax 26.5%, excise tax 18.6%).
Expenditures: UM 26,801,000,000 (administrative expenses 35.8%; defense
12.1%; interest on debt 7.8%).
Tourism (1988): receipts from visitors U.S.$14,000,000; expenditures by na-
tionals abroad U.S.$27,000,000.
Land use (1990): forested 4.3%; meadows and pastures 38.3%; agricultural
and under permanent cultivation 0.2%; desert 57.2%.
Production (metric tons except as noted). Agriculture, forestry, fishing (1991):
sorghum 59,000, rice 52,000, pulses 21,000, dates 14,000, vegetables (including melons) 8,000, roots and tubers 6,000 (of which sweet potatoes 3,000,
yams 3,000), millet 4,000, corn [maize] 1,000; livestock (number of live
animals) 4,200,000 sheep, 3,310,000 goats, 1,360,000 cattle, 920,000 camels,
153,000 asses, 18,000 horses, 4,000,000 chickens; roundwood (1989) 12,000
cu m; fish catch (1990) 91,000. Mining and quarrying (1989): iron ore
(gross weight) 11,263,000; gypsum 6,000. Manufacturing (1990): cow's milk
97,000; meat 44,000, of which fresh beef and veal 17,000, fresh mutton and
lamb 6,000, goat meat 5,000; hides and skins 4,720; cheese 1,841; butter
680. Construction (1984): 42,478 sq m. Energy production (consumption):
electricity (kW-hr; 1990) 140,000,000 (140,000,000); coal (metric tons; 1990)
none (6,000); crude petroleum (barrels; 1990) none (6,250,000); petroleum
products (metric tons; 1990) 730,000 (796,000); natural gas, none (n.a.).
Household income and expenditure. Average household size (1980) 5.0; income per household: n.a.; sources of income: n.a.; expenditure (1983)[2]:
food and beverages 61.0%; housing 24.0%; clothing and footwear 5.2%.

Gross national product (at current market prices; 1990): U.S.$987,000,000
(U.S.$500 per capita).

Structure of gross domestic product and labour force

	1988 in value UM '000,000	1988 % of total value	1987 labour force	1987 % of labour force
Agriculture	21,082	29.0	380,800	66.0
Mining	4,981	6.9		
Manufacturing	8,483	11.7	57,700	10.0
Public utilities	4,093	5.6		
Construction				
Transportation and communications	3,342	4.6		
Trade and finance	8,577	11.8	138,500	24.0
Services	3,891	5.4		
Pub. admin., defense	10,620	14.6		
Other (indirect taxes net of subsidies)	7,566	10.4	—	—
TOTAL	72,635	100.0	577,000	100.0

Population economically active (1990): total 678,000; activity rate of total
population 33.5% (participation rates: over age 10, 49.7%; female 22.1%;
unemployed [1988] 50.0%).

Price and earnings indexes (1985 = 100)

	1985	1986	1987	1988	1989	1990	1991[3]
Consumer price index	100.0	107.4	116.2	117.7	133.0	141.7	147.5
Earnings index	...	...	...	...	...	...	...

Public debt (external, outstanding; 1990): U.S.$1,859,000,000.

Foreign trade

Balance of trade (current prices)

	1984	1985	1986	1987	1988	1989
UM '000,000	−1,855	+10,110	+9,404	+3,395	+4,576	+8,277
% of total	6.5%	21.3%	17.7%	5.7%	6.4%	12.4%

Imports (1989): UM 29,174,000,000 (1988; machinery and transport equipment
51.0%, food 30.6%, consumer goods 9.0%, crude petroleum and petroleum
products 7.0%). *Major import sources:* France 42.6%; Spain 8.2%; West
Germany 6.4%; United States 6.0%; The Netherlands 5.5%; Thailand 5.2%;
China 4.3%; Algeria 3.9%; Belgium 2.5%; Japan 1.7%.
Exports (1989): UM 37,451,000,000 (fish 58.6%, iron ore 31.3%). *Major ex-
port destinations:* Japan 31.4%; France 11.8%; Belgium 10.2%; Italy 10.1%;
U.S.S.R 9.1%; Spain 7.0%; Côte d'Ivoire 6.6%; United Kingdom 3.0%;
United States 2.0%; Panama 0.3%.

Transport and communications

Transport. Railroads (1990): route length 428 mi, 689 km; passenger-mi
4,350,000[4], passenger-km 7,000,000[4]; short ton-mi cargo 5,393,000,000, metric ton-km cargo 7,873,000,000. Roads (1989): total length 4,696 mi, 7,558
km (paved 23%). Vehicles (1990): passenger cars 10,000; trucks and buses
5,000. Merchant marine (1991): vessels (100 gross tons and over) 125; total
deadweight tonnage 22,843. Air transport (1988)[5]: passenger-mi 129,597,000,
passenger-km 208,567,000; short ton-mi cargo 24,126,000, metric ton-km
cargo 35,223,000; airports (1992) with scheduled flights 10.
Communications. Daily newspapers (1990): total number 1; total circulation,
n.a. Radio (1991): total number of receivers 250,000 (1 per 8.2 persons).
Television (1991): total number of receivers 1,100 (1 per 1,861 persons).
Telephones (1989)[6]: 4,581 (1 per 431 persons).

Education and health

Education (1988–89)

	schools	teachers	students	student/ teacher ratio
Primary (age 6–11)	1,121	3,135	158,800	50.7
Secondary (age 12–17)	44[7]	1,873	37,370	20.0
Voc., teacher tr.[4]	6[7]	185	2,529	13.7
Higher	7	268[4]	5,808	20.2[4]

Educational attainment: n.a. *Literacy* (1990): percentage of total population
age 15 and over literate 34.0%; males literate 47.1%; females literate 21.4%.
Health (1988): physicians 187 (1 per 10,128 persons); hospital beds 1,556 (1
per 1,217 persons); infant mortality rate per 1,000 live births (1991) 94.
Food (1988–90): daily per capita caloric intake 2,447 (vegetable products 81%,
animal products 19%); 106% of FAO recommended minimum requirement.

Military

Total active duty personnel (1992): 9,600 (army 93.7%, navy 4.2%, air force
2.1%). *Military expenditure as percentage of GNP* (1989): 4.3% (world 4.9%);
per capita expenditure U.S.$22.

[1]New constitution took effect July 21, 1991; multiparty bicameral elections were held
in March 1992. [2]Nouakchott only. [3]First quarter. [4]1984. [5]Includes part of Air Afrique
traffic. [6]Number of subscribers. [7]1986.

Mauritius

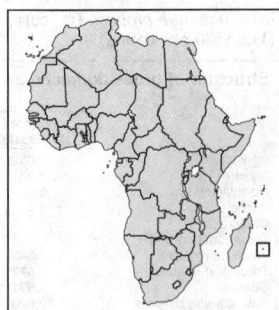

Official name: Republic of Mauritius.
Form of government: republic[1] with one legislative house (Legislative Assembly [70[2]]).
Chief of state: President.
Head of government: Prime Minister.
Capital: Port Louis.
Official language: English.
Official religion: none.
Monetary unit: 1 Mauritian rupee (Mau Re; plural Mau Rs) = 100 cents; valuation (Oct. 5, 1992) 1 U.S.$ = Mau Rs 14.60; 1 £ = Mau Rs 24.82.

Area and population

	area		population
Islands Districts	sq mi	sq km	1991 estimate[3]
Mauritius	720	1,865	1,054,546
Black River	100	259	41,819
Flacq	115	298	119,721
Grand Port	100	260	102,308
Moka	89	231	67,594
Pamplemousses	69	179	100,896
Plaines Wilhems	78	203	324,172
Port Louis	17	43	142,645
Rivière du Rempart	57	148	90,974
Savanne	95	245	64,417
Rodrigues	40	104	37,782
Agalega Cargados Carajos Shoals (Saint Brandon)	27	71	500
TOTAL	788[4]	2,040[4]	1,092,828

Demography

Population (1992)[5]: 1,081,000.
Density (1992): persons per sq mi 1,371.2, persons per sq km 529.7.
Urban-rural (1991)[6]: urban 40.7%; rural 59.3%.
Sex distribution (1991): male 49.80%; female 50.20%.
Age breakdown (1990)[6]: under 15, 29.6%; 15–29, 29.0%; 30–44, 22.0%; 45–59, 11.3%; 60–74, 6.5%; 75 and over, 1.6%.
Population projection[5]: (2000) 1,157,000; (2010) 1,260,000.
Doubling time: 50 years.
Ethnic composition (1988): Indo-Pakistani 68.0%; Creole (mixed Caucasian, Indo-Pakistani, and African) 25.0%; Chinese 3.0%; white 3.0%; other 1.0%.
Religious affiliation (1983)[6]: Hindu 52.5%; Roman Catholic 25.7%; Muslim 12.9%; Protestant 4.4%; Buddhist 0.4%; other 4.1%.
Major cities (1991): Port Louis 142,645; Beau Bassin–Rose Hill 95,711; Curepipe 66,790; Quatre Bornes 66,572; Vacoas-Phoenix 57,227.

Vital statistics

Birth rate per 1,000 population (1991): 20.7 (world avg. 26.4); (1985) legitimate 72.8%; illegitimate 27.2%.
Death rate per 1,000 population (1991): 6.6 (world avg. 9.2).
Natural increase rate per 1,000 population (1991): 14.1 (world avg. 17.2).
Total fertility rate (avg. births per childbearing woman; 1989)[6]: 2.2.
Marriage rate per 1,000 population (1990)[6]: 10.6.
Divorce rate per 1,000 population (1989)[6]: 0.7.
Life expectancy at birth (1986–88)[6]: male 64.7 years; female 72.2 years.
Major causes of death per 100,000 population (1990)[6]: diseases of the circulatory system 273.8; diseases of the respiratory system 60.1; malignant neoplasms (cancers) 60.0; symptoms, signs, and ill-defined conditions 49.0.

National economy

Budget (1991–92). Revenue: Mau Rs 10,981,800,000 (tax revenue 90.1%, of which import and stamp duties 43.1%, income tax 14.8%, sales tax 8.6%). Expenditures: Mau Rs 10,070,000,000 (social services 31.9%, of which education, art, and culture 13.1%, social security 9.9%, health 7.7%; public-debt service 31.8%).
Land use (1989): forested 30.8%; meadows and pastures 3.8%; agricultural and under permanent cultivation 57.3%; other 8.1%.
Tourism (1990): receipts from visitors U.S.$264,000,000; expenditures by nationals abroad U.S.$94,000,000.
Gross national product (at current market prices; 1990): U.S.$2,422,000,000 (U.S.$2,250 per capita).

Structure of gross domestic product and labour force

	1991			
	in value Mau Rs '000,000[7]	% of total value	labour force[8, 9]	% of labour force
Agriculture	3,890	11.2	45,300	16.2
Mining	40	0.1	200	0.1
Manufacturing	8,377	24.1	108,300	38.6
Construction	2,455	7.1	10,400	3.7
Public utilities	640	1.8	3,400	1.2
Transportation and communications	3,770	10.8	13,600	4.9
Trade	6,225	17.9	18,100	6.4
Finance	4,040	11.6	...	...
Pub. admin., defense	3,773	10.9	67,200	24.0
Services	1,555	4.5		
Other	...	...	13,800	4.9
TOTAL	34,765	100.0	280,300	100.0

Production (metric tons except as noted). Agriculture, forestry, fishing (1990): sugarcane 5,548,000, green tea 29,610, potatoes 17,820, tomatoes 11,570, bananas 6,140, black tea 6,000, cabbages 4,000, onions 3,000, corn (maize) 2,265, peanuts (groundnuts) 1,755, pineapples 1,355, tobacco 789; livestock (number of live animals) 95,000 goats, 33,000 cattle, 10,000 pigs, 7,000 sheep; roundwood 27,000 cu m; fish catch (1989) 17,194. Manufacturing (1990): clothing 97,624,000[10]; raw sugar 624,302; molasses 168,023; manufactured tea 5,751; beer and stout 281,243 hectolitres. Construction (1990): residential 887,230 sq m; nonresidential 227,340 sq m. Energy production (consumption): electricity (kW-hr; 1990) 770,000,000 (770,000,000); coal (metric tons; 1990) none (75,000); crude petroleum, none (none); petroleum products (metric tons; 1990) none (286,000); natural gas, none (none).
Public debt (external, outstanding; 1990): U.S.$805,000,000.
Population economically active (1990): total 454,000; activity rate of total population 42.7% (participation rates [1987]: ages 15–64, 69.8%; female 34.2%; unemployed 11.0%).

Price and earnings indexes (1985 = 100)

	1985	1986	1987	1988	1989	1990	1991[11]
Consumer price index	100.0	101.6	102.2	111.5	125.6	142.6	151.8
Monthly earnings index[9]	100.0	106.3	112.8	143.3	169.8	179.4	208.8

Household income and expenditure. Average household size (1990) 4.5[6]; income per household (1979) Mau Rs 15,540 (U.S.$2,430); sources of income (1984): salaries and wages 53.1%, entrepreneurial income 32.4%, transfer payments 7.3%, interest and dividends 4.3%, other 2.9%; expenditure (1980–81)[12]: food, beverages, and tobacco 50.4%, clothing and footwear 10.5%, housing 10.4%, transportation 10.0%, energy 6.4%, health care 3.0%, other 9.3%.

Foreign trade[13]

Balance of trade (current prices)

	1985	1986	1987	1988	1989	1990
U.S.$'000,000	− 258.0	+ 58.2	− 16.2	− 167.8	− 211.1	− 280.0
% of total	2.9%	4.5%	0.9%	7.7%	9.6%	10.6%

Imports (1990): Mau Rs 24,018,700,000 (manufactured goods classified chiefly by material 34.8%, machinery and transport equipment 26.5%, food 10.9%, mineral fuels and lubricants 8.1%, chemicals 6.7%, inedible crude materials excluding fuels 3.2%, animal and vegetable oils and fats 1.0%). *Major import sources:* France 14.7%; South Africa 8.8%; United Kingdom 7.1%; Germany 7.0%; Japan 6.1%; China 4.6%; United States 4.6%.
Exports (1990): Mau Rs 17,568,600,000 (clothing and textiles 51.7%, sugar 29.1%, molasses 0.7%, tea 0.5%). *Major export destinations:* United Kingdom 35.8%; France 22.7%; United States 13.1%; Germany 8.7%; Italy 4.5%; Belgium-Luxembourg 2.3%; Reunion 1.8%.

Transport and communications

Transport. Railroads: none. Roads (1990): total length 1,119 mi, 1,801 km (paved 93%). Vehicles (1990): passenger cars 29,402; buses 1,929. Merchant marine (1991): vessels (100 gross tons and over) 37; total deadweight tonnage 115,466. Air transport (1990)[14]: passenger-mi 898,271,000, passenger-km 1,466,877,000; short ton-mi cargo 124,844,000, metric ton-km cargo 182,270,000; airports (1992) with scheduled flights 1.
Communications. Daily newspapers (1991): total number 7; total circulation 82,000; circulation per 1,000 population 77. Radio (1991): 250,000 receivers (1 per 4.3 persons). Television (1991): 128,111 receivers (1 per 8.4 persons). Telephones (1990): 76,468[6] (1 per 14 persons).

Education and health

Education (1990)

	schools	teachers	students	student/ teacher ratio
Primary (age 5–12)	283	6,507	137,491	21.1
Secondary (age 12–20)	124	3,728	78,110	21.0
Voc., teacher tr.	7[10]	69[15]	518[10]	...
Higher	2	382[16]	2,179[16]	5.7[16]

Educational attainment (1983). Percentage of population age 25 and over having: no formal education 24.2%; incomplete primary 28.1%; primary 23.2%; incomplete secondary 13.1%; secondary 7.7%; higher 3.6%; other 0.1%. *Literacy* (1983)[6]: total population age 15 and over literate 501,262 (81.8%); males literate 267,835 (89.0%); females literate 233,427 (74.8%).
Health (1990): physicians 950 (1 per 1,118 persons); hospital beds 2,900 (1 per 366 persons); infant mortality rate per 1,000 live births 20.4.
Food (1987): daily per capita caloric intake 2,680 (1987–89; vegetable products 88%, animal products 12%); 124% of FAO recommended minimum requirement.

Military

Total active duty personnel: none; however, a special 800-person police mobile unit ensures internal security. *Military expenditure as percentage of GNP* (1989): 0.9% (world 4.9%); per capita expenditure U.S.$4.

[1]Mauritius became a republic on March 12, 1992. [2]Includes 8 nonelective seats. [3]January 1. [4]Detail does not add to total given because of rounding. [5]Based on 1990 census figures. [6]Island of Mauritius only. [7]At factor cost. [8]Employed persons in establishments employing 10 or more persons. [9]March. [10]1988. [11]December. [12]Current weights of CPI components; Island of Mauritius only. [13]Import figures are f.o.b. in balance of trade and c.i.f. for commodities and trading partners. [14]Air Mauritius only. [15]1982. [16]1989.

Mexico

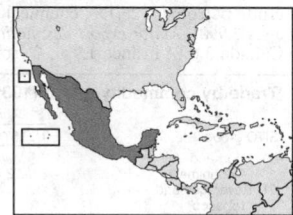

Official name: Estados Unidos Mexicanos (United Mexican States).
Form of government: federal republic with two legislative houses (Senate [64]; Chamber of Deputies [500]).
Chief of state and head of government: President.
Capital: Mexico City.
Official language: Spanish.
Official religion: none.
Monetary unit: 1 peso (Mex$) = 100 centavos; valuation (Oct. 5, 1992) 1 U.S.$ = Mex$3,013; 1 £ = Mex$5,122.

Area and population		area		population
		sq mi	sq km	1990 census
States	**Capitals**			
Aguascalientes	Aguascalientes	2,112	5,471	719,659
Baja California Norte	Mexicali	26,997	69,921	1,660,855
Baja California Sur	La Paz	28,369	73,475	317,764
Campeche	Campeche	19,619	50,812	535,185
Chiapas	Tuxtla Gutiérrez	28,653	74,211	3,210,496
Chihuahua	Chihuahua	94,571	244,938	2,441,873
Coahuila	Saltillo	57,908	149,982	1,972,340
Colima	Colima	2,004	5,191	428,510
Durango	Durango	47,560	123,181	1,349,378
Guanajuato	Guanajuato	11,773	30,491	3,982,593
Guerrero	Chilpancingo	24,819	64,281	2,620,637
Hidalgo	Pachuca	8,036	20,813	1,888,366
Jalisco	Guadalajara	31,211	80,836	5,302,689
México	Toluca	8,245	21,355	9,815,795
Michoacán	Morelia	23,138	59,928	3,548,199
Morelos	Cuernavaca	1,911	4,950	1,195,059
Nayarit	Tepic	10,417	26,979	824,643
Nuevo León	Monterrey	25,067	64,924	3,098,736
Oaxaca	Oaxaca	36,275	93,952	3,019,560
Puebla	Puebla	13,090	33,902	4,126,101
Querétaro	Querétaro	4,420	11,449	1,051,235
Quintana Roo	Chetumal	19,387	50,212	493,277
San Luis Potosí	San Luis Potosí	24,351	63,068	2,003,187
Sinaloa	Culiacán	22,521	58,328	2,204,054
Sonora	Hermosillo	70,291	182,052	1,823,606
Tabasco	Villahermosa	9,756	25,267	1,501,744
Tamaulipas	Ciudad Victoria	30,650	79,384	2,249,581
Tlaxcala	Tlaxcala	1,551	4,016	761,277
Veracruz	Jalapa (Xalapa)	27,683	71,699	6,228,239
Yucatán	Mérida	14,827	38,402	1,362,940
Zacatecas	Zacatecas	28,283	73,252	1,276,323
Federal District				
Distrito Federal	—	571	1,479	8,235,744
TOTAL		756,066	1,958,201	81,249,645

Demography

Population (1992): 84,439,000.
Density (1992): persons per sq mi 111.7, persons per sq km 43.1.
Urban-rural (1990): urban 71.3%; rural 28.7%.
Sex distribution (1990): male 49.10%; female 50.90%.
Age breakdown (1990): under 15, 38.3%; 15–29, 29.4%; 30–44, 16.6%; 45–59, 8.9%; 60–74, 4.5%; 75 and over, 1.7%; unspecified 0.6%.
Population projection: (2000) 95,490,000; (2010) 111,360,000.
Doubling time: 27 years.
Ethnic composition (1981): mestizo 55.0%; Amerindian 29.0%; Caucasian 15.0%; black 0.5%; other 0.5%.
Religious affiliation (1990): Roman Catholic 89.7%; Protestant (including Evangelical) 4.9%; Jewish 0.1%; other 2.1%; none 3.2%.
Major cities (1990): Mexico City 8,236,960; Guadalajara 1,628,617; Ciudad Netzahualcóyotl 1,259,543; Monterrey 1,064,197; Puebla 1,054,921; León 872,453; Juárez 797,679; Tijuana 742,686; Mérida 557,340; Chihuahua 530,487.
Place of birth (1990): 93.1% native-born; 6.9% foreign-born and unknown.
Mobility (1980). Population living in the same state as in 1970: 89.1%; different state 10.9%.
Households. Total households (1992) 17,152,000; distribution by size (1980): 1 person 5.4%, 2 persons 10.2%, 3 persons 12.4%, 4 persons 14.3%, 5 persons 13.5%, 6 persons 11.7%, 7 or more persons 32.5%. Family households (1983): 13,996,700 (94.6%); nonfamily 798,900 (5.4%).
Immigration (1987): permanent immigrants admitted 72,649.
Emigration (1990): legal immigrants into the United States 679,000.

Vital statistics

Birth rate per 1,000 population (1990): 31.2 (world avg. 27.1); (1983) legitimate 72.5%; illegitimate 27.5%.
Death rate per 1,000 population (1990): 5.0 (world avg. 9.8).
Natural increase rate per 1,000 population (1990): 26.2 (world avg. 17.3).
Total fertility rate (avg. births per childbearing woman; 1990): 3.7.
Marriage rate per 1,000 population (1991)[1]: 7.9.
Divorce rate per 1,000 population (1991)[1]: 2.0.
Life expectancy at birth (1990): male 66.5 years; female 73.1 years.
Major causes of death per 100,000 population (1990): accidents 71.9; diseases of the circulatory system 70.8; diseases of the respiratory system 30.3; conditions originating in the perinatal period 28.2; infectious and parasitic diseases 27.1.

Social indicators

Access to services (1992). Proportion of dwellings having: electricity 89.3%; piped water supply 81.0%; drained sewage 66.1%.

Educational attainment (1990). Percentage of population age 15 and over having: no primary education 13.4%; some primary 22.8%; completed primary 19.3%; some secondary 42.5%; other 2.0%.

Distribution of income (1983)				
percentage of household income by quintile				
1	2	3	4	5 (highest)
4.0	8.8	14.2	22.4	50.6

Quality of working life. Average workweek (1991): 45.5[2] hours. Annual rate (1986) per 100,000 insured workers for: temporary disability 9,077; indemnification for permanent injury 281; death 23. Labour stoppages (1988): 68, involving 4,750 workers. Average duration of journey to work: n.a. Method of transport: n.a. Rate per 1,000 workers of discouraged (unemployed no longer seeking work): n.a.
Social participation. Eligible voters participating in last national election (1988): *c.* 50%. Population participating in voluntary work: n.a. Trade union membership in total work force: n.a. Practicing religious population in total affiliated population (1970): weekly 10% of urban dwellers, 25% of rural dwellers; yearly 55% of urban dwellers, 73% of rural dwellers.
Social deviance (1991). Criminal cases tried by local authorities per 100,000 population for: murder 60.3; rape 22.4; other assault 301.0; theft 703.8. Incidence per 100,000 in general population of: alcoholism, n.a.; drug and substance abuse, n.a.[3]; suicide 1.54[4].
Leisure (1985). Favourite leisure activities (average daily paid attendance): cinema 582,416; sporting events 31,518; live theatre 16,400; museums and archaeological sites 12,169; bullfights 3,049.
Material well-being (1985). Households possessing: radio 96%; television 73%; washing machine 33%; automobile 29%; telephone 27%; refrigerator 23%.

National economy

Gross national product (1990): U.S.$214,500,000,000 (U.S.$2,490 per capita).

Structure of gross domestic product and labour force				
	1991		1990	
	in value Mex$'000,000,000	% of total value	labour force	% of labour force
Agriculture	76,127.0	8.9	5,300,114	22.0
Mining	19,796.6	2.3	260,515	1.1
Manufacturing	189,399.8	22.2	4,493,279	18.7
Construction	33,366.0	3.9	1,594,961	6.6
Public utilities	12,317.3	1.5	154,469	0.6
Transportation and communications	71,947.8	8.4	1,045,392	4.3
Trade	228,004.1	26.7	3,875,100	16.1
Finance	98,610.6	11.6	791,932	3.3
Pub. admin., defense } Services	133,492.1	15.7	928,358 / 4,155,421	3.9 / 17.3
Other	−10,278.2[5]	−1.2[5]	1,463,742[6]	6.1[6]
TOTAL	852,783.1	100.0	24,063,283	100.0

Budget (1991). Revenue: Mex$147,703,000,000,000 (income taxes 29.2%, value-added taxes 22.7%, petroleum revenues 21.0%, import duties 6.6%). Expenditures: Mex$148,404,000,000,000 (interest on public debt 29.2%, revenue sharing with state governments 18.0%, wages and salaries 18.0%, transfers 13.8%).
Public debt (external, outstanding; 1992): U.S.$76,087,100,000.
Tourism (1992): receipts from visitors U.S.$6,641,000,000; expenditures by nationals abroad U.S.$3,964,700,000.

Manufacturing, mining, and construction enterprises (1988)				
	no. of enterprises	no. of employees ('000)	yearly wages as a % of avg. of all wages[7]	value added (Mex$'000,000)
Manufacturing	138,835	2,640.5	166.2	20,950,900
Metal products	26,414	759.3	...	6,605,300
Chemicals	4,948	354.9	...	4,228,000
Food, beverages, and tobacco	50,454	543.7	130.0	3,378,700
Textiles and apparel	16,621	423.3	122.8	2,414,800
Iron and steel	871	100.4	...	1,332,400
Nonmetallic mineral products	14,343	150.9	...	1,177,700
Paper and printing	7,762	141.4	...	1,127,900
Wood and wood products	15,951	135.4	...	497,000
Nonelectrical machinery and transport equipment	8	8	...	8
Electrical machinery	8	8	...	8
Other manufactures	1,471	31.1	...	189,200
Mining	2,073	153.0	198.2	1,643,800
Construction	5,308	342.4	131.8	1,414,800

Production (metric tons except as noted). Agriculture, forestry, fishing (1992): sugarcane 35,332,000, corn (maize) 13,630,000, sorghum 5,287,000, wheat 3,583,000, oranges 2,329,000, bananas 1,685,000, mangoes 1,182,000, dry beans 858,000, lemons 765,000, avocados 699,000, soybeans 626,000, cantaloupes 621,000, apples 542,000, barley 485,000, grapes 457,000, rice 280,000, pineapples 277,000, strawberries 85,000, cottonseed 57,000, walnuts 22,000; livestock (number of live animals) 32,417,000 cattle, 13,840,000 pigs, 10,644,000 goats, 6,750,000 turkeys, 6,173,000 horses[9], 6,003,000 sheep[9], 3,188,000 asses[9], 3,186,000 mules[9], 246,000,000 chickens[9]; roundwood (1990) 22,205,000 cu m; fish catch 1,125,756, of which sardines 323,832. Mining and quarrying (metal content of ores; 1991): iron ore 6,391,000; zinc 301,685; copper 267,039; lead 158,831; manganese 79,000; silver 2,207; gold 7.58; (nonmetals; 1991) salt 7,483,124; gypsum 2,237,889; sulfur 1,791,000; fluorite 360,000; barite 192,000. Manufacturing (value added in U.S.$'000,000; 1990): food and beverages 12,311; chemical products 9,335; machinery and transport equipment 7,362, of which transport equipment 3,598, electrical machinery 1,963; textiles 3,942; iron and steel products 3,371; metal products 2,162; printed and published materials 1,696; wearing apparel and footwear 1,692; rubber products 1,659; paper and paper products 1,515. Construction (gross value of new construction, in Mex$'000,000; 1985): residential 154,835; nonresidential 168,096.

Trade and service enterprises (1985)

	no. of establishments	no. of employees	yearly wage as a % of avg. of all wages[7]	annual income (Mex$'000,000)
Trade	618,059	1,780,700	...	14,348,200
Wholesale	30,264	329,100	...	5,205,700
Retail	587,795	1,451,600	...	9,142,500
Boutiques (excluding food products)	223,601	600,200	...	3,022,900
Food and tobacco speciality stores	339,736	588,500	...	2,050,800
Automobile, tire, and auto parts dealers	16,768	104,400	...	1,737,600
Small supermarkets and grocery stores	4,512	96,400	...	1,227,300
Gasoline stations	2,395	23,900	...	708,700
Other	783	38,200	...	395,200
Services	341,436	1,401,500	85.2	3,476,900
Professional services	21,040	193,000	77.9	645,700
Food and beverage services	109,108	341,400	...	620,600
Transp. and travel agencies	3,058	41,000	133.4	353,400
Lodging	7,819	111,500	...	283,900
Automotive repair	55,850	148,500	...	209,800
Educational services (private)	8,227	124,200	134.3	166,000
Medical and social assistance	38,606	101,000	206.4	151,700
Amusement services (cinemas and theatres)	2,915	29,500	148.9	144,500
Recreation	8,323	41,000	...	139,500
Other repair	36,031	64,200	...	86,500
Commercial and professional organizations	3,209	41,900	77.9	67,400
Other	47,250	164,300	49.9	607,900

Energy production (consumption): electricity (kW-hr; 1992) 131,501,000,000 (1990; 122,477,000,000); coal (metric tons; 1990) 10,004,000 (10,369,000); crude petroleum (barrels; 1992) 975,000,000 (1990; 463,869,000); petroleum products (metric tons; 1990) 73,676,000 (77,166,000); natural gas (cu m; 1990) 44,745,000,000 (45,453,000,000).

Population economically active (1990): total 24,063,283; activity rate of total population 29.6% (participation rates: ages 15–64, 49.8%; female 23.5%; unemployed 2.7%).

Price and earnings indexes (1985 = 100)

	1985	1986	1987	1988	1989	1990	1991
Consumer price index	100.0	186.2	431.7	924.6	1,109.6	1,405.4	1,723.8
Monthly earnings index	100.0	175.7	411.5	873.0	1,166.8	1,522.6	1,965.7

Household income and expenditure. Average household size (1992) 4.8; income per household (1989) Mex$3,461 (U.S.$1,384); sources of income (1983): wages and salaries 52.4%, property and entrepreneurship 23.6%, transfer payments 5.6%, other 18.4%; expenditure (1989): food, beverages, and tobacco 37.3%, housing (includes household furnishings) 22.6%, transportation and communications 9.9%, clothing and footwear 8.0%, recreation and entertainment 5.3%, health and medical services 3.6%.

Financial aggregates[10]

	1987	1988	1989	1990	1991	1992 (8 mo.)
Exchange rate, Mex$ per:						
U.S. dollar	1,378.2	2,273.1	2,461.5	2,812.6	3,018.4	3,091.3
£	2,258.7	4,049.3	4,036.1	5,020.0	5,114.2	
SDR	1,782.1	3,054.9	3,470.7	4,190.3	4,392.9	4,568.7
International reserves (U.S.$)						
Total (excl. gold; '000,000)	12,464	5,279	6,329	9,863	17,726	18,858[11]
SDRs ('000,000)	706	394	383	417	586	350
Reserve pos. in IMF ('000,000)	—	—	—	—	—	—
Foreign exchange	11,758	4,885	5,946	9,446	17,140	18,316[11]
Gold ('000,000 fine troy oz)	2.54	2.56	1.03	0.92	0.92	0.79[11]
% world reserves	0.27	0.27	0.11	0.10	0.10	0.09[11]
Interest and prices						
Treasury bill rate	103.07	61.95	45.01	34.76	19.28	13.60[11]
Balance of payments (U.S.$'000,000)						
Balance of visible trade,	+8,433	+1,752	−645	−4,433	−11,063	...
of which:						
Imports, f.o.b.	12,222	18,905	23,410	−31,271	38,184	...
Exports, f.o.b.	20,655	20,657	22,765	26,838	27,121	...
Balance of invisibles	+12,401	−691	−4,603	−16,153	−24,346	...
Balance of payments, current account	+3,968	−2,443	−3,958	−7,117	−13,283	...

Land use (1990): forested 22.3%; meadows and pastures 39.0%; agricultural and under permanent cultivation 13.0%; other 25.7%.

Foreign trade

Balance of trade (current prices)

	1985	1986	1987	1988	1989	1990
Mex$'000,000,000	+2,249.1	+3,178.3	+11,794.1	+4,635.0	−863.8	−7,778.9
% of total	24.6%	18.7%	25.6%	5.2%	6.0%	4.8%

Imports (1991): U.S.$38,184,000,000 (metallic products, machinery, and equipment 52.9%; chemical products 8.9%; food, beverages, and tobacco 6.8%; iron and steel 5.7%; textiles and clothing 3.7%). *Major import sources:* U.S. 65.6%; Germany 6.1%; Japan 4.7%; France 2.5%; Brazil 2.1%; Canada 1.8%; Italy 1.6%; Spain 1.5%.
Exports (1991): U.S.$31,254,000,000 (metallic products, machinery, and equipment 28.0%, of which automobile 11.6%, machinery and electrical 5.6%;

crude petroleum 26.1%; chemical products 6.3%; processed food and beverages 3.9%). *Major export destinations:* U.S. 58.7%; Japan 4.0%; Spain 3.7%; Canada 3.6%; France 1.9%; Germany 1.7%; U.K. 1.0%; Brazil 0.6%.

Trade by commodity group (1989)

	imports		exports	
SITC group	U.S.$'000,000	%	U.S.$'000,000	%
00 Food and live animals	2,785	12.6	2,481	10.8
01 Beverages and tobacco	91	0.4	285	1.2
02 Crude materials, excluding fuels	1,926	8.7	1,099	4.8
03 Mineral fuels, lubricants, and related materials	908	4.1	7,784	33.9
04 Animal and vegetable oils, fats, and waxes	320	1.5	—	—
05 Chemicals and related products, n.e.s.	3,026	13.7	1,542	6.7
06 Basic manufactures	3,178	14.4	3,255	14.2
07 Machinery and transport equipment	7,429	33.6	5,616	24.4
08 Miscellaneous manufactured articles	2,262	10.3	873	3.8
09 Goods not classified by kind	160	0.7	—	—
TOTAL[12]	22,085	100.0	22,974	100.0

Direction of trade (1991)

	imports		exports	
	U.S.$'000,000	%	U.S.$'000,000	%
Western Hemisphere	35,185	74.8	32,795	84.4
United States	33,276	70.8	28,969	74.5
Latin America and the Caribbean	1,523	3.2	1,695	4.4
Canada	386	0.8	2,131	5.5
Europe	6,840	14.5	3,561	9.2
EEC	5,935	12.6	3,332	8.6
EFTA	770	1.6	171	0.4
U.S.S.R.	20	—	3	—
Other Europe	115	0.3	55	0.2
Asia	4,603	9.8	2,339	6.0
Japan	2,822	6.0	1,583	4.1
Africa	157	0.3	58	0.1
Other	248	0.6	115	0.3
TOTAL	47,033	100.0	38,868	100.0

Transport and communications

Transport. Railroads (1992): route length 16,363 mi, 26,334 km; passenger-mi 2,765,000,000, passenger-km 4,450,000,000; short ton-mi cargo 23,562,000,000, metric ton-km cargo 34,400,000,000. Roads (1992): total length 151,309 mi, 243,509 km (paved 35%[13]). Vehicles (1990): passenger cars 6,819,305; trucks and buses 3,063,185. Merchant marine (1991): vessels (100 gross tons and over) 649; total deadweight tonnage 1,612,359. Air transport (1991)[14]: passenger-mi 10,839,100,000, passenger-km 17,443,800,000; short ton-mi cargo 1,182,031,000, metric ton-km cargo 1,725,742,000; airports (1992) 54.
Communications. Daily newspapers (1986): total number 392; total circulation 11,256,000; circulation per 1,000 population 142. Radio (1991): 16,325,000 receivers (1 per 5.1 persons). Television (1991): 12,350,000 receivers (1 per 6.7 persons). Telephones (1992): 11,128,000 (1 per 7.6 persons).

Education and health

Education (1992–93)

	schools	teachers	students	student/ teacher ratio
Primary (age 6–12)	86,636	481,466	14,500,000	30.1
Secondary (age 12–18)	25,131	352,865	5,980,000	16.9
Voc., teacher tr.	6,571	77,347	1,076,700	13.9
Higher	1,832	128,212	1,256,100	9.8

Literacy (1990): total population age 15 and over literate 43,354,067 (87.4%); males literate 21,575,645 (90.2%); females literate 21,778,422 (84.8%).
Health: physicians (1987) 130,000 (1 per 600 persons); hospital beds (1990) 63,100 (1 per 1,298 persons); infant mortality rate per 1,000 live births (1988) 46.6.
Food (1988–90): daily per capita caloric intake 3,062 (vegetable products 82%, animal products 18%); 131% of FAO recommended minimum requirement.

Military

Total active duty personnel (1992): 175,000 (army 74.3%, navy 21.1%, air force 4.6%). *Military expenditure as percentage of GNP* (1989): 0.5% (world 4.9%); per capita expenditure U.S.$11.

---

[1]Federal District only. [2]Manufacturing only. [3]Through 1982, cannabis remained the most abused drug. [4]1987. [5]Imputed bank service charge. [6]Includes 659,870 unemployed. [7]1984. [8]Included in Metal products. [9]1991. [10]Exchange rates and treasury bill rates are expressed in period averages; international reserves are expressed in end-of-period rates. [11]End of May. [12]Totals include adjustments of unspecified nature. [13]1989. [14]All scheduled traffic of Mexicana and AeroMexico airlines.

Micronesia, Federated States of

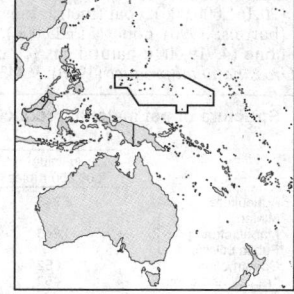

Official name: Federated States of Micronesia.
Political status: federal republic in free association with the United States with one legislative house (National Congress [14])[1].
Head of state and government: President.
Capital: Palikir.
Official language: none.
Official religion: none.
Monetary unit: 1 U.S. dollar (U.S.$) = 100 cents; valuation (Oct. 5, 1992) 1 £ = U.S.$1.70.

Area and population

States Major Islands	area		population
	sq mi	sq km	1990 estimate
Chuuk (Truk)	49.1	127.2	53,700
Wenn (Moen) Islands	7.0	18.1	14,218[2]
Kosrae	42.3	109.6	7,200
Kosrae Island	42.3	109.6	7,200
Pohnpei	133.3	345.2	33,100
Pohnpei Island	129.0	334.1	30,000
Yap	45.9	118.9	13,900
Yap Island	38.7	100.2	6,951[2]
TOTAL	270.8[3]	701.4[3]	107,900

Demography

Population (1992): 114,000.
Density (1992): persons per sq mi 421.0, persons per sq km 162.5.
Urban-rural (1980): urban 19.4%; rural 80.6%.
Sex distribution (1980): male 51.12%; female 48.88%.
Age breakdown (1980): under 15, 46.4%; 15–29, 26.8%; 30–44, 12.6%; 45–59, 8.5%; 60–74, 4.5%; 75 and over, 1.2%.
Population projection: (2000) 142,000; (2010) 177,000.
Doubling time: 26 years.
Ethnic composition (1980): Trukese 41.1%; Pohnpeian 25.9%; Mortlockese 8.3%; Kosraean 7.4%; Yapese 6.0%; Ulithian, or Woleaian, 4.0%; Pingelapese, or Mokilese, 1.2%; Western Trukese 1.0%; Palauan 0.4%; Filipino 0.2%; other 4.5%.
Religious affiliation: Christianity is the predominant religious tradition, with the Kosraeans, Pohnpeians, and Trukese being mostly Protestant and the Yapese mostly Roman Catholic.
Major cities (1980): Wenn (Moen) 10,351; Tol 6,705; Kolonia 5,549.

Vital statistics

Birth rate per 1,000 population (1985): 30.6 (world avg. 27.1); legitimate, n.a.; illegitimate, n.a.
Death rate per 1,000 population (1985)[4]: 3.6 (world avg. 9.8).
Natural increase rate per 1,000 population (1985): 27.0 (world avg. 17.3).
Total fertility rate (avg. births per childbearing woman; 1990): 5.0.
Marriage rate per 1,000 population: n.a.
Divorce rate per 1,000 population: n.a.
Life expectancy at birth (1985)[4]: male 64.0 years; female 68.1 years.
Major causes of death per 100,000 population (1985)[4]: diseases of the cerebrovascular system 85.7; major infectious diseases 39.6, of which intestinal diseases 14.3, septicemia 8.9; pneumonia, influenza, and tuberculosis 29.7; malignant and benign neoplasms (cancers) 23.1; homicide, suicide, and accidents 22.0.

National economy

Budget (1986). Revenue: U.S.$51,189,000 (U.S. Department of the Interior 75.7%, domestic taxes and other local revenue sources 19.5%, other U.S. government grants and federal program funds 4.8%). Expenditures: U.S.$13,208,000.
Public debt (external, outstanding): n.a.
Tourism (1990): number of visitors 20,475.
Production (metric tons except as noted). Agriculture, forestry, fishing: n.a.; however, Micronesia's major crops include coconuts (from which more than 4,000 tons of copra is produced), breadfruit, cassava, sweet potatoes, and a variety of tropical fruits (including bananas); livestock comprises mostly pigs and poultry; fish catch (1990) 3,640, of which skipjack tuna 600. Mining and quarrying: quarrying of sand and aggregate for local construction only. Manufacturing: n.a.; however, copra and coconut oil[5] are the most important products; the manufacture of handicrafts and personal items (clothing, mats, boats, etc.) by individuals is also important. Construction: n.a. Energy production (consumption): electricity (kW-hr; 1990) 40,000,000 (40,000,000); coal, none (n.a.); crude petroleum, none (n.a.); petroleum products[6] (metric tons; 1988) none (52,000); natural gas, none (n.a.).
Household income and expenditure. Average household size (1980) 7.0; average annual income per household, n.a.; sources of income (as percentage of workers over age 16): wage and salary workers (government) 51.5%, wage and salary workers (private) 22.8%, self-employed persons 2.7%, primarily subsistence workers 5.7%; expenditure (1985): food and beverages 73.5%.
Land use (1984)[6]: forested 22.5%; meadows and pastures 13.5%; agricultural and under permanent cultivation 33.5%; other 30.5%.

Gross national product (at current market prices; 1989): U.S.$150,000,000 (U.S.$1,500 per capita).

Structure of gross domestic product and labour force

	1983		1980	
	in value U.S.$'000,000	% of total value	labour force	% of labour force
Agriculture and fishing	44.9	42.2	197	2.0
Trade	12.7	11.9	864	8.8
Public administration	31.5	29.6	1,765	18.0
Manufacturing			115	1.2
Construction			945	9.6
Transportation, communications, and public utilities	17.4	16.3	472	4.8
Finance			121	1.2
Services			3,086	31.5
Other			2,233[7]	22.8[7]
TOTAL	106.5	100.0	9,798	100.0[3]

Population economically active (1982): total 9,798; activity rate of total population 13.4% (participation rates: over age 16, 26.1%; female 29.8%; unemployed 17.1%).
Price and earnings indexes: n.a.

Foreign trade

Balance of trade (current prices)

	1983	1984	1985	1986	1987	1988
U.S.$'000,000	−54.94	−35.1	−37.5	−41.9	−41.2	−65.4
% of total	88.4%	90.1%	89.9%	90.2%	96.9%	93.4%

Imports (1988): U.S.$67,701,000 (food, beverages, and tobacco 41.4%; manufactured goods 28.1%; machinery and transport equipment 13.5%; mineral fuels 6.0%; chemicals 5.2%). *Major import sources:* United States 36.2%; South Pacific Region 26.1%; Japan 22.0%; Australia 3.9%.
Exports (1988): U.S.$2,289,000 (copra 25.6%; manufactured goods 12.8%; animal and vegetable oils 2.2%). *Major export destinations:* Japan 58.2%; South Pacific Region 32.7%; United States 0.6%.

Transport and communications

Transport. Railroads: none. Roads (1990): total length 140 mi, 226 km (paved 17%). Vehicles: passenger cars, trucks, and buses, n.a. Merchant marine: n.a. Air transport: n.a.; airports (1991) with scheduled flights 4.
Communications. Daily newspapers: there are no private newspapers. Radio (1991): total number of receivers 70,000 (1 per 1.6 persons). Television (1991): total number of receivers 7,000 (1 per 16 persons). Telephones (1986): 1,556 (1 per 61 persons).

Education and health

Education (1983–84)

	schools	teachers	students	student/ teacher ratio
Elementary (age 6–12)	151	1,051	23,345	22.2
Secondary (age 13–18)	14	314	4,159	13.2
College[8]	...	...	920	...

Educational attainment (1980). Percentage of population age 25 and over having: no formal schooling 24.8%; some primary education 38.2%; primary 11.7%; some secondary 7.7%; secondary 9.6%; higher 8.0%. *Literacy* (1980): total population age 15 and over literate 30,074 (76.7%); males literate 13,710 (67.0%); females literate 16,364 (87.2%).
Health (1985): physicians 36[9] (1 per 2,540 persons); hospital beds 325 (1 per 280 persons); infant mortality rate per 1,000 live births (1987) 23.3[4].
Food: daily per capita caloric intake, n.a.

Military

External security is provided by the United States.

[1]On Nov. 3, 1986, the United States unilaterally terminated the UN trusteeship it held over the Federated States of Micronesia (FSM), thus formally initiating their free-association political status. On Dec. 22, 1990, the United Nations Security Council joined the Trusteeship Council, which had endorsed the termination of the trusteeship in May 1986. [2]1985. [3]Detail does not add to total given because of rounding. [4]Registered deaths only. [5]In 1985 FSM exported 2,503 metric tons of coconut oil to the United States. [6]Includes all areas formerly constituting the U.S. Trust Territory of the Pacific Islands. [7]Includes 1,673 unemployed. [8]In 1985, 1,200 students were enrolled in colleges and universities in the United States. [9]Excludes medical officers.

Moldova

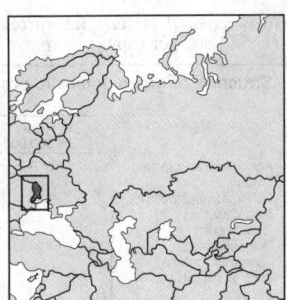

Official name: Republica Moldova (Republic of Moldova).
Form of government: unitary multiparty republic with a single legislative body (Parliament [380[1]]).
Head of state: President.
Head of government: Prime Minister.
Capital: Chişinău (Kishinyov).
Official language: Romanian.
Official religion: none.
Monetary unit: 1 ruble = 100 kopecks; valuation (Oct. 5, 1992) free rate, 1 U.S.$ = 316.82 rubles; 1 £ = 538.59 rubles.

Area

Administrative subdivisions

Cities	area sq km[2]	Rural districts	area sq km[2]	Rural districts	area sq km[2]
Bălţi	...	Anenii Noi	830	Hinceşti	
Cahul	...	Basarabeasca	660	(Kotovsk)	1,350
Chişinău		Brinceni	810	Ialoveni	...
(Kishinyov)	160	Cahul	800	Leova	720
Dubăsari	...	Cainari	...	Nisporeni	760
Orhei	...	Călăraş	760	Ocniţa	660
Rîbniţa	...	Camenca	820	Orhei	1,100
Soroca	...	Cantemir	860	Rezina	670
Tighina (Bendery)	...	Căuşeni	1,120	Rîbniţa	850
Tiraspol	...	Ciadîr-Lunga	720	Rişcani	1,000
Ungheni	...	Cimişlia	1,170	Sîngerei	...
		Comrat	840	Slobozia	960
		Criuleni	850	Şoldăneşti	...
		Donduşeni	890	Soroca	870
		Drochia	780	Ştefan-Vodă	
		Dubăsari	670	(Suvorovo)	1,030
		Edineţ	860	Străşeni	760
		Făleşti	1,070	Taraclia	...
		Floreşti	830	Teleneşti	860
		Glodeni	760	Ungheni	1,070
		Grigoriopol	820	Vulcăneşti	930
				TOTAL	33,700[3]

Demography

Population (1992): 4,394,000.
Density (1992): persons per sq mi 338.0, persons per sq km 130.4.
Urban-rural (1991): urban 47.5%; rural 52.5%.
Sex distribution (1991): male 47.70%; female 52.30%.
Age breakdown (1989): under 15, 27.9%; 15–29, 22.9%; 30–44, 21.0%; 45–59, 15.6%; 60–74, 9.7%; 75 and over, 2.9%.
Population projection: (2000) 4,707,000; (2010) 5,147,000.
Doubling time: 87 years.
Ethnic composition (1989): Moldovan 64.5%; Ukrainian 13.8%; Russian 13.0%; Gagauz 3.5%; Jewish 2.0%; Bulgarian 1.5%; other 1.7%.
Religious affiliation: believers are predominantly Eastern (Moldovan) Orthodox.
Major cities (1991): Chişinău (Kishinyov) 753,500; Tiraspol 186,000; Bălţi 164,900; Tighina (Bendery) 141,500; Rîbniţa 62,900.

Vital statistics

Birth rate per 1,000 population (1990): 17.7 (world avg. 27.1); (1989) legitimate 89.6%; illegitimate 10.4%.
Death rate per 1,000 population (1990): 9.7 (world avg. 9.8).
Natural increase rate per 1,000 population (1990): 8.0 (world avg. 17.3).
Total fertility rate (avg. births per childbearing woman; 1989): 2.5.
Marriage rate per 1,000 population (1990): 9.4.
Divorce rate per 1,000 population (1990): 3.0.
Life expectancy at birth (1990): male 65.2 years; female 72.0 years.
Major causes of death per 100,000 population (1989): diseases of the circulatory system 452.2; malignant neoplasms (cancers) 131.6; accidents and violence 105.3; diseases of the digestive system 85.4; diseases of the respiratory system 64.2; infectious and parasitic diseases 12.4; endocrine and metabolic disorders 8.3; diseases of the nervous system 8.2.

National economy

Budget (1991). Revenue: 6,403,100,000 rubles (tax revenue 86.3%, of which turnover tax 44.2%, enterprise profits tax 26.8%, individual income tax 7.8%, sales tax 7.1%; nontax revenue 13.7%, of which remainder from previous budget 2.7%, various fees 1.5%, revaluation of inventory 1.4%). Expenditures: 6,401,400,000 rubles (social welfare and culture 50.9%, of which education 21.4%, social security 15.3%, health 12.2%, culture and art 2.0%; national economy 38.2%; transfers to union budget 3.4%; government administration 1.7%).
Public debt (external, outstanding): n.a.
Tourism: receipts from visitors, n.a.; expenditures by nationals abroad, n.a.
Production (metric tons except as noted). Agriculture, forestry, fishing (1990): sugar beets 2,155,000, grain 2,011,000, vegetables (except potatoes) 1,282,000, fruit (except grapes) 1,074,000, grapes 1,040,000, potatoes 304,000, sunflower seeds 209,000, tobacco 62,000; livestock (number of live animals) 1,776,000 pigs, 1,281,900 sheep and goats, 1,060,700 cattle, 23,614,000 poultry; roundwood 125,000 cu m; fish catch, n.a. Mining and quarrying: n.a. Manufacturing (1991; '000,000 rubles): food 3,244; machinery and equipment 2,435; textiles 2,400; building materials 397; wood products 389; chemicals 272; electricity 264; ferrous metals 110. Construction (1990): 433,400,000 rubles.

Energy production (consumption): electricity (kW-hr; 1990) 15,690,000,000 (20,161,000,000); coal (metric tons; 1990) none (4,576,000); crude petroleum (barrels; 1990) none (51,625,000); petroleum products (metric tons; 1990) none (4,919,000); natural gas (cu m; 1990) none (4,004,000,000).
Gross national product (1990): 9,443,000,000 rubles (2,200 rubles per capita)[4].

Structure of net material product and labour force

	1990			
	in value '000,000 rubles	% of total value	labour force	% of labour force
Agriculture	3,943	41.7	673,000	32.5
Mining				
Manufacturing	3,245	34.4	456,000	22.0
Public utilities				
Construction	852	9.0	172,000	8.3
Transp. and commun.	452	4.8	70,000	3.4
Trade	871	9.2	148,000	7.1
Finance	—	—		
Pub. admin., defense	—	—	519,000	25.1
Services	—	—		
Other	80	0.9	33,000	1.6
TOTAL	9,443	100.0	2,071,000	100.0

Population economically active (1990): total 2,071,000; activity rate of total population 47.4% (participation rates [1989]: ages 16–59 [male], 16–54 [female] 86.3%; female 50.0%; unemployed 4.2%).
Price and earnings indexes: n.a.
Land use: n.a.
Household income and expenditure. Average household size (1989) 3.4; income per household (1990) 4,000 rubles; sources of income (1990): salaries and wages 69.1%, pensions and stipends 12.2%, income from sale of agricultural products 6.7%, financial receipts 4.3%, other 7.7%; expenditure (1990): food and consumer goods 73.4%, services 6.7%, other 19.9%.

Foreign trade

Balance of trade (current prices)

	1987	1988	1989	1990
'000,000 rubles	−287.2	−1,023	−1,155	−284.7
% of total	2.6%	9.2%	9.6%	2.3%

Imports (1990): 6,461,400,000 rubles (machinery and equipment 28.8%, textiles 20.2%, chemicals 11.3%, energy products 8.6%, food products 7.1%, ferrous metals 4.8%, agricultural products 4.2%, wood pulp and paper 3.5%). Major import sources: former Soviet republics 77.3%, of which Russian Federation 38.7%, Ukraine 17.2%, Belarus 8.6%, Uzbekistan 5.3%, Lithuania 2.7%, Latvia 2.4%, Kazakhstan 2.4%; other countries 22.7%.
Exports (1990): 6,176,700,000 (food products 44.2%, textiles 19.6%, machinery and equipment 16.9%, agricultural exports 7.3%, chemical products 3.4%, wood and paper products 1.4%, electric power 1.3%, ferrous metals 1.1%, building materials 1.0%, other industries 3.8%). Major export destinations: former Soviet republics 94.8%, of which Russian Federation 61.6%, Ukraine 14.1%, Belarus 7.2%, Uzbekistan 3.4%, Kazakhstan 2.9%, Latvia 2.4%, Lithuania 2.4%, other former Soviet republics 0.8%; other countries 5.2%.

Transport and communications

Transport. Railroads (1991): length 715 mi, 1,150 km; passenger-mi 5,515,000,000, passenger-km 8,875,000,000; short ton-mi cargo 10,278,300,000, metric ton-km cargo 15,007,000,000. Roads (1991): total length 6,400 mi, 10,300 km (paved 94%). Vehicles (1988): passenger cars 177,100; trucks and buses, n.a. Merchant marine: vessels (100 gross tons and over) n.a.; total deadweight tonnage, n.a. Air transport (1990): passenger-mi 1,461,000,000, passenger-km 2,352,000,000; short ton-mi cargo 13,000,000, metric ton-km cargo 19,000,000; airports (1992) with scheduled flights 1.
Communications. Daily newspapers (1990): total number 240; total circulation 309,000,000; circulation per 1,000 population 71. Radio and television (1990): total number of receivers 1,767,000 (1 per 2.5 persons). Telephones (1990): 538,700 (1 per 8.1 persons).

Education and health

Education (1990–91)

	schools	teachers	students	student/ teacher ratio
Primary (age 7–13)				
Secondary (age 14–17)	1,664	54,300	743,500	13.7
Voc., teacher tr.				
Higher	9	...	54,700	...

Educational attainment (1989). Percentage of population age 15 and over having: no formal schooling or some primary education 24.5%; some secondary 20.4%; completed secondary or some postsecondary 46.4%; higher 8.7%. *Literacy:* n.a.
Health (1991): physicians 17,400 (1 per 251 persons); hospital beds 56,400 (1 per 77 persons); infant mortality rate per 1,000 live births 19.0.
Food: daily per capita caloric intake, n.a.

Military

Total active duty personnel (1992): 12,000 (army 100%). *Military expenditure as percentage of GDP* (1992): 18.4% (world, c. 5.0%); expenditure, n.a.

[1]Total seats at 1990 elections, including 10 left vacant at those elections and, subsequently, by withdrawal of more than 100 representatives from constituencies in the unilaterally proclaimed Gagauz and Transdniester republics. [2]One sq km is equal to approximately 0.3861 sq mi. [3]Total includes 3,190 sq km (1,230 sq mi) not distributable by administrative subdivision. [4]No equivalent U.S.$ value is offered, as Soviet GNP data are very speculative.

Mongolia

Official name: Mongol Uls (Mongolia).
Form of government: unitary multiparty republic with one legislative house (People's Great Khural [76]).
Chief of state: President.
Head of government: Prime Minister.
Capital: Ulaanbaatar (Ulan Bator).
Official language: Khalkha Mongolian.
Official religion: none.
Monetary unit: 1 tugrik = 100 möngös; valuation (Oct 5, 1992) 1 U.S.$ = 40.00 tugriks; 1 £ = 68.00 tugriks.

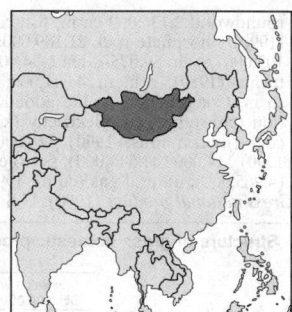

Area and population

Provinces	Capitals	area sq mi	area sq km	population 1989 census
Arhangay	Tsetserleg	21,000	55,000	84,700
Bayan-Ölgiy	Ölgiy	18,000	46,000	90,900
Bayanhongor	Bayanhongor	45,000	116,000	74,600
Bulgan	Bulgan	19,000	49,000	51,900
Dornod	Choybalsan	47,700	123,500	80,800
Dornogovĭ	Saynshand	43,000	111,000	57,000
Dundgovĭ	Mandalgovi	30,000	78,000	49,300
Dzavhan	Uliastay	32,000	82,000	88,500
Govĭ-Altay	Altay	55,000	142,000	62,700
Hentiy	Öndörhaan	32,000	82,000	73,800
Hovd	Hovd	29,000	76,000	76,500
Hövsgöl	Mörön	39,000	101,000	101,800
Ömnögovĭ	Dalandzadgad	64,000	165,000	42,400
Övörhangay	Arvayheer	24,000	63,000	96,500
Selenge	Sühbaatar	16,000	42,000	86,900
Sühbaatar	Baruun-Urt	32,000	82,000	50,900
Töv	Dzuunmod	31,000	81,000	100,000
Uvs	Ulaangom	27,000	69,000	83,900
Autonomous municipalities				
Darhan	—	100	200	85,800
Erdenet	—	300	800	56,100
Ulaanbaatar	—	800	2,000	548,400
TOTAL		604,800[1]	1,566,500	2,043,400

Demography

Population (1992): 2,182,000.
Density (1992): persons per sq mi 3.6, persons per sq km 1.4.
Urban-rural (1990): urban 58.0%; rural 42.0%.
Sex distribution (1989): male 49.90%; female 50.10%.
Age breakdown (1989): under 15, 41.9%; 15–29, 29.2%; 30–44, 14.6%; 45–59, 8.5%; 60 and over, 5.8%.
Population projection: (2000) 2,552,000; (2010) 3,104,000.
Doubling time: 25 years.
Ethnic composition (1979): Khalkha Mongol 77.5%; Kazakh 5.3%; Dörbed Mongol 2.8%; Bayad 2.0%; Buryat Mongol 1.9%; Dariganga Mongol 1.5%; other 9.0%.
Religious affiliation: although formal freedom of worship exists, all traditional religious practice (lamaistic Buddhism, shamanism, Islam, and others) has been greatly reduced during the 20th century; reliable data on the current situation do not exist.
Major cities (1991): Ulaanbaatar (Ulan Bator) 575,000; Darhan 90,000; Erdenet 56,200[2].

Vital statistics

Birth rate per 1,000 population (1989): 36.0 (world avg. 27.1); legitimate, n.a.; illegitimate, n.a.
Death rate per 1,000 population (1989): 8.0 (world avg. 9.8).
Natural increase rate per 1,000 population (1989): 28.0 (world avg. 17.3).
Total fertility rate (avg. births per childbearing woman; 1990): 4.7.
Marriage rate per 1,000 population (1989): 7.8.
Divorce rate per 1,000 population (1989): 0.5.
Life expectancy at birth (1990): male 61.2 years; female 63.8 years.
Major causes of death per 100,000 population: n.a.; however, in the 1980s, major causes of mortality included diseases of the respiratory system, diseases of the cardiovascular system, malignant neoplasms (cancers), diseases of the digestive system, and injuries, accidents, and poisonings.

National economy

Budget (1990). Revenue: 7,375,000,000 tugriks (turnover tax 59.7%, deductions from profits 33.8%, social insurance contributions 3.5%, income tax 0.7%). Expenditures: 7,375,000,000 tugriks (economy 47.2%, social and cultural services 40.5%, defense 8.0%, administration and other 4.3%).
Public debt (external; 1991): U.S.$16,800,000,000.
Tourism (1990): number of international arrivals 147,200.
Production (metric tons except as noted). Agriculture, forestry, fishing (1990): cereals 718,300, potatoes 131,100, vegetables 41,700; livestock (number of live animals) 14,831,900 sheep, 5,028,200 goats, 2,773,900 cattle, 2,200,100 horses, 557,900 camels, 171,000 pigs[3]; roundwood 2,390,000 cu m; fish catch (1989) 254. Mining and quarrying (1989): copper 165,000; molybdenum 1,200. Manufacturing (1990): cement 440,800; flour 187,000; bread 63,000; meat 53,900; plywood 3,400 cu m; woolen cloth 1,065,800 sq m; leather shoes 4,800,000 pairs; soft drinks 200,000 hectolitres; vodka 69,000 hectolitres; bricks 205,300,000 units; sheepskin coats 136,900 units. Construction (1988): residential 461,000 sq m; nonresidential 176,000 sq m. Energy production (consumption): electricity (kW-hr; 1990) 3,600,000,000 (3,760,000,000); coal

(metric tons; 1990) 7,890,000 (7,240,000); crude petroleum, none (n.a.); petroleum products (metric tons; 1990) none (706,000); natural gas, none (n.a.).
Gross national product (1990): U.S.$240,700,000 (U.S.$112 per capita).

Structure of gross domestic product and labour force

	1989 in value '000,000 tugriks	% of total value	labour force	% of labour force
Agriculture	1,722.9	16.1	186,000	29.4
Mining and manufacturing	2,919.8	27.2	119,600	18.9
Construction	617.2	5.8	41,700	6.6
Transp. and commun.	903.8	8.4	47,000[4]	7.4[4]
Trade	2,327.4	21.7	57,100[4]	9.0[4]
Services[5]	1,285.4	12.0	133,400	21.1
Other	954.4[6]	8.9[6]	48,400	7.6
TOTAL	10,730.9	100.0[1]	633,200	100.0

Population economically active (1990): total 648,700; activity rate of total population 30.9% (participation rates: ages 15–64 [1985] 82.2%; female [1987] 52.4%; unemployed [1991] 10.0%).

Price and earnings indexes (1985 = 100)

	1984	1985	1986	1987	1988	1989
Consumer price index	99.4	100.0	99.0	99.0	99.0	99.0
Monthly earnings index	99.0	100.0	100.4	101.0	101.3	102.9

Household income and expenditure. Average family size (1989) 4.8; income per household: n.a.; sources of income (1989): wages and salaries 75.1%[7], transfer payments 15.1%, self-employment 3.4%, other 6.4%; expenditure (1989): products 82.0%, services 18.0%.
Land use (1989): forested 8.9%; meadows and pastures 79.3%; agricultural and under permanent cultivation 0.9%; other 10.9%.

Foreign trade

Balance of trade (current prices)

	1985	1986	1987	1988	1989	1990
'000,000 rubles	− 272	− 283	− 259	− 251	− 162	− 176
% of total	22.7%	22.8%	21.2%	20.2%	14.4%	16.6%

Imports (1990): 139,400,000 tugriks (1989; machinery and transport equipment 29.6%; fuels, minerals, and metals 27.3%; consumer goods 21.9%; food products 12.5%; chemical products and rubber 8.7%). *Major import sources* (1989): U.S.S.R. and socialist countries 95.6%; capitalist countries 4.1%.
Exports (1990): 99,700,000 tugriks (1989; minerals and metals 42.8%; raw materials and food products 35.7%; consumer goods 17.5%; construction materials 4.0%). *Major export destinations* (1989): U.S.S.R. and socialist countries 93.1%; capitalist countries 6.7%.

Transport and communications

Transport. Railroads (1991): length 1,445 mi, 2,325 km; passenger-km 578,000,-000[3]; metric ton-km cargo 5,960,000,000[3]. Roads (1988): total length 30,600 mi, 49,200 km (paved 2%). Vehicles: n.a. Merchant marine: vessels (100 gross tons and over) none. Air transport (1988): passenger-km 532,400,000; metric ton-km cargo 10,600,000; airports (1992) with scheduled flights 1.
Communications. Daily newspapers (1990): total number 2; total circulation 222,000; circulation per 1,000 population 106. Radio (1991): total number of receivers 275,000 (1 per 7.8 persons). Television (1991): total number of receivers 120,000 (1 per 18 persons). Telephones (1990): 66,400 (1 per 32 persons).

Education and health

Education (1990–91)

	schools	teachers	students	student/ teacher ratio
Primary and secondary (age 8–18)	665	21,900	459,400	21.0
Voc., teacher tr.	44	1,200[8]	29,100	17.7[8]
Higher	8	1,465	13,829	9.4

Educational attainment (1989). Percentage of population age 10 and over having: primary education 33.7%; some secondary 31.9%; complete secondary 16.9%; vocational secondary 9.4%; some higher and complete higher 8.1%.
Literacy (1989): total population age 10 and over literate 97.9%.
Health: physicians 6,233 (1 per 345 persons); hospital beds 27,080 (1 per 79 persons); infant mortality rate per 1,000 live births 64.0.
Food (1987–89): daily per capita caloric intake 2,449 (vegetable products 62%, animal products 38%); 101% of FAO recommended minimum requirement.

Military

Total active duty personnel (1991): 14,500 (army 96.6%; navy, none; air force 3.4%). *Military expenditure as percentage of GNP:* n.a.; per capita expenditure (1989) U.S.$122. The last elements of the U.S.S.R.'s 67,000-person garrison (1988) were withdrawn in September 1992.

---

[1]Detail does not add to total given because of rounding. [2]1990. [3]1989. [4]Trade includes communications. [5]Services includes finance, public administration, and defense. [6]Other includes depreciation of fixed capital. [7]Includes income from agricultural cooperatives. [8]1988–89.

Morocco

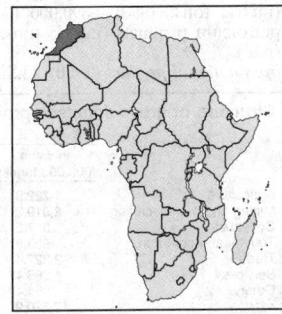

Official name: al-Mamlakah al-Maghribīyah (Kingdom of Morocco).
Form of government: constitutional monarchy with one legislative house (Chamber of Representatives [306]).
Head of state and government: King.
Capital: Rabat.
Official language: Arabic.
Official religion: Islam.
Monetary unit: 1 Moroccan dirham (DH) = 100 Moroccan francs; valuation (Oct. 5, 1992) 1 U.S.$ = DH 7.94; 1 £ = DH 13.50.

Area and population

Provinces	Capitals	area sq mi	area sq km	population 1992 estimate
Agadir	Agadir	2,282	5,910	807,000
Azilal	Azilal	3,880	10,050	419,000
Béni Mellal	Béni Mellal	2,732	7,075	936,000
Ben Slimane	Ben Slimane	1,066	2,760	204,000
Boulemane	Boulemane	5,558	14,395	156,000
Chaouen (Chefchaouen)	Chaouen (Chefchaouen)	1,680	4,350	363,000
Essaouira	Essaouira	2,446	6,335	428,000
Fès	Fès	2,085	5,400	1,029,000
Figuig	Figuig	21,618	55,990	108,000
Guelmim	Guelmim	11,100	28,750	168,000
al-Hoceima	al-Hoceima	1,371	3,550	371,000
Ifrane	Ifrane	1,278	3,310	116,000
el-Jadida	el-Jadida	2,317	6,000	928,000
el-Kelaa des Srarhna	el-Kelaa des Srarhna	3,888	10,070	684,000
Kénitra	Kénitra	1,832	4,745	920,000
Khémisset	Khémisset	3,207	8,305	473,000
Khénifra	Khénifra	4,757	12,320	442,000
Khouribga	Khouribga	1,641	4,250	547,000
Marrakech	Marrakech	5,697	14,755	1,525,000
Meknès	Meknès	1,542	3,995	753,000
Nador	Nador	2,367	6,130	796,000
Ouarzazate	Ouarzazate	16,043	41,550	649,000
Oujda	Oujda	7,992	20,700	974,000
er-Rachidia	er-Rachidia	23,006	59,585	503,000
Safi	Safi	2,813	7,285	848,000
Settat	Settat	3,764	9,750	790,000
Sidi Kacem	Sidi Kacem	1,568	4,060	602,000
Tangier	Tangier	461	1,195	566,000
Tan-Tan	Tan-Tan	6,678	17,295	55,000
Taounate	Taounate	2,156	5,585	603,000
Taroudannt	Taroudannt	6,355	16,460	658,000
Tata	Tata	10,010	25,925	107,000
Taza	Taza	5,799	15,020	715,000
Tétouan	Tétouan	2,326	6,025	864,000
Tiznit	Tiznit	2,687	6,960	381,000
Prefectures				
Ain Chok–Hay Hassani	—			452,000
Ain Sebaa–Hay Mohammadi	—			587,000
Ben Msik–Sidi Othmane	—	623	1,615	984,000
Casablanca-Anfa	—			1,069,000
Mohammadia–Znata	—			219,000
Rabat	—			690,000
Salé	—	492	1,275	656,000
Skhirate-Temara	—			199,000
TOTAL		177,117	458,730	25,344,000

Demography

Population (1992): 26,239,000.
Density (1992): persons per sq mi 148.1, persons per sq km 57.2.
Urban-rural (1992): urban 49.5%; rural 50.5%.
Sex distribution (1990): male 50.15%; female 49.85%.
Age breakdown (1990): under 15, 40.5%; 15–29, 28.3%; 30–44, 16.8%; 45–59, 8.4%; 60–74, 4.8%; 75 and over, 1.2%.
Population projection: (2000) 31,410,000; (2010) 37,360,000.
Doubling time: 29 years.
Ethnic composition (1986): Arab 70%; Berber 30%; other, less than 1%.
Religious affiliation (1982): Muslim (mostly Sunnī) 98.7%; Christian 1.1%.
Major cities (1982): Casablanca 2,139,204; Rabat 518,616; Fès 448,823.

Vital statistics

Birth rate per 1,000 population (1990–95): 32.6 (world avg. 26.4).
Death rate per 1,000 population (1990–95): 8.3 (world avg. 9.2).
Natural increase rate per 1,000 population (1990–95): 24.3 (world avg. 17.2).
Total fertility rate (avg. births per childbearing woman; 1990): 4.7.
Life expectancy at birth (1990): male 61.6 years; female 65.0 years.
Major causes of death (1989)[1]: childhood diseases 22.9%; circulatory diseases 15.4%; accidents 7.3%; infectious and parasitic diseases 6.3%; cancers 5.6%.

National economy

Budget (1992). Revenue: DH 73,427,000,000 (indirect taxes 21.8%; extraordinary revenue 21.4%; customs duties 19.8%; stamp duties 4.0%). Expenditures: DH 73,317,000,000 (current expenditure 81.5%, of which debt payments 30.6%; investment expenditure 18.5%).
Public debt (external, outstanding; 1990): U.S.$19,971,000,000.
Tourism: receipts from visitors (1990) U.S.$1,293,000,000; expenditures by nationals abroad (1989) U.S.$153,000,000.
Production (metric tons except as noted). Agriculture, forestry, fishing (1990): wheat 3,711,000, sugar beets 2,978,000, barley 2,138,000, sugarcane 1,092,000, tomatoes 940,000, potatoes 880,000; livestock (number of live animals) 17,500,000 sheep, 6,071,000 goats, 3,400,000 cattle, 39,000,000 chickens;

roundwood 2,136,000 cu m; fish catch (1989) 520,354. Mining and quarrying (1990): phosphate rock 21,189,000; barite 370,000[2]; iron ore 120,000; fluorite 105,000[2]; salt 89,075[2]; lead 74,400; zinc 17,500; copper 14,500. Manufacturing (1989): cement 4,641,000; refined sugar 751,979; carpets 1,642,914 sq m. Construction (value added in DH; 1989): 9,217,000. Energy production (consumption): electricity (kW-hr; 1990) 9,628,000,000 (9,628,000,000); coal (metric tons; 1990) 526,000 (1,762,000); crude petroleum (barrels; 1990) 114,000 (41,544,000); petroleum products (metric tons; 1990) 4,752,000 (4,965,000); natural gas (cu m; 1990) 50,741,000 (50,741,000).
Gross national product (1990): U.S.$23,788,000,000 (U.S.$950 per capita).

Structure of gross domestic product and labour force

	1990 in value DH '000,000	1990 % of total value	1982 labour force	1982 % of labour force
Agriculture	32,414	15.5	2,351,629	39.2
Mining	5,607	2.7	63,360	1.1
Manufacturing	39,089	18.7	930,615	15.5
Construction	11,418	5.5	437,464	7.3
Public utilities	15,074	7.2	22,465	0.4
Transp. and commun.	13,794	6.6	140,981	2.3
Trade	41,590	19.9 }	498,130	8.3
Finance	...	...		
Pub. admin., defense	25,643	12.3	532,803	8.9
Services }	24,084	11.5	474,109	7.9
Other			547,704[3]	9.1[3]
TOTAL	208,713	100.0[4]	5,999,260	100.0

Population economically active (1990)[5]: total 3,895,126; activity rate 32.5% (participation rates: over age 15, 49.6%; female 26.1%; unemployed 15.4%).

Price index (1985 = 100)

	1985	1986	1987	1988	1989	1990	1991
Consumer price index	100.0	108.7	111.7	114.3	117.9	126.0	136.1
Earnings index[6]	100.0	100.0	100.0	109.9	120.9	152.7	...

Household income and expenditure. Average household size (1982) 5.8; expenditure (1972–73)[7]: food 54.0%, clothing 8.5%, housing 7.0%, transportation 6.9%.
Land use (1989): forested 17.8%; meadows 46.8%; agricultural 20.7%.

Foreign trade[8]

Balance of trade (current prices)

	1986	1987	1988	1989	1990	1991
DH '000,000	−9,390	−8,707	−5,853	−14,130	−16,755	−13,327
% of total	17.5%	15.7%	9.0%	20.0%	19.3%	15.1%

Imports (1991): DH 55,888,000,000 (1990; capital goods 26.8%; crude oil 14.3%; consumer goods 11.6%; food, beverages, and tobacco 8.4%). *Major import sources* (1990): France 22.9%; Spain 8.4%; Italy 6.8%; W.Ger. 6.3%.
Exports (1991): DH 37,532,000,000 (1990; food 24.8%; phosphates 9.7%). *Major export destinations* (1990): France 31.5%; Spain 9.2%; Italy 6.9%.

Transport and communications

Transport. Railroads (1990): route length 1,893 km[2]; passenger-km 2,232,000,000; metric ton-km cargo 5,112,000,000. Roads (1990): total length 59,450 km (paved 49%). Vehicles (1990): passenger cars 666,158; trucks and buses 280,789. Merchant marine (1991): vessels (100 gross tons and over) 480; total deadweight tonnage 600,905. Air transport (1989): passenger-km 2,700,000,000; metric ton-km cargo 35,016,000; airports (1992) 16.
Communications. Daily newspapers (1989): total number 11; total circulation 360,000[9], circulation per 1,000 population 15[9]. Radio (1991): 4,500,000 receivers (1 per 5.7 persons). Television (1991): 1,210,000 receivers (1 per 21.2 persons). Telephones (1990): 402,000 (1 per 62 persons).

Education and health

Education (1990–91)

	schools	teachers	students	student/teacher ratio
Primary (age 7–12)	4,052	87,839	2,483,691	28.3
Secondary (age 13–17)[10]	1,080	69,915	1,121,193	16.0
Vocational[11]	562	5,359	68,802	12.8
Higher	35	7,713	225,001	29.2

Educational attainment (1982). Percentage of population age 25 and over having: no formal education 47.8%; some primary education 47.8%; some secondary 3.8%; higher 0.6%; not specified 2.3%. *Literacy* (1990): total population over age 15 literate 49.5%; males 61.3%; females literate 38.0%.
Health (1990): physicians 5,665 (1 per 4,415 persons); hospital beds 26,066[12] (1 per 959 persons); infant mortality rate (1990–95) 68.0.
Food (1987–89): daily per capita caloric intake 3,005 (vegetable products 94%, animal products 6%); 124% of FAO recommended minimum requirement.

Military

Total active duty personnel (1991): 195,500 (army 89.5%, navy 3.6%, air force 6.9%). *Military expenditure as percentage of GNP* (1989): 5.5% (world 4.9%); per capita expenditure U.S.$48.

---

[1]Registered deaths of urban population only. [2]1989. [3]Unemployed, not previously employed only. [4]Detail does not add to total given because of rounding. [5]Urban labour force only, representing the total urban employed and unemployed. [6]Based on minimum hourly wage of workers 18 years of age and older; values reflect adjustments made to the minimum wage during the year. [7]Weights of consumer price index components. [8]Import figures are f.o.b. in balance of trade. [9]For 8 newspapers only. [10]Public institutions only. [11]Excludes teacher training. [12]Public only.

Mozambique

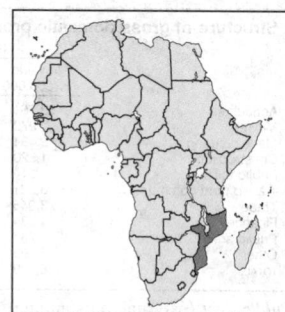

Official name: República de Moçambique (Republic of Mozambique).
Form of government: unitary republic[1] with a single legislative house (Assembly of the Republic [249]).
Chief of state and head of government: President.
Capital: Maputo.
Official language: Portuguese.
Official religion: none.
Monetary unit: 1 metical (Mt., plural meticais) = 100 centavos; valuation (Oct. 5, 1992) 1 U.S.$ = Mt. 2,712; 1 £ = Mt. 4,611.

Area and population

Provinces	Capitals	area sq mi	area sq km	population 1991 estimate
Cabo Delgado	Pemba	31,902	82,625	1,202,221
Gaza	Xai-Xai	29,231	75,709	1,401,485
Inhambane	Inhambane	26,492	68,615	1,156,958
Manica	Chimoio	23,807	61,661	609,512
Maputo	Maputo	9,944	25,756	840,757
Nampula	Nampula	31,508	81,606	2,841,416
Niassa	Lichinga	49,828	129,055	686,650
Sofala	Beira	26,262	68,018	1,427,493
Tete	Tete	38,890	100,724	734,561
Zambézia	Quelimane	40,544	105,008	2,619,281
City				
Maputo	—	232	602	931,591
TOTAL LAND AREA		308,642[2]	799,379	
INLAND WATER		5,019	13,000	
TOTAL		313,661[2]	812,379	14,451,925[3]

Demography

Population (1992)[3]: 14,842,000.
Density (1992)[4]: persons per sq mi 48.1, persons per sq km 18.6.
Urban-rural (1980): urban 13.2%; rural 86.8%.
Sex distribution (1990)[5]: male 49.32%; female 50.68%.
Age breakdown (1990)[5]: under 15, 44.0%; 15–29, 26.2%; 30–44, 15.4%; 45–59, 9.2%; 60–74, 4.4%; 75 and over, 0.8%.
Population projection: (2000) 18,574,000; (2010) 23,892,000.
Doubling time: 26 years.
Ethnolinguistic composition (1983): Makua 47.3%; Tsonga 23.3%; Malawi 12.0%; Shona 11.3%; Yao 3.8%; Swahili 0.8%; Makonde 0.6%; Portuguese 0.2%; other 0.7%.
Religious affiliation (1980): traditional beliefs 47.8%; Christian 38.9%, of which Roman Catholic 31.4%; Muslim 13.0%; other 0.3%.
Major cities (1991): Maputo 931,591; Beira 298,847; Nampula 250,473.

Vital statistics

Birth rate per 1,000 population (1990–95): 44.0 (world avg. 26.4).
Death rate per 1,000 population (1990–95): 17.0 (world avg. 9.2).
Natural increase rate per 1,000 population (1990–95): 27.0 (world avg. 17.2).
Total fertility rate (avg. births per childbearing woman; 1990–95): 6.2.
Marriage rate per 1,000 population (1974): 0.7.
Divorce rate per 1,000 population (1973): 0.01.
Life expectancy at birth (1990–95): male 46.9 years; female 50.2 years.
Major infectious diseases (certified cases per 100,000 population; 1980): measles 227.4; pulmonary tuberculosis 55.9; viral hepatitis 19.2; leprosy 13.8; cholera 4.6; tetanus 4.5.

National economy

Budget (1990). Revenue: Mt. 298,000,000,000 (indirect taxes 45.9%, customs taxes 21.9%, individual income tax 17.8%). Expenditures: Mt. 693,200,000,-000 (defense and security 19.6%, wages and salaries 9.4%).
Production (metric tons except as noted). Agriculture, forestry, fishing (1991): cassava 3,690,000, coconut 420,000, sugarcane 330,000, corn (maize) 327,000, sorghum 155,000, peanuts (groundnuts) 115,000, bananas 80,000; livestock (number of live animals) 1,370,000 cattle, 380,000 goats, 118,000 sheep, 106,-000 pigs, 22,000,000 chickens; roundwood (1990) 16,036,000 cu m; fish catch (1990) 35,000. Mining and quarrying (1992): marine salt 46,900[6]; bauxite 8,000; copper 133[6, 7]; garnet 2,250 kg; gemstones 15,000 carats. Manufacturing (1990): cement 76,767; wheat flour 49,368; raw sugar 33,141; soap 8,843; cotton threads 4,676; beer 352,900 hectolitres; cigarettes 414,000,000 units; poplin 3,664,000 sq m. Construction (1974): residential 247,000 sq m; nonresidential 121,000 sq m. Energy production (consumption): electricity (kW-hr; 1990) 485,000,000 (810,000,000); coal (metric tons; 1990) 40,000 (58,000); crude petroleum (1990) none (none[8]); petroleum products (metric tons; 1990) none[8] (262,000); natural gas, none (none).
Population economically active (1980): total 5,671,290; activity rate of total population 48.6% (participation rates: over age 15, 87.3%; female 52.4%; unemployed 1.7%).

Price and earnings indexes (1985 = 100)

	1984	1985	1986	1987	1988	1989	1990
Consumer price index	77.4	100.0	138.7	365.2	548.2	778.9	1,145.0
Earnings index	...	...	...	...	...	...	...

Public debt (external, outstanding; 1991): U.S.$5,187,000,000.
Household income and expenditure. Average household size (1980) 4.2; income per household: n.a.; sources of income: n.a.; expenditure: n.a.
Gross national product (at current market prices; 1990): U.S.$1,208,000,000 (U.S.$80 per capita).

Structure of gross domestic product and labour force

	1990 in value Mt. '000,000	1990 % of total value	1980 labour force	1980 % of labour force
Agriculture	637,000	37.3	4,754,831	83.8
Mining	} 390,000[9]	} 22.9[9]	73,425	1.3
Manufacturing			273,369	4.8
Construction	225,000	13.2	42,121	0.7
Public utilities	...	...	10	10
Transportation and communications	162,400	9.5	77,025	1.4
Trade and finance			112,244	2.0
Pub. admin., defense	} 292,200	} 17.1	243,449[10]	4.3[10]
Services				
Other			94,826[11]	1.7[11]
TOTAL	1,706,700[2]	100.0	5,671,290	100.0

Tourism: n.a.
Land use (1990): forested 18.2%; meadows and pastures 56.1%; agricultural and under permanent cultivation 4.0%; other 21.7%.

Foreign trade[12]

Balance of trade (current prices)

	1985	1986	1987	1988	1989	1990
U.S.$'000,000	−347	−464	−528	−612	−670	−648
% of total	69.3%	74.6%	73.1%	74.8%	76.1%	71.8%

Imports (1989): U.S.$775,000,000 (foodstuffs 22.1%, capital equipment 18.8%, machinery and spare parts 13.3%, crude petroleum and derivatives 7.5%). *Major import sources:* South Africa 23.2%; U.S.S.R. 9.8%; United States 7.1%; Portugal 6.8%; Italy 6.0%.
Exports (1990): U.S.$126,400,000 (shrimps 34.3%, cashew nuts 11.3%, cotton 6.9%, sugar 6.3%, timber 1.3%). *Major export destinations:* Spain 17.9%; United States 11.6%; Japan 10.4%; Portugal 5.6%.

Transport and communications

Transport. Railroads (1988): route length (1991) 1,857 mi, 2,988 km; passenger-mi 46,800,000, passenger-km 75,300,000; short ton-mi cargo 158,800,-000, metric ton-km cargo 231,800,000. Roads (1989): total length 16,215 mi, 26,095 km (paved 20%). Vehicles (1990): passenger cars 87,500; trucks and buses 24,000. Merchant marine (1991): vessels (100 gross tons and over) 114; total deadweight tonnage 29,942. Air transport (1990): passenger-mi 344,133,000, passenger-km 553,829,000; short ton-mi cargo 41,532,000, metric ton-km cargo 60,636,000; airports (1992) with scheduled flights 7.
Communications. Daily newspapers (1991): total number 2; total circulation 49,000; circulation per 1,000 population 3.3. Radio (1991): total number of receivers 500,000 (1 per 29 persons). Television (1991): total number of receivers 35,000 (1 per 418 persons). Telephones (1990): 66,000 (1 per 217 persons).

Education and health

Education (1988)

	schools	teachers	students	student/teacher ratio
Primary (age 5–9)[13]	3,647	21,410	1,199,669	56.0
Secondary (age 10–16)[14]	207	3,422	107,080	31.3
Voc., teacher tr.	32	968	10,604	10.9
Higher	2	457	2,562	5.6

Educational attainment (1980). Percentage of population age 25 and over having: no formal schooling 80.7%; primary education 18.2%; secondary 0.9%; higher 0.2%. *Literacy* (1990): percentage of total population age 15 and over literate 32.9%; males literate 45.1%; females literate 21.3%.
Health (1988): physicians 342 (1 per 43,536 persons); hospital beds 12,129 (1 per 1,227 persons); infant mortality rate per 1,000 live births (1990–95) 130.0.
Food (1988–90): daily per capita caloric intake 1,805 (vegetable products 97%, animal products 3%); 77% of FAO recommended minimum requirement.

Military

Total active duty personnel (1992): 50,200 (army 89.6%, navy 2.4%, air force 8.0%). *Military expenditure as percentage of GNP* (1989): 9.7% (world 4.9%); per capita expenditure U.S.$8.

---

[1]Mozambique adopted a new multiparty constitution, which became effective on Nov. 30, 1990; multiparty elections are planned for 1993. [2]Detail does not add to total given because of rounding. [3]Excludes refugees in nearby countries. [4]Density is based on land area. [5]Includes refugees in nearby countries. [6]1990. [7]Metal content only. [8]Internal disorder and a lack of foreign exchange have brought importation of crude petroleum and the production of refined petroleum products practically to a halt. [9]Includes fishing industry. [10]Services includes Public utilities. [11]Unemployed. [12]Import figures are c.i.f. [13]Includes initiation classes in which pupils learn Portuguese. [14]Includes the two stages of secondary education and the upper-level primary stage.

Myanmar (Burma)

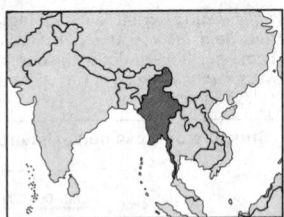

Official name: Pyidaungzu Myanma
  Naingngandaw (Union of Myanmar).
Form of government: military regime[1].
Head of state and government:
  Chairman of the State Law and Order
  Restoration Council.
Capital: Yangôn (Rangoon).
Official language: Burmese.
Official religion: none.
Monetary unit: 1 Myanmar kyat
  (K) = 100 pyas; valuation (Oct. 5,
  1992) 1 U.S.$ = K 6.65; 1 £ = K 11.31.

Area and population		area		population
				1983
Divisions	**Capitals**	sq mi	sq km	census
Irrawaddy (Ayeyarwady)	Bassein (Pathein)	13,567	35,138	4,994,061
Magwe (Magway)	Magwe (Magway)	17,305	44,820	3,243,166
Mandalay	Mandalay	14,295	37,024	4,577,762
Pegu (Bago)	Pegu (Bago)	15,214	39,404	3,799,791
Sagaing	Sagaing	36,535	94,625	3,862,172
Tenasserim (Tanintharyi)	Tavoy (Dawei)	16,735	43,343	917,247
Yangôn	Yangôn (Rangoon)	3,927	10,171	3,965,916
States				
Chin	Hakha	13,907	36,019	368,949
Kachin	Myitkyinā	34,379	89,041	904,794
Karen	Pa-an (Hpa-an)	11,731	30,383	1,055,359
Kayah	Loi-kaw	4,530	11,733	168,429
Mon	Moulmein (Mawlamyine)	4,748	12,297	1,680,157
Rakhine (Arakan)	Sittwe (Akyab)	14,200	36,778	2,045,559
Shan	Taunggyi	60,155	155,801	3,716,841
TOTAL		261,228	676,577	35,307,913[2]

Demography

Population (1992): 43,466,000.
Density (1992): persons per sq mi 166.4, persons per sq km 64.2.
Urban-rural (1991): urban 25.0%; rural 75.0%.
Sex distribution (1988): male 49.57%; female 50.43%.
Age breakdown (1988): under 15, 36.8%; 15–29, 29.5%; 30–44, 17.1%; 45–59, 10.3%; 60 and over, 6.3%.
Population projection: (2000) 51,129,000; (2010) 60,567,000.
Doubling time: 37 years.
Ethnic composition (1983): Burman 69.0%; Shan 8.5%; Karen 6.2%; Rakhine 4.5%; Mon 2.4%; Chin 2.2%; Kachin 1.4%; other 5.8%.
Religious affiliation (1983): Buddhist 89.4%; Christian 4.9%; Muslim 3.8%; tribal religions 1.1%; Hindu 0.5%; other 0.3%.
Major cities (1983): Yangôn (Rangoon) 2,513,023; Mandalay 532,949; Moulmein (Mawlamyine) 219,961; Pegu (Bago) 150,528; Bassein (Pathein) 144,096.

Vital statistics

Birth rate per 1,000 population (1991): 32.0 (world avg. 26.4).
Death rate per 1,000 population (1991): 13.0 (world avg. 9.2).
Natural increase rate per 1,000 population (1991): 19.0 (world avg. 17.2).
Total fertility rate (avg. births per childbearing woman; 1991): 4.1.
Marriage rate per 1,000 population: n.a.
Divorce rate per 1,000 population: n.a.
Life expectancy at birth (1991): male 60.0 years; female 63.5 years.
Major causes of death per 100,000 population (1978): pneumonia 16.1; heart diseases 10.5; enteritis and other diarrheal diseases 10.0; tuberculosis 9.4; malignant neoplasms (cancers) 6.5; cerebrovascular disease 4.1; malaria 3.5.

National economy

Budget (1990–91). Revenue: K 8,929,000,000 (revenue from taxes 50.4%, receipts from state economic enterprises 49.6%). Expenditures: K 14,235,-000,000 (current expenditures 78.8%, capital expenditures 21.2%).
Tourism (1990): receipts from visitors U.S.$5,000,000; expenditures by nationals abroad U.S.$1,000,000.
Production (metric tons except as noted). Agriculture, forestry, fishing (1991): rice 13,201,000, sugarcane 2,143,000, peanuts (groundnuts) 505,000, pulses 484,000, plantains 241,000, sesame seeds 231,000, corn (maize) 190,000, onions 172,000, millet 138,000, potatoes 136,000, seed cotton 64,000, tobacco leaves 40,000, jute 29,000; livestock (number of live animals) 9,310,000 cattle, 2,250,000 pigs, 2,080,000 buffalo, 1,320,000 sheep and goats, 4,000,000 ducks, 24,000,000 chickens; roundwood (1990) 23,182,000 cu m; fish catch (1990) 743,818. Mining and quarrying (1990–91): copper concentrates 31,500; gypsum 30,536; refined lead 2,750; tin concentrates 676; refined silver 190,000 troy oz. Manufacturing (value of production in '000,000 kyats; 1987–88): food and beverages 23,549.8; clothing and wearing apparel 1,606.6; industrial raw materials 1,468.9; construction materials 1,120.9; transport vehicles 719.0; personal goods 327.8. Construction (units; 1987–88)[3]: residential 1,193; nonresidential 1,483. Energy production (consumption): electricity (kW-hr; 1990) 2,601,000,000 (2,601,000,000); coal (metric tons; 1990) 78,000 (118,000); crude petroleum (barrels; 1990) 6,376,000 (6,376,000); petroleum products (metric tons; 1990) 566,000 (567,000); natural gas (cu m; 1990) 1,075,000,000 (1,075,000,000).
Household income and expenditure. Average household size (1983) 5.2; average annual income per household: n.a.; sources of income: n.a.; expenditure (1978)[4]: food and beverages 64.4%, clothing and footwear 8.0%, fuel and light 7.8%, household rent and repairs 3.8%, tobacco 3.7%, other 12.3%.
Gross national product (at current market prices; 1989–90): U.S.$16,330,000,-000 (U.S.$400 per capita).

Structure of gross domestic product and labour force				
	1990–91		1989–90	
	in value K '000,000	% of total value	labour force	% of labour force
Agriculture	68,761	59.2	10,614,000	67.6
Mining	970	0.8	78,000	0.5
Manufacturing	9,484	8.2	1,137,000	7.2
Construction	1,520	1.3	174,000	1.1
Public utilities	514	0.4	17,000	0.1
Transp. and commun.	3,021	2.6	385,000	2.5
Trade	23,945	20.6	1,405,000	8.9
Finance	234	0.2 }	956,000	6.1
Public admin., services	4,287	3.7 }		
Other	3,493	3.0	935,000	6.0
TOTAL	116,229	100.0	15,701,000	100.0

Public debt (external, outstanding; 1990): U.S.$4,415,000,000.
Population economically active (1989–90): total 15,701,000; activity rate of total population 38.2% (participation rates: ages 15–64 [1983] 64.2%; female [1987–88] 35.3%; unemployed [1987–88] 4.3%).

Price and earnings indexes (1985 = 100)							
	1985	1986	1987	1988	1989	1990	1991
Consumer price index	100.0	109.3	136.4	158.3	201.3	236.8	313.2
Monthly earnings index[5]	100.0	101.7	113.5	199.2	277.6	...	...

Land use (1990): forested 49.3%; meadows and pastures 0.5%; agricultural and under permanent cultivation 15.3%; other 34.9%.

Foreign trade[6]

Balance of trade (current prices)						
	1986	1987	1988	1989	1990	1991
K '000,000	+160.0	−173.5	−346.8	+274.9	+485.0	−1,055.4
% of total	3.8%	5.6%	14.2%	10.6%	13.5%	16.7%

Imports (1989–90): K 3,500,000,000 (machinery and equipment 51.4%, industrial raw materials 31.4%, consumer goods 17.1%). *Major import sources* (1988–89): Japan 40.3%; EEC 36.5%; Southeast Asian countries 7.6%; eastern European countries 3.0%; North America 1.7%.
Exports (1989–90): K 3,632,400,000 (agricultural products 31.5%, forest products 23.8%, minerals and gems 8.7%, animal and marine products 4.5%). *Major export destinations* (1988–89): Southeast Asian countries 23.4%; India 16.9; China 9.1%; EEC 7.0%; African countries 6.9%; Japan 5.0%.

Transport and communications

Transport. Railroads (1990–91): route length 1,949 mi, 3,137 km; passenger-mi 2,781,000,000, passenger-km 4,476,000,000; short ton-mi cargo 395,000,-000, metric ton-km cargo 576,000,000. Roads (1988): total length 14,579 mi, 23,463 km (paved 38%). Vehicles (1989): passenger cars 27,000; trucks and buses 42,000. Merchant marine (1991): vessels (100 gross tons and over) 154; total deadweight tonnage 1,525,615. Air transport (1987–88): passenger-mi 133,270,000, passenger-km 214,471,000; short ton-mi cargo 1,470,000, metric ton-km cargo 2,146,000; airports (1992) with scheduled flights 20.
Communications. Daily newspapers (1990): total number 6; total circulation 498,000; circulation per 1,000 population 12. Radio (1991): total receivers 3,200,000 (1 per 13 persons). Television (1991): total receivers 1,000,000 (1 per 43 persons). Telephones (1988): 80,568 (1 per 501 persons).

Education and health

Education (1990–91)	schools	teachers	students	student/ teacher ratio
Primary (age 5–9)	36,499	198,909	5,423,500	27.3
Secondary (age 10–15)	2,920	67,503	1,262,100	18.7
Voc., teacher tr.	101	2,079	25,100	12.1
Higher	31	5,974	218,800	36.6

Educational attainment (1983). Percentage of population age 25 and over having: no formal schooling 55.8%; primary education 39.4%; secondary 4.6%; religious 0.1%; postsecondary 0.1%. *Literacy* (1983): total population age 15 and over literate 16,472,494 (78.5%); males literate 8,816,031 (85.8%); females literate 7,656,463 (71.6%).
Health (1990–91): physicians 12,427 (1 per 3,389 persons); hospital beds 26,294 (1 per 1,602 persons); infant mortality rate per 1,000 live births (1991) 62.
Food (1988–90): daily per capita caloric intake 2,454 (vegetable products 96%, animal products 4%); 114% of FAO recommended minimum requirement.

Military

Total active duty personnel (1992): 286,000 (army 92.7%, navy 4.2%, air force 3.1%). *Military expenditure as percentage of GNP* (1989): 3.7% (world 4.9%); per capita expenditure U.S.$15.

[1]Multiparty elections were held on May 27, 1990, for seats in a 492-seat National Assembly; although the opposition party, the National League for Democracy, won a majority of the seats, the military government has refused to hand over power. [2]Includes 7,710 persons not distributed by area. [3]Construction Corporation activity only. [4]Based on 24 rural townships. [5]Wages in manufacturing. [6]Import figures are f.o.b. in balance of trade and c.i.f. in commodities and trading partners.

Namibia[1]

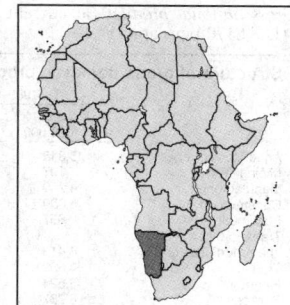

Official name: Republic of Namibia.
Political status: unitary multiparty republic with one legislative house (National Assembly [72[2]]).
Head of state and government: President.
Capital: Windhoek.
Official language: English.
Official religion: none.
Monetary unit[3]: 1 Namibian dollar (Nam$) = 100 cents; valuation (Oct. 5, 1992) 1 U.S.$ = Nam$2.84; 1 £ = Nam$4.82.

Area and population[4]

Districts	Capitals	area sq mi	area sq km	population 1992 estimate
Caprivi	—	7,541	19,532	92,000
Erongo	—	24,602	63,719	98,500
Hardap	—	42,428	109,888	80,000
Karas	—	62,288	161,324	73,000
Khomas	—	14,210	36,804	161,000
Kunene	—	55,697	144,254	58,500
Ohangwena	—	4,086	10,582	178,000
Okavango	—	16,763	43,417	136,000
Omaheke	—	32,714	84,731	55,600
Omusati	—	5,265	13,637	158,000
Oshana	—	2,042	5,290	159,000
Oshikoto	—	10,273	26,607	176,000
Otjozondjupa	—	40,667	105,327	85,000
TOTAL		318,580[5]	825,580[5]	1,511,600[5]

Demography

Population (1992): 1,512,000.
Density (1992): persons per sq mi 4.5, persons per sq km 1.7.
Urban-rural (1991): urban 32.8%; rural 67.2%.
Sex distribution (1991): male 49.78%; female 50.22%.
Age breakdown (1990): under 15, 45.7%; 15–29, 25.5%; 30–44, 15.0%; 45–59, 8.6%; 60–74, 4.3%; 75 and over, 0.9%.
Population projection: (2000) 1,820,000; (2010) 2,458,000.
Doubling time: 23 years.
Ethnic composition (1989): Ovambo 49.8%; Kavango 9.3%; Herero 7.5%; Damara 7.5%; white 6.4%; Nama 4.8%; other 14.7%.
Religious affiliation (1981): Lutheran 51.2%; Roman Catholic 19.8%; Dutch Reformed 6.1%; Anglican 5.0%; other 17.9%.
Major cities (1988): Windhoek 114,500; Swakopmund 15,500; Rundu 15,000; Rehoboth 15,000; Keetmanshoop 14,000.

Vital statistics

Birth rate per 1,000 population (1990–95): 41.6 (world avg. 26.4).
Death rate per 1,000 population (1990–95): 10.6 (world avg. 9.2).
Natural increase rate per 1,000 population (1990–95): 31.0 (world avg. 17.2).
Total fertility rate (avg. births per childbearing woman; 1990–95): 5.7.
Life expectancy at birth (1990–95): male 57.5 years; female 60.0 years.
Major causes of death per 100,000 population: n.a.; however, major diseases include malaria, tuberculosis, and trypanosomiasis (sleeping sickness).

National economy

Budget (1991–92). Revenue: R 2,806,000,000 (customs and excise taxes 42.8%, of which general sales tax 13.9%; individual income taxes 10.7%; mining taxes 4.4%; nontax revenues 3.7%). Expenditures: R 3,120,000,000 (education 18.6%; health and welfare 16.9%; finance 10.3%; national defense 5.2%).
Tourism (1981): receipts U.S.$45,960,000; expenditures, n.a.
Production (metric tons except as noted). Agriculture, forestry, fishing (1991): roots and tubers 275,000, corn (maize) 50,000, millet 50,000, fruits 36,000, vegetables and melons 33,000, sorghum 8,000, pulses 7,000, wool 1,200, karakul pelts 770,627 units[6]; livestock (number of live animals) 2,131,000 cattle, 6,700,000 sheep, 1,900,000 goats; fish catch (1990) 289,770. Mining and quarrying (1991): diamonds 1,187,000 carats, mostly gem quality; zinc 68,098; lead 33,367; copper 31,928; uranium 2,900; silver 2,926,000 troy oz; gold 59,510 troy oz. Manufacturing (1991): n.a.; products include cut gems (primarily diamonds), fur products (karakul), processed foods (fish, meats, and dairy products), textiles, carved wood products, refined metals (copper and lead). Construction (value of buildings completed in R '000,000; 1990): residential 44.6; nonresidential 92.4. Energy production (consumption): electricity (kW-hr; 1989) 1,181,000,000 (n.a.); coal, none (n.a.); crude petroleum, none (n.a.).
Population economically active: total (1988) c. 230,000; activity rate of total population, c. 18% (participation rates [1984]: ages 15–64, c. 56%; female 20.4%; unemployed [1988] c. 20%).

Price and earnings indexes (1985 = 100)[7]

	1984	1985	1986	1987	1988	1989	1990
Consumer price index	89.3	100.0	113.4	127.7	144.1	165.9	185.7
Earnings index	...	...	...	...	...	...	...

Household income and expenditure. Average household size (1981) 4.8; average annual income per household (1980) R 3,223 (U.S.$4,143); sources of income (1989): wages and salaries 70.0%, income from property 24.4%, transfer payments 5.2%; expenditure: n.a.

Public debt (external, outstanding; 1989): U.S.$1,880,000,000.
Gross national product (1989): U.S.$1,350,000,000 (U.S.$1,030 per capita).

Structure of gross domestic product and labour force

	1990 in value R '000,000	1990 % of total value	1988 labour force[8, 9]	1988 % of labour force[8, 9]
Agriculture	750.0	15.4	36,071	19.5
Mining	1,050.0	21.6	10,062	5.5
Manufacturing	303.0	6.2	9,442	5.1
Construction	113.0	2.3	12,657	6.8
Public utilities	96.0	2.0	1,273	0.7
Transp. and commun.	318.0	6.5	7,880	4.3
Trade	605.0	12.4	29,394	15.9
Finance	365.0	7.5	4,327	2.3
Services	98.0	2.0	25,167	13.6
Public admin., defense	1,019.0	20.9	48,520	26.3
Other	151.0	3.1	...	...
TOTAL	4,868.0	100.0[5]	184,793	100.0

Land use (1990): forested 22.0%; meadows and pastures 46.2%; agricultural and under permanent cultivation 0.8%; other 31.0%.

Foreign trade

Balance of trade (current prices)

	1984	1985	1986	1987	1988	1989
R '000,000	−82.9	324.2	511.7	97.0	179.5	332.0
% of total	3.6%	11.3%	14.8%	2.8%	4.4%	6.6%

Imports (1989): R 2,339,600,000 (1988; chemical and petroleum products 21.5%; food and agricultural products 17.1%; machinery and transport equipment 6.6%; other 46.2%). *Major import sources:* South Africa (75–100%).
Exports (1989): R 2,671,600,000 (minerals 75.9%, of which diamonds 30.5%; agricultural products 11.0%, of which cattle 5.8%, karakul pelts 0.9%). *Major export destinations* (1986): U.S. 25%; South Africa 19%; Japan 15%.

Transport and communications

Transport. Railroads: length (1990) 1,480 mi, 2,382 km; passenger-km 6,500,000; metric ton-km 1,198,000,000. Roads (1991): total length 26,570 mi, 42,760 km (paved 11%). Number of registered motor vehicles (1986): 103,715. Merchant marine (1991): vessels (100 gross tons and over) 1; total deadweight tonnage, n.a. Air transport (1990)[10]: passenger-km 561,565,000; metric ton-km cargo 3,309,000; airports (1992) with scheduled flights 11.
Communications. Daily newspapers (1991): total number 5; total circulation 49,500; circulation per 1,000 population 36. Radio (1987): 210,000 receivers (1 per 5.7 persons). Television (1991): 27,000 receivers (1 per 49 persons). Telephones (1987): 69,273 (1 per 17 persons).

Education and health

Education (1988)

	schools	teachers	students	student/ teacher ratio
Primary (age 6–12) }	1,118	12,525	286,836 }	22.9
Secondary (age 13–19)			77,770 }	
Voc., teacher tr.	9	81[11]	1,200[11]	14.8[11]
Higher	1	170[6]	4,200[6]	24.7[6]

Educational attainment (1977). Percentage of labour force having: no formal schooling 59.8%; primary education 33.2%; secondary 5.0%; higher 2.0%.
Literacy (1985): total population age 15 and over literate 474,000 (72.5%); males literate 239,000 (74.2%); females literate 235,000 (70.8%).
Health (1988): physicians 281 (1 per 4,450 persons); hospital beds 7,540 (1 per 166 persons); infant mortality rate per 1,000 live births (1990–95) 97.
Food (1979–81): daily per capita caloric intake 2,197 (vegetable products 77%, animal products 23%); 96% of FAO recommended minimum requirement.

Military

Total active duty personnel (1992): 7,500 (army 98.7%, navy 1.3%). *Military expenditure as percentage of GNP* (1984): 7.7% (world 5.9%); per capita expenditure U.S.$113.

---

[1]On March 21, 1990, Namibia achieved independence, its constitution (approved Feb. 9, 1990) became effective, the 72-member Constituent Assembly (elected Nov. 7–11, 1989) became the National Assembly, and a president (elected Feb. 6, 1990, by the Constituent Assembly) was sworn in. [2]Seventy-two elected and up to six appointed members. [3]As of June 1992, the Namibian dollar circulates at par and concurrently with the South African rand. [4]Excludes area and population of Walvis Bay (in August 1992 Namibia and South Africa agreed to the future joint administration of Walvis Bay). [5]Detail does not add to total given because of rounding. [6]1987. [7]Windhoek only. [8]Employed persons only. [9]Formal sector only. [10]Namib Air only. [11]1982.

Nepal

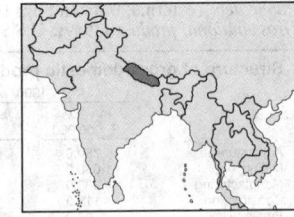

Official name: Nepāl Adhirājya
(Kingdom of Nepal).
Form of government: constitutional
monarchy with two legislative houses
(National Council [60[1]]; House of
Representatives [205]).
Chief of state: King.
Head of government: Prime Minister.
Capital: Kāthmāndu.
Official language: Nepālī.
Official religion: Hinduism.
Monetary unit: 1 Nepalese rupee
(NRs) = 100 paisa (pice); valuation
(Oct. 5, 1992) 1 U.S.$ = NRs 46.55;
1 £ = NRs 79.13.

Area and population		area		population
		sq mi	sq km	1990 estimate
Development regions Zones	Capitals			
Eastern	Dhankūtā	10,987	28,456	4,750,000
Koshī		3,733	9,669	1,885,000
Mechī		3,165	8,196	1,268,000
Sāgarmāthā		4,089	10,591	1,597,000
Central	Kāthmāndu	10,583	27,410	6,068,000
Bāgmatī		3,640	9,428	2,093,000
Janakpur		3,733	9,669	2,052,000
Nārāyanī		3,210	8,313	1,923,000
Western	Pokharā	11,351	29,398	3,884,000
Dhawalāgiri		3,146	8,148	508,000
Gandakī		4,740	12,275	1,320,000
Lumbinī		3,465	8,975	2,056,000
Mid-western	Surkhet	16,362	42,378	2,469,000
Bherī		4,071	10,545	1,153,000
Karnālī		8,244	21,351	281,000
Rāptī		4,047	10,482	1,035,000
Far-western	Dipāyal	7,544	19,539	1,746,000
Mahākālī		2,698	6,989	1,022,000
Setī		4,846	12,550	724,000
TOTAL		56,827	147,181	18,917,000

Demography

Population (1992): 19,795,000.
Density (1992): persons per sq mi 348.3, persons per sq km 134.5.
Urban-rural (1987): urban 8.3%; rural 91.7%.
Sex distribution (1991): male 51.63%; female 48.37%.
Age breakdown (1986): under 15, 42.2%; 15–29, 25.6%; 30–44, 17.3%; 45–59, 10.0%; 60–74, 4.2%; 75 and over, 0.7%.
Population projection: (2000) 23,176,000; (2010) 27,807,000.
Doubling time: 29 years.
Ethnic composition (1981): Nepalese 58.4%; Bihārī (including Maithilī and Bhojpurī) 18.7%; Tharu 3.6%; Tamang 3.5%; Newār 3.0%; other 12.8%.
Religious affiliation (1981): Hindu 89.5%; Buddhist 5.3%; Muslim 2.7%; Jain 0.1%; other 2.4%.
Major cities (1981): Kāthmāndu 235,160; Birātnagar 93,544; Lalitpur 79,875; Bhaktapur 48,472; Pokharā 46,642.

Vital statistics

Birth rate per 1,000 population (1991): 39.0 (world avg. 26.4).
Death rate per 1,000 population (1991): 15.0 (world avg. 9.2).
Natural increase rate per 1,000 population (1991): 24.0 (world avg. 17.2).
Total fertility rate (avg. births per childbearing woman; 1991): 5.6.
Marriage rate per 1,000 population: n.a.
Divorce rate per 1,000 population: n.a.
Life expectancy at birth (1990): male 55.4 years; female 52.6 years.
Major causes of death per 100,000 population: n.a.; however, the leading causes of mortality are infectious and parasitic diseases, diseases of the respiratory system, diseases of the nervous system, diseases of the circulatory system, and injuries and poisoning.

National economy

Budget (1990–91). Revenue: NRs 12,356,600,000 (import duties 23.9%, foreign grants 20.3%, general sales tax 14.6%, excise taxes 10.0%, administrative fees and charges 9.1%, income taxes 7.9%, property taxes 4.3%). Expenditures: NRs 18,989,000,000 (transportation and communications 12.6%, education 10.9%, agriculture 9.6%, interest payments 8.3%, general public services 8.0%, housing 6.8%, defense 5.9%, health 4.7%).
Tourism (1990): receipts from visitors U.S.$57,000,000; expenditures by nationals abroad U.S.$45,000,000.
Land use (1990): forested 18.1%; meadows and pastures 14.6%; agricultural and under permanent cultivation 19.4%; other 47.9%.
Production (metric tons except as noted). Agriculture, forestry, fishing (1991): rice 3,600,000, corn (maize) 1,235,000, sugarcane 1,106,000, wheat 836,000, potatoes 738,000, pulses 279,000, millet 220,000, barley 28,000, jute 16,000, tobacco 7,000; livestock (number of live animals) 6,350,000 cattle, 5,355,000 goats, 3,101,000 buffalo, 925,000 sheep, 575,000 pigs; roundwood (1990) 18,217,000 cu m; fish catch (1990) 14,546. Mining and quarrying (1989): limestone 289,743; magnesite 27,978; talc 6,728; garnet 25,000 kg. Manufacturing (1989–90): cement 101,179; sugar 29,996; soap 11,943; jute goods 7,473; tea 984; cigarettes 6,137,000,000 units; shoes 710,000 pairs. Construction: n.a. Energy production (consumption): electricity (kW-hr; 1990) 739,000,000 (771,000,000); coal (metric tons; 1990) none (35,000); petroleum products (metric tons; 1990) none (174,000); natural gas, none (none).

Gross national product (at current market prices; 1990): U.S.$3,289,000,000 (U.S.$170 per capita).

Structure of gross domestic product and labour force				
	1989–90		1984–85	
	in value NRs '000,000	% of total value	labour force	% of labour force
Agriculture	45,848	54.0	...	79.0
Mining	107	0.1	...	...
Manufacturing	4,200	4.9	...	3.6
Construction	5,680	6.7	...	8.2[2]
Public utilities	657	0.8	...	[3]
Transportation and communications	4,413	5.2	...	[2]
Trade	4,059	4.8	...	2.9
Finance	6,524	7.7	...	
Services	6,787	8.0	...	6.3
Other	6,636[4]	7.8[4]	...	
TOTAL	84,911	100.0		100.0

Population economically active (1986): total 7,760,155; activity rate of total population 45.5% (participation rates: ages 15–64, 82.5%; female 34.7%; unemployed [1980] 5.5%).

Price and earnings indexes (1985 = 100)						
	1985	1986	1987	1988	1989	1990	1991
Consumer price index	100.0	119.0	131.8	143.6	156.3	169.2	195.5
Earnings index	...	...	...	...	...	...	...

Public debt (external, outstanding; 1990): U.S.$1,545,000,000.
Household income and expenditure (1984–85). Average household size 6.1; income per household NRs 14,796 (U.S.$853); sources of income: self-employment 63.4%, wages and salaries 25.1%, rent 7.5%, other 4.0%; expenditure: food and beverages 61.2%, housing 17.3%, clothing 11.7%, health care 3.7%, education and recreation 2.9%, transportation and communications 1.2%, other 2.0%.

Foreign trade[5]

Balance of trade (current prices)						
	1986	1987	1988	1989	1990	1991
NRs '000,000	−6,275.7	−7,659.6	−10,780	−10,796	−13,037	−17,059
% of total	51.0%	52.8%	54.6%	56.2%	51.4%	46.5%

Imports (1988–89): NRs 16,263,714,000 (machinery and transport equipment 29.8%; basic manufactured goods 28.7%; chemicals 9.4%; food and live animals, chiefly for food 8.2%; crude materials except fuels 7.3%; mineral fuels 6.9%). *Major import sources* (1987–88): India 33.1%; Japan 13.9%; Singapore 8.8%; West Germany 5.4%; South Korea 4.6%; China 3.7%.
Exports (1988–89): NRs 4,195,297,000 (basic manufactures 47.3%; food and live animals, chiefly for food 13.8%; crude materials except fuels 6.0%; animal and vegetable oils 2.4%). *Major export destinations* (1987–88): India 38.1%; United States 23.0%; West Germany 16.5%; United Kingdom 6.2%; Italy 1.7%; Belgium 1.4%.

Transport and communications

Transport. Railroads (1989–90): route length 33 mi, 53 km; passengers carried 1,100,000; freight handled 13,000 metric tons. Roads (1989): total length 4,354 mi, 7,007 km (paved 41%). Vehicles (1978): passenger cars 14,201; trucks and buses 9,988. Merchant marine: none. Air transport[6] (1989): passenger-mi 254,000,000, passenger-km 408,000,000; short ton-mi cargo 7,455,000, metric ton-km cargo 10,884,000; airports (1992) with scheduled flights 5.
Communications. Daily newspapers (1988): total number 28; total circulation 122,000[7]; circulation per 1,000 population, 6.7[7]. Radio (1991): 600,000 receivers (1 per 32 persons). Television (1990): 35,100 receivers (1 per 539 persons). Telephones (1989): 44,514 (1 per 415 persons).

Education and health

Education (1988–89)	schools	teachers	students	student/ teacher ratio
Primary (age 6–10)	13,514	57,204	2,108,739	36.9
Secondary (age 11–15)	5,535	21,132	612,943	29.0
Vocational[8]	5	117	648	5.5
Higher[8]	116	4,165	67,555	16.2

Educational attainment (1981). Percentage of population age 25 and over having: no formal schooling 41.2%; primary education 29.4%; secondary 22.7%; higher 6.8%. *Literacy* (1991): total population age 15 and over literate 4,255,000 (37.7%); males literate 2,975,000 (51.7%); females literate 1,280,000 (23.3%).
Health (1989–90): physicians 951 (1 per 19,644 persons); hospital beds 4,717 (1 per 3,960 persons); infant mortality rate per 1,000 live births (1991) 98.
Food (1988–90): daily per capita caloric intake 2,205 (vegetable products 94%, animal products 6%); 100% of FAO recommended minimum requirement.

Military

Total active duty personnel (1992): 35,000 (army 99.4%, air force 0.6%). *Military expenditure as percentage of GNP* (1989): 1.2% (world 4.9%); per capita expenditure U.S.$2.

[1]Includes 10 members nominated by the King. [2]Construction includes transportation and communications. [3]Less than 0.05%. [4]Includes indirect taxes. [5]Import figures are f.o.b. in balance of trade and c.i.f. for commodities and trading partners. [6]International flights only. [7]Circulation for 22 dailies only. [8]1985–86.

Netherlands, The

Official name: Koninkrijk der Nederlanden (Kingdom of The Netherlands).
Form of government: constitutional monarchy with a parliament (States General) comprising two legislative houses (First Chamber [75]; Second Chamber [150]).
Chief of state: Monarch.
Head of government: Prime Minister.
Seat of government: The Hague.
Capital: Amsterdam.
Official language: Dutch.
Official religion: none.
Monetary unit: 1 Netherlands guilder (f.) = 100 cents; valuation (Oct. 5, 1992) 1 U.S.$ = f. 1.58; 1 £ = f. 2.69.

Area and population		area		population
				1990[1]
Provinces	Capitals	sq mi	sq km	estimate
Drenthe	Assen	1,025	2,654	441,028
Flevoland	Lelystad	549	1,422	211,507
Friesland	Leeuwarden	1,295	3,353	599,151
Gelderland	Arnhem	1,935	5,011	1,804,209
Groningen	Groningen	906	2,346	553,862
Limburg	Maastricht	838	2,170	1,103,960
Noord-Brabant	's-Hertogenbosch	1,910	4,946	2,189,481
Noord-Holland	Haarlem	1,029	2,665	2,376,015
Overijssel	Zwolle	1,289	3,339	1,020,424
Utrecht	Utrecht	514	1,331	1,015,515
Zeeland	Middelburg	692	1,792	355,947
Zuid-Holland	The Hague	1,123	2,908	3,219,839
TOTAL LAND AREA		13,103[2]	33,937	
INLAND WATER		3,060	7,926	
TOTAL		16,163	41,863	14,892,574[3]

Demography

Population (1992): 15,163,000.
Density[4] (1992): persons per sq mi 1,157.2, persons per sq km 446.8.
Urban-rural (1990): urban 88.5%; rural 11.5%.
Sex distribution (1990): male 49.41%; female 50.59%.
Age breakdown (1990): under 15, 18.2%; 15–29, 24.6%; 30–44, 23.7%; 45–59, 16.2%; 60–74, 11.9%; 75 and over, 5.4%.
Population projection: (2000) 15,885,000; (2010) 16,403,000.
Doubling time: not applicable; vital rates and net migration in near balance.
Ethnic composition (by nationality; 1990): Netherlander 95.8%; Turkish 1.2%; Moroccan 0.9%; German 0.3%; other 1.8%.
Religious affiliation (1986): Roman Catholic 36.0%; Dutch Reformed Church 18.5%; Reformed Churches 8.4%; other 4.5%; no religion 32.6%.
Major cities (1990): Amsterdam 695,162; Rotterdam 579,179; The Hague 441,506; Utrecht 230,358; Eindhoven 191,467.

Vital statistics

Birth rate per 1,000 population (1990): 13.2 (world avg. 27.1); legitimate 88.6%; illegitimate 11.4%.
Death rate per 1,000 population (1990): 8.6 (world avg. 9.8).
Natural increase rate per 1,000 population (1990): 4.6 (world avg. 17.3).
Total fertility rate (avg. births per childbearing woman; 1989): 1.6.
Marriage rate per 1,000 population (1989): 6.1.
Divorce rate per 1,000 population (1989): 1.9.
Life expectancy at birth (1989): male 73.7 years; female 79.7 years.
Major causes of death per 100,000 population (1989): malignant neoplasms (cancers) 238.6, of which lung cancer 57.6; ischemic heart diseases 153.2; cerebrovascular diseases 82.6; accidents, poisonings, and violence 37.9.

National economy

Budget (1990). Revenue: f. 175,165,000,000 (income and corporate taxes 43.7%, value-added taxes 21.2%, excise and import taxes 6.9%, natural-gas royalties 3.0%). Expenditures: f. 201,403,000,000 (social security and public health 22.6%, education and culture 16.7%, debt service 11.4%, defense 7.2%, transportation 5.9%).
Public debt (1990): U.S.$187,562,000,000.
Tourism (1990): receipts from visitors U.S.$3,615,000,000; expenditures by nationals abroad U.S.$7,340,000,000.
Production (metric tons except as noted). Agriculture, forestry, fishing (1990): sugar beets 8,623,000, potatoes 7,036,000, wheat 1,076,000, barley 219,000; livestock (number of live animals) 13,915,000 pigs, 4,926,000 cattle, 1,702,000 sheep; roundwood 1,411,000 cu m; fish catch (1989) 421,613. Manufacturing (value of sales in f. '000,000; 1987): foodstuffs 67,300; chemicals and chemical products 36,700; electrical machinery 23,500; petroleum products 16,700; transport equipment 12,200. Construction (buildings completed by value in f. '000; 1990): residential 10,805,000; nonresidential 15,009,000. Energy production (consumption): electricity (kW-hr; 1990) 71,866,000,000 (81,-074,000,000); coal (metric tons; 1990) none (15,809,000); crude petroleum (barrels; 1990) 24,212,000 (327,560,000); petroleum products (metric tons; 1990) 52,638,000 (29,183,000); natural gas (cu m; 1990) 80,272,000,000 (45,298,000,000).
Household income and expenditure (1989). Average household size 2.5; income per household (1985) f. 80,000 (U.S.$24,000); sources of income: wages 50.1%, transfer payments 28.4%, self-employment 21.5%; expenditure: food,

beverages, and tobacco 18.1%, rent 14.3%, medical care 12.2%, transportation and communications 11.1%, education and recreation 9.6%, household furnishings and appliances 8.1%, clothing and footwear 6.6%, other 20.0%.
Gross national product (at current market prices; 1990): U.S.$258,804,000,000 (U.S.$14,931 per capita).

Structure of gross domestic product and labour force				
	1989		1990	
	in value f. '000,000	% of total value	labour force	% of labour force
Agriculture	21,080	4.8	289,000	4.2
Mining	13,820	3.1	11,000	0.2
Manufacturing	95,720	21.6	1,185,000	17.2
Construction	27,620	6.2	409,000	6.0
Public utilities	9,000	2.0	41,000	0.6
Transp. and commun.	32,230	7.3	382,000	5.6
Trade	73,030	16.4	1,104,000	16.1
Finance	[5]	[5]	646,000	9.4
Pub. admin., defense	[5]	[5]	2,229,000	32.4
Services	189,210[5]	42.6[5]		
Other	−17,950[6]	−4.0[6]	574,000[7]	8.4[7]
TOTAL	443,760	100.0	6,872,000[2]	100.0[2]

Population economically active (1990): total 6,872,000; activity rate of total population 46.0% (participation rates: ages 15–64, 66.7%; female 39.2%; unemployed 7.5%).

Price and earnings indexes (1985 = 100)						
	1985	1986	1987	1988	1989	1990	1991
Consumer price index	100.0	100.1	99.4	100.1	101.2	103.7	107.7
Hourly earnings index	100.0	101.6	103.0	104.3	105.7	108.8	112.7

Land use (1989): forested 8.8%; meadows and pastures 31.6%; agricultural and under permanent cultivation 27.5%; other 32.1%.

Foreign trade

Balance of trade (current prices)						
	1986	1987	1988	1989	1990	1991
f. '000,000	20,386	13,201	17,647	19,217	22,345	26,131
% of total	5.5%	3.6%	4.5%	4.4%	4.9%	5.6%

Imports (1991): f. 234,609,000,000 (machinery and transport equipment 32.8%, of which transport equipment 9.5%; foodstuffs, beverages, and tobacco 12.0%; chemicals and chemical products 10.7%; mineral fuels 9.8%; metals and metal products 7.4%; textiles 7.2%; raw materials, oils, and fats 5.3%). *Major import sources:* Germany 26.4%; Belgium-Luxembourg 14.6%; U.K. 8.9%; U.S. 8.0%; France 7.8%.
Exports (1991): f. 248,809,000,000 (machinery and transport equipment 24.7%, of which transport equipment 6.0%; foodstuffs, beverages, and tobacco 20.6%; chemicals and chemical products 16.9%; mineral fuels 10.4%; metals and metal products 6.9%; textiles 4.9%). *Major export destinations:* Germany 30.9%; Belgium-Luxembourg 15.0%; France 11.2%; U.K. 9.8%; Italy 6.7%.

Transport and communications

Transport. Railroads (1990): length 2,828 km[8]; passenger-km 11,064,000,000; metric ton-km cargo 3,072,000,000. Roads (1990): total length 116,309 km (paved 88%). Vehicles (1990): passenger cars 5,509,000; trucks and buses 555,000. Merchant marine[9] (1991): vessels (100 gross tons and over) 1,249; total deadweight tonnage 4,848,023. Air transport (1990): passenger-km 28,356,000,000; metric ton-km cargo 2,207,800,000; airports (1992) 5.
Communications. Daily newspapers (1990): total number 45; total circulation 4,944,000; circulation per 1,000 population 332. Radio (1991): total number of receivers 12,146,299 (1 per 1.2 persons). Television (1991): total number of receivers 5,000,000 (1 per 3.0 persons). Telephones (1986): 9,080,000 (1 per 1.6 persons).

Education and health

Education (1989–90)				
	schools	teachers[10]	students	student/ teacher ratio
Primary (age 6–12)	9,443	82,562	1,540,000	...
Secondary (age 12–18)	1,284	94,441	697,000	...
Voc., teacher tr.	1,245	15,869	546,000	...
Higher	478	30,952[11]	329,000	...

Educational attainment (1985). Percentage of population[12] ages 25–64 having: primary education 16.7%; secondary 61.8%; higher 20.0%; other 1.5%.
Literacy (1990): virtually 100% literate.
Health (1990): physicians 36,042 (1 per 415 persons); hospital beds (1989) 90,532 (1 per 164 persons); infant mortality rate per 1,000 live births 7.1.
Food (1987–89): daily per capita caloric intake 3,303 (vegetable products 66%, animal products 34%); 118% of FAO recommended minimum requirement.

Military

Total active duty personnel (1991): 101,400 (army 63.2%, navy 16.4%, air force 15.8%, other[13] 4.6%). *Military expenditure as percentage of GNP* (1989): 2.9% (world 4.9%); per capita expenditure U.S.$431.

[1]January 1. [2]Detail does not add to total given because of rounding. [3]Includes 1,636 persons having no fixed municipality of residence. [4]Based on land area only. [5]Services includes Finance and Pub. admin., defense. [6]Imputed bank service charge. [7]Includes 516,000 unemployed persons. [8]1989. [9]Includes Netherlands Antilles and Aruba. [10]1988–89. [11]1985–86. [12]Economically active population (4,612,000) only. [13]Includes 3,900 military police.

Netherlands Antilles

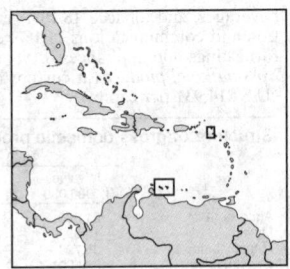

Official name: Nederlandse Antillen (Netherlands Antilles).
Political status: nonmetropolitan territory of The Netherlands with one legislative house (States of the Netherlands Antilles [22])[1].
Chief of state: Dutch Monarch represented by governor.
Head of government: Prime Minister.
Capital: Willemstad.
Official language: Dutch.
Official religion: none.
Monetary unit: 1 Netherlands Antillean guilder (NA f.) = 100 cents; valuation (Oct. 5, 1992) 1 U.S.$ = NA f. 1.79; 1 £ = NA f. 3.04.

Area and population		area		population
Island councils	Capitals	sq mi	sq km	1992[2] estimate
Leeward Islands				
Bonaire	Kralendijk	111	288	11,139
Curaçao	Willemstad	171	444	143,816
Windward Islands				
Saba	The Bottom	5	13	1,116
Sint Eustatius, or Statia	Oranjestad	8	21	1,781
Sint Maarten (Dutch part only)	Philipsburg	13	34	33,459
TOTAL		308	800	191,311

Demography

Population (1992): 191,000.
Density (1992): persons per sq mi 620.1, persons per sq km 238.8.
Urban-rural (1985)[3]: urban 92.4%; rural 7.6%.
Sex distribution (1992[2]): male 49.03%; female 50.97%.
Age breakdown (1990[2]): under 15, 26.2%; 15–29, 26.1%; 30–44, 24.0%; 45–59, 13.8%; 60–74, 7.1%; 75 and over, 2.8%.
Population projection: (2000) 194,000; (2010) 198,000.
Doubling time: 56 years.
Ethnic composition (1980)[3]: Netherlands Antillean (Dutch/Spanish/black/Amerindian) creole 84.0%; white 6.1%; other West Indian 4.9%; Suriname creole 2.9%; other 2.1%.
Religious affiliation (1981): Roman Catholic 83.8%; Protestant 10.2%, of which Lutheran/Reformed tradition 3.3%, Methodist 3.2%, Seventh-day Adventist 1.5%; Jewish 0.3%; nonreligious 2.6%; other 3.1%.
Major cities (1985): Willemstad (urban area) 125,000; Philipsburg 6,000[4].

Vital statistics

Birth rate per 1,000 population (1991): 18.3 (world avg. 26.4); (1988[5]) legitimate 51.6%; illegitimate 48.4%.
Death rate per 1,000 population (1991): 5.8 (world avg. 9.2).
Natural increase rate per 1,000 population (1991): 12.5 (world avg. 17.2).
Total fertility rate (avg. births per childbearing woman; 1984)[3]: 3.4.
Marriage rate per 1,000 population (1991): 6.4.
Divorce rate per 1,000 population (1991): 2.5.
Life expectancy at birth (1981)[6]: male 71.1 years; female 75.8 years.
Major causes of death per 100,000 population (1987)[7]: diseases of the circulatory system 205.5; malignant neoplasms (cancers) 150.6; respiratory diseases 41.0; endocrine and metabolic diseases 31.9; accidents 29.0; conditions originating in the perinatal period 17.5.

National economy

Budget (1991). Revenue: NA f. 338,100,000 (taxes 71.8%, of which taxes on goods and services 32.4%, import duties 26.1%, property taxes 2.7%; nontax revenue 28.2%). Expenditures: NA f. 351,400,000 (current expenditures 94.3%, of which goods and services 19.1%, debt service 10.4%, transfer payments 9.2%; capital expenditures 5.7%).
Production (metric tons except as noted). Agriculture, forestry, fishing (value of production in NA f. '000; 1982): eggs 3,863, fruits and vegetables 2,850[8], pork 1,250, goat meat 555; livestock (number of live animals; 1991) 14,000 goats, 6,000 cattle, 4,000 sheep, 3,000 pigs; roundwood, n.a.; fish catch (1990) 8,500. Mining and quarrying (1990): unrefined salt 354,000[9]; limestone 360,000. Manufacturing (1985): residual fuel oil 6,900,000[10]; ship repair NA f. 48,000,000[11]; Curaçao liqueur 780 hectolitres; other manufactures include electronic parts, cigarettes, textiles, and rum. Construction (number of buildings completed; 1991)[6]: residential 547; nonresidential 173. Energy production (consumption): electricity (kW-hr; 1990) 735,000,-000 (735,000,000); coal, none (none); crude petroleum (barrels; 1990) none (82,300,000); petroleum products (metric tons; 1990) 10,365,000 (1,276,000); natural gas, none (none).
Land use (1990): forested, negligible; meadows and pastures, negligible; agricultural and under permanent cultivation 10.0%; other (dry savanna) 90.0%.
Household income and expenditure. Average household size (1981) 3.7; income per household: n.a.; sources of income: n.a.; expenditure (1986)[12, 13]: transportation and communications 23.6%, food 19.0%, housing 16.8%, household furnishings 10.2%, clothing and footwear 8.4%, recreation and education 6.6%, health 2.3%, beverages and tobacco 2.2%, other 10.9%.
Gross national product (at current market prices; 1991). U.S.$1,490,000,000 (U.S.$7,800 per capita).

Structure of gross domestic product and labour force

	1988			
	in value NA f. '000,000	% of total value	labour force	% of labour force
Agriculture } Mining }	22.5	0.9	540	0.7
Manufacturing	139.6	5.9	4,524	6.2
Construction	226.8	9.5	5,404	7.4
Public utilities	127.8	5.4	1,274	1.8
Transportation and communications	335.8	14.0	4,690	6.4
Trade	632.3	26.4	15,890	21.8
Finance	325.2	13.6	4,596	6.3
Pub. admin., defense	482.5	20.2 }	21,259	29.2
Services	256.6	10.7 }		
Other	−156.9[14]	−6.6[14]	14,729[15]	20.2[15]
TOTAL	2,392.2	100.0	72,906	100.0

Population economically active (1988): total 72,906; activity rate of total population 38.4% (participation rates: ages 15–64, 43.1%[16]; female 43.1%; unemployed 20.4%).

Price and earnings indexes (1985 = 100)							
	1984	1985	1986	1987	1988	1989	1990
Consumer price index	99.6	100.0	101.3	105.1	107.8	112.0	116.2
Monthly earnings index[17]	95.5	100.0	89.3	84.6	...	...	...

Public debt (1991): U.S.$375,400,000.
Tourism: receipts from visitors (1991) U.S.$450,400,000; expenditures by nationals abroad (1983)[3] U.S.$107,000,000.

Foreign trade

Balance of trade (current prices)					
	1985	1986	1987	1988	1989	1990
NA f. '000,000	−603	−124	−59	−214	+19	−227
% of total	9.1%	3.6%	1.2%	5.0%	0.4%	3.4%

Imports (1990)[13]: NA f. 3,842,857,000 (crude petroleum and petroleum products 70.4%, machinery and transport equipment 9.7%, food and live animals 5.2%, chemicals 3.0%). *Major import sources:* Venezuela 59.2%; United States 12.3%; The Netherlands 5.7%; Ecuador 5.5%; Mexico 2.5%.
Exports (1990)[13]: NA f. 3,217,861,000 (crude petroleum and petroleum products 96.5%, chemicals 1.4%, machinery and transport equipment 0.6%). *Major export destinations:* United States 30.6%; Dominican Republic 7.4%; Venezuela 4.6%; Colombia 3.2%; Cuba 3.2%; Brazil 3.2%.

Transport and communications

Transport. Railroads: none. Roads (1989): total length 525 mi, 845 km (paved, n.a.). Vehicles (1992[2]): passenger cars 55,136; trucks and buses 12,511. Merchant marine (1990): vessels (100 gross tons and over) 103[3]; total deadweight tonnage, n.a. Air transport (1982)[18]: passenger-mi 234,-000,000, passenger-km 377,000,000; short ton-mi cargo 1,243,000, metric ton-km cargo 1,815,000; airports (1992) with scheduled flights 5.
Communications. Daily newspapers (1990): total number 10; total circulation 95,000; circulation per 1,000 population 499. Radio (1991): 125,000 receivers (1 per 1.5 persons). Television (1991): 32,000 receivers (1 per 5.5 persons). Telephones (1991): 58,076 (1 per 3.3 persons).

Education and health

Education (1990–91)	schools	teachers	students	student/ teacher ratio
Primary (age 6–12)	86	1,077	22,410	20.8
Secondary (age 12–17)	23	552	8,075	14.6
Voc., teacher tr.	38	431	6,354	14.7
Higher[19]	2	80	700	8.8

Educational attainment (1981). Percentage of population age 25 and over having: no formal schooling or some primary education 29.7%; completed primary 31.5%; completed vocational or secondary 37.6%; completed higher 1.2%. *Literacy* (1981): total population age 15 and over literate 154,860 (93.8%); males literate 73,400 (94.2%); females literate 81,460 (93.4%).
Health (1992): physicians 273 (1 per 701 persons); hospital beds 1,436 (1 per 133 persons); infant mortality rate per 1,000 live births (1989) 6.3.
Food (1988–90): daily per capita caloric intake 2,681 (vegetable products 68%, animal products 32%); 111% of FAO recommended minimum requirement.

Military

Total active duty personnel (1992): none; external security is maintained by The Netherlands via a Dutch naval contingent stationed in the Netherlands Antilles.

[1]Aruba withdrew from the Netherlands Antilles on Jan. 1, 1986, becoming an autonomous member of the Kingdom of The Netherlands, the same status as the whole of the Netherlands Antilles. [2]January 1. [3]Includes Aruba. [4]1981 census. [5]Excludes Sint Eustatius. [6]Curaçao only. [7]Excludes Sint Maarten. [8]Mostly tomatoes, beans, cucumbers, gherkins, melons, and lettuce grown on hydroponic farms; aloes grown for export, divi-divi pods, and sour orange fruit are nonhydroponic crops. [9]1988. [10]1989. [11]Foreign income in 1986. [12]Weights of consumer price index components. [13]Curaçao and Bonaire only. [14]Less imputed bank service charges. [15]Unemployed. [16]1986. [17]Average nonagricultural wage. [18]ALM Airlines only. [19]1986–87.

New Caledonia

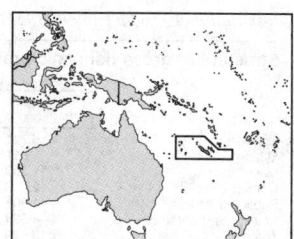

Official name: Territoire de la
Nouvelle-Calédonie et Dépendances
(Territory of New Caledonia and
Dependencies).
Political status: overseas territory
(France) with one legislative house
(Territorial Congress [54]).
Chief of state: President of France.
Head of government: High
Commissioner (for France); President
of the Territorial Congress (for New
Caledonia).
Capital: Nouméa.
Official language: French.
Official religion: none.
Monetary unit: 1 franc of the
Comptoirs français du Pacifique
(CFPF) = 100 centimes; valuation
(Oct. 5, 1992) 1 U.S.$ = CFPF 84.71;
1 £ = CFPF 144.00.

Area and population

Regions	Capitals	area sq mi	area sq km	population 1989 census
Loyauté	...	765	1,981	17,912
Nord	...	3,700	9,583	34,526
Sud	...	2,707	7,012	111,735
TOTAL		7,172	18,576	164,173

Demography

Population (1992): 174,000.
Density (1992): persons per sq mi 24.3, persons per sq km 9.4.
Urban-rural (1989): urban 59.4%; rural 40.6%.
Sex distribution (1989): male 51.08%; female 48.92%.
Age breakdown (1989): under 15, 32.6%; 15–29, 28.5%; 30–44, 19.8%; 45–59, 12.1%; 60–74, 5.4%; 75 and over, 1.6%.
Population projection: (2000) 199,000; (2010) 230,000.
Doubling time: 39 years.
Ethnic composition (1989): Melanesian 44.8%; European 33.6%; Wallisian 8.6%; Indonesian 3.2%; Tahitian 2.9%; Vietnamese 1.5%; Ni-Vanuatu 1.0%; other 4.4%.
Religious affiliation (1989): Roman Catholic 59.2%; Sunnī Muslim 3.0%; other (mostly Protestant) 37.8%.
Major cities (1989)[1]: Nouméa 65,110; Mont-Doré 16,370; Dumbéa 10,052; Païta 6,049.

Vital statistics

Birth rate per 1,000 population (1989): 23.9 (world avg. 27.1); legitimate 48.1%; illegitimate 51.9%.
Death rate per 1,000 population (1989): 6.0 (world avg. 9.8).
Natural increase rate per 1,000 population (1989): 17.9 (world avg. 17.3).
Total fertility rate (avg. births per childbearing woman; 1989): 3.0.
Marriage rate per 1,000 population (1989): 5.2.
Divorce rate per 1,000 population (1989): 1.1.
Life expectancy at birth (1989): male 66.5 years; female 71.8.
Major causes of death per 100,000 population (1981)[2]: diseases of the circulatory system 45.0; traumas 31.6; malignant neoplasms (cancers) 23.5; infectious and parasitic diseases 10.9; ill-defined conditions 94.2.

National economy

Budget (1991). Revenue: CFPF 56,704,000,000 (current revenue 98.5%, of which indirect taxes 49.9%, direct taxes 27.2%, French government grants 9.4%; development revenue 1.5%). Expenditures: CFPF 55,781,000,000 (current expenditure 84.9%, of which social and cultural services 67.7%, administrative 10.3%, public debt 3.8%; development expenditure 15.1%).
Public debt (external, outstanding; 1989): U.S.$313,000,000.
Production (metric tons except as noted). Agriculture, forestry, fishing (1990): yams 12,000, coconuts 8,000, fruits (excluding melons) 7,000, sweet potatoes 4,000, vegetables (including melons) 4,000, cassava 4,000, sweet potatoes 4,000, potatoes 2,000, bananas and plantains 2,000; livestock (number of live animals) 124,000 cattle, 39,000 pigs, 18,000 goats, 1,000,000 chickens; roundwood 12,000 cu m; fish catch 8,996. Mining and quarrying (metric tons; 1991): nickel ore 5,640,000 (ferronickel [metal content] 34,411, nickel matte [metal content] 9,041); chromite ore (1990) 11,031 (concentrate 6,207). Manufacturing (metric tons; 1988): cement (1991) 90,490; soap 381; crude vegetable oil 164; copra cake 108; beer 65,141 hectolitres. Construction (dwellings completed; 1991): 772 units. Energy production (consumption): electricity (kW-hr; 1990) 1,144,000,000 (1,144,000,000); coal (metric tons; 1990) none (164,000); crude petroleum, none (none); petroleum products (metric tons; 1990) none (357,000); natural gas, none (none).
Population economically active (1989): total 65,945; activity rate of total population 40.2% (participation rates: over age 20, 65.7%; female 37.5%; unemployed 7.9%).

Price and earnings indexes (1985 = 100)[3]

	1985	1986	1987	1988	1989	1990	1991
Consumer price index	100.0	99.5	100.9	104.5	108.8	110.3	113.9
Earnings index[4]	100.0	100.6	101.5	104.6	106.7	109.9	113.5

Land use (1989): forested 38.7%; meadows and pastures 15.4%; agricultural and under permanent cultivation 1.1%; other 44.8%.
Gross national product (at current market prices; 1987): U.S.$1,606,000,000 (U.S.$10,140 per capita).

Structure of gross domestic product and labour force

	1988 in value CFPF '000,000	1988 % of total value	1989 labour force	1989 % of labour force
Agriculture	3,575	1.6	7,763	11.8
Mining	11,667	5.2	910	1.4
Manufacturing	51,351	22.9	4,668	7.1
Construction	10,712	4.8	4,476	6.8
Public utilities	5,723	2.5	576	0.9
Transportation and communications	8,806	3.9	3,087	4.7
Trade	46,794	20.8	9,454	14.3
Finance }	32,009	14.3	2,475	3.8
Services }			12,587	19.1
Pub. admin., defense	53,861	24.0	9,429	14.3
Other	...	...	10,520	15.9
TOTAL	224,498	100.0	65,945	100.0[5]

Household income and expenditure. Average household size (1989) 4.0; average annual income per household (1980–81) CFPF 1,627,000 (U.S.$18,598)[6]; sources of income (1986): wages and salaries 59.0%, self-employment 19.6%, transfer payments 21.4%; expenditure (1981): food 27.5%, transportation 15.1%, housing 13.3%, household furnishings 11.4%, recreation 6.4%, other 26.3%.
Tourism (1990): receipts from visitors U.S.$150,000,000; expenditures by nationals abroad, n.a.

Foreign trade

Balance of trade (current prices)[7]

	1986	1987	1988	1989	1990	1991
CFPF '000,000	−36,164	−34,691	+496	−10,708	−42,998	−42,881
% of total	40.3%	37.7%	0.4%	6.4%	32.9%	31.8%

Imports (1991): CFPF 88,798,000,000 (machinery and electrical goods 21.0%, food 17.0%, transportation equipment 14.5%, mineral products 9.7%, metal and metal products 7.0%, chemicals and chemical products 6.8%). *Major import sources:* France 45.7%; Australia 9.7%; United States 7.0%; Japan 5.8%; New Zealand 3.7%.
Exports (1991): CFPF 45,917,000,000 (ferronickel and nickel matte 68.8%, nickel ore 21.2%, nonmineral products 10.0%). *Major export destinations* (1987): France 44.0%; Japan 19.1%; West Germany 8.6%; United States 7.5%; India 4.5%.

Transport and communications

Transport. Railroads: none. Roads (1989): total length 3,580 mi, 5,762 km (paved 22%). Vehicles (1989): passenger cars 50,000; trucks and buses 18,000. Merchant marine (1991): vessels (100 gross tons and over) 17; deadweight tonnage, n.a. Air transport (1990)[8]: passenger-mi 79,655,000, passenger-km 128,193,000; short ton-mi cargo 332,000[9], metric ton-km cargo 485,000[9]; airports (1992) with scheduled flights 10.
Communications. Daily newspapers (1991): total number 1; total circulation 18,000; circulation per 1,000 population 106. Radio (1991): total number of receivers 90,000 (1 per 1.9 persons). Television (1991): total number of receivers 35,500 (1 per 4.8 persons). Telephones (1990): 28,776[10] (1 per 5.8 persons).

Education and health

Education (1990)

	schools	teachers	students	student/teacher ratio
Primary (age 6–10)	279	1,696	34,242	20.2
Secondary (age 11–17)	44 }	1,685	14,237 }	12.5
Vocational	29 }		6,765 }	
Higher	6	141[11]	1,207	8.6

Educational attainment (1989). Percentage of population age 6 and over having: no formal schooling 5.2%; primary education 52.5%; secondary 37.8%; higher 4.5%. *Literacy* (1989): total population age 15 and over literate 33,288 (57.9%); males literate 16,807 (57.4%); females literate 16,421 (58.3%).
Health (1990): physicians 216 (1 per 776 persons); hospital beds 1,118 (1 per 150 persons); infant mortality rate per 1,000 live births (1989) 11.2.
Food (1987–89): daily per capita caloric intake 2,863 (vegetable products 80%, animal products 20%); 126% of FAO recommended minimum requirement.

Military

Total active duty personnel (1991): 3,800 French troops. *Military expenditure as percentage of GNP:* n.a.

[1]Populations cited are for communes that make up Grand Nouméa. [2]Public health facilities only. [3]All figures are end-of-year. [4]Based on minimum hourly wage. [5]Detail does not add to total given because of rounding. [6]Average European household CFPF 2,243,000 (U.S.$25,640); Melanesian CFPF 777,000 (U.S.$8,882). [7]Import figures are c.i.f. [8]Air Calédonie only. [9]1988. [10]Subscribers. [11]1989.

New Zealand

Official name: New Zealand (English); Aotearoa (Maori).
Form of government: constitutional monarchy with one legislative house (House of Representatives [97]).
Chief of state: British Monarch, represented by Governor-General.
Head of government: Prime Minister.
Capital: Wellington.
Official languages: English; Maori.
Official religion: none.
Monetary unit: 1 New Zealand dollar ($NZ) = 100 cents; valuation (Oct. 5, 1992) 1 U.S.$ = $NZ 1.84; 1 £ = $NZ 3.13.

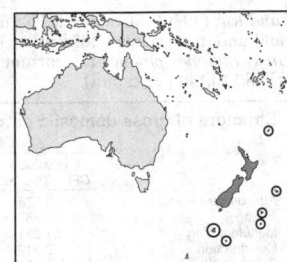

Area and population	area		population
Islands			1991
Regional Councils	sq mi	sq km	census[1]
North Island	44,702	115,777	2,549,707
Auckland	...	...	953,058
Bay of Plenty	...	...	208,030
Gisborne	...	...	44,302
Hawkes Bay	...	...	139,104
Manawatu-Wanganui	...	...	226,298
Northland	...	...	131,547
Taranaki	...	...	107,112
Waikato	...	...	338,405
Wellington	...	...	401,851
South Island	58,384	151,215	877,235
Canterbury	...	...	441,091
Nelson-Marlborough	...	...	113,073
Otago	...	...	185,225
Southland	...	...	102,269
West Coast	...	...	35,577
Remainder[2, 3]	...	...	854
Offshore islands[4]	322	854	...
Stewart Island[5]	674	1,746	...
Chatham Islands[6]	372	963	...
TOTAL	104,454	270,534	3,427,796

Demography

Population (1992): 3,481,000.
Density (1992): persons per sq mi 33.3, persons per sq km 12.9.
Urban-rural (1991): urban 75.9%; rural 24.1%.
Sex distribution (1991): male 49.29%; female 50.71%.
Age breakdown (1991): under 15, 23.2%; 15–29, 24.6%; 30–44, 22.4%; 45–59, 14.4%; 60–74, 10.9%; 75 and over, 4.5%.
Population projection: (2000) 3,802,000; (2010) 4,128,000.
Doubling time: 70 years.
Ethnic composition (1991): New Zealand European 73.8%; New Zealand Maori 9.6%; Pacific Island Polynesian 3.6%; multiethnic 4.5%; other and not specified 8.5%.
Religious affiliation (1991): Anglican 21.4%; Presbyterian 16.0%; Roman Catholic 14.8%; Methodist 4.1%; nonreligious 19.7%; other 24.0%.
Major cities (1991): Auckland 315,925; Christchurch 292,537; Manukau 225,928; North Shore 151,330; Wellington 149,598.

Vital statistics

Birth rate per 1,000 population (1991): 17.8 (world avg. 26.4); legitimate 64.3%; illegitimate 35.7%.
Death rate per 1,000 population (1991): 7.9 (world avg. 9.2).
Natural increase rate per 1,000 population (1991): 9.9 (world avg. 17.2).
Total fertility rate (avg. births per childbearing woman; 1991): 2.2.
Marriage rate per 1,000 population (1990): 6.9.
Divorce rate per 1,000 population (1989): 0.3.
Life expectancy at birth (1991): male 72.0 years; female 77.9 years.
Major causes of death per 100,000 population (1987): diseases of the circulatory system 380.7, of which ischemic heart disease 230.1; malignant neoplasms (cancers) 193.7; diseases of the respiratory system 87.1; accidents 60.3; diseases of the digestive system 22.1; metabolic diseases 15.0.

National economy

Budget (1989–90). Revenue: $NZ 28,234,000,000 (1988–89; income tax 59.9%, goods and services tax 16.5%, interest and profits 9.8%, sales tax 7.0%). Expenditures: $NZ 25,686,200,000 (social services 40.1%, debt service and investment 18.4%, education 15.7%, health 14.7%, administration 11.9%).
National debt (fiscal year 1991): U.S.$25,822,000,000.
Tourism (1990): receipts U.S.$900,000,000; expenditures U.S.$996,000,000.
Production (metric tons except as noted). Agriculture, forestry, fishing (1991): barley 367,100, corn (maize) 176,000, wheat 173,700, peas 63,900, oats 60,300; livestock (number of live animals) 55,941,000 sheep, 8,085,000 cattle, 790,000 goats, 385,000 pigs; roundwood (1989) 10,557,000 cu m; fish catch (1990) 565,440. Mining and quarrying (1990): limestone 3,082,000; iron ore and sand concentrate 2,367,000; serpentine 21,000; gold 4,963 kg; silver 4,837 kg. Manufacturing (1990–91): wood pulp 1,348,700; chemical fertilizers 994,000; cement 581,000; beer 362,656,000 litres; carbonated soft drinks 162,748,000 litres; footwear 4,022,000 pairs. Construction ($NZ '000; 1990–91): residential 2,430,000; nonresidential 599,700. Energy production (consumption): electricity (kW-hr; 1990) 30,158,000,000 (30,158,000,000); coal (metric tons; 1990) 2,415,000 (2,015,000); crude petroleum (barrels; 1990) 13,963,000 (32,743,000); petroleum products (metric tons; 1990) 4,347,000 (4,260,000); natural gas (cu m; 1990) 4,605,900,000 (4,605,900,000).

Gross national product (1990): U.S.$43,185,000,000 (U.S.$12,680 per capita).

Structure of gross domestic product and labour force				
	1988–89		1992	
	in value $NZ '000,000	% of total value	labour force	% of labour force
Agriculture	5,771	9.0	152,900	9.4
Mining	611	1.0	3,500	0.2
Manufacturing	11,790	18.5	239,400	14.8
Construction	2,215	3.5	78,200	4.8
Public utilities	1,301	2.0	12,200	0.8
Transp. and commun.	4,534	7.1	87,800	5.4
Trade	10,879	17.1	312,200	19.3
Finance	14,637	22.9	154,800	9.6
Pub. admin., defense } Services	8,346	13.1	415,600	25.7
Other	3,721[7]	5.8[7]	163,600[8]	10.1[8]
TOTAL	63,805	100.0	1,620,200	100.0[9]

Population economically active (1991[1]): total 1,623,900; activity rate 47.3% (participation rates: over age 15, 64.0%; female 43.5%; unemployed 9.8%).

Price and earnings indexes (1985 = 100)							
	1986	1987	1988	1989	1990	1991	1992[10]
Consumer price index	113.2	131.0	139.4	147.3	156.3	160.4	161.8
Weekly earnings index	116.4	125.7	141.6	147.3	153.7	157.6	158.7

Household income and expenditure. Average household size (1991) 2.9; annual income per household (1989–90) $NZ 39,800 (U.S.$23,760); sources of income (1987–88): wages and salaries 68.7%, transfer payments 14.1%, self-employment 8.1%; expenditure (1989–90): housing 22.7%, transportation 18.3%, food 16.6%, household durable goods 13.6%, clothing 4.6%.
Land use (1990): forested 27.4%; meadows and pastures 50.3%; agricultural and under permanent cultivation 1.5%; other 20.8%.

Foreign trade

Balance of trade (current prices)						
	1986	1987	1988	1989	1990	1991
$NZ '000,000	+578.6	+927.9	+3,215.0	+1,380.6	+1,351.2	+3,310.6
% of total	2.6%	4.0%	13.6%	4.8%	4.4%	11.0%

Imports (1991–92): $NZ 14,215,800,000 (minerals, chemicals, and plastics 25.5%; machinery 24.4%; transport equipment 14.8%; basic manufactures 8.6%; food and live animals 7.4%; metals and metal products 6.8%; textiles, clothing, and footwear 6.5%). *Major import sources:* Australia 22.2%; U.S. 18.3%; Japan 15.2%; U.K. 6.2%.
Exports (1991–92): $NZ 17,875,700,000 (food and live animals 49.5%; basic manufactures 22.7%; minerals, chemicals, and plastics 9.3%; metals and metal products 7.1%). *Major export destinations:* Australia 19.0%; Japan 15.3%; U.S. 12.8%; U.K. 6.5%; South Korea 4.3%; Malaysia 2.6%; Germany 2.3%.

Transport and communications

Transport. Railroads (1990): length 2,627 mi, 4,227 km; passenger-km (1984) 458,160,000; short ton-mi cargo (1988–89) 1,837,000,000, metric ton-km cargo 2,682,000,000. Roads (1991): total length 57,771 mi, 92,974 km (paved 56%). Vehicles (1990): passenger cars 1,557,074; trucks and buses 310,671. Merchant marine (1991): vessels (100 gross tons and over) 142; total deadweight tonnage 319,038. Air transport (1990): passenger-mi 6,591,000,000, passenger-km 10,608,000,000; short ton-mi cargo 227,000,000, metric ton-km cargo 332,000,000; airports (1992) 36.
Communications. Daily newspapers (1989): total number 34; total circulation 1,031,000; circulation per 1,000 population 306. Radio (1991): 3,100,000 receivers (1 per 1.1 persons). Television (1991): 1,100,000 receivers (1 per 3.1 persons). Telephones (1988): 2,403,000 (1 per 1.4 persons).

Education and health

Education (1990)	schools	teachers	students	student/ teacher ratio
Primary (age 5–12)[11]	2,455	22,140	421,259	19.0
Secondary (age 13–17)	336	14,683	229,273	15.6
Voc., teacher tr.	32	4,498	56,771	12.6
Higher[12]	7	3,761	78,919	21.0

Educational attainment (1987). Percentage of population age 25 and over having: primary and some secondary education 51.9%; secondary 35.8%; higher 6.9%; not specified 5.4%. *Literacy:* virtually 100.0%.
Health (1989): physicians 9,453 (1 per 359 persons); hospital beds 29,352 (1 per 114 persons); infant mortality rate per 1,000 live births (1991): 8.3.
Food (1988–90): daily per capita caloric intake 3,461 (vegetable products 59%, animal products 41%); 131% of FAO recommended minimum.

Military

Total active duty personnel (1992): 10,900 (army 44.0%, navy 22.0%, air force 34.0%). *Military expenditure as percentage of GNP* (1989): 2.2% (world 4.9%); per capita expenditure U.S.$258.

[1]Provisional; March 5. [2]Includes the population of Kermadec Islands and persons on oil rigs. [3]Includes the population of Chatham Islands county and Campbell Island. [4]Excludes islands in Regional Councils. [5]Part of Southland Regional Council. [6]Chatham Islands county remains outside any Regional Council. [7]Includes import duties less imputed bank service charges. [8]Includes 161,600 unemployed. [9]Detail does not add to total given because of rounding. [10]Second quarter. [11]Includes 79 composite schools that provide both primary and secondary education. [12]Universities only.

Nicaragua

Official name: República de Nicaragua
(Republic of Nicaragua).
Form of government: unitary multiparty
republic with one legislative house
(National Assembly [92[1]]).
Head of state and government:
President.
Capital: Managua.
Official language: Spanish.
Official religion: none.
Monetary unit: 1 córdoba oro C\$[2] = 100
centavos; valuation (Oct. 5, 1992)
1 U.S.\$ = C\$5.00; 1 £ = C\$8.50.

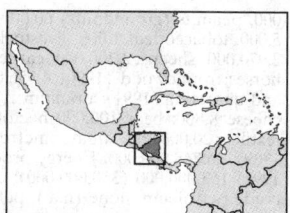

Area and population		area		population
Departments[3]	Capitals	sq mi	sq km	1990 estimate
Boaco	Boaco	1,649	4,271	117,900
Carazo	Jinotepe	424	1,097	150,000
Chinandega	Chinandega	1,849	4,789	330,500
Chontales	Juigalpa	2,442	6,324	129,600
Estelí	Estelí	839	2,173	169,100
Granada	Granada	383	992	162,600
Jinotega	Jinotega	3,722	9,640	175,600
León	León	2,024	5,243	344,500
Madriz	Somoto	622	1,612	88,700
Managua	Managua	1,300	3,368	1,026,100
Masaya	Masaya	267	690	230,800
Matagalpa	Matagalpa	2,675	6,929	322,300
Nueva Segovia	Ocotal	1,388	3,594	122,100
Río San Juan	San Carlos	2,857	7,402	52,200
Rivas	Rivas	846	2,190	149,800
Zelaya	Bluefields	23,180	60,035	298,900
TOTAL LAND AREA		46,467	120,349	
INLAND WATER[3]		3,990	10,333	
TOTAL		50,457	130,682	3,870,700

Demography

Population (1992): 4,131,000.
Density (1992)[4]: persons per sq mi 89.9, persons per sq km 34.3.
Urban-rural (1990): urban 59.8%; rural 40.2%.
Sex distribution (1990): male 50.12%; female 49.88%.
Age breakdown (1990): under 15, 45.8%; 15–29, 27.6%; 30–44, 15.0%; 45–59, 7.3%; 60–74, 3.6%; 75 and over, 0.7%.
Population projection: (2000) 5,261,000; (2010) 6,824,000.
Doubling time: 23 years.
Ethnic composition (1985): mestizo (Spanish/Indian) 77.0%; white 10.0%; black 9.0%; Amerindian 4.0%.
Religious affiliation (1990): Roman Catholic 90.7%; other (mostly Baptist, Moravian, and Pentecostal) 9.3%.
Major cities (1985): Managua 682,111; León 100,982; Granada 88,636; Masaya 74,946; Chinandega 67,792.

Vital statistics

Birth rate per 1,000 population (1991): 37.0 (world avg. 26.4).
Death rate per 1,000 population (1991): 7.0 (world avg. 9.2).
Natural increase rate per 1,000 population (1991): 30.0 (world avg. 17.2).
Total fertility rate (avg. births per childbearing woman; 1991): 4.7.
Marriage rate per 1,000 population (1988): 2.1.
Divorce rate per 1,000 population (1988): 0.4.
Life expectancy at birth (1991): male 60.0 years; female 65.0 years.
Major causes of death per 100,000 population (registered only; 1987): diseases of the circulatory system 69.8; infectious and parasitic diseases 64.9; deaths from war operations and homicide 51.0; diseases of the respiratory system 48.7; accidents 33.3.

National economy

Budget (1991). Revenue: U.S.\$440,000,000 (current and development revenue 79.3%, foreign loans 20.7%). Expenditures: U.S.\$499,000,000.
Production (metric tons except as noted). Agriculture, forestry, fishing (1991): sugarcane 3,018,000, corn (maize) 245,000, rice 140,000, bananas 114,000, seed cotton 75,000, cassava 71,000, sorghum 70,000, oranges 68,000, plantains 63,000, dry beans 56,000, coffee 28,000, sesame seed 13,000; livestock (number of live animals) 1,680,000 cattle, 709,000 pigs; roundwood (1990) 4,077,000 cu m; fish catch (1990) 2,766, of which crustaceans 1,803. Mining and quarrying (1989): gold 39,000 troy oz. Manufacturing (value of production in C\$'000,000; 1988[5]): processed foods 1,556; beverages 1,204; metal products 694; textiles 640; chemicals and chemical products 572; nonmetal mineral products 361; clothing 285; tobacco products 247. Construction (buildings completed; 1988): 41,600 cu m. Energy production (consumption): electricity (kW-hr; 1990) 1,038,000,000 (1,238,000,000); coal, none (none); crude petroleum (barrels; 1990) none (3,592,000); petroleum products (metric tons; 1990) 460,000 (628,000); natural gas, none (none).
Population economically active (1991): total 1,386,300; activity rate of total population 34.7% (participation rates: over age 15, 62.0%; female 33.2%; unemployed [1992] 60.0%).

Price and earnings indexes (1988 = 100)					
	1988	1989	1990	1991	1992
Consumer price index	100.0	4,146	326,086	27,174,000	27,174,000[6]
Monthly earnings index[7]	100.0	6,141	...	...	...

Gross national product (at current market prices; 1988): U.S.\$1,661,000,000 (U.S.\$460 per capita).

Structure of gross domestic product and labour force				
	1990		1987	
	in value C\$'000,000,000[8]	% of total value	labour force	% of labour force
Agriculture	348,342	30.2	365,200	32.4
Mining	6,713	0.6	3,000	0.3
Manufacturing	182,990	15.9	90,500	8.0
Construction	40,170	3.5	16,800	1.5
Public utilities	13,659	1.2	7,800	0.7
Transportation and communications	48,141	4.2	20,900	1.8
Trade	256,976	22.3	94,600	8.4
Finance, real estate	69,406	6.0	18,700	1.7
Pub. admin., defense	133,730	11.6	77,400	6.9
Services[9]	51,559	4.5	148,500	13.2
Other	—	—	282,900[10]	25.1[10]
TOTAL	1,151,686	100.0	1,126,300	100.0

Public debt (external, outstanding; 1990): U.S.\$7,920,000,000.
Household income and expenditure. Average household size (1980) 6.9; income per household: n.a.; sources of income: n.a.; expenditure: n.a.
Tourism (1990): receipts from visitors U.S.\$12,000,000; expenditures by nationals abroad U.S.\$2,000,000.
Land use (1990): forested 28.5%; meadows and pastures 45.5%; agricultural and under permanent cultivation 10.7%; other 15.3%.

Foreign trade

Balance of trade (current prices)					
	1986	1987	1988	1989	1990	1991
U.S.\$'000,000	– 609.6	– 622.7	– 270.4	– 234.9	– 343.5	– 395.8
% of total	55.2%	50.9%	33.1%	29.0%	34.8%	35.3%

Imports (1990): U.S.\$664,700,000 (nondurable consumer goods 23.2%, petroleum products 16.4%, capital goods for transport 14.6%, capital goods for industry 11.9%). *Major import sources* (1991): United States 21.3%; former U.S.S.R. 10.2%; Cuba 8.0%; Costa Rica 7.8%; Guatemala 7.3%; Venezuela 7.1%.
Exports (1990): U.S.\$321,200,000[11] (coffee 21.0%, meat 20.0%, cotton 11.4%, sugar 10.8%, bananas 7.2%). *Major export destinations* (1991): United States 16.4%; Germany 14.4%; Japan 11.0%; Canada 11.0%; Italy 7.8%.

Transport and communications

Transport. Railroads (1991): route length 186 mi, 300 km; (1988) passenger-mi 15,800,000, passenger-km 25,400,000; short ton-mi cargo 46,600,000, metric ton-km cargo 68,000,000. Roads (1988): total length 9,319 mi, 14,997 km (paved 10%). Vehicles (1990): passenger cars 31,111; trucks and buses 42,974. Merchant marine (1991): vessels (100 gross tons and over) 25; total deadweight tonnage 3,013. Air transport (1990)[12]: passenger-mi 68,800,000, passenger-km 110,700,000; short ton-mi cargo 2,451,000, metric ton-km cargo 3,579,000; airports (1992) with scheduled flights 1[13].
Communications. Daily newspapers (1991): total number 3; total circulation 113,000; circulation per 1,000 population 28. Radio (1991): 880,000 receivers (1 per 4.5 persons). Television (1991): 210,000 receivers (1 per 19 persons). Telephones (1990): 47,000 (1 per 82 persons).

Education and health

Education (1989)	schools	teachers	students	student/ teacher ratio
Primary (age 7–12)	3,840	18,746	595,612	31.8
Secondary (age 13–18)	...	4,768[14]	143,954	24.0[14]
Voc., teacher tr.	...	1,170	17,258	14.8
Higher[15, 16]	4	1,591	34,166	21.5

Educational attainment (1971). Percentage of population age 25 and over having: no formal schooling 53.9%; some primary and complete primary education 41.7%; some secondary and complete secondary education 4.4%.
Literacy (1986): total population age 15 and over literate 74.0%.
Health (1988): physicians 1,789 (1 per 2,024 persons); hospital beds 4,762 (1 per 761 persons); infant mortality rate per 1,000 live births (1991) 60.0.
Food (1984–86): daily per capita caloric intake 2,472 ([17]vegetable products 84%, animal products 16%); 110% of FAO recommended minimum requirement.

Military

Total active duty personnel (1992): 14,700 (army 88.4%, navy 3.4%, air force 8.2%). *Military expenditure as percentage of central government expenditure* (1991): 16.0%.

[1]Includes two unsuccessful 1990 presidential candidates meeting special conditions. [2]The córdoba oro, introduced in August 1990, circulated simultaneously with the new córdoba until April 30, 1991, when the new córdoba ceased to be legal tender; on April 30, 1 córdoba oro equaled 5,000,000 new córdobas. The new córdoba had been introduced in February 1988 at the rate of 1 new córdoba to 1,000 (old) córdobas. [3]Lakes and lagoons are excluded from the areas of departments. [4]Based on land area. [5]At prices of 1983 in old córdobas. [6]June. [7]Registrants of Nicaraguan Institute of Social Security and Welfare. [8]At current prices in new córdobas. [9]Includes restaurants, hotels, and business services. [10]Mostly underemployed informal workers. [11]Estimated exports (1991) U.S.\$266,000,000 (cotton 16.5%, coffee 13.9%, bananas 10.2%, fish 6.6%, gold 2.8%). [12]Aeronica only. [13]International only; domestic scheduled air service not available. [14]1988. [15]Universities only. [16]1990. [17]1979–81.

Niger

Official name: République du Niger
  (Republic of Niger).
Form of government: interim regime[1]
with a single provisional legislative
body (High Council of the
Republic [15]).
Chief of state: President.
Head of government: Prime Minister.
Capital: Niamey.
Official language: French.
Official religion: none.
Monetary unit: 1 CFA franc
  (CFAF) = 100 centimes;
  valuation (Oct. 5, 1992)
  1 U.S.$ = CFAF 238.75;
  1 £ = CFAF 405.88.

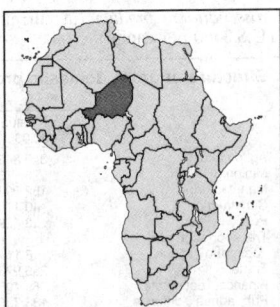

Area and population

Departments	Capitals	area sq mi	area sq km	population 1988 census[2]
Agadez	Agadez	244,869	634,209	205,232
Diffa	Diffa	54,138	140,216	187,230
Dosso	Dosso	11,970	31,002	1,018,058
Maradi	Maradi	14,896	38,581	1,386,549
Tahoua	Tahoua	41,188	106,677	1,306,948
Tillabéry	Tillabéry	34,863	90,293	1,715,118
Zinder	Zinder	56,151	145,430	1,409,417
TOTAL		458,075	1,186,408	7,228,552

Demography

Population (1992): 8,281,000.
Density (1992): persons per sq mi 18.1, persons per sq km 7.0.
Urban-rural (1988): urban 15.3%; rural 84.7%.
Sex distribution (1988): male 49.53%; female 50.47%.
Age breakdown (1988): under 15, 48.7%; 15–29, 24.8%; 30–44, 14.6%; 45–59,
  6.8%; 60–74, 3.6%; 75 and over, 1.5%.
Population projection: (2000) 10,656,000; (2010) 14,484,000.
Doubling time: 21 years.
Ethnic composition (1988): Hausa 52.8%; Zerma-Songhai 21.0%; Tuareg
  10.6%; Fulani 9.8%; Kanuri-Nanga 4.5%; Teda 0.5%; Arab 0.3%; Gurma
  0.3%; other 0.2%.
Religious affiliation (1988): Muslim, primarily Sunnī, 98.6%; other, mostly
  traditional beliefs, 1.4%.
Major cities (1988): Niamey 392,169; Zinder 119,838; Maradi 109,386; Tahoua
  49,941; Agadez 49,361.

Vital statistics

Birth rate per 1,000 population (1990–95): 51.3 (world avg. 26.4).
Death rate per 1,000 population (1990–95): 18.7 (world avg. 9.2).
Natural increase rate per 1,000 population (1990–95): 32.6 (world avg. 17.2).
Total fertility rate (avg. births per childbearing woman; 1990): 7.1.
Marriage rate per 1,000 population: n.a.
Divorce rate per 1,000 population: n.a.
Life expectancy at birth (1990–95): male 44.9 years; female 48.1 years.
Major causes of death (1984): n.a.; however, among selected major causes
  registered at medical facilities are measles, diarrhea, meningitis, malaria,
  pneumonia, tetanus, viral hepatitis, and poliomyelitis.

National economy

Budget (1990)[3]. Revenue: CFAF 237,686,000,000 (foreign loans 28.6%, external aid and gifts 23.7%, import duties 10.4%, sales taxes 10.0%, personal income taxes 8.8%, corporate and business taxes 4.3%). Expenditures: CFAF
  237,686,000,000 (amortization of public debt 16.3%, agriculture 15.7%, education 10.3%, transportation and communications 8.8%, housing 8.4%,
  health 5.2%, defense 5.2%).
Public debt (external, outstanding; 1990): U.S.$1,293,000,000.
Tourism (1989): receipts from visitors U.S.$13,000,000; expenditures by na-
  tionals abroad U.S.$32,000,000.
Gross national product (at current market prices; 1990): U.S.$2,365,000,000
  (U.S.$310 per capita).

Structure of gross domestic product and labour force

	1989 in value CFAF '000,000	1989 % of total value	1988 labour force	1988 % of labour force
Agriculture	245,602	36.3	1,793,450	77.8
Mining	43,020	6.4		
Manufacturing	59,978	8.8	86,270	3.7
Construction	26,748	4.0		
Public utilities	17,465	2.6		
Transportation and communications	22,924	3.4		
Trade and finance	107,894	15.9	354,820	15.4
Pub. admin., defense	90,687	13.4		
Services	62,611	9.2		
Other	—	—	71,610	3.1
TOTAL	676,929	100.0	2,306,150	100.0

Production (metric tons except as noted). Agriculture, forestry, fishing (1991):
  millet 1,853,000, sorghum 472,000, pulses 387,000, roots and tubers 251,000,
  vegetables and melons 141,000, sugarcane 140,000, onions 80,000, rice 71,-

000, peanuts (groundnuts) 60,000, wheat 12,000, corn (maize) 6,000, cotton
5,000, tobacco leaf 1,000; livestock (number of live animals) 4,800,000 goats,
2,970,000 sheep, 2,200,000 cattle, 415,000 asses, 360,000 camels, 305,000
horses; roundwood (1990) 4,956,000 cu m; fish catch (1989) 4,751. Mining
and quarrying (1991): uranium 2,777. Manufacturing (1988): cement 40,000;
cheese 8,800; beer 100,000 hectolitres; beverages 98,000 hectolitres; cotton
textiles 20,000,000 square metres. Construction (value added in CFAF;
1989): 26,748,000,000. Energy production (consumption): electricity (kW-hr;
1990) 163,000,000 (350,000,000); coal (metric tons; 1990) 158,000 (158,000);
crude petroleum, none (n.a.); petroleum products (metric tons; 1990) none
(190,000); natural gas, none (n.a.).
Population economically active (1988): total 2,366,720; activity rate of total
  population 32.7% (participation rates: over age 10, 53.5%; female 20.7%;
  unemployed, n.a.).

Price and earnings indexes (1985 = 100)

	1985	1986	1987	1988	1989	1990	1991
Consumer price index	100.0	96.8	90.3	89.0	86.5	85.8	79.1
Hourly earnings index[4]	100.0	100.0	100.0	100.0	100.0	100.0	100.0

Household income and expenditure. Average household size (1988) 6.4; income per household: n.a.; sources of income (1977): self-employment 59.5%,
  family 30.1%, salary or wages 4.8%, employer 0.7%; expenditure (1983):
  food and beverages 50.5%, household expenses 19.1%, clothing 7.3%.
Land use (1990): forested 1.6%; meadows and pastures 7.0%; agricultural
  and under permanent cultivation 2.8%; other 88.6%.

Foreign trade[5]

Balance of trade (current prices)

	1985	1986	1987	1988	1989	1990
CFAF '000,000	−46,300	−11,400	−12,000	−20,900	−20,900	−5,000
% of total	17.1%	4.7%	5.2%	8.6%	8.4%	2.8%

Imports (1989): CFAF 134,800,000,000 (raw materials and machinery 42.5%,
  consumer goods 36.6%, cereals 12.2%, petroleum products 6.0%). *Major
  import sources:* France 32.1%; Côte d'Ivoire 10.7%; West Germany 4.9%;
  Japan 4.5%; Italy 4.0%; Nigeria 3.5%; The Netherlands 3.5%.
Exports (1989): CFAF 113,900,000,000 (uranium 71.5%, live animals 10.5%,
  cowpeas 5.2%). *Major export destinations:* France 64.9%; Nigeria 11.4%;
  Spain 8.4%; Canada 2.6%; Côte d'Ivoire 0.8%.

Transport and communications

Transport. Railroads (1991): none[6]. Roads (1988): total length 24,836 mi,
  39,970 km (paved 8%). Vehicles (1989): passenger cars 16,000; trucks and
  buses 18,000. Air transport (1988)[7]: passenger-mi 129,597,000, passenger-km
  208,567,000; short ton-mi cargo 24,126,000, metric ton-km cargo 35,223,000;
  airports (1992) with scheduled flights 1.
Communications. Daily newspapers (1991): total number 1; total circulation
  5,000; circulation per 1,000 population 0.6. Radio (1991): total number of
  receivers 400,000 (1 per 20 persons). Television (1991): total number of
  receivers 25,000 (1 per 321 persons). Telephones (1985): 11,824 (1 per 563
  persons).

Education and health

Education (1988)

	schools	teachers	students	student/ teacher ratio
Primary (age 7–12)[8]	2,215	8,462	344,848	40.8
Secondary (age 13–19)	64[9]	2,282	63,379	27.8
Voc., teacher tr.	8[10]	161	2,437	15.1
Higher	3	341[11]	4,506	11.1[11]

Educational attainment (1988). Percentage of population age 25 and over
  having: no formal schooling 85.0%; Koranic education 11.2%; primary education 2.5%; secondary 1.1%; higher 0.2%. *Literacy* (1988): percentage
  of total population age 15 and over literate 10.8%; males literate 16.7%;
  females literate 5.4%.
Health: physicians (1985) 160 (1 per 38,500 persons); hospital beds (1979)
  3,261 (1 per 1,633 persons); infant mortality rate per 1,000 live births
  (1990–95) 124.0.
Food (1987–89): daily per capita caloric intake 2,297 (vegetable products 94%,
  animal products 6%); 98% of FAO recommended minimum requirement.

Military

Total active duty personnel (1992): 3,300 (army 97.0%, air force 3.0%). *Military
  expenditure as percentage of GNP* (1989): 1.3% (world 4.9%); per capita
  expenditure U.S.$3.

[1]1989 constitution suspended August 1991; transitional government from November
1991 to February 1993. A referendum on a new constitution was scheduled for Dec.
26, 1992, with legislative and presidential elections in early 1993. [2]De jure. [3]Figures
refer to recurrent and capital revenues and expenditures; in 1992 recurrent revenues
and expenditures were balanced at CFAF 106,000,000,000, a 27% drop from 1991.
[4]Guaranteed minimum wage for professionals. [5]Import figures are c.i.f. in balance
of trade, commodities, and trading partners. [6]Niger is a cofounder of the Common
Benin-Niger Organization for Railroads and Transport, currently maintaining rail operations only in Benin but having the purpose of extending rail services from the sea
at Cotonou, Benin, to Dosso and, ultimately, Niamey, Niger; in the interim, freight
transported between the two countries is carried by truck. [7]Air Afrique. [8]1989. [9]1980–
81. [10]1980. [11]Université de Niamey and École Nationale d'Administration du Niger
only.

Nigeria

Official name: Federal Republic of
Nigeria.
Form of government: federal republic;
temporarily governed (pending
restoration of civilian governmental
apparatus by 1993) by Armed Forces
Ruling Council (AFRC).
Head of state and government:
President.
Capital: Abuja (Federal
Capital Territory)[1].
Official language: English.
Official religion: none.
Monetary unit: 1 Nigerian naira
(₦) = 100 kobo; valuation (Oct. 5,
1992) 1 U.S.$ = ₦18.42; 1 £ = ₦31.31.

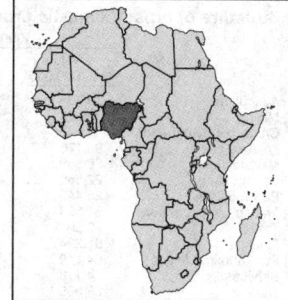

Area and population

States	Capitals	area sq mi	area sq km	population 1991 census
Abia	Umuahia	10,516[2]	27,237[2]	2,297,978
Adamawa	Yola	35,286[3]	91,390[3]	2,124,049
Akwa Ibom	Uyo	2	2	2,359,736
Anambra	Awka	6,824	17,675	2,767,903
Bauchi	Bauchi	24,944	64,605	4,294,413
Benue	Makurdi	17,442[4]	45,174[4]	2,780,398
Borno	Maiduguri	44,942[5]	116,400[5]	2,596,589
Cross River	Calabar	2	2	1,865,604
Delta	Asaba	13,707[6]	35,500[6]	2,570,181
Edo	Benin City	6	6	2,159,848
Enugu	Enugu	2	2	3,161,295
Imo	Owerri	4,575	11,850	2,485,499
Jigawa	Dutse	16,712[7]	43,285[7]	2,829,929
Kaduna	Kaduna	27,122[8]	70,245[8]	3,969,252
Kano	Kano	7	7	5,632,040
Katsina	Katsina	8	8	3,878,344
Kebbi	Birnin Kebbi	39,589[9]	102,535[9]	2,062,226
Kogi	Lokoja	4	4	2,099,046
Kwara	Ilorin	25,818	66,869	1,566,469
Lagos	Ikeja	1,292	3,345	5,685,781
Niger	Minna	25,111	65,037	2,482,367
Ogun	Abeokuta	6,472	16,762	2,338,570
Ondo	Akure	8,092	20,959	3,884,485
Osun	Oshogbo	14,558[10]	37,705[10]	2,203,016
Oyo	Ibadan	10	10	3,488,789
Plateau	Jos	22,405	58,030	3,283,704
Rivers	Port Harcourt	8,436	21,850	3,983,857
Sokoto	Sokoto	9	9	4,392,391
Taraba	Jalingo	3	3	1,480,590
Yobe	Damaturu	5	5	1,411,481
Federal Capital Territory				
Abuja	Abuja	2,824	7,315	378,671
TOTAL		356,669[11]	923,768	88,514,501

Demography

Population (1992): 89,666,000.
Density (1992): persons per sq mi 251.4, persons per sq km 97.1.
Urban-rural (1990): urban 35.2%; rural 64.8%.
Sex distribution (1990): male 49.53%; female 50.47%.
Age breakdown (1990): under 15, 47.4%; 15–29, 26.0%; 30–44, 14.4%; 45–59,
8.0%; 60–74, 3.5%; 75 and over, 0.7%.
Population projection: (2000) 105,885,000; (2010) 130,344,000.
Doubling time: 22 years.
Ethnic composition (1983): Hausa 21.3%; Yoruba 21.3%; Igbo (Ibo) 18.0%;
Fulani 11.2%; Ibibio 5.6%; Kanuri 4.2%; Edo 3.4%; Tiv 2.2%; Ijaw 1.8%;
Bura 1.7%; Nupe 1.2%; other 8.1%.
Religious affiliation (1980): Christian 49.0%, of which Protestant 26.3%, Ro-
man Catholic 12.1%, African indigenous 10.6%; Muslim 45.0%; other 6.0%.
Major cities (1992): Lagos 1,347,000; Ibadan 1,295,000; Kano 699,900; Ogbo-
mosho 660,600; Oshogbo 441,600; Ilorin 430,600.

Vital statistics

Birth rate per 1,000 population (1990–95): 46.5 (world avg. 26.4).
Death rate per 1,000 population (1990–95): 14.0 (world avg. 9.2).
Natural increase rate per 1,000 population (1990–95): 32.5 (world avg. 17.2).
Total fertility rate (avg. births per childbearing woman; 1990–95): 6.6.
Life expectancy at birth (1990–95): male 50.8 years; female 54.3 years.
Major causes of death per 100,000 population: n.a.

National economy

Budget (1991). Revenue: ₦35,200,000,000 (petroleum profit tax 39.2%; import
duties 12.7%; company income tax 5.0%). Expenditures: ₦22,100,000,000
(recurrent expenditure 56.6%, of which debt service 39.1%, defense 3.9%,
police 2.8%, education 2.3%; capital expenditure 43.4%).
Production (metric tons except as noted). Agriculture, forestry, fishing (1991):
cassava 20,000,000, yams 16,000,000, sorghum 4,800,000, millet 4,200,000, rice
3,185,000, corn (maize) 1,900,000, plantains 1,314,000, sugarcane 1,250,000,
peanuts (groundnuts) 1,219,000; livestock (number of live animals) 36,000,-
000 goats, 24,000,000 sheep, 14,500,000 cattle; roundwood (1990) 107,732,000
cu m; fish catch (1990) 316,328. Mining and quarrying (1991): limestone
1,435,405; marble 52,379. Manufacturing (value added in U.S.$'000,000;
1990): food and beverages 703; textiles 373; chemical products 165; metal
products 160; machinery and transport equipment 159; paper products
62; rubber and plastic products 61. Construction (dwellings completed;
1982): 31,038. Energy production (consumption): electricity (kW-hr; 1990)

9,945,000,000 (9,845,000,000); coal (metric tons; 1990) 90,000 (55,000); crude
petroleum (barrels; 1990) 647,940,000 (73,140,000); petroleum products (metric tons; 1990) 8,993,000 (10,276,000); natural gas (cu m; 1990) 3,668,000,000
(3,688,000,000).
Tourism (1990): receipts U.S.$21,000,000; expenditures U.S.$51,000,000.
Gross national product (1990): U.S.$31,285,000,000 (U.S.$270 per capita).

Structure of gross domestic product and labour force

	1991 in value ₦'000,000	1991 % of total value	1986 labour force	1986 % of labour force
Agriculture	37,000	39.2	13,259,000	43.1
Mining	12,000	12.7	6,800	0.1
Manufacturing	7,800	8.3	1,263,700	4.1
Construction	1,800	1.9	545,600	1.8
Public utilities	500	0.5	130,400	0.4
Transp. and commun.	3,200	3.4	1,111,900	3.6
Trade	12,400	13.1	7,417,400	24.1
Finance	8,500	9.0	120,100	0.4
Pub. admin., defense	8,400	8.9 }	4,902,100	15.9
Services	2,800	3.0 }		
Other	...	...	2,008,500[12]	6.5[12]
TOTAL	94,400	100.0	30,765,500	100.0

Public debt (external, outstanding; Dec. 31, 1991): U.S.$32,849,000,000.
Population economically active (1986): total 30,765,500; activity rate 31.1%
(participation rates: ages 15–64, 58.8%; female 33.3%; unemployed 4.1%).

Price and earnings indexes (1985 = 100)

	1985	1986	1987	1988	1989	1990	1991
Consumer price index	100.0	105.7	117.7	181.8	273.5	293.7	331.9
Earnings index	...	...	...	...	...	...	...

Household income and expenditure. Avg. household size (1983) 5.0; annual income per household (1981) ₦2,300 (U.S.$3,745)[13]; sources of income (1979):
self-employment 49.4%, wages 36.2%, interest 5.4%, rent 4.7%, transfer
payments 4.3%; expenditures (1979): food 53.0%, fuel and light 11.4%,
clothing 6.0%, transportation 4.7%, household goods 3.8%, other 21.1%.
Land use (1990): forested 13.1%; pastures 43.9%; agricultural 35.5%; other
7.5%.

Foreign trade

Balance of trade (current prices)

	1985	1986	1987	1988	1989	1990
₦'000,000	+4,049	+3,043	+15,401	+8,283	+29,730	+68,587
% of total	22.0%	21.8%	35.2%	14.2%	34.5%	45.4%

Imports (1991): ₦89,488,200,000 (machinery and transport equipment 41.1%;
manufactured goods [mostly iron and steel products, textiles, and paper
products] 23.5%; chemicals 17.1%; food 8.7%; mineral fuels 0.5%). *Major
import sources:* Germany 13.8%; U.K. 13.6%; U.S. 11.8%; France 8.9%.
Exports (1991): ₦121,533,700,000 (crude petroleum 96.2%; cocoa beans 1.4%;
rubber 0.8%; chemicals 0.1%; other significant exports include cocoa products, textiles, and cashew nuts). *Major export destinations:* U.S. 40.7%; Spain
12.6%; Germany 8.6%; Netherlands 5.0%, France 5.0%; Italy 4.0%.

Transport and communications

Transport. Railroads (1987): length 3,505 km; passenger-km 3,808,277,000;
metric ton-km cargo 1,743,000,000. Roads (1984): total length 124,000 km
(paved 48%). Vehicles (1990): passenger cars 785,000; trucks and buses
625,000. Merchant marine (1991): vessels (100 gross tons and over) 259;
total deadweight tonnage 718,616. Air transport (1991): passenger-km 774,-
844,000; metric ton-km cargo 21,675,000; airports (1992) 14.
Communications. Daily newspapers (1990): total number 24; total circulation
1,553,000[14]; circulation per 1,000 population 18[14]. Radio (1991): 10,000,000
receivers (1 per 12 persons). Television (1991): 4,100,000 receivers (1 per 30
persons). Telephones (1988): 722,070 (1 per 117 persons).

Education and health

Education (1989–90)

	schools	teachers	students	student/ teacher ratio
Primary (age 6–12)	34,904	344,221	12,712,087	36.9
Secondary (age 12–17)	5,594[15]	136,677	2,723,791	19.9
Voc., teacher tr.	376[15]	15,738[16]	391,583[16]	24.9[16]
Higher[15, 17]	48	3,235	55,068	17.0

Literacy (1990): total population age 15 and over literate 29,538,200 (50.7%);
males literate 17,792,300 (62.3%); females literate 11,745,000 (39.5%).
Health (1986): physicians 16,003 (1 per 6,573 persons); hospital beds 90,668
(1 per 1,160 persons); infant mortality rate (1990–95) 96.0.
Food (1988–90): daily per capita caloric intake 2,200 (vegetable products 97%,
animal products 3%); 93% of FAO recommended minimum requirement.

Military

Total active duty personnel (1992): 76,000 (army 81.6%, navy 5.9%, air force
12.5%). *Military expenditure as percentage of GNP* (1989): 0.5% (world 4.9%).

[1]The transfer of the capital from Lagos to Abuja in the Federal Capital Territory was
completed in 1992. [2]Abia includes Akwa Ibom, Cross River, and Enugu. [3]Adamawa
includes Taraba. [4]Benue includes Kogi. [5]Borno includes Yobe. [6]Delta includes Edo.
[7]Jigawa includes Kano. [8]Kaduna includes Katsina. [9]Kebbi includes Sokoto. [10]Osun
includes Oyo. [11]Detail does not add to total given because of rounding. [12]Includes
1,263,600 unemployed persons. [13]Urban households only. [14]For 15 newspapers only.
[15]1987–88. [16]1988–89. [17]For colleges of education only.

Norway

Official name: Kongeriket Norge
(Kingdom of Norway).
Form of government: constitutional
monarchy with one legislative house
(Parliament [165]).
Chief of state: King.
Head of government: Prime Minister.
Capital: Oslo.
Official language: Norwegian.
Official religion: Evangelical Lutheran.
Monetary unit: 1 Norwegian krone
(NKr) = 100 øre; valuation (Oct. 5,
1992) 1 U.S.$ = NKr 5.75;
1 £ = NKr 9.78.

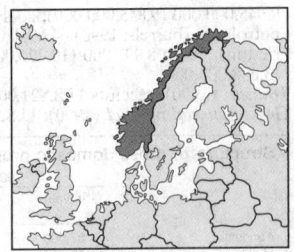

Area and population		area[1]		population
Counties	Capitals	sq mi	sq km	1992[2] estimate
Akershus	—	1,898	4,917	421,510
Aust-Agder	Arendal	3,557	9,212	97,828
Buskerud	Drammen	5,763	14,927	225,712
Finnmark	Vadsø	18,779	48,637	75,251
Hedmark	Hamar	10,575	27,388	187,542
Hordaland	Bergen	6,036	15,634	414,038
Møre og Romsdal	Molde	5,832	15,104	238,810
Nordland	Bodø	14,798	38,327	239,856
Nord-Trøndelag	Steinkjer	8,673	22,463	127,491
Oppland	Lillehammer	9,753	25,260	182,479
Oslo	Oslo	175	454	467,090
Østfold	Moss	1,615	4,183	238,373
Rogaland	Stavanger	3,529	9,141	341,838
Sogn og Fjordane	Leikanger	7,195	18,634	106,834
Sør-Trøndelag	Trondheim	7,271	18,831	252,872
Telemark	Skien	5,913	15,315	163,020
Troms	Tromsø	10,021	25,954	147,979
Vest-Agder	Kristiansand	2,811	7,281	145,954
Vestfold	Tønsberg	856	2,216	199,553
TOTAL		125,050	323,878	4,274,030[3]

Demography

Population (1992): 4,283,000.
Density (1992): persons per sq mi 34.3, persons per sq km 13.2.
Urban-rural (1990): urban 75.0%; rural 25.0%.
Sex distribution (1991): male 49.44%; female 50.56%.
Age breakdown (1991): under 15, 19.0%; 15–29, 22.9%; 30–44, 22.1%; 45–59,
15.1%; 60–74, 13.8%; 75 and over, 7.1%.
Population projection: (2000) 4,426,000; (2010) 4,550,000.
Doubling time: not applicable; doubling time exceeds 100 years.
Ethnic composition (by country of citizenship; 1991): Norway 96.6%; Den-
mark 0.4%; Sweden 0.3%; United Kingdom 0.3%; Pakistan 0.3%; United
States 0.2%; Vietnam 0.2%; other 1.7%.
Religious affiliation (1980): Lutheran 87.9%; nonreligious 3.2%; other 8.9%.
Major cities (1992)[4]: Oslo 467,090; Bergen 215,967; Trondheim 139,660; Sta-
vanger 99,764; Baerum 91,851.

Vital statistics

Birth rate per 1,000 population (1991): 14.3 (world avg. 26.4); (1990) legiti-
mate 61.4%; illegitimate 38.6%.
Death rate per 1,000 population (1991): 10.5 (world avg. 9.2).
Natural increase rate per 1,000 population (1991): 3.8 (world avg. 17.2).
Total fertility rate (avg. births per childbearing woman; 1990): 1.9.
Marriage rate per 1,000 population (1990): 5.2.
Divorce rate per 1,000 population (1990): 2.4.
Life expectancy at birth (1990): male 73.4 years; female 79.8 years.
Major causes of death per 100,000 population (1990): ischemic heart disease
265.1; malignant neoplasms (cancers) 232.5; cerebrovascular disease 132.5.

National economy

Budget (1992). Revenue: NKr 304,389,000,000 (social-security taxes 26.5%,
value-added taxes 21.4%, taxes on interest and dividends 12.0%, ordinary
income tax 4.4%, taxes on petroleum income and activity 3.4%). Expenditures: NKr 316,046,000,000 (social security and welfare 25.3%, health 8.4%,
debt service 5.5%).
Public debt (1990): U.S.$23,430,000,000.
Tourism (1990): receipts from visitors U.S.$1,506,000,000; expenditures by
nationals abroad U.S.$3,413,000,000.
Production (metric tons except as noted). Agriculture, forestry, fishing (1991):
barley 740,000, oats 601,000, potatoes 484,000, wheat 224,000; livestock (number of live animals) 1,029,600 sheep[5], 967,700 cattle, 721,700 pigs; roundwood
(1990) 11,794,000 cu m; fish catch 1,957,550, of which capelin 564,000, herring 379,398, cod 166,225, mackerel 150,000. Mining and quarrying (1991)[6]:
iron ore 2,028,000, zinc 17,520[7], copper 17,400, lead 3,000[7]. Manufacturing
(value added in NKr '000,000; 1990): machinery and equipment 26,605, of
which transport equipment 6,433, electrical equipment 4,698; food products
15,308; paper and paper products 13,572; chemical products 11,253; wood
and wood products 5,353. Construction (1991): residential 2,696,000 sq m;
nonresidential 2,228,000 sq m. Energy production (consumption): electricity
(kW-hr; 1990) 121,601,000,000 (105,651,000,000); coal (metric tons; 1990)
311,000 (779,000); crude petroleum (barrels; 1990) 622,051,000 (99,218,000);
petroleum products (metric tons; 1990) 13,069,000 (7,761,000); natural gas
(cu m; 1990) 19,883,000,000 (1,746,000,000).
Gross national product (1990): U.S.$98,079,000,000 (U.S.$23,120 per capita).

Structure of gross domestic product and labour force				
	1990		1991	
	in value NKr '000,000	% of total value	labour force	% of labour force
Agriculture	19,306	2.9	116,000	5.5
Mining	3,275	0.5	21,000	1.0
Crude petroleum and natural gas	95,170	14.4	...	...
Manufacturing	90,589	13.7	294,000	13.8
Construction	27,568	4.2	130,000	6.1
Public utilities	25,445	3.8	21,000	1.0
Transp. and commun.	57,555	8.7	162,000	7.6
Trade	73,301[8]	11.1[8]	354,000	16.7
Finance	61,294	9.3	153,000	7.2
Pub. admin., defense	104,149	15.7	} 869,000[9]	} 40.9[9]
Services	64,113	9.7		
Other	39,905	6.0		
TOTAL	661,669[10]	100.0	2,126,000[10]	100.0[10]

Population economically active (1991): total 2,126,000; activity rate of total
population 49.6% (participation rates [1990]: ages 16–64, 77.1%; female
43.6%; unemployed [1991] 5.5%).

Price and earnings indexes (1985 = 100)							
	1985	1986	1987	1988	1989	1990	1991
Consumer price index	100.0	107.2	116.5	124.3	130.0	135.4	140.0
Hourly earnings index	100.0	110.0	128.0	135.0	141.0	149.6	157.2

Household income and expenditure. Average household size (1990) 2.4; consumption expenditure per household (1989) NKr 158,900 (U.S.$23,000);
sources of income (1989): wages and salaries 59.9%, social security 21.6%,
self-employment and property income 17.0%; expenditure (1990): housing
18.9%, food 18.4%, transportation 12.6%, clothing and footwear 7.6%,
household furniture and equipment 6.8%, beverages and tobacco 6.7%.
Land use (1989): forested 27.1%; meadows and pastures 0.4%; agricultural
and under permanent cultivation 2.9%; built-up and other 69.6%.

Foreign trade

Balance of trade (current prices)						
	1986	1987	1988	1989	1990	1991
NKr '000,000	− 12,403	− 3,645	− 2,976	+ 27,248	+ 48,231	+ 59,565
% of total	4.4%	1.2%	1.0%	7.9%	12.9%	15.9%

Imports (1991): NKr 165,181,000,000 (machinery and transport equipment
38.3%, of which ships 6.6%, road vehicles 4.9%; metals and metal products
7.0%, of which iron and steel 3.8%; food products 5.2%, of which fruits
and vegetables 1.5%; petroleum products 3.1%, of which crude petroleum
0.9%). *Major import sources:* Sweden 15.4%; Germany 14.1%; U.K. 8.7%;
Denmark 7.3%.
Exports (1991): NKr 220,316,000,000 (fuels and fuel products 48.5%, of which
crude petroleum 36.5%, natural gas 7.4%; metals and metal products 11.4%,
of which aluminum 4.9%; machinery and transport equipment 7.7%; food
products 7.3%, of which fish 6.5%). *Major export destinations:* U.K. 26.5%;
Germany 11.1%; Sweden 10.3%; The Netherlands 7.9%.

Transport and communications

Transport. Railroads (1990): route length 4,182 km; passenger-km 2,116,000,-
000; metric ton-km cargo 2,617,000,000. Roads (1991): total length 88,800
km (paved 70%). Vehicles (1991): passenger cars 1,614,623; trucks and
buses 383,128. Merchant marine (1991): vessels (100 gross tons and over)
2,577; total deadweight tonnage 40,950,168. Air transport (1990): passenger-
km 7,664,588,000; metric ton-km cargo 831,113,000; airports (1992) 47.
Communications. Daily newspapers (1991): total number 61; total circulation
2,163,000; circulation per 1,000 population 508. Radio (1991): 3,300,000 receivers (1 per 1.3 persons). Television (1991): 1,465,858 receivers (1 per 2.9
persons). Telephones (1990)[11]: 2,132,290 (1 per 2.0 persons).

Education and health

Education (1990–91)				
	schools	teachers	students	student/ teacher ratio
Primary (age 7–12)	3,406	33,961	475,344	14.0
Secondary (age 13–18) and vocational	843	20,647	237,053	11.5
Higher	227	7,556	137,982	18.3

Educational attainment (1990). Percentage of population age 16 and over
having: lower secondary education 32.2%; higher secondary 49.0%; higher
18.8%. *Literacy* (1990): virtually 100% literate.
Health (1990): physicians (1991) 13,826 (1 per 309 persons); hospital beds
25,201 (1 per 168 persons); infant mortality rate per 1,000 live births 7.0.
Food (1987–89): daily per capita caloric intake 3,338 (vegetable products 65%,
animal products 35%); 125% of FAO recommended minimum requirement.

Military

Total active duty personnel (1991): 32,700 (army 48.6%, navy 22.3%, air force
29.1%). *Military expenditure as percentage of GNP* (1989): 3.3% (world avg.
4.9%); per capita expenditure U.S.$691.

[1]Excludes Svalbard and Jan Mayen (24,360 sq mi [63,080 sq km]). [2]January 1.
[3]Includes the Norwegian population of Svalbard and Jan Mayen registered as residents in municipalities on the mainland. [4]Population of municipalities. [5]One year and
over. [6]Metal content of ore. [7]1990. [8]Includes hotels. [9]Includes 116,000 unemployed.
[10]Detail does not add to total given because of rounding. [11]Main lines only.

Oman

Official name: Salṭanat 'Umān (Sultanate of Oman).
Form of government: monarchy[1].
Head of state and government: Sultan.
Capital: Muscat.
Official language: Arabic.
Official religion: Islam.
Monetary unit: 1 rial Omani (RO) = 1,000 baizas; valuation (Oct. 5, 1992) 1 RO = U.S.$2.63 = £1.54.

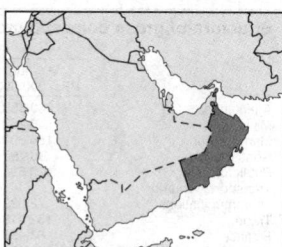

Area and population

Regions[4]	Centres[5]	area[2] sq mi	sq km	population[3] 1990 estimate
al-Bāṭinah	ar-Rustāq; Ṣuḥār	5,320	13,770	416,200
al-Dākhilīyah	Nizwā; Samā'il	29,770	77,110	197,400
al-Janūbīyah	Salālah	45,370	117,510	146,900
Masqaṭ	Muscat	1,420	3,670	410,000
Musandam	Khaṣab	590	1,530	21,400
ash-Sharqīyah	Ibrā; Ṣūr	16,190	41,920	206,500
az-Ẓāhirah	al-Buraymī; 'Ibri	19,490	50,490	131,600
TOTAL		118,150	306,000	1,530,000

Demography

Population (1992): 1,640,000.
Density (1992): persons per sq mi 13.9, persons per sq km 5.4.
Urban-rural (1990): urban 10.6%; rural 89.4%.
Sex distribution (1990): male 52.40%; female 47.60%.
Age breakdown (1990): under 15, 43.1%; 15–29, 24.4%; 30–44, 21.7%; 45–59, 7.7%; 60–74, 2.6%; 75 and over, 0.5%.
Population projection: (2000) 2,176,000; (2010) 3,106,000.
Doubling time: 20 years.
Ethnic composition (1990): Omani Arab 73.5%; Pakistani (mostly Baluchi) 21.0%; other 5.5%.
Religious affiliation (1984): Muslim 86%; Hindu 13%; other 1%.
Major cities (1990): Muscat 85,000[6]; Nizwā 62,880; Samā'il 44,721; Salālah 10,000[6].

Vital statistics

Birth rate per 1,000 population (1991): 41.0 (world avg. 26.4).
Death rate per 1,000 population (1991): 6.0 (world avg. 9.2).
Natural increase rate per 1,000 population (1991): 35.0 (world avg. 17.2).
Total fertility rate (avg. births per childbearing woman; 1990): 7.0.
Marriage rate per 1,000 population: n.a.
Divorce rate per 1,000 population: n.a.
Life expectancy at birth (1991): male 65.0 years; female 68.0 years.
Morbidity (reported cases of illness per 100,000 population; 1989): influenza 6,823; malaria 1,235; chicken pox 1,156; mumps 1,048; dysentery 376; measles 294; bacillary dysentery 206; infectious hepatitis 96; tuberculosis 33; brucellosis 15.

National economy

Budget (1992). Revenue: RO 1,627,700,000 (oil revenue 78.4%; gas revenue 4.2%; other 17.4%). Expenditures: RO 1,932,700,000 (civil ministries 48.3%, of which [1990] education 8.8%, general public services 7.0%, fuel and energy 5.7%, health 3.9%; defense 34.4%; interest paid on loans 5.1%).
Public debt (external, outstanding; 1990): U.S.$2,783,000,000.
Gross national product (at current market prices; 1990): U.S.$9,503,000,000 (U.S.$6,327 per capita).

Structure of gross domestic product and labour force

	1990 in value RO '000,000	% of total value	labour force	% of labour force
Agriculture	126.9	3.1	146,400	27.7
Mining	2,068.0	50.6	2,800	0.5
Manufacturing	151.1	3.7	32,800	6.2
Construction	124.7	3.1	104,800	19.8
Public utilities	51.2	1.3	4,100	0.8
Transportation and communications	132.2	3.2	14,500	2.7
Trade	467.1	11.4	87,500	16.5
Finance	293.3	7.2	9,400	1.8
Pub. admin., defense	656.7	16.1	81,000	15.3
Services	83.7	2.0	45,800	8.7
Other	−70.9[7]	−1.7[7]	—	—
TOTAL	4,084.0	100.0	529,100	100.0

Tourism (1990): receipts from visitors U.S.$69,000,000; expenditures by nationals abroad U.S.$47,000,000.
Household income and expenditure. Average household size (1986) 3.7; income per household: n.a.; sources of income: n.a.; food expenditure (1978): meat and eggs 20.6%, cereals 15.2%, fruits and nuts 12.4%, vegetables 11.9%, dairy products 10.3%, other foods 29.6%.
Production (metric tons except as noted). Agriculture, forestry, fishing (1991): vegetables and melons 159,000 (of which watermelons 27,000), dates 125,-000, mangoes 33,000, bananas 24,000, onions 9,000, potatoes 5,000, papayas 3,000, tobacco leaf 2,000, wheat 1,000; livestock (number of live animals) 725,000 goats, 280,000 sheep, 138,000 cattle, 90,000 camels, 3,000,000 chickens; fish catch (1990) 120,239[8]. Mining and quarrying (1990): copper 15,200; silver 2,500 kg; gold 20 kg. Manufacturing: major products include refined

petroleum products, cement blocks and floors, furniture, aluminum products, electric wire and cable, spark plugs, household utensils, fertilizers, and fibreglass products. Construction (1989): number of residential permits 3,408; nonresidential permits 353. Energy production (consumption): electricity (kW-hr; 1990) 5,345,000,000 (5,345,000,000); coal, none (none); crude petroleum (barrels; 1990) 249,420,000 (23,638,000); petroleum products (metric tons; 1990) 3,226,000 (1,586,000); natural gas (cu m; 1990) 2,722,356,000 (2,722,356,000).
Population economically active (1990)[9]: total 680,850; activity rate of total population 39.9% (participation rates: ages 15–64 [1986] 60.9%; female [1986] 7.5%; unemployed, n.a.).

Price and earnings indexes (1985 = 100)

	1985	1986	1987	1988	1989	1990	1991[10]
Consumer price index[11]	100.0	107.1	109.8	111.6	113.2	114.7	118.4
Earnings index	...	...	...	...	...	...	...

Land use (1990): meadows and pastures 4.7%; agricultural and under permanent cultivation 0.3%; other (mostly desert and developed area) 95.0%.

Foreign trade[12]

Balance of trade (current prices)

	1985	1986	1987	1988	1989	1990
RO '000,000	+555.0	+113.0	+707.0	+385.0	+646.0	+1,034
% of total	19.3%	5.5%	31.9%	17.6%	26.2%	34.3%

Imports (1990): RO 1,031,000,000 (machinery and transport equipment 36.1%; manufactured goods 18.4%; food and live animals 16.0%; miscellaneous manufactured articles 10.4%; chemicals 5.8%; minerals, fuels, lubricants, and related materials 4.0%). *Major import sources* (1989): United Arab Emirates 24.2%; Japan 15.7%; United Kingdom 11.7%; United States 8.4%; West Germany 5.5%.
Exports (1990): RO 2,110,000,000 (petroleum 91.7%; reexports 5.1%; other commodities 3.2%). *Major export destinations* (1989): Japan 37.2%; South Korea 26.7%; Taiwan 8.6%; Singapore 3.9%; United Kingdom 3.4%; China 3.2%; United States 3.1%.

Transport and communications

Transport. Railroads: none. Roads (1991): total length 17,053 mi, 27,438 km (paved 18%). Vehicles (1990): private vehicles 96,559, commercial vehicles 70,231. Merchant marine (1991): vessels (100 gross tons and over) 27; total deadweight tonnage 11,941. Air transport (1991)[13]: passenger-mi 1,042,000,-000, passenger-km 1,676,000,000; short ton-mi cargo 35,100,000, metric ton-km cargo 51,245,000; airports (1992) with scheduled flights 6.
Communications. Daily newspapers (1991): total number 4; total circulation 61,500; circulation per 1,000 population 39. Radio (1991): total number of receivers 900,000 (1 per 1.7 persons). Television (1991): total number of receivers 1,000,033 (1 per 1.6 persons). Telephones (1990): 107,409[14] (1 per 14 persons).

Education and health

Education (1989–90)

	schools	teachers	students	student/ teacher ratio
Primary (age 6–14)	671	12,344	304,207	24.6
Secondary (age 15–17)	128	2,219	36,617	16.5
Voc., teacher tr.	25	728	5,596	7.7
Higher	5	482	3,925	8.1

Educational attainment: n.a. *Literacy* (1990): total population age 6 and over literate 41%; males literate 58%; females literate 24%.
Health (1990): physicians 1,393 (1 per 1,078 persons); hospital beds 3,952 (1 per 380 persons); infant mortality rate per 1,000 live births (1991) 40.
Food: daily per capita caloric intake, n.a.

Military

Total active duty personnel (1992): 35,700 (army 81.8%, navy 8.4%, air force 9.8%); foreign troops 3,700. *Military expenditure as percentage of GNP* (1989): 20.3% (world 4.9%); per capita expenditure U.S.$1,085.

---

[1]The sultan is assisted by an appointed 60-member advisory council consisting of 59 governorate representatives and the sultan's representative, who leads the body. [2]No survey of surface area has ever been carried out in the Sultanate of Oman. [3]The first census of Oman has been scheduled for 1993; figures given represent official 1990 estimates of the Omani government. [4]Regions are divided into 59 wilāyat (provinces). [5]Centres of the regions are not administrative capitals. [6]1982. [7]Net imputed bank service charges. [8]Fish landed. [9]Non-Omani workers constitute approximately 55–60% of the labour force. [10]Average of first two quarters. [11]Applies to food and beverages in the capital area only. [12]Import figures are c.i.f. [13]One-fourth apportionment of international flights of Gulf Air. [14]Number of subscribers.

Pakistan

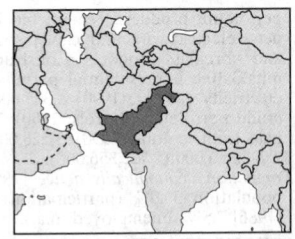

Official name: Islām-ī Jamhūrīya-e Pākistān (Islamic Republic of Pakistan).
Form of government: multiparty, federal Islamic republic with two legislative houses (Senate [87]; National Assembly [217]).
Chief of state: President.
Chief of government: Prime Minister.
Capital: Islāmābād.
Official language: Urdū.
Official religion: Islam.
Monetary unit: 1 Pakistan Rupee (PRs) = 100 paisa; valuation (Oct. 5, 1992) 1 U.S.$ = PRs 25.06; 1 £ = PRs 42.60.

Area and population

Provinces	Capitals	area[1] sq mi	sq km	population 1983 estimate[2]
Balochistān	Quetta	134,051	347,190	4,611,000
North-West Frontier	Peshāwar	28,773	74,521	11,658,000
Punjab	Lahore	79,284	205,344	50,460,000
Sindh	Karāchi	54,407	140,914	20,312,000
Federally Administered Tribal Areas	...	10,509	27,220	2,329,000
Federal Capital Area Islāmābād	...	350	906	359,000
TOTAL		307,374	796,095	89,729,000

Demography

Population (1992): 130,129,000.
Density (1992): persons per sq mi 383.1, persons per sq km 147.9.
Urban-rural (1987): urban 32.0%; rural 68.0%.
Sex distribution (1991): male 52.50%; female 47.50%.
Age breakdown (1987): under 15, 46.0%; 15–29, 24.6%; 30–44, 14.0%; 45–59, 9.3%; 60–74, 4.8%; 75 and over, 1.3%.
Population projection: (2000) 162,409,000; (2010) 205,496,000.
Doubling time: 23 years.
Linguistic composition (1981): Punjābī 48.2%; Pashto 13.1%; Sindhī 11.8%; Saraiki 9.8%; Urdū 7.6%; other 9.5%.
Religious affiliation (1981): Muslim 96.7%; Christian 1.6%; Hindu 1.5%; other 0.2%.
Major cities (1981): Karāchi 5,208,132; Lahore 2,952,689; Faisalābād 1,104,209; Rāwalpindi 794,843; Islāmābād 204,364.

Vital statistics

Birth rate per 1,000 population (1991): 40.5 (world avg. 26.4).
Death rate per 1,000 population (1991): 10.8 (world avg. 9.2).
Natural increase rate per 1,000 population (1991): 29.7 (world avg. 17.2).
Total fertility rate (avg. births per childbearing woman; 1991): 5.4.
Marriage rate per 1,000 population (1975–80): 10.7.
Divorce rate per 1,000 population (1975–80): 0.3.
Life expectancy at birth (1991): male 59.3 years; female 60.7 years.
Major causes of death (percentage of total deaths; 1987): malaria 18.2%; childhood diseases 12.1%; diseases of digestive system 9.8%; diseases of respiratory system 9.2%; infection of intestinal tract 7.7%.

National economy

Budget (1991–92). Revenue: PRs 212,551,700,000 (custom duties 28.0%, excise taxes 13.3%, general turnover tax 11.3%, income taxes 11.1%). Expenditures: PRs 185,648,700,000 (public-debt service 43.5%, defense 38.2%, education and health 3.0%, subsidies 2.9%, grants to local authorities 2.9%).
Production (metric tons except as noted). Agriculture, forestry, fishing (1990–91): sugarcane 35,989,000, wheat 15,105,000, rice 3,265,000, cotton 1,634,000, corn (maize) 1,185,000, gram 583,000, jowar 256,000; livestock (number of live animals; 1989–90) 35,400,000 goats, 17,600,000 cattle, 14,700,000 buffalo, 9,200,000 sheep, 1,000,000 camels, 184,700,000 poultry; roundwood (1990) 26,587,000 cu m; fish catch (1990) 479,036. Mining and quarrying (1990–91): limestone 9,017,000; rock salt 744,000; gypsum 458,000; silica sand 143,000; chromite 25,000. Manufacturing (1990–91): cement 7,800,000; chemical fertilizers 2,957,000, of which urea 2,050,000; refined sugar 1,934,000; cotton yarn 1,041,000; vegetable products 656,000; chemicals 321,048[3]; jute textiles 97,400; paper and paperboard 96,854[3]; cotton textiles 292,000,000 sq m; cigarettes 29,890,000,000 units; motor-vehicle tires 952,000 units; bicycles 429,000 units. Construction (value in PRs; 1984): residential 8,490,000,000; nonresidential 14,579,000,000. Energy production (consumption): electricity (kW-hr; 1990) 43,899,000,000 (43,899,000,000); coal (metric tons; 1990) 2,751,000 (3,616,000); crude petroleum (barrels; 1990) 19,485,000 (46,920,-000); petroleum products (metric tons; 1990) 5,733,000 (10,116,000); natural gas (cu m; 1990) 12,264,000,000 (12,264,000,000).
Tourism (1990): receipts from visitors U.S.$156,000,000; expenditures by nationals abroad U.S.$429,000,000.
Household income and expenditure (1988). Average household size 6.3; income per household PRs 25,572 (U.S.$1,420); sources of income: self-employment 56.0%, wages and salaries 22.0%, other 22.0%; expenditure: food 47.0%, housing 12.0%, clothing and footwear 8.0%, other 33.0%.
Gross national product (at current market prices; 1990): U.S.$42,649,000,000 (U.S.$380 per capita).

Structure of gross domestic product and labour force

	1990–91 in value PRs '000,000[5]	% of total value	labour force	% of labour force
Agriculture	230,388	22.7	16,260,000	49.6
Mining	6,262	0.6	} 4,080,000	12.4
Manufacturing	154,091	15.2		
Construction	36,790	3.6	2,030,000	6.2
Public utilities	28,898	2.8	190,000	0.6
Transportation and communications	72,822	7.2	1,550,000	4.7
Trade	152,416	15.0	3,790,000	11.5
Finance	63,458	6.2		
Pub. admin., defense	75,459	7.4	} 4,910,000[4]	15.0[4]
Services	67,223	6.6		
Other	128,921	12.7		
TOTAL	1,016,728	100.0	32,810,000	100.0

Population economically active (1990–91): total 32,810,000; activity rate of total population 26.4% (participation rates: ages 15–64, 50.3%; female 11.4%; unemployed 3.1%).

Price and earnings indexes (1985 = 100)

	1985	1986	1987	1988	1989	1990	1991
Consumer price index	100.0	103.5	108.4	117.9	127.2	138.7	147.8
Monthly earnings index	100.0	105.3	...	...	...	...	...

Public debt (external, outstanding; 1990): U.S.$15,338,000,000.
Land use (1990): forested 4.6%; meadows and pastures 6.5%; agricultural and under permanent cultivation 26.9%; built-on, wasteland, and other 62.0%.

Foreign trade[6]

Balance of trade (current prices)

	1986	1987	1988	1989	1990	1991
PRs '000,000	−25,214	−19,938	−27,036	−37,093	−24,896	−28,537
% of total	18.3%	12.1%	14.2%	16.1%	9.3%	8.4%

Imports (1990–91): PRs 171,052,400,000 (petroleum products 22.1%, specialized machinery 8.4%, road vehicles 5.8%, vegetable oil and fats 5.4%, organic chemicals 3.8%, manufactured fertilizers 3.5%, iron and steel manufactures 3.3%, power-generating machinery 3.2%). *Major import sources:* Japan 13.0%; U.S. 11.8%; Germany 7.3%; Saudi Arabia 6.3%; China 5.1%; U.K. 4.9%; Malaysia 4.0%; Italy 3.5%; Singapore 3.2%.
Exports (1990–91): PRs 138,341,700,000 (ready-made garments 17.7%, cotton 7.8%, rice 5.7%, leather and leather goods 4.6%, fresh fish 1.9%, petroleum products 1.6%, professional instruments 1.4%, fruits and vegetables 0.9%). *Major export destinations:* U.S. 10.8%; Germany 8.5%; Japan 8.3%; U.K. 7.3%; Hong Kong 6.0%; France 3.8%; Italy 3.8%; Saudi Arabia 3.6%.

Transport and communications

Transport. Railroads (1990–91): route length 5,453 mi, 8,775 km; passenger-mi 12,460,000,000, passenger-km 20,052,000,000; short ton-mi cargo 4,529,-000,000, metric ton-km cargo 6,612,000,000. Roads (1990–91): total length 87,040 mi, 140,077 km (paved 46%). Vehicles (1989): passenger cars 738,059; trucks and buses 171,519. Merchant marine (1991): vessels (100 gross tons and over) 74; total deadweight tonnage 513,061. Air transport (1990): passenger-km 9,384,000,000; metric ton-km cargo 428,484,000; airports (1992) with scheduled flights 35.
Communications. Daily newspapers (1989): total number 271; total circulation 1,106,035; circulation per 1,000 population 9. Radio (1991): total number of receivers 10,000,000 (1 per 13 persons). Television (1991): total number of receivers 2,080,000 (1 per 61 persons). Telephones (1989–90): 922,500 (1 per 131 persons).

Education and health

Education (1990–91)

	schools	teachers	students	student/ teacher ratio
Primary (age 5–9)	127,575	218,300	8,856,000	40.6
Secondary (age 10–14)	13,604	184,200	3,397,000	18.4
Voc., teacher tr.	930	8,722	108,000	12.4
Higher	733	26,050	658,900	25.3

Educational attainment (1981). Percentage of population age 25 and over having: no formal schooling 78.9%; some primary education 8.7%; some secondary 10.5%; postsecondary 1.9%. *Literacy* (1981): total population age 15 and over literate 11,938,790 (25.6%); males literate 8,709,162 (36.0%); females literate 3,229,628 (15.2%).
Health (1990): physicians 51,883 (1 per 2,364 persons); hospital beds 71,897 (1 per 1,706 persons); infant mortality rate per 1,000 live births 113.0.
Food (1988–90): daily per capita caloric intake 2,280 (vegetable products 87%, animal products 13%); 99% of FAO recommended minimum requirement.

Military

Total active duty personnel (1992): 580,000 (army 88.8%, navy 3.4%, air force 7.8%). *Military expenditure as percentage of GNP* (1989): 6.8% (world 4.9%); per capita expenditure U.S.$21.

[1]Excludes the Pakistani-occupied part of Jammu and Kashmir. [2]Provincial estimates exclude and 1991 estimate includes Afghan refugees and residents of Pakistani-occupied Jammu and Kashmir. [3]1989–90. [4]Includes unemployed. [5]At factor cost of 1980–81. [6]Import figures are f.o.b. in balance of trade and c.i.f. for commodities and trading partners.

Panama

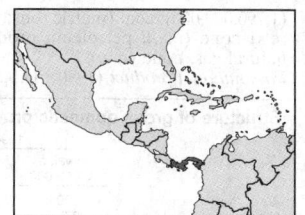

Official name: República de Panamá (Republic of Panama).
Form of government: multiparty republic with one legislative house (Legislative Assembly [67]).
Head of state and government: President assisted by Vice Presidents.
Capital: Panama City.
Official language: Spanish.
Official religion: none.
Monetary unit: 1 balboa (B) = 100 cents; valuation (Oct. 5, 1992) 1 U.S.$ = B 1.00; 1 £ = B 1.70.

Area and population		area		population
				1990
Provinces	Capitals	sq mi	sq km	census[1, 2]
Bocas del Toro	Bocas del Toro	3,376	8,745	93,361
Chiriquí	David	3,341	8,653	370,227
Coclé	Penonomé	1,902	4,927	173,190
Colón	Colón	1,888	4,890	168,294
Darién[3]	La Palma	6,437	16,671	43,832
Herrera	Chitré	904	2,341	93,681
Los Santos	Las Tablas	1,470	3,806	76,947
Panamá	Panama City	4,590	11,887	1,072,127
Veraguas	Santiago	4,339	11,239	203,626
Special territory				
Comarca de San Blas	El Porvenir	910	2,357	34,044
TOTAL		29,157	75,517[4]	2,329,329

Demography

Population (1992): 2,515,000.
Density (1992): persons per sq mi 86.3, persons per sq km 33.3.
Urban-rural (1990): urban 52.9%; rural 47.1%.
Sex distribution (1990): male 50.61%; female 49.39%.
Age breakdown (1990): under 15, 34.8%; 15–29, 29.2%; 30–44, 18.2%; 45–59, 10.3%; 60–74, 5.5%; 75 and over, 2.0%.
Population projection: (2000) 2,893,000; (2010) 3,324,000.
Doubling time: 37 years.
Ethnic composition (1987): mestizo 60.0%; black and mulatto 20.0%; white 10.0%; Amerindian 8.0%; Asian 2.0%.
Religious affiliation (1985): Roman Catholic 84.0%; Protestant 4.8%; Muslim 4.5%; Baha'i 1.1%; Hindu 0.3%; other 5.3%.
Major cities (1990): Panama City 411,549; San Miguelito 242,529[5]; David 65,635[6]; Colón 54,469; Barú 45,669[6].

Vital statistics

Birth rate per 1,000 population (1991): 26.0 (world avg. 26.4); (1985) legitimate 28.1%; illegitimate 71.9%.
Death rate per 1,000 population (1991): 5.0 (world avg. 9.2).
Natural increase rate per 1,000 population (1991): 21.0 (world avg. 17.2).
Total fertility rate (avg. births per childbearing woman; 1991): 3.0.
Marriage rate per 1,000 population (1990): 4.2.
Divorce rate per 1,000 population (1990): 0.6.
Life expectancy at birth (1991): male 72.0 years; female 76.0 years.
Major causes of death per 100,000 population (1990): diseases of the circulatory system 94.4, of which ischemic heart diseases 40.9, cerebrovascular disease 32.3; malignant neoplasms (cancers) 48.4; accidents 23.9; homicide and violence 14.8.

National economy

Budget (1992). Revenue: B 1,453,789,000 (current revenue 82.9%, of which indirect taxes 25.6%, direct taxes 21.0%, income from state enterprises 12.0%; development revenue 17.1%, of which loans 12.5%). Expenditures: B 1,453,789,000 (current transfers 19.2%; development expenditure 14.1%; education 12.9%; internal debt payments 12.7%; external debt payments 10.6%; health 7.8%).
Public debt (external, outstanding; 1990): U.S.$3,758,000,000.
Production (metric tons except as noted). Agriculture, forestry, fishing (1990): sugarcane 1,291,000, bananas 1,250,000, rice 180,000, corn (maize) 115,000, oranges 34,000, tomatoes 29,000, coffee 13,000, tobacco 2,000; livestock (number of live animals) 1,502,000 cattle, 240,000 pigs; roundwood 1,872,000 cu m; fish catch (value of production in B '000): shrimps 34,300, lobster 4,700, fish 3,200. Mining and quarrying (1989): limestone 400,000[7]; salt 18,000. Manufacturing (value added in B '000; 1988): food products 172,600; beverages 60,300; tobacco products 23,500; paper and paper products 20,900; wearing apparel 19,100; plastic products 17,500. Construction (value of construction in B '000; 1990): residential 22,900; nonresidential 24,600. Energy production (consumption): electricity (kW-hr; 1990) 2,901,000,000 (3,015,000,000); coal (metric tons; 1990) none (35,000); crude petroleum (barrels; 1990) none (8,722,000); petroleum products (metric tons; 1990) 1,121,000 (740,000); natural gas (cu m; 1990) none (60,428,000).
Population economically active (1989): total 820,042[2, 8]; activity rate of total population 34.6% (participation rates: ages 15–69, 60.5%; female 33.2%; unemployed [1992] 28.0%[9]).

Price and earnings indexes (1985 = 100)						
	1985	1986	1987	1988	1989	1990	1991
Consumer price index	100.0	100.0	101.0	101.0	101.0	102.0	103.0
Weekly earnings index	100.0	99.3	102.0	101.5	99.9	...	...

Household income and expenditure. Average household size (1990) 4.4; median income per household (1980) B 2,950 (U.S.$2,950); sources of income (1979): wages and salaries 85.3%, transfers 9.2%, other 5.5%; expenditure (1978): food 47.3%, housing and energy 12.7%, household furnishings 8.5%, transportation 6.8%, health care 4.9%, other 19.8%.
Gross national product (1990): U.S.$4,414,000,000 (U.S.$1,830 per capita).

Structure of gross domestic product and labour force				
	1991		1989	
	in value B '000,000[10]	% of total value	labour force[2, 8]	% of labour force[2, 8]
Agriculture	230.5	11.3	208,400	25.4
Mining	3.3	0.2	315	—
Manufacturing	193.0	9.4	80,671	9.8
Construction	67.8	3.3	32,385	3.9
Public utilities	80.9	4.0	10,156	1.2
Transp. and commun.	518.7[11]	25.4[11]	43,354	5.3
Trade	247.5	12.1	118,214	14.4
Finance, real estate	293.2	14.4	31,225	3.8
Pub. admin., defense	250.1	12.2	221,845	27.1
Services	203.1	9.9 }		
Other	−45.3[12]	−2.2[12]	73,477[13]	9.0[13]
TOTAL	2,042.7[4]	100.0	820,042	100.0[4]

Tourism (1990): receipts from visitors U.S.$167,000,000; expenditures by nationals abroad U.S.$99,000,000.
Land use (1989): forested 43.9%; meadows and pastures 20.4%; agricultural and under permanent cultivation 7.6%; other 28.1%.

Foreign trade[14, 15]

Balance of trade (current prices)						
	1985	1986	1987	1988	1989	1990
B '000,000	−903.4	−763.0	−817.6	−393.6	−570.6	−999.1
% of total	57.4%	52.8%	54.0%	41.3%	49.0%	59.5%

Imports (1990): B 1,489,100,000 (mineral fuels 16.7%, chemicals and chemical products 12.7%, machinery and apparatus 11.7%, textiles and wearing apparel 9.0%). *Major import sources:* U.S. 33.8%; Colón Free Zone 18.4%; Ecuador 11.1%; Japan 5.0%; Costa Rica 2.9%.
Exports (1990): B 321,200,000 (bananas 27.8%, shrimps 13.8%, raw sugar 11.8%, clothing 5.0%, coffee 4.3%). *Major export destinations:* U.S. 42.3%; Germany 16.3%; Costa Rica 9.1%; Italy 4.8%; Puerto Rico 2.8%.

Transport and communications

Transport. Railroads (1990): route length 250 mi, 402 km; passengers carried 77,003; short ton-mi cargo 7,165,000[16], metric ton-km cargo 10,460,000[16]. Roads (1991): total length 6,223 mi, 10,015 km (paved 30%). Vehicles: passenger cars (1990) 186,943; trucks and buses (1989) 49,169. Merchant marine (1991): vessels (100 gross tons and over) 4,953; total deadweight tonnage 72,169,724. Panama Canal traffic (1989): oceangoing transits 13,389; cargo 154,306,000 metric tons. Air transport (1990)[17]: passenger-mi 121,582,000, passenger-km 195,667,000; short ton-mi cargo 1,658,000, metric ton-km cargo 2,421,000; airports (1992) with scheduled flights 8.
Communications. Daily newspapers (1990): total number 5; total circulation 144,000; circulation per 1,000 population 60. Radio (1991): 450,000 receivers (1 per 5.5 persons). Television (1991): 204,539 receivers (1 per 12 persons). Telephones (1990): 256,116 (1 per 9.4 persons).

Education and health

Education (1990)				
	schools	teachers	students	student/teacher ratio
Primary (age 6–11)	2,512	12,969	324,594	25.0
Secondary (age 12–17) } Voc., teacher tr.	347	10,066	191,251	19.0
Higher	8	3,451	53,235	15.4

Educational attainment (1980). Percentage of population age 25 and over having: no formal schooling 17.4%; incomplete primary education 27.3%; complete primary education 23.4%; secondary 23.5%; higher 8.4%. *Literacy* (1990): total population age 15 and over literate 1,385,000 (88.1%); males literate 705,000 (88.1%); females literate 680,000 (88.2%).
Health (1990): physicians 2,748 (1 per 880 persons); hospital beds 7,319 (1 per 330 persons); infant mortality rate per 1,000 live births (1991) 21.0.
Food (1987–89): daily per capita caloric intake 2,537 (vegetable products 83%, animal products 17%); 110% of FAO recommended minimum requirement.

Military

Total active duty personnel (1991): 11,000-member national police force replaced military forces abolished by constitutional amendment in 1991. U.S. forces in former Canal Zone 9,900. *Military expenditure as percentage of GNP* (1989): 3.4% (world 4.9%); per capita expenditure U.S.$59.

[1]Final figure not adjusted for underenumeration. [2]Excludes nonresidents in former Canal Zone. [3]Includes Comarca Emberá (1990 pop. 16,746) created in 1983 for dispersed Amerindians. [4]Detail does not add to total given because of rounding. [5]Population of urban district. [6]Population of the cabecera, the seat, or "head," of the municipality. [7]1988. [8]Excludes indigenous areas and institutional households. [9]Excludes 20% underemployment. [10]At prices of 1970. [11]Includes trans-Panamanian oil pipeline, commission of Panama Canal, and all activities of Colón Free Zone. [12]Net of imputed bank service charges and import fees. [13]Includes 25,296 not adequately defined and 48,181 unemployed without previous employment. [14]Import figures are f.o.b. in balance of trade and c.i.f. in commodities and trading partners. [15]Excludes Colón Free Zone (1990 imports f.o.b. B 2,676,600,000; 1990 reexports f.o.b. B 3,086,300,000). [16]Chiriqui Land Company Railways; 1987. [17]Scheduled traffic of COPA only.

Papua New Guinea

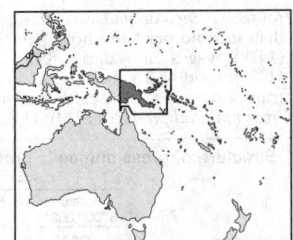

Official name: Independent State of
Papua New Guinea.
Form of government: constitutional
monarchy with one legislative house
(National Parliament [109]).
Chief of state: British Monarch
represented by Governor-General.
Head of government: Prime Minister.
Capital: Port Moresby.
Official language: English.
Official religion: none.
Monetary unit: 1 Papua New Guinea
kina (K) = 100 toea; valuation
(Oct. 5, 1992) 1 U.S.$ = K 0.97;
1 £ = K 1.65.

Area and population

Provinces	Administrative centres	area		population 1990 census[1]
		sq mi	sq km	
Central	Port Moresby (Central)	11,400	29,500	140,584
Eastern Highlands	Goroka	4,300	11,200	299,619
East New Britain	Rabaul	6,000	15,500	184,408
East Sepik	Wewak	16,550	42,800	248,308
Enga	Wabag	4,950	12,800	238,357
Gulf	Kerema	13,300	34,500	68,060
Madang	Madang	11,200	29,000	270,299
Manus	Lorengau	800	2,100	32,830
Milne Bay	Alotau (Samarai)	5,400	14,000	157,288
Morobe	Lae	13,300	34,500	363,535
National Capital District	Port Moresby	100	240	193,242
New Ireland	Kavieng	3,700	9,600	87,194
North Solomons (Bougainville)	Arawa (Buka)	3,600	9,300	159,500[2]
Oro (Northern)	Popondetta	8,800	22,800	96,762
Sandaun (West Sepik)	Vanimo	14,000	36,300	135,185
Simbu (Chimbu)	Kundiawa	2,350	6,100	183,801
Southern Highlands	Mendi	9,200	23,800	302,724
Western	Daru	38,350	99,300	108,705
Western Highlands	Mount Hagen	3,300	8,500	291,090
West New Britain	Kimbe	8,100	21,000	127,547
TOTAL		178,704[3]	462,840	3,689,038[4]

Demography

Population (1992): 3,834,000.
Density (1992): persons per sq mi 21.5, persons per sq km 8.3.
Urban-rural (1990)[1]: urban 15.2%; rural 84.8%.
Sex distribution (1990)[1]: male 52.09%; female 47.91%.
Age breakdown (1985): under 15, 41.6%; 15–29, 27.5%; 30–44, 16.0%; 45–59, 9.3%; 60–74, 4.5%; 75 and over, 1.0%.
Population projection: (2000) 4,568,000; (2010) 5,692,000.
Doubling time: 32 years.
Ethnic composition (1983): New Guinea Papuan 84.0%; New Guinea Melanesian 15.0%; other 1.0%.
Religious affiliation (1980): Protestant 58.4%; Roman Catholic 32.8%; Anglican 5.4%; traditional beliefs 2.5%; Bahā'ī 0.6%; other 0.3%.
Major cities (1990)[1]: Port Moresby 193,242; Lae 80,655; Madang 27,057; Wewak 23,224; Goroka 17,855.

Vital statistics

Birth rate per 1,000 population (1991): 34.0 (world avg. 26.4); legitimate, n.a.; illegitimate, n.a.
Death rate per 1,000 population (1991): 12.0 (world avg. 9.2).
Natural increase rate per 1,000 population (1991): 22.0 (world avg. 17.2).
Total fertility rate (avg. births per childbearing woman; 1991): 5.3.
Marriage rate per 1,000 population: n.a.
Life expectancy at birth (1990): male 54.0 years; female 56.0 years.
Major causes of death per 100,000 population (1984): pneumonia 27.6; conditions originating from perinatal period 10.9; malaria 9.3; diarrheal diseases 9.0; meningitis 7.7; tuberculosis 6.7.

National economy

Budget (1991). Revenue: K 1,054,200,000 (foreign grants 20.9%, personal income tax 20.1%, import duties 19.3%, nontax revenue 15.7%, company tax 9.6%, excise duties 9.2%). Expenditures: K 1,139,600,000 (administrative 41.2%, transfers to provincial governments 27.3%, interest payments 8.9%, capital works 7.4%).
Public debt (external, outstanding; 1990): U.S.$1,503,000,000.
Tourism (1990): receipts from visitors U.S.$28,000,000; expenditures by nationals abroad U.S.$42,000,000.
Land use (1989): forested 84.4%; agricultural and under permanent cultivation 0.9%; meadows and pastures 0.2%; other 14.5%.
Production (metric tons except as noted). Agriculture, forestry, fishing (1990): bananas 1,200,000, coconuts 900,000, sweet potatoes 510,000, sugarcane 430,000, taro 215,000, yams 210,000, palm oil 143,000, copra 116,000, cassava 112,000, coffee 67,000, palm kernels 57,000, cocoa 40,000, pineapples 12,000, tea 8,000; livestock (number of live animals) 1,840,000 pigs, 103,000 cattle, 14,000 goats, 3,000,000 chickens; roundwood 8,188,000 cu m; fish catch (1989) 25,244. Mining and quarrying (1990): copper 196,500; silver 101,400 kg; gold 32,800 kg. Manufacturing (value added, in K; 1985): food, beverages, and tobacco 162,558,000; metals, metal products, machinery, and equipment 47,493,000; wood and wood products 29,807,000. Construction (value in K[5]; 1986): residential K 19,369,000; nonresidential K 55,675,000. Energy production (consumption): electricity (kW-hr; 1990) 1,790,000,000

(1,790,000,000); coal (metric tons; 1990) none (1,000); crude petroleum (barrels) none (n.a.); petroleum products (metric tons; 1990) none (743,000); natural gas, none (n.a.).
Gross national product (1990): U.S.$3,372,000,000 (U.S.$860 per capita).

Structure of gross domestic product and labour force

	1990		1980	
	in value K '000,000	% of total value	labour force[6]	% of labour force[6]
Agriculture	899.8	28.8	564,500	77.0
Mining	377.9	12.1	4,300	0.6
Manufacturing	370.6	11.9	14,000	1.9
Construction	177.4	5.7	21,600	2.9
Public utilities	51.3	1.6	2,800	0.4
Transp. and commun. }	498.3	16.0	17,400	2.4
Trade			25,100	3.4
Finance	...	...	4,500	0.6
Pub. admin., defense	554.3	17.8	77,100	10.5
Services }	191.0	6.1	1,500	0.2
Other				
TOTAL	3,120.6	100.0	732,800	100.0[3]

Population economically active (1980)[6]: total 732,800; activity rate 24.6% (participation rates: over age 10, 35.2%; female 39.8%; unemployed 12.8%[7]).

Price and earnings indexes (1985 = 100)

	1985	1986	1987	1988	1989	1990	1991
Consumer price index	100.0	105.5	109.0	114.9	120.9	128.4	137.3
Weekly earnings index[8]	100.0	104.5	109.5	112.8	118.6	122.4	129.9

Household income and expenditure. Average household size (1980) 4.6; income per household (1975–76) K 2,771 (U.S.$3,483); sources of income (1970): wages and salaries 57.3%, transfer payments 1.1%, self-employment and other 41.6%; expenditure (1987)[9]: food and beverages 40.9%, transportation and communications 13.0%, housing 12.5%, clothing and footwear 6.2%, heating and lighting 4.9%, services and other 22.5%.

Foreign trade[10]

Balance of trade (current prices)

	1986	1987	1988	1989	1990	1991
K '000,000	−45.0	+174.4	+214.7	−47.2	+38.5	−52.7
% of total	2.7%	8.3%	9.4%	2.1%	1.8%	2.0%

Imports (1990): K 1,206,700,000 (1989; machinery and transport equipment 41.6%; basic manufactures 20.1%; food and live animals 15.1%; chemicals 6.3%; mineral fuels, lubricants, and related materials 5.1%). *Major import sources* (1989): Australia 40.4%; Japan 17.7%; U.S. 9.5%; Singapore 6.2%; New Zealand 4.5%; U.K. 3.4%; W.Ger. 2.8%.
Exports (1990): K 1,087,800,000 (copper ore and concentrates 35.4%; gold 35.3%; coffee 8.6%; timber 5.7%; cocoa beans 2.8%; palm oil and copra 1.9%). *Major export destinations:* Japan 28.0%; Australia 26.1%; W.Ger. 16.0%; South Korea 9.2%; U.K. 4.3%; U.S. 2.4%.

Transport and communications

Transport. Railroads: none. Roads (1986): total length 12,263 mi, 19,736 km (paved 6%). Vehicles (1988): passenger cars 17,532; trucks and buses 29,021. Merchant marine (1991): vessels (100 gross tons and over) 85; total deadweight tonnage 30,967. Air transport (1990): passenger-mi 388,000,000, passenger-km 624,000,000; short ton-mi cargo 10,093,000, metric ton-km cargo 14,736,000; airports (1992) with scheduled flights 98.
Communications. Daily newspapers (1988): total number 2; total circulation 65,000; circulation per 1,000 population 18. Radio (1991): 235,000 receivers (1 per 16 persons). Television (1991): 10,000 receivers (1 per 375 persons). Telephones (1988): 72,223 (1 per 49 persons).

Education and health

Education (1989)

	schools	teachers	students	student/ teacher ratio
Primary (age 7–12)	2,692	13,171	417,818	31.7
Secondary (age 13–16)	122[11]	2,306	57,676	25.0
Voc., teacher tr.	112[11]	751	9,331	12.4
Higher[11]	2	902	6,397	7.1

Educational attainment (1990). Percentage of population age 25 and over having: no formal schooling 82.6%; some primary education 8.2%; completed primary 5.0%; some secondary 4.2%. *Literacy* (1990): total population age 15 and over literate 52.0%; males literate 64.9%; females literate 37.8%.
Health: physicians (1987) 283 (1 per 11,904 persons); hospital beds (1984) 14,661 (1 per 222 persons); infant mortality rate (1991) 59.0.
Food: daily per capita caloric intake (1987) 2,145 (1980–82; vegetable products 90%, animal products 10%); (1984) 82% of FAO recommended minimum requirement.

Military

Total active duty personnel (1991): 3,800 (army 89.5%, navy 7.9%, air force 2.6%). *Military expenditure as percentage of GNP* (1989): 1.4% (world 4.9%); per capita expenditure U.S.$13.

---

[1]Preliminary results; excludes North Solomons and five census divisions. [2]Estimate. [3]Detail does not add to total given because of rounding. [4]Includes noncitizens. [5]Completed new buildings. [6]Citizens of Papua New Guinea over age 10 involved in "money-raising activities" only. [7]1977; in six urban centres. [8]Minimum wage of urban labourers. [9]Weights of retail price index components. [10]Import figures are f.o.b. in balance of trade and c.i.f. for commodities and trading partners. [11]1986.

Paraguay

Official name: República del Paraguay (Republic of Paraguay).
Form of government: multiparty republic with two legislative houses (Senate [36]; Chamber of Deputies [72]).
Head of state and government: President.
Capital: Asunción.
Official language: Spanish.
Official religion: Roman Catholicism.
Monetary unit: 1 Paraguayan Guaraní (G) = 100 céntimos; valuation (Oct. 5, 1992) 1 U.S.$ = G1,543; 1 £ = G2,624.

Area and population

Regions Departments	Capitals	area sq mi	area sq km	population 1990 estimate
Occidental		95,338	246,925	65,800
Alto Paraguay	Fuerte Olimpio	17,754	45,982	10,100
Boquerón	Dr. Pedro P. Peña	18,034	46,708	16,900
Chaco	Mayor Pablo Lagerenza	14,041	36,367	300
Nueva Asunción	General Eugenio A. Garay	17,359	44,961	300
Presidente Hayes	Pozo Colorado	28,150	72,907	38,200
Oriental		61,710	159,827	4,213,700
Alto Paraná	Ciudad del Este	5,751	14,895	373,300
Amambay	Pedro Juan Caballero	4,994	12,933	97,700
Asunción	Asunción	45	117	607,700
Caaguazú	Coronel Oviedo	4,430	11,474	462,500
Caazapá	Caazapá	3,666	9,496	132,000
Canindiyú	Salto del Guairá	5,663	14,667	120,800
Central	Asunción	952	2,465	769,100
Concepción	Concepción	6,970	18,051	181,500
Cordillera	Caacupé	1,910	4,948	222,200
Guairá	Villarrica	1,485	3,846	179,800
Itapúa	Encarnación	6,380	16,525	371,600
Misiones	San Juan Bautista	3,690	9,556	97,500
Ñeembucú	Pilar	4,690	12,147	83,300
Paraguarí	Paraguarí	3,361	8,705	230,700
San Pedro	San Pedro	7,723	20,002	284,000
TOTAL		157,048	406,752	4,279,500

Demography

Population (1992): 4,519,000.
Density (1992): persons per sq mi 28.8, persons per sq km 11.1.
Urban-rural (1990): urban 47.5%; rural 52.5%.
Sex distribution (1988): male 50.63%; female 49.37%.
Age breakdown (1988): under 15, 40.6%; 15–29, 28.4%; 30–44, 17.4%; 45–59, 8.2%; 60–74, 4.3%; 75 and over, 1.1%.
Population projection: (2000) 5,538,000; (2010) 6,928,000.
Doubling time: 26 years.
Ethnic composition (1980): mestizo (Spanish-Guaraní) 90.8%; Amerindian 3.0%; German 1.7%; other 4.5%.
Religious affiliation (1980): Roman Catholic 96.0%; Protestant 2.1%; other 1.9%.
Major cities (1990): Asunción 607,706; San Lorenzo 123,737[1]; Ciudad del Este 110,584; Concepción 62,577[1]; Encarnación 44,064.

Vital statistics

Birth rate per 1,000 population (1990): 34.1 (world avg. 27.1); (1985) legitimate 68.7%[2]; illegitimate 31.3%[2].
Death rate per 1,000 population (1990): 6.5 (world avg. 9.8).
Natural increase rate per 1,000 population (1990): 27.6 (world avg. 17.3).
Total fertility rate (avg. births per childbearing woman; 1990–95): 4.3.
Marriage rate per 1,000 population (1990): 1.8[2].
Divorce rate per 1,000 population: n.a.
Life expectancy at birth (1990–95): male 65.1 years; female 69.5 years.
Major causes of death per 100,000 population (1986): diseases of the circulatory system 157.5; infectious and parasitic diseases 60.7; malignant neoplasms (cancers) 48.3; diseases of the respiratory system 43.4.

National economy

Budget (1991). Revenue: G901,740,000,000 (taxes on goods and services 34.8%, customs duties 16.4%, income on fixed assets 13.8%, income tax 10.4%, sales tax 8.1%, pension funds 5.2%, alcohol tax 3.7%, real estate taxes 1.8%). Expenditures: G1,247,251,300,000 (education 11.8%, defense 11.4%, interior 8.2%, agriculture 6.7%, public works 5.7%).
Public debt (external, outstanding; 1991): U.S.$1,832,000,000.
Production (metric tons except as noted). Agriculture, forestry, fishing (1991): cassava 3,900,000, sugarcane 2,300,000, soybeans 1,304,000, corn (maize) 980,000, seed cotton 750,000, oranges 367,000, bananas 311,000, lint cotton 259,000, sweet potatoes 85,000; livestock (number of live animals) 8,260,000 cattle, 2,450,000 pigs, 17,000,000 chickens; roundwood (1990) 8,430,000 cu m; fish catch (1990) 12,500. Mining and quarrying (1989): limestone 500,-000[3]; kaolin 74,000; gypsum 4,500. Manufacturing (value of production in G'000,000; 1988): woven cotton fabric 164,329; processed meat 129,222; soft drinks 47,621; beer 38,580; gasoline 23,308; sugar 22,986; wheat flour 21,043; soybean flour 20,626; naphtha 17,287; cement 14,275. Construction (1985): residential 60,800 sq m; nonresidential 163,200 sq m. Energy production (consumption): electricity (kW-hr; 1990) 2,434,000,000 (1,837,000,000); coal, none (none); crude petroleum (barrels; 1990) none (2,555,000); petroleum products (metric tons; 1990) 342,000 (537,000); natural gas, none (none).

Tourism (1990): receipts from visitors U.S.$112,000,000; expenditures by nationals abroad U.S.$105,000,000.
Gross national product (1990): U.S.$4,796,000,000 (U.S.$1,110 per capita).

Structure of gross domestic product and labour force

	1990 in value G'000,000	1990 % of total value	1982 labour force	1982 % of labour force
Agriculture	1,798,724	27.8	445,518	42.9
Mining	23,064	0.4	1,406	0.1
Manufacturing	1,118,679	17.3	124,658	12.0
Construction	353,068	5.5	69,900	6.7
Public utilities	161,823	2.5	2,605	0.3
Transp. and commun.	249,873	3.8	30,524	2.9
Trade	1,880,670	29.0	85,961	8.3
Finance	123,309	1.9	18,019	1.7
Pub. admin., defense	} 765,224	} 11.8	174,228	16.8
Services				
Other			86,444	8.3
TOTAL	6,474,434	100.0	1,039,258[4]	100.0

Population economically active (1982): total 1,039,258; activity rate 51.5% (participation rates: ages 15–64, 57.5%; female 19.7%; unemployed [1989] 9.2%).

Price and earnings indexes (1985 = 100)

	1985	1986	1987	1988	1989	1990	1991
Consumer price index	100.0	131.7	160.5	124.1	248.7	343.7	427.1
Earnings index							

Household income and expenditure. Average household size (1982) 5.2; sources of income (1987): wages and salaries 39.4%, transfer payments 2.5%, other 58.1%; expenditure (1980): food 48.7%, housing 16.4%, clothing 9.7%, household durable goods 6.2%, transportation and communications 4.5%.
Land use (1989): forested 34.7%; meadows and pastures 53.1%; agricultural and under permanent cultivation 5.6%; other 6.6%.

Foreign trade

Balance of trade (current prices)

	1985	1986	1987	1988	1989	1990
G'000,000	−75,892	−150,210	−115,975	+28,520	+376,875	−234,684
% of total	28.2%	44.9%	21.8%	4.5%	22.5%	10.9%

Imports (1991): U.S.$1,275,387,000 (machinery and transport equipment 41.1%, of which transport equipment 7.6%; fuels and lubricants 10.1%; tobacco and beverages 8.7%; chemicals and pharmaceuticals 6.2%; iron products 3.8%). Major import sources: Brazil 18.4%; United States 14.5%; Japan 12.9%; Argentina 11.9%; United Kingdom 4.4%; Germany 4.3%; Algeria 3.0%.
Exports (1991): U.S.$737,096,000 (cotton fibres 43.3%; soybeans 21.3%; processed meat 7.5%; timber 6.1%; vegetable oil 3.3%, of which tung oil 1.1%; perfume oils 2.6%; tobacco 1.0%). Major export destinations: Brazil 27.6%; The Netherlands 14.9%; Argentina 6.1%; Italy 5.3%; Germany 4.9%; Switzerland 4.8%; United States 4.6%.

Transport and communications

Transport. Railroads (1988): route length 274 mi, 441 km; passenger-mi 13,573,000, passenger-km 21,843,000; short ton-mi cargo 13,580,000, metric ton-km cargo 19,826,000. Roads (1988): total length 15,957 mi, 25,681 km (paved 9%). Vehicles (1990): passenger cars 117,067; buses 3,375. Merchant marine (1991): vessels (100 gross tons and over) 38; total deadweight tonnage 38,514. Air transport (1990): passenger-mi 355,019,000, passenger-km 571,349,000; short ton-mi cargo 2,427,000, metric ton-km cargo 3,543,000; airports (1992) with scheduled flights 1.
Communications. Daily newspapers (1991): total number 6; total circulation 123,000[5]; circulation per 1,000 population 28. Radio (1991): 775,000 receivers (1 per 5.7 persons). Television (1991): 350,000 receivers (1 per 13 persons). Telephones (1990): 128,394 (1 per 33 persons).

Education and health

Education (1989–90)

	schools	teachers	students	student/teacher ratio
Primary (age 7–12)	4,411	31,590	656,877	20.8
Secondary (age 13–18)[6]	812	9,444[3]	165,373	17.4[3]
Higher	2	2,694[1]	28,677	...

Educational attainment (1982). Percentage of population age 25 and over having: no formal schooling 13.6%; primary education 64.7%; secondary 15.5%; higher 3.4%; not stated 2.8%. Literacy (1990): percentage of total population age 15 and over literate 90.1%; males literate 92.1%; females literate 88.1%.
Health (1989): physicians 4,128 (1 per 1,008 persons); hospital beds 4,596 (1 per 931 persons); infant mortality rate per 1,000 live births (1990–95) 39.0.
Food (1988–90): daily per capita caloric intake 2,684 (vegetable products 82%, animal products 18%); 116% of FAO recommended minimum requirement.

Military

Total active duty personnel (1992): 16,500 (army 75.7%, navy 18.2%, air force 6.1%). Military expenditure as percentage of GNP (1989): 1.4% (world 4.9%); per capita expenditure U.S.$13.

[1]1985. [2]Civil Registry records only. [3]1988. [4]Detail does not add to total. [5]For four newspapers only. [6]Includes vocational education and teacher training.

Peru

Official name: República del Perú (Spanish) (Republic of Peru).
Form of government[1]: unitary multiparty republic with one legislative house (Congress [80][2]).
Head of state and government: President.
Capital: Lima.
Official languages: Spanish; Quechua.
Official religion: Roman Catholicism.
Monetary unit[3]: 1 nuevo sol = 100 céntimos; valuation (Oct. 5, 1992) 1 U.S.$ = 1.52 nuevo sol; 1 £ = 2.58 nuevo soles.

Area and population

Departments	Capitals	area sq mi	area sq km	population 1991 estimate
Amazonas	Chachapoyas	15,154	39,249	352,100
Ancash	Huaraz	13,529	35,041	1,006,200
Apurímac	Abancay	8,068	20,896	376,400
Arequipa	Arequipa	24,458	63,345	939,900
Ayacucho	Ayacucho	16,917	43,815	586,800
Cajamarca	Cajamarca	13,136	34,023	1,250,100
Cusco	Cusco	27,758	71,892	1,056,600
Huancavelica	Huancavelica	8,545	22,131	380,500
Huánuco	Huánuco	14,565	37,722	629,200
Ica	Ica	8,235	21,328	527,400
Junín	Huancayo	17,147	44,410	1,106,500
La Libertad	Trujillo	9,573	24,795	1,211,800
Lambayeque	Chiclayo	5,495	14,231	902,900
Lima	Lima	13,437	34,802	6,431,800
Loreto	Iquitos	142,414	368,852	667,500
Madre de Dios	Puerto Maldonado	32,889	85,183	50,800
Moquegua	Moquegua	6,105	15,813	132,400
Pasco	Cerro de Pasco	9,776	25,320	298,900
Piura	Piura	13,858	35,892	1,413,800
Puno	Puno	27,804	72,012	1,032,500
San Martín	Moyobamba	19,789	51,253	481,900
Tacna	Tacna	6,171	15,983	209,300
Tumbes	Tumbes	1,803	4,669	143,900
Ucayali	Pucallpa	39,541	102,411	236,800
Constitutional Province				
Callao	Callao	57	147	572,300
TOTAL		496,224	1,285,216[4]	21,998,300

Demography

Population (1992): 22,454,000.
Density (1992): persons per sq mi 45.2, persons per sq km 17.5.
Urban-rural (1992): urban 71.3%; rural 28.7%.
Sex distribution (1992): male 50.32%; female 49.68%.
Age breakdown (1991): under 15, 37.2%; 15–29, 29.1%; 30–44, 17.7%; 45–59, 10.0%; 60–74, 4.9%; 75 and over, 1.1%.
Population projection: (2000) 26,276,000; (2010) 31,047,000.
Doubling time: 28 years.
Ethnic composition (1981): Quechua 47.1%; mestizo 32.0%; white 12.0%; Aymara 5.4%; other Amerindian 1.7%; other 1.8%.
Religious affiliation (1989): Roman Catholic 92.5%; Protestant 5.5%.
Major cities (1990): Lima 6,115,700; Arequipa 621,700; Callao 572,300; Trujillo 532,000; Chiclayo 419,600; Piura 315,800.

Vital statistics

Birth rate per 1,000 population (1990): 32.8 (world avg. 27.1); (1977) legitimate 57.8%; illegitimate 42.2%.
Death rate per 1,000 population (1990): 8.3 (world avg. 9.9).
Natural increase rate per 1,000 population (1990): 24.5 (world avg. 17.2).
Total fertility rate (avg. births per childbearing woman; 1990): 4.2.
Marriage rate per 1,000 population (1982): 6.0[5].
Life expectancy at birth (1990): male 61.5 years; female 65.3 years.
Major causes of death per 100,000 population (1983): respiratory diseases 111.0, infectious diseases 101.1; diseases of the circulatory system 59.7; accidents, poisoning, and violence 30.7; malignant neoplasms 30.3.

National economy

Budget (1990). Revenue: I/. 38,460,000,000,000[3] (tax on goods and services 44.1%, tax on external trade 26.2%, income taxes 10.0%, nontax revenues 2.6%). Expenditures: I/. 74,826,000,000,000[3] (general public services 50.2%, education 16.2%, public order and safety 12.3%, defense 11.2%, health 5.1%, agriculture 2.1%, transportation and communications 2.0%).
Public debt (external, outstanding; 1990): U.S.$13,341,000,000.
Tourism (1990): receipts U.S.$353,000,000; expenditures U.S.$571,000,000.
Production (metric tons except as noted). Agriculture, forestry, fishing (1991): sugarcane 7,000,000, potatoes 1,450,000, rice 814,000, corn (maize) 669,000, plantains 580,000, cassava 440,000, seed cotton 176,000, coffee 82,000; livestock (number of live animals) 11,250,000 sheep, 3,630,000 cattle, 2,250,000 pigs, 60,000,000 chickens; roundwood (1990) 8,096,000 cu m; fish catch (1990) 6,875,072. Mining and quarrying (1990): iron ore 2,200,000; zinc 585,119; copper 317,706; lead 188,937; silver 1,781. Manufacturing (1991): cement 2,137,000; wheat flour 610,861; refined sugar 562,134; animal feed 531,693; evaporated milk 120,052; cooking oil 111,048; light beer 6,750,060 hectolitres; motor vehicles 2,474 units. Construction (value added in I/. '000[3]; 1985): buildings 9,753,500[6]. Energy production (consumption): electricity (kW-hr; 1990) 13,817,000,000 (13,817,000,000); coal (metric tons; 1990) 145,000 (140,000); crude petroleum (barrels; 1990) 51,086,000 (56,908,000);

petroleum products (metric tons; 1990) 7,395,000 (5,766,000); natural gas (cu m; 1990) 499,808,000 (499,808,000).
Gross national product (1990): U.S.$25,149,000,000 (U.S.$1,160 per capita).

Structure of gross domestic product and labour force

	1990 in value U.S.$'000,000	% of total value	labour force	% of labour force
Agriculture	2,478	8.8	2,605,000	34.0
Mining	628	2.2	183,900	2.4
Manufacturing	8,453	29.9	804,500	10.5
Construction	2,284	8.1	283,500	3.7
Public utilities	191	0.7	23,000	0.3
Transp. and commun.	1,055	3.7	337,100	4.4
Trade	4,333	15.3	1,195,200	15.6
Finance	...	...	183,900	2.4
Services	8,848[7]	31.3[7]	2,045,700[8]	26.7[8]
TOTAL	28,270	100.0	7,661,800	100.0

Population economically active (1990): total 7,661,800; activity rate of total population 34.3% (participation rates: over age 15, 56.4%; female [1985–86] 38.3%; unemployed [1986] 8.2%).

Price and earnings indexes (1985 = 100)

	1985	1986	1987	1988	1989	1990	1991
Consumer price index	100.0	177.9	330.7	2,536	88,733	6,727[9]	34,274[9]
Monthly earnings index[10]	100.0	199.8	379.2	1,405.9	39,141.0	...	...

Household income and expenditure (1986). Average household size 5.2; income per household I/. 39,392[3] (U.S.$2,824); sources of income: n.a.; expenditure: food 55.4%, rent and utilities 10.4%, transportation 8.6%, clothing 7.5%, education 6.9%, household durables 4.6%, health 4.6%, other 2.0%.
Land use (1990): forest 53.4%; pasture 21.2%; agricultural 2.9%; other 22.5%.

Foreign trade

Balance of trade (current prices)

	1986	1987	1988	1989	1990	1991
U.S.$'000,000	+106.6	–307.8	+127.9	+1,523.9	+585.3	–165
% of total	2.2%	5.5%	2.4%	27.6%	9.8%	2.4%

Imports (1991): U.S.$3,494,000,000 (raw and intermediate materials 50.0%, machinery and transport equipment 28.3%, consumer goods 19.0%). *Major import sources:* U.S. 21.3%; Colombia 6.4%; Argentina 5.8%; W.Ger. 5.1%; Japan 5.1%; Brazil 5.0%; Ecuador 4.3%.
Exports (1991): U.S.$3,329,000,000 (copper 22.2%, fish flour 14.0%, zinc 9.7%, petroleum and derivatives 5.1%, lead 4.9%, gold 4.1%, coffee 3.6%). *Major export destinations:* U.S. 14.7%; Japan 5.9%; W.Ger. 3.9%; China 3.0%; U.K. 2.8%; Colombia 1.9%; Brazil 1.8%; Venezuela 1.7%.

Transport and communications

Transport. Railroads (1991): route length 2,157 mi, 3,472 km; passenger-km 319,772,000; metric ton-km cargo 826,848,000. Roads (1990): total length 43,460 mi, 69,942 km (paved 11%). Vehicles (1990): passenger cars 368,155; trucks and buses 237,395. Merchant marine (1991): vessels (100 gross tons and over) 618; total deadweight tonnage 788,414. Air transport (1990): passenger-km 2,034,246,000; metric ton-km cargo 199,793,000; airports (1992) 22.
Communications. Daily newspapers (1986): total number 70; total circulation 1,427,000[11]; circulation per 1,000 population 71[11]. Radio (1991): 4,400,000 receivers (1 per 5.2 persons). Television (1991): 2,080,000 receivers (1 per 11 persons). Telephones (1990): 779,306 (1 per 28 persons).

Education and health

Education (1991)

	schools[12]	teachers	students	student/ teacher ratio
Primary (age 6–11)	28,860	138,455	4,053,801	29.3
Secondary (age 12–16)	6,462	96,969	1,996,181	20.6
Voc., teacher tr.	1,524	11,289	312,669	27.7
Higher	493	44,361	751,234	16.9

Educational attainment (1981). Percentage of population age 25 and over having: no formal schooling 20.1%; less than primary education 33.2%; primary 21.1%; secondary 20.8%; higher 4.8%. *Literacy* (1991): total population age 15 and over literate 89.3%; males 95.9%; females 82.6%.
Health (1990): physicians (1989) 21,856 (1 per 997 persons); hospital beds 35,715 (1 per 625 persons); infant mortality rate 80.7.
Food (1988–90): daily per capita caloric intake 2,037 (vegetable products 86%, animal products 14%); 87% of FAO recommended minimum requirement.

Military

Total active duty personnel (1992): 112,000 (army 67.0%, navy 19.6%, air force 13.4%). *Military expenditure as percentage of GNP* (1987): 4.9% (world 5.4%); per capita expenditure U.S.$106.

[1]On April 5, 1992, the President of Peru dissolved the legislature, suspended the Constitution, and took control of the government. [2]Interim legislative body elected November 1992. [3]A new currency, the nuevo sol, was introduced in January 1991, replacing the inti (abbrev.: I/.) at the rate of one million intis for one nuevo sol. It was in effect from July 1, 1991, when new bills and coins became available. [4]Detail does not add to total given because of rounding. [5]Excludes Indian jungle population; based on incomplete information. [6]Includes new construction and capital repairs. [7]Includes finance, public administration, and other. [8]Includes public administration and other. [9]1985 = 0.1. [10]Estimate for Lima metropolitan area only. [11]Partial circulation. [12]1990.

Philippines

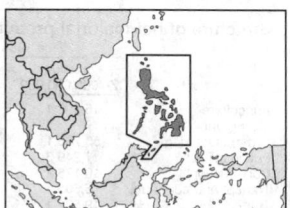

Official name: Republika ng Pilipinas (Pilipino); Republic of the Philippines (English).
Form of government: unitary republic with two legislative houses (Senate [24]; House of Representatives [200[1]]).
Chief of state and head of government: President.
Capital: Manila.
Official languages: Pilipino; English.
Official religion: none.
Monetary unit: 1 Philippine peso (₱) = 100 centavos; valuation (Oct. 5, 1992) 1 U.S.$ = ₱ 24.29; 1 £ = ₱ 41.30.

Area and population	area		population
Regions	sq mi	sq km	1990 census[2]
Bicol	6,808	17,633	3,911,000
Cagayan Valley	10,362	26,838	2,342,000
Central Luzon	7,039	18,231	6,191,000
Central Mindanao	8,994	23,293	3,121,000
Central Visayas	5,773	14,951	4,593,000
Cordillera	7,063	18,294	1,149,000
Eastern Visayas	8,275	21,432	3,048,000
Ilocos	4,958	12,840	3,548,000
National Capital Region	246	636	7,832,000
Northern Mindanao	10,937	28,328	3,503,000
Southern Mindanao	12,237	31,693	4,453,000
Southern Tagalog	18,117	46,924	8,261,000
Western Mindanao	7,214	18,685	3,145,000
Western Visayas	7,808	20,223	5,379,000
TOTAL	115,800[3]	300,000[3]	60,477,000[3]

Demography

Population (1992): 63,609,000.
Density (1992): persons per sq mi 549.3, persons per sq km 212.0.
Urban-rural (1991): urban 43.2%; rural 56.8%.
Sex distribution (1990): male 50.23%; female 49.77%.
Age breakdown (1990): under 15, 38.6%; 15–29, 28.6%; 30–44, 18.1%; 45–59, 9.3%; 60–74, 4.4%; 75 and over, 1.0%.
Population projection: (2000) 74,609,000; (2010) 86,493,000.
Doubling time: 29 years.
Ethnic composition (by mother tongue of households; 1980): Tagalog 29.7%; Cebuano 24.2%; Ilocano 10.3%; Hiligaynon Ilongo 9.2%; Bicol 5.6%; Samar-Leyte 4.0%; Pampango 2.8%; Pangasinan 1.8%; other 12.5%[3].
Religious affiliation (1980): Roman Catholic 84.1%; Aglipayan (Philippine Independent Church) 6.2%; Muslim 4.3%; Protestant 3.9%; other 1.5%.
Major cities (1990): Manila 1,876,194; Quezon City 1,587,140; Caloocan 615,726; Cebu 610,000; Makati 465,896.

Vital statistics

Birth rate per 1,000 population (1991): 31.2 (world avg. 26.4); (1982) legitimate 93.9%; illegitimate 6.1%.
Death rate per 1,000 population (1991): 7.3 (world avg. 9.2).
Natural increase rate per 1,000 population (1991): 23.9 (world avg. 17.2).
Total fertility rate (avg. births per childbearing woman; 1991): 4.0.
Marriage rate per 1,000 population (1989): 5.0.
Life expectancy at birth (1991): male 62.7 years; female 66.5 years.
Major causes of death per 100,000 population (1986): pneumonia 90.4; heart diseases 69.9; tuberculosis 54.6; vascular diseases 52.5; malignant neoplasms (cancers) 32.8; diarrhea 19.4; accidents 18.5; malnutrition 11.0.

National economy

Budget (1991). Revenue: ₱ 206,381,000,000 (taxes on goods and services 37.2%, income taxes 26.5%, customs duties 25.4%, nontax revenues 10.6%). Expenditures: ₱ 254,384,000,000 (debt service 29.7%, education 15.5%, power, water, transport, and communications 10.5%, defense 10.2%, general public services 10.2%, agriculture 8.5%, health 4.0%).
Tourism (1990): receipts from visitors U.S.$1,306,000,000; expenditures by nationals abroad U.S.$111,000,000.
Production (metric tons except as noted). Agriculture, forestry, fishing (1990): sugarcane 24,800,000, coconuts 10,185,000, rice 9,319,000, corn (maize) 4,854,000, bananas 3,803,000, copra 2,072,000, cassava 1,850,000, centrifugal sugar 1,740,000, pineapples 1,170,000, sweet potatoes 670,000; livestock (number of live animals) 7,990,000 pigs, 2,765,000 buffalo, 2,193,000 goats, 1,629,000 cattle, 70,000,000 chickens; roundwood 38,559,000 cu m; fish catch (1989) 2,098,787. Mining and quarrying (1990): nickel ore 608,115; chromite 234,621; copper 182,139; silver 47,518 kilograms; gold 29,234 kilograms. Manufacturing (value added in producers' prices ₱ '000,000; 1988)[4]: food items 76,560; petroleum products 18,637; footwear and wearing apparel 16,262; industrial chemicals 14,663; textiles 13,148; electrical machinery 10,712; basic metal processing 10,030; beverages 7,250; tobacco 5,930. Construction (authorized; 1988): residential 3,486,000 sq m; nonresidential 3,222,000 sq m. Energy production (consumption): electricity (kW-hr; 1990) 26,327,000,000 (26,327,000,000); coal (metric tons; 1990) 1,173,000 (2,222,000); petroleum (barrels; 1990) 1,785,000 (84,214,000); petroleum products (metric tons; 1990) 10,127,000 (10,524,000); natural gas, n.a. (n.a.).
Public debt (external, outstanding; 1990): U.S.$24,587,000,000.
Gross national product (1990): U.S.$43,954,000,000 (U.S.$730 per capita).

Structure of gross domestic product and labour force	1990			
	in value ₱ '000,000	% of total value	labour force	% of labour force
Agriculture	261,900	23.2	10,185,000	41.5
Mining	17,000	1.5	133,000	0.5
Manufacturing	279,000	24.7	2,188,000	8.9
Construction	49,700	4.4	974,000	4.0
Public utilities	26,200	2.3	91,000	0.4
Transp. and commun.	59,800	5.3	1,137,000	4.6
Trade	223,900	19.8	3,146,000	12.8
Finance	80,500	7.1	444,000	1.8
Services	131,900	11.7	4,220,000	17.2
Other	...	...	2,008,000[5]	8.2[5]
TOTAL	1,129,800[3]	100.0	24,525,000[3]	100.0[3]

Population economically active (1990): total 24,525,000; activity rate 40.3% (participation rates: ages 15–64, 66.1%; female 37.0%; unemployed 8.1%).

Price index (1985 = 100)							
	1986	1987	1988	1989	1990	1991	1992[6]
Consumer price index	100.8	104.6	113.7	127.6	145.7	172.9	188.1

Household income and expenditure. Average household size (1990) 5.3; income per family (1989) ₱ 72,057 (U.S.$3,315); sources of income (1989): wages and self-employment 92.3%, pensions, social security, and related benefits 7.7%; expenditure (1989): food, beverages, and tobacco 57.0%, household furnishings and operations 14.2%, clothing 5.8%, fuel and power 4.1%, transportation and communications 2.6%.
Land use (1989): forested 35.4%; meadows and pastures 4.2%; agricultural and under permanent cultivation 26.7%; other 33.7%.

Foreign trade[7]

Balance of trade (current prices)						
	1986	1987	1988	1989	1990	1991
₱ '000,000	−2,974	−22,368	−24,023	−57,713	−86,604	−89,465
% of total	1.5%	8.8%	7.5%	14.6%	17.0%	15.6%

Imports (1990): U.S.$12,206,200,000 (petroleum and petroleum products 14.3%, nonelectrical machinery 7.7%, electrical machinery 6.0%, iron and steel 4.7%, inedible crude materials 4.4%, motor vehicles and parts 4.2%, cereals and cereal preparations 3.9%, inorganic chemicals 1.2%). *Major import sources:* United States 19.4%; Japan 18.3%; Taiwan 6.6%; Hong Kong 4.5%; Saudi Arabia 4.5%; West Germany 4.4%; Singapore 4.0%; South Korea 3.9%; United Arab Emirates 3.8%; Australia 3.0%.
Exports (1990): U.S.$8,186,000,000 (clothing 8.3%, electrical machinery and parts 7.8%, coconut products 6.1%, metalliferous ores and metal scrap 4.4%, nonferrous metals 3.6%, copper ore and concentrates 2.5%, bananas 1.8%). *Major export destinations:* United States 36.5%; Japan 19.7%; West Germany 4.8%; The Netherlands 4.4%; United Kingdom 4.3%; Hong Kong 4.0%; Singapore 2.9%; South Korea 2.8%; Taiwan 2.6%.

Transport and communications

Transport. Railroads (1990): route length 658 mi, 1,059 km; passenger-mi 164,000,000, passenger-km 264,000,000; short ton-mi cargo 25,000,000, metric ton-km cargo 36,000,000. Roads (1989): total length 98,841 mi, 159,069 km (paved 14%). Vehicles (1990): passenger cars 454,554; trucks and buses 783,262. Merchant marine (1991): vessels (100 gross tons and over) 1,465; total deadweight tonnage 14,258,160. Air transport[8] (1991): passenger-mi 5,783,000,000, passenger-km 9,307,000,000; short ton-mi cargo 183,138,000, metric ton-km cargo 267,377,000; airports (1992) with scheduled flights 31.
Communications. Daily newspapers (1984): total number (1988) 29; circulation 2,379,145; circulation per 1,000 population 44. Radio (1991): 4,000,000 receivers (1 per 16 persons). Television (1991): 7,000,000 receivers (1 per 8.9 persons). Telephones (1989): 986,117 (1 per 60 persons).

Education and health

Education (1989–90)	schools	teachers	students	student/ teacher ratio
Primary (age 7–12)	34,382	315,585	10,284,861	32.6
Secondary (age 13–16)	5,523	118,805	3,961,639	33.3
Voc., teacher tr.	945	15,386	291,600	19.0
Higher	810	70,012[9]	1,225,315	22.6[9]

Educational attainment (1980). Percentage of population age 25 and over having: no grade completed 11.7%; elementary education 53.8%; secondary 18.8%; college 15.2%; not stated 0.5%. *Literacy* (1980): total population age 15 and over literate 25,139,700 (88.7%); males literate 12,772,200 (89.9%); females literate 12,367,500 (87.5%).
Health: physicians (1985) 51,461 (1 per 1,062 persons); hospital beds (1988) 85,943 (1 per 683 persons); infant mortality rate (1991) 42.
Food (1987–89): daily per capita caloric intake 2,342 (vegetable products 89%, animal products 11%); 104% of FAO recommended minimum requirement.

Military

Total active duty personnel (1991): 106,500 (army 63.8%, navy 21.6%, air force 14.6%). *Military expenditure as percentage of GNP* (1989): 2.2% (world 4.9%); per capita expenditure U.S.$16.

[1]Excludes 50 nonelective seats allotted to sectoral interests, of which only a small number have been filled. [2]Preliminary results. [3]Detail does not add to total given because of rounding. [4]Manufacturing establishments with 10 or more workers. [5]Mostly unemployed. [6]June. [7]Import figures are f.o.b. in balance of trade and c.i.f. for commodities and trading partners. [8]Philippines Airlines only. [9]1987–88.

Poland

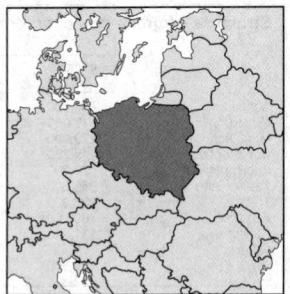

Official name: Rzeczpospolita Polska (Republic of Poland).
Form of government: unitary multiparty republic with two legislative houses (Senate [100]; Diet [460]).
Chief of state: President.
Head of government: Prime Minister.
Capital: Warsaw.
Official language: Polish.
Official religion: none.
Monetary unit: 1 złoty (Zl) = 100 groszy; valuation (Oct. 5, 1992)
1 U.S.$ = Zl 14,199; 1 £ = Zl 24,139.

Area and population

Provinces	Capitals	area sq mi	area sq km	population 1991[1] estimate
Biała Podlaska	Biała Podlaska	2,065	5,348	305,300
Białystok	Białystok	3,882	10,055	692,800
Bielsko	Bielsko Biala	1,430	3,704	900,200
Bydgoszcz	Bydgoszcz	3,996	10,349	1,110,800
Chełm	Chełm	1,493	3,866	247,200
Ciechanów	Ciechanów	2,456	6,362	428,400
Częstochowa	Częstochowa	2,387	6,182	776,700
Elbląg	Elbląg	2,356	6,103	478,900
Gdańsk	Gdańsk	2,855	7,394	1,431,600
Gorzów	Gorzów Wielkopolski	3,276	8,484	500,700
Jelenia Góra	Jelenia Góra	1,690	4,378	517,900
Kalisz	Kalisz	2,514	6,512	710,800
Katowice	Katowice	2,568	6,650	3,988,800
Kielce	Kielce	3,556	9,211	1,126,700
Konin	Konin	1,984	5,139	469,200
Koszalin	Koszalin	3,270	8,470	508,200
Kraków	Kraków	1,256	3,254	1,231,600
Krosno	Krosno	2,202	5,702	495,000
Legnica	Legnica	1,559	4,037	515,800
Leszno	Lèszno	1,604	4,154	386,800
Łódź	Łódź	588	1,523	1,139,500
Łomża	Łomża	2,581	6,684	346,700
Lublin	Lublin	2,622	6,792	1,016,400
Nowy Sącz	Nowy Sącz	2,153	5,576	697,900
Olsztyn	Olsztyn	4,759	12,327	753,000
Opole	Opole	3,295	8,535	1,018,600
Ostrołęka	Ostrołęka	2,509	6,498	397,300
Piła	Piła	3,168	8,205	480,700
Piotrków	Piotrków Trybunalski	2,419	6,266	642,600
Płock	Płock	1,976	5,117	516,400
Poznań	Poznań	3,147	8,151	1,334,100
Przemyśl	Przemyśl	1,713	4,437	406,800
Radom	Radom	2,816	7,294	751,100
Rzeszów	Rzeszów	1,698	4,397	723,700
Siedlce	Siedlce	3,281	8,499	651,400
Sieradz	Sieradz	1,880	4,869	408,200
Skierniewice	Skierniewice	1,529	3,960	419,300
Słupsk	Słupsk	2,878	7,453	413,800
Suwałki	Suwałki	4,050	10,490	470,600
Szczecin	Szczecin	3,854	9,981	972,100
Tarnobrzeg	Tarnobrzeg	2,426	6,283	599,100
Tarnów	Tarnów	1,603	4,151	670,300
Toruń	Toruń	2,065	5,348	659,100
Wałbrzych	Wałbrzych	1,609	4,168	740,900
Warszawa	Warszawa	1,463	3,788	2,421,600
Włocławek	Włocławek	1,700	4,402	429,400
Wrocław	Wrocław	2,427	6,287	1,128,800
Zamość	Zamość	2,695	6,980	490,400
Zielona Góra	Zielona Góra	3,424	8,868	660,000
TOTAL		120,727	312,683	38,183,200

Demography

Population (1992): 38,429,000.
Density (1992): persons per sq mi 318.3, persons per sq km 122.9.
Urban-rural (1992): urban 62.0%; rural 38.0%.
Sex distribution (1992): male 48.83%; female 51.17%.
Age breakdown (1990): under 15, 25.3%; 15–29, 21.0%; 30–44, 23.9%; 45–59, 15.1%; 60–74, 10.6%; 75 and over, 4.1%.
Population projection: (2000) 39,700,000; (2010) 41,348,000.
Ethnic composition (1990): Polish 98.7%; Ukrainian 0.6%; other 0.7%.
Religious affiliation (1992): Roman Catholic 93.5%; Orthodox 1.5%.
Major cities (1991): Warsaw 1,654,500; Łódź 846,500; Kraków 750,600.

Vital statistics

Birth rate per 1,000 population (1991): 14.3 (world avg. 26.4); (1985) legitimate 95.0%; illegitimate 5.0%.
Death rate per 1,000 population (1991): 10.6 (world avg. 9.2).
Natural increase rate per 1,000 population (1991): 3.7 (world avg. 17.2).
Total fertility rate (avg. births per childbearing woman; 1991): 2.1.
Marriage rate per 1,000 population (1991): 6.1.
Divorce rate per 1,000 population (1991): 0.9.
Life expectancy at birth (1990): male 66.5 years; female 75.5 years.
Major causes of death per 100,000 population (1990): diseases of the circulatory system 534.2; malignant neoplasms (cancers) 191.3.

National economy

Budget (1991). Revenue: Zl 210,885,100,000,000 (turnover tax 29.0%, income tax 25.5%). Expenditures: Zl 241,857,700,000,000 (social benefits and programs 20.5%, interest on debts 18.9%).
Public debt (external, outstanding; 1990): U.S.$39,474,000,000.
Tourism (1990): receipts U.S.$266,000,000; expenditures U.S.$220,000,000.
Gross national product (1990): U.S.$64,480,000,000 (U.S.$1,700 per capita).

Structure of net material product and labour force

	1989 in value Zl '000,000,000	1989 % of total value	1991 labour force	1991 % of labour force
Agriculture	15,593.1	14.5	4,961,200	30.1
Mining and manufacturing	53,765.1	50.2	4,403,500	26.7
Public utilities	1,249.3	1.2	...	...
Construction	10,175.2	9.5	1,090,900	6.6
Transp. and commun.	5,505.5	5.1	895,500	5.4
Trade	19,582.1	18.3	1,459,000	8.9
Finance	—	—	...	...
Public administration	—	—	...	...
Services	—	—	424,900	2.6
Other	1,333.5[2]	1.2[2]	3,241,500	19.7
TOTAL	107,203.8	100.0	16,476,500	100.0

Production (metric tons except as noted). Agriculture (value added in Zl '000,000; 1991): potatoes 9,180,900, wheat 7,024,600, industrial crops 4,992,200, rye 2,624,400, barley 2,606,900; livestock (number of live animals; 1990) 19,464,000 pigs, 10,049,000 cattle; roundwood (1990) 19,622,000 cu m; fish catch (1990) 473,011. Mining and quarrying (1990): copper 341,300; zinc 143,000; lead 68,900; aluminum 45,800; silver 832. Manufacturing (value of production in Zl '000,000,000; 1991): machinery and transport equipment 5,909.0; chemicals 1,731.3; food 964.2; textiles 236.6. Construction (1990): 101,013 units, of which residential 51,858. Energy production (consumption): electricity ('000,000 kW-hr; 1990) 136,337 (135,297); coal ('000 metric tons; 1990) 215,000 (188,800); crude petroleum (barrels; 1990) 1,187,000 (94,457,-000); petroleum products ('000 metric tons; 1990) 10,183 (11,863); natural gas ('000,000 cu m; 1990) 2,508 (9,546).
Population economically active (1988): total 18,452,230; activity rate of total population 48.7% (participation rates: ages 18–64 [male], 18–59 [female] 82.4%; female [18–59] 45.4%; unemployed [1991] 11.4%).

Price and earnings indexes (1985 = 100)

	1986	1987	1988	1989	1990	1991	1992[3]
Consumer price index	117.7	147.4	236.1	828.9	5,684.3	9,680.2	12,336.4
Monthly earnings index	121.1	147.0	270.4	1,035.7	4,817.7	7,696.9	...

Household income and expenditure. Average household size (1991): 3.6; average annual income (1991) Zl 40,521,000 (U.S.$3,830); sources of income: wages 80.4%, self-employment 1.8%, other 17.8%; expenditure (1991): food and beverages 47.9%, clothing 9.5%, recreation 7.1%, housing 9.9%.
Land use (1990): forest 28.0%; meadow 13.0%; agric. 47.1%; other 11.9%.

Foreign trade

Balance of trade (current prices)

	1986	1987	1988	1989	1990	1991
Zl '000,000,000	+152	+361	+740	+4,612	+51,935	−6,543
% of total	3.7%	5.9%	6.6%	13.4%	25.1%	2.0%

Imports (1991): Zl 164,259,300,000,000 (machinery and transport equipment 37.6%, fuel and power 18.8%, chemicals 12.6%, food 10.4%, consumer goods 6.1%). *Major import sources* (1991): Germany 26.5%; U.S.S.R. 14.1%; Austria 6.3%; The Netherlands 4.9%; Italy 4.5%.
Exports (1991): Zl 157,715,900,000,000 (machinery and transport equipment 22.4%, iron and steel products 15.9%, chemicals 11.6%, fuel and power 10.7%, food 10.0%, light-industrial products 6.1%). *Major export destinations* (1991): Germany 29.4%; U.S.S.R. 11.0%; U.K. 7.1%; The Netherlands 5.2%; Czechoslovakia 4.6%; Austria 4.5%.

Transport and communications

Transport. Railroads (1991): length 25,848 km; passenger-km 40,115,000,000; metric ton-km cargo 65,146,000,000. Roads (1991): total length 363,116 km (paved 62%). Vehicles (1991): passenger cars 5,261,000; trucks and buses 1,137,000. Merchant marine (1991): vessels (100 gross tons and over) 673; total deadweight tonnage 4,432,017. Air transport (1991): passenger-km 3,589,000,000; metric ton-km cargo 45,000,000; airports (1992) 12.
Communications. Daily newspapers (1991): 48; circulation 6,200,500. Radio (1991): 10,400,000 (1 per 3.7 persons). Television (1991): 10,000,000 (1 per 3.8 persons). Telephones (1990): 5,039,000 (1 per 7.5 persons).

Education and health

Education (1991–92)

	schools	teachers	students	student/ teacher ratio
Primary (age 7–14)	18,578	321,500	5,302,700	16.5
Secondary (age 15–18)	1,565	26,600	548,800	20.6
Voc., teacher tr.	8,826	89,500	1,677,000[4]	...
Higher	117	63,200	423,500	6.7

Educational attainment (1988). Percentage of population age 15 and over having: no formal schooling or less than full primary education 6.4%; primary 38.8%; secondary 48.3%; higher 6.5%. *Literacy* (1988): 98.7%.
Health (1992): physicians 81,641 (1 per 471 persons); hospital beds 249,737 (1 per 154 persons); infant mortality rate per 1,000 live births (1991) 15.0.
Food (1988–90): daily per capita caloric intake 3,426 (vegetable products 66%, animal products 34%); 131% of FAO recommended minimum.

Military

Total active duty personnel (1992): 296,500 (army 65.5%, navy 6.5%, air force 28.0%). *Military expenditure as percentage of GNP* (1989): 8.9% (world 4.9%); per capita expenditure U.S.$408.

[1]January 1. [2]Other material activities. [3]First quarter. [4]1990–91.

Portugal

Official name: República Portuguesa (Republic of Portugal).
Form of government: parliamentary state with one legislative house (Assembly of the Republic [230]).
Chief of state: President.
Head of government: Prime Minister.
Capital: Lisbon.
Official language: Portuguese.
Official religion: none.
Monetary unit: 1 escudo (Esc) = 100 centavos; valuation (Oct. 5, 1992) 1 U.S.$ = Esc 125.74; 1 £ = Esc 213.75.

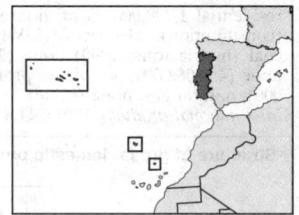

Area and population

Continental Portugal Districts	Capitals	area sq mi	area sq km	population 1991 census
Aveiro	Aveiro	1,084	2,808	656,000
Beja	Beja	3,948	10,225	167,900
Braga	Braga	1,032	2,673	746,100
Bragança	Bragança	2,551	6,608	158,300
Castelo Branco	Castelo Branco	2,577	6,675	214,700
Coimbra	Coimbra	1,524	3,947	427,600
Évora	Évora	2,854	7,393	173,500
Faro	Faro	1,915	4,960	340,100
Guarda	Guarda	2,131	5,518	187,800
Leiria	Leiria	1,357	3,515	427,800
Lisboa	Lisbon (Lisboa)	1,066	2,761	2,063,800
Portalegre	Portalegre	2,342	6,065	134,300
Porto	Porto	925	2,395	1,622,300
Santarém	Santarém	2,605	6,747	442,700
Setúbal	Setúbal	1,955	5,064	713,700
Viana do Castelo	Viana do Castelo	871	2,255	248,700
Vila Real	Vila Real	1,671	4,328	237,100
Viseu	Viseu	1,933	5,007	401,000
Azores (Açores)				
Autonomous Region[1]	Ponta Delgada	868	2,247	236,700
Madeira Autonomous				
Region	Funchal	306	794	253,000
TOTAL		35,672[2]	92,389[2]	9,853,000[3]

Demography

Population (1992): 9,844,000.
Density (1992): persons per sq mi 276.0, persons per sq km 106.5.
Urban-rural (1990): urban 33.6%; rural 66.4%.
Sex distribution (1990): male 48.31%; female 51.69%.
Age breakdown (1987): under 15, 22.7%; 15–29, 24.6%; 30–44, 18.8%; 45–59, 16.5%; 60–74, 12.6%; 75 and over, 4.8%.
Population projection: (2000) 9,756,000; (2010) 9,642,000.
Nationality (1989): Portuguese 99.0%; Cape Verdean 0.3%; Brazilian 0.1%; Spanish 0.1%; British 0.1%; American 0.1%; other 0.3%.
Religious affiliation (1981): Christian 96.0%, of which Roman Catholic 94.5%, Protestant 0.6%, other Christian (mostly Apostolic Catholic and Jehovah's Witness) 0.9%; nonreligious 3.8%; Jewish 0.1%; Muslim 0.1%.
Major cities (1988[1]): Lisbon 830,500; Porto 350,000; Amadora 95,518.

Vital statistics

Birth rate per 1,000 population (1990): 11.8 (world avg. 27.1); legitimate 85.5%; illegitimate 14.5%.
Death rate per 1,000 population (1990): 10.4 (world avg. 9.8).
Natural increase rate per 1,000 population (1990): 1.4 (world avg. 17.3).
Total fertility rate (avg. births per childbearing woman; 1990–95): 1.7.
Marriage rate per 1,000 population (1990): 7.3.
Divorce rate per 1,000 population (1990): 0.9.
Life expectancy at birth (1987–88): male 70.6 years; female 77.6 years.
Major causes of death per 100,000 population (1990): circulatory diseases 461.3, of which cerebrovascular diseases 249.7, ischemic heart disease 96.2; malignant neoplasms (cancers) 184.2; respiratory diseases 75.7.

National economy

Budget (1990). Revenue: Esc 3,439,600,000,000 (indirect taxes 37.4%, direct taxes 22.8%, property income 3.1%). Expenditures: Esc 3,408,800,000,000 (1988; education 12.4%, health 9.8%, defense 6.6%, administration 5.3%, public works 2.8%).
Public debt (1990): U.S.$46,984,000,000.
Production (metric tons except as noted). Agriculture, forestry, fishing (1991): grapes 1,450,000, potatoes 948,000, tomatoes 894,000, corn (maize) 677,000, wheat 323,000, olives 296,000, rice 153,000, cork 109,262[4], oats 80,000; livestock (number of live animals) 5,673,000 sheep, 2,664,000 pigs, 1,375,000 cattle; roundwood 10,443,000 cu m; fish catch (1990) 321,891. Mining and quarrying (1991): copper pyrites 650,199; kaolin 39,186[5]; tungsten 1,619. Manufacturing (value of production in Esc '000,000; 1989): cotton and synthetic fibres 222,717; refined petroleum 148,274; clothing 138,659; motor vehicles 113,924; knitted fabrics 105,339; dairy products 90,282; iron and steel 70,919; cement 57,720; alcoholic beverages 47,489. Construction (1990): residential 4,197,912 sq m; nonresidential 2,045,167 sq m. Energy production (consumption): electricity (kW-hr; 1990) 28,529,000,000 (28,566,000,000); coal (metric tons; 1990) 281,000 (4,397,000); crude petroleum (barrels; 1990) none (76,796,000); petroleum products (metric tons; 1990) 10,061,000 (9,696,000); natural gas, none (n.a.).
Gross national product (1990): U.S.$50,692,000,000 (U.S.$4,890 per capita).

Structure of gross domestic product and labour force

	1990 in value Esc '000,000	1990 % of total value	1991 labour force	1991 % of labour force
Agriculture	490,787	6.3	796,700	16.4
Mining	} 2,275,815	29.2	32,400	0.7
Manufacturing			1,137,600	23.4
Construction	585,382	7.5	370,200	7.6
Public utilities	250,629	3.2	47,200	1.0
Trade	1,352,031	17.4	726,300	15.0
Pub. admin., defense	} 1,653,845	21.2	1,087,400	22.4
Services				
Transp. and commun.	462,412	5.9	216,800	4.5
Finance	720,037	9.2	209,000	4.3
Other	...	...	228,400[6]	4.7[6]
TOTAL	7,790,937[3]	100.0[3]	4,852,000	100.0

Population economically active (1991): total 4,852,000; activity rate of total population 49.2% (participation rates [1990]: ages 15–64, 68.9%; female 43.1%; unemployed 4.7%).

Price and earnings indexes (1985 = 100)

	1985	1986	1987	1988	1989	1990	1991
Consumer price index	100.0	111.8	122.2	133.9	150.8	170.9	190.3
Daily earnings index	100.0	117.4	133.5	152.5	176.4	...	...

Household income and expenditure. Average household size (1981) 3.8; income per household: n.a.; sources of income (1990): wages and salaries 44.9%, property and entrepreneurial income 33.9%, transfer payments 21.2%; expenditure (1986): food 34.7%, transportation and communications 15.4%, clothing and footwear 10.3%, cafes and hotels 9.7%, housing 5.0%, health 4.5%, recreation 4.3%, other 16.1%.
Tourism (1990): receipts from visitors U.S.$3,556,000,000; expenditures by nationals abroad U.S.$867,000,000.
Land use (1990): forested 32.3%; meadows and pastures 9.2%; agricultural and under permanent cultivation 34.5%; other 24.0%.

Foreign trade

Balance of trade (current prices)

	1986	1987	1988	1989	1990	1991
Esc '000,000	−255,500	−457,800	−580,000	−705,000	−918,600	−1,067,800
% of total	9.4%	15.2%	16.0%	15.2%	16.4%	18.5%

Imports (1991): Esc 3,766,438,000,000 (machinery and transport equipment 36.2%, of which road vehicles 13.2%; chemicals and chemical products 9.2%; textiles 6.5%; office machines 2.9%). *Major import sources:* Spain 15.8%; Germany 14.8%; France 11.9%; Italy 10.2%; U.K. 7.5%; The Netherlands 6.1%.
Exports (1991): Esc 2,346,856,000,000 (textiles and wearing apparel 22.1%; machinery and transport equipment 19.6%, of which electrical equipment 6.3%; footwear 8.4%; cork and wood products 4.7%; chemicals and chemical products 4.7%). *Major export destinations:* Germany 19.1%; Spain 15.0%; France 14.4%; U.K. 10.8%.

Transport and communications

Transport. Railroads (1991): route length 2,229 mi, 3,588 km; passenger-km 5,700,000,000; metric ton-km cargo 1,788,000,000. Roads (1981): total length 32,282 mi, 51,953 km (paved 86%). Vehicles (1990): passenger cars 3,208,286; trucks and buses 189,822[7]. Merchant marine (1991): vessels (100 gross tons and over) 337; total deadweight tonnage 1,425,777. Air transport (1990): passenger-km 6,882,800,000; metric ton-km cargo 166,605,000; airports (1992) 13.
Communications. Daily newspapers (1991): total number 30; total circulation 525,000[8]; circulation per 1,000 population 50[8]. Radio (1991): 2,475,000 receivers (1 per 4.2 persons). Television (1991): 1,789,703 receivers (1 per 5.8 persons). Telephones (1991): 2,859,361 (1 per 3.6 persons).

Education and health

Education (1991–92)

	schools	teachers	students	student/ teacher ratio
Primary (age 5–11)	11,439	63,657	1,013,474	15.9
Secondary (age 12–19)	1,116	73,196	856,916	11.7
Vocational	116[9]	1,500[9]	60,077	19.4[9]
Higher[10]	231	15,108	182,283	12.1

Educational attainment (1981). Percentage of population age 25 and over having: no formal schooling 4.4%; primary education 76.2%; secondary 19.0%; postsecondary 0.1%; higher 0.3%. *Literacy* (1990): total population age 15 and over literate 6,769,270 (86.8%); males literate 3,208,634 (86.7%); females literate 3,560,636 (86.9%).
Health (1990): physicians 28,016 (1 per 352 persons); hospital beds 42,920 (1 per 230 persons); infant mortality rate per 1,000 live births (1990): 11.0.
Food (1988–90): daily per capita caloric intake 3,342 (vegetable products 76%, animal products 24%); 136% of FAO recommended minimum requirement.

Military

Total active duty personnel (1992): 58,300 (army 56.1%, navy 26.2%, air force 17.7%). *Military expenditure as percentage of GNP* (1989): 3.3% (world 4.9%); per capita expenditure U.S.$141.

[1]Comprises three districts not shown separately. [2]Includes 156 sq mi (404 sq km) of inland water. [3]Detail does not add to total given because of rounding. [4]1986. [5]1990. [6]Mostly unemployed. [7]1987. [8]For 24 newspapers only. [9]Public schools only. [10]Includes teacher colleges.

Puerto Rico

Official name: Estado Libre Asociado de Puerto Rico (Commonwealth of Puerto Rico).
Political status: self-governing commonwealth in association with the United States, having two legislative houses (Senate [29[1]]; House of Representatives [53][1]).
Chief of state: President of the United States.
Head of government: Governor.
Capital: San Juan.
Official languages: Spanish.
Official religion: none.
Monetary unit: 1 U.S. dollar (U.S.$) = 100 cents; valuation (Oct. 5, 1992) 1£ = U.S.$1.70.

Population (1990 census)

Municipio	population	Municipio	population	Municipio	population
Adjuntas	19,451	Fajardo	36,882	Naguabo	22,620
Aguada	35,911	Florida	8,689	Naranjito	27,914
Aguadilla	59,335	Guánica	19,984	Orocovis	21,158
Agunas Buenas	25,424	Guayama	41,588	Patillas	19,633
Aibonito	24,971	Guayanilla	21,581	Peñuelas	22,515
Añasco	25,234	Guaynabo	92,886	Ponce	187,749
Arecibo	93,385	Gurabo	28,737	Quebradillas	21,425
Arroyo	18,910	Hatillo	32,703	Rincón	12,213
Barceloneta	20,947	Hormigueros	15,212	Río Grande	45,648
Barranquitas	25,605	Humacao	55,203	Sabana Grande	22,843
Bayamón	220,262	Isabela	39,147	Salinas	28,335
Cabo Rojo	38,521	Jayuya	15,527	San Germán	34,962
Caguas	133,447	Juana Díaz	45,198	San Juan	437,745
Camuy	28,917	Juncos	30,612	San Lorenzo	35,163
Canóvanas	36,816	Lajas	23,271	San Sebastián	38,799
Carolina	177,806	Lares	29,015	Santa Isabel	19,318
Cataño	34,587	Las Marías	9,306	Toa Alta	44,101
Cayey	46,553	Las Piedras	27,896	Toa Baja	89,454
Ceiba	17,145	Loíza	29,307	Trujillo Alto	61,120
Ciales	18,084	Luquillo	18,100	Utuado	34,980
Cidra	35,601	Manatí	38,692	Vega Alta	34,559
Coamo	33,837	Maricao	6,206	Vega Baja	55,997
Comerío	20,265	Maunabo	12,347	Vieques	8,602
Corozal	33,095	Mayagüez	100,371	Villalba	23,559
Culebra	1,542	Moca	32,926	Yabucoa	36,483
Dorado	30,759	Morovis	25,288	Yauco	42,058
				TOTAL	3,522,037

Demography

Area: 3,515 sq mi, 9,104 sq km.
Population (1992): 3,581,000.
Density (1992): persons per sq mi 1,018.8, persons per sq km 393.3.
Urban-rural (1985): urban 70.7%; rural 29.3%.
Sex distribution (1985): male 48.68%; female 51.32%.
Age breakdown (1980): under 15, 31.6%; 15–29, 26.5%; 30–44, 18.4%; 45–59, 12.3%; 60–74, 8.3%; 75 and over, 2.9%.
Population projection: (2000) 3,832,000; (2010) 4,169,000.
Doubling time: 61 years.
Ethnic composition (1980): white 80.0%; black 20.0%.
Religious affiliation (1984): Roman Catholic 85.3%; Protestant 4.7%; other 10.0%.
Major cities (municipio; 1990): San Juan 437,745; Bayamón 220,262; Ponce 187,749; Carolina 177,806; Caguas 133,447.

Vital statistics

Birth rate per 1,000 population (1990): 18.3 (world avg. 27.1); (1983) legitimate 75.6%; illegitimate 24.4%.
Death rate per 1,000 population (1990): 6.9 (world avg. 9.8).
Natural increase rate per 1,000 population (1990): 11.4 (world avg. 17.3).
Total fertility rate (avg. births per childbearing woman; 1988): 2.4.
Marriage rate per 1,000 population (1989): 9.1.
Divorce rate per 1,000 population (1985): 4.5.
Life expectancy at birth (1990–95): male 72.5 years; female 79.2 years.
Major causes of death per 100,000 population (1985): circulatory diseases 262.5, of which ischemic heart disease 102.1, diseases of pulmonary circulation 64.2; malignant neoplasms 106.1; respiratory diseases 78.6.

National economy

Budget (1992). Revenue: U.S.$5,857,000,000 (income taxes 36.2%, excise taxes 15.4%, service charges 5.5%, property taxes 1.1%, other receipts 41.8%). Expenditures: U.S.$5,607,000,000 (education 30.3%, public safety and protection 11.4%, welfare 10.8%, health 10.7%, debt service 6.2%).
Public debt (outstanding; 1991): U.S.$12,834,800,000.
Tourism: receipts from visitors (1991) U.S.$1,445,200,000; expenditures by nationals abroad (1990) U.S.$647,000,000.
Production (in U.S.$'000,000 except as noted). Agriculture, forestry, fishing (gross farm income; 1991): milk 201.8, vegetables 97.4, poultry 85.3, pork 56.8, coffee 50.5, beef 45.1, fruit 42.3, eggs 18.9, sugar 18.0; livestock (number of live animals; 1990) 600,000 cattle, 206,000 pigs; roundwood, n.a.; fish catch (1989) 1,953 metric tons. Mining (value of production; 1984): stone 28. Manufacturing (value added in U.S.$'000,000; 1991): chemicals, pharmaceuticals, and allied products 5,742; machinery and metal products 3,120; food products 1,467; clothing 473; printing and publishing 161; stone, clay, and glass products 159. Construction (new buildings authorized; 1985):

residential 1,798,000 sq m; nonresidential 41,000 sq m. Energy production (consumption): electricity (kW-hr; 1990) 15,328,000,000 (15,328,000,000); coal (metric tons; 1990) none (200,000); crude petroleum (barrels; 1990) none (45,808,000); petroleum products (metric tons; 1990) 5,210,000 (7,045,-000); natural gas, none (none).
Gross national product (1991): U.S.$22,831,000,000 (U.S.$6,429 per capita).

Structure of gross domestic product and labour force

	1991			
	in value U.S.$'000,000	% of total value	labour force	% of labour force
Agriculture	469.8	1.5	32,000	2.9
Manufacturing	12,672.4	39.0	155,000	14.2
Mining } Construction	764.2	2.4	... 52,000	... 4.8
Public utilities } Transp. and commun.	2,671.9	8.2	16,000 39,000	1.5 3.6
Trade	4,850.9	14.9	184,000	16.9
Finance, real estate	4,152.1	12.8	30,000	2.8
Pub. admin., defense } Services	3,537.7 3,125.2	10.9 } 9.6 }	415,000	38.1
Other	224.7[2]	0.7[2]	166,000[3]	15.2[3]
TOTAL	32,469.0[4]	100.0	1,090,000[4]	100.0

Population economically active (1991): total 1,090,000; activity rate 30.7% (participation rates: ages 16–64, 45.8%; female 37.1%[5]; unemployed 15.2%).

Price and earnings indexes (1985 = 100)

	1985	1986	1987	1988	1989	1990	1991
Consumer price index	100.0	99.2	100.7	104.0	107.7	112.0	117.8
Hourly earnings index[6]	100.0	103.5	...	...	...	...	...

Household income and expenditure. Average family size (1990) 3.3; income per family (1990) U.S.$23,930; sources of income (1991): wages and salaries 59.3%, transfers 25.5%, self-employment 6.2%, rent 4.6%, other 4.4%; expenditure (1991): food and beverages 24.6%, housing and energy 12.8%, transportation 12.4%, household furnishings 11.3%, health care 10.9%, clothing 8.7%, recreation 7.9%, education 3.2%, other 8.2%.
Land use (1989): forested 20.0%; meadows and pastures 37.7%; agricultural and under permanent cultivation 14.4%; other 27.9%.

Foreign trade

Balance of trade (current prices)

	1986	1987	1988	1989	1990	1991
U.S.$'000,000	+1,472	+1,354	+1,327	+2,312	+3,584	+5,419
% of total	6.8%	5.9%	5.3%	7.6%	10.6%	14.6%

Imports (1991): U.S.$15,904,300,000 (chemicals [all forms] 23.2%; food 12.7%; electrical machinery 8.6%; petroleum and petroleum products 7.8%; non-electrical machinery 7.3%; transport equipment 5.3%; wood, paper, and printed products 5.3%). *Major import sources* (1990): U.S. 68.7%; Venezuela 4.4%; Japan 3.2%; Dominican Republic 2.0%; The Bahamas 1.8%; U.K. 1.0%.
Exports (1991): U.S.$21,323,000,000 (chemicals and chemical products 46.2%; electrical machinery 13.2%; food 12.4%; computers 10.9%). *Major export destinations* (1990): U.S. 86.9%; Dominican Republic 2.0%; U.S. Virgin Islands 1.4%; U.K. 0.8%; The Netherlands 0.7%.

Transport and communications

Transport. Railroads (1988)[7]: length 59 mi, 96 km. Roads (1986): total length 5,810 mi, 9,351 km (paved 87%). Vehicles (1989–90): passenger cars 1,315,587; trucks 205,565. Merchant marine: n.a. Air transport (1990–91): passenger arrivals 4,245,137, passenger departures 4,262,164; cargo loaded and unloaded 222,172[8] metric tons; airports (1992) with scheduled flights 7.
Communications. Daily newspapers (1991): total number 4; total circulation 473,000; circulation per 1,000 population 133. Radio (1991): 2,000,000 receivers (1 per 1.8 persons). Television (1990): 830,000 receivers (1 per 4.4 persons). Telephones (1985): 772,006 (1 per 4.3 persons).

Education and health

Education (1985–86)

	schools	teachers	students	student/ teacher ratio
Primary (age 5–12)	1,542	18,359	427,582	23.3
Secondary (age 13–18)	395	13,612	334,661	24.6
Voc., teacher tr.	52	...	149,191	...
Higher	45	9,045	156,818	17.3

Educational attainment (1987). Percentage of population age 25 and over having: some primary education 47.8%; some secondary 12.7%; complete secondary 21.1%; higher 18.4%. *Literacy* (1980): total population age 15 and over literate 89.1%; males literate 89.7%; females literate 88.5%.
Health (1984): physicians 7,560 (1 per 433 persons); hospital beds 12,493 (1 per 262 persons); infant mortality rate per 1,000 live births (1989) 14.3.
Food: daily per capita caloric intake, n.a.

Military

Total active duty personnel (1986): 3,600 U.S. personnel.

[1]Includes (1992; each house) two special at-large seats above usual legally mandated membership of body that were created under a constitutional provision to limit majority party's control of either house to two-thirds. [2]Statistical discrepancy. [3]Unemployed. [4]Detail does not add to total given because of rounding. [5]1990. [6]Manufacturing sector only. [7]Privately owned railway for sugarcane transport only. [8]Handled by the Luis Muñoz Marín International Airport only.

Qatar

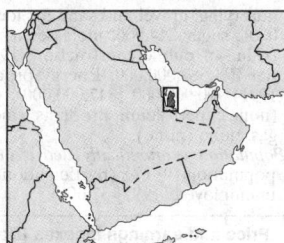

Official name: Dawlat Qaṭar (State of Qatar).
Form of government: monarchy (emirate)[1]; Islamic law is the basis of legislation in the state.
Head of state and government: Emir.
Capital: Doha.
Official language: Arabic.
Official religion: Islam.
Monetary unit: 1 riyal (QR) = 100 dirhams; valuation (Oct. 5, 1992) 1 U.S.$ = QR 3.67; 1 £ = QR 6.25.

Area and population		area		population[2]
		sq mi	sq km	1986 census
Municipalities	Capitals			
ad-Dawḥah (Doha)	—	51	132	217,294
al-Ghuwayrīyah	al-Ghuwayrīyah	241	622	1,629
Jarayān al-Bāṭinah	Jarayān al-Bāṭinah	1,434	3,715	2,727
al-Jumaylīyah	al-Jumaylīyah	990	2,565	7,217
al-Khawr	al-Khawr	385	996	8,993
ar-Rayyān	ar-Rayyān	343	889	91,996
ash-Shamāl	Madinat ash-Shamāl	348	901	4,380
Umm Ṣalāl	Umm Ṣalāl Muḥammad	190	493	11,161
al-Wakrah	al-Wakrah	430	1,114	23,682
TOTAL		4,412	11,427	369,079

Demography

Population (1992): 520,000.
Density (1992): persons per sq mi 117.9, persons per sq km 45.5.
Urban-rural (1990): urban 89.5%; rural 10.5%.
Sex distribution (1986): male 67.15%; female 32.85%.
Age breakdown (1986): under 15, 27.8%; 15–29, 29.3%; 30–44, 32.3%; 45–59, 8.6%; 60 and over, 2.0%.
Population projection: (2000) 657,000; (2010) 830,000.
Doubling time: 33 years.
Ethnic composition (1983): South Asian 34%; Qatari 20%; other Arab 25%; Iranian 16%; other 5%.
Religious affiliation (1980): Muslim 92.4% (mostly Sunnī); Christian 5.9%; Hindu 1.1%; Bahā'ī 0.2%; other 0.4%.
Major cities (1986): Doha 217,294; ar-Rayyān 41,603; al-Wakrah 13,159; Umm Sa'īd 6,094.

Vital statistics

Birth rate per 1,000 population (1990): 22.7 (world avg. 27.1); legitimate, n.a.; illegitimate, n.a.
Death rate per 1,000 population (1990): 1.8 (world avg. 9.8).
Natural increase rate per 1,000 population (1990): 20.9 (world avg. 17.3).
Total fertility rate (avg. births per childbearing woman; 1990): 5.7.
Marriage rate per 1,000 population (1989): 3.1.
Divorce rate per 1,000 population (1989): 1.0.
Life expectancy at birth (1986): male 65.2 years; female 67.6 years.
Major causes of death per 100,000 population (1989): diseases of the circulatory system 52.5; injuries and poisoning 43.3; neoplasms (including benign neoplasms) 20.1; certain conditions originating in the perinatal period 15.2; diseases of the respiratory system 8.0; diseases of the digestive system 7.0; endocrine, metabolic, and nutritional diseases and immunity disorders 6.3; signs, symptoms, and ill-defined conditions 16.9.

National economy

Budget (1991–92). Revenue: QR 8,438,000,000 (1989–90; crude oil 85.0%). Expenditures: QR 11,706,000,000 (wages and salaries 36.8%; state capital development projects 17.9%, of which electricity and water 7.0%, housing and public buildings 6.7%, social and health services 1.9%, education 0.5%).
Production (metric tons except as noted). Agriculture, forestry, fishing (value of production in QR '000; 1991): forage 97,316, milk and dairy products 95,-712, vegetables and other crops (except cereals) 77,271, beef 36,031, poultry meat 29,868, fruits and dates 23,629, eggs 14,257, cereals 2,713; livestock (number of live animals; 1991) 132,000 sheep, 80,000 goats, 23,000 camels, 10,000 cattle; roundwood, n.a.; fish catch (1990) 5,702. Mining and quarrying (1987): limestone 900,000; gypsum 248,000; sand and gravel 6,000; phosphate rock 1,986; salt 81. Manufacturing (value added in QR '000; 1988): chemicals and petroleum products 1,957,084; clothing and textiles 95,804; paper and paper products 88,172; food, beverages, and tobacco 74,888; fabricated metal products and machinery 71,228; furniture and wood products 63,750. Construction (1986): residential 391,400 sq m; nonresidential 167,600 sq m. Energy production (consumption): electricity (kW-hr; 1990) 4,624,000,000 (4,624,000,000); coal, none (n.a.); crude petroleum (barrels; 1990) 144,357,-000 (21,621,000); petroleum products (metric tons; 1990) 4,119,000 (905,000); natural gas (cu m; 1990) 5,434,970,000 (5,434,970,000).
Tourism (1987): receipts and expenditures, n.a.; total number of tourists staying in hotels 100,761.
Population economically active (1986): total 201,182; activity rate of total population 54.5% (participation rates: over age 15, 76.0%; female 9.8%; unemployed 0.5%).

Price and earnings indexes (1985 = 100)							
	1984	1985	1986	1987	1988	1989	1990
Consumer price index	98.1	100.0	101.6	104.3	109.1	112.7	116.1
Earnings index	...	...	...	...	...	...	...

Gross national product (at current market prices; 1990): U.S.$6,962,000,000 (U.S.$15,860 per capita).

Structure of gross domestic product and labour force				
	1991		1986	
	in value QR '000,000	% of total value	labour force	% of labour force
Agriculture	215	0.9	6,283	3.1
Oil sector	8,250	34.0	4,807	2.4
Manufacturing	3,120	12.8	13,914	6.9
Construction	950	3.9	40,523	20.1
Public utilities	415	1.7	5,266	2.6
Transportation	697	2.9	7,357	3.7
Trade	1,528	6.3	21,964	10.9
Finance	2,610	10.7	3,157	1.6
Pub. admin., defense	} 6,504	} 26.8	96,466	48.0
Services			} 1,445[3]	} 0.7[3]
Other				
TOTAL	24,289	100.0	201,182	100.0

Household income and expenditure. Average household size (1986) 6.4; income per household: n.a.; sources of income (1988): wages and salaries 80.8%, rents and royalties 10.6%, self-employment 5.6%, other 3.0%; expenditure (1988): housing 26.6%, food 24.5%, transportation 13.0%, recreation and personal effects 11.1%, clothing 9.1%, education 4.3%, energy and water 1.9%, health 1.0%.
Public debt (external, outstanding; 1989): U.S.$1,100,000,000.
Land use (1990): meadows and pastures 5.3%; agricultural and under permanent cultivation 0.5%; built-up, desert, and other 94.2%.

Foreign trade

Balance of trade (current prices)						
	1984	1985	1986	1987	1988	1989
QR '000,000	+8,015	+7,130	+2,730	+3,224	+2,253	+4,827
% of total	48.6%	46.2%	25.4%	28.7%	19.8%	33.9%

Imports (1991): QR 6,261,200,000 (machinery and transport equipment 42.4%; manufactured goods 19.0%; food and live animals 15.2%; chemicals and chemical products 6.2%; beverages and tobacco 1.2%). *Major import sources:* Japan 13.6%; United Kingdom 11.8%; United States 11.6%; Germany 8.5%; Italy 5.6%; France 5.2%; United Arab Emirates 4.3%; Saudi Arabia 4.1%; Australia 3.5%.
Exports (1990): QR 12,847,000,000 (crude petroleum, petroleum products, and liquefied gas 84.1%; non-oil exports 15.9%). *Major export destinations* (1989): Japan 54.4%; Thailand 5.0%; Singapore 4.0%; South Korea 3.6%; United Arab Emirates 3.4%; Italy 2.7%; India 2.7%; Saudi Arabia 2.5%.

Transport and communications

Transport. Railroads: none. Roads (1988): total length 671 mi, 1,080 km (paved 63%). Vehicles (1990): passenger cars 115,149; trucks and buses 47,228. Merchant marine (1991): vessels (100 gross tons and over) 64; total deadweight tonnage 724,330. Air transport (1991)[4]: passenger-mi 1,042,000,-000, passenger-km 1,676,000,000; short ton-mi cargo 35,100,000, metric ton-km cargo 51,245,000; airports (1992) with scheduled flights 1.
Communications. Daily newspapers (1989): total number 4; total circulation 51,500[5]; circulation per 1,000 population 147[5]. Radio (1991): total number of receivers 250,000 (1 per 1.8 persons). Television (1990): total number of receivers 160,000 (1 per 2.8 persons). Telephones (1989): 134,823 (1 per 3.1 persons).

Education and health

Education (1988–89)	schools	teachers	students	student/ teacher ratio
Primary (age 6–11)	97	2,589	48,097	18.6
Secondary (age 12–17)	78	2,115	22,178	10.5
Vocational	3	104	924	8.9
Higher[6]	1	504	5,637	11.2

Educational attainment (1986). Percentage of population age 25 and over having: no formal education 53.3%, of which illiterates 24.3%; primary 9.8%; preparatory (lower secondary) 10.1%; secondary 13.3%; postsecondary 13.3%; other 0.2%. *Literacy* (1986): total population age 15 and over literate 201,733 (75.7%); males literate 149,980 (76.8%); females literate 51,753 (72.5%).
Health (1989): physicians 752 (1 per 568 persons); hospital beds 1,069 (1 per 399 persons); infant mortality rate per 1,000 live births (1990) 31.0.
Food: daily per capita caloric intake, n.a.

Military

Total active duty personnel (1992): 7,500 (army 80.0%, navy 9.3%, air force 10.7%). *Military expenditure as percentage of GNP* (1985): 46.9% (world 5.7%); per capita expenditure U.S.$6,700.

[1]Provisional constitution of 1970 provided limited constitutional forms but has not been fully implemented. [2]Total population excludes 2,784 Qataris residing abroad. [3]Unemployed. [4]One-fourth apportionment of international flights of Gulf Air. [5]1986. [6]1989–90.

Réunion

Official name: Département de la Réunion (Department of Reunion).
Political status: overseas department (France) with two legislative houses (General Council [45]; Regional Council [45]).
Chief of state: President of France.
Heads of government: Commissioner of the Republic (for France); President of General Council (for Réunion); President of Regional Council (for Réunion).
Capital: Saint-Denis.
Official language: French.
Official religion: none.
Monetary unit: 1 franc (F) = 100 centimes; valuation (Oct. 5, 1992) 1 U.S.$ = F 4.78; 1 £ = F 8.12.

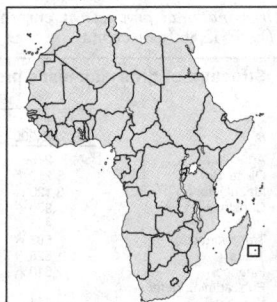

Area and population

Arrondissements	Capitals	area sq mi	area sq km	population 1990 census
Saint-Benoît	Saint-Benoît	284	736	85,132
Saint-Denis	Saint-Denis	164	423	207,158
Saint-Paul	Saint-Paul	180	467	113,071
Saint-Pierre	Saint-Pierre	339	878	192,462
TOTAL		970[1, 2]	2,512[1, 2]	597,823

Demography

Population (1992): 623,000.
Density (1992): persons per sq mi 642.3, persons per sq km 248.0.
Urban-rural (1990): urban 73.4%; rural 26.6%.
Sex distribution (1990): male 49.22%; female 50.78%.
Age breakdown (1990): under 15, 31.3%; 15–29, 29.5%; 30–44, 19.6%; 45–59, 11.5%; 60–74, 6.2%; 75 and over, 1.9%.
Population projection: (2000) 718,000; (2010) 857,000.
Doubling time: 39 years.
Ethnic composition (1983): mixed race 63.5%; East Indian 28.2%; Chinese 2.2%; French 1.9%; East African 1.1%; other 3.1%.
Religious affiliation (1990): Roman Catholic 89.6%; Muslim 2.0%; other 8.4%.
Major cities (1990): Saint-Denis 100,926; Le Port 29,190; Le Tampon 27,300; Saint-André 25,237; Saint-Pierre 23,899.

Vital statistics

Birth rate per 1,000 population (1990): 23.5 (world avg. 27.1); legitimate 47.3%; illegitimate 52.7%.
Death rate per 1,000 population (1990): 5.4 (world avg. 9.8).
Natural increase rate per 1,000 population (1990): 18.1 (world avg. 17.3).
Total fertility rate (avg. births per childbearing woman; 1990): 2.6.
Marriage rate per 1,000 population (1990): 6.4.
Divorce rate per 1,000 population (1990): 1.3.
Life expectancy at birth (1990): male 69.0 years; female 78.3 years.
Major causes of death per 100,000 population (1988): diseases of the circulatory system 180.0; malignant neoplasms (cancers) 88.9; accidents and violence 69.0; diseases of the digestive system 58.9; diseases of the respiratory system 41.4.

National economy

Budget (1991). Revenue: F 3,779,000,000 (receipts from the French central government and local administrative bodies 49.4%, new loans 13.1%). Expenditures: F 3,779,000,000 (current expenditures 65.2%, development expenditures 34.8%).
Public debt (external, outstanding; 1989)[3]: U.S.$63,000,000.
Tourism (1990): receipts U.S.$140,000,000; expenditures, n.a.
Gross national product (at current market prices; 1988): U.S.$1,871,000,000 (U.S.$3,230 per capita).

Structure of gross domestic product and labour force

	1988 in value F '000,000	1988 % of total value	1990 labour force	1990 % of labour force
Agriculture	2,108[4]	8.8[4]	11,256	4.8
Manufacturing	1,933[4]	8.1[4]	10,087	4.3
Construction	1,756	7.4	16,519	7.1
Public utilities	527	2.2	1,316	0.6
Transportation and communications	1,581	6.6	7,309	3.1
Trade, restaurants	4,216	17.7	17,689	7.6
Finance, real estate, insurance	4,919	20.6	27,630	11.8
Pub. admin., defense, and services	6,822	28.6	54,382	23.3
Other			87,378[5]	37.4[5]
TOTAL	23,860[6]	100.0	233,566	100.0

Production (metric tons except as noted). Agriculture, forestry, fishing (1990): sugarcane 2,007,000[7], pineapples 8,370, pe-tsai (Chinese cabbage) and black nightshade 8,059, bananas 7,000, onions 5,203, eggplant 3,174, pimento 380, ginger 95, tobacco 90[7], vanilla 30, geranium essence 23; livestock (number of live animals) 100,000 pigs, 44,000 goats, 19,000 cattle; roundwood 32,000 cu m; fish (value of catch in F '000,000) lobster 27, other 33. Mining and

quarrying: gravel and sand for local use. Manufacturing (1991): cement 336,-000[8]; sugar 214,500; molasses 65,900[8]; rum 89,800 hectolitres. Construction (value of public construction; 1988): residential F 258,200,000; nonresidential F 1,587,000,000. Energy production (consumption): electricity (kW-hr; 1991) 990,000,000 (847,000,000); coal, none (none); crude petroleum, none (none); petroleum products (metric tons; 1990) none (299,000); natural gas, none (none).
Population economically active (1990): total 233,566; activity rate of total population 39.1% (participation rates: ages 15–64, 60.4%; female 41.1%; unemployed [1992] 37.0%).

Price and earnings indexes (December 1985 = 100)[9]

	1986	1987	1988	1989	1990	1991	1992[10]
Consumer price index	101.9	104.8	106.4	111.6	116.1	119.6	121.7
Monthly earnings index[11]	100.1	102.0	105.0	108.0	110.6	112.2	113.7

Household income and expenditure. Average household size (1990) 3.8; income per household (1987) F 90,000 (U.S.$14,970); sources of income (1987): wages and salaries and self-employment 67.5%, transfer payments 29.7%, other 2.8%; expenditure (1986–87): transportation and communications 24.9%, food and beverages 22.4%, housing 11.8%, recreation and education 10.1%, clothing and footwear 7.9%, household furnishings 6.0%, other 16.9%.
Land use (1989): forested 35.2%; meadows and pastures 4.4%; agricultural and under permanent cultivation 20.8%; other 39.6%.

Foreign trade

Balance of trade (current prices)

	1986	1987	1988	1989	1990	1991
F '000,000	−6,930	−7,865	−8,781	−10,067	−10,747	−11,925
% of total	78.8%	81.6%	80.6%	83.1%	84.1%	87.5%

Imports (1990): F 11,322,300,000 (food and agricultural products 18.5%, electrical and nonelectrical machinery 15.5%, transport equipment 15.3%, chemical products 8.7%, mineral lubricants 7.5%). Major import sources: France 68.3%; other EEC countries 11.7%; Madagascar 1.0%; Mauritius 0.9%.
Exports (1990): F 999,900,000 (sugar 74.7%, electrical and nonelectrical machinery 6.5%, lobster 2.6%, rum 1.8%, essential oils 1.6%). Major export destinations: France 83.0%; Madagascar 3.2%; other EEC countries 2.7%; Mauritius 1.5%.

Transport and communications

Transport. Railroads (1984): route length 384 mi[12], 614 km[12]; traffic, n.a. Roads (1989): total length 1,690 mi, 2,719 km (paved, n.a.[13]). Vehicles (1990): passenger cars 145,000; trucks and buses 50,000. Merchant marine (1991): vessels (100 gross tons and over) 7; total deadweight tonnage, n.a. Air transport (1991): passenger arrivals 405,586, passenger departures 405,278; cargo unloaded 11,470 metric tons, cargo loaded 3,019 metric tons; airports (1992) with scheduled flights 1.
Communications. Daily newspapers (1990): total number 3; total circulation 59,000; circulation per 1,000 population 98. Radio (1991): total number of receivers 150,000 (1 per 4.1 persons). Television (1991): total number of receivers 90,000 (1 per 6.8 persons). Telephones (1990): 162,385 (1 per 3.7 persons).

Education and health

Education (1990–91)

	schools	teachers	students	student/teacher ratio
Primary (age 6–10)	360	...	73,639	20.7[14]
Secondary (age 11–17) } Voc., teacher tr.	91[15]	...	79,574	...
Higher[16]	1	137	4,607	33.6

Educational attainment (1986–87). Percentage of population age 25 and over having: no formal schooling 18.8%; primary education 44.3%; lower secondary 21.6%; upper secondary 11.0%; higher 4.3%. Literacy (1986–87): total population age 15 and over literate 298,965 (78.2%); males literate 141,006 (75.9%); females literate 157,959 (80.3%).
Health (1990): physicians 933 (1 per 638 persons); hospital beds 3,237 (1 per 184 persons); infant mortality rate per 1,000 live births (1990–95) 12.0.
Food (1988–90): daily per capita caloric intake 3,082 (vegetable products 81%, animal products 19%); 136% of FAO recommended minimum requirement.

Military

Total active duty personnel (1991): 3,300 French troops[17].

[1]Includes 3 sq mi (8 sq km) not distributed by arrondissement. [2]Indian Ocean islets administered by France from Réunion are excluded from total. Areas of these islets, which have no permanent population, are: Îles Glorieuses 1.7 sq mi (4.3 sq km), Île Juan de Nova 1.9 sq mi (4.8 sq km), Île Tromelin 0.3 sq mi (0.8 sq km), Bassas da India 0.1 sq mi (0.2 sq km), Île Europa 7.8 sq mi (20.2 sq km). [3]Includes long-term private debt not guaranteed by the government. [4]Agriculture includes derivatives of sugar; Manufacturing excludes derivatives of sugar. [5]Includes 86,118 unemployed. [6]Detail does not add to total given because of rounding. [7]1991. [8]1990. [9]Indexes refer to December. [10]March. [11]Based on minimum-level wage of public employees. [12]For sugar industry only. [13]Road network was extensively damaged by a 1987 cyclone. [14]Includes preprimary. [15]1991–92. [16]University only. [17]Includes troops stationed on Mayotte.

Romania

Official name: România (Romania).
Form of government: unitary republic
with two legislative houses (Senate
[143]; Assembly of Deputies [341[1]]).
Chief of state: President.
Head of government: Prime Minister.
Capital: Bucharest.
Official language: Romanian.
Official religion: none.
Monetary unit: 1 Romanian leu (plural
lei) = 100 bani; valuation (Oct. 5, 1992)
1 U.S.$ = 440.65 lei; 1 £ = 749.10 lei.

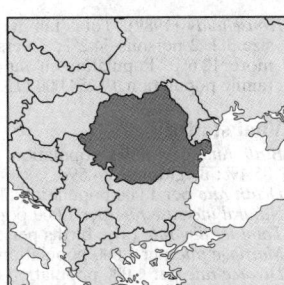

Area and population		area		population
				1992[2]
Counties	Capitals	sq mi	sq km	census
Alba	Alba Iulia	2,406	6,231	414,200
Arad	Arad	2,954	7,652	487,400
Argeş	Piteşti	2,626	6,801	680,600
Bacău	Bacău	2,551	6,606	736,100
Bihor	Oradea	2,909	7,535	634,100
Bistriţa-Năsăud	Bistriţa	2,048	5,305	327,200
Botoşani	Botoşani	1,917	4,965	458,900
Brăila	Brăila	1,824	4,724	392,100
Braşov	Braşov	2,066	5,351	642,500
Buzău	Buzău	2,344	6,072	516,300
Călăraşi	Călăraşi	1,959	5,074	338,800
Caraş-Severin	Reşiţa	3,283	8,503	375,200
Cluj	Cluj-Napoca	2,568	6,650	735,100
Constanţa	Constanţa	2,724	7,055	748,000
Covasna	Sfîntu Gheorghe	1,431	3,705	232,600
Dîmboviţa	Tîrgovişte	1,559	4,036	559,900
Dolj	Craiova	2,862	7,413	761,100
Galaţi	Galaţi	1,708	4,425	639,900
Giurgiu	Giurgiu	1,356	3,511	313,100
Gorj	Tîrgu Jiu	2,178	5,641	400,100
Harghita	Miercurea-Ciuc	2,552	6,610	347,700
Hunedoara	Deva	2,709	7,016	548,000
Ialomiţa	Slobozia	1,718	4,449	304,000
Iaşi	Iaşi	2,112	5,469	806,800
Maramureş	Baia Mare	2,400	6,215	538,500
Mehedinţi	Drobeta-Turnu Severin	1,892	4,900	332,100
Mureş	Tîrgu Mureş	2,585	6,696	607,300
Neamţ	Piatra Neamţ	2,274	5,890	577,600
Olt	Slatina	2,126	5,507	521,000
Prahova	Ploieşti	1,812	4,694	873,200
Sălaj	Zalău	1,486	3,850	266,300
Satu Mare	Satu Mare	1,701	4,405	400,100
Sibiu	Sibiu	2,093	5,422	452,800
Suceava	Suceava	3,303	8,555	700,800
Teleorman	Alexandria	2,224	5,760	482,300
Timiş	Timişoara	3,356	8,692	700,300
Tulcea	Tulcea	3,255	8,430	270,200
Vaslui	Vaslui	2,045	5,297	457,800
Vîlcea	Rîmnicu Vîlcea	2,203	5,705	436,300
Vrancea	Focşani	1,878	4,863	392,600
Muncipality				
Bucharest	Bucharest	703	1,820	2,351,000
TOTAL		91,699[3]	237,500	22,760,500

Demography

Population (1992): 23,332,000.
Density (1992): persons per sq mi 254.4, persons per sq km 98.2.
Urban-rural (1992): urban 54.4%; rural 45.6%.
Sex distribution (1989): male 49.34%; female 50.66%.
Age breakdown (1989): under 15, 23.9%; 15–29, 22.4%; 30–44, 20.8%; 45–59, 17.6%; 60–74, 11.3%; 75 and over, 4.0%.
Population projection: (2000) 24,028,000; (2010) 24,928,000.
Ethnic composition (1990): Romanian 78.3%; Hungarian 10.8%; Gypsy 9.9%; German 0.9%; Jewish 0.1%.
Religious affiliation (1980): Romanian Orthodox 70.0%; Greek Orthodox 10.0%; Muslim 1.0%; atheist 7.0%; other 3.0%; none 9.0%.
Major cities (1992): Bucharest 2,064,474; Constanţa 350,476; Iaşi 342,994; Timişoara 334,278; Cluj-Napoca 328,008.

Vital statistics

Birth rate per 1,000 population (1990): 13.6 (world avg. 27.1).
Death rate per 1,000 population (1990): 10.6 (world avg. 9.8).
Natural increase rate per 1,000 population (1990): 3.0 (world avg. 17.3).
Total fertility rate (avg. births per childbearing woman; 1989): 2.2.
Marriage rate per 1,000 population (1990): 8.3.
Divorce rate per 1,000 population (1990): 1.4.
Life expectancy at birth (1987–89): male 66.5 years; female 72.4 years.
Major causes of death per 100,000 population (1989): diseases of the circulatory system 617.6; benign and malignant neoplasms (cancers) 141.6.

National economy

Budget (1989)[4]. Revenue: 348,421,300,000 lei (turnover tax 43.2%, share in profit of state enterprises 15.4%, income tax 14.4%, state and social insurance 12.7%). Expenditures: 288,425,500,000 lei (national economy 56.1%, social services 37.4%, defense 4.1%).
Tourism (1990): receipts U.S.$106,000,000; expenditures U.S.$103,000,000.
Production (metric tons except as noted). Agriculture (1991): corn (maize) 10,493,000, wheat 5,442,000, sugar beets 4,687,000, potatoes 1,900,000, grapes 849,000, cabbages 780,000, oats 258,000, dry onions 180,000, soybeans 179,-000; livestock (number of live animals) 14,062,000 sheep, 12,003,000 pigs, 5,381,000 cattle, 1,005,000 goats, 121,000,000 chickens; roundwood (1990)

17,321,000 cu m; fish catch (1990) 127,659. Mining and quarrying (1990): bauxite 3,000,000; iron ore 600,000; lead 30,000. Manufacturing (1991): raw steel 7,115,500; chemical fertilizers 1,091,626; sulfuric acid 745,400; aluminum and aluminum alloys 167,451; synthetic rubber 54,583; television sets 389,227 units. Construction (1989): residential 5,409,000 sq m. Energy production (consumption): electricity (kW-hr; 1990) 64,161,100,000 (73,782,000,000); coal (metric tons; 1990) 38,183,200 (51,700,000); crude petroleum (barrels; 1990) 59,095,000 (175,685,000); petroleum products (metric tons; 1990) 21,705,000 (12,951,000); natural gas (cu m; 1990) 28,335,600,000 (30,832,500,000).
Public debt (external, outstanding; 1990): none.
Gross national product (1990): U.S.$38,025,000,000 (U.S.$1,640 per capita).

Structure of net material product and labour force				
	1989		1990	
	in value '000,000 lei	% of total value	labour force	% of labour force
Agriculture	93,282	15.2	3,096,900	28.6
Mining, manufacturing, and public utilities	362,697	59.1	4,015,100	37.0
Construction	44,800	7.3	653,100	6.0
Transp. and commun.	47,255	7.7	752,300	6.9
Trade	5	5	678,500	6.3
Pub. admin.	—	—}	1,395,500	12.9
Services	—	—		
Other	65,666[5]	10.7[5]	248,100	2.3
TOTAL	613,700	100.0	10,839,500	100.0

Population economically active (1990): total 10,839,500; activity rate 46.7% (participation rates: ages 15–64, 68.9%; female 42.6%).

Price and earnings indexes (1985 = 100)							
	1986	1987	1988	1989	1990	1991	1992[6]
Consumer price index	102.2	103.3	106.2	107.0	111.5	306.0	956.4
Annual earnings index	101.4	102.0	104.6	108.7	120.2	265.2	703.1

Household income and expenditure. Average household size (1984) 3.1; income per household (1989) 73,500 lei (U.S.$4,940); sources of income (1982): wages 62.6%; expenditure (1989): food 51.1%, housing 16.4%, clothing 15.7%.
Land use (1990): forest 27.8%; pasture 20.5%; agricultural 43.6%; other 8.1%.

Foreign trade[7]

Balance of trade (current prices)						
	1986	1987	1988	1989	1990	1991
U.S.$'000,000	+1,679	+2,179	+3,750	+2,050	−3,244	−1,123
% of total	9.4%	11.6%	19.7%	10.8%	21.7%	12.0%

Imports (1991): lei 405,710,300,000 (1989; mineral fuels 41.1%, machinery and transport equipment 40.4%, chemicals 4.7%). *Major import sources* (1990): U.S.S.R. 23.6%; West Germany 11.4%; Saudi Arabia 8.3%; Iran 5.9%; U.S. 4.6%; Poland 4.3%; Egypt 3.6%.
Exports (1990): lei 320,303,300,000 (1989; machinery and transport equipment 56.7%, fuels 11.0%, chemicals 7.0%). *Major export destinations* (1990): U.S.S.R. 25.2%; West Germany 10.2%; Italy 8.8%; U.S. 5.8%; France 3.4%; Czechoslovakia 3.2%; Turkey 2.8%; China 2.6%.

Transport and communications

Transport. Railroads (1991): length 6,887 mi, 11,083 km; passenger-km 25,-428,000,000; metric ton-km cargo 37,848,000,000. Roads (1992): length 95,099 mi, 153,014 km (paved 51%). Vehicles (1992): cars 1,397,118; trucks and buses 332,273. Merchant marine (1991): vessels (100 gross tons and over) 469; total deadweight tonnage 5,772,388. Air transport (1991): passenger-km 3,842,000,000; metric ton-km cargo 78,000,000; airports (1992) 14.
Communications. Daily newspapers (1990): total number 36; total circulation 3,120,300; circulation per 1,000 population 134. Radios (1989): 3,262,757 (1 per 7.1 persons). Televisions (1990): 4,003,242 (1 per 5.8 persons). Telephones (1990): 3,022,934 subscribers (1 per 7.7 persons).

Education and health

Education (1989–90)				
	schools	teachers	students	student/ teacher ratio
Primary (age 6–13)	13,357	141,732	2,891,810	20.4
Secondary (age 14–17)	981	42,519	1,346,315	31.7
Vocational	837	12,419[8]	306,126	...
Higher	44	11,696	164,507	14.1

Educational attainment (1977). Percentage of population age 25 and over having: primary education 55.6%; secondary 39.8%; postsecondary 4.6%.
Literacy (1983): 95.8%.
Health (1989): physicians 49,054 (1 per 472 persons); hospital beds 216,295 (1 per 107 persons); infant mortality rate per 1,000 live births (1990) 26.9.
Food (1988–90): daily per capita caloric intake 3,081 (vegetable products 78%, animal products 22%); 116% of FAO recommended minimum.

Military

Total active duty personnel (1992): 200,000 (army 80.5%, navy 9.5%, air force 10.0%). *Military expenditure as percentage of GNP* (1989): 6.1% (world 4.9%); per capita expenditure U.S.$299.

[1]Includes 13 nonelective seats. [2]Preliminary results of Jan. 7, 1992, census. [3]Detail does not add to total given because of rounding. [4]Actual figures. [5]Includes trade and other material activities. [6]August. [7]Import figures are f.o.b. in balance of trade and c.i.f. for commodities and trading partners. [8]1987–88.

Russia

Official name: Rossiyskaya Federatsiya (Russian Federation).
Form of government: federal multiparty republic with a single policy-making body (Congress of People's Deputies [1,068]) and its standing parliament (Supreme Soviet [252]).
Head of state: President.
Head of government: Prime Minister.
Capital: Moscow.
Official language: Russian.
Official religion: none.
Monetary unit: 1 ruble = 100 kopecks; valuation (Oct. 5, 1992) free rate, 1 U.S.$ = 316.82 rubles; 1 £ = 538.39 rubles.

Area and population		area		population
		sq mi	sq km	1991 estimate
Republics	**Capitals**			
Adygea	Maykop	2,900	7,600	437,400
Bashkortostan	Ufa	55,400	143,600	3,983,900
Buryatia	Ulan-Ude	135,600	351,300	1,056,000
Checheno-Ingushetia[1]	Grozny	7,400	19,300	1,306,800
Chukchi	Anadyr	284,800	737,700	153,700
Chuvashia	Cheboksary	7,100	18,300	1,346,200
Dagestan	Makhachkala	19,400	50,300	1,854,200
Gorno-Altay	Gorno-Altaisk	35,700	92,600	196,600
Kabardino-Balkaria	Nalchik	4,800	12,500	777,700
Kalmykia	Elista	29,400	76,100	328,600
Karachay-Cherkessia	Cherkessk	5,400	14,100	427,100
Karelia	Petrozavodsk	66,600	172,400	799,400
Khakassia	Abakan	23,900	61,900	577,100
Komi	Syktyvkar	160,600	415,900	1,264,700
Koryak	Palana	116,400	301,500	39,600
Mari El	Ioshkar-Ola	9,000	23,200	758,000
Mordvinia	Saransk	10,100	26,200	964,100
Nenets	Naryan-Mar	68,100	176,400	54,900
North Ossetia	Vladikavkaz	3,100	8,000	642,500
Russia	Moscow	3,077,100	7,969,100	122,368,300
Tatarstan	Kazan	26,300	68,100	3,679,400
Tuva	Kyzyl-Orda	65,800	170,500	306,600
Udmurtia	Izhevsk	16,300	42,100	1,628,300
Yakut-Sakha	Yakutsk	1,198,200	3,103,200	1,108,600
Yamalo-Nenets	Salekhard	289,700	750,300	492,600
Autonomous okrugs				
Agin-Buryat	Aginskoye	7,300	19,000	77,800
Khanty-Mansi	Khanty-Mansiysk	202,000	523,100	1,314,200
Taymyr (Dolgano-Nenets)	Dudinka	332,900	862,100	53,700
Ust-Ordynsky Buryat	Ust-Ordynsky	8,600	22,400	138,300
Autonomous oblasts				
Evenki	Tura	296,400	767,700	25,100
Komi-Permyak	Kudymkar	12,700	32,900	161,100
Yevreyskaya (Jewish)	Birobidzhan	13,900	36,000	220,200
TOTAL		6,592,800[2]	17,075,400	148,542,700

Demography

Population (1992): 149,469,000.
Density (1992): persons per sq mi 22.7, persons per sq km 8.8.
Urban-rural (1991): urban 73.9%; rural 26.1%.
Sex distribution (1991): male 46.90%; female 53.10%.
Age breakdown (1989): under 15, 23.1%; 15–29, 22.0%; 30–44, 21.9%; 45–59, 17.6%; 60–74, 11.2%; 75 and over, 4.2%.
Population projection: (2000) 155,096,000; (2010) 161,976,000.
Doubling time: not applicable; doubling time exceeds 100 years.
Ethnic composition (1989): Russian 81.5%; Tatar 3.8%; Ukrainian 3.0%; Chuvash 1.2%; Bashkir 0.9%; Belorussian 0.8%; Mordovian 0.7%; Chechen 0.6%; German 0.6%; other 6.9%.
Religious affiliation: believers are predominantly Russian Orthodox; there are Roman Catholic, Protestant, Muslim, Jewish, and Buddhist minorities.
Major cities (1991): Moscow 8,801,500; St. Petersburg 4,466,800; Novosibirsk 1,446,300; Nizhny Novgorod 1,445,000; Yekaterinburg 1,375,400; Samara 1,257,300; Omsk 1,166,800; Chelyabinsk 1,148,300; Rostov-na-Donu 1,127,600; Kazan 1,107,300; Perm 1,100,400.

Other principal cities (1991)					
	population		population		population
Arkhangelsk	428,200	Krasnoyarsk	924,400	Sochi	341,500
Astrakhan	511,900	Kurgan	369,600	Tambov	334,400
Barnaul	606,800	Kursk	433,300	Tolyattigrad	654,700
Bryansk	458,900	Lipetsk	498,700	Tomsk	506,600
Cheboksary	449,300	Magnitogorsk	445,500	Tula	543,600
Chita	377,000	Murmansk	472,900	Tver	455,300
Grozny	401,400	Naberezhnye Chelny	513,000	Tyumen	494,200
Irkutsk	640,500	Nizhny Tagil	439,200	Ufa	1,097,000
Ivanovo	482,200	Novokuznetsk	601,900	Ulan-Ude	362,400
Izhevsk	646,800	Orenburg	556,500	Vladimir	376,000
Kaliningrad	408,100	Oryol	345,200	Vladivostok	648,000
Kaluga	366,300	Penza	551,500	Volgograd	1,007,300
Kemerovo	520,700	Saransk	347,000	Voronezh	900,000
Khabarovsk	613,300	Saratov	911,100	Vyatka	491,200
Krasnodar	631,200	Simbirsk	667,700	Yaroslavl	638,100

Mobility (1989). Population living in the same residence as in 1988: 78.8%; different residence, same oblast 11.5%; different republic 9.7%.
Emigration (1990): 103,609.

Households

Households (1989). Total family households 40,246,000; average household size 3.2; 2 persons 34.2%; 3 persons 28.0%; 4 persons 25.2%; 5 persons or more 12.6%. Population in family households: 128,787,000 (87.0%), nonfamily population 19,254,000 (13.0%).

Vital statistics

Birth rate per 1,000 population (1990): 13.4 (world avg. 27.1); legitimate 85.4%; illegitimate 14.6%.
Death rate per 1,000 population (1990): 11.2 (world avg. 9.8).
Natural increase rate per 1,000 population (1990): 2.2 (world avg. 17.3).
Total fertility rate (avg. births per childbearing woman; 1990): 1.9.
Marriage rate per 1,000 population (1990): 1.9.
Divorce rate per 1,000 population (1990): 3.8.
Life expectancy at birth (1990): male 63.9 years; female 74.3 years.
Major causes of death per 100,000 population (1989): diseases of the circulatory system 598.0; malignant neoplasms (cancers) 187.4; accidents, poisoning, and violence 125.8, of which suicide 25.7, murder 12.5; diseases of the respiratory system 58.2; diseases of the digestive system 27.5; infectious and parasitic diseases 12.6; diseases of the nervous system 6.9; endocrine and metabolic disorders 6.5.

Social indicators

Educational attainment (1989). Percentage of population age 15 and over having: primary or no formal education 19.4%; some secondary 21.0%; secondary and some postsecondary 48.3%; higher and postgraduate 11.3%.
Distribution of income: n.a.
Quality of working life (1990). Average workweek: 40 hours. Annual rate per 100,000 workers of: injury or accident 569; industrial illness 5.3; death 11.2. Proportion of labour force insured for damages or income loss resulting from: injury 100%; permanent disability 100%; death 100%. Average days lost to labour stoppages per 1,000 workdays (1990): 2.9. Average duration of journey to work: n.a. Rate per 1,000 workers of discouraged: n.a.
Access to services (1990). Proportion of dwellings having access to: electricity, virtually 100%; safe public water supply 94%; public sewage collection 92%; central heating 92%; bathroom 87%; gas 72%; hot water 79%.
Social participation. Eligible voters participating in last national election: 96%. Population participating in voluntary work, n.a. Trade union membership in total work force (1989): 100%. Practicing religious population in total affiliated population: n.a.
Social deviance. Offense rate per 100,000 population (1990) for: murder 10.5; rape 10.1; serious bodily injury 41.2; burglary and housebreaking 64.2; larceny-theft 436.6. Incidence per 100,000 in general population (1990) of: alcoholism 1,790.6; substance abuse 23.6; suicide 26.4.
Leisure. Favourite leisure activities (annual attendance): n.a.
Material well-being (1990). Goods possessed per 100 households: automobile 17; radio receiver 110; television receiver 121; refrigerator 106; air conditioner, virtually none; washing machine 79; camera 43; motorcycle 19; bicycle 47; tape recorder 64.

National economy

Budget (1992). Revenue: 3,285,000,000 rubles (foreign activity 30.2%; value-added tax 29.6%; enterprise profits tax 15.3%; royalty on oil 4.7%; royalty on gas 4.7%; individual income tax 3.5%; excise taxes 3.5%; tax on mineral extraction, natural resources, and timber 2.3%). Expenditures: 3,111,600,000 rubles (social welfare and culture 28.1%, of which social benefits 8.2%; debt services 27.2%, of which foreign debt 17.4%; defense 13.2%; national economy 13.1%; subsidies 6.2%).
Gross national product (at current market prices; 1990): 446,600,000,000 rubles (3,000 rubles per capita)[3].

Structure of net material product and labour force				
	1990			
	in value '000,000 rubles	% of total value	labour force	% of labour force
Agriculture	88,500	19.9	9,845,000	12.5
Mining Manufacturing Public utilities	187,600	42.2	22,107,000	28.1
Construction	56,500	12.7	7,018,000	8.9
Transp. and commun.	30,700	6.9	5,778,000	7.3
Trade	67,100	15.1	5,545,000	7.1
Finance	—	—	401,000	0.5
Pub. admin., defense	—	—	882,000	1.1
Services	—	—	27,106,000	34.5
Other	14,200	3.2	—	—
TOTAL	444,600	100.0	78,682,000	100.0

Public debt (external, outstanding; 1991): U.S.$7,000,000,000.
Tourism: receipts from visitors, n.a.; expenditures by nationals abroad, n.a.
Production (metric tons except as noted). Agriculture, forestry, fishing (1990): corn (maize) 189,000,000, wheat 49,600,000, sugar beets 32,300,000, potatoes 30,800,000, hay 30,700,000, barley 27,800,000, fodder crops 17,200,000, rye 16,400,000, oats 12,300,000, vegetables (other than potatoes) 10,300,000, peas 4,300,000, sunflower seeds 3,400,000, millet 1,900,000, rice 896,000, buckwheat 809,000; livestock (number of live animals; 1991): 57,000,000 cattle, 55,200,000 sheep, 38,300,000 pigs, 6,000,000 goats, 2,600,000 horses; roundwood 92,100,000 cu m; fish catch, n.a. Mining and quarrying (1990): iron ore 107,000,000. Manufacturing (1990): crude steel 89,600,000; rolled steel 63,700,000; pig iron 59,400,000; mineral fertilizers 15,979,000; cement 15,000,000; sulfuric acid 12,800,000; synthetic resins and plastics 3,258,000; caustic soda 2,258,000; detergents 876,000; synthetic fibres 673,500; soap 417,000; cotton fabrics 5,624,000,000 sq m; silk fabrics 1,051,000,000 sq m; linen fabrics 603,000,000 sq m; wool fabrics 466,000,000 sq m; carpets

43,500,000 sq m; ceramic tiles 22,600,000 sq m; leather 12,490,000 sq m; tableware 552,000,000 pieces; fur hats 9,700,000 pieces; cigarettes 151,-000,000,000 units; watches 60,100,000 units; tires 13,100,000 units; washing machines 5,419,000 units; television receivers 4,717,000 units; vacuum cleaners 4,470,000 units; refrigerators 3,774,000 units; bicycles 3,671,000 units; tape recorders 3,408,000 units; cameras 1,856,000 units; sewing machines 1,754,000 units; passenger cars 1,103,000 units; motorcycles 765,000 units; video recorders 454,000 units; machine tools 16,700 units; robots 1,200 units; furniture 5,779,000,000 rubles; agricultural machinery 2,143,000,000 rubles; chemical equipment 675,000,000 rubles; oil equipment 192,000,000 rubles; forge press machines 60,000,000 rubles; pharmaceuticals 2,522,000 rubles; leather footwear 385,000,000 pairs; rubber footwear 123,000,000 pairs; beer 33,000,000 hectolitres; vodka and liquors 13,800,000 hectolitres; champagne 10,400,000 hectolitres; grape wine 7,570,000 hectolitres; brandy 592,000 hectolitres. Construction (1990): residential 60,500,000 sq m.

Manufacturing, mining, and construction enterprises (1990)

	no. of enter-prises	no. of employees	monthly wages as a % of avg. of all wages	value added ('000,000 rubles)
Manufacturing				
Machinery and metal products	5,252	9,652,000	98.2	...
Fuel and energy	1,419	1,346,000	133.3	...
Metallurgy	408	1,272,000	124.3	...
Chemicals, petrochemicals, pulp, and paper	4,602	2,921,000	94.1	...
Light industry	4,515	2,288,000	80.0	...
Food	5,902	1,610,000	100.1	...
Other industries	2,729	3,018,000	...	...
Building materials	2,074	7,018,000	108.2	...

Energy production (consumption): electricity (kW-hr; 1991) 1,046,000,000 (1990; 1,073,800,000): by source (1990): thermal 73.7%, hydroelectric 15.4%, nuclear 10.9%; coal (metric tons; 1991) 353,300,000 (n.a.); crude petroleum (barrels; 1991) 3,379,000,000 (1,554,000,000); petroleum products, n.a. (n.a.); natural gas (cu m; 1991) 643,000,000,000 (413,000,000,000); peat (metric tons; 1990) 5,200,000 (n.a.); oil shale (metric tons; 1990) 4,600,000 (n.a.).
Service enterprises: n.a.
Population economically active (1990): total 78,682,000; activity rate of total population 53.0% (participation rates [1989]: ages 16–59 [male], 16–54 [female] 89.6%; female 52.4%; unemployed 9.0%).

Price and earnings indexes (1985 = 100)

	1985	1986	1987	1988	1989	1990	1991
Consumer price index	100.0	...	...	...	...	...	...
Monthly earnings index	100.0	103.2	107.3	116.8	128.4	147.4	263.2

Land use (1990): forested c. 45.2%; meadows and pastures 5.6%; agricultural and under permanent cultivation 7.8%; other 41.4%.
Household income and expenditure. Average household size (1989) 3.2; income per household: n.a.; sources of income (1990): wages and salaries 77.7%, pensions and stipends 13.2%, other 9.1%; expenditure (1990): food and nonalcoholic beverages 31.0%, clothing and footwear 22.3%, taxes and other financial payments 11.1%, culture 10.2%, furniture and household appliances 9.4%, alcoholic beverages 3.8%, housing 2.7%.

Foreign trade

Balance of trade (current prices)

	1987	1988	1989	1990	1991
'000,000,000 rubles	...	...	...	−6.2%	...
% of total	...	...	...	6.9%	...

Imports (1990): 47,800,000,000 rubles (machinery and transport equipment 41.2%, miscellaneous manufactured articles 18.0%, food 14.7%, textiles 10.4%, mineral fuels and lubricants 7.1%, raw materials excluding fuels 4.4%). *Major import sources:* foreign countries 52.7%; former Soviet republics 47.3%.
Exports (1990): 41,600,000,000 rubles (mineral fuels and lubricants 51.4%, machinery and transport equipment 17.5%, textiles 16.8%, raw materials excluding fuels 4.6%, miscellaneous manufactured articles 4.1%, chemicals and related products 3.8%). *Major export destinations:* former Soviet republics 70.0%; other countries 30.0%.

Trade by commodity group (1990)

	imports		exports	
SITC group	'000,000 rubles	%	'000,000 rubles	%
00 Food and live animals	7,000	14.7	700	1.7
02 Raw materials, excluding fuels	2,100	4.4	1,900	4.6
03 Mineral fuels, lubricants, and related materials	3,400	7.1	21,400	51.4
05 Chemicals and related products	2,000	4.2	1,600	3.8
65 Textile yarn, fabrics, and related materials	5,000	10.4	7,000	16.8
07 Machinery and transport equipment	19,700	41.2	7,300	17.5
08 Miscellaneous manufactured articles	8,600	18.0	1,700	4.1
09 Goods not classified by kind	...	...	...	...
TOTAL	47,800	100.0	41,600	100.0[2]

Direction of trade (1990)

	imports		exports	
	'000,000 rubles	%	'000,000 rubles	%
Former Soviet republics	22,600	47.3	29,100	70.0
Other countries	25,200	52.7	12,500	30.0
TOTAL	47,800	100.0	41,600	100.0

Transport and communications

Transport. Railroads (1990): length 99,900 mi, 160,800 km; passenger-mi 169,-696,000,000, passenger-km 273,100,000,000; short ton-mi cargo 1,698,000,000, metric ton-km cargo 2,479,000,000. Roads (1991): total length 549,000 mi, 884,000 km (paved 74%). Vehicles (1991): passenger cars 8,964,000; trucks and buses 484,000. Merchant marine: vessels (100 gross tons and over) n.a.; total deadweight tonnage, n.a. Air transport (1990): passenger-mi 95,132,-000,000, passenger-km 153,100,000,000; short ton-mi cargo 2,755,000, metric ton-km cargo 2,500,000; airports (1992) with scheduled flights 58.

Distribution of traffic (1990)

	cargo carried ('000,000 tons)	% of national total	passengers carried ('000,000)	% of national total
Intercity transport			32,014	63.9
Road	2,941	46.6	28,626	57.1
Rail	2,140	33.9	3,201	6.4
Sea and river	678	10.7	96	0.2
Air	3	...	91	0.2
Pipeline	558	8.8	—	—
Urban transport			18,105	36.1
Road	—	—	557	1.1
Rail	—	—	17,548	35.0
TOTAL	6,320	100.0	50,119	100.0

Communications. Daily newspapers (1990): total number 4,808; total circulation 166,000,000; circulation per 1,000 population 112. Radio (1991): total number of receivers 49,700,000 (1 per 3 persons). Television (1991): total number of receivers 55,000,000 (1 per 2.7 persons). Telephones (1991): 23,400,000 (1 per 6.3 persons).

Education and health

Education (1990–91)

	schools	teachers	students	student/ teacher ratio
Primary (age 6–13) } Secondary (age 14–17) }	67,600	1,506,000	20,851,000	13.8
Voc., teacher tr.	2,603	...	2,270,000	...
Higher	514	...	1,648,000	...

Literacy: total population age 15 and over literate, n.a.; males literate, n.a.; females literate, n.a.
Health (1991): physicians 671,700 (1 per 221 persons); hospital beds 1,931,000 (1 per 77 persons); infant mortality rate per 1,000 live births 17.4.
Food (1992): daily per capita caloric intake 2,100 (vegetable products, n.a., animal products, n.a.); 82% of FAO recommended minimum requirement: n.a.

Military

Total active duty personnel (1992): 2,200,000 (Commonwealth of Independent States [CIS] centrally controlled 8.2%, Russian general purpose [army] 63.6%, navy 14.5%, air force 13.6%). *Military expenditure as percentage of GNP* (1991): 7.9% (U.S. 5.1%); per capita expenditure U.S.$353.

[1]The Chechen-Ingush republic split into two separate republics June 4, 1992. [2]Detail does not add to total given because of rounding. [3]No equivalent U.S.$ value is offered, as Soviet GNP data are very speculative.

Rwanda

Official name: Repubulika y'u Rwanda (Rwanda); République Rwandaise (French) (Republic of Rwanda).
Form of government: transitional[1] government with one legislative house (National Development Council [70]).
Chief of state: President.
Head of government: Prime Minister.
Capital: Kigali.
Official languages: Rwanda; French.
Official religion: none.
Monetary unit: 1 Rwanda franc (RF); valuation (Oct. 5, 1992) 1 U.S.$ = RF 140.21; 1 £ = RF 239.15.

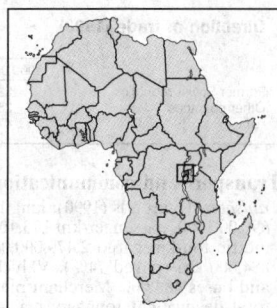

Area and population

Prefectures	Capitals	area sq mi	area sq km	population 1991 census
Butare	Butare	709	1,837	766,839
Byumba	Byumba	1,838	4,761	783,350
Cyangugu	Cyangugu	712	1,845	515,129
Gikongoro	Gikongoro	794	2,057	464,585
Gisenyi	Gisenyi	791	2,050	734,697
Gitarama	Gitarama	845	2,189	851,516
Kibungo	Kibungo	1,562	4,046	655,368
Kibuye	Kibuye	658	1,705	470,747
Kigali	Kigali	1,204	3,118	1,156,651
Ruhengeri	Ruhengeri	642	1,663	766,112
TOTAL		9,757[2]	25,271	7,164,994

Demography

Population (1992): 7,347,000.
Density (1992): persons per sq mi 722.5, persons per sq km 279.0.
Urban-rural (1991): urban 5.4%; rural 94.6%.
Sex distribution (1991): male 48.67%; female 51.33%.
Age breakdown (1990): under 15, 49.0%; 15–29, 26.1%; 30–44, 13.5%; 45–59, 7.5%; 60–74, 3.3%; 75 and over, 0.6%.
Population projection: (2000) 9,356,000; (2010) 12,657,000.
Doubling time: 21 years.
Ethnic composition (1983): Hutu 90%; Tutsi 9%; Twa 1%.
Religious affiliation (1988): Roman Catholic 65%; traditional beliefs 17%; Protestant 9%; Muslim 9%.
Major cities (1991): Kigali 232,733; Ruhengeri 29,578; Butare 28,645; Gisenyi 21,918.

Vital statistics

Birth rate per 1,000 population (1990–95): 50.0 (world avg. 26.4); (1978) legitimate 94.9%; illegitimate 5.1%.
Death rate per 1,000 population (1990–95): 15.6 (world avg. 9.2).
Natural increase rate per 1,000 population (1990–95): 34.4 (world avg. 17.2).
Total fertility rate (avg. births per childbearing woman; 1990–95): 8.0.
Marriage rate per 1,000 population (1984)[3]: 2.5.
Divorce rate per 1,000 population: n.a.
Life expectancy at birth (1990–95): male 48.8 years; female 52.2 years.
Major causes of death per 100,000 population (1984)[4]: complications of pregnancy, childbirth, and birth injury 192.4; infectious and parasitic diseases (including malaria, typhoid, trypanosomiasis [sleeping sickness], pneumonia, tuberculosis, bacillary dysentery and amebiasis, diphtheria, meningococcal infection, and poliomyelitis) 11.8; diseases of the digestive system 10.3; diseases of the nervous system 10.1; accidents, poisoning, and violence 5.2.

National economy

Budget (1988–89). Revenue: RF 27,500,000,000 (1984; import and export duties 39.6%, taxes on goods and services 25.3%, income tax 18.1%, property taxes 1.9%). Expenditures: RF 27,500,000,000 (1987; education 19.9%, debt repayment 16.6%, defense 9.9%, infrastructure 6.6%, health 4.6%, agriculture 1.1%).
Public debt (external, outstanding; 1991): U.S.$958,000,000.
Production (metric tons except as noted). Agriculture, forestry, fishing (1991): plantains 3,030,000, roots and tubers 1,725,000 (of which sweet potatoes 850,000, cassava 560,000, potatoes 240,000), cereals 330,000 (of which sorghum 205,000, corn [maize] 104,000), coffee 43,000, tea 12,000, tobacco 4,000; livestock (number of live animals) 1,150,000 goats, 630,000 cattle, 394,000 sheep, 139,000 pigs; roundwood (1990) 5,842,000 cu m; fish catch (1990) 2,504. Mining and quarrying (1990): cassiterite (tin ore) 1,048; wolframite (tungsten ore) 289; gold (1989) 25,600 troy oz. Manufacturing (1990): cement 51,000[5]; lye soap 9,535; sugar 2,969; beer 84,267,000 bottles; lemonade 39,430,000 bottles; plastic footwear 163,770 pairs; blankets 406,876 units; matches 70,942,000 boxes. Construction (1981): residential 59,600 sq m; nonresidential 34,400 sq m. Energy production (consumption): electricity (kW-hr; 1990) 176,000,000 (195,000,000); coal, none (n.a.); petroleum products (metric tons; 1990) none (129,000); natural gas (cu m; 1990) 153,762 (153,762).
Tourism (1990): receipts from visitors U.S.$10,000,000; expenditures by nationals abroad U.S.$23,000,000.
Land use (1990): forested 22.5%; meadows and pastures 18.7%; agricultural and under permanent cultivation 46.8%; other 12.0%.
Population economically active (1987): total 3,430,000; activity rate of total population 49.9% (participation rates: over age 10, 77.7%; female 73.5%; unemployed, n.a.).

Price and earnings indexes (1985 = 100)

	1985	1986	1987	1988	1989	1990	1991
Consumer price index	100.0	98.9	103.0	106.0	107.1	111.6	133.5
Earnings index	...	...	...	...	...	...	...

Gross national product (at current market prices; 1990): U.S.$2,214,000,000 (U.S.$310 per capita).

Structure of gross domestic product and labour force

	1988 in value RF '000,000	1988 % of total value	1987 labour force	1987 % of labour force
Agriculture	67,430	37.9	3,149,000	91.8
Mining	350	0.2		
Manufacturing	24,980	14.0		
Construction	12,240	6.9	113,000	3.3
Public utilities	1,170	0.7		
Transportation and communications	12,640	7.1		
Trade	22,660	12.7		
Finance	14,550	8.2	168,000	4.9
Pub. admin., defense	15,660	8.8		
Services				
Other	6,240	3.5		
TOTAL	177,930[2]	100.0	3,430,000	100.0

Household income and expenditure. Average household size (1991) 4.7; average annual income per household (1983) RF 122,870 (U.S.$1,300); sources of income (1977): self-employment (profits, interest, etc.) 71.0%, salaries and wages 16.5%, transfers 9.5%; expenditure (1982)[6]: food 44.2%, housing 13.2%, clothing and footwear 11.4%, transportation 10.3%, household equipment 8.4%.

Foreign trade[7]

Balance of trade (current prices)

	1986	1987	1988	1989	1990	1991
RF '000,000	−4,860	−10,562	−11,403	−10,918	−6,834	−15,181
% of total	12.9%	37.1%	40.7%	41.7%	27.0%	39.6%

Imports (1990): RF 23,057,370,000 (machinery and transport equipment 20.9%, of which machinery 17.0%, transport equipment 3.9%; mineral fuels and lubricants 13.7%; food, beverages, and tobacco 11.9%; construction materials 5.7%). *Major import sources:* Belgium-Luxembourg 19.4%; Kenya 16.6%; Germany 11.1%; France 7.7%; Japan 6.8%; The Netherlands 3.6%; Italy 2.5%; United Kingdom 2.3%; Switzerland 1.5%; Canada 1.1%.
Exports (1990): RF 8,478,288,000 (coffee 66.7%; tea 17.9%). *Major export destinations:* Germany 21.5%; Belgium-Luxembourg 13.6%; The Netherlands 12.7%; United Kingdom 8.4%; United States 5.3%; Ireland 2.7%; Italy 2.3%.

Transport and communications

Transport. Railroads: none. Roads (1990): total length 8,185 mi, 13,173 km (paved 9%). Vehicles (1990): passenger cars 7,868; trucks and buses 2,048. Merchant marine: none. Air transport (1987): passenger arrivals 42,000, passenger departures 47,000; metric ton cargo loaded 20,120; metric ton cargo unloaded 16,500; airports (1992) with scheduled flights 3.
Communications. Daily newspapers (1991): total number 1; total circulation per 1,000 population 14. Radio (1991): total number of receivers 630,000 (1 per 11 persons). Television: none. Telephones (1990): 14,136 (1 per 497 persons).

Education and health

Education (1989–90)

	schools	teachers	students	student/teacher ratio
Primary (age 7–15)	1,671	18,524	1,058,529	57.1
Secondary (age 16–19)	...	4,022[8]	65,323	...
Higher	3[9]	646	3,389	5.2

Educational attainment (1978). Percentage of population age 25 and over having: no formal schooling 76.9%; some primary education 16.8%; complete primary education 4.0%; some secondary and complete secondary education 2.0%; some postsecondary vocational and higher education 0.3%. *Literacy* (1990): percentage of total population age 15 and over literate 50.2%; males literate 63.9%; females literate 37.1%.
Health (1984): physicians 177[10] (1 per 33,170 persons); hospital beds 9,046 (1 per 649 persons); infant mortality rate per 1,000 live births (1990–95) 112.0.
Food (1988–90): daily per capita caloric intake 1,913 (vegetable products 97%, animal products 3%); 82% of FAO recommended minimum requirement.

Military

Total active duty personnel (1992): 5,200 (army 96.2%, navy, none, air force 3.8%). *Military expenditure as percentage of GNP* (1988): 1.6% (world 5.0%); per capita expenditure U.S.$5.

---

[1]Multiparty constitution became effective June 10, 1991; no timetable for elections existed as of October 1992. [2]Detail does not add to total given because of rounding. [3]Excludes marriages not registered in court. [4]In hospitals only. [5]1988. [6]Weights of consumer price index components. [7]Imports f.o.b. in balance of trade and c.i.f. in commodities and trading partners. [8]Includes vocational and teacher training. [9]1985. [10]Excludes foreign physicians.

Saint Kitts and Nevis

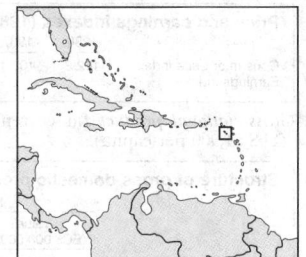

Official name: Federation of Saint Kitts and Nevis[1].
Form of government: constitutional monarchy with one legislative house (National Assembly [15[2]]).
Chief of state: British Monarch represented by Governor-General.
Head of government: Prime Minister.
Capital: Basseterre.
Official language: English.
Official religion: none.
Monetary unit: 1 Eastern Caribbean dollar (EC$)=100 cents; valuation (Oct. 5, 1992) 1 U.S.$=EC$2.70; 1 £=EC$4.59.

Area and population

Islands[3]	Capitals	area sq mi	area sq km	population 1989 estimate
Nevis[4]	Charlestown	36.0	93.2	10,080
St. Kitts	Basseterre	68.0	176.2	31,880
TOTAL		104.0	269.4	41,960

Demography

Population (1992): 43,100.
Density (1992): persons per sq mi 414.4, persons per sq km 160.0.
Urban-rural (1990): urban 48.9%; rural 51.1%.
Sex distribution (1988): male 51.24%; female 48.76%.
Age breakdown (1988): under 15, 32.1%; 15–29, 27.3%; 30–44, 18.0%; 45–59, 10.3%; 60–74, 8.5%; 75 and over, 3.8%.
Population projection: (2000) 43,000; (2010) 45,000.
Doubling time: 60 years.
Ethnic composition (1988): black 86.0%; mixed 11.0%; white 2.0%; Indo-Pakistani 1.0%.
Religious affiliation (1985): Protestant 76.4%, of which Anglican 36.2%, Methodist 32.3%, Roman Catholic 10.7%; other 12.9%.
Major towns (1985): Basseterre 18,500; Charlestown 1,700.

Vital statistics

Birth rate per 1,000 population (1989): 22.5 (world avg. 27.1); (1983) legitimate 19.2%; illegitimate 80.8%.
Death rate per 1,000 population (1989): 11.0 (world avg. 9.8).
Natural increase rate per 1,000 population (1989): 11.5 (world avg. 17.3).
Total fertility rate (avg. births per childbearing woman; 1991): 2.6.
Marriage rate per 1,000 population: n.a.
Divorce rate per 1,000 population: n.a.
Life expectancy at birth (1991): male 64.0 years; female 71.0 years.
Major causes of death per 100,000 population (1985): diseases of the circulatory system 443.2, of which cerebrovascular disease 220.5, diseases of pulmonary circulation and other heart disease 122.7; malignant neoplasms (cancers) 95.5; diseases of the respiratory system 81.8; infectious and parasitic diseases 50.0; ill-defined conditions 102.3.

National economy

Budget (1990). Revenue: EC$103,300,000 (tax revenue 68.8%, of which import duties 19.5%, income taxes 19.3%, consumption taxes 17.4%, nontax revenue 28.1%; foreign grants 1.9%; development revenue 1.2%). Expenditures: EC$106,100,000 (current expenditure 90.9%; development expenditure 9.1%).
Production (metric tons except as noted). Agriculture, forestry, fishing (1990): sugarcane 168,500, coconuts 2,000, fruits 1,000, vegetables 1,000, potatoes 304; livestock (number of live animals) 15,000 sheep, 10,000 goats, 5,000 cattle, 4,000 pigs; roundwood, n.a.; fish catch (1989) 1,100. Mining and quarrying: excavation of sand for local use. Manufacturing: raw sugar 19,-500[5]; molasses 8,800[6]; aerated beverages 35,000 hectolitres[7]; beer 16,000 hectolitres[8]; other manufactures include garments, electronic components, plastics, and ethanol. Construction: n.a. Energy production (consumption): electricity (kW-hr; 1990) 37,000,000 (37,000,000); coal, none (none); crude petroleum, none (none); petroleum products (metric tons; 1990) none (21,-000); natural gas, none (none).
Gross national product (at current market prices; 1990): U.S.$133,000,000 (U.S.$3,330 per capita).

Structure of gross domestic product and labour force

	1990 in value EC$'000,000[9]	1990 % of total value	1984 labour force[10]	1984 % of labour force[10]
Agriculture	29.1	8.5	4,380	29.6
Mining	1.7	0.5	—	—
Manufacturing	46.6	13.6	2,170	14.7
Construction	41.8	12.2	400	2.7
Public utilities	3.9	1.1	1,030	7.0
Transportation and communications	49.2	14.3	450	3.0
Trade, restaurants	80.8	23.5	940	6.3
Finance, real estate	45.9	13.4	280	1.9
Pub. admin., defense	57.9	16.8 }	4,700	31.7
Services	12.3	3.6 }		
Other	−25.4[11]	−7.4[11]	460	3.1
TOTAL	343.7[12]	100.0[12]	14,810	100.0

Household income and expenditure. Average household size (1980) 3.7; income per household: n.a.; sources of income: n.a.; expenditure (1978)[13]: food, beverages, and tobacco 55.6%, household furnishings 9.4%, housing 7.6%, clothing and footwear 7.5%, fuel and light 6.6%, transportation 4.3%, other 9.0%.
Population economically active (1980): total 17,125; activity rate of total population 39.5% (participation rates: ages 15–64, 69.5%; female 41.0%; unemployed[14]).

Price and earnings indexes (1985=100)

	1985	1986	1987	1988	1989	1990	1991
Consumer price index	100.0	100.0	101.0	101.2	106.3	110.8	115.5
Earnings index	...	...	...	...	...	...	...

Public debt (external, outstanding; end of 1990): U.S.$35,100,000.
Tourism (1990): receipts from visitors U.S.$63,000,000; expenditures by nationals abroad U.S.$4,000,000.
Land use (1989): forested 17.0%; meadows and pastures 3.0%; agricultural and under permanent cultivation 39.0%; other 41.0%.

Foreign trade[15]

Balance of trade (current prices)

	1985	1986	1987	1988	1989	1990
EC$'000,000	−83.5	−101.9	−139.0	−177.4	−199.5	−208.5
% of total	43.2%	42.9%	47.9%	54.5%	56.4%	60.9%

Imports (1988): EC$251,500,000 (food and live animals 15.6%, nonelectrical machinery 13.1%, road vehicles 7.1%, metal manufactures 6.8%, refined petroleum 4.8%). *Major import sources:* United States 47.4%; United Kingdom 18.1%; Trinidad and Tobago 6.5%; Canada 4.2%; Japan 3.8%.
Exports (1988)[16]: EC$74,100,000 (sugar 32.0%, electronic components 23.6%, knitted undergarments 18.0%, power-generating equipment 7.5%, beverages 4.1%). *Major export destinations:* United States 62.3%; United Kingdom 21.8%; Trinidad and Tobago 4.3%; Antigua and Barbuda 2.3%; Netherlands Antilles 1.6%.

Transport and communications

Transport. Railroads (1990): length 22 mi, 36 km[17]. Roads (1990): total length 186 mi, 300 km (paved 41%). Vehicles (1986): passenger cars 3,600; trucks and buses 700. Merchant marine (1991): vessels (100 gross tons and over) 1; total deadweight tonnage 550. Air transport: passenger arrivals (1987) 98,263; passenger departures (1982) 52,410; cargo handled, n.a.; airports (1992) with scheduled flights 2.
Communications (1991). Daily newspapers[18]: none. Radio: total number of receivers 25,000 (1 per 1.7 persons). Television: total number of receivers 9,500 (1 per 4.5 persons). Telephones (1990): 9,367 (1 per 4.6 persons).

Education and health

Education (1989–90)

	schools	teachers	students	student/ teacher ratio
Primary (age 5–12)	33	341	7,442	21.8
Secondary (age 13–17) }	7	294	4,176	14.2
Vocational				
Higher	...	37[19]	211	5.2[19]

Educational attainment (1980). Percentage of population age 25 and over having: no formal schooling 1.1%; primary education 29.6%; secondary 67.2%; higher 2.1%. *Literacy* (1985): 90.0%.
Health (1990): physicians 27 (1 per 1,593 persons); hospital beds 258 (1 per 167 persons); infant mortality rate per 1,000 live births (1989): 22.2.
Food (1987–89): daily per capita caloric intake 2,614 (vegetable products 76%, animal products 24%); 108% of FAO recommended minimum requirement.

Military

Total active duty personnel (1987): the 300-member police force includes an 80-member paramilitary unit.

[1]Saint Christopher and Nevis and Federation of Saint Christopher and Nevis are both officially acceptable, variant, short- and long-form names of the country. [2]Includes four nonelective seats. [3]Parish subdivisions of both islands are for statistical purposes only. [4]Nevis has full internal self-government. The Nevis legislature is subordinate to the National Assembly only with regard to external affairs and defense. [5]1991. [6]1987. [7]1988. [8]1989. [9]At factor cost. [10]Employed persons only. [11]Less imputed bank service charges. [12]Detail does not add to total given because of rounding. [13]Weights of consumer price index components. [14]Official data not available. Unemployment rates were thought to be low in 1990 and 1991 because of labour shortages in construction and the sugar industry. [15]Imports c.i.f.; exports f.o.b. [16]Exports (1989): EC$77,200,000 (domestic exports 88.4%, of which sugar 41.1%, electronic components c. 30.0%; reexports [mostly machinery and equipment] 11.6%). [17]Light railway serving the sugar industry on Saint Kitts. [18]Total circulation of one weekly newspaper and one twice-weekly newspaper is 12,000. [19]1987–88.

Saint Lucia

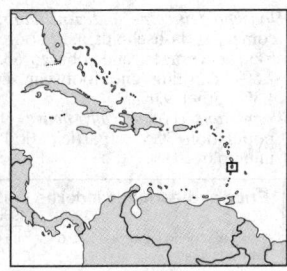

Official name: Saint Lucia.
Form of government: constitutional monarchy with two legislative houses (Senate [11]; House of Assembly [17]).
Chief of state: British Monarch represented by Governor-General.
Head of government: Prime Minister.
Capital: Castries.
Official language: English.
Official religion: none.
Monetary unit: 1 Eastern Caribbean Dollar (EC$) = 100 cents; valuation (Oct. 5, 1992) 1 U.S.$ = EC$2.70; 1 £ = EC$4.59.

Area and population		area		population
Administrative regions	Capitals	sq mi	sq km	1991 census
Anse-la-Raye	Anse-la-Raye	22	57	6,834
Babonneau	Babonneau	17	44	8,285
Castries	Castries	28	73	45,768
Dennery	Dennery	26	67	11,168
Gros Islet	Gros Islet	22	57	11,446
Micoud	Micoud	30	78	15,088
Soufrière	Soufrière	27	70	14,088
Vieux Fort	Vieux Fort	36	93	20,631
TOTAL		238[1]	617[1]	133,308

Demography

Population (1992): 135,000.
Density (1992): persons per sq mi 567.2, persons per sq km 218.8.
Urban-rural (1990): urban 46.4%; rural 53.6%.
Sex distribution (1991): male 48.49%; female 51.51%.
Age breakdown (1991): under 15, 36.8%; 15–29, 29.4%; 30–44, 16.3%; 45–59, 8.7%; 60–74, 6.3%; 75 and over, 2.5%.
Population projection: (2000) 143,000; (2010) 155,000.
Doubling time: 40 years.
Ethnic composition (1985): black 87.0%; mixed 9.1%; East Indian 2.6%; white 1.3%.
Religious affiliation (1991): Roman Catholic 79.0%; Protestant 15.5%, of which Seventh-day Adventist 6.5%, Pentecostal 3.0%; other 5.5%.
Major city (1991): Castries 11,147.

Vital statistics

Birth rate per 1,000 population (1990): 23.2 (world avg. 27.1); legitimate 10.0%; illegitimate 90.0%.
Death rate per 1,000 population (1990): 5.6 (world avg. 9.8).
Natural increase rate per 1,000 population (1990): 17.6 (world avg. 17.3).
Total fertility rate (avg. births per childbearing woman; 1990): 3.4.
Marriage rate per 1,000 population (1989): 2.7.
Divorce rate per 1,000 population (1989): 0.3.
Life expectancy at birth (1990): male 68.6 years; female 74.4 years.
Major causes of death per 100,000 population (1990): diseases of the circulatory system 209.5, of which ischemic heart diseases 109.7, hypertensive disease 58.8, cerebrovascular disease 35.0; malignant neoplasms (cancers) 48.3; diseases of the respiratory system 33.7; ill-defined conditions 81.3.

National economy

Budget (1991–92). Revenue: EC$464,900,000 (current revenue 64.9%; grants and loans for development expenditures 35.1%). Expenditures: EC$476,600,000 (current expenditures 55.3%, of which education 11.5%, health 6.3%, debt servicing 5.6%; development expenditures 44.7%).
Public debt (external, outstanding; end of 1990): U.S.$58,200,000.
Tourism: receipts from visitors (1991) U.S.$174,000,000; expenditures by nationals abroad (1990) U.S.$21,000,000.
Production. Agriculture, forestry, fishing (export value in EC$'000 except as noted; 1990): bananas 155,000[2], breadfruit 642, pepper 599, mangoes 498, cacao beans 338, plantains 248, ginger 82; livestock (number of live animals) 16,000 sheep, 13,000 cattle, 12,000 pigs, 12,000 goats; roundwood, n.a.; fish catch 573 metric tons. Mining and quarrying: excavation of sand for local construction and pumice. Manufacturing (value of production in EC$'000; 1990): alcoholic beverages and tobacco 26,113, of which rum 6,306; paper products and cardboard boxes 16,362[3]; garments 14,309; refined coconut oil 9,097; raw coconut oil 7,034; copra 5,810; other manufactures include electronic components. Construction (buildings approved; 1990): residential 70,000 sq m; nonresidential 18,300 sq m. Energy production (consumption): electricity (kW-hr; 1990) 126,900,000 (111,800,000); coal, none (none); crude petroleum, none (none); petroleum products (metric tons; 1990) none (53,000); natural gas, none (none).
Household income and expenditure. Average household size (1991) 4.0; income per household: n.a.; sources of income: n.a.; expenditure (1984)[4]: food 46.8%, housing 13.5%, clothing and footwear 6.5%, transportation and communications 6.3%, household furnishings 5.8%, fuel and light 4.5%, recreation and education 3.2%, beverages and tobacco 2.8%, health care 2.3%, other 8.3%.
Population economically active (1980): total 42,200; activity rate of total population 37.2% (participation rates: ages 15–64, 69.9%; female 39.1%; unemployed [1990] 13.0%).

Price and earnings indexes (1985 = 100)							
	1986	1987	1988	1989	1990	1991	1992[5]
Consumer price index	102.2	109.4	110.3	115.1	120.0	127.4	133.4
Earnings index	...	...	...	...	...	...	...

Gross national product (at current market prices; 1990): U.S.$286,000,000 (U.S.$1,900 per capita).

Structure of gross domestic product and labour force				
	1990[6]		1985	
	in value EC$'000,000	% of total value	labour force	% of labour force
Agriculture	115.8	13.8	...	33.9
Mining	6.1	0.7	...	0.2
Manufacturing	67.4	8.0	...	10.4
Construction	50.5	6.0	...	3.2
Public utilities	26.7	3.2	...	1.4
Transportation and communications	141.6	16.8	...	4.5
Trade, restaurants	202.4	24.1	...	18.5
Finance, real estate	112.8	13.4	...	2.6
Pub. admin., defense	123.0	14.6 }	...	25.3
Services	29.7	3.5 }		
Other	−34.6[7]	−4.1[7]	...	
TOTAL	841.4	100.0	...	100.0

Land use (1989): forested 13.0%; meadows and pastures 5.0%; agricultural and under permanent cultivation 30.0%; other 52.0%.

Foreign trade[8]

Balance of trade (current prices)						
	1985	1986	1987	1988	1989	1990
EC$'000,000	−197.0	−194.0	−268.9	−275.1	−446.6	−388.7
% of total	41.2%	30.2%	38.5%	35.0%	43.1%	36.1%

Imports (1990): EC$732,400,000 (machinery and transport equipment 21.4%, of which road vehicles 6.7%, electrical machinery and appliances 4.7%; food and live animals 19.4%, of which meat and meat preparations 5.5%; crude petroleum and petroleum products 6.7%; paper and paperboard 5.8%). *Major import sources:* United States 34.2%; Caricom countries 17.9%, of which Trinidad and Tobago 9.4%; United Kingdom 14.2%; Japan 6.2%; Canada 3.0%.
Exports (1990): EC$343,700,000 (bananas 58.1%; clothing 15.3%; paper and paperboard 4.8%; beer and ale 3.7%; refined coconut oil 2.5%). *Major export destinations* (1989)[9]: United Kingdom 52.2%; Caricom countries 19.7%, of which Barbados 4.7%, Dominica 3.3%; United States 19.4%; Italy 7.2%.

Transport and communications

Transport. Railroads: none. Roads (1989): total length 500 mi, 805 km (paved 56%). Vehicles (1989): passenger cars 6,500; trucks and buses 4,000. Merchant marine (1991): vessels (100 gross tons and over) 7; total deadweight tonnage, 2,070. Air transport (1990): passenger arrivals 223,467, passenger departures 226,630; cargo unloaded 1,480 metric tons, cargo loaded 2,766 metric tons; airports (1992) with scheduled flights 2.
Communications. Daily newspapers: none[10]. Radio (1991): total number of receivers 90,000 (1 per 1.7 persons). Television (1991): total number of receivers 25,000 (1 per 6 persons). Telephones (1990): 13,751[11] (1 per 11 persons).

Education and health

Education (1989–90)				
	schools	teachers	students	student/ teacher ratio
Primary (age 5–11)	83	1,112	32,636	29.3
Secondary (age 12–16)	13	376	6,771	18.0
Voc., teacher tr. } Higher	1	...	763	...

Educational attainment (1980). Percentage of population age 25 and over having: no formal schooling 17.5%; primary education 74.4%; secondary 6.8%; higher 1.3%. *Literacy* (1990): about 80%.
Health (1990): physicians 60 (1 per 2,521 persons); hospital beds 534 (1 per 283 persons); infant mortality rate per 1,000 live births (1989) 17.7.
Food (1987–89): daily per capita caloric intake 2,582 (vegetable products 76%, animal products 24%); 107% of FAO recommended minimum requirement.

Military

Total active duty personnel (1987):[12].

[1]Total includes the uninhabited 30 sq mi (78 sq km) Central Forest Reserve. [2]1991. [3]Export production only. [4]Weights of consumer price index components. [5]March. [6]At factor cost. [7]Less imputed bank service charges. [8]Imports c.i.f.; exports f.o.b. [9]Domestic exports only totaling EC$208,200,000. [10]Three newspapers published once or twice a week have a total circulation (1990) of 18,000. [11]Number of subscribers. [12]The police force includes a specially trained 80-member paramilitary unit.

Saint Vincent and the Grenadines

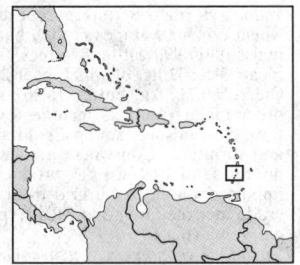
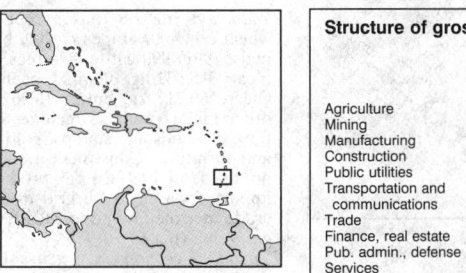

Official name: Saint Vincent and the Grenadines.
Form of government: constitutional monarchy with one legislative house (House of Assembly [21][1]).
Chief of state: British Monarch represented by Governor-General.
Head of government: Prime Minister.
Capital: Kingstown.
Official language: English.
Official religion: none.
Monetary unit: 1 Eastern Caribbean Dollar (EC$) = 100 cents; valuation (Oct. 5, 1992) 1 U.S.$ = EC$2.70; 1 £ = EC$4.59.

Area and population	area		population
	sq mi	sq km	1991 census[3]
Constituencies[2]			
Island of Saint Vincent[4]			
Barrouallie	14.2	36.8	5,222
Bridgetown	7.2	18.6	7,528
Calliaqua	11.8	30.6	20,689
Chateaubelair	30.9	80.0	6,056
Colonarie	13.4	34.7	7,864
Georgetown	22.2	57.5	7,347
Kingstown (city)	1.9	4.9	15,670
Kingstown (suburbs)	6.4	16.6	10,872
Layou	11.1	28.7	5,949
Marriaqua	9.4	24.3	8,843
Sandy Bay	5.3	13.7	2,802
Saint Vincent Grenadines			
Northern Grenadines[5]	9.0	23.3	5,830
Southern Grenadines[5]	7.5	19.4	2,926
TOTAL	150.3	389.3[6]	107,598

Demography

Population (1992): 109,000.
Density (1992): persons per sq mi 725.2, persons per sq km 280.0.
Urban-rural[7] (1991): urban 24.7%; rural 75.3%.
Sex distribution (1991): male 50.17%; female 49.83%.
Age breakdown (1985): under 15, 37.4%; 15–29, 32.7%; 30–44, 14.9%; 45–59, 7.5%; 60–74, 5.6%; 75 and over, 1.9%.
Population projection: (2000) 116,000; (2010) 125,000.
Doubling time: 40 years.
Ethnic composition (1986): black 65.5%; mulatto 19.0%; East Indian 5.5%; white (mostly Portuguese) 3.5%; Amerindian/black 2.0%; other 4.5%.
Religious affiliation (1980): Protestant 77.3%, of which Anglican 36.0%, Methodist 20.4%, Seventh-day Adventist 4.1%, Plymouth Brethren 3.9%; Roman Catholic 19.3%; other 3.4%.
Major city (1991): Kingstown 15,670.

Vital statistics

Birth rate per 1,000 population (1990): 23.9 (world avg. 27.1); legitimate, n.a.; illegitimate, n.a.
Death rate per 1,000 population (1990): 6.4 (world avg. 9.8).
Natural increase rate per 1,000 population (1990): 17.5 (world avg. 17.3).
Total fertility rate (avg. births per childbearing woman; 1991): 2.8.
Marriage rate per 1,000 population (1990): 4.7.
Divorce rate per 1,000 population (1990): 0.7.
Life expectancy at birth (1991): male 68.0 years; female 72.0 years.
Major causes of death per 100,000 population (1990): diseases of the circulatory system 224.5, of which hypertensive disease 72.6, cerebrovascular disease 55.7, diseases of pulmonary circulation and other forms of heart disease 45.3; malignant neoplasms (cancers) 89.6; diseases of the respiratory system 37.7.

National economy

Budget (1989–90). Revenue: EC$144,700,000 (current revenue 94.6%, of which consumption taxes on imported goods 27.6%, income taxes 23.0%, customs duties 15.9%; development revenue 5.4%). Expenditures: EC$155,400,000 (current expenditure 80.8%, of which education 16.3%, health 14.0%, public works 5.6%, police and defense 5.6%; development expenditure 19.2%).
Public debt (external, outstanding; 1990): U.S.$51,700,000.
Tourism: receipts from visitors (1991) U.S.$53,000,000; expenditures by nationals abroad (1990) U.S.$5,000,000.
Production (metric tons except as noted). Agriculture, forestry, fishing (1991): bananas 80,000, coconuts 20,000, eddoes and dasheens[8] 5,200[9], sweet potatoes 4,000, plantains 2,000, lemons and limes 1,000, ginger 834[9], arrowroot starch 56[9], soursops, guavas, and papaws are other important fruits; livestock (number of live animals) 15,000 sheep, 9,000 pigs, 8,000 cattle; roundwood, n.a.; fish catch (1990) 8,370, of which squids and octopuses 4,393. Mining and quarrying: sand and gravel for local use. Manufacturing (value added in EC$'000; 1988): beverages and tobacco products 9,686; food products 9,499; textiles, clothing, and footwear 3,872; metal products and electrical machinery 2,510. Construction (gross floor area planned; 1990): 96,800 sq m. Energy production (consumption): electricity (kW-hr; 1990) 51,300,000 (47,400,000); coal, none (none); crude petroleum, none (none); petroleum products (metric tons; 1990) none (26,000); natural gas, none (none).
Gross national product (1990): U.S.$184,000,000 (U.S.$1,610 per capita).

Structure of gross domestic product and labour force				
	1990[10]		1980	
	in value EC$'000,000	% of total value	labour force	% of labour force
Agriculture	83.5	19.3	8,928	25.7
Mining	1.1	0.3	108	0.3
Manufacturing	37.7	8.7	1,781	5.1
Construction	38.7	8.9	3,549	10.2
Public utilities	21.6	5.0	402	1.2
Transportation and communications	90.2	20.8	1,882	5.4
Trade	61.3	14.2	2,566	7.4
Finance, real estate	47.4	10.9	351	1.0
Pub. admin., defense	70.8	16.3 }	7,579	21.8
Services	8.3	1.9 }		
Other	−27.4[11]	−6.3[11]	7,593[12]	21.9[12]
TOTAL	433.2	100.0	34,739	100.0

Population economically active (1980): total 34,739; activity rate of total population 35.5% (participation rates: over age 15, 60.9%; female 36.1%; unemployed [1992] 25–50%).

Price and earnings indexes (1985 = 100)							
	1985	1986	1987	1988	1989	1990	1991
Consumer price index	100.0	101.2	104.1	104.4	108.1	117.9	120.6
Annual earnings index	100.0	107.0	...	...	...	...	...

Household income and expenditure. Average household size (1991) 3.9; income per household (1988) EC$4,579 (U.S.$1,696); sources of income: n.a.; expenditure (1981)[13]: food and beverages 59.8%, clothing 7.7%, household furnishings 6.6%, housing 6.3%, energy 6.2%, other 13.4%.
Land use (1990): forested 36.0%; meadows and pastures 5.0%; agricultural and under permanent cultivation 28.0%; other 31.0%.

Foreign trade[14]

Balance of trade (current prices)						
	1985	1986	1987	1988	1989	1990
EC$'000,000	−43.1	−63.2	−125.1	−99.9	−142.8	−144.1
% of total	11.2%	15.5%	30.7%	17.8%	26.2%	24.4%

Imports (1990): EC$367,400,000 (basic manufactures 23.9%, food products 21.7%, machinery and transport equipment 21.7%). *Major import sources:* United States 36.0%; United Kingdom 17.7%; Trinidad and Tobago 12.5%; Barbados 4.1%; Canada 3.9%.
Exports (1990): EC$223,300,000 (domestic exports 94.0%, of which bananas 53.9%, flour 8.7%, varieties of taro roots 4.3%, reexports 6.0%). *Major export destinations:* United Kingdom 54.0%; Trinidad and Tobago 12.1%; United States 10.4%; Saint Lucia 6.2%.

Transport and communications

Transport. Railroads: none. Roads (1990): total length 633 mi, 1,019 km (paved 43%). Vehicles (1991): passenger cars 5,350; trucks and buses 2,814. Merchant marine (1991): vessels (100 gross tons and over) 698; total deadweight tonnage 4,221,099. Air transport (1990): passenger arrivals 102,473, passenger departures 103,517; airports (1992) with scheduled flights 5.
Communications. Daily newspapers: none[15]. Radio (1991): total number of receivers 55,000 (1 per 2.0 persons). Television (1991): total number of receivers 17,500 (1 per 6.2 persons). Telephones (1990): 16,837 (1 per 6.4 persons).

Education and health

Education (1989–90)	schools	teachers	students	student/ teacher ratio
Primary (age 5–11)	64	1,153[16]	24,366	21.5
Secondary (age 12–18)	21	396[16]	6,909	18.7
Voc., teacher tr.	2	...	295	...

Educational attainment (1980). Percentage of population age 25 and over having: no formal schooling 2.4%; primary education 88.0%; secondary 8.2%; higher 1.4%. *Literacy* (1983): total population age 15 and over literate 54,000 (85.0%).
Health: physicians (1989) 40 (1 per 2,650 persons); hospital beds (1987) 404 (1 per 258 persons); infant mortality rate per 1,000 live births (1988–90 avg.) 21.3.
Food (1988–90): daily per capita caloric intake 2,460 (vegetable products 85%, animal products 15%); 102% of FAO recommended minimum requirement.

Military

Total active duty personnel (1987): 570-member police force includes 80-member paramilitary unit. *Military expenditure as percentage of central government expenditure* (1988–89): 5.9%[17].

[1]Includes six nonelective seats. [2]For statistical purposes and the election of legislative representatives. [3]Preliminary. [4]For local administration, the island of Saint Vincent is divided into 5 parishes; population by parish is not available. [5]Both a constituency and a parish. [6]Detail does not add to total given because of rounding. [7]Urban defined as Kingstown and suburbs. [8]Varieties of taro roots. [9]1990. [10]At factor cost. [11]Less imputed bank service charges. [12]Not adequately defined. [13]Weights of consumer price index components. [14]Imports c.i.f.; exports f.o.b. [15]Circulation data not available for weekly newspapers. [16]1990–91. [17]May not agree with military expenditure as percentage of GNP because of different bases used.

San Marino

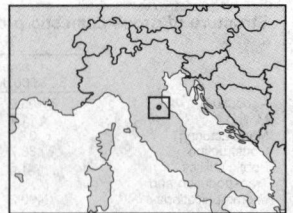

Official name: Serenissima Repubblica di San Marino (Most Serene Republic of San Marino).
Form of government: unitary multiparty republic with one legislative house (Great and General Council [60]).
Head of state and government: Captains-Regent (2).
Capital: San Marino.
Official language: Italian.
Official religion: none.
Monetary unit: 1 Italian lira (Lit; plural lire) = 100 centesimi; valuation (Oct. 5, 1992) 1 U.S.$ = Lit 1,315; 1 £ = Lit 2,236.

Area and population

Castles	Capitals	area sq mi	area sq km	population 1991[1] estimate
Acquaviva	Acquaviva	1.88	4.86	1,175
Borgo Maggiore	Borgo	3.48	9.01	4,769
Chiesanuova	Chiesanuova	2.11	5.46	750
Città	San Marino	2.74	7.09	4,185
Domagnano	Domagnano	2.56	6.62	2,021
Faetano	Faetano	2.99	7.75	736
Fiorentino	Fiorentino	2.53	6.56	1,576
Montegiardino	Montegiardino	1.28	3.31	632
Serravalle/Dogano	Serravalle	4.07	10.53	7,264
TOTAL		23.63[2]	61.19	23,108

Demography

Population (1992): 23,600.
Density (1992): persons per sq mi 998.7, persons per sq km 385.7.
Urban-rural (1991[1]): urban 90.1%; rural 9.9%.
Sex distribution (1991[1]): male 49.05%; female 50.95%.
Age breakdown (1991[1]): under 15, 16.1%; 15–29, 24.9%; 30–44, 22.7%; 45–59, 17.6%; 60–74, 13.1%; 75 and over, 5.6%.
Population projection: (2000) 25,100; (2010) 27,200.
Doubling time: not applicable; natural population growth is negligible, averaging only 0.3% during 1986–90.
Ethnic composition (1992): Sammarinesi 80.4%; Italian 18.7%; other 0.9%.
Religious affiliation (1980): Roman Catholic 95.2%; no religion 3.0%; other 1.8%.
Major cities (1991[1]): Serravalle/Dogano 4,643; San Marino 2,339; Borgo Maggiore 2,176; Murata 1,396; Domagnano 989.

Vital statistics

Birth rate per 1,000 population (1987–91): 10.6 (world avg. 26.4); (1985) legitimate 95.2%; illegitimate 4.8%.
Death rate per 1,000 population (1987–91): 7.3 (world avg. 9.2).
Natural increase rate per 1,000 population (1991): 3.3 (world avg. 17.2).
Total fertility rate (avg. births per childbearing woman; 1984): 1.3.
Marriage rate per 1,000 population (1986): 6.8.
Divorce rate per 1,000 population (1989): 1.0.
Life expectancy at birth (1980–85): male 70.7 years; female 76.2 years.
Major causes of death per 100,000 population (1987–91): diseases of the circulatory system 335.9; malignant neoplasms (cancers) 240.5; accidents, violence, and suicide 48.1.

National economy

Budget (1991). Revenue: Lit 379,337,000,000 (mainly receipts from postage stamp sales, tourism, and customs duties [collected by Italy and paid as a subsidy]). Expenditures: Lit 379,337,000,000 ([3]finance and economic planning 31.0%, internal affairs 11.3%, health and social security 9.0%, education and culture 7.1%, public works 6.3%).
Public debt: n.a.
Tourism: number of tourist arrivals (1991) 3,112,995; receipts from visitors (1983) U.S.$56,454,000; expenditures by nationals abroad, n.a.
Land use (1985): agricultural and under permanent cultivation 74%; meadows and pastures 22%; forested, built-on, wasteland, and other 4%.
Gross national product (at current market prices; 1987): U.S.$188,000,000 (U.S.$8,590 per capita).

Structure of labour force (1992[1])

	labour force	% of labour force
Agriculture	296	2.2
Manufacturing	4,495	33.7
Construction and public utilities	1,058	8.0
Transportation and communications	231	1.7
Trade	2,232	16.7
Finance and insurance	294	2.2
Services		
Public administration and defense	4,233	31.8
Other	493[4]	3.7[4]
TOTAL	13,332	100.0

Production (metric tons except as noted). Agriculture, forestry, fishing[3]: wheat *c.* 4,400, grapes *c.* 700, barley *c.* 500; livestock (number of live animals; 1991) 990 cattle, 874 pigs, 82 sheep. Manufacturing (1991): processed meats 385,637 kg, of which beef 260,877 kg, pork 105,389 kg, veal 17,012 kg; cheese 90,717 kg; butter 16,307 kg; yogurt 8,348 kg; milk 1,210,836 litres; other major products include textiles, cement, paper, leather, bricks, pottery, tiles, postage stamps, gold and silver jewelry, paints, synthetic rubber, and furniture. Construction (new units completed; 1991): residential 129; nonresidential 69. Energy production (consumption): all electrical power is imported via electrical grid from Italy, consumption n.a.; coal, none (n.a.); crude petroleum, none (n.a.); petroleum products, none (n.a.); natural gas, none (n.a.).
Population economically active (1992[1]): total 13,332; activity rate of total population 53.3% (participation rates: ages 15–64, 72.9%; female 40.8%; unemployed 3.7%).

Price and earnings indexes (1985 = 100)

	1985	1986	1987	1988	1989	1990	1991[5]
Consumer price index	100.0	107.9	114.6	120.7	127.4	135.9	141.4
Earnings index	...	...	...	...	...	...	...

Household income and expenditure. Total number of households (1991[1]): 8,210; average household size 2.8; income per household: n.a.; sources of income: n.a.; expenditure (1985)[6]: food, beverages, and tobacco 30.4%; transportation and communications 14.5%; housing, fuel, and electrical energy 9.7%; clothing and footwear 8.8%; recreation, entertainment, education, and culture 8.1%; furniture, appliances, and goods and services for the home 7.5%; health and sanitary services 5.1%; other goods and services 15.9%.

Foreign trade

Balance of trade: n.a. San Marino and Italy form a single customs area; separate figures for San Marino are not available.
Imports (1990): manufactured goods of all kinds, oil, and gold. *Major import source:* Italy.
Exports (1990): wine, wheat, woolen goods, furniture, wood, ceramics, building stone, dairy products, meat, and postage stamps. *Major export destination:* Italy.

Transport and communications

Transport. Railroads: none (nearest rail terminal is at Rimini, Italy, 17 mi [27 km] northeast). Roads (1987): total length 147 mi, 237 km. Vehicles (1992): passenger cars 21,188; trucks and buses 3,450. Merchant marine: vessels (100 gross tons and over) none. Air transport: airports with scheduled flights, none; there is, however, a heliport that provides passenger and cargo service between San Marino and Rimini, Italy, during the summer months.
Communications. Daily newspapers (1990): 5; circulation per 1,000 population, n.a. Radio (1991): total number of receivers 12,535 (1 per 1.9 persons). Television (1987): total number of receivers 7,000 (1 per 3.2 persons). Telephones (1988): 15,700 (1 per 1.5 persons).

Education and health

Education (1991–92)

	schools	teachers	students	student/ teacher ratio
Primary (age 6–10)	14	218	1,200	5.5
Secondary (age 11–18)	3	129	841	6.5
Voc., teacher tr.	...	...	317	...
Higher	...	...	332[7, 8]	...

Educational attainment (1992). Percentage of the adult labour force having: basic literacy or primary education 26.1%; secondary 40.0%; some postsecondary 28.4%; higher degree 5.5%. *Literacy* (1986): total population age 15 and over literate 18,135 (98.0%); males literate 8,957 (98.2%); females literate 9,178 (97.7%).
Health (1987): physicians 60 (1 per 375 persons); hospital beds 149 (1 per 151 persons); infant mortality rate per 1,000 live births (1987–91) 13.1.
Food (1986–88): daily per capita caloric intake 3,571 (vegetable products 73%, animal products 27%); 142% of FAO recommended minimum requirement.

Military

Total active duty personnel (1991): none[9]. *Military expenditure as percentage of national budget* (1987): 0.9% (world 5.4%); per capita expenditure (1987) U.S.$82.

[1]January 1. [2]Detail does not add to total given because of rounding. [3]Early 1980s. [4]Unemployed. [5]May. [6]Weighting coefficients for component expenditures are those of the 1985 official Italian consumer price index. [7]1986–87. [8]In Italy. [9]Defense is provided by a public security force of about 50; all fit males 16–55 constitute a militia.

São Tomé and Príncipe

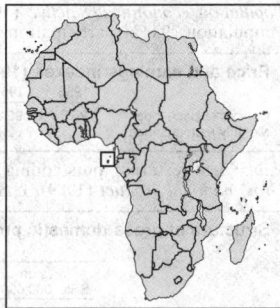

Official name: República democrática de São Tomé e Príncipe (Democratic Republic of São Tomé and Príncipe).
Form of government: multiparty[1] republic with one legislative house (National People's Assembly [55]).
Chief of state: President.
Head of government: Prime Minister.
Capital: São Tomé.
Official language: Portuguese.
Official religion: none.
Monetary unit: 1 dobra (Db) = 100 cêntimos; valuation (Oct. 5, 1992) 1 U.S.$ = Db 239.58; 1 £ = Db 407.28.

Area and population

Islands Districts	Capitals	area sq mi	area sq km	population 1984 estimate
Príncipe		55	142	5,671
Paguê	Santo António	55	142	5,671
São Tomé		332	859	98,693
Aqua Grande	São Tomé	7	17	34,997
Cantagalo	Santana	46	119	11,270
Caué	São João Angolares	103	267	4,972
Lemba	Neves	88	229	8,537
Lobata	Guadalupe	41	105	12,717
Mé-zóchi	Trinidade	47	122	26,200
TOTAL		386	1,001	104,364

Demography

Population (1992): 126,000.
Density (1992): persons per sq mi 325.2, persons per sq km 125.4.
Urban-rural (1988): urban 40.5%; rural 59.5%.
Sex distribution (1981): male 49.72%; female 50.28%.
Age breakdown (1981): under 15, 46.3%; 15–29, 25.0%; 30–44, 11.6%; 45–59, 10.0%; 60–74, 5.3%; 75 and over, 1.8%.
Population projection: (2000) 151,000; (2010) 191,000.
Doubling time: 28 years.
Ethnic composition: mestiços, angolares (descendants of Angolan slaves), forros (descendants of freed slaves), serviçais (alien contract labourers), tongas (children of serviçais), and Europeans.
Religious affiliation (1991): Roman Catholic, about 80.8%; remainder mostly Protestant, predominantly Seventh-day Adventist and an indigenous Evangelical Church.
Major city (1984): São Tomé 34,997.

Vital statistics

Birth rate per 1,000 population (1989): 35.0 (world avg. 27.1); (1977) legitimate 9.8%; illegitimate 90.2%.
Death rate per 1,000 population (1989): 10.2 (world avg. 9.8).
Natural increase rate per 1,000 population (1989): 24.8 (world avg. 17.3).
Total fertility rate (avg. births per childbearing woman; 1990): 5.4.
Marriage rate per 1,000 population: n.a.
Divorce rate per 1,000 population: n.a.
Life expectancy at birth (1990): male 64.0 years; female 67.0 years.
Major causes of death per 100,000 population (1987): malaria 160.6; direct obstetric causes 76.7; pneumonia 74.0; influenza 61.5; anemias 47.3; hypertensive disease 32.1.

National economy

Budget (1988). Revenue: Db 975,000,000 (indirect taxes 44.4%; income from property 16.0%; nondurable goods 11.3%; direct taxes 10.2%). Expenditures: Db 1,115,000,000 (current expenditure 82.4%, of which wages and salaries 45.5%; capital expenditure 17.6%).
Tourism (1990): receipts from visitors U.S.$1,000,000; expenditures by nationals abroad U.S.$2,000,000.
Production (metric tons except as noted). Agriculture, forestry, fishing (1991): coconuts 42,000, cassava 5,000, fruits (other than melons) 4,000, cacao 3,000, copra 3,000, bananas 3,000, palmetto 3,000[2], vegetables and melons 3,000, cereals 1,000, taro 742[3], palm kernel 500; livestock (number of live animals) 4,000 goats, 4,000 cattle, 3,000 pigs, 2,000 sheep; roundwood (1990) 9,000 cu m; fish catch 2,996, principally marine fish and shellfish. Mining and quarrying: some quarrying to support local construction industry. Manufacturing (1987): bread 2,459; soap 604; coconut oil 330; ice 191[4]; palm oil 177; limes 22[4]; corn (maize) flour 18[4]; sawn wood 3,272 cu m; beer 28,540 hectolitres; bottled water 13,750 hectolitres; soft drinks 10,460 hectolitres; other products include clothing, bricks, and clay products. Construction (1972): buildings authorized 44 (5,561 sq m, of which residential 3,698, mixed residential-commercial 1,361, commercial 502). Energy production (consumption): electricity (kW-hr; 1990) 15,000,000 (15,000,000); coal, none (n.a.); crude petroleum, none (n.a.); petroleum products (metric tons; 1990) none (22,000); natural gas, none (n.a.).
Household income and expenditure. Average household size: n.a.; income per household: n.a.; sources of income: n.a.; expenditure: n.a.
Public debt (external, outstanding; 1991): U.S.$142,000,000.
Population economically active (1987): total 20,912; activity rate of total population 18.5% (participation rates [1981]: ages 15–64, 61.1%; female 32.4%; unemployed 30.7%[3]).

Earnings indexes (1981 = 100)

	1981	1982	1983	1984	1985	1986
Agricultural sector	100.0	93.6	98.5	103.0	97.2	96.3
Nonagricultural sectors	100.0	101.4	100.7	107.7	107.7	123.8

Gross national product (at current market prices; 1990): U.S.$47,000,000 (U.S.$380 per capita).

Structure of gross domestic product and labour force

	1987 in value U.S.$'000,000	% of total value	labour force	% of labour force
Agriculture	8	25.8	8,448	40.4
Mining	...	...		
Manufacturing	3	9.7	1,129[5]	5.4[5]
Public utilities	1	3.2		
Construction	3	9.7	742	3.5
Transportation and communications	4	12.9	455	2.2
Trade	3	9.7	5	5
Finance	...	...	5	5
Pub. admin., defense	9	29.0	3,708	17.7
Services	...	...		
Other	...	...	6,430[6]	30.7[6]
TOTAL	31	100.0	20,912	100.0[7]

Land use (1990): meadows and pastures 1.0%; agricultural and under permanent cultivation 38.6%; forest, built-on, wasteland, and other 60.4%.

Foreign trade[8]

Balance of trade (current prices)

	1983	1984	1985	1986	1987	1988
Db '000,000	−543.6	−732.1	−765.2	−252.6	−268.4	−127.4
% of total	42.6%	40.4%	54.8%	26.9%	25.8%	8.3%

Imports (1988): Db 1,733,000,000 (food and other agricultural products 35.2%, capital goods 30.5%, intermediate goods 27.8%, mineral fuels and lubricants 6.5%). *Major import sources* (1987): Portugal 33.7%; East Germany 12.1%; Spain 11.3%; Angola 8.8%; West Germany 8.4%; France 6.5%; The Netherlands 5.4%; Norway 4.2%; Belgium-Luxembourg 3.5%.
Exports (1988): Db 927,000,000 (cacao 95.4%, copra 4.0%, coconuts 0.3%, pulses 0.3%). *Major export destinations:* West Germany 52.3%; East Germany 20.2%; The Netherlands 12.7%.

Transport and communications

Transport. Railroads: none. Roads (1988): total length 236 mi, 380 km (paved 66%). Vehicles (1975): passenger cars 1,774; trucks and buses 265. Merchant marine (1991): vessels (100 gross tons and over) 3; total deadweight tonnage 1,172. Air transport (1985): passenger-mi 3,800,000, passenger-km 6,100,000; short ton-mi cargo 70,000, short ton-km cargo 100,000; airports (1992) with scheduled flights 2.
Communications. Daily newspapers: none; 2 government weeklies (circulation, n.a.). Radio (1991): total number of receivers 31,000 (1 per 4.0 persons). Television: none. Telephones (1988): 2,800 (1 per 42 persons).

Education and health

Education (1989)

	schools	teachers	students	student/ teacher ratio
Primary (age 6–13)	64	559	19,822	35.5
Secondary (age 14–18)	11[9]	318	7,446	23.4
Voc., teacher tr.	2[9]	18[10]	289	...
Higher	...	...	700[11]	...

Educational attainment (1981). Percentage of population age 25 and over having: no formal schooling 56.6%; incomplete primary education 18.0%; primary 19.2%; incomplete secondary 4.6%; complete secondary 1.3%; postsecondary 0.3%. *Literacy* (1981): total population age 15 and over literate 28,114 (54.2%); males literate 17,689 (70.2%); females literate 10,425 (39.1%).
Health (1987): physicians 40 (1 per 2,819 persons); hospital beds (1983) 640 (1 per 158 persons); infant mortality rate per 1,000 live births (1989) 72.
Food (1988–90): daily per capita caloric intake 2,153 (vegetable products 95%, animal products 5%); 92% of FAO recommended minimum requirement.

Military

Total active duty personnel (1992): a gendarmerie of about 900 men was to be established in the early 1990s. *Military expenditure as percentage of GNP* (1980): 1.6% (world 5.4%); per capita expenditure U.S.$6.

[1]Multiparty system effective as of January 1991 elections. [2]1988. [3]1987. [4]1983. [5]Manufacturing includes Trade and Finance. [6]Unemployed. [7]Detail does not add to total given because of rounding. [8]Import figures are c.i.f. [9]1984–85. [10]Vocational teachers only. [11]Students abroad, 1982–83.

Saudi Arabia

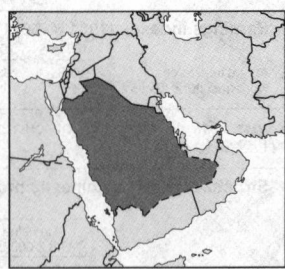

Official name: al-Mamlakah
al-ʿArabīyah as-Saʿūdīyah (Kingdom
of Saudi Arabia).
Form of government: monarchy.
Head of state and government: King.
Capital: Riyadh.
Official language: Arabic.
Official religion: Islam.
Monetary unit: 1 Saudi riyal
(SRls) = 100 halalah; valuation (Oct.
5, 1992) 1 U.S.$ = SRls 3.79;
1 £ = SRls 6.44.

Area and population		area		population
Regions				1985
Administrative Districts	**Capitals**	sq mi	sq km	estimate
al-Gharbīyah (Western)	—	...	...	3,043,189
al-Bāḥah	al-Bāḥah	...	...	...
al-Madīnah	Medina (al-Madīnah)	...	...	...
Makkah	Mecca (Makkah)	...	...	...
al-Janūbīyah (Southern)	—	...	...	625,017
ʿAsīr	Abha	...	...	...
Jīzān	Jīzān	...	...	...
Najrān	Najrān	...	...	...
ash-Shamālīyah (Northern)	—	...	...	679,476
al-Ḥudūd ash-Shamālīyah				
(Northern Borders)	ʿArʿar	...	...	...
al-Jawf	Sakākah	...	...	...
al-Qurayyāt	an-Nabk	...	...	...
Tabūk	Tabūk	...	...	...
ash-Sharqīyah (Eastern)		...	...	3,030,765
ash-Sharqīyah (Eastern)	ad-Dammām	...	...	...
al-Wūsṭā (Central)		...	...	3,632,092
Ḥāʾil	Ḥāʾil	...	...	...
al-Qasīm	Buraydah	...	...	...
ar-Riyāḍ	Riyadh (ar-Riyāḍ)	...	...	...
TOTAL		865,000	2,240,000	11,010,539

Demography

Population (1992): 15,267,000.
Density (1992): persons per sq mi 17.6, persons per sq km 6.8.
Urban-rural (1990): urban 77.3%; rural 22.7%.
Sex distribution (1990): male 54.35%; female 45.65%.
Age breakdown (1990): under 15, 45.3%; 15–29, 24.4%; 30–44, 18.0%; 45–59, 8.2%; 60–74, 3.4%; 75 and over, 0.7%.
Population projection: (2000) 20,697,000; (2010) 29,557,000.
Doubling time: 23 years.
Ethnic composition (1983): Saudi 82.0%; Yemeni 9.6%; other Arab 3.4%; other 5.0%.
Religious affiliation (1980): Muslim (mostly Sunnī) 98.8%; Christian 0.8%; other 0.4%.
Major cities (1980): Riyadh (ar-Riyāḍ) 1,308,000[1]; Jiddah 1,500,000[2]; Mecca (Makkah) 550,000; aṭ-Ṭāʾif 300,000.

Vital statistics

Birth rate per 1,000 population (1991): 36.6 (world avg. 26.4).
Death rate per 1,000 population (1991): 6.3 (world avg. 9.2).
Natural increase rate per 1,000 population (1991): 30.3 (world avg. 17.2).
Total fertility rate (avg. births per childbearing woman; 1991): 6.7.
Marriage rate per 1,000 population: n.a.
Divorce rate per 1,000 population: n.a.
Life expectancy at birth (1991): male 65.0 years; female 68.0 years.
Major causes of death per 100,000 population: n.a.; however, major diseases include cholera, cerebrospinal meningitis, yellow fever, typhoid, tuberculosis, lung infections, and asphyxia.

National economy

Budget (1992). Revenue: SRls 151,000,000,000 (1990; oil revenues 72.8%). Expenditures: SRls 181,000,000,000 (defense and security 30.0%, education 17.2%, health and social development 6.7%, transportation and communications 4.6%, economic resource development 4.4%).
Production (metric tons except as noted). Agriculture, forestry, fishing (1991): wheat 4,000,000, dates 505,000, tomatoes 435,000, watermelons 426,000, barley 375,000, grapes 103,000, cucumbers and gherkins 101,000, eggplants 74,000, pumpkins, squash, and gourds 64,000, potatoes 39,000, carrots 21,000, onions 17,000; livestock (number of live animals) 5,692,000 sheep, 3,350,000 goats, 390,000 camels, 176,000 cattle, 103,000 asses, 80,000,000 chickens; fish catch (1990) 46,427. Mining and quarrying (1989): gypsum 375,000; lime 12,000. Manufacturing (1985): cement 10,633,500; methanol 1,287,000; steel rods and bars 948,000; ethylene 927,900; urea 825,000; ethylene glycol 310,-000; industrial ethanol 200,000; ethylene dichloride 190,000; styrene 125,000; caustic soda 125,000; nitrogen 82,000; citric acid 75,000; oxygen 55,000; melamine 14,000. Construction (value added in SRls; 1990): 31,800,000,000. Energy production (consumption): electricity (kW-hr; 1990) 47,400,000,000 (47,400,000,000); coal, n.a. (n.a.); crude petroleum (barrels; 1990) 2,350,-912,000 (557,270,000); petroleum products (metric tons; 1990) 84,916,000 (36,396,000); natural gas (cu m; 1990) 28,223,000,000 (28,223,000,000).
Tourism: receipts from visitors (1989) U.S.$2,050,000,000; expenditures by nationals abroad (1988) U.S.$2,000,000,000.
Pilgrims to Mecca from abroad (1989): 774,560.
Land use (1990): forested 0.6%; meadows and pastures 39.5%; agricultural and under permanent cultivation 1.1%; other, built-on, and waste 58.8%.

Population economically active (1986): total 3,032,000; activity rate of total population 29.8% (participation rates: ages 15–64, 51.5%; female 3.2%).

Price and earnings indexes (1985 = 100)						
	1986	1987	1988	1989	1990	1991	1992[3]
Consumer price index	96.8	95.3	96.2	97.1	99.1	104.0	102.9
Monthly earnings index	...	...	...	...	...	...	...

Public debt (external, outstanding; 1989): U.S.$1,187,000,000.
Gross national product (1989): U.S.$89,986,000,000 (U.S.$6,230 per capita).

Structure of gross domestic product and labour force				
	1990			
	in value SRls '000,000	% of total value	labour force	% of labour force
Agriculture	22,200	6.4	569,200	9.9
Mining	1,700	0.5	3,500	0.1
Oil sector	122,300	35.0	46,800	0.8
Manufacturing	33,100	9.5	374,900	6.5
Construction	31,800	9.1	944,100	16.4
Public utilities	−800	−0.2	126,900	2.2
Transp. and commun.	21,700	6.2	262,300	4.5
Trade	28,200	8.1	898,300	15.6
Finance	23,000	6.6	99,000	1.7
Pub. admin., defense	56,200	16.1	624,800	10.8
Services and other	9,900	2.8	1,822,000	31.6
TOTAL	349,300	100.0[4]	5,771,800	100.0[4]

Household income and expenditure. Average household size (1986) 6.6; income per household: n.a.; sources of income: n.a.; expenditure (1980)[5]: food 52.2%, housing 17.2%, clothing 6.6%, furniture and utensils 5.9%, transportation and communications 4.5%, health care 2.1%.

Foreign trade[6]

Balance of trade (current prices)						
	1985	1986	1987	1988	1989	1990
SRls '000,000,000	+20.2	+8.6	+16.5	+15.1	+32.3	+82.1
% of total	11.3%	6.1%	10.5%	9.0%	17.9%	32.8%

Imports (1990): SRls 90,139,000,000 (transport equipment 20.5%, machinery and appliances 16.4%, textiles and clothing 8.8%, metals and metal articles 8.7%, chemicals 8.0%, precious stones and jewelry 6.9%). *Major import sources:* U.S. 16.7%; Japan 15.3%; U.K. 11.3%; W.Ger. 7.4%; Switzerland 6.6%; Italy 4.6%; France 4.0%; South Korea 3.3%; The Netherlands 2.3%; Taiwan 2.2%; Belgium 1.7%; Turkey 1.2%.
Exports (1990): SRls 166,339,000,000 (crude petroleum 74.1%, other 25.9%). *Major export destinations:* U.S. 24.0%; Japan 19.0%; Singapore 5.4%; France 4.8%; The Netherlands 4.7%; Bahrain 3.9%; South Korea 3.8%; Italy 3.6%; Taiwan 3.4%; Brazil 3.3%; India 2.5%; United Arab Emirates 1.8%.

Transport and communications

Transport. Railroads (1989): route length 555 mi, 893 km; passenger-mi 75,-186,000, passenger-km 121,000,000; short ton-mi cargo 548,639,000, metric ton-km cargo 801,000,000. Roads (1990): total length 75,506 mi, 121,516 km (paved 43%). Vehicles (1990): passenger cars 2,350,000; trucks and buses 2,150,000. Merchant marine (1991): vessels (100 gross tons and over) 309; total deadweight tonnage 1,999,497. Air transport (1990): passenger-mi 9,984,000,000, passenger-km 16,068,000,000; short ton-mi cargo 417,554,000, metric ton-km cargo 609,619,000; airports (1992) with scheduled flights 25.
Communications. Daily newspapers (1989): total number 10; total circulation 664,300; circulation per 1,000 population 49. Radio (1991): 5,000,000 receivers (1 per 2.9 persons). Television (1991): 4,500,000 receivers (1 per 3.3 persons). Telephones (1988): 1,069,325 (1 per 12.7 persons).

Education and health

Education (1988–89)	schools	teachers	students	student/ teacher ratio
Primary (age 6–12)	8,631	105,937	1,694,394	16.0
Secondary (age 13–18)	4,153	52,818	739,088	14.0
Voc., teacher tr.[7]	32	3,295	31,354	9.5
Higher	82	9,631	115,006	11.9

Educational attainment (1986). Percentage of population age 25 and over having: no formal schooling 31.8%; primary, secondary, or higher education 68.2%. *Literacy* (1990): percentage of population age 15 and over literate 62.4%; males literate 73.1%; females literate 48.1%.
Health (1990): physicians 22,688 (1 per 623 persons); hospital beds 39,500 (1 per 358 persons); infant mortality rate per 1,000 live births (1991) 69.0.
Food (1988–90): daily per capita caloric intake 2,929 (vegetable products 84%, animal products 16%); 121% of FAO recommended minimum requirement.

Military

Total active duty personnel (1992): 102,000 (army 71.6%, navy 10.8%, air force 17.6%). *Military expenditure as percentage of GNP* (1989): 16.0% (world 4.9%); per capita expenditure U.S.$897.

[1]1981 estimate. [2]1983 estimate. [3]September. [4]Detail does not add to total given because of rounding. [5]Urban middle-income households only. [6]Import figures are f.o.b. in balance of trade and c.i.f. in commodities and trading partners. [7]1987–88.

Senegal

Official name: République du Sénégal (Republic of Senegal).
Form of government: multiparty republic with one legislative house (National Assembly [120]).
Head of state and government: President assisted by Prime Minister.
Capital: Dakar.
Official language: French.
Official religion: none.
Monetary unit: 1 CFA franc (CFAF) = 100 centimes; valuation (Oct. 5, 1992) 1 U.S.$ = CFAF 238.75; 1 £ = CFAF 405.88.

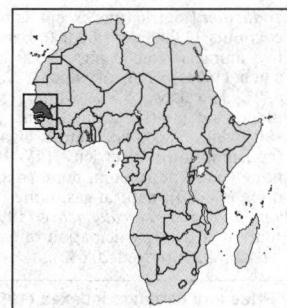

Area and population		area		population
				1988
Regions	Capitals	sq mi	sq km	census
Dakar	Dakar	212	550	1,571,614
Diourbel	Diourbel	1,683	4,359	620,197
Fatick	Fatick	3,064	7,935	507,651
Kaolack	Kaolack	6,181	16,010	805,859
Kolda	Kolda	8,112	21,011	593,199
Louga	Louga	11,270	29,188	507,572
Saint-Louis	Saint-Louis	17,034	44,117	656,941
Tambacounda	Tambacounda	23,012	59,602	383,572
Thiès	Thiès	2,549	6,601	937,412
Ziguinchor	Ziguinchor	2,834	7,339	398,067
TOTAL		75,951	196,712	6,982,084

Demography

Population (1992): 7,691,000.
Density (1992): persons per sq mi 101.3, persons per sq km 39.1.
Urban-rural (1988): urban 38.6%; rural 61.4%.
Sex distribution (1988): male 48.65%; female 51.35%.
Age breakdown (1988): under 15, 47.5%; 15–29, 26.1%; 30–44, 13.6%; 45–59, 7.8%; 60 and over, 5.0%.
Population projection: (2000) 9,519,000; (2010) 12,424,000.
Doubling time: 23 years.
Ethnic composition (1988): Wolof 43.5%; Fulani- (Peul-) Tukulor 24.1%; Serer 14.9%; Diola 5.3%; Malinke 4.3%; other 7.9%.
Religious affiliation (1988): Sunnī Muslim 94.0%; Christian, predominantly Roman Catholic 4.9%; traditional beliefs and other 1.1%.
Major cities (1992): Dakar 1,729,823; Thiès 201,350; Kaolack 179,894; Ziguinchor 148,831; Saint-Louis 125,717.

Vital statistics

Birth rate per 1,000 population (1991): 44.0 (world avg. 26.4).
Death rate per 1,000 population (1991): 13.0 (world avg. 9.2).
Natural increase rate per 1,000 population (1991): 31.0 (world avg. 17.2).
Total fertility rate (avg. births per childbearing woman; 1991): 6.2.
Marriage rate per 1,000 population: n.a.
Divorce rate per 1,000 population: n.a.
Life expectancy at birth (1991): male 54.0 years; female 56.0 years.
Major causes of death (percentage of officially confirmed deaths from infectious diseases only; 1988): malaria 44.8%; tetanus 17.8%; meningitis 15.3%; tuberculosis of respiratory system 10.4%.

National economy

Budget (1991–92). Revenue: CFAF 660,900,000,000 (1990; current revenue 86.0%, of which import duties 28.0%, personal and corporate income taxes 17.0%, value-added taxes 16.9%, personal property taxes 3.1%; aid, grants, and subsidies 13.9%). Expenditures: CFAF 660,900,000,000 (1990; debt service 22.4%; public services 16.0%; agriculture 13.9%; education 11.0%; defense 6.1%; transportation and communications 4.9%; public order and security 4.5%; industry 3.2%; health 2.3%).
Public debt (external, outstanding; 1990): U.S.$3,891,000,000.
Production (metric tons except as noted). Agriculture, forestry, fishing (1991): sugarcane 820,000, peanuts (groundnuts) 700,000, millet 560,000, paddy rice 160,000, corn (maize) 106,000, sorghum 85,000, cotton 41,000; livestock (number of live animals; 1991) 4,000,000 sheep, 2,813,000 cattle, 1,200,000 goats, 547,000 pigs; roundwood (1990) 4,480,000 cu m; fish catch (1989) 268,781. Mining and quarrying (1991): calcium phosphate 1,740,500; cement 503,300; aluminum phosphate 119,300[1]. Manufacturing (1988): peanut oil 202,200; wheat flour 103,600; nitrogenous fertilizers 68,000; soap 32,900; fresh fish 26,800; sugar 22,200; cotton fibres 19,200; canned fish 14,006; carbonated beverages 238,000 hectolitres; beer 170,000 hectolitres; footwear 561,400 pairs. Construction (authorized; 1988): residential 253,300 sq m; nonresidential 24,900 sq m. Energy production (consumption): electricity (kW-hr; 1990) 684,000,000 (684,000,000); coal, none (n.a.); crude petroleum (barrels; 1990) none (5,882,000); petroleum products (metric tons; 1990) 694,000 (704,000); natural gas, none (n.a.).
Population economically active (1990): total 3,146,000; activity rate of total population 42.9% (participation rates [1988]: over age 10, 46.2%; female 26.0%; unemployed 12.0%).

Price and earnings indexes (1985 = 100)							
	1985	1986	1987	1988	1989	1990	1991
Consumer price index	100.0	106.4	101.8	99.9	100.4	100.7	98.9
Hourly earnings index[2]	100.0	100.0	100.0	100.0	104.7	109.5	...

Household income and expenditure[3]. Average household size (1988) 8.8; average annual income per household (1975) CFAF 1,105,800 (U.S.$5,160); sources of income (1975): wages and salaries 51.6%, remittances and gifts 17.5%, pensions, social security, and related benefits 12.5%, other 18.4%; expenditure (1979): food and tobacco 57.5%, housing, maintenance, and utilities 18.4%, clothing 11.9%, transport 5.4%, other 6.8%.
Gross national product (at current market prices; 1990): U.S.$5,260,000,000 (U.S.$710 per capita).

Structure of gross domestic product and labour force				
	1990		1982	
	in value CFAF '000,000,000	% of total value	labour force[4]	% of labour force
Agriculture	326.5	20.5	10,654	9.1
Mining			1,918	1.6
Manufacturing	248.0	15.6	30,736	26.4
Public utilities			3,221	2.8
Construction	46.2	2.9	8,402	7.2
Transp. and commun.	150.5	9.5	24,789	21.2
Trade	388.6	24.5	14,648	12.6
Finance			7,921	6.8
Services	428.7	27.0	14,339	12.3
Pub. admin., defense				
Other	...	...	...	...
TOTAL	1,588.5	100.0	116,628	100.0

Tourism (1990): receipts from visitors U.S.$152,000,000; expenditures by nationals abroad U.S.$105,000,000.
Land use (1990): forested 54.8%; meadows and pastures 16.1%; agricultural and under permanent cultivation 12.2%; other 16.9%.

Foreign trade

Balance of trade (current prices)						
	1984	1985	1986	1987	1988	1989
CFAF '000,000,000	−203.1	−100.1	−93.0	−130.3	−169.6	−168.4
% of total	30.3%	21.4%	18.7%	28.8%	35.5%	27.6%

Imports (1989): CFAF 389,541,000,000 (petroleum products 17.1%; agricultural and industrial equipment 13.8%; rice 9.8%; transport equipment and parts 5.9%; pharmaceutical products 3.3%; paper and paper products 3.3%; wheat and wheat products 3.2%; dairy products 3.1%). *Major import sources:* France 31.8%; United States 7.3%; Italy 5.3%; Nigeria 5.0%; Côte d'Ivoire 4.7%; Spain 4.1%; Thailand 3.6%; Gabon 3.6%; West Germany 3.2%; The Netherlands 3.2%; Japan 3.1%; Pakistan 3.0%.
Exports (1989): CFAF 221,147,000,000 (peanut oil 14.2%; petroleum products 13.6%; crustaceans, mollusks, and shellfish 11.9%; phosphates 10.0%; canned fish 7.4%; fresh fish 6.6%). *Major export destinations:* France 35.0%; India 10.1%; Italy 6.7%; Mali 4.6%; Japan 4.1%; Spain 3.9%; The Netherlands 3.2%; Côte d'Ivoire 2.7%; Philippines 2.5%; Cameroon 1.8%; United Kingdom 1.3%; Greece 1.3%.

Transport and communications

Transport. Railroads (1992): length 562 mi, 904 km; (1987–88) passenger-mi 24,882,000, passenger-km 40,043,468; short ton-mi cargo 276,213,000, metric ton-km cargo 403,289,000. Roads (1988): total length 8,772 mi, 14,117 km (paved 27%). Vehicles (1989): passenger cars 90,000; trucks and buses 37,000. Merchant marine (1991): vessels (100 gross tons and over) 167; total deadweight tonnage 38,668. Air transport (1990)[5]: passenger-mi 144,276,000, passenger-km 232,329,000; short ton-mi cargo 26,971,000, metric ton-km cargo 39,374,000; airports (1992) with scheduled flights 9.
Communications. Daily newspapers (1990): total number 1; total circulation 45,000; circulation per 1,000 population 6.2. Radio (1991): total number of receivers 850,000 (1 per 8.8 persons). Television (1991): total number of receivers 60,000 (1 per 125 persons). Telephones (1991): 50,000 (1 per 150 persons).

Education and health

Education (1990–91)	schools	teachers	students	student/ teacher ratio
Primary (age 6–12)	2,458	13,394	708,299	52.9
Secondary (age 13–18)	321	4,791[6]	173,490	34.8[6]
Vocational	13	259[6]	6,435	24.6[6]
Higher	18	770[1]	18,862	19.3[1]

Educational attainment (1988). Percentage of population age 6–34 having: no formal schooling 62.6%; primary education 25.7%; secondary 8.4%; higher 0.8%; other 2.5%. *Literacy* (1988): percentage of total population age 15 and over literate 28.6%; males literate 38.8%; females literate 19.4%.
Health (1988): physicians 407 (1 per 17,072 persons); hospital beds 6,127 (1 per 1,134 persons); infant mortality rate per 1,000 live births (1991) 86.0.
Food (1987–89): daily per capita caloric intake 2,374 (vegetable products 91%, animal products 9%); 100% of FAO recommended minimum requirement.

Military

Total active duty personnel (1992): 9,700 (army 87.6%, navy 7.2%, air force 5.2%). *Military expenditure as percentage of GNP* (1989): 2.0% (world 4.9%); per capita expenditure U.S.$12.

[1]1988. [2]January 1; index refers to the *S.M.I.G.* (*salaire minimum interprofessionnel garanti*), a form of minimum professional wage. [3]Traditional African households in Dakar. [4]Wage earners, excluding armed forces only. [5]Air Afrique only. [6]1989.

Seychelles

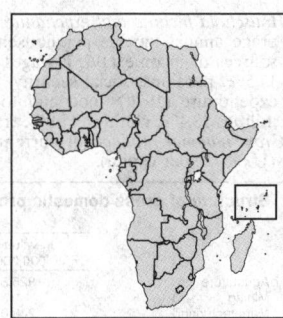

Official name: Repiblik Sesel (Creole);
Republic of Seychelles (English);
République des Seychelles (French).
Form of government: unitary
single-party[1] republic with one
legislative house (People's Assembly
[25[2]]).
Head of state and government:
President.
Capital: Victoria.
Official languages[3]: Creole; English;
French.
Official religion: none.
Monetary unit: 1 Seychelles rupee
(SR) = 100 cents; valuation (Oct. 5,
1992) 1 U.S.$ = SR 4.83;
1 £ = SR 8.30.

Area and population		area		population
				1987
Island Groups	Capital	sq mi	sq km	census
Central (Granitic) group				
La Digue and satellites	—	6	15	1,926
Mahé and satellites	Victoria	61	158	61,183
Praslin and satellites	—	16	42	5,002
Silhouette	—	8	20	191
Other islands	—	2	4	0
Outer (Coralline) islands	—	83	214	296
TOTAL		175[4]	453	68,598

Demography

Population (1992): 71,000.
Density (1992): persons per sq mi 405.7, persons per sq km 156.7.
Urban-rural (1990): urban 59.3%; rural 40.7%.
Sex distribution (1989): male 49.96%; female 50.04%.
Age breakdown (1989): under 15, 35.1%; 15–29, 31.5%; 30–44, 15.3%; 45–59, 9.2%; 60–74, 6.5%; 75 and over, 2.4%.
Population projection: (2000) 75,200; (2010) 80,900.
Doubling time: 43 years.
Ethnic composition (1983): Seychellois Creole (mixture of Asian, African, and European) 89.1%; Indian 4.7%; Malagasy 3.1%; Chinese 1.6%; English 1.5%.
Religious affiliation (1987): Roman Catholic 88.6%; other Christian (mostly Anglican) 8.5%; Hindu 0.4%; other 2.5%.
Major city (1987): Victoria 24,325.

Vital statistics

Birth rate per 1,000 population (1991): 24.2 (world avg. 26.4); (1989) legitimate 27.2%; illegitimate 72.8%.
Death rate per 1,000 population (1991): 7.7 (world avg. 9.2).
Natural increase rate per 1,000 population (1991): 16.5 (world avg. 17.2).
Total fertility rate (avg. births per childbearing woman; 1990): 2.8.
Marriage rate per 1,000 population (1984): 6.0.
Divorce rate per 1,000 population (1985): 0.7.
Life expectancy at birth (1991): male 65.0 years; female 75.0 years.
Major causes of death per 100,000 population (1985–89): diseases of the circulatory system 263.5, of which cerebrovascular disease 57.4; malignant neoplasms (cancers) 116.9; diseases of the respiratory system 77.1, of which pneumonia 49.0; accidents and adverse effects 44.4; infectious and parasitic diseases 42.9; diseases of the digestive system 40.5.

National economy

Budget (1992). Revenue: SR 1,172,000,000 (customs taxes and duties 42.6%, transfers from Social Security Fund 11.9%, business taxes 10.7%, dividends and interest 9.2%, administrative fees 7.0%, grants 5.7%). Expenditures: SR 1,185,500,000 (debt service 16.9%, capital projects 12.7%, education 11.5%, defense 8.0%, social security 7.2%, health 6.5%, tourism and transport 5.1%).
Tourism (1991): receipts from visitors U.S.$97,190,000; expenditures by nationals abroad U.S.$12,200,000.
Land use (1989): forested 18.5%; agricultural and under permanent cultivation 22.2%; built-on, wasteland, and other 59.3%.
Gross national product (at current market prices; 1989): U.S.$285,000,000 (U.S.$4,170 per capita).

Structure of gross domestic product and labour force				
	1990			
	in value SR '000,000[5]	% of total value	labour force[6]	% of labour force
Agriculture	80.0	4.4	2,199	9.4
Mining and manufacturing	168.5	9.2	4,302	18.3
Construction	77.4	4.2		
Public utilities	35.4	1.9	...	...
Transportation and communications	804.7[7]	44.0[7]	3,731	15.9
Trade	206.4	11.3	3,325	14.1
Finance	160.2	8.8		
Public admin., defense	247.9	13.6	8,937	38.0
Services	46.0	2.5		
Other	...	...	1,018	4.3
TOTAL	1,826.6[4]	100.0[4]	23,512	100.0

Production (metric tons except as noted). Agriculture, forestry, fishing (1990): coconuts 11,000, copra 2,000, bananas 2,000, tea 241[8]; livestock (number of live animals) 15,000 pigs, 5,000 goats, 2,000 cattle, 185,200[9] chickens; fish catch (1991) 5,746, of which (1989) jack 36.9%, snapper 20.8%, mackerel 6.7%, kawakawa 5.3%. Mining and quarrying (1985): guano 4,500. Manufacturing (1991): canned tuna 3,571; beer and stout 58,910 hectolitres; soft drinks 56,000 hectolitres; cigarettes 69,400,000 units. Energy production (consumption): electricity (kW-hr; 1991) 105,500,000 (105,500,000); coal, none (n.a.); petroleum, none (n.a.); petroleum products (metric tons; 1990) none (54,000); natural gas, none (n.a.).
Population economically active (1991): total 23,957; activity rate of total population 34.0% (participation rates [1985]: ages 15 and over, 57.4%[10]; female 42.4%; unemployed 20.6%).

Price and earnings indexes (1985 = 100)							
	1985	1986	1987	1988	1989	1990	1991
Consumer price index	100.0	100.3	102.9	104.7	106.4	110.6	112.7
Monthly earnings index	100.0	...	...	...	...	...	...

Public debt (external, outstanding; 1990): U.S.$146,000,000.
Household income and expenditure. Average household size (1987) 4.5; average annual income per household (1978) SR 18,480 (U.S.$2,658); sources of income: wages and salaries 77.2%, self-employment 3.8%, transfer payments 3.2%; expenditure (1983–84): food and beverages 53.9%, housing 13.6%, energy and water 9.1%, household and personal goods 6.6%, transportation 6.4%, clothing and footwear 4.2%, recreation 1.4%.

Foreign trade

Balance of trade (current prices)						
	1986	1987	1988	1989	1990	1991
SR '000,000	−447.2	−511.6	−546.4	−627.8	−692.3	−660.0
% of total	66.1%	67.3%	61.7%	63.9%	53.4%	56.7%

Imports (1991): SR 911,875,000 (manufactured goods 27.2%, of which metal manufactures 5.0%, paper products 2.3%; machinery and transport equipment 23.1%, of which electrical machinery and parts 4.6%, communications equipment 4.2%; mineral fuels, lubricants, and related materials 21.9%, of which petroleum products 20.7%; food and live animals 17.0%, of which cereals 4.5%, fish, crustaceans, and mollusks 3.2%, vegetables and fruits 3.1%; chemicals 6.0%; beverages and tobacco 2.2%; other 2.6%). *Major import sources:* South Africa 12.9%; Singapore 11.7%; United Kingdom 11.5%; Bahrain 10.8%; France 8.8%; Kuwait 5.4%; Japan 5.2%; United States 2.5%.
Exports (1991): SR 251,888,000[11] (petroleum products 60.2%[12]; canned tuna 25.1%; fish 7.0%; cinnamon bark 0.4%; copra 0.4%; food, beverages, tobacco, and chemicals 0.4%[12]). *Major export destinations*[13]: United Kingdom 51.2%; France 23.2%; Réunion 13.4%; Pakistan 1.2%.

Transport and communications

Transport. Railroads: none. Roads (1990): total length 191 mi, 308 km (paved 67%). Vehicles (1989): passenger cars 4,072; trucks and buses 1,321. Merchant marine (1991): vessels (100 gross tons and over) 8; total deadweight tonnage 2,661. Air transport (1991): passenger arrivals 98,000, passenger departures 101,000; metric ton cargo unloaded 2,387, metric ton cargo loaded 760; airports (1992) with scheduled flights 1.
Communications. Daily newspapers (1990): total number 1; total circulation 3,200; circulation per 1,000 population 47. Radio (1991): total number of receivers 30,000 (1 per 2.3 persons). Television (1991): total number of receivers 8,200 (1 per 8.3 persons). Telephones (1988): 13,937 (1 per 4.8 persons).

Education and health

Education (1992)				student/
	schools	teachers	students	teacher ratio
Primary (age 6–15)	25[14]	664	12,979	19.5
Secondary (age 16–18)	4[9]	520	7,406	14.2
Voc., teacher tr.	1[9]	179	1,684	9.4

Educational attainment (1987). Percentage of population age 12 and over having: no formal schooling 7.8%; primary education 51.5%; some secondary 12.2%; complete secondary 13.4%; vocational 9.9%; postsecondary 3.1%; unspecified 2.1%. *Literacy* (1987): total population age 12 and over literate 42,461 (84.8%); males literate 20,691 (83.4%); females literate 21,770 (86.1%).
Health (1991): physicians 71 (1 per 992 persons); hospital beds 411 (1 per 171 persons); infant mortality rate per 1,000 live births 12.9.
Food (1987–89): daily per capita caloric intake 2,340 (vegetable products 97%, animal products 3%); 100% of FAO recommended minimum requirement.

Military

Total active duty personnel (1991): 1,300 (army 76.9%, navy 15.4%, air force 7.7%). *Military expenditure as percentage of GNP* (1989): 4.2% (world 4.9%); per capita expenditure U.S.$206[15].

---

[1]Multiparty system approved December 1991; referendum on a new constitution scheduled for November 1992 with legislative and presidential elections to follow in December. [2]Includes two nonelected members. [3]As of July 1981, Creole replaced English and French as the prescribed national language, but, per official source, "all are still considered official languages." [4]Detail does not add to total given because of rounding. [5]At prices of 1989. [6]Excludes self-employed and domestic workers. [7]Includes import duties. [8]1991. [9]1986. [10]1987. [11]Includes SR 165,825,000 of reexports. [12]Items reexported. [13]Domestic export only. [14]1988. [15]At prices of 1987.

Sierra Leone

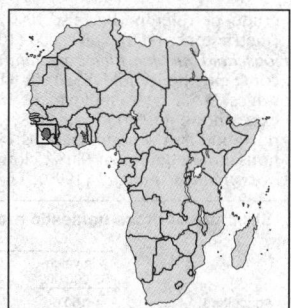

Official name: Republic of
 Sierra Leone.
Form of government: military regime[1].
Head of state and government:
 Chairman, Supreme Council of
 State.
Capital: Freetown.
Official language: English.
Official religion: none.
Monetary unit: 1 leone (Le) = 100
 cents; valuation (Oct. 5, 1992)
 1 U.S.$ = Le 493.38; 1 £ = Le 838.75.

Area and population		area		population
Provinces				**1985**
Districts	**Capitals**	**sq mi**	**sq km**	**census**[2]
Eastern Province	Kenema	6,005	15,553	960,551
Kailahun	Kailahun	1,490	3,859	233,839
Kenema	Kenema	2,337	6,053	337,055
Kono	Sefadu	2,178	5,641	389,657
Northern Province	Makeni	13,875	35,936	1,262,226
Bombali	Makeni	3,083	7,985	315,914
Kambia	Kambia	1,200	3,108	186,231
Koinaduga	Kabala	4,680	12,121	183,286
Port Loko	Port Loko	2,208	5,719	329,344
Tonkolili	Magburaka	2,704	7,003	247,451
Southern Province	Bo	7,604	19,694	740,510
Bo	Bo	2,015	5,219	268,671
Bonthe (incl. Sherbro)	Bonthe	1,339	3,468	105,007
Moyamba	Moyamba	2,665	6,902	250,514
Pujehun	Pujehun	1,585	4,105	116,318
Western Area[3]	Freetown	215	557	554,243
TOTAL		27,699	71,740	3,517,530

Demography

Population (1992): 4,373,000.
Density (1992): persons per sq mi 157.9, persons per sq km 61.0.
Urban-rural (1990): urban 32.2%; rural 67.8%.
Sex distribution (1990): male 49.12%; female 50.88%.
Age breakdown (1985): under 15, 41.4%; 15–29, 26.1%; 30–44, 17.1%; 45–59,
 10.3%; 60–74, 4.5%; 75 and over, 0.6%.
Population projection: (2000) 5,437,000; (2010) 7,172,000.
Doubling time: 26 years.
Ethnic composition (1983): Mende 34.6%; Temne 31.7%; Limba 8.4%; Kono
 5.2%; Bullom-Sherbro 3.7%; Fulani 3.7%; Kuranko 3.5%; Yalunka 3.5%;
 Kissi 2.3%; other 3.4%.
Religious affiliation (1980): traditional beliefs 51.5%; Sunnī Muslim 39.4%;
 Protestant 4.7%; Roman Catholic 2.2%; Anglican 1.2%; other 1.0%.
Major cities (1985): Freetown 469,776; Koidu–New Sembehun 80,000; Bo
 26,000; Kenema 13,000; Makeni 12,000.

Vital statistics

Birth rate per 1,000 population (1990–95): 48.1 (world avg. 26.4); legitimate,
 n.a.; illegitimate, n.a.
Death rate per 1,000 population (1990–95): 21.6 (world avg. 9.2).
Natural increase rate per 1,000 population (1990–95): 26.5 (world avg. 17.2).
Total fertility rate (avg. births per childbearing woman; 1990–95): 6.5.
Marriage rate per 1,000 population: n.a.
Divorce rate per 1,000 population: n.a.
Life expectancy at birth (1990–95): male 41.4 years; female 44.6 years.
Major causes of death per 100,000 population: n.a.; however, the major dis-
 eases are malaria, tuberculosis, leprosy, whooping cough, measles, tetanus,
 and diarrhea.

National economy

Budget (1990–91). Revenue: Le 18,499,000,000 (taxes 91.5%, grants 6.8%,
 nontax revenue 1.7%). Expenditures: Le 22,662,000,000 (recurrent expenditure 82.8%, development expenditure 17.2%).
Tourism (1990): receipts from visitors U.S.$19,000,000; expenditures by na-
 tionals abroad U.S.$7,000,000.
Production (metric tons except as noted). Agriculture, forestry, fishing (1991):
 rice 386,000, cassava 90,000, sugarcane 70,000, palm oil 58,700, pulses
 39,000, palm kernels 30,300, plantains 28,000, taros 28,000, coffee 26,000,
 cacao beans 24,000, millet 22,000, sorghum 22,000, tomatoes 21,000, peanuts
 (groundnuts) 21,000, sweet potatoes 11,000, corn (maize) 11,000; livestock
 (number of live animals) 330,000 cattle, 330,000 sheep, 184,000 goats, 52,000
 pigs, 6,000,000 chickens; roundwood (1990) 3,088,000 cu m; fish catch (1990)
 50,000. Mining and quarrying (1991): bauxite 1,180,000; rutile (a titanium
 ore) 154,800; diamonds 251,534 carats; gold 829 oz. Manufacturing (1990):
 salt 17,369[4]; nails 1975; beer and stout 59,590 hectolitres; mineral water 6,010
 hectolitres[5]; paint 2,000 litres; cigarettes 1,159,000,000 units[5]. Construction
 (value added in Le; 1988): 500,000,000. Energy production (consumption):
 electricity (kW-hr; 1990) 224,000,000 (224,000,000); coal, none (n.a.); crude
 petroleum (barrels; 1990) none (2,089,000); petroleum products (metric
 tons; 1990) 259,000 (213,000); natural gas, none (n.a.).
Household income and expenditure. Average household size (1983) 4.7; average
 annual income per household (1984): U.S.$320; sources of income (1984):
 self-employment 61.6%, wages and salaries 27.9%, other 10.5%; expenditure
 (1986): food, beverages, and tobacco 67.7%, housing 14.1%, transportation
 and communications 8.2%, clothing and footwear 2.8%, furniture, furnish-

ings, and household durable goods 2.2%, recreation, entertainment, and
 education 1.4%, health 1.1%.
Public debt (external, outstanding; 1990): U.S.$606,000,000.
Gross national product (at current market prices; 1990): U.S.$981,000,000
 (U.S.$240 per capita).

Structure of gross domestic product and labour force				
	1988			
	in value Le '000,000	% of total value	labour force[6]	% of labour force[6]
Agriculture	11,190.0	39.5	7,262	10.4
Mining	2,794.9	9.9	5,845	8.3
Manufacturing	1,355.0	4.8	8,616	12.3
Construction	500.0	1.8	7,259	10.3
Public utilities	99.2	0.4	2,713	3.9
Transportation and communications	2,567.0	9.1	7,718	11.0
Trade	5,870.0	20.7 }	5,058	7.2
Finance	2,607.9	9.2 }		
Pub. admin., defense	878.5	3.1 }	25,714	36.6
Services	417.0	1.5 }		
Other	...	...	...	...
TOTAL	28,279.5	100.0	70,185	100.0

Population economically active (1985): total 1,352,000; activity rate of total
 population 36.9% (participation rates: ages 15–64, 62.9%; female 33.7%;
 unemployed [registered; 1986] 9.0%).

Price index (1985 = 100)							
	1985	1986	1987	1988	1989	1990	1991
Consumer price index	100.0	180.9	504.1	676.9	1,088.5	2,296.2	4,654.0

Land use (1990): forested 28.8%; meadows and pastures 30.8%; agricultural
 and under permanent cultivation 9.1%; other 31.3%.

Foreign trade

Balance of trade (current prices)						
	1985	1986	1987	1988	1989	1990
Le '000,000	–149.8	–172.4	+752.8	–1,260.3	–1,327.9	+1,475.9
% of total	12.1%	4.6%	8.8%	15.9%	7.4%	3.6%

Imports (1990): Le 22,133,600,000 (1989; machinery and transport equipment
 33.5%; food and live animals 27.1%; basic manufactured goods 13.8%;
 minerals, fuels, and lubricants 11.6%; chemicals 3.6%). *Major import sources*
 (1985): U.K. 14.2%; W.Ger. 11.0%; China 10.1%; U.S. 5.9%; Japan 5.7%;
 The Netherlands 5.3%; France 3.2%.
Exports (1990): Le 20,914,700,000 (1989; rutile 47.0%; bauxite 18.2%; diamonds 14.8%; cacao 6.5%; coffee 5.7%). *Major export destinations* (1989):
 U.S. 26.6%; U.K. 22.3%; The Netherlands 11.8%; W.Ger. 8.6%; Switzerland
 2.5%.

Transport and communications

Transport. Railroads (1985): length 52 mi, 84 km. Roads (1989): total length
 4,660 mi, 7,500 km (paved 20%). Vehicles (1989): passenger cars 29,012;
 trucks and buses 10,173. Merchant marine (1991): vessels (100 gross tons and
 over) 59; total deadweight tonnage 12,817. Air transport (1985)[7]: passenger-
 mi 68,290,000, passenger-km 109,903,000; short ton-mi cargo 1,400,000, metric ton-km cargo 2,044,000; airports (1992) with scheduled flights 1.
Communications. Daily newspapers (1990): total number 2; total circulation
 10,000; circulation per 1,000 population 2.4. Radio (1991): 900,000 receivers
 (1 per 4.7 persons). Television (1991): 25,000 receivers (1 per 170 persons).
 Telephones (1990): 26,550 (1 per 160 persons).

Education and health

Education (1988–89)				
	schools	teachers	students	student/ teacher ratio
Primary (age 5–11)	2,262	12,972	433,604	33.4
Secondary (age 12–18)	232	5,263	104,452	19.8
Voc., teacher tr.[8]	16	475	6,086	12.8
Higher[8]	2	324	2,314	7.1

Educational attainment (1974). Percentage of population age 5 and over
 having: no formal schooling 81.3%; primary education 12.1%; secondary
 5.9%; higher 0.7%. *Literacy* (1990): total population age 15 and over literate
 478,300 (20.7%); males literate (30.7%); females literate (11.3%).
Health: physicians (1988) 300 (1 per 13,150 persons); hospital beds 4,025 (1
 per 980 persons); infant mortality rate per 1,000 live births (1985–90) 154.
Food (1988–90): daily per capita caloric intake 1,899 (vegetable products 96%,
 animal products 4%); 83% of FAO recommended minimum requirement.

Military

Total active duty personnel (1992): 6,150 (army 97.6%, navy 2.4%, air force,
 none). *Military expenditure as percentage of GNP* (1988): 0.7% (world 5.0%);
 per capita expenditure U.S.$1.

---

[1]Constitutional government overthrown April 1992; legislature dissolved May 1992.
[2]Preliminary figures exclude adjustment for underenumeration; adjusted total is
3,700,000. [3]Not officially a province; the administration of the Western Area is split
among Greater Freetown (the city and its suburbs) and other administrative bodies.
[4]1988. [5]1989. [6]Registered employment only. [7]International flights only. [8]1985–86.

Singapore

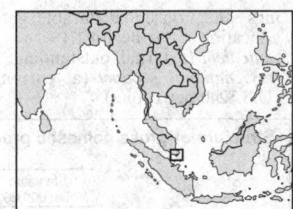

Official name: Hsin-chia-p'o
  Kung-ho-kuo (Mandarin Chinese);
  Republik Singapura (Malay);
  Singapore Kudiyarasu (Tamil);
  Republic of Singapore (English).
Form of government: unitary multiparty
  republic with one legislative house
  (Parliament [87][1]).
Chief of state: President.
Head of government: Prime Minister.
Capital: Singapore.
Official languages: Chinese; Malay;
  Tamil; English.
Official religion: none.
Monetary unit: 1 Singapore dollar
  (S$) = 100 cents; valuation (Oct. 5,
  1992) 1 U.S.$ = S$1.60; 1 £ = S$2.71.

Population (1990 census)

Census division[2]	population	Census division[2]	population	Census division[2]	population
Alexandra	27,245	Henderson	18,445	Nee Soon East	58,651
Aljunied	51,669	Hong Kah Central	48,379	Nee Soon South	49,771
Ang Mo Kio	35,814	Hong Kah North	33,265	Pasir Panjang	35,824
Ayer Rajah	44,977	Hong Kah South	37,900	Paya Lebar	41,903
Bedok	22,032	Hougang	36,774	Potong Pasir	32,992
Boon Lay	39,249	Jalan Besar	28,298	Punggol	68,270
Boon Teck	22,652	Jalan Kayu	34,907	Queenstown	19,676
Braddell Heights	47,738	Joo Chiat	35,777	Radin Mas	35,730
Brickworks	10,593	Jurong	74,696	Sembawang	28,039
Bukit Batok	44,918	Kaki Bukit	32,782	Serangoon Gardens	44,702
Bukit Gombak	46,149	Kallang	34,178	Siglap	36,022
Bukit Merah	18,666	Kampong Chai Chee	33,928	Tampines East	41,474
Bukit Panjang	95,827	Kampong Glam	29,481	Tampines North	73,634
Bukit Timah	47,056	Kampong Kembangan	33,510	Tampines West	38,833
Buona Vista	23,873	Kampong Ubi	40,682	Tanah Merah	32,314
Cairnhill	48,445	Kebun Baru	36,878	Tanglin	43,544
Changi	50,003	Kim Keat	28,538	Tanjong Pagar	29,217
Changkat	41,995	Kim Seng	23,683	Teck Ghee	26,622
Cheng San	27,821	Kolam Ayer	22,420	Telok Blangah	29,157
Chong Boon	32,174	Kreta Ayer	29,631	Thomson	71,345
Chong Pang	38,613	Kuo Chuan	26,968	Tiong Bahru	27,468
Chua Chu Kang	43,465	Leng Kee	28,886	Toa Payoh	22,811
Clementi	37,635	Macpherson	23,764	Ulu Pandan	42,923
Eunos	52,976	Marine Parade	31,003	West Coast	46,052
Fengshan	27,285	Moulmein	33,872	Whampoa	18,285
Geylang Serai	36,800	Mountbatten	23,891	Yio Chu Kang	28,589
Geylang West	34,560	Nee Soon Central	47,032	Yuhua	32,733
				TOTAL	3,016,379

Demography

Area: 240 sq mi, 622 sq km.
Population (1992): 2,792,000[3].
Density (1992): persons per sq mi 11,633.3, persons per sq km 4,488.7.
Urban-rural: urban 100.0%.
Sex distribution (1991): male 50.60%; female 49.40%.
Age breakdown (1991): under 15, 23.2%; 15–29, 26.4%; 30–44, 28.4%; 45–59, 12.8%; 60 and over, 9.2%.
Population projection: (2000) 3,006,000; (2010) 3,179,000.
Doubling time: 51 years.
Ethnic composition (1991): Chinese 77.7%; Malay 14.2%; Indian[4] 7.1%.
Religious affiliation (1991): Buddhist, Taoist, and other traditional beliefs 53.9%; Muslim 15.4%; Christian 12.6%; Hindu 3.6%; nonreligious 14.5%.
Major cities: Singapore has no separately defined cities within its borders.

Vital statistics

Birth rate per 1,000 population (1991): 17.3 (world avg. 26.4).
Death rate per 1,000 population (1991): 4.7 (world avg. 9.2).
Natural increase rate per 1,000 population (1991): 12.6 (world avg. 17.2).
Total fertility rate (avg. births per childbearing woman; 1991): 1.7.
Marriage rate per 1,000 population (1991): 9.0.
Divorce rate per 1,000 population (1990): 1.3.
Life expectancy at birth (1988): male 70.3 years; female 75.8 years.
Major causes of death per 100,000 population (1990): malignant neoplasms (cancers) 119.0; cardiovascular diseases 116.4; cerebrovascular diseases 60.4; diseases of the respiratory system 50.2; diabetes mellitus 12.1.

National economy

Budget (1991–92). Revenue: S$17,225,700,000 (tax revenue 63.2%, development fund account 20.0%, nontax revenue 13.3%, sinking fund account 3.4%). Expenditures: S$15,809,400,000 (administration 28.7%, defense 23.4%, debt servicing 16.9%, government development 14.2%, grants 9.6%).
Public debt (external, outstanding; 1989): U.S.$3,853,000,000.
Production (metric tons except as noted). Agriculture, forestry, fishing (1990): vegetables 8,000, fruits 1,000; livestock (number of live animals) 1,000,000 ducks, 4,000,000 chickens; fish catch (1991) 11,022. Mining and quarrying (value added in S$; 1990): granite 53,600,000. Manufacturing (value added in S$; 1990): electronic products and components 7,693,200,000; transport equipment 1,617,700,000; petroleum refining and petroleum products 1,587,400,000; fabricated metal products 1,234,500,000; nonelectrical machinery 1,165,900,000; industrial chemicals and gases 1,117,800,000; paints, pharmaceuticals, and chemical products 1,109,500,000. Construction (1990): residential 14,170 units; nonresidential 2,226,000 sq m. Energy production (consumption): electricity (kW-hr; 1990) 15,617,600,000 (14,194,300,000);

crude petroleum (barrels; 1990) none (299,511,000); petroleum products (metric tons; 1990) 34,396,000 (10,490,000).
Household income and expenditure. Average household size (1984) 3.9; income per household S$20,800 (U.S.$9,700); sources of income (1977–78): wages 75.4%, self-employment 18.7%, transfer payments 2.0%, other 3.9%; expenditure (1989): food 20.8%, recreation and education 14.5%, transportation and communications 14.4%, rent and utilities 9.3%, furniture and household equipment 9.0%, clothing and footwear 7.4%, health 4.1%.
Gross national product (1990): U.S.$33,512,000,000 (U.S.$12,310 per capita).

Structure of gross domestic product and labour force

	1991			
	in value S$'000,000[5]	% of total value	labour force[6]	% of labour force[6]
Agriculture	160.6	0.3	4,300	0.3
Quarrying	94.7	0.2	400	...
Manufacturing	17,431.4	28.6	429,600	28.2
Construction	3,690.5	6.1	99,000	6.5
Public utilities	1,281.1	2.1	7,100	0.5
Transp. and commun.	8,723.5	14.3	152,900	10.0
Trade	10,672.0	17.5	345,300	22.7
Finance	16,691.7	27.4	163,300	10.7
Services	6,173.5	10.1	322,300	21.1
Other	−4,023.1[7]	−6.6[7]	...	...
TOTAL	60,895.9	100.0	1,524,300[8]	100.0

Population economically active (1990): total 1,347,399; activity rate of total population 49.8% (participation rates: ages 15 and over, 63.1%; female 39.0%; unemployed 1.7%).

Price and earnings indexes (1985 = 100)

	1985	1986	1987	1988	1989	1990	1991
Consumer price index	100.0	98.6	99.1	100.6	103.0	106.6	110.2
Weekly earnings index	100.0	...	...	...	...	...	...

Land use (1989): forested 4.9%; agricultural 1.6%; other 93.5%.
Tourism (1990): receipts from visitors U.S.$4,362,000,000; expenditures by nationals abroad U.S.$1,381,000,000.

Foreign trade[9]

Balance of trade (current prices)

	1986	1987	1988	1989	1990	1991
S$'000,000	−3,384	−4,265	−4,159	−4,143	−8,559	−5,770
% of total	3.3%	3.4%	2.6%	2.3%	4.3%	2.7%

Imports (1991): S$114,194,900,000 (crude petroleum 10.0%, office machines 7.1%, telecommunications apparatus 6.6%, petroleum products 4.0%, electric power machinery 3.3%). *Major import sources:* Japan 21.3%; United States 15.8%; Malaysia 15.2%; Saudi Arabia 5.1%; Taiwan 4.1%; China 3.4%.
Exports (1991): S$101,879,500,000 (office machines 17.3%, petroleum products 13.9%, telecommunications apparatus 9.7%, clothing 3.0%, optical instruments 2.1%). *Major export destinations:* United States 19.7%; Malaysia 15.0%; Japan 8.7%; Hong Kong 7.2%; Thailand 6.3%; West Germany 4.2%.

Transport and communications

Transport. Railroads (1991): length 26 km. Roads (1990): total length 2,836 km (paved 97%). Vehicles (1991): passenger cars 300,116; trucks and buses 127,687. Merchant marine (1991): vessels (100 gross tons and over) 854; total deadweight tonnage 13,719,636. Air transport (1991): passenger-km 33,462,000,000; metric ton-km cargo 1,854,000,000; airports (1992) 1.
Communications. Daily newspapers (1990): total number 8; total circulation 813,484; circulation per 1,000 population 301. Radio (1991): 662,000 receivers (1 per 4.1 persons). Television (1991): 550,000 receivers (1 per 4.9 persons). Telephones (1988): 1,271,000 (1 per 2.1 persons).

Education and health

Education (1990)

	schools	teachers	students	student/ teacher ratio
Primary (age 6–11)	208	10,006	257,932	25.8
Secondary (age 12–18)	192	9,197	191,459	20.8
Voc., teacher tr.	23	1,558	29,102	18.7
Higher	7	4,615	55,562	12.0

Educational attainment (1980). Percentage of population age 25 and over having: no schooling or without primary six certificate 43.7%; primary education 38.3%; secondary 14.6%; postsecondary 3.4%. *Literacy* (1989): total population age 10 and over literate 1,982,523 (87.6%); males literate 1,070,594 (93.3%); females literate 911,929 (81.7%).
Health (1989): physicians 3,397 (1 per 779 persons); hospital beds 9,716 (1 per 272 persons); infant mortality rate per 1,000 live births (1991) 5.5.
Food (1987–89): daily per capita caloric intake 3,249 (vegetable products 77%, animal products 23%); 141% of FAO recommended minimum requirement.

Military

Total active duty personnel (1991): 55,500 (army 81.1%, navy 8.1%, air force 10.8%). *Military expenditure as percentage of GNP* (1989): 5.1% (world 4.9%); per capita expenditure U.S.$557.

[1]Includes six nonelected members. [2]The census divisions have no administrative function. [3]De jure population. [4]Includes Sri Lankan. [5]At prices of 1985. [6]Employed only. [7]Imputed bank service charges. [8]Detail does not add to total given because of rounding. [9]Import figures are f.o.b. in balance of trade and c.i.f. for commodities and trading partners.

Slovenia

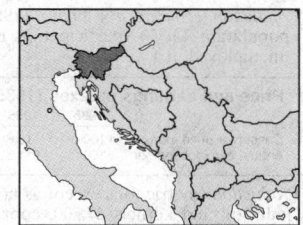

Official name: Republika Slovenija
 (Republic of Slovenia).
Form of government: multiparty
 republic with two legislative
 houses (State Council [40]; State
 Assembly [90]).
Head of state: President.
Head of government: Prime Minister.
Capital: Ljubljana.
Official language: Slovene.
Official religion: none.
Monetary unit: tolar; valuation
 (Oct. 12, 1992) 1 Yugoslav dinar
 (Din) = 0.42 tolars; 1 U.S.$ = 84.84
 tolars; 1 £ = 144.65 tolars.

Area and population (1991 census)

Districts	area sq km[1]	population	Districts	area sq km[1]	population
Ajdovščina	352	22,830	Metlika	108	8,197
Brežice	268	24,700	Mozirje	508	16,533
Celje	230	66,443	Murska Sobota	692	63,716
Čerknica	483	15,197	Nova Gorica	605	58,860
Črnomelj	486	18,301	Novo Mesto	759	59,171
Domžale	240	44,404	Ormož	212	17,656
Dravograd	105	8,582	Pesnica	169	18,137
Gornja Radgona	210	21,334	Piran	45	16,761
Grosuplje	421	28,282	Postojna	492	20,072
Hrastnik	58	11,096	Ptuj	645	68,846
Idrija	425	17,221	Radlje ob Dravi	346	17,026
Ilirska Bistrica	480	14,687	Radovljica	641	34,578
Izola	28	13,806	Ravne na Koroškem	304	27,499
Jesenice	375	32,108	Ribnica	256	12,733
Kamnik	289	28,927	Ruše	209	15,654
Kočevje	766	18,479	Šentjur pri Celju	240	19,317
Koper	273	45,218	Sevnica	293	18,784
Kranj	453	72,814	Šežana	698	23,838
Krško	345	28,615	Škofja Loka	512	38,622
Lasko	250	19,012	Slovenj Gradec	286	21,135
Lenart	204	17,144	Slovenska Bistrica	369	32,541
Lendava	256	26,120	Slovenske Konjice	222	22,206
Litija	328	18,986	Šmarje pri Jelšah	400	31,807
Ljubljana-Bežigrad	46	58,243	Tolmin	939	20,999
Ljubljana-Center	5	28,921	Trbovlje	58	19,372
Ljubljana-Moste Polje	152	72,235	Trebnje	308	17,731
Ljubljana-Šiška	156	83,310	Tržič	155	15,095
Ljubljana-Vič Rudnik	543	80,582	Velenje	182	42,688
Ljutomer	179	18,817	Vrhnika	169	19,458
Logatec	173	9,827	Zagorje ob Savi	147	16,825
Maribor	359	153,053	Žalec	349	39,688
			TOTAL	20,256	1,974,839

Demography

Population (1992): 1,985,000.
Density (1992): persons per sq mi 253.9, persons per sq km 98.0.
Urban-rural (1981): urban 48.9%; rural 51.1%.
Sex distribution (1981): male 48.56%; female 51.44%.
Age breakdown (1981): under 15, 23.0%; 15–29, 24.2%; 30–44, 20.6%; 45–59, 17.8%; 60–74, 10.1%; 75 and over, 4.3%.
Population projection: (2000) 2,055,000; (2010) 2,145,000.
Doubling time: not applicable; doubling time exceeds 100 years.
Ethnic composition (1981): Slovene 90.5%; Croat 2.9%; Serb 2.2%; Bosnian 0.7%; Magyar 0.5%; other 3.2%.
Religious affiliation (1991): most believers are Christians and are predominantly adherents of the Roman Catholic Church; other Christians are members of the Slovene Old Catholic Church, a few Protestant denominations, and the Eastern Orthodox Church; there are also small Islamic and Jewish communities.
Major cities (1991): Ljubljana 323,291; Maribor 153,053; Kranj 72,814; Ptuj 68,846; Celje 66,443.

Vital statistics

Birth rate per 1,000 population (1990): 12.1 (world avg. 27.1).
Death rate per 1,000 population (1990): 9.9 (world avg. 9.8).
Natural increase rate per 1,000 population (1990): 2.2 (world avg. 17.3).
Total fertility rate (avg. births per childbearing woman): n.a.
Marriage rate per 1,000 population (1989): 5.0.
Divorce rate per 1,000 population (1989): 1.1.
Life expectancy at birth (1980–82): male 67.0 years; female 75.0 years.
Major causes of death per 100,000 population (1989): circulatory diseases 426.2; cancers 206.6; accidents 94.9; respiratory diseases 73.9; digestive diseases 58.8.

National economy

Budget (1990–91). Revenue: Din 68,000,000,000. Expenditures: n.a.
Tourism (1990): receipts U.S.$852,000,000; expenditures, n.a.
Production (metric tons except as noted). Agriculture, forestry, fishing (1991): potatoes 407,000, corn (maize) 339,000, wheat 181,000, grapes 104,000, plums 8,000; livestock (number of live animals) 588,000 pigs, 533,000 cattle, 20,000 sheep, 12,766,000 poultry; roundwood (1990) 2,435,000 cu m; fish catch (1990) 6,912, of which freshwater 888. Mining and quarrying (1990): lead-zinc ore 137,000; kaolin and dolomite 14,000; pyrite concentrate 7,000; silver (refined) 1,400. Manufacturing (1990): cement 1,143,000; steel bars 167,000; aluminum ingots 100,000; soap and detergents 52,000; cold rolled steel 43,000; cotton yarn 19,000; hosiery 29,000,000 pairs; leather footwear 11,042,-

000 pairs; kitchen ranges 352,000 units; refrigerators 342,000 units; bicycles 238,000 units; televisions 191,000 units; telephones 109,000 units; passenger cars 74,000 units. Construction (residential units constructed; 1990): 7,759. Energy production (consumption): electricity (kW-hr; 1990) 12,399,000,000 (10,505,000,000); coal (metric tons; 1990) 5,583,000 (n.a.); crude petroleum (barrels; 1990) 22,200 (n.a.); petroleum products (metric tons; 1990) 571,700 (n.a.); natural gas (cu m; 1990) 24,000,000 (n.a.).
Gross national product (1990): U.S.$20,300,000,000 (U.S.$10,312 per capita).

Structure of gross material product and labour force

	1989		1990	
	in value Din '000,000	% of total value	labour force	% of labour force
Agriculture	2,599	6.2	19,434	2.5
Mining Manufacturing }	25,734	61.9	385,497	49.0
Construction	2,453	5.9	50,979	6.5
Public utilities	427	1.0	14,267	1.8
Transp. and commun.	1,909	4.6	46,419	5.9
Trade	6,721	16.2	97,981	12.5
Finance			36,934	4.7
Pub. admin., defense Services Other }	1,733	4.2 }	134,525	17.1
TOTAL	41,576	100.0	786,036[2]	100.0[2]

Population economically active (1991): total 747,000; activity rate of total population 37.8% (participation rates: ages 15–64, n.a.; female [1990] 47.2%; unemployed 12.3%).

Price and earnings indexes (1985 = 100)

	1984	1985	1986	1987	1988	1989	1990
Consumer price index	56	100	196	455	1,370	18,900	123,000
Earnings index[3]	91	100	114	108	96	113	79

Land use (1990): forest 50.3%; pasture 32.2%; agricultural 12.0%; other 5.5%.
Household income and expenditure. Average household size (1991) 2.8; income per household (1990) Din 161,589 (U.S.$14,277); sources of income (1990): wages 59.4%, transfers 17.5%, self-employment 14.5%, other 8.6%; expenditure (1988): food 27.6%, transportation 12.8%, housing 9.5%, clothing 8.9%, energy 6.6%, education and entertainment 5.9%, household durable goods 5.4%, drink and tobacco 4.7%, health care 4.2%.

Foreign trade

Balance of trade (current prices)

	1985	1986	1987	1988	1989	1990
Din '000,000	0.8	– 5.7	5.0	99.0	638.0	– 6,336.0
% of total	0.7%	3.0%	1.2%	6.3%	3.6%	6.4%

Imports (1990): Din 53,017,000,000 (raw materials and semifinished goods 33.1%; basic manufactures 23.4%; consumer goods 18.8%, of which food, beverages, and tobacco 4.2%, clothing and footwear 2.4%, medicines and pharmaceuticals 1.3%; machinery 11.7%, of which electrical motors 2.7%; mineral fuels 7.0%; transport equipment 2.0%). *Major import sources* (1991): Germany 23.2%; U.S. 18.1%; Italy 15.8%; France 9.0%; Austria 9.0%.
Exports (1990): Din 46,681,000,000 (machinery and transport equipment 38.1%; chemicals 8.9%; medicines and pharmaceuticals 4.7%; clothing and footwear 4.5%; furniture 3.8%). *Major export destinations* (1991): Germany 22.2%; Italy 19.1%; U.S.S.R. 13.3%; France 9.8%; Austria 5.4%; U.S. 4.6%.

Transport and communications

Transport. Railroads (1990): length, n.a.; passengers transported 19,970,000; cargo transported 19,303,000 tons. Roads (1991): total length 9,045 mi, 14,553 km (paved 72%). Vehicles (1990): passenger cars 583,923; trucks and buses 35,661. Merchant marine (1990): fishing vessels 42. Air transport (1991): passenger-mi 359,000,000, passenger-km 577,000,000; short ton-mi cargo 832,900,000, metric ton-km cargo 1,216,000; airports (1992) with scheduled flights 1.
Communications. Daily newspapers (1990): total number 3; total circulation 220,000; circulation per 1,000 population 112. Radio (1989): 687,000 receivers (1 per 2.9 persons). Television (1989): 528,500 receivers (1 per 3.7 persons). Telephones (1990): 656,932 (1 per 3.0 persons).

Education and health

Education (1990–91)

	schools	teachers	students	student/ teacher ratio
Primary (age 7–14)	822	12,402	226,463	18.3
Secondary (age 15–18)	145	6,633	94,062	14.2
Higher	28	2,555	33,574	13.1

Educational attainment (1981). Percentage of population age 15 and over having: less than full primary education 26.0%; primary 32.5%; secondary 34.5%; post-secondary and higher 5.9%. *Literacy* (1981): total population age 10 and over literate 1,584,500 (99.2%); males 99.3%; females 99.1%.
Health (1990): physicians (1989) 4,071 (1 per 481 persons); hospital beds 13,753 (1 per 143 persons); infant mortality rate per 1,000 live births 8.9.

Military

Total active duty personnel (1991): 60,000 (army 100%). *Military expenditure as percentage of GNP:* n.a.

[1]One sq km is equal to approximately 0.3861 sq mi. [2]Excludes 32,000 workers in the private sector. [3]Based on worker real net personal income.

Solomon Islands

Official name: Solomon Islands.
Form of government: constitutional monarchy with one legislative house (National Parliament [38]).
Chief of state: British Monarch represented by Governor-General.
Head of government: Prime Minister.
Capital: Honiara.
Official language: English.
Official religion: none.
Monetary unit: 1 Solomon Islands dollar (SI$) = 100 cents; valuation (Oct. 5, 1992) 1 U.S.$ = SI$2.97; 1 £ = SI$5.04.

Area and population		area		population
		sq mi	sq km	1991 estimate
Provinces	**Capitals**			
Central Islands	Tulagi	497	1,286	20,914
Guadalcanal	Honiara	2,060	5,336	60,692
Isabel	Buala	1,597	4,136	16,526
Makira	Kira Kira	1,231	3,188	25,307
Malaita	Auki	1,631	4,225	86,710
Temotu	Santa Cruz	334	865	16,500
Western	Gizo	3,595	9,312	64,732
Capital Territory				
Honiara	—	8	22	36,919
TOTAL		10,954[1]	28,370	328,300

Demography

Population (1992): 339,000.
Density (1992): persons per sq mi 30.9, persons per sq km 11.9.
Urban-rural (1986): urban 15.7%; rural 84.3%.
Sex distribution (1991): male 51.73%; female 48.27%.
Age breakdown (1991): under 15, 46.4%; 15–29, 27.2%; 30–44, 14.5%; 45–59, 7.8%; 60–74, 3.5%; 75 and over, 0.6%.
Population projection: (2000) 433,000; (2010) 569,000.
Doubling time: 20 years.
Ethnic composition (1986): Melanesian 94.2%; Polynesian 3.7%; other Pacific Islander 1.4%; European 0.4%; Asian 0.2%; other 0.1%.
Religious affiliation (1986): Christian 96.7%, of which Protestant 77.5%, Roman Catholic 19.2%; Baha'i 0.4%; traditional beliefs 0.2%; other and no religion 2.7%.
Major cities (1986)[2]: Honiara 35,288[3]; Gizo 3,727; Auki 3,262; Kira Kira 2,585; Buala 1,913.

Vital statistics

Birth rate per 1,000 population (1991): 40.0 (world avg. 26.4).
Death rate per 1,000 population (1991): 5.0 (world avg. 9.2).
Natural increase rate per 1,000 population (1991): 35.0 (world avg. 17.2).
Total fertility rate (avg. births per childbearing woman; 1991): 6.2.
Marriage rate per 1,000 population: n.a.
Divorce rate per 1,000 population: n.a.
Life expectancy at birth (1980–84): male 59.9 years; female 61.4 years.
Major causes of death per 100,000 population: n.a.; however, major diseases include malaria, tuberculosis, and leprosy[4].

National economy

Budget (1991). Revenue: SI$154,000,000 (taxes on foreign trade 46.8%, income taxes 29.2%, nontax revenue 14.3%, foreign grants 9.7%). Expenditures: SI$214,000,000 (administrative 33.2%, interest payments 12.6%, capital expenditure 10.7%).
Tourism (1990): receipts from visitors U.S.$4,000,000; expenditures by nationals abroad U.S.$11,000,000.
Land use (1989): forested 91.5%; meadows and pastures 1.4%; agricultural and under permanent cultivation 2.0%; other 5.1%.
Gross national product (at current market prices; 1990): U.S.$187,000,000 (U.S.$580 per capita).

Structure of gross domestic product and labour force				
	1991			
	in value SI$'000[5]	% of total value	labour force[6]	% of labour force
Agriculture	75,900	31.2	7,704	28.9
Mining	...	...	52	0.2
Manufacturing	16,100	6.6	2,061	5.8
Construction			1,071	4.0
Public utilities			341	1.3
Transportation and communications	19,700	8.1	1,580	5.9
Trade	31,300	12.9	2,849	10.7
Finance			781	2.9
Pub. admin., defense	55,700	22.9	3,290	12.4
Services			6,902	25.9
Other	44,300	18.2	...	...
TOTAL	243,000	100.0[1]	26,631	100.0[1]

Household income and expenditure. Average household size (1986) 6.4; average annual income per household (1983) SI$1,010[7] (U.S.$1,160); sources of income (1983): wages and salaries 74.1%, self-employment, remittances, gifts, and other assistance 25.9%; expenditure (1990)[8]: food 51.1%, drinks and tobacco 13.7%, housing 8.8%, transportation 8.4%, clothing 3.9%.

Population economically active (1986): total 39,210[6]; activity rate of total population 13.7% (participation rates: ages 15–60, 98.6%; female 25.4%; unemployed, n.a.).

Price and earnings indexes (1985 = 100)						
	1985	1986	1987	1988	1989	1990	1991
Consumer price index	100.0	113.6	126.1	147.2	169.1	183.9	211.6
Annual earnings index[6]	100.0	111.6	121.3	194.2	248.8	216.9	262.8

Production (metric tons except as noted). Agriculture, forestry, fishing (1991): palm oil and kernels 27,500, copra 23,700, cacao beans 4,600, coconut oil 3,200; livestock (number of live animals; 1990) 52,000 pigs, 13,000 cattle; roundwood 329,000 cu m; fish catch 49,500. Mining and quarrying (1989): gold 1,157 troy oz. Manufacturing (1991): processed fish 36,900; sawn timber 14,500 cu m; other major industries include soap and tobacco manufacturing, weaving, wood carving, fibreglass products, boatbuilding, and leatherworking. Construction (gross value in SI$; 1980): residential 1,858,000; nonresidential 693,000. Energy production (consumption): electricity (kW-hr; 1990) 30,000,000 (30,000,000); coal, none (n.a.); petroleum products (metric tons; 1990) none (53,000); natural gas, none (n.a.).
Public debt (external, outstanding; 1990): U.S.$108,000,000.

Foreign trade

Balance of trade (current prices)						
	1985	1986	1987	1988	1989	1990
SI$'000	+1,142	+10,562	−6,646	−32,710	−45,920	−18,340
% of total	0.6%	4.8%	2.5%	8.7%	11.7%	5.0%

Imports (1991): SI$142,300,000 (machinery and transport equipment 32.5%, manufactured goods 22.8%, mineral fuels and lubricants 20.6%, food 14.9%). *Major import sources* (1990): Australia 35.3%; Japan 16.3%; Singapore 14.4%; other Asian countries 11.3%; New Zealand 9.3%; United Kingdom 1.5%.
Exports (1991): SI$226,500,000 (fish products 47.0%, timber products 23.6%, palm oil products 7.8%, cacao beans 5.9%, copra 5.4%). *Major export destinations* (1990): Japan 39.2%; United Kingdom 23.4%; other Asian countries 14.2%; Australia 4.6%; The Netherlands 1.4%.

Transport and communications

Transport. Railroads: none. Roads (1987)[9]: total length 1,300 mi, 2,100 km (paved 8%). Vehicles (1986): passenger cars 1,350; trucks and buses 2,026. Merchant marine (1991): vessels (100 gross tons and over) 35; total deadweight tonnage 5,771. Air transport (1987): passenger-mi 7,000,000, passenger-km 12,000,000; short ton-mi cargo 25,000[10], metric ton-km cargo 37,000[10]; airports (1992) with scheduled flights 20.
Communications. Daily newspapers[11]: none. Radio (1990): total number of receivers 70,000 (1 per 4.6 persons). Television: none. Telephones (1989): 7,000 (1 per 44 persons).

Education and health

Education (1989)	schools	teachers	students	student/ teacher ratio
Primary (age 7–12)	468	2,248	51,436	22.9
Secondary (age 13–18)	20	307	5,556	18.1
Voc., teacher tr.[12]	2	63	465	7.4
Higher	—	—	—	—

Educational attainment (1986)[13]. Percentage of population age 25 and over having: no schooling 44.4%; primary education 46.2%; secondary 6.8%; higher 2.6%. *Literacy* (1976): total population age 15 and over literate 55,500 (54.1%); males 33,600 (62.4%); females 21,900 (44.9%).
Health: physicians (1988) 31 (1 per 9,852 persons); hospital beds (1986) 1,479 (1 per 193 persons); infant mortality rate per 1,000 live births (1991) 39.0.
Food (1987–89): daily per capita caloric intake 2,191 (vegetable products 90%, animal products 10%); 96% of FAO recommended minimum requirement.

Military

Total active duty personnel: no military forces are maintained, but a police force of 475 provides internal security.

[1]Detail does not add to total given because of rounding. [2]Ward populations. [3]1990. [4]Reported cases of these diseases in 1986 were: malaria 72,108, tuberculosis 337, and leprosy 260. [5]At 1984 factor cost. [6]Population employed in the monetary sector only. [7]Public-service earnings. [8]Retail price index components. [9]Includes 500 mi (800 km) of privately maintained roads mainly for plantation use. [10]1984. [11]In 1988 there were three weekly newspapers with a combined circulation of 10,000. [12]1986. [13]Indigenous population only.

Somalia[1]

Official name: Jamhuuriyadda Dimuqraadiga Soomaaliya (Somali); Jumhūrīyah aṣ-Ṣūmāl ad-Dīmuqrāṭīyah (Arabic) (Somali Democratic Republic).
Form of government: republic[2].
Chief of state: interim President.
Head of government: Prime Minister.
Capital: Mogadishu.
Official languages: Somali; Arabic.
Official religion: Islam.
Monetary unit: 1 Somali shilling (So.Sh.) = 100 cents; valuation (Oct. 5, 1992) 1 U.S.$ = So.Sh. 2,615; 1 £ = So.Sh. 4,446.

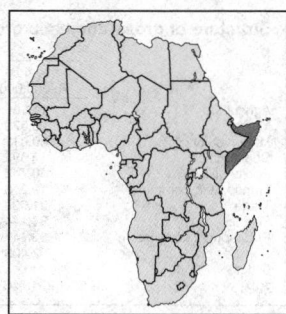

Area and population

Regions	Capitals	area sq mi	area sq km	population 1980 estimate
Bakool	Xuddur	10,000	27,000	148,700
Banaadir	Mogadishu (Muqdisho)	400	1,000	520,100
Bari	Boosaaso	27,000	70,000	222,300
Bay	Baydhabo	15,000	39,000	451,000
Galguduud	Dhuusamarreeb	17,000	43,000	255,900
Gedo	Garbahaarrey	12,000	32,000	235,000
Hiiraan	Beledweyne	13,000	34,000	219,300
Jubbada Dhexe	Bu'aale	9,000	23,000	147,800
Jubbada Hoose	Kismaayo	24,000	61,000	272,400
Mudug	Gaalkacyo	27,000	70,000	311,200
Nugaal	Garoowe	19,000	50,000	112,200
Sanaag	Ceerigaabo	21,000	54,000	216,500
Shabeellaha Dhexe	Jawhar	8,000	22,000	352,000
Shabeellaha Hoose	Marka	10,000	25,000	570,700
Togdheer	Burao	16,000	41,000	383,900
Woqooyi Galbeed	Hargeysa	17,000	45,000	655,000
TOTAL		246,000[3]	637,000	5,074,000

Demography[4]

Population (1992): 7,872,000.
Density (1992): persons per sq mi 32.0, persons per sq km 12.4.
Urban-rural (1990): urban 36.4%; rural 63.6%.
Sex distribution (1990): male 47.70%; female 52.30%.
Age breakdown (1990): under 15, 47.0%; 15–29, 23.4%; 30–44, 16.6%; 45–59, 8.6%; 60–74, 3.7%; 75 and over, 0.7%.
Population projection: (2000) 9,736,000; (2010) 13,114,000.
Doubling time: 24 years.
Ethnic composition (1983): Somali 98.3%; Arab 1.2%; Bantu 0.4%; other 0.1%.
Religious affiliation (1980): Sunnī Muslim 99.8%; Christian 0.1%; other 0.1%.
Major cities (1981): Mogadishu 500,000; Hargeysa 70,000; Kismaayo 70,000; Berbera 65,000; Marka 60,000.

Vital statistics[4]

Birth rate per 1,000 population (1985–90): 50.1 (world avg. 27.1); legitimate, n.a.; illegitimate, n.a.
Death rate per 1,000 population (1985–90): 20.2 (world avg. 9.8).
Natural increase rate per 1,000 population (1985–90): 29.9 (world avg. 17.3).
Total fertility rate (avg. births per childbearing woman; 1985–90): 6.6.
Marriage rate per 1,000 population: n.a.
Divorce rate per 1,000 population: n.a.
Life expectancy at birth (1985–90): male 43.4 years; female 46.6 years.
Major causes of death per 100,000 population: n.a.; however, major diseases include leprosy, malaria, tetanus, and tuberculosis.

National economy

Budget (1991). Revenue: So.Sh. 151,453,000,000 (domestic revenue sources, principally indirect taxes and import duties 60.4%; external grants and transfers 39.6%). Expenditures: So.Sh. 141,141,000,000 (general services 46.9%; economic and social services 31.2%; debt service 7.0%).
Tourism: receipts from visitors (1986) U.S.$8,000,000; expenditures by nationals abroad (1983) U.S.$13,000,000.
Production (metric tons except as noted). Agriculture, forestry, fishing (1991): sugarcane 240,000, sorghum 140,000, bananas 110,000, corn (maize) 100,000, vegetables 60,000, roots and tubers 51,000, sesame seed 40,000, beans 12,000, dates 10,000, rice 5,000, seed cotton 3,000, peanuts (groundnuts) 2,000; livestock (number of live animals) 20,500,000 goats, 13,800,000 sheep, 6,860,000 camels, 4,900,000 cattle; roundwood (1990) 7,133,000 cu m; fish catch (1990) 17,500. Mining and quarrying (1988): salt 30,000. Manufacturing (value added in So.Sh. '000,000; 1988): food 794; cigarettes and matches 562; hides and skins 420; paper and printing 328; plastics 320; chemicals 202; beverages 144. Construction (value added in So.Sh.; 1991): 51,100,000,000. Energy production (consumption): electricity (kW-hr; 1990) 230,000,000 (230,000,000); coal, none (n.a.); crude petroleum (barrels; 1990) n.a. (1,642,000); petroleum products (metric tons; 1990) 209,000 (264,000); natural gas, none (n.a.).
Household income and expenditure. Average household size (1980) 4.9; income per household: n.a.; sources of income: n.a.; expenditure (1983)[5]: food and tobacco 62.3%, housing 15.3%, clothing 5.6%, energy 4.3%, other 12.5%.
Public debt (external, outstanding; 1991): U.S.$1,880,000,000.
Gross national product (at current market prices; 1990): U.S.$946,000,000 (U.S.$150 per capita).

Structure of gross domestic product and labour force

	1991 in value So.Sh. '000,000	1991 % of total value	1987 labour force	1987 % of labour force
Agriculture	867,500	64.5	1,893,000	71.8
Mining	2,700	0.2		
Manufacturing	59,200	4.4	251,000	9.5
Construction	51,100	3.8		
Public utilities	9,400	0.7		
Transportation and communications	80,700	6.0		
Trade	125,000	9.3		
Finance	45,700	3.4	493,000	18.7
Pub. admin., defense	80,700	6.0		
Services	30,900	2.3		
Other	–8,100	–0.6		
TOTAL	1,344,900[3]	100.0	2,637,000	100.0

Population economically active (1987): total 2,637,000; activity rate of total population 42.3% (participation rates: over age 10, 63.1%; female 48.7%; unemployed, n.a.).

Price and earnings indexes (1985 = 100)

	1983	1984	1985	1986	1987	1988	1989[6]
Consumer price index	38.0	72.6	100.0	135.8	174.0	316.6	707.1
Earnings index	...	...	...	...	...	...	...

Land use (1990): forested 14.4%; meadows and pastures 68.5%; agricultural and under permanent cultivation 1.7%; other 15.4%.

Foreign trade[7]

Balance of trade (current prices)

	1986	1987	1988	1989	1990	1991
U.S.$'000,000	–317	–262	–224	–252	–328	–336
% of total	63.8%	59.1%	65.9%	60.3%	62.1%	58.3%

Imports (1991): U.S.$456,000,000 (1988; petroleum 33.1%, agricultural inputs [including fertilizers, pesticides, and seeds] 20.9%, food 10.5%, machinery and transport equipment 9.7%, manufactured raw materials 5.8%, construction materials 2.7%). *Major import sources* (1990): Italy 30.8%; The Netherlands 8.8%; Bahrain 6.0%; United Kingdom 5.9%; Djibouti 5.9%; China 4.9%; Germany 4.7%; Thailand 4.6%.
Exports (1991): U.S.$120,000,000 (live animals 56.7%, bananas 26.7%). *Major export destinations* (1990): Italy 28.7%; Saudi Arabia 23.4%; Yemen 19.1%; United Arab Emirates 10.7%.

Transport and communications

Transport. Railroads: none. Roads (1985): total length 10,697 mi, 17,215 km (paved 15%). Vehicles (1990): passenger cars 20,000; trucks and buses 12,000. Merchant marine (1991): vessels (100 gross tons and over) 27; total deadweight tonnage 18,900. Air transport (1989): passenger-mi 154,000,000, passenger-km 248,000,000; (1988) short ton-mi cargo 1,355,000, metric ton-km cargo 1,978,000; airports (1992) with scheduled flights, n.a.
Communications. Daily newspapers (1990): total number 1; total circulation, n.a. Radio (1991): total number of receivers 400,000 (1 per 19 persons). Television (1987): total number of receivers 3,000 (1 per 2,270 persons). Telephones (1988): 8,000 (1 per 882 persons).

Education and health

Education (1986–87)

	schools	teachers	students	student/ teacher ratio
Primary (age 6–14)	1,125	8,208	171,830	20.9
Secondary (age 15–18)	82	2,109	42,764	20.3
Voc., teacher tr.	21	498	4,809	9.7
Higher	1	262[8]	1,692	...

Educational attainment: n.a. *Literacy* (1990): percentage of total population age 15 and over literate 24.1%; males literate 42.7%; females literate 14.0%.
Health: physicians (1987) 323 (1 per 19,071 persons); hospital beds (1985) 5,536 (1 per 1,053 persons); infant mortality rate per 1,000 live births (1985–90) 132.
Food (1988–90): daily per capita caloric intake 1,874 (vegetable products 69%, animal products 31%); 81% of FAO recommended minimum requirement.

Military

Total active duty personnel (1992): following the 1991 revolution, no national armed forces had yet been formed. *Military expenditure as percentage of GNP* (1986): 3.2% (world 5.5%); per capita expenditure U.S.$6.

---

[1]Proclamation of a "Somaliland Republic" by the Somali National Congress May 18, 1991, on territory corresponding to the former British Somaliland (which unified with the former Italian Trust Territory of Somalia to form Somalia in 1960) has received no international recognition. The new entity would represent about a quarter of Somalia's territory and a quarter to a third of its population. [2]No effective central government in December 1992. [3]Detail does not add to total given because of rounding. [4]Population size, structure, and vital rates are as assessed by the United Nations in 1990, prior to the outbreak of civil war in early 1991. Data do not account for emigration of up to 1,000,000 refugees to surrounding countries (September 1992), massive internal refugee displacements, or estimated excess mortality of over 300,000 from starvation, violence, and disease during 1991–92. Total de facto population may be as low as 4,500,000 in late 1992. [5]Capital city only. [6]Third quarter. [7]Imports are c.i.f. [8]1980–81.

South Africa[1]

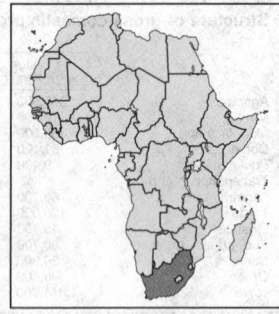

Official name: Republiek van
Suid-Afrika (Afrikaans); Republic of
South Africa (English).
Form of government: multiparty
republic with three legislative houses
(House of Assembly [178]; House
of Representatives [85]; House of
Delegates [45])[2, 3].
Head of state and government: State
President.
Capitals: Pretoria (executive);
Bloemfontein (judicial); Cape Town
(legislative).
Official languages: Afrikaans; English.
Official religion: none.
Monetary unit: 1 rand (R) = 100 cents;
valuation (Oct. 5, 1992)
1 U.S.$ = R 2.84; 1 £ = R 4.82.

Area and population[4]		area		population
		sq mi	sq km	1991 census
Provinces	**Capitals**			
Cape[5]	Cape Town	247,638	641,379	5,514,420
Natal	Pietermaritzburg	21,344	55,281	2,074,134
Orange Free State	Bloemfontein	49,166	127,338	1,929,392
Transvaal	Pretoria	87,658	227,034	8,630,396
National states				
Gazankulu	Giyani	2,535	6,565	688,681
KaNgwane	Louieville	1,476	3,823	445,976
KwaNdebele	KwaMhlangu	1,253	3,244	298,790
KwaZulu	Ulundi	13,928	36,074	4,507,038
Lebowa	Lebowakgomo	8,430	21,833	2,101,490
Qwaqwa	Phuthaditjhaba	253	655	313,874
TOTAL		433,680[6]	1,123,226	26,504,191[7]

Demography

Population (1992): 32,063,000.
Density (1992): persons per sq mi 73.9, persons per sq km 28.5.
Urban-rural (1991)[8]: urban 60.3%; rural 39.7%.
Sex distribution (1991)[8]: male 48.82%; female 51.18%.
Age breakdown (1991)[8]: under 15, 32.1%; 15–29, 29.4%; 30–44, 20.7%; 45–59, 10.5%; 60–74, 5.7%; 75 and over, 1.6%.
Population projection: (2000) 37,391,000; (2010) 44,785,000.
Doubling time[9]: 27 years.
Ethnic composition (1990): black 70.2%, of which Zulu *c.* 25.0%, Sotho (comprising 3 subgroups) *c.* 25.0%, Xhosa *c.* 10.0%, Tsonga *c.* 5.0%, Swazi *c.* 4.0%; white 16.3%; Coloureds 10.4%, of which Cape Malays 1.3%; Asian Indians 3.1%.
Religious affiliation (1991): Christian 67.9%, of which black independent churches 22.2%, Afrikaans Reformed 12.2%, Roman Catholic 7.8%, Methodist 6.2%, Anglican 4.0%, Lutheran 2.5%; Hindu 1.3%; Muslim 1.1%; not specified 28.1%; other 1.6%.
Major cities (metropolitan area; 1985): Cape Town 776,617 (1,911,521); Durban 634,301 (982,075); Johannesburg 632,369 (1,609,408)[10]; Pretoria 443,059 (822,925).

Vital statistics

Birth rate per 1,000 population (1991)[9]: 34.0 (world avg. 26.4).
Death rate per 1,000 population (1991)[9]: 8.0 (world avg. 9.2).
Natural increase rate per 1,000 population (1991)[9]: 26.0 (world avg. 17.2).
Total fertility rate (avg. births per childbearing woman; 1991)[9]: 4.4.
Life expectancy at birth (1991)[9]: male 61.0 years; female 67.0 years.
Major causes of death per 100,000 population (1988): malignant neoplasms (cancers) 70.2; diseases of the respiratory system 69.6; infectious and parasitic diseases 68.3; homicide and violence 55.4; accidents 49.1; cerebrovascular disease 47.6; ischemic heart diseases 40.2.

National economy

Budget (1991–92). Revenue: R 74,966,000,000 (income taxes 59.8%, sales taxes 25.9%). Expenditures: R 94,944,000,000 (education 15.7%, interest on debt 13.6%, economic services 10.6%, defense 10.3%, health 9.7%).
National debt (end of year, 1991): U.S.$41,767,000,000.
Production (in R '000,000 except as noted). Agriculture, forestry, fishing (in value of production; 1989–90): poultry and eggs 2,561, corn (maize) 2,495, beef 2,167, dairy products 1,588, temperate fruits 995, sugar 943, sheep and goat meat 832, wheat 800, wool 745, grapes 523; roundwood 19,361,000 cu m[9]; fish catch 878,580 metric tons[9, 11]. Mining and quarrying (in value of sales; 1990): gold 18,994, coal 8,149, platinum-group metals 2,322, iron ore 1,077, copper 1,064, diamonds 1,057[12], manganese 848, lime and limestone 423, chrome 421, nickel 269. Manufacturing (in value added; 1990): food and beverages 7,810; chemicals 6,614; iron and steel 6,013; transport equipment 5,148; metal products 4,376; paper and paper products 4,234; petroleum products 2,858; electrical apparatus 2,394; textiles 2,040. Construction (1989): residential 6,234,883 sq m; nonresidential 2,058,979 sq m. Energy production (consumption)[9, 13]: electricity (kW-hr; 1990) 164,518,000,000 (161,748,000,-000); coal (metric tons; 1990) 175,579,000 (132,979,000); crude petroleum (barrels; 1990) none (115,081,000); petroleum products (metric tons; 1990) 13,747,000 (10,530,000).
Land use (1990)[9]: forested 3.7%; meadows and pastures 66.6%; agricultural and under permanent cultivation 10.8%; other 18.9%.
Gross national product (1990)[9]: U.S.$90,410,000,000 (U.S.$2,520 per capita).

Structure of gross domestic product and labour force				
	1990		1991[8]	
	in value R '000,000	% of total value	labour force	% of labour force
Agriculture	11,886	5.1	1,004,986	9.8
Mining	25,079	10.7	679,981	6.7
Manufacturing	60,018	25.6	1,260,324	12.3
Construction	7,396	3.2	460,111	4.5
Public utilities	10,742	4.6	88,018	0.9
Transp. and commun.	19,276	8.2	437,385	4.3
Trade	31,620	13.5	1,218,145	11.9
Finance	34,144	14.5	444,598	4.4
Pub. admin., defense	32,147	13.7 }	2,339,345	22.9
Services	2,408	1.0 }		
Other	...	...	2,282,410	22.3
TOTAL	234,716	100.0[6]	10,215,303	100.0

Tourism (1990): receipts U.S.$1,029,000,000; expenditures U.S.$1,065,000,000.
Population economically active (1990): total 11,073,000; activity rate of total population 36.0% (participation rates: ages 20–64 [1985] 68.3%; female 33.2%; unemployed [1988] 9.8%).

Price and earnings indexes (1985 = 100)							
	1986	1987	1988	1989	1990	1991	1992[14]
Consumer price index	118.7	136.7	155.4	178.2	203.8	235.0	259.4
Monthly earnings index[15]	113.9	131.5	154.0	180.0	...	...	...

Household income and expenditure. Average household size (1983) 4.5; average annual income per household (1980) R 8,829 (U.S.$11,349); sources of income (1990): wages and salaries 76.0%, transfer payments 4.7%, other 19.3%; expenditure (1990): food 35.5%, transportation and communications 15.0%, clothing and footwear 9.4%, household goods 8.7%.

Foreign trade

Balance of trade (current prices)					
	1986	1987	1988	1989	1990	1991
R '000,000	+15,246	+15,167	+9,643	+13,888	+16,861	+18,476
% of total	22.1%	20.9%	10.9%	13.5%	16.0%	16.0%

Imports (1991): R 48,339,000,000 (machinery and apparatus 14.9%, transport equipment 14.1%, chemicals and chemical products 11.2%, textiles and clothing 5.2%). *Major import sources* (1990): Germany 19.7%; U.K. 11.8%; U.S. 11.4%; Japan 9.8%; not specified 25.6%.
Exports (1991): R 66,815,000,000 (gold 29.4%, base metals and metal products 14.4%, mineral fuels [mostly coal] 11.6%, precious stones [mostly diamonds] 10.1%). *Major export destinations* (1990): Switzerland 9.0%; U.K. 8.1%; Japan 6.4%; The Netherlands 5.4%; not specified 48.4%.

Transport and communications

Transport. Railroads (1990): route length 15,793 mi, 25,417 km; passenger-km 12,740,000,000[16]; metric ton-km cargo 100,437,000,000[16]. Roads (1990): length 115,420 mi, 185,751 km (paved 30%). Vehicles (1990): passenger cars 3,316,706; trucks and buses 1,461,573. Merchant marine (1991): vessels 231; total deadweight tonnage 283,756. Air transport (1991)[17]: passenger-km 8,369,687,000; metric ton-km cargo 190,926,000; airports (1992) 41[9].
Communications. Daily newspapers (1990): total number 19; total circulation 1,486,425; circulation per 1,000 population 48. Radio (1991): 10,000,000 receivers (1 per 3.8 persons). Television (1991): 3,445,000 receivers (1 per 11 persons). Telephones (1990): 5,017,000 (1 per 6.1 persons).

Education and health

Education (1990)	schools	teachers	students	student/ teacher ratio
Primary (age 6–12) } Secondary (age 13–17) }	20,348	245,525	7,027,068	28.6
Voc., teacher tr.	214	9,922	205,682	20.7
Higher[18]	17	40,156	286,910	7.1

Educational attainment (1985)[19]. Percentage of population age 25 and over having: no formal schooling 24.8%; incomplete primary education 41.6%; complete primary 4.8%; some secondary 22.1%; complete secondary 4.4%; higher 2.3%. *Literacy* (1984)[9]: percentage of adult population literate 50%; white 93%; Asian 69%; Coloured 62%; black 32%.
Health: physicians (1990) 23,379 (1 per 1,320 persons); hospital beds (1987) 141,790 (1 per 205 persons); infant mortality rate (1991) 51.0[9].
Food (1988–90)[9]: daily per capita caloric intake 3,133 (vegetable products 87%, animal products 13%); 128% of FAO recommended minimum.

Military

Total active duty personnel (1992): 72,400 (army 68.9%, navy 6.2%, air force 13.8%, intraservice medical service 11.1%). *Military expenditure as percentage of GNP* (1989): 4.4% (world 4.9%); per capita expenditure U.S.$125.

[1]Data exclude the South African-recognized republics of Bophuthatswana, Transkei, and Venda unless otherwise footnoted. [2]For representation of whites, Coloureds, and Asians, respectively. [3]Including 4, 2, and 2 nonelective seats, respectively. [4]Bophuthatswana, Ciskei, Transkei, and Venda had an area of 39,610 sq mi (102,589 sq km) in 1986 and a population of 6,780,000 in 1992. [5]Includes exclave of Walvis Bay. [6]Detail does not add to total given because of rounding. [7]Preliminary unadjusted figures; the 1991 census, adjusted for underenumeration, was estimated at 31,281,551. [8]Based on preliminary unadjusted census. [9]Includes Bophuthatswana, Ciskei, Transkei, and Venda. [10]1985 population of the 14 districts constituting the Witwatersrand region was 3,572,171. [11]1989. [12]1986. [13]Includes Botswana, Lesotho, Namibia, and Swaziland. [14]March. [15]Manufacturing only. [16]1989–90. [17]SAA only. [18]Universities only. [19]Includes Ciskei.

Spain

Official name: Reino de España
  (Kingdom of Spain).
Form of government: constitutional
  monarchy with two legislative
  houses (Senate [250[1]]; Congress of
  Deputies [350]).
Chief of state: King.
Head of government: Prime Minister.
Capital: Madrid.
Official language: Spanish.
Official religion: none.
Monetary unit: 1 peseta (Pta) = 100
  céntimos; valuation (Oct. 5, 1992)
  1 U.S.$ = Ptas 100.47;
  1 £ = Ptas 170.80.

Area and population

Autonomous communities	Capitals	area		population
		sq mi	sq km	1991 census[2]
Andalucía	Seville	33,694	87,268	6,859,958
Aragón	Zaragoza	18,398	47,650	1,178,521
Asturias	Oviedo	4,079	10,565	1,091,093
Baleares (Balearic Islands)	Palma de Mallorca	1,936	5,014	702,770
Canarias (Canary Islands)	Santa Cruz de Tenerife	2,796	7,242	1,456,474
Cantabria	Santander	2,042	5,289	523,633
Castilla–La Mancha	Toledo	30,591	79,230	1,650,083
Castilla y León	Valladolid	36,368	94,193	2,537,495
Cataluña	Barcelona	12,328	31,930	5,959,929
Extremadura	Mérida	16,063	41,602	1,050,490
Galicia	Santiago de Compostela	11,365	29,434	2,709,743
La Rioja	Logroño	1,944	5,034	261,634
Madrid	Madrid	3,087	7,995	4,845,851
Murcia	Murcia	4,370	11,317	1,032,275
Navarra	Pamplona	4,023	10,421	516,333
País Vasco (Basque Country)	Vitoria (Gasteiz)	2,803	7,261	2,093,415
Valencia	Valencia	8,998	23,305	3,831,197
TOTAL SPAIN		194,885	504,750	38,300,894
Enclaves in Northern Morocco				
Ceuta	—	7.1	18.5	68,288
Melilla	—	5.4	14.0	56,497
Other enclaves (plazas de soberanía)	—	0.26	0.66	...
TOTAL		194,897.79[3]	504,783.16	38,425,679

Demography

Population (1992): 39,085,000[4].
Density (1992): persons per sq mi 200.5, persons per sq km 77.4.
Urban-rural (1990): urban 78.4%; rural 21.6%.
Sex distribution (1992): male 49.10%; female 50.90%.
Age breakdown (1992): under 15, 18.4%; 15–29, 25.1%; 30–44, 20.6%; 45–59, 16.5%; 60–69, 10.1%; 70 and over, 9.3%.
Population projection: (2000) 39,879,000; (2010) 40,317,000.
Doubling time: not applicable; doubling time exceeds 100 years.
Ethnolinguistic composition (1989): Spanish 72.3%; Catalan 16.3%; Galician 8.1%; Basque 2.3%; other 1.0%.
Religious affiliation (1980): Roman Catholic 97.0%; Protestant 0.4%; nonreligious and atheist 2.6%.
Major cities (1991)[5]: Madrid 2,909,792; Barcelona 1,623,542; Valencia 752,909; Seville 659,126; Zaragoza 586,219.

Vital statistics

Birth rate per 1,000 population (1990): 10.2 (world avg. 27.1); (1988) legitimate 92.0%; illegitimate 8.0%.
Death rate per 1,000 population (1989): 8.5 (world avg. 9.8).
Natural increase rate per 1,000 population (1989): 1.7 (world avg. 17.3).
Total fertility rate (avg. births per childbearing woman; 1990–95): 1.7.
Marriage rate per 1,000 population (1990): 5.5.
Life expectancy at birth (1990–95): male 74.4 years; female 80.3 years.
Major causes of death per 100,000 population (1987): circulatory diseases 340.9; malignant neoplasms (cancers) 184.1; respiratory diseases 65.7.

National economy

Budget (1992[6]). Revenue: Ptas 12,577,000,000,000 (direct taxes 49.8%; indirect taxes 38.5%, of which value-added tax on products 24.6%; other taxes on production 11.7%). Expenditures: Ptas 13,702,000,000,000 (current transfers between public administrations 51.8%; wages and salaries 17.8%).
Production (metric tons except as noted). Agriculture, forestry, fishing (1990): barley 9,415,000, sugar beets 7,223,000, grapes 6,481,000, potatoes 5,399,000, wheat 4,760,000, corn (maize) 3,051,000, tomatoes 2,928,000, oranges 2,567,000, onions 1,063,000; livestock (number of live animals) 27,400,000 sheep, 16,910,000 pigs, 5,331,000 cattle, 3,200,000 goats; roundwood 17,758,000 cu m; fish catch (1989) 974,536. Mining and quarrying (metal content in metric tons; 1990): iron ore 3,012,000, zinc 252,700, lead 112,800. Manufacturing (value added, in Ptas '000,000; 1990): machinery and transport equipment 2,040,206; food products 1,493,404; chemical products 884,878; paper products 616,134; wood and cork products 345,187; clothing and footwear 312,705; textiles 308,653. Construction (1990): dwellings 281,059. Energy production (consumption): electricity (kW-hr; 1990) 150,622,000,000 (150,202,000,000); coal (metric tons; 1990) 35,813,000 (45,578,000); crude petroleum (barrels; 1990) 5,967,000 (380,239,000); petroleum products (metric tons; 1990) 46,774,000 (38,304,000); natural gas (cu m; 1990) 2,137,747,000 (9,448,105,000).

Gross national product (1990): U.S.$429,404,000,000 (U.S.$10,920 per capita).

Structure of gross domestic product and labour force

	1989		1990	
	in value Ptas '000,000	% of total value	labour force	% of labour force
Agriculture	2,226,400	5.0	1,685,900	11.2
Mining			480,800	3.2
Manufacturing	12,244,600	27.2	2,632,300	17.5
Public utilities			152,300	1.0
Construction	3,723,200	8.3	1,433,500	9.5
Transp. and commun.	...	...	772,300	5.1
Trade			3,076,100	20.5
Finance	26,871,300	59.7	725,100	4.8
Services			2,978,300	19.8
Pub. admin., defense				
Other	−80,500[7]	−0.2[7]	1,083,500[8]	7.2[8]
TOTAL	44,985,000	100.0	15,019,900[3]	100.0[3]

Public debt (1992[9]): Ptas 22,726,000,000,000 (U.S.$229,000,000,000).
Tourism (1990): receipts from visitors U.S.$18,593,000,000; expenditures by nationals abroad U.S.$4,254,000,000.
Population economically active (1991): total 15,073,100; activity rate of total population 38.6% (participation rates [1990]: ages 16–64, 64.9%; female 35.1%; unemployed 16.3%).

Price and earnings indexes (1985 = 100)

	1985	1986	1987	1988	1989	1990	1991
Consumer price index	100.0	108.8	114.5	120.0	128.2	136.8	144.9
Monthly earnings index	100.0	110.1	119.7	129.1	136.3	148.2	160.3

Household income and expenditure. Average household size (1983) 2.8; income per household (1983) Ptas 1,250,000 (U.S.$8,700); sources of income (1988): wages and salaries 47.8%, profits and self-employment 32.1%, social security 15.5%; expenditure (1987): food 25.2%, housing 14.0%, transportation 13.2%, clothing and footwear 9.5%, household goods and services 7.1%.
Land use (1989): forested 31.4%; meadows and pastures 20.4%; agricultural and under permanent cultivation 40.7%; other 7.5%.

Foreign trade

Balance of trade (current prices)

	1986	1987	1988	1989	1990	1991
Ptas '000,000	−814.5	−1,493.0	−1,954.7	−2,722.0	−2,765.4	−2,724.3
% of total	9.7%	15.1%	17.2%	20.6%	19.7%	19.6%

Imports (1991): Ptas 9,672,149,000,000 (machinery 13.8%; energy products 10.8%, of which crude petroleum 10.7%; agricultural products 10.2%; transportation equipment 9.2%). *Major import sources:* Germany 16.2%; France 15.2%; Italy 10.0%; U.K. 7.5%; Japan 4.7%.
Exports (1991): Ptas 6,225,665,000,000 (transport equipment 20.2%; agricultural products 15.0%; machinery 8.1%). *Major export destinations:* France 20.0%; Germany 13.9%; Italy 11.4%; U.K. 7.7%.

Transport and communications

Transport. Railroads (1991): route length 12,563 km; passenger-km 15,228,000,000; metric ton-km cargo 10,668,000,000. Roads (1990): length 324,166 km (paved 74%). Vehicles (1990): cars 11,995,640; trucks and buses 2,446,852. Merchant marine (1991): vessels 2,305; deadweight tonnage 5,831,699. Air transport (1990): passenger-km 22,116,000,000; metric ton-km cargo 785,952,000; airports (1992) with scheduled flights 25.
Communications. Daily newspapers (1991): total number 110; total circulation 3,005,000[10]; circulation per 1,000 population 77[10]. Radio (1991): 12,600,000 receivers (1 per 3.2 persons). Television (1991): 17,240,000 receivers (1 per 2.3 persons). Telephones (1987): 15,476,776 (1 per 2.5 persons).

Education and health

Education (1988–89)

	schools	teachers	students	student/ teacher ratio
Primary (age 6–11)	20,251	118,693	3,156,183	26.6
Secondary (age 12–18)	22,633	200,633	3,611,860	18.3
Vocational	2,668	63,236	1,234,045	19.5
Higher	789	55,504	1,101,297	19.8

Educational attainment (1981). Percentage of population age 25 and over having: less than primary education 46.1%, of which illiterate or no formal schooling 34.5%; primary 34.0%; lower secondary 9.3%; upper secondary 3.3%; higher 7.1%. *Literacy* (1988–89): total population age 15 and over literate 94.7%; males literate 97.0%; females literate 92.5%.
Health: physicians (1989) 143,803 (1 per 275 persons); hospital beds (1987) 195,772 (1 per 198 persons); infant mortality rate (1990) 7.7.
Food (1987–89): daily per capita caloric intake 3,567 (vegetable products 69%, animal products 31%); 145% of FAO recommended minimum requirement.

Military

Total active duty personnel (1991): 257,400 (army 70.7%, navy 15.5%, air force 13.8%). *Military expenditure as percentage of GNP* (1989): 2.1% (world 4.9%); per capita expenditure U.S.$200.

[1]208 seats are directly elected; 42 seats are indirectly elected by the parliaments of the autonomous communities. [2]Preliminary 1991 census; underenumeration estimated at about one million. [3]Detail does not add to total given because of rounding. [4]Estimate based on 1981 census. [5]For *municipios*, which may contain rural population. [6]Preliminary. [7]Import taxes and imputed bank service charges. [8]Includes 700,700 unemployed persons not previously employed. [9]June. [10]For 82 newspapers only.

Sri Lanka

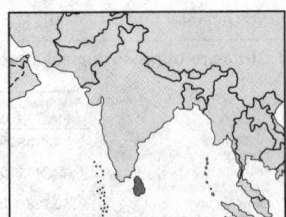

Official name: Sri Lankā Praja-
thanthrika Samajavadi Janarajaya
(Sinhalese); Ilangai Jananayaka
Socialisa Kudiarasu (Tamil)
(Democratic Socialist Republic of Sri
Lanka).
Form of government: unitary multiparty
republic with one legislative house
(Parliament [225]).
Head of state and government:
President.
Capitals: Colombo (administrative)
and Sri Jayewardenepura Kotte
(legislative).
Official languages: Sinhalese; Tamil.
Official religion: none.
Monetary unit: 1 Sri Lanka rupee
(SL Rs) = 100 cents; valuation
(Oct. 5, 1992) 1 U.S.$ =
SL Rs 44.06; 1 £ = SL Rs 74.90.

Area and population		area		population
Districts	Capitals	sq mi	sq km	1990 estimate
Amparai	Amparai	1,705	4,415	474,000
Anuradhapura	Anuradhapura	2,772	7,179	705,000
Badulla	Badulla	1,104	2,861	701,000
Batticaloa	Batticaloa	1,102	2,854	409,000
Colombo	Colombo	270	699	1,935,000
Galle	Galle	638	1,652	932,000
Gampaha	Gampaha	536	1,387	1,518,000
Hambantota	Hambantota	1,007	2,609	510,000
Jaffna	Jaffna	396	1,025	863,000
Kalutara	Kalutara	617	1,598	934,000
Kandy	Kandy	749	1,940	1,236,000
Kegalle	Kegalle	654	1,693	743,000
Kilinochchi	Kilinochchi	494	1,279	99,000
Kurunegala	Kurunegala	1,859	4,816	1,410,000
Mannar	Mannar	771	1,996	129,000
Matale	Matale	770	1,993	414,000
Matara	Matara	495	1,283	765,000
Monaragala	Monaragala	2,177	5,639	344,000
Mullaitivu	Mullaitivu	1,010	2,617	91,000
Nuwara Eliya	Nuwara Eliya	672	1,741	530,000
Polonnaruwa	Polonnaruwa	1,271	3,293	314,000
Puttalam	Puttalam	1,186	3,072	589,000
Ratnapura	Ratnapura	1,264	3,275	923,000
Trincomalee	Trincomalee	1,053	2,727	311,000
Vavuniya	Vavuniya	759	1,967	114,000
TOTAL		25,332	65,610	16,993,000

Demography

Population (1992): 17,464,000.
Density (1992): persons per sq mi 689.4, persons per sq km 266.2.
Urban-rural (1991): urban 21.6%; rural 78.4%.
Sex distribution (1989): male 50.97%; female 49.03%.
Age breakdown (1989): under 15, 35.3%; 15–29, 29.5%; 30–44, 18.0%; 45–59, 10.6%; 60–74, 5.2%; 75 and over, 1.4%.
Population projection: (2000) 19,190,000; (2010) 21,261,000.
Doubling time: 46 years.
Ethnic composition (1981): Sinhalese 74.0%; Tamil 18.2%; Sri Lankan Moor 7.1%; other 0.7%.
Religious affiliation (1981): Buddhist 69.3%; Hindu 15.5%; Muslim 7.6%; Christian 7.5%; other 0.1%.
Major cities (1990): Colombo 615,000; Dehiwala–Mount Lavinia 196,000; Moratuwa 170,000; Jaffna 129,000; Sri Jayewardenepura Kotte 109,000.

Vital statistics

Birth rate per 1,000 population (1991): 21.2 (world avg. 26.4); (1982) legitimate 94.6%; illegitimate 5.4%.
Death rate per 1,000 population (1991): 5.8 (world avg. 9.2).
Natural increase rate per 1,000 population (1991): 15.4 (world avg. 17.2).
Total fertility rate (avg. births per childbearing woman; 1991): 2.6.
Marriage rate per 1,000 population (1989): 8.4.
Divorce rate per 1,000 population (1988): 0.2.
Life expectancy at birth (1991): male 69.1 years; female 73.4 years.
Major causes of death per 100,000 population (1986): diseases of the circulatory system 101.9; violence and poisoning 77.8; diseases of the nervous system 45.3; respiratory diseases 36.1; infectious and parasitic diseases 32.2; malignant neoplasms (cancers) 27.7.

National economy

Budget (1991). Revenue: SL Rs 74,640,000,000 (sales and turnover tax 29.7%, import duties 24.5%, excise taxes 14.3%, income taxes 10.5%, nontax revenue 10.0%). Expenditures: SL Rs 135,190,000,000 (public-debt service 16.6%, transfer payments 16.2%, administration 12.7%, defense 8.7%, transport 5.2%, education 4.7%, power 3.9%, food and cooperatives 3.8%).
Public debt (external, outstanding; 1990): U.S.$4,709,000,000.
Tourism (1990): receipts U.S.$125,000,000; expenditures U.S.$79,000,000.
Production (metric tons except as noted). Agriculture, forestry, fishing (1991): rice 2,397,000, coconuts 1,800,000, sugarcane 860,000, cassava 410,000, tea 241,000, copra 110,000, rubber 102,000, sweet potatoes 80,000; livestock (number of live animals) 1,814,000 cattle, 981,000 buffalo, 526,000 goats; roundwood (1990) 9,129,000 cu m; fish catch (1990) 165,397. Mining and

quarrying (1989): quartz stone 961,000; limestone 608,000; clays 101,000; salt 100,000; titanium concentrate 80,000; gemstones U.S.$14,000,000. Manufacturing (value added, in SL Rs; 1990): textiles and apparel 27,930,000,000; food, beverages, and tobacco 21,955,000,000; petrochemicals 21,215,000,000; nonmetallic mineral products 7,554,000,000. Construction (1990): residential, 6,262 units completed. Energy production (consumption): electricity (kW-hr; 1990) 3,150,000,000 (3,150,000,000); crude petroleum (barrels; 1990) none (12,732,000); petroleum products (metric tons; 1990) 1,684,000 (1,264,000).
Gross national product (1990): U.S.$7,988,000,000 (U.S.$470 per capita).

Structure of gross domestic product and labour force				
	1990			
	in value SL Rs '000,000	% of total value	labour force	% of labour force
Agriculture	76,504	26.3	2,851,056	40.9
Mining	7,098	2.4	161,351	2.3
Manufacturing	43,128	14.8	868,500	12.5
Construction	21,541	7.4	183,398	2.6
Public utilities	3,652	1.3	13,409	0.2
Transp. and commun.	28,655	9.9	246,781	3.5
Trade	61,812	21.3	510,451	7.3
Finance	20,363	7.0	49,467	0.7
Pub. admin., defense	15,840	5.5 }	980,266	14.1
Services	11,902	4.1 }		
Other	—	—	1,104,109[1]	15.9[1]
TOTAL	290,495	100.0	6,968,788	100.0

Population economically active: total (1990) 6,968,788; activity rate 43.2% (participation rates: ages 15 and over 61.5%; female 37.3%; unemployed 14.4%).

Price and earnings indexes (1985 = 100)						
	1985	1986	1987	1988	1989	1990	1991
Consumer price index	100.0	108.0	116.3	132.6	147.9	179.7	201.6
Average wage index[2]	100.0	105.4	110.7	138.4	159.4	189.1	211.3

Household income and expenditure (1989). Average household size (1981) 5.2; income per household SL Rs 67,400 (U.S.$1,900); sources of income: wages 50.5%, property income and self-employment 40.0%, transfers 9.5%; expenditure: food and beverages 58.4%, transportation 14.2%, clothing 6.3%, housing and energy 4.7%, household furnishings 4.6%.
Land use (1990): forested 32.2%; meadows and pastures 6.8%; agricultural and under permanent cultivation 29.4%; other 31.6%.

Foreign trade

Balance of trade (current prices)						
	1986	1987	1988	1989	1990	1991
SL Rs '000,000	– 12,773	– 13,146	– 17,058	– 15,135	– 17,485	– 29,612
% of total	15.8%	13.8%	15.4%	11.9%	9.9%	14.9%

Imports (1990): SL Rs 107,727,500,000 (machinery and transport equipment 15.4%, petroleum products 13.3%, textiles 10.2%, sugar 4.8%, wheat 3.5%). *Major import sources:* Japan 12.1%; Iran 8.3%; U.S. 7.7%; Taiwan 5.8%; U.K. 5.1%; South Korea 4.8%; China 4.5%; Hong Kong 4.5%.
Exports (1990): SL Rs 79,480,800,000 (tea 24.9%, rubber 3.9%, precious and semiprecious stones 3.7%, desiccated coconut 1.8%, cinnamon 1.5%). *Major export destinations:* U.S. 24.8%; W.Ger. 6.4%; U.K. 5.8%; Japan 5.2%; Belgium 4.9%; Iran 3.3%; Egypt 3.0%; Singapore 2.5%.

Transport and communications

Transport. Railroads (1990): route length 1,453 km; passenger-km 2,484,700,-000; metric ton-km cargo 167,000,000. Roads (1990): total length 25,952 km (paved 81%). Vehicles (1990): passenger cars 173,519; trucks and buses 146,004. Merchant marine (1991): vessels (100 gross tons and over) 78; total deadweight tonnage 513,057. Air transport (1991): passenger-km 3,486,000,-000; metric ton-km cargo 98,700,000; airports (1992) 1.
Communications. Daily newspapers (1990): total number 15; total circulation 748,400; circulation per 1,000 population 44. Radio (1991): 2,200,000 receivers (1 per 7.8 persons). Television (1991): 700,000 receivers (1 per 25 persons). Telephones (1990): 166,000 (1 per 102 persons).

Education and health

Education (1990)				
	schools	teachers	students	student/ teacher ratio
Primary (age 5–10)	2,797	71,495	2,081,957	29.1
Secondary (age 11–17)	7,128	109,907	2,111,908	19.2
Voc., teacher tr.	25	641	18,971	29.6
Higher	34	2,171	41,951	19.3

Educational attainment (1981). Percentage of population age 25 and over having: no schooling 15.5%; less than complete primary education 12.1%; complete primary 52.3%; postprimary 14.7%; secondary 3.0%; higher 1.1%; unspecified 1.3%. *Literacy* (1986): percentage of population age 15 and over literate 84.3%; males literate 88.3%; females literate 80.1%.
Health (1990): physicians 2,571 (1 per 6,609 persons); hospital beds 47,738 (1 per 356 persons); infant mortality rate per 1,000 live births (1991) 25.
Food (1988–90): daily per capita caloric intake 2,246 (vegetable products 95%, animal products 5%); 101% of FAO recommended minimum.

Military

Total active duty personnel (1992): 105,900 (army 84.0%, navy 8.4%, air force 7.6%). *Military expenditure as percentage of GNP* (1989): 3.2% (world 4.9%); per capita expenditure U.S.$13.

[1]Includes unemployed. [2]Agricultural minimum rates.

Sudan, The

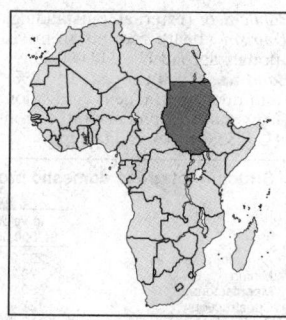

Official name: Jumhūrīyat as-Sūdān (Republic of the Sudan).
Form of government: military regime with one transitional legislative house (National Transitional Assembly [300])[1].
Head of state and government: Chairman, Revolutionary Command Council for National Salvation.
Capital: Khartoum.
Official language: Arabic.
Official religion: [2].
Monetary unit: 1 Sudanese pound[3] (LSd) = 100 piastres; valuation (Oct. 5, 1992) 1 U.S.$ = LSd 99.82; 1 £ = LSd 169.70.

Area and population

States	Capitals	area		population
		sq mi	sq km	1983 census
A'ālī an-Nīl (Upper Nile)	Malakāl	92,198	238,792	1,599,605
Baḥr al-Ghazāl (Bahr el-Ghazal)	Wāw	77,566	200,894	2,265,510
Dārfūr (Darfur)	al-Fāshir	196,404	508,684	3,093,699
al-Istiwā'īyah (Equatoria)	Jūbā	76,436	197,969	1,406,181
al-Kharṭūm (Khartoum)	Khartoum	10,875	28,165	1,802,299
Kurdufān (Kordofan)	al-Ubayyiḍ	146,817	380,255	3,093,294
ash-Shamālīyah (Northern)	ad-Dāmir	183,800	476,040	1,083,024
ash-Sharqīyah (Eastern)	Kassalā	128,987	334,074	2,208,209
al-Wusṭā (Central)	Wad Madanī	53,675	139,017	4,012,543
TOTAL		966,757[4]	2,503,890	20,564,364

Demography

Population (1992): 29,971,000.
Density (1992): persons per sq mi 31.0, persons per sq km 12.0.
Urban-rural (1990): urban 22.0%; rural 78.0%.
Sex distribution (1990): male 50.23%; female 49.77%.
Age breakdown (1990): under 15, 45.2%; 15–29, 26.1%; 30–44, 15.5%; 45–59, 8.6%; 60–74, 3.9%; 75 and over, 0.7%.
Population projection: (2000) 37,607,000; (2010) 49,040,000.
Doubling time: 23 years.
Ethnic composition (1983): Sudanese Arab 49.1%; Dinka 11.5%; Nuba 8.1%; Beja 6.4%; Nuer 4.9%; Azande 2.7%; Bari 2.5%; Fur 2.1%; Shilluk 1.7%; Lotuko 1.5%; other 9.5%.
Religious affiliation (1980): Sunnī Muslim 73.0%; traditional beliefs 16.7%; Christian 9.1%, of which Roman Catholic 4.4%, crypto-Christian 2.6%, Anglican 1.8%, Orthodox groups 0.2%; nonreligious 1.0%; other 0.2%.
Major cities (1983): Omdurman 526,287[5]; Khartoum 476,218[5]; Khartoum North 341,146[5]; Port Sudan (1990) c. 215,000[6]; Wad Madanī (1987) c. 145,000.

Vital statistics

Birth rate per 1,000 population (1991): 44.0 (world avg. 26.4).
Death rate per 1,000 population (1991): 13.0 (world avg. 9.2).
Natural increase rate per 1,000 population (1991): 31.0 (world avg. 17.2).
Total fertility rate (avg. births per childbearing woman; 1991): 6.4.
Marriage rate per 1,000 population: n.a.
Divorce rate per 1,000 population: n.a
Life expectancy at birth (1991): male 52.0 years; female 54.0 years.
Major causes of death per 100,000 population: n.a.[7].

National economy

Budget (1990–91). Revenue: LSd 14,457,000,000 (1987–88; tax revenue 60.9%, nontax revenue 39.1%). Expenditures: LSd 13,900,000,000 (current expenditures c. 68.0%, development budget c. 32.0%).
Tourism (1990): receipts from visitors U.S.$5,000,000; expenditures by nationals abroad U.S.$15,000,000.
Population economically active (1983)[8]: total 6,342,981; activity rate of total population 35.1% (participation rates: ages 15–64, 57.4%; female 29.1%; unemployed, n.a.).

Price and earnings indexes (1985 = 100)

	1984	1985	1986	1987	1988	1989	1990
Consumer price index	68.8	100.0	124.4	150.7	247.1	403.9	660.9[9]
Earnings index	...	...	...	...	...	...	...

Production (metric tons except as noted). Agriculture, forestry, fishing (1991): sugarcane 4,500,000, sorghum 2,941,000, wheat 680,000, millet 308,000, seed cotton 273,000, peanuts (groundnuts) 193,000, cottonseed 162,000, yams 128,000, sesame seeds 97,000, cotton lint 91,000, gum arabic 30,200[10]; livestock (number of live animals) 21,028,000 cattle, 20,700,000 sheep, 15,277,000 goats, 2,757,000 camels; roundwood (1990) 22,827,000 cu m; fish catch (1990) 38,848. Mining and quarrying (1989): salt 91,000; chromite concentrate 25,000; gold 20,900 troy oz. Manufacturing (1989): wheat flour 733,900; refined sugar 356,200; cement 171,200; plastics 12,195[11]; yarn 9,700[11]; perfumes 2,500[11]; textiles 58,600,000 m[11]; cigarettes 1,300,000,000 units; tires and tubes 256,300 units. Construction: n.a. Energy production (consumption): electricity (kW-hr; 1990) 1,327,000,000 (1,327,000,000); coal, none (none); crude petroleum (barrels; 1990) none (7,440,000); petroleum products (metric tons; 1990) 836,000 (1,036,000); natural gas, none (none).
Gross national product (1988): U.S.$10,094,000,000 (U.S.$420 per capita).

Structure of gross domestic product and labour force

	1988–89		1983	
	in value LSd '000,000	% of total value	labour force[8]	% of labour force[8]
Agriculture	26,450	36.0	4,028,705	63.5
Mining	} 6,030	} 8.2	6,534	0.1
Manufacturing			266,693	4.2
Construction	3,330	4.5	139,282	2.2
Public utilities	1,320	1.8	43,728	0.7
Transportation and communications	...	...	215,474	3.4
Trade and finance	...	...	314,676	5.0
Pub. admin., defense	8,630	11.7	} 550,409	} 8.7
Services	27,800	37.8		
Other	...	...	777,480[12]	12.2[12]
TOTAL	73,560	100.0	6,342,981	100.0

Household income and expenditure. Average household size (1980) 5.3; income per household: n.a.[13]; sources of income: n.a.; expenditure (1983): food and beverages 63.6%, housing 11.5%, household goods 5.5%, clothing and footwear 5.3%, health care 4.1%, energy 3.8%.
Public debt (external, outstanding; 1990): U.S.$9,440,000,000.
Land use (1990): forested 18.9%; meadows and pastures 46.3%; agricultural and under permanent cultivation 5.4%; desert and other 29.4%.

Foreign trade[14]

Balance of trade (current prices)

	1986	1987	1988	1989	1990	1991
LSd '000,000	−1,569	−1,116	−2,482	−2,991	−3,009	−5,760
% of total	48.5%	27.2%	35.1%	33.1%	39.3%	59.7%

Imports (1989): LSd 6,014,000,000 (basic manufactures 23.1%, machinery 17.1%, transport equipment 13.3%, chemicals and medicines 7.6%, wheat and wheat flour 5.4%, coffee and tea 4.2%). *Major import sources* (1991)[15]: Saudi Arabia 13.5%; United Kingdom 10.3%; Italy 8.5%; Germany 7.8%; China 7.6%; United States 7.2%; Japan 4.1%.
Exports (1989): LSd 3,023,000,000 (cotton 44.6%, sesame seeds 11.0%, gum arabic 10.4%, sorghum 9.8%, livestock 6.4%, hides and skins 3.8%). *Major export destinations* (1991)[16]: Thailand 17.3%; former U.S.S.R. 10.9%; Saudi Arabia 10.0%; Italy 9.5%; Germany 8.8%; Japan 7.8%; France 5.1%.

Transport and communications

Transport. Railroads (1988): route length (1990) 2,936 mi, 4,725 km; passenger-mi 414,000,000, passenger-km 667,000,000; short ton-mi cargo 434,000,000, metric ton-km cargo 633,000,000. Roads (1985): total length 6,599 km (paved 59%). Vehicles (1990): passenger cars 116,473; trucks and buses 56,949. Merchant marine (1991): vessels (100 gross tons and over) 16; total deadweight tonnage 62,244. Air transport (1991)[17]: passenger-mi 264,500,000, passenger-km 425,600,000; short ton-mi cargo 7,758,000, metric ton-km cargo 11,327,000; airports (1992) with scheduled flights 12.
Communications. Daily newspapers (1990): total number 5; total circulation 590,000[18]; circulation per 1,000 population 21[18]. Radio (1991): 6,000,000 receivers (1 per 4.9 persons). Television (1991): 250,000 receivers (1 per 117 persons). Telephones (1988): 76,347 (1 per 338 persons).

Education and health

Education (1990–91)

	schools	teachers	students	student/ teacher ratio
Primary (age 7–12)	8,109	60,674	2,165,566	35.7
Secondary (age 13–18)	2,514	25,134	446,981	17.8
Voc., teacher tr.	96	1,906	33,685	17.7
Higher	20	3,397	58,566	17.2

Educational attainment: n.a. Literacy (1990): total population age 15 and over literate 3,750,000 (27.1%); males 2,940,000 (42.7%); females 810,000 (11.7%).
Health (1986): physicians 2,405[19] (1 per 10,130 persons); hospital beds 18,571 (1 per 1,311 persons); infant mortality rate (1991) 85.
Food (1988–90): daily per capita caloric intake 2,043 (vegetable products 83%, animal products 17%); 87% of FAO recommended minimum.

Military

Total active duty personnel (1992): 82,500[20] (army 90.9%, navy 1.8%, air force 7.3%). *Military expenditure as percentage of GNP* (1989): 2.2% (world 4.9%); per capita expenditure U.S.$12.

[1]Initial seats filled February 1992; all seats are to be occupied by early 1993. [2]Islam was being imposed in 1992. [3]A new currency, the Sudanese dinar (introduced on May 18, 1992, at a value equal to 10 Sudanese pounds), will gradually replace the Sudanese pound. [4]Detail does not add to total given because of rounding. [5]Khartoum urban agglomeration: 1990 est. (including Omdurman and Khartoum North) 1,950,000; 1992 est. (including Omdurman, Khartoum North, squatters, and displaced persons from southern Sudan) c. 3,000,000–4,000,000. [6]Excluding about 300,000 refugees from Eritrea. [7]According to UN estimates 7,600,000 Sudanese were threatened with starvation in 1992. [8]Excludes nomads, the homeless, and institutionalized persons. [9]Average of 2nd and 3rd quarters. [10]1990. [11]1986–87. [12]Includes 592,759 unemployed not previously employed. [13]Average annual income of paid worker (1992) U.S.$216. [14]Imports c.i.f.; exports f.o.b. [15]Based on estimated imports of LSd 7,704,000,000. [16]Based on estimated exports of LSd 1,944,000,000. [17]Sudan Airways only. [18]Four newspapers only. [19]Government-employed only. [20]Excludes 85,000-member Islamic paramilitary group.

Suriname

Official name: Republiek Suriname
(Republic of Suriname).
Form of government: multiparty
republic with one legislative house
(National Assembly [51]).
Head of state and government:
President.
Capital: Paramaribo.
Official language: Dutch.
Official religion: none.
Monetary unit: 1 Suriname guilder
(Sf) = 100 cents; valuation (Oct.
5, 1992) 1 U.S.$ = Sf 1.79;
1 £ = Sf 3.03.

Area and population		area		population
				1980
Districts	**Capitals**	sq mi	sq km	census[1]
Brokopondo	Brokopondo	8,278	21,440	20,249
Commewijne	Nieuw Amsterdam	1,587	4,110	14,351
Coronie	Totness	626	1,620	2,777
Marowijne	Albina	17,753	45,980	23,402
Nickerie	Nieuw Nickerie	24,946	64,610	34,480
Para	Onverwacht	378	980	14,867
Saramacca	Groningen	9,042	23,420	10,335
Suriname	...	629	1,628	166,494
Town district				
Paramaribo	Paramaribo	12	32	67,905
TOTAL		63,251[2]	163,820[2]	354,860

Demography

Population (1992): 404,000.
Density (1992): persons per sq mi 6.4, persons per sq km 2.5.
Urban-rural (1988): urban 65.2%; rural 34.8%.
Sex distribution (1990): male 49.53%; female 50.47%.
Age breakdown (1991): under 15, 33.9%; 15–29, 32.8%; 30–44, 17.4%; 45–59, 9.8%; 60–74, 4.9%; 75 and over, 1.2%.
Population projection: (2000) 408,000; (2010) 416,000.
Doubling time: 41 years.
Ethnic composition (1983): Indo-Pakistani 37.0%; Suriname Creole 31.3%; Javanese 14.2%; Bush Negro 8.5%; Amerindian 3.1%; Chinese 2.8%; Dutch 1.4%; other 1.7%.
Religious affiliation (1983): Hindu 26.0%; Roman Catholic 21.6%; Muslim 18.6%; Protestant (mostly Moravian) 18.0%; other 15.8%.
Major cities (1980): Paramaribo 192,109[3]; Nieuw Nickerie 6,078; Meerzorg 5,355; Marienburg 3,633.

Vital statistics

Birth rate per 1,000 population (1988): 23.2 (world avg. 27.1); legitimate, n.a.; illegitimate, n.a.
Death rate per 1,000 population (1988): 6.1 (world avg. 9.8).
Natural increase rate per 1,000 population (1988): 17.1 (world avg. 17.3).
Total fertility rate (avg. births per childbearing woman; 1990–95): 2.6.
Marriage rate per 1,000 population (1985): 6.1.
Divorce rate per 1,000 population (1985): 1.5.
Life expectancy at birth (1985–90): male 67.1 years; female 72.1 years.
Major causes of death per 100,000 population (1985): diseases of the circulatory system 149.1, of which ischemic heart disease 51.6, diseases of pulmonary circulation and other forms of heart disease 41.9; malignant neoplasms (cancers) 48.0; diseases of the respiratory system 42.2; ill-defined conditions 67.6.

National economy

Budget (1989). Revenue: Sf 836,600,000 (direct taxes 37.8%; indirect taxes 27.5%; bauxite levy 22.9%; grants 6.0%; aid 5.7%). Expenditures: Sf 1,206,-500,000 (current expenditures 94.8%, of which general public services 46.6%, transfers 12.1%, debt service 11.2%; capital expenditures 5.2%).
Production (metric tons except as noted). Agriculture, forestry, fishing (1991): rice 190,000, bananas 49,000, sugarcane 45,000, oranges 14,000, coconuts 11,000, plantains 8,000, cassava 3,000, tomatoes 3,000, cucumbers 3,000, palm oil 1,500; livestock (number of live animals) 90,000 cattle, 25,000 pigs; roundwood 149,000 cu m; fish catch 4,000. Mining and quarrying (1990): bauxite 3,267,000; gold 707 troy oz. Manufacturing (1988): cement 33,933; aluminum 9,800; palm oil 1,667; alumina 1,632; sugar 307; plywood 1,338 cu m; shoes 115,123 pairs; soft drinks 296,280 hectolitres; beer 98,870 hectolitres; cigarettes 501,000,000 units. Construction (buildings authorized; 1985): residential Sf 46,500,000; nonresidential Sf 8,100,000. Energy production (consumption): electricity (kW-hr; 1990) 1,350,000,000 (1,350,000,000); hard coal (metric tons; 1989) none (1,000); crude petroleum (barrels; 1990) 1,705,000 (1,096,000); petroleum products (metric tons; 1990) none (437,-000); natural gas, none (none).
Population economically active (1985): total 99,240; activity rate of total population 25.9% (participation rates [1980]: ages 10–64, 38.7%; female 27.2%; unemployed [1989] 15.6%).

Price and earnings indexes (1985 = 100)						
	1984	1985	1986	1987	1988	1989	1990
Consumer price index[4]	90.1	100.0	118.7	182.0	195.4	196.9	239.7
Earnings index	...	...	...	...	...	...	...

Public debt (external, outstanding; 1986): U.S.$69,600,000.
Tourism (1990): receipts from visitors U.S.$11,000,000; expenditures by nationals abroad U.S.$12,000,000.
Land use (1990): forested 95.3%; meadows and pastures 0.1%; agricultural and under permanent cultivation 0.4%; other 4.2%.
Gross national product (at current market prices; 1990): U.S.$1,365,000,000 (U.S.$3,050 per capita).

Structure of gross domestic product and labour force				
	1988		1985	
	in value Sf '000,000[5]	% of total value	labour force	% of labour force
Agriculture, forestry	233.9	11.1	16,700	16.8
Mining	79.7	3.8	4,600	4.7
Manufacturing	250.8	11.9	10,960	11.1
Construction	127.4	6.0	2,800	2.8
Public utilities	113.8	5.4	1,420	1.4
Transportation and communications	160.2	7.6	3,830	3.9
Trade	378.6	18.0	12,840	12.9
Finance, real estate	400.6	19.0	2,100	2.1
Pub. admin., defense	506.8	24.0	40,190	40.5
Services	36.8[6]	1.7[6]	3,800	3.8
Other	−178.9	−8.5	...	...
TOTAL	2,109.7	100.0	99,240	100.0

Household income and expenditure. Average household size (1980) 3.9; income per household: n.a.; sources of income (1975): wages and salaries 74.6%, transfer payments 3.2%, other 22.2%; expenditure (1968–69)[4]: food and beverages 40.0%, household furnishings 12.3%, clothing and footwear 11.0%, transportation and communications 9.5%, recreation and education 8.4%, energy 6.9%, housing 4.4%, other 7.5%.

Foreign trade

Balance of trade (current prices)						
	1985	1986	1987	1988	1989	1990
Sf '000,000	+54.1	−5.0	+17.3	+103.6	+218.3	+91.5
% of total	4.8%	0.6%	1.6%	14.3%	24.8%	10.9%

Imports (1988): Sf 626,300,000 (machinery and transport equipment 23.6%, fuels and lubricants 14.4%). *Major import sources:* United States 26.6%; Netherlands Antilles 18.0%; The Netherlands 16.7%; Trinidad and Tobago 8.3%; Brazil 4.9%.
Exports (1988): Sf 744,300,000 (alumina 71.9%, rice 9.6%, shrimps 7.5%, bananas 4.9%, aluminum 3.6%, bauxite 0.1%). *Major export destinations:* The Netherlands 23.6%; United States 21.2%; Norway 19.4%; Brazil 9.4%; West Germany 6.1%.

Transport and communications

Transport. Railroads (1987): length 104 mi, 167 km; passengers, not applicable; cargo, n.a. Roads (1990): total length 5,688 mi, 9,153 km (paved 29%). Vehicles (1990): passenger cars 36,755; trucks and buses 14,473. Merchant marine (1991): vessels (100 gross tons and over) 24; total deadweight tonnage 15,721. Air transport (1988)[7]: passenger-mi 344,729,000, passenger-km 554,759,000; short ton-mi cargo 15,735,000, metric ton-km cargo 22,973,000; airports (1992) with scheduled flights 3.
Communications. Daily newspapers (1991): total number 1; total circulation 18,000; circulation per 1,000 population 43. Radio (1991): total number of receivers 247,741 (1 per 1.7 persons). Television (1991): total number of receivers 40,000 (1 per 10 persons). Telephones (1990): 48,149 (1 per 8.4 persons).

Education and health

Education (1986–87)				
	schools	teachers	students	student/ teacher ratio
Primary (age 6–11)	301	3,984	59,633	14.9
Secondary (age 12–18)	89	1,588	23,217	14.6
Voc., teacher tr.[8]	64	1,283	15,996	12.5
Higher	1	187	1,198	6.4

Educational attainment: n.a. *Literacy* (1990): total population age 15 and over literate 262,700 (94.9%); males literate 128,700 (95.1%); females literate 134,000 (94.7%).
Health (1985): physicians 219 (1 per 1,798 persons); hospital beds 1,964 (1 per 200 persons); infant mortality rate per 1,000 live births 27.6.
Food (1988–90): daily per capita caloric intake 2,436 (vegetable products 86%, animal products 14%); 108% of FAO recommended minimum requirement.

Military

Total active duty personnel (1992): 1,800[9] (army 77.8%, navy 13.9%, air force 8.3%). *Military expenditure as percentage of GNP* (1989): 3.0% (world 4.9%); per capita expenditure U.S.$100.

[1]Preliminary. [2]Area excludes 6,809 sq mi (17,635 sq km) of territory disputed with Guyana. [3]1988. [4]For Paramaribo and environs. [5]At factor cost. [6]Imputed bank service charges. [7]SLM (Suriname Airways) only. [8]1984–85. [9]All services are part of the army.

Swaziland

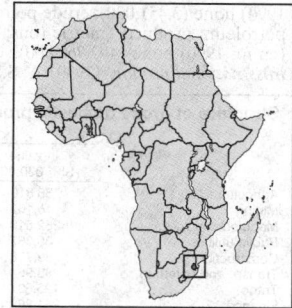

Official name: Umbuso weSwatini (Swazi); Kingdom of Swaziland (English).
Form of government[1]: monarchy with two legislative houses (Senate [20[2]]; House of Assembly [50[2]]).
Head of state and government: King, assisted by Prime Minister.
Capitals: Mbabane (administrative); Lobamba (royal and legislative).
Official languages: Swazi; English.
Official religion: none.
Monetary unit: 1 lilangeni[3] (plural emalangeni [E]) = 100 cents; valuation (Oct. 5, 1992) 1 U.S.$ = E 2.84; 1 £ = E 4.82.

Area and population

Districts	Capitals	area sq mi	area sq km	population 1986 census[4]
Hhohho	Mbabane	1,378	3,569	178,936
Lubombo	Siteki	2,296	5,947	153,958
Manzini	Manzini	1,571	4,068	192,596
Shiselweni	Nhlangano	1,459	3,780	155,569
TOTAL		6,704	17,364	681,059

Demography

Population (1992): 826,000.
Density (1992): persons per sq mi 123.2, persons per sq km 47.6.
Urban-rural (1988): urban 30.4%; rural 69.6%.
Sex distribution (1986): male 47.22%; female 52.78%.
Age breakdown (1986): under 15, 47.3%; 15–29, 26.6%; 30–44, 13.4%; 45–59, 7.4%; 60–74, 3.4%; 75 and over, 1.3%; unknown 0.6%.
Population projection: (2000) 1,089,000; (2010) 1,501,000.
Doubling time: 20 years.
Ethnic composition (1983): Swazi 84.3%; Zulu 9.9%; Tsonga 2.5%; Indian 0.8%; Pakistani 0.8%; Portuguese 0.2%; other 1.5%.
Religious affiliation (1980): Christian 77.0%, of which Protestant 37.3%, Roman Catholic 10.8%; African indigenous 28.9%; traditional beliefs 20.9%; other 2.1%.
Major cities (1986): Manzini 52,000; Mbabane 38,290; Nhlangano 4,107; Piggs Peak 3,223; Siteki 2,271.

Vital statistics

Birth rate per 1,000 population (1990–95): 46.7 (world avg. 26.4); legitimate, n.a.; illegitimate, n.a.
Death rate per 1,000 population (1990–95): 11.1 (world avg. 9.2).
Natural increase rate per 1,000 population (1990–95): 35.6 (world avg. 17.2).
Total fertility rate (avg. births per childbearing woman; 1990–95): 6.5.
Marriage rate per 1,000 population: n.a.
Divorce rate per 1,000 population: n.a.
Life expectancy at birth (1990–95): male 56.2 years; female 59.8 years.
Major causes of death (1985)[5]: respiratory diseases 11.3%; infectious intestinal diseases 10.4%; circulatory diseases 7.5%; tuberculosis 7.1%; malnutrition 6.5%; accidents and injuries 6.0%; perinatal conditions 5.6%.

National economy

Budget (1992–93). Revenue: E 910,100,000 (receipts from Customs Union of Southern Africa 52.0%; tax on income and profits 35.9%; sales tax 11.5%; foreign-aid grants 5.1%; property income 4.9%; fees, services, and fines 1.2%). Expenditures: E 1,010,200,000 (recurrent expenditure 68.1%, of which education 18.1%, general administration 17.6%, economic services 9.4%, justice and police 6.1%, health 5.9%, defense 5.1%, public-debt payments 2.7%).
Land use (1990): forested 6.0%; meadows and pastures 68.9%; agricultural and under permanent cultivation 11.9%; other 13.2%.
Tourism (1990): receipts from visitors U.S.$25,000,000; expenditures by nationals abroad U.S.$14,000,000.
Gross national product (at current market prices; 1990): U.S.$645,000,000 (U.S.$820 per capita).

Structure of gross domestic product and labour force

	1988 in value E '000	1988 % of total value	1986 labour force	1986 % of labour force
Agriculture	183,100	13.8	30,197	18.8
Mining	16,000	1.2	5,245	3.3
Manufacturing	265,100	20.0	14,742	9.2
Construction	37,100	2.8	7,661	4.8
Public utilities	34,700	2.6	1,315	0.8
Transp. and commun.	82,200	6.2	7,526	4.7
Trade	141,700	10.7	12,348	7.7
Finance	154,000	11.6	1,931	1.2
Pub. admin., defense	198,900	15.0 }	32,309	20.1
Services	32,900	2.5 }		
Other	179,400[6]	13.6[6]	47,081[7]	29.4[7]
TOTAL	1,325,100	100.0	160,355	100.0

Population economically active (1986): total 160,355; activity rate of total population 23.5% (participation rates: ages 15 and over, 44.1%; female 34.2%; unemployed 27.0%).

Price and earnings indexes (1985 = 100)

	1984	1985	1986	1987	1988	1989	1990
Consumer price index	83.5	100.0	111.8	125.7	140.4	151.5	168.1
Earnings index	...	...	...	...	...	...	...

Public debt (external, outstanding; 1991): U.S.$269,000,000.
Production (metric tons except as noted). Agriculture, forestry, fishing (1991): sugarcane 3,900,000, corn (maize) 153,000, citrus fruits 66,200, seed cotton 30,000, lint cotton 10,000, roots and tubers 10,000 (of which potatoes 6,000, sweet potatoes 4,000), pulses 5,000; livestock (number of live animals) 740,200 cattle, 320,000 goats, 35,000 sheep, 24,000 pigs, 1,000,000 chickens; roundwood (1990) 2,223,000 cu m; fish catch (1990) 110. Mining and quarrying (1991): asbestos 13,888; diamonds 57,420 carats. Manufacturing (value added in E; 1987): food and beverages 119,550,000, of which sugarcane milling 66,650,000, beverage processing 31,770,000; paper and paper products 71,650,000; textiles and garments 16,510,000; wood and wood products 9,270,000; machinery and equipment 7,700,000; nonmetallic mineral products 6,330,000. Construction (value in E; 1991)[8]: residential 27,800,000; nonresidential 48,000,000. Energy production (consumption): electricity (kW-hr; 1990) 150,000,000 (1986; 650,000,000); coal (metric tons; 1989) 165,122 (28,454); crude petroleum, n.a. (n.a.); petroleum products, n.a. (n.a.); natural gas, n.a. (n.a.).
Household income and expenditure. Average household size (1986) 5.3; annual income per household (1985) E 332 (U.S.$151); sources of income (1985): wages and salaries 44.3%, transfers 12.2%, self-employment 9.9%, rent 0.8%, other 32.8%; expenditure (1985): food and beverages 29.7%, household durable goods 17.7%, transportation and communications 12.3%, clothing and footwear 18.6%, rent and fuel 6.9%, recreation 4.6%.

Foreign trade[9]

Balance of trade (current prices)

	1986	1987	1988	1989	1990	1991
E '000,000	−40.6	−110.2	−57.3	−56.7	−100.6	−109.7
% of total	3.0%	6.8%	2.8%	2.1%	3.3%	3.4%

Imports (1989): E 1,524,513,000 (1989–90; machinery and transport equipment 29.1%; minerals, fuels, and lubricants 15.5%; foodstuffs 12.9%; chemicals 7.2%). *Major import sources* (1989–90): South Africa 91.3%; Switzerland 1.5%; United Kingdom 0.9%; Japan 0.9%; West Germany 0.8%.
Exports (1989): E 1,206,917,000 (sugar 32.2%; wood and wood products 15.4%; asbestos, coal, and diamonds 5.7%; cotton 2.7%; yarns 2.4%). *Major export destinations:* South Africa 44.7%; Canada 7.3%; United States 4.3%; United Kingdom 3.4%; Mozambique 3.2%.

Transport and communications

Transport. Railroads (1987): length 320 mi, 515 km; passengers, n.a.; short ton-mi cargo 73,300,000[10], metric ton-km cargo 107,000,000[10]. Roads (1989): total length 1,740 mi, 2,801 km (paved 26%). Vehicles (1991): passenger cars 25,333; trucks and buses 8,603. Merchant marine: none; landlocked state. Air transport (1984)[11]: passenger-mi 13,977,000, passenger-km 22,494,000; short ton-mi cargo 1,508,000, metric ton-km cargo 2,201,000; airports (1992) with scheduled flights 1.
Communications. Daily newspapers (1991): total number 2; total circulation 19,000; circulation per 1,000 population 24. Radio (1991): total number of receivers 60,000 (1 per 13 persons). Television (1991): total number of receivers 12,500 (1 per 64 persons). Telephones (1989): 24,419 (1 per 31 persons).

Education and health

Education (1990)

	schools	teachers	students	student/ teacher ratio
Primary (age 6–13)	497	5,083	166,454	32.7
Secondary (age 14–18)	135	2,213	41,128	18.6
Voc., teacher tr.[12]	7	181	1,280	7.1
Higher[12]	1	178	1,270	7.1

Educational attainment (1986). Percentage of population age 25 and over having: no formal schooling 42.1%; some primary education 23.9%; complete primary 10.5%; some secondary 19.2%; complete secondary and higher 4.3%. *Literacy* (1986): total population age 15 and over literate 240,171 (67.0%); males literate 112,578 (69.0%); females literate 127,593 (65.0%).
Health (1984): physicians 80 (1 per 7,971 persons); hospital beds 1,608 (1 per 396 persons); infant mortality rate per 1,000 live births (1990–95) 107.0.
Food (1988–90): daily per capita caloric intake 2,634 (vegetable products 91%, animal products 9%); 114% of FAO recommended minimum requirement.

Military

Total active duty personnel (1983): 2,657. *Military expenditure as percentage of GNP* (1989): 1.7% (world 4.9%); per capita expenditure U.S.$13.

[1]The government announced on Oct. 9, 1992, that a new constitution would be forthcoming. [2]Includes 10 nonelective seats. [3]The lilangeni is at par with the South African rand. [4]Preliminary. [5]Percentage of deaths of known cause at government, mission, and private hospitals. [6]Includes imputed bank service charges and indirect taxes. [7]Includes 43,925 unemployed. [8]Urban areas under the jurisdiction of the Manzini and Mbabane town councils only. [9]Import figures are f.o.b. in balance of trade and c.i.f. in commodities and trading partners. [10]1984. [11]Royal Swazi National Airways only. [12]1986–87.

Sweden

Official name: Konungariket Sverige (Kingdom of Sweden).
Form of government: constitutional monarchy and parliamentary state with one legislative house (Parliament [349]).
Chief of state: King.
Head of government: Prime Minister.
Capital: Stockholm.
Official language: Swedish.
Official religion: Church of Sweden (Lutheran).
Monetary unit: 1 Swedish krona (SKr) = 100 ore; valuation (Oct. 5, 1992) 1 U.S.$ = SKr 5.35; 1 £ = SKr 9.10.

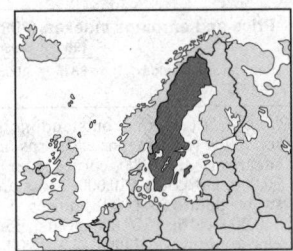

Area and population

Counties	Capitals	area sq mi	area sq km	population 1992[1] estimate
Älvsborg	Vänersborg	4,400	11,395	444,259
Blekinge	Karlskrona	1,136	2,941	151,168
Gävleborg	Gävle	7,024	18,191	289,339
Göteborg och Bohus	Göteborg	1,985	5,141	742,550
Gotland	Visby	1,212	3,140	57,883
Halland	Halmstad	2,106	5,454	257,874
Jämtland	Östersund	19,090	49,443	136,009
Jönköping	Jönköping	3,839	9,944	309,738
Kalmar	Kalmar	4,313	11,170	241,383
Kopparberg	Falun	10,886	28,194	290,388
Kristianstad	Kristianstad	2,350	6,087	291,468
Kronoberg	Växjö	3,266	8,458	178,612
Malmöhus	Malmö	1,907	4,938	786,757
Norrbotten	Luleå	38,191	98,913	264,834
Örebro	Örebro	3,289	8,519	273,608
Östergötland	Linköping	4,078	10,562	406,100
Skaraborg	Mariestad	3,065	7,937	278,162
Södermanland	Nyköping	2,340	6,060	256,818
Stockholm	Stockholm	2,505	6,488	1,654,511
Uppsala	Uppsala	2,698	6,989	273,918
Värmland	Karlstad	6,789	17,584	284,187
Västerbotten	Umeå	21,390	55,401	253,835
Västernorrland	Härnösand	8,370	21,678	261,280
Västmanland	Västerås	2,433	6,302	259,438
TOTAL LAND AREA		158,661[2]	410,929	
INLAND WATER		15,071	39,035	
TOTAL		173,732[2]	449,964	8,644,119

Demography

Population (1992): 8,673,000.
Density (1992)[3]: persons per sq mi 54.7, persons per sq km 21.1.
Urban-rural (1985): urban 83.4%; rural 16.6%.
Sex distribution (1991): male 49.40%; female 50.60%.
Age breakdown (1991[1]): under 15, 18.0%; 15–29, 20.7%; 30–44, 21.2%; 45–59, 17.4%; 60–74, 14.7%; 75 and over, 8.0%.
Population projection: (2000) 8,938,000; (2010) 9,157,000.
Ethnic composition (1991[1]): Swedish 90.8%; Finnish 2.5%; other 6.7%.
Religious affiliation (1991): Church of Sweden 88.9% (nominally; about 30% nonpracticing); Roman Catholic 1.7%; Pentecostal 1.1%; other 8.3%.
Major cities (1992): Stockholm 679,364; Göteborg 432,112; Malmö 234,796; Uppsala 170,743; Linköping 124,352.

Vital statistics

Birth rate per 1,000 population (1991): 14.4 (world avg. 26.4); (1990) legitimate 53.0%; illegitimate 47.0%.
Death rate per 1,000 population (1991): 11.0 (world avg. 9.2).
Natural increase rate per 1,000 population (1991): 3.3 (world avg. 17.2).
Total fertility rate (avg. births per childbearing woman; 1989): 2.0.
Marriage rate per 1,000 population (1991): 4.2.
Divorce rate per 1,000 population (1991): 2.3.
Life expectancy at birth (1986–90): male 74.4 years; female 80.2 years.
Major causes of death per 100,000 population (1988): heart disease 481.3; malignant neoplasms (cancers) 240.0; cerebrovascular disease 115.9.

National economy

Budget (1991–92). Revenue: SKr 464,632,000,000 (value-added and excise taxes 48.2%, income and capital gains taxes 14.2%, nontax revenue 13.7%, social-security contributions 12.3%, property taxes 5.1%). Expenditures: SKr 470,107,900,000 (health and social affairs 26.7%, education and culture 13.2%, interest on national debt 12.8%, defense 8.0%).
Public debt (1991): U.S.$96,374,000,000.
Tourism (1990): receipts from visitors U.S.$2,895,000,000; expenditures by nationals abroad U.S.$6,066,000,000.
Production (metric tons except as noted). Agriculture, forestry, fishing (1990): sugar beets 2,775,500, wheat 2,242,900, barley 2,122,600, oats 1,584,200, potatoes 1,186,100; livestock (number of live animals) 2,077,500 pigs, 1,718,400 cattle, 405,000 sheep; roundwood 51,500,000 cu m; fish catch 240,708, of which Baltic herring 86,841. Mining and quarrying (1990): iron ore 12,878,000[4]; zinc 159,800[4]; lead 84,200[4]; copper 73,400[4]. Manufacturing (value added, in SKr '000,000; 1989): machinery and transport equipment 133,377; paper and paper products 49,081; food and beverages 28,292; wood and wood products 19,374; textiles and wearing apparel 5,602. Construction (1990): 58,426 dwellings completed. Energy production (consumption): electricity (kW-hr; 1990) 146,535,000,000 (144,647,000,000); coal (metric tons;

1990) none (3,451,000); crude petroleum (barrels; 1990) 22,000 (122,500,000); petroleum products (metric tons; 1990) 15,780,000 (12,824,000); natural gas (cu m; 1990) none (492,760,000).
Gross national product (1990): U.S.$202,498,000,000 (U.S.$23,680 per capita).

Structure of gross domestic product and labour force

	1990 in value SKr '000,000	1990 % of total value	1991 labour force	1991 % of labour force
Agriculture	36,810	3.1	143,000	3.2
Mining	5,162	0.4	11,000	0.2
Manufacturing	262,510	22.3	890,000	19.6
Public utilities	35,367	3.0	37,000	0.8
Construction	89,778	7.6	312,000	6.9
Transp. and commun.	83,964	7.1	318,000	7.0
Trade	125,637	10.7	624,000	13.7
Finance	251,862	21.4	397,000	8.7
Pub. admin., defense } Services	334,697	28.5	1,698,000	37.4
Other	−50,450[5]	−4.3[5]	115,000[6]	2.5[6]
TOTAL	1,175,337	100.0[2]	4,545,000	100.0

Population economically active (1991): total 4,545,000; activity rate of total population 52.7% (participation rates [1990]: ages 16–64 84.8%; female 48.0%; unemployed [1991] 2.5%).

Price and earnings indexes (1985 = 100)

	1985	1986	1987	1988	1989	1990	1991
Consumer price index	100.0	104.2	108.6	114.9	122.3	135.1	147.8
Hourly earnings index	100.0	107.2	115.1	123.1	137.4	...	...

Household income and expenditure. Average household size (1985) 2.2; income per household (1985) SKr 125,900 (U.S.$14,635); sources of income (1989): wages and salaries 60.1%, transfer payments 22.8%, self-employment 8.2%; expenditure (1989): housing and energy 23.1%, food 21.9%, transportation 17.6%, education and recreation 10.3%.
Land use (1989): forested 68.1%; meadows and pastures 1.4%; agricultural and under permanent cultivation 6.9%; other 23.6%.

Foreign trade

Balance of trade (current prices)

	1986	1987	1988	1989	1990	1991
SKr '000,000	37,910	29,827	31,208	31,178	26,105	6,730
% of total	7.7%	5.6%	5.4%	4.9%	4.0%	1.2%

Imports (1991): SKr 298,810,000,000 (machinery and transport equipment 37.2%, of which transport equipment 10.8%, electrical machinery 9.7%; chemicals 10.3%; food 6.7%; clothing 5.9%). *Major import sources:* Germany 18.8%; U.S. 8.6%; U.K. 8.3%; Denmark 7.8%; Norway 7.7%; Finland 7.0%.
Exports (1991): SKr 332,770,000,000 (machinery and transport equipment 42.7%, of which transport equipment 14.8%, electrical machinery 8.8%; paper products 11.4%; chemicals 8.5%; wood and wood pulp 6.1%; iron and steel products 5.8%). *Major export destinations:* Germany 15.2%; U.K. 9.3%; Norway 8.4%; U.S. 8.0%; Denmark 7.1%; Finland 5.7%.

Transport and communications

Transport. Railroads (1990): length 6,960 mi, 11,202 km; passenger-mi 3,363,000,000, passenger-km 5,412,000,000; short ton-mi cargo 12,526,000,000, metric ton-km cargo 18,288,000,000. Roads (1989): total length 83,060 mi, 133,673 km (paved 71%). Vehicles (1991): passenger cars 3,605,200; trucks and buses 325,100. Merchant marine (1991): vessels (100 gross tons and over) 684; total deadweight tonnage 3,758,288. Air transport (1990): passenger-mi 4,511,000,000, passenger-km 7,260,000,000; short ton-mi cargo 139,112,000, metric ton-km cargo 203,100,000; airports (1992) 42.
Communications. Daily newspapers (1990): total number 177; total circulation 4,916,000; circulation per 1,000 population 574. Radio (1991): 7,271,556 receivers (1 per 1.2 persons). Television (1991): 3,750,000 receivers (1 per 2.3 persons). Telephones (1983): 7,410,000 (1 per 1.1 persons).

Education and health

Education (1990–91)

	schools	teachers	students	student/ teacher ratio
Primary (age 7–12)	4,649	100,030	881,523	8.8
Secondary (age 13–18)	489	30,114	292,047	9.7
Higher[7]	...	27,523[8]	272,718	9.9

Educational attainment (1979). Percentage of population age 25 and over having: lower secondary education 7.3%; higher secondary 35.7%; some postsecondary 15.4%. *Literacy* (1988): virtually 100%.
Health: physicians (1989) 26,577 (1 per 320 persons); hospital beds (1988) 55,331 (1 per 148 persons); infant mortality rate per 1,000 live births (1990) 5.6.
Food (1987–89): daily per capita caloric intake 2,945 (vegetable products 62%, animal products 38%); 109% of FAO requirement.

Military

Total active duty personnel (1991): 63,000 (army 69.0%, navy 19.1%, air force 11.9%). *Military expenditure as percentage of GNP* (1989): 2.6% (world 4.9%); per capita expenditure U.S.$574.

---

[1]January 1. [2]Detail does not add to total given because of rounding. [3]Density based on land area only. [4]Metal content of ore. [5]Includes statistical discrepancies less imputed bank service charges. [6]Unemployed. [7]1989–90. [8]Includes graduate assistants.

Switzerland

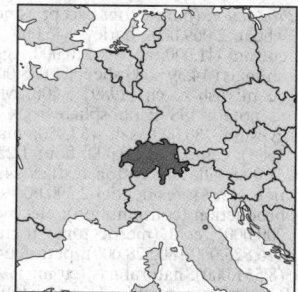

Official name: Confédération Suisse (French); Schweizerische Eidgenossenschaft (German); Confederazione Svizzera (Italian) (Swiss Confederation).
Form of government: federal state with two legislative houses (Council of States [46]; National Council [200]).
Head of state and government: President.
Capitals: Bern (administrative); Lausanne (judicial).
Official languages: French; German; Italian.
Official religion: none.
Monetary unit: 1 Swiss Franc (Sw F) = 100 centimes; valuation (Oct. 5, 1992) 1 U.S.$ = Sw F 1.23; 1 £ = Sw F 2.09.

Area and population		area		population
				1991[1]
Cantons	Capitals	sq mi	sq km	estimate
Aargau	Aarau	542	1,405	496,280
Appenzell Ausser-Rhoden[2]	Herisau	94	243	51,470
Appenzell Inner-Rhoden[2]	Appenzell	66	172	13,573
Basel-Landschaft[2]	Liestal	165	428	230,112
Basel-Stadt[2]	Basel	14	37	191,787
Bern	Bern	2,335	6,049	945,573
Fribourg	Fribourg	645	1,670	207,751
Genève	Geneva	109	282	375,957
Glarus	Glarus	264	684	37,648
Graubünden	Chur	2,744	7,106	170,411
Jura	Delémont	323	837	65,697
Luzern	Luzern	576	1,492	319,525
Neuchâtel	Neuchâtel	308	797	160,609
Nidwalden[2]	Stans	107	276	32,628
Obwalden[2]	Sarnen	189	491	28,813
Sankt Gallen	Sankt Gallen	778	2,014	420,268
Schaffhausen	Schaffhausen	115	298	71,697
Schwyz	Schwyz	351	908	110,526
Solothurn	Solothurn	305	791	226,655
Thurgau	Frauenfeld	391	1,013	205,946
Ticino	Bellinzona	1,085	2,811	286,725
Uri	Altdorf	416	1,076	33,650
Valais	Sion	2,018	5,226	248,313
Vaud	Lausanne	1,243	3,219	583,625
Zug	Zug	92	239	84,908
Zürich	Zürich	668	1,729	1,150,546
TOTAL		15,943	41,293	6,750,693[3]

Demography

Population (1992): 6,911,000.
Density (1992): persons per sq mi 433.5, persons per sq km 167.4.
Urban-rural (1991): urban 59.7%; rural 40.3%.
Sex distribution (1991): male 48.86%; female 51.14%.
Age breakdown (1991): under 15, 17.2%; 15–29, 22.1%; 30–44, 23.0%; 45–59, 18.3%; 60–74, 12.7%; 75 and over, 6.7%.
Population projection: (2000) 7,028,000; (2010) 7,049,000.
Ethnolinguistic composition (1990): German 63.0%; French 17.6%; Italian 9.4%; Yugoslav 2.1%; Spanish 1.7%; Romansch 0.8%; other 5.4%.
Religious affiliation (1990): Roman Catholic 47.2%; Protestant 43.5%; Muslim 1.5%; Jewish 0.3%; other 7.5%.
Major cities (1991[1]): Zürich 341,276 (841,052[4]); Basel 171,036 (360,350[4]); Geneva 167,167 (394,783[4]); Bern 134,629 (299,466[4]); Lausanne 123,159.

Vital statistics

Birth rate per 1,000 population (1991): 12.6 (world avg. 26.4); (1990) legitimate 93.9%; illegitimate 6.1%.
Death rate per 1,000 population (1991): 9.0 (world avg. 9.2).
Natural increase rate per 1,000 population (1991): 3.6 (world avg. 17.2).
Total fertility rate (avg. births per childbearing woman; 1990): 1.6.
Marriage rate per 1,000 population (1991): 6.8.
Life expectancy at birth (1989–90): male 74.0 years; female 80.8 years.
Major causes of death per 100,000 population (1990): heart disease 280.2, of which ischemic 152.4, other 127.8; malignant neoplasms (cancers) 244.0.

National economy

Budget (1991). Revenue: Sw F 33,902,000,000 (indirect taxes 50.0%, direct taxes 38.1%, nontax revenue 11.9%). Expenditures: Sw F 33,829,000,000 (current expenditures 87.3%, capital expenditures 12.7%).
National debt (end of year 1990): SwF 40,569,000,000.
Tourism (1990): receipts from visitors U.S.$6,839,000,000; expenditures by nationals abroad U.S.$5,989,000,000.
Production (metric tons except as noted). Agriculture, forestry, fishing (1991): milk 3,850,000, sugar beets 897,000, potatoes 725,000, wheat 574,000, barley 357,000, apples 190,000, grapes 178,000; livestock (number of live animals) 1,829,000 cattle, 1,723,000 pigs; roundwood (1990) 6,778,000 cu m; fish catch (1990) 4,176. Mining (1990): salt 400,000. Manufacturing (value added in U.S.$'000,000; 1990): nonelectrical machinery 7,544; food products 5,832; electrical goods and electronics 5,713; industrial chemicals 4,800; printing and publishing 4,222; metal products 3,944. Construction (in Sw F '000,-000; 1990): residential 21,876; nonresidential 34,375. Energy production (consumption)[5]: electricity (kW-hr; 1990) 55,846,000,000 (53,738,000,000); coal (metric tons; 1990) none (332,000); crude petroleum (barrels; 1990) none (21,983,000); petroleum products (metric tons; 1990) 2,890,000 (11,-257,000); natural gas (cu m; 1990) 3,600,000 (1,945,000,000).
Gross national product (1990): U.S.$219,337,000,000 (U.S.$32,790 per capita).

Structure of gross domestic product and labour force				
	1985		1990	
	in value Sw F '000,000	% of total value	labour force	% of labour force
Agriculture	8,180	3.6	197,500	5.5
Manufacturing	58,625 }	25.7	880,600	24.7
Mining			24,900	0.7
Public utilities	5,023	2.2 }		
Construction	17,325	7.6	339,700	9.5
Transp. and commun.	14,763	6.5	216,700	6.1
Trade	39,742	17.4	733,500	20.6
Finance, insurance[6]	36,994	16.2	443,900	12.5
Pub. admin., defense	26,065	11.4 }	641,900	18.0
Services	27,933	12.3 }		
Other	−6,700[7]	−2.9[7]	84,300	2.4
TOTAL	227,950	100.0	3,563,000[8]	100.0[8]

Population economically active (1990): total 3,563,000[8]; activity rate of total population 52.6% (participation rates: age 15 and over [1988] 62.9%; female 37.2%; unemployed [July 1991–June 1992] 2.0%).

Price and earnings indexes (1985 = 100)							
	1986	1987	1988	1989	1990	1991	1992[9]
Consumer price index	100.8	102.2	104.1	107.4	113.2	119.8	124.9
Hourly earnings index	103.9	106.5	110.4	114.8	121.7	130.9	...

Household income and expenditure. Average household size (1981) 2.5; average income per household (1982) Sw F 61,000 (U.S.$30,045); sources of income (1989): wages 64.5%, transfer payments 14.5%, other 21.0%; expenditure (1989): food 20.7%, housing 14.6%, transportation and communications 12.2%, education and recreation 10.6%, beverages and tobacco 7.7%.
Land use (1990): forested 26.4%; meadows and pastures 40.5%; agricultural and under permanent cultivation 10.4%; other 22.7%.

Foreign trade[10]

Balance of trade (current prices)						
	1986	1987	1988	1989	1990	1991
Sw F '000,000	−5,781	−6,950	−7,519	−9,998	−7,397	−6,144
% of total	4.1%	4.9%	4.8%	5.6%	4.0%	3.4%

Imports (1990): Sw F 96,611,000,000 (machinery and electronics 20.5%, of which industrial machinery 8.3%; chemical products 11.0%; agricultural products 8.4%; motor vehicles 7.6%). *Major import sources:* Germany 33.8%; France 11.1%; Italy 10.5%; U.S. 6.1%; U.K. 5.3%; Japan 4.4%.
Exports (1990): Sw F 88,256,900,000 (industrial machinery 20.2%; pharmaceuticals 9.1%; watches and clocks 7.7%; electrical machinery and electronics 6.0%; precision instruments 5.3%). *Major export destinations:* Germany 22.1%; France 9.9%; Italy 8.9%; U.S. 7.9%; U.K. 7.4%; Japan 4.8%.

Transport and communications

Transport. Railroads[11]: length (1989) 3,120 mi, 5,021 km; passenger-km (1991) 12,384,000,000; metric ton-km cargo (1991) 8,112,000,000. Roads (1990): total length 44,179 mi, 71,099 km. Vehicles (1990): passenger cars 3,011,673; trucks and buses 285,564. Merchant marine (1991): vessels (100 gross tons and over) 21; total deadweight tonnage 486,525. Air transport (1991)[12]: passenger-km 15,163,000,000; metric ton-km cargo 944,647,000; airports (1992) with scheduled flights 6.
Communications. Daily newspapers (1991): total number 106; total circulation 3,139,755; circulation per 1,000 population 458. Radio (1991): 2,685,031 receivers (1 per 2.6 persons). Television (1991): 2,412,473 receivers (1 per 2.8 persons). Telephones (1990): 6,152,834 (1 per 1.1 persons).

Education and health

Education (1990–91)				
	schools	teachers	students	student/teacher ratio
Primary (age 7–12)	...	...	404,154	...
Secondary (age 13–19)	...	...	384,780	...
Voc., teacher tr.	...	...	218,780	...
Higher	...	...	137,492	...

Educational attainment (1988). Percentage of Swiss (resident alien) population age 30 and over having completed: lower secondary education or less 33.9% (45.2%); upper secondary 47.5% (31.2%); higher 18.6% (23.6%).
Literacy: virtually 100.0%.
Health (1989): physicians 21,200 (1 per 317 persons); hospital beds 57,256 (1 per 117 persons); infant mortality rate (1991) 6.8.
Food (1988–90): daily per capita caloric intake 3,508 (vegetable products 61%, animal products 39%); 130% of FAO recommended minimum.

Military

Total active duty personnel (1992): 1,600[13]. *Military expenditure as percentage of GNP* (1989): 2.1% (world 4.9%); per capita expenditure U.S.$566.

[1]January 1. [2]Demicanton; functions as a full canton. [3]Includes 1,127,109 resident aliens. [4]Population of urban agglomeration. [5]Includes Liechtenstein. [6]Includes consulting services. [7]Imputed bank charges less import duties. [8]Labour force includes 954,940 foreign workers. [9]August. [10]Import figures are f.o.b. in balance of trade and c.i.f. in commodities and trading partners. [11]Swiss Federal Railways. [12]Swissair only. [13]Excludes 565,000 army reservists and 60,000 air corps reservists.

Syria

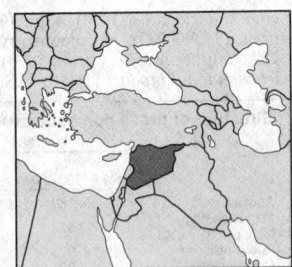

Official name: al-Jumhūrīyah al-ʿArabīyah as-Sūrīyah (Syrian Arab Republic).
Form of government: unitary multiparty[1] republic with one legislative house (People's Council [250]).
Head of state and government: President.
Capital: Damascus.
Official language: Arabic.
Official religion: none[2].
Monetary unit: 1 Syrian pound (LS) = 100 piastres; valuation (Oct. 5, 1992) 1 U.S.\$ = LS 20.96; 1£ = LS 35.64.

Area and population

Governorates	Capitals	area sq mi	area sq km	population 1992 estimate
Darʿā	Darʿā	1,440	3,730	568,000
Dayr az-Zawr	Dayr az-Zawr	12,765	33,060	565,000
Dimashq	Damascus	6,962	18,032	2,824,000[3]
Ḥalab	Aleppo	7,143	18,500	2,677,000
Ḥamāh	Ḥamāh	3,430	8,883	1,046,000
al-Ḥasakah	al-Ḥasakah	9,009	23,334	965,000
Ḥimṣ	Homs	16,302	42,223	1,209,000
Idlib	Idlib	2,354	6,097	870,000
al-Lādhiqīyah	Latakia	887	2,297	783,000
al-Qunayṭirah	al-Qunayṭirah	719[4]	1,861[4]	41,000
ar-Raqqah	ar-Raqqah	7,574	19,616	485,000
as-Suwaydāʾ	as-Suwaydāʾ	2,143	5,550	281,000
Ṭarṭūs	Ṭarṭūs	730	1,892	644,000
Municipality				
Damascus	—	41	105	[3]
TOTAL		71,498[4]	185,180[4]	12,958,000

Demography

Population (1992): 12,958,000.
Density (1992): persons per sq mi 181.1, persons per sq km 69.9.
Urban-rural (1990): urban 50.4%; rural 49.6%.
Sex distribution (1990): male 50.60%; female 49.40%.
Age breakdown (1990): under 15, 48.3%; 15–29, 27.1%; 30–44, 13.7%; 45–59, 6.7%; 60–74, 3.4%; 75 and over, 0.8%.
Population projection: (2000) 16,876,000; (2010) 22,923,000.
Doubling time: 19 years.
Ethnic composition (1981): Arab 88.8%; Kurdish 6.3%; other 4.9%.
Religious affiliation (1980): Muslim (mostly Sunnī) 89.6%; Christian 8.9%; other 1.5%.
Major cities (1992): Damascus 1,451,000; Aleppo 1,445,000; Homs 518,000; Latakia 284,000; Ḥamāh 254,000.

Vital statistics

Birth rate per 1,000 population (1990–95): 42.5 (world avg. 26.4).
Death rate per 1,000 population (1990–95): 5.7 (world avg. 9.2).
Natural increase rate per 1,000 population (1990–95): 36.8 (world avg. 17.2).
Total fertility rate (avg. births per childbearing woman; 1990–95): 6.3.
Marriage rate per 1,000 population (1988)[5]: 7.5.
Divorce rate per 1,000 population (1988)[5]: 0.7.
Life expectancy at birth (1990–95): male 65.2 years; female 69.2 years.
Major causes of death per 100,000 population (1981): diseases of the circulatory system 60.7; accidents and adverse effects 18.3; infectious and parasitic diseases 15.1.

National economy

Budget (1992). Revenue: LS 93,043,000,000 (taxes and duties 38.0%, foreign revenues 21.0%). Expenditures: LS 93,043,000,000 (defense 26.3%, administration 17.5%, education 12.2%, agriculture and irrigation 10.1%, health 3.1%).
Tourism (1990): receipts from visitors U.S.\$244,000,000; expenditures by nationals abroad U.S.\$190,000,000.
Land use (1989): steppe and pasture 43.4%; cultivable 29.9%; forested 3.9%; other 22.8%.
Gross national product (1990): U.S.\$12,404,000,000 (U.S.\$1,020 per capita).

Structure of gross domestic product and labour force

	1989 in value LS '000,000	% of total value	labour force	% of labour force
Agriculture	48,591	23.9	675,107	22.0
Mining	24,993	12.3	9,924	0.3
Manufacturing	18,035	8.9	454,459	14.8
Construction	8,771	4.3	357,865	11.7
Public utilities	−166	−0.1	29,220	1.0
Transportation and communications	22,165	10.9	184,570	6.0
Trade	45,496	22.4	373,835	12.2
Finance	8,131	4.0	40,636	1.3
Pub. admin.	23,176	11.4 }		
Services	3,940	1.9 }	825,953	26.9
Other	95	0.1	117,263	3.8
TOTAL	203,227	100.0	3,068,832	100.0

Production (metric tons except as noted). Agriculture, forestry, fishing (1990): wheat 2,069,000, barley 846,000, grapes 496,000, tomatoes 482,000, seed cotton 441,000, apples 210,000, eggplants 123,000; livestock (number of live animals) 14,395,000 sheep, 1,078,000 goats, 800,000 cattle; roundwood 51,000 cu m; fish catch (1989) 5,600. Mining and quarrying (metric tons except as noted; 1989): phosphate rock 2,256,000,000; sand and gravel 8,000,000; gypsum 180,000; salt 137,950; marble 18,000 cu m. Manufacturing (tons; 1988): cement 3,330,000; flour 1,221,000; fertilizers 95,000; glass and pottery 51,000; silk and cotton textiles 24,000; sugar 20,000; soap 16,000. Construction (1988): residential 2,390,000 sq m; nonresidential 339,000 sq m. Energy production (consumption): electricity (kW-hr; 1990) 10,600,000,000 (10,600,-000,000); coal (metric tons) none (n.a.); crude petroleum (barrels; 1990) 156,825,000 (80,528,000); petroleum products (metric tons; 1990) 10,836,000 (8,551,000); natural gas (cu m; 1990) 281,897,000 (281,897,000).
Population economically active (1989): total 3,068,832; activity rate of total population 26.2% (participation rates: ages 15–64 [1986] 46.7%; female 15.4%; unemployed 3.8%).

Price and earnings indexes (1985 = 100)

	1985	1986	1987	1988	1989	1990	1991
Consumer price index	100.0	136.1	217.0	292.0	325.3	388.4	418.2
Annual earnings index[6]	100.0	132.7					

Public debt (external, outstanding; 1990): U.S.\$4,005,000,000.
Average household size (1986): 5.7; income per household: n.a.; sources of income: n.a.; expenditure (1970)[7]: food 48.8%, housing 17.7%, clothing and footwear 9.1%, household durable goods 5.1%, fuel and light 4.6%, transportation and communications 3.8%, education and recreation 3.1%.

Foreign trade

Balance of trade (current prices)

	1985	1986	1987	1988	1989	1990
LS '000,000	−7,857	−4,626	−10,418	−7,879	12,140	22,661
% of total	37.9%	30.8%	25.5%	20.7%	21.9%	31.4%

Imports (1990): LS 24,712,000,000 (1989; food, beverages, and tobacco 21.1%; machinery and equipment 17.6%; chemicals and chemical products 16.8%; basic metals industries 11.9%; textiles 8.1%; paper and paper products 2.0%). *Major import sources:* France 12.6%; Germany 9.6%; United States 8.4%; Turkey 7.6%; Italy 6.9%; China 4.4%; U.S.S.R. 3.7%; Belgium-Luxembourg 3.4%; Japan 3.2%.
Exports (1990): LS 47,373,000,000 (1989; crude petroleum and petroleum products 39.2%; textiles, wearing apparel, and leather 29.3%; chemicals and chemical products 11.8%; food, beverages, and tobacco 6.0%). *Major export destinations:* U.S.S.R. 44.3%; France 10.7%; Italy 9.9%; Germany 8.6%; Saudi Arabia 5.8%; Lebanon 4.3%; United Kingdom 2.3%; Iran 1.6%.

Transport and communications

Transport. Railroads (1991): route length 948 mi, 1,525 km; passenger-mi 813,000,000, passenger-km 1,308,000,000; short ton-mi cargo 847,000,000, metric ton-km cargo 1,236,000,000. Roads (1990): total length 18,475 mi, 29,732 km (paved 78%). Vehicles (1989): passenger cars 117,570; trucks and buses 138,603. Merchant marine (1991): vessels (100 gross tons and over) 79; total deadweight tonnage 179,327. Air transport (1991): passenger-mi 719,000,000, passenger-km 1,157,000,000; short ton-mi cargo 9,873,000, metric ton-km cargo 14,414,000; airports (1992) with scheduled flights 5.
Communications. Daily newspapers (1990): total number 9; total circulation 236,400; circulation per 1,000 population 19.5. Radio (1991): 2,850,000 receivers (1 per 4.4 persons). Television (1991): 700,000 receivers (1 per 17.9 persons). Telephones (1989): 685,000 (1 per 17 persons).

Education and health

Education (1989–90)

	schools	teachers	students	student/ teacher ratio
Primary (age 6–11)	9,524	90,272	2,357,981	26.1
Secondary (age 12–18)	2,077	42,623	856,942	20.1
Voc., teacher tr.	238	8,920	56,094	6.3
Higher	44	4,605[8]	203,979	...

Educational attainment (1984). Percentage of population age 10 and over having: no schooling 32.0%; knowledge of reading and writing 28.4%; primary education 31.3%; secondary 4.9%; certificate 2.0%; higher 1.9%.
Literacy (1990): percentage of population age 15 and over literate 64.5%; males literate 78.3%; females literate 50.8%.
Health (1988): physicians 8,420 (1 per 1,347 persons); hospital beds 13,505 (1 per 840 persons); infant mortality rate per 1,000 live births (1990–95) 39.0.
Food (1987–89): daily per capita caloric intake 3,074 (vegetable products 88%, animal products 12%); 124% of FAO recommended minimum requirement.

Military

Total active duty personnel (1991): 404,000 (army 74.3%, navy 1.0%, air force 24.7%). *Military expenditure as percentage of GNP* (1989): 11.6% (world 4.9%); per capita expenditure U.S.\$186.

[1]Parties ideologically compatible with the Baʿth Party. [2]Islam is required to be the religion of the head of state and is the basis of the legal system. [3]Governorate includes Damascus (Dimashq) municipality. [4]Includes territory in the Golan Heights recognized internationally as part of Syria (located between the 1949 Israel-Syria Armistice line [west] and the 1974 UN Disengagement of Forces zone [east]) that has been occupied by Israel since 1967. Israel's unilateral annexation of this territory in December 1981 has received no international recognition. [5]Syrian Arabs only. [6]Public sector only. [7]Weights of consumer price index components for Damascus only. [8]1986–87.

Taiwan

Official name: Chung-hua Min-kuo
(Republic of China).
Form of government: multiparty
republic with a National Assembly
(403[1]) and Legislative Yuan (220[1]).
Chief of state: President.
Head of government: Premier.
Capital: Taipei.
Official language: Mandarin Chinese.
Official religion: none.
Monetary unit: 1 New Taiwan dollar
(NT$) = 100 cents; valuation (Oct. 5,
1992) 1 U.S.$ = NT$25.26;
1 £ = NT$42.95.

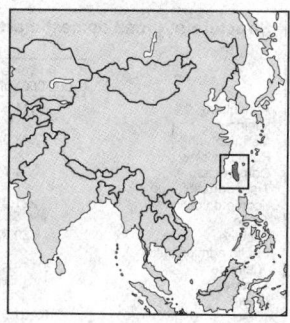

Area and population[2]

Counties	Capitals	area sq mi	area sq km	population 1992 estimate[3, 4]
Chang-hua	Chang-hua	415	1,074	1,255,352
Chia-i	Chia-i	734	1,902	554,365
Hsin-chu	Hsin-chu	551	1,428	380,466
Hua-lien	Hua-lien	1,787	4,629	353,701
I-lan	I-lan	825	2,137	454,010
Kao-hsiung	Feng-shan	1,078	2,793	1,134,723
Miao-li	Miao-li	703	1,820	551,226
Nan-t'ou	Nan-t'ou	1,585	4,106	539,415
P'eng-hu	Ma-kung	49	127	95,096
P'ing-tung	P'ing-tung	1,072	2,776	897,328
T'ai-chung	Feng-yuan	792	2,051	1,294,090
T'ai-pei	Hsin-ying	778	2,016	1,037,794
T'ai-pei	Pan-ch'iao	792	2,052	3,120,553
T'ai-tung	T'ai-tung	1,357	3,515	256,124
T'ao-yüan	T'ao-yüan	471	1,221	1,390,517
Yün-lin	Tou-liu	498	1,291	752,348
Municipalities				
Chia-i	—	23	60	258,274
Chi-lung	—	51	133	356,501
Hsin-chu	—	40	104	329,738
Kao-hsiung	—	59	154	1,398,041
T'ai-chung	—	63	163	779,370
T'ai-nan	—	68	176	690,292
Taipei	—	105	272	2,712,644
TOTAL		13,900[5]	36,000	20,592,048[5]

Demography

Population (1992): 20,727,000.
Density (1992): persons per sq mi 1,491.2, persons per sq km 575.6.
Urban-rural[4] (1990): urban 74.5%; rural 25.5%.
Sex distribution[3, 4] (1992): male 51.62%; female 48.38%.
Age breakdown[4] (1990): under 15, 27.1%; 15–29, 27.8%; 30–44, 23.1%; 45–59, 12.3%; 60–74, 7.9%; 75 and over, 1.8%.
Population projection: (2000) 22,621,000; (2010) 25,234,000.
Doubling time: 67 years.
Ethnic composition (1986): Taiwanese 84.0%; mainland Chinese 14.0%; aborigine 2.0%.
Religious affiliation (1980): Chinese folk-religionist 48.5%; Buddhist 43.0%; Christian 7.4%; Muslim 0.5%; other 0.6%.
Major cities[3, 4] (1992): Taipei 2,716,663; Kao-hsiung 1,396,984; T'ai-chung 777,059; T'ai-nan 689,509; Chi-lung 356,139.

Vital statistics

Birth rate per 1,000 population (1991): 15.6 (world avg. 26.4); (1991)[4] legitimate 97.6%; illegitimate 2.4%.
Death rate per 1,000 population (1991): 5.2 (world avg. 9.2).
Natural increase rate per 1,000 population (1991): 10.4 (world avg. 17.2).
Total fertility rate[4] (avg. births per childbearing woman; 1990): 1.8.
Marriage rate per 1,000 population (1991): 7.9.
Divorce rate per 1,000 population (1991): 1.4.
Life expectancy at birth (1990): male 71.3 years; female 76.8 years.
Major causes of death[4] per 100,000 population (1990): malignant neoplasms 91.6; cerebrovascular diseases 70.1; accidents and suicide 68.9; heart disease 56.9; diabetes 19.6; liver diseases 17.8; hypertension disease 14.8.

National economy

Budget (1990)[6]. Revenue: NT$1,198,602,000,000 (income taxes 18.8%, surplus of public enterprises 10.1%, land tax 8.8%, commodity tax 7.1%, customs duties 6.8%). Expenditures: NT$1,155,543,000,000 (administration and defense 29.1%, economic development 25.3%, education 19.6%).
Production (metric tons except as noted). Agriculture, forestry, fishing (1990): sugarcane 5,580,953, rice 1,806,596, citrus fruits 528,941, corn (maize) 339,-436, pineapples 234,629, bananas 201,440, sweet potatoes 199,830; livestock (number of live animals; 1990) 8,565,250 pigs, 172,990 goats and sheep, 132,-362 cattle; timber 113,830 cu m; fish catch 1,455,495. Mining and quarrying (1990): silver 3,926 kilograms; gold 72 kilograms. Manufacturing (1991): cement 19,398,604; steel ingots 3,072,514; paperboard 2,855,974; fertilizers 1,993,512; synthetic fibre 1,774,754; polyvinyl chloride plastics 978,435; electronic calculators 31,474,361 units; sewing machines 3,480,000 units; microcomputer systems 2,465,597 units; colour televisions 2,456,361 units; videotape recorders 725,391 units. Construction (1991): total residential and nonresidential 32,008,000 sq m. Energy production (consumption): electricity (kW-hr; 1991) 89,639,000,000 (54,361,200,000[7]); coal (metric tons; 1990) 472,050 (3,202,000[8]); crude petroleum (barrels; 1986) 704,700 (n.a.); natural gas (cu m; 1990) 1,128,877,000 (n.a.).

Gross national product (1991): U.S.$180,162,000,000 (U.S.$8,790 per capita).

Structure of gross domestic product and labour force[4]

	1991 in value NT$'000,000	% of total value	labour force[9]	% of labour force
Agriculture	170,789	3.6	1,092,000	12.8
Mining	19,109	0.4	19,000	0.2
Manufacturing	1,613,728	34.3	2,611,000	30.5
Construction	231,488	4.9	719,000	8.4
Public utilities	126,004	2.7	37,000	0.4
Transp. and commun.	289,286	6.1	457,000	5.3
Trade	739,334	15.7	1,725,000	20.1
Finance	909,708	19.3	360,000	4.2
Pub. admin., defense	536,462	11.4 }	1,418,000	16.6
Services	294,279	6.3 }		
Other	−219,670[10]	−4.7[10]	130,000[11]	1.5[11]
TOTAL	4,710,517	100.0	8,569,000[5]	100.0

Public debt (foreign; 1990): U.S.$3,265,000,000.
Tourism (1990): receipts from visitors U.S.$1,740,000,000.
Population economically active (1990): total 10,236,324; activity rate 50.5% (participation rates: age 15–64, 72.5%; female 38.5%; unemployed 1.7%).

Price and earnings indexes (1985 = 100)[4]

	1985	1986	1987	1988	1989	1990	1991
Consumer price index	100.0	100.7	101.2	102.5	107.0	111.5	115.5
Monthly earnings index[12]	100.0	110.1	121.0	134.2	153.8	176.1	195.7

Household income and expenditure (1990). Average household size 4.0; income per household NT$627,511 (U.S.$23,147[13]); sources of income: wages 60.5%, self-employment 20.3%, transfer payments 5.9%, other 13.3%; expenditure: food and tobacco 32.3%, rent, fuel, and power 24.6%, recreation and education 13.4%, transportation and communications 8.8%, clothing and footwear 5.9%, health care 4.8%, household furnishings 4.3%, other 5.9%.
Land use (1980): forested 55.0%; agricultural 25.2%; other 19.8%.

Foreign trade

Balance of trade (current prices)

	1986	1987	1988	1989	1990	1991
NT$'000,000	590,181	592,545	306,852	359,832	330,980	350,013
% of total	24.4%	21.0%	9.7%	11.5%	10.1%	9.4%

Imports (1991): NT$1,690,772,000,000 (electronic machinery 16.2%, nonelectrical machinery 13.3%, chemicals 11.4%, iron and steel 7.5%, road motor vehicles 6.3%, crude petroleum 5.1%). *Major import sources:* Japan 30.0%; U.S. 22.5%; Germany 4.8%; Australia 3.2%; Hong Kong 3.1%; Korea 2.8%.
Exports (1991): NT$2,040,785,000,000 (data-processing equipment 5.9%, outer garments 4.0%, radio transmission equipment 3.9%, plastic articles 3.6%, footwear 2.9%, athletic equipment 2.3%, synthetic fabrics 1.4%). *Major export destinations:* U.S. 29.3%; Hong Kong 16.3%; Japan 12.1%; Germany 5.1%; Singapore 3.2%; The Netherlands 2.9%.

Transport and communications

Transport. Railroads (1991): track length 4,600 km; passenger-km 8,621,000,-000; metric ton-km cargo 1,960,600,000. Roads (1990): total length 19,479 km (paved 86%). Vehicles (1991): passenger cars 2,636,228; trucks and buses 653,869. Merchant marine (1991): vessels (100 gross tons and over) 664; total deadweight tonnage 9,013,306. Air transport (1991): passenger-km 29,036,000,000; metric ton-km cargo 3,862,661,000; airports (1992) 12.
Communications. Daily newspapers (1988): total number 93; total circulation 4,000,000; circulation per 1,000 population 202. Radio (1991): 13,600,000 receivers (1 per 1.5 persons). Television (1991): 6,660,000 receivers (1 per 3.1 persons). Telephones (1990): 8,432,000 (1 per 2.4 persons).

Education and health

Education (1990–91)

	schools	teachers	students	student/ teacher ratio
Primary (age 6–12)	2,487	82,583	2,354,113	28.5
Secondary (age 13–18)	870	66,557	1,369,190	20.6
Vocational	216	17,703	449,111	25.4
Higher	121	27,579	576,623	20.9

Educational attainment (1990). Percentage of population age 25 and over having: no formal schooling 2.0%; less than complete primary education 7.9%; primary 32.9%; incomplete secondary 21.7%; secondary 22.4%; some college 7.1%; higher 6.0%. *Literacy* (1990): population age 15 and over literate 13,746,772 (92.4%); males 7,428,003 (96.3%); females 6,318,769 (87.9%).
Health (1990): physicians 22,293 (1 per 910 persons); hospital beds 89,151 (1 per 227 persons); infant mortality rate per 1,000 live births 5.3.
Food: daily per capita caloric intake (1990) 3,020 (1988: vegetable products 77%, animal products 23%); 118% of FAO recommended minimum.

Military

Total active duty personnel (1991): 370,000 (army 73.0%, navy 8.1%, air force 18.9%). *Military expenditure as percentage of GNP* (1989): 5.4% (world 4.9%); per capita expenditure U.S.$397.

[1]Occupied seats as of Dec. 21, 1991. [2]Excludes Fukien (Kinma) area; population in 1990, 48,339. [3]End of March. [4]For Taiwan area only, excluding Quemoy and Matsu. [5]Detail does not add to total given because of rounding. [6]General government. [7]By industry only. [8]1986. [9]Civilian employed persons only. [10]Import duties less imputed bank service charge. [11]Unemployed. [12]In manufacturing. [13]Based on the average exchange rate.

Tajikistan

Official name: Jumhurii Tojikiston (Republic of Tajikistan).
Form of government: unitary republic with a transitional Parliament (80).
Head of state and government: acting president, assisted by a State Council.
Capital: Dushanbe.
Official language: Tajik (Tojik).
Official religion: none.
Monetary unit: 1 ruble = 100 kopecks; valuation (Oct. 5, 1992) free rate, 1 U.S.$ = 315.78 rubles; 1 £ = 538.59 rubles.

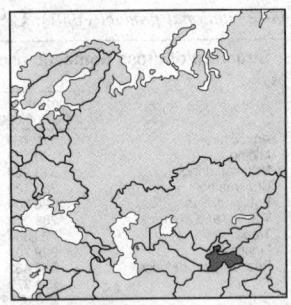

Area and population		area		population
		sq mi	sq km	1991 estimate
Autonomous republic	**Capitals**			
Badakhshan	Khorog	24,600	63,700	167,100
Provinces				
Khudzhand	Khudzhand	10,100	26,100	1,635,900
Kulyab	Kulyab	4,600	12,000	668,100
Kurgan-Tyube	Kurgan-Tyube	4,900	12,600	1,113,500
Regions under republican jurisdiction	—	11,000	28,400	1,181,800
City				
Dushanbe	—	100	300	591,900
TOTAL		55,300	143,100	5,358,300

Demography

Population (1992): 5,568,000[1].
Density (1992): persons per sq mi 100.8, persons per sq km 38.9.
Urban-rural (1991): urban 31.4%; rural 68.6%.
Sex distribution (1990): male 49.70%; female 50.30%.
Age breakdown (1989): under 15, 42.9%; 15–29, 28.1%; 30–44, 13.8%; 45–59, 9.0%; 60–74, 4.6%; 75 and over, 1.6%.
Population projection: (2000) 7,041,000; (2010) 8,948,000.
Doubling time: 21 years.
Ethnic composition (1989): Tajik 62.3%; Uzbek 23.5%; Russian 7.6%[1]; Tatar 1.4%; Kyrgyz 1.3%; Ukrainian 0.8%; German 0.6%; other 2.5%.
Religious affiliation (1990): believers are predominantly Sunnī Muslim (Ḥanafīyah).
Major cities (1989): Dushanbe 582,400; Khudzhand (formerly Leninabad) 164,500; Kulyab 79,300; Kurgan-Tyube 58,400; Ura-Tyube 47,700.

Vital statistics

Birth rate per 1,000 population (1990): 38.8 (world avg. 27.1); (1989) legitimate 93.0%; illegitimate 7.0%.
Death rate per 1,000 population (1990): 6.2 (world avg. 9.8).
Natural increase rate per 1,000 population (1990): 32.6 (world avg. 17.3).
Total fertility rate (avg. births per childbearing woman; 1989): 5.1.
Marriage rate per 1,000 population (1989): 9.2.
Divorce rate per 1,000 population (1989): 1.5.
Life expectancy at birth (1990): male 67.0 years; female 72.1 years.
Major causes of death per 100,000 population (1989): diseases of the circulatory system 197.5; diseases of the respiratory system 138.8; infectious and parasitic diseases 81.2; malignant neoplasms (cancers) 51.9; violence, poisoning, and accidents 48.4; diseases of the digestive system 23.0; diseases of the nervous system 8.9; endocrine and metabolic disorders 6.9.

National economy

Production (metric tons except as noted). Agriculture, forestry, fishing (1990): seed cotton 842,100, vegetables (except potatoes) 528,000, grain 318,000, fruit (except grapes) 220,200, potatoes 207,000, grapes 189,500; livestock (number of live animals) 3,358,900 sheep and goats, 1,349,200 cattle, 210,000 pigs; roundwood, n.a.; fish catch, n.a. Mining and quarrying: n.a. Manufacturing (1989): cement 1,111,000; cotton yarn 129,000; vegetable oil 93,200; mineral fertilizers 88,100; copper cable 16,200; canned food 374,000,000 units; bricks 320,000,000 units; refrigerators 170,500 units; leather footwear 10,800,000 pairs; woven cotton fabrics 125,000,000 m; reinforced concrete 1,169,000 cu m; carpets and rugs 10,800,000 sq m; lighting equipment 8,900,000 rubles. Construction (1990): residential 1,735,000 sq m. Energy production (consumption): electricity (kW-hr; 1991) 17,500,000,000 (n.a.); coal (metric tons; 1991) 300,000 (n.a.); crude petroleum (barrels; 1991) 733,000 (n.a.); petroleum products, n.a. (n.a.); natural gas (cu m; 1991) 100,000,000 (n.a.).
Population economically active (1990): total 2,468,300; activity rate of total population 46.1% (participation rates [1989]: ages 16–59 [male], 16–54 [female] 78.1%; female 39.0%; unemployed 2.0%).

Price and earnings indexes (1985 = 100)					
	1986	1987	1988	1989	1990
Consumer price index	...	...	...	...	...
Monthly earnings index	102.7	105.1	112.2	119.2	131.1

Tourism: receipts from visitors, n.a.; expenditures by nationals abroad, n.a.
Gross national product (at current market prices; 1991): 9,616,800,000 rubles (1,800 rubles per capita)[2].

Structure of gross domestic product and labour force				
	1990			
	in value '000,000 rubles	% of total value	labour force[3]	% of labour force[3]
Agriculture	2,014.6	38.3	831,000	42.9
Mining				
Manufacturing	1,503.0	28.5	260,700	13.5
Public utilities				
Construction	771.7	14.7	160,800	8.3
Transportation and communications	221.0	4.2	64,700	3.3
Trade			145,400	7.5
Finance	750.7	14.3	—	—
Public administration, defense	—	—	38,800	2.0
Services	—	—	436,900	22.5
Other	—	—	—	—
TOTAL	5,261.0	100.0	1,938,300	100.0

Budget (1991). Revenue: 5,457,000,000 rubles (union transfers 46.6%, turnover tax 17.5%, enterprise profits tax 11.1%, individual income tax 6.1%, sales tax 4.0%, duties and local taxes 3.1%). Expenditures: 5,020,000,000 rubles (social welfare and culture 62.5%, national economy 26.2%).
Public debt (external, outstanding): n.a.
Land use: n.a.
Household income and expenditure. Average household size (1989) 6.1; income per household: n.a.; sources of income: n.a.; expenditure: n.a.

Foreign trade

Balance of trade (current prices)	
	1991
'000,000 rubles	512.0
% of total	6.3%

Imports (1991): 3,815,600,000 rubles (no breakdown available). *Major import sources:* former Soviet republics 90.8%; other 9.2%.
Exports (1991): 4,327,600,000 rubles (no breakdown available). *Major export destinations:* former Soviet republics 91.2%; other 8.8%.

Transport and communications

Transport. Railroads (1990): length 553.6 mi, 891.0 km; passenger-mi 6,094,400,000, passenger-km 9,808,000,000; short ton-mi cargo 7,617,000,000, metric ton-km cargo 11,121,000,000. Roads (1990): total length 8,324,000 mi, 13,396,000 km (paved 93%). Vehicles (1988): passenger cars 209,100; trucks and buses, n.a. Merchant marine: vessels (100 gross tons and over) n.a.; total deadweight tonnage, n.a. Air transport (1989): passenger-mi 3,214,600,000, passenger-km 5,173,400,000; short ton-mi cargo 22,124,000, metric ton-km cargo 32,300,000; airports (1991) with scheduled flights 1.
Communications. Daily newspapers (1990): total number 74; total circulation 1,598,000; circulation per 1,000 population 298.2. Radio (1989): total number of receivers 860,000 (1 per 6.2 persons). Television (1989): total number of receivers 815,000 (1 per 6.6 persons). Telephones (1989): 273,100 (1 per 19.6 persons).

Education and health

Education (1989–90)	schools	teachers	students	student/ teacher ratio
Primary (age 6–13)	3,101	...	1,258,000	...
Secondary (age 14–17)				
Voc., teacher tr.	...	...	...	...
Higher	10	...	65,586	...

Educational attainment (1989). Percentage of population age 25 and over having: primary education or no formal schooling 16.3%; some secondary 21.1%; completed secondary and some postsecondary 55.1%; higher 7.5%.
Literacy: n.a.
Health (1990): physicians 14,500 (1 per 362 persons); hospital beds 56,500 (1 per 93 persons); infant mortality rate per 1,000 live births 40.7.
Food: daily per capita caloric intake, n.a.

Military

Total active duty personnel (1992): 13,000 under joint Commonwealth of Independent States- (CIS-) Tajik control (army 100%). *Military expenditure as percentage of GNP:* n.a.; per capita expenditure, n.a.

[1]Excluding adjustment for some 100,000 Russian refugees who have emigrated from the predominantly Muslim state. [2]No equivalent U.S.$ value is offered, as Soviet GNP data are very speculative. [3]State sector.

Tanzania

Official name: Jamhuri ya Muungano wa Tanzania (Swahili); United Republic of Tanzania (English).
Form of government: republic[1] with one legislative house (National Assembly [255[2]]).
Head of state and government: President.
Seat of government: Dar es Salaam[3] (Capital designate, Dodoma).
Official languages: Swahili; English.
Official religion: none.
Monetary unit: 1 Tanzanian shilling (T Sh) = 100 cents; valuation (Oct. 5, 1992) 1 U.S.$ = T Sh 319.44; 1 £ = T Sh 543.04.

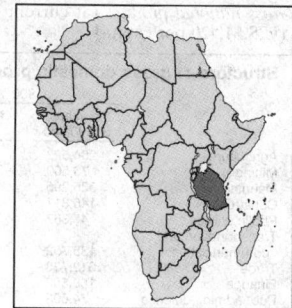

Area and population

Regions	Capitals	area sq mi	area sq km	population 1988 census
Arusha	Arusha	31,778	82,306	1,351,675
Coast	Dar es Salaam	12,512	32,407	638,015
Dar es Salaam	Dar es Salaam	538	1,393	1,360,850
Dodoma	Dodoma	15,950	41,311	1,237,819
Iringa	Iringa	21,955	56,864	1,208,914
Kagera	Bukoba	10,961	28,388	1,326,183
Kigoma	Kigoma	14,300	37,037	854,817
Kilimanjaro	Moshi	5,139	13,309	1,108,699
Lindi	Lindi	25,501	66,046	646,550
Mara	Musoma	7,555	19,566	970,942
Mbeya	Mbeya	23,301	60,350	1,476,199
Morogoro	Morogoro	27,336	70,799	1,222,737
Mtwara	Mtwara	6,451	16,707	889,494
Mwanza	Mwanza	7,564	19,592	1,878,271
Pemba North	Wete	222	574	137,399
Pemba South	Chake Chake	128	332	127,640
Rukwa	Sumbawanga	26,500	68,635	694,974
Ruvuma	Songea	24,517	63,498	783,327
Shinyanga	Shinyanga	19,607	50,781	1,772,549
Singida	Singida	19,051	49,341	791,814
Tabora	Tabora	29,402	76,151	1,036,293
Tanga	Tanga	10,351	26,808	1,283,636
Zanzibar North	Mkokotoni	182	470	97,028
Zanzibar South and Central	Koani	330	854	70,184
Zanzibar West	Zanzibar	89	230	208,327
TOTAL LAND AREA		341,217[4]	883,749	
INLAND WATER		22,800	59,050	
TOTAL		364,017[4]	942,799	23,174,336

Demography

Population (1992): 25,809,000.
Density (1992)[5]: persons per sq mi 75.6, persons per sq km 29.2.
Urban-rural (1990): urban 32.8%; rural 67.2%.
Sex distribution (1990): male 49.44%; female 50.56%.
Age breakdown (1990): under 15, 49.1%; 15–29, 25.6%; 30–44, 13.9%; 45–59, 7.6%; 60–74, 3.2%; 75 and over, 0.6%.
Population projection: (2000) 32,292,000; (2010) 42,732,000.
Doubling time: 21 years.
Ethnic composition (1983): Nyamwezi and Sukuma 21.1%; Swahili 8.8%; Hehet and Bena 6.9%; Makonde 5.9%; Haya 5.9%; other 51.4%.
Religious affiliation (1984): Christian 34%; Muslim 33%; traditional beliefs and other 33%.
Major cities (1988): Dar es Salaam 1,360,850; Mwanza 223,013; Dodoma 203,833; Tanga 187,634; Zanzibar 157,634.

Vital statistics

Birth rate per 1,000 population (1991): 49.5 (world avg. 26.4).
Death rate per 1,000 population (1991): 15.2 (world avg. 9.2).
Natural increase rate per 1,000 population (1991): 34.3 (world avg. 17.2).
Total fertility rate (avg. births per childbearing woman; 1991): 7.0.
Life expectancy at birth (1991): male 50.0 years; female 55.0 years.
Major causes of death per 100,000 population: n.a.; however, the major diseases include malaria, bilharziasis, tuberculosis, and sleeping sickness.

National economy

Budget (1991–92). Revenue: T Sh 215,162,000,000[6] (1986–87; sales tax 46.4%, income tax 21.2%, customs and excise tax 11.7%). Expenditures: T Sh 227,973,000,000 (1986–87; public administration 25.5%, defense 20.1%, economic services 16.4%, education 3.7%).
Public debt (external, outstanding; 1990): U.S.$4,704,000,000.
Tourism (1990): receipts from visitors U.S.$65,000,000; expenditures by nationals abroad (1988) U.S.$19,000,000.
Production (metric tons except as noted). Agriculture (1991): cassava 6,266,-000, corn (maize) 2,332,000, sugarcane 1,420,000, bananas 750,000, plantains 750,000, rice 664,000, sorghum 480,000, coconuts 370,000, sweet potatoes 291,000, dry beans 270,000, millet 270,000, potatoes 200,000, seed cotton 190,000, mangoes 187,000, cottonseed 124,000, unshelled peanuts (groundnuts) 65,000; livestock (number of live animals) 13,138,000 cattle, 8,814,000 goats, 3,556,000 sheep, 282,000 pigs, 20,000,000 chickens; roundwood (1990) 34,276,000 cu m; fish catch (1990) 377,000. Mining and quarrying (1989): salt 20,010; diamonds 150,000 carats. Manufacturing (1987): cement 489,-000; meats 220,000; hides and skins 39,500; wheat 24,743; soap 22,029; fertilizer 19,276; iron sheets 17,214; rolled steel 9,668; aluminum 2,024; tex-

tiles 39,064,000 sq m. Construction: n.a. Energy production (consumption): electricity (kW-hr; 1990) 885,000,000 (885,000,000); coal (metric tons; 1990) 4,000 (4,000); crude petroleum (barrels; 1990) none (4,081,000); petroleum products (metric tons; 1990) 524,000 (624,000).
Gross national product (1990): U.S.$2,779,000,000 (U.S.$120 per capita).

Structure of gross domestic product and labour force

	1989 in value T Sh '000,000	1989 % of total value	1987 labour force	1987 % of labour force
Agriculture	207,059	51.2	9,528,000	82.4
Mining	1,129	0.3		
Manufacturing	30,353	7.5		
Construction	5,904	1.5	538,000	4.7
Public utilities	4,831	1.2		
Transp. and commun.	23,345	5.8		
Trade	53,572	13.3		
Finance			1,497,000	13.0
Pub. admin., defense	77,962	19.3		
Services				
Other			...	...
TOTAL	404,155	100.0[4]	11,563,000	100.0[4]

Population economically active (1987): total 11,563,000; activity rate of total population 47.8% (participation rates: over age 10, 75.1%; female 46.0%).

Price and earnings indexes (1985 = 100)

	1986	1987	1988	1989	1990	1991	1992[7]
Consumer price index	132.4	172.1	225.8	288.9	359.4	415.9	503.5
Monthly earnings index	...	...	...	...	...	...	...

Household income and expenditure. Avg. household size (1988) 5.2; income per household: n.a.; sources of income: n.a.; expenditures (1981): food 54.3%, clothing 10.8%, housing 8.6%, energy 6.6%, transportation 6.4%.
Land use (1990): forested 46.2%; meadows and pastures 39.5%; agricultural and under permanent cultivation 3.8%; other 10.5%.

Foreign trade

Balance of trade (current prices)

	1985	1986	1987	1988	1989	1990
T Sh '000,000	−10,314	−12,505	−31,947	−43,191	−44,161	−88,440
% of total	51.0%	36.0%	46.3%	43.2%	49.2%	35.3%

Imports (1990): T Sh 169,439,000,000 (1987; machinery 25.6%, transport equipment 17.0%, metals 11.1%, fuel 9.4%, food 6.7%). *Major import sources* (1988): U.K. 16.2%; West Germany 10.5%; Japan 10.5%; Italy 8.5%; Sweden 3.8%; The Netherlands 3.5%; Denmark 3.4%; U.S. 3.2%; Yugoslavia 1.1%.
Exports (1990): T Sh 80,999,000,000 (1988; coffee 25.9%, cotton 23.6%, sisal 1.4%). *Major export destinations* (1988): West Germany 22.6%; U.K. 16.6%; The Netherlands 6.9%; Singapore 5.9%; Italy 5.2%; Japan 4.8%; Finland 3.1%; Portugal 3.1%; U.S. 2.8%; France 2.5%.

Transport and communications

Transport. Railroads (1990): length 3,569 km; passenger-km 3,420,000,000[8]; metric ton-km cargo 1,248,000,000[8]. Roads (1989): length 82,114 km (paved 4.2%). Vehicles (1990): passenger cars 45,000; trucks and buses 55,000. Merchant marine (1991): vessels (100 gross tons and over) 38; deadweight tonnage 47,539. Air transport (1991)[9]: passenger-km 280,462,000; metric ton-km 4,380,000; airports (1992) with scheduled flights 19.
Communications. Daily newspapers: total number (1989) 2; total circulation 180,000; circulation per 1,000 population 7.6. Radio (1991): 4,000,000 receivers (1 per 6.3 persons). Television (1991): 80,000 receivers (1 per 314 persons). Telephones (1990): 140,131 (1 per 174 persons).

Education and health

Education (1989)

	schools	teachers	students	student/ teacher ratio
Primary (age 7–13)[10]	10,431	98,392	3,258,601	33.1
Secondary (age 14–19)	288[11]	7,863	145,748	18.5
Voc., teacher tr.	63[11]	1,015	13,263	13.1
Higher	4	1,206	5,254	4.4

Educational attainment (1978). Percentage of population age 10 and over having: no schooling 48.6%; some primary education 40.7%; completed primary 8.7%; secondary and higher 1.9%. *Literacy* (1978): percentage of total population age 15 and over literate 46.3%; males literate 62.2%; females literate 31.4%; estimated total literacy in 1987: 94.0%.
Health (1984): physicians 1,065 (1 per 19,775 persons); hospital beds 22,800 (1 per 924 persons); infant mortality rate per 1,000 live births (1991) 105.
Food (1988–90): daily per capita caloric intake 2,195 (vegetable products 94%, animal products 6%); 95% of FAO recommended minimum requirement.

Military

Total active duty personnel (1992): 46,800 (army 96.2%, navy 1.7%, air force 2.1%). *Military expenditure as percentage of GNP* (1989): 4.1% (world 4.9%); per capita expenditure U.S.$5.

---

[1]Multiparty system officially approved May 1992; future date of multiparty elections not announced as of October 1992. [2]Includes 180 directly elected, 35 indirectly elected, 15 presidential nominees, and 25 ex officio members. [3]Government in process of being transferred from Dar es Salaam to Dodoma; legislative branch meets in Dodoma. [4]Detail does not add to total given because of rounding. [5]Based on land area. [6]Includes foreign grants and loans. [7]First quarter. [8]1989. [9]Air Tanzania only. [10]Excludes Pemba and Zanzibar. [11]1986–87.

Thailand

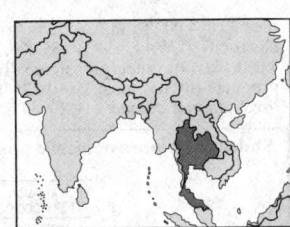

Official name: Muang Thai, or Prathet
Thai (Kingdom of Thailand).
Form of government: constitutional
monarchy with two legislative
houses (Senate [270]; House of
Representatives [360]).
Chief of state: King.
Head of government: Prime Minister[1].
Capital: Bangkok.
Official language: Thai.
Official religion: Buddhism.
Monetary unit: 1 Thai baht (B) = 100
stangs; valuation (Oct. 5, 1992)
1 U.S.$ = B 25.18; 1 £ = B 42.80.

Area and population	area		population
			1990
Regions	sq mi	sq km	census[2]
Bangkok Metropolis	604	1,565	5,876,000
Central[3]	39,512	102,336	12,072,000
Northeastern	65,195	168,854	19,037,000
Northern	65,500	169,644	10,583,000
Southern	27,303	70,715	6,964,000
TOTAL	198,115[4]	513,115[4]	54,532,000

Demography

Population (1992): 56,801,000.
Density (1992): persons per sq mi 286.7, persons per sq km 110.7.
Urban-rural (1990): urban 18.7%; rural 81.3%.
Sex distribution (1990): male 49.57%; female 50.43%.
Age breakdown (1990): under 20, 44.3%; 20–39, 34.2%; 40–59, 15.4%; 60–69,
3.9%; 70 and over, 2.2%.
Population projection: (2000) 65,534,000; (2010) 76,656,000.
Doubling time: 50 years.
Ethnic composition (1983): Thai 79.5%, of which Siamese 52.6%, Lao 26.9%;
Chinese 12.1%; Malay 3.7%; Khmer 2.7%; other 2.0%.
Religious affiliation (1989): Buddhist 94.3%; Muslim 4.0%; Christian 0.5%;
other 1.2%.
Major cities (1989): Bangkok 5,876,000[5]; Nonthaburi 227,492; Nakhon
Ratchasima 206,605; Chiang Mai 167,000[5]; Khon Kaen 131,472.

Vital statistics

Birth rate per 1,000 population (1991): 20.9 (world avg. 26.4).
Death rate per 1,000 population (1991): 6.7 (world avg. 9.2).
Natural increase rate per 1,000 population (1991): 14.2 (world avg. 17.2).
Total fertility rate (avg. births per childbearing woman; 1991): 2.4.
Marriage rate per 1,000 population (1990): 8.4.
Divorce rate per 1,000 population (1990): 0.8.
Life expectancy at birth (1991): male 64.4 years; female 68.5 years.
Major causes of death per 100,000 population (1989)[6]: diseases of the heart
155.2; malignant neoplasms (cancers) 113.5; accidents, poisonings, and vio-
lence 101.2; tuberculosis of respiratory system 23.7; pneumonia 22.1; diar-
rheal disease 8.2.

National economy

Budget (1990–91). Revenue: B 387,500,000,000 (taxes 89.7%, state enterprises
4.6%, sale of property and services 3.6%). Expenditures: B 387,500,000,000
(economic services 22.1%, education 19.1%, defense 16.3%, debt service
15.1%, public utilities and health 13.5%, internal security 5.0%, general
administration 3.8%).
Public debt (external, outstanding; 1990): U.S.$13,488,000,000.
Production (metric tons except as noted). Agriculture, forestry, fishing (1991):
sugarcane 42,000,000, cassava 21,000,000, rice 18,800,000, corn (maize)
4,150,000, bananas 1,613,000[5], rubber 1,250,000, coconuts 920,000, soybeans
525,000, dry beans 310,000, sorghum 230,000[5], cabbages 194,000[5]; livestock
(number of live animals; 1990) 5,669,000 cattle, 5,350,000 buffalo, 4,900,000
pigs, 108,000,000 chickens; roundwood (1990) 37,686,000 cu m; fish catch
(1989) 2,822,530. Mining and quarrying (1991): limestone 19,516,000; gypsum
7,196,000; zinc ore 496,000; barite 92,974; fluorite 60,619; lead ore 39,245; tin
concentrates 14,937. Manufacturing (1990): cement 18,053,899; refined sugar
3,382,934; synthetic fibre 225,017; jute products 152,263; motorcycles 715,115
units. Construction (1990): residential 16,343,000 sq m; nonresidential 13,-
449,000 sq m. Energy production (consumption): electricity (kW-hr; 1990)
46,175,000,000 (46,796,000,000); coal (metric tons; 1990) 12,421,000 (12,-
639,000); crude petroleum (barrels; 1990) 8,650,000 (81,164,000); petroleum
products (metric tons; 1990) 12,614,000 (19,588,000); natural gas (cu m;
1990) 5,498,000,000 (5,498,000,000).
Land use (1989): forested 27.9%; meadows and pastures 1.5%; agricultural
and under permanent cultivation 43.3%; other 27.3%.
Tourism (1990): receipts from visitors U.S.$4,326,000,000; expenditures by
nationals abroad U.S.$854,000,000.
Population economically active (1989): total 29,469,600; activity rate of total
population 53.5% (participation rates: over age 13, 76.2%; female 45.4%;
unemployed [1990] 4.9%).

Price and earnings indexes (1985 = 100)							
	1985	1986	1987	1988	1989	1990	1991
Consumer price index	100.0	101.8	104.4	108.4	114.2	121.0	127.9
Earnings index	...	...	...	...	...	...	...

Gross national product (at current market prices; 1990): U.S.$79,044,000,000
(U.S.$1,420 per capita).

Structure of gross domestic product and labour force				
	1990		1989	
	in value B '000,000	% of total value	labour force[7]	% of labour force
Agriculture	254,523	12.4	16,500,900	56.0
Mining	73,500	3.6	56,800	0.2
Manufacturing	535,396	26.1	3,172,900	10.8
Construction	146,817	7.2	1,017,900	3.4
Public utilities	47,367	2.3	114,700	0.4
Transportation and communications	138,752	6.8	715,400	2.4
Trade	312,738	15.2	3,102,000	10.5
Finance	188,882	9.2		
Pub. admin., defense	74,603	3.6	3,022,300	10.3
Services	278,630	13.6		
Other	...	...	1,766,700	6.0
TOTAL	2,051,208	100.0	29,469,600	100.0

Household income and expenditure (1990). Average household size 4.1; average annual income per household B 67,452 (U.S.$2,636); sources of income:
wages and salaries 35.8%, self-employment 34.2%, transfer payments 5.8%,
other 24.2%; expenditure: food, tobacco, and beverages 38.4%, housing
23.8%, transportation and communications 13.3%, clothing 6.1%, medical
and personal care 5.5%, education and recreation 3.6%, other 9.3%.

Foreign trade[8]

Balance of trade (current prices)						
	1986	1987	1988	1989	1990	1991
B '000,000	−10,133	−1,900	−59,529	−71,417	−172,323	−139,742
% of total	2.1%	0.3%	6.9%	6.5%	12.7%	8.8%

Imports (1991): B 959,408,000,000 (electrical power equipment and machinery
33.5%, mineral fuels and lubricants 9.2%, iron and steel 7.8%, chemicals 7.8%, transport equipment 6.3%, precious stones 5.6%). *Major import
sources:* Japan 29.4%; United States 10.6%; Singapore 8.0%; Germany
5.6%; Taiwan 4.8%; South Korea 4.2%; Malaysia 3.2%; China 3.0%; United
Kingdom 2.3%.
Exports (1991): B 723,112,000,000 (electrical power equipment and machinery
22.9%, textiles and apparel 13.1%, fish and fish preparations 10.3%, precious stones 5.3%, cereals 4.8%, rubber and rubber articles 4.4%, footwear
3.3%). *Major export destinations:* United States 21.3%; Japan 18.1%; Singapore 8.1%; Germany 5.2%; Hong Kong 4.7%; The Netherlands 4.4%;
United Kingdom 3.6%; France 2.5%; Malaysia 2.4%.

Transport and communications

Transport. Railroads (1990)[9]: route length 2,399 mi, 3,861 km; passenger-mi
7,215,119,000, passenger-km 11,611,631,000; short ton-mi cargo 2,254,274,-
000, metric ton-km cargo 3,291,185,000. Roads (1989): total length 45,499 mi,
73,223 km (paved 53%). Vehicles (1989): passenger cars 655,927; trucks and
buses 1,523,361. Merchant marine (1991): vessels (100 gross tons and over)
333; total deadweight tonnage 1,066,880. Air transport (1991): passenger-mi
11,368,000,000, passenger-km 18,295,000,000; short ton-mi cargo 593,950,000,
metric ton-km cargo 867,152,000; airports (1992) with scheduled flights 24.
Communications. Daily newspapers (1988): total number 40; total circulation
4,750,000; circulation per 1,000 population 90. Radio (1991): 10,000,000 receivers (1 per 5.6 persons). Television (1991): 3,300,140 receivers (1 per 17
persons). Telephones (1990): 1,324,522 receivers (1 per 41 persons).

Education and health

Education (1988)	schools	teachers	students	student/ teacher ratio
Primary (age 7–12)	34,073	349,210	6,518,540	18.7
Secondary (age 13–18)	1,437[10]	103,377	1,734,687	16.8
Voc., teacher tr.	1,528[10]	19,775	336,420	17.0
Higher	62[10]	30,905[11]	1,026,952[11]	33.2[11]

Educational attainment (1980). Percentage of population age 25 and over
having: no formal schooling 20.5%; primary education 67.3%; secondary
9.3%; postsecondary 2.9%. *Literacy* (1985): total population age 15 and
over literate 28,451,390 (88.8%); males literate 14,877,240 (93.2%); females
literate 13,574,150 (84.5%).
Health (1989): physicians 12,713 (1 per 4,227 persons); hospital beds 89,982
(1 per 597 persons); infant mortality rate per 1,000 live births (1991) 25.0.
Food (1987–89): daily per capita caloric intake 2,312 (vegetable products 91%,
animal products 9%); 104% of FAO recommended minimum requirement.

Military

Total active duty personnel (1991): 283,000 (army 67.1%, navy 17.7%, air
force 15.2%). *Military expenditure as percentage of GNP* (1989): 2.7% (world
4.9%); per capita expenditure U.S.$34.

---

[1]The interim constitution requires that future prime ministers be elected members
of Parliament. [2]Preliminary results. [3]Excluding Bangkok Metropolis. [4]Detail does
not add to total given because of rounding. [5]1990. [6]Imputed rates calculated from
registered deaths. [7]August; economically active persons 13 years and over. [8]Import
figures are f.o.b. in balance of trade and c.i.f. for commodities and trading partners.
[9]Traffic data refer to fiscal year ending September 30. [10]1980. [11]1985.

Togo

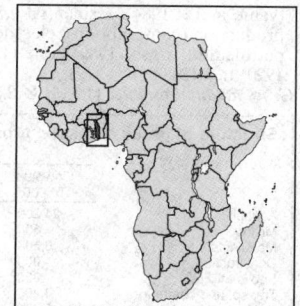

Official name: République Togolaise (Republic of Togo).
Form of government: transitional regime with one interim legislative body (High Council of the Republic [79])[1].
Chief of state: President.
Head of government: Prime Minister.
Capital: Lomé.
Official language: French.
Official religion: none.
Monetary unit: 1 CFA franc (CFAF) = 100 centimes; valuation (Oct. 5, 1992) 1 U.S.$ = CFAF 238.75; 1 £ = CFAF 405.88.

Area and population

Regions Prefectures	Capitals	area sq mi	area sq km	population 1981 census
Centrale	Sokodé			269,174
Sotouboua	Sotouboua	2,892	7,490	128,617
Tchamba	Tchamba	2	2	44,912
Tchaoudjo	Sokodé	2,198[2]	5,692[2]	95,645
De la Kara	Kara			432,626
Assoli	Bafilo	362	938	32,444
Bassar	Bassar	2,444	6,330	118,345
Binah	Pagouda	180	465	50,077
Doufelgou	Niamtougou	432	1,120	66,120
Kéran	Kandé	653	1,692	44,762
Kozah	Kara	419	1,085	120,878
Des Plateaux	Atakpamé			561,656
Amou	Amlamé	1,692[3]	4,382[3]	72,951
Haho	Notsé	1,412	3,658	109,995
Kloto	Kpalimé	1,077	2,790	106,429
Ogou	Atakpamé	2,372	6,145	163,906
Wawa	Badou	3	3	108,375
Des Savanes	Dapaong			326,826
Oti	Sansanné-Mango	1,453	3,762	77,747
Tône	Dapaong	1,869	4,840	249,079
Maritime	Lomé			1,039,700
Golfe	Lomé	133	345	438,110
Lacs	Aného	275	712	140,006
Vo	Vogan	290	750	150,313
Yoto	Tabligbo	483	1,250	100,387
Zio	Tsévié	1,289	3,339	210,884
TOTAL		21,925	56,785	2,700,982[4]

Demography

Population (1992): 3,701,000.
Density (1992): persons per sq mi 168.8, persons per sq km 65.2.
Urban-rural (1990): urban 25.7%; rural 74.3%.
Sex distribution (1990): male 49.45%; female 50.55%.
Age breakdown (1990): under 15, 45.3%; 15–29, 26.0%; 30–44, 15.0%; 45–59, 8.7%; 60 and over, 5.0%.
Population projection: (2000) 4,668,000; (2010) 6,238,000.
Doubling time: 20 years.
Ethnic composition (1981): Ewe-Adja 43.1%; Tem-Kabre 26.7%; Gurma 16.1%; Kebu-Akposo 3.8%; Ana-Ife (Yoruba) 3.2%; non-African 0.3%; other 6.8%.
Religious affiliation (1991): traditional beliefs 50.0%; Roman Catholic 26.0%; Muslim 15.0%; Protestant 9.0%.
Major cities (1983): Lomé 366,476; Sokodé 48,098[5]; Kpalimé 27,669[5].

Vital statistics

Birth rate per 1,000 population (1991): 49.0 (world avg. 26.4).
Death rate per 1,000 population (1991): 13.0 (world avg. 9.2).
Natural increase rate per 1,000 population (1991): 36.0 (world avg. 17.2).
Total fertility rate (avg. births per childbearing woman; 1991): 7.1.
Marriage rate per 1,000 population (1979): 2.3.
Life expectancy at birth (1991): male 54.0 years; female 58.0 years.
Morbidity (reported cases of illness per 100,000 population; 1978): infectious and parasitic diseases 26,926; diseases of the respiratory system 9,296; diseases of the digestive system 8,007; accidents, poisoning, and trauma 7,172.

National economy

Budget (1991). Revenue: CFAF 92,500,000,000 (1990; tax revenue 92.9%, nontax revenue 7.1%). Expenditures: CFAF 92,500,000,000 (1990; general public services 25.4%, education 23.1%, defense 14.9%, debt service 14.1%, economic services 7.4%, health 5.2%).
Production (metric tons except as noted). Agriculture, forestry, fishing (1991): cassava 500,000, yams 433,000, corn (maize) 236,000, sorghum 106,000, millet 70,000, cottonseed 55,000, rice 34,000, peanuts (groundnuts) 33,000, pulses 20,000, bananas 16,000, coconuts 14,000, palm oil 14,000, oranges 12,000, coffee 12,000, tomatoes 9,000, cacao beans 8,000; livestock (number of live animals) 1,741,000 goats, 1,200,000 sheep, 500,000 pigs, 250,000 cattle, 6,000,000 chickens; roundwood (1990) 910,000 cu m; fish catch (1989) 16,458. Mining and quarrying (1988): phosphate rock 3,464,000; salt 600,000[6]; marble 5,000[7]. Manufacturing (1987): cement 370,000; wheat flour 58,000; beer 452,000 hectolitres; soft drinks 149,000 hectolitres; footwear 29,000 pairs[8]. Construction (value added in CFAF; 1987): 14,200,000,000. Energy production (consumption): electricity (kW-hr; 1990) 41,000,000 (350,000,000); crude petroleum, none (n.a.); petroleum products (metric tons; 1990) none (125,000).
Gross national product (1990): U.S.$1,474,000,000 (U.S.$410 per capita).

Structure of gross domestic product and labour force

	1988 in value CFAF '000,000	1988 % of total value	1987 labour force	1987 % of labour force
Agriculture	138,400	34.4	926,000	70.6
Mining	25,800	6.4		
Manufacturing	32,300	8.0		
Construction	14,000	3.5	142,000	10.8
Public utilities	11,600	2.9		
Transp. and commun.	27,300	6.8		
Trade	90,800	22.5		
Finance	...		244,000	18.6
Pub. admin., defense	33,100	8.2		
Services	29,400	7.3		
TOTAL	402,800[9]	100.0	1,312,000	100.0

Population economically active: total (1990) 1,430,000; activity rate of total population 40.5% (participation rates [1985]: ages 15–64, 69.5%; female 37.5%; unemployed [1980] 2.3%).

Price and earnings indexes (1985 = 100)

	1984	1985	1986	1987	1988	1989	1990
Consumer price index	101.8	100.0	104.1	104.2	104.0	103.2	104.2
Hourly earning index[10]	100.0	100.0	100.0	105.5	105.5	105.5	105.5

Household income and expenditure. Average household size (1980) 5.6; average annual income per household CFAF 102,000 (U.S.$452); sources of income: n.a.; expenditure (1970): food and beverages 60.9%, housing 9.9%, transportation 8.2%, clothing 7.7%, household durable goods 3.9%.
Public debt (external, outstanding; 1990): U.S.$1,052,000,000.
Tourism (1990): receipts from visitors U.S.$23,000,000; expenditures by nationals abroad U.S.$46,000,000.
Land use (1990): forested 29.4%; meadows and pastures 32.9%; agricultural and under permanent cultivation 12.3%; other 25.4%.

Foreign trade[11]

Balance of trade (current prices)

	1983	1984	1985	1986	1987	1988
CFAF '000,000,000	−46.2	−34.9	−8.7	−29.7	−36.2	−52.5
% of total	27.2%	17.3%	3.8%	13.2%	19.8%	26.7%

Imports (1990): CFAF 160,500,000,000 (1987; machinery and transport equipment 27.2%, food products 14.6%, cotton yarn and fabrics 11.3%, chemicals 10.5%, refined petroleum products 7.3%). *Major import sources* (1987): France 32.7%; The Netherlands 9.3%; W.Ger. 8.8%; U.K. 7.1%; Côte d'Ivoire 5.5%; Japan 5.0%; U.S. 3.6%.
Exports (1988): CFAF 72,209,000,000 (1987; calcium phosphates 45.8%, coffee 12.6%, cotton [ginned] 11.8%, cocoa beans 11.4%, machinery and transport equipment 6.2%). *Major export destinations* (1987): The Netherlands 14.8%; France 7.7%; Spain 7.4%; U.S. 7.3%; Italy 7.0%; U.S.S.R. 6.6%; Canada 5.7%; U.K. 5.5%.

Transport and communications

Transport. Railroads (1991): length 326 mi, 525 km; passenger-km 109,000,000[7]; metric ton-km cargo 11,000,000[7]. Roads (1990): total length 7,545 km (paved 24%). Vehicles (1990): passenger cars 4,920; trucks and buses 389. Merchant marine (1991): vessels (100 gross tons and over) 8; total deadweight tonnage 34,126. Air transport (1989)[12]: passenger-km 32,344,000; metric ton-km cargo 5,753,000; airports (1992) with scheduled flights 1.
Communications. Daily newspapers (1990): total number 2; total circulation 10,000[13]; circulation per 1,000 population 2.9[13]. Radio (1991): 700,000 receivers (1 per 5.1 persons). Television (1991): 23,000 receivers (1 per 156 persons). Telephones (1990): 21,032 (1 per 169 persons).

Education and health

Education (1988)

	schools	teachers	students	student/ teacher ratio
Primary (age 6–11)[14]	2,429	10,426	569,388	54.6
Secondary (age 12–18)	358[15]	4,003[16]	103,835	27.1[16]
Vocational	18[16]	357	5,956	16.7
Higher[17]	1[16]	276	7,732	28.0

Educational attainment (1981). Percentage of population age 15 and over having: no formal schooling 76.5%; primary education 13.5%; secondary 8.7%; higher 1.3%. *Literacy* (1985): total population age 15 and over literate 631,700 (39.1%); males literate 401,800 (51.7%); females literate 229,900 (27.5%).
Health: physicians (1985) 230 (1 per 12,992 persons); hospital beds (1982) 3,655 (1 per 752 persons); infant mortality rate (1991) 110.0.
Food (1987–89): daily per capita caloric intake 2,141 (vegetable products 94%, animal products 6%); 92% of FAO recommended minimum requirement.

Military

Total active duty personnel (1992): 5,250 (army 91.4%, navy 3.8%, air force 4.8%). *Military expenditure as percentage of GNP* (1989): 3.3% (world 4.9%); per capita expenditure U.S.$12.

[1]Multiparty system introduced in April 1991, but single-party transitional government will run the country until multiparty elections (which remain unscheduled) are held in 1993. [2]Tchaoudjo includes Tchamba. [3]Amou includes Wawa. [4]Total includes 71,000 persons not counted separately. [5]1981. [6]1982. [7]1986. [8]Excludes rubber. [9]Detail does not add to total given because of rounding. [10]January 1 figures. [11]Import figures are f.o.b. in balance of trade and c.i.f. for commodities and trading partners. [12]Air Afrique only. [13]For one daily only. [14]1989. [15]1984. [16]1987. [17]Universities only.

Tonga

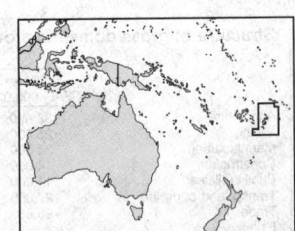

Official name: Pule'anga Fakatu'i 'o Tonga (Tongan); Kingdom of Tonga (English).
Form of government: constitutional monarchy with one legislative house (Legislative Assembly [31][1]).
Head of state and government: King assisted by Privy Council.
Capital: Nuku'alofa.
Official languages: Tongan; English.
Official religion: none.
Monetary unit: 1 pa'anga[2] (T$) = 100 seniti; valuation (Oct. 5, 1992) 1 U.S.$ = T$1.38; 1 £ = T$2.35.

Area and population		area		population
Divisions				1986
Districts	**Capitals**	sq mi	sq km	census
'Eua	'Ohonua	33.7	87.4	4,393
'Eua Fo'ou		...	...	1,995
'Eua Motu'a		...	...	2,398
Ha'apai	Pangai	42.5	110.0	8,979
Foa		...	...	1,409
Ha'ano		...	...	892
Lulunga		...	...	1,588
Mu'omu'a		...	...	897
Pangai		...	...	2,840
'Uiha		...	...	1,353
Niuas	Hihifo	27.7	71.7	2,379
Niua Fo'ou		...	...	763
Niua Toputapu		...	...	1,616
Tongatapu	Nuku'alofa	100.6	260.5	63,614
Kolofo'ou		...	...	15,782
Kolomotu'a		...	...	13,117
Kolovai		...	...	4,023
Lapaha		...	...	6,992
Nukunuku		...	...	5,790
Tatakamotonga		...	...	6,778
Vaini		...	...	11,132
Vava'u	Neiafu	46.0	119.2	15,170
Hahake		...	...	2,292
Hihifo		...	...	2,095
Leimatu'a		...	...	2,875
Motu		...	...	1,387
Neiafu		...	...	5,273
Pangaimotu		...	...	1,248
TOTAL LAND AREA		289.5[3]	749.9[3]	
INLAND WATER		11.4	29.6	
TOTAL		300.9	779.5	94,535

Demography

Population (1992): 97,300.
Density (1992)[4]: persons per sq mi 336.1, persons per sq km 129.8.
Urban-rural (1986): urban 30.7%; rural 69.3%.
Sex distribution (1986): male 50.30%; female 49.70%.
Age breakdown (1986): under 15, 40.6%; 15–29, 29.0%; 30–44, 13.8%; 45–59, 10.2%; 60–74, 5.0%; 75 and over, 1.4%.
Population projection: (2000) 101,000; (2010) 106,000.
Doubling time: 30 years.
Ethnic composition (1986): Tongan 95.5%; part Tongan 2.8%; other 1.7%.
Religious affiliation (1986): Free Wesleyan 43.0%; Roman Catholic 16.0%; Mormon 12.1%; Free Church of Tonga 11.0%; Church of Tonga 7.3%; other 10.6%.
Major cities (1984): Nuku'alofa (1986) 21,383; Mu'a 4,047; Neiafu 3,948; Haveluloto 3,136; Pangai-Hihifo 2,179.

Vital statistics

Birth rate per 1,000 population (1990): 30.4 (world avg. 27.1).
Death rate per 1,000 population (1990): 7.1 (world avg. 9.8).
Natural increase rate per 1,000 population (1990) 23.3 (world avg. 17.3).
Total fertility rate (avg. births per childbearing woman; 1988): 4.0.
Marriage rate per 1,000 population (1985): 6.6.
Divorce rate per 1,000 population (1985): 0.6.
Life expectancy at birth (1980–85): male 61.0 years; female 64.8 years.
Major causes of death per 100,000 population (1988)[5]: diseases of the circulatory system 112.2; malignant neoplasms 59.8; diseases of the respiratory system 37.7; infectious diseases 30.4; injuries and poisoning 18.9.

National economy

Budget (1992–93). Revenue: T$50,600,000 (foreign-trade taxes 49.4%, government services revenue 18.2%, indirect taxes 12.4%, direct taxes 8.6%, interest and rent 8.4%). Expenditures: T$50,570,000 (education 17.6%, general administration 17.5%, law and order 11.6%, public works and communications 11.5%, health 11.4%, public debt 7.5%, agriculture 4.9%).
Tourism: receipts from visitors (1991) U.S.$7,699,000; expenditures by nationals abroad (1990) U.S.$1,000,000.
Production (metric tons except as noted). Agriculture, forestry, fishing (1991): yams 33,000, taro 27,000, coconuts 25,000, cassava 15,000, sweet potatoes 14,000, vegetables (including melons) 14,000, fruits (excluding melons) 13,000, copra 1,000; livestock (number of live animals) 60,000 pigs, 10,000 cattle, 9,000 goats, 6,000 horses; roundwood (1990) 5,000 cu m; fish catch (1990) 2,630. Mining and quarrying (1982): coral 150,000; sand 25,000. Manufacturing (output in T$; 1990): food products and beverages 6,279,000; wearing apparel and footwear 3,351,000; metal products 1,672,000; paper and paper products 1,586,000; chemical products 1,347,000. Construction

(value in T$; 1984): residential 9,552,300; nonresidential 11,377,100. Energy production (consumption): electricity (kW-hr; 1990) 22,000,000 (22,000,000); petroleum (barrels; 1989) none (154,000); petroleum products (metric tons; 1990) n.a. (24,000).
Gross national product (1990): U.S.$100,000,000 (U.S.$1,010 per capita).

Structure of gross domestic product and labour force				
	1988–89		1986	
	in value T$'000[6]	% of total value	labour force	% of labour force
Agriculture	24,200	33.7	10,429	42.9
Mining	600	0.8	27	0.1
Manufacturing	6,500	9.1	622	2.6
Construction	4,000	5.6	1,741	7.2
Public utilities	800	1.1	326	1.3
Transp. and commun.	4,400	6.1	1,176	4.8
Trade	6,900	9.6	1,612	6.6
Finance	2,900	4.0	465	1.9
Pub. admin., defense } Services	12,500	17.4	5,492	22.6
Other	9,000[7]	12.5[7]	2,434	10.0
TOTAL	71,800	100.0[8]	24,324	100.0

Public debt (external, outstanding; 1990): U.S.$47,000,000.
Population economically active (1986): total 24,324; activity rate 25.8% (participation rates: ages 15–64, 44.7%; female 21.5%; unemployed 9.1%).

Price and earnings indexes (1985 = 100)						
	1985	1986	1987	1988	1989	1990	1991
Consumer price index	100.0	121.7	127.4	140.0	145.8	159.9	176.8
Earnings index	...	...	...	...	...	...	...

Household income and expenditure. Average household size (1986) 6.3; income per household: n.a.; sources of income: n.a.; expenditure (1984)[9]: food 49.3%, household operations 13.3%, housing 10.5%, tobacco and beverages 7.0%, transportation 5.8%, clothing and footwear 5.6%.
Land use (1990): forested 11.1%; meadows and pastures 5.6%; agricultural and under permanent cultivation 66.7%; other 16.6%.

Foreign trade

Balance of trade (current prices)					
	1986	1987	1988	1989	1990	1991
T$'000,000	− 47.7	− 58.0	− 50.3	− 54.0	− 49.8	− 42.1
% of total	72.7%	74.4%	70.9%	73.5%	62.1%	47.4%

Imports (1991): T$76,800,000 (food and live animals 21.5%, machinery and transport equipment 19.0%, mineral fuels 15.8%, basic manufactures 15.5%, chemicals 8.1%). *Major import sources:* New Zealand 29.6%; Australia 25.5%; Fiji 15.5%; U.S. 9.1%; Japan 9.0%.
Exports (1991): T$20,600,000 (squash 60.2%, vanilla beans 14.1%, coconut products 1.9%). *Major export destinations:* Japan 60.2%; U.S. 13.1%; Australia 8.7%; New Zealand 7.8%.

Transport and communications

Transport. Railroads: none. Roads (1991): total length 433 km (paved 65%). Vehicles (1989): passenger cars 1,433, commercial vehicles 2,784. Merchant marine (1991): vessels (100 gross tons and over) 17; total deadweight tonnage 51,018. Air transport (1990): passenger-km 5,897,000; metric ton-km cargo 12,000; airports (1992) with scheduled flights 6.
Communications. Daily newspapers (1988): total number 1; total circulation 7,000; circulation per 1,000 population 73. Radio (1988): total number of receivers 79,716 (1 per 1.2 persons). Television: total number of receivers, n.a.[10]. Telephones (1990): 5,212 (1 per 18 persons).

Education and health

Education (1990)	schools	teachers	students	student/ teacher ratio
Primary (age 6–11)	115	689	16,522	24.0
Secondary (age 12–18)	57[11]	767	13,877	18.1
Voc., teacher tr.	9	65	872	13.4
Higher	1[12]	17[13]	705[13]	41.5[13]

Educational attainment (1976). Percentage of population age 25 and over having: no formal schooling 0.4%; incomplete primary education 37.3%; complete primary 12.4%; lower secondary 45.6%; secondary 0.1%; postsecondary 0.1%; higher 0.6%; special education 2.4%; other 1.1%. *Literacy* (1976): total population age 15 and over literate 46,456 (92.8%); males 23,372 (92.9%); females 23,084 (92.8%).
Health (1989): physicians 45 (1 per 2,130 persons); hospital beds 307 (1 per 312 persons); infant mortality rate per 1,000 live births (1988) 49.0.
Food (1988–90): daily per capita caloric intake 2,967 (vegetable products 81%, animal products 19%); 130% of FAO recommended minimum requirement.

Military

Total active duty personnel (1991): Tonga has a national police (defense) force of about 300. *Military expenditure as percentage of GNP* (1989): 4.9% (world 4.9%); per capita expenditure U.S.$21.

[1]Includes 13 nonelective seats. [2]The pa'anga is now linked to an international basket of currencies rather than to the Australian dollar. [3]Total includes 39.0 sq mi (101.1 sq km) of uninhabited islands. [4]Density is based on land area. [5]Excludes deaths from non-intestinal infectious diseases. [6]At constant 1981–82 prices. [7]Includes indirect taxes less subsidies. [8]Detail does not add to total given because of rounding. [9]Current weight of consumer price index components. [10]Tonga has no authorized television service, but a "pirate" station began transmitting in mid-1984. [11]1987. [12]1986. [13]1985.

Trinidad and Tobago

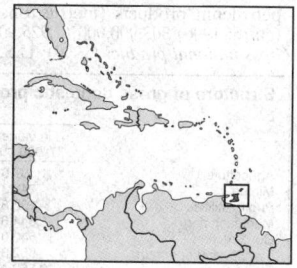

Official name: Republic of Trinidad and Tobago.
Form of government: multiparty republic with two legislative houses (Senate [31]; House of Representatives [36]).
Chief of state: President.
Head of government: Prime Minister.
Capital: Port of Spain.
Official language: English.
Official religion: none.
Monetary unit: 1 Trinidad and Tobago dollar (TT$) = 100 cents; valuation (Oct. 5, 1992) 1 U.S.$ = TT$4.25; 1 £ = TT$7.23.

Area and population

Counties	Capitals	area sq mi	area sq km	population 1990 census[1]
Caroni	Chaguanas	214.0	554.3	177,109
Nariva/Mayaro	Rio Claro	352.0	911.7	36,781
St. Andrew/St. David	Sangre Grande	361.7	936.8	62,944
St. George	...	350.4	907.5	445,620
St. Patrick	Siparia	251.0	650.1	120,129
Victoria	Princes Town	314.1	813.5	210,833
Unitary State				
Tobago[2]	Scarborough	116.2	301.0	50,282
Cities				
Port of Spain	—	3.7	9.6	50,878
San Fernando	—	2.5	6.5	30,092
Boroughs				
Arima	—	4.7	12.2	29,695
Point Fortin	—	9.8	25.4	20,025
TOTAL		1,980.1	5,128.4[3]	1,234,388

Demography

Population (1992): 1,261,000.
Density (1992): persons per sq mi 636.8, persons per sq km 245.9.
Urban-rural (1990): urban 69.1%; rural 30.9%.
Sex distribution (1990): male 50.07%; female 49.93%.
Age breakdown (1990): under 15, 31.3%; 15–29, 26.9%; 30–44, 21.5%; 45–59, 12.2%; 60 and over, 8.1%.
Population projection: (2000) 1,362,000; (2010) 1,500,000.
Doubling time: 50 years.
Ethnic composition (1986): black 43.0%; East Indian 36.0%; mixed 16.0%; white 2.0%; Chinese 1.0%; other 2.0%.
Religious affiliation (1980): Roman Catholic 32.2%; Protestant 27.6%, of which Anglican 14.4%, Presbyterian 3.7%, Pentecostal 3.4%; Hindu 24.3%; Muslim 5.9%; nonreligious 1.0%; unknown 6.0%; other 3.0%.
Major cities (1990): Port of Spain 50,878; San Fernando 30,092; Arima 29,695; Point Fortin 20,025; Scarborough 6,089[4].

Vital statistics

Birth rate per 1,000 population (1989): 20.7 (world avg. 27.1); (1979) legitimate 56.9%; illegitimate 43.1%.
Death rate per 1,000 population (1989): 6.8 (world avg. 9.8).
Natural increase rate per 1,000 population (1989): 13.9 (world avg. 17.3).
Total fertility rate (avg. births per childbearing woman; 1990): 2.8.
Marriage rate per 1,000 population (1989): 5.6.
Divorce rate per 1,000 population (1989): 0.9.
Life expectancy at birth (1990–95): male 69.7 years; female 74.7 years.
Major causes of death per 100,000 population (1989): diseases of the circulatory system 263.9, of which ischemic heart diseases 116.5, cerebrovascular disease 81.8; diabetes mellitus 85.9; malignant neoplasms (cancers) 83.0.

National economy

Budget (1991): Revenue: TT$6,704,200,000 (petroleum-sector corporate taxes 27.6%, value-added taxes 15.7%, individual income taxes 13.6%, import duties 8.1%, royalties from petroleum sector 7.6%). Expenditures: TT$6,-809,600,000 (current expenditures 88.8%; development expenditures 11.2%).
Tourism (1990): receipts from visitors U.S.$95,000,000; expenditures by nationals abroad U.S.$122,000,000.
Production (metric tons except as noted). Agriculture, forestry, fishing (1990): sugarcane 1,301,000[5], coconuts 40,000, rice 13,500, oranges 7,000, bananas 6,000, grapefruit 4,000, corn (maize) 3,000, cocoa 2,111, coffee 1,944; livestock (number of live animals) 80,000 cattle, 70,000 pigs, 50,000 goats; roundwood 72,000 cu m; fish catch 3,200[6]. Mining and quarrying (1991): natural asphalt 21,000. Manufacturing (1991): anhydrous ammonia and urea (nitrogenous fertilizers) 2,465,600; cement 485,600; methanol 452,800; steel billets 439,700; steel wire rods 364,100; raw sugar 110,400[7]; beer 303,600 hectolitres; rum 142,700 proof hectolitres. Construction (buildings authorized; 1990): residential 210,600 sq m; nonresidential 27,200 sq m. Energy production (consumption): electricity (kW-hr; 1990) 3,466,000,000 (3,105,000,000); coal, none (none); crude petroleum (barrels; 1991) 52,404,000 (33,989,000[8]); petroleum products (metric tons; 1991) 5,359,000 (976,000[8]); natural gas (cu m; 1991) 5,381,600,000 (5,065,000,000).
Land use (1989): forested 43.1%; meadows and pastures 2.1%; agricultural and under permanent cultivation 23.4%; other 31.4%.
Gross national product (at current market prices; 1990): U.S.$4,458,000,000 (U.S.$3,470 per capita).

Structure of gross domestic product and labour force

	1991 in value TT$'000,000	1991 % of total value	1990 labour force	1990 % of labour force
Agriculture[9]	537	2.6	50,700	10.8
Petroleum[10], natural gas, quarrying	4,810	22.9	21,200	4.5
Manufacturing[11]	2,059	9.8	47,000	10.1
Construction	1,936	9.2	64,800	13.9
Public utilities	355	1.7	8,500	1.8
Transp. and commun.	2,002	9.6	31,000	6.6
Trade	2,982	14.2	81,000	17.3
Finance, real estate	2,033	9.7	28,300	6.1
Pub. admin., defense	2,517	12.0 }	133,500	28.6
Services	1,387	6.6 }		
Other	360[12]	1.7[12]	1,600	0.3
TOTAL	20,978	100.0	467,700[3]	100.0

Public debt (external, outstanding; 1990): U.S.$2,508,000,000.
Population economically active (1990): total 467,700; activity rate of total population 38.1% (participation rates: ages 15–64, 61.5%; female 34.0%; unemployed [1991] 18.8%).

Price and earnings indexes (1985 = 100)

	1985	1986	1987	1988	1989	1990	1991[13]
Consumer price index	100.0	107.7	119.3	128.5	143.2	159.0	164.7
Weekly earnings index	100.0	101.8	106.2	108.0	108.8	115.2	119.3

Household income and expenditure. Average household size (1990) 4.1; income per household (1988): TT$17,083 (U.S.$4,444); sources of income: n.a.; expenditure (1981–82): food and beverages 27.7%, housing 22.7%, clothing and footwear 15.5%, transportation 13.2%, household furnishings 8.8%, other 12.1%.

Foreign trade[14]

Balance of trade (current prices)

	1986	1987	1988	1989	1990	1991
TT$'000,000	+129	+877	+1,114	+1,517	+3,480	+1,359
% of total	1.3%	9.1%	11.4%	12.7%	24.5%	8.8%

Imports (1990): TT$5,362,000,000 (nondurable consumer goods 22.8%, of which food 14.3%; capital goods 20.2%, of which industrial machinery 11.6%; crude petroleum and petroleum products 9.8%). *Major import sources* (1991): United States 38.9%; EEC 14.7%, of which United Kingdom 7.4%; Venezuela 14.0%; Japan 5.6%; Canada 4.9%.
Exports (1990): TT$8,842,000,000 (crude petroleum and petroleum products 66.7%; ammonia 8.2%; iron and steel bar rods 5.1%; urea 2.9%; methanol 1.9%; sugar 1.5%). *Major export destinations* (1991): United States 49.3%; Caricom 12.3%, of which Barbados 3.2%; EEC 9.2%, of which United Kingdom 2.3%.

Transport and communications

Transport. Railroads: none. Roads (1987): total length 4,906 mi, 7,895 km (paved 46%). Vehicles (1989): passenger cars 269,238; trucks and buses 68,759. Merchant marine (1991): vessels (100 gross tons and over) 48; total deadweight tonnage 12,549. Air transport (1990)[15]: passenger-mi 1,694,000,-000, passenger-km 2,726,000,000; short ton-mi cargo 9,850,000[6], metric ton-km cargo 14,381,000[6]; airports (1992) with scheduled flights 2.
Communications. Daily newspapers (1990): total number 4; total circulation 172,801; circulation per 1,000 population 140. Radio (1991): 700,000 receivers (1 per 1.8 persons). Television (1991): 250,000 receivers (1 per 5.0 persons). Telephones (1990): 216,039 (1 per 5.7 persons).

Education and health

Education (1989–90)

	schools	teachers	students	student/ teacher ratio
Primary (age 5–11)	472	6,839	189,623	27.7
Secondary (age 12–16) }	100[16]	4,878	99,133	20.3
Voc., teacher tr. }				
Higher[17]	1	346	4,090	11.8

Educational attainment (1980). Percentage of population age 25 and over having: no formal schooling 7.1%; primary education 66.5%; secondary 21.7%; higher 2.7%; other 2.0%. *Literacy* (1985): total population age 15 and over literate 751,600 (96.1%).
Health (1990): physicians 802 (1 per 1,543 persons); hospital beds[18] 3,894 (1 per 318 persons); infant mortality rate per 1,000 live births (1989) 10.2.
Food (1987–89): daily per capita caloric intake 2,913 (vegetable products 83%, animal products 17%); 120% of FAO recommended minimum requirement.

Military

Total active duty personnel (1991): 2,650 (army 100.0%). *Military expenditure as percentage of GNP* (1989): 1.6% (world 4.9%); per capita expenditure U.S.$48.

[1]Preliminary data. [2]Attained full internal self-government in 1987. [3]Detail does not add to total given because of rounding. [4]1980. [5]1991. [6]1992. [7]1990. [8]Includes sugar industry. [9]Includes refined petroleum. [10]Excludes refined petroleum and sugar industries. [12]Net of value-added taxes less imputed bank service charges. [13]Average through September. [14]Exports f.o.b.; imports c.i.f. [15]BWIA only. [16]1988–89. [17]1990–91; University of the West Indies, St. Augustine campus. [18]Includes nursing homes.

Tunisia

Official name: al-Jumhūrīyah
at-Tūnisīyah (Republic of Tunisia).
Form of government: multiparty
republic with one legislative house
(Chamber of Deputies [141]).
Chief of state: President.
Head of government: Prime Minister.
Capital: Tunis.
Official language: Arabic.
Official religion: Islam.
Monetary unit: 1 dinar (D) = 1,000
millimes; valuation (Oct. 5, 1992)
D 1.00 = U.S.$1.19 = £0.70.

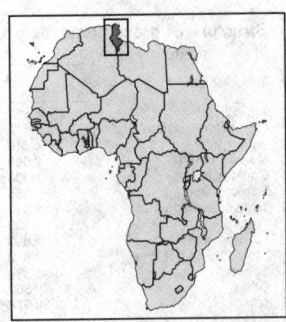

Area and population

Governorates	Capitals	area sq mi	area sq km	population 1990 estimate
Aryānah	Aryānah	602	1,558	533,300
Bājah	Bājah	1,374	3,558	299,100
Banzart	Banzart	1,423	3,685	447,300
Bin 'Arūs	Bin 'Arūs	294	761	306,600
Jundūbah	Jundūbah	1,198	3,102	403,100
al-Kāf	al-Kāf	1,917	4,965	269,500
Madanīyīn	Madanīyīn	3,316	8,588	349,800
al-Mahdīyah	al-Mahdīyah	1,145	2,966	311,500
al-Munastīr	al-Munastīr	393	1,019	327,200
Nābul	Nābul	1,076	2,788	530,300
Qābis	Qābis	2,770	7,175	276,300
Qafṣah	Qafṣah	3,471	8,990	277,300
al-Qaṣrayn	al-Qaṣrayn	3,114	8,066	354,800
al-Qayrawān	al-Qayrawān	2,591	6,712	488,600
Qibilī	Qibilī	8,527	22,084	114,800
Ṣafāqis	Ṣafāqis	2,913	7,545	665,300
Sīdī Bū Zayd	Sīdī Bū Zayd	2,700	6,994	337,500
Silyānah	Silyānah	1,788	4,631	243,200
Sūsah	Sūsah	1,012	2,621	389,400
Taṭāwīn	Taṭāwīn	15,015	38,889	118,700
Tawzar	Tawzar	1,822	4,719	76,800
Tūnis	Tunis (Tūnis)	134	346	824,000
Zaghwān	Zaghwān	1,069	2,768	129,600
TOTAL		59,664	154,530	8,073,900[1]

Demography

Population (1992): 8,413,000.
Density (1992): persons per sq mi 141.0, persons per sq km 54.4.
Urban-rural (1985): urban 53.0%; rural 47.0%.
Sex distribution (1990): male 50.72%; female 49.28%.
Age breakdown (1990): under 15, 37.3%; 15–29, 28.6%; 30–44, 16.4%; 45–59, 10.2%; 60–74, 5.8%; 75 and over, 1.7%.
Population projection: (2000) 9,779,000; (2010) 11,288,000.
Doubling time: 28 years.
Ethnic composition (1983): Arab 98.2%; Berber 1.2%; French 0.2%; Italian 0.1%; other 0.3%.
Religious affiliation (1980): Sunnī Muslim 99.4%; Christian 0.3%; Jewish 0.1%; other 0.2%.
Major cities (commune; 1989): Tunis 620,149; Ṣafāqis 221,770; Aryānah 131,-403; Ettadhamen 111,793; Sūsah 101,071.

Vital statistics

Birth rate per 1,000 population (1990): 25.4 (world avg. 27.1); (1974) legitimate 99.8%; illegitimate 0.2%.
Death rate per 1,000 population (1990): 6.4 (world avg. 9.8).
Natural increase rate per 1,000 population (1990): 19.0 (world avg. 17.3).
Total fertility rate (avg. births per childbearing woman; 1990–95): 3.4.
Marriage rate per 1,000 population (1990): 6.9.
Divorce rate per 1,000 population (1990): 1.5.
Life expectancy at birth (1990–95): male 66.4 years; female 68.7 years.
Major causes of death per 100,000 population: n.a.; however, of approximately 9,000 deaths[2] for which a cause was reported in 1988, complications of pregnancy and childbirth 25.0%; diseases of the circulatory system 20.7%; infectious and parasitic diseases 19.7%; accidents and poisonings 10.9%.

National economy

Budget (1990). Revenue: D 2,780,147,000 (indirect taxes 58.0%, investment 18.7%, direct taxes 14.5%). Expenditures: D 2,745,980,000 (finance 28.8%, education 20.3%, national economy 11.8%, interior affairs 9.3%, health 8.5%, defense 6.3%, agriculture 4.2%).
Tourism (1990): receipts from visitors U.S.$953,000,000; expenditures by nationals abroad U.S.$179,000,000.
Land use (1989): forested 4.0%; meadows and pastures 18.9%; agricultural and under permanent cultivation 30.3%; other 46.8%.
Production (metric tons except as noted). Agriculture, forestry, fishing (1990): wheat 895,000, barley 596,000, tomatoes 530,000, watermelons 450,000, olives 330,000, sugar beets 289,000, potatoes 217,000, oranges 140,000, grapes 130,-000, dates 75,000, alfalfa 70,000[3], almonds 52,000; livestock (number of live animals) 5,966,000 sheep, 1,280,000 goats, 622,000 cattle; roundwood 3,249,-000 cu m; fish catch (1989) 95,091. Mining and quarrying (1991): phosphate rock 6,707,000[4]; iron ore 280,000; zinc 4,900; lead 700. Manufacturing (1990): cement 4,311,000; phosphoric acid 1,080,000; flour 563,900; crude steel 192,000[5]; mineral water 577,000 hectolitres. Construction (1982): residential building authorized 2,679,000 sq m. Energy production (consumption): electricity (kW-hr; 1990) 5,536,000,000 (5,506,000,000); coal (metric tons; 1990) none (15,000); crude petroleum (barrels; 1990) 34,893,000 (9,065,000);

petroleum products (metric tons; 1990) 1,658,000 (3,005,000); natural gas (cu m; 1990) 303,900,000 (2,925,900,000).
Gross national product (1990): U.S.$11,592,000,000 (U.S.$1,420 per capita).

Structure of gross domestic product and labour force

	1990 in value D '000,000	1990 % of total value	1989 labour force	1989 % of labour force
Agriculture	1,587.0	14.5	543,100	23.0
Mining	749.3	6.8 }	36,600	1.6
Public utilities	163.8	1.5		
Manufacturing	1,644.6	15.0	422,300	17.9
Construction	540.0	4.9	295,200	12.5
Transp. and commun.	662.3	6.0		
Trade	2,552.4	23.2 }	349,000	14.8
Finance				
Pub. admin., defense	1,831.0	16.7 }	465,400	19.7
Services				
Other	1,256.0[6]	11.4[6]	249,000[7]	10.5[7]
TOTAL	10,987.0[1]	100.0	2,360,600	100.0

Public debt (external, outstanding; 1990): U.S.$6,716,000,000.
Population economically active (1989): total 2,360,000, activity rate of total population 28.8% (participation rates: ages 15–64, 42.2%; female 20.9%; unemployed 13.4%).

Price and earnings indexes (1985 = 100)

	1985	1986	1987	1988	1989	1990	1991
Consumer price index	100.0	105.8	113.4	120.6	129.5	138.3	149.7
Monthly earnings index	...	...	...	...	...	...	...

Household income and expenditure. Average household size (1989) 6.1; income per household: n.a.; sources of income: n.a.; expenditure (1985): food and beverages 39.0%, household durable goods 11.2%, housing 10.7%, transportation 9.0%, recreation 7.1%, clothing and footwear 6.0%, energy 5.1%, health care 3.0%, education 1.8%, other 7.1%.

Foreign trade

Balance of trade (current prices)

	1986	1987	1988	1989	1990	1991
D '000,000	−737.3	−569.9	−898.9	−1,089.8	−1,439.7	−1,037.5
% of total	20.8%	13.9%	17.9%	16.3%	18.9%	13.1%

Imports (1991): D 4,998,400,000 (1990; textiles 10.6%, iron and steel products 3.4%, plastic materials 2.9%, wheat 2.6%, sulfur 2.5%). *Major import sources:* France 28.0%; Italy 16.7%; Germany 13.7%; Belgium 5.1%; U.S. 4.6%; Spain 3.0%; Japan 2.2%; The Netherlands 2.1%.
Exports (1991): D 3,785,100,000 (1990; clothing and accessories 25.2%, petroleum and petroleum products 17.1%, phosphoric acid 4.0%, olive oil 3.5%, fish and crustaceans 3.3%, phosphates 3.1%). *Major export destinations:* France 22.7%; Italy 17.6%; Germany 14.8%; Belgium 5.6%; Libya 5.3%; Spain 3.3%; The Netherlands 2.4%.

Transport and communications

Transport. Railroads (1990): route length 1,343 mi, 2,162 km; passenger-mi 635,000,000, passenger-km 1,019,000,000; short ton-mi cargo 1,256,000,000, metric ton-km cargo 1,834,000,000. Roads (1989): total length 18,133 mi, 29,183 km (paved 60%). Vehicles (1989): passenger cars 321,101; trucks and buses 208,596. Merchant marine (1991): vessels (100 gross tons and over) 71; total deadweight tonnage 439,822. Air transport (1991): passenger-mi 875,000,000, passenger-km 1,408,000,000; short ton-mi cargo 12,200,000, metric ton-km cargo 17,800,000; airports (1992) 5.
Communications. Daily newspapers (1991): total number 6; total circulation 230,000[8]; circulation per 1,000 population 28[8]. Radio (1991): 1,700,000 receivers (1 per 4.8 persons). Television (1991): 650,000 receivers (1 per 13 persons). Telephones (1988): 333,185 (1 per 24 persons).

Education and health

Education (1990–91)

	schools	teachers	students	student/ teacher ratio
Primary (age 6–11)	3,841	50,280	1,405,665	28.0
Secondary (age 12–18)	585	24,474	564,540	23.1
Voc., teacher tr.[9, 10]	...	237	3,839	16.2
Higher	...	3,901[11]	68,534	14.0[11]

Educational attainment (1989). Percentage of population age 25 and over having: no formal schooling 54.9%; primary 26.9%; secondary 14.3%; higher 3.4%; unspecified 0.5%. *Literacy* (1989): total population age 10 and over literate 62.8%; males literate 73.6%; females literate 51.7%.
Health (1989): physicians 4,313 (1 per 1,834 persons); hospital beds 15,644 (1 per 506 persons); infant mortality rate per 1,000 live births (1990–95) 44.0.
Food (1987–89): daily per capita caloric intake 3,081 (vegetable products 91%, animal products 9%); 129% of FAO recommended minimum requirement.

Military

Total active duty personnel (1991): 35,000 (army 77.1%, navy 12.9%, air force 10.0%). *Military expenditure as percentage of GNP* (1989): 2.8% (world 4.9%); per capita expenditure U.S.$34.

---

[1]Detail does not add to total given because of rounding. [2]Recorded deaths from urban areas only, including complete figures for Tunis. [3]1988. [4]1990. [5]1989. [6]Indirect taxes less subsidies. [7]Includes 218,300 unemployed. [8]Circulation for 4 dailies only. [9]1987–88. [10]Teacher training only. [11]1988–89.

Turkey

Official name: Türkiye Cumhuriyeti
 (Republic of Turkey).
Form of government: multiparty
 republic with one legislative
 house (Turkish Grand National
 Assembly [450]).
Chief of state: President.
Head of government: Prime Minister.
Capital: Ankara.
Official language: Turkish.
Official religion: none.
Monetary unit: 1 Turkish lira (LT) = 100
 kurush; valuation (Oct. 5, 1992)
 1 U.S.$ = LT 7,511;
 1 £ = LT 12,768.

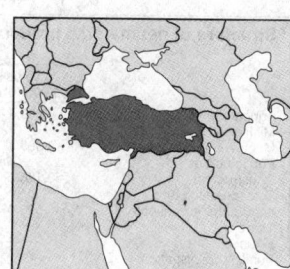

Area and population

Geographic regions[1]	area		population
	sq mi	sq km	1990 census
Akdeniz kıyısı (Mediterranean Coast)	22,933	59,395	5,443,867
Batı Anadolu (West Anatolia)	29,742	77,031	3,864,661
Doğu Anadolu (East Anatolia)	68,074	180,180	6,867,415
Güneydoğu Anadolu (Southeast Anatolia)	15,347	35,880	2,699,776
İç Anadolu (Central Anatolia)	91,254	236,347	13,096,179
Karadeniz kıyısı (Black Sea Coast)	31,388	81,295	6,827,304
Marmara ve Ege kıyıları (Marmara and Aegean coasts)	33,035	85,560	11,698,384
Trakya (Thrace)	9,175	23,764	5,975,449
TOTAL	300,948	779,452	56,473,035

Demography

Population (1992): 58,584,000.
Density (1992): persons per sq mi 194.7, persons per sq km 75.2.
Urban-rural (1990): urban 61.3%; rural 38.7%.
Sex distribution (1990): male 51.32%; female 48.67%.
Age breakdown (1990): under 15, 34.6%; 15–29, 29.1%; 30–44, 18.2%; 45–59, 11.1%; 60–74, 5.5%; 75 and over, 1.5%.
Population projection: (2000) 69,694,000; (2010) 78,524,000.
Doubling time: 32 years.
Ethnic composition (1983): Turkish 85.7%; Kurdish 10.6%; Arab 1.6%; Circassian 0.3%; Turkmen 0.3%; Georgian 0.2%; other 1.3%.
Religious affiliation (1986): Sunnī Muslim c. 90.0%; Alevi (nonorthodox Shī'ah sect) c. 9.6%; Christian c. 0.4%, of which Eastern Orthodox c. 0.2%.
Major cities (1990): Istanbul 6,620,241; Ankara 2,559,471; İzmir 1,757,414; Adana 916,150; Bursa 834,576; Gaziantep 603,434; Konya 513,346.

Vital statistics

Birth rate per 1,000 population (1991): 28.0 (world avg. 26.4).
Death rate per 1,000 population (1991): 6.0 (world avg. 9.2).
Natural increase rate per 1,000 population (1991): 22.0 (world avg. 17.2).
Total fertility rate (avg. births per childbearing woman; 1991): 3.6.
Marriage rate per 1,000 population (1989): 7.9.
Divorce rate per 1,000 population (1989): 0.5.
Life expectancy at birth (1991): male 68.0 years; female 72.0 years.
Major causes of death per 100,000 population: n.a.; however, of the 150,475 deaths (approximately 30% of total deaths[2]) for which a cause was reported in 1989, diseases of the circulatory system represented 41.2%; malignant neoplasms (cancers) 10.1%; accidental death 3.3%; pneumonia 3.1%.

National economy

Budget (1991). Revenue: LT 99,105,000,000,000 (direct taxes 41.1%; indirect taxes 38.0%; nontax revenue 9.5%; grants 8.5%). Expenditures: LT 130,865,-000,000,000 (current expenditures 85.5%, of which personnel 37.3%, debt service 18.4%, transfers 21.3%; investment expenditures 14.5%).
Public debt (external, outstanding; 1990): U.S.$37,737,000,000.
Tourism (1991): receipts from visitors U.S.$2,654,000,000; expenditures by nationals abroad U.S.$592,000,000.
Production (in '000 metric tons except as noted). Agriculture, forestry, fishing (1991): wheat 20,400, sugar beets 15,097, barley 7,800, potatoes 4,600, grapes 3,500, corn (maize) 2,100, apples 1,900, cottonseed 984, sunflower seeds 800, oranges 770, olives 720, lentils 700, cotton (lint) 616, hazelnuts 320, tobacco 243, sultana raisins 130; livestock (number of live animals; 1990) 31,500,000 sheep, 11,600,000 cattle; roundwood (1990) 15,524,000 cu m; fish catch (1989) 457,116. Mining (1989)[3]: coal 1,733; crude petroleum 741; boron minerals 472; chrome 251. Manufacturing (1989)[3]: refined petroleum 6,371; spinning and weaving of textiles 4,921; food products 4,445; iron and steel 3,727; industrial chemicals 2,680; paints, soaps, and pharmaceuticals 2,273. Construction (buildings completed; 1990): residential 25,692,000 sq m; nonresidential 7,477,000 sq m. Energy production (consumption): electricity (kW-hr; 1991) 60,219,000,000 ([1990] 56,813,000,000); coal (metric tons; 1991) 42,947,000 ([1990] 52,227,000); crude petroleum (barrels; 1990) 20,764,000 (171,595,000); petroleum products (metric tons; 1990) 20,370,000 (19,870,000); natural gas (cu m; 1990) 181,952,000 (3,065,322,000).
Household income and expenditure (1987). Average household size (4.8); income per household LT 3,680,500 (U.S.$4,294); sources of income: self-employment 51.4%, wages and salaries 24.1%, rent and interest 13.7%, transfers 10.8%; expenditure: food and beverages 33.1%, housing 14.7%, clothing 12.3%, household furnishings 11.5%.
Gross national product (at current market prices; 1990): U.S.$91,742,000,000 (U.S.$1,630 per capita).

Structure of gross domestic product and labour force

	1991			
	in value LT '000,000'000[4]	% of total value	labour force	% of labour force
Agriculture	99,376	17.4	9,603,000	46.4
Mining	10,860	1.9	133,000	0.6
Manufacturing	111,236	19.5	2,722,000	13.1
Construction	37,387	6.6	882,000	4.3
Public utilities	14,334	2.5	14,000	0.1
Transportation and communications	84,115	14.7	785,000	3.8
Trade	100,152	17.5	2,104,000	10.2
Finance, real estate	42,076	7.4	406,000	1.9
Pub. admin., defense	58,879	10.3 }	2,587,000	12.5
Services	12,281	2.2 }		
Other	—	—	1,471,000[5]	7.1[5]
TOTAL	570,696	100.0	20,707,000	100.0

Population economically active (1990): total 20,235,000; activity rate of total population 35.5% (participation rates: ages 15–64, 61.3%[6]; female 32.7%[6]; unemployed 11.8%[7]).

Price and earnings indexes (1985 = 100)

	1986	1987	1988	1989	1990	1991	1992[8]
Consumer price index	134.6	186.9	327.8	535.2	857.9	1,423.9	2,075.0
Daily earnings index[9]	132.0	206.3	344.1	766.4	1,429.6	3,574.1	...

Land use (1989): forested 26.2%; meadows and pastures 11.2%; agricultural and under permanent cultivation 36.2%; other 26.4%.

Foreign trade[10]

Balance of trade (current prices)

	1986	1987	1988	1989	1990	1991
U.S.$'000,000	−2,960	−3,204	−1,900	−3,316	−8,140	−6,349
% of total	16.5%	13.6%	7.5%	12.5%	23.9%	18.9%

Imports (1991): U.S.$21,047,000,000 (nonelectrical machinery 17.9%; crude petroleum 11.7%; iron and steel 9.5%; electrical and electronic equipment 9.3%; transport equipment 7.3%). *Major import sources:* Germany 15.3%; United States 10.6%; Italy 8.8%; Saudi Arabia 8.7%; France 5.8%; United Kingdom 5.5%; U.S.S.R. 5.2%; Japan 5.2%.
Exports (1991): U.S.$13,593,000,000 (textiles 32.3%, of which clothing 21.4%; agricultural products 18.1%; iron and steel 10.6%; manufactured agricultural products 8.1%). *Major export destinations:* Germany 28.0%; Italy 8.2%; United States 7.6%; U.S.S.R. 5.7%; France 5.6%; United Kingdom 5.5%; Iran 4.2%.

Transport and communications

Transport. Railroads (1991): route length (1990) 5,238 mi, 8,429 km; passenger-mi 3,994,000,000, passenger-km 6,428,000,000; short ton-mi cargo 5,445,000,000, metric ton-km cargo 7,950,000,000. Roads (1990): total length 228,296 mi, 367,409 km (paved [1988] 14%). Vehicles (1990): passenger cars 1,857,889; trucks and buses 800,848. Merchant marine (1991): vessels (100 gross tons and over) 880; total deadweight tonnage 7,043,622. Air transport (1991)[11]: passenger-mi 2,620,000,000, passenger-km 4,216,000,000; short ton-mi cargo 53,095,000, metric ton-km cargo 77,518,000; airports (1992) with scheduled flights 12.
Communications. Daily newspapers (1991)[12]: total number 31; total circulation 4,151,000; circulation per 1,000 population 72. Radio (1991): total number of receivers 7,100,000 (1 per 8.1 persons). Television (1991): total number of receivers 10,530,000 (1 per 5.4 persons). Telephones (1991): 8,172,000 (1 per 7.0 persons).

Education and health

Education (1989–90)

	schools	teachers	students	student/ teacher ratio
Primary (age 6–10)	51,170	224,672	6,848,083	30.5
Secondary (age 11–16)	7,185	109,720	2,790,266	25.4
Voc., teacher tr.	2,542	49,504	830,716	16.8
Higher	387	32,029	644,835	20.1

Educational attainment (1985). Percentage of population age 25 and over having: no formal schooling 40.1%; primary education 44.4%; secondary 11.6%; higher 3.9%. *Literacy* (1990): total population age 15 and over literate 29,400,000 (80.7%); males literate 16,800,000 (89.7%); females literate 12,600,000 (71.1%).
Health (1990): physicians 50,639 (1 per 1,108 persons); hospital beds 120,738 (1 per 465 persons); infant mortality rate per 1,000 live births (1991) 54.0.
Food (1987–89): daily per capita caloric intake 3,170 (vegetable products 92%, animal products 8%); 126% of FAO recommended minimum requirement.

Military

Total active duty personnel (1991): 579,200 (army 81.1%, navy 9.0%, air force 9.9%). *Military expenditure as percentage of GNP* (1989): 4.1% (world 4.9%); per capita expenditure U.S.$57.

---

[1]Administratively divided into 73 provinces. [2]Province and district centres only. [3]Value added in LT '000,000,000. [4]At factor cost. [5]Unemployed. [6]1989. [7]1992. [8]February. [9]Private sector only. [10]Imports are f.o.b. in balance of trade and c.i.f. in commodities and trading partners. [11]Turkish Airlines only. [12]Principal daily newspapers in Istanbul, Ankara, and 5 other large cities.

Turkmenistan

Official name: Türkmenistan
Jumhuriyäti (Republic of
Turkmenistan).
Form of government: republic with a
single legislative body (Majlis[1] [50]).
Head of state and government:
President.
Capital: Ashkhabad (Ashgabat).
Official language: Turkmen.
Official religion: none.
Monetary unit: 1 ruble = 100 kopecks;
valuation (Oct. 5, 1992) free rate,
1 U.S.$ = 316.82 rubles;
1 £ = 538.59 rubles.

Area and population

Provinces	Capitals	area		population
		sq mi	sq km	1991 estimate
Balkan	Nebit-Dag	90,300	233,900	925,500
Chardzhou	Chardzhou	36,200	93,800	774,700
Mary	Mary	33,500	86,800	859,500
Tashauz	Tashauz	28,400	73,600	738,000
City				
Ashkhabad (Ashgabat)	—			416,400
TOTAL		188,500[2]	488,100	3,714,100

Demography

Population (1992): 3,859,000.
Density (1992): persons per sq mi 20.5, persons per sq km 7.9.
Urban-rural (1991): urban 45.4%; rural 54.6%.
Sex distribution (1989): male 49.30%; female 50.70%.
Age breakdown (1989): under 15, 40.5%; 15–29, 28.8%; 30–44, 15.5%; 45–59,
9.1%; 60–74, 4.7%; 75 and over, 1.4%.
Population projection: (2000) 4,585,000; (2010) 5,491,000.
Doubling time: 26 years.
Ethnic composition (1989): Turkmen 72.0%; Russian 9.5%; Uzbek 9.0%;
Kazakh 2.5%; Tatar 1.1%; other 5.9%.
Religious affiliation: believers are predominantly Sunnī Muslim (Şūfī).
Major cities (1991): Ashkhabad 416,400; Chardzhou 166,400; Tashauz 117,000;
Mary 94,900; Nebit-Dag 89,100.

Vital statistics

Birth rate per 1,000 population (1990): 34.2 (world avg. 27.1); (1989) legiti-
mate 96.5%; illegitimate 3.5%.
Death rate per 1,000 population (1990): 7.0 (world avg. 9.8).
Natural increase rate per 1,000 population (1990): 27.2 (world avg. 17.3).
Total fertility rate (avg. births per childbearing woman; 1989): 4.3.
Marriage rate per 1,000 population (1989): 9.8.
Divorce rate per 1,000 population (1989): 1.4.
Life expectancy at birth (1990): male 62.9 years; female 69.7 years.
Major causes of death per 100,000 population (1989): diseases of the cir-
culatory system 275.3; diseases of the respiratory system 160.6; infectious
and parasitic diseases 79.3; malignant neoplasms (cancers) 65.1; accidents,
poisoning, and violence 62.4; diseases of the digestive system 32.2; diseases
of the nervous system 9.1; endocrine and metabolic disorders 8.0.

National economy

Budget (1991). Revenue: 6,489,000,000 rubles (nontax revenue 69.6%, of
which corporation profit transfer 23.9%, union transfers 21.7%; tax revenue
30.4%, of which turnover tax 10.3%, company profit tax 8.0%, individual
income tax 5.4%, sales tax 4.8%). Expenditures: 5,597,000,000 rubles (social
and cultural affairs 56.9%, of which social security 26.7%, education and
science 19.7%, health 9.4%; national economy 39.0%; government administration 2.7%).
Public debt (external, outstanding): n.a.
Tourism: n.a.
Production ('000,000 rubles except as noted). Agriculture, forestry, fishing
(1990): seed cotton 2,223, vegetables 139, grain 91, fruit 52; livestock (number of live animals; 1989) 5,083,000 sheep and goats, 807,000 cattle, 268,000
pigs; roundwood 4,000,000 cu m; fish catch, n.a. Mining and quarrying
(1989): sulfur 5,547,000; sodium sulphate 261,000. Manufacturing (1990):
light industry 2,028, of which textiles 1,745; fuel 989; food 700; building
materials 285; electricity 250; machinery and metalworking equipment 246;
chemicals and petroleum products 192; paper products 64; pharmaceuticals
12; printing 8. Construction (1991): 5,949,200,000 rubles. Energy production
(consumption): electricity (kW-hr; 1991) 17,171,400,000 (8,337,000,000); coal:
n.a. (n.a.); crude petroleum (barrels; 1989) 42,601,960 (n.a.); petroleum
products (metric tons; 1991) 7,131,800,000 (2,024,300,000); natural gas (cu
m; 1991) 84,300,000,000 (9,500,000,000).
Land use: n.a.
Household income and expenditure. Average household size (1989) 5.6; income per household: n.a.; sources of income (1991): salaries and wages
61.9%, pensions and grants 26.0%, income from agriculture sales 9.4%,
nonwage income of workers 2.7%; expenditure (1991): food and clothing
79.4%, services 10.1%, taxes and other payments 10.5%.
Gross national product (at current market prices; 1991): 13,771,000,000 rubles
(3,700 rubles per capita)[3].

Structure of net material product and labour force

	1991		1989	
	in value '000,000 rubles	% of total value	labour	% of labour force
Agriculture	6,389.7	46.4	674,800	42.6
Mining				
Manufacturing }	2,699.1	19.6	168,000	10.6
Public utilities				
Construction	3,126.1	22.7	151,300	9.5
Transportation and and communications	578.4	4.2	63,500	4.0
Trade	—	—	90,000	5.7
Finance	—	—	...	...
Public administration, defense	—	—	...	...
Services	—	—	410,400	25.9
Other	977.7	7.1	27,400	1.7
TOTAL	13,771.0	100.0	1,585,400	100.0

Population economically active (1991): total: 1,585,400; activity rate of total
population 42.7% (participation rates [1989]: ages 16–59 [male], 16–54 [fe-
male] 84.2%; female [1990] 52.2%; unemployed [1991] 20–25%).

Price and earnings indexes (1985 = 100)

	1985	1986	1987	1988	1989	1990	1991
Consumer price index	100.0	101.0	102.0	107.0	112.4	125.0	195.2
Monthly earnings index	100.0	101.0	103.8	109.0	115.7	127.5	196.1

Foreign trade

Balance of trade (current prices)

	1987	1988	1989	1990	1991
'000,000 rubles	−477	−284	−676	−971	+898
% of total	8.9%	5.1%	11.3%	15.5%	6.1%

Imports (1991): 5,938,000,000 rubles (detail, n.a.). *Major import sources:* former Soviet republics 91.8%; foreign countries 8.2%.
Exports (1991): 7,836,000,000 rubles (detail, n.a.). *Major export destinations:*
former Soviet republics.

Transport and communications

Transport. Railroads (1990): length 1,317 mi, 2,120 km; passengers 9,000,-
000; short ton cargo 37,600,000, metric ton-km cargo 34,100,000. Roads
(1990): total length 8,300 mi, 13,400 km (paved 86%). Vehicles (1988):
passenger cars 170,600; trucks and buses, n.a. Merchant marine: vessels
(100 gross tons and over) n.a.; total deadweight tonnage, n.a. Air transport
(1989): passenger-mi 2,021,000,000, passenger-km 3,253,000,000; short ton-
mi cargo 222,000,000, metric ton-km cargo 324,200,000; airports (1992) with
scheduled flights 1.
Communications. Daily newspapers (1989): total number 66; total circulation
1,141,000; circulation per 1,000 population 307. Radio and television (1990):
total number of receivers 1,967,000 (1 per 1.9 persons). Telephones (1989):
251,800 (1 per 15 persons).

Education and health

Education (1989–90)

	schools	teachers	students	student/ teacher ratio
Primary (age 6–13)	398 }	55,200	710,600 }	15.0
Secondary (age 14–17)	1,324		115,000	
Voc., teacher tr.	92	...	35,000	...
Higher	9	...	42,000	...

Educational attainment (1989). Percentage of population age 25 and over
having: primary education or no formal schooling 13.6%; some secondary
21.3%; completed secondary and some postsecondary 56.8%; higher 8.3%.
Literacy: n.a.
Health (1990): physicians 13,200 (1 per 274 persons); hospital beds 42,000 (1
per 86 persons); infant mortality rate per 1,000 live births 45.2.
Food: daily per capita caloric intake, n.a.

Military

Total active duty personnel: CIS-joint control 34,000 (100% army). *Military
expenditure as a percentage of GNP:* n.a.

---

[1]Constitution of May 18, 1992, provided for transitional status of former Supreme
Soviet as Majlis (from May 19) until a permanent representative body, the People's
Council (Khalk Maslakhaty) could be constituted. [2]Detail does not add to total given
because of rounding. [3]No equivalent U.S.$ value is offered, as Soviet GNP data
are very speculative.

Tuvalu

Official name: Tuvalu.
Form of government: constitutional monarchy with one legislative house (Parliament [12]).
Chief of state: British Monarch, represented by Governor-General.
Head of government: Prime Minister.
Capital: Fongafale, on Funafuti atoll.
Official language: none.
Official religion: none.
Monetary unit[1]: 1 Tuvalu Dollar = 1 Australian Dollar ($T = $A) = 100 Tuvalu and Australian cents; valuation (Oct. 5, 1992) 1 U.S.$ = $A 1.38; 1 £ = $A 2.35.

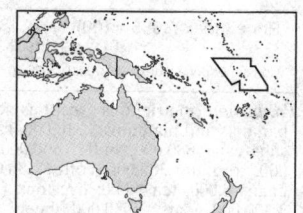

Area and population

Islands[2]	area		population
	sq mi	sq km	1985 census
Funafuti	0.91	2.36	2,810
Nanumaga	1.00	2.59	672
Nanumea	1.38	3.57	879
Niulakita	0.16	0.41	74
Niutao	0.82	2.12	904
Nui	1.27	3.29	604
Nukufetau	1.18	3.06	694
Nukulaelae	0.64	1.66	315
Vaitupu	1.89	4.90	1,231
TOTAL	9.25	23.96	8,229[3, 4]

Demography

Population (1992): 9,500.
Density (1992): persons per sq mi 1,027.0, persons per sq km 396.5.
Urban-rural (1985): urban 34.2%; rural 65.8%.
Sex distribution (1991): male 46.00%; female 54.00%.
Age breakdown (1979): under 15, 33.8%; 15–29, 31.0%; 30–44, 14.3%; 45–59, 13.2%; 60–74, 6.1%; 75 and over, 1.6%.
Population projection: (2000) 11,000; (2010) 14,000.
Doubling time: 35 years.
Ethnic composition (1979): Tuvaluan (Polynesian) 91.2%; mixed (Polynesian/Micronesian/other) 7.2%; European 1.0%; other 0.6%.
Religious affiliation (1979): Church of Tuvalu (Congregational) 96.9%; Seventh-day Adventist 1.4%; Bahā'ī 1.0%; Roman Catholic 0.2%; other 0.5%.
Major locality (1990): Fongafale, on Funafuti atoll, 3,432.

Vital statistics

Birth rate per 1,000 population (1990): 30.0 (world avg. 27.1); (1989) legitimate 82.2%; illegitimate 17.8%.
Death rate per 1,000 population (1990): 10.0 (world avg. 9.8).
Natural increase rate per 1,000 population (1990): 20.0 (world avg. 17.3).
Total fertility rate (avg. births per childbearing woman; 1990): 3.1.
Marriage rate per 1,000 population: n.a.
Divorce rate per 1,000 population: n.a.
Life expectancy at birth (1990): male 60.0 years; female 63.0 years.
Major causes of death per 100,000 population (1985): diseases of the digestive system 170.0; diseases of the circulatory system 150.0; diseases of the respiratory system 120.0; diseases of the nervous system 120.0; malignant neoplasms (cancers) 70.0; infectious and parasitic diseases 40.0; endocrine and metabolic disorders 20.0; ill-defined conditions 430.0; in 1992 the leading causes of death included liver diseases, meningitis, tuberculosis, and still and perinatal deaths; other health problems included acute respiratory infections, diarrhea, filariasis, conjunctivitis, fish poisoning, diabetes, rheumatism, and hypertension.

National economy

Budget (1990). Recurrent revenue: $A 5,301,000 (local sources [including fisheries licenses, import duties, sales tax, and income and company taxes] 77.4%; Tuvalu Trust Fund[5] 22.6%). Expenditures: $A 10,826,000[6] (1987; capital [development] expenditures 68.9%, of which marine transport 20.7%, education 13.0%, fisheries 5.6%, health 3.1%; current expenditures 31.1%).
Gross domestic product (at current market prices; 1990): U.S.$8,750,000 (U.S.$967 per capita).

Structure of gross domestic product and labour force

	1990		1979	
	in value $A	% of total value	labour force[7]	% of labour force[7]
Agriculture, fishing, forestry	2,699,000	24.1	38	1.0
Mining	302,000	2.7	1	—
Manufacturing[8]	358,000	3.2	62	1.6
Construction	1,635,000	14.6	224	5.6
Public utilities	235,000	2.1	14	0.3
Transportation and communications	403,000	3.6	107	2.7
Trade, hotels, and restaurants	1,669,000	14.9	98	2.4
Finance	997,000	8.9	11	0.3
Pub. admin., defense } Services	2,901,000	25.9	177	4.4
			170	4.2
Unemployed	—	—	162	4.0
Noncash economy	—	—	2,946[9]	73.5[9]
TOTAL	11,199,000	100.0	4,010	100.0

Production (metric tons except as noted). Agriculture[10], forestry, fishing (1991): coconuts 4,000, fruits 1,000, hens' eggs 16[11], other agricultural products include breadfruit, pulaka (taro), bananas, pandanus fruit, sweet potatoes, and pawpaws; livestock (number of live animals) 12,000 pigs[12]; forestry, n.a.; fish catch 1,460, of which tuna 71.2%. Mining and quarrying: n.a.[13]. Manufacturing (1984): copra 840 metric tons; handicrafts and baked goods are also important. Construction: n.a.; however, the main areas of construction activity are road works, coastal protection, government facilities, and water-related infrastructure projects. Energy production (consumption): electricity (kW-hr; 1987) 3,000,000 (3,000,000); coal, none (none); crude petroleum, none (none); petroleum products, none (n.a.); natural gas, none (none).
Public debt: n.a.
Tourism (1990): number of visitors 567; receipts from visitors $A 169,700; hotel occupancy 95%.
Population economically active (1979)[7]: total 4,010; activity rate of total population 55.2% (participation rates: over age 15, 81.1%; female 51.3%; unemployed 4.0%).

Price and earnings indexes (1986 = 100)

	1984	1985	1986	1987	1988	1989	1990
Consumer price index	...	...	100.0	111.0	113.3	116.3	123.2
Earnings index[14]	...	...	100.0	102.5	105.0	110.0	112.5

Household income and expenditure. Average household size (1979) 6.4; average annual income per household $A 2,575; sources of income: agriculture and other 61.2%, cash economy only 17.9%, agriculture only 14.9%, other 6.0%; expenditure (1987)[15]: food 45.5%, housing and household operations 11.5%, transportation 10.5%, alcohol and tobacco 10.5%, clothing 7.5%, other 14.5%.
Land use (1983): agricultural and under permanent cultivation 75%[16]; other 25%.

Foreign trade

Balance of trade (current prices)

	1984	1985	1986	1987	1988	1989
$A '000	−3,637	−3,969	−4,076	−4,946	−6,780	−5,158
% of total	85.4%	92.7%	99.9%	99.9%	99.7%	99.5%

Imports (1989): $A 5,170,000 (1986; food and live animals 29.5%, manufactured goods 25.2%, machinery and transport equipment 15.1%, petroleum and petroleum products 13.8%, beverages and tobacco 7.0%, chemicals 6.6%). *Major import sources* (1986): Australia 40.6%; New Zealand 10.9%; United Kingdom 5.1%; Japan 3.0%; United States 1.0%.
Exports (1990): $A 30,400 (1986; copra 86.4%). *Major export destinations:* n.a.

Transport and communications

Transport. Railroads: none. Roads (1985): total length 5 mi, 8 km (paved, none). Vehicles[17]: passenger cars, n.a.; trucks and buses, n.a. Merchant marine (1991): vessels (100 gross tons and over) 2; total deadweight tonnage 798. Air transport (1977): passenger arrivals (Funafuti) 1,443; cargo, n.a.; airports (1992) with scheduled flights 1.
Communications. Daily newspapers: none. Radio (1991): total number of receivers 3,000 (1 per 3.1 persons). Television: none. Telephones (1987): 160 (1 per 54 persons).

Education and health

Education (1987)

	schools	teachers	students	student/ teacher ratio
Primary (age 5–11)	11	64	1,364	21.3
Secondary (age 12–18)	1	15[18]	243	...
Vocational[18]	8	16	354	22.1
Higher	—	—	—	—

Educational attainment (1979). Percentage of population age 25 and over having: no formal schooling 0.4%; primary education 93.0%; secondary 6.1%; higher 0.5%. *Literacy* (1990): total population literate in Tuvaluan 8,593 (95.0%); literacy in English estimated at 45.0%.
Health (1990): physicians 4 (1 per 2,261 persons); hospital beds 30 (1 per 302 persons); infant mortality rate per 1,000 live births 78.6.
Food: daily per capita caloric intake, n.a.

Military

Total active duty personnel (1987): there is a police force of 32 men.

[1]The value of the Tuvalu Dollar is pegged to the value of the Australian Dollar, which is also legal currency in Tuvalu. [2]Local government councils have been established on all islands except Niulakita. [3]Total includes 46 persons unaccounted for in island populations. [4]De facto population; about 1,500 Tuvaluans live abroad, mainly in Nauru or on foreign fishing vessels. [5]The Tuvalu Trust Fund was capitalized in 1987 with $A 27.7 million to replace recurrent grant aid from the United Kingdom; the Fund was valued at $A 36 million in late 1991. [6]Figure includes $A 5,200,000 of capital expenditures, paid for, primarily, by foreign-aid contributions that are not part of recurrent revenue. [7]Based on indigenous de facto population only. [8]Including cottage industry. [9]Mostly subsistence fishermen and handicraft workers. [10]Because of poor soil quality, only limited subsistence agriculture is possible on the islands. [11]1989. [12]Other livestock include goats. [13]Research into the mineral potential of Tuvalu's maritime exclusive economic zone (289,500 sq mi [750,000 sq km] of the Pacific Ocean) is currently being conducted by the South Pacific Geo-Science Commission. [14]Average minimum wage. [15]Weights of consumer price index components. [16]Capable of supporting coconut palms, pandanus, and breadfruit. [17]There are several cars, tractors, trailers, and light trucks on Funafuti; a few motorcycles are in use on most islands. [18]1982–83.

Uganda

Official name: Republic of Uganda.
Form of government: transitional
  military regime with one interim
  legislative body (National Resistance
  Council [278[1]])[2].
Head of state and government:
  President assisted by Prime Minister.
Capital: Kampala.
Official language: English; Swahili.
Official religion: none.
Monetary unit: 1 Uganda
  shilling (U Sh) = 100 cents;
  valuation (Oct. 5, 1992)
  1 U.S.$ = U Sh 1,192;
  1 £ = U Sh 2,026.

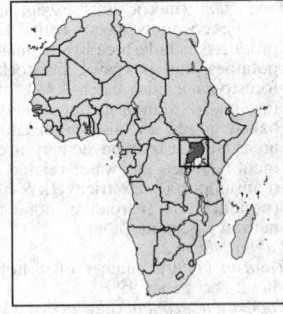

Area and population

Regions Districts	Capitals	area sq mi	area sq km	population 1991 census[3]
Central				
Kalangala	—	...	...	16,400
Kampala	Kampala	70	180	773,500
Kiboga	—	...	...	140,800
Luwero	Luwero	3,550	9,200	449,200
Masaka	Kasawa Bukoto	6,310	16,330	831,300
Mpigi	Mpigi	2,400	6,220	915,400
Mubende	Bageza	3,980	10,310	497,500
Mukono	Kawuga Mukono	5,500	14,240	816,200
Rakai	Byakabanda	1,920	4,970	382,000
Eastern				
Iganga	Bulamogi	5,060	13,110	944,000
Jinja	Jinja	280	730	284,900
Kamuli	Namwendwa	1,680	4,350	480,700
Kapchorwa	Kaptanya	670	1,740	116,300
Kumi	Kumi	1,100	2,860	237,000
Mbale	Bunkoko	980	2,550	706,600
Pallisa	—	...	...	355,000
Soroti	Soroti	3,880	10,060	430,900
Tororo	Sukulu	1,780	4,550	554,000
Northern				
Apac	Apac	2,510	6,490	460,700
Arua	Olaki	3,020	7,830	624,600
Gulu	Bungatira	4,530	11,740	338,700
Kitgum	Labongo	8,230	16,140	350,300
Kotido	Kotido	5,100	13,210	190,700
Lira	Lira	2,800	7,250	498,300
Moroto	Katikekile	5,450	14,110	171,500
Moyo	Moyo	1,930	5,010	178,500
Nebbi	Nebbi	1,120	2,890	315,900
Western				
Bundibugyo	Busaru	900	2,340	116,000
Bushenyi	Bumbaire	2,080	5,400	734,800
Hoima	Hoima	3,820	9,900	197,800
Kabale	Rubale	960	2,490	412,800
Kabarole	Karambe	3,230	8,360	741,400
Kasese	Rukoki	1,240	3,200	343,000
Kibaale	—	...	...	219,300
Kisoro	—	...	...	184,900
Masindi	Nyangeya	3,720	9,640	253,500
Mbarara	Kakika	4,190	10,840	929,600
Rukungiri	Kagunga	1,060	2,750	388,000
TOTAL LAND AREA		76,080	197,040	
INLAND WATER[4]		16,990	44,000	
TOTAL		93,070[5]	241,040[5]	16,582,700[5]

Demography

Population (1992): 17,194,000.
Density (1992)[6]: persons per sq mi 226.0, persons per sq km 87.3.
Urban-rural (1991): urban 11.3%; rural 88.7%.
Sex distribution (1991): male 49.00%; female 51.00%.
Age breakdown (1985): under 15, 48.5%; 15–29, 25.8%; 30–44, 14.1%; 45–59,
  7.4%; 60–74, 3.6%; 75 and over, 0.6%.
Population projection: (2000) 20,958,000; (2010) 26,842,000.
Doubling time: 19 years.
Ethnic composition (1983): Ganda 17.8%; Teso 8.9%; Nkole 8.2%; Soga
  8.2%; Gisu 7.2%; Chiga 6.8%; Lango 6.0%; Rwanda 5.8%; other 31.1%.
Religious affiliation (1980): Roman Catholic 49.6%; Protestant 28.7%; Muslim
  6.6%; other 15.1%.
Major cities (1991): Kampala 773,000; Jinja 61,000; Mbale 54,000.

Vital statistics

Birth rate per 1,000 population (1990–95): 51.5 (world avg. 26.4).
Death rate per 1,000 population (1990–95): 14.1 (world avg. 9.2).
Natural increase rate per 1,000 population (1990–95): 37.4 (world avg. 17.2).
Total fertility rate (avg. births per childbearing woman; 1990–95): 7.3.
Life expectancy at birth (1990–95): male 51.4 years; female 54.7 years.
Major causes of death per 100,000 population: n.a.

National economy

Budget (1990–91). Revenue: U Sh 127,929,000,000 (sales and excise taxes
  36.6%; customs duties 35.7%, of which export tax on coffee 9.5%; income
  taxes 9.5%). Expenditures: U Sh 163,119,700,000 (current expenditures
  79.2%, of which security 51.7%, education 16.5%, public services 16.2%,
  health 5.5%; capital expenditures 20.8%).
Tourism: receipts from visitors (1990) U.S.$10,000,000; expenditures by na-
  tionals abroad U.S.$8,000,000.
Population economically active (1991): total 8,363,000; activity rate of total
  population 49.9% (participation rates: ages 15–64, 78.9%[7]; female 41.6%[8]).

Price index (1985 = 100)

	1985	1986	1987	1988	1989	1990	1991
Consumer price index	100.0	261.0	783.0	2,519.0	3,743.0	4,983.0	6,382.0

Production (metric tons except as noted). Agriculture, forestry, fishing (1991):
  bananas and plantains 8,310,000; cassava 3,350,000, sweet potatoes 1,800,000,
  sugarcane 880,000, millet 600,000, corn (maize) 600,000, dry beans 400,-
  000, sorghum 380,000, coffee 180,000, peanuts (groundnuts) 173,000, cacao
  beans 8,000, tea 8,000; livestock (number of live animals) 5,000,000 cattle,
  3,300,000 goats, 1,950,000 sheep; roundwood (1990) 15,142,000 cu m; fish
  catch (1990) 245,200. Mining and quarrying (1990): tungsten (wolfram) 37.1;
  tin ore 24.6; gold 2,322 troy oz. Manufacturing (1990): soap 30,600; sugar
  28,900; cement 14,960; animal feed 15,000; metal products 1,300; footwear
  319,000 pairs; fabrics 8,200,000 sq m; 1,289,700,000 cigarettes; beer 194,000
  hectolitres. Construction: n.a. Energy production (consumption): electricity
  (kW-hr; 1990) 603,000,000 (493,000,000); petroleum products (metric tons;
  1990) none (267,000).
Gross national product (1990): U.S.$3,814,000,000 (U.S.$220 per capita).

Structure of gross domestic product and labour force

	1990 in value U Sh '000,000	1990 % of total value	1987 labour force	1987 % of labour force
Agriculture	363,273	35.4	6,240,000	82.6
Manufacturing and mining	69,891	6.8		
Construction	73,860	7.2	385,000	5.1
Public utilities	9,538	0.9		
Transp. and commun.	102,342	10.0		
Trade	220,557	21.5		
Finance	53,520	5.2	929,000	12.3
Pub. admin., defense	100,737	9.8		
Services	33,364	3.2		
TOTAL	1,027,082	100.0	7,554,000	100.0

Household size. Average household size (1983) 4.8; income per household:
  n.a.; expenditure (1989–90)[9]: food 57.1%, rent, education, and health 15.7%,
  fuel and lighting 7.3%, transportation 5.9%, clothing 5.5%.
Land use (1990): forested 27.9%; meadows and pastures 9.0%; agricultural
  and under permanent cultivation 33.6%; other 29.5%.
Public debt (external, outstanding; 1990): U.S.$2,301,000,000.

Foreign trade

Balance of trade (current prices)

	1986	1987	1988	1989	1990	1991
U Sh '000,000	+2,226	−19,051	−55,716	−23,471	−48,013	+23,012
% of total	22.3%	41.0%	48.9%	17.4%	27.1%	8.5%

Imports (1991): U Sh 137,250,000,000 (1984; sugar 16.0%, motor vehicles
  10.8%, clothing and fabrics 9.6%, construction materials 8.0%, food 5.4%).
  Major import sources: Kenya 23.3%; U.K. 15.0%; Japan 9.3%; Germany
  6.9%.
Exports (1991): U Sh 146,661,000,000 (1990; unroasted coffee 79.6%, cotton
  3.3%, tea 1.2%). *Major export destinations:* The Netherlands 21.5%; France
  16.2%; U.S. 11.9%; Spain 11.1%; Germany 10.9%; Italy 7.9%.

Transport and communications

Transport. Railroads (1990): route length 1,240 km; passenger-km 109,000,-
  000; metric ton-km cargo 103,000,000. Roads (1986): total length 28,332
  km (paved 22%). Vehicles (1990): passenger cars 35,492; trucks and buses
  14,902. Merchant marine (1991): vessels (100 gross tons and over) 3; total
  deadweight tonnage 8,600[10]. Air transport (1990)[11]: passenger-km 67,000,-
  000; metric ton-km cargo 3,000,000; airports (1992) 1.
Communications. Daily newspapers (1990): total number 6; total circulation
  63,800; circulation per 1,000 population 3.7. Radio (1991): 3,500,000 receivers (1 per 5.1 persons). Television (1991): 90,000 receivers (1 per 197
  persons). Telephones (1990): 57,185 (1 per 286 persons).

Education and health

Education (1989)

	schools	teachers	students	student/ teacher ratio
Primary (age 5–11)	7,905	75,561	2,633,764	34.8
Secondary (age 12–15)	774	13,356	240,334	18.0
Voc., teacher tr.	136	2,081	23,179	11.1
Higher	9	934[12]	5,778	8.8[12]

Educational attainment (1969). Percentage of population age 25 and over
  having: no formal schooling, or less than one full year 58.2%; primary education 33.9%; lower secondary 5.0%; upper secondary 2.5%; higher 0.4%.
Literacy (1990): population age 15 and over literate 4,586,000 (48.3%); males
  literate 2,900,000 (62.2%); females literate 1,686,000 (34.9%).
Health: physicians (1984) 700 (1 per 20,300 persons); hospital beds (1989)
  20,136 (1 per 817 persons); infant mortality rate (1990–95) 94.0.
Food (1988–90): daily per capita caloric intake 2,178 (vegetable products 94%,
  animal products 6%); 93% of FAO recommended minimum requirement.

Military

Total active duty personnel (1992): 70,000 (army 100%). *Military expenditure
  as percentage of GNP* (1988): 1.5% (world 5.0%); per capita U.S.$4.

[1]Includes 68 nonelective seats. [2]Constitution of 1967 suspended July 1985. [3]Preliminary.
[4]Includes swamps. [5]Detail does not add to total given because of rounding. [6]Based
on land area. [7]1985. [8]1987. [9]Kampala and Entebbe only. [10]1988. [11]Uganda Airlines only. [12]1984.

Ukraine

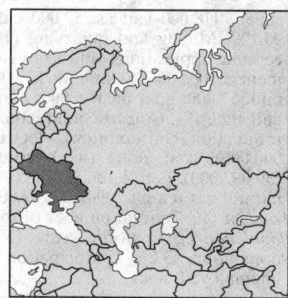

Official name: Ukrayina (Ukraine).
Form of government: unitary multiparty republic with a single legislative body (Supreme Council [450]).
Head of state: President.
Head of government: Prime Minister.
Capital: Kiev (Kyyiv).
Official language: Ukrainian.
Official religion: none.
Monetary unit: 1 ruble = 100 kopecks; valuation (Oct. 5, 1992) free rate, 1 U.S.$ = 316.82 rubles; 1 £ = 538.59 rubles.

Area and population

		area		population
		sq mi	sq km	1991 estimate
Autonomous republic	**Capitals**			
Crimea (Krym)	Simferopol	10,400	27,000	2,549,800
Provinces				
Cherkasy	Cherkasy	8,100	20,900	1,530,900
Chernihiv	Chernihiv	12,300	31,900	1,405,800
Chernivtsi	Chernivtsi	3,100	8,100	938,600
Dnipropetrovsk	Dnipropetrovsk	12,300	31,900	3,908,700
Donetsk	Donetsk	10,200	26,500	5,346,700
Ivano-Frankivsk	Ivano-Frankivsk	5,400	13,900	1,442,900
Kharkiv	Kharkiv	12,100	31,400	3,194,800
Kherson	Kherson	11,000	28,500	1,258,700
Khmelnytsky	Khmelnytsky	8,000	20,600	1,520,600
Kirovohrad	Kirovohrad	9,500	24,600	1,245,300
Kyyiv (Kiev)	Kiev	11,200	28,900	4,589,800
Luhansk	Luhansk	10,300	26,700	2,871,100
Lviv	Lviv	8,400	21,800	2,764,400
Mykolayiv	Mykolayiv	9,500	24,600	1,342,400
Odessa	Odessa	12,900	33,300	2,635,300
Poltava	Poltava	11,100	28,800	1,756,900
Rivne	Rivne	7,800	20,100	1,176,800
Sumy	Sumy	9,200	23,800	1,430,200
Ternopil	Ternopil	5,300	13,800	1,175,100
Vinnytsya	Vinnytsya	10,200	26,500	1,914,400
Volyn	Volodymyr-Volynsky	7,800	20,200	1,069,000
Zakarpatska	Uzhhorod	4,900	12,800	1,265,900
Zaporizhzhya	Zaporizhzhya	10,500	27,200	2,099,600
Zhytomyr	Zhytomyr	11,600	29,900	1,510,700
TOTAL		233,100	603,700	51,944,400

Demography

Population (1992): 52,135,000.
Density (1992): persons per sq mi 223.7, persons per sq km 86.4.
Urban-rural (1991): urban 67.5%; rural 32.5%.
Sex distribution (1991): male 46.44%; female 53.56%.
Age breakdown (1991): under 15, 21.5%; 15–29, 21.0%; 30–44, 20.6%; 45–59, 18.5%; 60–69, 10.7%; 70 and over, 7.7%.
Population projection: (2000) 52,558,000; (2010) 53,245,000.
Ethnic composition (1989): Ukrainian 72.7%; Russian 22.1%; Jewish 0.9%; Belorussian 0.9%; Moldovan 0.6%; Bulgarian 0.5%; Polish 0.4%; other 1.9%.
Religious affiliation: believers are predominantly Ukrainian Orthodox; there is a Ukrainian Catholic minority.
Major cities (1991): Kiev 2,643,400; Kharkiv 1,622,800; Dnipropetrovsk 1,189,300; Donetsk 1,160,700; Odessa 1,127,700.

Vital statistics

Birth rate per 1,000 population (1990): 12.7 (world avg. 27.1); legitimate 88.8%; illegitimate 11.2%.
Death rate per 1,000 population (1990): 12.1 (world avg. 9.8).
Natural increase rate per 1,000 population (1990): 0.6 (world avg. 17.3).
Total fertility rate (avg. births per childbearing woman; 1990): 1.9.
Marriage rate per 1,000 population (1990): 9.3.
Divorce rate per 1,000 population (1990): 3.7.
Life expectancy at birth (1990): male 66.0 years; female 75.0 years.
Major causes of death per 100,000 population (1989): circulatory diseases 668.2; cancers 191.5; accidents 101.2; respiratory diseases 74.4; diseases of the digestive system 30.1; infectious diseases 11.6.

National economy

Budget (1992). Revenue: 289,300,000,000 rubles (detail not available). Expenditure: 289,300,000,000 rubles (current expenditure 97.0%, of which education and health 25.3%, environmental 12.8%, social services 11.6%, indexation of government wages 11.3%, subsidies 9.4%, defense 6.1%; capital expenditure 3.0%).
Production (metric tons except as noted). Agriculture, forestry, fishing (1990): sugar beets 44,264,000, wheat 30,374,000, potatoes 16,765,000, barley 9,169,000, corn (maize) 4,737,000, sunflower seeds 2,725,000; livestock (number of live animals) 24,623,000 cattle, 19,427,000 pigs, 8,419,000 sheep and goats; roundwood 10,500,000 cu m; fish catch 1,100,000. Mining and quarrying (1990): iron ore 105,900,000; manganese 7,100,000. Manufacturing (1990): synthetic fibres 191,400,000; crude steel 52,600,000; pig iron 44,900,000; cement 22,510,000; steel pipes 6,500,000; sugar 5,200,000; computers 1,746,300,000 rubles; agricultural machinery 946,200,000 rubles; coal equipment 847,000,000 rubles; metal-cutting equipment 560,200,000 rubles; automated machinery 482,600,000 rubles; chemical equipment 302,100,000 rubles; leather goods 281,900,000 rubles; forge press machines 237,100,000 rubles; optical instruments 168,000,000 rubles; textile machinery 18,600,000 rubles. Construction (1990): residential 17,458,000 sq m. Energy production

(consumption): electricity (kW-hr; 1991) 279,000,000,000 (n.a.); coal (metric tons; 1991) 135,600,000 (n.a.); crude petroleum (barrels; 1991) 35,900,000 (n.a.); natural gas (cu m; 1991) 28,100,000,000 (n.a.).
Gross national product (at current market prices; 1990): 189,500,000,000 rubles (3,600 rubles per capita)[1].

Structure of net material product and labour force

	1989		1990	
	in value '000,000 rubles	% of total value	labour value	% of labour force
Agriculture	50,800	26.8	6,128,000	25.3
Mining	} 80,900	} 42.7	6,772,000	28.0
Manufacturing				
Public utilities			878,000	3.6
Construction	21,200	11.2	1,882,000	7.8
Transp. and commun.	11,800	6.2	1,732,000	7.2
Trade	19,800	10.4	1,753,000	7.2
Finance	—	—	128,000	0.5
Pub. admin., defense	—	—	287,000	1.2
Services	—	—	4,134,000	17.1
Other	5,000	2.6	516,000	2.1
TOTAL	189,500	100.0[2]	24,210,000	100.0

Population economically active (1990): total 24,210,000; activity rate of total population 46.6% (participation rates [1989]: ages 16–59 [male], 16–54 [female] 88.4%; female 54.5%; unemployed 3.1%).

Price and earnings indexes (1985 = 100)

	1985	1986	1987	1988	1989	1990
Consumer price index	100.0	104.0	107.0	116.0	130.0	152.0
Monthly earnings index	100.0	102.6	104.7	113.3	123.6	137.8

Land use (1990): forested 14.3%; meadows and pastures 12.2%; agricultural and under permanent cultivation 55.6%; other 17.9%.
Household income and expenditure. Average household size (1990) 3.2; income per household (1990) 4,800 rubles; sources of income (1990): wages 61.2%, pensions 14.2%, sales of agricultural products 13.1%, financial receipts 4.7%, other 6.8%; expenditure (1990): food and nonalcoholic beverages 32.8%, consumer goods 27.4%, of which furniture and household appliances 4.2%, entertainment and culture 4.3%, alcoholic beverages 3.3%, housing 1.7%.

Foreign trade

Balance of trade (current prices)

	1987	1988	1989	1990	1991
'000,000,000 rubles	−6.2	−2.9	−6.5	−8.1	−12.1
% of total	6.6%	3.0%	6.3%	8.1%	10.6%

Imports (1991): 63,100,000,000 rubles (1990; machinery 34.8%, textiles 18.0%, chemicals 10.6%, food 7.4%, oil and gas 7.3%, ferrous metals 5.0%). *Major import sources:* Western countries 69.0%, of which Spain 12.3%, Britain 10.9%, Germany 10.6%, Italy 4.1%; former Soviet republics 31.0%.
Exports (1991): 51,000,000,000 rubles (1990; machinery 39.2%, ferrous metals 16.6%, food 14.7%, chemicals 8.5%, textiles 5.0%). *Major export destinations:* Western countries 51.0%; former Soviet republics 49.0%.

Transport and communications

Transport. Railroads (1991): length 22,799 km; passenger-km 76,000,000,000; metric ton-km cargo 474,000,000,000. Roads (1991): total length 167,800 km (paved 94%). Vehicles (1988): passenger cars 2,920,000. Air transport (1990): passenger-km 16,100,000,000; metric ton-km cargo 125,000,000; airports (1992) 20.
Communications. Daily newspapers (1990): total number 1,787; total circulation 24,919,000; circulation per 1,000 population 48. Radio (1991): total number of receivers 14,520,000 (1 per 4.1 persons). Television (1991): total number of receivers 17,024,000 (1 per 3.0 persons). Telephones (1991): 6,908,000 (1 per 7.5 persons).

Education and health

Education (1990–91)

	schools	teachers	students	student/ teacher ratio
Primary (age 6–13) Secondary (age 14–17) }	21,825	532,000	6,939,000	13.0
Voc., teacher tr.	742	...	757,000	...
Higher	149	...	881,300	...

Educational attainment (1989). Percentage of population age 15 and over having: some primary education 6.8%; completed primary 13.8%; some secondary 18.4%; completed secondary 31.1%; some postsecondary 19.5%; higher 10.4%. *Literacy:* n.a.
Health (1991): physicians 227,200 (1 per 229 persons); hospital beds 700,300 (1 per 74 persons); infant mortality rate per 1,000 live births 12.8.

Military

Total active duty personnel (1992): 230,000 (army 65.2%, air force and air defense 34.8%). The Black Sea Fleet of the former U.S.S.R. (headquarters: Sevastopol, Ukraine) remained to be divided with Russia and Georgia at year-end. Commonwealth of Independent States- (CIS-) controlled Strategic Nuclear Forces constituted a third military establishment during a two-year transition period.

[1]No equivalent U.S.$ value is offered, as Soviet GNP data are very speculative. [2]Detail does not add to total given because of rounding.

United Arab Emirates

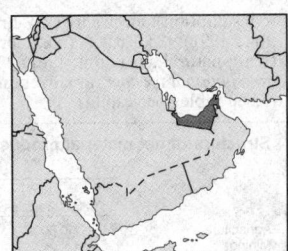

Official name: al-Imārāt al-ʿArabīyah al-Muttaḥidah (United Arab Emirates).
Form of government: federation of seven emirates with one appointive advisory body (Federal National Council [40[1]]).
Chief of state: President.
Head of government: Prime Minister.
Capital: Abu Dhabi[2].
Official language: Arabic.
Official religion: Islam.
Monetary unit: 1 U.A.E. dirham (Dh) = 100 fils; valuation (Oct. 5, 1992) 1 U.S.$ = Dh 3.71; 1 £ = Dh 6.30.

Area and population		area		population
				1985
Emirates	Capitals	sq mi	sq km	census
Abu Dhabi (Abū Ẓaby)	Abu Dhabi	26,000	67,350	670,125
ʿAjmān (Ajman)	ʿAjmān	100	250	64,318
Dubayy (Dubai)	Dubayy	1,510	3,900	419,104
Al-Fujayrah (Fujairah)	Al-Fujayrah	440	1,150	54,425
Raʾs al-Khaymah (Ras al-Khaimah)	Raʾs al-Khaymah	660	1,700	116,470
Ash-Shāriqah (Sharjah)	Ash-Shāriqah	1,000	2,600	268,722
Umm al-Qaywayn (Umm al-Qaiwain)	Umm al-Qaywayn	290	750	29,229
TOTAL		30,000	77,700	1,622,393

Demography

Population (1992): 1,989,000.
Density (1992): persons per sq mi 66.3, persons per sq km 25.6.
Urban-rural (1990): urban 77.8%; rural 22.2%.
Sex distribution (1990): male 67%; female 33%.
Age breakdown (1990): under 15, 30.6%; 15–29, 19.8%; 30–44, 33.8%; 45–59, 12.6%; 60–74, 2.6%; 75 and over, 0.6%.
Population projection: (2000) 2,332,000; (2010) 2,724,000.
Doubling time: 43 years.
Ethnic composition (1983): Arab 87.1%, of which Arab from United Arab Emirates 30.7%; Pakistani and Indian 9.1%; Persian 1.7%; Baluchi 0.8%; African 0.8%; British 0.2%; American 0.1%; other 0.2%.
Religious affiliation (1980): Muslim 94.9% (Sunnī 80%, Shīʿī 20%); Christian 3.8%; other 1.3%.
Major cities (1980): Dubayy 266,000; Abu Dhabi 722,143[3]; ash-Shāriqah 125,000; al-ʿAyn 102,000; Raʾs al-Khaymah 42,000.

Vital statistics

Birth rate per 1,000 population (1990–95): 20.3 (world avg. 26.4); legitimate, n.a.; illegitimate, n.a.
Death rate per 1,000 population (1990–95): 3.9 (world avg. 9.2).
Natural increase rate per 1,000 population (1990–95): 16.4 (world avg. 17.2).
Total fertility rate (avg. births per childbearing woman; 1990): 4.3.
Marriage rate per 1,000 population (1989): 2.0[4].
Divorce rate per 1,000 population (1989): 1.1[4].
Life expectancy at birth (1990–95): male 69.8 years; female 74.1 years.
Major causes of death per 100,000 population (1989)[4]: accidents and poisoning 43.7; diseases of the circulatory system 34.3; malignant neoplasms (cancers) 13.7; respiratory diseases 8.1.

National economy

Budget (1992). Revenue: Dh 15,900,000,000 (1989; grants 89.3%, general taxes 4.5%, nontax revenue 6.2%). Expenditures: Dh 17,300,000,000 (1989; defense 43.9%, education 15.0%, public safety 13.5%, health 6.9%, economic services 4.3%).
Gross national product (at current market prices; 1990): U.S.$31,613,000,000 (U.S.$16,614 per capita).

Structure of gross domestic product and labour force				
	1989		1986	
	in value Dh '000,000	% of total value	labour force	% of labour force
Agriculture	1,748	1.7	44,124	5.0
Mining	39,073	39.0	18,100	2.0
Manufacturing	8,646	8.6	57,029	6.4
Construction	9,194	9.2	221,003	24.8
Public utilities	2,211	2.2	17,233	1.9
Transportation and communications	5,169	5.2	65,896	7.4
Trade	10,895	10.9	121,278	13.6
Finance	12,061	12.0	27,831	3.1
Pub. admin., defense	11,979	12.0 }	318,447	35.7
Services	2,618	2.6 }		
Other	−3,442[5]	−3.4[5]	—	—
TOTAL	100,152	100.0	890,941	100.0[6]

Public debt (external, outstanding; 1989): U.S.$9,300,000,000.
Production (metric tons except as noted). Agriculture, forestry, fishing (1991): dates 72,000, tomatoes 35,000, melons 33,000 (of which watermelons 20,000), cabbages 19,000, eggplants 16,000, pumpkins and squash 16,000, lemons and limes 12,000, mangoes 9,000, cauliflowers 9,000, cucumbers 5,000, green peppers 4,000; livestock (number of live animals) 590,000 goats, 270,000

sheep, 118,000 camels, 53,000 cattle, 7,000,000 chickens; fish catch (1990) 95,129. Mining and quarrying (1988): lime 45,000; also marble, shale for ceramic applications, and aggregate for cement. Manufacturing (1991): cement 5,200,000[7]; aluminum 239,000; mutton and lamb meat 22,000; goat's milk 17,000; goat meat 6,000; cow's milk 6,000; beef and veal 3,000; butter and ghee 174. Construction (value added in Dh; 1989): 9,298,000,000. Energy production (consumption): electricity (kW-hr; 1990) 13,590,000,000 (13,590,000,000); coal, none (n.a.); crude petroleum (barrels; 1990) 762,653,000 (59,092,000); petroleum products (metric tons; 1990) 13,170,000 (6,479,000); natural gas (cu m; 1990) 20,199,000,000 (16,990,000,000).
Tourism (1987): total number of tourist arrivals 18,000.
Population economically active (1986): total 891,000; activity rate of total population 53.2% (participation rates: ages 15–64, 76.7%; female 6.6%; unemployed, n.a.).

Price and earnings indexes (1985 = 100)							
	1981	1982	1983	1984	1985	1986	1987
Consumer price index[8]	107.7	119.0	113.5	97.3	100.0	97.0	93.6
Monthly earnings index	...	...	...	...	...	...	...

Household income and expenditure. Average household size (1986) 6.8; income per household: n.a.; sources of income: n.a.; expenditure: n.a.
Land use (1990): forested, none; meadows and pastures 2.4%; agricultural and under permanent cultivation 0.5%; built-up, wasteland, and other 97.1%.

Foreign trade

Balance of trade (current prices)					
	1984	1985	1986	1987	1988	1989
Dh '000,000	+27,238	+23,249	+36,707	+25,928	+19,090	+27,420
% of total	36.7%	31.8%	46.1%	33.9%	28.9%	28.1%

Imports (1989): Dh 35,080,000,000 (1987; machinery and transport equipment 30.5%, basic manufactures 16.8%, food and live animals 15.8%, chemicals 6.9%, mineral fuels 4.0%, crude minerals 1.8%). *Major import sources:* Japan 15.0%; United Kingdom 9.4%; United States 8.4%; West Germany 7.6%; Italy 4.7%; France 3.7%; Thailand 3.4%; Saudi Arabia 3.1%; China 2.9%; The Netherlands 2.5%; Australia 2.5%; Singapore 2.3%; Belgium-Luxembourg 1.2%; Switzerland 1.2%; Turkey 1.2%.
Exports (1989): Dh 62,500,000,000 (crude petroleum 65.6%, nonpetroleum exports and reexports 34.4%). *Major export destinations:* Japan 32.1%; Singapore 4.8%; India 4.4%; South Korea 4.3%; United States 3.9%; Oman 3.0%; Australia 2.4%; France 1.8%; Italy 1.7%; United Kingdom 1.4%; West Germany 1.2%; Brazil 1.1%; Bangladesh 0.8%; The Netherlands 0.6%; Belgium-Luxembourg 0.6%; Iran 0.4%; Iraq 0.3%.

Transport and communications

Transport. Railroads: none. Roads (1984): total length 2,709 mi, 4,360 km (paved [1981] 61%). Vehicles (1990): passenger cars 302,000; trucks and buses 157,000. Merchant marine (1991): vessels (100 gross tons and over) 279; total deadweight tonnage 1,360,904. Air transport (1991)[9]: passenger-mi 2,411,000,000, passenger-km 3,880,000,000; short ton-mi cargo 98,625,000, metric ton-km cargo 143,990,000; airports (1992) with scheduled flights 4.
Communications. Daily newspapers (1991): total number 9; total circulation 246,600[10]; circulation per 1,000 population 127[10]. Radio (1991): total number of receivers 400,000 (1 per 4.9 persons). Television (1991): total number of receivers 170,000 (1 per 11 persons). Telephones (1990): 367,333 (1 per 5.2 persons).

Education and health

Education (1989–90)	schools	teachers	students	student/ teacher ratio
Primary (age 6–11) }	354[11]	11,921	215,532	18.1
Secondary (age 12–18) }		7,614	94,979 }	12.6
Vocational	9[12]		690 }	
Higher[13]	1	478	7,655	16.0

Educational attainment (1975). Percentage of population age 25 and over having: no formal schooling 72.2%; primary education 5.2%; secondary 16.6%; higher 6.0%. *Literacy* (1986): total population age 15 and over literate 858,149 (73.0%); males literate 657,579 (74.5%); females literate 200,570 (68.4%).
Health (1991): physicians 1,840 (1 per 1,057 persons); hospital beds 4,400 (1 per 442 persons); infant mortality rate per 1,000 live births (1990–95) 22.0.
Food (1987–89): daily per capita caloric intake 3,295 (vegetable products 77%, animal products 23%); 136% of FAO recommended minimum requirement.

Military

Total active duty personnel (1992): 54,500 (army 91.7%, navy 3.7%, air force 4.6%). *Military expenditure as percentage of GNP* (1989): 5.3% (world 4.9%); per capita expenditure U.S.$695.

---

[1]All appointed seats. [2]Provisional. [3]1988. [4]Registered; Abu Dhabi Emirate only. [5]Less imputed bank service charges and indirect taxes net of subsidies. [6]Detail does not add to total given because of rounding. [7]1989. [8]City of Abu Dhabi only. [9]Emirates (airline) and one-fourth apportionment of international flights of Gulf Air only. [10]Based on seven dailies only. [11]1987–88. [12]1985–86. [13]1988–89.

United Kingdom

Official name: United Kingdom of
Great Britain and Northern Ireland.
Form of government: constitutional
monarchy with two legislative houses
(House of Lords [1,191]; House of
Commons [651]).
Chief of state: Sovereign.
Head of government: Prime Minister.
Capital: London.
Official language: English.
Official religion: Churches of England
and Scotland "established" (protected
by the state, but not "official")
in their respective countries; no
established church in Northern
Ireland or Wales.
Monetary unit: 1 pound sterling
(£) = 100 new pence; valuation
(Oct. 5, 1992) 1 £ = U.S.$1.70;
1 U.S.$ = £0.59.

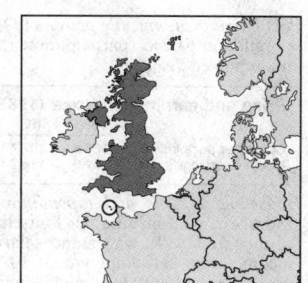

Population projection: (2000) 59,021,000; (2010) 59,962,000.
Doubling time: not applicable; doubling time exceeds 100 years.
Ethnic composition (1986): white 94.2%; Asian Indian 1.4%; West Indian
1.0%; Pakistani 0.8%; African 0.2%; Chinese 0.2%; Bangladeshi 0.2%; Arab
0.1%; other and not stated 1.9%.
Religious affiliation (1980): Christian 86.9%, of which Anglican 56.8%, Roman
Catholic 13.1%, Presbyterian 7.0%, Methodist 4.3%, Baptist 1.4%; Muslim
1.4%; Jewish 0.8%; Hindu 0.7%; Sikh 0.4%; nonreligious 8.8%; other 1.0%.
Major cities (1991): Greater London 6,377,900; Birmingham 934,900; Glasgow 689,200[7]; Leeds 674,400; Sheffield 499,700; Bradford 449,100; Liverpool
448,300; Edinburgh 434,500[7]; Manchester 406,900; Bristol 370,300.
Place of birth (1985): native-born 93.5% (50,720,000); foreign-born 5.9%, of
which Ireland 1.0%, India 0.7%, Caribbean 0.5%, Pakistan 0.4%; not stated
0.6%.
Mobility (1981). Population living in the same residence as 1980: 90.9%;
different residence, same country (of the U.K.) 8.2%; different residence,
different country within the U.K. 0.4%; from outside the U.K. 0.5%.
Households (1988–89)[8, 9]. Average household size 2.5 (3.1); 1 person 26%
(20%), 2 persons 34% (26%), 3 persons 16% (16%), 4 persons 16% (17%), 5
persons 5% (10%), 6 or more persons 2% (11%). Family households (1987):
17,836,500 (77.4%), nonfamily 5,208,500 (22.6%, of which 1-person 9.9%).
Immigration (1990): permanent residents 267,000, from Australia, New
Zealand, and Canada 20.2%, U.S. 6.7%, Bangladesh, India, and Sri Lanka
4.9%, Pakistan 3.4%, South Africa 2.2%.

Area and population

Countries	Capitals	area sq mi	area sq km	population 1991[1] census
England	London	50,363	130,439	46,161,000[2]
Counties				
Avon	Bristol	520	1,346	919,800
Bedfordshire	Bedford	477	1,235	514,200
Berkshire	Reading	486	1,259	716,500
Buckinghamshire	Aylesbury	727	1,883	619,500
Cambridgeshire	Cambridge	1,316	3,409	640,700
Cheshire	Chester	899	2,329	937,300
Cleveland	Middlesbrough	225	583	541,100
Cornwall[3]	Truro	1,376	3,564	469,300
Cumbria	Carlisle	2,629	6,810	486,900
Derbyshire	Matlock	1,016	2,631	914,600
Devon	Exeter	2,591	6,711	998,200
Dorset	Dorchester	1,025	2,654	645,200
Durham	Durham	941	2,436	589,800
East Sussex	Lewes	693	1,795	670,600
Essex	Chelmsford	1,418	3,672	1,495,600
Gloucestershire	Gloucester	1,020	2,643	520,600
Greater London[4]	London	610	1,579	6,377,900
Greater Manchester[4]	Manchester	497	1,287	2,454,800
Hampshire	Winchester	1,458	3,777	1,511,900
Hereford & Worcester	Worcester	1,516	3,927	667,800
Hertfordshire	Hertford	631	1,634	951,500
Humberside	Hull	1,356	3,512	835,200
Isle of Wight	Newport	147	381	126,600
Kent	Maidstone	1,441	3,731	1,485,100
Lancashire	Preston	1,183	3,064	1,365,100
Leicestershire	Leicester	986	2,553	860,500
Lincolnshire	Lincoln	2,284	5,915	573,900
Merseyside[4]	Liverpool	252	652	1,376,800
Norfolk	Norwich	2,073	5,368	736,400
North Yorkshire	Northallerton	3,208	8,309	698,700
Northamptonshire	Northhampton	914	2,367	572,900
Northumberland	Newcastle upon Tyne	1,943	5,032	300,600
Nottinghamshire	Nottingham	836	2,164	980,600
Oxfordshire	Oxford	1,007	2,608	553,800
Shropshire	Shrewsbury	1,347	3,490	401,600
Somerset	Taunton	1,332	3,451	459,100
South Yorkshire[4]	Barnsley	602	1,560	1,248,500
Staffordshire	Stafford	1,049	2,716	1,020,300
Suffolk	Ipswich	1,466	3,797	629,900
Surrey	Kingston upon Thames	648	1,679	998,000
Tyne and Wear[4]	Newcastle upon Tyne	208	540	1,087,000
Warwickshire	Warwick	765	1,981	477,000
West Midlands[4]	Birmingham	347	899	2,499,300
West Sussex	Chichester	768	1,989	692,800
West Yorkshire[4]	Wakefield	787	2,039	1,984,700
Wiltshire	Trowbridge	1,344	3,480	553,300
Northern Ireland[5]	Belfast	5,452	14,120	1,570,000
Scotland	Edinburgh	30,418	78,783	4,957,300[2]
Regions				
Borders	Newton Saint Boswells	1,814	4,698	102,600
Central	Stirling	1,042	2,700	268,000
Dumfries and Galloway	Dumfries	2,481	6,425	147,100
Fife	Glenrothes	509	1,319	339,300
Grampian	Aberdeen	3,379	8,752	493,200
Highland	Inverness	10,092	26,137	209,400
Lothian	Edinburgh	683	1,770	723,700
Strathclyde	Glasgow	5,318	13,773	2,218,200
Tayside	Dundee	2,951	7,643	385,300
Island areas[6] (TOTAL)	—	2,149	5,566	70,700
Wales	Cardiff	8,019	20,768	2,798,500
Counties				
Clwyd	Mold	937	2,427	401,900
Dyfed	Carmarthen	2,227	5,768	341,600
Gwent	Newport	531	1,376	432,300
Gwynedd	Caernarvon	1,494	3,869	238,600
Mid Glamorgan	Cardiff	393	1,018	526,500
Powys	Llandrindod Wells	1,960	5,077	116,500
South Glamorgan	Cardiff	161	416	383,300
West Glamorgan	Swansea	316	817	357,800
TOTAL		94,251	244,110	55,486,800

Demography

Population (1992)[1]: 57,561,000.
Density (1992): persons per sq mi 610.7, persons per sq km 235.8.
Urban-rural (1985): urban 91.5%; rural 8.5%.
Sex distribution (1991): male 48.82%; female 51.18%.
Age breakdown (1991): under 15, 19.2%; 15–29, 22.5%; 30–44, 21.0%; 45–59,
16.6%; 60–74, 13.7%; 75 and over, 7.0%.

Vital statistics

Birth rate per 1,000 population (1991): 13.8 (world avg. 26.4); (1990) legiti-
mate 72.1%; illegitimate 28.7%.
Death rate per 1,000 population (1991): 11.2 (world avg. 9.2).
Natural increase rate per 1,000 population (1991): 2.6 (world avg. 17.2).
Total fertility rate (avg. births per childbearing woman; 1990): 1.8.
Marriage rate per 1,000 population (1989): 6.8.
Divorce rate per 1,000 population (1989): 2.9.
Life expectancy at birth (1987–89): male 72.4 years; female 78.0 years.
Major causes of death per 100,000 population (1990): diseases of the circu-
latory system 515.3, of which ischemic heart disease 295.3, cerebrovascular
disease 133.1; malignant neoplasms (cancers) 280.9; diseases of the respiratory system 123.9, of which pneumonia 56.8; accidents and violence 37.1;
diseases of the digestive system 36.4; diseases of the endocrine system 17.7,
of which diabetes mellitus 14.8; diseases of the genitourinary system 14.6.

Social indicators

Educational attainment (1981). Percentage of population age 25 and over
having: primary or secondary education only 89.7%; some postsecondary
4.8%; bachelor's or equivalent degree 4.9%; higher university degree 0.6%.

Distribution of disposable income (1989)

percentage of household income by quintile

1	2	3	4	5 (highest)
7.1	11.6	16.3	22.2	42.8

Quality of working life (1987). Average workweek (hours; 1989): male 44.0,
female 30.3 (overtime[10]: male 8.6%, female 2.1%). Annual rate per 100,000
workers for: injury or accident 707.4; industrial diseases 0.5[11]; death 1.4.
Proportion of labour force (employed persons) insured for damages or
income loss resulting from: injury 100%; permanent disability 100%; death
100%. Average days lost to labour stoppages per 1,000 employee workdays
1991: 0.2. Principal means of transport to work (1985–86): private automobile 67%, public transportation 17%, foot 6%, bicycle 6%, other 4%.
Access to services (1987). Proportion of households having access to: bath or
shower 98%; toilet 98%; central heating 73%.
Social participation. Eligible voters participating in last national election:
77.7%. Population age 16 and over participating in voluntary work (1986):
20%. Trade union membership in total work force (1989) 35.6%.
Social deviance (1991)[12]. Offense rate per 100,000 population for: theft and
handling stolen goods 4,796.8; burglary 2,118.4; violence against the person
330.6; fraud and forgery 303.7; robbery 78.7; sexual offense 51.1. Incidence
per 100,000 population of: notified drug addicts 9.1[13]; suicide 8.1.
Leisure (1990). Favourite leisure activities (hours weekly): watching television
23.5; listening to radio 10.1; reading 2.6[14]; cultural activities 1.5[14].
Material well-being (1989). Households possessing: automobile 67%, telephone 87%, television receiver 98% (colour 93%), refrigerator 95%, central
heating 78%, washing machine 86%, videocassette recorder 60%.

National economy

Gross national product (at current market prices; 1990): U.S.$923,959,000,000
(U.S.$16,070 per capita).

Structure of gross domestic product and labour force

	1991 in value £'000,000	% of total value	labour force	% of labour force
Agriculture	8,772	1.8	272,000	1.0
Mining	28,273[15]	5.7[15]	437,000[15]	1.5[15]
Manufacturing	104,283	21.0	4,758,000	16.8
Construction	33,686	6.8	960,000	3.4
Public utilities	[15]	[15]	[15]	[15]
Transp. and commun.	34,755	7.0	1,313,000	4.6
Trade	73,024	14.7	4,596,000	16.2
Finance	88,179	17.7	2,595,000	9.1
Pub. admin., defense	84,429	17.0	1,891,000	6.7
Services	33,915	6.8	4,845,000	17.0
Other	7,685[16]	1.5[16]	6,743,000[17]	23.7[17]
TOTAL	497,001	100.0	28,410,000	100.0

Budget (1991–92). Revenue: £201,463,000,000 (income tax 39.4%, taxes on expenditures 30.7%, social-security contributions 17.1%). Expenditures: £213,-204,000,000 (1990–91; social-security benefits 35.0%, national health service 13.5%, defense 13.5%, debt interest 10.8%, education and science 4.1%).
Total national debt (March 1990): £185,870,000,000.

Financial aggregates

	1986	1987	1988	1989	1990	1991	1992[18]
Exchange rate:							
U.S. dollar per £	1.47	1.64	1.78	1.64	1.78	1.77	1.92
SDRs per £	1.20	1.32	1.34	1.22	1.36	1.31	1.33
International reserves (U.S.$)							
Total (excl. gold; '000,000,000)	18.42	41.72	44.10	34.77	35.85	41.89	43.25
SDRs ('000,000,000)	1.55	1.38	1.32	1.14	1.25	1.31	1.34
Reserve pos. in IMF ('000,000,000)	1.98	1.78	1.67	1.64	1.68	1.85	1.84
Foreign exchange ('000,000,000)	14.89	38.56	41.12	31.99	32.93	38.73	40.08
Gold ('000,000 fine troy oz)	19.01	19.01	19.00	18.99	18.97	18.89	18.68
% world reserves	2.0	2.0	2.0	2.0	2.0	2.0	2.0
Interest and prices							
Central bank discount (%)	...	...	...	...	...	...	...
Govt. bond yield (%) long term	9.87	9.48	9.36	9.58	11.08	9.92	9.16[19]
Industrial share prices (1985=100)	124.1	163.8	147.6	176.5	173.3	190.2	213.3[20]
Balance of payments (U.S.$'000,000)							
Balance of visible trade,	−12,801	−17,962	−36,994	−39,157	−32,400	−17,990	...
Imports, f.o.b.	119,272	148,247	180,527	190,898	214,693	201,081	...
Exports, f.o.b.	106,472	130,285	143,534	151,741	182,293	183,091	...
Balance of invisibles	16,104	17,354	17,417	15,323	13,468	10,944	...
Balance of payments, current account	158	−7,373	−26,956	−31,289	−27,676	−9,447	...

Tourism (1991): receipts from visitors U.S.$12,873,000,000; expenditures by nationals abroad U.S.$17,648,000,000.

Manufacturing, mining, and construction enterprises (1989)

	no. of enter-prises[13]	no. of employees	annual wages as a % of avg. of all wages[14]	annual value added (£'000,000)
Manufacturing				
Food, beverages, and tobacco	8,916	598,000	103.0	13,268
Transport equipment	4,233	529,000	...	13,103
Electrical and data-processing equipment	9,644	590,000	96.8	12,650
Mechanical engineering	23,322	590,000	108.4	12,622
Paper and paper products; printing and publishing	21,495	469,000	133.8	11,469
Chemical engineering	3,137	296,000	118.1	11,394
Rubber and plastic	4,785	237,000	118.1	4,704
Metal manufacturing	1,186	141,000	102.8	4,236
Timber and wood products	13,794	215,000	98.1	3,478
Clothing and footwear	11,207	320,000	85.6	3,288
Textiles	4,466	216,000	79.2	2,962
Mineral-oil processing	123	15,000	118.1	1,960
Mining				
Extraction of coal, mineral oil, and natural gas	...	121,000	118.1	9,330
Extraction of minerals other than fuels	793	19,100[13]	103.1	742.3[13]
Construction	185,854	1,160,000	...	20,426

Production (metric tons except as noted). Agriculture, forestry, fishing (1991): wheat 14,300,000, barley 7,700,000, sugar beets 7,340,000, potatoes 6,700,-000, turnips and rutabagas 3,451,000[21, 22], corn (maize) 3,151,000, rapeseed 1,330,000, cabbage 765,000, oats 527,000; livestock (number of live animals) 29,954,000 sheep, 11,846,000 cattle, 7,379,000 pigs; roundwood (1990) 6,455,-000 cu m; fish catch (1990) 803,536. Mining: iron ore 13,200[23]; zinc 5,600[22]; tin 2,300; lead 2,200. Manufacturing (total sales in £'000,000; 1990): motor vehicles and parts 13,061; aerospace equipment 7,753[24]; electronic data-processing and telecommunications equipment 6,403; basic electrical equipment 3,504; mechanical lifting and handling equipment 2,626; constructional steelwork 2,617; boilers 2,078. Construction (value in £; 1990[8]): residential 6,884,000,000; nonresidential 21,470,000,000, of which commercial 10,390,-000,000, industrial 5,243,000,000.

Retail trade enterprises (1989)

	no. of enter-prise	no. of employees	weekly wage as a % of all wages	annual turnover (£'000,000)[25]
Food and grocery, of which	67,775	809,000	...	38,341
large grocery	69	504,000	...	27,935
other grocery	24,921	106,000	...	4,128
meats	14,295	68,000	...	2,586
Household goods, of which	45,678	319,000	...	19,827
electrical and musical goods	11,945	94,000	...	6,791
furniture	10,956	72,000	...	4,691
Drink, confectionery, and tobacco, of which	48,893	259,000	...	11,180
tobacco and confectionery	42,785	219,000	...	8,664
Clothing and footwear, of which	30,170	296,000	...	11,068
women's, girls', and infants' wear	15,811	113,000	...	4,040
footwear	3,934	82,000	...	2,337
men's and boys' wear	3,938	37,000	...	1,933
Pharmaceuticals	8,590	80,000	...	3,781
Mail order	15	31,000	...	3,444

Energy production (consumption): electricity (kW-hr; 1990) 318,979,000,000 (330,922,000,000); coal (metric tons; 1990) 89,303,000 (100,249,000); crude petroleum (barrels; 1990) 656,722,000 (568,604,000); petroleum products (metric tons; 1990) 81,919,000 (79,470,000); natural gas (cu m; 1990) 53,895,-000,000 (61,895,000,000).

Population economically active (1991): total 28,410,000; activity rate of total population 51.2% (participation rates: ages 15–64, 61.1%[13]; female 47.8%; unemployed 7.9%).

Price and earnings indexes (1985=100)

	1986	1987	1988	1989	1990	1991	1992[26]
Consumer price index	103.4	107.7	113.0	121.8	133.4	141.2	144.1
Monthly earnings index	107.9	116.7	126.4	137.9	150.9	164.0	170.7

Household income and expenditure (1991). Average household size 2.3[12]; average annual income per household (1989) £15,800 (U.S.$25,900); sources of income (1989): wages and salaries 62.3%, social-security benefits 10.8%, income from self-employment 10.7%, rent, dividends, and interest 10.0%; expenditure (1990): food and beverages 18.2%, transport and vehicles 17.7%, housing 14.3%, household goods 6.5%, clothing 5.9%, energy 3.5%.
Land use (1990): forested 9.9%; meadows and pastures 46.3%; agricultural and under permanent cultivation 27.6%; other 16.2%.

Foreign trade

Balance of trade (current prices)

	1986	1987	1988	1989	1990	1991
£'000,000	−12,801	−17,926	−37,446	−39,157	−31,131	−17,990
% of total	5.7%	6.4%	11.5%	11.4%	7.8%	4.7%

Imports (1991): £118,871,400,000 (machinery and transport equipment 36.3%, of which road vehicles 8.6%, data-processing equipment 6.4%; petroleum and petroleum products 9.9%; chemicals and chemical products 9.2%, of which organic chemicals 2.2%; food and live animals 8.7%, of which vegetables and fruits 2.5%, meat and meat preparations 1.6%; paper and paperboard 3.2%; textile yarn and fabrics 3.1%; iron and steel products 2.2%; nonferrous metals 2.1%). *Major import sources:* Germany 14.9%; U.S. 11.5%; France 9.3%; The Netherlands 8.4%; Japan 5.7%; Italy 5.4%; Belgium-Luxembourg 4.6%; Ireland 3.7%; Norway 3.6%; Switzerland 3.2%.
Exports (1991): £104,818,400,000 (machinery and transport equipment 41.6%, of which road vehicles 8.2%, data-processing equipment 6.3%, power-generating machinery and equipment 4.8%, machinery specialized for particular industries 3.7%; chemicals and chemical products 13.2%, of which organic chemicals 3.3%; petroleum and petroleum products 6.5%; nonmetallic mineral manufactures 3.0%; iron and steel products 2.9%; professional, scientific, and controlling instruments 2.9%). *Major export destinations:* Germany 14.0%; France 11.1%; United States 10.8%; The Netherlands 7.9%; Italy 5.9%; Belgium-Luxembourg 5.6%; Ireland 5.0%; Spain 4.1%; Sweden 2.4%; Japan 2.2%; Switzerland 2.0%.

Transport and communications

Transport. Railroads (1991)[27]: length 23,518 mi[7], 37,849 km[7]; passenger-mi 20,620,000,000, passenger-km 33,184,000,000; short ton-mi cargo 10,947,000,-000, metric ton-km cargo 15,982,000,000. Roads (1990)[8]: total length 222,472 mi, 358,034 km (paved 100%). Vehicles (1991)[8]: passenger cars 19,737,000; trucks and buses 2,773,000. Merchant marine (1991): vessels (100 gross tons and over) 1,949; total deadweight tonnage 8,299,700. Air transport (1990): passenger-mi 49,448,000,000, passenger-km 79,579,600,000; short ton-mi cargo 1,636,100,000, metric ton-km cargo 2,388,700,000; airports (1992) with scheduled flights 56.
Communications. Daily newspapers (1990): total number 99; total circulation 22,253,500; circulation per 1,000 population 388. Radio (1990): 57,456,832 receivers (1 per 1.0 person). Television (1991): 19,546,000 licenses (1 per 2.9 persons). Telephones (1984): 29,517,991 receivers (1 per 1.9 persons).

Education and health

Education (1989–90)[28]

	schools	teachers	students	student/teacher ratio
Primary (age 5–10)	24,268	216,160	4,617,737	21.4
Secondary (age 11–19)	4,876	234,290	3,395,700	14.5
Voc., teacher tr.[29, 30]	724	93,000[31]	539,710	...
Higher[32, 33]	50	49,377	352,574	7.1

Literacy (1990): total population literate, virtually 100%[34].
Health (1981): physicians 92,172 (1 per 611 persons); hospital beds (1987) 388,700 (1 per 146 persons); infant mortality rate (1991) 7.4.
Food (1988–90): daily per capita caloric intake 3,270 (vegetable products 66%, animal products 34%); 130% of FAO recommended minimum requirement.

Military

Total active duty personnel (1992): 293,500 (army 49.5%, navy 21.2%, air force 29.3%). *Military expenditure as percentage of GNP* (1989): 4.2% (world 4.9%); per capita expenditure U.S.$605.

[1]1992 estimate includes, and 1991 preliminary census excludes, adjustment for under-enumeration of about 5%. [2]Detail does not add to total given because of rounding. [3]Includes separately administered Isles of Scilly (area 6 sq mi [16 sq km]; pop. 2,900). [4]Geographic entity only; since April 1, 1986, the administrative functions of the former metropolitan county councils have been dispersed among other local authorities. [5]Comprises 26 local government districts not shown separately. [6]Includes three separately administered island groups (Orkney 377 sq mi [976 sq km], pop. 19,300; Shetland 553 sq mi [1,432 sq km], pop. 22,400; Western Isles 1,119 sq mi [2,898 sq km], pop. 31,000). [7]1990. [8]Great Britain only. [9]Figures in parentheses are for Northern Ireland (1984). [10]1986. [11]1982. [12]England and Wales only. [13]1988. [14]1984. [15]Mining includes Public utilities. [16]Plus rent; less imputed bank service charges. [17]Includes 2,241,000 unemployed and 3,298,000 self-employed not distributed by sector. [18]July. [19]June. [20]May. [21]Primarily for fodder. [22]1987. [23]Metal content. [24]1989. [25]Includes value-added taxes. [26]March. [27]British Rail only. [28]Public sector only. [29]Third level. [30]1987–88. [31]1984–85. [32]Universities only. [33]1990–91. [34]A survey in 1986–87, however, puts the number of functional illiterates at 9–12% of the adult population.

United States

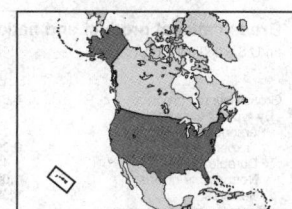

Official name: United States of America.
Form of government: federal republic with two legislative houses (Senate [100]; House of Representatives [435[1]]).
Head of state and government: President.
Capital: Washington, D.C.
Official language: English.
Official religion: none.
Monetary unit: 1 dollar (U.S.$) = 100 cents; valuation (Oct. 5, 1992) 1 U.S.$ = £0.59; 1 £ = U.S.$1.70.

Area and population

States	Capitals	area[2]		population
		sq mi	sq km	1992 estimate
Alabama	Montgomery	51,705	133,915	4,136,000
Alaska	Juneau	591,004	1,530,693	587,000
Arizona	Phoenix	114,000	295,259	3,832,000
Arkansas	Little Rock	53,187	137,754	2,399,000
California	Sacramento	158,706	411,407	30,867,000
Colorado	Denver	104,091	269,594	3,470,000
Connecticut	Hartford	5,018	12,997	3,281,000
Delaware	Dover	2,045	5,294	689,000
Florida	Tallahassee	58,664	151,939	13,488,000
Georgia	Atlanta	58,910	152,576	6,751,000
Hawaii	Honolulu	6,471	16,760	1,160,000
Idaho	Boise	83,564	216,430	1,067,000
Illinois	Springfield	57,871	149,885	11,631,000
Indiana	Indianapolis	36,413	94,309	5,662,000
Iowa	Des Moines	56,275	145,752	2,812,000
Kansas	Topeka	82,277	213,096	2,523,000
Kentucky	Frankfort	40,410	104,659	3,755,000
Louisiana	Baton Rouge	47,752	123,677	4,287,000
Maine	Augusta	33,265	86,156	1,235,000
Maryland	Annapolis	10,460	27,091	4,908,000
Massachusetts	Boston	8,284	21,455	5,998,000
Michigan	Lansing	97,102	251,493	9,437,000
Minnesota	St. Paul	86,614	224,329	4,480,000
Mississippi	Jackson	47,689	123,514	2,614,000
Missouri	Jefferson City	69,697	180,514	5,193,000
Montana	Helena	147,046	380,847	824,000
Nebraska	Lincoln	77,355	200,349	1,606,000
Nevada	Carson City	110,561	286,352	1,327,000
New Hampshire	Concord	9,279	24,032	1,111,000
New Jersey	Trenton	7,787	20,168	7,789,000
New Mexico	Santa Fe	121,593	314,924	1,581,000
New York	Albany	52,735	136,583	18,119,000
North Carolina	Raleigh	52,669	136,412	6,843,000
North Dakota	Bismarck	70,702	183,117	638,000
Ohio	Columbus	44,787	115,998	11,016,000
Oklahoma	Oklahoma City	69,956	181,185	3,212,000
Oregon	Salem	97,073	251,418	2,977,000
Pennsylvania	Harrisburg	46,043	119,251	12,009,000
Rhode Island	Providence	1,212	3,139	1,005,000
South Carolina	Columbia	31,113	80,582	3,603,000
South Dakota	Pierre	77,116	199,730	711,000
Tennessee	Nashville	42,144	109,152	5,024,000
Texas	Austin	266,807	691,027	17,656,000
Utah	Salt Lake City	84,899	219,887	1,813,000
Vermont	Montpelier	9,614	24,900	570,000
Virginia	Richmond	40,767	105,586	6,377,000
Washington	Olympia	68,139	176,479	5,136,000
West Virginia	Charleston	24,232	62,758	1,812,000
Wisconsin	Madison	66,215	171,496	5,007,000
Wyoming	Cheyenne	97,809	253,324	466,000
District				
Dist. of Columbia	—	69	179	589,000
TOTAL		3,679,192[3]	9,529,063	255,082,000[3]

Demography

Population (1992)[4]: 255,414,000.
Density (1992): persons per sq mi 69.4, persons per sq km 26.8.
Urban-rural (1990): urban 75.2%; rural 24.8%.
Sex distribution (1991): male 48.77%; female 51.23%.
Age breakdown (1991): under 15, 21.9%; 15–29, 22.7%; 30–44, 24.4%; 45–59, 14.3%; 60–74, 11.4%; 75 and over, 5.3%.
Population projection: (2000) 269,207,000; (2010) 283,566,000.
Doubling time: 88 years.
Composition by race (1990): white 80.3%; black 12.1%; other races 7.6%.
Religious affiliation (1990): Christian 86.5%, of which Protestant 52.7%, Roman Catholic 26.2%, other Christian 7.6%; Muslim 1.9%; Jewish 1.8%; nonreligious 7.5%; other 2.3%.
Mobility (1989–90). Population living in the same residence as in 1987: 82.0%; different residence, same county 11.0%; different county, same state 3.0%; different state 3.0%; moved from abroad 1.0%.
Households (1991). Total households 94,312,000 (married-couple families 52,147,000 [55.3%]). Average household size 2.6; 1 person 25.0%, 2 persons 32.0%, 3 persons 17.0%, 4 persons 15.5%, 5 or more persons 10.5%. Family households: 66,322,000 (70.3%); nonfamily 27,990,000 (29.7%), of which 1-person 25.0%.
Immigration (1990[5]): permanent immigrants admitted 1,536,483, from Mexico 44.2%, El Salvador 5.2%, Philippines 4.1%, Vietnam 3.2%, Dominican Republic 2.7%, Jamaica 2.2%, Guatemala 2.1%, South Korea 2.1%, China 2.1%, India 2.0%, U.S.S.R. 1.7%, Iran 1.6%, Colombia 1.6%, Poland 1.3%. Refugee arrivals (1989): 80,400.

Major cities (1990): New York 7,322,564; Los Angeles 3,485,398; Chicago 2,783,726; Houston 1,630,553; Philadelphia 1,585,577; San Diego 1,110,549; Detroit 1,027,974; Dallas 1,006,877; Phoenix 983,403; San Antonio 935,933.

Other principal cities (1990)

	population		population		population
Akron	223,019	Fort Worth	447,619	Oklahoma City	441,719
Albuquerque	384,736	Fresno	354,202	Omaha	335,795
Anaheim	266,406	Honolulu	365,272	Pittsburgh	369,879
Anchorage	226,338	Indianapolis	741,952	Portland (Ore.)	437,319
Arlington (Tex.)	261,721	Jacksonville	672,971	Riverside	226,505
Atlanta	394,017	Jersey City	228,537	Rochester (N.Y.)	231,636
Aurora (Colo.)	222,103	Kansas City (Mo.)	435,146	Sacramento	369,365
Austin	465,622	Las Vegas	258,295	St. Louis	396,685
Baltimore	736,014	Lexington (Ky.)	225,366	St. Paul	272,235
Baton Rouge	219,531	Long Beach	429,433	St. Petersburg	238,629
Birmingham	265,968	Louisville	269,063	San Francisco	723,959
Boston	574,283	Memphis	610,337	San Jose	782,248
Buffalo	328,123	Mesa	288,091	Santa Ana	293,742
Charlotte	395,934	Miami	358,548	Seattle	516,259
Cincinnati	364,040	Milwaukee	628,088	Tampa	280,015
Cleveland	505,616	Minneapolis	368,383	Toledo	332,943
Colorado Springs	281,140	Nashville	510,784	Tucson	405,390
Columbus	632,910	New Orleans	496,938	Tulsa	362,307
Corpus Christi	257,453	Newark	275,221	Virginia Beach	393,069
Denver	467,610	Norfolk	261,229	Washington, D.C.	606,900
El Paso	515,342	Oakland	372,242	Wichita	304,011

Place of birth (1990): native-born 227,078,000 (91.3%); foreign-born 21,632,000 (8.7%), of which Mexico 4,447,000, Germany (East and West) 1,163,000, Philippines 998,000, Canada 871,000, United Kingdom 765,000, Cuba 751,000, South Korea 663,000, Italy 640,000, Vietnam 556,000, China 543,000, India 463,000, Japan 422,000, Poland 397,000, U.S.S.R. 337,000, Portugal 219,000, Greece 189,000, other 8,208,000.

Vital statistics

Birth rate per 1,000 population (1992[6]): 16.2 (world avg. 26.4); (1990) legitimate 76.6%; illegitimate 23.4%.
Death rate per 1,000 population (1992[6]): 8.5 (world avg. 9.2).
Natural increase rate per 1,000 population (1992[6]): 7.7 (world avg. 17.2).
Total fertility rate (avg. births per childbearing woman; 1989): 2.0.
Marriage rate per 1,000 population (1992[6]): 9.4; median age at first marriage (1991): men 26.3 years, women 24.1 years.
Divorce rate per 1,000 population (1992[6]): 4.7.
Life expectancy at birth (1990): white male 72.6 years, black and other male 68.4 years; white female 79.3 years, black and other female 76.3 years.
Major causes of death per 100,000 population (12 months ending April 1992): cardiovascular diseases 359.2, of which ischemic heart disease 188.4, other forms of heart disease 77.1, cerebrovascular diseases 56.8, atherosclerosis 6.5, other cardiovascular diseases 9.9; malignant neoplasms (cancers) 203.0; diseases of the respiratory system 62.6, of which pneumonia 29.5; accidents and adverse effects 34.6, of which motor-vehicle accidents 16.9; diabetes mellitus 19.3; acquired immune deficiency syndrome (AIDS) 12.1; suicide 11.5; homicide 10.6; chronic liver disease and cirrhosis 9.7.
Morbidity rates of infectious diseases per 100,000 population (1990): gonorrhea 276.6; chicken pox 120.1; syphilis 20.1; salmonellosis 19.5; acquired immune deficiency syndrome (AIDS) 16.7; hepatitis A (infectious) 12.6; measles (rubeola) 11.7; shigellosis 10.9; tuberculosis 10.3; hepatitis B (serum) 8.5; aseptic meningitis 4.8.
Incidence of chronic health conditions per 1,000 population (1989): chronic sinusitis 138.3; arthritis 127.3; deformities or orthopedic impairments 114.9; hypertension 113.6; hay fever 86.9; hearing impairment 83.1; heart conditions 75.9; chronic bronchitis 49.2; asthma 47.7; hemorrhoids 47.2.

Social indicators

Educational attainment (1991). Percentage of population age 25 and over having: less than full primary education 6.2%; primary 4.4%; less than full secondary 11.0%; secondary 38.6%; some postsecondary 18.4%; 4-year higher degree and more 21.4%. Number of earned degrees (1989–90): bachelor's degree 1,017,252; master's degree 319,749; doctor's degree 35,586; first-professional degrees (in fields such as medicine, theology, and law) 74,150.

Distribution of income (1991)

percentage of national household income by quintile

1	2	3	4	5 (highest)
4.4	10.7	16.6	24.1	44.2

Quality of working life (1991). Average workweek: 34.3 hours (9.6% overtime[7]). Annual rate per 100,000 workers for (1990): injury or accident 1,800; death 10.5. Proportion of labour force insured for damages or income loss resulting from: injury, permanent disability, and death (1988) 56.6%. Average days lost to labour stoppages per 1,000 workdays (1989): 0.7. Average duration of journey to work (1979): 22.5 minutes (private automobile 85.7%, public transportation 5.9%, bicycle or motorcycle 1.3%, foot 3.9%, work at home 2.3%, other 0.9%). Rate per 1,000 workers of discouraged (unemployed no longer seeking work; 1991): 8.1.
Access to services (1987). Proportion of dwellings having access to: electricity virtually 100.0%; safe public water supply 98.6%; public sewage collection 99.2%; public fire protection, n.a.
Social participation. Eligible voters participating in last presidential election (1992): 54.0%. Population age 16 and over participating in voluntary work (1989): 20.4%. Trade union membership in total work force (1991): 16.1%. Practicing religious population in total affiliated population (church attendance; 1987): once a week 47%; once in six months 67%; once a year 74%.
Social deviance (1991). Offense rate per 100,000 population for: murder 9.8; rape 42.3; robbery 272.7; aggravated assault 433.3; motor-vehicle theft 659.0;

burglary and housebreaking 1,252.0; larceny-theft 3,228.8; drug-abuse violation 309.2; drunkenness 260.1. Drug and substance users (population age 26 and over; 1988): alcohol 54.8%; marijuana 3.9%; cocaine 0.9%; tranquilizers 0.6%; analgesics 0.4%; stimulants 0.5%; hallucinogens, n.a.; heroin, n.a. Rate per 100,000 population of suicide (1992): 11.5.

Crime rates per 100,000 population in metropolitan areas (1991)

| | violent crime | | | | |
	total	murder	rape	robbery	assault
Atlanta	987.9	13.0	54.3	417.8	502.8
Baltimore	1,255.0	14.8	51.3	573.6	615.2
Boston	832.3	5.6	30.3	263.0	533.3
Chicago	...	16.9	...	779.1	780.9
Dallas	1,333.6	23.9	71.4	518.0	720.3
Detroit	1,001.2	16.8	69.9	392.9	521.6
Houston	1,076.6	22.9	55.9	501.2	496.6
Los Angeles	1,795.9	20.5	45.5	750.2	979.8
Miami	2,194.9	18.2	62.0	1,067.9	1,046.9
Minneapolis	470.0	3.8	56.1	166.1	243.9
New York	2,044.2	25.7	35.7	1,175.7	807.2
Philadelphia	759.0	11.4	35.6	384.3	327.7
Pittsburgh	429.1	3.3	33.9	183.6	208.3
St. Louis	937.5	16.5	28.1	317.3	575.6
San Francisco	983.7	9.2	35.8	502.5	436.1
Washington, D.C.	785.1	18.1	32.3	360.9	373.8

| | property crime | | | | |
	total	burglary	larceny	auto theft	arson[8]
Atlanta	7,329.1	1,720.8	4,632.8	975.5	69.2
Baltimore	6,011.7	1,367.4	3,802.6	841.8	84.9
Boston	4,642.7	1,051.0	2,590.9	1,000.8	30.0[9]
Chicago	6,150.6	1,275.8	3,826.9	1,047.8	85.6
Dallas	8,705.7	2,116.6	5,261.6	1,327.6	140.3
Detroit	6,055.2	1,232.7	3,703.7	1,118.8	147.3
Houston	7,112.0	1,888.4	3,559.8	1,663.8	115.2
Los Angeles	5,826.6	1,427.1	2,936.2	1,463.4	163.8
Miami	10,591.1	2,569.4	6,236.3	1,785.4	45.4
Minneapolis	5,102.9	1,020.0	3,576.7	506.1	90.1
New York	6,440.2	1,406.0	3,320.4	1,713.8	83.0
Philadelphia	4,095.6	915.5	2,337.3	842.8	82.2[9]
Pittsburgh	3,073.4	713.5	1,679.6	680.3	133.4
St. Louis	5,367.1	1,451.7	3,252.0	663.5	148.4
San Francisco	5,806.9	1,067.8	3,709.5	1,029.6	49.7
Washington, D.C.	5,113.5	954.4	3,458.3	700.8	36.4

Leisure (1976). Favourite leisure activities (weekly hours): watching television 9.6; social time 7.6; reading 3.7; cultural activities 1.5; recreation 1.2.
Material well-being (1991). Occupied dwellings with householder possessing: automobile 84.9%[9]; telephone 93.6%; radio receiver 99.0%[10]; television receiver 98.2%[10]; refrigerator 99.8%[11]; air conditioner 63.7%[11]; washing machine 74.9%[11]; videocassette recorder 71.9%; cable television 58.9%.
Recreational expenditures (1990): U.S.$256,600,000,000 (television and radio receivers 20.5%; nondurable toys and sports equipment 11.0%; sports supplies 10.8%; magazines and newspapers 8.1%; golfing, bowling, and other participatory activities 7.5%; books and maps 6.0%, spectator amusements 4.4%, of which theatre and opera 1.6%, spectator sports 1.4%, movies 1.3%; flowers, seeds, and potted plants 3.7%).

National economy

Budget (1993). Revenue: U.S.$1,162,900,000,000 (individual income tax 43.6%, social-insurance taxes and contributions 38.2%, corporation income tax 9.6%, other 8.6%). Expenditures: U.S.$1,503,900,000,000 (social security and medicare 29.0%, defense 18.5%, interest on debt 14.0%, income security 13.5%, health 7.1%, other 17.9%).
Total national debt (1992): U.S.$4,002,800,000,000.

Manufacturing, mining, and construction enterprises (1991)

	no. of enterprises[11]	no. of employees	hourly wage as a % of all wages	value added (U.S.$'000,000)[10]
Manufacturing				
Transportation equipment	10,500	1,891,100	142.7	146,916
Electric and electronic machinery	15,962	1,598,300	103.7	106,984
Food and related products	20,624	1,671,900	95.8	140,973
Machinery, except electrical	52,135	2,006,900	117.7	132,166
Chemical and related products	12,109	1,072,400	135.7	157,032
Fabricated metal products	36,105	1,358,800	108.3	79,952
Paper and related products	6,342	688,200	123.2	59,823
Instruments and related products	10,326	980,000	112.8	81,666
Primary metals	6,771	725,700	129.1	53,367
Rubber and plastic products	14,515	863,700	97.5	49,889
Stone, clay, and glass products	16,166	523,900	110.1	34,140
Apparel and related products	22,872	1,010,300	65.5	33,034
Lumber and wood	33,982	678,900	89.4	28,597
Textile-mill products	6,412	672,300	80.3	26,542
Petroleum and coal products	2,254	158,800	164.9	27,214
Furniture and fixtures	11,613	472,000	84.8	21,645
Miscellaneous manufacturing industries	16,544	366,300	85.7	20,096
Tobacco products	138	49,100	161.5	22,561
Leather and leather products	2,193	124,700	69.5	4,587
Mining				
Oil and gas extraction	22,910	394,100	130.9	80,049[11]
Coal mining	3,905	135,100	165.3	17,068[11]
Metal mining	1,027	56,200	143.9	4,610[11]
Nonmetallic, except fuels	5,775	104,900	115.5	9,233[11]
Construction				
General contractors and operative builders	157,600	1,151,800	128.3	33,802[11]
Heavy construction contractors	36,600	728,500	133.0	44,940[11]
Special trade contractors	342,000	2,804,300	138.8	117,480[11]

Gross national product (at current market prices; 1991): U.S.$5,694,900,000,000 (U.S.$22,540 per capita).

Gross national product and national income

(in U.S.$'000,000,000)

	1987	1988	1989	1990	1991
Gross national product	4,515.6	4,873.7	5,200.8	5,465.1	5,677.5
By type of expenditure					
Personal consumption expenditures	3,009.4	3,238.2	3,450.1	3,657.3	3,887.7
Durable goods	423.4	457.5	474.6	480.3	446.1
Nondurable goods	1,001.3	1,060.0	1,130.1	1,193.7	1,251.5
Services	1,584.7	1,720.7	1,845.5	1,983.3	2,190.1
Gross private domestic investment	699.5	747.1	771.2	741.0	721.1
Fixed investment	671.2	720.8	742.9	746.1	731.3
Changes in business inventories	28.3	26.2	28.3	−5.0	−10.2
Net exports of goods and services	−114.7	−74.1	−46.1	−31.2	−21.8
Exports	449.7	552.0	626.2	672.8	598.2
Imports	564.3	626.1	672.3	704.0	620.0
Government purchases of goods and services	921.4	962.5	1,025.6	1,098.1	1,090.5
Federal	381.3	380.3	400.1	424.0	447.3
State and local	540.2	582.3	625.6	674.1	643.2
By major type of product					
Goods output	1,788.4	1,935.1	2,072.7	2,143.3	2,182.5
Durable goods	780.5	860.2	906.6	928.0	888.4
Nondurable goods	1,007.9	1,074.9	1,166.0	1,215.2	1,294.1
Services	2,292.4	2,488.6	2,671.2	2,864.2	3,030.3
Structures	434.8	450.0	456.9	457.4	464.7
National income (incl. capital consumption adjustment)	3,660.3	3,984.9	4,223.3	4,418.4	4,544.2
By type of income					
Compensation of employees	2,686.4	2,905.1	3,079.0	3,244.2	3,390.8
Proprietors' income	323.4	354.2	379.3	402.5	368.0
Rental income of persons	13.7	16.3	8.2	6.9	−10.4
Corporate profits	337.6	311.6	275.2	298.3	346.3
Net interest	328.6	371.8	324.0	466.7	449.5
By industry division (excl. capital consumption adjustment)					
Agriculture, forestry, fishing	92.6	94.7	101.0	103.4	90.9
Mining and construction	229.4	248.3	261.5	267.3	246.8
Manufacturing	719.7	782.2	803.8	806.5	841.0
Durable	426.7	453.7	465.6	461.5	464.2
Nondurable	293.0	328.6	338.2	345.0	376.8
Transportation	119.9	131.2	136.6	144.0	140.8
Communications	80.3	87.4	87.4	92.8	95.3
Public utilities	80.8	86.8	90.2	92.0	99.0
Wholesale and retail trade	526.5	569.5	607.5	638.8	669.3
Finance, insurance, real estate	512.7	562.0	613.8	647.5	685.0
Services	713.1	799.9	883.0	963.4	1,002.5
Government and government enterprise	529.3	566.9	41.7	648.4	699.5
Other	29.0	33.5	37.6	41.7	17.4

Structure of gross domestic product and labour force

| | 1989 | | 1991 | |
	in value U.S.$'000,000,000	% of total value	labour force[12]	% of labour force[12]
Agriculture	113	2.2	3,647,000	2.9
Mining	80	1.5	794,000	0.6
Manufacturing	966	18.7	21,994,000	17.3
Construction	248	4.8	8,100,000	6.4
Public utilities	156	3.0	1,630,000	1.3
Transportation and communications	306	5.9	6,978,000	5.5
Trade	825	16.0	25,900,000	20.4
Finance	897	17.4	13,941,000	11.0
Public administration, defense	619	12.0 }	43,002,000	33.9
Services	971	18.8 }		
Other	−18[13]	−0.3[13]	881,000[14]	0.7[14]
TOTAL	5,163	100.0	126,867,000	100.0

Business activity (1988): number of businesses 18,896,000 (sole proprietorships 72.4%, active corporations 18.9%, active partnerships 8.7%), of which services 7,748,000, wholesaling and retailing 3,578,000; business receipts $10,939,800,000,000 (active corporations 89.6%, sole proprietorships 6.1%, active partnerships 4.3%), of which wholesaling and retailing $3,204,900,000,000, services $997,600,000,000; net profit $553,800,000,000 (active corporations 74.6%, sole proprietorships 22.8%, partnerships 2.6%), of which services $103,200,000,000, wholesaling and retailing $59,400,000,000. New business concerns and business failures (1991): total number of new incorporations 628,567; total failures 87,113, of which commercial service 22,644, retail trade 16,953; failure rate per 10,000 concerns (1990) 75; current liabilities of failed concerns $87,750,600,000, of which manufacturing and mining $11,103,300,000, retail trade $6,984,300,000; average liability $1,007,300. Business expenditures for new plant and equipment (1991): total $528,390,000,000, of which trade, services, and communications $246,320,000,000, manufacturing businesses $182,810,000,000 (nondurable goods 57.5%, durable goods 42.5%), public utilities $66,570,000,000, transportation $22,660,000,000, mining $10,020,000,000.
Production (metric tons except as noted). Agriculture, forestry, fishing (1991): corn (maize) 189,867,000, milk 67,373,000, soybeans 54,039,000, wheat 53,915,000, sugarcane 28,332,000, sugar beets 25,263,000, potatoes 18,970,000, sorghum 14,720,000, tomatoes 11,379,000, barley 10,113,000, oranges 7,258,000, rice 7,006,000, cottonseed 6,132,000, grapes 4,944,000, apples 4,477,000, oats 3,520,000, onions 2,277,000, peanuts (groundnuts) 2,242,000, peaches and pears 2,140,000, grapefruit 2,048,000, sunflower seeds 1,637,000, dry beans 1,495,000, green peas 1,330,000, carrots 1,262,000, cucumbers 565,000, sweet potatoes 522,000, pineapples 504,000, cauliflower 354,000, almonds 335,700; livestock (number of live animals) 98,896,000 cattle, 54,427,000 pigs, 11,200,000 sheep, 1,780,000 goats, 1,623,000,000 poultry; roundwood (1990) 501,000,000 cu m; fish catch 4,302,000, of which Alaska pollock 1,295,000, menhaden 897,000, Pacific salmon 355,000, crabs 295,000, Pacific cod 251,-

000, shrimp 145,000, sea herring 104,000, clams 60,000. Mining and quarrying (1991): iron ore 54,000,000; phosphate rock 47,000,000; lime 15,200,000; gypsum 13,900,000; aluminum 4,100,000; copper 1,630,000; feldspar 573,000; zinc 520,000; lead 480,000; magnesium 130,000; molybdenum 60,000; tin 13,000; uranium 3,400; silver 1,800; gold 300. Manufacturing (1991): crude steel 79,206,000; paper and paperboard 72,149,000; wood pulp 57,895,000; pig iron 44,001,000; sulfuric acid 39,288,000; coke 21,814,000; nitrogenous and phosphate fertilizers 17,616,000; phosphoric acid 11,196,000; newsprint 5,630,000; cheese 5,525,500; synthetic rubber 1,918,270[10]; butter 1,212,300; machine tools U.S.$1,893,950,000; cotton fabric 3,682,000,000 sq m; carpets and rugs 1,068,400,000 sq m; footwear 168,633,000 pairs; motor-vehicle tires 202,390,000 units; automobile batteries 66,585,000 units; major household appliances 40,997,000 units, of which 7,273,000 refrigerators, 7,234,000 microwave ovens, 6,197,000 washing machines, 4,313,000 clothes dryers, 4,002,000 food disposals, 3,936,000 water heaters, 2,807,000 air conditioners; television receivers 19,649,000 units; radio receivers 18,530,000 units. Construction (1991): private U.S.$290,706,000,000, of which residential U.S.$157,835,000,000, commercial and industrial U.S.$70,760,000,000, other U.S.$62,111,000,000; federal, state, and local U.S.$110,249,000,000.

Retail and wholesale trade and services (1991)

	no. of establish-ments[8]	no. of employees	hourly wage as a % of all wages	annual sales (U.S.$'000,000)
Retail trade	1,495,000	19,259,000	67.3	1,821,500
Automotive dealers	85,700	1,996,000	87.8	374,500
Food stores	183,900	3,203,900	71.7	370,600
General merchandise group stores	35,800	2,426,100	68.1	217,600
Eating and drinking places	391,500	6,465,400	50.1	189,500
Gasoline service stations	105,800	627,300	62.4	128,500
Building materials, hardware, garden supply, and mobile home dealers	71,200	745,900	79.2	92,700
Apparel and accessory stores	147,500	1,153,400	63.9	95,600
Furniture, home furnishings, equipment stores	104,600	801,200	86.0	90,100
Drugstores and proprietary stores	50,600	614,000	69.5	74,900
Liquor stores	31,700	117,100	121.2[8]	21,400
Wholesale trade[15]	466,700	6,069,000	107.9	1,741,600
Durable goods	292,800	3,525,000	111.5	846,500
Machinery, equipment, and supplies	114,400	774,000	110.5	156,200
Motor vehicles, automotive equipment	43,000	445,700	98.8	154,400
Electrical goods	35,300	477,200	113.6	113,700
Metals and minerals, except petroleum	11,100	133,400	112.7	76,300
Lumber and other construction materials	19,100	211,400	104.2	52,600
Hardware, plumbing, heating equipment and supplies	23,100	269,600	105.1	41,300
Furniture and home furnishings	14,500	141,500	99.3	28,100
Sporting, recreational, photographic, and hobby goods	8,900	88,300[8]	108.0[8]	25,200[10]
Miscellaneous durable goods	23,400	291,500	86.9	107,600
Nondurable goods	173,900	2,544,000	102.9	895,100
Groceries and related products	42,100	845,000	104.3	254,400
Petroleum and petroleum products	16,700	188,200	99.5	138,700
Farm-products raw materials	12,600	235,000	77.7	118,000
Apparel and accessories	16,900	198,100	101.2	60,700
Paper and paper products	16,800	241,300	107.7	48,600
Drugs, drug proprietaries, and druggists' sundries	4,900	187,000	121.9	54,200
Beer, wine, and distilled alcoholic beverages	5,800	146,600	122.0	47,100
Chemicals and allied products	12,700	136,000	122.8	44,800
Miscellaneous nondurable goods	15,300	483,800	86.8	128,600
Services[15, 16]	1,626,017	28,323,000	98.9	1,170,200
Business	251,900	5,086,700	94.4	345,100
Health, except hospitals	406,753	8,177,000	106.1	245,700
Legal	138,222	910,300	140.6	91,100
Engineering, architectural, and surveying	62,299	748,000	149.9	79,600
Hotels, motels, and other lodging places	46,793	1,595,400	69.3	63,700
Amusement and recreation, including motion pictures	99,480	1,515,800	96.0	77,100
Automotive repair, services, garages	151,218	882,400	86.7	74,500
Personal	185,443	1,108,200	69.4	65,200
Accounting, auditing, and bookkeeping	69,773	514,900	119.2	34,200
Miscellaneous repair services	65,532	337,600	102.2	31,800

Energy production (consumption): electricity (kW-hr; 1991) 2,822,000,000,000 (2,759,000,000,000); coal (metric tons; 1991) 993,600,000 (888,400,000); crude petroleum (barrels; 1991) 2,690,050,000 (4,799,750,000); petroleum products (metric tons; 1991) 758,400,000 (828,600,000); natural gas (cu m; 1991) 506,025,000,000 (553,597,000,000). Domestic production of energy by source (1991): coal 31.9%, natural gas 27.3%, crude oil 23.1%, nuclear power 8.4%, hydroelectric power 4.3%, other 5.0%.

Energy consumption by source (1991): petroleum and petroleum products 40.1%, natural gas 24.7%, coal 23.1%, nuclear energy 8.0%, hydroelectric power 3.8%, other 0.3%; by end use: industrial 36.4%, residential and commercial 36.3%, transportation 27.3%.

Household income and expenditure. Average household size (1991) 2.6; average (mean) annual income per household (1991) U.S.$37,900; sources of income (1990): wages and salaries 63.8%, transfer payments 15.0%, self-employment 8.7%, other 12.5%; expenditure (1991)[17]: food 15.9%, health 14.9%, housing 14.8%, transportation 11.3%, clothing 5.4%, household durable goods 4.4%, energy 3.0%.

Selected household characteristics (1991). Total number of households 94,312,000, of which (by race and Spanish origin[18]) white 85.6%, black 11.3%, other 1.6%, Spanish origin 6.6%; (by location; 1992) in metropolitan areas 77.9%, outside metropolitan areas 22.1% (farms 1.6%); (by tenure; 1991) owned 60,395,000 (64.0%), rented 33,917,000 (36.0%); family households 66,322,000, of which married couple 78.6%, female head with children under age 18, 10.3%, other 11.1%; nonfamily households 27,990,000, of which female householder 56.6%, male 43.4%, persons living alone 84.3%. Work disability status of householder (1988): having no work disability 91.4%, having work disability 8.6%.

Financial aggregates

	1986	1987	1988	1989	1990	1991	1992[19]
Exchange rate, U.S.$ per:							
£[20]	1.47	1.64	1.78	1.64	1.78	1.77	1.94
SDR[20]	1.17	1.29	1.34	1.28	1.36	1.37	1.46
International reserves (U.S.$)[21]							
Total (excl. gold; '000,000,000)	37.45	34.72	36.74	63.55	72.26	66.66	67.42
SDRs ('000,000,000)	8.39	10.28	9.64	9.95	10.99	11.24	12.19
Reserve pos. in IMF ('000,000,000)	11.73	11.35	9.75	9.05	9.08	9.49	9.76
Foreign exchange ('000,000,000)	17.33	13.09	17.36	44.55	52.19	45.93	45.46
Gold ('000,000 fine troy oz)	262.04	262.38	261.87	261.93	261.91	261.91	261.93
% world reserves	27.49	27.69	27.62	27.78	27.84	27.86	28.11
Interest and prices							
Central bank discount (%)[21]	5.5	6.0	6.5	7.0	6.5	3.5	3.0
Govt. bond yield (%)[20]	7.06	7.67	8.24	8.56	8.25	6.81	4.72
Industrial share prices[20] (1985 = 100)	126.2	159.2	147.6	178.2	188.1	214.6	236.2
Balance of payments ($'000,000,000)							
Balance of visible trade	−145.05	−159.49	−126.97	−115.71	−108.84	−73.44	−20.79[22]
Imports, f.o.b.	−368.41	−409.77	−447.31	−477.38	−497.55	−489.40	−131.40[22]
Exports, f.o.b.	223.36	250.28	320.34	361.67	388.71	415.96	110.61[22]
Balance of invisibles	−0.37	−0.71	0.60	14.51	18.38	69.75	4.86[22]
Balance of payments, current account	−145.42	−160.20	−126.37	−101.20	−90.46	−3.69	−15.93[22]

Population economically active (1991): total 126,867,000[12]; activity rate of total population 50.2% (participation rates: ages 15–64, 73.7%; female 45.0%; unemployed 6.6%).

Price and earnings indexes (1985 = 100)

	1986	1987	1988	1989	1990	1991	1992
Consumer price index	101.9	105.7	109.9	115.2	121.4	126.6	129.9
Hourly earnings index	102.1	103.9	106.7	109.8	113.6	117.3	120.0

Average employee earnings

	average hourly earnings in U.S.$		average weekly earnings in U.S.$	
	July 1991	July 1992	July 1991	July 1992
Manufacturing				
Durable goods	11.80	12.03	480.26	495.64
Lumber and wood products	9.30	9.46	370.14	384.08
Furniture and fixtures	8.76	9.00	339.01	357.30
Stone, clay, and glass products	11.43	11.68	480.06	498.74
Primary metal industries	13.45	13.77	568.94	593.49
Fabricated metal products	11.22	11.39	455.53	470.41
Machinery, except electrical	12.16	12.49	500.99	520.83
Electrical and electronic equipment	10.75	11.05	428.93	448.63
Transportation equipment	14.84	15.12	617.34	621.43
Instruments and related products	11.65	11.93	467.17	481.97
Miscellaneous manufacturing	8.83	9.11	342.60	358.02
Nondurable goods	10.47	10.73	417.75	430.27
Food and kindred products	9.90	10.18	399.96	409.24
Tobacco manufactures	18.16	18.38	697.34	700.28
Textile mill products	8.27	8.60	335.76	350.88
Apparel and other textile products	6.80	6.94	250.24	256.78
Paper and allied products	12.81	13.13	553.39	568.53
Printing and publishing	11.47	11.76	427.83	443.35
Chemicals and allied products	14.11	14.49	596.85	618.72
Petroleum and coal products	16.87	17.70	740.59	768.18
Rubber and miscellaneous plastics products	10.08	10.39	408.24	427.03
Leather and leather products	7.12	7.28	268.42	280.28
Nonmanufacturing				
Metal mining	15.04	15.37	640.70	657.84
Coal mining	17.24	17.12	730.98	700.21
Oil and gas extraction	13.52	14.01	592.18	606.63
Nonmetallic minerals, except fuels	11.96	12.29	544.18	566.57
Construction	13.94	14.05	538.08	546.55
Transportation and public utilities	13.26	13.43	515.81	526.46
Wholesale trade	11.13	11.38	424.05	434.72
Retail trade	6.94	7.10	203.34	208.03
Finance, insurance, and real estate	10.34	10.73	368.10	381.99
Hotels, motels, and tourist courts	6.99	7.28	215.29	227.14
Health services	11.01	11.39	358.93	374.73
Legal services	14.54	14.98	501.63	521.30
Miscellaneous services	14.70	15.45	524.79	576.29

Tourism (1991): receipts from visitors U.S.$45,551,000,000; expenditures by nationals abroad U.S.$39,418,000,000; number of foreign visitors (1990) 13,418,000 (5,383,000 from western Europe, 3,830,000 from Asia, 1,283,000 from Central America and the Caribbean, 1,016,000 from South America); number of nationals traveling abroad 15,990,000[10] (8,043,000[10] to Europe and the Mediterranean, 1,519,000[10] to Latin America[23]).

Land use (1990): forested 32.0%; meadows and pastures 26.3%; agricultural and under permanent cultivation 20.7%; other 21.0%.

Foreign trade

Balance of trade (current prices)

	1985	1986	1987	1988	1989	1990	1991
U.S.$'000,000,000	−117.7	−138.3	−152.1	−118.5	−109.4	−101.7	−99.2
% of total	21.2%	23.3%	23.0%	15.5%	13.1%	11.4%	9.8%

Imports (1991): U.S.$487,129,000,000 (machinery and transport equipment 43.3%, of which motor vehicles and parts 13.8%; basic and miscellaneous manufactures 28.9%, mineral fuels and lubricants 11.2%; chemicals and related products 5.0%; food and live animals 4.5%). *Major import sources:* Japan 18.8%; Canada 18.7%; Mexico 6.4%; Germany 5.4%; Taiwan 4.7%; China 3.9%; United Kingdom 3.8%; South Korea 3.5%; France 2.7%; Italy 2.4%; Saudi Arabia 2.3%; Singapore 2.0%; Hong Kong 1.9%.
Exports (1991): U.S.$421,730,000,000 (machinery and transport 44.4%, of which motor vehicles and parts 7.0%; basic and miscellaneous manufactures 18.6%; chemicals and related products 10.2%; food and live animals 7.0%; mineral fuels and lubricants 2.9%). *Major export destinations:* Canada 20.2%; Japan 11.4%; Mexico 7.9%; United Kingdom 5.2%; Germany 5.1%; South Korea 3.7%; France 3.6%; The Netherlands 3.2%; Taiwan 3.1%; Belgium-Luxembourg 2.6%; Australia 2.0%; Singapore 2.1%.

Trade by commodity group (1991)

	imports		exports	
SITC Group	U.S.$'000,000	%	U.S.$'000,000	%
00 Food and live animals	21,952.3	4.5	29,555.0	7.0
01 Beverages and tobacco	4,822.6	1.0	6,750.3	1.6
02 Crude materials, excluding fuels	13.079.0	2.7	25,462.0	6.0
03 Mineral fuels, lubricants, and related materials	54,342.7	11.2	12,033.2	2.9
04 Animal and vegetable oils, fat, and waxes	856.7	0.2	1,147.1	0.3
05 Chemicals and related products, n.e.s.	24,168.7	5.0	42,966.7	10.2
06 Basic manufactures	57,418.9	11.8	35,566.0	8.4
07 Machinery and transport equipment	210,786.5	43.3	187,359.9	44.4
08 Miscellaneous manufactured articles	83,389.6	17.1	43,162.2	10.2
09 Goods not classified by kind	16,312.0	3.3	37,727.6	8.9
TOTAL	487,129[24]	100.0[3]	421,730	100.0[3]

Direction of trade (1991)

	imports		exports	
	U.S.$'000,000	%	U.S.$'000,000	%
Africa	14,130	2.9	6,097	1.4[3]
South Africa	1,733	0.4	2,086	0.5
Other	12,397	2.5	4,011	1.0
Americas	152,474	31.3	148,467	35.2
Canada	91,141	18.7	85,103	20.2
Caribbean countries and Central America	6,286	1.3	10,491	2.5
Mexico	31,194	6.4	33,276	7.9
South America	23,853	4.9	19,597	4.6
Asia	211,417	43.4	133,353	31.6
Japan	91,583	18.8	48,147	11.4
Other Asia	119,834	24.6	85,206	20.2
Europe	103,498	21.2[4]	123,288	29.2
EEC	86,481	17.8	103,209	24.5
Other Western Europe	15,207	3.1	15,293	3.6
U.S.S.R.	813	0.2	3,578	0.8
Eastern Europe	997	0.2	1,208	0.3
Oceania	5,510	1.1	9,696	2.3
Australia	4,010	0.8	8,416	2.0
Other Oceania	1,500	0.3	1,280	0.3
Other	—	—	829	0.2
TOTAL	487,129[24]	100.0[3]	421,730	100.0[3]

Transport and communications

Transport. Railroads (1990): length 144,000 mi, 232,000 km; passenger-mi 13,297,000,000, passenger-km 21,400,000,000; short ton-mi cargo 1,180,382,-000,000, metric ton-km cargo 1,723,329,000,000. Roads (1990): total length 3,879,322 mi, 6,243,163 km (paved 58%). Vehicles (1990): passenger cars 143,549,627; trucks and buses 45,105,000. Merchant marine (1991): vessels (100 gross tons and over) 6,222; total deadweight tonnage 30,064,259. Air transport (1990): passenger-mi 335,867,000,000, passenger-km 540,526,000,-000; short ton-mi cargo 10,600,000,000, metric ton-km cargo 15,476,000,000; airports (1990) with scheduled flights 834. Certified route passenger/cargo air carriers (1990) 60; operating revenue (U.S.$'000,000; 1990) 75,967, of which domestic 57,991, international 17,976; operating expenses 77,882, of which domestic 59,004, international 18,878.

Intercity passenger and freight traffic by mode of transportation (1990)

	cargo traffic ('000,000,000 ton-mi)	% of nat'l total	passenger traffic ('000,000,000 passenger-mi)	% of nat'l total
Rail	1,071	37.5	13	0.6
Road	735	25.7	1,683	81.9
Inland water	462	16.2	—	—
Air	11	0.4	358	17.4
Pipeline	577	20.2	—	—
TOTAL	2,855[3]	100.0	2,054	100.0[3]

Communications. Daily newspapers (1992): total number 1,755; total circulation (1990) 62,300,000; circulation per 1,000 population (1990) 249. Radio (1991): total number of receivers 520,000,000 (1 per 0.5 persons). Television (1991): total number of receivers 215,000,000 (1 per 1.2 persons). Telephones (1990; access lines): 127,178,122 (1 per 2.0 persons).

Other communications media (1990)

Print	titles		titles
Books (new)	53,446	Home economics	90
of which		Industrial arts	106
Agriculture	562	Journalism and communications	90
Art	1,569	Labour and industrial relations	70
Biography	2,193	Law	273
Business	1,569	Library and information sciences	118
Education	1,054	Literature and language	158
Fiction	5,941	Mathematics and science	238
General works	2,332	Medicine	182
History	2,563	Philosophy and religion	130
Home economics	949	Physical education and recreation	151
Juvenile	5,413	Political science	136
Language	586	Psychology	138
Law	1,096	Sociology and anthropology	149
Literature	2,298	Zoology	94
Medicine	3,447		
Music	375	Cinema[9]	
Philosophy, psychology	2,058	Feature films	489
Poetry, drama	1,128		
Religion	2,586		traffic
Science	3,288		(units, '000)
Sociology, economics	7,971	Electronic[25]	
Sports, recreation	1,077	Telegrams	53,000
Technology	2,690	Domestic	42,000
Travel	701	International	11,000
Periodicals[8]	3,731	Telex	69,559
of which			
Agriculture	153		(pieces of mail)
Business and economics	262		
Chemistry and physics	170	Post	
Children's periodicals	78	Mail	166,875,000,000
Education	203	Domestic	166,077,000,000
Engineering	265	International	798,000,000
Fine and applied arts	145		
General interest	181		
History	151		

Education and health

Education (1990–91)

	schools	teachers	students	student/ teacher ratio
Primary (age 6–13)	} 101,050	1,387,625	26,305,999	19.0
Secondary and vocational (age 14–17)		967,142	14,206,244	14.7
Higher, including teacher-training colleges	3,406	825,700	8,175,012	9.9

Literacy (1980): total population age 15 and over literate 166,497,565 (95.5%); males literate 79,161,126 (95.7%); females literate 87,336,439 (95.3%); other studies indicate adult "functional" literacy may not exceed 85%.
Health (1989): physicians 629,000 (1 per 391 persons), specialties in internal medicine 16.0%, general practice 11.5%, pediatrics 6.6%, general surgery 6.2%, psychiatry 5.7%, obstetrics and gynecology 5.5%, anesthesiology 4.2%, orthopedics 3.1%, pathology 2.6%, ophthalmology 2.6%, radiology 1.4%, other 34.6%; nurses 1,666,000 (1 per 148 persons); dentists 168,000 (1 per 1,472 persons); hospital beds 1,224,000 (1 per 202 persons), of which non-federal 91.8% (community hospitals 83.0%, psychiatric 14.2%, long-term general and special 2.4%), federal 8.2%; infant mortality rate per 1,000 live births (1991) 10.3.
Food (1988–90): daily per capita caloric intake 3,642 (vegetable products 70%, animal products 30%); 138% of FAO recommended minimum requirement. Per capita consumption of major food groups (pounds annually; 1990): dairy products 570.6; grains 185.4; sweeteners 137.5; potatoes 127.2; red meat 112.3; fresh vegetables 111.0; fresh fruits 92.3; poultry products 63.6; fats and oils 62.7; fish and shellfish 15.5.

Military

Total active duty personnel (1992): 1,913,750 (army 35.2%, navy 28.6%, air force 26.1%, marines 10.1%). *Military expenditure as percentage of GNP* (1989): 5.8% (world 4.9%); per capita expenditure U.S.$1,222. *Military aid* (1990): total $4,893,000,000 (Middle East and South Asia 86.7%, of which Israel 36.6%, Egypt 24.5%, Turkey 10.2%, Greece 7.1%, Pakistan 4.7%, Jordan 1.4%; Latin America 4.8%, of which El Salvador 1.7%, Colombia 1.5%, Honduras 0.4%, Dominican Republic 0.4%; East Asia 3.1%, of which Philippines 2.9%, Thailand 0.1%; Africa 2.3%, of which Morocco 0.9%, Tunisia 0.6%; Europe 1.8%, of which Portugal 1.8%; international organizations 1.3%).

[1]Excludes 5 nonvoting delegates. [2]Total area excluding U.S. share of Great Lakes is 3,618,770 sq mi (9,372,571 sq km). [3]Detail does not add to total given because of rounding. [4]Includes military personnel residing overseas. [5]Fiscal year ending September 30. [6]Year ending May 1992. [7]October 1991; excludes construction and mining. [8]1989. [9]1988. [10]1990. [11]1987. [12]Excludes armed forces overseas. [13]Statistical discrepancy. [14]Includes unemployed persons not previously employed. [15]Number of establishments is for 1987. [16]Annual sales is for 1990. [17]Personal-consumption expenditure. [18]Persons of Spanish origin may be of any race. [19]August. [20]Annual average. [21]End of year. [22]Second quarter. [23]Includes Central and South America. [24]Includes statistical discrepancy. [25]1986.

Uruguay

Official name: República Oriental del Uruguay (Oriental Republic of Uruguay).
Form of government: republic with two legislative houses (Senate [31][1]; Chamber of Representatives [99]).
Head of state and government: President.
Capital: Montevideo.
Official language: Spanish.
Official religion: none.
Monetary unit: 1 Uruguayan new peso (NUr$) = 100 centésimos; valuation (Oct. 5, 1992) 1 U.S.$ = NUr$3,271; 1 £ = NUr$5,561.

Area and population

Departments	Capitals	area sq mi	area sq km	population 1985 census
Artigas	Artigas	4,605	11,928	69,145
Canelones	Canelones	1,751	4,536	364,248
Cerro Largo	Melo	5,270	13,648	78,416
Colonia	Colonia del Sacramento	2,358	6,106	112,717
Durazno	Durazno	4,495	11,643	55,077
Flores	Trinidad	1,986	5,144	24,739
Florida	Florida	4,022	10,417	66,474
Lavalleja	Minas	3,867	10,016	61,466
Maldonado	Maldonado	1,851	4,793	94,314
Montevideo	Montevideo	205	530	1,311,976
Paysandú	Paysandú	5,375	13,922	103,763
Río Negro	Fray Bentos	3,584	9,282	48,644
Rivera	Rivera	3,618	9,370	89,475
Rocha	Rocha	4,074	10,551	66,601
Salto	Salto	5,468	14,163	108,487
San José	San José de Mayo	1,927	4,992	89,893
Soriano	Mercedes	3,478	9,008	79,439
Tacuarembó	Tacuarembó	5,961	15,438	83,498
Treinta y Tres	Treinta y Tres	3,679	9,529	46,869
TOTAL LAND AREA		67,574	175,016	
INLAND WATER		463	1,199	
TOTAL		68,037	176,215	2,955,241

Demography

Population (1992): 3,130,000.
Density[2] (1992): persons per sq mi 46.3, persons per sq km 17.9.
Urban-rural (1990): urban 85.5%; rural 14.5%.
Sex distribution (1990): male 48.74%; female 51.26%.
Age breakdown (1990): under 15, 25.8%; 15–29, 23.0%; 30–44, 18.9%; 45–59, 15.8%; 60–74, 11.9%; 75 and over, 4.6%.
Population projection: (2000) 3,274,000; (2010) 3,453,000.
Doubling time: 83 years.
Ethnic composition (1980): mixed Spanish-Italian 85.9%; mestizo 3.0%; Italian 2.6%; Jewish 1.7%; mulatto 1.2%; other 5.6%.
Religious affiliation (1980): Christian 62.9%, of which Roman Catholic 59.5%; Jewish 1.7%; nonreligious and atheist 35.1%; other 0.3%.
Major cities (1985): Montevideo 1,311,976; Salto 80,823; Paysandú 76,191; Las Piedras 58,288; Rivera 57,316.

Vital statistics

Birth rate per 1,000 population (1990): 18.3 (world avg. 27.1); (1983) legitimate 73.8%; illegitimate 26.2%.
Death rate per 1,000 population (1990): 9.9 (world avg. 9.8).
Natural increase rate per 1,000 population (1990): 8.4 (world avg. 17.3).
Total fertility rate (avg. births per childbearing woman; 1990–95): 2.3.
Marriage rate per 1,000 population (1987): 7.2.
Divorce rate per 1,000 population (1987): 1.5.
Life expectancy at birth (1985–90): male 68.9 years; female 75.3 years.
Major causes of death per 100,000 population (1989): diseases of the circulatory system 371.6; malignant neoplasms (cancers) 220.9; respiratory diseases 70.8; accidents 48.3; diseases of the digestive system 41.1.

National economy

Budget (1991). Revenue: NUr$3,714,341,000,000 (direct taxes 75.9%, receipts from foreign trade 11.7%). Expenditures: NUr$3,636,941,000,000 (social security and welfare 56.7%, general public services 15.7%, interest on public debt 9.5%, capital investments 9.4%, subsidies 5.5%).
Public debt (external, outstanding; 1990): U.S.$2,949,000,000.
Tourism (1990): receipts U.S.$261,000,000; expenditures U.S.$111,000,000.
Production (metric tons except as noted). Agriculture, forestry, fishing (1990): sugarcane 682,800, wheat 542,400, rice 347,300, sugar beets 208,500, barley 202,600, corn (maize) 112,300; livestock (number of live animals) 25,220,000 sheep, 8,723,000 cattle, 480,000 horses; roundwood 3,295,000 cu m; fish catch 88,936. Mining and quarrying (1989): hydraulic cement 513,000; gypsum 110,000. Manufacturing (value added in NUr$'000,000; 1987): food products (excluding beverages) 73,085; textiles 47,375; petroleum products 47,053; chemicals and chemical products 40,322; beverages 33,906; transport equipment 32,641; tobacco products 19,829; leather products 17,540; paper and paper products 15,729. Construction (approvals; 1988): residential 277,425 sq m; nonresidential 31,380 sq m. Energy production (consumption): electricity (kW-hr; 1990) 7,372,000,000 (6,042,000,000); coal, none (none); crude petroleum (barrels; 1990) none (8,796,000); petroleum products (metric tons; 1990) 1,084,000 (1,164,000); natural gas, none (n.a.).
Gross national product (1990): U.S.$7,929,000,000 (U.S.$2,560 per capita).

Structure of gross domestic product and labour force

	1990 in value NUr$'000,000	1990 % of total value	1985 labour force	1985 % of labour force
Agriculture	1,046,277	10.9	170,183	14.5
Mining	19,308	0.2	1,771	0.1
Manufacturing	2,677,705	27.8	214,945	18.3
Construction	341,567	3.5	64,385	5.4
Public utilities	275,583	2.9	17,377	1.5
Transp. and commun.	571,805	5.9	59,289	5.0
Trade	1,140,808	11.9	139,242	11.9
Finance	1,274,416	13.2	42,688	3.6
Pub. admin., defense	886,721	9.2	369,260	31.4
Services	1,991,353	20.7		
Other	−601,877[3]	−6.2[3]	97,668[4]	8.3[4]
TOTAL	9,623,666	100.0	1,176,808	100.0

Population economically active (1985): total 1,176,808; activity rate 39.8% (participation rates: ages 20–64, 65.5%; female 33.2%; unemployed [1988] 8.3%).

Price and earnings indexes (1985 = 100)

	1985	1986	1987	1988	1989	1990	1991
Consumer price index	100.0	176.4	288.5	467.9	844.4	1,794	3,624
Monthly earnings index[5]	100.0	186.7	319.8	524.8	946.1	1,844	...

Household income and expenditure. Avg. household size (1985) 3.3; avg. annual income per household (1985) NUr$266,261 (U.S.$2,625); sources of income: wages 53.5%, self-employment 17.0%, transfer payments and other 29.5%[6]; expenditure (1982–83)[7]: food 39.9%, housing 17.6%, transportation and communications 10.4%, health care 9.3%, clothing 7.0%, durable goods 6.3%, recreation 3.1%, education 1.3%, personal effects and other 5.1%.
Land use (1989): forested 3.8%; meadows and pastures 77.3%; agricultural and under permanent cultivation 7.5%; other 11.4%.

Foreign trade[8]

Balance of trade (current prices)

	1986	1987	1988	1989	1990	1991
U.S.$'000,000	+305.2	+99.6	+300.3	+478.8	+435.4	+44.9
% of total	16.3%	4.4%	12.0%	17.6%	14.8%	1.4%

Imports (1991): U.S.$1,621,988,000 (machinery and appliances 21.3%; mineral products 15.5%; chemical products 14.3%; transport equipment 11.3%; synthetic plastics, resins, and rubber 7.4%; textile products 5.4%; base metals and products 5.2%). *Major import sources:* Brazil 22.8%; Argentina 17.4%; United States 12.1%; Germany 4.9%; France 3.2%.
Exports (1991): U.S.$1,540,926,000 (textiles and textile products 26.6%; live animals and live-animal products 24.0%; hides and skins 13.7%; vegetable products 13.0%; food, beverages, and tobacco 4.3%; synthetic plastics, resins, and rubber 2.7%). *Major export destinations:* Brazil 24.0%; Argentina 11.2%; United States 10.2%; Germany 8.6%; Italy 3.9%.

Transport and communications

Transport. Railroads (1988): route length 3,006 km; passenger-km (1987) 140,600,000; metric ton-km cargo 212,500,000. Roads (1985): length 52,000 km (paved 23%). Vehicles (1988): passenger cars 252,329; trucks and buses 144,728. Merchant marine (1991): vessels (100 gross tons and over) 91; deadweight tonnage 156,618. Air transport (1990): passenger-km 471,000,000; metric ton-km cargo 2,600,000; airports (1992) 7.
Communications. Daily newspapers (1988): total number 33; total circulation 694,000[9]; circulation per 1,000 population 227[9]. Radio (1991): total receivers 1,800,000 (1 per 1.7 persons). Television (1991): total receivers 700,000 (1 per 4.4 persons). Telephones (1989): 528,674 (1 per 5.8 persons).

Education and health

Education (1989)

	schools	teachers	students	student/teacher ratio
Primary (age 6–11)	2,735	19,391	359,455	18.5
Secondary (age 12–17)	293	13,571[10, 11]	196,851	...
Vocational	95[11]	...	56,084	...
Higher	2	5,925[11]	63,777	10.5[11]

Educational attainment (1985). Percentage of population age 25 and over having: no formal schooling 7.5%; less than primary education 26.6%; primary 31.2%; secondary 19.9%; higher 14.8%. *Literacy* (1985): population age 15 and over literate 95.0%; males 975,200 (94.5%); females 1,074,300 (95.4%).
Health (1990): physicians 9,061 (1 per 341 persons); hospital beds (1983) 23,400 (1 per 127 persons); infant mortality rate 20.4.
Food (1987–89): daily per capita caloric intake 2,697 (vegetable products 65%, animal products 35%); 101% of FAO recommended minimum requirement.

Military

Total active duty personnel (1991): 22,900 (army 69.9%, navy 15.3%, air force 14.8%). *Military expenditure as percentage of GNP* (1988): 2.2% (world 5.0%); per capita expenditure U.S.$55.

---

[1]Includes the vice president who serves as ex officio presiding officer. [2]Based on land area. [3]Includes indirect taxes less subsidies. [4]Includes unemployed not previously employed. [5]Salaried employees only. [6]Urban only. [7]Weights of consumer price index components in Montevideo. [8]Import figures are f.o.b. in balance of trade and c.i.f. for commodities and trading partners. [9]Partial circulation only. [10]Public only. [11]1988.

Uzbekistan

Official name: Ozbekistan Jumhuriyäti (Republic of Uzbekistan).
Form of government: multiparty republic with a single legislative body (Supreme Soviet [550]).
Head of state: President.
Head of government: Prime Minister.
Capital: Tashkent (Toshkent).
Official language: Uzbek.
Official religion: none.
Monetary unit: 1 ruble = 100 kopecks; valuation (Oct. 5, 1992) free rate, 1 U.S.$ = 316.82 rubles; 1 £ = 538.59 rubles.

Area and population

Autonomous Republic	Administrative centres	area sq mi	area sq km	population 1991[1] estimate
Karakalpakstan	Nukus	63,700	164,900	1,273,800
Provinces				
Andizhan (Andijan)	Andizhan	1,600	4,200	1,795,100
Bukhara	Bukhara	54,900	142,100	1,708,000
Dzhizak (Djizak)	Dzhizak	7,900	20,500	780,000
Fergana	Fergana	2,700	7,100	2,226,400
Kashka Darya	Karshi	11,000	28,400	1,697,700
Khorezm	Urgench	2,400	6,300	1,068,500
Namangan	Namangan	3,100	7,900	1,557,800
Samarkand	Samarkand	9,500	24,500	2,386,200
Surkhan Darya	Termez	8,000	20,800	1,335,900
Syr Darya	Gulistan	2,000	5,100	580,300
Tashkent (Toshkent)	Tashkent	6,000	15,600	4,298,500
TOTAL		172,700[2]	447,400	20,708,200

Demography

Population (1992): 21,363,000.
Density (1992): persons per sq mi 123.7, persons per sq km 47.7.
Urban-rural (1991): urban 40.3%; rural 59.7%.
Sex distribution (1989): male 49.40%; female 50.60%.
Age breakdown (1989): under 15, 40.8%; 15–29, 28.4%; 30–44, 15.0%; 45–59, 9.3%; 60–74, 4.7%; 75 and over, 1.8%.
Population projection: (2000) 26,044,000; (2010) 32,453,000.
Doubling time: 25 years.
Ethnic composition (1989): Uzbek 71.4%; Russian 8.3%; Tajik 4.7%; Kazakh 4.1%; Tatar 2.4%; Kara-Kalpak 2.1%; Crimean Tatar 1.0%; Korean 0.9%; Kyrgyz 0.9%; Ukrainian 0.8%; Turkmen 0.6%; other 2.8%.
Religious affiliation (1990): believers are predominantly Sunnī Muslim (Hanafīyah).
Major cities (1991): Tashkent 2,119,900; Samarkand 394,600; Namangan 319,200; Andizhan 298,300; Bukhara 249,600.

Vital statistics

Birth rate per 1,000 population (1990): 33.7 (world avg. 27.1); (1989) legitimate 95.8%; illegitimate 4.2%.
Death rate per 1,000 population (1990): 6.1 (world avg. 9.8).
Natural increase rate per 1,000 population (1990): 27.6 (world avg. 17.3).
Total fertility rate (avg. births per childbearing woman; 1989): 4.0.
Marriage rate per 1,000 population (1989): 10.0.
Divorce rate per 1,000 population (1989): 1.5.
Life expectancy at birth (1990): male 66.2 years; female 72.6 years.
Major causes of death per 100,000 population (1989): diseases of the circulatory system 251.3; diseases of the respiratory system 119.3; accidents, poisoning, and violence 60.1; malignant neoplasms (cancers) 55.9; infectious and parasitic diseases 44.5; diseases of the digestive system 27.1; diseases of the nervous system 9.1; endocrine and metabolic disorders 6.5.

National economy

Budget (1992). Revenue: 74,700,000,000 rubles (price differential tax 36.1%, turnover tax 26.2%, excise tax 12.7%, corporate income tax 12.7%, individual income tax 5.5%). Expenditures: 86,200,000,000 rubles (social and cultural affairs 27.3%, subsidies 24.7%, national economy 18.9%).
Public debt (external, outstanding; 1991): U.S.$2,000,000,000.
Tourism: n.a.
Production (metric tons except as noted). Agriculture, forestry, fishing (1989): seed cotton 5,292,000, vegetables (except potatoes) 2,584,600, melons and watermelons 931,800, fruit (except grapes) and berries 548,300, rice 483,700, corn (maize) 460,600, grapes 416,100, wheat 341,700, potatoes 324,600, barley 246,100, beans 5,100; livestock (number of live animals; 1990) 8,785,600 sheep and goats (of which 4,930,800 Karakul, 747,500 goats), 4,180,200 cattle, 742,900 pigs, 97,400 horses; roundwood (1990) 15,000 cu m; fish catch, n.a. Mining and quarrying: n.a. Manufacturing (1989): cement 6,193,600; milk 2,929,300; sulfuric acid 2,389,700; mineral fertilizers 1,899,900; ammonia 1,872,800; cotton fibre 1,580,800; steel 1,079,700; pig iron 895,700; meat 477,800; detergents 211,500; plastics and resins 163,900; cardboard 56,100; synthetic fibre 50,600; paper 25,700; wool 24,400; jute 22,000; eggs 2,429,100 units; bricks 2,162,900 units; Karakul pelts 1,483,000 units; tractors 23,700 units; cotton cloth 521,200,000 m; carpets and rugs 7,122,000 cu m; footwear 44,200,000 pairs. Construction (1989): 4,447,000,000 rubles, of which residential 795,000,000 rubles. Energy production (consumption): electricity (kW-hr; 1992) 57,400,000,000 (54,800,000,000); coal (metric tons;

1992) 6,200,000 (10,400,000); crude petroleum (barrels; 1992) 20,663,000 (61,865,000); petroleum products, n.a. (n.a.); natural gas (cu m; 1992) 41,600,000,000 (37,800,000,000).
Gross national product (at current market prices; 1989): 21,200,000,000 rubles (1,100 rubles per capita)[3].

Structure of net material product and labour force

	1991 in value '000,000 rubles	% of total value	labour force[4]	% of labour force[4]
Agriculture	19,879.0	43.2	1,977,000	29.1
Mining				
Manufacturing }	15,246.2	33.2	1,200,000	17.6
Public utilities				
Construction	4,905.7	10.7	714,000	10.5
Transp. and commun.	1,930.5	4.2	251,000	3.7
Trade	4,001.7	8.7	462,000	6.8
Finance	—	—	...	...
Pub. admin., defense	—	—	...	...
Services	—	—	2,067,000	30.4
Other	—	—	129,000	1.9
TOTAL	45,963.1	100.0	6,800,000	100.0

Population economically active (1991): total 8,976,800; activity rate of total population 43.0% (participation rates [1989]: ages 16–59 [male], 16–54 [female] 78.2%; female 43.8%; unemployed [1990] 3.9%).

Price and earnings indexes (1985 = 100)

	1985	1986	1987	1988	1989	1990	1991
Consumer price index	100.0	...	...	...	...	126.6	117.2
Earnings index	...	...	...	...	...	...	...

Land use (1989): forested 4.2%; meadows and pastures 52.5%; agricultural and under permanent cultivation 10.1%; other 33.2%.
Household income and expenditure. Average household size (1989) 5.5; income per household (1991) 12,900 rubles; sources of income (1991): wages and salaries 48.2%, subsidies, grants, and nonwage income 40.1%, other 11.7%; expenditure (1991): food and consumer goods 82.3%, other 17.7%.

Foreign trade

Balance of trade (current prices)

	1987	1988	1989	1990
'000,000,000 rubles	−3.9	−1.2	−3.5	−3.7
% of total	20.8%	8.5%	17.0%	18.4%

Imports (1991): 20,200,000,000 rubles (foodstuffs and agricultural commodities 47.2%; consumer goods 43.5%; raw materials and processed industrial goods 4.9%; machinery and transport equipment 4.3%). *Major import sources:* mostly former Soviet republics.
Exports (1991): 19,600,000,000 rubles (raw materials and processed industrial goods 64.0%, of which cotton 33.6%; chemical products, fertilizers, and rubber 14.0%; fuel, mineral raw materials, and metals 4.5%; foodstuffs and agricultural commodities 4.4%; machinery and transport equipment 2.5%). *Major export destinations:* mostly former Soviet republics.

Transport and communications

Transport. Railroads (1990): length 4,225 mi, 6,800 km; passenger-mi 2,485,500,000, passenger-km 4,000,000,000; short ton-mi cargo 40,137,800,000, metric ton-km cargo 58,600,000,000. Roads (1990): total length 55,431 mi, 89,207 km (paved 83%). Vehicles (1988): passenger cars 790,800; trucks and buses, n.a. Merchant marine: vessels (100 gross tons and over) n.a.; total deadweight tonnage, n.a. Air transport (1990): passenger-mi 6,835,100,000, passenger-km 11,000,000,000; short ton-mi cargo 47,672,000,000, metric ton-km cargo 69,600,000,000; airports (1992) with scheduled flights 1.
Communications. Daily newspapers (1990): total number 279; total circulation 5,158,400; circulation per 1,000 population 249.1. Radio (1990): total number of receivers 3,690,000 (1 per 5.6 persons). Television (1990): total number of receivers 3,180,000 (1 per 6.5 persons). Telephones (1990): 1,659,100 (1 per 14.8 persons).

Education and health

Education (1989–90)

	schools	teachers	students	student/ teacher ratio
Primary (age 6–13)	1,467 }	352,600	283,000 }	13.0
Secondary (age 14–17)	6,571		4,584,100	
Voc., teacher tr.	244	...	277,300	...
Higher	44	...	331,600	...

Educational attainment (1989). Percentage of population age 25 and over having: primary education or no formal schooling 13.3%; some secondary 19.8%; completed secondary and some postsecondary 57.7%; higher 9.2%.
Literacy: n.a.
Health (1990): physicians 73,700 (1 per 281 persons); hospital beds 254,900 (1 per 81.2 persons); infant mortality rate per 1,000 live births 34.6.
Food: daily per capita caloric intake, n.a.

Military

Total active duty personnel (1992): CIS-joint control forces 15,000. *Military expenditure as percentage of GNP:* n.a.; per capita expenditure, n.a.

---

[1]January 1. [2]Detail does not add to total given because of rounding. [3]No equivalent U.S.$ value is offered, as Soviet GNP data are very speculative. [4]State sector only.

Vanuatu

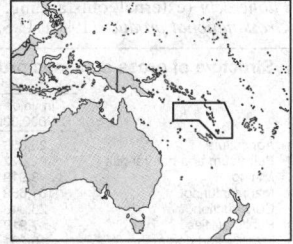

Official name: Ripablik blong Vanuatu (Bislama); République de Vanuatu (French); Republic of Vanuatu (English).
Form of government: republic with a single legislative house (Parliament [46]).
Chief of state: President.
Head of government: Prime Minister.
Capital: Vila.
Official languages: Bislama; French; English.
Official religion: none.
Monetary unit: vatu (VT); valuation (Oct. 5, 1992) 1 U.S.$ = VT 112.94; 1 £ = VT 192.00.

Area and population

Local Government Regions	Capitals	area sq mi	area sq km	population 1989 census[1]
Ambrym	Eas	257	666	7,000
Ambae/Maéwo	Longana	270	699	11,000
Banks/Torres	Sola	341	882	5,970
Efaté	Vila	356	923	31,000
Épi	Ringdove	172	446	3,700
Malekula	Lakatoro	793	2,053	19,250
Paama	Liro	23	60	1,690
Pentecost	Loltong	193	499	11,240
Santo/Malo	Luganville	1,640	4,248	25,350
Shepherd	Morua	33	86	3,980
Taféa	Isangel	629	1,628	22,450
TOTAL		4,707	12,190	142,630

Demography

Population (1992): 154,000.
Density (1992): persons per sq mi 32.7, persons per sq km 12.6.
Urban-rural (1989): urban 18.4%[2]; rural 81.6%.
Sex distribution (1989): male 51.60%; female 48.40%.
Age breakdown (1989)[3]: under 15, 45.5%; 15–29, 26.6%; 30–44, 15.2%; 45–59, 8.4%; 60–74, 3.7%; 75 and over, 0.6%.
Population projection: (2000) 177,000; (2010) 208,000.
Doubling time: 23 years.
Ethnic composition (1989): Ni-Vanuatu 98.0%; other 2.0%.
Religious affiliation (1989): Christian 77.2%, of which Presbyterian 35.8%, Roman Catholic 14.5%, Anglican 14.0%, Seventh-day Adventist 8.2%; Custom 4.6%; other 12.5%; nonreligious 1.7%; unknown 4.0%.
Major towns (1989): Vila (Port-Vila) 19,400; Luganville (Santo) 6,900; Port Olry 884[4]; Isangel 752[4].

Vital statistics

Birth rate per 1,000 population (1991): 36.0 (world avg. 26.4).
Death rate per 1,000 population (1991): 5.0 (world avg. 9.2).
Natural increase rate per 1,000 population (1991): 31.0 (world avg. 17.2).
Total fertility rate (avg. births per childbearing woman; 1991): 6.2.
Marriage rate per 1,000 population (1985): c. 7.4.
Divorce rate per 1,000 population (1985): less than 0.7.
Life expectancy at birth (1985): male 61.1 years; female 59.3 years.
Major causes of death per 100,000 population (1985)[5]: infectious and parasitic diseases 69.3; diseases of the respiratory system 60.5; diseases of the circulatory system 37.6; accidents and violence 23.6; malignant neoplasms (cancers) 22.9; ill-defined conditions 117.3.

National economy

Budget (1989). Revenue: VT 4,154,700,000 (taxes on international trade 58.6%; taxes on goods and services 22.7%; nontax revenue 16.8%). Expenditures: VT 7,287,200,000 (manufacturing, mining, and construction 21.4%; public services 13.7%; education 12.6%; transportation and communications 10.5%; agriculture 6.7%; health 6.6%).
Tourism (1988): receipts from visitors U.S.$18,000,000; expenditures by nationals abroad U.S.$2,000,000.
Land use (1989): forested 1.3%; meadows and pastures 2.1%; agricultural 11.9%; limestone, volcanic rock, and other 84.7%.
Production (metric tons except as noted). Agriculture, forestry, fishing (1990): coconuts 300,000, copra 45,000, roots and tubers 40,000, vegetables and melons 8,000, cacao beans 2,000, bananas 1,000, corn (maize) 1,000; livestock (number of live animals) 129,000 cattle, 82,000 pigs, 14,000 goats; roundwood 63,000 cu m; fish catch (1989) 3,340. Mining and quarrying (1985): small quantities of coral-reef limestone, crushed stone, sand, and gravel. Manufacturing (value added in '000 VT; 1984): food, beverages, and tobacco 358,000; wood products 96,000; fabricated metal products 60,000; paper products, including printing and publishing 48,800; nonmetallic mineral products 24,600; handicrafts 14,600; textiles, clothing, and leather 12,900. Construction (approvals in Vila and Luganville; 1991): residential 6,845 sq m; nonresidential 3,235 sq m. Energy production (consumption): electricity (kW-hr; 1990) 26,000,000 (26,000,000); coal, none (none); crude petroleum, none (none); petroleum products (metric tons; 1990) none (22,000); natural gas, none (none).
Population economically active (1989): total 66,957; activity rate of total population 47.0% (participation rates: ages 15–64, 85.0%; female 46.3%; unemployed 0.5%).

Price and earnings indexes (1985 = 100)

	1985	1986	1987	1988	1989	1990	1991
Consumer price index	100.0	103.9	118.3	132.2	142.7	151.1	160.6
Earnings index	...	...	...	...	...	...	...

Public debt (external, outstanding; 1990): U.S.$26,000,000.
Gross national product (at current market prices; 1990): U.S.$167,000,000 (U.S.$1,060 per capita).

Structure of gross domestic product and labour force

	1990 in value VT '000,000	1990 % of total value	1989 labour force	1989 % of labour force
Agriculture	3,582	20.0	40,889	61.1
Mining	...	...	1	—
Manufacturing	1,050	5.9	891	1.3
Construction	1,033	5.8	1,302	1.9
Public utilities	339	1.9	109	0.2
Transportation and communications	1,517	8.5	1,030	1.5
Trade	5,772	32.2	2,712	4.0
Finance	1,743	9.7	646	1.0
Pub. admin., defense	1,985	11.1 }	7,891	11.8
Services	1,278	7.1 }		
Other	–400[6]	–2.2[6]	11,486	17.2
TOTAL	17,899	100.0	66,957	100.0

Household income and expenditure (1985)[2]. Average household size (1989) 5.1; income per household U.S.$11,299; sources of income: wages and salaries 59.0%, self-employment 33.7%; expenditure (1987)[7]: food and beverages 45.5%, clothing and footwear 14.1%, housing 10.2%, transportation 9.8%.

Foreign trade[8]

Balance of trade (current prices)

	1985	1986	1987	1988	1989	1990
U.S.$'000,000	–33.6	–38.0	–43.4	–42.5	–44.2	–65.8
% of total	47.3%	68.3%	61.3%	58.0%	61.7%	70.4%

Imports (1991): VT 9,174,000,000 (machinery and transport equipment 24.7%; basic manufactures 18.4%; food and live animals 15.6%; mineral fuels 14.2%; chemical products 6.6%; beverages and tobacco 3.9%). *Major import sources:* Australia 38.2%; New Zealand 11.3%; Fiji 10.1%; Japan 8.1%; France 7.4%; New Caledonia 6.6%; Singapore 5.0%; Hong Kong 3.9%.
Exports (1991): VT 1,810,000,000 (domestic exports 91.7%, of which copra 29.1%, beef and veal 19.9%, cocoa beans and preparations 15.0%, seashells 5.4%, timber 3.9%; reexports 8.3%). *Major export destinations[9]:* Japan 22.5%; Australia 15.7%; The Netherlands 14.6%; France 7.5%; New Caledonia 4.7%.

Transport and communications

Transport. Railroads: none. Roads (1984): total length 660 mi, 1,062 km; (paved 24%). Vehicles (1990): passenger cars 4,200; trucks and buses 2,800. Merchant marine (1991): vessels (100 gross tons and over) 287; total deadweight tonnage 3,328,686. Air transport (1990): domestic passenger arrivals 96,009, international passenger arrivals 44,547; international cargo unloaded 536 metric tons, international cargo loaded (1987) 133 metric tons; airports (1992) with scheduled flights 28.
Communications. Daily newspapers: none. Radio (1991): total number of receivers 20,000 (1 per 7.5 persons). Television (1987): total number of receivers 1,000 (1 per 136 persons). Telephones (1986): 3,240 (1 per 44 persons).

Education and health

Education (1989)

	schools	teachers	students	student/teacher ratio
Primary (age 6–11)	263	970	25,000	25.8
Secondary (age 11–18)	21[10]	169	3,065	18.1
Voc., teacher tr.[11]	...	...	...	...
Higher[12]	...	...	...	...

Educational attainment (1989). Percentage of population age 6 and over having: no formal schooling or less than one year 22.3%, some primary education 52.6%, lower-level secondary 18.3%, upper-level secondary and higher 4.8%, not stated 2.0%. *Literacy* (1979): total population age 15 and over literate 32,120 (52.9%); males 18,550 (57.3%); females 13,570 (47.8%).
Health (1990): physicians 20 (1 per 7,345 persons); hospital beds 364 (1 per 404 persons); infant mortality rate per 1,000 live births (1991) 36.0.
Food (1987–89): daily per capita caloric intake 2,552 (vegetable products 82%, animal products 18%); 112% of FAO recommended minimum requirement.

Military

Total active duty personnel: Vanuatu has a paramilitary force of about 300.

[1]Provisional results. [2]Vila and Luganville only. [3]For indigenous population only. [4]1979. [5]Deaths reported to the Ministry of Health only. [6]Imputed bank service charges. [7]Weights of consumer price index components. [8]Imports c.i.f.; exports f.o.b. [9]Destination of domestic exports only. [10]1986. [11]Included with Secondary. [12]A centre of the University of the South Pacific in Vila was completed in May 1989.

Venezuela

Official name: República de Venezuela (Republic of Venezuela).
Form of government: federal multiparty republic with two legislative houses (Senate [49][1]; Chamber of Deputies [201]).
Head of state and government: President.
Capital: Caracas.
Official language: Spanish.
Official religion: none.
Monetary unit: 1 bolívar (B, plural Bs) = 100 céntimos; valuation[2] (Oct. 5, 1992) 1 U.S.$ = Bs 69.49; 1 £ = Bs 118.14.

Area and population

States	Capitals	area sq mi	area sq km	population 1990 census
Anzoátegui	Barcelona	16,700	43,300	924,074
Apure	San Fernando de Apure	29,500	76,500	305,132
Aragua	Maracay	2,700	7,014	1,194,982
Barinas	Barinas	13,600	35,200	456,246
Bolívar	Ciudad Bolívar	91,900	238,000	968,695
Carabobo	Valencia	1,795	4,650	1,558,608
Cojedes	San Carlos	5,700	14,800	196,526
Falcón	Coro	9,600	24,800	632,513
Guárico	San Juan de Los Morros	25,091	64,986	525,737
Lara	Barquisimeto	7,600	19,800	1,270,196
Mérida	Mérida	4,400	11,300	615,503
Miranda	Los Teques	3,070	7,950	2,026,229
Monagas	Maturín	11,200	28,900	503,176
Nueva Esparta	La Asunción	440	1,150	280,777
Portuguesa	Guanare	5,900	15,200	625,576
Sucre	Cumaná	4,600	11,800	722,707
Táchira	San Cristóbal	4,300	11,100	859,861
Trujillo	Trujillo	2,900	7,400	520,292
Yaracuy	San Felipe	2,700	7,100	411,980
Zulia	Maracaibo	24,400	63,100	2,387,208
Other federal entities				
Amazonas	Puerto Ayacucho	67,900	175,750	60,207
Delta Amacuro	Tucupita	15,500	40,200	91,085
Dependencias Federales	—	50	120	2,245
Distrito Federal	Caracas	745	1,930	2,265,874
TOTAL		**352,144**[3]	**912,050**	**19,405,429**

Demography

Population (1992): 20,184,000.
Density (1992): persons per sq mi 57.3, persons per sq km 22.1.
Urban-rural (1990): urban 84.0%; rural 16.0%.
Sex distribution (1990): male 49.74%; female 50.26%.
Age breakdown (1990): under 15, 38.3%; 15–29, 28.1%; 30–44, 18.6%; 45–59, 9.3%; 60–74, 4.5%; 75 and over, 1.2%.
Population projection: (2000) 24,072,000; (2010) 29,157,000.
Doubling time: 28 years.
Ethnic composition (1981): mestizo 69%; white 20%; black 9%; Indian 2%.
Religious affiliation (1987): Roman Catholic 91.7%; other 8.3%.
Major cities (1990): Caracas 1,290,087; Maracaibo 1,206,726; Valencia 955,005; Barquisimeto 723,587; Maracay 538,616; Petare 531,926.

Vital statistics

Birth rate per 1,000 population (1990): 29.9 (world avg. 27.1); (1974) legitimate 47.0%; illegitimate 53.0%.
Death rate per 1,000 population (1990): 4.7 (world avg. 9.8).
Natural increase rate per 1,000 population (1990): 25.2 (world avg. 17.3).
Total fertility rate (avg. births per childbearing woman; 1990): 3.6.
Marriage rate per 1,000 population (1990): 5.5.
Divorce rate per 1,000 population (1987): 1.2.
Life expectancy at birth (1990): male 67.0 years; female 73.3 years.
Major causes of death per 100,000 population (1990): heart diseases 75.3; malignant neoplasms (cancers) 49.3; accidents 38.1; perinatal problems 32.4; cerebrovascular diseases 27.8; pneumonia 15.1.

National economy

Budget (1990). Revenue: Bs 758,217,000,000 (oil revenues 77.6%, tax revenues 12.2%, nontax revenues 8.9%, internal borrowing 1.3%). Expenditures: Bs 754,557,000,000 (operating expenses 83.7%, public-debt service 14.3%).
Tourism (1990): receipts U.S.$359,000,000; expenditures U.S.$945,000,000.
Production (metric tons except as noted). Agriculture, forestry, fishing (1990): sugarcane 7,000,000, corn (maize) 1,150,000, bananas 1,130,000, plantains 500,000, rice 400,000, sorghum 376,000, cassava 350,000, coffee 70,000, cacao 16,000; livestock (number of live animals) 13,819,000 cattle; roundwood 1,501,000 cu m; fish catch (1989) 327,031. Mining and quarrying (1991): iron ore 19,959,000; bauxite 2,100,000; aluminum ore 605,000; gold 80,400 troy ounces. Manufacturing (value added in Bs '000; 1989): base metals 44,641,000; food products 36,476,000; chemicals 35,537,000; beverages 19,-123,000; metal products 13,114,000; textiles 11,984,000; electrical machinery and equipment 10,894,000; tobacco 10,747,000; nonmetallic minerals 9,446,-000. Construction (in Bs; 1990): residential 14,092,000,000; nonresidential 87,917,000,000. Energy production (consumption): electricity (kW-hr; 1990) 61,000,000,000 (61,000,000,000); coal (metric tons; 1990) 1,864,000 (200,000); crude petroleum (barrels; 1990) 770,567,000 (336,074,000); petroleum products (metric tons; 1990) 48,145,000 (16,448,000); natural gas (cu m; 1990) 17,711,000,000 (17,711,000,000).

Public debt (external, outstanding; 1990): U.S.$26,027,000,000.
Gross national product (1990): U.S.$50,574,000,000 (U.S.$2,560 per capita).

Structure of gross domestic product and labour force

	1990 in value Bs '000,000[4]	% of total value	labour force	% of labour force
Agriculture	25,858	5.5	855,590	11.9
Petroleum and natural gas	82,572	17.5 }	69,686	1.0
Mining	3,919	0.8 }		
Manufacturing	101,652	21.5	1,142,015	15.9
Construction	23,346	4.9	647,301	9.0
Public utilities	7,919	1.7	71,850	1.0
Transp. and commun.	16,291	3.4	428,107	6.0
Trade	73,831	15.6	1,497,085	20.9
Finance	...	...	421,307	5.9
Pub. admin., defense	43,875	9.3 }	2,006,594	28.0
Services	90,259	19.1 }		
Other	3,509	0.7	33,782	0.5
TOTAL	473,031	100.0	7,173,317	100.0[3]

Population economically active (1990): total 7,173,317; activity rate 36.1% (participation rates: over age 15, 59.1%; female [1989] 29.8%; unemployed 9.9%).

Price and earnings indexes (1985 = 100)

	1985	1986	1987	1988	1989	1990	1991
Consumer price index	100.0	111.5	142.9	185.0	340.9	480.1	644.3
Monthly earnings index[5]	100.0	105.4	115.4	139.3	207.8	309.5	...

Household income and expenditure: average household size (1981) 5.3; average annual income per household (1981) Bs 42,492 (U.S.$9,899); sources of income: n.a.; expenditure (1987): food 32.0%, transportation and communications 14.9%, household furnishings and maintenance 12.0%, rent and utilities 8.8%, clothing 7.5%, education and recreation 6.6%, medical care 5.9%.
Land use (1989): forested 34.5%; meadows and pastures 20.0%; agricultural and under permanent cultivation 4.4%; other 41.1%.

Foreign trade

Balance of trade (current prices)

Bs '000,000	1986	1987	1988	1989	1990	1991
	+11,429	+7,510	−65,434	+232,261	+529,115	+286,500
% of total	7.8%	3.2%	18.2%	33.5%	46.7%	20.1%

Imports (1990): U.S.$6,607,792,000 (machinery and transport equipment 33.3%, chemicals 14.3%, basic metal manufactures 9.9%, vegetable products 5.8%, mineral products 5.3%, paper products 4.2%). *Major import sources:* U.S. 45.4%; W.Ger. 9.9%; Italy 4.8%; Brazil 3.9%; Japan 3.8%; France 3.5%; U.K. 3.0%.
Exports (1990): U.S.$18,044,254,000 (crude petroleum and petroleum products 79.7%, iron ore 1.8%). *Major export destinations:* U.S. 47.3%; Puerto Rico 4.2%; The Netherlands 3.9%; W.Ger. 3.7%; Japan 2.8%; Canada 2.6%.

Transport and communications

Transport. Railroads (1990): route length 226 mi, 363 km; passenger-km 64,-065,349; metric ton-km cargo 35,469,794. Roads (1990): total length 48,174 mi, 77,529 km (paved 34%). Vehicles (1990): passenger cars 1,582,000; trucks and buses 464,000. Merchant marine (1991): vessels (100 gross tons and over) 278; total deadweight tonnage 1,437,092. Air transport (1990): passenger-km 4,032,000,000; metric ton-km cargo 114,960,000; airports (1992) with scheduled flights 32.
Communications. Daily newspapers (1988): total number 56; total circulation 2,225,000[6]; circulation per 1,000 population 119[6]. Radio (1991): 8,100,000 receivers (1 per 2.4 persons). Television (1991): 3,700,000 receivers (1 per 5.3 persons). Telephones (1988): 1,749,325 (1 per 10 persons).

Education and health

Education (1989–90)

	schools	teachers	students	student/teacher ratio
Primary (age 7–12)	12,601	171,431	3,036,219	17.7
Secondary (age 13–17)[7]	1,454	62,660[8]	1,114,563	17.2[8]
Higher	85	39,489	528,473	13.4

Educational attainment (1990). Percentage of population age 10 and over having: no formal schooling 9.5%; primary education 45.7%; secondary 35.9%; higher 8.9%. *Literacy* (1990): total population age 15 and over literate 13,371,743 (92.2%); males 6,742,992 (93.5%); females 6,628,751 (91.1%).
Health (1990): physicians (1989) 32,616 (1 per 576 persons); hospital beds 52,010 (1 per 370 persons); infant mortality rate per 1,000 live births 25.9.
Food (1987–89): daily per capita caloric intake 2,620 (vegetable products 84%, animal products 16%); 106% of FAO recommended minimum.

Military

Total active duty personnel (1991): 75,000 (army 76.0%, navy 14.7%, air force 9.3%). *Military expenditure as percentage of GNP* (1989): 1.0% (world 4.9%); per capita expenditure U.S.$22.

---

[1]In addition, three former presidents hold lifetime membership. [2]Venezuela's three-tiered system of official exchange rates was replaced on March 14, 1989, by a unified market-determined exchange rate. The free-market rate governs as a luxury-goods rate. [3]Detail does not add to total given because of rounding. [4]At 1984 prices. [5]Blue-collar workers. [6]Circulation data refer to 36 dailies only. [7]Includes vocational and teacher training. [8]1987–88.

Vietnam

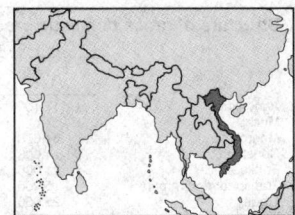

Official name: Cong Hoa Xa Hoi Chu Nghia Viet Nam (Socialist Republic of Vietnam).
Form of government: socialist republic with one legislative house (National Assembly [395]).
Chief of state: President.
Head of government: Prime Minister.
Capital: Hanoi.
Official language: Vietnamese.
Official religion: none.
Monetary unit: 1 dong (D) = 10 hao = 100 xu; valuation (Oct. 5, 1992) 1 U.S.$ = D 10,881; 1 £ = D 18,497.

Area and population

Regions Provinces	Capitals	area sq mi	area sq km	population 1991 estimate
Dong bang song Cuu Long		15,280	39,575[1]	14,882,600
An Giang	Long Xuyen	1,322	3,424	1,849,700
Ben Tre	Ben Tre	868	2,247	1,264,300
Can Tho	Can Tho	2,379[2]	6,161[2]	1,695,000
Dong Thap	Cao Lamh	1,265	3,276	1,401,600
Kien Giang	Rach Gia	2,410	6,243	1,266,000
Long An	Tan An	1,675	4,338	1,177,100
Minh Hai	Bac Lieu	2,969	7,689	1,642,600
Soc Trang		[2]	[2]	1,123,900
Tien Giang	My Tho	903	2,339	1,557,400
Tra Vinh	... }	1,489	3,857	901,100
Vinh Long				1,003,900
Dong bang song Hong		4,813	12,466[1]	13,275,600
Ha Tay	...	827	2,143	2,130,000
Hai Hung	Hai Duong	985	2,552	2,554,500
Haiphong (MUNICIPALITY)	—	581	1,504	1,516,900
Hanoi (CAPITAL)	—	361	934	2,095,000
Nam Ha	... }	1,471	3,810	2,473,700
Ninh Binh				800,100
Thai Binh	Thai Binh	588	1,524	1,705,400
Dong Nam Bo		9,067[1]	23,484[1]	8,194,200
Ba Ria–Vung Tau	...	754	1,954	532,100
Dong Nai	Bien Hoa	2,266	5,868	1,742,400
Ho Chi Minh City (MUNICIPALITY)		807	2,090	4,075,700
Song Be	Thu Dau Mot	3,686	9,546	1,017,000
Tay Ninh	Ho Chi Minh City	1,555	4,027	827,000
Duyen hai mien trung		17,693	45,824[1]	6,995,600[1]
Binh Dinh	Quy Nhon	2,346	6,076	1,295,000
Binh Thuan	...	4,410[3]	11,422[3]	823,600
Khanh Hoa	Nha Trang	2,030	5,258	871,700
Ninh Thuan	...	[3]	[3]	412,000
Phu Yen	Tuy Hoa	2,017	5,223	670,500
Quang Nam–Da Nang	Da Nang	4,629	11,988	1,832,300
Quang Ngai	Quang Ngai	2,261	5,856	1,090,400
Khu Bon cu		19,760	51,178	9,054,200
Ha Tinh	...	2,338	6,055	1,234,500
Nghe An	...	6,321	16,371	2,561,900
Quang Binh	Dong Hoi	3,082	7,983	693,200
Quang Tri	Dong Ha	1,773	4,592	490,800
Thanh Hoa	Thanh Hoa	4,312	11,168	3,152,900
Thua Thien-Hue	Hue	1,934	5,009	742,400
Mien nui va trung du		39,745	102,938[1]	11,542,800
Bac Thai	Thai Nguyen	2,511	6,503	1,082,600
Cao Bang	Cao Bang	3,261	8,445	591,500
Ha Bac	Bac Giang	1,782	4,615	2,172,900
Ha Giang	...	2,240	5,802	489,900
Hoa Binh	...	1,781	4,613	722,900
Lai Chau	Lai Chau	6,618	17,140	467,600
Lang Son	Lang Son	3,153	8,167	643,600
Lao Cai	...	3,106	8,045	491,500
Quang Ninh	Hai Duong	2,293	5,939	848,200
Son La	Son La	5,487	14,210	726,800
Tuyen Quang	...	3,023	7,830	597,200
Vinh Phu	Viet Tri	1,862	4,823	2,097,700
Yen Bai	...	2,628	6,807	610,400
Tay Nguyen		21,455[1]	55,569	2,688,900
Dac Lac	Buon Me Thoat	7,645	19,800	1,072,300
Gia Lai	...	5,899	15,278	773,800
Kon Tum	...	3,984	10,318	149,800
Lam Dong	Da Lat	3,929	10,173	693,000
TOTAL		127,813	331,033	67,678,700[4]

Demography

Population (1992): 69,052,000.
Density (1992): persons per sq mi 540.2; persons per sq km 208.6.
Urban-rural (1989): urban 20.1%; rural 79.9%.
Sex distribution (1991): male 49.07%; female 50.93%.
Age breakdown (1989): under 15, 39.0%; 15–29, 28.7%; 30–44, 16.0%; 45–59, 9.1%; 60–74, 5.6%; 75 and over, 1.6%.
Population projection: (2000) 81,094,000; (2010) 95,700,000.
Ethnic composition (1989): Vietnamese 87.1%; Tho (Tay) 1.8%; Chinese (Hoa) 1.5%; Tai 1.5%; Khmer 1.4%; Muong 1.4%; Nung 1.1%; other 4.2%.
Religious affiliation (1980): Buddhist 55.3%; Roman Catholic 7.0%.
Major cities (1992): Ho Chi Minh City 4,075,700; Hanoi 2,095,000.

Vital statistics

Birth rate per 1,000 population (1991): 29.5 (world avg. 26.4).
Death rate per 1,000 population (1991): 8.1 (world avg. 9.2).
Natural increase rate per 1,000 population (1991): 21.4 (world avg. 17.2).
Total fertility rate (avg. births per childbearing woman; 1991): 3.7.
Life expectancy at birth (1991): male 63.0 years; female 67.0 years.
Morbidity (cases of reportable infectious disease per 100,000 population; 1983): influenza 837.0; diarrhea 686.4; malaria 349.8; dengue fever 249.7.

National economy

Budget (1990). Revenue: D 6,490,000,000,000 (transfers from state enterprises 49.9%, foreign sources 18.0%, taxes 15.0%). Expenditures: D 8,090,000,000,000 (current expenditures 65.7%, capital expenditures 23.0%).
Public debt (external, outstanding; 1989): U.S.$15,072,000,000.
Gross national product (1990): U.S.$15,200,000,000 (U.S.$230 per capita).

Structure of gross domestic product and labour force

	1991 in value D '000,000,000	% of total value	labour force	% of labour force
Agriculture	23,563.3	51.7	22,608,600	72.7
Mining, manufacturing	10,370.7	22.8	3,400,000	10.9
Construction	2,014.9	4.4	821,200	2.6
Transp. and commun.	878.4	1.9	537,000	1.7
Trade	8,148.3	18.0	1,724,100	5.5
Finance	...	...	106,500	0.3
Pub. admin.	...	... }	1,194,000	3.8
Services	...	...		
Other	575.3	1.2	699,600	2.3
TOTAL	45,550.9	100.0	31,091,000	100.0[1]

Tourism: receipts from visitors (1989) U.S.$59,000,000.
Production (metric tons except as noted). Agriculture, forestry, fishing (1991): rice 19,428,000, sugarcane 5,940,000, cassava 3,000,000, sweet potatoes 2,105,000, bananas 1,250,000, coconuts 1,000,000, corn (maize) 652,000; livestock (number of live animals) 12,583,000 pigs, 3,282,000 cattle, 2,929,000 buffalo, 111,000,000 poultry; roundwood (1990) 29,209,000 cu m; fish catch (1990) 850,000. Mining and quarrying (1989): phosphate rock 500,000; salt 300,000; gypsum 25,000; bauxite 6,000; zinc 5,000. Manufacturing (1991): cement 3,177,000; chemical fertilizers 434,000; sugar 344,000; steel 130,000; paper 103,000; textiles 277,000,000 sq m; bricks 3,566,500,000 units[5]; bicycles 108,000 units[5]. Construction: n.a. Energy production (consumption): electricity (kW-hr; 1990) 8,722,000,000 (8,722,000,000); coal (metric tons; 1990) 5,000,000 (4,380,000); crude petroleum (barrels; 1990) 19,816,000 (294,000); petroleum products (metric tons; 1990) 38,000 (2,971,000).
Population economically active (1989): total 30,521,019; activity rate 47.4% (participation rates: ages 15–64, 79.9%; female 51.7%; unemployed 5.8%).
Household income and expenditure. Average household size (1989) 4.8; income per household (1990)[6] D 577,008 (U.S.$93); expenditure (1990): food 62.4%, clothing 5.0%, household goods 4.6%, education 2.9%, housing 2.5%.
Land use (1990): forest 30.3%; pasture 1.0%; agricultural 20.3%; other 48.4%.

Foreign trade

Balance of trade (current prices)

	1985	1986	1987	1988	1989	1990
U.S.$'000,000	−844	−1,370	−1,330	−1,472	−827	−765
% of total	36.1%	46.6%	43.6%	46.7%	18.7%	15.4%

Imports (1990): U.S.$2,865,000,000 (1985; fuel and raw materials 44.7%, machinery 23.2%, wheat flour and food products 17.2%). *Major import sources* (1985): U.S.S.R. 69.2%; Japan 8.2%; Singapore 7.0%; Hong Kong 3.0%.
Exports (1990): U.S.$2,100,000,000 (1985; raw materials 46.0%, handicrafts 24.1%, agricultural products 9.5%). *Major export destinations* (1985): U.S.S.R. 51.1%; Hong Kong 13.8%; Japan 9.1%; Singapore 8.6%.

Transport and communications

Transport. Railroads (1991): length 3,220 km; passenger-km 1,913,000,000[5]; metric ton-km cargo 847,000,000[5]. Roads (1991): total length 88,000 km (paved 11%[7]). Vehicles (1976): passenger cars 100,000; trucks and buses 200,000. Merchant marine (1991): vessels (100 gross tons and over) 230; total deadweight tonnage 871,708. Air transport (1988): passenger-km 10,240,000,000; metric ton-km cargo 6,000,000[8]; airports (1992) 4.
Communications. Daily newspapers (1990): 4; total circulation 525,000[9]; circulation per 1,000 population 7.9[9]. Radio (1991): 7,000,000 receivers (1 per 9.7 persons). Television (1991): 2,200,000 receivers (1 per 31 persons). Telephones (1988): 116,000 (1 per 544 persons).

Education and health

Education (1990–91)

	schools	teachers	students	student/ teacher ratio
Primary and secondary (age 7–18)	16,516	434,800	11,882,500	27.3
Vocational	268	10,400	135,400	13.0
Higher	106	21,900	129,600	5.9

Educational attainment (1989). Percentage of population 25 and over having: no formal education (illiterate) 16.6%; some primary 46.6%; complete primary 23.5%; secondary 6.5%; postsecondary and higher 6.8%. *Literacy* (1989): persons 15 and over literate 87.6%; males 93.0%; females 82.8%.
Health (1990): physicians 23,300 (1 per 2,843 persons); hospital beds 165,516 (1 per 400 persons); infant mortality rate per 1,000 live births (1991) 48.
Food (1984–86): daily per capita caloric intake 2,259 (vegetable products 94%, animal products 6%); 104% of FAO recommended minimum requirement.

Military

Total active duty personnel (1992): 857,000 (army 81.7%, navy 4.9%, air force 13.4%). *Military expenditure as percentage of GNP* (1986): 19.4% (world 5.5%); per capita expenditure U.S.$44.

[1]Detail does not add to total given because of rounding. [2]Can Tho includes Soc Trang. [3]Binh Thuan includes Ninh Thuan. [4]Total includes 1,044,800 persons in special enumeration groups not distributed in province and region estimates. [5]1990. [6]Wage workers and government officials only. [7]1988. [8]1985. [9]For three newspapers only.

Western Samoa

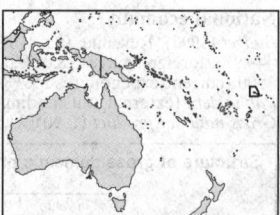

Official name: Malo Sa'oloto Tuto'atasi o Samoa i Sisifo (Samoan); Independent State of Western Samoa (English).
Form of government: constitutional monarchy[1] with one legislative house (Legislative Assembly [48][2]).
Chief of state: Head of State.
Head of government: Prime Minister.
Capital: Apia.
Official languages: Samoan; English.
Official religion: none.
Monetary unit: 1 tala (WS$, plural tala) = 100 sene; valuation (Oct. 5, 1992) 1 U.S.$ = WS$2.44; 1 £ = WS$4.15.

Area and population

Islands	area		population
Political Districts	sq mi	sq km	1986 census
Savaii	659	1,707	44,930
Fa'aseleleaga			...
Gaga'emauga			...
Gaga'ifomauga			...
Palauli			...
Satupa'itea			...
Vaisigano			...
Upolu	432	1,119	112,228
A'ana			...
Aiga-i-le-Tai			...
Atua			...
Tuamasaga			...
Vaa-o-Fonoti			...
TOTAL	1,093[3]	2,831[3]	157,158[4]

Demography

Population (1992): 160,000.
Density (1992): persons per sq mi 146.4, persons per sq km 56.5.
Urban-rural (1986): urban 20.5%; rural 79.5%.
Sex distribution (1986): male 52.96%; female 47.04%.
Age breakdown (1986): under 15, 41.2%; 15–29, 30.8%; 30–44, 13.3%; 45–59, 9.1%; 60–74, 4.4%; 75 and over, 1.2%.
Population projection: (2000) 165,000; (2010) 171,000.
Doubling time: 25 years.
Ethnic composition (1982): Samoan (Polynesian) c. 88%; Euronesian c. 10%; European c. 2%.
Religious affiliation (1986): Congregational 47.2%; Roman Catholic 22.3%; Methodist 15.1%; Mormon 8.6%; other 6.8%.
Major city (1981): Apia 33,170.

Vital statistics

Birth rate per 1,000 population (1991): 34.0 (world avg. 26.4); (1978) legitimate 43.5%; illegitimate 56.5%.
Death rate per 1,000 population (1991): 6.0 (world avg. 9.2).
Natural increase rate per 1,000 population (1991): 28.0 (world avg. 17.2).
Total fertility rate (avg. births per childbearing woman; 1991): 4.5.
Marriage rate per 1,000 population (1989)[5]: 5.3.
Divorce rate per 1,000 population (1989)[5]: 0.2.
Life expectancy at birth (1991): male 64.0 years; female 69.0 years.
Major causes of death per 100,000 population (1985)[5]: diseases of the circulatory system 42.0; malignant neoplasms (cancers) 18.2; diseases of the respiratory system 13.2; infectious and parasitic diseases 8.8; diabetes mellitus 5.6.

National economy

Budget (1990). Revenue: WS$121,100,000 (tax revenue 74.6%, of which taxes on international trade 43.2%, income tax 17.4%, taxes on goods and services 13.5%; nontax revenue 25.5%, of which rents, royalties, and interest 6.9%). Expenditures: WS$158,700,000 (development expenditure 59.2%; current expenditure 40.8%).
Public debt (external, outstanding; 1990): U.S.$80,000,000.
Production (metric tons except as noted). Agriculture, forestry, fishing (1990): coconuts 190,000, taro 41,000, copra 26,000, bananas 24,000, papayas 12,000, mangoes 7,000, pineapples 6,000, avocados 2,000, cacao 2,000, milk 1,000; livestock (number of live animals) 55,000 pigs, 30,000 cattle, 1,000,000 chickens; roundwood 131,000 cu m; fish catch (1989) 3,500. Mining and quarrying: n.a. Manufacturing (1985): coconut oil 11,766, copra meal 6,098, sawn wood 21,000 cu m[6]; other products include coconut cream, beverages, tobacco products, aluminum products, concrete blocks, handicrafts, and kava. Construction (permits issued in WS$; 1989): residential 4,600,000; commercial, industrial, and other 8,000,000. Energy production (consumption): electricity (kW-hr; 1990) 50,000,000 (50,000,000); coal, none (n.a.); crude petroleum, none (n.a.); petroleum products (metric tons; 1990) none (41,000).
Household income and expenditure. Average household size (1981) 5.1; income per household (1972) WS$1,518 (U.S.$2,200); sources of income (1972): wages 49.4%, self-employment 22.8%, remittances, gifts, and other assistance 18.0%, land rent 8.7%, other 1.1%; expenditure (1987)[7]: food 58.8%, transportation 9.0%, housing and furnishings 5.1%, fuel and light 5.0%, clothing 4.2%, other goods and services 1.9%, other 16.0%.
Gross national product (at current market prices; 1990): U.S.$121,000,000 (U.S.$730 per capita).

Structure of gross domestic product and labour force

	1989		1986	
	in value WS$'000	% of total value	labour force	% of labour force
Agriculture	117,100	47.1	29,023	63.6
Mining	...	...	1,587	3.5
Manufacturing	31,600	12.7		
Construction	4,600	1.9	62	0.1
Public utilities	11,000	4.4	855	1.9
Transp. and commun.	5,200	2.1	1,491	3.3
Trade	25,600	10.3	1,710	3.7
Finance	...	...	842	1.8
Pub. admin., defense, government services	31,000	12.5	9,436	20.7
Other services	22,300	9.0	629	1.4
Other				
TOTAL	248,400	100.0	45,635	100.0

Population economically active (1986): total 45,635; activity rate of total population 28.5% (participation rates: ages 15–64 [1981] 48.6%; female 18.8%).

Price and earnings indexes (1985 = 100)

	1985	1986	1987	1988	1989	1990	1991
Consumer price index	100.0	107.2	110.6	120.0	127.7	147.2	145.2
Monthly earnings index	...	...	...	...	...	...	...

Tourism: receipts from visitors (1990) U.S.$20,000,000; expenditures by nationals abroad (1989) U.S.$2,000,000.
Land use (1989): forested 47.3%; meadows and pastures 0.4%; agricultural and under permanent cultivation 43.1%; other 9.2%.

Foreign trade[8]

Balance of trade (current prices)

	1986	1987	1988	1989	1990	1991
WS$'000	−72,388	−94,240	−111,729	−109,249	−137,300	−196,994
% of total	60.6%	65.4%	64.0%	65.4%	77.0%	83.9%

Imports (1990): WS$193,418,000 (1983; food 21.3%, machinery 21.0%, petroleum products 18.4%, miscellaneous manufactured articles 7.4%, chemicals 5.9%, animal oils and fats 0.5%). *Major import sources* (1988): Australia 23.3%; New Zealand 20.7%; Singapore 11.1%; Japan 8.9%; United States 4.5%; West Germany 1.8%.
Exports (1990): WS$20,494,000 (coconut oil 37.2%[9], taro 17.1%, coconut cream 12.3%[9], copra 5.4%, cocoa 2.4%, timber 0.1%). *Major export destinations:* New Zealand 33.5%; American Samoa 21.3%; West Germany 18.2%; Australia 11.3%; United States 5.8%.

Transport and communications

Transport. Railroads: none. Roads (1987): total length[10] 1,296 mi, 2,085 km (paved 19%). Vehicles (1989): passenger cars 2,514; trucks and buses 3,048. Merchant marine (1991): vessels (100 gross tons and over) 7; total deadweight tonnage 6,501. Air transport: passengers, n.a.; cargo, n.a.; airports (1992) with scheduled flights 2.
Communications. Daily newspapers: none. Radio (1991): 75,000 receivers (1 per 2.1 persons). Television (1987): 6,000 receivers (1 per 26 persons). Telephones (1988): 5,455 (1 per 29 persons).

Education and health

Education (1986–87)

	schools	teachers	students	student/ teacher ratio
Primary (age 5–11)	164[11]	1,511[12]	40,755	27.0
Secondary (age 12–18)	38[13]	492	11,395	23.2
Voc., teacher tr.	4[11]	37	228	6.2
Higher[11]	6	25	271	10.8

Educational attainment (1981). Percentage of population age 25 and over having: some primary education 16.5%; complete primary 24.5%; some secondary 52.1%; complete secondary 3.1%; higher 2.0%; unknown 1.8%.
Literacy (1981): virtually 100%.
Health: physicians (1990) 44 (1 per 3,584 persons); hospital beds (1989) 644 (1 per 255 persons); infant mortality rate per 1,000 live births (1991) 47.0.
Food (1987–89): daily per capita caloric intake 2,509 (vegetable products 81%, animal products 19%); 110% of FAO recommended minimum requirement.

Military

No military forces are maintained; New Zealand is responsible for defense.

[1]According to the constitution, the current Head of State, paramount chief HH Malietoa Tanumafili II, will hold office for life. Upon his death, the monarchy will functionally cease, and future Heads of State will be elected by the Legislative Assembly. [2]Includes the Head of State as an ex officio member. [3]Total includes 2 sq mi (5 sq km) of uninhabited islands. [4]The provisional total for the 1991 census is 159,862. [5]Registered only. [6]1990. [7]Consumer price index components. [8]Import figures are f.o.b. in balance of trade and c.i.f. in commodities and trading partners. [9]1988. [10]Total length includes 733 mi (1,180 km) of plantation roads. [11]1983. [12]Includes some secondary teachers. [13]1982.

Yemen

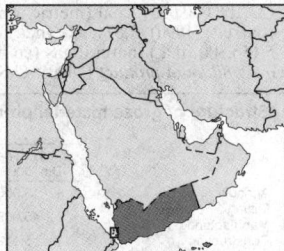

Official name: al-Jumhūrīyah al-Yamanīyah (Republic of Yemen).
Form of government: transitional administration[1] with one legislative house (House of Representatives [301]).
Head of state: President assisted by Presidential Council.
Head of government: Prime Minister assisted by Council of Ministers.
Capital: Ṣan'ā'.
Official language: Arabic.
Official religion: Islam.
Monetary unit: 1 Yemen rial (YRls) = 100 fils; 1 Yemeni dinar (YD) = 1,000 fils; valuation (Oct. 5, 1992) 1 U.S.$ = YRls 16.50 = YD 0.46; 1 £ = YRls 28.00 = YD 0.79.

The Republic of Yemen was formed on May 22, 1990, by the union of the former Yemen Arab Republic (North Yemen) and People's Democratic Republic of Yemen (South Yemen).

Area and population

Governorates	Capitals	area sq mi	area sq km	population 1986 estimate[2]
North Yemen				
al-Baydā'	al-Baydā'	4,310	11,170	381,000
Dhamār	Dhamār	3,430	8,870	813,000
Ḥajjah	Ḥajjah	3,700	9,590	898,000
al-Ḥudaydah	al-Ḥudaydah	5,240	13,580	1,294,000
Ibb	Ibb	2,480	6,430	1,512,000
al-Jawf	al-Jawf	...	...	87,000
al-Maḥwīt	al-Maḥwīt	830	2,160	322,000
Ma'rib	Ma'rib	15,400	39,890	121,000
Ṣa'dah	Ṣa'dah	4,950	12,810	344,000
Ṣan'ā'	Ṣan'ā'	7,840	20,310	1,857,000
Ta'izz	Ta'izz	4,020	10,420	1,644,000
South Yemen				
Abyān	Zinjibār	8,297	21,489	434,000
'Adan	Aden	2,695	6,980	407,000
Ḥaḍramawt	al-Mukallā	59,991	155,376	686,000
Laḥij	Laḥij	4,928	12,766	382,000
al-Mahrah	al-Ghaydah	25,618	66,350	85,000
Shabwah	'Atāq	28,536	73,908	226,000
TOTAL		182,278[3, 4]	472,099[3]	11,494,000[4]

Demography

Population (1992): 12,147,000.
Density (1992)[5]: persons per sq mi 59.2, persons per sq km 22.8.
Urban-rural (1990): urban 28.9%; rural 71.1%.
Sex distribution (1990): male 48.96%; female 51.04%.
Age breakdown (1990): under 15, 49.6%; 15–29, 27.8%; 30–44, 11.4%; 45–59, 7.2%; 60–74, 3.4%; 75 and over, 0.6%.
Population projection: (2000) 14,878,000; (2010) 19,173,000.
Doubling time: 20 years.
Ethnic composition (1986): predominantly Arab.
Religious affiliation (1980): Muslim 99.9%, of which Sunnī 53.0%, Shī'ī 46.9%; other 0.1%.
Major cities (1986): Ṣan'ā' 427,150; Aden 318,000[6]; Ta'izz 178,043; al-Ḥudaydah 155,110; al-Mukallā 59,100[6].

Vital statistics

Birth rate per 1,000 population (1991): 51.3 (world avg. 26.4).
Death rate per 1,000 population (1991): 16.2 (world avg. 9.2).
Natural increase rate per 1,000 population (1991): 35.1 (world avg. 17.2).
Total fertility rate (avg. births per childbearing woman; 1991): 7.4.
Marriage rate per 1,000 population: n.a.
Life expectancy at birth (1991): male 49.0 years; female 51.0 years.
Major causes of death per 100,000 population: n.a.; however, major diseases include malaria, tuberculosis, leprosy, and intestinal infections.

National economy

Budget (1991–92 est.). Revenue: YRls 45,778,000,000 (1990[7]; tax revenue 59.8%, property income 30.4%). Expenditures: YRls 58,114,000,000 (defense 21.9%, education 14.3%, general public services 6.3%, health 3.5%).
Tourism: receipts from visitors (1990) U.S.$20,000,000; expenditures by nationals abroad (1989) U.S.$81,000,000.
Production (metric tons except as noted). Agriculture, forestry, fishing (1991): watermelons 170,000, tomatoes 170,000, potatoes 168,000, grapes 145,000, sorghum 132,000, wheat 77,000, onions 72,000, bananas 52,000, papayas 50,000, millet 20,000; livestock (number of live animals) 3,800,000 sheep, 3,400,000 goats, 1,180,000 cattle, 690,000 asses, 180,000 camels, 24,000,000 chickens; roundwood (1990) 324,000 cu m; fish catch (1990) 89,149. Mining and quarrying (1989): salt 230,000; gypsum 63,000. Manufacturing (1988)[8]: flour 23,700; wheat bran 10,500; canned tomatoes 1,265; cotton lint 800; foam rubber 715; soft drinks 49,000,000 bottles; beer 5,200,000 litres; textiles 2,600,000 metres; cigarettes 1,166,000,000 units. Construction: n.a. Energy production (consumption): electricity (kW-hr; 1990) 1,740,000 (1,740,000); coal, none (n.a.); crude petroleum (barrels; 1990) 68,148,000 (31,691,000); petroleum products (metric tons; 1990) 4,026,000 (2,722,000).

Gross national product (at current market prices; 1989): U.S.$7,203,000,000 (U.S.$640 per capita).
Population economically active (1986): total 2,043,237; activity rate of total population 19.6% (participation rates: 15–64, 41.2%; female 12.1%).

Structure of gross domestic product and labour force

	1988 in value YD '000,000	1988 % of total value	1986 labour force	1986 % of labour force
Agriculture	52.5	14.8	1,151,348	56.3
Mining	}		11,771	0.6
Manufacturing	29.8	8.4	94,913	4.6
Public utilities	}		160,952	7.9
Construction	39.0	11.0	32,852	1.6
Transp. and commun.	35.0	9.8	107,611	5.3
Trade	46.8	13.2	248,979	12.2
Finance	10.3	2.9	8,757	0.4
Pub. admin., defense	} 106.7	30.0	226,054	11.1
Services	}			
Other	35.2	9.9	...	...
TOTAL	355.3	100.0	2,043,237	100.0

Public debt (external, outstanding; 1989): U.S.$4,919,000,000.
Household income and expenditure. Average household size (1986) 5.6; income per household: n.a.; sources of income: n.a.; expenditure: n.a.

Price index (1985 = 100)[10]

	1985	1986	1987	1988	1989	1990
Consumer price index	100.0	121.1	140.3	155.2	178.8	240.0

Land use (1990): forested 7.7%; meadows and pastures 30.4%; agricultural and under permanent cultivation 3.0%; other 58.9%.

Foreign trade

Balance of trade (current prices)[7]

	1982	1983	1984	1985	1986	1987
YRls '000,000	−8,235	−9,439	−8,449	−7,782	−8,466	−13,460
% of total	78.4%	83.1%	79.0%	77.2%	78.4%	90.4%

Imports (1987)[7]: U.S.$1,370,700,000 (food and live animals 31.6%, basic manufactured goods 28.6%, machinery and transport equipment 21.9%, chemical products 9.3%, raw materials 5.8%, beverages and tobacco 2.4%). *Major import sources:* Japan 12.0%; United States 10.8%; The Netherlands 10.0%; West Germany 7.1%; France 6.3%; Italy 5.3%; Saudi Arabia 5.3%.
Exports (1987)[7]: U.S.$69,000,000 (coffee 16.6%, cigarettes 15.6%, biscuits 13.6%, leather 12.5%, grapes 8.6%, sesame seeds 4.2%). *Major export destinations:* Saudi Arabia 53.6%; South Yemen 24.0%; Italy 8.2%; Japan 4.0%.

Transport and communications

Transport. Railroads: none. Roads (1986): total length 39,152 km (paved [1991] 9%[7]). Vehicles (1990): passenger cars 145,390; trucks and buses 219,105. Merchant marine (1991): vessels (100 gross tons and over) 39; deadweight tonnage 13,653. Air transport (1990): passenger-km 1,032,248,000; metric ton-km cargo 11,661,000; airports (1992) with scheduled flights 12.
Communications. Daily newspapers (1988)[7]: total number 2; total circulation 120,000; circulation per 1,000 population 16. Radio (1991): 325,000 receivers (1 per 36 persons). Television (1991): 300,000 receivers (1 per 39 persons). Telephones (1988): 70,000 (1 per 157 persons).

Education and health

Education (1990–91)[7]

	schools	teachers	students	student/teacher ratio
Primary (age 7–12)	7,313[11]	35,350	1,291,372	36.5
Secondary (age 13–18)	942[12]	12,106	394,578	32.6
Voc., teacher tr.	73[12]	1,247	26,119	20.9
Higher[11]	1	470	23,457	49.9

Educational attainment (1975)[7]. Percentage of population age 10 and over having: no formal schooling 82.6%; reading ability only 5.3%; reading and writing ability 10.6%; primary education 0.8%; secondary education 0.2%; higher 0.1%; not specified 0.4%. *Literacy* (1990): percentage of total population age 15 and over literate 38.5%; males literate 53.3%; females literate 26.3%.
Health (1986): physicians 1,886 (1 per 5,531 persons); hospital beds 10,485 (1 per 995 persons); infant mortality rate per 1,000 live births (1991) 121.0.
Food (1986–88): daily per capita caloric intake 2,284 (vegetable products 90%, animal products 10%); 94% of FAO recommended minimum requirement.

Military

Total active duty personnel (1992): 63,500 (army 94.5%, navy 2.4%, air force 3.1%). *Military expenditure as percentage of GNP* (1988): 12.4% (world 5.0%); per capita expenditure U.S.$71.

---

[1]The termination of the transitional regime was slated for April 1993. [2]Based on North Yemen's 1986 census results and South Yemen's 1986 estimates. [3]North Yemen claimed a major part of the undemarcated eastern boundary with Saudi Arabia, which increased the total area to 205,356 sq mi (531,869 sq km). [4]Detail does not add to total given because of rounding. [5]Based on the higher total area estimate of 205,356 sq mi (531,869 sq km). [6]1984. [7]Yemen Arab Republic only. [8]Democratic Republic of Yemen only. [9]Includes import duties and indirect taxes. [10]Urban areas only. [11]1988–89. [12]1985–86.

Yugoslavia

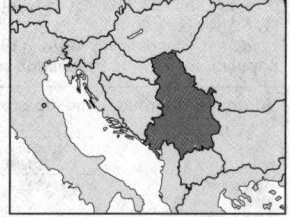

Official name: Federativna Republika Jugoslavija (Federal Republic of Yugoslavia).
Form of government: federal multiparty republic with two legislative houses (Chamber of Republics [40]; Chamber of Citizens [138]).
Chief of state: President.
Head of government: Prime Minister.
Capital: Belgrade.
Official language: Serbo-Croatian.
Official religion: none.
Monetary unit: 1 New Yugoslav dinar (Din) = 100 paras; valuation (Oct. 5, 1992) 1 U.S.\$ = Din 225.41; 1 £ = Din 383.20.

Area and population		area		population
				1991
Republics	**Capitals**	sq mi	sq km	census
Montenegro	Podgorica	5,333	13,812	616,327
Serbia	Belgrade	21,609	55,968	5,753,825
Autonomous provinces[1]				
Kosovo	Priština	4,203	10,887	1,954,747
Vojvodina	Novi Sad	8,304	21,506	2,012,605
TOTAL		39,449	102,173	10,337,504

Demography

Population (1992): 10,394,000.
Density (1992): persons per sq mi 263.5, persons per sq km 101.7.
Urban-rural (1981): urban 48.0%; rural 52.0%.
Sex distribution (1981): male 49.70%; female 50.30%.
Age breakdown (1981): under 15, 24.2%; 15–29, 23.8%; 30–44, 19.9%; 45–59, 19.4%; 60–74, 9.1%; 75 and over, 3.2%.
Population projection: (2000) 10,761,000; (2010) 11,239,000.
Doubling time: not applicable; doubling time exceeds 100 years.
Ethnic composition (1981): Serb 62.6%; Albanian 13.5%; Montenegrin 5.5%; Magyar 3.9%; Bosnian 3.0%; Croat 1.6%; Gypsy 1.1%; other 8.8%.
Religious affiliation (1991): most believers are affiliated with the Serbian Orthodox Church; there are also Muslim, Roman Catholic, and Protestant minorities.
Major cities (1991)[2]: Belgrade 1,553,854; Novi Sad 264,533; Niš 247,898; Kragujevac 178,881; Leskovac 160,948.

Vital statistics

Birth rate per 1,000 population (1990): 14.6 (world avg. 27.1).
Death rate per 1,000 population (1990): 9.3 (world avg. 9.8).
Natural increase rate per 1,000 population (1990): 5.3 (world avg. 17.3).
Total fertility rate (avg. births per childbearing woman): n.a.
Marriage rate per 1,000 population (1989): 6.8.
Divorce rate per 1,000 population (1989): 1.2.
Life expectancy at birth (1980–82): male 68.2 years; female 73.2 years.
Major causes of death per 100,000 population (1989): diseases of the circulatory system 524.3; malignant neoplasms (cancers) 148.3; accidents, violence, and poisoning 49.3; diseases of the respiratory system 47.7; diseases of the digestive system 26.3.

National economy

Budget (1991–92). Revenue: Din 132,000,000,000 (financed largely by the National Bank and foreign reserves). Expenditures: Din 132,000,000,000 (subsidies to enterprises 50%, defense 42%, administration 8%).
Tourism (1991): total tourist nights 14,540,000.
Production (metric tons except as noted). Agriculture, forestry, fishing (1991): corn (maize) 7,482,000, wheat 4,109,000, potatoes 849,000, grapes 550,000, plums 373,000; livestock (number of live animals) 4,354,000 pigs, 3,044,000 sheep, 2,092,000 cattle, 30,213,000 poultry; roundwood (1990) 4,351,000 cu m; fish catch (1990) 8,110, of which freshwater 7,649. Mining and quarrying (1990): copper ore 26,463,000; lead-zinc ore 1,573,000; quartz sand 1,467,000; bauxite 941,000; lime 671,000; marl 398,000; refined silver 86,000; salt 44,000; asbestos ore 26,000; antimony ore 20,000; feldspar 13,000; chromium 12,000. Manufacturing (1990): wheat flour 1,146,000; hot-rolled iron strips 1,051,000; crude steel 1,012,000; sulfuric acid 886,000; copper concentrate 542,000; alumina 269,000; copper anodes 174,000; steel bars 149,000; unwrought lead 70,000; welded pipes 55,000; polyvinyl chloride powder 51,000; linoleum flooring 48,036; refined lead 48,000; frozen fruit 39,075; drawn wire 37,000; cotton yarn 32,500; frozen vegetables 31,227; roofing shingles 27,000; nails and screws 21,000; cured meats 18,776; cosmetics 16,712; medicines 15,199; ferroalloys 12,000; blown glassware 9,900; knitted clothing 8,326; roller bearings 6,689; household ceramics 4,553; asbestos fibre 1,353; soaps and detergents 1,285; pharmaceutical products 801; parquet flooring 1,301,000 cu m; silk 21,000,000 sq m; carpeting 15,836,000 sq m; flat glass 9,465,000 sq m; liquor 38,769,000 hectolitres; hosiery 89,000,000 pairs; leather footwear 26,191,000 pairs; light bulbs 50,000,000 units; furniture 2,799,000 units; refrigerators 215,000 units; bicycles 191,000 units; kitchen ranges 190,000 units; gasoline engines 182,000 units; automobiles 179,000 units; television receivers 144,000 units; telephones 73,000 units; diesel engines 32,000 units; tractors 31,224 units; radios 24,000 units; automobile tires 12,089 units; trucks 8,400 units; buses 651 units; railway-goods cars 356 units; locomotives 4 units. Construction (residential units constructed; 1990): 41,547. Energy production (consumption): electricity (kW-hr; 1990) 40,948,000,000

(33,108,000,000); coal (metric tons; 1990) 45,531,000 (n.a.); crude petroleum (barrels; 1990) 7,874,000 (n.a.); petroleum products (metric tons; 1990) 5,156,300 (n.a.); natural gas (cu m; 1990) 646,000,000 (n.a.).
Gross national product (1990): U.S.\$31,867,000,000 (U.S.\$3,093 per capita).

Structure of gross material product and labour force				
	1989		1990	
	in value Din '000,000	% of total value	labour force[3]	% of labour force[3]
Agriculture	13,966	16.5	134,689	5.1
Mining	} 45,065	53.3	1,127,761	42.7
Manufacturing				
Construction	5,112	6.0	205,766	7.8
Public utilities	965	1.1	55,026	2.1
Transp. and commun.	5,304	6.3	175,261	6.6
Trade	12,108	14.3	347,451	13.2
Finance			94,662	3.6
Pub. admin., defense	} 2,076	2.5	} 500,300	18.9
Services				
Other				
TOTAL	84,596	100.0	2,640,916	100.0

Population economically active (1991): total 2,525,000; activity rate of total population 24.4% (participation rates: ages 15–64, n.a.; female [1990] 39.1%; unemployed, n.a.).

Price and earnings indexes (1985 = 100)							
	1984	1985	1986	1987	1988	1989	1990[4]
Consumer price index	58	100	218	410	1,210	16,450	113,000
Monthly earnings index[5]	98	100	108	99	93	122	94

Land use (1990): forested 29.5%; meadows and pastures 20.7%; agricultural and under permanent cultivation 35.7%; other 14.1%.
Household income and expenditure. Average household size (1991) 3.2; income per household (1990) Din 88,569 (U.S.\$7,826); sources of income (1990): wages and salaries 51.5%, transfer payments 17.9%, self-employment 14.8%, other 15.8%; expenditure (1988): food 38.3%, fuel and light 8.1%, clothing and footwear 8.0%, transportation and communications 7.2%, housing 6.7%, beverages and tobacco 4.9%, household durable goods 4.4%, education and entertainment 4.1%, health care 3.4%.

Foreign trade

Balance of trade (current prices)					
	1985	1986	1987	1988	1989	1990
Din '000,000	−12	−10	−8	−27	−1,375	−21,587
% of total	5.4%	3.1%	1.3%	1.2%	4.5%	17.4%

Imports (1991): Din 104,591,000,000 (machinery and transport equipment 22.7%, of which road vehicles 6.8%; mineral fuels and lubricants 19.0%; chemicals 13.7%; manufactured goods 10.4%, of which textiles 3.2%; food and live animals 8.4%, of which beverages 0.8%). *Major import sources:* Germany 20.2%; former U.S.S.R. 12.6%; Italy 10.6%; U.S. 4.1%; Austria 3.9%.
Exports (1991): Din 89,707,000,000 (manufactured goods 49.9%, of which clothing 14.2%, iron and steel 5.4%, textile products 4.3%; machinery and transport equipment 19.6%; food and live animals 11.8%, of which fruits and vegetables 3.7%; chemicals 9.1%). *Major export destinations:* Germany 23.1%; former U.S.S.R. 17.8%; Italy 14.0%; U.S. 4.4%; Romania 4.3%.

Transport and communications

Transport. Railroads (1990): length, n.a.; passengers transported 50,954,000; cargo transported 49,599,000 tons. Roads (1991): total length 28,595 mi, 46,019 km (paved 59%). Vehicles (1990): passenger cars 1,407,490; trucks and buses 132,482. Merchant marine (1990): fishing vessels 227. Air transport: n.a.; airports (1992) with scheduled flights 7.
Communications. Daily newspapers (1990): total number 12; total circulation 1,006,000; circulation per 1,000 population 98. Radio (1989): 2,240,000 receivers (1 per 4.6 persons). Television (1989): 1,961,000 receivers (1 per 5.2 persons). Telephones (1990): 1,838,947 (1 per 5.6 persons).

Education and health

Education (1990–91)				
	schools	teachers	students	student/ teacher ratio
Primary (age 7–14)	5,075	65,099	1,238,480	19.0
Secondary (age 15–18)	565	28,609	407,405	14.2
Higher	147	12,633	157,232	12.4

Educational attainment (1981). Percentage of population age 15 and over having: less than full primary education 44.6%; primary 24.4%; secondary 24.7%; postsecondary and higher 5.7%. *Literacy* (1981): total population age 10 and over literate 7,411,500 (89.2%); males literate 4,236,900 (95.4%); females literate 3,174,600 (83.2%).
Health (1990): physicians (1989) 20,920 (1 per 490 persons); hospital beds 62,283 (1 per 165 persons); infant mortality rate per 1,000 live births 24.2.
Food: daily per capita caloric intake, n.a.

Military

Total active duty personnel (1992): 135,000 (army 74.1%, navy 4.4%, air force 21.5%). *Military expenditure as percentage of GNP:* n.a.

---

[1]The autonomous provinces are administratively part of the Republic of Serbia. [2]Populations refer to municipal areas, not cities proper. [3]Excludes 66,000 workers in the private sector. [4]On Jan. 1, 1990, the new dinar, equal to 10,000 old dinars, was introduced. [5]Based on worker real net personal income.

Zaire

Official name: République du Zaïre (Republic of Zaire).
Form of government: Unitary republic[1] with one legislative house (National Assembly [222]).
Chief of state: President.
Head of government: Prime Minister.
Capital: Kinshasa.
Official language: French.
Official religion: none.
Monetary unit: 1 zaïre (Z) = 100 makuta (singular likuta) = 10,000 sengi; valuation (Oct. 5, 1992) 1 U.S.$ = Z 962,941; 1 £ = Z 1,637,000.

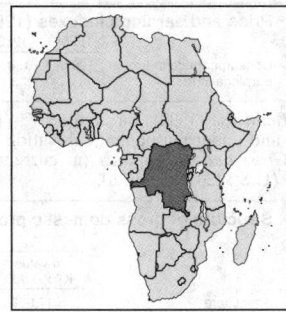

Area and population

Regions	Capitals	area sq mi	area sq km	population 1991 estimate
Bandundu	Bandundu	114,154	295,658	4,617,000
Bas-Zaïre	Matadi	20,880	54,078	2,485,000
Equateur	Mbandaka	155,712	403,292	4,312,000
Haute-Zaïre	Kisangani	194,302	503,239	5,073,000
Kasai-Occidental	Kananga	60,605	156,967	2,982,000
Kasai-Oriental	Mbuji-Mayi	64,949	168,216	3,338,000
Kinshasa	—	3,848	9,965	3,804,000
Maniema	Kindu	50,916[2]	131,871[2]	[3]
Nord-Kivu	Goma	23,188[2]	60,057[2]	6,728,000[3]
Shaba	Lubumbashi	191,845	496,877	5,207,000
Sud-Kivu	Bukavu	25,048[2]	64,875[2]	[3]
TOTAL		905,446[4]	2,345,095	38,543,000[4]

Demography

Population (1992): 41,151,000.
Density (1992): persons per sq mi 45.5, persons per sq km 17.6.
Urban-rural (1985): urban 44.2%; rural 55.8%.
Sex distribution (1984): male 49.18%; female 50.82%.
Age breakdown (1985): under 15, 45.2%; 15–29, 26.0%; 30–44, 15.5%; 45–59, 8.7%; 60–74, 3.9%; 75 and over, 0.7%.
Population projection: (2000) 53,118,000; (2010) 72,538,000.
Doubling time: 22 years.
Ethnic composition (1983): Luba 18.0%; Kongo 16.1%; Mongo 13.5%; Rwanda 10.3%; Azande 6.1%; Bangi and Ngale 5.8%; Rundi 3.8%; Teke 2.7%; Boa 2.3%; Chokwe 1.8%; Lugbara 1.6%; Banda 1.4%; other 16.6%.
Religious affiliation (1980): Roman Catholic 48.4%; Protestant 29.0%; indigenous Christian 17.1%; traditional beliefs 3.4%; Muslim 1.4%; other 0.7%.
Major cities (1991): Kinshasa 3,804,000; Lubumbashi 739,082; Mbuji-Mayi 613,027; Kisangani 373,397; Kananga 371,862.

Vital statistics

Birth rate per 1,000 population (1990–95): 45.3 (world avg. 26.4).
Death rate per 1,000 population (1990–95): 13.0 (world avg. 9.2).
Natural increase rate per 1,000 population (1990–95): 32.3 (world avg. 17.2).
Total fertility rate (avg. births per childbearing woman; 1990–95): 6.1.
Marriage rate per 1,000 population (1977)[5]: 0.07.
Divorce rate per 1,000 population (1977): 0.02.
Life expectancy at birth (1990–95): male 52.3 years; female 55.7 years.
Major causes of death per 100,000 population (1977)[6]: measles 9.6; meningitis 1.1; influenza 0.4; whooping cough 0.3.

National economy

Budget (1991). Revenue: Z 2,257,000,000,000 (revenue from mining 30.4%, external trade taxes 26.8%, income tax 18.6%, petroleum tax 15.8%, other revenue 8.4%). Expenditures: Z 2,357,000,000,000 (service of external and internal debt 28.4%, capital expenditure 20.5%, administration 20.0%).
Tourism (1990): receipts from visitors U.S.$7,000,000; expenditures by nationals abroad U.S.$16,000,000.
Production (metric tons except as noted). Agriculture, forestry, fishing (1991): cassava 18,227,000, plantains 1,820,000, sugarcane 1,180,000, corn (maize) 906,000, bananas 510,000, peanuts (groundnuts) 435,000, sweet potatoes 377,000, rice 365,000, yams 300,000, mangoes 210,000, papayas 208,000, oranges 155,000, pineapples 145,000, dry beans 122,000, coffee 102,000, seed cotton 77,000, palm kernels 75,000, dry peas 62,000, avocados 46,000, carrots 45,000, tomatoes 40,000, onions 31,000, cabbage 28,000, cucumbers 25,000, natural rubber 10,000; livestock (number of live animals) 3,070,000 goats, 1,600,000 cattle, 910,000 sheep, 830,000 pigs, 21,000,000 chickens; roundwood (1990) 38,904,000 cu m; fish catch (1990) 162,000. Mining and quarrying (1991): copper 291,500; zinc 25,200; cobalt 8,800; cassiterite 2,176[7]; wolframite 16[7]; gold 4,500 kg; diamonds 16,800,000 carats. Manufacturing (1988): cement 400,000; palm oil 182,000[8]; sulfuric acid 152,000; corn flour 89,685[9]; sugar 71,000[8]; soap 47,109; animal feedstuff 20,000; explosives 19,500; plastics 7,586[9]; iron and steel products 5,875; paint 2,458; medicine 45[9]; printed fabrics 44,370,000 sq m; cigarettes 5,236,000,000 units; tires 102,000 units; bicycles 5,830 units; automobiles 2,038 units; beer 4,590,000 hectolitres; carbonated beverages 1,923,000 hectolitres; leather shoes 2,954,000 pairs. Construction (1985): residential 20,000 sq m; nonresidential 39,000 sq m. Energy production (consumption): electricity (kW-hr; 1990) 6,155,000,000 (6,048,000,000); coal (metric tons; 1990) 126,000 (169,000); crude petroleum (barrels; 1990) 10,321,000 (2,672,000); petroleum products (metric tons; 1990) 260,000 (883,000); natural gas, none (n.a.).
Household income and expenditure. Average household size (1982) 6.0; average annual income per household Z 1,200 (U.S.$209); sources of income:

n.a.; expenditure (1985): food 61.7%, housing and energy 11.5%, clothing and footwear 9.7%, transportation 5.9%, furniture and utensils 4.9%, medical care 2.6%, recreation and education 2.0%.
Gross national product (1990): U.S.$8,117,000,000 (U.S.$230 per capita).

Structure of gross domestic product and labour force

	1988 in value Z '000,000	1988 % of total value	1987 labour force	1987 % of labour force
Agriculture	162,672.4[10]	26.1[10]	8,413,000	67.4
Mining	131,413.9	21.1		
Manufacturing	9,977.0	1.6		
Construction	12,558.3[11]	2.0[11]	1,847,000	14.8
Public utilities	24,166.2	3.9		
Transp. and commun.	3,378.0	0.5		
Trade	108,300.1	17.4		
Finance				
Pub. admin., defense	139,478.2	22.4	2,222,000	17.8
Services				
Other	30,877.4[12]	5.0[12]		
TOTAL	622,821.5	100.0	12,482,000	100.0

Public debt (external, outstanding; 1990): U.S.$8,851,000,000.
Population economically active (1987): total 12,482,000; activity rate 38.4% (participation rates: over age 10, 57.4%; female 40.8%; unemployed, n.a.).

Price and earnings indexes (1985 = 100)

	1985	1986	1987	1988	1989	1990	1991
Consumer price index	100.0	144.4	258.0	510.5	1,041.7	1,888.4	42,575
Annual earnings index	100.0	...	...	...	...	...	...

Land use (1990): forested 76.9%; meadows and pastures 6.6%; agricultural and under permanent cultivation 3.5%; other 13.0%.

Foreign trade

Balance of trade (current prices)

	1985	1986	1987	1988	1989	1990
Z '000,000	+13,339.7	+13,228	+36,258	+86,582	+198,966	+168,029
% of total	16.4%	11.3%	19.8%	26.0%	26.3%	13.3%

Imports (1990): Z 1,106,500,000,000 (1987; machinery and transport equipment 45.5%, of which mining equipment 32.0%, transport equipment 7.8%; food, beverages, and tobacco 14.6%; energy 13.8%; consumer goods 7.4%; minerals 5.4%; chemical products 4.4%; textiles and clothing 3.7%). *Major import sources:* Belgium-Luxembourg 25.4%; France 11.3%; China 10.6%; Germany 10.0%; U.S. 9.8%; Japan 2.7%.
Exports (1990): Z 1,537,200,000,000 (copper 47.6%; diamonds 11.4%; crude petroleum 10.8%; coffee 5.7%). *Major export destinations:* Belgium-Luxembourg 54.4%; U.S. 12.5%; France 6.9%; Germany 6.2%; Italy 4.1%; Japan 1.7%.

Transport and communications

Transport. Railroads (1989)[13]: length 3,193 mi, 5,138 km; passenger-mi 162,000,000, passenger-km 260,000,000; short ton-mi cargo 1,186,000,000, metric ton-km cargo 1,732,000,000. Roads (1989): total length 91,000 mi, 146,500 km (paved 12%). Vehicles (1985): passenger cars 24,253; trucks and buses 60,528. Merchant marine (1991): vessels (100 gross tons and over) 30; total deadweight tonnage 75,932. Air transport (1991)[14]: passenger-mi 89,627,000, passenger-km 144,242,000; short ton-mi cargo 14,415,000, metric ton-km cargo 21,046,000; airports (1992) with scheduled flights 24.
Communications. Daily newspapers (1988): total number 7; total circulation 45,000; circulation per 1,000 population 1.4. Radio (1991): 3,400,000 receivers (1 per 10 persons). Television (1991): 20,000 receivers (1 per 1,748 persons). Telephones (1988): 32,116 (1 per 1,026 persons).

Education and health

Education (1987–88)

	schools	teachers	students	student/ teacher ratio
Primary (age 6–11)	10,817	113,468[15]	4,356,516	36.6[15]
Secondary (age 12–17)	4,276[16]	49,153[16]	507,944	21.7[16]
Voc., teacher tr.	[16]	[16]	558,407	[16]
Higher	...	3,506	52,800	15.1

Educational attainment: n.a. *Literacy* (1990): percentage of total population age 15 and over literate 71.8%; males literate 83.6%; females literate 60.7%.
Health (1985): physicians 1,318 (1 per 23,193 persons); hospital beds 64,071 (1 per 476 persons); infant mortality rate per 1,000 live births (1985–90) 83.
Food (1988–90): daily per capita caloric intake 2,130 (vegetable products 97%, animal products 3%); 96% of FAO recommended minimum requirement.

Military

Total active duty personnel (1992): 29,100 (army 89.4%, navy 4.5%, air force 6.1%). *Military expenditure as percentage of GNP* (1988): 2.6% (world 5.0%); per capita expenditure U.S.$7.

---

[1]Military-dominated regime as of October 1992; transitional government pending. [2]Estimate. [3]Nord-Kivu includes Manlema and Sud-Kivu. [4]Detail does not add to total given because of rounding. [5]Registered marriages only. [6]Infectious diseases only. [7]1990. [8]1991. [9]1987. [10]Includes Z 103,323,500,000 in the subsistence sector. [11]Includes Z 12,083,100,000 in the subsistence sector. [12]Import taxes and duties less imputed bank service charge. [13]Traffic statistics are for services operated by the Zaire National Railways (SNCZ), which controls more than 90% of the country's total rail facility. [14]Air Zaïre only. [15]1986–87. [16]Secondary includes Voc., teacher tr.

Zambia

Official name: Republic of Zambia.
Form of government: multiparty republic with one legislative house (National Assembly [150[1]]).
Head of state and government: President.
Capital: Lusaka.
Official language: English.
Official religion: none.
Monetary unit: 1 Zambian kwacha (K) = 100 ngwee; valuation (Oct. 5, 1992) 1 U.S.$ = K 196.65; 1 £ = K 334.31.

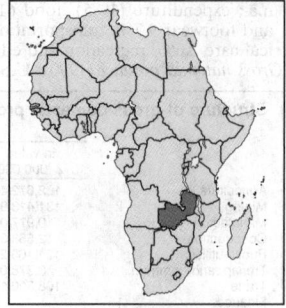

Area and population

Provinces	Capitals	area sq mi	area sq km	population 1990 census
Central	Kabwe	36,446	94,395	725,611
Copperbelt	Ndola	12,096	31,328	1,579,542
Eastern	Chipata	26,682	69,106	973,818
Luapula	Mansa	19,524	50,567	526,705
Lusaka	Lusaka	8,454	21,896	1,207,980
Northern	Kasama	57,076	147,826	867,795
North-Western	Solwezi	48,582	125,827	383,146
Southern	Livingstone	32,928	85,283	946,353
Western	Mongu	48,798	126,386	607,497
TOTAL		290,586	752,614	7,818,447

Demography

Population (1992): 8,303,000.
Density (1992): persons per sq mi 28.6, persons per sq km 11.0.
Urban-rural (1990): urban 42.0%; rural 58.0%.
Sex distribution (1990): male 49.16%; female 50.84%.
Age breakdown (1986): under 15, 47.0%; 15–29, 25.8%; 30–44, 14.6%; 45–59, 8.3%; 60 and over, 4.3%.
Population projection: (2000) 10,753,000; (2010) 14,855,000.
Doubling time: 19 years.
Ethnolinguistic composition (1980): Bemba peoples 36.2%; Maravi (Nyanja) peoples 17.6%; Tonga peoples 15.1%; North-Western peoples 10.1%; Barotze peoples 8.2%; Mambwe peoples 4.6%; Tumbuka peoples 4.6%; other 3.6%.
Religious affiliation (1980): Christian 72.0%, of which Protestant 34.2%, Roman Catholic 26.2%, African Christian 8.3%; traditional beliefs 27.0%; Muslim 0.3%; other 0.7%.
Major cities (1990): Lusaka 982,362; Ndola 376,311; Kitwe 338,207; Mufulira 152,944.

Vital statistics

Birth rate per 1,000 population (1990–95): 50.3 (world avg. 26.4); legitimate, n.a.; however, marriage is both early and universal, suggesting that legitimate births are a relatively high proportion of all births.
Death rate per 1,000 population (1990–95): 12.4 (world avg. 9.2).
Natural increase rate per 1,000 population (1990–95): 37.9 (world avg. 17.2).
Total fertility rate (avg. births per childbearing woman; 1990–95): 7.2.
Marriage rate per 1,000 population: n.a.
Divorce rate per 1,000 population: n.a.
Life expectancy at birth (1990–95): male 54.4 years; female 56.5 years.
Major causes of death per 100,000 population: n.a.; however, among nearly 7,000,000 visits to outpatient clinics in 1982, almost two-thirds of the reported illnesses were related to nutritional deficiencies and infectious and parasitic diseases.

National economy

Budget (1992). Revenue: K 79,902,000,000 (customs duties and excise taxes 62.6%, income tax 24.8%, mineral revenue 5.4%). Expenditures: K 64,813,000,000 (1989; economic services 35.0%, education 10.9%, health 7.2%, community services 2.4%).
Production (metric tons except as noted). Agriculture, forestry, fishing (1991): corn (maize) 1,448,000, sugarcane 1,350,000, cassava 270,000, fruits and vegetables 183,000 (of which onions 30,000, tomatoes 30,000, oranges 4,000), seed cotton 69,000, wheat 68,000, soybeans 61,000, peanuts (groundnuts) 45,000, sorghum 40,000, millet 31,000, sweet potatoes 28,000, pulses 26,000, sunflower seeds 23,000, tobacco 5,000; livestock (number of live animals) 3,045,000 cattle, 540,000 goats, 230,000 pigs, 65,000 sheep, 16,000,000 chickens; roundwood (1990) 12,221,000 cu m; fish catch (1990) 64,484. Mining and quarrying (1991): copper 421,590; zinc 9,717; cobalt 4,674; lead 3,670; gold 4,147 troy oz[2]. Manufacturing (1987): cement 375,000; sulfuric acid 304,000; raw sugar 130,000; cigarettes 1,500,000,000 units. Construction (value in K; 1985): buildings 151,100,000; other construction 43,200,000. Energy production (consumption): electricity (kW-hr; 1990) 7,771,000,000 (6,291,000,000); coal (metric tons; 1990) 377,000 (372,000); crude petroleum (barrels; 1990) none (3,960,000); petroleum products (metric tons; 1990) 486,000 (425,000); natural gas, none (n.a.).
Household income and expenditure. Average household size (1981) 5.8; average annual income per household (1981) K 1,041 (U.S.$908); sources of income (1981): wages and salaries 94.0%, other 6.0%; expenditure (1977): food 37.7%, housing 11.0%, clothing 8.3%, transportation 4.3%, education 2.1%, health 1.0%.
Population economically active (1990): total 2,716,000; activity rate of total population 34.9% (participation rates: ages 15–64, 60.1%[3]; female 28.2%[3]; unemployed 17.4%[4]).

Price and earnings indexes (1985 = 100)

	1985	1986	1987	1988	1989	1990	1991
Consumer price index	100.0	154.0	224.3	346.9	793.5	1,674.4	3,224.9
Earnings index	...	...	...	...	...	...	...

Land use (1990): forested 38.8%; meadows and pastures 40.4%; agricultural and under permanent cultivation 7.1%; other 13.7%.
Gross national product (at current market prices; 1990): U.S.$3,391,000,000 (U.S.$420 per capita).

Structure of gross domestic product and labour force

	1990 in value K '000,000	1990 % of total value	1990 labour force	1990 % of labour force
Agriculture	17,956	16.7	1,872,000	68.9
Mining	8,808	8.2	56,800	2.1
Manufacturing	45,914	42.7	50,900	1.9
Construction	3,739	3.5	29,100	1.1
Public utilities	494	0.5	8,900	0.3
Transportation and communications	4,304	4.0	25,600	0.9
Trade	15,377[5]	14.3[5]	30,700	1.1
Finance	6,101	5.7	24,200	0.9
Public admin., defense	} 5,598	} 5.2	111,600	4.1
Services				
Other	−689[6]	−0.6[6]	506,100	18.6
TOTAL	107,602	100.0[7]	2,716,000[7]	100.0[7]

Public debt (external, outstanding; 1989): U.S.$4,095,000,000.
Tourism (1989): receipts from visitors U.S.$12,000,000; expenditures by nationals abroad U.S.$98,000,000.

Foreign trade

Balance of trade (current prices)

	1985	1986	1987	1988	1989	1990
K '000,000	−124.0	−1,373.3	+1,431.1	+2,888.1	+7,753.2	+7,787.0
% of total	4.0%	18.2%	10.2%	17.3%	26.6%	11.0%

Imports (1990): K 27,307,900,000 (1988; machinery and transport equipment 38.3%; basic manufactures 19.8%; chemicals 16.9%; mineral fuels, lubricants, and electricity 12.3%; food 3.8%). *Major import sources:* South Africa 16.9%; United Kingdom 12.2%; Germany 11.6%; United States 10.2%; Japan 6.7%.
Exports (1990): K 33,802,600,000 (1988; copper 85.2%; cobalt 6.1%; zinc 1.6%; tobacco 0.3%; lead 0.2%). *Major export destinations* (1988): United States 10.3%; Japan 3.5%; United Kingdom 2.5%; West Germany 1.5%; South Africa 0.7%.

Transport and communications

Transport. Railroads (1988): length 1,345 mi, 2,164 km; passenger-mi 472,000,000, passenger-km 759,000,000; short ton-mi cargo 520,000,000, metric ton-km cargo 752,000,000. Roads (1991): total length 23,214 mi, 37,359 km (paved 18%). Vehicles (1982): passenger cars 105,783; trucks and buses 94,780. Merchant marine: vessels (100 gross tons and over) none. Air transport (1991): passenger-mi 200,000,000, passenger-km 322,000,000; short ton-mi cargo 27,309,000, metric ton-km cargo 39,870,000; airports (1992) with scheduled flights 8.
Communications. Daily newspapers (1989): total number 2; total circulation 139,000; circulation per 1,000 population 17. Radio (1991): total number of receivers 1,660,380 (1 per 5.3 persons). Television (1991): total number of receivers 200,000 (1 per 44 persons). Telephones (1990): 99,840 (1 per 78 persons).

Education and health

Education (1989)

	schools	teachers	students	student/ teacher ratio
Primary (age 7–13)	3,489	28,881[8]	1,446,847	47.0[8]
Secondary (age 14–18)	480	5,786[9]	161,349[9]	27.9[9]
Voc., teacher tr.	26	846	8,218	9.7
Higher	2	320	6,247	19.5

Educational attainment (1980). Percentage of population age 25 and over having: no formal schooling 54.7%; some primary education 34.4%; some secondary 10.5%; higher 0.4%. *Literacy* (1990): population age 15 and over literate 3,131,000 (72.8%); males literate 1,676,000 (80.8%); females literate 1,455,000 (65.3%).
Health: physicians (1984) 798 (1 per 8,437 persons); hospital beds (1989) 22,461 (1 per 349 persons); infant mortality rate per 1,000 live births (1990–95) 72.0.
Food (1988–90): daily per capita caloric intake 2,016 (vegetable products 95%, animal products 5%); 87% of FAO recommended minimum requirement.

Military

Total active duty personnel (1992): 24,000 (army 83.3%, navy, none, air force 16.7%). *Military expenditure as percentage of GNP* (1989): 1.4% (world 4.9%); per capita expenditure U.S.$8.

[1]President may appoint a maximum of eight additional members. [2]1990. [3]1985. [4]1987. [5]Includes import duties. [6]Includes imputed bank service charges. [7]Detail does not add to total given because of rounding. [8]1986. [9]1988.

Zimbabwe

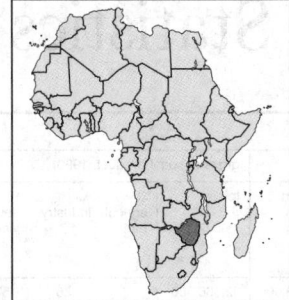

Official name: Republic of Zimbabwe.
Form of government: multiparty
republic with one legislative house
(House of Assembly [150[1]]).
Head of state and government:
President.
Capital: Harare.
Official language: English.
Official religion: none.
Monetary unit: 1 Zimbabwe dollar
(Z$) = 100 cents; valuation (Oct. 5,
1992) 1 U.S.$ = Z$5.08; 1 £ = Z$8.63.

Area and population		area		population
				1982
Provinces	Capitals	sq mi	sq km	census
Manicaland	Mutare	13,463	34,870	1,103,837
Mashonaland Central	Bindura	10,534	27,284	560,847
Mashonaland East	Marondera	9,627	24,934	1,496,500
Mashonaland West	Chinhoyi	23,346	60,467	854,098
Masvingo (Victoria)	Masvingo	17,108	44,310	1,029,504
Matabeleland North	Bulawayo	28,393	73,537	962,064
Matabeleland South	Gwanda	25,633	66,390	515,298
Midlands	Gweru	22,767	58,967	1,086,284
TOTAL		150,873[2]	390,759	7,608,432

Demography

Population (1992): 9,871,000.
Density (1992): persons per sq mi 65.4, persons per sq km 25.3.
Urban-rural (1988): urban 26.4%; rural 73.6%.
Sex distribution (1987): male 49.07%; female 50.93%.
Age breakdown (1987): under 15, 44.9%; 15–29, 29.2%; 30–44, 14.6%; 45–59,
7.3%; 60–74, 3.1%; 75 and over, 0.9%.
Population projection: (2000) 11,943,000; (2010) 14,739,000.
Doubling time: 23 years.
Ethnolinguistic composition (1982): African 97.6%, of which Shona-speak-
ing Bantu 70.8%; Ndebele-speaking Bantu 15.8%; European 2.0%; Asian
0.1%; other 0.3%.
Religious affiliation (1980): Christian 44.8%, of which Protestant (including
Anglican) 17.5%, African indigenous 13.6%, Roman Catholic 11.7%; ani-
mist 40.4%; other 14.8%.
Major cities (1987): Harare 863,000; Bulawayo 495,317[3]; Chitungwiza 229,000;
Gweru 78,940[3]; Mutare 75,358[3].

Vital statistics

Birth rate per 1,000 population (1990–95): 39.9 (world avg. 26.4).
Death rate per 1,000 population (1990–95): 8.9 (world avg. 9.2).
Natural increase rate per 1,000 population (1990–95): 31.0 (world avg. 17.2).
Total fertility rate (avg. births per childbearing woman; 1989): 5.1.
Marriage rate per 1,000 population: n.a.
Divorce rate per 1,000 population: n.a.
Life expectancy at birth (1987): male 57.9 years; female 61.4 years.
Major causes of death per 100,000 population: n.a.; major causes of death
include malnutrition, measles, pneumonia, malaria, and diarrheal diseases.

National economy

Budget (1992–93). Revenue: Z$10,886,355,000 (income tax 39.2%; customs
duties 22.0%; sales tax 15.3%; international grants 7.3%; excise tax 5.5%;
revenue from investments and property 3.8%). Expenditures: Z$12,905,-
519,100 (recurrent expenditures 84.4%, of which goods and services 42.8%,
transfer payments 41.6%).
Population economically active (1986–87): total 3,260,000; activity rate of total
population 38.3% (participation rates: over age 15, 76.5%; female 36.6%;
unemployed 7.2%[4]).

Price and earnings indexes (1985 = 100)							
	1985	1986	1987	1988	1989	1990	1991
Consumer price index	100.0	114.3	128.6	138.1	155.9	183.0	227.5
Monthly earnings index	100.0	118.3	126.4	...	...	...	...

Production (metric tons except as noted). Agriculture, forestry, fishing (1991):
sugarcane 2,793,000, corn (maize) 1,586,000, wheat 253,000, tobacco leaves
178,000, vegetables (including melons) 151,000, cottonseed 125,000, peanuts
(groundnuts) 107,000, soybeans 97,000, sorghum 68,000; livestock (number
of live animals) 5,950,000 cattle, 2,450,000 goats, 721,000 sheep, 340,000 pigs,
10,000,000 chickens; roundwood (1990) 7,893,000 cu m; fish catch (1990)
25,000 metric tons. Mining and quarrying (value of production in Z$; 1990):
gold 505,200,000; nickel 236,100,000; asbestos 161,900,000; coal 156,300,000;
copper 85,000,000; chrome 55,800,000. Manufacturing (value in Z$; 1986–
87): foodstuffs 1,295,600,000; chemicals and petroleum products 994,400,-
000; beverages and tobacco 666,800,000; textiles, canvas, and yarns 595,-
100,000; clothing and footwear 364,400,000; paper, printing, and publishing
293,400,000; transport equipment 175,700,000; nonmetallic mineral products
174,700,000; wood and furniture 161,000,000; metal and metal products
108,300,000; other manufactured goods 52,000,000. Construction (Z$; 1988):
residential 148,670,000; industrial 66,136,000; commercial 65,926,000. Energy
production (consumption): electricity (kW-hr; 1990) 9,559,000,000 (10,433,-
000,000); coal (metric tons; 1990) 4,958,000 (4,968,000); crude petroleum,
none (none); petroleum products (metric tons; 1990) none (563,000); natural
gas, none (none).

Public debt (external, outstanding; 1990): U.S.$2,751,000,000.
Household income and expenditure. Average household size (1980) 5.8; income per household Z$1,689 (U.S.$2,628); sources of income: n.a.; expenditure (1987): food, beverages, and tobacco 30.1%, household durable goods
11.1%, clothing, footwear, and textiles 10.3%, energy 7.3%, housing 6.5%,
transportation 6.1%, education 6.0%, health service 3.8%, recreation 0.6%.
Gross national product (1990): U.S.$6,313,000,000 (U.S.$640 per capita).

Structure of gross domestic product and labour force				
	1990			
	in value Z$'000,000	% of total value	labour force[5]	% of labour force[5]
Agriculture	1,686	12.9	290,400	24.3
Mining	1,071	8.2	50,900	4.3
Manufacturing	3,436	26.4	198,500	16.6
Construction	289	2.2	75,800	6.3
Public utilities	434	3.3	8,500	0.7
Transp. and commun.	978	7.5	52,900	4.4
Trade	1,499	11.5	95,400	8.0
Finance	851	6.5	17,400	1.5
Pub. admin., defense	977	7.5	94,500	7.9
Services	1,808[6]	13.9[6]	309,700	25.9
Other	6	6	—	—
TOTAL	13,029	100.0[2]	1,194,000	100.0[2]

Land use (1990): forested 49.5%; meadows and pastures 12.5%; agricultural
and under permanent cultivation 7.3%; other 30.7%.
Tourism (1990): receipts from visitors U.S.$47,000,000.

Foreign trade

Balance of trade (current prices)						
	1985	1986	1987	1988	1989	1990
Z$'000,000	349.0	529.9	629.7	896.5	...	– 296.8
% of total	10.8%	13.9%	15.3%	17.8%	...	3.4%

Imports (1990): Z$4,528,200,000 (machinery and transport equipment 37.3%,
of which transport equipment 11.6%; fuels 15.6%, of which petroleum
products 12.2%; chemicals 15.5%; manufactured goods 14.4%, of which
bars, rods, and sections 1.9%, paper and paperboard 1.3%). *Major import
sources:* South Africa 19.9%; United Kingdom 11.5%; United States 11.4%;
Germany 7.3%; Japan 4.6%; Botswana 3.5%; France 2.1%; Switzerland
2.0%; The Netherlands 1.9%.
Exports (1990): Z$4,231,000,000 (domestic exports 85.4%, of which tobacco
17.0%; gold sales 13.8%; ferroalloys 9.0%; corn [maize] 6.1%; nickel metal
5.8%; cotton 4.9%; asbestos 4.1%; sugar 2.9%; copper 1.6%). *Major export
destinations[7]:* Germany 10.1%; United Kingdom 9.3%; South Africa 7.6%;
United States 5.6%; Botswana 5.0%; Japan 4.7%; Malawi 4.1%; Italy 3.9%;
The Netherlands 3.7%; Mozambique 3.1%; Zambia 3.0%.

Transport and communications

Transport. Railroads (1989): route length 1,714 mi, 2,759 km; passenger-mi
540,842,000, passenger-km 870,403,000; short ton-mi cargo 7,255,000, metric
ton-km cargo 10,592,000. Roads (1989): total length 52,964 mi, 85,237 km
(paved 19%). Vehicles (1990): passenger cars 178,000; trucks and buses
82,000. Merchant marine: none. Air transport (1989): passenger-mi 440,551,-
000, passenger-km 709,000,000; short ton-mi cargo 8,489,000, metric ton-km
cargo 12,394,000; airports (1992) with scheduled flights 8.
Communications. Daily newspapers (1991): total number 2; total circulation
195,300; circulation per 1,000 population 20. Radio (1991): 522,000 receivers
(1 per 18 persons). Television (1991): 137,090 receivers (1 per 70 persons).
Telephones (1990): 300,955 (1 per 32 persons).

Education and health

Education (1989)				
	schools	teachers	students	student/ teacher ratio
Primary (age 7–13)	4,532	58,000	2,333,340	40.2
Secondary (age 14–19)	1,517	25,000	670,552	26.8
Voc., teacher tr.[8]	21	1,224	41,688	34.0
Higher	1	561[8]	9,288	...

Educational attainment (1986–87). Percentage of employed population age
15 and over having: no formal schooling 24.5%; primary 42.9%; secondary
and tertiary 31.7%. *Literacy* (1985): total population age 15 and over literate 3,413,000 (76.0%); males literate 1,846,000 (81.5%); females literate
1,567,000 (66.8%).
Health: physicians (1987) 1,243 (1 per 6,951 persons); hospital beds (1985) 19,-
913 (1 per 411 persons); infant mortality rate per 1,000 live births (1989) 67.
Food (1988–90): daily per capita caloric intake 2,256 (vegetable products 93%,
animal products 7%); 94% of FAO recommended minimum requirement.

Military

Total active duty personnel (1992): 48,500 (army 94.8%, air force 5.2%). *Military expenditure as percentage of GNP* (1989): 6.3% (world 4.9%); per capita
expenditure U.S.$38.

---

[1]Includes 30 nonelective seats. [2]Detail does not add to total given because of
rounding. [3]1982. [4]Does not take into consideration seasonal unemployment of communal workers. [5]Wage-earning workers only. [6]Services includes imputed bank service
charges. [7]Excludes gold sales and reexports. [8]1988.

Comparative National Statistics

World and regional summaries

region/bloc	area and population, 1992						gross national product, 1990						labour force, 1990		
	area		population			population projection, 2010	total (U.S.$ '000,000)	% agriculture	% industry	% services	growth rate, 1980–90	GNP per capita (U.S.$)	total ('000)	% male	% female
	square miles	square kilometres	total ('000)	per sq mi	per sq km										
World	52,447,900	135,839,420	5,436,358,000	103.7	40.0	7,069,828,000	22,566,380	7	36	57	2.8	4,290	2,363,545	63.9	36.1
Africa	11,677,460	30,244,380	656,108,000	56.2	21.7	1,052,581,000	398,840	19	36	45	1.6	640	242,784	65.6	34.4
Central Africa	2,549,210	6,602,420	77,751,000	30.5	11.8	135,975,000	34,280	23	34	43	3.2	470	26,428	64.7	35.3
East Africa	2,471,310	6,400,630	203,170,000	82.2	31.7	350,200,000	48,250	32	23	45	2.7	250	85,082	58.8	41.2
North Africa	3,284,090	8,505,750	151,659,000	46.2	17.8	222,546,000	151,650	15	38	47	1.4	1,050	40,016	84.6	15.4
Southern Africa	1,034,140	2,678,610	44,312,000	42.8	16.5	64,078,000	96,080	5	44	51	1.7	2,260	14,532	64.3	35.7
West Africa	2,238,710	6,057,170	179,216,000	76.6	29.6	279,782,000	68,580	37	29	34	0.7	400	76,726	63.8	36.2
Americas	16,296,840	42,208,670	734,444,000	45.1	17.4	922,073,000	6,956,600	3	31	66	3.0	9,770	293,723	66.5	33.5
Anglo-America[3]	8,368,970	21,675,560	283,274,000	33.8	13.1	319,888,000	5,990,750	2	30	68	3.2	21,630	135,438	58.7	41.3
Canada	3,849,670	9,970,610	27,737,000	7.2	2.8	36,182,000	542,770	3	33	64	3.3	20,160	13,360	60.2	39.8
United States	3,679,190	9,529,060	255,414,000	69.4	26.8	283,566,000	5,445,830	2	30	68	3.2	21,790	122,005	58.6	41.4
Latin America	7,927,870	20,533,110	451,170,000	56.9	22.0	602,185,000	965,850	10	37	53	1.5	2,220	158,285	73.1	26.9
Caribbean	90,650	234,760	34,618,000	381.9	147.5	42,077,000	71,880	9	41	50	−0.1	2,140	13,813	66.9	33.1
Mexico	756,070	1,958,200	84,439,000	111.7	43.1	111,360,000	214,500	9	30	61	1.1	2,620	30,487	72.9	27.1
Central America	201,660	522,310	29,901,000	148.3	57.2	45,996,000	28,890	19	20	61	1.0	1,020	9,520	78.5	21.5
South America	6,879,490	17,817,840	302,212,000	43.9	17.0	402,752,000	650,580	11	39	50	1.9	2,230	104,465	73.6	26.4
Andean Group	2,109,990	5,464,900	108,835,000	51.6	19.9	150,197,000	156,670	10	40	50	1.6	1,500	34,715	75.6	24.4
Brazil	3,286,500	8,512,000	151,381,000	46.1	17.8	200,067,000	402,790	10	39	51	2.7	2,760	55,026	72.6	27.4
Other South America	1,483,000	3,840,940	41,996,000	28.3	10.9	52,488,000	91,120	14	39	47	−0.4	2,230	14,724	72.4	27.6
Asia	12,321,460	31,912,350	3,291,269,000	267.1	103.1	4,297,919,000	5,272,810[4]	9[4]	40[4]	51[4]	4.7[4]	1,700[4]	1,436,522[4]	64.7[4]	35.3[4]
Eastern Asia	4,546,950	11,776,530	1,385,183,000	304.6	117.6	1,631,024,000	4,048,640	6	42	52	5.0	3,000	775,590	57.4	42.6
China	3,696,120	9,572,900	1,165,888,000	315.4	121.8	1,387,729,000	415,880	27	42	31	9.5	370	669,693	56.7	43.3
Japan	145,880	377,840	124,330,000	852.3	329.1	129,410,000	3,140,950	3	42	55	4.1	25,430	62,202	62.1	37.9
South Korea	38,330	99,260	43,663,000	1,139.1	439.9	49,683,000	231,130	9	45	46	10.1	5,390	18,664	66.2	33.8
Other Eastern Asia	666,620	1,726,530	51,302,000	77.0	29.7	64,202,000	260,670	5	39	56	7.4	5,230	25,031	58.8	41.2
South Asia	1,970,120	5,102,540	1,187,486,000	602.7	232.7	1,665,070,000	374,670	31	28	41	5.3	330	411,136	77.4	22.6
India	1,222,560	3,166,410	889,703,000	727.7	281.0	1,223,483,000	294,820	31	29	40	5.4	350	322,944	74.8	25.2
Pakistan	339,700	879,810	130,129,000	383.1	147.9	205,496,000	42,650	26	25	49	6.3	350	33,698	87.5	12.5
Other South Asia	407,860	1,056,320	167,654,000	411.1	158.7	236,091,000	37,210	39	19	42	3.5	230	54,494	86.2	13.8
Southeast Asia	1,735,190	4,494,140	452,797,000	260.9	100.8	605,886,000	328,990	19	38	43	4.9	760	189,297	63.0	37.0
ASEAN	1,185,040	3,069,270	326,896,000	275.9	106.5	430,920,000	302,490	16	39	45	5.4	960	132,060	65.6	34.4
Non-ASEAN	550,150	1,424,870	125,901,000	228.8	88.4	174,966,000	26,510	46	26	28	0.4	220	57,237	57.1	42.9
Southwest Asia	4,069,200	10,539,140	265,803,000	65.3	25.2	395,939,000	520,500[4]	13[4]	35[4]	52[4]	1.9[4]	2,780[4]	60,499[4]	76.2[4]	23.8[4]
Central Asia	1,542,150	3,994,400	52,331,000	33.9	13.1	75,185,000	[4]	[4]	[4]	[4]	[4]	[4]	[4]	[4]	[4]
Gulf Cooperation Council	1,024,580	2,653,640	21,137,000	20.6	8.0	36,998,000	171,520	5	50	45	−0.8	8,290	6,511	91.7	8.3
Iran	632,460	1,638,060	59,570,000	94.2	36.4	91,537,000	139,120	21	21	58	2.7	2,490	15,253	82.0	18.0
Other Southwest Asia	869,910	2,253,040	132,765,000	152.6	58.9	192,219,000	209,860[4]	14[4]	32[4]	54[4]	4.2[4]	1,900[4]	38,735[4]	71.3[4]	28.7[4]
Europe	8,868,320	22,968,920	727,234,000	82.0	31.7	762,033,000	9,593,090[4]	9[4]	37[4]	54[4]	1.9[4]	12,160[4]	378,335[4]	57.7[4]	42.3[4]
Eastern Europe	7,437,080	19,261,960	348,057,000	46.8	18.1	371,418,000	3,263,560[4]	19[4]	42[4]	39[4]	1.0[4]	7,920[4]	208,749[4]	53.0[4]	47.0[4]
Russia	6,592,850	17,075,400	149,469,000	22.7	8.8	161,976,000	2,660,000[4]	20[4]	42[4]	38[4]	1.3[4]	9,190[4]	146,634[4]	52.0[4]	48.0[4]
Other Eastern Europe	844,230	2,186,560	198,588,000	235.2	90.8	209,442,000	603,560[4]	13[4]	45[4]	42[4]	−0.2[4]	4,920[4]	62,115[4]	55.4[4]	44.6[4]
Western Europe	1,431,240	3,706,960	379,177,000	264.9	102.3	390,615,000	6,329,530	3	35	62	2.4	16,790	169,586	63.6	36.4
EFTA	517,360	1,339,960	33,018,000	63.8	24.6	34,286,000	802,210	4	36	60	2.5	24,640	15,917	58.1	41.9
European Community	912,670	2,363,810	345,358,000	378.4	146.1	355,374,000	5,517,360	3	35	62	2.3	16,050	153,330	64.1	35.9
France	210,030	543,970	57,289,000	272.8	105.3	61,784,000	1,099,750	4	29	67	2.2	19,380	25,404	60.1	39.9
Germany	137,820	356,960	79,122,000	574.1	221.7	79,579,000	1,411,350	2	39	59	2.2	17,850	38,981	60.7	39.3
Italy	116,320	301,280	57,158,000	491.4	189.7	56,270,000	970,620	4	33	63	2.4	17,030	23,339	68.1	31.9
Spain	194,900	504,780	39,085,000	200.5	77.4	40,317,000	429,400	5	39	56	3.1	11,020	14,456	75.5	24.5
United Kingdom	94,250	244,110	57,730,000	612.5	236.5	59,962,000	923,960	2	36	63	2.7	16,090	27,766	61.4	38.6
Other EC	159,350	412,710	54,974,000	345.0	133.2	57,462,000	682,290	5	31	64	1.8	12,510	23,384	66.5	33.5
Other Western Europe	1,210	3,190	801,000	660.9	251.1	955,000	9,960	4	23	73	3.9	12,730	339	68.1	31.9
Oceania	3,283,820	8,505,100	27,303,000	8.3	3.2	35,222,000	345,040	5	31	64	2.9	13,030	12,181	63.0	37.0
Australia	2,966,150	7,682,300	17,562,000	5.9	2.3	22,125,000	290,520	4	31	65	3.2	17,040	7,963	61.9	38.1
Pacific Ocean Islands	317,670	822,800	9,741,000	30.7	11.8	13,097,000	54,520	10	26	64	1.5	5,780	4,218	65.0	35.0

[1]Refers only to the long-term external public and publicly guaranteed debt of the 114 countries that report under the World Bank's Debtor Reporting System (DRS).   [2]Continent and regional totals may

Africa

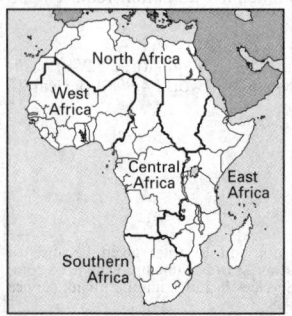

Americas

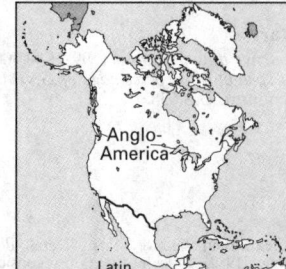

Asia

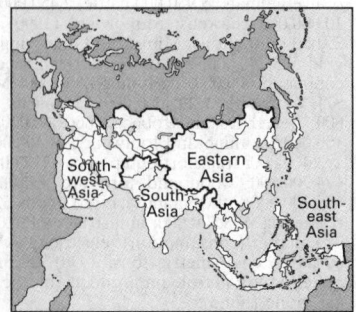

pop. per 1,000 ha of arable land, 1990	electricity consumption (kW-hr per capita), 1990	trade (U.S.$'000,000), 1991			debt (U.S.$ '000,000), 1990[1]		life expectancy (years)		health			food (% FAO recommended minimum), 1988–90	literacy (%)		region/bloc
		imports (c.i.f.)	exports[2] (f.o.b.)	balance[2]	total	% of GNP	male	female	pop. per doctor	infant mortality per 1,000 births	pop. having safe water (%)		male	female	
3,890	2,218	3,577,700	3,454,400	−123,300	982,418	30.6	63.5	67.5	740	62.5	74	115	80.8	68.0	World
3,820	485	98,645	90,582	−8,063	226,643	82.0	53.1	56.2	4,660	90.4	46	103	56.4	37.3	Africa
3,340	173	6,529	5,640	−889	29,692	88.5	50.8	54.3	14,330	88.4	34	95	71.6	47.7	Central Africa
4,600	134	14,350	11,929	−2,421	36,526	86.5	50.6	54.1	13,150	104.1	34	90	53.3	40.0	East Africa
4,040	648	37,654	38,108	+454	96,317	75.3	59.6	61.3	2,070	58.8	63	121	60.9	33.9	North Africa
2,850	3,952	18,235	13,365	−4,870	1,133	27.9	59.4	65.3	1,680	56.2	45	125	52.4	52.8	Southern Africa
3,490	107	21,877	19,231	−2,646	62,975	91.6	49.8	53.0	9,290	102.7	51	95	49.8	28.4	West Africa
1,950	5,727	777,762	759,642	−18,120	320,126	30.2	67.8	73.8	530	39.8	87	124	90.7	88.9	Americas
1,180	12,742	633,571	612,625	−20,946	—	—	72.1	78.9	410	8.7	100	136	95.7	95.3	Anglo-America[3]
590	18,149	123,421	120,799	−2,622	—	—	73.3	80.0	450	7.1	100	122	95.6	95.7	Canada
1,330	12,170	509,300	490,741	−18,559	—	—	72.0	78.8	400	8.9	100	138	95.7	95.3	United States
3,320	1,407	144,191	144,094	−97	320,126	30.2	65.1	70.6	670	51.0	79	114	86.9	83.8	Latin America
7,250	1,457	18,410	17,246	−1,164	10,187	55.5	66.6	70.5	570	55.2	68	114	86.8	83.8	Caribbean
3,540	1,367	49,244	46,973	−2,271	76,204	33.1	67.8	73.9	600	46.6	71	131	89.5	85.1	Mexico
5,160	483	8,767	15,870	+7,103	22,507	80.2	63.4	68.0	1,460	47.2	59	104	77.1	69.8	Central America
2,970	1,504	67,770	64,005	−3,765	211,229	26.9	64.4	69.9	660	52.5	84	110	87.1	84.7	South America
5,620	1,307	30,471	28,581	−1,890	76,542	47.5	64.3	69.7	910	52.6	78	98	91.3	86.4	Andean Group
2,890	1,643	23,420	22,491	−929	82,098	16.1	63.5	69.1	690	57.0	96	114	81.8	80.6	Brazil
1,410	1,501	13,879	12,933	−946	52,589	46.4	67.6	73.5	370	32.0	57	128	95.1	94.5	Other South America
6,760	882	911,776[4]	840,820[4]	−70,956[4]	333,267	21.8	63.3	66.0	1,010	63.4	71	109	77.5[4]	58.5[4]	Asia
13,030	1,303	549,442	506,676	−42,766	63,133	10.5	69.0	72.6	640	30.0	75	114	89.0	73.0	Eastern Asia
12,150	546	63,957	62,812	−1,145	45,319	12.5	68.4	71.4	640	32.0	72	112	87.0	68.0	China
29,980	6,944	236,633	213,095	−23,538	—	—	75.9	81.8	610	4.6	98	125	100.0	100.0	Japan
21,950	2,775	81,114	70,764	−10,350	17,814	7.5	67.4	75.4	1,010	12.8	78	120	99.1	93.5	South Korea
11,740	3,298	167,738	160,005	−7,733	—	—	69.1	74.6	540	23.1	97	120	97.1	91.9	Other Eastern Asia
5,510	300	38,948	37,586	−1,362	95,705	27.0	58.0	58.8	2,580	88.0	70	99	58.0	31.2	South Asia
5,160	336	21,687	19,852	−1,835	61,097	21.8	58.1	59.1	2,420	80.0	75	101	61.8	33.7	India
6,040	358	8,431	8,825	+394	16,532	41.7	59.3	60.7	1,990	113.0	50	99	36.0	15.2	Pakistan
7,830	78	8,830	8,909	+79	18,076	53.0	56.2	55.6	6,070	102.7	61	91	52.0	28.1	Other South Asia
7,300	384	184,006	164,362	−19,644	103,260	35.6	59.7	63.4	3,090	66.4	50	114	87.7	76.1	Southeast Asia
7,750	491	181,119	161,751	−19,368	97,761	36.4	59.5	63.1	2,970	67.6	56	114	88.0	76.2	ASEAN
6,330	97	2,887	2,611	−276	5,499	26.0	60.2	64.0	3,450	63.3	37	114	86.9	76.0	Non-ASEAN
2,530	2,145	139,380[4]	129,395[4]	−9,985[4]	71,169	24.9	63.9	68.5	620	57.9	86	129	76.9[4]	57.0[4]	Southwest Asia
1,170	4,130	[4]	[4]	[4]			65.3	72.5	270	34.0	100	132	[4]	[4]	Central Asia
8,830	4,718	63,683	60,875	−2,808	2,205	24.7	66.0	69.0	680	58.6	94	123	72.8	49.9	Gulf Cooperation Council
3,970	1,026	21,688	19,675	−2,013	1,797	1.3	64.0	65.0	2,880	66.0	78	130	64.5	43.3	Iran
3,130	1,407	54,009[4]	48,655[4]	−5,354[4]	67,167	48.7	63.0	68.3	740	61.5	83	128	83.7[4]	64.7[4]	Other Southwest Asia
2,380	5,978	1,742,141[4]	1,678,701[4]	−63,440[4]	100,303	30.0	69.3	76.9	300	12.4	98	134	98.7[4]	97.9[4]	Europe
1,150	5,598	121,041[4]	113,397[4]	−7,644[4]	85,749	31.1	65.5	74.4	260	17.0	97	132	98.6[4]	98.0[4]	Eastern Europe
1,130	7,241	54,239[4]	49,304[4]	−4,935[4]	—	—	63.9	74.3	210	17.4	100	132	99.0[4]	99.0[4]	Russia
2,150	4,371	66,802[4]	64,093[4]	−2,709[4]	85,749	31.1	66.7	74.5	320	16.6	95	133	97.8[4]	95.5[4]	Other Eastern Europe
4,730	6,330	1,675,339	1,613,000	−62,339	14,554	25.0	72.7	79.2	340	7.8	100	135	98.8	97.9	Western Europe
4,090	13,203	215,484	210,276	−5,208	—	—	73.2	79.8	360	6.5	99	122	100.0	100.0	EFTA
4,800	5,689	1,456,438	1,399,603	−56,835	14,432	25.8	72.6	79.2	340	7.9	100	136	98.7	97.7	European Community
3,150	6,661	232,902	230,637	−2,265	—	—	72.7	80.9	380	7.4	100	143	98.9	98.7	France
6,610	7,391	390,114	358,632	−31,482	—	—	72.1	78.7	350	7.8	100	132	100.0	100.0	Germany
6,270	4,407	182,697	163,864	−18,833	—	—	73.2	79.7	230	8.5	100	139	97.8	96.4	Italy
2,500	3,833	94,003	87,618	−6,385	—	—	73.3	79.7	260	8.0	100	141	97.0	92.5	Spain
8,690	5,761	209,933	191,277	−18,656	—	—	72.4	78.0	610	7.3	100	130	100.0	100.0	United Kingdom
5,220	4,863	346,789	367,575	+20,786	14,432	25.8	72.3	78.5	360	8.6	98	138	97.2	95.5	Other EC
23,640	3,286	3,417	3,121	−296	122	5.0	72.9	78.1	530	8.8	100	130	98.3	98.1	Other Western Europe
530	7,171	54,934	48,642	−6,292	2,078	41.5	69.5	75.3	530	24.9	89	125	94.3	91.5	Oceania
350	9,161	41,501	36,985	−4,516	—	—	73.3	79.6	440	8.1	99	124	99.5	99.5	Australia
12,300	3,664	13,433	11,657	−1,776	2,078	41.5	62.9	67.2	830	41.1	69	127	83.4	74.0	Pacific Ocean Islands

contain undistributable detail.   [3]Anglo-America includes Canada, the United States, Greenland, Bermuda, and St. Pierre and Miquelon.   [4]Data for Russia refer to all 15 republics of the former U.S.S.R.

Europe

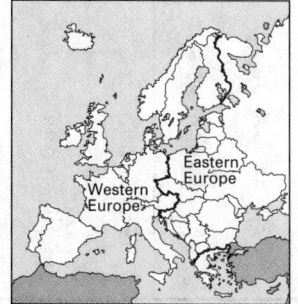

Eastern Europe

Oceania

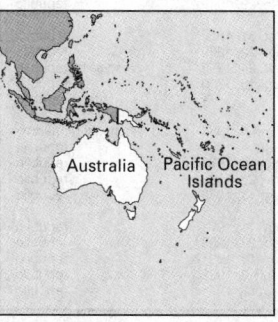

Government and international organizations

This table summarizes principal facts about the governments of the countries of the world, their branches and organs, the topmost layers of local government comprising each country's chief administrative subdivisions, and the participation of their central governments in the principal intergovernmental organizations of the world.

In this table "date of independence" may refer to a variety of circumstances. In the case of the newest countries, those that attained full independence after World War II, the date given is usually just what is implied by the heading—the date when the country, within its present borders, attained full sovereignty over both its internal and external affairs. In the case of longer established countries, the choice of a single date may be somewhat more complicated, and grounds for the use of several different dates often exist. The reader should refer to *Macropædia* and *Micropædia* articles on national histories and relevant historical acts. In cases of territorial annexation or dissolution, the date given here refers either to the final act of union of a state composed of smaller entities or to the final act of separation from a larger whole (*e.g.*, the separation of Bangladesh from Pakistan in 1971).

The date of the current, or last, constitution is in some ways a less complicated question, but governments sometimes do not, upon taking power, either adhere to existing constitutional forms or trouble to terminate the previous document and legitimize themselves by the installation of new constitutional forms. Often, however, the desire to legitimize extraconstitutional political activity by associating it with existing forms of long precedent leads to partial or incomplete modification, suspension, or abrogation of a consti-

tution, so that the actual day-to-day conduct of government may be largely unrelated to the provisions of a constitution still theoretically in force. When a date in this column is given in italics, it refers to a document that has been suspended, abolished by extraconstitutional action, or modified extensively.

The characterizations adopted under "type of government" represent a compromise between the forms provided for by the national constitution and the more pragmatic language that a political scientist might adopt to describe these same systems. For an explanation of the application of these terms in the Britannica World Data, *see* the Glossary at page 541.

The positions denoted by the terms "chief of state" and "head of government" are usually those identified with those functions by the constitution. The duties of the chief of state may range from largely ceremonial responsibilities, with little or no authority over the day-to-day conduct of government, to complete executive authority as the effective head of government. In certain countries, an official of a political party or a revolutionary figure outside the constitutional structure may exercise the powers of both positions.

Membership in the legislative house(s) of each country as given here includes all elected or appointed members, as well as ex officio members (those who by virtue of some other office or title are members of the body), whether voting or nonvoting. The legislature of a country with a unicameral system is shown as the upper house in this table.

The number of administrative subdivisions for each country is listed down to the second level. A single country may, depending on its size, complexity, and historical antecedents, have as many as five levels of administrative

Government and international organizations

country	date of independence[a]	date of current or last constitution[b]	type of government	executive branch[c] chief of state	executive branch[c] head of government	legislative branch[d] upper house (members)	legislative branch[d] lower house (members)	admin. subdivisions first-order (number)	admin. subdivisions second-order (number)	seaward claims territorial (nautical miles)	seaward claims fishing/ economic (nautical miles)
Afghanistan	Aug. 19, 1919	*Nov. 30, 1987*	republic[1]	——interim president LC——		—	—	31	185	—	—
Albania	Nov. 28, 1912	April 29, 1991[2]	republic	president	prime minister	140	—	27	...	12	3
Algeria	July 5, 1962	Feb. 23, 1989	republic[1]	president HSC	prime minister	60[5]	—	48	1,541	12	12
American Samoa	—	July 1, 1967	territory (U.S.)	U.S. president	governor	18	21	3	15	12	200
Andorra	Dec. 6, 1288		coprincipality	[7]	chief executive	28	—	7	...	—	—
Angola	Nov. 11, 1975	Aug. 27, 1992	republic	——president——		220	—	18	157	20	200
Antigua and Barbuda	Nov. 1, 1981	Nov. 1, 1981	constitutional monarchy	British monarch	prime minister	17	17	30	...	12	200
Argentina	July 9, 1816	July 9, 1853	federal republic	——president——		46	254	24	...	200	3
Armenia	Sept. 23, 1991	April 1978	republic	president	prime minister	260	—	37[8]	...	—	—
Aruba	—	Jan. 1, 1986	integral part of Neth.	Dutch monarch	[9]	21	—	...	...	12	200
Australia	Jan. 1, 1901	July 9, 1900	federal parl. state[11]	British monarch	prime minister	76	148	8	*c.* 900	3	200
Austria	Oct. 30, 1918	Oct. 1, 1920	federal republic	president	chancellor	63	183	9	99	—	—
Azerbaijan	Aug. 30, 1991	April 1978	republic	president	prime minister	360	—	2[8]	61[8]	...	...
Bahamas, The	July 10, 1973	July 10, 1973	constitutional monarchy	British monarch	prime minister	16	49	—	—	3	200
Bahrain	Aug. 15, 1971	June 1973	monarchy (emirate)	emir	prime minister	x	—	1	—	3	12
Bangladesh	March 26, 1971	Dec. 16, 1972	republic	president	prime minister	330	—	4	64	12	200
Barbados	Nov. 30, 1966	Nov. 30, 1966	constitutional monarchy	British monarch	prime minister	21	28	—	—	12	200
Belarus	Aug. 25, 1991	April 1978	republic	chairman SS	prime minister	360	—	6[8]	118[8]	—	—
Belgium	Oct. 4, 1830	Feb. 7, 1831	constitutional monarchy	monarch	prime minister	185	212	9	589	12	12
Belize	Sept. 21, 1981	Sept. 21, 1981	constitutional monarchy	British monarch	prime minister	8	28	6	—	3	3
Benin	Aug. 1, 1960	Dec. 2, 1990	republic	——president——		64	—	6	86	200	200
Bermuda	—	June 8, 1968	colony (U.K.)	British monarch	[13]	11	40	11	—	12	200
Bhutan	March 24, 1910	—	[14]	——king——		150	—	18	36	—	—
Bolivia	Aug. 6, 1825	Feb. 2, 1967	republic	——president——		27	130	9	108	—	—
Bosnia and Hercegovina	March 3, 1992	1990	republic[15]	president	prime minister	240	—	100[8]	...	...	...
Botswana	Sept. 30, 1966	Sept. 30, 1966	republic	——president——		15[5]	40	21	...	—	—
Brazil	Sept. 7, 1822	Oct. 5, 1988	federal republic	——president——		81	503	27	4,493	200	200
Brunei	Jan. 1, 1984	*Sept. 29, 1959*	monarchy (sultanate)	——sultan——		21[5]	—	4	...	12	200
Bulgaria	Oct. 5, 1908	July 12, 1991	republic	president	prime minister	240	—	9	273	12	200
Burkina Faso	Aug. 5, 1960	June 11, 1991[2]	republic	president	prime minister	107	—	30	250	—	—
Burundi	July 1, 1962	March 13, 1992	republic[1]	——president[16]——		...	—	15	113	—	—
Cambodia	Nov. 9, 1953	Oct. 23, 1991[17]	republic	[18]		117	—	22	...	12	200
Cameroon	Jan. 1, 1960	June 2, 1972	republic[1]	president	prime minister	180	—	10	49	50	3
Canada	July 1, 1867	April 17, 1982	federal parl. state[11]	Canadian GG[19]	prime minister	110[20]	295	12	...	12	200
Cape Verde	July 5, 1975	Sept. 28, 1990	republic	president	prime minister	79	—	14	31	12[21]	200[21]
Cayman Islands	—	Aug. 22, 1972	colony (U.K.)	British monarch	governor	20	—	...	...	3	200
Central African Republic	Aug. 13, 1960	Nov. 21, 1986	republic	president	prime minister	...[5]	52	17	52	—	—
Chad	Aug. 11, 1960	Feb. 28, 1991[2]	republic	president	prime minister	31[5]	—	14	53	—	—
Chile	Sept. 18, 1810	March 11, 1981	republic	——president——		48	120	13	51	12	200
China	1523 BC	Dec. 4, 1982	people's republic	president	premier SC	2,978	—	30	336	12	3
Colombia	July 20, 1810	July 5, 1991	republic	——president——		102	161	33	1,019	12	200
Comoros	July 6, 1975	Oct. 1, 1978	federal Islamic republic	——president——		42	—	3	7	12	200
Congo	Aug. 15, 1960	March 15, 1992[22]	republic	president	prime minister	60	125	15	47	200	3
Cook Islands	—	Aug. 4, 1965	territory (N.Z.)[23]	British monarch	prime minister	15[5]	24	14	44	12	200
Costa Rica	Sept. 15, 1821	Nov. 9, 1949	republic	——president——		57	—	7	81	12	200
Côte d'Ivoire	Aug. 7, 1960	Oct. 31, 1960	republic	president	prime minister	175	—	34	163	12	200
Croatia	June 25, 1991	Dec. 22, 1990	republic	president	prime minister	...	138	102[8]	...	12	200
Cuba	May 20, 1902	Feb. 24, 1976	socialist republic	——president——		510	—	15	169	12	200
Cyprus[24]	Aug. 16, 1960	Aug. 16, 1960	republic	——president——		80[25]	—	5	...	12	3
Czechoslovakia	Oct. 28, 1918	[26]	federal republic[27]	president	prime minister	150	150	2	12	—	—
Denmark	*c.* 800	June 5, 1953	constitutional monarchy	monarch	prime minister	179	—	16	273	3	200
Djibouti	June 27, 1977	Sept. 4, 1992[22]	republic	——president——		65	—	5	13	12	200
Dominica	Nov. 3, 1978	Nov. 3, 1978	republic	president	prime minister	31	—	27	...	12	200
Dominican Republic	Feb. 27, 1844	Nov. 28, 1966	republic	——president——		30	120	30	136	6	200
Ecuador	May 24, 1822	Aug. 10, 1979	republic	——president——		77	—	21	169	200	200
Egypt	Feb. 28, 1922	Sept. 11, 1971	republic	president	prime minister	454	—	26	176	12	200
El Salvador	Jan. 30, 1841	Dec. 20, 1983	republic	——president——		84	—	14	261	200	200
Equatorial Guinea	Oct. 12, 1968	Nov. 16, 1991[22]	republic[1]	president	prime minister	41	—	7	18	12	200
Estonia	Aug. 20, 1991	July 3, 1992	republic	president	prime minister	101	—	21	...	12	200
Ethiopia	*c.* 1000 BC	July 1991[2]	republic	——president[16]——		87[28]	—	14	...	12	3

subordination or it may have none at all. Each level of subordination may have several kinds of subdivisions.

Finally, in the second half of the table are listed the memberships each country maintains in the principal international intergovernmental organizations of the world. This part of the table may also be utilized to provide a complete membership list for each of these organizations as of Dec. 1, 1992.

Notes for the column headings

a. The date may also be either that of the organization of the present form of government or the inception of the present administrative structure (federation, confederation, union, etc.).
b. Constitutions whose dates are in italic type had been wholly or substantially suspended or abolished as of late 1992.
c. For abbreviations used in this column see the list on the facing page.
d. When a legislative body has been adjourned or otherwise suspended, figures in parentheses indicate the number of members in the legislative body as provided for in constitution or law. If the provision for the legislative body in the constitution has been abrogated then the space has been marked with an "X".
e. Vatican City also a member.

f. States contributing funds to or receiving aid from UNICEF in 1991.
g. Palestine (Liberation Organization) also a member.

International organizations, conventions

ACP	African, Caribbean, and Pacific (Lomé IV) convention
ADB	Asian Development Bank
ASEAN	Association of South East Asian Nations
CARICOM	Caribbean Community and Common Market
EC	The European Communities
ECOWAS	Economic Community of West African States
EEC	European Economic Community
FAO	Food and Agriculture Org.
GATT	General Agreement on Tariffs and Trade
GCC	Gulf Cooperation Council
I-ADB	Inter-American Development Bank
IAEA	International Atomic Energy Agency
IBRD	International Bank for Reconstruction and Development
ICAO	International Civil Aviation Org.
ICJ	International Court of Justice
IDA	International Development Assn.
IDB	Islamic Development Bank
IFC	International Finance Corporation
ILO	International Labour Org.
IMF	International Monetary Fund
IMO	International Maritime Org.
ITU	International Telecommunication Union
LAS	League of Arab States
OAS	Organization of American States
OAU	Organization of African Unity
OPEC	Organization of Petroleum Exporting Countries
SPC	South Pacific Commission
UNCTAD	United Nations Conference on Trade and Development
UNESCO	United Nations Educational Scientific and Cultural Org.
UNICEF	United Nations Children's Fund
UNIDO	United Nations Industrial Development Org.
UPU	Universal Postal Union
WHO	World Health Org.
WIPO	World Intellectual Property Org.
WMO	World Meteorological Org.

Abbreviations used in the executive-branch column

CCRNS	Revolutionary Command Council for National Salvation
CM	Council of Ministers
CTRN	Transitional Committee for National Recovery
FC	Federal Council
GG	Governor-General
GPC	General People's Committee
HSC	High State Council
LC	Leadership Council
MC	Military Council
PC	Presidential Council
PNDC	Provisional National Defense Council
StC	State Council
SLORC	State Law and Order Restoration Council
SuC	Supreme Council
SCS	Supreme Council of State
SS	Supreme Soviet

United Nations (date of admission)	UNCTAD[e]	UNICEF[a,f]	ICJ	FAO	GATT	IAEA[e]	IBRD	ICAO	IDA	IFC	ILO	IMF	IMO	ITU[e]	UNESCO	UNIDO	UPU[e]	WHO[e]	WIPO[e]	WMO	Commonwealth of Nations	ASEAN	EC	GCC	LAS[g]	OAS	OAU	SPC	ACP	ADB	CARICOM	ECOWAS	EEC	I-ADB	IDB[g]	OPEC	country
1946	●	●	●	●	●	●	●	●	●	●	●	●		●	●	●	●	●	●	●										●					●		Afghanistan
1955	●	●	●	●	●[4]	●	●	●	●	●	●	●	●	●	●	●	●	●	●	●																	Albania
1962	●	●	●	●	●[6]	●	●	●	●	●	●	●	●	●	●	●	●	●	●	●					●		●								●	●	Algeria
—														●				●										●									American Samoa
—																																					Andorra
1976	●	●	●	●	●[6]	●	●	●	●	●	●	●	●	●	●	●	●	●		●							●		●								Angola
1981	●	●	●	●	●[6]		●	●	●	●	●	●	●	●	●	●	●[6]	●		●	●					●				●		●					Antigua and Barbuda
1945	●	●	●	●	●[4]	●	●	●	●	●	●	●	●	●	●	●	●	●		●						●								●			Argentina
1992					●[4]													●																			Armenia
—															●[10]																						Aruba
1945	●	●	●	●	●	●	●	●	●	●	●	●	●	●	●	●	●	●	●	●	●							●		●				●			Australia
1955	●	●	●	●	●	●	●	●	●	●	●	●	●	●	●	●	●	●	●	●										●				●			Austria
1992														●				●																			Azerbaijan
1973	●	●	●	●	●[6]		●	●	●	●	●	●	●	●	●	●	●	●		●	●					●			●		●			●			Bahamas, The
1971	●	●	●	●	●[6]		●	●	●	●	●	●	●	●	●	●	●	●		●				●	●										●		Bahrain
1974	●	●	●	●	●	●	●	●	●	●	●	●	●	●	●	●	●	●		●	●									●					●		Bangladesh
1966	●	●	●	●	●		●	●	●	●	●	●	●	●	●	●	●	●		●	●					●			●		●			●			Barbados
1945	●	●	●	●			●	●	●	●	●	●	●	●	●	●	●	●	●	●																	Belarus
1945	●	●	●	●	●	●	●	●	●	●	●	●	●	●	●	●	●	●	●	●			●							●			●	●			Belgium
1981	●	●	●	●			●	●	●	●	●	●	●	●	●	●	●	●		●	●					●			●		●			●			Belize
1960	●	●	●	●			●	●	●	●	●	●	●	●	●	●	●	●		●							●		●			●			●		Benin
—														●				●																			Bermuda
1971	●	●	●	●			●		●			●		●	●	●	●	●		●										●							Bhutan
1945	●	●	●	●			●	●	●	●	●	●	●	●	●	●	●	●		●						●								●			Bolivia
1992																		●																			Bosnia and Hercegovina
1966	●	●	●	●			●	●	●	●	●	●		●	●	●	●	●		●	●						●		●					●			Botswana
1945	●	●	●	●	●		●	●	●	●	●	●	●	●	●	●	●	●		●						●								●			Brazil
1984	●	●	●	●	●[6]		●	●			●	●	●	●	●		●	●		●	●	●								●					●		Brunei
1955	●	●	●	●	●[6]	●	●	●	●	●	●	●	●	●	●	●	●	●	●	●																	Bulgaria
1960	●	●	●	●	●		●	●	●	●	●	●	●	●	●	●	●	●		●							●		●			●			●		Burkina Faso
1962	●	●	●	●			●	●	●	●	●	●	●	●	●	●	●	●		●							●		●					●			Burundi
1955	●	●	●	●			●	●	●	●	●	●	●	●	●	●	●	●		●										●							Cambodia
1960	●	●	●	●	●		●	●	●	●	●	●	●	●	●	●	●	●		●							●		●					●			Cameroon
1945	●	●	●	●	●	●	●	●	●	●	●	●	●	●	●	●	●	●	●	●	●					●				●				●			Canada
1975	●	●	●	●	●[6]		●	●	●	●	●	●	●	●	●	●	●	●		●							●		●			●			●		Cape Verde
—																		●			●																Cayman Islands
1960	●	●	●	●	●		●	●	●	●	●	●		●	●	●	●	●		●							●		●					●			Central African Republic
1960	●	●	●	●	●		●	●	●	●	●	●		●	●	●	●	●		●							●		●					●			Chad
1945	●	●	●	●	●		●	●	●	●	●	●	●	●	●	●	●	●		●						●								●			Chile
1945	●	●	●	●	●[6]	●	●	●	●	●	●	●	●	●	●	●	●	●	●	●																	China
1945	●	●	●	●	●		●	●	●	●	●	●	●	●	●	●	●	●		●						●								●			Colombia
1975	●	●	●	●			●	●	●	●	●	●	●	●	●	●	●	●		●					●		●		●						●		Comoros
1960	●	●	●	●			●	●	●	●	●	●	●	●	●	●	●	●		●							●		●					●			Congo
—																		●										●									Cook Islands
1945	●	●	●	●			●	●	●	●	●	●	●	●	●	●	●	●		●						●								●			Costa Rica
1960	●	●	●	●			●	●	●	●	●	●	●	●	●	●	●	●		●							●		●					●			Côte d'Ivoire
1992																		●																			Croatia
1945	●	●	●	●				●			●		●	●	●	●	●	●		●							●							●			Cuba
1960	●	●	●	●	●[6]		●	●	●	●	●	●	●	●	●	●	●	●		●	●												●[10]				Cyprus[24]
1945	●	●	●	●	●		●	●	●	●	●	●	●	●	●	●	●	●	●	●																	Czechoslovakia
1945	●	●	●	●	●		●	●	●	●	●	●	●	●	●	●	●	●	●	●			●							●			●	●			Denmark
1977	●	●	●	●			●	●	●	●	●	●	●	●	●	●	●	●		●					●		●		●						●		Djibouti
1978	●	●	●	●	●[6]		●	●	●	●	●	●	●	●	●	●	●	●		●	●					●			●		●			●			Dominica
1945	●	●	●	●			●	●	●	●	●	●	●	●	●	●	●	●		●						●							●[4]	●			Dominican Republic
1945	●	●	●	●			●	●	●	●	●	●	●	●	●	●	●	●		●						●								●[10]			Ecuador
1945	●	●	●	●	●		●	●	●	●	●	●	●	●	●	●	●	●		●					●		●							●			Egypt
1945	●	●	●	●	●		●	●	●	●	●	●	●	●	●	●	●	●		●						●								●			El Salvador
1968	●	●	●	●	●[6]		●	●	●	●	●	●		●	●	●	●	●		●							●		●					●			Equatorial Guinea
1991					●[4]									●				●																			Estonia
1945	●	●	●	●			●	●	●	●	●	●	●	●	●	●	●	●		●							●							●			Ethiopia

membership in international organizations	country
UN organs★ and affiliated intergovernmental organizations	

Government and international organizations (continued)

country	date of independence[a]	date of current or last constitution[b]	type of government	executive branch[c]		legislative branch[d]		admin. subdivisions		seaward claims	
				chief of state	head of government	upper house (members)	lower house (members)	first-order (number)	second-order (number)	territorial (nautical miles)	fishing/ economic (nautical miles)
Faeroe Islands	—	April 1, 1948	part of Danish realm	Danish monarch [29]		32	—	7	50	3	200
Fiji	Oct. 10, 1970	July 25, 1990	republic	president	prime minister	34	70	15	—	12[21]	200[21]
Finland	Dec. 6, 1917	July 17, 1919	republic	president	prime minister	200	—	12	460	4	12
France	August 843	Oct. 4, 1958	republic	president	prime minister	321	577	22	96	12	200
French Guiana	—	Feb. 28, 1983	overseas dept. (Fr.)	French president [30]		19	31	2	21	12	200
French Polynesia	—	Sept. 6, 1984	overseas territory (Fr.)	French president [31]		41	—	5	48	12	200
Gabon	Aug. 17, 1960	March 26, 1991	republic	president	prime minister	120	—	9	37	12	200
Gambia, The	Feb. 18, 1965	April 24, 1970	republic	president		50	—	7	35	12	200
Gaza Strip	—	—	Israeli military	—	area commander	—	—	3	—	—	—
Georgia	April 9, 1991	1921[32]	republic	president	prime minister	234	—	...	65[8]	...	...
Germany	May 5, 1955	May 23, 1949	federal republic	president	chancellor	68	662	16	543	...	200
Ghana	March 6, 1957	April 28, 1992[22, 33]	republic[1]	chairman PNDC		...	...	10	110	12	200
Gibraltar	—	May 30, 1969	colony (U.K.)	British monarch	governor	18	—	—	—	3	200
Greece	Feb. 3, 1830	June 11, 1975	republic	president	prime minister	300	—	13	52	6	[3]
Greenland	—	May 1, 1979	part of Danish realm	Danish monarch [34]		27	—	3	18	3	200
Grenada	Feb. 7, 1974	Feb. 7, 1974	constitutional monarchy	British monarch	prime minister	13	15	9	—	12	200
Guadeloupe	—	Feb. 28, 1983	overseas dept. (Fr.)	French president [30]		42	41	3	34	12	200
Guam	—	Aug. 1, 1950	territory (U.S.)	U.S. president	governor	21	—	19	—	12	200
Guatemala	Sept. 15, 1821	Jan. 14, 1986	republic	president		116	—	22	330	12	200
Guernsey	—	Jan. 1, 1949[26]	crown dependency (U.K.)	British monarch[35]	bailiff	60	—	1	2	3	200
Guinea	Oct. 2, 1958	Dec. 23, 1990[2]	republic	president CTRN		15[28]	—	31	175	12	200
Guinea-Bissau	Sept. 10, 1974	May 16, 1984	republic[1]	president	prime minister	150	—	9	37	12	200
Guyana	May 26, 1966	Oct. 6, 1980	cooperative republic	president		65	—	10	26	12	200
Haiti	Jan. 1, 1804	March 29, 1987	republic[36]	president[37]	prime minister	27	83	9	...	12	200
Honduras	Nov. 5, 1838	Jan. 20, 1982	republic	president		128	—	18	289	12	200
Hong Kong	—	[26]	crown colony (U.K.)	British monarch	governor	60	—	...	19	3	[3]
Hungary	Nov. 16, 1918	Oct. 18, 1989[2]	republic	president	prime minister	394	—	20	168	—	—
Iceland	June 17, 1944	June 17, 1944	republic	president	prime minister	63	—	...	201	12	200
India	Aug. 15, 1947	Jan. 26, 1950	federal republic	president	prime minister	245	545	32	474	12	200
Indonesia	Aug. 17, 1945	Aug. 17, 1945	republic	president		1,000	500	27	296	12[21]	200[21]
Iran	Oct. 7, 1906	Dec. 2–3, 1979	Islamic republic	president[38]		270	—	24	196	12	50[39]
Iraq	Oct. 3, 1932	Sept. 22, 1968[32]	republic	president		250	—	18	96	12	[3]
Ireland	Dec. 6, 1921	Dec. 29, 1937	republic	president	prime minister	60	166	32	81	3	200
Isle of Man	—	1961[26]	crown dependency (U.K.)	British monarch[35]	chief minister	10	24	24	—	3	200
Israel	May 14, 1948	June 1950[26]	republic	president	prime minister	120	—	6	232	6	[3]
Italy	March 17, 1861	Jan. 1, 1948	republic	president	prime minister	325	630	20	94	12	[3]
Jamaica	Aug. 6, 1962	Aug. 6, 1962	constitutional monarchy	British monarch	prime minister	21	60	13	—	12	[3]
Japan	c. 660 BC	May 3, 1947	constitutional monarchy	emperor	prime minister	252	512	47	3,268	12[40]	200
Jersey	—	Jan. 1, 1949[26]	crown dependency (U.K.)	British monarch[35]	bailiff	58	—	1	—	3	200
Jordan	May 25, 1946	Jan. 8, 1952	constitutional monarchy	king[16]		40	80	8	...	3	[3]
Kazakhstan	Dec. 16, 1991	June 2, 1992[41]	republic	president	prime minister	360	—	17[8]	211[8]	—	—
Kenya	Dec. 12, 1963	Dec. 12, 1963	republic	president		202	—	8	40	12	200
Kiribati	July 12, 1979	July 12, 1979	republic	president		41	—	6	23	12	200
Korea, North	Sept. 9, 1948	Dec. 27, 1972	socialist republic	president	premier	687	—	13	172	12	200
Korea, South	Aug. 15, 1948	Feb. 25, 1988	republic	president	prime minister	299	—	15	204	12[42]	12
Kuwait	June 19, 1961	Nov. 16, 1962	const. mon. (emirate)	emir[16]		50	—	5	—	12	[3]
Kyrgyzstan	Aug. 31, 1991	April 1978	republic	president	prime minister	350	—	2[8]	40[8]	—	—
Laos	Oct. 23, 1953	Aug. 15, 1991	republic	president	prime minister	79	—	17	...	—	—
Latvia	Aug. 21, 1991	Nov. 7, 1922[26]	republic	chairman SuC	prime minister	201	—	33	49	...	...
Lebanon	Nov. 26, 1941	Sept. 21, 1990	republic	president	prime minister	128	—	...	...	12	[3]
Lesotho	Oct. 4, 1966	Oct. 4, 1966	monarchy	king	chairman MC	(33)	(60)	10	...	—	—
Liberia	July 26, 1847	Jan. 6, 1986	republic[43]	president		51[28]	—	...	...	200	[3]
Libya	Dec. 24, 1951	March 2, 1977	socialist state[44]	rev. leader	sec. GPC	750	—	13	...	12[45]	[3]
Liechtenstein	July 12, 1806	Oct. 5, 1921	constitutional monarchy	prince	head of gov't.	25	—	11	—	—	—
Lithuania	Sept. 6, 1991	March 11, 1990[32]	republic	head of state	prime minister	141	—	55	81	...	...
Luxembourg	May 10, 1867	Oct. 17, 1868	constitutional monarchy	grand duke	prime minister	21[5]	60	3	12	—	—
Macau	—	May 10, 1990	special terr. (Port.)	governor		23	—	2	5	6	12
Macedonia	Sept. 1991[46]	Nov. 17, 1991	republic	president	prime minister	120	—	30[8]	—	—	—
Madagascar	June 26, 1960	Aug. 19, 1992[22]	republic[1]	[47]	prime minister	(137)	—	6	111	12	200
Malawi	July 6, 1964	July 6, 1966	republic	president		146	—	3	24	—	—
Malaysia	Aug. 31, 1957	Aug. 31, 1957	fed. const. monarchy	paramount ruler	prime minister	69	180	15	131	12	200
Maldives	July 26, 1965	Nov. 11, 1968	republic	president		48	—	19	202	21, 48	48
Mali	Sept. 22, 1960	Feb. 14, 1992	republic	president	prime minister	129	—	8	46	—	—
Malta	Sept. 21, 1964	Dec. 13, 1974	republic	president	prime minister	65	—	1	—	12	25
Marshall Islands	Dec. 22, 1990	May 1, 1979	republic[49]	president		12[5]	33	26	—	12	200
Martinique	—	Feb. 28, 1983	overseas dept. (Fr.)	French president [30]		45	41	3	34	12	200
Mauritania	Nov. 28, 1960	July 21, 1991	republic	president		56	79	13	...	70	200
Mauritius	March 12, 1968	March 12, 1992	republic	president	prime minister	70	—	11	105	12	200
Mayotte	—	Dec. 24, 1976	terr. collectivity (Fr.)	French president [50]		17	—	17	—	12	200
Mexico	Sept. 16, 1810	Feb. 5, 1917	federal republic	president		64	500	32	2,378	12	200
Micronesia	Dec. 22, 1990	May 10, 1979	federal republic[49]	president		14	—	4	—	12	200
Moldova	Aug. 27, 1991	April 1978	republic	president	prime minister	380	—	...	40[8]	—	—
Monaco	Feb. 2, 1861	Dec. 17, 1962	constitutional monarchy	prince	min. of state	18	—	5	—	12	[3]
Mongolia	March 13, 1921	Feb. 12, 1992	republic	president	prime minister	76	—	21	380	—	—
Morocco	March 2, 1956	Sept. 4, 1992[22]	constitutional monarchy	king[16]		306	—	43[51]	...	12	200
Mozambique	June 25, 1975	Nov. 30, 1990	republic	president		249	—	11	143	12	200
Myanmar (Burma)	Jan. 4, 1948	Jan. 4, 1974	republic	chairman SLORC		(492)	—	14	314	12	200
Namibia	March 21, 1990	March 21, 1990	republic	president		72	—	13	—	12	200
Nauru	Jan. 31, 1968	Jan. 31, 1968	republic	president		18	—	14	—	12	200
Nepal	Nov. 13, 1769	Nov. 9, 1990	constitutional monarchy	king	prime minister	60	205	14	75	—	—
Netherlands, The	March 30, 1814	Feb. 17, 1983	constitutional monarchy	monarch	prime minister	75	150	12	647	12	200
Netherlands Antilles	—	Dec. 29, 1954	integral part of Neth.	Dutch monarch [9]		22	—	5	—	12	200
New Caledonia	—	[26]	overseas territory (Fr.)	French president [53]		54	—	3	32	12	200
New Zealand	Sept. 26, 1907	June 30, 1852[26]	constitutional monarchy	British monarch	prime minister	97	—	14	73	12	200
Nicaragua	April 30, 1838	Jan. 9, 1987	republic	president		92	—	16	134	200	200

membership in international organizations

United Nations (date of admission) · UN organs★ and affiliated intergovernmental organizations · Commonwealth of Nations · regional multipurpose · economic · country

UN (adm.)	UNCTAD★e	UNICEF★f	ICJ★	FAO	GATT	IAEAe	IBRD	ICAO	IDA	IFC	ILO	IMF	IMO	ITUe	UNESCO	UNIDO	UPUe	WHO	WIPOe	WMO	Commonwealth	ASEAN	EC	GCC	LASg	OAS	OAU	SPC	ACP	ADB	CARICOM	ECOWAS	EEC	I-ADB	IDBg	OPEC	country
—																	•																				Faeroe Islands
1970	•	•	•	•	•6	•	•	•	•	•	•	•	•	•	•	•	•	•	•	•	•							•	•	•							Fiji
1955	•	•	•	•	•	•	•	•	•	•	•	•	•	•	•	•	•	•	•	•			•											•			Finland
1945	•	•	•	•	•	•	•	•	•	•	•	•	•	•	•	•	•	•	•	•			•					•		•			•	•			France
—																	•																				French Guiana
—																	•			•								•									French Polynesia
1960	•	•	•	•	•	•	•	•	•	•	•	•	•	•	•	•	•	•	•	•							•		•	•					•	•	Gabon
1965	•	•	•	•	•	•	•	•	•	•	•	•	•	•	•	•	•	•	•	•	•						•		•	•		•			•		Gambia, The
—																																					Gaza Strip
1992						•						•					•	•		•																	Georgia
1973	•	•	•	•	•	•	•	•	•	•	•	•	•	•	•	•	•	•	•	•			•							•			•	•			Germany
1957	•	•	•	•	•	•	•	•	•	•	•	•	•	•	•	•	•	•	•	•	•						•		•	•		•					Ghana
—																							•														Gibraltar
1945	•	•	•	•	•	•	•	•	•	•	•	•	•	•	•	•	•	•	•	•			•										•				Greece
—																	•																				Greenland
1974	•	•	•	•	•6	•	•	•	•	•	•	•	•	•	•	•	•	•	•	•	•					•			•		•						Grenada
—																	•																				Guadeloupe
—																	•											•									Guam
1945	•	•	•	•	•	•	•	•	•	•	•	•	•	•	•	•	•	•	•	•						•			•					•			Guatemala
—																	•																				Guernsey
1958	•	•	•	•	•	•	•	•	•	•	•	•	•	•	•	•	•	•	•	•							•		•	•		•			•		Guinea
1974	•	•	•	•	•6	•	•	•	•	•	•	•	•	•	•	•	•	•	•	•							•		•	•		•			•		Guinea-Bissau
1966	•	•	•	•	•	•	•	•	•	•	•	•	•	•	•	•	•	•	•	•	•					•			•		•4			•			Guyana
1945	•	•	•	•	•6	•	•	•	•	•	•	•	•	•	•	•	•	•	•	•						•			•		•4			•			Haiti
1945	•	•	•	•	•	•	•	•	•	•	•	•	•	•	•	•	•	•	•	•						•			•					•			Honduras
—														•10																•							Hong Kong
1955	•	•	•	•	•	•	•	•	•	•	•	•	•	•	•	•	•	•	•	•																	Hungary
1946	•	•	•	•	•	•	•	•	•	•	•	•	•	•	•	•	•	•	•	•																	Iceland
1945	•	•	•	•	•	•	•	•	•	•	•	•	•	•	•	•	•	•	•	•	•									•							India
1950	•	•	•	•	•	•	•	•	•	•	•	•	•	•	•	•	•	•	•	•		•								•						•	Indonesia
1945	•	•	•	•		•	•	•	•	•	•	•	•	•	•	•	•	•	•	•															•	•	Iran
1945	•	•	•	•		•	•	•	•	•	•	•	•	•	•	•	•	•	•	•					•										•	•	Iraq
1955	•	•	•	•	•	•	•	•	•	•	•	•	•	•	•	•	•	•	•	•			•										•				Ireland
—																	•																				Isle of Man
1949	•	•	•	•	•	•	•	•	•	•	•	•	•	•	•	•	•	•	•	•														•			Israel
1955	•	•	•	•	•	•	•	•	•	•	•	•	•	•	•	•	•	•	•	•			•							•			•	•			Italy
1962	•	•	•	•	•	•	•	•	•	•	•	•	•	•	•	•	•	•	•	•	•					•			•		•			•			Jamaica
1956	•	•	•	•	•	•	•	•	•	•	•	•	•	•	•	•	•	•	•	•										•				•			Japan
—																	•																	•			Jersey
1955	•	•	•	•	•	•	•	•	•	•	•	•	•	•	•	•	•	•	•	•					•										•		Jordan
1992					•10	•	•					•			•		•	•		•																	Kazakhstan
1963	•	•	•	•	•	•	•	•	•	•	•	•	•	•	•	•	•	•	•	•	•						•		•	•							Kenya
—					•6												•	•		•	•							•	•	•							Kiribati
1991	•	•	•	•		•		•			•			•	•	•	•	•		•										•							Korea, North
1991	•	•	•	•		•	•	•	•	•	•	•	•	•	•	•	•	•	•	•										•							Korea, South
1963	•	•	•	•	•	•	•	•	•	•	•	•	•	•	•	•	•	•	•	•				•	•										•	•	Kuwait
1992						•	•					•			•		•	•		•																	Kyrgyzstan
1955	•	•	•	•		•	•	•	•	•	•	•	•	•	•	•	•	•	•	•										•							Laos
1991	•	•	•	•		•	•					•			•		•	•		•																	Latvia
1945	•	•	•	•		•	•	•	•	•	•	•	•	•	•	•	•	•	•	•					•										•		Lebanon
1966	•	•	•	•	•	•	•	•	•	•	•	•	•	•	•	•	•	•	•	•	•						•		•	•							Lesotho
1945	•	•	•	•	•	•	•	•	•	•	•	•	•	•	•	•	•	•	•	•							•		•	•		•					Liberia
1955	•	•	•	•		•	•	•	•	•	•	•	•	•	•	•	•	•	•	•					•		•								•	•	Libya
1990			•														•	•		•														•			Liechtenstein
1991	•					•						•			•		•	•		•																	Lithuania
1945	•	•	•	•	•	•	•	•	•	•	•	•	•	•	•	•	•	•	•	•			•										•				Luxembourg
—													•10				•			•																	Macau
—																		•																			Macedonia
1960	•	•	•	•	•	•	•	•	•	•	•	•	•	•	•	•	•	•	•	•							•		•	•							Madagascar
1964	•	•	•	•	•	•	•	•	•	•	•	•	•	•	•	•	•	•	•	•	•						•		•	•							Malawi
1957	•	•	•	•	•	•	•	•	•	•	•	•	•	•	•	•	•	•	•	•	•	•								•					•		Malaysia
1965	•	•	•	•	•	•	•	•	•	•	•	•	•	•	•	•	•	•	•	•	•									•					•		Maldives
1960	•	•	•	•	•6	•	•	•	•	•	•	•	•	•	•	•	•	•	•	•							•		•	•		•			•		Mali
1964	•	•	•	•	•	•	•	•	•	•	•	•	•	•	•	•	•	•	•	•	•									•			•10				Malta
1991	•			•			•					•					•	•		•								•		•							Marshall Islands
—																	•																				Martinique
1961	•	•	•	•	•	•	•	•	•	•	•	•	•	•	•	•	•	•	•	•					•		•		•	•					•		Mauritania
1968	•	•	•	•	•	•	•	•	•	•	•	•	•	•	•	•	•	•	•	•	•						•		•	•							Mauritius
—																																					Mayotte
1945	•	•	•	•	•	•	•	•	•	•	•	•	•	•	•	•	•	•	•	•						•					•4			•			Mexico
1991	•			•			•					•					•	•		•								•		•							Micronesia
1992					•4	•	•					•			•		•	•		•																	Moldova
—														•	•		•	•		•																	Monaco
1961	•	•	•	•	•	•	•	•	•	•	•	•	•	•	•	•	•	•	•	•										•							Mongolia
1956	•	•	•	•	•	•	•	•	•	•	•	•	•	•	•	•	•	•	•	•					•		•								•		Morocco
1975	•	•	•	•	•	•	•	•	•	•	•	•	•	•	•	•	•	•	•	•							•		•	•							Mozambique
1948	•	•	•	•	•	•	•	•	•	•	•	•	•	•	•	•	•	•	•	•										•							Myanmar (Burma)
1990	•	•	•	•		•	•	•	•	•	•	•		•	•	•	•	•		•	•						•		•	•							Namibia
—																	•				•52							•	•	•							Nauru
1955	•	•	•	•	•6	•	•	•	•	•	•	•	•	•	•	•	•	•	•	•										•							Nepal
1945	•	•	•	•	•	•	•	•	•	•	•	•	•	•	•	•	•	•	•	•			•							•			•	•			Netherlands, The
—														•10			•			•																	Netherlands Antilles
—																	•											•									New Caledonia
1945	•	•	•	•	•	•	•	•	•	•	•	•	•	•	•	•	•	•	•	•	•							•		•							New Zealand
1945	•	•	•	•	•	•	•	•	•	•	•	•	•	•	•	•	•	•	•	•						•								•			Nicaragua

Government and international organizations (continued)

country	date of independence[a]	date of current or last constitution[b]	type of government	executive branch[c] chief of state	head of government	legislative branch[d] upper house (members)	lower house (members)	admin. subdivisions first-order (number)	second-order (number)	seaward claims territorial (nautical miles)	fishing/economic (nautical miles)
Niger	Aug. 3, 1960	*Sept. 24, 1989*	republic[1]	president	prime minister	15	—	8	35	—	—
Nigeria	Oct. 1, 1960	*Oct. 1, 1979*	federal republic[1]	president	president	91[54]	593[54]	31	589	30	200
Northern Mariana Is.	—	Jan. 9, 1978	commonwealth (U.S.)	U.S. president	governor	9	15	4	—	3	200
Norway	June 7, 1905	May 17, 1814	constitutional monarchy	king	prime minister	165	—	19	448	4	200
Oman	Dec. 20, 1951	—	monarchy (sultanate)	—— sultan ——		60[5]	—	59	—	12	200
Pakistan	Aug. 14, 1947	Aug. 14, 1973	federal Islamic republic	president	prime minister	87	217	5[55]	17[55]	12	200
Palau	—	Jan. 1, 1981	trust territory (U.S.)	high commissioner	president	14	16	16	—	3	200
Panama	Nov. 3, 1903	Oct. 11, 1972[32]	republic	—— president[56] ——		67	—	11	67	200	3
Papua New Guinea	Sept. 16, 1975	Sept. 16, 1975	constitutional monarchy	British monarch	prime minister	109	—	20	...	12[21]	200[21]
Paraguay	May 14, 1811	June 22, 1992	republic	—— president ——		36	72	20	206	—	—
Peru	July 28, 1821	*July 28, 1980*	republic	—— president ——		80[28]	—	25	185	200	200
Philippines	July 4, 1946	Feb. 11, 1987	republic	—— president ——		24	200[57]	14	73	48	200[21]
Poland	Nov. 10, 1918	July 22, 1952	republic	president	prime minister	100	460	49	2,904	12	200
Portugal	c. 1140	April 25, 1976	parliamentary state	president	prime minister	230	—	22	305	12	200
Puerto Rico	—	July 25, 1952	commonwealth (U.S.)	U.S. president	governor	29	53	78	...	12	200
Qatar	Sept. 3, 1971	July 1970[32]	monarchy	—— emir ——		35[5]	—	9	—	3	58
Réunion	—	Feb. 28, 1983	overseas dept. (Fr.)	French president	[30]	45	45	4	24	12	200
Romania	May 21, 1877	Dec. 13, 1991	republic	president	prime minister	143	341	41	260	12	200
Russia	Dec. 8, 1991	July 7, 1992[59]	federal republic	president	prime minister	1,068	252	86[8]	1,846[8]	...	...
Rwanda	July 1, 1962	June 10, 1991	republic[1]	president		70	—	10	143	—	—
St. Kitts and Nevis	Sept. 19, 1983	Sept. 19, 1983	constitutional monarchy	British monarch	prime minister	15	—	1	—	12	200
St. Lucia	Feb. 22, 1979	Feb. 22, 1979	constitutional monarchy	British monarch	prime minister	11	17	8	—	12	200
St. Vincent	Oct. 27, 1979	Oct. 27, 1979	constitutional monarchy	British monarch	prime minister	21	—	7	—	12	200
San Marino	855	Oct. 8, 1600	republic	—— captains-regent (2) ——		60	—	9	—	—	—
São Tomé and Príncipe	July 12, 1975	Sept. 10, 1990	republic	president	prime minister	55	—	2	7	12[21]	200[21]
Saudi Arabia	Sept. 23, 1932	—	monarchy	—— king ——		—	—	14	...	12	3
Senegal	Aug. 20, 1960	March 7, 1963	republic	—— president[16] ——		120	—	10	30	12	200
Seychelles	June 29, 1976	June 5, 1979	republic	—— president ——		25	—	...	...	12	200
Sierra Leone	April 27, 1961	*Oct. 1, 1991*	republic	—— chairman SCS ——		(127)	—	...	...	200	3
Singapore	Aug. 9, 1965	June 3, 1959	republic	president		87	—	...	...	3	12
Slovenia	June 25, 1991	Dec. 23, 1991	republic	president	prime minister	40[60]	90[60]	58	...	...	...
Solomon Islands	July 7, 1978	July 7, 1978	constitutional monarchy	British monarch	prime minister	38	—	8	—	12[21]	200[21]
Somalia	July 1, 1960	July 1, 1960	republic[61]	president	prime minister	...	...	...	...	200	200
South Africa	May 31, 1910	Sept. 3, 1984	republic	—— state president ——		308[62]	—	4[63]	—	12	200
Bophuthatswana	Dec. 6, 1977[64]	Dec. 6, 1977	republic	—— president ——		108	—	12	76	—	—
Ciskei	Dec. 4, 1981[64]	*Dec. 4, 1981*	republic	—chairman of military committee—		(87)	—	7	42	—	—
Transkei	Oct. 26, 1976[64]	*Dec. 1963*	republic	—— head of military council ——		(150)	—	9	28	—	—
Venda	Sept. 13, 1979[64]	*Sept. 13, 1979*	republic	—— head of state ——		(92)	—	4	28	—	—
Spain	1492	Dec. 29, 1978	constitutional monarchy	king	prime minister	250	350	17	50	12	200
Sri Lanka	Feb. 4, 1948	Sept. 7, 1978	republic	—— president ——		225	—	25	...	12	200
Sudan, The	Jan. 1, 1956	*Oct. 10, 1985*	republic	—— president CCRNS ——		300[28]	—	9	66	12	3
Suriname	Nov. 25, 1975	Nov. 25, 1987	republic	—— president ——		51	—	9	—	12	200
Swaziland	Sept. 6, 1968	*Sept. 6, 1968*	monarchy	—— king[16] ——		(20)	(50)	4	40	—	—
Sweden	before 836	Jan. 1, 1975	constitutional monarchy	king	prime minister	349	—	24	284	12	200
Switzerland	Sept. 22, 1499	May 29, 1874	federal state	—— president FC ——		46	200	26	3,003	—	—
Syria	April 17, 1946	March 14, 1973	republic	—— president ——		250	—	14	59	35	3
Taiwan	Oct. 25, 1945	Dec. 25, 1947	republic	president	premier	403	161[60]	3	21	24	200
Tajikistan	Sept. 9, 1991	April 1978	republic	president	prime minister	80[28]	—	3[8]	45[8]	—	—
Tanzania	Dec. 9, 1961	April 25, 1977	republic	—— president ——		255	—	25	99	12	200
Thailand	1350	Dec. 9, 1991	constitutional monarchy	king	prime minister	270	360	73	655	12	200
Togo	April 27, 1960	Sept. 27, 1992[22]	republic[1]	president	prime minister	79[28]	—	5	21	30	200
Tonga	June 4, 1970	Nov. 4, 1875	constitutional monarchy	—— monarch[65] ——		31	—	5	23	12	200
Trinidad and Tobago	Aug. 31, 1962	July 27, 1976	republic	president	prime minister	31	36	11	...	12	200
Tunisia	March 20, 1956	June 1, 1959	republic	president	prime minister	141	—	23	245	12	3
Turkey	Oct. 29, 1923	Nov. 7, 1982	republic	president	prime minister	450	—	73	829	12[66]	200[67]
Turkmenistan	Oct. 27, 1991	May 18, 1992	republic	—— president ——		50	—	3[8]	41[8]	—	—
Tuvalu	Oct. 1, 1978	Sept. 15, 1986	constitutional monarchy	British monarch	prime minister	12	—	8	—	12	200
Uganda	Oct. 9, 1962	*Sept. 8, 1967*	republic[1]	—— president[16] ——		278[28]	—	38	...	—	—
Ukraine	Aug. 24, 1991	April 1978	republic	president	prime minister	450	—	25[8]	479[8]	...	...
United Arab Emirates	Dec. 2, 1971	Dec. 2, 1971[32]	federation of emirates	president	prime minister	40[5]	—	7	—	12	200
United Kingdom	Oct. 14, 1066	[68]	constitutional monarchy	monarch	prime minister	1,191[5]	651	3[69]	82	3	200
United States	July 4, 1776	March 4, 1789	federal republic	—— president ——		100	435[70]	51	3,141	12	200
Uruguay	Aug. 25, 1828	Feb. 15, 1967	republic	—— president ——		31	99	19	...	200	200
Uzbekistan	Aug. 31, 1991	July 1992[41]	republic	president	prime minister	550	—	11[8]	149[8]	—	—
Vanuatu	July 30, 1980	July 30, 1980	republic	president	prime minister	46	—	11	...	12[21]	200[21]
Venezuela	July 5, 1811	Jan. 23, 1961	federal republic	—— president ——		52	201	24	286	12	200
Vietnam	Sept. 2, 1945	April 15, 1992	socialist republic	president	prime minister	395	—	53	...	12	200
Virgin Islands (U.S.)	—	July 22, 1954	territory (U.S.)	U.S. president	governor	15	—	2	—	12	200
West Bank	—	—	Israeli military	—	area commander	—	—	7	—	—	—
Western Sahara	—	—	annexture of Morocco			—	—	4	8	12	—
Western Samoa	Jan. 1, 1962	Oct. 28, 1960	[72]	head of state	prime minister	48	—	...	...	12	200
Yemen	December 1918	May 16, 1991	republic[1]	president PC	prime minister CM	301	—	17	...	12	...
Yugoslavia	Dec. 1, 1918	April 27, 1992	federal republic	president	prime minister	40	138	2	2	—	—
Zaire	June 30, 1960	Feb. 15, 1978	republic[1]	president	prime minister	222	—	11	41	12	200
Zambia	Oct. 24, 1964	August, 1991	republic	—— president ——		150[57]	—	9	53	—	—
Zimbabwe	April 18, 1980	April 18, 1980	republic	—— president ——		150	—	8	...	—	—

[1]Transitional government. [2]Transitional constitution. [3]Territorial sea claim assumed to claim fishing/economic rights within the same zone. [4]Observer status. [5]Body with limited or no legislative authority. [6]Full membership pending. [7]President of France and Bishop of Urgel, Spain. [8]1990. [9]Executive responsibilities divided between (for The Netherlands) the governor and (locally) the prime minister. [10]Associate member. [11]Formally a constitutional monarchy. [12]Defined by equidistant line. [13]Executive responsibilities divided between (for the U.K.) the governor and (locally) the premier of the Cabinet. [14]Resembles a constitutional monarchy without a formal constitution. [15]Central government has ineffective control because of war. [16]Assisted by the prime minister. [17]Cambodia Peace Accord. [18]Executive responsibilities divided between (for the UN) the head of the UN Transitional Authority in Cambodia and (locally) the chairman of the Supreme National Council assisted by delegation heads. [19]Governor-general can exercise all the powers of the reigning monarch of the Commonwealth. Royal assent to the monarch is a matter of choice. [20]Temporarily increased from 104. [21]Measured from claimed archipelagic baselines. [22]Date of referendum approving new constitution. [23]Self-governing state in free association with New Zealand. [24]Republic of Cyprus only. [25]56 seats occupied. [26]Evolving body of constitutional law. [27]Czechoslovakia will be divided into two independent countries as of Jan. 1, 1993. [28]Interim legislature. [29]Executive responsibilities divided between (for Denmark) the state commissioner and (locally) the head of the home government. [30]Executive responsibilities divided among (for France) the commissioner and (locally) the president of the General Council and president of the Regional Council. [31]Executive responsibilities divided between (for France) the high commissioner and (locally) the president of the Council of Ministers. [32]Provisional constitution. [33]Constitution scheduled to take effect Jan. 7, 1993. [34]Executive responsibilities divided between (for Denmark) the high commissioner and (locally) the prime minister. [35]Represented by the lieutenant governor. [36]Military-dominated extraconstitutional regime. [37]Office declared vacant June 1992. [38]Shares coexecutive authority with spiritual leader.

membership in international organizations

United Nations (date of admission)	UN organs★ and affiliated intergovernmental organizations																				Commonwealth of Nations	regional multipurpose							economic								country
	UNCTAD★[e]	UNICEF★[f]	ICJ★	FAO	GATT	IAEA[e]	IBRD	ICAO	IDA	IFC	ILO	IMF	IMO	ITU[e]	UNESCO	UNIDO	UPU[e]	WHO	WIPO[e]	WMO		ASEAN	EC	GCC	LAS[g]	OAS	OAU	SPC	ACP	ADB	CARICOM	ECOWAS	EEC	I-ADB	IDB[g]	OPEC	
1960	●	●	●	●	●	●	●	●	●	●	●	●		●	●	●	●	●	●	●							●		●			●			●		Niger
1960	●	●	●	●	●	●	●	●	●	●	●	●	●	●	●	●	●	●		●	●						●		●			●				●	Nigeria
—																	●											●									Northern Mariana Is.
1945	●	●	●	●	●	●	●	●	●	●	●	●	●	●	●	●	●	●	●	●										●				●			Norway
1971	●	●	●	●			●	●	●	●		●	●	●	●	●	●	●		●				●	●										●		Oman
1947	●	●	●	●	●	●	●	●	●	●	●	●	●	●	●	●	●	●	●	●	●									●					●		Pakistan
—		●															●											●									Palau
1945	●	●	●	●		●	●	●	●	●	●	●	●	●	●	●	●	●	●	●						●								●			Panama
1975	●	●	●	●	●[6]		●	●	●	●	●	●	●	●	●	●	●	●		●	●							●	●	●							Papua New Guinea
1945	●	●	●	●	●[6]	●	●	●	●	●	●	●		●	●	●	●	●	●	●						●								●			Paraguay
1945	●	●	●	●	●	●	●	●	●	●	●	●	●	●	●	●	●	●	●	●						●								●			Peru
1945	●	●	●	●	●	●	●	●	●	●	●	●	●	●	●	●	●	●	●	●		●								●							Philippines
1945	●	●	●	●	●	●	●	●	●	●	●	●	●	●	●	●	●	●	●	●																	Poland
1955	●	●	●	●	●	●	●	●		●	●	●	●	●	●	●	●	●	●	●			●										●	●			Portugal
—																	●	●[10]													●[4]						Puerto Rico
1971	●		●	●	●[6]	●	●	●			●	●	●	●	●	●	●	●	●	●				●	●										●	●	Qatar
—																	●																				Réunion
1955	●	●	●	●	●	●	●	●	●	●	●	●	●	●	●	●	●	●	●	●																	Romania
1991	●	●				●					●	●	●	●	●	●	●	●	●	●																	Russia
1962	●	●	●	●	●		●	●	●	●	●	●		●	●	●	●	●	●	●							●		●								Rwanda
1983	●	●	●	●	●[6]		●		●			●			●	●	●	●			●					●			●		●						St. Kitts and Nevis
1979	●	●	●	●	●[6]		●	●	●	●	●	●	●		●	●	●	●		●	●					●			●		●						St. Lucia
1980	●	●	●	●	●[6]		●	●	●			●	●	●	●	●	●	●			●					●			●		●						St. Vincent
1992	●	●	●					●			●	●		●	●		●	●																			San Marino
1975	●	●	●	●	●[6]		●	●	●		●	●		●	●	●	●	●		●							●		●								São Tomé and Príncipe
1945	●	●	●	●		●	●	●	●	●	●	●	●	●	●	●	●	●	●	●				●	●										●	●	Saudi Arabia
1960	●	●	●	●	●	●	●	●	●	●	●	●	●	●	●	●	●	●	●	●							●		●			●			●		Senegal
1976	●	●	●	●	●[6]		●	●		●	●	●	●		●	●	●	●		●	●						●		●								Seychelles
1961	●	●	●	●	●	●	●	●	●	●	●	●	●	●	●	●	●	●	●	●	●						●		●			●			●		Sierra Leone
1965	●	●	●		●	●	●	●		●	●	●	●	●			●	●	●	●	●	●								●							Singapore
1992																		●																			Slovenia
1978	●	●	●	●	●[6]		●	●	●	●	●	●	●	●			●	●		●	●							●	●	●							Solomon Islands
1960	●	●	●	●			●	●	●	●	●	●	●	●	●	●	●	●	●	●					●		●		●						●		Somalia
1945	●		●		●	●	●	●	●	●		●		●				●	●																		South Africa
—																																					Bophuthatswana
—																																					Ciskei
—																																					Transkei
—																																					Venda
1955	●	●	●	●	●	●	●	●	●	●	●	●	●	●	●	●	●	●	●	●			●							●			●	●			Spain
1955	●	●	●	●	●	●	●	●	●	●	●	●	●	●	●	●	●	●	●	●	●									●							Sri Lanka
1956	●	●	●	●		●	●	●	●	●	●	●	●	●	●	●	●	●	●	●					●		●		●						●		Sudan, The
1975	●	●	●	●	●		●	●			●	●	●	●	●	●	●	●	●	●						●			●		●[4]			●			Suriname
1968	●	●	●	●	●[6]		●	●	●	●	●	●		●	●	●	●	●	●	●	●						●		●								Swaziland
1946	●	●	●	●	●	●	●	●	●	●	●	●	●	●	●	●	●	●	●	●										●				●			Sweden
—	●	●	●	●	●	●	●	●			●	●	●	●	●	●	●	●	●	●										●				●			Switzerland
1945	●	●	●	●		●	●	●	●	●	●	●	●	●	●	●	●	●		●					●										●		Syria
—					●[4]																									●							Taiwan
1992												●						●																			Tajikistan
1961	●	●	●	●	●	●	●	●	●	●	●	●	●	●	●	●	●	●	●	●	●						●		●								Tanzania
1946	●	●	●	●	●	●	●	●	●	●	●	●	●	●	●	●	●	●	●	●		●								●							Thailand
1960	●	●	●	●	●		●	●	●	●	●	●	●	●	●	●	●	●	●	●							●		●			●					Togo
—	●	●		●	●[6]		●	●	●	●		●		●	●	●	●	●			●							●	●	●							Tonga
1962	●	●	●	●	●		●	●	●	●	●	●	●	●	●	●	●	●	●	●	●					●			●		●			●			Trinidad and Tobago
1956	●	●	●	●	●	●	●	●	●	●	●	●	●	●	●	●	●	●	●	●					●		●								●		Tunisia
1945	●	●	●	●	●	●	●	●	●	●	●	●	●	●	●	●	●	●	●	●										●			●[10]		●		Turkey
1992					●[4]							●						●																			Turkmenistan
—		●			●[6]										●		●				●[52]							●	●								Tuvalu
1962	●	●	●	●	●	●	●	●	●	●	●	●		●	●	●	●	●	●	●	●						●		●						●		Uganda
1945	●	●			●[4]	●					●	●		●	●	●	●	●	●	●																	Ukraine
1971	●	●	●	●	●[6]	●	●	●	●	●	●	●	●	●	●	●	●	●	●	●				●	●										●	●	United Arab Emirates
1945	●	●	●	●	●	●	●	●	●	●	●	●	●	●		●	●	●	●	●	●		●					●		●			●	●			United Kingdom
1945	●	●	●	●	●	●	●	●	●	●	●	●	●	●		●	●	●	●	●						●		●		●				●			United States
1945	●	●	●	●	●	●	●	●		●	●	●	●	●	●	●	●	●	●	●						●								●			Uruguay
1992												●						●																			Uzbekistan
1981	●	●	●	●			●	●	●	●		●	●	●		●	●	●		●	●							●	●	●							Vanuatu
1945	●	●	●	●	●	●	●	●		●	●	●	●	●	●	●	●	●	●	●						●					●[4]			●		●	Venezuela
1977	●	●	●	●		●	●	●	●	●	●	●	●	●	●	●	●	●	●	●										●							Vietnam
—																	●																				Virgin Islands (U.S.)
—																																					West Bank
—																											●[71]										Western Sahara
1976	●	●	●	●			●		●	●		●		●	●		●	●			●							●	●	●							Western Samoa
1947	●	●	●	●			●	●	●	●	●	●	●	●	●	●	●	●	●	●					●										●		Yemen
[73]	●		●	●	●	●	●	●	●	●	●	●	●	●	●	●	●	●	●	●														●			Yugoslavia
1960	●	●	●	●	●	●	●	●	●	●	●	●	●	●	●	●	●	●	●	●							●		●								Zaire
1964	●	●	●	●	●	●	●	●	●	●	●	●		●	●	●	●	●	●	●	●						●		●								Zambia
1980	●	●	●	●	●	●	●	●	●	●	●	●		●	●	●	●	●	●	●	●						●		●								Zimbabwe

[39]Sea of Oman only; median line boundaries in the Persian Gulf. [40]3 nautical miles in 5 straits. [41]Draft constitution approved by legislature. [42]3 nautical miles in Korean Strait. [43]Interim administration of Economic Community of West African States established on Nov. 10, 1990. [44]Formally a *jamahiriya,* translated as "the masses of people." [45]Based on Gulf of Sidra closing line (32°30′ N), in part. [46]Limited international recognition as of November 1992. [47]Chief of state: president; chief of the transitional regime: president of the High State Authority. [48]Zone defined by geographic coordinates. [49]Self-governing state having free-association security provisions with the United States. [50]Executive responsibilities divided between (for France) the commissioner and (locally) the president of the General Council. [51]Excludes Western Sahara. [52]Special member. [53]Executive responsibilities divided between (for France) the high commissioner and (locally) the president of the Territorial Congress. [54]Elected July 1992; to be seated in 1993. [55]Excluding six federally administered tribal areas. [56]Assisted by vice presidents. [57]Elective seats only. [58]Limits of continental shelf or median line boundaries. [59]Date of presidential decree strengthening the role of the Security Council. [60]Pending elections. [61]No effective central government in November 1992. [62]Total of 3 legislative houses. [63]Excludes national states. [64]Recognized by South Africa and each other only. [65]Assisted by Privy Council. [66]Black Sea and Mediterranean Sea; 6 nautical miles in Aegean Sea. [67]Black Sea only. [68]Based on evolving body of statutes and common law. [69]England and Wales form a single administrative entity. [70]Excludes 5 nonvoting delegates. [71]Membership held by the Sahrawi Arab Democratic Republic. [72]Mixed political system approximating a constitutional monarchy. [73]Yugoslavia's seat in the UN General Assembly was not recognized as of Sept. 15, 1992.

Area and population

This table provides the area and population for each of the countries of the world and for all but the smallest political dependencies having a permanent civilian population. The data represent the latest published and unpublished data for both the surveyed area of the countries and their populations, the latter both as of a single year (1992) to provide the best comparability and as of the most recent census to provide the fullest comparison of certain demographic measures that are not always available in estimated form between successive national censuses. The 1992 midyear estimates represent a combination of national, United Nations (UN) or other international organizations, and *Encyclopædia Britannica* estimates so as to give the best fit to available published series, to take account of unpublished information received in correspondence, and to incorporate the results of very recent censuses for which published analyses are not yet available.

One principal point to bear in mind when studying these statistics is that all of them, whatever degree of precision may be implied by the exactness of the numbers, are estimates—all of varying, and some of suspect, accuracy—even when they *contain* a very full enumeration. The United States—which has a long tradition both of census taking and of the use of the most sophisticated analytical tools in processing the data—is unable to determine within 2.1% (the estimated 1990 undercount) its total population nationally. And that is an *average* underenumeration. In states and larger cities, where enumeration of particular populations, both legal and illegal, is most difficult, the accuracy of the enumerated count may be off as much as 4% at a state level and as much as 10% for a single city. The accuracy of census operations may approach 0.25% of civil population registers, as in the case of China. Other census operations are inherently less accurate than the Chinese. For example, Ethiopia's first-ever census in 1984 resulted in figures that were 30% or more above prevailing estimates; Nigeria's 1991 census corrected decades of miscounts and was far below prevailing estimates. An undercount of 2 to 8% is more typical, but census operations that can assure results of 30% or more above or below prevailing estimates can still represent well-founded benchmarks from which future planning may proceed. The editors have tried to take account of the range of variation and accuracy in published data, but it is difficult to establish a value for many sources of inaccuracy unless some country or agency has made a conscientious effort to establish both the relative accuracy (precision) of its estimate and the absolute magnitude of the quantity it is trying to measure—for example, the number of people in Cambodia who died at the hands of the Khmer Rouge. Was it 1,000,000 or 2,000,000? If a figure of 1,000,000 is adopted, what is its accuracy: ± 1%, 10%, 50%? Are the original data complete or incomplete, analytically biased or unbiased, in good agreement with other published data, or isolated and inferential?

Many similar problems exist and in endless variations: What is the extent of southern European immigration to western Europe in search of jobs? How many refugees from Afghanistan, Mozambique, or Ethiopia are there in surrounding countries? How many undocumented aliens are there in the United States? How many Palestinians are there in the Middle East (they are politically inconvenient to enumerate everywhere)? How many Amerindians exist (remain, preserving their original language and a mode of life unassimilated by the larger national culture) in the countries of South America? How many people have died or emigrated as a result of the civil violence in Central America?

Area and population

country	area			population (latest estimate)					population (latest census)				
	square miles	square kilo- metres	rank	total midyear 1992	rank	density		% annual growth rate 1987–92	census year	total	male (%)	female (%)	urban (%)
						per sq mi	per sq km						
Afghanistan	251,825	652,225	41	18,052,000	47	71.7	27.7	4.9	1979	13,051,358[1]	51.4	48.6	15.1
Albania	11,100	28,748	140	3,357,000	123	302.4	116.8	1.8	1989	3,182,417	51.5	48.5	35.5
Algeria	919,595	2,381,741	11	26,401,000	35	28.7	11.1	2.7	1987[3]	23,038,942	50.1	49.9	49.7
American Samoa	77	199	205	49,600	205	644.2	249.2	3.3	1990	46,773	51.4	48.6	33.4
Andorra	181	468	191	57,100	202	315.5	122.0	3.2	1990	54,507	53.1	46.9	66.2[4]
Angola	481,354	1,246,700	24	10,609,000	64	22.0	8.5	2.8	1970	5,673,046	52.1	47.9	14.2
Antigua and Barbuda	171	442	193	64,000	200	374.3	144.8	0.0	1991	63,880	47.4[5]	52.6[5]	30.8[2]
Argentina	1,073,518	2,780,400	8	33,070,000	31	30.8	11.9	1.4	1991	32,608,687	49.0	51.0	86.3[6]
Armenia	11,500	29,800	139	3,426,000	122	297.9	115.0	1.1	1989	3,287,677	49.3	50.7	67.8
Aruba	75	193	206	69,100	198	921.3	358.0	2.8	1981	60,312	48.6	51.4	...
Australia	2,966,200	7,682,300	6	17,562,000	48	5.9	2.3	1.6	1991	16,849,496	49.6	50.4	85.4[7]
Austria	32,378	83,859	115	7,857,000	84	242.7	93.7	0.7	1991	7,812,100	47.4[8]	52.6[8]	55.1[8]
Azerbaijan	33,400	86,600	113	7,237,000	89	216.7	83.6	1.0	1989	7,037,867	48.7	51.3	53.8
Bahamas, The	5,382	13,939	156	264,000	172	49.1	18.9	1.8	1990	255,095	49.0	51.0	54.4[6]
Bahrain	267	692	184	531,000	159	1,988.8	767.3	3.0	1981	350,798	58.4	41.6	80.7
Bangladesh	55,598	143,998	94	110,602,000	9	1,989.3	768.1	1.8	1991	107,992,940	51.5	48.5	15.7[8]
Barbados	166	430	194	259,000	174	1,560.2	602.3	0.3	1990[3]	257,082	47.7	52.3	44.7[9]
Belarus	80,200	207,600	85	10,321,000	68	128.7	49.7	0.4	1989	10,199,709	46.9	53.1	65.5
Belgium	11,787	30,528	137	10,021,000	71	850.2	328.3	0.3	1991	9,978,681	48.9	51.1	96.9[9]
Belize	8,867	22,965	148	196,000	178	22.1	8.5	2.5	1991	184,340	51.0[10]	49.0[10]	47.3[10]
Benin	43,450	112,600	101	4,928,000	103	113.4	43.8	3.1	1992	4,855,349	47.9[11]	52.1[11]	26.5[11]
Bermuda	21	54	212	60,300	201	2,871.4	1,116.7	0.8	1991[12]	58,460	48.5	51.5	100.0
Bhutan	18,150	47,000	129	1,511,000	142	83.3	32.1	2.4	1980	1,165,000	51.4[13]	48.6[13]	3.9[13]
Bolivia	424,164	1,098,581	28	7,739,000	85	18.2	7.0	2.8	1988	6,405,100	49.7	50.3	51.3
Bosnia and Hercegovina	19,741	51,129	126	4,397,000	109	222.7	86.0	0.6	1991	4,365,639	49.7[8]	50.3[8]	36.2[8]
Botswana	224,607	581,730	47	1,359,000	144	6.1	2.3	3.4	1991	1,325,291	47.1[8]	52.9[8]	23.9
Brazil	3,286,500	8,511,996	5	151,381,000	5	46.1	17.8	1.9	1991	146,154,502	49.4	50.6	67.6[6]
Brunei	2,226	5,765	165	268,000	171	120.4	46.5	3.1	1991	260,863	53.4[8]	46.6[8]	59.4[8]
Bulgaria	42,855	110,994	103	8,985,000	76	209.7	81.0	0.0	1985	8,948,649	49.5	50.5	64.8
Burkina Faso	105,946	274,400	73	9,515,000	73	89.8	34.7	2.7	1985[3]	7,964,705	48.1	51.9	11.7
Burundi	10,740	27,816	143	5,657,000	95	526.7	203.4	2.8	1990[3]	5,356,266	48.5	51.5	5.5[9]
Cambodia	70,238	181,916	89	8,974,000	77	127.8	49.3	2.4	1981	6,684,000	50.0[15]	50.0[15]	10.3[15]
Cameroon	179,714	465,458	53	12,622,000	61	70.5	27.2	3.4	1987	10,493,655	49.0[16]	51.0[16]	38.0
Canada	3,849,674	9,970,610	2	27,737,000	33	7.2	2.8	1.5	1991	27,296,859	49.3[7]	50.7[7]	77.1[9]
Cape Verde	1,557	4,033	167	346,000	169	222.2	85.8	1.3	1990	336,798	48.0	52.0	44.8
Cayman Islands	102	264	203	28,100	212	275.5	106.4	4.2	1989	25,355	48.8	51.2	100.0
Central African Republic	240,324	622,436	43	2,930,000	126	12.2	4.7	2.3	1988	2,688,426	49.1	50.9	46.7[9]
Chad	495,755	1,284,000	21	5,961,000	93	12.0	4.6	2.5	1975	4,029,917	47.7	52.3	16.0
Chile	292,135	756,626	38	13,599,000	57	46.6	18.0	1.6	1992	13,231,803	49.0[17]	51.0[17]	82.2[17]
China	3,696,100	9,572,900	3	1,165,888,000	1	315.4	121.8	1.9	1990	1,133,682,501	51.6	48.4	26.4
Colombia	440,831	1,141,748	27	34,252,000	30	77.7	30.0	2.0	1985	30,062,193	49.5	50.5	67.0[2]
Comoros	719	1,862	173	497,000	161	691.2	266.9	3.4	1980	335,150	49.9	50.1	23.2
Congo	132,047	342,000	63	2,692,000	130	20.4	7.9	5.4	1984[3]	1,909,248	48.7	51.3	52.0
Cook Islands	91	236	204	17,100	214	187.9	72.5	0.7	1986	19,369	52.2	47.8	...
Costa Rica	19,730	51,100	127	3,161,000	124	160.2	61.9	2.5	1984	2,416,809	50.0	50.0	43.9
Côte d'Ivoire	123,847	320,763	68	12,951,000	59	104.6	40.4	3.9	1975	6,702,866	51.8	48.2	32.0
Croatia	21,829	56,538	125	4,808,000	104	220.3	85.0	0.4	1991	4,784,265	48.4[8]	51.6[8]	50.8[8]
Cuba	42,804	110,861	104	10,848,000	63	253.4	97.9	1.0	1981	9,723,605	50.6	49.4	69.0
Cyprus	3,572	9,251	162	756,000	153	211.6	81.7	1.1	1982[3]	642,731	49.7	50.3	63.5
Czechoslovakia	49,382	127,899	98	15,605,000	52	316.0	122.0	0.2	1991	15,567,666	48.7	51.3	65.5[6]
Denmark	16,638	43,093	131	5,167,000	100	310.6	119.9	0.2	1991[18]	5,146,469	49.3	50.7	87.0[9]
Djibouti	8,950	23,200	147	557,000	158	62.2	24.0	3.5	1960–61	81,200	...	...	75.0[19]
Dominica	290	750	182	71,500	195	246.6	95.3	-0.4	1991	71,794	50.0	50.0	...
Dominican Republic	18,704	48,443	128	7,471,000	87	399.4	154.2	2.2	1981	5,647,977	50.1	49.9	52.0
Ecuador	104,505	270,667	74	10,607,000	65	101.5	39.2	2.1	1990	9,648,189	49.7	50.3	55.4

Still, much information is accurate, well founded, and updated regularly. The sources of these data are censuses; national population registers (cumulated periodically); registration of migration, births, deaths, and so on; sample surveys to establish demographic conditions; and the like.

The statistics provided for area and population by country are ranked, and the population densities based on those values are also provided. The population densities, for purposes of comparison within this table, are calculated on the bases of the 1991 midyear population estimate as shown and of total area of the country. Elsewhere in individual country presentations the reader may find densities calculated on more specific population figures and more specialized area bases: land area for Finland (because of its many lakes) or ice-free area for Greenland (most of which is ice cap). The data in this section conclude with the estimated average annual growth rate for the country (including both natural growth and net migration) during the five-year period, 1987–92.

In the section containing census data, information supplied includes the census total (usually de facto, the population actually present, rather than de jure, the population legally resident, who might be anywhere); the male–female breakdown; the proportion that is urban (according to the country's own definition of the term "urban," which differs very much from country to country); and finally an analysis of the age structure of the population by 15-year age groups. This last analysis may be particularly useful in distinguishing the type of population being recorded—young, fast-growing nations show a high proportion of people under 30 (some countries like Jordan or Mayotte have more than 50% of their population under 15 years), while other nations (for example Sweden, which suffered no age-group losses in World War II) exhibit quite uniform proportions.

Finally, a section is provided giving the population of each country at 10-year intervals from 1940 to 2010. The data for years past represent the best available analysis of the published data by the country itself, by the demographers of the United Nations, or by the editors of Britannica. The projections for 2000 and 2010 similarly represent the best fit of available data through the early 1990s with projected population structure and growth rates during the next two decades. The evidence of the last 20 years with respect to similar estimates published around 1970, however, shows how cloudy is the glass through which these numbers are read. In 1970 no respectable Western analyst would have imagined proposing that mainland China could achieve the degree of birth control that it apparently has since then (as evidenced by the results of 1982 and 1990 censuses); on the other hand, even the Chinese admit that their methods have been somewhat Draconian and that they have already seen some backlash in terms of higher birth rates among those who have so far postponed larger families. How much is "some" by 2000? Compound that problem with all the social, economic, political, and biological factors that can affect 220 countries' populations, and the difficulty facing the prospective compiler of such projections may be appreciated.

Specific data about the vital rates affecting the data in this table may be found in great detail in both the country statistical boxes in "The Nations of the World" section and in the *Vital statistics, marriage, family* table, beginning at page 786.

Percentages in this table for male and female population will always total 100.0, but percentages by age group may not, for reasons such as nonresponse on census forms, "don't know" responses (which are common in countries with poor birth registration systems), and the like.

age distribution (%)						population (by decade, '000s)								country
0–14	15–29	30–44	45–59	60–74	75 and older	1940	1950	1960	1970	1980	1990	2000 projection	2010 projection	
44.5	26.9	15.8	8.6	3.6	0.6	...	8,150	9,829	12,431	14,985	15,862	25,088	30,627	Afghanistan
35.4[2]	29.3[2]	17.0[2]	11.3[2]	5.4[2]	1.6[2]	1,088	1,215	1,607	2,136	2,672	3,250	3,796	4,315	Albania
43.9	28.0	13.9	8.4	4.2	1.6	7,688	8,956	10,800	14,330	18,666	25,012	32,584	40,288	Algeria
38.1	29.0	18.1	9.4	4.3	1.1	13	19	20	27	33	47	61	76	American Samoa
17.4	26.4	27.0	15.4	10.1	3.7	5	6	8	19	33	54	73	100	Andorra
41.7	23.2	17.0	7.4	3.8	1.0	3,738	4,131	4,816	5,588	7,722	10,020	13,400	18,082	Angola
44.0[5]	24.2[5]	12.0[5]	11.7[5]	—8.0[5]—		34	45	55	66	64	64	64	64	Antigua and Barbuda
30.4[6]	23.9[6]	18.8[6]	15.1[6]	9.0[6]	2.8[6]	14,169	17,150	20,611	23,788	27,820	32,195	36,461	40,687	Argentina
30.3	25.7	20.8	13.6	6.4	3.2	1,320	1,354	1,867	2,520	3,067	3,335	3,968	4,445	Armenia
25.9	30.6	21.3	12.7	7.4	2.1	31	51	57	61	60	64	72	75	Aruba
22.1	24.2	23.4	15.0	11.1	4.4	7,079	8,219	10,315	12,552	14,741	17,045	19,705	22,125	Australia
19.9[8]	23.6[8]	20.1[8]	17.1[8]	13.2[8]	6.1[8]	6,684	6,935	7,048	7,447	7,549	7,718	8,091	8,201	Austria
32.8	29.7	16.8	12.8	5.7	2.2	3,274	2,896	3,895	5,172	6,165	7,134	8,324	9,445	Azerbaijan
38.1[6]	27.8[6]	17.9[6]	9.8[6]	5.1[6]	1.3[6]	70	79	113	169	210	256	298	337	Bahamas, The
32.9	34.5	20.0	8.8	3.1	0.7	90	127	162	215	337	503	654	825	Bahrain
46.6[8]	24.6[8]	14.9[8]	8.2[8]	—5.7[8]—		41,259	45,482	54,699	68,171	88,792	106,626	128,043	153,761	Bangladesh
28.9[6]	32.3[6]	14.2[6]	11.2[6]	—13.3[6]—		179	209	232	235	249	257	266	274	Barbados
23.0	22.4	20.6	18.0	11.5	4.5	9,046	7,745	8,190	9,040	9,650	10,260	10,697	11,110	Belarus
18.2	21.8	22.5	16.9	14.1	6.6	8,301	8,639	9,153	9,690	9,859	9,967	10,236	10,512	Belgium
46.2[6]	27.1[6]	11.8[6]	8.4[6]	4.7[6]	1.8[6]	56	68	90	120	146	187	230	269	Belize
48.7[11]	22.2[11]	13.6[11]	—14.8[11]—			...	2,046	2,273	2,693	3,459	4,630	6,369	8,745	Benin
22.7[6]	27.5[6]	22.2[6]	15.7[6]	9.0[6]	2.9[6]	31	37	43	53	55	59	65	70	Bermuda
39.2[14]	26.5[14]	16.3[14]	10.9[14]	—7.1[14]—		500	726	853	1,045	1,165	1,442	1,812	2,266	Bhutan
41.1	25.9	17.0	9.5	4.7	1.3	2,508	2,765	3,405	4,265	5,579	7,322	9,668	12,699	Bolivia
27.5[8]	29.0[8]	19.2[8]	15.8[8]	6.3[8]	2.0[8]	...	2,662	3,240	3,703	4,107	4,347	4,601	4,871	Bosnia and Hercegovina
56.5[8]	19.9[8]	10.2[8]	6.6[8]	3.4[8]	3.4[8]	278	407	490	581	905	1,270	1,782	2,500	Botswana
39.1[6]	28.6[6]	16.4[6]	10.0[6]	—5.9[6]—		41,525	52,901	71,539	93,139	121,286	145,891	173,850	200,067	Brazil
38.5[8]	32.7[8]	16.4[8]	7.9[8]	—4.5[8]—		36	48	84	129	185	252	334	432	Brunei
20.8	20.0	21.3	20.1	13.5	4.2	6,344	7,251	7,867	8,490	8,862	8,991	9,007	9,035	Bulgaria
48.3	23.4	13.4	8.7	4.7	1.4	3,036	3,584	4,350	5,412	6,599	9,012	11,884	15,549	Burkina Faso
42.4[11]	29.4[11]	13.4[11]	8.2[11]	4.8[11]	1.8[11]	1,887	2,435	2,908	3,350	4,120	5,339	7,036	8,824	Burundi
43.8[15]	24.9[15]	16.8[15]	9.8[15]	4.1[15]	0.6[15]	3,400	4,346	5,433	6,938	6,400	8,592	10,448	11,988	Cambodia
43.4[16]	24.3[16]	16.6[16]	9.9[16]	4.3[16]	1.5[16]	...	4,467	5,297	6,610	8,653	11,833	16,701	23,665	Cameroon
21.4[7]	25.8[7]	23.0[7]	14.9[7]	10.9[7]	4.1[7]	11,693	13,737	17,909	21,324	24,067	26,929	31,215	36,182	Canada
46.0[6]	27.6[6]	9.1[6]	9.0[6]	6.3[6]	2.0[6]	181	148	199	272	296	337	383	436	Cape Verde
22.7	28.4	26.8	13.1	6.4	2.6	7	7	8	11	17	27	31	36	Cayman Islands
43.2	27.5	15.0	9.2	4.1	0.8	991	1,311	1,500	1,793	2,257	2,793	3,528	4,449	Central African Republic
40.6	28.3	17.2	9.5	—4.4—		2,351	2,658	3,064	3,652	4,477	5,678	7,337	9,491	Chad
31.9[17]	29.1[17]	19.1[17]	11.7[17]	6.3[17]	1.9[17]	5,063	6,091	7,585	9,368	11,104	13,173	15,272	17,182	Chile
27.7	31.0	20.7	12.1	6.9	1.7	530,000	556,613	667,070	818,316	981,242	1,133,683	1,291,894	1,387,729	China
36.1	31.2	17.2	9.5	4.6	1.4	9,091	11,268	15,321	20,884	26,906	32,978	39,397	45,645	Colombia
47.2	23.2	14.8	7.6	5.1	1.8	179	148	177	245	333	463	659	933	Comoros
44.7	27.2	13.3	9.1	4.6	0.7	...	815	960	1,182	1,631	2,264	3,511	4,934	Congo
37.8	29.1	14.1	11.6	5.7	1.5	13	15	18	18	18	17	17	17	Cook Islands
37.9	31.5	15.8	9.2	4.4	1.2	619	862	1,236	1,731	2,285	3,015	3,711	4,366	Costa Rica
44.5	27.0	16.7	7.8	2.8	1.2	2,350	2,775	3,799	5,515	8,194	11,997	17,600	25,503	Côte d'Ivoire
20.9[8]	23.3[8]	20.2[8]	19.9[8]	11.0[8]	3.9[8]	...	3,851	4,140	4,411	4,588	4,770	4,960	5,157	Croatia
30.3	27.6	19.1	12.1	8.2	2.7	4,566	5,752	7,019	8,565	9,724	10,631	11,502	12,181	Cuba
25.0	26.6	20.1	13.8	—14.5—		413	494	573	615	627	740	826	923	Cyprus
24.3[6]	22.9[6]	19.8[6]	17.2[6]	11.5[6]	4.3[6]	14,713	12,389	13,654	14,334	15,274	15,549	15,829	16,114	Czechoslovakia
17.0	22.6	22.3	17.6	13.4	6.9	3,832	4,271	4,581	4,929	5,123	5,141	5,184	5,171	Denmark
38.0[19]	34.0[19]	17.0[19]	—11.0[19]—			44	60	78	158	355	525	706	949	Djibouti
39.8[8]	28.6[8]	11.9[8]	9.2[8]	7.4[8]	3.1[8]	45	51	60	70	75	72	80	92	Dominica
40.6	30.1	15.1	8.7	—5.5—		1,759	2,313	3,160	4,343	5,648	7,168	8,621	9,903	Dominican Republic
38.8	28.5	17.3	9.0	4.7	1.7	2,546	3,307	4,421	5,958	8,123	10,161	12,417	14,467	Ecuador

Area and population (continued)

country	area			population (latest estimate)					population (latest census)				
	square miles	square kilo-metres	rank	total midyear 1992	rank	density		% annual growth rate 1987-92	census year	total	male (%)	female (%)	urban (%)
						per sq mi	per sq km						
Egypt	385,229	997,739	30	55,979,000	21	145.3	56.1	2.7	1986	48,205,049	51.1	48.9	43.9
El Salvador	8,124	21,041	149	5,460,000	98	672.1	259.5	1.6	1971	3,554,648	49.6	50.4	39.4
Equatorial Guinea	10,831	28,051	142	367,000	166	33.9	13.1	2.4	1983	300,000	48.3	51.7	28.2
Estonia	17,413	45,100	130	1,592,000	141	91.4	35.3	0.5	1989	1,572,916	46.9	53.1	71.6
Ethiopia	483,123	1,251,282	22	54,077,000	22	111.9	43.2	3.1	1984	42,184,966	49.8	50.2	10.2
Faeroe Islands	540	1,399	175	47,600	206	88.1	34.0	0.4	1992[18]	47,316	52.0	48.0	...
Fiji	7,056	18,274	153	748,000	154	106.0	40.9	0.7	1986	715,375	50.7	49.3	38.7
Finland	130,559	338,145	64	5,033,000	101	38.5	14.9	0.4	1985	4,910,619	48.4	51.6	76.2
France	210,026	543,965	48	57,289,000	18	272.8	105.3	0.5	1990	56,625,026	48.7	51.3	74.3[9]
French Guiana	33,399	86,504	114	123,000	186	3.7	1.4	4.5	1990	114,808	52.1	47.9	73.4[17]
French Polynesia	1,544	4,000	168	206,000	177	133.4	51.5	2.4	1988	188,814	52.1	47.9	55.0
Gabon	103,347	267,667	76	1,253,000	146	12.1	4.7	3.4	1960-61	448,564	47.1	52.9	45.7[9]
Gambia, The	4,127	10,689	160	921,000	151	223.2	86.2	3.1	1983	695,886	49.7	50.3	21.2
Gaza Strip	140	363	197	670,000	156	4,785.7	1,845.7	3.8	1988[18]	588,500	50.2	49.8	...
Georgia	26,900	69,700	120	5,482,000	97	203.8	78.7	0.4	1989	5,443,359	47.2	52.8	55.7
Germany	137,822	356,957	62	79,122,000	12	574.1	221.7	0.4	1987[20]	61,077,042	48.0	52.0	85.5[2]
Ghana	92,098	238,533	81	15,237,000	54	165.4	63.9	2.6	1984	12,296,081	49.3	50.7	32.0
Gibraltar	2.2	5.8	216	31,800	209	14,454.5	5,482.8	1.6	1981[21]	26,479	52.2	47.8	...
Greece	50,949	131,957	96	10,288,000	70	201.9	78.0	0.4	1991	10,264,156	49.0	51.0	58.1[8]
Greenland	840,000	2,175,600	14	56,600	203	0.1	0.0	0.9	1991[18]	55,533	53.8	46.2	80.1
Grenada	134	348	199	90,900	192	678.4	261.2	0.2	1991	90,691	49.4	50.6	25.3[5]
Guadeloupe	687	1,780	174	400,000	163	582.2	224.7	1.8	1990	387,034	48.9	51.1	48.5[9]
Guam	209	541	188	139,000	183	665.1	256.9	2.1	1990	133,152	53.3	46.7	38.2
Guatemala	42,042	108,889	105	9,442,000	75	224.6	86.7	2.8	1981[3]	6,043,559	49.8	50.2	34.3
Guernsey	30	78	210	64,200	199	2,140.0	823.1	1.6	1991[22]	58,867	48.1	51.9	...
Guinea	94,926	245,857	78	7,232,000	90	76.2	29.4	2.5	1983	5,781,014	48.6	51.4	26.0
Guinea-Bissau	13,948	36,125	135	1,015,000	149	72.8	28.1	2.1	1979	767,739	48.2	51.8	14.0
Guyana	83,044	215,083	84	748,000	155	9.0	3.5	-0.2	1980	758,619	49.5	50.5	30.5[13]
Haiti	10,695	27,700	144	6,764,000	92	632.4	244.2	2.0	1982	5,053,792	48.5	51.5	20.6
Honduras	43,277	112,088	102	4,996,000	102	115.4	44.6	3.3	1988	4,376,839	49.6	50.4	43.7[9]
Hong Kong	415	1,075	177	5,799,000	94	13,974.3	5,395.5	0.8	1991[3]	5,674,114	51.1	48.9	93.1[7]
Hungary	35,920	93,033	110	10,318,000	69	287.2	110.9	-0.3	1990	10,375,323	48.1	51.9	61.8
Iceland	39,699	102,819	106	261,000	173	6.6	2.5	1.2	1991[18]	259,581	50.2	49.8	90.7
India	1,222,243	3,165,596	7	889,700,000	2	727.9	281.1	2.1	1991	844,324,222	51.9	48.1	25.7
Indonesia	741,052	1,919,317	16	184,796,000	4	249.4	96.3	1.8	1990	179,321,641	49.9	50.1	30.9
Iran	632,457	1,638,057	18	59,570,000	15	94.2	36.4	3.3	1986[3]	49,445,010	51.1	48.9	54.3
Iraq	167,975	435,052	58	18,838,000	45	112.1	43.3	3.1	1987	16,335,199	51.4	48.6	70.2
Ireland	27,137	70,285	119	3,519,000	120	129.7	50.1	-0.1	1991	3,523,401	49.7	50.3	57.1[9]
Isle of Man	221	572	187	70,700	197	319.9	123.6	1.5	1991[3]	69,788	48.3	51.7	51.1
Israel[24]	7,992	20,700	150	5,239,000	99	655.5	253.1	3.4	1983[3,25]	4,037,620	49.8	50.2	86.9
Italy	116,324	301,277	71	57,158,000	19	491.4	189.7	0.1	1991	57,103,833	48.6	51.4	66.5[13]
Jamaica	4,244	10,991	159	2,445,000	133	576.1	222.5	0.8	1991	2,366,067	49.1[17]	50.9[17]	47.8[17]
Japan	145,883	377,835	61	124,330,000	8	852.3	329.1	0.4	1990	123,611,541	49.1	50.9	76.7[26]
Jersey	45	116	209	84,800	193	1,884.4	731.0	0.9	1991	84,082	48.6	51.4	...
Jordan[27]	34,342	88,946	112	3,636,000	118	105.9	40.9	5.0	1979	2,132,997	52.3	47.7	59.5
Kazakhstan	1,049,200	2,717,300	9	17,008,000	51	16.2	6.3	0.9	1989	16,536,511	48.5	51.5	57.2
Kenya	224,961	582,646	46	26,985,000	34	120.0	46.3	4.1	1979	15,327,061	49.7	50.3	15.1
Kiribati	313	811	179	74,700	194	238.7	92.1	2.2	1990	72,298	49.6	50.4	34.8
Korea, North	47,400	122,762	99	22,227,000	40	468.9	181.1	1.8	28	28	49.9[9]	50.1[9]	67.9[9]
Korea, South	38,326	99,263	108	43,663,000	24	1,139.3	439.9	1.0	1990[3]	43,520,199	51.9	48.1	74.4
Kuwait	6,880	17,818	154	1,190,000	147	173.0	66.8	...	1985	1,697,301	56.9	43.1	100.0
Kyrgyzstan	76,600	198,500	86	4,533,000	105	59.2	22.8	1.7	1989	4,290,442	48.9	51.1	38.2
Laos	91,400	236,800	83	4,409,000	108	48.2	18.6	2.9	1985	3,584,803	49.0	51.0	15.9[2]
Latvia	24,900	64,500	123	2,685,000	131	107.8	41.6	0.2	1989	2,680,029	46.6	53.4	71.1
Lebanon	3,950	10,230	161	2,803,000	127	709.6	274.0	1.0	1970	2,126,325	50.8	49.2	60.1
Lesotho	11,720	30,355	138	1,854,000	139	158.2	61.1	2.6	1986[3]	1,577,536	48.2	51.8	16.0
Liberia	38,250	99,067	109	2,780,000	129	72.7	28.1	3.4	1984	2,101,628	50.6	49.4	38.8
Libya	678,400	1,757,000	17	4,447,000	107	6.6	2.5	3.0	1984	3,637,488	53.6	46.4	75.8[3]
Liechtenstein	62	160	208	29,600	211	477.4	185.0	1.3	1980	25,215	49.6	50.4	...
Lithuania	25,213	65,301	122	3,801,000	116	150.8	58.2	0.9	1989	3,689,779	47.4	52.6	68.0
Luxembourg	999	2,586	170	387,000	164	387.4	149.7	0.9	1991	384,062	48.8[8]	51.2[8]	84.3[9]
Macau	6.9	18.0	215	367,000	167	53,188.4	20,388.9	3.8	1991	355,693	48.5	51.5	96.4
Macedonia	9,928	25,713	146	2,050,000	136	206.5	79.7	0.6	1991	2,033,964	50.7	49.3[8]	53.9[8]
Madagascar	226,658	587,041	45	12,803,000	60	56.5	21.8	3.3	1974-75	7,603,790	50.0	50.0	16.3
Malawi	45,747	118,484	100	9,484,000	74	207.3	80.0	3.7	1987	7,982,607	48.6	51.4	8.5[29]
Malaysia	127,584	330,442	65	18,630,000	46	146.0	56.4	2.4	1980	13,136,109	50.2	49.8	34.2
Maldives	115	298	201	230,000	175	2,000.0	771.8	3.4	1990	213,215	51.3	48.7	25.9
Mali	482,077	1,248,574	23	8,464,000	79	17.6	6.8	1.8	1987	7,696,348	48.9	51.1	22.0
Malta	122	316	200	360,000	168	2,950.8	1,139.2	0.9	1985	345,418	49.2	50.8	94.3[30]
Marshall Islands	70	181	207	50,000	204	714.3	276.2	4.1	1988	43,380	51.1	48.9	64.5
Martinique	436	1,128	176	369,000	165	846.3	327.1	1.1	1990	359,579	48.4	51.6	74.7[9]
Mauritania	398,000	1,030,700	29	2,108,000	135	5.3	2.0	3.0	1976-77	1,419,939	50.1	49.9	21.9
Mauritius	788	2,040	172	1,081,000	148	1,371.8	529.9	0.9	1983	1,002,178	49.8	50.2	41.7[31]
Mayotte	144	373	196	97,400	190	676.4	261.1	5.4	1991	94,410	51.3[26]	48.7[26]	59.7[26]
Mexico	756,066	1,958,201	15	84,439,000	14	111.7	43.1	1.6	1990	81,249,645	49.1	50.9	71.3
Micronesia	271	701	183	114,000	187	420.7	162.6	3.3	1980	73,160	51.1	48.9	19.4
Moldova	13,000	33,700	136	4,394,000	110	338.0	130.4	0.6	1989	4,337,592	47.5	52.5	46.9
Monaco	0.75	1.95	217	30,300	210	40,400.0	15,538.5	1.0	1990	29,972	47.5	52.5	100.0
Mongolia	604,800	1,566,500	19	2,182,000	134	3.6	1.4	1.8	1989	2,043,100	48.9	51.1	57.1
Morocco	177,117	458,730	55	26,239,000	36	148.1	57.2	2.5	1982	20,419,555[32]	50.1	49.9	42.7
Mozambique	313,661	812,379	36	14,842,000	56	47.3	18.3	1.9	1980	12,130,000	48.7	51.3	13.2
Myanmar (Burma)	261,228	676,577	40	43,446,000	25	166.4	64.2	2.1	1983	35,313,905	49.6	50.4	24.0
Namibia	317,818	823,144	35	1,431,000	143	4.5	1.7	3.0	1991	1,401,711	49.2[8]	50.8[8]	26.0[8]
Nauru	8.2	21.2	214	9,600	216	1,170.7	452.8	2.0	1983	8,042	52.1[29,33]	47.9[29,33]	—
Nepal	56,827	147,181	93	19,795,000	44	348.3	134.5	2.4	1981	15,022,839	51.2	48.8	6.4

| age distribution (%) | | | | | | population (by decade, '000s) | | | | | | | | country |
0–14	15–29	30–44	45–59	60–74	75 and older	1940	1950	1960	1970	1980	1990	2000 projection	2010 projection	
39.5	26.4	16.9	10.6	5.2	1.0	16,942	20,461	26,085	33,329	40,546	53,153	65,556	77,251	Egypt
46.2	25.1	15.2	8.2	4.3	1.0	1,550	1,931	2,527	3,534	4,508	5,299	6,604	8,099	El Salvador
41.7	25.1	15.7	11.2	5.3	1.0	...	211	244	291	255	350	448	573	Equatorial Guinea
22.2	21.4	21.0	18.5	11.7	5.1	1,054	1,101	1,216	1,365	1,481	1,583	1,647	1,699	Estonia
46.6	22.7	15.6	8.9	4.5	1.7	...	16,675	20,024	24,068	38,439	50,987	68,496	92,040	Ethiopia
24.5	23.4	21.1	14.7	11.3	4.9	27	31	35	39	43	48	49	51	Faeroe Islands
38.2	29.5	17.8	9.6	3.8	0.8	218	289	394	520	634	732	826	917	Fiji
19.4	22.6	24.0	16.6	12.5	5.0	3,698	4,009	4,430	4,606	4,780	4,986	5,064	5,036	Finland
19.1	22.6	22.8	15.6	12.8	7.1	41,300	41,736	45,684	50,770	53,880	56,735	59,245	61,784	France
33.4	27.3	23.2	10.2	4.4	1.5	30	27	33	49	69	117	151	194	French Guiana
36.0	29.7	18.9	10.4	4.1	0.9	50	62	84	109	151	197	240	285	French Polynesia
35.4[2]	24.1[2]	18.1[2]	13.1[2]	7.5[2]	1.8[2]	442	469	486	504	806	1,172	1,612	2,052	Gabon
43.8	26.5	15.7	7.3	——5.7——		193	232	357	458	632	874	1,132	1,446	Gambia, The
49.5	——39.6——			——10.9——		...	...	...	370	451	623	838	1,107	Gaza Strip
24.8	24.1	19.2	17.5	10.8	3.6	3,612	3,527	4,160	4,708	5,075	5,460	5,777	6,101	Georgia
14.6	24.0	20.1	20.6	13.6	7.2	57,400	68,373	72,673	77,772	78,304	79,070	79,330	79,579	Germany
45.0	26.4	14.6	8.1	4.1	1.8	3,636	5,297	6,958	8,789	11,222	14,470	18,733	24,253	Ghana
21.4	22.2	22.3	17.7	12.6	3.8	14	23	24	26	30	31	36	42	Gibraltar
23.7[8]	21.5[8]	19.2[8]	18.7[8]	12.3[8]	4.6[8]	7,319	7,566	8,327	8,793	9,702	10,219	10,406	10,463	Greece
26.0	28.5	24.7	14.1	——6.6——		19	23	33	41	50	56	61	63	Greenland
39.4[13]	31.2[13]	10.1[13]	9.2[13]	7.3[13]	2.8[13]	71	76	90	95	89	91	92	94	Grenada
24.9	29.5	21.4	12.5	8.3	3.4	180	206	265	320	327	389	442	507	Guadeloupe
30.0	30.0	22.6	10.8	5.5	1.1	22	59	67	85	107	134	160	187	Guam
44.9	26.8	14.8	8.5	3.9	1.1	2,201	3,024	4,005	5,263	6,783	8,920	11,809	15,242	Guatemala
17.0	23.3	22.2	16.8	13.5	7.2	44	44	45	51	55	62	73	85	Guernsey
43.1[2]	26.2[2]	16.3[2]	9.6[2]	4.2[2]	0.7[2]	...	3,245	3,660	4,388	5,407	6,876	8,879	11,451	Guinea
44.3	25.5	15.1	8.2	4.7	2.2	341	411	520	653	787	973	1,200	1,480	Guinea-Bissau
40.8	30.5	14.0	8.8	4.4	1.2	344	423	560	702	759	754	728	807	Guyana
39.2	26.9	15.6	10.0	5.4	2.9	2,827	3,261	3,807	4,535	5,370	6,486	8,003	8,876	Haiti
48.1[23]	25.8[23]	13.9[23]	7.8[23]	3.6[23]	0.9[23]	1,146	1,390	1,873	2,553	3,316	4,681	6,249	7,872	Honduras
23.0	25.0	26.2	——25.8——			1,786	1,974	3,074	3,942	5,063	5,705	6,167	6,660	Hong Kong
21.3	19.4	22.5	17.9	13.4	5.6	9,280	9,338	9,984	10,353	10,693	10,366	10,097	9,828	Hungary
24.9	24.8	22.2	13.3	10.2	4.6	121	143	176	204	228	255	276	293	Iceland
39.5[8]	25.9[8]	17.4[8]	10.7[8]	——6.5[8]——		317,000	357,561	442,344	554,911	687,057	853,094	1,041,543	1,223,483	India
40.8[6]	27.0[6]	16.4[6]	10.2[6]	4.5[6]	1.1[6]	70,500	75,449	92,701	119,467	146,449	178,249	211,288	238,174	Indonesia
45.5	26.4	13.6	9.1	4.2	1.2	14,000	16,913	21,554	28,359	38,783	55,928	71,894	91,537	Iran
45.2	27.2	14.2	7.0	3.7	1.4	3,745	5,180	6,847	9,356	13,043	17,751	23,947	30,834	Iraq
28.9[7]	24.7[7]	18.8[7]	12.8[7]	——14.8[7]——		2,958	2,969	2,834	2,954	3,421	3,526	3,492	3,458	Ireland
17.3	20.7	20.4	17.0	15.3	9.2	52	55	49	52	64	69	77	86	Isle of Man
32.6	26.4	18.0	12.3	9.4	3.1	...	...	2,114	2,958	3,896	4,739	6,275	6,581	Israel[24]
21.4[8]	22.4[8]	20.0[8]	18.7[8]	12.7[8]	4.7[8]	43,840	46,769	50,223	53,565	56,235	57,003	57,274	56,270	Italy
38.4[17]	28.8[17]	13.8[17]	9.4[17]	6.9[17]	2.6[17]	1,212	1,403	1,629	1,891	2,133	2,403	2,602	2,813	Jamaica
21.5[26]	20.7[26]	23.9[26]	19.2[26]	10.8[26]	3.9[26]	73,075	83,200	93,419	103,720	116,807	123,537	126,894	129,410	Japan
15.5	24.9	23.9	17.0	11.9	6.8	51	57	63	71	76	83	91	100	Jersey
51.6	23.4	13.4	7.4	3.1	1.1	...	1,095	1,384	1,795	2,181	3,282	4,790	6,760	Jordan[27]
31.9	26.3	19.4	13.2	6.9	2.3	6,148	6,703	9,996	13,110	14,939	16,742	19,006	21,748	Kazakhstan
51.4	24.8	13.2	7.0	3.0	0.6	4,470	6,018	8,115	11,225	16,667	24,872	37,505	56,629	Kenya
40.3	27.5	17.3	9.2	4.8	0.9	29	33	41	49	57	72	87	103	Kiribati
28.6[9]	34.6[9]	19.8[9]	10.5[9]	5.2[9]	1.3[9]	...	9,740	10,568	14,388	17,999	21,412	25,491	28,491	Korea, North
25.4	29.9	23.2	13.7	6.3	1.6	...	21,147	25,142	32,976	38,124	42,869	46,789	49,683	Korea, South
36.8	28.3	24.1	8.6	1.8	0.4		145	292	748	1,370	2,143	...		Kuwait
37.5	27.0	16.3	10.9	6.2	2.1	1,528	1,740	2,173	2,965	3,630	4,395	5,403	6,545	Kyrgyzstan
44.2	25.2	14.4	9.9	4.9	1.4	1,075	1,949	2,382	2,962	3,292	4,170	5,435	6,710	Laos
21.4	21.7	20.3	19.2	12.0	5.3	1,886	1,949	2,129	2,374	2,543	2,684	2,768	2,853	Latvia
42.6	23.8	16.7	9.1	——7.7——		965	1,443	1,857	2,469	2,669	2,701	3,327	3,898	Lebanon
40.7	25.1	16.6	10.7	5.6	1.3	566	766	885	1,043	1,358	1,760	2,282	2,958	Lesotho
43.2	28.2	14.7	7.7	4.4	1.8	...	758	1,004	1,393	1,864	2,607	3,602	4,933	Liberia
49.7[3]	25.3[3]	13.7[3]	7.4[3]	3.2[3]	0.6[3]	900	1,029	1,349	1,982	3,054	4,206	5,559	6,990	Libya
23.0	26.5	24.1	14.1	9.2	3.1	11	14	16	21	26	29	33	39	Liechtenstein
22.6	23.8	20.0	17.9	10.9	4.8	2,925	2,567	2,779	3,148	3,439	3,737	3,935	4,110	Lithuania
18.5[8]	23.7[8]	21.2[8]	18.7[8]	12.8[8]	5.1[8]	296	296	314	339	364	382	400	409	Luxembourg
24.6	26.9	29.4	9.5	7.3	2.3	375	188	169	221	235	341	493	713	Macau
29.1[8]	27.1[8]	19.6[8]	14.8[8]	7.1[8]	2.2[8]	...	1,229	1,392	1,629	1,900	2,024	2,157	2,298	Macedonia
44.4	25.7	14.2	10.0	4.6	1.1	4,034	4,230	5,309	6,742	8,785	12,004	16,627	22,827	Madagascar
44.6[29]	25.7[29]	14.2[29]	9.0[29]	4.3[29]	2.0[29]	1,696	3,033	3,481	4,511	6,137	8,831	12,493	17,069	Malawi
39.5	29.1	16.5	9.2	4.6	1.1	...	6,187	7,908	10,466	13,764	17,756	22,140	25,986	Malaysia
46.9	26.7	12.3	9.0	4.0	0.8	81	82	106	128	155	216	286	369	Maldives
46.1	23.9	15.0	8.9	4.9	1.2	3,388	3,426	4,224	5,690	6,816	8,130	9,790	11,744	Mali
24.1	23.2	23.2	15.4	10.5	3.8	270	308	329	326	324	354	377	393	Malta
51.0	24.5	14.6	5.5	3.6	0.8	...	11	15	22	31	46	68	100	Marshall Islands
23.1	28.9	20.5	13.5	9.7	4.3	200	222	252	287	326	361	404	452	Martinique
45.7[13]	26.1[13]	14.8[13]	8.7[13]	4.0[13]	0.6[13]	666	781	970	1,245	1,483	1,988	2,665	3,572	Mauritania
32.6	31.7	17.8	10.9	5.7	1.3	428	479	662	824	957	1,062	1,157	1,260	Mauritius
50.2[26]	24.7[26]	13.4[26]	6.9[26]	3.4[26]	1.4[26]	16	17	25	35	52	89	130	188	Mayotte
38.3	29.4	16.6	8.9	4.5	1.7	19,815	25,828	34,993	48,934	69,655	81,883	95,490	111,360	Mexico
46.4	26.8	12.6	8.5	4.5	1.1	...	30	40	57	77	108	142	177	Micronesia
27.9	22.9	21.0	15.6	9.7	2.9	2,468	2,341	3,004	3,595	4,001	4,365	4,707	5,147	Moldova
12.3	16.7	21.2	20.4	17.9	10.8	20	22	23	24	27	30	32	32	Monaco
41.9	29.2	14.6	8.5	——5.8——		750	747	931	1,248	1,663	2,098	2,552	3,104	Mongolia
42.2	28.3	14.1	9.2	4.8	1.5	7,750	8,953	11,640	15,126	19,082	25,009	31,410	37,360	Morocco
44.4	26.7	15.9	8.7	3.6	0.7	...	6,458	7,584	9,390	12,103	14,161	18,350	23,604	Mozambique
40.7	27.7	15.0	10.5	——6.1——		...	17,832	21,746	27,102	33,821	41,675	51,129	60,567	Myanmar (Burma)
44.0[13]	26.0[13]	15.5[13]	9.3[13]	4.3[13]	0.9[13]	336	405	522	761	1,002	1,348	1,820	2,458	Namibia
44.1[29,33]	33.1[29,33]	11.4[29,33]	8.5[29,33]	1.9[29,33]	1.0[29,33]	3	4	5	7	8	9	11	13	Nauru
41.4	25.5	17.4	10.0	4.7	1.0	7,000	8,000	9,180	11,232	14,642	18,910	23,176	27,807	Nepal

Area and population (continued)

country	area			population (latest estimate)					% annual growth rate 1987–92	population (latest census)				
	square miles	square kilo-metres	rank	total midyear 1992	rank	density				census year	total	male (%)	female (%)	urban (%)
						per sq mi	per sq km							
Netherlands, The	16,163	41,863	132	15,163,000	55	938.1	362.2	0.7	1992[18]	15,129,150	49.4	50.6	89.0[34]
Netherlands Antilles	308	800	180	191,000	179	620.1	238.8	0.2	1981	171,620	48.3	51.7	...
New Caledonia	7,172	18,576	152	174,000	180	24.3	9.4	1.9	1989	164,173	51.1	48.9	59.4
New Zealand	104,454	270,534	75	3,481,000	121	33.3	12.9	0.8	1991	3,434,949	49.3	50.7	75.9
Nicaragua	50,464	130,700	97	4,131,000	113	81.9	31.6	3.4	1971	1,877,952	48.3	51.7	48.0
Niger	458,075	1,186,408	26	8,281,000	82	18.1	7.0	3.3	1988[3]	7,228,552	49.6	50.4	15.4
Nigeria	356,669	923,768	32	89,666,000	10	251.4	97.1	2.1	1991	88,514,501	50.3	49.7	16.1[35]
Northern Mariana Islands	184	477	190	44,800	207	243.5	93.9	6.0	1990	43,345	52.6	47.4	28.0
Norway	125,050	323,878	67	4,283,000	112	34.3	13.2	0.5	1990	4,247,546	49.4	50.6	75.0[9]
Oman	118,150	306,000	70	1,640,000	140	13.9	5.4	4.1	[28]	[28]	52.4[9]	47.6[9]	10.6[9]
Pakistan	339,697	879,811	34	130,129,000	7	383.1	147.9	3.2	1981[36]	84,253,644	52.5	47.5	28.3
Palau	188	488	189	15,700	215	83.5	32.2	2.0	1990	15,122	53.8	46.2	59.6
Panama	29,157	75,517	117	2,515,000	132	86.3	33.3	2.0	1990	2,329,329	50.6	49.4	49.7[6]
Papua New Guinea	178,704	462,840	54	3,834,000	115	21.5	8.3	2.2	1990	3,529,538[37]	52.0[37]	48.0[37]	15.2[37]
Paraguay	157,048	406,752	59	4,519,000	106	28.8	11.1	2.9	1982	3,035,360	50.1	49.9	42.8
Peru	496,225	1,285,216	20	22,454,000	39	45.2	17.5	2.1	1981	17,005,210	49.7	50.3	64.9
Philippines	115,800	300,000	72	63,609,000	14	549.3	212.0	2.3	1990	60,684,887	50.2[6]	49.8[6]	37.3[6]
Poland	120,727	312,683	69	38,429,000	29	318.3	122.9	0.4	1988	37,878,641	48.7	51.3	61.2
Portugal	35,672	92,389	111	10,429,000	66	292.4	112.9	0.3	1981[3]	9,833,014	48.2	51.8	29.7
Puerto Rico	3,515	9,104	163	3,581,000	119	1,018.8	393.3	0.8	1990	3,522,037	48.7[6]	51.3[6]	66.8[6]
Qatar	4,412	11,427	158	520,000	160	117.9	45.5	5.3	1986	369,079	67.2	32.8	88.0[2]
Réunion	970	2,512	171	623,000	157	642.3	248.0	1.8	1990	597,828	49.2	50.8	63.9[9]
Romania	91,699	237,500	82	23,332,000	38	254.4	98.2	0.3	1992	22,760,500	49.3[29]	50.7[29]	54.4
Russia	6,592,800	17,075,400	1	149,469,000	6	22.7	8.8	0.5	1989	147,400,537	46.9	53.1	73.6
Rwanda	10,169	26,338	145	7,347,000	88	722.5	279.0	3.1	1991	7,164,994	48.7	51.3	7.7[9]
St. Kitts and Nevis	104	269	202	43,100	208	414.4	160.2	– 0.4	1980	43,309	48.1	51.9	37.1
St. Lucia	238	617	186	135,000	184	567.2	218.8	0.8	1991	133,308	48.5	51.5	...
St. Vincent and the Grenadines	150	389	195	109,000	188	726.7	280.2	0.8	1991	107,598	50.2	49.8	25.7[13]
San Marino	24	61	211	23,600	213	983.3	386.9	0.8	1976	19,149	50.4	49.6	90.0[9]
São Tomé and Príncipe	386	1,001	178	126,000	185	326.4	125.9	2.3	1981	96,611	49.7	50.3	...
Saudi Arabia	865,000	2,240,000	13	15,267,000	53	17.6	6.8	4.0	1974	6,726,466	53.2	46.8	65.9[13]
Senegal	75,951	196,712	87	7,691,000	86	101.3	39.1	2.6	1988	6,928,405	48.7	51.3	38.6
Seychelles	175	453	192	71,000	196	405.7	156.7	0.7	1987	68,598	49.7	50.3	35.5
Sierra Leone	27,699	71,740	118	4,373,000	111	157.9	61.0	2.6	1985	3,517,530	49.6	50.4	28.3[2]
Singapore	240	622	185	2,792,000	128	11,633.3	4,488.7	1.8	1990[3]	2,705,115	50.6	49.4	100.0
Slovenia	7,821	20,256	151	1,985,000	138	253.8	98.0	0.4	1991	1,974,839	48.6[8]	51.4[8]	48.9[8]
Solomon Islands	10,954	28,370	141	339,000	170	30.9	11.9	2.8	1986	285,176	51.9	48.1	9.3[16]
Somalia	246,000	637,000	42	7,872,000	83	32.0	12.4	2.9	1975	4,089,203	50.1	49.9	25.4
South Africa[38]	473,290	1,225,815	25	38,842,000	28	82.1	31.7	2.0	1985[39]	27,722,100	51.2	48.8	55.9[40]
Bophuthatswana	16,988	44,000	—	2,056,000	—	121.0	46.7	2.4	1980	1,287,814	46.9[5]	53.1[5]	14.2[5]
Ciskei	2,996	7,760	—	854,000	—	285.0	110.1	1.9	1985	831,636	47.3	52.7	49.8
Transkei	16,855	43,653	—	3,303,000	—	196.0	75.7	1.8	1980	2,334,946	41.2[5]	58.8[5]	3.2[5]
Venda	2,771	7,176	—	567,000	—	204.6	79.0	2.9	1985	459,986	41.0[6]	59.0[6]	2.1[6]
Spain	194,898	504,783	51	39,085,000	27	200.5	77.4	0.2	1991[3]	38,425,679	49.1[8]	50.9[8]	72.8[13]
Sri Lanka	25,332	65,610	121	17,464,000	49	689.4	266.2	1.3	1981	14,848,364	50.8	49.2	21.5
Sudan, The	966,757	2,503,890	10	29,971,000	32	31.0	12.0	3.5	1983	20,564,364	50.8	49.2	20.6[2]
Suriname	63,251	163,820	91	404,000	162	6.4	2.5	0.6	1980	354,860	49.5	50.5	44.8[13]
Swaziland	6,704	17,364	155	826,000	152	123.2	47.6	3.4	1986	681,059	47.2	52.8	22.8
Sweden	173,732	449,964	56	8,673,000	78	49.9	19.3	0.6	1991[18]	8,644,096	49.4	50.6	83.1[6]
Switzerland	15,943	41,293	133	6,911,000	91	433.5	167.4	0.9	1980[41]	6,365,960	48.9	51.1	57.1
Syria	71,498	185,180	88	12,958,000	58	181.2	70.0	3.4	1981	9,052,628	51.1	48.9	47.1
Taiwan	13,969	36,179	134	20,727,000	42	1,483.8	572.9	1.1	1980[3]	17,968,797	52.2	47.8	70.6[13]
Tajikistan	55,300	143,100	95	5,568,000	96	100.7	38.9	2.7	1989	5,108,576	49.7	50.3	32.6
Tanzania	364,017	942,799	31	25,809,000	37	70.9	27.4	2.8	1988	23,174,336	48.9	51.1	13.8[42]
Thailand	198,115	513,115	50	56,801,000	20	286.7	110.7	1.9	1990	54,532,300	49.6	50.4	18.7
Togo	21,925	56,785	124	3,701,000	117	168.8	65.2	2.9	1981	2,719,567	48.7	51.3	15.2
Tonga	301	781	181	97,300	191	323.3	124.7	0.5	1986[3]	94,649	50.3	49.7	30.7
Trinidad and Tobago	1,980	5,128	166	1,261,000	145	636.9	245.9	1.2	1990	1,234,388	50.1	49.9	56.9[13]
Tunisia	59,664	154,530	92	8,413,000	80	141.0	54.4	1.9	1984	6,975,450	50.8	49.2	52.8
Turkey	300,948	779,452	37	58,584,000	16	194.7	75.2	2.2	1990	56,473,035	50.4[26]	49.6[26]	45.9[26]
Turkmenistan	188,500	488,100	52	3,859,000	114	20.5	7.9	2.6	1989	3,533,925	49.3	50.7	45.4
Tuvalu	9.3	24.0	213	9,500	217	1,021.5	395.8	2.0	1985	8,229	47.4	52.6	...
Uganda	93,070	241,040	80	17,194,000	50	184.7	71.3	2.5	1991	16,582,674	49.5[6]	50.5[6]	8.1[6]
Ukraine	233,100	603,700	44	52,135,000	23	223.7	86.4	0.3	1989	51,706,746	46.3	53.7	66.9
United Arab Emirates	30,000	77,700	116	1,989,000	137	66.3	25.6	2.9	1985	1,622,464	64.9	35.1	80.8[6]
United Kingdom	94,251	244,110	79	57,730,000	17	612.5	236.5	0.3	1981[43]	56,379,000	48.6	51.4	89.6
United States	3,679,192	9,529,063	4	255,414,000	3	69.4	26.8	1.0	1990	249,246,000	48.7	51.3	75.2
Uruguay	68,037	176,215	90	3,130,000	125	46.0	17.8	0.6	1985	2,955,241	48.7	51.3	86.2
Uzbekistan	172,700	447,400	57	21,363,000	41	123.7	47.7	2.2	1989	19,905,158	49.3	50.7	40.7
Vanuatu	4,707	12,190	157	154,000	182	32.7	12.6	2.4	1989	142,630	51.6	48.4	17.7
Venezuela	352,144	912,050	33	20,184,000	43	57.3	22.1	2.4	1990	19,405,429	49.7	50.3	85.7[8]
Vietnam	127,246	329,566	66	69,052,000	13	542.7	209.5	2.0	1989	64,411,713	48.7	51.3	20.1
Virgin Islands (U.S.)	136	352	198	103,000	189	757.4	292.6	0.5	1990	95,947	47.8[6]	52.2[6]	29.6[6]
West Bank	2,270	5,900	164	989,000	150	435.7	167.6	3.0	1988[18]	895,400	50.3	49.7	...
Western Sahara	97,344	252,120	77	209,000	176	2.1	0.8	2.5	1970	76,425	...	...	...
Western Samoa	1,093	2,831	169	160,000	181	146.4	56.5	0.3	1991	159,682	53.0[7]	47.0[7]	20.5[7]
Yemen	205,356	531,869	49	12,147,000	62	59.2	22.8	2.6	1986[44]	9,274,173[45]	47.3[8]	52.7[8]	10.2[8]
Yugoslavia	39,449	102,173	107	10,394,000	67	263.5	101.7	0.4	1991	10,337,504	49.7[8]	50.3[8]	46.8[8]
Zaire	905,446	2,345,095	12	41,151,000	26	45.4	17.5	3.2	1984	29,671,407	49.2	50.8	36.6[2]
Zambia	290,586	752,614	39	8,303,000	81	28.6	11.0	3.3	1990	7,818,447	49.2	50.8	42.0
Zimbabwe	150,873	390,759	60	9,871,000	72	65.4	25.3	2.7	1982	7,608,432	49.3	50.7	23.0

[1]Settled population only. [2]1985 estimate. [3]Data are for de jure population. [4]1991 estimate. [5]1970 census. [6]1980 census. [7]1986 census. [8]1981 census. [9]1990 census. [10]1990 quick-count. [11]1979 census. [12]Excludes institutional population. [13]1980 estimate. [14]1982 estimate. [15]1962 census. [16]1976 census. [17]1982 census. [18]Civil register; not a census. [19]1983 estimate. [20]Former West Germany only. [21]Excludes visitors, transients, and family members of British servicemen. [22]Data exclude Alderney (population 2,297) and Sark (population 604). [23]1974 census. [24]Excluding territory occupied after 1967. [25]Includes East Jerusalem and Israeli residents in the occupied territories. [26]1985 census. [27]Excluding West Bank. [28]No census ever taken. [29]1977

age distribution (%)						population (by decade, '000s)								country
0–14	15–29	30–44	45–59	60–74	75 and older	1940	1950	1960	1970	1980	1990	2000 projection	2010 projection	
18.2[34]	24.1[34]	24.0[34]	16.3[34]	11.9[34]	5.5[34]	8,834	10,027	11,417	12,958	14,150	14,952	15,885	16,403	Netherlands, The
30.0	29.9	19.5	11.3	6.7	2.6	77	112	136	163	171	190	194	198	Netherlands Antilles
32.6	28.6	19.8	12.1	5.4	1.6	53	59	79	110	140	168	199	230	New Caledonia
23.2	24.6	22.4	14.4	10.9	4.5	1,636	1,908	2,372	2,820	3,169	3,417	3,802	4,128	New Zealand
48.1	25.6	14.1	7.4	3.8	1.1	825	1,109	1,472	1,972	2,771	3,871	5,261	6,824	Nicaragua
46.7[2]	25.6[2]	14.9[2]	8.0[2]	3.9[2]	0.9[2]	1,700	2,291	2,913	4,016	5,568	7,779	10,656	14,484	Niger
43.0[35]	31.9[35]	16.5[35]	5.1[35]	2.5[35]	1.0[35]	...	33,320	42,366	56,346	69,875	86,015	105,885	130,344	Nigeria
23.8	33.5	30.7	9.1	2.3	0.5	48	6	9	10	17	44	50	58	Northern Mariana Islands
18.8	22.9	22.1	15.1	13.9	7.2	2,973	3,265	3,581	3,877	4,086	4,241	4,426	4,550	Norway
44.3[2]	24.8[2]	18.0[2]	8.9[2]	3.5[2]	0.6[2]	...	413	505	654	984	1,530	2,165	3,063	Oman
44.5	23.9	15.4	9.3	5.3	1.6	28,300	39,513	49,955	65,706	85,299	122,626	162,409	205,496	Pakistan
30.3	27.8	22.8	10.5	6.4	2.2	25	6	9	11	12	15	18	21	Palau
34.8	29.2	18.2	10.2	5.5	2.0	620	893	1,148	1,531	1,956	2,418	2,893	3,324	Panama
43.0[6]	25.9[6]	17.0[6]	10.4[6]	3.5[6]	0.2[6]	1,308	1,613	1,920	2,419	2,966	3,671	4,568	5,692	Papua New Guinea
41.1	28.1	15.4	9.1	4.8	1.5	1,111	1,351	1,774	2,351	3,147	4,277	5,538	6,928	Paraguay
41.2	27.9	15.6	9.3	4.4	1.6	6,784	7,632	9,931	13,193	17,295	21,550	26,276	31,047	Peru
42.0[6]	28.5[6]	15.6[6]	8.6[6]	4.3[6]	1.0[6]	16,459	20,988	27,561	36,850	48,286	60,921	74,609	86,493	Philippines
25.4	21.2	23.3	15.5	10.4	4.2	31,500	24,824	29,561	32,526	35,578	38,118	39,700	41,348	Poland
25.5	23.5	18.0	17.2	11.9	3.9	7,696	8,405	8,826	9,040	9,766	10,362	10,699	11,046	Portugal
31.6[6]	26.4[6]	18.5[6]	12.3[6]	8.3[6]	2.9[6]	1,878	2,218	2,360	2,721	3,204	3,528	3,832	4,169	Puerto Rico
27.8	29.3	32.3	8.6	1.6	0.4	...	47	59	151	229	487	657	830	Qatar
29.5	29.8	20.3	11.7	6.5	2.1	221	244	338	447	507	601	718	857	Réunion
25.7[29]	23.7[29]	19.6[29]	17.1[29]	10.9[29]	3.0[29]	15,907	16,311	18,407	20,799	22,201	23,161	24,028	24,928	Romania
23.1	22.0	21.9	17.6	11.2	4.2	110,098	105,018	119,906	130,392	138,936	148,292	155,096	161,976	Russia
45.6	28.6	12.4	8.4	3.9	0.9	1,910	2,120	2,742	3,728	5,112	6,916	9,356	12,657	Rwanda
37.2	30.4	9.5	9.4	10.0	3.5	43	49	51	46	43	43	43	45	St. Kitts and Nevis
36.8	29.4	16.3	8.7	6.3	2.5	70	79	86	101	122	132	143	155	St. Lucia
41.7[13]	33.3[13]	11.5[13]	7.3[13]	5.2[13]	1.0[13]	61	67	80	86	99	107	116	125	St. Vincent and the Grenadines
24.4	23.0	19.9	17.4	11.4	3.9	10	13	15	19	21	23	25	27	San Marino
46.3	25.0	11.6	10.0	5.3	1.8	60	60	64	74	94	120	151	191	São Tomé and Príncipe
46.7	23.9	15.2	7.9	——6.3——		...	3,201	4,075	5,745	9,372	14,134	20,697	29,557	Saudi Arabia
47.5	26.1	13.6	7.8	——5.0——		1,857	2,600	3,076	4,267	5,651	7,292	9,519	12,424	Senegal
33.6	30.3	15.3	10.7	7.1	2.9	32	34	42	54	64	70	75	81	Seychelles
40.7[23]	24.8[23]	17.4[23]	9.2[23]	——7.9[23]——		1,700	1,809	2,165	2,692	3,336	4,151	5,437	7,172	Sierra Leone
23.2	27.3	27.7	12.7	6.9	2.2	751	1,022	1,639	2,075	2,282	2,705	3,006	3,179	Singapore
23.0[8]	24.2[8]	20.6[8]	17.9[8]	10.1[8]	4.0[8]	...	1,473	1,580	1,718	1,886	1,968	2,055	2,145	Slovenia
47.3	25.7	13.9	8.1	——4.9——		94	104	125	163	230	319	433	569	Solomon Islands
45.6	24.9	15.5	7.4	——5.4——		...	2,423	2,935	3,668	5,345	7,497	9,736	13,114	Somalia
37.1	28.5	18.1	10.1	4.7	1.5	10,353	12,458	15,925	22,460	29,799	37,346	45,453	54,661	South Africa[38]
52.6[5]	21.3[5]	10.4[5]	——13.6[5]——		2.1[5]	...	...	...	...	1,335	1,969	2,445	2,995	Bophuthatswana
44.9	26.2	15.0	6.9	5.5	1.5	...	...	...	...	682	817	1,015	1,244	Ciskei
43.7[5]	21.5[5]	13.3[5]	——20.3[5]——		1.2[5]	...	...	...	...	2,336	3,163	3,928	4,812	Transkei
43.3[5]	20.3[5]	12.4[5]	——22.7[5]——		1.3[5]	...	...	...	...	345	543	674	825	Venda
25.6[8]	23.2[8]	17.9[8]	17.6[8]	11.4[8]	4.2[8]	25,757	27,868	30,303	33,779	37,581	38,959	39,879	40,317	Spain
35.3	29.6	17.9	10.6	5.2	1.4	5,972	7,678	9,889	12,514	14,747	16,993	19,190	21,261	Sri Lanka
45.1[2]	26.1[2]	15.6[2]	8.7[2]	3.8[2]	0.7[2]	8,500	9,322	11,256	14,090	19,449	28,311	37,607	49,040	Sudan, The
39.3	29.5	13.8	10.0	4.5	2.8	193	215	247	292	355	403	410	417	Suriname
47.3	26.6	13.4	7.4	3.4	1.3	154	253	320	409	559	770	1,089	1,501	Swaziland
18.2	20.5	20.8	17.8	14.5	8.1	6,371	7,041	7,498	8,081	8,310	8,559	8,938	9,157	Sweden
19.2	23.1	22.0	17.4	12.7	5.6	4,234	4,715	5,429	6,270	6,385	6,796	7,028	7,049	Switzerland
48.5	25.8		8.3	3.7	1.2	2,597	3,495	4,561	6,305	8,704	12,116	16,876	22,923	Syria
32.1	32.1	16.5	12.6	5.7	1.0	5,987	7,619	10,668	14,583	17,705	20,279	22,621	25,234	Taiwan
42.9	28.1	13.8	9.0	4.6	1.6	1,525	1,532	2,083	2,942	3,967	5,303	7,041	8,948	Tajikistan
46.2[42]	24.9[42]	14.4[42]	8.5[42]	4.5[42]	1.6[42]	...	7,892	10,073	13,273	18,441	24,403	32,292	42,732	Tanzania
28.8	30.4	21.2	12.3	5.7	1.6	15,296	20,010	26,392	35,745	45,044	54,799	65,534	76,656	Thailand
49.8	24.8	13.1	6.8	3.3	2.0	834	1,201	1,465	1,954	2,614	3,493	4,668	6,238	Togo
40.6	29.0	13.8	10.1	5.0	1.4	37	50	65	80	92	96	101	106	Tonga
34.2[6]	30.9[6]	16.3[6]	10.0[6]	6.2[6]	1.7[6]	503	668	828	941	1,082	1,237	1,362	1,500	Trinidad and Tobago
39.7	28.8	14.2	10.7	5.4	1.2	2,887	3,530	4,221	5,137	6,392	8,074	9,779	11,288	Tunisia
37.1[26]	26.3[26]	17.1[26]	12.6[26]	——6.9[26]——		17,723	20,809	27,509	35,321	44,438	56,098	69,694	78,524	Turkey
40.5	28.8	15.5	9.1	4.7	1.4	1,302	1,211	1,594	2,189	2,860	3,668	4,585	5,491	Turkmenistan
31.8[11]	31.7[11]	15.2[11]	13.2[11]	6.3[11]	1.7[11]	4	5	5	6	8	9	11	14	Tuvalu
47.8[13]	26.0[13]	14.0[13]	8.0[13]	3.5[13]	0.6[13]	4,233	5,969	7,551	9,806	12,777	16,364	20,958	26,842	Uganda
21.5	21.0	20.6	18.5	10.7	7.7	41,340	36,906	42,783	47,317	50,033	51,892	52,558	53,245	Ukraine
31.9[2]	24.9[2]	32.1[2]	8.7[2]	1.9[2]	0.5[2]	...	70	90	223	1,015	1,903	2,332	2,724	United Arab Emirates
20.6	22.8	19.4	16.9	14.4	5.8	48,226	50,290	52,372	55,632	56,330	57,411	59,021	59,962	United Kingdom
22.6[6]	27.4[6]	19.1[6]	15.2[6]	11.3[6]	4.4[6]	132,594	152,271	180,671	204,879	227,722	249,924	269,207	283,566	United States
26.6	22.8	18.3	16.5	11.4	4.3	1,974	2,194	2,531	2,824	2,914	3,094	3,274	3,453	Uruguay
40.8	28.4	15.0	9.3	4.7	1.8	6,551	6,314	8,559	11,973	15,975	20,515	26,044	32,453	Uzbekistan
45.3[11]	27.5[11]	15.0[11]	7.7[11]	3.4[11]	1.1[11]	43	52	65	86	115	147	177	208	Vanuatu
40.5[8]	29.9[8]	15.8[8]	8.7[8]	4.0[8]	1.1[8]	3,740	5,009	7,502	10,604	15,024	19,260	24,072	29,157	Venezuela
39.0	28.7	16.0	9.1	5.6	1.6	20,209	22,725	30,172	41,063	53,722	66,233	81,094	95,701	Vietnam
36.0[6]	24.2[6]	21.5[6]	11.1[6]	5.7[6]	1.4[6]	25	27	32	75	97	102	107	113	Virgin Islands (U.S.)
47.4	——40.0——			——12.6——		...	...	...	608	721	932	1,192	1,505	West Bank
42.9	27.2	16.3	7.4	4.4	1.8	...	14	32	76	155	199	256	329	Western Sahara
41.1[7]	30.9[7]	13.3[7]	9.1[7]	4.4[7]	1.2[7]	61	82	111	143	155	165	171	171	Western Samoa
45.7[8]	23.2[8]	15.1[8]	10.5[8]	4.7[8]	0.8[8]	...	4,529	5,538	6,276	8,854	11,546	14,879	19,173	Yemen
24.2[8]	23.8[8]	19.9[8]	19.4[8]	9.1[8]	3.2[8]	...	7,131	8,050	8,910	9,866	10,304	10,761	11,239	Yugoslavia
45.2[2]	25.9[2]	15.5[2]	8.7[2]	3.9[2]	0.7[2]	10,370	13,055	16,151	21,368	27,406	38,616	53,118	72,538	Zaire
49.0[6]	24.8[6]	13.1[6]	7.4[6]	3.5[6]	0.9[6]	1,484	2,440	3,141	4,189	5,634	7,783	10,753	14,855	Zambia
51.0	26.3	13.4	6.5	1.2	1.6	1,940	2,730	3,840	5,308	7,100	9,369	11,943	14,739	Zimbabwe

census. [30]1967 census. [31]Island of Mauritius only. [32]Including 163,868 in Western Sahara. [33]Indigenous population only. [34]1991 civil register. [35]1963 census. [36]Excludes Afghan refugees and residents of Pakistani-occupied Jammu and Kashmir. [37]Excludes North Solomons Province. [38]Includes black national states shown separately. [39]Excludes Bophuthatswana, Ciskei, Transkei, and Venda. [40]1985 estimate; includes Bophuthatswana, Ciskei, Transkei, and Venda. [41]Includes resident aliens; excludes seasonal workers. [42]1978 census. [43]Includes residents abroad and foreign military personnel; excludes visitors. [44]Former Yemen Arab Republic only. [45]Includes 1,168,199 nationals abroad.

Major cities and national capitals

The following table lists the principal cities or municipalities (those exceeding 100,000 in population [50,000 for Anglo-America]) of the countries of the world, together with figures for each national capital (indicated by a ★), regardless of size.

Most of the populations given refer to a so-called city proper, that is, a legally defined, incorporated, or chartered area defined by administrative boundaries and by national or state law. Some data, however, refer to the municipality, or commune, similar to the medieval city-state in that the city is governed together with its immediately adjoining, economically dependent areas, whether urban or rural in nature. Some countries define no other demographic or legal entities within such communes or municipalities, but many identify a centre, seat, head (*cabecera*), or locality that corresponds to the most densely populated, compact, contiguous core of the municipality. Because the amount of work involved in carefully defining these "centres" may be considerable, the necessary resources usually exist only at the time of a national census (generally 5 or 10 years apart). Between censuses, therefore, it may be possible only to track the growth of the municipality as a whole. Thus, in order to provide the most up-to-date data for cities in this table, figures referring to municipalities or communes may be given (identified by the abbreviation "MU"), even though the country itself may define a smaller, more closely knit city proper. Specific identification of municipalities is provided in this table *only* when

the country also publishes data for a more narrowly defined city proper; it is *not* provided when the sole published figure is the municipality, whether or not this is the proper local administrative term for the entity.

Problems also exist in the identification of cities in terms of named legal entities. There is, for example, a single municipality (*commune*) named Brussel (Brussels) at the centre of the Brussels agglomeration in Belgium; the *commune* numbers only about 136,000 population, while the agglomeration, which is understood by most people to constitute the city, numbers nearly a million. Both are shown so as to apprise the reader of the existence of a problem.

For certain countries, more than one form of the name of the city is given, usually to permit recognition of recent place name changes or of *forms* of the place name likely to be encountered in press stories if the title of the city's entry in the *Encyclopædia Britannica* is spelled according to a different romanization or spelling policy. Chinese names, *e.g.*, are given first in their Wade-Giles spelling (the scholarly system used by Britannica) and then, parenthetically, in their Pinyin spelling, the official Chinese system now encountered in press reports, official documents, and maps.

Sources for this data were usually the national census and statistical abstracts of the countries concerned, supplemented by correspondence with most national statistical offices to solicit unpublished data.

Major cities and national capitals

country / city	population	country / city	population	country / city	population	country / city	population	country / city	population
Afghanistan (1988 est.)		Paraná	277,338	Mymensingh	185,517	**Brazil** (1980)		Santa Maria	151,202
Herāt	177,300	Posadas	219,824	Naogaon	100,794	Americana	121,794	Santarém	101,534
★ Kābul	1,424,400	Quilmes	509,445	Nārāyanganj	268,952	Anápolis	160,520	Santo Andre	549,278
Kandahār (Qandahār)	225,500	Resistencia	218,438[2]	Nawābganj	121,205	Aracaju	288,106	Santos	411,023
Mazār-e Sharīf	130,600	Río Cuarto	217,717	Pābna	104,479	Araçatuba	113,486	São Bernardo	
		Rosario	875,664[2]	Rājshāhi	299,671	Barra Mansa	123,421	do Campo	381,261
Albania (1989)		Salta	373,857	Rangpur	203,931	Bauru	178,861	São Caetano do	
★ Tiranë	239,400	San Fernando	144,761	Saidpur	102,030	Belém	758,117	Sul	163,030
		San Isidro	299,022	Tangail	104,387	Belo Horizonte	1,442,483	São Carlos	109,231
Algeria (1987)		San Juan	119,399	Tongi	154,175	Blumenau	144,819	São Gonçalo	221,278
★ Algiers	1,507,241	San Justo	946,715[2]			★ Brasília	411,305	São João de Meriti	210,548
Annaba	305,526	San Luis	121,146	**Barbados** (1990)		Campina Grande	222,229	São José	
Batna	181,601	San Miguel de		★ Bridgetown	6,070	Campinas	566,517	do Rio Prêto	171,982
Béchar	107,311	Tucumán	473,014			Campo Grande	282,844	São José dos	
Bejaïa	114,534	San Salvador de		**Belarus** (1991 est.)		Campos	174,218	Campos	268,073
Biskra	128,280	Jujuy	124,950[2]	Baranovichi	166,700	Canoas	214,115	São Luís	182,466
Blida (el-Boulaida)	170,935	Santa Fe	442,214	Bobruysk	223,000	Carapicuiba	185,763	São Paulo	7,033,529
ech-Cheliff	129,976	Santiago del Estero	201,709	Borisov	150,200	Caruaru	137,636	São Vicente	192,770
Constantine		Tigre	256,005	Brest	277,000	Cascavel	100,351	Sorocaba	254,718
(Qacentina)	440,842	Tres de Febrero	349,221	Gomel	503,300	Caxias do Sul	198,824	Taubaté	155,371
Mostaganem	114,037	Vicente López	289,142	Grodno	284,800	Contagem	111,697	Teresina	339,264
Oran (Wahran)	628,558			★ Minsk	1,633,600	Cuiabá	167,894	Uberaba	180,296
Sétif	170,182	**Armenia** (1991 est.)		Mogilyov	363,000	Curitiba	843,733	Uberlândia	230,400
Sidi bel Abbès	152,778	Kirovakan	169,000[3]	Mozyr	103,000	Diadema	228,594	Vitória	144,143
Skikda	128,747	Kumayri (Leninakan)	120,000[4]	Orsha	125,300	Divinopolis	108,344	Vitória da	
Tébessa	107,559	★ Yerevan	1,283,000	Pinsk	123,800	Duque de Caxias	306,057	Conquista	125,717
Tlemcen (Tilimsen)	126,882			Vitebsk	361,500	Feira de Santana	225,003	Volta Redonda	177,772
		Aruba (1986 est.)				Florianópolis	153,547		
American Samoa		★ Oranjestad	19,800	**Belgium** (1991)		Fortaleza	648,815	**Brunei** (1991)	
(1990)				Antwerp	467,518	Franca	143,630	★ Bandar Seri	
★ Pago Pago	3,519	**Australia** (1991)[5, 6]		Brugge (Bruges)	117,063	Goiânia	703,263	Begawan	21,484
		Adelaide	1,023,617	★ Brussels	136,424	Governador			
Andorra (1990)		Brisbane	1,334,746	Agglomeration	954,045	Valadares	173,699	**Bulgaria** (1991 est.)	
★ Andorra la Vella	20,437	★ Canberra	278,894	Charleroi	206,214	Guarulhos	395,117	Burgas	204,915
		Geelong	145,323	Ghent	230,246	Imperatriz	111,818	Pleven	138,323
Angola (1990 est.)		Gold Coast	157,859	Liège (Luik)	194,596	Ipatinga	105,083	Plovdiv	379,083
★ Luanda	1,544,400	Hobart	181,838	Namur	103,443	Itabuna	129,938	Ruse	192,365
Lubango	105,000[1]	Melbourne	3,022,157	Schaerbeek	102,702	Jacareí	103,652	Shumen	110,754
		Newcastle	427,703			João Pessoa	290,424	★ Sofia	1,141,142
Antigua and Barbuda		Perth	1,143,265	**Belize** (1990 est.)		Joinville	217,074	Sliven	112,220
(1986 est.)		Sunshine Coast	126,142	★ Belmopan	5,256	Juàzeiro do Norte	125,248	Stara Zagora	164,553
★ Saint John's	36,000	Sydney	3,538,970			Juiz de Fora	299,728	Tolbukhin	115,786
		Wollongong	236,010	**Benin** (1982 est.)		Jundiaí	210,015	Varna	314,913
Argentina (1991; MU)				★ Cotonou (official)	487,020	Lages	108,768		
Almirante Brown	449,105	**Austria** (1991)		★ Porto-Novo (de facto)	208,258	Limeira	137,812	**Burkina Faso** (1985)	
Avellaneda	346,620	Graz	232,155			Londrina	258,054	Bobo Dioulasso	228,668
Bahía Blanca	271,467	Innsbruck	114,996	**Bermuda** (1991)		Maceió	376,479	★ Ouagadougou	441,514
Berazategui	243,690	Linz	202,855	★ Hamilton	1,100	Manaus	613,068		
★ Buenos Aires	2,960,976	Salzburg	143,971			Marília	103,904	**Burundi** (1989)	
Caseros	340,343[2]	★ Vienna	1,533,176	**Bhutan** (1987 est.)		Maringá	158,047	★ Bujumbura	240,525
Catamarca	110,489			★ Paro (administrative)	3,000[7]	Mauá	205,817	Gitega	100,333
Concordia	138,905	**Azerbaijan** (1991 est.)		★ Thimphu (official)	15,000	Mogi das Cruzes	122,265		
Córdoba	1,179,067	★ Baku (Baky)	1,080,500			Montes Claros	151,881	**Cambodia** (1989 est.)	
Corrientes	267,742	Gyandzha	282,200	**Bolivia** (1989 est.)		Mossoró	118,007	★ Phnom Penh	800,000
Esteban Echeverría	276,017	Sumgait	236,200	Cochabamba	403,600	Natal	376,552		
Florencio Varela	253,554			El Alto	307,400	Nilópolis	103,033	**Cameroon** (1987)	
Formosa	165,700	**Bahamas, The** (1990)		★ La Paz	473,856	Niterói	386,185	Bafoussam	113,000
General San Martín	407,506	★ Nassau	172,196	(administrative)	669,400	Nova Iguaçu	491,802	Bamenda	110,000
General Sarmiento	646,891			Oruro	176,700	Novo Hamburgo	132,066	Douala	810,000
Godoy Cruz	141,553[2]	**Bahrain** (1988 est.)		Potosí	110,700	Olinda	266,392	Garoua	142,000
Guaymallén	157,334[2]	★ al-Manāmah	151,500	Santa Cruz	529,200	Osasco	473,856	Maroua	123,000
La Matanza	1,121,164			★ Sucre (judicial)	105,800	Passo Fundo	103,121	Nkongsamba	112,000
La Plata	542,567	**Bangladesh** (1991)				Pelotas	197,092	★ Yaoundé	649,000
La Rioja	106,281	Barisāl	163,481	**Bosnia and Hercegovina**		Petrópolis	149,427		
Lanús	466,755	Chittagong	1,363,998	(1991; MU)		Piracicaba	179,395	**Canada** (1991)	
Lomas de Zamora	572,769	Comilla	143,282	Banja Luka	195,139	Ponta Grossa	171,111	Barrie	62,728
Mar del Plata	414,696[2]	Dhākā (Dacca)	3,397,187	★ Sarajevo	525,980	Porto Alegre	1,108,883	Beauport	69,158
Mendoza	121,696	Dinājpur	126,189			Porto Velho	101,644	Brampton	234,445
Merlo	390,031	Jamālpur	101,242	**Botswana** (1991)		Presidente Prudente	127,623	Brantford	81,997
Moreno	287,188	Jessore	160,198	★ Gaborone	133,791	Recife	1,184,215	Burlington	129,575
Morón	641,541	Khulna	545,849			Ribeirão Prêto	300,704	Burnaby	158,858
						Rio Claro	135,957		
						Rio de Janeiro	5,090,700		
						Rio Grande	124,706		
						Salvador	1,506,602		

country city	population
Calgary	710,677
Cambridge	92,772
Charlesbourg	70,788
Chicoutimi	62,670
Chilliwack	50,228
Dartmouth	67,798
Delta	88,978
East York	102,696
Edmonton	616,741
Etobicoke	309,993
Guelph	87,976
Halifax	114,455
Hamilton	318,499
Hull	60,707
Jonquiere	57,933
Kamloops	67,057
Kelowna	75,950
Kingston	56,597
Kitchener	168,282
Laval	314,398
Lethbridge	60,974
London	303,165
Longueuil	129,874
Markham	153,811
Mississauga	463,388
Moncton	57,010
Montreal	1,017,666
Montreal-Nord	85,516
Nanaimo	60,129
Niagara Falls	75,399
North Bay	55,405
North York	562,564
Oshawa	129,344
★ Ottawa	313,987
Peterborough	68,371
Prince George	69,653
Quebec	167,517
Red Deer	58,134
Regina	179,178
Richmond	126,624
Saint Catharines	129,300
Saint-Hubert	74,027
Saint John	74,969
Saint John's	95,770
Saint-Laurent	72,402
Sainte-Foy	73,133
Sarnia-Clearwater	74,167
Saskatoon	186,058
Sault Sainte Marie	81,476
Scarborough	524,598
Sherbrooke	76,429
Sudbury	92,884
Surrey	245,173
Thunder Bay	113,746
Toronto	635,395
Vancouver	471,844
Verdun	61,307
Victoria	71,228
Waterloo	71,181
Windsor	191,435
Winnipeg	616,790
York	140,525
Cape Verde (1990)	
★ Praia	61,797
Cayman Islands (1989)	
★ George Town	12,921
Central African Republic (1988)	
★ Bangui	451,690
Chad (1992 est.)	
Moundou	117,500
★ N'Djamena	687,800
Sarh	129,600
Chile (1991 est.; MU)	
Antofagasta	221,200
Arica	194,588
Calama	117,577
Chillán	162,201
Concepción	311,537
Coquimbo	116,685
Curicó	109,139
Iquique	152,113
La Serena	118,106
Los Angeles	136,520
Osorno	136,223
Puente Alto	198,336
Puerto Montt	125,061
Punta Arenas	125,030
Quilpué	111,553
Rancagua	200,361
San Bernardo	199,935
★ Santiago	3,604,056[8]
(Greater Santiago; administrative)	5,342,913
Talca	182,854
Talcahuano	251,135
Temuco	249,225
Valdívia	123,580
★ Valparaíso (legislative)	295,954
Viña del Mar	312,306
China (1990)[9]	
A-ch'eng (Acheng)	197,595
A-k'o-su (Aksu)	164,092
An-ch'ing (Anqing)	250,718
An-k'ang (Ankang)	142,170
An-shan (Anshan)	1,203,986
An-shun (Anshun)	174,142
An-ta (Anda)	136,446
An-yang (Anyang)	420,332
Canton (Guangzhou)	2,914,281
Chan-chiang (Zhanjiang)	400,997
Ch'ang-chi (Changji)	132,260
Chang-chia-k'ou (Zhangjiakou)	529,136
Ch'ang-chih (Changzhi)	317,144
Ch'ang-chou (Changzhou)	531,470
Chang-chou (Zhangzhou)	181,424
Ch'ang-ch'un (Changchun)	1,679,270
Ch'ang-sha (Changsha)	1,113,212
Ch'ang-shu (Changshu)	181,805
Ch'ang-te (Changde)	301,276
Chao-ch'ing (Zhaoqing)	194,784
Ch'ao-chou (Chaozhou)	313,469
Ch'ao-hsien (Chaoxian)	123,676
Chao-tung (Zhaodong)	179,976
Ch'ao-yang (Chaoyang)	222,394
Chen-chiang (Zhenjiang)	368,316
Cheng-chou (Zhengzhou)	1,159,679
Ch'eng-te (Chengde)	246,799
Ch'eng-tu (Chengdu)	1,713,255
Chi-an (Ji'an)	148,583
Chi-hsi (Jixi)	683,885
Chi-lin (Jilin)	1,036,858
Chi-nan (Jinan)	1,480,915
Chi-ning (Jining) (*Inner Mongolia*)	163,552
Chi-ning (Jining) (*Shantung*)	265,248
Ch'i-t'ai-ho (Qitaihe)	214,957
Ch'i-tung (Qidong)	126,872
Chia-hsing (Jiaxing)	211,526
Chia-mu-ssu (Jiamusi)	493,409
Chiang-men (Jiangmen)	230,587
Chiang-yin (Jiangyin)	213,659
Chiang-yu (Jiangyou)	175,753
Chiao-hsien (Jiaoxian)	153,364
Chiao-nan (Jiaonan)	121,397
Chiao-tso (Jiaozuo)	409,100
Ch'ien-chiang (Qianjiang)	205,504
Ch'ih-feng (Chifeng)	350,077
Chin-ch'ang (Jinchang)	105,287
Chin-ch'eng (Jincheng)	136,396
Chin-chou (Jinzhou)	569,518
Ch'in-chou (Qinzhou)	114,586
Chin-hsi (Jinxi)	357,052
Chin-hua (Jinhua)	144,280
Ch'in-huang-tao (Qinhuangdao)	364,972
Ch'ing-chou (Qingzhou)	128,258
Ch'ing-tao (Qingdao)	1,459,195
Ching-te-chen (Jingdezhen)	281,183
Ch'ing-yüan (Qingyuan)	164,641
Chiu-chiang (Jiujiang)	291,187
Chiu-t'ai (Jiutai)	180,130
Chou-k'ou (Zhoukou)	146,288
Chou-shan (Zhoushan)	156,317
Chu-ch'eng (Zhucheng)	102,134
Ch'ü-ching (Qujing)	178,669
Ch'u-chou (Quzhou)	112,373
Chu-chou (Zhuzhou)	409,924
Chu-hai (Zhuhai)	164,747
Ch'u-hsien (Chuxian)	125,341
Chu-ma-tien (Zhumadian)	123,232
Ch'üan-chou (Quanzhou)	185,154
Chung-shan (Zhongshan)	278,829
Chungking (Chongqing)	2,266,772
Feng-ch'eng (Fengcheng)	193,784
Fo-shan (Foshan)	303,160
Fu-chin (Fujin)	103,104
Fu-chou (Fuzhou) (*Fukien*)	874,809
Fu-chou (Fuzhou) (*Kiangsi*)	121,949
Fu-hsin (Fuxin)	635,473
Fu-ling (Fuling)	173,878
Fu-shun (Fushun)	1,202,388
Fu-yang (Fuyang)	179,572
Fu-yü (Fuyu)	192,981
Ha-mi (Hami)	161,315
Hai-ch'eng (Haicheng)	205,560
Hai-k'ou (Haikou)	280,153
Hai-la-erh (Hailar)	180,650
Hai-lun (Kailun)	133,565
Hai-ning (Haining)	100,478
Han-chung (Hanzhong)	169,930
Han-tan (Handan)	837,552
Hang-chou (Hangzhou)	1,099,660
Harbin	2,443,398
Heng-shui (Hengshui)	104,269
Heng-yang (Hengyang)	487,148
Ho-fei (Hefei)	733,278
Ho-kang (Hegang)	522,747
Ho-pi (Hebi)	212,976
Ho-tse (Heze)	189,293
Ho-yuan (Heyuan)	120,101
Hsi-ch'ang (Xichang)	134,419
Hsi-ning (Xining)	551,776
Hsia-men (Xiamen)	368,786
Hsiang-fan (Xiangfan)	410,407
Hsiang-t'an (Xiangtan)	441,968
Hsiao-kan (Xiaogan)	166,280
Hsiao-shan (Xiaoshan)	162,930
Hsien-ning (Xianning)	136,811
Hsien-t'ao (Xiantao)	222,884
Hsien-yang (Xianyang)	352,125
Hsin-hsiang (Xinxiang)	473,762
Hsin-t'ai (Xintai)	281,248
Hsin-yang (Xinyang)	192,509
Hsin-yu (Xinyu)	173,524
Hsing-ch'eng (Xingcheng)	102,384
Hsing-hua (Xinghua)	161,910
Hsing-t'ai (Xingtai)	302,789
Hsü-ch'ang (Xuchang)	208,815
Hsü-chou (Xuzhou)	805,695
Hsuan-ch'eng (Xuancheng)	112,673
Hu-chou (Huzhou)	218,071
Hu-ho-hao-t'e (Hohhot)	652,534
Hua-tien (Huadian)	175,873
Huai-an (Huai'an)	131,149
Huai-hua (Huaihua)	126,785
Huai-nan (Huainan)	703,934
Huai-pei (Huaibei)	366,549
Huai-yin (Huaiyin)	239,675
Huang-shan (Huangshan)	102,628
Huang-shih (Huangshi)	457,601
Hui-chou (Huizhou)	161,023
Hun-chiang (Hunjiang)	482,043
Hung-hu (Honghu)	190,772
I-ch'ang (Yichang)	371,601
I-cheng (Yizheng)	109,268
I-ch'un (Yichun)	795,789
I-ch'un (Yichun) (*Kiangsi*)	151,585
I-hsing (Yixing)	200,824
I-ning (Yining)	177,193
I-pin (Yibin)	241,019
I-yang (Yiyang)	185,818
Jen-ch'iu (Renqiu)	114,256
Jih-chao (Rizhao)	185,048
Jui-an (Rui'an)	156,468
K'ai-feng (Kaifeng)	507,763
K'ai-li (Kaili)	113,958
K'ai-yuan (Kaiyuan)	124,219
Kan-chou (Ganzhou)	220,129
Kashgar (Kashi)	174,570
Ko-chiu (Gejiu)	214,294
K'o-la-ma-i (Karamay)	197,602
K'u-erh-le (Korla)	159,344
Kuang-shui (Guangshui)	102,770
Kuang-yüan (Guangyuan)	182,241
Kuei-hsien (Guixian)	114,025
Kuei-lin (Guilin)	364,130
K'uei-t'un (Kuitun)	118,553
Kuei-yang (Guiyang)	1,018,619
K'un-ming (Kunming)	1,127,411
K'un-shan (Kunshan)	102,052
Kung-chu-ling (Gongzhuling)	226,569
Lai-chou (Laizhou)	198,664
Lai-wu (Laiwu)	246,833
Lai-yang (Laiyang)	137,080
Lan-chou (Lanzhou)	1,194,640
Lang-fang (Langfang)	148,105
Lao-ho-k'ou (Laohekou)	123,366
Le-shan (Leshan)	341,128
Lei-yang (Leiyang)	130,115
Leng-shui-chiang (Lengshuijiang)	137,994
Lhasa	106,885
Li-ling (Liling)	108,504
Li-yang (Liyang)	109,520
Liang-ch'eng (Liangcheng)	156,307
Liao-ch'eng (Liaocheng)	207,844
Liao-yang (Liaoyang)	492,559
Liao-yüan (Liaoyuan)	354,141
Lien-yüan (Lianyuan)	118,858
Lien-yün-kang (Lianyungang)	354,139
Lin-ch'ing (Linqing)	123,958
Lin-fen (Linfen)	187,309
Lin-ho (Linhe)	133,183
Lin-i (Linyi)	324,720
Liu-chou (Liuzhou)	609,320
Liu-p'an-shui (Liupanshui)	363,954
Lo-ho (Luohe)	126,438
Lo-yang (Luoyang)	759,752
Long-yen (Longyan)	134,481
Lou-ti (Loudi)	128,418
Lu-an (Lu'an)	144,248
Lu-chou (Luzhou)	262,892
Lung-ching (Longjing)	139,417
Lung-k'ou (Longkou)	148,362
Ma-an-shan (Ma'anshan)	305,421
Man-chou-li (Manzhouli)	120,023
Mao-ming (Maoming)	178,683
Mei-ho-k'ou (Meihekou)	209,038
Mei-hsien (Meixian)	132,156
Mi-shan (Mishan)	132,744
Mien-yang (Mianyang)	262,947
Mu-tan-chiang (Mudanjiang)	571,705
Nan-ch'ang (Nanchang)	1,086,124
Nan-ch'ung (Nanchong)	180,273
Nan-ning (Nanning)	721,877
Nan-p'ing (Nanping)	195,064
Nan-t'ung (Nantong)	343,341
Nan-yang (Nanyang)	243,303
Nanking (Nanjing)	2,090,204
Nei-chiang (Neijiang)	256,012
Ning-po (Ningbo)	552,540
O-ch'eng (Echeng)	190,123
Pai-ch'eng (Baicheng)	217,987
Pai-yin (Baiyin)	204,970
P'an-chih-hua (Panzhihua) (Tu-k'ou [Dukou])	415,466
P'an-shan (Panshan)	362,773
Pang-pu (Bengbu)	449,245
Pao-chi (Baoji)	337,765
Pao-ting (Baoding)	483,155
Pao-t'ou (Baotou)	983,508
Pei-an (Bei'an)	204,899
Pei-hai (Beihai)	112,673
Pei-p'iao (Beipiao)	194,301
★ Peking (Beijing)	5,769,607
Pen-hsi (Benxi)	768,778
Pin-chou (Binzhou)	133,555
P'ing-hsiang (Pingxiang)	425,579
P'ing-ting-shan (Pingdingshan)	410,775
P'ing-tu (Pingdu)	150,123
Po-chou (Bozhou)	106,346
P'u-ch'i (Puqi)	117,264
P'u-yang (Puyang)	175,988
San-men-hsia (Sanmenxia)	120,523
San-ming (Sanming)	160,691
San-ya (Sanya)	102,820
Sha-shih (Shashi)	281,352
Shan-t'ou (Shantou)	578,630
Shan-wei (Shanwei)	107,847
Shao-hsing (Shaoxing)	179,818
Shao-kuan (Shaoguan)	350,043
Shao-yang (Shaoyang)	247,227
Shang-chih (Shangzhi)	215,373
Shang-ch'iu (Shangqiu)	164,880
Shang-jao (Shangrao)	132,455
Shanghai	7,496,509
Shen-chen (Shenzhen)	350,727
Shen-yang (Shenyang)	3,603,712
Shih-chia-chuang (Shijiazhuang)	1,068,439
Shih-ho-tzu (Shihezi)	299,676
Shih-shou (Shishou)	104,571
Shih-tsui-shan (Shizuishan)	257,862
Shih-yen (Shiyan)	273,786
Shuang-ch'eng (Shuangcheng)	142,659
Shuang-ya-shan (Shuangyashan)	386,081
Sian (Xi'an)	1,959,044
Ssu-p'ing (Siping)	317,223
Su-ch'ien (Suqian)	105,021
Su-chou (Suzhou) (*Anhwei*)	151,862
Su-chou (Suzhou) (*Kiangsu*)	706,459
Sui-hua (Suihua)	227,881
Sui-ning (Suining)	146,086
Ta-an (Da'an)	138,963
Ta-ch'ing (Daqing)	657,297
Ta-hsien (Daxian)	188,101
Ta-li (Dali)	136,554
Ta-lien (Dalian)	1,723,302
Ta-t'ung (Datong)	798,319
T'ai-an (Tai'an)	350,696
T'ai-chou (Taizhou)	152,442
T'ai-yüan (Taiyuan)	1,533,884
Tan-chiang (Danjiang)	103,211
Tan-tung (Dandong)	523,699
Tan-yang (Danyang)	169,603
T'ang-shan (Tangshan)	1,044,194
T'ao-nan (Taonan)	150,168
Te-chou (Dezhou)	195,485
Te-yang (Deyang)	182,488
T'eng-hsien (Tengxian)	315,083
T'ieh-fa (Tiefa)	131,807
T'ieh-li (Tieli)	265,683
T'ieh-ling (Tieling)	254,842
T'ien-men (Tianmen)	186,332
T'ien-shui (Tianshui)	244,974
Tientsin (Tianjin)	4,574,689
Tsa-lan-t'un (Zalantun)	130,031
Ts'ang-chou (Cangzhou)	242,708
Tsao-chuang (Zaozhuang)	380,846
Tsao-yang (Zaoyang)	162,198
Tsitsihar (Qiqihar)	1,070,051
Tsun-i (Zunyi)	261,862
Tu-chiang-yen (Dujiangyan)	123,357
Tu-yun (Duyun)	132,971
Tun-hua (Dunhua)	235,100
T'ung-ch'uan (Tongchuan)	280,657
T'ung-hua (Tonghua)	324,600
Tung-kuan (Dongguan)	308,669
T'ung-liao (Tongliao)	255,129
T'ung-ling (Tongling)	228,017
Tung-t'ai (Dongtai)	192,247
Tung-ying (Dongying)	281,728
Tz'u-hsi (Cixi)	107,329
Tzu-hsing (Zixing)	110,048
Tzu-kung (Zigong)	393,184
Tzu-po (Zibo)	1,138,074
Wa-fang-tien (Wafangdian)	251,733
Wan-hsien (Wanxian)	156,823
Wei-fang (Weifang)	428,522
Wei-hai (Weihai)	128,888
Wei-nan (Weinan)	140,169
Wen-chou (Wenzhou)	401,871
Wen-teng (Wendeng)	133,910
Wu-chou (Wuzhou)	210,452
Wu-hai (Wuhai)	264,081
Wu-han (Wuhan)	3,284,229
Wu-hsi (Wuxi)	826,833
Wu-hu (Wuhu)	425,740
Wu-lan-hao-t'e (Ulanhot)	159,538
Wu-lu-mu-ch'i (Ürümqi)	1,046,898
Wu-wei (Wuwei)	133,101
Ya-k'o-she (Yakeshi)	377,869
Yang-chiang (Yangjiang)	215,196
Yang-chou (Yangzhou)	312,892
Yang-ch'üan (Yangquan)	362,268
Yen-an (Yan'an)	113,277
Yen-ch'eng (Yancheng)	296,831
Yen-chi (Yanji)	230,892
Yen-t'ai (Yantai)	452,127
Yin-ch'uan (Yinchuan)	356,652
Ying-k'ou (Yingkou)	421,589
Yü-lin (Yulin)	144,467
Yü-men (Yumen)	109,234
Yü-shu (Yushu)	131,861
Yü-tz'u (Yuci)	191,356
Yu-yao (Yuyao)	114,065
Yüan-chiang (Yuanjiang)	107,004
Yüeh-yang (Yueyang)	302,800
Yun-ch'eng (Yuncheng)	108,359
Yung-an (Yong'an)	111,762
Colombia (1985)	
Armenia	180,221
Barrancabermeja	137,406
Barranquilla	896,649
Bello	206,297
Bucaramanga	341,513
Buenaventura	160,342
Cali	1,323,944
Cartagena	491,368
Cúcuta	357,026
Floridablanca	137,975
Ibagué	269,495
Itagüí	135,797
Manizales	275,067

Major cities and national capitals (continued)

country city	population
Medellín	1,418,554
Montería	157,466
Neiva	178,130
Palmira	175,186
Pasto	197,407
Pereira	233,271
Popayán	141,964
Santa Marta	177,922
★ Santafé de Bogotá, D.C.	3,974,813
Sincelejo	120,537
Soledad	164,494
Valledupar	142,771
Villavicencio	161,166
Comoros (1988 est.)	
★ Moroni	22,000
Congo (1992 est.)	
★ Brazzaville	937,579
Pointe-Noire	576,206
Cook Islands (1986)	
★ Rarotonga Island	9,678
Costa Rica (1991 est.)	
★ San José	299,456
Côte d'Ivoire (1984 est.)	
★ Abidjan	1,850,000
Bouaké	220,000
Yamoussoukro	120,000
Croatia (1991; MU)	
Osijek	164,589
Rijeka	205,842
Split	206,559
★ Zagreb	930,753
Cuba (1989 est.)	
Bayamo	121,926
Camagüey	278,958
Cienfuegos	119,300
Guantánamo	197,868
★ Havana	2,077,938
Holguín	222,794
Las Tunas	115,208
Matanzas	112,123
Pinar del Río	116,500
Santa Clara	190,735
Santiago de Cuba	397,024
Cyprus (1990 est.)[5]	
Limassol	132,100
★ Nicosia	168,800[10]
Czechoslovakia (1991)	
Bratislava	441,453
Brno	387,986
Košice	234,840
Liberec	101,934
Olomouc	105,690
Ostrava	327,553
Plzen	173,129
★ Prague	1,212,010
Denmark (1990 est.)	
Ålborg	113,599
Århus	200,188
★ Copenhagen	1,337,114[5]
Odense	138,986
Djibouti (1988 est.)	
★ Djibouti	290,000
Dominica (1991)	
★ Roseau	20,755
Dominican Republic (1986 est.)	
La Romana	101,350
Santiago de los Caballeros	308,400
★ Santo Domingo	1,600,000
Ecuador (1990)	
Ambato	124,166
Cuenca	194,981
Guayaquil	1,508,444
Machala	144,197
Manta	125,505
Portoviejo	132,937
★ Quito	1,100,847
Santo Domingo	114,422
Egypt (1986)	
Alexandria	3,170,000[11]
Aswān	191,461
Asyūṭ	273,191
Banhā	115,571
Banī Suwayf	151,813

country city	population
Būr Saʿīd (Port Said)	461,000[11]
★ Cairo	6,452,000[11]
Damanhūr	190,840
al-Fayyūm	212,523
Hulwan (Helwan)	352,300[12]
al-Ismāʿīlīyah	212,567
al-Jīzah (Giza)	2,156,000[11]
Kafr ad-Dawwar	195,102
Kafr ash-Shaykh	102,910
al-Maḥallah al-Kubrā	358,844
al-Manṣūrah	316,870
al-Minyā	179,136
Qinā	119,794
Sawhāj	132,965
Shibīn al-Kawm	132,751
Shubrā al-Khaymah	811,000[11]
as-Suways (Suez)	392,000[11]
Ṭanṭā	334,505
al-Uqṣur (Luxor)	125,404
az-Zaqāzīq	245,496
El Salvador (1987 est.; MU)	
Mejicanos	112,066
San Miguel	183,449
★ San Salvador	481,397
Santa Ana	232,210
Equatorial Guinea (1983)	
★ Malabo	31,630
Estonia (1991 est.)	
★ Tallinn	481,500
Tartu	115,300
Ethiopia (1989 est.)	
★ Addis Ababa	1,732,080
Asmera	342,706
Dire Dawa	121,887
Faeroe Islands (1992 est.)	
★ Tórshavn	16,226
Fiji (1986)	
★ Suva	69,665
Finland (1992 est.)	
Espoo	175,806
★ Helsinki	496,311
Oulu	102,032
Tampere	174,266
Turku	159,541
Vantaa	102,032
France (1990; MU)	
Aix-en-Provence	126,854
Amiens	136,358
Angers	146,163
Besançon	119,194
Bordeaux	213,274
Boulogne-Billancourt	101,971
Brest	153,099
Caen	115,624
Clermont-Ferrand	140,167
Dijon	151,636
Grenoble	153,973
Le Havre	197,219
Le Mans	148,465
Lille	178,301
Limoges	136,407
Lyon	422,444
Marseille	807,726
Metz	123,920
Montpellier	210,866
Mulhouse	109,905
Nancy	102,410
Nantes	251,133
Nice	345,625
Nîmes	133,607
Orléans	107,965
★ Paris	2,175,110
Perpignan	108,049
Reims	185,164
Rennes	203,533
Rouen	105,470
Saint-Étienne	201,695
Strasbourg	255,937
Toulon	170,167
Toulouse	365,933
Tours	133,403
Villeurbanne	119,848
French Guiana (1990)	
★ Cayenne	37,097
French Polynesia (1988)	
★ Papeete	23,555
Gabon (1987 est.)	
★ Libreville	352,000
Port-Gentil	164,000

country city	population
Gambia, The (1986 est.)	
★ Banjul	44,188[13]
Serekunda	102,600
Gaza Strip (1988 est.)	
Gaza (Ghazzah)	57,000
Georgia (1991 est.)	
Batumi	137,500
Kutaisi	238,200
Rustavi	161,900
Sukhumi	120,000
★ Tbilisi	1,279,000
Germany (1991 est.)	
Aachen	241,861
Augsburg	256,877
Bergisch Gladbach	104,037
Berlin	3,433,695
Bielefeld	319,037
Bochum	396,486
★ Bonn	292,234
Bottrop	118,936
Braunschweig	258,833
Bremen	551,219
Bremerhaven	130,446
Chemnitz	294,244
Cologne (Köln)	953,551
Cottbus	125,891
Darmstadt	138,920
Dortmund	599,055
Dresden	490,571
Duisburg	535,447
Düsseldorf	575,794
Erfurt	208,989
Erlangen	102,440
Essen	626,973
Frankfurt am Main	644,865
Freiburg im Breisgau	191,029
Fürth	103,362
Gelsenkirchen	293,714
Gera	129,037
Göttingen	121,831
Hagen	214,449
Halle	310,234
Hamburg	1,652,363
Hamm	179,639
Hannover	513,010
Heidelberg	136,796
Heilbronn	115,843
Herne	178,132
Hildesheim	105,291
Ingolstadt	105,489
Jena	102,518
Karlsruhe	275,061
Kassel	194,268
Kiel	245,567
Koblenz	108,733
Krefeld	244,020
Leipzig	511,079
Leverkusen	160,919
Lübeck	214,758
Ludwigshafen	162,173
Magdeburg	278,807
Mainz	179,486
Mannheim	310,411
Moers	104,595
Mönchengladbach	259,436
Mülheim an der Ruhr	177,681
Munich (München)	1,229,026
Münster	259,438
Neuss	147,019
Nürnberg	493,692
Oberhausen	223,840
Offenbach am Main	114,992
Oldenburg	143,131
Osnabrück	163,168
Paderborn	120,680
Pforzheim	112,944
Potsdam	139,794
Recklinghausen	125,060
Regensburg	121,691
Remscheid	123,155
Reutlingen	103,687
Rostock	248,088
Saarbrücken	191,694
Salzgitter	114,355
Schwerin	127,447
Siegen	107,039
Solingen	162,928
Stuttgart	570,699
Ulm	108,930
Wiesbaden	256,885
Witten	104,701
Wolfsburg	126,708
Wuppertal	378,312
Würzburg	125,953
Zwickau	118,914
Ghana (1988 est.)	
★ Accra	949,113
Kumasi	385,192
Sekondi-Takoradi	103,653
Tamale	151,069
Tema	109,975

country city	population
Gibraltar (1990 est.)	
★ Gibraltar	30,681[14]
Greece (1991)	
★ Athens	748,110
Iráklion	117,167
Kallithéa	110,738
Larissa	113,426
Pátrai (Patras)	155,180
Peristérion	145,854
Piraiévs (Piraeus)	169,622
Thessaloníki	377,951
Greenland (1991 est.)	
★ Nuuk (Godthåb)	12,181
Grenada (1991)	
★ Saint George's	4,439
Guadeloupe (1990)	
★ Basse-Terre	14,107
Guam (1990)	
★ Agana	1,139
Guatemala (1990 est.)	
★ Guatemala City	1,076,725
Guernsey (1991)	
★ St. Peter Port	16,648
Guinea (1983)	
★ Conakry	705,280
Guinea-Bissau (1988 est.)	
★ Bissau	125,000
Guyana (1986 est.)	
★ Georgetown	150,368
Haiti (1992 est.)	
★ Port-au-Prince	752,600
Honduras (1989 est.)	
San Pedro Sula	300,400
★ Tegucigalpa	608,100[15]
Hong Kong (1992 est.)	
Hong Kong	5,799,000[14]
Hungary (1991 est.)	
★ Budapest	2,018,035
Debrecen	213,927
Győr	129,598
Kecskemét	103,568
Miskolc	194,033
Nyíregyháza	114,596
Pécs	170,023
Szeged	176,135
Székesfehérvár	109,106
Iceland (1991 est.)	
★ Reykjavík	99,623
India (1991)	
Abohar	107,016
Ādoni	135,718
Agartala	157,636
Āgra	899,195
Ahmadābād	2,872,865
Ahmadnagar	181,015
Āizawl	154,343
Ajmer	401,930
Akola	327,946
Alandur	125,009
Alīgarh	479,978
Allahābād	806,447
Alleppey	174,606
Alwar	206,107
Ambāla	119,535
Ambattur	223,332
Amrāvati	433,746
Amritsar	709,456
Amroha	136,893
Anand	110,144
Anantapur	174,792
Āra (Arrah)	156,871
Āsānsol	261,836
Aurangābād	572,634
Āvadi	180,291
Baharampur	115,036
Bahraich	135,352
Bally	181,978
Bālurghāt	119,829
Bangalore	2,650,659
Bānkura	114,927
Barāhanagar	223,770
Bārāsat	107,365
Barddhamān (Burdwān)	244,789
Bareilly	583,473

country city	population
Barrackpore	133,429
Basīrhāt	101,652
Bathinda (Bhatinda)	159,144
Beāwar	105,357
Belgaum	325,639
Bellary	245,758
Bhāgalpur	254,993
Bharatpur	148,506
Bharūch (Broach)	132,312
Bhātpāra	304,298
Bhāvnagar	400,636
Bhilainagar	389,601
Bhīlwāra	183,791
Bhīmavaram	125,495
Bhind	109,731
Bhiwandi	378,546
Bhiwāni	121,449
Bhopāl	1,063,662
Bhubaneshwar	411,542
Bhusāwal	144,804
Bīd (Bhīr)	112,351
Bīdar	107,542
Bihār Sharīf	200,976
Bijāpur	186,846
Bīkaner	415,355
Bilāspur	190,911
Bokāro	350,540
Bombay (Greater)	9,909,547
Brahmapur	210,585
Budaun	116,706
Bulandshahr	126,737
Burhānpur	172,809
Burnpur	174,704
Calcutta	4,388,262
Calicut (Kozhikode)	419,531
Chandannagar	122,351
Chandīgarh	502,992
Chandrapur	225,841
Chhapra	136,824
Chittoor	133,233
Cochin	564,038
Coimbatore	853,402
Cuddalore	143,774
Cuddapah	121,422
Cuttack	402,390
Darbhanga	218,274
Dāvangere	265,971
Dehra Dūn	270,028
Delhi	7,174,755
Dewās	163,699
Dhānbād	151,334
Dhūle (Dhūlia)	277,957
Dibrugarh	118,374
Dindigul	182,293
Durg	150,513
Durgāpur	415,986
Elūru	212,918
Erode	158,774
Etāwah	124,032
Faizābād	125,012
Farīdābād	613,828
Farrukhābād-cum-Fatehgarh	193,624
Fatehpur	117,203
Fīrozābād	215,089
Gadag-Betigeri	133,918
Gāndhīdhām	104,392
Gāndhīnagar	121,746
Gangānagar	161,377
Gaya	291,220
Ghāziābād	460,949
Gonda	106,078
Gondia	109,271
Gorakhpur	489,850
Gudivāda	101,635
Gulbarga	303,139
Guna	100,389
Guntakal	107,560
Guntūr	471,020
Gurgaon	120,790
Guwāhāti (Gauhāti)	577,591
Gwalior	692,982
Hābra	100,142
Haldīa	100,109
Haldwāni-cum-Kāthgodam	102,744
Hālisahar	113,670
Hāpur	146,591
Haridwār (Hardwār)	148,882
Hāthras	113,653
Hindupur	104,635
Hisār (Hissār)	172,873
Hoshiārpur	122,528
Howrah (Hāora)	946,732
Hubli-Dhārwād	647,640
Hugli-Chunchura	142,388
Hyderābād	2,991,884
Ichalkaranji	214,835
Imphāl	196,268
Indore	1,086,673
Ingrāj Bāzār	139,018
Jabalpur	739,961
Jaipur	1,454,678
Jalandhar (Jullundur)	519,530
Jalgaon	241,603
Jālna	174,958
Jammu	206,135[11]
Jāmnagar	325,475

country city	population
Jamshedpur	461,212
Jaunpur	136,287
Jhānsi	301,304
Jodhpur	648,621
Jūnāgadh	130,132
Kākināda	279,875
Kalyān	1,014,062
Kāmārhāti	266,625
Kānchipuram	145,028
Kānchrāpāra	100,059
Kānpur	1,958,282
Karīmnagar	148,349
Karnāl	173,742
Katihār	135,348
Khammam	127,812
Khandwa	145,111
Kharagpur	189,010
Kolhāpur	405,118
Kota	536,444
Krishnanagar	120,918
Kukatpalle	185,378
Kulti-Barākar	108,930
Kumbakonam	139,449
Kurnool	236,313
Lātūr	197,164
Lucknow	1,592,010
Ludhiāna	1,012,062
Machilīpatnam (Masulipatam)	159,007
Madras	3,795,028
Madurai	951,696
Mahbūbnagar	116,775
Mālegaon	342,431
Mālkājgiri	126,066
Mandya	119,970
Mangalore	272,819
Māngo	110,024
Mathura	226,850
Maunāth Bhanjan	136,447
Medinīpur (Midnāpore)	125,098
Meerut	752,078
Miraj	121,564
Mirzāpur-cum-Vindhyāchal	169,368
Modinagar	102,307
Moga	108,213
Morādābād	416,836
Morena	147,095
Munger (Monghyr)	150,042
Murwāra (Katni)	163,699
Muzaffarnagar	240,057
Muzaffarpur	240,450
Mysore	480,006
Nadiād	166,852
Nāgercoil	189,482
Nāgpur	1,622,225
Naihāti	132,032
Nānded	274,626
Nandyāl	120,171
Nāshik (Nāsik)	646,896
Navadwīp	125,247
Navsāri	125,980
Nellore	316,445
★ New Delhi	294,149
Neyveli	117,471
Nizāmābād	240,924
Noida	167,440
North Barrackpore	100,513
North Dum Dum	151,298
Ongole	100,544
Pālghāt	122,964
Pāli	136,797
Pallavaram	111,194
Pānihāti	275,359
Pānīpat	191,010
Parbhani	190,235
Pathānkot	142,862
Patiāla	253,341
Patna	916,980
Pīlībhīt	106,329
Pimpri-Chinchwad	515,962
Pondicherry	202,648
Porbandar	116,546
Proddatūr	133,860
Pune	1,559,558
Puri	124,835
Pūsa	122,086
Quilon	139,717
Qutubullapur	105,380
Rāe Bareli	130,101
Rāichūr	157,477
Rāiganj	151,454
Raipur	437,887
Rāj Nāndgaon	125,394
Rājahmundry	326,071
Rājapālaiyam	114,042
Rājkot	556,137
Rāmagundam	213,962
Rāmpur	242,752
Rānchi	598,498
Ratlām	183,370
Raurkela Steel Township	215,489
Rewa	128,918
Rishra	102,649
Rohtak	215,844
Sāgar	195,106
Sahāranpur	373,904
Salem	363,934
Sambalpur	130,766
Sambhal	150,012
Sāngli	193,181
Satna	156,321
Shāhjahānpur	237,663
Shāntipur	109,911
Shiliguri (Silīguri)	226,677
Shillong	130,691
Shimoga	178,882
Shivpuri	108,271
Sholāpur (Solapur)	603,870
Shrīrāmpur	137,087
Sīkar	148,235
Silchar	115,045
Sirsa	112,542
Sitāpur	120,595
Sonīpat	142,992
South Dum Dum	230,507
Srīnagar	586,038[11]
Sūrat	1,496,943
Surendranagar	105,973
Tāmbaram	106,590
Tellicherry	103,577
Tenāli	143,836
Thāne (Thāna)	796,620
Thanjāvūr	200,216
Tiruchchirāppalli	386,628
Tirunelveli	135,762
Tirupati	174,393
Tirupper (Tiruppūr)	235,076
Tiruvannāmalai	108,291
Tiruvottiyūr	167,851
Titāgarh	113,831
Tonk	100,020
Trivandrum	523,733
Tumkūr	138,598
Tuticorin	205,105
Udaipur	307,682
Ujjain	366,787
Ulhāsnagar	368,822
Uluberia	155,188
Unnāo	107,246
Uttarpāra-Kotrung	100,867
Vadodara (Baroda)	1,021,084
Vārānasi (Benares)	925,962
Vellore	172,467
Vijayawāda	701,351
Vishākhapatnam	750,024
Vizianagaram	159,461
Warangal	446,760
Wardha	102,974
Yamunanagar	144,250
Yavatmāl (Yeotmāl)	108,591
Indonesia (1980)	
Ambon	208,898
Balikpapan	280,675
Bandung	1,462,637
Banjarmasin	381,286
Bogor	247,409
Cilacap	113,893
Cimahi	105,940
Cirebon	223,776
Denpasar	261,263
★ Jakarta	6,503,449
Jambi	230,373
Jayapura	149,618
Jember	140,105
Kediri	221,836
Madiun	150,562
Magelang	123,484
Malang	511,780
Manado	217,159
Mataram	141,387
Medan	1,378,955
Padang	480,922
Palembang	787,187
Pekalongan	132,558
Pekanbaru	186,262
Pematangsiantar	150,376
Pontianak	304,778
Probolinggo	100,296
Purwokerto	105,395
Samarinda	264,718
Semarang	1,026,671
Sukabumi	109,994
Sumba	355,073
Surabaya	2,027,913
Surakarta	469,888
Tanjung Karang-Telukbetung	284,275
Tasikmalaya	165,297
Tegal	131,728
Telukbetang	284,275
Ujung Pandang	709,038
Yogyakarta	398,727
Iran (1986)	
Ahvāz	579,826
Āmol	118,242
Arāk	265,349
Ardabīl	281,973
Bābol	115,320
Bakhtarān	560,514
Bandar 'Abbās	201,642
Borūjerd	183,879
Bushire	120,787
Dezfūl	151,420
Gorgān	139,430
Hamadan	272,499
Isfahan (Eşfahān)	986,753
Karaj	275,100
Kāshān	138,599
Kermān	257,284
Khorramābād	208,592
Khvoy	115,343
Malāyer	103,640
Masjed Suleymān	104,787
Meshed (Mashhad)	1,463,508
Neyshābūr	109,285
Orūmīyeh	300,746
Qazvīn	248,591
Qom	543,139
Rasht	290,897
Sabzevār	129,103
Sanandaj	204,537
Shīrāz	848,289
Tabrīz	971,482
★ Tehrān	6,042,584
Yazd	230,483
Zāhedān	281,923
Zanjān	215,261
Iraq (1985 est.)	
al-Amārah	131,758
★ Baghdad	3,841,268[16]
Ba'qūbah	114,516
Basra	616,700
al-Ḥillah	215,249
Irbīl	333,903
Karbalā'	184,574
Kirkūk	570,000[17]
Mosul	570,926
an-Najaf	242,603
an-Nasiriyah	138,842
ar-Ramādī	137,388
as-Sulaymaniyah	279,424
Ireland (1991)	
Cork	127,024
★ Dublin	477,675
Isle of Man (1991)	
★ Douglas	22,214
Israel (1990 est.)	
Bat Yam	133,200
Beersheba (Be'er Sheva')	113,800
Bene Beraq	111,800
Haifa (Ḥefa)	223,600
Ḥolon	148,400
★ Jerusalem (Yerushalayim, Al-Quds)	504,100
Netanya	120,300
Petaḥ Tiqwa	135,400
Ramat Gan	116,100
Rishon le-Ẓiyyon	129,400
Tel Aviv–Yafo	321,700
Italy (1991 est.; MU)	
Ancona	103,268
Bari	353,032
Bergamo	117,886
Bologna	411,803
Bolzano	100,380
Brescia	196,766
Cagliari	211,719
Catania	364,176
Catanzaro	103,802
Cosenza	104,483
Ferrara	140,600
Florence (Firenze)	408,403
Foggia	159,541
Forlì	109,755
Genoa (Genova)	701,032
La Spezia	103,008
Latina	103,630
Lecce	102,344
Livorno	171,265
Messina	274,846
Milan (Milano)	1,432,184
Modena	177,501
Monza	123,188
Naples (Napoli)	1,206,013
Novara	103,349
Padua (Padova)	218,186
Palermo	734,238
Parma	173,991
Perugia	150,576
Pescara	128,553
Piacenza	103,536
Pisa	101,500
Prato	166,688
Ravenna	136,724
Reggio di Calabria	178,496
Reggio nell'Emilia	131,880
Rimini	130,896
★ Rome (Roma)	2,791,354
Salerno	151,374
Sassari	120,011
Siracusa	125,444
Taranto	244,033
Terni	109,809
Torre del Greco	102,647
Trento	102,124
Trieste	231,047
Turin (Torino)	991,870
Venice (Venezia)	317,837
Verona	258,946
Vicenza	109,333
Jamaica (1991)	
★ Kingston	103,771
Japan (1991 est.)	
Abiko	121,524
Ageo	197,925
Aizuwakamatsu	119,289
Akashi	275,399
Akishima	106,126
Akita	303,805
Amagasaki	498,038
Anjō	144,729
Aomori	162,477
Asahikawa	361,631
Asaka	104,757
Ashikaga	168,012
Atsugi	200,673
Beppu	129,977
Chiba	834,545
Chigasaki	203,848
Chōfu	198,696
Daitō	126,558
Ebina	107,904
Fuchu	211,350
Fuji	223,862
Fujieda	120,982
Fujinomiya	117,624
Fujisawa	354,679
Fukui	253,470
Fukuoka	1,249,320
Fukushima	279,127
Fukuyama	367,322
Funabashi	535,572
Gifu	410,619
Habikino	116,486
Hachinohe	241,009
Hachiōji	474,698
Hadano	158,212
Hakodate	308,289
Handa	101,591
Hamamatsu	549,962
Higashi-Kurume	113,601
Higashi-Murayama	135,065
Higashi-Ōsaka	517,237
Hikone	100,379
Himeji	457,579
Hino	167,126
Hirakata	392,392
Hiratsuka	248,363
Hirosaki	174,624
Hiroshima	1,090,048
Hitachi	202,465
Hōfu	118,121
Ibaraki	254,542
Ichihara	262,739
Ichikawa	443,378
Ichinomiya	263,912
Ikeda	104,383
Ikoma	101,005
Imabari	122,588
Iruma	139,592
Ise	103,808
Isesaki	117,525
Ishinomaki	122,789
Itami	186,073
Iwaki	356,746
Iwakuni	109,258
Iwatsuki	107,856
Izumi	146,380
Joetsu	130,107
Kadoma	142,204
Kagoshima	536,895
Kakamigahara	130,764
Kakogawa	242,608
Kamakura	174,019
Kanazawa	444,024
Kariya	122,203
Kashihara	116,417
Kashiwa	308,447
Kasugai	268,506
Kasukabe	191,268
Katsuta	111,471
Kawachi-Nagano	110,570
Kawagoe	308,082
Kawaguchi	443,985
Kawanishi	141,280
Kawasaki	1,187,034
Kiryū	125,636
Kisarazu	124,774
Kishiwada	188,694
Kita-Kyūshū	1,021,816
Kitami	107,746
Kobe	1,488,619
Kochi	317,877
Kodaira	166,693
Kofu	201,259
Koganei	107,430
Kokubunji	102,253
Komaki	129,267
Komatsu	106,211
Koriyama	316,833
Koshigaya	288,489
Kumagaya	154,203
Kumamoto	630,926
Kurashiki	415,476
Kure	215,102
Kurume	230,004
Kushiro	205,624
Kyōto	1,458,563
Machida	352,500
Maebashi	287,710
Matsubara	135,811
Matsudo	458,893
Matsue	143,586
Matsumoto	202,011
Matsuyama	446,979
Matsuzaka	119,191
Minakoyojō	130,157
Minō	122,917
Misato	131,162
Mishima	106,230
Mitaka	166,659
Mito	236,039
Miyazaki	289,080
Moriguchi	156,867
Morioka	235,895
Muroran	118,220
Musashino	139,165
Nagano	348,791
Nagaoka	186,536
Nagareyama	142,351
Nagasaki	443,823
Nagoya	2,158,784
Naha	303,480
Nara	351,985
Narashino	152,752
Neyagawa	257,097
Niigata	487,856
Niihama	129,151
Niiza	139,789
Nishinomiya	426,711
Nobeoka	129,581
Noda	116,048
Numazu	211,824
Obihiro	169,242
Odawara	194,916
Ōgaki	148,772
Ōita	412,860
Okayama	597,238
Okazaki	311,906
Okinawa	106,825
Ōme	128,784
Ōmiya	410,694
Ōmuta	149,214
Ōsaka	2,613,199
Ōta	141,573
Otaru	163,475
Ōtsu	262,953
Oyama	144,875
Saga	169,869
Sagamihara	542,000
Sakai	808,072
Sakata	100,857
Sakura	148,815
Sapporo	1,696,056
Sasebo	243,960
Sayama	158,972
Sendai	930,520
Seto	126,722
Shimizu	241,088
Shimonoseki	261,388
Shizuoka	472,666
Sōka	208,604
Suita	343,696
Suzuka	175,920
Tachikawa	154,105
Takamatsu	329,777
Takaoka	175,538
Takarazuka	203,536
Takasaki	237,615
Takatsuki	360,770
Tama	146,487
Tokorozawa	307,174
Tokushima	263,887
Tokuyama	110,762
★ Tokyo	8,154,404
Tomakomai	162,477
Tondabayashi	113,709
Tottori	143,293
Toyama	322,470
Toyohashi	343,064
Toyokawa	112,713
Toyonaka	408,305
Toyota	337,122
Tsu	159,724
Tsuchiura	129,380
Tsukuba	146,540
Ube	175,355
Ueda	120,058
Uji	178,921
Urawa	427,690
Urayasu	117,956
Utsunomiya	430,967
Wakayama	396,620
Yachiyo	150,710
Yaizu	112,849
Yamagata	249,615
Yamaguchi	130,451

Major cities and national capitals (continued)

country city	population	country city	population	country city	population	country city	population	country city	population
Yamato	198,733	Taejŏn	1,062,084	**Martinique** (1990)		**Mozambique** (1991 est.)		Ilawe-Ekiti	166,900
Yao	278,022	Ŭijŏngbu	212,368	★ Fort-de-France	100,080	Beira	298,847	Ilesha	342,400
Yatsushiro	107,923	Ulsan	682,978			Chimoio	108,818	Ilobu	180,100
Yokkaichi	277,502	Wŏnju	173,013	**Mauritania** (1988)		★ Maputo (Lourenço		Ilorin	430,600
Yokohama	3,250,887	Yŏsu	173,164	★ Nouakchott	393,325	Marques)	931,591	Inisa	108,300
Yokosuka	434,957					Matala	337,239	Iseyin	197,100
Yonago	131,697	**Kuwait** (1985)		**Mauritius** (1990 est.)		Nacala	125,208	Iwo	335,200
Zama	114,467	Ḩawallī	145,215	★ Port Louis	141,870	Nampula	250,473	Jos	185,600
		★ Kuwait (al-Kuwayt)	44,224			Quelimane	146,206	Kaduna	309,600
Jersey (1991)		as-Sālimīyah	153,220	**Mayotte** (1985)		Tete	112,221	Kano	699,900
★ St. Helier	28,123			★ Mamoudzou	7,325			Katsina	186,900
		Kyrgyzstan (1991 est.)				**Myanmar (Burma)** (1983)		Kumo	134,000
Jordan (1990 est.)		★ Bishkek (Frunze)	641,400	**Mexico** (1980)		Bassein (Pathein)	144,096	Lafia	110,900
★ Amman	1,213,300	Osh	238,200	Acapulco	301,902	Mandalay	532,949	★ Lagos	1,347,000
az-Zarqā'	514,980			Aguascalientes	293,152	Monywa	106,843	Maiduguri	289,100
Irbid	314,680	**Laos** (1985)		Atizapán de Zaragoza		Moulmein		Makurdi	111,410
		★ Vientiane	178,203	(Ciudad López		(Mawlamyine)	219,961	Minna	125,900
Kazakhstan (1991 est.)				Mateos)	188,497	Pegu (Bago)	150,528	Mushin	301,500
Aktyubinsk	266,600	**Latvia** (1991 est.)		Campeche	128,434	Sittwe (Akyab)	107,621	Offa	178,400
★ Alma-Ata (Almaty)	1,156,200	Daugavpils	129,000	Celaya	141,675	Taunggye	108,231	Ogbomosho	660,600
Aqtau (Shevchenko)	169,000	Liēpāja	114,900	Chihuahua	385,603	★ Yangôn (Rangoon)	2,513,023	Oka	129,600
Atyrau (Guryev)	156,700	★ Rīga	910,200	Ciudad Madero	132,444			Ondo	153,500
Chimkent	438,800			Ciudad Obregón	165,572	**Namibia** (1988 est.)		Onitsha	336,600
Dzhambul	312,300	**Lebanon** (1985 est.)		Ciudad Victoria	140,161	★ Windhoek	114,500	Oshogbo	441,600
Dzhezkazgan	111,100	★ Beirut (Bayrūt)	1,910,000[5, 11]	Coatzacoalcos	127,170			Owo	166,100
Ekibastuz	138,900	an-Nabaţīyah	100,000	Cuernavaca	192,770	**Nauru** (1983)		Oyo	237,400
Karaganda	608,600	Sidon (Şaydā)	100,000	Culiacán	304,826	★ Yaren	559	Port Harcourt	371,000
Kokchetav	143,300	Tripoli (Ţarābulus)	500,000	Ensenada	120,483			Sapele	126,000
Kustanay	233,900	Zahlah	200,000	Durango	257,915	**Nepal** (1981)		Shagamu	106,000
Kzyl-Orda	158,200			Gómez Palacio	116,967	★ Kāthmāndu	235,160	Shaki	161,200
Pavlodar	342,500	**Lesotho** (1986)		Guadalajara	1,626,152			Shomolu	133,700
Petropavlovsk	248,300	★ Maseru	109,382[5]	Guadalupe	370,524	**Netherlands, The**		Sokoto	185,500
Rudny	128,800			Hermosillo	297,175	(1991 est.)		Warri	114,100
Semipalatinsk	344,700	**Liberia** (1984)		Irapuato	170,138	Amersfoort	101,974	Zaria	345,200
Taldy-Kurgan	136,100	★ Monrovia	421,058	Jalapa	204,594	★ Amsterdam (capital)	702,444	
Temirtau	213,100			Juárez	544,496	Apeldoorn	148,204	**Northern Mariana Is.**
Tselinograd	286,000	**Libya** (1988 est.)		León	593,002	Arnhem	131,703	(1990)
Uralsk	214,000	Banghāzi	446,250	Los Mochis	122,531	Breda	124,794	★ Saipan	38,896
Ust-Kamenogorsk	332,900	Misrātah	121,669	Matamoros	188,745	Dordrecht	110,473	
		★ Tripoli (Ţarābulus)	591,062	Mazatlán	199,830	Eindhoven	192,895	**Norway** (1992 est.; MU)
Kenya (1984 est.)				Mérida	400,142	Enschede	146,509	Bergen	215,967
Kisumu	167,100	**Liechtenstein** (1991 est.)		Mexicali	341,559	Groningen	168,702	★ Oslo	467,090
Mombasa	425,600	★ Vaduz	4,870	★ Mexico City	8,236,960[18]	Haarlem	149,474	Trondheim	139,660
★ Nairobi	1,504,900[11]			Minatitlán	106,765	Leiden	111,949	
Nakuru	101,700	**Lithuania** (1991 est.)		Monclova	115,786	Maastricht	117,417	**Oman** (1982 est.)
		Kaunas	433,200	Monterrey	1,090,009	Nijmegen	145,782	★ Muscat	85,000
Kiribati (1990)		Klaipéda	208,300	Morelia	297,544	Rotterdam	582,266	
★ Bairiki	2,226	Panevėžys	131,200	Nezahualcóyotl	1,341,230	★ The Hague (seat of		**Pakistan** (1981)
		Šiauliai	149,000	Nuevo Laredo	201,731	government)	444,242	Bahāwalpur	180,263
Korea, North		★ Vilnius	597,700	Oaxaca	154,223	Tilburg	158,846	Chiniot	105,559
(1987 est.)				Orizaba	114,848	Utrecht	231,231	Dera Ghāzi Khān	102,007
Anju	186,000	**Luxembourg** (1991)		Pachuca	110,351	Zaanstad	130,705	Faisalābād
Ch'ŏngjin	520,000	★ Luxembourg	75,622	Poza Rica	166,799			(Lyallpur)	1,104,209
Haeju	195,000			Puebla	835,759			Gujrānwāla	658,753
Hamhŭng-Hungnam	701,000	**Macau** (1986 est.)		Querétaro	215,976	**Netherland Antilles**		Gujrāt	155,058
Hŭich'ŏn	163,000	★ Macau (Santo Nome		Reynosa	194,693	(1985 est.)		Hyderābād	751,529
Kaesŏng	120,000	de Deus)	416,200	Saltillo	284,937	★ Willemstad	125,000[5]	★ Islāmābād	204,364
Kanggye	211,000			San Luis Potosí	362,371			Jhang	195,558
Kimch'aek		**Macedonia** (1991; MU)		San Nicolás de los		**New Caledonia** (1989)		Jhelum	106,462
(Songjin)	179,000	★ Skopje (Skopije)	563,301	Garza	280,696	★ Nouméa	65,110	Karāchi	5,208,132
Kusŏng	177,000			Tampico	267,957			Kasūr	155,523
Namp'o	370,000	**Madagascar** (1990 est.)		Tepic	145,741	**New Zealand** (1991)		Lahore	2,952,689
★ P'yŏngyang	2,355,000	★ Antananarivo	802,390	Tijuana	429,500	Auckland	315,925	Lahore
Sinp'o	158,000	Fianarantsoa	124,489	Tlaquepaque	133,500	Christchurch	292,537	Cantonment	237,000
Sinŭiju	289,000	Mahajanga	121,967	Toluca	199,778	Dunedin	116,524	Lārkāna	123,890
Sunch'ŏn	356,000	Toamasina	145,431	Torreón	328,086	Hamilton	101,276	Mardān	147,977
Tanch'ŏn	284,000			Tuxtla	131,096	Manukau	225,928	Mīrpur Khās	124,371
Tŏkch'ŏn	217,000	**Malaŵi** (1987)		Uruapan	122,828	North Shore	151,330	Multān	730,070
Wŏnsan	274,000	Blantyre	333,120	Veracruz	284,822	Waitakere	136,600	Nawābshāh	102,139
		★ Lilongwe		Villahermosa	158,216	★ Wellington	149,598	Okāra	153,483
Korea, South (1990)		(administrative)	223,318	Zapopan	345,390			Peshāwar	566,248
Andong	116,932	★ Zomba (legislative)	43,250			**Nicaragua** (1985 est.)		Quetta	285,719
Ansan	252,157			**Micronesia**		León	100,982	Rahīm Yār Khān	119,036
Anyang	480,668	**Malaysia** (1980)		★ Palikir	—	★ Managua	682,111	Rāwalpindi	794,843
Ch'angwŏn	323,138	Ipoh	293,849					Sāhiwāl	150,954
Chech'ŏn	102,037	Johor Baharu	246,395	**Moldova** (1991 est.)		**Niger** (1988)		Sargodha	291,362
Cheju	232,687	Kelang	192,080	Beltsy	164,900	Maradi	112,965	Sheikhūpura	141,168
Chinhae	120,207	Kota Baharu	167,872	Bendery	141,500	★ Niamey	398,265	Siālkot	302,009
Chinju	258,365	★ Kuala Lumpur	565,329	★ Chişinău		Zinder	120,892	Sukkur	190,551
Ch'ŏnan	211,382	Kuala Terengganu	180,296	(Kishinyov)	676,700			Wāh Cantonment	122,335
Ch'ŏngju	497,429	Kuantan	131,547	Tiraspol	186,000	**Nigeria** (1992 est.)		
Chŏnju	517,104	Petaling Jaya	207,805			Aba	270,500	**Palau** (1990)
Ch'unch'ŏn	174,153	Pinang (George		**Monaco** (1990)		Abeokuta	386,800	★ Koror	9,018
Ch'ungju	129,994	Town)	248,241	★ Monaco	29,972[14]	★ Abuja (capital		
Hanam	101,278	Port Kelang	192,080			designate)	298,300[19]	**Panama** (1990)
Inch'ŏn	1,818,293	Seremban	132,911	**Mongolia** (1989)		Ado-Ekiti	325,300	★ Panama City	411,549
Iri	203,401	Taiping	146,002	★ Ulaanbaatar (Ulan		Akure	146,900	San Miguelito	242,529
Kangnŭng	152,605			Bator)	548,400	Awka	100,700	
Kimhai	106,166	**Maldives** (1990)				Benin City	207,200	**Papua New Guinea**
Kumi	206,101	★ Male	55,130	**Morocco** (1982)		Bida	113,600	(1987 est.)
Kunsan	218,216			Agadir	110,479	Calabar	157,800	★ Port Moresby	152,100
Kuri	109,418	**Mali** (1992 est.)		Casablanca		Deba Habe	125,300	
Kwangju	1,144,695	★ Bamako	745,787	(Dar el-Beida)	2,139,204	Ede	277,900	**Paraguay** (1990 est.)
Kwangmyŏng	328,803			Fès (Fez)	448,823	Effon-Alaiye	138,600	★ Asunción	607,706
Kyŏngju	141,895	**Malta** (1991 est.)		Kenitra	188,194	Enugu	286,100	Ciudad del Este	110,584
Masan	496,639	★ Valletta	9,199	Khouribga	127,181	Gusau	143,000	
Mokp'o	253,423			Marrakech	439,728	Ibadan	1,295,000	**Peru** (1990 est.)
P'ohang	318,595	**Marshall Is.** (1988 est.)		Meknès	319,783	Ife	268,600	Arequipa	621,700
Puch'ŏn	667,777	★ Majuro	17,649	Mohammedia	105,120	Ijebu-Ode	141,600	Ayacucho	101,600
Pusan	3,797,566			Oujda	260,082	Ikare	127,500	Callao	588,600
Shihŭng	107,190			★ Rabat	518,616	Ikerre	221,400	Chiclayo	419,600
Sŏngnam	540,764			Safi	197,309	Ikire	111,500	Chimbote	296,600
★ Seoul (Sŏul)	10,627,790			Salé	289,391	Ikirun	164,300	Cuzco	275,000
Sunch'ŏn	167,209			Tanger	266,346	Ikorodu	167,300	Huancayo	207,600
Suwŏn	644,968			Tétouan	199,615	Ila	238,900	Ica	152,300
Taegu	2,228,834							

country / city	population
Iquitos	269,500
Juliaca	134,700
★ Lima	421,570
Metro Lima-Callao	6,115,700
Piura	315,800
Pucallpa	153,000
Sullana	154,800
Tacna	150,200
Trujillo	532,000
Philippines (1990)	
Angeles	236,000
Bacolod	364,000
Bago	124,000
Baguio	183,000
Batangas	184,000
Butuan	228,000
Cabanatuan	173,000
Cadiz	120,000
Cagayan de Oro	340,000
Calbayog	113,000
Caloocan	746,000
Cebu	610,000
Cotabato	127,000
Dagupan	122,000
Davao	850,000
General Santos	250,000
Iligan	227,000
Iloilo	311,000
Lapu-Lapu	146,000
Las Piñas	286,000
Legaspi	121,000
Lipa	160,000
Lucena	151,000
Makati	452,000
Malabon	277,000
Mandaluyong	247,000
Mandaue	180,000
★ Manila	1,587,000
Metro Manila	7,832,000
Marikina	308,000
Muntilupa	278,000
Naga	115,000
Navotas	186,000
Olongapo	192,000
Ormoc	129,000
Pagadian	107,000
Parañaque	300,000
Pasay	354,000
Pasig	395,000
Quezon City	1,632,000
Roxas	103,000
San Carlos (*Negros Occidental*)	106,000
San Carlos (*Pangasinan*)	124,000
San Juan del Monte	127,000
San Pablo	161,000
Surigao	100,000
Tacloban	138,000
Tagig	267,000
Toledo	120,000
Valenzuela	340,000
Zamboanga	444,000
Poland (1992 est.)	
Białystok	272,100
Bielsko-Biała	184,100
Bydgoszcz	382,000
Bytom	231,800
Chorzów	131,500
Czestochowa	258,300
Dąbrovo Górnicza	137,200
Elbląg	126,500
Gdańsk	465,400
Gdynia	251,500
Gliwice	214,800
Gorzów Wielkopolski	124,600
Grudziadz	102,600
Jastrzębie-Zdrój	104,000
Kalisz	106,400
Katowice	366,500
Kielce	214,200
Koszalin	109,300
Kraków	750,600
Legnica	105,600
Łódź	846,500
Lublin	352,200
Olsztyn	163,900
Opole	128,900
Płock	124,500
Poznań	590,100
Radom	229,300
Ruda Śląska	171,400
Rybnik	144,600
Rzeszów	153,900
Słupsk	102,000
Sosnowiec	259,500
Szczecin	413,600
Tarnów	121,600
Toruń	202,400
Tychy	139,600
Wałbrzych	141,100
★ Warsaw (Warszawa)	1,654,500
Włocławek	122,300
Wodzisław Śląskie	112,000
Wrocław	643,100
Zabrze	205,500
Zielona Góra	114,300
Portugal (1991)	
★ Lisbon	677,790
Porto	350,000[20]
Puerto Rico (1990; MU)	
Bayamón	220,262
Caguas	133,447
Carolina	177,806
Mayagüez	100,371
Ponce	187,749
★ San Juan	437,745
Qatar (1986)	
★ Doha	217,294
Réunion (1990)	
★ Saint-Denis	100,926
Romania (1992)	
Arad	190,088
Bacău	204,495
Baia Mare	148,815
Botoşani	126,204
Brăila	234,706
Braşov	323,835
★ Bucharest	2,064,474
Buzău	148,247
Cluj-Napoca	328,008
Constanţa	350,476
Craiova	303,520
Drobeta-Turnu Severin	115,526
Focşani	101,296
Galaţi	325,788
Iaşi	342,994
Oradea	220,848
Piatra Neamţ	123,175
Piteşti	179,479
Ploieşti	252,073
Rîmnicu Vîlcea	113,356
Satu Mare	131,859
Sibiu	169,696
Suceava	114,355
Timişoara	334,278
Tirgu Mureş	163,625
Russia (1991 est.)	
Abakan	157,300
Achinsk	122,000
Almetyevsk	132,700
Angarsk	268,500
Anzhero-Sudzhensk	107,000
Arkhangelsk	428,200
Armavir	178,300
Arzamas	111,800
Astrakhan	511,900
Balakovo	202,100
Balashikha	137,600
Barnaul	606,800
Belgorod	311,400
Berezniki	200,700
Biysk	234,600
Blagoveshchensk	214,300
Bratsk	259,400
Bryansk	458,900
Cheboksary	436,000
Chelyabinsk	1,148,300
Cherepovets	315,900
Cherkessk	117,000
Chita	377,000
Dimitrovgrad	127,000
Dzerzhinsk	286,700
Elektrostal	153,000
Engels	183,600
Glazov	106,000
Grozny	401,400
Irkutsk	640,500
Ivanovo	482,200
Izhevsk	646,800
Kaliningrad	408,100
Kaliningrad (*Moscow oblast*)	161,500
Kaluga	366,300
Kamensk-Uralsky	210,500
Kamyshin	124,400
Kansk	109,900
Kazan	1,107,300
Kemerovo	520,700
Khabarovsk	613,300
Khimki	138,100
Kineshma	104,900
Kirov	491,200
Kiselyovsk	126,900
Kislovodsk	121,300
Kolomna	163,500
Kolpino	144,500
Komsomolsk-na-Amure	318,800
Kostroma	281,800
Kovrov	161,900
Krasnodar	631,200
Krasnoyarsk	924,400
Kurgan	369,600
Kursk	433,300
Kuznetsk	100,200
Leninsk-Kuznetsky	133,400
Lipetsk	460,100
Lyubertsy	164,900
Magadan	154,900
Magnitogorsk	444,500
Makhachkala	333,500
Maykop	170,400
Mezhdurechensk	107,500
Miass	169,700
Michurinsk	109,400
★ Moscow	8,801,500
Murmansk	472,900
Murom	126,000
Mytishchi	153,900
Naberezhnye Chelny (Brezhnev)	513,100
Nakhodka	164,500
Nalchik	240,600
Neftekamsk	110,500
Nevinnomyssk	123,300
Nizhnekamsk	196,200
Nizhnevartovsk	247,400
Nizhny Novgorod (Gorky)	1,445,000
Nizhny Tagil	439,200
Noginsk	122,700
Norilsk	169,000
Novgorod	233,800
Novocheboksarsk	119,900
Novocherkassk	188,500
Novokuybyshevsk	115,400
Novokuznetsk	601,900
Novomoskovsk (*Tula oblast*)	145,800
Novorossiysk	188,600
Novoshakhtinsk	107,300
Novosibirsk	1,446,300
Novotroitsk	107,600
Obninsk	103,700
Odintsovo	128,400
Oktyabrsky	106,700
Omsk	1,166,800
Orekhovo-Zuyevo	136,800
Orenburg	556,500
Orsk	275,600
Oryol	345,200
Penza	551,500
Perm	1,100,400
Pervouralsk	143,700
Petropavlovsk-Kamchatsky	272,900
Petrozavodsk	278,200
Podolsk	208,500
Prokopyevsk	273,100
Pskov	207,500
Pyatigorsk	131,100
Rostov-na-Donu	1,027,600
Rubtsovsk	172,500
Ryazan	527,200
Rybinsk (Andropov)	252,600
Saint Petersburg (Leningrad)	4,466,800
Salavat	151,400
Samara (Kuybyshev)	1,257,300
Saransk	319,600
Sarapul	110,600
Saratov	911,100
Serov	106,800
Serpukhov	141,200
Severodvinsk	254,100
Shakhty	227,700
Shchyolkovo	109,600
Smolensk	349,800
Sochi	341,500
Solikamsk	110,200
Stary Oskol	182,700
Stavropol	328,500
Sterlitamak	252,200
Surgut	261,100
Syktyvkar	224,000
Syzran	174,900
Taganrog	293,600
Tambov	334,400
Tolyatti (Toliatti)	654,700
Tomsk	506,600
Tula	543,600
Tver (Kalinin)	455,300
Tyumen	494,200
Ufa	1,097,000
Ukhta	112,100
Ulan-Ude	362,400
Ulyanovsk	667,700
Usolye-Sibirskoye	106,800
Ussuriysk	160,200
Ust-Ilimsk	112,200
Velikiye Luki	115,400
Vladikavkaz (Ordzhonikidze)	306,000
Vladimir	355,600
Vladivostok	648,000
Volgodonsk	188,100
Volgograd	1,007,300
Vologda	289,200
Volzhsky	278,400
Vorkuta	117,400
Voronezh	900,000
Votkinsk	104,500
Yakutsk	193,300
Yaroslavl	638,100
Yekaterinburg (Sverdlovsk)	1,375,400
Yelets	121,300
Yoshkar-Ola	274,600
Yuzhno-Sakhalinsk	164,000
Zagorsk	115,600
Zelenograd	162,700
Zhukovsky	101,300
Zlatoust	210,700
Rwanda (1991)	
★ Kigali	232,733
St. Kitts and Nevis (1985 est.)	
★ Basseterre	18,500
St. Lucia (1990)	
★ Castries	11,147
St. Vincent and The Grenadines (1991)	
★ Kingstown	15,670
San Marino (1991 est.)	
★ San Marino	2,339
São Tomé and Príncipe (1984 est.)	
★ São Tomé	34,997
Saudi Arabia (1980 est.)	
ad-Dammām	200,000
Jiddah	1,500,000[21]
Mecca (Makkah)	550,000
Medina (al-Madinah)	290,000
★ Riyadh (ar-Riyad)	1,308,000[17]
aṭ-Ṭā'if	300,000
Senegal (1992 est.)	
★ Dakar	1,729,823
Kaolack	179,894
St.-Louis	125,717
Thiès	201,350
Ziguinchor	148,831
Seychelles (1987)	
★ Victoria	24,325
Sierra Leone (1985)	
★ Freetown	469,776
Singapore (1992 est.)[14]	
★ Singapore	2,792,000
Slovenia (1991; MU)	
★ Ljubljana	323,291
Maribor	153,053
Solomon Islands (1986)	
★ Honiara	30,499
Somalia (1985 est.)	
★ Mogadishu	700,000
South Africa (1985)	
★ Bloemfontein (judicial)	104,381
Boksburg	110,832
★ Cape Town (legislative)	776,617
Metro Cape Town	1,911,521
Durban	634,301
Metro Durban	982,075
Germiston	116,718
Johannesburg	632,369
Metro Johannesburg	1,609,408
Pietermaritzburg	133,809
Port Elizabeth	272,844
★ Pretoria (executive)	443,059
Metro Pretoria	822,925
Roodepoort	141,764
Soweto	864,000[20]
Bophuthatswana	
★ Mmabatho	...
Ciskei (1986 est.)	
★ Bisho	2,850
Mdantsane	242,823
Transkei (1984 est.)	
★ Umtata	80,000
Venda (1985)	
★ Thohoyandou	10,166
Spain (1991; MU)	
Albacete	128,718
Alcalá de Henares	159,355
Alcorcón	139,641
Algeciras	101,063
Alicante	261,255
Almería	153,288
Badajoz	121,924
Badalona	206,585
Baracaldo	104,883
Barcelona	1,623,542
Bilbao	368,710
Burgos	160,381
Cádiz	153,550
Cartagena	166,736
Castellón de la Plana	133,180
Córdoba	300,229
Coruña, La	245,459
Donostia (San Sebastián)	169,933
Elche	181,658
Fuenlabrada	144,723
Getafe	138,704
Gijón	259,054
Granada	254,034
Hospitalet de Llobregat	269,241
Huelva	141,041
Jaén	101,938
Jerez de la Frontera	182,939
La Laguna	109,485
Leganés	171,400
León	144,137
Lleida (Lérida)	111,880
Logroño	121,066
★ Madrid	2,909,792
Málaga	512,136
Mataró	101,501
Móstoles	192,018
Murcia	318,838
Ourense (Orense)	101,623
Oviedo	194,919
Palma (de Mallorca)	296,754
Palmas de Gran Canaria, Las (Is. Canarias)	342,030
Pamplona	179,251
Sabadell	184,460
Salamanca	162,544
Santa Coloma de Gramanet	132,173
Santa Cruz de Tenerife	189,317
Santander	189,069
Sevilla (Seville)	659,126
Tarragona	110,003
Terrassa	154,300
Valencia	752,909
Valladolid	328,365
Vigo	274,629
Vitoria (Gasteiz)	204,961
Zaragoza (Saragossa)	586,219
Sri Lanka (1990 est.)	
★ Colombo (administrative)	615,000
Dehiwala-Mount Lavinia	196,000
Jaffna	129,000
Kandy	104,000
Moratuwa	170,000
★ Sri Jayawardenepura Kotte (legislative and judicial)	109,000[22]
Sudan, The (1983)	
Juba	116,000[23]
★ Khartoum	476,218
Khartoum North	341,146
Nyala	111,693
Omdurman	526,287
Port Sudan	206,727
al-Qaḍārif	116,876
al-Ubayyiḍ	140,024
Wad Madanī	141,065
Waw	116,000[23]
Suriname (1986 est.)	
★ Paramaribo	77,558
Swaziland (1986)	
★ Mbabane	38,290
Sweden (1992 est.; MU)	
Borås	102,387
Göteborg	432,112
Helsingborg	109,907
Jönköping	112,277
Linköping	124,352
Malmö	234,796
Norrköping	120,756
Örebro	122,042
★ Stockholm	679,364
Uppsala	170,743
Västerås	120,354
Switzerland (1991 est.)	
Basel (Bâle)	171,036
★ Bern (Berne)	134,629
Geneva (Genève)	167,167
Lausanne	123,159
Zürich	341,276

Major cities and national capitals (continued)

country / city	population
Syria (1992 est.)	
Aleppo (Ḥalab)	1,445,000
★ Damascus (Dimashq)	1,451,000
Dayr az-Zawr	125,000
Ḥamāh	229,000
al-Ḥasakah	106,000
Homs (Ḥims)	518,000
Latakia (al-Ladhiqiyah)	284,000
al-Qāmishlī	151,000
ar-Raqqah	130,000
Taiwan (1991 est.)	
Chang-hua	215,224
Chi-lung (Keelung)	352,919
Chia-i	257,597
Chung-ho	374,339
Chung-li	269,804
Feng-shan (Kao-hsiung-hsien)	290,777
Fêng-yüan	151,642
Hsin-chu	324,426
Hsin-chuang	299,174
Hsin-tien	225,517
Hua-lien	107,552
Kao-hsiung	1,386,723
Pan-ch'iao (T'ai-pei-hsien)	538,954
P'ing-tung	210,801
San-chu'ung	375,996
T'ai-chung	761,802
T'ai-nan	683,251
T'ai-tung	108,196
★ Taipei (T'ai-pei)	2,719,659
T'ao-yuan	241,263
Yung-ho	249,736
Tajikistan (1991 est.)	
★ Dushanbe	582,400
Khodzhent (Leninabad)	164,500
Tanzania (1988)	
★ Dar es Salaam	1,360,850
Mbeya	194,000[24]
Mwanza	252,000[24]
Tabora	214,000[24]
Tanga	187,634
Zanzibar	157,634
Thailand (1989 est.)	
★ Bangkok	5,876,000[25]
Chiang Mai	164,382
Hat Yai	139,357
Khon Kaen	131,472
Nakhon Ratchasima	206,605
Nakhon Sawan	107,907
Nonthanburi	227,492
Togo (1983 est.)	
★ Lomé	366,476
Tonga (1986)	
★ Nuku'alofa	21,383
Trinidad and Tobago (1990)	
★ Port-of-Spain	50,878
Tunisia (1989)	
Aryānah	131,403
Ettadhamen	111,793
Ṣafāqis (Sfax)	221,770
Sūsah	101,071
★ Tunis	620,149
Turkey (1990)	
Adana	916,150
Adapazari	171,225
Adıyaman	100,045
★ Ankara	2,559,471
Antakya	123,871
Antalya	378,208
Aydın	107,011
Balıkesir	170,589
Batman	147,347
Bursa	834,576
Çorum	116,810
Denizli	204,118
Diyarbakır	381,144
Edirne	102,345
Elazığ	204,603
Erzurum	242,391
Eskişehir	413,082
Gaziantep	603,434
Gebze	159,116
İçel	422,357
İskenderun	154,807
Isparta	112,117
Istanbul	6,620,241
İzmir	1,757,414
İzmit	256,882
Kahramanmaraş	228,129
Karabük	105,373
Kayseri	421,362
Kırıkkale	185,431
Konya	513,346
Kütahya	130,944
Malatya	281,776
Manisa	158,928
Ordu	102,107
Osmaniye	122,307
Samsun	303,979
Sivas	221,512
Tarsus	187,508
Trabzon	143,941
Urfa (Şanlıurfa)	276,528
Uşak	105,270
Van	153,111
Zonguldak	116,725
Turkmenistan (1991 est.)	
★ Ashkhabad (Ashgabat)	412,200
Chardzhou	166,400
Tashauz	117,000
Tuvalu (1985 est.)	
★ Funafuti	2,810
Uganda (1991)	
★ Kampala	773,463
Ukraine (1991 est.)	
Berdyansk	135,000
Bila Tserkva (Belaya Tserkov)	204,000
Cherkasy (Cherkassy)	302,000
Chernihiv (Chernigov)	306,000
Chernivtsi (Chernovtsy)	259,000
Dniprodzerzhynsk (Dneprodzerzhinsk)	284,000
Dnipropetrovsk (Dnepropetrovsk)	1,189,000
Donetsk	1,121,000
Horlivka (Gorlovka)	337,000
Ivano-Frankivsk (Ivano-Frankovsk)	226,000
Kamyanets-Podilsky (Kamenets-Podolsky)	105,000
Kerch	178,000
Kharkiv (Kharkov)	1,623,000
Kherson	365,000
Khmelnytsky (Khmelnitsky)	245,000
★ Kiev (Kyyiv)	2,635,000
Kirovohrad	278,000
Komunarsk	126,000
Kostyantynivka (Konstantinovka)	108,000
Kramatorsk	201,000
Krasny Luch	113,000
Kremenchuk (Kremenchug)	241,000
Kryvy Rih (Krivoy Rog)	724,000
Luhansk (Voroshilovgrad)	504,000
Lutsk	210,000
Lviv (Lvov)	802,000
Lysychansk (Lisichansk)	126,000
Makiyivka (Makeyevka)	424,000
Mariupol (Zhdanov)	522,000
Melitopol	177,000
Mykolayiv (Nikolayev)	512,000
Nikopol	159,000
Odesa (Odessa)	1,101,000
Oleksandriya (Aleksandriya)	105,000
Pavlohrad	134,000
Poltava	320,000
Rivne (Rovno)	239,000
Sevastopol	366,000
Severodonetsk	133,000
Simferopol	353,000
Slovyansk (Slavyansk)	137,000
Stakhanov	113,000
Sumy	301,000
Ternopil (Ternopol)	218,000
Uzhhorod	123,000
Vinnytsya (Vinnitsa)	381,000
Yenakiyeve (Yenakiyevo)	120,000
Yevpatoriya	111,000
Zaporizhzhya (Zaporozhye)	897,000
Zhytomyr (Zhitomir)	298,000
United Arab Emirates (1989 est.)	
★ Abu Dhabi (Abū Ẓaby)	363,432
Al-'Ayn	176,441
Dubai (Dubayy)	585,189
Sharjah (ash-Shāriqah)	125,123[26]
United Kingdom (1981)	
Aberdeen	190,465
Belfast	354,400
Birmingham	1,024,118
Blackburn	110,254
Blackpool	149,012
Bolton	143,921
Bournemouth	148,382
Bradford	295,048
Brighton	137,985
Bristol	420,234
Cardiff	266,267
Coventry	322,573
Derby	220,681
Dudley	187,367
Dundee	174,345
Edinburgh	420,169
Glasgow	765,030
Gloucester	108,150
Huddersfield	148,544
Ipswich	131,131
Kingston upon Hull	325,485
Leeds	451,841
Leicester	328,835
Liverpool	544,861
★ London	6,677,928
Luton	164,743
Manchester	448,604
Middlesbrough	159,421
Newcastle upon Tyne	203,591
Newport	116,658
Northampton	155,694
Norwich	173,286
Nottingham	277,203
Oldbury/Smethwick	153,461
Oldham	107,830
Oxford	119,909
Peterborough	114,733
Plymouth	242,560
Poole	124,974
Portsmouth	177,905
Preston	168,405
Reading	198,341
Rotherham	123,312
St. Helens	114,822
Sheffield	477,257
Slough	106,822
Southampton	214,802
Southend-on-Sea	156,969
Stockport	136,792
Stoke-on-Trent	275,168
Sunderland	195,896
Sutton Coldfield	103,097
Swansea	175,172
Swindon	128,493
Walsall	178,852
West Bromwich	154,531
Wolverhampton	265,631
York	126,377
United States (1990)	
Abilene (Texas)	106,654
Akron (Ohio)	223,019
Alameda (Calif.)	76,459
Albany (Ga.)	78,122
Albany (N.Y.)	101,082
Albuquerque (N.M.)	384,736
Alexandria (Va.)	111,183
Alhambra (Calif.)	82,106
Allentown (Pa.)	105,090
Altoona (Pa.)	51,881
Amarillo (Texas)	157,615
Anaheim (Calif.)	266,406
Anderson (Ind.)	59,459
Anchorage (Alaska)	226,338
Anderson (Ind.)	59,459
Ann Arbor (Mich.)	109,592
Antioch (Calif.)	62,195
Appleton (Wis.)	65,695
Arlington (Texas)	261,721
Arlington (Va.)	170,936
Arlington Heights (Ill.)	75,460
Arvada (Colo.)	89,235
Asheville (N.C.)	61,607
Atlanta (Ga.)	394,017
Aurora (Colo.)	222,103
Aurora (Ill.)	99,581
Austin (Texas)	465,622
Bakersfield (Calif.)	174,820
Baldwin Park (Calif.)	69,330
Baltimore (Md.)	736,014
Baton Rouge (La.)	219,531
Battle Creek (Mich.)	53,540
Bayonne (N.J.)	61,444
Baytown (Texas)	63,850
Beaumont (Texas)	114,323
Beaverton (Ore.)	53,310
Bellevue (Wash.)	86,874
Bellflower (Calif.)	61,815
Bellingham (Wash.)	52,179
Berkeley (Calif.)	102,724
Bethlehem (Pa.)	71,428
Billings (Mont.)	81,151
Binghamton (N.Y.)	53,008
Birmingham (Ala.)	265,968
Bloomington (Ill.)	51,972
Bloomington (Ind.)	60,633
Bloomington (Minn.)	86,335
Boca Raton (Fla.)	61,492
Boise City (Idaho)	125,738
Bossier City (La.)	52,721
Boston (Mass.)	574,283
Boulder (Colo.)	83,312
Bridgeport (Conn.)	141,686
Bristol (Conn.)	60,640
Brockton (Mass.)	92,788
Broken Arrow (Okla.)	58,043
Brooklyn Park (Minn.)	56,381
Brownsville (Texas)	98,962
Bryan (Texas)	55,002
Buena Park (Calif.)	68,784
Buffalo (N.Y.)	328,123
Burbank (Calif.)	93,643
Burnsville (Minn.)	51,288
Camarillo (Calif.)	52,303
Cambridge (Mass.)	95,802
Camden (N.J.)	87,492
Canton (Ohio)	84,161
Cape Coral (Fla.)	74,991
Carlsbad (Calif.)	63,126
Carrollton (Texas)	82,169
Carson (Calif.)	83,995
Cedar Rapids (Iowa)	108,751
Cerritos (Calif.)	53,240
Champaign (Ill.)	63,502
Chandler (Ariz.)	90,533
Charleston (S.C.)	80,414
Charleston (W.V.)	57,287
Charlotte (N.C.)	395,934
Chattanooga (Tenn.)	152,466
Chesapeake (Va.)	151,976
Cheyenne (Wyo.)	50,008
Chicago (Ill.)	2,783,726
Chicopee (Mass.)	56,632
Chino (Calif.)	59,682
Chula Vista (Calif.)	135,163
Cicero (Ill.)	67,436
Cincinnati (Ohio)	364,040
Clarksville (Tenn.)	75,494
Clearwater (Fla.)	98,784
Cleveland (Ohio)	505,616
Cleveland Heights (Ohio)	54,052
Clifton (N.J.)	71,742
Clovis (Calif.)	50,323
College Station (Texas)	52,456
Colorado Springs (Colo.)	281,140
Columbia (Mo.)	69,101
Columbia (S.C.)	98,052
Columbus (Ga.)	179,278
Columbus (Ohio)	632,910
Compton (Calif.)	90,454
Concord (Calif.)	111,348
Coon Rapids (Minn.)	52,978
Coral Springs (Fla.)	79,443
Corona (Calif.)	76,095
Corpus Christi (Texas)	257,453
Costa Mesa (Calif.)	96,357
Council Bluffs (Iowa)	54,315
Cranston (R.I.)	76,060
Dallas (Texas)	1,006,877
Daly City (Calif.)	92,311
Danbury (Conn.)	65,585
Danville (Va.)	53,056
Davenport (Iowa)	95,333
Dayton (Ohio)	182,044
Daytona Beach (Fla.)	61,921
Dearborn (Mich.)	89,286
Dearborn Heights (Mich.)	60,838
Decatur (Ill.)	83,885
Denton (Texas)	66,270
Denver (Colo.)	467,610
Des Moines (Iowa)	193,187
Des Plaines (Ill.)	53,223
Detroit (Mich.)	1,027,974
Diamond Bar (Calif.)	53,672
Dothan (Ala.)	53,589
Downey (Calif.)	91,444
Dubuque (Iowa)	57,546
Duluth (Minn.)	85,493
Durham (N.C.)	136,611
East Lansing (Mich.)	50,677
East Orange (N.J.)	73,552
East Providence (R.I.)	50,380
Eau Claire (Wis.)	56,856
Edmond (Okla.)	52,315
El Cajon (Calif.)	88,693
El Monte (Calif.)	106,209
El Paso (Texas)	515,342
Elgin (Ill.)	77,010
Elizabeth (N.J.)	110,002
Elyria (Ohio)	56,746
Encinitas (Calif.)	55,386
Erie (Pa.)	108,718
Escondido (Calif.)	108,635
Euclid (Ohio)	54,875
Eugene (Ore.)	112,669
Evanston (Ill.)	73,233
Evansville (Ind.)	126,272
Everett (Wash.)	69,961
Fairfield (Calif.)	77,211
Fall River (Mass.)	92,703
Fargo (N.D.)	74,111
Farmington Hills (Mich.)	74,652
Fayetteville (N.C.)	75,695
Flint (Mich.)	140,761
Florissant (Mo.)	51,206
Fontana (Calif.)	87,535
Fort Collins (Colo.)	87,758
Fort Lauderdale (Fla.)	149,377
Fort Smith (Ark.)	72,798
Fort Wayne (Ind.)	173,072
Fort Worth (Texas)	447,619
Fountain Valley (Calif.)	53,691
Fremont (Calif.)	173,339
Fresno (Calif.)	354,202
Fullerton (Calif.)	114,144
Gainesville (Fla.)	84,770
Galveston (Texas)	59,070
Garden Grove (Calif.)	143,050
Garland (Texas)	180,650
Gary (Ind.)	116,646
Gastonia (N.C.)	54,732
Glendale (Ariz.)	148,134
Glendale (Calif.)	180,038
Grand Prairie (Texas)	99,616
Grand Rapids (Mich.)	189,126
Great Falls (Mont.)	55,097
Greeley (Colo.)	60,536
Green Bay (Wis.)	96,466
Greensboro (N.C.)	183,521
Greenville (S.C.)	58,282
Gresham (Ore.)	68,235
Hamilton (Ohio)	61,368
Hammond (Ind.)	84,236
Hampton (Va.)	133,793
Harrisburg (Pa.)	52,376
Hartford (Conn.)	139,739
Haverhill (Mass.)	51,418
Hawthorne (Calif.)	71,349
Hayward (Calif.)	111,498
Henderson (Nev.)	64,942
Hesperia (Calif.)	50,418
Hialeah (Fla.)	188,004
High Point (N.C.)	69,496
Hollywood (Fla.)	121,697
Honolulu (Ha.)	365,272
Houston (Texas)	1,630,553
Huntington (W.V.)	54,844
Huntington Beach (Calif.)	181,519
Huntington Park (Calif.)	56,065
Huntsville (Ala.)	159,789
Independence (Mo.)	112,301
Indianapolis (Ind.)	731,327
Inglewood (Calif.)	109,602
Iowa City (Iowa)	59,738
Irvine (Calif.)	110,330
Irving (Texas)	155,037
Jackson (Miss.)	196,637
Jacksonville (Fla.)	672,971
Janesville (Wis.)	52,133
Jersey City (N.J.)	228,537
Joliet (Ill.)	76,836
Kalamazoo (Mich.)	80,277
Kansas City (Kan.)	149,767
Kansas City (Mo.)	435,146
Kenner (La.)	72,033
Kenosha (Wis.)	80,352
Kettering (Ohio)	60,569
Killeen (Texas)	63,535
Knoxville (Tenn.)	165,121
La Crosse (Wis.)	51,003
La Habra (Calif.)	51,266
La Mesa (Calif.)	52,931
Lafayette (La.)	94,440
Lake Charles (La.)	70,580
Lakeland (Fla.)	70,576
Lakewood (Calif.)	73,557
Lakewood (Colo.)	126,481
Lakewood (Ohio)	59,718
Lancaster (Calif.)	97,291
Lancaster (Pa.)	55,551
Lansing (Mich.)	127,321
Laredo (Texas)	122,899
Largo (Fla.)	65,674
Las Cruces (N.M.)	62,126
Las Vegas (Nev.)	258,295
Lawrence (Kan.)	65,608
Lawrence (Mass.)	70,207
Lawton (Okla.)	80,561
Lexington (Ky.)	225,366
Lincoln (Neb.)	191,972
Little Rock (Ark.)	175,795

[1]1984 estimate. [2]City proper; 1980 census. [3]1987 estimate. [4]1989 census. [5]Population refers to widest officially defined agglomeration or metropolitan area. [6]Population of the statistical division containing the city. [7]1982 estimate. [8]1982 census. [9]Excludes the agricultural population of the named civil division. [10]Excludes population of Lefkoşa (Turkish-occupied Nicosia), estimated at 37,400 in 1985. [11]1990 estimate. [12]1986 estimate. [13]1983 census. [14]No separate areas within the state are distinguished administratively as cities. [15]Population includes Comayagüela. [16]1987 census.

country city	population	country city	population	country city	population	country city	population	country city	population
Livermore (Calif.)	56,741	Overland Park (Kan.)	111,790	San Leandro (Calif.)	68,223	Waterloo (Iowa)	66,467	**Vietnam** (1989)	
Livonia (Mich.)	100,850	Owensboro (Ky.)	53,549	San Mateo (Calif.)	85,486	Waukegan (Ill.)	69,392	Bien Hoa	190,086[27]
Lodi (Calif.)	51,874	Oxnard (Calif.)	142,216	Sandy (Utah)	75,058	Waukesha (Wis.)	56,958	Cam Rahn	114,041
Long Beach (Calif.)	429,433	Palm Bay (Fla.)	62,632	Santa Ana (Calif.)	293,742	West Allis (Wis.)	63,221	Can Tho	208,326
Longmont (Colo.)	51,555	Palmdale (Calif.)	68,842	Santa Barbara (Calif.)	85,571	West Covina (Calif.)	96,086	Da Nang	370,670
Longview (Texas)	70,311	Palo Alto (Calif.)	55,900	Santa Clara (Calif.)	93,613	West Haven (Conn.)	54,021	Haiphong	456,049
Lorain (Ohio)	71,245	Pasadena (Calif.)	131,591	Santa Clarita (Calif.)	110,642	West Palm Beach		★ Hanoi	1,088,862
Los Angeles (Calif.)	3,485,398	Pasadena (Texas)	119,363	Santa Fe (N.M.)	55,859	(Fla.)	67,643	Ho Chi Minh City	
Louisville (Ky.)	269,063	Passaic (N.J.)	58,041	Santa Maria (Calif.)	61,284	West Valley City		(Saigon)	3,169,135
Lowell (Mass.)	103,439	Paterson (N.J.)	140,891	Santa Monica (Calif.)	86,905	(Utah)	86,976	Hong Gai	123,073
Lubbock (Texas)	186,206	Pawtucket (R.I.)	72,644	Santa Rosa (Calif.)	113,313	Westland (Mich.)	84,724	Hue	211,085
Lynchburg (Va.)	66,049	Pembroke Pines		Santee (Calif.)	52,902	Westminster (Calif.)	78,118	Long Xuyen	217,171
Lynn (Mass.)	81,245	(Fla.)	65,452	Sarasota (Fla.)	50,961	Westminster (Colo.)	74,625	My Tho	101,496[27]
Lynwood (Calif.)	61,945	Pensacola (Fla.)	58,165	Savannah (Ga.)	137,560	Wheaton (Ill.)	51,464	Nam Dinh	165,649
McAllen (Texas)	84,021	Peoria (Ariz.)	50,618	Schaumburg (Ill.)	68,586	Whittier (Calif.)	77,671	Nha Trang	213,687
Macon (Ga.)	106,612	Peoria (Ill.)	113,504	Schenectady (N.Y.)	65,566	Wichita (Kan.)	304,011	Qui Nhon	160,091
Madison (Wis.)	191,262	Philadelphia (Pa.)	1,585,577	Scottsdale (Ariz.)	130,069	Wichita Falls (Texas)	96,259	Thai Nguyen	126,066
Malden (Mass.)	53,884	Pico Rivera (Calif.)	59,177	Scranton (Pa.)	81,805	Wilmington (Del.)	71,529	Thanh Hoa	103,981[27]
Manchester (N.H.)	99,567	Pine Bluff (Ark.)	57,140	Seattle (Wash.)	516,259	Wilmington (N.C.)	55,530	Viet Tri	116,140
Medford (Mass.)	57,407	Phoenix (Ariz.)	983,403	Shreveport (La.)	198,525	Winston-Salem (N.C.)	143,485	Vinh	154,040[27]
Melbourne (Fla.)	59,646	Pittsburgh (Pa.)	369,879	Simi Valley (Calif.)	100,217	Worcester (Mass.)	169,759	Vung Tau	124,634
Memphis (Tenn.)	610,337	Plano (Texas)	128,713	Sioux City (Iowa)	80,505	Wyoming (Mich.)	63,891		
Merced (Calif.)	56,216	Plantation (Fla.)	66,692	Sioux Falls (S.D.)	100,814	Yakima (Wash.)	54,827	**Virgin Islands** (U.S.)	
Meriden (Conn.)	59,479	Pleasanton (Calif.)	50,553	Skokie (Ill.)	59,432	Yonkers (N.Y.)	188,082	(1990)	
Mesa (Ariz.)	288,091	Plymouth (Minn.)	50,889	Somerville (Mass.)	76,210	Yorba Linda (Calif.)	52,422	★ Charlotte Amalie	12,331
Mesquite (Texas)	101,484	Pomona (Calif.)	131,723	South Bend (Ind.)	105,511	Youngstown (Ohio)	95,732		
Miami (Fla.)	358,548	Pompano Beach (Fla.)	72,411	South Gate (Calif.)	86,284	Yuma (Ariz.)	54,923	**West Bank** (1987 est.)	
Miami Beach (Fla.)	92,639	Pontiac (Mich.)	71,166	South San Francisco				Nābulus	106,944
Midland (Texas)	89,443	Port Arthur (Texas)	58,724	(Calif.)	54,312	**Uruguay** (1985)		★ —	—
Midwest City (Okla.)	52,267	Port St. Lucie (Fla.)	55,866	Southfield (Mich.)	75,728	★ Montevideo	1,251,647		
Milpitas (Calif.)	50,686	Portland (Maine)	64,358	Sparks (Nev.)	53,367			**Western Sahara**	
Milwaukee (Wis.)	628,088	Portland (Ore.)	437,319	Spokane (Wash.)	177,196	**Uzbekistan** (1991 est.)		(1982)	
Minneapolis (Minn.)	368,383	Portsmouth (Va.)	103,907	Springfield (Ill.)	105,227	Amalyk	116,400	★ El Aaiún (Laayoune)	93,875
Mission Viejo (Calif.)	72,820	Providence (R.I.)	160,728	Springfield (Mass.)	156,983	Andizhan	298,300		
Mobile (Ala.)	196,278	Provo (Utah)	86,835	Springfield (Mo.)	140,494	Angren	132,600	**Western Samoa** (1991)	
Modesto (Calif.)	164,730	Pueblo (Colo.)	98,640	Springfield (Ohio)	70,487	Bukhara	249,600	★ Apia	32,859
Monroe (La.)	54,909	Quincy (Mass.)	84,985	Stamford (Conn.)	108,056	Chirchik	158,400		
Montebello (Calif.)	59,564	Racine (Wis.)	84,298	Sterling Heights		Dzhizak	110,900	**Yemen** (1986)	
Monterey Park (Calif.)	60,738	Raleigh (N.C.)	207,951	(Mich.)	117,810	Fergana	226,500	★ Aden (economic)	318,000[1]
Montgomery (Ala.)	187,106	Rancho Cucamonga		Stockton (Calif.)	210,943	Karshi	168,000	Al-Ḥudaydah	155,110
Mount Prospect (Ill.)	53,170	(Calif.)	101,409	Suffolk (Va.)	52,141	Kokand	175,000	★ Ṣan'ā' (political)	427,185
Mount Vernon (N.Y.)	67,153	Rapid City (S.D.)	54,523	Sunnyvale (Calif.)	117,229	Margilan	124,900	Ta'izz	178,430
Mountain View (Calif.)	67,460	Reading (Pa.)	78,380	Sunrise (Fla.)	64,407	Namangan	319,200		
Muncie (Ind.)	71,035	Redding (Calif.)	66,462	Syracuse (N.Y.)	163,860	Navoi	111,600	**Yugoslavia**	
Napa (Calif.)	61,842	Redlands (Calif.)	60,394	Tacoma (Wash.)	176,664	Nukus	179,600	(1991; MU)	
Naperville (Ill.)	85,351	Redondo Beach		Tallahassee (Fla.)	124,773	Samarkand	370,500	★ Belgrade (Beograd)	1,553,854
Nashua (N.H.)	79,662	(Calif.)	60,167	Tampa (Fla.)	280,015	★ Tashkent		Niš	247,898
Nashville (Tenn.)	488,374	Redwood City (Calif.)	66,072	Taylor (Mich.)	70,811	(Toshkent)	2,113,300	Novi Sad	264,533
National City (Calif.)	54,249	Reno (Nev.)	133,850	Tempe (Ariz.)	141,865	Urgench	130,400	Priština	148,656[28]
New Bedford (Mass.)	99,922	Rialto (Calif.)	72,388	Terre Haute (Ind.)	57,483			Subotica	150,666
New Britain (Conn.)	75,491	Richardson (Texas)	74,840	Thornton (Colo.)	55,031	**Vanuatu** (1989)			
New Haven (Conn.)	130,474	Richmond (Calif.)	87,425	Thousand Oaks		★ Vila	19,311	**Zaire** (1991 est.)	
New Orleans (La.)	496,938	Richmond (Va.)	203,056	(Calif.)	104,352			Boma	246,207
New Rochelle (N.Y.)	67,265	Riverside (Calif.)	226,505	Toledo (Ohio)	332,943	**Venezuela** (1990 est.)		Bukavu	209,566
New York City (N.Y.)	7,322,564	Roanoke (Va.)	96,397	Topeka (Kan.)	119,883	Acarigua	130,627[11]	Kananga	371,862
Newark (N.J.)	275,221	Rochester (Minn.)	70,745	Torrance (Calif.)	133,107	Barcelona	106,061	Kikwit	182,850
Newport Beach (Calif.)	66,643	Rochester (N.Y.)	231,636	Trenton (N.J.)	88,675	Barinas	152,853	★ Kinshasa	3,804,000
Newport News (Va.)	170,045	Rochester Hills (Mich.)	61,766	Troy (Mich.)	72,884	Barquisimeto	602,622	Kisangani	373,397
Newton (Mass.)	82,585	Rockford (Ill.)	139,426	Troy (N.Y.)	54,269	Baruta	292,618[5]	Kolwezi	544,497
Niagara Falls (N.Y.)	61,840	Rosemead (Calif.)	51,638	Tucson (Ariz.)	405,390	Cabimas	197,613[5]	Likasi	279,839
Norfolk (Va.)	261,229	Roseville (Mich.)	51,412	Tulsa (Okla.)	367,302	★ Caracas	1,824,892	Lubumbashi	739,082
Norman (Okla.)	80,071	Royal Oak (Mich.)	65,410	Tuscaloosa (Ala.)	77,759	Catia la Mar	136,250[11]	Matadi	172,926
North Charleston		Sacramento (Calif.)	369,365	Tustin (Calif.)	50,689	Ciudad Bolívar	225,846	Mbandaka	165,623
(S.C.)	70,218	Saginaw (Mich.)	69,512	Tyler (Texas)	75,450	Ciudad Guayana		Mbuji-Mayi	613,027
North Little Rock		St. Charles (Mo.)	54,555	Union City (Calif.)	53,762	(San Felix			
(Ark.)	61,741	St. Clair Shores		Union City (N.J.)	58,012	de Guayana)	536,506[11]	**Zambia** (1990)	
Norwalk (Calif.)	94,279	(Mich.)	68,107	Upland (Calif.)	63,374	Coro	124,616	Chingola	167,954
Norwalk (Conn.)	78,331	St. Joseph (Mo.)	71,852	Utica (N.Y.)	68,637	Cumaná	212,492	Kabwe	166,519
Oak Lawn (Ill.)	56,182	St. Louis (Mo.)	396,685	Vacaville (Calif.)	71,479	Guacara	122,701[11]	Kitwe	338,207
Oak Park (Ill.)	53,648	St. Paul (Minn.)	272,235	Vallejo (Calif.)	109,199	Guarenas	186,506[11]	Luanshya	146,275
Oakland (Calif.)	372,242	St. Petersburg (Fla.)	238,629	Victoria (Texas)	55,076	Los Teques	143,519	★ Lusaka	982,362
Oceanside (Calif.)	128,398	Salem (Ore.)	107,786	Vineland (N.J.)	54,780	Maracaibo	1,207,513	Mufulira	152,944
Odessa (Texas)	89,699	Salinas (Calif.)	108,777	Virginia Beach (Va.)	393,069	Maracay	354,428	Ndola	376,311
Ogden (Utah)	63,909	Salt Lake City (Utah)	159,936	Visalia (Calif.)	75,636	Maturín	207,382		
Oklahoma City		San Angelo (Texas)	84,474	Vista (Calif.)	71,872	Mérida	167,992	**Zimbabwe** (1987 est.)	
(Okla.)	444,719	San Antonio (Texas)	935,933	Waco (Texas)	103,590	Petare	531,866[11]	Bulawayo	495,317[8]
Olathe (Kan.)	63,352	San Bernardino		Walnut Creek (Calif.)	60,569	Pozuelos	106,151[11]	Chitungwiza	229,000
Omaha (Neb.)	335,795	(Calif.)	164,164	Waltham (Mass.)	57,878	San Cristóbal	220,697	★ Harare	863,000
Ontario (Calif.)	133,179	San Buenaventura		Warren (Mich.)	144,864	Turmero	211,368[11]		
Orange (Calif.)	110,658	(Ventura) (Calif.)	92,575	Warren (Ohio)	50,793	Valencia	903,076		
Orem (Utah)	67,561	San Diego (Calif.)	1,110,549	Warwick (R.I.)	85,427	Valera	111,114[5]		
Orlando (Fla.)	164,693	San Francisco (Calif.)	723,959	★ Washington, D.C.	606,900				
Oshkosh (Wis.)	55,006	San Jose (Calif.)	782,248	Waterbury (Conn.)	108,961				

---

[17]1981 estimate.   [18]Distrito Federal; 1990 preliminary census.   [19]Federal Capital Territory; 1991 estimate.   [20]1988 estimate.   [21]1983 estimate.   [22]Population refers to Kotte only.   [23]1980 estimate.
[24]1985 estimate.   [25]1990 preliminary census.   [26]1980 census.   [27]1979 census.   [28]1981 census.

Language

This table presents data on the principal language communities of each of the countries of the world. The countries, and the principal languages used in each, are listed alphabetically; a bullet (●) indicates those languages that are designated as official by each country. The sum of the estimated populations for each language community and of the "Other" group equals the 1992 population of the country given in the "Area and population" table.

The estimates represent, so far as national data collection systems permit, the distribution of mother tongues (a mother tongue being the language spoken first and, usually, most fluently by an individual). Many countries do not collect data on this basis, however, and for these countries a variety of techniques have been used to approximate mother-tongue distribution. Some countries compile data on ethnic or "national" groups; for such countries ethnic distribution was often assumed to conform roughly to the distribution of language communities. This approach, however, must be used with caution, because a minority population is not always free to educate its children in its own language and because better economic opportunities often draw minority group members into the majority-language community. For some countries, a given individual may only be visible in national statistics as a passport-holder of a foreign nation, however long he may remain resident. Such persons, often guest workers, have sometimes had to be assumed to be speakers of the principal language of their home country. For example, since The Netherlands does not collect language data, holders of Moroccan passports were assumed to be speakers of Arabic (although perhaps a quarter of them might be of Berber heritage). For other countries, the language mosaic may be so complex, the language communities so minute in size, scholarly study so inadequate, or the census base so obsolete that it was possible only to assign percentages to groups of related languages, despite their mutual unintelligibility (Papuan and Melanesian languages in Papua New Guinea, for instance). For some countries in the Americas, so few speakers of any single indigenous language remain that it was necessary to combine these groups as *Amerindian* so as to give a fair impression of their aggregate size within their respective countries.

No systematic attempt has been made to account for populations that may legitimately be described as bilingual, unless the country itself collects data on that basis, as does Bolivia or the Comoros, for example. Where a nonindigenous official or excolonial language constitutes a lingua franca of the country, however, speakers of the language as a second tongue are shown in italics, even though very few may speak it as a mother tongue. No comprehensive attempt has been made to distinguish between degrees of dialectal variance among communities *usually* classified as belonging to the same language, though this *was* possible for some countries—*e.g.*, between French and Occitan (the dialect of southern France) or among the various dialects of Chinese.

In giving the names of Bantu languages, grammatical particles specific to a language's autonym (name for itself) have been omitted (the form *Rwanda* is used here, for example, rather than *kinyaRwanda,* and *Tswana* instead of *seTswana*). Parenthetical alternatives are given for a number of languages that differ markedly from the name of the people speaking them (such as Kurukh, spoken by the Oraon tribes of India) or that may be combined with other groups sometimes distinguishable in national data but appearing here under the name of the largest member—*e.g.*, "Tamil (and other Indian languages)" combining data on South Asian Indian populations in Singapore. The term *creole* as used here refers to distinguishable dialectal communities related to a national, official, or former colonial language (such as the French creole that survives in Mauritius from the end of French rule in 1810).

Language

Major languages by country	Number of speakers
Afghanistan[1]	
● Dari (Persian), of which	
Chahar Aimak	520,000
Hazāra	1,570,000
Tajik	3,670,000
Nūristāni	150,000
● Pashto	9,430,000
Turkmen	370,000
Uzbek	1,570,000
Other (including other Dari)	770,000
Albania[1]	
● Albanian	3,289,000
Greek	62,000
Other	6,000
Algeria[1]	
● Arabic	21,800,000
Berber	4,480,000
French	*5,300,000*
Other	130,000
American Samoa	
● English	1,000
English (lingua franca)	*49,000*
● Samoan	45,000
Other	3,000
Andorra[2]	
● Catalan	16,000
French	4,000
Portuguese	4,000
Spanish	28,000
Other	4,000
Angola[1]	
Ambo (Ovambo)	250,000
Chokwe	450,000
Herero	80,000
Kongo	1,400,000
Luchazi	250,000
Luimbe-Nganguela	570,000
Lunda	130,000
Luvale (Luena)	380,000
Mbunda	130,000
Mbundu	2,290,000
Nyaneka-Humbe	570,000
Ovimbundu	3,940,000
● Portuguese	*3,700,000*
Other	160,000
Antigua and Barbuda	
● English	...
English/English Creole	63,000
Other	1,000
Argentina	
Amerindian languages	370,000
Italian	580,000
● Spanish	31,760,000
Other	370,000
Armenia	
● Armenian	3,200,000
Azerbaijani	90,000
Other	140,000
Aruba	
● Dutch	...
Papiamento	58,000
Other	6,000
Australia	
Aboriginal languages	46,000
Arabic/Lebanese	130,000
Chinese	160,000
Dutch	76,000
● English	15,167,000
French	63,000
German	133,000
Greek	325,000
Hungarian	37,000
Italian	493,000
Maltese	70,000
Polish	81,000
Russian	26,000
South Slavic languages	216,000
Spanish	86,000
Turkish	39,000
Vietnamese	72,000
Other	342,000
Austria	
Czech	7,000
● German	7,512,000
Hungarian	16,000
Serbo-Croatian	144,000
Slovene	20,000
Turkish	61,000
Other	9,700
Azerbaijan	
Armenian	340,000
● Azerbaijani	5,960,000
Lezgian	160,000
Russian	550,000
Other	230,000
Bahamas, The	
● English	...
English/English Creole	228,000
French (Haitian) Creole	36,000
Bahrain[2]	
● Arabic	380,000
Other	150,000
Bangladesh[1]	
● Bengali	108,090,000
Chakmā	410,000
Gāro	100,000
Khāsī	90,000
Marma (Magh)	210,000
Mro	30,000
Santhālī	80,000
Tripuri	80,000
Other	1,520,000
Barbados	
Bajan (English Creole)	233,000
● English	26,000
Belarus	
● Belorussian	6,780,000
Russian	3,300,000
Ukrainian	130,000
Other	110,000
Belgium[2]	
Arabic	160,000
● Dutch	5,940,000
● French	3,280,000
● German	90,000
Italian	240,000
Spanish	50,000
Turkish	90,000
Other	170,000
Belize	
Black Carib (Garífuna)	13,000
● English	98,000
English Creole (lingua franca)	*150,000*
German	3,000
Mayan languages	19,000
Spanish	61,000
Spanish (lingua franca)	*120,000*
Benin[1]	
Adja	540,000
Bariba	420,000
Dendi	110,000
Djougou	150,000
Fon	1,930,000
● French	*760,000*
Fulani (Peul)	270,000
Houéda (Péda)	420,000
Somba (Otamary)	320,000
Yoruba (Nago)	590,000
Other	180,000
Bermuda	
● English	56,000
Other	4,000
Bhutan[1]	
Assamese	200,000
● Dzongkha (Bhutiä)	940,000
Nepāli (Gurung, Rai, and Limbŭ)	270,000
Other	100,000
Bolivia	
● Aymara	171,000
Guaraní	2,000
● Quechua	406,000
● Spanish	3,411,000
Spanish-Aymara	1,459,000
Spanish-Guaraní	25,000
Spanish-Quechua	1,912,000
Spanish-others	137,000
Other	218,000
Bosnia and Hercegovina	
● Serbo-Croatian	4,330,000
Other	40,000
Botswana[1]	
● English	...
Khoikhoin (Hottentot)	34,000
Ndebele	18,000
San (Bushmen)	47,000
Shona	169,000
Tswana	1,026,000
Other	66,000
Brazil[1]	
Amerindian languages	260,000
German	830,000
Italian	640,000
Japanese	730,000
● Portuguese	147,520,000
Other	1,410,000
Brunei	
Chinese	25,000
English	10,000
● Malay	122,000
Malay-Chinese	2,000
Malay-English	77,000
English-Chinese	6,000
Malay-Chinese-English	11,000
Other	14,000
Bulgaria[1]	
Armenian	30,000
● Bulgarian	7,660,000
Macedonian	220,000
Romany	230,000
Russian	20,000
Turkish	760,000
Other	50,000
Burkina Faso[1,3]	
● French	*570,000*
Fulani	790,000
Hausa	10,000
Mande	840,000
Busansi (Bisa)	190,000
Dyula	70,000
Marka (Soninke)	230,000
Samo	270,000
Songhai	140,000
Tamashek (Tuareg)	320,000
Voltaic (Gur)	7,340,000
Bobo	650,000
Gurunsi (Grusi)	490,000
Gurma	460,000
Lobi	660,000
Mossi	4,570,000
Senufo	500,000
Other	70,000
Burundi[1]	
● French	*380,000*
● Rundi	5,510,000
Hutu	4,630,000
Tutsi	760,000
Twa	50,000
Other[4]	150,000
Cambodia[1]	
Cham	210,000
Chinese	280,000
● Khmer	8,440,000
Other[5]	40,000
Cameroon[1]	
Chadic	
Buwal (Bura)	250,000
Hausa	150,000
Kotoko	140,000
Mandara (Wandala)	720,000
Masana (Masa)	500,000
● English	...
● French	*1,910,000*
Niger-Congo	
Adamawa-Eastern	
Chamba	300,000
Gbaya	150,000
Mbum	170,000
Benue-Congo	
Bamileke (Medumba)-Widikum (Mogha-mo)-Bamum (Mum)	2,350,000
Basa (Bassa)	140,000
Duala	1,380,000
Fang (Pangwe)-Beti-Bulu	2,490,000
Ibibio (Efik)	20,000
Jukun	80,000
Lundu	350,000
Maka	620,000
Tikar	940,000
Tiv	330,000
Wute	40,000
Kwa	
Igbo	70,000
West Atlantic	
Fulani	1,220,000
Saharan	
Kanuri	40,000
Semitic	
Arabic	120,000
Other	100,000
Canada	
● English	16,775,000
● French	6,737,000
English-French	363,000
English-other	574,000

Major languages by country	Number of speakers
French-other	39,000
English-French-other	50,000
Aboriginal (Amerindian and Eskimo [Inuktitut]) languages	200,000
Arabic	44,000
Chinese	291,000
Czech	25,000
Danish	22,000
Dutch	136,000
Filipino (Pilipino)	47,000
Finnish	28,000
German	480,000
Greek	122,000
Hungarian	75,000
Italian	499,000
Polish	136,000
Portuguese	169,000
Punjābī	69,000
Russian	28,000
Serbo-Croatian	44,000
Spanish	92,000
Ukrainian	227,000
Vietnamese	44,000
Yiddish	25,000
Other	394,000
Cape Verde	
Crioulo (Portuguese Creole)	346,000
● Portuguese	...
Cayman Islands	
● English	28,000
Central African Republic[1]	
Banda	840,000
Baya (Gbaya)	720,000
● French	340,000
Kare	70,000
Mbaka	130,000
Mbum	120,000
Ngbandi	310,000
Sango (lingua franca)	730,000
Sara	200,000
Zande (Azande)	290,000
Other	260,000
Chad[1]	
● Arabic	1,560,000
Dagu	140,000
● French	780,000
Hausa	140,000
Kanuri	140,000
Kotoko	120,000
Masa	140,000
Masalit, Maba, and Mimi	370,000
Mbum	390,000
Mubi	250,000
Sara, Bagirmi, and Kreish	1,820,000
Tama	370,000
Teda (Tubu)	440,000
Other	100,000
Chile[1]	
Amerindian languages (mostly Araucanian [Mapuche])	930,000
● Spanish	12,460,000
Other	210,000
China[1]	
Achang	30,000
Bulang (Blang)	90,000
Ch'iang (Qiang)	200,000
Chinese (Han)	1,072,100,000
Cantonese (Yüeh [Yue])	54,000,000
Hakka	40,000,000
Hsiang (Xiang)	51,000,000
Kan (Gan)	26,000,000
● Mandarin	767,000,000
Min	44,000,000
Wu	91,000,000
Chingpo (Jingpo)	120,000
Chuang (Zhuang)	15,930,000
Daghur (Daur)	120,000
Evenk (Ewenki)	30,000
Gelo	450,000
Hani (Woni)	1,290,000
Hui	8,850,000
Kazakh	1,140,000
Korean	1,980,000
Kyrgyz	150,000
Lahu	420,000
Li	1,140,000
Lisu	590,000
Manchu	10,100,000
Maonan	70,000
Miao	7,610,000
Mongol	4,940,000
Mulam	160,000
Nakhi (Naxi)	290,000
Nu	30,000
Pai (Bai)	1,640,000
Pumi	30,000
Puyi (Chung-chia)	2,620,000
Salar	90,000
She	650,000
Shui	360,000
Sibo (Xibe)	180,000
Tai (Dai)	1,050,000
Tajik	30,000
Tibetan	4,720,000
Tu	200,000
T'u-chia (Tujia)	5,870,000
Tung (Dong)	2,590,000
Tung-hsiang (Dongxiang)	380,000
Uighur	7,420,000
Wa (Va)	360,000
Yao	2,190,000
Yi	6,760,000
Other	920,000
Colombia[1]	
Amerindian languages	290,000
Arawakan	30,000
Cariban	20,000
Chibchan	140,000
Other	90,000
English Creole	40,000
● Spanish	33,920,000
Comoros	
● Arabic	...
Comorian	373,000
Comorian-French	64,000
Comorian-Malagasy	27,000
Comorian-Arabic	8,000
Comorian-Swahili	2,000
Comorian-French-other	19,000
● French	30,000
Other	2,000
Congo[1]	
Bubangi	30,000
● French	700,000
Kongo	1,240,000
Kota	20,000
Lingala (lingua franca)	...
Maka	40,000
Mbete	120,000
Mboshi	280,000
Monokutuba (lingua franca)	1,400,000
Punu	70,000
Sango	70,000
Teke	420,000
Other	130,000
Cook Islands	
● English	...
● Maori	16,000
Other	1,000
Costa Rica	
Chibchan languages	9,000
Bribrí	6,000
Cabécar	3,000
Chinese	6,000
English Creole	63,000
● Spanish	3,082,000
Côte d'Ivoire[1]	
Akan (including Baule and Anyi)	5,360,000
● French	4,500,000
Kru (including Bete)	2,160,000
Malinke (including Dyula and Bambara)	1,920,000
Southern Mande (including Dan and Guro)	1,320,000
Voltaic ([Gur] including Senufo and Lobi)	2,040,000
Other	150,000
Croatia	
● Serbo-Croatian	4,580,000
Other	190,000
Cuba	
● Spanish	10,737,000
Cyprus[1]	
● Greek	550,000
● Turkish	180,000
Other	30,000
Czechoslovakia[1]	
Bulgarian	5,000
● Czech	8,447,000
German	53,000
Greek	3,000
Hungarian	588,000
Moravian	1,364,000
Polish	62,000
Romany	114,000
Russian	6,000
Ruthenian	19,000
Silesian	45,000
● Slovak	4,831,000
Ukrainian	20,000
Other	45,000
Denmark[2]	
● Danish	5,005,000
English	15,000
German	8,000
Iranian languages	9,000
Norwegian	10,000
South Slavic languages	10,000
Swedish	8,000
Turkish	30,000
Other	70,000
Djibouti[1]	
Afar	110,000
● Arabic	30,000
● French	50,000
Somali	340,000
Gadaboursi	80,000
Issa	190,000
Issaq	70,000
Other	70,000
Dominica	
● English	3,000
French Creole	50,000
French Creole-English	19,000
Dominican Republic	
French (Haitian) Creole	150,000
● Spanish	7,320,000
Ecuador	
Quechua (and other Indian languages)	740,000
● Spanish	9,860,000
Egypt[1]	
● Arabic	55,310,000
Other	670,000
El Salvador	
● Spanish	5,487,000
Equatorial Guinea[1]	
Bubi	54,000
Fang	264,000
French	...
● Spanish	...
Other[6]	49,000
Estonia	
● Estonian	980,000
Russian	550,000
Other	50,000
Ethiopia[1]	
● Amharic	20,390,000
Gurage	1,770,000
Oromo (Galla)	19,110,000
Tigrinya	4,660,000
Other	8,150,000
Faeroe Islands	
● Danish	...
● Faeroese	48,000
Fiji[1]	
● English	...
Fijian	366,000
Hindī	345,000
Other	37,000
Finland	
● Finnish	4,707,000
● Swedish	299,000
Other	27,000
France	
Arabic[7]	1,450,000
English[7]	80,000
● French[7, 8, 9]	53,650,000
Basque[7]	80,000
Breton	570,000
Catalan (Rousillonais)	210,000
Corsican	170,000
Dutch (Flemish)	100,000
German (Alsatian)	1,300,000
Occitan	1,550,000
Italian[7]	260,000
Polish[7]	50,000
Portuguese[7]	660,000
Spanish[7]	220,000
Turkish[7]	200,000
Other[7]	730,000
French Guiana	
Amerindian languages	4,000
English Creole	2,000
● French	...
French Creoles	112,000
Other	6,000
French Polynesia[10]	
Chinese	11,000
● French	166,000
Polynesian languages	188,000
Other	40,000
Gabon[1]	
Fang	440,000
● French	420,000
Kota	40,000
Mbete	180,000
Mpongwe (Onyènè)	190,000
Punu, Sira, Nzebi	210,000
Teke	20,000
Other	170,000
Gambia, The	
Dyola	100,000
● English	...
Fulani	170,000
Malinke	370,000
Soninke	80,000
Wolof	130,000
Other	70,000
Gaza Strip	
Arabic	659,000
Hebrew	...
Other	11,000
Georgia	
Abaza	90,000
Armenian	380,000
Azerbaijani	300,000
● Georgian	3,920,000
Ossetian	130,000
Russian	490,000
Other	170,000
Germany[2]	
● German	74,260,000
Greek	290,000
Italian	520,000
Polish	270,000
Portuguese	70,000
Southern Slavic languages	610,000
Spanish	130,000
Turkish	1,610,000
Vietnamese	60,000
Other	1,300,000
Ghana[1]	
Akan	7,990,000
● English	...
Ewe	1,810,000
Ga-Adangme	1,180,000
Gurma	510,000
Hausa (lingua franca)	9,100,000
Mole-Dagbani (Mossi)	2,410,000
Other	1,330,000
Gibraltar	
● English	11,000
Spanish	12,000
Other	10,000
Greece[1]	
Albanian	60,000
● Greek	9,830,000
Macedonian	160,000
Turkish	90,000
Other	150,000
Greenland[1]	
● Danish	9,000
● Greenlandic	48,000
Grenada	
● English	...
English/English Creole	91,000
Guadeloupe	
French Creole/French	380,000
● French	...
Other	20,000
Guam	
● Chamorro	41,000
Chinese	2,000
Chuukese (Trukese)	2,000
● English	52,000
English (lingua franca)	138,000
Japanese	3,000
Korean	4,000
Palauan	2,000
Philippine languages	28,000
Other	5,000
Guatemala	
Black Carib (Garífuna)	20,000
Mayan languages	3,310,000
Cakchiquel	840,000
Kekchí	460,000
Mam	260,000
Quiché	960,000
● Spanish	6,110,000
Guernsey	
English	64,000
French	...
Guinea[1]	
● French	610,000
Mande	3,690,000
Kpelle	340,000
Loma	170,000
Malinke	1,680,000
Susu	800,000
Yalunka	210,000
Other	500,000
West Atlantic	3,530,000
Basari-Koniagi	80,000
Fulani (Peul)	2,790,000
Kissi	430,000
Other	220,000
Other	10,000
Guinea-Bissau	
Balante	148,000
Crioulo (Portuguese Creole)	43,000
Crioulo-Portuguese	23,000
Crioulo-other (except Portuguese)	303,000
Fulani	168,000
Malinke	70,000
Mandyako	50,000
Pepel	28,000
● Portuguese	—
Portuguese-other (except Crioulo)	82,000
Other	99,000
Guyana	
Amerindian languages	14,000
Arawakan	5,000
Cariban	9,000
● English	...
English Creoles	584,000
Other (includes Caribbean Hindī and English)	150,000
Haiti	
● French	60,000
French-Haitian (French) Creole	820,000
● Haitian (French) Creole	5,890,000
Honduras	
Black Carib (Garífuna)	102,000
English Creole	16,000
Miskito	14,000
● Spanish	4,861,000
Other	2,000
Hong Kong	
Chinese	
● Cantonese	5,142,000
Cantonese (lingua franca)	5,560,000
Chiu Chau	81,000
Fukien (Min)	110,000
Hakka	93,000
Putonghua (Mandarin)	64,000
Putonghua (lingua franca)	1,050,000
Sze Yap	23,000
● English	128,000
English (lingua franca)	1,830,000
Filipino (Pilipino)	6,000
Japanese	12,000
Other	140,000
Hungary[1]	
German	170,000
● Hungarian	9,970,000
Romanian	20,000
Romany	410,000
Slovak	110,000
South Slavic languages	30,000
Other	20,000

Language (continued)

Major languages by country	Number of speakers

Iceland[2]
- ● Icelandic — 245,000
- Other — 16,000

India
Austro-Asiatic
- Ho — 1,050,000
- Kharia — 260,000
- Khasi — 830,000
- Korku — 470,000
- Munda — 460,000
- Mundari — 980,000
- Santali — 5,490,000
- Savara (Sora) — 310,000

Dravidian
- Gondi — 2,550,000
- Kannada — 35,110,000
- Khond — 270,000
- Koya — 320,000
- Kui — 660,000
- Kurukh (Oraon) — 1,650,000
- Malayalam — 33,890,000
- Tamil — 58,400,000
- Telugu — 70,800,000
- Tulu — 1,800,000
- English — 300,000
- ● English (lingua franca) — 22,000,000

Indo-Iranian (Indo-Aryan)
- Assamese — 14,560,000
- Bengali — 67,250,000
- Bhili (Bhilodi) — 5,810,000
- Barel — 400,000
- Bhilali — 400,000
- Dogri — 1,990,000
- Gujarati — 43,330,000
- Halabi — 690,000
- ● Hindi — 344,950,000
- Anga (Angika) — 700,000
- Baghelkhandi — 400,000
- Bagri — 1,700,000
- Banjari — 800,000
- Bhojpuri — 23,300,000
- Bundelkhandi — 600,000
- Chhattisgarhi — 10,900,000
- Garhwali — 2,100,000
- Gojri — 500,000
- Harauti — 500,000
- Khortha (Khotta) — 800,000
- Kumauni — 2,000,000
- Lamani (Banjari) — 2,000,000
- Magahi (Magadhi) — 10,800,000
- Maithili — 10,000,000
- Malvi — 1,000,000
- Mandeali — 400,000
- Marwari — 7,700,000
- Mewari — 1,300,000
- Nagpuri — 500,000
- Nimadi — 1,300,000
- Pahari — 2,100,000
- Rajasthani — 3,400,000
- Sadani (Sadri) — 1,300,000
- Surgujia — 900,000
- Hindi (lingua franca) — 400,000,000
- Kashmiri — 4,150,000
- Khandeshi — 1,550,000
- Kisan — 200,000
- Konkani — 2,070,000
- Marathi — 64,800,000
- Nepali (Gorkhali) — 1,640,000
- Oriya — 29,880,000
- Punjabi — 24,270,000
- Sindhi — 2,540,000
- Kachchi — 800,000
- Urdu — 46,120,000

Sino-Tibetan
- Adi — 160,000
- Ao — 140,000
- Garo — 530,000
- Lushai (Mizo) — 500,000
- Meithei (Manipuri) — 1,180,000
- Nissi — 180,000
- Tripuri — 640,000
- Other — 14,990,000

Indonesia
- ● Bahasa Indonesia — 22,210,000
- Balinese — 3,770,000
- Banjarese — 2,480,000
- Batak — 3,940,000
- Bugi — 3,550,000
- Javanese — 74,100,000
- Madurese — 8,890,000
- Minang — 4,660,000
- Sundanese — 28,180,000
- Other — 33,020,000

Iran[1]
- Armenian — 280,000
- Iranian languages — 43,620,000
- Bakhtyari (Luri) — 990,000
- Baluchi — 1,340,000
- ● Farsi (Persian) — 26,870,000
- Farsi (lingua franca) — 48,700,000
- Gilaki — 3,110,000
- Kurdish — 5,380,000
- Luri — 2,540,000
- Mazandarani — 2,120,000
- Other — 1,280,000

Semitic languages — 1,410,000
- Arabic — 1,270,000
- Other — 140,000

Turkic languages — 13,120,000
- Afshari — 670,000
- Azerbaijani — 9,900,000
- Qashqa'i — 750,000
- Shahsavani — 350,000
- Turkish (mostly Pishagchi, Bayat, and Qajar) — 420,000
- Turkmen — 920,000
- Other — 120,000
- Other — 440,000

Iraq[1]
- ● Arabic — 14,530,000
- Assyrian — 150,000
- Kurdish — 3,570,000
- Persian — 150,000
- Turkish — 60,000
- Turkmen — 260,000
- Other — 110,000

Ireland
- ● English — 3,340,000
- ● Irish — 180,000

Isle of Man
- ● English — 71,000

Israel
- ● Arabic — 963,000
- English — 63,000
- French — 43,000
- German — 35,000
- ● Hebrew — 3,603,000
- Hungarian — 29,000
- Romanian — 82,000
- Russian — 90,000
- Spanish — 45,000
- Yiddish — 112,000
- Other — 174,000

Italy[1]
- Albanian — 120,000
- Catalan — 30,000
- French — 310,000
- German — 310,000
- Greek — 40,000
- ● Italian — 54,350,000
- Rhaetian — 740,000
- Friulian — 720,000
- Ladin — 20,000
- Sardinian — 1,530,000
- Slovene — 120,000
- Other — 240,000

Jamaica
- ● English — 650,000
- English Creoles — 1,710,000
- Hindi and other Indian languages — 50,000
- Other — 30,000

Japan[2]
- Chinese — 150,000
- English — 60,000
- ● Japanese — 123,150,000
- Korean — 690,000
- Philippine languages — 50,000
- Other — 130,000

Jersey
- English — 85,000
- ● French — ...
- Jersey Norman French — 6,000

Jordan[1]
- ● Arabic — 3,610,000
- Other — 30,000

Kazakhstan
- German — 540,000
- ● Kazakh — 6,680,000
- Russian — 8,050,000
- Tatar — 230,000
- Uighur — 180,000
- Ukrainian — 340,000
- Uzbek — 330,000
- Other — 650,000

Kenya[1]
Bantu
- Bajun (Rajun) — 60,000
- Basuba — 110,000
- Embu — 320,000
- Gusii (Kisii) — 1,660,000
- Kamba — 3,040,000
- Kikuyu — 5,640,000
- Kuria — 160,000
- Luhya — 3,730,000
- Mbere — 110,000
- Meru — 1,480,000
- Nyika (Mijikenda) — 1,290,000
- Pokomo — 70,000
- Swahili — 10,000
- ● Swahili (lingua franca) — 18,000,000
- Taita — 270,000

Cushitic
Oromo
- Boran — 120,000
- Gabbra — 50,000
- Gurreh — 150,000
- Orma — 60,000
Somali
- Degodia — 160,000
- Ogaden — 50,000
- Somali — 280,000

Nilotic
- Kalenjin — 2,910,000
- Luo — 3,440,000
- Masai — 420,000
- Sambur — 130,000
- Teso — 230,000
- Turkana — 360,000

Semitic
- Arabic — 70,000
- Other[11] — 600,000

Kiribati[1]
- ● English — ...
- Kiribati (Gilbertese) — 73,900
- Tuvaluan (Ellice) — 400
- Other — 500

Korea, North[1]
- Chinese — 40,000
- ● Korean — 22,190,000

Korea, South[1]
- Chinese — 40,000
- ● Korean — 43,650,000

Kuwait
- ● Arabic — ...
- Other — ...

Kyrgyzstan
- ● Kyrgyz — 2,380,000
- Russian — 1,160,000
- Uzbek — 580,000
- Other — 410,000

Laos[1]
- ● Lao-Lu (Lao) — 2,950,000
- Lao-Soung (Miao [Hmong] and Man [Yao]) — 230,000
- Lao-Tai (Tai) — 350,000
- Lao-Theng (Mon-Khmer) — 730,000
- Other[12] — 150,000

Latvia
- ● Latvian — 1,400,000
- Russian — 1,130,000
- Other — 160,000

Lebanon[1]
- ● Arabic — 2,610,000
- Armenian — 170,000
- French — 670,000
- Other — 30,000

Lesotho[1]
- ● English — ...
- ● Sotho — 1,580,000
- Zulu — 280,000

Liberia[1]
- ● English — 560,000
- Krio (English Creole) — 2,500,000
- Kwa (Kru)
  - Bassa — 385,000
  - Belle — 14,000
  - Dey — 10,000
  - Grebo — 249,000
  - Krahn — 105,000
  - Kru — 204,000
- Mande (Northern)
  - Gbandi — 78,000
  - Kpelle — 540,000
  - Loma — 157,000
  - Mandingo — 142,000
  - Mende — 22,000
  - Vai — 99,000
- Mande (Southern)
  - Gio — 218,000
  - Mano — 197,000
- West Atlantic (Mel)
  - Gola — 110,000
  - Kissi — 112,000
  - Other — 137,000

Libya[1]
- ● Arabic — 4,270,000
- Berber — 130,000
- Other[13] — 40,000

Liechtenstein[2]
- ● German — 26,800
- Other — 2,800

Lithuania
- ● Lithuanian — 3,050,000
- Polish — 230,000
- Russian — 440,000
- Other — 80,000

Luxembourg[2]
- Belgian — 9,000
- ● French — 13,000
- ● German — 9,000
- Italian — 21,000
- ● Luxemburgian — 286,000
- Portuguese — 31,000
- Spanish — 2,000
- Other — 17,000

Macau[1]
- ● Chinese (Cantonese) — 470,000
- ● Portuguese — ...
- Other — 10,000

Macedonia
- Albanian — 420,000
- ● Macedonian — 1,420,000
- Romany — 40,000
- Serbo-Croatian — 70,000
- Turkish — 70,000
- Other — 20,000

Madagascar[1]
- ● French — 1,300,000
- ● Malagasy — 12,670,000
- Other — 130,000

Malawi[1]
- Chewa (Maravi) — 5,530,000
- ● English — 470,000
- Lomwe — 1,740,000
- Ngoni — 630,000
- Yao — 1,250,000
- Other — 320,000

Malaysia
- Bajau — 120,000
- Chinese — 1,080,000
- Chinese-others — 610,000
- Dusan — 190,000
- ● English — 90,000
- English-others — 210,000
- English (lingua franca) — 5,700,000
- Iban — 440,000
- Iban-others — 70,000
- ● Malay — 8,030,000
- Malay-others — 2,850,000
- Tamil — 720,000
- Tamil-others — 10,000
- Other — 4,190,000

Maldives
- ● Divehi (Maldivian) — 230,000

Mali[1]
- Bambara — 2,690,000
- Bobo — 200,000
- Dogon — 340,000
- Dyula — 250,000
- ● French — 670,000
- Fulani — 1,180,000
- Malinke — 560,000
- Senufo — 1,010,000
- Songhai — 610,000
- Soninke — 740,000
- Tamashek (Tuareg) — 620,000
- Other — 260,000

Malta[1]
- ● English — 8,000
- ● Maltese — 345,000
- Other — 8,000

Marshall Islands[2]
- ● English — ...
- ● Marshallese — 48,400
- Other — 1,600

Martinique
- French Creole/French — 357,000
- ● French — ...
- Other — 12,000

Mauritania[1]
- ● Arabic — ...
- French — 120,000
- Fulani — 20,000
- Hassaniyah Arabic — 1,720,000
- Soninke — 60,000
- Tukulor — 110,000
- Wolof — 140,000
- Zenaga — 20,000
- Other — 30,000

Mauritius
- Bhojpuri — 213,000
- ● English — 2,000
- French — 39,000
- French Creole — 600,000
- Hindi — 120,000
- Marathi — 13,000
- Tamil — 38,000
- Telugu — 17,000
- Urdu — 26,000
- Other — 13,000

Mayotte[14]
- Maharais (local dialect of Comorian Swahili) — 87,000
- Other Comorian Swahili dialects — 36,000
- Malagasy — 40,000
- ● French — 31,000
- Arabic — 2,000
- Other — 4,000

Mexico
Amerindian languages — 6,660,000
- Amuzgo — 35,000
- Aztec (Nahuatl) — 1,514,000
- Chatino — 37,000
- Chinantec — 137,000
- Chocho — 16,000
- Chol — 164,000
- Chontal — 47,000
- Cora — 15,000
- Cuicatec — 16,000
- Huastec — 153,000
- Huave — 15,000
- Huichol — 25,000
- Kanjobal — 19,000
- Mame — 19,000
- Mayo — 47,000
- Mazahua — 169,000
- Mazatec — 207,000
- Mixe — 117,000
- Mixtec — 486,000
- Otomi — 360,000
- Popoluca — 40,000
- Purepecha — 119,000
- Tarahumara — 69,000
- Tepehua — 11,000
- Tepehuan — 23,000
- Tlapanec — 87,000
- Tojolabal — 47,000
- Totonac — 263,000
- Triqsi — 19,000
- Tzeltal — 334,000
- Tzotzil — 296,000
- Yaqui — 13,000
- Yucatec (Mayan) — 895,000
- Zapotec — 495,000
- Zoque — 56,000
- Other — 298,000
- ● Spanish — 77,780,000
- Spanish-Amerindian languages — 5,420,000

Micronesia
- Chuukese (Trukese) — 47,400
- ● English — 600
- Kosraean — 8,300
- Mortlockese — 8,700
- Palauan — 500
- Pohnpeian — 27,100
- Woleaian — 4,200
- Yapese — 6,600
- Other — 10,700

Moldova
- Gagauz — 140,000
- ● Moldavian — 2,720,000
- Russian — 1,020,000
- Ukrainian — 380,000
- Other — 140,000

Monaco[2]
- English — 2,000
- ● French — 12,000
- Italian — 5,000
- Monegasque — 5,000
- Other — 6,000

Mongolia[1]
- Bayad — 43,000
- Buryat — 41,000
- Dariganga — 34,000
- Dörbed — 62,000
- Dzakhchin — 27,000
- Kazakh — 115,000
- ● Khalkha (Mongolian) — 1,691,000
- Ould — 12,000

Major languages by country	Number of speakers
Torgut	12,000
Uryankhai	26,000
Other	120,000
Morocco[1]	
● Arabic	17,060,000
Berber	8,660,000
Other[5]	520,000
Mozambique	
Chopi	430,000
Chuabo	860,000
Koti	50,000
Lomwe	1,170,000
Makonde	290,000
Makua	4,170,000
Marendje	520,000
Mwani	70,000
Ngulu	10,000
Nsenga	30,000
Nyanja	500,000
Nyungwe	340,000
Phimbi	20,000
● Portuguese	180,000
Ronga	550,000
Sena	1,400,000
Shona	980,000
Swahili	10,000
Swazi	10,000
Tonga	290,000
Tsonga	1,860,000
Tswa	900,000
Yao	250,000
Zulu	10,000
Other	100,000
Myanmar (Burma)[1]	
● Burmese	29,970,000
Chin	950,000
Kachin (Chingpo)	590,000
Karen	2,700,000
Kayah	180,000
Mon	1,050,000
Rakhine (Arakanese)	1,960,000
Shan	3,680,000
Other	2,380,000
Namibia[1]	
Bergdama (Damara)	108,000
East Caprivian (mostly Lozi)	53,000
● English	120,000
Herero	108,000
Kavango (Okavango)	133,000
Nama	69,000
Ovambo (Ambo [Kwanyama])	712,000
San (Bushmen)	41,000
Other	207,000
Nauru	
Chinese	800
English	700
Kiribati (Gilbertese)	1,700
● Nauruan	5,500
Tuvaluan (Ellice)	800
Nepal	
Indo-Aryan languages	
Bhojpurī	1,510,000
Dhanwar	20,000
Hindī (Awadhī dialect)	310,000
Maithilī	2,200,000
● Nepālī (Eastern Pahāṛī)	11,550,000
Rājbansī	80,000
Tharu	720,000
Tibeto-Burman languages	
Bhutiā (Sherpa)	100,000
Gurung	230,000
Limbū	170,000
Magar	280,000
Newārī	590,000
Rai and Kirāntī	290,000
Sunwar	10,000
Tamāng	690,000
Thakali	10,000
Other	1,040,000
Netherlands, The[2]	
Arabic	143,000
● Dutch	14,523,000
Dutch and Frisian	420,000
Turkish	180,000
Other	317,000
Netherlands Antilles	
● Dutch	...
English	15,000
Papiamento	164,000
Other	11,000
New Caledonia[1]	
● French	58,000
Melanesian languages	80,000
Polynesian languages (mostly Wallisian)	20,000
Other	16,000
New Zealand	
● English	3,251,000
● Maori	111,000
Other	118,000
Nicaragua	
English Creole	41,000
Misumalpan languages	
Miskito	163,000
Sumo	10,000
● Spanish	3,914,000
Other	4,000
Niger	
Arabic	20,000
● French	1,200,000
Fulani (Fulfulde)	860,000
Hausa	4,440,000
Hausa (lingua franca)	5,800,000
Kanuri	350,000
Songhai, Zerma, and Dendi	1,740,000
Tamashek (Tuareg)	770,000
Teda (Tubu)	50,000
Other	60,000
Nigeria[1]	
Arabic	300,000
Bura	1,400,000
Edo	3,000,000
● English (lingua franca)	13,000,000
English Creole (lingua franca)[15]	31,000,000
Fulani	10,100,000
Hausa	19,100,000
Hausa (lingua franca)	45,000,000
Ibibio	5,000,000
Igbo (Ibo)	16,100,000
Ijaw	1,600,000
Kanuri	3,700,000
Nupe	1,100,000
Tiv	2,000,000
Yoruba	19,100,000
Other	7,000,000
Northern Mariana Islands	
Carolinian	2,100
Chamorro	13,400
Chinese	3,200
Chuukese (Trukese)	1,000
● English	2,100
English (lingua franca)	40,600
Japanese	900
Korean	2,900
Palauan	1,500
Philippine languages	15,300
Other	2,300
Norway[2]	
Danish	17,000
English	24,000
● Norwegian	4,139,000
Swedish	12,000
Other	92,000
Oman	
● Arabic (Omani)	1,190,000
Baluchī	300,000
Farsi (Persian)	50,000
Swahili	30,000
Urdū	40,000
Other	20,000
Pakistan	
Baluchī	3,920,000
Brāhūī	1,560,000
Pashto	17,100,000
Punjābī	
Punjābī	62,680,000
Hindko	3,160,000
Sindhī	
Sindhī	15,320,000
Siraikī	12,790,000
● Urdū	9,890,000
Other[11]	3,710,000
Palau	
Chinese	300
● English	500
English (lingua franca)	15,600
● Palauan	12,900
Philippine languages	1,500
Other	600
Panama	
Amerindian languages	210,000
Bokotá	4,000
Chibchan	187,000
Cuna	51,000
Guaymí	134,000
Teribe	2,000
Chocó	19,000
Embera	16,000
Waunama	3,000
Chinese	8,000
English Creoles	339,000
● Spanish	1,956,000
Other[11]	3,000
Papua New Guinea[1]	
● English	60,000
Melanesian languages	770,000
Papuan languages	2,990,000
Tok Pisin (English Creole)	2,540,000
Other[16]	80,000
Paraguay	
German	39,000
Guaraní	1,813,000
Guaraní-Spanish	2,198,000
Portuguese	143,000
● Spanish	293,000
Other	33,000
Peru	
Aymara	210,000
● Quechua	1,780,000
● Spanish	17,110,000
Spanish-Aymara	370,000
Spanish-Quechua	3,330,000
Spanish-others	330,000
Other	300,000
Philippines	
Aklanon	620,000
Bicol	4,430,000
Bolinao (Zambal)	270,000
Cebuano	15,520,000
Chavacano	330,000
Chinese	160,000
Davaweno	190,000
● English (lingua franca)	33,000,000
● Filipino (Pilipino; Tagalog)	15,150,000
Hamtikanon	520,000
Hiligaynon/Ilongo	6,360,000
Ibanag	370,000
Ifugao	200,000
Ilocano	7,080,000
Kankanai	230,000
Maguindanao	760,000
Manobo	200,000
Maranao	910,000
Masbate	470,000
Pampango	2,180,000
Pangasinan	1,430,000
Romblon	260,000
Samal	370,000
Samar-Leyte (Waray-Waray)	2,940,000
Subanon	210,000
Sulu-Moro (Tau Sug)	500,000
Other	1,940,000
Poland	
Belorussian	190,000
German	500,000
● Polish	37,510,000
Ukrainian	230,000
Portugal[2]	
● Portuguese	10,330,000
Other	100,000
Puerto Rico	
English	14,000
● Spanish	2,086,000
Spanish-English	1,526,000
Other	51,000
Qatar[2]	
● Arabic	210,000
Other[17]	310,000
Réunion	
● French	190,000
French Creole	570,000
Other[18]	60,000
Romania	
Bulgarian	9,000
German	359,000
Hebrew	26,000
Hungarian	1,808,000
● Romanian	20,786,000
Romany	82,000
Russian	19,000
Serbo-Croatian	42,000
Slovak	21,000
Tatar	23,000
Turkish	23,000
Ukrainian	56,000
Other	77,000
Russia	
Adyghian	120,000
Armenian	370,000
Avar	540,000
Azerbaijani	290,000
Bashkir	1,000,000
Belorussian	440,000
Buryat	370,000
Chechen	900,000
Chuvash	1,400,000
Dargin	350,000
Georgian	90,000
German	360,000
Ingush	210,000
Kabardinian	380,000
Kalmyk	160,000
Karachay	150,000
Kazakh	570,000
Komi	240,000
Komi-Permyak	110,000
Kumyk	280,000
Lak	100,000
Lezgian	250,000
Mari	540,000
Moldavian	120,000
Mordovinian	750,000
Ossetian	380,000
Romany	130,000
● Russian	129,430,000
Tabasaran	90,000
Tatar	4,800,000
Tuvinian	210,000
Udmurt	510,000
Ukrainian	1,900,000
Uzbek	100,000
Yakut	360,000
Other	1,470,000
Rwanda	
● French	500,000
● Rwanda	7,350,000
St. Kitts and Nevis	
● English	...
English/English Creole	43,000
St. Lucia	
● English	28,000
English/French Creole	110,000
St. Vincent and the Grenadines	
● English	...
English/English Creole	108,000
Other	1,000
San Marino[1]	
● Italian	23,600
São Tomé and Príncipe	
Crioulo (Portuguese Creole)	126,000
● Portuguese	...
Saudi Arabia[1]	
● Arabic	14,500,000
Other	760,000
Senegal[1]	
Dyola (Diola)	430,000
● French	390,000
Fulani (Peul)-Tukulor	1,790,000
Malinke (Mandingo)	360,000
Serer	1,140,000
Wolof	3,380,000
Wolof (lingua franca)	5,490,000
Other	630,000
Seychelles	
English	2,000
French	1,000
● Seselwa (French Creole)	66,000
Other	3,000
Sierra Leone[1]	
● English	...
Krio (English Creole [lingua franca])	
Mande	2,190,000
Kono-Vai	230,000
Kuranko	150,000
Mende	1,510,000
Susu	60,000
Yalunka	150,000
West Atlantic	2,100,000
Bullom-Sherbro	160,000
Fulani	160,000
Kissi	100,000
Limba	370,000
Temne	1,390,000
Other	80,000
Singapore[1]	
● Bahasa Malaysia	395,000
Chinese	2,169,000
● English	1,044,000
● Mandarin Chinese	...
● Tamil (and other Indian languages)	197,000
Other	31,000
Slovenia	
Serbo-Croatian	140,000
● Slovene	1,800,000
Other	40,000
Solomon Islands[1]	
● English	...
Melanesian languages	290,000
Papuan languages	29,000
Polynesian languages	13,000
Other[19]	7,000
Somalia[1]	
● Arabic	...
English	...
● Somali	7,740,000
Other	130,000
South Africa[20]	
● Afrikaans	6,080,000
● English	3,370,000
Nguni	16,860,000
Ndebele	790,000
Swazi	910,000
Xhosa	6,770,000
Zulu	8,370,000
Sotho	9,520,000
North Sotho	3,380,000
South Sotho	2,610,000
Tswana (Western Sotho)	3,540,000
Tsonga	1,320,000
Venda	750,000
Other	930,000
Bophuthatswana[21]	
● Afrikaans	...
● English	...
Nguni	290,000
North Ndebele	50,000
South Ndebele	40,000
Swazi	30,000
Xhosa	90,000
Zulu	70,000
Sotho	1,590,000
North Sotho	130,000
South Sotho	80,000
● Tswana	1,370,000
Tsonga	140,000
Venda	10,000
Other	20,000
Ciskei[21]	
● English	...
● Xhosa	840,000
Other	20,000
Transkei[21]	
● English	...
● Xhosa	3,110,000
Other	190,000
Venda[21]	
● Afrikaans	...
● English	...
● Venda	510,000
Other	60,000
Spain[2]	
Basque (Euskera)	890,000
● Castilian Spanish	28,270,000
Catalan (Català)	6,370,000
English	100,000
Galician (Gallego)	3,190,000
Other	270,000
Sri Lanka	
English	10,000
English-Sinhalese	960,000
English-Sinhalese-Tamil	630,000
English-Tamil	200,000
● Sinhalese	10,520,000
Sinhalese-Tamil	1,630,000
● Tamil	3,420,000
Other	60,000
Sudan, The[1]	
● Arabic	14,790,000
Azande	810,000
Bari	740,000
Beja	1,910,000

Language (continued)

Major languages by country	Number of speakers	Major languages by country	Number of speakers	Major languages by country	Number of speakers	Major languages by country	Number of speakers	Major languages by country	Number of speakers
Dinka	3,460,000	Gogo	1,010,000	**Tuvalu**		**Uruguay**		Romanian	60,000
Fur	620,000	Ha	890,000	● English	...	● Spanish	3,020,000	Romany	100,000
Lotuko	440,000	Haya	1,520,000	Kiribati (Gilbertese)	700	Other	110,000	● Serbo-Croatian	7,980,000
Nubian	2,430,000	Hehet	1,770,000	Tuvaluan (Ellice)	8,800			Slovak	70,000
Nuer	1,470,000	Iramba	740,000			**Uzbekistan**		Vlach	140,000
Shilluk	520,000	Luguru	1,270,000	**Uganda**[1]		Crimean Tatar	190,000	Other	190,000
Other	2,790,000	Luo	210,000	Bantu		Karakalpak	420,000		
		Makonde	1,520,000	Ganda (Luganda)	3,060,000	Kazakh	810,000	**Zaire**[1]	
Suriname		Masai	250,000	Gisu	1,230,000	Korean	110,000	Azande	2,180,000
● Dutch	...	Ngoni	340,000	Gwere	490,000	Kyrgyz	150,000	Boa	840,000
English	...	Nyakyusa	1,390,000	Kiga (Chiga)	1,180,000	Russian	2,320,000	Chokwe	650,000
Sranantonga	170,000	Nyamwezi (Sukuma)	5,450,000	Konjo	240,000	Tajik	950,000	● French	*2,800,000*
Sranantonga-other	170,000	Shambala	1,100,000	Nkole	1,410,000	Tatar	400,000	Kongo	5,740,000
Other (mostly Hindī, Javanese, and Saramacca)	90,000	● Swahili	2,280,000	Nyoro	560,000	Turkish	110,000	Kongo (lingua franca)	*11,000,000*
		Swahili (lingua franca)	*23,000,000*	Rundi	530,000	Turkmenian	120,000	Lingala (lingua franca)	*25,000,000*
Swaziland[1]		Tatoga	190,000	Rwanda	1,000,000	Ukrainian	80,000	Luba	6,430,000
● English	...	Yao	630,000	Soga	1,410,000	● Uzbek	15,240,000	Lugbara	580,000
● Swazi	740,000	Other	3,970,000	Swahili (lingua franca)	*6,000,000*	Other	470,000	Mongo	4,820,000
Zulu	20,000			Toro	550,000			Ngala and Bangi	2,070,000
Other[22]	60,000	**Thailand**[1]		Central Sudanic		**Vanuatu**		Rundi	1,380,000
		Chinese	6,890,000	Lugbara	660,000	● Bislama (English Creole)	*130,000*	Rwanda	3,670,000
Sweden[2]		Karen	200,000	Madi	240,000	● English	...	Swahili (lingua franca)	*18,000,000*
Arabic	49,000	Malay	2,070,000	English	...	● French	*50,000*	Teke	980,000
Danish	43,000	Mon-Khmer languages	1,530,000	Nilotic		Melanesian languages	151,000	Other	6,430,000
English	31,000	Khmer	720,000	Acholi	800,000	Other	3,000		
Finnish	215,000	Kuy	610,000	Alur	290,000			**Zambia**[23]	
German	45,000	Other	200,000	Karamojong	350,000	**Venezuela**		Bemba group	3,010,000
Iranian languages	43,000	Thai languages	45,530,000	Kuman	180,000	● Amerindian languages	200,000	Aushi (Ushi)	140,000
Norwegian	51,000	Lao	15,270,000	Lango	1,040,000	Goajiro	70,000	Bemba	2,070,000
Polish	37,000	● Thai (Siamese)	29,860,000	Padhola	280,000	Warrau (Warao)	30,000	Bisa	120,000
South Slavic languages	45,000	Other	390,000	Teso	1,530,000	Other	100,000	Lala	230,000
Spanish	53,000	Other	590,000	Other	170,000	● Spanish	19,550,000	Lamba	190,000
● Swedish	7,856,000					Other	440,000	Other	250,000
Turkish	27,000	**Togo**[1]		**United Arab Emirates**[2]				● English	...
Other	177,000	● French	*640,000*	● Arabic	840,000	**Vietnam**[1]		Lozi (Barotse) group	680,000
		Gur (Voltaic) languages		Other[17]	1,150,000	Bahnar	150,000	Lozi (Barotse)	500,000
Switzerland		Gurma	600,000			Chinese (Hoa)	1,030,000	Luyi (Luyana)	130,000
● French	1,273,000	Tem-Kabre	990,000	**United Kingdom**		Hre	90,000	Nkoya	50,000
● German	4,496,000	Kwa languages		● English	56,160,000	Jarai	240,000	Other	10,000
● Italian	675,000	Ana-Ife (Yoruba)	120,000	Scots-Gaelic	80,000	Khmer	930,000	Mambwe group	380,000
Romansch	55,000	Ewe-Adja	1,600,000	Welsh	550,000	Man (Yao)	460,000	Lungu	80,000
Other	412,000	Kebu-Akposo	140,000	Other	940,000	Miao (Meo or Hmong)	540,000	Mambwe	130,000
		Other	260,000			Muong	940,000	Mwanga (Winawanga)	150,000
Syria[1]				**United States**		Nung	750,000	Other	10,000
● Arabic	11,500,000	**Tonga**		American Indian or Alaska Native languages	440,000	Rhadé	190,000	North-Western group	840,000
Armenian	360,000	● English	...	Arabic	280,000	Tai	1,060,000	Chokwe	50,000
Kurdish	820,000	● Tongan	96,000	Armenian	120,000	Tho (Tay)	1,230,000	Kaonde	230,000
Other	270,000	Other	2,000	Asian Indian languages	320,000	● Vietnamese	60,170,000	Luchazi	50,000
				Chinese	770,000	Other	1,310,000	Lunda	220,000
Taiwan		**Trinidad and Tobago**		Czech	140,000			Luvale (Luena)	170,000
Austronesian languages	330,000	● English	...	Dutch	180,000	**Virgin Islands (U.S.)**		Mbunda	120,000
Ami	124,000	English Creole	1,261,000	● English	225,820,000	● English	84,000	Nyanja (Maravi) group	1,460,000
Atayal	79,000	French Creole	...	Finnish	80,000	French	3,000	Chewa	440,000
Bunun	38,000	Hindi	...	French	1,910,000	Spanish	14,000	Ngoni	160,000
Paiwan	60,000	Spanish	...	German	1,920,000	Other	3,000	Nsenga	380,000
Puyuma	8,000			Greek	490,000			Nyanja (Maravi)	430,000
Rukai	8,000	**Tunisia**		Hungarian	210,000	**West Bank**		Other	50,000
Saisiyat	4,000	● Arabic	5,880,000	Italian	1,920,000	Arabic	950,000	Tonga (Ila-Tonga) group	1,250,000
Tsou	6,000	Arabic-French	2,210,000	Japanese	410,000	Hebrew	30,000	Ila	70,000
Yami	4,000	Arabic-French-English	270,000	Korean	340,000			Lenje	150,000
Hakka Chinese	2,100,000	Arabic-other	10,000	Lithuanian	80,000	**Western Sahara**		Soli	60,000
● Mandarin Chinese	2,730,000	Other-no Arabic	20,000	Norwegian	130,000	Arabic	209,000	Tonga	910,000
South Fukien Chinese (Min)	15,550,000	Other	20,000	Persian	130,000			Other	70,000
Other	20,000			Philippine languages	610,000	**Western Samoa**		Tumbuka group	380,000
		Turkey[1]		Polish	960,000	● English	1,000	Senga	70,000
Tajikistan		Arabic	930,000	Portuguese	430,000	● Samoan	75,000	Tumbuka	310,000
Russian	540,000	Kurdish	6,200,000	Russian	210,000	Samoan-English	82,000	Other	300,000
● Tajik	3,460,000	● Turkish	50,180,000	Serbo-Croatian	180,000				
Uzbek	1,290,000	Other	1,270,000	Slovak	100,000	**Yemen**[1]		**Zimbabwe**	
Other	280,000			Spanish	14,230,000	● Arabic	11,910,000	● English	220,000
		Turkmenistan		Swedish	120,000	Other	240,000	Ndebele (Nguni)	1,600,000
Tanzania[1]		Russian	460,000	Thai	110,000			Nyanja	220,000
Chaga (Chagga), Pare	1,270,000	● Turkmenian	2,780,000	Ukrainian	140,000	**Yugoslavia**		Shona	7,120,000
● English	*3,900,000*	Uzbek	330,000	Vietnamese	250,000	Albanian	1,410,000	Other	710,000
		Other	290,000	Yiddish	370,000	Hungarian	390,000		
				Other	1,220,000				

[1]Figures given represent ethnolinguistic groups. [2]Data refer to nationality (usually resident aliens holding foreign passports). [3]Majority of population speak Moré (language of the Mossi); Dyula is language of commerce. [4]Swahili also spoken. [5]French also spoken. [6]Pidgin English and Portuguese Creole also spoken. [7]Based on "nationality" at 1982 census. [8]Includes naturalized citizens. [9]French is the universal language throughout France; traditional dialects and minority languages are retained regionally in the approximate numbers shown, however. [10]Data reflect multilingualism; total 1992 population is 206,000. [11]English also spoken. [12]English and French also spoken. [13]English and Italian also spoken. [14]Data reflect ability to speak the language, not mother tongue; 1992 population estimate is 97,000. [15]Includes speakers of standard English. [16]English and Hiri (Police Motu) also spoken. [17]Mostly Pakistanis, Indians, and Iranians. [18]Gujarātī and Chinese also spoken. [19]Solomon Islands Pidgin (English) is the lingua franca. [20]Includes the Black national states also shown separately. [21]Excludes adjustment for significant elements of change such as territorial transfers and migration. [22]Afrikaans and Portuguese also spoken. [23]Groups are officially defined geographic divisions; elements comprising them are named by language.

Religion

The following table presents statistics on religious affiliation for each of the countries of the world. An assessment was made for each country of the available data on distribution of religious communities within the total population; the best available figures, whether originating as census data, membership figures of the churches concerned, or estimates by external analysts in the absence of reliable local data, were applied as percentages to the estimated 1992 midyear population of the country to obtain the data shown below.

Several concepts govern the nature of the available data, each useful separately but none the basis of any standard of international practice in the collection of such data. The word "affiliation" was used above to describe the nature of the relationship joining the religious bodies named and the populations shown. This term implies some sort of formal, usually documentary, connection between the religion and the individual (a baptismal certificate, a child being assigned the religion of its parents on a census form, maintenance of one's name on the tax rolls of a state religion, etc.) but says nothing about the nature of the individual's personal religious practice, in that the individual may have lapsed, never been confirmed as an adult, joined another religion, or may have joined an organization that is formally atheist.

The user of these statistics should be careful to note that not only does the nature of the affiliation (with an organized religion) differ greatly from country to country, but the social context of religious practice does also. A country in which a single religion has long been predominant will often show more than 90% of its population to be *affiliated,* while in actual fact, no more than 10% may actually *practice* that religion on a regular basis. Such a situation often leads to undercounting of minority religions (where someone [head of household, communicant, child] is counted at all), blurring of distinctions seen to be significant elsewhere (a Hindu country may not distinguish Protestant [or even Christian] denominations; a Christian country may not distinguish among its Muslim or Buddhist citizens), or double-counting in countries where an individual may conscientiously practice more than one "religion" at a time.

Until 1989 communist countries had for long consciously attempted to ignore, suppress, or render invisible religious practice within their borders. Countries with large numbers of adherents of traditional, often animist, religions and belief systems usually have little or no formal methodology for defining the nature of local religious practice. On the other hand, countries with strong missionary traditions, or good census organizations, or few religious sensitivities may have very good, detailed, and meaningful data.

The most authoritative work available is DAVID B. BARRETT (ed.), *World Christian Encyclopedia* (1982); it examines both the theoretical and practical problems of collecting and analyzing religious statistics, assembles a mine of national detail, and establishes a basis for further study.

Religion

Religious affiliation	1992 population	Religious affiliation	1992 population	Religious affiliation	1992 population	Religious affiliation	1992 population	Religious affiliation	1992 population
Afghanistan		**Azerbaijan**		**Botswana**		Roman Catholic	970,000	Muslim (mostly Sunnī)	180,000
Sunnī Muslim	15,160,000	*Believers are predominantly*		traditional beliefs	640,000	traditional beliefs	350,000	other (mostly Christian)	30,000
Shī'ī Muslim	2,710,000	*Shī'ī Muslim; Sunnī Muslim*		Protestant	360,000	other	160,000		
other	180,000	*(Hanafīyah) minority.*		African Christian	160,000			**Czechoslovakia**	
				Roman Catholic	130,000	**Chad**		Roman Catholic	7,230,000
Albania		**Bahamas, The**		other	40,000	Muslim	2,630,000	Slovak Evangelical	330,000
Muslim	690,000	Protestant	146,000			traditional beliefs	1,360,000	Evangelical Church of	
Christian[1]	180,000	Anglican	53,000	**Brazil**		Roman Catholic	1,250,000	Czech Brethren	190,000
atheist	630,000	Roman Catholic	50,000	Roman Catholic	132,910,000	Protestant	690,000	Greek Catholic	190,000
nonreligious	1,860,000	other	15,000	Protestant	9,230,000	other	40,000	Czechoslovak	
				Afro-American Spiritist	3,030,000			Hussite	170,000
Algeria		**Bahrain**		Spiritist	2,570,000	**Chile**		Reformed Christian	90,000
Sunnī Muslim	26,160,000	Shī'ī Muslim	320,000	atheist and		Roman Catholic	10,980,000	Eastern Orthodox	50,000
other	240,000	Sunnī Muslim	140,000	nonreligious	2,120,000	Protestant	830,000	Silesian Evangelical	50,000
		other	80,000	other	1,500,000	other	1,800,000	atheist and	
American Samoa								nonreligious	4,680,000
Congregational	28,000	**Bangladesh**		**Brunei**		**China**		other	2,680,000
Roman Catholic	10,000	Muslim	95,840,000	Muslim	178,000	nonreligious	690,200,000		
other	11,000	Hindu	13,420,000	other	90,000	Chinese folk-		**Denmark**	
		other	1,342,000			religionist	234,300,000	Evangelical Lutheran	4,592,000
Andorra				**Bulgaria**		atheist	139,900,000	other	575,000
Roman Catholic	52,000	**Barbados**		*Believers are predominantly*		Buddhist	70,000,000		
other	6,000	Anglican	103,000	*Bulgarian Orthodox; Muslim*		Muslim	28,000,000	**Djibouti**	
		Protestant	66,000	*minority.*		other	3,500,000	Sunnī Muslim	524,000
Angola		other	90,000					Christian[2]	33,000
Roman Catholic	7,290,000			**Burkina Faso**		**Colombia**			
Protestant	2,100,000	**Belarus**		traditional beliefs	4,260,000	Roman Catholic	32,130,000	**Dominica**	
traditional beliefs	1,010,000	*Believers are predominantly*		Muslim	4,090,000	other	2,120,000	Roman Catholic	55,000
other	210,000	*affiliated with the Belorussian*		Christian[2]	1,160,000			other	17,000
		Orthodox Church; Roman				**Comoros**			
Antigua and Barbuda		*Catholic minority.*		**Burundi**		Sunnī Muslim	496,000	**Dominican Republic**	
Anglican	28,000			Roman Catholic	4,430,000	Christian	1,000	Roman Catholic	6,780,000
Protestant	27,000	**Belgium**		traditional beliefs	760,000			other	690,000
Roman Catholic	7,000	Roman Catholic	9,020,000	other	470,000	**Congo**			
other	2,000	other	1,000,000			Roman Catholic	1,450,000	**Ecuador**	
				Cambodia		Protestant	660,000	Roman Catholic	9,860,000
Argentina		**Belize**		Buddhist	7,930,000	African Christian	380,000	other	750,000
Roman Catholic	30,080,000	Roman Catholic	122,000	other	1,050,000	other	200,000		
other	2,980,000	Anglican	23,000					**Egypt**	
		other	51,000	**Cameroon**		**Cook Islands**		Sunnī Muslim	50,400,000
Armenia				Roman Catholic	4,430,000	Congregational	11,400	Christian (mostly	
Believers are predominantly		**Benin**		Muslim	2,790,000	Roman Catholic	3,000	Coptic[3])	5,600,000
affiliated with the Armenian		traditional beliefs	3,030,000	traditional beliefs	2,730,000	other	2,700		
Apostolic Church (Eastern		Roman Catholic	910,000	Protestant	2,230,000			**El Salvador**	
Orthodox); Roman Catholic		Muslim	750,000	other	480,000	**Costa Rica**		Roman Catholic	5,040,000
and Muslim minorities.		other	240,000			Roman Catholic	2,800,000	other	450,000
				Canada		other	360,000		
Aruba		**Bermuda**		Roman Catholic	13,130,000			**Equatorial Guinea**	
Roman Catholic	57,000	Anglican	23,000	Protestant	8,140,000	**Côte d'Ivoire**		Roman Catholic	300,000
other	8,000	Methodist	10,000	Anglican	2,810,000	traditional beliefs	10,600,000	other	80,000
		Roman Catholic	8,000	Eastern Orthodox	420,000	Muslim	3,500,000		
Australia		other	19,000	Jewish	340,000	Roman Catholic	2,600,000	**Estonia**	
Anglican	4,190,000			Muslim	110,000	Protestant	900,000	*Believers are predominantly*	
Roman Catholic	4,570,000	**Bhutan**		Sikh	80,000			*affiliated with the Evangeli-*	
Uniting Church		Buddhist	1,050,000	Hindu	80,000	**Croatia**		*cal Lutheran Church of*	
and Methodist	1,330,000	Hindu	370,000	nonreligious	2,050,000	Roman Catholic	3,660,000	*Estonia; Russian Orthodox*	
Presbyterian	630,000	other	90,000	other	580,000	Eastern Orthodox	530,000	*and Protestant minorities.*	
other Protestant	1,090,000					Muslim	60,000		
Orthodox	480,000	**Bolivia**		**Cape Verde**		other	540,000	**Ethiopia**	
nonreligious	2,230,000	Roman Catholic	7,160,000	Roman Catholic	322,000			Ethiopian Orthodox	28,390,000
other	3,030,000	other	580,000	Protestant	24,000	**Cuba**		Muslim (mostly	
						Roman Catholic	4,300,000	Sunnī)	16,980,000
Austria		**Bosnia and Hercegovina**		**Cayman Islands**		nonreligious	5,280,000	traditional beliefs	6,160,000
Roman Catholic	6,630,000	*Believers are predominantly*		Presbyterian	10,000	atheist	690,000	other	2,540,000
Evangelical Lutheran	440,000	*Sunnī Muslim, Serbian*		Church of God	7,000	other	570,000		
atheist and		*Orthodox, and Roman*		other	12,000			**Faeroe Islands**	
nonreligious	470,000	*Catholic.*				**Cyprus**		Evangelical Lutheran	35,000
other	320,000			**Central African Republic**		Greek Orthodox	550,000	other	12,000
				Protestant	1,440,000				

Religion (continued)

Religious affiliation	1992 population
Fiji	
Christian (mostly Methodist and Roman Catholic)	396,000
Hindu	286,000
Muslim	59,000
other	8,000
Finland	
Evangelical Lutheran	4,420,000
other	613,000
France	
Roman Catholic	43,770,000
nonreligious	6,990,000
atheist	1,950,000
Muslim	1,720,000
other	2,870,000
French Guiana	
Roman Catholic	97,000
other	26,000
French Polynesia	
Protestant	96,000
Roman Catholic	81,000
other	29,000
Gabon	
Roman Catholic	820,000
Protestant	240,000
African Christian	150,000
other	50,000
Gambia, The	
Muslim (mostly Sunnī)	880,000
other	40,000
Gaza Strip	
Muslim (mostly Sunnī)	663,000
other	7,000
Georgia	
Believers are predominantly affiliated with the Georgian Orthodox Church; Muslim minority.	
Germany	
Evangelical Lutheran	31,810,000
Roman Catholic	27,960,000
Muslim	1,690,000
other (mostly nonreligious or unaffiliated)	17,660,000
Ghana	
Protestant	3,810,000
traditional beliefs	3,260,000
Roman Catholic	2,850,000
African Christian	2,440,000
Muslim	2,390,000
Anglican	320,000
other	170,000
Gibraltar	
Roman Catholic	24,000
other	8,000
Greece	
Greek Orthodox	10,040,000
Muslim	150,000
other	100,000
Greenland	
Evangelical Lutheran	56,000
other	1,000
Grenada	
Roman Catholic	54,000
Anglican	16,000
other	21,000
Guadeloupe	
Roman Catholic	370,000
other	30,000
Guam	
Roman Catholic	111,000
Protestant	22,000
other	6,000
Guatemala	
Roman Catholic	7,080,000
Protestant	2,360,000
Guernsey	
Anglican	42,000
other	22,000

Religious affiliation	1992 population
Guinea	
Muslim	6,150,000
traditional beliefs	580,000
other	510,000
Guinea-Bissau	
traditional beliefs	660,000
Muslim	300,000
Christian	50,000
Guyana	
Hindu	277,000
Protestant	121,000
Anglican	107,000
Roman Catholic	85,000
Muslim	65,000
other	93,000
Haiti	
Roman Catholic	5,430,000
Baptist	660,000
Pentacostal	240,000
other	430,000
Honduras	
Roman Catholic	4,250,000
Protestant	500,000
other	250,000
Hong Kong	
Buddhist and Taoist	4,280,000
Roman Catholic	270,000
Protestant	220,000
other	1,030,000
Hungary	
Roman Catholic	6,610,000
Protestant	2,410,000
nonreligious and atheist	1,160,000
other	140,000
Iceland	
Evangelical Lutheran	241,000
other	20,000
India[4]	
Hindu	713,900,000
Muslim	98,100,000
Sikh	17,000,000
Roman Catholic	9,800,000
Protestant	8,300,000
Buddhist	6,100,000
Jain	4,200,000
other	6,500,000
Indonesia	
Muslim	160,620,000
Protestant	11,940,000
Roman Catholic	5,780,000
Hindu	3,590,000
Buddhist	1,810,000
other	1,050,000
Iran	
Shī'ī Muslim	53,290,000
Sunnī Muslim	4,590,000
other	1,000,000
Iraq	
Shī'ī Muslim	11,590,000
Sunnī Muslim	6,400,000
other	850,000
Ireland	
Roman Catholic	3,275,000
other	244,000
Isle of Man	
Anglican	44,000
other	27,000
Israel	
Jewish	4,270,000
Muslim (mostly Sunnī)	750,000
other	210,000
Italy	
Roman Catholic	48,020,000
nonreligious	7,860,000
atheist	1,500,000
other	410,000
Jamaica	
Protestant	1,220,000
Anglican	170,000
Roman Catholic	120,000
other	950,000

Religious affiliation	1992 population
Japan	
Shintoist[5]	107,910,000
Buddhist[5]	91,770,000
Christian	1,480,000
other	11,420,000
Jersey	
Anglican	52,000
Roman Catholic	20,000
other	13,000
Jordan	
Sunnī Muslim	3,380,000
other	250,000
Kazakhstan	
Believers are predominantly Sunnī Muslim (Ḥanafīyah); Christian minorities (mainly Russian Orthodox and Baptist).	
Kenya	
Roman Catholic	7,120,000
Protestant	5,210,000
traditional beliefs	5,100,000
African Christian	4,750,000
Anglican	1,940,000
Muslim	1,620,000
other	1,240,000
Kiribati	
Roman Catholic	40,000
Congregational	29,000
other	6,000
Korea, North	
atheist and nonreligious	15,090,000
traditional beliefs	3,470,000
Ch'ŏndogyo	3,090,000
other	580,000
Korea, South	
Buddhist	15,850,000
Confucian	10,680,000
Protestant	10,190,000
Roman Catholic	2,250,000
Wonbulgyo	1,140,000
Ch'ŏndogyo	1,010,000
Taejong	490,000
other	2,050,000
Kuwait	
Kuwaiti nationals are predominantly Sunnī Muslim; Shī'ī Muslim minority.	
Kyrgyzstan	
Believers are predominantly Sunnī Muslim (Ḥanafīyah).	
Laos	
Buddhist	2,550,000
traditional beliefs	1,480,000
other	380,000
Latvia	
Believers are predominantly affiliated with the Latvian Evangelical Lutheran Church; Russian Orthodox, Roman Catholic, and Protestant minorities.	
Lebanon	
Shī'ī Muslim	1,020,000
Sunnī Muslim	660,000
Maronite Christian	560,000
Druze	190,000
Greek Orthodox	150,000
Greek Catholic	100,000
Armenian Christian	100,000
other	30,000
Lesotho	
Roman Catholic	810,000
Protestant	550,000
other	490,000
Liberia	
Christian	1,880,000
traditional beliefs	510,000
Muslim	380,000
Libya	
Sunnī Muslim	4,310,000
other	130,000
Liechtenstein	
Roman Catholic	26,000
other	4,000

Religious affiliation	1992 population
Lithuania	
Believers are predominantly Roman Catholic; Russian Orthodox and Protestant minorities.	
Luxembourg	
Roman Catholic	364,000
other	23,000
Macau	
Buddhist	220,000
nonreligious	224,000
other	44,000
Macedonia	
Believers are predominantly affiliated with the Macedonian Orthodox Church; Sunnī Muslim minority.	
Madagascar	
Christian[2]	6,530,000
traditional beliefs	6,020,000
other	260,000
Malawi	
Christian[2]	6,120,000
traditional beliefs	1,800,000
Muslim	1,540,000
other	30,000
Malaysia	
Muslim	9,860,000
Buddhist	3,220,000
Chinese folk-religionist	2,160,000
Hindu	1,300,000
Christian	1,190,000
other	890,000
Maldives	
Sunnī Muslim	230,000
Mali	
Muslim	7,600,000
traditional beliefs	760,000
Christian	80,000
Malta	
Roman Catholic	356,000
other	4,000
Marshall Islands	
Believers are predominantly Protestant (mainly Congregational); Roman Catholic minority.	
Martinique	
Roman Catholic	330,000
other	40,000
Mauritania	
Sunnī Muslim	2,100,000
other	10,000
Mauritius	
Hindu	570,000
Roman Catholic	280,000
Muslim	140,000
Protestant	50,000
other	40,000
Mayotte	
Sunnī Muslim	94,000
Christian	3,000
Mexico	
Roman Catholic	75,730,000
Protestant and Evangelical Catholic	4,130,000
Jewish	70,000
nonreligious	2,740,000
other	1,770,000
Micronesia	
Believers are about equally Roman Catholic and Protestant (mainly Congregational).	
Moldova	
Believers are predominantly Russian Orthodox.	
Monaco	
Roman Catholic	27,000
other	3,000
Mongolia	
atheist and nonreligious	1,430,000

Religious affiliation	1992 population
traditional beliefs	670,000
other	70,000
Morocco	
Muslim (mostly Sunnī)	25,900,000
other	340,000
Mozambique	
traditional beliefs	7,180,000
Roman Catholic	4,720,000
Muslim	1,950,000
other	1,180,000
Myanmar (Burma)	
Buddhist	38,880,000
Christian	2,130,000
Muslim	1,660,000
traditional beliefs	500,000
Hindu	220,000
other	70,000
Namibia	
Lutheran	733,000
Roman Catholic	283,000
Dutch Reformed	87,000
Anglican	72,000
other	256,000
Nauru	
Congregational	5,200
other	4,400
Nepal	
Hindu	17,720,000
Buddhist	1,050,000
Muslim	530,000
other	500,000
Netherlands, The	
Roman Catholic	5,460,000
Dutch Reformed Church (NHK)	2,880,000
Reformed Churches	1,210,000
Muslim	420,000
nonreligious	4,850,000
other	340,000
Netherlands Antilles	
Roman Catholic	160,000
other	31,000
New Caledonia	
Roman Catholic	103,000
other	71,000
New Zealand	
Anglican	740,000
Presbyterian	560,000
Roman Catholic	510,000
Methodist	140,000
Baptist	70,000
Ratana	50,000
Mormon	50,000
nonreligious	680,000
other	670,000
Nicaragua	
Roman Catholic	3,750,000
other	380,000
Niger	
Sunnī Muslim	6,620,000
traditional beliefs	1,660,000
Nigeria	
Muslim	40,350,000
Protestant	23,580,000
Roman Catholic	10,850,000
African Christian	9,500,000
traditional beliefs	5,020,000
other	360,000
Northern Mariana Islands	
Believers are predominantly Roman Catholic.	
Norway	
Evangelical Lutheran (Church of Norway)	3,764,000
other	519,000
Oman	
Muslim	1,390,000
other	230,000
Pakistan	
Muslim (mostly Sunnī)	125,960,000
Christian	2,030,000

Religious affiliation	1992 population
Hindu	1,960,000
other	170,000
Palau	
Roman Catholic	6,400
Protestant	3,900
traditional beliefs	3,900
other	1,500
Panama	
Roman Catholic	2,110,000
other	400,000
Papua New Guinea	
Protestant	2,240,000
Roman Catholic	1,260,000
Anglican	210,000
other	130,000
Paraguay	
Roman Catholic	4,340,000
other	180,000
Peru	
Roman Catholic	21,560,000
other	1,880,000
Philippines	
Roman Catholic	53,500,000
Aglipayan	3,940,000
Muslim	2,740,000
Protestant	2,230,000
other	1,200,000
Poland	
Roman Catholic	36,370,000
Polish Orthodox	880,000
other	1,180,000
Portugal	
Roman Catholic	9,860,000
other	570,000
Puerto Rico	
Roman Catholic	3,050,000
other	530,000
Qatar	
Muslim (mostly Sunnī)	480,000
other	40,000
Réunion	
Roman Catholic	560,000
other	60,000
Romania	
Romanian Orthodox	16,330,000
Greek Orthodox	2,330,000
atheist	1,630,000
Muslim	230,000
nonreligious	2,100,000
other	700,000

Russia
Believers are predominantly affiliated with the Russian Orthodox Church; Roman Catholic, Protestant, Muslim, Jewish, and Buddhist minorities.

Religious affiliation	1992 population
Rwanda	
Roman Catholic	4,780,000
traditional beliefs	1,840,000
Protestant	660,000
Muslim	70,000
St. Kitts and Nevis	
Anglican	14,000
Methodist	12,000
other	17,000
St. Lucia	
Roman Catholic	107,000
other	28,000

Religious affiliation	1992 population
St. Vincent and the Grenadines	
Anglican	45,000
Methodist	23,000
Roman Catholic	13,000
other	28,000
San Marino	
Roman Catholic	23,000
other	1,000
São Tomé and Príncipe	
Roman Catholic	100,000
Protestant	30,000
Saudi Arabia	
Muslim (mostly Sunnī)	15,080,000
other	180,000
Senegal	
Sunnī Muslim	7,270,000
Christian	380,000
other	90,000
Seychelles	
Roman Catholic	63,000
other	8,000
Sierra Leone	
traditional beliefs	2,250,000
Sunnī Muslim	1,720,000
other	390,000
Singapore	
Buddhist and Taoist	1,505,000
Muslim	429,000
Protestant	218,000
Roman Catholic	135,000
Hindu	99,000
nonreligious	391,000
other	15,000

Slovenia
Believers are predominantly Roman Catholic.

Religious affiliation	1992 population
Solomon Islands	
Protestant	142,000
Anglican	115,000
Roman Catholic	65,000
other	17,000
Somalia	
Sunnī Muslim	7,860,000
other	20,000
South Africa[6]	
Christian	21,770,000
Protestant	10,850,000
Dutch (Afrikaans) Reformed Churches	3,910,000
Nederduitse Gereformeerde	3,450,000
Gereformeerde	170,000
Nederduitsch Hervormde	290,000
other Protestant	6,940,000
Methodist	2,000,000
Presbyterian	440,000
United Congregational	400,000
Lutheran	800,000
Apostolic Faith Mission of South Africa	430,000
New Apostolic Church	150,000
other Apostolic	440,000
Baptist	270,000
Pentecostal Protestant	80,000
African Protestant Church	40,000

Religious affiliation	1992 population
Full Gospel	220,000
Pentecostal	20,000
Salvation Army	30,000
Seventh-day Adventist	100,000
Swiss	40,000
Assemblies of God	160,000
other	1,310,000
Roman Catholic	2,490,000
Anglican	1,280,000
Greek Orthodox	30,000
Black independent churches	7,110,000
Zion Christian Church	1,490,000
other	5,620,000
Mormon	10,000
Hindu	420,000
Muslim	360,000
Jewish	70,000
other beliefs	30,000
nonreligious	390,000
not stated	9,020,000
Bophuthatswana	
Christian	1,860,000
traditional beliefs	200,000
Ciskei	
Christian	610,000
traditional beliefs	240,000
Transkei	
Christian[2]	2,310,000
traditional beliefs	990,000
Venda	
traditional beliefs	440,000
Christian	120,000
Spain	
Roman Catholic	37,680,000
other	1,410,000
Sri Lanka	
Buddhist	12,070,000
Hindu	2,700,000
Muslim	1,320,000
Roman Catholic	1,200,000
other	140,000
Sudan, The	
Sunnī Muslim	21,880,000
traditional beliefs	5,010,000
Christian[2]	2,730,000
other	360,000
Suriname	
Hindu	111,000
Roman Catholic	92,000
Muslim	79,000
Protestant	76,000
other	46,000
Swaziland	
Christian[2]	640,000
traditional beliefs	170,000
other	20,000
Sweden	
Church of Sweden (Lutheran)	7,712,000
other	961,000
Switzerland	
Roman Catholic	3,290,000
Protestant	3,060,000
other	560,000
Syria	
Muslim (mostly Sunnī)	11,610,000
Christian[2]	1,150,000
other	190,000
Taiwan	
Chinese folk-religionist	10,050,000
Buddhist	8,910,000
Christian[2]	1,530,000
other	220,000

Tajikistan
Believers are predominantly Sunnī Muslim (Hanafīyah).

Religious affiliation	1992 population
Tanzania	
Muslim	9,000,000
Christian	8,400,000
traditional beliefs	8,400,000
Thailand	
Buddhist	53,600,000
Muslim	2,240,000
Christian	300,000
other	650,000
Togo	
traditional beliefs	2,180,000
Roman Catholic	800,000
Sunnī Muslim	450,000
Protestant	250,000
other	30,000
Tonga	
Free Wesleyan	42,000
Roman Catholic	16,000
other	39,000
Trinidad and Tobago	
Roman Catholic	406,000
Hindu	307,000
Anglican	181,000
Protestant	168,000
other	199,000
Tunisia	
Sunnī Muslim	8,360,000
other	60,000
Turkey	
Muslim (mostly Sunnī)	58,120,000
other	470,000

Turkmenistan
Believers are predominantly Sunnī Muslim (Șūfī).

Religious affiliation	1992 population
Tuvalu	
Congregational	9,200
other	300
Uganda	
Roman Catholic	8,530,000
Anglican	4,500,000
traditional beliefs	2,170,000
Muslim (mostly Sunnī)	1,130,000
other	870,000

Ukraine
Believers are predominantly affiliated with the Ukrainian Orthodox Church; Roman Catholic minority.

Religious affiliation	1992 population
United Arab Emirates	
Sunnī Muslim	1,590,000
Shī'ī Muslim	320,000
other	80,000
United Kingdom	
Christian[2]	50,170,000
Roman Catholic	75,600,000
Church of England	32,790,000
Protestant	8,660,000
Muslim	810,000
Jewish	460,000
nonreligious	5,080,000
other	1,210,000
United States[7]	
Christian[2]	220,810,000
Protestant	130,130,000
Roman Catholic	66,970,000
Anglican	4,420,000
Eastern Orthodox	740,000

Religious affiliation	1992 population
other Christian	6,790,000
other Christian (denomination not stated)	11,750,000
Muslim	4,850,000
Jewish	4,570,000
Buddhist	590,000
Hindu	330,000
New-Religionist	150,000
Baha'i	50,000
nonreligious	19,100,000
agnostic	1,740,000
other (mostly not stated)	3,220,000
Uruguay	
Roman Catholic	1,830,000
other	1,300,000

Uzbekistan
Believers are predominantly Sunnī Muslim (Hanafīyah).

Religious affiliation	1992 population
Vanuatu	
Presbyterian	54,000
Anglican	22,000
Roman Catholic	22,000
other	49,000
Venezuela	
Roman Catholic	18,490,000
other	1,700,000
Vietnam	
Buddhist	38,200,000
atheist and nonreligious	12,880,000
Roman Catholic	4,840,000
other	13,160,000
Virgin Islands (U.S.)	
Protestant	47,000
Roman Catholic	35,000
other	21,000
West Bank	
Muslim (mostly Sunnī)	790,000
Jewish	120,000
Christian and other	80,000
Western Sahara	
Sunnī Muslim	209,000
Western Samoa	
Congregational	75,000
Roman Catholic	34,000
other	49,000
Yemen	
Muslim	12,130,000
other	20,000

Yugoslavia
Believers are predominantly affiliated with the Serbian Orthodox Church; Muslim, Roman Catholic, and Protestant minorities.

Religious affiliation	1992 population
Zaire	
Roman Catholic	17,320,000
Protestant	10,380,000
African Christian	6,120,000
traditional beliefs	1,220,000
other	740,000
Zambia	
Christian[2]	5,980,000
traditional beliefs	2,240,000
other	80,000
Zimbabwe	
Christian[2]	5,730,000
traditional beliefs	4,000,000
other	140,000

[1]Albanian Christians are mostly Eastern Orthodox and Roman Catholic.   [2]Includes affiliated and nominal Christians.   [3]Official 1986 census figure is 5.9 percent.   [4]Excludes Assam.   [5]Many Japanese practice both Shintoism and Buddhism.   [6]Excludes black republics listed separately.   [7]For additional denominational detail, see the article WORLD AFFAIRS (North America): United States.

Vital statistics, marriage, family

This table provides some of the basic measures of the factors that influence the size, direction, and rates of population change within a country. The accuracy of these data depends on the effectiveness of each respective national system for registering vital and civil events (birth, death, marriage, etc.) and on the sophistication of the analysis that can be brought to bear upon the data so compiled.

Data on birth rates, for example, depend not only on the completeness of registration of births in a particular country but also on the conditions under which those data are collected: Do all births take place in a hospital? Are the births reported comparably in all parts of the country? Are the records of the births tabulated at a central location in a timely way with an effort to eliminate inconsistent reporting of birth events, perinatal mortality, etc.? Similar difficulties attach to death rates but with the added need to identify "cause of death." Even in a developed country such identifications are often left to nonmedical personnel, and in a developing country with, say, only one physician for every 10,000 population there will be too few physicians to perform autopsies to assess accurately the cause of death after the fact and also too few to provide ongoing care at a level where records would permit inference about cause of death based on prior condition or diagnosis.

Calculating natural increase, which at its most basic is simply the difference between the birth and death rates, may be affected by the differing degrees of completeness of birth and death registration for a given country. The total fertility rate may be understood as the average number of children that would be borne per woman if all childbearing women lived to the end of their childbearing years and bore children at each age at the average rate for that age. Calculating a meaningful fertility rate requires analysis of changing age structure of the female population over time, changing mortality rates among mothers and their infants, and changing medical practice at births, each improvement of natural survivorship or medical support leading to greater numbers of live-born children and greater numbers of children who survive their first year (the basis for measurement of infant mortality, another basic indicator of demographic conditions and trends within a population).

As indicated above, data for causes of death are not only particularly difficult to obtain, since many countries are not well equipped to collect the data, but are also difficult to assess, as their accuracy may be suspect and their meaning may be subject to varying interpretation. Take the case of a citizen of a less developed country who dies of what is clearly a lung infection: Was the death complicated by chronic malnutrition, itself complicated by a parasitic infestation, these last two together so weakening the subject that he died of an infection that he might have survived had his general health been better? Similarly, in a developed country: Someone may die from what is identified in an autopsy as a cerebrovascular accident, but if that accident occurred in a vascular system that was weakened by diabetes, what was the actual cause of death? Statistics on causes of death seek to identify the "underlying" cause (that which sets the final train of events leading to death in motion) but often must settle for the most proximate cause or symptom. Even this kind of analysis may be misleading for those charged with interpreting the data with a view to ordering health-care priorities for a particular country. The eight groups of causes of death utilized here include most, but not all, of the detailed

Vital statistics, marriage, family

country	vital rates						causes of death (rate per 100,000 population)								
	year	birth rate per 1,000 population	death rate per 1,000 population	infant mortality rate per 1,000 live births	rate of natural increase per 1,000 population	total fertility rate	year	infectious and parasitic diseases	malignant neoplasms (cancers)	endocrine and metabolic disorders	diseases of the nervous system	diseases of the circulatory system	diseases of the respiratory system	diseases of the digestive system	accidents, poisonings, and violence
Afghanistan	1991	44.0	20.0	164.0	24.0	6.3		...	...	...	...	...	...	...	...
Albania	1989	24.7	5.7	28.2[2]	19.0	3.0		...	...	...	...	...	...	...	...
Algeria	1988	33.2	4.9	39.9	28.3	4.7		...	...	...	...	...	...	...	...
American Samoa	1989	38.2	3.8	8.0	34.4	5.4	1989	6.6[4]	72.5	13.2[5]	...	92.3[6]	33.0[7]	...	44.0
Andorra	1990	12.2	3.7	4.9[9]	8.5	3.1		...	...	...	...	...	...	...	...
Angola	1990–95	46.6	18.6	127.0	28.0	6.3		...	...	...	...	...	...	...	...
Antigua and Barbuda	1988	14.1	4.6	21.2[2]	9.5	1.9[10]	1988	14.0	44.5	25.4	7.6	237.5	44.5	15.2	5.1
Argentina	1991	20.0	9.0	31.0	11.0	2.7	1987	29.9	140.4	25.4	8.8	357.7	52.5	38.3	53.0
Armenia	1990	22.5	6.2	18.6	16.3	2.6[13]	1990	13.0[13]	98.3	14.2[13]	4.0[13]	305.9	50.3	21.7	55.6
Aruba	1990	17.3	6.4	9.6[13]	10.9	1.8[14]	1989	9.8	118.7	45.5	4.9	243.8	29.3	29.3	13.0
Australia	1991	14.8	6.9	8.1[10]	7.9	1.9[10]	1988	4.4	178.8	16.4	13.0	333.1	54.6	25.1	51.3
Austria	1990	11.6	10.7	7.9	0.9	1.4	1990	4.2	250.4	28.9	16.5	552.3	54.4	52.7	72.2
Azerbaijan	1990	26.4	6.2	23.0	20.2	2.8[13]	1989	42.1	72.1	8.6	9.7	292.4	88.9	25.6	42.1
Bahamas, The	1990	19.2	4.5	26.3	14.7	2.2[15]	1988	11.8	94.4	57.4	14.2	154.3	35.0	33.4	69.6
Bahrain	1991	27.9	3.7	17.0	24.2	4.7[10]	1988	2.4	34.1	14.6	2.2	110.0	15.0	3.8	23.7
Bangladesh	1990	32.8	11.3	98.0[13]	21.5	4.2[13]		...	...	...	...	...	...	...	...
Barbados	1991	16.4	8.8	10.9[16]	7.6	1.8[13]	1988	19.8	160.7	79.8	15.2	338.9	47.9	36.6	44.0
Belarus	1990	13.9	10.7	11.9	3.2	2.0[13]	1990	7.1	171.8	7.1[17]	9.7	545.8	73.6	22.2	100.5
Belgium	1990	12.4	10.5	6.9[9]	1.9	1.6[18]	1987	8.5	272.4	24.3	32.3	429.5	77.9	39.0	69.4
Belize	1991	38.0	5.0	36.0	33.0	4.7	1982–84[19]	42.9	34.0	19.2	8.3	123.1	50.6	15.4	33.3
Benin	1991	49.0	16.0	119.0	33.0	7.0		...	...	...	...	...	...	...	...
Bermuda	1990	16.2	7.5	7.2	8.7	1.8[13]	1989	...	178.0	...	...	343.0	31.0	...	61.0
Bhutan	1989	38.3	16.4	127.0	21.9	5.5[14]		...	...	...	...	...	...	...	...
Bolivia	1988	42.8	14.1	102.0	28.7	6.1[2]		...	...	...	...	...	...	...	...
Bosnia and Hercegovina	1990	14.1	6.4	15.2	7.7	...	1989	9.9	122.6[20]	12.6	11.9	344.1	29.0	29.2	47.1
Botswana	1990–95	43.9	9.5	58.0	34.4	6.4		...	...	...	...	...	...	...	...
Brazil	1990–95	26.1	7.5	57.0	18.6	3.2	1986[22]	37.2	52.4	13.0	6.7	156.2	48.3	22.0	69.2
Brunei	1989	27.6	3.3	9.0	24.3	3.4	1986	5.3	27.0	...	...	80.0	23.4	...	39.8
Bulgaria	1991	10.7	12.2	16.7	-1.5	1.6	1990	5.9	167.3	20.5	6.2	743.3	71.8	36.6	61.9
Burkina Faso	1990–95	47.0	17.1	127.0	29.9	6.5		...	...	...	...	...	...	...	...
Burundi	1991	47.0	15.0	111.0	32.0	6.9		...	...	...	...	...	...	...	...
Cambodia	1989	41.8	16.9	131.0	24.9	4.6		...	...	...	...	...	...	...	...
Cameroon	1990–95	47.3	13.3	86.0	34.0	6.9		...	...	...	...	...	...	...	...
Canada	1989	14.9	7.3	7.1	7.6	1.7[3]	1989	4.7	195.7	21.9	17.9	296.2	61.6	27.2	52.7
Cape Verde	1987	32.1	7.7	51.0[14]	24.4	5.3[18]	1980	153.7	43.8	20.6	16.5	135.8	72.3	27.7	30.1
Cayman Islands	1990	17.9	4.0	6.1	13.9	1.6[13]	1986–90[19]	10.6	90.0	8.2[5]	...	199.7	30.3[23]	4.1	58.9
Central African Republic	1990–95	45.1	16.3	95.0	28.8	6.2		...	...	...	...	...	...	...	...
Chad	1990–95	43.3	17.9	122.0	25.4	5.8		...	...	...	...	...	...	...	...
Chile	1988	23.3	5.8	18.9	17.5	2.7[24]	1987	19.2	104.3	11.2	7.9	154.4	63.0	36.4	67.0
China	1990	21.0	6.3	32.0[14]	14.7	2.2[13]	1989[25]	23.0	113.1	7.0[17]	4.1	204.8	121.5	27.2	56.5
Colombia	1990–95	25.8	6.9	37.0	18.9	2.9	1990[22]	25.5	82.6	16.5	9.7	192.9	52.8	22.9	158.5
Comoros	1991	47.0	12.0	87.0	35.0	7.0		...	...	...	...	...	...	...	...
Congo	1990–95	46.1	13.2	65.0	32.9	6.3		...	...	...	...	...	...	...	...
Cook Islands	1986	24.0	5.2	21.7	18.8	4.1[27]	1976–78	54.0	38.0	27.0	0.0	197.0	110.0	18.0	49.0
Costa Rica	1990	27.4	3.8	15.3	23.6	3.0	1989	11.9	81.2	15.6	7.7	110.1	37.8	20.3	22.1
Côte d'Ivoire	1991	48.0	12.0	97.0	36.0	6.8		...	...	...	...	...	...	...	...
Croatia	1990	11.9	11.4	10.0	0.5	...	1989	12.0	222.2[20]	15.6	7.9	581.5	32.1	54.7	86.5
Cuba	1990	17.5	6.5	11.1[13]	11.0	1.9	1988	9.1	127.8	22.9	9.7	291.4	58.1	22.9	81.5
Cyprus	1990	19.0	8.5	10.5	10.5	2.4[3]		...	...	...	...	...	...	...	...
Czechoslovakia	1990	13.4	11.7	11.3	1.7	2.0	1990	3.6	245.7	19.8	9.2	648.3	60.0	50.4	82.9
Denmark	1990	12.4	11.9	7.5	0.5	1.5	1990	8.0	292.3	20.7[17]	13.0	529.1	90.1	40.9	73.7
Djibouti	1990–95	45.8	16.4	112.0	29.4	6.5		...	...	...	...	...	...	...	...
Dominica	1990	19.9	7.4	18.4	12.5	2.6[15]	1985	13.2	72.3	18.4	17.1	213.1	46.0	21.0	27.6
Dominican Republic	1991	27.0	7.0	60.0	20.0	3.1	1985	51.4	27.4	12.3	8.6	100.3	35.4	22.3	33.7
Ecuador	1988	35.4	7.6	63.0	27.8	4.7[24]	1988	61.1	48.4	12.1	9.6	83.7	56.2	25.9	63.7

causes classified by the World Health Organization and would not, thus, aggregate to the country's crude death rate for the same year. Among the lesser causes excluded by the present classification are: benign neoplasms; nutritional disorders; anemias; mental disorders; kidney and genitourinary diseases not classifiable under the main groups; maternal deaths (for which data *are* provided, however, in the "Health services" table); diseases of the skin and musculoskeletal systems; congenital and perinatal conditions; and general senility and other ill-defined (ill-diagnosed) conditions, a kind of "other" category.

Expectation of life is probably the most accurate single measure of the quality of life in a given society. It summarizes in a single number all of the natural and social stresses that operate upon individuals in that society. The number may range from as few as 40 years of life in the least developed countries to as much as 80 years for women in the most developed nations. The lost potential in the years separating those two numbers is prodigious, regardless of how the loss arises—wars and civil violence, poor public health services, or poor individual health practice in matters of nutrition, exercise, stress management, and so on.

Data on marriages and marriage rates probably are less meaningful in terms of international comparisons than some of the measures mentioned above because the number, timing, and kinds of social relationships that substitute for marriage depend on many kinds of social variables—income, degree of social control, heterogeneity of the society (race, class, language communities), or level of development of civil administration (if one must travel for a day or more to obtain a legal civil ceremony, one may forgo it). Nevertheless, the data for a single country say specific things about local practice in terms of the age at which a man or woman typically marries, and the overall rate will at least define the number of legal civil marriages, though it cannot say anything about other, less formal arrangements (here the figure for the legitimacy rate for children in the next section may identify some of the societies in which economics or social constraints may operate to limit the number of marriages that are actually confirmed on civil registers). The available data usually include both first marriages and remarriages after annulment, divorce, widowhood, or the like.

The data for families provide information about the average size of a family unit (individuals related by blood or civil register) and the average number of children under a specified age (set here at 15 to provide a consistent measure of social minority internationally, though legal minority depends on the laws of each country). When well-defined family data are not collected as part of a country's national census or vital statistics surveys, data for households are substituted on the assumption that most households worldwide represent families in some conventional sense. In the older countries of Europe and North America increasing numbers of households are composed of unrelated individuals (unmarried heterosexual couples, aged [or younger] groups sharing limited [often fixed] incomes for reasons of economy, or homosexual couples); such arrangements are not yet so common in the rest of the world that they represent great numbers overall. Very few census programs, even in developed countries, make adequate provision for distinguishing these households.

expectation of life at birth (latest year)		nuptiality, family, and family planning														country
		marriages			age at marriage (latest)						families (F), households (H) (latest)					
		year	total number	rate per 1,000 popu- lation	groom (percent)			bride (percent)			families (households)		children		induced abortions		
male	female				19 and under	20–29	30 and over	19 and under	20–29	30 and over	total ('000)	size	number under age 15	percent legitimate	number	ratio per 100 live births	
44.0	43.0	...	...	...	...	...	...	...	...	...	H 2,110	H 6.2	H 2.8[1]	...	...	...	Afghanistan
72.0	79.0	1989	27,655	8.6	1.2	78.2	20.6	20.0	74.9	5.1	F 675	F 4.7	...	...	...	...	Albania
65.8	66.3	1988	139,930	5.9	0.7[3]	67.1[3]	32.2[3]	29.8[3]	61.4[3]	8.8[3]	H 3,322	H 6.9	H 3.0	...	...	...	Algeria
69.0	74.0	1989	317	7.0	5.6[8]	65.5[8]	28.8[8]	24.5[8]	60.5[8]	15.0[8]	H 4	H 7.1	H 2.9	72.0	...	...	American Samoa
74.0	81.0	1988	125	2.5	...	...	...	...	...	...	...	...	...	...	...	...	Andorra
44.9	48.1	...	...	...	...	...	...	...	...	...	...	H 4.8	...	...	...	...	Angola
70.0	73.0	1988	382	4.9	1.0[11]	37.4[12]	61.6	3.7[11]	52.4[12]	43.9	H 15	H 4.2	H 1.9	23.4	...	...	Antigua and Barbuda
68.0	74.0	1983	177,010	6.0	5.6	71.5	22.9	26.0	58.6	15.4	H 7,104	H 3.9	H 1.2	67.5	...	...	Argentina
67.9	73.4	1989	27,257	7.8	2.7	77.0	20.3	34.0	54.2	11.8	H 559	H 4.7	H 1.8	92.1	26,141	34.7	Armenia
71.6	76.8	1990	504	7.7	...	...	...	...	...	...	H 15	H 4.0	...	63.2	...	...	Aruba
73.3	79.6	1989	117,176	7.0	1.3	59.7	39.0	6.9	65.0	28.1	F 4,140	F 3.1	F 0.5	80.0	...	...	Australia
72.5	79.0	1990	45,212	5.9	1.9	62.9	35.2	7.5	69.1	23.4	H 3,023	H 2.5	H 0.6	76.4	...	...	Austria
66.9	74.8	1989	71,874	10.4	1.2	80.4	18.4	24.8	63.9	11.3	H 1,381	H 4.8	H 1.7	97.5	42,134	23.2	Azerbaijan
69.0	76.0	1989	2,131	8.6	0.8	55.7	43.5	7.3	60.7	32.0	H 68	H 3.8	...	42.3	...	...	Bahamas, The
71.0	76.0	1989	3,033	6.2	1.7	70.5	27.8	27.0	61.3	11.7	H 67	H 6.5	H 2.2	...	...	...	Bahrain
56.4	55.4	1987	1,150,000	11.6	...	...	...	...	...	...	H 19,700	H 5.3	...	...	...	...	Bangladesh
71.9	76.9	1989	2,047	8.0	0.2	43.2	56.6	1.7	58.7	39.6	H 67	H 3.7	H 1.5	26.9	...	...	Barbados
63.9	74.7	1989	97,929	9.6	4.1	74.7	21.2	26.2	55.6	18.2	H 2,796	H 3.2	H 0.8	92.1	250,905	163.5	Belarus
72.4	79.1	1988	59,075	6.0	1.4	74.5	24.1	9.3	73.6	17.7	F 3,613	F 2.7	F 0.5	90.8	...	...	Belgium
67.0	72.0	1988	1,072	6.0	...	...	...	...	...	...	H 33	H 5.2	H 2.4	45.2	822	12.1	Belize
49.0	52.0	1980–85	...	12.8	...	...	...	...	...	...	...	H 5.4	...	...	...	...	Benin
73.0	79.0	1990	905	15.2	0.2[13]	40.6[13]	59.2[13]	2.1[13]	49.9[13]	48.0[13]	H 18	H 2.7	H 0.7	66.7	92	11.0	Bermuda
49.2	47.8	...	...	...	...	...	...	...	...	...	...	H 5.4	...	...	...	...	Bhutan
51.0	55.0	1980	26,990	4.8	8.3	75.1	16.6	26.1	55.4	18.5	H 1,050	H 4.4	H 1.8	80.9	...	...	Bolivia
68.0	73.0	1990	31,449	7.0	2.3[13]	76.0[13]	21.7[13]	28.5[13]	59.3[13]	12.2[13]	H 1,203	H 3.6	H 1.1[21]	...	...	...	Bosnia and Hercegovina
52.7	59.3	1986	1,638	1.5	—	33.0	67.0	5.0	69.2	25.8	H 125	H 5.7	H 2.0	28.8	17	0.1	Botswana
63.5	69.1	1988	951,236	6.7	7.7	70.2	22.1	32.0	53.3	14.7	F 31,888	F 4.2	...	...	...	...	Brazil
72.6	76.4	1986	1,673	7.4	5.6	72.5	21.9	12.5	58.9	28.6	H 23	H 5.8	H 2.5	99.6	...	...	Brunei
68.0	74.7	1991	50,300	5.6	5.9[13]	74.6[13]	19.5[13]	36.8[13]	51.4[13]	11.8[13]	F 2,627	F 2.7	F 0.7	89.5	132,021	117.6	Bulgaria
47.6	50.9	...	...	...	...	...	...	...	...	...	...	H 4.9	...	...	...	...	Burkina Faso
50.0	54.0	...	...	...	...	...	...	...	...	...	...	H 4.6	...	...	...	...	Burundi
46.5	49.4	...	...	...	...	...	...	...	...	...	...	H 5.6	...	...	...	...	Cambodia
53.5	56.5	...	...	...	...	...	...	...	...	...	...	H 5.2	...	...	...	...	Cameroon
73.3	80.0	1988	187,728	7.2	1.2	59.5	39.3	5.7	65.7	28.6	F 6,735	F 3.1	F 0.8	83.8	63,585	17.2	Canada
63.0	67.0	1988	1,040	3.2	2.3	62.4	35.3	17.0	61.1	21.9	F 59	F 5.1	...	55.2	...	...	Cape Verde
—77.1—		1990	274	10.0	2.9	42.7	54.4	8.0	50.7	41.3	H 4	H 3.8	H 1.1	58.8	...	...	Cayman Islands
48.0	53.0	...	...	...	...	...	...	...	...	...	...	H 4.3	...	...	...	...	Central African Republic
45.9	49.1	...	...	...	...	...	...	...	...	...	...	H 3.9	...	...	...	...	Chad
68.1	75.1	1989	103,710	8.0	4.9	74.6	20.5	20.8	65.5	13.7	H 1,690	H 4.5	H 2.0	68.2	2,346	1.0	Chile
68.4	71.4	1989	9,351,912	8.5	...	...	...	...	...	...	H 241.3[26]	H 4.3	...	...	10,500,000	47.7	China
66.4	72.3	1980	102,448	3.8	6.4	69.6	24.0	31.5	56.5	12.0	F 4,772	F 5.4	F 2.5	75.2	...	...	Colombia
54.0	59.0	...	...	...	...	...	...	...	...	...	...	H 5.6	...	...	...	...	Comoros
52.1	57.3	...	...	...	...	...	...	...	...	...	H 326	H 4.7	H 2.0	...	...	...	Congo
64.0	70.0	1988	122	8.6	5.7	54.1	40.2	7.4	62.3	30.3	H 3	H 5.6	H 2.4	...	...	...	Cook Islands
72.9	77.6	1989	21,622	7.4	9.2[27]	69.3[27]	21.5[27]	36.2[27]	51.1[27]	12.7[27]	F 472	F 5.0	F 1.7	62.8	...	...	Costa Rica
52.0	56.0	...	...	...	...	...	...	...	...	...	...	H 4.5	...	...	...	...	Côte d'Ivoire
67.0	74.0	1990	27,916	6.0	1.2[13]	72.4[13]	26.4[13]	19.5[13]	64.8[13]	15.7[13]	H 1,527	H 3.1	H 0.7[21]	...	...	...	Croatia
72.7	76.1	1988	82,431	7.9	8.7	58.2	33.1	25.6	50.1	24.3	F 2,002	F 4.2	H 1.6	...	155,325	82.7	Cuba
73.9	78.3	1989	5,597	8.1	0.8	70.5	28.7	17.8	66.0	16.2	F 160	H 3.5	H 1.1	99.6	...	...	Cyprus
68.9	75.1	1989	117,787	8.4	6.9	71.4	21.7	29.7	55.6	14.7	H 5,288	H 2.9	H 0.9	92.7	160,285	76.9	Czechoslovakia
72.0	77.7	1990	31,513	6.1	0.8	43.7	55.5	1.9	56.7	41.4	F 2,800	F 1.8	F 0.2	55.3	20,589	32.5	Denmark
47.4	50.7	1982	2,500	6.7	...	...	...	...	...	...	...	H 5.6	...	96.8	...	...	Djibouti
73.0	79.0	...	...	...	...	...	...	...	...	...	H 18	H 4.3	H 2.2	35.0	...	...	Dominica
65.0	69.0	1987	15,642	2.3	8.0[27]	63.0[27]	29.0[27]	29.7[27]	51.0[27]	19.3[27]	H 753	H 5.1	H 2.5	32.8	562	0.5	Dominican Republic
63.4	67.6	1987	61,301	6.2	11.8	65.4	22.8	34.4	51.8	13.8	...	H 5.1	...	67.9	...	...	Ecuador

Vital statistics, marriage, family (continued)

country	vital rates						causes of death (rate per 100,000 population)								
	year	birth rate per 1,000 population	death rate per 1,000 population	infant mortality rate per 1,000 live births	rate of natural increase per 1,000 population	total fertility rate	year	infectious and parasitic diseases	malignant neoplasms (cancers)	endocrine and metabolic disorders	diseases of the nervous system	diseases of the circulatory system	diseases of the respiratory system	diseases of the digestive system	accidents, poisonings, and violence
Egypt	1988	37.5	8.5	45.1[2]	29.0	5.4[2]	1987	98.9	22.0	9.1	13.6	314.4	140.7	45.8	39.1
El Salvador	1991	34.0	7.0	47.0	27.0	4.0	1988	41.8	28.9	9.9[28]	1.9	70.9	30.4	26.1[28]	49.3
Equatorial Guinea	1990	43.0	16.0	117.0[18]	27.0	5.5	...	...	...	...	...	...	...	...	...
Estonia	1990	14.1	12.3	12.3	1.8	2.2[13]	1989	8.1	205.3	7.3	8.7	722.6	30.0	27.7	110.8
Ethiopia	1990–95	48.4	18.3	122.0	30.1	6.8	...	...	...	...	...	...	...	...	...
Faeroe Islands	1989	19.7	7.8	16.1	11.9	2.8	1989	8.4	120.3	10.6[5]	2.1	398.8	61.2	6.3	48.5
Fiji	1988	26.8	5.0	27.0	21.8	3.1	1985	31.3	53.3	29.1[5]	2.7[17]	190.8	43.1	13.3	48.5
Finland	1990	13.2	10.1	5.8[13]	3.1	1.7[15]	1989	6.5	196.6	11.8	17.6	490.1	67.2	35.2	94.3
France	1991	13.0	9.2	7.4	3.8	1.8	1989	12.1	246.6	23.9	19.7	318.8	63.4	49.3	85.8
French Guiana	1990	31.0	5.1	22.7[29]	25.9	3.7[15]	1984	55.2	62.7	10.1[5]	3.8[17]	152.9	25.1	33.8	104.0
French Polynesia	1990	27.4	4.6	10.4	22.8	3.9	1984	21.2	67.7	10.0	19.4	120.1	36.5	17.7	58.9
Gabon	1990–95	43.4	16.0	94.0	27.4	5.3	...	...	...	...	...	...	...	...	...
Gambia, The	1990–95	44.9	19.5	132.0	25.4	6.2	...	...	...	...	...	...	...	...	...
Gaza Strip	1991	43.0	6.0	41.0	37.0	6.9	...	...	...	...	...	...	...	...	...
Georgia	1990	17.0	8.4	15.9	8.6	2.1[13]	1989	13.5	98.6	12.0	4.1	553.2	51.4	32.1	58.2
Germany	1989	11.4	11.5	7.8	−0.1	...	1989	7.2	260.7	27.3	15.1	585.6	66.8	52.7	56.4
Ghana	1990–95	43.5	11.9	81.0	31.6	6.3	...	...	...	...	...	...	...	...	...
Gibraltar	1989	17.3	7.1	6.0	10.2	2.4	1987	17.0	203.9	—	—	601.4	34.0	23.8	3.4
Greece	1989	10.1	9.3	9.8	0.8	1.8	1989	6.1	191.6	10.0	3.1	477.8	48.1	25.5	49.3
Greenland	1989	21.8	8.2	21.5	13.6	2.4	1989	28.8	151.2	1.8[5]	3.6[17]	162.0	75.6	19.8	232.2
Grenada	1989	33.0	8.3	29.0[15]	24.7	3.0[10]	1984	13.5	90.5	62.9	11.4	290.3	54.1	39.5	47.9
Guadeloupe	1990	19.4	6.0	9.2[13]	13.4	2.3[13]	1987	21.7	118.0	25.9	2.7	216.0	29.1	40.7	74.6
Guam	1988	27.4	3.8	9.9	23.6	3.1	1988	8.6	69.0	20.4[5]	0.8[33]	158.3	25.1[23]	14.9	44.7
Guatemala	1989	39.4	7.3	43.6	32.1	5.6	1984	211.5	29.8	29.6	9.0	57.2	145.7	21.7	52.0
Guernsey	1990	12.7	10.1	1.3	2.6	1.6[13]	1990	8.4	314.3	11.8	15.1	430.3	112.6	30.3	20.2
Guinea	1990–95	47.0	21.0	134.0	26.0	6.5	...	...	...	...	...	...	...	...	...
Guinea-Bissau	1991	42.0	18.0	140.0	24.0	6.0	...	...	...	...	...	...	...	...	...
Guyana	1991	23.0	7.0	51.0	16.0	2.7	1984	19.3	37.1	33.3	11.6	202.5	39.8	74.0	56.5
Haiti	1991	43.0	15.0	106.0	28.0	6.3	...	...	...	...	...	...	...	...	...
Honduras	1989	38.0	7.0	64.0	31.0	5.0	1983	46.6	12.4	5.3	7.8	48.4	26.3	16.7	42.2
Hong Kong	1991	12.0	5.0	7.0	7.0	1.4[14]	1990	18.4	149.9	5.6[17]	4.0	142.1	86.2	21.4	29.9
Hungary	1990	12.1	14.0	14.8	−1.9	1.8	1990	9.2	297.8	20.7	11.2	736.8	64.1	87.0	128.1
Iceland	1990	18.7	6.7	5.9	12.0	2.3	1990	4.3	178.0	5.5	12.5	292.9	79.6	11.4	49.4
India	1990	29.9	9.6	80.0	20.3	3.7[15]	...	...	...	...	...	...	...	...	...
Indonesia	1991	32.2	11.7	90.0	20.5	3.7	...	...	...	...	...	...	...	...	...
Iran	1991	44.0	9.0	66.0	35.0	6.5	...	...	...	...	...	...	...	...	...
Iraq	1991	46.0	7.0	80.0	39.0	7.2	...	...	...	...	...	...	...	...	...
Ireland	1990	15.1	9.1	9.1	6.0	2.4[18]	1989	5.7	208.7	15.8	16.2	426.7	124.2	24.3	42.6
Isle of Man	1991	12.8	14.1	3.4	−1.3	1.8[13]	1991	15.8	332.4	—	—	633.3	273.7	18.6	70.2
Israel	1991	21.3	6.3	9.0[13]	15.0	2.8[10]	1988	11.3	123.7	21.7	9.1	275.9	43.5	17.8	44.0
Italy	1990	9.8	9.3	8.5	0.5	1.4[18]	1988	3.9	248.3	35.2	16.7	411.8	60.1	51.8	49.8
Jamaica	1991	24.7	5.5	27.0[13]	19.2	2.4[10]	1984	29.8	90.1	33.2	14.0	215.3	35.3	20.4	19.3
Japan	1990	10.0	6.7	4.6[13]	3.3	1.6[13]	1990	9.8	177.2	9.5	5.3	248.1	81.5	30.9	45.3
Jersey	1990	13.4	9.6	6.0[13]	3.8	1.3[13]	...	...	...	...	...	...	...	...	...
Jordan	1991	46.0	5.0	38.0	41.0	7.1	...	...	...	...	...	...	...	...	...
Kazakhstan	1990	21.7	7.7	26.4	14.0	2.8[13]	1989	24.6	131.1	6.3	6.1	333.9	79.4	24.6	99.9
Kenya	1990–95	47.0	9.7	63.0	37.3	6.8	...	...	...	...	...	...	...	...	...
Kiribati	1991	33.0	12.0	63.0	21.0	4.2	...	...	...	...	...	...	...	...	...
Korea, North	1991	24.3	5.5	30.0	18.8	2.5	1986	19.4	69.0	3.0[17]	6.5	224.9	46.7	51.6	38.2
Korea, South	1991	15.5	5.8	12.8[10]	9.7	1.6[10]	1989	13.2	86.4[20]	8.8[17]	4.6	132.6	19.5	38.7	66.3
Kuwait	1989	25.9	2.3	14.0	23.6	3.9	1987	6.7	25.5	6.9	1.3	73.6	16.5	4.9	31.4
Kyrgyzstan	1990	29.3	7.0	30.0	22.3	3.8[13]	1989	31.4	73.2	5.3	7.9	284.2	143.7	28.7	86.0
Laos	1989	40.3	15.8	106.0	24.5	6.7[10]	...	...	...	...	...	...	...	...	...
Latvia	1990	14.1	13.0	13.7	1.1	2.0[13]	1989	12.8	207.7	7.5	6.6	731.2	37.5	26.5	130.0
Lebanon	1990–95	29.6	7.7	40.0	21.9	3.4	...	...	...	...	...	...	...	...	...
Lesotho	1990–95	40.2	11.0	89.0	29.2	5.8	...	...	...	...	...	...	...	...	...
Liberia	1990–95	46.7	14.1	126.0	32.6	6.7	...	...	...	...	...	...	...	...	...
Libya	1988	46.0	7.0	82.0[24]	39.0	6.6	...	...	...	...	...	...	...	...	...
Liechtenstein	1991	14.3	6.4	0.0	7.9	...	1991	13.7	154.1	6.8[5]	...	273.9	30.8	10.3	30.8
Lithuania	1990	15.3	10.7	10.3	4.6	2.0[13]	1989	8.7	179.2	5.7	8.0	594.3	47.0	22.0	117.4
Luxembourg	1990	12.9	9.9	7.3	3.0	1.6	1989	5.0	253.1	18.8	17.2	501.1	66.0	55.2	65.5
Macau	1990	15.3	3.3	8.4	12.0	1.5[14]	1990	11.9	73.1	7.2	1.6	145.2	52.5	14.5	31.8
Macedonia	1990	16.9	7.0	35.3	9.9	...	1989	20.3	102.4[20]	13.3	5.1	346.2	49.8	18.2	34.5
Madagascar	1990–95	44.9	12.6	110.0	32.3	6.5	...	...	...	...	...	...	...	...	...
Malawi	1990–95	55.4	19.0	138.0	36.4	7.6	1986[36]	711	27	25	60	50	265	34	78
Malaysia	1990	28.0	4.6	12.6	23.4	3.5[13]	1981[37]	55.0	53.3	9.0[5]	5.6[17]	122.8	38.9	12.8	70.8
Maldives	1990	41.0	6.0	48.0	35.0	6.5[15]	1987	61.7	—	—	—	151.3	57.0	—	2.6
Mali	1991	51.0	21.0	114.0	30.0	7.0	...	...	...	...	...	...	...	...	...
Malta	1990	15.2	7.7	11.3	7.5	1.9[24]	1990	7.6	152.3	31.4	8.5	385.6	60.0	30.2	28.2
Marshall Islands	1991	47.0	8.0	30.3	39.0	7.1	1985	35.5	32.7	38.2	27.3	70.9	109.1	13.6	49.1
Martinique	1990	17.9	6.1	8.1[9]	11.8	1.9[13]	1987	20.6	123.3	31.8	10.7[27]	199.5	30.1	30.4	55.6
Mauritania	1991	49.6	17.5	94.0	32.1	7.2	...	...	...	...	...	...	...	...	...
Mauritius	1990	21.0	6.5	20.4	14.5	1.9[3]	1990	16.1	58.9[20]	40.9[17]	7.0	269.9	60.4	27.6	46.5
Mayotte	1987	51.0	13.0	96.0	38.0	6.8[13]	...	...	...	...	...	...	...	...	...
Mexico	1990	31.5	5.3	46.6[14]	26.2	3.2[14]	1986	57.3	44.2	34.9	7.6	90.1	51.3	39.2	77.0
Micronesia	1989	34.0	5.0	26.0	29.0	5.0	1984	20.4	27.1	6.8	4.5	53.2	47.5	5.7	23.8
Moldova	1990	17.7	9.7	19.0	8.0	2.5[13]	1989	12.4	131.6	8.3	8.2	452.2	64.2	85.4	105.3
Monaco	1988	22.9	18.5	9.0[13]	4.4	1.2[13]	...	...	...	...	...	...	...	...	...
Mongolia	1989	36.0	8.0	64.4	28.0	4.8	...	...	...	...	...	...	...	...	...
Morocco	1990–95	32.6	8.3	68.0	24.3	4.7	...	...	...	...	...	...	...	...	...
Mozambique	1990–95	44.0	17.0	130.0	27.0	6.2	...	...	...	...	...	...	...	...	...
Myanmar (Burma)	1991	32.0	13.0	62.0	19.0	4.1	...	...	...	...	...	...	...	...	...
Namibia	1990–95	41.6	10.6	97.0	31.0	5.7	...	...	...	...	...	...	...	...	...
Nauru	1989	21.0	5.0	41.0	16.0	2.5	1976–81[19]	33.0	38.0	24.0	13.0	89.0	16.0	53.0	116.0
Nepal	1991	39.0	15.0	98.0	24.0	5.6	...	...	...	...	...	...	...	...	...

| expectation of life at birth (latest year) | | nuptiality, family, and family planning | | | | | | | | | | | | | | | country |
male	female	marriages year	total number	rate per 1,000 population	groom 19 and under	groom 20–29	groom 30 and over	bride 19 and under	bride 20–29	bride 30 and over	families total ('000)	size	children number under age 15	percent legitimate	induced abortions number	ratio per 100 live births	
59.0	60.0	1989	463,000	8.9	8.5[27]	61.5[27]	30.0[27]	46.9[27]	42.3[27]	10.8[27]	H 9,733	H 4.9	H 2.1	100.0	...	...	Egypt
63.0	68.0	1988	21,295	4.0	6.6	56.5	36.9	23.0	51.9	25.1	H 686	H 5.4	H 2.4	32.0	...	...	El Salvador
48.0	52.0											H 4.5					Equatorial Guinea
65.8	75.0	1989	12,644	8.0	6.8	63.1	30.1	23.0	51.6	25.4	H 427	H 3.1	H 0.8	74.8	28,428	117.0	Estonia
45.4	48.7	...										H 4.5			...	...	Ethiopia
73.3	79.6	1989	230	4.9	1.0[2]	68.8[2]	30.2[2]	8.8[2]	70.7[2]	20.5[2]	F 14	F 3.0	F 0.9	55.9	26	3.3	Faeroe Islands
68.3	72.8	1986	6,289	8.8	6.8	69.9	23.3	30.1	57.3	12.6	F 97	F 6.0	F 2.5	82.7	...	...	Fiji
70.8	78.9	1989	25,043	5.0	1.6[2]	62.6[2]	35.8[2]	6.2[2]	68.5[2]	25.3[2]	F 1,163	F 2.5	F 0.9	80.8	12,995	20.5	Finland
72.7	80.9	1991	280,450	4.9	0.5[14]	64.9[14]	34.6[14]	4.2[14]	71.0[14]	24.8[14]	H 20,899	H 2.7	H 1.0	71.8	166,510	21.6	France
63.4	69.7	1990	466	4.0	0.6[28]	45.3[28]	54.1[28]	6.8[28]	55.3[28]	37.9[28]	H 33	H 3.4	H 1.2	17.9	388	16.8	French Guiana
66.1	71.3	1990	987	4.9	11.3[2,30]	75.8[2,30]	12.9[2,30]	41.5[2,30]	52.5[2,30]	6.0[2,30]	H 40	H 4.7	H 1.7	41.5	...	...	French Polynesia
51.9	55.2	...									H 136	H 4.0					Gabon
43.4	46.6	...									H 123	H 4.9	H 3.4				Gambia, The
65.0	67.0																Gaza Strip
69.0	76.3	1989	38,288	7.0	5.7	66.2	28.1	27.8	55.7	16.5	H 1,244	H 4.1	H 1.1	82.3	68,883	75.6	Georgia
72.1[31]	78.7[31]	1988	534,903	6.9	1.1	62.4	36.5	6.5	69.6	23.9	F 22,882[31]	F 2.7[31]	F 0.5[31]	84.5	169,624	19.0	Germany
54.2	57.8										H 2,355	H 4.9	H 2.2				Ghana
71.4	75.5	1989	212	6.9							H 7	H 3.8	H 1.0	97.1	...	...	Gibraltar
72.6	77.6	1986	58,933	5.9	1.7	64.5	33.8	25.8	58.6	15.6	H 2,990	H 3.3	H 0.7	97.9	180	0.2	Greece
60.4	66.3	1989	396	7.1	0.5[2]	45.7[2]	53.8[2]	3.4[2]	60.3[2]	36.3[2]	F 28	F 1.9	F 0.5	28.3	800	73.4	Greenland
69.0	74.0										H 24	H 3.7	H 2.2	22.5			Grenada
70.0	77.0	1989	1,854	4.9	0.6[3]	56.8[3]	42.6[3]	8.8[3]	67.5[3]	23.7[3]	H 112	H 3.4	H 0.9	40.0	561	8.7	Guadeloupe
69.5	75.6	1987	1,512	12.0	0.6	57.5	41.9	2.9	65.1	32.0	H 31	H 4.0	H 1.3	67.8	...	...	Guam
59.7	64.4	1988	46,155	5.4	15.9	55.7	28.4	41.5	38.0	20.5	H 1,102	H 5.5	H 2.7	34.8	...	...	Guatemala
...	...	1990	403	6.8							H 21	H 2.7	H 0.5	80.2			Guernsey
44.0	45.0										H 1,064	H 4.7					Guinea
41.9	45.1										H 124	H 4.1	H 2.8	11.3			Guinea-Bissau
61.0	68.0										H 150	H 5.1	H 2.1	61.4			Guyana
52.0	55.0										H 1,147	H 4.4	H 1.8				Haiti
63.0	67.0	1983	19,875	4.9	7.7	65.1	27.2	27.9	58.5	13.6	H 463	H 5.7	H 2.8				Honduras
75.0	81.0	1990	47,188	8.1	0.6[13]	50.6[13]	48.8[13]	3.3[13]	66.2[13]	30.5[13]	H 1,582	H 3.4	H 0.7	94.5	17,600	25.2	Hong Kong
65.1	73.7	1989	65,712	6.2	5.6	71.1	23.3	27.9	56.2	15.9	F 3,058	F 2.9	F 0.8	86.9	90,508	89.5	Hungary
75.7	80.3	1990	1,154	4.5	0.4	58.8	40.8	1.7	69.4	28.9	H 85	H 2.9	H 1.3	44.8	670	14.7	Iceland
58.1	59.1										H 97,093	H 5.5	H 2.4		582,161	2.4	India
55.6	58.9	1987–88	1,178,850	6.8							H 34,507	H 4.9	H 2.0				Indonesia
64.0	65.0	1987	346,647	6.8							H 9,759	H 5.1	H 2.2				Iran
46.0	57.0	1988	145,885	8.5	4.0[8]	49.1[8]	46.9[8]	23.9[8]	47.2[8]	28.9[8]	H 2,128	H 6.9	H 3.2				Iraq
71.0	76.7	1990	17,490	5.0	1.3[14]	73.3[14]	25.4[14]	4.9[14]	80.4[14]	14.7[14]	H 726	H 3.9	H 1.3	85.5	...	...	Ireland
...	...	1991	448	6.4	1.1	52.9	46.0	5.8	56.0	38.2				72.6			Isle of Man
73.9	77.5	1990	31,199	6.7	3.4[14]	74.7[14]	21.9[14]	23.9[14]	65.3[14]	10.8[14]	H 1,189	H 3.6	H 1.2	98.8	15,216	15.1	Israel
73.2	79.7	1990	312,585	5.4	1.7[3]	75.2[3]	23.1[3]	18.7[3]	70.1[3]	11.2[3]	F 17,615	F 3.2	F 0.7	93.7	187,618	34.0	Italy
71.4	75.8	1990	13,037	5.4							F 509	F 4.3	F 2.0	14.9			Jamaica
75.9	81.8	1989	708,316	5.8	1.1[30]	61.3[30]	37.6[30]	3.4[30]	79.5[30]	17.1[30]	F 22,240	F 5.4	F 1.2	99.0	466,876	38.0	Japan
...	...										H 29	H 2.6	H 0.4	88.1	313	29.2	Jersey
70.0	73.0	1989	31,508	8.1	5.0	74.7	20.3	40.2	54.3	5.5	H 375	H 6.9	H 3.4				Jordan
64.2	73.2	1989	165,380	10.0	3.8	76.0	20.2	26.0	58.2	15.8	H 3,824	H 4.0	H 1.4	88.0	358,124	93.7	Kazakhstan
59.0	63.0										H 1,938	H 6.2	H 2.7				Kenya
52.0	58.0	1988	352	5.2							H 10	H 6.1	F 2.0				Kiribati
66.0	72.0	1987	188,007	9.3							H 4,054	H 4.8	H 1.7				Korea, North
67.4	75.4	1989	309,872	7.3	0.3	77.1	22.6	2.7	89.5	7.8	H 11,357	H 3.8	H 1.0	99.5	...	...	Korea, South
72.0	76.0	1988	10,283	5.3	4.1	70.9	25.0	34.0	56.2	9.8	H 246	H 7.4	H 1.6				Kuwait
64.5	72.8	1989	41,790	9.7	2.2	82.4	15.4	29.8	59.5	10.7	H 856	H 4.2	H 1.9	87.3	87,212	66.3	Kyrgyzstan
47.8	50.8											H 5.3					Laos
64.2	74.6	1989	24,496	9.1	6.5	63.5	30.0	22.7	51.8	25.5	H 732	H 3.1	H 0.8	84.1	48,957	125.8	Latvia
65.1	69.0										H 405	H 5.3	H 2.2				Lebanon
54.0	63.0										H 330	H 4.8	H 2.0				Lesotho
54.0	57.0										H 474	H 5.0					Liberia
59.1	62.5										F 383	F 5.4	F 2.9				Libya
66.1	72.9	1991	183		1.1[11]	54.1[34]	44.8[35]	2.2[11]	72.7[34]	25.1[35]	H 8	H 3.0	H 0.7	92.3			Liechtenstein
66.9	76.3	1989	34,630	9.3	6.1	71.5	22.4	22.5	58.5	19.0	H 1,000	H 3.2	H 0.8	93.3	50,117	89.8	Lithuania
70.6	77.9	1990	2,312	6.1	1.5	58.9	39.6	6.9	66.8	26.3	H 145	H 2.8	H 0.5	87.1			Luxembourg
75.1	80.3	1989	1,728	3.9	0.2	54.7	45.1	2.5	74.7	22.8	H 50	H 4.8	H 1.8	99.3			Macau
68.0	72.0	1990	15,973	7.5	4.2[13]	79.0[13]	16.8[13]	27.5[13]	64.3[13]	8.2[13]	H 435[21]	H 4.4[21]	H 1.3[21]				Macedonia
54.0	57.0										H 1,709	H 4.7					Madagascar
48.4	49.7											H 4.5					Malawi
68.8	73.3											H 5.2					Malaysia
66.0	64.1										H 23	H 6.1	H 2.7				Maldives
45.0	47.0	1983	21,785	2.8							H 1,364	H 5.6					Mali
73.7	78.1	1990	2,498	7.0	2.6	77.1	20.3	11.6	76.9	11.5	H 76	H 3.6	H 1.2	98.2			Malta
59.6	62.6										H 5	H 8.7					Marshall Islands
71.0	77.0	1989	1,617	4.8	0.1[14]	46.8[14]	53.1[14]	3.3[14]	61.5[14]	35.2[14]	H 107	H 3.3	H 0.8	33.9	1,753	30.6	Martinique
44.0	50.0										H 246	H 5.0					Mauritania
64.7	72.2	1989	11,197	10.7	1.7	60.6	37.7	22.7	60.3	17.0	F 155	F 5.3	F 2.0	72.8			Mauritius
54.0	58.0										H 10	H 4.7	H 2.3	89.2			Mayotte
67.8	73.9	1985	553,000	7.1	17.3	63.5	19.2	40.7	46.9	12.4	H 16,203	H 1.9	H 1.9	72.5			Mexico
68.0	73.0										H 11	H 7.0					Micronesia
65.2	72.0	1989	39,928	9.4	3.9	76.3	19.8	31.6	52.5	15.9	H 1,144	H 3.4	H 1.1	89.6	90,860	110.5	Moldova
72.0	80.0	1987		7.5							H 14	H 2.2	H 0.3	96.8			Monaco
61.2	63.8	1989	16,100	7.8							F 428	F 4.8					Mongolia
61.6	65.0										H 2,819	H 5.8	H 2.5				Morocco
46.9	50.2										F 1,860	F 4.4	F 2.0	73.1			Mozambique
60.0	63.5											H 5.2					Myanmar (Burma)
57.5	60.0											H 4.8					Namibia
64.0	69.0										H 1	H 8.0	H 2.6				Nauru
55.4	52.6											F 5.8	H 2.2				Nepal

Vital statistics, marriage, family (continued)

country	vital rates						causes of death (rate per 100,000 population)								
	year	birth rate per 1,000 population	death rate per 1,000 population	infant mortality rate per 1,000 live births	rate of natural increase per 1,000 population	total fertility rate	year	infectious and parasitic diseases	malignant neoplasms (cancers)	endocrine and metabolic disorders	diseases of the nervous system	diseases of the circulatory system	diseases of the respiratory system	diseases of the digestive system	accidents, poisonings, and violence
Netherlands, The	1990	13.2	8.6	7.1	4.6	1.6	1989	5.3	238.6	31.6	18.5	348.4	70.6	31.5	37.9
Netherlands Antilles	1989	18.5	6.4	6.3	12.1	3.4[28,38]	1987[39]	...	150.6	31.9	10.8	205.4	41.0	21.1	41.6
New Caledonia	1989	23.9	6.0	11.2	17.9	3.0									
New Zealand	1991	17.8	7.9	8.3	9.9	2.2	1987	4.7	193.7	15.0	14.6	380.7	87.1	22.1	60.3
Nicaragua	1991	37.0	7.0	65.0	30.0	4.7	1978	52.3	13.5	2.9	4.5	62.1	18.6	14.2	59.2
Niger	1990–95	51.3	18.7	124.0	32.6	7.1	...	...	...	...	...	...	...	...	...
Nigeria	1990–95	46.5	14.0	96.0	32.5	6.6	...	...	...	...	...	...	...	...	...
Northern Mariana Islands	1987	45.6	5.5	4.1	40.1	4.2[41]	1987	18.7	70.2[20]	23.4	14.0	135.7	70.2	9.4	145.1
Norway	1991	14.2	10.5	6.9[10]	3.6	1.9[10]	1989	7.1	231.9	15.6	16.9	501.2	105.2	33.1	66.3
Oman	1991	41.0	6.0	40.0	35.0	6.7	...	...	...	...	...	...	...	...	...
Pakistan	1991	40.5	10.8	113.0[10]	29.7	5.4	...	...	...	...	...	...	...	...	...
Palau	1988	24.9	6.5	26.0	18.4	3.2[3]	1985–86	15.3	92.1[20]	19.2[17]	11.5	176.5	99.8	34.5	95.9
Panama	1991	26.0	5.0	21.0	21.0	3.0	1990	12.6	48.4	9.7[5]	1.7[33]	94.4	12.4	6.3	41.6
Papua New Guinea	1991	34.0	12.0	59.0	22.0	5.3	...	...	...	...	...	...	...	...	...
Paraguay	1990–95	33.0	6.4	39.0	26.6	4.3	1986[42]	60.7	48.3	20.8	8.8	157.5	43.4	17.9	40.3
Peru	1990	32.8	8.3	80.7	24.5	4.2	1983	101.1	30.3	17.3	11.4	59.7	111.0	24.9	30.7
Philippines	1991	31.2	7.3	45.0[14]	23.9	4.0	1984	179.8	30.2	13.4	...	100.6	...	...	16.8
Poland	1990	14.3	10.2	15.9[13]	4.1	2.1	1990	8.1	191.3	16.0	9.1	534.2	41.1	31.5	78.2
Portugal	1989	11.5	9.3	12.2	2.2	1.8[24]	1990	7.9	184.2	32.8	8.7	461.3	75.7	46.8	68.3
Puerto Rico	1990	18.3	6.9	14.3[13]	11.4	2.4[14]	1989	15.3	109.0	79.0	13.4	249.4	75.7	40.3	61.4
Qatar	1989	31.8	2.5	31.0[14]	29.3	4.7	1986	9.3	20.4[20]	6.9[17]	2.4	50.0	10.6	6.1	41.0
Réunion	1990	23.1	5.3	12.0[18]	17.8	2.6	1988	12.3	88.4	23.5[17]	16.9	180.0	41.4	58.9	69.0
Romania	1990	13.6	10.7	26.9	2.9	2.2[13]	1989	11.7	141.6	9.7[17]	16.4	617.6	105.7	53.5	74.7
Russia	1990	13.4	11.2	17.4	2.2	1.9	1989	12.6	187.4	6.5	6.9	598.0	58.2	27.5	125.8
Rwanda	1990–95	50.0	15.6	112.0	34.4	8.0	...	...	...	...	...	...	...	...	...
St. Kitts and Nevis	1989	22.5	11.0	22.2	11.5	2.6[15]	1985	50.0	95.5	20.5[5]	11.4	443.2	81.8	25.0	29.5
St. Lucia	1990	23.2	5.6	17.7	17.6	3.4	1990	27.8	48.3	25.8	6.6	209.5	33.7	28.4	36.4
St. Vincent and the Grenadines	1990	23.9	6.4	21.3[9]	17.5	2.8[15]	1990	20.8	89.6	36.8	22.6	244.5	37.7	17.9	48.1
San Marino	1987–91	10.6	7.3	13.1	3.3	1.3[28]	1987–91[19]	0.9	246.0	2.75	0.0[33]	343.5	20.6	10.7	49.2
São Tomé and Príncipe	1990	38.0	8.0	72.0	30.0	5.4	1987	240.7	19.6	5.3[5]	2.7[33]	143.5	86.5	15.2	14.3
Saudi Arabia	1991	36.6	6.3	69.0	30.3	6.7	...	...	...	...	...	...	...	...	...
Senegal	1990–95	43.9	16.1	80.0	27.8	6.2	...	...	...	...	...	...	...	...	...
Seychelles	1990	24.0	8.1	13.0	15.9	2.8	1985–89[19]	42.9	116.9	10.6	7.9	263.5	77.1	40.5	67.0
Sierra Leone	1990–95	48.1	21.6	143.0	26.5	6.5	...	...	...	...	...	...	...	...	...
Singapore	1990	18.5	4.8	6.7	13.7	1.8	1989	16.3	122.3	16.7	4.1	189.4	80.8	13.5	33.9
Slovenia	1990	12.5	9.9	8.9	2.6	...	1989	8.6	206.6[20]	11.2	7.3	426.2	73.9	58.8	94.9
Solomon Islands	1988	44.5	9.9	72.0[10]	34.6	7.2	...	...	...	...	...	...	...	...	...
Somalia	1990–95	46.8	18.1	122.0	28.7	6.6	...	...	...	...	...	...	...	...	...
South Africa	1991	34.0	8.0	51.0	26.0	4.4	...	...	...	...	...	...	...	...	...
Bophuthatswana	1982	...	...	89.0	...		...	...	...	...	...	...	...	...	...
Ciskei	1982	...	...	89.0	...		...	...	...	...	...	...	...	...	...
Transkei	1982	...	...	89.0	...		...	...	...	...	...	...	...	...	...
Venda	1982	...	...	89.0	...		...	...	...	...	...	...	...	...	...
Spain	1989	10.4	8.4	8.0[14]	2.0	1.7[24]	1987	8.5	184.1	26.5	10.0	340.9	68.7	47.3	45.0
Sri Lanka	1991	21.2	5.8	25.0	15.4	2.6	1986	32.2	27.7	9.0	45.3	101.9	36.1	15.5	77.8
Sudan, The	1991	44.0	13.0	85.0	31.0	6.4	...	...	...	...	...	...	...	...	...
Suriname	1990–95	24.5	5.6	28.0	18.9	2.6	1985	34.5	48.0	25.1	6.3	149.1	42.2	28.2	67.6
Swaziland	1990–95	46.7	11.1	107.0	35.6	6.5	...	...	...	...	...	...	...	...	...
Sweden	1991	14.4	11.0	5.6[10]	3.4	2.0[13]	1988	8.3	240.0	20.7	12.8	597.2	92.4	35.9	62.1
Switzerland	1991	12.6	9.0	6.8	3.6	1.6[10]	1991	12.0	244.0	24.1[17]	17.4	417.4	77.2	27.1	78.9
Syria	1990–95	42.5	5.7	39.0	36.8	6.3	1981[22]	21.5	11.9	7.2	13.1	86.2	18.9	8.2	26.8
Taiwan	1991	15.6	5.2	5.3[10]	10.4	1.8[10]	1990	...	91.6	19.6[5]	...	141.7[43]	28.9[44]	17.8[45]	68.9[46]
Tajikistan	1990	38.8	6.2	40.7	32.6	5.1[13]	1989	81.2	51.9	6.9	8.9	197.5	138.8	23.0	48.4
Tanzania	1991	49.5	15.2	105.0	34.7	7.0	...	...	...	...	...	...	...	...	...
Thailand	1990–95	20.0	6.5	24.0	13.5	2.2	1989[47]	79.1	129.8	...	38.5	200.0	48.8	72.7	103.5
Togo	1991	49.0	13.0	110.0	36.0	7.1	...	...	...	...	...	...	...	...	...
Tonga	1990	30.4	7.1	49.0[14]	23.3	4.0[14]	1980	53.5	46.9	13.1	3.3	61.1	41.5	17.5	14.2
Trinidad and Tobago	1989	20.7	6.8	10.2	13.9	2.8[10]	1988	15.2	84.2	92.3	11.0	245.1	44.3	23.6	51.2
Tunisia	1990	25.4	6.4	44.0[18]	19.0	3.4[18]	...	...	...	...	...	...	...	...	...
Turkey	1991	28.0	6.0	54.0	22.0	3.6	1988[48]	38.8	82.9	8.6[5]	3.1[17]	390.5	29.5	15.1	30.9
Turkmenistan	1990	34.2	7.0	45.2	27.2	4.3[13]	1989	79.3	65.1	8.0	9.1	275.3	160.6	32.2	62.4
Tuvalu	1991	29.0	10.0	33.0	19.0	3.1	1985	40.0	70.0	20.0	120.0	150.0	120.0	170.0	...
Uganda	1990–95	51.5	14.1	94.0	37.4	7.3	...	...	...	...	...	...	...	...	...
Ukraine	1990	12.7	12.1	12.8	0.6	1.9	1990	11.6	196.3	6.7[17]	7.4	644.7	60.5	31.3	107.7
United Arab Emirates	1991	30.0	3.0	23.0	27.0	4.9	...	...	...	...	...	...	...	...	...
United Kingdom	1991	13.8	11.2	7.3	2.6	1.8[10]	1990	4.9	280.8	19.1	22.2	515.3	123.8	36.3	37.1
United States	1991	16.2	8.5	8.9	7.7	2.0	1991	23.3[49]	203.6	19.7[5]	0.3[33]	358.5	64.8[23]	15.8	57.7
Uruguay	1990	18.3	9.9	20.4	8.4	2.3[18]	1989	18.0	220.9	24.4	15.4	371.6	70.8	41.1	63.7
Uzbekistan	1990	33.7	6.1	34.6	27.6	4.0[13]	1990	44.5	55.9	6.5	9.1	251.3	119.3	24.7	60.1
Vanuatu	1989	40.0	7.5	53.0	32.5	6.2[14]	1985[50]	69.3	22.9	16.2	11.8	37.6	60.5	12.5	23.6
Venezuela	1989	27.5	4.4	22.9	23.1	3.3	1987	30.4	51.6	15.5	7.4	110.5	32.3	17.9	59.7
Vietnam	1991	29.5	8.1	48.0	21.4	3.7	1979	48.0	54.0	...	...	123.8	...	...	...
Virgin Islands (U.S.)	1988	22.0	5.0	13.1	17.0	2.6[13]	1988	13.5	63.5	39.6[5]	1.0[33]	193.6	28.1[23]	18.7	73.9
West Bank	1991	36.0	6.0	40.0	30.0	4.8	...	...	...	...	...	...	...	...	...
Western Sahara	1991	48.0	23.0	177.0	25.0	7.3	...	...	...	...	...	...	...	...	...
Western Samoa	1991	34.0	6.0	47.0	28.0	4.5	...	...	...	...	...	...	...	...	...
Yemen	1991	51.3	16.2	121.0	35.1	7.4	...	...	...	...	...	...	...	...	...
Yugoslavia	1990	14.6	9.3	24.2	5.3	...	1989	12.7	148.3[20]	20.1	7.3	524.3	47.7	26.3	49.3
Zaire	1990–95	45.3	13.0	75.0	32.3	6.1	...	...	...	...	...	...	...	...	...
Zambia	1990–95	50.3	12.4	72.0	37.9	7.2	...	...	...	...	...	...	...	...	...
Zimbabwe	1990–95	39.9	8.9	55.0	31.0	5.3	...	...	...	...	...	...	...	...	...

[1]Excludes nomadic tribes. [2]1987. [3]1986. [4]Septicemia only. [5]Diabetes mellitus only. [6]Cerebrovascular disease, heart disease, hypertension, and arteriosclerosis only. [7]Chronic obstructive pulmonary diseases, pneumonia, and influenza only. [8]1982. [9]1988–90 average. [10]1990. [11]Under 21 years of age. [12]21–29 years of age. [13]1989. [14]1988. [15]1991. [16]1989–90 average. [17]Includes nutritional disorders. [18]1990–95. [19]Average annual rates for the period. [20]Includes benign neoplasms. [21]1981. [22]Estimates based on about 75 percent of total deaths. [23]Bronchitis, pneumonia, influenza, and chronic obstructive pulmonary diseases only. [24]1985–90. [25]Estimates based on selected urban and rural areas. [26]Millions of households. [27]1985. [28]1984. [29]1985–88 average.

expectation of life at birth (latest year)		nuptiality, family, and family planning															country
		marriages			age at marriage (latest)						families (F), households (H) (latest)						
					groom (percent)			bride (percent)			families (households)		children		induced abortions		
male	female	year	total number	rate per 1,000 population	19 and under	20–29	30 and over	19 and under	20–29	30 and over	total ('000)	size	number under age 15	percent legitimate	number	ratio per 100 live births	
73.7	80.2	1989	90,248	6.1	0.5	62.4	37.1	3.7	71.5	24.8	H 5,565	H 2.6	H 0.6	88.6	17,300	9.7	Netherlands, The
71.1	75.8	1982	959	5.6	4.0	77.0	18.9	22.2	61.1	16.7	H 41	H 3.7	H 2.1	51.6	...	...	Netherlands Antilles
66.5	71.8	1987	729	4.5	0.5	54.5	45.0	10.2	61.9	27.9	...	H 4.1	...	48.1	...	...	New Caledonia
72.0	77.9	1989	22,733	6.8	1.2	58.7	40.1	5.5	66.0	28.5	H 1,178	H 2.9	H 0.7	64.3	10,200	17.6	New Zealand
60.0	65.0	1988	7,530	2.1	18.1[11, 27]	—81.9[27, 40]—		48.2[11, 27]	—51.8[27, 40]—		...	H 6.9	...	...	...	...	Nicaragua
44.9	48.1	...	...	...	...	...	...	...	...	...	H 1,130	H 6.4	...	...	...	...	Niger
50.8	54.3	...	...	...	...	...	...	...	...	...	H 14,441	H 5.0	...	...	...	...	Nigeria
59.0	64.0	1987	685	31.2	2.5	50.2	47.3	5.7	70.4	23.9	H 7	H 4.6	H 1.5	53.9	...	...	Northern Mariana Islands
73.4	79.8	1990	21,926	5.2	0.9[13]	58.7[13]	40.4[13]	4.9[13]	69.3[13]	25.8[13]	F 1,981	F 2.1	F 0.4	61.4	15,551	25.5	Norway
65.0	68.0	...	...	...	...	...	...	...	...	...	H 350	H 3.7	...	...	...	...	Oman
59.3	60.7	...	...	...	...	...	...	...	...	...	...	H 6.5	...	...	...	...	Pakistan
59.1	62.8	...	...	...	...	...	...	...	...	...	H 3	H 5.0	H 1.6	...	...	...	Palau
72.0	76.0	1990	10,187	4.2	3.6[13]	55.0[13]	41.4[13]	15.6[13]	55.8[13]	28.6[13]	H 524	H 4.4	H 1.5	28.1	12	—	Panama
54.0	56.0	...	...	...	...	...	...	...	...	...	H 674	H 4.6	...	...	...	...	Papua New Guinea
65.1	69.5	1987	17,741	4.5	3.8	64.4	31.8	34.0	46.5	19.5	H 345	H 5.2	...	68.7	...	...	Paraguay
61.5	65.3	1982	109,200	6.0	5.5	60.4	34.1	25.9	51.4	22.6	H 3,099	H 5.2	...	57.8	...	...	Peru
62.7	66.5	1988	393,514	6.7	8.3	69.7	22.0	26.0	61.0	13.0	F 9,566	F 5.7	F 2.4	93.9	...	...	Philippines
66.8	75.5	1989	255,700	6.7	4.2[14]	76.0[14]	19.8[14]	19.9[14]	65.7[14]	14.4[14]	F 9,435	F 3.6	F 0.9	95.0	105,333	17.9	Poland
70.6	77.6	1988	71,098	6.9	5.0	75.5	19.5	21.0	66.2	12.8	H 2,954	H 3.8	H 0.8	85.5	...	...	Portugal
71.5	78.4	1989	31,642	8.9	11.4	57.3	31.3	23.7	52.3	24.0	F 563	F 4.1	F 1.8	75.6	...	...	Puerto Rico
65.2	67.6	1989	1,330	3.2	5.1	74.7	20.2	37.5	55.2	7.3	H 61	H 6.4	...	...	...	...	Qatar
69.0	78.3	1990	3,831	6.4	1.4[2]	67.8[2]	30.8[2]	14.8[2]	66.8[2]	18.4[2]	H 158	H 3.8	H 1.1	47.3	4,302	31.7	Réunion
66.5	72.4	1989	177,943	7.7	4.6	72.7	22.7	29.9	55.8	14.3	H 7,115	H 3.1	...	...	992,265	315.3	Romania
63.9	74.3	1989	1,384,307	9.4	5.8	66.9	27.3	27.4	49.0	23.6	H 40,426	H 3.2	H 0.8	86.5	4,242,028	196.3	Russia
48.8	52.2	1982	14,313	2.6	...	...	...	...	...	...	H 894	H 5.2	...	94.9	...	...	Rwanda
64.0	71.0	...	...	...	...	...	...	...	...	...	H 12	H 3.7	H 1.4	19.2	...	...	St. Kitts and Nevis
68.6	74.4	1989	395	2.7	0.8	34.4	64.8	3.5	45.1	51.4	H 25	H 4.6	H 2.0	10.0	...	...	St. Lucia
68.0	72.0	1990	503	4.7	0.5[3]	41.6[3]	57.9[3]	6.4[3]	59.5[3]	34.1[3]	H 20	H 4.8	H 2.0	...	...	...	St. Vincent and the Grenadines
70.7	76.2	1989	169	7.4	0.6	75.1	24.3	5.3	85.3	9.5	F 8	F 2.8	F 0.5	95.2	...	...	San Marino
64.0	67.0	...	...	...	...	...	...	...	...	...	...	...	...	9.8	...	...	São Tomé and Príncipe
65.0	68.0	...	...	...	...	...	...	...	...	...	H 1,513	H 6.6	...	...	...	...	Saudi Arabia
48.3	50.3	...	...	...	...	...	...	...	...	...	H 1,167	H 4.8	...	...	...	...	Senegal
67.3	74.2	1987	622	9.4	1.0	54.2	44.8	6.4	65.1	28.5	H 13	H 4.8	H 1.9	27.2	9	0.5	Seychelles
41.4	44.6	...	...	...	...	...	...	...	...	...	H 749	H 4.7	...	...	...	...	Sierra Leone
70.3	75.8	1988	24,853	9.4	0.4	66.5	33.1	5.1	79.1	15.8	H 510	H 3.9	H 1.3	...	21,226	48.7	Singapore
67.0	75.0	1990	9,131	4.7	0.7[13]	75.3[13]	24.0[13]	13.2[13]	73.3[13]	13.5[13]	H 642	H 3.1	H 0.7[21]	...	...	...	Slovenia
59.9	61.4	...	...	...	...	...	...	...	...	...	F 41	F 5.6	F 2.3	...	...	...	Solomon Islands
45.4	48.6	...	...	...	...	...	...	...	...	...	...	H 4.9	...	...	...	...	Somalia
61.0	67.0	...	...	...	...	...	...	...	...	...	...	H 4.5	...	75.9	...	...	South Africa
—57.0—		...	...	...	...	...	...	...	...	...	...	...	...	...	...	...	Bophuthatswana
—57.0—		...	...	...	...	...	...	...	...	...	H 144	H 6.2	...	...	...	...	Ciskei
—57.0—		...	...	...	...	...	...	...	...	...	...	...	...	...	...	...	Transkei
—57.0—		...	...	...	...	...	...	...	...	...	H 70	H 5.4	...	...	...	...	Venda
73.3	79.7	1989	215,840	5.6	2.6[14]	76.4[14]	21.0[14]	11.6[14]	77.0[14]	11.4[14]	F 10,665	F 3.5	...	90.9	...	...	Spain
69.1	73.4	1989	141,533	8.4	0.5[27]	71.1[27]	28.4[27]	16.9[27]	73.0[27]	10.1[27]	H 2,721	H 5.2	H 1.9	94.6	...	...	Sri Lanka
52.0	54.0	...	...	...	...	...	...	...	...	...	H 3,471	H 5.3	...	...	...	...	Sudan, The
67.8	72.8	1988	2,200	5.5	...	...	...	...	...	...	...	H 3.9	...	...	...	...	Suriname
56.2	59.8	...	...	...	...	...	...	...	...	...	H 112	H 5.0	...	...	1,145	...	Swaziland
74.4	80.2	1990	40,477	4.7	0.4	46.8	52.8	2.2	60.2	37.6	H 3,670	H 2.2	H 0.5	53.0	37,585	33.5	Sweden
74.0	80.8	1990	46,603	6.8	0.2	53.3	46.5	2.4	67.9	29.7	H 2,500	H 2.5	...	93.9	...	...	Switzerland
65.2	69.2	1988	101,946	7.5	...	...	...	...	...	...	F 1,151	H 6.2	F 2.4	...	...	...	Syria
71.3	76.8	1990	143,886	7.1	1.5	62.3	36.2	6.0	77.7	16.3	H 5,093	H 4.0	H 1.0	97.8	...	...	Taiwan
67.0	72.1	1989	47,616	9.2	2.1	86.8	11.1	39.0	54.3	6.7	H 799	H 6.1	H 2.7	93.0	54,494	27.2	Tajikistan
50.0	55.0	...	...	...	...	...	...	...	...	...	H 3,435	H 5.1	H 2.3	...	...	...	Tanzania
65.1	69.2	1989	406,134	7.3	...	...	...	...	...	...	H 10,418	H 5.3	H 1.9	...	...	...	Thailand
54.0	58.0	...	...	...	...	...	...	...	...	...	H 479	H 5.6	...	...	...	...	Togo
61.0	64.8	1985	645	6.6	...	...	...	...	...	...	F 15	F 6.1	F 2.7	80.6	...	...	Tonga
69.7	74.7	1989	6,794	5.6	2.8	59.6	37.6	18.1	58.1	23.8	H 301	H 4.1	H 1.3	56.9	9	—	Trinidad and Tobago
66.4	68.7	1990	55,300	6.9	1.1[2]	66.3[2]	32.6[2]	24.6[2]	63.6[2]	11.8[2]	H 1,313	H 5.5	...	99.8	23,300	10.9	Tunisia
68.0	72.0	1989	450,763	7.9	8.5[14]	75.9[14]	15.6[14]	36.1[14]	56.5[14]	7.4[14]	H 9,730	H 5.2	H 2.0	...	...	...	Turkey
62.9	69.7	1989	34,890	9.8	3.0	87.4	9.6	16.1	77.1	6.8	H 598	H 5.6	H 2.4	96.5	39,068	31.3	Turkmenistan
61.0	63.0	...	...	...	...	...	...	...	...	...	H 1	H 6.4	H 2.2	82.2	...	...	Tuvalu
51.4	54.7	...	...	...	...	...	...	...	...	...	H 2,766	H 4.8	...	...	...	...	Uganda
66.0	75.0	1989	489,330	9.5	5.5	70.2	24.3	32.9	46.7	20.4	H 14,507	H 3.2	H 0.8	89.2	1,058,414	153.2	Ukraine
69.0	74.0	...	...	...	...	...	...	...	...	...	H 247	H 6.8	...	...	...	...	United Arab Emirates
72.4	78.0	1989	392,042	6.8	2.1	60.5	37.4	7.6	64.6	27.8	H 21,672	H 2.7	H 1.7	72.1	180,622	23.2	United Kingdom
72.0	78.8	1991	2,371,000	9.4	4.5[14]	54.1[14]	41.4[14]	11.8[14]	55.7[14]	32.5[14]	F 63,558	F 2.6	F 1.0	76.6	1,354,000	35.5	United States
68.9	75.3	1987	21,812	7.2	7.2	63.3	29.5	24.7	54.2	21.1	H 863	H 3.3	H 0.9	73.8	...	...	Uruguay
66.2	72.6	1989	200,681	10.0	2.3	87.4	10.3	37.9	55.2	6.9	H 3,415	H 5.5	H 2.4	95.8	226,276	33.8	Uzbekistan
61.1	59.3	...	...	...	...	...	...	...	...	...	H 28	H 5.1	H 2.2	...	...	...	Vanuatu
66.9	73.1	1989	111,970	5.8	11.6	62.9	25.5	31.5	52.3	16.2	H 2,707	H 5.3	H 2.2	47.0	...	...	Venezuela
63.0	67.0	...	...	...	...	...	...	...	...	...	H 12,958[51]	H 4.8[51]	H 1.9[51]	...	...	...	Vietnam
66.7	70.7	1987	1,906	18.0	4.5	50.9	44.6	1.0	38.4	60.6	H 32	H 3.1	H 1.0	38.4	...	...	Virgin Islands (U.S.)
67.0	69.0	...	...	...	...	...	...	...	...	...	...	...	...	...	...	...	West Bank
39.0	41.0	...	...	...	...	...	...	...	...	...	...	...	...	...	...	...	Western Sahara
64.0	69.0	1989	833	5.3	0.5	52.7	46.8	8.6	61.3	30.1	F 20	F 7.8	F 3.8	43.5	...	...	Western Samoa
49.0	51.0	...	...	...	...	...	...	...	...	...	H 1,848	H 5.6	...	...	...	...	Yemen
68.2	73.2	1990	65,029	6.2	2.4[13]	68.8[13]	28.8[13]	23.6[13]	60.7[13]	15.7[13]	H 2,711[21]	H 3.7[21]	H 0.9[21]	...	...	...	Yugoslavia
52.3	55.7	...	...	...	...	...	...	...	...	...	...	H 6.0	...	...	...	...	Zaire
54.4	56.5	...	...	...	...	...	...	...	...	...	H 1,370	H 4.4	H 2.1	...	...	...	Zambia
59.0	62.6	...	...	...	...	...	...	...	...	...	...	H 5.8	...	95.8	...	...	Zimbabwe

[30]First marriages only. [31]Former West Germany only. [32]1983. [33]Meningitis only. [34]21–30 years of age. [35]Over 31 years of age. [36]Estimates based on reported inpatient deaths only, about 10 percent of total deaths. [37]Estimates based on about 35 percent of total deaths. [38]Includes Aruba. [39]Excludes Sint Maarten. [40]Over 21 years of age. [41]1976–80 average. [42]Reporting areas only. [43]Cerebrovascular disease, heart disease, and hypertension only. [44]Pneumonia, bronchitis, emphysema, and asthma only. [45]Chronic liver disease and cirrhosis only. [46]Accidents only. [47]Estimates based on about 25 percent of total deaths. [48]Estimates based on about 30 percent of total deaths. [49]Of which AIDS, 11.4. [50]Registered events only. [51]Private households only.

National product and accounts

The national product and accounts table furnishes, for most of the countries of the world, breakdowns of (1) gross national product (GNP) and its global and per capita growth rates (1980–90), (2) principal accounting and industrial components of gross domestic product (GDP), (3) recent growth rates of real GDP, and (4) principal elements of each country's balance of payments, including international goods trade, invisibles, and tourism payments.

Measures of national output. The two most commonly used measures of national output (except for the accounting systems of centrally planned economies) are GDP and GNP. Each of these measures represents an aggregate value of goods and services produced by a specific country. The GDP, the more basic of these, is a measure of the total value of goods and services produced entirely within a given country. The GNP, the more comprehensive value, is composed of both domestic production, GDP, *and* the net income from current (short-term) transactions with other countries. When the income received from other countries is greater than payments to them, a country's GNP is greater than its GDP. In theory, if all national accounts could be equilibrated, the global summation of GDP would equal GNP.

In the first section of the table, data are provided for the nominal GNP. ("Nominal" refers to value in current prices for the year indicated and is distinguished from a "real" valuation, which is one adjusted to eliminate the effect of recent inflation [most often] or, occasionally, of deflation between two given dates.) Both the total and per capita values of this product are denominated in U.S. dollars for ease of comparison. Beside these are given figures for average annual growth of total and per capita real GNP. GNP per capita provides a rough measure of annual national income per person, but values should be compared cautiously, as they are subject to a number of distortions, notably of exchange rate, but also of purchasing power parity (the differing ability [by more than an exchange rate] of any two currencies to purchase comparable goods in their respective domestic markets), and in the existence of elements of national production that do not enter the monetary economy in such a way as to be visible to fiscal authorities (*e.g.,* food, clothing, or housing produced and consumed within families or communal groups or services exchanged).

In a number of countries with centrally planned economies, the conventional concept for the aggregated national income/product is net material product (NMP), which includes only material goods and "productive" services. These NMP accounts are not directly comparable to the GDP values presented in this table for market economies. The GDP value is more comprehensive and includes a number of sectors (especially personal and financial services) excluded from the NMP value. Estimated GNPs have been supplied for most countries (including the centrally planned), based either on the country's own, or on external, analysis.

The internal structure of the national product. GDP/GNP values allow comparison of the relative size of national economies, but further information is provided when these aggregates are analyzed according to their component kinds of expenditure, cost components, and industrial sectors of origin.

There are three major domestic components of GDP expenditure: private

National product and accounts

country	gross national product (GNP)		average annual growth rates, 1980–90			gross domestic product (GDP) by type of expenditure, 1989 (%)					cost components of gross domestic product (GDP), 1989 (%)			
	nominal, 1990 ('000,000 U.S.$)	per capita, 1990 (U.S.$)	real GNP (%)	population (%)	real GNP per capita (%)	private	government	gross domestic investment	exports	imports	indirect taxes net of subsidies	consumption of fixed capital	compensation of employees	net operating surplus
Afghanistan	3,100[1]	220[1]	...	0.6	...	...	...	...	...	...	...	...	...	...
Albania	4,100	1,280	...	2.0	...	...	...	...	...	...	...	...	...	...
Algeria	51,585	2,060	2.7	3.0	-0.3	50	18	29	16	-14	19[7]	9[7]	38[7]	34[7]
American Samoa	190[9]	4,860[9]	...	3.7	...	...	...	...	...	...	...	...	...	...
Andorra	727[10]	13,550[10]	...	4.9	...	...	...	...	...	...	...	...	...	...
Angola	5,996[5]	620[5]	8.8	2.6	6.2	41	35	16	42	-35	9	11	43	47[11]
Antigua and Barbuda	363	4,600	5.2	0.0	5.2	70[12]	19[12]	36[12]	75[12]	-100[12]	16[12]		—84[12]—	
Argentina	76,491	2,370	-0.5	1.5	-2.0	—80—		9	20	-8	87	11	34[7]	57[7,11]
Armenia	...	...	...	0.8	...	—70[2]—		44[2]	—14[2]—		...	...	...	...
Aruba	730[5,10]	11,840[5,10]	...	0.6	...	66[12]	21[12]	17[12]	—3[12]—		...	...	...	...
Australia	290,522	17,080	3.2	1.5	1.7	59	16	26	16	-18	12	15	50	24
Austria	147,016	19,240	2.1	0.2	1.9	55	18	26	40	-39	14	12	52	22
Azerbaijan	...	...	...	1.5	...	—73[2]—		13[2]	—13[2]—		...	...	...	...
Bahamas, The	2,913	11,510	3.6	2.0	1.6	46	15	22	72	-55	16[1]	—	11[1]	73[1]
Bahrain	3,120[5]	6,380[5]	-0.1	4.1	-4.2	41	27	13	98	-79	3	17	48	33
Bangladesh	22,579	200	3.7	1.8	1.9	89	9	11	7	-17	...	...	...	...
Barbados	1,680	6,540	1.7	0.3	1.4	67	18	19	42	-47	...	...	...	...
Belarus	...	...	...	0.6	...	74[2,6]	22[2,6]	26[2,6]	68[2,6]	-71[2,6]	...	...	...	...
Belgium	154,688	15,440	1.4	0.1	1.3	62	14	20	77	-73	9	9	52	30
Belize	373	1,970	5.3	2.6	2.7	63	22	26	58	-71	12[16]	9[16]	—79[16]—	
Benin	1,716	360	2.2	3.0	-0.8	84	12	12	20	-28	4	11	20	76[11]
Bermuda	1,642	27,790	...	0.8	...	69	12	16	61	-58	...	...	...	...
Bhutan	273	190	9.7	2.2	7.5	67[1]	14[1]	39[1]	30[1]	-50[1]	2[1]	9[1]	—89[1]—	
Bolivia	4,526	620	0.0	2.8	-2.8	82	13	6	28	-29	...	...	...	...
Bosnia and Hercegovina	...	...	...	0.6	...	...	...	...	...	...	...	...	...	...
Botswana	2,561	2,040	9.9	3.4	6.5	31	20	27	62	-41	7[12]	15[12]	28[12]	50[12]
Brazil	402,788	2,680	2.7	2.0	0.7	58	14	25	8	-5	9		—91—	
Brunei	3,302[5,10]	13,260[5,10]	...	3.3	...	...	...	...	...	...	...	...	...	...
Bulgaria	47,783	5,310	...	0.1	...	58[16]	11[16]	24[16]	—7[16]—		...	...	...	...
Burkina Faso	2,955	330	4.1	3.2	0.9	95[20]	17[20]	3[20]	30[20]	-44[20]	7[20]		—93[20]—	
Burundi	1,151	210	4.2	2.6	1.6	82	14	17	10	-22	12[1]	4[1]	22[1]	63[1]
Cambodia	890[5,10]	130[5,10]	...	3.0	...	...	...	...	...	...	...	...	...	...
Cameroon	11,223	940	2.9	3.2	-0.3	66	10	26	16	-17	12[9]	5[9]	26[9]	57[9]
Canada	542,774	20,450	3.3	1.0	2.3	58	19	23	25	-25	11	11	55	22
Cape Verde	331	890	5.7	1.3	4.4	86[1]	19[1]	37[1]	15[1]	-56[1]	9[20]		—91[20]—	
Cayman Islands	357[5]	13,770[5]	...	4.6	...	62	14	23	66	-66	16	8	57	20
Central African Republic	1,194	390	1.4	2.2	-0.8	83[12]	18[12]	9[12]	22[12]	-33[12]	...	...	...	...
Chad	1,074	190	5.8	2.4	3.4	90	23	11	22	-46	8[12]		—92[12]—	
Chile	25,504	1,940	2.8	1.7	1.1	67	10	20	37	-34	13[9]	12[9]	33[9]	42[9]
China	415,884	370	9.5	1.5	8.0	59[2]	9[2]	36[2]	15[2]	-16[2]	...	...	...	...
Colombia	40,805	1,240	3.1	2.1	1.0	66	10	20	18	-14	11	11	38	51[11]
Comoros	227	480	2.8	3.4	-0.6	73[20]	27[20]	23[20]	16[20]	-40[20]	8[20]		—92[20]—	
Congo	2,296	1,010	3.2	3.3	-0.1	53	19	16	48	-35	14	19	32	35
Cook Islands	40[1,10]	2,200[1,10]	...	-0.6	...	...	...	...	...	...	...	...	...	...
Costa Rica	5,342	1,910	3.0	2.8	0.2	61	16	27	34	-39	13	2	49	36
Côte d'Ivoire	8,920	730	0.2	3.9	-3.7	69	16	7	35	-27	19[20]		—81[20]—	
Croatia	...	...	...	0.3	...	...	...	...	...	...	...	...	...	...
Cuba	20,900	2,000	...	0.9	...	95[2]	9[2]	18[2]	—21[2]—		...	...	...	...
Cyprus	5,633	8,040	6.0	1.4	4.6	62	13	29	52	-58	9	11	—81—	
Czechoslovakia	124,334	7,940	...	0.2	...	72[2]	9[2]	16[2]	—2[2]—		...	...	...	...
Denmark	113,515	22,090	2.1	0.0	2.1	53	25	18	35	-32	15	9	54	22
Djibouti	196[12]	430[12]	...	4.0	...	80[20]	36[20]	23[20]	39[20]	-79[20]	21[20]		—79[20]—	
Dominica	160	1,940	4.3	1.2	3.1	79	19	36	39	-72	18		—82—	
Dominican Republic	5,847	820	1.9	2.4	-0.5	76	7	21	32	-36	10[1]	6[1]	—84[1]—	
Ecuador	10,112	960	1.9	2.3	-0.4	71	9	22	27	-29	12	11	14	74[11]

consumption (analyzed in greater detail in the "Household budgets and consumption" table), government spending, and gross domestic investment. The fourth, nondomestic, component of GDP expenditure is net foreign trade; values are given for both exports (a positive value) and imports (a negative value, representing obligations to other countries). The sum of these five percentages, excluding statistical discrepancies and rounding, should be 100% of the GDP.

The structure of GDP as accounted by cost components here comprises four general categories: indirect taxes (excise or value-added taxes), net of subsidies; consumption of fixed capital (depreciation); and two income categories: (a) compensation of employees (salaries, wages, etc.) and (b) net operating surplus ("profits," interests, rent, etc.).

The distribution of GDP for ten industrial sectors is aggregated into three major industrial groups:

1. The primary sector, composed of agriculture (including forestry and fishing) and mineral production (including fossil fuels).
2. The secondary sector, composed of manufacturing, construction, and public utilities.
3. The tertiary sector, which includes transportation and communications, trade (wholesale and retail), financial services (including banking, real estate, insurance, and business services), other (community, social, and personal) services, and government services.

Percentages in this section of the table may not add to 100 because the value of each economic sector is calculated as a percentage of the total GDP, which may contain adjustments that are not distributed by sector.

Average annual growth rate of real GDP. These columns show average annual growth rates of real product for the decade from 1975 to 1985, as well as for the five years from 1985 to 1990. Real GDP growth rates indicate the change in total output achieved by each country during the periods indicated excluding inflation.

Balance of payments (external account transactions). The external account records the sum (net) of all economic transactions of a current nature between one country and the rest of the world. The account shows a country's net of overseas receipts and obligations, including not only the trade of goods and services but also such invisible items as interest and dividends, short- and long-term investments, tourism, transfers to or from overseas residents, etc. Each transaction gives rise either to a foreign claim for payment, recorded as a deficit (e.g., from imports, capital outflows), or a foreign obligation to pay, recorded as a surplus (e.g., from exports, capital inflows) or a domestic claim on another country. Any international transaction automatically creates a deficit in the balance of payments of one country and a surplus in that of another. Values are given in U.S. dollars for comparability.

Tourist trade. Net income or expenditure from tourism (in U.S. dollars for comparability) is often a significant element in a country's balance of payments. Receipts from foreign nationals reflect payments for goods and services from foreign currency resources by tourists in the given country. Expenditures by nationals abroad are also payments for goods and services, but in this case made by the residents of the given country as tourists abroad.

origin of gross domestic product (GDP) by economic sector, 1989 (%)										avg. annual growth rate of real GDP (%)		balance of payments, 1991 (current external transactions; '000,000 U.S.$)			tourist trade, 1990 ('000,000 U.S.$)		country
primary		secondary			tertiary					1975–1985	1985–1989	net transfers		current balance of payments	receipts from foreign nationals	expenditures by nationals abroad	
agri-culture	mining	manu-factur-ing	con-struc-tion	public util-ities	transp., commu-nications	trade	finan-cial svcs.	other svcs.	govt.			goods-merchan-dise	invisibles				
52[2]	3	25[2,3]	8[2]	3	4[2]	9[2]		2[2]		1.0[2]	−5.9[2,4]	−371[5]	229[5]	−142[5]	1	1	Afghanistan
33[2]	3	45[2,3]	6[2]	3		16[2]				4.5[2]	...	−179[6]	...	...	...	...	Albania
9	20[8]	17	16	8	5	13		19		6.1	...	4,187[6]	−2,767[6]	1,420[6]	64	149	Algeria
...	...	...	...	...	...	...	...	...	...	...	...	−70[5]	...	...	10	...	American Samoa
...	...	...	...	...	...	...	...	...	...	...	...	−1,151[6]	...	...	...	...	Andorra
13	34	4	4		4	10	1	29		2.5	7.2	1,276[6]	...	...	...	...	Angola
5	7[8]	3	14	8	16	26		39		4.5	8.2[4]	−286	251	−35	250	17	Antigua and Barbuda
15	3	22	2	5	12	13	8	19		0.0	0.3	4,691	−7,191	−2,500	903	1,171	Argentina
14[2]	3	50[2,3]	21[2]	3	4[2]	4[2]		6[2]		6.7[2]	0.9[2]	...	...	...	...	...	Armenia
...	...	...	...	...	...	...	...	...	...	...	...	−398[6]	261[6]	−137[6]	353	40	Aruba
4	5	16	7	3	7	18	21	16	4	2.9	3.2	3,431	−13,501	−10,070	3,797	4,120	Australia
3	13	27[13]	7	3	6	16	16	4	14	2.4	3.0	−12,049	11,797	−252	13,017	7,476	Austria
31[2]	3	43[2,3]	12[2]	3	3[2]	4[2]		7[2]		...	−2.3[2]	...	...	...	...	...	Azerbaijan
4[12]	3	10[3,12]	3[12]	3	11[12]	26[12]	12[12]	16[12]	17[12]	4.5	2.6[14]	−921[6]	741[6]	−180[6]	1,333	196	Bahamas, The
1	18	18	7	2	11	10	16	5	22	4.7	2.1[4]	−193	−545	−738	110	77	Bahrain
38	—	8	6	1	11	8	2	22	4	4.0	4.1	−1,587[6]	1,190[6]	−397[6]	11	78	Bangladesh
4	1	7	6	3	7	28	12	3	15	2.3	2.2	−452[5]	449[5]	−3[5]	494	45	Barbados
26[2]	3	45[2,3]	11[2]	3	4[2]	5[2]		10[2]		5.2[2]	3.9[2,14]	...	...	...	...	...	Belarus
2	—	23	6	3	7	33		29		1.7	3.3	630[6,15]	3,918[6,15]	4,548[6,15]	3,575	5,664	Belgium
22	—	12	7	3	11	18	10	8	12	2.3	9.2	−64[5]	45[5]	−19[5]	91	8	Belize
36	1	9	3	1	7	17		11	10	4.5	−0.3[4]	−132[1]	49[1]	−83[1]	47	12	Benin
...	...	...	...	...	...	...	...	...	...	1.8	2.6	−481[6]	447[6]	−34[6]	481	104	Bermuda
44[1]	1[1]	6[1]	8[1]	10[1]	5[1]	7[1]		20[1]		8.3	8.3[14]	−32[5]	41[5]	9[5]	2	...	Bhutan
22	15	11	3	1	7	11	13	4	13	0.1	1.7	−44	−218	−262	98	60	Bolivia
15[17]	13	54[13,17]	7[17]	1[17]	7[17]	15[17]		3[17]		3.6[17]	0.3[14,17]	...	...	...	...	...	Bosnia and Hercegovina
3	51	4	3	2	2	16	5	2	13	11.9	9.2	147[6]	−11[6]	138[6]	65	39	Botswana
8	1	27	8	2	5	7		41		3.9	2.0	16,112[5]	15,087[5]	1,025[5]	1,444	1,559	Brazil
21	36[1]	9[1]	31	1	5[1]	12[1]		33[1]		3.0	0.2[4]	684[5]	...	...	35	...	Brunei
13[2]	—	57[2,18]	9[2]	18	9[2]	9[2]		22,19		−0.6	−1.3	115[6]	...	...	394	...	Bulgaria
38	1[8]	10	2	8	6	6		18		4.1	7.0[4]	−289[6]	178[6]	−111[6]	9	35	Burkina Faso
48	1[8]	10	2	8	3	8		15		4.8	3.3	−116[6]	60[6]	−56[6]	4	16	Burundi
...	...	...	...	...	...	...	...	...	...	...	...	−115[1]	...	...	...	...	Cambodia
21	16[8]	11	6	8	7	14		19		9.0	−1.9[4]	621[1]	−1,050[1]	−429[1]	21	283	Cameroon
3	4	19	7	3	8	12	16	22	6	3.4	3.0	5,929	−31,458	−25,529	6,374	8,390	Canada
21[20]	—	5[20]	20[20]	3[20]	12[20]	25[20]	4[20]	1[20]	9[20]	4.4	4.4[4]	−99[5]	109[5]	10[5]	...	...	Cape Verde
1	1	2	10	3	13	21	31	6	10	...	11.2[14]	−284[6]	...	...	326	...	Cayman Islands
42	4[8]	7	4	8	4	20		16		0.5	1.7	−712[6]	−4[20]	−75[20]	9	41	Central African Republic
35	1[8]	18	1	8	2	29		8		−5.0	3.0[14]	−85[5]	29[5]	−56[5]	12	36	Chad
7	12[8]	23	4	8	6	18		25		3.5	6.1	1,575	−1,483	92	548	426	Chile
32[21]	...	48[21]	6[21]	...	4[21]	11[21]	...	...		8.2	7.5[21]	8,743	5,022	13,765	2,218	470	China
16	7	21	7	2	8	14	11	5	8	3.8	4.6	3,037	−486	2,551	362	515	Colombia
34[20]	...	12[20]	10[20]	3[20]	4[20]	21[20]		16[20]		4.2	...	−276	186	−96	2	6	Comoros
14	28	6	2	2	14	9		25		8.8	−0.9[14]	571	−791	−220	7	75	Congo
...	...	...	...	...	...	...	...	...	...	1.0	9.6[14]	−32[5]	...	...	16	...	Cook Islands
20	13	22[13]	4	3	8	17	13	4	9	2.7	4.6	−468[6]	−116[6]	−584[6]	275	148	Costa Rica
28	3[8]	14	3	8	9	14		21		3.7	−0.1[4]	1,419[6]	−2,702[6]	−1,283[6]	48	246	Côte d'Ivoire
14[17]	13	43[13,17]	7[17]	1[17]	14[17]	19[17]		4[17]		2.8[17]	0.0[14,17]	...	...	...	...	...	Croatia
16[22]	4[22]	39[22]	9[22]	3[22]	8[22]	20[22]		1[19,22]		5.7[2]	−1.4[2,14]	−3,579[5]	...	...	268	...	Cuba
7	—	15	9	2	9	20	14	6	12	8.1	6.4	−1,458[6]	1,504[6]	46[6]	1,258	162	Cyprus
10[2]	3	58[2,3]	11[2]	3	5[2]	16[2]		2,19		0.7	2.7	−121	1,029	908	470	636	Czechoslovakia
5	1	19	7	2	8	15	18	5	23	2.6	1.5	4,859	−2,678	2,181	3,322	3,676	Denmark
4	2[8]	7	6	8	10	12		31		1.4	...	−190[6]	...	...	6	...	Djibouti
27	1	7	6	3	15	12	13	3	19	5.4	5.7[14]	−44[6]	18[6]	−26[6]	25	4	Dominica
15	5[8]	17	10	8	8	15		31		3.2	2.0	−1,058[6]	999[6]	−59[6]	750	144	Dominican Republic
17	13	16	4	2	8	15	11	3	8	4.3	2.0	644	−1,111	−467	193	176	Ecuador

National product and accounts   (continued)

country	gross national product (GNP)		average annual growth rates, 1980–90			gross domestic product (GDP) by type of expenditure, 1989 (%) consumption		gross domestic invest-ment	foreign trade		cost components of gross domestic product (GDP), 1989 (%) indirect taxes net of subsidies	consump-tion of fixed capital	compen-sation of employ-ees	net operating surplus
	nominal, 1990 ('000,000 U.S.$)	per capita, 1990 (U.S.$)	real GNP (%)	popu-lation (%)	real GNP per capita (%)	private	govern-ment		exports	imports				
Egypt	31,381	600	4.7	2.7	2.0	80	13	23	22	-38	7[12]		93[12]	
El Salvador	5,767	960	0.8	1.6	-0.8	82	12	16	13	-24	5	4	91	
Equatorial Guinea	136	330	...	3.2	...	64	22	21	26	-33	...	...	...	...
Estonia	...	...	...	0.7	...	60	14	33	-7-					
Ethiopia	6,041	120	1.9	2.9	-1.0	70	25	13	12	-20	9[20]		91[20]	
Faeroe Islands	662[5,10]	13,850[5,10]	...	0.9	...	53	25	19	34	-31	12[20]	11	62[20]	26[11,20]
Fiji	1,326	1,770	1.3	1.4	-0.1	70	14	16	58	-58	10[20]	8[20]	42[20]	40[20]
Finland	129,823	26,070	3.6	0.4	3.2	52	20	28	24	-25	13	15	54	19
France	1,099,750	19,480	2.2	0.5	1.7	60	18	22	23	-23	13	13	52	23
French Guiana	179[20]	1,820[20]	...	5.4	...	...								
French Polynesia	2,480[5,10]	12,920[5,10]	...	2.7	...	54[12]	39[12]	33[12]	8[12]	-35[12]	...	...	...	...
Gabon	3,654	3,220	0.8	3.8	-3.0	45	20	29	48	-41	18	14	35	34
Gambia, The	229	260	3.0	3.3	-0.3	81[20]	17[20]	21[20]	50[20]	-70[20]	16	10	74	
Gaza Strip	270	430	...	3.3	...	152[12]	14[12]	34[12]	47[12]	-148[12]				
Georgia	...	...	...	0.7	...	80[2]	11[2]	19[2]	-1[2]					
Germany[24]	1,411,346	22,730	2.2	0.2	2.0	54	19	21	35	-28	10	12	52	25
Ghana	5,824	390	2.8	2.6	0.2	89	10	10	17	-26	9[7]	57	86[7]	
Gibraltar	280[5]	10,080[5]	...	0.4	...									
Greece	60,245	6,000	1.2	0.5	0.7	69	22	20	24	-32	11	9	40	39
Greenland	500[1]	9,000[1]	...	1.0	...									
Grenada	199	2,120	5.8	0.6	5.2	71	19	33	50	-73	...	...	...	...
Guadeloupe	1,170[20]	3,200[20]	...	1.8	...	92[12]	35[12]	21[12]	8[12]	-56[12]				
Guam	1,000	7,000	...	2.3	...									
Guatemala	8,309	900	0.7	2.8	-2.1	84	8	14	17	-22				
Guernsey[25]	1,431	23,020	5.4	1.2	4.2									
Guinea	2,756	480	...	2.4	...	76[20]	9[20]	18[20]	33[20]	-35[20]	12[20]		88[20]	
Guinea-Bissau	176	180	3.7	2.1	1.6	93[1]	12[1]	29[1]	13[1]	-47[1]	13[20]		87[20]	
Guyana	293	370	-2.7	0.0	-2.7	63[1]	32[1]	25[1]	82[1]	-103[1]	15[20]	4[20]	81[20]	
Haiti	2,400	370	-0.4	1.9	-2.3	88	11	15	19	-33	...	...	...	
Honduras	3,020	590	2.2	3.3	-1.1	74	16	13	21	-24	11	3	43	42
Hong Kong	66,666	11,540	7.0	1.2	5.8	58	7	27	136	-128	5[1]	11	47[1]	48[1,11]
Hungary	63,432	6,120	1.3	-0.3	1.4	64	11	21	44	-40	11[1]	9[1]	49[1]	29[1]
Iceland	5,456	21,150	2.4	1.1	1.3	60	19	19	37	-34	20	11	51	15
India	294,816	350	5.4	2.2	3.2	65	13	23	7	-8	11[1]	14[1]	75[1]	
Indonesia	101,151	560	6.3	2.0	4.3	53	9	34	26	-23	7	5	88	
Iran	139,120	2,450	2.7	3.7	-1.0	63[1]	13[1]	19[1]	3[1]	-3[1]	2[1]	9[1]	89[1]	
Iraq	35,000[5]	1,940[5]	...	3.1	...	53	30	22	22	-28	2[1]	9[1]	33[1]	56[1]
Ireland	33,467	9,550	1.4	0.3	1.1	57	15	18	67	-57	12	10	50	28
Isle of Man	490[1]	7,570[1]	...	0.0	...									
Israel	50,866	10,970	3.2	2.0	1.2	59	29	16	34	-38	15	15	49	20
Italy	970,619	16,850	2.4	0.2	2.2	62	17	21	19	-20	8	12	45	35
Jamaica	3,606	1,510	0.7	1.2	-0.5	60	14	29	47	-51	15	8	44	34
Japan	3,140,948	25,430	4.1	0.6	3.5	56	9	32	15	-12	7	15	54	24
Jersey	2,693	32,330	...	1.0	...									
Jordan	3,924	1,240	-0.4	3.8	-4.2	79	22	18	53	-71	16[20]	8[20]	42[20]	35[20]
Kazakhstan	...	...	...	1.1	...	...	...	...	...	...	...	...	...	...
Kenya	8,958	370	4.2	4.1	0.1	61	19	25	23	-29	14	11	37	50[11]
Kiribati	54	760	3.6	2.4	1.2	70	45	31	22	-70	12[12]	12[12]	52[12]	25[12]
Korea, North	21,000[5]	990[5]	...	1.8	...	...	...	...	...	...	...	...	...	...
Korea, South	231,132	5,400	10.1	1.2	8.9	53	10	34	34	-31	11	10	44	35
Kuwait	33,089[5]	16,160[5]	2.2	4.6	-2.4	47	24	20	55	-45	—	7[9]	31[9]	62[9]
Kyrgyzstan	...	...	...	1.9	...	61	20	40	-22-		—	16	50	34
Laos	848	200	3.7	2.4	1.3	...								
Latvia	...	...	...	0.5	...									
Lebanon	1,800[9]	690[9]	...	0.1	...	110	44	10	32	-96	2[16]		98[16]	
Lesotho	832	470	1.8	2.6	-0.8	126	21	50	20	-117	22		78	
Liberia	1,030[20]	440[20]	...	3.4	...	63[1]	12[1]	10[1]	39[1]	-28[1]	4[20]		96[20]	
Libya	23,333[5]	5,310[5]	-5.4	3.3	-8.7	39[20]	33[20]	24[20]	35[20]	-31[20]	3[9]	6[9]	36[9]	55[9]
Liechtenstein	580[20]	21,000[20]	...	1.2	...	...	...	...						
Lithuania	...	...	...	0.8	...	54	20	34	-8-					
Luxembourg	10,875	28,770	4.3	0.4	3.9	55	16	26	103	-101	14	11	61	14
Macau	3,690[10]	8,010[10]	...	6.0	...	34	8	19	84	-45	...	...	...	...
Macedonia	...	...	...	0.6	...									
Madagascar	2,710	230	0.5	3.2	-2.7	73	13	14	14	-14	13[20]		87[20]	
Malawi	1,662	200	3.3	3.7	-0.4	84	16	15	18	-33	10		90	
Malaysia	41,524	2,340	5.1	2.6	2.5	52	14	30	74	-70	13		87	
Maldives	96	440	10.0	3.3	6.7	59[1]	4[1]	28[1]	-91-		...	...	...	...
Mali	2,292	270	3.8	1.8	2.0	83	11	22	17	-34	8[20]		92[20]	
Malta	2,342	6,630	3.1	0.9	2.2	64	18	29	81	-92	11	5	43	41
Marshall Islands	63[5,10]	1,500[5,10]	...	4.2	...						10[16]	4[16]	51[16]	36[16]
Martinique	1,429[20]	4,100[20]	...	1.0	...	83[12]	32[12]	18[12]	11[12]	-44[12]	...	...	...	...
Mauritania	987	500	0.6	3.0	-2.4	75[20]	21[20]	21[20]	59[20]	-76[20]	13[20]		87[20]	
Mauritius	2,422	2,250	6.4	1.0	5.4	66	12	29	67	-75	16	11	39	44[11]
Mayotte	...	...	...	4.7	...									
Mexico	214,500	2,490	1.1	1.6	-0.5	68	8	23	16	-15	9	11	25	55
Micronesia	99[5]	980[5]	...	3.4	...	...	...	...	...	...	...	...	...	...
Moldova	...	...	...	0.9	...									
Monaco	...	...	...	1.2	...									
Mongolia	1,352[1]	660[1]	...	2.4	...									
Morocco	23,788	950	4.3	2.7	1.6	64	16	24	23	-28	15[20]		85[20]	
Mozambique	1,208	80	-1.5	1.6	-3.1	98	18	32	21	-69	6[20]		94[20]	
Myanmar (Burma)	16,330[34]	400[34]	...	2.1	...	89[1]		13[1]	3[1]	-5[1]	8[9]	9[20]	38[20]	44[20]
Namibia	1,511[5]	1,190[5]	...	2.7	...	56	28	17	55	-56	13	4	44	38
Nauru	90[5]	10,000[5]	...	1.6	...	...	...	...	...	...	...	...	...	...
Nepal	3,289	170	4.5	2.6	1.9	82	11	20	13	-25	6[20]	4[20]	90[20]	

Column groupings: **origin of gross domestic product (GDP) by economic sector, 1989 (%)** — primary (agriculture, mining); secondary (manufacturing, construction, public utilities); tertiary (transp./communications, trade, financial svcs., other svcs., govt.). **avg. annual growth rate of real GDP (%)** — 1975–1985, 1985–1990. **balance of payments, 1991 (current external transactions; '000,000 U.S.$)** — net transfers (goods-merchandise, invisibles), current balance of payments. **tourist trade, 1990 ('000,000 U.S.$)** — receipts from foreign nationals, expenditures by nationals abroad.

agriculture	mining	manufacturing	construction	public utilities	transp., communications	trade	financial svcs.	other svcs.	govt.	1975–1985	1985–1990	goods-merchandise	invisibles	current balance of payments	receipts from foreign nationals	expenditures by nationals abroad	country
20	[13]	21[13]	5	4	10	25		4	11	8.0	5.0	−6,699[6]	6,883[6]	184[6]	1,994	166	Egypt
12	—	18	3	2	4	34	8	10	8	−0.4	1.9	−663[5]	293[5]	−370[5]	69	104	El Salvador
54	[13]	1[13]	6	3	2	8	26			−6.0	1.4[14]	−11[5]	−8[5]	−19[5]	...	...	Equatorial Guinea
26[2]	3	44[2,3]	12[2]	3	7[2]	1[2]	11[2]			4.2[2]	1.0[2]	...	...	...	...	...	Estonia
41	—	12	4	1	7	10	4	7	11	1.1	5.5[14]	−362[5]	218[5]	−144[5]	25	10	Ethiopia
5	1	19	7	2	8	15	19	5	22	2.5	1.4	4[5]	−93[5]	−89[5]	...	...	Faeroe Islands
19	7[8]	9	4	8	10	21	28			1.4	3.7	−97[6]	104[6]	7[6]	230	32	Fiji
6	—	23	10	2	8	12	18	6	17	2.9	3.4	768[6]	−7,450[6]	−6,682[6]	1,169	2.765	Finland
6	[13]	19[13]	5	2	6	14	6	23	16	2.3	3.1	−10,139	3,991	−6,148	20,187	12,424	France
...	...	...	...	...	...	...	...	...	...			−653[6]			...	...	French Guiana
5[6]	[13]	7[6,13]	6[6]	2[6]	...	23[6]	...	29[6]	29[6]	5.2	5.2[14]	−817[6]	...	...	142	...	French Polynesia
10	31	6	5	2	8	12	4	11	7	−2.1	...	1,711[6]	−1,487[6]	224[6]	4	143	Gabon
31	—	6	4	—	10	21	6	2	10	1.8	3.8[14]	−30[6]	64[6]	34[6]	26	8	Gambia, The
22[12]	[13]	13[12,13]	22[12]	23	43[12,23]					2.8	...	−235[20]	219[20]	−16[20]	6[20]	10[20]	Gaza Strip
28[2]	3	40[2,3]	14[2]	3	4[2]	5[2]	8[2]			6.1[2]	−4.8[2]	...	...	...	...	...	Georgia
2[6]	3[6]	32[6]	6[6]	...	6[6]	9[6]	12[6]	17[6]	11[6]	2.2	3.1	23,060	−43,710	−20,650	10,683	29,836	Germany[24]
50	4[8]	11	2	8	5	25	11			0.3	4.8	−308	79	−229	82	13	Ghana
...	...	...	...	...	...	...	...	...	...			−279[6]	...	...	112	...	Gibraltar
17	2	17	6	2	8	16		8	18	2.8	1.7	−10,178[6]	6,641[6]	−3,537[6]	2,575	1,088	Greece
...	...	...	...	...	...	...	...	...	...			15[6]			...	...	Greenland
20	—	6	11	3	15	20	11	3	17	4.9	5.5	−80[6]	52[6]	−28[6]	38	7	Grenada
...	...	...	...	...	...	...	...	...	...	2.3	...	−1,550[6]	...	...	231	...	Guadeloupe
...	...	...	...	...	...	...	...	...	...	...	...	...	...	...	936	589	Guam
28	...	15	2	2	7	25	9	6	7	2.2	3.0	−358[5]	−9[5]	−367[5]	185	139	Guatemala
...	...	...	...	...	...	...	...	...	...			...	...	151[5]	...	...	Guernsey[25]
28[6]	24[6]	4[6]	6[6]	16	4[6]	22[6]	11[6]			2.9	4.2[4]	177[6]	...	...	...	...	Guinea
46[1]	—	7[1]	6[1]	11	4[1]	24[1]	8[1]			1.7	...	−37[1]	...	...	...	...	Guinea-Bissau
33	2	7[20]	6	20	5	5	5	2	11	−3.9	−2.7	5[9]	−102[9]	−97[9]	30	...	Guyana
33	2	15	6	1	2	17	6	3	12	2.3	0.6	−138	128	−10	75	32	Haiti
21	2	16	5	3	7	13	16	13	6	4.1	3.1	3[5]	−305[5]	−302[5]	29	38	Honduras
—		17	5	2	9	23	29	14		8.9	7.8	−1,685	...	...	5,032	...	Hong Kong
21	[13]	35[13]	7	2	10	9	16			0.0	1.7	187	83	270	1,000	600	Hungary
17[6]	—	14[6]	9[6]	5[6]	8	11[6]	17[6]	7[6]	17[6]	4.1	2.7	80[6]	−240[6]	−160[6]	122	218	Iceland
33	2	18	6	2	7	13	8	6	6	4.5	6.2	−6,110[6]	−716[6]	−6,826[6]	1,437	425	India
23	13	18	5	1	5	17	17			6.2	6.3	4,667	−9,152	−4,485	1,879	886	Indonesia
23[1]	5[1]	7[1]	6[1]	1[1]	6[1]	25[1]	1[1]	14[1]	11[1]	1.4	−4.8[4]	101[1]	−1,969[1]	−1,868[1]	62	396	Iran
16	23[8]	12	6	8	7	11	29			2.9	5.8[4]	5,733[5]	...	...	55	...	Iraq
12[1]	26	37[1,26]	26	26	18[1]		27[1]		6[1]	3.4	4.4	3,971[6]	−3,050[6]	921[6]	1,447	1,159	Ireland
3[9]	—	16[9]	10[9]	3[9]	11[9]	12[9]	30[9]	24[9]	8[9]	−1.7	...	...	...	...	36[12]	...	Isle of Man
3	13	19[13]	5	3	9	12	23	4	24	2.6	3.8	−4,566	3,702	−864	1,382	1,485	Israel
4	3	20	5	5	6	18	11	3	12	3.2	3.0	723[6]	−13,456[6]	−12,733[6]	19,738	13,826	Italy
5	10	20	12	3	7	21	14	5	8	−1.6	3.5	−468[6]	205[6]	−263[6]	740	54	Jamaica
3	—	29	10	3	7	13[27]	17	15[27]	8	4.4	4.7	103,090	−30,180	72,910	3,578	24,928	Japan
5	—	2			93					...	...	...	...	...	526	...	Jersey
8	7[8]	10	5	8	9	14	48			8.6	0.3	−773[5]	1,158[5]	385[5]	500	419	Jordan
34[2]	3	30[2,3]	19[2]	3	9[2]	5[2]	32[2]			2.7[2]	2.1[2]	...	...	...	...	...	Kazakhstan
27	—	10	6	1	6	10	14	1	13	4.7	5.9[14]	−998[5]	521[6]	−477[6]	443	38	Kenya
49	3[8]	1	4	8	11	9	24			−11.5	0.9[4]	−16[1]	221	6[1]	2	...	Kiribati
...	...	...	...	...	...	...	...	...	...	...	...	−800[6]	...	...	...	...	Korea, North
10	1	31	10	2	7	12	14	7	7	7.7	10.2	−2,004[6]	−168[6]	−2,172[6]	3,559	3,166	Korea, South
1	41	14	2	−1	4	8	12	19		−2.7	3.8[4]	5,872[5]	3,717[5]	9,589[5]	80	2,315	Kuwait
42[2]	3	33[2,3]	12[2]	3	4[2]		9[2]			4.0[2]	5.0[2,28]	...	...	...	...	...	Kyrgyzstan
59[1]	—	7[1]	10[1]	2[1]	5[1]	8[1]	2[1]	6[1]		...	...	−162[5]	...	...	...	...	Laos
24[2]	3	45[2,3]	10[2]	3	7[2]	14[2]				3.5[2]	3.5[2]	...	...	...	...	...	Latvia
9	5[8]	13	3	8	4	28	38			−9.4	−22.5[14]	−3,223	...	...	...	...	Lebanon
15	—	12	14	1	4	8	27			4.7	6.2[14]	−718	782	64	9	15	Lesotho
35[20]	14[20]	7[20]	3[20]	2[20]	8[20]	6[20]	12[20]	3[20]	12[20]	0.0	1.9[4]	...	−181[20]	−118[20]	6[12]	...	Liberia
5	28	8	13	2	6	7	9	1	21	−3.1	...	3,780[6]	−1,550[6]	2,230[6]	6	424	Libya
...	...	...	...	...	...	...	...	...	...	...	...	454[5]	...	...	...	...	Liechtenstein
32[2]	3	36[2,3]	13[2]	3	5[2]	14[2]				...	3.9[2]	...	...	...	...	...	Lithuania
2	—	28	6	2	6	16	14	15	13	2.4	4.3	15	15	15	290	...	Luxembourg
...	...	...	...	...	...	...	3[17]	...	...		8.0	161[6]	...	...	139	708	Macau
17[17]	13	55[13,17]	5[17]	1[17]	6[17]	13[17]	3[17]			3.1[17]	1.0[14,17]	...	...	...	...	...	Macedonia
42[20]	—	12[20]	4[20]	1[20]	8[20]	13[20]	8[20]		12[20]	0.2	...	−15	−127[5]	−128[5]	43	34	Madagascar
37	—	12	4	2	6	11	10	4	15	3.1	3.1	44[1]	−97[1]	−53[1]	8	3	Malawi
20	10	25	3	2	7	11	9	2	12	6.8	6.7	−262	−4,099	−4,361	1,657	4,473	Malaysia
25	2	6[18]	8	18	5	17	4	23	9	11.5[29]	9.3	−59[6]	61[6]	2[6]	85	19	Maldives
41[1]	7[1]	7[1]	4[1]	1[1]	4[1]	20[1]	5[1]		7[1]	1.8	7.6[30]	−88[6]	−6[6]	−94[6]	32	67	Mali
4	—	27	4[31]	3	6	14	13	9	23[32]	6.5	6.1[14]	−461[5]	458[5]	−3[5]	496	134	Malta
—	...	...	...	7[33]	6[33]	84[33]	2[33]					...	...	...	...	...	Marshall Islands
...	...	12[1]	6[1]		5[1]	12[1]		5	15	3.9	...	−1,464[6]	...	...	240	...	Martinique
29[1]	7[1]	12[1]	...	...	5[1]	12[1]	4	10	15	2.0	4.0[30]	995	−1,185	−195	15	31	Mauritania
12	—	25	6	2	11	18	12	4	10	4.2	7.6	−271[6]	151[6]	−120[6]	264	94	Mauritius
...	...	...	...	...	...	...	...	...	...	...	...	−53[6]	...	...	...	...	Mayotte
8	3	25	4	1	8	27	11	10	6	4.1	1.3	−11,063	−2,220	−13,283	5,324	5,379	Mexico
...	...	...	...	...	...	...	...	...	...	...	...	...	...	...	...	...	Micronesia
40[2]	[13]	34[2,13]	10[2]	2[2]	4[2]	10[2]	12[2]			3.8[2]	3.6[2]	...	...	...	...	...	Moldova
...	...	...	...	...	...	...	...	...	...	...	...	...	...	...	...	...	Monaco
16	[13]	27[13]	6	...	8	22	12			6.1[2]	...	−41[1]	...	...	...	...	Mongolia
16	3	18	5	7	7	13	3	10	12	3.9	4.5[14]	−2,071[6]	1,871[6]	−200[6]	1,259	184	Morocco
37[6]	[13]	23[6,13]	13[6]	...	10[6]	...	17[6]			−4.0	3.1[4]	−648[6]	...	...	...	...	Mozambique
51	1	9	2	1	4	23	1	9		5.8	−2.0	−290[12]	−412	−294[12]	5	1	Myanmar (Burma)
11	29	5	3	2	6	12	1	7	20	0.0	2.0[14]	795	−1,165	−375	...	...	Namibia
...	...	...	...	...	...	...	...	...	...	...	...	...	...	...	...	...	Nauru
52	—	6	9	1	5	4	7	8		3.8	4.6	−449[6]	160[6]	−289[6]	57	45	Nepal

National product and accounts   (continued)

country	gross national product (GNP) nominal, 1990 ('000,000 U.S.$)	per capita, 1990 (U.S.$)	average annual growth rates, 1980–90 real GNP (%)	popu-lation (%)	real GNP per capita (%)	gross domestic product (GDP) by type of expenditure, 1989 (%) consumption private	govern-ment	gross domestic invest-ment	foreign trade exports	imports	cost components of gross domestic product (GDP), 1989 (%) indirect taxes net of subsidies	consump-tion of fixed capital	compen-sation of employ-ees	net operating surplus
Netherlands, The	258,804	17,330	1.9	0.6	1.3	59	15	21	58	−54	10	11	52	28
Netherlands Antilles	1,370[5]	7,060[5]	...	1.1	...	...	...	...	...	...	...	...	...	...
New Caledonia	1,606[20]	10,140[20]	...	1.8	...	45	31	20	32	−29	5[1]	9[1]	47[1]	39[1]
New Zealand	43,185	12,680	1.4	0.8	0.6	61	17	19	29	−27	15	8	44	33
Nicaragua	1,661[1]	460[1]	...	3.4	...	55[20]	36[20]	10[20]	13[20]	−15[20]	...	...	...	...
Niger	2,365	310	−1.3	3.4	−4.7	73	17	13	24	−28	7[7]	9[7]	18[7]	66[7]
Nigeria	31,285	270	0.2	3.2	−3.4	62	6	10	45	−22	4[7]	2[7]	29[7]	65[7]
Northern Mariana Is.	256[10, 12]	12,360[10, 12]	...	9.8	...	...	...	...	...	...	...	...	...	...
Norway	98,079	23,120	3.1	0.4	2.7	50	21	24	42	−38	11	16	53	20
Oman	7,756[5]	5,220[5]	7.1	4.3	2.8	44	32	14	41	−32	3[6]	11	34[1]	66[1, 11, 36]
Pakistan	42,649	380	6.3	3.7	2.6	73	15	18	14	−21	11	6	—83—	
Palau	32[10, 12]	2,290[10, 12]	...	2.3	...	...	...	...	...	...	5[12]	5[12]	62[12]	28[12]
Panama	4,414	1,830	0.1	2.1	−2.0	67	22	2	34	−25	7	9	51	33
Papua New Guinea	3,372	860	1.9	2.2	−0.3	64	25	23	41	−53	10	10	42	37
Paraguay	4,796	1,110	1.9	3.1	−1.2	76	7	24	34	−40	6	10	27	57
Peru	25,149	1,160	0.2	2.6	−2.4	68	10	20	13	−11	4	7	24	64
Philippines	43,954	730	0.9	2.4	−1.5	73	9	18	25	−26	8	9	—83—	
Poland	165,870	4,350	−0.5	0.7	−1.2	57[1]	8[1]	33[1]	23[1]	−20[1]	...	...	44	42[11]
Portugal	50,692	4,890	3.0	0.6	2.4	64	16	30	37	−46	14	11	43	46
Puerto Rico	21,346	6,470	2.3	1.2	1.1	68	14	17	72	−71	5	6	43	46
Qatar	6,962	15,860	−6.6	6.7	−13.3	32[20]	44[20]	14[20]	41[20]	−32[20]	1[12]	—99[12]—		
Réunion	3,400[20]	5,990[20]	...	1.7	...	83[1]	33[1]	23[1]	5[1]	−43[1]	10	11	56	34[11]
Romania	73,700	3,180	...	0.4	...	64	4	27	—6—		20	14	66	
Russia	2,660,000[39]	9,190[39]	...	0.7	...	...	...	...	...	...	...	...	...	...
Rwanda	2,214	310	1.0	3.1	−2.1	79	15	16	9	−18	9[1]	7[1]	25[1]	59[1]
St. Kitts	133	3,330	4.8	−0.1	4.9	78	22	32	56	−87	14[7]	—86[7]—		
St. Lucia	286	1,900	6.3	2.1	4.2	62[16]	25[16]	35[16]	64[16]	−86[16]	...	...	...	...
St. Vincent	184	1,610	6.9	1.3	5.6	61	20	30	66	−77	...	...	...	...
San Marino	393[10]	17,000[10]	...	0.8	...	...	...	...	...	...	...	...	...	...
São Tomé and Príncipe	47	380	−1.5	2.5	−4.0	72[1]	21[1]	16[1]	58[1]	−67[1]	...	...	...	...
Saudi Arabia	86,898[5]	6,020[5]	−0.8	4.2	−5.0	49	33	22	37	−41	−0.2[1]	11	46[1]	54[1, 11]
Senegal	5,260	710	3.0	2.6	0.4	68	16	20	29	−33	18[20]	—82[20]—		
Seychelles	318	4,670	3.2	1.0	2.2	65	27	22	48	−62	23[1]	7[1]	36[1]	34[1]
Sierra Leone	981	240	0.9	2.2	−1.3	80	6	10	19	−16	5[12]	7[12]	16[12]	72[12]
Singapore	33,512	12,310	7.0	1.7	5.3	47	11	35	—8—		...	...	...	...
Slovenia	...	...	...	0.4	...	...	...	...	...	...	...	...	...	...
Solomon Islands	187	580	7.0	3.3	3.7	69	31	33	52	−85	14[20]	7[20]	48[20]	32[20]
Somalia	946	150	1.1	3.4	−2.3	95	11	40	8	−55	3[20]	—97[20]—		
South Africa	90,410	2,520	1.5	2.3	−0.8	56	19	21	29	−23	11	17	51	21
Bophuthatswana	1,736[16, 42]	950[16, 42]	...	...	...	...	...	...	...	...	...	...	...	...
Ciskei	377[9]	490[9]	...	...	...	...	...	...	...	...	...	...	...	...
Transkei	1,471[16, 42]	470[16, 42]	...	...	...	...	...	...	...	...	...	...	...	...
Venda	201[16, 42]	490[16, 42]	...	...	...	...	...	...	...	...	...	...	...	...
Spain	429,404	10,920	3.1	0.6	2.5	63	14	26	19	−22	8	11	45	35
Sri Lanka	7,971	470	3.9	1.4	2.5	74	14	21	28	−37	14	6	44	35
Sudan, The	10,094[1]	420[1]	...	3.8	...	81	10	15	9	−15	8[7]	11[7]	34[7]	47[7]
Suriname	1,365	3,050	−2.6	1.5	−4.1	23	32	23	41	−30	8[1]	8[1]	55[1]	29[1]
Swaziland	645	820	4.5	3.3	1.2	73	31	19	74	−97	15[20]	7[20]	45[20]	34[20]
Sweden	202,498	23,680	2.1	0.3	1.8	52	26	21	32	−32	12	11	60	17
Switzerland	219,337	32,790	2.3	0.6	1.7	58	13	30	38	−38	6	11	62	21
Syria	12,404	990	1.4	3.4	−2.0	57	16	15	36	−24	3	4	—93—	
Taiwan	160,897	7,930	8.0	1.4	6.6	53	16	23	50	−43	11	8	51	29
Tajikistan	...	...	...	2.9	...	...	...	...	...	...	...	...	...	...
Tanzania	2,779	120	2.3	2.8	−0.5	95	10	25	18	−49	13	3	10	74
Thailand	79,044	1,420	7.6	2.0	5.6	59	10	31	36	−39	13	9	27	51
Togo	1,474	410	1.8	2.9	−1.1	73	12	23	35	−42	21[20]	—79[20]—		
Tonga	100	1,010	2.1	0.5	1.6	96[7]	18[7]	28[7]	—41[7]—		11[7]	3[7]	37[7]	48[7]
Trinidad and Tobago	4,458	3,470	−4.3	1.4	−5.7	58	20	17	39	−34	5	11	56	27
Tunisia	11,592	1,420	3.4	2.4	1.0	65	17	23	43	−47	12	11	—78—	
Turkey	91,742	1,630	5.5	2.4	3.1	61	16	23	23	−23	9	6	—85—	
Turkmenistan	...	...	...	2.5	...	...	...	...	...	...	...	...	...	...
Tuvalu	4.6[5]	530[5]	...	1.9	...	...	...	...	...	...	...	...	...	...
Uganda	3,814	220	4.1	3.0	1.1	95	10	24	18	−49	65[12]	—35[12]—		
Ukraine	...	...	...	0.4	...	...	...	...	...	...	...	...	...	...
United Arab Emirates	31,613	19,860	−3.1	6.5	−9.6	42	20	23	59	−45	−2	15	26	60
United Kingdom	923,959	16,070	2.7	0.2	2.5	64	20	20	24	−28	14	11	56	19
United States	5,445,825	21,700	3.2	0.9	2.3	67	18	17	9	−11	8	12	60	20
Uruguay	7,929	2,560	−0.3	0.6	−0.9	72	13	9	24	−18	15	3	—82—	
Uzbekistan	...	...	...	2.5	...	...	...	...	...	...	...	...	...	...
Vanuatu	167	1,060	2.4	2.5	−0.1	62	29	36	36	−63	22[20]	11	42[20]	35[11, 20]
Venezuela	50,574	2,560	0.7	2.5	−1.8	65	10	13	34	−21	3	7	34	55
Vietnam	14,200[5]	210[5]	...	2.1	...	...	...	...	...	...	...	...	...	...
Virgin Islands (U.S.)	1,246[10, 20]	11,740[10, 20]	2.3	0.5	1.8	...	...	...	...	...	...	...	...	...
West Bank	1,000[1]	1,000[1]	...	2.6	...	97[12]	9[12]	31[12]	21[12]	−57[12]	...	...	...	...
Western Sahara	...	...	...	2.5	...	...	...	...	...	...	...	...	...	...
Western Samoa	121	730	2.0	0.2	1.8	...	...	...	...	...	...	...	...	...
Yemen	7,203[5]	640[5]	...	2.7	...	82	22	15	14	−33	9	3	—88—	
Yugoslavia	124,344[45]	5,220[45]	−0.2[45]	0.7[45]	−0.9[45]	47[45]	14[45]	43[45]	25[45]	−29[45]	5[45]	12[45]	—83[45]—	
Zaire	8,117	230	1.6	2.2	−0.6	52	20	24	50	−45	...	...	...	...
Zambia	3,391	420	0.7	3.9	−3.2	77	14	9	29	−29	5[1]	14[1]	30[1]	50[1]
Zimbabwe	6,313	640	2.6	2.8	−0.2	69	17	17	35	−29	15	11	52[20]	37[11, 20]

[1]1988. [2]Net material product. [3]Manufacturing includes mining and public utilities. [4]1985–88. [5]1989. [6]1990. [7]1983. [8]Mining includes public utilities. [9]1985. [10]GDP. [11]Net operating surplus includes consumption of fixed capital. [12]1986. [13]Manufacturing includes mining. [14]1985–89. [15]Data refer to the Belgium-Luxembourg Economic Union (BLEU). [16]1984. [17]Social product. [18]Manufacturing includes public utilities. [19]Activities in the material sphere not elsewhere specified. [20]1987. [21]National income. [22]Global social product. [23]Tertiary sector includes public utilities. [24]Data refer to former West Germany only, except balance of payments. [25]Excludes Alderney and Sark. [26]Manufacturing includes mining, construction, and public utilities. [27]Services includes

agri-culture	mining	manu-facturing	con-struction	public utilities	transp., communications	trade	financial svcs.	other svcs.	govt.	1975–1985	1985–1990	goods-merchandise	invisibles	current balance of payments	receipts from foreign nationals	expenditures by nationals abroad	country
4	3	20	6	2	7	13	18	11	11	1.8	2.7	11,972	-2,766	9,206	3,615	7,340	Netherlands, The
19	—	13[9]	10[9]	3[9]	12[9]	18[9]	16[9]	6[9]	24[9]	1.9[35]	...	-762[5]	772[5]	10[5]	460	...	Netherlands Antilles
2	26[8]	5	5	8	4	21	—37—			-0.2	...	-409[6]	...	...	150	...	New Caledonia
9	1	18	3	2	7	17	23	—13—		1.6	0.3	831[6]	-2,222[6]	-1,391[6]	1,072	1,335	New Zealand
29	1	16	3	1	5	30	6	4	5	-1.8	-4.0	-483[1]	-232[1]	-715[1]	12	2	Nicaragua
34	10[8]	8	5	[8]	4	15	—24—			1.7	...	-58[5]	-53[5]	-111[5]	15	32	Niger
40	14	10	1	—	4	18	4	3	6	-0.7	5.6	4,441	-3,238	1,203	25	57	Nigeria
...	...	...	...	...	...	...	...	...	...						300	...	Northern Mariana Is.
3	11	15	5	4	8	12	9	10	16	4.0	1.5	8,955	-3,934	5,021	1,506	3,413	Norway
4	46	4	3	1	3	12	9	2	17	13.6	1.7[4]	2,969[6]	-1,874[6]	1,095[6]	69	47	Oman
27	1	16	4	3	7	18	7	7	10	6.4	6.0	-2,699[6]	1,121[6]	-1,578[6]	156	429	Pakistan
16[9]	—	11[9]	1[9]	9	3[9]	19[9]	4[9]	29	36[9]	0.2[37]		-279[9]	...	...	...	...	Palau
11	—	8	2	5	20	12	21	9	17	4.6	-1.4	-938	962	24	167	99	Panama
28	12	11	5	2	5	10[27]	6	—18[27]—		1.2	1.2	-23[5]	-332[5]	-355[5]	28	42	Papua New Guinea
30	—	17	6	2	4	27	2	—12—		6.3	3.9	39[6]	52[6]	91[6]	112	105	Paraguay
8	2	21	7	1	4	24	13	—21—		0.6	-1.8	391[6]	-1,397[6]	-674[6]	353	571	Peru
23	2	25	4	2	5	19	7	—12—		2.8	5.1	-3,211	2,177	-1,034	1,306	111	Philippines
15[2]	13	50[2,13]	9[2]	1[2]	5[2]	18[2]	—12,19—			-0.2	-1.4	1,410[6]	-576[6]	834[6]	266	220	Poland
6	13	29[13]	6	3	6	20	8	8	13	3.1	4.7	-7,752	8,495	743	3,556	867	Portugal
2	31	42	2[31,38]	7[38]	13	12	10	13	3.3	5.5	1,730	-5,131	-3,401	1,367	647	Puerto Rico
1	29	13	5	2	.3	6	10	—34—		0.0	...	1,326[5]	...	...	...	...	Qatar
7	28	9	6	8	5	15	—54—			5.1	...	-1,896[6]	...	...	140	...	Réunion
15[2]	3	59[2,3]	7[2]	3	72	—11[2,19]—				-0.1	-2.2	-1,220	36	-1,184	106	103	Romania
19[2]	3	45[2,3]	13[2]	2	6[2]	14[2]	—3[2]—			3.9[2]	1.2[2]	...	...	...	270[39]	...	Russia
38	1[8]	15	7	8	7	13	—17—			5.0	0.4[4]	-125[6]	176	-108[6]	10	23	Rwanda
9	—	16	12	1	14	21	12	4	18	2.9	6.5	-79[6]	29[6]	-50[6]	63	4	St. Kitts
12	4[8]	7	7	8	8	20	—31—			4.6	4.7[40]	-162	81	-81	154	21	St. Lucia
17	—	9	9	7	19	13	10	2	18	6.3	7.1[40]	-45	36	-9	54	5	St. Vincent
...	...	...	...	...	...	...	...	...	...						...	...	San Marino
26[20]	...	10[20]	10[20]	3[20]	13[20]	10[20]	—29[20]—			1.8		-6[6]	-2[6]	-8[6]	1	2	São Tomé and Príncipe
7	28	8	10	—	7	8	7	13	9	3.7	2.9[14]	22,793[6]	-26,900[6]	-4,107[6]	1,884	2,000[20]	Saudi Arabia
23	3[8]	17	7	8	10	15	—24—			2.0	4.3[4]	-264[6]	139[6]	-125[6]	152	105	Senegal
4[6]	13	9[6,13]	4[6]	2[6]	44[6]	11[6]	9[6]	3[6]	14[6]	2.5	2.3[4]	-128	132	4	120	20	Seychelles
40	10[8]	6	2	8	9	20	—15—			1.4	2.4	-21[5]	2[5]	-19[5]	19	7	Sierra Leone
—	—	29	5	2	14	18	30	—10—		7.3	8.0	-4,218	8,426	4,208	4,362	1,381	Singapore
8[17]	13	53[13,17]	9[17]	1[17]	9[17]	18[17]	—3[17]—			3.0[17]	-0.4[14,17]	...	...	...	...	...	Slovenia
49[6]	—	3[6]	4[6]	1[6]	7[6]	9[6]	3[6]	—24[6]—		6.8	3.4[14]	-8	-29	-37	4	11	Solomon Islands
65[41]	—	4[41]	4[41]	1[41]	6[41]	9[41]	3[41]	2[41]	4[41]	1.4	3.2[4]	-279[5]	125[5]	-157[5]	8[12]	...	Somalia
5[6]	11[6]	26[6]	3[6]	5[6]	8[6]	13[6]	15[6]	1[6]	14[6]	2.6	1.6	6,267	-3,603	2,664	815	1065	South Africa
...	...	...	...	...	...	...	...	...	...								Bophuthatswana
8[16]	—	13[16]	10[16]	—	9[16]	3[16]	7[16]	—50[16]—									Ciskei
...	...	...	...	...	...	...	...	...	...								Transkei
...	...	...	...	...	...	...	...	...	...								Venda
5[1]	3	30[1,3]	9[1]	3	—60[1]—					1.7	4.5	-31,738	15,736	-16,002	18,593	4,254	Spain
23	1	17	7	2	10	18	6	2	8	5.3	3.4	-736	179	-557	125	79	Sri Lanka
36	1[3]	8[13]	5	2	—38—				12	-0.1	4.1[30]	-322[6]	-476[6]	-369[6]	5	15	Sudan, The
11[1]	4[1]	12[1]	6[1]	5[1]	8[1]	18[1]	19[1]	21	24[1]	0.8	1.5[14]	92[6]	-60[6]	32[6]	11	12	Suriname
21[20]	2[20]	24[20]	5[20]	1[20]	6[20]	9[20]	10[20]	3[20]	18[20]	3.6	4.2[4]	-75[6]	87[6]	12[6]	25	14	Swaziland
3	—	24	7	3	7	12	21	—27—		1.6	2.0	5,979	-9,222	-3,243	2,895	6,066	Sweden
4[9]	19	25[9]	8[9]	2[9]	7[9]	17[9]	10[9]	14[9]	9[9]	1.5	2.8	-6,377	12,868	6,491	6,839	5,989	Switzerland
24	12	9	4	—	11	22	4	2	11	4.1	2.1	2,159[6]	-332[6]	1,827[6]	244	190	Syria
5	—	36	5	3	6	15	17	6	10	8.6	8.9	15,690	-3,676	12,014	1,740	...	Taiwan
37[2]	3	27[2,3]	15[2]		—17[2]—					3.7[2]	1.8[2]	...	...	...	...	...	Tajikistan
51	—	8	1	1	6	13	—19—			2.0	3.9	-779[6]	353[6]	-426[6]	65	19	Tanzania
15	3	25	7	2	7	15	8	13	4	6.8	9.9	-6,751[6]	-531[6]	-7,282[6]	4,326	854	Thailand
34[1]	6[1]	8[1]	3[1]	3[1]	7[1]	23[1]	...	7[1]	8[1]	1.3	2.9[4]	-105[6]	5[6]	-100[6]	23	46	Togo
41[7]	—	5[7]	4[7]	7	6[7]	15[7]	6[7]	—22[7]—		6.6	...	-41	37	-4	9	1	Tonga
3	19	12	10	2	9	20	11	6	12	2.0	-1.9	988[6]	-558[6]	430[6]	95	122	Trinidad and Tobago
12	8	14	5	2	7	20	4	4	12	5.2	3.3	-874	683	-191	953	179	Tunisia
17	2	25	4	4	11	18	3	5	6	3.8	6.0	-7,326	7,598	272	3,308	520	Turkey
43[2]	3	23[2,3]	18[2]	3	6[2]	—9[2]—				1.9[2]	2.7[2]	...	...	...	...	...	Turkmenistan
11[9]	—	2[9]	10[9]	2[9]	1[9]	11[9]	—64[9]—			...		3[20]	...	...	...	...	Tuvalu
69	13	5[13]	2	—	4	12	5		—4	-1.4	5.3	-313[6]	50[6]	-263[6]	10	8	Uganda
28[2]	3	43[2,3]	10[2]	3	5[2]	12[2]	—2[2]—			3.4[2]	2.4[2,14]	...	...	...	...	...	Ukraine
2	38	9	10	2	5	11	12	2	12	6.6	-2.1[14]	7,469[1]	...	...	...	...	United Arab Emirates
1	5[8]	22	7	8	7	14	20	7	16	1.8	3.2	-17,990	8,544	-9,446	15,000	19,106	United Kingdom
2[1]	2[1]	20[1]	5[1]	3[1]	6[1]	16[1]	17[1]	18[1]	12[1]	3.2	2.7	-73,600	64,940	-8,660	40,579	38,671	United States
9	4[3]	19	3	2	6	10	14	12[43]	10	0.7	3.6	61	44	105	261	111	Uruguay
42[2]	3	26[2,3]	14[2]	3	5[2]	—12[2]—				4.4[2]	3.0[2,14]	...	...	...	...	...	Uzbekistan
19	—	5	6	2	8	32	—17—		12	5.1	1.7	-66[6]	74[6]	8[6]	25	1	Vanuatu
6	17	22	5	2	6	14	—19—		9	1.0	2.8	4,791	-3,128	1,663	359	945	Venezuela
42[2,20]	3	33[2,3,20]	32[2,20]	3	1[2,20]	19[2,20]	—32,19,20—			3.7[2]		-765[6]	...	...	85	...	Vietnam
...	...	...	...	...	...	...	...	...	...	-0.4	...	-1,312[20]	...	...	707	...	Virgin Islands (U.S.)
33[12]	13	8[12,13]	14[12]	23	—46[12,23]—					4.8	...	-391[20]	525[20]	134[20]	10[20]	46[20]	West Bank
...	...	...	...	...	...	...	...	...	...								Western Sahara
31[12]	4[12]	15[12]	2[12]	1[12]	6[12]	18[12]	10[12]	4[12]	9[12]	1.3		-105[6]	5[6]	-100[6]	20	2	Western Samoa
20	5	12	4	2	13	15	9	1	14	6.2[44]	7.1[30,44]	-1,117[5]	121[5]	-996[5]	20	81	Yemen
18[17]	13	46[13,17]	6[17]	1[17]	8[17]	16[17]	—3[17]—			3.2[17]	0.6[14,17]	512[45]	-1,673[45]	-1,161[45]	2,774[45]	149[45]	Yugoslavia
26[1]	21[1]	2[1]	2[1]	4[1]	1[1]	17[1]	—22[1]—			-0.1	...	600[6]	-1,243[6]	-643[6]	7	16	Zaire
14	12	35	1	1	5	18	4	—11—		0.2	1.5[4]	566[5]	-749[5]	-183[5]	6	98	Zambia
13	7	26	2	3	7	11	7	19	8	0.2	1.5	501[1]	-384[1]	117[1]	47	58	Zimbabwe

restaurants and hotels. [28]1978–90. [29]1976–85. [30]1985–87. [31]Construction includes mining. [32]Government includes public utilities. [33]1981. [34]1989–90. [35]Includes Aruba. [36]Net operating surplus includes indirect taxes net of subsidies. [37]1983–85. [38]Transportation and communications includes public utilities. [39]Data refer to former U.S.S.R. [40]1986–89. [41]1991. [42]At prices of 1978. [43]Services includes mining. [44]Former Yemen Arab Republic only. [45]Data refer to Yugoslavia as constituted prior to 1991.

Employment and labour

This table provides international comparisons of the world's national labour forces—giving their size; composition by demographic component and employment status; and structure by industry.

The table focuses on the concept of "economically active population," which the International Labour Organisation (ILO) defines as persons of all ages who are either employed or looking for work. In general, "economically active population" does not include students, persons occupied solely in domestic duties, retired persons, persons living entirely on their own means, and persons wholly dependent on others. Persons engaged in illegal economic activities—smugglers, prostitutes, drug dealers, bootleggers, black marketeers, and others—also fall outside the purview of the ILO definition. Countries differ markedly in their treatment, as part of the labour force, of such groups as members of the armed forces, inmates of institutions, the unemployed (both persons seeking their first job and those previously employed), seasonal and international migrant workers, and persons engaged in informal, subsistence, or part-time economic activities. Some countries include all or most of these groups among the economically active, while others may treat the same groups as inactive.

Three principal structural comparisons of the economically active total are given in the first part of the table: (1) participation rate, or the proportion of the economically active who possess some particular characteristic, is given for women and for those of working age (usually ages 15 to 64), (2) activity rate, the proportion of the total population who *are* economically active, is given for both sexes and as a total, and (3) employment status, usually (and here) grouped as employers, self-employed, employees, family workers (usually unpaid), and others.

Each of these measures indicates certain characteristics in a given national labour market; none should be interpreted in isolation, however, as the meaning of each is influenced by a variety of factors—demographic structure and change, social or religious customs, educational opportunity, sexual differentiation in employment patterns, degree of technological development, and the like. Participation and activity rates, for example, may be high in a particular country because it possesses an older population with few children, hence a higher proportion of working age, or because, despite a young population with many below working age, the economy attracts eligible immigrant workers, themselves almost exclusively of working age. At the same time, low activity and participation rates might be characteristic of a country having a young population with poor employment possibilities or of a country with a good job market distorted by the presence of large numbers of "guest" or contract workers who are not part of the domestic labour force. An illiterate woman in a strongly sex-differentiated labour force is likely to begin and end as a family or

Employment and labour

| country | year | economically active population | | | | | | | | | | distribution by economic sector | | | |
| | | total ('000) | participation rate (%) | | activity rate (%) | | | employment status (%) | | | | agriculture, forestry, fishing | | manufacturing; mining, quarrying; public utilities | |
			female	ages 15–64	total	male	female	employers, self-employed	employees	unpaid family workers	other	number ('000)	% of econ. active	number ('000)	% of econ. active
Afghanistan	1979	3,941	7.9	49.1	30.3	54.2	4.9	...	...	...	...	2,369	60.1	494	12.5
Albania	1989[3]	1,458	45.8	74.5[4]	45.6	48.0	43.1	...	...	...	...	799	54.8	279	19.1
Algeria	1987	5,341	9.2	44.3	23.6	42.4	4.4	16.8	61.7	2.6	18.9	725	13.6	622	11.6
American Samoa	1990	14.2	41.1	52.6[6]	30.4	34.8	25.7	2.1	92.6	0.2	5.1	0.3	2.3	4.8	33.7
Andorra	1989	25	45.6	74.3	55.1	...	...	...	...	...	...	0.3	1.2	2.7	11.0
Angola	1987	3,839	39.5	62.3[8]	41.9	51.6	32.5	...	...	...	...	2,741	71.4	384[9]	10.0[9]
Antigua and Barbuda	1985	32	40.1	56.2[11, 12]	42.6	53.3	32.9	12.3[13]	69.9[13]	0.6[13]	17.2[13]	2.1[14, 15]	9.0[14, 15]	2.1[14, 15]	9.1[14, 15]
Argentina	1990	12,305	27.9	59.6	38.1	55.4	21.0	25.1[16]	71.2[16]	3.3[16]	0.4[16]	1,201[16]	12.0[16]	2,136[16]	21.3[16]
Armenia	1990	2,044	49.4	79.9[18]	61.3	...	...	...	...	...	...	117	5.7	453	22.2
Aruba	1981	26	36.7	62.0	43.2	56.1	30.9	...	...	...	...	0.04[3]	0.2[3]	2.5[3]	10.6[3]
Australia	1990[20]	8,459	41.4	73.6	49.8	58.4	41.2	14.0	78.3	0.8	6.9	448	5.3	1,485	17.7
Austria	1990[20]	3,536	41.0	67.6	45.8	56.5	36.0	10.2	86.0	3.8	—	271	7.7	1,005	28.4
Azerbaijan	1990	3,242	42.6[21]	71.8[18]	45.4	...	...	...	...	...	...	...	...	...	...
Bahamas, The	1989	127	47.3	70.5[16]	51.2	55.5	47.1	76.5	11.1	0.3	12.1	5.0	3.9	6.1	4.8
Bahrain	1988	322	12.4	74.7	54.2	73.2	19.1	9.5[23]	85.9[23]	0.1[23]	4.6[23]	6	1.7	38	12.0
Bangladesh	1985–86	30,920	10.4	50.8	30.4	53.6	6.5	37.6	42.8	17.9	1.7	17,463	56.5	3,160	10.2
Barbados	1991[20]	122	47.8	76.4	49.0	53.6	44.9	8.8[14]	76.4[14]	0.2[14]	14.6[14]	5.7	4.7	11.9	9.7
Belarus	1989	5,327	49.0	77.2	52.5	57.2	48.3	...	...	...	...	985[24, 25]	18.9[24, 25]	1,593[24, 25]	30.9[24, 25]
Belgium	1990	4,179	41.6	66.3[21, 26]	41.7	50.1	34.1	12.7	73.9	3.4	10.0	100	2.4	820	19.6
Belize	1983–84	47	32.5	63.0[16]	29.6	39.5	19.5	23.4	55.1	7.5	14.0	13.1	27.6	4.9	10.3
Benin	1987	2,026	48.1	73.2[8]	47.8	50.4	45.2	...	...	...	...	1,291	63.7	163[9]	8.1[9]
Bermuda	1991	35.2	48.2[25]	76.0[12]	59.7[25]	63.5[25]	56.1[25]	7.7[16]	88.6[16]	0.5[16]	3.2[16]	0.6[27]	1.7[27]	1.4[27]	3.9[27]
Bhutan	1985	632	32.9	69.0	44.6	58.0	30.3	...	...	...	...	531[16]	92.5[16]	16[9, 16]	2.8[9, 16]
Bolivia	1990	2,276	23.8	54.5	31.1	48.1	14.6	48.4[29]	34.3[29]	15.8[29]	1.4[29]	869[29]	42.3[29]	263[29]	12.8[29]
Bosnia and Hercegovina	1990[24]	1,026	36.9		22.7			...	...	...	...	39	3.8	519	50.5
Botswana	1985[20]	368	53.0	72.7	37.0	38.1	36.0	2.1	33.5	39.0	25.3	159	43.2	20	5.4
Brazil	1988[20]	61,048	35.1	66.9[30]	43.2	57.1	29.7	25.3	63.6	7.3	3.8	14,233	23.3	9,982	16.4
Brunei	1986	86	30.7	60.4	38.2	51.3	24.2	7.4[23]	88.4[23]	0.6[23]	3.6[23]	3.1	3.5	8.0	9.3
Bulgaria	1985	4,686	47.7	75.7	52.4	55.1	49.6	0.3	98.2	—	1.5	772	16.5	1,778	37.9
Burkina Faso	1985	4,067	48.9	85.2	51.1	54.2	48.1	...	...	...	...	3,754	92.3	114[9]	2.8[9]
Burundi	1991	2,780	52.6	91.4	52.9	51.6	54.2	35.6[31]	5.6[31]	58.4[31]	0.4[31]	2,246[31]	92.9[31]	40[31]	1.6[31]
Cambodia	1985	3,602	40.5	71.4	49.5	59.2	39.8	...	...	...	...	2,454[16]	74.4[16]	220[9, 16]	6.7[9, 16]
Cameroon	1987	4,269	38.5	66.3[4, 33]	39.4	48.6	30.3	60.2[14]	14.6[14]	18.0[14]	7.1[14]	2,901[4]	74.0[4]	180[4]	4.6[4]
Canada	1991[20]	13,757	45.0	75.9	52.1	58.2	46.2	8.8	90.1	0.5	0.6	476	3.5	2,447	17.8
Cape Verde	1980	67	30.5	42.9	22.5	34.1	12.7	24.1	65.1	1.1	9.6	22.1	33.2	2.7	4.1
Cayman Islands	1991	16.7	48.4	81.6[30]	64.0	68.6	59.8	15.0	79.1	—5.9—		0.2	1.4	0.5	3.2
Central African Republic	1987	1,378	46.4	71.2[8]	48.9	53.9	44.2	...	...	...	...	907	65.8	94[9]	6.8[9]
Chad	1987	1,859	21.5	51.2[8]	35.3	56.2	15.0	...	...	...	...	1,439	77.4	117[9]	6.3[9]
Chile	1991[20]	4,794	30.7	56.7	36.6	51.8	22.0	26.0	65.4	3.3	5.3	867	18.1	872	18.2
China	1987[20]	584,569	44.5	76.8[30]	54.7	59.6	49.7	...	...	...	...	414,740	71.0	95,977	16.4
Colombia	1985	9,558	32.8	49.4[34]	34.3	46.6	22.3	...	...	...	...	2,412[16]	28.5[16]	1,231[16]	14.5[16]
Comoros	1985	117	26.2	53.1	29.6	43.5	15.6	47.6[16]	25.6[16]	—26.8[16]—		53[16]	53.3[16]	4.1[16]	4.2[16]
Congo	1984	563	45.6	54.0	29.5	33.0	26.2	64.3	31.4	1.2	3.1	294	52.2	50	8.8
Cook Islands	1986	6.7	33.9	69.1	40.5	51.5	28.6	7.7	74.4	6.7	11.2	1.2	17.7	0.7	9.9
Costa Rica	1991	1,066	29.9	58.7[33]	37.1	52.7	21.9	24.8	70.2	4.1	0.9	265	24.8	215	20.2
Côte d'Ivoire	1988	4,263	32.3	66.6	39.4	52.2	26.0	...	...	...	...	2,452[4]	60.5[4]	409[4, 9]	10.1[4, 9]
Croatia	1990[24]	1,509	43.2		32.2			...	...	...	...	69	4.6	632	41.9
Cuba	1988	4,570	36.1	56.9[30]	43.7	55.4	31.7	4.8[23]	94.1[23]	0.2[23]	0.9[23]	602[24]	18.4[24]	726[24]	22.2[24]
Cyprus	1990[35]	277	37.7	72.9	48.1	60.1	36.2	23.5[21]	72.2[21]	1.3[21]	3.0[21]	36[21]	13.6[21]	251[21]	19.0[21]
Czechoslovakia	1990	7,843	44.3	78.9[16]	50.1	57.3	43.2	0.1[16]	91.2[16]	8.5[16]	0.2[16]	928	11.8	2,882	36.7
Denmark	1990	2,912	46.1	82.7	56.7	62.1	51.5	9.0	88.8	1.8	0.4	156	5.4	602	20.7
Djibouti	1987	165	39.4	64.3[8]	43.7	51.8	34.9	...	...	...	...	127	76.9	14[9]	8.5[9]
Dominica	1989	30.6	41.8	62.3	37.5	47.1	29.3	29.2	50.6	1.9	18.3	7.7	25.2	3.6	11.8
Dominican Republic	1981	1,915	28.9	53.6	33.9	48.1	19.7	36.5	51.3	3.3	8.9	420	22.0	243	12.7
Ecuador	1990	3,360	26.4	55.7	34.8	51.5	18.3	45.7	42.5	4.4	7.4	1,036	30.8	404	12.0
Egypt	1986	13,395	10.9	46.2	27.7	48.1	6.2	28.2	58.4	2.7	10.7	4,767	35.7	1,651	12.4
El Salvador	1980[20]	1,593	34.8	62.4	35.4	47.5	24.0	28.2	59.2	10.9	1.7	637	40.0	262	16.4
Equatorial Guinea	1983	103	35.7	66.7	39.2	52.5	26.9	29.0	16.0	29.9	25.1	59.4	57.9	1.8	1.8
Estonia	1989	856	50.0	79.7	54.7	58.5	51.3	...	...	...	...	100	11.7	270	31.5
Ethiopia	1991	22,343	40.0	69.1	40.5	48.4	32.6	58.5[38]	6.5[38]	34.0[38]	1.0[38]	16,101[38]	88.3[38]	312[38]	1.7[38]

traditional agricultural worker. Loss of working-age men to war, civil violence, or emigration for job opportunities may also affect the structure of a particular labour market.

The distribution of the economically active population by employment status reveals that a large percentage of economically active persons in some less developed countries falls under the heading "employers, self-employed." This occurs because the countries involved have poor, largely agrarian economies in which the average worker is a farmer who tills his own small plot of land. In countries with well-developed economies, "employees" will usually constitute the largest portion of the economically active.

Caution should be exercised when using the economically active data to make intercountry comparisons, as countries often differ in their choices of classification schemes, definitions, and coverage of groups and in their methods of collection and tabulation of data. The population base containing the economically active population, for example, may range, in developing countries, from age 9 or 10 with no upper limit to, in developed countries, age 18 or 19 upward to a usual retirement age of from 55 to 65, with sometimes a different range for each sex. Data on female labour-force participation, in particular, often lack comparability. In many less developed countries, particularly those dominated by the Islamic faith, a cultural bias favouring traditional roles for women results in the under-counting of economically active women. In other less developed countries, particularly those in which subsistence workers are deemed economically active, the role of women may be overstated.

The second major section of the table provides data on the distribution by economic (also conventionally called industrial) sector of the "economically active population." The data usually include such groups as unpaid family workers, members of the armed forces, and the unemployed, the last distributed by industry as far as possible.

The categorization of industrial sectors is based on the divisions listed in the *International Standard Industrial Classification of All Economic Activities*. The "other" category includes persons whose activities were not adequately defined and the unemployed who were not distributable by industrial sector.

A substantial part of the data presented in this table is summarized from various issues of the ILO's *Year Book of Labour Statistics*, which compiles its statistics both from official publications and from information submitted directly by national census and labour authorities. The editors have supplemented and updated ILO statistical data with information from Britannica's holdings of relevant official publications and from direct correspondence with national authorities.

construction		transportation, communications		trade, hotels, restaurants		finance, real estate		public administration, defense		services		other		country
number ('000)	% of econ. active	number ('000)	% of econ. active	number ('000)	% of econ. active	number ('000)	% of econ. active	number ('000)	% of econ. active	number ('000)	% of econ. active	number ('000)	% of econ. active	
51	1.3	66	1.6	138	3.5	1	1	1	1	749[1]	19.0[1]	78[2]	2.0[2]	Afghanistan
49	3.4	44	3.0	49	3.3	1	1	1	1	220[1]	15.1[1]	17	1.2	Albania
690	12.9	216	4.1	391	7.3	143	2.7	5	5	1,180[5]	22.1[5]	1,374	25.7	Algeria
1.2	8.3	0.8	5.5	1.8	13.0	0.3	2.1	1.4	10.0	2.8	19.8	0.7[7]	5.1[7]	American Samoa
2.9	11.8	...	...	6.0	24.2	1.3	5.4	2.6	10.3	4.1	16.7	0.1	0.5	Andorra
9	9	10	10	10	10	10	10	10	10	714[10]	18.6[10]	—	—	Angola
2.6[14,15]	11.1[14,15]	2.6[14,15]	11.1[14,15]	5.2[14,15]	22.4[14,15]	0.8[14,15]	3.4[14,15]	5	5	7.9[5,14,15]	33.9[5,14,15]	—	—	Antigua and Barbuda
1,003[16]	10.0[16]	460[16]	4.6[16]	1,702[16]	17.0[16]	396[16]	3.9[16]	5	5	2,399[5,16]	23.9[5,16]	736[17]	7.3[17]	Argentina
162	7.9	88	4.3	88	4.3	18	0.9	8	0.4	41.3	20.2	697[19]	34.1[19]	Armenia
1.9[3]	8.0[3]	1.3[3]	5.4[3]	7.7[3]	32.7[3]	1.0[3]	4.4[3]	5	5	9.1[3,5]	38.5[3,5]	0.02[3]	0.1[3]	Aruba
628	7.5	563	6.7	1,695	20.1	934	11.1	345	4.1	2,075	24.6	241[17]	2.9[17]	Australia
302	8.5	222	6.3	661	18.7	225	6.4	5	5	816[5]	23.1[5]	35[17]	1.0[17]	Austria
...	...	...	...	...	...	...	...	...	...	...	...	...	...	Azerbaijan
9.9	7.8	8.9	7.0	36.3	28.5	8.6	6.7	5	5	35.8[5]	28.1[5]	16.9[22]	13.3[22]	Bahamas, The
91	28.1	18	5.7	49	15.2	14	4.2	5	5	107[5]	33.1[5]			Bahrain
647	2.1	1,321	4.3	3,833	12.4	367	1.2	5	5	2,563[5]	8.3[5]	1,567[17]	5.1[17]	Bangladesh
8.3	6.1	4.7	3.8	16.1	13.2	4.0	3.3	5	5	41.8[5]	34.2[5]	29.8[22]	24.4[22]	Barbados
570[24,25]	11.0[24,25]	238[24,25]	4.6[24,25]	382[24,25]	7.4[24,25]	1	1	1	1	1,281[1,24,25]	25.2[1,24,25]	100[24,25]	2.0[24,25]	Belarus
236	5.6	257	6.2	634	15.2	328	7.8	5	5	1,389[5]	33.2[5]	415[22]	9.9[22]	Belgium
2.0	4.2	2.0	4.3	4.6	9.6	0.6	1.2	6.3	13.2	7.3	15.5	6.6[7]	14.0[7]	Belize
9	9	10	10	10	10	10	10	10	10	572[10]	28.2[10]			Benin
3.4	9.7	2.7	7.6	9.5	27.1	4.6	13.0	2.4	6.8	6.4	18.0	4.3[28]	12.1[28]	Bermuda
9	9	10	10	10	10	10	10	10	10	27[10,16]	4.7[10,16]			Bhutan
110[29]	5.4[29]	108[29]	5.3[29]	260[29]	12.6[29]	33[29]	1.6[29]	5	5	375[5,29]	18.3[5,29]	36[17,29]	1.8[17,29]	Bolivia
75	7.3	69	6.7	131	12.8	39	3.8	5	5	155[5]	15.1[5]			Bosnia and Hercegovina
9	2.5	3	0.7	16	4.3	3	0.8	5	5	65[5]	17.7[5]	93[22]	25.3[22]	Botswana
3,726	6.1	2,210	3.6	6,789	11.1	3,496	5.7	5	5	18,293[5]	30.0[5]	2,319[7]	3.8[7]	Brazil
9.4	10.9	6.9	8.0	8.0	9.3	4.3	5.0	5	5	38.6[5]	44.6[5]	8.1[22]	9.3[22]	Brunei
407	8.7	315	6.7	397	8.5	25	0.5	5	5	993[5]	21.2[5]	1	—	Bulgaria
9	9	10	10	10	10	10	10	10	10	199[10]	4.9[10]			Burkina Faso
15[31]	0.6[31]	6[31]	0.3[31]	21[31]	0.9[31]	1.3[31]	0.1[31]	6[31]	0.2[31]	75[31]	3.1[31]	8[31,32]	0.3[31,32]	Burundi
9	9	10	10	10	10	10	10	10	10	625[10,16]	18.9[10,16]	—	—	Cambodia
67[4]	1.7[4]	52[4]	1.3[4]	154[4]	3.9[4]	8[4]	0.2[4]	5	5	293[4,5]	7.5[4,5]	228[4,22]	5.8[4,22]	Cameroon
891	6.5	995	7.2	2,395	17.4	801	5.8	822	6.0	4,849	35.2	81[7]	0.6[7]	Canada
18.9	28.3	3.4	5.1	3.9	5.9	0.2	0.3	2.1	3.2	13.2	19.8	—	—	Cape Verde
2.7	16.0	1.2	7.3	5.1	30.2	2.8	16.6	0.7	4.3	3.3	19.9	0.2[2]	1.1[2]	Cayman Islands
9	9	10	10	10	10	10	10	10	10	378[10]	27.4[10]	—	—	Central African Republic
9	9	10	10	10	10	10	10	10	10	303[10]	16.3[10]	—	—	Chad
322	6.7	308	6.4	775	16.2	228	4.8	5	5	1,168[5]	24.4[5]	254[22]	5.3[22]	Chile
13,298	2.3	10,898	1.9	20,785	3.6	1,268	0.2	9,704	1.7	17,414	3.0	487	0.1	China
242[16]	2.9[16]	353[16]	4.2[16]	1,262[16]	14.9[16]	278[16]	3.3[16]	5	5	1,998[5,16]	23.6[5,16]	691[16,17]	8.2[16,17]	Colombia
3.3[16]	3.3[16]	2.1[16]	2.1[16]	1.9[16]	1.9[16]	0.2[16]	0.2[16]	2.4[16]	2.4[16]	4.6[16]	4.7[16]	28[16]	27.8[16]	Comoros
25	4.5	29	5.1	67	11.8	3	0.5	5	5	85[5]	15.1[5]	10	2.0	Congo
0.4	6.7	0.6	9.3	1.1	16.7	0.2	3.1	5	5	2.1[5]	30.5[5]	0.4[22]	6.0[22]	Cook Islands
69	6.5	46	4.3	166	15.5	39	3.6	5	5	247[5]	23.2[5]	19[17]	1.8[17]	Costa Rica
9	9	10	10	10	10	10	10	10	10	1,192[4,10]	29.4[4,10]	—	—	Côte d'Ivoire
119	7.9	125	8.3	238	15.8	61	4.0	5	5	266[5]	17.6[5]	—	—	Croatia
322[24]	9.9[24]	224[24]	6.9[24]	371[24]	11.4[24]	21[24]	0.6[24]	169[20,24]	5.2[20,24]	777[24]	23.8[24]	52[24]	1.6[24]	Cuba
22[21]	8.4[21]	13[21]	5.1[21]	54[21]	20.5[21]	14[21]	5.2[21]	5	5	47[5,21]	18.0[5,21]	27[21,36]	10.2[21,36]	Cyprus
856	10.9	528	6.7	836	10.7	37	37	152	1.9	1,604[37]	20.4[37]	59	0.7	Czechoslovakia
201	6.9	198	6.8	429	14.7	257	8.8	5	5	1,019[5]	35.0[5]	52[17]	1.8[17]	Denmark
9	9	10	10	10	10	10	10	10	10	24[10]	14.6[10]	—	—	Djibouti
2.6	8.5	1.6	5.2	2.9	9.5	0.7	2.3	5	5	5.7[5]	18.6[5]	5.4[36]	17.6[36]	Dominica
81	4.3	40	2.1	192	10.0	22	1.2	5	5	363[5]	18.9[5]	553[17]	28.9[17]	Dominican Republic
197	5.9	131	3.9	477	14.2	81	2.4	5	5	838[5]	24.9[5]	196[17]	5.8[17]	Ecuador
864	6.5	656	4.9	860	6.4	237	1.8	5	5	2,632[5]	19.7[5]	1,682[22]	12.6[22]	Egypt
80	5.0	66	4.1	256	16.1	16	1.0	5	5	250[5]	15.7[5]	27[32]	1.7[32]	El Salvador
1.9	1.9	1.8	1.7	3.1	3.0	0.4	0.4	5	5	8.4[5]	8.2[5]	25.8[22]	25.2[22]	Equatorial Guinea
73	8.5	73	8.5	75	8.8	4	0.5	19	2.2	182	21.3	60	7.0	Estonia
46[38]	0.3[38]	77[38]	0.4[38]	696[38]	3.8[38]	15[38]	0.1[38]	5	5	933[5,38]	5.1[5,38]	562[2,38]	0.3[2,38]	Ethiopia

Employment and labour (continued)

country	year	economically active population total ('000)	participation rate (%) female	participation rate (%) ages 15–64	activity rate (%) total	activity rate (%) male	activity rate (%) female	employment status (%) employers, self-employed	employment status (%) employees	employment status (%) unpaid family workers	employment status (%) other	distribution by economic sector agriculture, forestry, fishing number ('000)	agriculture, forestry, fishing % of econ. active	manufacturing; mining, quarrying; public utilities number ('000)	manufacturing; mining, quarrying; public utilities % of econ. active
Faeroe Islands	1977	17.6	27.2	64.0	41.9	58.2	23.9	11.9	86.1	...	2.0	3.3	18.8	3.9	21.9
Fiji	1986	241	21.2	56.0	33.7	52.4	14.5	33.6	42.2	16.3	7.9	106	44.1	22	9.0
Finland	1991	2,559	47.0	75.5	51.1	55.7	46.7	12.9	85.3	0.7	1.1	208	8.1	545	21.3
France	1991[20]	24,609	43.3	65.1	43.3	50.3	36.7	12.6	77.1	1.0	9.3	1,257	5.1	4,841	19.7
French Guiana	1990	48.7	38.2	67.2	42.4	50.4	33.8	11.2	59.7	5.0	24.1	4[14]	11.4[14]	2[14]	5.9[14]
French Polynesia	1988	75	37.1	64.8	39.9	48.2	30.9	13.0	55.0	4.0	28.0	7.6	10.0	5.4	7.2
Gabon	1987	607	38.1	59.5[8]	44.0	55.3	33.1	...	...	...	...	425	70.0	76[9]	12.5[9]
Gambia, The	1983	326	46.3	78.2	47.3	51.1	43.6	0.5	78.0	14.3	7.1	240	73.7	9	2.9
Gaza Strip	1989	101	3.1	33.6[30]	16.5	31.9	1.0	...	...	...	...	18.4	18.2	12.5[39]	12.4[39]
Georgia	1988	2,463	45.9[21]	90.1[18, 21]	45.2	...	...	...	...	...	...	640	26.0	887	36.0
Germany[40]	1990	30,327	40.6	71.6	49.6	60.8	39.2	8.0	90.2	1.8	—	961	3.2	9,283	30.6
Ghana	1984	5,580	51.2	82.5[30]	45.4	44.9	45.8	67.7	15.7	12.2	4.4	3,311	59.3	631	11.3
Gibraltar	1990	14.2	34.5	71.5[23]	47.2[16]	60.3[16]	33.1[16]	6.6[23]	89.7[23]	...	3.6[23]	—	...	1.1	8.1
Greece	1990[20]	4,000	37.1	57.7[29]	39.6[29]	50.8[29]	28.7[29]	32.4	50.6	12.0	5.0	893	22.3	808	20.2
Greenland	1976	21.4	33.4	63.5[30]	43.1	53.0	31.4	12.6	82.5	0.4	4.5	3.2	15.1	3.3	15.3
Grenada	1988	38.9	48.6	72.7[41]	39.9	42.9	37.2	...	...	...	...	5.6	14.3	3.3	8.6
Guadeloupe	1990	172	45.5	66.4	44.5	49.6	39.7	13.2	53.7	2.0	31.1	9.4[42]	7.2[42]	6.8[42]	5.3[42]
Guam	1990	66.1	37.4	75.7[6]	49.7	58.4	39.7	2.4	94.4	0.1	3.1	0.5	0.8	3.5	5.3
Guatemala	1989[20]	2,898	25.5	57.7[30]	33.5	50.8	16.7	32.7	47.6	16.2	3.5	1,416	48.9	405	14.0
Guernsey[43]	1991	30.2	43.2	74.2	51.2	60.6	42.6	13.7	86.3	—	...	2.4	7.8	2.4	7.9
Guinea	1983	1,823	39.4	63.5	39.1	48.7	30.1	36.2	15.6	37.6	10.6	1,424	78.1	27	1.5
Guinea-Bissau	1988	279	3.3	41.0[31]	30.0	60.1	1.9	...	...	...	...	153[31]	71.9[31]	3[31]	1.5[31]
Guyana	1987[44]	270	29.9	60.4	35.7	50.9	21.0	14.3[16]	63.8[16]	1.9[16]	20.0[16]	50[16]	20.4[16]	41[16]	16.8[16]
Haiti	1990	2,679	40.0	64.8	41.1	50.3	32.3	59.1	16.5	10.4	14.0	1,535	57.3	178	6.6
Honduras	1991[20]	1,567	29.8	57.9[30]	39.1	56.4	22.7	34.3	44.2	10.4	11.1	551	35.2	230	14.7
Hong Kong	1991[20]	2,799	37.4	69.9	50.1	61.8	38.0	10.6	86.6	1.0	1.8	22	0.8	734	26.2
Hungary	1991	4,669	45.5	65.7[25]	45.1	51.1	39.5	9.0	79.1	2.4	9.5	819	17.5	1,388	29.7
Iceland	1989[45]	126	31.5[11]	79.1[46]	49.7	...	...	...	...	...	...	13	...	24	19.3
India	1981[47]	260,275	27.0	60.7[31]	39.1	55.2	21.9	8.8	16.3	3.6	71.3	172,713	66.4	28,846	11.1
Indonesia	1989	75,508	39.9	67.7	42.6	51.2	34.0	42.4	26.2	28.6	2.8	41,284	54.7	7,909	10.5
Iran	1986	12,855	10.3	46.8	26.0	45.6	5.5	36.9	41.5	3.9	17.7	3,209	25.0	1,584	12.3
Iraq	1987	3,956	11.6	43.2[30]	24.2	41.6	5.8	25.4[48]	59.5[48]	11.4[48]	3.7[48]	493	12.5	348	8.8
Ireland	1989	1,292	30.7	58.6	36.8	51.0	22.6	18.7	77.0	1.8	2.5	163	12.6	231	18.1
Isle of Man	1991	33.2	42.3	73.2	47.6	56.9	38.9	15.8	80.1	...	4.1	1.2	3.7	3.9	11.6
Israel	1991[20]	1,770	41.1	57.8	35.3	41.7	28.9	16.9[25]	72.4[25]	1.1[25]	9.6[25]	56	3.1	357	20.1
Italy	1990[20]	24,075	37.2	64.4[49]	42.0	54.3	30.3	21.6	63.2	3.6	11.5	1,895	7.9	4,986	20.7
Jamaica	1991	1,077	46.6	71.6[25, 50]	44.2	47.2	41.2	34.1	47.2	2.7	16.0	248	23.0	107	9.9
Japan	1991	65,050	40.8	70.7	52.5	63.3	42.0	13.2	76.9	7.5	2.4	4,270	6.6	15,890	24.4
Jersey	1991	47.5	43.2	66.9[30]	56.5	66.1	47.5	12.6	84.0	...	3.4	2.2	4.7	3.8	8.0
Jordan	1988	644	11.4	43.2	22.8	39.3	5.3	22.8[31]	67.2[31]	0.8[31]	9.2[31]	33	5.1	55	8.6
Kazakhstan	1989[24]	6,495	54.0	80.4[18]	39.1	...	...	...	...	...	...	1,220	18.8	1,640	25.3
Kenya	1987	8,836	40.5	66.2[8]	40.2	47.8	32.6	...	...	...	...	6,919	78.3	654[9]	7.4[9]
Kiribati	1990	32.6	46.4	75.6[30]	45.1	48.9	41.4	71.9	25.3	...	2.8	23.1	71.0	0.9	2.8
Korea, North	1985	9,084	46.0	75.3	44.6	48.6	40.6	...	...	...	...	3,355[16]	42.8[16]	2,373[9, 16]	30.3[9, 16]
Korea, South	1991[20]	19,012	40.3	63.5	44.1	52.5	35.8	27.7	59.4	10.7	2.3	3,102	16.3	5,071	26.7
Kuwait	1988	730	24.3	61.5	38.9	53.5	21.0	5.9[4]	92.4[4]	0.1[4]	1.5[4]	9	1.3	69	9.4
Kyrgyzstan	1989[24]	1,429	48.6	81.3[18]	33.0	...	...	...	...	...	...	474	33.2	400	28.0
Laos	1985	2,014	45.3	84.2	48.9	53.1	44.6	...	...	...	...	1,393[16]	75.7[16]	130[9, 16]	7.1[9, 16]
Latvia	1989	1,470	50.0	80.0	55.1	59.3	51.5	...	...	...	...	248	16.9	374	25.4
Lebanon	1988	904	16.6	44.0	26.5	43.9	8.9	...	...	...	...	132[42]	19.1[42]	131[42]	18.9[42]
Lesotho	1976	424	32.3	56.1	34.8	48.9	21.7	7.5	49.9	36.8	5.8	99	23.3	141	33.2
Liberia	1984	704	41.0	56.3	33.5	39.1	27.8	59.1	21.6	14.4	5.0	481	68.3	31	4.4
Libya	1989	994	8.1[4]	47.6[4]	24.1[51]	42.3[51]	3.5[51]	23.7[51]	69.6[51]	4.2[51]	2.6[51]	192	19.2	144	14.5
Liechtenstein	1991	14.7	37.7	70.8	50.0	63.7	37.0	9.1	87.3	3.6	—	0.3	2.4	5.1	34.4
Lithuania	1989	1,926	48.9	76.9	52.4	56.6	48.6	...	...	...	...	122	6.3	507	26.3
Luxembourg	1991[52]	165	35.6	61.7	42.8	56.3	29.9	9.1	87.9	1.5	1.5	6	3.4	32	19.2
Macau	1990[20]	228	41.3	61.5[8, 23]	50.5	60.6	40.8	10.5	84.5	1.9	3.1	0.4	0.2	75	32.6
Macedonia	1990[24]	507	37.3	...	23.8	...	...	...	...	...	...	42	8.3	224	44.1
Madagascar	1987	4,687	39.9	65.8[8]	44.4	53.4	35.4	...	...	...	...	3,651	77.9	462[9]	9.9[9]
Malawi	1987	3,300	51.5	89.4	41.3	41.2	41.5	69.9	13.4	11.3	5.4	2,700	81.8	104	3.2
Malaysia	1990[20]	6,685	35.5	63.5	37.6	48.2	26.9	25.6[29]	61.9[29]	12.5[29]	—	1,889[29]	30.6[29]	1,059[29]	17.1[29]
Maldives	1990	56	19.9	50.2	26.5	41.3	10.8	39.7	49.3	4.5	6.5	14.1	25.0	9.4	16.6
Mali	1976	2,266	17.0	53.2	35.4	60.2	11.8	45.8	4.1	42.5	7.5	1,862	82.2	27	1.2
Malta	1989	131	25.1	45.9[4]	37.2	56.4	18.4	14.1[11]	77.4[11]	...	8.5[11]	3	2.5	38	29.0
Marshall Islands	1980	4.4	25.2	30.0[12]	14.3	20.8	7.4	3.3	78.1	0.3	18.4	0.1	1.0	0.4[54]	9.4[54]
Martinique	1990	165	47.5	68.1	45.9	49.8	42.2	9.5	56.9	1.5	32.1	10.4[42]	7.1[42]	7.1[42]	4.9[42]
Mauritania	1987	577	21.5	47.2[8]	31.0	49.2	13.2	...	...	...	...	389	66.0	59[9]	10.0[9]
Mauritius	1991[55]	463	35.2	68.0	44.5	57.9	31.2	9.0[11]	60.8[11]	0.6[11]	29.6[11]	81	17.5	146	31.5
Mayotte	1985	22.3	40.1	68.9	33.4	39.2	27.3	48.0	30.1	13.0	8.9	12.3	55.0	0.9	3.8
Mexico	1990	24,063	23.5	49.8	29.6	46.2	13.6	24.9	66.2	2.4	6.5	5,300	22.0	4,908	20.4
Micronesia	1980	9.8	29.8	26.1[12]	13.4	18.4	8.2	2.7	74.4	0.1	22.7	0.2	2.0	0.6[54]	6.0[54]
Moldova	1990	2,071	50.0[21]	86.3[18]	47.7	...	...	...	...	...	...	673	32.5	456	22.0
Monaco	1990	12.6	39.7	...	42.0	53.2	31.8	17.4	75.1	0.3	7.2	—	0.3	2.7	21.8
Mongolia	1987	946	45.5[4]	82.2[4]	46.9[4]	50.9[4]	42.8[4]	...	...	...	...	561	59.3	122	12.9
Morocco	1982	5,999	19.7	49.8	29.3	47.1	11.6	27.1	40.5	17.6	14.8	2,352	39.2	1,016	16.9
Mozambique	1980	5,671	52.4	87.3[30]	48.6	47.6	49.5	44.4[13]	40.0[13]	14.5[13]	1.1[13]	4,755	83.8	347	6.1
Myanmar (Burma)	1989–90[20]	15,701	35.3[11]	64.2[11]	40.2[11]	52.4[11]	28.2[11]	...	...	...	...	10,614[56]	67.6[56]	1,232	7.8
Namibia	1985	477	23.9	55.4	30.8	47.3	14.6	...	...	...	...	185[16]	43.4[16]	93[9, 16]	21.8[9, 16]
Nauru	1977	2.2	...	...	30.5	...	...	...	...	...	...	...	...	...	...
Nepal	1990	8,585	34.7	82.5[42]	45.4	57.5	32.6	86.2[23]	9.1[23]	2.5[23]	2.2[23]	6,244[23]	91.1[23]	37[23]	0.5[23]
Netherlands, The	1991	7,011	39.7	67.6	46.6	56.9	36.5	8.8	82.7	1.5	7.0	293	4.2	1,227	17.5
Netherlands Antilles	1988[20]	73	43.1	59.5[42]	38.5	45.1	32.3	...	...	...	...	0.5	0.7	5.8	8.0
New Caledonia	1989	66	37.5	70.7[49]	40.2	49.1	30.8	16.3	64.3	1.6	17.8	7.8	11.8	6.2	9.3
New Zealand	1991[20]	1,592	43.6	70.8	47.1	53.9	40.6	16.8	68.9	1.3	13.0	142	8.9	247	15.5
Nicaragua	1991	1,386	33.2	62.0[30]	34.7	47.8	22.3	...	...	...	...	365[58]	32.4[58]	101[58]	9.0[58]

construction		transportation, communications		trade, hotels, restaurants		finance, real estate		public administration, defense		services		other		country
number ('000)	% of econ. active	number ('000)	% of econ. active	number ('000)	% of econ. active	number ('000)	% of econ. active	number ('000)	% of econ. active	number ('000)	% of econ. active	number ('000)	% of econ. active	
2.0	11.1	1.9	11.1	2.1	11.9	0.3	1.9	5	5	3.5[5]	20.1[5]	0.6	3.2	Faeroe Islands
12	4.9	13	5.5	26	10.8	6	2.5	5	5	37[5]	15.2[5]	20[22]	8.2[22]	Fiji
217	8.5	183	7.2	379	14.8	206	8.1	124	4.8	663	25.9	33[32]	1.3[32]	Finland
1,581	6.4	1,405	5.7	3,778	15.4	2,227	9.1	5	5	6,982[5]	28.4[5]	2,537[22]	10.3[22]	France
3[14]	8.8[14]	1.3[14]	4.2[14]	2[14]	6.2[14]	4[14]	11.3[14]	5	5	10[5,14]	31.3[5,14]	7[14,22]	20.9[14,22]	French Guiana
5.5	7.4	2.8	3.7	10.3	13.7	1.2	1.5	5	5	21.5[5]	28.6[5]	21.1[22]	28.0[22]	French Polynesia
9	9	10	10	10	10	10	10	10	10	106[10]	17.5[10]	—	—	Gabon
4	1.3	8	2.5	17	5.1	1	1	1	1	22[1]	6.8[1]	25	7.7	Gambia, The
28.5	28.2	4.6	4.5	17.9	17.7	37	37	10.8	10.7	6.0[37,39]	5.9[37,39]	2.4[7]	2.4[7]	Gaza Strip
...	...	197	8.0	172	7.0	...	...	74	3.0	493	20.0	—	—	Georgia
1,848	6.1	1,624	5.4	4,632	15.3	2,373	7.8	5	5	7,723[5]	25.5[5]	1,883[7]	6.2[7]	Germany[40]
65	1.2	123	2.2	792	14.2	27	0.5	98	1.7	376	6.7	158[7]	2.8[7]	Ghana
2.2	15.4	0.7	4.6	3.2	22.4	1.4	9.9	5	5	4.4[5]	31.0[5]	1.2[36]	8.6[36]	Gibraltar
260	6.5	259	6.5	672	16.8	187	4.7	5	5	721[5]	18.0[5]	201[32]	5.0[32]	Greece
3.1	14.6	1.8	8.6	2.7	12.6	0.3	1.6	5	5	6.3[5]	29.5[5]	0.6	2.8	Greenland
3.5	9.1	1.7	4.4	5.4	13.9	0.8	2.0	5	5	5.9[5]	15.3[5]	12.7[22]	32.5[22]	Grenada
8.8[42]	6.8[42]	4.0[42]	3.1[42]	9.6[42]	7.4[42]	18.7[42]	14.5[42]	5	5	31.4[5,42]	24.3[5,42]	40.6[7,42]	31.4[7,42]	Guadeloupe
8.0	12.1	4.5	6.8	11.5	17.5	3.9	6.0	17.7	26.7	14.5	21.9	2.0[7]	3.1[7]	Guam
114	3.9	72	2.5	375	12.9	38	1.3	5	5	417[5]	14.4[5]	60[22]	2.1[22]	Guatemala
3.2	10.5	1.4	4.5	7.4	24.6	5.8	19.3	1.9	6.4	5.3	17.7	0.4	1.3	Guernsey[43]
9	0.5	29	1.6	37	2.0	4	0.2	5	5	138[5]	7.5[5]	156	8.5	Guinea
2[31]	0.8[31]	2[31]	1.1[31]	5[31]	2.4[31]	0.2[31]	0.1[31]	5	5	26[5,31]	12.3[5,31]	21[31]	10.0[31]	Guinea-Bissau
7[16]	2.8[16]	9[16]	3.8[16]	15[16]	6.2[16]	3[16]	1.2[16]	30[16]	12.1[16]	29[16]	11.9[16]	61[16,22]	24.7[16,22]	Guyana
28	1.0	21	0.8	353	13.2	5	0.2	5	5	155[5]	5.8[5]	404[22]	15.1[22]	Haiti
81	5.2	44	2.8	235	15.0	24	1.5	5	5	224[5]	14.3[5]	177[36]	11.3[36]	Honduras
224	8.0	273	9.8	731	26.1	229	8.2	5	5	535[5]	19.1[5]	50[7]	1.8[7]	Hong Kong
329	7.0	418	8.9	558	11.9	1	1	1	1	1,157[1]	24.8[1]	—	—	Hungary
12	9.8	...	...	19	14.9	...	...	...	...	37	29.8	20	15.9	Iceland
3,864	1.5	6,207	2.4	12,638	4.9	1,822	0.7	5	5	18,515[5]	7.1[5]	15,670	6.0	India
1,829	2.4	2,192	2.9	10,891	14.4	397	0.5	5	5	8,969[5]	11.7[5]	2,138[22]	2.8[22]	Indonesia
1,207	9.4	631	4.9	876	6.8	114	0.9	5	5	3,051[5]	23.7[5]	2,183[22]	17.0[22]	Iran
341	8.6	224	5.7	216	5.4	27	0.7	5	5	1,955[5]	49.4[5]	352[32]	8.9[32]	Iraq
72	5.6	66	5.1	192	14.8	86	6.6	5	5	275[5]	21.3[5]	206[22]	15.9[22]	Ireland
3.4	10.3	2.4	7.3	6.1	18.4	4.4	13.1	5	5	10.4[5]	31.4[5]	1.4[7]	4.1[7]	Isle of Man
96	5.4	97	5.5	224	12.7	161	9.1	5	5	583[5]	32.9[5]	198[22]	11.2[22]	Israel
1,859	7.7	1,146	4.8	4,537	18.8	895	3.7	5	5	5,986[5]	24.9[5]	2,771[22]	11.5[22]	Italy
55	5.1	36	3.3	174	16.1	40	3.7	5	5	243[5]	22.6[5]	175[22]	16.2[22]	Jamaica
6,040	9.3	3,780	5.8	14,330	22.0	5,370	8.3	5	5	13,710[5]	21.1[5]	1,640[22]	2.5[22]	Japan
4.4	9.3	2.4	5.0	6.8	14.4	7.4	15.6	3.1	6.5	15.7	33.1	1.6[22]	3.4[22]	Jersey
51	7.9	52	8.1	76	11.8	18	2.8	5	5	358[5]	55.6[5]	—	—	Jordan
766	11.8	698	10.7	532	8.2	40	0.6	96	1.5	1,503	23.1	—	—	Kazakhstan
9	9	10	10	10	10	10	10	10	10	1,264[10]	14.3[10]	—	—	Kenya
0.3	1.0	0.9	2.8	1.3	4.1	0.4	1.4	2.1	6.5	2.3	7.0	1.1[22]	3.4[22]	Kiribati
9	9	10	10	10	10	10	10	10	10	2,110[10,16]	26.9[10,16]	—	—	Korea, North
1,543	8.1	985	5.2	4,082	21.5	1,017	5.3	5	5	2,775[5]	14.6[5]	436[7]	2.3[7]	Korea, South
115	15.7	38	5.2	83	11.4	22	3.0	5	5	384[5]	52.6[5]	11[2]	1.5[2]	Kuwait
...	...	79	5.5	93	6.5	40	2.8	...	...	288	20.2	55	3.9	Kyrgyzstan
9	9	10	10	10	10	10	10	10	10	316[10,16]	17.2[10,16]			Laos
114	7.8	105	7.1	122	8.3	...	...	17	1.2	236	16.1	254	17.3	Latvia
43[42]	6.2[42]	48[42]	7.0[42]	115[42]	16.5[42]	24[42]	3.5[42]	5	5	200[5,42]	28.8[5,42]	—	—	Lebanon
12	2.9	4	1.1	8	2.0	0.3	0.1	5	5	74[5]	17.6[5]	84	19.9	Lesotho
4	0.6	14	2.0	47	6.7	1	1	1	1	63[1]	9.0[1]	64[22]	9.1[22]	Liberia
156	15.7	79	7.9	53	5.3	15	1.5	308	31.0	48	4.8	—	—	Libya
1.2	8.3	0.5	3.1	1.7	11.3	1.1	7.2	0.6	4.1	4.2	28.5	0.1[36]	0.7[36]	Liechtenstein
194	10.1	116	6.0	145	7.5	...	...	22	1.1	327	17.0	493	25.6	Lithuania
15	9.3	11	6.9	32	19.7	21	12.8	21	12.6	22	13.4	2[7]	1.5[7]	Luxembourg
19	8.5	10	4.5	48	20.9	8	3.3	5	5	61[5]	26.7[5]	8[22]	3.3[22]	Macau
48	9.4	26	5.2	64	12.5	14	2.8	5	5	90[5]	17.5[5]	—	—	Macedonia
9	9	10	10	10	10	10	10	10	10	574[10]	12.2[10]	—	—	Madagascar
52	1.6	17	0.5	103	3.1	7	0.2	5	5	137[5]	4.2[5]	180[22]	5.5[22]	Malawi
340[29]	5.5[29]	266[29]	4.3[29]	1,120[29]	18.1[29]	231[29]	3.7[29]	844[29]	13.7[29]	427[29]	6.9[29]	—	—	Malaysia
3.2	5.6	5.3	9.4	8.9	15.7	1.1	1.9	5	5	11.8[5]	21.0[5]	2.7[53]	4.7[53]	Maldives
8	0.3	12	0.5	45	2.0	0.2	—	49	2.1	124	5.5	139	6.1	Mali
6	4.5	9	7.0	13	9.6	5	3.5	5	5	53[5]	40.3[5]	57	3.7[7]	Malta
0.4	8.4	54	54	0.5	12.3	—	0.7	0.6	13.4	1.6	36.4	0.8[22]	18.4[22]	Marshall Islands
6.9[42]	4.7[42]	5.9[42]	4.0[42]	12.4[42]	8.5[42]	19.3[42]	13.2[42]	5	5	32.9[5,42]	22.6[5,42]	51.1[7,42]	35.0[7,42]	Martinique
9	9	10	10	10	10	10	10	10	10	142[10]	24.0[10]	—	—	Mauritania
24	5.2	32	6.9	61	13.2	11	2.4	5	5	94[5]	20.3[5]	14[22]	3.1[22]	Mauritius
2.0	8.9	0.6	2.6	0.6	2.7	0.9	4.0	5	5	2.9[5]	13.0[5]	2.3[22]	10.1[22]	Mayotte
1,595	6.6	1,045	4.3	3,875	16.1	792	3.3	5	5	5,084[5]	21.1[5]	1,464[36]	6.1[36]	Mexico
0.9	9.6	54	54	0.9	8.8	0.1	1.2	1.8	18.0	3.1	31.5	2.2[22]	22.8[22]	Micronesia
172	8.3	70	3.4	148	7.1	1	1	1	1	519[1]	25.1[1]	33	1.6	Moldova
0.7	5.3	...	...	2.5	20.2	1.0	8.0	2.8	22.4	1.9	14.9	0.9[36]	7.1[36]	Monaco
31	3.2	42	4.4	45	4.8	1	1	1	1	115[1]	12.2[1]	31	3.2	Mongolia
437	7.3	141	2.3	498	8.3	37	37	533	8.9	474[37]	7.9[37]	548[2]	9.1[2]	Morocco
42	0.7	7.7	1.4	112	2.0	1	1	1	1	243[1]	4.3[1]	95[7]	1.7[7]	Mozambique
174	1.1	385	2.5	1,405	8.9	1	1	1	1	956[1]	6.1[1]	935[57]	6.0[57]	Myanmar (Burma)
9	9	10	10	10	10	10	10	10	10	148[10,16]	34.7[10,16]	—	—	Namibia
...	...	...	...	...	...	...	...	...	...	...	...	...	...	Nauru
2[23]	—	7[23]	0.1[23]	109[23]	1.6[23]	10[23]	0.1[23]	5	5	314[5,23]	4.6[5,23]	127[23]	1.9[23]	Nepal
418	6.0	403	5.7	1,138	16.2	682	9.7	5	5	2,313[5]	33.0[5]	537[22]	7.7[22]	Netherlands, The
5.4	7.4	4.7	6.4	15.9	21.8	4.6	6.3	5	5	21.3[5]	29.3[5]	14.7[22]	20.2[22]	Netherlands Antilles
4.5	6.8	3.1	4.7	9.5	14.3	2.5	3.8	5	5	22.0[5]	33.4[5]	13.5[7]	16.0[7]	New Caledonia
85	5.3	85	5.3	284	17.9	161	10.1	5	5	368[5]	23.1[5]	219[22]	13.8[22]	New Zealand
17[58]	1.5[58]	21[58]	1.8[58]	95[58]	8.4[58]	19[58]	1.7[58]	77[58]	6.9[58]	149[58]	13.2[58]	283[58,59]	25.1[58,59]	Nicaragua

Employment and labour (continued)

country	year	economically active population											distribution by economic sector			
		total ('000)	participation rate (%)		activity rate (%)			employment status (%)				agriculture, forestry, fishing		manufacturing; mining, quarrying; public utilities	
			female	ages 15–64	total	male	female	employers, self-employed	employees	unpaid family workers	other	number ('000)	% of econ. active	number ('000)	% of econ. active
Niger	1988[60]	2,367	20.7	61.7[8]	33.9	54.3	13.9	49.5	5.0	41.6	3.9	1,793	75.9	72	3.0
Nigeria	1988[20]	30,766	33.3	58.8	31.1	41.1	20.9	64.6	18.8	10.7	5.9	13,259	43.1	1,401	4.6
Northern Mariana Islands	1990	26.6	43.2	83.3[6]	61.3	66.2	55.9	1.4	96.1	0.2	2.3	0.6	2.3	6.0	22.5
Norway	1991	2,126	45.3	76.3[6]	49.9	55.2	44.7	8.5	84.5	1.3	5.7	120	5.6	350	16.5
Oman	1988	644	6.3	57.2	38.2	60.7	5.9	...	...	...	...	399	62.0	33	5.1
Pakistan	1991–92[20]	32,814	14.2	50.8	28.0	46.4	8.2	41.2	32.4	20.2	6.2	14,592	44.5	4,062	12.4
Palau	1990	6.1	36.9	64.1[6]	40.2	47.1	32.1	2.5	89.5	0.2	7.8	0.4	7.1	0.2	3.0
Panama	1989[20]	820	33.2	60.5[33]	34.6	45.8	23.2	28.6	60.1	5.4	5.9	208	25.4	91	11.1
Papua New Guinea	1980[61]	733	39.8	35.2[8]	24.6	28.3	20.5	72.7	26.4	—	0.9	564	77.0	21	2.9
Paraguay	1982	1,039	19.7	57.5	34.3	54.8	13.6	43.1	37.7	9.2	9.9	446	42.9	129	12.4
Peru	1990	7,662	38.3[62]	56.4[30]	34.3	...	...	39.8[23]	41.8[23]	8.4[23]	10.0[23]	2,605	34.0	1,011	13.2
Philippines	1990[20]	24,525	37.0	66.1	39.7	50.5	29.9	35.2	42.0	14.7	8.1	10,185	41.5	2,412	9.8
Poland	1988	18,452	45.4	71.7	48.7	54.5	43.2	14.2	75.1	10.7	—	5,133	27.8	5,245	28.4
Portugal	1990[20]	4,949	43.1	68.9	47.8	56.7	39.7	24.5	67.4	3.3	4.8	846	17.1	1,240	25.1
Puerto Rico	1992[20]	1,096	37.7	51.8[6]	30.6	39.2	22.5	14.0	84.5	0.7	0.8	39	3.6	205	18.7
Qatar	1986	201	9.8	76.0	54.5	73.2	16.2	1.8	97.7	—	0.5	6.3	3.1	24.0	11.9
Réunion	1990[20]	234	41.1	60.3	39.1	46.8	31.6	10.4[14]	56.3[14]	1.1[14]	32.2[14]	17[14]	10.1[14]	8[14]	4.7[14]
Romania	1990	10,840	46.1	68.9	46.7	51.0	42.6	9.2	72.9	...	17.9	3,097	28.6	4,015	37.0
Russia	1989	77,283	48.5	77.1	52.6	57.9	47.9	...	...	...	...	9,845[25]	12.5[25]	22,107[25]	28.1[25]
Rwanda	1989	3,143	53.5	94.3[46]	46.3	44.6	48.0	38.8[46]	7.2[46]	53.8[46]	0.2[46]	2,833	90.1	52	1.7
St. Kitts and Nevis	1980	17.1	41.0	69.5	39.5	48.4	31.2	9.7	78.5	0.4	11.4	4.5	26.1	3.8	22.3
St. Lucia	1980	42.2	39.1	69.9	37.2	47.1	28.0	21.0	55.8	1.6	21.6	10.7	25.5	3.7	8.7
St. Vincent	1980	35	36.1	60.9[30]	35.5	46.6	25.0	18.0[13]	82.5[13]	1.5[13]	...	8.9	25.7	2.3	6.6
San Marino	1991	13.3	40.8	72.9	53.3	61.8	44.4	21.7	77.8	0.6	...	0.3	2.2	4.5	33.7
São Tomé and Príncipe	1981	31	32.4	61.1	31.7	43.1	20.4	15.8	79.4	0.1	4.7	16	53.9	1.9	6.2
Saudi Arabia	1988	5,369	3.6	59.1	36.3	54.9	3.6	...	...	...	...	192	3.6	595	11.1
Senegal	1990	2,433	26.0	46.2[8]	33.5	50.9	17.0	...	...	...	...	...	...	...	...
Seychelles	1989	29	42.5	74.3	44.0	50.7	37.3	10.7[23]	76.6[23]	0.3[23]	12.4[23]	2.3[4,63]	9.5[4,63]	2.3[4,63]	9.6[4,63]
Sierra Leone	1987	1,405	33.3	53.0[8]	37.0	50.3	24.1	...	...	...	...	908	64.7	231[9]	16.4[9]
Singapore	1991[20]	1,554	39.8	63.1[25,30]	56.3	67.0	45.3	12.0	85.0	1.1	1.9	4	0.3	437	28.1
Slovenia	1990[24]	786	46.8	...	40.2	...	...	...	...	...	...	19	2.5	400	50.9
Solomon Islands	1986[64]	39	25.6	24.9[65]	13.7	19.7	7.3	29.6	68.6	—	1.8	18	46.0	3.4	8.7
Somalia	1987	2,637	39.3	75.1[8]	42.3	52.0	32.8	...	...	...	...	1,893	71.8	251[9]	9.5[9]
South Africa	1991	10,215	41.0	68.3[4,49]	38.9	47.0	31.1	4.0[16]	89.4[16]	...	6.6[16]	1,180[4]	13.6[4]	2,215[4]	25.5[4]
Bophuthatswana	1980[66]	333	...	...	25.2	...	...	...	...	...	...	157	47.2	54	16.2
Ciskei	1980[66]	140	...	...	20.5	...	...	...	...	...	...	11	7.9	31	21.9
Transkei	1980[66]	554	...	...	23.8	...	...	...	...	...	...	420	75.9	30	5.4
Venda	1985[66]	67	42.2	31.3	14.6	20.2	10.5	...	...	...	...	9.2	13.8	4.3	6.4
Spain	1991[20]	15,073	35.5	60.0[6]	38.9	51.4	27.0	17.3	71.7	4.3	6.7	1,541	10.2	3,216	21.3
Sri Lanka	1990	6,969	37.3	61.5[30]	43.2	54.4	32.1	24.2	49.8	11.6	14.4	2,851	40.9	1,043	15.0
Sudan, The	1983[60]	6,343	29.1	57.4	35.1	50.0	20.4	59.2[51]	25.3[51]	9.9[51]	5.6[51]	4,029	63.5	317	5.0
Suriname	1980[20,67]	81	28.1	39.5	22.8	33.0	12.7	11.3	83.5	2.1	3.8	7.5	9.2	13.8	17.0
Swaziland	1987	330	39.4	62.6[8]	41.3	50.6	32.1	...	...	...	...	235	71.3	35[9]	10.7[9]
Sweden	1991[20]	4,552	48.0	83.9[6]	52.9	55.7	50.1	8.3	88.7	0.3	2.7	143	3.1	938	20.6
Switzerland	1991	3,600	38.3	70.7[16]	52.4	65.6	39.5	9.7[16]	90.3[16]	...	...	197	5.5	894	24.8
Syria	1989[20]	3,069	15.4	46.7[42]	26.2	43.4	8.3	8.9	54.1	22.3	14.7	675	22.0	494	16.1
Taiwan	1990	10,236	38.0	72.5	50.3	60.4	39.5	20.4	68.7	9.2	1.7	2,179	21.3	3,078	30.1
Tajikistan	1990	2,468	39.0	78.1[18]	46.1	...	...	...	...	...	...	831[24]	42.9[24]	261[24]	13.5[24]
Tanzania	1987	11,563	48.5	75.1[8]	47.8	49.7	46.0	...	...	...	...	9,528	82.4	538[9]	4.7[9]
Thailand	1989[20,68]	29,470	45.4	79.1[23]	53.5	58.4	48.7	31.0	31.5	26.8	10.7	16,501[56]	56.0[56]	3,344	11.3
Togo	1987	1,312	37.0	61.7[8]	41.3	52.6	30.2	70.3[23]	10.4[23]	11.3[23]	8.0[23]	926	70.6	142[9]	10.8[9]
Tonga	1986	24	21.0	43.6	25.1	39.4	10.6	10.2	47.0	32.1	10.6	10.6	44.7	0.9	3.9
Trinidad and Tobago	1990	468	34.0	61.5	37.7	50.0	25.5	18.0	78.1	3.1	0.8	51	10.8	77	16.4
Tunisia	1989	2,361	20.9	52.8	29.8	46.5	12.7	20.9	54.9	7.4	16.8	510	21.6	418	17.7
Turkey	1991[20]	21,045	31.1	59.6	37.5	51.4	23.4	28.7	37.4	31.1	2.8	9,524	45.3	2,911	13.8
Turkmenistan	1991	1,585	52.2[25]	84.2[18]	42.7	...	...	...	...	...	...	675	42.6	168	10.6
Tuvalu	1979[69]	4.0	51.3	81.1[30]	55.2	57.6	53.1	0.3	22.2	—77.5—	...	...	1.0	0.1	1.9
Uganda	1987	7,554	41.6	70.1[8]	45.0	52.8	37.2	...	...	...	...	6,236	82.6	385[9]	5.1[9]
Ukraine	1989	26,160	49.2	80.6[49]	50.8	56.0	46.4	...	...	...	...	6,128[25]	25.3[25]	7,650[25]	31.6[25]
United Arab Emirates	1988	726	10.4	69.0	47.0	67.6	12.9	6.8[16]	92.7[16]	0.1[16]	0.5[16]	37	5.0	68	9.4
United Kingdom	1990	28,436	42.8	75.7	50.3	58.4	42.6	13.1	81.4	...	5.5	569	2.0	5,898	20.7
United States	1991[71]	126,867	45.0	73.7	50.3	56.8	44.2	8.3	90.7	0.3	0.7	3,647	2.9	24,418	19.2
Uruguay	1990	1,242	40.6	55.9[73]	40.1	48.9	31.8	22.3[4]	70.8[4]	1.8[4]	5.1[4]	45	3.6	281	22.6
Uzbekistan	1991	8,976	43.8	78.2[18]	43.0	...	...	...	...	...	...	1,977[24]	29.1[24]	1,200[24]	17.6[24]
Vanuatu	1989	67	46.3	85.0	47.0	49.0	44.9	...	...	...	...	39.3[31]	76.8[31]	1.1[31]	2.2[31]
Venezuela	1990[20]	7,246	31.5	61.1	36.5	49.6	23.2	28.1	59.7	2.3	9.9	856	11.8	1,284	17.7
Vietnam	1989	30,521	51.7	79.9	47.4	47.0	47.7	...	...	...	...	20,471	67.1	3,390	11.1
Virgin Islands (U.S.)	1980	38.1	45.5	65.1	39.4	44.9	34.4	7.1	86.4	0.3	6.2	0.5	1.2	3.8	10.0
West Bank	1989	189	10.7	40.3[30]	18.4	36.7	4.5	...	...	...	...	37.1	19.6	28.9[9]	15.3[9]
Western Sahara	...	...	...	...	...	...	...	...	...	...	...	...	...	...	...
Western Samoa	1981	42	15.0	48.6	26.5	43.5	8.3	21.1	43.5	35.0	0.4	25	60.4	1.2	2.9
Yemen	1988	3,029	31.6	52.6	26.4	36.8	16.4	...	...	...	...	2,152	71.1	129	4.3
Yugoslavia	1990[24]	2,641	38.6	...	25.1	...	...	...	...	...	...	135	5.1	1,183	44.8
Zaire	1987	12,482	36.2	57.4[8]	38.4	49.6	27.5	...	...	...	...	8,419	67.5	1,847[9]	14.8[9]
Zambia	1987	2,411	28.5	51.5[8]	33.6	48.1	19.1	22.9[16]	42.5[16]	3.6[16]	31.0[16]	1,691	70.2	259[9]	10.7[9]
Zimbabwe	1986–87	3,260	47.8	76.5[30]	42.1	44.8	39.6	...	...	...	...	2,110	64.7	179	5.5

[1]Services includes finance, real estate and public administration, defense. [2]Unemployed, not previously employed only. [3]Employed persons only. [4]1985. [5]Services includes public administration, defense. [6]Ages 16–64. [7]Unemployed only. [8]Over age 10. [9]Manufacturing; mining, quarrying; public utilities includes construction. [10]Services includes transportation, communications; trade, hotels, restaurants; finance, real estate; and public administration, defense. [11]1983. [12]Over age 16. [13]1970. [14]1982. [15]Wage earners and self-employed only. [16]1980. [17]Includes unemployed, not previously employed. [18]Ages 16–59 (male) and 16–54 (female). [19]Includes self-employed and unemployed. [20]Excludes armed forces. [21]1989. [22]Mostly unemployed. [23]1981. [24]State sector only. [25]1990. [26]Ages 15–64 (male) and 15–59 (female). [27]Agriculture includes mining, quarrying. [28]Mostly employees of international companies and unemployed. [29]1988. [30]Over age 15. [31]1979. [32]Mostly unemployed, not previously employed. [33]Ages 15–69. [34]Over age 12. [35]Republic of Cyprus only. [36]Includes unemployed. [37]Services includes finance, real estate. [38]1984.

construction		transportation, communications		trade, hotels, restaurants		finance, real estate		public administration, defense		services		other		country
number ('000)	% of econ. active	number ('000)	% of econ. active	number ('000)	% of econ. active	number ('000)	% of econ. active	number ('000)	% of econ. active	number ('000)	% of econ. active	number ('000)	% of econ. active	
14	0.6	15	0.6	208	8.8	2	0.1	5[5]	5	130[5]	5.5[5]	132[36]	5.6[36]	Niger
546	1.8	1,112	3.6	7,417	24.1	120	0.4	5[5]	5	4,902[5]	15.9[5]	2,009[22]	6.5[22]	Nigeria
5.8	21.7	1.4	5.3	5.3	19.8	1.0	3.8	1.4	5.3	4.5	16.9	0.6[7]	2.3[7]	Northern Mariana Islands
142	6.7	166	7.8	369	17.4	156	7.3	5[5]	5	768[5]	36.1[5]	54[32]	2.5[32]	Norway
52	8.0	26	4.0	23	3.6	1	0.2	5[5]	5	110[5]	17.1[5]			Oman
2,036	6.2	1,615	4.9	4,072	12.4	277	0.8	5[5]	5	4,081[5]	12.4[5]	2,079[22]	6.3[22]	Pakistan
0.9	14.2	0.4	6.6	1.1	18.7	0.2	2.9	0.8	13.7	1.6	26.1	0.5[7]	7.8[7]	Palau
32	3.9	43	5.3	118	14.4	31	3.8	5[5]	5	222[5]	27.1[5]	73[32]	9.0[32]	Panama
22	2.9	1.7	2.4	25	3.4	4	0.6	5[5]	5	77[5]	10.5[5]	2	0.2	Papua New Guinea
70	6.7	31	2.9	86	8.3	18	1.7	5[5]	5	174[5]	16.8[5]	86[17]	8.3[17]	Paraguay
284	3.7	337	4.4	1,195	15.6	184	2.4	5[5]	5	2,046[5]	26.7[5]	—	—	Peru
974	4.0	1,137	4.6	3,145	12.8	444	1.8	5[5]	5	4,220[5]	17.2[5]	2,008[22]	8.2[22]	Philippines
1,465	7.9	1,235	6.7	1,493	8.1	322	1.7	5[5]	5	3,558[5]	19.3[5]	—	—	Poland
385	7.8	212	4.3	726	14.7	208	4.2	5[5]	5	1,098[5]	22.2[5]	231[22]	4.7[22]	Portugal
81	7.4	40	3.6	216	19.7	27	2.5	5[5]	5	480[5]	43.8[5]	9[2]	0.8[2]	Puerto Rico
40.5	20.1	7.4	3.7	22.0	10.9	3.2	1.6	5[5]	5	96.5[5]	47.9[5]	1.4[32]	0.7[32]	Qatar
11[14]	6.5[14]	6[14]	3.4[14]	14[14]	8.3[14]	16[14]	9.4[14]	5[5]	5	45[5,14]	25.8[5,14]	55[14,22]	31.9[14,22]	Réunion
653	6.0	752	6.9	679	6.3	44	0.4	5[5]	5	1,352[5]	12.5[5]	248	2.3	Romania
7,018[25]	8.9[25]	5,778[25]	7.3[25]	5,545[25]	7.1[25]	401[25]	0.5[25]	882[25]	1.1[25]	27,106[25]	34.5[25]	—	—	Russia
38	1.2	7	0.2	80	2.5	3	0.1	5[5]	5	120[5]	3.8[5]	9	0.3	Rwanda
0.4	2.5	0.3	1.6	1.3	7.3	0.8	4.7	1.0	5.7	2.9	17.0	2.2[22]	12.8[22]	St. Kitts and Nevis
2.6	6.3	1.5	3.5	2.8	6.5	0.5	1.1	2.4	5.6	7.9	18.8	10.1[22]	24.0[22]	St. Lucia
3.5	10.2	1.9	5.4	2.6	7.4	0.4	1.0	5[5]	5	7.6[5]	21.8[5]	7.6	21.9	St. Vincent
1.1	7.9	0.2	1.7	2.2	16.7	0.3	2.2	2.1	15.7	2.1	16.0	0.5[7]	3.7[7]	San Marino
1.8	5.9	1.0	3.4	2.0	6.5	0.2	0.5	2.4	7.8	3.5	11.3	1.4[7]	4.6[7]	São Tomé and Príncipe
1,181	22.0	321	6.0	964	18.0	151	2.8	5[5]	5	1,965[5]	36.6[5]	—	—	Saudi Arabia
...	...	...	...	...	...	...	...	...	...	...	...	...	...	Senegal
1.1[4,63]	4.4[4,63]	2.3[4,63]	9.4[4,63]	3.1[4,63]	12.8[4,63]	0.8[4,63]	3.4[4,63]	5[5]	5	3.6[4,5,63]	15.0[4,5,63]	8.6[4,36,63]	35.8[4,36,63]	Seychelles
9	9	10	10	10	10	10	10	10	10	266[10]	18.9[10]	—	—	Sierra Leone
99	6.4	153	9.8	345	22.2	163	10.5	5[5]	5	322[5]	20.7[5]	30[22]	1.9[22]	Singapore
51	6.5	46	5.9	98	12.5	37	4.7	5[5]	5	135[5]	17.1[5]	—	—	Slovenia
2.2	5.6	2.0	5.1	3.3	8.4	0.6	1.4	5[5]	5	9.4[5]	23.9[5]	0.3	0.8	Solomon Islands
9	9	10	10	10	10	10	10	10	10	493[10]	18.7[10]	—	—	Somalia
556[4]	6.4[4]	418[4]	4.8[4]	942[4]	10.8[4]	339[4]	3.9[4]	446[4]	5.1[4]	1,520[4]	17.5[4]	1,077[4,22]	12.4[4,22]	South Africa
22	6.6	7	2.2	23	6.8	1.2	0.4	5[5]	5	52[5]	15.7[5]	17	5.0	Bophuthatswana
6	4.1	5	3.8	14	10.0	1.2	0.9	5[5]	5	33[5]	23.9[5]	38	27.5	Ciskei
15	2.7	4	0.6	11	2.1	1.1	0.2	5[5]	5	49[5]	8.9[5]	23	4.2	Transkei
7.1	10.7	2.6	3.8	5.4	8.1	1.3	1.9	5[5]	5	17.4[5]	26.0[5]	19.6	29.3	Venda
1,519	10.1	776	5.2	2,908	19.3	790	5.2	5[5]	5	3,342[5]	22.2[5]	982[32]	6.5[32]	Spain
183	2.6	247	3.5	510	7.3	49	0.7	5[5]	5	980[5]	14.1[5]	1,104[22]	15.8[22]	Sri Lanka
139	2.2	215	3.4	294	4.6	21	0.3	5[5]	5	550[5]	8.7[5]	777[32]	12.3[32]	Sudan, The
3.8	4.7	2.9	3.6	11.4	14.1	2.0	2.4	5[5]	5	36.2[5]	44.7[5]	3.4	4.2	Suriname
9	9	10	10	10	10	10	10	10	10	60[10]	18.0[10]	—	—	Swaziland
312	6.9	318	7.0	624	13.7	397	8.7	5[5]	5	1,692[5]	37.2[5]	127[22]	2.7[22]	Sweden
332	9.2	219	6.1	730	20.3	383	10.7	5[5]	5	805[5]	22.4[5]	39[7]	1.1[7]	Switzerland
358	11.7	185	6.0	374	12.2	41	1.3	5[5]	5	826[5]	26.9[5]	117[2]	3.8[2]	Syria
447	4.4	442	4.3	1,575	15.4	313	3.1	1,381	13.5	652	6.4	171[22]	1.7[22]	Taiwan
161[24]	8.3[24]	65[24]	3.3[24]	145[24]	7.5[24]	...	...	39[24]	2.0[24]	437[24]	22.5[24]	—	—	Tajikistan
9	9	10	10	10	10	10	10	10	10	1,497[10]	13.0[10]	—	—	Tanzania
1,018	3.5	715	2.4	3,102	10.5	1	1	1	1	3,022[1]	10.3[1]	1,766[22]	6.0[22]	Thailand
9	9	10	10	10	10	10	10	10	10	245[10]	18.6[10]	—	—	Togo
1.7	7.2	1.1	4.7	1.5	6.4	0.4	1.9	5[5]	5	5.1[5]	21.4[5]	2.3[22]	9.8[22]	Tonga
65	13.9	31	6.6	81	17.3	28	6.0	5[5]	5	134[5]	28.5[5]	2	0.3	Trinidad and Tobago
248	10.5	96	4.1	217	9.2	15	0.7	5[5]	5	444[5]	18.8[5]	412[22]	17.5[22]	Tunisia
876	4.2	781	3.7	2,173	10.3	414	2.0	5[5]	5	2,675[5]	12.7[5]	1,553[7]	7.4[7]	Turkey
151	9.5	64	4.0	90	5.7	1	1	1	1	410[1]	25.9[1]	27	1.7	Turkmenistan
0.2	5.6	0.1	2.7	0.1	2.4	—	0.3	0.2	4.4	0.2	4.2	3.1[36,70]	77.5[36,70]	Tuvalu
9	9	10	10	10	10	10	10	10	10	933[10]	12.4[10]	—	—	Uganda
1,882[25]	7.8[25]	1,732[25]	7.2[25]	1,753[25]	7.2[25]	128[25]	0.5[25]	287[25]	1.2[25]	4,134[25]	17.1[25]	516[25]	2.1[25]	Ukraine
130	18.0	47	6.5	96	13.3	26	3.6	5[5]	5	321[5]	44.2[5]	—	—	United Arab Emirates
1,805	6.3	1,546	5.4	5,445	19.1	3,143	11.1	2,190	7.7	5,981	21.0	1,556[7]	5.5[7]	United Kingdom
8,100	6.4	6,978	5.5	25,900[72]	20.4[72]	13,941	11.0	5[5]	5	43,002[5,72]	33.9[5,72]	880[32]	0.7[32]	United States
83	6.7	72	5.8	220	17.7	57	4.6	5[5]	5	456[5]	36.7[5]	29[2]	2.3[2]	Uruguay
714[24]	10.5[24]	251[24]	3.7[24]	462[24]	6.8[24]	1	1	1	1	2,067[1,24]	30.4[1,24]	129[24]	1.9[24]	Uzbekistan
1.1[31]	2.2[31]	1.3[31]	2.6[31]	2.2[31]	4.3[31]	0.3[31]	0.6[31]	5[5]	5	5.5[5,31]	10.7[5,31]	0.3[31]	0.6[31]	Vanuatu
647	8.9	428	5.9	1,497	20.7	421	5.8	5[5]	5	2,007[5]	27.7[5]	106[32]	1.5[32]	Venezuela
581	1.9	576	1.9	1,880	6.2	90	0.3	305	1.0	1,374	4.5	1,854[22]	6.1[22]	Vietnam
3.7	9.7	2.8	7.4	9.0	23.8	2.6	6.7	4.1	10.8	9.2	24.2	2.3[7]	6.2[7]	Virgin Islands (U.S.)
47.7	25.2	9.5	5.0	25.9	13.7	37	37	21.8	11.5	9.7[37,39]	5.1[37,39]	8.3[7]	4.4[7]	West Bank
...	...	...	...	...	...	...	...	...	...	...	...	...	...	Western Sahara
2.3	5.5	1.4	3.3	1.8	4.4	1.3	3.1	1.8	4.4	6.4	15.4	0.3	0.6	Western Samoa
178	5.9	90	3.0	84	2.8	4	0.1	5[5]	5	391[5]	12.9[5]	—	—	Yemen
206	7.8	175	6.6	347	13.2	95	3.6	5[5]	5	500[5]	18.9[5]	—	—	Yugoslavia
9	9	10	10	10	10	10	10	10	10	2,216[10]	17.7[10]	—	—	Zaire
9	9	10	10	10	10	10	10	10	10	461[10]	19.1[10]	—	—	Zambia
51	1.6	76	2.3	128	3.9	24	0.7	5[5]	5	397[5]	12.5[5]	277[22]	8.5[22]	Zimbabwe

[39]Services includes public utilities.   [40]Former West Germany only.   [41]Ages 15–65.   [42]1986.   [43]Excludes Alderney and Sark.   [44]Data are for persons aged 15–64 only.   [45]Workers covered by compulsory social insurance only.   [46]1978.   [47]Excludes Assam.   [48]1977.   [49]Ages 20–64.   [50]Ages 14–64.   [51]1973.   [52]Excludes about 20,000 foreign border workers.   [53]Includes unemployed, previously employed.   [54]Manufacturing; mining; quarrying; public utilities includes transportation, communications.   [55]Island of Mauritius only.   [56]Includes unemployed seasonal agricultural workers.   [57]Includes underemployed seasonal nonagricultural workers.   [58]1987.   [59]Mostly underemployed informal workers.   [60]Excludes nomadic population.   [61]Citizens over age 10 involved in money-raising activities only.   [62]1985–86.   [63]Excludes self-employed and domestic workers.   [64]Wage earners only.   [65]Over age 14.   [66]Excludes migrant workers in South Africa.   [67]Excludes unemployed.   [68]February survey.   [69]De facto indigenous population only.   [70]Mostly workers in the noncash economy.   [71]Excludes armed forces overseas.   [72]Services includes hotels.   [73]Over age 20.

Agriculture and land use

This table provides data on the structure of national agricultural sectors from the perspective of farms and farmland use. The data are taken mainly from national agricultural censuses and surveys, supplemented by reports of the United Nations Food and Agriculture Organization's (FAO's) *World Census of Agriculture*. Many of these national censuses, of course, are taken under guidelines established by the FAO for the *World Census of Agriculture* programs (the 1990 census is the fifth and will include national censuses taken during the decade 1986–95). It represents a cooperative effort by FAO member countries to collect agricultural data within a general framework that permits international harmonization of concepts and definitions; transfer of technical expertise; and increased effectiveness in the collection, analysis, publication, and policy-related use of such statistics. More than 100 countries were expected to participate in the 1990 census.

All agricultural statistics are subject to quality-control problems, including errors or biases arising from such factors as incomplete or inaccurate lists of holdings, ambiguous questions, respondents who inadvertently or willfully give inaccurate information, failure to record data for all parts of fragmented holdings, respondents' misunderstandings of the definitions of land use and cropping methods, or a failure to report livestock temporarily absent from the holding on public or common pasture land or in transit. Frequently, subjects studied, classificational schemes, and definitions vary

from the FAO guidelines (economic planners need different information about a commercial, high-technology, multicrop agricultural sector than they do for a family-subsistence, low-technology, one-crop sector). When a complete census of agriculture is impossible, a sample survey may be taken. This is a limited census of a predetermined number of carefully screened holdings. From these results, nationwide projections may be prepared.

With respect to the first section of the table, number and size of farms, many countries impose a minimum size limit for holdings that may be covered in their census reports, and this cutoff, if not sufficiently low, can result in a substantial undercount of smaller holdings; conversely Soviet-bloc nations often publish statistics only on state collective or cooperative farms and exclude privately held plots of land, even though in some instances these provide a significant fraction of agricultural output.

The land tenure statistics classify farms according to the rights under which the farmer holds the land. Owner-operated includes two types of ownership: outright ownership in which the holder has title and has the right to determine use and transfer of the land; and ownerlike possession in which the holder lacks the legal title but uses it under perpetual lease, hereditary tenure, or leases of 30 years or more with nominal, or no, rent. Farms classed as owner-operated are divided into individual and family, corporate or state, and socialized or collective proprietorships. Rented

Agriculture and land use

country	year	number of farms ('000)	average (ha)	size class (%) under 1 ha	1–5 ha	5–10 ha	10–20 ha	20–50 ha	50–200 ha	over 200 ha	owner-operated individual/family	corporate/state	socialized/collective	rented (including share-croppers)	tribal/communal	other[b]
Afghanistan	1981	126[1]	3.5[1]	44.8[1]	35.2[1]	—	— 20.0[1] —	—	—	—	55.1[1]	—	— 100.0 —	—	25.1[1]	—	19.8[1]
Albania	1989	0.5	1,182[2]									—	— 100.0 —	—	—	—
Algeria	1987	899[5]	6.2[5]	1.1[5]	12.7[5]	15.8[5]	21.7[5]	25.6[5]	18.0[5]	5.1[5]	...	...	...	...	...	...
American Samoa	1990	1.1	2.9	44.7[6]	40.0[7]	— 13.8[8] —			1.6[9]		93.9	—	—	2.2	—	3.9
Andorra	—															
Angola	1970–71	1,067	3.9	3.3	13.5	9.3	11.3	13.7	19.2	29.7	80.5	1.1	—	—	18.2	0.2
Antigua and Barbuda	1984	2.3	2.1	61.7	33.8	2.9	0.6	0.6	0.4	—	32.1[11]	— 22.9[11] —		40.5[11]	—	4.5[11]
Argentina	1974	510	399	— 19.4 —		8.2	9.5	16.7	25.1	21.1	73.8[11]	—	—	11.7[11]	—	14.5[11]
Armenia	1990	...	...	...	...	...	...	...	...	...	...	...	...	...	...	...
Aruba	...	...	...	...	...	...	...	...	...	...	...	...	...	...	...	...
Australia	1991	126	3,604[12]	— 15.1 —					9.6[13]	75.3[14]	...	...	...	...	...	...
Austria	1980[16]	303	24.2	3.7	31.0	17.3	21.0	21.2	5.2	0.6	59.0	—	—	2.3	—	38.7
Azerbaijan	1990	...	...	...	...	...	...	...	...	...	...	...	...	...	...	...
Bahamas, The	1978	4.2	8.5	55.2[6]	30.1[7]	— 12.3[8] —		1.1[17]	0.4[18]	1.0[19]	74.9	0.6	—	4.0	—	20.5
Bahrain	1980	0.8	4.4	19.4	52.9	17.4	8.2	2.0	— 0.1 —		37.9	0.1	—	62.0	—	—
Bangladesh	1983–84	10,045	0.9	70.3	27.0[20]	2.5[21]	— 0.2[22] —				53.2[23]	...	...	0.5[23]	...	46.3[23]
Barbados	1969	0.2	95.8	...	...	...	...	...	...	...	...	...	...	...	...	...
Belarus	1990	...	...	...	...	...	...	...	...	...	...	...	...	...	...	...
Belgium	1988	89[24]	15.2[24]	— 38.9[24] —		14.9[24]	19.9[24]	20.9[24]	— 5.4[24] —		27.7[11,25]	—	0.8[11,25]	71.5[11,25]	—	—
Belize	1974	8.9	26.7	— 69.4 —			16.7	8.6	4.4	0.9	43.6	56.4	—	—	—	—
Benin	1983	...	...	...	...	...	...	...	...	...	...	...	...	...	...	...
Bermuda	1990	0.08[26]	3.1[26]	...	...	...	...	...	...	...	...	...	...	...	...	...
Bhutan	1984	160	0.8	51.3[6,27]	42.9[7,27]	— 5.8[27,28] —					...	...	...	...	...	...
Bolivia	1984	315	72.1	25.3	42.1	12.1	6.8	6.1	4.9	2.8	70.3	—	—	2.0	4.3	23.3
Bosnia and Hercegovina[29]	1981	540	...	33.4	48.9	13.7	2.3	— 0.6 —			100.0	—	—	—	—	—
Botswana	1985	81.0	3.2	32.1	49.9	12.6	— 5.4 —				—	0.6	—	—	99.4	—
Brazil	1985	5,835	64.5	11.1	28.6	13.2	14.0	15.6	12.4	4.9	63.2	—	—	17.9	—	18.4[31]
Brunei	1964	6.3	2.6	44.1[6]	40.4[7]	— 15.5[28] —					52.3	1.0	—	22.0	—	24.7
Bulgaria	1991	2.2[4,33]	2,467[4,33]	...	...	...	...	...	...	...	—	84.6[4,11]	—	15.4[4]	—	—
Burkina Faso	1984	1,860	4.8	...	...	...	...	...	...	...	...	...	...	...	...	...
Burundi	1983	...	...	...	...	...	...	...	...	...	...	...	...	...	...	...
Cambodia	1962[34]	840	3.6	30.7	54.9	10.4	3.4	— 0.6 —			...	...	...	...	...	...
Cameroon	1973	926	1.6	42.7	53.8	3.2	0.3	—	—	—	2.4	—	—	5.2	59.5	32.9
Canada	1986	293	231	1.6[6]	3.4[7]	12.1[35]	29.7[36]	14.6[37]	— 38.6[38] —		—	— 63.7[11] —		36.3[11]	—	—
Cape Verde	1979	...	...	...	...	...	...	...	...	...	...	...	...	...	...	...
Cayman Islands	1984	0.2	...	—	5.0	80.0	—	10.0	3.0	2.0	—	— 90.0 —		— 10.0 —		
Central African Republic	1974	283	1.7	32.2	65.2	2.5	—	—	—	—	0.3[11]	—	—	0.1[11]	98.6[11]	1.2[11]
Chad	1973	366	2.6	19.7	69.5	10.0	— 0.8 —		—	—	...	...	...	...	...	...
Chile	1975–76	306	94.1	16.0	32.5	13.4	12.3	11.8	9.2	4.8	—	— 84.0 —		7.2	— 8.8 —	
China	1987	1,650[41]	...	...	...	...	...	...	...	...	—	10.0[42]	90.0[42]	—	—	—
Colombia	1971	1,177	26.3	22.8	36.7	13.6	10.0	8.5	6.3	2.1	68.7	—	—	5.8	4.1	21.4
Comoros	1982	...	...	...	...	...	...	...	...	...	...	...	...	...	...	...
Congo	1986	143[5]	1.4[5]	37.3[5]	62.2[5]	0.5[5]	—	—	—	—	91.7[11]	8.3[11]	—	—	—	—
Cook Islands	1975[43]	1.1	2.3	...	...	...	...	...	...	...	...	...	...	...	...	...
Costa Rica	1973	82	38.3	23.3	25.5	11.2	10.8	15.2	10.7	3.3	97.9	1.7	—	0.1	—	0.3
Côte d'Ivoire	1975	550	5.0	9.5	54.4	24.9	9.4	1.7	0.1	—	...	...	...	...	...	...
Croatia[29]	1981	569	...	30.7	51.1	14.7	2.3	— 0.3 —			100.0	—	—	—	—	—
Cuba	1988	1.8[33]	1,047[33]	...	...	...	...	...	...	...	—	—	79.0	—	—	—
Cyprus	1985	48.0	3.8	24.4	56.8	15.0	2.9	— 0.9 —			6.0[11]	30.8[11]	63.2[11]	9.4	—	11.6[44]
Czechoslovakia	1980	1,391	8.1	89.9[45]	— 9.9[46] —			— 0.2[47] —			6.0[11]	30.8[11]	63.2[11]	—	0.6	—
Denmark	1991[48]	77	35.9	— 2.7 —		15.2	23.4	37.7	— 20.9 —		—	— 64.4[24] —		— 35.6[24] —		
Djibouti	1987–88	1.2	0.4	*c.* 100	...	...	...	...	...	...	...	...	...	...	...	...
Dominica	1986–88	1.9	1.9	89[49]	— 9[50] —			— 2 —			33	—	—	15	—	52
Dominican Republic	1981	385	6.3	16.0	65.7	8.5	5.4	2.6	1.5	0.3	53.2	18.5	4.5	1.6	—	17.4
Ecuador	1974	517	15.4	27.8	38.8	10.6	8.0	8.2	5.6	0.9	70.3	0.3	—	7.7	7.4	14.3
Egypt	1985	3,546	0.7	95.5[51]	2.4[52]	— 2.1[53] —			0.1[54]		...	...	...	...	...	...
El Salvador	1970–71	271	5.4	48.9	37.9	5.8	3.4	2.6	1.2	0.2	41.5	—	—	28.2	6.3	24.1
Equatorial Guinea	...	...	...	...	...	...	...	...	...	...	...	...	...	...	...	...
Estonia	1990	...	...	...	...	...	...	...	...	...	...	...	...	...	...	...
Ethiopia	1976–77	4,893	1.4	49.9	46.5	3.4	0.2	—	—	—	98.4	1.6	—	—	—	—

includes sharecropping; communal/tribal includes types of customary or traditional arrangements in which title or goods do not change hands. "Other" usually includes farms held under multiple forms of tenure.

Statistics on types of farms by commodities produced refer to FAO categories. The terms "mainly crops" and "mainly livestock" indicate that more than half of the for-sale production was that indicated.

The section on technology provides some measures of the role modern technology plays in the farm activities of each country (although, of course, irrigation may employ technology developed in ancient times). Ratios referred to area mean area of "arable" (cultivated and cultivable) land, roughly "cropland," less area of permanent crops (see below).

The classification of farmland by economic use is also subject to differing treatment internationally. For purposes of this table, "cropland" comprises: (1) land under temporary crops (those requiring replanting after each harvest), (2) land under permanent crops (those not requiring replanting, including tree, bush and shrub, and vine crops), and (3) land temporarily (less than five years) fallow (unused, but capable of being returned to cultivation with no special preparation). "Meadows and pastures" includes land (both permanent and temporary use) whose principal purpose is the raising of animal fodder or forage. "Woodland and forest" includes both natural and planted tracts of timber, whether harvested or not. "Other"

comprises: (1) mixed and multiple use lands, (2) residue of farmland holdings not classifiable according to categories listed above (including areas of farm buildings, roads, ornamental gardens, flooded land, wasteland, etc.), (3) land not classified by respondents in census, or (4) detail not distinguishable as one of categories above by reason of its summarization in a published source. When "cropland" is indicated to compose 100 percent of farmland, it should usually be understood to mean only that woodland, pasture, etc., are not part of the published data, rather than that those classes of land use do not exist.

Measurements of area are given in hectares (1 hectare is equal to 2.471 acres). A kilogram (kg) is equal to 2.205 pounds (1 kg/ha = 0.89 lb/ac). The following notes further define the column headings:
a. All properties used wholly or partly for agricultural production. A property need not have agricultural land to be considered a farm; piggeries, hatcheries, and poultry batteries are farms because they engage in agricultural production, i.e., raise livestock and produce livestock products.
b. All forms of tenure not included in the preceding categories. Includes land operated by schools, religious bodies, squatters, seasonally by nomads, and built-on, waste, and similar types of alienation.
... Not available, or no agricultural census or survey ever taken.
—None, less than half the smallest unit shown, or not applicable.

mainly crops	mainly live-stock	mixed/other	tractors (per 1,000 ha)	electri-city (% of farms having)	irriga-tion (% of land irrig.)	artificial fertilizer (kg/ha)	total ('000 ha)	% of total land area	perma-nent crops	tempo-rary crops	fallow	total crop-land	mead-ows and pastures	wood-land and forest	other	country
...	...	...	0.1	...	34	7	39,810	61.0	1.8	46.3	51.9	19.9	75.4	4.8	—	Afghanistan
61.5[3]	32.0[3]	6.5[3]	20.8	...	73	158	1,111[4]	40.0[4]	17.6	—82.4—		64.3[4]	35.7[4]	...	...	Albania
...	...	...	13.9	...	5	23	39,701	16.7	7.6	51.0	41.4	19.2	78.3	—	2.5	Algeria
55.7[3]	44.3[3]	—	7.0	38.5	...	...	3.2	16.4	—88.7—		11.3	71.4	5.3	...	23.3	American Samoa
...	...	...	...	...	...	...	...	2.0	...	...	...	...	...	...	...	Andorra
...	...	...	3.4	...	89[10]	4	4,180	3.4	36.8	63.2	...	1.7	82.0	...	16.2	Angola
32.9	44.1	23.0	29.8	...	...	...	2.5	9.0	26.0	57.1	16.9	62.6	36.0	—1.4—		Antigua and Barbuda
10.6	78.9	10.5	8.1	...	7	5	203,345	73.1	...	...	...	10.6	78.9	4.8	5.7	Argentina
...	...	...	27.2	...	...	...	1,300	43.3	...	...	...	38.5	53.8	—	7.7	Armenia
...	...	...	...	...	...	...	...	...	...	...	...	...	...	...	...	Aruba
24.1	56.0	19.9	6.8	...	4	29	466,800[12]	60.8[12]	0.3[15]	—99.7[15]—		10.0[15]	—90.0[15]—			Australia
...	...	...	236	...	—	208	7,326	87.4	6.6	87.4	6.0	21.3	26.0	41.5	11.2	Austria
...	...	...	24.2	...	...	...	4,200	48.3	...	...	...	38.1	52.4	—	9.5	Azerbaijan
...	...	...	9.6	...	10[10]	...	36.2	2.6	23.3	59.9	16.8	23.3	6.9	25.7	44.0	Bahamas, The
...	...	...	...	21.3	...	...	3.5	5.2	50.7	49.3	...	45.9	...	...	54.1	Bahrain
91.3[23]	8.7[23]	—	0.6	...	30	83	9,117	63.5	2.1[23]	96.3[23]	1.5[23]	88.7[23]	...	—11.3[23]—		Bangladesh
...	...	...	18.6	...	...	94	19.8	45.9	...	...	...	13.7	—86.3—			Barbados
...	...	...	20.8	...	...	...	9,300	44.9	...	...	...	65.6	33.3	—	1.1	Belarus
...	2.5	...	151.7	...	—	519	1,362	44.6	1.6	97.8	0.6	52.8	47.2	—	...	Belgium
...	...	...	24.5	...	5	80	233	10.0	13.1	81.1	5.8	36.5	15.9	36.1	11.6	Belize
...	...	...	0.1	...	—	4	3,300	29.3	...	...	...	100.0	—	—	—	Benin
...	...	...	22.9	...	...	...	2.4	4.4	18.6	72.9	8.5	91.1	8.9	—	—	Bermuda
...	...	...	...	...	30	1	156	3.4	11.7	—88.3—		100.0	—	—	—	Bhutan
...	...	...	1.4	...	5	1	22,670	20.6	—55.0—		45.0	6.9	47.7	39.0	6.4	Bolivia
...	...	...	...	...	...	...	2,525	49.4	8.9	70.9	20.2	44.2	55.4	—	0.4	Bosnia and Hercegovina[29]
13.6	27.9	58.5	3.6	...	—	1	343[30]	5.9[30]	—	100.0[30]	—	83.5[30]	...	...	...	Botswana
80.0[32]	16.2[32]	3.8[32]	10.4	4.1[32]	4	47	376,287	44.5	18.2[30]	66.9[30]	14.9[30]	15.8[30]	47.8[30]	24.2[30]	12.2[30]	Brazil
...	...	...	24.3	...	33	100	16.4	2.8	78.0	22.0	—	54.8	0.1	16.4	28.7	Brunei
54.4[3]	45.6[3]	—	13.8	...	33	194	6,159	55.6	6.3	—93.7—		75.4	24.6	...	...	Bulgaria
...	...	...	0.04	...	...	4	8,919	32.6	...	...	...	...	...	...	...	Burkina Faso
...	...	...	0.1	...	6	2	2,388	85.8	—73.8—		26.2	56.7	37.7	5.6	...	Burundi
...	...	...	0.5	...	3	1	2,984	16.5	94.9	3.5	1.6	96.1	—	3.9	...	Cambodia
...	...	...	0.2	...	—	6[24]	1,490	3.3	...	...	...	100.0	—	—	—	Cameroon
52.2	44.4	3.4	16.8	...	1.8	46	67,826	7.4	—79.6—		20.4	61.5	5.2	—33.3—		Canada
...	...	...	0.4	...	5	—	25[39]	6.2[39]	20.8[39]	79.1[39]	...	100.0[39]	—	—	—	Cape Verde
2.4	7.1	90.5	90.0	...	85[8]	1	...	...	...	...	...	...	...	...	...	Cayman Islands
...	...	...	0.1	...	...	2	491	0.8	11.8	88.2	—	100.0	—	—	—	Central African Republic
...	...	...	0.05	...	—	2	23,877[40]	45.8[40]	50.0[40]	—50.0[40]—		23.7[40]	76.3[40]	...	...	Chad
...	...	...	8.6	...	30	74	28,759	38.0	24.4	36.6	38.9	11.5	42.3	20.7	25.5	Chile
...	...	...	9.3	...	49	260	166,902	17.4	4.1	—95.9—		100.0	—	—	—	China
...	...	...	9.1	...	13	87	30,993	27.0	30.6	27.6	41.8	24.7	56.4	...	18.9	Colombia
...	...	...	...	...	...	...	83	44.3	56.4	—43.6—		100.0	—	—	—	Comoros
6.2[3]	93.8[3]	—	4.9	...	3	4	226	0.7	14.8	85.2	...	100.0	—	—	—	Congo
...	...	...	134	...	...	...	...	...	55.9	21.9	22.2	100.0	—	—	—	Cook Islands
...	...	...	22.5	...	41	191	3,122	60.0	42.2	57.8	—	15.7	49.9	22.9	11.4	Costa Rica
...	...	...	1.4	...	3	11	2,753	8.6	65.9	34.1	...	100.0	—	—	—	Côte d'Ivoire
...	...	...	...	...	...	...	3,220	57.0	8.8	81.8	9.4	50.4	48.5	—	1.1	Croatia[29]
...	...	...	29.5	...	34	179	8,679	78.3	...	...	...	33.9	32.1	31.9	2.1	Cuba
72.7	27.3	...	131	...	34	137	210	35.6	34.7	54.3	11.0	74.9	—25.1—			Cyprus
34.3	24.4	41.3	28.2	100.0	6	312	6,924	54.1	2.6	—97.4—		75.3	24.7	...	...	Czechoslovakia
49.1	22.4	28.5	65.1	...	17	237	2,770	65.3	...	98.9	...	80.2	19.8	...	...	Denmark
...	...	...	...	...	...	...	6	0.3	...	6.8	...	100.0	—	—	—	Djibouti
...	...	...	12.9	...	...	176	20	26.3	...	...	...	...	...	...	...	Dominica
44.0	56.0	—	2.3	60.0	23	41	2,412	49.8	38.0	40.2	21.8	34.1	51.6	13.0	0.9	Dominican Republic
67.8	12.4	19.8	5.1	...	33	32	7,955	29.6	32.8	51.5	15.7	32.8	32.2	29.0	6.0	Ecuador
...	...	...	22.8	...	112	400	2,731[55]	3.0[55]	3.5[55]	96.5[55]	...	100.0[55]	—	—	—	Egypt
95.3	4.7	—	6.0	...	21	133	1,452	69.0	25.1	58.6	16.4	44.9	38.2	11.6	5.3	El Salvador
...	...	...	0.8	...	...	...	...	...	...	...	...	...	...	...	...	Equatorial Guinea
...	...	...	18.5	...	...	...	1,400	31.1	...	...	...	78.6	21.4	—	...	Estonia
...	...	...	0.3	...	1	4	6,971	5.7	7.4	76.8	15.8	86.9	9.1	...	4.0	Ethiopia

Agriculture and land use (continued)

country	farms (latest census of agriculture)[a]			size of holding							tenure (% of farms)					
	year	number of farms ('000)	average (ha)	size class (%)							owner-operated			rented (including share-croppers)	tribal/ communal	other[b]
				under 1 ha	1–5 ha	5–10 ha	10–20 ha	20–50 ha	50–200 ha	over 200 ha	individual/ family	corporate/ state	socialized/ collective			
Faeroe Islands	...	...	...	...	...	...	...	...	...	...	...			3.5	95.1	1.4
Fiji	1978–79	66	4.2	64.3	20.6	8.1	3.7	2.1	—1.2—		—	—78.6—	—	21.4		
Finland	1990[56]	199	12.8	—	34.6	21.5	23.9	17.6	—2.4—		—	—78.6—	—	21.4		
France	1988	1,017	26.6[30]	8.8	18.6	11.0	16.4	28.3	—16.9—		65.2[42]			33.5[42]	—	1.2[42]
French Guiana	1988	4.5	4.6	16.5	73.6	6.0	1.5	—2.4—			...			...		...
French Polynesia	1987	5.6	...	37.7		...62.3...					36.5			6.3	—	57.1
Gabon	1975	71	1.0	68.0	—32.0—		—	—			81.8			0.3	5.3	12.5
Gambia, The	1989–90	...	...	...	...	...	...	...	...	...	...			...		...
Gaza Strip	1968	...	...	...	...	...	...	...	...	...	...			...		...
Georgia	1990	...	...	...	...	...	...	...	...	...	...			...		...
Germany[57]	1990[2]	630	18.7	12.5[49]	17.7[58]	16.8	20.6	24.8	—7.6—		39.5[55]			6.7[55]	—	53.8[55]
Ghana	1970	805	3.2	36.6	48.7	9.0	3.9	1.8	—		...			...		...
Gibraltar	—															
Greece	1981	999	3.5	24.7	54.2	15.0	4.7	1.2	—0.2—		...			...		...
Greenland	—															
Grenada	1981	8	1.7	88.3[49]	6.9[59]	3.3[60]	0.7	0.4[17]	—0.3[61]—		—	—73.2—	—	14.1		12.7
Guadeloupe	1988	17	2.8	32.1	58.3	7.0	1.6	—0.9—			46.6[62]			19.1[62]		34.3[62]
Guam	1987	0.4	15.1	42.2[26]	33.9[7]	—19.4[8]—		—4.6[9]—			64.4			4.3	—	31.3
Guatemala	1979	600	6.8	39.7[64]	49.8[65]	8.2[66]	2.0[67]	—0.2[68]—			—	—74.0[69]—	—	6.3[69]	5.8[69]	13.9[69]
Guernsey	1991	0.102	16.2	6.7[70]	24.0[70]	23.1[70]	—46.1[70]—				32.4[11,24]			67.6[11,24]		...
Guinea	1984–85[2]	...	2.4	...	...	...	...	...	...	...	...			...		...
Guinea-Bissau	1961	87	3.0	13.4	73.3	10.0	3.0	0.3	—			90.0				10.0
Guyana	1964	...	...	...	...	...	...	...	...	...	...			...		...
Haiti	1971	617	1.4	58.7	37.5	—3.8—					66.6			25.0		8.4
Honduras	1974	195	13.5	17.3	46.6	14.5	9.8	7.8	3.3	0.8	99.7	0.1	—		0.2	
Hong Kong	1986	11	0.3	97.5	2.3	0.1	—0.1—					—9.0—		77.0		14.0
Hungary	1990	1,412	...	90.0[72]	—9.9[72]—		—0.1[72]—				6.8[73]	13.3[73]	74.5[73]			
Iceland	1981	7.0	...	15.7	9.3	11.7	23.7	35.8	—3.7—		...			...		...
India	1976–77	81,569	2.0	54.6	35.8	6.6	2.4	0.5	—0.1—		92.7	—	—	1.2	—	6.1
Indonesia	1987	19,501[55]	c.1[55]	70.7[55]	—29.3[55]—						74.8[5]	—5	—5	3.2[5]	—5	22.1[5]
Iran	1982	...	...	...	...	...	...	...	...	...	...			...		...
Iraq	1979	470	13.3	25.9[75]	27.6[76]	23.2[77]	11.5[78]	9.4	1.9[79]	0.5[80]	52.5[10]			40.9[10]		6.6[10]
Ireland	1986	279[32]	25.0[70]	2.7[32]	—37.8[32]—		—52.4[32]—		7.1[32]		...			...		...
Isle of Man	1987	0.8	59.7	—25.8[81]—		14.0[82]	18.2[17]	23.4[18]	18.5[19]		72.4			27.6		...
Israel	1981	52	11.3	26.5	57.6	8.3	4.0	2.0	—1.8—		84.0		1.4			14.6
Italy	1982	3,269	7.2	18.0[83]	30.2[83]	37.7[83]	3.1[83]	9.2[83]	1.8[83]		81.5[32]			6.7[32]		11.8[32]
Jamaica	1978–79	184	2.9	32.5[84]	60.7[85]	4.8[60]	0.9	0.4[17]	0.3[18]	0.4[19]	99.5[86]	0.2[86]		—		0.3[86]
Japan	1990	3,835	1.4	68.5	29.4	—2.1—					79.4[32]			...		20.6[32]
Jersey	1990	0.6	11.1	—45.0[87]—		16.4[88]	19.7[89]	—19.0[90]—			31.4[27]			68.6[27]		...
Jordan	1983	57	6.3	25.3	44.6	15.6	8.6	4.5	1.3	0.1	80.5			13.1	0.3	6.1
Kazakhstan	1990	...	...	...	...	...	...	...	...	...	...			...		...
Kenya	1976–79	2,750	2.5	65.5	27.3	2.7[92]	3.4	—4.4[93]—			...			...		...
Kiribati	...	...	...	...	...	...	...	...	...	...	...			...		...
Korea, North	...	...	...	...	...	...	...	...	...	...	...			...		...
Korea, South	1990[2]	1,767	1.2	60.8[24]	—39.2[24]—						82.5[32]			17.4[32]		0.1[32]
Kuwait	1985–86	1.9	2.4	48.6[32]	25.4[32]	10.2[32]	8.7[32]	4.0[32]	3.1[32]	—	95.3					4.7
Kyrgyzstan	1990	...	...	...	...	...	...	...	...	...	...			...		...
Laos	1983	...	...	...	...	...	...	...	...	...	...			...		...
Latvia	1990	...	...	...	...	...	...	...	...	...	...			...		...
Lebanon	1970	143	4.3	47.7	—44.5—		—6.5—		1.2	0.1	...			...		...
Lesotho	1986	207	2.0[32]	27.0[32]	67.5[32]	—5.5[32]—					...			...		...
Liberia	1971[94]	122	3.0	52.8	31.0	12.0	—3.7—		—0.5—		40.0[11]	—	—	—	43.3[11]	16.7[11]
Libya	1974	144	14.0	12.7	34.1	20.6	17.4	12.0	—3.2—		...			...		...
Liechtenstein	1985	0.45	8.7	30.8	27.9	13.4	13.2	13.6	—1.1—		85.5			11.7	—	2.8
Lithuania	1990	...	...	...	...	...	...	...	...	...	...			...		...
Luxembourg	1991	3.7	37	8.9	17.4	8.4	9.5	25.1	—30.8—		49.9[11]	—0.5[11]—		49.6[11]		...
Macau	—															
Macedonia[29]	1981	176	...	44.7	43.0	6.7	1.2	—0.2—			100.0			—	—	...
Madagascar	1984–85	1,453	1.3	54.8	44.2	1.0	0.2	—0.1—			—	—87.3[11]—		4.9[11]		7.4[11]
Malawi	1980–81[95]	1,136	1.2	54.9	40.1[96]	—5.0[97]—					...			...		...
Malaysia	1980[98]	920[99]	2.2[99,100]	...	...	...	...	...	...	...	53.2[32,99]	18.2[32,101]	...	19.6[32,99]	...	9.0[32,99]
Maldives	1985	...	...	...	...	...	...	...	...	...	...			...		...
Mali	1982–83	562	4.0	20.1	54.1	17.4	—8.4—				96.8[103]	3.2				...
Malta	1983	12	1.1	67.8	30.0	2.0	—0.2—				16.0			70.4		13.6[44]
Marshall Islands	—															
Martinique	1988	16.0	2.3	64.9	28.2	4.0	1.6	—1.4—			...			...		...
Mauritania	1984–85	100	2.0	49.2	41.0[20]	7.0[60]	2.0	0.5[17]	—0.3[61]—		68.4			4.4	10.4	17.0
Mauritius	1980	32.5	1.1	61.3	36.2	1.9	0.3	0.2	—0.1—		95.8			4.2	—	...
Mayotte	1987	5.9[55]	1.7[91]	...	...	...	...	...	...	...	...			...		...
Mexico	1970[104]	2,848	49	23.5	39.4	21.1	8.8	2.7	2.9	1.5	—	—97.6—	—	1.0		1.5
Micronesia	...	...	...	...	...	...	...	...	...	...	...			...		...
Moldova	1990	...	...	...	...	...	...	...	...	...	...			...		...
Monaco	—															
Mongolia	1985	0.3	385,000	29.8[5]	44.0[5]	14.9[5]	7.7[5]	3.0[5]	—0.7[5]—		—	16.0[105]	84.0[105]	—		—
Morocco	1985–86	1,900[91]	3.9[91]	...	...	...	...	...	...	...	...			...		...
Mozambique	1973	1,605	3.1	—89.7[101]—		—10.0[102]—		—0.3—			0.2	0.1	—		99.7	—
Myanmar (Burma)	1987–88	4,308[106]	2.3[106]	61.2[49,106]	24.7[59,106]	11.5[106]	2.5[82,106]	—0.8[9,106]—			...			...		...
Namibia	1983	...	...	...	...	...	...	...	...	...	...			...		...
Nauru	—															
Nepal	1981–82	2,194	1.1	66.7	29.9	2.7	—0.7—				97.5			1.6	—	0.9
Netherlands, The	1988[48]	130	15.5	10.5	22.3	17.1	21.5	24.4	—4.2—		—31.5[11]—		—	12.2[11]		56.4[11]
Netherlands Antilles	...	...	...	...	...	...	...	...	...	...	...			...		...
New Caledonia	1983–84	12.7	23	71.2[49]	13.8[58]	3.7	2.3	2.5	3.8	2.8	...			...		...
New Zealand	1991	80.4	217	—12.5[26]—		10.3[26]	8.4[26]	—46.5[26]—		22.3[26]	85.7[26]	10.9[26]				3.4[26]
Nicaragua	1984	...	...	—26.2—			—30.6—			43.3	62.3[11]	19.3[11]	18.6[11]			

farmland use

activity (% of farms)			technology (latest)				land in farms		land use (%) — cropland							
mainly crops	mainly livestock	mixed/other	tractors (per 1,000 ha)	electricity (% of farms having)	irrigation (% of land irrig.)	artificial fertilizer (kg/ha)	total ('000 ha)	% of total land area	permanent crops	temporary crops	fallow	total cropland	meadows and pastures	woodland and forest	other	country
...	...	...	...	...	...	...	...	...	...	...	...	...	...	...	...	Faeroe Islands
...	...	...	28.3	...	1	72	277	15.2	...	...	...	...	...	...	...	Fiji
52.3	——47.6——		99.5	100.0[32]	3	214	12,338	40.5	0.3[32]	97.6[32]	2.1[32]	18.4	1.0	58.0	22.6	Finland
35.8	37.9	26.3	84.1	...	6	319	33,649[4]	61.8[4]	7.4[4]	90.6[4]	2.0[4]	53.6[4]	34.1[4]	8.2[4]	4.1[4]	France
...	...	...	28.3	...	...	152	24.6	0.3	3.1	53.8	43.0	60.0	40.0	...	...	French Guiana
...	...	...	31.0	...	19.4	15	36.8	10.4	90.0	7.1	2.9	62.0	8.5	1.9	27.6	French Polynesia
...	...	...	5.0	...	...	2	73.0	0.3	...	...	...	...	...	...	...	Gabon
...	...	...	0.2	...	7	20	176.4	16.5	...	100.0	...	100.0	...	...	...	Gambia, The
...	...	...	45.3	...	53	...	19.3	53.2	74.6	25.4	...	100.0	...	...	...	Gaza Strip
...	...	...	30.4	...	...	...	3,200	45.7	...	...	...	25.0	62.5	—	12.5	Georgia
...	...	...	133	...	4	433	11,867	47.7	2.3	——97.3——		63.1	36.7	—	—	Germany[57]
...	...	...	3.5	...	1	4	2,574	10.8	61.4	38.6	—	100.0	—	—	—	Ghana
...	...	...	...	...	...	...	...	...	...	...	...	...	...	...	...	Gibraltar
...	...	...	65.4	...	41	233	3,546	26.9	29.2	61.1	9.7	98.1	1.9	...	...	Greece
...	c. 100	...	...	...	...	...	...	...	...	...	...	...	...	...	...	Greenland
...	...	...	5.6	...	...	...	13.9	40.2	...	...	...	...	...	...	...	Grenada
...	...	...	76.2	...	14	355	143.4	84.1	16.2	46.7	37.1	33.3	18.6	48.1	...	Guadeloupe
72.2[63]	17.2[63]	10.5[63]	15.0	68.7	...	69	5.3	9.8	——51.2[27]——		48.8[27]	17.8[27]	34.3[27]	——47.9[27]——	...	Guam
...	67.6	...	3.0	...	6	69	4,147	38.1	27.6	——72.4——		42.0	27.3	27.2	3.4	Guatemala
...	...	...	...	...	...	...	2	26.2	—	100.0	—	10.5	89.5	—	—	Guernsey
...	...	...	0.4	...	4	1	1,600[71]	6.5	...	...	...	...	...	...	...	Guinea
...	...	...	0.2	...	...	...	169	4.7	...	...	...	...	...	...	...	Guinea-Bissau
...	...	...	7.5	...	27	29	10,652	26.2	...	...	...	8.4	91.6	...	...	Guyana
...	...	...	0.4	...	14	2	1,579	57.0	...	...	...	54.4	33.3	12.3	...	Haiti
...	...	...	2.2	...	6	22	2,630	23.5	15.4[25]	34.6[25]	50.0[25]	52.0[25]	48.0[25]	...	...	Honduras
56.3	37.3	6.4	1.2	...	33	100.0[26]	7.3	6.8	7.4	37.0	55.6	100.0	...	...	...	Hong Kong
43.4[3]	44.3[3]	12.3[3]	10.0	...	3	272	8,236	88.5	3.4	96.6	...	60.6	14.4	20.6	4.4	Hungary
...	...	...	1,625	87.0[39]	...	2,917	...	...	...	...	...	...	...	...	...	Iceland
...	...	...	5.6	...	26	65	163,343	49.7	——88.3[74]——		11.7[74]	96.0[74]	1.5[74]	——2.5[74]——	...	India
86.8[5]	—[5]	13.2[5]	1.1	...	48	117	48,583	25.3	27.0	45.2	27.8	60.7	5.1	18.9	15.3	Indonesia
87.9	11.2	0.8	8.1	...	41	73	104,900	63.8	4.9	62.0	33.2	14.2	85.8	...	...	Iran
...	...	...	7.3	...	49	38	5,732	13.1	3.0	62.4	34.6	87.2	0.7	0.2	11.9	Iraq
...	...	...	174	...	...	698	5,692	82.6	0.5	99.5	...	9.5	69.5	——21.0——		Ireland
...	...	...	...	...	...	...	48	83.3	3.5	——96.5——		12.8	87.2	...	...	Isle of Man
...	...	...	82.6	...	63	233	584	28.2	22.0	——78.0——		70.5	19.1	...	10.4	Israel
...	...	...	156	...	34	254	23,632	78.4	26.3[83]	73.7[83]	...	52.4[83]	21.2[83]	17.1[83]	9.3[83]	Italy
...	...	...	14.7	...	17	109	603[86]	54.8[86]	22.2[86]	72.2[86]	5.6[86]	41.3[86]	21.6[86]	13.5[86]	23.6[86]	Jamaica
80.8[30]	——19.2[30]——		494	...	69	415	5,243	13.9	9.1	——90.9——		95.5	—	——36.6——	4.5	Japan
85.1[91]	14.9[91]	—	...	...	...	...	6.5	56.2	——98.9——		1.1	63.4	...	...	...	Jersey
58.2[63,83]	14.9[63,83]	26.9[63,83]	18.4	1.5	18	73	364	4.1	13.3	63.0	23.7	87.7	1.0	0.3	11.0	Jordan
...	...	...	6.2	...	...	...	197,600	72.7	...	...	...	18.0	81.9	...	0.1	Kazakhstan
...	...	...	5.0	...	3	51	6,922	11.9	11.5	——88.5——		71.0	23.8	1.9	3.3	Kenya
...	...	...	...	...	...	...	...	...	...	...	...	...	...	...	...	Kiribati
...	...	...	42.4	...	82	338	...	...	...	...	...	...	...	...	...	Korea, North
82.3[3]	17.7[3]	—	15.8	...	68	411	2,109	21.2	6.7	——93.3——		100.0	—	—	—	Korea, South
36.7	61.8	1.5	30.0	100.0	50	194	44.5	0.3	30.2	69.8	—	100.0	—	—	—	Kuwait
...	...	...	19.6	...	3	...	10,100	51.0	...	...	...	13.9	85.1	—	1.0	Kyrgyzstan
...	...	...	1.0	...	14	2	1,680	7.1	2.3	——97.7——		52.4	47.6	—	—	Laos
...	...	...	22.4	...	...	...	2,500	38.5	...	...	...	68.0	32.0	—	—	Latvia
77.0[63]	8.1[63]	14.9[63]	14.4	...	41	75	275[30]	27.0[30]	36.7[30]	39.7[30]	23.6[30]	100.0[30]	—	—	—	Lebanon
37.3	—	62.7	5.6	...	...	14	372[32]	12.3[32]	...	89.6[32]	10.4[32]	98.8[32]	...	...	1.2[32]	Lesotho
...	...	...	3.0	...	2	9	370[73]	3.8[73]	66.2[73]	33.8[73]	...	98.3[73]	...	1.7[73]	...	Liberia
...	...	...	17.7	...	13	41	8,800[73]	5.1[73]	——33.3[73]——		66.7[73]	20.5[73]	79.5[73]	—	—	Libya
23.9	61.6	14.5	106	...	...	...	3.7	23.1	1.6	——98.4——		30.4	66.0	2.5	1.1	Liechtenstein
...	...	...	21.2	...	...	...	3,400	52.3	...	...	...	67.6	32.4	—	—	Lithuania
25.5	55.8	18.7	155	...	...	...	137	53.1	2.5	97.5	0.5	40.6	50.0	7.5	1.9	Luxembourg
...	...	...	...	...	...	...	...	...	...	...	...	...	...	...	...	Macau
...	...	...	1.1	...	35	3	1,320	51.3	9.3	65.4	25.3	46.4	53.4	—	1.2	Macedonia[29]
...	...	...	...	...	...	...	2,044	3.5	15.4	84.6	—	100.0	—	...	...	Madagascar
22.1	...	77.9	0.6	...	0.8	21	1,332	14.1	0.2	99.8	—	94.8	—	5.2	—	Malawi
...	...	...	11.5[102]	...	33[102]	151[102]	4,100[27]	31.2[27]	84.8[27]	15.2[27]	—	100.0[27]	—	...	...	Malaysia
...	...	...	...	...	...	...	19	63.5	...	...	...	...	...	...	...	Maldives
...	...	...	0.4	...	10	6	2,277	1.8	—	100.0	—	100.0	—	...	...	Mali
...	...	...	37.3	...	8	56	13.0	41.2	5.0	——95.0——		87.5	—	——12.5——		Malta
...	...	...	...	...	...	...	...	...	...	...	...	...	...	...	...	Marshall Islands
...	...	...	96.0	...	60	1,018	95.6	86.9	23.2	36.1	40.7	39.8	20.1	40.1	—	Martinique
...	...	...	1.7	...	6	16	194	0.2	...	56.2	43.8	100.0	...	...	...	Mauritania
...	...	...	3.5	...	17	266	171	91.5	5.9	94.1	—	62.2	4.4	33.4	...	Mauritius
...	...	...	...	...	...	...	14.6	39.0	33.3	66.7	—	100.0	—	...	...	Mayotte
88.8	8.3	2.9	7.3	...	22	71	139,868	72.7	6.3	58.1	35.6	16.5	53.3	14.2	16.0	Mexico
61.4[3]	15.7[3]	22.9[3]	7.4	45	0	...	5.8	12.2	——9.3——		90.7	32.9	30.2	——36.9——	—	Micronesia
...	...	...	29.6	...	...	...	2,500	73.5	...	...	...	68.0	12.0	—	20.0	Moldova
...	...	...	...	...	...	...	...	...	...	...	...	...	...	...	...	Monaco
...	...	...	8.4	...	6	14	124,587	79.6	—	66.8	33.2	0.9	99.1	...	...	Mongolia
...	...	...	4.0	...	15	35	8,062	17.6	6.6	72.9	20.5	100.0	—	...	...	Morocco
...	...	...	2.0	...	4	1	13,626	17.8	——44.9——		55.1	55.0	45.0	...	...	Mozambique
...	...	...	1.0	...	11	11	12,560	18.6	3.0	79.5	17.5	97.0	3.0	...	...	Myanmar (Burma)
...	...	...	4.5	...	0.6	...	662	0.8	0.3	——99.7——		100.0	—	...	...	Namibia
...	...	...	...	...	...	...	...	...	...	...	...	...	...	...	...	Nauru
...	...	...	1.1	...	36	24	2,464	16.7	1.3	97.1	1.6	94.0	1.7	0.6	3.7	Nepal
32.3	54.9	12.9	217	...	61	705	2,012	48.1	3.5	95.8	0.7	44.6	55.4	...	...	Netherlands, The
...	...	...	2.5	...	...	...	...	...	...	...	...	...	...	...	...	Netherlands Antilles
...	...	...	132	...	...	20	293	15.8	51.7	34.8	13.5	6.5	93.5	...	...	New Caledonia
13.9	65.5	20.6	159	...	56	760	17,450	64.5	13.0[4]	87.0[4]	—	1.9[4]	98.1[4]	...	...	New Zealand
...	...	...	2.3	...	8	57	5,651	47.7	...	...	...	...	...	...	...	Nicaragua

Agriculture and land use   (continued)

country	farms (latest census of agriculture)[a]														
	year	number of farms ('000)	size of holding								tenure (% of farms)				
			average (ha)	size class (%)							owner-operated			rented (including share-croppers)	tribal/ com-munal	other[b]
				under 1 ha	1–5 ha	5–10 ha	10–20 ha	20–50 ha	50–200 ha	over 200 ha	individual/ family	corporate/ state	socialized/ collective			
Niger	1980[2]	699	4.9	3.8	54.1	37.8	—	— 4.3 —			...	...	...	...	...	...
Nigeria	1971	...	...	92.0	7.8	0.2	—	—	—	—	...	...	...	...	...	...
Northern Mariana Is.	1990	0.1	49.1	26.1[107]	35.3[108]	— 24.4[8] —		— 14.3 —			56.3	...	...	23.5	...	20.2
Norway	1989	183	10.2	6.4[52]	11.3[53]	12.7	16.6	23.7	22.2	7.1	—	— 65.4 —		34.6	—	—
Oman	1978–79	83	1.0	70.5	25.0	2.8	1.3[106]	0.3[107]	0.1	—	...	...	...	...	...	...
Pakistan	1980	4,070	4.7	17.2	56.2	17.4	6.5	— 2.7 —			64.1[11]	0.3[11]	—	35.6[11]	—	—
Palau	...	...	...	...	...	...	...	...	...	...	...	...	...	...	...	...
Panama	1980	153	14.7	41.0	25.0	9.3	9.0	9.0	5.6	1.0	23.2	—	—	2.0	—	74.8[31]
Papua New Guinea	1985[111]	0.8	483	— 26.8[50] —				28.3[55]	44.9[55]		26.9[11, 55]	71.0[11, 55]	—	2.1[11, 55]	—	—
Paraguay	1981	249	88	8.6	27.4	19.9	22.7	14.5	4.4	2.5	54.5	0.4	—	9.2	—	35.9[31]
Peru	1984	1,574	9.5	24.1	47.7	13.2	6.7	5.5	— 2.8 —		75.5	—	—	0.8	6.8	16.9
Philippines	1980	3,420	2.6	22.7	63.3	10.5	— 3.5 —				58.3	—	—	27.4	—	14.3
Poland	1989	3,952	4.8	52.0[49]	19.5[58]	17.5	— 10.9 —			0.1	76.2[11]	—	23.8[11]	...	—	...
Portugal	1979	784	6.6	44.5	41.9	7.7	3.3	1.5	0.7	0.4	68.1	—	—	8.7	—	23.2
Puerto Rico	1987	20	17.2	— 48.7[112] —		19.5[113]	16.7[114]	6.7[115]	— 8.3[61] —		— 77.5 —			7.1	—	15.4
Qatar	1990	0.8	7.0	20.5	41.8	18.0	12.6	5.8	— 1.4 —		...	...	...	...	...	...
Réunion	1988–89	15	4.1	35.6	47.9	12.5	2.7	— 1.3 —			46.1[5]	—	—	22.5[5]	—	31.4[5]
Romania	1987	4.2[26, 33]	2,700[26, 33]	...	...	...	...	...	...	...	—	13.7[11, 26]	60.8[11, 26]	—	—	25.5[11, 26]
Russia	1990	...	...	...	...	...	...	...	...	...	...	...	...	...	...	...
Rwanda	1984	1,112	1.2	56.8	26.8[116]	— 16.4[117] —					50.9	—	—	1.4	—	47.7[44]
St. Kitts and Nevis	1981	...	...	...	...	...	...	...	...	...	46.8[11]	48.0[11]	—	5.2[11]	—	...
St. Lucia	1986	12	2.0	75.9[49]	10.3[59]	4.9[60]	0.9	0.3[17]	0.2[18]	0.4[19]	72.0	—	—	15.5	—	12.5
St. Vincent	1985–86	8[57]	1.8[62]	48.0[62, 84]	40.7[62, 118]	8.5[59, 62]	2.4[8, 62]	— 0.5[9, 62] —			62.0[62]	—	—	8.8[62]	—	19.2[62]
San Marino	1975	0.7	7.0	21.3	47.8	— 24.7 —		5.1	— 1.1 —		39.9[11]	15.5[11]	—	29.9[11]	—	14.7[11]
São Tomé and Príncipe	1964	11.1	8.7	88.5	9.8	0.7	0.2	0.2	0.2	0.4	77.2	—	—	20.5	—	2.3
Saudi Arabia	1982–83	212	10.1	36.6	35.8	11.3	8.2	5.0	2.6	0.5	85.9	—	—	2.6	—	11.5
Senegal	1976	362	7.0	— 99.4 —					— 0.6 —		...	—	0.6	...	—	99.4
Seychelles	1977	4.9	1.5	...	...	...	...	...	...	...	...	...	...	...	...	...
Sierra Leone	1971	286	1.8	38.8	55.0	— 6.1 —		— 0.1 —			93.6	—	—	6.4	—	—
Singapore	1973	16	0.8	77.4	22.2	0.3	— 0.1 —				7.4	—	—	88.8	—	3.8
Slovenia[29]	1981	192	...	31.8	34.0	17.0	11.7	— 4.7 —			100.0	—	—	—	—	—
Solomon Islands	1975[99]	92	1.0	...	...	...	...	...	...	...	...	...	...	...	100.0	...
Somalia	1984	198	3.6	...	...	...	...	...	...	...	99.9	0.1	—	—	.	—
South Africa	1978	72	1,193	...	...	...	...	...	...	...	...	...	...	...	...	...
Bophuthatswana	1976	...	...	...	...	...	...	...	...	...	...	...	...	...	...	...
Ciskei	1986	...	...	...	...	...	...	...	...	...	...	...	...	...	...	...
Transkei	1976	...	...	...	...	...	...	...	...	...	...	...	...	...	...	...
Venda	1976	53.3	9.3	...	...	...	...	...	...	...	...	...	...	...	...	...
Spain	1982	2,375	18.7	26.4	37.1	14.0	10.2	7.1	3.9	1.3	75.4	—	...	4.0	—	20.6
Sri Lanka	1982	1,817	1.1	77.5[6]	— 22.2[119] —		0.1[120]	0.1[17]	— 0.1[61] —		77.1[5]	6.4[5]	0.1[5]	14.4[5]	—	2.0[5]
Sudan, The	1982	...	...	...	...	...	...	...	...	...	22.3	2.2	—	28.0	42.0	5.5
Suriname	1981	22	7.5	21.9[86]	61.2[86]	11.1[86]	3.6[86]	1.6[86]	0.3[86]	0.3[86]	20.2[86]	0.9[86]	—	49.5[86]	—	29.4[86]
Swaziland	1972	39	19.5	26.2	60.4	— 12.0 —				1.4	86.1	—	—	3.4	—	10.5
Sweden	1990[48]	97	29.5	—	15.5	19.7	21.6	27.3	15.0	0.9	47.7[24]	—	—	15.4[24]	—	36.8[24, 44]
Switzerland	1985	119	9.1	23.1	18.7	14.6	27.5	15.2	0.9	—	36.2[30]	—	0.8[30]	58.5[30]	—	4.5[30]
Syria	1988	444	8.9	16.7	36.8[20]	22.8[60]	13.1	8.5	2.0[121]	0.2[122]	65.8[11, 97]	1.8[11]	32.5[11]	—	—	—
Taiwan	1989	723	1.2	72.6	27.4	...	...	...	...	...	86.4	—	—	3.7	—	9.9
Tajikistan	1990	...	...	...	...	...	...	...	...	...	...	...	...	...	...	...
Tanzania	1986–87	3,626	0.9[2]	70.1	28.8	1.0	— 0.1 —				87.3[62]	—	—	3.6[62]	—	9.1[62]
Thailand	1988	4,877	3.7	14.3	72.0[123]	— 13.1[124] —		— 0.5[125] —			87.0	—	—	3.6	—	9.3
Togo	1982–83	263	1.5	48.8	38.6[96]	— 12.7[97] —					70.7[11]	—	—	21.1[11]	8.2[11]	—
Tonga	1985	10.1	3.3	18.9	67.9	12.7	—	0.5	—	—	—	— 97.2 —		—	—	2.8
Trinidad and Tobago	1982	30.6	4.3	35.1	50.7	9.6	4.1	—	0.4	0.1	52.1	—	—	36.5	—	11.4
Tunisia	1988	376	13.6	— 45.7 —		20.6	17.9	11.4	— 4.4 —		...	...	...	...	...	...
Turkey	1980	3,651	6.2	15.8	46.3	20.2	11.6	5.3	0.8	—	88.6	—	—	12.1	—	1.2
Turkmenistan	1990	...	...	...	...	...	...	...	...	...	...	...	...	...	...	...
Tuvalu	1976	1.5	1.7	...	...	...	...	...	...	...	99.9	—	—	—	0.1	—
Uganda	1964	1,171	3.9	20.7	59.8	11.2	— 8.3 —				97.4	—	—	—	—	2.6
Ukraine	1990	...	...	...	...	...	...	...	...	...	...	...	...	...	...	...
United Arab Emirates	1986–87	17.9	2.3	45.4	38.8[127]	— 15.9[128] —					...	...	...	...	...	...
United Kingdom	1991	241	107.3[129]	5.8[49, 130]	8.3[58, 130]	12.6[130]	16.4[130]	24.9[130]	26.1[130]	5.8[130]	— 73.1[130, 131] —			26.9[130, 131]	—	...
United States	1987	2,088	187.0	— 8.7[85] —		— 19.8[8] —			30.9[132]	22.9[133]	17.7[134]	52.8	6.1	—	11.5	—	29.2
Uruguay	1986	57	280.5	—	9.0	13.0	12.8	16.0	22.8	26.3	— 59.1[30] —			17.3[30]	—	23.6[30]
Uzbekistan	1990	...	...	...	...	...	...	...	...	...	...	...	...	...	...	...
Vanuatu	1983–84	27	6.9	...	...	...	...	...	...	...	65.3[30]	34.7[30]		...	...	...
Venezuela	1984–85	381	82.0	8.3	36.3	15.7	13.0	10.4	9.3	7.1	61.5[135]	...	—	6.1[135]	...	31.3[31, 135]
Vietnam	1991	31[33]	28.0[2]	...	...	...	...	...	...	...	— 100 —			—	—	—
Virgin Islands (U.S.)	1987	0.3	27.0	30.0[136]	30.3[137]	12.0	13.9	6.0	3.7[138]	4.1[139]	75.3	—	—	8.6	—	16.1
West Bank	1965	55	3.4	49.8	34.4	10.6	4.0	1.0	0.2	0.0	7.16	—	—	6.4	—	22.0
Western Sahara	1983	...	...	...	...	...	...	...	...	...	...	...	...	...	...	...
Western Samoa	1989	11	6.1	...	...	...	...	...	...	...	...	...	...	...	86.0	14.0
Yemen[140]	1977–83	591	2.3	57.5	30.9	7.4	3.3	0.8	0.1	—	90.3[11]	—	—	9.4[11]	—	0.3[11]
Yugoslavia	1981	1,198	...	24.7	48.8	19.9	4.4	— 0.7 —			100.0	—	—	—	—	—
Zaire	1970	2,538	2.3	41.6	57.3	1.0	0.2	—	—	—	4.2	0.1	—	—	95.6	0.1
Zambia	1971	768	3.1	50.5	45.2	— 3.8 —		— 0.5 —			...	...	...	—	98.0	—
Zimbabwe	1974	765	38.7	— 16.7[81] —			52.8[143]	29.8[144]	— 0.7[14] —		— 2.0 —			—	98.0	—

---

[1]1967. [2]Cultivated area only. [3]Based on value of output by sector. [4]1987. [5]1973. [6]Less than 1.2 ha. [7]1.2 to 4.0 ha. [8]4.0 to 20 ha. [9]20 ha or more. [10]Percentage of farms having irrigation. [11]Based on area, not number, of holdings. [12]1989–90. [13]50 to 100 ha. [14]100 ha or more. [15]1987–88. [16]Excluding holdings without land. [17]20 to 40 ha. [18]40 to 81 ha. [19]81 ha or more. [20]1.0 to 4.0 ha. [21]4.0 to 10.1 ha. [22]10.1 ha or more. [23]1977. [24]1989. [25]1979. [26]1985. [27]1982. [28]4.0 ha or more. [29]Holdings and tenure refer to private holdings only; land use 1990. [30]1980. [31]Almost all squatters. [32]1970. [33]State farms and cooperatives only. [34]Precollectivization. [35]4.0 to 28 ha. [36]28 to 100 ha. [37]100 to 160 ha. [38]160 ha or more. [39]Irrigated land only. [40]1968. [41]1984. [42]1971. [43]Rarotonga only. [44]Owned and rented holdings. [45]Less than 0.5. [46]0.5 to 50 ha. [47]50 to 1000 ha. [48]Arable area only. [49]Less than 2.0 ha. [50]2.0 to 20 ha. [51]2.1 ha or less. [52]2.1 to 4.2 ha. [53]4.2 to 21 ha. [54]21 ha or more. [55]1983. [56]Excludes holdings of less than 1.0 ha. [57]Former West Germany only. [58]2.0 to 5.0 ha. [59]2.0 to 10 ha. [60]4.0 to 10 ha. [61]40 ha or more. [62]1972. [63]Commercial farms only. [64]Less than 0.7 ha. [65]0.7 to 7.1 ha. [66]7.1 to 45 ha. [67]45 to 452 ha. [68]452 ha or more. [69]Excludes holdings of 0.04 ha (500 sq m) or less. [70]1974. [71]1990. [72]1991. [73]1981. [74]Excludes state of Punjab. [75]Less than 2.5 ha. [76]2.5 to 7.5 ha. [77]7.5 to 12.5 ha. [78]12.5 to 20 ha. [79]50 to 250 ha. [80]250 ha or more. [81]Less than 8.0 ha. [82]8.0 to

mainly crops	mainly livestock	mixed/other	tractors (per 1,000 ha)	electricity (% of farms having)	irrigation (% of land irrig.)	artificial fertilizer (kg/ha)	total ('000 ha)	% of total land area	permanent crops	temporary crops	fallow	total cropland	meadows and pastures	woodland and forest	other	country
...	...	...	0.05	...	0.9	1	3,407	2.9	...	...	...	...	...	...	...	Niger
64.3[3]	35.7[3]	—	0.4	...	3	10	34,290	37.1	—20.0—		80.0	31.4	27.5	41.1	...	Nigeria
24.3[3]	70.6[3]	3.9[3]	22	45	...	...	5.8	12.2	...	...	...	32.9	30.2	—36.9—		Northern Mariana Is.
...	...	...	176	...	11	269	20,570	63.5	0.4	98.5	1.0	4.3	0.6	34.2	60.9	Norway
...	...	...	8.6	...	87	111	83	0.3	68.6	31.4	—	49.2	—50.8—			Oman
...	...	...	9.0	...	80	83	19,109	24.0	—83.7—		16.3	93.8	...	0.6	5.6	Pakistan
																Palau
...	...	...	14.2	0.5[42]	7	67	2,259	29.3	21.6	43.3	35.0	24.6	57.4	15.6	2.4	Panama
...	...	...	34.8	...	...	22	386	0.8	100.0	...	...	33.7	26.4	...	39.9	Papua New Guinea
33.0	—67.0—		5.1	...	3	4	21,941	53.9	4.2	76.6	19.2	12.6	47.5	38.5	1.4	Paraguay
4.9	93.0	2.1	4.9	6.5	37	58	14,893	11.6	24.1	75.9	...	27.1	47.5	19.8	5.6	Peru
98.2	1.5	0.3	2.0	...	36	63	9,034	30.1	57.5	42.5	—	86.3	6.8	—6.9—		Philippines
53.8[3]	46.2[3]	—	80.0	...	0.7	398	18,720	59.9	1.9	—98.1—		78.3	21.7			Poland
...	...	...	26.2	...	22	138	5,183	56.1	26.1	44.6	29.3	52.6	3.2	34.5	9.7	Portugal
61.0	33.4	5.6	55.5	...	57	...	349	39.3	—70.4—		29.6	28.0	46.4	19.1	6.6	Puerto Rico
50.4[3]	49.6[3]	...	18.4	...	100	120	5.7	0.5	25.2	74.8	...	100.0	—	—	...	Qatar
...	...	...	47.9	...	13	243	212.6	84.4	2.6	44.1	53.3	53.9	4.8	41.3	...	Réunion
...	...	...	15.3	...	35	138	14,759	61.9	4.0	96.0	—	77.9	22.1	...	...	Romania
...	...	...	10.4	...	...	...	213,700	12.5	...	...	...	61.7	37.5	...	0.8	Russia
...	...	...	0.1	—	—	1	1,350	51.3	—85.6—		14.4	63.7	10.6	5.2	20.5	Rwanda
...	...	...	27.0	...	...	...	12	45.3	31.5	—68.5—		58.1	—41.9—			St. Kitts and Nevis
25.0[70]	—75.0[70]—		17.4	...	20	...	23	38.0	68.5[70]	—31.5[70]—		57.9[70]	10.2[70]	26.4[70]	5.5[70]	St. Lucia
...	...	...	19.5	...	25	...	17.9	34.8	64.3	16.1	19.6	84.3	15.7	...	...	St. Vincent
...	...	...	...	...	...	...	4.7	76.5	60.9	6.5	32.6	69.2	6	8.2	16.4	San Marino
...	...	...	62.0	...	6	...	96	100.0	99.4	—0.6—		38.3	...	59.7	2.0	São Tomé and Príncipe
...	...	...	1.7	...	39	428	2,135	1.0	4.1	18.7	77.2	88.5	—11.5—			Saudi Arabia
...	...	...	0.1	...	3	5	11,338	59.1	0.1	—99.9—		22.4	77.6	...	...	Senegal
1.8	32.4	65.8	39.0	...	...	...	7.5	27.8	89.6	—10.4—		100.0	...	...	...	Seychelles
50.3	—49.7—		0.3	...	2	2	2,732	38.1	20.7	—79.3—		19.3	80.7	...	...	Sierra Leone
12.5	6.2	81.3	29.5	...	100	2,800	5.6[41]	9.0[41]	75.0	25.0	—	66.7	...	33.3	...	Singapore
...	...	...	...	...	...	...	866	42.8	19.0	80.0	1.0	35.2	64.7	—	0.1	Slovenia[29]
43.4	—56.6—		...	...	...	...	93	3.4	40.0	45.2	14.8	100.0	—	—	—	Solomon Islands
20.0	60.0	20.0	2.1	...	11	2	...	...	...	...	...	...	—	—	—	Somalia
...	...	...	14.8	...	9	63	85,447	70.2	5.9	—94.1—		11.9	79.7	1.3	7.1	South Africa
...	...	...	...	...	1	...	3,839	94.8	...	87.1	...	2.4	97.6	...	...	Bophuthatswana
...	...	...	...	...	—	3	770	95.3	9.7	80.3	—	10.0	90.0	...	...	Ciskei
...	...	...	...	...	...	...	622	14.9	...	...	...	100.0	100.0	—	—	Transkei
...	...	...	0.3	...	1	4.8	500	64.9	25.4	63.6	11.0	9.2	90.8	...	—	Venda
...	...	...	46.4	...	22	130	44,312	87.8	23.8	55.8	20.4	40.9	12.5	21.7	24.9	Spain
...	...	...	31.9	...	60	110	2,009	30.6	56.4	43.6	—	86.0	1.0	2.7	8.8	Sri Lanka
33.0[86]	12.5[86]	54.5[86]	22.3	...	15	4	31,500	13.3	0.8	88.7	10.5	23.8	76.2	...	...	Sudan, The
39.7	—60.3—		20.5	...	100	29	165	1.0	15.0	53.0	32.0	40.4	23.1	19.1	17.4	Suriname
17.3[111]	39.5[111]	33.9[111]	64.1	...	39	46	766,775	44.6	2.0	81.1	16.9	19.7	60.6	12.0	7.7	Swaziland
35.5[30]	—64.5[30]—		...	...	4	137	8,253	21.7	...	91.0	9.0	34.8	4.0	50.3	10.9	Sweden
...	...	...	281	...	6	454	1,203	29.1	6.7	66.2	27.1	36.1	53.4	10.5	...	Switzerland
...	...	...	11.7	...	14	50	6,065	32.8	—77.3—		22.7	91.7	...	...	8.3	Syria
41.9	30.3	27.8	...	...	38	400[84]	2,827	78.5	27.5	72.5	—	31.7	...	65.7	2.4	Taiwan
...	...	...	44.1	...	...	...	4,300	30.1	...	...	...	18.6	76.7	...	4.7	Tajikistan
44.1	4.7	51.2	4.5	...	4	8	7,545[62]	8.5[62]	19.1[62]	72.5[62]	8.4[62]	49.8[62]	10.2[62]	24.7[62]	15.3[62]	Tanzania
...	...	...	7.9	...	22	39	14,178	27.6	13.5	—86.5—		93.8	0.9	2.1	3.2	Thailand
...	...	...	0.3	...	0.5	8	406	7.1	17.3[23]	—82.7[23]—		71.0[23]	29.0[23]	...	...	Togo
...	...	...	6.8	...	...	2	33	44.5	—62.7—		37.3	81.2	6.7	10.1	1.9	Tonga
63.7[126]	—36.3[126]—		35.4	40.7	30	18	132	25.8	55.9	—44.1—		62.3	4.4	6.1	27.2	Trinidad and Tobago
...	...	...	8.5	...	9	21	9,449	61.1	31.1	48.3	20.6	78.2	21.8	...	...	Tunisia
11.5	2.5	86.0	27.1	...	9	58	30,732	39.9	17.5	71.0	11.5	85.4	7.3	1.7	5.4	Turkey
...	...	...	40.1	...	...	...	35,800	73.4	...	...	...	3.4	96.1	—	0.5	Turkmenistan
																Tuvalu
...	...	...	0.9	...	—	—	2,262	11.3	29.8	70.2	—	100.0	—	—	—	Uganda
...	...	...	12.8	...	...	...	41,400	68.5	...	...	...	80.7	16.9	—	2.4	Ukraine
...	...	...	...	...	17	138	17.5[91]	0.2[91]	64.8[91]	18.2[91]	17.1[91]	97.6[91]	...	1.3[91]	1.1[91]	United Arab Emirates
...	...	...	77.3	...	2	358	18,498	75.8	0.7	98.3	1.0	35.8	60.4	—3.8—		United Kingdom
40.7	55.4	3.8	24.9	68.8	10	93	390,316	41.0	1.0	90.5	8.5	46.0	42.5	8.3	3.2	United States
37.1[30]	58.7[30]	4.2[30]	28.2	...	9	52	15,882	90.7	3.1	—96.9—		8.8	85.3	4.2	1.7	Uruguay
...	...	...	40.4	...	...	...	26,600	59.4	...	...	...	16.9	81.2	...	1.9	Uzbekistan
92.2	7.2	0.6	2.9	...	...	...	183	15.0	62.5	3.0	34.5	84.9	15.1	...	...	Vanuatu
27.6	9.0	63.4	14.8	...	8	178	31,278	34.3	19.0[135]	59.0[135]	22.0[135]	13.2[135]	57.0[135]	22.8[135]	7.0[135]	Venezuela
74.5[3]	25.5[3]	—	6.3	...	32	90	9,060	27.4	7.4	—92.6—		100.0	...	...	...	Vietnam
48.3	40.8	10.9	48.0	15.4	...	...	7.2	20.9	18.3	13.7	68.0	10.7	75.3	10.3	3.7	Virgin Islands (U.S.)
...	...	...	14.1[27]	...	5	...	185[30]	31.4[30]	62.2[30]	37.8[30]	—	100.0[30]	...	...	...	West Bank
...	...	...	...	...	...	...	5,002	18.8	—	—	—	—	100.0	—	—	Western Sahara
...	...	...	0.6	...	...	...	70[83]	24.8[83]	71.2[83]	28.8[83]	—	93.8[83]	6.2[83]	...	...	Western Samoa
35.5[11,141]	56.9[11,141]	7.6[11,141]	1.8	...	23	7	1,351	0.1	6.7	69.7	23.6	98.8	...	...	1.2	Yemen[140]
12.7[86,142]	—87.3[86,142]—		151	...	2	147	6,238	61.1	8.8	89.3	1.9	65.4	34.0	...	0.6	Yugoslavia
92.3	—9.7—		0.1	...	—	1	5,897	2.6	7.7	—92.3—		70.6	20.1	2.0	7.3	Zaire
15.8	9.7	74.5	1.1	...	0.6	16	938	1.3	4.5	—95.5—		14.2	38.1	...	47.7	Zambia
1.8[11,91]	26.7[11,91]	71.5[11,91]	7.5	...	8	59	29,620	76.6	2.5	—97.5—		34.5	65.7	...	...	Zimbabwe

20 ha. [83]1975. [84]Less than 0.4 ha. [85]0.4 to 4.0 ha. [86]1969. [87]Less than 4.5 ha. [88]4.5 to 9.0 ha. [89]9.0 to 18 ha. [90]18 ha or more. [91]1978. [92]5.0 to 8.0 ha. [93]8.0 ha or more. [94]Excludes temporary rangeland available for agricultural use to subsistence farms. [95]Excludes large commercial farms. [96]1.0 to 3.0 ha. [97]3.0 ha or more. [98]West Malaysia except as noted. [99]Smallholder farms only. [100]Average size of estate farm is 400 ha. [101]Based on number of households on estates. [102]All Malaysia. [103]Includes rented farms. [104]Includes 1,828,000 holdings in 22,700 communes (ejidos). [105]In area, state lands constitute 80.6% of Mongolia's agricultural cooperatives 19.4%. [106]Family farms only. [107]Less than 0.8 ha. [108]0.8 to 4.0 ha. [109]10 to 25 ha. [110]25 to 50 ha. [111]Large holdings only. [112]1.0 to 3.9 ha. [113]3.9 to 7.9 ha. [114]7.9 to 19.7 ha. [115]19.7 ha to 40 ha. [116]1.0 to 2.0 ha. [117]0.4 to 2.0 ha. [119]1.2 to 12 ha. [120]12 to 20 ha. [121]50 to 300 ha. [122]300 ha or more. [123]1.0 to 6.4 ha. [124]6.4 to 22.4 ha. [125]22.4 ha or more. [126]1963. [127]1.0 to 7.5 ha. [128]7.5 ha or more. [129]Full-time operations only. [130]1988. [131]Excludes Northern Ireland. [132]20 to 72 ha. [133]72 to 202 ha. [134]202 ha or more. [135]1971. [136]Less than 3.0 ha. [137]3.0 to 10 ha. [138]100 to 260 ha. [139]260 ha or more. [140]Former Yemen Arab Republic only. [141]1976. [142]Data refer to Yugoslavia as constituted prior to 1991. [143]8.0 to 16 ha. [144]416 to 100 ha.

Crops and livestock

This table provides comparative data for selected categories of agricultural production for the countries of the world. The data are taken mainly from the United Nations Food and Agriculture Organization's (FAO) annual *Production Yearbook*.

The FAO depends largely on questionnaires supplied to each country for its statistics, but, where no official or semiofficial responses are returned, the FAO makes estimates, using incomplete, unofficial, or other similarly limited data. And, although the FAO provides standardized guidelines upon which many nations have organized their data collection systems and methods, persistent, often traditional, variations in standards of coverage, methodology, and reporting periods reduce the comparability of statistics that *can* be supplied on such forms. FAO data are based on calendar-year periods; that is, data for any particular crop refer to the calendar year in which the harvest (or the bulk of the harvest) occurred.

In spite of the often tragic food shortages in a number of countries in recent years, worldwide agricultural production is probably more often underreported than overreported. Many countries do not report complete domestic production; the former Soviet bloc, for example, excepting Czechoslovakia, long published statistics only for collective or cooperative production and excluded the production of privately held plots of land that in some instances represented a significant part of total agricultural production. Some countries report only crops that are sold commercially and ignore crops produced for family or communal subsistence.

Methodological problems attach to much smaller parts of the agricultural whole, however. The FAO's cereals statistics relate, ideally, to weight or volume of crops harvested for dry grain (excluding cereal crops used for grazing; harvested for hay; or harvested green for food, feed, or silage). Some countries, however, collect the basic data they report to the FAO on sown or cultivated areas instead and calculate production statistics from estimates of yield. Millet and sorghum, which in many European and North American countries are used primarily as livestock or poultry feed, may be reportable by such countries as animal fodder only, while elsewhere many nations use the same grains for human consumption and report them as cereals. Statistics for tropical fruits are frequently not compiled by producing countries, and coverage is not uniform, with some countries reporting only commercial fruits and others including those consumed for

Crops and livestock

country	grains production ('000 metric tons) 1979–81 average	1991	grains yield (kg/hectare) 1979–81 average	1991	roots and tubers[a] production ('000 metric tons) 1979–81 average	1991	yield (kg/hectare) 1979–81 average	1991	pulses[b] production ('000 metric tons) 1979–81 average	1991	yield (kg/hectare) 1979–81 average	1991	fruits[c] production ('000 metric tons) 1979–81 average	1991	vegetables[d] production ('000 metric tons) 1979–81 average	1991
Afghanistan	4,060	2,724	1,337	1,161	265	223	14,881	16,767	41	35	989	967	807	647	516	488
Albania	916	559	2,500	2,281	112	65	6,967	7,222	23	14	376	401	135	97	338	248
Algeria	1,958	3,623	656	1,161	540	1,000	6,878	8,333	52	45	431	317	1,197	1,073	824	1,948
American Samoa	...	...	...	...	3	4	4,829	5,810	...	...	...	...	2	1	...	...
Andorra	...	...	...	...	...	...	...	...	...	...	...	...	...	...	...	...
Angola	379	381	533	386	1,820	2,060	3,562	3,927	42	40	385	303	432	425	224	227
Antigua and Barbuda	...	...	1,809	1,833	...	...	4,673	5,077	...	...	...	...	9	8	1	2
Argentina	24,457	20,351	2,183	2,632	2,328	3,150	14,087	20,388	239	274	918	1,186	6,258	5,507	2,279	2,831
Armenia	200[3]	200[4]	1,840[3]	1,840[4]	291[3,5]	213[4,5]	14,600[3,5]	9,500[4,5]	...	...	...	...	...	...	...	390[4]
Aruba	...	...	...	...	...	...	...	...	...	...	...	...	...	...	...	...
Australia	21,164	17,212	1,322	1,347	844	1,166	23,445	30,326	142	1,345	895	992	2,182	2,490	1,052	1,596
Austria	4,391	4,921	4,130	5,378	1,356	791	25,387	24,868	23	120	2,876	3,458	951	985	666	471
Azerbaijan	1,200[3]	1,400[4]	2,390[3]	2,340[4]	190[3,5]	185[4,5]	800[3,5]	7,800[4,5]	...	...	...	...	...	...	...	856[4]
Bahamas, The	1	1	1,142	1,262	2	2	8,998	9,242	1	1	1,238	1,309	12	12	28	27
Bahrain	...	...	...	...	...	...	19,048	9,706	—	—	917	875	35	21	15	11
Bangladesh	20,983	29,655	1,938	2,546	1,705	1,100	10,062	6,627	637	507	646	706	1,304	1,251	1,066	1,224
Barbados	2	2	2,538	2,500	11	7	11,653	8,247	1	1	1,209	1,254	3	3	10	7
Belarus	5,400[3]	7,000[4]	1,860[3]	2,660[4]	11,559[3,5]	8,591[4,5]	15,400[3,5]	13,500[4,5]	...	...	...	...	...	...	...	749[4]
Belgium[8]	2,069	2,467	4,861	6,776	1,468	1,950	39,246	44,318	7	19	3,080	4,233	382	363	956	1,592
Belize	27	24	1,924	1,440	3	4	20,000	21,875	1	2	526	686	72	148	3	5
Benin	366	534	698	821	1,363	2,120	7,449	9,264	34	54	445	539	142	163	121	221
Bermuda	...	...	...	...	1	1	9,041	20,636	...	...	...	...	1	—	2	3
Bhutan	159	105	1,439	1,072	40	53	6,767	10,250	2	2	592	800	29	67	11	9
Bolivia	663	1,010	1,183	1,581	1,061	1,467	5,151	7,184	20	30	1,014	1,097	532	875	317	370
Bosnia and Hercegovina	...	...	...	...	...	338[4,5]	...	5,870[4,5]	...	...	...	...	...	185[4,9]	...	...
Botswana	35	45	203	251	7	7	5,513	5,385	19	14	622	467	9	11	16	16
Brazil	30,805	35,991	1,496	1,755	27,265	27,761	11,570	12,551	2,206	2,788	464	495	18,607	31,348	4,089	5,738
Brunei	3	1	1,640	1,625	1	1	1,470	2,813	...	...	...	...	5	5	8	8
Bulgaria	8,130	8,918	3,853	3,973	376	503	10,175	11,838	68	78	984	1,052	1,975	1,305	2,021	1,666
Burkina Faso	1,166	2,234	575	841	131	111	8,783	5,826	176	183	376	389	56	71	76	118
Burundi	219	342	1,081	1,563	1,052	1,411	6,956	7,746	324	200	941	943	1,164	1,668	151	220
Cambodia	1,438	2,450	1,056	1,332	178	112	6,569	5,333	17	45	635	1,000	121	249	323	470
Cameroon	866	1,003	849	1,211	1,663	1,946	3,994	5,148	105	76	542	514	1,715	1,549	370	453
Canada	42,728	55,969	2,174	2,600	2,626	2,781	23,818	24,100	194	884	1,544	1,665	697	750	1,747	2,061
Cape Verde	4	4	365	175	15	18	3,146	3,302	4	9	286	450	12	11	5	6
Cayman Islands	...	...	...	...	—	—	4,345	3,945	...	...	...	...	1	—	...	...
Central African Republic	103	165	529	1,191	1,106	760	3,270	3,536	7	15	556	1,000	163	194	44	64
Chad	508	891	587	680	424	665	4,505	5,599	59	60	434	435	97	114	59	74
Chile	1,742	2,866	2,124	4,054	901	851	10,262	14,105	171	159	843	1,230	1,657	2,676	1,760	1,688
China	286,591	392,919	3,029	4,286	144,326	147,291	13,592	15,141	6,648	6,915	1,223	1,566	8,864	22,992	80,016	118,604
Colombia	3,339	3,948	2,452	2,451	4,144	4,494	11,043	11,899	128	160	604	693	3,905	5,202	1,362	1,696
Comoros	19	19	1,082	1,290	57	64	3,660	5,534	5	7	1,237	839	36	55	3	4
Congo	15	26	780	813	678	845	6,683	7,738	5	10	572	812	218	282	33	43
Cook Islands	...	...	...	...	11	11	30,158	28,919	...	...	...	...	14	12	2	2
Costa Rica	337	256	2,498	2,875	45	93	5,764	8,321	12	33	498	477	1,362	1,948	58	116
Côte d'Ivoire	856	1,292	858	910	3,414	4,292	5,154	5,780	8	8	667	667	1,549	1,499	317	452
Croatia	...	...	...	...	...	608[4,5]	...	7,880[4,5]	...	...	...	...	...	574[4,9]	...	...
Cuba	551	526	2,458	2,381	997	770	6,092	4,858	12	26	306	351	810	1,539	466	586
Cyprus	87	65	1,793	1,065	182	188	23,108	22,059	6	2	1,054	1,015	359	435	101	133
Czechoslovakia	9,762	11,853	3,798	4,893	3,388	2,713	16,730	16,155	137	316	1,692	2,378	644	929	1,017	1,199
Denmark	7,346	9,115	4,040	5,985	913	1,511	26,904	37,762	14	410	3,420	4,183	124	53	263	305
Djibouti	...	...	833	2,750	...	...	...	...	...	...	...	...	...	...	13	22
Dominica	—	—	1,427	1,364	26	26	11,093	9,479	...	...	467	450	46	50	7	7
Dominican Republic	447	363	3,004	3,211	214	235	5,783	6,976	73	96	958	951	1,333	1,629	209	299
Ecuador	686	1,583	1,633	1,981	552	492	9,595	5,623	39	61	547	729	3,767	4,338	243	367
Egypt	8,131	13,670	4,052	5,516	1,330	1,096	18,336	21,971	283	381	2,000	2,414	2,310	4,720	7,312	6,530
El Salvador	719	729	1,702	1,635	27	40	12,350	14,805	41	67	850	869	257	290	96	161
Equatorial Guinea	...	...	...	...	53	81	2,926	2,613	...	...	...	...	11	17	...	...
Estonia	800[3]	1,000[4]	2,080[3]	2,410[4]	929[3,5]	617[4,5]	14,500[3,5]	13,600[4,5]	...	...	...	...	...	...	...	105[4]
Ethiopia	5,804	6,420	1,186	1,237	1,631	2,078	3,703	3,641	962	763	1,061	778	201	231	501	594

subsistence as well. Figures on wild fruits and berries are seldom included in national reports at all. FAO vegetable statistics include vegetables and melons grown for human consumption only. Some countries do not make this distinction in their reports, and some exclude the production of kitchen gardens and small family plots, although in certain countries, such small-scale production may account for 20 to 40 percent of total ouput.

Livestock statistics may be distorted by the timing of country reports. Ireland, for example, takes a livestock enumeration in December that is reported the following year and that appears low against data for otherwise comparable countries because of the slaughter and export of animals at the close of the grazing season. It balances this, however, with a June enumeration, when numbers tend to be high. Milk production as defined by the FAO includes whole fresh milk, excluding milk sucked by young animals but including amounts fed by farmers or ranchers to livestock, but national practices vary. Certain countries do not distinguish between milk cows and other cattle, so that yield per dairy cow must be estimated. Some countries do not report egg production statistics (here given in metric tons), and external estimates must be based on the numbers of chickens

and reported or assumed egg-laying rates. Other countries report egg production by number, and this must be converted to weight, using conversion factors specific to the makeup by species of national poultry flocks.

Metric system units used in the table may be converted to English system units as follows:

metric tons $\times$ 1.1023 = short tons
kilograms $\times$ 2.2046 = pounds
kilograms per hectare $\times$ 0.8922 = pounds per acre.

The notes that follow, keyed by references in the table headings, provide further definitional information.
a. Includes such crops as potatoes and cassava.
b. Includes beans and peas harvested for dry grain only. Does not include green beans and green peas.
c. Excludes melons.
d. Includes melons, green beans, and green peas.
e. From milk cows only.
f. From chickens only.

livestock													country
cattle		sheep		hogs		chickens		milke		yield		eggsf		
stock ('000 head)		stock ('000 head)		stock ('000 head)		stock ('000 head)		production ('000 metric tons)		yield (kg/animal)		production (metric tons)		
1979–81 average	1991	1979–81 average	1991	1979–81 average	1991	1979–81 average	1991	1979–81 average	1991	1979–81 average	1991	1979–81 average	1991	
3,723	1,650	18,667	13,500	...	...	6,000	7,000	552	340	491	430	14,000	14,200	Afghanistan
606	650	1,232	1,600	174	170	3,000	5,000	296	283	1,326	1,252	9,957	8,100	Albania
1,356	1,443	13,111	13,350	4	5	18,000	24,000	514	596	975	1,045	20,217	175,000	Algeria
...	...	...	...	10	11	491	502	—	—	800	800	34	30	American Samoa
...	...	...	...	...	...	...	...	...	...	...	...	...	...	Andorra
3,117	3,100	225	280	400	495	5,000	6,000	146	148	500	502	3,650	3,900	Angola
14	16	12	13	4	4	621	802	6	6	977	1,058	138	120	Antigua and Barbuda
55,620	50,080	31,473	27,552	3,751	4,464	38,000	45,000	5,311	6,200	1,746	2,214	253,731	323,700	Argentina
8006	600	2,2006,7	1,2007	2006	300	11,1006	9,400	5393	4324	...	1,7654	25,0003	24,3004	Armenia
...	...	...	...	...	...	...	...	...	...	...	...	...	...	Aruba
26,161	23,430	134,871	162,774	2,416	2,530	46,000	62,000	5,590	6,578	2,989	4,066	197,870	187,000	Australia
2,553	2,584	193	309	3,906	3,688	15,000	13,000	3,434	3,355	3,509	3,565	96,804	93,000	Austria
1,8006	1,800	5,4006,7	5,4007	2006	200	20,7006	29,100	8973	9704	...	1,7464	40,9003	46,2004	Azerbaijan
4	5	35	40	18	20	1,000	2,000	3	3	1,000	1,000	356	420	Bahamas, The
6	15	7	8	...	...	—	1,000	6	19	2,703	2,620	3,238	2,750	Bahrain
25,053	23,500	750	900	...	...	59,000	60,000	833	750	221	206	39,745	40,000	Bangladesh
23	21	52	56	44	45	1,000	2,000	7	13	1,294	1,303	1,489	1,600	Barbados
6,8006	7,000	6006,7	4007	4,6006	5,100	39,2006	50,600	6,3063	7,4574	...	3,2204	154,3003	171,7004	Belarus
3,104	3,000	110	166	5,083	6,421	29,000	35,000	4,042	3,900	3,877	4,382	200,655	185,000	Belgium8
50	51	3	4	16	26	—	1,000	4	7	1,021	1,032	1,034	1,430	Belize
810	955	972	970	455	730	11,000	25,000	12	16	120	130	7,860	18,000	Benin
1	1	...	...	2	2	561	502	2	1	2,836	2,917	435	495	Bermuda
299	413	10	59	55	73	1251	...	26	29	257	257	159	330	Bhutan
4,570	5,600	9,050	12,300	1,553	2,340	7,000	19,000	71	118	1,396	1,405	22,500	33,500	Bolivia
...	853	...	1,317	...	617	...	10,607	...	9214	...	...	...	27,5584	Bosnia and Hercegovina
2,906	2,500	147	320	5	16	1,000	2,000	90	105	350	350	627	792	Botswana
116,645	152,000	18,414	20,300	34,102	35,000	426,000	570,000	11,378	15,300	712	793	765,117	1,400,000	Brazil
3	1	...	...	11	14	1,000	2,000	...	...	...	...	1,787	3,000	Brunei
1,782	1,475	10,358	7,938	3,803	4,187	39,000	28,000	1,843	1,756	2,638	3,059	131,679	111,219	Bulgaria
2,760	2,900	1,855	3,339	198	520	11,000	22,000	81	83	175	177	7,448	15,400	Burkina Faso
614	435	301	365	44	103	3,000	4,000	37	26	350	350	2,356	3,116	Burundi
831	2,150	—	—	205	1,610	3,000	8,000	14	17	170	170	5,400	13,500	Cambodia
3,521	4,700	2,167	3,550	1,139	1,414	8,000	18,000	88	117	500	500	8,400	12,000	Cameroon
13,328	12,369	729	780	9,709	10,516	96,000	114,000	7,354	7,340	4,137	5,400	330,863	319,600	Canada
12	19	1	6	40	86	591	1,000	1	1	500	500	65	400	Cape Verde
5	2	...	...	...	...	161	212	...	...	...	...	84	5	Cayman Islands
1,662	2,677	84	135	243	426	2,000	3,000	20	36	170	170	966	1,332	Central African Republic
4,360	4,400	2,620	1,983	9	15	3,000	4,000	118	113	270	270	2,850	3,690	Chad
3,650	3,300	6,059	6,650	1,068	1,300	18,000	29,000	1,111	1,490	1,561	1,910	66,046	91,000	Chile
52,567	81,407	101,864	112,820	313,660	363,975	860,000	2,077,000	1,143	4,816	1,854	1,670	2,325,749	6,845,000	China
24,110	24,875	2,399	2,745	2,013	2,700	30,000	43,000	2,187	3,600	965	1,043	176,972	267,000	Colombia
60	47	8	14	...	...	2431	3622	3	4	500	500	564	640	Comoros
64	68	69	108	28	52	1,000	2,000	3	3	1,500	1,500	825	1,200	Congo
...	...	...	...	17	17	631	...	...	...	...	...	77	60	Cook Islands
2,183	1,741	2	3	223	224	5,000	4,000	318	430	1,067	1,341	16,760	17,500	Costa Rica
664	1,064	1,020	1,150	315	369	17,000	27,000	12	20	110	119	10,253	16,600	Côte d'Ivoire
...	757	...	753	...	1,620	...	16,612	...	9224	...	...	...	47,8874	Croatia
5,166	4,920	356	385	1,417	1,900	24,000	28,000	1,045	1,070	1,579	1,911	98,936	110,000	Cuba
22	52	290	325	162	289	2,000	3,000	33	106	3,601	4,885	5,309	8,500	Cyprus
4,935	4,923	883	1,030	7,694	7,090	46,000	47,000	5,830	5,826	3,140	3,552	243,327	266,230	Czechoslovakia
2,970	2,220	55	111	9,699	9,489	15,000	16,000	5,126	4,620	4,920	6,228	77,130	84,000	Denmark
52	170	452	420	...	...	...	...	...	...	...	...	...	...	Djibouti
7	9	6	8	8	5	981	1172	3	5	1,000	1,000	177	158	Dominica
1,918	2,250	65	120	298	435	12,000	28,000	427	420	1,742	1,714	19,267	33,000	Dominican Republic
2,987	4,200	1,148	1,250	3,417	2,125	33,000	56,000	924	1,505	1,446	1,750	43,056	56,900	Ecuador
1,906	3,500	1,791	4,900	20	110	28,000	35,000	648	1,140	674	814	78,100	128,000	Egypt
1,234	1,243	4	5	455	320	5,000	5,000	268	327	958	1,130	36,822	39,000	El Salvador
4	5	33	36	4	5	1201	1952	...	...	...	...	116	180	Equatorial Guinea
8006	800	2006,7	1007	1,1006	1,000	6,8006	6,500	1,1933	1,2084	...	4,0564	25,8003	26,7004	Estonia
26,000	30,000	23,250	23,000	18	20	52,000	58,000	615	752	197	206	73,140	79,120	Ethiopia

Crops and livestock (continued)

country	grains — production ('000 metric tons) 1979–81 avg	grains — production 1991	grains — yield (kg/hectare) 1979–81 avg	grains — yield 1991	roots and tubers[a] — production 1979–81 avg	roots and tubers[a] — production 1991	roots and tubers[a] — yield 1979–81 avg	roots and tubers[a] — yield 1991	pulses[b] — production 1979–81 avg	pulses[b] — production 1991	pulses[b] — yield 1979–81 avg	pulses[b] — yield 1991	fruits[c] — production 1979–81 avg	fruits[c] — production 1991	vegetables[d] — production 1979–81 avg	vegetables[d] — production 1991
Faeroe Islands	...	...	...	...	1	2	13,684	13,977	...	...	540	600	...	...	...	...
Fiji	19	35	2,004	2,265	24	62	7,945	12,818	...	...	...	...	11	14	6	7
Finland	2,993	3,399	2,511	3,318	629	672	15,578	18,566	13	28	2,182	2,527	107	89	130	210
France	46,091	60,442	4,700	6,543	6,735	6,300	28,465	37,059	340	3,294	3,304	4,690	14,255	10,313	6,864	7,945
French Guiana	1	29	1,159	5,370	13	18	10,842	10,112	...	...	...	...	2	7	3	16
French Polynesia	...	...	...	...	19	13	12,245	10,720	...	...	...	...	4	8	6	7
Gabon	11	21	1,718	1,458	372	430	6,289	6,815	—	—	528	650	181	260	22	31
Gambia, The	78	108	1,189	1,089	6	6	3,000	3,000	4	4	267	267	4	4	7	8
Gaza Strip	4	1	2,793	471	5	20	18,333	20,000	—	—	3,071	—	200	150	61	85
Georgia	600[3]	700[4]	2,010[3]	2,470[4]	393[3,5]	294[4,5]	11,700[3,5]	10,600[4,5]	...	...	...	...	...	...	...	443[4]
Germany	32,043	39,270	8,061	11,702	19,465	10,225	49,631	56,186	116	175	4,618	5,710	4,447	3,103	3,205	3,511
Ghana	726	1,436	807	1,221	3,183	5,897	6,721	6,111	14	21	101	102	966	1,320	299	452
Gibraltar	...	...	...	...	...	...	...	...	...	...	...	...	...	...	...	...
Greece	4,951	5,167	3,090	3,411	1,041	1,102	16,378	20,000	94	49	1,262	1,465	3,437	3,795	3,636	3,946
Greenland	...	...	...	...	...	...	...	...	...	...	...	...	...	...	...	...
Grenada	—	—	949	1,000	3	3	4,582	5,249	1	1	1,607	1,078	29	22	2	2
Guadeloupe	—	—	1,200	1,200	22	23	8,459	11,024	—	—	514	600	115	112	17	22
Guam	—	—	3,000	1,392	2	2	13,756	14,070	...	...	...	...	2	2	2	4
Guatemala	1,117	1,301	1,604	1,897	52	60	3,535	5,042	77	121	844	823	734	810	277	366
Guernsey	...	...	...	...	...	...	...	...	...	...	...	...	...	...	...	...
Guinea	678	888	958	981	644	732	7,116	6,318	42	62	646	885	639	756	410	420
Guinea-Bissau	102	165	711	1,484	47	50	5,986	6,250	2	2	971	920	44	50	21	20
Guyana	267	253	2,907	3,226	16	32	6,626	7,273	1	1	487	591	41	69	9	12
Haiti	419	335	1,009	1,015	689	829	3,778	4,151	90	99	471	558	1,007	959	281	273
Honduras	492	734	1,170	1,358	21	32	4,896	6,848	38	110	518	711	1,675	1,568	95	169
Hong Kong	—	—	1,712	2,000	—	1	25,407	23,097	...	...	...	...	3	4	189	114
Hungary	13,001	15,505	4,519	5,593	1,507	1,229	15,894	27,190	127	333	1,547	2,173	2,389	2,262	1,841	2,078
Iceland	...	...	...	...	11	12	11,858	12,000	...	...	...	...	...	...	1	2
India	138,182	195,109	1,324	1,897	16,777	22,049	12,926	15,964	10,509	14,007	461	582	20,409	28,388	41,379	54,358
Indonesia	33,611	50,732	2,835	3,843	16,153	19,026	9,054	11,818	352	508	882	1,383	4,943	6,542	2,434	4,112
Iran	8,930	14,626	1,132	1,478	1,269	2,500	14,436	16,666	247	309	799	627	3,215	6,744	5,009	7,625
Iraq	1,803	1,248	832	254	96	176	18,464	17,600	36	10	802	583	1,161	1,169	1,880	2,295
Ireland	2,009	2,084	4,733	6,260	822	650	20,799	29,954	—	7	3,444	4,667	21	22	283	216
Isle of Man	...	...	...	...	...	...	...	...	...	...	...	...	...	...	...	...
Israel	239	167	1,840	1,874	201	229	36,551	37,506	8	9	955	1,137	1,913	2,000	762	1,104
Italy	18,025	19,043	3,548	4,336	2,962	2,258	18,274	18,614	321	208	1,335	1,381	20,661	17,632	13,401	14,676
Jamaica	7	3	1,667	1,548	230	245	11,666	12,786	8	6	882	899	332	375	104	102
Japan	14,318	13,165	5,252	5,443	5,342	5,804	22,838	24,584	108	155	1,254	1,570	6,330	5,281	15,230	15,022
Jersey	...	...	...	...	...	...	...	...	...	...	...	...	...	...	...	...
Jordan	91	68	571	406	9	45	16,866	20,000	8	6	588	636	90	234	437	647
Kazakhstan	20,100[3]	28,500[4]	790[3]	1,220[4]	1,952[3,5]	2,324[4,5]	9,900[3,5]	11,300[4,5]	...	...	...	...	...	...	...	1,136[4]
Kenya	2,281	2,747	1,364	1,397	1,257	1,560	7,993	8,211	185	240	430	343	650	944	490	642
Kiribati	...	...	...	...	9	8	8,011	7,879	...	...	...	...	5	5	4	5
Korea, North	9,001	10,080	5,964	6,315	1,909	2,490	12,486	12,769	280	330	849	930	851	1,330	2,636	4,459
Korea, South	8,073	7,905	4,764	5,777	1,655	794	17,765	20,620	56	41	940	1,111	997	1,893	9,070	10,205
Kuwait	—	—	3,087	5,667	...	...	16,934	15,000	...	...	...	...	1	—	36	—
Kyrgyzstan	1,300[3]	1,500[4]	2,400[3]	2,800[4]	309[3,5]	365[4,5]	12,800[3,5]	13,600[4,5]	...	...	...	...	...	...	...	487[4]
Laos	1,056	1,460	1,402	2,157	184	319	10,114	8,507	17	35	1,728	2,333	89	137	184	230
Latvia	1,300[3]	1,600[4]	1,770[3]	2,360[4]	1,468[3,5]	1,016[4,5]	14,500[3,5]	12,700[4,5]	...	...	...	...	...	...	...	170[4]
Lebanon	41	71	1,307	1,829	130	201	16,923	15,388	10	16	968	1,182	704	989	347	533
Lesotho	198	125	977	622	6	8	15,526	15,000	8	7	536	305	16	19	21	27
Liberia	254	110	1,251	786	346	348	6,894	6,641	3	3	500	500	121	130	64	71
Libya	225	298	430	674	97	148	6,671	8,132	9	13	1,079	1,119	203	298	527	752
Liechtenstein	...	...	...	...	11	124[4]	18,742	17,974[4]	...	...	...	...	...	...	...	...
Lithuania	2,500[3]	3,300[4]	2,070[3]	3,010[4]	1,921[3,5]	1,573[4,5]	13,900[3,5]	14,000[4,5]	...	...	...	...	...	...	...	295[4]
Luxembourg[8]	...	...	...	...	...	...	...	...	...	...	...	...	...	...	...	...
Macau	...	...	...	...	4	7	11,174	13,273	...	...	...	...	4	3	2	1
Macedonia	...	...	...	...	...	754[4,5]	...	5,650[4,5]	...	...	...	...	...	353[4,9]	...	...
Madagascar	2,178	2,352	1,664	1,873	2,267	3,149	5,704	6,413	53	47	852	815	719	781	283	330
Malawi	1,341	1,679	1,161	1,147	562	508	4,458	3,181	204	271	609	583	375	452	212	255
Malaysia	2,061	1,586	2,827	2,422	468	530	8,895	9,232	...	...	...	...	925	1,109	310	322
Maldives	—	—	806	1,000	7	8	5,176	5,084	—	—	600	625	8	10	15	19
Mali	1,064	2,232	790	993	123	145	8,349	8,485	47	57	338	200	13	15	173	258
Malta	8	9	3,252	3,431	21	18	8,948	10,938	1	1	2,333	2,333	11	12	47	52
Marshall Islands	...	...	...	...	...	...	...	...	...	...	...	...	...	...	...	...
Martinique	...	...	...	...	22	25	6,997	9,960	...	...	...	...	178	285	27	24
Mauritania	48	117	384	908	7	6	2,888	1,787	29	21	407	365	15	16	7	8
Mauritius	1	2	2,536	2,889	12	19	17,368	19,502	1	2	491	750	6	8	26	42
Mayotte	...	...	...	...	...	...	...	...	...	...	...	...	...	...	...	...
Mexico	20,692	23,056	2,152	2,330	1,120	1,127	12,906	15,089	1,311	1,661	719	743	7,316	9,605	3,860	4,840
Micronesia	...	...	...	...	...	...	...	...	...	...	...	...	...	...	...	...
Moldova	2,400[3]	2,500[4]	3,230[3]	3,400[4]	399[3,5]	295[4,5]	8,900[3,5]	7,200[4,5]	...	...	...	...	...	...	...	1,177[4]
Monaco	...	...	...	...	...	...	...	...	...	...	...	...	...	...	...	...
Mongolia	320	591	573	1,040	50	96	7,878	10,787	...	4	292	1,000	3	—	26	22
Morocco	3,583	8,648	811	1,575	503	928	14,169	17,405	229	439	571	741	1,600	2,304	1,320	3,204
Mozambique	649	546	603	342	3,712	3,821	4,194	3,869	59	78	381	263	327	356	184	195
Myanmar (Burma)	12,984	13,667	2,521	2,583	167	221	8,087	8,627	365	484	588	695	838	966	1,872	2,182
Namibia	90	114	468	488	203	275	9,242	9,167	6	7	944	1,077	31	36	28	33
Nauru	...	...	...	...	...	...	...	...	...	...	...	...	...	...	...	...
Nepal	3,640	5,919	1,615	1,957	349	863	5,455	7,816	140	279	536	605	404	504	517	1,075
Netherlands, The	1,280	1,205	5,696	6,827	6,329	6,735	37,752	38,398	24	83	3,145	4,368	535	356	2,527	3,591
Netherlands Antilles	1[1]	2[2]	653[1]	714[2]	...	...	...	...	...	...	...	...	...	...	...	...
New Caledonia	3	1	2,134	1,244	21	22	5,691	5,703	—	—	772	667	9	9	3	5
New Zealand	785	906	4,077	5,052	220	311	26,301	29,948	63	58	2,965	3,045	363	825	382	493
Nicaragua	392	455	1,475	1,665	28	96	9,107	12,114	39	56	576	611	313	306	47	55

livestock														country
cattle		sheep		hogs		chickens		milk[e]				eggs[f]		
stock ('000 head)		stock ('000 head)		stock ('000 head)		stock ('000 head)		production ('000 metric tons)		yield (kg/animal)		production (metric tons)		
1979–81 average	1991	1979–81 average	1991	1979–81 average	1991	1979–81 average	1991	1979–81 average	1991	1979–81 average	1991	1979–81 average	1991	
2	2	67	67	...	...	...	...	...	...	...	...	...	...	Faeroe Islands
153	158	...	...	14	15	1,000	3,000	54	62	1,701	1,699	1,976	2,050	Fiji
1,747	1,315	107	57	1,430	1,290	9,000	6,000	3,236	2,477	4,572	5,618	77,967	66,900	Finland
23,825	21,446	12,133	11,490	11,472	12,239	177,000	213,000	26,720	26,000	2,634	2,956	849,667	942,000	France
6	19	3	4	6	11	121[1]	100[2]	—	—	2,080	2,143	292	250	French Guiana
8	7	2	—	24	32	2,000	2,000	2	2	2,771	2,215	923	1,300	French Polynesia
5	28	105	165	126	162	2,000	2,000	—	1	250	259	1,050	1,500	Gabon
293	410	136	175	10	11	280[1]	1,000	5	7	175	175	402	813	Gambia, The
5	4	15	10	...	...	1,000	3,000	11	6	4,185	4,000	2,265	4,800	Gaza Strip
1,600[6]	1,300	2,000[6,7]	1,600[7]	900[6]	900	18,800[6]	21,800	656[3]	660[4]	...	1,619[4]	35,070[3]	36,100[4]	Georgia
20,672	19,488	3,147	3,240	34,768	30,819	137,000	106,000	31,724	29,300	7,882	9,993	1,123,574	912,000	Germany
804	1,300	1,942	2,500	379	620	11,000	11,000	16	25	130	130	12,203	12,720	Ghana
...	...	...	...	...	...	...	...	...	...	...	...	...	...	Gibraltar
929	634	8,040	9,759	944	1,143	30,000	27,000	666	690	1,867	2,248	122,540	138,000	Greece
...	...	20	22	...	...	...	...	...	...	...	...	...	...	Greenland
6	4	14	11	8	7	252[1]	260[2]	1	1	769	800	948	920	Grenada
91	65	3	5	44	36	420[1]	390[2]	1	2	507	500	778	900	Guadeloupe
1	—	...	...	13	15	127[1]	218[2]	...	...	...	...	1,071	679	Guam
1,886	1,695	615	675	737	1,110	14,000	10,000	263	150	749	732	39,947	63,500	Guatemala
4	3	...	...	...	...	...	...	8	9	3,514	4,389	...	...	Guernsey
1,753	1,800	436	518	39	33	7,000	13,000	41	42	185	185	7,420	13,860	Guinea
290	410	177	245	256	293	—	1,000	9	12	170	170	300	576	Guinea-Bissau
189	230	115	130	115	80	13,000	15,000	13	56	832	933	3,900	4,200	Guyana
1,000	1,400	89	92	1,533	930	5,000	13,000	20	20	229	233	2,943	3,600	Haiti
1,980	2,388	5	8	418	740	5,000	8,000	271	310	652	881	18,947	24,700	Honduras
7	2	...	...	520	304	6,000	6,000	4	2	3,022	2,179	2,737	1,900	Hong Kong
1,936	1,571	2,960	1,865	8,232	8,000	62,000	45,000	2,559	2,625	3,727	5,000	250,000	230,000	Hungary
60	73	838	700	11	19	247[1]	307[2]	121	117	3,635	3,656	3,000	3,800	Iceland
186,500	198,400	44,987	55,700	9,433	10,450	160,000	380,000	13,420	27,000	530	871	682,000	1,357,000	India
6,502	10,350	4,124	5,750	3,234	6,800	168,000	590,000	79	329	762	1,037	177,767	400,000	Indonesia
5,450	6,800	31,672	45,000	17	...	97,000	165,000	1,125	1,428	700	700	155,333	278,000	Iran
1,630	1,400	10,842	7,800	...	...	26,000	50,000	290	225	750	750	48,362	35,000	Iraq
6,043	6,029	2,374	6,001	1,122	1,069	8,000	9,000	4,729	5,527	3,178	3,984	35,000	30,000	Ireland
...	32[10]	...	147[10]	...	8[10]	...	71[10]	...	...	...	...	...	...	Isle of Man
299	331	243	375	96	100	25,000	24,000	702	965	6,817	8,874	91,675	106,000	Israel
8,697	8,647	9,120	11,575	8,885	9,520	138,000	138,000	10,546	10,000	3,478	3,448	659,163	707,000	Italy
279	300	4	2	210	250	5,000	8,000	48	49	1,000	1,000	15,500	16,500	Jamaica
4,261	4,863	13	32	9,851	11,335	284,000	335,000	6,526	8,180	4,526	6,127	1,998,041	2,466,000	Japan
7	6[4]	...	...	...	...	...	...	...	...	...	...	...	...	Jersey
29	29	950	1,400	...	...	28,000	47,000	18	35	1,000	1,912	19,000	22,200	Jordan
8,700[6]	9,800	35,200[6,7]	35,700[7]	3,100[6]	3,200	48,100[6]	59,900	4,629[3]	5,642[4]	...	2,367[4]	169,700[3]	196,500[4]	Kazakhstan
10,418	13,700	5,100	6,550	89	105	17,000	25,000	958	2,189	460	470	19,968	42,000	Kenya
...	...	...	...	10	9	154[1]	220[2]	...	...	...	...	105	126	Kiribati
945	1,350	292	390	2,100	3,300	18,000	21,000	55	90	2,244	2,368	103,833	148,000	Korea, North
1,728	2,126	7	5	2,115	4,528	41,000	74,000	449	1,848	4,864	6,059	255,786	489,000	Korea, South
17	—	250	—	...	...	9,000	—	24	—	2,653	3,300	8,573	60	Kuwait
1,000[6]	1,200	10,000[6,7]	10,000[7]	300[6]	400	10,300[6]	13,900	717[3]	1,185[4]	...	3,034[4]	22,100[3]	33,500[4]	Kyrgyzstan
437	865	...	...	1,117	1,390	5,000	8,000	6	10	200	200	22,167	34,000	Laos
1,400[6]	1,400	200[6,7]	200[7]	1,800[6]	1,400	11,200[6]	10,300	1,766[3]	1,893[4]	...	3,379[4]	38,000[3]	38,500[4]	Latvia
64	57	137	205	18	45	19,000	24,000	85	60	2,290	2,857	41,275	53,000	Lebanon
582	540	1,183	1,470	75	75	1,000	1,000	20	24	290	290	789	828	Lesotho
39	38	200	220	103	120	2,000	4,000	1	1	130	130	2,336	4,032	Liberia
164	150	5,046	5,500	...	...	6,000	55,000	63	140	1,499	1,556	16,233	34,650	Libya
6	6	2	3	3	3	43[1]	...	9	13	3,310	4,702	—	...	Liechtenstein
2,200[6]	2,300	100[6,7]	100[7]	2,600[6]	2,400	13,900[6]	16,800	2,731[3]	3,157[4]	...	3,538[4]	49,500[3]	59,800[4]	Lithuania
...	...	...	...	3	1	353[1]	450[2]	...	...	...	...	575	645	Luxembourg[8]
—	287	...	2,297	...	179	...	5,729	...	185[4]	...	...	...	27,559[4]	Macau
10,147	10,265	695	753	1,090	1,461	18,000	22,000	443	472	259	270	12,327	17,420	Madagascar
817	1,150	84	230	192	280	8,000	9,000	35	49	458	461	10,503	11,270	Malawi
532	658	65	200	1,869	2,400	51,000	148,000	25	30	549	641	96,767	211,500	Malaysia
...	...	...	...	...	...	...	...	...	...	...	...	...	...	Maldives
5,670	5,000	6,247	5,850	48	61	12,000	22,000	139	122	245	245	6,720	11,880	Mali
13	22	5	6	12	102	1,000	1,000	29	24	4,111	3,810	6,256	6,800	Malta
...	...	...	...	...	...	...	...	...	...	...	...	...	...	Marshall Islands
57	35	76	63	37	49	...	...	5	3	754	694	1,500	450	Martinique
1,262	1,360	5,098	4,200	...	...	3,000	4,000	85	98	350	350	2,720	4,420	Mauritania
27	34	10	7	7	10	2,000	2,000	25	25	2,500	2,500	2,800	4,200	Mauritius
...	...	...	...	...	...	...	...	...	...	...	...	...	...	Mayotte
27,706	29,847	6,484	6,003	16,895	15,902	177,000	246,000	6,949	6,925	1,284	1,237	636,256	1,141,381	Mexico
...	...	...	...	...	...	...	...	...	...	...	...	...	...	Micronesia
1,200[6]	1,100	1,200[6,7]	1,300[7]	2,000[6]	1,800	17,800[6]	24,600	1,245[3]	1,512[4]	...	3,972[4]	46,000[3]	53,000[4]	Moldova
...	...	...	...	...	...	...	...	...	...	...	...	...	...	Monaco
2,452	2,849	14,261	15,083	32	185	165[1]	300[2]	210	203	355	262	983	1,265	Mongolia
3,362	3,500	15,228	14,000	7	9	24,000	41,000	753	990	640	535	72,900	93,000	Morocco
1,400	1,370	106	118	120	165	17,000	22,000	63	68	170	170	9,400	12,800	Mozambique
8,565	9,310	235	280	2,263	2,250	23,000	24,000	283	456	245	220	31,435	34,780	Myanmar (Burma)
2,403	2,131	4,117	6,700	37	51	—	1,000	68	71	412	410	113	130	Namibia
...	...	...	...	2	3	3[1]	...	...	...	...	...	8	20	Nauru
6,893	6,350	730	925	375	575	6,000	7,000	190	260	325	377	14,300	18,000	Nepal
5,071	4,830	856	1,702	10,058	13,788	81,000	101,000	11,832	11,220	5,025	6,148	540,409	645,600	Netherlands, The
2	1	8	4	7	3	100[1]	135[2]	4	2	1,250	1,000	517	400	Netherlands Antilles
113	122	4	3	16	38	...	1,000	3	4	600	600	887	1,650	New Caledonia
8,063	8,200	67,393	57,000	433	433	7,000	10,000	6,586	7,973	3,306	3,366	56,855	46,020	New Zealand
2,373	1,680	3	4	625	709	3,000	7,000	225	161	767	634	28,833	25,500	Nicaragua

Crops and livestock (continued)

country	grains production ('000 metric tons)		grains yield (kg/hectare)		roots and tubers[a] production ('000 metric tons)		roots and tubers[a] yield (kg/hectare)		pulses[b] production ('000 metric tons)		pulses[b] yield (kg/hectare)		fruits[c] production ('000 metric tons)		vegetables[d] production ('000 metric tons)	
	1979–81 average	1991	1979–81 average	1991	1979–81 average	1991	1979–81 average	1991	1979–81 average	1991	1979–81 average	1991	1979–81 average	1991	1979–81 average	1991
Niger	1,702	2,415	440	372	212	251	7,210	7,153	292	387	269	177	37	44	142	141
Nigeria	7,480	14,200	1,264	1,206	18,926	37,602	8,823	10,827	647	1,559	444	777	2,062	2,662	2,906	3,965
Northern Mariana Islands	...	...	...	...	...	...	...	...	...	...	...	...	...	...	...	...
Norway	1,129	1,467	3,634	4,491	524	484	25,884	25,866	...	...	...	...	117	109	189	170
Oman	2	5	982	2,143	1	5	13,663	24,091	...	...	...	...	109	189	105	159
Pakistan	17,200	21,198	1,608	1,783	423	755	10,495	10,407	595	806	397	527	2,570	3,980	2,083	3,725
Palau	...	...	...	...	...	...	...	...	...	...	...	...	...	...	...	...
Panama	252	299	1,469	1,759	76	78	8,496	6,695	5	6	412	381	1,208	1,302	44	60
Papua New Guinea	4	3	2,087	1,695	1,125	1,267	6,952	6,530	2	2	500	500	1,327	1,688	286	363
Paraguay	659	1,508	1,538	1,837	2,080	3,968	13,100	15,862	69	55	803	868	827	950	218	226
Peru	1,422	1,757	1,933	2,357	2,477	2,350	7,574	8,095	111	99	856	921	1,483	1,406	720	856
Philippines	11,088	14,325	1,633	2,043	3,100	2,788	6,632	6,858	37	37	652	786	6,816	6,848	3,477	4,253
Poland	18,466	27,861	2,345	3,196	39,508	29,038	16,808	16,785	216	668	1,232	1,954	1,584	1,874	4,553	5,521
Portugal	1,210	1,403	1,102	1,535	1,141	972	8,947	7,937	76	63	228	283	2,055	2,145	1,529	1,975
Puerto Rico	6	—	8,925	5,000	39	25	6,470	6,268	6	2	916	690	296	267	28	42
Qatar	1	3	2,623	3,733	—	—	13,367	6,000	...	1	...	1,443	6	8	18	24
Réunion	12	13	5,064	6,500	11	19	13,133	12,857	...	...	2,626	1,443	26	49	14	29
Romania	18,109	19,270	2,854	3,186	4,317	1,900	14,728	8,089	115	163	258	1,533	2,952	2,022	4,168	2,607
Russia	92,000[3]	116,700[4]	1,300[3]	1,850[4]	38,439[3,5]	30,848[4,5]	10,403[3,5]	9,900[4,5]	...	...	...	...	...	...	...	10,328[4]
Rwanda	271	330	1,134	1,187	1,743	1,725	8,809	6,952	221	250	727	839	2,162	3,089	169	132
St. Kitts and Nevis	...	...	...	...	2	1	3,649	3,322	—	—	1,000	1,000	1	1	1	1
St. Lucia	—	—	703	696	10	11	4,246	4,192	—	—	2,187	2,500	90	186	1	1
St. Vincent and the Grenadines	1	1	3,294	3,535	24	21	8,071	4,970	—	—	913	1,007	35	87	1	2
San Marino	...	...	...	...	...	...	...	...	...	...	...	...	...	...	...	...
São Tomé and Príncipe	1	1	1,538	2,000	14	19	12,701	14,222	...	...	...	...	4	5	3	3
Saudi Arabia	303	4,476	820	5,026	3	39	9,930	15,000	6	7	1,813	1,825	480	641	684	1,630
Senegal	850	914	690	813	43	85	4,344	3,712	21	12	398	346	75	106	82	130
Seychelles	...	...	...	...	—	—	5,000	5,000	...	...	...	...	2	2	1	2
Sierra Leone	542	442	1,249	1,011	126	129	3,727	4,201	31	39	579	655	128	156	153	188
Singapore	...	...	...	...	2	—	11,330	16,800	...	...	...	...	9	1	39	8
Slovenia	...	...	...	...	...	413[4,5]	...	13,670[4,5]	...	...	...	...	...	241[4,9]	...	...
Solomon Islands	13	—	3,513	...	87	109	15,048	16,979	2	2	840	1,200	11	15	5	6
Somalia	305	251	474	552	39	51	10,863	10,406	10	12	494	300	182	304	27	60
South Africa[11]	14,036	10,945	1,896	2,003	793	1,303	11,435	14,640	110	119	1,051	1,152	3,139	3,813	1,662	1,950
Bophuthatswana[11]	...	...	...	...	...	...	...	...	...	...	...	...	...	...	...	...
Ciskei[11]	...	...	...	...	...	...	...	...	...	...	...	...	...	...	...	...
Transkei[11]	...	...	...	...	...	...	...	...	...	...	...	...	...	...	...	...
Venda[11]	...	...	...	...	...	...	...	...	...	...	...	...	...	...	...	...
Spain	14,709	19,195	1,986	2,459	5,670	5,382	15,986	19,466	365	215	704	713	12,603	12,542	8,547	10,377
Sri Lanka	2,132	2,440	2,464	2,969	717	577	9,685	9,203	47	72	845	727	1,718	832	535	1,081
Sudan, The	2,962	3,993	655	634	296	158	3,329	2,990	99	110	1,260	1,060	763	844	795	903
Suriname	258	190	3,972	3,451	3	3	5,301	11,633	—	—	849	750	52	74	6	28
Swaziland	92	159	1,345	1,930	13	10	1,993	2,289	3	5	576	1,061	121	129	12	12
Sweden	5,407	5,092	3,595	4,480	1,191	1,233	28,914	26,869	32	103	2,248	2,475	207	167	228	298
Switzerland	843	1,281	4,883	6,200	924	725	37,834	37,958	1	9	3,354	4,140	724	499	306	307
Syria	3,069	3,279	1,156	1,438	279	295	15,302	15,526	180	127	799	686	733	1,475	2,973	1,885
Taiwan	3,565[1]	3,303[2]	4,264[1]	5,272[2]	2,341[1]	5,430[2]	15,146[1]	13,889[2]	32[1]	40[2]	944[1]	1,887[2]	1,639[1]	2,165[2]	2,387[1]	3,531[2]
Tajikistan	300[3]	300[4]	1,440[3]	1,310[4]	165[3,5]	207[4,5]	16,800[3,5]	14,300[4,5]	...	...	...	...	...	...	...	528[4]
Tanzania	3,010	3,826	1,063	1,226	6,158	6,766	9,491	7,796	315	424	454	484	1,953	2,057	973	1,111
Thailand	20,314	24,279	1,910	2,047	15,512	20,518	14,226	13,491	342	474	685	752	6,304	5,750	2,711	2,521
Togo	301	447	729	836	922	953	8,722	8,013	23	20	238	211	41	48	65	168
Tonga	...	...	...	...	91	90	5,934	5,685	...	...	...	...	14	13	7	14
Trinidad and Tobago	13	17	3,167	2,821	20	9	12,206	9,973	4	3	1,638	1,365	57	60	30	16
Tunisia	1,146	2,554	828	1,546	127	220	12,905	12,941	89	93	560	614	518	623	1,044	1,512
Turkey	25,232	31,051	1,869	2,256	2,957	4,600	16,679	22,439	817	1,866	1,140	885	7,682	9,391	13,340	19,058
Turkmenistan	300	400[4]	2,170[3]	2,360[4]	18[3,5]	354[4,5]	7,000[3,5]	7,800[4,5]	...	...	...	...	...	1	...	411[4]
Tuvalu	...	...	...	...	...	...	...	...	...	...	...	...	...	...	...	...
Uganda	1,171	1,652	1,555	1,537	3,548	5,395	5,823	6,461	252	533	697	775	6,300	8,358	290	415
Ukraine	37,900	51,000[4]	2,340[3]	3,490[4]	20,013[3,5]	16,732[4,5]	12,300[3,5]	11,700[4,5]	...	...	...	...	62	121	...	6,666[4]
United Arab Emirates	3	7	5,606	4,667	2	6	14,558	14,146	...	...	...	...	...	...	130	204
United Kingdom	18,840	22,649	4,791	6,467	6,601	6,700	32,891	41,358	240	722	3,168	3,297	524	502	3,762	3,532
United States	301,405	279,923	4,150	4,511	15,487	19,496	28,933	33,137	1,457	1,746	1,633	1,966	26,531	24,668	25,471	32,227
Uruguay	1,012	1,098	1,644	2,351	197	256	5,497	7,474	5	6	909	997	273	424	172	182
Uzbekistan	2,400	1,900[4]	2,020[3]	1,880[4]	305[3,5]	336[4,5]	9,700[3,5]	8,000[4,5]	...	...	...	...	...	...	...	2,843[4]
Vanuatu	1	1	513	538	32	51	19,630	10,200	...	...	...	...	10	19	6	9
Venezuela	1,550	2,324	1,904	2,465	602	644	7,906	8,060	37	67	509	615	2,048	2,594	401	472
Vietnam	12,225	20,084	2,049	2,949	6,284	5,386	6,592	8,311	117	203	558	674	2,578	4,012	2,578	4,012
Virgin Islands (U.S.)	...	...	...	...	...	...	...	...	...	...	...	...	...	...	...	...
West Bank	...	...	...	...	...	...	...	...	...	...	...	...	...	...	...	...
Western Sahara	1[1]	2[2]	708[1]	741[2]	...	...	...	...	...	...	...	...	...	...	...	...
Western Samoa	...	...	...	...	39	42	6,952	6,530	...	...	...	...	53	51	—	1
Yemen	913	298	1,041	477	133	168	11,992	11,831	80[12]	53[12]	1,087[12]	1,197[12]	173	317	335	574
Yugoslavia	...	...	...	...	...	138[4,5]	...	34,510[4,5]	...	...	...	...	...	888[4,9]	...	...
Zaire	900	1,359	807	755	13,595	19,038	6,901	7,542	155	193	604	613	2,624	3,070	479	560
Zambia	990	1,603	1,676	2,308	205	302	3,465	3,864	7	26	340	488	76	107	209	280
Zimbabwe	2,273	2,054	1,359	1,327	76	124	3,823	4,805	23	51	566	695	108	151	136	153

livestock								milk[e]		yield		eggs[f]		country
cattle		sheep		hogs		chickens		production				production		
stock ('000 head)		stock ('000 head)		stock ('000 head)		stock ('000 head)		('000 metric tons)		(kg/animal)		(metric tons)		
1979–81 average	1991	1979–81 average	1991	1979–81 average	1991	1979–81 average	1991	1979–81 average	1991	1979–81 average	1991	1979–81 average	1991	
3,343	2,200	2,979	2,970	31	38	10,000	19,000	97	125	200	380	6,800	8,670	Niger
12,267	14,500	9,000	24,000	1,000	4,000	92,000	170,000	354	360	288	300	180,000	225,000	Nigeria
1	—	...	...	1	2	15[1]	20[2]	—	—	713	717	20	20	Niue
989	953	2,033	2,211	675	715	4,000	4,000	1,926	1,928	5,125	5,621	44,665	52,577	Norway
141	138	114	280	...	...	—	3,000	18	18	420	420	710	6,050	Oman
15,268	17,785	22,580	30,160	...	...	54,000	192,000	2,189	3,449	864	1,183	96,367	238,300	Pakistan
...	...	...	...	...	...	...	...	...	...	...	...	...	...	Palau
1,425	1,399	...	...	205	256	5,000	9,000	94	126	988	1,126	14,553	12,050	Panama
130	105	2	4	870	1,000	2,000	3,000	—	—	228	106	1,815	3,000	Papua New Guinea
5,966	8,260	387	460	1,090	2,450	12,000	17,000	163	230	1,903	1,901	26,025	36,000	Paraguay
3,958	3,630	14,565	11,250	2,083	2,250	37,000	60,000	796	786	1,298	1,257	59,700	117,000	Peru
1,885	1,677	30	30	7,712	8,007	53,000	65,000	13	15	994	1,034	201,285	267,000	Philippines
12,494	8,844	4,105	3,234	20,343	21,868	77,000	52,000	16,250	15,050	2,778	3,202	488,642	380,000	Poland
1,332	1,375	4,440	5,673	3,367	2,664	17,000	18,000	750	1,550	2,123	3,846	62,008	95,600	Portugal
497	599	6	7	225	209	7,000	12,000	420	388	2,324	4,396	21,902	14,723	Puerto Rico
9	10	48	132	61	81	1,000	2,000	4	3	1,561	1,500	281	3,400	Qatar
20	19	2	2			3,000	4,000	5	6	526	612	2,413	2,200	Réunion
6,351	5,381	15,766	14,062	10,926	12,003	92,000	121,000	3,987	3,150	1,914	1,544	323,833	370,000	Romania
58,100[6]	57,000	65,000[6,7]	58,200[7]	36,000[6]	38,300	563,700[6]	659,800	48,731[3]	55,715[4]	...	2,781[4]	2,021,300[3]	2,228,600[4]	Russia
625	630	303	394	124	139	1,000	1,000	61	88	510	596	860	2,600	Rwanda
5	5	14	15	2	2	74[1]	85[2]	...	...	...	...	297	350	St. Kitts and Nevis
10	12	13	16	10	12	128[1]	250[2]	1	1	1,390	1,435	497	534	St. Lucia
8	8	13	15	6	9	139[1]	178[2]	1	2	1,362	1,348	530	590	St. Vincent and the Grenadines
...	...	...	...	...	...	...	...	...	...	...	...	...	...	San Marino
3	4	2	2	2	3	70[1]	100[2]	—	—	170	170	148	172	São Tomé and Príncipe
374	176	2,888	5,692	...	...	19,000	80,000	64	225	443	2,601	41,967	164,000	Saudi Arabia
2,424	2,813	1,966	4,000	176	547	8,000	14,000	87	101	357	360	6,353	12,000	Senegal
3	2	...	...	10	18	109[1]	290[2]	1	—	519	523	811	1,968	Seychelles
349	330	268	330	36	52	4,000	6,000	18	17	350	350	4,669	6,900	Sierra Leone
1	—	...	...	1,017	380	14,000	4,000	...	...	...	...	26,870	16,200	Singapore
...	533	...	20	...	588	...	12,766	...	596[4]	...	...	...	19,296[4]	Slovenia
23	13	...	...	45	53	133[1]	143[2]	1	1	600	900	284	288	Solomon Islands
4,437	4,900	10,467	13,800	9	10	3,000	3,000	477	497	414	390	2,320	2,680	Somalia
13,647	13,512	31,625	32,580	1,339	1,490	30,000	40,000	2,553	2,515	2,809	2,734	159,952	191,100	South Africa[11]
...	...	...	...	...	...	...	...	...	...	...	...	...	...	Bophuthatswana[11]
...	...	...	...	...	...	...	...	...	...	...	...	...	...	Ciskei[11]
...	...	...	...	...	...	...	...	...	...	...	...	...	...	Transkei[11]
...	...	...	...	...	...	...	...	...	...	...	...	...	...	Venda[11]
4,608	5,126	14,721	24,500	10,392	16,100	51,000	51,000	5,984	6,200	3,255	4,133	665,560	657,000	Spain
1,662	1,814	27	31	71	102	6,000	10,000	182	147	448	219	28,857	48,400	Sri Lanka
18,376	21,028	17,628	20,700	3	10	27,000	33,000	1,352	2,299	500	480	31,745	34,333	Sudan, The
46	98	3	10	19	30	5,000	7,000	7	18	1,209	1,935	2,638	3,100	Suriname
658	750	32	35	17	24	1,000	1,000	36	42	252	271	272	320	Swaziland
1,928	1,675	392	406	2,711	2,175	13,000	11,000	3,452	3,242	5,257	6,382	113,633	106,000	Sweden
2,008	1,829	350	409	2,113	1,723	6,000	6,000	3,653	3,850	4,194	4,923	43,186	36,100	Switzerland
778	786	9,311	15,321	1	1	15,000	15,000	504	775	1,353	2,279	68,759	65,000	Syria
130[1]	105[2]	...	...	3,267[1]	6,674[2]	24,760[1]	76,979	46[1]	203	3,426[1]	4,398	59,462[1]	178,500[2]	Taiwan
1,200[6]	1,400	2,900[6,7]	3,300[7]	100[6]	200	6,300[6]	8,200	527[3]	575[4]	...	2,579[4]	19,100[3]	27,800[4]	Tajikistan
12,616	13,138	3,754	3,556	160	282	18,000	20,000	374	463	160	160	35,302	40,040	Tanzania
4,228	6,052	25	178	3,344	5,000	60,000	114,000	19	178	1,950	2,297	104,667	127,600	Thailand
229	250	592	1,220	231	500	2,000	6,000	7	7	225	225	1,677	5,520	Togo
10	10	...	...	105	60	121[1]	130[2]	—	—	2,106	1,500	229	280	Tonga
77	60	10	14	59	50	7,000	9,000	6	12	1,169	1,500	7,433	8,000	Trinidad and Tobago
583	631	4,651	6,290	4	6	24,000	41,000	216	396	1,064	1,087	36,383	53,900	Tunisia
15,467	11,377	46,199	40,553	13	12	55,000	65,000	3,449	2,865	579	585	217,164	375,000	Turkey
6,000[6]	800	4,500[6,7]	5,500[7]	200[6]	300	5,300[6]	7,400	332[3]	436[4]	...	2,555[4]	13,000[3]	15,400[4]	Turkmenistan
...	...	...	...	6	12	10[1]	21[2]	...	...	...	...	11	15	Tuvalu
5,063	5,000	1,152	1,950	242	850	13,000	19,000	354	437	350	350	10,587	15,200	Uganda
25,400[6]	24,600	9,000[6,7]	8,400[7]	19,800[6]	19,400	233,600[6]	246,100	21,862[3]	24,508[4]	...	2,940[4]	750,800[3]	764,600[4]	Ukraine
26	53	132	270	...	...	2,000	7,000	4	6	446	305	2,533	8,750	United Arab Emirates
13,321	11,846	21,643	29,954	7,856	7,379	116,000	122,000	15,917	15,022	4,755	5,200	834,000	646,270	United Kingdom
112,152	98,896	12,670	11,200	64,045	54,427	1,068,000	1,520,000	58,139	67,373	5,377	6,744	4,123,566	4,005,400	United States
10,965	8,889	19,219	25,986	327	215	6,000	9,000	811	900	1,442	1,500	16,903	22,100	Uruguay
3,500[6]	4,600	9,000[6,7]	9,200[7]	500[6]	700	25,600[6]	36,000	2,448[3]	3,034[4]	...	2,578[4]	83,200[3]	115,200[4]	Uzbekistan
91	123	...	...	68	60	131[1]	180[2]	2	3	201	245	237	320	Vanuatu
10,527	13,368	333	525	2,156	1,971	41,000	55,000	1,353	1,591	1,161	1,383	128,745	107,250	Venezuela
1,646	3,282	...	...	9,396	12,583	55,000	82,000	26	40	800	800	55,250	100,000	Vietnam
8	8	4	3	5	3	57[1]	49[2]	3	2	3,477	2,746	196	130	Virgin Islands (U.S.)
...	...	...	...	...	...	...	...	...	...	...	...	...	...	West Bank
...	...	17[1]	25[2]	...	...	...	1,000[2]	...	...	...	...	...	...	Western Sahara
26	31	...	...	56	57	...	1,000	1	1	1,000	1,000	152	196	Western Samoa
973	1,180	3,002	3,800	...	...	6,000	24,000	79	98	234	250	7,220	17,500	Yemen
...	2,097	...	3,044	...	4,354	...	30,213	...	2,015	...	...	...	92,018	Yugoslavia
1,159	1,600	726	910	685	830	15,000	21,000	6	7	827	896	7,247	8,100	Zaire
2,238	3,045	29	65	217	230	18,000	16,000	60	82	300	300	27,893	34,800	Zambia
5,378	5,950	481	550	155	340	9,000	10,000	152	250	1,435	2,000	11,100	13,050	Zimbabwe

[1]1975–77. [2]1986. [3]1981–85. [4]1990. [5]Potatoes only. [6]1981. [7]Includes goats. [8]Belgium includes Luxembourg. [9]Tree fruits and grapes only. [10]1987. [11]South Africa includes Bophuthatswana, Ciskei, Transkei, and Venda. [12]Former Yemen Arab Republic only.

Extractive industries

Extractive industries are generally defined as those exploiting *in situ* natural resources and include such activities as mining, forestry, fisheries, and agriculture; the definition is often confined, however, to nonrenewable resources only. For the purposes of this table, agriculture is excluded; it is covered in the two tables immediately preceding.

Extractive industries are divided here into three parts: mining, forestry, and fisheries. These major headings are each divided into two main subheadings, one that treats production and one that treats foreign trade. The production sections are presented in terms of volume except for mining, and the trade sections are presented in terms of U.S. dollars. Volume of production data usually imply output of primary (unprocessed) raw materials only, but, because of the way national statistical information is reported, the data may occasionally include some processed and manufactured materials as well, since these are often indistinguishably associated with the extractive process (sulfur from petroleum extraction, cured or treated lumber, or "processed" fish). This is also the case in the trade sections, where individual national trade nomenclatures may not distinguish some processed and manufactured goods from unprocessed raw materials.

Mining. In the absence of a single international source publication or standard of practice for reporting volume or value of mineral production, single-country sources predominantly have been used to compile mining production figures, supplemented by U.S. Bureau of Mines data, by the United Nations' *Industrial Statistics Yearbook* (2 vol.), and by industry sources, especially *Mining Journal*'s *Mining Annual Review*. Each country

has its own methods of classifying mining data, which do not always accord with the principal mineral production categories adopted in this table—namely, "metals," "nonmetals," and "energy." The available data have therefore been adjusted to accord better with the definition of each group. Included in the "metal" category are all ferrous and nonferrous metallic ores, concentrates, and scrap; the "nonmetal" group includes all nonmetallic minerals (stone, clay, precious gems, etc.) except the mineral fuels; the last group, "energy," is composed predominantly of the natural hydrocarbon fuels, though it may also include manufactured gas.

The contribution (value) of each national mineral sector to its country's gross domestic product is given, as is the distribution by group of that contribution (to gross domestic product and to foreign trade), although statistics regarding the value of mineral production are less readily available in country sources than those regarding trade or volume of minerals produced. Figures for value added by mineral output, though not always available, were sought first, as they provide the most consistent standard to compare the importance of minerals both within a particular national economy and among national mineral sectors worldwide. Where value added to the gross domestic product was not available, gross value of production or sales was substituted and the exception footnoted. Figures for value of production are reported here in millions of U.S. dollars to permit comparisons to be made from country to country. Comparisons can also be made as to the relative importance of each mineral group within a given country.

Extractive industries

country	mining % of GDP, 1990	mineral production (value added) year	total ('000,000 U.S.$)	metals[a]	non-metals[b]	energy[c]	trade (value) year	exports total ('000,000 U.S.$)	metals[a]	non-metals[b]	energy[c]	imports total ('000,000 U.S.$)	metals[a]	non-metals[b]	energy[c]
Afghanistan	...	1988[1]	16.2	—	17.7	82.3	1986	148.9[2]	—	—	100.0[2]	0.3	—	100.0	—
Albania	...	...	...				...	...				...			
Algeria	18.1[3]	1987	9,569.7	——2.4——		97.6	1988	6,081.8	0.4	0.4	99.2	130.3	9.2	26.4	64.4
American Samoa	...	1987	...	—	100.0	—	1989	0.1	100.0	—	—	0.1	—	—	100.0
Andorra	...						1990	0.3	—	100.0	—	26.9	—	95.1	4.9
Angola	33.9[4]	1989	2,609.0	—	4.9	95.1	1989	2,249.1	—	10.9	89.1	—			100.0
Antigua and Barbuda	2.3[5]	1988	6.2	—	100.0	—	1984	—				1.1	—	—	100.0
Argentina	2.6	1989	3,813.2	2.7	4.9	92.4	1988	52.9	36.9	20.1	43.0	500.4	32.8	7.4	59.8
Armenia	...														
Aruba	...	1990	...	—	100.0	—									
Australia	5.0[6]	1990–91	14,669.6	37.5[7]	7.1[7]	55.4[7]	1989	6,939.4	36.7	5.1	58.2	1,335.4	6.9	23.0	70.1
Austria	0.3	1988	626.0	8.5	22.2	69.3	1989	294.4	41.5	58.1	0.4	2,151.2	24.8	10.8	64.4
Azerbaijan	...						1990	620.8	14.9	5.9	79.2	...			
Bahamas, The	...	1988[1]	11.3	—	100.0	—	1988	1,397.0	—	1.3	98.7	1,075.6	—	—	100.0
Bahrain	17.5[4]	1989	628.7	—	1.2[8]	98.8[8]	1988	56.1	5.5	33.0	61.5	1,082.8	0.3	1.7	98.0
Bangladesh	—	1989–90	2.6	—	0.3[9]	99.7[9]	1987	—	—	—	—	211.7	0.2	11.5	88.3
Barbados	0.6	1990	9.0	——100.0——			1988	0.2	—	100.0	—	4.9	—	28.0	72.0
Belarus	...						1990	1,177.4	14.2	14.7	71.1	2,180.6	47.8	5.5	46.7
Belgium	0.3	1990	502.7	—	44.6[10]	55.4[10]	1989[11]	8,517.1	6.7	92.0	1.3	15,351.4	16.4	51.9	31.7
Belize	0.2[4]	1989	0.4	—	100.0	—	1986	—				0.9	—	—	100.0
Benin	0.9[4]	1989	13.8[12]	——100.0[12]——			1989	4.8	—	—	100.0	2.0[13]	—	100.0[13]	—
Bermuda	...						1985	0.3[14]	73.2[14]	26.8[14]	—	1.7	—	42.0	58.0[15]
Bhutan	0.8[5]	1988	2.4	——100.0——			1987	1.5	13.8	85.9	0.3[15,16]	0.9	—	9.7	90.3[15,16]
Bolivia	11.8	1990	843.4	——56.5[5]——		43.5[5]	1987	410.2	39.0	0.2	60.8	1.2[8]	—	100.0[8]	—
Bosnia and Hercegovina	...														
Botswana	50.9[7]	1988–89	1,277.0	12.5[1,13]	86.6[1,13]	0.9[1,13]	[17]					...			
Brazil	1.9	1990	6,972.0	25.3[1,14]	22.1[1,14]	52.6[1,14]	1988	2,020.6	85.3	14.2	0.5	5,606.6	6.3	3.4	90.3
Brunei	36.1[5]	1988	1,068.6[18]	...	...	...	1988	1,780.0	—	—	100.0	13.9	2.5	97.5	—
Bulgaria	0.4[5]	1988	128.8	...	...	...						2.3	—	100.0	—
Burkina Faso	0.1[3]	1987	0.3	—	100.0	—	1983	—	—	—	—				
Burundi	0.1[3]	1987	1.0	...	100.0	—	1989	0.7[10]	—	100.0[10]	—	2.6	—	100.0	—
Cambodia	...	1990	...	—	100.0	—	1982	3.8	100.0	—	—	...			
Cameroon	12.6[3]	1987	1,714.0[12]	...	100.0	—	1987	142.1	—	—	100.0	37.2	76.6	23.4	—
Canada	3.9	1988	21,053.1	32.0	8.2	59.8	1989	13,800.8	28.6	9.9	61.5	6,067.9	28.4	9.8	61.8
Cape Verde	0.3[3]	1987	0.4	—	100.0	—	1988	0.1	20.3	79.7	—	1.0[10]	—	—	100.0[10]
Cayman Islands	0.6[4]	1989	3.6	—	100.0	—	1990	—	—	—	—	27.2[15,16]	—	1.9	98.1[15,16]
Central African Republic	2.4[3]	1988	20.4[19]	——100.0[19]——			1987	44.5	—	100.0	—	1.4[20]	—	100.0[20]	—
Chad	0.5[3]	1987	5.0	—	100.0	—	1988	4.1	100.0	—	—	0.8[21]	—	100.0[21]	—
Chile	8.5	1990	3,086.7	...	...	...	1988	1,213.0	96.1	3.9	—	533.6	0.5	7.2	92.3
China	...	1989	10,951.4	11.2	13.9	74.9	1987	4,146.3	3.9	8.7	87.4	553.5	94.9	5.1	—
Colombia	7.0	1990	3,666.9	...	...	...	1988	1,121.2	0.8	8.1	91.1	61.1	39.6	60.4	—
Comoros	...	1990	...	—	100.0	—	1983	0.1	—	100.0	—	3.8	—	100.0	—
Congo	27.9[4]	1989	677.7[12]	...	...	...	1986	785.6	1.7	5.9	92.4	0.1[20]	—	42.1[20]	57.9[20]
Cook Islands	0.1[8]	1986	...	—	100.0	—	1984	—				86.5	—	19.1	80.9
Costa Rica	...						1986	—							
Côte d'Ivoire	1.2[3]	1987	115.0[12]	...	...	...	1985	37.2	6.4	0.9	92.7	313.1	0.2	3.6	96.2
Croatia	...														
Cuba	...						1987	431.4	83.6	1.8	14.6	1,257.3	—	1.8	98.2
Cyprus	0.3[4]	1989	11.2	6.2	93.8	—	1989	2.6	41.1	58.9	—	113.1	—	10.3	89.7
Czechoslovakia	2.3[14]	1989	1,868.4	9.4	6.6	84.0	1987	627.2[16]	2.5	12.1	85.4[16]	7,150.1[15,16]	8.5	3.0	88.5[15,16]
Denmark	1.1	1989	862.9	—	18.8	81.2	1989	543.2	29.8	11.6	58.6	1,155.2	3.7	9.8	86.5
Djibouti	—[3]	1987	...	—	100.0	—	1989	—				14.6[21]	0.2	9.7	90.1[21]
Dominica	0.7[4]	1989	1.1	—	100.0	—	1985	—				0.6	—	16.9	83.1
Dominican Republic	4.0	1990	227.4	91.6[1,21]	8.4[1,21]	—	1985	1.3	20.8	79.2	—	367.2	14.7	—	85.3
Ecuador	10.4	1989	1,058.6	——6.5[23]——		93.5[16]	1989	1,041.2	—	0.4	99.6	12.1	—	99.8	0.2

Since the data for value of mineral production are obtained mostly from country sources, there is some variation (from a standard calendar year) in the time periods to which the data refer. In addition, the time period for which production data are available does not always correspond with the year for which mineral trade data are available.

The Standard International Trade Classification (SITC), Revision 3, was used to determine the commodity groupings for foreign trade statistics. The actual trade data for these groups is taken largely from the United Nations' *International Trade Statistics Yearbook* (2 vol.) and national sources.

Forestry. Data for the production and trade sections of forestry are based on the Food and Agriculture Organization (FAO) of the United Nations' *Yearbook of Forest Products*. Production of roundwood (all wood obtained in removals from forests) is the principal indicator of the volume of each country's forestry sector; this total is broken down further (as percentages of the roundwood total) into its principal components: fuelwood and charcoal, and industrial roundwood. The latter group was further divided to show its principal component, sawlogs and veneer; lesser categories of industrial roundwood could not be shown for reasons of space. These included pitprops (used in mining, a principal consumer of wood) and pulpwood (used in papermaking and plastics). Value of trade in forest products is given for both imports and exports, although exports alone tend to be the significant indicator for producing countries, while imports of wood are rarely a significant fraction of the trade of most importing countries.

Fisheries. Data for nominal (live weight) catches of fish, crustaceans, mollusks, etc., in all fishing areas (marine areas and inland waters) are taken from the FAO *Yearbook of Fishery Statistics (Catches and Landings)*. Total catch figures are given in metric tons; the catches in inland waters and marine areas are given as percentages of the total catch, as are the main kinds of catch—fish, crustaceans, and mollusks. The total catch figures exclude marine mammals, such as whales and seals; and such aquatic animal products as corals, sponges, and pearls; but include frogs, turtles, and jellyfish. The subtotals by kind of catch, however, exclude the last group, which do not belong taxonomically to the fish, crustaceans, or mollusks.

Figures for trade in fishery products (including processed products and preparations like oils, meals, and animal feeding stuffs) are taken from the FAO's *Yearbook of Fishery Statistics (Fishery Commodities)*. Value figures for trade in fish products are given for both imports and exports.

The following notes further define the column headings:

a. Includes ferrous and nonferrous metallic ores, concentrates, and scraps, such as iron ore, bauxite and alumina, copper, zinc, gold (except unwrought or semimanufactured), lead, or uranium.

b. Includes natural fertilizers; stone, sand, and aggregate; and pearls, precious and semiprecious stones, worked and unworked.

c. Includes hydrocarbon solids, liquids, and gases.

1 cubic metre = 35.3147 cubic feet
1 metric ton = 1.1023 short tons

forestry, 1990						fisheries, 1990								country
production of roundwood				trade (value '000 U.S.$)		catch (nominal)						trade (value, '000 U.S.$)		
total ('000 cubic metres)	fuelwood, charcoal (%)	industrial roundwood (%)		exports	imports	total ('000 metric tons)	by source (%)		by kind of catch (%)			exports	imports	
		total	sawlogs, veneer				marine	inland	fish	crustaceans	mollusks			
6,465	76.2	23.8	13.2	...	29,018	1.5	—	100.0	100.0	—	—	...	70	Afghanistan
2,330	69.0	31.0	31.0	710	445	12.0	55.2	44.8	81.3	1.7	17.0	5,904	...	Albania
2,162	87.9	12.1	0.9	...	371,654	91.1	99.6	0.4	96.3	2.9	0.8	590	6,775	Algeria
...	...	...	...	...	...	0.1	100.0	—	100.0	—	—	305,947	3,204	American Samoa
...	...	...	...	...	...	—	—	100.0	100.0	—	—	...	...	Andorra
6,448	85.9	14.1	1.0	...	256	106.9	92.5	7.5	99.9	0.1	—	3,490	63,400	Angola
...	...	...	...	...	...	2.2	100.0	—	90.9	9.1	—	495	1,070	Antigua and Barbuda
10,819	40.0	60.0	23.7	36,579	151,293	555.6	98.1	1.9	92.3	1.9	5.8	318,679	8,150	Argentina
...	...	...	...	...	...	...	...	...	...	...	...	...	...	Armenia
...	...	...	...	...	...	0.8	100.0	—	100.0	—	—	130	4,520	Aruba
20,326	14.2	85.8	43.1	405,966	1,435,597	210.4	98.0	2.0	66.6	18.0	14.4	524,870	344,031	Australia
17,280	15.5	84.5	61.9	2,960,135	1,309,759	4.8	—	100.0	100.0	—	—	2,903	148,750	Austria
...	...	...	...	...	...	...	...	...	...	...	...	...	...	Azerbaijan
115	—	100.0	13.0	...	42,904	7.5	99.4	0.6	18.4	77.0	4.4	32,800	5,800	Bahamas, The
—	—	—	—	...	36,164	8.3	100.0	—	75.7	22.9	1.4	2,170	3,140	Bahrain
30,936	97.1	2.9	1.5	...	12,007	847.8	29.9	70.1	90.6	9.3	—	174,905	10	Bangladesh
...	...	...	...	...	15,121	3.0	100.0	—	100.0	—	—	312	6,310	Barbados
...	...	...	...	...	...	...	...	...	...	...	...	...	...	Belarus
4,682[11]	12.2[11]	87.8[11]	59.8[11]	2,130,792[11]	2,719,575[11]	41.6	98.4	1.6	94.2	3.4	2.4	228,939[11]	753,676[11]	Belgium
188	67.0	33.0	33.0	2,445	3,253	1.5	99.9	0.1	27.6	62.9	9.3	5,209	519	Belize
5,038	94.8	5.2	0.6	...	1,869	41.7	21.3	78.7	81.0	19.0	—	780	2,030	Benin
...	...	...	...	...	...	0.5	—	97.6	2.4	—	—	...	8,344	Bermuda
3,224	91.4	8.6	7.4	13,145	...	1.0	—	100.0	100.0	—	—	...	...	Bhutan
1,597	84.0	16.0	15.2	22,160	4,060	7.4	—	100.0	100.0	—	—	95	1,780	Bolivia
5,379	...	...	...	...	...	3.6	—	100.0	...	...	...	...	...	Bosnia and Hercegovina
1,389	93.8	6.2	...	...	9,415	1.9	—	100.0	100.0	—	—	480	2,490	Botswana
259,243	71.9	28.1	15.5	1,750,981	299,402	800.0	73.8	26.2	89.1	10.2	0.7	153,017	88,310	Brazil
294	26.9	73.1	70.1	30	6,775	2.3	94.4	5.6	75.8	23.6	0.6	350	7,180	Brunei
4,099	37.0	63.0	25.4	45,375	101,240	56.1	84.8	15.2	90.1	—	9.9	17,170	2,500	Bulgaria
8,745	95.5	4.5	...	...	9,409	7.0	—	100.0	100.0	—	—	...	5,800	Burkina Faso
4,212	98.8	1.2	0.1	...	2,355	17.4	—	100.0	100.0	—	—	...	46	Burundi
5,929	90.4	9.6	1.9	94	100	105.0	38.0	62.0	97.6	2.4	—	...	...	Cambodia
14,216	77.0	23.0	17.4	99,833	35,412	77.6	74.2	25.8	83.2	16.8	—	8,230	46,670	Cameroon
155,475	4.4	95.6	64.7	17,993,024	1,930,601	1,624.3	96.9	3.1	85.1	7.0	7.9	2,269,808	620,315	Canada
...	...	...	...	...	963	7.0	100.0	—	99.1	0.9	—	3,860	260	Cape Verde
...	...	...	...	...	...	0.4	100.0	—	28.2	71.8	—	12,820	2,257	Cayman Islands
3,490	87.5	12.5	4.9	29,994	468	13.0	—	100.0	100.0	—	—	...	1,520	Central African Republic
4,033	85.9	14.1	...	...	591	115.0	—	100.0	100.0	—	—	...	...	Chad
18,708	35.5	64.5	39.6	749,883	77,000	5,195.4	100.0	—	97.1	0.5	2.0	866,397	4,100	Chile
277,015[22]	67.0[22]	33.0[22]	16.6[22]	692,137[22]	3,834,615[22]	12,095.4	56.7	43.3	77.0	9.6	12.5	1,622,123	163,945	China
19,384	86.2	13.8	10.1	20,060	104,056	101.1	62.0	38.0	87.7	11.6	0.7	117,774	43,556	Colombia
...	...	...	...	...	...	8.0	100.0	—	99.4	0.6	—	—	660	Comoros
3,644	57.0	43.0	22.2	106,087	4,500	48.2	45.5	54.5	99.9	0.1	—	3,020	19,160	Congo
...	...	...	...	...	...	1.2	100.0	—	68.9	0.5	28.1	...	140	Cook Islands
4,127	71.8	28.2	22.8	21,895	40,020	21.1	97.3	2.7	54.5	44.0	0.8	56,534	11,866	Costa Rica
12,654	77.1	22.9	17.0	236,147	27,200	108.9	70.5	29.5	97.6	2.4	—	174,722	136,700	Côte d'Ivoire
4,877	...	...	...	...	...	45.3	77.0	23.0	...	...	...	...	...	Croatia
3,134	80.5	19.5	6.2	1,847	193,411	188.2	87.6	12.4	88.0	6.9	4.6	101,101	38,907	Cuba
68	29.4	70.6	52.9	430	66,911	2.7	97.3	2.7	88.2	0.1	11.7	4,497	23,539	Cyprus
17,854	10.0	90.0	49.4	427,733	106,079	22.4	—	100.0	100.0	—	—	6,930	93,138	Czechoslovakia
2,107	20.3	79.7	46.0	392,650	1,730,909	1,517.2	97.6	2.4	92.9	0.7	6.4	2,165,497	1,116,108	Denmark
...	...	...	...	...	1,587	0.4	98.2	1.8	98.2	1.8	—	...	954	Djibouti
...	...	...	...	...	1,452	0.7	100.0	—	100.0	—	—	...	1,362	Dominica
982	99.4	0.6	0.4	...	51,266	20.0	91.2	8.8	53.2	7.2	39.6	563	16,700	Dominican Republic
10,157	65.6	34.4	30.6	24,373	157,834	391.1	99.5	0.5	77.8	22.0	0.2	488,594	—	Ecuador

Extractive industries (continued)

country	% of GDP, 1990	mining — production year	total ('000,000 U.S.$)	metals[a]	non-metals[b]	energy[c]	trade year	exports total ('000,000 U.S.$)	metals[a]	non-metals[b]	energy[c]	imports total ('000,000 U.S.$)	metals[a]	non-metals[b]	energy[c]
Egypt	15.9[3]	1988	1,960.0	0.4	6.7	92.9	1988	1,256.6	0.4	—	99.6	522.0	24.3	26.1	49.6
El Salvador	0.2	1990	8.1	100.0	—	—	1986	1.7	—	100.0	—	204.1	—	4.2	95.8
Equatorial Guinea	...	...	...	...	...	...	1983	1.3	100.0	—	—	...	...	...	...
Estonia	...	...	...	...	...	...	...	...	...	...	...	91.9	...	4.2	95.8
Ethiopia	0.1[7]	1988–89	6.9	—	100.0	—	1988	...	...	...	...	...	...	...	...
Faeroe Islands	0.1[5]	1988	1.2	—	—	100.0	1989	0.5	—	100.0	—	2.4	—	100.0	—
Fiji	2.8[5]	1985	12.1	94.9	5.1	—	1987	0.2	89.5	10.5	—	3.0	—	45.5	54.5
Finland	0.3	1990	400.7	32.7	67.3	—	1989	132.1	42.0	49.9	8.1	2,345.4	19.3	10.5	70.2
France	0.5[4]	1989	4,733.5	5.6	20.8	73.6	1989	2,433.2	61.5	28.1	10.4	15,233.7	12.8	8.0	79.2
French Guiana	...	1990	...	—	100.0	—	1989	...	—	—	100.0	1.3	—	—	100.0
French Polynesia	...	...	...				1986	21.1	0.3	99.7	—	7.6	—	63.7	36.3
Gabon	47.8	1990	1,904.1	8.9[14]	0.1[14]	91.0[14]	1986	1,285.1	7.5	—	92.5	6.5[14]	—	100.0[14]	—
Gambia, The	—	1989–90	...	—	100.0	—	1986	3.3	—	100.0	—	...	...	...	...
Gaza Strip	—	...	...				[25]	[25]				...	...	...	...
Georgia	...	...	...				1990	275.2	74.7	9.9	15.4	547.0	55.8	12.4	31.8
Germany	3.4[4, 26]	1988[26]	11,838.1	0.5	19.9	79.6	1989[26]	3,847.6	45.2	31.1	23.7	19,573.9	26.3	8.8	64.9
Ghana	1.8	1990	109.8	97.7[14]	2.3[14]	—	1988	76.8	27.8	72.2	—	331.8[13]	4.8[13]	0.5[13]	94.7[13]
Gibraltar	...	...	...				1986	1.0	—	100.0	—	0.3	—	100.0	—
Greece	1.4[4]	1988	593.6	12.7	34.5	52.8	1989	314.7	47.4	37.8	14.8	972.0	7.7	7.8	84.5
Greenland	...	1990	...	100.0	—	—	1989	77.3	100.0	—	—	2.2	—	80.9	19.1
Grenada	0.4[4]	1989	0.5	—	100.0	—	1986	...	...	...	...	1.2	—	38.7	61.3
Guadeloupe	...	1990	...	—	100.0	—	1989	1.1	100.0	—	—	1.7	—	—	100.0
Guam	...	1987[1]	2.3	—	100.0	—	1988[27]	—	100.0[27]	—	—	...	...	...	...
Guatemala	0.3	1990	25.3[12]	...	...	...	1988	14.4	—	—	100.0	345.9[10]	—	1.1[10]	98.9[10]
Guernsey	...	...	...				...	...				...			
Guinea	23.9	1990	764.5[29]	—	100.0[29]	—	1988	481.8	88.7	11.3	—	0.3[10]	100.0[10]	—	—
Guinea-Bissau	—[5]	1988	0.1	—	100.0	—	1986	1.0	—	100.0	—	1.3[20]	—	89.5[20]	10.5[20]
Guyana	13.0	1990	33.2[30]	—	100.0	—	1986	75.6	98.7	1.3	—	1.1	—	100.0	—
Haiti	0.1	1990	2.5	100.0	—	—	1983	8.5[31]	100.0[31]	—	—	17.0[13]	100.0[13]	—	—
Honduras	1.1	1990	57.1	—	100.0	—	1987	5.4	100.0	—	—	88.8	—	2.0	98.0
Hong Kong	—[4]	1988	33.1	—	100.0	—	1989	1,371.5	27.2	72.1	0.7	2,530.4	6.6	78.2	15.2
Hungary	8.1[14]	1989	939.5	4.8	4.3	90.9	1989	365.0[16]	30.7	—	69.3[16]	762.2[15, 16]	8.6	9.8	81.6[15, 16]
Iceland	...	1990	...	—	100.0	—	1989	8.8	—	100.0	—	52.0	69.5	20.4	10.1
India	2.2[32]	1988–89	5,513.8	8.6	10.3	81.1	1987	2,551.8	18.5	81.2	0.3	4,749.5	7.9	39.5	52.6
Indonesia	13.1[4]	1989	12,276.4	—	6.5[3]	93.5[3]	1989	8,582.9	8.2	0.6	91.2	1,273.6	35.1	14.9	50.0
Iran	4.6[6]	1988–89	13,858.7	—	8.2[1, 33]	91.8[1, 33]	1987	9,417.7	0.1	0.1	99.8	23.9	14.9	24.8	60.3
Iraq	19.5[5]	1988	10,905.3[12]	—	100.0	—	1986	8,784.3	—	0.4	99.6	4.6	23.5	74.9	1.6
Ireland	...	1987	333.2[34]	17.7	80.8	1.5[34]	1989	508.5	89.1	3.4	7.5	609.2	17.1	8.5	74.4
Isle of Man	...	1990	...	—	100.0	—	...	...				...			
Israel	...	1985–86	248.4	...	...	...	1989	3,358.2	0.4	97.9	1.7	3,791.5	0.1	78.5	21.4
Italy	...	1987	2,473.6	5.9	19.2	74.9	1989	746.4	35.8	51.4	12.8	16,277.7	17.0	7.4	75.6
Jamaica	10.0	1990	395.3	99.1	0.9	—	1988	418.8	99.8	0.2	—	8.8	0.4	—	99.6
Japan	0.3[4]	1988	1,771.4	7.5	36.6	55.9	1989	564.2	42.6	56.4	1.0	43,094.5	21.7	11.0	67.3
Jersey	...	...	...				...	...				...			
Jordan	4.7[5]	1988	168.5	—	100.0	—	1988	395.4	0.9	99.1	—	387.5	—	10.5	89.5
Kazakhstan	...	...	...				...	...				...			
Kenya	0.2[4]	1989	18.1	0.8[13]	99.2[13]	—	1987	24.2	8.6	90.0	1.4	310.2	1.0	1.7	97.3
Kiribati	—	1990	...	...	...	...	1987	0.03	98.6	1.4	—	0.04	—	67.4	32.6
Korea, North	...	...	...				...	...				...			
Korea, South	0.5	1988	1,350.7	3.9	24.9	71.2	1989	182.2	21.8	75.8	2.4	9,677.4	25.2	4.8	70.0
Kuwait	40.9[4]	1989	9,441.8	—	—	100.0	1987	4,911.2	0.3	—	99.7	75.8	—	41.3	58.7
Kyrgyzstan	...	...	...				...	...				...			
Laos	...	1990	...	—	100.0	—	1983	0.7[31]	100.0[31]	—	—	...	...	...	...
Latvia	...	...	...				1990	111.2	58.9	38.0	3.1	607.9	47.2	6.9	45.9
Lebanon	...	...	...				1986	45.8	28.3	71.7	—	28.9	2.2	78.3	19.5
Lesotho	0.4[4]	1989	1.7	—	100.0	—	[17]	...	...	...	...	...	...	...	...
Liberia	9.9[5]	1988	115.0[36]	—	100.0[36]	—	1988	194.1	65.3	33.6	1.1	...	...	...	...
Libya	27.8[4]	1989	6,873.2	—	0.7[20]	99.3[20]	1988	6,227.5	—	—	100.0	86.7[14]	80.1[14]	19.9[14]	—
Liechtenstein	...	...	...				...	...				...			
Lithuania	...	...	...				1990	344.8	4.9	16.9	78.2	927.7	30.0	4.2	65.8
Luxembourg	0.1[4]	1989	6.4	—	100.0	—	[11]	...	...	...	...	...	...	...	...
Macau	...	1989	1.9	—	100.0	—	1989	...	...	...	...	19.3	—	74.2	25.8
Macedonia	...	...	...				...	...				...			
Madagascar	0.3[5]	1987	6.0	—	100.0	—	1986	18.0	36.0	64.0	—	2.3	—	58.9	41.1
Malawi	...	1986	0.1	—	100.0	—	1985	...	...	...	...	6.1	—	60.5	39.5
Malaysia	9.7	1990	5,922.8	...	...	...	1988	3,294.5	5.0	1.7	93.3	503.7	44.6	24.4	31.0
Maldives	1.8	1990	1.9	—	100.0	—	1985	...	...	...	...	1.5	—	100.0	—
Mali	1.1[4]	1989	22.3	—	100.0	—	1986	11.5	—	100.0	—	23.4	—	39.3	60.7
Malta	...	1988	3.1	—	100.0	—	1989	8.6	69.7	29.5	0.8	3.7	—	—	100.0
Marshall Islands	...	...	...				1982	—				...			
Martinique	...	1990	...	—	100.0	—	1989	1.2	56.4	—	44.6	87.6	—	—	100.0
Mauritania	9.4[4]	1989	95.0	—	100.0	—	1988	172.1	93.6	0.3	6.1	0.3[8]	—	100.0[8]	—
Mauritius	0.1	1990	2.4	—	100.0	—	1987	14.6	—	100.0	—	18.8	0.8	80.2	19.0
Mayotte	...	...	...				...	...				...			
Mexico	2.3	1989	5,476.7[16]	9.2	7.8	83.0[16]	1989	8,000.8	3.6	4.0	92.4	629.0	43.2	32.9	23.9
Micronesia	...	...	...				...	...				...			
Moldova	...	...	...				1990	75.1	54.4	45.6	—	664.5	40.0	12.6	47.4
Monaco	...	...	...				...	...				...			
Mongolia	...	...	...				...	...				...			
Morocco	3.2	1989	580.8	—	93.6[5]	6.4[5]	1989	621.6	15.9	84.1	—	959.3	0.2	14.3	85.5
Mozambique	0.2[3]	1987[1]	3.4	0.4	79.7	19.9	1984	1.7	71.6	—	28.4	21.0	—	100.0	—
Myanmar (Burma)	0.9[32]	1989–90	69.8[18]	...	...	...	1988	18.2	53.5	46.5	—	...	...	...	...
Namibia	29.1[4]	1989	481.0	—	100.0	—	1983	593.0	64.0	36.0	—	[17]	[17]	[17]	[17]
Nauru	...	1990	...	—	100.0	—	1987	90.9	—	100.0	—	...	...	...	...
Nepal	0.2[7]	1988–89	4.7	...	...	...	1986	0.4	—	100.0	—	2.7	14.3	85.7	—

forestry, 1990						fisheries, 1990								country
production of roundwood				trade (value '000 U.S.$)		catch (nominal)						trade (value, '000 U.S.$)		
total ('000 cubic metres)	fuelwood, charcoal (%)	industrial roundwood (%)		exports	imports	total ('000 metric tons)	by source (%)		by kind of catch (%)			exports	imports	
		total	sawlogs, veneer				marine	inland	fish	crusta-ceans	mollusks			
2,248	95.4	4.6	—	...	2,742,127	313.0	24.0	76.0	98.1	1.6	0.3	11,450	68,970	Egypt
4,566	96.8	3.2	2.0	2,725	21,800	13.2	73.4	26.6	54.0	42.6	3.4	17,291	1,587	El Salvador
607	73.6	26.4	26.4	18,700	...	4.0	90.0	10.0	81.1	11.3	3.8	245	1,720	Equatorial Guinea
														Estonia
42,549	95.9	4.1	0.1	...	3,483	5.0	40.0	60.0	100.0	—	—	...	70	Ethiopia
						282.9	100.0	—	94.3	2.7	3.0	369,778	10,328	Faeroe Islands
307	12.1	87.9	86.6	22,775	7,804	35.0	87.1	12.9	78.0	3.4	14.9	33,941	24,628	Fiji
41,647	7.2	92.8	41.5	9,391,773	602,515	97.4	90.1	9.9	100.0	—	—	15,481	132,027	Finland
44,718	23.4	76.6	51.2	3,628,456	6,066,580	896.8	94.6	5.4	66.4	2.7	30.9	931,193[24]	2,809,033[24]	France
254	26.0	74.0	70.5	2,169	1,087	5.7	98.5	1.5	34.0	66.0	—	41,743	4,407	French Guiana
...		...	...	...	14,695	3.0	99.4	0.6	96.6	3.2	0.2	—	7,100	French Polynesia
3,789	67.7	32.3	32.3	136,774	3,655	22.0	90.9	9.1	80.2	19.8	—	3,859	12,144	Gabon
928	97.7	2.3	1.5	...	235	16.8	83.9	16.1	91.6	8.3	0.1	2,870	5,320	Gambia, The
...	...	...	...	...	...	0.5	100.0	—	100.0	—	—	...	...	Gaza Strip
...	...	...	...	...	...	104.0	...	...	...	...	...	...	...	Georgia
84,707	5.2	94.8	68.0	6,329,540	12,353,599	390.6	86.1	13.9	90.0	2.1	7.9	674,403	1,614,845	Germany
17,169	93.6	6.4	4.2	76,526	5,129	391.8	85.2	14.8	98.7	0.8	0.5	22,838	30,310	Ghana
						...	100.0	—	...	...	...	...	...	Gibraltar
2,037	66.1	33.9	26.8	97,817	998,786	140.0	92.9	7.1	86.2	3.8	10.0	82,877	190,015	Greece
—						138.2	100.0	—	47.1	52.9	—	375,906	1,929	Greenland
...		...	...	...	...	1.8	100.0	—	97.5	0.8	1.4	—	665	Grenada
17	88.2	11.8	11.8	...	15,820	8.5	99.5	0.5	91.5	2.2	6.1	250	18,712	Guadeloupe
						0.6	67.7	32.3	100.0	—	—			Guam
7,822	98.5	1.5	1.3	18,326	69,410	6.9	62.3	37.7	61.9	37.9	0.2	17,980	3,185	Guatemala
						[28]	[28]	[28]	[28]	[28]	[28]	5,495		Guernsey
4,034	85.6	14.4	4.5	800	1,056	32.0	92.2	7.8	100.0	—	—	...	4,090	Guinea
567	74.4	25.6	7.1	350	310	5.4	96.3	3.7	79.3	20.6	0.1	1,502	540	Guinea-Bissau
225	7.1	92.9	83.6	2,694	2,356	36.9	97.8	2.2	89.5	10.5	—	20,710	...	Guyana
5,840	95.9	4.1	3.8	...	4,584	7.5	96.7	3.3	97.3	2.7	—	2,025	5,505	Haiti
6,165	86.5	13.5	11.9	31,061	137,921	15.4	98.9	1.1	27.7	41.6	30.7	56,450	1,380	Honduras
193	100.0	...	...	705,535	1,752,273	234.5	97.4	2.6	89.5	5.6	4.9	693,755	1,111,838	Hong Kong
6,604	44.6	55.4	30.7	135,289	340,176	33.9	—	100.0	100.0	—	—	17,938	43,733	Hungary
				...	59,293	1,507.6	100.0	—	97.1	2.1	0.8	1,240,299	17,056	Iceland
274,460	91.1	8.9	6.7	16,337	290,967	3,790.6	60.8	39.2	91.8	7.1	1.1	504,865	...	India
171,532	82.2	17.8	16.0	3,137,780	330,157	3,080.5	74.2	25.8	88.0	9.5	2.0	978,650	30,850	Indonesia
6,727	36.5	63.5	4.0	...	192,806	250.0	80.0	20.0	95.9	3.8	0.3	53,120	13,800	Iran
155	67.7	32.3	12.9	...	117,556	14.0	25.0	75.0	100.0	—	—	...	...	Iraq
1,527	3.3	96.7	58.9	131,906	485,435	230.5	99.7	0.3	87.0	3.8	9.2	269,345	100,738	Ireland
...	...	...	...	...	...	4.0	100.0	—	21.7	1.6	76.7	...	...	Isle of Man
113	11.5	88.5	31.9	25,666	404,075	26.1	38.4	61.6	98.7	0.9	0.4	6,346	82,677	Israel
8,038	46.1	53.9	30.3	1,816,926	6,711,969	525.2	89.1	10.9	54.8	6.6	38.6	238,524[35]	2,458,086[35]	Italy
215	6.0	94.0	60.5	...	54,239	10.4	68.1	31.9	98.7	1.2	—	2,470	26,820	Jamaica
29,813	1.7	98.3	61.6	1,562,832	12,844,677	10,353.6	98.0	2.0	82.6	1.7	14.7	807,456	10,568,292	Japan
9	55.6	44.4	—	9,267	60,949	3.0[28]	100.0[28]	—	14.3[28]	81.6[28]	4.1[28]	4,037	...	Jersey
						0.1	3.2	96.8	100.0	—	—	140	10,360	Jordan
...	...	...	...	...	...	...	...	...	...	...	...	...	...	Kazakhstan
35,580	95.0	5.0	1.3	4,054	23,594	142.4	5.5	94.5	99.3	0.6	0.1	17,468	655	Kenya
						30.0	100.0	—	85.8	0.7	13.5	778	256	Kiribati
4,692	87.2	12.8	12.8	...	24,750	1,750.1	93.7	6.3	100.0	—	—	52,040	—	Korea, North
6,598	68.1	31.9	16.2	478,401	2,378,890	2,750.0	98.8	1.2	64.8	3.8	29.8	1,363,296	384,738	Korea, South
...	...	...	...	20,152	102,443	4.5	100.0	—	60.9	39.1	—	15,080	26,270	Kuwait
...	...	...	...	...	...	...	...	...	...	...	...	...	...	Kyrgyzstan
4,139	92.4	7.6	5.1	10,251	200	20.0	—	100.0	100.0	—	—	...	...	Laos
...	...	...	...	...	...	...	...	...	...	...	...	...	...	Latvia
467	96.8	3.2	3.2	2,451	70,374	1.5	94.7	5.3	97.4	1.3	1.3	...	...	Lebanon
613	100.0	—	—	...	4,588	—	—	100.0	100.0	—	—	—	2,300	Lesotho
6,056	80.7	19.3	16.6	78,264	1,942	16.0	78.1	21.9	97.1	2.8	—	1,770	7,795	Liberia
643	83.4	16.6	9.8	...	75,754	7.8	100.0	—	100.0	—	—	940	10,500	Libya
...	...	...	...	...	...	—	—	100.0	100.0	...	...	37	37	Liechtenstein
...	...	...	...	...	...	...	...	...	...	...	...	...	...	Lithuania
11	11	11	11	11	11	—	—	100.0	100.0	—	—	11	11	Luxembourg
...	...	...	...	1,034	11,156	2.6	100.0	—	51.1	46.3	2.6	6,309	18,580	Macau
1,064	...	...	...	...	...	1.6	—	100.0	...	...	...	...	...	Macedonia
8,096	90.0	10.0	5.8	534	8,546	106.7	70.0	30.0	89.4	10.3	0.1	36,330	450	Madagascar
8,215	95.1	4.9	1.0	1,993	8,058	80.0	—	100.0	100.0	—	—	380	775	Malawi
51,035	17.1	82.9	80.4	3,040,884	483,372	602.5	97.6	2.4	75.7	13.4	9.5	229,514	145,831	Malaysia
				...	3,374	78.3	100.0	—	99.0	—	—	32,450	...	Maldives
5,589	93.6	6.4	0.2	...	1,915	65.0	—	100.0	100.0	—	—	760	2,220	Mali
...	...	...	...	...	37,814	0.7	100.0	—	97.6	1.4	1.0	458	12,733	Malta
						0.2	100.0	—	100.0	—	—	170	212	Marshall Islands
12	83.3	16.7	16.7	...	24,201	3.4	97.5	2.5	94.8	4.4	—	460	26,257	Martinique
12	58.3	41.7	8.3	...	3,033	91.0	93.4	6.6	56.1	0.3	43.6	149,000	480	Mauritania
27	59.3	40.7	22.2	...	33,158	14.7	99.7	0.3	97.1	0.5	2.4	10,900	17,518	Mauritius
...	...	...	...	...	...	0.8[8]	...	...	...	...	...	...	...	Mayotte
22,205	69.9	30.1	16.4	13,884	403,605	1,401.0	86.1	13.9	85.9	5.6	8.4	361,432	42,163	Mexico
...	...	...	...	...	...	3.6	99.9	0.1	99.0	0.4	0.3	220	280	Micronesia
...	...	...	...	...	...	...	...	...	...	...	...	...	...	Moldova
...	...	...	...	...	...	—	100.0	—	100.0	—	—	24	24	Monaco
2,390	56.5	43.5	43.5	...	6,800	0.1	—	100.0	100.0	—	—	—	2,370	Mongolia
2,136	64.7	35.3	7.9	60,719	226,094	565.5	99.7	0.3	85.8	1.0	14.2	522,251	2,537	Morocco
16,036	93.7	6.3	0.3	923	950	35.0	99.2	0.8	81.7	17.7	0.6	42,195	9,636	Mozambique
23,182	76.7	23.3	17.9	148,084	4,721	743.8	80.6	19.4	99.1	0.9	—	13,000	...	Myanmar (Burma)
38	[38]	[38]	[38]	[38]	[38]	289.8	100.0	—	99.8	0.2	—	17	17	Namibia
...	...	...	...	...	...	—	100.0	—	100.0	—	—	...	...	Nauru
18,217	96.9	3.1	3.1	...	7,165	14.5	—	100.0	100.0	—	—	...	...	Nepal

Extractive industries (continued)

country	mining						trade (value)								
	% of GDP, 1990	mineral production (value added)					year	exports					imports			
		year	total ('000,000 U.S.$)	by kind (%)				total ('000,000 U.S.$)	by kind (%)			total ('000,000 U.S.$)	by kind (%)		
				metals[a]	non-metals[b]	energy[c]			metals[a]	non-metals[b]	energy[c]		metals[a]	non-metals[b]	energy[c]
Netherlands, The	2.9[4]	1989	6,516.7	—	2.1[3]	97.9[3]	1989	4,275.3	28.7	11.4	59.9	10,044.9	12.8	8.1	79.1
Netherlands Antilles	...	1985	10.3	—	100.0	—	1987	114.9[8]	2.3[8]	13.8[8]	83.9[8]	100.4	—	—	100.0
New Caledonia	23.1[5]	1988	466.8	100.0	—	—	1991	400.0[39]	100.0[39]	—	—	12.8[8, 15]	—	13.3[8]	86.7[8, 15]
New Zealand	1.0[7]	1988–89	422.9	—14.3—		85.7	1989	138.4	23.8	9.0	67.2	608.1	20.9	15.4	63.7
Nicaragua	0.6	1990	13.4	—100.0—		—	1986	3.8	100.0	—	—	92.8	—	6.9	93.1
Niger	6.7[3]	1987	164.3	—100.0—		—	1985	164.9	100.0	—	—	—	—	—	—
Nigeria	13.8[4]	1989	15,410.7	—	4.1	95.9	1986	5,451.9	0.2	0.2	99.6	70.3	21.9	78.1	—
Northern Mariana Islands	—		—				...		...	...			...	...	
Norway	11.0[4]	1989	10,388.9	0.8	1.4	97.8	1989	11,098.2	2.1	1.4	96.5	1,535.9	74.4	10.8	14.8
Oman	45.8[4]	1989	3,845.5	—	1.1	98.9	1989	3,500.7	—0.1—		99.9	10.9	—	100.0	—
Pakistan	0.6[6]	1990–91	279.9	—22.0[1, 40]—		78.0[1, 40]	1988	16.2	78.3	21.7	—	615.7	20.8	6.9	72.3
Palau	—	1985	—				1984	—	100.0	—	—	4.6[16]	—	—	100.0[16]
Panama	0.1	1990	4.5	—100.0—		—	1989	120.9	4.0	94.6	1.4	121.8	4.7	0.1	95.2
Papua New Guinea	11.7[4]	1989	412.1	100.0	—	—	1987	596.9	100.0	—	—	3.9	—	100.0	—
Paraguay	0.5	1990	34.7	—	100.0	—	1988	...	...	...	...	70.3	—	3.9	96.1
Peru	2.2	1989	951.9	—64.4[42]—		35.6	1987	603.7	95.9	0.3	3.8	50.6	27.2	31.7	41.1
Philippines	1.7[4]	1989	757.4	83.7	—16.3—		1988	411.5	93.0	1.8	5.2	1,210.6	9.2	5.5	85.3
Poland	5.4[14]	1989	1,558.7	10.8	23.4	65.8	1987	1,432.0	0.6	22.5	76.9	1,837.1	12.5	8.8	78.7
Portugal	...	1986	129.2	14.4	77.7	7.9	1989	409.5	65.7	34.1	0.2	1,737.4	2.9	7.9	89.2
Puerto Rico	0.1[7]	1989–90	29.9	—	100.0	—	1986[27]	50.7	2.4	95.9	1.7	52.1	0.4	28.8	70.8
Qatar	29.4[4]	1989	1,955.2[18]	...	100.0	...	1989	2,211.4[16]	0.1	0.3	99.6[16]	49.1[15, 16]	62.8	16.0	21.2[15, 16]
Réunion	...	1990	—	...	...	...	1989	—	—	—	—	6.9	—	—	100.0
Romania	...	1989	1,268.6	23.5	14.0	62.5	...	...	...	...	...	...	...	...	...
Russia[44]	...	1989[1]	90,630.0	21.6	12.4	65.8	1984	52,690.0[45]	10.3	1.4	88.3[45]	10,070.0[45]	59.3	2.7	38.0[45]
Rwanda	0.3[3]	1988	4.6	100.0	—	—	1986	3.2	100.0	—	—	8.5	—	100.0	—
St. Kitts and Nevis	0.4[4]	1989	0.4	—	100.0	—	1988	—	—	—	—	0.1	—	—	100.0
St. Lucia	0.6[3]	1987	1.0	—	100.0	—	1986	—	—	—	—	1.5	—	—	100.0
St. Vincent	0.3[4]	1989	0.4	—	100.0	—	1983	—	—	—	—	—	—	—	—
San Marino	...			...	...	...	...	...	...	...	...	...	...	...	...
São Tomé and Príncipe	0.2[8]	1986	0.1	—	100.0	—	1983	—	—	—	—	—	—	—	—
Saudi Arabia	27.6[4]	1989	22,389.1	—2.1—		97.9	1989	20,083.7	0.4	0.6	99.0	190.6	65.6	34.4	—
Senegal	1.4[3]	1987	52.0	—	100.0	—	1987	51.5	1.5	98.0	0.5	99.1	—	19.4	80.6
Seychelles	...	1989	—	—	100.0	—	1985	0.3[21]	0.4[21]	99.6[21]	—	0.2	1.0	—	99.0
Sierra Leone	9.9[5]	1988	86.0	—100.0—		—	1986	112.6	57.0	43.0	—	0.1	—	100.0	—
Singapore	0.1	1990	44.9	—	100.0	—	1989	307.0	66.0	33.9	0.1	4,972.1	3.0	3.2	93.8
Slovenia	...			...	...	...	...	...	...	...	...	...	...	...	...
Solomon Islands	−0.3	1990	−1.1	—100.0—		—	1987	1.0[47]	100.0[47]	—	—	0.2	—	74.9	25.1
Somalia	0.2[48]	1991	9.0	—	100.0	—	1988	—	—	—	—	—	—	—	—
South Africa	10.7	1989	9,012.6	—86.6—		13.4	1989[17]	4,143.7[49]	33.5	22.6	43.9[49]	193.7[49]	26.0	74.0	—[49]
Bophuthatswana	...			...	...	...	...	...	...	...	...	...	...	...	...
Ciskei	...			...	...	...	...	...	...	...	...	...	...	...	...
Transkei	0.1[8]	1986	0.4	...	...	...	...	...	...	...	...	...	...	...	...
Venda	3.9[3]	1987	8.5	—	—	100.0	...	...	...	...	...	...	...	...	...
Spain	1.4[21]	1988	2,743.6	8.9	26.6	64.5	1989	617.9	45.9	52.6	1.5	9,010.2	17.3	5.0	77.7
Sri Lanka	2.4	1990	117.2[50]	—100.0[50]—		—	1987	92.1	10.2	89.8	—	292.2	6.0	12.4	81.6
Sudan, The	0.1[3]	1987	6.0	—100.0—		—	1988	—	—	—	—	4.4[8]	...	...	100.0[8]
Suriname	3.7	1990	54.9	99.8[1, 21]	0.2[1, 21]	—	1988	237.4	100.0	—	—	[17]	[17]	[17]	[17]
Swaziland	1.2[5]	1988	7.1	—	100.0	—	1986	17.2	—	70.0	30.0	3,303.4	20.7	8.3	71.0
Sweden	0.4[4]	1989	680.8	76.8	23.2	—	1989	879.5	83.5	13.8	2.7	3,919.3	2.4	80.4	17.2
Switzerland	1.1[10]	1990		—	100.0	—	1989	2,875.1	6.3	93.5	0.2				
Syria	10.9[4]	1989	2,226.5[12]	—	—100.0[12]—		1989	814.2	...	...	100.0	122.2	0.7	11.7	87.6
Taiwan	0.4	1990	671.2	—	78.5	21.5	1990	424.3	...	...	...	6,548.6	—36.0—		64.0
Tajikistan	...			...	...	...	...	...	...	...	...	...	...	...	...
Tanzania	0.3[4]	1989	7.9	...	...	...	1987	4.1	—	100.0	—	85.4	—	20.2	79.8
Thailand	3.5[4]	1989	2,413.6	3.3	67.6	29.1	1987	589.7	5.1	86.1	8.8	1,530.5	12.1	20.6	67.3
Togo	6.4[5]	1988	86.6	—	100.0	—	1988	121.4	—	100.0	—	1.7	—	100.0	—
Tonga	0.6[10]	1985	0.3	—	100.0	—	1987	—	—	—	—	0.2	—	40.1	59.9
Trinidad and Tobago	30.5	1990	1,552.5	—	1.2[5]	98.8[5]	1989	514.4	—	1.8	98.2	87.9	46.7	12.0	41.3
Tunisia	8.0[4]	1989	798.3	—9.1[8]—		90.9[8]	1989	627.7	4.0	10.2	85.8	370.6	3.6	49.5	46.9
Turkey	1.3	1989	1,607.7	10.4	22.8	66.8	1989	955.0	17.4	29.2	53.4	3,865.4	20.0	2.4	77.6
Turkmenistan	...			...	...	...	...	...	...	...	...	...	...	...	...
Tuvalu	—	1990	—	...	...	...	1986	—	—	—	—	—	—	—	100.0
Uganda	—[4]	1989	0.2	...	...	...	1988	0.5	100.0	—	—	—	—	—	—
Ukraine	...			...	...	...	1990	7,590.9	80.2	4.5	15.3	10,662.0	35.9	2.7	61.4
United Arab Emirates	39.0[4]	1989	10,643.7[18]	—	—100.0[18]—		1986	9,043.3	0.3	0.1	99.6	33.3	19.7	79.5	0.8
United Kingdom	3.3[3]	1988[1]	25,509.6	—	5.2	94.8	1989	11,525.0	10.1	35.5	54.4	13,019.3	19.8	28.7	51.5
United States	1.7[5]	1988	80,400.0	2.6[3]	6.5[3]	90.9[3]	1989	13,136.7	41.6	21.7	36.7	51,176.9	8.2	12.7	79.1
Uruguay	0.2	1990	16.5	—	100.0	—	1988	3.2	—	100.0	—	132.3	6.0	9.2	84.8
Uzbekistan	...			...	...	...	...	...	...	...	...	...	...	...	...
Vanuatu	...	1990	—	—	100.0	—	1986	—	—	—	—	0.3	—	—	100.0
Venezuela	13.0	1989	7,818.0	2.9	1.1	96.0	1988	3,881.1	1.8	—	98.2	296.1	64.0	33.7	2.3
Vietnam	...			...	...	...	...	...	...	...	...	...	...	...	...
Virgin Islands (U.S.)	...	1987[1]	2.7	—	100.0	—	1986[27]	0.3	18.3	81.7	—	966.5	...	0.2	99.8
West Bank	...			...	...	...	1986[29]	11.8[25, 51]							
Western Sahara	—			...	...	52	...	...	...	...	...	...	...	...	...
Western Samoa	...	1990	—	...	...	...	1983	—[53]	100.0[53]	—	—	0.2	—	81.6	18.4
Yemen	5.0[4]	1989	376.6	—	—100.0—		1985[54]	0.4	—	100.0	—	86.5[16]	—	—	100.0[16]
Yugoslavia	2.3[4, 55]	1988[55]	1,784.2	25.7	16.4	57.9	1988[55]	110.2[15]	58.5	8.6	32.9[15]	3,151.2[15]	9.0	9.0	82.0[15]
Zaire	21.1[5]	1988	702.7	65.2[21, 56]	27.8[21, 57]	7.0[21, 58]	1988	280.8	3.4	51.1	45.5				
Zambia	12.5[4]	1989	421.9	96.1[3]	3.9[3]	—	1988	20.7	—	100.0	—	29.0	81.8	18.2	—
Zimbabwe	8.2	1990	437.5	68.8[1, 8]	18.5[1, 8]	12.7[1, 8]	1986	75.8	14.0	83.4	2.6				

[1]Gross value of production (output). [2]1987–88 average. [3]1987. [4]1989. [5]1988. [6]1990–91. [7]1988–89. [8]1986. [9]1987–88. [10]1985. [11]Belgium includes Luxembourg. [12]Mostly crude petroleum. [13]1982. [14]1983. [15]Includes coke and briquettes. [16]Includes petroleum products. [17]South Africa includes Botswana, Lesotho, Namibia, and Swaziland. [18]Mostly crude petroleum and natural gas. [19]Mostly diamonds, some gold. [20]1980. [21]1984. [22]China includes Taiwan. [23]Includes coal mining. [24]France includes Monaco. [25]West Bank includes Gaza Strip. [26]Former West Germany only. [27]Trade with the United States only. [28]Jersey includes Guernsey. [29]Mostly bauxite and diamonds. [30]Mostly bauxite. [31]1982–83 average. [32]1989–90. [33]1982–83. [34]Excludes crude petroleum and natural gas. [35]Italy includes San Marino. [36]Mostly iron ore. [37]Switzerland includes Liechtenstein. [38]South Africa includes Namibia. [39]Mostly nickel. [40]1985–86. [41]Excludes

forestry, 1990 — production of roundwood total ('000 cubic metres)	fuelwood, charcoal (%)	industrial roundwood total (%)	industrial roundwood sawlogs, veneer	trade exports ('000 U.S.$)	trade imports ('000 U.S.$)	fisheries, 1990 — catch total ('000 metric tons)	by source (%) marine	inland	by kind of catch (%) fish	crustaceans	mollusks	trade exports ('000 U.S.$)	trade imports ('000 U.S.$)	country
1,411	10.7	89.3	33.7	2,540,762	4,741,958	438.3	98.8	1.2	72.8	1.7	23.1	1,332,900	843,510	Netherlands, The
...	...	...	...	...	12,136	1.2	100.0	—	100.0	—	—	170	9,380	Netherlands Antilles
12	—	100.0	91.7	...	9,807	4.8	100.0	—	59.1	11.0	2.7	4,520	3,620	New Caledonia
11,998	0.4	99.6	57.1	858,077	153,517	565.4	100.0	—	87.0	0.6	12.3	439,191	36,166	New Zealand
4,077	78.4	21.6	20.4	2,569	10,566	2.8	94.6	5.4	34.8	65.2	—	8,627	—	Nicaragua
4,956	93.8	6.2	—		5,360	3.4	—	100.0	100.0	—	—	—	1,000	Niger
107,732	92.7	7.3	5.2	1,680	33,083	316.3	68.8	31.2	97.9	2.1	—	14,585	155,850	Nigeria
...	...	...	...	...	...	0.3	100.0	—	99.4	0.6	—	25	...	Northern Mariana Islands
11,794	7.8	92.2	44.9	1,590,671	663,956	1,747.1	100.0	—	95.9	3.7	0.4	2,059,754	237,376	Norway
...	...	...	...	...	46,878	120.2	100.0	—	97.4	1.5	1.1	50,700	2,050	Oman
26,587	90.1	9.9	8.4	...	154,210	479.0	76.4	23.6	93.2	6.0	0.8	93,509	263	Pakistan
...	...	...	...	...	...	1.4	100.0	—	99.3	0.7	—	550	...	Palau
1,872	91.2	8.8	5.6	3,988	76,979	161.7	99.8	0.2	91.6	5.8	2.6	88,935[41]	9,597[41]	Panama
8,188	67.6	32.4	30.3	115,500	5,504	25.0	41.7	58.3	95.2	4.8	—	10,600	45,595	Papua New Guinea
8,430	63.2	36.8	31.9	24,971	13,055	12.5	—	100.0	100.0	—	—	20	360	Paraguay
8,096	87.2	12.8	11.6	2,558	104,914	6,875.1	99.5	0.5	99.0	0.2	0.8	505,822	1,405	Peru
38,559	87.0	13.0	5.6	123,119	173,662	2,208.8	73.5	26.5	84.6	5.1	10.1	395,960	84,808	Philippines
19,622	14.1	85.9	44.3	227,826	85,829	473.0	90.5	9.5	93.0	0.3	6.7	192,156	45,295	Poland
10,443	5.7	94.3	39.7	1,245,940	533,376	321.9	99.2	0.8	91.9	0.6	7.5	279,923	606,040	Portugal
...	...	...	...	...	...	2.1	94.5	5.5	81.9	12.2	5.9	...[43]	...[43]	Puerto Rico
32	96.9	3.1	...	...	18,015	5.7	100.0	—	96.5	2.9	0.6	—	3,950	Qatar
...	...	...	...	...	46,105	2.0	99.9	0.1	82.9	15.6	—	6,254	30,241	Réunion
17,321	22.2	77.9	40.0	313,550	105,210	127.7	62.3	37.7	100.0	—	—	160	18,930	Romania
364,600	22.1	77.9	40.0	3,074,548	1,018,867	10,389.0	90.6	9.4	94.1	3.5	2.3	933,448	152,985	Russia[44]
5,842	95.9	4.1	0.5	...	3,184	2.5	—	100.0	100.0	—	—	...	200	Rwanda
...	...	...	...	...	...	1.7	100.0	—	88.2	11.8	—	230[46]	850[46]	St. Kitts and Nevis
...	...	...	...	...	...	1.0	99.7	0.3	99.7	0.3	—	15	2,840	St. Lucia
...	...	...	...	...	2,984	8.4	100.0	—	46.5	1.0	52.5	19,270	595	St. Vincent
...	...	...	...	...	...	—	—	100.0	100.0	—	—	...[35]	...[35]	San Marino
9	—	100.0	100.0	...	...	3.6	100.0	—	99.1	0.1	0.8	...	1,200	São Tomé and Príncipe
...	...	...	...	...	336,701	46.4	96.9	3.1	88.7	11.0	0.3	6,390	61,790	Saudi Arabia
4,480	86.2	13.8	0.4	...	21,920	299.7	94.3	5.7	92.5	1.9	5.6	335,245	37,380	Senegal
...	...	...	...	...	...	5.4	100.0	—	98.8	0.7	0.5	11,840	5,025	Seychelles
3,088	95.5	4.5	0.6	146	1,028	50.0	70.0	30.0	96.0	2.1	1.9	16,250	1,150	Sierra Leone
...	...	...	...	663,302	747,548	13.3	99.5	0.5	75.8	11.4	12.8	414,810	381,582	Singapore
2,435	...	...	...	...	...	6.9	87.2	12.8	...	...	...	...	...	Slovenia
449	30.7	69.3	69.3	17,240	767	55.8	100.0	—	99.7	—	0.1	22,080	197	Solomon Islands
7,133	98.7	1.3	0.4	...	2,170	17.5	97.7	2.3	97.7	2.3	—	14,770	10	Somalia
19,361[38]	36.6[38]	63.4[38]	23.1[38]	495,141[38]	231,596[38]	536.4	99.6	0.4	97.3	1.1	1.6	107,470[17]	115,206[17]	South Africa
														Bophuthatswana
														Ciskei
														Transkei
														Venda
17,758	14.6	85.4	27.8	970,601	2,515,795	1,458.1	98.0	2.0	77.8	2.2	20.0	743,506	2,360,853	Spain
9,129	91.9	8.1	1.4	600	28,771	165.4	81.1	18.9	96.9	3.1	—	22,544	45,089	Sri Lanka
22,827	90.6	9.4	0.2	...	12,475	38.8	2.9	97.1	100.0	—	—	80	2,300	Sudan, The
149	12.1	87.9	70.5	840	9,671	4.0	96.5	3.5	79.2	20.8	—	2,920	140	Suriname
2,223	25.2	74.8	14.3	76,741	655	0.1	—	100.0	100.0	—	—	17	17	Swaziland
55,854	7.9	92.1	41.1	9,099,059	1,133,510	260.1	97.7	2.3	98.4	1.1	0.5	173,434	445,434	Sweden
6,778	12.9	87.1	72.8	1,294,468	2,465,790	4.2	—	100.0	100.0	—	—	11,009[37]	390,226[37]	Switzerland
51	25.5	74.5	37.3	113	115,100	5.8	27.5	72.5	99.4	0.6	—	50	840	Syria
191	17.7	82.3	...	...	...	1,455.5	78.6	21.4	...	...	...	589,980[5]	118,195[5]	Taiwan
														Tajikistan
34,276	94.1	5.9	0.9	1,539	15,700	377.0	12.5	87.5	99.4	0.4	0.1	6,575	305	Tanzania
37,686	91.8	8.2	1.3	101,551	1,002,371	2,650.0	92.5	7.5	77.4	8.8	13.1	2,264,936	794,423	Thailand
910	78.9	21.1	2.0	...	2,525	15.8	97.3	2.7	99.3	0.7	—	560	14,550	Togo
5	—	100.0	100.0	...	2,027	2.6	100.0	—	100.0	—	—	1,016	350	Tonga
72	30.6	69.4	66.7	458	54,396	3.3	100.0	—	87.3	12.7	—	2,423	4,278	Trinidad and Tobago
3,249	94.9	5.1	0.5	5,415	158,410	92.1	100.0	—	83.4	1.8	14.8	107,820	2,671	Tunisia
15,524	63.1	36.9	21.9	41,699	244,022	382.2	89.1	10.9	87.5	2.0	10.5	69,527	27,838	Turkey
														Turkmenistan
...	...	...	...	...	...	1.5	100.0	—	100.0	—	—	...	...	Tuvalu
15,142	87.1	12.9	0.5	...	1,166	245.2	—	100.0	100.0	—	—	...	...	Uganda
...	...	...	...	...	...	1,100.0	...	...	...	...	...	...	...	Ukraine
...	...	...	...	...	...	95.1	100.0	—	99.9	0.1	—	16,893	18,232	United Arab Emirates
6,455	4.0	96.0	58.1	1,813,516	10,217,343	803.5	98.0	2.0	87.3	5.0	6.1	961,982	1,511,161	United Kingdom
501,000	17.1	82.9	51.0	12,607,198	14,966,360	5,856.0	95.6	4.4	78.5	7.7	13.3	3,019,857[43]	5,573,221[43]	United States
3,295	92.2	7.8	2.9	7,066	11,358	90.8	99.8	0.2	98.8	—	1.2	71,226	3,417	Uruguay
...	...	...	...	...	...	...	...	...	...	...	...	...	...	Uzbekistan
63	38.1	61.9	61.9	1,900	202	3.4	100.0	—	65.6	9.0	23.9	310	730	Vanuatu
1,501	50.6	49.4	47.7	...	200,838	332.3	94.3	5.7	84.9	3.7	11.4	85,800	1,295	Venezuela
29,209	82.7	17.3	11.1	...	8,707	850.0	71.8	28.2	88.1	8.1	3.8	229,184	...	Vietnam
...	...	...	...	...	...	0.8	100.0	—	90.6	7.2	2.2	...	...	Virgin Islands (U.S.)
...	...	...	...	...	...	...	100.0	—	...	...	...	...	...	West Bank
														Western Sahara
131	53.4	46.6	44.3	1,478	16,665	3.6	100.0	—	97.5	1.1	1.4	105	950	Western Samoa
324	100.0	—	—	29	10,499	89.1	100.0	—	90.6	3.8	5.5	10,790	2,320	Yemen
4,351	...	...	...	...	...	8.1	5.7	94.3	...	...	...	36,761[55]	114,165[55]	Yugoslavia
38,904	92.7	7.3	1.0	17,032	3,666	162.0	1.2	98.8	100.0	...	...	...	61,480	Zaire
12,221	94.6	5.4	1.4	...	5,465	64.5	—	100.0	100.0	—	—	570	94	Zambia
7,893	79.4	20.6	6.5	4,169	5,765	25.0	—	100.0	100.0	—	—	...	2,510	Zimbabwe

the Free Zone of Colón and the Canal Zone. [42]Includes coal mining. [43]United States includes Puerto Rico. [44]Data refer to the former U.S.S.R. [45]Includes refined petroleum and electricity. [46]Includes Anguilla. [47]Gold only. [48]1991. [49]Excludes crude petroleum. [50]Mostly precious and semiprecious stones. [51]Exports of stone and marble to Jordan only. [52]Accounts for 5% to 6% of 1988 phosphate production of Morocco. [53]1983–84 average. [54]Former Yemen Arab Republic only. [55]Data refer to Yugoslavia as constituted prior to 1991. [56]Includes coal and nonmetals other than diamonds. [57]Diamonds only. [58]Crude petroleum only.

Manufacturing industries

This table provides a summary of manufacturing activity by industrial sector for the countries of the world, providing figures for total manufacturing value added, as well as the percentage contribution of 29 major branches of manufacturing activity to the gross domestic product. U.S. dollar figures for total value added by manufacturing are given but should be used with caution because of uncertainties with respect to national accounting methods, purchasing power parities, price structures and preferments, exchange rates, and so on, especially for countries having inconvertible currencies.

Manufacturing activity is classified here according to a modification of the International Standard Industrial Classification (ISIC), revision 2, published by the United Nations. A summary of the 2-, 3-, and 4-digit ISIC codes (groups) defining these 29 sectors follows, providing definitional detail beyond that possible in the column headings.

The collection and publication of national manufacturing data is usually carried out by one of three methods: a full census of manufacturing (usually done every 5 to 10 years for a given country), a periodic survey of manufacturing (usually taken at annual or other regular intervals between censuses), and the onetime sample survey (often limited in geographical, sectoral or size of enterprise coverage). The full census is, naturally, the most complete, but, since up to 10 years may elapse between such censuses,

it is sometimes necessary to substitute a survey of more recent date but less complete coverage. In certain instances, in order to provide the most timely data, the estimate series maintained by the United National Industrial Development Organization (UNIDO) in Vienna for its *Industry and Development Global Report* and other studies has been used. Data for the republics of the former U.S.S.R. were adapted from interim assessments published (1992) by the International Monetary Fund (IMF).

ISIC code (-s)	Products manufactured
31	Food, beverages, and tobacco
311+312	food including prepared animal feeds
313	alcoholic and nonalcoholic beverages
314	tobacco manufactures
32	Textiles, wearing apparel, and leather goods
321	spinning of textile fibres, weaving and finishing of textiles, knitted articles, carpets, rope, etc.
322	wearing apparel (including leather clothing; excluding knitted articles and footwear)
323+324	leather products (including footwear; excluding wearing apparel), leather substitutes, and fur products

Manufacturing industries

country	year	total manufacturing value added (U.S.$'000-000)	food (311+312)	beverages (313)	tobacco manufactures (314)	textiles (exc. wearing apparel) (321)	wearing apparel (322)	leather and fur products (323+324)	wood products (exc. furniture) (331)	wood furniture (332)	paper, paper products (341)	printing and publishing (342)	industrial chemicals (351)	paints, soaps, etc. (352 exc. 3522)	drugs and medicines (3522)
Afghanistan	1988–89[1]	435	18.3	1.9	—	8.0	0.4	16.7	—0.5—		0.9	4.9	4.8	0.2	2.7
Albania	1989[2,3]	...	—28.3—			...	...	...	—6.0[4]—		...—[4]		—6.7—		
Algeria	1990	6,163	13.9	3.2	3.8	6.5	5.2	3.8	3.7	1.7	4.5	0.5	0.5	—3.3—	
American Samoa	1988[5]	354													
Andorra	1989[6]	22	0.6	20.6	—	—	45.9	0.2	—0.4—		2.3	0.7	...	0.2	...
Angola	1989	319	20.0	—12.2—		—11.6—			—3.7—		—0.3—		9.1[7]	[7]	[7]
Antigua and Barbuda	1989	12	...	...	...	...	...	...	...	...	...	...	...	...	...
Argentina	1988	37,218	16.3	3.9	1.6	7.7	1.8	1.7	1.0	0.9	2.8	2.3	5.6	—6.3—	
Armenia	1990[2,3]	1,772	8.8	9.6	—	—30.9—		28.7	...	...	—	—	...	...	...
Aruba	1982	20	...	...	...	...	...	...	...	...	...	...	...	...	...
Australia	1988–89	28,111	13.1	3.2	0.5	3.2	2.7	0.9	3.9	2.1	3.0	8.5	2.9	—3.9—	
Austria	1988[9]	25,111	7.4	2.7	5.1	4.3	1.9	1.0	2.2	3.3	4.2	3.8	5.0	1.8	1.7
Azerbaijan	1990[10]	546	9.5			—19.2—			—	—	—	—	1.7	—	
Bahamas, The	1987[9]	101	18.1	41.6	—	0.2	1.9	—	...	3.7[12]	0.2	12.3	[13]	0.8	11.2
Bahrain	1982[9,14]	904											56.6		
Bangladesh	1987–88[9,15]	839	12.4	0.2	15.0	28.6	0.7	4.0	0.7	0.3	2.6	0.8	8.6	4.1	7.3
Barbados	1990	122	28.1	13.2	1.7	0.8	7.4	—	—	1.7	0.8	9.9	—	—2.5—	
Belarus	1990[2,3]	...	—15.2—			—18.4—			—4.6[4]—		—[4]		9.4[7]	[7]	[7]
Belgium	1989	33,465	16.7	1.9	0.6	4.8	2.1	0.4	0.8	3.8	2.4	3.3	10.8	—2.9—	
Belize	1984[16]	22	56.7	28.8	4.9	—	6.1	—	...	...	—	—	2.0	—	...
Benin	1986	56	—62.5—			—8.8—			—3.4—		—4.0—		[17]	[17]	[17]
Bermuda	...	...	...	...	...	...	...	...	...	...	...	...	...	...	...
Bhutan	1989	19	...	...	...	...	...	...	...	...	...	...	...	...	...
Bolivia	1990	648	22.4	7.6	0.9	2.2	1.7	1.5	1.7	1.4	0.2	2.9	0.6	—3.4—	
Bosnia and Hercegovina	1989	4,252	8.3	0.9	1.1	3.5	10.5	6.5	—12.0—		3.3	1.0	7.3[18]	[18]	[18]
Botswana	1990	136	34.1	19.3	—	7.4	3.0	0.7	0.7	0.7	1.5	1.5	1.5	—3.0—	
Brazil	1988	111,289	9.9	1.0	0.6	6.7	2.8	3.0	1.2	0.9	3.3	2.2	6.4	—6.4—	
Brunei	1988	279	...	...	...	...	...	...	...	...	...	...	...	...	...
Bulgaria	1990[19]	17,161[20]	11.5	1.9	2.3	6.6	4.5	2.9	1.6	2.2	0.8	0.7	2.9	—3.8—	
Burkina Faso	1990	254	45.8	15.4	0.8	17.0	2.0	3.6	—	1.6	—	1.2	0.8	—	
Burundi	1990	102	44.4	28.3	14.1	1.0	2.0	...	...	...	—	1.0	3.0	—1.0—	
Cambodia	1988[2,3]	25[21]	—70.2—			—10.3—			...	...	...	...	...	...	...
Cameroon	1990	1,406	36.5	15.9	2.5	3.6	1.3	0.6	4.3	2.0	0.8	0.7	2.1	—5.0—	
Canada	1988[9]	107,703	10.0	2.8	0.8	2.7	2.4	0.5	4.4	1.8	9.3	5.9	4.8	3.0	1.9
Cape Verde	1986[3]	24	—45.5—		8.3	—	...	...	—20.8—		—	—	—	—	...
Cayman Islands	1989	11	...	...	...	...	...	...	...	...	...	...	...	...	...
Central African Republic	1990	26	32.0	16.0	28.0	—28.0	-4.0	...	20.0	4.0	—	8.0	4.0	—8.0—	
Chad	1986[3]	73	...	...	...	32.2[23]	—	—	...	...	—	—	...	...	...
Chile	1986[9,24]	4,496	18.3	4.5	1.7	4.5	1.8	1.5	2.4	0.5	7.3	2.3	1.7	3.9	2.3
China	1989	111,510	4.9	2.5	6.2	11.4	2.2	0.9	0.7	0.5	2.2	1.1	9.3	0.9	2.0
Colombia	1989	7,971	16.1	12.3	2.2	10.2	3.0	1.9	0.7	0.5	3.6	3.0	6.7	—7.1—	
Comoros	1987	22	...	...	—	...	...	...	...	...	...	...	...	...	...
Congo	1990	97	12.4	15.5	7.2	8.2	2.1	6.2	9.3	5.2	1.0	1.0	1.0	—2.1—	
Cook Islands	1986	1.7	...	...	...	...	...	...	...	...	...	...	...	...	...
Costa Rica	1989[9]	926	32.1	12.5	1.7	3.1	3.1	1.7	2.1	2.6	4.2	3.9	3.5	3.5	2.1
Côte d'Ivoire	1990	1,546	19.4	6.3	2.7	9.6	0.5	2.7	4.6	1.4	...	...	1.3	—6.7—	
Croatia	1989	8,364	13.0	2.3	1.1	4.5	7.7	5.7	—6.5—		2.4	1.5	11.0[18]	[18]	[18]
Cuba	1990[19]	5,687	16.4	6.1	44.5	1.9	1.6	1.2	0.8	0.7	0.2	1.5	1.1	—4.6—	
Cyprus[25]	1990	792	12.7	9.6	5.4	4.2	14.3	5.3	5.3	4.6	1.7	4.5	0.4	3.0	0.6
Czechoslovakia	1989	15,456	7.2	1.8	0.2	6.8	1.8	2.6	2.1	1.2	2.5	0.9	5.7	0.3	0.8
Denmark	1989[16,26]	18,949	18.2	3.3	1.2	2.8	1.2	0.4	2.1	2.7	2.8	6.9	4.7	2.2	4.3
Djibouti	1986	5.2	...	...	...	...	...	...	...	...	...	...	...	...	...
Dominica	1989[16,27]	9.0	...	...	...	...	...	...	...	...	...	...	...	...	...
Dominican Republic	1990	1,530	29.4	14.0	6.9	4.5	0.9	3.4	0.2	2.0	2.9	1.9	1.5	—3.7—	
Ecuador	1988[9,15]	1,016	30.9	3.8	1.2	9.9	1.0	0.9	1.9	1.1	3.0	3.0	3.0	3.7	1.5
Egypt	1988–89[16,28]	12,980	22.1	1.8	3.5	15.5	0.6	0.7	0.6	1.4	1.2	1.5	3.1	4.0	2.2
El Salvador	1990	1,068	37.8	14.8	4.0	5.7	—5.7—		1.5	2.2[12]	1.5	1.5	—5.4—		
Equatorial Guinea	1989	1.7	...	...	...	...	...	...	...	...	...	...	...	...	...
Estonia	1988[2,3]	8,795	—25.3—			—28.2—			—9.4[4]—		—[4]		...	...	...
Ethiopia	1987–88[15]	754	17.4	22.9	7.9	13.0	1.3	5.7	1.0	0.6	0.8	2.4	0.3	—2.9—	

ISIC code (-s)	Products manufactured
33	Wood and wood products
331	sawlogs, wood products (excluding furniture), cane products, and cork products
332	wood furniture
34	Paper and paper products, printing and publishing
341	wood pulp, paper, and paper products
342	printing, publishing, and bookbinding
35	Chemicals and chemical, petroleum, coal, rubber, and plastic products
351	basic industrial chemicals (including fertilizers, pesticides, and synthetic fibres)
352 minus 3522	chemical products not elsewhere specified (including paints, varnishes, and soaps and other toiletries)
3522	drugs and medicines
353 + 354	refined petroleum and derivatives of petroleum and coal
355	rubber products
356	plastic products (excluding synthetic fibres)
36	Glass, ceramic, and nonmetallic mineral products
361 + 362	pottery, china, glass, and glass products
369	bricks, tiles, cement, cement products, plaster products, etc.

ISIC code (-s)	Products manufactured
37	Basic metals
371	iron and steel
372	nonferrous basic metals and processed nickel and cobalt
38	Fabricated metal products, machinery and equipment
381	fabricated metal products (including cutlery, hand tools, fixtures, and structural metal products)
382 minus 3825	nonelectrical machinery and apparatus not elsewhere specified
3825	office, computing, and accounting machinery
383 minus 3832	electrical machinery and apparatus not elsewhere specified
3832	radio, television, and communications equipment (including electronic parts)
384 minus 3843	transport equipment not elsewhere specified
3843	motor vehicles (excluding motorcycles)
385	professional and scientific equipment; photographic and optical goods; watches and clocks
39	Other manufactured goods
390	jewelry, musical instruments, sporting goods, artists' equipment, toys, etc.

			(36)		(37)		(38)								(39)	country
refined petroleum and products	rubber products	plastic products	pottery, china, and glass	bricks, tiles, cement, etc.	iron and steel	non-ferrous metals	fabricated metal products	nonelectrical machinery	office equip., computers	electrical equip.	radio, television	transport equip. exc. motor vehicles	motor vehicles	professional equip.	jewelry, musical instruments	
(353+354)	(355)	(356)	(361+362)	(369)	(371)	(372)	(381)	(382 exc. 3825)	(3825)	(383 exc. 3832)	(3832)	(384 exc. 3843)	(3843)	(385)	(390)	
—	—	2.1	1.1	6.6	0.4	—	—	16.4					0.1	—	37.1	Afghanistan
2.6	0.5	1.2	1.2	8.9	13.7	0.8	7.9	1.4		3.7		5.4		0.9	1.4	Albania
...	...	...	...	...	...	...	...	...		...		...		...	...	Algeria
—	0.1	4.6	0.2	0.1	0.8	1.6	...	...		...		...		...	...	American Samoa
...	...	...	...	...	...	...	...	3.3		14.6		...		2.4	1.3	Andorra
20.0	7	7	11.3		1.9		5.0					4.7		8	0.3[8]	Angola
13.1	1.2	1.4	1.5	3.2	5.8	1.0	6.3	2.8		4.0		7.0		0.4	0.3	Antigua and Barbuda
...	3.2	...	—	3.5	...	...	0.8	11.4							0.3	Argentina
...	...	...	...	...	...	...	...	...		...		...		...	—	Armenia
...	...	...	...	...	...	...	...	...		...		...		...	...	Aruba
0.9	1.1	3.2	2.2	3.2	6.0	4.6	9.0	4.6		6.2		3.3	5.8	0.9	1.0	Australia
2.1	1.2	1.6	1.9	4.9	7.3	1.7	7.9	9.4		8.6	2.4	1.0	3.9	0.8	0.9	Austria
31.8[11]	—	—	—	0.1	2.1	0.4	...	35.2							—	Azerbaijan
−1.9[13]	...	0.8	0.1	0.3	6.4	...	...			0.9	0.4				3.2	Bahamas, The
35.9	...	...	...	...	...	7.5	...	...		...		...		...		Bahrain
7.1	0.2	0.2	0.7	0.7	1.3	...	1.3	0.2		1.9		0.9		—	0.1	Bangladesh
5.0	2.5	2.5	0.8	3.3	—	—	9.1	4.1		4.1		2.5		—	—	Barbados
4.7	7	7	...	3.8	...	...	37.5								—	Belarus
1.5	0.9	4.3	1.8	2.1	4.6	2.2	7.1	7.8		7.3		7.3		0.5	2.2	Belgium
—	...	...	...	...	—	—	1.1	...		0.3					—	Belize
17	17	17	10.1				5.0								0.7	Benin
...	...	...	...	...	...	...	...	...		...		...		...	...	Bermuda
36.1	0.2	0.6	0.8	4.3	0.8	7.9	0.9	0.5		0.3		0.6		0.2	0.3	Bhutan
−0.7	0.2	18	2.4		5.8	7.0	11.6	5.8		6.3		7.1		0.2	0.3	Bolivia
															0.3	Bosnia and Hercegovina
—	0.7	0.7	...	...	—	—	4.4	1.5		1.5		1.5		—	16.3	Botswana
7.0	2.1	2.7	0.9	3.5	7.3	2.3	4.2	9.2		7.9		6.5		0.9	1.1	Brazil
...	...	...	...	...	...	...	...	...		...		...		...	...	Brunei
1.2	2.5	0.9	1.1	2.6	3.1	1.1	2.9	20.9		7.9		5.2		2.6	6.4	Bulgaria
—	2.0	0.8	—	—	0.8	0.4	0.4	0.4		0.4		1.2			5.5	Burkina Faso
...	...	...	...	1.0	...	...	4.0	—		—		...		—		Burundi
...	...	...	...	...	...	...	...	...		...		...		...	...	Cambodia
0.9	1.8	4.6	1.6	1.3	6.8	4.6	0.6	0.9		0.9		0.9		...	0.6	Cameroon
2.4	1.2	2.4	0.7	2.6	3.7	4.1	5.7[22]	5.3	1.2	2.9	3.3	2.9	9.2	0.8	1.4	Canada
												10.8[22]			—	Cape Verde
...	...	...	...	...	...	...	...	...		...		...		...	...	Cayman Islands
...	...	...	...	...	...	...	...	...		...		4.0		...	8.0	Central African Republic
															...	Chad
5.8	1.0	1.5	0.9	2.8	5.3	22.6	3.2	1.4		1.2	0.2	0.3	0.7	0.1	0.1	Chile
3.4	1.7	1.9	6.8		7.7	2.5	3.3	12.4		5.3	3.4	4.1		1.0	1.8	China
1.9	1.6	2.8	2.0	4.5	4.7	0.5	3.3	1.7		3.7		4.2		0.9	1.1	Colombia
1.0	1.0	—	2.1	3.1	...	...	8.2	3.1		4.1		6.2		—	—	Comoros
—	...	...	...	...	...	...	...	...		...		...		...	—	Congo
...	...	...	...	...	...	...	...	...		...		...		...	...	Cook Islands
6.0	2.0	...	0.3	2.6	...	...	2.2	1.6		1.4	2.2	1.1	0.4	...	0.3	Costa Rica
15.4	0.1	—	0.3	1.7	0.2	0.1	6.7	0.3		1.6		16.9			1.5	Côte d'Ivoire
4.0	1.0	18	3.9		2.1	1.8	7.6	8.4		6.6		8.7			0.3	Croatia
0.9	1.4	1.4	0.5	1.8	0.6	1.1	1.2	2.8		0.9		3.7		0.2	3.8	Cuba
3.4	0.2	3.2	0.5	9.0	...	...	6.6	3.0		1.3		0.3	0.8		2.4	Cyprus[25]
3.4	1.3	0.2	2.6	3.7	12.4	1.7	4.6	18.5		6.6		9.3		0.6	1.3	Czechoslovakia
1.7	0.6	2.6	0.8	4.3	1.2	0.3	7.8	12.8		3.0	2.6	4.4		2.9	2.1	Denmark
—	—	...	...	...	—	...	—	...		...		...		...	...	Djibouti
																Dominica
12.0	0.9	2.3	0.7	3.6	2.1	0.1	4.8	0.7		1.1		0.1		0.1	0.3	Dominican Republic
4.7	1.1	4.1	2.1	7.1	2.1	0.6	5.1	0.4		4.2	0.6		1.7	0.7	0.5	Ecuador
3.2	0.4	1.8	1.5	7.4	5.3	8.0	4.0	3.7		1.4	0.8	1.4	2.2	0.7	0.1	Egypt
6.3	0.5		5.2		2.6		0.9	0.7		1.7		0.3		8	1.6[8]	El Salvador
2.7	...	...	...	3.9	...	...	...	...		...		...		...	...	Equatorial Guinea
...	...	...	...	...	...	...	...	15.8							—	Estonia
12.8	1.6	1.5	0.1	2.6	1.5	—	1.6	—		0.1		—	1.9		—	Ethiopia

Manufacturing industries (continued)

country	year	total manufacturing value added (U.S.$'000-000)	(31) food (311+312)	beverages (313)	tobacco manufactures (314)	(32) textiles (exc. wearing apparel) (321)	wearing apparel (322)	leather and fur products (323+324)	(33) wood products (exc. furniture) (331)	wood furniture (332)	(34) paper, paper products (341)	printing and publishing (342)	(35) industrial chemicals (351)	paints, soaps, etc. (352 exc. 3522)	drugs and medicines (3522)
Faeroe Islands	1988[3, 16]	186	50.2[29]	...	...	...	—3.8—		0.1	5.6	1.3	2.3	3.5	...	5.2	...
Fiji	1987	118	60.7	—7.1—	...											
Finland	1989[16, 32]	24,334	9.2	2.3	0.5	1.7	1.7	0.6	5.3	2.0	16.0	7.6	5.1	1.6	1.0
France	1989[9, 33]	204,448	10.4	1.8	0.7	3.3	2.4	1.0	1.3	1.5	2.5	5.0	4.6	2.9	1.6
French Guiana	1981[3]	12	—43.5—			—	—	—	...	...	...	...	...	...	...
French Polynesia	1989[3]	174	—26.2—		—	...	...	—	...	...	...	...	—	—2.5—	
Gabon	1990	360	11.9	4.7	4.1	0.6	0.8	—	8.8	1.1	0.6	0.8	1.9		
Gambia, The	1990	18	58.8	5.9	—	5.9	—	—	...	5.9	...	5.9	...	...	...
Gaza Strip	1987[3, 34]	84	—15.5—			12.4[35]	16.8	[35]	—13.7[4]—		—4—		6.2[7]	[7]	[7]
Georgia	1990[3, 10]	9,352	—43.6—			—23.0—			—1.1[4]—		—4—		...	...	...
Germany[37]	1988[9, 26]	426,933	4.9	2.2	2.3	2.4	1.1	0.5	16.1	0.7	2.4	1.9	7.7	3.4	2.1
Ghana	1990	607	9.2	14.6	14.9	5.6	0.2	0.3	...	...	0.7	1.1	0.3	—6.7—	
Gibraltar	...	...	...	...	...	...	...	...	...	...	...	...	...	...	...
Greece	1990	11,305	14.4	4.9	1.9	14.0	6.4	2.1	2.6	1.3	2.0	2.0	3.6	—4.6—	
Greenland	1987[38]	125	99.9	—	—	—	—	0.1	—	—	—	—	—	—	—
Grenada	1989[16, 39]	7.7	...	...	—	—	—	—	...	...	...	...	...	...	...
Guadeloupe	1982[3]	86	25.0	26.3[40]	...	...	...	—	...	...	...	...	...	...	...
Guam	1986	9.1	...	...	...	...	...	—	...	...	...	...	...	...	...
Guatemala	1988[9, 32]	842	24.1	5.3	2.5	6.5	3.2	2.7	1.2	0.6	1.4	4.8	4.9	9.1	6.8
Guernsey	1991[10]	53	—	—	—	—2.9—			—	—	—	10.8	—	—	7.3
Guinea	1990	115	...	...	...	...	...	...	...	...	...	...	...	...	...
Guinea-Bissau	1988	11	...	...	...	...	...	...	...	...	...	...	...	...	...
Guyana	1990[41]	23	...	...	...	...	...	...	...	...	...	...	[42]	[42]	[42]
Haiti	1987–88[9]	155	30.7	3.0	4.3	—13.9—			...	...	—	...	...	...	...
Honduras	1989	589	31.0	9.9	4.6	4.1	2.8	0.9	6.2	1.7	3.3	2.7	0.6	4.1	1.5
Hong Kong	1988[9]	10,795	2.8	1.6	1.9	15.3	21.1	1.1	0.4	0.6	2.0	5.7	0.6	0.7	0.3
Hungary	1989	7,109	7.4	1.8	0.5	4.6	2.6	1.6	1.0	1.6	1.7	2.0	7.3	0.3	5.3
Iceland	1990	939	35.9	2.9	...	3.3	1.9	1.4	0.1	5.5	1.3	8.3	1.6	—1.9—	
India	1986–87[16, 43]	16,379	9.3	1.0	1.8	14.1	0.7	0.6	0.5	0.1	1.9	1.9	7.4	3.7	3.4
Indonesia	1990	9,912	8.4	1.0	10.7	9.5	1.8	0.7	9.6	0.3	1.1	1.4	5.2	—4.3—	
Iran	1988	44,515	6.0	2.0	0.3	13.7	0.3	1.6	0.9	0.3	1.9	0.8	1.7	—4.8—	
Iraq	1989	5,849	9.1	2.8	3.9	6.0	1.0	1.5	—	0.3	2.7	1.5	4.3	—15.0—	
Ireland	1988[16, 44]	11,501	21.4	5.3	1.1	2.3	1.8	0.3	1.0	0.6	1.3	3.7	3.2	1.4	10.1
Isle of Man	1985–86[3, 16]	45	—16.9—			...	...	...	...	...	...	...	...	...	...
Israel	1988[9, 32]	8,966	13.6	1.5	0.2	3.6	4.0	0.8	1.2	1.5	2.7	4.4	7.4[45]	2.5	1.5
Italy	1987[26]	112,376	5.6	2.2	0.5	7.5	3.7	2.6	1.1	1.9	2.5	3.8	—10.7—		
Jamaica	1990	589	21.9	12.9	11.7	0.7	3.4	1.5	0.3	4.4	3.9	2.0	2.4	—10.5—	
Japan	1989[46]	872,035	7.6	1.2	0.2	3.2	1.3	0.4	1.6	1.0	2.6	5.3	4.5	2.5	2.9
Jersey	1990	42	...	...	...	...	...	...	—3.5—		2.9	2.2	...	—21.0—	
Jordan	1989[3]	631	9.4	3.8	11.4	2.5	1.9	1.0	...	...	...	...	...	...	...
Kazakhstan	...	...	...	...	...	...	...	...	...	...	...	...	...	...	...
Kenya	1990	942	29.5	7.6	2.4	6.2	2.9	1.6	2.2	1.4	4.0	3.1	2.3	—6.6—	
Kiribati	1988	0.60	...	...	—	...	...	—	...	...	...	...	...	...	...
Korea, North	...	...	...	...	...	...	...	...	...	...	...	...	...	...	...
Korea, South	1988[9, 32]	66,089	5.7	2.2	3.5	9.6	4.0	1.7	0.8	0.8	2.3	2.2	3.8	2.5	2.2
Kuwait	1989	2,317	6.3	1.6	—	0.5	3.8	—	0.4	1.2	0.9	2.3	2.8	—0.7—	
Kyrgyzstan	1990[3, 10]	81	—5.9—			—3.5—			...	...	...	...	...	...	...
Laos	1988	40	—24.9—			12.7	3.1	2.1	—5.6[4]—		—4—		7.2[7]	[7]	[7]
Latvia	1990[2, 3]	18,399	...	...	...	...	...	...	...	...	...	...	...	...	...
Lebanon	1987	483	...	...	...	...	...	...	...	1.2	...	2.0	...	—2.1—	
Lesotho	1990[3]	70	—47.2—		...	—39.8—		0.3	...	4.5	0.6	1.3	0.4	—7.2—	
Liberia	1985[2, 9, 26]	64	10.8	42.7		3.2	0.7	7.1	0.4	0.5	0.7	0.7	10.9	—2.0—	
Libya	1989	936	7.4	3.2	8.0	...	...	...	...	...	...	...	...	...	...
Liechtenstein	...	...	...	...	...	...	...	...	...	...	...	...	...	...	...
Lithuania	1989[3]	5,511	—21.6—			—34.7—			—9.2[4]—		—4—		6.8[7]	[7]	[7]
Luxembourg	1990	2,156	2.2	2.5	0.5	1.8	0.3	—	0.1	0.1	1.5	1.7	13.0	—4.9—	
Macau	1989	468	1.0	0.5	—	22.1	46.0	2.8	0.3	1.1	0.8	1.7	—	0.4	0.8
Macedonia	1989	2,095	7.3	3.2	6.4	14.3	15.4	6.8	—3.7—		0.9	0.7	7.6[18]	[18]	[18]
Madagascar	1990	129	16.5	16.5	1.6	33.9	1.6	3.1	...	...	3.9	0.8	—	—5.5—	
Malawi	1990	137	11.0	5.9	4.4	14.7	0.7	3.7	2.2	0.7	2.2	5.9	11.0	—22.8—	
Malaysia	1988[16]	6,209	14.0	2.0	2.3	3.6	2.9	0.1	6.2	0.7	1.5	2.7	11.3	2.4	0.4
Maldives	1990	5.8	...	...	...	...	...	...	—	...	—	0.8	0.8	—0.8—	
Mali	1990	122	13.9	1.6	10.7	41.8	10.7	—	—	—	1.0	5.5	0.6	—3.1—	
Malta	1988	453	10.4	9.6	1.6	2.5	17.2	2.5	0.4	4.5	—	5.5	...	...	...
Marshall Islands	1981[1]	0.16	39.7	—	—	—	—	—	—	8.8	—	51.5	—	—	—
Martinique	1982[3]	133	23.9	13.0[40]	...	...	...	—	...	...	...	...	...	...	...
Mauritania	1988[3]	113	68.0[29]	...	...	...	...	—	...	...	...	...	...	...	...
Mauritius	1990	511	14.5	4.7	1.4	5.3	47.4	1.6	0.8	0.8	0.6	2.3	2.9	—2.2—	
Mayotte	1990	...	...	...	...	...	...	...	...	...	...	...	...	...	...
Mexico	1986[9, 49]	19,708	5.9	8.4	2.7	3.2	0.8	1.1	0.2	0.3	2.3	0.7	8.7	2.8	1.8
Micronesia	...	...	...	...	...	...	...	...	...	...	...	...	...	...	...
Moldova	1990[3]	5,549	—8.2—			—38.7—			—3.8[4]—		—4—		3.5[7]	[7]	[7]
Monaco	...	...	...	...	...	...	...	...	...	...	...	...	...	...	...
Mongolia	1989[2, 3]	2,436[51]	—21.3—			13.6	5.5	10.9	—7.8—		...	1.0	...	...	...
Morocco	1990[19]	1,824	19.1	3.8	2.8	13.8	2.7	2.9	2.2	0.3	3.6	2.1	9.9	—6.1—	
Mozambique	1988	292	28.6	9.2	5.4	18.2	4.1	1.4	1.3	0.8	2.9	2.2	0.5	—5.1—	
Myanmar (Burma)	1984–85[3]	731	—38.8—			—9.4—			...	...	...	3.4	...	...	...
Namibia	1989	80	...	...	...	...	...	...	...	...	...	...	...	...	...
Nauru	1985	—	...	...	...	...	...	...	...	...	...	...	...	4.9	1.1
Nepal	1989–90[3, 9, 15]	206	14.3	5.9	16.2	16.5	8.4	1.5	1.0	0.5	1.5	0.8	...	4.9	1.1
Netherlands, The	1990	54,388	15.0	2.2	1.4	2.1	0.7	0.4	1.2	1.2	3.0	7.9	9.8	—3.5—	
Netherlands Antilles	1985	77	...	...	...	...	...	...	...	...	...	...	...	...	...
New Caledonia	1988[3]	474	—5.8—			...	...	...	...	...	...	...	...	...	...
New Zealand	1988–89[9]	6,712	22.8	—3.7—		3.7	—5.1—		—6.7—		6.6	7.6	3.3	—2.9—	
Nicaragua	1985[9, 52]	1,441	27.2	23.2	6.5	7.2	2.3	3.4	1.1	0.4	0.3	2.3	2.3	4.6	1.1

refined petroleum and products (353+354)	rubber products (355)	plastic products (356)	(36) pottery, china, and glass (361+362)	bricks, tiles, cement, etc. (369)	(37) iron and steel (371)	non-ferrous metals (372)	(38) fabricated metal products (381)	nonelectrical machinery (382 exc. 3825)	office equip., computers (3825)	electrical equip. (383 exc. 3832)	radio, television (3832)	transport equip. exc. motor vehicles (384 exc. 3843)	motor vehicles (3843)	profes-sional equip. (385)	(39) jewelry, musical instruments (390)	country
...	0.5	1.8	...	2.1[31]	[31]	...	3.1	—1.2—				21.8[30]	...	...	...	Faeroe Islands
												1.2			0.4	Fiji
2.6	0.5	1.3	0.9	3.9	3.9	1.8	6.6	10.0	0.7	3.6	2.8	3.0	1.9	1.2	0.6	Finland
6.3	1.4	2.4	1.3	3.1	3.4	2.4	7.0	—9.7—		—9.4—		3.5	8.2	1.7	1.1	France
		...					...								...	French Guiana
							—41.7—								...	French Polynesia
15.5	0.3	0.3	0.8	11.6	2.2	2.2	9.4	—1.4—		—6.6—		—7.7—		0.6	3.6	Gabon
—	—	—	...	13.9											17.6	Gambia, The
			...	0.9	—20.6[36]—						36				...	Gaza Strip
1.2[11]	7	7			5.8	0.7	—14.7—									Georgia
3.5	1.3	2.8	1.2	2.3	3.9	1.5	6.8	12.8	1.9	6.6	7.2	1.4	11.1	1.6	0.5	Germany[37]
13.0	0.5	0.7	0.3	3.1	0.2	8.2	2.3	—0.8—				—0.3—	0.2		—	Ghana
...	...	...	...	...	...	...	...					...			...	Gibraltar
3.8	1.1	2.8	1.3	6.1	2.7	3.2	5.4	—1.9—		—3.4—		—6.9—		0.1	1.3	Greece
												...				Greenland
—	...	...	...	...	—	...	...	...	...	...	...	...	...	...	...	Grenada
...	...	...	...	...	...	...	...	...	...	...	...	...	...	...	...	Guadeloupe
		...														Guam
1.1	2.3	3.6	3.4	5.9	3.1	0.1	2.8	0.7	0.1	2.4	0.4	0.1	0.2	0.2	0.5	Guatemala
—	—	11.8		2.8	—			—7.7—			50.2	4.5	—		2.0	Guernsey
...	...	...	...	...	...	...	...	...	...	...	...	...	...	...	...	Guinea
...	...	...	...	...	...	...	...	...	...	...	...	...	...	...	...	Guinea-Bissau
															...	Guyana
42	42	42	—	5.1	...	—	—23.6—							—	13.6	Haiti
1.9	2.2	4.3	0.2	7.0	0.9	0.2	5.0	0.9		1.1	0.5	0.2	0.3	0.2	1.6	Honduras
0.1	0.2	7.8	0.3	0.5	0.3	0.3	7.0	3.2	2.3	4.2	9.0	2.1	0.1	4.7	3.7	Hong Kong
3.8	1.4	1.9	2.0	2.8	6.4	4.3	4.0	—10.7—		4.0	7.5	2.6	3.8	5.1	2.0	Hungary
—	1.7	2.6	0.7	4.5	1.2	2.7	3.2	—7.6—		—3.2—		—7.2—		0.2	1.2	Iceland
5.3	2.8	0.9	0.8	4.0	9.8	0.7	2.5	8.2	0.1	6.1	1.8	3.8	5.3	0.8	0.6	India
17.7	2.8	1.3	1.4	2.8	8.0	—	3.1	—0.7—		—2.5—		—5.3—			0.4	Indonesia
21.6	1.5	2.2	1.2	8.5	4.2	1.7	4.1	—5.6—		—5.7—		—8.8—		0.5	0.1	Iran
24.9	0.4	0.9	0.9	12.4	0.4	—	1.8	—3.6—		—4.9—		—1.8—			—	Iraq
0.3	0.8	2.1	1.5	3.6	0.8	0.1	3.2	2.9	12.7	2.8	9.0	1.5	0.7	3.9	0.7	Ireland
...	...	...	...	...	...	...	...					...				Isle of Man
45	0.7	4.3	0.5	2.8	0.9	0.7	13.2	1.7	1.2	2.7	17.5	5.3	0.9	1.5	1.2	Israel
1.3	1.7	3.2	—6.6—		5.3	1.4	5.4	11.1	1.3	6.7	2.5	3.2	6.8	0.9	0.4	Italy
11.4	0.5	0.3	1.4	4.4	1.2	—	1.4	—0.3—		—0.7—		—2.0—			0.8	Jamaica
0.9	1.2	3.5	1.4	3.0	5.7	1.4	6.8	10.0	3.4	6.4	8.9	1.1	9.1	1.4	1.5	Japan
...	...	...	...	...	...	...	...					...				Jersey
9.4	0.2	2.5	—15.4—		—5.4[47]—		47	—5.2—		—1.5—		—0.2—		0.5	0.1	Jordan
...	...	...	...	...	...	...	...	...	...	...	...	...	...	...	...	Kazakhstan
1.3	4.6	2.0	0.6	3.5	0.7	—	5.2	—0.6—		—4.5—		—5.6—		0.1	1.5	Kenya
—	...	...													...	Kiribati
...	...	...	...	...	...	...	...	...	...	...	...	...	...	...	...	Korea, North
3.2	3.2	2.7	1.2	3.2	5.9	1.3	4.9	5.4	0.9	8.9	6.3	1.9	6.2	1.3	2.3	Korea, South
63.9	0.2	1.0	0.3	6.3	0.6	0.1	3.8	—1.2—		—0.9—		—0.8—		0.3	0.2	Kuwait
					1.2	62.4	—24.7—								...	Kyrgyzstan
...	...	...					...	...	...	...	...	...	...	...	...	Laos
0.4	7	7	0.6	3.2	1.4	0.1	—26.3—								...	Latvia
...	...	...	...	...	...	...	...					...			...	Lebanon
—	...	...	...	4.1	1.6	...	...								...	Lesotho
—	—	0.6	0.2	20.7	—	—	9.5	—0.3—		—0.7—					—	Liberia
30.8	—	0.5	0.1	21.6	—	—	0.3	—		—		—			1.9	Libya
...	...	...	...	...	...	...	...					...			...	Liechtenstein
9.5	7	7		6.7	...		—39.4—								...	Lithuania
0.2	8.0	2.3	4.2	5.8	29.5	2.8	9.8	—6.2—		—1.4—		—0.6—		0.5	0.1	Luxembourg
—	—	0.6	1.2	—	—	—	1.4	0.2	—	1.1	0.1	0.9	—	0.7	16.3	Macau
-1.4	0.2	18	—6.1—		5.8	3.7	5.1	—2.5—		—8.1—		—3.7—		...	0.1	Macedonia
5.5	0.8	0.8	—	2.4	—	—	3.1	—		—2.4—		—1.6—			—	Madagascar
—	1.5	2.2	—	1.5	—	—	7.4	—0.7—		—		—1.4—				Malawi
2.0	8.2	2.1	1.1	5.0	2.6	0.7	3.1	2.8	—	2.3	14.4	1.0	2.7	0.9	0.8	Malaysia
0.8	—	—	—	0.8	—	—									...	Maldives
							4.1	—1.6—		—1.6—		—9.8—			—	Mali
—	3.5	1.8	0.4	2.1	—	48	4.0[48]	—1.3—		2.8	14.1	3.9	—	3.6	3.6	Malta
															...	Marshall Islands
...	...	...	...	...	...	...	...	...	...	...	...	...	...	...	...	Martinique
															...	Mauritania
—	0.2	1.4	—	1.6	1.0	...	2.3	—0.6—		—1.4—		—0.8—		2.9	3.5	Mauritius
...	...	...	...	...	...	...	...					...			...	Mayotte
11.7	1.8	1.2	1.9	2.8	7.6	3.2	2.9	2.6	0.7	3.2	3.2	1.0	17.2	0.3	0.3	Mexico
3.9[50]	7	7	...	5.1											...	Micronesia
					—0.5—		—29.5—								...	Moldova
...	...	...	...	...	...	...	...					...			...	Monaco
4.3	...	...	0.5	12.0	...	12.9	4.1								...	Mongolia
...	1.4	0.9	0.4	11.4	0.5	0.3	7.5	—1.5—		—4.0—		—2.4—		0.1	0.1	Morocco
0.8	2.5	1.2	0.9	2.9	0.8	0.4	2.7	—0.8—		—4.3—		—2.6—		0.1	0.1	Mozambique
...	...	...		10.0				—1.4—		—1.1—		—5.3—			...	Myanmar (Burma)
...	...	...	...	...	...	...	...					...			...	Namibia
—	1.0	1.8		11.3	3.6	—	2.5	—		0.7	0.7				—	Nauru
															0.8	Nepal
4.2	0.5	2.3	0.5	3.3	2.2	2.2	8.8	—8.5—		—11.6—		—5.4—		1.4	0.7	Netherlands, The
...	...	...	...	...	...	...	...					...			...	Netherlands Antilles
						78.1		—5.6—							...	New Caledonia
3.9	1.0	2.9	—3.8—		—3.5—		7.2	—5.5—		—3.7—		—4.6—		0.4	1.3	New Zealand
8.1	0.6	2.0	0.3	1.8	0.1	—	4.1	0.3	—	0.4	0.1	0.2	0.1	—	0.2	Nicaragua

Manufacturing industries (continued)

country	year	total manufacturing value added (U.S.$'000,000)	food (311+312)	beverages (313)	tobacco manufactures (314)	textiles exc. wearing apparel (321)	wearing apparel (322)	leather and fur products (323+324)	wood products exc. furniture (331)	wood furniture (332)	paper, paper products (341)	printing and publishing (342)	industrial chemicals (351)	paints, soaps, etc. (352 exc. 3522)	drugs and medicines (3522)
Niger	1988	188	...	...	...	...	...	...	...	...	...	...	...	...	...
Nigeria	1990	2,171	13.1	19.4	1.7	17.2	0.2	2.4	0.2	0.8	2.9	2.8	0.6	—7.0—	
Northern Mariana Islands	1987[1,3]	58	—3.3—			26.0	—62.7[53]—		...	...		1.3	...	...	...
Norway	1990[32]	13,504	9.7	—8.4—		1.4	0.4	0.2	4.6	1.8	5.8	10.2	6.0	1.5	1.4
Oman	1990[3]	393	...	...	...	...	...	...	...	...	...	...	...	...	...
Pakistan	1986–87	3,975	13.9	1.5	14.4	17.0[55]	0.9	1.1	0.2	0.1	0.9	1.1	8.0	3.1	3.5
Palau	1983	0.13	...	...	...	...	...	...	...	...	...	...	...	...	...
Panama	1988[9,32]	485	35.6	12.4	4.8	0.8	3.9	1.5	0.5	0.8	4.3	4.3	1.4	5.0	2.0
Papua New Guinea	1989	451	48.4	13.1	4.9	—	0.4	...	11.6	2.0	1.1	2.4	1.1	—1.1—	
Paraguay	1990	630	26.9	8.1	1.6	5.7	0.3	8.7	15.5	1.9	0.3	4.7	1.4	—0.9—	
Peru	1987[9,32]	8,438	12.8	13.0	1.8	10.3	2.5	1.5	1.0	0.8	2.4	3.3	3.1	4.2	1.8
Philippines	1987[3,9,57]	4,056	19.5	12.3	11.4	3.9	3.9	0.3	2.0	0.7	2.8	1.1	3.3	3.3	3.9
Poland	1989	31,742	6.2	8.7	1.0	9.5	3.3	2.9	2.0	2.0	1.5	0.7	3.7	1.6	1.0
Portugal	1987[9,60]	7,530	10.9	2.9	2.0	15.7	4.4	3.1	3.5	0.8	7.8	3.6	5.0	3.3	2.0
Puerto Rico	1987[3]	13,709	4.7	9.4	...	0.6	5.0	1.5	0.3	0.6	0.7	2.0	0.8	3.5	38.8
Qatar	1987[9,26]	577	4.6	0.7	...	0.1	—5.3—		3.0	0.7	—	4.2	33.7	—0.1—	
Réunion	1988[3]	323	51.0	7.0[40]	...	...	...	...	...	...	...	...	...	...	...
Romania	1989	22,218	9.2	5.0	0.1	10.4	6.6	3.8	3.8	2.4	0.8	0.4	1.0	1.9	0.8
Russia[63]	1989	503,500[20]	16.9	1.8	0.5	7.6	4.7	1.5	1.3	1.1	0.8	0.7	4.0	—1.9—	
Rwanda	1990	180	32.6	19.3	8.8				4.4	0.6	1.1	1.1	7.7	—	
St. Kitts and Nevis	1990	11	...	...	...	...	...	...	...	...	...	...	...	...	...
St. Lucia	1990[2,64]	63	35.7	41.5	...		22.8							0.1	
St. Vincent	1988[3,16]	14	24.9	—25.4—			10.1		—1.9—		—5.3—		...	...	...
San Marino	1978	47	—7.2—				9.5		—5.8—		—5.0—		[66]	[66]	[66]
São Tomé and Príncipe	1988	0.77	...			—			—		—		—		
Saudi Arabia	1988	15,452	4.6	0.6	1.0	1.2	1.4	0.9	0.9	0.5	0.8	0.8	...	...	...
Senegal	1990	367	39.7	4.1	4.1	8.4	3.3	1.6	0.3	0.3	0.8	2.4	4.3	—1.6—	
Seychelles	1989	26	—79.6—				—0.6—		—2.1—		—6.0—		[67]	[67]	[67]
Sierra Leone	1985–86[15]	43	—60.6—				—0.5—		—15.8—		—0.5—		[67]	[67]	[67]
Singapore	1990[16]	11,749	2.6	1.3	0.7	0.5	2.4	0.2	0.5	0.8	1.5	4.1	5.2	—5.2—	
Slovenia	1989	7,943	8.1	1.7	0.4	5.0	7.8	3.8	—6.1—		4.1	1.3	11.2[18]	[18]	[18]
Solomon Islands	1990[16,70]	6.7	...	...	...	...	...	...	...	...	...	...	...	...	...
Somalia	1988	18	26.5	4.8	18.7	3.3	0.4	14.0	...	0.1	—10.9—		—6.7—		
South Africa	1989[16]	19,984	8.5	4.3	0.6	3.6	2.7	1.8	1.3	1.0	6.4	2.9	5.8	—11.0[71]—	
Bophuthatswana	1985	120	...	...	...	...	...	...	...	...	...	...	...	...	...
Ciskei	1980[16]	36	...	...	...	...	...	...	...	...	...	...	...	...	...
Transkei	1986[3,16,72]	49	—37.0—				—35.0—		—12.0—		...		...		
Venda	1985[16]	12	—70.7—				—19.4—		—4.8—		—		—		
Spain	1988[16,26]	65,922	11.8	4.8	1.2	4.2	2.5	1.7	2.4	1.6	2.6	4.5	5.2	3.2	2.2
Sri Lanka	1988[9,32]	780	20.1	10.4	21.0	8.1	10.1	1.6	1.0	0.1	2.6	1.5	0.4	2.6	0.4
Sudan, The	1988	354	44.1	2.3	12.7	9.3	0.3	2.5	0.3	0.3	1.7	2.3	0.8	—4.0—	
Suriname	1989[2,16,64]	348	46.7	20.1	7.1	...	1.8	1.1	5.0	1.1	2.9	1.8	...	—6.3—	
Swaziland	1990	112	50.0	4.5	—	...	...	...	2.7	1.8	26.4	8.2	...	—0.9—	
Sweden	1988[16,32]	44,029	8.0	1.2	0.4	1.4	0.5	0.2	4.9	1.2	10.0	6.3	4.1	2.4	2.4
Switzerland	1990	57,332	10.2	2.0	0.6	3.0	2.0	0.8	3.9	2.6	2.4	7.4	8.4	—6.7—	
Syria	1988	1,284	16.0	2.9	11.1	21.7	1.2	6.5	1.3	3.4	0.3	0.7	0.4	—4.5—	
Taiwan	1990	53,669	5.7	—5.7—		6.9	4.1	1.5	—1.6—		—5.1—		—8.8—		
Tajikistan	1990[2]	7,617	—19.9—				—47.5—		—1.3[4]—		—4—		[73]	[73]	[73]
Tanzania	1989	104	22.3	8.7	6.8	10.7	1.0	4.9	1.9	1.0	2.9	3.9	3.9	—1.9—	
Thailand	1989	16,591	16.3	7.2	3.5	9.6	7.0	0.9	1.9	1.1	3.0	0.7	2.6	—5.7—	
Togo	1989[3]	115	—50.8—				—14.1—		—7.1—		—3.8—		[42]	[42]	[42]
Tonga	1989–90[1,3]	12	—40.3—				—22.5—						—0.8—		2.2
Trinidad and Tobago	1987[15]	423	28.5	9.6	8.0	1.0	2.7	0.8	0.8	1.2	6.1	4.9	1.9	—8.3—	
Tunisia	1990	1,821	7.5	5.9	2.5	6.7	11.8	2.8	1.0	1.4	1.8	1.4	8.8	2.2	1.9
Turkey	1988[9,75]	18,579	8.4	2.7	5.3	11.5	2.9	1.6	0.7	0.3	1.8	1.3	8.8	2.2	1.9
Turkmenistan	1990[2,3]	7,780	—15.4—			38.4	—6.2—		—1.6[4]—		—4—		[76]	[76]	[76]
Tuvalu	1989	0.16	...	...	...	...	...	...	...	...	...	...	...	...	...
Uganda	1988[3]	193	—17.0—			...	...	...	...		...		...		
Ukraine	1989[3,10]	70,914	—17.5—				—6.1—		—0.9[4]—		—4—		8.7[7]	[7]	[7]
United Arab Emirates[77]	1988	1,002[78]	—6.0—				—2.0—		—2.1—		—1.6—		[79]	[79]	[79]
United Kingdom	1989	180,241	8.7	2.5	0.9	2.7	2.3	0.7	1.4	1.8	3.0	7.4	5.9	1.9	3.0
United States	1989	1,308,103	8.2	1.9	1.4	2.1	2.5	0.4	2.3	1.6	4.7	7.5	6.2	2.3	2.6
Uruguay	1987[9,32]	1,938	16.6	7.7	4.5	10.8	3.3	5.0	0.5	0.2	3.6	2.2	2.1	3.6	3.5
Uzbekistan			...	...	...	...	...	...	...	...	...	...	...	...	...
Vanuatu	1985[3]	4.6	33.8	8.8	—		—8.7—		—5.4—		—17.2—		...		
Venezuela	1988[32]	9,965	10.6	5.5	3.1	3.5	1.8	1.2	0.5	0.7	2.5	2.1	4.2	—6.1—	
Vietnam	1989[50,80]	5,533	—28.2—				—17.7[81]—		—[82]—		[82]	[81]	—9.9—		
Virgin Islands (U.S.)	[83]		...	...	...	...	...	...	...	...	...	...	...	...	...
West Bank	1987[3,34]	237	—40.7—				—9.8—		4.0	—5.1—		...		[84]	[84]	[84]
Western Sahara		...	...	...	...	...	...	...	...	...	...	...	...	...	...
Western Samoa	1988[85]	16	51.4	14.3	20.1	—			—		10.9	—	...	3.3	...
Yemen[86]	1986	540	—51.9—				—8.7—		—3.9—		—0.5—		[87]	[87]	[87]
Yugoslavia	1989	12,986	18.1	2.7	0.8	4.9	9.2	4.3	—3.8—		1.5	1.1	8.7[18]	[18]	[18]
Zaire	1990	64	11.1	20.6	11.1	6.3	3.2	6.3	1.6	1.6	—	1.6	14.3		
Zambia	1990	678	11.1	11.9	6.3	8.7	6.6	1.5	0.7	1.8	1.2	1.6	7.4	—8.7—	
Zimbabwe	1990	2,098	10.8	16.1	5.3	7.8	4.7	3.8	1.5	1.0	3.0	3.3	4.7	—5.9—	

[1]Gross output in value of sales. [2]Gross output of production. [3]Percentage breakdown by ISIC category is incomplete. [4]33 includes 34. [5]Export production of canned tuna and related products to the United States. [6]Value of manufactured exports (excluding duty-free reexports). [7]351 includes 352, 355, and 356. [8]390 includes 385. [9]In producer's prices. [10]Value of manufactured exports. [11]Includes crude petroleum and natural gas. [12]Includes metal furniture. [13]353 + 354 includes 351. [14]Three largest sectors only. [15]Establishments employing 10 or more persons. [16]In factor values. [17]Sector 35 equals 5.5%. [18]351 includes 352 and 356. [19]Excludes petroleum refining. [20]In constant prices of 1980. [21]Excludes fabricated metal products. [22]384 minus 3843 includes 381. [23]Cotton fibre only. [24]Establishments employing 50 or more persons and all public establishments. [25]Republic of Cyprus only. [26]Establishments employing 20 or more persons. [27]Primarily soap. [28]Private establishments employing 10 or more persons and all public establishments. [29]Processed fish only. [30]Ship repair only. [31]369 includes 371. [32]Establishments employing five or more persons. [33]Excludes wine. [34]Data refer to "Revenue" (mostly value of sales). [35]321 includes 323 + 324. [36]37 includes 38. [37]Former West Germany only. [38]Value of external sales by public enterprises. [39]Primarily beverages. [40]Rum, including processed sugar and molasses. [41]Includes public utilities. [42]Sector 35 equals 5.9%. [43]Establishments with electric power and 10 or more employees or without electric power and 20 or more employees. [44]Establishments employing three or more persons. [45]351 includes 353 + 354. [46]Establishments employing four or more persons. [47]37 includes 381. [48]381 includes 372.

Column groups: (36) = pottery, china, and glass (361+362) and bricks, tiles, cement, etc. (369); (37) = iron and steel (371) and non-ferrous metals (372); (38) = fabricated metal products (381) through professional equip. (385); (39) = jewelry, musical instruments (390).

refined petroleum and products (353+354)	rubber products (355)	plastic products (356)	pottery, china, and glass (361+362)	bricks, tiles, cement, etc. (369)	iron and steel (371)	non-ferrous metals (372)	fabricated metal products (381)	nonelectrical machinery (382 exc. 3825)	office equip., computers (3825)	electrical equip. (383 exc. 3832)	radio, television (3832)	transport equip. exc. motor vehicles (384 exc. 3843)	motor vehicles (3843)	professional equip. (385)	jewelry, musical instruments (390)	country
3.0	1.6	1.2	0.6	5.8	1.8	2.6	7.4	1.3		2.1		3.9		...	0.4	Niger
...	...[53]	...[53]	4.9												0.7	Nigeria
															...	Northern Mariana Islands
1.9	0.4	2.1	0.8	2.7	2.6	6.1	5.8	10.8	0.9	3.2	2.3	6.5	1.1	0.6	0.7	Norway
9.5[54]															...	Oman
8.7	1.0	0.6	0.8	7.7	7.5	—	0.8	1.9		2.5		2.4		0.1	0.3	Pakistan
															...	Palau
...[56]	0.4	3.6	1.1	3.2	...	0.9	2.4	0.1		0.6		1.4	0.1	0.5	8.4[56]	Panama
—	—	0.4	0.7	1.6	...	—	6.7	1.3		0.7		2.4		0.2	0.3	Papua New Guinea
12.7	—	1.9	0.6	4.3	...	0.5	1.9	0.2		0.2		1.3		0.2	0.3	Paraguay
13.1	1.4	3.3	1.1	2.8	1.4	2.6	3.4	2.1	0.1	3.2	2.2	0.7	2.7	0.4	1.1	Peru
11.9	1.6	0.9	1.4	0.4[58]	3.2	0.3	1.3[59]	1.1	0.1	1.6	3.9	0.8	0.7	0.3	0.7	Philippines
5.0	1.0	1.1	1.6	2.2	6.6	3.4	5.1	11.0	0.5	3.9	3.5	4.5	4.1	0.8	1.5	Poland
2.3[61]	1.1	2.0	3.4	5.4	2.7	0.5	4.4	2.3	0.2	3.3	2.4	1.9	2.6	0.3	0.2	Portugal
1.8	1.1	1.3	0.4		0.5		1.3	1.4	4.2	5.4	7.5	3.5		4.4	0.7	Puerto Rico
27.8	—	0.8	—	6.2	7.6	—	4.9								0.2	Qatar
																Réunion
2.3	1.3	1.1	1.7	3.0	4.3	—	5.9	11.4	0.9	5.0		2.7	2.7	2.5	8.9[62]	Romania
4.2	1.1	0.6	0.9	3.6	3.3	1.9	2.3	25.8		3.0		3.8		3.2	3.7	Russia[63]
9.4				13.3			9.4	0.6		0.6		0.6			...	Rwanda
																St. Kitts and Nevis
																St. Lucia
...	...	0.4					6.6[65]			...[65]	...[65]				...	St. Vincent
[66]	[66]	[66]	12.3				26.2								22.6	San Marino
																São Tomé and Príncipe
71.7	...	5.7	—	5.3	0.2	0.1	1.2	0.8		0.9		1.0			0.4	Saudi Arabia
5.2	...	—	5.2	8.4	—	—	8.2	2.7		0.8		3.8			—	Senegal
...[67]	...[67]	...[67]			—	[68]	2.4								—	Seychelles
...[67]	...[67]	...[67]	6.8[68]		—	[68]	4.1								7.7	Sierra Leone
7.5	0.3	2.2	0.2	1.2	1.2	0.3	5.8	5.5	[69]	4.0	36.1[69]	7.6		1.9	1.3	Singapore
0.5	1.9	[18]	3.1		3.4	2.1	7.6	7.5		14.8		8.7			0.7	Slovenia
—	—	—													—	Solomon Islands
—	—	10.7		2.1			1.5	—							—	Somalia
...[71]	1.3	1.9	1.3	3.8	10.0	3.6	6.8	5.6		4.2		1.5	7.0	0.7	2.4	South Africa
																Bophuthatswana
																Ciskei
...	...	...		1.0	—	—	12.0								...	Transkei
...	...	...		2.2	—	—	2.9								...	Venda
2.9	2.0	2.4	1.8	4.9	4.5	1.9	5.9	5.7	0.5	4.0	2.1	1.8	10.6	0.4	0.8	Spain
1.5	3.9	1.1	2.2	3.8	0.9		1.4	0.3		0.7	0.1	0.7	0.2		3.2	Sri Lanka
2.0	2.0	1.1	0.3	1.1	—	4.5	4.0			2.5		1.7			0.3	Sudan, The
	0.2	0.3	4.2		—	—	—					1.0	—		0.2	Suriname
							3.6	0.9		0.9						Swaziland
1.4	0.9	1.6	0.8	2.1	4.6	1.5	8.3	9.9	1.3	3.7	4.1	3.3	11.6	1.6	0.4	Sweden
2.6	0.9	2.6	1.2	1.6	1.9	1.9	6.9	13.1		10.0				5.2	0.3	Switzerland
7.2	1.0	0.9	1.7	6.3	—	0.6	5.0	2.1		3.1		0.5			1.5	Syria
5.0	1.4	6.4	3.9		6.8		5.5	4.1		14.5		7.3		1.3	4.4	Taiwan
[73]	[73]	[73]	0.5	3.5		11.7	9.9								—	Tajikistan
2.9	4.9	—	—	1.0	2.9	1.9	4.9	1.0		2.9		7.8			7.6	Tanzania
7.3	3.3	1.3	1.6	2.5	1.6	0.7	2.0	1.9		2.9		7.5		0.3	7.6	Thailand
[42]	[42]	[42]	10.9		2.2	—	4.3								...	Togo
																Tonga
7.6	2.5	2.6	7.0		3.8[74]	—	8.3	0.2		3.2		0.1	4.9	[8]	1.6[8]	Trinidad and Tobago
0.9	0.8	2.2	1.4	19.1	7.7	0.4	8.3	3.5				1.8		0.1	0.5	Tunisia
13.0	1.7	1.0	3.1	4.6	8.4	2.2	3.1	4.4		2.3	2.4	0.6	4.7	0.2	0.2	Turkey
[76]	[76]	[76]	0.3	6.3											...	Turkmenistan
—	—	—		...											...	Tuvalu
																Uganda
2.0[11]	[7]	[7]		1.6	18.2	2.2	40.8								...	Ukraine
[79]	[79]	[79]	3.2			—	4.1									United Arab Emirates[77]
1.8	1.2	3.1	1.6	3.5	2.8	1.0	5.3	11.5	2.3	4.0	5.2	5.8	6.1	1.4	1.3	United Kingdom
2.0	1.1	2.5	0.9	1.7	2.4	1.8	6.1	7.7	2.5	3.5	4.7	5.9	5.9	6.0	1.5	United States
10.7	3.1	2.2	2.2	1.8	0.9	0.2	3.3	0.7	0.1	2.6	0.5	1.5	5.9	0.1	0.4	Uruguay
																Uzbekistan
					11.1											Vanuatu
25.9	1.0	2.4	1.2	2.7	5.6	7.3	3.8	2.2		3.2		1.9		0.3	0.6	Venezuela
5.7	...		16.8[82]		1.6		15.8								...	Vietnam
[84]	[84]	[84]	9.3		7.0[47]		[47]									Virgin Islands (U.S.)
																West Bank
																Western Sahara
																Western Samoa
[87]	[87]	[87]	15.3		—	—	8.7	—		—		—		—	1.8	Yemen[86]
0.7	2.5	[18]	3.7		2.7	3.3	9.2	7.2		7.5		7.8			0.4	Yugoslavia
1.6		1.6			—	—	4.8	1.6		1.6		1.6			7.9	Zaire
1.6	5.0	0.9	0.4	7.2	1.0	0.3	5.3	3.1		4.6		2.7			0.3	Zambia
0.7	1.6	2.6	0.4	0.6	7.9	0.6	...	2.5		—		—		0.5	0.7	Zimbabwe

[49]Data include estimated figure for refined petroleum. [50]Includes electricity. [51]Total (1989) manufacturing value added equaled U.S.$770,000,000. [52]Establishments employing 30 or more persons. [53]322 and 323+324 includes 355+356. [54]Refined petroleum only. [55]Includes ginning and baling of fibres. [56]390 includes 353+354. [57]Establishments employing 10 or more persons with average monthly sales of U.S.$48,600. [58]Excludes cement. [59]Excludes metal furniture. [60]Some sector data are limited to establishments with 10 or more employees; other coverage may be limited to conform with disclosure rules. [61]Excludes derivatives. [62]Includes waterworks and supply. [63]Data refer to former U.S.S.R. [64]Selected industries only. [65]381 includes 383. [66]Sector 35 equals 11.4%. [67]Sector 35 equals 4.1%. [68]36 includes 37. [69]3832 includes 3825. [70]Excludes fish processing and sawmilling. [71]352 includes 353+354. [72]Percentage breakdown based on 1985 gross output of production of large industrial enterprises, equaling U.S.$89,000,000. [73]Sector 35 equals 5.6%. [74]371 includes 381. [75]Private establishments employing 25 or more persons and all public establishments. [76]Sector 35 equals 4.5%. [77]Abu Dhabi emirate only. [78]Total (1987) manufacturing value added for the United Arab Emirates equals U.S.$2,153,000,000. [79]Sector 35 equals 81.1%. [80]Includes mining. [81]32 includes 342. [82]36 includes 33 and 341. [83]Data withheld for reasons of confidentiality. [84]Sector 35 equals 15.1%. [85]Percentage breakdown based on 1984 gross output of large industrial enterprises, equaling U.S.$24,000,000. [86]Former Yemen Arab Republic only. [87]Sector 35 equals 9.2%.

Energy

This table provides data about the commercial energy supplies (reserves, production, consumption, and trade) of the various countries of the world, together with data about oil pipeline networks and traffic. Many of the data and concepts used in this table are adapted from the United Nations' *Energy Statistics Yearbook*.

Electricity. Total installed electrical power capacity comprises the sum of the rated power capacities of all main and auxiliary generators in a country. "Total installed capacity" (kW) is multiplied by 8,760 hours per year to yield "Total production capacity" (kW-hr).

Production of electricity comprises the total gross production of electricity by publicly or privately owned enterprises and also that generated by industrial establishments for their own use, but usually excludes consumption by the utility itself. Measured in millions of kilowatt-hours (kW-hr), annual production of electricity ranges generally between 50% and 60% of total production capacity. The data are further analyzed by type of generation: fossil fuels, hydroelectric power, and nuclear fuel.

The great majority of the world's electrical and other energy needs are met by the burning of fossil hydrocarbon solids, liquids, and gases, either for thermal generation of electricity or in internal combustion engines. Many renewable and nontraditional sources of energy are being developed worldwide (wood, biogenic gases and liquids, tidal, wave, and wind power, geothermal and photothermal [solar] energy, and so on), but collectively these sources are still negligible in the world's total energy consumption.

For this reason only hydroelectric and nuclear generation are considered here separately with fossil fuels.

Trade in electrical energy refers to the transfer of generated electrical output via an international grid. Total electricity consumption (residential and nonresidential) is equal to total electricity requirements less transformation and distribution losses.

Coal. The term coal, as used in the table, comprises all grades of anthracite, bituminous, subbituminous, and lignite that have acquired or may in the future, by reason of new technology or changed market prices, acquire an economic value. These types of coal may be differentiated according to heat content (density) and content of impurities. Most coal reserve data are based on proved recoverable reserves only, of all grades of coal. Exceptions are footnoted, with proved in-place reserves reported only when recoverable reserves are unknown. Production figures include deposits removed from both surface and underground workings as well as quantities used by the producers themselves or issued to the miners. Wastes recovered from mines or nearby preparation plants are excluded from production figures.

Natural gas. This term refers to any combustible gas (usually chiefly methane) of natural origin from underground sources. The data for production cover, to the extent possible, gas obtained from gas fields, petroleum fields, or coal mines that is actually collected and marketed. (Much natural gas in Middle Eastern and North African oil fields is

Energy

country	electricity installed capacity, 1990 ('000 kW)	production, 1990 capacity ('000,000 kW-hr)	production, 1990 amount ('000,000 kW-hr)	power source, 1990 fossil fuel (%)	hydro-power (%)	nuclear fuel (%)	trade, 1990 exports ('000,000 kW-hr)	imports ('000,000 kW-hr)	consumption amount 1990 ('000,000 kW-hr)	per capita 1990 (kW-hr)	residential 1988 (%)	non-residential 1988 (%)	coal reserves, latest ('000,000 metric tons)	production, 1990 ('000 metric tons)	consumption, 1990 ('000 metric tons)
Afghanistan	494	4,327	1,128	32.3	67.7	—	—	—	1,128	68	...	...	66	143	143
Albania	777	6,807	4,100	12.2	87.8	—	650	—	3,450	1,063	...	...	15[2]	2,400	2,640
Algeria	4,657	40,795	15,994	99.2	0.8	—	270	210	15,934	638	...	...	43	10	1,210
American Samoa	33	289	90	100.0	—	—	—	—	90	2,368	27.5[4]	72.5[4]	—	—	...
Andorra	...	...	...	...	...	...	...	...	...	...	...	...	—	—	...
Angola	617	5,405	1,840	26.1	73.9	—	—	—	1,840	184	27.5[3]	72.5[3]	—	—	—
Antigua and Barbuda	26	228	95	100.0	—	—	—	—	95	1,250	42.4[5]	57.6[5]	—	—	—
Argentina	17,128	150,041	50,907	50.1	35.6	14.3	54	890	51,743	1,601	47.7	52.3	130	270	1,407
Armenia	2,810	24,616	10,377	85.0	15.0	—	...	1,699	12,076	3,621	...	...	—	50	570
Aruba	90	788	375	100.0	—	—	—	—	375	6,250	...	...	—	—	—
Australia	36,782	322,210	154,571	90.4	9.6	—	—	—	154,571	9,161	30.1[3]	69.9[3]	90,940	205,666	96,054
Austria	16,839	147,510	50,414	35.5	64.5	—	7,298	6,839	49,955	6,588	23.1[3]	83.4[3]	65	2,510	6,282
Azerbaijan	...	...	23,300	...	...	...	...	...	...	...	...	...	—	—	—
Bahamas, The	401	3,513	950	100.0	—	—	—	—	950	3,755	33.6[5]	66.4[5]	—	—	—
Bahrain	1,040	9,110	3,490	100.0	—	—	—	—	3,490	6,764	...	...	—	—	—
Bangladesh	2,520	22,075	8,057	89.0	11.0	—	—	—	8,057	70	47.1	52.9	1,054[2]	—	558
Barbados	140	1,226	468	100.0	—	—	—	—	468	1,835	31.2	68.8	...	...	...
Belarus	...	...	38,700	...	...	...	...	13,044	51,744	5,029	...	...	—	—	1,500
Belgium	14,140	123,866	70,215	38.8	0.4	60.8	8,509	4,785	66,491	6,754	26.9[6]	73.1[6]	410	2,357	16,911
Belize	23	201	105	100.0	—	—	—	—	105	561	...	...	—	—	—
Benin	15	131	5	100.0	—	—	—	195	200	43	...	...	—	—	—
Bermuda	170	1,489	490	100.0	—	—	—	—	490	8,448	41.4[4]	58.6[4]	—	—	—
Bhutan	353	3,092	1,564	0.4	99.6	—	1,395	3	172	113	29.2[4]	69.8[4]	...	2	18
Bolivia	735	6,439	1,955	34.3	65.7	—	—	6	1,961	268	75.4	24.6	—	—	—
Bosnia and Hercegovina	3,441	30,140	14,632	79.1	20.9	—	289	858	15,201	3,497	21.8[1]	78.2[1]	...	...	...
Botswana	8	8	522[8,9]	8	8	8	8	828[8,9]	8	8	...	...	3,500	400[6,8]	8
Brazil	52,892	463,334	222,195	5.7	93.3	1.0	1,741	26,545	246,999	1,643	42.9	57.1	1,245	4,595	15,436
Brunei	382	3,346	1,215	100.0	—	—	—	—	1,215	4,568	55.3[5]	44.7[5]	—	—	—
Bulgaria	9,975	87,381	41,300	64.2	5.5	30.3	600	5,000	45,700	5,072	41.2[4]	58.8[4]	3,730	31,659	37,959
Burkina Faso	59	517	155	100.0	—	—	—	—	155	17	...	...	—	—	—
Burundi	43	377	106	1.9	98.1	—	—	13	119	22	...	...	—	—	—
Cambodia	35	307	70	57.1	42.9	—	—	—	70	8	...	...	—	—	—
Cameroon	627	5,493	2,705	2.6	97.4	—	—	—	2,705	229	...	...	—	1	1
Canada	104,140	912,266	481,791	23.3	61.6	15.1	18,236	17,781	481,336	18,149	28.8[5]	71.2[5]	6,966	68,331	49,180
Cape Verde	7	61	36	100.0	—	—	—	—	36	97	...	...	—	—	—
Cayman Islands	56	491	225	100.0	—	—	—	—	225	9,000	54.4	45.6	—	—	—
Central African Republic	43	377	95	18.9	81.1	—	—	—	95	31	...	...	4	...	...
Chad	31	272	82	100.0	—	—	—	—	82	14	...	...	—	—	—
Chile	4,079	35,732	18,372	50.6	49.4	—	—	—	18,372	1,395	32.9	67.1	1,181	2,223	3,760
China	98,600	863,736	618,000	82.1	17.9	—	40	1,500	619,460	546	6.2	93.8	730,700	1,080,000	1,064,460
Colombia	9,407	82,405	36,000	24.4	75.6	—	—	225	36,225	1,098	65.3	34.7	9,666	19,000	5,300
Comoros	5	44	16	87.5	12.5	—	—	—	16	29	...	...	—	—	—
Congo	149	1,305	398	—	100.0	—	—	63	461	203	...	...	—	—	—
Cook Islands	6	53	16	100.0	—	—	—	—	16	889	...	...	—	—	—
Costa Rica	933	8,173	3,609	2.6	97.4	—	126	289	3,772	1,251	73.3	26.7	—	—	—
Côte d'Ivoire	1,173	10,275	2,365	32.8	67.2	—	—	—	2,365	197	36.7	63.3	—	—	—
Croatia	3,272	28,660	8,748	56.5	43.5	—	331	1,307	9,724	2,046	51.0[1]	49.0[1]	...	...	200
Cuba	3,988	34,935	16,245	99.5	0.5	—	—	—	16,245	1,531	52.7	47.3	—	—	—
Cyprus	471	4,126	1,975	100.0	—	—	—	—	1,975	2,817	74.0	26.0	—	—	108
Czechoslovakia	20,740	181,682	89,345	67.8	5.3	26.9	7,000	10,300	92,645	5,913	23.6[4]	76.4[4]	5,370	108,291	108,291
Denmark	9,133	80,005	25,724	97.5	0.1	2.4[10]	4,925	11,973	32,772	6,372	32.5[6]	67.5[6]	63[1]	—	10,112
Djibouti	38	333	175	100.0	—	—	—	—	175	428	...	...	—	—	—
Dominica	8	70	30	46.7	53.3	—	—	—	30	366	53.5[5]	46.5[5]	—	—	—
Dominican Republic	1,447	12,676	5,325	84.0	16.0	—	—	—	5,325	743	...	...	—	—	1[10]
Ecuador	1,657	14,515	6,327	21.4	78.6	—	—	—	6,327	598	67.2	32.8	23	...	...

flared [burned] because it is often not economical to capture and market it.) Manufactured gas is generally a by-product of industrial operations such as gasworks, coke ovens, and blast furnaces. It is usually burned at the point of production and rarely enters the marketplace. Production of manufactured gas is, therefore, only reported as a percentage of domestic gas consumption.

Crude petroleum. Crude petroleum is the liquid product obtained from oil wells; the term also includes shale oil, tar sand extract, and field or lease condensate. Production and consumption data in the table refer, so far as is possible, to the same year so that the relationship between national production and consumption patterns can be clearly seen; both are given in barrels.

Proved reserves are that oil remaining underground in known fields whose existence has been "proved" by the evaluation of nearby producing wells or by seismic tests in sedimentary strata known to contain crude petroleum, and that is judged recoverable within the limits of present technology and economic conditions (prices). The published proved reserve figures do not necessarily reflect the true reserves of a country, because government authorities or corporations often have political or economic motives for withholding or altering such data.

The estimated exhaustion rate of petroleum reserves is an extrapolated ratio of published proved reserves to the current rate of withdrawal/production. Present world published proved reserves will last about 40 to 45 years at the present rate of withdrawal, but there are large country-to-country variations above or below the average.

Data on petroleum and refined product pipelines are provided because of the great importance to both domestic and international energy markets of this means of bringing these energy sources from their production or transportation points to refineries, intermediate consumption and distribution points, and final consumers. Their traffic may represent a very significant fraction of the total movement of goods within a country. Available data for petroleum pipelines are often incomplete and their basis varies internationally, some countries reporting only international shipments, others reporting domestic shipments of 50 kilometres or more, and so on.

For data in the hydrocarbons portions of the table (coal, natural gas, and petroleum), extensive use has been made of a variety of international sources, such as those of the United Nations, the International Energy Agency (of the Organization for Economic Cooperation and Development), the World Energy Conference (in its *Survey of Energy Resources* [triennial]); the U.S. Department of Energy (especially its *International Energy Annual*); and of various industry surveys, such as those published by the *International Petroleum Encyclopedia*, the *Oil and Gas Journal*, the *Petroleum Economist*, and *World Oil*.

| natural gas | | | | | | crude petroleum | | | | | | | country |
| published proved reserves, 1992 ('000,000,000 cu m) | production | | consumption | | | reserves, 1992 | | production, 1991 ('000,000 barrels) | consumption, 1990 ('000,000 barrels) | refining capacity, 1992 ('000 barrels per day) | pipelines (latest) | | |
	natural gas, 1991 ('000,000 cu m)	manufactured gas, 1990 (% of total gas consumption)	amount, 1990 ('000,000 cu m)	residential, 1988 (%)	non-residential, 1988 (%)	published proved ('000,000 barrels)	years to exhaust proved reserves				length (km)	traffic ('000,000 metric ton-km)	
100	300[1]	...	1,888	...	...	...	...	—	—	—	...	...	Afghanistan
19	696	...	397	...	...	165	15	11	19	40	200	...	Albania
3,299	45,876	30.7	19,034	26.8[3]	73.2[3]	9,200	32	291	176	465	6,910	...	Algeria
...	...	...	...	...	...	...	...	—	—	—	...	...	American Samoa
...	...	...	...	...	...	...	...	—	—	—	...	...	Andorra
51	578	10.9	167	...	...	1,818	10	180	12	32	179	...	Angola
...	...	...	...	...	...	...	...	—	—	—	—	—	Antigua and Barbuda
579	21,161	11.1	25,279	47.2	52.8	1,570	9	178	171	696	6,990	—	Argentina
...	170[1]	...	4,882	...	...	...	...	—	...	...	...	...	Armenia
...	...	...	...	...	...	...	...	—	—	—	...	...	Aruba
2,136	21,430	30.5	18,099	...	...	1,524	8	198	204	703	3,000	...	Australia
11	1,322	18.7	5,631	25.7[3]	74.3[3]	85	9	9	55	210	725	5,319	Austria
170	11,655	...	...	...	...	3,300	38	86	...	380	...	1,705	Azerbaijan
...	...	...	...	...	...	...	...	—	...	...	...	...	Bahamas, The
170	4,517	4.5	5,151	...	...	84	6	14	90	243	72	...	Bahrain
725	4,960	0.3	4,392	35.9	64.1	0.5	2	0.3	9	31	—	—	Bangladesh
0.2	20[1]	...	29	61.0	39.0	3	7	0.4	2	3	—	—	Barbados
...	210	...	15,400	...	...	...	...	11	...	...	...	...	Belarus
—	14[1]	25.3	12,111	43.4[6]	56.6[6]	...	...	...	185[7]	602	1,328	1,011	Belgium
...	...	...	...	...	...	...	...	...	...	...	...	...	Belize
—	...	...	...	...	...	20	13	1.5	—	—	—	—	Benin
...	...	...	...	...	...	...	...	—	—	—	—	—	Bermuda
...	...	...	...	...	...	...	...	—	—	—	...	...	Bhutan
127	3,027	21.3	745	—	100.0	119	15	8	7	45	2,380	...	Bolivia
...	...	...	...	...	...	...	...	...	...	...	...	...	Bosnia and Hercegovina
...	...	...[8]	...	...	...	...	...	—	...[8]	—	—	—	Botswana
115	3,480	62.3	3,484	—	100.0	2,800	12	232	427	1,406	5,804	...	Brazil
317	8,271	1.2	2,063	...	...	1,350	25	55	—	10	553	...	Brunei
7	10[1]	10.3	6,660	...	...	15	10	1.5	60	300	611	—	Bulgaria
...	...	...	...	...	...	...	...	—	—	—	—	—	Burkina Faso
...	...	...	...	...	...	...	...	—	—	—	...	—	Burundi
...	...	...	...	...	...	...	...	—	—	—	...	—	Cambodia
110	—	100.0	...	...	...	400	7	55	14	42	—	—	Cameroon
2,739	115,356	24.2	63,863	20.6[3]	79.4[3]	5,588	10	556	521	1,905	23,564	99,908	Canada
...	...	...	...	...	...	...	...	—	—	—	...	—	Cape Verde
...	...	...	...	...	...	...	...	...	...	...	...	—	Cayman Islands
...	...	...	...	...	...	...	...	—	—	—	...	—	Central African Republic
...	...	...	...	...	...	...	...	—	—	—	...	—	Chad
116	844	32.0	1,859	51.6	48.4	300	50	6	45	143	1,540	...	Chile
1,002	15,398	16.1	15,258	...	...	24,000	23	1,022	801	2,200	7,600	...	China
110	4,066	15.3	4,726	8.9	91.1	1,935	12	160	87	274	4,935	...	Colombia
...	...	...	...	...	...	...	...	—	—	—	...	—	Comoros
74	2	50.4	2	...	...	830	15	57	5	21	25	...	Congo
—	—	...	...	...	...	...	...	—	...	...	...	...	Cook Islands
...	—	14.3	...	...	...	...	...	—	3	15	176	...	Costa Rica
99	—	63.7	—	—	—	100	143	0.7	20	69	—	—	Côte d'Ivoire
...	1,989[1]	...	...	...	...	...	...	15[1]	...	...	1,911	3,482	Croatia
3	311[1]	89.3	31	—	100.0	100	20	5	50	280	—	—	Cuba
—	—	63.5	—	—	—	...	...	—	5	19	—	—	Cyprus
14	592	25.0	14,758	...	...	15	14	1.1	91	455	2,948	8,902	Czechoslovakia
115	3,780	19.7	2,020	...	...	755	15	51	56	186	688	1,898	Denmark
...	...	...	...	...	...	...	...	—	—	—	—	—	Djibouti
...	...	38.5	...	...	...	...	...	—	—	—	...	...	Dominica
...	...	35.5	...	...	...	...	...	—	10	48	104	...	Dominican Republic
110	102	35.5	100	—	—	1,550	14	107	42	142	2,158	...	Ecuador

Energy (continued)

country	electricity installed capacity, 1990 ('000 kW)	production, 1990 capacity ('000,000 kW-hr)	production, 1990 amount ('000,000 kW-hr)	power source, 1990 fossil fuel (%)	power source, 1990 hydro-power (%)	power source, 1990 nuclear fuel (%)	trade, 1990 exports ('000,000 kW-hr)	trade, 1990 imports ('000,000 kW-hr)	consumption amount, 1990 ('000,000 kW-hr)	consumption per capita, 1990 (kW-hr)	consumption resi-dential, 1988 (%)	consumption non-resi-dential, 1988 (%)	coal reserves, latest ('000,000 metric tons)	coal pro-duction, 1990 ('000 metric tons)	coal con-sump-tion, 1990 ('000 metric tons)
Egypt	11,738	102,825	39,550	79.5	20.5	—	—	—	39,550	754	30.3	69.7	53	—	1,340
El Salvador	740	6,482	2,296	8.9	72.9	18.2[10]	9	11	2,298	438	67.3	32.7	...	...	...
Equatorial Guinea	5	44	18	88.9	11.1	—	—	—	18	51	...	...	...	...	...
Estonia	...	...	17,181	...	...	...	8,477	1,475	10,179	6,433	...	...	...	...	...
Ethiopia	393	3,443	906	13.0	79.7	7.3[10]	—	—	906	18	...	...	11	...	—
Faeroe Islands	91	797	232	64.7	35.3	—	—	—	232	4,936	...	...	...	...	...
Fiji	200	1,752	435	23.0	77.0	—	—	—	435	569	26.5	73.5	...	—	14
Finland	13,220	115,807	54,508	44.7	20.1	35.2	360	11,113	65,261	13,118	18.6[3]	81.3[3]	...	—	6,227
France	103,410[11]	905,872[11]	419,584[11]	11.5[11]	13.7[11]	74.8[11]	52,112[11]	6,674[11]	374,146[11]	6,661[11]	30.3[6]	69.7[6]	258	13,251[11]	28,656[11]
French Guiana	108	946	335	100.0	—	—	—	—	335	3,418	...	58.7[3, 12]	...	...	...
French Polynesia	79	692	275	74.5	25.5	—	—	—	275	1,335	...	...	...	...	...
Gabon	279	2,444	915	23.0	77.0	—	—	—	915	781	52.2	47.8	...	...	...
Gambia, The	13	114	67	100.0	—	—	—	—	67	78	...	...	...	...	...
Gaza Strip	...	...	...	...	...	...	...	...	...	...	...	...	...	...	...
Georgia	...	...	14,200	...	...	...	...	...	...	...	...	...	...	700	...
Germany	123,160	1,078,882	572,002	68.1	3.4	28.5	26,200	27,500	573,302	7,250	26.3[6, 13]	73.7[6, 13]	80,069	463,885	474,459
Ghana	1,187	10,398	5,288	1.0	99.0	—	285	—	5,003	333	...	...	...	—	3
Gibraltar	27	237	82	100.0	—	—	1	—	81	2,700	...	...	...	—	—
Greece	8,508	74,530	35,002	94.3	5.7	—	619	1,330	35,713	3,555	30.6[6]	69.4[6]	3,000	51,896	53,119
Greenland	87	762	220	100.0	—	—	—	—	220	3,929	35.3	64.7	—	—	—
Grenada	9	79	51	100.0	—	—	—	—	51	600	46.8[5]	53.2[5]	...	...	...
Guadeloupe	319	2,794	684	100.0	—	—	—	—	684	1,994	...	32.9[12]	...	...	...
Guam	302	2,646	800	100.0	—	—	—	—	800	6,780	36.9[6]	63.1[6]	...	...	...
Guatemala	696	6,097	2,325	10.1	89.9	—	—	—	2,325	253	27.0[2]	73.0[3]	...	...	...
Guernsey	...	...	217	100.0	—	—	...	...	217	5.108	...	...	...	...	...
Guinea	176	1,542	518	66.2	33.8	—	—	—	518	90	...	...	...	...	...
Guinea-Bissau	7	61	17	100.0	—	—	—	—	17	18	...	...	...	...	...
Guyana	114	999	220	97.7	2.3	—	—	—	220	276	32.5[14]	67.5[14]	...	...	...
Haiti	153	1,340	475	31.6	68.4	—	—	—	475	73	...	...	13[2]	...	...
Honduras	290	2,540	1,105	19.9	80.1	—	2	165	1,268	247	52.2	47.8	21[2]	...	...
Hong Kong	8,342	73,076	28,938	100.0	—	—	1,797	—	27,141	4,639	67.0	33.0	—	—	8,932
Hungary	6,603	57,842	28,411	51.0	0.6	48.4	—	11,127	39,538	3,747	30.7[4]	69.3[4]	4,461	17,578	17,891
Iceland	957	8,383	4,610	0.1	93.8	6.1[10]	—	—	4,610	18,221	20.9[3]	79.1[3]	...	—	70
India	75,995	665,716	286,035	74.8	23.1	2.1	95	1,000	286,940	336	42.0	58.0	62,548	211,296	218,939
Indonesia	11,480	100,565	44,260	79.3	20.2	0.5[10]	—	—	44,260	240	55.0	45.0	3,000	7,327	3,499
Iran	17,554	153,773	56,000	88.2	11.8	—	—	—	56,000	1,026	21.1[9]	78.9[9]	193	1,300	1,700
Iraq	9,000	78,840	29,160	97.9	2.1	—	—	—	29,160	1,541	...	...	...	...	...
Ireland	3,807	33,349	14,515	93.2	6.8	—	—	—	14,515	3,902	41.4[6]	58.6[6]	14	35	3,034
Isle of Man	...	...	188[5]	100.0	—	—	390	—	172[4]	2,530[4]	48.1[6]	51.9[6]	...	...	...
Israel	4,135	36,223	20,730	100.0	—	—	—	—	20,340	4,422	69.8	30.2	...	—	3,708
Italy	56,548[15]	495,360[15]	216,891[15]	82.3[15]	16.2[15]	1.5[5, 15]	922[15]	35,577[15]	251,546[15]	4,407[15]	25.0[6]	75.0[6]	39	1,014[15]	20,768[15]
Jamaica	732	6,412	2,730	95.2	4.8	—	—	—	2,730	1,112	24.1	75.9	...	—	—
Japan	194,763	1,706,124	857,273	65.0	11.2	23.6	—	—	857,273	6,944	20.8[3]	79.2[3]	873	8,277	113,113
Jersey	...	...	390	...	...	...	...	...	390	5,749	...	...	...	...	...
Jordan	1,048	9,180	3,688	99.5	0.5	—	—	—	3,688	920	60.6	39.4	...	...	...
Kazakhstan	...	...	86,128	...	...	...	...	32,677	118,805	7,040	...	...	25,000	130,315	...
Kenya	723	6,333	3,044	5.6	83.3	11.1[10]	—	171	3,215	134	35.7	64.3	...	—	151
Kiribati	2	18	7	100.0	—	—	—	—	7	106	...	...	...	...	...
Korea, North	9,500	83,220	53,500	40.7	59.3	—	—	—	53,500	2,457	...	...	661	53,700	56,150
Korea, South	24,056	210,731	118,738	50.1	5.4	44.5	—	—	118,738	2,775	33.4	66.6	158	17,217	43,405
Kuwait	6,790	59,480	20,610	100.0	—	—	—	—	20,610	10,108	91.9	8.1	...	...	...
Kyrgyzstan	...	...	14,903	...	...	...	—	—	—	—	...	...	...	—	3,997
Laos	225	1,971	870	5.2	94.8	—	520	13	363	88	...	...	...	...	...
Latvia	...	...	6,647	...	...	...	3,555	7,138	10,230	2,477	...	...	...	...	...
Lebanon	870	7,621	4,735	88.4	11.6	—	—	38	4,773.	1,767	...	...	...	...	...
Lesotho	8	8	8	8	8	8	8	8	8	8	...	...	...	8	8
Liberia	332	2,908	565	56.6	43.4	—	—	—	565	219	...	...	...	...	...
Libya	4,100	35,916	19,000	100.0	—	—	—	—	19,000	4,180	...	...	...	—	5
Liechtenstein	17	17	17	17	17	17	17	17	17	17	...	...	...	—	17
Lithuania	...	...	28,405	98.5	1.5	—	16,513	4,539	16,430	4,396	...	...	...	...	...
Luxembourg	1,238	10,845	1,374	40.3	59.7	—	746	4,614	5,242	14,054	15.3[6]	84.7[6]	...	—	197
Macau	183	1,603	790	100.0	—	—	2	91	879	1,835	75.0[5]	25.0[5]	...	—	—
Macedonia	1,657	14,515	5,755	91.5	8.5	—	52	185	5,888	2,909	27.4[1]	72.6[1]	...	...	...
Madagascar	220	1,927	566	43.8	56.2	—	—	—	566	47	...	...	1,075[2]	—	13
Malawi	185	1,621	587	2.4	97.6	—	—	—	587	67	52.3	47.7	12	—	19
Malaysia	5,037	44,124	24,723	71.2	28.8	—	76	19	24,666	1,379	54.8	45.2	4	120	1,860
Maldives	5	44	29	100.0	—	—	—	—	29	135	50.9[4]	49.1[4]	...	...	...
Mali	87	762	214	19.6	80.4	—	—	—	214	23	...	...	...	...	...
Malta	250	2,190	1,100	100.0	—	—	—	—	1,100	3,116	25.1[9]	74.9[9]	...	—	300
Marshall Islands	...	...	...	...	.	...	...	...	...	...	...	...	...	...	...
Martinique	110	964	615	100.0	—	—	—	—	615	1,804	...	40.9[12]	...	...	6
Mauritania	105	920	140	82.1	17.9	—	—	—	140	69	...	...	...	—	6
Mauritius	313	2,742	770	89.0	11.0	—	—	—	770	712	...	...	...	—	75
Mayotte	8	70	17	100.0	—	—	—	—	13	147	...	...	...	...	...
Mexico	29,274	256,440	122,477	73.2	20.6	6.2[10]	1,950	600	121,127	1,367	17.4[9]	82.6[9]	1,886	10,004	10,369
Micronesia	...	...	...	...	...	...	...	...	...	...	...	...	...	...	...
Moldova	...	...	15,690	...	...	...	...	4,471	20,161	4,619	...	...	...	—	4,576
Monaco	11	11	11	11	11	11	11	11	11	11	...	...	...	...	...
Mongolia	901	7,893	3,600	100.0	—	—	—	160	3,760	1,717	29.8[4]	70.2[4]	24,000[2]	7,890	7,240
Morocco	2,362	20,691	9,628	87.3	12.7	—	—	—	9,628	384	63.2	36.8	45	526	1,762
Mozambique	2,358	20,656	485	89.7	10.3	—	—	325	810	52	...	...	240	40	58
Myanmar (Burma)	1,116	9,776	2,601	52.2	47.8	—	—	—	2,601	62	...	59.1[3, 12]	2	78	118
Namibia	8	8	8	8	8	8	8	8	8	8	...	...	...	8	8
Nauru	10	88	29	100.0	—	—	—	—	29	3,222	...	...	...	...	...
Nepal	277	2,427	739	3.7	96.3	—	26	58	771	40	58.6	41.4	...	—	35

| natural gas | | | | | | crude petroleum | | | | | | | country |
| published proved reserves, 1992 ('000,000,000 cu m) | production | | consumption | | | reserves, 1992 | | production, 1991 ('000,000 barrels) | consumption, 1990 ('000,000 barrels) | refining capacity, 1992 ('000 barrels per day) | pipelines (latest) | | |
	natural gas, 1991 ('000,000 cu m)	manufactured gas, 1990 (% of total gas consumption)	amount, 1990 ('000,000 cu m)	residential, 1988 (%)	non-residential, 1988 (%)	published proved ('000,000 barrels)	years to exhaust proved reserves				length (km)	traffic ('000,000 metric ton-km)	
351	7,481	15.4	6,525	36.3	63.7	4,500	14	323	167	523	1,767	...	Egypt
—	—	57.8	—	—	—	...	...	—	5	16	—	—	El Salvador
24	...	...	...	...	...	...	...	...	...	...	...	—	Equatorial Guinea
...	...	...	...	...	...	...	...	...	...	...	...	...	Estonia
25	—	100.0	—	—	—	...	...	—	5	18	—	—	Ethiopia
...	...	...	...	...	...	...	...	...	...	...	...	—	Faeroe Islands
...	...	...	...	...	...	...	...	...	...	...	...	—	Fiji
...	...	21.5	2,729	0.6[6]	99.4[6]	...	...	—	68	241	—	—	Finland
37	3,441	19.9[11]	35,735[11]	32.4[6]	67.6[6]	171	8	21	530[11]	1,816	7,546	22,969	France
...	...	...	...	...	...	...	...	...	...	...	...	...	French Guiana
...	...	...	...	...	...	...	...	...	...	...	...	...	French Polynesia
13	102	5.5	100	—	100.0	730	7	108	8	24	284	...	Gabon
...	...	...	...	...	...	...	...	...	...	...	...	...	Gambia, The
...	...	...	...	...	...	...	...	...	—	—	—	—	Gaza Strip
...	45	...	...	...	...	...	...	1.2	...	...	...	—	Georgia
248	27,363	22.5	82,862	36.6[6,13]	63.4[6,13]	449	17	27	701	2,062	7,590	14,136	Germany
—		85.6				0.5	...	...	7	27	—	—	Ghana
...	...	...	...	...	...	...	...	...	...	...	...	...	Gibraltar
1	102	104.2	101	...	...	41	7	6	103	396	573	...	Greece
...	...	...	...	...	...	...	...	...	...	...	...	...	Greenland
...	...	...	...	...	...	...	...	...	...	...	...	—	Grenada
...	—	100.0	...	—	—	...	...	—	—	—	—	—	Guadeloupe
...	...	...	...	...	...	...	...	...	...	...	...	...	Guam
0.3	...	10.1	...	...	...	35	25	1.4	5	16	275	...	Guatemala
...	...	...	...	...	...	...	...	...	...	...	...	...	Guernsey
24	...	...	...	...	...	...	...	—	—	—	—	—	Guinea
...	...	...	...	...	...	...	...	...	...	...	...	—	Guinea-Bissau
...	...	...	...	...	...	...	...	...	...	...	...	—	Guyana
...	—	...	...	...	...	...	...	...	...	...	...	—	Haiti
...	...	33.4	...	...	...	...	...	—	2	14	—	—	Honduras
—		65.6	—	—	—			—			—	—	Hong Kong
106	5,222	9.6	10,446	14.0[6]	86.0[6]	159	11	14	39	220	1,834	3,367	Hungary
...	...	...	...	...	...	...	...	...	...	...	...	...	Iceland
730	13,493	22.7	10,303	53.7	46.3	6,127	26	236	394	1,122	5,200	...	India
2,952	38,585	30.3	11,155	...	100.0	11,846	23	523	273	860	2,961	...	Indonesia
17,000	22,116	6.0	22,416	—	100.0[5]	62,500	51	1,220	262	720	9,800	...	Iran
3,098	612	55.0	1,153	...	...	100,000	980	102	137	319	5,075	...	Iraq
48	2,509	4.2	2,321	13.9[6]	86.1[6]	—		—	13	56	—	—	Ireland
...	...	...	...	...	...	...	...	...	...	...	...	—	Isle of Man
0.3	50[1]	107.1	31	—	100.0	1.3	13	0.1	59	208	998	...	Israel
322	20,162	17.2[15]	40,519[15]	45.6[6]	54.4[6]	692	21	33	539[15]	2,386	3,851	8,980	Italy
—		37.3				...	...	—	7	34	10	—	Jamaica
33	1,606	41.4	48,874	61.3[6]	38.7[6]	60	12	5	1,382	4,612	406	...	Japan
...	...	...	...	...	...	...	...	...	...	...	...	...	Jersey
3	110[1]	90.8	—	...	...	5	50	0.1	19	100	209	...	Jordan
...	7,885	...	...	...	...	...	...	189	...	...	3,400	22,300	Kazakhstan
—	—	103.7	...	...	...	...	...	—	16	90	483	...	Kenya
...	...	...	...	...	...	...	...	...	...	...	...	...	Kiribati
...	...	...	...	...	...	...	...	—	21	42	37	...	Korea, North
—	—	29.0	3,243	...	...	...	...	—	306	1,163	455	...	Korea, South
1,373	428	41.0	7,277	18.4	81.6	95,210	1,360	70	202	819	917	...	Kuwait
...	1,103	...	...	...	...	...	...	1.7	...	...	...	...	Kyrgyzstan
...	...	...	...	...	...	...	...	—	—	—	136	—	Laos
...	...	...	...	...	...	...	...	—			1,555	—	Latvia
—		24.2	...	...	...			—	9	38	72	—	Lebanon
		8	—			...	...	—	8	—	—	—	Lesotho
—	—	50.5[16]						—		15	—	—	Liberia
1,218	6,470	5.7	8,273	...	...	22,800	42	548	110	348	4,826	...	Libya
—		17	17			...	...	—	17		—	...	Liechtenstein
...	...		...	...				—			...	...	Lithuania
...	—	45.6	452	48.0[6]	52.0[6]			—	7	—	48	...	Luxembourg
...	...	...	...	...	...	...	...	...	...	...	...	—	Macau
...								—	...	...	—	—	Macedonia
2	—	50.5	...	...	...			—	1.2	16	—	—	Madagascar
...	...	...	...	...	...	...	...	...	...	...	...	—	Malawi
1,672	16,560	19.0	3,402	14.0	86.0	3,045	13	230	69	210	1,307	...	Malaysia
...	...	...	...	...	...	...	...	...	...	...	...	...	Maldives
—	—	—						—	—	—	—	—	Mali
—								—			—	—	Malta
...	...	...	...	...	...	...	...	...	...	...	...	—	Marshall Islands
—	—	250.2	...	...	...			—	4	12	—	—	Martinique
...	...	84.8	...	...	...			—	6	—	—	—	Mauritania
...	...	...	...	...	...	...	...	...	...	...	...	...	Mauritius
...	...	...	...	...	...	...	...	...	...	...	...	—	Mayotte
2,025	38,217	26.3	23,206	3.9[9]	96.1[9]	51,298	51	1,014	464	1,574	38,350	...	Mexico
...	...	...	...	...	...	...	...	...	...	...	...	...	Micronesia
...	—	...	4,004	...	...			—	52	...	...	...	Moldova
...		11	11					—	11	—	—	—	Monaco
...								—			—	—	Mongolia
1	60[1]	42.1	51	—	100.0	2	7	0.3	43	155	362	...	Morocco
65	—	—									595	...	Mozambique
265	988	0.4	1,075	...	100.0[5]	50	13	4	6	32	1,343	...	Myanmar (Burma)
59		8	—	...	...			—	8		—	—	Namibia
...	...	...	...			...	...	—	—	—	—	—	Nauru
...		—	—			...	...	—			—	...	Nepal

Energy (continued)

country	electricity installed capacity, 1990 ('000 kW)	production, 1990 capacity ('000,000 kW-hr)	production, 1990 amount ('000,000 kW-hr)	power source, 1990 fossil fuel (%)	power source, 1990 hydro-power (%)	power source, 1990 nuclear fuel (%)	trade, 1990 exports ('000,000 kW-hr)	trade, 1990 imports ('000,000 kW-hr)	consumption amount, 1990 ('000,000 kW-hr)	consumption per capita, 1990 (kW-hr)	consumption resi-dential, 1988 (%)	consumption non-resi-dential, 1988 (%)	coal reserves, latest ('000,000 metric tons)	coal pro-duction, 1990 ('000 metric tons)	coal con-sump-tion, 1990 ('000 metric tons)
Netherlands, The	17,441	152,783	71,866	94.9	0.2	4.9	471	9,679	81,074	5,423	25.0[5]	75.0[5]	497	—	15,809
Netherlands Antilles	200	1,752	735	100.0	—	—	—	—	735	3,910	...	...	...	—	...
New Caledonia	230	2,015	1,144	59.7	40.3	—	—	—	1,144	6,850	...	...	2	—	164
New Zealand	7,504	65,735	30,158	21.2	72.8	6.0[10]	—	—	30,158	8,891	37.5[5]	62.5[5]	117	2,415	2,015
Nicaragua	395	3,460	1,038	46.8	25.3	27.9[10]	10	210	1,238	320	69.1	30.9	...	...	...
Niger	63	552	163	100.0	—	—	—	187	350	45	60.4	39.6	70	158	158
Nigeria	4,040	35,390	9,945	77.7	22.3	—	100	—	9,845	91	80.5	19.5	190	90	55
Northern Mariana Islands	...	...	...	...	...	...	...	...	...	...	...	...	...	—	...
Norway	27,195	238,228	121,601	0.4	99.6	—	16,233	283	105,651	25,083	27.0[3]	73.0[3]	10	311	779
Oman	1,531	13,412	5,345	100.0	—	—	—	—	5,345	3,559	...	...	...	...	...
Pakistan	9,137	80,040	43,899	60.7	38.6	0.7	—	—	43,899	358	63.0	37.0	102	2,751	3,616
Palau	...	...	...	...	...	...	...	...	...	...	...	...	...	...	...
Panama	992	8,690	2,901	23.7	76.3	—	90	204	3,015	1,247	26.8[9]	73.2[9]	—	—	35
Papua New Guinea	490	4,292	1,790	74.3	25.7	—	—	—	1,790	462	27.5	72.5	—	—	1
Paraguay	5,800	50,808	2,434	0.2	99.8	—	600	3	1,837	430	...	...	...	...	...
Peru	4,137	36,240	13,817	24.2	75.8	—	—	—	13,817	641	40.0	60.0	1,060	145	140
Philippines	6,869	60,172	26,327	56.2	23.1	20.7[10]	—	—	26,327	422	55.1	44.9	82	1,173	2,222
Poland	30,703	268,958	136,337	97.6	2.4	—	11,477	10,437	135,297	3,521	33.5[4]	66.5[4]	40,400	215,000	188,800
Portugal	7,381	64,658	28,529	67.4	32.6	—	1,696	1,733	28,566	2,777	36.4[3]	63.6[3]	36	281	4,397
Puerto Rico	4,230	37,055	15,328	98.1	1.9	—	—	—	15,328	4,405	31.0[9]	69.0[9]	...	—	200
Qatar	1,410	12,352	4,624	100.0	—	—	—	—	4,624	12,565	83.0	17.0	...	...	...
Réunion	175	1,533	817	38.7	61.3	—	—	—	817	1,366	...	...	...	...	...
Romania	22,903	200,630	64,306	82.9	17.1	—	—	9,476	73,782	3,170	23.6[4]	76.4[4]	3,970[1]	44,500	51,700
Russia	213,300	1,868,500	1,082,200	73.7	15.4	10.9	36,300[18]	360[18]	1,690,060[18]	5,856[18]	21.6[4, 18]	78.4[4, 18]	265,582[18]	731,000[18]	703,200[18]
Rwanda	60	526	176	2.3	97.7	—	3	22	195	27	...	...	...	...	...
St. Kitts and Nevis	15	131	37	100.0	—	—	—	—	37	841	...	...	...	...	...
St. Lucia	22	193	104	100.0	—	—	—	—	104	693	26.6[4]	73.4[4]	...	...	...
St. Vincent and the Grenadines	14	123	48	25.0	75.0	—	—	—	48	414	45.3[5]	54.7[5]	...	...	...
San Marino	15	15	15	15	15	15	15	15	15	15	...	...	...	15	15
São Tomé and Príncipe	6	53	15	46.7	53.3	—	—	—	15	124	...	...	...	...	...
Saudi Arabia	18,510	162,148	47,400	100.0	—	—	—	—	47,400	3,354	69.3	30.7	...	...	...
Senegal	231	2,024	684	100.0	—	—	—	—	684	93	...	...	...	...	...
Seychelles	22	193	85	100.0	—	—	—	—	85	1,232	...	...	...	...	...
Sierra Leone	126	1,104	224	100.0	—	—	—	—	224	54	...	...	...	—	—
Singapore	3,400	29,784	15,618	100.0	—	—	—	—	15,618	5,736	48.0	52.0	...	—	3
Slovenia	2,701	23,660	12,399	38.7	24.0	37.3	29	7	12,377	6,288	18.0[1]	82.0[1]	...	...	...
Solomon Islands	12	105	30	100.0	—	—	—	—	30	94	78.4	21.6	...	...	...
Somalia	60	526	230	100.0	—	—	—	—	230	31	...	...	...	...	...
South Africa	25,890[8]	226,796[8]	164,518[8]	97.1[8]	0.5[8]	2.4[8]	3,100[8]	330	161,748[8]	3,952[8]	...	...	55,333	175,579[8]	132,979[8]
Bophuthatswana	...	...	...	...	...	...	...	...	...	...	...	...	...	...	...
Ciskei	...	...	...	...	...	...	...	...	...	...	...	...	...	...	...
Transkei	...	...	...	...	...	...	...	...	...	...	...	...	...	...	...
Venda	...	...	...	...	...	...	...	...	...	...	...	...	...	...	...
Spain	43,273	379,071	150,622	46.6	17.4	36.0	3,628	3,208	150,202	3,833	16.7[3]	83.2[3]	770	35,813	45,578
Sri Lanka	1,289	11,292	3,150	0.2	99.8	—	—	—	3,150	183	61.8	38.2	...	—	—
Sudan, The	500	4,380	1,327	29.4	70.6	—	—	—	1,327	53	...	...	...	—	1
Suriname	415	3,635	1,350	18.9	81.1	—	—	—	1,350	3,199	...	...	...	—	...
Swaziland	8	8	8	8	8	8	8	8	8	8	18.7[14]	81.3[14]	1,820	8	...
Sweden	34,189	299,496	146,535	3.6	49.9	46.5	14,672	12,784	144,647	17,130	26.4[3]	73.6[3]	1	—	3,451
Switzerland	16,300[17]	142,788[17]	55,846[17]	2.1[17]	55.5[17]	42.4[17]	22,862[17]	20,754[17]	53,738[17]	8,097[17]	26.6[6]	73.4[6]	...	—	332[17]
Syria	3,717	32,561	10,600	54.9	45.1	—	—	—	10,600	846	21.2[6]	78.8[6]	...	—	...
Taiwan	16,883	147,895	82,350	51.8	9.9	38.3	—	—	74,345	3,666	27.9	72.1	171	472	...
Tajikistan	...	...	17,500	...	...	...	...	...	...	...	...	...	...	300	...
Tanzania	439	3,846	885	30.8	69.2	—	—	—	885	32	...	...	200	4	4
Thailand	9,722	85,165	46,175	89.2	10.8	—	31	652	46,796	840	51.8	48.2	914	12,421	12,639
Togo	34	298	41	87.8	12.2	—	—	289	330	93	...	...	...	...	...
Tonga	7	61	22	100.0	—	—	—	—	22	232	...	...	...	...	...
Trinidad and Tobago	985	8,629	3,480	100.0	—	—	—	—	3,480	2,717	40.9	59.1	—	—	15
Tunisia	1,524	13,350	5,536	99.3	0.7	—	30	—	5,506	673	43.9	56.1	...	...	...
Turkey	16,316	142,928	57,544	59.7	40.2	0.1[10]	907	176	56,813	1,017	14.2[9]	85.8[9]	6,104	46,592	52,227
Turkmenistan	...	...	17,171	...	...	...	8,834	...	8,337	2,216	...	...	...	...	...
Tuvalu	...	...	...	...	...	...	...	...	...	...	...	...	...	...	...
Uganda	162	1,419	603	1.2	98.8	—	110	—	493	26	...	...	...	...	...
Ukraine	55,600	485,000	279,000	...	...	...	43,900	15,500	248,200	4,782	...	...	...	135,600	...
United Arab Emirates	4,660	40,822	13,590	100.0	—	—	—	—	13,590	8,553	...	...	...	...	...
United Kingdom	73,059	639,997	318,979	77.2	2.2	20.6	47	11,990	330,922	5,761	35.4[6]	64.6[6]	3,800	89,303	100,249
United States	775,396	6,792,469	3,031,058	70.8	9.6	19.0	20,526	22,506	3,033,038	12,170	34.9[6]	65.1[6]	215,241	944,040	832,606
Uruguay	1,681	14,726	7,372	13.6	86.4	—	1,330	—	6,042	1,953	63.4	36.6	...	—	...
Uzbekistan	...	...	56,325	...	...	...	2,157	—	54,168	2,640	...	...	...	6,200	10,400
Vanuatu	11	96	26	100.0	—	—	—	—	26	165	...	...	...	...	...
Venezuela	18,647	163,348	61,000	38.9	61.1	—	—	—	61,000	3,091	47.2	52.8	417	1,864	200
Vietnam	1,320	11,563	8,722	38.4	61.6	—	—	—	8,722	131	36.4[4]	63.6[4]	165	5,000	4,380
Virgin Islands (U.S.)	316	2,768	980	100.0	—	—	—	—	980	8,448	40.2[5]	59.8[5]	...	...	...
West Bank	...	...	...	...	...	...	...	...	...	...	...	...	...	...	...
Western Sahara	56	491	85	100.0	—	—	—	—	85	478	...	...	...	...	...
Western Samoa	19	166	50	60.0	40.0	—	—	—	50	298	...	...	...	...	...
Yemen	800	7,008	1,740	100.0	—	—	—	—	1,740	151	...	...	1[1]	...	...
Yugoslavia	16,470[19]	144,277[19]	44,371	67.7[19]	23.4[19]	8.9[19]	2,407	392	42,356	4,111	26.0[1]	74.0[1]	16,570[19]	75,848[19]	79,069[19]
Zaire	2,831	24,800	6,155	2.5	97.5	—	112	5	6,048	170	...	89.[13, 12]	600	126	169
Zambia	2,436	21,339	7,771	0.5	99.5	—	1,500	20	6,291	744	33.5	66.5	55	377	372
Zimbabwe	2,038	17,853	9,559	63.1	36.9	—	5	879	10,433	1,075	44.1	55.9	734	4,958	4,968

natural gas						crude petroleum							country
published proved reserves, 1992 ('000,000,000 cu m)	production		consumption			reserves, 1992		production, 1991 ('000,000 barrels)	consumption, 1990 ('000,000 barrels)	refining capacity, 1992 ('000 barrels per day)	pipelines (latest)		
	natural gas, 1991 ('000,000 cu m)	manufactured gas, 1990 (% of total gas consumption)	amount, 1990 ('000,000 cu m)	residential, 1988 (%)	non-residential, 1988 (%)	published proved ('000,000 barrels)	years to exhaust proved reserves				length (km)	traffic ('000,000 metric ton-km)	
1,970	82,674	17.2	45,298	46.8[5]	53.4[5]	145	6	24	328	1,219	1,383	4,560	Netherlands, The
—	—	166.7	...	...	...	...	...	—	82	470	—	—	Netherlands Antilles
...	...	...	...	...	...	...	...	—	...	...	...	...	New Caledonia
98	4,157	6.2	4,225	4.8[5]	95.2[5]	180	12	15	33	95	310	...	New Zealand
—	—	93.4	—	—	—	...	...	—	4	16	56	...	Nicaragua
...	...	...	...	...	...	...	...	—	...	...	...	...	Niger
2,965	3,251	1.7	3,710	—	100.0	17,900	26	678	71	433	5,042	...	Nigeria
...	...	...	...	...	...	...	...	...	...	...	...	...	Northern Mariana Islands
2,737	24,610	45.7	2,464	...	...	7,609	11	680	99	288	53	9,618	Norway
280	2,583	6.9	2,722	...	...	4,250	17	257	24	80	1,300	—	Oman
640	14,402	1.4	12,264	42.0	58.0	162	6	25	47	121	1,135	...	Pakistan
...	...	...	...	...	...	...	...	—	...	...	...	...	Palau
—	...	19.5	61	—	—	...	...	—	9	40	130	...	Panama
227	—	—	—	—	—	200	...	—	...	...	—	—	Papua New Guinea
—	—	30.0	...	...	...	...	...	—	3	8	—	—	Paraguay
200	1,283	29.3	564	61.3	38.7	382	9	42	57	189	800	...	Peru
47	—	59.1	—	—	—	38	35	1.1	84	287	357	...	Philippines
130	4,132	36.3	11,875	...	...	30	43	0.7	95	333	2,346	17,661	Poland
—	—	64.4	—	—	—	—	—	—	77	294	69	—	Portugal
—	—	32.1	...	...	...	...	...	—	46	123	—	—	Puerto Rico
4,587	7,167	28.8	5,435	—	100.0	3,729	26	142	21	60	235	—	Qatar
...	...	...	...	...	...	...	...	—	...	...	—	—	Réunion
105	27,340	12.3	30,191	...	...	1,150	24	47	179	657	4,229	6,654	Romania
52,482[18]	811,565[18]	8.7[18]	690,844[18]	...	...	57,000[18]	15[18]	3,745[18]	3,336[18]	12,300[18]	68,400	1,240,000	Russia
57	0.2	—	0.2	...	...	...	...	—	...	...	—	—	Rwanda
...	...	...	...	...	...	...	...	—	—	—	—	—	St. Kitts and Nevis
...	...	...	...	...	...	...	...	—	—	—	—	—	St. Lucia
...	...	...	...	...	...	...	...	—	—	—	—	—	St. Vincent and the Grenadines
...	...	15	15	...	...	...	...	—	—	—	—	—	San Marino
...	...	...	...	...	...	...	...	—	15	—	—	—	São Tomé and Príncipe
5,226	45,024	53.9	28,223	9.8[6]	90.2[6]	261,937	87	3,001	552	1,863	6,550	...	Saudi Arabia
—	—	10.0	—	—	—	...	...	—	6	24	—	—	Senegal
...	...	...	...	...	...	...	...	—	...	...	—	—	Seychelles
...	...	...	...	...	...	...	...	—	2	10	—	—	Sierra Leone
—	—	468.5	—	—	—	...	...	—	300	893	—	—	Singapore
...	24[1]	—	...	...	...	...	...	—	...	...	593	128	Slovenia
...	—	—	...	...	...	...	...	—	...	...	—	—	Solomon Islands
6	—	—	...	...	...	...	...	—	1.6	10	15	...	Somalia
51	—	100.0[8]	...	...	...	—	—	—	115[8]	431	2,679	...	South Africa
...	...	...	...	...	...	...	...	—	—	—	—	—	Bophuthatswana
...	~	...	...	...	...	...	...	—	—	—	...	...	Ciskei
...	...	...	...	...	...	...	...	—	—	—	...	...	Transkei
...	...	...	...	...	...	...	...	—	—	—	...	...	Venda
21	1,332	44.7	5,483	...	...	21	3	8	380	1,321	2,059	4,664	Spain
—	—	79.2	—	—	—	...	...	—	13	50	62	...	Sri Lanka
85	—	63.7	...	...	...	300	...	...	7	22	815	...	Sudan, The
—	...	—	...	...	...	38	25	1.5	1	...	—	—	Suriname
—	...	8	...	...	...	...	...	—	9	...	—	—	Swaziland
—	—	41.1	500	...	...	...	...	—	121	435	—	—	Sweden
—	—	12.2[17]	1,992[17]	38.3[6]	61.7[6]	...	...	—	22[17]	132	314	1,110	Switzerland
181	1,331	30.3	282	...	...	1,700	10	173	81	237	1,819	...	Syria
19	1,300[1]	...	...	...	...	4	6	0.7	...	543	615	...	Taiwan
...	100	...	...	...	...	...	...	0.7	...	...	...	...	Tajikistan
116	—	100.0	—	—	—	...	...	—	4	17	982	...	Tanzania
385	7,515	13.4	5,498	—	100.0	262	15	17	81	221	67	...	Thailand
...	...	...	...	...	...	...	...	—	...	...	—	—	Togo
...	...	...	...	...	...	...	...	—	—	—	—	—	Tonga
252	4,661	3.7	5,532	2.2	97.8	535	10	53	34	246	1,051	...	Trinidad and Tobago
85	405	8.7	1,379	10.0	90.0	1,700	45	38	9	34	883	...	Tunisia
20	201	41.1	3,212	...	...	540	17	32	167	704	4,059	55,492	Turkey
326	84,300	...	9,500	...	...	740	...	43	...	...	...	...	Turkmenistan
...	...	...	...	...	...	...	...	—	—	—	—	—	Tuvalu
...	...	...	...	...	...	...	...	—	...	...	—	—	Uganda
...	28,100	...	...	...	...	...	...	36	...	...	—	200,000	Ukraine
5,460	32,955	18.5	16,990	...	...	98,100	112	878	59	193	830	...	United Arab Emirates
545	55,331	14.7	61,964	52.7[6]	47.3[6]	3,994	6	649	569	1,856	3,926	9,836	United Kingdom
4,794	526,356	19.2	523,454	33.4[9]	66.6[9]	26,250	10	2,691	4,928	15,327	275,800	871,618	United States
—	—	94.2	—	—	—	...	...	—	9	29	—	—	Uruguay
...	41,600	...	37,800	...	...	...	...	21	62	...	176	200	Uzbekistan
...	...	...	...	...	...	...	...	—	...	...	—	—	Vanuatu
3,115	28,393	17.9	17,711	7.7	92.3	59,100	69	855	336	1,171	6,850	...	Venezuela
3	3	—	3	...	...	500	21	24	...	...	150	...	Vietnam
—	—	100.0	—	—	—	...	...	...	120	545	—	—	Virgin Islands (U.S.)
...	...	...	...	...	...	...	...	—	—	—	—	—	West Bank
...	...	...	...	...	...	...	...	—	—	—	—	—	Western Sahara
...	...	...	...	...	...	...	...	—	...	...	—	—	Western Samoa
198	...	42.7	...	...	...	4,000	55	73	33	115	456	—	Yemen
82[19]	2,676[19]	20.7[19]	5,560[19]	—	—	240[19]	11[19]	21[19]	115[19]	609[19]	1,398	894	Yugoslavia
30	—	9.2	—	—	—	187	19	10	3	17	390	...	Zaire
...	—	100.0	—	—	—	...	...	—	4	24	1,724	...	Zambia
...	—	90.6	—	—	—	...	...	—	...	...	8	...	Zimbabwe

[1]1990. [2]Estimated reserves in place. [3]1981. [4]1985. [5]1984. [6]1983. [7]Belgium includes Luxembourg. [8]South Africa includes Botswana, Lesotho, Namibia, and Swaziland. [9]1982. [10]Geothermally generated electricity. [11]France includes Monaco. [12]Transportation and industry only; excludes agricultural, commercial, and public-service sectors. [13]Data refer to former West Germany only. [14]1980. [15]Italy includes San Marino. [16]1989. [17]Switzerland includes Liechtenstein. [18]Data refer to former U.S.S.R. [19]Data refer to Yugoslavia as constituted prior to 1991.

Transportation

This table presents data on the transportation infrastructure of the various countries and dependencies of the world and on their commercial passenger and cargo traffic. Most states have roads and airports, with services corresponding to the prevailing level of economic development. A number of states, however, lack railroads or inland waterways because of either geographic constraints or lack of development capital and technical expertise. Pipelines, one of the oldest means of bulk transport if aqueducts are considered, are today among the most narrowly developed transportation modes worldwide for shipment of bulk materials. Because the principal contemporary application of pipeline technology is to facilitate the shipment of hydrocarbon liquids and gases, coverage of pipelines will be found in the "Energy" table. It is, however, also true that pipelines now find increasing application for slurries of coal or other raw materials.

While the United Nations' *Statistical Yearbook* and *Monthly Bulletin of Statistics* provide much data on infrastructure and traffic and have established basic definitions and classifications for transportation statistics, the number of countries covered is limited. Several commercial publications maintain substantial data bases and publishing programs for their particular areas of interest: highway and vehicle statistics are provided by the International Road Federation's annual *World Road Statistics;* the International Union of Railways' *International Railway Statistics* and Jane's *World Railways* provide similar data for railways; Lloyd's *Register of Shipping Statistical Tables* summarizes the world's merchant marine; the *Official Airline Guide,* the International Civil Aviation Organization's *Digest of Statistics: Commercial Air Carriers,* and the International Air Transport Association's *World Air Transport Statistics* have also been used to supplement and update data collected by the UN. Because several of these agencies are commercially or insurance-oriented, their data tend to be more complete, accurate, and timely than those of intergovernmental organizations, which depend on periodic responses to questionnaires or publication of results in official sources. All of these international sources have been extensively supplemented by national statistical sources to provide additional data. Such diversity of sources, however, imposes limitations on the comparability of the statistics from country to country because the basis and completeness of data collection and the frequency and timeliness of analysis and publication may vary greatly. Data shown in italic are from 1987 or earlier.

The categories adopted in the table also have special problems of comparability. Total road length is subject to wide international variation of interpretation, as "roads" can mean anything from mere tracks to highly developed highways. Each country also has individual classifications that differ according to climate, availability of road-building materials, traffic patterns, administrative responsibility, and so on. "Paved roads," by contrast, is a much more tightly definable category, but the proportion of paved to total roads may be distorted by the less comparable total road statistics. Automobile and truck and bus fleet statistics, which are usually

Transportation

| country | roads and motor vehicles (latest) | | | | | | | | railroads (latest) | | | | | |
	roads length mi	roads length km	paved (percent)	auto-mobiles	trucks and buses	persons per vehicle	cargo short ton-mi ('000,000)	cargo metric ton-km ('000,000)	track length mi	track length km	passengers passenger-mi ('000,000)	passengers passenger-km ('000,000)	cargo short ton-mi ('000,000)	cargo metric ton-km ('000,000)
Afghanistan	11,930	19,200	47	36,000	34,000	227	1,993	2,910	6	10	...	...	...	...
Albania	10,377	16,700	40	3,500	11,200	146	869	1,269	425	684	468	752	462	674
Algeria	50,734	81,648	59	750,000	500,000	20	2,148	3,136	2,384[2]	3,836[2]	1,225	1,972	2,012	2,937
American Samoa	217	350	43	4,447	445	9.3	...	...	—	—	—	—	—	—
Andorra	137	220	80	34,168	4,523	1.4	...	...	—	—	—	—	—	—
Angola	45,118	72,611	11	130,000	45,000	57	...	...	1,739[2]	2,798[2]	203	326	1,178	1,720
Antigua and Barbuda	724	1,165	33	13,500	3,500	4.7	...	...	—	—	—	—	—	—
Argentina	131,338	211,369	27	4,283,700	1,500,800	5.6	...	...	21,198[2]	34,115[2]	6,351	10,221	6,172	9,011
Armenia	4,800	7,700	99	230,100	...	...	3,200	4,672	511	823	196	316	3,345	4,884
Aruba	236	380	100	24,109	1,027	2.5	...	...	—	—	—	—	—	—
Australia	503,474	810,264	38	7,672,300	2,104,300	1.7	32,964	48,127	22,222[2,9]	35,763[2,9]	1,359	2,187	34,264	50,024
Austria	66,598	107,180	100	2,991,284	261,906	2.4	5,949	8,685	4,137	6,658	5,570[9]	8,964[9]	8,811[9]	12,864[9]
Azerbaijan	22,800	36,700	87	235,600	...	...	5,660	8,264	1,299	2,090	3,025	4,869	...	...
Bahamas, The	2,548	4,100	40	70,000	15,000	3.0	...	...	—	—	—	—	—	—
Bahrain	1,624	2,614	75	90,000	8,000	5.0	...	...	—	—	—	—	—	—
Bangladesh	120,100	193,283	4	41,401	53,200	1,127	...	...	1,706[2]	2,745[2]	3,150	5,070	440	643
Barbados	977	1,573	95	38,832	8,628	5.4	...	...	—	—	—	—	—	—
Belarus	29,900	48,100	94	498,700	...	...	15,321	22,369	3,472	5,587	10,268	16,524	57.0	83.2
Belgium	85,672	137,876	94	3,833,294	401,902	2.4	17,172	25,071	2,162[2]	3,479[2]	4,063	6,539	5,720	8,352
Belize	1,600	2,575	13	11,040	2,328	14	...	...	—	—	—	—	—	—
Benin	5,241	8,435	12	25,000	13,000	122	...	...	395	635	85.5	137.6	121.1	176.8
Bermuda	120	193	100	19,500	3,500	2.6	...	...	—	—	—	—	—	—
Bhutan	1,600	2,500	72	2,590	1,367	348	...	...	—	—	—	—	—	—
Bolivia	25,875	41,642	4	261,082	55,887	23	1,133	1,654	2,269[2]	3,652[2]	241	388	371	541
Bosnia and Hercegovina	13,153	21,168	54	438,080	50,578	8.9	2,708	3,954	646	1,039	...	...	...	...
Botswana	9,300	15,000	13	25,000	35,000	21	...	...	443	714	160	257	0.5	0.8
Brazil	1,037,780	1,670,148	10	14,995,837	1,609,764	8.7	178,359	260,400	18,711[2]	30,113[2]	9,965	16,037	74,955	109,433
Brunei	1,366	2,199	50	99,997	17,512	2.1	...	...	12[17]	19[17]	—	—	—	—
Bulgaria	22,942	36,922	92	1,276,751	145,417	6.3	9,468	13,823	2,672	4,300	4,842	7,793	9,680	14,132
Burkina Faso	8,161	13,134	12	12,000	13,000	360	...	...	308[2]	495[2]	422	680	322	470
Burundi	3,905	6,285	18	12,698	12,793	209	...	...	—	—	—	—	—	—
Cambodia	9,200	14,800	18	4,000	7,100	737	...	...	403	649	33.6	54.0	6.9	10.0
Cameroon	32,444	52,214	6	93,000	82,000	68	175	255	686[2]	1,104[2]	284	457	514	751
Canada	546,514	879,530	32	12,811,318	3,458,368	1.6	29,033	42,388	56,771	91,365	725	1,166	163,978	239,404
Cape Verde	3,489	5,615	29	13,027	4,356	19	...	...	—	—	—	—	—	—
Cayman Islands	110	177	68	8,750	1,250	2.7	...	...	—	—	—	—	—	—
Central African Republic	14,564	23,438	2	12,000	10,000	127	2.8	4.1	—	—	—	—	—	—
Chad	24,855	40,000	1	8,500	6,500	378	...	...	—	—	—	—	—	—
Chile	49,457	79,593	14	706,641	310,000	13	...	...	2,778[2]	4,470[2]	669	1,076	1,077	1,572
China	630,282	1,014,342	85	1,664,010	4,171,855	194	231,148	337,470	41,581	66,918	162,550	261,600	725,560	1,059,300
Colombia	80,229	129,117	8	1,098,895	230,481	24	15	22	2,011[2]	3,236[2]	88	141	268	391
Comoros	466	750	53	1,000	4,000	84	...	...	—	—	—	—	—	—
Congo	6,835	11,000	5	27,000	21,000	47	46	67	494	795	270	434	320	467
Cook Islands	174	280	...	689	728	12	...	...	—	—	—	—	—	—
Costa Rica	22,093	35,556	15	168,814	108,256	11	1,385	2,022	402[2]	647[2]	35.2	56.6	102.7	150.0
Côte d'Ivoire	41,900	67,500	7	170,000	92,000	46	...	...	410[2]	660[2]	634[20]	1,021[20]	396[20]	578[20]
Croatia	19,928	32.071	73	865,516	72,043	5.1	2,561	3,739	1,519	2,444	...	...	...	...
Cuba	28,932	46,555	27	229,500	184,600	25	1,208	1,763	3,009	4,843	1,796	2,891	1,655	2,416
Cyprus	6,104	9,824	43	165,433	68,494	2.4	...	...	—	—	—	—	—	—
Czechoslovakia	45,486	73,203	90	3,242,262	333,336	4.3	8,139	11,881	8,147	13,111	11,969	19,263	31,027	49,933
Denmark	44,156	71,063	100	1,590,345	301,350	2.7	7,260	10,600	1,763	2,838	3,139	5,051	1,234	1,801
Djibouti	1,906	3,067	10	13,000	2,000	34	...	...	66	106	182	293	81.5	119
Dominica	470	756	...	2,700	1,550	17	...	...	—	—	—	—	—	—
Dominican Republic	11,000	17,000	17	114,000	72,000	38	...	...	88	142	...	...	...	...
Ecuador	23,386	37,636	17	272,282	41,231	32	178	259	600[2]	965[2]	39.3	63.3	5.6	8.2

based upon registration, are relatively accurate, though some countries round off figures, and unregistered vehicles may cause substantial undercount. There is also inconsistent classification of vehicle types; in some countries a vehicle may serve variously as an automobile, a truck, or a bus, or even as all three on certain occasions. Relatively few countries collect and maintain commercial road traffic statistics.

Data on national railway systems are generally given for railway track length rather than the length of routes, which may be multitracked. Siding tracks usually are not included, but some countries fail to distinguish them. The United States data include only class 1 railways, which account for about 94 percent of total track length. Passenger traffic is usually calculated from tickets sold to fare-paying passengers. Such statistics are subject to distortion if there are large numbers of nonpaying passengers, such as military personnel, or if season tickets are sold and not all the allowed journeys are utilized. Railway cargo traffic is calculated by weight hauled multiplied by the length of the journey. Changes in freight load during the journey should be accounted for but sometimes are not, leading to discrepancies.

Merchant fleet and tonnage statistics collected by Lloyd's registry service for vessels over 100 gross tons are quite accurate. Cargo statistics, however, reflect the port and customs requirements of each country and the reporting rules of each country's merchant marine authority (although these, increasingly, reflect the recommendations of the International Mar-

itime Organization); often, however, they are only estimates based on customs declarations and the count of vessels entered and cleared. Even when these elements are reported consistently, further uncertainties may be introduced because of ballast, bunkers, ships' stores, or transshipped goods included in the data.

Airport data are based on scheduled flights reported in the commercial *Official Airline Guide* and are both reliable and current. The comparability of civil air traffic statistics suffers from differing characteristics of the air transportation systems of different countries; data for an entire country may be two to three years behind those for a single airport.

Outside of Europe, where standardization of data on inland waterways is necessitated by the volume of international traffic, comparability of national data declines markedly. Calculations as to both the length of a country's waterway system (or route length of river, lake, and coastal traffic) and the makeup of its stock of commercially significant vessels (those for which data will be collected) are largely determined by the nature and use of the country's hydrographic net—its seasonality, relief profile, depth, access to potential markets—and inevitably differ widely from country to country. Data for coastal or island states may refer to scheduled coastwise or interisland traffic.

merchant marine		international cargo (latest)		air	traffic (latest)				canals and inland waterways (latest)				country
fleet, 1991 (vessels over 100 gross tons)	total dead-weight tonnage, 1991 ('000)			airports with scheduled flights, 1992	passengers		cargo		length		cargo		
		loaded metric tons ('000)	off-loaded metric tons ('000)		passenger-mi ('000,000)	passenger-km ('000,000)	short ton-mi ('000,000)	metric ton-km ('000,000)	mi	km	short ton-mi ('000,000)	metric ton-km ('000,000)	
—	—	—	—	1	121[1]	195[1]	9.9[1]	14.4[1]	750	1,200	...	...	Afghanistan
24	81.0	1,090	644	1	...	...	...	...	27	43	...	...	Albania
148	1,093.4	52,270	13,900	25	1,397[3]	2,248[3]	7.3[3]	10.6[3]	...	...	...	...	Algeria
3	[4]	355	747	3	...	...	...	...	...	...	...	...	American Samoa
—	—	—	—	—	—	—	—	—	—	—	—	—	Andorra
111	122.4	19,900	1,230	16	606[5]	975[5]	23.2[5]	33.9[5]	805	1,295	...	...	Angola
241	811.2	30	117	2	110	177	...	...	...	...	...	...	Antigua and Barbuda
490	2,540.8	25,596	7,440	63	5,163[6]	8,431[6]	127[6]	186[6]	6,800	11,000	19,326	28,215	Argentina
...	...	...	...	2	3,453	5,557	33.6	49.0	...	...	...	...	Armenia
103[7]	[8]	...	...	1	...	...	...	...	...	...	...	...	Aruba
714	3,645.0	287,928	31,200	441	16,270	26,184	745	1,088	5,200	8,368	...	...	Australia
32	233.6	2,538	6,607	6	1,773	2,853	36.4	53.1	277	446	1,139	1,663	Austria
...	...	...	...	1	3,025	4,869	...	...	...	...	...	...	Azerbaijan
973	28,798.2	9,450	10,782	23	135[10]	218[10]	0.1	0.2	...	...	...	...	Bahamas, The
93	262.0	13,465	3,400	1	963[11]	1,549[11]	30.3[11]	44.3[11]	...	...	...	...	Bahrain
308	620.4	948	6,156	7	1,368	2,201	64.3	93.9	5,000	8,046	...	...	Bangladesh
35	7.8	201	519	1	93[12]	149[12]	0.8[13]	1.1[13]	...	...	...	...	Barbados
...	...	...	...	1	3,575	5,754	34.0	49.0	...	...	1,236	1,805	Belarus
268	3,052.9	27,852	61,560	4	4,705	7,572	472	689	1,269	2,043	3,645	5,322	Belgium
3[14]	0.3[14]	173	225	8	...	...	...	...	513	825	...	...	Belize
13[14]	4.6[14]	86	1,100	1	129.6[15]	208.6[15]	24.1[15]	35.2[15]	...	...	...	...	Benin
100	5,193.8	121	498	1	...	...	...	...	...	...	...	...	Bermuda
—	—	—	—	1	2.7	4.4	...	...	...	...	...	...	Bhutan
1	15.8	...	...	19	795	1,280	21.9	32.0	6,214	10,000	90	132	Bolivia
...	...	...	...	1	...	...	...	...	...	...	...	...	Bosnia and Hercegovina
—	—	—	—	7	38.9[16]	62.6[16]	2.1[16]	3.1[16]	...	...	...	...	Botswana
669	9,855.4	160,848	57,204	100	11,088	17,844	1,653	2,525	31,069	50,000	56,030	81,803	Brazil
48	348.0	14,500	1,210	1	278	448	6.8	9.9	130	209	...	...	Brunei
226	1,962.3	5,512	21,978	3	2,336	3,759	30.9	45.1	292	470	0.3	0.5	Bulgaria
...	...	...	...	2	129.6	208.6	24.1	35.2	...	...	...	...	Burkina Faso
1	0.4	39	182	2	...	...	...	...	...	...	...	...	Burundi
3	3.8	10	100	1	...	...	...	...	2,300	3,700	...	...	Cambodia
45	39.7	1,320	2,448	5	360	580	76	111	1,299	2,090	...	...	Cameroon
1,204	2,928.8	155,220	66,150	106	28,655	46,116	991	1,447	1,860	3,000	...	...	Canada
41	31.5	170	490	8	76.4	122.9	1.6	2.3	...	...	...	...	Cape Verde
155	539.0	785	707	2	...	...	...	...	...	...	...	...	Cayman Islands
—	—	—	—	1	144[18]	232[18]	12.1[18]	17.7[18]	500	800	...	...	Central African Republic
—	—	—	—	1	144	232	12.1	17.7	1,240	2,000	...	...	Chad
387	874.9	20,220	10,848	16	1,852	2,980	473	690	450	725	5,629	8,218	Chile
2,382	21,110.0	92,340	74,172	84	13,546	21,800	548	800	86,100	138,600	766,218	1,118,660	China
100	466.1	21,636	6,108	65	2,445	3,935	460	672	8,900	14,300	2	3	Colombia
7	4.0	11	103	4	...	...	...	...	...	...	...	...	Comoros
22	10.8	9,400	686	14	129.6	208.6	24.1	35.2	696	1,120	...	...	Congo
6	...	10	32	6	...	...	...	...	...	...	...	...	Cook Islands
29	10.1	1,600	1,811	9	658[19]	1,059[19]	24.8[19]	36.1[19]	454	730	...	...	Costa Rica
51	98.6	4,760	4,910	7	52.4[18]	84.4[18]	5.2[18]	7.6[18]	609	980	...	...	Côte d'Ivoire
...	...	...	...	1	...	...	...	...	...	...	494	721	Croatia
401	1,009.5	2,628	2,760	11	1,908	3,070	23.8	34.8	149	240	...	...	Cuba
1,359	36,527.0	1,944	4,344	1	1,399	2,252	22.1	32.2	...	...	...	...	Cyprus
24	577.8	...	...	7	1,459	2,348	39.5	57.7	295	475	3,029	4,422	Czechoslovakia
425	8,221.1[21]	14,676	29,460	12	2,646[22]	4,258[22]	84.4[22]	123.2[22]	259	417	1,233	1,800	Denmark
8	0.4	409	840	3	...	...	...	...	...	...	...	...	Djibouti
7	3.2	37	58	2	...	...	...	...	...	...	...	...	Dominica
29	11.3	2,515	4,210	5	154.0	247.9	2.7	4.0	...	...	...	...	Dominican Republic
158	525.6	8,402	2,518	14	772	1,243	43.3	63.2	932	1,500	...	...	Ecuador

Transportation (continued)

country	roads length mi	roads length km	paved (percent)	auto-mobiles	trucks and buses	persons per vehicle	cargo short ton-mi ('000,000)	cargo metric ton-km ('000,000)	track mi	track km	passenger-mi ('000,000)	passenger-km ('000,000)	cargo short ton-mi ('000,000)	cargo metric ton-km ('000,000)
Egypt	28,272[23]	45,500[23]	68[23]	826,915	550,649	38	21,394	31,235	3,176	5,110	21,671	34,876	1,965	2,868
El Salvador	7,764	12,495	14	75,000	80,000	34	...	...	374[2]	602[2]	3.7	6.0	25.7	37.5
Equatorial Guinea	1,667	2,682	19	5,500	3,500	39	...	...	—	—	—	—	—	—
Estonia	28,000	45,000	98	198,300	...	...	3,089	4,510	640	1,030	1,069	1,721	4,614	6,736
Ethiopia	24,533	39,482	20	42,250	21,000	751	...	...	486[25]	782[25]	185	297	88	128
Faeroe Islands	269	433	...	14,232	3,445	2.7	...	...	—	—	—	—	—	—
Fiji	2,996	4,821	13	40,253	27,589	11	...	...	370[17]	595[17]	—	—	—	—
Finland	47,477	76,407	61	1,926,326	271,082	2.3	18,014	26,300	3,646[2]	5,867[2]	1,645	2,647	5,230	7,635
France	500,576	805,600	92	23,550,000	4,740,000	2.0	100,687	147,000	21,388[2]	34,421[2]	39,512	63,588	35,294	51,528
French Guiana	706	1,137	40	23,520	1,689	4.1	...	...	—	—	—	—	—	—
French Polynesia	492	792	33	37,000	15,000	3.7	...	...	—	—	—	—	—	—
Gabon	4,286	6,898	11	22,000	16,000	31	...	...	403	648	21	34	126	184
Gambia, The	1,483	2,386	32	6,500	1,500	109	...	...	—	—	—	—	—	—
Gaza Strip	...	...	...	18,116	3,937	28	...	...	—	—	—	—	—	—
Georgia	21,000	33,900	87	427,400	...	...	4,168	6,085	976	1,570	10.6	17.0	...	...
Germany	386,037	621,267	...	35,512,083	2,764,191	2.1	117,437	171,455	56,562	91,028	40,131	64,585	83,857	122,429
Ghana	23,702	38,145	20	57,897	30,125	160	873	1,275	592[2]	953[2]	172	278	86.9	127
Gibraltar	27	43	100	17,861	1,338	1.6	...	...	—	—	—	—	—	—
Greece	80,800	130,000	79	1,729,683	792,945	4.1	...	...	1,540[2]	2,479[2]	939.5	1,512	443	648
Greenland	50	80	...	1,990	1,557	16	...	...	—	—	—	—	—	—
Grenada	650	1,046	66	4,784	981	16	...	...	—	—	—	—	—	—
Guadeloupe	1,301	2,093	80	95,962	28,134	2.7	...	...	—	—	—	—	—	—
Guam	419	674	100	52,923	15,754	1.9	...	...	—	—	—	—	—	—
Guatemala	8,297	13,352	26	125,000	100,000	39	...	...	570[2]	917[2]	6.3	10.1	29.2	42.7
Guernsey	...	...	...	34,918	6,143	1.5	...	...	—	—	—	—	—	—
Guinea	17,600	28,400	4	13,500	13,000	259	...	...	411[2]	662[2]	...	...	...	...
Guinea-Bissau	2,100	3,500	15	3,300	2,400	171	...	...	—	—	—	—	—	—
Guyana	3,540	5,697	11	24,000	9,000	23	...	...	55[17]	88[17]	...	...	...	...
Haiti	2,485	4,000	15	33,000	22,000	118	...	...	—	—	—	—	—	—
Honduras	7,066	11,371	21	88,982	18,049	44	...	...	583	939	4.9	7.9	264	386
Hong Kong	950	1,529	100	236,747	132,595	16	...	...	21	34	1,573	2,532	49	72
Hungary	18,480	29,741	99	1,912,200	223,900	4.9	8,986	13,120	8,221	13,230	7,085	11,403	11,474	16,752
Iceland	7,070	11,378	20	119,731	14,450	1.9	318	464	—	—	—	—	—	—
India	1,224,000	1,970,000	49	2,391,000	1,396,000	225	144,000	210,000	38,509[2]	61,975[2]	177,000	284,800	160,200	233,900
Indonesia	155,538	250,314	43	1,372,673	1,533,152	62	17,000	25,000	4,090	6,583	5,771	9,288	2,186	3,192
Iran	86,599	139,368	48	2,008,000	472,000	23	46,750	68,250	2,779[2]	4,473[2]	2,953	4,752	5,454	7,963
Iraq	28,305	45,554	84	744,252	295,744	18	...	...	1,484[2]	2,389[2]	271	436	223	326
Ireland	57,354	92,303	94	796,408	147,213	3.7	3,400	5,000	1,749	2,814	761	1,224	403	589
Isle of Man	357	574	58	39,392	4,443	1.5	...	...	37[2]	59[2]	...	...	...	...
Israel	8,075	12,996	100	786,266	157,886	5.0	...	...	323[2]	520[2]	94.9	152.7	710.7	1,038
Italy	187,904	302,403	100	27,300,000	2,427,000	1.9	111,541	162,847	12,153	19,559	28,282	45,516	14,589	21,300
Jamaica	10,212	16,435	29	95,000	17,000	21	...	...	211[2]	339[2]	22.5	36.1	71.5	104.4
Japan	692,639	1,114,697	69	36,621,085	22,234,567	2.1	168,556	246,088	17,059	27,454	229,172	368,817	17,217	25,136
Jersey	...	...	...	60,747	7,293	1.2	...	...	—	—	—	—	—	—
Jordan	3,733	6,007	100	173,077	65,687	14	19,133	27,934	490[2]	788[2]	3.7	6.0	338	493
Kazakhstan	102,500	164,900	64	734,800	...	...	30,670	44,777	9,040	14,550	11,700	18,800	281	410
Kenya	34,000	54,700	15	150,000	150,000	83	134	196	1,885[2]	3,034[2]	428	688	1,369	1,999
Kiribati	398	640	5	307	130	147	...	...	—	—	—	—	—	—
Korea, North	14,290	23,000	2	...	...	...	...	...	3,122	5,024	...	...	...	...
Korea, South	34,659	55,778	61	2,074,922	1,308,385	13	5,921	8,645	4,012	6,456	18,559	29,868	9,230	13,476
Kuwait	2,655	4,273	100	499,388	110,663	3.5	...	...	—	—	—	—	—	—
Kyrgyzstan	11,900	19,100	86	173,800	...	...	3,858	5,632	490	789	...	...	...	...
Laos	8,681	13,971	21	18,000	4,000	190	...	...	—	—	—	—	—	—
Latvia	49,200	79,100	49	241,700	...	...	4,009	5,853	1,500	2,400	3,582	5,765	...	...
Lebanon	4,579	7,370	85	473,372	49,560	5.0	...	...	259	417	5.3	8.6	29	42
Lesotho	2,930	4,715	12	6,363	15,379	73	...	...	1	2	—	—	—	—
Liberia	5,011	8,064	9	8,000	4,000	217	...	...	304[2]	490[2]	...	...	1,746[17]	2,549[17]
Libya	11,992	19,300	56	448,000	322,000	5.3	...	...	12	19	—	—	—	—
Liechtenstein	201	323	...	16,891	1,673	1.5	...	...	—	—	—	—	—	—
Lithuania	39,800	64,000	86	...	...	...	5,025	7,336	1,951	3,139	2,246	3,615	13,191	19,258
Luxembourg	3,163	5,091	99	183,404	12,009	2.0	164	239	169[2]	272[2]	171	276	490	720
Macau	60	97	100	27,639	5,335	14	...	...	—	—	—	—	—	—
Macedonia	6,581	10,591	48	230,993	22,594	8.0	1,819	2,655	431	693	...	...	...	...
Madagascar	30,792	49,555	11	46,636	33,156	150	220	321	549[2]	883[2]	126	202	140	205
Malawi	7,590	12,215	22	16,118	17,394	254	—	—	495[2]	797[2]	69.4	111.6	48.4	70.6
Malaysia	32,623	52,501	68	1,845,618	407,133	7.9	...	...	1,381	2,222	1,141[36]	1,836[36]	962[36]	1,404[36]
Maldives	...	...	...	623	813	150	...	...	—	—	—	—	—	—
Mali	11,185	18,000	8	29,436	7,556	209	...	...	401	646	454.8	731.9	296.0	432.2
Malta	990	1,593	91	104,863	19,951	2.8	...	...	—	—	—	—	—	—
Marshall Islands	...	...	...	763	80	43	...	...	—	—	—	—	—	—
Martinique	1,050	1,690	75	135,269	7,328	2.3	...	...	—	—	—	—	—	—
Mauritania	4,696	7,558	23	10,000	5,000	133	...	...	428[2]	689[2]	4.4	7.0	5,393	7,873
Mauritius	1,119	1,801	93	29,402	1,929	34	...	...	—	—	—	—	—	—
Mayotte	143	230	49	—1,528—		40	...	...	—	—	—	—	—	—
Mexico	147,300	237,057	35	6,941,104	2,828,479	8.2	73,455	107,243	16,380[2]	26,361[2]	3,358	5,404	23,300	34,000
Micronesia	140	226	17	...	...	...	...	...	—	—	—	—	—	—
Moldova	6,400	10,300	94	177,100	...	...	4,319	6,305	715	1,150	5,515	8,875	10,279	15,007
Monaco	31	50	100	17,000	3,800	1.4	...	...	1	2	...	...	...	...
Mongolia	30,600	49,200	2	...	...	...	1,438	2,099	1,445	2,325	359	578	4,082	5,960
Morocco	36,940	59,450	49	669,637	282,945	26	830	1,212	1,176[2]	1,893[2]	1,387	2,232	3,501	5,112
Mozambique	16,215	26,095	20	87,500	24,000	127	...	...	1,857	2,988	46.8	75.3	158.8	231.8
Myanmar (Burma)	14,579	23,463	38	30,000	43,000	571	71	103.7	1,949[2]	3,137[2]	2,781	4,476	395	576
Namibia	26,570	42,760	11	—122,331—		11	...	...	1,481	2,383	...	...	3,356	4,900
Nauru	10	16	100	—1,448—		6.3	...	...	3[17]	5[17]	...	...	4.7	6.8
Nepal	4,354	7,007	41	14,201	9,988	574	984	1,437	33[2]	53[2]	...	...	...	...

| merchant marine | | | | air | | | | | canals and inland waterways (latest) | | | | country |
fleet, 1991 (vessels over 100 gross tons)	total dead-weight tonnage, 1991 ('000)	international cargo (latest) loaded metric tons ('000)	off-loaded metric tons ('000)	airports with sched-uled flights, 1992	traffic (latest) passengers passenger-mi ('000,000)	passenger-km ('000,000)	cargo short ton-mi ('000,000)	metric ton-km ('000,000)	length mi	km	cargo short ton-mi ('000,000)	metric ton-km ('000,000)	
444	1,852.5	10,596	23,808	10	3,250	5,230	90.4	132	2,175	3,500	1,715	2,504	Egypt
12		265	1,550	1	662[24]	1,066[24]	3.2[24]	4.6[24]	...	...	...	...	El Salvador
2	6.7	100	60	1	4	7	0.7	1.0	...	...	...	...	Equatorial Guinea
...	...	...	...	1	722	1,162	7.5	11.0	...	...	...	...	Estonia
27	84.3	610	3,100	29	999	1,608	115.0	167.9	...	...	...	...	Ethiopia
196	[21]	370	378	1	...	...	...	...	...	...	...	...	Faeroe Islands
62	49.6	585	595	17	548	882	17.4	25.3	126	203	...	...	Fiji
266	875.9	26,616	32,280	25	6,116	9,842	95.2	139	4,148	6,675	2,761	4,031	Finland
761	5,677.7[26]	61,812	177,036	66	24,531[27]	39,479[27]	2,545[27]	3,715[27]	9,278	14,932	5,200	7,600	France
4	[28]	59	342	8	...	...	...	...	286	460	...	...	French Guiana
40	[28]	24	648	36	...	...	...	...	...	...	...	...	French Polynesia
28	30.0	8,890	610	18	276.7	445.3	17.9	26.1	994	1,600	...	...	Gabon
9	1.7	155	210	1	...	...	...	...	250	400	...	...	Gambia, The
—	...	...	...	—	...	...	...	...	—	...	...	...	Gaza Strip
...	...	...	...	1	3,291	5,296	...	...	...	...	...	...	Georgia
1,552	7,323.6	47,496	107,952	39	62,809	101,082	3,064	4,473	4,686	7,541	38,401	56,061	Germany
160	121.0	1,485	2,640	3	253.3	407.6	45.8	66.8	795	1,280	75	110	Ghana
44	2,695.1	4	380	1	...	...	...	...	—	—	...	...	Gibraltar
1,863	41,691.7	21,576	38,532	33	4,824	7,764	84.2	123	50	80	585	854	Greece
90	[21]	283	291	18	16.3	26.3	0.23	0.34	...	...	...	...	Greenland
3	0.5	35	58	2	...	...	...	...	...	...	...	...	Grenada
17	[28]	336	1,368	5	...	...	...	...	...	...	...	...	Guadeloupe
3	[4]	86	177	1	...	...	...	...	...	...	...	...	Guam
7	0.9	3,172	1,820	2	132	213	6.2	9.0	162	260	...	...	Guatemala
—	...	...	...	1	...	...	...	...	...	...	...	...	Guernsey
26	2.8	9,920	690	1	17.9	28.8	1.7	2.5	805	1,295	...	...	Guinea
19	1.8	32	285	2	6	9	0.7	1.0	...	...	...	...	Guinea-Bissau
81	11.0	1,715	665	1	134	216	1.9	2.8	3,700	6,000	...	...	Guyana
3	0.4	164	684	2	...	...	...	...	60	100	...	...	Haiti
846	1,225.1	1,328	1,151	9	321[29]	516[29]	2.0[29]	3.0[29]	289	465	...	...	Honduras
355	10,024.1	27,972[30]	59,616[30]	1	...	...	...	...	...	...	...	...	Hong Kong
17	151.0	...	...	1	1,053	1,695	5.8	8.4	1,008	1,622	9,901	14,455	Hungary
392	118.5	1,230	1,783	21	1,147	1,846	23.7	34.6	...	...	58	84	Iceland
890	10,528.5	22,800	43,320	98	10,264	16,518	454	663	10,054	16,180	...	...	India
1,991	3,130.8	109,560	30,840	116	7,896	12,708	290	424	13,409	21,579	17,000	25,000	Indonesia
401	8,382.9	87,392	13,782	18	3,455	5,561	78.1	114	562	904	...	...	Iran
138	1,589.9	97,830	8,638	3	976	1,570	37.4	54.6	631	1,015	...	...	Iraq
187	203.0	5,993	16,425	11	2,364	3,804	296	432	...	...	...	...	Ireland
114	...	6	203	1	...	...	...	...	...	...	...	...	Isle of Man
58	654.2	7,704	12,384	7	4,363[31]	7,021[31]	569[31]	831[31]	...	...	...	...	Israel
1,652	11,720.0	41,832	226,692	30	14,139[32]	22,754[32]	800.3[32]	1,168[32]	1,500	2,400	94	137	Italy
12	21.3	6,549	4,477	6	806	1,297	14.9	21.7	...	...	...	...	Jamaica
10,063	39,691.7	84,312	711,612	71	59,268	95,383	9,064	13,233	1,100	1,770	145,638	212,628	Japan
—	—	...	...	1	...	...	...	...	...	...	...	...	Jersey
4	135.5	8,868	6,168	2	1,729	2,782	174	254	...	...	19,202	28,035	Jordan
...	...	...	...	5	8,259	13,291	62.0	90.0	...	...	2,638	3,851	Kazakhstan
30	11.6	2,260	5,170	16	919[33]	1,479[33]	120[33]	175[33]	...	...	...	...	Kenya
7	2.7	16	24	18	5.3	8.6	0.5	0.8	3	5	...	...	Kiribati
98	749.2	630	5,386	1	...	...	...	...	1,400	2,253	...	...	Korea, North
2,136	12,227.1	51,984	208,476	12	11,625	18,708	1,708	2,494	1,000	1,609	11,382	16,617	Korea, South
197	2,293.2	61,778	7,123	1	1,186	1,908	198	289	...	...	...	...	Kuwait
...	...	...	...	1	2,304	3,708	...	...	...	...	...	...	Kyrgyzstan
1	1.5	—	—	12	11	18	1.4	2.0	2,850	4,587	...	...	Laos
...	...	...	...	1	2,011	3,237	...	...	...	...	200	292	Latvia
164	424.6	148	1,120	2	934	1,503	16.4	24.0	...	...	...	...	Lebanon
—	—	—	—	8	17.4	28.0	0.5	0.7	—	—	—	—	Lesotho
1,605	93,640.4	22,200	1,430	1	11	17	0.07	0.1	...	...	...	...	Liberia
129	1,469.7	49,420	7,449	11	1,223[34]	1,968[34]	7.1[34]	10.3[34]	...	...	...	...	Libya
—	—	...	...	—	...	...	...	...	...	...	...	...	Liechtenstein
...	...	...	...	3	1.5	2.4	15.8	23.0	...	...	112	164	Lithuania
51	2,854.3	—	—	1	79.5	128	606.9	886.1	23	37	208	304	Luxembourg
6	[35]	750	3,905	—	—	—	—	—	...	...	...	...	Macau
—	—	...	...	1	...	...	...	...	...	...	...	...	Macedonia
86	90.7	540	792	52	319	513	52.5	76.7	...	...	...	...	Madagascar
1	0.3	...	...	5	49	79	9.8	14.3	891	1,434	6.7	9.8	Malawi
508	2,541.9	17,964	31,512	38	7,400	11,909	394	575	4,534	7,296	...	...	Malaysia
42	61.4	23	72	1	...	...	...	...	...	...	...	...	Maldives
—	—	—	—	1	68	110	0.4	0.6	1,128	1,815	18	27	Mali
702	11,853.0	96	2,472	1	561	903	3.3	4.8	...	...	...	...	Malta
28	[4]	26	117	24	...	...	...	...	...	...	...	...	Marshall Islands
6	[28]	1,092	1,260	1	...	...	...	...	...	...	...	...	Martinique
125	22.8	8,960	610	10	129.6	208.6	24.1	35.2	...	...	...	...	Mauritania
37	115.5	890	1,315	1	898	1,467	124.8	182.3	...	...	...	...	Mauritius
1	[28]	...	...	1	...	...	...	...	...	...	...	...	Mayotte
649	1,612.4	132,336	44,856	78	10,215[37]	16,440[37]	1,046[37]	1,527[37]	1,800	2,900	...	...	Mexico
17	[4]	...	...	4	...	...	...	...	...	...	...	...	Micronesia
—	—	...	...	1	1,461	2,352	13.0	19.0	...	...	217	317	Moldova
—	—	...	...	1	—	—	...	...	...	...	...	...	Monaco
...	...	...	...	1	331	532	7.3	10.6	247	397	2.9	4.3	Mongolia
480	600.9	32,052	22,224	16	1,700	2,700	24.0	35.0	...	...	2,622	3,828	Morocco
114	29.9	2,460	3,100	7	344	554	41.5	60.6	2,330	3,750	...	...	Mozambique
154	1,525.6	672	708	20	133.3	214.5	1.5	2.1	7,954	12,800	236.5	345.3	Myanmar (Burma)
1	[28]	483	260	11	...	...	...	...	...	...	...	...	Namibia
3	13.7	1,644	64	1	148[38]	238[38]	1.1[38]	1.6[38]	...	...	...	...	Nauru
—	—	—	—	5	254[34]	408[34]	7.5[34]	10.9[34]	...	...	...	...	Nepal

Transportation (continued)

country	roads and motor vehicles (latest)								railroads (latest)					
	roads		paved (percent)	motor vehicles			cargo		track length		traffic			
	length			auto-mobiles	trucks and buses	persons per vehicle	short ton-mi ('000,000)	metric ton-km ('000,000)	mi	km	passengers		cargo	
	mi	km									passenger-mi ('000,000)	passenger-km ('000,000)	short ton-mi ('000,000)	metric ton-km ('000,000)
Netherlands, The	72,271	116,309	88	5,509,000	555,000	2.5	15,131	22,091	1,757	2,828	6,875	11,064	2,104	3,072
Netherlands Antilles	510	820	...	68,000	15,000	2.3	...	...	—	—	—	—	—	—
New Caledonia	3,580	5,762	22	53,000	19,000	2.3	...	...	—	—	—	—	—	—
New Zealand	57,771	92,974	56	1,557,074	310,671	1.8	...	...	2,627	4,227	285	458	1,837	2,682
Nicaragua	9,319	14,997	10	31,111	42,974	52	...	...	186[2]	300[2]	15.8	25.5	46.6	68.0
Niger	24,836	39,970	8	16,000	18,000	221	...	...	—	—	—	—	—	—
Nigeria	77,000	124,000	48	785,000	625,000	61	...	...	2,178	3,505	2,366	3,808	566.7	827.4
Northern Mariana Islands	186	300	18	16,170	5,602	2.0	...	...	—	—	—	—	—	—
Norway	55,253	88,922	69	1,614,623	383,128	2.1	5,467	7,981	2,600[2]	4,184[2]	1,327	2,136	1,612	2,354
Oman	17,053	27,438	18	140,000	75,266	7.0	...	...	—	—	—	—	—	—
Pakistan	87,040	140,077	46	738,059	171,519	131	...	...	5,453[2]	8,775[2]	12,460	20,052	4,529	6,612
Palau	16	26	...	—— 1,687 ——		7.2	...	...	—	—	—	—	—	—
Panama	6,223	10,015	30	176,708	49,169	10	...	...	250[2]	402[2]	...	...	...	...
Papua New Guinea	12,263	19,736	6	17,532	29,021	76	...	...	—	—	—	—	—	—
Paraguay	15,957	25,681	9	75,000	35,000	39	...	...	274[2]	441[2]	13.5	21.8	13.6	19.8
Peru	43,460	69,942	11	395,000	230,000	34	...	...	2,157[2]	3,472[2]	415	668	636	929
Philippines	98,841	159,069	14	454,554	783,262	49	...	...	658[2]	1,059[2]	164	264	25	36
Poland	225,629	363,116	62	5,260,646	1,136,721	6.0	34,110	49,800	16,297	26,228	31,300	50,373	57,213	83,530
Portugal	43,605	70,176	86	1,605,000	593,000	4.7	6,884	10,051	2,229[2]	3,588[2]	3,519	5,664	1,088	1,588
Puerto Rico	5,810	9,351	87	1,315,587	205,565	2.3	...	...	—	—	—	—	—	—
Qatar	671	1,080	63	88,000	39,000	3.6	...	...	—	—	—	—	—	—
Réunion	1,690	2,719	81	145,000	50,000	3.1	...	...	384[2]	614[2]	—	—	—	—
Romania	45,246	72,816	51	1,292,283	370,685	14	19,859	28,994	6,887	11,083	18,279	29,417	39,215	57,253
Russia	549,000	884,000	74	8,964,000	484,000	16	205,045	299,360	99,900	160,800	169,696	273,100	1,698	2,479
Rwanda	8,185	13,173	9	7,868	2,048	697	140	200	—	—	—	—	—	—
St. Kitts and Nevis	186	300	41	3,600	700	10	...	...	—	—	—	—	—	—
St. Lucia	500	805	56	6,500	4,000	13	...	...	—	—	—	—	—	—
St. Vincent and the Grenadines	534	859	59	5,350	2,814	13	...	...	—	—	—	—	—	—
San Marino	147	237	...	19,360	3,159	1.0	...	...	—	—	—	—	—	—
São Tomé and Príncipe	236	380	66	1,774	265	41	...	...	—	—	—	—	—	—
Saudi Arabia	89,897	144,676	43	2,350,000	2,150,000	3.1	...	...	555[2]	893[2]	75.2	121	549	801
Senegal	8,772	14,117	27	92,000	43,000	54	375	547	713	1,147	24.9	40.0	276.2	403.3
Seychelles	191	308	67	4,301	1,484	12	...	...	—	—	—	—	—	—
Sierra Leone	4,660	7,500	20	35,870	11,789	87	36	53	52	84	...	...	...	...
Singapore	1,762	2,836	97	300,116	127,687	6.5	...	...	16	26	...	...	...	...
Slovenia	9,045	14,553	72	583,923	35,661	3.2	2,645	3,861	849	1,366	...	...	...	...
Solomon Islands	1,300	2,100	8	1,350	2,026	84	...	...	—	—	—	—	—	—
Somalia	10,697	17,215	15	20,000	12,000	234	...	...	—	—	—	—	—	—
South Africa	115,420	185,751	30	3,316,706	1,461,570	6.5	1,053	1,538	15,793[2]	25,417[2]	7,916	12,740	68,794	100,437
Bophuthatswana	3,900	6,300	21	...	...	...	...	...	165	265	...	...	...	...
Ciskei	1,867	3,004	15	...	...	...	...	...	60	96	...	...	...	...
Transkei	5,591	8,998	11	...	...	...	...	...	190	306	...	...	...	...
Venda	1,305	2,100	15	...	...	...	...	...	8	13	...	...	...	...
Spain	201,427	324,166	74	12,010,717	2,385,213	2.7	113,413	165,580	7,806[2]	12,563[2]	9,619	15,480	7,710	11,256
Sri Lanka	16,126	25,952	81	173,519	146,004	53	3,373	4,925	903[2]	1,453[2]	1,544	2,485	114	167
Sudan, The	4,100	6,599	59	116,473	56,949	163	...	...	2,936[2]	4,725[2]	414	667	434	633
Suriname	5,687	9,153	26	36,755	14,473	7.9	...	...	104	167	...	...	...	...
Swaziland	1,740	2,801	26	24,899	8,120	23	...	...	320	515	...	...	73	107
Sweden	83,060	133,673	71	3,605,200	325,100	2.2	17,809	26,000	6,960	11,202	3,363	5,412	12,526	18,288
Switzerland	44,179	71,099	96	3,011,673	285,564	2.1	4,552	6,646	3,120	5,021	7,695	12,384	5,556	8,112
Syria	18,475	29,732	78	117,570	138,603	46	1,075	1,570	948[2]	1,525[2]	813	1,308	847	1,236
Taiwan	12,104	19,479	86	2,636,228	653,869	6.2	5,497	8,025	2,858	4,600	5,357	8,621	1,343	1,961
Tajikistan	8,324	13,396	93	209,100	...	...	3,518	5,136	554	891	6,094	9,808	7,617	11,121
Tanzania	51,023	82,114	4	45,000	55,000	244	...	...	2,218	3,569	2,125	3,420	857	1,248
Thailand	45,499	73,223	53	655,927	1,523,361	25	...	...	2,399[2]	3,861[2]	7,215	11,612	2,254	3,291
Togo	4,688	7,545	24	25,000	15,000	85	...	...	326	525	68	109	8	11
Tonga	269	433	65	1,433	2,784	23	...	...	—	—	—	—	—	—
Trinidad and Tobago	4,906	7,895	46	272,000	70,000	3.6	...	...	—	—	—	—	—	—
Tunisia	18,133	29,183	60	321,101	208,596	15	678	990	1,343[2]	2,162[2]	635	1,019	1,256	1,834
Turkey	228,297	367,409	14	1,884,599	900,848	20	45,008	65,710	5,238[2]	8,430[2]	3,994	6,428	5,445	7,950
Turkmenistan	8,300	13,400	86	170,600	...	...	3,283	4,793	1,317	2,120	...	...	37.6	54.9
Tuvalu	5	8	—	...	...	...	...	...	—	—	—	—	—	—
Uganda	17,605	28,332	22	35,496	14,094	326	...	...	770[2]	1,240[2]	67.7	109	70.5	103
Ukraine	104,300	167,800	94	2,920,000	...	...	54,580	79,685	14,167	22,799	47,200	76,000	324,700	474,000
United Arab Emirates	2,709	4,360	61	302,000	157,000	4.1	...	...	—	—	—	—	—	—
United Kingdom	221,529	356,517	100	19,742,000	2,861,000	2.5	94,111	137,400	23,518[51]	37,849[51]	25,000	40,000	11,800	17,300
United States	3,875,665	6,237,290	90	143,081,443	44,179,104	1.3	784,677	1,145,609	172,893	278,245	12,897	20,756	1,154,973	1,686,232
Uruguay	32,311	52,000	23	252,329	144,728	7.7	500	730	1,868[2]	3,006[2]	87.4	140.6	146	213
Uzbekistan	55,431	89,207	83	790,800	...	...	15,037	21,954	4,200	6,800	2,500	4,000	40,100	58,600
Vanuatu	660	1,062	24	4,200	2,800	21	...	...	—	—	—	—	—	—
Venezuela	48,156	77,500	34	1,615,000	459,000	9.1	...	...	226[2]	363[2]	23.4	37.6	26.4	38.6
Vietnam	53,250	85,700	11	...	...	...	1,182	1,726	2,000	3,218	2,179	3,506	695	1,015
Virgin Islands (U.S.)	532	856	100	32,886	7,289	2.4	...	...	—	—	—	—	—	—
West Bank	...	...	...	40,033	14,324	16	...	...	...	...	...	...	...	...
Western Sahara	3,790	6,100	8	6,284	424	20	...	...	...	...	...	...	...	...
Western Samoa	1,296	2,085	19	2,514	3,048	29	...	...	—	—	—	—	—	—
Yemen	31,764	51,119	10	162,961	237,028	29	...	...	—	—	—	—	—	—
Yugoslavia	28,595	46,019	59	1,407,490	132,482	6.7	14,929[54]	21,796[54]	5,945[54]	9,567[54]	7,178[54]	11,552[54]	16,124[54]	23,541[54]
Zaire	91,031	146,500	12	100,000	90,000	203	...	...	3,193	5,138	162[55]	260[55]	1,186[55]	1,732[55]
Zambia	23,214	37,359	17	98,000	67,000	47	...	...	1,345	2,164	472	759	515	752
Zimbabwe	52,964	85,237	19	178,000	82,000	36	...	...	1,714[2]	2,759[2]	541	870	7.3	10.6

[1]Bakhtar Afghan Airlines only. [2]Route length. [3]Air Algérie international flights only. [4]United States data includes American Samoa, Guam, Puerto Rico, and the U.S. Virgin Islands. [5]TAAG-Angola Airlines only. [6]Aerolineas Argentinas only. [7]Includes Netherlands Antilles. [8]Included with The Netherlands. [9]Government railways only. [10]Bahamasair only. [11]Apportionment of ¼ of international flights of Gulf Air (jointly run by Bahrain, Oman, Qatar, and United Arab Emirates) only. [12]Caribbean Airways only. [13]Caribbean Air Cargo only. [14]1990. [15]Cotonou airport traffic only. [16]Air Botswana only. [17]For industrial purposes only. [18]Air Afrique only. [19]Lasca only. [20]Traffic between Ouagadougou, Burkina Faso, and Abidjan, Côte d'Ivoire. [21]Includes Faeroe Islands and Greenland. [22]Apportionment of ²⁄₇ of SAS operations only. [23]National roads only. [24]TACA airlines only. [25]Includes 100 km of the Chemin de Fer Djibouti-Ethiopien (CDE) in Djibouti. [26]Includes

fleet, 1991 (vessels over 100 gross tons)	total dead-weight tonnage, 1991 ('000)	international cargo (latest)		airports with scheduled flights, 1992	traffic (latest)				length		cargo		country
		loaded metric tons ('000)	off-loaded metric tons ('000)		passengers		cargo		mi	km	short ton-mi ('000,000)	metric ton-km ('000,000)	
					passenger-mi ('000,000)	passenger-km ('000,000)	short ton-mi ('000,000)	metric ton-km ('000,000)					
1,122	4,848.0[39]	90,504	286,716	5	17,620	28,356	1,512	2,208	3,939	6,340	4,723	6,896	Netherlands, The
127	[8]	12,852	9,174	4	234[40]	377[40]	1.2[40]	1.8[40]	...	...	...	...	Netherlands Antilles
17	[28]	1,224	873	10	79.7[41]	128[41]	0.34[41]	0.54[41]	...	...	...	...	New Caledonia
136	319.0	14,952	7,860	36	6,591	10,608	227	332	1,000	1,609	1,503	2,195	New Zealand
25	3.0	328	1,603	1	68.8	110.7	2.5	3.6	1,379	2,220	...	...	Nicaragua
—	—	—	—	1	129.6	208.6	24.1	35.2	186	300	...	...	Niger
259	718.6	65,700	9,900	13	159	256	21.0	30.6	5,328	8,575	...	...	Nigeria
2	[4]	...	...	3	...	...	...	...	...	...	...	...	Northern Mariana Islands
2,577	40,950.1	89,100	18,900	47	3,676[22]	5,916[22]	102.0[22]	148.9[22]	980	1,577	5,924	8,649	Norway
27	11.9	29,230	2,450	6	1,042[11]	1,676[11]	35.1[11]	51.2[11]	...	...	...	...	Oman
74	513.1	5,388	19,644	35	5,831	9,384	293	428	...	...	...	...	Pakistan
4	[4]	2	56	1	...	...	...	...	...	...	...	...	Palau
4,953	72,169.7	100,032	63,288	8	122	196	1.7	2.4	497	800	...	...	Panama
85	31.0	2,331	1,834	98	388	624	10.1	14.7	6,798	10,940	...	...	Papua New Guinea
38	38.5	...	...	1	355	571	2.4	3.5	1,900	3,100	...	...	Paraguay
618	788.4	8,851	5,020	22	1,264	2,034	137	200	5,300	8,600	...	...	Peru
1,465	14,258.2	14,112	31,656	31	5,783[42]	9,307[42]	183[42]	267[42]	2,000	3,219	...	...	Philippines
673	4,432.0	24,912	12,960	12	2,753	4,430	39.0	57.0	2,484	3,997	708	1,034	Poland
331	1,425.8[34]	7,334	18,958	17	4,277	6,883	547	799	510	820	...	...	Portugal
20	[4]	4	4	7	...	...	...	...	...	...	...	...	Puerto Rico
64	724.3	14,085	2,345	1	963[11]	1,549[11]	30.3[11]	44.3[11]	...	...	...	...	Qatar
7	[28]	300	800	1	...	...	...	...	...	...	...	...	Réunion
469	5,772.4	8,652	21,396	14	1,140	1,834	109	159	1,071	1,724	1,432	2,090	Romania
...	...	...	...	58	95,132	153,100	2,755	4,022	...	...	146,543	213,949	Russia
—	...	...	...	3	...	...	...	...	...	...	...	...	Rwanda
1	0.6	31	38	2	...	...	...	...	...	...	...	...	St. Kitts and Nevis
7	2.1	151	238	2	...	...	...	...	...	...	...	...	St. Lucia
698	4,221.1	79	131	5	...	...	...	...	...	...	...	...	St. Vincent and the Grenadines
—	—	—	—	—	—	—	—	—	...	...	...	...	San Marino
3	1.2	12	22	2	3.8	6.1	0.07	0.1	...	...	...	...	São Tomé and Príncipe
309	1,999.5	150,666	42,546	25	9,984	16,068	418	610	...	...	...	...	Saudi Arabia
167	38.7	2,465	2,690	9	129.6[34]	208.6[34]	24.1[34]	35.2[34]	560	900	...	...	Senegal
8	2.7	7	260	1	...	...	...	...	...	...	...	...	Seychelles
59	12.8	1,200	510	2	68.3[43]	109.9[43]	1.4[43]	2.0[43]	500	800	447	652	Sierra Leone
854	13,719.6	89,700	116,484	1	20,792	33,462	1,270	1,854	...	...	...	...	Singapore
...	...	...	...	1	359	577	833	1,216	...	...	...	...	Slovenia
35	5.8	280	356	20	7[44]	12[44]	0.02[44]	0.04[44]	...	...	...	...	Solomon Islands
27	18.9	317	1,210	5	84.6	136.1	1.4	2.0	...	...	...	...	Somalia
231	283.8	95,904	13,560	41	5,201[45]	8,370[45]	131[45]	191[45]	...	...	...	...	South Africa
—	—	—	—	1	...	...	...	...	...	...	...	...	Bophuthatswana
—	—	—	—	1	...	...	...	...	...	...	...	...	Ciskei
—	—	—	—	1	—	—	—	—	...	...	...	...	Transkei
—	—	—	—	1	...	...	...	...	...	...	...	...	Venda
2,305	5,831.7	39,684	129,528	31	15,319	24,653	2,006	2,929	649	1,045	21,836[46]	31,880[46]	Spain
78	513.1	4,188	6,708	1	2,166	3,486	67.6	98.7	267	430	...	...	Sri Lanka
16	62.2	1,390	3,480	12	366[47]	589[47]	8.8[47]	12.9[47]	3,300	5,310	...	...	Sudan, The
24	15.7	5,345	1,252	3	345[48]	555[48]	15.7[48]	23.0[48]	746	1,200	...	...	Suriname
—	—	—	—	1	14	22	1.5	2.2	—	—	—	—	Swaziland
684	3,578.3	45,480	53,460	42	4,511[49]	7,260[49]	139[49]	203[49]	1,275	2,052	4,795	7,000	Sweden
21	486.5	...	...	6	9,422	15,163	647	945	40	65	108	158	Switzerland
79	179.3	16,224	5,076	5	719	1,157	9.9	14.4	418	672	...	...	Syria
644	9,013.3	114,462	186,600	12	18,042	29,036	2,646	3,863	...	...	...	...	Taiwan
...	...	...	...	1	3,214	5,173	22.1	32.3	...	...	...	...	Tajikistan
38	47.5	770	3,100	19	174	280	3.0	4.4	...	...	...	...	Tanzania
333	1,066.9	26,126	26,586	24	11,368	18,295	594	867	2,300	3,701	...	...	Thailand
8	34.1	805	750	1	20.1	32.3	3.9	5.8	—	—	...	...	Togo
17	51.0	21	105	6	3.7	5.9	0.01	0.02	...	...	...	...	Tonga
48	12.5	7,736	4,076	2	1,694[50]	2,726[50]	9.9[50]	14.4[50]	...	...	...	...	Trinidad and Tobago
71	439.8	5,916	10,056	5	875	1,408	12.2	17.8	...	...	...	...	Tunisia
880	7,043.6	42,072	76,920	12	2,620	4,216	53.1	77.5	750	1,200	35	51	Turkey
...	...	...	...	1	2,021	3,253	222	324	...	...	...	...	Turkmenistan
2	0.8	...	...	1	...	...	...	...	...	...	...	...	Tuvalu
3	...	...	...	1	118	190	14	20	...	...	...	...	Uganda
...	...	...	...	20	10,000	16,100	85.6	125	...	...	8,168	11,925	Ukraine
279	1,360.9	63,380	8,973	4	2,411[11]	3,880[11]	98.6[11]	144[11]	...	...	...	...	United Arab Emirates
1,835	8,299.7	128,316	171,588	56	50,786	81,732	1,844	2,692	1,424	2,291	39,500	57,700	United Kingdom
6,143	30,064.3[34]	389,568[52]	448,860[52]	834	467,096	751,720	10,275	15,001	25,482	41,009	489,321	714,396	United States
91	156.6	670[53]	1,415[53]	7	293	471	1.8	2.6	1,000	1,600	...	...	Uruguay
...	...	...	...	1	6,800	11,000	47,700	69,600	...	...	...	...	Uzbekistan
287	3,328.7	77	74	28	—	—	—	—	...	...	...	...	Vanuatu
278	1,437.1	82,082	17,566	32	2,505	4,032	78.8	115	4,400	7,100	...	...	Venezuela
230	871.7	305	1,486	4	6,363	10,240	4.1	6.0	11,000	17,702	...	...	Vietnam
2	[4]	105.5	648.3	4	...	...	...	...	...	...	...	...	Virgin Islands (U.S.)
—	—	—	—	—	...	...	...	...	...	...	...	...	West Bank
...	...	45	15	1	...	...	...	...	...	...	...	...	Western Sahara
7	6.5	108	60	2	...	...	...	...	...	...	...	...	Western Samoa
39	13.7	1,836	7,189	12	641	1,032	8.0	11.7	...	...	...	...	Yemen
462[54]	5,173.1[54]	7,296[54]	26,772[54]	14[54]	5,375[54]	8,651[54]	92.5[54]	135[54]	1,616[54]	2,600[54]	3,430[54]	5,007[54]	Yugoslavia
30	75.9	2,500	1,400	26	303[56]	487[56]	35.7[56]	52.1[56]	9,300	15,000	678	990	Zaire
—	—	—	—	8	144.3	232.2	6.6	9.7	1,398	2,250	...	...	Zambia
—	—	—	—	8	441	709	8.5	12.4	...	...	...	...	Zimbabwe

French overseas territories.   [27]Air France, UTA, and Air Inter only.   [28]Included with France.   [29]TAN and SAHSA airlines only.   [30]Includes transshipments.   [31]El Al only.   [32]Alitalia only.   [33]Kenya Airways only.   [34]International traffic only.   [35]Included with Portugal.   [36]Peninsular Malaysia and Singapore.   [37]Aeronaves de Mexico and Mexicana only.   [38]Air Nauru only.   [39]Includes Netherlands Antilles and Aruba.   [40]Antillean Airlines only.   [41]Air Caledonie only.   [42]PAL only.   [43]Sierra Leone Airlines international traffic only.   [44]Solair only.   [45]SAA only.   [46]Coastal shipping only.   [47]Sudan Airways only.   [48]Suriname Airways only.   [49]Apportionment of 3/7 of SAS operations only.   [50]BWIA international traffic only.   [51]British Railways only; excludes Northern Ireland.   [52]Includes Puerto Rico.   [53]Port of Montevideo only.   [54]Data refer to Yugoslavia as constituted prior to 1991.   [55]Zaire National Railways only.   [56]Air Zaire only.

Communications

The "Communications" table has been redesigned for 1993. It combines the most important subject matter on publishing (books, periodicals, pamphlets, and newspapers) from *Britannica World Data*'s former "Cultural institutions" table with comparably important elements (on post offices, telecommunications [radio, television, and telephones], and cinema) from the previous "Communications" table, so as to achieve a better-integrated presentation of all these media. Virtually all the states of the world have a variety of communications media and services available to their citizens: book publishing and newspapers (although only daily papers are included in this table); postal services; radio and television broadcast systems; telephones; and cinema. Unfortunately, the availability of information about the structure and volume of these national services and sectors often runs behind the capabilities of the services themselves. Certain countries publish no official information; others publish data analyzed according to a variety of fiscal, calendar, religious, or other years; still others, while they possess such data almost simultaneously with the end of the business year, may not see them published except in company or parastatal reports of limited distribution. Even when such data are published in national statistical summaries, it may be only after a delay of up to several years.

The data also differ in their completeness and reliability. Figures for book production, for example, generally include all works published in separate bindings except advertising works, timetables, telephone directories, price lists, catalogs of businesses or exhibitions, musical scores, maps, atlases, and the like. The figures include government publications, school texts, theses, offprints, series works, and illustrated works, even those consisting principally of illustrations. Figures refer to works actually published during the year of survey, usually by a registered publisher, and deposited for copyright. A book is defined as a work of 49 or more pages, a pamphlet as a work of from 5 to 48 pages. A work published simultaneously in more than one country is counted as having been published in each. Newspaper statistics are especially difficult to collect and compare. Newspapers continually are founded, cease publication, merge, or change frequency of publication. Data on circulation, sales, and readership are often incomplete, slow to be aggregated at the national level, or regarded as proprietary. In some countries circulation data are virtually nonexistent. In others no daily newspaper exists.

Post office statistics are compiled mainly from the Universal Postal Union's annual summary *Statistique des services postaux*. Postal services, unlike the other media discussed earlier, tend most often to be operated by a single national service, to cover a country completely, and to record traffic data according to broadly similar schemes (although the details of *classes* of mail handled may differ). Some countries do not enumerate

Communications

country	publishing (latest)							daily newspapers (latest)		
	number of titles			number of copies ('000)						
	books		periodicals	pamphlets	books		periodicals	pamphlets	number	total circulation ('000)	circulation per 1,000 population
	total	school textbooks			total	school textbooks					
Afghanistan	...	...	71	...	...	...	...	...	14	151	10
Albania	1,651	...	143	...	8,066	...	3,477	...	2	135	42
Algeria	551	39	26	167	...	...	...	...	6	1,400	56
American Samoa	...	...	...	...	...	...	...	...	3	9	222
Andorra	45	1	15	...	...	...	15	...	—	—	—
Angola	14	...	...	...	130	...	...	...	4	112	14
Antigua and Barbuda	...	...	...	...	...	...	...	...	1	6	75
Argentina	4,836	...	...	...	...	...	...	...	194	...	...
Armenia	817[9]	...	76	9	10,100[9]	...	28,800	9	82	1,678	503
Aruba	...	...	...	...	...	...	...	...	5	...	...
Australia	6,644	469	...	4,319	...	...	...	...	71	6,689	405
Austria	8,912	...	2,549	550	...	...	...	...	30	...	...
Azerbaijan	829[9]	...	91	9	12,500[9]	...	49,100	9	154	2,900	416
Bahamas, The	...	...	...	...	...	...	...	...	3	35	141
Bahrain	46	...	...	...	...	...	...	...	5	...	...
Bangladesh	1,209	...	41	...	...	...	163	...	68	918	9
Barbados	18	...	52	69	...	...	...	...	2	41	161
Belarus	2,006[9]	...	129	9	94,800[9]	...	54,100	9	220	5,400	528
Belgium	6,150	...	12,222	672	...	...	...	...	35	2,121	213
Belize	12	...	...	...	156	...	...	...	—	—	—
Benin	...	...	...	...	...	...	...	...	1	12	3
Bermuda	...	...	...	...	...	...	...	...	1	18	305
Bhutan	...	...	...	...	...	...	...	...	—	—	—
Bolivia	365	...	106	82	365	...	...	46	16	...	...
Bosnia and Hercegovina	966	...	92	...	7,540	...	1,887	...	4	135	31
Botswana	134	18	20	155	...	...	153	...	1	35	28
Brazil	13,973	...	3,782	3,675	...	...	980	...	288	...	...
Brunei	16	8	4	...	52	34	...	...	—	—	—
Bulgaria	3,746	1,060	994	797	50,037	13,953	6,091	7,950	17	2,396	267
Burkina Faso	4	...	32	...	9	...	...	...	2	9	0.9
Burundi	37	9	...	17	274	229	...	174	1	20	4
Cambodia	...	...	...	...	...	...	...	...	...	...	...
Cameroon	...	...	58	...	...	...	127	...	1	66	5
Canada	12,750	...	1,444	...	...	...	38,540	...	110	5,800	221
Cape Verde	9	—	...	1	9	—	...	1	...	...	...
Cayman Islands	...	...	...	...	...	...	...	...	1	6	262
Central African Republic	...	...	...	...	...	...	...	...	1	0.2	0.1
Chad	...	...	10	...	...	...	...	...	1	2	0.3
Chile	1,716	...	255	634	...	...	...	...	39	840	67
China	74,968	...	6,078	...	5,864,460	...	1,840,000	...	78	...	...
Colombia	1,486	214	...	...	...	...	...	...	31	1,317	40
Comoros	...	...	...	...	...	...	...	...	—	—	—
Congo	...	...	21	...	...	...	64	...	2	16	7
Cook Islands	...	...	3	...	...	...	4	...	1	2	100
Costa Rica	186	...	274	12	...	...	163	...	6	308	105
Côte d'Ivoire	46	13	12	...	3,766	3,517	325	...	2	130	11
Croatia	2,239	...	352	...	12,220	...	6,357	...	9	636	133
Cuba	1,735	1,043	108	469	44,032	21,968	2,894	6,501	19	1,614	155
Cyprus	435	33	59	126	422	132	237	169	11	90	162
Czechoslovakia	8,205	2,956	942	1,089	71,359	17,490	25,362	9,234	30	5,100	327
Denmark	7,291	...	209	3,471	...	...	7,283	...	46	1,853	361
Djibouti	...	...	...	...	...	...	...	...	1	4	8
Dominica	...	...	...	...	...	...	...	...	—	—	—
Dominican Republic	...	...	277	...	...	...	...	1,320	8	257	37
Ecuador	...	...	...	...	...	...	...	...	26	...	...
Egypt	1,311	256	241	140	20,096	14,267	1,696	2,967	18	...	...
El Salvador	15	6	...	...	63	21	...	...	6	270	52
Equatorial Guinea	17	...	...	—	17	...	...	...	2	...	...
Estonia	1,628[9]	...	161	9	18,900[9]	...	40,300	9	111	2,556	1,620
Ethiopia	347	170	3	213	...	...	14	...	3	47	0.9

domestic traffic or may record only international traffic requiring handling charges.

Data for some kinds of communications apparatus and traffic are relatively easy to collect; telephones, for example, even mobile, must be installed, and service recorded so that it may be charged. But in most countries radios may be purchased by anyone and turned on whenever desired; car radios are seldom enumerated or licensed separately. As a result, data on distribution and use of radio and television apparatus may be collected in a variety of ways—on the basis of numbers of subscribers, licenses issued, periodic sample surveys, census or housing surveys, or private consumer surveys. Statistics on commercial cinema attendance (usually those of the United Nations Educational, Scientific and Cultural Organization [Unesco] or national data) may refer to a variety of screening facilities, including fixed, mobile, or drive-in facilities.

The *Statistical Yearbook* of Unesco contains extensive data on book publishing, newspapers, radio and television, and cinema that have been collected from standardized questionnaires. The quality and recency of its data, however, depend on the completion and timely return of each questionnaire by national authorities, and response rates depend on a variety of factors. In general, however, response rates for inquiries by international organizations in communications are better than in other fields because these organizations and the responsible authorities in each country must conduct day-to-day business and, hence, have a better ongoing relationship. The commercially published annual *World Radio TV Handbook* (A. G. Sennitt, editor) is a valuable source of information on broadcast media and has complete and timely coverage. It depends on data received from broadcasters, but, because some do not respond, local correspondents and monitors are used in many countries, and some unconfirmed or unofficial data are included as estimates. The statistics on telephones are derived mainly from the UN-affiliated International Telecommunication Union's (ITU's) *Yearbook of Common Carrier Telecommunication Statistics* and from a variety of national and regional intergovernmental sources. A number of countries report incomplete telephone data: the national total may exclude figures for some telephone companies, or some portion of the national territory; some countries supply statistics only on telephone exchange lines; some island states report only radio telephones. A number of countries omit data on public coin-box telephones; their statistics thus reflect an undercount.

... Not available.

—None, nil, or not applicable.

post offices, 1990				radio, 1991		television, 1991		telephones, 1990		cinema (latest) annual attendance		country
number	persons per office	pieces of mail handled ('000)	pieces of mail handled per capita	receivers (all types; '000)	persons per receiver	receivers (all types; '000)	persons per receiver	receivers ('000)	persons per receiver	number ('000,000)	per 1,000 population	
358[1]	41,400[1]	36,981[1,2]	2.5[1,2]	1,400	12	100	169	31[3]	443[3]	...	...	Afghanistan
613[4]	5,020[4]	13,763[4]	4.5[4]	525	6.3	246[5]	135[5]	4.8[6]	580[6]	6.9	2,160	Albania
2,828	8,840	401,378	16	5,500	4.7	1,600	16	1,103	23	21.0	880	Algeria
...	...	...	...	20	2.4	8.0	6.0	7.3[7]	5.0[7]	...	...	American Samoa
...	...	3,483[8]	90[8]	10	5.5	6.0[4]	8.1[4]	21[3]	1.9[3]	...	...	Andorra
133	64,700	9,268	1.1	450	23	50	206	77[1]	125[1]	3.2	370	Angola
...	...	...	...	75	1.1	2	28	11[3]	7.2[3]	...	...	Antigua and Barbuda
5,117	6,290	449,721[1,2]	14[1,2]	21,582	1.5	7,165	4.5	4,622	7.0	25.3	800	Argentina
931[10]	3,580[10]	63,500[11]	19[11]	401[5]	8.3[5]	722[5]	4.6[5]	595[12]	6.0[12]	13.4	4,020	Armenia
...	...	...	...	40	1.6	19	3.4	36	1.8	...	...	Aruba
4,361	3,910	3,493,185	205	20,000	0.9	7,000	2.5	8,727[13]	1.8[13]	39.8	2,360	Australia
2,665[1,14]	2,860[1,14]	3,406,656[1]	450[1]	4,700	1.7	2,688	2.9	4,541	1.7	10.2	1,340	Austria
1,967[10,15]	3,550[10,15]	122,000[11]	17[11]	3,682[15]	1.9[15]	...	...	...	...	45.7	6,550	Azerbaijan
128[1]	1,960[1]	60,526[1]	240[1]	200	1.3	50	5.2	140	1.8	...	...	Bahamas, The
11	45,700	48,233[16,17,18]	96[16,17,18]	250	2.1	186	2.8	153	3.3	1.0	2,100	Bahrain
7,985[1]	13,100[1]	255,292[1]	2.4[1]	4,500	25	350	320	249	433	302.3	3,000	Bangladesh
16	16,100	18,756	73	200	1.3	69	3.7	118	2.2	...	...	Barbados
4,233[10,15]	2,400[10,15]	302,000[11]	29[11]	2,658[1]	3.8[1]	3,122[1]	3.3[1]	1,635	6.3	121.0	11,800	Belarus
1,821	5,470	3,378,640	340	4,521	2.2	4,200	2.4	5,429	1.8	16.1	1,630	Belgium
112[7]	1,520[7]	3,096[7]	18[7]	100	1.9	12	16	16	12	...	...	Belize
193	24,000	4,548	1.0	350	14	16	292	16	293	1.3	330	Benin
16[1]	3,680[1]	18,200[1,16,17,18]	310[1,16,17,18]	100	0.6	30	2.0	51	1.2	0.2	3,630	Bermuda
84	17,200	3,750	2.6	22	67	...	...	1.9[7]	675[7]	...	...	Bhutan
216	33,900	12,923	1.8	4,000	1.9	610	12	194[5]	37[5]	4.6	650	Bolivia
656	6,630	128,886	30	733[5]	5.9[5]	629[5]	6.9[5]	727	6.0	4.3	1,000	Bosnia and Hercegovina
164[1]	7,490[1]	61,618[1]	50[1]	1,100	1.2	8.0[4]	143[4]	50	27	...	...	Botswana
11,495	12,800	2,723,347[19]	18[19]	60,000	2.6	30,000	5.1	14,125	10	91.3	680	Brazil
13	19,700	7,513	29	100	2.6	100	2.6	49[1]	5.2[1]	2.3	11,900	Brunei
3,141	2,860	563,612[18]	63[18]	2,000	4.5	2,300	3.9	2,515[1]	3.6[1]	68.0	7,750	Bulgaria
145	62,200	3,552[1,2]	0.4[1,2]	200	46	42	223	18[15]	485[15]	6.0	720	Burkina Faso
44	121,000	5,023	0.9	500	11	4.5	1,210	10	523	0.1	24	Burundi
...	...	...	...	800	11	70	125	7.3[20]	790[20]	...	...	Cambodia
1,595	7,420	...	...	2,000	6.1	5.0	2,450	61[15]	185[15]	...	...	Cameroon
16,734[1]	1,570[1]	9,004,547[1,19]	340[1,19]	22,600	1.2	16,000	1.7	20,126[4]	1.3[4]	78.8	3,040	Canada
62	5,430	2,068	6.1	50	6.8	...	...	7.8[15]	42[15]	...	...	Cape Verde
15[1]	1,730[1]	2,788[1]	110[1]	18	1.5	4.0[4]	5.7[4]	19	1.4	...	...	Cayman Islands
76[4]	35,500[4]	...	...	550	5.3	6.0[4]	449[4]	7.3[15]	370[15]	...	...	Central African Republic
88	64,500	3,660	0.6	1,250	4.7	5.0[4]	1,050[4]	8.0	716	...	...	Chad
1,118	11,800	229,499	17	4,250	3.1	3,200[1]	4.1[1]	1,096	12	13.8	1,100	Chile
51,233	22,100	5,509,676[17,19]	4.9[17,19]	121,212[5]	9.4[5]	126,000	9.1	12,735	90	16,878	15,300	China
1,678	19,700	220,456	6.7	33,253	1.0	5,500	6.1	2,909	11	41.0	1,290	Colombia
...	...	...	...	50	9.6	0.1[4]	4,190[4]	4.0[1]	113[1]	...	...	Comoros
124	18,300	2,582[16]	1.1[16]	250	9.3	5.8	404	26[1]	86[1]	...	...	Congo
127	1,430[7]	1,815[7]	110[7]	5.0	3.4	3.5	4.9	4.2	4.1	...	...	Cook Islands
316	9,540	54,443	18	255	12	611	5.1	450	6.8	0.2	76	Costa Rica
383	31,300	27,604[17]	2.3[17]	1,500	8.3	810	15	153	80	...	...	Côte d'Ivoire
1,087	4,390	324,474	68	1,105[5]	4.3[5]	1,027[5]	4.6[5]	1,101	4.3	8.1	1,690	Croatia
903[15]	11,500[15]	116,244[15]	11[15]	3,500	3.1	2,500	4.3	610	18	44.8	4,260	Cuba
774	730	46,696[16,17]	82[16,17]	270	2.1	234	2.5	370	1.5	...	...	Cyprus
5,958[14]	2,610[14]	1,529,163	98	10,500	1.5	5,720	2.7	4,278	3.6	70.6	4,550	Czechoslovakia
1,392	3,690	1,789,802	350	2,235	2.3	3,000	1.7	5,000	1.0	10.3	2,010	Denmark
5[8]	76,600[8]	1,623[8]	4.2[8]	30	18	14	39	15	37	...	...	Djibouti
63[8]	1,210[8]	2,051[8]	27[8]	45	1.9	5.2	16	15	4.9	...	...	Dominica
201[4]	33,300[4]	4,609[4]	0.7[4]	1,150	6.4	728	10	293[15]	24[15]	...	...	Dominican Republic
468	21,700	19,412	1.9	3,000	3.5	700	15	540	19	10.1	1,060	Ecuador
7,360	7,220	289,529	5.4	14,000	3.9	3,750	14	2,233	24	30.3	620	Egypt
309	17,100	20,928	3.9	1,935	2.8	500	11	250	21	...	...	El Salvador
201[1]	17,100[1]	...	...	100	3.6	2.5	143	2.0[4]	163[4]	...	...	Equatorial Guinea
...	...	73,400[11]	47[11]	926[1]	1.7[1]	605[1]	2.6[1]	304[7]	5.1[7]	15.0	9,510	Estonia
924	54,500	34,182	0.7	9,000	5.8	100	518	159	325	...	...	Ethiopia

Communications (continued)

country	publishing (latest) number of titles books total	school textbooks	periodicals	pamphlets	number of copies ('000) books total	school textbooks	periodicals	pamphlets	daily newspapers (latest) number	total circulation ('000)	circulation per 1,000 population
Faeroe Islands	148	...	...	...	...	...	...	...	—	40	56
Fiji	10	·6	...	3	20	12	...	6	2	40	56
Finland	7,697	547	6,941	2,400	...	...	195,381	...	54	2,596	521
France	40,115	1,282	22,443	...	...	...	...	...	114	...	...
French Guiana	...	...	7	...	...	...	6	...	2	5	45
French Polynesia	...	...	...	...	...	...	...	...	3	23	126
Gabon	...	...	...	...	...	...	...	...	1	15	14
Gambia, The	23	2	...	19	31	22	...	32	1	1	1.2
Gaza Strip	...	...	...	...	...	...	...	...	—	...	...
Georgia	1,659[9]	...	75	9	20,100[9]	...	29,700	9	147	3,677	679
Germany	71,998	3,810	8,111	...	...	...	296,143	...	395	32,655	420
Ghana	338	27	...	12	...	...	...	...	3	180	13
Gibraltar	...	...	15	...	...	...	4	...	2	3	100
Greece	4,651	...	309	...	...	...	...	...	145	...	...
Greenland	...	...	...	...	...	...	...	...	—	—	—
Grenada	...	...	...	...	...	...	...	...	—	—	—
Guadeloupe	...	...	45	...	...	...	142	...	1	20	50
Guam	...	...	...	...	...	...	...	...	1	20	152
Guatemala	...	...	...	...	...	...	...	...	8	...	...
Guernsey	...	...	...	...	...	...	...	...	1	16	277
Guinea	...	...	...	...	...	...	...	...	—	...	...
Guinea-Bissau	...	...	...	...	...	...	...	...	2	12	12
Guyana	9	—	...	35	...	...	...	...	1	58	77
Haiti	188	17	...	83	...	...	...	...	4	45	7
Honduras	...	...	...	...	...	...	...	...	6	218	49
Hong Kong	3,642	538	495	2,039	27,483	7,771	...	16,829	69	...	...
Hungary	7,599	1,147	1,559	1,032	108,420	24,185	13,390	15,259	31	2,510	237
Iceland	886	121	...	364	...	...	...	...	6	131	518
India	11,614	357	19,937	...	...	...	50,094	...	2,281	17,000	21
Indonesia	1,279	39	1,456	117	...	...	3,622	...	60	3,716	22
Iran	6,289	...	314	...	31,565	...	...	...	17	...	...
Iraq	82	...	...	...	452	...	...	...	7	522	30
Ireland	628	...	257	2,051	...	...	2,975	...	7	669	191
Isle of Man	...	...	...	...	...	...	...	...	—	—	—
Israel	2,038	291	807	176	8,872	3,961	...	...	28	1,611	350
Italy	20,672	1,555	9,158	1,975	186,594	49,222	3,958	13,818	73	6,005	105
Jamaica	23	3	...	48	...	...	...	...	3	122	51
Japan	36,346	1,657	2,138	...	315,225	2,117	36,293	...	125	51,908	429
Jersey	...	...	...	...	...	...	...	...	1	24	300
Jordan	...	...	29	...	...	...	36	...	5	230	73
Kazakhstan	2,055[9]	...	88	9	28,800[9]	...	33,300	9	450	6,700	403
Kenya	933	...	...	...	...	...	...	...	5	...	...
Kiribati	...	...	...	...	...	...	...	...	—	...	...
Korea, North	...	...	...	...	...	...	...	...	16	...	...
Korea, South	34,516	2,982	...	4,751	172,143	90,590	...	20,995	39	...	...
Kuwait	749	...	73	44	...	...	257	...	9	374	191
Kyrgyzstan	936[9]	...	50	9	9,700[9]	...	34,400	9	122	1,623	375
Laos	...	...	...	...	...	...	...	...	3	31	8
Latvia	1,564[9]	...	243	9	20,800[9]	...	68,300	9	172	4,296	1,622
Lebanon	...	...	...	...	...	...	...	...	39	...	...
Lesotho	...	...	2	...	...	...	11	...	3	17	10
Liberia	...	...	...	...	...	...	...	...	7	...	...
Libya	121	20	...	...	553	180	...	—	1	40	10
Liechtenstein	...	...	79	...	...	...	220	...	2	16	577
Lithuania	2,686[9]	...	135	9	23,700[9]	...	40,400	9	140	2,595	712
Luxembourg	362	13	430	158	...	...	...	...	5	144	380
Macau	...	...	11	...	...	...	...	...	8	242	568
Macedonia	559	...	74	...	1,683	...	347	...	2	47	23
Madagascar	88	20	121	58	343	61	261	388	6	69	6
Malawi	66	5	14	75	...	...	124	...	1	25	3
Malaysia	3,225	943	1,631	123	13,126	7,703	1,689	721	47	2,462	145
Maldives	...	...	64	...	...	...	70	...	2	2	11
Mali	160	76	...	...	92	56	...	...	1	40	5
Malta	262	16	336	124	...	...	...	...	3	67	192
Marshall Islands	...	...	...	...	...	...	...	...	—	—	—
Martinique	...	...	8	...	...	...	17	...	1	30	83
Mauritania	...	...	...	...	...	...	...	...	1	...	...
Mauritius	74	17	58	26	195	86	...	47	7	82	76
Mayotte	...	...	...	...	...	...	...	...	1	12	160
Mexico	3,490	107	203	...	...	...	27,203	...	392	11,256	142
Micronesia	...	...	...	...	...	...	...	...	—	—	—
Moldova	1,277[9]	...	68	9	19,800[9]	...	38,400	9	189	2,400	561
Monaco	48	...	...	...	541	...	...	...	—	—	—
Mongolia	889	...	38	...	6,923	...	633	...	2	173	84
Morocco	...	...	...	...	...	...	...	...	11	...	...
Mozambique	29	...	5	37	3,130	...	2,263	360	2	49	3
Myanmar (Burma)	673	...	...	...	...	...	...	...	6	498	12
Namibia	...	...	...	...	...	...	...	...	3	18	14
Nauru	...	...	...	...	...	...	...	...	—	—	—
Nepal	122	122	...	...	7,243	7,243	...	...	63	...	...
Netherlands, The	15,392	2,494	...	...	...	...	...	...	46	4,606	313
Netherlands Antilles	...	...	...	...	...	...	...	...	6	...	...
New Caledonia	11	...	15	3	...	...	27	...	1	19	118
New Zealand	1,601	14	5,788	1,851	...	...	...	...	34	1,031	306
Nicaragua	27	—	...	14	271	—	...	192	7	...	...

post offices, 1990				radio, 1991		television, 1991		telephones, 1990		cinema (latest)		country
number	persons per office	pieces of mail handled ('000)	pieces of mail handled per capita	receivers (all types; '000)	persons per receiver	receivers (all types; '000)	persons per receiver	receivers ('000)	persons per receiver	annual attendance number ('000,000)	per 1,000 population	
...	...	...	...	20	2.4	14	3.4	24[20]	2.0[20]	...	500	Faeroe Islands
260	2,810	19,477	27	450	1.6	10	73	73	10	...	...	Fiji
3,632[8]	1,340[8]	1,098,005[8]	230[8]	4,950	1.0	1,900	2.6	3,700	1.4	7.2	1,450	Finland
16,967[21]	3,430[21]	20,510,000[21]	350[21]	49,000	1.2	29,300	1.9	34,346[13]	1.6[13]	118.8	2,110	France
...	...	...	...	44[7]	2.1[7]	6.5	18	33[7]	2.9[7]	...	...	French Guiana
92	2,140	16,309	83	90	2.2	27	7.6	44[4]	4.3[4]	0.4	2,190	French Polynesia
52	22,500	6,478[2,16]	5.5[2,16]	250	4.8	40	30	26	57	0.1	95	Gabon
...	...	...	...	135	6.4	...	...	9.3[1]	92[1]	...	...	Gambia, The
...	...	...	...	...	...	...	...	...	...	...	...	Gaza Strip
...	...	138,000[11]	25[11]	...	...	...	...	...	...	47.0	8,680	Georgia
29,515[22]	2,120[22]	16,317,637[22]	260[22]	32,000	2.5	45,150	1.8	45,711[15]	1.7[15]	166.3	2,110	Germany
1,005	14,400	128,289	8.9	3,142	4.7	175	85	79	185	3.9	340	Ghana
4	7,710	12,699	410	17	1.8	7.0	4.5	17	1.9	0.17	5,830	Gibraltar
1,236[14]	8,270[14]	438,177	43	4,085	2.5	2,300	4.5	4,699	2.2	...	...	Greece
...	...	...	...	25	2.2	20	2.8	12[3]	4.4[3]	...	...	Greenland
...	...	...	...	80	1.2	30	3.2	27	3.4	...	...	Grenada
...	...	...	...	100	4.0	150	2.6	121	3.2	...	...	Guadeloupe
...	...	...	...	105	1.3	75	1.8	41[15]	3.1[15]	...	...	Guam
594	15,000	84,200	9.4	400	23	475	19	250	36	7.7	910	Guatemala
15	4,150	15,064[19]	240[19]	...	...	...	...	60[15]	1.0[15]	...	...	Guernsey
75	91,700	174	0.0	200	35	65	108	20	355	2.6	430	Guinea
24	40,500	...	...	35	28	...	...	3.07	297[7]	...	...	Guinea-Bissau
131[7]	5,760[7]	32,272[7]	43[7]	310	2.5	40	19	33[7]	23[7]	13.0	17,200	Guyana
125	51,900	1,420,307	220	3,000	2.2	25	265	50[15]	126[15]	2.1	380	Haiti
...	...	...	...	1,800	2.6	200	24	92	53	...	...	Honduras
162	35,200	863,815	150	3,000	1.9	1,749	3.3	3,280	1.7	58.5	10,290	Hong Kong
3,213	3,210	1,613,113	160	6,000	1.7	4,215	2.5	1,872	5.5	45.8	4,400	Hungary
122	2,090	63,181[17]	250[17]	155	1.7	76	3.4	125[8]	1.9[8]	1.2	4,750	Iceland
147,236	5,790	13,854,201	16	55,000	16	20,000	44	5,486	157	4,300.0	5,150	India
26,027	6,850	595,172	3.3	22,000	8.2	11,000	16	1,015[1]	174[1]	133.2	770	Indonesia
4,075[14]	13,700[14]	335,698	6.0	11,500	5.0	2,250	26	2,270	25	80.5	1,490	Iran
343	51,800	244,870[16]	14[16]	3,500	5.2	1,000	18	937[4]	18[4]	...	...	Iraq
2,103[15]	1,680[15]	...	...	2,000	1.8	991	3.6	942[13]	3.8[13]	11.6	3,290	Ireland
37[4]	1,730[4]	24,049[4]	370[4]	...	...	...	...	901	0.9[1]	...	...	Isle of Man
1,601	2,960	453,800[17]	96[17]	2,250	2.2	1,200	4.1	2,425	2.0	...	...	Israel
14,464	3,990	8,995,333	160	14,817	3.9	17,001	3.4	32,037	1.8	93.8	1,630	Italy
825	2,910	99,855[16,17]	42[16,17]	1,500	1.6	484	5.0	175	14	...	...	Jamaica
24,098	5,130	22,637,552	180	97,000	1.3	80,000	1.5	66,636[13]	1.8[13]	143.6	1,170	Japan
22	3,790	51,034	610	...	...	...	...	901	0.9[1]	...	...	Jersey
842	3,760	99,864	32	700	4.7	250	13	320	11	0.9	290	Jordan
...	...	379,000[11]	23[11]	4,189[15]	3.9[15]	4,573[15]	3.6[15]	1,967	8.5	207.0	12,500	Kazakhstan
1,025	24,300	296,071	12	4,200	6.2	260	100	383	66	...	...	Kenya
24	2,990	337	4.7	10	7.3	...	...	1.3[15]	53[15]	...	...	Kiribati
...	...	...	...	3,750	5.8	250	87	30[15]	700[15]	187.4	9,560	Korea, North
3,245	13,200	2,380,061	56	42.000	1.0	8,700	5.0	15,736	2.7	55.3	1,300	Korea, South
54[15]	36,300[15]	115,215[1,16,17,18]	56[1,16,17,18]	1,100[1]	1.9[1]	800[1]	2.6[1]	362[15]	5.5[15]	0.9	480	Kuwait
...	...	38,000[11]	8.6[11]	...	...	...	...	307	14	46.1	10,700	Kyrgyzstan
125	33,400	2,136	0.5	425	10	32	134	7.1	596	...	...	Laos
1,141[10]	2,350[10]	104,000[11]	39[11]	1,328[5]	2.0[5]	1,136[5]	2.4[5]	584[15]	4.3[15]	19.7	7,340	Latvia
...	...	...	...	2,150	1.3	838	3.3	150[4]	18[4]	...	...	Lebanon
140	12,600	77,615	44	420	4.3	50	36	19[15]	88[15]	...	...	Lesotho
44[15]	55,400[15]	26,803[1]	11[1]	600	4.5	45	60	28[4]	86[4]	...	...	Liberia
317	13,300	1,551,441[2,16,17,18]	370[2,16,17,18]	1,000	4.3	500	8.7	500[15]	8.0[15]	...	...	Libya
12	2,390	17,222[9]	600[9]	19[4]	1.5[4]	9.0[4]	3.1[4]	43[15]	0.7[15]	...	...	Liechtenstein
...	...	103,000[1,11]	28[1,11]	...	...	...	...	838	4.5	13.9	3,690	Lithuania
106	3,580	172,964	460	230	1.7	100	3.8	176[1]	2.1[1]	0.5	1,330	Luxembourg
25	18,400	11,541	25	250	1.9	70	6.8	111	3.1	2.7	6,400	Macau
257	7,880	38,401	19	365[5]	5.5[5]	331[5]	6.1[5]	357	5.7	2.1	1,060	Macedonia
9,354	1,280	51,681	4.3	1,500	8.3	130	95	44[15]	262[15]	3.0	280	Madagascar
263[13]	28,000[13]	113,975[13]	15[13]	1,060	8.6	...	...	50	179	...	...	Malawi
5,020	3,540	873,735	49	3,500	5.2	2,000	9.1	2,023	8.9	41.6	2,400	Malaysia
29	7,420	2,242[1]	11[1]	25	8.8	4.8	47	2.5[13]	75[13]	...	...	Maldives
88	92,600	5,660	0.7	150	55	10	830	15	564	...	...	Mali
44	8,050	49,667	140	90	4.0	132	2.7	179	2.0	0.3	860	Malta
...	...	...	...	...	...	...	...	0.8[15]	57[15]	...	...	Marshall Islands
...	...	...	...	60	6.1	45	8.1	159	2.3	1.1	3,150	Martinique
61[1]	31,700[1]	...	...	250	8.2	1.1	1,860	7.0	288	...	...	Mauritania
114	9,320	32,766	31	250	4.3	128	8.4	75	14	0.9	850	Mauritius
...	...	...	...	30	2.9	3.5	25	3.2	29	...	...	Mayotte
6,683	12,900	784,676	9.1	16,325	5.1	12,350	6.7	10,103	8.2	351.0	4,500	Mexico
...	...	...	...	70	1.6	7.0	16	...	...	...	...	Micronesia
1,359[4,10]	3,150[4,10]	86,000	20	1,419[4]	3.0[4]	1,155[4]	3.7[4]	538	8.1	43.0	9,850	Moldova
...	...	...	...	11	2.7	18	1.7	53	0.6	0.1	3,390	Monaco
424[15]	4,790[15]	12,820[15,17,18]	6.3[15,17,18]	275	7.8	120	18	63[1]	35[1]	20.1	9,720	Mongolia
1,278	19,600	215,107	8.6	4,500	5.7	1,210	21	475	53	30.2	1,240	Morocco
289	49,300	8,462	0.6	500	29	35	418	66	217	4.1	300	Mozambique
1,135	36,700	76,264	1.8	3,200	13	1,000	43	81[15]	501[15]	...	...	Myanmar (Burma)
...	...	...	...	210[4]	5.7[4]	27	49	72[15]	17[15]	...	...	Namibia
1[13]	8,500[13]	168[13]	20[13]	4.0	2.4	...	...	1.5[15]	5.9[15]	...	...	Nauru
2,232[1]	7,870[4]	...	...	600	32	250	78	67[1]	275[1]	...	...	Nepal
2,624[4]	5,580[4]	6,105,000[1]	410[1]	12,146	1.2	5,000	3.0	9,750[15]	1.5[15]	15.6	1,050	Netherlands, The
161	11,800[1]	17,427[1]	92[1]	125	1.5	35	5.5	50[1]	3.8[1]	...	...	Netherlands Antilles
264	630	18,596[16]	110[16]	90	1.9	36	4.8	32[8]	4.7[8]	0.2	1,260	New Caledonia
1,242[7]	2,670[7]	838,656[7,16]	250[7,16]	3,100	1.1	1,100	3.1	2,403[4]	1.4[4]	...	...	New Zealand
...	...	...	...	880	4.5	210	19	50[3]	64[3]	5.0	1,750	Nicaragua

Communications (continued)

country	publishing (latest)								daily newspapers (latest)		
	number of titles				number of copies ('000)				number	total circulation ('000)	circulation per 1,000 population
	books		periodicals	pamphlets	books		periodicals	pamphlets			
	total	school textbooks			total	school textbooks					
Niger	...	...	...	...	...	...	...	0.1	1	5	0.6
Nigeria	900	800	92	566	...	...	495	...	25	...	...
Northern Mariana Islands	...	...	...	...	...	...	...	...	—	—	...
Norway	4,301	...	7,150	1,030	...	...	...	...	61	2,163	510
Oman	...	...	19	...	...	...	117	...	4	62	42
Pakistan	...	...	282	...	...	...	7,674	...	271	1,106	9
Palau	...	...	...	...	...	...	...	...	—	—	—
Panama	...	...	18	...	...	...	...	...	5	144	60
Papua New Guinea	...	...	...	...	...	...	...	...	2	65	18
Paraguay	...	...	...	...	...	...	...	...	6	...	...
Peru	359	3	507	122	...	...	...	...	70	...	...
Philippines	997	120	1,177	75	...	...	6,916	...	38	3,298	56
Poland	8,466	395	3,031	1,820	176,903	38,619	44,599	38,690	48	6,715	185
Portugal	6,539	1,005	805	1,194	26,592	9,765	...	6,793	34	...	...
Puerto Rico	...	...	...	...	...	...	...	...	4	473	142
Qatar	461	252	13	...	...	...	320	...	4	52	147
Réunion	41	—	60	32	...	...	...	...	3	60	102
Romania	3,245	...	422	622	59,147	...	17,090	4,228	36	3,120	134
Russia	41,234[9]	...	3,681	[9]	1,553,100[9]	...	5,010,200	[9]	4,808	166,000	1,119
Rwanda	131	42	9	76	746	552	91	2,109	1	...	...
St. Kitts and Nevis	—	—	3	3	—	—	6	3	—	—	—
St. Lucia	44	25	...	19	89	84	...	7	—	—	—
St. Vincent	...	...	...	...	...	...	...	...	—	—	—
San Marino	...	...	16	...	...	...	...	...	5	...	...
São Tomé and Príncipe	...	...	...	...	...	...	...	...	—	—	—
Saudi Arabia	...	...	58	...	...	...	...	...	10	664	49
Senegal	42	8	123	...	169	70	381	...	1	45	6
Seychelles	...	...	2	...	...	...	2	...	1	3.2	47
Sierra Leone	16	16	...	...	...	...	...	...	2	10	2
Singapore	1,524	389	1,786	403	8,947	4,081	...	2,179	8	777	289
Slovenia	1,853	...	274	...	6,267	...	7,194	...	4	203	103
Solomon Islands	...	...	...	...	...	...	...	...	—	—	—
Somalia	...	...	...	...	...	...	...	...	1	...	...
South Africa	...	...	...	...	...	...	...	...	20	1,341	37
Bophuthatswana	...	...	...	...	...	...	...	...	—	—	—
Ciskei	...	...	...	...	...	...	...	...	—	—	—
Transkei	...	...	...	...	...	...	...	...	—	—	—
Venda	...	...	...	...	...	...	...	...	—	—	—
Spain	33,313	3,072	1,998	5,040	175,724	29,469	...	23,943	110	...	...
Sri Lanka	910	100	170	1,278	8,577	...	1,770	6,135	15	748	44
Sudan, The	...	...	10	...	...	...	136	...	2	120	4
Suriname	...	...	22	...	...	...	44	...	1	18	43
Swaziland	...	...	...	...	...	...	...	...	2	19	25
Sweden	11,197	408	46	...	...	...	4,947	...	179	4,965	585
Switzerland	8,549	208	3,079	4,721	...	...	...	...	104	3,188	471
Syria	119	1	...	...	553	...	...	...	7	244	21
Taiwan	16,156	...	4,134	...	...	...	...	...	93	4,000	202
Tajikistan	787[9]	...	36	[9]	12,000[9]	...	27,200	[9]	74	1,598	309
Tanzania	166	12	...	197	...	...	...	...	2	180	8
Thailand	11,097	1,027	976	120	...	...	...	...	40	4,750	87
Togo	...	...	...	...	...	...	...	...	2	...	...
Tonga	...	...	...	...	...	...	...	...	1	7	73
Trinidad and Tobago	...	...	...	...	...	...	...	...	4	173	140
Tunisia	293	...	...	...	879	...	...	...	6	230	33
Turkey	6,031	212	2,670	654	...	...	...	...	426	3,094	55
Turkmenistan	759[9]	...	33	[9]	7,600[9]	...	12,800	[9]	66	1,141	319
Tuvalu	...	...	...	...	...	...	...	...	—	—	—
Uganda	...	...	...	...	...	...	...	...	6	64	4
Ukraine	7,046[9]	...	185	[9]	170,500[9]	...	165,700	[9]	1,787	25,000	482
United Arab Emirates	152	152	...	...	2,815	2,815	...	...	9	356	193
United Kingdom	48,897	1,346	6,408	3,964	...	...	...	...	99	22,254	388
United States	50,000	...	11,593	...	...	...	...	...	1,626	63,000	251
Uruguay	386	40	465	419	536	60	...	473	33	...	...
Uzbekistan	2,080[9]	...	95	[9]	51,000[9]	...	171,800	[9]	279	6,600	322
Vanuatu	...	...	...	...	...	...	...	...	—	—	—
Venezuela	996	32	160	206	...	...	4,649	...	56	...	...
Vietnam	...	...	...	...	...	...	...	...	4	2,250	38
Virgin Islands (U.S)	...	...	...	...	...	...	...	...	2	25	241
West Bank	...	...	...	...	...	...	...	...	—	...	...
Western Sahara	...	...	...	...	...	...	...	...	—	—	—
Western Samoa	...	...	...	...	...	...	...	...	2	...	...
Yemen	...	...	...	...	...	...	...	...	2	120	11
Yugoslavia	4,180	...	569	...	15,805	...	13,516	...	15	1,002	97
Zaire	...	...	106	...	...	...	225	...	7	45	1
Zambia	454	215	...	...	...	...	...	...	2	139	17
Zimbabwe	183	36	...	154	...	...	...	...	2	206	22

post offices, 1990				radio, 1991		television, 1991		telephones, 1990		cinema (latest)		country
number	persons per office	pieces of mail handled ('000)	pieces of mail handled per capita	receivers (all types; '000)	persons per receiver	receivers (all types; '000)	persons per receiver	receivers ('000)	persons per receiver	annual attendance		
										number ('000,000)	per 1,000 population	
284	27,400	8,106	1.0	400	20	25	321	12[15]	630[15]	...	...	Niger
3,537	33,900	547,875	4.6	10,000	12	4,100	30	722[15]	115[15]	4.6	51	Nigeria
...	...	...	...	10.5	4.2	4.1	11	4.9[4]	4.4[4]	...	...	Northern Mariana Islands
2,620	1,620	1,917,579	450	3,300	1.3	1,466	2.9	2,579[3]	1.6[3]	12.4	2,930	Norway
71	21,200	28,116[2, 16, 17]	19[2, 16, 17]	900	1.7	1,000	1.6	80[4]	17[4]	...	...	Oman
12,193	10,100	746,669[19]	6.1[19]	10,000	13	2,080	61	740[15]	158[15]	25.3	230	Pakistan
...	...	...	...	9.0	1.7	1.6	9.7	1.5[15]	9.3[15]	...	...	Palau
268	9,020	19,360	8.0	450	5.5	205	12	256	9.5	...	...	Panama
114	34,200	36,478[2]	9.4[2]	235	16	10	375	63	59	...	...	Papua New Guinea
307	13,900	7,025	1.6	775	5.7	350	13	128	38	...	...	Paraguay
2,373	9,410	31,777[17]	1.4[17]	4,400	5.2	2,080	11	769	28	33.0	1,910	Peru
2,158	28,200	656,280	11	4,000	16	7,000	8.9	1,047	59	...	...	Philippines
8,041	4,740	1,061,805	28	10,400	3.7	10,000	3.8	5,232	7.3	69.5	1,830	Poland
7,306	1,420	707,310	68	2,475	4.2	1,790	5.8	2,769	3.7	16.9	1,650	Portugal
...	...	...	...	2,000	1.8	830	4.4	977[15]	3.4[15]	...	...	Puerto Rico
26	16,900	25,048[19]	57[19]	250	1.8	160	2.8	139	3.6	0.3	710	Qatar
...	...	...	...	150	4.1	90	6.8	168	3.6	...	...	Réunion
4,470	5,180	...	...	3,263[1]	7.1[1]	5,000	4.6	3,023	7.7	203.4	8,790	Romania
...	...	3,900,000[11]	26[11]	49,700[5]	3.0[5]	55,000[5]	2.7[5]	23,400[12]	6.3[12]	1,609.0	10,900	Russia
46	150,000	9,578	1.4	630	11	...	...	14	497	0.3	56	Rwanda
8	5,380	2,543	59	25	1.7	9.5	4.5	9.4	4.6	...	...	St. Kitts and Nevis
57	2,650	3,739	25	90	1.7	25	6.2	18[15]	7.4[15]	...	...	St. Lucia
54	2,160	...	...	55	2.1	18	6.7	17	6.4	...	...	St. Vincent
10	2,310	...	...	13	1.9	7.0[4]	3.2[4]	16[15]	1.5[15]	0.02	880	San Marino
11	10,900	302	2.5	31	4.0	...	...	2.8[15]	42[15]	...	...	São Tomé and Príncipe
609[14]	23,200[14]	356,378	25	5,000	2.9	4,500	3.3	1,069[15]	13[15]	...	...	Saudi Arabia
133	55,000	14,789	2.0	850	8.8	60	125	29[15]	246[15]	...	...	Senegal
...	...	...	...	30	2.3	8.2	8.3	14[15]	4.8[15]	...	...	Seychelles
102[1]	39,700[1]	8,306[1]	2.1[1]	900	4.7	25	170	35	122	...	...	Sierra Leone
534	5,040	466,461	170	662	4.1	550	4.9	1,200[15]	2.2[15]	30.7	20,600	Singapore
534	3,690	270,048	140	601[5]	3.3[5]	445[5]	4.4[5]	657	3.0	2.8	1,440	Slovenia
113	2,820	2,164[17]	6.8[17]	38	8.6	...	...	7.0[1]	46[1]	...	...	Solomon Islands
...	...	...	...	400	19	3.0[4]	2,270[4]	8.0[15]	882[15]	...	...	Somalia
...	...	...	...	10,000	3.8	3,445	11	5,077	6.1	26.0	680	South Africa
...	...	...	...	...	...	...	...	36[15]	52[15]	...	...	Bophuthatswana
343[3]	21,500[3]	...	...	...	...	...	...	23[15]	35[15]	...	...	Ciskei
192[7]	15,600[7]	...	...	...	...	6.0[15]	619[15]	7.2[7]	409[7]	...	...	Transkei
...	...	...	...	...	...	...	...	...	...	...	...	Venda
41,833	950	5,608,624	140	12,600	3.2	17,240	2.3	15,477[4]	2.5[4]	78.1	1,970	Spain
3,944	4,310	487,760	29	2,200	7.8	700	25	166	103	37.2	2,270	Sri Lanka
808	35,000	25,957	0.9	6,000	4.9	250	117	78[15]	343[15]	13.0	600	Sudan, The
...	...	...	...	250	1.7	40	10	48	8.4	...	...	Suriname
71	10,800	11,281	15	60	13	13	64	25	31	...	...	Swaziland
2,038	4,200	3,685,041[1, 23]	430[1, 23]	7,272	1.2	3,750	2.3	7,410[8]	1.1[8]	18.0	2,140	Sweden
3,742	1,820	5,046,893	740	2,685	2.6	2,412	2.8	6,153	1.1	12.8	1,900	Switzerland
585[1]	20,000[1]	20,857	1.7	2,850	4.4	700	18	695	18	6.9	590	Syria
12,700	1,600	1,718,709	85	13,600	1.5	6,660	3.1	7,835[1]	2.6[1]	64.2	3,200	Taiwan
775[1, 10]	6,680[1, 10]	49,000[11]	9.2[11]	860[1]	6.0[1]	815[1]	6.3[1]	273[1]	20[1]	41.6	8,030	Tajikistan
837	29,200	91,202	3.7	4,000	6.3	80	314	140	177	1.7	74	Tanzania
4,057	13,500	642,400	12	10,000	5.6	3,300	17	1,000[7]	53[7]	...	...	Thailand
416	8,400	...	...	700	5.1	23	156	21	169	...	...	Togo
...	...	...	...	75	1.3	...	...	4.0[3]	243[3]	...	...	Tonga
236	5,240	23,913	19	700	1.8	250	5.0	226	5.5	...	...	Trinidad and Tobago
703	11,500	171,026[17]	21[17]	1,700	4.8	650	13	410	20	...	...	Tunisia
40,447[14]	1,390[14]	1,542,296	27	7,100	8.1	10,530	5.4	8,517	6.7	25.8	510	Turkey
...	...	59,000[11]	16[11]	...	...	...	...	252[1]	15[1]	39.0	10,900	Turkmenistan
9[15]	970[15]	882[2, 15]	102[2, 15]	3.0	3.1	...	...	0.18	51	...	...	Tuvalu
284	58,100	14,213	0.9	3,500	5.1	90	197	57	290	...	...	Uganda
...	...	1,473,000[11]	28[11]	15,000[1]	3.5[1]	17,000[1]	3.0[1]	6,908[12]	7.5[12]	612.0	11,800	Ukraine
185	10,300	106,300	56	400	4.9	170	11	655	2.9	...	...	United Arab Emirates
20,638	2,780	16,412,000	290	70,000	0.8	20,000	2.9	29,518[3]	1.9[3]	94.6	1,650	United Kingdom
40,067	6,080	165,028,262[19]	680[19]	520,000	0.5	215,000	1.2	181,091[3]	1.3[3]	1,132.5	4,580	United States
361	8,570	34,418	11	1,800	1.7	700	4.4	579	5.4	6.2	2,110	Uruguay
...	...	200,000[11]	9.7[11]	3,690[1]	5.4[1]	3,180[1]	6.3[1]	1,659	15	149.0	7,410	Uzbekistan
...	...	...	...	20	7.5	1.0[4]	137[4]	3.2[7]	44[7]	...	...	Vanuatu
603	31,900	84,501	4.4	8,100	2.4	3,700	5.3	1,794	11	29.8	1,590	Venezuela
...	...	...	...	7,000	9.7	2,200	31	116[15]	544[15]	239.9	3,760	Vietnam
...	...	...	...	90	1.1	32	3.2	59	1.7	...	...	Virgin Islands (U.S.)
...	...	...	...	...	...	...	...	...	...	...	...	West Bank
...	...	...	...	...	...	...	...	...	...	...	...	Western Sahara
461[1]	3,430[1]	2,098[1, 16]	131[1, 16]	75	2.1	6.0[4]	26[4]	5.5[15]	30[15]	...	...	Western Samoa
406[1]	27,700[1]	17,624[1]	1.6[1]	325	36	300	39	70[15]	157[15]	...	...	Yemen
1,548	6,660	474,729	46	1,907[5]	5.4[5]	1,704[5]	6.0[5]	1,839	5.6	8.3	804	Yugoslavia
365	93,500	45,394[16]	1.3[16]	3,400	10	20	1,750	32[15]	1,026[15]	...	...	Zaire
427	19,800	88,264	10	1,660	5.3	200	44	100	79	...	...	Zambia
294	31,900	175,141	19	522	18	137	70	301	32	5.6	690	Zimbabwe

[1]1989. [2]Foreign-received and foreign-sent only. [3]1984. [4]1987. [5]1990. [6]1982. [7]1986. [8]1983. [9]Books includes pamphlets. [10]Includes telephone and telegraph offices. [11]Letters sent. [12]1991. [13]1985. [14]Permanent post offices only. [15]1988. [16]Excludes postcards. [17]Excludes small packets. [18]Excludes printed matter. [19]Domestic and foreign-sent only. [20]1981. [21]Includes overseas departments. [22]Former West Germany only. [23]Domestic only.

Trade: external

The following table presents comparative data on the international, or foreign, trade of the countries of the world. The table analyzes data for both imports and exports in two ways: (1) into several major commodity groups defined in accordance with the United Nations system called the Standard International Trade Classification (SITC) and (2) by direction of trade for each country with major world trading blocs and partners. These commodity groupings are defined by the SITC code numbers beneath the column headings. The single-digit numbers represent broad SITC categories (in the SITC, called "sections"); the double-digit numbers represent subcategories ("divisions") of the single-digit categories (27 is a subcategory of 2), the three-digit is a subcategory ("group") of the double-digit (667 is a subcategory of 66). Where a plus or minus sign is used before one of these SITC numbers, the SITC category or subcategory is being added to or subtracted from the aggregate implied by the total of the preceding sections. The SITC commodity aggregations used here are listed in the table at the end of this headnote. The full SITC commodity breakdown—some 3,118 basic headings—is presented in the 1986 United Nations publication *Standard International Trade Classification, Revision 3* (though many countries still report according to revision 2 and some according to revision 1).

The SITC was developed by the United Nations through its Statistical Commission as an outgrowth of the need for a standard system of aggregating commodities of external trade to provide international comparability of foreign trade statistics. All member nations of the United Nations are urged to use the SITC system as far as possible in reporting their external trade statistics. The United Nations Statistical Commission has defined external merchandise trade as "all goods whose movement into or out of the customs area of a country compiling the statistics adds to or subtracts from the material resources of the country." Goods passing through a country for transport only are excluded, but goods entering for reexport, or deposited (as in a bonded warehouse, or free trade area) for reimport, are included. Statistics in this table refer only to goods and exclude purely financial transactions that are covered in the "Finance" and "National product and accounts" tables.

For purposes of comparability of data, total value of imports and exports is given in this table in U.S. dollars. Conversions from other currencies are determined according to the average rates for the year for which data are supplied; these are mainly as calculated by the International Monetary Fund (IMF). The commodity categories are given in terms of percentages of the total value of the country's import or export trade (with the exclusions noted above). Value is based on transaction value: for imports, the

Trade: external

country	year	imports total value ('000,000 U.S.$)	food and agricultural raw materials (0+1+2−27−28+4)	mineral ores and concentrates (27+28+667)	fuels and other energy (3)	manufactured goods total[a] (5+6−667+7+8+9)	of which chemicals and related products (5)	of which machinery and transport equipment (7)	of which other[a] (6−667+8+9)	from European Economic Community (EEC)[b]	from United States	from Eastern Europe[c]	from Japan	from all other[d]
Afghanistan	1989[1]	821.7	—13.4[2]—		2.7	83.9[3]	2.2	46.2	35.4[3]	4.2[4]	0.4[4]	56.9[4]	8.3[4]	30.1[4]
Albania	1990	446.5	25.7	—24.5—		49.8	9.3	31.0	9.5	37.7[5]	...	27.9	0.1	34.4
Algeria	1988	7,396.7	32.5	0.6	2.3	64.5	13.1	27.5	24.0	58.7	10.8	3.0	4.3	23.2
American Samoa	1989[6]	377.9	65.1	—[2]	7.1	27.8[3]	1.2	6.7	20.0[3]	—	28.0	—	3.9	68.1
Andorra	1987	700.4	—28.3[2]—		3.7	68.0[3]	7.3	19.9	40.8[3]	84.9	2.8	0.2	6.3	5.9
Angola	1981	1,678.4	31.7	0.2	0.8	67.3	12.1	20.9	34.3	58.3	9.8	3.8	4.5	23.7
Antigua and Barbuda	1984	131.9	24.6	—	25.0	50.4	6.4	21.8	22.2	10.6	37.8	—	—	51.6
Argentina	1990	4,076.7	8.0	6.1	8.3	77.6	27.6	32.0	18.1	25.6	20.1	1.3	4.4	48.6
Armenia	1989	7,500.0[7]	...	...	...	...	...	...	...	...	...	...	...	...
Aruba	1988	330.9	22.3	0.1	7.6	70.0	8.0	19.7	42.3	22.8	40.7	0.1	3.7	32.8
Australia	1990	40,073.0	6.8	0.9	5.4	86.9	8.8	42.9	35.1	22.5	24.4	0.3	18.3	34.5
Austria	1991	50,832.0	8.2	1.3	6.0	84.6	9.7	39.1	35.7	67.8	4.0	6.0	4.8	17.4
Azerbaijan	1989	8,400.0[7]	...	...	...	...	...	...	...	...	...	...	...	...
Bahamas, The	1988	2,263.5	10.2	0.1	56.7	33.0	6.4	9.6	17.1	7.7	39.6	1.0	0.6	51.1
Bahrain	1990	3,711.5	9.1	0.3	53.2	37.4	8.1	11.9	17.4	17.6[4]	19.4[4]	...	7.0[4]	56.0[4]
Bangladesh	1987	2,572.7	33.2	1.0	13.8	52.0	8.3	17.2	26.5	13.1	9.1	2.8	12.0	63.0
Barbados	1990	698.5	19.9	0.4	14.3	65.4	10.1	24.2	31.1	19.1	33.8	0.1	5.3	41.7
Belarus	1989	27,000.0[7]	...	...	...	...	...	...	...	...	...	...	...	...
Belgium[8]	1991	120,639.2	12.6	8.7	8.4	70.4	11.5	26.0	32.9	72.8	4.8	1.6	2.2	18.6
Belize	1986	122.0	27.4	0.1	13.9	58.6	8.4	18.0	32.2	16.5	57.4	0.1	2.4	23.7
Benin	1984	288.2	—34.5[2]—		13.0	52.4[3]	7.4	14.1	31.0[3]	55.1	5.0	1.0	4.0	34.9
Bermuda	1990	540.6[9]	23.3	0.1	8.6	67.9	10.0	20.2	37.8	15.3	59.5	—	5.2	20.0
Bhutan	1983	39.0[10]	14.5	0.3	21.4	63.9	3.4	29.7	30.8	12.0	0.3	—	4.6	83.1[11]
Bolivia	1990	715.7	19.9[13]	0.1[13]	0.4[13]	79.6[13]	9.9[13]	41.2[13]	28.5[13]	15.0[13]	21.0[13]	1.1[13]	10.0[13]	52.9[13]
Bosnia and Hercegovina	...	...	...	...	...	...	...	...	...	...	...	...	...	...
Botswana	1988	1,193.8	14.9	1.6	6.1	77.4	6.7	37.5	33.2	10.1	2.1	—	0.7	87.0[14]
Brazil	1990	22,459.0	8.1[16]	3.4[16]	30.1[16]	58.4[16]	17.0[16]	28.9[16]	12.4[16]	20.8	21.1	0.3	6.0	51.8
Brunei	1986	653.3	21.0	0.8	1.0	77.1	7.0	38.0	32.2	23.8	12.2	—	17.7	46.3
Bulgaria	1990	13,099.9	7.8	—33.6[17]—		58.6[18]	5.2	46.2	7.2[18]	16.2	0.6	68.4	1.0	13.8
Burkina Faso	1987	434.3	—25.4[2]—		7.7	66.8[3]	13.5	27.2	26.1[3]	50.8	6.4	0.9	5.0	36.8
Burundi	1989	188.1	10.6	1.4	11.9	76.1	14.9	31.1	30.1	48.3	1.2	4.5	8.1	37.9
Cambodia	1989	215.0[4]		1.2[19]	30.2[19]		36.9[19]		1.9[4]	—[4]	96.1[4, 20]	1.7[4]	0.3[4]
Cameroon	1989	1,273.3	16.6	3.4	1.4	78.6	15.2	30.8	32.6	60.8	5.1	0.8	5.7	27.7
Canada	1990	116,453.5	7.7	1.8	6.2	84.2	6.7	50.3	27.3	11.5	64.6	0.4	7.0	16.6
Cape Verde	1988	106.5	29.9[19]	—[19]	12.0[19]	58.0[19]	6.7[19]	28.9[19]	22.4[19]	69.1	1.9	4.1	5.8	19.1
Cayman Islands	1991	267.4	25.8	0.4	10.1	63.7	5.9	25.8	32.0	6.3	75.2	...	3.1	15.4
Central African Republic	1989	159.1	20.1	0.7	6.7	72.6	14.0	33.2	25.3	56.7	1.3	0.3	7.6	34.2
Chad	1988	419.3	15.9[23]	0.6[23]	14.2[23]	69.3[23]	16.4[23]	28.8[23]	24.1[23]	19.0[4]	8.5[4]	...	2.2[4]	70.3[4]
Chile	1990	7,022.3	6.6	0.4	15.7	77.4	12.1	43.7	21.6	21.8	19.5	0.6	8.1	49.9
China	1991	63,791.4	11.7	2.0[2]	3.3	83.0[3]	14.5	30.7	37.7[3]	13.2	12.6	4.2	15.7	54.4
Colombia	1990	5,588.5	10.5	0.9	6.0	82.5	22.6	36.2	23.7	21.2	35.4	0.8	8.9	33.8
Comoros	1990	51.6	—47.1[2, 24]—		13.1[24]	39.8[3, 24]	3.5[24]	17.6[24]	18.8[3, 24]	73.0[4]	—[4]	...	5.0[4]	22.1[4]
Congo	1986	578.6	18.9	0.7	1.7	78.7	9.1	35.3	34.3	76.0	5.2	1.1	4.2	13.5
Cook Islands	1989	43.7	—29.3[2]—		11.8	58.9[3]	7.2	17.9	33.8[3]	6.0[5]	4.2	—	10.4	79.3
Costa Rica	1987	1,380.2	9.4	1.3	10.2	79.0	20.6	27.8	30.6	14.7	37.2	0.4	8.5	39.3
Côte d'Ivoire	1987	2,241.4	—24.0—		15.0	61.1	13.8	21.3	25.9	56.5	4.4	1.0	5.5	32.6
Croatia	...	...	...	...	...	...	...	...	...	...	...	...	...	...
Cuba	1987	7,611.5	14.2	0.3[2]	34.7	50.8[3]	5.8	30.7	14.3[3]	9.8	...	81.6	1.4	7.2
Cyprus	1990	2,563.7	15.8	0.6	10.5	73.1	8.0	30.6	34.6	53.7	7.1	6.2	11.5	21.5
Czechoslovakia	1989	14,988.0	13.8	2.9	17.3	65.9	9.3	36.9	19.6	25.6	0.4	47.2	0.5	26.3
Denmark	1991	32,187.5	15.5	0.5	7.0	77.0	11.3	31.5	34.1	52.8	6.3	2.7	3.9	34.4
Djibouti	1990	214.8	38.8	1.0	7.1	53.1	6.8	17.4	28.9	47.0	3.3	0.3	5.4	44.0
Dominica	1989	107.1	24.4	0.1	5.3	70.1	11.6	25.4	33.2	22.5	31.1	0.2	5.8	40.5
Dominican Republic	1985	1,247.9	13.7	0.3	35.2	50.7	11.7	23.2	15.9	10.3	34.7	—	4.6	48.6
Ecuador	1990	1,803.9	11.4	0.7	2.1	85.8	22.8	36.7	26.3	23.2	32.6	0.7	9.5	34.1
Egypt	1988	23,297.9	32.8	1.1	2.6	63.5	13.1	26.8	23.6	41.5	11.9	9.3	5.0	32.3
El Salvador	1989	1,289.7	17.0[13]	0.9[13]	11.4[13]	70.7[13]	19.2[13]	26.2[13]	25.3[13]	10.7	40.2	—	4.3	44.8
Equatorial Guinea	1984	25.0	—28.6[2]—		20.1	51.3[3]	4.3	25.4	21.6[3]	73.8[4]	0.7[4]	—[4]	0.8[4]	24.7[4]
Estonia[27]	1990	6,203.9	—16.5[2]—		7.2	76.3[3]	13.8	30.6	32.0[3]	...	0.6	91.5	0.5	7.4
Ethiopia	1988	1,085.0	19.1	0.4	9.9	70.6	8.9	44.3	17.4	48.2	10.9	12.3	7.9	20.7

value at which the goods were purchased by the importer plus the cost of transportation and insurance to the frontier of the importing country (c.i.f. [cost, insurance, and freight] valuation); for exports, the value at which the goods were sold by the exporter, including the cost of transportation and insurance to bring the goods onto the transporting vehicle at the frontier of the exporting country (f.o.b. [free-on-board] valuation).

The largest part of the information presented here comes from the United Nations' *Commodity Trade Statistics* (including microfiche format) and *International Trade Statistics Yearbook*. These publications, however, cannot always provide the most recent data for all countries listed in this table and must be supplemented by national and regional sources.

a. Also includes any unallocated commodities.
b. EEC of 12 countries (Belgium, Denmark, France, Germany, Greece, Ireland, Italy, Luxembourg, The Netherlands, Portugal, Spain, and the United Kingdom).
c. Includes Albania, Bulgaria, Czechoslovakia, Hungary, Poland, Romania, and former U.S.S.R.
d. May include value of trade shown as not available (...) in any of the four preceding columns. May include any unspecified areas or countries.
... Not available.

— None, less than 0.05%, or not applicable.
Detail may not add to 100.0 or indicated subtotals because of rounding.

SITC category codes:

0	food and live animals
1	beverages and tobacco
2	crude materials, inedible, except fuels
27	crude fertilizers and crude minerals (excluding coal, petroleum, and precious stones)
28	metalliferous ores and metal scrap
3	mineral fuels, lubricants, and related materials (including coal, petroleum, natural gas, and electric current)
4	animal and vegetable oils, fats, and waxes
5	chemicals and related products not elsewhere specified
6	manufactured goods classified chiefly by material
667	pearls, precious and semiprecious stones, unworked or worked
7	machinery and transport equipment
8	miscellaneous manufactured articles
9	commodities and transactions not classified elsewhere

exports									direction of trade (%)					country
total value ('000,000 U.S.$)	Standard International Trade Classification (SITC) categories (%)								to European Economic Community (EEC)[b]	to United States	to Eastern Europe[c]	to Japan	to all other[d]	
	food and agricultural raw materials (0+1+2 −27−28 +4)	mineral ores and concentrates (27+28 +667)	fuels and other energy (3)	manufactured goods										
				total[a] (5+6 −667 +7+8 +9)	of which chemicals and related products (5)	of which machinery and transport equipment (7)	of which other[a] (6−667 +8+9)							
235.9	—58.5[2]—		23.6	17.9[3]	...	...	...	11.0[4]	0.6[4]	72.9[4]	0.2[4]	15.2[4]	Afghanistan
267.4	37.9	—46.8—		15.3	1.5	0.8	13.0	23.1[5]	...	38.2	2.1	36.6	Albania
8,164.0	0.4	0.5	94.8	4.2	0.8	1.6	1.8	68.6	18.7	2.2	2.5	7.9	Algeria
307.5	100.0		—	—	—	—	—	—	100.0	—	—	—	American Samoa
24.6	—29.6[3]—		—	70.4[3]	7.2	10.9	52.4[3]	99.9	—	—	—	0.1	Andorra
1,874.5	5.4	12.1	82.1	0.4	—	—	0.4	27.9	37.2	0.6	1.3	32.9	Angola
17.6	6.2	—	11.5	82.3	7.5	30.1	44.7	3.4	17.9	—	—	78.7	Antigua and Barbuda
12,351.5	60.2	0.2	8.0	31.6	6.0	5.8	19.8	30.6	13.8	5.6	3.2	46.8	Argentina
6,100.0[7]	...	...	...	...	...	...	...	...	...	...	...	...	Armenia
30.5	54.0	1.2	0.2	44.5	7.1	7.9	29.5	5.6	22.3	—	—	72.1	Aruba
41,349.9	25.7	7.9	16.1	50.2	2.2	7.7	40.3	13.3	11.4	1.3	25.3	48.8	Australia
41,113.0	7.0	0.8	0.9	91.3	8.9	38.3	44.1	65.9	2.8	9.0	1.7	20.6	Austria
11,000.0[7]	...	...	...	...	...	...	...	...	...	...	...	...	Azerbaijan
2,163.8	2.8	0.8	77.7	18.7	16.8	0.8	1.2	2.2	79.6	—	2.2	16.0	Bahamas, The
3,760.9	0.2	0.2	83.4	16.2	3.2	0.4	12.6	2.1[4]	5.2[4]	...	10.0[4]	82.7[4]	Bahrain
1,194.5	25.2	—	1.3	73.6	0.3	1.4	71.9	24.1	31.9	4.8	5.5	33.6	Bangladesh
213.4	—27.4—		27.5	45.0	11.9	12.1	21.0	19.8	13.0	—	0.3	67.0	Barbados
33,000.0[7]	...	...	...	...	...	...	...	...	...	...	...	...	Belarus
117,841.1	11.7	7.2	3.9	77.1	14.1	27.0	36.0	75.2	3.8	1.2	1.2	18.6	Belgium[8]
92.6	69.7	—	2.9	27.4	0.9	3.6	23.0	28.4	56.5	1.0	0.1	14.1	Belize
166.7	—50.3[2]—		44.7	5.0[3]	0.3	1.2	3.5[3]	71.8	17.6	—	1.9	8.7	Benin
59.7	...	...	...	...	81.7	...	18.3	33.2	54.8	—	—	11.9	Bermuda
13.9[10]	32.1	...	...	67.9	16.5	...	51.4	0.4	—	—	0.2	99.4[12]	Bhutan
922.9	26.5	28.8	24.6	20.0	0.6	—	19.4	28.9	20.0	2.2	0.3	48.6	Bolivia
...	...	...	...	...	...	...	...	...	...	...	...	...	Bosnia and Hercegovina
1,472.8	5.8	87.8	0.1	6.4	0.6	2.3	3.4	2.8	0.3	—	0.1	96.9[15]	Botswana
31,412.8	31.1	9.4	2.2	57.3	5.9	18.5	32.9	30.8	23.7	1.8	7.4	36.2	Brazil
1,798.0	0.6	0.1	97.1	2.2	0.1	1.4	0.8	0.2	6.1	—	66.8	26.9	Brunei
13,410.6	16.3	—7.7[17]—		76.1[18]	5.8	59.1	11.2[18]	7.8	1.7	76.3	0.3	13.8	Bulgaria
155.0	—58.0[2]—		—	42.0[3]	0.5	9.7	31.8[3]	45.5	0.2	—	1.9	52.4	Burkina Faso
77.8	90.0	—	—	10.0	—	—	10.0	40.7[16]	0.1[16]	20.5[16]	5.4[16]	33.3[16]	Burundi
25.0[4]	82.9[19, 21]	...	—	...	...	...	...	4.0[4]	1.4[4]	78.8[4, 20]	9.2	6.5	Cambodia
1,281.6	54.5	0.2	18.0	27.3	1.6	5.2	20.5	66.6	10.0	1.6	1.5	29.3	Cameroon
126,896.9	17.6	4.2	10.0	68.2	5.2	37.2	25.7	8.1	75.0	0.8	5.5	10.5	Canada
3.2	90.0	1.8	—	8.2	2.4	2.0	3.8	93.5	0.3	—	—	6.1	Cape Verde
2.9	...	...	...	...	...	...	85.5[22]	...	21.7	...	...	...	Cayman Islands
140.3	54.3	43.2	—	2.5	0.2	0.2	2.0	89.2	0.6	—	—	10.2	Central African Republic
140.6	88.0	1.9[2, 17]	—	10.1[3, 18]	0.5	5.8	3.8[3, 18]	34.4[4]	0.1[4]	—	2.6[4]	62.9[4]	Chad
8,522.0	32.6	10.9	0.5	56.0	3.4	1.1	51.5	37.8	16.8	0.1	16.2	29.1	Chile
71,910.2	14.9	0.9[2]	6.7	77.5[3]	5.3	9.9	62.2[3]	9.4	8.6	2.8	14.3	64.9	China
6,765.0	37.2	1.7	36.9	24.2	3.4	1.3	19.6	26.4	44.4	0.9	3.8	24.5	Colombia
17.9	59.8	—	1.8	38.4	35.3	...	3.1	75.1[4]	19.2[4]	—	2.6[4]	3.1[4]	Comoros
776.9	8.4	1.4	89.1	1.2	0.1	0.5	0.6	41.6	54.2	0.5	0.1	3.5	Congo
2.8	—64.4—		1.1	35.6	0.6	6.1	28.9	...	1.2	—	32.1	66.1[25]	Cook Islands
1,121.5	71.9	0.8	1.1	26.3	4.7	3.0	18.5	27.4	45.3	1.6	1.1	24.6	Costa Rica
3,109.8	—77.3—		10.9	11.8	2.3	1.5	7.9	63.1	10.5	5.4	0.6	20.3	Côte d'Ivoire
...	...	...	...	...	...	...	...	...	...	...	...	...	Croatia
5,402.1	84.1	6.7[2]	6.8	2.5[3]	0.5	0.6	1.4[3]	10.2	—	81.5	1.4	6.8	Cuba
949.2	34.0	0.9	6.5	58.6	5.2	14.7	38.6	47.6	1.6	5.3	0.5	45.0	Cyprus
14,453.8	7.5	1.3	5.2	86.0	7.6	44.4	34.1	24.8	0.6	47.3	0.6	26.7	Czechoslovakia
35,733.1	31.4	0.6	4.2	63.9	9.4	25.8	28.7	54.2	4.7	3.1	3.6	34.4	Denmark
24.9	43.3	—	—	56.8	—	4.8	51.9	54.5	0.2	—	0.2	45.1	Djibouti
45.1	64.5	—	—	35.4	26.8	2.7	5.9	58.0	7.8	—	—	34.3	Dominica
738.5	75.7[26]	0.3[26]	—[26]	24.1[26]	4.0[26]	4.5[26]	15.6[26]	13.4	77.1	3.0	2.4	4.2	Dominican Republic
2,714.4	45.5	0.1	51.9	2.5	0.4	0.3	1.8	10.1	53.0	1.0	1.9	34.1	Ecuador
5,706.3	18.4	0.4	33.2	48.0	3.1	0.3	44.6	38.5	6.3	16.4	4.7	34.1	Egypt
556.8	73.8[13]	0.6[13]	1.3[13]	24.3[13]	6.2[13]	1.5[13]	16.6[13]	21.4	36.4	—	2.9	39.3	El Salvador
23.5	—76.5[2]—		0.2	23.3[3]	0.1	0.5	22.7[3]	83.8[4]	2.3[4]	—[4]	1.1[4]	12.8[4]	Equatorial Guinea
5,150.5	—28.7[2]—		4.2	67.1[3]	10.0	18.4	38.7[3]	...	0.1	97.8	—	2.1	Estonia[27]
421.1	94.0	0.2	3.0	2.8	1.2	—	1.6	44.8	9.8	7.5	12.2	25.7	Ethiopia

Trade: external (continued)

country	year	imports total value ('000,000 U.S.$)	Standard International Trade Classification (SITC) categories (%)							direction of trade (%)				
			food and agricultural raw materials (0+1+2−27−28+4)	mineral ores and concentrates (27+28+667)	fuels and other energy (3)	manufactured goods total[a] (5+6−667+7+8+9)	of which chemicals and related products (5)	of which machinery and transport equipment (7)	of which other[a] (6−667+8+9)	from European Economic Community (EEC)[b]	from United States	from Eastern Europe[c]	from Japan	from all other[d]
Faeroe Islands	1991	294.0	28.6	0.7	13.2	57.4	7.9	15.6	33.9	61.1	3.9	1.4	2.3	31.4
Fiji	1987	379.0	20.5	0.4	16.3	62.8	8.6	19.4	34.8	8.1	5.3	0.2	12.1	74.3
Finland	1991	21,692.7	8.4	3.1	13.4	75.2	11.6	34.7	28.9	45.9	6.9	10.7	6.0	30.5
France[28]	1990	233,163.2	12.4	1.4	9.6	76.6	10.7	34.1	31.8	59.8	8.1	2.2	4.0	25.8
French Guiana	1990	742.7	15.4	0.3	7.7	76.7	5.7	40.3	30.6	80.7	3.6	0.1	2.3	13.3
French Polynesia	1988	808.3	20.4	0.2	5.4	74.1	6.4	35.9	31.8	65.2	11.3	0.1	4.4	18.9
Gabon	1983	685.6	18.5	1.0	1.8	78.8	7.5	38.5	32.7	74.6	11.0	0.3	7.4	6.6
Gambia, The	1990	199.6	—40.5[2]—		8.7	50.8[3]	6.1	15.1	29.6[3]	53.1[4]	4.2[4]	3.9[4]	4.3[4]	34.6[4]
Gaza Strip	1990	36.5[30]	...	...	...	...	...	...	...	...	...	...	...	...
Georgia	1989	9,700.0[7]												
Germany	1991	389,024.4	12.4[32]	1.6[32]	8.3[32]	77.7[32]	8.6[32]	34.9[32]	34.2[32]	52.1	6.5	5.1	6.1	30.2
Ghana	1985	867.3	—8.0[2]—		29.2	62.8[3]	12.5	26.4	23.9[3]	50.6	6.3	0.3	6.6	36.2
Gibraltar	1988	257.9	—24.4[2]—		20.7	54.9[3]	4.3	21.4	29.2[3]	73.4[33]	5.4[33]		10.4[33]	10.8[33]
Greece	1990	19,734.6	18.8	1.0	7.7	72.5	10.5	31.0	31.0	64.3	3.7	4.0	5.9	22.1
Greenland	1991	402.8	20.6	0.4	12.0	67.1	5.1	20.1	41.8	76.0	2.7	0.3	4.0	17.0
Grenada	1987	88.7	—31.7[2]—		5.8	62.5[3]	9.5	23.2	29.8[3]	24.6	26.9	—	7.2	41.3
Guadeloupe	1990	1,681.0	21.1	0.3	5.4	73.2	8.1	31.1	34.1	78.5	4.1	0.2	2.2	15.1
Guam	1983	610.7	16.9	0.1	46.9	36.2	2.3	19.1	14.8	...	23.4	...	19.9	56.6
Guatemala	1987	1,448.8	12.4	5.2	12.8	69.7	19.4	26.5	23.8	16.9	36.9	1.2	6.3	38.7
Guernsey[35]	...	...												
Guinea	1988	491.2	—10.0[2,36]—		30.3[36]	59.7[3,36]	3.0[36]	39.8[36]	16.9[3,36]	62.1[4]	7.8[4]	7.1[4]	2.2[4]	20.7[4]
Guinea-Bissau	1984	38.7	20.1[36]	2.2[36]	6.2[36]	71.5[36]	5.6[36]	36.4[36]	29.5[36]	52.0	8.8	15.2	0.2	23.8
Guyana	1986	242.5	5.6[26]	0.5[26]	43.2[26]	50.7[26]	9.4[26]	23.2[26]	18.1[26]	20.1[4]	16.4[4]	0.5[4]	3.7[4]	59.3[4]
Haiti	1989[6]	313.7	—32.5[2]—		17.7	49.8[3]	9.2	17.0	23.5[3]	19.3[4]	46.9[4]	0.4[4]	6.8	26.6[4]
Honduras	1989	875.6	13.7	0.9	15.8	69.6	21.7	24.7	23.2	10.4	39.8	0.4	9.1	40.3
Hong Kong	1991	103,547.9	9.2	2.2	2.0	86.6	7.4	28.1	51.0	9.2	7.6	0.1	16.4	66.7
Hungary	1990	8,646.6	11.2	1.3[2]	14.2	73.3[3]	14.9	34.6	23.7[3]	37.0	2.6	27.9	2.1	30.4
Iceland	1990	1,659.4	11.0	3.4	9.8	75.8	8.1	35.1	32.5	49.9	14.4	6.5	5.6	23.6
India	1991[1]	23,799.2	7.2	14.2	27.3	51.3	12.9	17.6	20.7	28.3	10.7	5.4	7.5	48.1
Indonesia	1990	21,837.1	9.7	3.2	8.9	78.2	15.5	42.7	20.0	18.7	11.5	0.9	24.3	44.7
Iran	1989[1]	8,113.0	—19.9[2]—		4.2	75.9[3]	18.7	36.8	20.4[3]	46.1[4]	1.0[4]	3.6[4]	10.2	39.1[4]
Iraq	1989	11,730.0[4]	17.6[37]	0.2[37]	0.3[37]	81.9[37]	7.5[37]	39.8[37]	34.6[37]	31.6[4]	11.0[4]	11.9[4]	4.6[4]	40.9[4]
Ireland	1991	20,764.6	13.0	0.9	5.9	80.3	13.3	34.7	32.3	65.5	15.0	1.0	5.0	13.6
Isle of Man[35]	...	...												
Israel	1991	16,906.3[38]	9.4	16.5	7.8	66.3	9.2	31.3	25.9	47.7	19.3	1.1	4.3	27.6
Italy[39]	1990	180,056.6	17.4	2.2	10.5	69.9	11.1	30.1	28.7	57.5	5.1	3.6	2.3	31.4
Jamaica	1990	1,838.5	15.0	0.1	22.0	63.0	11.1	25.2	26.7	10.6	47.6	0.4	4.9	36.5
Japan	1991	236,736.7	21.6	5.6	23.1	49.7	7.4	16.7	25.7	13.4	22.5	1.7	—	62.4
Jersey	1980	537.1	23.9	0.4	9.3	66.5	6.5	24.8	35.2	84.9[40]	...	...	...	15.1
Jordan	1988	2,786.1	20.9	1.5	15.5	62.1	9.9	22.6	29.7	29.7	12.6	5.5	5.3	46.9
Kazakhstan	1989	24,900.0[7]	...											
Kenya	1987	1,739.3	9.5	0.5	20.1	70.0	17.8	34.3	17.8	43.5	7.1	0.5	10.9	38.1
Kiribati	1990	26.9	34.0	0.2	10.7	55.0	5.1	19.1	30.8	1.7	6.6	—	23.6	68.1
Korea, North	1990	2,540.0	...	...	...	...	...	...	...	4.8[4,42]	—[4,42]	54.7[4,42]		33.0[4,42]
Korea, South	1990	69,843.7	13.6	4.0	15.8	66.6	10.6	34.3	21.7	12.0	24.3	...	26.6	37.1
Kuwait	1989	6,302.2	20.2	0.4	1.0	78.4	7.5	29.5	41.4	29.9	13.2	1.6	12.9	42.4
Kyrgyzstan	1989	5,600.0[7]	...											
Laos	1989	250.0[4]	32.1[43]	0.2[43]	11.2[43]	56.4[43]	6.1[43]	25.7[43]	24.7[43]	3.2[4]	0.2[4]	50.8[4]	10.7[4]	35.1[4]
Latvia[27]	1990	10,819.2	—16.9[2]—		9.4	73.7[3]	11.6	31.3	30.9[3]	...	...	88.8[42]	...	11.2[42]
Lebanon	1990	2,450.0[4]	—17.3[2,26]—		3.6[26]	79.1[3,26]	7.8[26]	29.3[26]	42.0[3,26]	41.3[4]	4.4[4]	11.2[4]	4.0[4]	39.1[4]
Lesotho	1988	587.5	—27.0[2,44]—		8.1[44]	64.8[3,44]	7.5[44]	13.8[44]	43.5[3,44]	1.5[45]	0.2[45]	—[45]	—[45]	98.2[45,46]
Liberia	1984	363.2	25.5	0.9	19.8	53.9	6.7	26.8	20.5	40.0	22.3	1.1	8.1	28.5
Libya	1987	4,722.6	18.9	0.1	0.4	80.6	9.0	34.9	36.7	61.6	1.2	3.1	5.9	28.2
Liechtenstein	1990	707.8	4.4	0.3[2]	0.6	94.8[3]	5.5	28.7	60.7[3]	...	...	...	...	...
Lithuania[27]	1990	12,867.7	—14.7[2]—		15.3	70.0[3]	11.7	31.8	26.5[3]	4.8[5]	0.8	86.3	0.7	7.3
Luxembourg	1989	6,193.1	11.8	—12.6[2]—		75.6[3]	14.0	27.5	34.1[3]	91.1[47]	2.0	...	0.8	6.1
Macau	1990	1,532.5	15.3	0.7	4.6	79.4	6.0	15.2	58.2	8.4	5.1	0.4	11.5	74.6
Macedonia	...	...	...											
Madagascar	1986	373.6	17.0	0.4	23.1	59.5	11.7	28.8	19.0	45.4	10.7	10.0	6.5	23.8
Malawi	1988	409.1	9.1[19]	1.3[19]	13.3[19]	76.3[19]	20.2[19]	29.4[19]	26.8[19]	36.3	5.1	0.9	9.1	48.6
Malaysia	1991	36,768.1	7.4	1.6	4.2	86.9	7.6	53.8	25.5	13.6	15.3	0.4	26.1	44.6
Maldives	1990	137.7	—29.7—		15.8	54.6	4.8	21.7	28.0	13.8[4]	0.2[4]	—[4]	6.5[4]	79.5[4]
Mali	1987	374.1	—22.3[2]—		14.8	62.9[3]	15.0	22.1	25.8[3]	48.8	5.0	0.9	3.3	42.0
Malta	1989	1,494.0	13.4	0.6	6.4	79.6	7.0	40.7	31.8	74.0	3.9	2.1	3.1	16.9
Marshall Islands	1988	33.8	45.5	—[2]	10.7	43.7[3]	2.0	10.8	31.0[3]	—	51.3	—	17.6	31.1
Martinique	1990	1,740.0	19.1	0.2	9.9	70.8	9.5	31.7	29.6	79.6	2.4	0.1	2.1	15.8
Mauritania	1988	361.3	30.6	...	7.0	62.4	...	51.0	11.4	68.6[4]	4.2[4]	0.3[4]	1.7[4]	25.1[4]
Mauritius	1989	1,325.7	16.3	2.3	7.5	73.9	6.5	22.9	44.4	34.2	1.6	0.1	9.1	55.0
Mayotte	1990	60.2	—22.2—		5.2	72.6	9.9	36.4	26.3	68.7[48]	...	...	...	31.3
Mexico	1990	28,066.3	19.7	2.1	4.1	74.1	11.2	36.8	26.0	15.4	64.7	0.5	3.8	15.7
Micronesia	1988	67.7	—42.0[2]—		6.0	52.0[3]	5.2	13.5	33.2[3]	...	36.2	...	22.0	41.8
Moldova	1989	9,200.0[7]	...											
Monaco[28]	...													
Mongolia	1990	828.6	10.8[16]	—33.5[16,17]—		55.7[16,18]	7.0[16]	30.2[16]	18.5[16,18]	5.0[5]	—	87.4	1.1	6.6
Morocco	1990	6,922.0	15.8	4.7	16.9	62.6	10.6	29.3	22.7	54.6	6.3	4.9	1.8	32.5
Mozambique	1988	715.0	—37.3[2]—		8.5	54.2[3]	6.5	33.4	14.3[3]	43.2[4]	7.9	13.7[20]	4.0[4]	31.2[4]
Myanmar (Burma)	1991[1]	612.4[50]	—2.3[2,42]—		2.4[42]	95.3[3,42]	9.2[42]	60.2[42]	25.9[3,42]	11.0	...	1.9	16.5	67.4
Namibia	1989	894.0	...	...	27.5[26]	...	...	25.2[26]	...	...	...	...	...	...
Nauru	1989[52]	13.9	—33.7[2]—		0.4	65.9[3]	2.7	22.3	40.9[3]	...	...	...	...	...
Nepal	1990[53]	404.5	17.1	0.5	12.2	70.1	15.6	23.7	30.8	15.3	1.6	2.8	13.7	66.6
Netherlands, The	1991	125,479.5	15.3	1.6	9.5	73.6	10.4	31.8	31.4	64.3	7.8	1.7	3.6	22.5
Netherlands Antilles	1990[54]	2,145.8	—6.3[2]—		70.4	23.3[3]	3.0	9.7	10.6[3]	15.7[4]	4.2[4]	—[4]	3.5[4]	59.5[4]
New Caledonia	1989	763.9	—17.6[2]—		9.2	73.3[3]	6.2	39.5	27.5[3]	44.1[48]	10.4	...	5.3	40.2
New Zealand	1990	9,483.5	8.0	2.5	7.7	81.8	11.6	41.7	28.6	19.1	17.9	0.2	15.5	47.3
Nicaragua	1986	774.5	12.8	0.8	17.9	68.5	18.3	27.3	23.0	23.7	2.7	37.4	2.5	33.7

exports total value ('000,000 U.S.$)	SITC: food and agricultural raw materials (0+1+2 -27-28 +4)	SITC: mineral ores and concentrates (27+28 +667)	SITC: fuels and other energy (3)	manuf. goods total[a] (5+6 -667 +7+8 +9)	of which chemicals and related products (5)	of which machinery and transport equipment (7)	of which other[a] (6-667 +8+9)	direction: to EEC[b]	to United States	to Eastern Europe[c]	to Japan	to all other[d]	country
433.6	94.4	—	—	5.6	0.1	5.4		77.9	7.1	0.4	3.5	11.1	Faeroe Islands
322.5	63.2	0.1	9.0	27.6	0.9	3.2	23.5	35.0	5.5	0.1	3.0	56.4	Fiji
22,964.0	11.3	0.5	3.0	85.1	6.9	27.4	50.8	51.2	6.1	6.7	1.5	34.5	Finland
209,996.1	17.7	1.0	2.3	79.0	13.5	37.3	28.2	62.9	6.1	1.4	1.9	27.7	France[28]
89.7	67.8	0.3	—	31.8	1.7	18.7	11.4	75.9	3.0	—	0.6	20.5	French Guiana
74.7	5.9	31.3	—	62.8	1.6	38.6	22.6	40.0	18.9	—	22.5	18.6	French Polynesia
1,475.4	7.5	7.0	79.5	6.0	1.2	0.6	4.1	54.6	25.6	1.8	0.3	17.6	Gabon
40.6	44.6[29]	...	...	...	...	...	...	53.4[4]	1.2[4]	...	35.4[4]	10.0[4]	Gambia, The
12.4[31]	...	...	...	...	...	...	...	...	...	...	...	...	Gaza Strip
9,700.0[7]	...	...	...	...	...	...	...	...	...	...	...	...	Georgia
402,638.4	6.4[32]	0.8[32]	1.3[32]	91.5[32]	12.9[32]	48.4[32]	30.2[32]	54.1	6.3	5.6	2.5	31.5	Germany
616.0	—74.7[2]—			25.3[3]	—	—	25.3[3]	51.3	11.1	10.5	13.1	13.9	Ghana
82.1	—8.2[2]—		51.5	40.3[3]	2.8	18.1	19.4[3]	22.2	...	...	...	77.8[34]	Gibraltar
8,053.2	32.1	3.1	7.3	57.6	3.9	4.2	49.4	64.3	5.6	4.3	1.0	24.9	Greece
340.6	95.5	—	0.9	3.6	—	1.3	2.4	96.8	—	—	0.9	2.3	Greenland
31.6	91.3		—	8.7	0.4	—	8.3	64.7	4.8	—	—	30.5	Grenada
121.7	77.5	0.9	—	21.6	3.5	12.6	5.5	81.2	0.2	—	—	18.6	Guadeloupe
39.2	23.5	2.7	3.5	70.3	5.6	11.5	53.2	...	24.9	...	4.8	70.4	Guam
899.2	73.9	0.5	1.8	23.8	10.5	1.1	12.2	16.1	38.4	1.0	1.8	42.7	Guatemala
													Guernsey[35]
548.1	3.0[36]	96.8[36]	—[36]	0.2[36]	—[36]	—[36]	0.2[36]	48.5[4]	23.1[4]	20.4[4]	0.2[4]	7.8[4]	Guinea
18.9	87.1[36]	0.3[36]	—[36]	12.6[36]	0.3[36]	—[36]	12.3[36]	64.4	...	—	—	35.6	Guinea-Bissau
214.3	63.7	21.0[2,17]		15.3[3,18]	5.2	3.5	6.6[3,18]	42.6[4]	22.6[4]	1.9[4]	8.7[4]	24.2[4]	Guyana
160.6	—36.3[2]—		—	63.7[3]	...	...	...	38.7[4]	56.2	0.1[4]	1.2	3.7[4]	Haiti
1,199.1	85.1	—	0.3	14.5	1.2	0.2	13.1	29.0	41.8	6.2	7.9	15.1	Honduras
98,298.9	5.5	1.5	0.7	92.3	5.9	25.6	60.8	17.6	22.7	0.5	5.4	53.8	Hong Kong
9,587.7	25.6	1.5[2]	3.1	69.8[3]	12.4	25.6	31.7[3]	35.5	3.5	28.2	1.2	31.6	Hungary
1,586.4	80.3	0.7	—	19.0	0.1	2.1	16.8	67.8	9.9	2.9	6.0	13.4	Iceland
17,940.2	19.5	20.3	2.9	57.2	7.4	7.4	42.4	27.6	14.7	17.7	9.3	30.7	India
25,675.3	16.2	2.6	43.8	37.4	2.4	1.4	33.6	11.8	13.1	0.6	42.5	32.0	Indonesia
11,830.0	—4.2[2]—		91.4	4.5[3]	—	—	4.5[3]	41.5[4]	0.1[4]	13.8[4]	12.8[4]	31.9[4]	Iran
14,520.0[4]	0.5		99.5	—	—	—	—	23.2[4]	16.0[4]	16.6[4]	7.5[4]	36.6[4]	Iraq
24,272.3	24.2	1.8	0.6	73.4	17.7	29.4	26.3	74.3	8.7	0.8	2.3	14.0	Ireland
													Isle of Man[35]
11,893.2	10.3	29.0	0.6	60.2	14.7	23.8	21.7	35.9	30.2	0.9	6.1	26.8	Israel
168,554.2	7.0	0.4	2.0	90.6	6.5	37.5	46.5	58.5	7.6	2.9	2.3	28.7	Italy[39]
1,262.7	19.9	63.7	1.4	15.0	2.1	2.7	10.2	29.6	28.8	4.3	0.7	36.6	Jamaica
314,525.5	1.1	0.1	0.4	98.3	5.6	70.3	22.5	18.8	29.1	0.9	—	51.2	Japan
209.2	27.6	4.3[41]		68.0	1.2	31.1	35.7	67.3[40]	...	...	...	32.7	Jersey
1,035.7	9.7	39.5	0.1	50.8	24.8	5.8	20.1	9.7	1.0	3.8	1.9	83.5	Jordan
15,000.0[7]	...	...	...	...	...	...	...						Kazakhstan
960.1	70.1	2.5	13.1	14.4	4.1	2.5	7.8	42.5	5.4	0.7	0.9	50.4	Kenya
2.9	74.5	—	—	25.4	—	3.3	22.2	42.8	15.4	—	0.2	41.6	Kiribati
1,720.0	...	...	...	...	...	...	...	2.7[4,42]	—[4,42]	54.6[4,42]	14.9[4,42]	27.9[4,42]	Korea, North
65,015.7	4.6	0.3	1.1	94.0	3.9	39.3	50.9	13.6	29.9	—	19.4	37.1	Korea, South
11,476.0	0.7	0.2	91.0	8.2	2.4	2.5	3.3	22.7[4]	8.2[4]	1.3[4]	18.5[4]	49.3[4]	Kuwait
4,300.0[7]	...	...	...	...	...	...	...						Kyrgyzstan
125.0[4]	46.5[19]	3.4[19]	50.1[19]	—[19]	—[19]	—[19]	—[19]	2.5[4]	0.6[4]	20.0[4]	5.8[4]	71.1[4]	Laos
9,033.9	—26.2[2]—		1.8	72.0[3]	12.4	27.9	31.7[3]	...	...	97.3[42]	...	2.7[42]	Latvia[27]
540.0[4]	—14.4[2,26]—		—[26]	85.6[3,26]	1.1[26]	18.2[26]	66.2[3,26]	20.8[4]	4.2[4]	8.7[4]	0.7[4]	65.6[4]	Lebanon
64.1	—35.2[2]—		—	64.8[3]	1.5	0.9	62.4[3]	10.3[45]	0.1[45]	—	—[45]	89.6[45]	Lesotho
449.1	34.1	64.8	—	1.1	0.1	0.3	0.8	70.7	20.2	1.6	1.3	6.1	Liberia
8,766.1	—	—	96.8	3.2	3.2	—	—	79.3	—	8.8	—	11.9	Libya
1,252.8	3.9	—2	0.1	95.9[3]	7.8	46.3	41.8[3]	42.7	...	...	—	57.3	Liechtenstein
10,925.2	—24.1[2]—		10.4	65.5[3]	6.0	31.4	28.0[3]	2.1[5]	0.1	95.7	—	2.1	Lithuania[27]
5,402.0	6.0	—1.2[2]—		92.9[3]	17.5	15.4	59.9[3]	79.5[47]	4.8	...	1.0	14.8	Luxembourg
1,700.9	1.7	—	—	98.2	1.3	1.8	95.2	34.4	36.0	0.3	3.1	26.3	Macau
													Macedonia
316.6	84.6	5.7	2.2	7.5	1.3	1.9	4.4	59.2	14.8	2.6	10.9	12.4	Madagascar
280.0	95.0[19]	—[19]		5.0[19]	0.5[19]	—[19]	4.5[19]	49.5	11.3	0.6	11.8	26.8	Malawi
34,425.2	21.9	0.7	15.6	61.8	1.8	41.1	18.9	14.8	16.9	0.3	15.9	52.2	Malaysia
52.6	72.2	0.1	—	27.7	—	—	27.7	25.9	24.4	—	8.5	41.3	Maldives
179.0	—69.0[2]—			31.0[3]	...	...	...	9.4	—	12.4	1.0	77.2	Mali
858.0	3.6	1.0	1.8	93.6	1.5	49.7	42.5	73.5	5.4	1.7	0.1	19.3	Malta
2.1	100.0	—	—	—	—	—	—	—[26]	79.4[26]	—[26]	—[26]	20.6[26]	Marshall Islands
276.1	61.1	0.4	15.9	22.6	3.3	11.4	8.0	67.7	0.5	—	—	31.7	Martinique
446.8	63.8	32.1	—	4.1	...	...	...	36.1[4]	3.0	16.0[4]	31.9	13.0[4]	Mauritania
986.8	36.6	2.4	—	61.0	0.9	1.8	58.3	75.1	13.8	1.3	0.3	9.5	Mauritius
6.9	17.9[49]	—[49]	—[49]	82.1[49]	81.3[49]	—[49]	0.8[49]	70.2[19,48]	...	...	...	29.8[19]	Mayotte
26,811.7	13.2	2.4	36.8	47.5	6.8	25.1	15.7	12.6	70.3	0.1	5.6	11.5	Mexico
2.3	87.2	—	—	12.8	...	...	...	...	0.3	—	58.2	41.5	Micronesia
8,000.0[7]	...	...	...	...	...	...	...						Moldova
													Monaco[28]
592.6	39.0[16]	—41.7[16,17]—		15.8[16,18]	...	0.1[16]	15.7[16,18]	4.0[5]	0.1	90.7	1.2	4.0	Mongolia
4,231.4	29.0	13.4	3.6	54.0	19.4	5.0	29.5	65.1	1.9	2.0	3.9	27.1	Morocco
103.0	82.4	7.7[2,17]	1.3	8.7[3,18]	0.3	0.8	7.6[3,18]	28.7[5]	15.5	...	16.6	39.2	Mozambique
389.7[50]	—81.8[2,42]—		3.4[42]	14.8[3,42]	4.0[42]	0.2[42]	10.6[3,42]	2.8	...	...	7.2	90.0	Myanmar (Burma)
1,020.9	11.0	75.9	—	13.1	...	...	...	...	25.0[51]	...	15.0[51]	...	Namibia
80.3	—	99.8	—	0.2	—	—	0.2	...	...	...	...	...	Nauru
149.2	6.1	—	—	93.9	0.1	—	93.8	45.5	32.9	2.7	0.5	18.3	Nepal
133,074.3	24.9	1.2	9.9	63.9	16.1	23.5	24.3	76.7	3.9	1.7	0.9	16.8	Netherlands, The
1,792.7	—0.8[2]—		96.3	2.9[3]	1.4	0.6	0.8[3]	16.1[4]	41.1[4]	—[4]	1.3[4]	41.6[4]	Netherlands Antilles
671.6	—[49]	29.9[49]	—[49]	70.1[49]	—[49]	—[49]	70.1[49]	36.4[48]	6.2	—[4]	28.4	29.0	New Caledonia
9,469.9	63.0	0.5	3.8	32.7	5.2	7.1	20.4	18.4	13.1	2.0	16.1	50.4	New Zealand
233.6	94.2	—	—	5.8	2.5	—	3.3	53.6	—	3.7	16.9	25.8	Nicaragua

Trade: external (continued)

country	year	imports total value ('000,000 U.S.$)	food and agricultural raw materials (0+1+2-27-28+4)	mineral ores and concentrates (27+28+667)	fuels and other energy (3)	manufactured goods total[a] (5+6-667+7+8+9)	of which chemicals and related products (5)	of which machinery and transport equipment (7)	of which other[a] (6-667+8+9)	from European Economic Community (EEC)[b]	from United States	from Eastern Europe[c]	from Japan	from all other[d]
Niger	1985	344.5	——41.4[2]——		11.1	47.6[3]	8.1	20.5	19.0[3]	42.1	11.4	0.1	3.8	42.6
Nigeria	1987	3,918.7	12.8	2.7	0.4	84.1	16.9	38.2	29.0	56.4	8.3	5.0	9.0	21.3
Northern Mariana Islands	1989	313.7	16.6		19.2	64.1	2.8	28.8	32.6	—	24.6	—	15.5	60.0
Norway	1991	25,479.5	8.1	5.5	4.3	82.2	8.9	38.3	34.9	48.2	7.8	2.1	4.9	37.0
Oman	1990	2,681.3	18.9	0.4	4.0	76.8	6.6	36.2	34.0	27.9	9.4	0.2	17.0	45.5
Pakistan	1991[53]	7,646.8	18.1	2.2	22.9	56.7	16.3	27.2	13.2	23.7	11.8	1.9	13.0	49.7
Palau	1984	25.1[56]	28.9	0.1[2]	0.9[56]	70.0[3]	4.0	24.5	41.5[3]	—	41.8	—	38.2	20.0
Panama	1989	964.8	16.2	0.5	16.7	66.6	18.9	17.8	30.0	9.2	38.4	0.3	4.3	47.9
Papua New Guinea	1988	1,347.1	17.8	0.3	8.4	73.5	7.2	39.6	26.7	7.9	10.4	—	17.8	63.9
Paraguay	1990	1,348.6	8.1	0.3	14.2	77.3	8.2	44.5	24.6	14.8	12.7	0.2	15.5	57.0
Peru	1988	3,109.2	41.2	1.0	4.3	53.4	17.3	21.8	14.4	18.9	22.2	0.7	3.9	54.3
Philippines	1990	13,041.7	12.8	2.0	14.9	70.3	11.3	25.9	33.1	11.2	19.4	0.6	18.5	50.3
Poland	1989	10,277.3	17.0	3.1	12.7	67.2	10.9	33.4	22.9	38.7	1.4	27.7	1.4	30.9
Portugal	1990	25,185.7	15.4	0.8	10.9	73.0	9.2	36.4	27.3	69.2	3.9	0.4	2.6	23.9
Puerto Rico	1988[53]	11,859.1	19.7	0.6	10.7	69.0	15.6	23.7	29.7	6.5	66.8	0.1	4.9	21.7
Qatar	1989	1,326.0	20.3[16]	2.1[16]	0.7[16]	76.9[16]	6.5[16]	39.5[16]	30.9[16]	37.6	8.8	—	18.8	34.8
Réunion	1990	2,074.0	19.9	0.2	6.3	73.7	9.4	30.7	33.6	80.2	0.5	—	2.2	17.1
Romania	1989	9,122.4	6.9	——56.0[17]——		37.1[18]	5.5	25.5	6.1[18]	13.0	2.0	46.2	1.2	37.5
Russia[27]	1989	229,200.0	——21.8[2]——		3.0	75.2[3]	8.7	41.0	25.5[3]	—	—	49.0[57]	—	51.0
Rwanda	1986	352.0	16.7	2.4	13.7	67.2	5.3	29.6	32.3	44.9	3.7	0.4	13.0	38.1
St. Kitts and Nevis	1988	93.3	21.0	—	5.5	73.5	7.5	32.0	34.0	21.2	47.4	—	3.8	27.5
St. Lucia	1986	154.8	25.7	0.2	7.7	66.5	12.2	19.8	34.5	24.5	34.1	0.1	6.9	34.4
St. Vincent and the Grenadines	1987	98.0	25.3	0.3[2]	6.2	68.3[3]	13.3	19.7	35.3[3]	27.4	35.5	0.2	3.3	33.6
San Marino[39]		...	...	...	...	...	...	...	...	...	...	...	...	...
São Tomé and Príncipe	1988	21.7	——35.2——		6.5	58.3	...	30.5	27.8	63.1[4]	31.3[4]	...	1.1[4]	4.5[4]
Saudi Arabia	1990	24,069.0	14.5	0.8	0.2	84.5	9.3	37.4	37.9	34.1	16.7	0.9	15.3	32.9
Senegal	1990	1,620.4	30.5	1.9	16.0	51.7	9.7	21.3	20.7	56.1	5.3	1.2	3.6	33.7
Seychelles	1990	185.8	20.8	0.1	20.7	58.4	5.4	24.7	28.3	32.3	2.3	0.1	6.8	58.5
Sierra Leone	1986	151.8	——32.9[2]——		11.1	55.9[3]	8.8	27.1	20.1[3]	46.6	9.9	0.6	6.4	36.4
Singapore	1990	60,579.0	7.7	0.6	15.8	75.8	7.7	44.7	23.5	12.8	16.0	0.4	20.2	50.6
Slovenia		...	...	...	...	...	...	...	...	...	...	...	...	...
Solomon Islands	1989	113.1	——18.2[2]——		9.7	72.1[3]	4.3	36.4	31.4[3]	4.6	2.8	0.1	23.2	69.3
Somalia	1986	284.4	30.3	0.2	4.6	64.9	5.1	37.1	22.7	53.8	8.8	—	4.1	33.3
South Africa[58]	1990	17,477.0	8.5[19]	2.2[19]	0.6[19,59]	88.7[19,60]	12.2[19]	39.5[19]	37.0[19,60]	43.0[4]	12.6[4]	0.1[4]	9.7[4]	34.5[4]
Bophuthatswana[58]		...	...	...	...	...	...	...	...	...	...	...	...	...
Ciskei[58]		...	...	...	...	...	...	...	...	...	...	...	...	...
Transkei[58]		...	...	...	...	...	...	...	...	...	...	...	...	...
Venda[58]		...	...	...	...	...	...	...	...	...	...	...	...	...
Spain	1990	87,703.2	14.0	2.2	11.8	72.0	9.9	38.1	24.0	59.5	8.3	2.0	4.4	25.7
Sri Lanka	1990	2,632.8	20.9	3.5	12.6	63.0	11.8	19.3	32.0	14.8	7.9	0.9	12.4	64.1
Sudan, The	1988	1,060.7	——17.2[2]——		20.8	62.0[3]	10.5	26.9	24.6[3]	31.9	8.9	2.4	3.7	53.2
Suriname	1990	472.0	11.8	1.5	18.0	68.7	21.4	24.7	22.6	29.4	41.0	—	2.8	26.8
Swaziland	1989[1]	590.3	15.7	0.8	11.8	71.7	9.7	33.6	28.3	9.7	0.7	...	2.4	87.3[62]
Sweden	1990	54,566.5	8.1	1.4	9.1	81.4	9.5	38.6	33.3	55.2	8.7	2.7	5.1	28.3
Switzerland	1990	69,686.2	8.5	5.0	4.5	81.9	11.3	31.6	39.1	71.7	6.1	1.0	4.4	16.8
Syria	1989	2,097.5	28.8	0.7[2]	5.9	64.6[3]	16.8	17.6	30.2[3]	43.7	7.9	10.2	4.2	34.1
Taiwan	1990	54,716.3	12.4[16]	2.4[16]	7.9[16]	77.2[16]	12.7[16]	32.9[16]	31.6[16]	13.4	23.0	0.5	29.3	33.9
Tajikistan	1989	5,300.0[7]	...	...	...	...	...	...	...	...	...	...	...	...
Tanzania	1987	975.8	7.9	1.8[2]	13.4	77.0[3]	10.7	43.4	22.9[3]	49.3	3.6	0.4[4]	11.2	35.5
Thailand	1990	33,371.4	9.7	4.7	9.2	76.3	10.4	41.0	24.9	14.7	10.8	1.4	30.4	42.7
Togo	1990	581.4	23.6	0.6	8.3	67.5	12.4	22.6	32.6	56.6	5.3	0.6	4.3	33.2
Tonga	1988	55.2	33.3	0.3	9.7	56.7	6.5	21.9	28.3	1.9	7.6	—	7.6	82.9
Trinidad and Tobago	1990	1,261.6	20.5	4.8	11.4	63.3	13.9	22.7	26.7	15.6	40.5	0.2	3.5	40.2
Tunisia	1990	5,476.0	15.0	3.5	9.0	72.5	8.9	28.4	35.2	70.5	5.2	4.0	1.8	18.5
Turkey	1990	22,300.7	12.6	3.2	20.7	63.5	12.8	31.6	19.2	41.9	10.2	8.7	5.0	34.1
Turkmenistan	1989	4,600.0[7]	...	...	...	...	...	...	...	...	...	...	...	...
Tuvalu	1989	4.1	——12.8[2]——		12.8	49.0[3]	7.1	12.2	29.6[3]	5.4[51]	1.0[51]	—[51]	3.1[51]	90.6[51]
Uganda	1989	394.0	8.7[24]	0.7[24]	29.6[24]	61.0[24]	11.1[24]	26.8[24]	23.0[24]	43.3[4]	5.4[4]	—[4]	6.5[4]	44.9[4]
Ukraine[27]	1990	88,100.0	——9.9[2]——		22.5	67.6[3]	8.9	37.7	21.0[3]	...	...	81.9[57]	...	18.1
United Arab Emirates	1987	7,296.8	19.4	1.1	3.9	75.6	7.0	30.3	38.3	33.2	8.0	0.6	17.1	41.2
United Kingdom[35]	1991	210,331.0	13.4	2.9	6.4	77.3	9.2	36.3	31.8	51.6	11.5	1.3	5.7	29.9
United States[64]	1990	516,717.5	7.7	2.0	13.3	77.0	4.6	41.3	31.1	18.5	—	0.5	18.0	63.0
Uruguay	1990	1,414.5	10.8	1.2	18.1	69.9	20.4	30.2	19.3	19.6	9.9	3.7	3.2	63.7
Uzbekistan	1989	18,600.0[7]	...	...	...	...	...	...	...	...	...	...	...	...
Vanuatu	1989	67.9	——20.8[2]——		8.1	71.0[3]	6.9	31.1	33.1[3]	4.9[16]	—[16]	—[16]	9.4[16]	85.8[16]
Venezuela	1990	6,363.6	15.5	2.9	3.0	78.5	15.9	40.0	22.7	25.9	46.2	0.2	3.9	23.8
Vietnam	1989	3,056.0	17.2[19]	——44.7[19]——		38.1[19]	...	23.2[19]	14.9[19]	6.3[4]	0.4[4]	74.6[4]	6.1[4]	12.6[4]
Virgin Islands (U.S.)	1990	3,294.7	...	...	70.1	...	...	...	...	...	37.2	...	...	...
West Bank	1990	62.1[65]	...	...	...	...	...	...	...	...	...	...	...	...
Western Sahara		...	...	...	...	...	...	...	...	...	...	...	...	...
Western Samoa	1989	77.0	24.3[26]	0.3[26]	17.5[26]	57.9[26]	7.4[26]	22.9[26]	27.6[26]	8.7[4]	5.6	—[4]	12.8	72.9[4]
Yemen	1990	1,572.3	44.3	0.2[2]	9.0	46.5[3]	7.1	16.3	23.1[3]	32.1	5.5	5.1	4.1	53.2
Yugoslavia[67]	1990	18,915.2	16.7	2.5	16.9	63.9	12.9	26.6	24.4	45.5	4.5	22.1	2.2	25.7
Zaire	1989	849.3	——20.0[13]——		13.8[13]	66.2[13]	4.4[13]	45.5[13]	16.3[13]	66.1[4]	9.4[4]	0.2[4]	4.1[4]	20.1[4]
Zambia	1988	838.8	5.3	0.8[2]	13.4	80.5[3]	18.5	42.1	19.9[3]	28.5[4]	7.4	0.7[4]	7.8	55.6[4]
Zimbabwe	1990	1,852.0	6.3	1.2	15.6	77.0	15.5	37.4	24.1	27.5	11.4	0.7	4.6	55.8

[1]Year ending March. [2]Excluding precious stones, etc. (667). [3]Including precious stones, etc. (667). [4]Estimated based on trading partners' information. [5]Main countries only. [6]Year ending September 30. [7]Approximation based on estimates of foreign trade and of trade between the republics constituting the former U.S.S.R. [8]Figures for Belgium-Luxembourg Economic Union (Luxembourg is also shown separately). [9]Free-on-board valuation (f.o.b.). [10]1989–90 (year ending June 30): imports $101.1, exports $68.0. [11]Includes 82.1% from India (81.7% in 1989–90). [12]Includes 97.5% to India (92.5% in 1989–90). [13]1987. [14]Includes 77.8% from rest of Customs Union of Southern Africa. [15]Includes 73.9% to Switzerland. [16]1988. [17]Including metals. [18]Excluding metals. [19]1985. [20]Former U.S.S.R. only. [21]Rubber only. [22]Emigrants' effects. [23]1975. [24]1976. [25]Includes 61.2% to New Zealand. [26]1983. [27]All figures are estimates of total trade, including imports from and exports to other republics of the former U.S.S.R. [28]Figures for France include Monaco. [29]Groundnuts, groundnut products, and fish only. [30]Excluding imports from Israel ($380.5 million in 1987). [31]Excluding exports to Israel ($143.2 million in 1987). [32]January–September only. [33]Excluding petroleum products. [34]Includes 51.5% for ships' bunkers. [35]Figures for United Kingdom include Guernsey, Isle of Man, and Jersey (the latter is also shown separately). [36]1980. [37]1986; commercial imports only (excluding oil companies' imports). [38]Excluding imported military

total value ('000,000 U.S.$)	food and agricultural raw materials (0+1+2 −27−28 +4)	mineral ores and concentrates (27+28 +667)	fuels and other energy (3)	manufactured goods total[a] (5+6 −667 +7+8 +9)	of which chemicals and related products (5)	of which machinery and transport equipment (7)	of which other[a] (6−667 +8+9)	to European Economic Community (EEC)[b]	to United States	to Eastern Europe[c]	to Japan	to all other[d]	country
209.0	—96.5[2]—			3.4[3]	0.3	1.4	1.8[3]	72.9	0.1	—	6.0	21.0	Niger
7,383.4	3.7	—	95.4	0.9	0.2	—	0.7	41.4	47.0	—	0.1	11.5	Nigeria
130.5[55]	...	...	...	...	...	...	...	—	—	—	—	100.0	Northern Mariana Islands
33,984.2	9.3	1.2	48.8	40.7	6.3	14.7	19.6	66.2	4.7	1.2	1.9	26.0	Norway
5,215.0	1.9	0.2	91.4	6.6	0.3	3.6	2.6	3.5[4]	5.6[4]	—[4]	34.2[4]	56.8[4]	Oman
6,235.9	18.8	0.3	1.7	79.2	0.4	1.0	77.9	31.0	10.8	2.9	8.2	47.1	Pakistan
0.5	69.1	—	—	30.9	—	—	30.9	—	8.0	—	58.8	33.2	Palau
297.2	78.3	1.6	0.1	19.9	5.1	0.1	14.8	25.7	46.1	0.4	0.3	27.5	Panama
1,453.4	28.7	59.2	0.2	11.9	0.2	2.4	9.3	32.1	3.0	0.9	41.2	22.8	Papua New Guinea
958.7	90.0	—	—	9.9	3.2	0.1	6.6	31.7	4.3	—	0.3	63.7	Paraguay
2,506.5	29.4	28.4	6.7	35.5	2.3	1.5	31.6	33.4	23.9	2.5	10.8	29.4	Peru
8,186.0	20.5	4.6	2.2	72.6	3.2	12.5	57.0	17.7	37.8	0.2	19.8	24.5	Philippines
13,466.1	14.9	2.5	9.7	73.0	7.7	33.6	31.7	36.9	2.8	30.6	1.4	28.3	Poland
16,406.1	13.4	3.1	3.5	80.1	5.3	19.6	55.3	74.0	4.8	0.6	1.0	19.6	Portugal
13,952.8	16.9	1.0	2.2	79.9	39.8	19.7	20.4	3.3	88.0	—	0.1	8.5	Puerto Rico
2,686.8	...	...	82.0	18.0	12.4	—	5.6	4.4[4]	1.9[4]	—[4]	52.0[4]	41.7[4]	Qatar
185.6	82.9	0.3	0.2	16.7	2.6	8.5	5.6	85.7	—	—	3.1	11.1	Réunion
10,487.3	8.4	—32.1[17]—		59.5[18]	9.5	29.2	20.7[18]	30.6	5.4	33.5	1.6	28.9	Romania
174,100.0	—10.3[2]—		22.8	66.8[3]	9.4	35.3	22.1[3]	—	—	68.5[57]	—	31.5	Russia[27]
117.7	94.8	2.7	—	2.5	—	—	2.5	89.8[4]	2.6[4]	—[4]	1.0[4]	6.6[4]	Rwanda
27.4	42.0	—	0.9	57.0	0.1	34.2	22.8	22.3	62.3	—	—	15.4	St. Kitts and Nevis
82.9	75.6	—	0.1	24.4	0.3	4.7	19.3	69.2	12.1	—	—	18.7	St. Lucia
51.7	76.9	0.1[2]	—	23.0[3]	1.3	5.2	16.4[3]	39.6	15.0	—	—	45.3	St. Vincent and the Grenadines
...	...	...	...	...	...	...	...	...	...	...	...	...	San Marino[39]
11.6	100.0	—	—	—	—	—	—	85.2[5]	10.4[4]	...	—[4]	4.4[4]	São Tomé and Príncipe
44,416.3	0.9	0.4	90.3	8.4	5.7	1.1	1.6	19.7[42]	26.3[42]	—[42]	17.8[42]	36.2[42]	Saudi Arabia
782.6	55.8	9.3	12.4	22.5	14.9	2.4	5.2	53.3	0.1	—	2.0	44.6	Senegal
38.6	31.8	—	63.8	4.4	...	...	...	31.8[42]	2.5[42]	—[42]	0.4[42]	65.3[42]	Seychelles
145.0	31.4[44]	66.4[44]	1.5[44]	0.7[44]	—[44]	—[44]	0.7[44]	24.4	15.1	0.3	—	60.2	Sierra Leone
52,526.4	7.8	0.6	18.2	73.5	6.3	50.1	17.1	14.4	21.3	1.0	8.7	54.6	Singapore
...	...	...	...	...	...	...	...	...	...	...	...	...	Slovenia
74.8	93.9	0.6	—	5.5	—	—	5.5	28.0	0.1	...	33.2	38.6	Solomon Islands
80.4	93.3	0.1	0.1	6.5	—	0.6	5.8	17.1	0.1	0.1	—	82.6	Somalia
23,628.0	8.6[19]	11.5[19]	8.9[19]	71.1[19,61]	2.8[19]	2.5[19]	65.8[19,61]	24.9[4]	7.5[4]	0.1[4]	6.7[4]	60.8[4]	South Africa[58]
...	...	...	...	...	...	...	...	...	...	...	...	...	Bophuthatswana[58]
...	...	...	...	...	...	...	...	...	...	...	...	...	Ciskei[58]
...	...	...	...	...	...	...	...	...	...	...	...	...	Transkei[58]
...	...	...	...	...	...	...	...	...	...	...	...	...	Venda[58]
55,632.3	16.8	1.0	5.2	77.0	8.4	38.8	29.8	69.4	5.8	1.1	1.1	22.6	Spain
1,912.2	39.7	10.0	1.5	48.8	1.0	2.8	45.0	25.7	25.8	3.3	5.4	39.9	Sri Lanka
509.1	97.2	0.5	—	2.3	—	—	2.3	31.6	3.2	2.6	11.1	51.4	Sudan, The
472.6	15.7	74.0	1.2	9.0	—	0.3	8.7	36.9	11.4	—	6.8	45.0	Suriname
467.6	75.5[16]	3.5[16]	1.0[16]	20.0[16]	0.6[16]	1.0[16]	18.4[16]	28.3[16]	2.3[16]	—[16]	1.8[16]	67.6[16]	Swaziland
57,434.0	9.4	1.7	3.0	85.9	7.5	43.3	35.2	54.2	8.6	1.9	2.1	33.2	Sweden
63,796.7	3.5	5.1	0.1	91.3	21.2	31.5	38.6	58.1	8.0	2.6	4.8	26.6	Switzerland
3,005.8	15.2	1.5	39.2	44.1	11.8	0.5	31.7	31.9	2.4	41.0	0.1	24.6	Syria
67,020.4	6.5[16]	0.2[16]	0.6[16]	92.7[16]	3.5[16]	35.2[16]	54.0[16]	16.0	32.3	0.2	12.4	39.0	Taiwan
4,000.0[7]	...	...	...	...	...	...	...	...	...	...	...	...	Tajikistan
309.9	78.1	1.7	2.8	17.4	1.4	0.9	15.1	41.5	2.1	2.1[4]	3.7	50.6[4]	Tanzania
23,068.7	33.8	4.3	0.8	61.0	2.0	22.0	37.0	21.6	22.7	1.1	17.2	37.4	Thailand
267.9	44.5	44.6	—	10.9	0.4	0.7	9.8	40.5	1.1	5.9	0.1	52.4	Togo
8.2	65.8	—	—	34.2	—	2.2	32.0	0.5	16.4	—	4.4	78.6	Tonga
2,080.4	5.6	0.5	67.1	26.8	14.1	1.9	10.7	8.3	56.9	—	0.8	34.1	Trinidad and Tobago
3,498.4	11.9	1.9	17.3	68.9	14.5	7.8	46.5	77.8	0.9	1.5	0.3	19.5	Tunisia
12,959.4	25.5	2.7	2.3	69.6	5.8	6.6	57.2	53.3	7.5	6.4	1.8	31.0	Turkey
4,200.0[7]	...	...	...	...	...	...	...	...	...	...	...	...	Turkmenistan
0.1[13]	100.0[51]	—	—	—	—	—	—			—	—	100.0[63]	Tuvalu
249.5	98.5	—	—	1.4	—	1.2	0.2	68.3	14.1[4]	0.6	3.4	13.6[4]	Uganda
75,200.0	—10.9[2]—		6.8	82.3[3]	7.5	46.1	28.6[3]	...	...	82.3[57]	—	17.7	Ukraine[27]
15,948.0[4]	2.0[51]	0.2[51]	89.9[51]	8.0[51]	0.5[51]	2.5[51]	5.0[51]	9.0[4]	4.1[4]	—[4]	31.1[4]	55.8[4]	United Arab Emirates
185,465.8	8.5	2.7	6.8	82.0	13.1	41.6	27.3	56.5	10.8	1.0	2.2	29.5	United Kingdom[35]
392,627.4	15.1	2.1	3.1	79.6	10.1	46.5	23.1	25.0	—	1.1	12.4	61.6	United States[64]
1,708.4	60.0	0.3	—	39.7	7.7	2.0	30.0	24.7	9.4	6.7	1.2	58.0	Uruguay
18,000.0[7]	...	...	...	...	...	...	...	...	...	...	...	...	Uzbekistan
22.1	92.1[49]	—[49]	—[49]	7.9[49]	—[49]	—[49]	7.9[49]	57.5[49]	0.1[49]	—[49]	18.4[49]	24.0[49]	Vanuatu
17,227.3	2.5	0.8	81.0	15.7	2.1	1.7	11.9	12.4[42]	51.6[42]	—[42]	4.0[42]	31.9[42]	Venezuela
1,502.0	—55.5[19]—			44.5[19]	...	...	...	5.8[4]	—[4]	55.0[4]	19.0[4]	20.2[4]	Vietnam
2,820.7	...	...	90.3[13]	...	...	...	...	...	93.8	...	...	...	Virgin Islands (U.S.)
28.4[66]	...	...	...	...	...	...	...	...	...	...	...	...	West Bank
...	...	...	...	...	...	...	...	...	...	...	...	...	Western Sahara
12.8	88.4	—	—	11.6	—	—	11.6	27.6	8.1	—	0.4	63.9	Western Samoa
693.0	9.8	0.4	88.8	1.0	0.1	—	0.9	36.6	37.2	1.0	1.7	23.4	Yemen
14,391.0	11.7	2.5	2.5	83.4	9.7	30.0	43.6	47.1	4.8	26.9	0.3	20.9	Yugoslavia[67]
1,254.4	17.7	56.2[17]	11.6	14.4[18]	0.2	0.8	13.4[18]	74.5[4]	11.6[4]	0.1[4]	2.1[4]	11.6[4]	Zaire
1,190.0	...	92.7[17]	...	...	...	...	7.3[18]	36.7[4]	3.0[4]	0.7[4]	23.3[4]	36.3[4]	Zambia
1,470.4	51.3	6.9	0.7	41.1	1.7	3.7	35.7	41.1	6.5	0.6	5.5	46.3	Zimbabwe

goods valued at $1,195.8 million in 1990. [39]Figures for Italy include San Marino. [40]United Kingdom only. [41]Including coins. [42]1989. [43]1974. [44]1984. [45]1981. [46]Includes 97.1% from rest of Customs Union of Southern Africa. [47]Excluding former East Germany. [48]France only. [49]Domestic exports only. [50]Excluding border trade. [51]1986. [52]Based on trade with Australia and New Zealand only. [53]Year ending June 30. [54]Curaçao and Bonaire only. [55]All reexports. [56]Excluding bulk imports of fuels. [57]Other republics of the former U.S.S.R. only. [58]Figures for South Africa refer to Customs Union of Southern Africa (includes South Africa, Botswana, Lesotho, Namibia, and Swaziland, also shown separately; also Bophuthatswana, Ciskei, Transkei, and Venda). [59]Excluding crude oil. [60]Including crude oil (included in "special transactions" accounting in total for 17.7%). [61]Including gold (included in "special transactions" accounting in total for 51.2%). [62]Includes 74.0% from South Africa. [63]All to the South Pacific region in 1985. [64]Figures for United States include American Samoa, Guam, Puerto Rico, and Virgin Islands (U.S.), also shown separately. [65]Excluding imports from Israel ($580.7 million in 1987). [66]Excluding exports to Israel ($160.5 million in 1987). [67]Data refer to Yugoslavia as constituted prior to 1991.

Trade: domestic

The following table presents data relating to domestic wholesale and retail trade for the countries of the world. The section on wholesale trade is based for the most part on establishments engaged primarily in selling goods to retailers and distributors for resale or to purchasers who buy for business and farm uses. The retail trade section is based on businesses engaged in selling merchandise for personal or household consumption; restaurants are, when possible, included, hotels excluded.

The data presented here are based on information from a variety of country and international sources. The country sources include statistical abstracts, correspondence, annual reports, and censuses of business and trade. Among the more useful international sources are the various compilations of the United Nations dealing with domestic trade and Euromonitor's *International Marketing Data and Statistics 1991*.

Since there is no single published source or common international methodology for the compilation of data on wholesale and retail trade, nor a single current year on which, by common agreement, the various national reports would be based, allowance must be made for variations in the meaning and recency of the information provided for any single country and for its comparability internationally. Variations occur in part because of the ways in which countries define wholesale and retail trade; the conventional free-enterprise distinction between wholesale and retail activity (of a single enterprise or an entire national trade sector) may not exist in the business practice of some countries. Variations also exist in the kind and level of detail reported. For example, countries may design surveys differently according to the size (number of employees, sales, surface area)

of establishments surveyed, their profitability, or other less direct criteria, such as ownership or location. The depth of analysis to which the data are subjected may also vary. The structure of a national trade sector is also affected by the degree of government involvement, which may range from total control of wholesale distribution in some socialist countries, to partial involvement in some strategic sectors, or to relative noninvolvement in fully private trade sectors of capitalist countries. In some smaller countries data may refer to a single trading enterprise.

At the table's extreme left, preceding the year to which the trade data refer, the combined value of the country's wholesale and retail trade as a percentage of gross domestic product or net material product is given. Unless otherwise noted, GDP data include restaurants and exclude hotels.

Both the wholesale and retail sections of the table provide similar detail: establishments or outlets, employees, sales, and derived values for relationships among these measures; the retail section provides an additional breakdown of sales by an end-use classification of retail sales outlets.

Although all sales figures are given in U.S. dollars, the comparability of these dollar figures may differ considerably; for instance, the purchasing power of various national currencies in domestic transactions may bear only a distant relationship to the exchange rate of the same currency in international transactions, especially for countries having nonconvertible currencies. The price of goods may also vary, depending on the degree to which they are subject to direct subsidies and artificial cost controls such as tax, investment, or free-trade preferences by a central government seeking to influence social or economic conditions.

Trade: domestic

country	domestic trade as percentage of GDP, 1989	year	wholesale trade					retail trade		
			establishments[a]	employees[b]	sales[c] (U.S.$'000,000)	employees per establishment	sales per establishment (U.S.$'000)	outlets[a]	employees[b]	sales[c] (U.S.$'000,000)
Afghanistan	8.9[1,2,3]	1981–82	...	4	...	...	...	...	126,100[4]	...
Albania	9.5[5]	1990	...	4	...	...	...	11,140[6]	41,000[4]	1,260[6]
Algeria	14.2[7]	1986	...	4	...	...	...	3,600[8,9]	390,990[2,4,7]	16,200
American Samoa	...	1990	149[10]	255	...	...	...	572[10]	1,495	...
Andorra	25.2[11]	1988	...	...	...	...	...	592[12]	7,227	...
Angola	12.7[2,13]	1973	4	...	...	...	...	29,138[4]	...	...
Antigua and Barbuda	24.9[2,14]	1980	25	350	...	14.0	...	199	1,000	23[15]
Argentina	13.3	1974	45,700	275,000[16]	...	6.0[16]	...	445,798[18]	930,000[16,18]	15,540[15]
Armenia	4.3	...	...	...	...	...	...	...	...	...
Aruba	37.2[2,11]	1990	...	723	...	...	...	...	5,700	19
Australia	18.2[2]	1989–90	39,319[20]	361,000[16,20]	84,798[12]	9.2[16,20]	2,157[12]	160,160[13]	928,500[13,16]	65,082
Austria	16.1[2]	1989	17,149	174,000	60,464	10.2	3,526	33,601	239,000	28,796
Azerbaijan	...	...	...	...	...	...	...	...	...	...
Bahamas, The[22]	26.2[2,13]	1980	23	1,066	143	46.3	6,235	132	4,059	460[13]
Bahrain	10.2[2]	1983	4	4	...	...	...	255[4]	12,551[4]	1,601
Bangladesh	7.9[2,14]	1985	...	4	...	...	...	271,000	3,610,000[4]	5,500[13]
Barbados	27.6[2]	1986	...	4	...	...	...	1,911[23]	25,300[4]	264[15]
Belarus	12.0	1990	...	...	...	...	...	...	382,000	...
Belgium	17.3[2,14]	1984	60,589	160,600	65,110	2.6	1,075	135,534	193,500	20,957
Belize	16.4[2]	1983	...	4	...	...	...	...	4,558[4]	33[13]
Benin	19.2[2,13]	1979	...	...	...	...	...	170[8]	1,910[13,16]	150[15]
Bermuda	32.8[24]	1985	60[24]	820	...	...	...	310[13,24]	4,342[16]	116[18,21]
Bhutan	6.3[2]	1982	...	4	...	...	...	...	9,000[4,16]	...
Bolivia	11.2	1989	...	4	...	...	...	...	244,907[4]	1,570[13]
Bosnia and Hercegovina	...	1989	...	...	18,469	...	...	...	...	18,065
Botswana	16.4[14]	1983–84	205	3,500	494[15]	...	...	1,660	10,700	165[15]
Brazil	7.1	1984	45,969[25]	370,000[25]	91,331[25]	8.0[25]	1,987[25]	1,030,000	3,450,000	40,090
Brunei	12.4[2,14]	1986	4	4	...	4	...	833[4,29]	4,261[4,29]	...
Bulgaria	8.4[1,2,14]	1987	...	7,700[30]	...	...	...	41,339[18]	79,820[18]	34,700[18]
Burkina Faso	12.3[7]	1975	...	4	...	...	...	...	19,354[4,16]	...
Burundi	8.1[14]	1981	...	...	...	...	...	...	...	210[13]
Cambodia	...	...	...	...	...	...	...	...	...	...
Cameroon	25.8[2,13]	1980	...	...	...	...	...	1,312[8]	13,776[13,16]	1,430[13]
Canada	11.5[31]	1989	...	4	169,270[13]	...	...	...	2,082,000[4,13]	158,920
Cape Verde	21.3[13]	1980	...	4	...	...	...	...	3,851[4]	...
Cayman Islands	21.5[2,14]	1989	...	235	...	...	...	...	1,905	...
Central African Republic	19.6[14]	1989	113	302	...	2.7	...	14,543	23,078	...
Chad	25.9[13]	1983	...	4	...	4	...	...	1,661[4,8,32]	497[4]
Chile	18.1[31]	1983	561[8]	15,300[8]	2,312[8]	27.2[8]	4,121[8]	1,125[13,18]	21,700[13,18]	1,403[13,18]
China	10.6[2]	1989	99,000	1,550,000[16]	...	15.6[16]	...	8,413,000[18]	20,330,000[16,18]	215,171[18]
Colombia	11.0[31]	1985	...	...	...	...	...	1,110[34]	49,000[34]	8,600[13]
Comoros	12.2[2,35]	1980	...	4	...	...	...	...	1,873[4,8]	...
Congo	14.4	1984	...	4	...	...	...	...	13,240[4]	...
Cook Islands	24.0[5]	1982[36]	4	4	4	4	4	109[4]	369[4]	31[4]
Costa Rica	20.0[31]	1975	332[37]	4,073[37]	35[37]	12.3[37]	104[37]	9,713	26,486	475[25]
Côte d'Ivoire	18.2[2,25]	1981	...	...	...	...	...	2,023[8]	16,720[8]	1,800[13]
Croatia	...	1989	...	...	38,117	...	...	...	...	39,231
Cuba	20.1[1]	1987	...	...	14,440	...	...	56,916[30]	230,000[7,16]	11,831
Cyprus	21.3[2,31]	1986	1,559[21]	12,400	225	5.3[21]	720[21]	8,474[21]	20,100[16,18]	268[18]
Czechoslovakia	16.2[1,2]	1990	63,110[30]	251,000[30]	40,083[30]	4.0[30]	635[30]	62,667[10]	258,127	21,235
Denmark	14.8[2]	1989	16,858[14]	141,299[14]	42,807	8.4[14]	2,455[14]	29,111[14]	124,867[14]	20,866
Djibouti	10.8[13]	1985	28	371[11]	...	...	...	431	1,877[11]	...
Dominica	11.5[2]	1983	...	4	...	...	...	...	1,597[4,24]	790[13]
Dominican Republic	14.3[31]	1983	670	...	3,136	...	4,681	11,220[11]	...	1,259[11]
Ecuador	14.9	1983	402	15,900	1,396	39.6	3,473	501	17,400	2,550[13]

The data on distribution of retail sales by kind of consumer goods may have their origin in several different types of data or analysis. One country may aggregate sales data by kind of establishment only (this may be perfectly satisfactory in a country of small, independent outlets); another may aggregate data directly by kind of goods (most easily done in a country with well-developed statistical, tax-reporting, and commercial systems). Other countries may find it impolitic to publish data that reflect the poverty of their distribution network or their supply of consumer goods and may aggregate or publish data for only a few sectors: food or nonfood goods, for example. For countries with only a few trading enterprises in a particular sector, detail must often be withheld to preserve the confidentiality of individual businesses.

The notes that follow further define the column headings.

a. The number of establishments or outlets refers to economic units that operate at a single physical location in one principal kind of activity, whether singly owned or part of a multiunit firm. Such units are not necessarily identical with a company or enterprise.

b. Number of employees refers to full-time and part-time paid workers, including salaried managers and officers; it usually excludes owner-operators, partners, vendors, and unpaid relatives.

c. Total sales (also called turnover) includes the value of merchandise sold for cash or credit; amounts received from customers for layaway purchases; receipts from rental or leasing of vehicles, equipment, tools, instruments, etc.; receipts for delivery, installation, maintenance, repair, alteration, storage, and other services.

d. Outlets engaged primarily in the sale of food and nonalcoholic beverages, such as grocery stores, meat and fish markets, and bakeries.

e. Outlets engaged primarily in the sale of clothing and shoes; also includes outlets that sell accessory items, such as millinery, furs, and leather goods.

f. Outlets engaged primarily in the sale of home furnishings, including furniture, draperies, floor coverings, household appliances, and home entertainment equipment.

g. Outlets that primarily serve food and drink, including restaurants, lunchrooms, cafeterias, social caterers, refreshment places, contract feeders, ice cream parlors, and bars and taverns.

h. Outlets engaged primarily in the sale of pharmaceuticals, cosmetics, and perfumes.

i. Outlets engaged primarily in the sale of building materials, hardware, garden supplies, paint, electrical supplies, and farm equipment.

j. Outlets engaged primarily in the sale of motor vehicles, motorcycles, bicycles, and tires, batteries, and other automotive supplies and parts; includes service stations.

k. Outlets engaged in the sale of multiple lines of merchandise, such as department stores, variety stores, and rural general stores.

l. Miscellaneous specialized outlets such as those engaged primarily in the sale of liquors, sporting goods, books, jewelry, photographic and optical goods, gifts, flowers, tobacco products, home fuels, and newspapers.

retail trade (continued)									employees per outlet	sales per outlet (U.S.$'000)	population per outlet	country
percentage breakdown of sales												
food[d]	clothing, shoes[e]	home furnishings[f]	eating, drinking[g]	drugs, pharma-ceuticals[h]	building materials[i]	automobile parts[j]	general merchandise[k]	other[l]				
...	...	...	...	...	...	...	...	...	...	...	...	Afghanistan
61.9				38.1					...	113[6]	277[6]	Albania
...	...	...	...	...	...	...	...	...	5.0[8,9]	...	5,146[8,9]	Algeria
...	...	...	...	...	...	...	...	...	...	...	90[10]	American Samoa
...	...	...	...	...	...	...	...	...	3.8[12]	...	39[12]	Andorra
...	...	...	...	...	...	...	...	...	...	...	...	Angola
...	...	...	...	...	...	...	...	...	5.0	100	378	Antigua and Barbuda
...	...	...	...	...	...	...	...	...	2.1[16,18]	...	58[18]	Argentina
...	...	...	...	...	...	...	...	...	...	...	...	Armenia
...	...	...	...	...	...	...	...	...	...	...	...	Aruba
36.9	8.7	3.0	18.0[2]	4.0	9.2	...	11.6	8.6	5.8[13,16]	387[13]	100[13]	Australia
30.0[21]	14.5[21]	10.3[21]	...	4.8[21]	...	13.7[21]	10.1[21]	16.6[21]	7.1	857	227	Austria
...	...	...	...	...	...	...	...	...	...	...	...	Azerbaijan
24.4[11]	7.7[11]	7.1[11]	—	3.7[11]	8.4[11]	30.1[11]	7.6[11]	11.0[11]	30.8	1,881	1,026	Bahamas, The[22]
...	...	...	...	...	...	...	...	...	49.2[4]	...	1,507[4]	Bahrain
...	...	...	...	...	...	...	...	...	...	...	...	Bangladesh
...	...	...	...	...	...	...	...	...	...	...	130[23]	Barbados
...	...	...	...	...	...	...	...	...	...	...	...	Belarus
35.1				64.9					1.4	155	73	Belgium
...	...	...	...	...	...	...	...	...	...	...	...	Belize
...	...	...	...	...	...	...	...	...	11.3[13,16]	387[13]	19,871[13]	Benin
...	...	...	...	...	...	...	...	...	11.0[15,18]	...	178[8,24]	Bermuda
...	...	...	...	...	...	...	...	...	...	...	...	Bhutan
...	...	...	...	...	...	...	...	...	...	...	...	Bolivia
...	...	...	...	...	...	...	...	...	...	...	...	Bosnia and Hercegovina
...	...	...	...	...	...	...	...	...	6.4	99.4	604	Botswana
15.0[26]	7.2	13.0[27]	...	4.7	[27]	27.3[28]	19.3	13.5	3.4	39	129	Brazil
...	...	...	...	...	...	...	...	...	5.1[4,29]	...	279[4,29]	Brunei
50.9	10.9	3.4	...	5.9	...	...	0.2	28.7	1.9[18]	839[18]	217[18]	Bulgaria
...	...	...	...	...	...	...	...	...	...	...	...	Burkina Faso
...	...	...	...	...	...	...	...	...	...	...	...	Burundi
...	...	...	...	...	...	...	...	...	...	...	...	Cambodia
...	...	...	...	...	...	...	...	...	10.5[8,16]	...	6,481[8]	Cameroon
23.7	6.3	6.1	...	4.5	...	36.2	10.9	12.3	...	...	...	Canada
...	...	...	...	...	...	...	...	...	...	...	...	Cape Verde
...	...	...	...	...	...	...	...	...	...	...	...	Cayman Islands
...	...	...	...	...	...	...	...	...	1.6	...	187	Central African Republic
...	...	...	...	...	...	...	...	...	...	...	...	Chad
28.3[11]	33	5.0[11]	1.6[11]	5.4[11]	4.7[11]	18.0[11]	17.1[11,33]	19.9[11]	19.3[13,18]	1,247[13,18]	10,210[13,18]	Chile
54.5	16.3	4.3[27]	...	3.4	[27]	2.9	18.6		2.4[16,18]	26[18]	131[18]	China
...	...	...	...	...	...	...	...	...	44.1[34]	1,522[34]	...	Colombia
...	...	...	...	...	...	...	...	...	...	...	...	Comoros
...	...	...	...	...	...	...	...	...	...	...	...	Congo
...	...	...	...	...	...	...	...	...	3.4[4]	284[4]	84[4]	Cook Islands
37.7	13.5	6.9	...	8.2	7.0	15.1	5.9	5.7	2.7	59	202	Costa Rica
...	...	...	...	...	...	...	...	...	8.3[8]	...	4,257[8]	Côte d'Ivoire
...	...	...	...	...	...	...	...	...	...	...	...	Croatia
37.0	...	...	28.8	3.4	...	2.8	...	28.0	4.0[7,16]	184[30]	177[30]	Cuba
21.9[30]	17.7[30]	8.6[30]	...	3.2[30]	9.0[30]	29.7[30]	...	9.9[30]	1.0[21]	124[21]	77[21]	Cyprus
42.9	15.1	12.8	...	3.6	2.9	10.0	...	12.7	4.2[10]	362[10]	249[10]	Czechoslovakia
55.3	6.7	4.8	...	...	2.2	16.6	3.7	10.7	4.3[14]	770[14]	176[14]	Denmark
...	...	...	...	...	...	...	...	...	...	...	998	Djibouti
...	...	...	...	...	...	...	...	...	...	...	...	Dominica
...	...	...	...	...	...	...	...	...	...	112[11]	519[11]	Dominican Republic
24.2[25]	29.1[25]	8.1[25]	3.0[25]	4.8[25]	4.0[25]	17.8[25]	3.4[25]	5.6[25]	34.7	2,131	79	Ecuador

Trade: domestic (continued)

country	domestic trade as percentage of GDP, 1989	year	wholesale trade					retail trade		
			establishments[a]	employees[b]	sales[c] (U.S.$'000,000)	employees per establishment	sales per establishment (U.S.$'000)	outlets[a]	employees[b]	sales[c] (U.S.$'000,000)
Egypt	24.6[2,3]	1983–84	2,552	45,500[16]	4,492	18.0[16]	1,760	2,545	55,800[16]	29,700[13]
El Salvador	34.8[2,31]	1983	396	6,400	1,038	16.2	2,621	1,416	10,700	485
Equatorial Guinea	8.4	1983	...	36	...	...	...	...	2,701	...
Estonia	...	1990	...	...	...	...	...	...	70,000	...
Ethiopia	9.6[2]	1984	375[8,39]	3,200[8,39]	...	8.5[8,39]	...	7,416[8,39]	17,100[8,39]	273
Faeroe Islands	16.0[14]	1987	78	4	19	...	241	430	1,484[2,4,25]	38
Fiji	14.2[2,14]	1986	234	2,852[12]	277	12.2[12]	1,183	1,036	5,493[12]	306
Finland	11.7[2]	1990	10,001[21]	82,719[21]	57,307	8.3[21]	2,622[21]	39,403[10]	149,757[10]	40,071
France	13.6	1989	192,080	1,105,679	317,219[14]	5.8	1,800[14]	552,945	1,274,477	295,850
French Guiana	12.3[23]	1988	139	4	...	...	...	588	2,737[4,13]	...
French Polynesia	22.7[31]	1986	4	4	...	...	...	947[4]	5,038[4]	...
Gabon	12.1[2,31]	1982	...	...	...	...	...	...	12,683[4,12,24]	...
Gambia, The	21.5	1983	...	4	...	...	...	...	3,732[4]	...
Gaza Strip	...	1986	...	4	...	...	...	...	13,400[4]	...
Georgia	6.0	...	...	...	...	...	...	...	...	...
Germany[40]	9.0	1988	41,909[13]	1,003,900[16]	460,420	23.6[13,16]	8,715[13]	168,230[13]	2,152,800	298,693
Ghana	18.8[14]	1983	460[41]	1,100[41]	115[41]	2.4[41]	250[41]	1,500	16,000	252[13]
Gibraltar		1990	...	678	...	...	...	...	1,986	...
Greece	12.8[2]	1984	23,218	73,812	...	3.2	...	184,892	301,318	12,263[5]
Greenland	8.0[22]	1989	...	4	141	...	...	...	2,214[4,7]	158
Grenada	19.7[2]	1983	...	4	4	...	...	...	2,813[4,24]	6[4]
Guadeloupe	17.0[2,11]	1988	4	4	...	...	...	7,408[4]	9,561[4,13]	212[25]
Guam	51.5[11]	1987	94	1,392	245	14.8	1,274	804	7,344	786
Guatemala	24.4[31]	1985	...	4	...	...	...	88,200[11]	178,741[4]	1,200[13]
Guernsey		1991	...	642	...	...	...	...	2,573	...
Guinea	21.9[31]	1979	...	4	...	...	...	...	12,808[4,40]	...
Guinea-Bissau	23.9[2,14]	1979	4	4	...	...	...	685[4,41]	5,085[4]	44[4,29]
Guyana	6.0[14]	1980	...	4	...	...	...	147[8]	14,690[4]	93[15]
Haiti	17.1	1983	...	4	...	...	...	653[8,35]	303,353[4]	500[13]
Honduras	13.4[31]	1984	...	4	...	...	...	...	107,292[4]	401[15]
Hong Kong	22.7	1989	16,103	70,899	12,811	4.4	796	51,102	192,358	18,022
Hungary	8.7[1]	1990	206[11]	122,600[11]	13,121[24]	595[24]	...	106,632	334,800[14]	17,066
Iceland	11.4	1988	1,509[15,42]	5,132[24]	598[25,42]	...	...	1,892[42]	9,162[42,43]	1,502[42]
India	12.5[3]	1980	4	4	...	...	...	3,132,000[4,18]	3,615,000[4,18]	108,300[15]
Indonesia	17.0[2]	1980	4	4	...	4	4	54,632[4]	85,400[4]	3,451[4]
Iran	26.9[2,14]	1972–73	18,210	31,688	2,429	1.7	133	218,132	80,055	37,350[13]
Iraq	10.8[2,14]	1975–76	1,532[29]	2,700[29]	...	1.8[29]	...	77,766[29]	106,800[29]	11,378[15]
Ireland	11.2[2,7]	1988	3,972	39,101	11,420	9.8	2,875	31,699	89,680	10,952
Isle of Man	12.0[15]	1981	...	775	...	...	...	...	3,146	...
Israel	11.6[2]	1983	3,836[41]	44,700[8]	...	8.7[41]	...	43,112	91,200[13]	10,578
Italy	18.5[2]	1983	...	4	...	...	...	1,033,725	1,369,200[4]	122,978
Jamaica	21.7[2,31]	1979	...	...	...	...	...	10,150[25]	125,100[30]	1,457[15]
Japan	12.7	1988	435,492	4,327,688[16]	3,484,100	9.9[16]	8,000	1,619,599[18]	6,850,478[16,18]	889,253[18]
Jersey	...	1986	...	855	...	...	...	...	7,046	...
Jordan	16.9[14]	1989	390	2,895	278	7.4	713	32,470	124,929	2,065
Kazakhstan	...		...	...	...	...	...	...	...	...
Kenya	9.7	1985	3,079[7]	27,481	4	13.6	...	5,033[7]	34,628	1,085[13]
Kiribati	13.5	1987	...	4	...	...	...	30	1,127[4,30]	3.8
Korea, North	...		...	...	...	...	...	...	...	...
Korea, South	11.9	1990	90,621	502,476	70,389	5.5	777	1,040,490[2]	2,356,800[2]	76,057[2]
Kuwait	8.9	1986	3,124	25,829	3,625	8.3	1,160	14,472	58,517	5,935
Kyrgyzstan	...		...	...	...	...	...	...	...	...
Laos	10.3	...	...	...	...	...	...	...	...	...
Latvia	...		...	...	...	...	...	...	...	...
Lebanon	34.2[7]	1986	...	7	...	...	...	...	114,706[4]	1,662[15]
Lesotho	7.7		...	...	...	...	...	...	...	...
Liberia	5.5[2,13]	1984	...	4	...	...	...	...	46,850[4]	115[13]
Libya	6.8	1973	1,126	4,148[16]	...	3.7[16]	...	26,825	44,605[16]	9,205[15]
Liechtenstein	...	1975	67	216	...	3.2	...	228	740	...
Lithuania	...		...	...	...	...	...	...	...	...
Luxembourg	15.9	1989	1,437	9,117	4,390	6.3	3,055	3,711	15,692	1,013
Macau	...	1981	...	482[16]	...	...	...	...	13,652[16]	...
Macedonia	...	1989	...	...	9,522	...	...	...	...	9,238
Madagascar	29.0[2,37]	1976	1,104	...	...	...	...	1,570	...	696[24]
Malawi	12.1[31]	1984	439	23,000	522	52	1,189	500	8,600	127
Malaysia	10.7	1980	19,663	116,200	15,461	5.9	786	95,993	73,000	8,200[13]
Maldives	17.1[2]	1977	...	4	...	...	...	...	1,341[4,16]	5[13]
Mali	12.9[2,7]	1979	...	4	...	...	...	...	5,200[4]	...
Malta	14.2[2]	1983	3	4	1.0	...	333	4[13]	11,936[4,8]	2.3
Marshall Islands	83.7[24]	1980	...	148[16]	...	...	...	...	395[2,16]	...
Martinique	17.4[2,11]	1983	...	4	...	...	...	...	3,518[4,28]	234
Mauritania	12.8[2,20]	1971[8]	23	100	102	4.3	4,445	59	700	103
Mauritius	13.6[2,31]	1986	4	4	4	4	4	207[2,4,8]	10,107[2,4,8]	164[2,4,8]
Mayotte	...	1983	4	4	4	...	4	41[4]	597[4,7]	27[4]
Mexico	11.0[31]	1975	11,652	130,939[16]	6,739	11.2[16]	578	463,612	987,089[16]	31,000[13]
Micronesia	29.6[15]	1980	...	348[16]	...	...	...	...	489[2,16]	...
Moldova	7.9	1990	...	...	...	...	...	...	148,000	...
Monaco	...	1975	...	273	...	...	...	...	1,439	...
Mongolia	21.7	1983[4,45]	...	...	...	...	...	4,828	21,100	1,235[30]
Morocco	12.4[31]	1972	...	...	...	...	...	4,000[8]	20,000[8]	5,750[13]
Mozambique	...	1980	...	4	...	...	...	...	63,058[4]	...
Myanmar (Burma)	22.8[2]	1983	...	...	...	...	...	...	...	2,116
Namibia	12.3	1977	222	5,035	377	22.7	1,698	1,248	7,569	254
Nauru	...		...	...	...	...	...	...	...	...
Nepal	5.3[2,3]	1983	...	4	...	...	...	...	119,000[4,16,24]	736

retail trade (continued)									employees per outlet	sales per outlet (U.S.$'000)	population per outlet	country
percentage breakdown of sales												
food[d]	clothing, shoes[e]	home furnishings[f]	eating, drinking[g]	drugs, pharmaceuticals[h]	building materials[i]	automobile parts[j]	general merchandise[k]	other[l]				
...	...	...	...	...	...	...	...	...	21.9[16]	1,278	17,756	Egypt
11.9[9,38]	7.6[9,38]	16.2[9,38]	...	7.9[9,38]	6.3[9,38]	12.4[9,38]	28.2[9,38]	9.5[9,38]	7.6	342	3,336	El Salvador
...	...	...	...	...	...	...	...	...	...	...	...	Equatorial Guinea
...	...	...	...	...	...	...	...	...	...	...	...	Estonia
15.9	45.2	...	...	...	7.9	9.8	10.5	10.7	2.3[8,39]	27[8,39]	55,200[8,39]	Ethiopia
...	...	...	...	...	...	...	...	...		89	109	Faeroe Islands
10.3	6.9	6.3	...	3.2	17.1	9.4	37.7	9.1	5.3[12]	295	645	Fiji
30.9	5.5	1.8	...	2.7	8.4	24.7	20.5	5.5	4.0[10]	887[10]	126[10]	Finland
35.6	14.3	15.6	...	4.8	...	15.2	7.7	6.8	2.3	535	109	France
											156	French Guiana
...	...	...	...	...	...	...	...	...	5.3[4]	...	188[4]	French Polynesia
50.5	9.6	...	...	...	33.8	6.1	...	...				Gabon
...	...	...	...	...	...	...	...	...	...	...	...	Gambia, The
...	...	...	...	...	...	...	...	...				Gaza Strip
...	...	...	...	...	...	...	...	...				Georgia
28.6	13.2	7.1	...	7.0	...	16.6	22.1	5.4	12.5[13,16]	1,322[13]	363[13]	Germany[40]
...	...	...	...	...	...	...	...	...	1.1	108[41]	7,993	Ghana
...	...	...	...	...	...	...	...	...				Gibraltar
60.0[5]	18.1[5]	9.5[5]	...	...	...	...	...	12.4[5]	1.6	...	54	Greece
...	...	...	...	...	...	...	...	...				Greenland
...	...	...	...	...	...	...	...	...				Grenada
...	...	...	...	...	...	...	...	...				Guadeloupe
11.6	10.9	4.9	8.0	0.3	5.2	26.9	3.3	28.9	9.1	978	147	Guam
...	...	...	...	...	...	...	...	...			83[11]	Guatemala
...	...	...	...	...	...	...	...	...				Guernsey
...	...	...	...	...	...	...	...	...				Guinea
...	...	...	...	...	...	...	...	...	0.8[4,41]	...	1,080[4,41]	Guinea-Bissau
9.7	18.9	13.8	4.5	2.8	17.7	18.6	...	14.0	...	743	5,884	Guyana
...	...	...	...	...	...	...	...	...			7,034[8,35]	Haiti
...	...	...	...	...	...	...	...	...				Honduras
17.7[14]	9.9[14]	...	20.2[14]	...	...	2.6[14]	...	49.7[14]	3.8	353	111	Hong Kong
38.2	9.0	4.6	...	0.9	19.8	6.1	...	21.4	3.6[14]	160	97	Hungary
24.6[41]	8.8[41]	10.1[41]	—	5.6[41]	—	—	31.1[41]	19.8[41]	4.8[42,43]	794[42]	132[42]	Iceland
...	...	...	...	...	...	...	...	...	1.2[4,18]	...	219[4,18]	India
...	...	...	...	...	...	...	...	...	1.6[4]	63[4]	2,681[4]	Indonesia
...	...	...	...	...	...	...	...	...	0.4	...	141	Iran
...	...	...	...	...	...	...	...	...	1.4[29]	...	148[29]	Iraq
40.6	9.1	1.4	10.4	2.9	5.1	21.6	2.8	6.1	2.8	345	112	Ireland
...	...	...	...	...	...	...	...	...				Isle of Man
22.0	7.0	11.0	...	...	...	10.0	6.0	44.0	2.1	245	95	Israel
50.8	15.1	...	...	3.4	...	...	...	30.7	...	119	55	Italy
...	...	...	...	...	...	...	...	...			214[25]	Jamaica
27.8	9.7	5.0	—	...	...	10.3	14.6	32.6	4.2[16,18]	549[18]	7.8[18]	Japan
...	...	...	...	...	...	...	...	...				Jersey
21.7	10.2	13.2	...	3.4	11.1	23.3	12.0	5.1	3.8	63	94	Jordan
...	...	...	...	...	...	...	...	...				Kazakhstan
...	...	...	...	...	...	...	...	...	7.0	128[2,4]	4,057[7]	Kenya
...	...	...	...	...	...	...	...	...	...	127	2,226	Kiribati
...	...	...	...	...	...	...	...	...				Korea, North
29.4[23,26]	13.1[23]	8.9[23]	18.9[23]	5.0[23]	2.4[23]	5.4[23]	1.2[23]	15.6[23]	2.3[2]	73[2]	41[2]	Korea, South
10.7	12.2	14.1	...	2.0	6.8	26.7	13.1	14.4	4.0	410	124	Kuwait
...	...	...	...	...	...	...	...	...				Kyrgyzstan
...	...	...	...	...	...	...	...	...				Laos
...	...	...	...	...	...	...	...	...				Latvia
...	...	...	...	...	...	...	...	...				Lebanon
...	...	...	...	...	...	...	...	...				Lesotho
...	...	...	...	...	...	...	...	...				Liberia
...	...	...	...	...	...	...	...	...	1.7[16]	...	84	Libya
...	...	...	...	...	...	...	...	...	3.2	...	105	Liechtenstein
...	...	...	...	...	...	...	...	...				Lithuania
28.9[26]	12.0	11.8	...	4.5	...	35.5	...	7.3	4.2	273	102	Luxembourg
...	...	...	...	...	...	...	...	...				Macau
...	...	...	...	...	...	...	...	...				Macedonia
...	...	...	...	...	...	...	...	...	...	...	4,977	Madagascar
...	...	...	...	...	...	...	...	...	17.2	254	14,196	Malawi
32.9[44]	7.3[44]	10.8[44]	...	2.5[44]	1.1[44]	33.3[28,44]	4.4[44]	7.7[44]	0.8	64	143	Malaysia
...	...	...	...	...	...	...	...	...				Maldives
...	...	...	...	...	...	...	...	...				Mali
...	...	...	...	...	...	...	...	...		578[8]	83,378[8]	Malta
...	...	...	...	...	...	...	...	...				Marshall Islands
...	...	...	...	...	...	...	...	...				Martinique
...	...	...	...	...	...	...	...	...	11.9	1,742	20,300	Mauritania
...	...	...	...	...	...	...	...	...	48.8[2,4,8]	792[2,4,8]	4,976[2,4,8]	Mauritius
...	...	...	...	...	...	...	...	...		652[4]	1,477[4]	Mayotte
17.8	7.3	5.8	...	2.8	7.3	24.5	16.6	17.9	2.1[16]	41	138	Mexico
...	...	...	...	...	...	...	...	...				Micronesia
...	...	...	...	...	...	...	...	...				Moldova
...	...	...	...	...	...	...	...	...				Monaco
...	...	...	...	...	...	...	...	...	4.3	225	372	Mongolia
...	...	...	...	...	...	...	...	...	5.0[8]	...	c. 4,000[8]	Morocco
...	...	...	...	...	...	...	...	...				Mozambique
...	...	...	...	...	...	...	...	...				Myanmar (Burma)
31.4	11.9	5.3	...	2.8	1.7	...	41.9	5.0	5.9	196	713	Namibia
...	...	...	...	...	...	...	...	...				Nauru
...	...	...	...	...	...	...	...	...				Nepal

Trade: domestic (continued)

country	domestic trade as percentage of GDP, 1989	year	wholesale trade					retail trade		
			establish-ments[a]	employees[b]	sales[c] (U.S.$'000,000)	employees per establishment	sales per establishment (U.S.$'000)	outlets[a]	employees[b]	sales[c] (U.S.$'000,000)
Netherlands, The	16.4	1989	43,800	285,300[7]	144,198	7.1[7]	3,290	83,100	372,700[7]	46,858
Netherlands Antilles	18.3[30]	1986	...	4	...	...	...	...	16,390[4]	149[15, 19]
New Caledonia	20.8[14]	1981	...	...	...	...	...	324	4,524[4]	...
New Zealand	17.1[2]	1991	8,263[46]	76,664[46]	16,295[46]	9.3[46]	1,972[46]	29,961[18, 46]	116,301[18, 46]	16,610
Nicaragua	30.4	1987	...	4	...	...	...	20,610[11]	94,600[4]	790[13]
Niger	13.2[2]									
Nigeria	17.9[2]	1983[8]	154	16,000	2,220	104	14,415	421	20,000	2,202
Northern Mariana Islands	...	1987	28	187	49	6.7	1,777	383	2,304	155
Norway	11.7[2]	1989	16,907	107,357[43]	47,533	6.4[43]	2,811	38,260	128,176[43]	23,962
Oman	12.2	1986	4	4	...	...	...	25,840[2, 4, 10]	123,000[4]	2,449[15]
Pakistan	15.0[2, 31]	1983	...	...	...	...	...	276,701[35]	501,773[16, 35]	12,848
Palau	...	1983	...	114[11]	...	...	...	...	226[2, 16]	...
Panama	11.6	1982[48]	560	13,115	1,491	23.4	2,662	7,561	15,765[8]	1,334
Papua New Guinea	9.8	1985	...	4	...	...	...	...	25,100[4, 25]	669[2]
Paraguay	27.4[2]	1983	...	...	...	...	...	...	91,900[16, 41]	2,645[13]
Peru	24.1[2]	1973	4,210	34,100	2,163	8.1	514	103,010	72,200	8,500[13]
Philippines	19.8[2, 6]	1981	20,642	122,717	4,538	5.9	220	279,968	241,872	4,836
Poland	18.3[1, 2]	1990	...	119,600[30, 43]	33,482[30]	...	...	469,709	606,700[30, 43]	27,976
Portugal	19.7[14]	1983	4,522	135,400[16]	9,260	29.9[16]	2,048	4,889	74,400[16]	3,057
Puerto Rico	15.5[31]	1985	2,327	18,000	7,365	7.7	3,165	35,918	127,000	7,206
Qatar	6.0	1988	128	2,792	68	21.8	535	5,893[2]	22,421[2]	1,048
Réunion	17.7[14]	1988	4	4	...	...	...	6,409[4]	21,562[4]	...
Romania	5.5[1, 2, 14]	1989	...	...	...	...	...	82,035	465,200	19,926
Russia	4.8	...	...	...	...	...	...	...	...	...
Rwanda	15.8[2, 7]	1978	...	4	...	...	...	...	8,014[2, 4]	350[13]
St. Kitts and Nevis	23.1[2, 14]	1984	...	4	...	...	...	...	940[4]	...
St. Lucia	24.1[31]	1980	...	4	...	...	...	...	4,770[2, 4, 16]	...
St. Vincent	14.2[2, 6]		...	...	...	...	...	...	...	...
San Marino	...	1988	102[13]	4	...	...	...	867[13]	1,704[4]	...
São Tomé and Príncipe	9.7[7]	1981	...	4	...	...	...	...	1,994[4]	...
Saudi Arabia	8.4	1981	4,460	31,481[16]	...	7.1[16]	...	80,266	174,187[16]	36,574[15]
Senegal	21.1[14]	1982	...	4	...	4	...	510[41]	24,789[4]	664[15]
Seychelles	11.3[31]	1985	4	4	...	4	...	131[4]	1,298[4]	...
Sierra Leone	10.0[13]	1983–84	...	...	...	...	...	...	7,211[4, 40]	177[15]
Singapore	17.5[2, 31]	1983	20,103	98,900	30,772	4.9	1,531	15,500[13, 18]	63,000[13, 18]	5,618[13, 18]
Slovenia	...	...	...	...	29,509	...	...	...	...	22,738
Solomon Islands	9.0[31]	1986	...	4	...	...	...	405	3,546[4]	139
Somalia	9.3[31]		...	...	...	...	...	...	...	...
South Africa[49]	13.5[2, 31]	1989	...	...	38,682	...	...	58,100[25]	373,200[25]	22,913
Bophuthatswana[49]	...	1979[4]	...	...	...	...	...	1,248	4,195	110
Ciskei[49]	...	1979[4]	...	...	...	...	...	682	1,632	36
Transkei[49]	...	1977[4]	...	...	...	...	...	...	5,580[16]	...
Venda[49]	...	1978[4]	...	...	...	...	...	485	...	...
Spain	20.5[2, 30]	1984	40,000[23]	...	...	...	...	710,865[23]	1,400,000[23]	54,777
Sri Lanka	21.3[2, 31]	1983[8]	190	15,000	...	78.9	...	1,348	44,300	1,116[4, 21]
Sudan, The	14.6[7]	1981	...	4	...	...	...	...	...	3,278
Suriname	8.3[14]	1984	...	4	...	...	...	13,000[17]	12,840[4]	110[13]
Swaziland	10.4[2, 13]	1984	67	1,000	...	14.9	...	656	3,700	23[13]
Sweden	11.6	1989	31,960[21]	167,800[21]	37,518[21]	5.2[21]	1,174[21]	61,039	224,228[7]	30,391
Switzerland	17.4[30]	1985	15,019	143,470	...	9.6	...	53,465	259,674	23,620[21]
Syria	24.1[2, 14]	1983	2,827[35]	...	...	...	...	75,865[35]	110,000[16, 35]	7,330[13]
Taiwan	15.3[2, 31]	1987	55,654[15]	169,100	7,572[30]	2.9[15]	101[15]	355,760[15]	181,200	14,291[30]
Tajikistan	17.0		...	...	...	...	...	...	138,300	...
Tanzania	13.3[2]	1983	...	...	...	...	...	1,620[8]	16,524[8]	3,975[13]
Thailand	15.5	1985[8, 52]	3,290	20,251	3,955	6.2	1,202	8,648	42,508	1,363
Togo	22.5[14]	1980	...	...	...	...	...	181[8]	1,815[8]	112
Tonga	14.8[2, 15]	1976	...	14[16]	...	...	...	...	654[16]	...
Trinidad and Tobago	13.4[2, 31]	1977	124	6,786	509	54.7	4,102	370	15,986	1,670[13]
Tunisia	20.5[2, 14]	1984	...	...	...	...	...	...	153,860[4, 30]	2,814
Turkey	17.6	1985	49,428	181,067[16]	18,820	3.7[16]	381	369,133	696,967[16]	21,957
Turkmenistan	...	1990	...	...	...	...	...	...	87,500	4,150
Tuvalu	11.1[30]	1979	...	4	...	...	...	...	113[4, 16]	...
Uganda	20.5[31]	1977	226	4,100	...	18.1	...	251	3,200	5,285[24]
Ukraine	6.1	1991	...	...	...	...	...	...	...	70,800
United Arab Emirates	11.8[2, 14]	1983	4	4	...	4	...	13,906[2, 4, 41]	121,278[4, 41]	5,910[13]
United Kingdom	14.7[2, 31]	1989	114,963[14]	877,000[10]	365,007[14]	8.4[10]	3,175[14]	350,013[16, 53]	2,439,211[16, 53]	194,420[18, 53]
United States	16.1[14]	1990	469,539[7]	5,609,024[7]	1,790,264	11.9[7]	5,377[7]	1,503,593[7]	17,779,942[7]	1,826,293
Uruguay	11.9[31]	1984	...	...	...	...	...	...	462,000	5,397[18]
Uzbekistan	...	1991	...	...	...	...	...	...	462,000	...
Vanuatu	34.2[7]	1983[55]	18	187[16]	...	10.4[16]	...	256	1,439[16]	...
Venezuela	14.1	1979	...	...	...	...	...	...	161,596	12,345[13]
Vietnam	18.5[1, 7]	1979	2,400[56]	4	...	...	...	56	447,000[4, 13]	7,485[41]
Virgin Islands (U.S.)	...	1987	84	1,322	211	15.7	2,509	1,311	8,529	703
West Bank	...	1986	...	4	...	...	...	...	23,000[4]	...
Western Sahara	...		...	...	...	...	...	...	...	...
Western Samoa	11.9[13]	1981	...	4	...	...	...	...	1,821[2, 4]	...
Yemen[57]	11.9[7]	1986	...	4	...	...	...	...	201,606[4]	2,195[15]
Yugoslavia[58]	17.7[1]	1990	8,979	50,579	5,107	5.6	569	68,773	244,593	19,563
Zaire	17.4[14]	1981	...	...	...	...	...	3,036[8]	33,398[8]	3,300[15]
Zambia	18.5[2]	1974	494[8]	15,500[8]	977[8]	31.4[8]	1,978[8]	1,636[8]	13,700[8]	768[15]
Zimbabwe	10.8	1985	...	4	...	...	...	...	78,800[4]	693

[1]Percentage of net material product. [2]Includes hotels. [3]1988–89. [4]Retail-trade data include wholesale trade. [5]1978. [6]Excludes retail-trade network of the agricultural cooperatives. [7]1987. [8]Data refer to larger establishments only. [9]1971. [10]1989. [11]1982. [12]1972. [13]1986. [14]1988. [15]1983. [16]All persons engaged, including proprietors. [17]1973. [18]Excludes restaurants (eating and drinking establishments). [19]Netherlands Antilles includes Aruba. [20]1981–82. [21]1984. [22]Data refer to New Providence Island only. [23]1979. [24]1981. [25]1980. [26]Includes alcohol and tobacco. [27]Home furnishings includes building materials. [28]Includes all fuels. [29]Privately owned establishments only. [30]1985. [31]1990. [32]1976. [33]General merchandise includes clothing and shoes. [34]For 12 major cities only. [35]1975. [36]Rarotonga only. [37]Wholesalers selling directly to the public only. [38]Selected outlets in urban areas only. [39]Excludes Addis Ababa and Asmera. [40]Former West

retail trade (continued)

percentage breakdown of sales									employees per outlet	sales per outlet (U.S.$'000)	population per outlet	country
food[d]	clothing, shoes[e]	home furnishings[f]	eating, drinking[g]	drugs, pharmaceuticals[h]	building materials[i]	automobile parts[j]	general merchandise[k]	other[l]				
41.9	11.3	12.2	...	2.0	4.1	17.0	...	11.5	4.47	564	179	Netherlands, The
												Netherlands Antilles
									...	...	439	New Caledonia
23.9	5.7	6.8	14.9	3.2	2.3	30.6	4.4	8.2	3.9[18,46]	346[18,46]	106[18,46]	New Zealand
											143[11]	Nicaragua
...	...	...	...	...	...	...	...	...	47.5	5,230	226,615	Niger
27.0	[47]	2.3	8.8	...	7.2	[47]	4.7	50.0[47]	6.0	406	56	Nigeria
35.0[24]	10.1	7.3	...		4.9	26.9	4.3	8.4	3.4[43]	626	110	Northern Mariana Islands
											188[2,4,5]	Norway
												Oman
64.0	12.0	4.0	...				...	20.0	1.8[12,35]		273[35]	Pakistan
												Palau
33.5[9]	10.9[9]	9.5[9]	...				...	46.1[9]	13.9[8]	176	270	Panama
			7.1[2]			26.0		66.9				Papua New Guinea
...	...	...	...		...	...		...	...	...	...	Paraguay
									0.7	20	145	Peru
25.4[26]	12.3	6.7	...	...	11.3	29.5[28]	...	14.8	0.9	17	177	Philippines
31.1[41]	9.9[41]	11.1[41]	...	2.0[41]	4.9[41]	6.7[41]	...	34.3[41]	2.4[30,42]	60	81	Poland
21.5[5]	14.1[5]	11.2[5]	...	3.3[5]	5.6[5]	35.2[5]	9.1[5]		15.3[16]	625	2,047	Portugal
30.5[11]	9.9[11]	4.5[11]	7.5[11]	4.3[11]	5.9[11]	23.2[11]	8.9[11]	5.3[11]	3.5	201	91	Puerto Rico
9.0	9.6	13.2	...	2.7	7.2	29.7	9.1	19.5	3.8	177	70	Qatar
									3.4		90[4]	Réunion
30.0[25]	10.0[25]	5.9[25]	25.0[25]	1.6[25]	0.8[25]	...	...	26.7[25]	5.7	243	282	Romania
												Russia
...	...	...	...		...	...		...	...	...	...	Rwanda
												St. Kitts and Nevis
												St. Lucia
												St. Vincent
											26[13]	San Marino
...	...	...	...		...	...		...	...	...	...	São Tomé and Príncipe
									2.2[16]	...	120	Saudi Arabia
									11.0[8]	...	11,839[8]	Senegal
									9.9[4]	...	498[4]	Seychelles
												Sierra Leone
1.2	4.3	10.2	10.5	0.7	0.3	22.1	50.7		4.1[13]	362[13]	178[13]	Singapore
												Slovenia
...	...	...	...		...	...		...	...	...	...	Solomon Islands
												Somalia
43.7	16.5	9.4	3.8	4.0	...	...	14.2	8.4	6.4[25]	383[25]	c. 540[25]	South Africa[49]
									3.4	88	1,041	Bophuthatswana[49]
									2.4	53	972	Ciskei[49]
												Transkei[49]
											621	Venda[49]
39.2	10.5	16.7	...	...	...	4.2[50]	...	29.4	2.0[23]	119[23]	52[23]	Spain
									32.9		11,436	Sri Lanka
												Sudan, The
												Suriname
52.5[13]	25.1[13]	22.4[13]	...				...		5.6		969	Swaziland
42.3	13.7	16.7	...	2.1	...	...	12.5	12.7	3.17	498	139	Sweden
46.4[21]	13.5[21]	...	4.0[21]				...	36.1[21]	4.9		122	Switzerland
16.0	2.5	...	...	3.5	12.3	39.5[51]	3.5	22.7	1.4[16,35]	...	97[35]	Syria
21.5[24]	3.2[24]	8.8[24]	...	4.1[24]	3.1[24]	8.7[24,28]	3.1[24]	47.5[24]	0.3[15]	33[15]	52[15]	Taiwan
												Tajikistan
									10.0[8]	...	12,600[8]	Tanzania
2.6	4.0	3.1	3.8	0.9	14.9	36.8	19.8	14.1	4.9	157	5,895	Thailand
									10.0[8]	...	15,600[8]	Togo
												Tonga
18.6	...	8.5	2.7	...	10.7	28.2	15.3	15.9	43.2	1,467	2,798	Trinidad and Tobago
												Tunisia
25.0	11.5	15.3	...	2.4	4.8	32.3	0.8	7.9	1.9	60[16]	136	Turkey
												Turkmenistan
												Tuvalu
									12.7	...	47,200	Uganda
												Ukraine
											49[2,4,40]	United Arab Emirates
34.9	10.0	17.9[2]	10.0	[54]	[27]	...	17.9	9.3[54]	7.0[18,53]	555[18,53]	164[18,53]	United Kingdom
20.3	5.2	5.0	10.2	3.8	5.2	28.2	11.6	10.5	11.8[7]	912[7]	162[7]	United States
												Uruguay
												Uzbekistan
									5.6[16]	...	484	Vanuatu
50.2	10.1	7.6	...		...	5.0	...	27.1				Venezuela
									25.0[56]	...	26,300[56]	Vietnam
17.6	7.9	6.4	12.0	2.3	4.8	11.4	1.9	35.7	6.5	536	81	Virgin Islands (U.S.)
												West Bank
												Western Sahara
												Western Samoa
												Yemen[57]
34.8	16.5	...	...	...	4.9	1.2	...	42.6	3.6	3,219	346	Yugoslavia[58]
									11.0[8]	...	9,676[8]	Zaire
									8.4[8]	359[8]	2,873[8]	Zambia
									...	...	...	Zimbabwe

Germany only. [41]1977. [42]Excludes fuels, automobiles, alcohol and tobacco, and building materials. [43]Full-time equivalents. [44]Peninsular Malaysia only. [45]State- and cooperative-owned establishments, including public catering. [46]1982–83. [47]Other includes clothing, shoes, and automobile parts. [48]Excludes Colón Free Trade Zone. [49]South Africa includes Bophuthatswana, Ciskei, Transkei, and Venda. [50]Motor vehicles only. [51]Includes machinery, transport equipment, and petroleum products. [52]Excludes combined wholesale/retail outlets. [53]Great Britain only. [54]Miscellaneous includes pharmaceuticals. [55]Urban establishments only. [56]State sector only. [57]Former Yemen Arab Republic only. [58]Data refer to Yugoslavia as constituted prior to 1991.

Finance

This table presents major statistical aggregates comprising national financial structure or constituting a basis for certain international financial comparisons. It includes such data as international reserves, money supply, central banking activity and discount rates, commercial (or "deposit money") banking activity, and external indebtedness of the central government. The country models are broadly similar and permit comparison of internal structure and external position at a high level of generalization.

One of the principal financial criteria of the relative economic position of a country is the size of its international reserves. International reserves as represented in this table comprise the sum of a country's (1) reserve position in the International Monetary Fund (IMF), a quota subscribed in the country's own currency, constituting a level up to which transactions may be effected within the IMF system, (2) holdings of foreign exchange, (3) holdings of gold, and (4) holdings of Special Drawing Rights (SDRs; an unconditional credit allocation, within a quota system set by the IMF, of currency needed by a country to maintain stability of foreign exchange transactions or markets). At appropriate accounting intervals these four elements are valued in a single unit of account (the SDR) and summed. The portion of this reserve total comprised by foreign exchange is very significant as an indication of the country's international liquidity (ability to pay its debts immediately in hard, or convertible, currencies). The ratio of external debt to total reserves, however, is less susceptible of interpretation in isolation: a low ratio, for example, may characterize the situation of a country with little need to borrow or of one with substantial debt but also

the means to repay it. Much higher ratios, on the other hand, may be manageable, despite small reserves, if a country's export earnings are also high.

The section on money supply for the country, both as a total and as a per capita amount, refers to one particular measure of money in circulation: M1, the sum of money in private sector demand deposit accounts and outside banks in circulation; it is distinguished from a broader measure of supply, M2, which is roughly M1 plus "quasi-money" (the time, savings, and foreign-currency deposits of residents).

The section of the table outlining banking activity and the principal monetary aggregates encompasses both central bank authorities and commercial (deposit) banks. For both, the principal component aggregates are grouped under assets and liabilities. For certain countries, the four principal aggregates under assets and liabilities do not comprise the entire total, and the percentages shown, therefore, may add to less than 100% (occasionally more, when the net of other liabilities [capital, reserves, undistributed profits, checks, and other transit items] is negative, reducing the total against which these percentages are calculated). The items excluded by the choice of categories are the least significant worldwide but may be important locally; they include such items as quasi-money, money seasonally adjusted, unused bank overdrafts, and so on. In the case of the central bank authority, data are also provided for the central bank discount rate, generally the controlling interest rate for banking and commercial activity in the country.

The largest share of assets in the case of both central and commercial

Finance

country	international reserves, 1992[a]			money supply, 1991[b]		central bank authority, 1991[b]									
	total ('000,000 SDRs)	% foreign exchange	ratio of external debt to total reserves, 1990[b]	stock ('000,000,000 national currency)	M1 per capita	assets (%)				liabilities (%)				central bank discount rate, 1992[a]
						claims on government	claims on private sector	claims on banks	claims on foreign assets	reserve money	government deposits	foreign liabilities	capital accounts	
Afghanistan	199	78.4	16.3[1,2]	351.025[3]	22,100[3]	93.9[3,4]	0.1[3]	0.5[3]	5.5[3]	73.6[3]	5.3[3]	6.3[3]	3.0[3]	...
Albania	...	...	...	...	...	...	...	...	...	...	...	...	...	...
Algeria	1,084	81.6	24.8	324.5	12,500	41.1	—	44.4	14.5	65.6	2.4	10.0	—	...
American Samoa	...	...	...	...	...	...	...	...	...	...	...	...	...	...
Andorra	...	...	...	...	...	...	...	...	...	...	...	...	...	...
Angola	...	...	...	...	...	...	...	...	...	...	...	...	...	...
Antigua and Barbuda	23[6]	100.0[6]	5.9[1,7]	0.168	2,620	33.7	—	1.4	64.9	99.5	0.1	—	—	7.0[6,8]
Argentina	4,769[6]	94.1[6]	9.6	2.706[3]	80[3]	29.6[9]	—	37.0[9]	33.3[9]	40.7[9]	—	22.2[9]	7.4[9]	7[10]
Armenia	...	...	...	...	...	...	...	...	...	...	...	...	...	...
Aruba	99	97.0	...	0.314	4,860	...	...	...	100.0	72.9	6.1	—	22.8	9.5
Australia	10,009	92.8	...	49.983	2,870	18.9	—	—	81.1	65.2	6.4	0.2	—	6.3
Austria	8,634	86.2	...	265.8	33,900	3.6	—	33.2	63.3	73.7	0.1	—	29.2	8.0
Azerbaijan	...	...	...	18.535	2,590	...	...	...	...	...	...	...	...	...
Bahamas, The	143[6]	94.4[6]	3.8[1,2]	0.355	1,350	41.4	—	0.8	57.9	69.5	4.7	—	26.9	7.5
Bahrain	961	94.4	1.2[1,2]	0.305	580	—	—	—	100.0	26.1	32.0	1.1	34.5	3.7[11]
Bangladesh	1,114	99.0	18.1	70.804	650	12.1[4]	—	38.8	49.1	54.0	2.0	29.5	4.9	8.5
Barbados	101	100.0	5.2[1,2]	0.495	1,920	46.3	—	16.9	36.9	57.8	15.3	30.6	6.2	18.0
Belarus	...	...	...	35.985	3,490	...	...	...	...	...	...	...	...	20.0
Belgium	9,383	80.6	...	1,217.0[3]	122,000[3]	6.1	—	—	93.9	53.9	—	—	—	8.5
Belize	47	95.7	2.0	0.118	620	17.2	—	—	82.8	67.9	—	11.7	—	12.0
Benin	144	97.9	19.4	116.7	24,400	22.8	—	38.9	38.3	77.7	12.9	6.1	—	11.0
Bermuda	...	...	...	0.052[3,12]	870[3,12]	...	...	...	...	...	...	...	...	...
Bhutan	69[6]	98.6[6]	0.9	0.750	500	—	—	2.1	97.9	68.8	5.0	—	—	8.0[10]
Bolivia	207	84.5	17.4	1.447	190	64.9[4]	—	15.4	19.7	18.3	54.0	17.4	3.4	22.5[10]
Bosnia and Hercegovina	...	...	...	...	...	...	...	...	...	...	...	...	...	...
Botswana	2,831	98.7	0.2	0.614	460	—	—	—	100.0	9.3	55.6	—	19.0	14.0
Brazil	11,234	98.9	10.7	...	...	85.5[4]	—	2.0	12.5	8.3	8.5	66.3	2.0	1,449
Brunei	...	...	...	...	...	...	...	...	...	...	...	...	...	...
Bulgaria	...	...	...	...	...	...	...	...	...	...	...	...	...	...
Burkina Faso	247	94.7	2.5	111.6	12,000	17.8	—	8.5	73.8	81.6	4.6	10.5	—	11.0
Burundi	101	96.0	8.1	23.233[3]	4,390[3]	29.5[4]	0.6	8.2	61.8	33.1	13.8	22.0	21.3	7.0[2]
Cambodia	...	...	...	...	...	...	...	...	...	...	...	...	...	...
Cameroon	34	70.6	177.2	429.9	34,500	77.8	—	18.8	3.4	48.4	10.5	37.6	0.9	10.8[6]
Canada	10,644	81.6	...	100.5	3,650	32.0	—	—	68.0	99.1	—	—	—	5.0
Cape Verde	60[7]	100.0[7]	...	7.538	21,900	43.7[4]	25.5	2.0	28.9	48.6	4.2	1.1	17.6	4.0[6,10]
Cayman Islands	...	...	...	0.050[3]	1,830[3]	...	...	...	...	...	...	...	...	...
Central African Republic	75	98.7	6.8	53.0	18,300	47.8	—	4.3	47.9	74.6	1.0	18.7	2.1	10.8[6]
Chad	81[6]	98.8[6]	3.4	68.9	11,700	21.7	—	30.8	47.5	74.8	0.4	16.7	1.9	10.8[6]
Chile	5,409	98.8	1.7	784.2	58,100	36.4[4]	1.5	28.2	33.9	52.2	9.3	13.5	8.5	19.7[10]
China	34,254	96.6	1.5	898.8	780	12.0	5.9	66.4	15.7	89.0	5.5	—	5.9	8.6[7,10]
Colombia	4,937	97.1	3.5	1,282.0[7]	41,500[7]	14.6	—	7.9	77.5	50.0	7.1	10.0	7.4	24.6[10]
Comoros	21[3]	100.0[3]	5.9	10.080	20,700	24.6	—	—	75.4	59.2	7.4	6.0	27.8	8.5[2]
Congo	3	100.0	625.7	112.2	47,300	63.7	—	33.5	2.8	70.7	5.2	20.4	1.6	10.8[6]
Cook Islands	...	...	...	...	...	...	...	...	...	...	...	...	...	...
Costa Rica	748	99.7	5.9	79.8	25,500	32.5[4]	—	13.3	54.2	66.9	7.0	92.3	6.5	27.0
Côte d'Ivoire	7	71.4	1,675.0	510.1	40,900	31.4	—	68.1	0.4	39.1	2.4	56.1	—	11.0
Croatia	...	...	...	...	...	...	...	...	...	...	...	...	...	...
Cuba	...	...	...	...	...	...	...	...	...	...	...	...	...	...
Cyprus	804	95.8	1.0	0.462	800	27.3	—	2.8	70.0	80.8	13.2	3.8	—	6.5
Czechoslovakia	1,497	88.2	...	371.4	23,800	...	...	...	...	...	...	...	...	9.0
Denmark	5,008	90.5	...	258.3	50,000	17.7	1.0	31.4	49.9	46.8	12.3	4.2	—	9.5
Djibouti	60	98.3	1.5	31.649	57,600	—	—	0.2	99.8	55.6	14.0	—	7.0	...
Dominica	12[6]	100.0[6]	5.4	0.074	1,030	43.6	—	—	56.4	84.9	—	15.1	—	6.5[8]
Dominican Republic	282	99.3	54.6	9.250	1,250	23.9	—	15.0	61.0	115.7	—	216.3	-9.8	...
Ecuador	566	96.1	11.4	852.9[3]	78,000[3]	58.9[4]	1.9	11.2	28.0	63.6	32.4	125.1	2.3	49.0

banks is usually either claims on government and government agencies or foreign assets and holdings, though some of the latter, such as the large outstanding loans to socialist and less developed countries, have become the chief liabilities. The chief liability of a central bank is usually reserve money (the currency and notes issued by the bank). When government deposits represent a substantial share, budgetary surpluses have usually been deposited by the central government. Large foreign liabilities imply extensive foreign investment. Among the deposit money banks, loans to the private sector normally represent the largest share of assets; occasionally, a trade- or banking-oriented country such as Belgium or Luxembourg will show major foreign assets. The chief liabilities of these banks will usually be savings deposits. If the country commands a high degree of confidence internationally, foreign liabilities may comprise a substantial share of liabilities.

Because the majority of the world's countries are in the less developed bloc, and because their principal financial concern is often external debt and its service, data are given for outstanding external public and publicly guaranteed long-term debt rather than for total public debt, which is the major concern in the developed countries. For comparability, the data are given in U.S. dollars. The volume of debt by itself does not create external payment problems. If the country's external debt service (interest payments plus principal repayment) needs can be met by a strong, dependable export market, by export of services, or, occasionally, by direct remittances from abroad (by residents working abroad and sending wages home in foreign

currencies, for example), no debt problem need exist. Countries whose debt service ratio (total debt service as a percent of exports of goods and services) is relatively high, however, must often base their external borrowing policy on maintenance of domestic conditions of strict efficiency and, sometimes, austerity. The failure to adhere to such policies may lead to eventual crises of financial liquidity, deflation, and slower growth.

Ideally, the data presented here should be obtained by utilizing a single international methodology to provide a universally comparable set of international statistics. No international agency, however, can collect such data for all countries because of differences, both overall and in detail, in national definitions of financial aggregates, in accounting methodology, and in the completeness with which it is possible to survey a country's financial activity. The greater part of the data presented in the table comes from the IMF's *International Financial Statistics* and the World Bank's *World Debt Tables*. These sources are supplemented by other recent data from national, regional, or other international sources. In a few cases the desired data are negligible or unavailable, as noted.

Detailed percentages may not add to 100.0 because of rounding, statistical discrepancy, or nonaccounting of negligible quantities.
— None, less than half the last significant figure, or not applicable.
... Not available.
a. Latest month.
b. Year-end.

deposit money banks, 1991[b] assets (%) loans to government	loans to private sector	reserves	foreign assets	liabilities deposits ('000,000,000 national currency)	composition (%) demand depos.	savings depos.	govt. depos.	foreign liabilities	external public debt outstanding, 1990[b] total ('000,000 U.S.$)	creditors (%) official	private	debt service total ('000,000 U.S.$)	repayment (%) principal	interest	debt service ratio (%)	country
1.4[3,4]	51.2[3]	31.1[3]	16.3[3]	51.160[3]	35.6[3]	49.4[3,5]	0.5[3]	0.6[3]	4,964[1,2]	...	...	411[1,2]	26.8[1,2]	73.2[1,2]	4.2[1,2]	Afghanistan
...	...	...	...	...	...	...	...	...	162[1,2]	...	...	71[1,2]	42.9[1,2]	57.1[1,2]	2.0[1,2]	Albania
8.3	84.5	1.2	6.0	385.8	34.5	23.4	3.0	43.5	24,316	28.4	71.6	8,070	76.3	23.7	58.1	Algeria
...	...	...	...	...	...	...	...	...	...	...	...	...	...	...	...	American Samoa
...	...	...	...	...	...	...	...	...	...	...	...	...	...	...	...	Andorra
...	...	...	...	...	...	...	...	...	7,152	46.7	53.3	222	59.9	40.1	6.9[2]	Angola
9.9[4]	65.9	8.9	15.3	0.870	12.6	59.3[5]	4.1	15.6	167[1,7]	...	...	15[1,7]	...	...	8.5[1,7]	Antigua and Barbuda
34.2[3]	53.0[3]	6.6[3]	6.2[3]	20.2[3]	2.2[3]	22.2[3,5]	5.7[3]	19.4[3]	46,146	24.0	76.0	3,792	43.9	56.1	25.2	Argentina
...	...	...	...	...	...	...	...	...	...	...	...	...	...	...	...	Armenia
2.9	59.2	9.7	28.2	1.167	20.8	48.0	2.2	23.5	...	...	...	...	...	...	...	Aruba
9.8[4]	83.9	1.3	5.0	309.835	11.2	55.2	0.9	16.5	...	...	...	...	...	...	...	Australia
30.8[4]	45.3	1.8	22.0	3,220.2	4.7	45.5	2.4	25.4	...	...	...	...	...	...	...	Austria
...	...	...	...	...	...	...	...	...	...	...	...	...	...	...	...	Azerbaijan
24.6[4]	86.2	8.3	−19.1	1.355	20.4	70.8[5]	2.6	—	563[1,2]	...	...	227[1,2]	76.2[1,2]	23.8[1,2]	12.4[1,2]	Bahamas, The
7.6	25.3	7.8	59.2	1.806	11.4	45.2	25.5	15.8	1,240[1,2]	...	...	170[1,2]	45.3[1,2]	54.7[1,2]	5.7[1,2]	Bahrain
23.0[4]	61.1	10.2	5.7	297.623	12.0	56.7	5.9	2.7	11,464	98.3	1.7	433	63.3	36.7	15.8	Bangladesh
22.3	62.2	6.4	9.0	1.974	14.9	62.4	5.4	14.2	569[1,2]	...	...	63[1,2]	50.8[1,2]	42.9[1,2]	12.1[1,2]	Barbados
...	...	...	...	...	...	...	...	...	...	...	...	...	...	...	...	Belarus
22.0[3,4]	21.9[3]	0.2[3]	55.9[3]	10,652.2[3]	5.5[3]	17.8[3,5]	—	69.7[3]	...	...	...	...	...	...	...	Belgium
11.1[4]	73.4	8.3	7.2	0.451	15.3	54.4	19.2	3.3	140.7	88.3	11.7	14.9	62.4	37.6	5.3[2]	Belize
4.5	54.0	32.9	8.6	159.7	42.2	19.8	18.5	11.5	1,262	75.2	24.8	10	50.0	50.0	4.8[2]	Benin
...	...	...	...	8.835[3]	...	...	...	...	403[1,2]	...	...	82[1,2]	56.1[1,2]	43.9[1,2]	10.5[1,2]	Bermuda
3.4[4]	15.5	63.4	17.7	1.976	25.5	32.8[5]	15.9	6.9	80.4	76.6	23.4	6.7	65.7	34.3	...	Bhutan
—	80.8	15.5	3.7	6.301	11.0	59.1[5]	2.1	6.0	3,683	91.3	8.7	285	59.3	40.7	28.6	Bolivia
...	...	...	...	...	...	...	...	...	...	...	...	...	...	...	...	Bosnia and Hercegovina
3.7[4]	60.4	26.4	9.5	1.620	28.1	66.9	—	3.0	509.8	95.2	4.8	98.2	62.9	37.1	4.4	Botswana
40.3[4,13]	41.4[13]	14.4[13]	3.8[13]	6.694[13]	10.9[13]	12.8[13]	1.4[13]	14.1[13]	82,098	31.3	68.7	4,941	55.0	45.0	14.6	Brazil
—14.2[13]—		0.5[13]	...	4.928[13]	—83.6[13]—				25[1,7]	...	...	2[1,7]	...	...	0.1[1,7]	Brunei
...	...	...	...	...	...	...	...	...	9,564	1.2	98.8	1,283	64.5	35.5	16.0	Bulgaria
8.9	64.1	21.2	5.8	171.6	26.7	29.7	29.9	10.1	750	94.9	5.1	28	64.3	35.7	5.2	Burkina Faso
21.4[4]	67.4	7.5	3.7	33.879	36.8	32.9	—	4.8	850	98.8	1.2	40	70.0	30.0	41.2	Burundi
...	...	...	...	...	...	...	...	...	1,400[1,2]	...	...	11[1,2]	0.0[1,2]	100.0[1,2]	29.7[1,2]	Cambodia
22.5	71.6	2.2	3.6	1,246.4	20.7	27.3	15.2	6.3	4,784	79.2	20.8	300	42.3	57.7	12.8	Cameroon
10.2[4]	77.0	1.5	11.2	453.1	17.4	53.4[5]	0.5	17.9	...	...	...	...	...	...	...	Canada
...	...	...	...	...	...	...	...	...	144.3	98.3	1.7	4.9	63.3	36.7	3.8	Cape Verde
...	...	...	...	283.185[2]	...	...	...	...	185[1,7]	...	...	26[1,7]	...	...	...	Cayman Islands
30.5[4]	61.8	2.0	5.7	43.0	25.0	15.1	12.3	8.0	815	97.4	2.6	14	35.7	64.3	6.2	Central African Republic
40.7[4]	46.1	1.4	11.8	68.4	28.3	6.0	19.1	9.5	430.4	98.0	2.0	6.5	49.2	50.8	2.2	Chad
4.6[4]	86.5	5.7	3.3	5,964.2	7.0	60.1[5]	5.1	16.4	10,339	50.1	49.9	1,570	30.2	69.8	14.9	Chile
—	77.1	18.3	4.6	2,464.3	20.5	37.7	—	4.4	45,319	31.9	68.1	5,904	57.1	42.9	8.7	China
3.9[7]	67.9[7]	21.8[7]	6.5[7]	2,577.4[7]	28.1[7]	31.7[5,7]	—	15.3[7]	14,680	58.2	41.8	3,116	60.2	39.8	33.2	Colombia
...	77.6	10.2	12.2	12.401	27.9	47.0	—	12.6	177.1	99.9	0.1	0.5	—	100.0	1.0	Comoros
31.3[4]	60.5	1.9	6.4	206.4	28.5	23.6	9.4	8.0	4,380	71.7	28.3	244	57.4	42.6	14.8	Congo
...	...	...	...	...	...	...	...	...	401[1,7]	...	...	0[1,7]	...	...	...	Cook Islands
6.6[4]	36.4	49.9	7.1	260.4	17.3	80.9[5]	1.4	2.6	3,076	77.2	22.8	432	60.9	39.1	21.1	Costa Rica
6.8	86.6	3.2	3.4	1,229.8	20.3	27.3	6.7	11.8	10,050	68.1	31.9	467	60.0	40.0	12.7	Côte d'Ivoire
...	...	...	...	...	...	...	...	...	...	...	...	...	...	...	...	Croatia
...	...	...	...	...	...	...	...	...	24,980[1,2]	...	...	343[1,2]	33.5[1,2]	66.5[1,2]	11.5[1,2]	Cuba
9.9	58.7	16.1	15.3	3.134	8.5	57.2	1.2	24.2	1,542	65.1	34.9	218	51.4	48.6	6.9	Cyprus
...	...	...	...	...	...	...	...	...	5,346	6.5	93.5	1,349	72.9	27.1	9.1	Czechoslovakia
12.4	50.5	2.3	34.7	835.3	27.9	29.6	—	33.5	...	...	...	...	...	...	...	Denmark
0.6[4]	46.0	0.8	52.5	76.290	27.2	38.7	1.4	16.8	144.6	99.9	0.1	9.8	79.6	20.4	5.3[2]	Djibouti
15.4[4]	58.8	10.4	15.4	0.401	10.7	54.5[5]	—	15.5	75.9	99.9	0.1	4.0	65.0	35.0	3.8	Dominica
10.0[4]	60.8	28.4	0.8	19.213	17.2	32.7	5.1	0.9	3,440	72.6	27.4	146	61.0	39.0	6.3	Dominican Republic
—	74.7[3]	19.7[3]	5.6[3]	1,227.8[3]	35.1[3]	34.5[3]	...	4.0[3]	9,854	41.2	58.8	872	54.0	46.0	26.8	Ecuador

Finance (continued)

country	international reserves, 1992[a]			money supply, 1991[b]		central bank authority, 1991[b]								central bank discount rate, 1992[a]
	total ('000,000 SDRs)	% foreign exchange	ratio of external debt to total reserves, 1990[b]	stock ('000,000,000 national currency)	M1 per capita	assets (%)				liabilities (%)				
						claims on government	claims on private sector	claims on banks	claims on foreign assets	reserve money	government deposits	foreign liabilities	capital accounts	
Egypt	4,282	97.9	12.2	28.337	510	62.6[4]	—	8.8	28.7	35.6	20.5	43.5	—	21.3[6]
El Salvador	278	94.2	4.3	4.872	900	53.5[4]	0.1	14.7	31.7	45.0	15.1	23.5	13.4	10.0[10]
Equatorial Guinea	6	—	...	2.6	7,280	81.9	—	—	18.1	14.2	1.9	58.8	1.9	10.8[6]
Estonia	...	...	...	...	...	...	...	...	...	...	...	...	...	...
Ethiopia	97	93.8	129.8	6.199	120	67.7	—	30.2	2.1	74.5	9.6	0.6	5.0	3.0
Faeroe Islands	...	...	...	...	...	...	...	...	...	...	...	...	...	...
Fiji	187	91.4	1.1	0.274	370	0.1[4]	—	—	99.9	47.3	1.6	—	20.1	8.0
Finland	4,943	91.1	...	129.769	25,800	2.5	5.6	28.9	62.9	66.4	—	0.1	12.2	9.5
France	27,115	81.7	...	1,622.0	28,400	11.6	0.6	25.9	61.9	53.4	13.4	10.3	32.0	9.5
French Guiana	...	...	...	4.654	39,400	...	...	...	...	...	...	...	...	...
French Polynesia	...	...	...	48.377	243,000	...	...	...	...	...	...	...	...	...
Gabon	167	98.2	10.7	195.4	159,000	28.5	—	13.9	57.6	59.2	15.0	21.9	1.3	10.8[6]
Gambia, The	47[6]	100.0[6]	5.5	0.394	430	3.3[4]	—	7.8	88.9	42.4	72.4	80.0	10.1	16.0
Gaza Strip	...	...	...	...	...	...	...	...	...	...	...	...	...	...
Georgia	...	...	...	...	...	...	...	...	...	...	...	...	...	...
Germany	48,124	85.0	...	575.0	7,270	6.9	—	62.7	30.4	77.5	3.1	11.8	—	8.8
Ghana	394[6]	95.4[6]	11.6	222.420	14,800	41.6[4]	—	1.6	56.9	27.5	15.5	91.1	—	20.0[6]
Gibraltar	...	...	...	...	...	...	...	...	...	...	...	...	...	...
Greece	3,282	94.1	6.4[1,2]	2,097.6	204,000	62.5	—	14.8	22.8	35.1	2.4	32.4	—	19.0
Greenland	...	...	...	...	...	...	...	...	...	...	...	...	...	...
Grenada	12[6]	100.0[6]	5.4	0.090	990	44.0	—	1.0	55.0	100.0	—	—	—	6.5[8]
Guadeloupe	...	...	...	6.497	16,600	...	...	...	...	...	...	...	...	...
Guam	...	...	...	...	...	...	...	...	...	...	...	...	...	...
Guatemala	485	98.6	7.5	3.843	410	9.3[4]	—	23.0	67.6	294.8	105.8	53.0	10.0	16.5[6]
Guernsey	...	...	...	...	...	...	...	...	...	...	...	...	...	...
Guinea	...	...	...	...	...	...	...	...	...	...	...	...	...	...
Guinea-Bissau	...	...	...	...	...	...	...	...	...	...	...	...	...	...
Guyana	90	98.9	59.4	7.466	9,960	18.8	—	—	81.2	50.7	—	413.5	-9.8	32.5[6]
Haiti	13[6]	92.3[6]	186.3	2.634[2]	410[2]	84.2[2,4]	8.3[2]	2.1[2]	5.4[2]	67.9[2]	5.5[2]	28.0[2]	6.7[2]	...
Honduras	141	99.3	77.0	2.277	460	43.8[4]	—	33.5	22.7	43.0	23.4	107.5	22.3	28.9
Hong Kong	...	...	...	128.497	22,400	...	...	...	...	...	...	...	...	...
Hungary	3,429	99.8	16.6	449.1[3]	43,400[3]	61.5[3]	0.4[3]	27.8[3]	10.3[3]	41.4[3]	4.5[3]	89.5[3]	—	27.0[6]
Iceland	386	98.4	...	24.595[3]	95,900[3]	28.4	1.0	8.3	62.4	49.3	16.7	2.8	—	16.5
India	4,822	90.1	29.8	1,040.0	1,180	79.1	—	7.6	13.3	71.9	0.1	6.7	11.1	12.0
Indonesia	7,595	97.6	5.9	26,693.0	146,000	13.0[4]	2.0	32.9	52.1	26.8	30.1	14.5	9.5	12.1[11]
Iran	...	...	...	7,929.3[3]	140,000[3]	94.2[3,4]	—	1.3[3]	4.5[3]	68.9[3]	15.8[3]	1.0[3]	1.8[3]	...
Iraq	...	...	...	...	...	...	...	...	...	...	...	...	...	...
Ireland	3,992	92.2	...	3.390	960	9.9	—	—	90.1	61.5	34.1	—	22.5	10.5
Isle of Man	...	...	...	...	...	...	...	...	...	...	...	...	...	...
Israel	5,121	99.8	3.1[1,2]	7.988	1,560	34.1	—	18.2	47.7	68.0	27.8	0.2	—	10.9
Italy	26,645	83.1	...	519,530.0	8,993,000	61.4	—	3.0	35.6	78.4	—	0.2	—	12.0
Jamaica	109	100.0	23.1	7.818	3,210	53.2	—	—	46.8	138.8	186.8	272.8	25.5	40.9[8]
Japan	50,110	84.0	...	131,040.0	1,056,000	38.0[4]	—	51.7	10.2	117.6	7.8	—	—	3.3
Jersey	...	...	...	...	...	...	...	...	...	...	...	...	...	...
Jordan	625	95.5	7.3	1.647	460	41.9	—	—	58.1	101.8	12.9	—	—	8.5[6]
Kazakhstan	...	...	...	...	...	...	...	...	...	...	...	...	...	...
Kenya	48	58.3	23.0	31.667	1,200	78.1	—	—	21.9	83.3	—	33.3	7.5	20.3
Kiribati	...	...	...	...	...	...	...	...	...	...	...	...	...	...
Korea, North	...	...	...	...	...	...	...	...	...	...	...	...	...	...
Korea, South	10,159	97.2	1.2	21,752.0	500,000	8.5[4]	—	60.8	30.7	47.0	16.6	0.1	—	7.0
Kuwait	2,290	85.6	0.2[1,2]	1.230	1,550	—	—	—	100.0	59.2	33.2	—	21.2	7.5
Kyrgyzstan	...	...	...	...	...	...	...	...	...	...	...	...	...	...
Laos	...	...	...	...	...	...	...	...	...	...	...	...	...	...
Latvia	...	...	...	...	...	...	...	...	...	...	...	...	...	...
Lebanon	795	55.8	0.5	689.4	249,000	5.7	0.5	4.3	89.6	18.0	6.5	0.1	1.4	18.0[6]
Lesotho	114	98.2	5.1	0.313	170	64.8	—	—	35.2	26.9	64.8	0.6	5.7	18.0
Liberia	6[2]	100.0[2]	...	0.227[2]	90[2]	98.2[2,4]	0.1[2]	0.7[2]	0.9[2]	32.1[2]	2.9[2]	48.2[2]	9.4[2]	8.1[2, 10]
Libya	4,514	84.3	0.6[1,2]	4.293	980	74.0	0.1	—	25.9	50.9	15.7	—	—	5.0[2]
Liechtenstein	...	...	...	...	...	...	...	...	...	...	...	...	...	...
Lithuania	...	...	...	...	...	...	...	...	...	...	...	...	...	11.0[6]
Luxembourg	...	...	...	80.6	209,000	...	...	...	...	...	...	...	...	6.0[10]
Macau	...	...	...	8.979[3]	19,200[3]	...	...	...	...	...	...	...	...	...
Macedonia	...	...	...	...	...	...	...	...	...	...	...	...	...	...
Madagascar	109[6]	100.0[6]	40.0	752.6	60,000	83.9[4]	—	5.5	10.6	30.0	45.0	202.0	0.6	11.5[2]
Malawi	48	93.8	9.9	0.634	70	59.6[4]	—	—	40.4	46.6	31.8	21.3	—	13.0
Malaysia	9,418	95.8	1.6	25.405[3]	1,410[3]	9.0[3]	—	—	91.0[3]	61.1[3]	17.6[3]	0.1[3]	—	7.4[6]
Maldives	16	93.8	2.7	0.404	1,800	61.0	—	0.2	38.8	86.4	15.1	2.1	8.2	7.0[6, 11]
Mali	212	95.3	12.0	107.4	12,900	24.5	—	16.9	58.6	93.5	2.2	14.0	—	11.0
Malta	878	89.4	0.1	0.407	1,130	—	—	—	100.0	98.3	3.9	—	—	5.5
Marshall Islands	...	...	...	...	...	...	...	...	...	...	...	...	...	...
Martinique	...	...	...	6.403	17,500	...	...	...	...	...	...	...	...	...
Mauritania	37	97.3	35.1	18.987	9,140	62.1	—	10.3	27.5	61.9	4.5	57.5	18.8	6.5[7]
Mauritius	681	96.2	1.0	6.677	6,200	18.6	—	1.8	79.6	67.4	0.1	0.5	2.2	8.3
Mayotte	...	...	...	0.621	6,490	...	...	...	...	...	...	...	...	...
Mexico	13,528	97.6	7.7	105,552.0	1,260,000	27.7	0.4	1.6	70.3	50.2	—	26.6	1.7	19.2[11]
Micronesia	...	...	...	...	...	...	...	...	...	...	...	...	...	...
Moldova	...	...	...	...	...	...	...	...	...	...	...	...	...	...
Monaco	...	...	...	...	...	...	...	...	...	...	...	...	...	...
Mongolia	...	...	...	...	...	...	...	...	...	...	...	...	...	...
Morocco	2,318	94.5	10.5	92.080	3,550	23.7	14.7	15.3	46.4	87.2	1.0	10.7	—	8.5[2]
Mozambique	...	...	...	...	...	...	...	...	...	...	...	...	...	...
Myanmar (Burma)	214	95.3	13.6	30.587[3]	730[3]	80.7[3]	—	16.5[3]	2.8[3]	80.0[3]	—	3.2[3]	—	9.0[6, 10]
Namibia	...	...	...	...	...	...	...	...	...	...	...	...	...	...
Nauru	...	...	...	...	...	...	...	...	...	...	...	...	...	...
Nepal	337	96.7	5.1	17.614	900	44.2	1.4	2.5	51.8	49.6	20.5	8.7	24.2	13.0[6]

loans to government	loans to private sector	reserves	foreign assets	deposits ('000,000,000 national currency)	demand depos.	savings depos.	govt. depos.	foreign liabilities	total ('000,000 U.S.$)	official	private	total ('000,000 U.S.$)	principal	interest	debt service ratio (%)	country
34.2[4]	20.0	14.4	31.3	134.095	9.5	52.3[5]	4.3	8.5	34,242	78.8	21.2	2,769	61.9	38.1	20.9	Egypt
5.9	65.7	24.3	4.1	13.079	17.5	68.1[5]	4.0	1.1	1,898	91.6	8.4	183	60.7	39.3	20.3	El Salvador
7.1[4]	78.4	5.3	9.3	15.9	9.8	4.4	6.9	3.8	206.0	91.4	8.6	1.1	54.5	45.5	2.2	Equatorial Guinea
...	...	...	...	...	...	...	...	...	...	...	...	...	...	...	...	Estonia
63.4[4]	9.8	21.0	5.8	5.372	40.8	40.7	3.3	3.0	3,116	90.1	9.9	188	76.6	23.4	30.6	Ethiopia
...	...	...	...	...	...	...	...	...	...	...	...	...	...	...	...	Faeroe Islands
15.0[4]	67.3	11.5	6.2	1.194	15.3	72.2	1.3	7.6	292.4	91.6	8.4	78.3	69.7	30.3	8.4	Fiji
0.6	78.0	4.7	16.7	599.429	20.3	24.1	1.9	36.9	...	...	...	...	...	...	...	Finland
6.5	67.9	0.8	24.8	9,698.0	14.0	26.3	—	28.0	...	...	...	...	...	...	...	France
...	...	...	...	...	...	...	...	...	45[1,7]	...	...	3[1,7]	...	...	2.6[1,7]	French Guiana
...	...	...	...	...	...	...	...	...	345[1,2]	...	...	321[1,2]	65.6[1,2]	34.4[1,2]	6.2[1,2]	French Polynesia
29.4[4]	58.3	6.5	5.8	391.8	33.8	28.7	10.1	10.2	2,945	76.0	24.0	128	41.4	58.6	4.9	Gabon
24.9[4]	51.6	16.9	6.7	0.583	36.3	43.8	—	0.4	304.2	93.9	6.1	40.2	70.0	30.0	22.1	Gambia, The
...	...	...	...	...	...	...	...	...	...	...	...	...	...	...	...	Gaza Strip
...	...	...	...	...	...	...	...	...	...	...	...	...	...	...	...	Georgia
16.1[4]	65.4	2.9	15.6	3,910.7	10.3	28.8	6.4	9.0	...	...	...	...	...	...	...	Germany
9.1[4]	38.3	18.2	34.4	306.9	38.7	30.8	5.8	13.2	2,670	91.5	8.5	180	68.3	31.7	18.2	Ghana
—39.7[3]—		0.2[3]	—	2.901[3]	—51.7[3]—			—	408[1,2]	...	...	47[1,2]	12.8[1,2]	87.2[1,2]	11.8[1,2]	Gibraltar
40.4	33.1	18.5	7.9	8,849.8	6.9	64.5	—	25.4	21,291[1,2]	...	...	2,945[1,2]	38.4[1,2]	61.6[1,2]	18.3[1,2]	Greece
...	...	...	...	...	...	...	...	...	...	...	...	...	...	...	...	Greenland
12.6[4]	66.2	9.9	11.2	0.435	11.3	65.2[5]	1.6	13.7	91.1	97.5	2.5	2.2	50.0	50.0	2.1[2]	Grenada
...	...	...	...	...	...	...	...	...	41[1,7]	...	...	6[1,7]	...	...	2.5[1,7]	Guadeloupe
...	...	...	...	...	...	...	...	...	...	...	...	...	...	...	...	Guam
21.4	53.7	24.7	0.2	9.334	18.8	75.2	0.5	1.4	2,179	81.9	18.1	163	53.4	46.6	10.3	Guatemala
...	...	...	...	...	...	...	...	...	...	...	...	...	...	...	...	Guernsey
...	...	...	...	...	...	...	...	...	2,230	95.5	4.5	52	69.2	30.8	6.0	Guinea
...	...	...	...	...	...	...	...	...	544.3	94.1	5.9	5.2	34.6	65.4	26.9	Guinea-Bissau
32.5[4]	28.8	28.4	10.3	23.375	16.0	60.9	—	3.9	1,663	91.0	9.0	137	46.7	53.3	55.2	Guyana
1.3[2]	60.5[2]	34.8[2]	3.4[2]	2.486[2]	30.9	60.1[2]	—	1.7[2]	745	94.0	6.0	11	45.5	54.5	3.3	Haiti
22.9[4]	65.5	8.7	2.9	5.347	21.3	46.4[5]	9.4	1.8	3,159	88.2	11.8	343	47.2	52.8	31.8	Honduras
...	...	...	...	5,619.9	...	...	...	...	8,066[1,2]	...	...	2,095[1,2]	52.9[1,2]	47.1[1,2]	3.0[1,2]	Hong Kong
2.6[3,4]	70.0[3]	22.2[3]	5.2[3]	1,353.8[3]	16.6[3]	34.2[3,5]	0.4[3]	7.7[3]	18,046	15.0	85.0	3,804	58.7	41.3	43.2	Hungary
9.9[3]	80.2[3]	7.6[3]	2.3[3]	195.182[3]	11.0[3]	52.9[3]	—	19.8[3]	...	...	...	...	...	...	...	Iceland
24.4	61.7	13.9	—	2,531.8	17.3	71.7	—	11.0	61,097	59.1	40.9	5,437	40.0	60.0	20.4	India
7.2[4]	77.1	8.2	7.4	149,117.0	11.5	48.8[5]	3.7	8.0	44,974	73.7	26.4	6,675	62.0	38.0	22.6	Indonesia
7.9[3]	51.2[3]	39.7[3]	1.2[3]	17,057.4[3]	35.3[3]	62.5[3]	—	0.7[3]	1,797	12.5	87.5	253	88.9	11.1	...	Iran
...	...	...	...	...	...	...	...	...	16,146[1,2]	...	...	2,288[1,2]	65.9[1,2]	34.1[1,2]	24.7[1,2]	Iraq
10.2	60.8	3.2	25.8	17.758	9.6	51.7	0.7	24.3	...	...	...	...	...	...	...	Ireland
...	...	...	...	...	...	...	...	...	...	...	...	...	...	...	...	Isle of Man
32.1	46.8	9.6	11.5	177.162	2.6	40.4	6.9	14.8	17,959[1,2]	...	...	3,689[1,2]	64.2[1,2]	35.8[1,2]	32.8[1,2]	Israel
16.1	61.3	12.6	10.0	1,066,310.0	40.5	45.3	—	17.6	...	...	...	...	...	...	...	Italy
8.5[4]	49.9	20.8	20.8	24.373	21.3	48.0	2.3	18.0	3,873	85.6	14.4	525	57.3	42.7	23.6	Jamaica
8.7[4]	77.8	1.3	12.2	709,620.0	13.1	53.1	—	15.3	...	...	...	...	...	...	...	Japan
...	...	...	...	...	...	...	...	...	...	...	...	...	...	...	...	Jersey
8.7	37.7	27.0	26.6	4.881	13.1	48.4	4.4	18.9	6,486	62.8	37.2	620	56.1	43.9	21.5	Jordan
...	...	...	...	...	...	...	...	...	...	...	...	...	...	...	...	Kazakhstan
21.4[4]	66.8	9.0	2.7	72.791	26.3	51.9[5]	7.3	1.9	4,810	81.2	18.8	471	59.9	40.1	21.1	Kenya
...	...	...	...	...	...	...	...	...	12[1,7]	...	...	0[1,7]	...	...	0.2[1,7]	Kiribati
...	...	...	...	...	...	...	...	...	3,708[1,2]	...	...	89[1,2]	60.7[1,2]	39.3[1,2]	240.5[1,2]	Korea, North
3.8	81.6	8.8	5.8	140,864.0	9.9	44.0[5]	5.0	7.5	17,814	52.0	48.0	4,806	73.6	26.4	6.2	Korea, South
—	77.4	0.4	22.2	7.967	9.8	51.3	1.0	3.8	610[1,2]	...	...	470[1,2]	88.5[1,2]	11.5[1,2]	8.3[1,2]	Kuwait
...	...	...	...	...	...	...	...	...	...	...	...	...	...	...	...	Kyrgyzstan
...	...	...	...	...	...	...	...	...	1,053	100.0	—	11	72.7	27.3	11.5	Laos
...	...	...	...	...	...	...	...	...	...	...	...	...	...	...	...	Latvia
19.8	30.2	4.3	45.8	6,624.2	3.0	72.6[5]	0.6	13.5	545.0	54.7	45.3	88.0	64.1	35.9	...	Lebanon
20.2[4]	33.1	22.9	23.8	0.828	33.3	41.7	3.2	3.8	371.8	91.1	8.9	22.0	65.5	34.5	2.4	Lesotho
13.0[2,4]	30.9[2]	47.6[2]	8.5[2]	0.400[2]	31.3[2]	18.5[2]	6.5[2]	10.8[2]	1,126	82.9	17.1	—	—	—	—	Liberia
—	66.4	31.1	2.5	3.967	57.5	28.2	3.8	7.5	2,607[1,2]	...	...	232[1,2]	48.3[1,2]	51.7[1,2]	4.7[1,2]	Libya
...	...	...	...	...	...	...	...	...	...	...	...	...	...	...	...	Liechtenstein
...	...	...	...	...	...	...	...	...	...	...	...	...	...	...	...	Lithuania
—	4.1	—	95.9	11,693.3	0.8	9.0	—	82.8	...	...	...	...	...	...	...	Luxembourg
—37.3[3]—		...	59.8[3]	56.790[3]	15.7[3]	37.2[3]	...	35.4[3]	251[1,2]	...	...	24[1,2]	29.2[1,2]	70.8[1,2]	1.8[1,2]	Macau
...	...	...	...	...	...	...	...	...	...	...	...	...	...	...	...	Macedonia
2.1	69.3	14.1	14.5	1,227.6	37.9	18.1	10.3	4.0	3,677	93.3	6.7	163	42.9	57.1	33.5	Madagascar
15.5[4]	66.0	17.4	1.2	1.005	34.4	56.4	—	5.3	1,366	95.6	4.4	75	57.3	42.7	19.3	Malawi
9.5	80.3	6.0	4.2	130.593	12.1	47.2	4.7	9.0	16,107	28.1	71.9	3,345	66.4	33.6	9.6	Malaysia
21.2[4]	30.8	31.5	16.5	0.803	14.3	37.5	2.7	18.7	63.9	94.1	5.9	7.0	71.4	18.6	4.1	Maldives
1.5	48.9	40.7	8.9	176.4	26.9	25.7	18.6	11.5	2,306	99.2	0.8	40	57.5	42.5	7.1	Mali
8.5	58.5	6.7	26.3	0.937	5.7	77.2	—	9.8	121.8	100.0	—	8.4	78.6	21.4	0.5[2]	Malta
...	...	...	...	...	...	...	...	...	...	...	...	...	...	...	...	Marshall Islands
...	...	...	...	...	...	...	...	...	27[1,7]	...	...	5[1,7]	...	...	1.2[1,7]	Martinique
0.2	85.5	10.9	3.5	37.083	30.9	16.1	0.1	34.3	1,898	97.9	2.1	41	70.7	29.3	8.3	Mauritania
13.6	52.5	26.9	7.1	29.193	11.2	79.7	—	0.5	739	84.4	15.6	78	55.1	44.9	4.4	Mauritius
...	...	...	...	...	...	...	...	...	...	...	...	...	...	...	...	Mayotte
21.5[4]	72.0	2.3	4.2	321,142.0	22.5	43.5[5]	4.5	17.9	76,204	29.8	70.2	7,980	32.8	67.2	18.3	Mexico
...	...	...	...	...	...	...	...	...	...	...	...	...	...	...	...	Micronesia
...	...	...	...	...	...	...	...	...	...	...	...	...	...	...	...	Moldova
...	...	...	...	...	...	...	...	...	...	...	...	...	...	...	...	Monaco
...	...	...	...	...	...	...	...	...	14,196[1,2]	...	...	130[1,2]	—	100.0[1,2]	115.0[1,2]	Mongolia
...	...	...	...	...	...	...	...	...	22,097	77.7	22.3	1,616	46.0	54.0	19.4	Morocco
...	...	...	...	...	...	...	...	...	4,053	85.0	15.0	16	50.0	50.0	5.3	Mozambique
93.8[4,7]	4.4[7]	1.8[7]	—	64.073[7]	1.6[7]	11.9[5,7]	8.5[7]	15.7[7]	4,446	94.4	5.6	58	77.6	22.4	28.6[7]	Myanmar (Burma)
...	...	...	...	1.961[2]	...	...	...	...	22[1,7]	...	...	0[1,7]	...	...	...	Namibia
...	...	...	...	...	...	...	...	...	141[1,7]	...	...	16[1,7]	...	...	...	Nauru
28.2[4]	47.4	8.9	15.5	33.870	12.7	68.6	—	4.5	1,557	93.1	6.9	57	54.4	45.6	14.2	Nepal

Finance (continued)

country	international reserves, 1992[a]			money supply, 1991[b]		central bank authority, 1991[b]								central bank discount rate, 1992[a]
	total ('000,000 SDRs)	% foreign exchange	ratio of external debt to total reserves, 1990[b]	stock ('000,000 national currency)	M1 per capita	assets (%)				liabilities (%)				
						claims on government	claims on private sector	claims on banks	claims on foreign assets	reserve money	government deposits	foreign liabilities	capital accounts	
Netherlands, The	13,930	81.1	...	129.7	8,580	9.6	—	4.7	85.7	61.5	5.0	—	—	8.5
Netherlands Antilles	143[6]	86.7[6]	4.3[1,2]	0.679	3,550	16.4	—	—	83.6	63.9	9.7	—	14.4	6.0[6]
New Caledonia	...	...	...	51.829	301,000	...	...	...	...	...	...	...	...	...
New Zealand	2,148	97.1	...	23.694[3]	6,910[3]	28.9[3]	—	3.0[3]	68.1[3]	16.2[3]	27.7[3]	37.6[3]	—	7.2
Nicaragua	...	...	...	...	...	54.2[13]	—	44.1[13]	1.7[13]	92.3[13]	9.7[13]	20.6[13]	0.1[13]	...
Niger	143	93.0	5.9	79.9	9,960	29.1	—	24.1	46.8	72.5	2.9	14.4	—	11.0
Nigeria	2,412	99.0	8.6	34.540[3]	400[3]	51.7[3]	0.5[3]	1.4[3]	41.0[3]	28.8[3]	30.3[3]	—	3.1[3]	17.5
Northern Mariana Islands	...	...	...	...	...	...	...	...	...	...	...	...	...	...
Norway	11,273	93.3	...	255.7	60,000	5.2	—	43.4	51.4	24.0	55.6	—	—	10.0
Oman	1,131	95.5	1.3	0.406	260	3.1	—	—	96.9	29.9	32.5	—	19.5	6.4[10]
Pakistan	719	89.8	42.1	305.978	2,390	63.8	—	24.4	11.9	76.9	4.5	13.4	—	10.0
Palau	...	...	...	...	...	...	...	...	...	...	...	...	...	...
Panama	299	98.3	11.6	0.557	230	60.9[4]	12.5	—	26.6	15.8	67.4	29.5	2.6	...
Papua New Guinea	245	98.8	3.7	0.417	110	45.1	—	—	54.9	29.5	30.8	10.0	40.1	10.0
Paraguay	703	89.6	2.5	840.091[3]	194,000[3]	18.2[3,4]	0.5[3]	9.5[3]	71.8[3]	75.4[3]	11.5[3]	0.9[3]	5.3[3]	...
Peru	1,736	96.1	11.6	0.570[3]	20[3]	0.4[3,4]	—	18.7[3]	80.8[3]	49.3[3]	0.1[3]	66.9[3]	8.0[3]	32.9
Philippines	2,316	94.0	22.6	107.7	1,710	19.4[4]	—	18.3	62.3	69.0	49.2	162.0	3.4	10.0
Poland	2,788	98.9	8.7	127,006.0	3,312,000	19.7[4]	—	47.8	32.5	69.6	7.1	14.0	0.6	40.0[6]
Portugal	18,262	95.4	0.9	2,872.5	276,000	7.8[4]	—	4.1	88.2	63.3	21.7	—	9.7	14.5
Puerto Rico	...	...	...	...	...	...	...	...	...	...	...	...	...	...
Qatar	512[6]	83.8[6]	0.3[1,2]	3.629	6,500	—	—	5.1	94.9	66.3	11.9	—	3.3	7.0[2,10]
Réunion	...	...	...	9.534	15,400	...	...	...	...	...	...	...	...	...
Romania	212	62.3	0.0	731.3	31,400	6.9	—	65.3	27.9	66.4	7.1	33.2	4.2	...
Russia	...	...	...	...	...	...	...	...	...	...	...	...	...	20.0
Rwanda	46	71.7	15.7	18.145	2,510	59.0	0.4	3.0	37.7	41.7	16.9	15.5	22.9	14.0
St. Kitts and Nevis	12[6]	100.0[6]	2.3	0.060	1,400	23.9	—	0.1	76.0	100.0	—	—	—	6.5[8]
St. Lucia	34[6]	97.1[6]	1.4	0.168	1,230	17.7	—	—	82.3	94.4	5.6	—	—	7.0[8]
St. Vincent and the Grenadines	16[6]	100.0[6]	2.1	0.061	560	18.6	—	—	81.4	94.3	5.7	—	—	6.5[8]
San Marino	...	...	...	...	...	...	...	...	...	...	...	...	...	...
São Tomé and Príncipe	...	...	...	...	...	...	...	...	...	...	...	...	...	...
Saudi Arabia	7,625	84.6	0.1[1,2]	101.9[3]	7,070[3]	—	—	—	100.0[3]	24.7[3]	10.5[3]	—	—	...
Senegal	8	62.5	227.2	215.5	28,800	47.4	—	51.7	1.0	48.6	1.7	31.7	—	11.0
Seychelles	16	93.8	8.9	0.266	3,770	42.3	—	5.0	52.8	78.7	11.6	—	5.3	9.5
Sierra Leone	10	90.0	101.0	25.091	5,810	77.8	—	—	22.2	103.5	4.4	749.9	—	55.0
Singapore	26,100	99.5	0.2[1,2]	16.436	5,920	—	—	—	100.0	21.9	36.2	—	—	2.9[11]
Slovenia	...	...	...	...	...	...	...	...	...	...	...	...	...	...
Solomon Islands	12	91.7	6.2	0.080	240	72.4	—	—	27.5	49.1	2.1	1.4	60.9	16.0[8]
Somalia	12[2]	100.0[2]	...	139.8[2]	18,900[2]	36.9[2,4]	—	43.9[2]	19.2[2]	74.2[2]	13.4[2]	238.0[2]	15.1[2]	45.0[3]
South Africa	1,336	82.0	...	49.864[3]	1,320[3]	26.7[3]	—	12.5[3]	60.7[3]	115.9[3]	62.3[3]	6.5[3]	...	16.0
Bophuthatswana	...	...	...	...	...	...	...	...	...	...	...	...	...	...
Ciskei	...	...	...	...	...	...	...	...	...	...	...	...	...	...
Transkei	...	...	...	...	...	...	...	...	...	...	...	...	...	...
Venda	...	...	...	...	...	...	...	...	...	...	...	...	...	...
Spain	50,911	96.8	...	16,573.0	424,000	26.8	—	13.7	59.5	103.0	1.6	—	6.5	13.0
Sri Lanka	562	98.8	11.6	39.596[3]	2,310[3]	70.0[3]	—	8.0[3]	22.0[3]	41.0[3]	5.7[3]	23.8[3]	16.5[3]	17.0
Sudan, The	3	100.0	832.4	18.899[2]	680[2]	97.8[2,4]	—	1.8[2]	0.4[2]	88.0[2]	—	58.9[2]	1.7[2]	...
Suriname	2	—	4.6[1,2]	2.886	6,850	98.2	0.5	—	1.4	88.7	0.4	3.0	1.6	...
Swaziland	205	95.6	1.2	0.212	260	—	—	2.0	98.0	28.8	51.7	1.2	5.1	13.0
Sweden	16,952	95.3	...	—	—	51.7	—	9.2	39.0	34.9	—	—	—	8.5
Switzerland	22,334	86.9	...	82.9	12,000	8.5	—	2.0	89.5	61.5	1.2	—	—	7.0
Syria	173[2]	82.7[2]	...	95.030[2]	7,970[2]	69.9[2,4]	—	6.6[2]	23.5[2]	61.7[2]	19.5[2]	36.0[2]	0.1[2]	5.0[2]
Taiwan	60,643	...	0.0[1,2]	2,165.3	105,000	0.2	—	9.6	90.2	47.8	6.1	—	—	5.9
Tajikistan	...	...	...	...	...	...	...	...	...	...	...	...	...	...
Tanzania	143[6]	100.0[6]	27.4	64.126[7]	2,740[7]	39.3[7]	—	49.7[7]	11.0[7]	40.9[7]	—	97.1[7]	—	15.5[2]
Thailand	13,679	98.0	0.9	222.4	3,950	9.5	—	9.8	80.7	36.5	30.2	—	35.1	11.0
Togo	239	99.2	3.1	78.5	21,800	27.8	—	5.6	66.6	77.5	1.7	13.6	—	11.0
Tonga	21	90.5	1.6	0.026	260	19.5	—	1.2	79.3	91.8	0.9	—	6.9	4.3[10]
Trinidad and Tobago	112	96.4	3.7	2.922	2,330	46.4	—	—	53.6	45.9	5.2	—	32.7	13.0
Tunisia	434	96.1	8.1	2.697	320	5.0	—	59.7	35.3	68.6	8.7	12.3	4.8	11.8[11]
Turkey	3,222	94.3	6.2	48,768.0	841,000	55.2[4]	—	4.2	40.7	38.8	1.4	55.5	2.3	45.0
Turkmenistan	...	...	...	13.060	4,210	...	...	...	...	...	...	...	...	...
Tuvalu	...	...	...	...	...	...	...	...	...	...	...	...	...	...
Uganda	32	100.0	52.3	...	...	92.1[4,14]	—	—	7.9[14]	91.0[14]	47.3[14]	69.3[14]	—	49.0
Ukraine	...	...	...	173.4	3,330	...	...	...	...	...	...	...	...	5.4[6]
United Arab Emirates	3,644	93.3	0.3[1,2]	13.012	6,620	—	—	0.2	99.8	54.1	34.1	1.2	8.4	...
United Kingdom	30,405	90.6	...	229.2	3,980	35.3	—	—	64.7	59.2	—	38.5	—	9.9[11]
United States	55,307	56.9	...	923.9	3,640	78.8	—	—	21.2	91.8	11.2	0.3	—	3.0
Uruguay	346	74.6	4.6	1,520.6	487,000	45.5[4]	1.3	19.4	33.8	17.5	31.6	42.1	—	210.5
Uzbekistan	...	...	...	...	...	...	...	...	...	...	...	...	...	...
Vanuatu	30	93.3	0.8	4.377	28,700	—	—	0.2	99.8	47.8	48.6	1.0	14.0	7.0[11]
Venezuela	7,421	93.2	2.8	347.6	17,400	22.3[4]	—	1.6	76.1	30.7	22.3	31.8	8.5	43.0
Vietnam	...	...	...	...	...	...	...	...	...	...	...	...	...	...
Virgin Islands (U.S.)	...	...	...	...	...	...	...	...	...	...	...	...	...	...
West Bank	...	...	...	...	...	...	...	...	...	...	...	...	...	...
Western Sahara	...	...	...	...	...	...	...	...	...	...	...	...	...	...
Western Samoa	52	96.2	1.3	0.043	270	1.1	—	9.5	89.4	44.8	44.6	0.3	—	6.5[10]
Yemen	299[3]	96.0[3]	11.9	29.086[2,15]	3,250[2,15]	94.1[2,15]	—	0.2[2,15]	5.8[2,15]	72.5[2,15]	9.7[2,15]	1.1[2,15]	0.4[2,15]	...
Yugoslavia	1,098	93.8	2.4	126.283[3]	5,290[3]	0.1[3]	—	33.2[3]	66.7[3]	138.2[3]	0.4[3]	34.8[3]	—	60.0
Zaire	132	99.2	39.3	18,056.0	510,000	79.6[4]	0.1	—	20.2	25.1	0.6	71.2	13.8	50.0[2]
Zambia	129[6]	100.0[6]	24.8	22.360	2,780	8.1	0.1	—	89.5	144.5	−186.7	793.2	—	37.0[6,8]
Zimbabwe	118	88.1	14.6	2.978	310	54.9[4]	—	—	45.1	51.2	—	72.2	—	21.0

| deposit money banks, 1991[b] | | | | | | | | | external public debt outstanding (long-term, disbursed only), 1990[b] | | | | | | | country |
| assets (%) | | | | liabilities | composition (%) | | | | total ('000,000 U.S.$) | creditors (%) | | debt service | | | | |
loans to government	loans to private sector	reserves	foreign assets	deposits ('000,000,000 national currency)	demand depos.	savings depos.	govt. depos.	foreign liabilities	total ('000,000 U.S.$)	official	private	total ('000,000 U.S.$)	repayment (%) principal	interest	debt service ratio (%)	country
13.2[4]	50.8	0.3	35.7	906.4	10.2	35.9[5]	—	29.7	...	...	...	...	...	...	...	Netherlands, The
2.2[4]	55.3	2.5	40.1	3.039	13.6	40.9[5]	1.7	38.9	1,013[1,2]	...	...	166[1,2]	57.8[1,2]	42.2[1,2]	7.4[1,2]	Netherlands Antilles
...	...	...	...	...	...	...	...	...	313[1,2]	...	...	34[1,2]	61.8[1,2]	38.2[1,2]	5.2[1,2]	New Caledonia
10.0[3]	80.1[3]	4.8[3]	5.1[3]	62.183[3]	36.4[3]	30.9[3]	—	17.8[3]	...	...	...	...	...	...	...	New Zealand
—	74.7[13]	25.2[13]	0.1[13]	1.044[13]	66.0[13]	18.2[5,13]	8.1[13]	0.2[13]	8,067	82.2	17.8	10	50.0	50.0	2.6	Nicaragua
11.8	54.2	29.3	4.7	138.9	25.0	30.3	19.7	25.2	1,326	91.3	8.7	14	57.1	42.9	3.7	Niger
15.2[3]	65.7[3]	8.0[3]	11.1[3]	59.789[3]	25.1[3]	38.5[3]	1.3[3]	0.4[3]	33,709	53.2	46.8	2,964	40.7	59.3	19.9	Nigeria
...	...	...	...	...	...	...	...	...	...	...	...	...	...	...	...	Northern Mariana Islands
14.8[4]	76.0	0.5	8.6	625.2	35.5	30.3[5]	4.4	15.6	...	...	...	...	...	...	...	Norway
8.8	66.1	6.0	19.0	1.414	13.4	58.7	10.5	2.8	2,205	15.3	84.7	743	76.2	23.8	12.6	Oman
26.3	53.2	11.6	8.9	437.121	35.8	21.2	1.5	20.2	16,532	95.9	4.1	1,360	63.5	36.5	17.1	Pakistan
...	...	...	...	...	...	...	...	...	...	...	...	...	...	...	...	Palau
1.4	24.0	—	74.7	11.608	4.3	18.4	—	67.7	3,987	37.7	62.3	140	35.7	64.3	2.6	Panama
16.9	78.7	1.6	2.8	1.374	20.0	62.2	2.9	10.4	1,509	68.9	31.1	260	66.9	33.1	16.8	Papua New Guinea
—	55.1[3]	24.4[3]	20.4[3]	986.199[3]	23.3[3]	61.4[3]	—	1.9[3]	1,736	69.4	30.6	187	59.9	40.1	11.6	Paraguay
37.5[3,4]	28.3[3]	16.9[3]	17.3[3]	1.6[3]	17.4[3]	37.0[3,5]	10.1[3]	8.2[3]	13,343	53.4	46.6	237	62.4	37.6	5.4	Peru
15.3[4]	43.0	22.0	19.7	533.3	6.0	60.5	3.0	10.3	24,108	62.8	37.2	2,177	46.8	53.2	16.4	Philippines
45.9[4]	26.6	12.3	15.2	375,766.0	18.7	40.7[5]	2.2	4.5	39,282	70.7	29.3	848	75.7	24.3	4.3	Poland
33.1[4]	44.4	14.9	7.5	12,372.2	17.2	39.8	4.4	23.0	14,432	23.9	76.1	4,317	76.7	23.3	15.9	Portugal
...	...	...	...	...	...	...	...	...	...	...	...	...	...	...	...	Puerto Rico
...	57.4	2.8	39.7	23.243	10.1	44.3	10.4	18.7	172[1,2]	...	...	62[1,2]	62.9[1,2]	37.1[1,2]	5.0[1,2]	Qatar
...	...	...	...	...	...	...	...	...	63[1,2]	...	...	15[1,2]	40.0[1,2]	60.0[1,2]	1.0[1,2]	Réunion
—	94.8[3]	0.9[3]	4.3[3]	955.8[3]	15.0[3]	29.3[3]	7.6[3]	6.3[3]	19	100.0	—	—	—	—	—	Romania
...	...	...	...	...	...	...	...	...	...	...	...	...	...	...	...	Russia
21.7[4]	41.9	17.6	18.8	28.898	29.7	51.5	9.7	3.6	692.3	99.5	0.5	15.8	60.8	39.2	10.5	Rwanda
21.8[4]	52.4	7.7	18.1	0.503	7.3	51.4[5]	16.2	14.6	36.1	100.0	—	2.6	38.5	61.5	...	St. Kitts and Nevis
5.3[4]	70.3	10.3	14.0	0.902	11.1	62.3[5]	13.7	9.8	60.3	95.7	4.3	5.7	56.1	43.9	...	St. Lucia
12.2[4]	51.1	11.7	25.0	0.473	8.8	53.8[5]	20.1	12.4	57.3	100.0	—	3.9	56.4	43.6	3.1[2]	St. Vincent and the Grenadines
...	...	...	...	...	...	...	...	...	...	...	...	...	...	...	...	San Marino
...	...	...	...	...	...	...	...	...	129.0	99.9	0.1	2.3	47.8	52.2	28.0	São Tomé and Príncipe
—	35.9	6.2	57.9	205.3	36.7	46.3[5]	0.7	13.6	1,187[1,2]	...	...	780[1,2]	94.1[1,2]	5.9[1,2]	3.4[1,2]	Saudi Arabia
6.3	76.6	13.7	3.3	519.3	21.6	30.5	16.0	9.6	2,953	93.9	6.1	210	61.0	39.0	14.9	Senegal
67.2[4]	14.6	8.9	9.2	1.029	14.8	56.0	4.4	6.9	151.2	76.7	23.3	18.2	61.0	39.0	7.3	Seychelles
10.6[4]	45.4	25.5	18.5	17.630	53.0	35.8	—	0.1	606	83.0	17.0	6	50.0	50.0	...	Sierra Leone
8.2	52.6	4.0	35.3	119.353	7.5	44.5	4.4	33.6	3,853[1,2]	...	...	728[1,2]	69.4[1,2]	30.6[1,2]	1.6[1,2]	Singapore
...	...	...	...	...	...	...	...	...	...	...	...	...	...	...	...	Slovenia
42.0	45.7	8.4	3.9	0.167	31.1	56.5	4.8	4.8	105.3	86.6	13.4	10.5	68.6	31.4	10.4	Solomon Islands
−12.4[2,4]	69.3[2]	27.1[2]	16.1[2]	129.6[2]	49.4[2]	13.8[2]	—	—	1,922	98.1	1.9	7	42.9	57.1	25.0[2]	Somalia
7.1[3]	88.5[3]	3.5[3]	0.9[3]	134.074[3]	30.6[3]	53.0[3]	...	5.0[3]	...	...	...	...	...	...	...	South Africa
...	...	...	...	...	...	...	...	...	...	...	...	...	...	...	...	Bophuthatswana
...	...	...	...	...	...	...	...	...	...	...	...	...	...	...	...	Ciskei
...	...	...	...	...	...	...	...	...	...	...	...	...	...	...	...	Transkei
...	...	...	...	...	...	...	...	...	...	...	...	...	...	...	...	Venda
19.5[4]	64.1	9.2	7.2	62,996.0	17.1	38.3	4.5	11.3	4,911	88.5	11.5	281	58.0	42.0	10.1	Spain
20.6[4]	55.0	11.0	13.4	139.574	15.5	45.5	6.2	18.3	...	...	...	...	...	...	...	Sri Lanka
1.6[2]	33.2[2]	48.8[2]	16.3[2]	14.871[2]	57.0[2]	17.4[2]	7.5[2]	4.1[2]	9,156	81.9	18.1	22	63.6	36.4	2.6	Sudan, The
5.9	47.1	46.0	1.0	3.841	44.5	44.6	1.0	4.2	54[1,2]	...	...	7[1,2]	57.1[1,2]	42.9[1,2]	2.0[1,2]	Suriname
—	73.3	14.1	12.6	0.893	17.7	47.3	23.5	3.3	251.2	97.3	2.7	52.4	79.8	20.2	5.7	Swaziland
6.4	73.0	1.1	19.5	1,397.8	—	42.4[5]	—	44.1	...	...	...	...	...	...	...	Sweden
2.8	69.5	1.1	26.6	750.7	5.2	39.2	—	23.8	...	...	...	...	...	...	...	Switzerland
57.6[3,4]	17.4[3]	15.3[3]	9.7[3]	114.693[3]	31.3[3]	24.5[3]	3.4[3]	9.0[3]	14,959	94.4	5.6	1,375	91.1	8.9	25.2	Syria
11.9[4]	68.2	15.3	4.6	7,685.4	23.1	57.2	5.2	5.0	2,751[1,2]	...	...	518[1,2]	50.2[1,2]	49.8[1,2]	1.1[1,2]	Taiwan
...	...	...	...	...	...	...	...	...	...	...	...	...	...	...	...	Tajikistan
84.0[4,7]	8.5[7]	5.2[7]	2.4[7]	94.862[7]	34.7[7]	24.9[7]	1.3[7]	84.3[7]	5,294	96.4	3.6	99	53.5	46.5	18.1	Tanzania
6.4[4]	87.2	2.9	3.5	2,051.7	3.4	78.5	2.5	6.0	12,572	63.8	36.2	3,301	73.4	26.6	10.5	Thailand
0.6	53.2	34.8	11.4	212.0	19.4	40.7	23.5	11.2	1,096	95.0	5.0	60	45.0	55.0	9.8	Togo
8.8[4]	40.1	51.2	—	0.082	22.7	36.2	13.4	—	49.2	80.5	19.5	2.1	42.9	57.1	3.7	Tonga
5.7[4]	75.0	15.1	4.1	10.167	20.1	68.5	1.6	1.7	1,808	29.2	70.8	297	55.2	44.8	12.8	Trinidad and Tobago
10.4[3]	81.1[3]	1.6[3]	6.9[3]	7.347[3]	21.3[3]	39.4[3]	5.6[3]	8.6[3]	6,506	80.5	19.5	1,308	69.5	30.5	22.2	Tunisia
25.8[4]	50.3	10.2	13.7	189,402.0	15.7	37.1	10.2	31.8	38,595	46.7	53.3	6,188	55.4	44.6	24.6	Turkey
...	...	...	...	...	...	...	...	...	...	...	...	...	...	...	...	Turkmenistan
...	...	...	...	...	...	...	...	...	...	...	...	...	...	...	...	Tuvalu
15.8[4]	41.4	17.6	25.2	155.991	50.4	19.8	1.4	7.8	2,301	88.1	11.9	62	74.2	25.8	34.8	Uganda
...	...	...	...	...	...	...	...	...	...	...	...	...	...	...	...	Ukraine
8.1[4]	37.3	4.7	49.8	139.482	6.0	38.3	7.8	18.5	1,473[1,2]	...	...	249[1,2]	51.8[1,2]	48.2[1,2]	2.1[1,2]	United Arab Emirates
1.2[4]	55.2	0.5	43.1	1,198.9	17.8	26.2[5]	—	47.1	...	...	...	...	...	...	...	United Kingdom
8.4[4]	82.4	2.6	6.7	4,473.1	14.4	53.1	1.5	8.4	...	...	...	...	...	...	...	United States
7.3[4]	29.8	19.0	43.8	19,023.9	3.6	46.0[5]	3.2	37.0	3,044	28.4	71.6	709	56.1	43.9	29.8	Uruguay
...	...	...	...	...	...	...	...	...	...	...	...	...	...	...	...	Uzbekistan
2.0[4]	22.2	3.5	72.3	28.051	11.4	69.7[5]	2.2	8.9	30.6	95.1	4.9	1.7	58.8	41.2	1.5	Vanuatu
5.7[4]	56.7	29.1	8.5	1,011.8	23.9	63.4[5]	2.3	5.8	24,643	7.9	92.1	3,517	26.2	73.8	17.0	Venezuela
...	...	...	...	...	...	...	...	...	15,072[1,2]	...	...	232[1,2]	11.6[1,2]	88.4[1,2]	30.1[1,2]	Vietnam
...	...	...	...	...	...	...	...	...	...	...	...	...	...	...	...	Virgin Islands (U.S.)
...	...	...	...	...	...	...	...	...	...	...	...	...	...	...	...	West Bank
...	...	...	...	...	...	...	...	...	...	...	...	...	...	...	...	Western Sahara
4.1[4]	44.6	46.5	4.8	0.142	20.5	53.5	1.7	2.1	91.7	98.6	1.4	4.6	73.9	26.1	5.1[2]	Western Samoa
5.5[2,4,15]	28.9[2,15]	59.8[2,15]	5.9[2,15]	18.473[2,15]	27.8[2,15]	44.8[2,15]	1.6[2,15]	11.6[2,15]	5,040	98.3	1.7	97	76.3	23.7	5.0	Yemen
—	63.6[3]	32.6[3]	3.8[3]	473.891[3]	15.5[3]	45.5[3,5]	4.2[3]	21.7[3]	13,492	53.7	46.3	2,042	38.0	62.0	6.6	Yugoslavia
0.9[4]	8.2	44.6	46.4	11,830.0	49.7	16.5[5]	1.5	21.3	8,851	90.0	10.0	144	35.4	64.6	6.2	Zaire
22.5	35.7	22.7	19.1	63.005	20.9	41.2	5.0	4.8	4,784	88.7	11.3	148	61.5	38.5	10.6	Zambia
16.4[4]	69.4	10.6	3.7	6.801	30.7	40.1	2.8	9.1	2,449	61.5	38.5	365	61.9	38.1	19.1	Zimbabwe

[1]Includes long-term private debt not guaranteed by the government. [2]1989. [3]1990. [4]Includes claims on nonfinancial government (public) enterprises and/or local governments. [5]Includes foreign currency deposits. [6]1991. [7]1988. [8]Treasury bill rate. [9]1984. [10]Short-term deposit rate. [11]Money market rate. [12]Notes and coins only. [13]1987. [14]1986. [15]Former Yemen Arab Republic only.

Housing and construction

The present table summarizes data about the housing stock and the construction industries of the countries of the world. The principal focus is on the elements that are most comparable internationally: the age of the housing (by decade, so far as possible), the legal tenure of the householder, construction of exterior walls, principal physical amenities, sanitary arrangements, and the amount of space both absolutely (total area of the average dwelling in square metres [1 square metre equals 1.20 square yards, or 10.76 square feet]) and relatively (persons per room). The data on construction characterize the industry in terms of: (1) the portion of national gross domestic product (GDP) represented by each country's construction industry, (2) the number of new dwelling units constructed annually, their area, and the rate (in years) required to replace the total national stock of dwellings shown on the extreme left of the table, and (3), for nonresidential construction, the number of buildings or portions of buildings built for nonresidential purposes and their area in square metres.

Because housing patterns differ greatly from country to country, the portion of each country's housing stock for which data are compared was defined as specifically as possible. In general, the numbers refer to permanent, private dwelling units that are usually occupied year-round, whether or not actually occupied on the date of the housing census or survey. That definition implies the exclusion of certain housing that is often part of national housing censuses: vacation homes, second homes occupied less than half the year, collective or communal dwellings, and so on. The housing unit to which the data on tenure refer may be either the individual dwelling or the household, according to the reporting practice of the country concerned.

The data are collected mostly from national housing censuses and surveys. The majority of countries combine the housing census with the population census at five- to ten-year intervals. Some countries, however, can conduct a meaningful housing census only in the capital city or in the few largest cities; others may be able to collect and process data for only a few of the most important housing characteristics even when national coverage is complete. These choices may be dictated by the lack of funding to collect data for the entire country or by the perception, particularly in a tropical, rural country where adequate dwellings can be built by hand, that no urgent housing problem exists. These choices may be complex, however, as

Housing and construction

country	housing stock			decade built (percent)					tenure[c] (percent)			construction of exterior walls (percent)			
	year	dwelling units[a]	median age[b] (years)	1949 or earlier	1950–59	1960–69	1970–79	1980 or later	owned	rented	collective, vacant, other	traditional materials	sawn/ framed wood	masonry or cement	other
Afghanistan	1979	3,940,000[1]	...	...	...	...	...	...	55.2	23.5	21.3	...	...	...	...
Albania	1989	675,456[5]	20.5	19.9	14.2	18.9	—46.5—		...	...	...	...	...	...	...
Algeria	1985	3,050,812[6]	...	—76.3[8]—			—23.7[8]—		63.0	24.6	12.4	...	...	...	...
American Samoa	1990	6,959	13.9	4.4	7.5	21.9	22.7	43.5	78.1	21.9	—	4.1[10]	56.3[10]	34.9[10]	4.7[10]
Andorra	1990	...	18.1	18.0	5.7	20.8	—55.5—		...	...	...	...	...	...	...
Angola	1970	...													
Antigua and Barbuda	1970	15,405[12]	11.1	23.3	31.4	46.1	—	—	55.9	40.4	3.7	...	...	...	...
Argentina	1980	10,096,888[14]	21.6	24.0	17.3	22.0	18.3	18.4	67.7	14.8	17.5	6.1	6.7	84.2	3.0
Armenia	1989	559,000[16]													
Aruba	1981	14,929	29.0	—62.4—		14.9	—22.7—		49.0	51.0	—	...	9.4	87.7	2.9
Australia	1986	6,450,152[14]	26.1[18]	37.9[18]	10.4[18]	18.6[18]	—33.1[18]—		69.1[16]	26.7[16]	5.1[16]				
Austria	1981	3,273,900[13]	63.6	44.5	13.3	19.4	—22.8—		47.7	36.2	16.1				
Azerbaijan	1989	1,381,000[16]													
Bahamas, The	1980	54,308	30.7	—54.7—		25.6	—19.7—		51.4	37.4	11.2	4.0[23]	32.3	54.7	9.0
Bahrain	1981	52,810	15.2	58.3	14.5	—27.2—			49.6	30.0	20.4	2.1[20]	...	95.1[20]	2.8[20]
Bangladesh	1981	14,785,048	...	...	...	...	...		89.7	5.0	5.3	20.0	11.6	5.0	63.4
Barbados	1980	67,138[16]	18.9	—51.3—		20.6	—28.1—		70.2	21.5	8.3	0.1	68.9[24]	26.3	4.7
Belarus	1989	2,796,000[16]													
Belgium	1981	3,599,977[12]	...	48.5[25]	17.9[26]	14.2[27]	8.2[28]	7.8[29]	59.2	35.8	4.9				
Belize	1980	27,298	...	24.6	30.0	—41.0—			56.1	27.2	16.7	7.5	73.4	14.0	5.1
Benin	1979	612,041													
Bermuda	1991	22,061	...	—56.0—		15.8	12.0	16.2	43.4	52.4	4.2	—	1.7[10,24]	95.1[10]	3.2[10]
Bhutan															
Bolivia	1988	1,318,800	...	...	...	47.4[19]			69.1	13.4	17.5	72.3	2.3	21.1	4.2
Bosnia and Hercegovina	1989	...													
Botswana	1981	170,262	...	...	...	...	...		59.9	17.1	23.0	65.5	—	28.0	6.5
Brazil	1988	33,167,108							65.0	20.2	14.8				
Brunei	1981	28,676							83.8	11.8	4.4	0.2	54.8	36.5	8.5
Bulgaria	1975	3,326,000[13]	17.9	—81.9—		11.1	—7.0—		77.3	22.7	—				
Burkina Faso	1985	1,274,546[16]													
Burundi	1979	938,000[37]							98.7	1.1	0.2				
Cambodia															
Cameroon	1976	1,390,896[12]							83.4	11.2	5.4	75.5	13.9	9.5	1.1
Canada	1986	10,079,442[14]	10.5	20.3[25]	20.0[38]	19.4[39]	—40.3[40]—		62.1	37.5	0.5				
Cape Verde	1980	59,919		—68.6—		—31.4—			...	15.4		57.7	...	36.5	5.8
Cayman Islands	1989	8,115[16]	...	—23.2—		—76.8—			53.1	40.6	6.3	—	24.6	75.1	0.3
Central African Republic	1975	405,399							...	...	...	82.2	7.1	2.5	8.2
Chad															
Chile	1982	2,510,275	20.4	—46.2—		21.1	—32.7—		63.1	18.7	18.2	13.0	44.4	41.6	1.0
China	1990	276,947,962							18.5[2,17]	81.5[2,17]					
Colombia	1985	5,266,581	20.6[42]	54.6[42]	26.2[42]	19.2[42]	—	—	67.6	23.6	8.8	16.7	7.0	75.6	0.7
Comoros	1980	81,791		5.3	7.7	21.3	—63.7—		87.4	3.1	9.5	73.5	1.8	16.9	7.8
Congo	1984	363,140[16]							61.0	34.6	4.4	15.0	20.0	52.8	12.2
Cook Islands	1986	3,667	14.0	11.6[18]	16.8[18]	48.6[18]	—23.0[18]—		85.3[19]	9.4[19]	5.3[19]				
Costa Rica	1984	500,788	...	...	...	36.4[42]			65.8	20.7	13.5	1.1	60.1	35.6	3.2
Côte d'Ivoire	1985	1,146,370[44]													
Croatia	1989														
Cuba	1981	2,363,364	24.6	23.2[45]	21.3[46]	21.6	—25.6—		...	...	...	1.4	37.1	61.5	—
Cyprus	1982	168,588	22.8	—39.9—		15.4	—44.7—		60.0	16.5	23.5	11.9	...	87.6	0.5
Czechoslovakia	1980	5,845,415[14]	36.7	20.8	15.1	20.3	24.6	—	44.7	41.7	13.6	—	2.9	93.8	3.3
Denmark	1991	2,374,970	36.6	44.3	10.0	16.4	18.1	11.2	53.8	44.5	1.7				
Djibouti	1982	25,000[47]	27.6	...					...	...	...	73.0[48]	22.5	4.5	
Dominica	1981	17,310[16]		58.4[30]	16.9[30]	21.1[30]	—3.6[30]—		64.7[30]	26.6[30]	8.7[30]	0.2[30]	88.8[30]	10.2[30]	0.8[30]
Dominican Republic	1981	1,125,785[12]							72.0	17.0	11.0	31.1	31.3	31.0	6.7
Ecuador	1990	2,335,551							68.1	22.6	9.3	13.9	9.3	57.7	19.1
Egypt	1986	9,732,728	...	—37.1[2]—		—62.9[2]—			64.0	27.2	8.8				
El Salvador	1971	680,456							56.7[43]	22.3[43]	21.0[43]	37.9	9.6	46.9	5.6
Equatorial Guinea	1983														
Estonia	1989	427,000[16]													
Ethiopia	1984	9,300,000													
Faeroe Islands	1977	11,172[22]	32.5	—60.1—		21.8	—15.0—		84.5	9.9	5.6	...	43.9	53.5	2.6
Fiji	1986	124,098							74.4	14.6	11.0	9.0	26.4	29.8	34.8
Finland	1988	2,111,751	16.9	—30.3—		16.7	26.6	26.4	67.7	24.2	8.1	14.0[22,50]	81.8[22,50]	—4.2[22,50]—	
France	1990	21,535,677	19.1[34]	—43.5[34,51]—		11.6[34,52]	27.3[34,53]	17.7[34,54]	54.4	39.6	6.0				
French Guiana	1990	33,285	...	...	...	23.2[30]			41.3	—58.7—		29.4[55]	—70.6—		

planners are always aware that much housing is physically inadequate to protect dwellers from the elements, is disadvantageously placed in relation to tainted or disease-infested water supply or to the outfall of unprocessed sewage, or is built of materials (mud, skins, thatch, etc.) that may harbour pests or disease. In the developed countries, median age and the distribution of physical amenities provide strong indicators of the quality and availability of housing.

The data for the construction industry refer to the most recent year in which a broad range of countries could be surveyed.

The broadest indication of total activity in a national construction industry is its contribution to the national gross domestic product, since that figure, in addition to construction of buildings, also includes civil engineering projects, such as dams, roads and other transportation infrastructure, recreational facilities, irrigation and land reclamation works, and the like. The scope of the data relating to construction of buildings may be limited in several respects. It may be confined to activity capable of being surveyed in the modern or urban sectors only, may be limited to private new construction only or to government and government-financed

activity only, or may refer to construction mortgaged or financed through certain organizations only. Depending on national data-collection systems, it usually excludes remodeling of old premises but may include extensions or enlargements of existing buildings. The data for new construction are usually of two principal types: authorized new construction or certification after construction that newly built structures meet building and fire codes and the like. Data for construction completed are naturally more meaningful but are not available for every country, necessitating the substitution of authorized construction data, which are usually available only for areas regulated by certain types of governmental authorities.

The following notes further define the column headings:
a. Data refer to permanent, private dwelling units that are usually occupied year-round, whether or not occupied on the census date.
b. Data are estimates unless specifically provided by a country source.
c. Data may be either for dwellings or for households, depending on country reporting practice.
d. Data may be either for construction completed or for construction authorized, depending on country reporting practice.

physical amenities (percent)			sewage disposal (percent)			space[b]			percent of GDP	new residential[d]			new nonresidential[d]		country
piped water	electricity	inside toilet or WC	closed public sewer or septic tank	open public sewer	other	average area (sq m)	rooms per dwelling unit	persons per room		total no. of dwellings	floor area ('000 sq m)	years to replace nat'l stock	number of units	floor area ('000 sq m)	
25.3[2]	66.5[2]	5.5[2]	5.5	77.9	16.6	...	5.5	2.1	8.2[3,4]	...	...	...	...	...	Afghanistan
44.6	...	29.9	...	...	...	...	...	...	6.4[3]	13,863[6]	...	29.9[6]	...	...	Albania
45.8[7]	73.3	...	51.0	22.8	26.2	...	2.8	2.5	17.3[6]	83,207[8]	...	36.7[9]	...	...	Algeria
96.2	94.4	93.4	68.5	—31.5—		...	4.5	1.6	...	218[9]	...	21.5[9]	14[10]	47.5[10]	American Samoa
...	...	—	...	...	...	...	...	...	19.9[11]	...	91[10]	...	...	...	Andorra
...	...	...	...	...	...	...	...	...	5.8[6]	...	585[10]	...	210[10]	164.5[10]	Angola
85.4	...	...	17.0	—83.0—		...	3.1	...	13.0[13]	764[9]	...	20.2[9]	...	...	Antigua and Barbuda
72.9	86.8	95.1	77.1	—22.9—		...	3.9	1.3	2.3	67,528[8]	...	105.2[15]	...	...	Argentina
...	...	...	...	...	...	...	4.3	1.1	14.6[11]	...	1,460	...	...	...	Armenia
98.7	98.7	89.2	...	...	...	...	4.3	1.1	8.2[17]	158[14]	...	94.5[14]	113[14]	...	Aruba
97.1[19]	98.4[20]	92.2[18]	99.0[18]	—1.0[18]—		...	5.1[18]	0.6[18]	7.4[21]	135,456	21,360[22]	43.0	23,340[22]	8,123[22]	Australia
95.0	...	85.5	94.3	...	5.7	76.5	4.3[9]	0.6[9]	6.8	39,300	3,662[15]	83.3	500[22]	100[22]	Austria
...	...	...	...	...	...	...	...	...	10.6[14]	...	2,848[11]	...	...	...	Azerbaijan
63.9	77.9	...	63.2	2.2	34.6	...	4.0	1.2	3.1	1,027[6]	...	52.9[6]	62[6]	...	Bahamas, The
97.5	98.2	...	44.7	...	55.3	...	3.0[20]	2.3[20]	7.1[3]	1,919[9]	...	27.5[9]	1,444[9]	...	Bahrain
56.8	6.6	2.6	1.5	—98.7—		...	2.0	2.9	6.0[4]	300,900[8]	...	49.1	...	...	Bangladesh
82.4	83.0	43.6	95.8	0.7	3.5	...	4.2	0.8	5.8	1,960[9]	...	34.3[9]	...	...	Barbados
...	...	...	...	...	...	...	...	...	11.8[11]	...	5,282	...	...	...	Belarus
93.9	100.0	76.1	62.5[30]	—37.5[30]—		82.1	5.0	0.5	5.7	49,801[15]	30,812[15,31]	72.3[15]	9,101[15]	47,465[15,31]	Belgium
60.1	59.4	19.7	21.1	—78.9—		...	2.5[32]	1.9[32]	12.0[11]	102[33]	6,185[34]	[33]	...	...	Belize
...	...	...	...	...	...	...	...	...	4.9[9]	...	...	...	...	...	Benin
97.4[10]	...	96.7[10]	96.7[10]	—3.3[10]—		...	3.2[10]	0.7[10]	4.9[35]	556[15]	...	36.6[15]	...	...	Bermuda
...	...	...	...	...	...	...	...	...	7.8[13]	...	...	...	1[1]	...	Bhutan
60.2	59.3	23.2	22.5	—77.5—		...	...	...	3.0	...	...	52.8[15]	...	...	Bolivia
66.2	94.2	53.2	...	...	...	56.0	...	...		25,445	...	...	...	...	Bosnia and Hercegovina
56.1	5.4	25.4	8.6	20.4	71.0	...	...	...	3.3[4]	...	96[6]	...	472[22]	132[6]	Botswana
72.1	85.9	...	60.1	—39.9—		...	5.1[10]	0.9[10]	8.4	115,914[6,33]	20,090[6]	[33]	5,017[22]	8,180[6]	Brazil
90.3	64.2	94.2	57.4	—42.6—		...	4.2	1.6	2.6[13]	195[34]	...	147.0[34]	5[34]	...	Brunei
74.6	99.8	33.2	33.2	—67.8—		...	2.5[36]	1.1[36]	9.4[3,13]	62,800	2,844[15]	53.0	...	...	Bulgaria
...	...	...	...	...	...	...	...	...	0.6[6]	...	...	...	...	...	Burkina Faso
11.0	0.6	...	1.6	—98.4—		37.2[17]	2.4[17]	0.6[17]	4.1[14]	...	...	...	...	...	Burundi
...	...	...	...	...	...	...	...	...	...	...	...	...	...	...	Cambodia
22.0	5.9	2.2	2.2	70.4	27.6	...	4.1	1.2	6.8[13]	...	230[1]	...	53[1]	51.1[1]	Cameroon
99.8[13]	100.0	99.4[13]	98.9[18]	—1.1—		...	5.7	0.5	6.5	218,304	...	44.0	14,846[22]	...	Canada
7.1	13.7	14.8	...	—3.4—	96.6	...	1.8	2.8	15.6[9]	...	31[17]	...	3[17]	0.5[17]	Cape Verde
99.0	96.9	95.9	96.9	—3.1—		...	4.7	0.7	8.9[3]	39[8]	...	...	...	...	Cayman Islands
...	...	...	...	...	...	...	1.1[38]	3.4[38]	2.66	...	734	...	16[34]	...	Central African Republic
...	...	...	...	...	...	...	...	...	1.6[6]	...	...	...	...	...	Chad
81.4	84.7	...	63.2	36.4	0.4	59.9[41]	3.6	1.3	5.8[11]	78,094	3,996[13]	32.1	...	1,552[13]	Chile
89.4[2,6]	...	25.2[2,6]	47.0[2,6]	—53.0[2,6]—		37.0[6]	2.2[6]	1.8[6]	5.9	...	1,048,013[13]	...	...	311,416[13]	China
70.5	78.5	77.9	69.6	—30.4—		103.7[41]	3.3	1.6	5.7[11]	74,996[6]	5,648[15]	70.2[6]	...	1,994[15]	Colombia
12.9	5.7	...	2.1	—97.9—		33.7	2.5	2.1	9.7[6]	...	...	...	...	...	Comoros
30.5	8.8	16.6	—86.2[2]—		13.8[2]	...	3.7[2]	1.7[2]	1.8	...	...	...	...	...	Congo
70.8	86.4	77.9	36.7[19]	—63.3[19]—		...	4.5	1.2	4.5[43]	...	...	...	24[22]	...	Cook Islands
86.9	97.3	...	66.5	—33.5—		...	4.0	1.4	3.3[11]	...	760[22]	...	2,868[22]	178[22]	Costa Rica
23.0	39.6	23.9	—68.5—		31.5	...	...	...	2.2[34]	...	...	...	...	...	Côte d'Ivoire
74.5	96.1	62.3	...	...	...	64.1	...	...		20,341	...	...	...	...	Croatia
74.1	82.9	45.2	60.9	9.3	30.1	73.2[41]	4.1	1.0	9.3	25,344[13]	1,800[13]	93.2[13]	469[22]	1,803[22]	Cuba
100.0	98.1	74.5	95.6	—4.4—		...	4.6	0.8	9.6[11]	6,639[6]	979[9]	25.4[6]	1,103[22]	411[22]	Cyprus
91.6	100.0	70.8	91.2	—8.8—		68.0	3.5	0.9	10.6	77,316[13]	4,223[6]	75.9[13]	...	...	Czechoslovakia
100.0	100.0	99.2[15]	98.6[18]	—1.4[18]—		107.8	3.8	0.6	6.6	25,392[15]	2,616[15]	90.8[15]	6,641[6]	6,648[15]	Denmark
45.0	58.0	82.0	26.0	23.0	51.0	...	1.9	6.9	2.19	100[31]	24.3[6]	...	26[6]	13.7[6]	Djibouti
91.1[1]	...	12.3[30]	12.3[30]	—87.7[30]—		...	2.8[30]	1.7[30]	5.8	...	...	...	...	...	Dominica
64.4	36.7[30]	14.1	52.1[30]	22.6[30]	25.3[30]	...	2.8[30]	1.5[30]	8.5[11]	...	648[6]	...	856[6]	508[6]	Dominican Republic
62.7[12]	77.7[12]	47.6[12]	39.5[12]	25.1[12]	35.4[12]	...	2.8	1.7	3.5	...	3,825[22]	...	596[22]	412.7[22]	Ecuador
73.1	87.0	...	...	...	...	...	3.3	1.5	5.0[16]	183,505[15]	...	53.0[15]	...	...	Egypt
48.0	34.1	6.3[20]	20.0[10]	—80.0[10]—		...	1.5[43]	3.3[43]	2.6[11]	...	341[22]	...	8[22]	0.7[22]	El Salvador
...	...	...	...	...	...	...	...	...	5.6	...	...	...	...	...	Equatorial Guinea
...	...	...	...	...	...	...	...	...	9.9[9]	...	468[11]	...	...	...	Estonia
...	...	...	...	...	...	...	...	2.7[49]	3.9[4]	...	158[22]	...	92[1]	46.9[1]	Ethiopia
99.7	99.5	95.0	89.7	8.1	2.2	...	5.5	1.1	9.0[13]	298[6]	...	37.5[6]	...	...	Faeroe Islands
73.7	48.5	56.0	35.4[7]	—64.6[7]—		...	3.3	1.8	3.6[13]	2,767[6]	24[15]	45.1[6]	105[6]	24[15]	Fiji
94.7	95.9[22,50]	92.1	96.1	—3.9—		73.8	3.5	0.6	9.8	65,397[11]	5,226[11]	45.4	32,886[19]	34,050[14,31]	Finland
99.7[13]	...	92.0[13]	73.8[44]	—26.2[44]—		77.0[43]	3.9	0.7	5.0[11]	286,668[13]	...	88.8[13]	...	47,887[13]	France
67.2	86.7	62.0	34.3[17]	—65.7[17]—		...	2.8	1.2	8.2[12]	667[17]	64[17]	31.6[17]	...	28.5[22]	French Guiana

Housing and construction (continued)

country	housing stock			decade built (percent)					tenure[c] (percent)			construction of exterior walls (percent)			
	year	dwelling units[a]	median age[b] (years)	1949 or earlier	1950-59	1960-69	1970-79	1980 or later	owned	rented	collective, vacant, other	traditional materials	sawn/ framed wood	masonry or cement	other
French Polynesia	1988	39,513	10.8	—11.3—		16.0	27.6	45.1	68.5	21.2	10.3	36.9	15.8	45.2	2.2
Gabon	1967	15,886[47]	...	—87.0—				13.0							
Gambia, The	1983	202,199	...	...	...	...	...	...	63.9	21.9	14.2	82.9	—	12.9	4.2
Gaza Strip	1985	66,819[58]	...	...	...	...	...	...	89.1[59]	7.6[59]	3.3[59]	...	...	...	...
Georgia	1989	1,244,000[16]	...	...	...	...	...	...							
Germany[60]	1987	27,524,000	...	30.6[51]	15.2[61]	23.6[62]	19.8[63]	10.8[64]	39.0	60.3	0.7	...	...	...	...
Ghana	1984	1,216,677	...	...	...	...	...	...	47.7[44]	25.3[44]	27.0[44]	...	...	...	...
Gibraltar	1986	7,846	...	...	...	...	...	...	5.9	94.1					
Greece	1981	3,999,332	29.2	30.2[25]	27.4[38]	20.7	—21.5—		73.1[67]	26.9[67]		...	...	...	...
Greenland	1987	18,143[13]	10.8[16]	11.9[19]	18.8[19]	46.5[19]	—22.8[19]—		39.3[22]	—60.7[22]—					
Grenada	1970	21,017[18]	18.3	48.0	29.0	22.2	—0.8—		76.5	14.0	9.5	0.4	80.8	17.8	1.0
Guadeloupe	1990	112,478	...			8.1[67]			62.6	—37.4—		29.5[55]	—70.5—		
Guam	1990	35,223	15.8	2.3	7.1	19.2	41.5	29.9	45.6	54.4		0.0	5.1	85.8	9.1
Guatemala	1981	1,259,598	12.5	—62.0—		10.0	—28.0—		64.7	11.3	24.0	55.6	21.1	19.3	4.0
Guernsey	1991	21,215[12]	...	...	...	...	...	...	68.4	31.6	—	...	...	...	...
Guinea	1983	674,152[16]	...	...	...	...	...	...	...	...	...	...	...	...	...
Guinea-Bissau	1979	123,936	...	...	...	...	...	...				95.7	0.1	2.3	1.9
Guyana	1980	149,734[16]	17.6	—43.5—		19.4	—37.1—		56.1	27.1	16.8		74.8	17.1	8.1
Haiti	1982	1,130,795	...	—75.9—			—24.1—		82.9[19]	4.8[19]	12.3[19]				
Honduras	1988	809,263	12.1[67]	—38.9[67]—		37.8[67]	—23.3[67]—		71.8[67]	16.5[67]	12.7[67]	61.0[67]	26.4[67]	11.7[67]	0.9[67]
Hong Kong	1991	1,580,072	...	—48.1[18]—		13.6[18]	—38.3[18]—		42.6	53.0	4.4	...	...	...	...
Hungary	1990	3,817,000	16.4	32.9[25]	11.8[46]	14.9	23.2	17.2	75.9	23.7	0.4	30.8[34]	14.3[34]	54.8[34]	0.1[34]
Iceland	1984	70,777	25.6	—46.0—			—54.1—		70.3[32]	—29.7[32]—				71.9[32]	
India	1981	142,954,921	...	...	...	...	...	...	84.6[20]	15.4[20]	—	...	...	...	...
Indonesia	1980	30,263,273[16]	...	...	...	...	...	...	87.0[20]	5.0[20]	8.0[20]	...	...	...	...
Iran	1986	8,211,375	...	—82.5[19]—			—17.5[19]—		77.0	12.2	9.8	28.8	0.7	69.2	1.3
Iraq	1956	741,000	...	...	...	...	...	...	83.0	12.8	4.2				
Ireland	1981	1,038,000[14]	47.2	—60.0—		12.8	—26.2—		67.9	20.9	11.2				
Isle of Man	1981	27,042	...	...	...	...	...	...	62.5	36.5	1.0				
Israel	1983	1,104,270	...	9.5[69]	—90.5[70]—				72.9	24.6	2.5				
Italy	1981	17,542,000	19.4	30.8[25]	19.7[26]	27.5[71]	—22.0[40]—		58.9	35.5	5.6	...	...	...	...
Jamaica	1982	517,297[16]	17.0	—33.6—		28.8	—39.6—		46.7	29.5	23.8	7.1	28.4	54.4	10.1
Japan	1988	37,454,000[16]	11.0	7.3[72]	—67.8[73]—		—24.9[40]—		61.4	37.2	1.4	—	73.1	25.5	1.4
Jersey	1991	28,775	...	...	...	...	...	...	49.6	48.0	2.4				
Jordan	1979	378,815[75]	...	...	...	...	...	...	62.6	30.8	6.6				
Kazakhstan	1989	3,824,000[16]	...	...	...	...	...	...	...	...	...	...	...	...	...
Kenya	1979	2,956,369[16]	...	...	...	...	...	...	...	...	...	...	...	...	...
Kiribati	1985	10,093[16]	...	...	...	...	...	...	68.2[43]	17.9[43]	13.9[43]	64.4[43]	—35.6[43]—		
Korea, North	1987	4,054,027[16]	...	...	...	...	...	...	...	...	...	...	...	...	...
Korea, South	1990	7,374,000	19.0[10]	26.1[10]	15.8[10]	18.2[10]	—39.2[10]—		83.8[22]	12.8[22]	3.4[22]	11.8[10]	38.8[10]	49.2[10]	0.2[10]
Kuwait	1985	228,781	14.5[10]	—12.2[10]—		38.8[10]	—34.5[10]—		38.2	53.6	8.2	46.5[50]	—	36.5[50]	17.0[50]
Kyrgyzstan	1989	856,000[16]	...	...	...	...	...	...	...	...	...	...	...	...	...
Laos	...	...	...	...	...	...	...	...	...	...	...	...	...	...	...
Latvia	1989	732,000[16]	...	...	...	...	...	...	...	...	...	...	...	...	...
Lebanon	1970	483,908[12]	...	30.1[76]	40.2[77]	—29.4—			...	...	...	...	...	...	...
Lesotho	1986[16]	317,161	...	...	...	...	...	...	...	...	...	...	...	...	...
Liberia	1974[47]	263.333	...	...	...	...	...	...	...	...	...	...	...	...	...
Libya	1984	569,679	...	...	...	...	...	...	62.5[42]	28.0[42]	9.5[42]				
Liechtenstein	1980	9,336	29.4	27.1[76]	15.0[77]	27.1	—30.8—		53.6	41.7	4.7				
Lithuania	1991	1,165,700[16]	...	...	...	...	...	...	...	...	...	...	...	...	...
Luxembourg	1981	128,281[16]	...	62.1[69]	11.8[78]	7.8	—18.3—		59.2	—40.8—					
Macau	1981	45,158	...	...	...	...	...	...	71.8[30]	28.2[30]	—	—	0.5[30]	99.3[30]	0.2[30]
Macedonia	1989	...	...	...	...	...	...	...	...	...	...	...	...	...	...
Madagascar	1975	1,671,473[16]	...	...	...	...	...	...	...	...	...	...	...	...	...
Malawi	1977	1,834,118	...	...	...	...	...	...	39.6	—60.4—					
Malaysia	1980	2,332,563	...	...	...	...	...	...	64.0	23.0	13.0	...	...	...	...
Maldives	1985	28,187	...	...	...	...	...	...	82.5	2.9	15.5	79.1	2.3		18.6
Mali	1987	1,366,907	...	...	...	...	...	...	...	...	...	...	...	...	...
Malta	1985	101,509	...	—81.8[80]—		—18.2[81]—			53.9	43.0	3.1	93.0[58]	...	92.9[58]	0.21[58]
Marshall Islands	1980	4,163	...	6.4	13.3	24.7	—55.5—		60.0	33.0	7.0	10.7	63.5	15.9	9.9
Martinique	1990	106,536	...	...	...	...	...	...	60.9	—39.1—		20.4[17]	—79.6[17]—		
Mauritania	1977	246,462[16]	...	...	...	...	...	...	...	...	...	...	...	...	...
Mauritius[82]	1983	191,676	...	—19.7—		24.3[83]	—56.0[84]—		66.0	18.6	15.4		4.2	66.8	28.9
Mayotte	1985	13,142	...	...	...	...	...	...	88.1[43]	6.2[43]	5.7[43]	67.7	—16.7—		15.6
Mexico	1990	16,197,802	...	—51.4[10]—		15.4[10]	—33.2[10]—		77.9	14.6	7.5	19.0	8.1	69.5	3.4
Micronesia	1980	11,562	...	3.8	5.2	21.3	—69.7—		51.8	39.2	9.0	6.0	41.8	14.6	37.6
Moldova	1989	1,144,000[16]	...	...	...	...	...	...	...	...	...	...	...	...	...
Monaco	1990	16,122	30.0	—39.5[51]—		13.0[52]	19.7[53]	27.8[55]	23.3	60.5	16.2	...	...	...	...
Mongolia	1969	242,000	...	...	...	...	...	...	100.0	—					
Morocco	1982	3,419,282[16]	...	...	...	...	...	...	40.8[2]	43.7[2]	15.5[2]	24.5	—	73.5	1.8
Mozambique	1980	2,712,439[16]	...	...	...	...	...	...	...	...	...	86.5	2.3	8.3	2.9
Myanmar (Burma)	1983	6,750,884	...	...	...	...	...	...	...	...	...	83.5	14.8	—	1.7
Namibia	...	...	...	...	...	...	...	...	...	...	...	...	...	...	...
Nauru	1977	508[86]	...	—88.6[86]—		—11.4[86]—			11.0[49]	80.6[49]	8.4[49]	...	...	...	...
Nepal	1981	2,585,154[16]	...	...	...	...	...	...	75.3[33,49]	10.7[33,49]	14.0[33,49]	...	...	...	...
Netherlands, The	1990	5,802,400	25.4	28.2	11.8	18.0	21.7	20.3	43.2[22]	56.8[22]	...	...	...	...	...
Netherlands Antilles	1981	41,101	21.0	—49.8—		19.7	—30.5—		45.3	54.7	...	—	21.6	75.7	2.7
New Caledonia	1989	44,047	...	—19.3—		—80.7—			56.4	29.7	13.9	6.4	11.7	61.7	20.2
New Zealand	1991	1,185,396	...	—64.1[18]—		19.2[18]	—16.2[18]—		72.4	22.7	4.9	...	...	...	...
Nicaragua	1971	330,422	...	...	...	...	...	...	64.4	20.3	15.3	30.8	45.6	21.8	1.8
Niger	1988	1,163,424[16]	...	...	...	...	...	...	...	...	...	66.5[75]	...	...	...
Nigeria	1961[47]	92,900	...	...	...	...	...	...	8.0	80.9	11.1	...	...	...	...
Northern Mariana Islands	1990	8,210	...	1.0	2.5	6.4	13.3	76.8	39.5	56.6	3.9	0.0	13.5	66.5	20.0
Norway	1990	1,769,000	25.3	44.1[25]	20.6[87]	17.8[88]	20.7[89]	16.0[90]	80.3	—19.7—		...	...	...	...
Oman	1982	2,469	...	...	...	...	...	...	...	...	...	...	...	...	...

| physical amenities (percent) | | | sewage disposal (percent) | | | space[b] | | | construction industry (1988) | | | | | | country |
piped water	electricity	inside toilet or WC	closed public sewer or septic tank	open public sewer	other sewer	average area (sq m)	rooms per dwelling unit	persons per room	percent of GDP	new residential[d] total no. of dwellings	floor area ('000 sq m)	years to replace nat'l stock	new nonresidential[d] number of units	floor area ('000 sq m)	
5.4	91.0	78.9	2.0[1]	67.0[1]	31.0[1]	...	3.8	1.3	6.1[11]	700[6]	85[56]	59.3[6]	156[6]	56	French Polynesia
...	50.5	...	...	...	...	...	3.0	1.3	6.2[11]	...	216[44]	...	75[57]	119.4[57]	Gabon
21.9	...	...	...	...	...	...	2.0	2.0	4.0[21]	...	...	...	14[44]	...	Gambia, The
97.2	93.5	97.3	...	...	...	144.3[41]	2.6	2.5	22.2[6]	1,247[6]	180[6]	53.6[6]	...	31.1[6]	Gaza Strip
...	...	...	...	...	...	...	...	...	11.0[11]	...	1,005	...	...	...	Georgia
100.0	99.7[65]	98.3	97.1[10]	—2.9[10]—		86.1[66]	4.4	0.5	5.6[11]	214,252	33,272	128.5	46,123[6]	30,090	Germany[60]
34.0[41]	...	...	...	...	...	...	...	...	2.5[13]	...	...	...	...	...	Ghana
96.7[18]	100.0[18]	98.8[18]	100.0[18]	—	—	...	3.2[18]	1.2[18]	...	...	...	...	...	...	Gibraltar
81.3[20]	89.0[20]	93.0[20]	...	...	...	138.4[9]	3.3[9]	0.9[20]	6.0	107,034[13]	37,507[13,31]	37.4[31]	11,471[19]	15,650[13]	Greece
62.7[19]	84.2[19]	39.1[19]	39.1[19]	—60.9[19]—		63.0[13]	2.8[22]	1.2[22]	23.3[10]	676[13]	48[6]	25.1[6]	...	12.3[22]	Greenland
86.5	...	23.0	23.0	—77.0—		...	2.9	1.6	10.8	...	...	...	...	...	Grenada
83.2	89.4	78.2	24.6[17]	—75.4[17]—		...	3.3	1.0	4.7[17]	676	...	126.7	...	166[9]	Guadeloupe
99.2	98.4	97.0	97.0	—3.0—		...	5.0	0.8	7.9[17]	417[6]	...	67.4[6]	500[6]	...	Guam
52.0	37.0	14.3	20.1	3.4	76.5	...	2.4	2.2	2.4	...	495[56]	...	...	56	Guatemala
96.5[19]	...	98.8	65.9	—34.1—		...	5.8[9]	0.5[9]	...	165	...	128.6	...	...	Guernsey
...	...	...	...	...	...	...	...	...	5.6[11]	...	...	...	...	...	Guinea
3.7	3.9	25.6	25.8	—74.2—		...	1.4	4.5	6.4[22]	...	...	...	...	...	Guinea-Bissau
38.1	69.0	29.0	10.4	—89.6—		...	2.9	1.8	5.2[11]	...	...	...	56[6]	...	Guyana
12.0[10]	1.1[20]	...	2.0	—98.0—		...	2.2[20]	2.1[20]	6.2	...	...	...	...	...	Haiti
55.0[10]	25.0[67]	13.0[67]	14.4[67]	—85.6[67]—		...	2.4[67]	2.3[67]	4.6	1,442[34]	214[9]	34	148[9]	98[9]	Honduras
85.7[18]	...	69.2[42]	65.4[42]	—34.6[42]—		53.2[20]	3.1[42]	2.8[42]	5.0	67,579[6]	1,367[11]	25.5[6]	303[6]	1,426[11]	Hong Kong
90.1	98.8[34]	75.9	85.5	—14.5—		52.3	2.6	1.0	6.6	50,600[13]	4,353[15]	78.3[13]	3,433[22]	21,886[22,31]	Hungary
99.1[32]	94.6[32]	93.6[32]	86.5[32]	—13.5[32]—		...	4.8[32]	0.9[32]	8.8[11]	...	...	...	...	926.5[31,35]	Iceland
67.0[42]	53.5[2,42]	20.0[42]	...	...	...	...	2.0[20]	2.6[20]	5.7[4]	...	...	...	13,908[34]	...	India
11.0	14.2	26.6	22.8[20]	—77.2[20]—		59.0	3.3	1.7[20]	5.3	...	...	...	...	...	Indonesia
73.7	83.7	43.6	...	...	...	60.0[19]	2.8	1.8	5.7[68]	124,891[22]	18,608[22]	65.0[22]	5,235[22]	1,466[22]	Iran
20.8	17.1	...	...	...	...	...	2.4	...	6.1[13]	...	11,521[6]	...	11,799[22]	1,176[6]	Iraq
94.8	94.7[20]	93.0	72.3[20]	—27.7[20]—		...	3.7[22]	1.0[22]	5.0[6]	20,000[14]	5,046[15]	51.9	...	840[9]	Ireland
...	...	96.8	...	...	...	...	...	0.4	9.8[6]	168[6]	...	161.0[6]	...	...	Isle of Man
96.5[20]	96.5[20]	98.8	99.0[67]	—1.0[67]—		125.5[41]	3.0	1.2	5.9[13]	20,436[13]	2,900[13]	54.0[13]	...	1,070[11]	Israel
98.7	99.0[20]	94.0	95.7[20]	—4.3[20]—		85.3	4.0[22]	0.8	5.3	167,076	81,294[15,31]	105.0	29,235	98,115[15,31]	Italy
76.9	48.6	35.2	...	...	...	...	2.4[30]	4.3	12.6[66]	4,115[11]	...	125.7[11]	...	...	Jamaica
94.0[1]	...	65.8	61.2[1]	—38.8[1]—		89.9	4.9	0.7	9.5	1,753,260[13]	151,284[13]	21.4[13]	...	104,508[13]	Japan
94.0[74]	...	93.0[18]	96.0[74]	...	...	...	5.6	0.5	...	354[6]	...	82.5[6]	...	...	Jersey
77.2	77.3	55.4[49]	15.7	—84.3—		...	...	...	5.6[13]	6,292[9]	1,709[9]	60.2[9]	820[9]	557[9]	Jordan
...	...	...	...	...	...	...	...	...	15.3[11]	...	7,871	...	...	...	Kazakhstan
...	...	...	...	...	...	...	...	...	5.6	...	136[9]	...	85[9]	184[9]	Kenya
...	...	...	...	...	...	...	...	...	4.9[13]	...	...	...	...	...	Kiribati
21.3[43]	23.7[43]	15.5[43]	...	...	...	...	...	...	...	...	...	...	...	...	Korea, North
44.6	49.9[30]	51.6	...	...	...	81.4	3.4	1.7	5.7	750,000	70,928	9.8	36,801[6]	45,491	Korea, South
53.9[10]	99.5[10]	...	35.9[10]	—64.1[10]—		...	4.0[10]	1.8[10]	2.3	9,735[37]	4,717[13]	23.5[37]	370[6]	279[13]	Kuwait
...	...	...	...	...	...	...	...	...	7.7[14]	...	1,560[11]	...	...	...	Kyrgyzstan
...	...	...	...	...	...	...	...	...	10.1[13]	...	...	...	...	...	Laos
...	93.4	82.9	...	...	...	...	...	...	9.1[13,10]	...	819[11]	...	...	...	Latvia
...	...	...	...	...	...	...	...	...	4.8[6]	...	4,938[6,56]	...	...	56	Lebanon
...	...	...	...	...	...	...	...	...	13.9	...	...	...	52[9]	...	Lesotho
...	...	...	...	...	...	...	2.3[22]	1.7	3.1[13]	...	...	...	...	...	Liberia
70.1[42]	72.1[42]	40.6[42]	40.6[42]	—59.4[42]—		...	3.3[42]	1.8[42]	12.7	...	...	...	...	...	Libya
96.5	96.6	86.7	90.2	—9.8—		102.0	3.0	1.4	...	...	360[11,31]	...	...	312[11,31]	Liechtenstein
...	...	...	...	...	...	...	...	...	...	15,300[12]	1,015[12]	...	...	...	Lithuania
99.4[30]	...	97.2	93.0[30]	—7.0[30]—		86.4[30]	5.4	0.5	6.4	1,940[15]	347[15]	66.1[15]	74[6]	38[15]	Luxembourg
95.7	99.3	68.9	...	...	...	...	3.2[34]	2.5[34]	...	7,591[11]	651[11]	5.9[11]	1,003[11]	406[11]	Macau
72.0	96.4	56.3	...	...	...	68.6	...	...	...	10,864	...	...	...	...	Macedonia
...	...	...	...	...	...	...	...	...	3.8[6]	...	24[6]	...	...	8.9[6]	Madagascar
12.4	15.7[58]	33.0[58]	33.0[58]	—67.0[58]—		...	2.1	1.7	3.8	121[33]	...	33	...	...	Malawi
65.0	64.4	...	56.4	4.4	39.2	...	2.3[30,79]	2.6[30,79]	3.3	...	8,809[9]	...	...	960[9]	Malaysia
...	53.4	...	16.3	—83.7—		...	3.6	1.9	8.4	680[6]	...	41.5[6]	...	...	Maldives
...	...	...	...	...	...	...	...	...	4.2[13]	...	...	...	...	...	Mali
98.0	98.0	98.8	98.0	15.4[58]	6.1[58]	...	3.2[58]	1.3[58]	...	2,132[6,50]	...	47.6[6,50]	2,319[6]	...	Malta
46.3	48.9	...	28.6	—71.4—		...	...	...	7.4[18]	...	...	...	...	...	Marshall Islands
90.2	90.3	84.6	41.8[17]	—58.2[17]—		...	3.4	1.0	3.6[6]	1,528[17]	...	55.8[17]	...	56.2[18]	Martinique
...	...	...	...	...	...	...	...	...	7.9[34]	...	...	...	...	...	Mauritania
99.1	93.2	48.9	51.1	—48.9—		...	3.6	1.4	7.0[11]	...	787[15]	...	552[6]	371[15]	Mauritius[82]
27.4[43]	...	4.4	54.7[43]	—45.3[43]—		...	4.1	2.5	...	616[9]	...	21.3[9]	...	...	Mayotte
79.4	87.5	45.0[10]	60.9	2.7	36.4	...	3.4	1.5	3.4[11]	...	...	...	61,386[18]	...	Mexico
40.0	28.3	...	8.0	—92.0—		...	...	...	...	...	...	...	...	...	Micronesia
...	...	...	...	...	...	...	...	...	...	...	1,594[11]	...	...	...	Moldova
100.0	100.0	96.2	98.4[44]	—1.6[44]—		...	2.8	0.8	...	...	...	...	...	...	Monaco
0.3	47.5	...	...	...	...	...	...	...	5.8	...	461	...	...	176	Mongolia
30.5	37.2	50.2	...	...	...	...	2.7	2.2	5.0[11]	51,911[9]	2,156[22]	65.9[9]	1,014[22]	457[22]	Morocco
12.7	4.2	...	...	...	...	...	...	...	13.2[11]	...	...	...	...	...	Mozambique
...	...	...	...	...	...	...	...	...	1.5[21]	1,193[33]	...	33	1,483	...	Myanmar (Burma)
...	...	...	...	...	...	...	...	...	2.6	...	...	...	...	...	Namibia
...	49.2	...	...	...	...	...	3.6[49]	1.6[49]	...	...	...	...	...	...	Nauru
47.7	30.2	6.1	...	...	...	...	3.7	2.0	7.7[4]	...	...	...	...	...	Nepal
100.0	98.0	100.0	90.0[6]	—10.0[6]—		...	4.1[22]	0.7[22]	6.2	97,384	35,616[22,31]	59.6	15,091[22]	49,968[22,31]	Netherlands, The
79.6	96.9	79.6	...	...	...	...	4.2	1.0	7.8[6]	415[9]	...	99.0[9]	483[9]	...	Netherlands Antilles
90.1	85.3	70.9	76.7	—23.3—		...	3.3	1.2	4.3[6]	710[11]	46[9]	62[11]	1[34]	...	New Caledonia
92.7[20]	...	97.1[20]	96.0[74]	...	...	126.3[41]	5.6	0.5	3.5[4]	19,092	2,543[6]	61.2	...	3,218[6]	New Zealand
27.9	40.9	19.3	19.2	—80.8—		...	2.2	2.1	3.0	...	43[9]	...	28[34]	19.6[34]	Nicaragua
...	...	...	...	...	...	...	...	...	2.1[6]	...	...	...	...	...	Niger
...	81.3	7.0	...	...	...	...	1.4	3.0	1.4	31,038[17]	...	...	1,592[10,22]	...	Nigeria
91.0	94.1[10]	79.5	81.7	—18.3—		...	3.6	1.1	...	...	...	...	...	...	Northern Mariana Islands
97.5[30]	...	94.6	86.8[10]	—13.2[10]—		103.5	4.1	0.6	5.2	21,689[14]	2,850[14]	82.2[14]	4,954[22]	4,483[13]	Norway
...	...	...	...	...	...	...	...	...	3.3	1,043[9]	...	...	266[9]	...	Oman

Housing and construction (continued)

country	year	dwelling units[a]	median age[b] (years)	1949 or earlier	1950-59	1960-69	1970-79	1980 or later	owned	rented	collective, vacant, other	traditional materials	sawn/framed wood	masonry or cement	other
				decade built (percent)					tenure[c] (percent)			construction of exterior walls (percent)			
Pakistan[91]	1980	12,587,648[16]	17.2	17.1[76]	36.7[92]	24.9[93]	—21.3[94]—		78.4	7.7	13.9	49.2	2.4	41.4[78]	7.1
Palau	1990	3,312	12.8	2.1	6.0	16.8	30.6	44.5	76.4	23.6	—	0.0	27.9	26.5	45.6
Panama	1980	530,445[11]	18.0	47.4	12.8	18.1	—21.7—		70.1	21.1	8.8	37.1	—	52.2	10.7
Papua New Guinea	1980	556,519[16]	...						40.0[44]	—60.0[44]—					
Paraguay	1982	580,810[12]	21.1	—56.0—		17.0	—27.0—		80.4	10.5	9.1	21.5	29.7	47.6	1.2
Peru	1981	4,049,000[14]	...	—30.9—			—69.1—		68.5	14.8	14.8	47.4	7.0	33.1	12.5
Philippines	1980	11,380,000[11,16]	...	—78.5[30]—			—21.5[30]—		80.2	12.4	7.4	36.3	33.6	23.8	6.3
Poland	1984	10,789,300[13]	...	35.0[72]	—33.7[73]—		—31.3[40]—		56.7	38.8	4.6	—14.1[43]—		—85.9[43]—	
Portugal	1981	3,235,630	33.7	—53.3—		17.5	—29.2—		72.1[11]	27.9[11]		—	0.7	61.0	38.3
Puerto Rico	1980	1,188,985[11]	15.8	12.2	15.0	31.6	—41.2—					—	19.7	77.4	2.9
Qatar	1986	64,543	...						21.9	72.0	6.1				
Réunion	1982	132,146[6]	...			21.2[67]			54.6	34.5	10.9				
Romania	1966	5,954,555	...												
Russia	1989	40,246,000[16]	...												
Rwanda	1978	1,055,950[16]	...												
St. Kitts and Nevis	1980	11,615[16]	24.2	—63.5—		17.9	—14.7—		54.7	29.5	15.8		75.7[22]	20.8	3.5
St. Lucia	1980	26,919	13.8	—36.8—		21.5	—41.7—		64.7	26.0	9.3	0.1	83.6[22]	12.4	3.9
St. Vincent and the Grenadines	1970	20,290[10,16]	...	—					74.7	16.5	7.9	8.9	64.1	26.1	0.8
San Marino	1979	8,384[11]	...						73.5	21.9	4.6				
São Tomé and Príncipe	1981	25,197[16,96]	...												
Saudi Arabia	...														
Senegal	1955[47,97]	13,000	...						—84.6—		15.4				
Seychelles	1977	12,315	...						46.6	—53.4—		4.1	57.2	38.7	...
Sierra Leone	...														
Singapore	1980	513,224	...	—63.2—			36.8		55.0	39.6	5.4	4.7		—95.3—	
Slovenia	1989														
Solomon Islands	1986	43,842[16]	...						27.4[19]	43.0[19]	29.6[19]				
Somalia	...														
South Africa	1970	1,354,520[98]	18.6	40.6	24.2	35.2	—								
Bophuthatswana	...														
Ciskei	...														
Transkei	1986	518,896[16]	...												
Venda	...														
Spain	1980	12,329,929[50]	39.4	39.2[99]	23.4[100]	18.5[39]	—18.9[40]—		57.2[34]	24.4[34]	18.3[34]				
Sri Lanka	1981	2,811,406	...						69.4	10.1	20.5				
Sudan, The	1966[2]	253,060	...						59.2	28.3	12.6	76.5	4.4	16.7	2.4
Suriname	1980	77,658	...	—52.4—			—47.6—					38.9[101]	—61.1[101]—		
Swaziland	1986	122,369	...									65.9	—34.1—		
Sweden	1990	3,830,037	20.0	33.2	14.2	22.4	22.2	10.6	55.9	40.0	4.1	98.7[10]			
Switzerland	1980	3,140,353[11]	...	—58.1—		22.6	—19.3—		29.9	67.1	3.0				
Syria	1987	1,836,195	...	—91.3[30]—			8.7[30]		81.6[30]	15.5[30]	2.8[30]				
Taiwan	1980	3,171,876[12]	15.3	13.8[25]	14.0[38]	42.4[102]	—29.8[94]—		79.1	11.8	9.1				
Tajikistan	1989	799,000[16]	...												
Tanzania	1978	3,554,793	...	—17.0—			—83.0—		75.4	19.4	5.2	83.0	—	16.3	0.7
Thailand	1980	12,224,400[11,16]	...	22.0[30]	25.0[30]	53.0[30]			83.4	9.1	7.5	15.1	70.0	6.3	8.6
Togo	1958-60[2]	22,274	...												
Tonga	1976	15,091[9,16]	22.5	—59.4[103]—		20.3[104]	—20.3[105]—		85.1	2.5	12.4	35.1	45.4	15.3	4.2
Trinidad and Tobago	1980	231,436	...	—56.3—		14.5	—29.2—		64.6	34.0	1.4	3.3	32.6	53.8	10.3[24]
Tunisia	1984	1,512,300[15]	...						78.9	12.6	8.5				
Turkey	1986	10,855,495	8.4	16.2[103]	6.2[106]	19.6[93]	—58.0[94]—		77.2	12.0	10.8	—28.8—		—71.2—	
Turkmenistan	1989	598,000[16]	...												
Tuvalu	1979	1,079	...						81.6	12.1	6.6	64.9	4.2	31.0	—
Uganda	...														
Ukraine	1989	14,057,000[16]	...												
United Arab Emirates	1980	153,009	15.0	0.8	1.3	11.4	—86.5—		36.2	45.2	18.6	2.9	7.3	87.3	2.5
United Kingdom[108]	1981	22,619,000[15]	32.6	54.0	13.0	16.6	—16.4—		66.6[15]	33.4[15]	—[15]				
United States	1990	102,263,678	25.0	32.9[29]	14.0[22]	16.6[22]	—36.5[22]—		64.2	35.8	—				
Uruguay	1985	852,400	...						59.0[109]	23.9	17.1				
Uzbekistan	1989	3,415,000[16]	...												
Vanuatu	1979	22,513	...						40.9[47]	25.7[47]	33.4[47]	61.4	7.7	13.6	17.2
Venezuela	1981	2,708,674	...						75.1	17.8	7.1	11.8	2.1	78.9	7.2
Vietnam	1989	12,958,041[16]	...												
Virgin Islands (U.S.)	1990	39,290	14.7	10.0[10]	8.9[10]	42.7[10]	—38.4[10]—		44.6	55.4	—				
West Bank	1985	119,165[58]	...						86.2[59]	11.5[59]	2.3[59]				
Western Sahara	1982	19,559	...						32.2[45]	62.3[45]	5.5[45]				
Western Samoa	1981	33,402	...						80.1	2.0	17.9	62.3	24.4	8.6	4.7
Yemen[110]	1975	863,109	...						85.3	7.0	7.7				
Yugoslavia[111]	1981	7,556,000[14]	...	31.1	12.7	26.8	—29.4—		67.1	25.0	7.9		—82.6—		17.4
Zaire	1967[47]	168,000	...						47.4	38.3	14.3				
Zambia	1980	1,128,356	...						78.8[112]	21.1[112]	—				
Zimbabwe	1969	925,581	...						65.1[98]	32.6[98]	2.3[98]	55.9[113]	—44.1[113]—		

[1]1983. [2]Urban only. [3]Percentage of net material product. [4]1988–89. [5]Families. [6]1987. [7]1977. [8]Average annual gain in housing stock during intercensal interval preceding last census. [9]1986. [10]1980. [11]1990. [12]Occupied dwellings only; may include seasonal and/or temporary housing. [13]1988. [14]1991. [15]1989. [16]Data refer to households. [17]1982. [18]1981. [19]1976. [20]1971. [21]1989–90. [22]1985. [23]Stucco. [24]Includes wood and brick, and wood and concrete. [25]1945 and earlier. [26]1946–61. [27]1962–70. [28]1971–75. [29]1976 and later. [30]1970. [31]Volume in cubic metres. [32]1960. [33]National coverage substantially incomplete; no meaningful replacement rate could be calculated. [34]1984. [35]1983–85 average. [36]1986–87. [37]Data refer to compound dwellings, which usually contain two or three dwelling units each. [38]1946–60. [39]1961–70. [40]1971 and later. [41]Average size of dwelling unit in year to which construction data refer. [42]1973. [43]1978. [44]1975. [45]1934–45. [46]1946–59. [47]Capital city only. [48]Includes corrugated steel. [49]1961. [50]Data refer to buildings. [51]1948 and earlier. [52]1949–61. [53]1962–74. [54]1975 and later. [55]Traditional houses, usually constructed of fragile tropical materials and lacking modern conveniences. [56]Residential includes nonresidential. [57]1933 and earlier. [58]1967. [59]Excludes refugee camps. [60]Former

piped water	electricity	inside toilet or WC	closed public sewer or septic tank	open public sewer	other	average area (sq m)	rooms per dwelling unit	persons per room	percent of GDP	total no. of dwellings	floor area ('000 sq m)	years to replace nat'l stock	number of units	floor area ('000 sq m)	country
20.3	30.6	25.1	...	...		...	1.9	3.3	3.6[95]	...	...	...	...	...	Pakistan[91]
87.9	75.7[10]	75.2	44.3	—55.7—		...	4.6	1.2	...	...	...	...	...	...	Palau
80.7	65.7	74.3	43.9	—56.1—		...	2.6	1.8	1.6	15,149[8]	...	35.0[6]	90[22]	142.5[22]	Panama
50.0	56.0	40.0	...	...		...	...	...	5.4	587[9]	...	...	...	...	Papua New Guinea
...	...	26.4	...	...		...	2.2[65]	2.4[65]	5.6	2,254[33]	61[19]	33	2,715[6]	365[6]	Paraguay
73.4	89.5	78.0	58.1	—41.9—		42.4	2.6	2.0	6.8	...	952[9]	...	...	...	Peru
41.4	46.0	35.0	44.1	—55.9—		...	2.4[65]	2.3[65]	4.4	...	2,124[22]	...	2,807[22]	2,170[22]	Philippines
69.7[43]	96.2[43]	41.4[43]	67.0[43]	—33.0[43]—		55.6	3.5	1.1	9.5[3]	189,600	13,856[6]	56.9	62,041[22]	...	Poland
73.4	77.6	67.7	75.5	—24.5—		75.4[41]	5.0[13]	0.8	6.3[13]	33,984	6,714	95.2	5,888[6]	1,691	Portugal
95.2	97.4	89.7	89.6	—10.4—		...	4.8	0.8	2.1[13]	11,710[6]	1,740[6]	82.8[6]	900[22]	41.0[22]	Puerto Rico
...	93.2	...	—50.5—		49.5	...	4.1	1.3	4.8	1,095[6]	391[9]	58.9[6]	258[9]	168[9]	Qatar
70.6	81.6	50.7	52.4	—47.6—		...	3.6	1.2	7.4[13]	8,499	...	16.6	...	...	Réunion
...	48.6	...	12.2	—87.8—		...	2.6	1.4	7.3[3]	60,400[15]	8,591[19]	98.6[15]	...	...	Romania
...	...	...	...	...		...	...	...	12.7[14]	...	61,694[11]	...	...	...	Russia
...	...	...	...	...		...	...	...	6.0[6]	435[34]	60[18]	...	63[34]	34[18]	Rwanda
46.3	57.5	33.5	31.8[31]	—68.2[31]—		...	3.0	1.1	9.1[13]	171[8]	...	68.0[8]	...	...	St. Kitts and Nevis
79.5	36.1[30]	...	11.0[2]	—89.0[30]—		...	3.2	1.6	7.9[6]	471[6,50]	18[36]	57.2[6,50]	121[9]	10.3[9]	St. Lucia
95.0[1]	...	...	22.0[1]	—78.0[1]—		...	2.8	1.8	8.9	465[6,56]	88[6,56]	...	56	56	St. Vincent and the Grenadines
99.8	100.0	98.3	98.3	—1.7—		...	4.5	0.8	...	128[11]	...	65.5[11]	101[11]	...	San Marino
...	...	...	...	...		...	...	...	9.7[6]	...	...	...	...	...	São Tomé and Príncipe
...	...	...	...	...		...	...	...	10.4	...	...	...	...	...	Saudi Arabia
87.7	95.9	...	...	...		...	2.3	1.5	7.6[6]	889[6,33]	257[6]	33	34[6]	33[6]	Senegal
77.5	46.8	33.1	33.1	—66.9—		...	3.6	1.4	4.2[11]	4,802[7,56]	...	...	46[9]	...	Seychelles
...	...	...	...	...		...	...	...	4.2[13]	...	...	...	...	...	Sierra Leone
90.6[30]	98.3	63.6[30]	63.6[30]	—36.4[30]—		...	1.8[30]	2.5[30]	5.3[11]	15,893[15]	9,222[19]	32.3[15]	992[19]	1,208[15]	Singapore
93.0	98.9	75.3	...	...		66.1	...	...	...	8,541	...	...	...	...	Slovenia
92.7[19]	79.6[19]	89.2	89.2[19]	—10.8[19]—		10.8[19]	2.3[19]	2.0[19]	4.3[11]	...	...	...	...	...	Solomon Islands
...	...	...	...	...		...	...	...	3.8[14]	...	...	...	...	...	Somalia
...	...	...	...	...		...	3.4		3.2[11]	39,266[15]	4,619[15]	34.5[15]	...	1,316[15]	South Africa
...	...	...	...	...		...	...	...	...	...	...	...	...	...	Bophuthatswana
...	...	...	...	...		...	...	...	...	...	...	...	...	...	Ciskei
...	...	...	...	...		...	...	...	...	...	...	...	...	...	Transkei
...	...	...	...	...		...	...	...	...	...	...	...	...	...	Venda
90.5	94.7	...	87.9	—12.1—		...	4.4[25]	...	8.9	230,160	...	53.6	...	...	Spain
18.2	14.9	4.7	4.7	—95.3—		18.6[30]	2.5	2.1	7.4[11]	59,637[9]	...	47.2[9]	...	...	Sri Lanka
63.9	26.4	70.2	2.6	—97.4—		...	2.2	2.5	4.5[4]	...	...	...	...	...	Sudan, The
62.9	82.0	40.4	19.6[101]	—80.4[101]—		...	2.1	1.9	6.0[13]	...	355[22,31]	...	161[22]	...	Suriname
42.5	11.6	21.4	...	...		...	...	...	3.5[6]	...	...	...	28[34]	...	Swaziland
99.0[22]	96.2[10]	98.0	96.3[10]	—3.7[10]—		...	3.4	0.6	7.2	58,426	...	65.6	...	3,818[34]	Sweden
100.0	...	93.3	92.2	—	7.8	86.0	3.8[9]	0.6[9]	7.6[22]	39,984[11]	...	78.5[11]	8,109[9]	...	Switzerland
40.2[1]	41.7[1]	...	36.0[1]	—64.0[1]—		93.0	3.0	2.0	4.6[13]	55,572[6]	2,390	33.0[6]	...	339	Syria
79.4	99.7	94.2	69.3	...		85.9	3.7	1.5	4.9[11]	...	31,256[56]	...	...	56	Taiwan
...	...	...	...	...		...	...	...	14.7[11]	...	1,753	...	...	...	Tajikistan
37.2	6.3	...	...	...		...	2.5	1.9	1.5	...	...	...	...	...	Tanzania
29.7[11]	89.3[11]	40.9	40.9[19]	9.8[19]	49.3[19]	...	1.9[19]	...	6.6	...	10,622	...	...	7,307	Thailand
4.1	10.3	...	—	—100.0—		...	1.8	3.4	3.5[13]	...	...	...	...	...	Togo
61.3	20.9	42.3	11.2	—88.8—		...	...	...	3.9	...	...	...	...	...	Tonga
64.3	83.3	41.1	41.0	—59.0—		...	3.3	1.4	77[11]	2,046[6,33]	362	33	69[9]	35	Trinidad and Tobago
26.4	63.4	43.3	69.2[15]	—30.8[15]—		...	1.9	2.4	4.4[13]	34,566[6]	...	38.0	...	...	Tunisia
68.0	56.8[38]	70.6	42.0	52.0	6.0	110.5[41]	2.4[22]	2.2[30]	4.0	250,480	27,561	43.3	3,933[9]	8,027	Turkey
...	...	...	...	...		...	...	...	22.7[14]	...	1,787[11]	...	...	...	Turkmenistan
...	...	...	...	...		...	...	...	9.6[22]	...	...	...	...	...	Tuvalu
65.4	7.4	37.3	...	...		...	...	...	2.3	...	...	...	65[65]	26.8[65]	Uganda
...	...	...	...	...		...	...	...	11.2[15]	...	17,464[11]	...	...	...	Ukraine
30.9[107]	24.2[107]	84.5	...	...		...	2.8	1.8	9.8[13]	...	...	...	133[34]	...	United Arab Emirates
...	...	99.0	...	...		...	3.8	0.6	6.9	206,682	...	109.4	...	...	United Kingdom[108]
98.5	96.9	98.2	99.2	—0.8—		147.1	5.2	0.5	4.8[13]	1,488,000	214,900[9]	68.7	...	140,100[9]	United States
88.9	84.7	73.3	...	92.0		...	3.4	1.7	2.7	...	160[22]	...	105[22]	21.4[22]	Uruguay
...	...	...	...	...		...	...	...	10.7[14]	...	9,908[11]	...	...	...	Uzbekistan
13.7	11.7	19.1	...	...		...	...	...	5.3[6]	...	5.7[9]	...	...	15.3[9]	Vanuatu
85.3	88.6	84.4	71.3	—28.7—		53.5[10]	3.9[20]	1.5[20]	4.9	91,666[9]	4,904[9]	29.5[9]	678[9]	1,067[9]	Venezuela
...	...	...	...	...		...	...	...	2.6[3,6]	...	...	...	53[34]	59.3[34]	Vietnam
96.3[10]	98.1[10]	86.0[10]	93.6[10]	—6.4[10]—		...	4.3	0.6	...	...	...	...	262[10]	...	Virgin Islands (U.S.)
75.2	91.2	90.1	...	...		127.2[41]	2.4	2.7	14.1[6]	5,740[6]	730[6]	20.8[6]	...	175.8[6]	West Bank
78.5	95.3	...	...	...		...	4.5	1.2	...	...	...	...	...	...	Western Sahara
80.7	37.7	71.0	16.6	—83.4—		...	3.9[19,97]	1.5[19,97]	1.9[6]	132[22]	...	...	118[22]	...	Western Samoa
5.7	4.6	...	...	...		...	2.0	2.8	4.5[6]	...	1,988[22]	...	...	...	Yemen[110]
67.8	95.7	53.3	...	...		60.7	2.6[22]	1.3[22]	6.2	116,236	12,883	56.4[6]	15,522[6]	1,197	Yugoslavia[111]
...	...	...	...	...		...	...	...	5.5[6]	...	20[22]	...	73[22]	39[22]	Zaire
12.4[112]	27.5[32]	15.1[112]	...		82.3[112]	...	1.9[112]	2.6[112]	1.4	1,222[33]	...	...	...	...	Zambia
...	9.3[113]	...	...	...		...	2.8	1.9	1.7	...	...	...	...	...	Zimbabwe

West Germany only. [61]1949–57. [62]1958–68. [63]1969–78. [64]1979 and later. [65]1972. [66]Excludes dwellings of less than 6 sq m. [67]1974. [68]1987–88. [69]1947 and earlier. [70]1948 to 1983. [71]1961–71. [72]1944 and earlier. [73]1945–70. [74]Minimum. [75]Includes nonconventional dwellings. [76]1946 and earlier. [77]1947–60. [78]1948–60. [79]Peninsular Malaysia only. [80]1957 and earlier. [81]1958–67. [82]Excluding Rodrigues and lesser outlying islands. [83]1960–68. [84]1969 and later. [85]1975–82. [86]Dwellings of indigenous population only. [87]1946–60. [88]1961–70. [89]1971–80. [90]1981 and later. [91]Excludes Islāmābād, North-West Frontier, and federally administered tribal areas. [92]1947–65. [93]1966–75. [94]1976 and later. [95]1990–91. [96]De jure population. [97]European-style dwellings only. [98]White, Coloured, and Asian dwellings only; excludes Bantu. [99]1940 and earlier. [100]1941–60. [101]1964. [102]1961–75. [103]1955 and earlier. [104]1956–66. [105]1966 and later. [106]1956–65. [107]1968. [108]Excludes Northern Ireland. [109]Preliminary. [110]Former Yemen Arab Republic only. [111]Data refer to Yugoslavia as constituted prior to 1991. [112]1969. [113]Bantu dwellings only.

Household budgets and consumption

This table provides international data on household income, on the consumption expenditure of households for goods and services, and on the principal object of such expenditure (in most countries), food consumption (by kind). For purposes of this compilation, income comprises pretax monetary payments and payment in kind. The first part of the table provides data on distribution of income by households and by sources of income; the second part analyzes the largest portion of income use—consumption expenditure. Such expenditure is defined as the purchase of goods and services to satisfy current wants and needs. This definition excludes income expended on taxes, debts, savings and investments, and insurance policies. The third and last part of the table focuses on food, which usually, and often by a wide margin, represents the largest share of consumer spending worldwide. The data provided include daily available calories per capita and consumption of major food groups.

For both sources of income and consumption expenditure, the primary basis of analysis for most countries is the household, an economic unit that can be as small as a single person or as large as an extended family. For some of the countries that do not compile information by household, the table provides data on personal income and personal expenditure, i.e., the income and expenditure of all the individuals constituting a society's households. When no expenditure data at all is available, the table reports the weights of each major class of goods and services comprising a given country's consumer (or retail) price index (CPI). The weighting of the components of the CPI usually reflects household spending patterns within the country or its principal urban or rural areas.

The data on distribution of income show, collectively for an entire country, the proportion of total income earned by households constituting the lowest quintile and highest decile (poorest 20% and wealthiest 10%) within the country. These figures show the degree to which either group represents a disproportionate share of poverty or wealth.

The data on sources of income illuminate patterns of economic structure in the gaining of an income. They indicate, for example, that in poor, agrarian countries income often derives largely from self-employment (usually farming) or that in industrial countries, with well-developed systems of salaried employment and social welfare, income derives mainly from wages and salaries and secondarily from transfer payments (see headnote a). Because household sizes and numbers of income earners vary so greatly internationally, and because the frequency and methodology of household and CPI surveys do not permit single-year comparisons for more than a few countries at once, no summary of total household income or expenditure was possible. Instead, U.S. dollar figures are supplied for per capita private final consumption expenditure (for a single, recent year) that are more comparable internationally and refer to the same date. The figures on distribution of consumption expenditure by end use reveal patterns of personal and family use of disposable income and indicate, inter alia, that in developing countries food may absorb 50% or more of disposable income, while in the larger household budgets of the developed countries, by contrast, food purchases may account for only 20–30% of spending. In either type of country, the cost of transportation often rivals that of housing, once the more basic need. Each category of expenditure betrays similar complexities of local habit, necessity, and aspiration.

The reader should exercise caution when using these data to make intercountry comparisons. Most of the information comes from single-country surveys, which often differ markedly in their coverage of economically or

Household budgets and consumption

country	income (latest) percent received by lowest 20% of households	highest 10% of households	by source (percent) wages, salaries	self-employment	transfer payments[a]	other[b]	consumption expenditure per capita private final, U.S.$ 1990	by kind or end use (percent of household or personal budget; latest) food[c]	housing[d]	clothing[e]	health care	energy, water	education
Afghanistan	...	...	20.7	28.0	8.2	43.1	100[1]	33.9	3.0	...	1.1	0.7	...
Albania	...	...	...	...	...	...	900	63.0	4.9	7.2	1.7	...	[2]
Algeria	...	...	...	...	...	...							
American Samoa	...	...	...	...	...	...	1,877[3]	32.9	20.4[4]	5.2	...	...	0.2
Andorra	...	...	...	...	...	...							
Angola	...	...					560[5]						
Antigua and Barbuda							2,170[6]	42.9	23.3	7.5	...	5.5	[2]
Argentina	4.4	35.2	...	...	...	...	1,670	38.2	9.3	8.0	7.9	9.0	2.6
Armenia	...	...	66.9	4.3	11.6	17.2	3,750						
Aruba	...	...						26.9	12.6	8.4	2.9	5.6	1.9
Australia	4.8	28.1	72.3	9.2	10.1	8.5	10,150	22.5	14.3	6.1	4.3	2.6	[2]
Austria	4.0	28.7	55.3	...	24.6	20.1	11,320	18.0	13.6	9.7	5.0	4.1	6.3
Azerbaijan	...	...											
Bahamas, The	3.6	32.1	...	...	...	...	3,950[7]	19.2	19.2	7.2	3.4	4.3	7.7
Bahrain	...	...					2,910[3]	32.4	21.2	5.9	2.3	2.2	2.3
Bangladesh	10.0	23.2	26.1	50.8	0.5	22.6	190	63.3	8.8	5.9	1.1	8.4	1.2
Barbados	6.8	...					4,490	43.2	13.1	5.1	...	6.2	...
Belarus	...	...	73.7	5.3	14.8	6.2	3,650						
Belgium	7.9[8]	21.5[8]	50.3	11.6	20.6	17.5	12,420	18.8	11.7	6.6	10.4	6.7	[2]
Belize			84.1	—15.9—			1,210	51.5[9]	2.3	11.1	3.4	6.0	1.5
Benin	8.0	39.0	...	...	...	...	360	37.0	10.0	14.0	5.0	2.0	4.0
Bermuda	7.2	24.7	72.2	6.7	2.4	18.7	12,690[10]	20.7[9]	21.8	6.0	6.8	4.5	[2]
Bhutan	...	...					110[3]	72.3	21.2			3.7	...
Bolivia	4.0	...					500	41.4	12.5	9.7	4.5	0.7	1.2
Bosnia and Hercegovina			53.2	12.0	18.2	16.6	1,890	44.7	1.6	8.3	3.4	7.8	[2]
Botswana	2.5	42.8	59.9	9.3	30.8	...	1,290[7]	39.5[9]	13.3[11]	5.6	2.3	11	[2]
Brazil	2.4	46.2					740	49.0[9,12]	8.6[12]	6.4[12]	5.3[12]	11.7[12]	2.2[12]
Brunei	...	...						45.1	5.0[11]	6.1	...	11	[2]
Bulgaria	9.7	22.5	52.8	12.0	17.7	17.5	1,790	39.6	7.4[11]	9.9	2.3	11	3.4
Burkina Faso	...	...					310	38.7[13]	5.1[13]	4.4[13]	5.2[13]	13.7[13]	[2]
Burundi	...	...					175	59.6[13]	4.4[13]	11.1[13]	...	5.8[13]	...
Cambodia	...	...											
Cameroon	...	...	34.7	51.3	10.4	3.6	750	33.6[13]	14.6[13]	16.3[13]	5.0[13]	...	...
Canada	5.7	24.1	65.4	7.2	14.1	13.3	12,960	14.1	22.2[11]	5.8	4.4	11	2.8
Cape Verde	...	...					880	63.4[13]	9.2[13]				
Cayman Islands	...	...											
Central African Republic	...	...					390	70.5[13]	0.6[13]	9.5[13]	1.0[13]	6.5[13]	...
Chad	8.0	30.0					190	45.3[13]	...	3.5[13]	11.9[13]	5.8[13]	...
Chile	4.4	34.8	40.8	...	8.1	51.2	1,280	41.9	13.3	7.6	...	...	[2]
China	8.5[15]	37.7[15,16]	81.2[17]	...	15.2[17]	3.6[17]	160	54.1[15]	14.4[15]	8.3[15]	...	4.4[15]	[2]
Colombia	4.0	37.1	46.1	36.7	9.6	7.6	710	39.2	11.3	5.7	5.4	1.3	1.6
Comoros	...	...	25.6	64.5	8.7	1.2	430	56.0	...	10.0	5.0	14.4	...
Congo	7.0	43.5					880	42.0	7.0	6.0	3.0	4.0	1.0
Cook Islands	...	...						58.4	3.1	12.4	...	...	...
Costa Rica	3.3	38.8					1,040	33.0	8.0	8.0	7.0	1.0	8.0
Côte d'Ivoire	5.0	36.3	44.9	49.9	—5.2—		600	48.0[13]	7.8[13]	10.1[13]	0.7[13]	8.5[13]	...
Croatia	...	...	40.2	40.8	12.1	6.9	5,050	37.8	2.9	8.6	4.3	7.6	[2]
Cuba	...	...	57.3	...	...	42.7	1,510[7]	26.7	...	...	...	2.5	...
Cyprus	7.9[17]	...					5,120	25.6	6.5	8.9	3.2	1.2	1.2
Czechoslovakia	10.0[18]	21.8[18]	55.3	—	13.7	31.0	1,380	26.1	...	8.7	...	...	...
Denmark	3.5	25.6	48.2	33.6	18.2	...	13,110	20.9[9]	21.6	5.4	1.9	6.0	[2]
Djibouti	...	...	51.6	36.0	10.5	1.9	1,030	50.3	6.4	1.7	2.4	13.1	...
Dominica	...	...					1,800[7]	43.1	16.1[4]	6.5	...	5.4	...
Dominican Republic	4.5[8]	41.7[8]	41.7	31.8	1.5	25.0	840	46.0	10.0	3.0	8.0	5.0	3.0
Ecuador	2.9	51.5	17.4	74.9	4.5	3.2	700	35.4	4.0	12.0	4.0	1.1	...

demographically stratified groups, in sample design, or in the methods employed for collection, classification, and tabulation of data. Further, the reference period of the data varies greatly; while a significant portion of the data is from 1980 or later, information for some countries dates from the 1970s. This older information is typeset in italic. Finally, intercountry comparisons of annual personal consumption expenditure may be misleading because of the distortions of price and purchasing power present when converting a national currency unit into U.S. dollars.

The table's food consumption data include total daily available calories per capita (food supply), which amounts to domestic production and imports minus exports, animal feed, and nonfood uses, and a percentage breakdown of the major food groups that make up food supply.

The data for daily available calories per capita provide a measure of the nutritional adequacy of each nation's food supply. The following list, based on estimates from the United Nations Food and Agriculture Organization (FAO), indicates the regional variation in recommended daily minimum nutritional requirements, which are defined by factors such as climatic ambience, physical activity, and average body weight: Africa (2,320 calories), Centrally Planned Asia (2,300 calories), Far East (2,240 calories), Latin America (2,360 calories), Near East (2,440 calories).

The breakdown of diet by food groups describes the character of a nation's food supply. A typical breakdown for a low-income country might show a diet with heavy intake of vegetable foods, such as cereals, potatoes, or cassava. In the high-income countries, a relatively larger portion of total calories derives from animal products (meat, eggs, and milk). The reader should note that these data refer to total national *supply* and do not reflect the differences that often exist within a single country.

In compiling this table, Britannica editors rely on both numerous national reports and principal secondary sources such as the World Bank's *World Development Report* (annual), the International Labour Organisation's *Statistical Sources and Methods, vol. 1 Consumer Price Indices* (2nd ed.); the UN's *Yearbook of National Accounts Statistics* (annual) and *National Accounts Statistics: Compendium of Income Distribution Statistics;* and the FAO's *Food Balance Sheets 1979–81* and *1984–86,* and *Review of Food Consumption Surveys—1985.*

The following terms further define the column headings:
a. Includes pensions, family allowances, unemployment payments, remittances from abroad, and social security and related benefits.
b. Includes interest and dividends, rents and royalties, and all other income not reported under the three preceding categories.
c. Includes alcoholic and nonalcoholic beverages and meals away from home when identifiable. Excludes tobacco except as noted.
d. Rent, maintenance of dwellings, and taxes only; excludes energy and water (heat, light, power, and water) and household durables (furniture, appliances, utensils, and household operations), shown separately.
e. Includes footwear.
f. Furniture, appliances, and utensils; usually includes expenditure on household operation.
g. Includes expenditure on cultural activities other than education.
h. May include data not shown separately in preceding categories, including meals away from home (*see* note c).
i. Represents pure fats and oils only.
j. Consists mainly of peas, beans, and lentils; spices; stimulants; sugars and honey; and nuts and oilseeds.

transportation, communications	household durable goods[f]	recreation[g]	personal effects, other[h]	daily available calories per capita (1987–89)	cereals	potatoes, cassava	meat, poultry	fish	eggs, milk	fruits, vegetables	fats, oils[i]	other[j]	country
...	...	...	61.3	...	*81.5*	*1.4*	*3.3*	—	*3.6*	*2.4*	*3.1*	*4.7*	Afghanistan
					66.4	*2.6*	*5.2*	*0.1*	*6.2*	*4.7*	*6.4*	*8.4*	Albania
3.8	6.0	3.8[2]	9.6	2,818	56.8	2.2	2.0	0.3	7.5	4.1	13.2	13.9	Algeria
15.1	[4]	1.1	25.1										American Samoa
...	...	...	...	3,567	23.8	5.5	18.0	1.5	9.4	6.7	15.9	19.1	Andorra
					35.3	*33.8*	*3.2*	*0.9*	*1.9*	*4.2*	*7.2*	*13.5*	Angola
10.0	...	...	*10.8*	2,295	31.2	0.9	14.0	2.2	10.6	7.9	13.4	19.7	Antigua and Barbuda
11.6	...	7.5	5.9	3,110	31.3	5.0	20.1	0.3	8.9	4.2	11.4	18.8	Argentina
...	...	...	...		...	...	...	...	...	...	...	...	Armenia
17.4	9.1	3.1	12.1		...	...	...	...	...	...	...	...	Aruba
15.1	7.4	11.8[2]	15.9	3,186	23.5	2.8	18.0	0.8	11.7	4.7	15.1	23.4	Australia
16.5	7.5	6.2	19.1	3,496	19.9	3.3	14.2	0.5	11.4	6.0	22.5	22.2	Austria
...	...	...	...										Azerbaijan
18.9	10.2	5.3	4.6	2,791	24.2	2.5	20.0	0.6	7.5	9.5	9.7	26.0	Bahamas, The
8.5	9.8	6.4	9.0		...	...	...	...	...	...	...	...	Bahrain
0.9	...	...	10.4	1,996	82.2	1.5	0.8	0.7	1.0	1.2	5.6	6.9	Bangladesh
4.6	9.6	...	16.2	3,247	32.8	4.0	15.3	1.9	7.5	2.6	10.5	25.3	Barbados
...	...	...	...		...	...	...	...	...	...	...	...	Belarus
13.1	10.3	6.4[2]	16.0	3,947	18.1	5.0	19.4	0.9	8.6	5.2	23.8	19.1	Belgium
6.5	10.1	2.2	5.4	2,660	34.1	2.2	9.7	0.4	9.7	8.6	10.9	24.4	Belize
14.0	5.0	...	9.0	2,245	36.3	35.0	2.7	0.6	1.1	3.2	10.3	10.9	Benin
17.1	14.7	8.4[2]	6.8	2,998	23.7	1.8	21.1	0.0	13.2	8.7	9.9	21.6	Bermuda
...	0.7	...	2.1		85.2	2.4	0.4	0.1	0.6	1.4	5.3	4.6	Bhutan
12.5	8.9	3.1	5.5	1,968	48.6	10.2	9.2	0.1	2.8	7.1	5.8	16.3	Bolivia
6.0	4.1	3.5[2]	2.3	3,620	...	...	...	...	...	...	...	...	Bosnia and Hercegovina
13.1	14.0	8.3[2]	3.9	2,368	62.4	0.9	4.2	0.3	7.3	1.4	4.7	18.9	Botswana
6.3[12]	...	2.1[12]	8.4[12]	2,722	38.9	6.8	6.4	0.4	6.4	4.9	10.6	25.6	Brazil
17.2	8.3	8.9[2]	9.4	2,824	48.5	0.9	9.4	2.1	6.5	4.3	8.4	19.9	Brunei
7.2	4.5	7.0	13.0	3,683	39.7	1.6	10.4	0.5	9.0	5.1	15.0	18.8	Bulgaria
18.6[13]	3.0[13]	2.3[2, 13]	9.0[13]	2,286	67.4	1.8	2.6	0.2	1.8	0.9	4.7	20.5	Burkina Faso
...	6.0[13]	...	13.1[13, 14]	1,995	25.4	23.6	0.9	0.1	0.6	7.7	1.2	40.5	Burundi
...	...	...	...		80.5	1.1	3.7	1.2	0.4	3.6	1.9	7.6	Cambodia
10.5[13]	...	5.1[13]	14.9[13]	2,195	33.5	20.1	3.6	1.3	0.8	9.4	10.9	20.3	Cameroon
15.3	9.7	8.6	17.1	3,462	20.4	3.3	14.2	1.0	9.5	5.8	21.2	24.5	Canada
...	...	...	20.7[13]	2,714	51.7	3.7	2.4	1.6	2.8	2.5	13.0	22.2	Cape Verde
...	...	...	...		...	...	...	...	...	...	...	...	Cayman Islands
4.1[13]	0.8[13]	1.3[13]	5.7[13]	2,004	26.0	38.9	7.2	0.4	0.3	5.2	6.0	15.9	Central African Republic
...	...	...	33.5[13]		57.2	11.2	3.2	1.6	2.6	2.9	3.3	18.0	Chad
11.8	*7.8*	8.2[2]	9.4	2,553	47.5	4.1	7.1	1.0	6.4	4.8	9.3	19.8	Chile
...	...	6.6[2, 15]	12.2[15]	2,634	70.8	6.0	7.4	0.6	1.2	2.6	4.7	6.8	China
13.0	5.6	4.7	12.2	2,571	32.1	8.5	6.8	0.3	6.2	9.1	9.5	27.6	Colombia
6.6	...	3.0	5.0	1,895	37.9	30.2	2.1	1.3	1.6	7.0	5.3	14.7	Comoros
17.0	4.0	...	16.0	2,603	18.5	43.8	2.3	3.5	1.0	7.3	11.6	11.8	Congo
5.7	9.6	...	10.8		...	...	...	...	...	...	...	...	Cook Islands
8.0	9.0	...	18.0	2,791	35.3	0.9	5.5	0.4	8.8	5.2	12.4	31.4	Costa Rica
12.2[13]	3.4[13]	0.6[13]	8.7[13]	2,580	39.6	26.8	2.9	1.3	1.9	7.9	9.2	10.5	Côte d'Ivoire
9.3	4.5	4.1[2]	1.5	3,620	...	...	...	...	...	...	...	...	Croatia
5.4	...	...	65.4	3,153	36.6	5.4	7.1	1.3	8.3	3.9	8.9	28.4	Cuba
16.1	10.6	6.1	20.6		*40.0*	*2.5*	*13.7*	*0.4*	*7.9*	*7.0*	*10.1*	*18.4*	Cyprus
...	...	...	65.2	3,609	29.4	4.0	14.2	0.5	10.1	4.2	17.5	20.3	Czechoslovakia
16.4	6.3	10.5[2]	11.0	3,622	20.2	3.6	24.2	1.6	9.5	4.2	16.0	20.6	Denmark
...	1.5	...	24.6		...	...	...	...	...	...	...	...	Djibouti
...	[4]	...	34.3	2,820	27.1	13.9	6.9	1.0	8.8	12.3	5.8	24.1	Dominica
4.0	8.0	...	13.0	2,342	32.9	2.4	4.6	0.6	4.3	15.1	14.2	25.8	Dominican Republic
11.7	8.8	...	23.0	2,518	38.0	3.4	5.2	1.7	7.4	13.9	9.9	20.5	Ecuador

Household budgets and consumption (continued)

country	income (latest)						consumption expenditure						
	percent received by		by source (percent)				per capita private final, U.S.$ 1990	by kind or end use (percent of household or personal budget; latest)					
	lowest 20% of households	highest 10% of households	wages, salaries	self-employment	transfer payments[a]	other[b]		food[c]	housing[d]	clothing[e]	health care	energy, water	education
Egypt	5.8	33.2	...	...	...	...	430	50.0	6.0	11.0	3.0	3.0	6.0
El Salvador	5.5[8]	29.5[8]	...	...	...	...	860	39.7	5.8	9.5	4.0	2.0	1.2
Equatorial Guinea	...	...	...	...	...	...	382	...	...	...	...	...	[2]
Estonia	...	...	70.1	8.6	14.6	6.8	5,070	29.2	...	11.7	...	...	[2]
Ethiopia	...	...	0.2	79.5	—	20.3	80	66.7[15]	0.5[15]	6.8[15]	3.1[15]	15.9[15]	2.5[15]
Faeroe Islands	...	...	...	...	...	...	...	40.9	11.0	8.0	...	18.9	...
Fiji	3.7	37.8	81.5	9.1	...	9.4	1,280	31.3	11.9[11]	10.2	2.2	[11]	[2]
Finland	3.7	26.9	61.6	13.1	21.0	4.3	14,350	21.4	13.8	5.4	3.9	3.3	[2]
France	6.3	25.5	52.4	21.2	26.1	0.3	12,650	19.3	19.3[11]	6.5	9.4	[11]	[2]
French Guiana	...	...	74.6		—25.4—		...	31.9[13]	18.4[11,13]	5.8[13]	4.3[13]	[11]	[2]
French Polynesia	...	...	54.4	28.3	15.3	2.0	4,310[19]	32.1	...	6.3	1.0	8.1	[2]
Gabon	3.3	54.4	...	...	...	...	2,435	54.7[9,13,20]	13.0[13,20]	17.5[13,20]	1.9[13,20]	...	...
Gambia, The	...	...	...	...	...	...	220	58.0[21]	5.1[21]	17.5[21]	...	5.4[21]	...
Gaza Strip	...	...	...	...	...	...	910[6]	...	...	...	...	...	...
Georgia	...	...	...	...	...	...	2,500	...	...	...	...	...	...
Germany	6.8[22]	23.4[22]	81.9[22]	10.3[22]	7.8[22]	...	12,720[22]	23.8[9,22]	20.9[22]	8.0[22]	3.3[22]	5.4[22]	[2]
Ghana	6.5	29.1	41.6[23]	47.1[23]	—	11.3[23]	350	57.4	11.5[11]	14.3	1.3	[11]	[2]
Gibraltar	...	...	...	...	...	...	...	39.1[9]	12.6	11.0	...	...	...
Greece	...	...	38.9	...	17.7	43.4	4,720	30.4	8.4	9.3	3.4	2.6	0.6
Greenland	...	...	...	...	...	...	...	29.5	8.9	7.6	...	7.1	...
Grenada	...	...	...	...	...	...	1,570	59.0	6.5	8.0	...	6.0	...
Guadeloupe	...	...	...	...	...	...	4,080[6]	29.8	8.2[4,11]	26.3	4.6	[11]	...
Guam	...	...	...	...	...	...	...	24.1	28.6	10.6	4.8	...	...
Guatemala	5.5	40.8	...	...	...	...	690	64.4	16.0[11]	3.1	0.6	[11]	0.3
Guernsey	...	...	...	...	...	...	...	23.7	12.1	7.5	...	8.2	...
Guinea	...	...	...	...	...	...	320	61.5	7.3[11]	7.9	11.1	[11]	...
Guinea-Bissau	...	...	...	...	...	...	220	...	...	...	...	...	...
Guyana	...	...	73.0	...	6.3	20.7	170	42.5[9]	21.4	8.6	...	5.2	[2]
Haiti	...	...	...	...	...	...	350	77.9	8.3	3.2	...	...	...
Honduras	3.2	50.6	58.8	[24]	1.8	39.4[24]	850	44.4	22.4[11]	9.0	7.0	[11]	[2]
Hong Kong	4.3[18]	37.3[18]	...	...	...	...	6,330[7]	16.5	15.7[11]	21.9	5.4	[11]	1.0
Hungary	10.9	18.7	58.2	...	38.7	3.1	1,950	41.5[9]	11.9	7.6	3.5	...	...
Iceland	4.7	27.3	74.2	2.4	16.1	7.3	14,260	21.1	11.2	10.4	1.7	2.5	0.3
India	8.1	26.7	42.2	39.7	...	18.1	270	53.5	7.0	11.5	2.6	4.3	1.3
Indonesia	8.8	26.5	42.1	41.5	2.5	13.9	320	61.3[9]	17.1[11]	5.1	...	[11]	...
Iran	3.8	41.7	40.8	28.2	4.5	26.5	4,750[7]	42.2[9]	29.2[11]	9.7	9.7	[11]	[2]
Iraq	2.1	...	23.9	33.9	23.0	18.6	1,710[10]	55.4[9]	7.9	10.3	2.4	4.1	...
Ireland	4.6	26.5	58.6	13.3	19.9	8.2	6,740	34.7	6.0	6.9	3.5	4.9	3.1
Isle of Man	6.4	26.6	64.1	6.6	16.9	12.4	...	31.0	7.9	7.0	...	11.0	...
Israel	8.4	23.1	87.9[17,20]	2.3[17,20]	—9.8[17,20]—	...	6,890	28.4[9]	16.4	8.4	...	4.3	...
Italy	6.8	25.3	42.0	28.0	19.6	10.4	11,750	21.7	10.6	9.6	6.3	3.6	0.9
Jamaica	5.4	33.4	66.1	19.3	14.6	...	880	35.7	5.7	4.6	2.8	4.9	0.2
Japan	10.9	31.6[16]	58.3	12.4	19.3	10.0	13,650	24.3	5.0	9.4	2.6	5.0	4.8
Jersey	...	...	...	...	...	...	...	28.3	14.9	8.3	...	6.5	...
Jordan	...	...	...	...	...	...	870	37.8	6.3[11]	5.5	4.0	[11]	3.3
Kazakhstan	...	...	...	...	...	...	...	...	...	...	...	...	...
Kenya	2.6	45.8	...	...	...	...	220	46.5	10.0	7.7	2.2	2.6	1.0
Kiribati	...	...	69.7	21.4	6.0	2.9	370[3]	64.0[9]	1.0	8.0	...	3.6	...
Korea, North	...	...	...	...	...	...	...	46.5[25]	0.6[25]	29.9[25]	...	3.3[25]	...
Korea, South	8.0[17,26]	24.5[17,26]	86.3	2.5	3.2	8.0	3,000	28.8	3.7	7.7	4.9	4.1	[2]
Kuwait	...	...	53.8	20.8	—25.4—		5,250	28.1[9]	15.5	8.1	0.7	9.6	[2]
Kyrgyzstan	...	...	...	...	...	...	2,370	...	...	...	...	...	...
Laos	...	...	...	...	...	...	140[7]	...	...	...	...	...	...
Latvia	...	...	75.7	3.8	8.5	12.0	3,950	28.5[20]	...	...	...	...	...
Lebanon	5.0	45.0	27.9	...	3.0	69.1	780[3]	42.8[13]	16.8[13]	8.6[13]	7.2[13]	4.5[13]	3.9[13]
Lesotho	...	...	22.4	27.8	44.7	5.1	390	33.4[9]	4.8[11]	21.9	1.8	[11]	[2]
Liberia	5.3	...	...	...	...	...	250[3]	34.4[13]	14.9[13]	13.8[13]	...	5.0[13]	[2]
Libya	10.1	...	...	...	...	...	3,749[3]	37.2[9]	32.2[11]	6.9	3.3	[11]	[2]
Liechtenstein	...	...	92.9[27]	7.1[27]	...	...	...	21.3[9]	18.0	6.6	7.7	4.4	[2]
Lithuania	...	...	68.2	1.8	12.5	17.5	4,360	...	...	...	...	...	...
Luxembourg	...	...	88.6	9.1	2.3	...	13,110	14.2	14.1	6.4	7.6	5.9	[2]
Macau	...	...	...	...	...	...	2,480[7]	44.3[9]	21.2	7.3	...	4.8	...
Macedonia	...	...	57.7	17.2	16.2	9.0	1,800	40.6	1.9	7.8	3.0	7.8	...
Madagascar	5.2	...	58.8[13,28]	14.1[13,28]	—	27.1[13,28]	250	59.0	6.0	6.0	2.0	6.0	4.0
Malawi	10.4	40.1	83.3	6.0	—	11.7	170	32.9[29]	13.3[29]	10.7[29]	...	...	...
Malaysia	4.6	34.8	...	...	...	...	1,280	28.7	10.2[11]	4.3	2.5	[11]	0.6
Maldives	...	...	...	...	...	...	270[7]	...	...	...	...	...	...
Mali	...	...	...	...	...	...	260	57.0	2.0	6.0	2.0	6.0	4.0
Malta	...	...	48.0	14.6	13.7	23.7	3,660[7]	29.2	3.8[30]	7.9	3.6	1.9[30]	[2]
Marshall Islands	...	...	...	...	...	...	...	57.7	15.6[4,11]	12.0	...	[11]	...
Martinique	...	...	74.2	...	...	25.8	4,840[6]	31.9	24.7[4,11]	7.2	5.5	[11]	[2]
Mauritania	...	...	...	...	...	...	460	61.0[13]	24.0[13]	5.2[13]	...	...	...
Mauritius	4.0	46.7	52.3	29.4	11.3	7.0	1,570	50.4[9]	4.0	10.4	3.0	6.4	2.9
Mayotte	...	...	...	...	...	...	...	79.6	—	...	...	7.1	...
Mexico	2.9	40.6	52.4	23.6	5.6	18.4	1,990	38.7[9]	37.0[11]	10.2	7.9	[11]	[2]
Micronesia	...	...	...	...	...	...	...	73.5	...	...	...	...	...
Moldova	...	...	69.1	6.7	12.6	11.6	2,640	...	...	...	...	...	...
Monaco	...	...	...	...	...	...	...	...	...	...	...	...	...
Mongolia	...	...	...	...	...	...	...	...	...	...	...	...	...
Morocco	9.8	25.4	...	...	...	...	640	40.0	7.0	11.0	4.0	2.0	6.0
Mozambique	...	...	...	...	...	...	80	...	...	...	...	...	...
Myanmar (Burma)	8.0	...	...	...	...	...	235[5]	49.1[13]	10.4[13]	15.3[13]	2.4[13]	4.0[13]	5.9[13]
Namibia	...	...	73.3	0.4	3.4	22.9	934[7]	...	...	...	...	...	...
Nauru	...	...	...	...	...	...	...	...	...	...	...	...	...
Nepal	3.1	50.7	39.2[13]	33.6[13]	—27.2[13]—		130	57.4[13]	11.4[11,13]	10.5[13]	4.2[13]	[11]	[2]

transportation, communications	household durable goods[f]	recreation[g]	personal effects, other[h]	food consumption									country
				daily available calories per capita (1987–89)	percent of total calories (latest) derived from:								
					cereals	potatoes, cassava	meat, poultry	fish	eggs, milk	fruits, vegetables	fats, oils[i]	other[j]	
4.0	3.0	...	14.0	3,326	60.5	1.6	2.5	0.3	2.0	6.3	13.7	13.1	Egypt
10.9	12.7	3.3	10.9	...	56.9	0.9	2.4	0.2	5.3	4.7	8.4	21.3	El Salvador
...	...	...	...	...	...	...	...	...	...	...	...	...	Equatorial Guinea
...	...	7.2[22]	51.9	...	...	...	...	...	...	...	...	...	Estonia
0.7[15]	2.1[15]	0.1[15]	1.6[15]	...	68.8	3.9	4.2	—	2.9	0.8	2.2	17.2	Ethiopia
...	6.6	...	14.6	...	29.3	5.5	15.8	3.9	7.0	3.3	18.0	17.2	Faeroe Islands
11.3	7.8	4.3[2]	21.0	2,871	38.7	7.3	4.9	3.5	4.1	1.8	10.7	29.1	Fiji
19.2	7.3	10.4[2]	15.3	3,144	24.2	5.2	16.3	2.2	14.3	4.4	13.7	19.7	Finland
16.7	7.9	7.6[2]	13.3	3,449	22.0	4.3	13.9	1.1	13.1	5.0	19.2	21.3	France
10.7[13]	5.3[13]	9.2[2,13]	14.4[13]	2,820	34.5	4.9	16.1	2.1	7.3	5.9	7.7	21.5	French Guiana
12.2	12.3	6.9[2]	21.1	2,785	36.5	5.1	10.9	2.1	5.6	4.4	12.7	22.8	French Polynesia
6.3[13,20]	...	...	6.6[13,20]	...	24.2	24.3	6.2	1.9	2.8	13.8	8.3	18.5	Gabon
...	...	...	14.0[21]	2,351	65.9	1.0	2.5	1.3	1.7	0.5	12.0	15.2	Gambia, The
...	...	...	...	...	50.4	1.6	4.2	0.2	4.9	9.0	13.8	15.9	Gaza Strip
...	...	...	...	...	...	...	...	...	...	...	...	...	Georgia
15.5[22]	8.7[22]	10.7[2,22]	3.7[22]	3,648	21.9	4.6	16.0	0.7	10.0	5.5	18.8	22.5	Germany
3.3	3.8	3.9[2]	4.5	2,246	26.2	41.2	1.9	2.2	0.2	9.7	9.5	9.2	Ghana
13.3	10.0	...	14.0	...	...	...	...	...	...	...	...	...	Gibraltar
13.4	3.2	5.4	23.3	3,793	29.5	3.6	12.9	0.9	10.3	8.7	17.5	16.7	Greece
7.7	9.3	12.4	17.5	...	...	...	...	...	...	...	...	...	Greenland
4.0	6.5	...	10.0	2,657	30.4	3.4	6.9	2.4	12.1	8.0	7.6	29.2	Grenada
13.3	4	5.2	12.6	2,720	33.2	3.6	12.1	3.2	7.7	8.0	10.7	21.5	Guadeloupe
18.0	...	5.1	8.8	...	...	...	...	...	...	...	...	...	Guam
7.0	5.0	0.9	2.7	2,229	59.9	0.6	1.9	0.0	4.6	2.4	6.5	23.9	Guatemala
15.7	8.3	...	24.7	...	...	...	...	...	...	...	...	...	Guernsey
5.1	2.9	4.1	0.1	2,193	49.0	13.5	1.6	0.6	1.1	13.3	12.0	8.9	Guinea
...	...	...	...	...	57.7	8.2	3.9	0.3	2.3	5.4	12.6	9.6	Guinea-Bissau
4.8	2.9	6.4[2]	8.2	2,739	52.6	2.4	3.6	2.9	4.0	4.1	5.6	24.8	Guyana
...	4.0	...	6.6	2,011	37.9	12.3	3.7	0.4	2.0	10.2	4.7	28.8	Haiti
3.0	8.3	2.4[2]	3.5	2,229	54.5	0.7	2.3	0.2	5.6	5.4	12.1	19.4	Honduras
8.3	12.3	9.2	9.7	2,817	37.0	0.7	21.4	2.8	4.7	4.7	12.7	16.0	Hong Kong
7.1	7.4	7.1	13.9	3,638	29.2	2.4	13.3	0.2	8.5	4.4	20.1	22.0	Hungary
18.6	11.1	8.2	14.9	3,518	23.5	2.9	14.4	6.5	16.7	3.2	10.4	22.3	Iceland
8.3	4.5	1.6	5.4	2,196	62.3	1.8	0.4	0.3	4.9	3.2	8.2	19.0	India
...	3.0	...	13.5	2,708	68.0	7.1	1.1	1.1	0.5	2.2	6.0	14.0	Indonesia
3.2	3.1	1.2[2]	1.7	...	64.1	1.2	3.8	—	2.8	4.7	8.4	15.0	Iran
5.3	6.2	1.2	7.2	...	60.6	0.5	3.9	0.2	3.6	6.3	5.9	19.0	Iraq
12.6	7.0	8.0	13.3	3,779	22.7	6.8	18.6	0.8	11.0	3.6	13.7	22.7	Ireland
14.9	5.7	...	22.5	...	...	...	...	...	...	...	...	...	Isle of Man
3.1	8.7	...	30.7	3,150	32.0	2.0	7.8	0.9	10.5	8.7	19.1	19.0	Israel
12.9	8.9	8.3	17.2	3,508	32.2	2.1	11.1	1.0	10.5	7.0	19.9	16.3	Italy
12.4	5.5	2.1	26.1	2,622	36.3	8.3	6.4	1.1	5.7	7.5	11.2	23.4	Jamaica
10.2	3.9	9.4	25.4	2,909	41.7	2.8	5.8	6.3	6.1	4.6	12.0	20.6	Japan
13.9	7.1	...	21.0	...	...	...	...	...	...	...	...	...	Jersey
5.8	4.8	2.9	29.6	...	61.8	1.6	3.7	0.3	5.2	2.9	9.1	15.4	Jordan
...	...	...	...	...	...	...	...	...	...	...	...	...	Kazakhstan
8.4	9.4	3.1	9.1	2,159	60.3	5.0	2.8	0.4	3.7	2.7	5.1	20.0	Kenya
8.0	2.9	...	12.5	2,956	24.7	16.5	2.5	5.9	1.0	5.6	10.0	33.8	Kiribati
...	3.8[25]	...	15.9	2,797	69.1	5.6	3.0	2.3	0.9	4.3	2.8	12.1	Korea, North
7.3	5.3	10.7[2]	27.5	2,853	59.6	0.8	4.4	3.8	2.0	6.4	8.0	15.1	Korea, South
13.7	11.2	5.2[2]	7.9	3,146	35.5	1.2	11.4	0.6	9.4	8.2	14.4	19.3	Kuwait
...	...	...	...	...	...	...	...	...	...	...	...	...	Kyrgyzstan
...	...	...	...	...	83.4	1.4	5.5	0.6	1.3	2.5	1.1	4.2	Laos
...	...	...	71.5[20]	2,490	...	...	...	...	...	...	...	...	Latvia
5.4[13]	2.6[13]	1.9[13]	6.3[13]	...	52.7	2.0	3.6	0.2	3.9	6.0	8.0	23.6	Lebanon
4.7	13.2	2.4[2]	17.8	2,326	76.2	0.5	3.7	0.2	1.9	1.6	2.6	13.3	Lesotho
...	6.1[13]	...	25.8[13]	2,404	47.4	20.0	2.0	1.1	0.6	4.8	16.5	7.5	Liberia
9.4	4.6	8.5[2]	2.5	3,350	43.3	1.4	7.7	0.3	6.7	7.8	18.0	14.9	Libya
13.3	5.8	16.3[2]	6.6	...	...	...	...	...	...	...	...	...	Liechtenstein
...	...	...	...	2,110	...	...	...	...	...	...	...	...	Lithuania
17.9	10.3	4.1[2]	19.0	3,947	18.1	5.0	19.4	0.9	8.6	5.2	23.8	19.1	Luxembourg
4.9	4.5	...	13.0	2,199	41.7	2.9	17.1	1.6	5.4	4.3	12.2	14.7	Macau
6.5	4.2	3.3[2]	1.8	3,620	...	...	...	...	...	...	...	...	Macedonia
4.0	1.0	...	12.0	2,177	59.4	19.5	6.5	0.4	0.6	4.3	2.3	7.0	Madagascar
17.6[29]	9.6[29]	...	15.9[29]	2,098	67.0	4.3	1.4	0.9	0.7	4.4	2.7	18.6	Malawi
20.9	7.7	11.0	14.1	2,754	45.9	2.8	6.6	2.1	5.2	3.9	14.1	19.3	Malaysia
...	...	...	...	...	42.5	6.4	0.8	12.4	—	6.3	7.7	23.9	Maldives
10.0	1.0	...	12.0	2,234	76.9	2.1	3.6	0.6	2.0	0.9	5.0	8.8	Mali
15.9	8.6	6.7[2]	22.4	3,238	31.4	1.1	11.9	1.0	11.7	6.0	15.6	21.3	Malta
...	4	...	14.7	...	...	...	...	...	...	...	...	...	Marshall Islands
14.2	4	5.0[2]	11.5	2,743	31.7	5.7	9.8	3.1	6.2	9.4	7.8	26.4	Martinique
...	...	...	9.8[13]	2,599	53.9	0.3	4.0	1.0	13.8	1.8	9.9	15.3	Mauritania
10.0	6.4	—	6.5	2,823	52.3	1.1	3.1	1.2	6.1	1.3	10.8	24.1	Mauritius
5.4	...	...	7.9	...	...	...	...	...	...	...	...	...	Mayotte
9.8	12.2	5.3[2]	17.6	3,048	48.7	0.7	8.0	0.6	6.3	3.5	11.2	21.1	Mexico
...	...	...	26.5	...	...	...	...	...	...	...	...	...	Micronesia
...	...	...	...	...	...	...	...	...	...	...	...	...	Moldova
...	...	...	...	3,449	22.0	4.3	13.9	1.1	13.1	5.0	19.2	21.3	Monaco
...	...	...	...	2,449	49.0	3.5	24.6	0.2	4.0	0.7	6.6	11.4	Mongolia
8.0	5.0	...	17.0	3,005	56.9	1.1	2.3	0.8	1.9	3.0	9.9	24.1	Morocco
...	...	...	...	1,665	31.9	42.5	1.8	0.3	0.9	2.0	12.3	8.3	Mozambique
3.8[13]	0.5[13]	1.1[13]	7.5[13]	2,474	76.4	0.5	2.0	1.2	1.1	2.6	6.6	9.7	Myanmar (Burma)
...	...	...	...	...	47.7	14.2	13.8	—	4.8	1.8	10.0	7.7	Namibia
...	...	...	...	...	...	...	...	...	...	...	...	...	Nauru
2.1[13]	—	7.9[2,13]	6.5[13]	2,074	81.4	2.7	1.5	0.0	4.1	0.9	4.3	5.2	Nepal

Household budgets and consumption (continued)

country	income (latest) percent received by		by source (percent)				consumption expenditure per capita private final, U.S.$ 1990	by kind or end use (percent of household or personal budget; latest)					
	lowest 20% of households	highest 10% of households	wages, salaries	self-employment	transfer payments[a]	other[b]		food[c]	housing[d]	clothing[e]	health care	energy, water	education
Netherlands, The	6.9	23.0	50.1	...	21.5	28.4	10,970	16.8	14.6	6.8	12.5	4.0	0.3
Netherlands Antilles	...	...	...	...	...	...	4,110[10]	21.2[9,31]	16.8[11,31]	8.4[31]	2.3[31]	[11]	[2]
New Caledonia	...	...	54.9	21.3	23.8	—	5,410[5]	37.0	15.7	7.0	2.5	0.7	[2]
New Zealand	5.1[18]	28.7[18]	68.7	8.1	14.1	9.1	7,720[7]	16.6	22.7	4.6	...	...	...
Nicaragua	3.1[15]	...	...	...	...	...	310	...	...	...	...	...	...
Niger	...	...	...	...	...	...	268[7]	50.5	19.1[4]	7.3	...	...	...
Nigeria	...	...	36.2	49.4	4.3	10.1	140	52.0	8.0	7.0	3.0	2.0	4.0
Northern Mariana Islands	...	...	...	...	...	...	...	36.9	7.4	...	3.1	6.3	3.7
Norway	2.6	26.6	59.9	9.9	23.1	7.1	12,590	26.1[9]	19.8[11]	7.8	4.7	[11]	[2]
Oman	...	...	...	...	...	...	2,280[7]	...	...	...	...	...	...
Pakistan	7.8	31.3	22.0	55.0	...	23.0	250	54.0	9.0	9.0	3.0	6.0	3.0
Palau	...	...	...	...	...	...	...	...	...	...	...	...	...
Panama	2.0	44.2	85.3	[24]	9.2	5.5[24]	1,310	47.3	12.7[11]	4.8	4.9	[11]	[2]
Papua New Guinea	...	...	57.3	[24]	1.1	41.6[24]	510	40.9	12.5[4]	6.2	...	4.9	...
Paraguay	...	...	33.9	[24]	2.5	63.6[24]	920	48.7	16.4	9.7	3.4	—	1.5
Peru	4.4	35.8	34.2	56.7	4.4	4.7	1,260	35.6[9]	0.6[11]	11.5	4.9	[11]	[2]
Philippines	5.5	32.1	— 91.0 —		9.0		520	57.8	...	5.3	...	3.1	...
Poland	9.7	21.0	82.1	...	17.9	14.7	900	45.8	10.6	16.9	2.6	1.7	...
Portugal	5.2	33.4	42.0	25.0	21.6	11.4	3,580	34.8	2.0	10.3	4.5	3.0	1.4
Puerto Rico	3.2	34.7	59.3	6.2	25.5	9.0	5,630[7]	23.0	15.6[11]	8.6	8.0	[11]	3.3
Qatar	...	...	80.8	5.6	...	13.6	3,600[3]	24.5	35.1[4]	9.1	1.0	1.9	4.3
Réunion	3.1[18]	51.4[18]	— 67.5 —		29.7	2.8	4,820[5]	22.4	11.8	7.9	2.2	2.2	[2]
Romania	...	...	62.6		— 37.4 —		1,180	51.1	16.4[4,11]	15.7	1.2	[11]	[2]
Russia	...	...	77.7	3.8	13.2	5.3	4,860	...	...	...	...	...	...
Rwanda	...	...	16.5	[24]	9.5	74.0[24]	240	30.0	10.0	11.0	3.0	6.0	4.0
St. Kitts and Nevis	...	...	...	...	...	...	2,580	55.6[9]	7.6	7.5	...	6.6	...
St. Lucia	...	...	...	...	...	...	740[19]	49.6[9]	13.5	6.5	2.3	4.5	[2]
St. Vincent and the Grenadines	...	...	...	...	...	...	890[3]	62.6[9]	6.3	7.7	...	6.2	...
San Marino	...	...	...	...	...	...	...	30.4[9]	9.7[11]	8.8	5.1	[11]	[2]
São Tomé and Príncipe	...	...	...	...	...	...	400	...	...	...	...	...	...
Saudi Arabia	...	...	...	...	...	...	2,680[7]	52.2[17,32]	17.2[17,32]	6.6[17,32]	2.1[17,32]	1.8[17,32]	1.1[17,32]
Senegal	5.5	45.4	51.6[13]		— 48.4[13] —		650	50.0	8.0	11.0	2.0	4.0	5.0
Seychelles	4.1	35.6	77.2	3.8	3.2	15.8	3,110	53.9	13.6	4.2	0.4	9.1	...
Sierra Leone	5.6	37.8	27.9	61.6	...	10.5	90	64.4[9]	15.1[11]	3.5	1.6	[11]	[2]
Singapore	5.1	33.5	75.4	18.7	2.0	3.9	5,130	18.9	9.3[11]	7.4	4.1	[11]	1.0
Slovenia	...	...	59.4	14.5	17.5	8.6	5,100	31.3	3.5	8.9	4.2	6.6	[2]
Solomon Islands	...	...	74.1		— 25.9 —		820[3]	51.0	12.5[3,11]	4.9	...	[11]	...
Somalia	...	...	...	...	...	...	17	62.3[9,13]	15.3[13]	5.6[13]	...	4.3[13]	...
South Africa	1.9	39.4	76.7	[24]	3.3	20.0[24]	1,700	33.2	10.7[11]	7.6	4.5	[11]	0.9
Bophuthatswana	...	...	...	...	...	...	...	...	...	...	...	...	...
Ciskei	...	...	...	...	...	...	...	38.6[9]	10.8	12.2	2.8	...	1.8
Transkei	3.4	43.8	...	...	...	...	...	...	...	...	...	...	...
Venda	...	...	56.2	4.8	32.9	6.1	...	51.2	4.3	11.2	0.5	4.5	1.9
Spain	6.9[8]	24.5[8]	47.8	24.6	19.2	8.4	7,870	22.0[9]	12.6[11]	9.0	3.6	[11]	[2]
Sri Lanka	4.8	43.0	50.5	[24]	9.5	40.0[24]	360	54.1	2.0	6.4	1.2	2.8	1.0
Sudan, The	4.0	34.6	...	...	...	...	760	63.5	11.5	5.3	4.1	3.8	[2]
Suriname	9.3	...	74.6	...	3.2	22.2	1,207	39.9[13]	4.4[13]	11.0[13]	3.6[13]	6.9[13]	2.6[13]
Swaziland	2.8	54.5	44.4	22.2	— 33.4 —		540[3]	33.5[9]	13.4[11]	6.0	1.8	[11]	[2]
Sweden	5.3	18.6	60.1	8.2	22.8	8.9	13,730	20.3	20.6	7.3	2.6	4.0	0.1
Switzerland	6.0[33]	27.0[33]	64.5	[24]	14.5	21.0[24]	19,050	27.8[9]	14.3	4.5	9.8	4.8	[2]
Syria	6.0	...	...	...	...	...	1,450	48.8[9]	17.7	9.1	...	4.6	[2]
Taiwan	8.4	22.8	60.5	20.3	5.9	13.3	4,221	29.8	21.0	5.9	4.8	3.6	5.1
Tajikistan	...	...	— 75.6 —		— 24.4 —		1,440	...	...	...	...	...	...
Tanzania	5.8	35.6	33.8	59.8	...	6.4	125[7]	53.8[9]	8.6	10.8	4.5	6.6	0.8
Thailand	5.1	42.8	37.5	50.4	0.5	11.6	830	32.5	6.9	13.7	7.0	1.7	0.4
Togo	8.0	30.5	...	...	...	...	320	60.9	9.9[11]	7.7	1.6	[11]	0.6
Tonga	...	...	...	...	...	...	860[19]	49.3	10.5	5.6	0.3	2.7	...
Trinidad and Tobago	2.6	33.6	...	...	...	...	2,130	27.7	22.7	15.5	2.2	1.1	1.5
Tunisia	4.1	37.6	...	...	...	...	940	39.0	10.7	6.0	3.0	5.1	1.8
Turkey	3.5[8]	41.5[8]	24.1	51.4	10.8	13.7	1,220	33.1	14.7	12.3	...	...	...
Turkmenistan	...	...	...	...	...	...	2,410	...	...	...	...	...	...
Tuvalu	...	...	17.9	76.1	...	6.0	...	55.5[9]	11.5[4]	7.5	...	...	...
Ukraine	...	...	70.5	5.3	15.7	8.5	2,760	...	...	...	...	...	...
Uganda	6.2	...	88.3[13,34]	1.8[13,34]	— 9.9[13,34] —		190	58.0[13,32]	...	14.0[13,32]	...	6.0[13,32]	...
United Arab Emirates	...	...	...	...	...	...	8,240	...	...	...	...	...	...
United Kingdom	7.2[8]	19.1[8]	61.8	13.3	12.7	12.2	10,860	18.9	15.9	6.2	1.3	3.6	0.8
United States	4.7	25.0	64.2	8.5	14.6	12.7	14,630	18.4	15.5	7.5	14.0	4.0	1.9
Uruguay	6.0[8,17]	29.3[8,17]	53.5	20.8	— 30.1 —		1,610	39.9	17.6[11]	7.0	9.3	[11]	1.3
Uzbekistan	...	...	— 70.9 —		13.6	15.5	2,150	...	...	...	...	...	...
Vanuatu	...	...	60.8	26.8	...	12.4	590[7]	50.2[9]	4.8	5.2	2.0	4.2	1.0
Venezuela	4.7	34.2	...	...	...	...	1,520	41.5[9]	7.6	9.4	[35]	1.9	[2]
Vietnam	...	...	...	...	...	...	...	25.3[36]	24.9[36]	5.4[36]	...	6.5[36]	...
Virgin Islands (U.S.)	...	...	65.7	2.6	13.0	12.7	...	...	...	...	...	...	...
West Bank	...	...	...	...	...	...	1,380[6]	...	...	...	...	...	...
Western Sahara	...	...	...	...	...	...	...	...	...	...	...	...	...
Western Samoa	...	...	49.4	22.8	...	27.8	710	58.8	5.1[4]	4.2	...	5.0	...
Yemen	...	...	...	...	...	...	580[7,37]	...	...	...	...	...	...
Yugoslavia[38]	6.1	26.6	32.3	[24]	16.0	51.7[24]	1,610	54.1[9]	1.9	11.6	3.7	7.9	[2]
Zaire	...	...	...	...	...	...	200	61.7	11.5[11]	9.7	2.6	[11]	[2]
Zambia	3.4	46.4	79.9	17.8	1.3	1.0	290	37.0	6.0	10.0	7.0	5.0	13.0
Zimbabwe	3.0	55.5	...	...	...	...	360	30.1[9]	6.5	10.3	3.8	7.3	6.0

[1]1982. [2]Recreation includes education. [3]1988. [4]Housing includes household durable goods. [5]1987. [6]1986. [7]1989. [8]Based on post-tax income. [9]Includes tobacco. [10]1985. [11]Housing includes energy, water. [12]Middle-income families in São Paulo. [13]Capital city only. [14]Includes wage taxes. [15]Rural only. [16]Highest 20 percent. [17]Urban areas only. [18]Based on post-tax per capita income. [19]1984. [20]Wage earners only. [21]Low-income population in Banjul and Kombo St. Mary only. [22]Former West Germany only. [23]Urban areas of Eastern Region only. [24]Other

transportation, communications	household durable goods f	recreation g	personal effects, other h	daily available calories per capita (1987–89)	cereals	potatoes, cassava	meat, poultry	fish	eggs, milk	fruits, vegetables	fats, oils	other i	country
11.3	8.2	9.6	15.9	3,163	18.2	5.0	11.7	0.5	13.7	5.3	23.5	22.1	Netherlands, The
23.6[31]	10.2[31]	6.6[2,31]	10.9[31]	2,827	30.6	3.2	16.8	2.1	9.2	7.5	13.3	17.4	Netherlands Antilles
10.4	11.4	5.4[2]	9.9	2,863	36.2	7.3	10.8	1.4	6.0	4.3	12.7	21.3	New Caledonia
18.3	13.6	...	24.2	3,389	20.7	3.0	18.0	1.6	13.0	6.2	14.6	22.9	New Zealand
...	...	...	...		40.5	1.2	6.1	0.4	7.7	5.1	9.7	29.3	Nicaragua
	4	...	23.1	2,297	68.5	3.8	3.3	0.0	2.7	1.5	3.6	16.4	Niger
4.0	6.0	...	14.0	2,306	44.4	26.6	1.7	0.4	0.6	3.8	10.0	12.6	Nigeria
18.2	7.5	4.0	12.9										Northern Mariana Islands
12.9	7.3	9.3[2]	12.1	3,338	26.8	4.9	11.7	2.3	13.7	4.6	17.5	18.4	Norway
...	...	...	...										Oman
1.0	5.0	...	10.0	2,197	58.5	0.4	2.4	0.2	5.7	2.7	15.5	14.6	Pakistan
													Palau
6.8	8.5	5.8[2]	9.2	2,537	38.8	2.9	8.7	1.6	5.3	5.1	14.2	23.6	Panama
13.0	4	...	22.5		15.4	34.5	6.3	1.9	0.6	23.7	4.4	13.2	Papua New Guinea
4.5	6.2	2.3	7.3	2,755	30.8	15.8	12.9	0.2	4.1	9.2	7.7	19.3	Paraguay
5.1	10.8	10.8[2]	20.7	2,244	45.4	8.3	5.4	1.2	5.2	4.1	7.6	22.8	Peru
2.3	13.5	...	18.0	2,342	62.2	4.9	5.1	3.2	1.7	4.6	5.0	13.3	Philippines
6.2	...	10.1	6.1	3,464	33.8	5.7	11.8	1.1	10.9	3.2	15.7	17.8	Poland
15.4	8.6	4.4	15.6	3,414	37.6	5.4	10.8	2.6	6.2	4.6	15.8	17.0	Portugal
13.9	7.4	4.0	16.2										Puerto Rico
13.0	4	—11.1—											Qatar
24.9	6.0	10.1[2]	12.5	3,072	45.6	1.9	10.7	1.7	4.6	3.4	13.5	18.6	Réunion
6.6	4	4.5[2]	4.5	3,252	41.9	4.1	8.0	0.8	9.0	7.0	12.6	16.6	Romania
...	...	...	...										Russia
9.0	9.0	...	18.0	1,945	13.1	30.2	1.2	0.0	1.6	13.1	2.5	38.3	Rwanda
4.3	9.4	...	9.0	2,614	31.3	4.9	11.5	1.7	8.2	3.3	12.8	26.2	St. Kitts and Nevis
6.3	5.8	3.2[2]	8.3	2,582	28.6	7.1	8.5	1.1	7.1	11.5	10.1	20.8	St. Lucia
3.7	6.6	...	6.9	2,618	36.2	11.0	8.7	0.8	4.0	4.1	8.4	26.9	St. Vincent and the Grenadines
14.5	7.5	8.1[2]	15.9	3,508	32.2	2.1	11.1	1.0	10.5	7.0	19.9	16.3	San Marino
...	...	...	...	2,380	38.7	13.1	1.6	2.0	1.3	2.9	17.8	22.5	São Tomé and Príncipe
4.5[17,32]	5.9[17,32]	...	8.6[17,32]	2,842	45.5	0.6	7.4	0.5	7.5	10.3	11.6	16.7	Saudi Arabia
6.0	2.0	...	12.0	2,374	68.1	1.2	4.0	2.5	2.9	1.2	6.6	13.4	Senegal
6.4	6.6	1.4	4.4	2,340	46.8	1.1	5.2	4.2	7.1	3.4	8.2	24.1	Seychelles
7.7	3.1	2.2[2]	4.0	1,841	54.4	6.0	1.2	1.7	0.5	3.9	19.9	12.4	Sierra Leone
14.4	9.0	13.5	22.4	3,249	35.1	2.8	16.1	2.6	5.5	7.2	6.6	24.1	Singapore
12.8	5.4	5.9[2]	1.0	3,620									Slovenia
6.6	...	...	25.0	2,191	25.9	35.3	3.2	5.4	1.0	3.0	8.2	18.0	Solomon Islands
...	...	...	12.1[13]	1,932	50.3	0.8	6.6	0.2	20.3	2.0	8.5	11.2	Somalia
15.6	10.5	5.8	11.2	3,104	54.0	1.5	8.1	0.6	4.4	2.5	9.0	20.0	South Africa
...	...	...	...		...	...	...	...	...	...	...	...	Bophuthatswana
													Ciskei
													Transkei
8.5	7.7	1.2	16.3										Venda
5.4	11.9	0.9	8.2										
15.7	6.6	6.5[2]	24.0	3,567	23.8	5.5	18.0	1.5	9.4	6.7	15.9	19.1	Spain
14.6	4.7	2.8	10.4	2,299	58.3	3.2	0.5	1.2	2.6	4.5	4.2	25.6	Sri Lanka
1.5	5.5	0.8[2]	4.0	2,028	51.7	1.1	5.8	0.1	12.4	3.5	9.3	16.3	Sudan, The
9.5[13]	12.3[13]	5.8[13]	4.0[13]	2,908	54.4	1.6	5.6	0.3	5.3	2.9	8.2	21.7	Suriname
8.8	12.8	3.3	20.4	2,612	52.5	0.7	6.1	0.0	3.5	2.9	7.0	27.4	Swaziland
18.3	6.6	9.7	10.5	2,945	20.7	4.4	10.4	2.1	16.3	4.8	20.3	21.0	Sweden
12.0	5.3	10.5[2]	11.0	3,565	20.6	2.5	18.2	0.6	12.9	6.0	16.8	22.3	Switzerland
3.8	5.1	3.1[2]	7.8	3,074	50.0	1.5	3.8	0.1	6.4	7.8	12.1	18.2	Syria
8.8	4.3	1.3	15.4										Taiwan
...	...	...	...										Tajikistan
6.4	6.3	1.6	0.6	2,209	47.4	20.1	2.3	1.3	1.9	8.5	5.7	12.8	Tanzania
10.9	8.0	3.6	15.3	2,312	61.1	2.5	4.9	1.7	1.3	5.9	3.0	19.6	Thailand
8.2	3.9	0.4	6.8	2,141	47.5	28.9	2.5	1.0	0.6	1.5	6.1	12.2	Togo
5.8	10.6	0.5	14.7	2,980	16.9	38.8	10.7	1.2	1.3	4.3	7.0	19.8	Tonga
13.2	8.8	1.4	5.9	2,913	37.3	4.2	5.9	0.9	8.9	3.9	13.1	25.8	Trinidad and Tobago
9.0	11.2	7.1	7.1	3,081	56.7	1.3	2.7	0.6	4.9	5.5	13.9	14.3	Tunisia
...	11.5	...	28.4	3,170	49.8	4.0	2.9	0.4	3.8	8.7	14.1	16.6	Turkey
													Turkmenistan
10.5	4	...	25.0										Tuvalu
													Ukraine
10.0[13,32]	...	...	12.0[13,32]	2,136	28.7	28.0	2.4	1.2	1.8	17.2	1.4	19.3	Uganda
...	...	...	...	3,295	33.4	1.2	9.2	1.0	8.3	15.4	11.3	20.1	United Arab Emirates
17.7	6.9	8.8	19.9	3,181	19.7	6.2	15.9	0.8	11.6	4.4	17.8	23.4	United Kingdom
12.3	7.7	7.7	11.0	3,676	19.7	2.6	18.7	0.7	11.5	5.4	17.0	24.3	United States
10.4	6.3	3.1	5.1	2,697	37.1	3.5	19.8	0.3	11.2	3.8	9.9	14.5	Uruguay
...	...	...	...										Uzbekistan
18.7	2.7	0.8	10.4	2,552	27.6	21.2	13.0	1.7	1.8	3.4	8.3	23.2	Vanuatu
5.2	3.6	4.8[2]	26.0[35]	2,620	37.5	2.2	9.2	0.9	9.0	6.2	13.7	21.4	Venezuela
...	...	...	...		72.9	8.6	4.8	2.2	0.1	2.6	2.0	6.8	Vietnam
11.7[36]	4.3[36]	...	21.9[36]										Virgin Islands (U.S.)
...	...	...	...		44.4	1.9	6.1	0.1	6.2	11.0	12.5	17.8	West Bank
...	...	...	...		...	...	...	...	...	...	...	...	Western Sahara
9.0	4	...	17.9	2,509	20.1	19.1	12.0	3.6	1.2	13.2	8.4	22.4	Western Samoa
...	...	...	...		65.8	1.4	4.0	0.6	3.7	3.8	6.1	14.6	Yemen
8.9	4.3	5.1[2]	2.5	3,620	44.2	2.5	8.0	0.3	8.0	3.7	16.3	17.0	Yugoslavia[38]
5.9	4.8	3.8[2]	...	2,061	16.9	55.7	2.0	0.9	0.2	7.1	7.4	9.8	Zaire
5.0	1.0	...	16.0	2,054	73.1	4.6	2.5	0.9	1.4	1.5	2.6	13.4	Zambia
6.1	11.1	0.6	18.2	2,288	59.6	1.4	2.8	0.2	1.5	1.1	9.8	23.5	Zimbabwe

includes self-employment.   [25]Workers and clerical workers only.   [26]Excludes single-person households and self-employed.   [27]Earned income only.   [28]Malagasy households only.   [29]Blantyre and Lilongwe only.   [30]Housing includes water.   [31]Curaçao and Bonaire only.   [32]Middle-income population only.   [33]Excludes transfers and property income.   [34]Unskilled African workers only.   [35]Personal effects, other includes health care.   [36]St. Thomas only.   [37]Former Yemen Arab Republic only.   [38]Data refer to Yugoslavia as constituted prior to 1991.

Health services

The provision of health services in most countries is both a principal determinant of the quality of life and a large and growing sector of the national economy. This table summarizes the basic indicators of health manpower; hospitals, by kind and utilization; mortality rates that are most indicative of general health services; external controls on health (adequacy of food supply and availability of safe drinking water); and sources and amounts of expenditure on health care. Each datum refers more or less directly to the availability or use of a particular health service in a country, and, while each may be an accurate measure at a national level, each may also conceal considerable differences in availability of the particular service to different segments of a population or regions of a country. In the United States, for example, the availability of physicians ranges from about one per 830 persons in the least well-served states to one per 310 in the best-served, with a rate of one per 170 in the national capital. Such disparities are even more pronounced in most other countries, unless the government has made some special effort to achieve a more even distribution of manpower and facilities. In addition, even when trained manpower exists and facilities have been created, the country may lose health professionals via the "brain drain" to foreign countries; or low levels of financial support at the national level may leave facilities underserved; or lack of good transportation may prevent those most in need from reaching a clinic or hospital that could help them.

Definitions and limits of data have been made as specific as possible in the compilation of this table. For example, despite wide variation worldwide in the nature of the qualifying or certifying process that permits an individual to represent himself as a physician, organizations such as the World Health Organization (WHO) try to maintain more consistent international standards for training and qualification. International statistics presented here for "physicians" refer to persons qualified according to WHO standards and exclude traditional health practitioners, whatever the local custom with regard to the designation "doctor." Statistics for health manpower in this table uniformly include all those actually working in the health service field, whether in the actual provision of services or in teaching, administration, research, or other tasks. One group of practitioners for whom this type of guideline works less well is that of midwives, whose training and qualifications vary enormously from country to country but who must be included, as they represent, after nurses, perhaps the largest and most important category of health auxiliary worldwide. The statistics here refer to those midwives working in some kind of institutional setting (a hospital, clinic, community health-care centre, or the like) and exclude rural noninstitutional midwives and traditional birth attendants.

Hospitals also differ considerably worldwide in terms of staffing and services. In this tabulation, the term hospital refers generally to a permanent facility offering inpatient services and/or nursing care and staffed by at least one physician. Establishments offering only outpatient or custodial care are excluded. These statistics are broken down into data for general hospitals (those providing care in more than one specialty), specialized facilities (with care in only one specialty), local medical centres, and rural health-care centres; the last two generally refer to institutions that provide a more limited range of medical or nursing care, often less than full-time. Hospital data are further analyzed into three categories of administrative classification: public, private nonprofit, and private for profit. Statistics on

Health services

country	year	physicians	dentists	nurses	pharmacists	midwives	population per physician	year	number	general	specialized	medical centres	rural	government	private nonprofit	private for profit	hospital beds per 10,000 pop.
										kinds (%)				**ownership (%)**			
Afghanistan	1987	2,957	329	2,135	206[1]	529[1]	4,797	1982	68	66.2	16.2	—	17.6	86.8	13.2	—	5
Albania	1989	5,570[6]	[6]	...	772[7]	9,936[7]	574[6]	1989	895	—17.9—		—82.1—		100.0	—	—	57
Algeria	1988	19,814	6,097	24,700[11]	1,811	3,800[11]	1,199	1988	264[12]	...	...	...	...				25[13]
American Samoa	1989	34	7	140	2	1	1,384	1990	1	100.0	—	—	—	100.0	—	—	27
Andorra	1988	112	...	...	2[14]	...	441	1988	1	100.0	—	—	—	100.0	—	—	23
Angola	1990	662	...	9,145	...	1,237[17]	15,136	1990	58	...	...	...	...				12
Antigua and Barbuda	1987	48	7	207	27[17]	...	1,606	1986	2	50.0	50.0	—	—	100.0	—	—	51
Argentina	1988	96,000	22,500	17,118	681[14]	...	328	1980	3,189	84.2	15.8	—	—	41.9	3.6	54.5	48[7]
Armenia	1990	14,519[6]	[6]	35,000[20]	...	20	246[6]	1990	181	...	...	...	...	100.0	—	—	85
Aruba	1990	69	18	491	10	3	918	1990	2	50.0	—	50.0	—	100.0	—	—	34
Australia	1986	36,610	5,721[1]	139,434[20]	9,800[21]	20	438	1990	1,071[19]	...	...	...	...	65.5[19]	—34.5[19]—		50
Austria	1991	23,238	3,317	30,842	2,024[22]	801	334	1991	320	39.7	60.3	—	—	...	...	...	103
Azerbaijan	1990	28,000[6]	[6]	70,400[20]	...	20	255[6]	1990	894	...	...	...	...	100.0	—	—	102
Bahamas, The	1988	303	31[14]	952[11]	37[24]	120[24]	809	1985	5	60.0	20.0	20.0	—	60.0	—40.0—		40[13]
Bahrain	1988	664	19[11]	1,148[11,20]	68[1]	20	713	1988	12	42.7	58.3	—	—	75.0	16.7	8.3	31
Bangladesh	1990	19,387	447[17]	9,274	...	7,485	5,500	1990	875	68.9[17]	5.1[17]	23.1[17]	2.9[17]	69.5	—30.5—		3
Barbados	1986	243	25[14]	760[14]	...	436[14]	1,042	1982	11	27.3	18.2	—	54.5	81.8	—	18.2	83[7]
Belarus	1990	41,400[6]	[6]	118,100[20]	...	20	248[6]	1990	874	...	...	...	...	100.0	—	—	132
Belgium	1990	32,984	7,050	91,263[1]	12,014	4,920[1]	302	1982	531	53.3	46.7	—	—	36.3	—63.7—		93[13]
Belize	1990	121	13	229	14	175[7]	1,543	1990	7	...	...	...	...	100.0	—	—	32
Benin	1983	238	13[24]	1,317	55[24]	323	16,025	1980	131	4.6	9.9	80.9	4.6	87.8	12.2	—	13[1]
Bermuda	1990	89	21	548	36	...	661	1989	2	50.0	50.0	—	—	...	...	...	68
Bhutan	1989	157	...	231[13]	18[13]	72[13]	8,969	1989	26	...	...	...	...	...	...	...	7
Bolivia	1987[31]	3,174	1,298	2,319	...	...	2,124	1987[32]	553	—14.8—		27.3	57.9	...	...	...	15
Bosnia and Hercegovina	1989	6,929	1,368	...	781	...	624	1989	...	...	...	...	...	...	...	...	46
Botswana	1986	156	14	1,530	10[24]	714[24]	7,185	1984	22	—63.6—		36.4	—	72.7	—27.3—		23
Brazil	1987	206,382	28,772	306,411[24]	6,094	2,526[24]	685	1987	28,972[11]	15.0[11]	4.6[11]	—80.4[11]—		58.9[11]	—41.1[11]—		36
Brunei	1990	171	30	870	8	173	1,473	1990	8	87.5	—	—	12.5	87.5	—12.5—		35
Bulgaria	1990	28,497	6,109	61,427	4,366	7,544	315	1990	256	74.6	25.4	—	—	...	...	...	98
Burkina Faso	1988	280	17	1,993	104	292	29,914	1988	66	3.0	—	83.4	13.6	100.0	—	—	7[14]
Burundi	1990	168[31]	10[7]	670[31]	29[7]	97[31]	31,777[31]	1988	264	—12.5—		—87.5—		87.5	—12.5—		19[23]
Cambodia	1988	303	...	1,818	130[14]	619	27,000	1988	188[32]	84.9[14]	15.1[14]	—	—	100.0	—	—	16
Cameroon	1986	833	17[1]	3,216[1]	96[1]	399[1]	12,540	1988	629	—27.0—		—73.0—		72.3	—27.7—		27[14]
Canada	1989	58,470	13,503[7]	241,955[7]	16,348[7]	...	449	1978	1,226	65.8	26.9	7.3	—	93.4	—	6.6	70[34]
Cape Verde	1987	77	3[24]	186[14]	7[24]	10[14]	4,208	1980	21	9.5	4.8	61.9	23.8	100.0	—	—	19[7]
Cayman Islands	1990	42	8	121	8[13]	14	669	1990	2	100.0	—	—	—	100.0	—	—	26
Central African Republic	1988	154	6	376	19	188	17,292	1988	133	—21.1—		—78.9—		79.7	—20.3—		15
Chad	1980	94	...	...	...	...	47,640	1978	4	100.0	—	—	—	—	—	100.0	8
Chile	1990	14,344	1,319[31,34]	...	203[31,34]	1,629[31,34]	919	1990	220	51.4[1]	19.0[1]	—	29.6[1]	83.2	—16.8—		33
China	1990	1,763,000[36]	...	1,056,000[34]	402,000[34]	59,000[34]	643[36]	1989	61,929	15.6	5.8	—78.6—		100.0	—	—	23
Colombia	1988	29,353	13,815	43,065	...	20	1,079	1983	946	—79.6—		—20.4—		82.1[24]	17.9[24]	—	17
Comoros	1984	31	4	168[20]	3	20	12,237	1980	17	17.7	—	23.5	58.8	100.0	—	—	23[1]
Congo	1989	567	...	2,500[1]	...	246[1]	3,873	1978	473	0.6	0.2	97.3	1.9	94.9	5.1	—	22[34]
Cook Islands	1986	15	8[1,31]	57[20]	2[21,31]	20	1,147	1981	8	12.5	—	—	87.5	100.0	—	—	89
Costa Rica	1989	3,686	790[14]	1,300[14]	702[14]	...	798	1980	39	48.7	28.2	—23.1—		92.3	—	7.7	22[23]
Côte d'Ivoire	1982	502	...	...	...	...	17,847	1988	...	...	...	...	...	...	...	...	9
Croatia	1989	10,160	2,157	...	1,886	...	466	1989	...	...	...	...	...	...	...	...	75
Cuba	1989	34,752	6,482	58,589	650[17]	...	303	1986	261	28.0	—47.1—		24.9	100.0	—	—	71[34]
Cyprus	1989[38]	1,172	417	2,450[20]	93[17]	20	480	1989[38]	124[1]	3.2[1]	—89.5[1]—		7.3[1]	12.1[1]	0.8[1]	87.1[1]	60
Czechoslovakia	1991	50,014	8,526	146,952[7]	7,375[7]	6,792[1]	311	1990	397	59.4	40.6	—	—	100.0	—	—	100
Denmark	1990	14,277	4,562	34,756	1,498[15]	915[11]	360	1990	127[1]	87.4[1]	12.6[1]	—	—	91.3[1]	8.7[1]	—	64
Djibouti	1989	97	10	359[14]	14	175[14]	5,258	1989[32]	13	—69.2—		30.8	—	100.0	—	—	27
Dominica	1990	37	4[13]	273[13,20]	12	20	1,947	1988	10	—30.0—		—70.0—		100.0	—	—	41[23]
Dominican Republic	1988	7,332	689	5,398	129[17]	...	934	1987	103	—44.7—		—55.3—		...	...	...	20
Ecuador	1984	11,033	4,292	14,794	...	...	826	1984	337	16.6	7.1	49.6	26.7	...	...	...	16[13]

number of beds refer to beds that are maintained and staffed on a full-time basis for a succession of inpatients to whom care is provided.

Data on hospital utilization refer to institutions defined as above. Admission and discharge, the two principal points at which statistics are normally collected, are the basis for the data on the amount and distribution of care by kind of facility. The data on numbers of patients exclude babies born during a maternal confinement but include persons who die before being discharged. The bed-occupancy and average length-of-stay statistics depend on the concept of a "patient-day," which is the annual total of daily censuses of inpatients. The bed-occupancy rate is the ratio of total patient-days to potential days based on the number of beds; the average length-of-stay rate is the ratio of total patient-days to total admissions. Bed-occupancy rates may exceed 100% because stays of partial days are counted as full days.

Two measures that give health planners and policy makers an excellent indication of the level of ordinary health care are those for mortality of children under age five and for maternal mortality. The former reflects the probability of a newborn infant dying before age five. The latter refers to deaths attributable to delivery or complications of pregnancy, childbirth, the puerperium (the period immediately following birth), or abortion.

Levels of nutrition and access to safe drinking water are two of the most basic limitations imposed by the physical environment in which health-care activities take place. The nutritional data are based on recommendations of the United Nations' Food and Agriculture Organization for the necessary daily intake (in calories) for a moderately active person of average size in a climate of a particular kind (fewer calories are needed in a hot

climate) to remain in average *good* health. Excess intake in the many developed countries ranges to more than 40% above the minimum required to maintain health (the excess usually being construed to diminish, rather than raise, health). The range of deficiency is less dramatic numerically but far more critical to the countries in which deficiencies are chronic, because the deficiencies lead to overall poor health (raising health service needs and costs), to decreased productivity in nearly every area of national economic life, and to the loss of social and economic potential through early mortality. By "safe" water is meant only water that has no substantial quantities of chemical or biological pollutants, *i.e.*, quantities sufficient to cause "immediate" health problems.

Two principal kinds of public health-care finance data are given: health insurance and central government expenditure. The data on insurance refer to public programs only and identify the mandated basis or extent of responsibility for costs or funding required under the relevant law of the principal participants (individuals, employers, and government). Data on public health-care expenditure refer to a consolidated statement of expenditure, budgetary and otherwise, by all elements of the central government but exclude expenditure by other levels (state, city, etc.). In a number of countries significant government expenditures for health-care services are made at these other levels, amounting to 2, 10, and sometimes 20 times the level of central government expenditure. These expenditures may include costs for national health insurance, family-planning programs, and workmen's compensation. Expenditures at the national level for social security are excluded.

admissions or discharges					mortality		popu-lation with access to safe water (latest) (%)	food supply (% of FAO require-ment) 1987–89	financing of public health care, latest year					country
rate per 10,000 pop.	by kinds of hospital (%)				bed occu-pancy rate (%)	aver-age length of stay (days)	under age 5 per 1,000 live newborn 1985–90	maternal mortality per 100,000 live births 1988–89			health-care insurance			public health expendi-tures (% of natl. budget)	public health expendi-tures per capita (U.S.$)	
	general	special-ized	medical centres	rural							indiv. (% of earn-ings)	em-ployer (% of payroll)	govt. (% of covered earnings)			
76[2]	52.8[2]	46.7[2]	—	0.5[2]	58.0[2]	8[2]	318	690[3]	21	86[4]	—	—	—	...	2.10[5]	Afghanistan
...	...	...	...	...	...	...	48	...	97	121[8]	—	8.0[9]	10	...	27.00[5]	Albania
568[14]	...	...	...	...	...	...	105	130[3]	71	117	1.5	15	—	...	35.30[5]	Algeria
965	100.0	—	—	—	38.4	4	30[16]	...	...	...	...	...	...	25.5	318.80	American Samoa
...	...	...	...	...	...	...	17[16]	...	100	...	...	...	...	...	...	Andorra
238	...	...	...	...	44.5[18]	16[18]	232	...	35	77[4]	...	...	...	...	11.00[5]	Angola
63[19]	...	...	...	...	49.9[19]	7[19]	27[16]	...	100	98	3.0[9]	5.0[9]	—	...	66.60[5]	Antigua and Barbuda
...	...	...	...	...	...	...	38	48.8[7]	57	132	3.0	6.0	—	2.0	15.80	Argentina
...	...	...	...	...	...	...	...	34.6	...	...	...	...	...	7.9	...	Armenia
...	...	...	...	...	...	...	27[16]	...	...	...	...	...	...	...	...	Aruba
...	...	...	...	...	...	...	10	4.9	99	120	15	—	10	12.8	550.20	Australia
2,493[23]	...	...	...	...	79.9[23]	12[23]	12	7.9	100	133	3.2[15]	3.2[15]	...	12.9	1,016.60	Austria
...	...	...	...	...	...	...	...	28.6	...	...	...	...	...	0.7	...	Azerbaijan
979[12]	77.0	—23.0—		—	...	...	27[16]	69.3[7]	100	115	1.7[9, 25]	7.1[9, 26]	—	13.4	274.30	Bahamas, The
1,274	...	...	...	...	80.0	7	32	7.9[7]	100	...	—	—	—	7.7	204.10	Bahrain
853[7]	...	...	...	...	...	...	188	600[3]	76	86	—	—	—	5.4	1.10	Bangladesh
842	93.9	4.6	—	1.5	89.8[12]	34[12]	14	26.7	100	134	0.7	0.7	—	11.9	263.10	Barbados
...	...	...	...	...	...	...	16	24.8	...	...	...	...	...	18.0	...	Belarus
1,552	91.0	9.0	—	—	85.3	19	12	3.4[17]	100	150	3.7	6.0	...	1.8	131.90	Belgium
...	...	...	...	...	...	...	...	43.2[27]	75	118	15	15	10	7.8	58.10	Belize
...	...	...	...	...	...	...	184	1,680[28]	35	98	—	0.2[29]	—	5.6	3.30	Benin
1,327	96.6	3.4	—	—	83.0	16	11[16]	...	...	118	...	...	...	14.5	678.90	Bermuda
3,796[13, 30]	...	...	...	...	...	...	196	1,710[3]	34	90[24]	...	...	...	5.3	4.20	Bhutan
...	...	...	...	...	...	...	171	480[3]	47	82	—	10.0	—	2.3	2.50	Bolivia
529[19]	...	...	...	...	82.4[19]	11[19]	...	56.0	...	...	...	...	...	...	...	Bosnia and Hercegovina
691[24]	89.1[24]	6.7[24]	4.2[24]	—	90.0[19]	10[19]	92	250[3]	58	102	—	—	—	4.8	35.90	Botswana
...	...	...	...	...	...	...	86	65.3[17]	96	114	15	15	15	7.2	78.70	Brazil
1,069[1]	98.5[1]	—	—	1.5[1]	38.0[1]	4[1]	...	...	100	126	—	—	—	3.4	186.40	Brunei
2,118[1]	...	...	...	...	84.4[1]	16[1]	19	18.7	99	147	—	30.0[9]	10	4.1	109.50	Bulgaria
...	...	...	...	...	...	...	235	810[3]	67	96	—	11.5[33]	—	5.2	1.80	Burkina Faso
109[11]	...	...	...	...	...	...	191	...	38	86	—	—	—	...	1.80[5]	Burundi
...	...	...	...	...	...	...	192	...	3	97[4]	...	...	...	...	...	Cambodia
...	...	...	...	...	...	...	153	300[3]	34	95	—	7.0[33]	—	3.4	6.50	Cameroon
1,677	93.9	6.0	0.1	—	75.7[1]	13[1]	9	4.1	100	130	15	15	15	5.5	253.50	Canada
...	...	...	...	...	...	...	86	107.4[24]	71	115	3.0	2.0	...	...	...	Cape Verde
1,250	100.0	—	—	—	62.0[35]	4[35]	27[16]	...	99	...	—	—	—	14.9	611.00	Cayman Islands
326[14]	...	...	...	...	41.9[14]	7[14]	223	600[3]	12	89	—	12.0[29, 33]	—	5.1	3.30	Central African Republic
...	...	...	...	...	...	...	223	960[3]	29	77[4]	—	6.0[33]	—	3.8	0.60	Chad
797[7]	84.9[24]	9.3[24]	—	5.8[24]	73.8[7]	8[7]	24	48.3[7]	89	105	15	...	...	5.9	30.40	Chile
182[11]	...	...	...	...	82.7[11]	16[11]	44	44[3]	72	112	—	37	...	...	4.00[5]	China
385[1]	...	...	...	...	59.3[1]	6[1]	68	86.1[11]	93	111	2.3	4.7	...	4.5	8.90	Colombia
...	...	...	...	...	...	...	127	50[3]	63	81	—	—	—	7.3	12.20	Comoros
...	...	...	...	...	...	...	115	900[3]	21	117	...	0.2	—	...	20.60[5]	Congo
1,352	70.7	—	—	29.3	43.6[19]	9[19]	30[16]	...	92	...	...	...	...	...	...	Cook Islands
1,192	77.8	16.7	—5.5—		75.7	8	22	18.4	91	125	5.5	9.3	0.8	19.0	66.90	Costa Rica
...	...	...	...	...	...	...	148	...	69	112	—	0.5	—	4.0	8.60	Côte d'Ivoire
733[19]	...	...	...	...	83.4[19]	12[19]	...	3.6	...	...	...	...	...	...	...	Croatia
1,619	32.3	—64.2—		3.5	74.4[1]	11[1]	18	38.8	82	136	—	10.0[9, 33]	10	...	52.40[5]	Cuba
729	96.1	1.2	—	2.7	71.6[19]	7[17, 19]	16	...	100	140[14]	...	...	...	6.4[38]	186.10[38]	Cyprus
1,727	95.2	4.8	—	—	73.0	15	16	9.6	100	146	—	50.0[9]	10	0.4	6.80	Czechoslovakia
2,158	98.3	1.7	—	—	82.4	9	9	8.1	100	135	—	—	10	1.1	91.70	Denmark
...	...	...	...	...	...	...	188[16]	740[3]	45	...	—	—	—	8.2	20.60	Djibouti
729[8]	...	...	...	...	...	...	33[16]	48.2[27]	77	117	3.0[9]	6.8[9]	—	8.8	22.70	Dominica
488	...	...	...	...	55.3	4	82	93.6[11]	63	104	2.5[9]	7.0[9]	2.5[9]	10.2	13.10	Dominican Republic
471	...	...	...	...	60.4	8	87	155.6	58	110	5.0[9]	7.0[9]	...	11.0	17.00	Ecuador

Health services (continued)

country	health personnel							hospitals		kinds (%)				ownership (%)			hospital beds per 10,000 pop.
	year	physicians	dentists	nurses	pharma-cists	midwives	popu-lation per physi-cian	year	number	gen-eral	spe-cial-ized	medical centres	rural	govern-ment	private non-profit	private for profit	
Egypt	1987	26,988	4,548	40,742	11,187	...	1,816	1982	1,521	32.3	13.2	15.9	38.6	83.1	3.8	13.1	20[34]
El Salvador	1991	4,080	800[13]	4,898[13]	597[14]	1,940	1,322	1989	42	45.2	14.3	40.5	—	69.0	—	31.0	10
Equatorial Guinea	1987	90	...	...	...	...	3,622	1982	...	...	...	...	...	...	...	...	112
Estonia	1990	7,200[6]	6	15,200[20]	...	20	220[6]	1990	125	...	...	...	...	100.0	...	...	120
Ethiopia	1986–87	1,241	16[24]	12,016[20]	282	20	36,660	1986–87	86	32.6[24]	18.6[24]	—	48.8[24]	88.4[24]	9.3[24]	2.3[24]	3
Faeroe Islands	1990	82	42	251[13]	10[13]	17	582	1990	3	33.3	—	—	66.7	100.0	—	—	75
Fiji	1990	300	47	1,651	44[24]	...	2,438	1986	25	...	...	...	...	...	...	...	24[23]
Finland	1989	9,871	3,794	36,904	7,060[17]	357	503	1989	439	86.1	13.9	—	—	...	...	...	135
France	1990	148,089	36,079[13]	299,098[13]	49,140[13]	10,356	382	1988	3,793	—91.2—		—	8.8	28.3	—71.7—	—	126
French Guiana	1987	237	51	499	33	29	374	1987	6	50.0	—	—	50.0	50.0	—50.0—	—	92
French Polynesia	1988	173	37	464[7]	29	20	1,085	1981	34	8.8	5.9	52.9	32.4	94.1	—	5.9	57[13]
Gabon	1984	565	...	...	...	...	2,000	1985	105	—26.7—		—73.3—		100.0	—	—	45
Gambia, The	1989	48	...	430	...	...	17,604	1989	7	...	...	...	...	57.1	—42.9—	—	10
Gaza Strip	1984	250	...	...	...	...	2,000	1987	7	...	...	...	...	85.7	14.3	—	16
Georgia	1990	32,100[6]	...	64,100[20]	...	20	170[6]	1990	422	...	...	...	...	100.0	...	...	110
Germany	1990	228,368	52,816	411,437	39,510	8,434	346	1990	3,585	...	...	...	...	42.1	—57.9—	—	105
Ghana	1989[31]	628	39	11,808	67	1,736	22,452	1991	121	90.9	9.1	—	—	60.3	—39.7—	—	13
Gibraltar	1990	29	2[13]	297[13]	3[13]	8[13]	1,064	1990	2	50.0	50.0	—	—	100.0	—	—	82
Greece	1988	32,145	9,206	25,639[7]	6,941	1,815[7]	315	1988	430	48.4	51.6	—	—	...	...	...	51
Greenland	1989	78	29[13]	537[13]	...	13[7]	710	1989	16	6.3	—	—	93.7	100.0	—	—	80
Grenada	1990	56	7	296	28	36	1,617	1982	39	7.7	7.7	69.2	15.4	100.0	—	—	36[23]
Guadeloupe	1986	491	114	1,169	153	95	682	1987	29[11]	...	...	...	...	37.9[11]	—62.1[11]—	—	101
Guam	1986	147	23[1]	594[20]	30[1]	20	823	1982	4	25.0	25.0	50.0	—	50.0	—50.0—	—	21[41]
Guatemala	1987	3,579	810[14]	9,093[14]	411[14]	...	2,356	1985	...	...	...	...	...	...	...	...	17[7]
Guernsey	1991	77	21[1]	592[1]	15[1]	31[1]	765	1991	1	100.0	—	—	—	100.0	—	—	91[1]
Guinea	1988	672	22	243	261	343	9,732	1988	38	—100.0—		...	...	100.0	—	—	6
Guinea-Bissau	1985	122	2[24]	674	3[24]	111	7,164	1981	17	11.8	—	—	88.2	100.0	—	—	19[8]
Guyana	1989	111	15	854	29	172	6,809	1979	55	20.0	12.7	27.3	40.0	87.3	3.6	9.1	29[7]
Haiti	1989	944	98	2,262[13]	...	...	6,083	1989	87	—77.8[21]—		22.2[21]—	—	61.1[21]	—38.9[21]—	—	8
Honduras	1990	2,900	459[13]	1,001[13]	792[13]	...	1,586	1990	46	59.1[1]	11.4[1]	—	29.5[1]	45.7	—54.3—	—	12
Hong Kong	1991[42]	6,545	1,526	21,404	720	981	896	1982	71	43.7	15.5	39.4	1.4	50.7	26.8	22.5	43[43]
Hungary	1990	33,905	4,267	51,518	4,504	2,695	306	1990	148	—75.3[44]—		—24.7[44]—		...	...	...	101
Iceland	1989	675	215	2,965	210	188	373	1988	41	56.1	41.5	2.4	—	...	...	...	100
India	1987[42]	331,630	9,598[14]	219,299	155,621[21]	181,323	2,418	1981	25,452	26.7	0.3	65.8	7.2	71.6	—28.4—	—	9[13]
Indonesia	1989	23,367	2,304[1]	76,636[20]	3,587[1]	20	7,427	1990	1,532	...	...	...	...	...	...	...	7
Iran	1989	18,350	3,600	43,291[7]	2,650[8]	2,202[8]	2,882	1982	581	71.1	15.5	9.8	3.6	66.4	13.9	19.7	15[34]
Iraq	1991	9,366	1,577	11,964[23]	1,552	2,267[1]	1,922	1990	177	72.9	27.1	—	—	...	...	...	18
Ireland	1984	5,180	1,131	25,261	2,068[24]	...	681	1990[12,45]	103	81.6	18.4	—	—	100.0	—	—	39
Isle of Man	1988	86	19[1,31]	750[1,31]	30[1]	611[1,31]	745	1986	3	33.3	33.3	—	33.3	100.0	—	—	109[21]
Israel	1987	11,895	2,900[8]	14,785[8]	2,540[8]	12,110[8]	345	1989	168	24.4	75.6	—	—	26.8	32.7	40.5	62
Italy	1988	255,110	3,697[17]	186,335[17,20]	43,500[24]	20	225	1989	1,681	75.0	25.0	—	—	62.6	—37.4—	—	69
Jamaica	1990	1,122[7]	64[31]	1,983[31]	64[31]	372[31]	2,095[7]	1987	36	83.3	16.7	—	—	80.6	—19.4—	—	25
Japan	1989	201,658	70,572	673,772	143,429	23,320	609	1989	10,081	89.2	10.8	—	—	66.6	—33.4—	—	135
Jersey	1990	89	41[1]	646[1]	22[1]	27[21]	936	1990	6	16.7	83.3	—	—	100.0	—	—	89
Jordan	1987	4,500	1,041	2,596[14,20]	800[14]	...	632	1987	56	80.0[14]	20.0[14]	—	—	39.0[14]	—61.0[14]—	—	20
Kazakhstan	1990	68,900[6]	6	207,300[20]	...	20	244[6]	1990	1,748	...	...	...	...	100.0	...	...	136
Kenya	1989	3,266	561	25,489	413	20	7,313	1989	558	—47.3—		—52.7—		...	...	...	14
Kiribati	1986	16	1[11]	125[11,20]	3[11]	20	4,104	1982	34	2.9	—	97.1	—	100.0	—	—	43[17]
Korea, North	1989	57,690	...	...	...	...	370	1982	7,924	19.3	12.4	—68.3—		...	...	...	135[34]
Korea, South	1990	42,554	9,619	89,032	37,118	7,643	1,007	1990	924	—60.2—		39.8	—	...	...	...	23
Kuwait	1989	2,949	382	9,764[13]	846	137[13]	695	1988	24	...	...	...	...	66.7	—33.3—	—	30[12]
Kyrgyzstan	1990	16,100[6]	6	46,000[20]	...	20	275[6]	1990	307	...	...	...	...	100.0	...	...	119
Laos	1985	558	...	6,753[20]	...	20	6,495	1985	...	...	...	...	...	...	...	...	27
Latvia	1990	13,200[6]	6	31,300[20]	...	20	203[6]	1990	204	...	...	...	...	100.0	...	...	147
Lebanon	1986	3,509	...	...	...	...	771	1982	...	...	...	...	...	...	...	...	38
Lesotho	1987	103	6[1]	452[1]	7[1]	...	15,728	1987	22	90.9	9.1	—	—	54.5	45.5	—	15
Liberia	1985	89	5	908	4[24]	443	24,600	1981	85[24]	...	...	...	...	60.0[24]	—40.0[24]—	—	15
Libya	1984	5,272	400[8]	5,924[8,20]	618[8]	20	690	1982	64	68.8	31.2	—	—	100.0	—	—	48
Liechtenstein	1990	28	12	...	2	...	1,031	1985	1	...	...	...	...	...	...	...	37
Lithuania	1990	17,100[6]	6	47,300[20]	...	20	219[6]	1990	197	...	...	...	...	100.0	...	...	123
Luxembourg	1990	766	198	1,469[21]	307	124[34]	498	1990	32	56.3	43.7	—	—	...	...	...	117
Macau	1990	329	18	594	5[21]	10[1]	1,176	1990	36	5.6	—	94.4	—	25.0	—75.0—	—	31
Macedonia	1989	4,331	1,094	...	404	...	464	1989	...	...	...	...	...	...	...	...	55
Madagascar	1985	1,189	100	3,323	37	1,638	8,610	1978	749	0.8	1.1	75.7	22.4	100.0	—	—	23[1]
Malaŵi	1984	262	12[8]	2,002[20]	12[8]	...	27,094	1987	395	12.2	0.8	—87.0—		59.2	—40.8—	—	16
Malaysia	1989	6,577	1,401	36,076	815[14]	14,525[8]	2,638	1989	264	...	...	...	...	38.6	—61.4—	—	22
Maldives	1990	40	1	137	13[11]	141[11]	5,377	1990	5	20.0	—	80.0	—	100.0	—	—	8
Mali	1983	349	15	2,058	58	305	20,602	1983	162	...	...	...	...	100.0	—	—	6
Malta	1991	805	98	3,905	440	274	444	1991	6	...	...	...	...	100.0	—	—	93
Marshall Islands	1985	17	2	51	...	...	2,217	1985	2	100.0	—	—	—	100.0	—	—	14
Martinique	1987	586	124	1,121	170	135	595	1988	...	...	...	...	...	...	...	...	86
Mauritania	1988	187	19	920	10	749	10,128	1988	16	...	...	...	...	100.0	—	—	8
Mauritius	1990	950	140	2,768[20]	127	20	1,118	1986	19	36.8	21.1	31.6	10.5	89.5	—10.5—	—	27[23]
Mayotte	1985	9	1	51	1	2	7,427	1985	2	100.0	—	—	—	100.0	—	—	12
Mexico	1987	130,000	4,925	108,486	...	...	600	1991[12]	726	86.0	14.0	—	—	...	...	...	13
Micronesia	1985	36	13	257	7	...	2,536	1990	4	100.0	—	—	—	100.0	—	—	36
Moldova	1990	17,400[6]	6	51,700[20]	...	20	251[6]	1990	334	...	...	...	...	100.0	...	...	131
Monaco	1990	80	32[1]	208[1]	56[1]	6[1]	366	1982	1	100.0	—	—	—	100.0	—	—	180[23]
Mongolia	1990[31]	6,233	200[17]	7,932[8]	400[17]	963[21]	345	1981	1,659	2.1	5.4	71.9	20.6	100.0	—	—	127[23]
Morocco	1990	5,711	701	22,925	1,697	87	4,379	1990[32]	203	31.0	—	69.0	—	100.0	—	—	11
Mozambique	1988	342	118	3,086	332	1,080	39,538	1988	238	4.2	0.8	84.5	13.5	100.0	—	—	9
Myanmar (Burma)	1989	11,951	850	8,521	80[21]	12,461	3,451	1989	614[1]	49.7[1]	2.4[1]	—	47.9[1]	100.0[1]	—	—	6
Namibia	1988	281	41	3,390	70	...	4,450	1988	61	...	...	...	...	...	...	...	60
Nauru	1980	11	...	...	...	...	700	1980	...	...	...	...	...	...	...	...	250
Nepal	1990	951	...	601	427[17]	2,379	19,644	1990	123	88.2[24]	11.8[24]	—	—	82.4[24]	17.6[24]	—	3

rate per 10,000 pop.	general	specialized	medical centres	rural	bed occupancy rate (%)	average length of stay (days)	under age 5 per 1,000 live newborn 1985–90	maternal mortality per 100,000 live births 1988–89	population with access to safe water (latest) (%)	food supply (% of FAO requirement) 1987–89	indiv. (% of earnings)	employer (% of payroll)	govt. (% of covered earnings)	public health expenditures (% of natl. budget)	public health expenditures per capita (U.S.$)	country
...	...	...	...	...	...	...	124	65.2[7]	73	133	1.0	4.0	—	2.8	11.70	Egypt
384	59.7	20.4	19.9	—	64.6	6	84	58.8[11]	39	105[4]	2.5	6.3	...	7.8	7.30	El Salvador
...	...	...	...	...	...	...	214	...	...	...	...	...	...	...	...	Equatorial Guinea
...	...	...	...	...	...	...	...	41.2	...	...	...	...	...	...	...	Estonia
...	...	...	...	...	...	...	252	...	19	74[4]	—	—	...	3.6	1.50	Ethiopia
1,812[17]	76.6[17]	—	—	24.3[17]	62.6	11[17]	10[16]	...	...	...	...	...	...	11.6	1,197.80	Faeroe Islands
886	...	...	...	...	72.6	7	31	41.1[11]	80	126	...	...	—	7.7	34.80	Fiji
2,271	97.2	2.8	—	—	81.6	18	7	11.1	95	116	1.7	1.5	10	10.8	726.70	Finland
2,243	...	...	—	—	83.0	16	10	8.5	100	137	5.9	12.6	...	15.2	1,115.10	France
2,060[17,32]	...	...	...	...	63.4[17,32]	9[17,32]	...	129.7[14]	...	125	...	...	...	...	...	French Guiana
1,472	70.9	...	3.2	25.9	51.7	8	30[16]	...	...	122	...	...	...	...	...	French Polynesia
258[21]	...	...	...	...	23.6[21]	13[21]	169	120[28]	68	108[4]	—	4.0	...	...	45.40[5]	Gabon
...	...	...	...	...	...	...	281	1,100[3]	75	99	...	...	...	8.0	8.20	Gambia, The
1,344	...	...	...	...	69.4	3	100[16]	...	...	...	...	...	...	...	...	Gaza Strip
...	...	...	...	...	...	...	...	54.9	...	...	...	...	...	...	...	Georgia
2,019	...	...	...	...	84.2	16	11	10.3	100	137	3.7[25,39]	3.7[25,39]	—	19.3[39]	1,138.90[39]	Germany
...	...	...	...	...	...	...	145	1,000[3]	57	98	5.0[9]	11.5[9]	—	9.0	4.50	Ghana
1,579	...	...	...	...	37.7	7	17[16]	...	...	...	...	...	...	13.2	641.60	Gibraltar
1,225	77.4	22.6	—	—	70.7	11	16	4.0	98	143	15	15	...	10.5	160.80	Greece
2,510	29.3	...	—	70.7	58.3	7	...	...	...	...	...	...	...	21.8	1,016.70	Greenland
749[40]	...	...	...	...	...	...	33[16]	65.4[7]	85	110	4.0[9]	4.0[9]	—	15.6	21.90	Grenada
2,420[14]	58.1[11,12]	41.9[11,12]	...	...	87.1[14]	15[14]	17	89.3[8]	...	112	...	...	...	...	...	Guadeloupe
738[41]	97.6[41]	2.4[41]	—	—	78.8[41]	8[41]	...	...	100	...	...	...	...	12.9	177.70	Guam
284	...	...	...	...	57.7	9	99	92.3	61	102	2.0	4.0	3.0	9.9	11.20	Guatemala
1,132	100.0	...	...	...	83.9[1]	28[1]	11	—	...	...	...	...	...	21.8	1,016.70	Guernsey
...	...	...	...	...	...	...	249	...	32	95	1.6	2.4	—	...	3.10[5]	Guinea
326	59.8	—	...	40.2	57.5	11	223	400[28]	21	110[4]	...	...	...	1.4	4.40	Guinea-Bissau
...	...	...	...	...	...	...	37	112.1[14]	61	121	4.8[9]	7.2[9]	—	5.7	28.00	Guyana
123[21]	...	...	...	...	...	...	170	230[3]	41	89	2.0[25]	2.0[25]	—	...	4.60[5]	Haiti
429[24]	75.6[24]	16.7[24]	—	7.7[24]	70.2[24]	8[24]	106	49.9[8]	50	99	2.5	5.0	2.5	9.1	19.30	Honduras
1,494	93.6	3.2	3.2	—	82.4	8	10	5.5	98	123	—	37	...	9.4	214.60	Hong Kong
2,219	...	...	...	...	77.7	13	19	15.4	98	138	10.0[9]	43.0[9]	10	7.9	131.60	Hungary
2,753	92.0	6.8	1.2	—	92.7	18	7	21.0[23]	100	132	2.0	—	10	24.9	1,498.80	Iceland
...	...	...	...	...	...	...	148	340[3]	75	99	2.3	5.0	...	1.6	1.00	India
...	...	...	...	...	...	...	117	450[3]	46	125	—	7.0	...	2.0	2.10	Indonesia
...	...	...	...	...	...	...	155	120[3]	78	130[4]	7.0[9]	20.0[9]	3.0[9]	8.5	104.30	Iran
645	...	...	...	...	42.4	4	94	...	87	122[4]	5.0[9]	12.0[9]	...	...	15.30[5]	Iraq
1,492	82.5	17.5	—	—	72.5	7	11	3.8	100	151	1.3	1.3	10	13.0	523.80	Ireland
1,274[21]	83.9[21]	7.0[21]	—	9.1[21]	81.2[21]	25[21]	10[16]	...	100	...	...	...	...	26.0	522.00	Isle of Man
1,669[19]	...	...	...	...	91.0[19]	5[19]	16	5.0	100	123	0.6	3.6	—	4.1	227.40	Israel
1,494	91.0	9.0	—	—	70.5	12	12	7.7	100	139	1.1	15.4	...	11.3	765.20	Italy
627	83.0	17.0	—	—	77.0	7	23	110[3]	72	117	2.5[9]	2.5[9]	...	7.8	44.40	Jamaica
643[1]	97.9[1]	2.1[1]	—	—	83.3[1]	56[1]	8	10.8	98	124	15	—	...	...	985.50[5]	Japan
1,724	88.9	11.1	—	—	86.8[8]	24[8]	10[16]	...	...	...	...	...	...	20.3	1,124.00	Jersey
1,061[17]	93.6[1]	6.4[1]	—	—	61.8[17]	4[17]	57	...	...	96	...	...	117[4]	5.8	26.10	Jordan
...	...	...	...	...	...	...	...	53.1	...	...	...	...	...	0.8	...	Kazakhstan
...	...	...	...	...	...	...	113	170[28]	30	93	...	...	...	5.4	5.70	Kenya
633	47.6	—	52.4	—	58.0	15	36[16]	...	44	130	—	—	—	13.0	32.10	Kiribati
...	...	...	...	...	...	...	31	41[3]	100	120	...	...	...	...	12.30[5]	Korea, North
519[46]	97.8	2.2	—	—	80.6[46]	13[46]	31	9.9	78	121	1.5[25]	1.5[25]	...	2.2	19.10	Korea, South
1,235	...	...	...	...	71.7[1]	8[1]	23	2.0[7]	100	130	...	—	—	7.4	359.00	Kuwait
...	...	...	...	...	...	...	...	42.6	...	...	...	...	...	3.3	...	Kyrgyzstan
...	...	...	...	...	...	...	160	...	24	118[4]	...	...	...	...	...	Laos
...	...	...	...	...	...	...	...	56.5	...	...	...	...	...	...	...	Latvia
...	...	...	...	...	...	...	49	...	93	132[4]	1.5	5.5	...	...	28.00[5]	Lebanon
221[19]	...	...	...	...	...	...	135	...	43	102	...	...	...	7.8	6.30	Lesotho
...	...	...	...	...	...	...	206	...	58	104	...	...	...	5.7	7.00	Liberia
719[13]	...	...	...	...	52.7[13]	13[13]	118	80[3]	97	142	1.5	1.4	2.2	...	165.60[5]	Libya
...	...	...	...	...	...	...	10[16]	...	...	...	...	...	...	...	...	Liechtenstein
...	...	...	...	...	...	...	...	28.7	...	...	...	...	...	...	...	Lithuania
1,985	92.6	7.4	—	—	82.9	18	10	23.6[7]	100	150	4.2	4.2	...	2.2	177.70	Luxembourg
635	...	...	...	...	57.6	10	31[16]	47.5[21]	...	96	...	...	...	...	...	Macau
646[19]	...	...	...	...	58.2[19]	9[19]	...	16.7	...	...	...	...	...	...	...	Macedonia
699[19]	...	...	...	...	57.9[19]	2[19]	90	240[3]	32	96	—	8.3[33]	—	4.2	1.90	Madagascar
436[11]	...	...	...	...	90.6[11]	8[11]	263	100[3]	56	90	...	...	...	7.4	3.90	Malawi
717[12]	...	...	...	...	...	...	35	59[3]	51	123	—	—	—	4.6	26.30	Malaysia
291[11]	...	...	...	...	57.5[11,47]	5[11,47]	...	645.6[7]	95	97[4]	...	...	...	18.4	68.00	Maldives
...	...	...	...	...	...	...	291	...	38	95	...	...	...	2.1	1.50	Mali
1,569[1]	...	...	...	...	83.7[1]	19[1]	13	35.8[11]	100	131	8.3[9]	8.3[9]	8.3[9]	8.8	198.80	Malta
...	...	...	...	...	...	...	36[16]	...	...	...	...	...	...	26.1	120.20	Marshall Islands
2,069	...	...	...	...	87.3	15	19	94.8[7]	...	113	...	...	...	...	...	Martinique
...	...	...	...	...	...	...	214	...	66	113	—	2.0	...	2.8	4.50	Mauritania
1,139[11,12]	...	...	...	...	84.5[12,24]	8[12,24]	28	99.2[7]	95	124	...	...	...	9.3	56.40	Mauritius
778	100.0	—	—	—	74.8	6	...	...	...	...	...	...	...	...	...	Mayotte
403	...	...	...	...	40.3	5[12]	68	65.2[21]	71	131	3.0	8.4	0.6	1.9	9.90	Mexico
2,171	100.0	—	—	—	...	...	36[16]	...	...	...	—	—	—	...	100.00	Micronesia
...	...	...	...	...	...	...	...	34.1	...	...	...	...	...	...	...	Moldova
2,630	100.0	—	—	—	77.6	14	10[16]	...	100	...	...	...	...	...	...	Monaco
2,508	25.9	33.0	1.1	40.0	89.1	14	58	100[3]	65	101	...	...	...	...	11.00[5]	Mongolia
238	93.6[44]	—	6.4[44]	—	52.9	9	118	300[3]	73	124	0.2	0.4	—	3.0	6.90	Morocco
92[19,24]	...	...	...	...	70.2[19,24]	9[19,24]	241	300[3]	24	71	...	...	...	6.6	3.20	Mozambique
289[1]	75.7[1]	10.1[1]	—	14.2[1]	78.1[1]	9[1]	85	140[3]	30	115	1.0	2.0	1.0	4.6	3.00	Myanmar (Burma)
...	...	...	...	...	...	...	176	...	...	83[4]	...	...	...	9.7	71.90	Namibia
...	...	...	...	...	...	...	36[16]	...	...	...	...	...	...	14.2	178.50	Nauru
54[13]	...	...	...	...	61.5[19,24]	7[19,24]	196	830[3]	36	94	—	—	...	4.7	1.20	Nepal

Health services (continued)

country	health personnel							hospitals		kinds (%)				ownership (%)			hospital beds per 10,000 pop.
	year	physicians	dentists	nurses	pharmacists	midwives	population per physician	year	number	general	specialized	medical centres	rural	government	private non-profit	private for profit	
Netherlands, The	1991	37,461	7,900	...	2,247	1,194	402	1990	249	67.9	32.1	—	—	...	...	...	60
Netherlands Antilles	1990	278	57	1,706	27[34]	8[34]	684	1990	11	36.4	36.4	27.2	—	...	...	...	79
New Caledonia	1990	216	64	283[21]	46	38	776	1981	38	10.5	7.9	39.5	42.1	92.1	—	7.9	67[23]
New Zealand	1989	9,453	1,238[7]	42,661[7, 20]	3,403[7]	20	359	1987	344	...	...	...	...	49.7	—50.3—		88[34]
Nicaragua	1988	1,789	277[7]	1,142[7]	...	...	2,024	1985	52	55.1	8.2	36.7		...	...	...	13[13]
Niger	1985	160	...	...	...	192	38,500	1979	...					...	...	...	6
Nigeria	1985	14,757	899	57,108	3,567	47,052	6,900	1985	11,588	6.6	0.5	—92.9—		81.4	—18.6—		9
Northern Mariana Islands	1986	23	4	103	2	2	1,324	1988	1	100.0	—	—	—	100.0	—	—	19
Norway	1991	13,826	5,084	58,561	3,041[8]	...	309	1990	365	20.0	80.0	—	—	...	...	...	59
Oman	1990	1,393	97	3,944	239	33[8]	1,078	1989	180	—28.3—		—71.7—		100.0	—	—	26[23]
Pakistan	1989	59,777	1,881	19,581	3,484	12,924	1,987	1989	9,534	—7.5—		—92.5—		88.0	—12.0—		5
Palau	1986[31]	10	3	82	1	...	1,396	1986	1	100.0	—	—	—	100.0	—	—	50
Panama	1990	2,748	506	2,466	...	...	880	1990	55	...	...	...	...	86.7[44]	—13.3[44]—		30
Papua New Guinea	1987	283	16[24]	3,941[14, 20]	9[24]	20	11,904	1980	390	5.1	—	53.6	41.2	46.2	53.8	—	45[14]
Paraguay	1988	2,536	195[14]	3,584[14]	...	...	1,593	1988	...					...	...	...	9
Peru	1989	21,856	5,331	15,796	6,113	3,437	997	1990	368	...	...	...	...	49.7[13]	—50.3[13]—		16
Philippines	1989	57,270	1,090[21, 31]	9,644[21, 31]	539[21, 31]	9,470[21, 31]	1,039	1985	1,814	...	...	...	...	34.4	—65.6—		15[34]
Poland	1991	81,674	18,219	207,654	13,978	23,868	468	1990	924	72.9	27.1	—	—	...	...	...	70
Portugal	1990	27,608	1,267	29,525[11]	5,656	824[11]	376	1989	621	24.8	13.7	61.5	—	86.3	—13.7—		46
Puerto Rico	1987	8,991	741[24]	14,392[24]	1,436[24]	199[24]	366	1988	67	...	...	...	...	...	...	...	40[17]
Qatar	1989	752	62[7]	1,418[7]	140[7]	70[21, 31]	568	1985	3	33.0	67.0	—	—	100.0	—	—	25[34]
Réunion	1990	933	232	2,180	201	131	638	1984	21	...	...	...	...	74.2[44]	—25.8[44]—		54[23]
Romania	1989[31]	41,938	7,116	81,031[1]	6,432	12,248[1]	552	1989	437[21]	56.8[21]	32.5[21]	—	10.8[21]	...	...	...	93
Russia	1990	694,700[6]	6	1,816,700[20]	...	20	214[6]	1990	12,762	...	...	...	...	100.0	—	—	137
Rwanda	1985[31]	178	9	559	9	464[8]	33,170	1985[34]	220	—13.6—		—86.4—		100.0	—	—	9
St. Kitts and Nevis	1990	27	5[7]	231[7]	7[11]	123[24]	1,593	1990	4	...	...	...	...	...	...	...	60
St. Lucia	1990	60	12[34]	246[34]	13[14]	...	2,521	1988	6	16.7	16.7	—	66.6	...	...	...	37
St. Vincent	1989	40	2	254	15[14]	...	2,650	1990	9[7]	11.1[7]	22.2[7]	11.1[7]	55.6[7]	88.9[7]	—11.1[7]—		39[7]
San Marino	1987	60	...	...	...	...	375	1987	...					...	...	...	66
São Tomé and Príncipe	1987	40	—	344[8]	1[8]	10[8]	2,819	1978	16	12.5	—	87.5	—	...	...	...	78
Saudi Arabia	1990	22,688	1,424[13]	38,434[13, 20]	1,237[13]	20	623	1990	285	...	...	...	...	77.5	—22.5—		28
Senegal	1988	407	58	934	200	474	17,072	1984	87	18.4	29.9	51.7	—	100.0	—	—	9[13]
Seychelles	1991	71	7	313	3	...	992	1991	7	14.3	14.3	71.4	—	100.0	—	—	65
Sierra Leone	1988	300	18[14]	1,318[14, 20]	14[14]	20	13,150	1988	219	—25.6—		—74.4—		...	...	...	10
Singapore	1989	3,397	593	9,237	557	571	779	1991	21	...	...	...	...	47.6	—52.4—		37[34]
Slovenia	1989	4,071	1,062	...	659	...	481	1989	...					...	...	...	72
Solomon Islands	1988	31	15[11]	464	...	...	9,852	1986	8	100.0	—	—	—	75.0	25.0	—	53
Somalia	1986	450	2	1,834	180	556	13,315	1985	...					...	...	...	9
South Africa	1990[42]	23,379	3,775	148,558	8,930	...	1,320	1987	737	...	...	...	...	...	...	...	49
Bophuthatswana	1989	178	...	6,039	...	...	10,750	1989	216	—5.6—		—94.4—		...	...	...	31
Ciskei	1986[31]	283	7	3,855	10	54	2,714	1986	97	5.2	1.0	92.8	1.0	99.0	1.0	—	41
Transkei	1985	240	...	...	...	...	12,220	1987	31	...	...	...	...	...	...	...	25
Venda	1991	46	...	1,160	...	...	12,320	1991	8	37.5	37.5	25.0	—	...	...	...	31
Spain	1990	148,717	10,347	158,497	36,590	6,321	262	1988	866	53.9	46.1	—	—	43.3	—56.7—		44
Sri Lanka	1990[31]	2,571	301[11]	8,317[13]	441[1]	3,255[11]	6,609	1990[12]	423	99.5[7]	0.5[7]	—	—	100.0	—	—	28
Sudan, The	1986[31]	2,405	334[21]	13,693[21]	58[21]	376[21]	10,130	1981	160	21.9	5.6	—	72.5	...	...	...	9
Suriname	1985	219	22[14]	1,400[14]	...	...	1,798	1980	17	29.4	17.6	47.1	5.9	58.8	29.4	11.8	50[11]
Swaziland	1984	80	13	377[8]	4[8]	...	7,971	1984	23	30.4	8.7	—60.9—		56.5	—43.5—		25
Sweden	1990	21,700	5,200	85,900[20]	5,080	20	394	1989	1,000[8]	10.3[8]	89.7[8]	—	—	...	...	...	63
Switzerland	1989	21,200	4,800	37,360[24]	...	...	317	1983	372	52.7	47.3	—	—	...	...	...	85[34]
Syria	1988	8,420	3,067	10,400	3,313	3,201	1,347	1988	213	80.3	19.7	—	—	23.0	—77.0—		12
Taiwan	1990	22,293	5,580	38,357	17,944	1,891	910	1990	827	...	...	...	...	11.5	—88.5—		44
Tajikistan	1990	14,500[6]	6	42,900[20]	...	20	370[6]	1990	365	...	...	...	...	100.0	—	—	105
Tanzania	1984	1,065	...	8,291[1]	...	2,887[1]	19,775	1982	3,032	4.9	—	87.2	7.9	...	...	...	11[14]
Thailand	1989	12,713	2,107	74,167	3,825	11,354	4,227	1989	1,011	91.6	8.4	—	—	76.6	—23.4—		17
Togo	1985	230	5[14]	1,116	50	712[14]	12,992	1979	65	10.8	4.6	61.5	23.1	96.9	3.1	—	13[1]
Tonga	1989	45	11	266	2	37	2,130	1989	4	...	...	...	...	...	...	...	32
Trinidad and Tobago	1988	1,025	129[11]	3,344[11, 20]	496[11]	20	1,213	1985	31	...	...	...	...	...	...	...	35[13]
Tunisia	1989	4,313	577	10,545	1,264[7]	...	1,834	1989[12]	130	6.2	2.3	—91.5—		100.0	—	—	20
Turkey	1990	50,639	10,514	44,904	15,792	30,415	1,108	1990	857	74.9	8.5	—16.6—		85.4	—14.6—		22
Turkmenistan	1990	13,200[6]	6	38,900[20]	...	20	281[6]	1990	347	...	...	...	...	100.0	—	—	113
Tuvalu	1987	4	2	31	1[11]	...	2,141	1985	8	11.1	—	—	88.9	100.0	—	—	36
Uganda	1984	700	17[21]	6,778[20, 21]	27[21]	20	20,300	1981	485	15.5	1.2	83.3	—	84.5	15.5	—	12[34]
Ukraine	1990	227,200[6]	6	607,200[20]	...	20	229[6]	1990	3,882	...	...	...	...	100.0	—	—	135
United Arab Emirates	1991	1,840	242[11]	6,090[11]	190[11]	...	1,057	1991	33	...	...	...	...	100.0	—	—	23
United Kingdom	1981	92,172	17,472	182,897	17,589	...	611	1988	2,501[21]	...	...	...	...	100.0	—	—	62[34]
United States	1989	612,000[13]	163,000	1,648,000	174,000	3,000[43]	404[13]	1988	6,780	85.5	14.5	—	—	27.2	47.8	25.0	51
Uruguay	1990	9,061	3,291[13]	...	886[13]	616[13]	341	1988	52	—26.9—		—	73.1	100.0	—	—	28
Uzbekistan	1990	73,700[6]	6	228,100[20]	...	20	281[6]	1990	1,373	...	...	...	...	100.0	—	—	123
Vanuatu	1990	20	2[1]	321	3[1]	...	7,345	1990	21	—23.8—		—76.2—		...	...	...	25
Venezuela	1989	32,616	7,945	52,260	5,615	...	590	1989	544	...	...	...	...	42.8	—57.2—		25
Vietnam	1989	21,300[6]	6	83,401[17]	12,100[7]	18,047[17]	3,040[6]	1984	10,768	14.6	6.5	78.9	—	100.0	—	—	34[34]
Virgin Islands (U.S.)	1985	167	...	...	...	...	622	1985	...					...	...	...	49
West Bank	1984	510	...	...	...	...	1,535	1987	16	...	...	...	...	56.3	—43.7—		16
Western Sahara[50]	1982	11	—	...	2	...	13,000	1982[32]	2	50.0	—	50.0	—	100.0	—	—	9
Western Samoa	1990	44	7[21]	344[21]	4[21]	42[21, 31]	3,584	1984	30	3.3	—	—	96.7	100.0	—	—	39[34]
Yemen	1986	1,886	52[51]	2,965[20, 51]	107[51]	20	5,531	1984[51]	34	63.3[1]	3.3[1]	—	33.3[1]	86.7[1]	13.3[1]	—	7[17]
Yugoslavia	1989	20,920	4,687	137,429[7, 52]	2,691	...	490	1989	...					...	...	...	61
Zaire	1985	1,318	58[41]	14,661[41]	414[41]	3,043[41]	23,193	1985	942[41]	37.3[41]	38.9[41]	23.8[41]	—	40.9[41]	44.6[41]	14.5[41]	21
Zambia	1984	798	42	5,167	44	1,392	8,437	1987	965	8.2	0.3	19.0	72.5	80.9	19.1	—	32[14]
Zimbabwe	1987	1,243	113	14,369	323	2,512	6,951	1985	1,202	3.7	1.3	—95.0—		72.5	—27.5—		24

[1]1982. [2]Excludes four specialized hospitals. [3]1980–88 UN estimate. [4]1986–88. [5]May include expenditures at the intermediate and local levels of government and/or the costs of additional services such as national health insurance and family-planning programs. [6]Physicians includes dentists. [7]1987. [8]1983. [9]Includes funds for old-age retirement, incapacitating disability, work injury, and life insurance. [10]Government provides remainder of the cost of benefits. [11]1985. [12]Government hospitals only. [13]1988. [14]1984. [15]Amounts vary internally. [16]Regional average. [17]1986. [18]Excludes specialized hospitals and medical centres. [19]General hospitals only. [20]Nurses includes midwives. [21]1981. [22]Number of pharmacies. [23]1990. [24]1980. [25]Minimum on a graduated scale. [26]Maximum on a graduated scale. [27]1982–87 average. [28]1980–87 UN estimate. [29]Employed women only. [30]Includes outpatients. [31]Government-employed health personnel only.

admissions or discharges					mortality				popu-lation with access to safe water (latest) (%)	food supply (% of FAO require-ment) 1987–89	financing of public health care, latest year					country
rate per 10,000 pop.	by kinds of hospital (%)				bed occu-pancy rate (%)	aver-age length of stay (days)	under age 5 per 1,000 live newborn 1985–90	maternal mortality per 100,000 live births 1988–89			health-care insurance			public health expendi-tures (% of natl. budget)	public health expendi-tures per capita (U.S.$)	
	general	special-ized	medical centres	rural							indiv. (% of earn-ings)	em-ployer (% of payroll)	govt. (% of covered earnings)			
1,055	97.7	2.3	—	—	79.3	16	9	5.3	100	118	4.2	14.5	...	11.7	1,153.30	Netherlands, The
...	...	...	...	...	...	...	27[16]	...	...	117	...	...	...	5.2	87.50	Netherlands Antilles
1,468	77.9	3.0	3.2	15.9	57.6	16	39[16]	...	...	126	...	...	...	...	...	New Caledonia
1,344[12]	...	...	...	...	77.7[12]	15[12]	12	12.7[7]	100	128	...	—	10	12.0	616.30	New Zealand
634	91.7		8.3	...	...	...	93	47.1[14]	54	105[4]	2.3	6.0	0.3	14.6	33.10	Nicaragua
...	...	...	...	...	...	...	228	420[3]	49	98	—	11.0[29,33]	—	5.3	4.80	Niger
...	...	...	...	...	...	...	173	800[3]	48	98	6.0[9]	6.0[9]	...	0.8	0.60	Nigeria
1,550	100.0	...	...	...	54.7	4	36[16]	...	...	...	...	...	...	...	511.60	Northern Mariana Islands
1,555	90.8	9.2	—	—	82.9	12	9	3.5	100	125	7.9[9]	17.2[9]	10	10.4	1,125.30	Norway
1,226	...	...	...	...	83.0[19]	5[19]	157	...	53	...	...	...	...	4.6	128.70	Oman
...	...	...	...	...	...	...	165	500[3]	50	95	—	7.0	—	0.9	0.60	Pakistan
1,233	...	...	...	...	...	...	36[16]	...	...	...	...	...	...	...	229.00	Palau
847	...	...	...	...	60.6	8	33	38.2[7]	84	110	1.0	8.0	—	17.9	98.10	Panama
253[19]	...	...	...	...	...	...	84	900[3]	34	98[4]	—	—	—	9.4	27.10	Papua New Guinea
...	...	...	...	...	...	...	61	379.5[17]	35	119	9.5[9]	13.0[9]	1.5[9]	4.3	4.90	Paraguay
416[1]	...	...	...	...	88.2[1]	14[1]	122	88.7[8]	61	95	3.0	6.0	—	5.5	17.00	Peru
...	...	...	...	...	...	...	72	105.5[21]	73	104	1.3	1.3	10	4.0	5.90	Philippines
1,242	...	...	...	...	71.6	15	19	10.7	89	132	—	38.0[9]	10	10.8	64.90	Poland
1,006	94.7		5.3	—	66.6	11	20	6.6	92	139	11.0[9]	24.5[9]	—	8.2	123.10	Portugal
1,156	...	...	...	...	66.2	7	17	19.5	...	...	...	...	...	...	...	Puerto Rico
1,328[21]	54.3[21]	45.7[21]	—	—	...	...	38	...	100	...	...	...	...	0.8	70.00	Qatar
...	...	...	...	...	...	...	14	...	...	135	...	...	...	...	...	Réunion
...	...	...	...	...	...	...	28	155.5	95	123	—	15	—	8.7	48.50	Romania
...	...	...	...	...	...	...	27[48]	49.0	100[48]	132[48]	—	4.4[9,25,48]	10[48]	...	264.10[5,48]	Russia
85[46]	...	...	...	...	42.8[46]	7[46]	205	210[3]	64	84	—	—	—	4.6	2.00	Rwanda
1,028[19,24]	...	...	...	...	58.9[19,24]	10[19,24]	27[16]	90.9[21]	100	108	5.0[9]	5.0[9]	—	12.4	84.20	St. Kitts and Nevis
955	...	...	...	...	...	...	33[16]	12.4[27]	67	107	5.0[9]	5.0[9]	...	...	...	St. Lucia
717[19]	...	...	...	...	64.1[19]	6[19]	33[16]	...	75	108	2.5[9]	3.0[9]	—	13.4	59.00	St. Vincent
1,435[24]	...	...	...	...	69.5[24]	11[24]	17[16]	...	...	...	...	...	...	...	...	San Marino
1,733	76.1	—	23.9	—	68.7	12	178[16]	76.7[7]	52	101	4.0[9]	6.0[9]	...	...	...	São Tomé and Príncipe
749[24]	...	...	...	...	...	...	98	...	97	117	—	—	—	...	212.00[5]	Saudi Arabia
...	...	...	...	...	...	...	222	600	54	100	3.0[26]	3.0[26]	—	4.0	4.40	Senegal
1,543[49]	...	...	...	...	70.8[49]	6[49]	188[16]	...	100	100	5.0[9]	10.0[9,25]	—	13.1	43.40	Seychelles
13[19,24]	...	...	...	...	77.1[19,24]	18[19,24]	291	450[3]	42	80	—	3.0	—	7.5	3.70	Sierra Leone
1,200[13]	...	...	...	...	73.0[21]	10[21]	11	6.9[7]	100	141	...	3.0	10	4.7	118.70	Singapore
968[19]	...	...	...	...	84.1[19]	10[19]	...	4.3	...	...	...	...	...	6.2	13.50	Slovenia
...	...	...	...	...	...	...	39[16]	10[3]	82	96	—	—	—	3.2	2.20	Solomon Islands
...	...	...	...	...	...	...	252	1,100[3]	35	84	—	—	—	9.4	69.40	Somalia
...	...	...	...	...	...	...	96	83[3]	...	127	—	—	10	5.4	26.00	South Africa
...	...	...	...	...	...	...	103[16]	...	...	...	...	...	...	...	...	Bophuthatswana
488	...	...	...	...	79.0	16	103[16]	...	...	...	...	...	...	...	...	Ciskei
632[17]	...	...	...	...	...	...	103[16]	...	...	...	...	...	...	...	...	Transkei
1,130[11]	...	...	...	...	102.4[11]	11[11]	103[16]	...	...	...	...	...	...	...	...	Venda
964	...	...	...	...	77.1	13	11	4.9[7]	100	145	4.8[9]	24.0[9]	...	12.8	376.20	Spain
1,506[13]	...	...	...	...	88.3[1]	6[1]	43	46.5[17]	41	104	...	...	...	6.7	9.50	Sri Lanka
81[19]	...	...	...	...	...	...	175	660[3]	21	86	—	—	—	1.3	0.80	Sudan, The
820	83.6	2.4	8.0	6.0	41.6	15	37	31.1[7]	68	129	—	—	—	3.7	48.90	Suriname
506	...	...	...	...	...	...	173	...	30	113	—	—	—	8.5	30.10	Swaziland
1,831	...	...	...	...	75.6	10	7	8.9	100	109	—	10.1	10	0.9	100.30	Sweden
1,278	85.9	14.1	—	—	80.8	24	8	3.7	100	133	15	—	10	13.1	384.70	Switzerland
474	...	...	...	...	57.9	5	63	280[3]	76	124	—	—	—	1.3	5.30	Syria
...	...	...	...	...	...	...	...	11.9[23]	...	...	1.4[9]	5.6[9]	2.8[9]	1.4	7.80	Taiwan
...	...	...	...	...	...	...	...	38.9	...	...	...	...	...	...	...	Tajikistan
706	66.5	—	13.1	20.4	...	...	174	340[3]	56	95	—	—	—	5.7	3.50	Tanzania
...	...	...	...	...	...	...	49	50[3]	66	104	—	—	—	6.8	14.60	Thailand
...	...	...	...	...	...	...	152	84[28]	71	93	—	2.0[29]	—	5.2	6.00	Togo
718[1]	...	...	...	...	56.8[1]	10[1]	30[16]	...	75	131	—	—	—	6.6	51.90	Tonga
...	...	...	...	...	...	...	23	63.0	98	120	2.8[9]	5.6[9]	—	8.9	178.20	Trinidad and Tobago
652[14]	...	...	...	...	65.5[14]	8[14]	99	310[3]	64	129	6.3	26.3	—	6.1	25.10	Tunisia
568	78.3[21]	19.1[21]	—	2.6[21]	44.1[21]	9[21]	92	210[3]	83	126	5.0	6.0	—	3.6	16.70	Turkey
...	...	...	...	...	...	...	...	55.2	...	...	...	...	...	1.4	...	Turkmenistan
1,368	40.9	—	—	59.1	51.5[19]	12.2[19]	36[16]	...	...	...	...	...	...	3.1	34.30	Tuvalu
...	...	...	...	...	...	...	169	300[3]	20	92	—	—	—	2.4	0.50	Uganda
...	...	...	...	...	...	...	17	32.7	...	...	...	...	...	...	...	Ukraine
1,032[1]	...	...	...	...	69.6[1]	7[1]	38	...	100	136	—	—	—	6.9	135.40	United Arab Emirates
1,434	...	...	...	...	80.6[17]	15[17]	11	7.5	100	126	5.0[9,25]	5.0[9,25]	10	14.6	739.10	United Kingdom
1,392	...	...	...	...	69.6	9	12	8.4	100	139	1.5	1.5	—	13.5	703.40	United States
392	...	...	...	...	67.4	17	30	25.3	85	101	3.0	4.0	—	4.5	31.50	Uruguay
...	...	...	...	...	...	...	...	42.8	...	...	...	...	...	...	...	Uzbekistan
912[24]	...	...	...	...	55.0	8[24]	39[16]	...	100	112	—	—	—	6.6	28.90	Vanuatu
...	...	...	...	...	...	...	43	55.0[7]	89	106	2.0	4.3[25]	1.5[9,25]	10.0	73.30	Venezuela
1,587	12.4	8.1	56.6	22.9	80.7	7	91	140[3]	46	103[4]	...	...	...	...	...	Vietnam
...	...	...	...	...	...	...	27[16]	...	...	...	...	...	...	15.7	327.30	Virgin Islands (U.S.)
963	...	...	...	...	80.5	5	100[16]	...	...	...	...	...	...	...	...	West Bank
226	98.2	—	1.8	—	36.9	5	105[16]	...	...	...	...	...	...	...	...	Western Sahara[50]
823	62.0	—	—	38.0	25.4	7	30[16]	...	83	110	—	—	—	7.1	20.80	Western Samoa
95	89.0	0.4	—	10.6	73.4	18	196	...	46	94[4]	—	—	—	3.9[51]	8.70[51]	Yemen
630[19]	...	...	...	...	76.0[19]	11[19]	28[52]	16.8	83[52]	143[52]	8.7[52]	15	15	4.3	140.00[5,52]	Yugoslavia
474[19,41]	...	...	...	...	71.6[19,41]	12[19,41]	161	800[3]	35	93	—	—	—	4.3	2.30	Zaire
1,249	75.7		24.3		68.5	7	127	150[3]	58	89	5.0[9,26]	5.0[9,25]	—	7.4	9.90	Zambia
767	40.8	25.7	33.5		64.1	7	113	480[3]	36	96	—	—	—	7.6	19.60	Zimbabwe

[32]Public sector only.   [33]Includes family allowances.   [34]1989.   [35]George Town Hospital only.   [36]Includes physicians practicing dentistry and 425,000 doctors of traditional Chinese medicine.   [37]Employer provides entire cost.   [38]Republic of Cyprus only.   [39]Former West Germany only.   [40]Excludes medical centres.   [41]1979.   [42]Registered personnel; all may not be present and working in the country.   [43]1991.   [44]Based on bed ownership.   [45]Excludes psychiatric hospitals.   [46]General and specialized hospitals only.   [47]Central Hospital only.   [48]Data refer to former U.S.S.R.   [49]Victoria Hospital only.   [50]Settlements of Smara, Boujdour, and El Aaiún only.   [51]Former Yemen Arab Republic only.   [52]Data refer to Yugoslavia as constituted prior to 1991.

Social protection

This table summarizes three principal areas of social protective activity for the countries of the world: social security, crime and law enforcement, and military affairs. Because the administrative structure, financing, manning, and scope of institutions and programmed tasks in these fields vary so greatly from country to country, no well-accepted or well-documented body of statistical comparisons exists in international convention to permit objective assessment of any of these subjects, either from the perspective of a single country or internationally. The data provided within any single subject area do, however, represent the most consistent approach to problems of international comparison found in the published literature for that field.

The provision of social security programs to answer specific social needs, for example, is summarized simply in terms of the existence or nonexistence of a specific type of benefit program because of the great complexity of national programs in terms of eligibility, coverage, term, age limits, financing, payments, and so on. Activities connected with a particular type of benefit often take place at more than one governmental level, through more than one agency at the same level, or through a mixture of public and private institutions. The data shown here are summarized from the U.S. Social Security Administration's *Social Security Programs Throughout the World* (biennial). A bullet symbol (●) indicates that a country has at least one program within the defined area; in some cases it may have several. A blank space indicates that no program existed providing the benefit shown; ellipses [...] indicate that no information was available as to whether a program existed.

Data given for social security expenditure as a percentage of total central governmental expenditure are taken from the International Monetary Fund's *Government Finance Statistics Yearbook,* which provides the most comparable analytic series on the consolidated accounts of central governments, governmentally administered social security funds, and independent national agencies, all usually separate accounting entities, through which these services may be provided in a given country.

Data on the finances of social security programs are taken in large part from the International Labour Office's *The Cost of Social Security* (triennial), supplemented by national data sources.

Figures for criminal offenses known to police, usually excluding civil offenses and minor traffic violations, are taken in part from Interpol's *International Crime Statistics* (biennial) and a variety of national sources. Statistics are usually based on the number of offenses reported to police, not the number of offenders apprehended or tried in courts. Attempted offenses are counted as the offense that was attempted. A person identified as having committed multiple offenses is counted only under the most serious offense. Murder refers to all acts involving the voluntary taking of life, including infanticide, but excluding abortion, or involuntary acts such as those normally classified as manslaughter. Assault includes "serious," or aggravated, assault—that involving injury, endangering life, or perpetrated with the use of a dangerous instrument. Burglary involves theft from the premises of another; although Interpol statistics are reported as "breaking and entering," national data may not always distinguish cases of forcible

Social protection

country	social security						finances								
	programs available, 1989					expenditures, 1989 (% of total central govt.)	year	receipts					expenditures			
	old-age, invalidity, death[a]	sickness and maternity[b]	work injury[c]	unemployment[d]	family allowances[e]			total ('000,000 natl. cur.)	insured persons (%)	employers (%)	government (%)	other (%)	total ('000,000 natl. cur.)	benefits (%)	administration (%)	other (%)
Afghanistan			●			...	...	...	...	...	...	...	...	...	...	...
Albania	●	●	●		●	...	1989						1,344.0			
Algeria	●	●	●		●	...	1987	17,632.0	...	...	...	...	16,378.0	94.1	5.6	0.3
American Samoa	●	...	...	...	...	...	1980	2.3	29.3	40.9	...	29.7	0.6	100.0	—	...
Andorra	...	...	...	...	...	...	1990	8,809.7	...	...	...	...	5,195.2	89.3	4.5	6.2
Angola	...	...	...	...	...	...										
Antigua and Barbuda	●	●	●		●	...	1983	13.0	29.2	48.7	—	22.1	4.2	66.1	33.9	...
Argentina	●	●	●	●	●	38.9[3]	1986	4,994.5	31.3	45.6	19.5	3.6	4,500.2	97.4	2.3	0.3
Armenia	●	●	●	●	●	...										
Aruba	●		●			9	1988	40.0	...	...	...	...	35.0	...	...	...
Australia	●	●	●	●	●	25.8	1986	24,310.5	1.8	12.5	84.8	0.9	23,896.9	98.8	1.2	—
Austria	●	●	●	●	●	45.2[10]	1986	368,562.0	29.5	46.8	21.2	2.5	361,191.0	96.2	2.4	1.4
Azerbaijan	●	●	●	●	●	...										
Bahamas, The	●	●	●			9.3[6]	1986	73.6	26.8	40.7	1.3	31.2	31.8	75.6	23.2	1.2
Bahrain	●		●			2.3[10]	1986	35.8	21.1	42.2	—	36.7	7.6	73.2	19.7	7.1
Bangladesh	...		●	...	...	9.8[10, 11]	1986	154.3	37.4	41.8	1.4	19.4	57.9	95.8	4.2	—
Barbados	●	●	●	●		19.8	1986	148.0	37.7	39.4	5.6	17.3	129.5	92.9	5.2	1.9
Belarus	●	●	●	●	●	...	1986	3,199.0	—	—	93.2	6.8	3,199.0	100.0	—	—
Belgium	●	●	●	●	●	41.3	1986	1,347,070.0	24.4	39.7	31.6	4.3	1,322,636.0	94.5	4.3	1.2
Belize	●	●	●			1.1[10]	1986	11.2	9.4	56.4	—	34.2	2.4	52.1	46.2	1.7
Benin	●		●		●	8.7[10, 12]	1986	4,539.2	15.9	78.4	—	5.7	3,906.3	65.5	3.0	1.0
Bermuda	●		●			...										
Bhutan	...	...	...	...	...	...	1990						26.0[10]			
Bolivia	●	●	●		●	13.6	1986	70,737,008.0	25.6	39.4	23.4	11.5	52,958.650.0	82.0	17.6	0.4
Bosnia and Hercegovina	●	●	●	●	●	...										
Botswana			●			1.6[10]	1988						33.0[10]			
Brazil	●	●	●	●	●	17.3	1986	201,807,600.0	38.5	53.5	3.8	4.2	184,814,900.0	91.7	6.4	1.9
Brunei	●		●			...	1984						39.5			
Bulgaria	●	●	●		●	16.1	1986	3,707.4	—	17.8	0.4	—	3,593.0	99.8	0.2	—
Burkina Faso	●		●		●	8.4[6, 10]	1986	8,057.5	15.6	64.3	—	20.1	2,060.4	99.2	—	0.8
Burundi	●		●			0.7[13]	1986	1,368.9	30.9	51.1	—	18.0	933.1	82.2	14.8	3.0
Cambodia	...	...	...	...	...	...										
Cameroon	●		●		●	6.5[10]	1986	56,770.0	14.0	68.2	—	17.8	19,869.0	100.0	—	—
Canada	●	●	●	●	●	28.6	1986	87,538.9	11.7	16.6	61.2	10.5	77,122.0	96.2	2.7	1.1
Cape Verde	●	●	●			...	1986	499.9	27.5	62.5	1.5	8.5	210.3	62.3	14.7	23.0
Cayman Islands	●	...	...	...	...	3.0[10]	1990	—					3.6[10]			
Central African Republic	●		●		●	6.2[2, 10]	1986	4,549.0	9.8	88.5	...	1.7	5,550.0	45.7	13.6	40.7
Chad	●		●		●	1.9[15]	1986	1,221.9	26.3	65.9[10]	—	7.8	841.4	41.4	55.3	3.3
Chile	●	●	●	●	●	29.2[3]	1986	588,205.0	30.1	2.0	48.9	19.0	425,099.0	92.0	7.4	0.6
China	●	●	●	●		...										
Colombia	●	●	●		●	19.6[2]	1986	169,872.0	21.5	56.5	1.7	20.2	133,837.0	51.6	42.3	6.1
Comoros	...	...	...	...	...	...	1983	40.7	100.0	—	—	—	54.3	17.4	62.3	20.3
Congo	...		●		●	0.4[18]	1983	15,272.8	12.1	80.2	—	7.7	7,256.7	66.6	21.3	12.1
Cook Islands	...	...	...	...	...	...										
Costa Rica	●	●	●		●	13.2	1986	23,387.4	25.5	49.2	2.7	22.6	18,080.1	81.8	3.8	14.4
Côte d'Ivoire	●		●		●	3.6[2]	1986	40,277.4	13.6	53.1	—	33.3	22,866.5	79.6	14.1	6.3
Croatia	●	●	●	●	●	...										
Cuba	●	●	●			...	1986	1,887.7	—	41.8	58.2	—	1,887.7	96.4	—	3.6
Cyprus[19]	●	●	●	●		18.5	1986	141.6	29.4	39.9	17.2	13.5	81.7	98.5	1.4	0.1
Czechoslovakia	●	●	●		●	20.6	1986	120,692.0	—	3.7	94.5	1.8	120,692.0	99.7	0.3	—
Denmark	●	...	●	●	●	36.4[3, 10]	1986	178,991.9	3.5	8.0	85.7	2.8	174,349.8	97.1	2.9	—
Djibouti	●	...	●		●	6.2[10, 14]	1979	1,352.2	...	...	...	...	1,115.7	...	...	...
Dominica	●	●	●			1.4[12]		12.3	24.9	...	...	26.5	4.4	68.0	32.0	—
Dominican Republic	●	●	●			3.3[3, 10]	1986	77.9	20.1	72.9	—	6.8	74.3	75.9	24.1	—
Ecuador	●	●	●			11.6[3, 10]	1986	101,137.5	16.4	24.3	11.0	48.3	41,625.0	88.1	11.9	—

entry. Automobile theft excludes brief use of a car without the owner's permission, "joyriding," and implies intent to deprive the owner of the vehicle permanently. Criminal offense data for certain countries refer to cases disposed of in court, rather than to complaints. Police manpower figures refer, for the most part, to full-time, paid professional staff, excluding clerical support and volunteer staff. Personnel in military service who perform police functions are presumed to be employed in their principal activity, military service.

The figures for military manpower refer to full-time, active-duty military service and exclude reserve, militia, paramilitary, and similar organizations. Because of the difficulties attached to the analysis of data on military manpower and budgets (including problems such as data withheld on national security grounds, or the publication of budgetary data specifically intended to hide actual expenditure, or the complexity of long-term financing of purchases of military matériel [how much was actually spent as opposed to what was committed, offset by nonmilitary transfers, etc.]), extensive use is made of the principal international analytic tools: publications such as those of the International Institute for Strategic Studies (*The Military Balance* and *Strategic Survey*) and the U.S. Arms Control and Disarmament Agency (*World Military Expenditures and Arms Transfers*), both annuals.

The data on military expenditures are from the sources identified above, as well as from the IMF's *Government Finance Statistical Yearbook* and country statistical publications.

The following notes further define the column headings:

a. Programs providing cash payments for *each* of the three types of long-term benefit indicated to persons (1) exceeding a specified working age (usually 50–65, often 5 years earlier for women) who are qualified by a term of covered employment, (2) partially or fully incapacitated for their usual employment by injury or illness, and (3) qualified by their status as spouse, cohabitant, or dependent minor of a qualified person who dies.

b. Programs providing cash payments (jointly, or alternatively, medical services as well) to occupationally qualified persons for *both* of the short-term benefits indicated: (1) illness and (2) maternity.

c. Programs providing cash or medical services to employment-qualified persons who become temporarily or permanently incapacitated (fully or partially) by work-related injury or illness.

d. Programs providing term-limited cash compensation (usually 40–75% of average earnings) to persons qualified by previous employment (of six months minimum, typically) for periods of involuntary unemployment.

e. Programs providing cash payments to families or mothers to mitigate the cost of raising children and to encourage the formation of larger families.

f. A police officer is a full-time, paid professional, performing domestic security functions. Data include administrative staff but exclude clerical employees, volunteers, and members of paramilitary groups.

g. Includes all active-duty personnel, regular and conscript, performing national security functions. Excludes reserves, paramilitary forces, border patrols, and gendarmeries.

crime and law enforcement (latest)					population per police officer[f]	military protection								country
offenses reported to the police per 100,000 population						manpower, 1992[g]		expenditure, 1989				arms trade, 1989 ('000,000 U.S.$)		
total	personal		property			total ('000)	per 1,000 population	total '000,000	per capita	% of central government expenditure	% of GDP or GNP	imports	exports	
	murder	assault	burglary	automobile theft										
...	...	...	...	...	540[1]	45.0	2.4	287[2]	21[2]	64.4[2]	7.7[2]	3,800	0	Afghanistan
...	...	...	...	...	550	40.0	11.9	157	49	11.4[3]	4.1	0	0	Albania
2,080	...	109.0	...	...	840	139.0	5.3	2,313	94	9.0[3]	5.1	575	0	Algeria
5,183	13.1	995.0	696.0	52.4	460	—	[4]	...	...	...	...	...	...	American Samoa
5,430	...	46.0	1,510.0	254.0	220	—	—	...	...	...	...	...	...	Andorra
237	10.9	0.8	...	0.1	14[5]	127.5	12.0	1,127[6]	161[6]	28.8[7]	23.9[6]	750	0	Angola
2,568	...	297.3	844.0	...	120	0.7[7]	8.9[7]	...	...	...	...	...	...	Antigua and Barbuda
637	8.5	0.6	—	110.4	1,270	65.0	2.0	1,854	58	12.0[8]	3.4	40	60	Argentina
363	6.1	7.0	...	...	...	...	...	...	...	...	...	...	...	Armenia
3,938	37.5	393.1	...	...	...	...	[4]	—	—	—	—	...	...	Aruba
6,773	4.5	369.6	1,962.8	770.6	450	67.9	3.9	6,153	368	9.2	2.3	675	80	Australia
6,007	2.3	1.8	1,151.6	26.7	470	52.0	6.6	1,402	184	2.8	1.1	100	40	Austria
201	...	...	...	...	...	...	...	...	...	...	...	...	...	Azerbaijan
6,836	52.6	115.8	2,580.4	...	155	0.7	2.7	9[2]	40[2]	2.5[2]	0.5[2]	...	...	Bahamas, The
1,878	0.6	624.3	63.5	...	180	6.2	11.6	196	389	13.1	6.5	50	0	Bahrain
16.8	2.0	2.1	4.4	0.3	2,560	107.0	1.0	323	3	15.1	1.6	120	0	Bangladesh
4,519	11.7	109.0	323.0	13.6	280	—	—	10	38	1.8	0.6	0	0	Barbados
650	2.9	7.0	...	...	...	125.0	36.5	...	...	...	...	...	...	Belarus
3,338	2.2	120.7	690.9	281.0	640	80.7	8.1	3,881	392	7.2	2.5	220	20	Belgium
1,869	...	573.8	420.2	...	290	0.7	3.4	4[2]	25[2]	4.0[2]	2.0[2]	...	...	Belize
1,234	...	...	...	...	3,250	4.4	0.9	33	7	19.4	2.0	0	0	Benin
7,413	10.8	154.6	2,092.3	...	370	—	[4]	—	—	—	—	...	...	Bermuda
...	...	...	...	...	...	4.0[11]	3.1[11]	...	...	...	...	...	...	Bhutan
...	...	...	...	...	...	31.5	4.1	182	27	25.3	4.0	10	0	Bolivia
558	...	...	...	...	...	67.0	15.2	...	...	...	...	...	...	Bosnia and Hercegovina
6,693	19.5	442.6	411.8	...	750	6.1	4.5	62	52	6.0	2.8	10	0	Botswana
116	...	...	...	...	...	296.7	2.0	5,731[3]	41[3]	2.3[3]	1.3[3]	160	50	Brazil
358	0.4	3.7	113.9	10.8	100	4.5	16.6	305[2]	1,398[2]	24.5[2]	8.1[2]	...	...	Brunei
...	...	...	...	...	...	107.0	11.9	5,885	656	29.7	11.9	290	160	Bulgaria
41	0.2	4.1	—	...	...	8.7	0.9	52[3]	6[3]	17.5[3]	2.1[3]	10	0	Burkina Faso
87	3.3	7.4	...	...	...	7.2	1.3	28	5	14.2	2.6	10	0	Burundi
...	...	...	...	...	1,980	135.0	15.0	...	...	...	...	490	0	Cambodia
...	0.2	0.1	0.2	0.3	1,170	11.7	0.9	148	14	6.6	1.3	5	0	Cameroon
11,442.6	5.7	134.3	1,331.7	382.7	8,640	84.0	3.0	10,840	413	8.8	2.0	190	410	Canada
...	...	...	...	...	110	1.3	3.8	12[14]	47[14]	13.5[14]	11.8[14]	5	0	Cape Verde
10,039	10.7	619.2	1,526.7	...	110	—	[4]	—	—	—	—	...	...	Cayman Islands
135	1.6	22.8	2.7	...	2,740[1]	6.5	2.2	18	6	6.6	1.7	0	0	Central African Republic
...	...	...	...	...	990	25.2	4.2	39[3]	8[3]	45.1[3]	4.3[3]	10	0	Chad
1,347	5.8	107.0	...	11.2	470	91.8	6.8	790	61	16.3[3]	3.4	120	160	Chile
201	1.9	4.1	17.5	...	1,360[16]	3,030.0	2.6	22,330	20	19.1	3.7	110	2,000	China
840	40.5	266.9	...	...	420	139.0	4.1	758	23	16.4	2.1	150	0	Colombia
...	...	...	...	...	960	—	[17]	...	...	...	...	...	...	Comoros
32	1.5	4.7	0.2	0.2	870	10.9	3.7	99[8]	49[8]	12.5[8]	5.1[8]	0	0	Congo
...	...	...	...	...	...	—	[4]	...	...	...	...	...	...	Cook Islands
868	5.3	11.1	232.4	23.1	480	7.5	2.4	22	8	1.6	0.5	...	...	Costa Rica
262	2.6	47.9	12.2	19.9	4,640	7.1	0.5	130	11	9.2[3]	1.5	0	0	Côte d'Ivoire
1,087	...	...	...	...	...	105.0	21.8	...	...	...	...	...	...	Croatia
...	...	...	...	...	650	175.0	16.1	1,377	131	10.2	3.9	1,200	5	Cuba
671	3.2	12.3	208.7	2.8	180	8.0	10.6	41	59	3.0	0.9	40	0	Cyprus[19]
1,911	2.0	89.4	621.5	95.7	640	145.8	9.3	8,361	534	21.7	6.8	460	875	Czechoslovakia
10,270	4.6	163.4	2,382.9	575.9	600	29.2	5.7	2,184	426	5.2	2.2	110	20	Denmark
487	4.8	67.0	14.4	9.8	...	3.8	6.8	27[2]	67[2]	22.4[2]	8.1[2]	...	...	Djibouti
22,432	9.3	47.0	1,025.0	11.0	300	—	—	...	...	...	...	...	...	Dominica
946	11.9	30.8	154.0	24.8	580	22.2	3.0	52	7	5.0	0.8	5	0	Dominican Republic
333	5.1	4.0	...	4.3	260	57.5	5.4	163	16	11.6	1.7	20	0	Ecuador

Social protection (continued)

country	old-age, invalidity, death[a]	sickness and maternity[b]	work injury[c]	unemployment[d]	family allowances[e]	expenditures, 1989 (% of total central govt.)	year	receipts total ('000,000 natl. cur.)	insured persons (%)	employers (%)	government (%)	other (%)	expenditures total ('000,000 natl. cur.)	benefits (%)	administration (%)	other (%)
Egypt	•	•	•	•	...	12.0	1988	2,633.0	38.6	61.4	—	—	2,596.0	...	...	...
El Salvador	•	•	•	...	...	2.2	1986	287.4	23.2	54.0	—	22.8	210.9	75.0	25.0	—
Equatorial Guinea	...	•	...	...	...	...	1983	43.0	4.7	95.3	—	—	20.0	30.0	70.0	—
Estonia	•	•	•	...	•	...										
Ethiopia	•	...	•	...	...	4.6[8]	1986	162.1	32.5	63.2	—	4.2	116.3	98.2	1.8	—
Faeroe Islands	•	...	...	...	•	...										
Fiji	•	...	•	...	...	4.0	1986	111.6	26.5	26.5	...	47.0	34.4	94.8	5.2	...
Finland	•	•	•	•	•	33.2[10]	1986	90,413.3	8.3	39.7	44.7	7.3	82,164.8	96.8	3.2	—
France	•	•	•	•	•	38.7[8]	1986	1,431,025.0	23.4	50.6	23.0	3.0	1,439,788.7	95.1	4.0	0.9
French Guiana	•	...	•	...	•	...	1987	597.8	...	...	...	...	653.7	...	...	...
French Polynesia	•	...	...	...	•	...	1988	14,902.3	...	...	...	...	13,640.5	...	...	...
Gabon	•	•	•	...	•	...	1986	37,788.0	8.3	84.8	—	6.9	42,326.0	80.7	15.1	4.2
Gambia, The	•	...	•	...	...	3.5[22]	1982	—	...	...	...	...	5.6	...	...	...
Gaza Strip	...	...	...	...	...	...										
Georgia	•	•	•	...	•	...										
Germany	•[23]	•[23]	•[23]	•[23]	•[23]	47.9[3,10,23]	1986[23]	459,340.0	36.6	35.0	25.8	2.6	451,885.0	97.2	2.8	—
Ghana	•	•	...	...	...	6.4[3]										
Gibraltar	•	•	...	•	•	...										
Greece	•	•	•	•	•	28.8[14]	1986	872,503.0	29.4	42.5	21.4	6.7	898,814.0	93.7	6.3	...
Greenland	•	...	...	...	...	...										
Grenada	•	•	...	...	...	5.0[10,13]	1986	15.2	27.7	57.9	—	14.4	6.0	91.0	9.0	...
Guadeloupe	•	...	•	...	•	...	1987	3,111.2	...	...	...	...	1,833.5	...	...	...
Guam	•	...	...	...	...	...	1989	...	...	...	...	...	7.3	...	...	...
Guatemala	•	•	•	...	...	5.2[10]	1986	209.0	26.9	55.9	—	17.2	134.4	86.0	10.9	3.1
Guernsey	...	...	...	...	...											
Guinea	•	•	•	...	•	...	1986	269.2	3.0	90.9	—	6.1	268.7	85.2	1.8	13.0
Guinea-Bissau	...	•	•	...	•	8.8[10]	1986	138.0	22.8	63.4	10.3	3.8	61.9	59.6	40.4	...
Guyana	•	•	•	...	...	3.7[7]	1986	200.2	17.3	21.4	0.7	60.6	62.1	80.2	18.2	1.6
Haiti	•	•	•	...	...	5.1[2]	1977	60.5	—26.6—		69.9	3.5	52.4	92.7	7.3	...
Honduras	•	•	•	...	...	4.5[12]	1986	166.2	23.9	40.8	3.3	32.0	76.8	84.6	15.4	...
Hong Kong	•	•	•	...	•	...	1989–90	...	...	...	...	...	4,155.0	87.0	13.0	—
Hungary	•	•	•	...	•	28.1	1986	149,400.0	21.1	78.9	...	...	142,939.0	99.3	0.7	—
Iceland	•	•	•	•	•[24]	3.5[8]	1988	9,413.0	—	21.0	79.0	...	45,577.0	98.1	1.9	...
India	•	•	•	•	...	...	1986	87,807.7	9.8	66.9	9.6	13.7	40,362.2	98.4	1.6	—
Indonesia	•	...	•	...	...	—	1986	97.9	17.3	58.1	—	24.6	92.2	12.5	19.4	68.1
Iran	•	•	•	•	•	14.5	1986	346,460.0	83.2	0.1	8.2	8.5	167,879.0	43.4	6.3	50.0
Iraq	•	•	•	•	•	...	1977	107.8	9.9	55.6	21.9	12.6	71.0	94.0	2.4	3.6
Ireland	•	•	•	•	•	26.8	1986	4,299.6	13.0	24.4	61.7	0.9	4,302.2	95.2	4.7	0.1
Isle of Man	•	•	•	•	•	37.0[25]	1985	...	...	...	...	...	14.4	...	...	...
Israel	•	•	•	•	•	20.4	1986	6,723.0	23.9	37.3	30.7	8.1	6,146.8	89.9	5.4	4.7
Italy	•	•	•	•	•	28.5[3]	1986	90,646.0	19.5	51.7	17.6	11.2	100,251.0	89.3	2.0	8.7
Jamaica	•	•	•	...	•	3.2[13]	1986	330.4	11.8	14.3	36.1	37.8	171.5	93.4	6.0	0.6
Japan	•	•	•	•	•	...	1986	50,525,725.0	27.2	30.6	26.8	15.4	40,145,652.0	94.6	1.7	3.7
Jersey	•	•	•	...	...	9.8	1990	56.9	—62.6—		23.4	14.0	47.5	...	...	...
Jordan	•	...	•	...	...	8.3	1986	53.6	28.7	55.3	—	16.0	9.5	77.4	14.0	8.6
Kazakhstan	•	•	•	...	•	...										
Kenya	•	...	•	...	...	0.1	1986	1,660.0	27.7	27.7	1.2	43.4	268.0	85.1	14.9	—
Kiribati	...	...	...	...	...											
Korea, North	...	•	...	...	...											
Korea, South	•	•	•	...	...	6.9	1990	1,286,000.0	31.6	68.4	—	...	2,037,000.0	...	...	...
Kuwait	•	...	•	...	•	8.5	1986	385.8	6.3	12.4	54.6	26.7	169.5	96.3	3.7	—
Kyrgyzstan	•	•	•	...	•	...										
Laos	•	•	•	...	...	...										
Latvia	•	•	•	...	•	...										
Lebanon	•	•	•	...	•	...										
Lesotho	...	...	•	...	...	1.0[11]	1988	...	...	...	...	...	5.3	...	...	...
Liberia	•	•	•	...	...	0.7[6]	1983	2.9	—	69.0	13.8	17.2	2.6	54.4	45.6	...
Libya	•	•	•	•	•	...	1977	192.9	9.1	28.7	58.7	3.5	128.2	96.2	3.2	0.5
Liechtenstein	•	•	•	•	•	...										
Lithuania	•	•	•	...	•	...										
Luxembourg	•	•	•	•	•	47.3	1986	59,427.9	24.7	34.2	34.5	6.6	51,643.0	96.8	2.7	0.5
Macau	•	...	...	...	...	...	1989	89.0	...	...	...	...	93.5	...	...	...
Macedonia	•	•	•	...	•	...										
Madagascar	•	...	•	...	•	10.3[28]	1986	10,288.2	22.2	77.8	—	—	10,075.3	87.0	13.0	—
Malawi	...	•	...	...	...	—	1986	...	...	...	...	...	5.4	...	...	...
Malaysia	•	...	•	...	...	3.8[8]	1986	6,304.0	21.6	40.5	2.5	35.4	1,589.3	93.9	6.1	...
Maldives	...	...	...	...	...	1.1	1989	—	...	...	...	...	6.4	...	...	...
Mali	•	•	•	...	•	3.0[3]	1986	8,128.8	16.6	74.3	—	9.1	7,924.6	63.7	34.7	1.6
Malta	•	•	•	•	•	33.5	1986	71.6	26.8	33.5	39.7	—	94.0	94.4	5.6	—
Marshall Islands	...	...	...	...	...	...										
Martinique	•	...	•	...	•	...	1988	2,332.2	...	...	...	...	3,706.2	...	...	...
Mauritania	•	...	•	...	•	3.7[12]	1986	584.6	6.3	87.7	—	6.0	583.3	81.8	18.2	...
Mauritius	•	•	•	•	•	15.1[10]	1986	993.8	9.6	35.0	37.7	17.7	654.1	95.1	4.1	0.8
Mayotte	...	...	...	...	...	...										
Mexico	•	•	•	...	...	9.4	1986	2,463,649.0	19.6	63.1	5.0	12.3	2,115,574.0	73.6	17.3	9.1
Micronesia	•	...	...	...	...	...										
Moldova	•	•	•	...	•	...										
Monaco	•	•	•	•	•	...										
Mongolia	•	•	•	...	•	...										
Morocco	•	•	•	...	•	6.9[8,10]	1986	3,660.7	27.6	41.2	—	31.2	2,506.5	94.5	3.5	1.9
Mozambique	•	...	...	...	...	...	1986	228.2	—	86.2	13.7	0.1	145.0	100.0	—	—
Myanmar (Burma)	•	•	...	...	...	0.3	1986	44.3	19.9	59.6	18.5	2.0	35.9	51.5	15.6	32.9
Namibia	...	...	...	...	...	...										
Nauru	•	•	•	...	...	...										
Nepal	...	...	•	...	...	0.7[11]	1985	—	...	...	...	...	59.3	...	...	...

crime and law enforcement (latest)					population per police officer[f]	military protection								country
offenses reported to the police per 100,000 population						manpower, 1992[9]		expenditure, 1989				arms trade, 1989 ('000,000 U.S.$)		
total	personal		property			total ('000)	per 1,000 population	total '000,000	per capita	% of central government expenditure	% of GDP or GNP	imports	exports	
	murder	assault	burglary	automobile theft										
3,314	1.6	0.7	...	3.4	580	410.0	7.3	3,499	67	10.7	5.0	600	370	Egypt
...	...	...	...	...	1,000	43.7	8.0	252	48	37.3	4.0	70	0	El Salvador
...	...	...	...	...	190	1.3	3.5	2[20]	9[20]	21.0[20]	...	10	0	Equatorial Guinea
1,213	5.6	20.5	...	...	...	2.0	1.3	...	...	...	...	...	...	Estonia
94	6.7	24.8	1.9	...	1,100	21	21	763	15	30.4	12.8	925	0	Ethiopia
...	...	...	...	...	...	—	[4]	...	...	...	...	...	0	Faeroe Islands
1,915	4.3	31.6	411.1	...	440	5.0	6.7	26	35	8.8[3]	2.2	0	0	Fiji
9,631	0.6	47.2	1,432.6	364.8	640	32.8	6.5	1,788	360	5.3	1.6	20	0	Finland
6,169	4.4	86.5	712.0	519.6	630	431.7	7.5	35,260	628	8.6	3.7	210	2,700	France
...	...	...	...	...	...	—	[4]	...	...	...	...	...	...	French Guiana
...	...	...	...	...	...	—	[4]	...	...	...	...	...	...	French Polynesia
323	2.2	25.3	62.2	20.9	1,290	4.8	3.8	140	132	12.4	4.5	20	0	Gabon
...	...	...	...	...	3,310	0.8	1.2	1	2	2.0	0.7	0	0	Gambia, The
4,355	...	...	...	...	...	—	—	—	—	—	—	...	...	Gaza Strip
...	...	...	...	...	...	...	...	...	...	...	...	...	...	Georgia
7,108[23]	3.9[23]	107.0[23]	1,749.1[23]	115.1[23]	...	447.0	5.6	33,600	544	9.5	2.8	875	1,200	Germany
864	2.0	95.9	4.7	...	620	7.2	0.5	30	2	3.1[3]	0.6	30	0	Ghana
10,039	—	860.2	...	...	170	—	[4]	...	...	...	...	...	...	Gibraltar
3,306	2.0	97.6	265.0	68.4	380	159.3	15.5	3,097	309	13.4	5.9	2,000	0	Greece
10,339	23.5	671.5	924.2	...	340	—	[4]	...	...	...	...	...	...	Greenland
2,679	10.0	880.0	153.0	...	230	—	—	...	...	...	...	...	...	Grenada
...	...	...	...	...	...	—	[4]	—	—	—	—	...	...	Guadeloupe
9,299	10.1	109.9	700.9	208.1	...	—	[4]	—	—	—	—	...	...	Guam
510	27.4	77.1	27.9	58.1	670	44.6	4.7	131	15	13.0	1.6	10	0	Guatemala
...	...	...	...	...	...	—	[4]	—	—	—	—	...	...	Guernsey
32.4	1.0	0.8	1.3	0.5	1,140	9.7	1.3	27[3]	4[3]	6.7[3]	1.2[3]	10	0	Guinea
...	...	...	...	...	...	9.2	9.1	3[8]	4[8]	4.1[8]	2.4[8]	10	0	Guinea-Bissau
1,980	15.6	28.1	434.7	...	190	2.0	2.7	6	8	3.6	2.7	0	0	Guyana
701	...	...	...	...	400	7.4	1.1	45	8	12.4	1.9	0	0	Haiti
...	9.4	7.7	...	3.3	1,040	16.8	3.4	150	32	15.5	3.2	30	0	Honduras
1,522	2.6	129.9	218.9	37.6	220	—	[4]	...	...	...	...	...	...	Hong Kong
3,287	3.1	66.0	742.9	77.6	710	80.8	7.8	4,064	384	20.1	6.3	30	50	Hungary
1,550	0.9	64.3	704.8	112.8	940	—	—	—	—	—	—	0	...	Iceland
187	3.5	...	19.3	...	820	1,265.0	1.4	8,174	10	13.6	3.1	3,500	0	India
134	0.9	6.2	28.4	6.0	1,340	283.0	1.5	1,510	8	8.2	1.7	90	0	Indonesia
76.6	0.5	47.7	...	...	...	528.0	8.9	21,120[11]	449[11]	34.1[11]	7.9[11]	1,300	0	Iran
91	1.7	21.7	40.8	1.4	140	382.5	20.3	16,710[11]	1,098[11]	50.8[22]	30.7[8]	1,900	60	Iraq
2,476	0.8	2.1	821.5	31.6	310	13.0	3.7	449	128	3.7	1.6	5	0	Ireland
...	...	...	...	...	...	—	[4]	...	...	...	...	...	...	Isle of Man
5,234	2.2	202.5	2,483.0	315.6	210	175.0	33.4	5,745	1,323	25.2	12.8	725	625	Israel
4,358	6.4	33.8	...	546.0	680	354.0	6.2	20,720	360	4.9	2.4	300	60	Italy
1,927	20.9	476.0	305.6	14.8	430	3.4	1.4	36	15	2.2[3]	1.1	5	0	Jamaica
1,397	1.0	15.7	184.3	27.6	480	246.0	2.0	28,410	231	6.0[3]	1.0	1,400	110	Japan
...	...	...	...	...	...	—	[4]	...	...	...	...	...	...	Jersey
625	1.9	13.6	44.4	12.3	630	99.4	27.3	548	175	32.7	12.7	190	5	Jordan
815	...	...	...	...	...	...	...	...	...	...	...	...	...	Kazakhstan
364	4.2	57.3	63.5	6.6	1,500	24.2	0.9	210	9	9.5	2.7	10	0	Kenya
285	12.4	5.5	73.3	...	330	—	—	...	...	...	...	...	...	Kiribati
...	...	...	...	...	460	1,132.0	50.9	6,000	285	40.7[3]	20.0	525	400	Korea, North
2,637	1.5	42.5	12.3	...	420	633.0	14.5	9,100	213	23.8	4.3	525	400	Korea, South
695	6.6	25.8	66.8	17.1	80	11.7	9.8	1,964	962	19.9	6.2	490	0	Kuwait
581	...	...	...	...	...	...	...	...	...	...	...	...	...	Kyrgyzstan
...	...	...	...	...	280	37.0	8.4	55[6]	156[6]	21.3[2]	10.5[2]	100	0	Laos
1,292	...	...	...	...	...	2.6	0.9	...	...	...	...	...	...	Latvia
366	13.2	14.1	65.7	67.3	530	36.8	13.1	429[7]	135[7]	20.0[7]	8.2[7]	10	10	Lebanon
1,896	51.1	204.3	201.3	...	1,130	2.0	1.1	11[8]	7[8]	9.4[8]	2.3[8]	0	0	Lesotho
1,007	2.9	5.7	...	...	1,570	—[26]	—[26]	58	23	13.3	4.8	10	0	Liberia
...	...	...	...	...	...	85.0	19.1	3,309	808	29.2	14.9	975	40	Libya
...	...	...	...	...	660	—	[27]	—	—	...	...	...	...	Liechtenstein
991	...	...	...	...	...	7.0	1.8	...	...	...	...	...	...	Lithuania
6,628	2.2	84.1	1,047.3	131.5	730	0.8	2.2	76	200	2.7[3]	0.9	10	5	Luxembourg
1,226	1.8	133.8	152.2	47.4	...	—	[4]	...	...	...	...	...	...	Macau
686	...	...	...	...	...	20.0	9.8	...	...	...	...	...	...	Macedonia
...	...	...	...	...	2,900	21.0	1.6	35	3	28.9	1.5	30	0	Madagascar
1,001	2.6	96.5	15.6	...	1,670	10.8	1.1	35	4	8.2	2.3	5	0	Malawi
451	1.9	14.3	97.7	18.4	760	127.5	7.0	1,039	61	10.0	2.9	70	0	Malaysia
2,353	1.9	3.3	36.1	...	35,710	—	[4]	...	...	...	...	...	...	Maldives
33	—	1.1	3.9	—	160	7.4	0.9	41	5	7.9[3]	2.0	10	10	Mali
2,802	10.4	50.6	1,907.1	367.1	230	1.7	4.6	22	62	2.4	1.1	0	0	Malta
2,273	...	...	...	...	400	—	[29]	...	...	...	...	...	...	Marshall Islands
4,284	7.3	104.6	711.9	101.8	...	—	[4]	—	—	—	—	...	...	Martinique
...	...	...	...	...	710	9.6	4.6	40	22	13.4	4.3	20	0	Mauritania
2,770	2.5	15.1	50.0	...	240	—	[4]	5	4	0.9	0.2	5	0	Mauritius
...	...	...	...	...	...	—	[4]	—	—	—	—	...	...	Mayotte
108	7.3	30.2	...	...	...	175.0	2.1	875	10	2.3	0.5	20	10	Mexico
...	...	...	...	...	...	—	[29]	...	...	...	...	...	...	Micronesia
...	...	...	...	...	...	...	...	...	...	...	...	...	...	Moldova
4,614	...	170.2	373.7	140.1	...	—	—	...	...	...	...	...	...	Monaco
...	...	...	...	...	120	15.5	7.1	259	122	...	...	0	0	Mongolia
769	1.5	170.5	...	...	840	195.5	7.5	1,203	48	21.1[8]	5.5	40	0	Morocco
...	...	...	...	...	...	50.2	3.4	107	8	40.7[3]	9.7	120	0	Mozambique
262	4.9	35.5	0.1	50.2	650	286.0	6.6	611	15	24.3[3]	3.7	20	0	Myanmar (Burma)
...	...	...	...	...	...	—	[4]	...	...	...	...	...	...	Namibia
...	25.0	400.0	100.0	...	110	—	—	...	...	...	...	...	...	Nauru
29.1	2.2	0.5	0.2	...	1,000	35.0	1.8	33	2	6.2	1.2	0	0	Nepal

Social protection (continued)

country	social security — programs available, 1989					expenditures, 1989 (% of total central govt.)	finances — year	receipts total ('000,000 natl. cur.)	insured persons (%)	employers (%)	government (%)	other (%)	expenditures total ('000,000 natl. cur.)	benefits (%)	administration (%)	other (%)
	old-age, invalidity, death[a]	sickness and maternity[b]	work injury[c]	unemployment[d]	family allowances[e]											
Netherlands, The	●	●	●	...	●	33.2	1986	140,734.0	38.0	33.4	15.6	13.0	122,791.0	97.0	3.0	...
Netherlands Antilles	●	●	●	...	...	15.2[8,9]	1990	115.1	100.0	...	...	...	125.5	...	...	...
New Caledonia	...	●	●	...	●	...	1987	15,834.0					14,598.0			
New Zealand	●	●	●	●	●	—	1986	9,645.5	1.6	3.1	92.5	2.9	9,534.5	97.4	2.4	0.2
Nicaragua	●	●	●	...	●	3.3[20]	1983	832.9	20.4	53.5	10.4	15.7	427.5	65.5	28.5	6.0
Niger	●	●	●	...	●	1.7[10,20]	1986	12,890.6	12.3	39.2	37.8	10.7	10,032.1	49.0	32.4	18.6
Nigeria	●	...	●	...	...	2.5[32]	1986	108.4	17.9	24.4	—	57.7	17.5	44.7	55.3 ·	—
Northern Mariana Islands	...	...	...	...	...											
Norway	●	●	●	●	●	38.0[10]	1986	157,853.7	17.5	24.6	55.7	2.2	153,249.6	99.0	1.0	—
Oman	...	...	...	...	...		1990						38.0[10]			
Pakistan	●	●	●	...	...	0.2[6]	1986	5,134.8	1.0	10.1	83.6	5.3	4,629.5	98.4	1.2	0.4
Palau	...	...	...	...	...											
Panama	●	●	●	●	...	20.0	1986	500.5	30.0	44.9	3.4	21.7	425.9	94.3	5.5	0.2
Papua New Guinea	●	...	●	...	...	0.5[3]	1983	45.0	40.5	32.1	8.0	19.4	9.4	82.3	9.7	8.0
Paraguay	●	●	●	...	●	13.3	1988	49,272.0					40,588.0			
Peru	●	●	●	...	●	0.2[7]	1986	7,041,677.0	31.1	68.9	—	—	6,136,672.0	39.5	51.6	8.9
Philippines	●	●	●	...	...	1.1	1986	10,705.0	18.6	26.5	—	54.9	4,244.8	86.9	13.1	—
Poland	●	●	●	●	●	...	1986	2,242,443.0	2.6	60.7	35.3	1.4	1,830,162.0	99.2	0.8	—
Portugal	●	●	●	●	●	24.0[8,10]	1986	494,527.0	24.6	66.0	7.0	2.4	459,353.8	95.4	4.6	—
Puerto Rico	●	●	●	●	●	...	1980						1,041.3	100.0	...	...
Qatar	...	...	...	...	...	...	1986	80.0	...	...	100.0	—	80.0	100.0	—	—
Réunion	...	...	...	...	...											
Romania	●	●	●	...	●	23.5	1983	72,064.9	...	54.0	46.0	—	63,927.5	100.0	...	...
Russia	●	●	●	●	●											
Rwanda	●	...	●	...	...	2.9[8,22]	1986	2,123.8	24.5	41.0	—	34.5	585.9	65.0	35.0	—
St. Kitts and Nevis	●	●	●	...	...	9.4[8,10]	1989	14.3					7.9			
St. Lucia	●	●	●	...	...	...	1986	14.6	28.6	28.6	—	42.8	3.4	61.4	38.6	—
St. Vincent and the Grenadines	●	●	●	...	...	2.3[3,10]	1989									
San Marino	●	●	●	...	●	...	1983	51,673.0	12.0	48.7	36.1	3.2	46,179.0	95.7	3.7	0.6
São Tomé and Príncipe	...	...	...	...	...	...	1986	46.4	37.7	56.3	—	6.0	23.7	100.0	—	—
Saudi Arabia	●	...	●	...	...	...										
Senegal	●	●	●	...	●	2.6[2,10]	1986	22,094.0	21.2	69.9	—	8.7	18,827.0	84.8	15.3	—
Seychelles	●	●	●	...	●	5.3[13]	1983	69.1	30.1	60.2	—	9.7	42.7	69.6	4.9	25.5
Sierra Leone	●	...	●	...	...	1.7[2]	1977	10.5	—26.7—		73.3	—	10.0	100.0	—	—
Singapore	●	●	●	...	...	2.0	1986	6,691.0	51.0	23.2	0.1	25.7	5,601.2	71.9	0.4	27.7
Slovenia	●	●	●	●	●											
Solomon Islands	●	...	●	...	...	0.6[3]	1986	13.7	27.9	41.8	—	30.3	6.8	40.8	11.5	47.7
Somalia	●	...	●	...	...	1.7[10,32]										
South Africa	●	●	●	●	...	...	1987	976.0	—	100.0	...	...	668.0	...	...	...
Bophuthatswana	...	...	...	...	...	...										
Ciskei	...	...	...	...	...	...	1984						21.9			
Transkei	...	...	...	...	...											
Venda	...	...	...	...	...											
Spain	●	●	●	●	●	34.8[3]	1986	5,893,481.0	16.4	54.0	27.1	2.5	5,801,152.0	95.0	2.7	2.3
Sri Lanka	●	●	●	...	...	12.6[10]	1986	10,432.8	20.9	24.2	32.2	22.7	4,022.6	98.8	1.1	0.1
Sudan, The	●	...	●	...	...	2.2[22]	1986	42.1	14.3	28.7	—	57.0	8.5	49.4	50.6	—
Suriname	●	...	●	...	●	6.0[6]	1983	125.8	35.8	26.5	36.6	1.1	106.3	98.1	1.9	—
Swaziland	●	...	●	...	...	0.4[10]	1986	10.7	31.4	31.4	—	37.2	3.9	45.8	54.2	—
Sweden	●	●	●	●	●	48.4	1986	318,641.9	1.8	38.5	49.2	10.5	291,962.1	95.9	4.1	—
Switzerland	●	●	●	●	●	49.9[2]	1986	37,602.7	45.1	23.2	26.3	5.4	35,691.2	91.5	2.8	5.7
Syria	●	...	●	...	...	2.2	1989	—	...	...	...	...	1,150.0	...	...	...
Taiwan	●	●	●	...	●	18.2[22,10]										
Tajikistan	●	●	●	●	●											
Tanzania	●	...	●	...	...	0.5[11]	1986	1,286.6	26.9	33.7	2.0	37.4	487.7	41.4	55.3	3.3
Thailand	●	...	●	...	...	3.4	1986	284.8	—	100.0	...	...	246.0	88.8	11.2	...
Togo	●	...	●	...	●	6.5[8]	1986	9,588.0	9.3	70.9	—	19.8	4,671.0	70.7	29.3	—
Tonga	...	...	...	...	...	1.1[10]										
Trinidad and Tobago	●	...	●	...	...	5.3[14]	1986	505.4	15.7	31.5	34.9	17.9	383.2	77.1	11.8	11.1
Tunisia	●	●	●	...	●	11.1	1989	325.3	36.9	63.1	—	—	358.3	90.1[13]	6.1[13]	3.9[13]
Turkey	●	●	●	...	...	0.5	1986	1,753,294.0	28.2	32.5	15.9	23.4	1,417,940.0	97.1	2.6	0.3
Turkmenistan	●	●	●	●	●											
Tuvalu	...	...	...	...	...	...	1981						0.1	67.6	32.4	—
Uganda	●	...	●	...	...	2.1[6]	1986	75.1	44.6	44.6	—	10.8	0.5	100.0	—	—
Ukraine	●	●	●	...	●	...	1986	16,835.0	...	...	94.7	5.3	16,835.0	100.0	—	—
United Arab Emirates	...	...	...	...	...	3.2[10]	1989	42.0	...	...	...	...	420.0[10]	...	...	...
United Kingdom	●	●	●	●	●	31.6[10]	1986	78,737.0	18.3	23.4	55.1	3.2	76,059.0	95.4	2.9	1.7
United States	●	●	●	●	●	20.5	1986	644,464.0	24.5	33.7	30.2	11.6	525,855.0	95.9	3.2	0.9
Uruguay	●	●	●	●	●	49.6[10]	1986	92,849.0	33.3	37.2	24.0	5.4	93,379.0	92.7	6.0	1.3
Uzbekistan	●	●	●	●	●											
Vanuatu	●	...	●	...	...	0.9[6]										
Venezuela	●	●	●	...	●	6.9[6]	1986	7,457.6	21.3	40.7	12.7	25.3	6,355.7	86.1	14.9	—
Vietnam	●	...	●	...	...											
Virgin Islands (U.S.)	...	...	...	...	...											
West Bank	...	...	...	...	...											
Western Sahara	...	...	...	...	...											
Western Samoa	●	...	●	...	...	—		—					—			
Yemen	●	...	●	...	...											
Yugoslavia	●	●	●	●	●	6.0[38]	1986[38]	2,777,651.0	63.3	32.2	3.4	1.1	2,732,679.0	90.3	1.9	7.8
Zaire	●	...	●	...	●	0.4[14]	1986	1,238.3	28.6	60.2	—	11.2	1,044.2	27.9	72.1	—
Zambia	●	...	●	...	...	1.5[3]	1986	179.2	28.4	28.4	—	43.2	67.7	40.6	59.4	—
Zimbabwe	...	...	●	...	...	2.5[8]	1983	167.0	25.9	7.6	64.2	2.3	112.2	93.7	6.2	0.1

[1]Rural areas only. [2]1984. [3]1988. [4]Political dependency; defense is the responsibility of the administering country. [5]Includes civilian militia. [6]1986. [7]1983. [8]1987. [9]Netherlands Antilles includes Aruba. [10]Includes welfare. [11]1985. [12]1979. [13]1977. [14]1981. [15]1976. [16]Local officers only. [17]Military defense is the responsibility of France. [18]1971. [19]Republic of Cyprus only. [20]1980. [21]Armed forces were demobilized with the overthrow of the government in May 1991. [22]1982. [23]Former West Germany. [24]Coverage is through tax system. [25]1988–89. [26]As a result of civil war, the

	crime and law enforcement (latest)					population per police officer[f]	military protection								country
	offenses reported to the police per 100,000 population						manpower, 1992[g]		expenditure, 1989				arms trade, 1989 ('000,000 U.S.$)		
	total	personal		property			total ('000)	per 1,000 population	total '000,000	per capita	% of central government expenditure	% of GDP or GNP	imports	exports	
		murder	assault	burglary	automobile theft										
	7,613	14.8	148.3	2,621.8	181.8	510	93.0	6.1	6,399	431	5.4	2.9	480	140	Netherlands, The
	5,146[30]	...	317.7	...	...	330	—	[4]	—	—	—	—	...	...	Netherlands Antilles
								[4]							New Caledonia
	13,247	4.1	136.9	2,477.6	1,026.4	630	10.9	3.1	847	258	5.6	2.2	50	0	New Zealand
	...	...	...	...	...	90[5]	14.7	3.6	5,225[8]	1,597[11]	26.2[8]	17.2[8]	430	0	Nicaragua
	32	0.2	2.5	1.0	0.1	2,350[31]	3.3	0.4	27	3	1.3	7.6	5	0	Niger
	312	...	...	...	...	1,140	76.0	0.8	130	1	2.4	0.5	5	20	Nigeria
	...	...	...	...	...		—	[4]	—	—			...	...	Northern Mariana Islands
	5,563	2.6	44.1	116.4	608.7	660	32.7	7.6	2,925	691	6.9	3.3	340	30	Norway
	162	...	...	...	...	430	35.7	21.8	1,552	1,085	41.4	20.3	60	0	Oman
	221	5.6	0.1	9.1	4.1	720	580.0	4.5	2,488	22	24.5	6.8	460	20	Pakistan
	...	...	...	323.0	...		—	[29]	...	...	...	...	...	...	Palau
	703	6.1	18.9	...	125.1	180	11.7	4.7	141	59	7.2[3]	3.4	5	0	Panama
	750.6	7.9	43.7	96.4	14.4	720	3.8	1.0	48	13	4.0	1.4	40	0	Papua New Guinea
	461	10.0	111.6	...	109.1	310	16.5	3.7	61	13	17.6[3]	1.4	0	0	Paraguay
	474	12.0	8.9	243.7	...	730	112.0	5.0	2,198[8]	106[8]	24.8[8]	4.9[8]	180	0	Peru
	230	30.1	41.8	...	1.2	1,160	106.5	1.7	960	15	12.1	2.2	70	0	Philippines
	2,311	2.8	50.5	1,027.7	...	370	296.5	7.7	15,480	410	23.4	8.9	625	400	Poland
	805	2.8	6.9	34.5	48.2	660	58.3	5.6	1,457	141	7.5	3.3	60	40	Portugal
	5,484	...	...	...	...	380	—	[4]	...	...	...	...	...	...	Puerto Rico
	358	3.0	54.7	1.5	7.8		7.5	14.4	608[20]	2,638[20]	20.1[8]	9.3[8]	0	0	Qatar
	...					220	—	[4]							Réunion
	276	3.4	3.0	45.7	6.7		200.0	8.6	6,916	299	16.9	6.1	20	70	Romania
	1,240	10.5	41.3	...	...		2,720.0	18.2	...	...	...	...	...	...	Russia
	327	6.1	58.9	4.0	...	4,650	5.2	0.7	37[3]	53	10.0[3]	1.6[3]	20	0	Rwanda
	15,468	...	...	...	...	300	—	—	...	...	...	...	...	...	St. Kitts and Nevis
	4,386	17.0	1,193.0	778.0	...	430	—	—	...	...	...	...	...	...	St. Lucia
	3,977	10.3	986.9	...	...	250	—	—	...	...	...	...	...	...	St. Vincent and the Grenadines
	...	...	...	...	...		—	—	...	...	...	...	...	...	San Marino
	558	4.0	...	...	...	400	—	—	1[20]	7[20]	2.5[20]	1.6[20]	5	0	São Tomé and Príncipe
	120	0.6	19.2	...	16.9	280	102.0	7.9	14,690	897	38.5	16.0	4,200	5	Saudi Arabia
	149	1.0	13.5	5.1	0.3	730	9.7	1.3	90	12	6.3	2.0	5	0	Senegal
	4,583	7.4	648.6	1,028.5	...	120	1.3	18.3	8[2]	124[2]	7.4[2]	5.6[2]	0	0	Seychelles
	...	...	...	...	...	600	6.2	1.4	6[3]	13	7.0[3]	0.7[3]	0	0	Sierra Leone
	1,507	1.5	4.7	126.2	15.9	230	55.5	19.9	1,475	550	18.9	5.1	120	70	Singapore
	1,930	...	...	...	...		15.0	7.6	...	...	...	...	...	...	Slovenia
	...	...	...	...	...	620									Solomon Islands
	144	1.5	8.0	31.2	...	540	—[33]	—[33]	43[6]	6[6]	30.0[6]	3.2[6]	30	0	Somalia
	...	...	...	...	...	870	72.4	1.9	3,786	98	13.5	4.4	100	0	South Africa
	...	...	...	...	...		...	...	...	...	...	...	...	...	Bophuthatswana
	...	...	...	...	...		...	...	...	...	...	...	...	...	Ciskei
	...	...	...	...	...		...	...	...	...	...	...	...	...	Transkei
	...	...	...	...	...		...	...	...	...	...	...	...	...	Venda
	2,635	2.4	26.2	1,212.0	342.8	580	217.0	5.6	7,775	199	5.7	2.1	750	130	Spain
	309	11.6	40.3	57.8	...	860	22.0	1.3	223	13	10.2	3.2	10	0	Sri Lanka
	509	30.5	60.3	107.7	6.9	740	82.5	2.8	339	13	11.7[3]	2.2	70	0	Sudan, The
	17,819	7.6	1,824.4	...	...		1.8	4.5	39	100	7.2	3.0	0	0	Suriname
	4,310	87.8	542.0	922.9	...	610	—	—	11	13	5.5	1.7	0	0	Swaziland
	14,188	7.0	36.2	1,801.8	879.0	330	60.5	8.8	4,875	574	6.5	2.6	70	575	Sweden
	5,275	3.2	50.0	1,076.0	1,504.6[34]	640	1.6	0.2	3,806	568	9.6[3]	2.1	300	600	Switzerland
	73	1.6	5.5	27.3	2.2	1,970	408.0	32.4	2,234	186	69.8	11.6	1,000	0	Syria
	481	...	...	...	...	720	360.0	17.4	8,060	397	30.3	5.4	430	10	Taiwan
	317	2.5	4.6	...	...		...	...	...	...	...	...	...	...	Tajikistan
	1,250	6.4	0.5	97.3	0.9	1,330	46.8	1.8	110	4	10.0	4.1	40	0	Tanzania
	1,449	9.5	21.8	25.0	4.2	530	283.0	5.0	1,843	33	17.7	2.7	240	0	Thailand
	11	...	...	...	...	1,970	5.3	1.4	43	12	16.3	3.3	5	0	Togo
	1,278	...	...	...	...	330	—	[35]	...	...	...	...	...	...	Tonga
	5,335	8.4	164.5	611.3	...	280	2.7	2.1	59	47	4.4	1.6	0	0	Trinidad and Tobago
	1,240	2.1	134.0	143.6	11.1	340	35.0	4.2	273	34	7.4	2.8	20	0	Tunisia
	134.3	1.7	55.8	...	9.5	1,570	560.3	9.6	3,150	56	17.2	4.1	1,100	0	Turkey
	...	...	...	...	...		...	...	...	...	...	...	...	...	Turkmenistan
	...	...	...	...	—	290	...	...	...	...	...	...	...	...	Tuvalu
	...	...	...	...	...	1,090	70.0	4.1	68[3]	4[3]	20.9[3]	1.5[3]	20	0	Uganda
	711	5.4	12.9	...	...		230.0	4.4	...	...	...	...	...	...	Ukraine
	1,496	1.8	5.4	...	...	140	54.5	27.4	1,471	695	40.7	5.3	850	5	United Arab Emirates
	8,986[36]	2.2[36]	353.5[36]	1,991.2[36]	977.4[36]	420	293.5	5.1	34,630	605	12.1	4.2	650	3,000	United Kingdom
	5,820	9.4	424.1	1,235.9	657.8	345	1,913.8	7.5	304,100	1,222	25.5	5.8	1,600	11,200	United States
	1,027	3.1	70.5	196.9	...	170	24.7	7.9	168[3]	57[3]	12.0[3]	2.2[3]	20	0	Uruguay
	420	5.1	15.6	...	...		...	...	...	...	...	...	...	...	Uzbekistan
	...	...	...	...	...	450	—	—	...	...	...	...	...	...	Vanuatu
	1,158	9.1	155.0	...	155.1	320	75.0	3.7	407	21	5.2	1.0	80	0	Venezuela
	...	...	...	...	...		857.0	12.4	2,400[6]	39[6]	40.7[6]	19.4[6]	1,300	0	Vietnam
	3,798	...	...	...	...	240	—	[4]	...	...	...	...	...	...	Virgin Islands (U.S.)
	2,226	...	...	...	...		—		...	...	...	...	...	...	West Bank
	...	...	...	...	...		—	[4]	—	—			...	...	Western Sahara
							—	[35]							Western Samoa
	...	...	...	...	...	1,940	63.5	5.2	566[3,37]	84[3,37]	30.0[3,37]	9.9[3,37]	650	0	Yemen
	1,135[38]	5.4[38]	35.5[38]	...	...	140[38]	135.0	13.0	2,126[38]	90[38]	53.4[38]	3.6[38]	120[38]	150	Yugoslavia
	...	...	...	...	...	910	54.1	1.3	49[3]	13	1.6[3]	0.8[3]	0	0	Zaire
	2,088	8.3	17.5	406.8	18.6	540	24.0	2.9	65	8	8.4	1.4	60	0	Zambia
	4,276	17.9	192.9	367.5	27.0	750	48.5	4.9	386	38	15.0	6.7	10	0	Zimbabwe

armed forces of Liberia have ceased to exist. [27]Military defense is the responsibility of Switzerland. [28]1974. [29]Military defense is the responsibility of the United States. [30]Curaçao only. [31]Includes paramilitary forces. [32]1978. [33]Following 1991 revolution, no National Armed Forces have yet been formed. [34]Includes bicycles and motorcycles. [35]Military defense is the responsibility of New Zealand. [36]England and Wales. [37]Former Yemen Arab Republic only. [38]Data refer to Yugoslavia as constituted prior to 1991.

Education

This table presents international data on education analyzed to provide maximum comparability among the different educational systems in use among the nations of the world. The principal data are, naturally, numbers of schools, teachers, and students, arranged by four principal levels of education—the first (primary); general second level (secondary); vocational second level; and third level (higher). Whenever possible, data referring to preprimary education programs have been excluded from this compilation. The ratio of students to teachers is calculated for each level. These data are supplemented at each level by a figure for enrollment ratio, an indicator of each country's achieved capability to educate the total number of children potentially educable in the age group usually represented by that level. At the first and second level this is given as a net enrollment ratio and at the third level as a gross enrollment ratio. Two additional comparative measures are given at the third level: students per 100,000 population and proportion (percentage) of adults age 25 and over who have achieved some level of higher or postsecondary education. Data in this last group are confined as far as possible to those who have completed their educations and are no longer in school. No enrollment ratio is provided for vocational training at the second level because of the great variation worldwide in the academic level at which vocational training takes place, in the need of countries to encourage or direct students into vocational programs (to support national development), and, most particularly, in the age range of students who normally constitute a national vocational system (some will be as young as 14, having just completed a primary cycle; others will be much older).

At each level of education, differences in national statistical practice, in national educational structure, public-private institutional mix, training and deployment of teachers, and timing of cycles of enrollment or completion of particular grades or standards all contribute to the problems of comparability among national educational systems.

Reporting the number of schools in a country is not simply a matter of counting permanent red-brick buildings with classrooms in them. Often the resources of a less developed country are such that temporary or outdoor facilities are all that can be afforded, while in a developed but sparsely settled country students might have to travel 80 km (50 mi) a day to find a classroom with 20 students of the same age, leading to the institution of measures such as traveling teachers, radio or televisual instruction at home under the supervision of parents, or similar systems. According to UNESCO definitions, therefore, a "school" is defined only as "a body of students . . . organized to receive instruction."

Such difficulties also limit the comparability of statistics on numbers of teachers, with the further complications that many at any level must work part-time, or that the institutions in which they work may perform a mixture of functions that do not break down into the tidy categories required by a table of this sort. In certain countries teacher training is confined to higher education, in others as a vocational form of secondary training, and so on. For purposes of this table, teacher training at the secondary level has been treated as vocational education. At the higher level, teacher training is classified as one more specialization in higher education itself.

The number of students may conceal great variation in what each country

Education

country	year	first level (primary)					general second level (secondary)					vocational second level[a]	
		schools	teachers[c]	students[d]	student/ teacher ratio	net enroll- ment ratio[b]	schools	teachers[c]	students[d]	student/ teacher ratio	net enroll- ment ratio[b]	schools	teachers[c]
Afghanistan	1989	553	16,756	586,014	35.0	19	819	5,715	271,000	47.4	...	33	556
Albania	1989	1,700	28,440	550,656	19.4	...	431	2,869	63,042	22.0	...	442[1]	7,498
Algeria	1991	12,240[2]	145,555	4,189,000	28.8	88	2,913[2]	120,886	2,175,000	18.0	53	713[3]	6,138
American Samoa	1989	122	503[5]	10,209	16.0[5]	...	7	215[5]	3,097	14.2[5]	...	1	16[5]
Andorra	1991	...	...	...	...	...	12	...	2,303	...	...	6	...
Angola	1989	6,308[7]	31,953	1,607,906	33.4	66	5,276[7]	3,870[3]	54,381	...	10	...	539[8]
Antigua and Barbuda	1989	45	414	9,097[1]	20.4[1]	...	13	273	4,413[1]	13.8[1]	...	2[9]	85[9]
Argentina	1987	21,025	252,259	4,906,907	19.5	...	1,987[10, 11]	111,421[11]	773,615[11]	6.9[11]	...	3,117[10, 11]	150,885[11]
Armenia	1990	1,397[12]	53,400[12]	597,900[12]	11.2[12]	...	12	12	12	12	...	70	...
Aruba	1990	29	317	6,640	20.9	...	10	166	2,988	18.0	...	16	221
Australia	1991	[14]	95,916[4]	1,786,500	18.4[4]	97	9,980[14]	103,298[4]	1,288,600	12.4[4]	79	2347[7, 15]	52,587[7, 15]
Austria	1991	3,386	29,404	371,971	12.7	93	2,013	57,548	436,931	7.6	...	939[4]	18,915[4]
Azerbaijan	1990	4,521[12]	...	1,449,000[12]	...	...	12	...	12	...	...	...	...
Bahamas, The	1991	100[17]	1,409[5]	27,264[17]	20.9[5]	...	37[17]	1,555[5]	23,616[17]	19.1[5]	...	...	...
Bahrain	1988	131	3,673	60,519	16.5	96	35	1,563	33,148	21.2	70	9	707
Bangladesh	1990	45,283	186,872	11,286,000	60.4	63	10,579	126,883	2,949,000	23.2	17	151	2,049
Barbados	1990	104	1,602	29,539	18.4	99	33	1,406	21,259	15.1	89	8[1]	79[1]
Belarus	1991	2,760	121,600[12]	1,474,000[12]	12.1[12]	...	2,611	12	12	12	...	145	...
Belgium	1989	4,608	71,064	755,609	10.6	97	2,123[20]	114,628[20]	825,920[20]	7.2[20]	89	457[20]	14,548[20]
Belize	1991	236	1,698	44,645	26.3	...	29	564	7,904	14.0	...	8	37[2, 9]
Benin	1988	2,879	13,821	482,451	34.9	52	151	2,711	90,184	33.3	13	13	687
Bermuda	1990	24	310	5,472	17.7	...	12	331	3,555	10.7	...	21	21
Bhutan	1988	150	1,513	42,446	28.1	...	30	695	16,350	23.5	...	5	21
Bolivia	1987	12,639	48,133	1,299,664	27.0	83	724	8,258	211,519	25.6	27	47	1,805
Bosnia and Hercegovina	1991	2,205	23,369	539,875	23.1	...	238	9,030	172,063	19.1	...	...	...
Botswana	1991	654	9,708	308,840	31.8	93	169	3,743	68,137	18.2	24	40	759
Brazil	1990	208,934	1,260,501	28,943,619	23.0	84	10,160	243,246	3,198,777	14.4	15	...	...
Brunei	1990	162	2,912	49,611	17.0	...	19	1,713	19,761	11.5	...	6	326
Bulgaria	1992	3,439[12]	72,719[12]	1,068,206[12]	14.7[12]	86	12	12	12	12	59	503	18,167
Burkina Faso	1990	2,362	8,572	472,979	55.2	28	113[1]	1,700[1]	82,931	33.7[1]	5	187	341
Burundi	1990	1,299	9,246	601,599	65.1	51	114	2,153	38,864	18.1	3	...	...
Cambodia	1991	4,617	40,821	1,321,573	32.4	...	463	13,105[2]	248,966	24.7[10]	...	13[10]	278[10]
Cameroon	1990	6,549	37,804	1,946,301	51.4	75	388[5]	11,400	366,528	32.2	15	220[5]	6,267
Canada	1991	15,507[12]	286,375[12]	5,129,060[12]	17.9[12]	96	12	12	12	12	93	...	...
Cape Verde	1988	545	1,892	62,727	33.2	95	16[5]	191	5,740	30.1	12	3[5]	77
Cayman Islands	1990	16[2]	303[2]	1,923	14.6	...	6[2]	24	2,134[24]	24	...	1[2]	22[2, 25]
Central African Republic	1990	1,003	3,581	323,661	90.4	46	46[27]	1,149[27]	47,212[27]	41.1[27]	...	27	27
Chad	1990	1,868	7,327	492,231	67.2	38	66[2]	1,422	54,751	38.5	...	25[5]	285[2]
Chile	1989	8,101	55,266	1,987,758	36.0	89	1,694[1]	...	607,709	...	58	1,262[1]	...
China	1990	938,394	6,332,000	142,136,000	22.4	100	87,631	3,033,000	45,860,000	15.1	...	13,146	459,000
Colombia	1988	37,948	136,549	4,044,220	29.6	69	6,134[27]	99,392[27]	2,076,455[27]	20.9[27]	...	27	27
Comoros	1990	257[1]	1,777[1]	64,737[1]	36.4[1]	55	32[28]	557	14,472	26.0	...	4[28]	41[5]
Congo	1990	1,604	7,704	492,595	63.9	...	238[1]	4,774	165,840	34.7	...	60[1]	1,965[1]
Cook Islands	1988	28	137	2,376	17.3	...	8[7]	146[7]	2,165	14.8[7]	...	...	...
Costa Rica	1990	3,268	13,651	435,205	31.9	86	179	5,808	125,738	21.6	36	77	2,076
Côte d'Ivoire	1985	5,796	33,500	1,214,511	36.3	...	218[29]	4,569[29]	272,911[5]	...	...	38[29]	1,947[28]
Croatia	1991	2,588	27,197	497,790	18.3	...	229	13,121	215,425	16.4	...	...	...
Cuba	1990	9,417	71,887	885,500	12.3	95	2,175	108,560	1,073,100	9.9	69	618	30,252
Cyprus[30]	1990	378	2,824	60,841	21.5	99	94[2]	3,145	40,073	12.7	84	12[2]	465
Czechoslovakia	1990	6,206	98,038	1,961,742	20.0	...	884	36,273	452,696	12.5	...	979	50,612
Denmark	1991	3,000[31]	62,700[2, 31]	632,174[31]	10.7[2, 31]	...	157[32]	7,500[2, 32]	71,876[33]	9.6[2, 32]	84	352	...
Djibouti	1990	66	707	30,778	43.5	37	32[27]	319[27, 33]	8,912[27]	...	13	27	27
Dominica	1991	65	439	12,836	29.2	...	9[1]	171[1]	5,030[4]	19.1[1]	...	27	27
Dominican Republic	1990	4,854[33]	21,850[33]	1,032,055[33]	47.2[33]	73	...	9,963[5]	426,962[5]	42.9[5]	...	...	108[5, 34]
Ecuador	1990	16,146[5]	60,608	1,843,819	30.4	...	2,027[5, 27]	36,730[1, 11]	504,481[1, 11]	13.7[1, 11]	...	27	16,838[1, 11]

defines as a particular educational "level." Many countries do, indeed, have a primary system composed of grades 1 through 6 (or 1 through 8) that passes students on to some kind of postprimary education. But the age of intake, the ability of parents to send their children or to permit them to finish that level, or the need to withdraw the children seasonally for agricultural work all make even a simple enrollment figure difficult to assess in isolation. All of these difficulties are compounded when a country has instruction in more than one language or when its educational establishment is so small that higher, sometimes even secondary, education cannot take place within the country. Enrollment figures in this table may, therefore, include students enrolled outside the country.

Student-teacher ratio, however, usually provides a good measure of the ratio of trained educators to the enrolled educable. In general, at each level of education both students and teachers have been counted on the basis of full-time enrollment or employment, or full-time equivalent when country statistics permit. At the primary and secondary levels, net enrollment ratio is the ratio of the number of children within the usual age group for a particular level who are actually enrolled to the total number of children in that age group ($\times$ 100). This ratio is usually less than (occasionally, equal to) 100 and is the most accurate measure of the completeness of enrollment at that particular level. It is not always, however, the best indication of utilization of teaching staff and facilities. Utilization, provided here for higher education only, is best seen in a gross enrollment ratio, which compares total enrollment (of all ages) to the population within the normal age limits for that level. For a country with substantial adult literacy or general

educational programs, the difference may be striking: typically, for a less developed country, even one with a good net enrollment ratio of 90 to 95, the gross enrollment ratio may be 20, 25, even 30% higher, indicating the heavy use made by the country of facilities and teachers at that level.

Literacy data provided here have been compiled as far as possible from data for the population age 15 and over for the best comparability internationally. Standards as to what constitutes literacy may also differ markedly; sometimes completion of a certain number of years of school is taken to constitute literacy; elsewhere it may mean only the ability to read or write at a minimal level testable by a census taker; in other countries studies have been undertaken to distinguish among degrees of functional literacy.

Finally, the data provided for public expenditure on education are complete in that they include all levels of public expenditure (national, state, local) but are incomplete for certain countries in that they do not include data for private expenditure; in some countries this fraction of the educational establishment may be of significant size. Occasionally data for external aid to education may be included in addition to domestic expenditure.

The following notes further define the column headings:
a. Usually includes teacher training at the second level.
b. Latest.
c. Full-time.
d. Full-time; may include students registered in foreign schools.

| students[d] | student/ teacher ratio | third level (higher) | | | | | | | literacy[b] | | | | public expenditure on education (percent of GNP)[b] | country |
		institutions	teachers[c]	students[d]	student/ teacher ratio	gross enroll- ment ratio[b]	students per 100,000 popula- tion[b]	percent of population age 25 and over with post- secondary education[b]	over age	total (%)	male (%)	female (%)		
8,537	15.4	5	198	1,419	7.5	1.3	115	3.2	15	29.4	44.1	13.9	1.8	Afghanistan
137,704	18.4	8[1]	1,659[1]	25,201[1]	15.1	8.5	814	...	15	100.0	100.0	100.0	...	Albania
165,182[4]	29.4[1]	15[3]	17,581[1]	250,813	12.3[1]	10.5	895	0.3	15	57.4	69.8	45.5	9.4	Algeria
157	9.8[5]	2	...	909	...	...	...	12.6	15	95.9	95.6	96.3	8.2	American Samoa
1,455	...	...	...	802[2, 6]	...	...	...	24.9	15	100.0	100.0	100.0	...	Andorra
6,087	...	17	316[7]	4,965[7]	15.7[7]	0.6	53	...	15	41.7	55.6	28.5	5.2	Angola
927[9]	10.9[9]	9	9	9	9	...	...	...	15	90.0	...	...	3.7	Antigua and Barbuda
1,207,200[11]	8.0[11]	1,540	69,985[7]	902,882[7]	12.9[7]	40.8	3,079	6.9	15	95.3	95.5	95.1	1.5	Argentina
45,900	...	14	...	68,400	...	...	...	71.5[13]	...	...	...	...	...	Armenia
2,578	11.7	1	20	180	9.0	...	...	...	15	95.0	...	...	...	Aruba
932,300[2]	...	95[1]	25,916[1]	485,100[4, 16]	16.2[2]	31.6	2,651	21.5	15	99.5	...	...	4.8	Australia
171,164[4]	9.0[4]	88[4]	13,013[4]	199,845[4]	15.4[4]	31.4	2,638	6.0	15	100.0	100.0	100.0	6.5	Austria
...	...	17	...	105,100	...	...	...	68.6[13]	...	...	...	...	...	Azerbaijan
...	...	1[18]	300[18]	2,200[18]	7.3[18]	...	...	...	15	95.0	...	...	4.4	Bahamas, The
7,478	10.6	4	539	5,529	10.3	14.9	1,175	3.8	15	77.4	82.1	69.3	5.4	Bahrain
24,000	11.7	459	16,564	548,492	33.1	3.6	329	1.3	15	35.3	47.1	22.0	2.2	Bangladesh
996[1]	12.6[1]	3	153[2]	4,242	8.6[2]	19.4	2,065	3.3	15	98.0[19]	...	...	6.9	Barbados
299,000	...	33	...	189,400	...	...	...	60.2[13]	...	...	...	...	...	Belarus
130,263[20]	9.0[20]	18	10,517	104,665	10.0	34.2	2,604	...	...	100.0	100.0	100.0	4.9	Belgium
1,726[11]	31.6[2, 9]	9	9	9	9	...	...	2.3	15	93.0	...	...	...	Belize
6,879	10.0	13	625[2]	8,883[2]	14.2[2]	2.3	198	...	15	23.4	31.7	15.6	5.1	Benin
21	21	1[21]	56[21]	498[21]	8.9[21]	...	...	7.4	15	96.9	96.7	97.0	3.2	Bermuda
21	21	2	150[21]	1,761[21]	11.7[21]	0.3	17	...	15	18.0	31.0	9.0	3.7	Bhutan
15,947	8.8	10	3,555	97,153	27.3	21.4	1,980	6.2	15	77.5	84.7	70.7	2.3	Bolivia
...	...	44	2,801	37,541	13.4	...	...	4.3[22]	10	85.5	96.5	76.7	...	Bosnia and Hercegovina
7,057	9.3	1	370	3,352	9.1	3.0	255	0.5	15	73.6	83.7	65.1	8.2	Botswana
...	...	918	145,585	1,540,080	10.6	11.2	1,045	5.0	15	81.2	81.8	80.6	3.7	Brazil
1,565	4.8	2	214	1,110	5.2	...	...	9.4	15	85.1	90.9	78.7	...	Brunei
254,480	14.0	86	23,960	175,557	7.3	26.2	1,756	...	15	95.5	...	...	5.5	Bulgaria
8,055	23.6	2	205	5,675	27.7	0.3	65	3.8	15	18.2	27.9	8.9	2.3	Burkina Faso
...	...	10	556	3,279	5.9	0.6	58	...	15	50.0	60.1	39.8	3.2	Burundi
7,334[10]	26.4[10]	7	180[23]	6,640	13.5[23]	...	...	...	15	48.0	...	...	...	Cambodia
90,633	14.5	5[5]	975[5]	19,586[5]	20.1[5]	3.0	242	...	15	54.1	66.3	42.6	3.3	Cameroon
...	...	270	63,570	856,520	13.5	65.6	5,034	37.4	14	95.6	95.6	95.7	7.0	Canada
673	8.7	...	...	...	...	—	...	0.5	15	47.4	61.4	38.6	2.9	Cape Verde
531[2, 26]	8.5[2]	1[2]	19[2, 25]	142[2, 26]	17.3[2]	...	...	2.9	15	97.5	97.5	97.6	...	Cayman Islands
27	27	1	134	2,534	18.9	1.3	107	0.1	15	37.7	51.8	24.9	2.9	Central African Republic
3,819	15.1[2]	4[5]	59	2,969	50.3	0.8	69	...	15	29.8	42.2	17.9	1.8	Chad
134,301	...	201[1]	15,131[10]	233,148[1]	...	18.8	1,843	7.1	15	93.4	93.5	93.2	3.6	Chile
5,194,000	11.3	1,075	395,000	2,063,000	5.2	1.7	194	1.0	15	77.7	87.0	68.0	2.4	China
27	27	235[5]	47,990[5]	457,680[5]	9.5[5]	13.7	1,466	...	15	86.7	87.5	85.9	2.9	Colombia
334[5]	14.6[5]	—	32	248	7.8	—	...	0.2	15	46.3	54.2	39.0	6.5	Comoros
20,722[1]	10.5	12[1]	641[1]	10,310[1]	16.1[1]	5.7	484	...	15	56.6	70.0	43.9	5.1	Congo
22	...	...	41[29]	360[29]	8.8[29]	...	...	2.1	...	91.8	92.1	91.4	...	Cook Islands
28,593	13.8	4[16]	6,451[16]	57,789[16]	9.0[16]	26.5	2,641	14.2	15	92.8	92.6	93.1	4.4	Costa Rica
25,328[7]	...	1[29]	1,204[3]	19,660[10]	...	2.6	200	...	15	53.8	66.9	40.2	6.9	Côte d'Ivoire
...	...	60	6,633	70,781	10.7	...	...	6.4[22]	10	94.4	97.5	91.6	...	Croatia
312,000	10.3	35	24,499	242,400	9.9	20.7	2,304	4.2	15	96.0	...	...	6.6	Cuba
3,146	6.8	26	481	5,852	12.2	13.0	844	...	15	94.5	...	...	3.6	Cyprus[30]
404,275	8.0	42	25,350	143,866	5.7	17.6	1,193	5.0	15	100.0	100.0	100.0	5.4	Czechoslovakia
240,267	...	94	...	126,221	...	31.5	2,466	...	...	100.0	100.0	100.0	7.6	Denmark
27	...	—	—	161[10]	...	...	...	...	20	33.7	...	...	2.7	Djibouti
...	...	2[1]	12[2]	68[2]	5.7[2]	...	...	1.7	15	94.4	...	...	5.7	Dominica
3,602[5, 34]	...	7[16]	5,319[16, 35]	86,504[16, 35]	16.3[16, 35]	18.6	1,929	2.3	15	83.3	84.8	81.8	1.5	Dominican Republic
260,850[1, 11]	15.5[1, 11]	21	12,856	206,541	16.1	29.0	1,914	7.6	15	89.8	91.6	88.0	2.6	Ecuador

Education (continued)

country	year	first level (primary)					general second level (secondary)					vocational second level[a]	
		schools	teachers[c]	students[d]	student/ teacher ratio	net enrollment ratio[b]	schools	teachers[c]	students[d]	student/ teacher ratio	net enrollment ratio[b]	schools	teachers[c]
Egypt	1990	14,767[36]	241,119[36]	6,155,100[36]	25.5[36]	...	6,558[36]	155,941[1]	3,123,233[1]	20.0[1]	...	519[37]	72,237
El Salvador	1989	4,160	25,318	1,016,181	40.1	70	468[27]	...	28,370	28.2[1,27]	15	27	...
Equatorial Guinea	1988	703	1,065	61,009	57.3	...	9	319	9,226	28.9	...	...	...
Estonia	1990	606[12]	17,952[12]	257,560[12]	12.7[12]	...	12	12	12	12	...	36	6,495
Ethiopia	1988	8,584[7]	65,993	2,855,846	43.3	28	1,209[7]	21,220	874,000	41.2	...	...	763
Faeroe Islands	1991	67[12]	611[2,12]	5,440[2]	14.0[2,12]	...	12	12	2,979[2]	12	...	9[1]	...
Fiji	1990	672[7]	4,272	143,553	33.6	98	140[7]	2,684	52,536	19.6	...	44[7]	369
Finland	1991	4,845[38]	42,165[2]	583,676[38]	13.9[2,38]	...	464[39]	6,178[2,39]	101,625[39]	16.1[2,39]	...	593	16,878[1]
France	1991	44,131	309,876	4,062,246	13.1	100	11,325[27]	413,304[27]	5,402,300[27]	13.1[27]	83	27	27
French Guiana	1988	84	...	11,342	...	...	11	...	6,541	...	...	8	...
French Polynesia	1990	278	2,503	44,734	17.9	...	32[27]	1,341[27]	20,159[27]	15.0[27]	...	27	27
Gabon	1987	992	4,229	195,049	46.1	...	518[8]	1,512	32,922	21.8	...	29[8]	759
Gambia, The	1989	232	2,451	73,620	30.0	62	11	281	3,624	12.9	...	18	540
Gaza Strip	1989	331[12]	4,429[12]	185,410[12]	41.9[12]	...	12	12	12	12	...	12	12
Georgia	1990	3,788[12]	...	924,700[12]	...	...	12	...	12	...	...	...	...
Germany	1990	38,294[12]	493,004[12,40]	8,962,461[12]	...	...	12	12	12	12	...	8,110	116,343
Ghana	1989	9,634	65,826	1,705,843	25.9	...	5,702[7]	43,112	763,167	17.7	...	137[7]	2,317
Gibraltar	1989	14	92	2,937	31.9	...	2	124	1,694	13.7	...	1	29
Greece	1988	8,178	39,125	868,335	22.2	98	2,765	44,887	708,549	15.8	85	506	7,435
Greenland	1990	90[2,12]	994[12]	7,674	9.1[12]	...	12	12	1,387	12	...	...	...
Grenada	1990	57[41]	768[41]	20,730[41]	27.0[41]	...	19	337	6,798	20.2	...	...	...
Guadeloupe	1991	222	2,069	39,290	19.0	...	75[27]	3,237[2,27]	49,846[2,27]	24.9[2,27]	...	27	27
Guam	1990	36	850	16,819	19.8	...	24	736	15,733	21.4	...	42	176[42]
Guatemala	1989	8,840	33,666	1,235,509	36.7	58	1,541[27]	17,313[27]	297,437[27]	17.2[27]	13	27	27
Guernsey	1992	22	231	4,469	19.3	...	8	286	3,521	12.3	...	1	228[25]
Guinea	1989	2,442	8,113	310,064	38.2	26	225[1]	3,868	71,346	18.4	7	35[1]	635[1]
Guinea-Bissau	1988	632[5]	3,065[5]	79,035	24.6[5]	45	12[7]	824[7]	5,505	7.5[7]	3	4[5]	107
Guyana	1990	423	3,948[7]	134,679[5]	28.5[7]	...	93	2,700[5]	73,418[5]	27.2[5]	...	8	176
Haiti	1990	5,625[2]	24,238	1,148,400	47.4	44	686	13,262	197,400	14.9	...	36[2]	491[2]
Honduras	1991	7,487	25,854	923,902	35.7	91	540	8,517	132,953	15.6	21	5[2]	581[2]
Hong Kong	1991	681	19,625[1]	524,919	27.3[1]	94	489	19,419[1]	433,208	25.0[1]	66	34[4]	2,488[1]
Hungary	1990	3,527	90,602	1,183,600	13.1	91	675	21,425	273,511	12.8	73	299	6,842
Iceland	1991	44	44	44	44	...	265[44]	3,200[44]	58,642[44]	18.3[44]	...	44	44
India	1990	550,700	1,601,717	97,318,114	60.8	...	214,380	2,311,837	49,402,664	21.4	...	...	...
Indonesia	1990[46]	146,558	1,140,886	26,528,590	23.3	99	28,745	703,099	8,473,299	12.1	41	3,880	111,448
Iran	1990	56,537	361,878	8,817,145	24.4	94	15,834[1]	240,102	4,456,342	18.6	48	1,088[1]	23,297
Iraq	1992	8,875	127,578	3,316,036	26.0	84	2,746	43,937	1,084,715	24.7	39	296	9,957
Ireland	1990	3,428	20,321[47]	560,833	...	89	493	11,630	213,788	18.4	79	352	7,118
Isle of Man	1989	32	240[37]	5,458	...	...	7	276[37]	4,908	...	...	1	...
Israel	1990	1,989	37,768[48]	611,671	16.2	...	710	43,548	393,508	9.0	...	383	...
Italy	1991	24,337	195,017	3,060,562	15.7	...	9,992	113,562	2,275,582	20.0	...	7,910	134,193
Jamaica	1991[33]	790[38]	9,693[38]	385,041[38]	48.7[38]	99	127[39]	7,721[39]	151,304[39]	19.6[39]	59	17[4]	821
Japan	1991	24,798	445,000	9,157,000	20.6	100	16,793	573,000	10,644,000	18.6	96	6,679	53,000
Jersey	1990	32	294[5]	5,794	19.2[5]	...	14	372[5]	4,405	12.3[5]	...	1	...
Jordan	1990	2,983	21,073	590,275	28.0	93	622	10,264[2]	357,754	11.5[2]	68	30	2,135
Kazakhstan	1990	8,064[12]	...	3,021,070[12]	...	...	12	...	12	...	...	...	...
Kenya	1990	14,691	163,609	5,389,300	32.9	91	2,654	28,056	640,635	22.8	...	24[34]	1,332[2,34]
Kiribati	1989	110	507	14,321	28.2	...	9	142	2,293	16.1	...	6	94
Korea, North	1987	4,792[7,12]	...	1,492,000	...	...	12	...	2,655,000	...	...	473[7]	...
Korea, South	1991	6,245	138,200	4,758,505	34.4	100	4,198[27]	187,620[27]	4,443,242[27]	23.9[27]	79	27	27
Kuwait	1992	203[35]	10,310	189,560	18.4	85	315[35]	21,585	270,580	12.5	...	34	617
Kyrgyzstan	1990	465	74,100[12]	931,300[12]	12.6[12]	...	1,334	12	12	12	...	109	...
Laos	1989	8,330	19,438	571,630	29.4	70	750	9,752	124,169	12.7	...	117[8]	2,049[1]
Latvia	1990	900[12]	...	353,300[12]	...	...	12	...	12	...	...	57	...
Lebanon	1986	2,130[3]	22,810[3]	399,029	...	...	1,405[3]	21,344[28]	279,849	...	...	181[3]	3,506[8]
Lesotho	1990	1,190	6,452	351,652	54.5	70	175	2,213	45,064	20.4	14	10	201
Liberia	1986	1,651[29]	9,099[29]	80,048	25.0[29]	...	419[29]	1,129[29]	43,273[5]	45.8[29]	...	6[29]	63[29]
Libya	1988	2,744[37]	41,515[8]	974,295	19.0	...	1,555[37]	30,524[8]	389,530	12.2	...	195[37]	3,051[8]
Liechtenstein	1991	14	115	1,892	16.4	...	8	80	1,092	13.6	...	1[2]	74[2]
Lithuania	1992	2,147[12]	42,897[12]	509,800[12]	11.9[12]	...	12	12	12	12	...	108	4,870
Luxembourg	1991	...	1,764[4,33]	26,612[33]	...	...	...	1,922[27,33]	7,594	...	60	...	27
Macau	1990	69	1,104	32,639	29.6	...	22	918	16,862	18.4	...	3[34]	20
Macedonia	1991	1,063	12,987	268,963	20.7	...	90	4,200	74,886	17.8	...	...	...
Madagascar	1990	13,555	37,932	1,512,312	39.9	64	1,142[2]	14,382	331,238	23.0	...	61[1]	1,630
Malawi	1990	2,624	20,580	1,325,453	64.4	50	94	1,096	29,326	26.8	...	13	250
Malaysia	1990	6,828	120,025	2,447,206	20.4	...	1,261	69,493	1,335,377	19.2	...	81	3,902
Maldives	1986	243	1,138	41,812	36.7	...	9	291	3,581	12.3	...	10	52
Mali	1990	1,320	7,581	323,354	42.7	19	331	3,411	51,818	15.2	...	...	...
Malta	1990	91	1,798	37,016	20.6	97	33	1,374	24,800	18.0	75	32	748
Marshall Islands	1989	89[7]	538	10,940	20.3	...	7[7]	95	1,862	19.6	...	...	...
Martinique	1989	210	2,004	32,986	16.4	...	75[5]	2,745[5,27]	31,234	16.5[5,27]	...	...	27
Mauritania	1989	1,121	3,135	158,800	50.7	...	44[7]	1,873	37,370	20.0	...	6[7]	185
Mauritius	1990	283	6,507	137,491	21.1	93	124	3,728	78,110	21.0	...	7[1]	69[3]
Mayotte	1990	88	427	19,078	44.7	...	4	66	2,280	34.5	...	2	17
Mexico	1993	86,636	481,466	14,500,000	30.1	100	25,131	352,865	5,980,000	16.9	44	6,571	77,347
Micronesia	1984	151	1,051	23,345	22.2	...	14	314	4,159	13.2	...	...	...
Moldova	1991	1,664[12]	54,300[12]	743,500[12]	13.7[12]	...	12	12	12	12	...	...	...
Monaco	1990	6[5]	735[12]	5,523[12]	7.5[12]	...	3[5]	12	12	12	...	...	...
Mongolia	1991	14	14	14	14	94	665[14]	21,900[14]	459,400[14]	21.0[14]	...	44	1,200[2]
Morocco	1991	4,052	87,839	2,483,691	28.3	55	1,080[33]	69,915[33]	1,121,193[33]	16.0[33]	29	562[50]	5,359[50]
Mozambique	1988	3,647[51]	21,410[51]	1,199,669[51]	56.0[51]	45	207[24]	3,422[24]	107,080[24]	31.3[24]	...	32	968
Myanmar (Burma)	1991	36,499	198,909	5,423,500	27.3	...	2,920	67,503	1,262,100	18.7	...	101	2,079
Namibia	1988	1,118[12]	12,525[12]	286,836	22.9[12]	...	12	12	77,770	12	...	9	81[3]
Nauru	1989	3	61	1,367	22.4	...	2	34	629	18.5	...	1	3
Nepal	1989	13,514	57,204	2,108,739	36.9	64	5,535	21,132	612,943	29.0	23	57[7]	117[7]

students[d]	student/ teacher ratio	third level (higher) institutions	third level (higher) teachers[c]	third level (higher) students[d]	student/ teacher ratio	gross enroll-ment ratio[b]	students per 100,000 popula-tion[b]	percent of population age 25 and over with post-secondary education[b]	literacy over age	literacy total (%)	literacy male (%)	literacy female (%)	public expenditure on education (percent of GNP)[b]	country
1,015,809	14.1	12[2,16]	33,106[16,36]	656,179[16]	...	19.6	1,762	4.1	15	48.4	62.9	33.8	6.8	Egypt
66,708	27	6[4,16]	2,637[4,16]	51,277[4,16]	19.4[4,16]	17.1	1,564	2.3	15	73.0	76.2	70.0	2.0	El Salvador
		5	133	1,542	11.6	6.1	...	1.1	15	62.8	77.8	48.6	...	Equatorial Guinea
19,915	3.1	6	2,977	26,279	8.8	...	...	...	15	...	...	...	...	Estonia
8,243	10.8	11[10]	1,699	31,204	18.4	0.8	70	...	15	4.8	9.3	0.5	4.4	Ethiopia
1,387[1]		1	20	100		...	...	...	15	100.0	100.0	100.0	...	Faeroe Islands
3,290	8.9	5[37]	320[7]	2,211[7]	6.9[7]	4.3	399	3.3	15	87.0	90.0	84.0	5.0	Fiji
164,249	9.0[1]	20	7,744[2]	110,646	14.0[2]	43.0	3,134	10.9	15	100.0	100.0	100.0	5.8	Finland
27	27	1,062[2]	53,110	1,698,643	32.0	37.2	2,842	...	15	98.8	98.9	98.7	5.3	France
3,778	...	...	...	...	...	...	...	6.4	16	82.0	82.5	81.3	19.2	French Guiana
27	27	4[2]	70[2]	701[2]	10.0[2]	...	...	...	15	95.0	94.9	95.0	9.7	French Polynesia
15,352	20.2	11[1,16]	363[1,16]	2,896[1,16]	8.0[1,16]	4.2	377	...	15	60.7	73.5	48.5	5.6	Gabon
12,982	24.0	9[8]	177[8]	1,489[8]	8.4[8]	—	...	...	15	27.2	39.0	16.0	4.0	Gambia, The
12	12	1[37]	30[3]	2,387[37]	...	...	...	9.5	...	...	...	...	...	Gaza Strip
...	...	19		93,100	...	...	...	72.5[13]	...	...	...	...	...	Georgia
2,557,881	22.0	312[35]	370,134[40]	1,782,739[35]	...	...	...	4.3	15	100.0	100.0	100.0	...	Germany
30,221	13.0	3[1]	1,160[5]	9,582[35]	...	1.5	127	3.5	15	60.4	70.0	50.9	3.4	Ghana
352[7]	14.1[7]	—				...	...	...	15	99.0	99.0	99.0	6.0	Gibraltar
117,193	15.8	82	12,760	189,173	14.8	28.0	2,104	7.4	15	93.2	97.6	89.1	2.7	Greece
2,297[2]	...	4	35[5]	200[1]	5.7[5]	...	...	...	15	100.0	100.0	100.0	...	Greenland
...	...	2	91	559	6.1	...	...	1.5	15	85.0	...	...	4.6	Grenada
27	27	1[2]		2,373[2]	...	...	...	5.2	15	90.1	89.7	90.5	15.0	Guadeloupe
1,095[42]	6.2[42]	1	206	2,208	10.7	...	...	34.4	15	96.4	96.4	96.5	8.5	Guam
27	27	5	4,346	69,532	16.0	8.6	741	3.0	15	60.3	69.7	51.7	1.8	Guatemala
4,952[26]	21.7	—				...	...	...	15	100.0	100.0	100.0	...	Guernsey
7,313	5.2[1]	10[1]	805[16]	6,245[16]	7.8[16]	1.4	122	...	15	24.0	34.9	13.4	3.3	Guinea
825	7.7	...				...	...	...	15	36.5	50.2	24.0	2.8	Guinea-Bissau
5,388	30.6	1[16]	370[16]	2,169[16]	5.8[16]	4.0	466	1.8	15	96.4	97.5	95.4	8.8	Guyana
3,012[2]	6.1	43	500[35,43]	6,300[35,43]	12.6[35,43]	1.2	107	0.7	15	53.0	59.1	47.4	1.8	Haiti
47,727	13.7[6]	5	2,740	34,333	12.5	9.7	901	3.3	15	73.1	75.5	70.6	4.9	Honduras
30,833[4]	18.5[1]	11	1,422[1]	67,373	32.4[1]	13.1	1,410	7.1	15	88.1	94.7	80.9	2.8	Hong Kong
201,702	29.5	57	16,319	100,868	6.2	14.7	956	7.0	15	98.9	99.2	98.6	6.0	Hungary
44	44	5	369[45]	5,450	14.0[45]	24.7	2,154	3.7	15	100.0	100.0	100.0	5.4	Iceland
...	...	6,600[2]	242,000[2]	3,820,000[2]	15.8[2]	6.4	581	2.5	15	48.2	61.8	33.7	3.2	India
1,410,073	12.7	792[1]	115,359[1]	1,179,489[1]	10.2[1]	...	600	1.2	15	77.6	85.6	70.0	0.9	Indonesia
212,100	9.1	85[1]	20,515[2]	315,657[2]	15.4[2]	6.9	610	7.8	15	54.7	64.5	43.3	3.1	Iran
152,903	15.4	20	10,520	197,786	18.8	13.8	1,188	...	15	59.7	69.8	49.3	3.8	Iraq
129,702	18.2	43	3,934[2]	61,323	16.0[2]	25.8	2,219	24.4	15	100.0	100.0	100.0	7.0	Ireland
425[35]	...	...				...	...	...	...	...	...	...	...	Isle of Man
110,967		7	6,479[1]	67,750		32.8	2,644	23.1	15	91.8	95.0	88.7	8.6	Israel
2,860,983	21.3	49	53,213[2]	1,222,645[2]	22.9[2]	28.6	2,379	4.1	15	97.1	97.8	96.4	5.0	Italy
14,898	18.1	15[2]	1,047[1]	19,173[4]	17.9[1]	5.0	556	2.0	15	98.4	98.2	98.6	6.6	Jamaica
1,242,000	23.4	1,169	151,000	2,763,000	18.3	30.7	2,184	31.7	15	100.0	100.0	100.0	4.8	Japan
283[5]						...	...	...	15	100.0	100.0	100.0	4.1	Jersey
26,525	12.4	55[2]	3,435	69,389	20.2	26.6	1,992	...	15	80.1	89.3	70.3	5.9	Jordan
...	...	55		285,600	...	...	...	64.0[13]	...	...	...	...	...	Kazakhstan
14,456[34]	13.4[2,34]	15		29,231	...	1.6	135	1.3	15	59.2	69.6	49.2	6.5	Kenya
610	6.5	—		85	—	—	—	...	15	90.0			8.7	Kiribati
220,000	...	281[7]	9,244[3]	301,000	...	...	...	3.6	15	99.0			3.6	Korea, North
27	27	560	43,821	1,518,512	34.7	39.2	3,841	14.2	15	96.3	99.1	93.5	3.6	Korea, South
2,872	4.7	1[2]	1,181[2]	17,988[2]	15.2[2]	17.9	1,384	11.1	15	73.0	77.1	66.7	5.0	Kuwait
38,923	...	9		59,265	...	...	...	30.0	...	...	...	...	...	Kyrgyzstan
16,293[1]	8.0[8]	9	503	5,253	10.4	1.6	141	...	15	83.9	92.0	75.8	1.0	Laos
38,100	...	10		45,600	...	...	...	...	15	80.1	87.8	73.1	...	Latvia
30,407	10.6[8]	18[3]	7,460[8]	70,510[8]	9.5[8]	27.7	2,634	...	15	...	...	...	...	Lebanon
2,348	11.7	1	133	1,273	9.6	3.9	333	0.6	15	73.6	62.4	84.5	4.0	Lesotho
2,322[29]	36.9[29]	3[29]	470[5]	5,095[5]	...	2.5	220	5.7	15	39.5	49.8	28.8	5.7	Liberia
70,335	10.0	6	1,340[29]	40,365	...	10.1	792	...	15	63.8	75.4	50.4	10.1	Libya
147[2]		—				...	...	11.2	15	100.0	100.0	100.0	...	Liechtenstein
46,200	9.5	14	9,003[1]	60,500	7.3[1]	...	...	...	...	...	...	...	...	Lithuania
11,430	...	...		4,957	...	3.1	245	...	15	100.0	100.0	100.0	4.7	Luxembourg
294	14.7	7	624	7,838	12.6	...	...	15.9	10	61.3	76.4	46.2	...	Macau
...	...	27	2,101	26,413	12.6	...	...	5.1	15	89.1	94.2	83.8	...	Macedonia
17,674	10.8	3	960	37,046	38.6	3.7	319	...	15	80.2	87.7	72.9	1.8	Madagascar
3,679	14.7	4	235	2,685	11.4	0.7	61	0.2	15	41.6	...	...	3.3	Malawi
39,187	10.0	43[2]	10,697[2]	108,845[2]	10.2[2]	6.6	638	1.9	15	78.4	86.5	70.4	5.6	Malaysia
462	8.9	—	—			...	...	0.4	15	90.4	90.6	90.1	...	Maldives
...	...	7[7]	499[7]	5,792[7]	11.6[7]	0.8	86	0.2	15	32.0	40.8	23.9	3.3	Mali
7,037	9.4	1	244	2,511	10.3	6.8	482	3.9	15	96.0	96.2	95.9	3.6	Malta
...	...	...				...	...	11.4	25	91.2	92.4	90.0	...	Marshall Islands
8,035	27	1	405[5]	2,743	30.5[5]	...	...	6.3	15	92.5	91.8	93.2	13.5	Martinique
2,529	13.7	7	268[10]	5,808	20.2[10]	3.4	287	...	15	34.0	47.1	21.4	4.9	Mauritania
518[1]	...	2	382[2]	2,179[2]	5.7[2]	2.0	203	3.6	15	81.8[49]	89.0[49]	74.8[49]	4.1	Mauritius
392	23.1	—				...	...	...	15	31.8	...	...	...	Mayotte
1,076,700	13.9	1,832	128,212	1,256,100	9.8	14.6	1,515	5.3	15	87.3	89.5	85.1	3.8	Mexico
...	...			920[5]	...	...	...	8.0	15	76.7	67.0	87.2	...	Micronesia
...	...	9		54,700	...	...	...	55.1[13]	...	...	...	...	...	Moldova
1,218[3]	...					...	...	6.8	...	...	...	...	...	Monaco
29,100	17.7[2]	8	1,465	13,829	9.4	21.8	...	8.1	10	97.9	...	...	7.0	Mongolia
68,802[50]	12.8[50]	35	7,713	225,001	29.2	10.5	983	0.6	15	49.5	61.3	38.0	7.3	Morocco
10,604	10.9	2	457	2,562	5.6	0.2	16	0.2	15	32.9	45.1	21.3	1.2	Mozambique
25,100	12.1	31	5,974	218,800	36.6	4.8	459	0.1	15	78.5	85.8	71.6	1.6	Myanmar (Burma)
1,200[3]	14.8[3]	1	170[5]	4,200[5]	24.7[5]	...	...	2.0	15	72.5	74.2	70.8	1.9	Namibia
30	10.0	1[52]		c. 200[52]		...	...	...	15	99.0			...	Nauru
648[7]	5.5[7]	116[7]	4,165[7]	67,555[7]	16.2[7]	6.2	523	6.8	15	37.7	51.7	23.3	2.8	Nepal

Education (continued)

country	year	first level (primary)					general second level (secondary)					vocational second level[a]	
		schools	teachers[c]	students[d]	student/teacher ratio	net enrollment ratio[b]	schools	teachers[c]	students[d]	student/teacher ratio	net enrollment ratio[b]	schools	teachers[c]
Netherlands, The	1990	9,443	82,562[2]	1,540,000	...	100	1,284	94,441[2]	697,000	...	82	1,245	15,869
Netherlands Antilles	1989	85[5]	1,231[5]	21,778	17.9[5]	...	23[5]	664[5]	8,698	14.2[5]	...	36[5]	50[7]
New Caledonia	1990	279	1,696	34,242	20.2	...	44	1,685[27]	14,237	12.5[27]	...	29	27
New Zealand	1990	2,455[53]	22,140[53]	421,259[53]	19.0	100	336	14,683	229,273	15.6	86	32	4,498
Nicaragua	1989	3,840	18,746	595,612	31.8	73	...	4,768[1]	143,954	...	23		1,170
Niger	1988	2,215[2]	8,462[2]	344,848[2]	40.8[2]	24	64[24]	2,282	63,379	27.8	4	8[29]	161
Nigeria	1989	34,904	344,221	12,712,087	36.9	...	5,594[1]	136,677	2,723,791	19.9	...	376[1]	9,646[1]
Northern Mariana Islands	1989	18	240	4,882	20.3	...	9[27]	163[27]	2,075[27]	12.7[27]	...	27	27
Norway	1991	3,406	33,961	475,344	14.0	98	843[27]	20,647[27]	237,053[27]	11.5[27]	85	27	27
Oman	1990	671	12,344	304,207	24.6	83	128	2,219	36,617	16.5	42	25	728
Pakistan	1991	127,575	218,300	8,856,000	40.6	...	13,604	184,200	3,397,000	18.4	...	930	8,722
Palau	1987	26	289[12]	2,784	13.1[12]	...	6	12	1,009	12	...	1[10]	36[10]
Panama	1990	2,512	12,969	324,594	25.0	90	347[27]	10,066[27]	191,251[27]	19.0[27]	48	27	27
Papua New Guinea	1989	2,692	13,171	417,818	31.7	...	127[7]	2,306	57,676	25.0	...	112[7]	751
Paraguay	1990	4,411	31,590	656,877	20.8	93	812[27]	9,444[2, 27]	165,373[27]	17.4[2, 27]	24	27	27
Peru	1991	28,860[4]	138,455	4,053,801	29.3	95	6,462[4]	96,969	1,996,181	20.6	42	1,524[4]	11,289
Philippines	1990	34,382	315,585	10,284,861	32.6	99	5,523	118,805	3,961,639	33.3	54	945	15,386
Poland	1992	18,578	321,500	5,302,700	16.5	97	1,565	26,600	548,800	20.6	76	8,826	89,500
Portugal	1992	11,439	63,657	1,013,474	15.9	92	1,116	73,196	856,916	11.7	37	116[33]	1,500[33]
Puerto Rico	1989[33]	1,145	33,357[12]	661,693[12]	19.8[12]	...	315	12	12	12	...	52[7]	...
Qatar	1989	97	2,589	48,097	18.6	96	78	2,115	22,178	10.5	71	3	104
Réunion	1991	360	...	73,639	20.7[41]	...	91[27, 57]	...	79,574[27, 57]	...	...	27	...
Romania	1990	13,357	141,732	2,891,810	20.4	...	981	42,519	1,346,315	31.7	...	837	12,419[1]
Russia	1991	67,600[12]	1,506,000[12]	20,851,000[12]	13.8[12]	...	12	12	12	12	...	2,603	...
Rwanda	1990	1,671	18,524	1,058,529	57.1	65	...	4,022[1, 27]	59,689[1, 27]	14.8[1, 27]	7	...	27
St. Kitts and Nevis	1990	33	341	7,442	21.8	...	7[27]	294[27]	4,176[27]	14.2[27]	...	27	27
St. Lucia	1990	83	1,112	32,636	29.3	...	13	376	6,771	18.0	...	1[9]	...
St. Vincent and the Grenadines	1990	64	1,153[35]	24,366	21.5	...	21	396[35]	6,909	18.7	...	2	...
San Marino	1992	14	218	1,200	5.5	...	3	129	841	6.5	...	...	...
São Tomé and Príncipe	1989	64	559	19,822	35.5	...	11[8]	318	7,446	23.4	...	2[8]	18[58]
Saudi Arabia	1989	8,631	105,937	1,694,394	16.0	56	4,153	52,818	739,088	14.0	31	32[1]	3,295[1]
Senegal	1991	2,458	13,394	708,299	52.9	48	321	4,791[2]	173,490	34.8[2]	13	13	259[2]
Seychelles	1992	25[1]	664	12,979	19.5	...	4[7]	520	7,406	14.2	...	1[7]	179
Sierra Leone	1989	2,262	12,972	433,604	33.4	...	232	5,263	104,452	19.8	...	12[8]	406[8]
Singapore	1990	208	10,006	257,932	25.8	100	192	9,197	191,459	20.8	...	23	1,558
Slovenia	1991	822	12,402	226,463	18.3	...	145	6,633	94,062	14.2	...	...	...
Solomon Islands	1989	468	2,248	51,436	22.9	...	20	307	5,556	18.1	...	27	63[7]
Somalia	1987	1,125	8,208	171,830	20.9	11	82	2,109	42,764	20.3	4	21	498
South Africa	1990	20,348[12]	245,525[12]	7,027,068[12]	28.6[12]	...	12	12	12	12	...	214	9,922
Bophuthatswana	1986	1,293	10,153[33]	498,585	35.1[33]	...	1,282[33]	16,178[33]	553,848[33]	34.2[33]	...	8[33]	261[33, 34]
Ciskei	1987	545	4,369	200,752	45.9	...	158	1,809	59,414	32.8	...	1	20
Transkei	1987	1,387	12,617	778,825	61.7	...	1,754	10,245	217,842	21.3	...	17[56]	349[56]
Venda	1986	400	4,039	139,822	34.6	...	155	2,081	51,078	24.5	...	1	42
Spain	1989	20,251	118,693	3,156,183	26.6	100	22,633	200,633	3,611,860	18.3	74	2,668	63,236
Sri Lanka	1990	2,797	71,495	2,081,957	29.1	100	7,128	109,907	2,111,908	19.2	...	25	641
Sudan, The	1991	8,109	60,674	2,165,566	35.7	...	2,514	25,134	446,981	17.8	...	96	1,906
Suriname	1987	301	3,984	59,633	15.0	99	89	1,588	23,217	14.6	40	64[8]	1,283[8]
Swaziland	1990	497	5,083	166,454	32.7	82	135	2,213	41,128	18.6	...	7[5]	181[5]
Sweden	1991	4,649	100,030	881,523	8.8	100	489	30,114	292,047	9.7	86	...	...
Switzerland	1991	...	...	404,154	...	...	...	...	384,780	...	...	...	...
Syria	1990	9,524	90,272	2,357,981	26.1	97	2,077	42,623	856,942	20.1	52	238	8,920
Taiwan	1991	2,487	82,583	2,354,113	28.5	...	870	66,557	1,369,190	20.6	...	216	17,703
Tajikistan	1990	3,101[12]	12	1,258,000[12]	12	...	12	12	12	12	...	12	12
Tanzania	1989	10,431[61]	98,392[61]	3,258,601[61]	33.1[61]	48	288[5]	7,863	145,748	18.5	...	63[5]	1,015
Thailand	1988	34,073	349,210	6,518,540	18.7	...	1,437[29]	103,377	1,734,687	16.8	...	1,528[29]	19,775
Togo	1988	2,429[2]	10,426[2]	569,388[2]	54.6[2]	72	358[10]	4,003[5]	103,835	27.1[5]	...	18[5]	357
Tonga	1990	115	689	16,522	24.0	...	57[5]	767	13,877	18.1	...	9	65
Trinidad and Tobago	1990	472	6,839	189,623	27.7	91	100[2, 27]	4,878[27]	99,133[27]	20.3[27]	71	27	27
Tunisia	1991	3,841	50,280	1,405,665	28.0	95	585	24,474	564,540	23.1	23		237[1, 34]
Turkey	1990	51,170	224,672	6,848,083	30.5	84	7,185	109,720	2,790,266	25.4	40	2,542	49,504
Turkmenistan	1990	398	55,200[12]	710,600	15.0[12]	...	1,324	12	115,000	12	...	92	...
Tuvalu	1987	11	64	1,364	21.3	100	1	15[37]	243	16.7[37]	...	8[37]	16[37]
Uganda	1988	7,905	75,561	2,632,764	34.8	53	297[10]	13,356	240,334	18.0	...	118[10]	2,081
Ukraine	1991	21,825[12]	532,000[12]	6,939,000[12]	13.0[12]	...	12	12	12	12	...	742	...
United Arab Emirates	1990	354[1, 12]	11,921	215,532	18.1	100	27	7,614[27]	94,979	12.6	...	9[7]	27
United Kingdom	1990[33]	24,268	216,160	4,617,737	21.4	99	4,876	234,290	3,395,700	14.5	79	724[1, 62]	93,000[8, 62]
United States	1990	83,425[12]	1,632,000	29,680,000[63]	18.2	95	12	1,112,000[27]	16,541,000[27]	14.9[27]	88	27	27
Uruguay	1989	2,735	19,391	359,455	18.5	88	293	13,571[1, 15]	196,851	...	55	95[1]	...
Uzbekistan	1990	1,467	352,600[12]	283,000	13.0[12]	...	6,571	12	4,584,100	12	...	244	...
Vanuatu	1989	263	970	25,000	25.8	...	21[11]	169[11]	3,065[11]	18.1[11]	...	11	11
Venezuela	1990	12,601	171,431	3,036,219	17.7	87	1,454[27]	62,660[1, 27]	1,114,563[27]	17.2[2, 27]	44	27	27
Vietnam	1989	14,424[12]	443,000[12]	12,204,000[12]	27.5[12]	88	12	12	12	12	...	277	10,700
Virgin Islands (U.S.)	1989[64]	41[5]	965	12,263	12.7	...	10[5]	799	9,741	12.2	...	3[7]	27[7]
West Bank[65]	1989	1,174[12]	9,226[12]	303,083[12]	32.8[12]	...	12	12	12	12	...	12	12
Western Sahara	1989[33]	27	596	14,794	24.8	...	18	577	9,218	16.0	...	...	...
Western Samoa	1986	164[37]	1,511[66]	31,412[5]	20.8	...	38[3]	513	20,168	39.3	...	4[37]	53
Yemen[67]	1991	7,313[2]	35,350	1,291,372	36.5	...	942[7]	12,106	394,578	32.6	...	73[7]	1,247
Yugoslavia	1991	5,075	65,099	1,238,480	19.0	...	565	28,609	407,405	14.2	...	...	...
Zaire	1988	10,817	113,468[5]	4,356,416	36.6[5]	60	4,276[27]	49,153[27]	507,944	21.7[27]	17	27	27
Zambia	1988	3,392	32,348	1,426,138	44.1	80	276[7]	5,627[7]	161,349	26.8[7]	15	28[7]	1,055[7]
Zimbabwe	1989	4,532	58,000	2,333,340	...	100	1,517	25,000	670,552	26.8	...	21[1]	1,224[1]

[1]1988. [2]1989. [3]1982. [4]1990. [5]1987. [6]Students registered abroad. [7]1986. [8]1985. [9]Vocational second level includes third level. [10]1984. [11]General second level includes teacher training at second level. [12]First level includes second level. [13]Percentage having completed secondary or more. [14]General second level includes first level. [15]Includes special education. [16]Universities only. [17]Data exclude 86 combined primary/secondary schools with 12,286 students. [18]College of the Bahamas only. [19]National literacy standard based solely on school attendance. [20]General second level includes some vocational and teacher training at the second level. [21]Third level includes vocational second level. [22]Age 15 and over. [23]University of Phnom Penh only. [24]Includes upper primary. [25]Includes part-time teachers. [26]Includes part-time teachers. [27]General second level includes vocational second level. [28]1981. [29]1980. [30]Republic of Cyprus only. [31]Includes preschool, primary, and lower secondary (to age 15). [32]Upper second level only (ages 16–18). [33]Public schools only. [34]Teacher training only. [35]1991. [36]Data exclude 1,147 primary and 1,057 secondary schools, as well as the university, in the El Azhar education system. [37]1983. [38]Includes lower-secondary students at all-age schools. [39]Excludes lower-secondary students. [40]Former West Germany only.

students[d]	student/teacher ratio	third level (higher) institutions	teachers[c]	students[d]	student/teacher ratio	gross enrollment ratio[b]	students per 100,000 population[b]	percent of population age 25 and over with postsecondary education[b]	literacy[b] over age	total (%)	male (%)	female (%)	public expenditure on education (percent of GNP)[b]	country
546,000	...	478[1]	30,952[7]	329,000	...	32.4	2,819	7.2	15	100.0	100.0	100.0	6.8	Netherlands, The
6,526	13.0[7]	2[7]	80[7]	578	8.8[7]	...	...	6.4	15	95.0	...	...	5.2	Netherlands Antilles
6,765	27	6	141[2]	1,207	9.9[2]	...	...	...	15	57.9	57.4	58.3	13.4	New Caledonia
56,771	12.6	7[16]	3,761[16]	78,919[16]	21.0[16]	40.7	3,591	6.9	15	100.0	100.0	100.0	5.9	New Zealand
17,258	14.8	4[4,16]	1,591[4,16]	34,166[4,16]	21.5[4,16]	8.4	768	...	15	74.0	...	...	3.9	Nicaragua
2,437	15.1	3	341[54]	4,506	11.1[54]	0.7	60	0.2	15	10.8	16.7	5.4	3.1	Niger
310,278[1]	32.2[1]	48[1,55]	3,235[1,55]	55,068[1,55]	17.0[1,55]	3.2	290	...	15	42.4	53.8	31.5	1.5	Nigeria
27	27	1	102	1,097	10.8	...	...	21.9	15	96.3	96.9	95.6	...	Northern Mariana Islands
27	27	227	7,556	137,982	18.3	36.0	2,858	18.8	15	100.0	100.0	100.0	7.5	Norway
5,596	7.7	5	482	3,925	8.1	4.1	308	...	6	41.0	58.0	24.0	3.7	Oman
108,000	12.4	733	26,050	658,900	25.3	4.8	448	1.9	15	25.6	36.0	15.2	2.6	Pakistan
382[10]	10.6[10]	...	...	...	...	...	...	16.8	25	92.7	94.4	91.0	...	Palau
27	27	8	3,451	53,235	15.4	21.9	2,199	8.4	15	88.1	88.1	88.1	6.2	Panama
9,331	12.4	27	902	6,397	7.1	2.0	146	...	15	52.0	64.9	37.8	4.7	Papua New Guinea
27	27	2	2,694[8]	28,677	...	8.0	750	3.4	15	90.1	92.1	88.1	1.5	Paraguay
312,669	27.7	493[4]	44,361	751,234	16.9	35.6	3,106	4.8	15	89.3	95.9	82.6	3.5	Peru
291,600	19.0	810	70,012[1]	1,225,315	22.6[1]	28.2	2,659	15.2	15	88.7	89.9	87.5	2.9	Philippines
1,677,000[35]	18.8[35]	117	63,200	423,500	6.7	20.3	1,328	6.5	15	98.7	99.2	98.3	4.6	Poland
60,077	19.4[33]	231[56]	15,108[56]	182,283[56]	12.1[56]	18.4	1,525	0.3	15	86.8	86.7	86.9	4.9	Portugal
149,191[7]	...	45	9,045	156,818	17.3	48.1	4,091	18.4	15	89.1	89.7	88.5	8.2	Puerto Rico
924	8.9	1[4]	504[4]	5,637[4]	11.2[4]	26.0	1,848	13.3	15	75.7	76.8	72.5	5.6	Qatar
27	...	1[16]	137[16]	4,607[16]	33.6[16]	...	...	4.3	15	78.2	75.9	80.3	15.1	Réunion
306,126	...	44	11,696	164,507	14.1	8.6	712	4.6	15	95.8	...	...	2.1	Romania
2,270,000	...	514	...	1,648,000	...	...	...	...	15	...	...	...	...	Russia
27	27	3[8]	646	3,389	5.2	0.6	48	...	15	50.2	63.9	37.1	4.2	Rwanda
27	27	...	37[1]	211[1]	5.2[1]	...	...	2.1	15	90.0	...	...	3.0	St. Kitts and Nevis
763[9]	...	9	...	9	...	...	...	1.3	15	80.0	...	...	7.2	St. Lucia
295	...	...	...	...	...	...	...	1.4	15	85.0	...	...	5.8	St. Vincent and the Grenadines
317	...	...	...	332[5,6]	...	...	...	...	15	98.0	98.2	97.7	...	San Marino
289	...	...	...	700[6,37]	...	...	...	0.3	15	54.2	70.2	39.1	4.3	São Tomé and Príncipe
31,354[1]	9.5[1]	82	9,631	115,006	11.9	12.2	951	...	15	62.4	73.1	48.1	7.6	Saudi Arabia
6,435	24.6[2]	18	770[16]	18,862	19.3[16]	3.0	253	0.8	15	28.6	38.8	19.4	3.7	Senegal
1,684	9.4	...	...	...	...	...	...	3.1	15	84.8	83.4	86.1	9.1	Seychelles
4,774[8]	11.8[8]	2[1]	373[1]	2,985[1]	8.0[1]	0.7	61	...	15	20.7	30.7	11.3	2.0	Sierra Leone
29,102	18.7	7	4,615	55,562	12.0	7.9	963	3.4	10	87.6	93.3	81.7	3.4	Singapore
...	...	28	2,555	33,574	13.1	...	...	5.9[22]	10	99.2	99.3	99.1	...	Slovenia
465	7.4	—	...	...	—	...	...	2.6	15	54.1	62.4	44.9	4.7	Solomon Islands
4,809	9.7	1	262[28]	1,692	...	3.0	...	...	10	54.8	60.9	47.9	0.4	Somalia
205,682	20.7	17[16]	40,156	286,910	7.1	...	...	2.3	15	50.0	...	...	3.8	South Africa
4,939[33]	13.0[33,34]	1	187	3,282	17.6	...	...	...	15	75.0	...	...	...	Bophuthatswana
174	8.7	3[59]	97[59]	1,677[59]	17.3[59]	...	...	...	15	72.0	...	...	...	Ciskei
6,363[56]	18.2[56]	1	203	3,988	19.6	...	...	...	...	...	...	...	...	Transkei
422	10.0	5	119[10]	5,135	24.0[10]	...	...	...	...	...	...	...	...	Venda
1,234,045	19.5	33[8]	55,504	1,101,297	19.8	31.5	2,655	7.1	15	94.7	97.0	92.5	4.3	Spain
18,971	29.6	34	2,171	41,951	19.3	4.2	400	1.1	15	84.3	88.3	80.1	3.0	Sri Lanka
33,685	17.7	20	3,397	58,566	17.2	2.9	246	...	15	27.1	42.7	11.7	4.0	Sudan, The
15,996	12.5[8]	...	373[8]	2,914[8]	7.2[8]	7.7	719	...	15	94.9	95.1	94.7	9.5	Suriname
1,280[5]	7.1[5]	1[5]	178[5]	1,270[5]	7.1[5]	3.9	316	...	15	67.0	69.0	65.0	6.2	Swaziland
...	...	...	27,523[4,60]	272,718[4]	9.9	31.3	2,196	15.4	15	100.0	100.0	100.0	7.3	Sweden
218,780	...	...	...	137,492	...	26.2	2,018	...	15	100.0	100.0	100.0	4.9	Switzerland
56,094	6.3	44	4,605[5]	203,979	...	19.9	1,737	1.3	15	79.9	89.7	69.3	4.1	Syria
449,111	25.4	121	27,579	576,623	20.9	...	2,225	6.0	15	92.4	96.3	87.9	3.6	Taiwan
...	...	10	...	65,586	...	...	...	62.6[13]	...	...	...	...	...	Tajikistan
13,263	13.1	4	1,206	5,254	4.4	0.3	20	...	15	85.0	...	...	3.7	Tanzania
336,420	17.0	62[29]	30,905[8]	1,026,952[8]	33.2[8]	16.1	1,734	2.9	15	88.8	93.2	84.5	3.2	Thailand
5,956	16.7	1[16]	276[16]	7,732[16]	26.6[16]	2.6	226	1.3	15	39.1	51.7	27.5	5.2	Togo
872	13.4	1[7]	178[7]	705[8]	41.5[8]	—	...	0.1	15	92.8	92.9	92.8	4.2	Tonga
27	27	1[4]	346[4]	4,090[4]	11.8[4]	6.0	563	2.9	15	96.1	...	...	4.9	Trinidad and Tobago
3,839[1,34]	...	7	3,901[2]	68,534	14.0[2]	7.9	784	3.4	15	62.8	73.6	51.7	6.3	Tunisia
830,716	16.8	387	32,029	644,835	20.1	12.7	1,253	3.9	15	80.7	89.7	71.1	1.8	Turkey
35,000	...	9	...	42,000	...	...	...	65.1[13]	...	...	...	...	...	Turkmenistan
354[37]	22.1[37]	—	...	...	...	...	...	...	15	95.5	95.5	95.5	...	Tuvalu
19,735	9.5	14[10]	934[10]	12,531[5]	8.8[10]	1.0	81	0.1	15	57.3	69.7	45.3	3.4	Uganda
757,000	...	149	...	881,300	...	...	...	29.9	15	...	...	...	...	Ukraine
690	27	1[2]	478[2]	7,655[2]	16.0[2]	8.5	487	...	15	73.0	74.5	68.4	2.1	United Arab Emirates
539,718[1,62]	...	50[4,16]	49,377[4,16]	352,574[4,16]	7.1[4,16]	23.5	1,954	11.0	15	100.0	100.0	100.0	4.7	United Kingdom
27	27	3,535[2]	755,000[2]	13,711,000	17.8[2]	59.6	5,596	32.2	15	95.5	95.7	95.3	6.8	United States
56,084	...	2	5,925[1]	63,777	10.5[1]	50.4	3,751	14.8	15	95.0	94.5	95.4	3.1	Uruguay
277,300	...	44	...	331,600	...	...	...	66.9[13]	15	...	...	...	...	Uzbekistan
11	11	...	...	...	...	...	—	...	15	52.9	57.3	47.8	5.5	Vanuatu
27	27	85	39,489	528,473	13.4	27.8	2,670	7.0	15	92.2	93.5	91.1	4.2	Venezuela
130,000	12.1	103	19,900	122,000	6.1	2.3	214	6.8	15	87.6	93.0	82.8	3.0	Vietnam
775[7]	28.7[7]	1[5]	975	757[5]	8.3[5]	...	...	17.6	15	90.0	...	...	7.5	Virgin Islands (U.S.)
12	12	4[37]	...	7,066[37]	...	...	...	8.1	...	...	...	...	...	West Bank[65]
...	...	...	...	...	...	...	...	...	...	...	...	...	...	Western Sahara
436	8.2	6[37]	37[37]	562[37]	15.2[37]	...	...	2.0	15	100.0	100.0	100.0	5.9	Western Samoa
26,119	20.9	1[2]	470[2]	23,457[2]	49.9[2]	2.9	274	...	15	38.5	53.3	26.3	6.1	Yemen[67]
...	...	147	12,633	157,232	12.4	...	...	5.7[22]	10	89.2	95.4	83.2	...	Yugoslavia
558,407	...	...	3,506	52,800	15.1	1.9	184	...	15	71.8	83.6	60.7	0.9	Zaire
8,950	9.2[7]	27	575[7]	3,729	6.7	2.0	178	0.4	15	68.6	79.5	58.1	5.5	Zambia
41,688[1]	34.0[1]	1	561[1]	9,288	13.7[1]	5.3	585	...	15	76.0	81.5	66.8	8.5	Zimbabwe

[41]Includes preschool.   [42]Postsecondary associate-degree program only.   [43]State University of Haiti only.   [44]General second level includes first level and vocational second level.   [45]Based on data for four schools only.   [46]Schools under the Department of Education and Culture only.   [47]National schools only.   [48]Teaching posts financed by the Ministry of Education and Culture only.   [49]Island of Mauritius only.   [50]Excludes teacher training.   [51]Includes Portuguese-language initiation classes.   [52]University of the South Pacific extension centre.   [53]Includes 79 composite schools that provide both primary and secondary education.   [54]Université de Niamey and Ecole Nationale d'Administration du Niger only.   [55]Colleges of education only.   [56]Includes postsecondary teacher training.   [57]1992.   [58]Vocational teachers only.   [59]Excludes the University of Fort Hare.   [60]Includes graduate assistants.   [61]Excludes Pemba and Zanzibar.   [62]Third-level vocational and teacher training.   [63]Includes some preschool.   [64]Excludes 42 private schools with 6,556 students.   [65]Excludes East Jerusalem.   [66]Includes some secondary teachers.   [67]Data are for the former Yemen Arab Republic only.

BIBLIOGRAPHY AND SOURCES

The following list indicates the principal sources used in the compilation of *Britannica World Data*. It is by no means a complete list, either for international or for national sources, but is indicative only of the range of materials to which reference has been made in preparing this compilation. For example, in addition to the kinds of works cited below, reference has also been made to the constitution of each country, to the publications of its central or commercial banks, to unpublished information received in correspondence from the countries, and to other more specialized sources.

International Statistical Sources

Asian Development Bank. *Asian Development Outlook* (annual); *Key Indicators of Developing Member Countries of ADB* (annual, with supplements).
Billboard Ltd. *World Radio TV Handbook* (annual).
Caribbean Development Bank. *Annual Report*.
Comité Monétaire de la Zone Franc. *La Zone Franc: Rapport* (annual).
Council for Mutual Economic Assistance (Comecon). *Statistichesky Yezhegodnik Stran-Chlenov Soveta Economicheskoy Vzaimopomoshchi* (Statistical Yearbook of the Council for Mutual Economic Assistance).
Eastern Caribbean Central Bank. *Report and Statement of Accounts* (annual).
Europa Publications Ltd. *Africa South of the Sahara* (annual); *Eastern Europe and the Commonwealth of Independent States*; *The Europa Year Book* (2 vol.); *The Far East and Australasia* (annual); *The Middle East and North Africa* (annual).
Food and Agriculture Organization. *Food Balance Sheets* (quinquennial); *Production Yearbook; Trade Yearbook; World Census of Agriculture* (decennial); *Yearbook of Fishery Statistics* (2 vol.); *Yearbook of Forest Products*.
FT Caribbean. *The Caribbean Handbook* (annual).
Her Majesty's Stationery Office. *The Commonwealth Yearbook*.
Instituts d'Émission d'Outre-Mer et des Départements d'Outre-Mer (France). *Rapport annuel, Bulletin trimestriel* (quarterly).
Inter-American Development Bank. *Economic and Social Progress in Latin America* (annual).
Inter-Parliamentary Union. *Chronicle of Parliamentary Elections and Developments* (annual); *World Directory of Parliaments* (annual).
International Air Transport Association. *World Air Transport Statistics* (annual).
International Bank for Reconstruction and Development/The World Bank. *World Bank Atlas* (annual); *World Debt Tables* (annual); *World Development Report* (annual).
International Civil Aviation Organization. *Civil Aviation Statistics of the World* (annual); *Digest of Statistics*.
International Institute for Strategic Studies. *The Military Balance* (annual).
International Labour Organisation. *Year Book of Labour Statistics; The Cost of Social Security: Basic Tables* (triennial).
International Monetary Fund. *Annual Report on Exchange Arrangements and Exchange Restrictions; Government Finance Statistics Yearbook; International Financial Statistics* (monthly, with supplements and yearbook).
International Road Federation. *World Road Statistics* (annual).
Jane's Publishing Co., Ltd. *Jane's World Railways* (annual).
Lloyd's Register of Shipping. *Lloyd's Register of Shipping: Statistical Tables* (annual).
Longman Group U.K. Ltd. *Keesing's Record of World Events* (monthly).

Macmillan Press Ltd. *The Statesman's Year-Book*.
Middle East Economic Digest Ltd. *Africa Economic Digest* (semimonthly); *Middle East Economic Digest* (semimonthly).
Mining Journal. *Mining Annual Review* (2 vol.).
Nordic Council. *Yearbook of Nordic Statistics*.
Official Airline Guides, Inc. *Official Airline Guide* (monthly).
Organization of Eastern Caribbean States. *Statistical Pocket Digest*.
Organization for Economic Cooperation and Development. *Economic Surveys* (annual); *Financing and External Debt of Developing Countries* (annual); *National Accounts of Developing Countries* (irreg.).
Oxford University Press. *World Christian Encyclopedia* (David B. Barrett, ed. [1982]).
PennWell Publishing Co. *International Petroleum Encyclopedia* (annual).
René Moreux et Cie. *Marchés tropicaux & Méditerranéens* (weekly).
South Pacific Commission. *Key Economic Indicators* (irreg.); *South Pacific Economies: Statistical Summary* (biennial).
United Nations (UN). *Demographic Yearbook; International Trade Statistics Yearbook* (2 vol.); *Energy Statistics Yearbook; Industrial Statistics Yearbook* (2 vol.); *Monthly Bulletin of Statistics; Population Studies* (irreg.); *National Accounts Statistics* (3 vol.; annual); *Population and Vital Statistics Report* (quarterly); *Statistical Yearbook; World Population Prospects 19*** (biennial).
UN: Conference on Trade and Development. *Handbook of International Trade and Development Statistics* (annual); *The Least Developed Countries* (annual).
UN: Economic Commission for Africa. *African Socio-Economic Indicators* (annual); *African Statistical Yearbook* (4 vol.); *Demographic and Related Socio-Economic Data Sheets for ECA Member States* (1986); *Survey of Economic and Social Conditions in Africa* (irreg.).
UN: Economic Commission for Europe. *Annual Bulletin of Housing and Building Statistics for Europe; Annual Bulletin of Transport Statistics for Europe*.
UN: Economic Commission for Latin America. *Economic Survey of Latin America and the Caribbean* (annual); *Statistical Yearbook for Latin America and the Caribbean*.
UN: Economic and Social Commission for Asia and the Pacific. *Foreign Trade Statistics of Asia and the Pacific* (annual); *Statistical Indicators for Asia and the Pacific* (quarterly); *Statistical Yearbook for Asia and the Pacific*.
UN: Economic and Social Commission for Western Asia. *Demographic and Related Socio-Economic Data Sheets* (irreg.); *Population Bulletin* (irreg.); *The Population Situation in the ESCWA Region* (irreg.); *Statistical Abstract of the Region of the Economic and Social Commission for Western Asia* (annual).
UN: Educational, Scientific, and Cultural Organization. *Statistical Yearbook*.
United Nations Industrial Development Organization. *Industry and Development: Global Report* (annual).
United States: Central Intelligence Agency, *The World Factbook;* Dept. of Commerce, *World Population Profile* (irreg.); Dept. of Energy, *International Energy Annual;* Dept. of Health and Human Services, *Social Security Programs Throughout the World* (biennial); Dept. of Interior, *Minerals Yearbook* (3 vol. in 8); Dept. of State, *Background Notes* (irreg.).
Vatican (Central Statistics Office of the Church). *Statistical Yearbook of the Church*.
World Energy Conference. *Survey of Energy Resources* (quinquennial).
World Health Organization. *World Health Statistics Annual; World Health Statistics Quarterly*.
World Tourism Organization. *World Tourism Statistics* (2 vol.; annual).

National Statistical Sources

Afghanistan. *First Seven-Year Economic and Social Development Plan, 1355–1361* (March 1976–March 1983); *Preliminary Results of the First Afghan Population Census, 1979*.
Albania. *Vjetari statistikor i R.P.S. të Shqipërisë* (Statistical Yearbook of the People's Socialist Republic of Albania [annual]).
Algeria. *Annuaire statistique; Recensement général de la population et de l'habitat, 1987*.
American Samoa. *American Samoa Statistical Digest* (annual); *Population of American Samoa* (ESCAP; Country Monograph Series No. 7.1 [1979]); *1990 Census of Population and Housing* (U.S.).
Andorra. *Estadístiques* (annual); *Recull Estadístic General de la Població Andorra 90*.
Angola. *Angola: an Introductory Economic Review* (A World Bank Country Study [1991]); *Informação Estatistica* (annual); *Perfil estatistico de Angola* (annual).
Antigua. *Statistical Yearbook*.
Argentina. *Anuario estadístico de la República Argentina; Boletín estadístico trimestral* (quarterly); *Censo nacional de población y vivienda, 1991; Encuesta permanente de hogares* (irreg.).
Armenia. *Statisticheskii Yezhegodnik Armenii* (Statistical Yearbook of Armenia).
Aruba. *Statistical Yearbook*.
Australia. *Census of Manufacturing Establishments; Summary of Operations by Industry Subdivision, Australia* (annual); *Foreign Trade Australia: Comparative and Summary Tables* (annual); *Monthly Summary of Statistics, Australia; National Income and Expenditure* (annual); *Social Indicators* (irreg.); *Year Book Australia; 1991 Census of Population and Housing*.
Austria. *Grosszählung 1991* (General Census 1991). *Österreichisches Jahrbuch* (annual); *Sozialstatistische Daten* (irreg.); *Statistisches Handbuch* (annual).
Azerbaijan. *Economic Review: Armenia* (IMF [1992]); *Narodnoye Khozyaystvo Azerbaydzhanskoy SSR* (National Economy of the Azerbaijan S.S.R. [annual]).
Bahamas, The. *Census of Population and Housing 1990 Quarterly Statistical Summary; Statistical Abstract* (annual); *Vital Statistics Report* (annual).
Bahrain. *Statistical Abstract* (annual); *1981 Census of Bahrain*.
Bangladesh. *Bangladesh Population Census, 1991; Population of Bangladesh* (ESCAP; Country Monograph Series No. 8 [1981]); *Statistical Yearbook of Bangladesh*.
Barbados. *Barbados Economic Report* (annual); *Monthly Digest of Statistics*.
Belarus. *Narodnoye Kozyaystvo Belorusskoy S.S.R.* (National Economy of the Belorussian S.S.R. [annual]).
Belgium. *Annuaire statistique de la Belgique; Recensement de la population et des logements au 1er mars 1991*.
Belize. *Abstract of Statistics* (annual); *Belize Economic Survey* (annual); *Belize Today: Development Plan 1990–94; Labour Force Survey (1983–84); 1980–81 Population Census of the Commonwealth Caribbean, Belize*.
Benin. *Annuaire statistique; Recensement des Entreprises 1980* (2 parts); *Recensement général de la population et de l'habitation* (1979).
Bermuda. *Bermuda Digest of Statistics* (annual); *Report of the Manpower Survey* (annual); *The 1991 Census of Population and Housing*.
Bhutan. *Bhutan: Development Planning in a Unique Environment* (A World Bank Country Study [1988]); *Statistical Yearbook of Bhutan* (annual).
Bolivia. *Bolivia en Cifras* (annual); *Censo Nacional de población y vivienda de 1976; Compendio Estadístico* (annual); *Estadísticas Económicas* (annual); *Estrategia de Desarrollo Económico y Social 1989–2000; Resumen estadístico* (annual).
Botswana. *National Development Plan 1985–91; 1981 Population and Housing Census*.

Brazil. *Anuário Econômico-Fiscal; Anuário Estatístico do Brasil; Censo Demografico 1991; Comercio Exterior do Brasil* (2 vol.; annual).
Brunei. *Brunei Statistical Yearbook; Population Survey 1986: Demographic Report; Report on the Census of Population, 1981.*
Bulgaria. *Prebroyavaneto na naselenieto kŭm 4.12.1985 godina* (Census of Population of Dec. 4, 1985); *Statisticheskii godishnikna Republika Bŭlgariya* (Statistical Yearbook of the Republic of Bulgaria).
Burkina Faso. *Annuaire Statistique; Recensement général de la population du 10 au 20 decembre 1985; Statistiques Sociales* (annual).
Burundi. *Annuaire statistique; Recensement général de la population, 1990.*
Cambodia. *Cambodia: A Country Study* (1990); *Intersectoral Basic Needs Assessment Mission to Cambodia* (Unesco; 1991); *Report of the Kampuchea Needs Assessment Study* (UNDP; 1989).
Cameroon. *Note annuelle de statistique; Recensement général de la population et de l'habitat 1987.*
Canada. *Canada Year Book* (biennial); *National Income and Expenditure Accounts* (quarterly); *Census Canada 1991: Population.*
Cape Verde. *Boletím Anual de Estatística; I.º Recenseamento Geral da População e Habìtação—1990.*
Cayman Islands. *Cayman Islands 1989 Census; Statistical Abstract of the Cayman Islands* (annual).
Central African Republic. *Annuaire statistique; Economic and Social Development Plan 1986–90; Recensement général de la population 1988.*
Chad. *Annuaire statistique; Chad: a Country Study* (1990).
Chile. *Chile XV censo nacional de población y de vivienda, 21 de abril 1982; Compendio estadístico* (annual); *Plan nacional indicativo de desarrollo* (quinquennial).
China, People's Republic of. *China: A Statistics Survey in 19**** (annual); *People's Republic of China Year-Book; Major Figures by 10 Percent Sampling on the 1982 Census of the People's Republic of China; Statistical Yearbook of China; Yearbook of the Encyclopedia of China.*
Colombia. *Colombia estadística* (2 vol.; annual); *XV Censo nacional de población y IV de vivienda* (1985).
Comoros. *Plan interimaire de développement économique et sociale (1983–1986); Recensement général de la population et de l'habitat 15 septembre 1980.*
Congo. *Annuaire statistique; Recensement Général de la Population et de l'Habitat de 1984.*
Cook Islands. *Cook Islands Census of Population and Dwellings, 1986; Cook Islands Quarterly Statistical Bulletin.*
Costa Rica. *Anuario estadístico; Censo de Población 1984; Plan Nacional de Desarrollo, 1986–90* (2 vol.).
Côte d'Ivoire. *Annuaire statistique; La Côte d'Ivoire en chiffres* (irreg.); *L'Économie Ivoirienne* (irreg.); *Enquête permanente aupres des menages: resultats provisoires 1985.*
Cuba. *Anuario estadístico; Censo de población y viviendas, 1981; Compendio estadístico de Cuba* (annual); *Cuba Half-Yearly Economic Report.*
Cyprus. *Census of Industrial Production* (annual); *Economic Report* (annual); *Statistical Abstract* (annual).
Czechoslovakia. *Statistická ročenka Československé Socialistické Republiky* (Statistical Yearbook of the Czechoslovak Socialist Republic); *Sčítání lidu, domů a bytů 1991* (Census of Population and Housing).
Denmark. *Folke- og boligtaellingen, 1981* (Population and Housing Census); *Statistisk årbog* (Statistical Yearbook).
Djibouti. *Annuaire statistique de Djibouti.*
Dominica. *Statistical Digest* (irreg.).
Dominican Republic. *República Dominicana en cifras* (annual); *VI Censo nacional de población y vivienda, 1981.*
Ecuador. *Encuesta anual de manufactura y minería; Serie estadística* (quinquennial); *Censo de población (V) y de vivienda (IV) 1990.*
Egypt. *Population, Housing, and Establishment Census, 1986; Statistical Yearbook.*
El Salvador. *Anuario estadístico* (8 vol.); *Censos económicos, 1979* (*Manufactura diversa; Agroindustrias; Comercio y servicios; Electricidad, construcción, transporte comercial*); *El Salvador en cifras* (annual).
Equatorial Guinea. *Censos Nacionales, I de Población y I de Vivienda—4 al 17 de Julio de 1983; Guinea en cifras* (irreg.).
Estonia. *Statistical Yearbook Estonia.*
Ethiopia. *Ethiopia 1984 Population and Housing Census; Ethiopia Statistical Abstract* (annual).
Faeroe Islands. *Årbog for Faerøerne* (Yearbook for the Faeroe Islands); *Rigsombudsmanden på Færøerne: Beretning* (annual).
Fiji. *Annual Employment Survey; Census of Industries* (annual); *Current Economic Statistics* (quarterly); *1986 Census of the Population.*
Finland. *Annual Statistics of Agriculture; Economic Survey* (annual); *1985 Population and Housing Census; Statistical Yearbook of Finland.*
France. *Annuaire statistique de la France; Données sociales* (triennial); *Recensement général de la population de 1990; Métropole; Tableaux de l'Economie Française* (annual).
French Guiana. *Recensement général de la population de 1990: logements-population-emplois, 973: Guyane; Tableaux economiques regionaux: Guyane* (annual).
French Polynesia. *Résultats du Recensement Général de la Population de la Polynésie Française, du 6 Septembre 1988; Tableaux de l'economie polynesienne* (irreg.); *Te avei'a: Bulletin d'information statistique* (monthly).
Gabon. *Situation économique, financière et sociale de la République Gabonaise* (annual).
Gambia, The. *Statistical Abstract* (annual?).
Gaza Strip. *Judaea, Samaria, and Gaza Area Statistics Quarterly; Palestinian Statistical Abstract* (annual).
Georgia. *Narodnoye Khozyaystvo Gruzinskoy SSR* (National Economy of the Georgian S.S.R. [annual]).
Germany. *Statistisches Jahrbuch für die Bundesrepublik Deutschland; Volkszählung vom 25. Mai 1987* (Census of Population).
Ghana. *Population Census of Ghana, 1984; Quarterly Digest of Statistics.*
Gibraltar. *Abstract of Statistics* (annual); *Census of Gibraltar, 1991.*
Greece. *Recensement des industries manufacturières: Artisanat, du commerce et autres services* (1978); *Recensement de la population et des habitations, 1991; Statistical Yearbook of Greece.*
Greenland. *Grønland* (annual); *Grønlands befolkning* (Greenland Population [annual]).
Grenada. *Abstract of Statistics* (annual).
Guadeloupe. *Recensement général de la population de 1990: logements-population-emplois, 971: Guadeloupe; Tableaux economiques regionaux: Guadeloupe* (annual).
Guam. *Guam Annual Economic Review; Census '90: Guam.*
Guatemala. *Censos nacionales, 1981: IX de población—IV de habitación.*
Guernsey. *Guernsey Census 1986; Statistical Digest* (annual).
Guinea. *Situation Économique et Conjoncturelle au 31 decembre 1985 et éléments sur la mise en oeuvre de la réform économique au cours du première trimestre 1986.*
Guinea-Bissau. *Boletim Trimestral de Estatística; Recenseamento Geral da População e da Habitação, 16 de Abril de 1979.*
Guyana. *Annual Statistical Abstract.*
Haiti. *Bulletin trimestriel de statistique; Dominican Republic and Haiti: Country Studies* (1991); *Résultats préliminaires du recensement général* (*Septembre 1982*).
Honduras. *Anuario estadístico; Censo nacional de Población y Vivienda 1988; Honduras en cifras* (annual); *Plan nacional de desarrollo, 1987–90.*
Hong Kong. *Annual Digest of Statistics; Hong Kong* (annual); *Hong Kong 1991 Population Census; Hong Kong in Figures* (annual); *Hong Kong Social and Economic Trends* (irreg.).
Hungary. *Statisztikai évkönyv* (Statistical Yearbook); *1990, Évi népszámlálás* (Census of Population).
Iceland. *Hagtidhindi* (monthly); *Landshagir* (Statistical Abstract of Iceland [irreg.]); *Verslunarskýrslur* (External Trade [annual]).
India. *Census of India, 1991; Economic Survey* (annual); *India: A Reference Annual; Statistical Abstract* (annual).
Indonesia. *Indonesia: An Official Handbook* (1989); *Hasil Sensus penduduk Indonesia, 1990* (Census of Population); *Statistical Yearbook of Indonesia.*
Iran. *National Census of Population and Housing, October 1986; A Statistical Reflection of the Islamic Republic of Iran* (annual); *Statistical Yearbook of the Islamic Republic of Iran.*
Iraq. *Iraq: A Country Study* (1990); *Statistical Abstract* (annual).
Ireland. *Census of Population of Ireland, 1991; National Income and Expenditure* (annual); *Statistical Abstract* (annual).
Isle of Man. *Census Report 1991; Isle of Man Digest of Economic and Social Statistics* (annual).
Israel. *1983 Census of Population and Housing; Statistical Abstract* (annual).
Italy. *Annuario di statistica agraria: Annuario di statistiche demografiche; Annuario di statistiche industriali; Annuario statistico dell'istruzione; Annuario statistico Italiano; Statistiche forestale* (annual); *Statistiche sociali* (1981); *13° Censimento generale della popolazione e delle Abitazioni 20 Ottobre 1991.*
Jamaica. *Economic and Social Survey* (annual); *Statistical Abstract* (annual); *Statistical Yearbook of Jamaica.*
Japan. *Establishment Census of Japan, 1981; Japan Statistical Yearbook; Statistical Indicators on Social Life* (annual); *1990 Population Census of Japan.*
Jersey. *Report of the Census for 1991; Statistical Digest* (annual).
Jordan. *Census 1979; Family Expenditure Survey* (1980); *National Accounts* (irreg.); *Statistical Yearbook.*
Kazakhstan. *Narodnoye Khozyaystvo Kazakhstana za 70 let: Statistichesky Sbornik* (National Economy of Kazakhstan over 70 years: Statistical Collection [annual]).
Kenya. *Economic Survey* (annual); *Kenya Statistical Digest* (quarterly); *Statistical Abstract* (annual).
Kiribati. *Annual Abstract of Statistics; Kiribati Population Census 1990; Sixth National Development Plan, 1987–1991.*
Korea, North. *North Korea: A Country Study* (1981).
Korea, South. *Korea Statistical Yearbook; Social Indicators in Korea* (irreg.); *The 5th Five-Year Economic and Development Plan, 1982–1986; 1990 Population and Housing Census.*
Kuwait. *Annual Statistical Abstract; Economic Report* (annual); *General Census of Population and Housing and Buildings 1985.*
Kyrgyzstan. *Narodnoye Khozyaystvo Kirgizskoy SSR* (National Economy of the Kirgiz S.S.R. [annual]).
Latvia. *Narodnoye Khozyaystvo Latvii* (National Economy of Latvia [annual]).
Lebanon. *Lebanon: A Country Study* (1989).
Lesotho. *Annual Statistical Bulletin; 1986 Population Census.*
Liberia. *Economic Survey* (annual); *1974 Census of Population and Housing.*
Libya. *The Five-Year Development Plan 1981–85; Libya Population Census, 1973; Statistical Abstract for Libya* (annual).
Liechtenstein. *Statistisches Jahrbuch; Volkszählung, 2 Dezember 1980* (Census of Population).
Lithuania. *Lithuania Statistics Yearbook.*
Luxembourg. *Annuaire statistique; Bulletin du STATEC* (monthly); *Recensement général de la population du 31 mars 1991.*
Macau. *Anuário Estatístico; Inquerito Industrial* (annual); *XIII Recenseamento Geral da População, 1991.*
Madagascar. *Recensement général de la population et des habitats, 1975; Situation économique* (annual).
Malaŵi. *Malawi Population and Housing Census, 1987; Malawi Statistical Yearbook; Malawi Yearbook.*
Malaysia. *Fifth Malaysia Plan, 1986–1990; Malaysia Official Year Book; Malaysian Annual Statistical Bulletin; 1980 Population and Housing Census.*
Maldives. *National Development Plan 1991–1993; Population and Housing Census of Maldives 1990; Statistical Year Book of Maldives.*
Mali. *Annuaire statistique du Mali; Comptes Economiques du Mali* (annual); *Recensement general de la population et de l'habitat (du 1*[er] *au 14 avril 1987).*
Malta. *Annual Abstract of Statistics; Census of Industrial Production Report for 19**** (annual); *Malta Year Book* (annual).
Marshall Islands. *Marshall Islands Statistical Abstract* (annual).
Martinique. *Annuaire statistique de la Martinique; Bulletin de statistique* (quarterly); *Recensement de la population de 1990: logements-population-emplois, 972: Martinique; Tableaux economiques regionaux: Martinique* (annual).
Mauritania. *Annuaire Statistique; Mauritania: A Country Study* (1990).
Mauritius. *Annual Digest of Statistics; 1983 Housing and Population Census of Mauritius.*
Mayotte. *Resultats du recensement de la population de la Collectivité territoriale de Mayotte 5 août 1985.*
Mexico. *Anuario estadístico; XI Censo general de población y vivienda, 1990; La Economia Mexicana en Cifras* (1990); *Informe de Gobierno: Estadístico* (annual).
Moldova. *Republica Moldova in Cifre* (annual).
Monaco. *Annuaire Officiel.*
Mongolia. *National Economy of the MPR, 1921–86* (1986; quinquennial?); *The Mongolian People's Republic: Towards a Market Economy* (1991).
Morocco. *Annuaire statistique du Maroc; Economic and Social Development Report, 1981; Recensement général de la population et de l'habitat de 1982.*

Mozambique. *Informação Estatística* (annual); *1° Recenseamento Geral da População, 1980.*
Myanmar (Burma). *Report to the Pyithu Hluttaw on the Financial, Social, and Economic Conditions for 19*** (annual); *1983 Population Census.*
Namibia. *Budget 19**-19*** (annual); *Population Census 1981; Statistical/Economic Review* (annual).
Nepal. *Census of Manufacturing Establishments of Nepal, 1981–82; Economic Survey* (annual); *Population Monograph of Nepal* (1987); *The Seventh Plan (1985–90); Statistical Pocket Book* (irreg.); *Statistical Yearbook of Nepal.*
Netherlands, The. *Statistical Yearbook of the Netherlands; 14e Algemene volkstelling, 28 februari 1971* (14th General Population Census).
Netherlands Antilles. *Tweede Algemene Volks- en Woningtelling Nederlandse Antillen: toestand per 1 Februari 1981; Statistical Yearbook of the Netherlands Antilles.*
New Caledonia. *Annuaire statistique; Enquête socio-économique, 1980–1981; Recensement de la population de la Nouvelle-Calédonie au 4 avril 1989; Tableaux de l'economie Caledonienne* (annual).
New Zealand. *1991 New Zealand Census of Population and Dwellings; New Zealand Official Yearbook.*
Nicaragua. *Anuario estadístico de Nicaragua; Nicaragua: A Country Study* (1982); *Plan Económico, 1987* (irreg.).
Niger. *Annuaire statistique; Les comptes de la nation* (triennial); *Plan de developpement economique et social du Niger 1987–91; 2ème Recensement général de la population 1988.*
Nigeria. *Annual Abstract of Statistics; Fourth National Development Plan* (1981); *Nigeria: A Country Study* (1981).
Norway. *Folke- og boligtelling 1990* (Population and Housing Census); *Industristatistikk* (annual); *Statistisk årbok* (Statistical Yearbook).
Oman. *Statistical Year Book; The Second Five-Year Plan of Development, 1981–1985.*
Pakistan. *Economic Survey* (annual); *Pakistan Statistical Yearbook; Population Census of Pakistan, 1981; Some Socio-Economic Trends* (annual); *10 Years of Pakistan in Statistics, 1972–1982* (1983).
Palau. *Abstract of Statistics* (annual); *Census '90: Republic of Palau.*.
Panama. *Indicadores económicos y sociales* (annual); *Censos nacionales de 1990: IX de población y V de vivienda, 13 de mayo de 1990; Panama en cifras* (annual); *Situacion económica: Cuentas nacionales* (annual); *Situacion económica: Industria* (annual).
Papua New Guinea. *Abstract of Statistics* (quarterly); *National Accounts Statistics—Statistical Bulletin* (quarterly); *Population of Papua New Guinea (ESCAP;* Country Monograph Series No. 7.2 [1982]); *Social Indicators of Papua New Guinea, 1980–85; Summary of Statistics* (annual); *1990 National Population Census.*
Paraguay. *Anuario estadístico del Paraguay; Censo nacional de población y vivienda, 1982.*
Peru. *Censos nacionales; VIII de población: III de vivienda, 12 de julio de 1981; Compendio estadístico* (2 vol.; annual); *Informe estadístico* (annual).
Philippines. *Philippine Statistical Yearbook; Philippine Yearbook; 1990 Census of Population and Housing.*
Poland. *Narodowy spis powszechny 1988* (Census of Population); *Rocznik statystyczny* (Statistical Yearbook).
Portugal. *Anuário Estatístico; Estatísticas Agricolas* (annual); *Estatísticas do Comercio Externo* (annual); *Estatísticas Demograficas* (annual); *Estatísticas Industriais* (2 vol.; annual); *Estatísticas Monetarias e Financeiras* (annual); *Recenseamento Agricola, 1979; XIII Recenseamento Geral da População: III Recenseamento Geral da Habitação, 1991.*
Puerto Rico. *Anuario estadístico; Estadisticas socioeconomicas* (annual); *Informe económico al gobernador* (Economic Report to the Governor [annual]); *1980 Census of Population* (U.S.).
Qatar. *Annual Statistical Abstract; Economic Survey of Qatar* (annual); *Qatar Year Book.*
Réunion. *Panorama de l'Économie de la Réunion* (annual); *Recensement général de la population de 1990: logements-population-emploi, 974; Réunion.*

Romania. *Anuarul statistic al României; Recensământul populației și al locuințelor, din 5 ianuarie 1977; Romania Yearbook.*
Russia. *Narodnoye Khozyaystvo Rossiyskoy SFSR* (National Economy of the Russian S.F.S.R. [annual]).
Rwanda. *Bulletin de Statistique: Supplement Annuel; IIIème Plan de Developpement Economique, Social et Culturel 1982–86; Recensement General de la Population et de l'Habitat 1991.*
St. Kitts and Nevis. *Annual Digest of Statistics; St. Christopher and Nevis: Economic Report* (World Bank Country Study) (1985).
St. Lucia. *Annual Statistical Digest.*
St. Vincent and the Grenadines. *Digest of Statistics* (annual); *Population and Housing Census 1991.*
San Marino. *Annuario statistico, 1981–84* (4 vol.?; irreg.); *3 Censimento generale dell agricoltura* (1977); *5 Censimento generale della popolazione* (1979).
Saudi Arabia. *The Statistical Indicator* (annual); *Statistical Summary* (Saudi Arabian Monetary Agency [annual]); *Statistical Year Book.*
Senegal. *Le Sénégal en chiffres* (irreg.); *Recensement de la Population et de l'Habitat 1988; Situation économique du Senegal* (annual).
Seychelles. *National Development Plan, 1990–94;* (2 vol.); *Statistical Abstract* (annual); *1987 Census Report.*
Sierra Leone. *Sierra Leone: 12 Years of Economic Achievement and Political Consolidation under the APC and Dr. Siaka Stevens, 1968–80.*
Singapore. *Census of Population, 1980; Report on the Census of Industrial Production* (annual); *Singapore Yearbook; Yearbook of Statistics Singapore.*
Solomon Islands. *Solomon Islands 1986 Population Census; Statistical Bulletin* (irreg.).
Somalia. *Statistical Abstract* (annual).
South Africa. *Population Census 1985; South Africa: Official Yearbook of the Republic of South Africa; South African Statistics* (biennial).
Spain. *Anuario estadístico; Censo de población de 1991.*
Sri Lanka. *Census of Population and Housing, 1981; Report on the Survey on Manufacturing Industries, 1979; Sri Lanka Year Book; Statistical Pocketbook of the Democratic Socialist Republic of Sri Lanka* (annual).
Sudan, The. *Third Population Census, 1983.*
Suriname. *General Population Census 1980; Statistisch Jaarboek van Suriname.*
Swaziland. *Annual Statistical Bulletin; Fourth Five-Year Development Plan (1986/87–90/91 Fiscal Years); Report on the 1986 Swaziland Population Census.*
Sweden. *Folk- och bostadsräkningen, 1990* (Population and Housing Census); *Statistisk årsbok för Sverige* (Statistical Abstract of Sweden [annual]).
Switzerland. *Recensement fédéral de la population, 1980; Statistisches Jahrbuch* (Statistical Yearbook).
Syria. *General Census of Housing and Inhabitants, 1981; Statistical Abstract* (annual).
Taiwan. *Industry of Free China* (monthly); *Social Indicators of the Republic of China* (annual); *Statistical Abstract* (annual); *Statistical Yearbook of the Republic of China; Taiwan Statistical Data Book* (annual); *Yearbook of Labor Statistics; 1980 Census of Population and Housing.*
Tajikistan. *Narodnoye Khozyaystvo Tadzhikskoy SSR* (National Economy of the Tadzhik S.S.R. [annual]).
Tanzania. *Tanzania Statistical Abstract* (irreg.); *1978 Population Census.*
Thailand. *Report of the Survey of Business Trade and Services* (biennial); *Foreign Trade Statistics* (monthly); *Report of the Industrial Survey, Whole Kingdom* (biennial); *Report of the Labor Force Survey: Whole Kingdom* (quarterly); *Statistical Handbook of Thailand* (annual); *Statistical Yearbook; 1990 Population and Housing Census.*
Togo. *Annuaire statistique du Togo; Eurostat Country Profile: Togo* (1991); *Plan de développement économique & social, 1981–1985; Recensement Général de la Population et de l'Habitat 1981.*
Tonga. *Population Census, 1986; Sixth Development Plan 1991–95; Statistical Abstract* (irreg.).

Trinidad and Tobago. *Annual Statistical Digest; 1990 Population and Housing Census.*
Tunisia. *Annuaire statistique de la Tunisie; Recensement général de la population et des logements, 30 mars 1984.*
Turkey. *Diş Ticaret İstatistikleri* (Annual Foreign Trade Statistics); *Genel Sanayi ve İşyerleri Sayımı* (Census of Industry and Business Establishments [1980]); *1990 Genel Nüfus Sayımı* (1990 Census of Population); *Genel Tarım Sayımı, 1980* (Census of Agriculture); *İnşaat İstatistikleri* (Construction Statistics [annual]); *Türkiye İstatistik Yıllığı* (Statistical Yearbook of Turkey).
Turkmenistan. *Narodnoye Khozyaystvo Turkmenskoy SSR* (National Economy of the Turkmen S.S.R. [annual]).
Ukraine. *Narodne Hospodarstvo Ukrayinskoyi RSR* (National Economy of the Ukrainian S.S.R. [annual]).
Union of Soviet Socialist Republics. *Narodnoye Khozyaystvo SSSR* (National Economy of the U.S.S.R. [annual]); *Promyshlennost SSSR* (Industry U.S.S.R. [irreg.]); *Soviet Union: a Country Study* (1991); *Trud v SSSR* (Labour in the U.S.S.R. [irreg.]); *Vsesoyuznaya perepis naseleniya 1989* (All-Union Census of Population 1989).
United Arab Emirates. *Statistical Yearbook* (Abu Dhabi).
United Kingdom. *Annual Abstract of Statistics; Britain: An Official Handbook* (annual); *National Income and Expenditure* (annual); *Census 1991; Report on the Census of Production: Summary Tables* (annual).
United States. *Agricultural Statistics* (annual); *Annual Energy Review; Current Population Reports* (Series P-20, P-23, P-25, P-26, P-27, P-28, P-60); *Digest of Education Statistics* (annual); *Minerals Yearbook* (3 vol.; annual); *National Transportation Statistics* (annual); *Statistical Abstract* (annual); *U.S. Exports: SIC-Based Products* (annual); *U.S. Imports: SIC-Based Products* (annual); *Vital and Health Statistics* (series 1–20); *1987 Census of Construction Industries; 1987 Census of Manufacturing; 1987 Census of Retail Trade; 1987 Census of Wholesale Trade; 1987 Census of Agriculture; 1990 Census of Population and Housing.*
Uruguay. *Anuario Estadístico; Censo General: VI de población: IV de viviendas, Octubre 1985. Encuesta Nacional de Hogares* (annual).
Uzbekistan. *Narodnoye Khozyaystvo Uzbekskoy SSR* (National Economy of the Uzbek S.S.R. [annual]).
Vanuatu. *National Population Census 1989; Second National Development Plan 1987–1991* (2 vol.); *Vanuatu Statistical Yearbook.*
Venezuela. *Anuario estadístico; Censo '90; Encuesta de hogares por muestreo* (annual); *Encuesta industrial* (annual).
Vietnam. *Nien Giam Thong Ke* (Statistical Yearbook); *Tong Dieu Tra Dan So Viet Nam—1989 (Vietnam Population Census—1989); Vietnam: a Country Study* (1989).
Virgin Islands of the United States. *Annual Report; Economic Review, 1986; 1990 Census of Population and Housing* (U.S.).
West Bank. *Judaea, Samaria, and Gaza Area Statistics Quarterly; Palestinian Statistical Abstract* (annual).
Western Sahara. *Recensement General de la Population et de l'Habitat* (1982 [Morocco]).
Western Samoa. *Annual Statistical Abstract; Census of Population and Housing, 1981.*
Yemen. *Country Presentation: Republic of Yemen* (1990); *The Yemens: Country Studies* (1986).
Yugoslavia. *Popis stanovištva, domaćinstava, stanova i poljoprivrednih gazdinstava 1991 godine* (Census of Population, Households, Housing, and Agricultural Holdings 1991); *Statistički godišnjak Jugoslavije* (Statistical Yearbook of Yugoslavia).
Zaire. *Annuaire statistique* (irreg.); *Conjoncture Economique* (semiannual); *Recensement Scientifique de la Population du 1er juillet 1984.*
Zambia. *Country Profile: Zambia 1985; Monthly Digest of Statistics; National Development Plan, 1989–93; 1990 Census of Population, Housing, Agriculture.*
Zimbabwe. *1982 Population Census: Main Demographic Features of the Population of Zimbabwe; Statistical Yearbook.*

Index

This index covers both *Britannica Book of the Year* (cumulative for ten years) and *Britannica World Data.*

Entries in dark type are titles of articles in the *Book of the Year;* an accompanying year in dark type gives the year the reference appears, and the accompanying page number in light type shows where the article appears. References for previous years are preceded by the year in dark type. For example, "Archaeology 93:96; 92:95; 91:125; 90:143; 89:125; 88:125; 87:141; 86:164; 85:165; 84:176" indicates that the article "Archaeology" appeared every year from 1984 through 1993. Other references that appear with a page number but without a year refer to references from the current yearbook.

Indented entries in light type that follow dark type article titles refer by page number to other places in the text where the subject of the article is discussed. Light type entries that are not indented refer by page number to subjects that are not themselves article titles. Names of people covered in biographies and obituaries are followed by the abbreviation "(biog.)" or "(obit.)" with the year in dark type and a page number in light type, *e.g.,* Ailey, Alvin (obit.) **90:**103, or Reagan, Ronald Wilson (biogs.) **89:**82; **88:**80; **87:**93; **86:**108; **85:**110; **84:**95. In cases where a person has both a biography and an obituary, the words appear as subentries under the main entry and are alphabetized accordingly, *e.g.:*
Berlin, Irving
  biography **89:**66
  obituary **90:**105
References to illustrations are by page number and are preceded by the abbreviation *il.*

The index uses word-by-word alphabetization (treating a word as one or more characters separated by a space from the next word). Names beginning with "Mc" and "Mac" are alphabetized as "Mac"; "St." is treated as "Saint."

A

Aamodt, Kjetil-André 308
AAUW: *see* American Association of University Women
ABB: *see* Asea Brown Boveri
ABB/Combustion Engineering 192
Abba (mus. group) 245
Abbott, Berenice (obit.) **92:**54
ABC: *see* American Bowling Congress
ABC (TV) 334
ABC Research 92
'Abd al-Wahab, Muhammad (obit.) **92:**54
Abdessalam, Belaid 380
Abdul, Paula (biog.) **91:**64
Abdul Rahman (obit.) **91:**86
Abdullah, Khalid 301
Abdullah, Musthaq 379
Abduvaliyev, Andrey 313
Abe, Nikken 268
Abe, Shintaro (obit.) **92:**54
Abel, Iorwith Wilbur (obit.) **88:**87
Abernathy, Ralph David (obit.) **91:**86
Abkhaz (people) 260
Abkhazia (Georgia) 436
  Islam 269
  Russia 452
Aborigine (people, Austr.)
  education 154
  prisons 119
aborigine (people, N. and S. Am.): *see* Native American peoples
abortion 175
  Germany 437
  Ireland 442
  religion 260
    United Methodist Church 265
  United States 467, 472
    court decisions 203
"Above The Mountains" (film) 238
Abruzzo, Ben (obit.) **86:**120
ABT: *see* American Ballet Theatre
Abu Dhabi (U.A.E.)
  Luxembourg 446
Abu Rishah, 'Umar (obit.) **91:**86
Abubakr III (obit.) **89:**88
A.C. Nielsen Co. 334
  see also Nielsen ratings
"Academic Federov" (ship) 502
Academy Award, *or* Oscar 237
ACC: *see* Air Combat Command
Accademia Italiana 103
Accola, Paul 308
ACE: *see* Advanced Computing Environment
ACE inhibitor: *see* angiotensin converting enzyme inhibitor
acquired immune deficiency syndrome: *see* AIDS
Acuff, Roy Claxton (obit.) **93:**54
ADA: *see* adenosine deaminase
ADA-deficient severe combined immunodeficiency, *or* SCID 213
Adami, Eddie Fenech 446
Adams, Ansel Easton (obit.) **85:**120
Adams, Bryan (biog.) **93:**33
Adams, Charles 264
Adams, Sir John Bertram (obit.) **85:**120
Adams, John Michael Geoffrey Manningham (obit.) **86:**120
Adams, Lorraine 255
Adams, Michael 290
Adamson, George (obit.) **90:**103

Addams, Charles Samuel (obit.) **89:**88
Aden: *see* Yemen, People's Democratic Republic of
adenosine deaminase, *or* ADA 213
Adler, Lawrence James (obit.) **89:**88
Adler, Stella (obit.) **93:**54
adoption
  court decisions 203
"Adoration of the Magi" (paint.) *il.* 103
advanced ceramics 185
Advanced Computing Environment, *or* ACE 200
Advanced Reactor Corp. 192
advertising 180
  beer 183
  magazines 256
  newspapers 254
  television and radio 334
"Aegean Sea" (Gr. tanker) 169
aerial sports **93:**279; **92:**305; **91:**305; **90:**321; **89:**306; **88:**308; **87:**346; **86:**380; **85:**374; **84:**150
aerospace 180
  ceramics 185
"Af en astmatisk kritikers bekendelser" (Jensen)
  Danish literature 220
AFDC: *see* Aid to Families with Dependent Children
Afewerke, Issayas (biog.) **92:**33
Afghanistan **93:**402; **92:**401; **91:**428; **90:**447; **89:**429; **88:**429; **87:**471; **86:**502; **85:**506; **84:**151
  refugees 254
  Soviet invasion (special report) 233
  see also WORLD DATA
'Aflaq, Michel (obit.) **90:**103
AFMA: *see* American Furniture Manufacturers Association
"Afn shvel" (journ.)
  Yiddish literature 224
African affairs **93:**354; **92:**348; **91:**378; **90:**399; **89:**382; **88:**382; **87:**421; **86:**453; **85:**456; **84:**153
  AIDS 285, 349
  agriculture and food supplies 84
  anthropology 94
  archaeology 98
  consumer affairs 114
  crime and law enforcement 115
  demography 251
  economic affairs 140
  fashion and dress 171
  Japan 399
  libraries 206
  mining 234
  motion pictures 240
  refugees 252, 253
  religion
    Churches of Christ 264
    Eastern Orthodoxy 261
  social security and welfare services 272
  special reports **92:**349; **85:**457
  wildlife conservation 169
  see also Middle Eastern and North African affairs *and* individual countries by name
African-American, *or* Afro-American: *see* black American
African elephant 166
African National Congress, *or* ANC 354, 370
  boycott 156
  demonstration *il.* 371
  race relations 260

African Unity, Organization of, *or* OAU 354
Senegal 368
Sierra Leone 369
Aga Khan Awards (arch.) 100
Agassi, Andre 311, *il.*
Agca, Mehmet Ali (biog.) **84:**75
Agriculture and Food Supplies 93:83; **92:**83; **91:**113; **90:**129; **89:**113; **88:**113; **87:**127; **86:**150; **85:**150; **84:**155
  Africa 354
    Sudan 373
  commodities markets 152
  international trade 144
  special reports **92:**167; **90:**140
  Western Europe 420
  see also WORLD DATA; famine *and* individual countries by name
Agriculture Modernization Law (Hond.) 486
Ahipeaud, Martial 359
Ahmann-Leighton, Christine 309
Ai Bei
  Chinese literature 224
AIA: *see* American Institute of Architects
aid: *see* relief
Aid to Families with Dependent Children, *or* AFDC 272
AIDS, *or* acquired immune deficiency syndrome 173
  advertisement *il.* 180
  books 257
  condom testing 114
  demography 252
  education 154
  France 434
  insurance 190
  Salvation Army 266
  special report **88:**206
  sports
    ice skating 304
    tennis 312
  United Nations 349
Aiken, George David (obit.) **85:**120
Ailey, Alvin (obit.) **90:**103
Air Combat Command, *or* ACC 226
air-launched cruise missile, *or* ALCM 226
air pollution
  Mexico 167, 487
  Scandinavian region 504
air traffic control 342
Airbus A320 181
Airbus A330 181, 341
Airbus A340 181, 342
Airbus Industrie 341
aircraft 181
  military affairs *il.* 227
airline 180
  airplane *il.* 181
  aviation 341, *il.* 342
  tourism 197
airport
  Spain *il.* 102
Aitken, Sir John William Maxwell (obit.) **86:**120
Aitken, Maria 338
Akalaitis, JoAnne (biog.) **92:**33
Akashi (bridge, Japan) 159
Akashi, Yasushi (biog.) **93:**33
  Cambodia 412
  Japan 399
Akayev, Askar 407
Akhromeyev, Sergey Fedorovich
  biography **85:**89
  obituary **92:**54
Akihito, *or* Heisei (biog.) **89:**65
  Japan 400
"Akutiske digte" (Poulsen)
  Danish literature 220
ALA: *see* American Library Association
Alabama, University of
  college football 295, *il.* 296
"Aladdin" (film) 237
Alamillo Bridge (bridge, Sp.) 159
Alaska (state, U.S.)
  Arctic region 503
  oil drilling 157
  oil spill case 118
  special report **92:**168
  welfare services 273
Alaska Highway 504
Albania **93:**424; **92:**418; **91:**468; **90:**485; **89:**468; **88:**468; **87:**513; **86:**541; **85:**547; **84:**168
  Albanian Orthodox Church 268
  economic affairs (special report) 144
  International Court of Justice 206
  Seventh-day Adventist Church 266
  see also WORLD DATA
Albanian Orthodox Church 268
Alberta (prov., Can.) 463
Albery, Sir Donald Arthur Rolleston (obit.) **89:**88
Albright, Ivan Le Lorraine (obit.) **84:**106
ALCM (U.S.): *see* air-launched cruise missile
alcoholic beverages: *see* beer; spirits; wine
Alda, Alan 340
Aldrich, Robert (obit.) **84:**106
Alegre, Norberto José d'Alva Costa 368
Aleixandre, Vicente (obit.) **85:**120
Aleksey II 262
  Roman Catholicism 267
Alemán, Miguel (obit.) **84:**106
Alessandri Rodríguez, Jorge (obit.) **87:**100
Alex Fraser Bridge (B.C., Can.) 159
Alexander, Kelly Miller, Sr. (obit.) **86:**120

Alexander, Lincoln (biog.) **86:**89
Alfa-Laval 93
Alfonsín, Raúl (biog.) **84:**75
Alfred Dunhill Cup (golf) 299
Alfredsson, Helen 298
Algeria **93:**380; **92:**378; **91:**404; **90:**424; **89:**407; **88:**407; **87:**448; **86:**479; **85:**483; **84:**168
  assassination 116
  Morocco 389
  pipeline construction 343
  refugees 252
  special report **92:**350
  women's role (special report) 95
  see also WORLD DATA
Algeripithecus 94
Ali, Salim (obit.) **88:**87
Alia, Ramiz (biog.) **86:**89
"All My Wives" (Su Tong)
  Chinese literature 224
"All the Pretty Horses" (McCarthy)
  American literature 216
Allais, Maurice (biog.) **89:**65
Allcock, Tony 305
"Allegories of Modernism" (art exhibit) 105
Allégret, Yves Edouard (obit.) **88:**87
Allen, Clabon Walter (obit.) **88:**87
Allen, George Herbert (obit.) **91:**86
Allen, Sir George Oswald Browning (obit.) **90:**103
Allen, Guy 306
Allen, John 166
Allen, Woody 236
Allen of Fallowfield, Alfred Walter Henry Allen (obit.) **86:**120
allergy 176
Alliance for Democracy and Progress (pol. party, Cent.Af.Rep.)
  Central African Republic 358
Allison, Davey 281
Allison, Fran (obit.) **90:**103
Allison, Joe
  college football 296
"All's Well That Ends Well" (play) 338
"Alma-Ata Declaration: Health for All by the Year 2000, The" (Warren) **90:**21
"Almanach du cinema" (encyc.)
  French literature 218
Almeida in Islington 339
Almendros, Nestor (obit.) **93:**54
Almirante, Giorgio (obit.) **89:**88
Almodóvar, Pedro (biog.) **91:**64
Alnæs, Karsten
  Norwegian literature 220
ALP: *see* Australian Labour Party
alpine skiing 308
Alsop, Joseph Wright (obit.) **90:**103
Alston, Walter Emmons (obit.) **85:**120
Althusser, Louis
  French literature 218
Altiatlasius
  anthropological discovery 94
Altman, Robert (Am. dir.) 236
Altman, Robert (Am. law.) 117
Altman, Sidney (biog.) **90:**81
aluminum
  Iceland 442
  mining 235
Alvarez, Luis Walter (obit.) **89:**88
Alvarez Bravo, Manuel 248
"Alvin" (Am. submarine)
  marine biology 210
Alzado, Lyle (obit.) **93:**54
Alzheimer's disease 175
AMA: *see* American Medical Association
Amado, Jorge
  Brazilian literature 222
Amalgamated Engineering and Electrical Union (U.K.) 201
"Amanda herzlos" (Becker)
  German literature 219
"Amant, L'" (film) 238
amateur radio, *or* ham radio 337
Amato, Giuliano (biog.) **93:**33
  Italy 444
Amazonia 165
Ameche, Alan Dante (obit.) **89:**88
Amelio, Gianni 238
Amazonia 165
American Association for the Advancement of Science 97
American Association of University Women, *or* AAUW
  education 154
American Ballet Theatre, *or* ABT 119
American Baptist Churches, General Board of the
  opposition to homosexuality 260
American Baptist Churches in the USA
  Tyson trial 264
American Booksellers Association 257
American Bowling Congress, *or* ABC 286
American Film and Video Festival 240
American Furniture Manufacturers Association, *or* AFMA 187
American Institute of Architects, *or* AIA 100
"American Journal of Archaeology" (journ.) 97
American League (baseball)
  statistical leaders 283
"American Legends: An Exhibition of Recent Works by Yousuf Karsh" (phot.) 248
American Library Association, *or* ALA 207
American literature 215

Chapaleufu, Indios
  polo 306
"Chaplin" (film) 237
Chapman, Graham (obit.) **90:**107
Chapman, Tracy (biog.) **89:**68
Char, René (obit.) **89:**91
Chara corallina
  botany 210
Charles, Prince of Belgium (obit.) **84:**111
Charles, Prince of Wales (biog.) **92:**36
  architecture 102
  newspapers 254
  United Kingdom 459
Charleson, Ian (obit.) **91:**90
"Charley's Aunt" (play) 341
Charlotte of Luxembourg (obit.) **86:**125
Charpak, Georges
  Nobel Prize 31
Chase, James Hadley (obit.) **86:**125
Chase, Lucia (obit.) **87:**103
Chatwin, Charles Bruce (obit.) **90:**107
Chavan, Yeshwantrao Balvantrao (obit.) **85:**126
Chávez, Julio César (biog.) **92:**36
  boxing 287
Checkland, Michael (biog) **88:**68
"Cheers" (TV program)
  advertising 180
cheese
  agriculture and food supplies 87
Cheiffou, Amadou
  Niger 367
"Chemical and Engineering News" (mag.) 186
chemical fertilizer
  gardening 172
chemical recycling
  plastics 194
chemicals 186
  plastics 194
  see also WORLD DATA
Chemistry 93:111; **92:**109; **91:**139; **90:**157; **89:**139; **88:**139; **87:**156; **86:**178; **85:**180; **84:**228
  Nobel Prize 31
Chen Boda (obit.) **90:**107
Chen Yonggui (obit.) **87:**103
Cheney, Richard Bruce (biog.) **90:**85
  Southeast Asian affairs 411
Cherenkov, Pavel Alekseyevich (obit.) **91:**90
Chernenko, Konstantin Ustinovich
  biography **85:**92
  obituary **86:**125
Chernobyl (Ukraine)
  nuclear industry 192
Chernomyrdin, Viktor *il.* 145
chess **93:**289; **92:**285; **91:**315; **90:**333; **89:**316; **88:**318; **87:**358; **86:**392; **85:**388; **84:**231
Chevalier, Haakon (obit.) **86:**125
Chevrolet
  automobiles 182
Chiang Ch'ing: *see* Jiang Qing
Chiang Ching-kuo
  biography **87:**81
  obituary **89:**91
Chiang Tse-min: *see* Jiang Zemin
Chiat/Day/Mojo Building
  architecture 101, *il.* 100
Chicago (Ill., U.S.)
  bridges 159
  clergy sex abuse 263
  flood 163
  museums 241
  rail-car rebuilding *il.* 343
  theatre 341
Chicago Blackhawks
  ice hockey 303
Chicago Bulls
  basketball 285
Chicago Cubs
  baseball 283
Chicago River
  flood 163
Chik, Han Kyung
  Presbyterian Churches 266
Chikatilo, Andrey
  crime 117
child
  court decisions 204
  development (special report) **89:**301
  environment 168
  gene therapy 213
  health and disease 173
  United States 272
    state laws 472
  welfare services 271
Child World (Am. co.)
  games and toys 188
"Children of the Rainbow" (book)
  education 472
Chile **93:**479; **92:**471; **91:**498; **90:**513; **89:**496; **88:**497; **87:**543; **86:**573; **85:**583; **84:**231
  dams 161
  education 156
  literature 221
  motion pictures 239
  soccer 294
  see also WORLD DATA
Chilstrom, Herbert Walfred (biog.) **88:**68
Chiluba, Frederick J. (biog.) **93:**37
  Zambia 376
Ch'in Pen-li: *see* Qin Benli
China **93:**394; **92:**392; **91:**418; **90:**438; **89:**421; **88:**421; **87:**463; **86:**493; **85:**498; **84:**233

agriculture and food supplies 89
anthropology 94
archaeology 98
arts and entertainment
  motion pictures 239
  television and radio 334
Buddhism 269
business and industry 179
  advertising 180
  chemicals 186
  man-made fibres 197
  mining 235
  nuclear industry 192
  silk 197
  tourism 198
  wool 196
dams 161
demography 250
economic affairs 140, 152
education 153
environment 167
international affairs
  Cuba 481
  Japan 400
  Kyrgyzstan 407
  South Korea 401
  Southeast Asia 411
    Brunei 412
    Vietnam 418
  United Kingdom 461
    Hong Kong 501
  military affairs 233
  race relations 258
  special report **86:**495
sports and games
  badminton 281
  diving 310
  ice skating 305
  table tennis 311
  see also WORLD DATA
Chinamano, Josiah (obit.) **85:**126
Chinese literature 224
"Chinese PEN, The" (Tai. pub.)
  Chinese literature 224
Chinese Student Protection Act (1992, U.S.)
  China 397
chip
  microelectronics 191
Chirac, Jacques René (biog.) **87:**81
Chissanó, Joaquim (biog.) **87:**81
  Mozambique 365, *il.* 366
Chiyonofuji (biog.) **86:**93
chlorofluorocarbon, *or* CFC
  environment 168
Choi Gak Kyu *il.* 401
cholesterol
  health and disease 174
Choonhavan, Chatichai (biog.) **89:**69
Chouinard, Julien (obit.) **88:**91
Chowdhury, Abu Sayeed (obit.) **88:**91
Chretien, Jean (biog.) **91:**67
Christensen, Lars Saabye
  Norwegian literature 220
Christensen, Lew (obit.) **85:**126
Christian Church, *or* Disciples of Christ 264
  United Church of Christ 267
Christian Democratic Party (pol. party, Slovenia)
  Slovenia 454
Christian Science: *see* Church of Christ, Scientist
Christianity 260
  Eastern Orthodoxy (special report) **93:**261
  Reformed Churches 266
  special reports **92:**261; **91:**289; **89:**290; **84:**602
Christie House (U.K.)
  art sales 106
"Christopher Columbus: The Discovery" (film) 236
"Chrome Suite, The" (Birdsell)
  English-Canadian literature 217
chromosomes
  health and disease 175
  Human Genome Project 212
Chronology of Events 93:9; **92:**9; **91:**16; **90:**33; **89:**17; **88:**17; **87:**55; **86:**66; **85:**24; **84:**45
chronostratigraphy 127
Chrysler Corporation 182, 183
Chuan Leekpai
  Thailand 417, *il.* 418
Chukotka, Republic of 503
Chung Ju Yung
  South Korea 401
Church, Frank Forrester (obit.) **85:**126
Church of . . . : *see under* substantive word, except as below
Church of Christ, Scientist 264
  religion 263
Church of God
  Pentecostal Churches 266
Church of Jesus Christ of Latter-day Saints, *or* Mormon 265
  Churches of Christ 264
Chuuk
  Federated States of Micronesia 497
Ciardi, John Anthony (obit.) **87:**103
cigarette: *see* smoking
Cilento, Sir Raphael West (obit.) **86:**125
cinema: *see* Motion Pictures
Circle in the Square 341
CIS: *see* Commonwealth of Independent States

CIS Joint General Purpose Forces, *or* CIS-JGPF
  military affairs 226
Ciskei
  South Africa 371
Cissé, Mohammed
  Benin 356
Citrine, Walter McLennan Citrine, 1st Baron (obit.) **84:**111
"City of Joy" (film) 237
"City Slickers" (film) 237
"ciudad ausente, La" (Piglia)
  Argentine literature 221
Civic Union (Russ.) 453
civil rights
  crime and law enforcement 118
  homosexuals 260, *il.* 472
  Syria 392
  United States 467, 473
civil war
  Afghanistan 403
  Africa 354
    Chad 358
    Ethiopia 360
    Rwanda 368
    Somalia 369
    Sudan 373
  agriculture and food supplies 83
  education affected 153
  El Salvador 483
  international law 204
  Iraq 385
  Laos 414
  military affairs 225
  new world order 6
  United Nations 348
"Civvies" (TV) 336
"Clabbered Dirt, Sweet Grass" (Paulsen)
  U.S. literature 216
Claire, Ina (obit.) **86:**125
Clancy, Tom (biog.) **89:**69
  books 257
Clapton, Eric
  popular music 244
Clark, Charles Manning Hope (obit.) **92:**58
Clark, Joe
  Canada 463
Clark, Kenneth Mackenzie Clark, Baron (obit.) **84:**111
Clark, Mark Wayne (obit.) **85:**126
Clark, Mary Higgins
  books 257
Clark, Michael (biog.) **85:**92
Clark, William Donaldson (obit.) **86:**126
Clarke, Kenny (obit.) **86:**126
Clarke, Thomas Ernest Bennett (obit.) **90:**108
classical music 241
Claude, Albert (obit.) **84:**112
"Clay & Star" (Sapinkopf and Belev)
  Bulgarian literature 223
Clean Air Act (U.S., 1990)
  environment 473
Clearly Canadian 185
Cleary, Phil
  Australia 494
Clegg, Sir Alec (obit.) **87:**104
Clegg, Hugh Anthony (obit.) **84:**112
Clemens, Roger (biog.) **87:**81
Clements, the Rev. George (biog.) **90:**86
Clifford, Clark McAdams (biog.) **92:**36
  Bank of Credit and Commerce International 117
climate
  Antarctica 502
  environment 164
  Oceanian affairs 493
  volcanic eruptions 128
Climate Change and Biodiversity Convention: *see* Convention on Protecting Species and Habitats
Clinton, Bill (biog.) **93:**37
  economic affairs 134
  education 154
  globalism 8
  Haitian boat people 253
  Middle Eastern affairs 378
    Saudi Arabian aircraft sale 391
  presidential election (special report) **93:**469
  race relations 260
  religion 263
  television and radio 334
  United States 465, 471
  welfare services 272
Clinton, Hilary
  presidential election (special report) **93:**470
Clodion
  art exhibitions 104
closed geodesics
  mathematics 225
Clovis culture
  archaeology 98
Clubb, Oliver Edmund (obit.) **90:**108
"Coach" (TV program)
  advertising 180
coal 158
  United Kingdom 201, 459
Coase, Ronald (biog.) **92:**30
Coates, Edith Mary (obit.) **84:**112
COBE: *see* Cosmic Background Explorer
Coca-Cola 185
cocaine
  special report **89:**144
Cochrane, Robert Greenhill (obit.) **86:**126

cockle, *or* Cerastoderma edule (mollusk)
  marine biology 210
cocoa
  agriculture and food supplies 88
cod
  Iceland 442
Code of Practice on Disputes Procedures
  Irish labour 201
Codelco (Chilean co.) 480
Codesa: *see* Convention for a Democratic South Africa
"Coeur en hiver, Un" (film) 238
coffee 88
  nicotine absorption 177
Cohen, Rod 240
Cohen, Stanley (biog.) **87:**82
Cohen, Wilbur Joseph (obit.) **88:**91
Cohn, Roy Marcus (obit.) **87:**104
Coho salmon
  endangered species (special report) **92:**167
coins: *see* Philately and Numismatics
cold-dark-matter hypothesis
  physics 249
Coldstream, Sir William Menzies (obit.) **88:**92
Cole, Lester (obit.) **86:**126
Cole, Natalie (biog.) **92:**37
Coleman, Ornette 243
Coleman, Roger
  execution 119
Coles, Charles (obit.) **93:**59
Colgate-Palmolive Co.
  advertising 180
"Collapse of the Junk Market: The Morning After, The" (special report) **91:**176
Collard, Antonius 304
"Collection for a King" (art exhibit) 105
college sports
  basketball 284
  football 295
Colley, George Joseph (obit.) **84:**112
Collins, Phil (biog.) **87:**82
Collins, Thomas LeRoy (obit.) **92:**58
Collor de Mello, Fernando (biog.) **91:**67
  Brazil 474, 478, *il.* 479
  crime 117
  Earth Summit *il.* 164
  Latin-American affairs (special report) **92:**465
Colombia **93:**480; **92:**472; **91:**499; **90:**514; **89:**497; **88:**498; **87:**544; **86:**575; **85:**584; **84:**238
  crime and law enforcement 116
  earthquakes 129
  literature 221
  oil discovery 157
  special report **89:**144
  see also WORLD DATA
Colorado (state, U.S.)
  gambling 473
  gay rights 468, 471
  Judaism 268
  Native American elected U.S. senator 260
colour
  gemstones 188
Coloured (people)
  South Africa 370
Coluche (obit.) **87:**104
"Columbia" (space shuttle) 273
Columbia River (riv., U.S.)
  hydrology 129
Columbus, Chris
  motion pictures 237
Columbus, Christopher
  art exhibitions 103
  gardening 172
  motion pictures 236
  race relations 259
  stamp commemorations 246
"Columbus and the Discovery of Japan" (play) 338
Columbus Lighthouse *il.* 483
Columbus quincentenary
  dance 122
  Dominican Republic 483
  John Paul II 267
  opera *il.* 243
  race relations 259
  Spain 454
  Spanish literature 221
  United Church of Christ 267
Colville, Sir John Rupert (obit.) **88:**92
Comelin, Jean-Paul 122
"Comic in the Tragic, The" (Heyblum)
  Yiddish literature 224
Commission on . . . : *see under* substantive word
commodity markets 152
  agriculture and food supplies 85
common agricultural policy, *or* CAP 420
  agriculture and food supplies 83, 89
  France 433
  Ireland 443
Commonwealth of Independent States, *or* CIS **93:**349
  Belarus 427
  India 406
  iron and steel 190
  military affairs 225
  Roman Catholicism 267
  Russia 451
  space exploration 273
  Turkmenistan 410
  Ukraine 457
Commonwealth of Nations **93:**349; **92:**344;

---

lamprey / Los Angeles 913

lamprey
  evolution 208
Lancaster, Sir Osbert (obit.) **87**:113
Lanchester, Elsa (obit.) **87**:113
Lancia (auto racing) 280
Land, Edwin Herbert (obit.) **92**:70
Land, Robert 304
land claims
  Arctic regions 504
Lander, Toni (obit.) **86**:135
Landis, John 236
Landon, Alfred Mossman (obit.) **88**:102
Landon, Michael (obit.) **92**:70
Landsbergis, Vytautas (biog.) **91**:74
"Landskap med kulehull" (Skagen)
  Norwegian literature 220
landslide 125
Lane, Dame Elizabeth Kathleen (obit.) **89**:100
Lang, Jack (biog.) **84**:88
Lange, David Russell (biog.) **85**:104
Lange, Jessica 340
Langer, Susanne Knauth (obit.) **86**:134
Laniarius liberatus: *see* Bulo Burti boubou
Lanoux, Armand Louis (obit.) **84**:121
Lansdale, Edward G. (obit.) **88**:102
Lansky, Meyer (obit.) **84**:121
Laos **93**:414; **92**:410; **91**:437; **90**:455; **89**:439; **88**:439; **87**:481; **86**:511; **85**:517; **84**:473
  see also WORLD DATA
LAPD (gov. agency, Los Angeles, Calif., U.S.): *see* Los Angeles Police Department
Lardner-Burke, Desmond William (obit.) **85**:135
Larger Fellowship, Church of the Unitarian Universalists 266
"largo invierno, El" (film): *see* "The Long Winter"
Larkin, Philip Arthur (obit.) **86**:134
Laroche, Guy (obit.) **90**:117
LaRouche, Lyndon Hermyle, Jr. (biog.) **87**:88
Larrain, Riccardo 239
Larrieu, Daniel 122
Lars, Byron 170
Larsen, Terje
  Norwegian literature 220
Larson, April 265
Lartigue, Jacques-Henri-Charles-Auguste (obit.) **87**:113
larvacean, *or* appendicularian (tunicate class)
  marine biology 210
laser 111
Lash, Joseph P. (obit.) **88**:102
Laskin, Bora (obit.) **85**:135
Lassiter, Luther (obit.) **89**:100
"Last Days of Chez Nous, The" (film) 237
"Last of the Mohicans, The" (film) 237
Latin-American affairs **93**:474; **92**:464; **91**:492; **90**:507; **89**:491; **88**:491; **87**:537; **86**:566; **85**:573; **84**:474
  agriculture and food supplies 84
  business and industry 178
  consumer affairs 113
  demography 251
  motion pictures 239
  refugees 253
  social security and welfare services 271
  special reports **92**:465; **89**:144; **86**:326, 567
  sports and games
    baseball 283
    soccer 294
  United Nations 349
  see also individual countries by name
Latin-American literature 221
Latino American (people): *see* Hispanic American
Lattimore, Owen (obit.) **90**:117
Lattimore, Richmond Alexander (obit.) **85**:135
Latvia **93**:445; **92**:434
  chess 289
  military affairs 225
  see also WORLD DATA
Laugesen, Peter
  Danish literature 220
launch vehicle (rocket system) 275
Laurence, Margaret (obit.) **88**:102
Laurent, Paul (obit.) **91**:100
Lavagetto, Harry Arthur (obit.) **91**:100
Law 93:203; **92**:202; **91**:231; **90**:249; **89**:232; **88**:234; **87**:264; **86**:289; **85**:290; **84**:476
  boxing 288
  child-support payment 272
  consumer affairs 113
  crime and law enforcement 118
  education 153
  environment 166
  prisons and penology 119
  race relations 259
  religion 260
  social security and welfare services 271
  United States 472
  see also individual countries by name
Law, Clara 239
Law, Roger (biog.) **87**:84
law enforcement: *see* Crime, Law Enforcement, and Penology
Lawford, Peter (obit.) **85**:136
lawn bowls **93**:305; **92**:301; **91**:331; **90**:350; **89**:332; **88**:334; **87**:378; **86**:413; **85**:407; **84**:215
lawn mower
  pollution 172
Lawson, Frederick Henry (obit.) **84**:122
Lawson, Nigel Thomas (biogs.) **89**:77; **84**:88
Layne, Bobby (obit.) **87**:113
LCMS: *see* Lutheran Church-Missouri Synod
LDCs: *see* less developed countries
Le Carré, John (biog.) **84**:88
Le Duan (obit.) **87**:114
Le Duc Tho (obit.) **91**:100
Le Gallienne, Eva (obit.) **92**:70
Le Luron, Thierry Jean-Gilles (obit.) **87**:114
Le Mans (Fr.)
  automobile racing 280
Le Mesurier, John (obit.) **84**:122
Le Pen, Jean-Marie (biog.) **85**:104
Le Poulain, Jean (obit.) **89**:100
Leach, Sir Edmund Ronald (obit.) **90**:117
lead
  health 168
  poisoning 176
Lean, Sir David (obit.) **92**:70
"Leap of Faith" (film) 237
leather 171
Leavett, Helen 248
Lebanon **93**:388; **92**:386; **91**:411; **90**:431; **89**:414; **88**:414; **87**:454; **86**:486; **85**:491; **84**:481
  crime 116
  United Nations 348
  see also WORLD DATA
LEC: *see* local exchange carrier
Leconte, Henri 311
Lederer, Jiri (obit.) **84**:122
Lederman, Leon Max (biog.) **89**:77
Lee, Amg 239
Lee, Jennie (obit.) **89**:100
Lee, Sang Chun 285
Lee, Spike (biog.) **90**:92
  "Malcolm X" 237, 467
Lee, Yuan Tseh (biog.) **87**:88
Lee Byung Chull (obit.) **88**:102
Lee Huan (biog.) **88**:76
Lee Kuan Yew 417
Lee Teng-hui (biogs.) **89**:77; **87**:88
  Taiwan 402
Lee *v.* Weisman (law case)
  school prayer 263
Leetch, Brian 303
Lefebvre, Marcel-François
  biography **89**:77
  obituary **92**:71
"Legacy of 1991: Phoenix or Empty Ashes?" (feature article) **92**:4
Léger, Paul-Emile (obit.) **92**:71
Lego Systems 188
Lehmann, Hermann (obit.) **86**:134
Lehmann, Rosamond Nina (obit.) **91**:100
Lehn, Jean-Marie (biog.) **88**:76
Leicester Haymarket 339
Leigh, Carolyn (obit.) **84**:122
Leiris, Michel Julien (obit.) **91**:100
Lekai, Laszlo Cardinal (obit.) **87**:114
Lekhanya, Justin Metsino (biog.) **87**:88
Leloir, Luis Federico (obit.) **88**:102
LeMay, Curtis Emerson (obit.) **91**:101
Lemieux, Mario (biog.) **92**:43
  ice hockey 303
Lemnitzer, Lyman Louis (obit.) **89**:100
LeMond, Greg (biog.) **90**:92
Lendl, Ivan (biog.) **87**:88
  tennis 312
Lenin Library (Moscow): *see* Russian State Library
Leno, Jay (biog.) **93**:43
  television 334
Lentini, Gianluigi 294
Lenzi, Mark 310
"Leon the Pig Farmer" (film) 237
Leonard, Elmore John (biog.) **86**:102
Leonard, Justin 299
Leone, Sergio (obit.) **90**:117
leopard pattern
  women's fashions 171
Leopold III (obit.) **84**:122
Lepage, Robert 338
Lerner, Alan Jay (obit.) **87**:114
Lerner, Maxwell Alan **93**:69
LeRoy, Mervyn (obit.) **88**:102
lesbian: *see* homosexuality
Lesotho **93**:363; **92**:359; **91**:388; **90**:408; **89**:391; **88**:392; **87**:430; **86**:462; **85**:468; **84**:483
  Commonwealth of Nations 349
  dams 162
  see also WORLD DATA
Lesotho Highlands Water Project
  tunnels 162
Lesourne, Jacques (biog.) **92**:43
less developed countries, *or* LDCs, *or* less industrialized countries, *or* Third World
  Africa 355
  business and industry 179
    plastics 194
    tobacco 197
  consumer affairs 114
  demography 250
  economic affairs 140
  environment 165
  health and disease 173
  international migration 252
  libraries 206
  social security and welfare services 271
Lester, Adrian 338
"Lethal Weapon 3" (film) 236
"Letter to the Bishops of the Catholic Church on Some Aspects of the Church Understood as Communion" 262
Lévesque, René (obit.) **88**:102
Levi, Primo (obit.) **88**:103
Levi-Montalcini, Rita (biog.) **87**:89
Levine, James (biog.) **84**:89
Levinson, Barry 237
Levy, David (biog.) **91**:75
Lewis, Carl (biog.) **84**:89
  track and field 313
Lewis, Flora
  "Legacy of 1991: Phoenix or Empty Ashes?" (feature article) **92**:4
Lewis, Juliette *il.* 237
Lewis, Lennox 287
Lewis, Saunders (obit.) **86**:134
Lewis, Steve 313
Lewis, Sir William Arthur (obit.) **92**:71
Lexcen, Ben
  biography **84**:89
  obituary **89**:100
"Lexington Herald-Leader" (Am. news.)
  Pulitzer Prize 255
LH cars 183
Li Jiu
  Chinese literature 224
Li Peng (biogs.) **89**:77; **86**:102
Li Xiannian (Li Hsien-nien)
  biography **84**:90
  obituary **93**:69
Liang Shih-Ch'iu (obit.) **88**:103
Liberace (obit.) **88**:103
Liberal Democrat Party (pol. party, Slovenia) 454
Liberal Party (Can.)
  constitutional reform 463
Liberia **93**:363; **92**:360; **91**:388; **90**:409; **89**:392; **88**:392; **87**:431; **86**:462; **85**:468; **84**:483
  nuns murdered 263
  rubber industry 194
  Sierra Leone 369
  United Nations 348
  see also WORLD DATA
Liberman, Yevsey Grigoryevich (obit.) **84**:122
Libertadores de America Cup
  soccer 294
Libraries 93:206; **92**:206; **91**:234; **90**:252; **89**:235; **88**:238; **87**:267; **86**:293; **85**:294; **84**:484
Library of Congress (U.S.) *il.* 206
Libya **93**:389; **92**:387; **91**:412; **90**:432; **89**:415; **88**:415; **87**:456; **86**:487; **85**:492; **84**:485
  airplane bombings 116, 348
    extradition of suspects 206
  Egypt 383
  special report **87**:457
  Tunisia 393
  water-supply project 129
  see also WORLD DATA
licensing
  French drivers 433
Lichty, George (obit.) **84**:122
Liechtenstein **93**:445; **92**:435; **91**:458; **90**:474; **89**:458; **88**:457; **87**:502; **86**:530; **85**:536; **84**:486
  see also WORLD DATA
Lied Jungle
  botanical gardens *il.* 111
Liepa, Maris-Rudolf Eduardovich (obit.) **90**:117
Lifar, Serge (obit.) **87**:114
"Life and Nothing More" (film) 239
life expectancy
  demography 252
life insurance 189
  consumer affairs 115
"Life Is a Dream" (play) 339
Life Sciences 93:207; **92**:207; **91**:235; **90**:253; **89**:236; **88**:238; **87**:269; **86**:294; **85**:295; **84**:487
  special report **86**:301
light bulb 158
light rail transit, *or* LRT 344
Light Rail Transit (Dallas, Tex., U.S.)
  tunnels 163
Lightner, Candy (biog.) **86**:102
Lightwood, Reginald (obit.) **86**:135
Liley, Sir Albert William (obit.) **84**:122
Lillie, Beatrice Gladys (obit.) **90**:117
Lilly, Art 306
Lim Yew Hock (obit.) **85**:136
Lima, Angelo
  stamp awards 245
Limbaugh, Rush
  books 258
  television and radio 335
Limbe Botanic Garden (Cameroon) 110
Limehouse Link road (London) 162
Lin Li
  swimming 309
Lincoln, Abraham
  Emancipation Proclamation 107
  "The Old Farmer's Almanac" 90
Lindros, Eric 303
Lindtberg, Leopold (obit.) **85**:136
Lineker, Gary Winston (biog.) **93**:43
linguistics
  Indo-Europeans 96
Linuche unguiculata (jellyfish) 210
Lipinski, Edward (obit.) **87**:114
Lipman, Maureen 338
Lipmann, Fritz Albert (obit.) **87**:114
Lipski, Jan Jozef (obit.) **92**:71
Lipton 185
Lipton, Eric 255
Lisbon Conference
  Greece 439
Lisbon Declaration
  Portugal 449
Lissouba, Pascal 359
Listach, Pat
  baseball 283
literacy 153
literary criticism
  U.S. literature 217
Literature 93:214; **92**:214; **91**:242; **90**:260; **89**:243; **88**:245; **87**:276; **86**:304; **85**:303; **84**:497
  Nobel Prize 30
  see also specific literatures by name
Lithuania **93**:445; **92**:435
  archaeology 98
  military affairs 225
  Olympic basketball 285
  see also WORLD DATA
"Litoral" (Ramos)
  Portuguese literature 222
Little, Brown (Am. publ.) 257
"Little Earthquakes" (recording) 245
"Little Hotel on the Side, A" (play) 341
Littler, Sir Emile (obit.) **86**:135
Liu Binyan (biog.) **87**:89
Liu Heng
  Chinese literature 224
"Live from Golgotha" (Vidal)
  U.S. literature 216
"Living End, The" (film) 237
Livingstone, Mary (obit.) **84**:123
Livingstone's fruit bat
  wildlife conservation 169
Lleras Camargo, Alberto (obit.) **91**:101
Llewellyn, Richard (obit.) **84**:123
Lloyd, Christopher
  television 334
Lloyd, Clive (biog.) **85**:104
Lloyd Webber, Andrew
  art acquisitions 106
  British theatre 337
Lloyd's of London
  insurance 189
Lloyd's Register
  shipbuilding 195
Lo-Johansson, (Karl) Ivar (obit.) **91**:101
local exchange carrier, *or* LEC 195
Locke, Bobby (obit.) **88**:103
Lockwood, Margaret Mary (obit.) **91**:101
Lodge, Henry Cabot (obit.) **86**:135
Loeffler, Robert 306
Loewe, Frederick (obit.) **89**:100
Loewy, Raymond Fernand (obit.) **87**:115
Lofton, James
  football 297
Lofton, Kenny
  baseball 283
Lofts, Norah (obit.) **84**:123
Logan, Joshua Lockwood (obit.) **89**:101
Lohmiller, Chip
  football 297
Lollapalooza
  popular music 245
Lombard League 443
  race relations 259
Lombard rate (econ.) 139
Lombardi Award
  college football 296
Lon Nol (obit.) **86**:135
London (U.K.)
  architecture 102
  art exhibitions 103
  car bomb 116, 461
  libraries 207
  theatre 338
  tourism 198
London, Artur (obit.) **87**:115
London, George (obit.) **86**:135
London Contemporary Dance Theatre 121
London Stock Exchange (U.K.) 151
London Zoo (U.K.) 110
Lonergan, The Rev. Bernard Joseph Francis (obit.) **85**:136
"Long Day Closes, The" (film) 237
long-playing record, *or* LP, *or* vinyl LP record
  popular music 244
long QT syndrome
  heart disease 175
long skirt
  women's fashions 170
"Long Winter, The," *or* "largo invierno, El" (film) 239
Longowal, Harchand Singh (obit.) **86**:135
Longtan Dam, *or* Lung-t'an Dam (China) 162
Loop, the (Chicago, Ill., U.S.)
  flood 163
López Bravo, Gregorio (obit.) **86**:136
Lorentz, Pare (obit.) **93**:70
Lorenz, Konrad Zacharias (obit.) **90**:117
Lorenzo, Frank (biog.) **89**:78
"Lorenzo il magnifico" (ballet) 122
Los Angeles (Calif., U.S.)
  race relations 260, 467
Los Angeles Police Department, *or* LAPD (gov. agency, Los Angeles, Calif., U.S.) 467
  misuse of force 118
  race relations 260

References giving only a page number in light type are for the current edition.

914 *Los Angeles / Mattel*

Los Angeles Public Library (Calif., U.S.) 207
Los Angeles riots: *see* riots and demonstrations
Losey, Joseph (obit.) **85**:136
"Lost in Yonkers" (play) 338
Lotus
pen computers 200
Louganis, Greg (biogs.) **89**:78; **84**:90
Louisiana (state, U.S.)
court decisions 204
energy 158
gambling 473
Hurricane Andrew 130
Loutit, John Freeman (obit.) **93**:70
Louvre Museum (Paris, Fr.) 104
"Love" (film) 238
Love, Davis, III 299
Loveless, Lea 309
"Loves of the Gods, The" (painting) 104
Lower, Arthur Reginald Marsden (obit.) **89**:101
Lowery, Nick
football 297
Loy, Douglas112
Loynaz, Dulce María
Spanish literature 221
LP: *see* long-playing record
LPGA: *see* Ladies' Professional Golf Association
LRT: *see* light rail transit
Lu Chen 305
Lubell, Samuel (obit.) **88**:103
Lucas, Fábio
Brazilian literature 222
Luce, Claire Boothe (obit.) **88**:103
"Lucifer's Daughter" (ballet) 122
Ludlam, Charles (obit.) **88**:104
Ludwig, Daniel Keith (obit.) **93**:70
Ludzhev, Dimitar 429
"lugar en el mundo, Un" (film) 239
Luhrmann, Baz 237
Luke, Keye (obit.) **92**:71
Lule, Yusufu Kirolde (obit.) **86**:136
"Lulu" (play) 339
Lundbye, Vagn
Danish literature 219
Lundkvist, Artur Nils (obit.) **92**:72
Lung-t'an Dam (China): *see* Longtan Dam
Luria, Salvador Edward (obit.) **92**:72
Lusinchi, Jaime (biog.) **85**:105
Lutheran Church-Missouri Synod, *or* LCMS 265
Lutheran Communion 265
religion 261
Lutheran World Federation 265
Lutyens, Agnes Elisabeth (obit.) **84**:123
Luxembourg **93**:445; **92**:435; **91**:458; **90**:474; **89**:458; **88**:458; **87**:502; **86**:530; **85**:537; **84**:513
see also WORLD DATA
"Lykkens sønn" (Wassmo)
Norwegian literature 220
Lymantria dispar: *see* gypsy moth
Lynch, David (biog.) **91**:75
Lynch, Sir Phillip Reginald (obit.) **85**:136
Lyons, Sir William (obit.) **86**:136
Lyubimov, Yury Petrovich (biog.) **85**:105
Greek theatre 339

M

M32 (galaxy)
astronomy 108
M51, *or* Whirlpool Galaxy
astronomy 108
M87, *or* Virgo A (galaxy)
astronomy 108
Maastricht Treaty, *or* Treaty on European Union, *or* Treaty of Economic and Monetary Union 419
Belgium 428
Denmark 431
games and toys 188
European unity 6
France 434
Germany 438
Greece 440
international law 205
Ireland 443
labour-management relations 201
Luxembourg 446
Netherlands 447
Portugal 449
special report **93**:421
United Kingdom 458
world affairs 344
"Mac" (film) 236
McAnally, Ray (obit.) **90**:118
"Macário" (play)
Brazilian literature 222
Macau 502
"Macbeth" (dance) 122
MacBeth, George Mann (obit.) **93**:70
McBride, Lloyd (obit.) **84**:123
McBride, Patricia (biog.) **90**:92
MacBride, Sean (obit.) **89**:101
McCarthy, Cormac
U.S. literature 215, *il.* 216
McCarthy, Mary Therese (obit.) **90**:118
McCarthy, Mike 293
McCarthy, William Joseph (biog.) **89**:78
McClintock, Barbara (obit.) **93**:70
McCloy, John Jay (obit.) **90**:118
MacColl, Ewan, *or* James Henry Miller (obit.) **90**:118
McCone, John Alex (obit.) **92**:72
McCracken, James Eugene (obit.) **89**:101
McCrea, Joel Albert (obit.) **91**:101
MacDonald, Carlton
college football 296
MacDonald, John Dann (obit.) **87**:115
MacDonald, Ross (obit.) **84**:123
McDonnell Douglas 180
McDowell, Marc 286
Macedo, Helder 222
Macedonia **93**:446
Greece 439
military affairs 226
see also WORLD DATA
McEnroe, John 311
MacEntee, Sean (obit.) **85**:136
McFarlane, Robert Carl (biog.) **84**:91
McGraw, Mike 255
McGriff, Fred
baseball 283
Machain, Humberto 116
Machel, Samora Moisès
biography **85**:105
obituary **87**:115
machinery and machine tools 191
ceramics 185
Machito (obit.) **85**:136
MacInnes, Helen Clark (obit.) **86**:136
McIntosh, Bob 302
Macintosh computer 199
McKay, Sir Alick Benson (obit.) **84**:123
McKay, Stan
Church of Canada 266
Mackay of Clashfern, Lord (biog.) **90**:93
McKell, Sir William John (obit.) **86**:136
McKellen, Sir Ian (biog.) **92**:43
British theatre 338
McKenna, Siobhan (obit.) **87**:115
McKenzie, Duke 288
MacKenzie, Kelvin (biog.) **93**:44
Mackintosh, Cameron 337, 340
McKissick, Floyd Bixler, Sr. (obit.) **92**:72
MacLaine, Shirley (biog.) **85**:106
McLaren, Norman (obit.) **88**:104
McLaren-Honda (auto racing) 279
McLaughlin, Audrey (biog.) **92**:44
MacLean, Alistair (obit.) **88**:104
Maclean, Donald Duart (obit.) **84**:123
McLean, Eileen 503
McLeay, Leo 494
MacLennan, John Hugh (obit.) **91**:101
Maclennon, Robert Adam Ross (biog.) **88**:77
MacLeod, John
college basketball 284
Macleod, Joseph Todd Gordon (obit.) **85**:136
MacLeod of Fuinary, George Fielden MacLeod (obit.) **92**:72
McMahon, Sir William (obit.) **89**:101
McMillan, Audray
football 297
McMillan, Edwin Mattison (obit.) **92**:72
MacMillan, Sir Kenneth (obit.) **93**:71
dance 121
Macmillan, Maurice Harold 1st Earl of Stockton, Viscount Macmillan of Ovenden: *see* Stockton, Maurice Harold Macmillan
McMillan, Terry 257
Macmillan and Co. (publ.) 257
MacMurray, Fred (obit.) **92**:72
McMurtry, Larry (biog.) **90**:93
McNall, Bruce 303
McNamara, Kevin (obit.) **88**:104
McNeill, James Charles (obit.) **88**:104
MacSharry, Ray 144
McTaggart, David (biog.) **86**:103
McTeer, Janet 338
McWilliam, Frederick Edward (obit.) **93**:71
Madagascar **93**:364; **92**:360; **91**:388; **90**:409; **89**:392; **88**:392; **87**:431; **86**:463; **85**:469; **84**:512
see also WORLD DATA
Madagascar Promotion Industrielle 364
Maddux, Greg
baseball 283
"Mademoiselle" (Am. mag.) 256
"Madness of George III, The" (play) 338
Madonna (biog.) **88**:77
books 258
popular music 245
madras
women's fashions 170
Madrid Hurtago, Miguel de la
special report **84**:523
Madsen, Svend Age
Danish literature 219
Mafia 118
Italy 445
Magaña Borjo, Álvaro Alfredo (biog.) **84**:91
magazines 255
advertising 180
photography 248
Maglie, Salvatore Anthony (obit.) **93**:71
magnesium
heart-attack treatment 174
magnetic resonance imaging, *or* MRI
schizophrenia research 176
Magnuson, Warren Grant (obit.) **90**:118
Magogo Sibilile Nantithi Ngangezinyge kaDinuzulu kaSenzangakhona, Princess Constance (obit.) **85**:137
Magritte, René 105
Mahaney, Kevin 308
Mahathir bin Mohamad, Datuk Seri (biog.) **87**:89
Southeast Asian affairs 411
Mahdi, Sadiq al- (biog.) **87**:89
Mahfouz, Naguib (biog.) **89**:79
Mahmood Iskandar ibni al-Marhum Sultan Ismail (biog.) **85**:106
Mahre, Phil (biog.) **84**:91
Maier, Carlo 122
mail order
special report **84**:250
maize: *see* corn
Major, John Roy (biogs.) **93**:44; **92**:44; **91**:75; **90**:93
race relations 259
United Kingdom 458
Western European affairs 420
Makhmalbaf, Mohsen 239
"Making of England, The" (art exhibit, U.K.) 105
Maktum, Rashid ibn Said al- (obit.) **91**:101
Maktum family
horse racing 301
Malamud, Bernard (obit.) **87**:115
Malawi **93**:364; **92**:361; **91**:389; **90**:410; **89**:392; **88**:392; **87**:431; **86**:463; **85**:469; **84**:514
agriculture and food supplies 84
Presbyterian Churches 266
wildlife conservation 169
see also WORLD DATA
Malaysia **93**:414; **92**:410; **91**:438; **90**:456; **89**:439; **88**:439; **87**:482; **86**:512; **85**:517; **84**:514
Australia 495
freight traffic 343
roads 162
wood products 198
Malcolm X
books 257
jazz 243
movies 467
"Malcolm X" (film) 237
United States 467
Malcuzynski, Karol (obit.) **85**:137
Maldini, Sergio
Italian literature 221
Maldives **93**:407; **92**:404; **91**:432; **90**:450; **89**:432; **88**:433; **87**:475; **86**:506; **85**:511; **84**:516
see also WORLD DATA
Maldonado, Candy
baseball 282
Malenkov, Georgy Maksimilianovich (obit.) **89**:101
Mali **93**:364; **92**:361; **91**:389; **90**:410; **89**:392; **88**:393; **87**:431; **86**:463; **85**:469; **84**:516
see also WORLD DATA
Malik, Adam (obit.) **85**:137
Maliki
women's role (special report) 95
Malkovich, John 338
Mall of America
architecture 101, *il.* 115
Mallarmé, Stéphane
French literature 218
Malone, Dan 255
Malone, Dumas (obit.) **87**:116
Malta **93**:446; **92**:435; **91**:458; **90**:474; **89**:458; **88**:458; **87**:502; **86**:531; **85**:537; **84**:517
see also WORLD DATA
Maltz, Albert (obit.) **86**:136
Malula, Joseph-Albert Cardinal (obit.) **90**:118
"Mama" (film) 239
Mambrety, Djibril Diop 240
Mamet, David (biog.) **86**:103
Mamoulian, Rouben (obit.) **88**:104
Man, Isle of
dependent states 500
"Män i min ålder" (Claesson)
Swedish literature 220
man-made fibres 197
Manahan, Anna Anderson (obit.) **85**:137
Mancham, James 368
Mandela, Nelson (biogs.) **91**:75; **86**:103
South Africa 370
Mandela, Winnie (biog.) **87**:89
South Africa 370
Mangope, Lucas 372
Manley, Edna Swithenbank (obit.) **88**:104
Manley, Michael 486
Mann, Michael 237
Mann, Sally
photography *il.* 248
Manning, Patrick 491
Manning, Preston (biog.) **92**:44
Mano, Jean-Luc 335
Mansell, Nigel (biog.) **93**:44
auto racing 281, 279
Mansour, Agnes Mary (biog.) **84**:91
Mantegna, Andrea 104
"Manuel Alvarez Bravo" (phot.) 248
manufacturing 134
Manx (lang.)
Isle of Man 500
Manzù, Giacomo (obit.) **92**:73
Maori (people)
New Zealand 498
Mapplethorpe, Robert (obit.) **90**:118
Mara, Ratu Sir Kamisese
Fiji 496
Maradona, Diego Armando (biog.) **87**:89
marathon running 315
Maravich, Pete (obit.) **89**:102
Marble, Alice (obit.) **91**:101
Marchand, Jean (obit.) **89**:102
Marchenko, Anatoly (obit.) **87**:116
"Marco e Mattio" (Vassalli)
Italian literature 221
Marcos, Ferdinand E. (obit.) **90**:119
Philippines 416
Marcus, Rudolph A.
Nobel Prize 31
Marechera, Dambudzo (obit.) **88**:104
Marella, Paolo Cardinal (obit.) **85**:137
Marfan's syndrome (path.) 175
Mari, Michele
Italian literature 220
"Maria Chapdelaine, ou le paradis retrouvé" (Gourdeau)
French-Canadian literature 219
Marías, Javier
Spanish literature 221
marine biology 210
environment 169
marine disasters 124
Marino, Dan (biog.) **85**:106
football 297
Maris, Roger Eugene (obit.) **86**:136
Marjolin, Robert Ernest (obit.) **87**:116
Mark Taper Forum (Los Angeles, Calif., U.S.) 341
"Mark und Bein" (Kempowski)
German literature 219
marketing
furniture 187
rubber tires 195
spirits 184
Markevitch, Igor (obit.) **84**:123
Markham, Beryl (obit.) **87**:116
markka (Fin. currency)
governmental policies 433
Markowitz, Harry M. (biog.) **91**:76
Marks, Johnny (obit.) **86**:136
marriage
demography 252
homosexual couples 261
Judaism 268
Marriott, John Willard (obit.) **86**:136
Mars Observer (spacecraft) 275
Marsalis, Branford
jazz 244
Marsalis, Wynton (biog.) **90**:93
Marsh, Michael 313
Marshall, Sir John Ross (obit.) **89**:102
Marshall, Penny
television news 336
Marshall Field's
Chicago flood *il.* 163
Marshall Islands **93**:497; **92**:488
see also WORLD DATA
Martha Graham Dance Company 119
Martin, Billy (obit.) **90**:119
Martin, John Joseph (obit.) **86**:137
Martin, Mary (obit.) **91**:102
Martin, Paul Joseph James (obit.) **93**:71
Martinez, Edgar
baseball 283
Martini, Cardinal Carlo Maria (biog.) **93**:44
Roman Catholicism 267
Martini Safari (auto racing) 280
Martinique (Fr.)
elections 500
Martino, Angel 309
Martins, Peter (biog.) **84**:92
Marvin, Lee (obit.) **88**:105
Maryland (state, U.S.)
education 472
race relations 260
welfare services 272
Masire, Ketumile 356
Mason, James Neville (obit.) **85**:137
mass media, *or* media
Hungary 441
see also books; magazines; newspapers; Television and Radio
mass murder: *see* massacre
Massachusetts (state, U.S.)
law and justice 473
nuclear energy 158
Massachusetts Institute of Technology
anti-trust law violation 156
massacre
archaeology 98
Liberia 263
South Africa 370, 372
police 118
race relations 260
Massey, Sir Harrie Stewart Wilson (obit.) **84**:124
Massey, Raymond (obit.) **84**:124
Masson, André (obit.) **88**:105
"Master Builder, The" (play) 340
"Master European Paintings from the National Gallery of Ireland" (art exhibit) 105
Masters, John (obit.) **84**:124
Masters Tournament (golf) 298
Masur, Kurt (biog.) **92**:45
Matchbox
miniature cars 188
Mathematics 93:225; **92**:225; **91**:253; **90**:271; **89**:254; **88**:256; **87**:287; **86**:319; **85**:316; **84**:519
Mathias, Sean 338
Matisse, Henri 105
Matsushita, Konosuke (obit.) **90**:119
Mattel (Am. co.) 188

Mauritania 93:365; 92:361; 91:389; 90:410;
 89:393; 88:393; 87:432; 86:463;
 85:469; 84:520
 see also WORLD DATA
Mauritius 93:365; 92:362; 91:389; 90:410;
 89:393; 88:393; 87:432; 86:464;
 85:470; 84:520
 see also WORLD DATA
"Maus" (Spiegelman) 258
Maxwell, Ian Robert
 biography 85:106
 crime and law enforcement 118
 Liechtenstein 445
 newspapers 254
 obituary 92:73
Maxwell, Kevin *il.* 117
Maxxum 9xi (phot.) 247
May Department Stores
 advertising 180
Mayagüez Indians 283
Mayan civilization
 archaeology 99
Maybray-King, Horace Maybray Maybray-
 King (obit.) 87:116
Mayer, Sir Robert (obit.) 86:137
Mayhew, Patrick 461
Mayor Zaragoza, Federico (biog.) 89:79
Mazankowski, Donald 465
Mazda 183
Mazowiecki, Tadeusz (biog.) 90:94
Mbasogo, Teodoro Obiang Nguema 359
M'Bow, Amadou Mahtar (biog.) 85:107
MDCs: *see* more developed countries
"Me: Stories of My Life" (Hepburn) 258
"Measure of Our Success: A Letter to
 My Children and Yours, A" (Edel-
 man) 257
Meciar, Vladimir 430
"Medea" (play) 339
Medeiros, Humberto Cardinal (obit.)
 84:124
Medellín drug cartel 116
media: *see* mass media
Medicaid 472
medical journal
 advertising 180
Médici, Emílio Garrastazú (obit.) 86:137
Medici, Lorenzo de' 103
medicine: *see* Health and Disease
"Mediterraneo" (film) 237
"Medusa's Head" (art exhibit) 105
Medwar, Sir Peter Brian (obit.) 88:105
Meech Lake accord
 Canada 463
megabat, *or* Megachiroptera
 primate origins 208
Mehren, Stein
 Norwegian literature 220
Mejía Victores, Oscar Humberto (biog.)
 84:92
Melen, Ferit (obit.) 89:102
Mellor, David
 British theatre 337
 United Kingdom 458
"Memoire tranquée" (film) 238
memory (elec.)
 microelectronics 191
men
 fashion 171
 gymnastics 299
"Men barnet i meg spør" (Brekke)
 Norwegian literature 220
Menasse, Robert 219
Menchú, Rigoberta
 Nobel Peace Prize 30
Mendez, Alberto 122
Menem, Carlos Saúl (biog.) 90:94
 Argentina 476
Menen, Aubrey (obit.) 90:119
Menghistu, Lemma (biog.) 89:102
meningitis (path.) 176
Mennin, Peter (obit.) 84:124
Menninger, Karl Augustus (obit.) 91:102
"Men's Piece" (dance) *il.* 120
menswear
 women's fashions 171
mental health 176
 special report 85:256
Mentschikoff, Soia (obit.) 85:137
Mercedes-Benz
 automobiles 182, 183
Mercer, Joseph (obit.) 91:102
Mercer, Mabel (obit.) 85:137
Mercosur: *see* Southern Cone Common
 Market
Mercury, Freddie (obit.) 92:73
mergers, corporate
 insurance 189
 special report 86:262
 stock exchanges 148
Merle, Carole 308
Merman, Ethel (obit.) 85:138
Merrill Lynch & Co. 148
Messerer, Asaf 122
Messiaen, Olivier-Eugène-Prosper-Charles
 (obit.) 93:71
Messier, Mark 303
Messmer, Otto (obit.) 84:124
metallo-carbohedrene, *or* met-car
 chemistry 111
metallurgy: *see* Mining
"Metaphysics as a Guide to Morals" (Mur-
 doch)
 British literature 214
meteorology 130
Methodist Churches 265
 religion 260

methotrexate (drug)
 juvenile rheumatoid arthritis 176
methyl tertiary butyl ether, *or* MTBE 186
Metropolitan Community Churches, Universal Fellowship of
 religion 261
Metropolitan Museum of Art (N.Y.C.,
 N.Y., U.S.) 240
 art exhibitions 104
Metsis, Yannis 122
Mewes, Emil 246
Mexico 93:486; 92:478; 91:505; 90:520;
 89:505; 88:504; 87:551; 86:582;
 85:577; 84:521
 archaeology 99
 Columbus quincentenary 259
 crime and law enforcement 116
 education 156
 environment 167
 gasoline explosion 157
 international affairs
 Canada 465
 North American Free Trade Agreement 90
 United States 467
 extradition treaty 203
 Vatican City State 263
 literature 221
 mining 234
 motion pictures 239
 roads 162
 social security and welfare services 272
 special report 84:523
 sports and games
 auto racing 279
 baseball 283
 see also WORLD DATA
Mexico, Gulf of
 pipeline damage 158
Mexico City (Mex.)
 air pollution 488
 Aztec graves 99
Mexico City Tigers 283
Meyendorff, John (obit.) 93:71
Meyer, Ray (biog.) 85:107
Meynkes (Katz), Hirsh-Dovid
 Yiddish literature 224
MFA: *see* Multi-fiber Agreement
MFDC: *see* Movement of Democratic
 Forces of Casamance
MIA: *see* missing-in-action
Miall, A. D. 127
Miami, University of (Coral Gables, Fla.,
 U.S.)
 college football 295, *il.* 296
Miami-Dade public library system
 Hurricane Andrew 207
Miami Dolphins
 football 296
Miandad, Javed 291
Michael (k. of Rom.)
 Romania 451
Michel, Hartmut (biog.) 89:79
Michel, Henri Jules (obit.) 87:116
Michelangelo
 computer viruses 200
Michelin
 rubber industry 195
Michelob (beer) 184
Michener, Daniel Roland (obit.) 92:73
Michigan (state, U.S.)
 race relations 467
 religion 261
Michigan, University of (Ann Arbor,
 Mich., U.S.)
 college sports
 basketball 284
 football 295
Micombero, Michel (obit.) 84:124
microbat, *or* Microchiroptera
 primate origins 208
microchip 192
microelectronics 191
Micronesia, Federated States of, *or*
 Caroline Islands 93:497; 92:489
micronutrients 85
Microsoft Corp.
 pen computers 199
Middle Eastern and North African affairs 93:377; 92:373; 91:401; 90:421;
 89:404; 88:404; 87:445; 86:476;
 85:481; 84:525
 archaeology 97
 capital punishment 119
 crime 116
 economic affairs 132
 literature 223
 military affairs 231
 motion pictures 239
 refugees 252
 religion
 Eastern Orthodoxy 261
 Islam 269
 special report 92:375
 see also particular Middle Eastern and
 North African countries
Middleton, Raymond Earl, Jr. (obit.)
 85:138
"Midsummer Night's Dream, A"
 (play) 338
Mifsud Bonnici, Carmelo (biog.) 86:103
migration, international: *see* international
 migration
Mihalovici, Marcel (obit.) 86:137
"Mikdamot" (Yizhar)
 Hebrew literature 223
Mikes, George (obit.) 88:105

Mikhailov, Aleksandr Aleksandrovich
 (obit.) 84:124
Miki, Takeo (obit.) 89:102
Mikulic, Branko (biog.) 87:90
Milanov, Zinka (obit.) 90:119
Milburn, Jackie (obit.) 89:103
Miles, Bernard James Miles (obit.) 92:73
Mili, Gjon (obit.) 85:138
Milingo, Archbishop Emmanuel (biog.)
 86:104
Military Affairs 93:225; 92:225; 91:253;
 90:271; 89:254; 88:256; 87:287;
 86:319; 85:317; 84:270
 Armenia 425
 Australia 495
 Austria 425
 Indonesia 413
 new world order 6
 Niger 366
 Pakistan 409
 Venezuela 491
 special reports 93:232; 92:231; 91:260;
 88:258; 86:326; 85:320; 84:281; 83:285
 see also war; civil war
milk
 health and disease 176
Milken, Michael R. (biog.) 91:76
Milland, Ray (obit.) 87:116
Miller, Arnold Ray (obit.) 86:137
Miller, Gordy 306
Miller, James Henry: *see* MacColl, Ewan
Miller, Jonathan Wolfe (biog.) 89:79
Miller, Merton H. (biog.) 91:76
Miller, Roger (obit.) 93:71
Miller, William Edward (obit.) 84:125
Mills, Wilbur Daigh (obit.) 93:71
Milne, Alasdair David Gordon (biog.)
 86:104
Milongo, André 359
Milosevic, Slobodan (biog.) 92:45
 education 155
 Yugoslavia 462
Milosovici, Lavinia 300, *il.* 299
Milosz, Czeslaw
 literature 223
Milstein, Nathan (obit.) 93:72
Milton Keynes Challenge (field
 hockey) 293
Miner, Steve 237
Mining 93:234; 92:234; 91:262; 90:280;
 89:263; 88:264; 87:298; 86:329;
 85:328; 84:530
 Angola's diamonds *il.* 189
 Chile 480
 disasters 125
 environment 165
 United Kingdom 158, 459
Ministers, Council of (EC)
 duty-free trade 114
mink
 furs 188
minke whale
 wildlife conservation 169
Minnelli, Vincente (obit.) 87:116
Minnesota (state, U.S.)
 new taxes 471
Minnesota Vikings 296
Minolta 247
minority groups: *see* race relations
Minotis, Alexis (obit.) 91:102
Mintoff, Dominic (biog.) 84:92
MINURSO (UN)
 Morocco 389
Minuteman III ICBM 226
Mir (space station) 274
Miró, Joan (obit.) 84:125
Miro, Pilar 239
Mirror Group Newspapers 254
Mishkutenok, Natalya 305
Miskine, Idriss (obit.) 85:138
missile
 special report 84:281
missing-in-action, *or* MIA (U.S. military)
 Cambodia 413
 Vietnam 419
Missionary Diocese of America
 Episcopal Church 266
Mississippi (state, U.S.)
 education 472
 welfare services 273
Mississippi River (riv., U.S.)
 hydrology 129
Mitchell, Clarence M., Jr. (obit.) 85:138
Mitchell, Dennis 299
Mitchell, James Alexander Hugh (obit.)
 86:137
Mitchell, Joan (obit.) 93:72
Mitchell, John Newton (obit.) 89:103
Mitchell, Kevin (biog.) 90:94
Mitchell, Leslie (obit.) 86:137
Mitchell, Peter Dennis (obit.) 93:72
mitochondrial DNA, *or* mtDNA
 anthropology 94
Mitsmakher, Sh.
 Yiddish literature 224
Mitsotakis, Konstantinos (biog.) 91:76
 Greece 439
Mitsubishi (Japanese corp.)
 automobile racing 280
 nuclear industry 193
Mitsuharu Inoue
 Japanese literature 224
Mitsuo, Kurotsuchi 239
Mitterrand, François Maurice (biogs.)
 89:80; 86:104
 France 433
 Kohl *il.* 420

Miyazawa, Kiichi (biog.) 92:45
 Japan 397, *il.* 399
Mo Yan
 Chinese literature 224
Moawad, René Anis (obit.) 90:119
Mobutu Sese Seko 375
"Moby Dick" (play) 337
Moch, Jules (obit.) 86:137
Mochrie, Dottie 299
Moczar, Mieczyslaw (obit.) 87:117
Modigliani, Franco (obit.) 86:104
"Modspil" (Wivel)
 Danish literature 220
Mogadishu (Som.) 369
Mohieddin, Ahmad Fuad (obit.) 85:138
Moi, Daniel Torotich Arap
 Kenya 362
Moldova 93:446
 Commonwealth of Independent
 States 350
 military affairs 225
 race relations 259
 Russia 452
 Ukraine 458
 see also WORLD DATA
molecular biology 211
molecule 111
Molotov, Vyacheslav Mikhaylovich (obit.)
 87:117
Momigliani, Arnaldo Dante (obit.) 88:105
Momoh, Joseph Saidu (biog.) 86:105
 Sierra Leone 369
Monaco 93:447; 92:436; 91:458; 90:475;
 89:459; 88:458; 87:503; 86:531;
 85:337; 84:534
 automobile racing 279
 see also WORLD DATA
Moncreiffe of that Ilk, Sir Rupert Iain Kay
 (obit.) 86:138
Mondale, Walter Frederick (biog.) 85:107
"Monday Night Football" (TV program)
 advertising 180
money markets
 Western Europe 419
Mongolia 93:401; 92:400; 91:427; 90:445;
 89:428; 88:428; 87:470; 86:501;
 85:506; 84:534
 Buddhism 269
 race relations 258
 see also WORLD DATA
Mongolian (people)
 race relations 258
Mongolian People's Revolutionary Party,
 or MPRP 402
Monk, Art
 football 297
mono-oxygenases
 detoxication 211
Monro, Matt (obit.) 86:138
Monsanto Company
 advertising 180
Monsen, Per (obit.) 86:138
Monsengwo Pasinya, Laurent 375
Monsoon 126
Montagnier, Luc (biog.) 93:44
 France 434
Montagu, Ivor (obit.) 85:138
Montaigne, Michel Eyquem de (Fr. phi-
 los.)
 French literature 218
Montana, Joe (biog.) 90:94
Montand, Yves (obit.) 92:74
Montecatini
 plastics 194
Montenegro
 Yugoslavia 462
Montgomerie, Colin 299
Montgomery, David 254
Montgomery, Fred
 college football 296
Montgomery, Greg
 football 297
Montreal (Que., Can.)
 Unitarian Universalists 266
Montreal Canadiens (ice hockey) 303
Monza 50-km race 280
Moon (Earth's satellite) 107
Moon, Warren
 football 297
Moore, Colleen (obit.) 89:103
Moore, Henry (obit.) 87:117
 art exhibitions 104
Moore, John Edward Michael (biog.) 88:77
Moore, Ronald
 college football 296
Moorehead, Alan McCrae (obit.) 84:125
Moorer, Michael 287
Morales, Pablo 309
Morante, Elsa (obit.) 86:138
Moravia, Alberto (obit.) 91:102
Morceli, Noureddine 314
more developed countries, *or* MDCs
 demography 250
Morecambe, Eric (obit.) 85:138
Moreira, Marcílio Marques 479
Moreno, José 293
Morgan, Gil 299
Moriarty, Joan-Denise 122
Morishita, Yoko (biog.) 86:105
Morley, Robert (obit.) 93:72
Mormon: *see* Church of Jesus Christ of
 Latter-day Saints
Morocco 93:389; 92:387; 91:413; 90:433;
 89:416; 88:416; 87:458; 86:488;
 85:493; 84:535
 anthropology 94
 United States 348

Pioneer Venus orbiter 275
pipeline 343
  explosion in Mexico 487
Piper, John Egerton Christmas (obit.)
  93:75
piracy
  Strait of Malacca 412
Pirelli (Eur. co.) 194
Pitman, Sir Isaac James (obit.) **86:**140
Pitohui dichrous: *see* hooded pitohui
Pitterman, Bruno (obit.) **84:**127
Pittsburgh Penguins (ice hockey) 303
Pittsburgh Pirates
  baseball 282
Pittsburgh Steelers 296
"Place of Greater Safety, A" (Mantel)
  British literature 215
Placido, Michele 238
"Plague, The" (film) 239
planet 108
Planeta Prize
  Spanish literature 221
Planned Parenthood *v.* Casey
  abortion rights 203
plant: *see* botany
plant hormone 210
Plante, Jacques (obit.) **87:**120
plastics 194
platform shoes
  women's fashions 171
"Player, The" (film) 236
Plaza Lasso, Galo (obit.) **88:**107
Pleasant Tap (race horse) 300
plimsoll
  men's fashions 171
Plimsoll, Sir James (obit.) **88:**107
PLO: *see* Palestine Liberation Organiza-
  tion
Plomley, Francis Roy (obit.) **86:**141
PNP (pol. party, Jam.): *see* People's Na-
  tional Party
Pocket Books (Am. publ.) 257
Podgorny, Nikolay Viktorovich (obit.)
  84:127
Podkrepa
  Bulgaria 429
Poelvoorde, Benoît 238
poetry
  British literature 215
  German literature 219
  U.S. literature 217
"Poet's Work, The" (Nathan and Quinn)
  literature 223
Poiret, Jean (obit.) **93:**75
Polacolor 64 Tungsten
  photography 247
Poland **93:**448; **92:**437; **91:**472; **90:**490;
  89:473; **88:**471; **87:**516; **86:**545;
  85:550; **84:**569
  economic affairs 141
    special report 143
  glass 189
  military affairs 230
  prisons and penology 118
  see also WORLD DATA
Polanyi, John Charles (biog.) **87:**92
polar regions: *see* Antarctica; Arctic re-
  gions
Polaroid 247
Polgar, Judit (biog.) **93:**47
Polgar, Sofia (biog.) **93:**47
Polgar, Zsuzsa (biog.) **93:**47
police
  crime and law enforcement 118
  dogs 208
  Dominican Republic 483
  Mafia assassinations 445
  Peru 489
  race relations 258
  South Africa 370
  United States 467
Policy Studies Institute (U.K.)
  television 335
Polisario Front, *or* Popular Front for the
  Liberation of Saguia el Hamra and
  Rio de Oro (pol. party, Af.)
  North African affairs 380
Polish literature 223
Political Bureau Standing Committee
  (China) *il.* 395
political correctness (special report) **92:**459
political crime 117
  Yemen 394
Political Parties 93:350; **92:**344; **91:**374;
  90:376; **89:**379; **88:**379; **87:**418;
  86:450; **85:**452; **84:**570
  race relations 260
  United States 471
  see also individual countries by name
political prisoners
  Aung San Suu Kyi 269
  China 395
  Iraq 384
  Kenya 362
  Panama 488
  South Africa 371
  Tunisia 392
Pollard, Fritz (obit.) **87:**120
Pollard, Jonathan Jay (biog.) **88:**79
pollution
  Chinese factory *il.* 167
  environment 164
  insurance 190
  lawn and garden tools 172
  special report **84:**364
  U.S. state governments 473
  see also air pollution

polo **93:**306; **92:**302; **91:**332; **90:**351;
  89:333; **88:**335; **87:**380; **86:**415;
  85:409; **84:**366
Polyakov, Eugene 122
polyester 197
polymer
  chemistry 113
  man-made fibres 197
polypropylene
  man-made fibres 197
  plastics 194
polyvinyl chloride 194
Pompeii (anc. city, It.)
  art exhibitions 103
Pomus, Jerome (obit.) **92:**76
Ponge, Francis (obit.) **89:**106
Ponnelle, Jean-Pierre (obit.) **89:**106
Ponomarenko, Sergey 305
Pons, Bobby Stanley (biog.) **90:**97
Ponsford, William Harold (obit.) **92:**76
Pont de Normandie (bridge, Fr.) 159
Ponting, Clive (biog.) **86:**107
pontoon
  Monaco 447
Poole, David (obit.) **92:**76
Popa, Vasko (obit.) **92:**77
Popcorn, Faith (biog.) **93:**47
Popieluszko, The Rev. Jerzy Aleksander
  (obit.) **85:**141
Popular Front for the Liberation of Saguia
  el Hamra and Rio de Oro (pol. party,
  Af.): *see* Polisario Front
popular music 244
**Populations and Population Movements
  93:**250; **92:**250; **91:**278; **90:**296;
  89:280; **88:**282; **87:**317; **86:**347;
  85:340; **84:**284
  international migration 252
  special reports **91:**279; **88:**318
  see also WORLD DATA
porcelain enamel 186
"Porcupine, The" (Barnes)
  British literature 214
pork production 87
Porter, Eliot Furness (obit.) **91:**106
Porter, Eric 338
Porter, Hal (obit.) **85:**142
Porter, Rodney Robert (obit.) **86:**141
Portland Trail Blazers
  basketball 285
"Portrait of a Lady with a Squirrel" (Holbein)
  art sales 106
Portugal **93:**449; **92:**439; **91:**460; **90:**476;
  89:460; **88:**460; **87:**504; **86:**533;
  85:539; **84:**574
  automobile racing 280
  literature 221
  Macau 502
  television 337
  see also WORLD DATA
Poseidon: *see* Franco-American Ocean To-
  pography Experiment (spacecraft)
"Posiolok kentavrov" (Kim)
  Russian literature 222
"Posledny poklon" (Astafyev)
  Russian literature 222
"Possessing the Secret of Joy"
  (Walker) 257
postal service
  Ireland 201
  magazine labels 256
Potter, Sally 237
Poulsen, Peter
  Danish literature 220
poultry production 87
Poundbury (U.K.)
  architecture 102
poverty
  consumer affairs 113
  special report **86:**374
  welfare services 272
Powell, Colin Luther (biog.) **90:**97
Powell, Michael 490
Powell, Michael Latham (obit.) **91:**106
Powell, Mike (biog.) **92:**47
Powell, William Horatio (obit.) **85:**142
power blower
  gardening 172
Power Systems
  electrical industry 187
Powerbook
  Macintosh computers 199
Pozer, John 238
PPV television: *see* pay-per-view television
Prague Festival Ballet
  dance 121
Pratolini, Vasco (obit.) **92:**77
prayer
  U.S. public school graduation 153, 263
PRCA: *see* Professional Rodeo Cowboys
  Association
Prebisch, Raúl (obit.) **87:**120
pregnancy 173
preimplantation diagnosis
  in vitro fertilization 175
Premadasa, Ranasinghe (biog.) **90:**97
  Sri Lanka 409
Preminger, Otto Ludwig (obit.) **87:**120
Premio Miguel de Cervantes
  Spanish literature 221
Presbyterian Church (U.S.A.) 266
  religion 260
  United Church of Christ 267
Prescription Drug User Fee Act (U.S.,
  1992)
  pharmaceuticals 193

Presley, Elvis
  stamp *il.* 246
Pressburger, Emeric (obit.) **89:**106
Presser, Jackie
  biography **84:**94
  obituary **89:**106
pressurized heavy water reactor, *or* PWR
  nuclear industry 192
Preston, Robert (obit.) **88:**107
Price, George 477
Price, Nick 299
Price, Sammy (obit.) **93:**75
Price, T. Rowe (obit.) **84:**127
"Price, The" (play) 340
Pridi Phanomyong (obit.) **84:**127
priesthood
  Anglican Communion 264
  Roman Catholicism 267
  women 261
Priestley, John Boynton (obit.) **85:**142
primate
  origins 94, 208
Prince 245
Prince, Harold 338
Prince of Wales Institute of Architecture
  (U.K.) 102
Prince William Sound (waterway, Alsk.,
  U.S.)
  law enforcement 118
  special report **84:**577
printing 194
Prison Reform Trust (U.K.)
  race relations 259
prisons and penology 118
  China 395
  Colombia 480
  Peru 489
  race relations 259
  special report **84:**577
  United States 204, 473
Pritchard, John Michael (obit.) **90:**121
Pritikin, Nathan (obit.) **86:**141
Pritzker, Abram Nicholas (obit.) **87:**120
Pritzker Prize (arch.) 100
privatization
  Africa
    Benin 356
  East Asia
    China 396
    Mongolia 402
  economic affairs 141
  Europe
    Bulgaria 429
    Czechoslovakia 192, 430
    Eastern Europe (special report) 143
    Greece 202
    Russia 453
    Ukraine 458
  Latin America
    Argentina 476
    Bolivia 478
    Brazil 478
    Chile 480
    Mexico 487
  social security and welfare services 271
  special reports **92:**465; **87:**194
Prix d'Amerique (Fr.)
  harness racing 302
Prix Fémina
  French literature 218
Prix Goncourt
  French literature 214, 218
Prix Médicis
  French literature 218
Prix Renaudot
  French literature 218
"Prize: The Epic Quest for Oil, Money,
  and Power, The" (Yergin)
  Pulitzer Prize 258
Pro Tunnel Tour
  motorboating 306
Proctor & Gamble
  advertising 180
product labeling: *see* labeling
product liability
  special report **86:**181
Professional Bowlers Association, *or*
  PBA 286
Professional Rodeo Cowboys Association,
  or PRCA 306
Progressive National Baptist Conven-
  tion 264
Prokovsky, André 122
Proposition 161, *or* "California Death with
  Dignity Act" 471
prosimian
  anthropology 94
protectionism
  special reports **88:**172; **86:**214
protein
  drug testing *il.* 193
  fossils 128
protest movement: *see* riots and demonstrations
Protestant churches 260, 264
  Eastern Orthodoxy 261
provincial jurisdiction
  Canada 464
Prøysen, Alf
  Norwegian literature 220
"prueba del laberinto, La" (Sánchez)
  Spanish literature 221
Pryce, Jonathan (biog.) **91:**79
PS (pol. party, Fr.): *see* Socialist Party
PSE: *see* Pacific Stock Exchange
public sector
  labour relations 202

Publishing 93:256; **92:**253; **91:**283; **90:**300;
  89:283; **88:**285; **87:**321; **86:**352;
  85:350; **84:**579
  classical music 243
  court decisions 203
  special reports **88:**288; **86:**355
  Unitarian Universalists 266
Pucci, Emilio (obit.) **93:**76
  fashion 171
Puckett, Kirby (biog.) **88:**79
  baseball 283
Puenzo, Luís 239
Puerto Rico
  boxing 288
  hotel project 500
Puig, Manuel (obit.) **91:**106
Pulitzer Prize
  fiction 258
  newspapers 255
  photography 248
pulmonary tuberculosis: *see* tuberculosis
pulsar 108
"Punch" (mag.) 256
"Pushing Hands" (film) 239
Putnam/Berkley (Am. publ.) 257
Putrament, Jerzy (obit.) **87:**120
Puttnam, David Terence (biog.) **87:**92
PWR: *see* pressurized heavy water reactor
"Pygmalion" (play) 338, 341
Pyke, Magnus (obit.) **93:**76

Q

Q survey
  advertising 180
Qabus ibn Sa'id
  Oman 390
Qaddafi, Muammar Muhammad al-, *or*
  Mu'ammar al-Qadhdhafi (biog.) **84:**95
  Egypt 383
  Libya 389
  special report **87:**457
QANTAS Boeing 747-400
  Australia 495
Qasimlu, Abd ar-Rahman
  Kurdish people (special report) **92:**375
Qatar **93:**390; **92:**388; **91:**414; **90:**434;
  89:416; **88:**416; **87:**459; **86:**489;
  85:494; **84:**585
  Bahrain 381
  Saudi Arabia 391
  see also WORLD DATA
Qiao Guanhua (obit.) **84:**127
Qin Benli, *or* Ch'in Pen-li (obit.) **92:**77
"Qiuyue" (film) 239
Qoboza, Percy (obit.) **89:**106
Quadros, Jânio da Silva (obit.) **93:**76
Quaker United Nations Office 266
Quakers: *see* Friends, Religious Society of
quark
  high-energy physics 250
"Quartier Mozart" (film) 240
Quayle, James Danforth (biogs.) **93:**47;
  89:81
  presidential election (special report)
  93:470
  television 334
Quayle, Sir John Anthony (obit.) **90:**122
Quebec (prov., Can.)
  constitutional reform 463
Quesada, Roberto
  Honduran literature 221
QuickSnap Panorama Flash
  photography 247
Quindlen, Anna 255
Quinn, Pat 303
quinone reductase
  anticarcinogens 212
Quirino, José 288
Qur'an
  women's role (special report) 95
Quwaiz, Abdullah al-
  Middle Eastern affairs 379

R

Rabi, Isidor Isaac (obit.) **89:**106
rabies 177
Rabin, Yitzhak (biog.) **93:**47
  Israel 386
  Middle Eastern affairs 377, *il.* 378
Rabinowitz, Louis Isaac (obit.) **85:**142
Rabuka, Sitiveni 496
Raby, Albert (obit.) **89:**106
RAC: *see* Royal Automobile Club
raccoon 177
Race Relations 93:258; **92:**258; **91:**287;
  90:304; **89:**287; **88:**291; **87:**326;
  86:359; **85:**335; **84:**585
  ethnic conflicts
    Eastern Europe 424
    Ethiopia 360
    Kazakhstan 406
    Kenya 362
    Russia 451
    Zaire 375
  New Zealand 498
  refugees 254
    Germany 8, 437
    international migration 252
    Malawi 364